Nations of the World

2016

Fifteenth Edition

Nations of the World

A Political, Economic & Business Handbook

Grey House Publishing
4919 Route 22
Amenia, NY 12501

Grey House Publishing

PUBLISHER: Leslie Mackenzie
EDITOR: Richard Gottlieb
EDITORIAL DIRECTOR: Laura Mars
MARKETING DIRECTOR: Jessica Moody
PRODUCTION MANAGER: Kristen Thatcher

Grey House Publishing, Inc.
4919 Route 22
Amenia, NY 12501
518.789.8700
FAX 518.789.0556
www.greyhouse.com
e-mail: books@greyhouse.com

World of Information

MANAGING DIRECTOR: Anthony Axon
PRODUCTION MANAGER: Sue Hewitt
EDITORIAL: Alfie Bullmore, Anthony Griffin, Sue Hewitt, Theo-Paul Ogier, Wlliam Snell Mendoza, Tash Stryder, Josh Townson, Noah von Heimendahl

World of Information
11 Clarendon Street
Cambridge CB1 1JU, UK
Tel: +44 (0) 1223.351584

First edition published 2000
Fifteenth Edition published 2016
Printed in Canada

Nations of the world: a political, economic & business handbook – 15th ed. (2016)

1. Almanacs, American. 2. Business travel – Handbooks, manuals, etc. 3. International trade – handbooks, manuals, etc.

HF1010.N37
658-dc21
ISBN: 978-1-61925-753-5

2001238305
softcover

Contents

Country Profiles

INTRODUCTION

The fifteenth edition of *Nations of the World: A Political, Economic & Business Handbook* profiles every nation and self-governing territory around the world. It offers political, economic and business information in an easy-to-access, single-volume format, supplemented by maps, charts and tables.

Nations of the World offers tremendous insight into current living conditions, social standings and economic climates of 235 nations. This past year (2015) has been quite a busy one for world elections and leadership changes, with 49 parliamentary and 29 heads of state elections. Two countries that made headlines in 2015 are Saudi Arabia, this being the first year that women were allowed to vote and run for office, and Myanmar, with an extraordinary win by the National Democratic Party. Other notable elections took place in Spain, Nigeria, Britain, Israel, and Argentina. Next year – 2016 – is shaping up to be just as busy, with 73 elections scheduled around the globe, not the least of which will be the closely-watched U.S. Presidential election.

According to the United Nations *World Economic Situation and Prospects 2015:*

> *The global economy continues to expand at only a moderate estimated pace of 2.6 percent in 2014. Recovery was hampered by some new challenges, including a number of unexpected shocks, such as the heightened geopolitical conflicts in different parts of the world. Most economies have seen a shift in gross domestic product (GDP) growth to a noticeably lower path compared to pre-crisis levels, raising the spectre of longer-term mediocre economic growth. In the developed economies, although some improvements are forecast for 2015 and 2016, significant downside risks persist, especially in the euro area and Japan. Growth rates in developing countries and economies in transition have become more divergent during 2014, with a sharp deceleration in a number of large emerging economies, particularly in Latin American and the Commonwealth of Independent States (CIS). A number of these economies have encountered various country-specific challenges, including structural imbalances and geopolitical tensions. In the outlook periods, the global economy is expected to expand at a slightly faster but still only moderate pace, with world gross product (WGP) projected to grow by 3.1 and 3.3 percent in 2015 and 2016 respectively.*

As economies and politics change, so do global markets, crucial to business worldwide. *Nations of the World* provides the understanding necessary to advance on the world stage in business, education, and recreation.

Every country profile has been reviewed and updated. Contributors worldwide have written thoughtful, comprehensive country essays. These international correspondents, true experts in their fields, have contributed to some of the most influential books and periodicals in the world. See the Contributor list following this Introduction.

Nations of the World, arranged alphabetically by country, is a reliable, careful compilation of essential information that is presented in a useful, organized format. This reference is critical for anyone doing business or traveling overseas. It has proved to be an important reference tool for students in secondary school through college, as well as for professionals in politics, the military, and reconstruction sectors.

Arrangement & Currency
The majority of country chapters start with a concise, independently written **Country Overview**. These overviews do not reflect the worldview of any particular government or intelligence agency. You will find current political and economic events, as well as an informed outlook toward the future. All chapters include: **Key Facts** -- official name(s), ruling parties, language, basic area, population, unemployment, and 2014 inflation figures; **Key Indicators** -- charted over five years that end in 2015, and include population, GNP, imports/exports, foreign debt, exchange rate; and **Risk Assessment** – rates politics, economy and general stability of the region. Most chapters include a **Map.**

A **Country Profile** includes detailed historical information in easy-to-follow chronological order, political structure and parties, and a detailed look at the country's population, labor market, media, trade, industry, agriculture and energy. Business travelers will learn about that country's time zones, banking practices, entry requirements, dress codes, climate, health issues, hotels, working hours and the best way to travel to and from. *Noted are countries in political crises, with advice to visitors.*

The **Business Directory** has contact numbers and web sites for hotels, travel information and chambers of commerce, plus dozens of other useful numbers and addresses.

Following the country profiles are **Regional Worldwide Overviews:** Global; Africa; Americas; Asia, Europe; Middle East. Like individual country chapters, these overviews offer an expertly written narrative on the region's current political and economic climate. These overviews include **Key Indicators, Currencies**, and a **Map** of the region.

Buyers of the print directory get Free Access to **Nations of the World Online**, where users can access individual Country Reports for download on http://gold.greyhouse.com. With online access, searching through this vast amount of text and finding specific country information has never been easier. Online access is available upon request to book buyers at no additional cost; use coupon at the back of the book.

With more than 2,000 pages of political, economic and business information, this thirteenth edition of *Nations of the World: A Political, Economic & Business Handbook* – in print and electronic formats – is a timely and immensely valuable reference acquisition to all public, academic and special library collections.

Praise for previous editions:

> *". . . a truly stunning go-to reference [with] fundamental nation facts . . . well-crafted, objectively expressed essays [and] comparative data."*
>
> Library Journal

> *". . . the most current information available for the political and economic state of the world's nations."*
>
> American Reference Books Annual

Contributors

Barry Baxter has spent most of his working life in Africa. He has worked as a journalist for 45 years, reporting from Botswana, South Africa, Zambia (and Northern Rhodesia), Zimbabwe (and Southern Rhodesia), Angola, Kenya, Tanzania and Uganda.

Daniel Brett is a freelance journalist contributing articles on agricultural economics, protest movements and trade-related issues in Africa and Latin America as well as the politics and economics of other developing countries.

Rick Butler is a freelance journalist specialising in Eastern Europe.

Shanjukta Ghosh is a graduate of Delhi University and writes on socioeconomic themes of the Indian subcontinent, with emphasis on high-technology.

Anthony Griffin is a UK-based journalist specialising in emerging markets, with an emphasis on Spanish speaking countries. He regularly contributes articles to British and international publications, on Europe and South America.

Aileen Herlihy, based in Australia, writes on health and welfare issues, with an emphasis on developing countries as well as Australia.

Niki Johnson is a research fellow at the Political Science Institute, Universidad de la República, Montevideo, Uruguay.

Ali Rafel al Mansour is an analyst based in the Middle East, who reports on the petroleum industry and OPEC.

Meldun Mawson is a Swedish writer who specialises in travel and tourism issues, and the social and cultural implications of political change in Latin America, as well as northern Europe.

Marianne Morse is a freelance political and economic country analyst. She edited the *Organization of American States – the next 50 years*.

Anita Parameswaran is a business analyst for a leading insurance company developing corporate strategy. She writes on North Africa and the Mediterranean.

Craig Stenhouse is a researcher specialising in Africa and the Middle East.

William R Thomson is a former director and vice president in charge of the Asia Development Bank's lending programmes in over 25 Asian and Pacific countries. He advises both international investment houses and governments on regional economic developments and investment opportunities.

José Luis Velasco lectures in Mexican politics and holds a doctorate in political science from Boston University. He is the author of *El Debate Actual Sobre el Federalismo Mexicano*, published by Instituto Mora.

Afghanistan

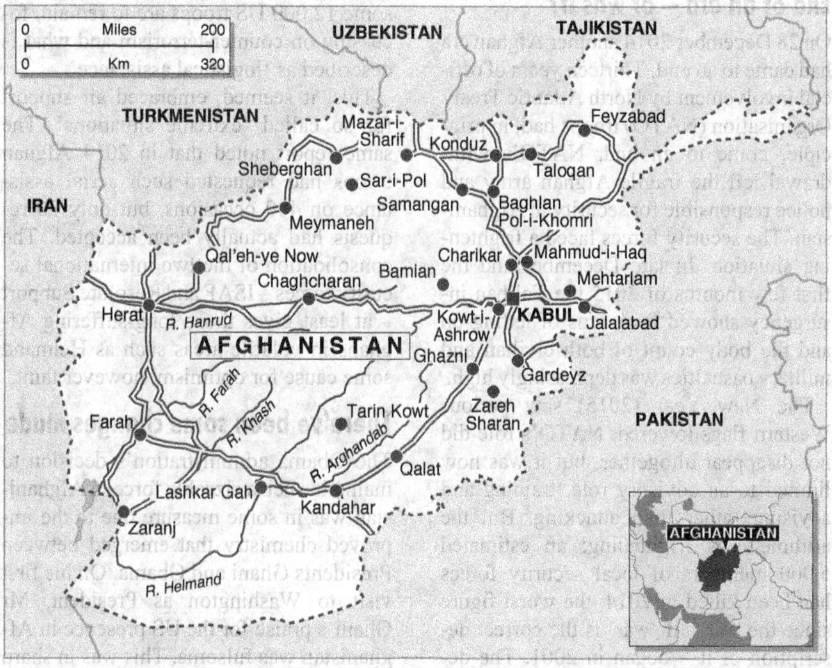

Expatriates say that 'Afghanistan is different'. And how! The investiture, on 29 September 2014, of Ashraf Ghani as Afghanistan's president brought to an end a six-month long political stalemate during which no governmental decisions or policies of consequence were implemented. President Ghani, who had once served as a World Bank official, took over from Hamid Karzai, having seen off the challenge of his electoral rival Abdullah Abdullah, who was parked in the uncertain, and novel, position of Chief Executive Officer, or *de facto* prime minister. Thus, in a *sui generis* form, there concluded a contentious electoral process largely characterised by the massive fraud seen in the second round, which had taken place in June 2014. The results of the voting on the second round, despite the efforts of the United Nations (UN) to produce an accurate audit of the eight million votes cast, were never published. Instead the result became classified as something of a state secret.

You vote, we'll count

Taking into consideration the host of tribal and political differences that had to be offset, the electoral agreement, pushed through by the US, was probably the best that Afghanistan could ever hope for. The secret results of the UN audit were accepted by the two opposing factions who were, it was assumed, given the alternative by US Secretary of State John Kerry of a withdrawal of whatever level of US military and civilian support was likely to be continued. The Kerry deal was in *realpolitik* terms a power sharing deal, but its critics saw it as little more than a carve-up.

The mystery surrounding the US brokered deal between the two candidates hinged on the fact that it was Mr Abdullah who appeared to have won the first round of voting on 5 April, gaining 45 per cent, substantially better than Mr Ghani, who could only muster 31 per cent. Since neither party had an absolute majority, the second round was required in which votes could only be cast for one or other of the two front runners. This round saw Mr Ghani dramatically leap-frog his rival, with 56 per cent of the votes. Strangely, the second round turnout increased by an estimated one million voters. Accusations abounded from both sides, with Mr Abdullah accusing both the Independent

KEY FACTS

Official name: The Islamic Republic of Afghanistan

Head of State: President Ashraf Ghani Ahmadzai (since 29 Sep 2014)

Head of government: Chief Executive Abdullah Abdullah (National Coalition of Afghanistan) (since 29 Sep 2014)

Ruling party: Members of the national assembly are elected as independent candidates

Area: 647,497 square km

Population: 31.28 million (2014)* (some 1 million Afghanis are still in exile in Pakistan and Iran)

Capital: Kabul

Official language: Pashtu and Dari (named as official languages in the 2004 constitution)

Currency: Afghani (Af) = 100 puls

Exchange rate: Af64.21 per US$ (Sep 2015)

GDP per capita: US$649 (2014)*

GDP real growth: 1.53% (2014)*

GDP: US$20.31 billion (2014)*

Inflation: 4.61% (2014)*

Balance of trade: -US$8.52 billion (2013) (Aghanistan's highest export is opium, which is not included in the IMF export figure)

* estimated figure

Election Commission and the government officials responsible of fraud. Mr Ghani responded by admitting that fraud had probably taken place on both sides. Mr Ghani's statement that his victory was due to the successful mobilisation of his fellow Pashtuns was probably nearer the mark.

All pull together?

In the immediate post investiture period, what was beyond doubt was the need for the government to create and maintain some sort of unity between the rival political factions. This, in a country so fragmented as Afghanistan, where the very concept of transparent elections had still to take hold, was an enormous challenge. None the less, at first sight it seemed that the two ex-ministers (President Ghani had been minister of finance, Mr Abdullah had been foreign minister) were on the same page. Nowhere was this more apparent than in the signature of the bilateral agreement with the United States for the creation of the Resolute Support Agreement (RSA) (see below). This theoretically interim agreement had been rejected by the outgoing and widely discredited, President Hamid Karzai.

The signing of the RSA was a relief for the beleaguered President Obama and his ever patient Secretary of State Kerry. Returning Afghanistan to some degree of normal functionality after thirteen years of the clearly corrupt and crony based Karzai rule was no small task. Cranking up the faltering economy was an immediate requirement, alongside gaining the upper hand in the never ending confrontation with the Taliban. President Ghani had indicated his willingness to meet with the Taliban. But the seemingly Westernised President Ghani, considered by most Afghan fundamentalists to be little more than Washington's lackey, has found himself floundering in the unstructured and erratic negotiating procedure he inherited from his wayward predecessor.

End of an era – or was it?

On 28 December 2014 another Afghan era had came to an end. Thirteen years of official involvement by North Atlantic Treaty Organisation (NATO) troops had, in principle, come to an end. NATO's withdrawal left the fragile Afghan army and police responsible for security in Afghanistan. The security forces faced a frightening situation. In late December and the first few months of 2015 the Taliban insurgency showed few signs of letting up and the body count of both civilian and military casualties was depressingly high.

The New Year (2015) saw various Western flags lowered. NATO's role did not disappear altogether, but it was now limited to an advisory role, training and advising rather than attacking. But the arithmetic is frightening: an estimated 5,000 members of local security forces had been killed in 2014, the worst figure since the war – if 'war' is the correct description of it – began in 2001. The depressing figure reflected the blunt fact that the Afghan troops – now numbering around 350,000 – were still both unreliable and largely untrained. The Taliban offensive in Helmand province was reported to have begun in June 2014, not long after the departure of US troops from the area.

The NATO 'advisory' troops are now known as the International Security Assistance Force (ISAF). According to a report in the London *Guardian*, some 17,000–18,000 international troops will continue to be stationed in Afghanistan. Of these, 12,000 will belong to a new NATO mission to Afghanistan to be called Resolute Support. On top of this, some 12,000 US troops are to remain, focussing on counter-terrorism and what is described as 'logistical assistance'.

This, it seemed, embraced air support for so called 'extreme situations'. The same report noted that in 2014 Afghan troops had requested such aerial assistance on 400 occasions, but only 30 requests had actually been accepted. The consolidation of the two international security forces – ISAF and Resolute Support – at least gives those long-suffering Afghans in volatile areas such as Helmand some cause for optimism, however faint.

There've been some changes made

The Obama administration's decision to maintain such a sizeable force in Afghanistan was in some measure due to the improved chemistry that emerged between Presidents Ghani and Obama. On his first visit to Washington as President, Mr Ghani's praise for the US presence in Afghanistan was fulsome. This was in sharp contrast to his predecessor's reluctance to acknowledge the US contribution. Whatever their exact role, the presence of the US and other NATO forces in Afghanistan throughout 2015 should enable Afghan forces to contain – if not properly counter – the Taliban offensive that could normally be expected in the summer months. And with any luck, it might boost recruitment efforts, which had slumped in late 2014.

What is doubtful, however, is whether any success in holding the Taliban at bay would persuade them to agree to negotiations. Perhaps the most important change in the tenor of Afhganistan's international relations lies not in Washington, but in the apparently improved relations with Pakistan. It was unclear whether Pakistan's support for the Taliban had been completely withdrawn following the horrendous attack on an army-run boys' school in Peshawar in December 2014 in which 141 people – mostly pupils – died. Certainly the attack caused many Pakistanis to reconsider their support for the Taliban. The dramatic rise of the so-called Islamic State in Syria and Iraq also gave the US reason not to leave Afghanistan as a potentially soft Islamic underbelly.

KEY INDICATORS — Afghanistan

	Unit	2011	2012	2013	2014	**2015
Population	m	*31.08	*29.82	30.66	*31.28	*32.01
Gross domestic product (GDP)	US$bn	18.20	20.30	20.13	*20.31	*21.53
GDP per capita	US$	585	681	659	*649	673
GDP real growth	%	5.7	14.0	3.7	*1.5	*3.5
Inflation	%	11.2	6.4	7.4	4.6	*6.7
Exports (fob) (goods)	US$m	430.7	619.9	620.9	–	–
Imports (fob) (goods)	US$m	6,709.9	9,392.2	9,145.5	–	–
Balance of trade	US$m	-6,279.2	-8,772.3	-8,524.6	–	–
Current account	US$m	398.0	798.0	1,515.0	*1,158.0	*660.0
Total reserves minus gold	US$m	–	5,982.5	6,441.9	6,680.7	–
Foreign exchange	US$m	–	5,788.0	6,260.0	–	–
Exchange rate	per US$	45.57	52.62	55.56	57.9	–

* estimated figure ** forecast figure

The cost of dragging Afghanistan from a backward Taliban controlled state towards something approaching the perceived standards of secular civilisation had been horrendous. One report in the London *Economist* put the figure at one trillion dollars, roughly US$30,000 for every single Afghan. This to achieve a mixed result. According to the *Economist*, the poverty rate has 'remained stuck at 36 per cent for a decade' and 'is even rising in places.' The Kharzai regime left Afghanistan more corrupt than ever and still languishing as Asia's poorest country. There were some successes: the *Economist* also pointed out that under the Taliban only three per cent of girls went to school, a figure which has risen to over 30 per cent according to the UN.

President Ghani's published agenda promises a lot – retrials for those allegedly involved in the collapse of the Kabul Bank (which saw some US$1 billion 'disappear'), land reform, a tightening of government expenditure. Easily said, but his country's vested interests are likely to provide substantial opposition.

The economy

Painting a positive picture of the Afghan economy is no easy matter. Preliminary estimates for 2014 suggested that growth had fallen to a mean two per cent, almost half the 3.7 per cent registered in 2013 and way down on the average growth figure of nine per cent registered in the period 2003–12. Much, if not all of the fall in 2014 could be attributed to the country's parlous political situation; investors and consumers all held back while they awaited the outcome of the April 2014 presidential election. At the same time, the US and NATO troop withdrawals not only knocked business confidence sideways, but in 2014 had already begun to show through in decreased purchases. Even the traditionally strong agriculture sector registered a mixed performance: although the harvest was good, it was only slightly up on the 2013 figure and the expectations for 2015 are less than strong. Inevitably, the generally indifferent economic performance resulted in a worryingly weak fiscal situation. Domestic revenues dropped by over three per cent, to 8.4 per cent in 2014, doing no more than reflect Afghanistan's generally unsatisfactory economic performance.

The IMF – ever optimistic

Despite this gloom, the International Monetary Fund (IMF) in an April 2015 Programme Note struck a somewhat more positive note, observing that in the previous decade, Afghanistan had made 'enormous progress' in reconstruction, development and in raising Afghanistan's per capita income. The Afghan authorities had, in the view of the IMF, taken steps to lay the foundation for economic stability and growth, to reduce poverty and to achieve social and development objectives despite a very difficult security situation and the challenges associated with building political and economic institutions. After such a glowing build-up, the IMF came down to earth by noting that 'security conditions, political uncertainty and weak institutions' continued to restrict growth and hold back improved social developments, (such as health and education). Rather ungraciously, in view of the vast sums provided, (and the vast sums that had simply 'disappeared') the IMF could only give what it described as 'the international community' a churlish and severely understated acknowledgement that 'substantial financial support' had been given and had been pledged for the medium term. Rather surprisingly, not once in the IMF's summary Programme Note does the word 'corruption' appear.

The IMF flatly concedes that Afghanistan is one of the poorest countries in the world, relying heavily on donor grants to fund development and security spending. Uncertainty surrounds the post-2014 likelihood of aid grants being maintained at earlier levels once the massive international military presence has been reduced. According to IMF figures, per capita income for 2014 was estimated at about US$660; Afghanistan ranked well below its neighbours on most human development indicators despite its progress toward meeting its social and development objectives and the Millennium Development Goals (MDGs). For example, child mortality had been reduced and school enrolment increased, albeit from very low levels – the enrolment rate for primary school is less than 40 per cent. The IMF reported that achievements in some areas were below expectation: more progress was needed in reducing the number of children under the age of five that were underweight; in increasing access to drinkable water and sanitation; and improving literacy rates for men and women aged 15 to 24. Overall, the low implementation rate of the development budget impeded more rapid progress toward poverty reduction. Despite these drawbacks, according to the IMF, Afghanistan has managed to become one of 20 fragile and conflict-affected states that have already met one or more the MDGs.

The ADB – more gloom?

In its more detailed end-2014 overview of the Afghan economy, the Asian Development Bank (ADB), also choosing to avoid alluding to the problem of widespread corruption, refers to the 'Protracted deadlock and political uncertainty' that had combined to limit economic growth in 2014. Growth was reported by the ADB to have fallen to 1.7 per cent from 3.4 per cent in 2013. On the supply side, expansion in industry and services fell by as much as half and, as already noted, agriculture remained flat, growing at about 1.0 per cent, as food production achieved its maximum potential for a third consecutive year. Opium production – a controversial issue for most international organisations and donor countries – rose by 17 per cent, although its farm-gate value of US$850 million was ten per cent less than in 2013. While opium is omitted from official gross domestic product (GDP) estimates, its earnings boost domestic demand and are a significant source of foreign exchange.

The ADB also noted that on the demand side, private consumption continued to be the main driver of growth, but at a much slower pace because of uncertainty and income lost in the retrenchment of spending by security forces mentioned above. The departure of large numbers of foreign ancillary workers meant that many restaurants and bars closed, not to mention hotels. Domestic investment had decreased with the number of newly registered firms falling to 2,086 from 3,895 in 2013. These figures included the number of registrations of foreign firms, which had halved to 98 from the previous year's 193.

According to the ADB, Afghanistan's level of ination fell markedly in the second half of 2014. Food inflation dropped to 2.9 per cent in December 2014 from 9.7 per cent a year earlier as prices for vegetables, oil and fats fell because of the ample available supply and lower international prices. Non-food inflation had also been declining since 2012, mainly because of falling property rents. Average ination in 2014 was 5.0 per cent, well down from the 7.4 per cent registered in 2013.

Afghanistan's fiscal policy had also come under immense pressure in 2014 when domestic revenue fell short of target by a large margin equal to US$527 million. Revenues amounted to only AF99.3 billion (US$1.75 billion), far below the budgeted target of AF128.8 billion (US$2.27 billion). Asked to fill the gap, development partners provided only US$118 million, leaving the government to finance the difference by drawing down treasury cash reserves. Domestic revenue financed only 43.9 per cent of the country's operating expenditures, 11.6 per cent less than in 2013. Weak revenue collection was partly due to the economic slowdown, but in the view of the ADB the deteriorating revenue performance since 2012 largely reflected weak governance in the tax and customs administration.

Afghanistan's Da Afghanistan Bank (central bank) monetary policy continued to be conducted through bi-weekly foreign exchange auctions. The fluctuation in foreign exchange reserves seen in mid-2014 reflected inconsistent foreign grant inflows and capital outflows in response to political and security concerns, but reserves largely stabilised toward the end of the year. Gross international reserves stood at US$7.4 billion at the end of December 2014, up slightly from the US$7.1 billion of a year earlier. The value of the national currency, the afghani, had steadily fallen since 2011 but was broadly stable in 2014, depreciating by less than one per cent against the US dollar to AF58.0. According to the ADB, broad money (M2) growth slowed to 8.3 per cent from 9.4 per cent a year earlier, as the expansion in demand deposits was only 3.7 per cent. Afghanis' preference for holding cash reflects the continued distrust and weak financial intermediation in the banking sector following the massive failure of the Kabul Bank in 2010.

The current account, including grants, was estimated to have been in surplus corresponding to 3.8 per cent of GDP in 2014, up from the 3.6 per cent seen in 2013. This improvement reflected increased earnings from transporting the military equipment of departing international security forces, as well as higher on-budget grants. Excluding grants, the current account was estimated to have been in deficit equal to 36.6 per cent of GDP, improving on 40.4 per cent in 2013 mainly because imports for grant-supported projects had fallen.

What are the prospects?

In the estimation of the ADB, the Afghan economy is projected to grow by 2.5 per cent in 2015, up from 1.7 per cent in 2014, as long as the political, security and business environment was adequately stable. Delays in naming the cabinet and the imminent prospect of parliamentary elections nationally due to take place by June 2015, consumer and investor enthusiasm looked likely to remain subdued. The fact that the agriculture sector performed at full potential in 2014 and winter snowfall was meagre, agricultural output was expected by the ADB to decline in 2015. Growth in industry and services was, however, projected to pick up in the second half of 2015 reflecting the hoped for increased political stability, but the demand for services was expected to suffer from the withdrawal of international security forces. Economic growth in 2016 was projected to edge up to 3.5 per cent on progress with political and security issues.

Risk assessment

Economy	Fair
Politics	Poor
Regional stability	Poor

Muslims in Afghanistan

% of population	99
Sunni (% of Muslim)	80
Shi'a (% of Muslim)	19

COUNTRY PROFILE

1838–42 First Afghan War when Britain invaded Afghanistan to counter the threat to British India from expanding Russian influence in Afghanistan and was defeated by fierce resistance from Afghanistan's many ethnic tribes.

1878–80 Second Afghan War after Britain invaded Afghanistan again; parts of the country were absorbed into British India. Russia also seized parts of Afghani territory.

1907 Russia signed an agreement with Britain, promising no further interference in Afghanistan.

1919 Third Afghan War, after which Britain recognised Afghanistan's independence. Amanullah Khan, independence leader, proclaimed himself Emir.

1926 Amanullah Khan proclaimed himself King; he attempted to modernise society by introducing social reforms.

1929 Amanullah fled after civil unrest over his reforms; Mohammed Nadir Shah was proclaimed King. He reunited a fragmented Afghanistan and took steps to modernise the country, though less obtrusively than Amanullah.

1933 Nadir Shah was assassinated and his son, Zahir Shah, became King; his reign lasted 40 years.

1956 Afghanistan built a close relationship with the Soviet Union, gaining arms supplies and undertaking trade.

1964 A constitutional monarchy was introduced, which led to political polarisation and power struggles.

1965 The Communist People's Democratic Party of Afghanistan (PDPA) was formed.

1973 General Mohammed Daud deposed and exiled King Zahir Shah. Afghanistan was declared a republic.

1978 General Daud was assassinated in the Saur (April) Revolution, a coup by the pro-Communists, led by the PDPA's leader, Noor Taraki, who was declared president.

1979 The Soviet Union invaded Afghanistan after the nationalist foreign minister, Hafizullah Amin, deposed Taraki. Amin was executed and replaced by the pro-Soviet Babrak Karmal. Numerous Afghan factions formed the Mujahidin and started a guerrilla war against the Soviet occupation forces. Backed by the US, Pakistan, China, Iran and Saudi Arabia, the Mujahidin inflicted heavy losses on Soviet troops.

1985 The Mujahidin gathered in Pakistan, forming an alliance against Soviet forces. Half of the Afghan population was displaced by the war.

1986 Babrak Karmal was replaced by Najibullah Ahmadzai, the head of the Afghani secret police, as head of the Soviet-backed regime.

1988 Afghanistan, USSR, the US and Pakistan signed peace accords.

1989 The Soviet Union withdrew its last troops from Afghanistan. Civil war continued as the Mujahidin refused to co-operate with the Najibullah regime.

1991 The US and Russia agreed to end military aid to both sides.

1992 Afghanistan was declared an Islamic republic after the capture of Kabul by Mujahidin factions and Najibullah was forced to seek the UN's protection in Kabul. Rival militias vied for power.

1993 Burhanuddin Rabbani, an ethnic Tajik, was proclaimed president, and Gulbuddin Hekmatyar, who was strongly backed by the US during the Soviet occupation, was appointed prime minister.

1994 The Pashtun-dominated Islamic fundamentalist Taliban, formed in Kandahar, south Afghanistan, emerged as the major challenge to the Rabbani government.

1995 The Taliban swept through southern Afghanistan.

1996 The Taliban captured Kabul and quickly imposed a strict version of *sharia* (Islamic law). Former president Najibullah was summarily executed and President Rabbani fled to join the anti-Taliban alliance in the north.

1997 Only Pakistan and Saudi Arabia recognised the Taliban as legitimate rulers of Afghanistan. Hostilities increased in the north between the Taliban and the militias

of the United National Islamic Front for the Salvation of Afghanistan (UNIFSA) (also known as the Northern Alliance).
1998 The Taliban captured Mazar i Sharif, the last major city that had been outside Taliban control; around 6,000 civilians were massacred following the city's capture. The US launched cruise missiles at suspected bases of Osama bin Laden, accused of bombing US embassies in Africa.
1999 The UN introduced economic sanctions against Afghanistan for harbouring bin Laden.
2001 The Afghan resistance leader, Commander Massoud, was assassinated. The giant statues of Buddha in Bamyan were destroyed by the Taliban. The US and Britain launched air strikes against the Taliban and al Qaeda, following the Taliban's refusal to hand over bin Laden, also blamed for masterminding the 11 September 2001 attacks on the twin towers in New York. Opposition forces seized Mazar i Sharif, then Kabul and other key cities. Afghan groups agreed an interim government in UN-sponsored talks in Bonn, Germany. The Taliban gave up Kandahar, its last stronghold, at the end of the year and Pashtun royalist, Hamid Karzai was sworn in as head of a 30-member interim power-sharing government.
2002 The first contingent of foreign peacekeepers arrived. Hamid Karzai was elected interim president by the *Loya Jirga* (a grand council of tribal leaders). Former monarch, Zahir Shah, returned to Kabul, but made no claim to the throne. He had been in exile for 29 years before his return. After 23 years, the Asian Development Bank resumed lending to Afghanistan.
2003 The afghani was re-valued. Afghanistan introduced a law banning armed factions from politics. NATO forces took control of security in Kabul.
2004 A new constitution preceded presidential elections, won by Hamid Karzai with 55 per cent of the vote. President Karzai was sworn in as Afghanistan's first democratically elected leader. Afghanistan was guaranteed US$8.2bn in aid until 2007.
2005 Parliamentary elections were held where the turnout was 36 per cent in Kabul and 53 per cent across the country.
2006 Resurgence of Taliban activity and fighting with coalition forces in the south, culminating in the fiercely fought Operation Mountain Thrust. Responsibility for security in the south passed to NATO. The Paris Club of international creditors forgave the greater part of the country's external debt.
2007 Former King Zahir Shar died. A *jirga* began in Kabul to discuss means of combating the Taliban. Russia cut around US$10 billion from Afghanistan's outstanding debt, accrued during the Soviet Union's occupation 1979–89. The Asian Development Bank approved a loan of over US$170 million to complete the circular highway connecting Kabul and other major cities, in particular the section between Herat in the west and Mazar i Sharif in the north. The completed road bypasses the warring territory of the south and facilitates trade with neighbouring northern and western countries.
2008 A US estimate was that the government controlled only 30 per cent of the country, and the Taliban about 10 per cent; the rest of the country was under the control of tribal chiefs. The government deny its control was so limited, claiming the tribal chiefs supported central government and provided security in its stead.
2009 The US deployed a further 17,000 reinforcements, to 'meet urgent security needs', adding to the 36,000 military personnel already deployed. The UN reported that 2,118 civilians had been killed in 2008, an increase of 39 per cent on the 2007 figure. Taliban insurgents were blamed for 55 per cent of the deaths while NATO and Afghan forces were held responsible for 39 per cent. In a UK-Afghan military operation on Taliban strongholds in Helmand province, US$71 million in heroin and drug manufacturing chemicals were seized, as well as factories making improvised bombs. Japan agreed to pay the salary of around 80,000 police officers, as well as fund teacher training and the construction of schools and hospitals. The presidents of Afghanistan and Pakistan agreed to increase military co-operation against Islamic extremists operating from strongholds in their shared border areas. Following an election campaign that lacked credibility due to accusations of widespread fraudulent activities, presidential elections took place on 20 August. Hamid Karzai won 49.67 per cent of the vote and his closest rival Abdullah Abdullah 30.59 per cent. In his first speech, after taking office President Karzai vowed to fight corruption. President Obama committed a further 30,000 US troops to be sent to Afghanistan, bringing US military strength to 100,000. Other foreign troops, around 32,000 at the end of 2009, were likely to be increased by 5,000.
2010 NATO launched a major offensive against the Taliban in the southern province of Helmand. General David Petraeus took command of the 130,000 strong international forces. A vital transit agreement was signed with Pakistan, allowing access to sea routes and the Indian market. President Karzai's timetable for transfer of control of security to domestic forces by 2014 was agreed at an international conference.. In parliamentary elections, 2,584 candidates stood for 249 seats in the Wolesi Jirga; all elected candidates were non-partisan.
2011 In June, in a move that was hoped to encourage the Taliban to join the political process, the UN announced it was splitting a sanctions blacklist for the Taliban and al Qaeda into two separate lists. Later in June, 'preliminary' talks between the US and the Taliban in Afghanistan took place. President Obama announced on that 10,000 US troops would leave Afghanistan in 2011 and a further 23,000 would leave by mid-2012. The remaining 70,000 are due to be withdrawn by 2014. In July France's President Sarkozy announced that 1,000 French troops would be withdrawn by the end of 2012. The half-brother of President Karzai was shot dead by the Taliban, in his home in Kandahar on 12 July. On 17 July Jan Mohammad Khan, an important tribal leader and aide to President Karzai, was killed in his home in Kabul. Bamiyan was the first province to be given responsibility for its own security on 18 July, when Nato handed over control to Afghan troops. 200 French troops that were part of a 4,000 military contingent stationed in the district of Surobi and the neighbouring Kapisa Province, were withdrawn from active service in the NATO mission in Afghanistan on 20 October. A further 200 were scheduled to be withdrawn by the end of December.
2012 The US defence secretary announced on 1 February that the US seeks to wind down combat operations in 2013. A declaration on 4 March by the religious advisory body, the *Ulema* (scholarly) Council, covered several aspects of the rights and role of women in Afghan society. It reiterated many of the edicts concerning women espoused by the Taliban, including the requirement to adopt the hijab, avoidance of men in social situations, including education, retail and commerce; acknowledging that women are secondary to men; respecting polygamy and confirming that women must at all times be accompanied by an acceptable male outside the home. Controversially, President Karzai welcomed the document while human rights and women's rights organisations said it was worrying and was a reversal of the progress of women's rights gained since 2001. The timing of the document and President Karzai's response were considered a part of the negotiations being undertaken with the Taliban. On 8 July, at a donor conference in Tokyo, US$16 billion (2012–16) was pledged in civilian aid and to safeguard Afghanistan's future. On 10 July, 200 French NATO troops began a

phased withdrawal. On 10 September, the US transferred its responsibility for the Bagram prison (and the more than 3,000 Taliban fighters) to Afghan authorities, although the US kept control of foreign prisoners. On 30 October, the date of the next presidential election was set for 5 April 2014. On 27 November, an independent audit report into the collapse of Kabul Bank stated that a fraud of almost US$900 million of corrupt loans benefitted just 19 people and companies, all part of the political elite. Foreign donors were forced to bail out the bank at a time of Afghanistan's fragile economy.

2013 In a ceremony attended by President Hamid Karzai and Nato Secretary General Anders Fogh Rasmussen the International Security Assistance Force (Isaf) forces handed over control of the last 95 districts to the Afghan National Army on 18 June. On the same day it was announced that talks between the US and the Taliban would take place in Doha, Qatar, on 20 June. Within hours, four US soldiers were killed in Bagram airbase by a rocket attack; a spokesman for the Taliban, Zabihullah Mujahid, said the rockets had been launched by militants. The attack emphasised the difficulties the talks will encounter with a far from unified group of insurgents. Although a condition of the talks is for the Taliban to renounce violence, there will not be a ceasefire. On 17 July President Karzai signed into law the composition and rules for the 2014 election commission, and a separate commission to adjudicate complaints about voter fraud and other irregularities. Mullah Omar, a Taliban leader who has been in hiding since 2001 and has a US$10 million bounty on his head, was reported by the BBC on 7 August saying that his fighters will not seek to monopolise power when foreign troops withdraw from Afghanistan in 2014. He said that the Taliban will try to reach an understanding with the Afghan people for 'an inclusive government based on Islamic principles'. Mullah Omar also reiterated his disdain for the elections, scheduled for next year, saying the poll ... '*de facto*, takes place in Washington... participation in such elections is only a waste of time, nothing more'. President Karzai visited Pakistan on 26/27 August for talks with President Sharif on restarting the peace process, including releasing senior Taliban members held in Pakistan jails. He called on Pakistan 'to facilitate peace talks' by providing opportunities for talks between the Afghan High Peace Council and the militants. The US consulate in Herat was attacked on 13 September. Herat is an important trading city in the west, close to the border with Iran. It has by and large escaped the violence of the south and east. In a move supported by the Afghan government Mullah Abdul Ghani Baradar, co-founder of the Afghan Taliban, was released from prison by Pakistan on 21 September. Afghanistan qualified for the cricket World Cup for the first time by beating Kenya in a qualifying round in Sharjah on 4 October. Latif Mehsud, a Pakistan Taliban leader and said to be a 'terrorist leader' wanted by the Americans for the Times Square bombing in 2010, was captured on the border with Pakistan in early October.

2014 The first round of the presidential election was held on 5 April between the eight remaining contestants. The result put Abdullah Abdullah (National Coalition of Afghanistan) ahead with 2,972,141 (45 per cent), followed by Ashraf Ghani Ahmadzai (Independent) with 2,084,547 (31.56 per cent). The result of the second round (held on 14 June) was published on 7 July, showing a turnaround to 4,485,888 votes in favour of Ashraf Ghani (56.44 per cent) and 3,461,639 votes for Abdullah Abdullah. Both parties alledged fraud and demanded a recount. An agreement on an audit of the votes was reached on 12 July, to start within 24 hours. President Karzai agreed to delay the inauguration of his successor until after the audit. A unity deal whereby Mr Ghani shares power with runner-up Abdullah Abdullah who becomes chief executive was finally reached. Mr Ghani was sworn in as President on 29 September.

2015 President Ashraf Ghani unveiled his unity cabinet on 12 January, three months after he was sworn in. However, parliament has to approve the ministers and a number of nominees, including Ghulam Jilani Popal (finance) and Yaqub Haidari (agriculture), either withdrew for various reasons, or were rejected. On 21 April 16 ministers were sworn in, making a total of 24 (out of 25, the defence minister still has to be annouced) finally giving Afghanistan a fully-fledged government. Most of the ministers are new to politics and are young, educated and come from professional backgrounds. There are four women in the cabinet for the first time, at the ministries of higher education, labour, women's affairs and counter-narcotics. With elections originally scheduled for 2015 and postponed, and after political squabbling, on 19 June the president issued a decree extending parliament's mandate until the elections could be held. On 30 July the Taliban confimed that their leader Mullah Omar was dead, although they did not report how or when he had died. On the same day Mullah Akhtar Mansoor was elected to succeed him. A number of attacks by the Taliban took place after the announcment, including in Kabul when over 50 people died in several attacks on the police, army and US special forces on Friday 7 August, and 29 in Kunduz on 9 August. The northern city of Kunduz was briefly taken and held by the Taliban at the end of September. The Afghan army retook the city.

Political structure

Constitution

On 4 January 2004, Afghanistan ratified a new constitution, establishing an Islamic republic, in which the president rules with a national assembly; women are recognised as equal citizens and have one-fifth of the lower house seats.

Independence date

19 August 1919

Form of state

Islamic republic

The executive

The president is the Head of State, leading a cabinet with two vice presidents and 25 ministers. The president possesses wide powers over military and legislative affairs.

National legislature

The National Assembly has two chambers. The Wolesi Jirga (House of the People) (lower) has 249 directly elected members for five-year terms with the number proportional to the populations of the provinces. Under the constitution, the Kuchi (nomad) community is allocated 10 seats; female candidates are also guaranteed seats. According to the constitution, the chamber may set up commissions to inquire into government actions, endorse and enforce legislation not approved by the president (providing it has a two-thirds majority), question ministers, decide on government development programmes and the budget and approve or reject government sponsored appointments. The Wolesi Jirga ratifies laws and approves the actions of the president.

The Meshrano Jirga (House of Elders) (upper house) has 102 members who are either indirectly elected or appointed representatives. Members must be aged over 35 years. One-third (34) are elected by district councils (one per district council) for three-year terms, one-third (34) by provincial councils (one per province) for four-year terms, and one-third (34) are nominated by the president for five-year terms.

Legal system

The 2004 constitution guarantees an independent judiciary, consisting of a Stera Mahkama (supreme court), high courts and appeal courts.

The president appoints the members of the supreme court, with the approval of the Wolesi Jirga.

Last elections
18 September 2010 (parliamentary); 6 April and 14 June 2014 (presidential first and second rounds)
Results: Presidential (2014): first round: Abdullah Abdullah (National Coalition of Afghanistan) 2,972,141 (45 per cent), Ashraf Ghani Ahmadzai (Independent) 2,084,547 (31.56 per cent), Zalmai Rassoul (Independent) 750,997 (11.37 per cent), Abdul Rasul Sayyaf (Islamic Dawa) 465,207 (7.04 per cent), Qutbuddin Hilal (Independent) 181,827 (2.75 per cent), Gul Agha Sherzai (Independent) 103,636 (1.57 per cent), Mohammad Daud Sultanzoy (Independent) 30,685 (0.45 per cent), Hedayat Amin Arsala (Independent) 15,506 (0.23 per cent).
Second round: Ashraf Ghani 4,485,888 (56.44 per cent), Abdullah Abdullah 3,461,639 (43.56 per cent). The result was disputed by both sides and an audit was agreed on 12 July, to be carried out immediately. However, Abdullah explicitly rejected the audit, claiming that it did not appropriately explain away the extra million votes Ghani received in the second round. By 19 September 2014 the opponents had agreed to a power sharing deal in which Ghani remains president, but Abdullah is given an important role as governmental chief executive.
Parliamentary: all 249 elected candidates elected were non-partisan.
Next elections
2019 (presidential); 2015 (parliamentary)

Political parties

Ruling party
Members of the national assembly are elected as independent candidates
Main opposition party
Jami'at e Islami (Islamic Society of Afghanistan) leads a loose alliance. Given the new democratic system, parties in Afghanistan are constantly influx and many leading politicians plan to form new parties in the coming years. Thus, it is difficult to definitively say who the opposition is at any one time.
31.28 million 2014* (some 1 million Afghanis are still in exile in Pakistan and Iran)

Population

The population is concentrated in the river basins and around the major cities. The central highlands and the arid south-western plateau are sparsely populated.
Afghanistan has almost 500,000 disabled people, many who have lost limbs as a result of mine explosions. In 2012, the UNHCR were concerned for 1.3 million Afghans, comprising asylum-seekers, refugees residing abroad, returning refugees and the estimated 400,000 internally displaced persons.

Last census: June 1979: 13,051,358 (excluding nomad population)
Population density: 40 inhabitants per square km (2010); 23 per cent urban population (Unicef)
Annual growth rate: 4.4 per cent, 1990–2010 (Unicef).
Internally Displaced Persons (IDP)
180,000–300,000 (UNHCR 2004)
Ethnic make-up
Pashtun (Pathan) (38 per cent), Tajik (25 per cent), Hazara (19 per cent), Uzbek (6 per cent), minority groups include Aimaks, Turkmen, Baluch and others (12 per cent).
The Pashtuns largely reside in south-eastern Afghanistan. Tajiks, Hazaras and Uzbeks are the main communities in northern and central Afghanistan.
Religions
Almost the entire population is Muslim (84 per cent Sunni Muslim, 15 per cent Shi'ite); Hindu, Sikh and Jewish minorities.

Education

The UN Educational, Scientific and Cultural Organisation (Unesco) assists the Afghan government in the education sector's reconstruction by promoting universal primary education, especially for girls, and the expansion of primary schooling with access to secondary education.
Unesco has extended its support for a computer centre at Kabul University, including Internet access for the young. It also funds the printing of text-books for all levels of education.
In January 2011 the minister of education, Farooq Wardak, was reported in the UK's *Times Educational Supplement* that a 'cultural change' meant the Taliban were 'no more opposing girls' education'.

Health

WHO continues to support the IDPs by providing essential medical supplies to clinics within the camps. There is provision for night health services and nutrition centres for malnourished children. Harsh winters in the region cause acute respiratory infections, while hot dry summers lead to diarrhoeal diseases.
Despite on-going security problems, UN relief agencies and the WHO provide emergency medical supplies and assistance to local hospitals.
In 2006, a large outbreak of polio in the volatile southern regions followed a drop in overall numbers of cases in previous years. The UN undertook immunisation of around 1.3 million children in the southern provinces of Kandahar and Helmand in 2007. The week-long campaign took place within the war zones while 10,000 health workers were given safe passage to undertake the operation. Despite this, Afghanistan in 2012 was one of only three remaining countries (with Pakistan and Nigeria) where polio is endemic.
Life expectancy: 48 years, 2010 (Unicef 2012)
Fertility rate/Maternal mortality rate: 6.3 births per woman, 2010 (Unicef)
Child (under 5 years) mortality rate (per 1,000): 99 per 1,000 live births (WHO 2012), 49 per cent of children aged under five were malnourished (World Bank).

Welfare

Many Afghans have fled the country due to war, drought and earthquakes. The UNHCR estimated that, at its peak, more than 3.7 million Afghans survive outside their homeland; between 1.1–1.5 million were internally displaced. Over 520,000 refugees returned in 2005, the largest group, of 453,000, came from camps in Pakistan. International agencies and the government have been working hard for their rehabilitation, as well as for the thousands who returned in previous years.
The WFP has been working with the Afghan government to rehabilitate irrigation systems and expand its activities to cover the reconstruction of schools, hospitals, roads and bridges.

Main cities

Kabul (capital, estimated population 3.0 million in 2012), Kandahar (368,099), Herat (308,203), Mazar-i-Sharif (267,147), Jalalabad (151,010), Kunduz (124,567), Balkh (87,052), Baglan (83,117).

Languages spoken

The languages spoken by Afghanistan's two largest ethnic groups are Dari (Afghan Persian) (50 per cent) and Pashtu (35 per cent). Turkic languages (primarily Uzbek and Turkmen) (11 per cent), 30 minor languages (primarily Baluchi and Pashai) (4 per cent). Farsi (Persian) is spoken by the Tajiks. Some speak a second language, including English, Russian, French or German.
The use of English began to grow after the arrival of NATO forces in 2005, as many jobs in government and non-governmental organisations (NGOs) required a level of use. By 2009 there were several hundred private schools teaching English to thousands of Afghan students.
Official language/s
Pashtu and Dari (named as official languages in the 2004 constitution)

Media

All material is subject to *Sharia* (Islamic law) and regulatory bodies are controlled by the government. However, since 2001 there has been a strong growth in broadcasting and print media, with five TV stations and over 300 newspapers published nationwide; in a country with a low literacy rate the radio is the principal medium for news and information.

Press

Print journalism does not match broadcast journalism for professionalism and research with opinions offered instead of investigation and hard facts. Self-censorship is widely practiced by older writers and violence towards journalists has curbed the focus necessary for news gathering. The market for newspapers and advertising revenue is so small that private newspapers must rely on political factions and individuals for sponsorship.

Dailies: State-owned publications, in Dari and Pashtu, include *Daily Anis Eslah*, *Arman-e Melli* and *Eslah*. English dailies include *Kabul Times*. Private newspapers in Dari and Pashtu include *Hewad*, *Eradeh*, *Shari'at*, *Daily Afghanistan* (www.dailyafghanistan.com), *Tolafghan* (www.tolafghan.com) and *Payam e Mojahed* (www.payamemojahed.com). English private dailies include *Daily Outlook Afghanistan* (www.outlookafghanistan.net) and *Daily Cheragh* (www.cheraghdaily.af).

Weeklies: In Dari and Pashtu, *Aina-e-Zan* (Women's Mirror). In English, *Kabul Weekly* is an independent newspaper funded by the UN. *Omaid Weekly* is published in the US and is one of the most widely read Afghani publications in the world.

Broadcasting

National Radio and Television Afghanistan (NRTA) is under the ministry of information and culture.

Radio: There are many radio stations broadcasting regionally. The government-owned Radio Afghanistan is national; it has competition from several foreign radio broadcasting services. Commercial radio stations including the popular Arman FM (www.arman.fm) with programmes in local languages and English, Radio Killid (www.thekillidgroup.com) and Rana FM (www.ranafm.org).

Television: The popularity of television is growing and some stations are providing local programming. The National Television Afghanistan (NTA) is government run; other national, free-to-air private stations include Tolo TV (www.tolo.tv) which shows foreign and domestic programmes, Ariana TV (www.arianatelevision.com) with news in Pashtu, Dari and English and Ayna TV is based in the northern provinces and broadcasts in four local languages.

Television is also provided by foreign entities including the US-based satellite networks Noor TV (www.noor-tv.com) and Payame Afghan TV (www.payameafghantv.com). Khorasan TV, is a local satellite network with Shamshad and Afghan TV (http://afghanistantv.org).

National news agency: BNA (Bakhtar News Agency)

Other news agencies: Pajhwok Afghan News: www.pajhwok.com
Afghan Islamic Press: www.afghanislamicpress.com

Economy

The economy has been in a state of renewal since 2001, after the fall of the authoritarian Taliban regime. Afghanistan has a strong agricultural sector, accounting for around 23.6 per cent of GDP (2014) (excluding the opium trade), although its level of productivity has been blighted by civil conflict, exploitation and under investment since the 1980s, leaving a legacy of degraded natural resources (particularly in forests and pastures) and fragmented rural institutions. Consequently, the level of productivity is low with inefficient production systems and poor management so that Afghanistan relies on international food aid to feed its population. It is estimated that introducing modern technologies would increase capacity by 7.5 million hectares of cultivated land, and with proper irrigation 20 per cent could be double-cropped.

Natural resources include minerals and hydrocarbons. Industrial manufacturing, which accounted for around 21.8 per cent of GDP in 2014, is mostly small-scale production of locally required products such as soap, furniture, textiles and shoes.

The informal economy is dominated by the illegal production and trade in opium, which creates an obstruction to government efforts to raise legitimate revenue through taxation. According the UN Opium Survey (published in November 2012), 3,700 tonnes of (wet) opium was produced in 2012 and in 2013 there was a 36 per cent rise in opium production. In 2014 production of opium had risen to 6,400 tonnes. Afghanistan is by far the world's largest opium producer, being responsible for around 90 per cent of the world's supply, and the US has reportedly spent in excess of US$7.6 billion trying to suppress the opium trade since ousting the Taliban government in 2001. The industry is a threat not just because of the substance itself but because much of the revenue is used to fund extremist militant groups. Trying to crack down on the industry can be damaging, however, as an estimated 411,000 people rely on the crop for employment and, although figures cannot be certain, the industry accounts for roughly 4 per cent of the nations GDP.

With increased spending by coalition forces, and international aid flowing into the country, Afghanistan's GDP growth was at an all-time high of 20.9 per cent in 2009, at a time of greatest economic recession worldwide. However in 2010, as domestic security deteriorated and world trade slowed, GDP growth fell back to 8.4 per cent and further to an estimated 5.7 per cent in 2011. Growth rocketed to 12 per cent in 2012 but this boom was short lived as GDP growth fell to 3.6 per cent in 2013 and further to 3.2 in 2014.

Inflation fell from a high of 26.8 per cent in 2008 (with a peak of 43 per cent in May 2008) to -12.2 per cent in 2009 as food prices fell and monetary policies introduced by government acted as deflationary pressures, and fell to 7.4 per cent in 2013 and further to 4 per cent in 2014.

Per capita income is low and despite having risen steadily from US$585 in 2011 to US$681 in 2012, it dipped slightly to US$665 in 2013 which was maintained at US$666 in 2014.

Corruption has been highlighted as one of Afghanistan's most insidious problems. The Corruptions Perceptions Index 2014 ranked Afghanistan as 172 out of 175 (1 being the least corrupt country), showing that corruption was rampant and entrenched in all areas of Afghan life. At the same time international donors voiced their criticism that anti-corruption measures were not producing tangible results and that if economic support was to be channelled through the government's budget, then measures for a strengthened financial system that cuts corruption and poor governance were required.

External trade

Much of the government's strategy for international trade is predicated on a future with secure, nationwide peace. It sees the future of Afghanistan as a hub for regional trade, with land links to surrounding countries.

The ministry of commerce and industry has undertaken negotiations in regional economic initiatives, which include the Economic Co-operation Organisation (ECO) and bilateral negotiations with neighbouring countries including Iran, India, Pakistan, Tajikistan and Uzbekistan. Plans include participation in the South Asia Free Trade Area (Safta) and the Central Asian Regional Economic Co-operation (Carec) programme. Afghanistan is also an observer member of the World Trade Organisation (WTO), and in mid-2015 was on track to become a full member.

A suggested oil pipeline through Afghanistan to Pakistan would link Central Asia with Pakistan; the project is due to be completed in 2017.

Imports
Afghanistan mainly imports capital goods including construction items needed to repair its neglected infrastructure, foodstuffs, textiles and petroleum products.
Main sources: Iran (19.4 per cent of total in 2014), Pakistan (17.3 per cent), China (13.5 per cent).

Exports
Opium, Afghanistan's largest, albeit illegal, export is primarily transported north through the Central Asian republics and on to Europe. Measures by foreign governments have been introduced in an attempt to eradicate the crop. Around 10 per cent of Afghan families rely on its production and as opium represents a large proportion of the country's exports this could lead to a serious drop in income if the campaign is successful.
Principal non-opium exports include hand-woven carpets, fruits and nuts, small scale industrial products, pelts and hides and semi-precious and precious stones. Afghanistan has been the world's largest exporter of raisins and a major producer of grapes, melons and other fruit.
Main destinations: Pakistan (33.0 per cent of total in 2014), India (28.0 per cent), Iran (5.8 per cent).

Agriculture
Farming
The population is returning to the countryside and some rural areas have been transformed by the return of Afghan refugees from Pakistan and Iran. However, the level of productivity is low with inefficient production systems and poor management so that Afghanistan relies on international food aid to feed its population. A severe drought in 2009 not only reduced harvests but also increased soil erosion. It is estimated that introducing modern technologies would increase capacity by 7.5 million hectares of cultivated land, and with proper irrigation 20 per cent could be double-cropped.
Twelve per cent of the total area is cultivated, another 10 per cent is pasture land and a further 5–6 per cent considered by some sources to have agricultural potential.
Most cultivated land is situated in river valleys or plains, which are often fertile; an estimated two-thirds of cultivated land is irrigated. Food output is frequently below what is required to feed the population. In total more than 12,000 out of 22,000 farming villages were abandoned or destroyed during the fighting of the 1990s.
Apart from the opium poppy, the main crops are wheat, fruit and vegetables, maize, rice, barley, cotton, sugar beet, sugar cane, oil seeds.
The livestock herd needs rebuilding. Livestock includes sheep, cattle, goats and poultry, with donkeys, horses, camels, mules and buffaloes kept as draught animals. Sheep provide a major source of protein and animal fat. Some 70 per cent of wool production, along with hides from karakul sheep, is exported.
After the fall of the Taliban, the farmers started to sow poppies again. In 2002, President Karzai banned opium poppy cultivation and trafficking, and offered farmers US$350 for each 0.2 hectare (ha) to be replanted with alternative crops. This was only a fraction of what the farmers could earn from the poppy crop. Around 6,250 tonnes of (wet) opium was produced in 2009, which was a fall of 1,190 tonnes from the high of 7,440 tonnes in 2007/08 – although the 2009 drought may have had more of an adverse effect on harvests than counter-narcotic measures. In 2010 the opium crop was devastated by disease, prices from traffickers rose sharply and as a result in 2011 opium production rose by 61 per cent. Afghanistan accounts for around 90 per cent of the world's opium trade. The UN reported that opium cultivation had reached a record level in 2012, with more than 200,000 hectares planted with the poppy for the first time. According the UN Opium Survey, 3,700 tonnes of (wet) opium was produced in 2012 and in 2013 there was a 36 per cent rise in opium production. In 2014 production of opium had risen to 6,400 tonnes. Afghanistan is by far the world's largest opium producer, being responsible for around 90 per cent of the world's supply, and the US has reportedly spent in excess of US$7.6 billion trying to suppress the opium trade since ousting the Taliban government in 2001. The industry is a threat not just because of the substance it self but because much of the revenue is used to fund extremist militant groups.
Trying to crack down on the industry can be damaging, however, as an estimated 411,000 people rely on the crop for employment and, although figures cannot be certain, the industry accounts for roughly 4 per cent of the nations GDP.

Forestry
Wooded land is limited to the eastern Hindu Kush region and along the Pakistani border. Many forests in these areas have been severely reduced due to trees being cut down and the wood smuggled out to surrounding countries.

Industry and manufacturing
Handmade Afghan carpets are identified as not only significant cultural products of the country, but also an important component of export trade. Developing the carpet industry is 'crucial' according to the minister of trade and industry in February 2012. Annual production of Afghan carpets is around two million square metres, of which 90 per cent are exported through neighbouring countries. As one of Afghanistan's main exports it is estimated that millions of people are directly and indirectly involved in the production of carpets, although carpet weavers and washers are often on low wages. The industry called for more government investment in workshops, factories and showrooms.

Tourism
The continuing instability in the country hinders the development of a tourist sector in Afghanistan, although given the right conditions there is considerable potential. The country has a wealth of cultural, heritage and natural sites which have been out-of-bounds for much of the war. But, despite the on-going fighting with the Taliban and Al Qaeda, Afghans still welcome visitors and there are escorted tours, for hardy travellers available either solely in Afghanistan or as part of a journey along the Silk Road. Restrictions on travel in the south apply and such destinations should be avoided. A number of luxury hotels are available in Kabul that offer tight security, nevertheless terrorists target foreigners and all visitors should adhere to instructions given by their respective diplomatic representatives.

Environment
In April 2009, the first national park, Band e Amir, featuring deep blue lakes and natural dams of travertine, was established near Bamyan Valley, the site of the giant, 1500-year old, Buddha statues destroyed by the Taliban in 2001.

Mining
Natural resources include copper, chromite, lead, zinc, iron, salt, lapis lazuli, emeralds, talc and barium sulphate.
Long-term mineral development projects include copper mining and smelting at Ainak and high-grade iron ore mining at Hajigak in northern Afghanistan.
A Chinese-owned mining company won a tender in November 2007 to develop one of the world's largest copper mines sited in Logar Province. It is estimated that the site has 13 million tonnes of copper. Australia, Canada, China and Russia all contested the tender, ultimately won by China Metallurgical Group with an investment of US$3 billion, making it the largest foreign investment and private business venture ever to have been undertaken in Afghanistan's history. However, developments with this project have been slow due security problems in the Logar province and corruption among Afghani officials.

Hydrocarbons
Proven hydrocarbon reserves were in excess of 1.5 billion barrels of oil and 49.55 billion cubic metres (cum) of natural gas in 2014, located in 29 fields in the north-western region of the country. Since then very little of these resources have been exploited and further exploration, using modern technologies, has been curtailed due to the geopolitical situation and the series of conflicts in Afghanistan. Potentially oil producing sedimentary sections have been located in the south of the country.

Little production of oil takes place in Afghanistan, however in 2014 the Afghani government was in the process of taking bids from foreign companies to start producing oil.

There are small deposits of coal. Production was just 724 tonnes in 2013.

Energy
The energy sector was badly damaged during the years of upheaval. Afghanistan has installed capacity of 490MW, generated by hydropower, of which only 271MW are available. Some border areas receive supplies from neighbouring countries. Electricity supply is only available to around 33 per cent of the population and interruptions and blackouts are frequent.

Banking and insurance
Afghanistan has six banks (four of which have almost no assets) and two commercial banks – Pashtani and Milli – with assets. In 2003, two banking laws were passed: the Central Banking Law and the Commercial Banking Law. The first laid the groundwork for the Central Bank to focus on monetary policy, pricing stability and oversight of the commercial markets; the second allowed for private ownership of commercial banks. Standard Chartered (UK), Microfinance Bank of Afghanistan and National Bank of Pakistan opened in 2004.

An International Monetary Fund (IMF) report in February 2011 into the operations of Kabul Bank, Afghanistan's largest private bank, recommended that it be put into receivership, which would help the government in its plan to stabilise financial services in the country. The IMF identified problems of corruption, bad loans and mismanagement that had resulted in hundreds of million of US dollars being lost. The IMF also urged the government to announce plans to deal with the scandal that had become public in 2010, to protect the rest of the banking system and that legal action should be taken against those responsible for the fraud. Abdul Qadeer Fitrat, central bank governor, resigned on 27 June saying he felt his life was in danger for investigating fraud at Kabul Bank. He said that he was being hindered in his investigations by the government, which in turn accused him of treason. On 27 November 2012, an independent audit report into the collapse of Kabul Bank stated that a fraud of almost US$900 million of corrupt loans benefitted just 19 people and companies, all part of the political elite. Foreign donors were forced to bail out the bank at a time of Afghanistan's fragile economy.

Central bank
Da Afghanistan Bank

Main financial centre
Kabul

Time
GMT plus 4.5 hours

Geography
Afghanistan is a landlocked country in south-western Asia. Its neighbours are Turkmenistan, Uzbekistan and Tajikistan to the north, Iran to the west, and Pakistan to the east and south. It also has a 76km border with the People's Republic of China to the north-east. The Hindu Kush mountains are in the north-east of the country.

There are three geographic areas: the central highlands (comprising over 60 per cent of the land), the arid southern region (25 per cent of the land) and the fertile northern plains.

Hemisphere
Northern

Climate
The climate is dry with large variations between day and night temperatures as well as swift seasonal changes. Maximum summer temperatures on the plains can reach 46 degrees Celsius (C), while the lowest winter temperatures, in the mountains, reach minus 26 degrees C; Kabul (at altitude 1,800 metres) has an average 16 to 33 degrees C in summer (July–August) and minus 8 to 2 degrees C in winter.

The rainy season is from October–April, although rainfall is very irregular; Kabul averages 335mm per annum.

Entry requirements
Passports
Required by all.

Visa
Required by all; application forms can be obtained via: www.embassyofafghanistan.org/main/consulate/visa.cfm or local embassies.

Business visas require a letter of introduction stating the purpose of visit and sponsorship information. A visa financial guarantee must be included with the application fee. For a multiply entry visa, a letter of introduction signed by the president of the organisation, must accompany the documentation.

Currency advice/regulations
Import and export of local currency is limited to Af500. Import of foreign currency is unlimited, although export of foreign currency is limited to the amount declared on arrival.

US dollars circulate widely. Travellers cheques are not readily accepted.

Customs
Alcohol is permitted for personal consumption.

All antiquities, carpets, furs and photography films require an export permit.

Prohibited imports
Illegal drugs, pornography; pork products in any form.

Cameras require an import permit.

Health (for visitors)
Mandatory precautions
Vaccination certificate for yellow fever if travelling from an infected areas.

Advisable precautions
Hepatitis A, anti-malarial precautions, polio, tetanus, typhoid. Diphtheria, hepatitis B, TB immunisations are recommended in some circumstances – seek further advice. Water precautions are necessary. There is a risk of rabies.

Emergency medical care is limited and visitors should ensure they have medical insurance that includes emergency evacuation. Hospitals and doctors require immediate cash payment before commencing treatment. The German Medical Diagnostic Center (www.medical-kabul.com), operates in Kabul, offering treatment that includes medical, radiological and pharmacy services. It does not offer emergency, obstetric or dental treatment.

Public hospitals are not up to Western standards and should be avoided. There are a limited number of private hospitals and some international aid groups operate medical facilities in cities and villages. Visitors should travel with all their necessary medications.

Hotels
Accommodation tends to be scarce and spartan. There are only a few international hotels in Kabul, including the Intercontinental Hotel, Bagh-I-Balla, Kabul and the Serena Hotel, Froshgah Street, Kabul.

Credit cards
Only Visa branded credit and debit cards are accepted at very limited outlets.

Public holidays (national)
Afghanistan uses the Persian calendar (although it used the Islamic calendar between 1999 and 2002). The Persian calendar has 12 months which differ from the Gregorian calendar: there are 31 days in each of the first six months of the Persian calendar, 30 days in each of the

next five months and 29 days in the last month, except in leap years when it has 30 days.
Persian year 1395: 20 March 2016 to 20 March 2017.
Dates of feasts vary according to the sighting of the new moon, so cannot be forecast exactly.

Fixed dates

21 Mar (Naw Roz/Persian New Year), 28 Apr (Islamic Revolution Day), 19 Aug (National Day).

Variable dates

Eid al Adha (three days), Ashura, Birth of the Prophet, First day of Ramadan, Eid al Fitr (three days).
Muslim holidays that occur on a Friday may be observed on Saturday.

Working hours

The weekend is Friday.

Banking

Sat–Wed: 0800–1200, 1300–1630; Thu: 0800–1330.

Business

Sat–Wed: 0800–1200, 1300–1630; Thu: 0800–1330.

Government

Sat–Thu: 0800–1600.

Shops

Commercial shops keep long but varying hours, usually Sat–Thu: 0700–2300.

Telecommunications

Mobile/cell phones

GSM 900/1800 services available in main cities only.

Electricity supply

220 volts AC, 60 cycle electrical system, using European round, two-prong plugs. Supplies may be seriously affected and power cuts frequent.

Weights and measures

Metric system (local units are also in use).

Social customs/useful tips

It is customary to shake hands on meeting and taking leave. Among men, embracing is a traditional form of greeting. Islamic conventions apply. When sitting cross-legged on sofas or cushions, soles of feet must not be shown.
Business meetings are usually conducted in English or Dari. Green or black tea, nuts and raisins are served. The form of greeting is *Salaam Aleykum* (peace be with you), followed by a firm handshake and placing the right hand over the heart. Several minutes are spent engaging in pleasantries about each other's countries. It is essential to build trust and to be patient.
Women should dress modestly in long skirts or trousers and avoid revealing tops and dresses.

Security

Foreign nationals are advised not to visit Afghanistan unless absolutely necessary. All visitors should register their presence with their diplomatic representative and keep up-to-date with local information on threat levels. Travel within the country should be kept to a minimum to lessen the risk of the threats posed by armed criminals and terrorists and between rival tribal armies.
Kidnapping, which is widespread, is the most serious threat to any visitor; seeking professional advice for security measures may be necessary.
Suicide-bombings have become more common and visitors must observe a high level of vigilance.
There is widespread danger from mines and unexploded ordinance throughout the country.
All street demonstrations and large gatherings should be avoided.

Getting there

The current security situation means that flights may be cancelled and roads closed at any time. It is advisable to check before travelling. The information that follows may also change.

Air

National airline: Ariana Afghan Airlines
International airport/s: Kabul airport (KBL), 16km from Kabul; facilites include a bank, bar and restaurant.
Airport tax: Departure tax: Af200

Surface

Road: There are links to Iran and Pakistan via the Asia Highway and to the CIS via road and rail. Hostilities have periodically closed the Pakistan route; check before travelling.
In August 2007, a road bridge spanning the River Pyanj in northern Afghanistan opened, linking Tajikistan and Afghanistan. The bridge, costing US$37m, was paid for by the US.
The Regional Road Corridor Improvement Project, estimated at US$18 billion, to improve Central Asian roads, airports, railway lines and seaports and provide a vital transit route between Europe and Asia was agreed on 3 November 2007. Six new transit corridors, between Afghanistan, Azerbaijan, China, Kazakhstan, Kyrgyzstan, Mongolia, Tajikistan and Uzbekistan, of mainly roads and rail links, will be constructed, or existing resources upgraded, by 2013. Half the costs with be provided by the Asian Development Bank and other multilateral organisations and the other half by participating countries.
Rail: Links exist between Kabul and the CIS.

Getting about

The current security situation means that flights may be cancelled and roads closed at any time. It is advisable to check before travelling. The information that follows may also change.

National transport

Air: Ariana Afghan Airlines flies a limited service to Herat and Mazar-e-sharif.
Road: Main centres are linked by paved roads but secondary roads vary in condition and by season. There are approximately 22,000km of roads.
Buses: Bus service are unreliable and dangerous for internal travel.
Rail: On 25 May 2010 a 75-kilometer stretch of railway line connecting Mazar-e-Sharif to the northern border with Uzbekistan was inaugurated; it is scheduled for completion by the end of 2010 and will connect to Uzbekistan's rail network and allow the easier transport of exports to regional markets in Europe and Asia.
Water: There are 1,200km of navigable inland waterways, including the Amu Darya River.

City transport

Taxis: Taxis are available from Kabul airport to the city centre. Tipping is not usual. Fares are negotiable and can be high for foreigners.
Buses, trams & metro: A limited number of buses are operating.

Car hire

International driving licences are required for those hire cars available.

BUSINESS DIRECTORY

The addresses listed below are a selection only. While World of Information makes every endeavour to check these addresses, we cannot guarantee that changes have not been made, especially to telephone numbers and area codes. We would welcome any corrections.

Telephone area codes

The international dialling code (IDD) for Afghanistan is + 93, followed by the area code and subscriber's number. Landline telephones are still unreliable. Some of the numbers below are mobile/cell numbers.

Herat	40	Kandahar	30
Jalalabad	60	Marez-E-Sherif	50
Kabul	20	Mobil phones	70

Chambers of Commerce

Afghan Chamber of Commerce and Industry, Mohammed Jan Khan Watt, Kabul (tel/fax: 290-196).

Banking

Afghanistan International Bank, House no 1608 Behind Amani High School, Wazir Akhbar Khan, Kabul (tel: 792 03158; fax: 202 103567).

Agricultural Development Bank, Jaddeh-Maiwand, Kabul.

Export Promotion Bank, Jaddah-Temorshahi, Kabul.

First Micro-finance Bank of Afghanistan, Street West of Park Shahr-i-Naw, Charahi Ansari, Kabul (tel: 0790 95705).

Industrial Promotion Bank, Shahr-i-naw, Kabul.

Mortgage and Construction Bank, Shahri-i-naw, Kabul.

National Bank of Pakistan, House No 2, Street No 10, Wazir Akbar Khan, Kabul (tel: 20-230 1660; fax: 20-230 1659).

Pashtany Tejaraty Bank, Mohmmad Jan Khan Watt, Kabul.

Standard Chartered Bank, P.O. Box 16019, House No. 10, Street No. 10 B, Wazir Akhbar Khan, Kabul (tel: 790 88888, 790 20833).

Central bank

Da Afghanistan Bank, Ibni Sina Watt, Kabul (tel: 240-7579).

Travel information

Ariana Afghan Airlines, PO Box 76, Ansari Watt, Kabul (tel: +873-762-523-844; fax: +873-762-523-846; internet: flyariana.com).

Kabul Airport, PO Box 76, Anseri Watt, Kabul.

Ministries

Ministry of Communications (internet: www.af-com-ministry.org).

Ministry of Finance (internet: www.mof.gov.af).

Ministry of Foreign Affairs: Malak Azghar Road, Kabul (tel: 210 0366; e-mail: contact@mfa.gov.af).

Ministry of Information and Culture, Mohammad Jan Khan Watt, beside Spinzar Hotel, Kabul (internet: www.moic.gov.af)

Ministry of Rural Rehabilitation and Development (internet: www.mrrd.gov.af).

Ministry of Agriculture, Irrigation and Livestock, Darulman, Kabul (internet: www.agriculture.gov.af).

Other useful addresses

Afghan Islamic Press, House 208, Qafila Road, Tahkal Payan, Peshawar, Pakistan (tel: (+92- 91) 570-1100; fax: (+92- 91) 570-3355; e-mail: aip@pes.comsats.net.pk).

Afghanistan Embassy (USA), 2341 Wyoming Avenue, NW, Washington DC 20008 (tel: (+1-202) 234-3770; fax: (+1-202) 328-3516; e-mail: info@embassyofafghanistan.org; internet: www.embassyofafghanistan.org)

Afghanistan Investment Support Agency, Opposite Ministry of Foreign Affairs, Kabul (tel/fax: 210-3404; internet: www.aisa.org.af).

Afghanistan Wireless Communication Corporation, Ministry of Communications Building, Mohammad Jan Khan Watt, Kabul (tel: 20-0000; fax: 20-0200; e-mail: info@afghan-wireless.com).

Arman FM (radio), PO Box 1045, Central Post Office, Kabul; House 3, St 12, Wazir Akbar Khan, Kabul (e-mail: info@arman.fm).

British Embassy, 15th Street, Roundabout Wazir Akbar, Khan, PO Box 334, Kabul (tel: 701-02000; fax: 701-02274; email: britishembassy.kabul@fco.gov.uk).

Fedex (Afghan Express), Karte 3, Khai Street, House 326, Kabul (tel: 25-00525; fax: 25-00524).

DHL Express, Street 10, Wazir Akbar Khan, House 310, Kabul (e-mail: kbl_hdesk@af.dhl.com).

TNT Express, Turabaz Khan Crossroads, Kabul.

National news agency: BNA (Bakhtar News Agency), www.bakhtarnews.com.af

Pajhwok Afghan News: www.pajhwok.com

Afghan Islamic Press: www.afghanislamicpress.com

Internet sites

Afghanistan Embassy (Australia): www.afghanembassy.net

Afghanistan Online: www.afghan-web.com

UN Development Business on-line subscription service: www.devbusiness.com

World Bank: www.worldbank.org/afghanistan

Albania

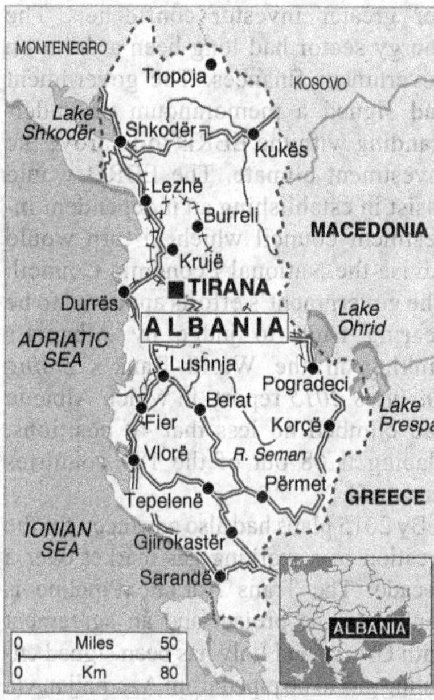

In late 2014, Jean-Claude Juncker of Luxembourg, then President-elect of the European Commission, exhorted the Albanian political class to co-operate to the maximum in a 'constructive way' and avoid any unnecessary polarisation. At the same time, Albania's Prime Minister Rama re-affirmed his government's wish to begin deep (and long overdue) reforms which would serve to accelerate Albania's entry process into the European Union (EU), which had been approved by a huge 77 per cent of Albania's 2.8 million electorate a year earlier.

Acccording to the *2014 Corruption Perception Index* published by the Berlin-based Transparency International, in 2014 Albania was considered the most corrupt country in Europe. None the less, Albania had made a formal application for membership of the EU in 2009 on the basis of a 2006 Stabilisation and Association agreement. At its meeting in June 2014, the European Council endorsed the European Commission's recommendation that Albania be granted official candidate status. In its 2014 Progress Report, published in October 2014, the European Commission stressed the need for sustained reform efforts in key priority areas, such as public administration and the judiciary, the fight against corruption and organised crime and the protection of fundamental rights, so that Albania could move toward the opening of accession negotiations.

The economy

Albania's unemployment level remained stubbornly high throughout 2014; weaknesses in the infrastructure and the widespread corruption continued to deter much foreign investment. In purely economic terms early 2015 was quite a critical period for the Albanian authorities. In late February 2015, the International Monetary Fund (IMF) authorised drawings of some €58.8 million (US$80.5 million), doubling the Fund's total disbursements for Albania to €117.7 million (US$161.2 million). Min Zhu, the Fund's deputy managing director put forward the IMF's view that 'Albania's economic recovery appears to be on track, even as downside risks persist.'

In a summary of its second and third reviews of the Albanian economy and responding to Albania's request for a waiver 'for the non-observance of performance criteria and the re-phasing of future disbursements', the IMF noted that economic recovery was underway, but that growth was below potential. High levels of non-performing loans (NPLs) had made Albania's banks risk-averse. Credit growth remained sluggish despite monetary easing. Despite this, the IMF affirmed that its programme was on track. The second review had been delayed because of the need to incorporate electricity reform in the programme and to allow time for conditions surrounding the Banka e Shqipërisë (Bank of Albania) (central bank) to normalise following the removal of its senior management. None the less, all the end-June (2014), end-September and available end-December quantitative performance criteria had been met. However, the continuous performance criterion on the accumulation of external arrears had not been observed due to a technical delay with one interest payment. An indicative target on new arrears accumulation was also missed by a small margin. Inflation had been slightly below the

KEY FACTS

Official name: Republika ë Shqipërisë (Republic of Albania)

Head of State: President Bujar Faik Nishani (PD) (from 11 Jun, inaugurated 24 Jul 2012)

Head of government: Prime Minister Edi Rama (PSS) (elected 23 Jun 2013)

Ruling party: Coalition: Aleanca për Shqipërinë Europiane (Alliance for a European Albania) consisting of 37 parties lead by the Partia Socialiste e Shqipërisë (PSS) (Socialist Party of Albania) and including Aleanca Socialiste për Integrim (ASI) (Socialist Alliance for Integration), Lëvizja Socialiste për Integrim (LSI) (Socialist Movement for Integration) and Partia Demokristiane e Shqipërisë (PDK) (Christian Democratic Party) (elected 23 Jun 2013)

Area: 28,748 square km

Population: 2.77 million (2014)*

Capital: Tirana

Official language: Tosk Albanian; the Albanian language is divided into two dialects – Gheg, north of the river Shkumbinit, and Tosk in the south.

Currency: Lek (L) = 100 qindarka

Exchange rate: L124.91 per US$ (Sep 2015)

GDP per capita: US$4,781 (2014)*

GDP real growth: 2.20% (2014)*

GDP: US$13.26 billion (2014)*

Labour force: 1.11 million (2013)

Unemployment: 14.00% (2014)*

Inflation: 1.63% (2014)*

Balance of trade: -US$2.52 billion (2014)*

* estimated figure

inner band prescribed under the inflation consultation clause. Several structural benchmarks were not met, but these were all expected to be completed in the first half of 2015.

Largely concurring with the IMF, in its 2014 *Transition Report* the London-based European Bank for Economic Reconstruction and Development (EBRD) noted that Albania's growth in the previous two years had slowed significantly, reflecting domestic challenges as well as inevitably lower foreign remittances and the economic problems encountered by a number of EU countries (notably Greece) with close links to Albania. In the first quarter of 2014 gross domestic product (GDP) growth was at an annual 1.6 per cent. Although disappointing, this figure was four percentage points higher that that registered two years earlier. Inflation had been suppressed by low levels of demand, low imported inflation and generally restrained domestic inflation which had resulted in levels staying within the Banka e Shqipërisë (Bank of Albania) (central bank)'s 2–4 per cent tolerance range. Reflecting this situation, the Bank had, according to the EBRD, implemented an expansionary monetary policy, in May 2014 cutting the base interest rate to its lowest level ever.

The EBRD noted that Albania's fiscal situation had worsened in 2013. The 2013 budget deficit had reached over 5 per cent of GDP, well above the targeted 3.5 per cent. The shortfall was in part due to problems with revenue collection as well as the rampant election expenditure seen in 2013. However, as confirmed by the IMF, the deficit was expected to narrow with improved tax collection and the introduction of higher tax rates. Albania's public debt had, according to the EBRD, reached around 70 per cent of GDP by the end of 2013.

The 2015 IMF disbursements referred to above were complimented by a further two loans from the World Bank, aimed at strengthening public finances and maintaining stability in the financial sector. The first use of the World Bank loans was to inject liquidity into the economy by clearing government arrears to the private sector, estimated to have been around €500 million (US$685 million) or some 5.4 per cent of GDP.

In the view of the EBRD, (and shared by the IMF), Albania's GDP growth was expected to improve slightly in 2014, but also sharing the IMF's view, the EBRD highlighted the 'downside risks.' In particular, the financial sector was exposed to both domestic and external risks. It was hoped that in 2015 the acquisition of EU membership candidate status would benefit the economy as would – to an unknown extent – the construction of the Trans Adriatic Pipeline.

The EBRD noted that little progress had occurred in terms of privatisation in the previous year. Although much of the economy was in private hands, there remained a number of larger companies where the state was a major shareholder – notably in energy, natural resources and telecommunications. The government had ambitiously announced plans to sell its stake in a minimum of 21 companies, including ten where the government was the major shareholder. Of these, the most attractive was the state's 16.8 per cent shareholding in Albtelecom.

For some time a fraught issue had been Albania's dispute with CEZ Group, the Czech (state-owned) monopoly power distribution company. It was hoped that the €95 million (US$130 million) settlement of relations with CEZ would trigger greater investor confidence. The energy sector had long been a drain on government finances. The government had signed a memorandum of understanding with the EBRD to improve the investment climate. The EBRD would assist in establishing an independent investment council which in turn would advise the National Economic Council. The government's efforts appeared to be bearing fruit, to judge by Albania's ranking in the World Bank's *Doing Business 2015* report, in which Albania had climbed no less that 40 positions, placing it 68 out of the 189 countries surveyed.

By 2015 plans had also advanced for the creation of a working gas market over a decade. The Trans Adriatic Pipeline is central to the project and an agreement with Greece and Italy has been signed enabling gas to be piped from Azerbaijan via Greece and Albania to Italy. The pipeline is expected to begin operations in 2018. Additionally, the construction of the proposed Ionian Adriatic Pipeline from Albania, through Montenegro and Bosnia to Croatia is expected to transform Albania into a regional gas hub.

The politics – Rama's Panorama

In 2013, Albania had seen its first successful, fully democratic, general election. This in itself was a huge achievement for one of Europe's most under-developed countries. The 'landslide' victory of the Partia Socialiste e Shqipërisë (PSS) (Socialist Party of Albania) lead by Edi Rama also marked the end of the overweening influence of former Prime Minister Sali Bersha. Mr Rama – in 2004 the winner of the City Mayors' World Mayor contest, when mayor of Tirana – was once a teacher at the Albanian Academy of Arts, a lively political site in its day. He had paid the price of criticising both sides of his country's political spectrum, leaving the so-called Democratic Party in 1990 later criticising both the socialists and the democrats in print and later paying the price of independence by being attacked and beaten almost to death. Mr Rama blamed supporters of the then President Sali Berisha. There followed a spell in

KEY INDICATORS — Albania

	Unit	2011	2012	2013	2014	**2015
Population	m	2.83	*2.82	*2.79	*2.77	*2.76
Gross domestic product (GDP)	US$bn	12.80	12.26	*12.92	*13.26	*12.40
GDP per capita	US$	3,992	4,354	*4,633	*4,781	*4,495
GDP real growth	%	2.0	1.3	*1.4	*2.2	*3.0
Inflation	%	3.4	2.0	1.9	*1.6	*1.8
Unemployment	%	13.3	13.0	*15.6	*14.0	*13.8
Exports (fob) (goods)	US$m	962.1	1,122.8	1,385.5	1,232.0	–
Imports (fob) (goods)	US$m	4,460.7	3,983.8	3,909.4	4,057.1	–
Balance of trade	US$m	-3,498.7	-2,861.0	-2,523.9	-2,519.0	–
Current account	US$m	-1,561.6	-1,138.0	*-1,377.0	*-1,841.0	*-194.2
Total reserves minus gold	US$m	26,467.9	2,515.7	2,712.3	2,604.2	–
Foreign exchange	US$m	2,566.7	2,423.1	2,599.7	–	–
Exchange rate	per US$	100.11	107.79	102.23	115.68	–

* estimated figure ** forecast figure

exile as a painter and sculptor in Paris, returning to Albania in 1998 when his father died,

In the 2009 election Mr Rama had accused the Democrats of cheating him of victory. Undaunted by his failure to gain election, in 2011 he claimed to have won a new term as mayor, but gerrymandering seemed to prevail when the Democrats managed to gain extra votes by the simple ploy of adding in votes cast in the wrong boxes. Things were to get worse when a January 2011 protest resulted in four Socialist supporters being shot dead by security forces apparently firing from the prime minister's office.

Expenditure on infrastructure projects were not, at the end of his electoral term in 2013, enough to keep Mr Berisha in office. He had probably been in office too long – for eight years – unable to keep a grip on the corruption scandals that prevailed and multiplied. One time Berish ally, Ilir Meta, the leader of a breakaway group from the Socialists that had fallen in with Mr Berisha in 2009, suddenly abandoned the Berisha camp to create an alliance with Mr Rama, to the dismay of a number of Socialists who suspected it would weaken any offensives against Mr Berisha's government. Mr Rama's sweeping election victory had meant that these attacks would no longer be necessary.

Risk assessment

Politics	Fair
Economy	Fair
Regional stability	Fair

Muslims in Albania

% of population	70
Sunni (% of Muslim)	95
Shi'a (% of Muslim)	5

COUNTRY PROFILE

1920s Italy withdrew from Albania and agreed to recognise its independence. Tirana was declared the capital city. Political instability followed. Prime Minister Ahmet Beg Zogu took the crown, proclaiming himself King Zog I.
1939 Italian troops under Benito Mussolini invaded Albania and King Zog fled.
1940 The Italians used Albania as their platform for the invasion of Greece.
1941 The Albanian Communist Party (ACP) was formed, with Enver Hoxha as its leader.
1943 German forces invaded and occupied Albania following surrender by the Italians.
1944 The Germans were forced out by Enver Hoxha's Communist resistance fighters. He proclaimed the constitution of the Democratic Government of Albania and became first secretary of the politburo. Albania became a Stalinist state and remained staunchly isolationist until the 1990s.
1945 The official language was based on Tosk Albanian.
1945–46 Tribunals were held which condemned thousands to death or imprisonment as 'war criminals' and 'enemies of the people'. Non-communists were purged from government positions.
1948 Albania broke its ties with Yugoslavia. The USSR began economic aid to Albania. The ACP was renamed the Partia e Punës (Party of Labour of Albania) (PLA).
1955 Albania became a founding member of the Warsaw Pact.
1961 Relations with the USSR soured when Albania supported China in the Sino-Soviet ideology dispute. Albania withdrew from the Council for Mutual Economic Assistance (Comecon).
1967 The Communist government outlawed religion, making Albania the world's only formal atheist state.
1968 Albania withdrew from the Warsaw Pact over the Soviet-led invasion of Czechoslovakia.
1976 A new constitution was adopted in which Albania declared itself the independent Peoples' Socialist Republic and reaffirmed its policy of self-reliance.
1985 Hoxha died and Ramiz Alia became first secretary of the politburo.
1989 Communist rule in Eastern Europe collapsed. Freedom of religion was restored.
1990 The PLA was renamed the Partia Socialiste ë Shqipërisë (PSS) (Socialist Party of Albania) and pursued a more liberal democratic ideology. Opposition parties were legalised. Thousands of people tried to flee the country when the right to travel abroad was granted.
1991 After an interim constitution was approved, multi-party elections were won by the PSS. Ramiz Alia was elected to the new post of executive president. Fatos Nano was forced to resign as head of government as the political and economic situation began to deteriorate. A caretaker government took power.
1992 The Partia Demokratike (ë Shqipërisë) (PD) (Democratic Party (of Albania)) won an overwhelming victory in parliamentary elections, ending five decades of communist rule. PD leader, Sali Berisha, was elected president.
Aleksander Meksi was appointed prime minister. Ramiz Alia, Fatos Nano and several others from the old Communist regime were tried and jailed for corruption.
1994 A national referendum rejected a new constitution, which would have given too much power to the president.
1995 Albania was admitted to the Council of Europe.
1996 The PD won a landslide victory in parliamentary elections, which were tainted by accusations of fraud.
1997 Leka, the son of King Zog, attempted to restore the monarchy but a referendum voted against it and he went abroad. Fraudulent pyramid investment schemes collapsed and many Albanians lost their life's savings, sparking weeks of rioting. President Berisha not only dismissed the prime minister and the head of the army but also closed down opposition newspapers and declared a state of emergency. The solution to the profound political crisis was fresh parliamentary elections in which the PSS were swept back into power and President Berisha resigned. The convictions of communist-era leaders were overturned; Fatos Nano was elected prime minister and Rexhep Majdani became president.
1998 Refugees from the war in Kosovo (Serbia) fled into Albania. Nano resigned due to protests over the economy, and was succeeded by Pandeli Majko. Voters approved Albania's first post-Communist constitution, which declared the country a parliamentary republic.
1999 There was a mass refugee exodus of Kosovans into Albania as thousands fled attacks by Serbian forces. Prime Minister Majko was succeeded by the Socialist, Ilir Meta.
2000 Albania joined the World Trade Organisation (WTO).
2001 Ilir Meta and the PSS won general elections.
2002 Prime Minister Ilir Meta resigned after failing to resolve an internal PSS feud with the president. Pandeli Majko became prime minister. Alfred Moisiu was elected president by parliament. Pandeli Majko resigned and Fatos Nano became prime minister again. The royal family returned from exile.
2003 Albania and the EU began Stabilisation and Association Agreement (SAA) talks.
2005 Albania signed a US$15 million deal with the US Occidental Petroleum Corporation for oil and natural gas drilling. The opposition PD won parliamentary elections and Sali Berisha became prime minister.
2006 The SAA with the EU was signed.
2007 Bamir Topi was elected president by parliament. Opposition parties had objected to his candidacy on the grounds that he was a representative of the ruling party.
2008. The electoral system was changed to the closed list proportional representation method.
2009 Albania joined Nato. Four coalition blocs contested parliamentary elections.

The AN government coalition, including the PD and Partia Republikane (RP) (Republican Party), Partia Demokrate e Re (PDR) (New Democratic Party) and the Partia për Drejtësi dhe Integrim (PDI) (Party for Justice and Integration), was sworn into office; Sali Berisha remained in office as prime minister.

2010 The first Albanian sale of government bonds; US$398 million of five-year bonds with a yield of 7 per cent, was managed by Deutsche Bank and J P Morgan Chase banks. Remittances were reported to represent 15 per cent of GDP, with most monies coming from Greece and Italy. The EU rejected Albania's application for candidate status; visa requirements for travel in EU were eased.

2011 In January, over 21,000 anti-government demonstrators rallied in Tirana protesting about corruption and alleged vote rigging of the 2009 elections; four people were killed by security forces. In May, violence broke out among political supporters following the announcement that the ruling PD's Lulzim Basha had beaten the incumbent PSS candidate Edi Rama in the 8 May mayoral election in Tirana. A census held on 1 October recorded a population of 2,831,741. In December, Leka Zogu, the self-proclaimed heir to the defunct throne of Albania, was buried in Tirana in an official ceremony attended by President Topi and Kosovo's President Atifete Jahjaga, and other political and religious leaders.

2012 On 6 January, the World Bank agreed to provide extra funding to ease the economic turmoil caused by the euro-zone debt crisis. Since 1991, Albania has been in receipt of US$1.4 billion in international aid and loans, to fund a number of infrastructure, education and public health services, plus anti-poverty programmes. On 11 June, after four rounds of voting, parliament elected Bujar Faik Nishani (Mehmeti) as president, with 73 votes (out of 140). President Nishani took office on 24 July. On 24 September, parliament voted to amend the constitution to curtail the right of immunity from prosecution for members of parliament, the judiciary and top officials. On 12 November the EU announced €81 million (US$105.1 million) had been allocated to assist Albania in a range of reforms to fight organised crime, as well as to finance infrastructure improvements.

2013 The Aleanca për Shqipërinë Europiane (Alliance for a European Albania) consisting of 37 parties ranging from far-left to right and lead by the Partia Socialiste e Shqipërisë (PSS) (Socialist Party of Albania) won the 23 June parliamentary elections with 57.63 per cent (84 seats, out of 140). Prime Minister Sali Berisha and his Partia Demokratike e Shqipërisë (PD) (Democratic Party of Albania), lead party in the 25-party Aleanca për Punësim, Mirëqenie dhe Integrim (Alliance for Employment, Prosperity and Integration), came in second with 39.46 per cent (56); the PD conceded defeat on 26 June in what was widely noted as a sign of political maturity. Turnout was 53.50 per cent. Leader of the PSS, Edi Rama, became prime minister. There were riots in Tirana after the US apparently asked the government to allow the destruction of Syria's chemicals to take place in Albania. Prime Minister Edi Rama said he would not permit it.

2014 In June UK prime minister, David Cameron, said he had dropped the UK's previous opposition to Albania's membership of the EU. As a result Albania was granted official candidate status.

2015 Local elections to elect mayors and other municipal members were held on 21 June, the first to be held since the number of municipalities had been reduced to 61. A joint OSCE/ODIHR election observation mission was invited to oversee the election. Their report on the election, published in September, raised concerns about the campaign, the process and the administration of justice related to electoral disputes, but praised the relatively calm atmosphere on election day and improvements in the language used by candidates during the contest.

Political structure

Constitution

Albania's communist constitution of 1976 was abrogated in 1991, when the democratic, Republic of Albania came into being under an interim constitution.

A new constitution was agreed by referendum and came into effect on 28 November 1998. It provides for multi-party elections and guarantees freedom of speech, religion, press, assembly and organisation.

Independence date

28 November 1912

Form of state

Unicameral parliamentary democratic republic

The executive

The president is head of state and shares control of the armed forces with the prime minister. The president is elected by parliament to a five-year term and is limited to two terms. The ballot is secret and the winning candidate must achieve a three-fifths majority. The president appoints the prime minister nominated by the party or coalition of parties that has a majority of seats in the Assembly. If the Assembly fails to approve the president's appointee three times, the president dissolves parliament. The prime minister and Council of Ministers are in charge of the country's economic, social and cultural affairs. The president and prime minister are jointly responsible for foreign relations and security affairs.

National legislature

The unicameral parliament, Kuvendi ë Shqipërisë (Assembly of Albania) has 140 members, elected for four-year terms. In November 2008 the electoral system was changed to the closed list proportional representative method. There are now 12 multi-party constituencies corresponding to the12 national administrative regions, wherein parties must win at least 3 per cent of the vote (and pre-election coalitions 5 per cent) before they can be placed on the closed list to become deputies of the assembly. The new system tends to favour leading political parties.

The Assembly meets twice a year. In addition to passing legislation, the Assembly also elects the president and approves the president's appointment of the prime minister and the prime minister's choices for the Council of Ministers.

Legal system

The court system is headed by the Supreme Court. Its members are appointed by the president to nine-year terms with the consent of the Assembly. Judges in appeals and district courts are appointed by the president upon the recommendations of the Higher Judicial Council, which is headed by the president and includes the chair of the Supreme Court and the minister of justice. A separate constitutional court rules on constitutional matters and consists of nine members appointed by the president with the Assembly's consent.

Last elections

30 May, 4, 8 and 11 June 2012 (presidential); 23 June 2013 (parliamentary)

Results: President: Bujar Nishani (PD) was elected in the fourth round of voting with 73 out of 76 votes cast.

Parliamentary: The Aleanca për Shqipërinë Europiane (Alliance for a European Albania) consisting of 37 parties ranging from far-left to right won with a total of 57.63 per cent of the vote (total 84 seats allocated, out of 140) (including the Partia Socialiste e Shqipërisë (PSS) (Socialist Party of Albania) 41.36 per cent (66 seats); Lëvizja Socialiste për Integrim (LSI) (Socialist Movement for Integration) 10.46 per cent (16); Aleanca Socialiste për Integrim (ASI) (Socialist Alliance for Integration) 0.85 per cent (1); Partia Demokristiane e Shqipërisë (PDK) (Christian Democratic Party) 0.46 per cent (1). Second was 25-party Aleanca për Punësim, Mirëqenie dhe Integrim (Alliance for Employment, Prosperity and Integration) with a total of 39.46 per cent (total allocated seats 56) (including the Partia Demokratike e Shqipërisë (PD) (

Democratic Party of Albania) 30.63 per cent (49 seats); Partia Republikane e Shqipërisë (PRS) (Republican Party) 3.02 per cent (3); Partia Drejtësi, Integrim dhe Unitet (PDIU) (Party for Justice, Unification and Unity) 2.61 per cent (4). No other parties won any seats. turnout was 53.50 per cent. Edi Rama, leader of the PSS became prime minister.

Next elections

2017 (parliamentary); July 2017 (presidential)

Political parties

Ruling party

Coalition: Aleanca për Shqipërinë Europiane (Alliance for a European Albania) consisting of 37 parties lead by the Partia Socialiste e Shqipërisë (PSS) (Socialist Party of Albania) and including Aleanca Socialiste për Integrim (ASI) (Socialist Alliance for Integration), Lëvizja Socialiste për Integrim (LSI) (Socialist Movement for Integration) and Partia Demokristiane e Shqipërisë (PDK) (Christian Democratic Party) (elected 23 Jun 2013)

Main opposition party

Partia Socialiste ë Shqipërisë (PSS) (Socialist Party of Albania)

2.77 million (2014)*

Population

Albania is the poorest country in south-east Europe.

Last census: 1 October 2011: 2,831,741 (provisional)

Population density: 120 inhabitants per square km. Urban population 52 per cent (2010 Unicef).

Annual growth rate: -0.1 per cent, 1990–2010 (Unicef).

Ethnic make-up

Albanians make up 97 per cent of the population. The largest ethnic minority group is the Greeks, who account for around 2 per cent of the total. Other groups include Macedonian, Montenegrin, Vlach and Gypsy (Romany) groups.

Religions

Muslim (70 per cent), Christian Orthodox (20 per cent) and Roman Catholic (10 per cent).

Education

Despite its many failings, the communist regime virtually eliminated illiteracy. However, since 1991 the situation has deteriorated markedly, with equipment and buildings in a parlous state. Although high attendance rates in primary schools have been maintained, enrolment in pre-primary schooling and at the secondary or tertiary level has declined. In Albania, the government has closed down a third of public kindergartens and pre-school attendance has dropped dramatically.

Unqualified teachers in elementary schools account for 10 per cent of teaching staff, and in the secondary schools, 8 per cent.

The government has an ongoing programme to replace equipment and reconstruct buildings in urban areas and is also focussing on teacher training and enrolment rates. The current structure of the sector has resulted in a misalignment between the supply and demand of education. Consequently, the government is also engaged in a school construction programme to provide facilities for those areas where there are currently no school facilities.

The total expenditure on education is around 3 per cent of GDP.

Literacy rate: 99 per cent adult rate; 99 per cent youth rate (15–24) (Unesco 2005).

Enrolment rate: 100 per cent (primary); 71.5 per cent (secondary) (World Bank).

Pupils per teacher: 18 in primary schools.

Health

Although Albania's modest healthcare sector functioned adequately during the communist era, it suffered from substantial underfunding. The government recognises the problem and plans to strengthen managerial capacities and to decentralise health planning. It will take many years to create a system capable of providing even basic healthcare.

HIV/Aids

Albania had been screened from the initial impact of the Aids epidemic by the isolation imposed by the former communist state. However, the country opened its borders following the advent of democratic government in 1991 and the first HIV case of HIV was detected in 1993. By 2003, 177 cases had been reported of which 37 had died of Aids. Between 2001–03 the percentage of HIV positive females increased and their numbers now match male infection rates.

Life expectancy: 77 years, 2010 (Unicef 2012)

Fertility rate/Maternal mortality rate: 1.5 births per woman, 2010 (Unicef 2012)

Child (under 5 years) mortality rate (per 1,000): 17 per 1,000 live births (WHO 2012); 14 per cent of children aged under five are malnourished (World Bank).

Welfare

Albania's social infrastructure is in a poor state. Never well developed, social disintegration in 1997 led to further deterioration of virtually all services as funds dried up.

The collapse of central government authority in 1997 has led to already poor tax collection rates falling further. Neither the funds nor the infrastructure exist to provide adequate welfare coverage. It has been estimated that more than one million people are living below the poverty line. The Albanian Institute of Statistics reported in late-1999 that over one-third of families have only one income source averaging US$64 per month.

The government is attempting to remedy this by introducing community-based social services for vulnerable groups and is in the process of reorganising the state pension system based on the actuarial model. The aim is to increase coverage in rural areas in order to reduce poverty.

Main cities

Tirana (capital, estimated population 587,135 in 2012), Durrës (Durrazzo) (168,254), Vlore (124,415), Elbasan (100,362), Shkoder (Scutari) (86,677), Korca (62,601), Fier (56,623), Berat (43,633), Kavaja (39,749), Lushnje (37,765).

Languages spoken

Greek, Romanian, Bulgarian, Serbian, Tosk and Gheg are also spoken.

English, Italian, German and French are also spoken in business circles.

Official language/s

Tosk Albanian; the Albanian language is divided into two dialects – Gheg, north of the river Shkumbinit, and Tosk in the south.

Media

Press freedom in Albania has been declared partly free by the US-based media watchdog, Freedom House, and the government has used criminal and tax laws to target and intimidate media sources it wishes to stifle.

Due to the country's poor infrastructure, mountainous terrain and low economic development, access to media can be poor.

Press

The print media is not sophisticated and tends towards sensationalism. Many newspapers are published by political parties and interest groups.

Dailies: In Albanian, policital party publications include *Rilindja Demokratike* (http://pages.albaniaonline.net/rd), and *Zeri i Popullit* (www.zeripopullit.com). Private newspapers include *Shekulli* (www.shekulli.com.al) the largest daily, *Gazeta Shqiptare* (www.balkanweb.com/gazetav4), *Koha Ditore* (www.koha.net), *Sot* (www.sot.com.al), *Korrieri* (www.korrieri.com) *Koha Jonë* (www.kohajone.com), are tabloids. In English, *Albanian Daily News* (www.albaniannews.com). And *Tirana Times* (www.tiranatimes.com).

Weeklies: In Albanian, general interest magazines include *Shqip* (www.shqip.al), and *Veriu Observer* (www.gazetaveriu.netfirms.com). *Sporti Shqiptar* (www.sportishqiptar.com.al) is a sports publication.
Business: In Albanian, *Biznesi* (www.biznesi.com.al) is a newspaper, *Monitor* (www.monitor.al) is a magazine. The Albanian Chamber of Commerce publishes *Probiznes News* (www.cci.gov.al) magazine.

Broadcasting
Radio Televizioni Shqiptar (RTSH) (www.rtsh.al) is the state broadcaster, operating from Tirana.
Radio: In Albanian, RTSH (http://rtsh.sil.at) operates three national stations, including an international service. There are two commercial national broadcasters, Plus 2 Radio (www.plus2radio.com.al) and Top Albania Radio (www.topalbaniaradio.com). Other local commercial radio stations include Radio Saranda (www.radiosaranda.com), Radio Planet (www.planet93fm.com) and Radio IMR (www.radio-ime.com), which has talk and information programmes.
There are foreign radio broadcasts received in foreign languages including, English, Italian, French and German.
Television: RTSH operates one national station; it also has a satellite service for expatriate communities in neighbouring countries. Funding is provided by government grants, subscription and commercial advertising. Programmes include news, current affairs and documentaries as well as popular shows. TV Arberia (www.telearberia.tv) is a private network.
National news agency: Albanian Telegraphic Agency (ATA)

Economy

Although the service sector accounts for over 63.4 per cent of the economy (2014), Albania is still a country where primary industries are important. Agriculture, including timber products, accounts for around 21.8 per cent of GDP and employs about 42 per cent of the workforce. Other industries include mining of ores, cement, chemical and energy production. Industry, especially manufacturing, accounts for around 15 per cent of GDP, with products geared for the export market.
GDP growth, which had been consistently high since 2000, fell from 7.5 per cent in 2008 to 3.3 per cent 2009 as the global economic crisis cut world trade. In 2010, while so many Western economies fell into recession Albania made a concerted effort to enhance the financial system and make progress towards a functioning market economy, according to an assessment by the European Union (EU), reporting on Albania's progress towards membership. Despite avoiding recession, growth had dropped to 1.6 per cent in 2012 before having dropped further to 1.4 per cent in 2013 and rising slightly to 1.9 per cent in 2014.
Albania is one of the poorest countries in Europe, despite poverty levels having fallen by almost 15 per cent since 2002; GDP per capita had never been higher than US$4,102 (in 2008), but with the downturn in the economy this fell steadily to US$3,715 in 2010. Per capita income is estimated to have risen to US$4,610 in 2013 and further to US$4,619 in 2014 (in current US$).
Foreign remittances are a very important part of the country's economy and amounted to US$1.1 billion in 2010 (10.9 per cent of GDP). They grew to US$1.2 billion in 2011 before increasing by an estimated 1.6 per cent in 2012. However, in the first 6 months remittances had dropped by 33 per cent on a year-on-year basis.
Full EU membership is not expected before 2020; however the EU has signed a Stabilisation and Association Agreement and continues to fund infrastructure improvements and was granted candidate status in June 2014. Other international financial institutions, such as the World Bank and IMF and the European Bank for Reconstruction and Development (EBRD) have all invested in projects of improvement. The rebuilding of the technical and physical infrastructure, from telecommunications to roads and railways, is a major priority. While the government encourages foreign investment in agriculture, agri-processing, manufacturing and export-oriented activities, poor basic services, such as electricity, discourage investor interest. Efforts to develop a larger tourist industry are also hindered by poor infrastructure and under-investment. Efforts to counter the grey economy include a simplified tax system and structural reforms. The EU has warned that measures to kerb corruption (Albania ranks 110 out of 175 on the corruption perception index) and organised crime must be robust and continuous in order to improve foreign investment confidence.
On 12 November 2012 the EU announced €81 million (US$105.1 million) had been allocated to assist Albania in a range of reforms to fight organised crime, as well as to finance infrastructure improvements.
On 6 January 2012, the World Bank had agreed to provide extra funding to mitigate the economic turmoil caused by the euro-zone debt crisis. Since 1991, Albania has been in receipt of over US$1.4 billion in international aid and loans, to fund a number of infrastructure, education and public health services, plus anti-poverty programmes.
Despite positive efforts on economic progress, keeping inflation under tighter control and some amount of growth, in 2013 the country's public debt equalled 60 per cent of GDP, rising to 72 per cent in 2014. Unemployment has been falling steadily in recent years however in 2014 still remained high at 18 per cent. Before the global economic crash in 2008 remittances were a significant asset to the economy, contributing some 15 per cent of GDP, now, however, their contribution dropped to 5.7 per cent in 2014.
Complex tax legislation and business regulations make Albania unattractive for FDI. Albania ranks 68 out of 189 in the ease of doing business index (2014) and as a result the government has attempted to undertake reforms in order to increase investment. However, although FDI has been increasing steadily since 2000, 2014 saw FDI drop to US$1.2 billion in 2014 from US$1.3 billion in 2013.

External trade

Albania is a signatory of the Central European Free Trade Agreement (CEFTA), along with Bosnia and Hercegovina, Croatia, Macedonia, Moldova, Montenegro and Serbia and Kosovo.
Albania, Macedonia and Bulgaria have a trilateral agreement to build a new Balkan oil pipeline (AMBO), from Burgas, on the Black Sea, to the port of Vlore, in southern Albania. Its estimated cost is US$1.2 billion with a supply target of 750,000 barrels per day, with the construction postponed until 2009; by mid-2015 construction was still awaiting a start date.
Albania made a formal application for the European Union in 2009, however full membership is not expected to take form until 2020, though it was awarded candidate status in June 2014.

Imports
Principal imports include machinery, capital goods, electrical and electronic goods, vehicles, minerals, fuels and oils.
Main sources: Italy (29.8 per cent of total in 2014), Greece (9.4 per cent), China (7.3 per cent).

Exports
Principal exports are minerals, including hydrocarbons and hydroelectricity, chrome products, copper wire, ferro-nickel ore and bitumen, chemicals and iron and steel. Major manufacturing plants include cement, textiles and footwear and food processing, plus engineering products.
Main destinations: Italy (52.0 per cent of total in 2014), Serbia (8.0 per cent), Spain (6.5 per cent)

Agriculture

Farming

Agriculture, formerly the largest sector in the economy, has declined to around 22 per cent of GDP, but remains an important social as well as economic factor in Albanian life. The sector, which employs about 42 per cent of the workforce, is dominated by small-scale subsistence farming, which is underdeveloped and poorly financed. There is minimal mechanisation and little use of fertilisers and pesticides. Despite government attempts to privatise farmland, outside financial assistance has been needed to develop farming.

Fishing

Albania's fish catch declined sharply following the collapse of Communism and has not recovered. The sector is in generally poor shape. The fishing fleet comprises ageing and poorly equipped vessels and there is a shortage of fishermen. Development of the marine fisheries, including rehabilitation and construction of ports and other infrastructure, is a government priority.

There is some freshwater fishing in rivers, lakes and reservoirs. Fish farming of marine and freshwater species is increasingly important. Internal consumption of fish has increased in recent years, leaving about half of the approximately 4,000 tonnes of production for export, mainly to Greece and Italy.

Forestry

Forests cover less than two-fifths of the land area, the equivalent of 991,000 hectares (ha).

The forest industry is small-scale and is based mainly on imported raw materials to meet domestic production needs.

Forestry is of little importance to GDP, with most timber production being used for domestic fuel. Timber processing and associated activities have been transferred to the private sector, but forest management remains in state hands.

Industry and manufacturing

The industrialisation policy of the Communist era was aimed at making Albania completely self-sufficient. Although this meant that Albania was one of the few countries in the world without any foreign debt, it also meant that the industrial sector relied on outdated and inefficient machinery, which produced poor quality goods unable to compete in international markets.

A side-effect of the search for higher productivity was a complete absence of environmental concerns, with industrial wastelands, oil slicks and abandoned equipment littering the country. Combined with thousands of broken concrete bunkers and derelict factories, Albania faces major, long-term environmental problems.

The industrial sector has experienced a disastrous decline in output since 1990. The sector is focused mainly on engineering, chemicals, metals, construction materials, food processing and other agro-allied industries. The sector employs around 20 per cent of the workforce and accounts for around 15 per cent of GDP. There is virtually no light industry.

Foreign investment is the key to reviving industrial output, and consequently the government has been attempting to portray Albania as a low-wage manufacturing base with extensive natural resources on Western Europe's doorstep. Foreign companies have become involved in rehabilitating and modernising Albania's chrome industry by taking over a number of steel plants and mines.

Tourism

In 2014, the travel and tourism industry contributed 21 per cent to GDP, a figure that is expected to fall by 2.1 per cent in 2015. The industry supplied employment to 19.2 per cent of the total workforce (182,000 jobs) but this is also expected to fall by 0.8 per cent in 2015 (to 182,500 jobs).

In 2014, investment in the sector was estimated to be US$160 million, which was 4.3 per cent of total investment. And this number is expected to rise 3.6 per cent in 2015 to combat the poor performance of the tourist industry. International visitor numbers were 3.0 million in the same year.

Attractions for visitors are typically Mediterranean beach resorts, unspoilt (undeveloped) countryside and historic sites. As the infrastructure grows and improves Albania as a destination for the less-seasoned European traveller will also develop.

Environment

Macedonia and Albania participate in the Lake Ohrid Conservation Project (LOCP) which is a bilateral project supported by the World Bank.

Mining

The mining sector contributes a total of as much as 20 per cent to GDP and employs some 15 per cent of the workforce.

Albania used to be the world's third-largest producer and second-largest exporter of chromium. The industry is undergoing rehabilitation. As with all areas of the Albanian economy, the mining sector suffers from obsolete technology and techniques, the disruption of supply lines and lack of management skills.

There are extensive reserves of copper, iron, zinc and nickel. In addition, there are smaller reserves of uranium, titanium-magnetite, gold and silver. Most of these reserves are in remote and mountainous areas of northern Albania, which increases production costs.

Hydrocarbons

The state-owned Albpetrol is responsible for policy, administration and exploitation of hydrocarbons in Albania, either solely or in partnership with foreign oil and gas companies.

Albania has the second-largest oil reserves in the Balkans, with considerable international interest in the industry. Two small oil fields, at Patos and Morinza, account for the majority of the country's oil production.

However, the extraction industry lacks the modern technology to fully exploit its reserves – many of the Russian, Chinese and Romanian-built oilrigs are over 40 years old, the majority in a poor state of repair.

A semi-products pipeline (180km) connects the three smallest refineries with Ballshi and the oilfields. There is also a 51km export pipeline from Ballshi to Vlora.

Armo the former state-owned oil refiner, with two facilities at Ballsh and Fier with total capacity of 26,000 barrels per day (bpd), was sold to a US-Swiss investment group in 2008. The 750,000bpd Albanian Macedonian Bulgarian Oil (Ambo) pipeline, to carry Russian and Caspian oil through the Baltic from the Black Sea port of Burgas in Bulgaria to Vlore on the Albanian Adriatic, via Macedonia – and avoiding the congested Turkish straits – was proposed in 2004 and endorsed in 2007 but by mid-2015 construction has yet to start.

Gas reserves lie mainly under the Kucove and Patos areas with the major gas fields being located at Diviak and Bubuline. Albania has an internal natural gas grid connecting some of the cities and natural gas fields. However most of the gas pipelines are corroding and require repairing.

Sufficient coal (of generally low quality) is produced for domestic consumption. Production is carried out at 21 mines in four basins run by various state-owned stock companies.

Energy

Total generating capacity was 1,878MW in 2014, generating around 4.73 billion kilowatt hours. The bulk of energy (around 90 per cent of total output) is produced from three hydropower plants in the north of Albania, although supplies are affected by drought conditions during summer.

There are small oil-fired power stations but imports have become prohibitively expensive. Two loans of US$21.6 million and US$35.3 million were provided by the World Bank in 2011, to ensure the repair and safeguard of the three hydroelectric power plants on the Drini River, which had been damaged by severe flooding in the winter of 2010–11.

On 15 June 2012 the official inauguration of the Ashta hydroelectric power plant took place. The plant became fully operational in March 2013 and has an installed capacity of 53MW, allowing generation of 242GWh per year. However, several foreign investors in the energy market have warned the government that a national strategy must be enacted to improve the connection of new power plants to the power grid.

Financial markets

Stock exchange

The Tirana Stock Exchange opened in mid-1996. Since the collapse of the pyramid schemes in 1997, it has been faced with the daunting task of rebuilding the confidence of potential investors.

Banking and insurance

The European Bank of Reconstruction and Development (EBRD) is involved in the development and privatisation of the banking system.

Albania's central bank is the Banka e Shqipërisë (Bank of Albania). It has the power to authorise the creation of and supervise new banks, including those with foreign capital.

Central bank

Banka e Shqipërisë (Bank of Albania)

Main financial centre

Tirana

Time

GMT plus one hour (daylight saving, late March to late October, GMT plus two hours)

Geography

Albania's 28,748 square km are split into three main areas: a coastal plain, mountains and an inland plain. Albania shares a border with Montenegro and Serbia (Kosovo) to the north, the Former Yugoslav Republic of Macedonia (FYROM) to the north-west and Greece to the south. The Adriatic and Ionian Seas are to the west. The country's Albanian name, Shqipëria, which translates as 'land of the eagles', reflects its remote and mountainous nature; mountains cover over 70 per cent of the land area. The highest mountain entirely within Albania is Mt Jezerce (2,694 metres) in the north, although Mt Korab on the border with FYROM reaches 2,751 metres.

The longest river, the Drini (285km), drains into Lake Ohrid on the border with FYROM. To the north, the Drini joins the Buna river, the only navigable waterway in Albania. There are three natural freshwater lakes in Albania, all of which share borders with either Greece, Montenegro or the FYROM. Numerous artificial lakes have been created by hydroelectric power stations damming rivers, the largest of which are in the north around Kukes and Skhodra.

Hemisphere

Northern

Climate

Albania has a Mediterranean climate, with long, hot and dry summers and cool, cloudy and wet winters. Autumn has humid weather brought by the warm sirocco wind. The high inland mountains can become cold during the winter months. July is the hottest month; November, December and April are the wettest months. It is warmest in the south-west and coldest in the north-east.

Dress codes

During the summer, light clothing is recommended, with warmer clothes essential during the winter months, particularly in mountainous regions.

Entry requirements

Passports

Required by all.

Visa

Not required by most citizens of Europe, North America, Australasia and a few Asian countries for visits up to 90 days. A US$10 entry tax is levied. (For a full list of exemptions visit www.mfa.gov.al/english/info2.asp.) An entry-exit form is issued at the border: the entry portion is handed in at passport control and the exit portion should be kept until departure.

Currency advice/regulations

The import and export of local currency is not permitted.

The import of foreign currencies is allowed without limitation, although all amounts must be declared on arrival. Export of foreign currency is allowed within the limits of the declaration given, less the amounts exchanged or spent. Keep exchange receipts.

Travellers cheques are accepted by banks and large tourist hotels. ATMs are available in Tirana and other main towns.

Customs

Personal items may be taken into Albania without incurring duty.

Health (for visitors)

Medical facilities are limited and medicine is in short supply. Doctors and hospitals generally expect immediate cash payment for health services. Health care is free for citizens of countries with reciprocal health agreements. Full medical insurance is advisable.

Mandatory precautions

A vaccination certificate for yellow fever is required if travelling from an infected area.

Advisable precautions

It is advisable to have immunisations against hepatitis A and B, typhoid and tetanus. Polio immunisation is not recommended for adults who received childhood inoculations. There is a risk of rabies. Access to clean water in the country is variable, and it is not usual to drink tap water.

Hotels

Hotel provision of all standards, including international hotels, is improving. Increasing numbers of hotels can be contacted directly by telephone. Bookings can be arranged online through Albania Holidays Ltd (www.albania-hotel.com).

Credit cards

Major international hotels in Tirana accept American Express, Mastercard and Diners Club (but not Visa). Cases of credit card fraud have been reported.

Public holidays (national)

Fixed dates

1 Jan (New Year's Day), 28 Nov (Independence and Liberation Day), 25 Dec (Christmas Day).

Variable dates

Orthodox Easter Monday, Labour Day (first Mon in May), Eid al Adha, Islamic New Year, Birth of the Prophet, Eid al Fitr.

Islamic year 1436 (25 Oct 2014–14 Oct 2015):: The Islamic year contains 354 or 355 days, with the result that Muslim feasts advance by 10–12 days against the Gregorian calendar. Dates of feasts vary according to the sighting of the new moon (*hilal*), so cannot be forecast exactly.

Working hours

Banking

Mon–Fri: 0800–1600.

Business

Mon–Fri: 0800–1600.

Government

Mon–Fri: 0700–1500.

Shops

Mon–Sat: 0800–1200, 1500–1900.

Social customs/useful tips

It is customary to shake hands on meeting and taking leave. Business cards are exchanged. Albanian business meetings are reasonably relaxed. Delays to negotiations can be expected as bureaucratic tendencies still exist.

Albanians are a naturally friendly and curious people with a good sense of humour, and are keen to talk to and meet foreigners.

Small gifts are appreciated. Round up the bill slightly when in restaurants.

Local body language customs: nodding the head up and down indicates no, and side to side indicates yes.

Security

It is advisable to be extremely cautious in Albania. Security has improved in recent years, but crime is still a serious problem and armed criminal gangs operate in most areas. There are a large number of semi-automatic weapons in private hands.

Travel to the north-eastern border areas between Albania and Kosovo is not recommended.
Avoid giving anything to women and children asking for money, as they target foreigners and will follow the compassionate whenever they see them again. Visitors should dress down and not display watches, cameras or other expensive items.

Getting there

Air

Albania is accessible by air from numerous European centres, including Athens, Bucharest, Budapest, Ioannina, Paris, Rome and Zurich.
National airline: Albanian Airlines.
International airport/s: Rinas Mother Teresa Airport (TIA), 25 km from Tirana.
Airport tax: US$10

Surface

Road: There are road links from all bordering countries, including Greece at Kakavia and Kristalopigi, and Kosovo (in Serbia) at Han-i-Hotit and Vrbnica, and Macedonia at Cafasan.
Rail: There are no passenger rail links between Albania and the rest of Europe and travel in some of the border regions is inadvisable.
Water: There are ferry services connecting Durrës and Vlora with Trieste, Ancona, Brindisi and Bari in Italy and Rijeka and Pula in Croatia. Others connect Durres to Kopa in Slovenia and Sarandra to Corfu.
Main port/s: Durrës, Vlora and Sarandra.

Getting about

National transport

Air: Ales Airlines (a private joint Italian-Albanian company licensed by the Albanian government) serves eight small airports across the country.
Road: Out of approximately 21,000km of roads, only 3,000km are paved. Road conditions can be unpredictable – narrow, unsurfaced and potholed, with the added risk of straying cattle or pedestrians. Mountain roads are often impassable. The roads are considered to be the worst in Europe.
Buses: Buses run frequently between Tirana and Durrës and other towns to the north and south. Tickets are sold on the bus.
Rail: The rail network is approximately 720km, single-track and unelectrified. Trains are diesel.

City transport

Taxis: The only city with a taxi service is Tirana. There are taxi transfers from Rinas airport to the city centre.
Buses, trams & metro: A flat-fare bus service operates in the main cities, including Tirana. Airport buses operate from the airport to the city centre every three hours. Journey duration is 30 minutes.

Car hire

Driving in Albania is only recommended for those with no other choice. An international driving permit or a national driving licence is required. It is advisable to hire a local car and driver through travel agencies. Traffic drives on the right.

BUSINESS DIRECTORY

The addresses listed below are a selection only. While World of Information makes every endeavour to check these addresses, we cannot guarantee that changes have not been made, especially to telephone numbers and area codes. We would welcome any corrections.

Telephone area codes

The international direct dialling code (IDD) for Albania is +355, followed by area code and subscriber's number:

Berat	32	Korca	82
Durrës	52	Shkoder	22
Elbasan	54	Tirana	4
Fier	34	Vlore	33

Useful telephone numbers

Police: 19
Fire: 18
Ambulance:17

Chambers of Commerce

Albanian British Chamber of Commerce and Industry, PO Box 1547, Tirana (tel: 227-000; fax: 230-636; e-mail: info:abcci.com).

American Chamber of Commerce in Albania, Rruga Deshmoret e 4 Shkurtit, Tirana (tel: 259-779; fax: 235-350; e-mail: info@amcham.com.al).

Korça Chamber of Commerce and Industry, Bulevard Republika, Korça (tel/fax: 824-457; e-mail: albchamber1@albchamber.com).

Tirana Chamber of Commerce and Industry, Rruga e Kavajes 6, Tirana (tel: 230-284; fax: 227-997; e-mail: ccitr@abissnet.com.al).

Union of Chambers of Commerce and Industry of Albania, Rruga e Kavajes 6, Tirana (tel: 230-283; fax: 227-997; e-mail: root@ccitr.tirana.al).

Banking

Albanian State Agricultural Bank, Tirana (tel: 27-738).

Albanian State Bank for Foreign Relations, Tirana.

Alpha Credit Bank, Deshmoret e Kombit Blvd 47, Tirana (Internet site: http://www.alpha.gr).

Arab Albanian Islamic Bank, Deshmoret e Kombit, Tirana (tel: 23-873).

Bankandertregtare (Intercommercial Bank), Tirana Tower, Rruga e Kavajes 59, Tirana (tel: 58-755/60; fax: 58-752; e-mail: icbs1@albaniaonline.net).

Banko Italo Albanese (Banka Italo Shqiptare) (Italian-Albanian Bank), Rruga e Barrikadave, Tirana (tel: 33-966; fax: 35-701).

Fefad Bank, Tirana (tel: 3-496, 37-958; fax: 33-481).

National Bank of Greece, Blvd. Deshmoret e Kombit, VEVE Business Centre, Tirana (tel: 33-621, 35-542).

National Commercial Bank of Albania, Tirana (tel: 50-955; fax: 50-960; e-mail: bkt@albmail.com).

Savings Bank of Albania, Rr Deshmoret e 4 Shkurti, 6 Tirana (tel: 24-540/051; fax: 23-587/695).

Tirana Bank, Blvd. Deshmoret e Kombit, NR55/1, Tirana (tel: 33-441).

Central bank

Banka e Shqiperise (Bank of Albania), Sheshi Skënderbej 1, Tirana (tel: 222-152; fax: 223-558; e-mail: public@bankofalbania.org).

Stock exchange

The Tirana Stock Exchange opened in mid-1996. Since the collapse of the pyramid schemes in 1997, it has been faced with the daunting task of rebuilding the confidence of potential investors.

Travel information

Lufthansa Tirana Rinas Airport Office (tel: 42-350/54/58; fax: 42-350/60).

Ministry of tourism

Ministry of Tourism, Blvd Deshmoret e Kombit, Tirana (tel: 28-123); fax: 27-922).

Ministries

Albanian Assembly, Kurvendi, Blvd Dëdhmotët e Kombit, nr 4, Tirana (tel: 42-37-418, 42-47-354,43-62-003; fax: 42-27-949; email: head-directory@parlament.al; internet: www.parlament.al).

Committee of Environmental Protection, Ministry of Health and Environmental Protection, Bulevari Bajran Curri, Tirana (tel: 42-682; 35-229; fax: 35-229).

Department of Economic Development and Foreign Aid Co-ordination, Tirana (tel: 28-467; fax: 28-363).

Industrialeksport – 4 Shkurti Street 6, Tirana (tel: 4550).

Institute of Statistics, Tirana (tel: 22-411; fax: 28-300).

Makinaimport (State Trade Organisation for the Import of Machinery), 4 Shkurti Street 6, Tirana (tel: 25-220, 25-221).

Mineralimpex (State Organisation for Export of Minerals), 4 Shkurti Street 6, Tirana (tel: 25-832, 23-848).

Ministry of Agriculture and Food, Blvd Dëdhmotët e Kombit Tirana (tel: 28-318, 32-675; fax: 23-806, 27-924).

Ministry of Energy and Mineral Resources (tel: 32-833; fax: 34-052).

Ministry of Finance and Economy, Dëdhmotët e Kombit, Tirana (tel: 28-405; fax: 28-494).

Ministry of Health and Environment, Ministria e Shendetesise, Tirana (tel and fax: 34-615).

Ministry of Industry, Transport and Trade, Sheshi Skenderbey, Tirana (tel: 25-353, 32-289; fax: 27-773, 616-835).

Ministry of Transport and Telecommunications, Sheshi Skenderbey, Tirana (tel: 25-353; tel/fax: 27-773/616/835).

National Agency for Privatisation (tel/fax: 27-937).

National Committee of Energy, Dëdhmotët e Kombit, Tirana (tel/fax: 28-475).

President's Office, Tirana (tel: 28-491; fax: 33-761).

Prime Minister's Office, Tirana (tel: 34-816; fax: 34-818).

Other useful addresses

Agroeksport – State Trade Organisation for the Export of Agricultural and Food Products, 4 Shkurti Street 6, Tirana (tel: 25-227, 25-229, 23-128).

Albanian Embassy (USA), 2100 S Street, NW, Washington DC (tel: (+1-202) 223-4942; fax: (+1-202) 628-7342).

Albanian Telecom, Myslim Shyri 42, Tirina (tel: 32-047; fax: 33-323).

Albkontrol (Organisation for Inspection of Exported and Imported Goods), Rruga Skënderbeu 15, Durrës (tel: 22-354; fax: 22-791).

Artimpex (State Organisation for Export), 4 Shkurti Street 6, Tirana.

British Embassy, Ruga Vaso Pasha 7/1, Tirana (tel: 34-973; fax: 34-975).

Bureau for the Registration of Patents & Trade Marks, Konferenca e Pezes Street 6, Tirana.

Business Economic Development Department, c/o Ministry of Industry and Trade, 3 Rruga Andon Zamo Cajupi, Tirana (tel: 34-673; fax: 34-658).

Foreign Investment Promotion Centre, Ekspozita Shqiperia Sot (Protokolli), Blvd Jeanne d'Arc, Tirana (tel: 27-626; fax: 28-439, 42-133).

Insig, Insurance Institute, Rruga e Dibres 91, Tirana (tel: 341-84, 341-69, 341-70; fax: 341-80, 238-38).

Small and Medium-Sized Enterprises (SME) Foundation, c/o Ministry of Industry and Trade, 3 Rruga Andon Zako Cajupi, Tirana (fax: 34-892); EU Expert (fax: 42-413, 34-609).

Transshqip (State Organisation for the Transport of Goods in Foreign Trade), 4 Shkurti Street 6, Tirana (tel: 23-076, 24-659).

US Embassy, 103 Rruga Elbasanit, Tirana (tel: 424-7285; fax: 423-2222; e-mail: wm_tirana@pd.state.gov).

National news agency: Albanian Telegraphic Agency (ATA)

Address: Bulevard Zhan D'Arc, 23, Tirane (tel: 251-152; fax: 234-230; internet: www.ata-al.net).

Internet sites

Albanian Daily News: www.albaniannews.com

Albanian parliament: parlament.al

Bank of Albania: www.bankofalbania.org

Algeria

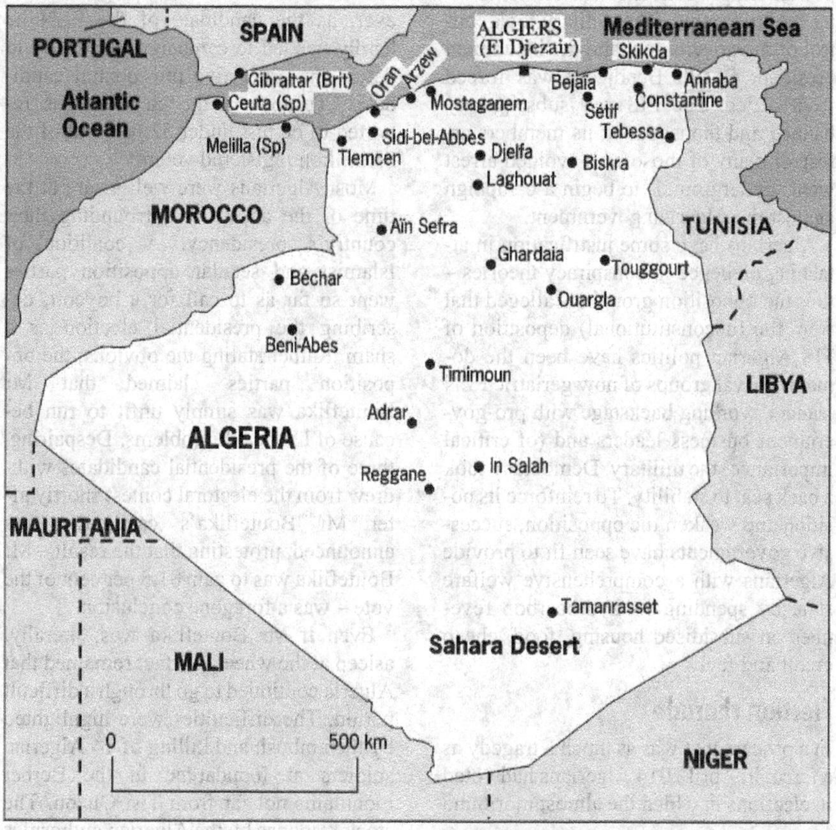

There was a sense of weary *déjà vu* in the streets of Algiers as 2015 wore on. Although Algeria's main ruling parties all claimed to be supporting the invalid President Abdelaziz Bouteflika there was widespread concern that falling oil prices were leaving Algeria with its first budget deficit. Mid-June 2015 saw a cabinet reshuffle when the 74 year old Abdelkader Bensaleh resigned from the Rassemblement National Démocratique (RND) (National Rally for Democracy), the subordinate ruling party with the Front de Libération Nationale (FLN) (National Liberation Front), which had led Algeria since its independence from France in 1962.

This 'enabling' departure allowed President Bouteflika's ultra loyal supporter and director of cabinet Ahmed Ouyahia, to lead the RND, unquestionably positioning him to run as a presidential successor. Amar Sadani, leader of the ruling FLN party, kept his position after President Bouteflika expressed support for him during the 2015 party congress.

The continued speculation and uncertainty over President Bouteflika's health (more bluntly, his life expectancy) since suffering a 'mini-stroke' in 2013 extended to whether he would even be able to remain in power until the end of his fourth term in 2019. Alongside the speculation came the internal debate as to who might replace the President, who had been in office since 1999.

Other contenders for the Presidency were rumoured to be the Prime Minister, Abdelmalek Sellal, who had only recently joined the FLN to boost support for his candidacy. Mr Sellal also has the advantage of being an intimate of President Bouteflika, for whom he served as election campaign leader in three elections. An equally high-profile presidential contender might be Lakhdar Brahimi, a

KEY FACTS

Official name: Al Jumhuriya al Jazairiya ad Dimucratiya ash Shabiya (Democratic and Popular Republic of Algeria)

Head of State: President Abdelaziz Bouteflika (since 1999; re-elected Apr 2004, 2009 and 17 April 2014)

Head of government: Prime Minister Abdelmalek Sellal (Independent) (from 29 Apr 2014)

Ruling party: Coalition led by Front de Libération Nationale (FLN) (National Liberation Front), (since 2002; re-elected 10 May 2012)

Area: 2,381,741 square km

Population: 38.70 million (2014)*

Capital: Algiers

Official language: Arabic

Currency: Algerian dinar (AD) = 100 centimes

Exchange rate: AD106.11 per US$ (Sep 2015)

GDP per capita: US$5,532 (2014)*

GDP real growth: 4.13% (2014)*

GDP: US$214.08 billion (2014)*

Labour force: 10.81 million (2010)

Unemployment: 10.60% (2014)*

Inflation: 2.92% (2014)

Oil production: 1.52 million bpd (2014)

Natural gas production: 83.30 billion cum (2014)

Balance of trade: US$9.45 billion (2014)

* estimated figure

former United Nations envoy who had gained prominence as a UN intermediary in Syria. Surprisingly, Algeria had managed to steer clear of the backwash from the 'Arab Spring' movement that had gained prominence in neighbouring Tunisia.

Algeria is a key North Atlantic Treaty Organisation (NATO) ally against Islamist militancy in the region. Although political violence in Algeria has declined since the 1990s, it was nevertheless taken aback by the bombing campaign carried out by a group calling itself al Qaeda in the Land of Islamic Maghreb (AQLIM). According to the British Broadcasting Corporation (BBC), the group was formerly known as the Salafist Group for Call and Combat and has its roots in an Islamist militia involved in the civil war in the 1990s. Although experts doubt whether AQLIM has direct operational links with al Qaeda elsewhere, its methods – which include suicide bombings – and its choice of targets, such as foreign workers and the UN headquarters in Algiers, follow the al Qaeda method. Of concern to the Algerian authorities is the way in which Islamist groups throughout the Sahara region are linking up under the umbrella of the new movement, reinforced by arms obtained during the Libyan civil war.

Algeria can no longer be considered a 'young' country. Many Algerians are still alive who saw the turmoil through which their country passed during the war of independence from France. Victory enabled the FLN to establish one-party rule, which persisted until the 1980s. Democracy collapsed into civil war when election results were 'cancelled' following the apparent victory of the Islamist party, the Front Islamique du Salut (FIS) (Islamic Salvation Front) in the parliamentary elections. The still ruling FLN, anticipating a loss of power, simply cancelled the elections after the first round. The military took control of the government and the incumbent president Chadli Bendjedid was forced from office. The FIS was subsequently banned and thousands of its members arrested; many of those who avoided arrest went 'underground' to begin a campaign against the Algerian government.

Algerians have some justification in attaching credence to conspiracy theories – thus the opposition groupings alleged that from the (unconstitutional) deposition of FIS Algerian politics have been the domain of rival groups of now geriatric FLN leaders, working backstage with pro-government business leaders and (of critical importance) the military. Democracy took a back seat to stability. To reinforce its position and weaken the opposition, successive governments have seen fit to provide Algerians with a comprehensive welfare state by spending its hydrocarbon revenues on subsidised housing, food, cheap credit and fuel.

Election charade

In a process that was as much a tragedy as a farce, in April 2014 Algerians had voted in elections in which the almost moribund incumbent President Abdelaziz Bouteflika sought a fourth term. Since the 77-year old Bouteflika suffered a stroke in 2013 he had rarely appeared in public. He did, however, manage to cast his vote, cutting a sorry figure in a wheelchair, apparently unaware of what was going on around him. Manifestly, Mr Bouteflika had not been an active campaigner. However, as the candidate of the FLN he hardly needed to campaign personally to defeat the other five presidential candidates. Turnout in the election was reported to be just under 52 per cent of the 23 million registered voters.

Most Algerians were well aware at the time of the absurdity surrounding their country's presidency. A coalition of Islamist and secular opposition parties went so far as to call for a boycott, describing the presidential election as a sham. Rather stating the obvious, the opposition parties claimed that Mr Bouteflika was simply unfit to run because of his health problems. Despairing, three of the presidential candidates withdrew from the electoral contest shortly after Mr Bouteflika's candidacy was announced, protesting that the result – Mr Bouteflika was to gain 81.5 per cent of the vote – was a foregone conclusion.

Even if Mr Bouteflika was, literally, asleep at the wheel, the fact remained that Algeria continued to go through a difficult period. The difficulties were highlighted by the ambush and killing of 14 Algerian soldiers at Iboudarene in the Berber mountains not far from Tisi Ouzou. The stock response by the Algerian authorities was to attribute the attack on the soldiers to al-Qa'eda in the Maghreb. That was the government's answer to a problem that its leader was clearly unable to grasp. The FLN's political masquerade was a cocktail of vested interests, ineptitude and paralysis. Underlying the obvious stalemate within the FLN, is a degree of self-deception creating a corresponding degree of muted despair among many Algerians.

The economy

Algeria has almost US$200 billion in foreign reserves and little by way of debt. But its oil and gas revenues fell 42 per cent in the first four months of 2015 and the government has suspended some major infrastructure projects and frozen some public sector hiring.

Algeria found itself at a delicate juncture after the 2014 fall in oil prices slashed the revenues that made up 95 per cent of its exports and more than half the state budget. Algeria's energy production had

KEY INDICATORS — **Algeria**

	Unit	2011	2012	2013	2014	**2015
Population	m	*35.95	*37.49	37.90	*38.70	*39.47
Gross domestic product (GDP)	US$bn	190.70	204.29	208.76	*214.08	*187.17
GDP per capita	US$	5,304	5,448	5,508	*5,532	*4,742
GDP real growth	%	2.5	3.3	2.8	*4.1	*2.6
Inflation	%	4.5	8.9	3.3	2.9	*4.0
Unemployment	%	10.0	11.0	9.8	10.6	*11.8
Oil output	'000 bpd	1,729.0	1,677.0	1,575.0	1,525.0	–
Natural gas output	bn cum	78.0	81.5	78.6	83.3	–
Exports (fob) (goods)	US$m	72,779.5	71,558.2	64,330.3	–	–
Imports (fob) (goods)	US$m	44,767.1	51,508.9	54,878.3	–	–
Balance of trade	US$m	28,012.4	20,049.3	9,452.1	–	–
Current account	US$m	19,393.3	12,290.0	835.0	-9,289.0	-29,358.0
Total reserves minus gold	US$m	176,177.0	191,297.0	194,712.0	179,618.0	–
Foreign exchange	US$m	173,910.0	189,010.0	192,357.0	–	–
Exchange rate	per US$	71.40	78.94	78.15	87.90	–

* estimated figure ** forecast figure

stagnated as foreign oil investors simply stayed away. According to the International Monetary Fund (IMF) in its December 2014 Country Report, Algeria's economic activity was projected to have picked up in 2014. The hydrocarbon sector, which had been shrinking in recent years, was expected to expand modestly, while non-hydrocarbon growth remained relatively robust. Inflation had fallen below Banque d'Algérie (the central bank)'s target, thanks to tighter monetary policy, but new pressures could emerge. Algeria's external and fiscal buffers remained large and the financial sector was generally healthy, if underdeveloped. However, in the view of the IMF, 'long-standing vulnerabilities' were coming to light. In 2014, for the first time in 15 years the current account recorded a deficit as stronger oil consumption and lower hydrocarbon prices weighed on exports while (largely investment-related) imports continued to grow. As was so often the case with 'oil rich' states, Algeria's economy remained overly dependent on the hydrocarbon sector and public spending and was therefore doubly vulnerable to any protracted decline in oil prices.

Unemployment had stabilised at high levels, especially among youth and women. The IMF considered that Algeria needed to consolidate macro-economic and financial stability. A full-fledged fiscal rule, combined with an ambitious consolidation effort over the medium term, would help put the fiscal stance on a sustainable path. The decline in inflation experienced since 2012 was a positive outcome that needed to be maintained with continued efforts to absorb liquidity and a more active use of interest rates. Algeria's exchange rate policy also needed to avoid deviations of the dinar from its equilibrium level and to support a 'deepening' of forex markets. An export-oriented strategy was needed to ensure external sustainability. Export diversification was imperative to ensure external sustainability and reduce Algeria's vulnerability to fluctuating oil prices. The IMF recommended that diversification policies should focus on maintaining economic stability and improving competitiveness, increasing openness to trade and capital flows, (particularly foreign direct investment (FDI)) and creating a more export-friendly business climate. The IMF suggested that additional reforms were needed to increase hydrocarbon exports, including reforms to increase production and phase-out implicit subsidies on energy and electricity, which were fuelling domestic consumption.

In short, Algeria's significant growth potential needed to be more fully realised. Reforms were needed to reduce the dominance of the public sector and transform the private sector into an engine for growth, supported by a deeper financial sector. To increase employment, Algeria will need better-functioning labour markets, a workforce equipped with more relevant skills and more effective labour market programmes. The IMF put gross domestic product (GDP) growth at 2.8 per cent in 2013 (lower than the African Development Bank's (AfDB) estimated 3.0 per cent, down from the 3.3 per cent of 2012, affected by a 5.5 per cent contraction in hydrocarbon production – the eighth consecutive year of decline – and lower public spending. Non-hydrocarbon sector growth remained stable at 7.1 per cent, supported by continued rapid growth in the agricultural and services sectors. Inflation declined from 8.9 per cent in 2012 to 3.3 per cent, reflecting the impact of fiscal consolidation, monetary policy tightening, softer international food prices and high base effects. Average inflation continued to decline in 2014, reaching 1.5 per cent in August, but was somewhat on the rise at 2.9 per cent on a year-on-year basis in December. The AfDB put the inflation rate at 3.3 per cent.

Algeria's current account surplus narrowed to 0.4 per cent of GDP in 2013, from 5.9 per cent in 2012. Hydrocarbon exports fell more than 10 per cent because of both softer prices and lower volumes. Imports grew by nearly 7 per cent, partly owing to the one-off effect of increased imports of petroleum products following the temporary shutdown of three refineries. Inflows of FDI investment remained weak, at less than one per cent of GDP and the level of foreign exchange reserves increased slightly, from US$191 billion to US$194 billion, mainly because of valuation effects. External debt stood at 1.6 per cent of GDP at end-2013.

Algeria's banking sector, in the view of the IMF, remained solvent and liquid. The overall capital adequacy ratio was 21.5 per cent in 2013, down slightly from 23.4 per cent in 2012. The ratio of non-performing loans (NPLs) improved from 11.5 per cent to 10.6 per cent, helped by the growth in credit. Nearly 70 per cent of NPLs were fully provisioned. Credit to the economy reached 45.2 per cent of non-hydrocarbon GDP in 2013, up from 41.3 per cent in 2012, remaining weak compared to other regional economies and other middle-income countries.

GDP growth increased to 4.1 per cent in 2014. The hydrocarbon sector recorded modest positive growth (0.4 per cent) for the first time in nine years, driven by the growth in domestic consumption and a less acute contraction in net hydrocarbon export volumes. Non-hydrocarbon growth slowed, however, owing to the poor wheat harvest and the slowdown in industrial activity. Inflation was 2.9 per cent, but bears watching closely, given the potential for new inflation pressures to emerge. Perhaps the largest cause for concern was the expectation that the current account showed a record a deficit (-4.0 per cent of GDP, estimate) for the first time since 1999. Over the medium term, current account deficits are expected to widen as lower oil prices outweigh any growth in hydrocarbon export volumes. Foreign exchange reserves decrease by some US$6 billion in 2014, reaching US$188 billion at the end of the year.

Energy

According to the US government Energy Information Administration (EIA), Algeria is the leading natural gas producer in Africa, the second-largest natural gas supplier to Europe and is among the top three oil producers in Africa. Algeria became a member of the Organisation of the Petroleum Exporting Countries (OPEC) in 1969, shortly after it began oil production in 1958. The economy is reliant on revenues generated from the hydrocarbon sector, which account for about 30 per cent of GDP, more than 95 per cent of export earnings and 60 per cent of budget revenues, according to the IMF. Oil and natural gas export revenues were almost US$63.8 billion in 2013, down from US$69.8 billion in the previous year, mainly because of lower export volumes, according to the Middle East Economic Survey (MEES). Hydrocarbon export revenue has permitted a comfortable level of foreign exchange reserves, which – according to the EIA – reached US$194 billion by the end of December 2013.

Oil and natural gas production have, according to the EIA, declined in recent years, mainly due to repeated project delays resulting from slow government approval, difficulties attracting investment, infrastructure gaps and technical problems. The Algerian government enacted new contractual and fiscal provisions in 2013 in the hope of attracting more FDI, particularly toward unconventional assets (especially shale oil and gas). In January 2014, the government launched its first licensing round since 2011. According to

PFC Energy, 31 blocks, of which 17 hold shale resources, were offered.

Algeria is estimated to hold the third-largest amount of shale gas resources in the world, according to the EIA, which estimates that Algeria contains 707 trillion cubic feet (tcf) and 5.7 billion barrels of recoverable shale gas and oil resources. However, industry analysts are cautious about the prospects of Algeria becoming a notable shale producer. An analysis by MEES points out the obstacles Algeria faces: remote location of the shale acreage, lack of infrastructure and accessibility to sites, water availability, lack of roads and pipelines to move materials and the need for more rigs because shale wells deplete quicker. A further disincentive was triggered by the 2013 attack on the In Amenas gas facility, which prompted security concerns about operating in Algeria's remote areas. Any major disruption to Algeria's hydrocarbon production would be detrimental to the local economy and, depending on the scale of lost production, could affect world oil prices. Also, unplanned cuts to natural gas output could affect European countries.

Algeria also relies on its own oil and natural gas production for (subsidised) domestic consumption. Natural gas and oil account for almost all of Algeria's total primary energy consumption. Domestic prices for oil products and natural gas are very low in Algeria by international standards, according to the IMF, which estimates that Algeria has the second-cheapest domestic price for natural gas in Africa, after Libya, as retail prices have not changed since 2005 and are now below operational costs. The IMF estimates that the cost of the subsidies on oil products and natural gas amounted to US$22.2 billion in 2012, or 10.7 per cent of GDP.

Natural gas accounts for 98 per cent of power generation in Algeria, according to the IMF. Like natural gas, electricity prices have also been unchanged since 2005. However, the cost of gaining an electricity connection can be time-consuming and costly. Nonetheless, more than 99 per cent of Algeria's population has access to electricity. Algeria's government is attempting to reduce the dependence on natural gas in the power sector by initiating more renewable energy projects. Soneglaz, Algeria's state electricity and gas utility, has signed contracts for solar projects and a wind farm pilot programme.

Algeria's national oil and natural gas company, , Entreprise Nationale Sonatrach (Sonatrach), dominates the country's hydrocarbon sector, owning roughly 80 per cent of all hydrocarbon production. By law, Sonatrach is given majority ownership of oil and natural gas projects in Algeria. Legislation drawn up in 2005 determines the involvement of international oil companies (IOCs) in upstream exploration and production, midstream transportation and the downstream sector. The original 2005 legislation was more favourable to foreign involvement than its 1986 predecessor. However, amendments to the bill were made in 2006 and some of the favourable terms were reversed, so that Sonatrach was granted a minimum equity stake of 51 per cent in any hydrocarbon project and a windfall profits tax was introduced for IOCs.

Unsurprisingly, Algeria has experienced difficulties attracting foreign investors, particularly at licencing rounds. In the country's seventh licencing round in 2008, only 4 of the available 16 blocks were awarded, 3 of 8 in 2009 and 2 of 10 in 2011. Analysts blame the lack of fiscal incentives for the failure to attract foreign investors to new projects, coupled with past Sonatrach corruption allegations. As noted above, the security situation has also been a concern. According to *BP Statistical Review of World Energy* of June 2015 (BP15) estimates, Algeria held an estimated 12.2 billion barrels of proved crude oil reserves, an estimate that has been unchanged for many years. All of Algeria's proved oil reserves are held onshore; there has been limited offshore exploration. The most oil reserves are in the Hassi Messaoud province, which contains the country's oldest and largest oil field, Hassi Messaoud, near the Libyan border. Hassi Messaoud is estimated to hold 3.9 billion barrels of proved and probable recoverable reserves, followed by the Hassi R'Mel field (3.7 billion barrels) and the Ourhoud field (1.9 billion barrels), according to the *Arab Oil & Gas Journal*.

Algeria produced an estimated average of 1.53 million bpd of oil in 2014, slightly higher than the previous year. Algerian oil fields produce high-quality light crude oil with very low sulphur and mineral content. Sonatrach operates the largest oil field in Algeria, Hassi Messaoud, which produced roughly 500,000bpd of crude oil in 2014, or more than 40 per cent of Algeria's total crude output. Other large producing areas in Algeria include the Ourhoud and the Hassi Berkine complex. Algeria's largest oil fields are mature. Field expansions and enhanced oil recovery techniques have kept the country's oldest fields at a steady rate of production, but this trend is slowly starting to reverse. The EIA projects that Algeria's crude oil output will decline in the short and medium term. Algeria does not have any major crude oil projects scheduled to come on stream. Algeria exports mostly light crude oil. The country's main crude grade is the Sahara blend, which is a blend of crudes produced at fields in the Hassi Messaoud region. In 2013, Algeria exported approximately 750,000bpd of crude oil, including condensate, according to estimates from EIA, Global Trade Atlas (GTA) and FACTs Global Energy. Most of Algeria's crude oil exports are sent to Europe (72 per cent), with the remainder sent to the Americas (18 per cent) and Asia and Oceania (10 per cent). The United States was one of Algeria's single largest markets for crude oil for almost a decade until 2013. US crude oil imports from Algeria have substantially declined.

According to BP15, as of December 2014, Algeria had 4.5 trillion cubic metres (tcm) of proved natural gas reserves, the tenth-largest natural gas reserves in the world and the second largest in Africa, behind Nigeria. Algeria's largest natural gas field, Hassi R'Mel, was discovered in 1956. Located in the centre of the country to the north-west of Hassi Messaoud, it holds proved reserves of about 85 trillion cubic feet (tcf), more than half of Algeria's total natural gas reserves. According to the *Arab Oil & Gas Journal*, Hassi R'Mel accounted for three-fifths of Algeria's gross natural gas production in 2012. The remainder of Algeria's natural gas reserves are located in associated and non-associated fields in the southern and south-eastern regions of the country.

As noted above, Algeria also holds vast shale gas resources, 707tcf of technically recoverable gas, the third-largest amount in the world after China and Argentina. The Ghadames Basin, encompassing eastern Algeria, southern Tunisia and western Libya, has been identified as a major shale gas basin. In May 2014, Algeria's Council of Ministers gave formal approval to allow shale oil and gas development. The Council of Ministers estimated that it would take 7 to 13 years to confirm Algeria's potential shale resources.

Risk assessment

Politics	Poor
Economy	Fair
Regional stability	Fair

Muslims in Algeria

% of population	99
Sunni (% of Muslims)	99
Shi'a (% of Muslims)	1

COUNTRY PROFILE

1830 Algeria was conquered by the French.
1831 The Légion Étrangère (French Foreign Legion) was established and based in Algeria to protect French colonial interests.
1848 Algeria became a *département* of France.
1954 The Front de Libération Nationale (FLN) (National Liberation Front) led the struggle for independence.
1962 Algeria gained independence and Ahmed ben Bella of the FLN was designated Algeria's first president.
1965 Ahmed ben Bella was ousted by Colonel Houari Boumédienne.
1976 Boumédienne won the presidential elections. He introduced a new constitution, which confirmed commitment to socialism, the FLN as the sole political party and Islam as the state religion. The constitution was approved by referendum. A programme of industrialisation began.
1973–76 Algeria supported the formation of the Frente Popular para la Liberación de Saguia el Hamra y Río de Oro (Polisario) (Popular Front for the Liberation of Saguia el Hamra y Río de Oro) in Spanish Sahara. The group wanted self-determination for Spanish Sahara (later known as Western Sahara). Spain handed the territory over to Morocco and Mauritania, Polisario announced the formation of the Saharawi Arab Democratic Republic (SADR) and formed a government-in-exile.
1977–85 Fighting continued between Moroccan military and Polisario forces. Morocco left the Organisation for African Unity (OAU) in protest at the SADR's admission to the body.
1988 Full diplomatic relations with Morocco were resumed.
1978 President Boumédienne died and the FLN candidate, Colonel Chadli Benjedid, was elected president; he was re-elected in 1984 and 1989.
1986–91 Rising inflation and unemployment, exacerbated by the collapse of oil and gas prices, led to strikes and violent demonstrations. A UN-monitored cease-fire began in Western Sahara.
1989 The National People's Assembly revoked the ban on new political parties and the Front Islamique du Salut (FIS) (Islamic Salvation Front) was founded.
1991 The FIS won the first round of the parliamentary elections and the second round was cancelled when it seemed certain the FIS would gain an absolute majority.
1992 Violent outbreaks followed the cancellation of the elections. The National People's Assembly was dissolved by presidential decree. President Chadli resigned and a five-member Haut Conseil d'Etat (HCE) (High Council of State) was instituted. The FIS was banned. A state of emergency was declared following clashes between FIS supporters and security forces. Mohammed Boudiaf, chairman of the HCE, was assassinated. The Armée Islamique du Salut (AIS) (Islamic Salvation Army), the military arm of the FIS, launched a campaign of guerrilla warfare.
1994 Liamine Zeroual became chairman of the HCE.
1995 Zeroual was elected president in the first multi-party democratic elections.
1997–98 The newly created Rassemblement Nationale Démocratique (RND) (National Democratic Rally) won the parliamentary elections.
1999 President Zeroual stood down (one year early) and Abdelaziz Bouteflika was elected president. A referendum approved Bouteflika's law on civil concord and thousands of members of the AIS and other armed groups were pardoned.
2000 Attacks continued by small groups of dissidents opposed to the civil accord. Ali Benflis became prime minister.
2001 The Berber community were granted greater cultural and political recognition following months of unrest in the Kabylie region.
2002 The Berber language, Tamazight, was officially recognised as a national language. Berber activists in Kabylie and several opposition parties elsewhere boycotted the parliamentary elections, which were won by the FLN.
2003 A major earthquake hit northern Algeria, the worst since 1980. The leader of the banned FIS and his deputy were freed from prison after serving 12-year sentences. President Bouteflika dismissed Ali Benflis as prime minister and appointed Ahmed Ouyahia in his place.
2004 President Bouteflika was re-elected and re-appointed Prime Minister Ouyahia.
2005 Nourredine Boudiafi, the head of the AIS, was arrested and his deputy killed. The government promised Berber leaders more investment in the Kabylie region and greater recognition for the Tamazight language. An official inquiry concluded that security forces abducted and killed over 6,000 citizens during civil unrest in the 1990s; the guerrilla campaign of the FIS was estimated to have killed 150,000 people. In a 'reconciliation' referendum there was overwhelming support for the government's granting of amnesty to many who were involved in the post-1992 killings.
2006 Ahmed Ouyahia resigned and Abdelaziz Belkhadem became prime minister. Measures to increase the state owned oil giant Sonatrach's role in oil and gas exploration and refining were introduced.
2007 The FLN won parliamentary elections, with a reduced majority, losing seats to its coalition partners in a low turnout. Prime Minister Belkhadem resigned and was re-appointed by the president.
2008 President Bouteflika appointed Ahmed Ouyahia as prime minister; he had previously served as prime minister 1996–98 and 2003–06. A referendum confirmed a change to the constitution allowing a president to run for a third-term in office. A census recorded a population of 34,452,759 people.
2009 President Bouteflika won a third term in office, with 90.2 per cent of the vote. His closest rival was Louisa Hanoune with 4.22 per cent. Algeria, Nigeria and Niger agreed to build a US$13 billion pipeline across the Sahara, taking Nigerian natural gas to the Mediterranean gas network.
2010 The Russian energy giant Gazprom, in partnership with the state-owned Sonatrach, began prospecting for natural gas in the Berkine basin, 500km south of Algiers. A published report warned that the Berber language (Tamazight) was in danger of dying out due to discrimination and neglect. According to research, the twentieth century was one of the driest periods, with multiple droughts in the Maghreb region. Parliament approved a US$1.48 billion fund for scientific research, in hopes of reversing the country's 'brain-drain'. Research programmes to benefit from further funding include agriculture, health and energy, with an emphasis on applied research and technology.
2011 Riots across the country in January following steep rises in food prices, were quelled by police at a cost of five dead, 800 injured (including 763 police officers) and thousands arrested. In response, the government cut import duties and taxes to curb prices that had risen by 30 per cent within 10 days. In February President Bouteflika announced that the 19-year state of emergency would be lifted. The decision had been forced on the regime, following widespread protests not only in Algeria but also in a number of other Arab countries. Africa's second metro (of 10 stations) opened in Algiers in November.
2012 Algeria's first post-independence president, Ahmed Ben Bella (1963–65) died on 11 April, aged 95 years. In parliamentary elections held on 10 May, the ruling FLN won 220 seats (out of 462), an increase of 84 seats over the 2007 elections. FLN's coalition partner, RND, increased their seats by seven to reach 68 in total. The newly formed Alliance de l'Algérie Vert (AAV) (Green Alliance), a

coalition of three Islamist political parties, led by Bouguerra Soltani, leader of the Algerian Hamas, won 48 seats. On 3 September, the president appointed Abdelmalek Sellal as prime minister, replacing Ahmed Ouyahia.
2013 On 16 January al-Qaeda-linked terrorists affiliated with a brigade led by Mokhtar Belmokhtar took over 800 people hostage at the Tigantourine gas facility near In Amenas. After four days, the Algerian special forces raided the site, in an effort to free the hostages. At least 39 foreign hostages were killed, an Algerian security guard and 29 militants. Some 685 Algerian workers and 107 foreigners were freed. Three militants were captured. President Abdelaziz Bouteflika suffered a mini-stroke on April 27; he was flown to hospital in Paris. The President returned on 16 July and although he was photographed meeting Prime Minister Sallal, he looked frail. There have been suggestions that the Constitutional Council should declare the position of president vacant so that an interim president can be appointed until elections can be held. However, in November the FLN endorsed Bouteflika as their presidential candidate.
2014 Despite his frailty and previously declaring that he would not stand again, President Bouteflika stood in the 17 April presidential election, winning with a resounding 8,332,598 (81.53 per cent) of the vote; turnout was 51.70 per cent. He was inaugurated as president for his fourth term on 28 April.
2015 Ahmed Ouyahia was elected as the new leader of Rassemblement National pour la Démocratie (RND) (National Rally for Democracy) in June. He would be a possible presidential contender.

Political structure

Constitution
The 1976 constitution has been amended three times.
In 1997, the government banned religion-based parties and imposed a law restricting the formation of political parties. All political parties must hold a founding conference attended by 400–500 delegates elected by 25,000 supporters from 25 of the country's 48 provinces. This policy is intended to limit the number of political parties and place at severe disadvantage all parties that lack funding – particularly those, such as the Front Islamique du Salut (FIS) (Islamic Salvation Front), without access to state funds.

Independence date
1962

Form of state
Republic

The executive
The head of state is the president, elected by universal suffrage for five years. He appoints a prime minister, who in turn appoints a government.
The president has the power to dissolve the government and request elections.

National legislature
The bicameral parliament consists of the 380-member Al Majlis al Sha'abi al Watani (Assemblée Populaire Nationale) (National People's Assembly) and the 144-member Al Majlis al Umma (Conseil de la Nation) (National Council). Members of the Majlis al Sha'abi al Watani are elected in multi-seat constituencies by proportional representation for five-year terms and include eight seats reserved for Algerian voters abroad; it holds legislative power. In the Majlis al Umma 96 members are elected by local councils and 48 are appointed by the president.

Legal system
The legal system is based on French and Islamic law.
The judicial system consists of 183 courts and 31 appeal courts organised on a regional basis.
There are three special criminal courts in Oran, Constantine and Algiers, which deal with economic crimes against the state (against which there is no appeal) – the Court of State Security which is composed of judges and army officers, the court of audit and the Supreme Court in Algiers, which is the ultimate judicial authority.
Algeria has not accepted International Court of Justice (ICJ) jurisdiction.

Last elections
17 April 2014 (presidential); 10 May 2012 (parliamentary)
Results: Presidential: Abdelaziz Bouteflika won with 8,332,598 (81.53 per cent) of the vote, Ali Benflis 1,244,918 (12.18 per cent), no other candidate won over 5 per cent; turnout was 51.70 per cent.
Parliamentary: Front de Libération Nationale (FLN) (National Liberation Front) won 208 seats (out of 462), Rassemblement National pour la Démocratie (RND) (National Rally for Democracy) 68, Alliance de l'Algérie Vert (AAV) (Green Alliance, coalition of three Islamist political parties) 49, Front des Forces Socialistes (FFS) (Socialist Forces Front) 27, Parti du Travail (PT) (Workers' Party) 24, Independents and 21 other political parties shared the remaining 86 seats. Turnout was 43.14 per cent.

Next elections
2019 (presidential); May 2017 (parliamentary)

Political parties

Ruling party
Coalition led by Front de Libération Nationale (FLN) (National Liberation Front), (since 2002; re-elected 10 May 2012)

Main opposition party
Parti du Travail (PT) (Workers' Party).

Population

37.90 million (2013)*
Last census: 16 April 2008: 34,745,000 (provision figure) (including 230,000 nomads)
Population density: 12 inhabitants per square km. Urban population 66 per cent (2010 Unicef).
Annual growth rate: 1.7 per cent, 1990–2010 (Unicef).

Internally Displaced Persons (IDP)
1.0 million (UNHCR 2004)

Ethnic make-up
The majority of Algerians are of Berber descent. The other significant ethnic group is Arab, although as a result of centuries of integration the two ethnic groups have become increasingly indistinguishable. The distinct Berber culture and language is best preserved in the north and eastern regions of Algeria.
The European population, most of whom are French, has declined from over one million before independence in 1962 to less than 50,000 in 2001.

Religions
Islam is the official religion. Approximately 99 per cent of the population is Sunni Muslim, while Christians make up about one per cent.

Education

Primary education lasts for six years. Secondary education, which begins at age 11, is divided into two courses of four years and three years. Approximately 13 per cent of students remain at tertiary level. Teaching is carried out in Arabic, although at higher levels French is widely used.
The government has encouraged girls to attend school to reduce the difference in literacy rates. A total of 86 per cent of girls are now educated to primary level, and 53 per cent to secondary level.
Total expenditure on education is 4–5 per cent of GDP.
Literacy rate: 69 per cent adult rate; 90 per cent youth rate (15–24) (Unesco 2005).
Compulsory years: 6 to 15.
Enrolment rate: 98 per cent gross primary enrolment of relevant age group (including repeaters); 63 per cent gross secondary enrolment (World Bank).
Pupils per teacher: 27 in primary schools.

Health

All Algerians are entitled to free medical care. Medicines are sold through the state monopoly at subsidised prices, and are provided free to children and the elderly, though there have been some cutbacks. Health indicators point to a deterioration

in public health, with infant mortality ratios and infectious diseases increasing. Health care infrastructure and personnel show considerable urban-rural disparities.
Life expectancy: 73 years, 2010 (Unicef 2012)
Fertility rate/Maternal mortality rate: 2.3 births per woman, 2010 (Unicef 2012)
Child (under 5 years) mortality rate (per 1,000): 20 per 1,000 live births (WHO 2012); 6 per cent of children aged under five are malnourished (World Bank).

Welfare

During the 1990s, unemployment rates increased dramatically, poverty doubled and the purchasing power of the middle class experienced a huge drop.
Government expenditure on social protection is relatively high, but the welfare system is criticised as unsustainable and inefficient. The most serious challenge to the government is tackling unemployment. The government continues to play a major role in providing housing and basic health services, particularly to urban populations. Substantial housing shortages have proven persistent, despite the deregulation efforts the government undertook to promote private sector construction.

Main cities

Algiers (El Djazair) (capital, estimated population 3.3 million in 2012), Oran (641,240), Constantine (465,138), Djelfa (373,547), Batna (324,897), Setif (324,502), Annaba (272,807), Sidi Bel Abbes (233,771), Tiaret (229,376).

Languages spoken

Arabic (modern standard), known as *Fus'ha*, is used in the courts, mosques, most of the media and in education.
About 80 per cent of Algerians speak the North African dialectal Arabic, *Darja*.
French is widely spoken, especially as a language of commerce.
In 2003, Tamazight (the Berber language) was categorised as a national language, but the Berbers want it to have equal status alongside Arabic as an official language. Tamazight belongs to the Afro-Asiatic family and is related to ancient Egyptian and Ethiopian. Berber groups and their dialects include: Kabyles (Taqbaylit), Kabylie region, Kabyle dialect; Chaouia (Ishawiyan), Eastern Algeria, Tashawit dialect; Mozabites (Imzabiyan), northern edge of Sahara, Tamzabit dialect; Tuaregs (Tamachaq), extreme south, Tuareg dialect.

Official language/s

Arabic

Media

Despite laws guaranteeing freedom of access to information and freedom of expression in accordance with the constitution journalists are regularly targeted by not only the authorities but also militant Islamists. There are libel laws with large fines and *Sharia* (Islamic law) that can curb the media's ability to question and investigate; self-censorship is prevalent. The law allows the formation of privately owned newspapers, but any new non-Arabic publication must first be approved by the independent Information Council.
In September 2011 the government announced sweeping media reforms to allow private radio and television stations to exist for the first time since independence in 1962.

Press

Most newspapers are in private ownership.
Dailies: In Arabic, *Ech Chaab* (www.ech-chaab.com) is state-owned, *Ech Chourouk* (www.echoroukonline.com) and *El Khabar* are privately owned, with English editions. In French, *El Moudjahid* (www.elmoudjahid-dz.com) is state-owned, *El Watan* (www.elwatan.com), *Liberte* (www.liberte-algerie.com), *La Tribune* (www.latribune-online.com), and *Le Soir d'Algeria* (www.lesoirdalgerie.com) an evening newspaper, are all privately owned. *Le jeune indépendant* (www.jeune-independant.com) is a publication for the young.
Weeklies: In French, a privately owned, current affairs magazine is *Algérie Actualité*, while *El Hakika* is an Arab tabloid.
Business: In French, there are three publications, *Le Maghreb* (www.lemaghrebdz.com), an influential daily along with *Liberte Economie* (www.liberte-economie.com), with wide ranging topics; *Le Journal d'Affaires* (www.lejournaldaffaires.com) is more informal.
Periodicals: In French and Arabic, *El Manchar* is a bi-monthly satirical magazine.

Broadcasting

All broadcasting is state controlled. National public broadcasting is provided by Radiodiffusion Télévision Algérienne (RTA).
Radio: Algerian Radio (www.algerian-radio.dz), operated by RTA, has 35 stations providing three radio networks with local and international services in Arabic, French and Tamazight. International services are also provided in Spanish and English.
Television: The state-run Enterprise Nationale de Télévision (ENTV) (www.entv.dz) provides services in Arabic and French with online programmes. Satellite programming is provided by ENTV through Canal Algérie and Thalitha. ENTV also has collaborative links with French-based Berbère TV (www.brtv.fr).
National news agency: Algerian Press Service (APS)
Other news agencies: Agence Algérienne d'Information (AAI) (in French): www.aai-online.com

Economy

With large reserves of hydrocarbons, 12.2 billion barrels of oil and 4.5 trillion cubic metres of natural gas at the end of 2014, the economy has been buoyed by strong exports that have provided a trade surplus. However, there is little investment in other sectors of the economy and without hydrocarbons it remains weak.
Algeria has benefited from the sharp rise in global oil prices since 2005, tripling its record foreign exchange reserves between 2000–06. Oil and gas accounts for almost 30 per cent of GDP, 60 per cent of budget revenues and 95 per cent of export earnings. It has been able to pay back around 50 per cent of its outstanding debts to its Paris Club creditors since the government introduced new hydrocarbon laws that opened up the market to redevelopment with deregulated oil and gas prices. However, the drop in the price of oil, to US$60 per barrel from around US$120, at the end of 2014, has seen Algeria use up much of their cash reserves to try and weather the storm. Though the crash has been less damaging in Algeria than other hydrocarbon rich nations, it has nonetheless caused many problems. The oil crash of 1986 saw Algeria come to the edge of bankruptcy and was one of the leading factors that led to the Algerian civil war which claimed some 200,000 lives. With this in mind, and the recent fears of the Arab spring, the government was unwilling to cut public services and so has had to heavily dip into their foreign currency reserves, which amount to about US$200 billion. The 2015 budget therefore increased by 15 per cent, pushing Algeria's debt to 22 per cent of GDP.
The IMF has warned that high revenue from oil production discourages growth elsewhere in the economy and the money from higher oil prices should be reinvested to diversify and expand the economy. The government embarked on a five-year US$55 billion spending programme in 2004 and the results have shown improvement in infrastructure and employment prospects. GDP growth averaged 2.8 per cent over 2007–10, and was 2.7 per cent in 2013 and rose again to 4 per cent in 2014. Growth in 2015 is unsure due to the drastic drop in oil prices. GDP grew steadily from US$134.3 billion in 2007 to US$160.8 billion in 2010, and up to US$206.1 billion in

2013. Per capita income had been rising steadily until 2008 when it was US$4,996, but in 2009 it dropped to US$3,954 before resuming an increase to US$4,539 in 2010 and to US$5,438 in 2013 and further to US$552.6 billion in 2014.

Foreign remittances in 2013 amounted to US$214 million (0.1 per cent of GDP).

Algeria has huge potential, mainly due to its rich natural resources, but also its strategic position close to the fast growing and fuel-hungry EU, to which Algeria has linked gas pipelines.

The government's policy of turning Algeria's command economy into a market economy has not been a particularly popular one. Industrial action in protest at the sale of public enterprises has continued and the IMF is cautious about the balance between deregulating the market and the sharp rise in job losses this would cause, against the long term good of the market. The public sector accounts for some 60 per cent of employment.

Government policy includes improving the investment climate in the tourist sector and the production of non-oil related goods. In reality, obstacles remain for non-oil trade, primarily due to fluctuating foreign currency exchange. A climate of unrest and violence has resulted in reluctance on the part of private investors to put money into Algeria.

Algeria is taking tentative steps towards breaking the stranglehold oil and gas has on its economy, but it remains to be seen if it can diversify at a time when windfall revenue from high oil prices negates the value of any other industry or business.

External trade

The strict control of imports has begun to be relaxed, although the government still has a strong influence over planning the economy, with hydrocarbon exports providing a trade surplus each year. Algeria has large gas and oil reserves and a ready market for its natural gas, with a major pipeline already connecting, through Spain, to the rest of Europe.

Algeria moved closer to full membership of the WTO at a meeting of its Working Party on membership in March 2014. As of mid-2015 it is not yet a full member. Changes to its foreign trade policy were discussed. However, in a bid to become a member Algeria must revise legislation on the importation of alcohol that may prove unpopular.

Algeria has an Association Agreement, including free trade, with the EU, signed in 2005, which provides for the gradual removal of import duties on industrial products

Imports

Principal imports are capital goods electrical and electronic goods, semi-finished goods, food and tobacco, transport equipment and raw materials.

Main sources: China (14.1 per cent of total in 2014), France (10.8 per cent), Italy (8.6 per cent).

Exports

Principal exports are hydrocarbons, chemical fertilisers, iron and steel, wine, tobacco and foodstuffs.

Main destinations: Spain (15.2 per cent total goods exports in 2014), Italy (13.2 per cent), France (11.0 per cent).

Agriculture

Farming

The sector employs about 11 per cent of the labour force and contributes around 9.3 per cent of GDP. Just over 238.2 million hectares (ha) are given over to agriculture, or around 17 per cent of total land available, of which 3.1 per cent are under arable and permanent crops and 13.8 per cent is pasture land.

Climatic conditions and the availability of water for irrigation directly affect crop yields. Despite extensive irrigation programmes and the dividing of state holdings into smaller units, agricultural output has failed to keep pace with the rate of population growth. Imports typically represent around 25 per cent of import costs. Government policy had been to reduce reliance on imported food, now, however, an open market is developing as state owned agricultural land is returned to private hands.

Underlying constraints to growth include soil erosion, desert encroachment, inefficient management in the state sector, poor marketing, recurrent droughts and the inability of farmers to secure loan finance due to problems with land security. Government plans to reduce dependence on imports by a series of measures, included investing in new technology, financial incentives for state and private sector farms to buy equipment, encouraging foreign investment, less interference in the private sector and tree planting to arrest desertification.

There has been a large increase in the number of vineyards now operating in Algeria, providing a boost in export revenue. Although wine consumption is banned under Islamic law, production has been increasing. It has provided a healthy income for farmers, in semi-arid regions, when other food crops have failed.

Main cash crops include grapes, oranges, olives, dates, tobacco, sugar beet and tomatoes. Hard and soft wheat and barley are grown for the home market, as are vegetables, and pulses.

Fishing

The fisheries sector largely consists of small-scale private sector operators, virtually all of whom do their fishing in the Mediterranean. Main catches include sardines, anchovies, sprats, tuna and shellfish.

The government plans to boost fisheries by modernising the Mediterranean ports, where most of the catch is landed. It has also set up a partnership with West African states for fishing in the Atlantic Ocean.

Forestry

Less than 2 per cent of Algeria's total land area is covered with forest or wooded land so that the country is one of the largest importers of wood in Africa.

Algeria's forest resources cover some 3.5 million hectares (ha), with the state monopoly processing some 272,000 cubic metres of wood annually. All of the forest and arable land is in a broad coastal strip, around 400km wide. As part of plans aimed at reducing desertification the government has established an extensive tract of plantation forests.

Other forestry products include sawn timber, wood-based panels and paper based on non-wood fibres. Most domestic demand for forest products is met through imports.

Industry and manufacturing

Industry represents 48.5 per cent of GDP and employs some 30 per cent of the labour force. Algeria's industrial sector is dominated by large, inefficient state-owned companies that have largely survived only due to the credit extended them by the country's state-owned banks. Government attempts to privatise these industries have been frustrated by a lack of investor interest and the fear that the possible mass redundancies which may result will cause further social instability.

The largest company in Algeria is the state-owned hydrocarbons concern, Société Nationale pour la Recherche, la Production, le Transport, la Transformation et la Commercialisation des Hydrocarbures (Sonatrach).

Production is dominated by heavy industries such as steel, petrochemicals, fertilisers and cement, but the focus of development is changing to light industry. Traditional agri-allied industries are also important, particularly textiles, food processing and tobacco and cigarette production. However past lack of investment and inefficiencies in these industries resulted in generally low productivity. In an effort to modernise the government has allowed some entities to be expanded, charge competitive prices and invest profits. Industry is opening up to more foreign involvement, particularly in large-scale projects such as motor vehicle assembly. Main constraints to development are shortages of vital inputs and skilled labour, high production and transport costs and maintenance problems. Industrial development is centralised in the northern coastal strip, but plans exist to extend industry to the high plateaux in the south.

Tourism

The Arab spring in 2011 has had an adverse affect on tourism across the Maghreb, including Algeria.

The tourist industry is small compared to neighbouring countries, but the government has intentions to grow the business. The country has cultural, coastal resorts and adventure tourism on offer, appealing primarily to European visitors. There were 1.91 million visitors to Algeria in 2009, which increased to 2.6 million in 2013, of which 71 per cent belonged to the Algerian diaspora, predominately from France.

In 2009 the government signed contracts with foreign and domestic interests for 283 new hotels with a total of 17,000 beds and 36,000 new jobs. In 2010 total accommodation was 90,000 beds, while there is a target of 160,000 beds by 2015. There are a good supply of airports and ports that could be utilised quickly, although the countrywide infrastructure still has to be redeveloped to expand tourism into the unspoiled Sahara region and seldom visited tribal areas.

In 2014 tourism contributed a total of 6.7 per cent to GDP, which is expected to rise by 5.8 per cent in 2015, and employed 7.1 per cent (747,000 jobs) of those in employment, which is also expected to rise by 4.6 per cent.

Algeria has seven Unesco World Heritage sites, including the Kasbah of Algiers, the Roman ruins of Djémila, Timgad and Tipasa, the traditional tenth century desert habitats, in the M'Zab valley, home of the Ibadites and the ruins of Al Qal'a, the first capital of the Hammadid emirs, founded in 1007. Lastly, the prehistoric rock cave paintings of Tassili n'Ajjer are found among a landscape of outstanding scenic interest.

Mining

The mining and hydrocarbons sector employs 4 per cent of the labour force and contributes 40 per cent to GDP.

Algeria is rich in minerals, including iron ore, uranium, zinc, phosphates, gold, antimony, bituminous coal, tungsten, manganese, lead, mercury and salt. The mining of iron ore and phosphate for feedstocks (for local steel and fertiliser production, respectively) and for export are the most important.

Also located near the Moroccan border are iron-ore reserves estimated at two billion tonnes. The remote location and the Western Sahara/Morocco conflict have so far prevented exploitation.

Hydrocarbons

At the end of 2014, oil reserves stood at 12.2 billion barrels; new oil discoveries, improved data on existing fields and a recent increase in exploration are likely to mean that Algeria's reserves will be revised upwards. Production in 2014 was 1.5 million barrels per day (bpd), an increase of 1.8 per cent on the 2013 figure, while domestic consumption was 395,000bpd, an increase of 1.6 per cent.

Approximately 90 per cent of Algeria's crude oil exports go to Western Europe, with Italy as the main market followed by Germany and France. The Netherlands, Spain and Britain are other important European markets. Algeria's Saharan blend oil, 45 degrees API with negligible (0.05 per cent) sulphur content, is considered among the highest quality in the world.

Algeria had a refining capacity 450,000bpd.

The state-run Sonatrach has responsibility for the oil and gas sectors including exploration, transportation, processing and marketing of hydrocarbons. It provides technical regulation and control including investment and development. In 2009 it let a contract with Swiss and Japanese engineering companies to construct new, and renovate existing, oil plants. The contracts, totalling over US$1.7 billion, provide large gas processing facilities at the Gassi Touil oil field as well as supply gas gathering plants and product pipelines. The project was completed in 2013.

The drop in the price of oil, to US$60 per barrel from around US$120, at the end of 2014, has seen Algeria use up much of their cash reserves to try and weather the storm. Though the crash has been less damaging in Algeria than other hydrocarbon rich nations, it has nonetheless caused many problems. The oil crash of 1986 saw Algeria come to the edge of bankruptcy and was one of the leading factors that led to the Algerian civil war which claimed some 200,000 lives. With this in mind, and the recent fears of the Arab spring, the government was unwilling to cut public services and so has had to heavily dip into their foreign currency reserves, which amount to about US$200 billion. The 2015 budget therefore increased by 15 per cent, pushing Algeria's debt to 22 per cent of GDP.

Natural gas reserves were 4.5 trillion cubic metres (cum) at the end of 2014, with production of 83.3 billion cum. They are Africa's second largest deposits of natural gas (after Nigeria). Sonelgaz (Sociètè Nationale de l'Electricité et du Gaz) (National Society for Electricity and Gas) is the state-owned company that has responsibility for the domestic distribution of electricity and natural gas. It has a quasi-monopoly over Algeria's international market in natural gas, as well as distribution and domestic sales of natural gas.

Exports of natural gas are destined to only five countries, with 27.56 billion cum exported to Italy alone, Spain received 12.05 billion cum, Portugal and Tunisia both imported around 1.3 billion cum and Slovenia 380,000 cum. The Medgaz (Algeria-Spain) sub-Mediterranean gas pipeline was completed in 2009. The gas stream went online in mid-2010, supplying 8 billion cum per annum. Another, the Galsi gas pipeline, is under construction between Algeria and northern Italy, which will also supply 8 billion cum per annum when completed in 2018. Existing gas pipelines include Pedro Duran Farell (Algeria-Spain) supplying 12 billion cum annually and the Trans-Mediterranean (Algeria-Tunisia-Italy-Slovenia) supplying 33.5 billion cum per year.

Algeria also exports liquefied natural gas (LNG) to many more destinations in Europe and the Far East. In 2013 Algeria exported a total of 14.9 billion cum of LNG.

In 2009, two major contracts were signed. The first between Algeria, Niger and Nigeria was to build a 2,580km trans-Sahara gas pipeline (TSGP) traversing all three countries, which is estimated will cost US$13 billion and transport up to 30 billion cum of natural gas, destined for Europe. Three foreign energy companies also expressed an interest in investing in the project – Russia's Gazprom, France's Total and the Anglo-Dutch Shell. Algeria also expressed an interest in Nigeria's upstream element of TSGP, which would utilise its existing gas pipeline network and storage facilities. The project is due to be finished in late 2015. The second was with Canada's SNC-Lavalin Group to build new gas handling facilities in eastern Algeria near Qartzites de Hamra that will process and treat around 10 billion cum of natural gas, generated from the four oil fields. The natural gas produced will be pumped to Arzew where it will be processed into 4.7 million tonnes per day of LNG for export.

Coal has become increasingly less important in the energy mix.

Energy

Total installed generating capacity was 51.2 billion kWh in 2014, of which 98 per cent was generated by oil and natural gas. Ongoing investment has included three new generating stations, a new power grid, incorporating high voltage power lines and, in 2008, the beginning of an 18-year contract with US General Electrics to improve efficiency, output and reliability of 51 gas turbines in 13 power stations. Société Nationale de l'Electricité et du Gaz (Sonelgaz) (National Society for Electricity and Gas) is the state-owned company that has responsibility for the distribution of electricity and natural gas.

Financial markets

Stock exchange

The Algiers stock exchange (Bourse d'Alger) was formally opened in 1999.

Banking and insurance

The Algerian banking sector is dominated by six state-owned banks. There is a total of 17 commercial banks and 10 financial institutions. The sector has been inefficient, with the large state banks acting mainly as depository institutions and financing loss-making public sector companies. In 2006 the government began financial sector reforms and by 2008 the 17 commercial banks had opened up to foreign investors and restructuring of the six public sector banks was underway. However, fallout from the subprime crisis in the United States led to the postponement in January 2008 of the sale of 51 per cent of Crédit Populaire d'Algérie. Algeria remains underbanked with some 26,000 people per branch and the government has confimed that it will continue with reforms.

Central bank

Banque d'Algérie.

Time

GMT plus one hour.

Geography

Algeria is the second largest country in Africa. With a total land area of 2.38 million square km, the country comprises three distinct regions: a narrow coastal plain, which has the most fertile soils and houses the majority of the country's population, agriculture and industry; the uplands of the Atlas mountain chain, which tend to be semi-arid steppe in the valleys; and the vast sandy desert to the south. Algeria has borders with Morocco to the west, Tunisia and Libya to the east and Niger, Mali and Mauritania to the south.

Hemisphere

Northern

Climate

The coastal region has a temperate Mediterranean climate, averaging 13 degrees Celsius (C) to 24 degrees C throughout the year and rising to a daytime high of 32 degrees C during the summer (June to September). The rainy season is October to May, with rains especially heavy from November to February. The desert is constantly inhospitable, with temperatures rising to 45 degrees C during the day, falling to 10 degrees C at night, and with very little rainfall.

Dress codes

Western-style dress is acceptable, with lightweight or safari suits recommended in summer. Women should not wear revealing clothes.

Entry requirements

Passports

Required by all

Visa

Visas are required by most nationals: visit http://algeria.embassyhomepage.com/ for details and application form or contact your local Algerian embassy. Visas are usually valid for 90 days.
Business visas must be accompanied by an invitation from an Algerian company (in duplicate).

Prohibited entry

Nationals of Israel

Currency advice/regulations

The import of foreign currency is unlimited, but must be declared on arrival; export of foreign currency is permitted up to the amount declared on arrival. Local currency may be imported and exported. Visitors are advised to change money through official sources only; it can sometimes be difficult to reconvert dinars to foreign currency. Declaration forms, issued on arrival, should be kept and used at each successive currency change to be surrendered on departure. Failure to comply with these regulations may mean visitors are liable to forfeit the currency. Travellers cheques can only be used in very limited outlets; US dollars and euros have most recognition.

Health (for visitors)

Mandatory precautions

A yellow fever and/or cholera vaccination certificate is required if arriving from infected or endemic areas.

Advisable precautions

Hepatitis A and B, diphtheria, TB, typhoid, tetanus and polio vaccinations are advisable. There is risk of malaria in some areas, therefore prophylaxis is recommended. There is also a rabies risk. Water precautions should be taken throughout the country. Bottled water is often hard to find, particularly in southern parts of the country.

Hotels

There is a limited range of hotels on offer; hotels are either high-luxury or modest one- two-star hotels. It is advisable to book well in advance as accommodation in Algiers is difficult to obtain.
The service charge is usually 15 per cent.

Credit cards

The use of credit cards are restricted to urban areas.

Public holidays (national)

The weekend in Algeria changed from the traditional Thursday-Friday Arab alignment to the Saturday-Sunday European align in August 2009.

Fixed dates

1 Jan (New Year's Day), 1 May (Labour Day), 19 Jun (Revolutionary Readjustment), 5 Jul (Independence Day), 1 Nov (Anniversary of the Revolution).

Variable dates

Eid al Adha (two days), Eid al Fitr (two days), Islamic New Year, Ashura, Prophet's Birthday.

Islamic year 1436 (25 Oct 2014–14 Oct 2015):: The Islamic year contains 354 or 355 days, with the result that Muslim feasts advance by 10–12 days against the Gregorian calendar. Dates of feasts vary according to the sighting of the new moon, so cannot be forecast exactly.

Working hours

The weekend in Algeria changed from the traditional Thursday-Friday Arab alignment to the Saturday-Sunday European align in August 2009.

Banking

Sun–Thur: 0900–1530.

Business

Sat–Tue: 0800–1200 and 1300–1700; Wed 0800–1200 and 1300–1600.

Government

Sat–Wed: 0800–1200 and 1400–1730; Thur 0800–1200.

Shops

Sat–Wed 0800–1230 and 1430–1800; Thu: 0800–1300.

Telecommunications

Mobile/cell phones

GSM 900/1800 services are available mostly in inhabited areas in the north and isolated towns in central and southern Algeria.

Electricity supply

Electricity supply varies from 127–220V; a compensator for use with electronic/computer equipement is advisable. A variety of plug fittings are used.

Social customs/useful tips

Business appointments should be made in advance. Business cards are exchanged after introductions. French-style courtesy should be adopted by visitors. Hospitality is regarded as very important, and visitors are usually entertained in restaurants and hotels. Wives seldom accompany their husbands to social engagements outside the home.
Care should taken to respect local customs, especially during the fasting month

of Ramadan (approximately 21 August–19 September 2009).

Security
Violence was endemic during the 1990s. Although there have been fewer violent incidents since 2000, visitors should still take precautions by avoiding travelling alone and avoid the provinces of Tamanrasset, Djanet and Illizi in the south-east, where tourists have been targetted for kidnapping. Incidents of assaults on foreigners have increased in some urban and rural areas and visitors should avoid carrying valuables and large sums of money.

Getting there
Air

National airline: Air Algérie
International airport/s: Algiers (Houari Boumédienne) (ALG), 20km from city. Facilities include duty-free shop, restaurant, bank, post office, shops, car hire.
Other airport/s: Annaba (Les Salines) (AAE), 12km from city; Constantine (Ain El-Bey) (CZL), 9km from city; Oran (Es Senia) (ORN), 10km from city.
Airport tax: None

Surface

Road: The border between Algeria and Morocco is closed and access is denied. Roads are good in the coastal and northern Sahara networks, while access to Mali, by the trans-Saharan highway, is unsealed and its use is subject to seasonal conditions.
Rail: A daily train service (the Trans-Maghreb) links Tunis with Algiers and Oran.
Water: Regular ferry services connect Algieria with France and Spain.
Main port/s: Algiers, Annaba, Arzew, Bejaia, Oran.

Getting about
National transport

Air: There are frequent services from Algiers to Annaba, Constantine and Oran provided by Air Algérie. Regular flights also link these towns with other principal centres. Fares are generally low for domestic flights but overbooking can occur, especially in summer.
Road: Main roads are in good condition generally, but desert routes are rarely maintained.
Buses: Long-distance coach services are operated by Société Nationale des Transports de Voyageurs (SNTV) and Altour. Bookings for long trips should be made well in advance.
Rail: The service is operated by Société Nationale des Transports Ferroviaires (SNTF). There are two classes; some services are air-conditioned and some have couchettes.

City transport

Taxis: Taxis are widely available in main centres; they are radio-controlled in Algiers. Taxis are identified by a local colour code. They are supposed to be metered, but owing to demand, usually operate without a meter and use a minimum fare system instead. A surcharge is imposed after dark. Tips are usually 10 per cent of fare.
Buses, trams & metro: State-owned service operates in Algiers. Can be overcrowded during rush hours. Daily and longer duration tickets are available.
A new metro in Algiers begin public operations in November 2011. Line One is 8.5km long and has 10 stations from Grande Poste in the city centre to Hai al Badr in Kouba southwest of the city. Stations open 0500–2300.

Car hire

Car hire is available in most main towns and at airports. An international driving licence and third-party insurance are required. The maximum speed limit is 50kph in towns and 100kph on main roads.

BUSINESS DIRECTORY
The addresses listed below are a selection only. While World of Information makes every endeavour to check these addresses, we cannot guarantee that changes have not been made, especially to telephone numbers and area codes. We would welcome any corrections.

Telephone area codes
The international dialling code (IDD) for Algeria is + 213 followed by the area code and subscriber's number:

Algiers	21	Ghardaia	29
Annaba	38	Oran	41
Béchar	49	Sétif	36
Boumerdes	24	Tiemcen	43
Constantine	31	Tindouf	49

Useful telephone numbers
Directory enquiries: 19
Telegrams: 13
Police: 17

Chambers of Commerce
Algerian Chambre de Commerce et d' Industrie, Palais Consulaire, 6 Boulevard Amilcar Cabral, Place des Martyrs, PO Box 100, 16003 Algiers (tel: 715-160; fax: 710-174; e-mail: caci@wissal.dz).

Constantine Chambre de Commerce et d' Industrie, 6 Rue de 24 Novembre 1954, PO Box 394, 25000 Constantine (tel: 935-923; fax: 937-807).

Dhara Chambre de Commerce et d' Industrie, 1 Avenue Benyahia Belcacem, PO Box 99, Mostaganem (tel: 216-709; fax: 216-578).

French Chambre de Commerce et Industrie en Algerie, Villa Clarac, 3 Rue des Cèdres, El Mouradia, Alger (tel: 606-496; fax: 609-509; e-mail: cfcia@cfcia.org).

Oran Chambre de Commerce et d' Industrie, 8 Boulevard de la Soummam, Oran (tel: 391-299; fax: 396-312).

Banking
Banque Al Baraka, Haï Bouteldja Houidif, Villa No 1 Rocade Sud, Ben Aknoun, Algiers (tel: 916-450; fax: 916-457; e-mail: info@albaraka-bank.com).

Banque de l'Agriculture et du Developpement Rural, 17 Boulevard Colonel Amirouche, Algiers (tel: 634-922; fax: 635-146).

Banque de Développement Local, 5 Rue Gaci Amar, Staoueli, Algiers (tel: 393-755; fax: 393-757).

Banque Extérieure d'Algérie, 3 Rue du Docteur Lucien Reynaud, Algiers (tel: 239-330; fax: 239-099; e-mail: dircom@bea.dz).

Banque Nationale d'Algérie, 8 Boulevard Ernesto Che Guevara, Algiers (tel: 714-719; fax: 712-424; e-mail: nb@bna.com.dz).

Caisse d'Epargne et de Prévoyance, 42 Rue Khelifa Boukhalfa, Algiers (tel: 713-395; fax: 714-131).

Crédit Populaire d'Algérie, 2 Boulevard Colonel Amirouche, Algiers (tel: 740-528; fax: 642-383).

Central bank

Banque d'Algérie, Villa Jolie, 38 Avenue Franklin Roosevelt, 16000 Algiers (tel: 230-023; fax: 260-856; e-mail: ba@bank-of-algeria.dz).

Stock exchange

The Algiers stock exchange (Bourse d'Alger) was formally opened in 1999.

Travel information
Air Algérie, 1 Place Maurice Audin, PO 483, 1600 Algiers (tel: 653-340; fax: 509-389; e-mail: contact@)airalgerie.dz).

Algiers-Houari Boumediene Airport, BP130 Dar El-Baida, 16100 Algiers (tel: 506-000; fax: 509-219; e-mail: hlamyl@hotmail.com).

Ministry of tourism

Ministry of Tourism and Handicraft, Rue des Frères Ziata, 16070 Algiers (tel: 792-301; fax: 792-632).

National tourist organisation offices

ONAT (Entreprise Nationale Algérienne du Tourisme), 126 bis Rue Didouche Mourad, Algiers (tel: 744-448; fax: 743-214; e-mail: onat@onat.dz.com).

Ministries

Prime Minister's Office, Rue Docteur Saadane, 16001 Algiers (tel: 732-300; fax: 717-927).

Ministry of Agriculture and Rural Development, 12 Boulevard Colonel Amirouche, 16001 Algiers (tel: 711-712; fax: 745-986).

Ministry of Commerce, Rue Docteur Saadane, 16001 Algiers (tel: 732-340; fax: 735-478).

Ministry of Communications and Culture, Palais de la Culture, El-Anassers, 16502 Algiers (tel: 679-420; fax: 684-459).

Ministry of Defence, Avenue Ali Khodja, Les Tagarins, 16030 Algiers (tel: 711-515).

Ministry of Education, 8 Avenue de Pékin, 16070 Algiers (tel: 605-560; fax: 606-757).

Ministry of Energy and Mines, 80 Avenue Ahmed Ghermoul, 16014 Algiers (tel: 673-300; fax: 650-997).

Ministry of Finance, Immeuble Mauretania, Place du Pérou, 16001 Algiers (tel: 711-366; fax: 736-450).

Ministry of Fisheries and Marine Resources, 4 Rue des Quatre Canons, 16001 Algiers (tel: 433-947; fax: 433-168).

Ministry of Foreign Affairs, Place Med Seddik Benyahia, 16070, Algiers (tel: 504-545; fax: 504-242).

Ministry of Health, Population and Hospital Reform, 125 Rue Abderrahmane Laala, 16075 Algiers (tel: 279-900; fax: 279-641).

Ministry of Higher Education and Scientific Research, 11 Rue Doudou Mokhtar, 16033 Algiers (tel: 912-323; fax: 912-113).

Ministry of Housing and Urbanism, 135 Rue Didouche Mourad, 16001 Algiers (tel: 740-722; fax: 747-664).

Ministry of Industry and Restructuring, Immeuble le Colisée, 4 Rue Ahmed Bey, 16030 Algiers (tel: 693-156; fax: 693-235; e-mail: info@mir-algeria.org).

Ministry of the Interior and Local Communities, Rue Docteur Saadane, 16001 Algiers (tel: 732-340; fax: 605-210).

Ministry of Justice, 8 Place Bir Hakem, 16030 Algiers (tel: 921-608; fax: 921-243).

Ministry of Labour and Social Protection, 44 Rue Med Belouizded, Belcourt, Algiers (tel: 683-366; fax: 745-306).

Ministry of Participation and Reforms Co-ordination (MPCR), Chemin Ibn Badis el Mouiz, 16030 Algiers (tel: 929-885; fax: 929-884).

Ministry of Post and Telecommunications, 4 Boulevard Krim Belkacem, 16027 Algiers (tel: 711-220; fax: 730-047).

Ministry of Public Works, 3 Rue du Caire, 16050 Algiers (tel: 689-500).

Ministry of Religious Affairs and Endowments, 4 Rue de Timgad, Algiers (tel: 608-555; fax: 600-936).

Ministry of Small and Medium Enterprises, Immeuble le Colisée, 4 Rue Ahmed Bey, 16030 Algiers (tel: 601-144; fax: 592-658).

Ministry of Transport, 119 rue Didouche Mourad, 16001 Algiers (tel: 740-699; fax: 646-637).

Ministry of Vocational Training and Professional Education, Route de Dély Ibrahim, 16033 Algiers (tel: 911-528; fax: 912-779).

Ministry of War Veterans, 9 Avenue Benarfa Mohamed, 16030 Algiers (tel: 922-355; fax: 922-739).

Ministry of Water Resources, 8 Place de Bir Hakem, 16030 Algiers (tel: 283-837; fax: 747-543).

Ministry of Youth and Sports, 3 Rue Mohamed Belouizdad, 16600 Algiers (tel: 683-350; fax: 657-778; e-mail: mjs@wissal.dz).

Other useful addresses

Algerian Embassy (USA), 2137 Wyoming Avenue, NW, Washington DC 20008 (tel: (+1-202) 265-2800; fax: (+1-202) 667-2174; e-mail: embalg.us@verizon.net).

APSI (investment promotion agency), Boulevard du 11 Décembre 1960, BP 336 El-Biar, 16030 Algiers (tel: 914-225; fax: 914-303; e-mail: apsi@wissal.dz).

British Embassy, 6 Avenue Souidani Boudiemaa, BP08 Alger-Gare, 16000, Algiers (tel: 230-068; fax: 230-067).

FINALEP (Algero-European Financial Participation Company), 11 Route Nationale, Staouéli, Algiers (tel: 393-494; fax: 392-020; e-mail: finalep@wissal.dz).

National Office of Statistics, 8/10 Rue des Moussebilines, BP 202 Ferhat Boussad, 16000 Algiers (tel: 744-100; fax: 743-839; e-mail: ons@onssiege.ons.dz).

SAFEX (Algerian fairs and exports company), Palais des Expositions, Pins Maritimes, BP 366 Alger Gare, Algiers (tel: 210-123; fax: 210-630; e-mail: safex@wissal.dz).

SNTF (national rail company), 21-23 Boulevard Mohamed V, Algiers (tel: 711-510; fax: 748-190).

Sonatrach (national oil and gas company), 10 Rue Djenane El-Malik, Hydra, 16035 Algiers (tel: 548-011; fax: 547-700; e-mail: sonatrach@sonatrach.dz).

US Embassy, 4 Chemin Cheikh Bachir El-Ibrahimi, BP 408 Alger-Gare, 16000, Algiers (tel: 691-255; fax: 693-979).

National news agency: Algerian Press Service (APS)

Address: Ave Des Frères Bouadou, Bir Mourad Rais, Algies (tel: 564-444; fax: 561-608; internet: www.aps.dz).

Agence Algérienne d'Information (AAI) (in French): www.aai-online.com

Internet sites

Africa news outlet: allafrica.com

African Development Bank: www.afdb.org

Algeria News Agency: www.aps.dz

Mbendi AfroPaedia: www.mbendi.co.za

American Samoa

COUNTRY PROFILE

1722 The Dutch navigator, Jacob Roggeveen, was the first European to sight the islands.
1831 The London Missionary Society arrived to convert native Samoans and established a British presence.
1872 The US gained exclusive use of the deep-water whaling port of Pago Pago.
1889 The Treaty of Berlin between Britain, the US and Germany promised an independent Samoan government.
1899 The Berlin Treaty was annulled by the Tripartite Treaty, which granted the US the right to all eastern islands of the Samoan group, giving Germany the remainder. In exchange, Britain gained control of Germany's rights in Tonga, Niue and the Solomon Islands (excluding Bougainville).
1900 American Samoa officially became a US territory. Traditional rights were protected in return for a military base and coaling station. Islanders became US nationals, but not citizens; they cannot vote in US elections.
1941 The US entered the Second World War and American Samoa became a strategic location, for the US Pacific Fleet.
1945 The US Marine Corps withdrew.
1951 The territory was transferred to the US Department of the Interior.
1956 The US appointed Peter Tali Coleman as the first Samoan governor; he went on to become the first popularly elected governor.
1960 The constitution was promulgated.
1967 A revised constitution was introduced, which guaranteed the rights of inhabitants on issues such as land ownership and civil rights.
2002 Following fears of overfishing in American Samoa's exclusive economic zone (EEZ), the Western Pacific Regional Fishery Management Council approved a decision to limit access of fleets to EEZ waters.
2003 Governor Tause Sunia died, his deputy Togiola Tulafono was appointed acting governor.
2004 Cyclone Heta caused devastation and President Bush declared the islands a federal disaster area. Incumbent, Acting Governor Tulafono won the gubernatorial elections.
2005 Cyclone Heta's damage to the Manu'a islands was estimated at US$2 million. The government-owned KVZK-TV re-launched Channel 5, which had been off-air since 1991. Travellers from American Samoa were required to obtain entry permits to enter Samoa. The governor introduced legislation to ban human trafficking and involuntary servitude.
2006 Eni Faleomavaega was re-elected for a tenth term as Territorial Delegate in elections to the US House of Representatives.
2007 Samoa agreed to waive the US$30 entry permit fee for all American Samoan nationals who could prove a Samoan ancestor.
2008 The run-off gubernatorial election was won by incumbent Togiola Tulfono .
2009 Togiola Tulfono became governor. An earthquake, of 8.3 magnitude, struck offshore in the Pacific Ocean and caused a devastating *tsunami* that swept over several Samoan islands, killing more than 140 people, including 25 in American Samoa. US federal aid was provided including emergency supplies. Later, a media report accused the administration of having previously squandered millions of dollars of funds, which had been allocated for a *tsunami* warning system. The system had only progressed to the planning stage, including for an island-wide siren warning system, before the US had halted funding in 2007, due to misspending by American Samoan officials.
2010 The resident population took part in the United States census, which, after personal details, included questions on race, housing and internet and mobile phone access. The population was recorded at 55,519. President Obama signed legislation to delay the increase in the minimum wage, scheduled for 2010 and 2011, in American Samoa. Congressman Eni Faleomavaega was re-elected for a twelfth term in office.
2011 In April, following agreements with the state and federal authorities on tax incentives and exemption plus a freeze on the increase in minimum wages, the Starkist cannery company announced that it would begin re-hiring 500 workers and gave a long-term commitment to stay in American Samoa and to increase production. Further discussions to improve the business environment for Starkist included state help to reduce energy costs and increased provision of cold-storage.

KEY FACTS

Official name: Territory of American Samoa

Head of State: President of the United States of America Barack Obama (from 2009; re-elected 6 Nov 2012)

Head of government: Governor Lolo Matalasi Moliga (from Jan 2013)

Area: 196 square km (five islands); Tutuila: 135 square km

Population: 54,719 (July 2012)*

Capital: Fagatogo (on Tutuila), usually known as Pago Pago

Official language: English and Samoan

Currency: US dollar (US$) = 100 cents

GDP real growth: 3.00%

* estimated figure

2012 Bilateral discussions resumed on 11 October between Samoa and American Samoa covering joint concerns in health, telecommunications, customs and utilities. The last such meetings had been held in 2007. On 26 July, President Obama signed the delayed law applying a minimum wage in American Samoa. In September, the last reading of the 2013 budget was approved by the senate, which agreed to a US$40 million reduction in public spending; the final budget was US$454.86 million. Six candidates contested gubernatorial elections on 6 November. Lolo Matalasi Moliga won 33.7 per cent of the vote and Faoa Aitofele Sunia 33.3 per cent. A run-off was held on 20 November in which Moliga won 52.9 per cent and Sunia 47.1 per cent. Governor elect Moliga takes office in January 2013.

2013 In July the American Samoa Visitor's Bureau reported that ocean explorer Jean Michel Cousteau would be arriving shortly to assess the potential economic potential of the Swains Islands' diverse marine life to attract tourist visitors. The Bureau is also working with potential tour operators throughout the islands to assist them in developing unique village level attractions. Tourism is a major employer as well as foreign exchange earner.

2014 Chief election officer, Tuaolo Fruean, has requested US$200,000 to finance the general election scheduled for 4 November when islanders will vote for their representative to the US House of Representatives and 20 members of the American Samoa legislature. A referendum on amending the constitution will be held at the same time. The amendment would give the Fono the authority to override the governor's veto instead of the US secretary of interior.

2015 In January the government launched a US$49-million project establishing the first locally-owned submarine cable company. The minister for communication, information and technology said the Samoa Submarine Cable Company would strengthen Samoa's communication links to the world.

Political structure

Constitution

The 1960 constitution was revised in 1967.

American Samoa is represented in the US by a senator and a non-voting representative.

American Samoans are not US citizens; they are classified as US nationals and have freedom of entry into the continental US, but no voting rights.

Form of state

American Samoa is an unincorporated and unorganised territory of the US, administered by the Office of Insular Affairs, US Department of the Interior.

The executive

Local executive power rests with a popularly elected governor and lieutenant governor, who serve four-year terms.

National legislature

The bicameral Fono (Legislative Assembly), consists of the House of Representatives (lower chamber), with 21 members elected for two-year terms, of which 20 members are elected in single seat constituencies and one, non-voting member for Swains Island, decided by public meeting; and the Senate (upper chamber) with 18 members, all *Matai* (local chiefs), elected for four-year terms, according to Samoan custom.

Legal system

High Court – the chief justice and associate justices are appointed by the US Secretary of the Interior.

Last elections

6 and 20 November 2012 (gubernatorial); 1 September 2010 (US House of Representatives)

Results: Gubernatorial (first round): Lolo Matalasi Moliga won 33.7 per cent of the vote Faoa Aitofele Sunia 33.3 per cent. Runoff: Moliga 52.9 per cent, Sunia 47.1 per cent.

US House of Representatives: Eni Faleomavaega (Democrat) won 56.3 per cent of the vote; Aumua Amata Coleman (Republican) 40.5 per cent; and Tuika Tuika (Independent) 3.3 per cent.

Next elections

November 2016 (gubernatorial)

Political situation

The relationship between American Samoa and the US has exercised the leadership of both countries. Under the constitution American Samoa is an unorganised territory, so the people of American Samoa are US nationals but not citizens and they cannot migrate for work to other US states and territories without visas. In 2007 the US imposed a minimum wage, under federal laws, that threatened the viability of the island's largest employers – two tuna canning factories – raising wages from the local norm of US$2.63–4.09 per hour, depending on the industry, to US$7.25 by 2009. Implementation of this was later delayed by the US. The US Congress, at the request of the American Samoan Congress representative, required three questions to be included in the 2008 political ballots: whether American Samoans should become US citizens, whether territorial senators should be elected by American Samoans and whether American Samoa should have its own federal district court and limited jurisdiction. Newly introduced, and some considered pre-emptive, measures to tighten immigration laws were also seen as another contentious issue that ignored the interests of local people. In March 2011, the Republican controlled US-Congress voted to rescind the voting rites of representations of American Samoa, effectively disenfranchising their electorate in policies that directly affect them.

Population

54,719 (July 2013)*

Last census: 1 April 2010: 55,519

Population density: 320 inhabitants per square km.

Annual growth rate: 1.6 per cent (2003)

Ethnic make-up

Samoan (Polynesian) (89 per cent), Tongan (4 per cent), Caucasian (2 per cent), others (5 per cent).

Religions

Approximately half the population are Christian Congregational, but Roman Catholics, Latter Day Saints and Protestants are also represented.

Education

Extra federal funds were provided in 2006 for schools with students from deprived backgrounds, aimed at those at risk of dropping out of education. There were also schemes for early reading and English learning, and support for children with disabilities. Specific funding for American Samoa of US$29.5 million will be added to improve the island's education system.

Compulsory years: Six to 18

Main cities

Fagatogo, (the capital, on Tutuila, is usually known as Pago Pago, estimated population 4,814 in 2012) Tafuna (9,756), Nu'uuli (6,345), Faleniu (3,426), Leone (2,902), Illi'ili (2,497), Aua (2,336), Pava'ia'i (2,000).

Languages spoken

English is used for business and commerce but Samoan, (closely related to Hawaiian), is in common use among the local population.

Official language/s

English and Samoan

Media

Press

There are only two national, locally based daily newspapers, the *Samoa News* (www.samoanews.com) and the *Samoa Observer* (www.samoaobserver.ws).

A new, locally printed, five day publication began in February 2006, the *American Samoa Tribune* is bilingual and owned by the Samoa Observer Newspaper Group.

Broadcasting

Radio: There are two commercial radio stations operating, both using their call signs, KKHJ 93FM (www.khjradio.com)

with music and general interest programming and KNWJ 104 FM (www.fm104.org) with religious programmes; both broadcast in English. Several radio station broadcasts can be picked up from Samoa.
Television: The government owned KVZK Television operates three channels, broadcasting for eight hours each day. KVZK is an affiliate of US broadcasters PBS, ABC and CBS. There are several privately owned cable TV stations including K34HI, a Fox affiliate, WVUV-LP an NBC affiliate, American Samoa Cablevision, a CNN affiliate and K11UU. K21GL broadcasts religious programmes.
TV signals, by SBC TV1, neighbouring Samoa's public, commercial broadcaster, can be received.
Other news agencies: ABC Pacific Beat: www.radioaustralia.net.au/pacbeat
Pacific Magazine: www.pacificmagazine.net

Economy

The economy is based on agriculture, fishing, fish processing and aid from the US. Since 2009 when the Chicken of the Sea tuna cannery closed, with the loss of over 2,000 jobs (12 per cent of a workforce of over 17,000), the economy has been precarious. The remaining tuna cannery, StarKist, laid off 600–800 workers in 2010 after minimum wage legislation was introduced by the US, increasing costs to the canning industry. President Obama later signed legislation delaying implementation of the increase and Star Kist re-hired workers and gave a guarantee to stay. Between them, the canneries had provided around 80 per cent of GDP. Other components of the economy such as agriculture and services, which each comprise a third of GDP, were unable to absorb the volume of unemployed workers which resulted in increased costs and welfare payments.
An agreement was reached in late 2010 for the Singapore-based, Tri Marine International company, to take over the closed Chicken of the Sea cannery. In 2015 a new cannery was opened and fish production and exports are expected to rise again, along with employment.
American Samoa's dependence on primary sectors has also meant the economy is particularly vulnerable to adverse weather conditions and disease. A devastating tsunami struck in 2009 and caused damage to property and crops on low lying lands. Reconstruction aided GDP growth through 2010, as US aid topped US$22.5 million.
Around half of the government's revenue is from US aid, making international support essential to the islands' development. Government efforts to attract investment to the territory and diversify the economy have had limited success. The islands' natural beauty is an obvious tourist attraction, making it a fast growing sector of the economy, not only for sun-worshipers but also more intrepid eco-tourists. There are 10-year tax incentives for new businesses in the area, attempting to attract light manufacturing and service based industries.
In January 2011 the Fono considered three possible revenue measures designed to cover the shortfall of US$7.2 million in government funding. They included an increase in business licences, higher import duties and a wage tax. The governor stated that without the new income, cuts to both work hours and the jobs of government workers were inevitable. In June 2011, the US Department of Homeland Security backed calls for American Samoa to be designated as 'high risk' over its accounting of government funds. This would mean a greater degree of scrutiny of all spending of federal funds, plus payments made in arrears would take longer to be paid.
US Army recruitment, which has been a considerable source of income and employment, has dropped in recent years. The fall is believed to have been due to the war in Iraq, which had negative publicity, arising from the death of a number of American Samoan military service personnel. In September 2012, the last reading of the 2013 budget was approved by the senate, which agreed to a US$40 million reduction in public spending; the final budget was US$454.86 million.

External trade

American Samoa benefits from duty free entry into the customs territory of the US. Fish cannery production is almost exclusively destined for the US domestic market.

Imports

Main imports are materials for the canneries, processed food, machinery and parts, timber and petroleum products.
Main sources: US, Australia and Samoa.

Exports

Main exports are canned tuna, small industrial products and handicrafts.
Main destinations: US, Indonesia and India.
Canned fish to the US is not counted as an export.

Agriculture

Farming

The soil is volcanic. About 10 per cent of the land area is cultivable, half of which is under permanent cultivation.

Fishing

Tuna and deep-sea fishing is important to the economy. American Samoa is the main processing site for the US tuna fishing fleet in the Pacific.

Forestry

Industry and manufacturing

The private sector is dominated by the fish processing industry, which employs one-third of the workforce. StarKist has the world's largest tuna cannery in American Samoa and has a 44 per cent US market share. The two other producers are BumbleBee and Chicken of the Sea (a Thai owned company). Between them they produce 80–90 per cent of American Samoa's principal export, the majority of which is directed to the US market. The tuna canneries export around US$470 million processed tuna annually. StarKist and Chicken of the Sea employ more than 5,150 people or 74 per cent of the private sector workforce. Sales from StarKist canneries are reported to have increased sharply in recent years. American Samoa is fighting to exclude tuna from the US/Thailand Free Trade Agreement (which has been on hold since the 2006 Thai coup d'état) in order to save around 3,000 jobs.
Since 2009 when the Chicken of the Sea tuna cannery closed, with the loss of over 2,000 jobs (12 per cent of a workforce of over 17,000), the economy has been precarious. The remaining tuna cannery, StarKist, laid off 600–800 workers in 2010 after minimum wage legislation was introduced by the US, increasing costs to the canning industry. An agreement was reached in late 2010 for the Singapore-based, Tri Marine International company, to take over the closed Chicken of the Sea cannery. In 2015 a new cannery was opened and fish production and exports are expected to rise again, along with employment.
Ecuador and Columbia are also a threat to the tuna canneries as they have the production capacity to supply the entire US market and wipe out the economy of American Samoa.
Other industries include textiles, meat canning, dairy produce, jewellery, handicrafts and tourism. There are also factories processing soap, liquor and perfume. The US government is trying to encourage joint ventures and other foreign investment for any product with a 30 per cent local content.
In May 2011, the government moved to take over the bankrupt MYD Samoa shipyard, for US$250,000. The government plans to invest in the shipyard and turn it into the South Pacific's key marine repair facility.

Tourism

Despite its obvious charms – blue lagoons, clean Pacific waters lapping against white sandy beaches and tropical weather to tempt any jaded traveller – American Samoa does not have a large tourist industry due to its remoteness and limited access, which has resulted in a lack of tourist infrastructure. Cruise ship arrivals have increased, but as they are based on the itineraries of foreign cruise liners visits are sporadic and result in economic feast and famine.

Ecotourism is a growing attraction.

In July 2013, ocean explorer Jean Michel Cousteau paid a visit to American Samoa to assess the economic potential of the Swains Islands' diverse marine life to attract tourist visitors. The Bureau is also working with potential tour operators throughout the islands to assist them in developing unique village level attractions. Tourism is a major employer as well as foreign exchange earner.

Mining

The only natural resources are pumice and pumicite.

Hydrocarbons

There are no known hydrocarbon reserves. Consumption of petroleum products, including refined oil, is typically over 4,000 barrels per day (bpd), all of which is imported.

American Samoa does not import nor produce natural gas or coal.

Energy

Total installed generating capacity was 45MW in 2011. The American Samoa Power Authority is responsible for electricity generation and supply. There are two oil-fired power stations supplied by imported petroleum products. Any generator using renewable sources of energy and privately run may sell surplus electricity back to the utility.

Banking and insurance

The Bank of Hawaii and the Amerika Samoa Bank provide 24-hour full banking services and correspond with banks in the US and the Pacific.

Time

GMT minus 11 hours

Geography

American Samoa comprises the seven islands of Tutuila, Ta'u, Olosega, Ofu, Aunu'u, Rose Atoll and Swains Island, lying in the southern central Pacific Ocean, about 3,700km (2,300 miles) south-west of Hawaii. Pago Pago has one of the best natural deepwater harbours in the region.

Hemisphere

Southern

Climate

Tropical with annual rainfall around three metres. There are two main seasons: rainy (November–April) and dry (May–October). Temperatures range from 20–32 degrees Celsius.

Entry requirements

Passports

Required by all except US citizens with proof of citizenship (all US nationals require a passport for re-entry to the US). Passports must be valid for at least 60 days beyond the intended length of stay.

Visa

US entry requirements apply. Visas required by all, except US citizens with proof of identity and foreign nationals from countries covered by the 'Visa Waiver Program', who are in possession of machine readable passports. All other visitors and passport holders must apply for a visa. Visas are valid for up to 90 days. A return/onward ticket is also required.

Further information can be found at http://travel.state.gov. More detailed information can be found at http://uscis.gov/graphics/services.

All visitors must have proof of adequate funds for up to 30 days and onward/return tickets. Entry to American Samoa does not give automatic entry to the US and visitors must apply separately through a US consulate.

Health (for visitors)

Mandatory precautions

Vaccination certificates required for yellow fever if travelling from infected area.

Advisable precautions

Vaccination for diphtheria, tuberculosis, hepatitis A and B, polio, tetanus and typhoid are advisable. There is a risk of rabies and dengue fever.

Public holidays (national)

Fixed dates

1 Jan (New Year's Day), 17 Apr (Flag Day), 4 Jul (Independence Day), 11 Nov (Veterans' Day), 25 Dec (Christmas Day).

Variable dates

Martin Luther King's Birthday (third Mon in Jan), Washington's Birthday (third Mon in Feb), Memorial Day (last Mon in May), Labour Day (first Mon in Sep), Columbus Day (second Mon in Oct), Thanksgiving Day (fourth Thu in Nov).

Working hours

Banking

Mon–Fri: 0900–1500; Sat: 0800–1200.

Business

Mon–Fri: 0730/0830–1730/1800; Sat: 0830–1200.

Government

Mon–Fri: 0730/0830–1730/1800; Sat: 0830–1200.

Shops

Mon–Fri: 0800–1700; Sat: 0800–1300.

Weights and measures

Imperial

Social customs/useful tips

Visitors should be sensitive to local conventions and respect local customs and practices. Care should be taken when dressed casually; bikinis and shorts are acceptable in hotels, but they are not considered appropriate when visiting urban and rural areas.

Getting there

Air

National airline: Hawaiian Airlines and Polynesian Airlines connect American Samoa to international air routes.

International airport/s: Pago Pago International (PPG), 11km from town; duty-free shop, restaurant and shops.

Airport tax: US$3, usually included in ticket price.

Surface

Main port/s: Pago Pago is an international port; it is one of the best natural deep water harbours in the region. It is served by a number of passenger cruise and cargo lines.

Getting about

National transport

Air: Samoa Air (possibly the only airline to charge by the passenger's weight) and Inter Island Air (a charter airline) serve the islands.

Road: There are approximately 150km of paved roads and 200km of unpaved or secondary roads, the majority of which are on Tutuila.

Buses: There is a local service operating between the airport and Pago Pago town centre. The 'aiga' bus service provides cheap travel between Pago Pago and outlying villages.

Water: A weekly service operates between Pago Pago and the Manu'a islands.

Car hire

An international driving licence or valid national driving licence is required. Minimum age of 21. Traffic drives on the right.

BUSINESS DIRECTORY

The addresses listed below are a selection only. While World of Information makes every endeavour to check these addresses, we cannot guarantee that changes have not been made, especially to telephone numbers and area codes. We would welcome any corrections.

Telephone area codes

The international direct dialling (IDD) code for American Samoa is +1 684, followed by subscriber's number.

Useful telephone numbers

Police, fire and ambulance911

Chambers of Commerce
American Samoa Chamber of Commerce, PO Box 2446, Pago Pago 96799 (tel: 699-6214; fax: 699-2219; e-mail: chamber@samoatelco.com).

Banking
Amerika Samoa Bank, PO Box 3790, Pago Pago 96799 (tel: 633-5053; fax: 633-5057).

Bank of Hawaii, PO Box 69, Pago Pago 96799 (tel: 633-4226; fax: 633-2918).

Central bank
Federal Reserve System, 20th Street and Constitution Avenue, NW, Washington DC 20551 (tel: (202) 452-3000; fax: (202) 452-3819).

Travel information
Flight information: (tel: 699-9101, 0800-2200).

Pago Pago International Airport, PO Box 1539, Pago Pago 96799 (tel: 699-9101/2/3; fax: 633-5281).

National tourist organisation offices
Office of Tourism, Convention Centre, Pago Pago, 96799 (tel: 633-1091/92/93; fax: 633-1094).

Ministries
Department of Commerce, Economic Development, American Samoa Government, Pago Page, American Samoa 96799 (tel: 84-633-5155; fax: 684-633-4195; email: Azodiacal@doc.asg.as

Other useful addresses
Office of Economic Development and Planning, Territorial Planning Commission, Pago Pago, 96799 (tel: 633-5156).

Office of the Governor, American Samoa Government, Pago Pago (tel: 633-4828; fax: 633-2269).

ABC Pacific Beat: www.radioaustralia.net.au/pacbeat

Pacific Magazine: www.pacificmagazine.net

Internet sites
Government website: http://americansamoa.gov/

Samoa News on-line: www.samoanews.com

US Office of Insular Affairs: www.doi.gov/oia

Andorra

KEY FACTS

Official name: Principat d'Andorra (Principality of Andorra)

Head of State: Co-Princes: Bishop of Seu d'Urgel (Spain), Joan Enric Vives i Sicília (from 2003) and President François Hollande (France); represented by Préfet Thierry Lataste (from 5 Jan 2015)

Head of government: Cap de Govern Antoni Marti Petit (from 11 May 2011)

Ruling party: Demòcrates per Andorra (Democrats for Andorra) (Democrats) (from 3 Apr 2011)

Area: 468 square km

Population: 78,115 (2011)

Capital: Andorra la Vella

Official language: Catalan

Currency: Euro (€) = 100 cents

Exchange rate: €0.89 per US$ (Sep 2015)

GDP per capita: US$44,952 (2008)

GDP real growth: 3.60% (2008)

Labour force: 42,220 (2008)

Unemployment: 7.00% (2008)

Inflation: 3.20% (2008)

Andorra's modest economy entered 2014 with a following wind. Much of the credit for this was due to the Principality's Cap de Govern (Head of government) Antoni Martí, who had fought hard to get a new law of foreign investment on to the statute book. Many of Andorra's legislators were sceptical of the new legislation's aspirations, described by Mr Martí as making Andorra 'Southern Europe's technological laboratory'. Andorra's sceptics – many of them traditionally gloomy Barcelona-based Catalans, dismissed the concept tacitly accepting that the principality was, by European standards, little more than a mountainous duty-free shop.

The Pujol problem

Andorra's attempts to change its image from money laundering to high technology suffered something of reverse when in July 2014 it emerged that the former Catalan leader in Barcelona's regional parliament, Jordi Pujol, had salted away in an Andorran bank account some €4 million (US$5.48 million) for a reported period of 23 years. Although the links between Barcelona's business and political elite may be less important and less obvious than was once the case, the revelations were as embarrassing for the Andorran authorities as they were for Barcelona, Catalonia's capital city. In its efforts to achieve independence from Spain, Catalonia had sought to claim the moral high ground over a Madrid government bogged down by corruption.

Cash drain, brain drain

Cap de Govern Martí identified the new foreign investment law as the Parlament's (Parliament) 'philosopher's stone' saying that 'we have no desire to become a marginalised 'island' on the edge of the European Union (EU).' The new legislation simplified the procedure for setting up a business in Andorra: the main change was that a majority Andorran shareholder was no longer required. By April 2014 the Andorran government reported that no less than 313 Spanish companies, 40 per cent of them from Barcelona (and most of the rest from Madrid) had established a presence in Andorra. According to the principality's grandly termed Secretary of State for Economic Diversification, Josep Maria Missé the initiative had generated an overall investment of €60 million. (US$8.22 million) – a large sum of money for a tiny economy. Mr Missé announced that up to the end of 2013, 58 per cent of the applications received were from Spanish based companies, although those received from French companies had increased dramatically, accounting for 27 per cent of new applications. An encouraging side-effect of the improved investment climate was that Andorra was beginning to catch up technologically. Ten per cent of the Spanish companies were from the technology sector. None the less the fact that tourism and business continued to dominate the Andorran economy was reflected by the fact that one third of the Spanish companies setting up in Andorra were from this sector, followed by the financial sector with 8 per cent and health and welfare, with 6 per cent. The interest of the Spanish financial sector was significant especially since Andorra had begun to shake off its classification by the Organisation for Economic Co-operation and Development (OECD) as a 'fiscal paradise' in 2011.

It is perhaps surprising that despite its size, the international ratings agencies continue to rank Andorra so highly. Canny management has meant that Andorra's private banking sector enjoys high solvency and liquidity ratios. Even after the negative effects of the global financial crisis, in 2011 the sector's total assets were put at around €14 billion (US$19.12 billion). According to the *Andorra Business* website, many Andorran banks own investment and insurance subsidiaries as well as foreign banking and asset management companies. International expansion has focussed on the Western Hemisphere – not only North America but also Central and South America and the Caribbean. The Andbanc group (Andorra's oldest firm of private bankers) is present in 12 countries, Crédit Andorra in eight and the Banca Privada d'Andorra in six. According to the London-based *Banker* magazine, although traditionally reliant on neighbouring Spain for their customer base, 'Andorra's banks have been forced to reassess their strategies in light of the country's – and the rest of Europe's – economic malaise.' Instead, they are targeting the Latin American market, as well as disillusioned clients of Swiss banks, attracted to a national banking sector renowned for its discretion and stability. Andbanc has been the fastest growing bank in Andorra; in 2013 net profits increased by 6.68 per cent, assets expanded by 15.2 per cent and return on equity reached a remarkable 18.79 per cent.

The Tax Man cometh

The development followed Andorra's declaration of willingness to exchange financial information with the Spanish authorities. The hard-pressed Spanish government sought to prevent tax evasion by Spanish individuals and businesses by quietly salting away profits and dividends in Andorra. Mr Martí confirmed that 'For some time the discussion of Andorra's fiscal transparency has been irrelevant.' In November 2013 Andorra took a significant step towards international acceptance and tax co-operation when it became the 60th signatory of the OECD's Multilateral Convention on Mutual Administrative Assistance on Tax Matters.

The process of regularisation of Andorra's international relations took a significant step forward in May 2013 with the announcement that legislation was to be placed on the statute book (in June 2013) providing for the novelty of income tax. Although the move was seen as an obvious means of bolstering state revenues, the fact that it followed an official visit to Paris by Mr Martí suggested that it was not only Spanish pressure that was influencing Andorran tax policies. While in Paris, Mr Martí met President Hollande, whose other (little known – and quaintly Ruritanian) official title is Prince of Andorra.

The new income tax, which is set to become effective in 2016, would apply to those living in the principality for a minimum of six months in a calendar year. The first €24,000 (US$32,900) earned would be tax free, with the next €16,000 (US$21,900) taxed at a modest five per cent. The balance of income exceeding the initial €40,000 (US$54,800) was to be taxed at 10 per cent. These rates could hardly be described as draconian, particularly as they are significantly less than those prevailing in most European and North American countries.

Ruritanian Andorra's population of 85,000 is for the most part clustered around the principality's main street, which in summer often becomes a carbon-monoxide filled traffic jam as tourists seek out tax-free bargains in clothing, cosmetics and tobacco. Parking – alongside breathing – becomes a nightmare in the enclosed valley. But in summer few tourists venture outside the crowded main street. In winter Andorra is a popular winter sports venue – with its added tax free advantages. Spanish number plates identify the origin of most of the winter visitors; those from Barcelona experience no language problems as Catalan is Andorra's official language as well as its lingua franca. Time was when a visibly Ruritanian Andorra would close its frontiers to Spain and France each night at 11.00 pm. This was easy enough to do as it simply meant locking the gate across each end of the principality's main road. Day trippers enjoying a late dinner found themselves obliged to spend the night in an Andorran hotel – if lucky. The less lucky could look forward to spending the night in their car.

Risk assessment

Politics	Fair
Economy	Good
Regional stability	Good

COUNTRY PROFILE

One of the world's smallest countries, Andorra is also one of the oldest nations in Europe, established by Charlemagne in 803 as a buffer state against a Muslim Spain.

803 Charlemagne captured the area from Spanish Muslims and his son, Louis the Pious, presented the area's inhabitants with a charter of liberties.

843 The Valls d'Andorra (Valleys of Andorra) were granted to Sunifred, Count of Urgell.

1278 Co-principality established between France (originally represented by a nominee of the king, then the emperor and latterly the president himself) and Spain (in the person of the Bishop of Seu d'Urgel).

1419 A parliament, the Consell de la Terra (Council of the Land), was established to represent the Andorran people.

1866 The Consell General de las Valls (Council of the Valleys) replaced the Council of the Land, during the year of the New Reform, which introduced democratisation to Andorra.

1933–34 The Council of the Valleys was temporarily dissolved by the courts. Elections were held and all men over 25 years were granted the right to vote.

1981 Constitutional reforms were enacted to move power away from the feudal co-princes and towards the parliament.

1983 Income tax was introduced following public spending needed for storm damage and a general recession.

1985 Universal suffrage was introduced.

1991 Andorra joined a customs union with the EU.

1993 Andorra introduced a new constitution, establishing the country as a sovereign parliamentary democracy, and a new 28-member parliament, the Consell General (General Council). The first elections were won by Agrupament Nacional Democratic (AND) (National Democratic Grouping).

1994 A coalition government was formed, led by Unió Liberal (UL). Marc Forné Molné of the Partit Liberal Andorra's (PLA) (Liberal Party of Andorra) was elected prime minister by the General Council.

2001 The PLA was re-elected.

2002 The Organisation for Economic Co-operation and Development (OECD) blacklisted Andorra as a tax haven with 'prejudicial' tax practices. The principality refused to agree to lift the secrecy surrounding its banking sector. Préfet Philippe Massoni was appointed representative of the President of France in Andorra.

2003 Joan Enric Vives Sicília succeeded Joan Martí Alanís as Bishop of Seu d'Urgel and *ex officio* co-prince of Andorra.

2004 An agreement on a Savings Tax Directive concerning tax withholding and savings between the EU and Andorra was reached.

2005 The ruling PLA won general elections and Albert Pintat Santolària was elected head of government.

2006 Measures to reform the economy and improve the country's reputation as a financial centre were adopted

2007 Nicolas Sarkozy, as president of the French Republic, became co-prince.

2009 Banking secrecy laws were reformed allowing Andorra's removal from the OECD blacklist. In parliamentary elections, the opposition PSD won 45.03 per cent of the vote, (14 seats out of 28). The ruling party contested the election as part of the Coalició Reformista (CR) (Reformist Coalition) (with three other parties) and together won 32.34 per cent (11 seats). Turnout was 75.3 per cent. Jaume Bartumeu (PSD) won after two rounds for elections of Cap de Govern (head of government).

2011 Early parliamentary elections were held on 3 April –called due to the failure by parliament to pass the budget and important legislation on value added tax (VAT). The opposition, Demòcrates per Andorra (Democrats for Andorra) (Democrats), a successor to the RF, won 71.4 per cent of the vote (20 seats out of 28),

PSD 21.4 per cent (six), Lauredian Union 7.1 per cent (two). Turnout was 74.1 per cent. In May, Antoni Marti, leader of the Democrats was elected prime minister by parliament, with 21 votes (out of 28).

2012 On 15 May, François Hollande as president of the French Republic became co-prince. On the same day, Préfet Sylvie Hubac was appointed representative of the President of France in Andorra. From 25 September street views of Andorra became available on Google Maps Street View.

2013 A new law governing the tax system and establishing a new fiscal framework was approved by the government on 15 August. The law is the culmination of a radical shake up of the tax system to bring Andorra into line with the rest of Europe.In October MEPs urged the European Commission to allow the three micro-states of Andorra, Monaco and San Marino to join the European Economic Area.

2014 Although Andorra's own euro coins were scheduled to go into circulation in March, they were not delivered until 23 December, in preparation for use in January 2015.

2015 Andorra's euro coinage went into circulation on 1 January.

Political structure

Constitution

The first written constitution was adopted 14 March 1993 after a referendum. The constitution allows Andorra to hold full sovereignty, to be able to form trade unions and political parties, and to have an independent judiciary. It can also decide its own foreign policy and join international organisations. Before the 1993 text there was do distinction between the executive, legislative and judiciary branches of Andorran politics, which was corrected.

Form of state

Andorra is a co-principality under the joint sovereignty of the President of France and the Spanish Bishop of Seu d'Urgel, who are represented locally by officials called *verguers*.

The executive

The co-princes (the Bishop of Seu d'Urgel and President of France), are titular heads of state. The country is governed by an administration formed by the party or coalition with the largest number of seats in the legislature.

National legislature

The unicameral General Council (Consell General, Consell General de les Valls) has 28 members, who serve for four-year terms, of which, 14 elected by proportional representation in a single national constituency and 14 are elected by seven *parroquies*, or parishes from a national list. The General Council elects the Cap de Govern (head of government) (subject to the approval by the co-princes), who is leader of the largest party and who presides over the executive council.

Legal system

Independent judiciary

Last elections

1 March 2015 (parliamentary)

Results: The vote in Andorra elections is split between constituencies and nationwide proportional representation. Both send 14 candidates to parliament. Parliamentary (constituency): Democrats for Andorra won 39.4 per cent and 10 seats (out of 14), PLA won 27.5 per cent and 4 seats. Two other parties gained the remaining vote but failed to win any seats Parliamentary (PR): DA won 37 per cent and 5 seats, PLA won 27.7 per cent and 4 seats, a left-leaning coalition won 23.5 per cent and 3 seats and The Social Democracy and Progress party won the remaining 11.7 per cent and 2 seats

Next elections

2019 (parliamentary)

Political parties

Ruling party

Demòcrates per Andorra (Democrats for Andorra) (Democrats) (from 3 Apr 2011)

Main opposition party

Partit Liberal d'Andorra (PLA) (Liberal Party of Andorra)

Population

78,115 (2011)

Last census: July 2000: 66,089

Population density: 147 people per square km. Urban population 88 per cent (2010 Unicef).

Annual growth rate: 2.4 per cent, 1990–2010 (Unicef).

Ethnic make-up

Of Andorra's total population, only about 33 per cent are natives with the right to vote. The rest include Spaniards (43 per cent), Portuguese (11 per cent), French (7 per cent), English, Australians, Moroccans and others (6 per cent).

Religions

Roman Catholicism is predominant.

Education

A range of universal, free public French, Spanish and Andorran lay schools provide education up to secondary level. Although schools are built and maintained by Andorran authorities, teachers are paid for the most part by France or Spain. The government provides free nursery schools, although supply falls short of demand. About 50 per cent of Andorran children attend the French primary schools, and the rest attend Spanish or Andorran schools. In July 1997, the University of Andorra was established, which serves principally as a centre for virtual studies, connected to Spanish and French universities. The only two graduate schools in Andorra are the Nursing School and the School of Computer Science.

Compulsory years: Four to 16

Health

Fertility rate/Maternal mortality rate: 2.4 births per woman, 2010 (Unicef 2012)

Child (under 5 years) mortality rate (per 1,000): 3 per 1,000 live births (WHO 2012)

Welfare

Social security in Andorra is based on a points system with two distinct programmes covering health and old-age insurance.

Health insurance covers illness, pregnancy, accidents at work, disability and death. Social security payments cover nearly 75 per cent and 90 per cent of expenditure relating to illness and hospitalisation respectively. There is no discrimination against disabled persons in employment, education, or in the provision of other state services.

Unemployment benefit includes 50 per cent of the average salary calculated in the first month and 66 per cent calculated from the second month onwards.

Pensions

People pay contributions towards their old-age pension and on retirement receive a pension proportional to the number of points collected. All salaried workers pay contributions to the Andorran Social Security Fund (CASS). Old-age pension is paid to those covered from the age of 65.

Family support

Maternity care and childbirth are fully covered by social security, while disability benefits are calculated in each individual case.

Main cities

Andorra la Vella (capital, estimated population 20,643 in 2012),
Escaldes-Engordany (17,008), Encamp (8,900), Sant Julià de Lòria (8,012), La Massana (5,192).

Languages spoken

French and Castilian

Official language/s

Catalan

Media

The constitution guarantees the freedom of speech and of the press.

Press

In Catalan, there are several newspapers including the *Diari d'Andorra* (www.diariandorra.ad), *Bondia* (www.bondia.ad), and *El Periodic d'Andorra* (www.elperiodico.com).

Broadcasting

Radio Televisio d'Andorra (RTVA) (www.rtvasa.ad) is the national

broadcaster; Spanish TV also broadcasts in Andorra (www.tvc.cat). All TV services are provided by digital technology.
Radio: Radio Nacional d'Andorra (RNA) is the only public station. Privately-owned commercial stations include Radio Valira, Andorra 1 (www.andorra1.ad) and Andorra 7 (www.andorra7radio.com). Radio signals from Spain and France can be picked up with ease.

Economy

With some 9 million visitors a year, Andorra is heavily reliant on the tourist sector, which accounts for around 80 per cent of GDP. Financial services, accounting for around 15 per cent of GDP, are an important magnet for foreign investment. Andorra is a tax haven with a banking system aimed at attracting foreign private funds, though this has recently come under pressure.
Andorra was removed from the Organisation for Economic Co-operation and Development's (OECD) list of unco-operative tax havens in 2009, following Andorra's agreement to operate equivalent measures in transparency and information exchange regarding taxation of income from savings as other EU member states. This began to erode Andorra's international status as a tax haven.
There is a very small-scale agriculture sector, given that in Andorra only some 5 per cent of land is arable; tobacco growing and sheep farming are the main sectors. Consequently, there is a heavy reliance on food imports. Light industry in Andorra consists almost entirely of tobacco products, handicrafts and furniture, which are the primary exports.
The most important activities of the service sector are commerce and the hotel trade, which employ almost 40 per cent of the workforce. There are insufficient modern and dynamic services, such as specialised services for businesses, and a reliance on traditional sectors limits the economy's potential.
Andorra is a member of the EU Customs Union and is treated as an EU member with no tariffs on manufactured goods when trading with EU members.
Andorra's reliance on tourism, as well as food and fuel imports, makes it vulnerable to the fluctuations in foreign markets. The reliance on foreign trade and tourism for their economy has meant that the economy has experienced negative growth in recent years, standing at -0.1 per cent in 2013 (most recent available figure), up from -1.8 per cent in 2012 as global conditions improved.

External trade

As a member of the European Union Customs Union with favourable excise duties Andorra is a major entrepôt for numerous European goods. However, Andorra is treated as a non-EU member and its agricultural products are subject to tariffs.
Spain and France are Andorra's main export partners and EU members take 99.5 per cent of total exports.
The nearly 3km long Envalira tunnel, between Andorra and France, runs under the highest mountain pass in Europe. It is one of the longest road tunnels in the world.
The volume of exports is typically under 5 per cent of GDP, a figure far below that of most OECD countries, indicating the unusual nature of the economy, based on retail sales to tourists.
Three-quarters of Andorra's revenue is free from import tariffs.

Imports

Main imports are foodstuffs, electricity, raw materials, manufactures and consumer goods.
Main sources: Spain (typically over 61 per cent of total), France (over 28 per cent), US (1 per cent)

Exports

Main exports include tobacco products and furniture.
Main destinations: Spain (typically over 70 per cent of total), France (over 15 per cent).

Agriculture

Farming

The agricultural sector is a small part of the economy, accounting for less than 1 per cent of GDP and typically employing less than 1 per cent of the working population.
Agricultural production is limited by a scarcity of arable land, and most food has to be imported. Milk is sourced domestically. Principal crops are tobacco and potatoes, rye, wheat, barley, oats. Some other vegetables are also grown.
The principal livestock activity is sheep husbandry.
The land used in agriculture is 2 per cent permanent crops, of which 56 per cent forest and woodland, 20 per cent irrigated land.

Fishing

Andorra imports fish from Spain for domestic needs. Trout are plentiful in streams.

Forestry

Logs are transported to Spain. Most reforestation is in pines.

Industry and manufacturing

The industrial sector, including the tourism industry, contributes around 80 per cent of economic activity. The small manufacturing sector primarily services tourism, but also includes cigarettes, cigars and furniture.

Tourism

The Andorran economy is heavily dependent on tourism with approximately 9 million visitors a year. It is very well known as a winter destination, with an established infrastructure catering for its many skiing tourists. During summer it caters for the active tourist and those favouring spa holidays. It also relies on day-trippers who visit the principality to shop for duty-free consumer and luxury items. The number of visitors not arriving from either Spain or France is typically below 50,000.
Despite the detrimental impact on tourism in Europe of the global economic crisis, Andorra did not experience either a drop in visitor numbers or weakness in business growth in the tourist industry during the late 2000s. This was probably due to the perception of Andorra as a destination of good value for money for most Europeans.

Environment

Current issues are deforestation and overgrazing of mountain meadows contributing to soil erosion. Natural hazards include snowslides and avalanches.

Mining

Forges in Andorra were once famed.
There are small amounts of iron ore and lead but access is a problem.
Even though Andorra has good hydroelectric facilities, around three-quarters of energy consumed is by imported oil from France and Spain. It does not import coal or natural gas.

Hydrocarbons

Even though Andorra has good hydroelectric facilities, around three-quarters of energy consumed is by imported oil from France and Spain. It does not import coal or natural gas.

Energy

Electricity demand is estimated at 500GWh, of which around 50 per cent is supplied by Endesa of Spain, and the remainder by Electricité de France (EDF) and the country's only hydroelectric plant. Installed generating capacity is estimated at 520MW.

Banking and insurance

The banking sector with its tax haven status contributes substantially to the economy. Seven commercial banks operate some 34 branches. Strict secrecy laws are maintained.
Andorra's financial service sector is benefiting from the eurozone which provides greater stability and enhanced opportunities. After being denounced as an unco-operative tax haven by the OECD in 2003, Andorra conceded to EU standards regarding taxation of income from savings. From 2005 Andorra has imposed a

withholding tax, up to 35 per cent, which is passed to the tax department of an EU citizen's country. Instead of informing the relevant EU country about the amount of money in savings accounts, the anonymity of the saver is preserved. In an effort to avoid joining the global list of non-co-operative tax havens, held by the Organisation of Economic Co-operation and Development (OECD), Andorra eased its banking laws to allow the sharing of bank data that cracks down on offshore tax evasion, eroding its status as a tax haven. Andorra has also agreed to supply information on tax fraud, for criminal or civil trials, and notify EU member states about additional malpractices.

Central bank

Time
GMT plus one hour (daylight saving, late March to late October, GMT plus two hours)

Geography
Andorra lies high in the eastern Pyrenees mountains in south-western Europe. The lowest elevation is 838 metres, reaching to nearly 3,000 metres at the peak of Coma Pedrosa. Andorra is landlocked, sharing borders with France and Spain.

Hemisphere

Northern

Climate
Warm summers and moderately cold winters; temperatures range from 0–30 degrees Celsius.

Entry requirements
Passports

Required by all except for nationals of France and Spain, who only require an identity card.

Visa

Not required, but the relevant regulations of Spain and France, depending on point of transit, should be followed. Stays of up to three months without a visa are allowed.

Currency advice/regulations

No currency restrictions.

Health (for visitors)
Mandatory precautions

None

Advisable precautions

Up-to-date tetanus, Measles-mumps-rubella, varicella and polio immunisations are recommended; also influenza if visiting Nov-Apr.

Hotels
Around 270 hotels, most with modern facilities.

Public holidays (national)
Fixed dates

1 Jan (New Year's Day), 6 Jan (Epiphany), 14 Mar (Constitution Day), 1 May (Labour Day), 24 Jun (St John's Day), 15 Aug (Assumption Day), 8 Sep (Mare de Déu de Meritxell, National Day), 1 Nov (All Saints Day), 4 Nov (St Charles Day), 8 Dec (Immaculate Conception), 24 Dec (Christmas Eve), 25–26 Dec (Christmas Holiday), 31 Dec (New Year's Eve).

Variable dates

Good Friday, Easter Monday, Ascension Day, Whit Monday.

Working hours
Banking

Mon–Fri: 0900–1300, 1500–1700; Sat: 0900–1200.

Business

Considerable variation in times, depending on whether following French or Spanish working practices.

Shops

Mon–Fri: 0900–2000; Sat: 0900–2100; Sun: 0900–1900.

Getting there
Air

International airport/s: The closest international airports are located in France (Toulouse-Blagnac, 180km) and Spain (Barcelona, 200km), connecting to inter- and intra-continental destinations. Approximately three hours drive. Regular shuttle bus services connect both airports with Andorra.

Surface

Road: From Spain: Barcelona-Andorra via Cervera; Barcelona-Andorra via Calaf; Barcelona-Andorra via Solsonal. Madrid-Andorra via Zaragoza. Buses run regularly from Barcelona and Madrid. Other road connections to Lleida, Puigcerdà, Tarragona and Girona. Mountainous roads exist over the Envalira pass to Perpignan, Tarbes and Toulouse. From France: Paris-Andorra via Aix-les-Thermes; Marseilles-Andorra via Perpignan; Biarritz via St Gaudens. A road runs from the Spanish to the French frontiers through Saint Julia, Andorra la Vella, Escaldes-Engordonay, Encamp, Camnillo and Soldeu.

Rail: From Spain: Barcelona to Puigcerda, then by bus to La Seu d'Urgel and Andorra. Madrid to Lleida, then bus to La Seu d'Urgel and Andorra. From France: Paris to Aix-les-Thermes or L'Hospitalet, then bus to Andorra; Perpignan to La Tour de Carol, then bus to Andorra .

Getting about
National transport

Road: There are 269km of roads, of which 198km are paved. Roads can be blocked by snow in winter and congestion in summer.

Buses: Constant minibus services link all the villages.

BUSINESS DIRECTORY
The addresses listed below are a selection only. While World of Information makes every endeavour to check these addresses, we cannot guarantee that changes have not been made, especially to telephone numbers and area codes. We would welcome any corrections.

Telephone area codes
The international direct dialling (IDD) code for Andorra is +376, followed by customer's number.

Useful telephone numbers
Mountain rescue: 112
Police: 110
Fire: 118
Ambulance: 118

Chambers of Commerce
Andorra Chamber of Commerce, Industry and Services, C/Prat de la Creu 8, Edifice le Mans 204, Andorra La Vella (tel: 809-292; fax: 809-293; e-mail: ccis@andorra.ad).

Banking
Banc Agricol i Comercial d'Andorra, Mossen Cinto 6, Andorra la Vella (tel: 821-333).

Banca Cassany SA, Avinguda Meritxell 39-41, Andorra la Vella.

Banc Internacional, Avinguda Meritxell 32, Andorra la Vella (tel: 820-037).

Banca Mora SA, Placa Coprinceps 2, Les Escaldes (tel: 820-607).

Banca Reig, Avinguda Meritxell, Andorra la Vella (tel: 822-618).

Credit Andorra, Avinguda Princep Benlloch 19, Andorra la Vella (tel: 820-326).

La Caixa, Pl Rebés, Andorra la Vella (tel: 820-015).

Central bank

European Central Bank (ECB), Kaiserstrasse 29, D-60311 Frankfurt am Main, Germany (tel: +49(69) 13-440; fax: +49(69) 1344-6000).

Travel information
Caseta d'Informació i Turisme (tourism kiosk opposite Restaurant Martí), Andorra la Vella (tel: 827-117).

Sindicat d'Iniciativa Oficina de Turisme (national tourist office at the top of Carrer Doctor Vilanova between Plaça del Poble and Plaça Rebés), Andorra la Vella (tel: 820-214).

Ministries
Government of Andorra, C/ Prat de la Creu 62, Andorra La Vella (tel: 829-345; internet: www.govern.ad).

Ministry of Finance, Andorra la Vella (tel: 829-245).

Ministry of Commerce, Industry and Agriculture, Andorra la Vella.

Ministry of Tourism and Environment, C/Prat de la Creu, Andorra la Vella (tel: 875-7 02; fax: 860-184; e-mail: turisme@andorra.ad)

Other useful addresses

French Embassy, C/ Les Canals 38-40, Andorra La Vella (tel: 820-809).

French Post Office, C/Bonaventura Armengol, Andorra la Vella (tel: 820-408).

General Syndic's Office (tel: 821-234).

Pas de la Casa Customs Post (Andorran frontier with France) (tel: 855-120).

Police, Andorra la Vella (tel: 821-222).

Sant Julia de Loria Customs Post (Andorran frontier with Spain) (tel: 841-090).

Servei de Telecomunicacions d'Andorra STA, Avinguda Meritxell 110, Andorra la Vella (tel: 821-021).

Sindicat d'Iniciativa de les Valls d'Andorra, c/Dr Vilanova, Andorra la Vella (tel: 820-214).

Spanish Embassy, C/ Prat de la Creu 34, Andorra La Vella (tel: 820-013).

Spanish Post Office, c/o Joan Maragall, Andorra la Vella (tel: 820-257).

Internet sites

Andorra information: http://www.visitandorra.com/en/home/

Angola

KEY FACTS

Official name: Republica de Angola (Republic of Angola)

Head of State: President José Eduardo dos Santos (since 1979, indirect election 26 Sep 2012)

Head of government: President José Eduardo dos Santos (indirect election 26 Sep 2012)

Ruling party: Movimento Popular de Libertação de Angola (MPLA) (Popular Movement for the Liberation of Angola) (from 1975; re-elected 31 Aug 2012)

Area: 1,246,700 square km

Population: 24.38 million (2014)*

Capital: Luanda

Official language: Portuguese

Currency: Kwanza (Kz) = 100 Lwei

Exchange rate: Kz126.00 per US$ (Sep 2015)

GDP per capita: US$5,273 (2014)*

GDP real growth: 4.22% (2014)*

GDP: US$128.56 billion (2014)*

Labour force: 7.98 million (2010)

Inflation: 7.30% (2014)

Oil production: 1.71 million bpd (2014)

Balance of trade: US$41.90 billion (2013)

* estimated figure

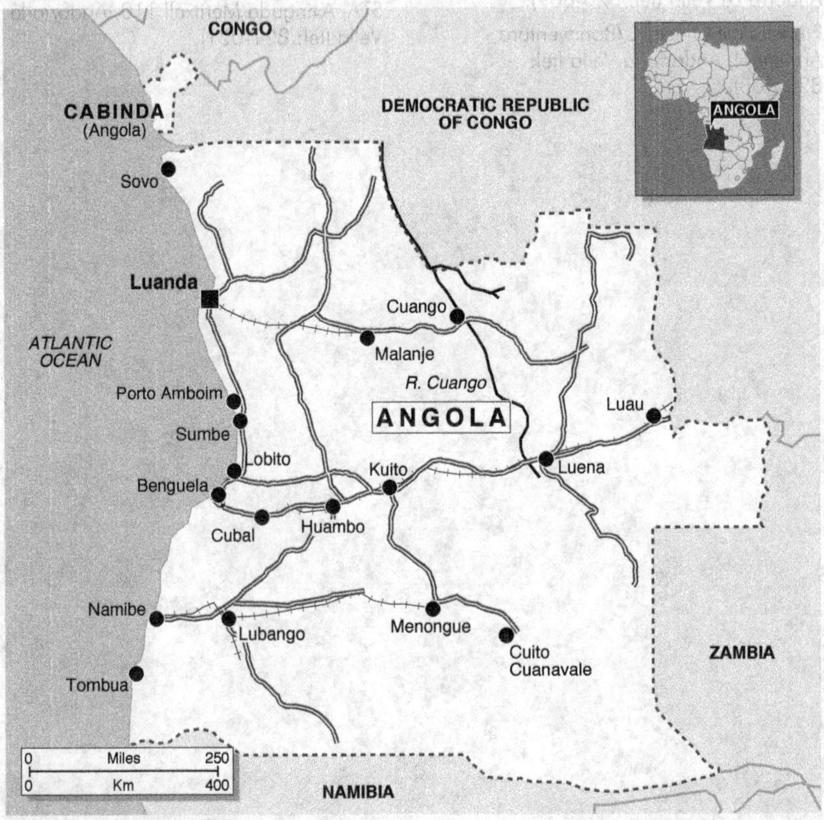

On 16 April 2015, a pilgrimage of the Angolan Christian sect the Seventh Day Light of the World Church to Mount Sumi led to the massacre of some 1,000 attendees. The event was shrouded in fear and mystery, and highlighted the extent to which the government sought to regulate the flow of information. The mass killing, that took place in Angola's central highland, was reported to be a retaliation from the police and defence forces following the death of eight police officers allegedly at the hands of members of the sect. These eight deaths were the result of a botched operation to arrest the leader of the sect, José Kalupeteka, during worship. The only traces of the thousands of victims who were camped in the hills were burnt-out vehicles, bullet ridden shacks and blood-splattered soil. The tragedy is added to a lengthy list of atrocities that have occurred in Angolan history.

Despite being the third-largest economy in sub-Saharan Africa, in terms of gross domestic product (GDP), around 36 per cent of Angolans live below the poverty line, according to the United Nations Development Programme. The latest 2012 estimate from the World Bank indicates that only 37 per cent of Angolans have access to electricity, leaving about 8 million people without access.

Angola has significant oil wealth, and is sub-Saharan Africa's second-largest oil producer. Therefore, the sharp decline in oil prices since June 2014 has severely affected the Angolan economy. In its end-of-mission statement following the completion of its August 2015 mission to Luanda, the International Monetary Fund (IMF) stated that a comfortable level of international reserves has allowed the economy to weather better the consequences of falling oil prices than in 2008–09. However with oil accounting for 95 per cent of exports and 75 per cent of fiscal revenue, the importance of diversifying the economy is underscored by recent developments.

The IMF expects the economic activity to slowdown as the industrial, construction and service sectors adjust to the lack of private consumption and public investment. Output growth is projected to average 3.5 per cent a year over 2015–16. There is acceleration in inflation reflecting loose monetary conditions in the first half of 2015 and the depreciation of the kwanza. Inflation is expected to have peaked by the end of 2015, and then fall gradually over time. The external accounts are weakening due to the decline in oil exports as well as the limited room for import substitution. The outlook is for a recovery in 2017, however, this is dependent on whether the current oil price situation remains.

The government reacted quickly to the changing oil prices by revising the 2015 budget, which will allow the central government deficit to fall to 3.5 per cent of GDP, down from 6.5 per cent in the previous year. Public debt on the other hand is moving in the other direction, expected to reach 57 per cent of GDP by the end of 2015. The IMF suggested in its review that the 2016 budget should be based on a conservative oil price assumption and be aimed at protecting spending on critical infrastructure needs and social assistance, while preserving fiscal discipline.

The review also stated that over the medium term, fiscal policy should be aimed at restoring fiscal buffers by reducing public debt and achieving fiscal consolidation through structural fiscal reforms. A priority is expanding the non-oil sector by rationalising tax incentives and giving more power to the tax administration agency Administração Geral Tributária (AGT). The IMF suggested monetary and exchange rate policies should be focused on containing inflation while maintaining an adequate amount of financial reserves.

Hydrocarbons

According to the Energy Information Administration (EIA), after Nigeria, Angola produces the second most oil in Sub-Saharan Africa, and its national company, Sonangol, is a shareholder in almost all oil and natural gas exploration and production projects countrywide. Companies from the US and Europe lead exploration in Angola; however, in recent years Chinese companies have been increasing their participation in the country. Reciprocally, Angola has been the second-largest supplier of crude oil to China since 2005, behind Saudi Arabia. Angolan oil also finds itself destined for the US, Europe and India. In recent years, however, US imports have declined in line with the increasing US production of similar quality crude grades.

Sonangol has a target production rate of 2.0 million barrels per day (bpd) by 2016, as new deep-water oil fields have been discovered and are scheduled to begin output. Crude oil targets in recent years have not been met, however, as Angola has continuously fallen short of its projected production, and in 2014 output declined. The industry is plagued by frequent technical problems, and there have been steep production decline rates at the older deep-water fields, which together have stopped total production reaching full potential.

Only small quantities of marketed natural gas are produced in Angola because almost all of the country's gross-production is flared or pumped back into oil wells. Angola has a new liquefied natural gas plant in Soyo, which – despite only coming online in 2013 – underwent a temporary closure in April 2014 due to chronic technical issues.

AfDB Report

The African Development Bank (AfDB) credited the deceleration of the economy to the above-mentioned temporary reduction in oil output as well as the sharp drop in international oil prices and a prolonged drought. Sound macroeconomic policies helped to keep the economic growth rate from dropping any lower than 4.5 per cent in 2014, which was a drop from 6.8 per cent in 2013. This trend, however, is expected to continue as the economy will suffer from expected lower oil prices over 2015/16, with a projected growth rate of 3.8 per cent in 2015. Following on from this, nevertheless, growth is projected to jump back to 4.6 per cent in 2016.

In its African Economic Outlook (AEO) report, the AfDB stated that growth and equitable development in Angola are constrained by the adverse business environment, inadequate governance and transparency in the management of public resources, weak quality and maintenance of physical infrastructure, limited quality of human resources, weak agriculture growth, inefficient public service delivery to the poor, and difficulties in managing income from non-renewables to create savings for future generations. High unemployment (particularly among the youth), significant poverty and high-income inequality increasingly add to the social pressures. Structural reforms are vital to diversify the economy and reduce the dependency on natural resources, increase productivity, improve the allocation of resources and facilitate the conditions for a faster rate of economic growth.

Angola has large and persistent regional inequalities, which have only been aggravated by 27 years of conflict – war that lead to a mass migration from rural to urban areas. The AfDB stated that the country's Public Investment Programme has helped improve regional allocation of

KEY INDICATORS **Angola**

	Unit	2011	2012	2013	2014	**2015
Population	m	*19.63	*20.21	*20.82	24.38	*25.11
Gross domestic product (GDP)	US$bn	100.90	115.33	*124.17	*128.56	*106.15
GDP per capita	US$	5,144	5,706	*5,245	*5,273	*4,227
GDP real growth	%	3.4	5.2	*6.8	*4.2	*4.5
Inflation	%	13.5	10.3	8.8	7.3	*8.4
Oil output	'000 bpd	1,746.0	1,784.0	1,801.0	1,712.0	–
Exports (fob) (goods)	US$m	67,310.3	71,091.2	68,246.5	–	–
Imports (fob) (goods)	US$m	20,228.5	23,716.9	26,344.0	–	–
Balance of trade	US$m	47,081.8	47,374.3	41,902.6	–	–
Current account	US$m	13,084.7	10,636.0	8,343.0	*-1,090.0	*-6,736.0
Total reserves minus gold	US$m	25,192.9	33,414.8	32,780.4	27,092.4	–
Foreign exchange	US$m	24,774.8	33,034.8	32,413.6	–	–
Exchange rate	per US$	93.10	95.66	97.62	102.87	–

* estimated figure ** forecast figure

public resources, but more efforts are required to improve the quality and availability of economic and social infrastructure. Knowing that economic isolation of regions and demographics might lead to spatial conflicts, the government introduced a series of tax breaks, accelerated provision of physical infrastructure in special economic zones and the development of aspects of the 2013–17 National Industrialisation Programme. Easy access to credit is being made available for small- and medium-sized businesses, and regional asymmetries are being reduced. The May 2014 population census will be used in the design of the National Population Policy, helping to anticipate the consequences of a growing population and its affect on natural resources.

Risk assessment

Politics	Fair
Economy	Fair
Regional stability	Good

COUNTRY PROFILE

1482 The Portuguese arrived in Angola, which became a staging post for trade with India and south-east Asia.

1575 The Portuguese founded Luanda. The country became a major source of slaves, who were transported to Brazil.

1836 The slave trade was abolished.

1885 The borders of Angola were set following the Berlin Conference of imperial powers who, with an eye on exploitable assets in Africa, agreed to formal boundaries. Angola provided Portugal with minerals and agricultural products.

1951 Angola's status changed from a colony to an overseas territory.

1956 The Movimento Popular de Libertação de Angola (MPLA) (Popular Movement for the Liberation of Angola) was founded as a guerrilla force fighting Portuguese rule.

1961 An uprising in which 50,000 Angolans were massacred led to increased repression by colonial security forces.

1962 The Frente Nacional para a Libertacao de Angola (FNLA) (National Front for the Liberation of Angola) was formed by refugees of the uprising, living mainly in what is now the Democratic Republic of Congo.

1966 The União Nacional de Independencia Total de Angola (Unita) (National Union for the Total Independence of Angola) was formed.

1972 The FNLA and MPLA assumed joint leadership of the liberation struggle.

1975 Angola gained independence from Portugal. Scheduled elections failed to take place when the MPLA took power. Unita and the FNLA formed an alliance aimed at defeating the MPLA government.

1979 José dos Santos (MPLA) became president, backed by the Soviet Union and Cuba. A civil war ensued, with Unita supported by the US and South Africa.

1988 An agreement between South Africa, Angola and Cuba was signed, all foreign troops to be withdrawn by mid-1991.

1990 A UN mission, to verify Cuban troop withdrawals, was initiated.

1991 The MPLA officially dropped its commitment to Marxism-Leninism in favour of social democracy. Cuban troops withdrew. The Bicesse Accords, sponsored by the UN and signed by the MPLA and Unita, recognised fundamental rights and duties based on the principles of the major international treaties on human rights and established multi-party politics.

1992 The first multi-party elections resulted in a coalition government formed by the MPLA and minor parties. The newly-legalised Unita lost and rejected the election results, ending the UN-brokered cease-fire.

1994 A cease-fire peace agreement, the *Lusaka Protocol*, was signed between the government and Unita.

1997 Unita joined the ruling MPLA in a power-sharing government of national unity, however, it did not disarm.

1998 Renewed hostilities between MPLA and Unita broke out.

2002 Jonas Savimbi, the leader of Unita, was killed by government forces. The Angolan government offered an amnesty for all Unita rebels who surrendered; ending the civil war. Fernando da Piedade Dias dos Santos (cousin of the José dos Santos) became prime minister.

2003 The World Bank approved a US$125 million assistance programme.

2004 More than 3,000 people were arrested in a crackdown on illegal diamond mining and trafficking (around 11,000 illegal migrants were deported in four months).

2006 A cease-fire was signed between the government and the armed militia, Fórum Cabindês para o Diálogo (FCD) (Cabinda Forum for Dialogue), in Cabinda, the rebel Angolan enclave, followed by the formal signing of a *Memorandum for Peace and Reconciliation* in Cabinda. Angola joined the Organisation of Petroleum Exporting Countries (OPEC) as a full member.

2008 The first parliamentary elections since 1992 were finally held; the ruling MPLA won 81.64 per cent of votes and 191 seats (out of 220). International observers reported that the election had not been free and fair and that there had been faults with the voting systems, particularly in Luanda. The president appointed Paulo Kassoma (MPLA) as the new prime minister.

2009 TAAG, the national airline, posted a loss of US$70 million after it had been banned from EU airspace in 2007. Later, the EU allowed TAAG to operate out of Portugal only and only with certain aircraft and under very strict conditions. Russian President Dmitry Medvedev paid an official visit to Angola.

2010 Parliament approved a new constitution that abolished direct presidential elections; the leader of the largest party in parliament assumes the post of head of state and will not be limited to a fixed number of terms in office. The opposition called it 'a complete fraud' that would lead to 'excessive executive power'. Vice President Fernando da Piedade Dias dos Santos was appointed as head of government (in a new post that replaced the office of prime minister). All restrictions on TAAG operating in the EU were lifted. A new voter registry was compiled.

2011 In March Angola committed 10.6 per cent of the total US$241.6 million set aside for telecommunications within the public investment programme, for the construction and launch of a Russian-built Angolan satellite in 2012. In June Angola and Russia signed a parliamentary protocol, aimed at sharing legislative and juridical experiences between their respective legislatures.

2012 In March a new political party was founded by Abel Chivukuvuku (former Unita parliamentary leader), the Ampla Convergência para a Salvação de Angola-Eleitoral Coligação (Casa-CE) (Broad Convergence for the Salvation of Angola-Electoral Coalition). On 17 July President dos Santos met an envoy of President Putin to discuss the Russian launch of the Angolan satellite (which by October was still in preparation). Parliamentary elections (only the third such conducted since 1979) were held on 31 August and were declared 'free and fair' by the African Union. The MPLA won an overwhelming majority of votes and seats in the legislature with 71.8 per cent of the vote (175 seats out of 220), which kept the existing government in office. The new government was sworn into office on 19 September; José Eduardo dos Santos was elected by parliament as president on 26 September.

2013 A severe drought in southern Angola was having a drastic affect by August, with drinking water supplies under threat and crops failing.

2014 Nigerian pirates have moved further afield to Angola. On January 18 they attacked an oil products tanker a few miles off the coast of Luanda, the capital and forced the vessel to sail hundreds of miles up the coast before offloading much of its

cargo close to the Niger Delta. A census, the first since 1970, took place during May. The result was 24.38 million, of which there were more women (51.6 per cent) than men (48.4 per cent) and the urban population outstripped the rural by 62.3 per cent to 37.7 per cent.
2015 Following an arrest of the leader of an unorthodox religious sect in Angola in mid-April, nine unarmed policemen who had come to arrest the leader, Jose Kalupeteka were killed. According to the government's opposition party, UNITA, the government responded by slaughtering 1,080 members of the sect with helicopter gunships mowing them down.

Political structure

Constitution

Parliament approved a new constitution on 21 January 2010, replacing the interim constitution formulated in 1975. The new constitution officially names the president as Head of State and government as well as commander-in-chief of the armed forces. Direct elections for the presidency were abolished with the majority party in parliament electing its leader as president. Presidential terms in office are limited to two five-year terms – although President Santos, if re-elected, could remain in office until 2022 as the two-term limit will not begin until the 2012 elections. The post of prime minister was abolished and all duties transferred to the office of vice president. The National Assembly can in future remove the president from office following approval by the Supreme Court. Land rights were rectified with the state assuming all land is owned by the state which can decide who may use it; only Angolan nationals and companies registered in Angola will have access to land rights.

Form of state

Presidential republic

The executive

The president is elected by the majority party in parliament and is Head of State and the executive, as well as commander-in-chief of the armed forces. Terms in office are limited to two five-year periods. Presidents appoint their own vice president.

National legislature

The unicameral Assembleia Nacional (National Assembly) has 220 seats, of which members are elected by proportional representation vote. The assembly is presumed to sit for five-year terms, but only two general elections have taken place since 1992.

Legal system

The Head of State appoints judges to the Constitutional and Supreme Courts and Head of the Court of Audits. The Judicial Proctorate is appointed for a four-year term of office and may be re-appointed for another four-year term.

Last elections

31 August 2012 (parliamentary); presidential elections abolished from 2010
Results: Parliamentary: Movimento Popular de Libertação de Angola (MPLA) (Popular Movement for the Liberation of Angola) won 71.8 per cent of the vote (175 seats out of 220), União Nacional de Independencia Total de Angola (Unita) (National Union for the Total Independence of Angola) 18.7 per cent (32), Ampla Convergência para a Salvação de Angola-Eleitoral Coligação (Casa-CE) (Broad Convergence for the Salvation of Angola-Electoral Coalition) 6 per cent (eight), Partido de Renovação Social (PRS) (Social Renewal Party) 1.7 per cent (three), Frente Nacional para a Libertacao de Angola (FNLA) (National Front for the Liberation of Angola) 1.13 per cent (two); four other political parties failed to win enough votes to obtain any seats. Turnout was 62.8 per cent.

Next elections

2019 (parliamentary).

Political parties

Ruling party

Movimento Popular de Libertação de Angola (MPLA) (Popular Movement for the Liberation of Angola) (from 1975; re-elected 31 Aug 2012)

Main opposition party

União Nacional de Independencia Total de Angola (Unita) (National Union for the Total Independence of Angola)

Population

24.38 million (2014)*
Last census: May 2014: 24.4 million; of which 51.6 per cent female, 48.4 per cent male. (Previous census December 1970: 5,646,166)
Population density: 19 inhabitants per square km. Urban population 62.3 per cent (2014 Census).
Annual growth rate: 3.1 per cent, 1990–2010 (Unicef).

Internally Displaced Persons (IDP)

450,000 (UNHCR 2004)

Ethnic make-up

37 per cent Ovimbundu, 25 per cent Mbundu, 13 per cent Bakongo, 2 per cent Mestico (mixed European and indigenous descent), 1 per cent European.

Religions

Traditional beliefs (47 per cent), Christianity (38 per cent), mainly Roman Catholic.

Education

Primary school enrolment has increased slowly, although the increase in male enrolment has been higher than for females. Education expenditure amounts to round 6 per cent of the national budget.
The government allocated US$40 million to hire the graduates of a Unesco scheme, which is set to train around 29,000 school teachers as part of a development programme.
Total expenditure on education is around 3 per cent of GDP.
Literacy rate: 66.8 per cent total; 53.8 per cent female; adult rates.
Compulsory years: 6 to 9
Enrolment rate: 74 per cent gross primary enrolment of relevant age group (including repeater) (World Bank)
Pupils per teacher: 29 in primary schools

Health

Public health has become a priority as Angola's human development indicators are poor, it is recognised to having a high rate of infant mortality and has to repair the damage done by 27 years of civil war. One in four children under aged five are likely to die of malaria, the single largest cause of child mortality.
Until the country can exploit its vast natural resources and raise the living standards of the population as a whole, it has to contend with inadequate numbers of doctors and antiquated medical equipment. Preventative care has been described as almost non-existent and primary care, outside former provincial capitals, limited to infrequent and inadequate drug supplies.
Most doctors, who work within the private sector, live in the capital, Luanda. The government has prepared a large package of incentives to encourage health workers to work in the provinces, however most measures are awaiting the financial resources to implement them.
There were cases of polio reported to the World Health Organisation – Global Polio Eradication Initiative in 2006; the country had previously been free of the disease and its re-emergence was due to infected travellers.
The border between Angola and the Democratic Republic of Congo (DRC) was closed on 6 January 2009 due to an outbreak of Ebola in the Luande Norte province of DRC.

HIV/Aids

In 2009 there were an estimted 200,000 living with HIV. While prevalence rates for countries in the region range between 25–40 per cent and the rate in Angola is only 2 per cent.
HIV prevalence: 2 per cent aged 15–49 in 2009 (World Bank)
Life expectancy: 51 years, 2010 (Unicef 2012)
Fertility rate/Maternal mortality rate: 5.4 births per woman, 2010 (Unicef 2012); 1,700 maternal deaths per 100,000 live births (World Bank).

Child (under 5 years) mortality rate (per 1,000): 164 per 1,000 live births (WHO 2012); 42 per cent of all children are underweight for their age (World Bank).

Welfare
In 2005 plans to return 22,000 refugees living in Zambia got underway, however by November only 35,000 were able to make the return and the programme was extended into early 2006. The numbers of internally displaced persons (IDPs) total over 100,000 and are unable to return home due to poor access and mine infestation and lack of administrative capacity with basic services virtually non-existent. Mine clearance is ongoing as one in every 415 Angolans has been disabled by landmines, but it is estimated in 2005 that six million more remain to be destroyed.

Main cities
Luanda (capital, estimated population 2.8 in 2012), Cabinda (455,468), Huambo (366,238), Lubango (274,141), Kuito (198,679), Malanje (173,327), Lobito (159,892), Benguela (144,116), Uíge (128,755), Namibe (101,317).

Languages spoken
Local languages: principally Ovimbundu, Kimbundu (the language of the Mbundu), Bakongo and Chokwe.

Official language/s
Portuguese

Media
While the constitution ensures freedom of expression the UNHCR considers Angola does not have press freedom as the government harasses private media outlets and uses anti-defamation laws to protect officials from reports deemed 'offensive'. There is also a special committee that has censorship authority over the media.

Press
There is only one national daily newspaper, operated by the government, in Portuguese *Jornal de Angola* (referred to as *JA*). Private, independent newspapers are all weekly, including *Angolense* (www.jornalangolense.com), *Semanário Angolense* (www.semanarioangolense.net), *Folha 8*, *A Capital*, *Actual*, *Cruzeiro do Sul* and *Agora*; *Diario de Luanda* is government-owned.

Broadcasting
National media is state-controlled. Independent media is largely based in major cities, particularly Luanda.

Radio: With high levels of illiteracy radio services are important sources of news and information; most households have radios. The state-run Radio Nacional de Angola (RNA) (www.rna.ao) is the only national radio service, which has a network of five stations broadcasting in Portuguese and local languages, as well as some foreign languages. Other private stations include Luanda Antena Comercial (www.nexus.ao/lac) and Radio Ecclesia (www.recclesia.org), based in Luanda, run by the Roman Catholic Church. As a frequent critic of the government it was denied permission to extend its service into other areas of the country in 2005.

Television: There is a limited national service operated by Televisão Popular de Angola (TPA) (www.tpa.ao).

Pay-TV is available through JumpTV (www.jumptv.com) which carries Portuguese TV programmes from RTP Internacional (RTPi) (http://programas.rtp.pt). TV Cabo (http://www.tvcabo.pt) is a satellite TV network providing international programmes. These services are almost exclusively based in Luanda.

National news agency: Angola Press (Angop): www.angolapress-angop.ao

Other news agencies: AngoNoticias (www.angonoticias.com).

Economy
Industry accounted for 57.0 per cent of GDP in 2014, of which around 7 per cent was manufacturing, services constituted 32.2 per cent of the economy and agriculture 10.8 per cent, of which subsistence farming for the majority of the population is still the norm.

Oil production is the dominant industry in Angola and exports constitute an estimated 63 per cent of GDP. Reserves were 12.7 billion barrels, and production 1.7 million bpd, at the end of 2014. Diamond mining is the only other major industry, with Angola being Africa's third largest producer.

GDP growth dropped dramatically from a record high of 22.6 per cent in 2007 to 2.4 per cent by 2009, as world trade almost ground to a halt and oil exports fell by about 5 per cent, however by 2013 Angola's GDP growth had risen to 8.4 per cent before dropping to 3.9 per cent in 2014. The current account balance was -US$1.9 billion in 2014. Inflation averaged 13.2 per cent over 2007–10 but was down to 7.3 per cent by 2014.

The government has undertaken a project to liberalise the economy but corruption is widespread and the government is highly inefficient, largely stemming from local patronage and the generally secretive nature of government.

In 2014, the UN Human Development Index (HDI) ranked Angola 149 (out of 187) for national development in health, education and income.

External trade
Angola signed a free trade agreement with the US in May 2009 and is a member of the World Trade Organisation (WTO). Angola is also a member of the Southern African Development Community (SADC).

Angola is the second largest exporter of petroleum in Africa (after Nigeria). Oil, combined with diamonds, accounts for 99.7 per cent of all exports. Angola has been criticised and warned that current accounting practices in the oil industry have led to widespread corruption with the loss of millions of dollars each year. Oil revenue is mainly used to finance government spending. Tradable goods exports account for only 0.3 per cent.

Angola is said to suffer from *Dutch Disease*, with all non-oil local industries being stifled by the otherwise mono-oil based economy.

Imports
Principal imports are refined petroleum products, electrical equipment, vehicles and spare parts, machinery, foodstuffs, medicines, textiles, consumer goods and military materials.

Main sources: China (23.7 per cent of total in 2014), Portugal (16.3 per cent), US (8.1 per cent)

Exports
Principal exports are crude oil, gas and derivatives (typically 92 per cent of total), diamonds (8 per cent), marble, coffee, sisal, fish and fish products, timber and cotton.

Main destinations: China (48.1 per cent of total in 2014), US (8.9 per cent), India (8.8 per cent)

Agriculture

Farming
Total agricultural land is 124.7 million hectares of which 43.3 per cent is pasture and 3.2 per cent arable.

Agriculture's share of GDP has slowly begun to rise, from 9 per cent in 2011 to 10.8 per cent in 2014, as production has increased, as more displaced persons and ex-combatants have returned to their farms. Production has been severely hampered by the lack of seed and animals, as well as fertilisers, equipment and vehicles, landmines, lack of infrastructure, reduced capabilities of institutions and little access to investment. International donors and financial institutions have provided relief funds and personnel to improve the situation.

Even so, food insecurity is widespread and around 50 per cent of the population is undernourished.

Of the major crops, only coffee is produced in exportable volumes, while the cultivation of sisal and cotton has virtually ceased. Several overseas companies are reportedly interested in rehabilitating sugar cane, cotton and sisal estates.

Livestock farming has been disrupted by insecurity, the neglect of veterinary services and recurrent droughts have affected much of the south and centre of Angola.

In 2012 a severe drought began in southern Angola and was having a drastic affect, with drinking water supplies under threat and crops failing. The effects of the drought were still apparent in mid-2015.

Fishing

The fishing sector represents less than 5 per cent of GDP. Government policy is aimed at increasing the amount of foreign fishing operations in territorial waters in order to increase foreign investment in the sector and increase licence revenue.

Angola's 1,600km coastline offers some of the richest fishing grounds in Africa, with the annual catch averaging 450,000 tonnes per year before independence. Production has shown a turnaround with an estimate of over 200,000 tonnes, largely due to increased government support for the sector.

In a meeting of African ministers in Namibia in 2005 members discussed illegal and unregulated fishing, which is estimated to cost Africa US$1 billion per annum in lost revenue and the threat to stocks and local artisan fishing. This figure had jumped up to US$1.3 billion by 2013.

Forestry

Angola has around 18 per cent forest cover with an additional 43 per cent of other wooded land. Most forests are semi-deciduous and located in the north of the country. There are a large number of mangrove forests around Luanda, and in the south and west the forests give way to savannah forest. Around 6.6 per cent of the country's forests are protected, although Angola is the only African country, which has not produced a forest law to bring forestry regulation up-to-date.

Angola has considerable timber resources. Valuable tree species, including rosewood, ebony, African sandalwood and mahogany, most of which can be found in the northern tropical forests that have not been commercially exploited since independence. In terms of wood products, Angola produces relatively small amounts of sawnwood, pulp and plywood panels. Most industrial roundwood is used for posts, poles and agricultural purposes. Average annual charcoal production is under 240,000 tonnes and woodfuel just under 3.5 million cubic metres.

Industry and manufacturing

The industrial sector, including diamond mining, oil production and other ancillary services, accounted for approximately 70.4 per cent of GDP in 2000 compared to 53 per cent of GDP in 1998 and employed around 12 per cent of the workforce. By 2014 the contribution had dropped back to 57.0 per cent.

Production is centred on food processing, brewing, sugar, textiles and tobacco products. Also important are light manufactures, electrical goods (eg radio production), construction materials, steel production, motor vehicles, detergents, bicycles and chemicals.

Activity is concentrated in Luanda, Lobito and Huambo. Output has been sluggish due to shortages of foreign exchange, poor management and a low-paid labour force.

About 60 per cent of total production is accounted for by nationalised industries. The government has embarked upon a privatisation programme involving some 200 state-owned enterprises in a variety of industrial sectors.

The diamond industry could receive a vital boom to the industry after De Beers has agreed to a joint mining venture with Endiama. Angola was seeking to become one of the top three diamond producers in the world, and increasing production by 4 million carrats between 2003 and 2006. However by 2014 they were still only the seventh largest diamond producer in the world.

Tourism

Angola has been expanding its tourism sector, in particular promoting holidays to coastal resorts and national parks and reserves. These had been off-limits during Angola's civil war and remained underdeveloped and hence able to adopt a new trend towards ecotourism when this became important. Tourism has enjoyed prolonged growth since the mid-1990s, even during the global economic crisis, which affected so many of Angola's competitors. However the industry is a much smaller sector of the economy than that of oil and natural gas extraction.

Travel and tourism was 3.6 per cent of GDP over 2014, a figure that has only varied by 0.42 per cent since 2001. The industry provided employment to 3.8 per cent of the workforce (163,500 jobs) over the same period. In 2008 a new government strategy to promote tourism had resulted in a marked increase in visitor numbers which had jumped from 294,000 in 2008 to 366,000 in 2009, and higher still to 425,000 in 2010 and up again to 537,000 in 2013.

Angola is in partnership with five of its southern African neighbours to establish a huge cross-border eco-tourism, game reserve and tourist resort. Angola has 13 national parks and reserves and has been underdeveloped since the 1960s so that once areas are designated free from landmines tourism can expand into virtually untamed territories.

Mining

Before independence, Angola was a major producer of iron ore, gold and copper. However, the major disruptions to the country's infrastructure and economy throughout the war have meant that the country's considerable base metal and gold resources have been barely exploited.

Diamonds (mostly of gemstone quality) were the country's second-largest foreign exchange earner in 2004. Endiama is the state-owned diamond mining company dealing with all aspects of diamond exploitation.

Before the ban on Angolan 'conflict' diamonds in 2000, Angola was the fourth-largest diamond producer in the world, producing some US$600 million of rough diamonds per year. By 2003 US$1 billion rough diamonds were sold through the official trading company Sodiam, however the true figure can only be estimated as illegal mining and smuggling from the former Unita-held territories is still a major problem. Without punitive measures to deter this lucrative trade, the revenue from diamonds cannot be fully measured or used.

The government is introducing a register and to licence the many artisan prospectors and control the wholesale price of diamonds, and to establish an export certification scheme to identify legitimate production and sales.

Angola also has deposits of phosphates (Cabinda site, estimated 100 million tonnes; Kindonakasi, estimated 50 million tonnes), gold (at Cassinga and Lombige), copper, lead and zinc (in Tetelo and Alto Zambeze). There are deposits of marble and black granite in southern Angola. The production of ornamental stones was predominantly of black granite which was exported mainly to Spain and Portugal. Angostone Construction and Ornamental Rocks Ltd mines red granite from mines in Cunene province. With an initial investment of US$1.5 million, Angostone is producing 150 cubic metres of red granite per month.

Hydrocarbons

Proven oil reserves were 12.7 billion barrels at the end of 2014, with production at 1.7 million barrels per day (bpd). Angola joined the Organisation of the Petroleum Exporting Countries (Opec) in 2007. Most oil fields are located offshore near the city of Soyo and the Angolan enclave of Cabinda. Onshore exploration has been hampered by the destruction of infrastructure and unexploded ordinance from Angola's 21-year civil war.

Oil revenue contributes over 80 per cent of public revenue and over 50 per cent of GDP. It is mainly used to finance

government spending, although it has been criticised and warned that its current accounting practices have led to widespread corruption with the loss of many millions of dollars each year. The Sociedade Nacional de Combustiveis de Angola (Sonangol) is the state-owned oil and gas company, which has a monopoly on exploration and production.
There is one refinery, in Luanda, which provided 39,000bpd with the balance of the modest domestic consumption of 62,000bpd met by imports. The construction of a new refinery in Lobito will provide products for domestic and regional African markets and is expected to be operational by 2017.
Proven natural gas reserves were 275 billion cubic metres (cum) in 2014, which was a significant increase on the 56 billion cum in 2007. The government is planning to increase the conversion of flared gas to liquefied natural gas (LNG) for export, with the construction of an LNG plant at Soyo, with an initial production capacity of five million tonnes (6.9 million cum).
Angola does not produce or import coal.

Energy
The state-owned monopoly Empresa Nacional de Electricidade (ENE) is responsible for all aspects of electricity production from generation to end-user supply. With the country's total electricity generating capacity at 1.2GW, only 38 per cent of the population has access to electricity and blackouts are frequent. Around 30 per cent of this is provided by thermal generation and about 70 per cent through hydroelectric dams. Much of the country's electricity generation and transmission infrastructure was damaged during the civil war. There are three separate regional power grids operating in the north, south and middle of Angola. Two new turbines and power lines for the Capanda hydroelectric dam on the Kwanza River have been installed. A new hydroelectric dam, to be located at Baynes, on the Kunene River, was agreed by the governments of Angola and Namibia in 2007 and construction is planned to begin by the end of 2015.

Banking and insurance
The central bank is the Banco Nacional de Angola (BNA) (National Bank of Angola). It issues, and is responsible for, all foreign exchange transactions in conjunction with the ministries of planning, commerce and finance. The banking sector has long been undercapitalised and economically inept. However, the sector has seen some foreign interest, with Portuguese banks such as Banco Fomento Exterior and Banco Totta e Azores opening branches in Luanda.
In 2005 the Banco de Poupança e Crédito (Bank for Savings and Credit) and World Vision International, began a programme of micro-credit, by offering 1,900 families at least US$200 and 79 small farmers associations up to US$10,000 for agricultural purposes.

Central bank
Banco Nacional de Angola (BNA) started functioning in late-1996 as the central bank, ceasing its commercial activities, as part of the government's financial reforms.

Main financial centre
Luanda

Time
GMT plus one hour

Geography
Angola lies on the west coast of Africa, bordered by the Democratic Republic of Congo (DRC) to the north, Zambia to the east and Namibia to the south.The Cabinda district is separated from the rest of the country by the estuary of the River Congo and DRC, with the Republic of Congo lying to its north.

Hemisphere
Southern

Climate
In Luanda and northern regions, October–April is hot and humid with usual temperatures ranging from 28–32 degrees Celsius (C), with a maximum of 34 degrees C. April–September is hot but less humid with daytime temperatures ranging from 25–30 degrees C and cool evenings. Southern regions are more temperate and rainfall can be frequent and heavy, particularly in April.

Dress codes
Informal dress is suitable for most occasions. Lightweight suits are recommended for business meetings. Visitors to the central and southern plateaux will need warm clothes at night, as will visitors to the coastal region during May to September.

Entry requirements
Passport and visa requirements are liable to change at short notice. It is advisable to check with the local Angolan Embassy/consulate at the outset.

Passports
Required by all. Passport must be valid for at least six months and contain two blank pages for stamping. Return or onward ticket is also required.

Visa
Required by all (except transit passengers remaining within the airport). Must be obtained in advance of arrival. Valid for 90 days. A proposed tourist *univisa* (a single visa to visit all 15-member states of SADC: Angola, Botswana, DRC, Lesotho, Madagascar, Malawi, Mauritius, Mozambique, Namibia, South Africa, Seychelles, Swaziland, Tanzania, Zambia and Zimbabwe) is expected to be in use by 2013. Visitors should check with the appropriate consulates to confirm start of *univisas* and their scope before beginning a tour of southern Africa.
A business visitor must provide a letter of invitation from a local Angolan company or institution and an own company letter stating purpose of visit.
An exit permit, provided by the same office which issued the visa, is also required.

Currency advice/regulations
There are no restrictions on the amount of foreign currency that can be taken into Angola, but it must be declared on arrival. The export of foreign currency is limited to US$5,000; the export of Angolan currency is prohibited

Customs
Many goods may not be imported without government authorisation and licensing.

Health (for visitors)
Mandatory precautions
Yellow fever vaccination certificate is required on arrival and may be demanded by some airlines before departure.

Advisable precautions
Hepatitis A and B, typhoid, tetanus, meningococcus and polio vaccinations are recommended. Malaria prophylaxis is essential. There is a rabies and cholera risk.
Water precautions must be taken.
Travel insurance, including emergency medical evacuation, is essential. All medication, with prescriptions, should be carried by travellers.

Hotels
Hotel accommodation is in short supply, although much existing capacity has been upgraded. Bookings should be made at least one month in advance of travel. Bookings cannot be made by airline companies or at airports.

Credit cards
American Express accepted at Presidente and Tivoli hotels. Generally, credit cards are not accepted.

Public holidays (national)
Fixed dates
1 Jan (New Year's Day), 4 Jan (Martyrs of the Colonial Repression Day), 4 Feb (Anniversary of Start of Liberation War), 8 Mar (Women's Day), 4 Apr (Peace and Reconciliation Day), 1 May (Labour Day), 25 May (Africa Day), 1 Jun (International Children's Day), 1 Aug (Armed Forces Day), 17 Sep (Nation's Founder and National Heroes Day), 2 Nov (All Souls Day), 11 Nov (Independence Day), 25 Dec (Christmas Day).

Variable dates
Good Friday, Easter Monday.

Working hours

Banking
Mon–Fri: 0830–1130, 1400–1530.

Business
Mon–Fri: 0830–1230, 1430–1800; Sat 0830–1230.

Government
Mon–Fri: 0800–1200, 1400–1700.

Telecommunications

Telephone/fax
Telephone and mobile phone usage and infrastructure are expanding, but international connections are unreliable. Angola Telecom is the country's public telecommunications company.

Electricity supply

220V AC, 50 cycles.

Social customs/useful tips

Travel permits may be required for travel outside Luanda province. Visitors are advised to carry spare passport photographs. Visitors should not attempt to photograph any public building, infrastructure or security forces or use binoculars in the vicinity.

Security

Travel by car in many parts of Luanda is relatively safe by day, but doors should be locked, windows closed and packages stored out of sight. Walking in Luanda after dark should be avoided.

There is the possibility of banditry and danger from landmines laid during the civil war. Frequent checkpoints and poor infrastructure contribute to unsafe travel on roads outside Luanda. Police and military personnel are heavily armed and can be unpredictable; their authority should not be challenged. No travel should be undertaken on roads outside the city after nightfall.

Throughout Angola, taking photographs or using binoculars near anything that could be perceived as being of military or security interest, including government buildings, could lead to problems with authorities and should be avoided at all costs.

Getting there

Air

National airline: TAAG (Linhas Aéreas de Angola). *In July 2007 the European Union banned TAAG from EU air space, due to safety concerns.*

International airport/s: Luanda-4 de Fevereiro (Code: LAD), 4km from city, restaurant. No taxis, public telephones or banking services.

Airport tax: None

Surface

Road: Road travel is not generally practicable, though access is now possible across the Namibian frontier to the south.

Rail: Rail travel to Angola is difficult due to regional conflict and war damage which has destroyed railways and bridges. The Benguela railway, which ran from the Zambian copperbelt to the port of Lobito, is being repaired.

Water: Angola has several ports along its Atlantic seaboard with the possibility of passenger traffic from other coastal African countries.

Main port/s: Cabinda, Lobito, Luanda, Namibe. Lobito and Luanda are being repaired.

Getting about

National transport

Air: Most of the country is only accessible by air. TAAG operates domestic flights connecting to main centres but these can be unreliable. There are separate helicopter services to the Cabinda enclave and some commercial companies, connected to the oil and diamond industries, who operate jet aircraft, may carry passengers. All passengers must carry authorisation to travel (*guia de marcha*), and business travellers should alert their embassy or representative of their travel plans.

Road: Angola's roads and bridges are gradually being restored. Landmines are a continuing danger, but traffic is now free to travel along the main roads between provincial capitals. The condition of roads ranges widely from reasonable to dire. Night travel is to be strictly avoided.

Buses: There are buses throughout the country but the service is poor and the buses are generally very crowded.

Taxis: Difficult to find and expensive. Travellers arriving by air will need to be met by their sponsors or by their hotel transport service.

Rail: The railway system is under repair, following the damage caused during the civil war. There are irregular passenger services on three routes from Luanda-Malanje, and Lobito-Dilolo, and Namibe-Menongue. Refreshements are available but no sleeping accommodation or air-conditioning is provided.

City transport

Taxis: Unregulated taxis should be avoided. No taxi service from airport to Luanda.

Buses, trams & metro: There are local city buses.

BUSINESS DIRECTORY

The addresses listed below are a selection only. While World of Information makes every endeavour to check these addresses, we cannot guarantee that changes have not been made, especially to telephone numbers and area codes. We would welcome any corrections.

Telephone area codes

Telephone direct dialling code for Angola is +244 followed by area code and subscriber's number.

Luanda 2

Chambers of Commerce

Angolan Chamber of Commerce and Industry, 14 Largo do Kinaxixi, PO Box 92, Luanda (tel: 344-506; fax: 344-629; e-mail: ccira@ebonet.net).

Banking

Banco de Comercio e Industria, 86 Avenida 4 de Fevereiro, Luanda (tel: 333-684; fax: 333-823; e-mail: secretariado@bci.ebonet.net).

Banco Comercial Angolano, 83A Avenida Comandante Valódia, PO Box 6900, Luanda (tel: 449-517; fax: 449-516; e-mail: bca@snet.co.ao).

Banco Africano de Investimentos, 34 Rua Major Kanhangulo, Luanda (tel: 337-369; fax: 335-486).

Banco de Poupança e Crédito, PO Box 1343, Luanda (tel: 233-9158).

Central bank

Banco Nacional de Angola, 151 Avenida 4 de Fevereiro, PO Box 1243, Luanda (tel: 332-633; fax: 390-579; e-mail: sec.gvb@bna.ao).

Travel information

Direcção de Emigração e Fronteiras de Angola (visa queries), Defa, Luanda (tel: 330-314, 330-019).

TAAG-Angola Airlines (Linhas Aéreas de Angola), Rua da Missão 123, CP 179, Luanda (tel: 332-485; fax: 393-548).

Ministry of tourism

Ministerio do Comercio e Turismo (Ministry of Commerce and Tourism), Largo 4 de Fevereiro 3, Luanda (tel: 338-741).

Ministries

Ministry of Agriculture and Rural Development, 2 Avenida Comandante Gika, CP 527 Luanda (tel: 322-694; fax: 323-217).

Ministry of Defence, Rua 17 de Setembro, Luanda (tel: 337-530; fax: 392-635).

Ministry of Education and Culture, Avenida Comandante Gika, CP 1281 Luanda (tel: 322-797; fax: 321-592).

Ministry of Energy and Water, 105 Avenida 4 de Fevereiro, CP 2229 Luanda (tel: 393-681; fax: 393-687).

Ministry of Ex-Servicemen and War Veterans, 2 Avenida Comandante Gika, CP 5466 Luanda (tel: 321-117; fax: 323-561).

Ministry of Family and Women's Advancement, Edifício Palácio de Vidro, Largo 4 de Fevereiro, 1242 Luanda (tel: 338-745; fax: 330-028).

Ministry of Finance, 127 Avenida 4 de Fevereiro, CP 592 Luanda (tel: 332-122; fax: 332-069).

Ministry of Fisheries and Environment, Edifício Atlantico, Avenida 4 de Fevereiro, CP 83 Luanda (tel: 390-690; fax: 333-814).

Ministry of Foreign Affairs, 8 Avenida Comandante Gika, CP 1500 Luanda (tel: 323-250; fax: 393-246).

Ministry of Geology and Mines, Avenida Comandante Gika, CP 1260 Luanda (tel: 326-724; fax: 321-655).

Ministry of Health, Rua 17 de Setembro, CP 1201 Luanda (tel: 322-797; fax: 321-592).

Ministry of Hotels and Tourism, Edifício Palácio de Vidro, Largo 4 de Fevereiro, CP 1242 Luanda (tel: 331-323; fax: 338-211).

Ministry of Industry, 25 Rua Cerqueira Lukoki, CP 594 Luanda (tel: 397-070; fax: 334-700).

Ministry of Information, 1 Avenida Comandante Valódia, CP 2608 Luanda (tel: 342-818; fax: 343-495).

Ministry of the Interior, 204 Avenida 4 de Fevereiro, CP 2723 Luanda (tel: 391-049; fax: 395-133).

Ministry of Justice, Rua 17 de Setembro, CP 2250 Luanda (tel: 330-327).

Ministry of Petroleum, Avenida 4 de Fevereiro, CP 1279 Luanda (tel: 337-440; fax: 372-373).

Ministry of Planning, Largo 17 de Setembro, Luanda (tel: 390-722; fax: 339-586).

Ministry of Posts and Telecommunications, 42 Avenida 4 de Fevereiro, CP 1459 Luanda (tel: 337-799; fax: 330-776).

Ministry of Public Administration, Employment and Social Security, 32 Rua 17 de Setembro, CP 1986 Luanda (tel: 338-654).

Ministry of Public Works and Town Planning, Rua Ed Mutamba, CP 1061 Luanda (tel: 336-717; fax: 333-814).

Ministry of Science and Technology, 25 Rua Cerqueira Lukoki, CP 1288 Luanda (tel: 338-987).

Ministry of Social Assistance and Reintegration, 117 Avenida dos Massacres, CP 102 Luanda (tel: 340-370; fax: 342-988).

Ministry of Territorial Administration, 8 Avenida Comandante Gika, Luanda (tel: 320-638; fax: 323-238).

Ministry of Trade, Edifício Palácio de Vidro, Largo 4 de Fevereiro, CP 1242 Luanda (tel: 338-737; fax: 370-804).

Ministry of Transport, 42 Avenida 4 de Fevereiro, Luanda (tel: 337-744; fax: 337-687).

Ministry of Youth and Sports, Avenida Comandante Gika, CP 5466 Luanda (tel: 321-117; fax: 323-561).

Other useful addresses

Angolan Embassy (USA), 2100 16th Street, NW, Washington DC 20009 (Tel: (+1-202) 785-1156; fax: (+1-202) 785-1258; e-mail: angola@angola.org).

ANGOP (news agency), CP 2181, Luanda (tel: 334-945).

Associação Comercial de Luanda, CP 1275, Edifício Palácio de Comércio, le Andar, Luanda (tel: 322-453).

DHL International Ltd, Avenida Che Guevara 52–52a, CP 1545 (tel: 390-326, 390-376, 392-082).

Direcção dos Servicos de Comércio, CP 1337, Largo Diogo Cão, Luanda.

Direcção dos Servicos de Estatistica (statistical agency), CP 1215, Luanda.

Direcção da Aviacao Civil (National Civil Aviation Directorate), Rua Frederich Engels, 92-6 andar, CP 569, Luanda (tel: 339-412, 338-196, 338-596).

Direcção dos Caminhos de Ferro (National Railways Directorate), Rua Major Kanhangulo, CP 1250, Luanda (tel: 370-061).

Direcção Nacional de Correios e Telecomunicacoes (National Posts and Telecommunications Directorate), Rua Frederich Engels, CP 1459, Luanda (tel: 339-750).

Direcção Nacional da Marinha Mercante e Portos (National Merchant Navy and Ports Directorate), Rua Rainha Ginga, 74-4 andar, Luanda (tel: 332-032, 339-847, 339-848).

Direcção Nacional dos Transportes Rodoviarios (National Road Transport Directorate), Rua Rainha Ginga, 74-1 andar, Luanda (tel: 339-390).

Empresa Nacional de Construcão de Obrías Industrials (National construction Company for Industrial Projects), Bairro do Cazenga, 5 Avenida Zona Industrial, CP 18612, Luanda (tel: 390-087, 391-478).

Empresa Nacional de Diamantes de Angola (Endiama), Rua Major Kanhangulo 100, CP 1247, Luanda (tel: 333 018; fax: 337 216; www.endiama.co.ao).

Empresa Nacional de Electricidada (ENE - National Electricity Company), Edeficio de Geologia e Minas 7, CP 772, Luanda (tel: 323-382, 337-498, 323-568, 321-498, 321-499).

Importang (state import agency), Calçada do Município 10, CP 1003, Luanda (tel: 392-787).

Institute Foreign Investment, Rue Serqueira Lukoki 25 (tel: 334-700).

Instituto Nacional do Cafe de Angola (INCA – National Coffee Institute of Angola), Rua Dr Alves Maciel 17-1D, Luanda (tel: 370-386).

Instituto Nacional de Estradas de Angola (National Roads Institute), Rua Amilcar Cabral 35-4, Caixa Postal 5667, Luanda (tel: 332-828, 391-536; fax: 335-754).

Radio Nacional de Angola, CP 1389, Luanda.

Sociedade Nacional de Combustiveis (SONANGOL-Angola National Fuels Company), Rua I Congresso do MPLA, Caixa Postal 1316, Luanda (tel: 334-143/9; fax: 333-542/6, 391-782).

Televisão Popular de Angola (TPA), CP 2002, Luanda.

US Embassy, 32 Rua Houari Boumedienne, Luanda (tel: 445-481; fax: 446-924).

National news agency: Angola Press (Angop): www.angolapress-angop.ao

AngoNoticias (www.angonoticias.com).

Internet sites

AllAfrica.com: www.allafrica.com

African Development Bank: www.afdb.org

Angola News: http://wn.com/angola_news

Jornal de Angola: www.jornaldeangola.com

Anguilla

COUNTRY PROFILE

Anguilla was originally settled about 1,500BC by Arawak Indians, who called it Mallıouhana, and later by Carib Indians.
1650 The British established a colony on Anguilla. The name Anguilla derives from the French word for 'eel': Anguille.
1745 and 1796 Anguilla repelled attacks by France.
1882 Anguilla became part of a larger colony governed from St Kitts.
1967 St Kitts-Nevis-Anguilla became a state, in association with the UK. (The status of an associated state allowed St Kitts-Nevis-Anguilla to become independent internally while the British government retained responsibility for external affairs and defence).
1969 Two brief Anguilla rebellions ended after British security forces were sent to install a British commissioner.
1971 The Anguilla Act was passed by the British parliament. A major provision of the Act stated that, should St Kitts-Nevis-Anguilla initiate legislative steps to terminate the status of association, Anguilla could be separated formally from the other islands.
1980 Anguilla separated from St Kitts-Nevis and became a British Dependent Territory.
1982 A new constitution gave Anguilla greater control over its internal affairs.
1994 The Anguilla United Party (AUP) was elected and its leader, Hubert Hughes, became chief minister.
1999 Hughes was re-elected, but lost his parliamentary majority when Victor Banks, leader of his coalition partner, the Anguilla Democratic Party (ADP), resigned.
2000 Hughes called a general election – four years early – in order to break the constitutional deadlock. Hughes and the ANP lost the election, which was won by the Anguilla United Front (AUF), coalition led by the Anguilla National Alliance (ANA) and the ADP; Osbourne Fleming (ANA) was appointed chief minister.
2002 Under UK legislation all British Dependent Territories became British Overseas Territories.
2005 The AUF coalition was re-elected. Andrew George was appointed governor.
2006 Wilhelm Bourne was appointed attorney general in succession to Ronald Scipio.
2007 A review of the constitution began.
2009 Anguilla Air Express, an executive air service to San Juan, Puerto Rico, began operations. Andrew George retired and Alistair Harrison replaced him as governor.
2010 In parliamentary elections the opposition Anguilla United Movement (AUM) won more seats (four seats out of seven) in the national assembly, despite winning fewer votes than the outgoing AUF, due to the voting system of first-past-the-post. Herbert Hughes (AUM) became chief minister.
2011 In January the chief minister renewed his call for Anguilla to be given independence from the UK, following an announcement in 2010 by Governor Harrison that he would not sign and pass the 2011 budget. In April the governor finally approved the 2011 budget. A census was undertaken on 11 May.
2012 The preliminary results of the census were published in January; the population was 13,542 people. On 2 May, the luxury Cap Juluca resort was sold at public auction to an investor syndicate. The new investment will include a renovated resort (costing up to US$80 million) with additional guest facilities and the sale of a limited number of residential villas.
2013 On 1 May Anguilla, along with Bermuda, the British Virgin Islands, the Cayman Islands, Montserrat and the Turks and Caicos Islands, signed a tax sharing agreement with the tax authorities of France, Germany, Italy, Spain and the UK.
2014 Overseas Territory representatives from the British Virgin Islands, Bermuda, Montserrat, the Cayman Islands and Anguilla met with United Kingdom business networking specialists, CaribDirect International Business Network (CIBN) in May. CIBN is an agency designed to facilitate and connect entrepreneurs and business people in the UK with Caribbean government and business representatives for trade and investment.
2015 In the general election held on 22 April the Anguilla United Front (AUF) won six out of the seven seats available. The seventh seat was won by an independent. Neither the Anguilla United Movement (AUM) or the Anguilla Progressive Party won any seats.

KEY FACTS

Official name: Anguilla

Head of State: Queen Elizabeth II; represented by Governor Christina Scott (from 23 Jul 2013)

Head of government: Chief Minister Victor Banks (AUF) (from 22 Apr 2015, sworn in 24 Apr)

Ruling party: Anguilla United Front (AUF) (from 22 Apr 2015)

Area: 96 square km (Anguilla 91 square km, Sombrero 5 square km)

Population: 14,000 (2014)* (13,542; 2011 preliminary census results)

Capital: The Valley

Official language: English

Currency: East Caribbean dollar (EC$) = 100 cents

Exchange rate: EC$2.70 per US$ (fixed rate)

GDP real growth: -5.10% (2012)*

GDP: US$280 (2012)*

Balance of trade: -US$123.36 million (2013)

Visitor numbers: 90,400 (2012)

* estimated figure

Political structure

Constitution

Anguilla Constitutional Order 1 April 1982 (amended 1990), gave greater control over its internal affairs.

Form of state

A self-governing, British Overseas Territory; residents have British citizenship (and by extension access to the European Union). Foreign affairs and defence are administered from the UK

The executive

Executive power rests with an appointed British governor, assisted by an executive council (chief minister, two *ex-officio* members and not more than three other ministers).

The governor, appointed from the UK, is responsible for defence and external affairs, but is required to consult the chief minister on matters relating to internal security, the police and civil service.

National legislature

The unicameral House of Assembly has 11 seats of which seven members elected for five-year terms in single-seat constituencies, plus two nominated members by the governor and two *ex-officio* members.

Legal system

The legal system is based on English common law. Anguilla is a member of the Eastern Caribbean Supreme Court, which is responsible for the high court and court of appeals. Final appeal rests with the Privy Council in the UK.

Last elections

22 April 2015 (parliamentary)

Results: Parliamentary: Anguilla United Front (AUF) 6 seats (out of 7) (85.7 per cent), independents 1 seat (14.3 per cent). Neither the Anguilla United Movement (AUM) or the Anguilla Progressive Party won any seats.

Next elections

2020 (parliamentary)

Political parties

Ruling party

Anguilla United Front (AUF) (from 22 Apr 2015)

Main opposition party

Anguilla United Front (AUF)

Political situation

The downturn in the global economy has had a severe negative effect on Anguilla, along with all of its neighbours. Not only has government revenue fallen, leading to spending cut backs, but the UK's Foreign and Commonwealth Overseas Territories office is demanding more commitment by the Anguillian government to good governance and public accountability. At the same time the US and EU want details of their citizens who may be possible tax evaders.

The AUF government's record was found wanting by the electorate when, in parliamentary elections held on 15 February, the opposition Anguilla United Movement (AUM) won more seats (four seats out of seven) in the national assembly, despite winning fewer votes than the outgoing AUF, due to the voting system of first-past-the-post. Herbert Hughes (AUM) became chief minister.

Approximately 4,000 Anguillans live in the USA.

Population

14,000 (2014)* (13,542; 2011 preliminary census results)

Last census: October 2001: 11,430

Population density: 104.5 inhabitants per sq km.

Annual growth rate: 3.3 per cent (2003)

Ethnic make-up

Mainly of African descent; some of Irish descent.

Religions

Anglican (40 per cent), Methodist (33 per cent), Seventh-Day Adventist (7 per cent), Baptist (5 per cent), Roman Catholic (3 per cent).

Main cities

The Valley (capital, estimated population 2,035 in 2012), North Side (2,592), The Quarter (1,737), Stoney Ground (1,545), The Farrington (1,199).

Languages spoken

Official language/s

English

Media

Press

The only local newspaper, *The Anguillan* (www.anguillian.com), is published weekly .

Dailies: *Chronicle* and *The Daily Herald* are published in St Martin and cover Anguillan news.

Periodicals: *What We Do in Anguilla* is an annual magazine with tourist information.

Broadcasting

Radio: The government-owned national radio station, Radio Anguilla, operates Radio Axa (www.radioaxa.com) with news, music and talk shows. There are several private radio stations including some with religious programming such as New Beginning Radio, The Caribbean Beacon and Voice of Creation. General interest stations include Klass FM (www.klass929.com), Heart Beat Radio (http://hbr1075.com) and Kool FM (www.koolfm103.com).

Television: The Caribbean Cable Communications operates Anguilla Television with two channels offering local and international programmes.

Other news agencies: Caribbean Net News: www.caribbeannetnews.com

Economy

With so few natural resources Anguilla's economy is dominated by high-end tourism (accounting for an estimated 61.2 per cent of GDP in 2014 and 63.4 per cent of total employment (4,500)), financial services, export of lobsters and remittances, as well as grants-in-aid from the UK and EU. Anguilla is largely reliant on imported fuel and food.

The economy was hit hard by the global economic crisis when GDP growth dropped from 17.3 per cent in 2007 to -0.3 per cent in 2008, and further still to -16.5 per cent in 2009. The economy was expected to recover in 2012, however, after a year of 0 per cent growth in 2011, the economy shrank by 3.6 per cent. Inflation, which had been 10.3 per cent at the height of the boom in 2007, fell to 1.2 per cent in 2008 and was estimated to be -2.2 per cent in 2010, with around 2.5 per cent in 2011 (most recent figure).

The global economic crisis drastically cut the number of visitors to Anguilla and resulted in a lower rating of its debt issue by the Caribbean Information and Credit Rating Services (CariCRIS), in 2009. The tourist and travel sector was expected to have attracted 13.2 per cent of total foreign direct investment (US$7.6 million (EC$20.6 million)) in 2014.

External trade

Anguilla is an associate member of both the Caribbean Community (Caricom) and the Organisation of Eastern Caribbean States (OECS). However, as a British Overseas Territory (BOT), Anguilla is constrained in its full participation of trading agreements as negotiated by either organisation.

Anguilla's international trade is largely confined to financial services and small-scale production of mechanical and engineering parts and marine crafts and agricultural products including seafood, livestock and foodstuffs.

Imports

Principal imports include petroleum, consumer goods, food products, chemicals, manufactures and textiles, vehicles.

Main sources: US (41.2 per cent in 2012), France (20 per cent), Italy (5.3 per cent).

Exports

Principal exports include lobsters, fish and other seafood, livestock, salt, rum and concrete blocks.

Main destinations: US (40.7 per cent in 2012), Azerbaijan (17.3 per cent), Switzerland (11 per cent).

Agriculture

Farming

The agriculture sector accounted for around 2.6 per cent of GDP in 2014.

There is mainly small-scale farming of peas, corn, sweet potatoes, okra and tropical fruits. The average cultivated plot is less than 0.25ha. Traditional livestock raising (goats, sheep, poultry) is important, with some animals raised for export.

Fishing

Lobster fishing is a major employer and principal earner of foreign exchange; 70 tonnes (t) are caught each year. The typical annual fish catch is 250t.

Industry and manufacturing

The industrial sector accounted for just under 24.4 per cent of GDP in 2014. The manufacturing sector is based primarily on boatbuilding, construction and fish processing.

Tourism

Tourism is an important component of the economy, in total accounting for an estimated 61.2 per cent of GDP in 2014 with direct revenue of US$178.1 million (EC$480.9 million). Tourism directly employs 22.4 per cent of the workforce (some 1,500 jobs), with 63.4 per cent of total employment having some involvement in the industry (around 4,500 jobs). The tourist and travel sector was expected to have attracted 13.2 per cent of total foreign direct investment (US$7.6 million (EC$20.6 million)) in 2014.

The number of visitors increased by 6.8 per cent in 2013 (latest figures), with a total of 69,068, up from 64,698 in 2012. Visitors from North America account for around 60 per cent of total arrivals, with European and other Caribbean islands providing the remainder.

In November 2010 the government began work on its Sustainable Tourism Master Plan 2010–2020 (STMP), which includes public consultation on the industry's future and development. Initial discussions focussed on Anguilla's prime attractions – pristine beaches and a clean environment, high quality accommodation, fine dining, relaxed atmosphere with a distinctive Caribbean flavour, peace and tranquillity, safety, friendly people and various degrees of exclusivity.

Hydrocarbons

There are no known hydrocarbon reserves; all needs are met by imports.

Energy

Total installed generating capacity is about 30MW. Anglec (Electricity Company) is responsible for generation, transmission and sales.

Financial markets

Stock exchange

Eastern Caribbean Securities Exchange (ECSE)

Banking and insurance

The seven members of the Organisation of Eastern Caribbean States (OECS), Antigua and Barbuda, Dominica, Grenada, Montserrat, St Kitts and Nevis, St Lucia and St Vincent and the Grenadines, share a common currency (the East Caribbean dollar (EC$)) and central bank. The British Virgin Islands and Anguilla are associate members.

The island's banking sector is well-regulated and internationally competitive. With a neutral tax jurisdiction and no foreign exchange restrictions, Anguilla's financial services sector has attracted a lot of foreign interest over the years. Around 5,000 companies are registered in Anguilla, with most of them classified as International Business Companies (IBCs).

As from 2005 Anguilla has adhered to an EU tax directive to inform EU citizens' tax departments about the amount of money in savings accounts and allow tax to be levied from the home country, rather than imposing a withholding tax, while retaining a saver's anonymity. Anguilla has also agreed to supply information on tax fraud, for criminal or civil trials, and notify EU member states about additional malpractices.

On 1 May 2013 Anguilla, along with Bermuda, the British Virgin Islands, the Cayman Islands, Montserrat and the Turks and Caicos Islands, signed a tax sharing agreement with the tax authorities of France, Germany, Italy, Spain and the UK.

Central bank

Eastern Caribbean Central Bank, St Kitts and Nevis.

Offshore facilities

The offshore financial services sector in Anguilla is the responsibility of the governor, with day-to-day regulation carried out by the government's financial services department. There are strict laws to combat money laundering and only banks with a previous good record can be licensed as offshore banks. Companies can be incorporated through the Anguilla Commercial Online Registration Network (ACORN).

Time

GMT minus four hours

Geography

Anguilla, a coralline island of 91 square km, is the most northerly of the Leeward Islands. It lies to the north-west of St Kitts and Nevis and 8km (5 miles) to the north of St Maarten, Netherlands Antilles. The island of Sombrero (48km north of Anguilla) is also included in the territory, as are several other uninhabited small islands.

Hemisphere

Northern

Climate

Subtropical with a mean annual temperature of 27 degrees Celsius. It is hottest from July–October, coolest from December–February. Cooling trade winds blow throughout the year. Rain mainly falls September–December.

Entry requirements

Passports

Required by all, except US nationals (all US nationals require a passport for re-entry to the US). Passports must be valid for at least six months after date of entry.

Visa

Required by all, except nationals of US, Canada, EU, Japan and a number of other countries visiting for no longer than six months. From May 2009 EU citizens may make a short-stay visit, for up to three months, without a visa. All visitors require onward or return tickets and sufficient funds for their stay.

Currency advice/regulations

There are no restrictions on the import of local and foreign currency, but it must be declared. The export of local and foreign currency is limited to the amount imported and declared. Travellers are advised to take travellers cheques in US dollars to avoid additional exchange rate charges.

Health (for visitors)

Mandatory precautions

Vaccination certificate for yellow fever required if arriving from an infected area.

Advisable precautions

Hepatitis A vaccination recommended. Water and food precautions advisable.

Hotels

Several high-quality hotels and a wide selection of villas and apartments.

10–15 per cent service charge is usually included in the bill, plus 10 per cent room tax.

Public holidays (national)

Fixed dates

1 Jan (New Year's Day), 1 May (Labour Day), 25 Dec (Christmas Day), 26 Dec (Boxing Day).

Variable dates

Good Friday, Easter Monday, Anguilla Day (May), Whit Monday, Queen's Official Birthday (Jun), August Monday (first Mon in Aug), August Thursday (first Thu in Aug), Constitution Day (Aug), Separation Day (third Mon in Dec).

Working hours

Banking

Mon–Thu: 0800–1500; Fri: 0800–1700.

Business

Mon–Fri: 0800–1200, 1300–1600.

Government

Mon–Fri: 0800–1200, 1300–1600.

Telecommunications

Mobile/cell phones

GSM 850/1900 services are available throughout the country.

Electricity supply

110/220V AC, 50 cycles

Getting there

Air

National airline: Air Anguilla.

Anguilla Air Express, an executive air service between San Juan, Puerto Rico and Anguilla, began in February 2009.

International airport/s: Wallblake (AXA), 3km from The Valley. Daily air service with St Maarten (Netherlands Antilles) and St Thomas (US Virgin Islands) and regular air services from Antigua, St Kitts and San Juan (Puerto Rico). Air taxi and charter services are available from Air Anguilla and Tyden Air.

Airport tax: Departure tax US$20.

Surface

Water: Tropical Shipping and Bernuth Lines sail from Miami to Anguilla. Frequent ferry services operate between Blowing Point and Marigot Bay, St Martin (French Antilles).

Main port/s: Road Bay, Sandy Ground; Blowing Point is a smaller port.

Getting about

National transport

Road: There is no public transport. Use taxis or car hire to travel. Anguilla has about 105km of roads, of which 65km are surfaced, but not to good standard. Public roads cover all parts of the island.

City transport

Taxis: Most generally used form of transport; readily available and inexpensive.

Car hire

Readily available. National licence needed to obtain temporary local licence. Drive on left.

BUSINESS DIRECTORY

The addresses listed below are a selection only. While World of Information makes every endeavour to check these addresses, we cannot guarantee that changes have not been made, especially to telephone numbers and area codes. We would welcome any corrections.

Telephone area codes

The international direct dialling code (IDD) for Anguilla is +1 264, followed by subscriber's number.

Useful telephone numbers

Police, ambulance, fire: 911

Chambers of Commerce

Anguilla Chamber of Commerce and Industry, PO Box 321, The Valley (tel/fax: 479-2839; e-mail: acoci@anguillanet.com).

Banking

Bank of Nova Scotia, PO Box 250, George Hill, The Valley (tel: 497-3333; fax: 497-3344).

Barclays Bank Plc (UK), PO Box 140, The Valley (tel: 497-2301/2304; fax: 497-2980).

Caribbean Commercial Bank (Anguilla) Ltd, PO Box 23, The Valley (tel: 497-2571/3; fax: 497-3570; e-mail: ccbaxa@anguillanet.com).

Caribbean Development Bank, PO Box 408, Wildey, st Michael, Barbados (1246) 431-1600; fax: (1246) 426-7269).

National Bank of Anguilla, PO Box 44, The Valley (tel: 497-2101/2104; fax: 497-3310).

Central bank

Eastern Caribbean Central Bank, Agency Office, PO Box 1385, Fairplay Commercial Complex, The Valley (tel: 497-5050; fax: 497-5150).

Stock exchange

Eastern Caribbean Securities Exchange (ECSE), www.ecseonline.com

Travel information

Air Anguilla, PO Box 110, The Valley (tel: 497-2643; fax: 497-2982).

National tourist organisation offices

Anguilla Tourist Board, PO Box 1388, The Valley (tel: 497-2759; fax: 497-2710; e-mail: atbtour@anguillanet.com; internet: www.charmingescapescollection.com).

Ministries

Ministries: all located at The Secretariat, The Valley (tel: 497-2451).

Ministry of Finance, PO Box 60, The Secretariat, The Valley (tel: 497-5881/3881; fax: 497-5872; e-mail: anguillafsd@anguillanet.com).

Office of the Governor, Government House, PO Box 60, The Valley (tel: 497-2621/2, 497-3312/3; fax: 497-3314/3151; e-mail: govthouse@anguillanet.com).

Office of the Chief Minister, The Secretariat, The Valley (tel: 497-2518; fax: 497-3389).

Office of the Minister of Finance, Planning and Economic Development, The Secretariat, The Valley (tel: 497-2545/2451; fax: 497-3761).

Other useful addresses

Agriculture Department (tel: 497-2615).

All Island Cable TV, George Hill, PO Box 336 (tel: 497-3600; fax: 497-3602).

Anguilla Electricity Co Ltd, PO Box 400, The Valley (tel: 497-5200; fax: 497-5440).

Cable & Wireless (WI) Ltd, Telecoms House, PO Box 77, The Valley (tel: 497-3100; fax: 497-2501; internet site: http://www.anguillanet.com).

Caribbean Beacon Radio, PO Box 690, The Valley (tel: 497-4340).

Government of Anguilla Financial Services Department, The Secretariat, The Valley (tel: 497-5881; fax: 497-5872; e-mail: anguillafsd@anguillafsd.com; internet site: http://www.anguillaoffshore.com).

Immigration Office (tel: 497-2451, Ext 129).

Radio Anguilla, The Secretariat, The Valley (tel: 497-2218; fax: 497-2751).

Caribbean Net News: www.caribbeannetnews.com

Antigua and Barbuda

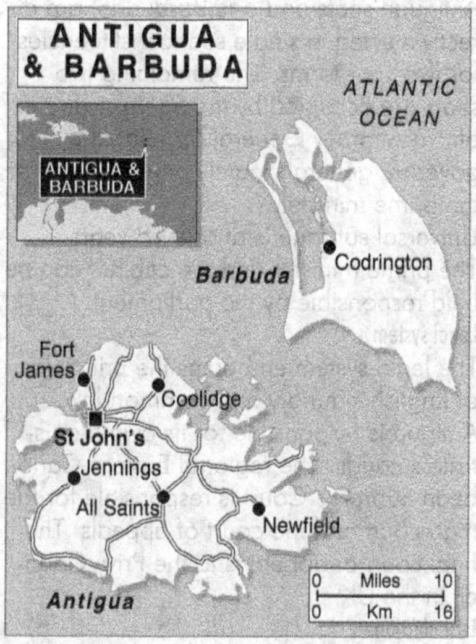

COUNTRY PROFILE

1493 Columbus sighted Antigua.
1632 Antigua and Barbuda was settled by the British.
1667 Control was passed to Great Britain after a brief period of French control.
1674 First sugar colony was set up in Antigua by Christopher Codrington.
1685 Codrington leased the island of Barbuda from the British crown and imported African slaves to help grow tobacco and sugar.
1834 The slaves of Antigua were freed.
1860 Barbuda reverted to the British crown.
1871–1956 Antigua and Barbuda were administered together as part of the Leeward Islands federation.
1946 Vere Bird formed the Antigua Labour Party (ALP).
1958–62 Antigua and Barbuda became a member of the short-lived Federation of the West Indies.
1967 The island of Antigua and its two dependencies, Barbuda and the uninhabited islet of Redonda, entered into a free association with other British dependencies in the Windward and Leeward Islands. Antigua became an associate member of the Commonwealth.
1969 A Barbuda separatist movement was formed
1972 The sugar industry was closed down.
1981 Antigua and Barbuda achieved full independence as a unitary state, but retained the monarchy. The ALP won the first post-independence elections with Bird becoming prime minister.
1990 Vere Bird Junior, son of the prime minister, was declared unfit for office by a judicial enquiry, which uncovered links with money laundering.
1993 Prime Minister Vere Bird Senor resigned and was replaced by his son, Lester.
1994 The ALP, led by Lester Bird won the general elections.
1995 Riots erupted over the imposition of new taxes. Ivor Bird, brother of the prime minister was convicted of smuggling cocaine into the country. Hurricane Luis struck the islands and destroyed 75 per cent of all homes.
1998 Six Russian-owned banks were closed down by the government, which accused them of money laundering.
1999 The ALP won the elections. Hurricane José caused severe damage to the country's infrastructure.
2001 After the adoption of a series of banking recommendations the islands were declared co-operative in the fight against international money laundering.
2002 The US$22 million Nevis Street pier was officially opened.
2004 The United Progressive Party (UPP) won parliamentary elections, ousting the ALP, which had dominated politics since the 1950s. Winston Baldwin Spencer was sworn in as prime minister.
2006 The dispute between Antigua and Barbuda and the US, involving the World Trade Organisation, over the US ban on internet gambling continued despite a WTO ruling in 2005 in favour of the islands. The newly constructed Parliament Building in St John's was dedicated.
2007 Louise Lake-Tack was sworn in as governor general. The WTO ordered the US to pay Antigua compensation for loss of earnings during the disputed online gambling.
2009 US financier Sir Allen Stanford was charged by US prosecutors for a US$7 billion investment (ponzi) fraud perpetrated through the Bank of Antigua. In parliamentary elections, the ruling UPP won nine out of 17 seats, the ALP seven, Barbuda People's Movement (BPM) one; the BPM voted with the government. Chief financial regulator, Leroy King, was

KEY FACTS

Official name: Antigua and Barbuda

Head of State: Queen Elizabeth II, represented by Governor General Dr Rodney Williams (from 14 Aug 2014)

Head of government: Prime Minister Gaston Browne (ABLP) (from 12 Jun 2014)

Ruling party: Antigua and Barbuda Labour Party (ABLP) (elected 12 Jun 2014)

Area: 280 square km (Antigua), 160 square km (Barbuda)

Population: 88,000 (2014)*

Capital: St John's (Antigua); Codrington (Barbuda)

Official language: English (Antiguan creole also spoken)

Currency: Eastern Caribbean dollar (EC$) = 100 cents

Exchange rate: EC$2.70 per US$ (Sep 2015)

GDP per capita: US$14,061 (2014)*

GDP real growth: 2.37% (2014)*

GDP: US$1.24 billion (2014)*

Inflation: 1.09% (2014)

Balance of trade: -US$430.18 million (2013)

Visitor numbers: 230,000 (2010)

* estimated figure

sacked by the government for allegedly collaborating with Sir Allen Stanford .
2010 Diplomatic relations were established between Antigua and Barbuda and Egypt.
2011 In January, Prime Minister Baldwin Spencer ratified the Revised Treaty of Basseterre, establishing the Organisation of Eastern Caribbean States (OECS) economic union. The trial of alleged swindler, Allen Stanford was postponed in January while he underwent a detoxification programme to rid him of heavy doses of anti-anxiety and anti-depressant drugs, which rendered him incompetent to stand trial. On 1 August citizens of the Organisation of Eastern Caribbean States (OECS) – Antigua and Barbuda, Dominica, Grenada, St Kitts and Nevis, St Lucia and St Vincent and the Grenadines – were granted freedom of movement, allowing them to reside, work, establish businesses and provide services throughout the organisation. During the Commonwealth Heads of Government summit, on 28 October, the 16 countries in which the British monarch is Head of State unanimously agreed to change the royal line of succession from that of first born son to the first born child (regardless of its gender). The change will be enacted after the succession of Prince William (currently second in line to the throne, after his father Prince Charles).
2012 Allan Stanford was convicted of fraud by a court in Texas (US) on 6 March. He had defrauded around 30,000 people of US$7 billion, with bogus investments through the Stanford International Bank in Antigua, using a corrupted finance official. Although investigators traced 30 bank accounts worldwide operated by Stanford they failed to locate any more than 8 per cent of the missing funds. On 14 June, the Texas court sentenced Stanford to 110 years in jail for defrauding investors.
2013 On 6 June the World Bank board of directors approved a US$10 million loan. The finance will support the government's efforts to improve public sector efficiency, strengthen capacity and institutions, and deliver better services to its citizens and residents.
2014 Antigua and Barbuda was removed from the OECD's 'grey list' in February. Finance and Economy Minister Harold Lovell stated that ' For Antigua and Barbuda to be labeled as compliant with international standards and practices is excellence news.' Court cases over constituent boundaries and voters lists delayed the general election due by 12 March. Campaigning for the election by the ruling UPP and opposition Antigua-Barbuda Labour Party (ABLP) never-the-less got underway in early February. Parliament was dissolved on 26 April in preparation for elections, which under the constitution must be held on or before 25 July. The elections were eventually held on 12 June and won by the opposition ABLP with 14 seats (out of 17). The UPP won just three seats and the Barbuda People's Movement (BPM) none. Voter turnout was 90 per cent.
2015 Members of the ruling ABLP walked out of the House of Representatives on 22 January in protest against an opposition member who attempted to disrupt the 2015 Budget Debate .

Political structure

Form of state
Independent state; it is a member of the Commonwealth.

The executive
The British monarch is the head of state, represented by a governor general who acts on the advice of the prime minister and the cabinet.

National legislature
The bicameral parliament has a 19-member House of Representatives (lower house), of which 17 members (16 Antiguan seats and one Barbudan) are directly elected in single seat constituencies for five-year terms. The remaining two seats are occupied by the Speaker and ex *officio* Attorney General appointed by the governor general, mainly on the advice of the prime minister.
Universal suffrage is at age 18 years.
The prime minister and the cabinet can be held responsible by the parliament.

Legal system
The legal system embodies the principles of English statutory and common law. Antigua is responsible for its own magistrate's courts. The regional Eastern Caribbean Supreme Court is responsible for the high court and the court of appeals. The final court of appeal is to the Privy Council in the UK.

Last elections
12 June 2014 (parliamentary)
Results: Parliamentary: the Antigua and Barbuda Labour Party (ABLP) won 14 seats (out of 17) (56.45 per cent), the United Progress Party (UPP) won 3 seats (41.95 per cent). Voter turnout was 90 per cent.

Next elections
2019 (parliamentary)

Political parties

Ruling party
Antigua and Barbuda Labour Party (ABLP) (elected 12 Jun 2014)

Main opposition party
United Progress Party (UPP)

Political situation
The government, in June 2009, sacked the Antigua and Barbuda chief financial regulator, Leroy King, following his arrest and expected extradition to the US. King was alleged to have accepted US$100,000 in bribes, while aiding US financier Sir Allen Stanford (charged in February 2009 by US prosecutors for a US$8 billion investment fraud perpetrated through the Bank of Antigua), by conducting sham audits and diverting the financial authority from looking closely at Stanford's business dealings.
In December 2009, US senate members lobbied the IMF and World Bank to deny bailout monies to Antigua and Barbuda until the government of the islands took responsibility for compensating US victims of Stanford's frauds.
In parliamentary elections held in March, the ruling UPP won nine out of 17 seats,

KEY INDICATORS — Antigua and Barbuda

	Unit	2011	2012	2013	2014	**2015
Population	m	*0.09	*0.09	*0.09	*0.09	*0.09
Gross domestic product (GDP)	US$bn	1.19	1.19	1.20	*1.24	*1.28
GDP per capita	US$	13,552	13,630	*13,734	*14,061	*14,349
GDP real growth	%	-0.5	2.8	1.8	*2.4	*1.9
Inflation	%	3.3	3.4	1.1	1.1	*1.2
Exports (fob) (goods)	US$m	43.5	59.0	64.2	–	–
Imports (fob) (goods)	US$m	427.0	483.6	494.4	–	–
Balance of trade	US$m	-383.5	-424.5	-430.2	–	–
Current account	US$m	-120.1	-167.0	-176.0	*-181.0	*-137.0
Total reserves minus gold	US$m	133.0	–	202.6	297.1	–
Foreign exchange	US$m	132.5	–	202.5	–	–
Exchange rate	per US$	2.70	2.70	2.70	2.70	–

* estimated figure ** forecast figure

the Antigua Labour Party (ALP) seven, Barbuda People's Movement (BPM) one; the BPM votes with the government.

Population
88,000 (2013)*
Last census: 27 May 2011: 86,295 (provisional)
Population density: 170 inhabitants per square km. Urban population 30 per cent (2010 Unicef).
Annual growth rate: 1.8 per cent, 1990–2010 (Unicef).

Ethnic make-up
The majority of the population is of African descent; the remainder is of British, Portuguese, Lebanese and Syrian origin.

Religions
Anglican (90 per cent), Methodist, Moravian, Roman Catholic, Pentecostal, Baptist and Seventh Day Adventists.

Education
Literacy rate: 90 per cent (2003)
Enrolment rate: Primary education 6–11 years: 50 per cent; secondary education 33 per cent; tertiary education 20–24 years 6 per cent (2003).

Health
Fertility rate/Maternal mortality rate: 1.8 births per woman, 2010 (Unicef 2012)
Child (under 5 years) mortality rate (per 1,000): 10 per 1,000 live births (WHO 2012)

Main cities
St John's (capital of Antigua, estimated population 21,993 in 2012), All Saints (5,125), Potters Village (3,331), Codrington (capital of Barbuda (1,325 in 2001).

Languages spoken
English patois is widely spoken. French also spoken by a small number of people.

Official language/s
English (Antiguan creole also spoken)

Media
Press
Dailies: There are two local newspapers including *Antigua Sun* (www.antiguasun.com), which also produces a Sunday edition, and *The Daily Observer* (www.antiguaobserver.com).

Broadcasting
The Antigua and Barbuda Broadcasting Service (ABS) (www.cmatt.com), provides radio and TV services.
Radio: There are several radio stations, including ABS Radio and private, commercial stations, Observer Radio (www.antiguaobserver.com), ZDK Liberty Radio (www.radiozdk.com) and VIBZFM (www.vibzfm.com). Crusader Radio (www.crusaderradio.com) is owned by the United Progressive political party and the Caribbean Radio Lighthouse (www.mannelli.com/lighthouse) is a Christian station.
Television: The government-owned ABS TV operates two channels and a cable service.
Other news agencies: Caribbean Net News: www.caribbeannetnews.com

Economy
High-end tourism dominates the economy of Antigua and Barbuda, accounting in total for 58.3 per cent of GDP in 2014, which leaves the economy vulnerable to external shocks. The global economic crisis cut tourist numbers until 2010, when numbers returned as the tourist industry made special offers to stimulate its core business. Financial services are also an important component of the economy, offering offshore banking services.
GDP growth recovered slightly from global economic crisis in 2012, reaching 4.0 per cent. However in 2013, growth dropped, shrinking to 0.5 per cent. GDP per capita has fallen, from a high of US$15,786 in 2008 to US$12,817 in 2010 and grew slowly into 2013 reaching US$13,838.
The necessary diversification of the economy is a difficult challenge as labour is attracted to the higher wages of the service sectors and away from agriculture and manufacturing industries. One area into which the islands have successfully diversified is the growing industry of internet gambling sites.
Agriculture is centred on the domestic market, but the lack of fresh water limits production. Manufacturing is limited to a *maquila* sector, producing principally bedding and electronic components.

External trade
Antigua and Barbuda is a member of the Caribbean Community (Caricom), which comprises a common market and customs union. It is also a member of the Eastern Caribbean Currency Union (ECCU) using the East Caribbean Dollar, and a member of the World Trade Organisation (WTO).
There is heavy dependence on imported food and energy. The large trading deficit is only partially offset by re-exports (mostly manufactured goods and fuel oil) and earnings from tourism and capital inflows.

Imports
Principal imports include chemicals, fuel and related materials, food and live animals, machinery and transport equipment, other manufactures.
Main sources: US (35.3 per cent of total in 2014), China (3.9 per cent), Trinidad & Tobago (3.1 per cent).

Exports
Principal exports include petroleum products while small-scale manufacturing enterprises produce bedding and handicrafts, and mechanical and electronic components for export.
Main destinations: US (27.1 per cent of total in 2014), UK (20.7 per cent), Curacao (7.3 per cent).

Re-exports
Petroleum

Agriculture
Farming
Agriculture accounted for 1.9 per cent of GDP in 2014. Farming is faced with several problems that could weaken its contribution to GDP still further. A limited water supply, soil depletion and drought cause hardship with workers turning to more lucrative employment in tourism and construction.
The majority of food grown is consumed locally. Fruit and sea-island cotton are grown for export.
Government policy is to encourage self-sufficiency in food. To expand agricultural production capacity, the government, with assistance from the European Development Fund, is promoting livestock development.
An agreement with Cuba has seen Antigua and Barbuda provided with technical assistance in a range of agricultural sectors, including tobacco, fertilisers, pesticides and irrigation.

Fishing
Fishing is mostly for local consumption however is a growth area. There are shrimp and lobster farms in operation with the catch each year over 300 tonnes (t). The typical annual fish catch is over 1,500t.

Industry and manufacturing
Activity is centred on food processing, galvanised sheet, paints and light industries (mainly assembly of household appliances, vehicles, garments, paper products). Industry contributed 18.5 per cent to GDP in 2014, of which the construction sector contributes about 13 per cent of total GDP. Construction activity has been dominated by housing and infrastructure repair as a result of hurricanes.

Tourism
Tourism is centred on luxury beach resorts that provide visitors with comprehensive, private and often secluded holidays.
The tourist industry is the leading component of economic activity, providing in total 58.3 per cent of GDP in 2014 (US$741 million). As revenue was US$207 million in 2008 the trend demonstrates the cut in tourist numbers due to the global economic crisis. Visitor numbers have fallen since the global economic crisis and have yet to recover to pre-recession levels. In 2013 visitor numbers stood at 237,000, compared to 673,00 in 2007. Around 53.0 per cent of

total employment was travel and tourism related in 2014 (16,500 jobs) with 15.9 per cent directly employed in the sector (5,000 jobs).
The growth in tourism has driven investment, which was estimated was US$124 million, or 42.0 per cent of total investment in 2014.

Mining
There are known deposits of high quality barytes, limestone and clay. Redonda island was once an important source of phosphates and guano.

Hydrocarbons
There are no known hydrocarbon reserves. Consumption of oil was 4,174 barrels per day (bpd) in 2013, all of which was imported.
In 2005, Antigua and Barbuda, plus a number of other Caribbean states, signed an agreement with Venezuela to establish PetroCaribe, a multi-national oil company to be owned by the participating states. PetroCaribe buys low-priced Venezuelan crude oil under long-term payment plans. Due to its economy worsening, in April 2015 Venezuela was considering reducing the subsidies for the PetroCaribe members, which would have large detrimental effects for Antigua and Barbuda whose economy relies largely on the cheap oil imports.

Energy
Total installed generating capacity was 27MW in 2013, producing 310 million kilowatt hours. The state-owned Antigua Public Utilities Authority (APUA) is responsible for, among other utilities, overseeing electricity; it generates, manages the transmission lines and distributes electricity.

Financial markets
Stock exchange
Eastern Caribbean Securities Exchange (ECSE)

Banking and insurance
The seven members of the Organisation of Eastern Caribbean States (OECS), Antigua and Barbuda, Dominica, Grenada, Montserrat, St Kitts and Nevis, St Lucia and St Vincent and the Grenadines, share a common currency (the East Caribbean dollar (EC$) and central bank. The British Virgin Islands and Anguilla are associate members.
Central bank
Eastern Caribbean Central Bank, St Kitts and Nevis.
Main financial centre
St John's
Offshore facilities
There is an offshore financial sector offering full tax haven facilities to international business companies, trusts, banks and insurance companies. A corporate income tax was introduced in 1999. The International Financial Sector Regulatory Authority has full oversight of the offshore sector. Service providers are required to report suspicious transactions to the authority under the money laundering legislation.

Time
GMT minus four hours

Geography
The country comprises three islands – Antigua, Barbuda and the uninhabited rocky islet of Redonda. They are situated along the outer edge of the Leeward Islands chain in the West Indies. Barbuda is the most northerly, 40km north of Antigua; Redonda is 40km south-west of Antigua. Guadeloupe lies to the south of the country, Montserrat to the south-west and St Kitts Nevis to the west.
Hemisphere
Northern

Climate
Tropical with temperature range from 21–32 degrees Celsius. Little variation throughout year, although driest from January–March.

Entry requirements
Passports
Required by all.
Visa
Not required for most countries. For a full list of those who may visit for business or tourism without a visa visit www.antigua-barbuda.com. Visits must not exceed six months and visitors must have onward/return tickets, confirmation of accommodation.
Currency advice/regulations
No restrictions on import or export of local or foreign currency, as long as amount is declared on arrival and not exceeded on departure.

Health (for visitors)
Mandatory precautions
Yellow fever vaccination certificate if arriving from an infected area.
Advisable precautions
Hepatitis A vaccination recommended. Water and food precautions advisable. Take medical kit.

Hotels
An 8.5 per cent room tax and 10 per cent service charge are added to hotel bills.

Public holidays (national)
Fixed dates
1 Jan (New Year's Day), 7 Oct (Merchant Holiday), 1 Nov (Independence Day), 9 Dec (VC Bird Day), 25 Dec (Christmas Day), 26 Dec (Boxing Day).
Variable dates
Good Friday, Easter Monday, Labour Day (first Mon in May), Whit Monday, Queen's Official Birthday (Jun), Caricom Day (Jul), Summer Carnival (first Mon and Tue in Aug).

Working hours
Banking
Mon–Thur: 0800–1300, 1500–1700; Fri: 0800–1200, 1500–1700.
Government
Mon–Fri: 0800–1200, 1300–1630. Offices close at 1500 on Fridays.
Shops
Mon–Sat: 0830–1200, 1300–1700. Many shops close Thur 1200.

Telecommunications
Mobile/cell phones
GSM 850/1900 services are available throughout the country.

Electricity supply
220/110V AC, 60Hz. American-style two-pin plugs. Some hotels also have outlets for 240V AC; in this case European-style two-pin plugs are used.

Getting there
Air
National airline: Antigua is a shareholder in LIAT, the regional Caribbean airline.
International airport/s: VC Bird International (ANU), 8km north-east of St John's; duty-free shop, restaurant, post office, car hire. A new, ultra modern, terminal was opened in August 2015, more than doubling the capacity of the airport.
Airport tax: Departure tax: US$20.
Surface
Main port/s: St John's Deepwater Harbour, Falmouth Harbour, English Harbour.

Getting about
National transport
Air: Scheduled daily services between Antigua and Barbuda.
Road: A network connects all main centres. Over 1,000km of roads, mainly all-weather.
Buses: Restricted service.
City transport
Taxis: Fixed rate system. Taxis are not metered and it is advisable to negotiate fares in advance.
Car hire
National or international licence required to obtain visitor's driving permit. Driving is on the left.

BUSINESS DIRECTORY
The addresses listed below are a selection only. While World of Information makes every endeavour to check these addresses, we cannot guarantee that changes have not been made, especially to telephone numbers and area codes. We would welcome any corrections.

Telephone area codes
The international direct dialling code (IDD) for Antigua and Barbuda is +1 268, followed by subscriber's number.

Chambers of Commerce
Antigua and Barbuda Chamber of Commerce and Industry, North and Popeshead Street, PO Box 774, St John's (tel: 462-0743; fax: 462-4575; email: chamcom@candw.org).

Banking
Antigua and Barbuda Development Bank, 27 St Mary's St, Box 1279, St John's (tel: 462-0838; fax: 462-0839).

Antigua and Barbuda Investment Bank Ltd, High St, Box 1679, St John's (tel: 462-0067/1653; fax: 462-0804).

Antigua Commercial Bank, St Mary's and Thames Sts, PO Box 95, St John's (tel: 462-1217/9/2085/1860/4; fax: 462-1220).

Bank of Antigua, 1000 Airport Blvd, Box 315, St John's (tel: 462-4283; fax: 462-0040).

Bank of Nova Scotia, High St, Box 342, St John's (tel: 480-1500; fax: 480-1554).

Barclays Bank plc, High Street, Box 225, St John's (tel: 485-5000; fax: 462-4910).

Caribbean Banking Corporation Ltd, High Street, Box 1324, St John's (tel: 462-4217; fax: 462-5040).

CIBC Caribbean Ltd, High St and Corn Alley, Box 28, St John's (tel: 462-0836/7/0998/1278).

Royal Bank of Canada, High and Market Sts, Box 252, St John's (tel: 462-0325/6; fax: 462-1304).

Swiss American National Bank of Antigua, High St, Box 1302, St John's (tel: 462-4460; fax: 462-0274).

Central bank
Eastern Caribbean Central Bank, Agency Office, PO Box 741, Factory Road, St John's (tel: 462—2489; fax: 462-2490).

Stock exchange
Eastern Caribbean Securities Exchange (ECSE)
www.ecseonline.com

Travel information
Antigua Hotels and Tourist Association (AHTA), Lower Redcliffe St, PO Box 454, St John's (tel: 462-0374/3703; fax: 462-3702; e-mail: ahta@candw.ag).

LIAT (1974) Ltd, PO Box 819, VC Bird International Airport (tel: 462-0700; fax: 462-4765).

Ministry of tourism
Ministry of Tourism, Culture and the Environment, New Administration Building, Queen Elizabeth Highway, St John's (tel: 462-0787; fax: 462-2836).

National tourist organisation offices
Antigua and Barbuda Department of Tourism, PO Box 363, Long and Thames Streets, St John's (tel: 462-0480, 462-0029; fax: 462-2483).

Ministries
Minister of State in the Prime Minister's Office and Leader of Government Business in the Senate, Queen Elizabeth Highway, St John's (tel: 462-5933; fax: 462-3225).

Ministry of Agriculture, Lands, Fisheries, Planning and Co-operatives, Nevis and Temple Sts, St John's (tel: 462-1543/5571; fax: 462-6104).

Ministry of Education, Youth, Sports and Community Development, Church St, St John's (tel: 462-4959; fax: 462-4970).

Ministry of Finance and Social Security, High St, St John's (tel: 462-4301; fax: 462-1622/5093).

Ministry of Foreign Affairs, Queen Elizabeth Highway, St John's (tel: 462-4956; fax: 462-3225/9377).

Ministry of Health and Civil Service Affairs, Cross St, St John's (tel: 462-8783; fax: 462-9308/5003).

Ministry of Justice and Legal Affairs, Nevis St, St John's (tel: 462-8867; fax: 462-2465).

Ministry of Labour and Home Affairs, c/o State Insurance Building, Redcliffe St, St John's (tel: 462-0567; 462-1595).

Ministry of Public Utilities, Public Works and Energy, St John's St, St John's (tel: 462-3851/4772; fax: 462-4622).

Ministry of Trade, Industry and Commerce Affairs, Redcliffe Street, St John's (tel: 462-4951; fax: 462-5003).

Other useful addresses
Antigua and Barbuda Embassy (USA), 3216 New Mexico Avenue, NW, Washington DC 20016 (tel: (+1-202) 362-5122; fax: (+1-202) 362-5225).

Antigua and Barbuda Investment Authority (ABIA), PO Box 80, Sagicor Financial Center, #9 Factory Road, St John's, (tel: 481-1000/1/2/3; fax: 481-1020; email: info-abia:antigua.gov.ag).

Antigua Public Utility Authority (APUA), PO Box 416, St Mary's Street, St John's (tel: 462-4990; fax: 462-2516).

British High Commission, PO Box 483, 11 Old Parham Road, St John's (tel: 462-0008/9, 463-0010).

Cable and Wireless Telex Bureau, St Mary's Street, St John's (tel: 462-0840/2).

Directorate of Offshore Gaming, 2nd Floor, Mutual Finance Centre, 9 Factory Rd, Room 216, PO Box 588, St John's (tel: 481-3300; fax: 481-3305; e-mail: director@antiguagaming.com; internet site: http://antiguagaming.d2g.com).

Free Trade & Processing Zone, PO Box 817, St John's (tel: 460-5552; fax: 460-5553; e-mail: ftpzone@candw.ag; internet site: http://www.antiguafreezone.com).

Industrial Development Board, 34 Newgate Street, St John's (tel: 462-1038; fax: 462-2836).

Caribbean Net News: www.caribbeannetnews.com

Internet sites
Daily Observer: www.antiguaobserver.com

East Caribbean Central Bank: www.eccb-centralbank.org

Argentina

KEY FACTS

Official name: República Argentina (Argentine Republic)

Head of State: President Cristina Fernández de Kirchner (FPV-PJ) (from 2007: re-elected 23 Oct 2011)

Head of government: President Cristina Fernández de Kirchner

Ruling party: Alianza Frente para la Victoria (FpV) (Front for Victory Alliance) (from 2005; re-elected Oct 2011)

Area: 2,766,889 square km

Population: 41.96 million (2014)* (40,177,096; 2010 census figure)

Capital: Buenos Aires

Official language: Spanish

Currency: Peso (P) = 100 centavos

Exchange rate: P9.33 per US$ (Sep 2015)

GDP per capita: US$12,873 (2014)*

GDP real growth: 0.47% (2014)*

GDP: US$540.16 billion (2014)*

Labour force: 11.77 million (2012)*

Unemployment: 7.25% (2014)*

Inflation: 10.62% (2013)*

Oil production: 629,000 bpd (2014)

Natural gas production: 35.40 billion cum (2014)

Balance of trade: US$9.48 billion (2014)*

Visitor numbers: 5.33 million (2011)

* estimated figure

Nota

Mauricio Macri won the second round of the presidential election held on 22 November by 51.6% of the vote to 48.3% for Daniel Scioli, the candidate favoured by outgoing president, Cristina Fernández. Mrs Fernández' plummeting popularity rating was said to be one of the reasons for Mr Scioli's defeat.

Not one to sit back and do nothing, Argentina's President Cristina Fernández de Kirchner entered her last year in office bent on strengthening her country's links with those countries she considered to be a thorn in the side of the United States – China, Russia, Venezuela and Iran. Late April 2015 saw her visiting Russia, in February she had been in China. This was seen by many as very much a last ditch effort to define Argentina's international alliances. Two of the candidates in the October presidential election – Messrs Sergio Massa and Mauricio Macri – had already gone on record that they would pursue a foreign policy to strengthen alliances with the European Union (EU) and the US. Mr Massa is the former mayor of the affluent Tigre municipality – effectively a wealthy outlying suburb of Buenos Aires. His position as mayor gave him a relatively high profile position to campaign from as well as useful links with Buenos Aires' rich and influential *bourgeoisie.* At one stage Mr Massa had appeared to be the front runner, but by the beginning of 2015 the playing field seemed to have levelled with Vice President Daniel Scioli, the former governor of Buenos Aires province, and Mr Macri, the mayor of the capital of Buenos Aires, coming up on the rails. Both Macri and Massa were perceived to take more centrist positions than President Fernández, which did not necessarily mean too much. As the 'official' (aka Peronist) candidate, Daniel Scioli kept his cards close to his chest, but it was thought that even he would need (perhaps rather than want) to improve relations with the US. Were Mr Scioli to win the election, it was thought that any swing in foreign relations would be slower, to some extent determined by Mrs Kirchner's continuing influence, if any.

Mrs Kirchner's concern not to be seen as a lame duck president in her final year probably accounted for the hyperactive note injected into Argentina's foreign relations. On the agenda for the Russian trip was the possibility of attracting Russian investment – via the Russian oil giant Gazprom – into the massive Vaca Muerta ('Dead Cow') oil and gas deposits (See 'Energy' below). Also under discussion was the construction, by Russia's nuclear engineering giant, Rusatom, of a nuclear energy plant. The fear of the opposition candidates was that Mrs Kirchner would enter into long-term agreements with Russia – as had already been the case with China with soya contracts.

Don't forget the Falklands

The febrile political thinking that pervaded the Casa Rosada in late 2014 and the first few months of 2015 had one other consequence. The political conflict between Argentina and Great Britain over the future of the Falkland Islands was back at the top of the agenda, 33 years after the beginning of the war that saw 649 casualties and 1,300 wounded. Argentina's latest move was a legal attempt to prevent five oil companies, three of them British, from exploring for oil some 200 kilometres from Falklands' shores. The legal move coincided with what turned out to be an unofficial visit by the Argentine Minister for Falklands' Affairs, Daniel Filmus. Mr Filmus announced that the purpose of his visit was to gain British public support for Argentina – something of a lost cause since the Falklands continued to strike a very patriotic chord with most of the UK's population.

Argentine concerns were inevitably heightened by the fact that the three British companies involved, Premier Oil, Falkland Oil and Gas and Rockhopper, had chosen the anniversary of the 1982 Argentine invasion to announce that they had struck oil. For her part, President Kirchner speaking in the southerly port of Ushaia at a memorial service for Argentina's war dead, promised to seek legal redress and to raise that matter of 'British aggression' in international fora. This caused the British government to summon the Argentine ambassador to the Foreign Office for an explanation.

Death of a prosecutor

For decades, the only certainty about Argentina's politics and economy has been its uncertainty. The most dramatic, not to say tragic, symbol of this uncertainty in early 2015 was the death, more probably the murder, of one Alberto Nisman, found dead in his smart Puerto Madero docklands apartment in Buenos Aires. Mr Nisman was the federal prosecutor responsible for investigating – in a final effort to resolve the matter – the 1994 bombing of a Jewish centre in Buenos Aires. Mr Nisman's report had the temerity to accuse President Kirchner and her advisors of attempting to suppress his investigation. On learning of his death Mrs Kirchner initially called it a suicide, later hinting at a plot by the intelligence services to rid them of a problem. In all respects, President Kirchner gave every impression of being on the back foot over the Nisman affair, publicly calling for a law to reform the country's intelligence services, replacing the current structure with one more closely controlled by the Presidency. Later, vague allegations were made by the president that somehow the Clarín news organisation were involved in Mr Nisman's death. Most Argentines will be pleased to see Mrs Kirchner leave the Casa Rosada in October 2015 when her second term of office ended.

The significance of Mr Nisman's death and of his controversial investigation, was that Iran had long been considered by many Argentines as responsible for the bombing massacre. According to the respected newspaper *Clarin*, Mr Nisman had accused Mrs Kirchner and her foreign minister, Hector Timerman, of trying to erase any evidence of Iran's role in the affair. The Kirchner administration's objective appeared to be the negotiation of favourable oil supply deals with Iran.

The popular outrage provoked by Mr Nisman's death certainly caught both the presidency and the government by surprise. In February 2015 an estimated 400,000 people took to the streets in Buenos Aires to protest, silently, that an injustice had been done. The march was organised by the federal prosecutors and its dignity contrasted sharply with Mrs Kirchner's near hysterical responses. What everyone in Buenos Aires knew, was that more than anything, the February march was to protest over the president's lack of rapport with her people and her headless chicken-like responses to the mounting number of crises that continued to confront an almost bankrupt country. By March 2015 President Kirchner's approval ratings had fallen below 30 per cent, reflecting the public's loss of confidence.

Let's default – again

Argentina is not a member of the International Monetary Fund (IMF). At the end of 2014 the IMF recognised the implementation by Argentina of all the specified actions the IMF had called for by

KEY INDICATORS — Argentina

	Unit	2011	2012	2013	2014	**2015
Population	m	*40.50	*41.03	*41.49	*41.96	*42.43
Gross domestic product (GDP)	US$bn	447.60	475.21	622.04	*540.16	*563.14
GDP per capita	US$	10,945	11,583	*14,992	*12,873	*13,271
GDP real growth	%	8.9	1.9	2.9	*0.5	*-0.3
Inflation	%	9.8	10.0	10.6	–	*18.6
Unemployment	%	7.2	7.2	*7.1	*7.3	*7.0
Oil output	'000 bpd	607.0	664.0	656.0	629.0	–
Natural gas output	bn cum	38.8	37.7	35.5	35.4	–
Exports (fob) (goods)	US$m	17,104.0	80,908.0	81,525.6	71,930.9	–
Imports (fob) (goods)	US$m	14,644.0	65,555.0	70,540.6	62,451.5	–
Balance of trade	US$m	2,460.0	15,353.6	10,985.1	9,479.4	–
Current account	US$m	-673.0	278.0	-5,006.0	*-4,680.0	*-9,656.0
Total reserves minus gold	US$m	49,056.0	39,920.0	28,143.0	29,017.0	–
Foreign exchange	US$m	45,773.0	36,765.0	24,981.0	–	–
Exchange rate	per US$	4.06	4.79	6.55	8.46	–

* estimated figure ** forecast figure

end-September 2014 and, importantly, the steps taken by the Argentine authorities to remedy the perceived inaccurate provision of data. The Argentine authorities had originally committed to implementing the IMF conditions by the end of February 2015. The next IMF report on the status of Argentina's implementation programme was due by mid-15 April 2015. Amongst others, the issues that had prevented the Argentine government and the IMF reaching agreement boiled down to a failure to finalise the likely levels of future Argentine primary surpluses and the extent to which Argentina should use its dollar reserves to pay monies owed to the Washington organisation. The more cynical observers considered that a fundamental problem was a philosophical divide between the parties.

A briefing on the current state of Argentina published in the London *Economist* in February 2014 noted that 'In the 43 years leading up to 1914 (the outbreak of the First World War) Argentina's gross domestic product (GDP) had grown at an annual rate of 6 per cent, the fastest in the world.' This may well have been the case, although some doubt has to be registered over the comparative accuracy of nineteenth-century economic statistics. At the time, according to the *Economist*, 'Argentina ranked among the ten richest countries in the world, after the likes of Australia, Britain and the United States, but ahead of France, Germany and Italy.' The caveat registered earlier needs to be repeated in the cases of France and Italy, both countries which have resorted to less than accurate statistics when it suited them to do so in the twentieth and even twenty-first centuries.

By the end of 2014 Argentina's economy looked pretty sickly. Foreign exchange reserves had fallen to around US$30 billion and the fall in international commodity prices meant that revenues had also fallen. Estimates put the likely economic shrinkage for 2015 at one per cent. Foreign direct investment (FDI), which had at least had been a positive figure – almost US$6 billion in 2013 – went into the red in 2014 as foreign firms wound down or sold their Argentine operations. As a result, over US$50 million left the country. The stalemate that followed Argentina's July 2014 default on its international debt, for the second time in 13 years, did little to improve affairs. In the 45 years since your correspondent first visited Argentina – in 1967 – Argentina's politics and its economy have appeared to follow a circular, rather than linear path. Defaults come and go, crises wax and wane. In 2014 the issue was attempts to resolve Argentina's perennial debt problems. In 2012 the Argentine authorities had appeared to have underestimated the tenacity of the United States legal system. At the time a New York court had ruled in favour of a group of hedge fund holders who had speculatively purchased Argentine debt at knock-down prices. According to the 2012 ruling, Argentina was obliged to pay in full any debt-holders who were not prepared to enter into 'new debt for old' arrangements. In the view of the Argentine government, the potential cost of the ruling was so high that in relative terms at least, default became a more attractive option. However, the debt swap option fell rather flat – one report suggested that only 4 per cent of debt holders had decided to accept and exchange their 2015 bonds.

There's the Economy – and there's the Real Economy

According to the United Nations Economic Commission for Latin America and the Caribbean (ECLAC/CEPAL) the Argentine economy slowed during 2014 due to what was described as 'the contractionary effect of the devaluation at the start of the year and the re-emergence of currency strains during the third quarter as a result of the 'legal setback' suffered by Argentina in its dispute with so-called vulture (ie'hedge') funds.' The slowdown in the Brazilian economy also had a negative effect. The adverse impact of these developments was particularly significant in the first quarter of the year, which saw a quarter-on-quarter contraction of 0.8 per cent in the seasonally adjusted GDP series. Activity was 0.5 per cent higher in the second quarter than in the first reflecting greater stability in the currency market, which saw a narrowing of the gap between the official exchange rate and the parallel (unofficial) rate.

However, according to ECLAC, the cumulative annual change to September 2014 in the monthly economic activity estimator (EMAE) was below zero (-0.1 per cent). ECLAC's view was that assuming the economic growth rate in the fourth quarter remained stable (ie zero), the GDP growth rate for 2014 was expected to be about -0.2 per cent (the IMF estimated 0.5 per cent).

ECLAC also considered that the growth projection for 2015, when Argentina's large currency repayments were to fall due (over US$10 billion in total), depended heavily on whether Argentina's access to international credit markets was restored. In ECLAC's view this was less to do with any unlikely influx of capital from abroad so much as its benevolent effect on exchange-rate expectations, always important in evaluating the Argentine economy. Were any resolution of the legal dispute with the vulture funds to be reached in early 2015, a moderate recovery could possibly be expected for the rest of the year, even yielding an annual growth rate of about one per cent..

ECLAC noted that in 2014 the Argentine authorities tried to offset the contractionary effects of January 2014's nominal peso devaluation (which saw the exchange rate depreciate by 26.3 per cent from the previous month and by as much as 64 per cent from the same month in 2013) by implementing an expansionary – populist – fiscal policy focused on assisting the most vulnerable, particularly recipients of the Universal Child Allowance (AUH).

The currency devaluation and interest-rate rise meant that in the second half of the year the currency gap narrowed and the stock of international reserves could be partly replenished. None the less, the possibly unexpected setback suffered in the legal dispute with the vulture funds in late June 2014 once again caused currency strains, reflected in the widening of the gap between the official exchange rate and the parallel rate, which reached 75 per cent in October after decreasing to 30 per cent during the second quarter. These strains eased in the fourth quarter following the introduction of measures aimed at neutralising any expectations of a devaluation: closer supervision of foreign-exchange operations involving securities, implementation of part of the US$11 billion currency swap agreement signed between the Banco Central de la República Argentina (central bank) and the People's Bank of China, specific agreements with leading exporters regarding foreign exchange settlement, issuance of securities tied to the dollar exchange rate and regulation of the deposit interest rate.

On the fiscal side, the government's policy in the first nine months of the year showed what ECLAC viewed as a 'counter-cyclical bias', manifested in a rate of primary spending growth (44 per cent) that outstripped growth in revenues (42.1 per cent) and nominal output (about 30 per cent). Capital spending, which averages about 12 per cent of all primary spending, rose by 46.8 per cent year on year as a result of increases in direct real investment and capital transfers to provincial and municipal governments, along with the boost given to financial investment (up 166 per cent year on year). Resorting to some degree of *legerdemain*, the Argentine government carried on using the public sector's own resources to defray the financing needs of the national treasury, essentially from the Fondo de Garantía de Sustentabilidad (FGS) (Sustainability Guarantee Fund) and the central bank, which between them provided funding equivalent to 2.9 per cent of GDP, more than twice as much as in the same period of 2013. In the case of the central bank, other important developments besides the remittance of profits were the transfer of international reserves to meet the country's external commitments and an increase in temporary advances to the national treasury, the stock of which rose from 4.5 per cent to 4.9 per cent of GDP between September 2013 and the same month in 2014.

Fear of inflation

Among other policies applied during 2014, ECLAC made special mention of the *Precios Cuidados* price watch programme, a commitment entered into by the government, supermarkets, distributors and their main suppliers to control the prices of a basket of mass consumption goods in order to restrain domestic price increases. The programme, which covered 320 products, was meant to reduce the impact of the devaluation on domestic prices. In August 2014 Congress passed a new pension fund moratorium law for people who had not met all the conditions for a retirement pension. This was estimated to affect about 470,000 new retirees. A new Hydrocarbons Act was passed in October 2014 (See 'Energy'), creating a new legal framework that provided for the exploitation of unconventional hydrocarbons with a view to attracting greater investmen. The lack of investment has been the major break on the sector in recent years.

Gloomier news during the first half of the year was that Argentina's balance-of-payments current account yielded a negative balance of US$2.8 billion, almost US$1.4 billion more than in the same period of 2013, mainly due to a drop in goods exports (-10.1 per cent) that was not fully offset by the decline in imports (-7.5 per cent). The figure recorded for foreign direct investment (FDI) flows yielded a negative balance of US$55 billion during the first half of 2014, some US$6 billion less than in 2013 largely owing to the inclusion in the figures of the divestment by the Spanish firm Repsol of its stake in YPF following the change of ownership resulting from the controversial expropriation of 51 per cent of the company's shares by the government.

The fall in the current account balance, the use of international reserves to pay off the external public debt and rising capital outflows caused international reserves to drop by about 8 per cent in the first 10 months of 2014 to some US$28 billion by late October. In mid-year 2014, the total external debt stock was 29 per cent of GDP, a rise of 6 percentage points on the same period the year before.

Economic information gathered by ECLAC showed demand falling across the board, with the exception of public consumption, which rose by 4 per cent. On the supply side, data showed an increase in services-producing sectors (1.2 per cent) and a slight decline (-0.6 per cent) in goods-producing sectors compared to the same period in 2013. Among the latter, manufacturing contracted by 1.1 per cent, mainly because of a decline in vehicle-making, which fell by over 20 per cent year on year, largely because of the drop in demand from Brazil. Construction also declined year on year (-2.1 per cent). ECLAC also noted that Argentina's inflation rate remained above the regional average and had increased from the previous year, essentially because of the accelerating depreciation of the nominal exchange rate. Figures from the new Índice de Precios al Consumidor Nacional urbano (IPCNu) (National Urban Consumer Price Index) produced by the Instituto Nacional de Estadística y Censos de la República Argentina (INDEC) (National Institute of Statistics and Censuses) showed prices rising by a cumulative 21.3 per cent over the first 10 months of the year. With a rise of 16.4 per cent, the food and beverages category increased by less than the overall index, a figure probably explained by the effects of the Precios Cuidados price watch programme. However, fuel prices rose by much more than the average, by over 40 per cent from January 2014.

Pay, as measured by the INDEC wage index, rose by 32.3 per cent year on year across the whole economy between January and September 2014, which was slightly above the increase in domestic prices. However, the nominal increase in private-sector pay was 29.8 per cent, which was below the level of price rises. The adjustable living minimum wage rose to P4,400 (US$47) in September 2014, 33.3 per cent up on the figure for the same month in 2013. Retirement benefits rose by 11.3 per cent in March and 17.2 per cent in September to give a cumulative annual increase of 30.5 per cent.

The unemployment rate was 7.5 per cent in the third quarter of 2014, an increase on the 6.8 per cent recorded in the same period of 2013, despite a drop in the labour participation rate from 46.1 per cent to 44.7 per cent. The slowdown in activity in 2014 was reflected by the employment rate, which fell by 1.6 percentage points, to 41.3 per cent, from the same quarter the year before.

International alignments

The same circular patterns seen in the domestic economy also emerge in Argentina's international economic relations. When the going gets tough, xenophobia often seems to be the preferred response. One report from a respected international consultancy put the number of foreign companies that had simply given up on Argentina, either leaving altogether or at least ceasing their operations until things improved, at around 40. In the 1960s it had been the British Motor Corporation that shut down after a promising start. The twenty-first century had seen the Spanish oil company Repsol's Argentine operations effectively nationalised and oil major Shell ludicrously held responsible for the vagaries of the Argentine peso.

Energy – Its our oil

According to an April 2015 report by the United States government Energy Information Administration (EIA), in 2013, Argentina was the largest dry gas producer and the fourth largest petroleum and other liquids producer in South America. Argentina's new hydrocarbons reform (referred to above), published on 31 October 2014, provided investors with offshore exploration opportunities and encouraged foreign ventures in unconventional explorations. As noted by the EIA, before the 2014 reform to the 1967 Hydrocarbon Law, Argentina's energy sector policies limited the industry's attractiveness to private investors, both restraining the profits of domestic producers and in a protectionist fashion, shielding consumers from rising prices. Domestic demand for energy grew rapidly while production of both petroleum and other liquids and natural gas declined – making Argentina a net hydrocarbons importer.

Aimed at incentivising foreign investment in the hydrocarbons sector and boosting domestic energy supplies, the new legislation aimed at reforming the national bidding process, increasing the frequency of offshore licencing rounds, allowing for longer exploitation periods and also offered tax exemptions to companies investing more than US$250 million over a three-year period. The reform was also expected to reinforce the national oil company Yacimientos Petrolíferos Fiscales' (YPF) position while reducing the impact of provincial oil companies.

Additionally, to limit the influence of the low oil prices seen in 2015, the Argentine ministry of economy had announced a reduction in oil exports tariffs. The Argentine government had also provided tax incentives to companies that formed partnerships with the state-owned energy company, Energía Argentina Sociedad Anónima's (ENARSA), for offshore exploration and offered higher gas prices for new gas production sold in the domestic market under the Gas Plus scheme.

According to the 2013 *Energy Balance* published by Argentina's Energy Secretariat, total primary energy production in Argentina for the year was 3.02 quadrillion Btu. Natural gas production accounted for approximately 51 per cent and production of crude oil represented 38 per cent of the total energy production portfolio. Hydroelectricity was the third largest primary energy source. Natural gas, which is used widely in the electricity, industrial and residential sectors, represented 53 per cent of total primary energy consumption in 2013 (3.22 quadrillion Btu). Oil was the primary fuel used in the transport sector, representing 33 per cent of total primary energy consumption. A smaller share of the country's total energy consumption can be attributed to nuclear, coal and hydropower, used for electricity generation, while other renewable resources are used to produce biofuels for transportation.

In January 2015, according to the *Oil and Gas Journal* (OGJ)Argentina held 2.4 billion barrels of proved crude oil reserves, a decrease of almost 0.5 billion barrels from the previous year. In 2014, total oil production was 711,000 barrels per day (bpd), of which 519,000bpd was from crude oil and 104,000bpd was from natural gas plant liquids.

YPF is Argentina's largest oil producer extracting oil from about 59 fields. The second-leading oil producer, with 18 per cent for total production in 2013, was Pan American Energy (PAE), which is owned by BP and the Bridas Corporation (itself a 50-50 joint venture between the China National Offshore Oil Corporation (CNOOC) and Bridas Energy Holdings). PAE currently operates one of Argentina's largest oil fields, the Cerro Dragón field. Chevron (US), Petrobras (Brazil) and China's Sinopec Group also have had significant presences in Argentina's upstream oil production.

Argentina had provend natural gas reserves of approximately 11.1 Trillion cubic feet (tcf) in January 2015, according to estimates from the OGJ, a decrease from 13.4tcf in 2014. Argentina also holds the world's second-largest shale gas reserves and Vaca Muerta, located in the Neuquen Basin, is Argentina's largest shale gas field with an estimated 308tcf of dry, wet and associated shale gas resources. According to OGJ, Total Austral, a subsidiary of Total SA (France), is Argentina's largest natural gas producer, accounting for about 30 per cent of the country's total domestic supply. YPF, Argentina's second-largest natural gas producer, accounts for over 23 per cent of the country's natural gas output. Other significant players in the natural gas sector include Pan American Energy, Petrobras (Brazil), Pluspetrol (Argentina), Tecpetrol (Argentina) and Apache Energy (US). Argentina produces more natural gas than total petroleum liquids. However, the country's natural gas output decreased for a seventh consecutive year to 1.3tcf of dry natural gas in 2013. The largest gas producing basins include Neuquén, Austral and Noroeste. Together, these three basins account for roughly 85 per cent of the country's natural gas production.

In 2013, Argentina imported 184 Billion cubic feet (bcf) of LNG from Bolivia via pipeline. Located on the Paraná River, the Escobar terminal is Argentina's sole LNG terminal. Argentina imported 244bcf of liquefied natural gas in 2013 via the terminal, of which the largest share of LNG came from Trinidad and Tobago. Although Argentina is a net importer of natural gas, it continues to export natural gas to its neighbours, principally Chile and, to a lesser extent, Uruguay.

The Falklands Factor – El Factor Malvinas

The fact that an estimated one billion barrels of crude oil are thought to be recoverable within an area less than 200 nautical miles from the Falkland Islands, a British territory, is for Mrs Kirchner an acute irritant. If successfully exploited, the find would be Britain's largest single hydrocarbons discovery outside the North Sea. Expectations had waxed and waned following the UK's Rockhopper Exploration and its partners' discovery in the Sea Lion field area in the North Falkland Basin. In 2015 Rockhopper's major shareholder, Premier Oil, decided to proceed with the field's development, which estimates suggested could produce up to 60,000bpd of high-quality crude by the end of the decade.

Quite apart from the logistic and climatic challenges, Premier would also have to cope with a possible tactical offensive by the Argentine government to prevent the field being developed by non-Argentine interests. This could involve legal action, extradition and embargoes. The low oil price prevailing in 2015 also meant that the field's economic viability could be called into question. However, a favourable factor is that in contrast to the high rates of taxation paid by oil companies in the North Sea, the tax rates in the Falklands are much lower. The rate of taxation is set by the islands' Governor. In mid-2015 the companies were paying a 9 per cent royalty on the oil produced and 26 per cent corporation tax, much less than the 60 per cent levied in the North Sea. It was also thought that Falklands oil was of high quality and would therefore only trade at a small discount to Brent, the global crude yardstick.

Risk assessment

Economy	Poor
Politics	Poor
Regional stability	Fair

COUNTRY PROFILE

1916–22 and 1928–30 President Hipolito Yrigoyen was Argentina's first popularly elected president. He was ousted in his second term by the armed forces.

1939–1945 Argentina was neutral during the Second World War and initially refused to break diplomatic relations with Japan and Germany.

1943 A military government, with pro-fascist sympathies, assumed power.

1944 Argentina broke diplomatic relations with Japan and Germany and declared war on them.

1946 General Juan Domingo Perón, a leading figure in the military government, won a free presidential election. He and his wife, Evita, became increasingly popular as social services spending grew. However, foreign exchange reserves built up during the Second World War were squandered by nationalising the railways and other public utilities. President Perón became increasingly repressive towards his critics and the Catholic Church.

1949 A new constitution strengthened the power of the president and criticising the government became a criminal offence,

leading to the jailing of Perón's opponents.
1951 Perón was re-elected with a large majority.
1952 Perón's populist wife, Evita, died of cancer and his grass roots support began to wane.
1955 An attempted coup by the navy was crushed by the army. However, the armed forces did seize power later and Perón was exiled. A series of unstable military and civilian governments in subsequent years saw the Perónists win the few elections held.
1973 Hector Campora was elected president, following a Perónist victory. He resigned following widespread civil disturbances and was succeeded by Juan Perón, who had returned from exile.
1974 Perón died and was succeeded by his third wife, Isabel María Estela Martínez Cartas de Perón (better known as Isabel Perón). The country sank into political and economic chaos.
1976 The armed forces overthrew the government and installed General Jorge Videla as president on 29 March.
1976–83 The military junta suppressed left-wing opposition groups and activists and up to an estimated 30,000 people 'disappeared' in the state-sponsored dirty war (Guerra Sucia), where violence and murder against citizens was undertaken by military and police forces, in extrajudicial activities.
1981 General Leopoldo Galtieri became president.
1982 The military invaded the Falkland Islands/Islas Malvinas, which lead to a conflict with the UK lasting ten weeks. Following Argentina's surrender its dead numbered over 700 and cost the economy billions of US dollars that all but collapsed and ended the military's power in office. General Bignone replaced Galtieri and instigated civilian elections.
1983 Raul Alfonsín of the Unión Cívica Radical (UCR) (Radical Civic Union) won the presidential elections.
1989 Perónist, Carlos Ménem, became president and began a programme of economic austerity in an effort to stabilise and restructure the ailing economy.
1990 Full diplomatic relations with the UK were restored, although Argentina continued to claim the Falkland Islands.
1992 The peso was introduced as a new currency and was pegged to the US dollar at a one-to-one rate.
1995 Ménem was re-elected president.
1997 International pressure was applied when a judge in Spain called for the arrest of senior military officers involved in human rights violations during the 'dirty war'. However a blanket national amnesty protected them.
1998 Argentine judges ordered arrests in connection with the abduction of hundreds of children of women arrested during the 'dirty war'. A protracted recession began.
1999 Fernando de la Rúa won the presidency; his centre-left Alianza para el Trabajo, la Justicia y la Educación (Alianza) (Alliance for Work, Justice and Education) failed to secure an absolute majority in the lower house of Congress but still had to deal with the economy which was US$114 billion in debt.
2000 The IMF granted a loan of US$40 million. Private Argentine aircraft and boats were again allowed to visit the Falkland Islands.
2001 The amnesty laws allowing members of the armed forces to escape prosecution for human rights abuses were overturned. The economy, devastated by years of recession and near to collapse led to public protests and a general strike against government spending cuts. The Perónists won the mid-term parliamentary elections and both houses of Congress came under opposition control. President Fernando de la Rúa resigned; Ramon Puerta took over briefly before Adolfo Rodríguez Saa became president. Saa's presidency lasted only until mass demonstrations against his austerity measures caused his resignation. Argentina defaulted on its public debt of US$132 billion. Eduardo Camaño became acting president.
2002 Perónist Eduardo Duhalde was elected president by the Legislative Assembly on 2 January. He became the fifth president in two weeks, initially for only a few months until elections were held. The peso was devalued breaking the link with the US dollar. The president was given the power to pass some laws without congressional approval for the next two years. The peso was floated.
2003 Carlos Saúl Menem withdrew from the presidential election leaving Néstor Kirchner to win by default.
2004 Former president Carlos Menem returned from exile in Chile to face allegations of fraud. The IMF accepted that its handling of Argentina's financial crisis in 2001 had aggravated the deepening recession and that it had continued to lend Argentina money when its debt burden had become unsustainable.
2005 Argentina's US$100 billion debt restructuring offer was accepted. The country hosted a thirty-four nation Summit of the Americas; violent protests accompanied proceedings.
2006 Argentina cleared its debt to the IMF. Price controls were extended in a bid to counter inflationary tendencies.
2007 Cristina Fernández de Kirchner (FPV), the wife of the former president Néstor Kirchner (2003–07), became president.
2008 Former president Fernando de la Rúa was charged with 'aggravated bribery' by a federal court. He was accused of bribing senators during the 2001 Congress debate to vote in favour of labour reforms.
2009 Argentina laid claim to 1.7 million square kilometres of ocean around its coast, up to Antarctica and including island chains governed by the UK, including Las Malvinas/Falkland Islands. In elections for 50 per cent of seats in the Chamber of Deputies, the ruling Perónist coalition, led by Frente para la Victoria (FPV) (Front for Victory) won 47 seats and lost its overall majority. The newly formed Acuerdo Cívico y Social (ACyS) (Civil and Social Agreement) (coalition of three parties and others) won a majority 41 seats in both chambers. President Kitchner remained in office as head of government. Former military leader Raynaldo Bignone and five other retired generals went on trial charged with kidnapping, torture, human rights violations and the disappearance and killing of hundreds of opponents of the regime in the late 1970s.
2010 The government was thwarted again in its attempt to tap US$6.5 billion of central bank funds to pay off debt when a court refused to allow the move. President Kitchner's original plan had been opposed by central bank governor, Martín Redrado, who was forced to resign. Argentina called on the UN to facilitate a meeting with the UK government to discuss sovereignty of Las Malvinas/Falkland Islands, just as UK-licensed oil exploration companies began exploratory drilling offshore of the islands. Long-term creditors agreed to accept new government bonds for two-thirds of the outstanding debt in a deal worth US$12 billion. This meant that Argentina had settled 92 per cent of its outstanding debt (from 2001) and expected to be able to borrow on the international money market at a better interest rate than any since 2001. Former president Néstor Kirchner died. A national census was conducted. Former military ruler Jorge Videla was sentenced to life in prison, for crimes against humanity.
2011 General Bignone, the last military leader of Argentina, was found guilty of human rights abuses during the 1976–83 junta rule and was sentenced to life in prison on 15 April; he had already been convicted in 2010 for abuses perpetrated while he was in charge of the country's second largest torture centre between 1978–79. Anti-tobacco legislation was approved by the lower house of assembly in June. Advertising and sponsorship was banned, as was smoking in bars, restaurants and the work place, as well as the

sale of single cigarettes and all sales to under 18 year olds. In June, the UK prime minister reaffirmed his government's determination not to negotiate over the sovereignty of Las Malvinas/Falkland Islands. On 21 June President Cristina Kirchner announced that she would stand for re-election in October. In presidential elections held on 23 October, seven candidates took part. The incumbent, Christina Fernández de Kirchner (FPV-PJ) won with 53.96 per cent. Her closest rival, Hermes Binner (PS), won 16.87 per cent.
2012 On 17 April, President Fernández declared that the publicly owned energy company YPF would be re-nationalised, through expropriation of 51 per cent of the shares owned by the Spanish energy company, Repsol. On 18 May, Repsol announced that it had cancelled its contract to provide liquefied natural gas (LNG) to Argentina. On 25 May the European Union filed a suit with the WTO against Argentina for import restrictions and difficulties in obtaining export licences. EU exports to Argentina are valued at around €8.3 billion (US$6.7 billion) annually. On 12 June, President Fernandez de Kirchner, while addressing the UN Committee on Decolonisation, demanded that the UK enter negotiations over the sovereignty of the Falkland Islands/Las Malvinas. Prime Minister Cameron (UK) responded on 13 June by saying there would be 'absolutely no negotiation' on sovereignty rights. Meanwhile the Falklands Islanders decided to conduct a referendum on its 'political status' in 2013. On 1 November, parliament lowered the voting age from 18 years to 16 years, to come into effect in elections due in 2013. On 2 August Buenos Aires province, in a largely symbolic move, banned all British merchant ships passing to or from the Islands from using its ports. The move was to prevent Falklands' ships flying the British Red Ensign (instead of their own Falklands' flag) from using the ports. In 2011 the trading bloc Mercosur had banned ships flying the Falkland's flag from all their ports.
2013 On 8 August President Fernandez restated Argentina's demand for sovereignty of the Falkland Islands when speaking at a UN Security Council (UNSC) meeting in New York. Argentina became a non-permanent member of the UNSC in January. She reiterated her demand that UN Resolution 2065 should be observed and that both parties should 'sit down and discuss' the issue. The UK says there is nothing to discuss since the Islanders had voted overwhelmingly in a referendum in March 2013 to remain British. Argentina lost another appeal, this time to a New York appeals court, to avoid repaying US$1.3 billion of debt dating back some 11 years. The appeals court did not order Argentina to repay the debt immediately, allowing a last appeal to the US Supreme Court, although it is considered unlikely that this will happen until 2014, which will be after the next elections in October this year. President Kirchner successfully underwent an operation to stop a bleed on her brain on 8 October. She is expected to remain off work for at least a month, including not campaigning for the 27 October elections, in which her ruling party, the FpV, risk loosing their majority in Congress. Although still facing a corruption investigation, Vice President Amado Boudou, will be in charge of the country during her leave. Mid-term elections to choose 127 members of the 257-member Chamber of Deputies and a third of the Senate's 72 members were held on 27 October. For the first time under-16 year olds were allowed to vote. Although Mrs Kirchner's FpV retained it's majority in both houses, it lost the important Buenos Aires province, where Sergio Massa's newly formed Frente Renovador (Renewal Front) list, won by 11.8 percentage points. Mr Massa was re-elected as Mayor of Tigre; he is considered a potential presidential candidate. YPF announced at the end of August that it has discovered oil and gas in the Patagonia region located in Santa Cruz province; the discovery holds the potential to produce 200,000 cubic meters of gas and 370 barrels of oil per day.
2014 The currency was devalued by 20 per cent on 24 January. Argentina made it to the final of the FIFA World Cup, loosing to Germant in the final played on 13 July. In August a judge in the US ruled in favour of a group of investors in Argentina's defaulted bonds from 2001. The ruling meant full repayment whenever Argentina made interest payments on securities issued in 2005 and 2010 debt restructurings. President Kirchner refused to comply with the order, saying it could lead to new claims of US$120 billion from other bondholders. A court ruling prevented Argentina from paying US$539 million in interest due by 30 July and in effect was forced into defaulting on the original deal. As the time for the 30 September interest payment approached a court first ruled that the monies deposited with Citigroup's Argentine branch for payment to the bondholders should be withheld, but later the judge gave a 30 day stay on the order so that he could reconsider his ruling.
2015 Alberto Nisman, who had been investigating the 1994 bombing of a Jewish centre in Buenos Aires which killed 85 people, was found shot dead in his apartment on 18 January. He was about to testify before a congressional hearing to outline his accusations against seniot government officialst. president Fernandez initially said Mr Nisman had committed suicide but by 26 January had confirmed he had been murdered and announced plans to disband Argentina's intelligence agency.

Political structure

Constitution

Under the 1853 constitution which was reinstated by the military government in 1955, power is separated into executive, legislative and judicial branches at federal and state level. Each of the 22 states has its own subordinated constitution, elects its own executive and legislature and establishes its own judiciary. In November 2012, the voting age was lowered from 18 years to 16 years, with its first usage during elections in 2013. Although voting is compulsory for adults aged 18–70 years, for those aged 16–17 it will be optional.

Form of state

Federal presidential democratic republic

The executive

Executive power is vested in the president, who is elected by popular vote every four years, with a limit of two terms in office.

National legislature

The Congreso Nacional (National Congress) consists of two chambers. The Cámara de Diputados de la Nación (Chamber of the Deputies of the Nation) has 256 members, elected by proportional representation for four-year terms; every two years half the seats are up for election. Deputies are elected through a closed-list proportional representation system, representing 24 multi-member districts. The chamber has exclusive rights to raise taxes.
The Senado de la Nación (Senate of the Nation) has 72 members, elected for six-year terms. Elected members are chosen from three-seat constituencies (23 provincial and the federal capital), two seats go to the party or coalition winning most votes and one seat to the second largest party or coalition. Every two years one-third of the constituencies are elected.
Universal suffrage is from aged 18 years and voting is mandatory (with some exceptions).

Legal system

The judiciary is independent of the government and forms the third 'pillar' of the constitution. Since 1998, federal judges have been elected and dismissed by a body comprising lawyers and academics. The election of judges was intended to reduce the endemic political influence that had previously affected the Argentine legal system, especially at the local level, for many years. There is a Supreme Court system at national and provincial levels.

Last elections
23 October 2011 (presidential and parliamentary (national congress 50 per cent of seats; Senate 24 seats in contention)); 27 October 2013 (chamber of deputies and senate: 50 per cent of seats contested every two years)
Results: Presidential: Christina Fernández de Kirchner (FPV-PJ) won 53.96 per cent, Hermes Binner (PS), 16.87 per cent, Ricardo Alfonsín (UCR) 11.15 per cent; four other candidates each won less than 9 per cent. Turnout was 78.89 per cent. Parliamentary (total seats after latest election): Alianza Frente para la Victoria (FpV) (Front for Victory Alliance) and allies 135 seats, Unión Civica Radical (UCR) (Radical Civic Union) 41, Peronismo Federal (PF) (Federal Peronism) 29, Partido Socialista (PS) Social Party 21, Propuesta Republicana (PRO) (Republican Proposal) 11, Coalición Civica (CC) (Civic Coalition) seven; other minor parties 13. Senate (total seats after latest election): Partido Justicialista (Justicialist Party) (JP-FpV) 30, UCR 17, PF 14, PS four; five other political parties occupy the remaining eight seats.

Next elections
25 October 2015 (chamber of deputies and senate: 50 per cent of seats contested every two years); 25 October 2015 (presidential).

Political parties
Ruling party
Alianza Frente para la Victoria (FpV) (Front for Victory Alliance) (from 2005; re-elected Oct 2011)

Main opposition party
Unión Cívica Radical (UCR) (Radical Civic Union)

Population
41.03 million (2012)*
More than a third of the country's population lives in and around Buenos Aires.
Last census: 27 October 2010: 40,177,096
Population density: 14 inhabitants per square km.Urban population 92 per cent (2010 Unicef).
Annual growth rate: 1.1 per cent, 1990–2010 (Unicef).

Ethnic make-up
White (97 per cent), principally descendants of Italian and Spanish immigrants. Minority groups include the Buenos Aires Jewish community and Anglo-Argentines throughout the country. The major indigenous nations are the Quechua of the north-west, the Mapuche of northern Patagonia and the Matacos, Tobas and others who inhabit the Chaco and north-eastern cities like Resistencia and Santa Fé.

Religions
Roman Catholic (92 per cent), Protestant (2 per cent), Jewish (2 per cent), others (4 per cent).

Education
Education is compulsory and free, so that Argentina has one of the highest literacy rates in Latin America. Secondary education consists of basic general education and polymodal education (multipurpose schools catering to ages between 15 and 18). In parallel to the polymodal cycle, there is a technical-,professional course, which leads after a further year's study to the title of *Técnico*. Higher education is provided by national and private universities, which are autonomous. There are 25 national universities. Technical institutes (Institutos de Formación Técnica) offer higher technical education, leading to the award of the *Título menor*. Professional courses are also available in a wide range of subjects.
Literacy rate: 97 per cent adult rate; 99 per cent youth rate (15–24) (Unesco 2005).
Compulsory years: 6 to 15
Enrolment rate: 120 per cent gross primary enrolment of relevant age group (including repeaters); 100 per cent gross secondary enrolment; 57 per cent in tertiary education (World Bank).
Pupils per teacher: 17 in primary schools

Health
Argentinians have the right to choose between the union-administered healthcare system, known as *obras sociales*, and private healthcare providers.
Most children receive immunisations against childhood diseases.

HIV/Aids
In 2009, there were an estimated 110,000 people living with HIV (Unicef 2012).
HIV prevalence: 0.5 per cent aged 15–49 in 2009 (Unicef 2012)
Life expectancy: 76 years, 2010 (Unicef 2012)
Fertility rate/Maternal mortality rate: 2.2 births per woman, 2010 (Unicef 2012); maternal deaths 38 per 100,000 live births (World Bank).
Child (under 5 years) mortality rate (per 1,000): 14 per 1,000 live births (WHO 2012); 5 per cent of children aged under five are malnourished (World Bank).

Welfare
The main portion of the Argentine social security system is borne by a pay-as-you-go system where employers' and employees' contributions fund payments. Workers must contribute 11 per cent of their pay regardless of whether workers participate in a private, or the public, social security system; employers must contribute the equivalent of 16 per cent of each workers' salary to the public system. Non-salaried workers must pay the full amount of 27 per cent of their income.
The whole social security system is adversely affected when employers fail to pay or withhold their social security contributions. However, the percentage of non-registered employees in Argentina is very high. According to non-official records of the Argentine Ministry of Labour, 20 out of 100 employees are non-registered employees, thus depriving them of pensions. Measures have been taken by the Argentine Social Security Authority (SSA) to force employers to register employees and contribute to the social security fund.
Ten of the country's largest private pension funds were nationalised in October 2008 at a cost of US$30 billion. The decision was taken to save the funds from the global financial turmoil.

Pensions
Argentina reformed its pension system in 1994 to a mixture of the old government-administered system and an individual retirement account programme administered by the Retirement and Pension Fund Administrators (AFJPs).
Argentina has retained the pay-as-you-go system. This system provides basic, universal old-age coverage (known as PBU) for all workers who reach retirement age and who have contributed for at least 30 years including a portion of the wealthiest Argentines' pensions. Payment of retirement benefits begin at age 65 for men and age 60 for women.

Main cities
Buenos Aires (capital, estimated population 13.0 million (m) in 2012), Córdoba (1.5m), Rosario (1.2m), Mendoza (933,601), Tucumán (850,106), La Plata (769,427), Mar del Plata (575,133), Skip (566,732), Santa Fe (518,102), San Juan (498,751).

Languages spoken
Italian, German and French are still maintained within their respective communities. English is generally spoken in business circles. There are 17 native Indian languages, the most widely spoken of which is Quechua.

Official language/s
Spanish

Media
Argentina has a sophisticated media industry with over 150 daily newspapers, based in cities or regionally, hundreds of private commercial radio stations and dozens of televisions stations. The

Supreme Court passed a ruling in late October 2013 upholding a bill passed in 2009 that stipulates, among other things, that a maximum of 24 audio-visual licences can be held by any one owner and bans TV networks from amassing over 35 per cent of the nation's viewers. It also means government has to approve the sale of all broadcast licences. The Clarin group, which has been involved in an open dispute against Cristina Kirchner's government since 2008 and had appealed against the law, is expected to be hardest hit by the ruling.

Press

Dailies: In Spanish, *La Nación* (www.lanacion.com.ar) is a respected publication, *Página 12* (www.pagina12.com.ar) has left-wing views, *La Prensa* (www.laprensa.com.ar), *La Razón* (www.larazon.com.ar) is a popular national broadsheet and *Clarín* (www.clarin.com). Regional newspapers includes *La Mañana de Córdoba* (www.lmcordoba.com.ar), *La Capital* (www.lacapital.com.ar) and *El Tábano* (www.eltabano.com).

In English, *Buenos Aires Herald* (www.buenosairesherald.com), has a business supplement and *Buenos Aires Times* (www.buenosairestimes.com).

Weeklies: In Spanish, *168 Horas* (http://168horas.com.ar), *Noticias* (www.noticias.uolsinectis.com.ar) has features on business and current affairs, *Foco* (www.foco.uol.com.ar). In German, *Argentinisches Tageblatt* (www.tageblatt.com.ar).

Business: In Spanish, major newspapers include *El Cronista* (www.cronista.com), *Negocio Nea* (www.negocionea.com.ar), *El Economista* (www.eleconomista.com.ar) and *Ambito Financiero* (www.ambitoweb.com) with an online edition in English. Business magazines include *Alzas y Bajas* (www.alzasybajas.com.ar), *Apertura* (www.apertura.com), *Bolsafe Valores* (www.bolsafevalores.com), *Edicion i* (www.edicioni.com), *El Gráfico* (www.elgrafico.uol.com.ar), *Estrategas* (www.revistaestrategas.com.ar), *Fortuna* (www.revista-fortuna.com.ar), *Gestion* (www.gestion.com.ar), *Merdado* (www.mercado.com.ar), *Prensa Economica* (www.prensaeconomica.com.ar) and *Realidad Economica* (www.iade.org.ar). Monthly magazines include *Tiempo Empresario* (www.tiempoempresario.com.ar) and *Negocios Magazine*.

Periodicals: There are numerous magazines available, covering all interests. *Viva Sophia* (www.vivisophia.com) is a monthly women's magazine.

Broadcasting

Radio: In Spanish, the national public radio is Radio Nacional (www.radionacional.gov.ar) with four channels. La Red (www.uol.com.ar) is a national, commercial network. Radio Intereconomía (www.intereconomia.com) has news and economic contents.

One of the most popular radio stations is based in Buenos Aires, Radio Rivadavia (www.rivadavia.com.ar) along with at least 40 other FM stations. All musical genres are broadcast, as well as news (Radio America, www.estoesamerica.com.ar), cultural (Radio Continental, www.continental.com.ar) and religious contents (Red Puerto Libre, www.redpuertolibre.com.ar).

Television: There are five national television networks operated through affiliates and many more local services. Canal 7 (www.canal7.com.ar) is the state-run national TV service specialising in cultural and educational programmes but with the lowest viewer numbers. Telefe (www.telefe.com) with the highest viewer figures produces local content programmes as well as showing internationally produced shows. Canal 13 (www.canaltrece.com.ar) is Telefe's rival, producing popular programmes as well as news and current affairs. America 2 (www.america2.com.ar) and Canal 9 (www.canal9.com.ar) are the remaining national networks.

Argentina has one of the world's highest take-up rate for cable television with over a dozen stations to choose from. Station contents can be specific to viewer interest such as sports, children's or lifestyle programming or general content.

National news agency: Telam: www.telam.com.ar

Other news agencies: Agencia DIB (in Spanish): www.dib.com.ar

Agencia Nova (in Spanish): www.agencianova.com

Clave Noticias (in Spanish): www.clavenoticias.com.ar

Noticias Argentinas (in Spanish): www.noticiasargentinas.com

Diarios y Noticias (DYN) (in Spanish): www.dyn.com.ar

Economy

Argentina has vast natural resources providing a good standard of living for the population. These include rich farmlands with yields destined for export, a diverse industrial base, an educated workforce and minerals such as petroleum and natural gas. The service sector, including its financial services and tourism, accounts for almost 60.1 per cent of GDP; industry constitutes over 29.5 per cent of GDP, of which manufacturing represents 15 per cent. Agriculture contributes 10.4 per cent of GDP, and uses the abundant agricultural produce (Argentina is a major global producer of soya beans, beef and wheat) in its food processing industry. Its mineral resources are used in chemical and pharmaceutical manufacturing, and iron, steel and aluminium production. Argentina has factories for motor vehicle and machinery assembly, as well as shipbuilding.

GDP growth was low in 2012 at 0.9 per cent, but jumped to 2.9 per cent in 2013. However, in 2014 the economy retracted into negative growth again as high government spending, public debt, a depleting currency, and an increase in the printing of it, left high inflation, 36.4 per cent, and a negative growth of -1.7 per cent.

An agreement (in 2009) between Argentina and China to swap US$10 billion worth of their currencies with each other allowed trade without recourse to the US dollar. Argentine business may buy Chinese imports directly in renminbi and the deal provides Argentina with hard cash.

World prices of Argentina's commodities hit an all-time high in 2008 and boosted the trade surplus to US$13.2 billion, allowing Argentina to build up official reserves of US$44.9 billion (August 2009), which permitted it to repay US$12 billion to creditors on loans defaulted in 2001. This brought the total percentage of loans repaid, as of June 2010, to 92 per cent. However, by July 2011, Argentina had still to pay some Paris Club debts, which were hindering it from borrowing on global capital markets; it had been isolated from these markets in 2001. Argentina's long history of economic crisis took shape again in 2014; heavy inflation and public debt saw the economy shrink again as Argentina, for a second time in thirteen years, had to default on paying back its debts. However, in July 2014 it was ordered by a US court to pay back the remainder of its creditors. It is still yet unclear what the full repercussions of this latest hurdle are, yet the scenes were not as disastrous or violent as those of 2001. This cycle that Argentina is struggling to break out of is seriously hampering economic gains and Argentina's ability to capitalise on its advantages.

Argentina is the second largest economy in South America (after Brazil).

External trade

The EU and Mercosur have had a trading agreement since 2006. Argentina typically has a trade surplus with the EU, over 66 per cent of which is made up of food and live animals (Argentina is consistently ranked third in the EU's total imports of agricultural products (including prepared foodstuffs)).

The European Union filed a suit with the WTO against Argentina for import restrictions and difficulties in obtaining export licences. EU exports to Argentina are valued at around €8.3 billion (US$6.7 billion) annually.
In 2004, twelve South American countries signed an agreement to launch the South American Community of Nations (CSN), modelled on the European Union. In 2007 the name was changed to Union of South American Nations (Unasur). Unasur seeked to integrate with the Andean Community of Nations and Mercosur in a single market by 2014, when tariffs on non-sensitive products are abolished with the remainder eliminated by 2019. However political tensions within the region have hampered the ongoing process and complete completion of the project is as yet unclear.
Argentine plans to form a closer trading relationship with China have been in existence for some time due to the increasing trade in soya, coupled with Chinese investment in Argentina.

Imports

Principal imports include metal manufactures, machinery and equipment, vehicles, chemicals and plastics.
Main sources: Brazil (20.3 per cent of total in 2014), China (6.5 per cent), US (5.9 per cent).

Exports

Mineral products, agricultural products, vehicles and parts, electrical machinery, live animals and related products, chemicals. Food processing particularly meat, flour and other canned items are the largest manufacturing activities. Argentina is the primary source of tannin and linseed oil worldwide.
Main destinations: Brazil (21.8 per cent of total in 2014), China (16.4 per cent),US (13.5 per cent).

Agriculture

Farming

The agricultural sector as a whole contributes around 10.4 per cent to GDP and employs 5 per cent of the workforce, with the sector being composed predominantly of individual farmers and small companies. Arable land covers 12 per cent of Argentina's total land area. The country is an important producer of food, particularly soya beans, meat and wheat. Together, vegetable products and livestock account for nearly a quarter of total exports. Overall, the country is the fifth largest agricultural exporter in the world, with the sector accounting for 60 per cent of all Argentina's exports. It is the largest exporter of soy oil, soy flour oil and sunflower, the second largest exporter of corn after the United States, the third largest exporter of meat and the fifth largest flour producer.
Argentina's meat consumption is the highest in Latin America, at over 50kg per person per annum. Argentina is the world's third-largest organic meat producer, with 90 per cent of organic produce destined for export markets, particularly the EU. In previous years agricultural profitability has been hit by low international commodity prices, rising production costs, subsidisation of international competitors and an over-valued exchange rate which has diminished competitiveness.
The worst drought since the 1970s created an agricultural emergency by January 2009, particularly in the provinces of Buenos Aires, Cordoba, La Pampa and Entre Rios, where 90 per cent of the wheat crop was lost nationwide, and 800,000 head of cattle died. The cattle industry declined as herds fell in numbers from 57 million in 2005 to 48.6 million in 2010 (the lowest level since 1964). Years of drought and the quota on beef exports, in operation since 2006, resulted in exports falling by 57 per cent in 2010 to 166,265 tonnes. Thought the agricultural sector is recovering, output is not that of pre-drought levels. For example, pre-drought exports to the EU amounted to just over €8 billion, after the drought exports to the EU have remained between €5 billion-€6 billion, thought they are on the increase.

Fishing

Argentina has increased its fishing production and exports of surplus stock are becoming a valuable export earner, especially when processed into oil and fish meal. Because of the Argentines' preference for beef, the domestic demand for fish is relatively weak. Principal fishing ports are Mar del Plata and Bahía Blanca. The typical annual fish catch is around 925,000 tonnes, including 550,000 tonnes marine fish and 350,000 tonnes shellfish.

Forestry

About 12 per cent of Argentina's total land is covered by forest, equivalent to 34.6 million hectares, and a further 6 per cent of other wooded land.
Argentina is not self-sufficient in forestry goods, with most of the domestic harvest going towards lumber. Pine and cedar used for pulp are harvested in the north-west of the country. Significant quantities of sawn goods, wood-based panels and chemical pulps are produced from domestic hardwoods and softwoods. A large quantity of paper is imported, although Argentina's pulp and paper industry relies mainly on domestic pulp production.

Industry and manufacturing

Argentina's main industrial centres are Cordoba and to a lesser extent Buenos Aires. Industry as a whole contributes approximately 29.5 per cent to GDP and employs 23 per cent of the workforce (2014).
Major sectors of production include food, textiles, machinery and transport equipment, consumer durables, industrial chemicals, metal working, engineering, paper, iron and steel and electrical equipment. The beef industry has given rise to a number of associated industries, including hides, leather, meat extracts and processed meats. Sectors that have gained in prominence in recent years include software and petrochemicals.
The automobile sector represents an important growth sector for the economy. In recent years the sector has suffered from poor consumer demand and an uncompetitive exchange rate. Many car assembly plants have been closed and operations have been transferred to Brazil, where labour costs are lower and there is a more lucrative domestic market. With the exception of the automobile industry however, the manufacturing sector has been boosted by the acceleration of economic integration within Mercusor.

Tourism

Tourism in Argentina has a wide variety of different activities, climates and terrains to offer visitors. Although the summer in the southern hemisphere (between December–February) offers the North American and European visitor a welcome break from a possible bleak winter, the majority of visitors to Argentina remain those from Brazil.
Tourist numbers have been dropping slightly, from 5.7 million in 2011 to 5.6 million in 2013 (latest figures. Employment in the industry had a total contribution of 9.7 per cent of the work force (1.7 million jobs) and total contribution to GDP 10.4 per cent in 2014, a figure that is forecast to rise by 1.3 per cent in 2015. The government recognised the importance of tourism to the economy by creating a Ministry of Tourism in July 2010, with the remit to represent an alternative development sector, which 'boosts employment and modifies regional economies'. Investment in travel and tourism in 2014 was estimated to be P51.3 billion (US$6.3 billion), 7 per cent of total investment in the country.
In April 2010, China and Argentina agreed to promote bilateral tourism exchange programmes and increase the number of Chinese tourists visiting for cultural events.

Environment
Argentina's diverse environments have created a number of different ecological challenges from heavy pollution in Buenos Aires, deforestation in subtropical provinces to overgrazing in Patagonia.

Mining
Iron ore is the principal mineral extracted, mostly in Río Negro province, but output is only sufficient to supply about half of the requirements of the country's largest blast furnace complex, the remainder being made up from imports. Other minerals extracted include lead, zinc, tin, and uranium.
Argentina's largest mining project is the Alumbrera copper and gold mine in Catamarca province, thought to be the ninth largest copper mine in the world. Annual production of some 15 tonnes of gold is also expected until the end of its 20-year life in 2019. In addition, the Cerro Vanguardia silver and gold mine produces approximately five tonnes of gold per year. Now a significant gold producer Argentina – which occupies a top twenty world position – has recently seen considerable production activity in the north-west of the country, where the Veladero mine is situated.

Hydrocarbons
Argentina had 2.3 billion barrels of proven oil reserves at the end of 2014, with production of 629,000 barrels per day (bpd), although production has fallen recently due to the lack of new capacity to offset declines in mature fields. Argentine became a net importer of oil in 2009, although it is the third-largest oil producer in Latin America. Domestic oil consumption was 662bpd in 2014, down 1.2 per cent on the 2013 figure.
In November 2011, Repsol confirmed that it had discovered its biggest ever shale-oil reserve in Neuquén province, with 927 million barrels of oil equivalent recoverable hydrocarbons.
On 17 April 2012 President Kirchner declared that the publicly owned YPF energy company would be re-nationalised, through expropriation of 51 per cent of the shares owned by the Spanish energy company, Repsol. The charge given was that Repsol has failed to invest in further exploration of hydrocarbons at a time when Argentina was in most need of reducing the country's energy bill (US$10 billion in 2011) and to recover sovereignty of Argentine natural assets. Repsol lost millions of dollars in the sale. The news resulted in warnings from the EU, saying the decision sent a 'very negative signal' to investors.
Proven gas reserves amounted to 300 billion cum in 2014, with production at 35.4 billion cum (a fall of 0.3 per cent from 2013). Gas has become the country's primary source of energy with consumption of 47.2 billion cum in 2014. Argentina became a net import of natural gas in 2008. Neuquén is the country's major gas field. YPF announced at the end of August 2014 that it had discovered oil and gas in the Patagonia region located in Santa Cruz province; the discovery holds the potential to produce 200,000 cubic meters of gas and 370 barrels of oil per day.
Argentina has total coal reserves of 130 million tonnes. It produces 340,000 tonnes per year and consumes around 1.54 million tonnes per year.
There are comprehensive pipeline links with surrounding countries. As traditional inland sites of oil and gas fields have matured the government has licensed offshore exploration sites.

Energy
As the third largest power producer in Latin America, Argentina has a fully deregulated and diversified market. Most of its electricity generation comes from hydropower, followed by natural gas. Argentina has over 25 million KW of installed generation.
Hydroelectricity is of prime importance to the energy sector, particularly the Yacyreta hydroelectric dam, which helps power Argentina and neighbouring Paraguay. The Salto Grande dam is also co-owned by a bordering country, Uruguay, and as is the case with the Yacyreta, power generated from the project is shared equally between the two nations.
Argentina relies on the Atucha I and Embalse nuclear power projects, both of which are operated by Nucleoelctrica Argentina SA. Construction of a third nuclear power station, Atucha II, was halted in 1999, although the government announced plans 2005 that it would invest US$700 million to complete the construction. However, the primary problem with Atucha II is technological obsolescence and discussions with the Atomic Energy of Canada Limited (AECL) to upgrade the design are ongoing. A feasibility study for a fourth nuclear power station began in 2006. Argentina has inactive uranium mines and is able to enrich uranium to process fuel rods but does not have a solution for spent radioactive waste from power plants.
Contracts were agreed between Canada-based Dynamotive and the province of Corrientes in 2008 for two 15.7 MW electricity generating stations, fuelled by biofuel from wood waste and other biomass residue.

Financial markets
Stock exchange
Bolsa de Comercio de Buenos Aires (BCDA) (Buenos Aires Stock Exchange)
Commodity exchange
MATba (Mercado a Témino de Buenos Aires)

Banking and insurance
The country's economic crisis of 2001 severely undermined Argentina's banking system, when the freezing of deposit accounts and the conversion of deposits into pesos undermined liquidity in the financial system. The value of assets deteriorated throughout 2002 as the peso lost value and government bonds fell to a fraction of their purchase price. Banks were unable to meet claims on deposits, while savers filed law suits against institutions for failing to honour their deposits. As such, the entire banking system teetered on the edge of collapse in 2003. This led to the closure of many local subsidiaries of foreign banks. However, Argentina's recent economic recovery has enabled the sector to rehabilitate itself somewhat, with an increase in money supply demand and a significant recovery on bank deposits and loans. The acceptance of the national government's debt restructuring plan in early 2005 has led to a much needed increase in foreign capital inflow and greater stability in the sector. Despite this gradual upturn the banking sector remains very sensitive to macroeconomic conditions and though the level of credit is growing, it remains at a slow rate.
A new Bank of the South, with a headquarters in Venezuela, will be launched in 2008 to provide an alternative source of development funding for the participating countries. Assets of US$7 billion will underpin its operations.
The governor of the central bank, Martin Redrado was forced by the government to resign in January 2010 after he had refused to pay US$6.5 billion of the country's debts from central bank reserves.
Central bank
Banco Central de la República Argentina
Main financial centre
Buenos Aires

Time
GMT minus three hours

Geography
Argentina is situated in the south-east of South America, facing the Atlantic Ocean to the east. Argentina is bounded by Chile to the west, Bolivia and Paraguay to the north and Brazil and Uruguay to the north-east. There are four main geographic provinces: the Andes, the lowland north, the Pampas and Patagonia.
The Andes Mountains line Argentina's western edge, forming the boundary with

Chile. The highest peak, Aconcagua, stands 6,960 metres (22,834 feet).
Gently rolling plains extend eastward from the base of the Andes and descend gradually to sea level. Open savannas alternate with almost impenetrable thorn forests in the western part of the region.
Vast, generally treeless plains of central Argentina gradually rise from the Atlantic coast to the Andes Mountains. These fertile plains are Argentina's breadbasket. They consist of the Humid Pampas along the coast and the Dry Pampas in the west and south.
Patagonia, south of the Pampas, is dry and desolate. The Patagonian steppes support flocks of sheep, the wool of which is exported to Europe.
The southernmost inhabited territory, Tierra del Fuego (Land of Fire), consists of various islands with the northern areas used for sheep farming, while the southern islands are mountainous and covered in glaciers and forests.

Hemisphere

Southern

Climate

Argentina's climate ranges from sub-tropical in the north to sub-antarctic in the south. The densely populated central zone (including Buenos Aires) is temperate. Summer, from December–March, is hot and humid with temperatures ranging from 26–35 degrees Celsius (C); autumn is April–May, with temperatures in the range 10–25 degrees C; winter is from June–August, with temperatures of 0–20 degrees C, when nights can be cold with temperatures below freezing; spring is from September–November, with temperatures of 12–25 degrees C.

Dress codes

Dress codes are fairly formal in Buenos Aires. Suits are worn for business appointments and, for men, jackets and ties are required for dining out and other social occasions. Casual clothing is often worn on the coast, but shorts and beachwear should be worn only at the beach or pool.

Entry requirements

Passports

Passports are required by all visitors except nationals of neighbouring countries with identity cards.

Visa

All business travellers are advised to contact an Argentine embassy for requirements, before departure.
Tourist visas are not required by most nationals of the Americas, Europe, Australasia and some Asian countries. Citizens of neighbouring countries of Argentina need only national identification cards.
In 2010 a presidential decree was passed requiring a 'reciprocity fee' to enter Argentina from citizens of the United States (US$131, multiple entries for 10 years), Canada (US$70, single entry) and Australia (US$100, multiple entry).
For further exemptions and details check with the appropriate embassy or consulate before departure.

Currency advice/regulations

There are no restrictions on the import and export of local or foreign currency.

Health (for visitors)

Mandatory precautions

None

Advisable precautions

Typhoid and hepatitis A vaccinations are recommended. Yellow fever vaccinations are advised for visitors to the north-eastern forest area. Malaria prophylaxis is advisable for visits to some lowland tropical areas. Water precautions should be taken outside main towns. There is some risk of dengue fever and anthrax outside urban areas.
Medical insurance is necessary and doctors often expect immediate cash payment before treatment. Take medical kit.

Hotels

Wide range available, graded from one to five stars. There is a 21 per cent tax, which may be included in hotel tariff.

Public holidays (national)

Fixed dates

1 Jan (New Year's Day), 1 May (Labour Day), 25 May (Anniversary of the 1810 Revolution), 19 Jun (Flag Day), 9 Jul (Independence Day), 8 Dec (Immaculate Conception), 25 Dec (Christmas Day), 31 Dec (New Year's Eve).

Variable dates

Maundy Thursday, Good Friday, Malvinas Day (first Mon in Apr), Death of General José San Martin (third Mon in Aug), Columbus Day (second Mon in Oct).

Working hours

Banking

Mon–Fri: 09/1000–1500.

Business

Mon–Fri: 0900–1300, 1500–1800.

Government

Mon–Fri: 0800–1700.

Shops

Mon–Fri: 0900–2200, Sat: 0900–1300.

Telecommunications

Mobile/cell phones

GSM 850/1900 services are available in highly populated areas only.

Electricity supply

220V AC, 50 cycles

Social customs/useful tips

The normal form of greeting is a handshake. In general, European practices are followed. Standards on punctuality differ though and visitors may be kept waiting. Commercial quotations should be made in US dollars.
In their public behaviour, Argentines are very conscious of civilities. It is considered polite to first extend a greeting like *buenos dias* (good day) or *buenas tardes* (good afternoon) if you are approaching a stranger to ask for information.
Same sex marriage became legal from July 2010.
Tough anti-tobacco legislation was approved by the lower house of assembly in June 2011; the Senate had already passed the legislation. Advertising and sponsorship will be banned, as will smoking in bars, restaurants and the work place and sale of single cigarettes and all sales to under 18 year olds.

Security

Although street crime is increasing in Argentina, personal security is a minor problem compared to other Latin American countries. Violent crime is rare in Buenos Aires. Travellers should take precautions against petty theft such as bag snatching, especially on trains.

Getting there

Air

National airline: Aerolíneas Argentinas.
International airport/s: Ministro Pistarini Ezeiza (EZE), 35km south-west of Buenos Aires; duty-free shop, restaurants, bank, car hire. A bus service operates to the city, every 30 minutes between 0500–2300, taking 45 minutes. Taxis are also available. A coach service also connects to Aeroparque Jorge Newbery airport for domestic flight connections.
Other airport/s: Aeroparque Jorge Newbery (AEP), 8km north-east of Buenos Aires, domestic terminal; duty-free shop, restaurant, bank, car hire.
Airport tax: International departures US$18; regional and to Uruguay US$8. International arrivals US$10. These levies are subject to inflation.

Surface

Road: There are well-maintained roads between all the neighbouring countries. Branches of the Pan-American Highway run from Buenos Aires to the borders of Bolivia, Brazil, Chile and Paraguay. Entry from Uruguay is possible via bridges over the Uruguay River at Puerto Colón, Puerto Unzué and the Salto Grande Dam. The long distances involved can make car journeys time-consuming: for example, the distance from Santiago in Chile to Buenos Aires is over 1,400 km.
Rail: The major direct route is north from Buenos Aires to Asunción in Paraguay. There are also direct rail links with Bolivia, Brazil and Chile. Services are often disrupted and delays can be expected.

Water: Ferry and hydrofoil services on the Río de la Plata link Colonia and Montevideo (Uruguay) with Buenos Aires. Ferries also operate from Paraguay on the Paraná River.

Main port/s: Buenos Aires, Ensenada (La Plata), Rosario and Bahía Blanca. There are numerous smaller ports and some specialised terminals (for oil, cereals, raw materials, etc).

Getting about

National transport

Air: Given the great distances involved, air travel is the logical method for reaching domestic destinations. Internal flights for Buenos Aires land at Aeroparque Jorge Newbery, 10 minutes from city centre by taxi.

An extensive domestic service is offered to regional airports and demand for services is high, so it is advisable to book flights in advance.

Road: The network has been improved in recent years and links major centres. Tolls are collected on major roads, which are privately-owned.

Buses: Long-distance bus services are operated by a number of companies, mostly centred on Buenos Aires, and are extensive (e.g. routes to Mar del Plata, Córdoba, San Martín de Los Andes, Mendoza). The Buenos Aires bus terminal is next to *Retiro*, the central rail station.

Rail: Travelling by train is generally cheaper, but slower, than travelling by bus. A comprehensive rail system links main towns. Long-distance Pullman services, with air-conditioning, sleeping facilities and restaurants, are recommended. It is advisable to book well in advance.

Water: There are regular sailings to Rosario and Corrientes via the Paraná River. River transport company Flota Fluvial operates services on the Plate, Paraná, Paraguay and Uruguay Rivers. Patagonian ports are also served, but sailings are irregular.

City transport

Taxis: Taxis, of which there are some 32,000 in Buenos Aires, generally have yellow roofs. They can be hailed or found on ranks and are metered within cities. For trips in the Buenos Aires centre which are less than six blocks, it is usually faster to walk than to take a taxi. Tips are not necessary, though generally expected from tourists.

There is also a widely available and much-used system of cars called *remises*, which offer a safer and more comfortable service. *Remises* are also available for travel to and from the airports, where they can be booked at separate counters. Journey time from Ezeiza airport to city centre is 40 minutes and 10 minutes from Aeroparque Jorge Newbery.

Buses, trams & metro: All major towns have good local services. In Buenos Aires there is a comprehensive public transport system with 'pay as you board' bus services, operating round the clock.

The Buenos Aires metro, known as *Subte*, has five lines and 80 stations; it operates from early morning to late at night. Tokens can be purchased at booking offices.

Ferry: The principal ferry connection in Buenos Aires is to Colonia in Uruguay and is frequented by tourists heading for the Uruguayan resort town of Punta del Este. River buses in the suburb of Tigre serve communities in the river delta and are a popular tourist attraction on weekends.

Car hire

Car hire is available in Buenos Aires and most main urban centres. An international driving licence, in addition to home licence, is advisable

BUSINESS DIRECTORY

The addresses listed below are a selection only. While World of Information makes every endeavour to check these addresses, we cannot guarantee that changes have not been made, especially to telephone numbers and area codes. We would welcome any corrections.

Telephone area codes

The international direct dialling code (IDD) for Argentina is +54, followed by area code and subscriber's number:

Bahía Blanca	291	Resistencia	3722
Balcarce	2266	Rio Cuarto	358
Buenos Aires	11	Rio Grande	2964
Catamarca	3833	Rosario	341
Córdoba	351	Salta	387
Formosa	3717	San Juan	264
Las Calera	351	San Lorenzo	3476
La Plata	221	San Miguel de	
Tucumen	381		
Mar Del Plata	223	San Pedro	3329
Mendoza	261	San Rafael	2627
Neuquén	299	Santa Fé	342
Paraná	343	Santa Rosa	2954

Useful telephone numbers

Fire: 107

Police: 101

Ambulance: 101

Chambers of Commerce

American Chamber of Commerce in Argentina, 1133 Viamonte, 1053 Buenos Aires (tel: 4371-4500; fax: 4371-8400; e-mail: amcham@amcham.com.ar).

Argentine Chamber of Commerce, 36 Avenida Leandro N Alem, 1003 Buenos Aires (tel: 5300-5000; fax: 5300-9058; e-mail: centroservices@cac.com.ar).

British-Argentine Chamber of Commerce, 457 Avenida Corrientes, 1043 Buenos Aires, CF (tel: 4394-2762; fax: 4394-3860; e-mail: info@ccab.com.ar).

Rosario Chamber of Commerce, 1868 Córdoba, 2000 Rosario (tel: 425-7147; fax: 425-7486; e-mail: ccer@commerce.com.ar).

Banking

Asociación de Bancos Argentinos (ADEBA), San Martín 1229, Piso 10, 1004 Buenos Aires, CF (tel: 4394-1430; fax: 4394-6340).

Banco Crédito-Op Cooperativo Ltdo, Reconquista 484, Zona postal 1003, Buenos Aires, CF (tel: 4394-0105/0122; fax: 4325-9104).

Banco de Crédito Argentino, Reconquista 2, Zona postal 1092, Buenos Aires, CF (tel: 4334-1181/89; fax: 4334-5618).

Banco de Galicia y Buenos Aires, Tte Gral Juan D Perón 407, Zona postal 1038, Buenos Aires, CF (tel: 4329-6000; fax: 4329-6100).

Banco de la Ciudad de Buenos Aires, Florida 302, Zona postal 1313, Buenos Aires, CF (tel: 4325-5881/89).

Banco de la Nación Argentina (BNA), Bartolomé Mitre 326, Zona postal 1036, Buenos Aires, CF (tel: 4347-6000; fax: 4347-8078); international banking division (tel: 4347-8092; fax: 4347-8078); foreign trade promotion (tel: 4347-8763; fax: 4347-8764).

Banco de la Pampa, Reconquista 319, Zona postal 1003, Buenos Aires, CF (tel: 4325-3410; fax: 4325-8750).

Banco de la Provincia de Buenos Aires, San Martín 137, Zona postal 1004, Buenos Aires, CF (tel: 4331-2561/3584; fax: 4331-5154).

Banco del Buen Ayre, Cerrito 740, Zona postal 1309, Buenos Aires, CF (tel: 4350-020/054; fax: 4837-890).

Banco del Sud, Maipú 277, Zona postal 1084, Buenos Aires, CF (tel: 4326-3313, 4326-2965; fax: 4325-3177).

Banco Francés del Rio de la Plata, Reconquista 165, Zona postal 1003, Buenos Aires, CF (tel: 4331-7071; fax: 4954-8009).

Banco General de Negocios, Esmeralda 120, Zona postal 1035, Buenos Aires, CF (tel: 4394-3003, 4394-2879; fax: 4394-2698).

Banco Hipotecario Nacional, Balcarce 167, Zona postal 1064, Buenos Aires, CF (tel: 4342-9732; fax: 4331-0620).

Banco Holandés Unido, Florida 361, Zona postal 1005, Buenos Aires, CF (tel: 4394-4553; fax: 4322-0839).

Banco Medefín UNB, 25 de Mayo 489, Zona postal 1339, Buenos Aires, CF (tel: 4313-4125; fax: 4312-9450).

Banco Quilmes, Tte Gral Juan D Perón 564, Zona postal 1038, Buenos Aires, CF (tel: 4331-8111/9; fax: 4334-5235).

Banco República, Sarmiento 336, Zona postal 1041, Buenos Aires, CF (tel: 4331-8385/87; fax: 4331-2130).

Banco Río de la Plata, Bartolomé Mitre 480, Zona postal 1036, Buenos Aires, CF (tel: 4331-7551, 4331-8361; fax: 4331-7551; internet site: http://www.bancorio.com.ar).

Banco Roberts, 25 de Mayo 258, Zona postal 1002, Buenos Aires, CF (tel: 4334-1723, 4334-6682; fax: 4334-6679).

Banco Sudameris, Tte Gral Juan D Perón 500, Zona postal 1038, Buenos Aires, F (tel: 4331-4061/9; fax: 4331-2793).

Banco Supervielle Société Générale, Reconquista 330, Zona postal 1003, Buenos Aires, CF (tel: 4394-4051/9).

Banco Tornquist, Bartolomé Mitre 531, Zona postal 1036, Buenos Aires, CF (tel: 4343-784/49; fax: 4342-6090).

Banco Velox, San Martín 298, Zona postal 1004, Buenos Aires, CF (tel: 394-0115/0665; fax: 4394-8255).

Banesto Banco Shaw, Sarmiento 355, Zona postal 1041, Buenos Aires, CF (tel: 4325-6500; fax: 4312-4743).

Caja Nacional de Ahorro y Seguro, Hipólito Yrigoyen 1750, Zona postal 1308, Buenos Aires, CF (tel: 4476-4216; fax: 4111-568).

Deutsche Bank, Bartolomé Mitre 401, Zona postal 1036, Buenos Aires, CF (tel: 4343-2511/9; fax: 4343-3536).

The First National Bank of Boston, Florida 99, Zona postal 1005, Buenos Aires, CF (tel: 4342-3051/61; fax: 4343-7303).

Lloyds Bank, Reconquista 101, Zona postal 1003, Buenos Aires, CF (tel: 4331-3551/9; fax: 4342-7487).

Central bank

Banco Central de la República Argentina, Reconquista 266, 1003 Buenos Aires (tel: 4348-3500; fax: 4334-6489).

Stock exchange

Bolsa de Comercio de Buenos Aires (BCDA) (Buenos Aires Stock Exchange) www.bcba.sba.com.ar/BCBA

Commodity exchange

MATba (Mercado a Témino de Buenos Aires) www.matba.com.ar

Travel information

Aerolíneas Argentinas, Paseo Colón 185, Zona postal 1063, Buenos Aires, CF (tel: 4320-2000; fax: 44317-3585; internet: www.austral.com.ar).

Austral Líneas Aéreas (ALA), Avda Corrientes 485, Piso 9, Zona postal 1398, Buenos Aires, CF (tel: 4340-7800, 4317-3605; fax: 4317-3992).

Ministry of tourism

Secretaría del Turismo, Presidencia de la Nación, Suípacha 1111, Piso 21, Zona potal 1360, Buenos Aires, CF (tel: 4312-5624, 4311-2089; fax: 4313-6834; internet site: http://www.sectur.gov.ar/eng/menu.htm).

National tourist organisation offices

Asociación Argentina de Agencias de Viaje y Turismo (Travel Agents' Association), Viamonte 640, Piso 10, Zona postal 1053, Buenos Aires, CF (tel: 4322-2804).

Ministries

Ministry of Culture and Education, Pizzurno 935, Zona postal 1020, Buenos Aires, CF (tel: 424-1551/9, 445-666, 448-110).

Ministry of Defence, Av. Paseo Colón 255, Zona postal 1063, Buenos Aires, CF (tel: 343-1561).

Ministry of Economy, Public Works and Services, Hipólito Yrigoyen 250, Zona posal 1310, Buenos Aires, CF (tel: 342-6411, 342-6421/9, 349-8814, 349-8810/2; fax: 331-0292, 331-2619, 331-2090; internet site: http://www.mecon.ar/default.htm).

Ministry of Foreign Affairs and International Trade, Reconquista 1088, Zona postal 1003, Buenos Aires, CF (tel: 331-0071, 312-1775, 312-3434; fax: 312-3593, 312-3423).

Ministry of the Interior, Balcarce 50, Zona postal 1064, Buenos Aires, CF (tel: 342-6081, 343-0880).

Ministry of Justice, Av Gral Gelly y Obes 2289, Piso 7, Zona postal 1425, Buenos Aires, CF (tel: 803-1051/3, 803-5453; fax: 803-3955).

Ministry of Labour and Social Security, Av L N Alem 650, Zona postal 1001, Buenos Aires, CF (tel: 311-3303, 311-2945).

Ministry of Public Health and Social Action, Av 9 de Julio 1925, Zona postal 1332, Buenos Aires, CF (tel: 381-8911, 381-8919).

Office of the President, Balcarce 50, Zona postal 1064, Buenos Aires, CF (tel: 331-5041, 303-608, 331-3183).

Other useful addresses

Administration of Agriculture and Agroindustrial Markets, Paseo Colón 922, Piso 1, Of 131, 1063 Buenos Aires (tel: 4349-2272/4; fax: 4349-2272).

Administration of Fish and Marine Resources, San Martín 459, Piso 2, 1004 Buenos Aires (tel: 4394-1869, 4394-5961).

Administration of Forestry Production, Av Paseo Colón 982, Piso 1, 1063 Buenos Aires (tel: 4349-2101, 4349-2103; fax: 4349-2108).

Administration of Geological and Mining Resources, Julio A Roca 651, Piso 8, 1322 Buenos Aires (tel: 4349-3131).

Administration of Livestock Markets, Paseo Colón 922, 1063 Buenos Aires (tel: 4349-2287, 4349-2294; fax: 4362-5144).

Administration of Markets of Non-Traditional Products, Paseo Colón 922, Buenos Aires (tel: 4362-1738, 4349-2280/2; fax: 4349-2280).

Administration of Mining Development, Av Julio A Roca 561, Piso 8, 1322 Buenos Aires (tel: 4349-3133).

Administration of Native Forestry Resources, San Martin 459, Piso 2, 1004 Buenos Aires (tel: 4394-1869).

Argentine Embassy (USA), 1600 New Hampshire Avenue, NW, Washington DC 20009 (tel: (+1-202) 238-6400; fax: (+1-202) 332-3171; e-mail: info@embajadaargentinaeeuu.org).

Argentine Industry Association, Av L N 1067, Piso 10, 1001 Buenos Aires (tel: 4313-2012, 4313-2512, 4313-2561; fax: 4313-2413).

Argentine Institute of Plant Sanitation and Quality, Av Paseo Colón 982, 1063 Buenos Aires (tel: 4313-8311).

Argentine Petrochemical Institute, Av Santa Fe 1480, Piso 5, Buenos Aires (tel: 4813-3436; fax: 4813-3436).

Argentine Petroleum Institute, Maipú 645, Piso 3, Primer Cuerpo, Buenos Aires (tel: 4322-3233, 4322-3652, 4322-3244; fax: 4322-3233).

Association of Importers and Exporters, Av Belgrano 124, Piso 1, 1092 Buenos Aires (tel: 4342-0010/9; fax: 4342-1312).

British Embassy, Dr Luis Agote 2412/52, Casilla de Correo 2050, 1425 Buenos Aires (tel: 4803-7070/1; fax: 4803-1731).

Bolsa de Comercio de Buenos Aires (Stock Exchange), Sarmiento 299, 1st Floor, AR 1353 Buenos Aires (tel: 4311-1174, 4311-5231, 4311-5235; fax: 4312-9332, 4312-6636).

Bureau of Export Promotion, Av Julio A Roca 651, Piso 6, 1322 Buenos Aires (tel: 4334-2975; fax: 4331-2266).

Centre for Business Promotion, Buenos Aires Stock Exchange, Sarmlento 299, Piso 1, 1353 Buenos Aires (tel: 4311-5231/4, 4313-4812, 4313-4544; fax: 4312-9332).

Customs Authority, Hipólito Yrigoyen 250 Of 606, 1310 Buenos Aires (tel: 4331-7330; fax: 4331-9839).

Department of Public Works and Transport, 250 Hipólito Yrigoyen Street, 11th Floor, Office 1141, PC 1310, Buenos Aires (tel/fax: 4349-7728; e-mail: arco@meyosp.mecon.ar).

Federal Board of Investment, San Martín 871, 1004 Buenos Aires (tel: 4313-5557; fax: 4313-1486).

Junta Nacional de Carnes (National Meat Board), San Martin 459, 104 Buenos Aires (tel: 4394-5161; fax: 4322-9357).

National Administration of Customs, Azopardo 350, 1328 Buenos Aires (tel: 4343-0661/9, 4343-0101/9).

National Administration of Fishing and Aquaculture, Av Paseo Colón 982, Anexo Jardin, Piso 1, 1063 Buenos Aires (tel: 4349-2330/1; fax: 4349-2332).

National Administration of Fuels, Av Paseo Colón 171, Piso 6, Of. 620, 1063 Buenos Aires (tel: 4319-8030/1).

National Commission of Telecommunications, Sarmiento 151, Piso 4, Of 435, 1041 Buenos Aires (tel: 4331-1203).

National Institute of Industrial Technology, Av L N Alem 1067, Piso 7, 1001 Buenos Aires (tel: 4313-3013).

National Institute of Mining Technology, Parque Tecnológico Migueletes, Casilla de Correo 327, 1650 San Martín (tel: 4754-5151, 4754-4141; fax: 4754-4070, 4754-8307).

National Institute of Statistics and Census, Dirección de Difusión Estadistics, Centro de Servicios Estadísticos, Av Julio A Roca 615, 1067 Buenos Aires (tel: 4349-9651).

National Viticulture Institute, Av Julio A Roca 651, Piso 5, Of 22, 1067 Buenos Aires (tel/fax: 4343-3816).

Public Works and Transport Department, 250 Hipólito Yrigoyen Street, 11th Floor, Office 1141, PC 1310, Buenos Aires (tel/fax: 4349-7728; e-mail: arco@meyosp.mecon.ar).

Secretariat of Agriculture, Livestock and Fisheries, Av Paseo Colón 982, 1063 Buenos Aires (tel: 4362-2365, 4362-5091, 4362-5946; fax: 4349-2504).

Secretariat of Energy, Av Paseo Colón 171, Piso 8 Of 803, 1063 Buenos Aires (tel: 4349-8003/5; fax: 4343-6404).

Secretariat of Finance, Hipólito Yrigoyen 250, 1310 Buenos Aires (tel: 4331-0731, 4342-2937, 4341-8900; fax: 4331-0292).

Secretariat of Industry, Av Junio A Roca 651, 1322 Buenos Aires (tel: 4334-5065, 4342-7822; fax: 4331-3218).

Secretariat of International Economic Relations, Reconquista 1088, 1003 Buenos Aires (tel: 4331-7281, 4331-1073; fax: 4312-0965).

Secretariat of Mining, Av Junio A Roca 561, Sector 9, 1322 Buenos Aires (tel: 4349-3212, 4349-3232; fax: 4343-3525).

Secretariat of Public Works and Communications, Sarmiento 151, 1041 Buenos Aires (tel: 4499-481; fax: 4312-1283).

Secretariat of Transportation, Av. 9 de Julio 1925, 1332 Buenos Aires (tel: 4381-1435, 4381-4007).

Secretariat of Trade and Investment, Hipólito Yrigoyen 250, 1310 Buenos Aires (tel: 4331-2208).

Sociedad Rural Argentina (one of the main associations of big landowners), Florida 460, 1005 Buenos Aires (tel: 4392-2030, 4322-2111).

Subsecretariat of Economic Planning, Hipólito Yrigoyen 250, Of 843, 1310 Buenos Aires (tel: 4349-5079; fax: 4349-5730).

Superintendencia de Seguros de la Nación (Insurance Superintendency), Av Julio A Roca 721, 1067 Buenos Aires (tel: 4306-653).

Telecom Argentina Stet-France Telecom SA, Maipú 1210, 9th Floor, Buenos Aires (tel: 4968-3604, 4968-3606).

Trade Information and Opportunities, Reconquista 1098, 1003 Buenos Aires (tel: 4315-1125; fax: 4311-1331).

Undersecretariat of Air, River and Maritime Transport, Hipólito Yrigoyen 250, 1310 Buenos Aires (tel: 4349-7205; fax: 4342-6365).

Undersecretariat of Interior Security, Balearce 50 Post box 1064, Buenos Aires (tel: 4342-9440 Ext 579; fax: 4331-7051).

Undersecretariat of Investments, Hipólito Yrigoyen 250, Piso 10 Of 1010, 1310 Buenos Aires (tel: 4349-8515/6, 4349-5037; fax: 4349-8522).

Undersecretariat of Medical and Sanitary Inspection, 9 de Julio 1925, Piso 10, Of 1003, 1332 Buenos Aires (tel: 4383-1811; fax: 4381-8912).

Unión Industrial Argentina (main private sector industrial association), Avenida Leandro N Alem 1067, 11 Piso, 1001 Buenos Aires (tel: 4313-2762).

US Embassy, Avenida Colombia 4300, 1425 Buenos Aires (tel: 5777-4533; fax: 5777-4240).

World Trade Centre Buenos Aires, Moreno 584, Piso 6, 1091 Buenos Aires (tel: 4331-3432, 4331-2604; fax: 4343-4270).

National news agency: Telam: www.telam.com.ar

Agencia DIB (in Spanish): www.dib.com.ar

Agencia Nova (in Spanish): www.agencianova.com

Clave Noticias (in Spanish): www.clavenoticias.com.ar

Noticias Argentinas (in Spanish): www.noticiasargentinas.com

Diarios y Noticias (DYN) (in Spanish): www.dyn.com.ar

Internet sites

Argentina: www.surdelsur.com

Buenos Aires: www.buenosaires.com

Tourism Secretariat: www.turismo.gov.ar

Armenia

Sadly – in April 2015 – the hundredth anniversary of the deaths of hundreds of thousands of Armenians passed by almost imperceptibly in most of the world. That such a tragedy could be so easily forgotten was in itself an indictment of human callousness. That this was the first time that the term 'genocide' became used to describe the tragedy was in itself a sad legacy. The massacre of so many Armenians came in the dog days of the once impressive Ottoman Empire.

As Turkey's colonial project faltered in the period before the First World War, so it was that thousands of Turks, rendered homeless by the wars in the Balkans and in the Caucasus began to return to the homeland. This wave of immigration created the growth of Turkish nationalism, promoting a change of ethos within Turkey; what had once been a hugely successful multicultural enterprise became more closely identified with Turkish nationalism and the establishment of an essentially Muslim (Sunni) nation state.

Whether there actually was a plan to wipe out the Armenian population, or whether the notion simply established itself is a matter of debate a century later. Most neutral historians favour the notion that in June 2015, a decision was certainly taken by the Turkish authorities to deport the civil Armenian population. Turkish historians allege that the deportations were triggered by Armenian insurrections. It is difficult to see how relatively small Armenian communities, often spread out through Turkey's remoter hinterland, could have posed a serious military threat to the Turkish state.

Before the First World War there were an estimated 1.8 million Armenians living in the Ottoman Empire. Conservative estimates put the number of Armenians that

KEY FACTS

Official name: Haikakan Hanrapetoutioun (Republic of Armenia)

Head of State: President Serge Sarkisian (since 1998; re-elected 18 Feb 2013)

Head of government: Prime Minister Hovik Abrahamian (since 13 April 2014)

Ruling party: Hayastani Hanrapetakan Kusaktsutyun (HHK) (Republican Party of Armenia) (from 2007; re-elected 6 May 2012)

Area: 29,800 square km

Population: 3.29 million (2014)*

Capital: Yerevan

Official language: Armenian

Currency: Dram (D) = Luma 100

Exchange rate: D485.18 per US$ (Sep 2015)

GDP per capita: US$3,121 (2014)*

GDP real growth: 3.43% (2014)*

GDP: US$10.28 billion (2014)*

Labour force: 1.13 million (2011)*

Unemployment: 18.00% (2014)*

Inflation: 3.11% (2014)

Balance of trade: -US$2.06 billion (2014)

* estimated figure

were murdered or simply disappeared at between one and one and a half million. Turkish historians have claimed that the term genocide is inappropriate because nowhere is there any record of an official decision to eliminate the Armenian population. Some of the arguments deployed in Turkey do seem a little arcane – such as the fact that during and after the deportations, funds were made available to Armenian communities (from missionaries and diplomatic sources) via the Ottoman banking system. Turkey also points out that in the major port of Izmir (Smirna) there were no deportations.

Turkey's claim is that that the Armenian population were collaborating with Turkey's enemies – notably the Russians – and had participated in numerous attacks on Turkish and Kurdish communities. One allegation is that in the latter months of 1914 and mid-1915 as many as 30,000 Muslims were murdered by Armenian gangs. Some Turkish historians admit that this figure may be exaggerated. Statistics are wheeled in by both sides of the argument to defend their case. Strangely, one statistic has it that in 1920 the Armenian Patriarch (religious leader) claimed that there were as many as 677,000 Armenians living in Anatolia.

Diaspora

The Armenian diaspora is spread throughout the Middle East, Russia, the US, France, Canada, Argentina and a host of other countries. The hope of many Armenians is that, sooner or later, Turkey will have to come clean and apologise for the events of the early twentieth century. Within Turkey there does seem to have been a wider acceptance that a crime was committed. However, this view sits uncomfortably with the increasingly hard-line Islamist political position of the recently elected President (and former Prime Minister) which continues to be one of rejection, silence and denial. Meanwhile, international diplomatic pressure continues to make itself felt; statements by Pope Francis have demanded that Turkey accept responsibility and even President Obama in a carefully worded statement has made his position clear. Even Turkey's Kurdish community seems to have come to terms with the need to accept responsibility. However, Turkey has had some success in avoiding the acceptance of the term genocide internationally. Of the 28 member states of the European Union, 17 still refuse to accept the term genocide and prominent members of the international academic and legal communities have referred to the accepted definition of genocide as limiting the definition to 'certain constitutional acts' supported by a clear and 'specific intention'. The latter is not always easily proven. However, whatever the *de jure* position, *de facto*, Armenians were massacred, murdered, forcefully deported. The intention may not have been enshrined constitutionally, but there would seem to be grounds for accepting that there existed an unwritten national wish to rid Turkey of almost all its Armenians.

One Sarkisian goes, the other stays

The resignation of Prime Minister Tigran Sarkisian in 3 April 2014 caught most Armenians by surprise. There had been rumours of his dismissal during his six years in power, but when he finally went, no-one was quite sure why. President Serge Sarkisian (no relation) had appointed his namesake (formerly chairman of the Central Bank of the Republic of Armenia), as prime minister after his election as president in 2008. Tigran Sarkisian was not known to have any political leanings although, according to Radio Free Europe, in the early 1990s he had been a member of the then opposition National Democratic Union. However, he joined the ruling Hayastani Hanrapetakan Kusaktsutyun (HHK) (Republican Party of Armenia) in November 2009, 18 months after being appointed. President Sarkisian re-appointed him to head the cabinet after his re-election for a second presidential term in February 2012.

Whether Tigran Sarkisian simply decided to go – possibly for health reasons – was one possibility. Another was that he had been offered a job with an international financial organisation. The former prime minister claimed to have submitted his resignation weeks earlier but had been asked by the president to reconsider. What was clear that there was no obvious replacement waiting in the wings. Other 'conspiracy' theories had it that the prime minister's alleged involvement in a corruption scandal was the reason. In 2013 allegations had surfaced of financial *legerdemain* to the tune of US$10.7 million by a prominent businessman Ashot Sukiasian. The misappropriated money seemed to have been deposited in an offshore bank account owned by a Cyprus company called Wlispera Holdings. Mr Sarkisian was identified as a co-owner of Wlispera, alongside Mr Sukiasian and others, an accusation he denied. Other theories had the prime minister locked in a power struggle with then parliamentary speaker Hovik Abrahamian. In an interview with radio Free Europe, the prime minister acknowledged that he faced competition from other members of the leadership. Mr Sarkisian's loyalty to the ruling HHK had certainly been called into question, possibly making him the obvious scapegoat for the government's more obvious shortcomings. Rumours also abounded that political unrest was bubbling beneath the surface and the resignation was designed to force the hand and possibly weaken, the opposition. Two of them, Ter-Petrossian's Armenian National Congress (HAK) and the Zharangutiun (Heritage) Party headed by US-born former foreign minister Raffi

KEY INDICATORS — Armenia

	Unit	2011	2012	2013	2014	**2015
Population	m	3.33	*3.28	*3.29	*3.29	*3.30
Gross domestic product (GDP)	US$bn	10.10	9.95	10.43	*10.28	*9.30
GDP per capita	US$	3,033	3,033	*3,173	*3,121	2,819
GDP real growth	%	4.4	7.1	3.5	*3.4	*-1.0
Inflation	%	7.7	2.5	5.8	3.1	*6.4
Unemployment	%	6.2	19.0	*18.5	*18.0	*17.9
Exports (fob) (goods)	US$m	1,455.8	1,588.0	1,643.2	1,698.2	–
Imports (fob) (goods)	US$m	3,561.3	3,656.0	3,996.1	3,753.6	–
Balance of trade	US$m	-2,105.4	-2,068.0	-2,352.9	-2,055.4	–
Current account	US$m	-1,136.5	-1,115.0	-839.0	*-949.0	-804.0
Total reserves minus gold	US$m	1,875.7	1,799.0	2,251.6	1,489.4	–
Foreign exchange	US$m	1,856.2	1,768.0	2,249.7	–	–
Exchange rate	per US$	369.71	406.44	401.47	474.97	–

* estimated figure ** forecast figure

Hovannisian, saw the next step as forcing the president too to step down. Meanwhile, following the resignation of the government, a new cabinet was formed in May 2014. Rather predictably, the new government affirmed its commitment to economic and social reforms, dealing with corruption and cracking down on tax evasion.

The stand-off between President Sarkisian and his most serious political rival, the leader of the opposition party Bargavach Hayastan (BHK) (Prosperous Armenia) Gagik Tsarukian, ended with the latter abandoning attempts to arouse popular support in a push for pre-term parliamentary and presidential elections. Instead, Mr Tsarukian asserted that Armenia's political problems should be resolved through peaceful, lawful and political means. Mr Tsarukian's change of heart appeared to have ended any alignment between the BHK and its opposition partners, the HAK and the Zharangutiun party. The Zharangutiun chairman Raffi Hovannisian declared that the alignment no longer existed. He added that he was open to co-operation with any political party or groups seeking regime change. Although the BHK claimed that the cause of the impasse was the government's planned constitutional reform, the BHK, the HAK and Zharangutiun remained convinced it was aimed at permitting President Sarkisian to remain in power as either prime minister or parliament speaker after his second presidential term ended in the spring of 2018.

From Russia – with little love

In October 2014, under pressure from a beleaguered President Putin of Russia, Armenia joined the Eurasian Economic Union (EEU), alongside Belarus, Kazakhstan and… Russia. EEU membership took effect from January 2015, ushering in Soviet style protectionism. Applying a circular logic, the EEU membership treaty should permit Armenia to exempt over 800 types of imported goods from the higher customs duties set by the EEU. Armenia is expected to adopt the EEU's tariffs by 2022. One attraction for Armenia was the possibility of lower (Russian) energy prices. There was also talk of increased investments from Russia, but little by way of any detail. Armenia's short term outlook is, in the view of the European Bank for Reconstruction and Development (EBRD), subject to uncertainty. The EBRD's Transition Report for 2014 notes that growth in 2014 and 2015 would probably maintain the same annual rates. The tense geopolitical situation and Armenia's trade and financial exposure to Russia could well have direct consequences. Possible good news was the possibility of Armenia substituting certain food items no longer available in Russia from the EU or from the US due to sanctions. However, according to the EBRD, a deeper integration into the global economy was a must for Armenia given its land-locked location, lack of resources and smallness. Traditionally, Armenia's biggest asset has been the initiative and enterprise of its people, something that was unlikely to flourish under the EEU environment.

The IMF

Armenia's economic environment has become more complex, particularly due to adverse external developments – slow growth in Russia and the EU and uncertainty regarding the crisis in Ukraine, including sanctions and counter-measures. A challenging domestic policy environment is also playing a role, most notably setbacks in the implementation of the pension reform. In spite of these challenges, the Fund-supported programme remains on track and its objectives highly relevant.

The International Monetary Fund (IMF) noted that Armenia's recovery from the 2009 crisis was is in place, but that significant challenges persisted. Co-operation between Armenia and the IMF has remained strong. An IMF supported programme was in place during 2010–13 and was completed with minor delays and few missed targets. More recently, a new 38-month arrangement was approved in March 2014 aimed at helping consolidate stability and buffers against possible external shocks and supporting growth through further reforms in the transition towards a dynamic emerging market economy. Beyond the programme relationship, Armenia and the IMF had maintained a continuous dialogue regarding policy challenges and Armenia's recent policy implementation has been consistent with previous IMF advice. In the view of the IMF, Armenia's economic environment had become more complex in 2014.

Externally, growth in Armenia's largest trading partners, both Russia and the EU, have been weaker than expected, affecting exports and remittances. The slowdown in Russia – driven by both structural and geopolitical developments, including sanctions, represented a particular challenge, along with the depreciation of the rouble. Domestically, the government has yet to overcome significant budget under-execution – particularly on capital expenditures – and the roll-out of the long-planned pension reform had experienced difficulties.

Armenia's new government, formed following the resignation of Prime Minister Tigran Sargsian, had merged the ministry of finance (MOF) and the state revenue committee (SRC); narrowing the scope of the pension reform after demonstrations and a ruling that some of its provisions were unconstitutional; implementation of an open skies policy in civil aviation; and concluding steps on accession to the Eurasian Economic Union (EEU).

Growth in the first half of 2014 was 2.7 per cent (*vis-à-vis* 3.5 per cent in 2013), as growth of exports and remittances slowed and government spending was lower than budgeted. The slowdown was broad-based, although construction, which had declined since the 2009 crisis, was relatively flat. Inflation through September was just 1.5 per cent, primarily driven by low food inflation.

Energy

Armenia's decision to participate in the EEU has paved the way for energy deals. Russia waived its 30 per cent export duties on natural gas, thereby setting a new as price for Armenia at US$189.00 per thousand cubic metres. The new arrangement took effect from 2014. In turn, Armenia transferred its remaining 20 per cent government stake in the gas monopoly, ArmRosGazprom, to Russia's Gazprom (thereby increasing Russia's stake to 100 per cent.) In addition, the Armenian authorities agreed to a 30-year immunity clause on changes to laws, regulations, decrees and corporate income tax rates that could negatively affect company finances. In January 2014 the US firm ContourGlobal signed an agreement with the Armenian government to acquite Vorotan High Cascade, a series of three hydroelectric plants totalling 405MW on the Vorotan River in Southern Armenia, for US$180 million. Under the terms of the agreement, ContourGlobal will invest US$70 million in the facility's modernisation over the next six years. The cascade accounts for some 15 per cent of Armenia's power generation capacity.

Risk assessment

Economy	Fair
Politics	Fair
Regional stability	Fair

COUNTRY PROFILE

At its height, the Armenian empire stretched from the Caspian Sea to the Mediterranean, before being incorporated into the Roman Empire in AD301. In the eleventh century, Armenia was incorporated into the Turkish Seljuk Empire.

1915 The Ottoman Empire killed around 1.5 million Armenians in response to the independence movement.

1916 Armenia was conquered by Russia. It joined an alliance with Georgia and Azerbaijan.

1918–20 Armenia was an independent republic for two years.

1920 Turkey and Russia invaded Armenia. An agreement with Russia led to Armenia proclaiming itself a socialist republic.

1922 Armenia was incorporated into the Union of Soviet Socialist Republics (USSR).

1923 Stalin drew the current recognised borders that placed the mainly ethnic Armenian Nagorno-Karabakh in Azerbaijan.

1930s The country suffered under Stalin's purges, but also underwent a period of industrial development.

1988–93 An earthquake in northern Armenia in 1988 killed 25,000 people. Nagorno-Karabakh demanded unification with Armenia, and conflict between Azerbaijan and Armenia began. It lasted intermittently for five years.

1990 The Pan-Armenian National Movement (PNM) won the parliamentary elections. A declaration of independence was made, but ignored by Moscow.

1991 The republic boycotted the Soviet referendum on the preservation of the USSR. In a referendum held shortly after the failed anti-Gorbachev coup in Moscow, 94 per cent voted for secession from the USSR. Levon Ter-Petrossian was elected president. Independence was formally proclaimed by the President. Armenia joined the Commonwealth of Independent States (CIS). The US recognised Armenia's independence.

1992 Armenia joined the UN. Conflict over Nagorno-Karabakh turned into full-scale war between Armenia and Azerbaijan.

1994 The war with Azerbaijan over Nagorno-Karabakh settled into an uneasy stalemate, with local Armenians backed by Armenian forces in control of the disputed enclave. A Russian-brokered cease-fire between Azerbaijan and Armenia was generally honoured.

1995 The first post-independence parliamentary elections resulted in victory for the ruling party, PNM. A constitution was approved by referendum which gave the president substantial powers, including the right to pass decrees.

1996 Levon Ter-Petrosian was re-elected president. There were protests over alleged electoral fraud.

1998 President Levon Ter-Petrosian was forced out of office after stating his wish to open negotiations with Azerbaijan. Robert Kocharian was elected president. The domestic political scene experienced growing instability and politically motivated violence. Deputy minister of defence, Colonel Vagram Khorkhoruni, was murdered. Arkady Gukasian was elected president of Nagorno-Karabakh.

1999 Prime Minister Vazgen Sargissian and other politicians were assassinated in the National Assembly. Aram Sargissian, the former prime minister's younger brother, was appointed to succeed him. The gunmen accused the government of leading Armenia into political and economic ruin.

2000 Andranik Margarian became prime minister and admitted that those affected by the 1988 earthquake were still living in a disaster zone. President Arkady Gukasian of Nagorno-Karabakh was seriously wounded in an assassination attempt.

2001 Armenia became a full member of the Council of Europe. There was no result in the US-brokered talks on Nagorno-Karabakh between the presidents of Azerbaijan and Armenia.

2002 The first meeting between the foreign ministers of Armenia, Azerbaijan and Turkey was held in Iceland to try to find a settlement for the Nagorno-Karabakh conflict.

2003 Incumbent Robert Kocharian won the second round of the presidential elections and the ruling Hayastani Hanrapetakan Kusaktsutyun (HHK) (Republican Party of Armenia), loyal to President Kocharian, won the parliamentary elections. There were criticisms of both elections. A referendum rejected constitutional amendments giving more power to the National Assembly. The death penalty was abolished.

2005 A referendum endorsed constitutional changes to strengthen parliament and limit presidential power.

2006 The Orinats Erkir party withdrew from the coalition government. Armenia, together with Azerbaijan and Georgia, signed a European Neighbourhood Policy co-operation agreement with the EU.

2007 Prime Minister Andranik Margarian died of a heart attack. Serge Sarkisian was appointed in his stead.

2008 Former prime minister Serge Sarkisian was elected as president with almost 53 per cent of the vote. The election 'mostly met international standards', according to the Organisation for Security and Co-operation in Europe (OSCE). However opposition members claimed the vote was rigged. President Sarkisian appointed Tigran Sarkisian (no relation) as prime minister.

2009 The first Yerevan municipal elections in nearly 20 years were held in which the HHK swept to victory (47.4 per cent). The two main opposition groups denounced the election as fraudulent. A rapprochement with Turkey included an official meeting in Switzerland.

2010 Following the US resolution describing Turkey's killing of Armenians during the First World War as genocide, Turkey's attitude to its negotiations with Armenia hardened. The accord of normalisation was suspended, following Turkey's demand that Armenia resolves its dispute with Azerbaijan concerning the territory of Nagorno-Karabakh. A deal was brokered by Russia, between Armenia and Azerbaijan for the return of prisoners captured during the Nagorno-Karabakh conflict.

2011 In June, Prime Minister Tigran Sarkisian announced that Armenia was ready to establish diplomatic relations with Turkey, without preconditions. At the same time he warned Azerbaijan that Armenia would defend its territory of Nagorno-Karabakh from foreign aggression. In June, under the auspices of Russian President Medvedev, the presidents of Azerbaijan and Armenia discussed a settlement agreement for Nagorno-Karabakh. Despite encouragement from world leaders, they failed to sign it and risked future conflict.

2012 In parliamentary elections held on 6 May the ruling HHK won 69 seats (out of 131), giving the party a majority to govern without forming a coalition. On 2 June Tigran Sarkisyan was reappointed as prime minister. In July, the minimum legal age for women to marry was raised from 17 to 18 years of age (matching the age for men). The date of the next presidential election was postponed until 3 February 2013.

2013 Incumbent president, Serge Sarkisian, comfortably won the 18 February presidential election with 59 per cent of the vote to 37 per cent for American born Raffi Hovannisian with 37 per cent. He was inaugurated on 9 April.

2014 Skirmishes between ethnic Armenians and Azerbaijani government forces in Nagorno-Karabakh enclave flared-up in late July/early August resulting in at least 15 deaths. A spokeswoman for the Iranian foreign ministry said that Iran was concerned about skirmishes between the two sides. On 4 September US secretary of state, John Kerry, met with President Sargsian and President Aliyev of Azerbaijan at the Nato Summit in Wales. They discussed efforts to resolve the conflict in Nagorno-Karabakh. Mr Kerry

expressed his strong concern for the recent violence along the Line of Contact, marking the deadliest period in the conflict since the 1994 cease-fire took effect.
2015 The 100th anniversary of the Armenian Genocide was commemorated on 24 April.

Political structure

Constitution

Although the country has had a directly elected president since 1991, a constitution was only approved by referendum in July 1995. It gave the president substantial powers, including the right to pass decrees.
In 2005 a referendum endorsed a number of constitutionals amendments, including reducing the power of the presidency, strengthening parliament and the judiciary, and enshrining in the constitution human rights provisions.

Independence date

21 September 1991.

Form of state

Multi-party republic: divided into various *marz* (provincial divisions).
It is a member of the Commonwealth of Independent States (CIS).

The executive

The president has broad powers. He is elected by direct universal suffrage for a period of five years and has the right to pass decrees.
Under the 1995 constitution, the president is not the head of the executive power, but rather directs that power, by forming the government, appointing (and dismissing) the prime minister and on the proposal of the latter, the cabinet ministers.
The president is not a member of the government, but chairs the sittings and ratifies all government decisions. In consultation with the prime minister, the president has the power to dissolve the National Assembly. The president is commander of the armed forces, represents the country in international negotiations, signs agreements and treaties and appoints the chief prosecutor. The president also appoints 4 members of the constitutional court and must be at least 35 years old.

National legislature

The unicameral Azgayin Zhoghov (National Assembly) is the supreme legislative body and comprises 131 deputies, of which 56 are elected in single seat constituencies and 75 by proportional representation through party-lists, assigned among those parties that win at least 5 per cent of the total number of votes.

Legal system

The highest appellate court is the Court of Appeal, which ensures uniformity in how the country's laws are applied through its final review of cases. The Court of Appeal's members are nominated by the Council of Justice, an administrative body created to ensure independence of the courts, and then appointed by the president. Armenia also has a Constitutional Court, which is charged with ensuring that legislative decisions and presidential decrees are consistent with the constitution. Of the Constitutional Court's nine members, five are appointed by the president and four by the National Assembly. The president of Armenia heads the Council of Justice. The minister of justice and the prosecutor general serve as deputy heads of the council.
In January 1999, a new civil code came into effect which creates the legal framework for property rights and contract enforcement, as well as the legal and institutional framework necessary for commercial banking activities. Despite this, the enforcement of laws and contracts remains weak.

Last elections

18 February 2013 (presidential); 6 May 2012 (parliamentary)
Results: Presidential: Serge Sarkisian won 59 per cent of the vote, Raffi Hovanessian 37 per cent.
Parliamentary: Hayastani Hanrapetakan Kusaktsutyun (HHK) (Republican Party of Armenia) 69 seats (out of 131), Bargavadj Hayastani Kusaktsutyun (BHK) (Prosperous Armenia) 36, Hay Azgayin Kongress (HAK) (Armenian National Congress, coalition of 13 political parties) seven, Hay Heghapokhakan Dashnaktsutiun (Dashnaks) (Armenian Revolutionary Federation) six, Orinats Erkir (OE) (Rule of Law) six, Zharangutyun (Heritage) five, independents two; three other political parties failed to win any seats. Turnout was 62.26 per cent.

Next elections

February 2018 (presidential); 2017 (parliamentary)

Political parties

Ruling party

Hayastani Hanrapetakan Kusaktsutyun (HHK) (Republican Party of Armenia) (from 2007; re-elected 6 May 2012)

Main opposition party

Hay Azgayin Kongress (HAK) (Armenian National Congress, coalition of 13 political parties)

Population

3.29 million (2013)*
The population is expected to reach 4.18 million by 2025.
Last census: October 2001: 3,002,594
Population density: 109 inhabitants per square km (2010). Urban population 64 per cent (2010 Unicef).
Annual growth rate: -0.7 per cent, 1990–2010 (Unicef).

Internally Displaced Persons (IDP)

50,000 (UNHCR)

Ethnic make-up

Armenians (93 per cent), Azerbaijanis (3 per cent), Russians (2 per cent); Kurdish and Yezidi minorities.

Religions

Armenian Apostolic Church (90 per cent), Armenian Catholic and Protestant (9 per cent), Russian and Greek Orthodox and Jewish.

Education

Primary education is followed by seven years of secondary school which is divided into a four-year first cycle (ages 12 to 16) and a three-year second cycle (ages 16 to 19). In the second cycle, students can opt between general or technical education. Higher education is provided by the Université Marien-Ngouabi, which is largely state subsidised. It has a yearly enrolment of about 12,000 students.
Literacy rate: 99 per cent, adult rates (Unesco 2005).
Compulsory years: 6 to 11
Enrolment rate: 96 per cent gross primary enrolment, 87 per cent gross secondary enrolment, of relevant age groups, (including repeaters) World Bank.
Pupils per teacher: 19 in primary schools.

Health

HIV/Aids

In 2009, there were an estimated 2,000 people living with HIV (Unicef 2012).
HIV prevalence: 0.1 per cent aged 15–49 in 2009 (Unicef 2012)
Life expectancy: 74 years, 2010 (Unicef 2012)
Fertility rate/Maternal mortality rate: 1.7 births per woman 2010 (Unicef 2012); maternal deaths 35 per 100,000 live births (World Bank).
Birth rate/Death rate: 6 deaths to 12 births per 1,000 people (World Bank).
Child (under 5 years) mortality rate (per 1,000): 16 per 1,000 live births (WHO 2012); 3 per cent of children aged under five are malnourished (World Bank).

Welfare

The poverty family allowance system is based on the principle of voluntary involvement and aims to target the most needy. Welfare issues concerning the elderly are crucial as almost 97 per cent of them need constant medication and 41 per cent need home care.

Pensions

In order to improve the state pension system, the government has increased the level of contributions for certain income groups. Under the state system, pensioners receive a uniform payment. There are no private pension funds.

Main cities
Yerevan (capital, estimated population 1.1 million in 2012, Gyumri (146,201), Vanadzor (105,406), Vagharshapat (57,836).

Languages spoken
Russian and Kurdish.

Official language/s
Armenian

Media
Despite censorship being prohibited in 2004 libel and defamation laws are often used to harass journalists, which has resulted in self-censorship particularly when reporting corruption and security matters particularly in Nagorno-Karabakh.

Press
The National Press Club (NPC) of Armenia formed is a self-governing, apolitical, non-profit, independent public organisation that aims to support free and democratic press in Armenia.
There are around 30 newspapers available but circulations are low with the largest being only 10,000. Productions costs have been traditionally high but following international aid a printing plant was opened and since 2005 has provided an alternative and competition for the semi-state-owned printing house. A number of publications have since increased their days of publishing and increased their circulations. Newspapers are generally owned by wealthy individuals or political parties.
Dailies: Most newspapers are published in Armenian, with Russian and English languages editions, including *Aravot* (http://new.aravot.am), a privately owned daily. Parliamentary publications include *Ayastani Anrapetutyun* (www.hhpress.am) and *Respublika Armenia* (www.ra.am). Political party publications include *Azg* (www.azg.am), *Yerkir* (http://yerkir.am), and *Aykakan Zhanamak* (www.hzh.am). In Russian, *Golos Armenii* (www.golos.am).
Weeklies: In Armenian, *Haykakan Zhamanak* is a popular weekly newspaper; with a Russian edition *Iravunk* (www.iravunk.com); with English editions *Eter* (www.eter.tv), *Lragir* (www.lragir.am), *Yerkir* (www.yerkir.am), and *168 Jam* (www.168.am). MFA Nagorno Karabakh (www.nkr.am) published in Stepanakert.

Broadcasting
Radio: The state-run Public Radio of Armenia (www.armradio.am) has two general interest stations, children's radio (http://lyunse.amradio.am) and (www.arevik.net) and an international service (http://int.armradio.am). There are a few private commercial radio stations including Hit FM (www.hit.am), Radio Van (www.radiovan.am) and City FM (www.cityfm.am).
Television: Television is the dominant media outlet. The state-run national service is provided by Public TV of Armenia (www.armtv.com) with local and imported shows most of which are translated into Armenian. Armenia TV (www.armeniatv.am) in the national commercial service. There are around 30 cable, digital and satellite TV stations broadcasting pay-to-view services.
National news agency: Armenpress
Other news agencies: Arka: www.arka.am
Arminfo: www.arminfo.info
Noyan Tapan: www.nt.am
Mediamax: www.mediamax.am

Economy
The industrial sector in Armenia contributed around 31.5 per cent of GDP in 2014, of which manufacturing accounted for around 10 per cent of total GDP. Industries include mining of gold, silver, base ores and minerals (marble and granite). Manufacturing includes processing imported diamonds and jewellery manufacturing, metal cutting and forge-pressing, instrument making, food processing, viniculture and alcohol distilling, vehicle assembly, clothing manufacturing and microelectronics. The service sector constitutes round 47 per cent of GDP; the major component of this is transport and storage, followed by energy and financial and banking services. Agriculture constitutes around 21.9 per cent of GDP.
GDP growth fell from a high of 13.7 per cent in 2007 to 6.9 per cent in 2008 and further, into recession, with negative growth of -14.2 per cent in 2009, as the global economic crisis took hold and international trade and commodity prices fell sharply, particularly in non-ferrous metals. However, in 2010 the economy recovered with a modest growth rate of 2.1 per cent, which rose to 4.4 per cent in 2011. The country experienced a high growth rate of 7.1 per cent in 2012 before dropping to an estimated 3.2 per cent in 2013. This has slightly improved to 3.4 per cent in 2014.
Foreign remittances in 2010 amounted to US$996 million (8.8 per cent of GDP), which rose to US$1.3 billion in 2011. By 2013, remittances accounted for 21.0 per cent of GDP, which was a 1.8 per cent increase on 2012. Remittances have, so far, averaged US$21.7 million in the four year period 2010–2014.
In 2014, the UN Human Development Index (HDI) ranked Armenia 87 (out of 187) for national development in health, education and income. Since 2000–10, Armenian progress has grown from below the average for European and Central Asian countries to slightly ahead of the average. In 2013, 32 per cent of the population lived below the national poverty line. This, following from similar figures in previous years, prompted the government to introduce programmes on social welfare to ameliorate the effect of the economic downturn on the most vulnerable, including family benefit payments, unemployment insurance, paid public works and pensions.
In 2009 the output of cut diamonds and their export was cut by 70 per cent (down to 70,600 carats) and rough cut diamond imports were down by 30 per cent as demand fell. However, as demand picked up in 2010, rough cut diamond imports also grew, with 20,000 carats imported in January alone. By 2013, the volume of diamond production was 94,498 carats, which was a 40 per cent increase on 2012 according to government figures. Armenia intends to increase the volume of diamond production by 300 per cent now that it eliminated a 6.5 per cent import custom duty from Russia.
Armenia has had to adapt in a world where it has to compete not only with other regional countries with similar prospects but with other much larger economies. The government has made structural reform a priority with efforts to make the economy a free market and encourage new sectors, which now include processed precious stones and jewellery production, information and communication technology and a nascent tourism industry. Older industries such as chemicals, electronic components, machinery, processed food, textiles and synthetic rubber, all of which are highly dependent on outside resources, are only being supported if they are viable and necessary to modern Armenia.

External trade
Armenia has regional trade agreements (RTAs) with eight neighbouring countries. It is a member of the World Trade Organisation (WTO) and benefits from the Aid for Trade scheme (sponsored by WTO), which offers trade related skills and financial infrastructure to developing countries.
On 19 October 2011, a free trade agreement (FTA) was signed by Russia with seven of its former Soviet republics: Armenia, Belarus, Kazakhstan, Kyrgyzstan, Moldova, Tajikistan and Ukraine. The FTA was ratified by all relevant parliaments before its instigation in 2012.
Armenia is a net exporter of electricity, supplying Georgia and the Nagorno-Karabakh region of Azerbaijan, although there has been external pressure applied to have its ageing nuclear power station closed down. Heavy industrial products have given way to light industrial products and agricultural produce for

export. All imported rough-cut diamonds are processed and exported. Precious metals, diamonds, pearls and other precious gems are worked into jewelry for export.
In total, the European Union imports almost three times as much Armenian goods and services each year as Russia, although Russia is Armenia's single largest trading partner.

Imports

Principal imports include natural gas and petroleum, foodstuffs, tobacco products, capital machinery, tools and rough-cut diamonds.
Main sources: Russia (25.7 per cent of total in 2014), China (10.0 per cent), Turkey (5.6 per cent).

Exports

Principal exports include electricity, diamonds, (other precious stones, pearls, lapis lazuli), precious metals and jewelry, base metals, mineral products, transport equipment, electrical equipment.
Main destinations: Russia (20.4 per cent of total in 2014), China (11.5 per cent), Germany (10.6 per cent).

Agriculture

Farming

Armenia is a major producer of grapes, vegetables, dairy products and some cotton and sheep breeding. Agriculture contributes around 21.9 per cent to GDP and employs about 45 per cent of the work force. Armenia was the first former Soviet republic to privatise agricultural land. There are around 335,000 family farms, which account for the bulk of agricultural output. Development has been inhibited by lack of private investment, an inadequate agricultural financing system and poor infrastructure.

Industry and manufacturing

The economy relies heavily on the industrial sector. Industry accounts for around 31.5 per cent of GDP and employs around 20 per cent of the workforce. Industry is mainly based on the extraction and processing of natural resources, particularly ores and chemicals.
Other industries are mechanical engineering, electronic generators, textiles, synthetic rubber, wine and cognac, mineral water and food processing.

Tourism

The tourist industry is based on Armenia's historic and cultural heritage, attracting its visitors from its diaspora in Russia, the US and Iran. Armenia is also the site of Mount Ararat, the location traditionally thought to be where Noah's Ark landed. The total contribution of travel and tourism to GDP in 2014 reached 12.7 per cent of GDP. This is forecaste to fall by 9.4 per cent in 2015 and rise by 2.6 per cent per annum from 2015–2025. This primary reflects the economic activity of hotels, travel agents and airlines.
The industry comprises 11.3 per cent of the total employment of the country. This is expected to fall by around 9.5 per cent in 2015, falling from 133,500 jobs to 121,000. This decrease could be due to economic weakening in countries that supply a lot of the visitors to Armenia, such as Turkey.

Mining

Mining accounts for around 13 per cent of GDP and employs 3 per cent of the workforce.
There are large deposits of copper, zinc, aluminium and other metals, including gold. Copper accounts for 38 per cent of the reserve, iron and molybdenum 25 per cent each; gold 7.3 per cent, silver 1.6 per cent and lead and zinc 3.1 per cent. Armenia is rich in varieties of building stone, such as marble, granite, tuffa, limestone and gypsum, and in semi-precious and ornamental stones, such as agates, jasper, amethyst and turquoise.
The major markets for Armenia's mining products are Belgium, Georgia, Iran, Liechtenstein, Switzerland and Germany.

Hydrocarbons

Armenia has no oil reserves and is completely dependent on imports of petroleum products, all of which are transported by rail or truck since there are currently no oil pipelines in Armenia. Oil imports amounted to 52,000 barrels per day (bpd) in 2014. Construction of a hydroelectric power station on the Aras River began in August 2012 after plans were discussed at a ministrial meeting in a 2008 when Iran and Armenia agreed to build a pipeline from Tabriz (Iran) to Eraskh (Armenia).
Armenia has no natural gas reserves. A 20-year agreement with Iran began in 2007, whereby 3.6 billion cubic metres (cum) of Iranian natural gas will be exchanged for Armenian electricity. The initial amount of 1.8 billion cum per annum will be doubled by 2019, with Armenia providing three kilowatts per one cum. A 137km gas pipeline was part of the agreement. Armenia imports some 2 billion cum of gas per year from Russia, via a pipeline from Georgia.
Imports of coal typically amount to around one million tonnes.

Energy

Installed electricity capacity was 3,472MW in 2013, generated by thermal, hydro and nuclear power. The ministry of energy oversees infrastructure projects and commercial energy companies providing electricity to end-users. There are 32 hydroelectric plants, which account for 34 per cent of production. Thermal power plants supply the remaining 26 per cent. Armenia is linked to Iran's grid, permitting two-way exchange of electricity. In December 2008 the energy minister announced the construction of a new nuclear power unit, at an estimated cost of US$5 billion, to provide 1,000MW, to be built by 2023. The plant will replace the existing Metsamor nuclear station, which was reopened in 1995 after its closure following the 1988 earthquake. Armenia has been under international pressure to close the plant. With a shared history, participation in Armenia's energy production by Russian companies is ongoing, including Rosatom (nuclear electricity generating).
Armenia and Iran are co-operating on development of renewable energy sources, including a new wind power plant with a capacity of 10.4MW.
In December 2011, an Iranian private consortium announced it would invest US$571 million in two power transmission lines between Armenia and Iran. The project will include an upgrade in the Aras River hydroelectric power plant to 1.7GW. In 2015 the project was still under construction.

Financial markets

Non-banking financial institutions (such as leasing organisations, insurance companies and investment funds) are either non-existent or at an early stage of development.
A Securities and Exchange Commission was established in November 1998.

Stock exchange

Armenia Stock Exchange (Armex)

Banking and insurance

The banking system in Armenia is growing but still experiences difficulties in attracting deposits (representing less than 10 per cent of GDP). Most lending is available at short maturities only and at high interest rates. The range of facilities and services on offer to customers is increasing. HSBC Armenia was one of the most active banks.
There are over 30 commercial banks in the country.

Central bank

Central Bank of the Republic of Armenia

Time

GMT plus three hours

Geography

Armenia is a landlocked country of high mountains and fertile valleys situated in south-west Transcaucasia. Georgia lies to the north of Armenia, to the west is the border with Turkey. Azerbaijan is to the east of the country – the ethnic Armenian enclave, Nagorno-Karabakh, is wholly within Azerbaijan – and to the south

Armenia has a short frontier with Iran. The autonomous republic of Nankhchivan, an Azerbaijani territory, is an enclave within southern Armenia. Lake Sevan is at an altitude of 1,924 metres and is surrounded by mountain ranges reaching 4,090 metres at Mount Aragats. Numerous rivers and streams flow from the mountains into the River Araks which marks the south-western border of the country, its basin forming a fertile lowland to the south of Yerevan – the Ararat Plain.

Hemisphere

Northern

Climate

Cool winters and hot summers characterise Armenia with the average January temperature in Yerevan at around 1 degree Celsius (C), while July averages 26 degrees C. Snow falls in early winter (November and December) and rain in April to June.

Annual rainfall in Yerevan averages 33cm but is much higher in mountain regions.

Entry requirements

Passports

Required by all. Must be valid at least four months after date of departure.

Visa

Required by all except nationals of CIS countries. An invitation is required for visits over 21 days.Visas can be obtained online: www.armeniaforeignministry.am/consular/visa.html.

Currency advice/regulations

There are no restrictions on import of local or foreign currency, but amounts over US$10,000 must be declared. Export of local or foreign currency unlimited, but cash restricted to US$10,000, amounts above which must be transferred through a bank.

Customs

Personal goods up to US$500 are duty-free. Advisable to declare valuables such as jewellery, cameras, computers and musical instruments.

Health (for visitors)

Mandatory precautions

None.

Advisable precautions

It is advisable to be in date for the following immunisations: tetanus (within 10 years), hepatitis A (moderate risk only); hepatitis B (if you need to spend more than six to eight weeks in the region); malaria precautions for western border areas only.

Any medicines required should be taken by the visitor. Take a medical kit including a disposable syringe. Food and water precautions should be observed.

Credit cards

Major credit cards and travellers cheques are accepted at the banks in Yerevan.

Public holidays (national)

Fixed dates

1–2 Jan (New Year), 6 Jan (Orthodox Christmas), 8 Mar (Women's Day), 7 Apr (Motherhood and Beauty Day), 24 Apr (Genocide Memorial Day), 9 May (Victory and Peace Day), 28 May (First Republic Day), 5 Jul (Constitution Day), 21 Sep (Independence Day), 7 Dec (Earthquake Memorial Day), 31 Dec (New Year's Eve).

Variable dates

Good Friday

Working hours

Banking

Mon–Fri: 0900–1800.

Business

Mon–Fri: 0900–1800.

Government

Mon–Fri: 0900–1730.

Shops

Mon–Fri: 0900–2000; Sat–Sun: 0900–1800.

Electricity supply

220V AC 50Hz

Weights and measures

Metric system

Social customs/useful tips

The Armenians are very hospitable and will invite strangers into their homes. Being unable to speak their language will not be a problem. Dress in rural areas should be modest.

Do not photograph military installations or equipment and seek permission to photograph religious buildings.

Security

Visitors should not travel to Nagorno-Karabakh in the west or the military occupied area surrounding it.

Getting there

Air

Armenia is increasingly accessible by air with flights from Europe, the Middle East and especially Moscow.

National airline: Armavia.

International airport/s: Zvartnots (EVN), 10km south-west of Yerevan; facilities include business and VIP halls plus duty-free shops, post office and cafés. The Asian Development Bank and the European Bank for Reconstruction and Development have agreed to assist in the construction of a new passenger terminal.in June 2013 Armenia International Airports agreed to an extensive resettlement plan for current residents.

Airport tax: A departure tax of US$20, excluding transit passengers.

Surface

Road: Access is from Georgia to the north and Iran to the south. Routes from Turkey and Azerbaijan are closed.

Rail: There is a service running from Batumi on the Black Sea, via Tbilisi and the Georgian border, to Yerevan. There are also connections fromTbilisi to Gyumri and to Vanadzor. The *gnatsk* is a through train, running on alternate days. Pre-booking is advised.

Getting about

National transport

Road: There are 7,705km (4,788 miles) of roads. The main roads are in reasonable condition, but local roads can be very poor.

Buses: Coaches operate between towns and city centres.

Rail: The railway system is aged and the service is unreliable.

City transport

Taxis: Taxis in Yerevan are unmetered. Expect to negotiate a fare to destination beforehand.

Buses, trams & metro: Vans (*marshrutnis*), charging a cheap flat fare, are the best way of travel in Yerevan. There is a short, single-line metro in Yerevan, which is cheap and efficient.

Car hire

Car rental services are available in Yerevan, but it is usual and advisable to hire a car and driver. Traffic drives on the right.

BUSINESS DIRECTORY

The addresses listed below are a selection only. While World of Information makes every endeavour to check these addresses, we cannot guarantee that changes have not been made, especially to telephone numbers and area codes. We would welcome any corrections.

Telephone area codes

The international direct dialling (IDD) code for Armenia is +374, followed by area code and subscriber's number:

Abovyan	222	Vanadzor	322
Gyumri	312	Yerevan	10

Chambers of Commerce

American Chamber of Commerce in Armenia, Hotel Armenia, 1 Amiryan Street, Yerevan 375010 (tel: 599-187; fax: 599-151; e-mail: amcham@arminco.com).

European Union Chamber of Commerce in Armenia, 8/1 Khorenatsi Street, Yerevan 375010 (tel: 547-760; fax: 547-780; e-mail: info@eucca.am).

Chamber of Commerce and Industry of the Republic of Armenia, 11 Khanjyan Street, Yerevan 375010 (tel: 560-184; fax: 587-871; e-mail: armcci@arminco.com).

Kotayk Marz Chamber of Commerce and Industry, 11 Sevani Street, Abovyan 378510 (tel: 26-035; fax: 233-97; e-mail: ccikotayk@ccikotayk.am).

Yerevan Chamber of Commerce and Industry, 11 Khanjyan Street, Yerevan 375010 (tel: 560-184; fax: 587-871; e-mail: yercci@arminco.com).

Banking

Ardshinbank of the Republic of Armenia, 3 Deghatan Street, Yerevan (tel: 560-611; fax: 151-155, 584-761).

Arminpex Bank, 2 Nalbandian Street, 375010 Yerevan (tel: 589-927, 567-183, 565-873; fax: 151-786, 151-815).

HSBC Armenia Bank, 1 Vramshapouh Arka Street, Yerevan (tel: 151-717; fax: 151-886).

Armeconombank, 32 G.Nzdehi Street, Yerevan 375026 (tel: 562-705, 531-115; fax: 151-149).

Armagrobank, 7a Movses Khorenacu Street, Yerevan 375015 (tel: 534-342; fax: 390-712-6).

Mellat, 1 P.Byusandy, Yerevan (tel: 581-354; fax: 151-811).

Prometeus, 19 Kochari Street, Yerevan 375012 (tel: 273-000; fax: 274-818).

Haykap, 22 Sarian Street, Yerevan 375002 (tel: 532-080; fax: 390-703-3).

Erebuni, 13 Khagakh- Don Street, Yerevan 375087 (tel: 577-256).

Credit - Yerevan, 2/8 Vramshapouh Arkay Street, Yerevan 375010 (tel: 589-065; fax: 580-083).

Central bank

Central Bank of Armenia, Vazgen Sargsyan Street 6, 375010 Yerevan (tel: 583-841; fax: 523-852); e-mail: mcba@cba.am).

Stock exchange

Armenia Stock Exchange (Armex) www.nasdaqomx.am/en/index.htm

Travel information

Armavia Airline Co Ltd, 3 Amiryan Street, 50 Mashtotsi Avenue, 0010 Yerevan(tel: 593-316; fax: 582-604; e-mail: armavia@infocom.am).

Levon Travel Bureau, 10 Sayat Nova Avenue, 375001 Yerevan (tel: 525-210; fax: 561-483; e-mail: tourism@levontravel.am).

National tourist organisation offices

Armenia Tourism Development Agency, 3 Nalbandyan Street, 0010 Yerevan (tel: 542-303; fax: 544-792; e-mail: help@armeniainfo.am).

Ministries

Ministry of Agriculture and Food Supplies, 1 Government House, Republican Square, 375010 Yerevan (tel: 524-641; fax: 151-086, 151-583).

Ministry of Communications, 22 Sarian Street, 375002 Yerevan (tel: 526-632; fax: 151-446; 151-151); Union Bldg, Republic Square, Yerevan 375010.

Ministry of Culture, Youth and Sports, 5 Toumanian Street, 375010 Yerevan (tel: 528-869, 561-920; fax: 523-930, 523-922, 526-869).

Ministry of Defence, Proshian Settlement, 60 G. Shaush Road, Yerevan (tel: 357-822; fax: 526-560).

Ministry of Ecology and Natural Resources, 35 Moskovian Street, 375012 Yerevan (tel: 530-741; fax: 534-902).

Ministry of Economical Structural Reform, 1 Government House, Republic Square, Yerevan 375010 (tel: 151-069).

Ministry of Education and Science, 13 Movses Khorenatsi Street, 375010 Yerevan (tel: 526-602; fax: 151-150).

Ministry of Energy, 1 Government House, Republican Square, 375010 Yerevan (tel: 521-964; fax: 151-036).

Ministry of Finance and Economy, 1 Melik-Adamian Street, 375010 Yerevan (tel: 527-082; fax: 151-154).

Ministry of Foreign Affairs, 2 Government House, Republican Square, 375010 Yerevan (tel: 523-531; fax: 151-042).

Ministry of Health, 8 Tumanian Street, 375001 Yerevan (tel: 582-413; fax: 151-097).

Ministry of Industry and Trade, Division of Tourism, 5 Hanrapetutjan Street, 375010 Yerevan (tel: 560-274, 560-780, 589-472, 587-706; fax: 526-577).

Ministry of Internal Affairs and National Security, 2 Nalbandian, 375025 Yerevan (tel: 529-733).

Ministry of Justice, 8 Parliament Street, 375010 Yerevan (tel: 582-157; fax: 565-640).

Ministry of Local Government Affairs, 2 Government House, Yerevan (tel: 525-274).

Ministry of Operational Affairs, 1 Government House, Republican Square, Yerevan 375010 (tel: 151-036; fax: 520-321).

Ministry of Privatisation and Foreign Investment, 1 Government House, Republic Square, Yerevan 375010 (tel: 520-351; fax: 151-036).

Ministry of Social Security, 18 Issahakian Street, 375025 Yerevan (tel: 526-831; fax: 151-920).

Ministry of Statistics and Data, State Registrar, Republican Square, 375010 Yerevan (tel: 524-213).

Ministry of Transport, 10 Zakiyan Street, 375015 Yerevan (tel: 563-391; fax: 525-268).

Ministry of Urban Planning and Construction, 1 Government House, Republican Square, Yerevan (tel: 589-080; fax: 151-036).

Prime Minister's Office, 1 Government House, Republican Square, 375101 Yerevan (tel: 520-360; fax: 151-035).

Other useful addresses

Armenian Embassy (USA), 2225 R Street, NW, Washington DC 20008 (tel: (+1-202) 319-1976; fax: (+1-202) 319-2982).

Armenian Foreign Trade Organisation, V/O Armentorg, Dom Pravitelstva, Ploschad Lenina, 375010 Yerevan.

Armenian Foundation for SMEs, 19 Khandjian Street, 375010 Yerevan (tel: 578-231; fax: 151-690; e-mail: smeda@arminco.com).

Armenian State Foreign Economic and Trade Association, Str 25 Hr Kochar, 375012 Yerevan (tel: 224-310; fax: 220-034).

Azat Mamoul (Dashnak News Agency), Yerevan (tel: 563-493; fax: 565-728).

British Embassy, 28 Charents Street, Yerevan (tel: 151-842; fax: 151-807).

Business Communication Centres, 6 Baghramian Avenue 2, 375009 Yerevan (tel: 222-145; fax: 151-934; e-mail: ggv@bcc.arminco.com).

Committee of Privatisation and Management of State Property, Ul Budakhian 1, 375014 Yerevan (tel: 280-120).

Department of Emergency Situations, Government House, Republican Square, Yerevan 375010 (tel: 531-612; fax: 151-036).

EC Energy Centre, Institute of Energy, Amaranotsayeen 127, Yerevan (tel/fax: 151-730).

Enterprise Development and Foreign Investment Promotion Armenian Agency (EDIPA), 23/1 Vramshapuh Arkah, Yerevan 375002 (tel: 538-929; fax: 151-149).

Secretariat of the Council of Ministers (tel: 520-360, 522-482; fax: 151-035, 141-036).

State Commission for Tax Inspection, Movses Khorenatsi, Yerevan 375010 (tel: 538-101, 538-073).

State Department for Statistics, State Register and Analysis of the Republic of Armenia, 3 Government House, Republic Square, Yerevan (tel: 524-213; fax: 521-921).

State TV and Radio, 5 Alex Manoogian, 375025 Yerevan (tel: 555-033).

TACIS (Technical Assistance to Commonwealth of Independent States), Ministry of Economy, 1 Government Building, Republic Square, Yerevan 10 (tel: 528-803; fax: 151-164).

US Embassy, 18 Baghramyan Avenue, Yerevan 375019 (tel: 520-791; fax: 520-800; e-mail: usinfo@arminco.com).

National news agency: Armenpress

Address: 4 Floor, 28 Isahakian Street, Yerevan 375009 (internet: www.armenpress.am).

Arka: www.arka.am

Arminfo: www.arminfo.info

Noyan Tapan: www.nt.am

Mediamax: www.mediamax.am

Internet sites

Armenian information: www.armgate.com

Armenia Yellow Pages: www.armenian.com

Arminfo News Agency: www.arminfo.am

Aruba

KEY FACTS

Official name: Aruba

Head of State: King William-Alexander of The Netherlands; Governor Fredis Refunjol (from 1 May 2004)

Head of government: Prime Minister Michiel (Mike) Godfried Eman (AVP) (from 31 Oct 2009)

Ruling party: Arubaanse Volks Partij (AVP) (Aruban People's Party) (from 25 Sep 2009; re-elected Sept 2013)

Area: 193 square km

Population: 106,113 (2011)* (101,848; 2010 census)

Capital: Oranjestad

Official language: Dutch

Currency: Aruban guilder (Af) = 100 cents (commonly called the florin)

Exchange rate: Af1.79 per US$ (Sep 2015)

GDP: US$2.58 billion (2011)*

Balance of trade: -US$1080.00 million (2013)*

Visitor numbers: 125 (2012)*

* estimated figure

COUNTRY PROFILE

1499 First European sighting of the islands of the Netherlands Antilles by Spanish mariners.
1636 Dutch took over; Spanish and Portuguese Jews escaping from persecution in Europe settled in the islands.
1800–02 British Protectorate.
1825 Gold discovered and mined until 1916.
1863 Slavery completely abolished.
1954 Internal autonomy was granted to Netherlands Antilles.
1986 Aruba seceded from Netherlands Antilles; both entities elected to remain part of the Kingdom of the Netherlands. Aruba has complete autonomy over its internal affairs; the Netherlands is constitutionally responsible for defence and external affairs.
2001 Movimiento Electoral di Pueblo (MEP) (People's Electoral Movement) won parliamentary elections and Nelson Oduber (MEP) became prime minister.
2003 A law was introduced in order to help fight money laundering more efficiently.
2004 Fredis Refunjol was sworn in as governor.
2005 MEP won parliamentary elections. The disappearance (and murder) of US-national, Natalee Holloway, caused an outcry in Alabama (her home state). A public protest began, calling for Aruba to be boycotted by all US tourists, for what was seen as an inept investigation and an accusation that Aruba's police service was incapable of protecting visitors. The risk to Aruba's tourist industry, with 930,000 US visitors spending US$2.3 million annually, prompted the US State Department to reassure its citizens and for the FBI to review the police case file. (A Dutch citizen, Joran van der Sloot, was arrested in Peru for killing a Peruvian student and convicted and sentenced to 28 years in prison in 2012; he was also suspected of killing Natalee Holloway).
2007 The chief prosecutor closed the official investigation into the case of Natalee Holloway (missing since 2005), even though at the time there had been no conviction.
2009 In parliamentary elections, the opposition Arubaanse Volks Partij (AVP) (Aruban People's Party) won 48 per cent of the vote (12 seats of 21), the incumbent MEP won 35.9 per cent (turnout was around 85 per cent). Mike Eman (AVP) took office as prime minister.
2010 The state-owned PetroChina began discussions to purchase the Aruba refinery, following an agreement by the US-based Valero Energy Corporation and the government resolving a long-standing dispute over business taxes. However, no agreement was reached.
2012 On 30 April, a memorandum of understanding was signed between PetroChina and the government to purchase the closed Valero Refinery (the second time PetroChina had made an approach, and again reached no conclusion). The US owners of the Valero Aruba Refinery announced on 4 September that it had decided to re-open and reorganise the facility as a refined oil products terminal, but with a reduced workforce. The refinery would be improved, but continue to supply diesel, petrol and jet fuel for domestic needs, and also act as a third-party terminal operation.
2013 the Central Bank of Aruba announced that it expected GDP to grow by 2.6 per cent in 2013, drive by growth in the tourism sector especially.
2014 On 23 July Fitch Ratings downgraded Aruba's long-term foreign and local currency issuer default ratings to BBB- from BBB. The following day minister of finance and government organisation, Juan David Yrausquin, said the Fitch report did not depict a true economic picture of Aruba. Prime Minister Mike Emanby began a hunger strike on 11 July after the Dutch government ordered the governor not to sign the Aruba budget for 2014, leaving the Aruba government furious about the Netherlands' interference.
2015 A decision was reached between the governments of The Netherlands, Aruba, Curaçao and St Maarten on 9 January whereby the four should work to agree a mechanism whereby future disagreements between the countries of the kingdom can be resolved. The result should be a proceedure to be followed to avoid disputes such as that between Aruba and the Netherlands over instructions as to its budget and St Maarten over problems with the reliability of politicians as candidates for ministerial posts.

Political structure

Form of state

Parliamentary democratic monarchy.
On 10 October 2010, the Caribbean islands of Curaçao and St Maarten joined Aruba (1986) as semi-autonomous countries within the Kingdom of the Netherlands; at the same time the Caribbean islands of Bonaire, St Eustatius and Saba became Bijzondere Gemeenten (special municipalities) of the Netherlands.

The executive

The Head of State is the monarch of The Netherlands, who is represented by a governor. The governor is appointed by the monarch, on the recommendation of the Aruban Council of Ministers.
Executive power is exercised by the governor and a prime minister who heads an eight-member council of ministers. The Council is accountable to the Staten (parliament).

National legislature

The unicameral parliament, Staten (Estates), has 21 members, elected for a four-year term by proportional representation.

Legal system

Aruba's judicial system, which has mainly been derived from the Dutch system, operates independently of the legislature and the executive. Jurisdiction, including appeal, lies with the Common Court of Justice of Aruba and the Supreme Court of Justice in The Netherlands.

Last elections

27 September 2013 (parliamentary)
Results: Arubaanse Volks Partij (AVP) (Aruban People's Party) won 57.3 per cent of the vote (13 seats out of 21), Movimiento Electoral di Pueblo (MEP) (People's Electoral Movement) 30.5 per cent (7), and Partido Democracia Real (PDR) (Real Democracy Party) 7.8 per cent (1). Turnout was 84.9 per cent.

Next elections

September 2017 (parliamentary)

Political parties

Ruling party

Arubaanse Volks Partij (AVP) (Aruban People's Party) (from 25 Sep 2009)

Main opposition party

Movimiento Electoral di Pueblo (MEP) (People's Electoral Movement)

Political situation

In 2009 Aruba and The Netherlands became embroiled in a governmental disagreement over who ultimately has power in Aruba. Under the auspices of the Kingdom Council of Minister, based in Willemstad (Holland), changes to the draft consensus of law establishing a joint court of justice and new constitutional relations were approved, after Aruba strongly objected then withdrew from talks. This provoked a series of complaints by Aruba that it had been sidelined as the only territory under consideration with direct concerns about the changes. By July, Aruba was threatening to take its complaint to the United Nation's Decolonisation Committee for adjudication, asserting the Netherlands would overrule its autonomy.
In October 2010 the Kingdom of the Netherlands was reconfigured to consist of the European country (including Caribbean municipal entities) and the Caribbean territories of Aruba, Curaçao and St. Martin.

Population

106,113 (2011)*
Last census: 29 September 2010: 101,848
Population density: 516 inhabitants per square km. Urban population: 51 per cent (1995—2001).
Annual growth rate: 0.2 per cent (2003)

Ethnic make-up

Carib and Arawak Indian, European and African heritage.

Religions

Roman Catholic (82 per cent), Protestant (8 per cent), Hindu, Muslim, Confucian, Jewish.

Education

Literacy rate: 97 per cent

Main cities

Oranjestad (capital, estimated population 28,849 in 2012), Sint Nicolas (15,293), Pos Chiquito (5,527), Palm Beach (Noord/Tanki Leendert) 5,371, Alto Vista (5,178).

Languages spoken

Papiamento is the local language. Dutch, English and Spanish are widely spoken.

Official language/s

Dutch

Media

Press

In Papiamento, from Oranjestad, *Diario* (http://news.diario-aruba.com), *Bon Dia* (www.bondia.com), *AWE Mainta* (www.awemainta.com) and *Solo di Pueblo* (www.solodipueblo.com) published in Santa Cruz. In Dutch, with an English edition, *Amigoe* (www.amigoe.com). In English, *Aruba Today* (www.arubatoday.com).

Broadcasting

Radio: In Papiamento, Dutch and English, Radio Kelkboom (www.watapana-aruba.com) broadcasts news, talk and music. There are several other commercial music and religious programme stations including Hit FM (www.hit94fm.com), Magic 96.5 (www.magic965.com), Mega 88FM (www.mega88fm.com) and Cool FM (www.coolaruba.com).
Television: Tele-Aruba (www.telearuba.aw) provides a comprehensive service with locally produced news, current affairs, educational, cultural and sports as well as imported programmes. There are several cable and satellite TV stations, some of which are also US affiliates, including Cable TVAruba (CTA) (www.cta.aw), Venevisión, Flamingo TV, ATV and Caribbean Super Station.
Other news agencies: The Governor of Aruba: www.kabga.aw
Caribbean Net News: www.caribbeannetnews.com

Economy

The service sector is the major component of the economy – contributing 83.2 per cent to GDP in 2014 – in particular tourism and financial services; the industrial sector is still important, as crude oil from regional sources is imported, refined and traded on. Construction, led by tourism, also provides employment and growth. Agriculture is largely composed of animal husbandry, as the island's soil is arid and unproductive. Other, less obvious sources of economic growth include trade in fine art and collectables.
After emerging out of recession due to global economic crisis and reach a growth of 3.7 per cent in 2011, GDP shrunk again in 2012 by 1.2 per cent. However following this double dip the economy turned around in 2013 and recorded a growth of 2.3 per cent. In response to experiencing biggest slump in any economy in the Caribbean in 2009, the Aruban government loosened its fiscal policies, cut a business tax and increased social payments to mitigate the impact of the recession.
Due to such a large part of the economy being reliant on the oil refining and tourism industries, the government is in the process of expanding over industries such as finance, technology and communications to protect the country from slumps in global tourism and oil. Offshore banking has become one of the mainstays of the economy.

External trade

Aruba is an Overseas Country and Territory (OCT) of The Kingdom of the Netherlands and benefits from free trade with any EU member. Aruba also has free trade agreements (FTA) with the US, Canada, Malaysia and India. Aruba has regional associations for trade with countries of the Economic Commission for Latin America and the Caribbean (Eclac), Caribbean Development Co-operation Committee (CDCC) and the Association of Caribbean States (ACS). Although not a member of the World Trade Organisation (WTO), Aruba uses developments

within the WTO to determine its trading practices.
Trans-shipment brings in important foreign exchange and Aruba offers free trade zones (situated near the harbour of Oranjestad and Barcadera) and activities, to foreign interests. Oil refining is an important industry, taking crude oil from regional sources for trading on.

Imports

Crude oil is imported for refining. Other products include foodstuffs, machinery, electrical equipment and chemicals.
Main sources: US (typically 50 per cent of total), The Netherlands (16 per cent), UK (5 per cent).

Exports

Main exports include refined petroleum products, live animals, animal products, art and collectables, machinery and electronic equipment and vehicles.
Main destinations: Panama (typically 24 per cent of total), The Netherlands Antilles (21 per cent), Colombia (18 per cent).

Re-exports

Refined oil and petroleum products.

Industry and manufacturing

Tourism is the dominant industry in Aruba. Industry accounts for over 16 per cent of the country's GDP.

Tourism

Aruba has many Caribbean attractions and offers diversions for holidaymakers including sports, natural history and leisure pastimes. Most visitors arrive from North America, plus Aruba has cultural ties to The Netherlands and northern South America.
Travel and tourism in total accounted for 88.4 per cent of GDP in 2014, with 32.5 per cent of total employment supported directly in the sector (16,500 jobs) and 90.8 per cent of total employment indirectly supported the industry. Visitor numbers steadily increased from 2009–12, as arrivals from the US returned following the global economic crisis. On 17 December 2014 the island welcomed its one millionth stay-over visitor in a year for the first time. Total stay-over visitors for 2014 were 1.07 million, a 9.5 per cent increase over 2013.
Over 300 cruise ships visit Aruba each year and the ministry of tourism is active in attracting more vessels to visit and 'enhance the experience' of passengers when they arrive. Construction of the new, 320-room Ritz-Carlton Hotel, sited in Palm Beach (considered one of the best Aruban locations for Caribbean beaches), was completed in 2012.

Hydrocarbons

There are no known hydrocarbons reserves. Consumption of oil was 5,970 barrels per day (bpd) in 2013, all of which was imported. Crude oil makes up over 95 per cent of all oil imported and is re-exported as refined oil; there is one refinery with a capacity of 275,000bpd. Oil exports are a major component of GDP and foreign exchange earnings.
The owners of the Valero Aruba Refinery announced in August 2014 that they would be 'abandoning' the facility, however Valero still operates owns and operates a terminal there. This was the second time the refinery was forced to be closed down due to low margins since 2009. Valero stated that it might continue operate the site as a terminal and storage operation.
Any use of natural gas or coal is commercially insignificant.

Energy

Total installed generating capacity was 266MW in 2013, generating over 980 million kilowatt hours. The state-owned, WEB Aruba NV is responsible for electricity generation, while NV Elmar is the sole provider of electricity on the island and responsible for transmission, distribution and sales.
The government is reviewing the installation of wind-powered generators.

Banking and insurance

The banking sector consists of six commercial banks, two of which are branches of banks established in The Netherlands and Curaçao, one is a subsidiary of a bank established in Curaçao and three have their head offices in Aruba.
Aruba is a signatory of an EU tax agreement that was introduced in July 2005. It has agreed to pass on, to the tax department of an EU citizen's country, information concerning the amount of money in savings accounts, to allow tax to be levied from the account holder's home country. Aruba has also agreed to supply information on tax fraud, for criminal or civil trials, and notify EU member states about additional malpractices.

Central bank

Centrale Bank van Aruba (CBA)

Offshore facilities

The offshore banking sector has great potential. The Central Bank has been better equipped to regulate the banking sector since the enactment of the State Ordinance on the Supervision of the Credit System, 1998.

Time

GMT minus four hours

Geography

Located in the Caribbean Sea north of Venezuela, Aruba is a flat island with large white sandy beaches and sparse vegetation. The highest point is Mount Jamanota which is 188 metres above sea level.

Hemisphere

Northern

Climate

Aruba lies outside the Caribbean's hurricane zone. It has an almost constant temperature of 27 degrees Celsius with cooling trade winds and an absence of tropical storms and hurricanes. Low levels of humidity and rainfall.

Entry requirements

Passports

Required by all, except nationals of US and Canada, who only need proof of citizenship, and of EU countries with EU Travel Cards. (NB citizens of Canada and US require passports for re-entry to their countries).
Passports must be valid for at least three months after arrival. A return or onward ticket and adequate funds are required.

Visa

Not required, except by nationals of former Communist and some other countries. For details, visit http://www.visitaruba.com/travel/toaruba/customs.html or contact the nearest embassy.

Currency advice/regulations

Import/export of Aruban currency is forbidden. No restriction on import of foreign currencies, but a licence is required for export.

Customs

Besides articles for personal use, persons aged over 18 are allowed 2 litres of alcohol and 200 cigarettes, 50 cigars and 250 grammes of tobacco.

Health (for visitors)

Mandatory precautions

Yellow fever vaccination certificate required if arriving from an infected area.

Advisable precautions

hepatitis A and B and typhoid vaccinations.

Hotels

There are numerous tourist hotels. It is advisable to book in advance. There is a 17.66 per cent service and government tax on room prices and a 10–15 per cent charge on food and drinks.

Public holidays (national)

Fixed dates

1 Jan (New Year's Day), 25 Jan (G F Croe's Day),18 Mar (National Anthem and Flag Day), 30 Apr (Queen's Day), 1 May (Labour Day), 25 Dec (Christmas Day), 26 Dec (Boxing Day).

Variable dates

Good Friday, Easter Monday, Ascension Day.

Working hours

Banking

Mon–Fri: 0800–1600.

Business
Mon–Fri: 0800–1200, 1300–1700.
Government
Mon–Fri: 0800–1200, 1300–1700. Sat: 0800–1200.
Shops
Mon–Sat: 0800–1800. Some shops close 1200–1400 every working day. Malls and shopping centres open 9.30–1800.

Telecommunications

Mobile/cell phones
GSM 900/1800 services are available, with coverage throughout the island.

Electricity supply

110/120V 60 cycles

Getting there

Air
Regular flights from US, Venezuela, Colombia and The Netherlands. In late 2013 it was reported that Tiara Air Aruba was owed so much by Venezuela that it was under financial stress.
International airport/s: Reina Beatrix (AUA), 2.5km from Oranjestad, duty-free shop, bar, restaurant, post office, car hire.
Airport tax: Except for transit passengers, US destinations US$36.75, all other international destinations US$33.50.
Surface
Main port/s: Oranjestad, Sint Nicolaas and Barcadera are deep-water harbours.

Getting about

National transport
Road: A well-developed road system connects all major towns.
Buses: Regular services in and around main centres. Also *jitney* services and sightseeing tours.
City transport
Taxis: Usually identified by 'TX' before the licence number. Taxis are not metered; fares are government-controlled according to destination.
Car hire
Prices are reasonable. An international licence is required. Driving is on the right.

BUSINESS DIRECTORY

The addresses listed below are a selection only. While World of Information makes every endeavour to check these addresses, we cannot guarantee that changes have not been made, especially to telephone numbers and area codes. We would welcome any corrections.

Telephone area codes

The international dialling code (IDD) for Aruba is +297, followed by subscriber's number.

Chambers of Commerce

Aruba Chamber of Commerce and Industry, 10 JE Irausquin Boulevard, PO Box 140, Oranjestad (tel: 582-1566; fax: 583-3962; businessinfo@arubachamber.com).

Banking

ABN-AMRO Bank NV, Caya GF Betico Croes 89, Oranjestad (tel: 821-515; fax: 821-856).

Aruba Bank NV, Caya GF Betico Croes 41, PO Box 192, Oranjestad (tel: 821-550; fax: 829-152).

Aruban Investment Bank NV, Middenweg 20, PO Box 1011, Oranjestad (tel: 827-327; fax: 827-461).

Banco di Caribe, Caya GF Croes 90, Oranjestad (tel: 832-168; fax: 832-422).

Caribbean Mercantile Bank NV, Caya GF Betico Croes 53, PO Box 28, Oranjestad (tel: 823-118; fax: 824-373).

First National Bank of Aruba NV, Caya GF Betico Croes 67, Oranjestad (tel: 833-221; fax: 821-756).

Interbank Aruba, Caya GF Betico Croes 38, Oranjestad (tel: 831-080; fax: 824-058).

Central bank
Centrale Bank van Aruba, JE Irausquin Boulevard 8, Oranjestad (tel: 525-2100; fax: 525-2101).

Travel information

Aruba Cruise Tourism, Royal Plaza Mall, Suite 230, LG Smith Blvd 94, Oranjestad (tel: 583-3648; email: info@ArubaByCruise.com; internet: www.arubabycruise.com).

Tiara Air Aruba, Sabana Blanco 70E, Suite 11, Oranjestad, Aruba (tel: 528 4272)

National tourist organisation offices
Aruba Tourism Authority, L G Smith Boulevard 172, Eagle (tel: 821-019; fax: 834-702).

Aruba Tourism Authority P R, A Schutte Str 2, Oranjestad (tel: 823-778, 823-779, 837-254; fax: 830-075; internet site: http://www.arubatourism.com).

Ministries

Ministry of Economic Affairs and Tourism, Government of Aruba, L G Smith Boulevard 76, Oranjestad (tel: 826-977; fax: 835-084).

Ministry of Finance, Oranjestad (tel: 823-237; fax: 827-116).

Ministry of Foreign Affairs, J E Irausquinplein 2A, Oranjestad (tel: 583-4705; fax: 583-8108)

Ministry of Public Works and Public Health, L G Smith Boulevard, Oranjestad (tel: 824-900; fax: 826-826).

Ministry of Traffic, Communications and Utilities, Oranjestad (tel: 824-900; fax: 835-985).

Cabinet of the Minister Plenipotentiary of Aruba, R J Schimmelpennincklaan 1, 2517 JN The Hague, The Netherlands (tel: (+3170) 356-6200; fax: (+3170) 356-6210).

Other useful addresses

Aruba Foreign Investment Agency, 85 Caya G F Betico Croes, Oranjestad (tel: 826-070; fax: 822-745).

Aruba Trade & Industry Association, Pedro Gallegostraat 6, PO Box 562, Oranjestad (tel: 827-593).

Department of Economic Affairs, Commerce and Industry, L G Smith Boulevard 160, Sun Plaza Building, Oranjestad (tel: 821-181, 821-482; fax: 834-494).

The Governor of Aruba: www.kabga.aw

Caribbean Net News: www.caribbeannetnews.com

Internet sites

Aruba government: www.aruba.com

Aruba online: www.arubatourism.com

Visit Aruba: www.visitaruba.com

Ascension Island

KEY FACTS

Official name: Ascension Island

Head of State: Queen Elizabeth II, represented by Governor and Commander-in-Chief, Mark Andrew Capes (from 29 Oct 2011) (resides in St Helena)

Head of government: Administrator of Ascension Island Marc Holland (from 24 Aug 2014)

Ruling party: Seven independent members represent constituents on an Island Council

Area: 88 square km

Population: 873 (2011)

Capital: Georgetown

Official language: English

Currency: St Helena Pound (£) = 100 pence

Exchange rate: £0.66 per US$ (Sep 2015)

COUNTRY PROFILE

1501 Ascension Island was sighted by the Portuguese mariner Juan da Nova.

1815 The UK took possession (on Napoleon's exile to St Helena) and established a garrison.

1823 Responsibility for the island was taken over by the Admiralty Board until 1922, when it became a dependency of St Helena.

1922–64 The Island was managed by the Eastern Telegraph Company (renamed Cable and Wireless in 1934).

1942 The US constructed a military airstrip by arrangement with the UK government and the island became an important transit point on the South African route between 1943–45.

1957 A US presence was re-established with the extension of the Eastern Test Range, and in 1967, a Nasa tracking station was built (since closed).

1964 In view of plans to establish BBC and Composite Signals Organisation (CSO) stations, an administrator was appointed.

1982 The island was re-garrisoned during the Falklands War and Ascension Island remains the intermediate stop for Royal Air Force (RAF) flights from the UK to the Falkland Islands.

1999 Geoffrey Fairhurst became the administrator.

2002 A referendum, in which 95 per cent of the islanders voted, agreed to the formation of an Island Council under the leadership of the administrator. Income tax and customs duties replaced the island's former tax-free status. Andrew Michael Kettlewell was appointed administrator. The first general election was held on 1 November.

2004 Michael Clancy became governor, resident in St Helena. Command of the renamed Ascension Island Base was transferred from Headquarters Strike Command (RAF High Wycombe), to the Permanent Joint Headquarters (PJHQ), Northwood, London.

2005 Michael Thomas Hill was appointed as the new administrator. Elections for the second Ascension Island Council were held.

2006 The Administrator's Office was renamed Administration Department.

2007 Six out of seven island councillors resigned in protest at a decision by the UK Foreign and Commonwealth Office (FCO) not to grant UK Right of Abode, Land Tenure, Fiscal Development and Social Development as previously announced, when taxation and democratic representation was introduced. The FCO had said that it wanted to create a settled society but the projected costs for the plans proved prohibitive and were rejected by the UK government. The Ascension Island Council was dissolved and business suspended for twelve months, with interim power reverting to the governor.

2008 The governor published a consultation document setting out a framework for the new Island Council and offering a period of consultation. Ross Denny became the new Administrator. An election for the Island Council was held.

2009 The FCO minister announced a new constitution for Ascension Island, which included a bill of rights and limits to the power of the governor. The Island council later voted in favour of the proposed changes.

2010 A formal meeting of the Island council discussed the €15.5 million (US$22.6 million) from the European Development Fund (EDF) (to be shared out between St Helena, Ascension Island and Tristan da Cunha) to provide finance for the road network. The UN dismissed the claim of sovereignty rights, by the UK government, over 200,000 square kilometres of seabed around Ascension Island; the UK was interested particularly in the oil and mineral rights.

2011 Administrator Ross Denny announced in June that Colin Wells would be his replacement as the new Administrator of Ascension Island from September. On 23 September, Governor Gurr's term in office ended when he retired and his replacement, Mark Andrew Capes took up the post on 29 October. Elections for the Island Council in October; seven independent candidates were elected. Colin Wells became the island administrator on 27 October.

2012 On 15 September, Mark Simmonds was appointed as the new minister for the South Atlantic British Overseas Territories.

2013 In June Ascension Island was transformed from a tranquil island to a hub of activity as it became a US support outpost for President Obama's 6-day visit to

Senegal, South Africa and Tanzania. Overall, more than 2 million kilos of cargo, 1,600 passengers and 103 aircraft transitted the island. On average, one military aircraft arrived or departed Ascension's airfield every 3.5 hours for 24 straight days, making the operation the largest movement of military equipment and personnel through Ascension Island since the Falklands War in 1982. At the peak of the operation, the influx of deployed troops increased the island's population by over 25 per cent. On 2 October Governor Capes announced that an election would be held on 31 October for the five members of the Ascension Island Council.

2014 Marc Holland was sworn in as the 19th Administrator of Ascension Island on 26 August.

2015 Black triggerfish, or simply 'blackfish' as the Ascension locals call them, are piranha like and whereas in nearly every imaginable tropical reef habitat around the world their numbers are modest, around Ascension Island, they literally swarm.

Political structure

Constitution

The Ascension Island is a dependency of St Helena, which is a British Overseas Territory. The governor of St Helena appoints an administrator, who is responsible for the daily management of Ascension Island.Constitutional changes led to the first Ascension Island council taking office on 1 November 2002.

The executive

The Ascension Island government (AIG) is headed by the administrator, under the jurisdiction of the governor of St Helena who has overall control of defence, external affairs, internal security and the public service. Local services are managed by the AIG; the UK government has overall responsibility for good governance and island security.

National legislature

A directly elected seven-seat Island Council, plus two *ex-officio* appointees, (a director of financial services and attorney general) advise the administrator on matters of law and policy.

Last elections

31 October 2013 (Island Council)

Results: The seven elected Councillors are independent members.

Political parties

Ruling party

Seven independent members represent constituents on an Island Council

873 (2011)

Population

There is no indigenous or permanent population, instead the community is comprised of contract workers and their families and military personnel.

Last census: March 1998: 712

Population density: 14 inhabitants per sq km.

Ethnic make-up

St Helenians, UK and US citizens.

Religions

Anglican and Roman Catholic

Main cities

There are no cities. Georgetown is the administrative capital and port (estimated population 560 in 2003). Two Boats village is a residential area; Traveller's Hill is the RAF garrison; Cat Hill is the US base.

Languages spoken

Official language/s

English

Media

Press

The only newspaper is *The Islander* (www.the-islander.org.ac), which is published weekly.

Broadcasting

The Ascension Island acts as a relay station for the BBC World Service (www.bbc.co.uk/worldservice) that broadcasts to Africa and provides radio programmes to the island along with the British Forces Broadcasting Service (BFBS) and the US military's Volcano Radio and TV services, which are also available to residents.

Economy

Ascension Island's main importance is as a military base and communications centre to the United Kingdom (UK). The cost of government net of revenue is about £1.85 million (US$3.0 million). Public services, public works, healthcare facilities and the pier head are funded by the military and commercial organisations on the island. They each contribute an agreed sum annually.

Tax and customs duties were introduced in 2002.

In 2013 a building project was begun to construct new homes to be owned by residents, with a view to increasing the population from under 900 to 1,500. The pier head facility has been improved for both public and commercial use.

Cable and Wireless plc operates an international satellite telecommunications service and the Ariane Earth Station on behalf of the European Space Agency (ESA). The BBC operates its Atlantic relay station broadcasting to Africa and South America.

The prospect of oil and natural gas around Ascension Island prompted the UK government to claim up to 200,000 square kilometres of the Atlantic Ocean for its mineral rights. But in June 2010, the United Nations Commission on the Limits of the Continental Shelf (CLCS) concluded that the volcanic shaft that is crowned by the Ascension Island was too slender to possess rights and the claim was dismissed. Under the UN Convention of the Sea, a state is allowed sovereignty across the ocean bed for up to 321km, if it can be demonstrated that there is continuity of the continental shelf.

Agriculture

Farming

There is no trace of industrial agriculture or fishing, however, the waters around Ascension Island are home to some very rare aquatic creatures. For example, there is a species of marteralia or flying squid that inhabit the waters around Ascension.

Fishing

There is a species of marteralia or flying squid that inhabit the waters around Ascension.

Tourism

The prospects for the tourist industry are limited due to the isolated nature of Ascension Island and the tourist infrastructure is minimal. However, for those that make the journey, diving is a popular pastime and the island is renowned for its wildlife. The only air access to the island is via Royal Air Force flights from the UK. By sea there are commercial ships; one is chartered to deliver supplies twice a year from Portland (UK) and another sails monthly from Cape Town (South Africa) and Walvis Bay (Namibia), via two other British South Atlantic territories (St Helena and Tristan de Cunha). This ship is operated under contract by Passenger Services Department, Andrew Weir Shipping Ltd (see travel information addresses).

Environment

In 2002, the British government gave £500,000 to the Royal Society for the Protection of Birds (RSPB) to clear the Island of rats and feral cats that were destroying the seabird population. Ascension Island is also an important breeding colony for the green turtle.

Hydrocarbons

Ascension Island relies entirely on imports of hydrocarbons. It imports around 200 barrels per day of oil.

Energy

Energy is produced by a number of means, including diesel and six wind turbines providing a generating capacity of over 270MW.

Banking and insurance

International banking facilities are available through the Bank of St Helena, including exchanging travellers' cheques and credit card facilities; foreign currency exchange is not offered.

Time
GMT

Geography
Ascension Island lies in the South Atlantic, north-west of St Helena. It is a rocky peak of volcanic origin with 44 craters. The last eruption took place about 600 years ago. The highest point is Green Mountain.

Hemisphere
Southern

Climate
The climate is sub-tropical. Showers occur throughout the year with slightly heavier rain in January–April.

Entry requirements
There is an £11 entry permit fee.

Visa
All visitors must have the Administrator's written permission to land, before beginning their visit. An Ascension Island Entry Permit form can be downloaded from www.ascension-island.gov.ac/visitors.htm and faxed for submission on (+247) 6152. Entry is only granted with evidence a full medical insurance policy, including medical evacuation.

Customs
Customs duties exist on alcohol, tobacco and petrol/diesel. Small amounts of personal goods are duty-free (see website above).

Hotels
A new consortium operates all public accommodation, including the Georgetown Obsidian Hotel (www.obsidian.co.ac, tel/fax: 6246, e-mail: accommodation@atlantis.co.ac).

Working hours
Banking
Mon–Fri: 0830–1500, except Thur: 0830–1230

Government
Mon–Fri: 0830–1230, 1330–1630.

Telecommunications
Telephone/fax
Direct satellite telephone

Getting there
Air
There is a twice-weekly RAF Tristar flight (Mondays and Thursdays) that departs from RAF Brize Norton, Oxfordshire. Bookings can be made through Passenger Services Department, Andrew Weir Shipping Ltd (see travel information addresses).

Surface
Water: The RMS *St Helena* operates twice a year from the UK (Portland) and monthly from Cape Town to Walvis Bay (Namibia), St Helena and Ascension Island. The ship is operated under contract by Passenger Services Department, Andrew Weir Shipping Ltd (see travel information addresses).

Main port/s: Georgetown

Getting about
Car hire
Cars can be hired for £20 per day.

BUSINESS DIRECTORY
The addresses listed below are a selection only. While World of Information makes every endeavour to check these addresses, we cannot guarantee that changes have not been made, especially to telephone numbers and area codes. We would welcome any corrections.

Telephone area codes
The international dialling code (IDD) for Ascension Island is +247 followed by subscriber's number.

Travel information
Passenger Services Department, Andrew Weir Shipping Ltd, Dexter House, 2 Royal Mint Court, London EC N4XX, UK (tel: +44 (0)207-575-6480; fax: +44 (0)207-575-6200; internet: www.aws.co.uk; e-mail: reservations@aws.co.uk).

St Helena Line, Andrew Weir Shipping (SA) Pty Ltd, 3rd Floor, BP Centre, Thibault Square, Cape Town, South Africa (tel: +27-21-425-1165; fax: +27-21-421-7485; e-mail: sthelenaline@mweb.co.za).

Miss Kerry Yon, Solomon and Co Plc (agents for St Helena Line), Jamestown, St Helena, South Atlantic (tel: +290-2523; fax: +290-2423; e-mail: solco.shipping@helanta.sh).

Ministries
The AIG telephone number is 7000, which will take the caller to a pre-recorded menu, from which the caller can identify and dial the extension of the contact required.

Administrator's Office, Islander Building, Georgetown (tel: 6311; fax: 6152; e-mail: andrew.kettlewell@ascension.gov.ac; internet site: http://www.ascension-island.gov.ac).

Chief Executive Officer, Ascension Island Works and Services Agency (AIWSA), Jamestown, St Helena (tel: 6346; fax: 6139; e-mail: chiefexecutive.aiwsa@atlantis.co.ac).

Other useful addresses
St Helena Government Representative, Suite 5, 30b Wimpole St, London W1G 8YB, UK (tel: +44 (0)207-224-5025; fax: +44 (0)207-224-5035).

St Helena Desk Officer, Foreign and Commonwealth Office, Room, King Charles Street, London SW1A 2AH, UK (tel: +44 (0)207-270-2695).

Miles Apart (books, maps, videos on South Atlantic Islands), 5 Harraton House, Exning, Newmarket, Suffolk CB8 7HF, UK (tel: +44 (0)1638-577-627: fax: +44 (0)1638-577-874); 5929 Avon Drive, Bethesda, Maryland 20814, USA (tel/fax: +1301-571-8942; e-mail: familycarter@msn.com).

The Islander, Fort Hayes, Georgetown (tel/fax: 6327; e-mail: the-islander@org.ac; internet site: http://www.the-islander.org.ac).

Internet sites
Andrew Weir Shipping: http://www.aws.co.uk

Ascension Island government: http://www.ascension-island.gov.ac

Australia

KEY FACTS

Official name: Commonwealth of Australia

Head of State: Queen Elizabeth II (since 1952), represented by Governor General Sir Peter Cosgrove (from 28 Mar 2014)

Head of government: Prime Minister Malcolm Turnbull (ALP) (elected party leader in snap poll 14 Sep 2015, sworn in 15 Sep 2015)

Ruling party: Liberal-National (LN) coalition (from 7 Sep 2013)

Area: 7,682,300 square km

Population: 23.59 million (2014)*

Capital: Canberra

Official language: English

Currency: Australian dollar (A$) = 100 cents

Exchange rate: A$1.43 per US$ (Sep 2015)

GDP per capita: US$61,219 (2014)*

GDP real growth: 2.71% (2014)*

GDP: US$1,444.19 billion (2014)

Labour force: 12.38 billion (2014)

Unemployment: 6.07% (2014)*

Inflation: 2.49% (2014)*

Oil production: 448,000 bpd (2014)

Natural gas production: 55.30 billion cum (2014)

Balance of trade: US$323.00 million (2014)*

* estimated figure

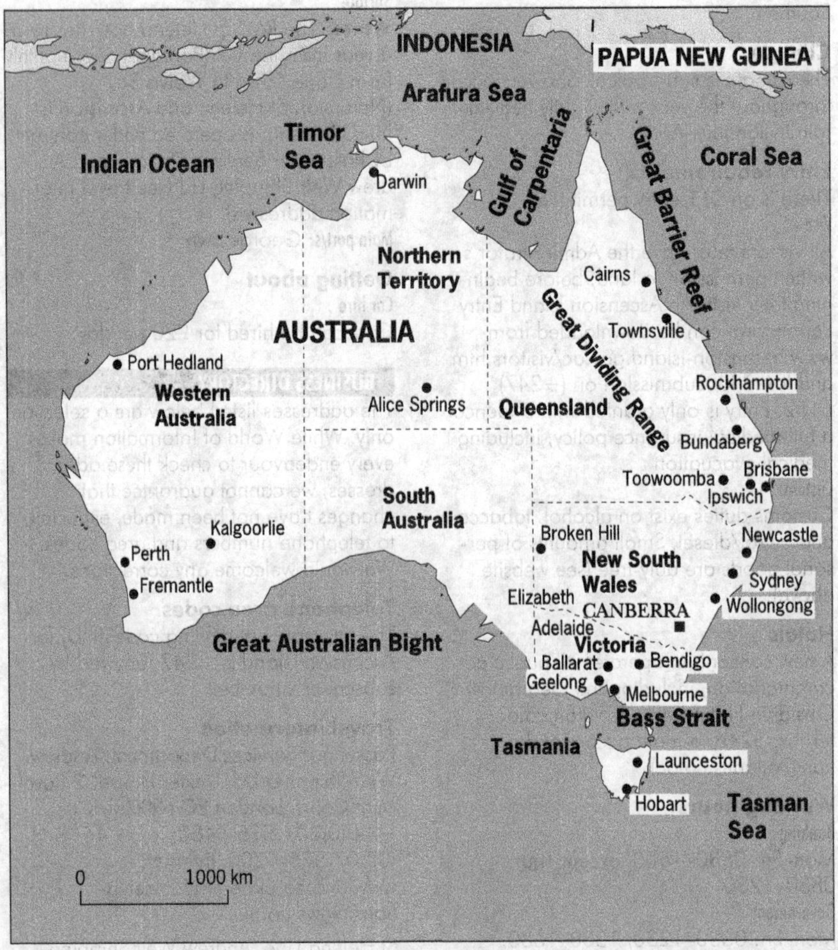

The writer, John Patrick O'Grady, once said of his fellow Australians 'There is no better way of life in the world than that of the Australian. I firmly believe this. The grumbling, growling, cursing, profane, laughing, beer drinking, abusive, loyal-to-his-mates Australian is one of the few free men left on this earth. He fears no one, crawls to no one, bludges on no one and acknowledges no master. Learn his way. Learn his language. Get yourself accepted as one of him; and you will enter a world that you never dreamed existed. And once you have entered it, you will never leave it.' The description has a ring of truth to it.

Governing... just

If Mr O'Grady's description is in any way accurate, it certainly explains why an ability to govern with a light touch has not always been the uppermost feature of Australia's leaders. A year and half after his election victory over the feuding Labor Party (the leaders of which were described by the author Germaine Greer thus: 'Gillard is as likeable as Rudd is charmless. She is self-deprecating; he is ludicrously vainglorious. She is a mistress of understatement; he is a ranter.') Prime Minister Tony Abbott (Liberal-National Coalition (LN)) certainly seemed to be as cack-handed as many of his predecessors. Inappropriate, off the cuff remarks had swiftly stamped him as a political laughing-stock. In early February Mr Abbott had managed to avoid a leadership contest when his Liberal Party voted against the idea by 61 votes to 39. The 22 vote margin hardly amounted to a vote of confidence. To many Liberal supporters it was merely a reflection of the lack of any obvious alternative.

Elsewhere in Australia, however, alternatives did exist. In late January 2015, the premier of Australia's Queensland state, Campbell Newman (Liberal Party), called a snap election reflecting fears that Mr Abbot's plummeting poll numbers risked eroding his party's grip at the local level and possibly endangering his political survival. He was right. The state's Labor Party leader, Annastacia Palaszczuk was sworn in as Queensland's premier, in a dramatic reversal of the political reversal seen at the last election when the Labor Party were swept out of power. However, it wouldn't be Australia if a close election result of this sort went unchallenged. The victory of Queensland's Labor Party was achieved after two weeks of legal wrangling between the parties over disqualified candidates and the losing Liberal-National (LN) insistence that it should continue as a caretaker government. The Queensland election gave Labor 44 seats to the LNP's 42 a massive swing away from the Newman government, deposed less than three years after what many considered to be the greatest electoral landslide in Australian political history in 2012 when Mr Newman's LN won 78 of the 89 seats in the Queensland legislative assembly.

The Queensland result did not bode well for Mr Abbott. Quite apart from his manifest political shortcomings, he also had to face the prospect of a faltering economy (see Economy below) which had pushed his national approval ratings to all-time lows. Two months after Mr Abbott's election victory, opinion polls had shown Labor to be ahead of the ruling Liberal-National coalition by a reported 52 points to 48, an almost exact reversal of the voting pattern in the election. Such an unprecedented swing was attributed, *inter alia*, to Mr Abbott's introduction of what one observer described as 'the worst budget in history'. Among other things, the budget was to create a proposed 16,000 public sector job losses.

Queensland premier Newman's surprise decision to call an election followed earlier defeats for Mr Abbott's Liberal-National coalition in state elections in Victoria and in a by-election that handed government in South Australia to the opposition Labor Party. As reported on the *Guardian Australia* website, Mr Newman's decision to call the election during parliament's summer break suggested a 'lack of confidence in Mr Abbott's ability to turn things around.'

The electorate's national disenchantment with the Abbott government had also seen the Labor Party rise in the opinion polls to take an 8 per cent lead over the NL according to a December 2014 opinion poll.

The economy

Australia, the world's biggest exporter of iron ore and coal, has been battered by a worldwide fall in commodity prices. In many respects the Australian economy's dependence on exported raw materials gives it more in common with Saudi Arabia than with South Korea. Australian manufacturing's total share of gross domestic product is 6.8 per cent. High-tech exports account of only 2.3 per cent of total exports, compared to 15.1 per cent in the United Kingdom and 16.3 per cent in Japan.

The writing began to appear on the wall for Australian manufacturing when the Japanese car manufacturer Mitsubishi closed its Australian factory in 2008. But worse was to follow, as three automotive giants – Toyota (Japan) Ford (US) and Holden (GM) (US) all announced that they would be ceasing to manufacture in Australia in 2017. The likely job-losses – mostly in Victoria and South Australia – were put at some 50,000.

A figure of this magnitude sits uncomfortably alongside another worrying statistic. Australia is among the world's most 'over- borrowed' countries, with an estimated 18 per cent of households coping with unacceptably high domestic debts – albeit for the most part in the shape of large mortgages.

Add to this gloomy scenario the fall in exports of raw materials and the picture takes on an almost alarming dimension. China's imports of coal from Australia and Indonesia, its top two suppliers, fell sharply in the first quarter of 2015, compared to the same period a year earlier, reflecting lower demand. Coal imports from Australia, excluding lignite, fell 27 per cent to 15.96 million tonnes in the first quarter from a year before, the General Administration of Customs data showed. Shipments in March 2015 fell by 15.9 per cent on the year to 5.35 million tonnes. Lower exports was only half the story. Lower demand inevitably meant lower prices. The fall in demand in China, the world's top consumer, had slashed prices by over 15 per cent in 2015, causing many mining companies to risk making losses.

In its February 2014 survey of the Australian economy, the International Monetary Fund (IMF) had noted that the Australian economy continued to be buoyed by strong emerging market demand for commodities. However, with the mining boom over its peak, a key requirement was to transition to broader-based growth and away from a one-dimensional dependency of raw materials. In the view of the IMF, 'strong policy frameworks could ease the transition, but an

KEY INDICATORS — Australia

	Unit	2011	2012	2013	2014	**2015
Population	m	22.73	*22.92	23.31	*23.59	*23.87
Gross domestic product (GDP)	US$bn	1,486.50	1,555.29	1,501.88	1,444.19	*1,252.27
GDP per capita	US$	65,497	67,856	64,429	*61,219	*52,454
GDP real growth	%	2.2	3.6	2.1	*2.7	*2.8
Inflation	%	3.1	1.8	2.5	*2.5	*2.0
Unemployment	%	5.0	5.2	5.7	*6.1	*6.4
Oil output	'000 bpd	484.0	458.0	416.0	448.0	–
Natural gas output	bn cum	45.0	49.0	42.9	55.3	–
Coal output	mtoe	230.8	241.1	269.1	280.8	–
Exports (fob) (goods)	US$m	271,844.0	257,909.0	254,800.0	240,788.0	–
Imports (fob) (goods)	US$m	243,498.0	262,983.0	250,523.0	240,464.0	–
Balance of trade	US$m	28,346.0	-5,073.0	4,278.0	323.0	–
Current account	US$m	-32,882.0	-64,002.0	-49,958.0	*-39,875.0	*-50,631.0
Total reserves minus gold	US$m	40,409.0	44,866.0	49,745.0	50,814.0	–
Foreign exchange	US$m	33,649.0	37,845.0	42,533.0	–	–
Exchange rate	per US$	0.96	0.96	1.12	1.22	–

* estimated figure ** forecast figure

improvement in productivity growth was also essential.'

The IMF in 2015 repeated the problem in straightforward terms. Australia's mining investment boom had passed its peak and the country was now confronting the need to generate broader-based growth. According to the IMF, the mining investment boom – which had accounted for almost half of Australia's GDP growth in the previous two years – had peaked and the economy was moving to the mining production and export phase. Mining-related investment was expected to drop sharply in the near term and a recovery in non-mining investment would be needed to underpin demand, suggested the IMF. Australia's economy was projected by the IMF to grow to about 3 per cent by 2016. While resource (raw materials) exports looked likely to expand rapidly and contribute to future growth, the outlook for the 'non-resource' sector was in the view of the IMF, more uncertain.

Australia's exchange rate was seen as moderately overvalued. In the first half of 2015 the Australian dollar (A$) had shown signs of rising against the US$ when stronger than anticipated inflation figures had quietened speculation that the Reserve Bank might cut interest rates. In the first three months of 2015, the underlying level of inflation – minus food and fuel – had stood at 0.7 per cent, up on the forecast 0.5 per cent as house prices continued to increase and travel and holiday costs rose. However, despite some recent depreciation, in early 2014 the IMF economists had considered that Australia's exchange rate was still moderately overvalued and was hindering non-mining activity. The main external risk to the Australian economy remained a slowdown in growth in China over the medium-term and a related fall in commodity prices. 'Australia's flexible exchange rate provides a buffer against shocks and the authorities have both monetary and fiscal policy space to react if the outlook deteriorates,' said Brian Aitken, the IMF mission chief to Australia.

In their report, the IMF economists took the view that Australia's fiscal position, with low debt and deficits, compared well to its advanced economy peers. The government's aim to return the budget to surplus over the coming decade would help rebuild fiscal buffers and increase the ability to deal with adverse shocks. But this aim appeared to be challenging in the light of current social spending commitments.

The IMF also thought that Australia's monetary policy should remain accommodative, with inflation within the target range, growth on the 'soft' side and the real exchange rate still strong. 'Monetary policy should act as the primary macro-economic tool for managing aggregate demand in the near term,' said Mr Aitken. The IMF report indicated that higher house prices would be expected to support demand through a more accommodative monetary policy. After several years of weak activity during which house prices lagged growth and construction activity was weak, there had been signs of a pick up.

The IMF report welcomed this revival in housing market activity, considering that it could contribute to near-term growth and begin to help address persistent structural supply shortages.

However, the IMF also thought that attention should be paid to the risks posed by a prolonged period of rapid price growth, which could give rise to over-optimism about future price increases, leading to overshooting. Should credit growth and transactions volume pick up sharply, the authorities should be prepared to take action, said the report. 'There are features of the Australian regulatory and supervisory approach to property lending which would limit the impact of a sharp decline in house prices on the financial system,' stated the report. The report also described Australia's banking sector as sound – balance sheets had strengthened over the previous year and stress tests showed that the major banks would be able to withstand a sizeable shock to output, terms of trade, rising unemployment and a fall in property prices. But the IMF economists also noted that the banks remain exposed to Australia's highly leveraged households.

The IMF economists drew attention to the fact that the increased role of the mining sector could make the economy more sensitive to terms-of-trade shocks. But, the floating exchange rate would play an essential role in buffering shocks by depreciating when terms of trade fall, making other tradeable goods and services more competitive. The IMF report noted that a key challenge in the future will be finding ways of increasing productivity to maintain growth. Against this background, stated the IMF, addressing infrastructure bottlenecks consistent with the government's deficit reduction goals is a priority. A shift to broader-based growth would also be helped by making the most of opportunities offered by a growing Asian middle class, which could support demand for Australia's services exports – in particular health, education, tourism and professional services.

Energy and minerals

It goes without saying that Australia – the 'lucky country', is rich in commodities, including fossil fuel and uranium reserves. It is also one of the few countries belonging to the Organisation for Economic Co-operation and Development (OECD) that is a significant net energy exporter, sending nearly 70 per cent of its total energy production (excluding energy imports) overseas, according to data from the Australian Bureau of Resource and Energy Economics (BREE). With the exception of crude oil and other liquids, Australia has a surplus of all other energy commodities. Australia was the world's second-largest coal exporter based on weight in 2012 and the third-largest exporter of liquefied natural gas (LNG) in 2013. Energy exports accounts for some 24 per cent of Australia's total export revenues, according to BREE. Australia also holds the world's largest recoverable reserves of uranium (about 32 per cent, based on 2012 data) and is the third-largest producer and exporter of uranium for nuclear-powered electricity, according to the World Nuclear Association. Nevertheless, Australia is a net importer of crude oil and refined petroleum products, although it does export some petroleum liquids.

Australia's (relatively – see above) stable political environment, its transparent regulatory structure, substantial hydrocarbon reserves and proximity to Asian markets make it an attractive place for foreign investment. The previous (Labor) Australian government had published an Energy White Paper in 2012 that outlined an energy policy that attempted to balance securing domestic energy at affordable prices with increasing exports to help supply Asia's growing demand for fuel. However, both of these options involve developing more energy infrastructure, attracting greater investment, creating efficient energy markets and pricing mechanisms for consumers and delivering cleaner and more sustainable energy. More recently, Australia's expanding energy industry has encountered the double whammy of escalating project costs and a shortage of labour. A complicating factor has also been the sharp fall in global oil prices. These factors, coupled with a bigger push for clean energy and stricter environmental regulations in some states, are all challenges that the domestic and international companies face in developing Australia's energy resources.

According to the *BP Statistical Review of World Energy* of June 2015 (BP15) Australia held more than 4.0 thousand million barrels of proved oil reserves in January 2015. *Geoscience Australia* reported that economic reserves, which included proved and probable commercial reserves, of nearly 3.8 billion barrels, composed of 0.9 billion barrels crude oil, 1.9 billion barrels condensates and 0.9 billion liquid petroleum gas (LPG) as of December 2012. Most Australian crude oil is a light, sweet grade, typically low in sulphur and wax and therefore higher in value than the heavier crudes. The majority of reserves are located off the coasts of the states of Western Australia, Victoria and the Northern Territory. Onshore basins, mostly found in the Cooper Basin, account for only 5 per cent of the oil resources. Western Australia (including the Bonaparte Basin which straddles Western Australia and the Northern Territory) has 72 per cent of the country's proven crude oil reserves, as well as 92 per cent of its condensate and 79 per cent of its LPG reserves. The two largest oil-producing basins are the Carnarvon Basin in north western Australia and the Gippsland Basin in south-eastern Australia. Carnarvon Basin production, which accounted for 61 per cent of total liquids production in 2013, is mostly exported and Gippsland Basin oil production, representing a 19 per cent share in 2013, is predominantly refined for domestic use.

The US government Energy Information Administration (EIA) reports that although Australia is not producing oil shale (defined as sedimentary rock containing solid organic content, such as kerogen and not equivalent to shale oil or tight oil) on a commercial basis, the country has resources of about 14 billion barrels of demonstrated or potential reserves (not economic or proved reserves), mostly located in Queensland, according to BREE. The majority of these reserves face technical and environmental challenges for commercial production. In 2008, the Queensland government issued a 20-year moratorium on oil shale mining at the McFarlane deposit and suspended other oil shale projects until the state had reviewed various technologies and environmentally safe methods of production. The state has since lifted bans on all production projects outside of the McFarlane deposit, but still reviews each project, applying strict environmental standards. Australia also holds shale oil or tight oil reserves, estimated to be around 18 billion barrels of technically recoverable reserves, located in various areas of Australia, according to a 2013 EIA study on world shale oil and natural gas resources.

Responsibility for Australia's management of oil exploration and production is divided between the states and the federal (Commonwealth) governments. Australia's states manage the applications for onshore exploration and production projects, while the Commonwealth shares jurisdiction over Australia's offshore projects with the adjacent state or territory. The Department of Resources, Energy and Tourism (RET) and the Ministerial Council on Energy (MCE) function as regulatory bodies over Australia's oil sector. As a result of the 2009 Montara field oil spill, Australia created a new offshore regulator to consolidate oversight for activity in this area in 2011. This new body, the National Offshore Petroleum Safety and Environmental Management Authority (NOPSEMA) oversees safety and the environmental performance of all offshore petroleum facilities.

International oil companies dominate the oil and natural gas exploration and development of Australia's hydrocarbon resources. Chevron is the largest foreign oil producer, supplying 96,000 barrels per day (bpd) in 2013. Other international oil companies actively investing in Australia's upstream hydrocarbon developments include Shell, ExxonMobil, ConocoPhillips, Inpex (Japan), Total, BHP Billiton and Apache Energy. There are some Australian companies, the largest being Woodside Petroleum and Santos that focus on upstream oil and gas developments. Other smaller domestic players in both the upstream and downstream markets include Origin Energy and Beach Energy.

In attempts to secure investment from international oil companies to develop many offshore blocks, Australia typically holds regular licensing rounds to release acreage for exploration each year. The 2011 round was the largest release held in a decade. The 2014 release offered 33 offshore blocks, including a second release of three blocks from the 2013 round, spanning four basins mostly in Western Australia and the Northern Territory. Western Australia held a separate licensing round in 2014 for five onshore blocks including those in the Canning Basin and in the Perth Basin and the state of Queensland called for cash tenders for another six onshore areas.

Production

Petroleum and other liquids production totalled 448,000 barrels per day (bpd) in 2014, of which about 44 per cent consisted of crude oil, 31 per cent lease condensates and 14 per cent liquid petroleum gas (LPG). The remaining 11 per cent comes from refining gains and biofuels. The share of crude in the total oil stream has declined over the past decade and has been gradually replaced by condensates and liquids associated with natural gas production. Australia's total liquids production peaked at 828,000bpd in 2000 and has declined overall since then. According to the Australian Petroleum Production and Exploration Association (APPEA), liquid fuels production will continue to decline over the long term unless more fields are discovered and Australia is able to tap into more deep-water fields. Production from new, smaller offshore fields has not been able to offset declines from mature basins. However, additional production from new condensate and other smaller projects are expected to compensate for overall production declines.

According to the EIA, Australia is a net importer of both crude oil and oil products because its consumption of both energy sources exceeds overall production. In 2013, net crude oil imports were 253,000bpd and net product imports were 325,000bpd, according to the Australia's Bureau of Statistics data. The country's northern and north-western regions rely on oil product imports resulting from the lack of sufficient regional refining capacity, while the eastern side imports crude oil for its refineries and domestic markets. Singapore supplies about 47 per cent of Australia's oil product imports, with the most of the remainder coming from refiners in Japan and South Korea. Most crude oil imports are from Malaysia, the United Arab Emirates and Indonesia, which altogether produced about 48 per cent of the total imports in 2013. Another 20 per cent of crude oil imports comes from West Africa, as Nigeria, Congo, and Gabon have increasingly supplied crude oil to Australia in recent years.

Natural gas

The EIA reported that Australia produces enough natural gas to cover its consumption and to be considered a leading gas exporter. Several recent discoveries and growing regional demand for gas have spurred more investment activity in the country's reserves. Australia's natural gas reserves vary by industry source and the category of commercial viability. According to the *BP Statistical Review of World Energy* of June 2015 (BP15), Australia's proved natural gas reserves were more than 132 trillion cubic feet (tcf) in January 2015.Most of the traditional gas resources (about 92 per cent) are located in the North West Shelf (NWS) offshore in the Carnarvon, Browse and Bonaparte basins.

Coal Bed Methane C(BM) proved and probable resources, primarily located in the north-eastern Queensland Province in the Bowen Basin and the Surat Basin, doubled over the 2009–12 period to 33tcf by 2012. *Geoscience Australia* anticipates the resource distribution of natural gas will shift from the offshore traditional gas production to CBM or other sources in the next two decades as key CBM developers are aggressively exploring and drilling in several areas. In addition to CBM resources, Australia had an estimated 437tcf of technically recoverable shale gas reserves in 2012, according to an EIA study. These resources are dispersed throughout the country in the inland Cooper Basin, the eastern Maryborough Basin, the offshore south-western Perth Basin and the north-western Canning Basin.

Natural gas production in Australia reached nearly 55.3 billion cubic metres (bcm) in 2014 and has climbed overall from less than 35.3bcm in 2004 as a result of new developments. Traditional natural gas is largely produced in the Carnarvon Basin offshore Northwestern Australia, the Cooper/Eromanga Basin in central Australia, the Gippsland Basin in the south-eastern Victoria Province and the Bonaparte Basin in the offshore joint production area shared between Australia and East Timor. The Carnarvon Basin supplied almost a third of the domestic natural gas market and the vast majority of the export market, according to APPEA. Victoria state comprised about 18 per cent of the total natural gas production. Queensland and New South Wales (NSW), Australia's main sources for CBM, made up roughly 15 per cent of natural gas production.

Major domestic and foreign companies operating in Australia include Santos, Woodside, Chevron, ConocoPhillips, ExxonMobil, Origin Energy, BG Group plc, Apache Corporation, INPEX Corporation, Total, Shell and Statoil. Chevron holds the largest amount of natural gas resources in Australia and the company has made 21 discoveries in the Carnarvon Basin since mid-2009, adding 10 trillion cubic feet to proved gas resources. The recent stream of CBM for LNG projects in Australia has also attracted Asian companies such as Sinopec, China National Offshore Oil Corporation (CNOOC), Tokyo Gas and China National Petroleum Corporation (CNPC) that are interested in purchasing both LNG for markets in China and Japan as well as the upstream assets required to supply these projects.

Risk assessment

Economy	Fair
Politics	Fair
Regional stability	Good

COUNTRY PROFILE

1778 Captain James Cook reached Australia and sailed the entire length of the East Coast. He claimed the land for Britain.

1788 British Naval captain, Arthur Phillip, founded a penal colony at Sydney. He had arrived with a fleet of 11 vessels and nearly 800 convicts.

1829 The Colony of Western Australia was established at Perth by Captain James Stirling.

1837 South Australia was established with Adelaide as its capital city.

1851 The discovery of gold in New South Wales sparked a wave of migration to Australia, known as the 'gold rush'. Within 10 years of the gold find, the population was estimated to have grown from 500,000 to 1.5 million. The Aborigines were treated badly.

1856 Australia became the first country to introduce the secret ballot for elections (known as the 'Australian ballot').

1877 The first Test cricket match between Australia and England was played in Melbourne.

1901 The Commonwealth of Australia was created. The former British colonies became the six states of Australia: New South Wales, Victoria, Queensland, Western Australia, South Australia and Tasmania. There are two self-governing states – the Northern Territory and the Australian Capital Territory.

1911 Canberra was founded as the capital city.

1914–1918 Australia fought alongside Britain during the First World War. Australian troops bore the brunt of the fighting in some theatres of war and suffered heavy casualties during the ill-fated beach landing at Gallipoli in Turkey in 1915.

1929–31 Following the Wall Street Crash, the Great Depression badly affected the Australian economy. Recovery was slow and uneven. The Labor government was defeated in the elections.

1939–45 Australia fought alongside Britain and the US during the Second World War. In 1942, Japanese aircraft bombed Darwin (Northern Territory), the only direct foreign attack on Australia since its creation.

1948 Australia began to promote immigration from Europe and between the 1940–70s more than a million people arrived, a third of which came from Britain.

1950 Australia participated in the Korean War.

1951 Australia, New Zealand and the US signed the Anzus Pact, a security pact for the South Pacific.

1963 The 'White Australia' policy of immigration restrictions was ended.

1965 Australia fought alongside the US in Vietnam. At the height of Australia's involvement, the task force numbered 8,500 troops.

1967 A national referendum approved changes to the constitution: the section which excluded Aboriginal people from the official census was removed and another change enabled the federal government to pass laws on Aboriginal issues.

1975 Australia restricted the immigration of non-skilled workers. The governor general, Sir John Kerr, dismissed Gough Whitlam's government following its repeated failure to pass the budget in the upper house of parliament. A caretaker government under Malcolm Fraser was installed.

1985 The issue of Aboriginal land rights was first addressed.

1986 Australia's legislative links with the UK were severed by the Australia Act, which abolished the UK parliament's residual legislative, executive and judicial controls over Australian state law.

1990 Bob Hawke and his Australian Labor Party (ALP) government narrowly won the federal election – the first ALP administration to win three consecutive elections.

1991 Paul Keating (ALP) succeeded Bob Hawke as prime minister.

1992 The Citizenship Act was amended to remove the obligation to swear an allegiance to the British Crown.

1993 The ALP won the general election with an increased majority. The Native Title Act granted the Aborigines compensation for the loss of land rights.

1996 The Liberal Party (LP)-National Party (NP) (referred to jointly as the Coalition) won a landslide victory in elections and John Howard, leader of the LP, took over as prime minister.

1998 The LP-NP coalition was re-elected at the general elections, but with a reduced majority.

1999 A national referendum opposed Australia becoming a republic by 55 per cent. After East Timor voted for independence from Indonesia, Australia led an

intervention force to counter pro-Indonesia militia violence.
2001 Howard won a third term in the federal elections after gaining support for his 'Pacific Solution' – the policy of refusing entry to asylum seekers and directing them to other countries in Asia-Pacific.
2002 There were riots in the Woomera desert detention camp for asylum seekers. Eighty-eight Australian citizens were killed in a night club bombing in Bali, Indonesia.
2003 Australia sent 2,000 troops to the Iraq War. The Senate passed a no-confidence motion in Prime Minister Howard over his handling of troops in Iraq. Australia headed a peacekeeping Regional Assistance Mission to Solomon Islands (Ramsi) force to the Solomon Islands.
2004 The first passenger train service (the Ghan) to cross Australia from Adelaide in the south to Darwin in the north began services. A parliamentary committee cleared the government of lying about the threat posed by weapons of mass destruction in Iraq. With an increased majority, John Howard won a fourth term as prime minister.
2006 Australia experienced its worst drought on record. Troops were sent to aid the Timor-Leste government against mutinying soldiers.
2007 Heavy rain began to fall in south-east Australia, breaking a six-year drought; however it did not rain in the Murray-Darling river system, the principal crop-growing region. In parliamentary elections the opposition ALP won 44.0 per cent of the vote (86 seats out of 150); Kevin Rudd became prime minister. One of his first acts was to sign the Kyoto Agreement on greenhouse gas emissions targets.
2008 The prime minister made a formal apology to indigenous Aboriginal peoples for former government policies, which included the forcible removal of Aboriginal children – 'the stolen generation' – from their families, in a policy of assimilation. Quentin Bryce, the first woman to hold the post, was sworn in as governor general of Australia.
2009 The worst forest fires ever recorded killed 173 people, injured around 500 and destroyed over 1,000 homes, with more badly damaged. Over 5,000 people were left homeless. The fires devastated 3,000 square km, including some towns in the state of Victoria. Arson was suspected to have caused a number of the fires. The Senate passed legislation setting a target of 20 per cent renewable sources of energy by 2020.
2010 Kevin Rudd was replaced as leader of the ALP, just months before a general election; deputy leader, Julia Gillard, was elected leader and automatically became prime minister. She called a snap general election and the result was a hung parliament – the ALP won 72 seats, the Coalition 73 seats, Greens one and independents four. Three independent members of parliament (MPs) supported the minority ALP government. Australia recorded 6,535 irregular maritime arrivals (IMAs) (asylum seekers and unauthorised migrants) during the year.
2011 At the beginning of January, after two months of heavy rains, major flooding in the State of Queensland caused widespread damage and mass evacuations. It was the worst recorded flooding since 1961 and steel and coal production were badly affected. By mid-January, floodwaters, which had inundated over 60 per cent of the state, were the worst in recorded history. Over 20 people were killed with over 70 missing in flash-floods. The capital, Brisbane, suffered flooding to its outer suburbs. Estimates were that the total damage would run to around US$13 billion in reconstruction. A bilateral agreement was signed in May between the governments of Australia and Malaysia for IMAs attempting to land in Australia to be held in camps in Malaysia until their applications for settlement are processed. Annually, around 900 IMAs are expected to be held in Malaysia. Talks were also underway with Papua New Guinea and Nauru to provide more IMA camps. In August, the High Court rejected government plans for a Malaysian IMA centre. The court said that Australia had signed treaties not to send asylum-seekers to another country that could not adequately protect them. The plan by the government to accommodate asylum seekers and illegal migrants in Malaysia, until their *bona fides* were determined, was discarded in October. During the Commonwealth Heads of Government summit, held in Perth, on 28 October, the 16 countries in which the British monarch is Head of State unanimously agreed to change the royal line of succession from that of first born son to the first born child (regardless of its gender). The change will be enacted after the succession of Prince William (currently second in line to the throne, after his father Prince Charles).
2012 On 30 July, Australia and New Zealand agreed to restore full diplomatic relations with Fiji as it moves towards democratic elections in 2014. On 13 August an independent panel recommended the reopening of overseas IMA camps and the government immediately began negotiations. On 20 August, the PNG government agreed to reopen the Manus Regional Asylum processing centre (on Manus Island), to be funded by the Australian government. Dismay from activists in Australia came when funds for the facility were drawn from the foreign aid budget. On 15 September, the first group of IMAs were flown to Nauru on 15 September, the first since the revival in farming out immigration detention facilities. The government began talks to open similar detention centres in PNG. The offshore centres are meant to deter refugee boats and people-smuggling.
2013 Months of infighting in the Labor party over who should lead them in to the September election resulted in a vote on 26 June which was won by Kevin Rudd with 57 votes to Mrs Gillard's 45. Mr Rudd was sworn in by Governor General Quentin Bryce the next day. On 4 August Prime Minister Rudd announced that the election would be brought forward to 7 September. In the first televised debate, held on 11 August, Prime Minister Rudd and opposition leader Tony Abbott debated the economy and immigration. A candidate for the One Nation Party withdrew her candidacy after she mistook Islam for a country in a TV interview. The treatment of asylum seekers was hotly debated in the run up to the election with both leaders proposing harsher treatment. Liberal Party leader Abbott launched his campaign on 26 August, vowing to control government spending and build a stronger economy by putting 'bulldozers on the ground and cranes into our skies'. The election was won convincingly by Tony Abbott's Liberal-National (LN) coalition with 89 seats (out of 150) (53.15 per cent) to the Australian Labor Party (ALP) 56 seats (46.85 per cent). Tony Abbott said he would work quickly to abolish the tax on carbon emissions and stop asylum-seekers arriving by boat. Kevin Rudd resigned as Labour leader on 10 September. Bill Shorten, who had been involved in the ousting of both Mr Rudd and Ms Gillard, announced he would be standing in the election to replace him. On 13 September former deputy prime minister Anthony Albanese announced he would also be standing. Mr Abbott announced his cabinet on 17 September, including Julie Bishop as finance minister and Mathias Cormann as finance minister. He was sworn in as prime minister on 18 September. Mr Abbott began his first overseas visit on 30 September, to Indonesia. Discussions were expected to centre on trade and Australia's controversial asylum policy of returning refugee boats to Indonesia. In October Mr Abbott was accused of expenses irregularities after he repaid the cost of travel to two weddings. Kevin Rudd announced his retirement from politics on 14 November.
2014 On 12 September Canberra lifted its terror alert level to 'high' as concern grew about Australian militants returning from fighting in Iraq and Syria. On 14

September Prime Minister Abbot announced Australia would deploy 600 troops to the United Arab Emirates to join the US-led international coalition gearing up for war against Islamic State (IS) militants.
After security officials received information that a terrorist group associated with the IS was planning to carry out 'demonstration killings' police carried out dawn raids in Sydney and Brisbane on 18 September. Fifteen arrests were made and Mr Abbot said that a major incident had been prevented. A lone gunman took some 30 people hostage in a café in central Sydney on 15 December. The siege ended a day later when poliece stormed the café; two hostages and the gunman were killed.
2015 In January the indigenous Barngarla people won a campaign, lasting nearly 20 years, for the law to recognise their right to traditional lands in South Australia. Although the Federal Court's ruling does not grant freehold it does now mean groups such as mining companies must in future negotiate with the Barngarla over proposed developments. The Bamgarla will also have rights allowing them to partake in traditional activities such as hunting, gathering, using bush medicine and protecting sacred sites. On 23 February Prime Minister Abbott announced moves to toughen citizenship laws for those involved in terrorism or inciting hatred, including suspending or revoking Australian citizenship for dual citizenship holders, and withdrawing some privileges from Australian citizens breaking anti-terror laws. A snap Liberal Party leadership election saw Malcolm Turnbull defeat Tony Abbot by 54 votes to 44 on 14 September. Mr Abbot tendered his resignation to the Governor General and Mr Turnbull was sworn in as Prime Minister on 15 September.

Political structure

Constitution

The Commonwealth of Australia is a constitutional monarchy with a parliamentary democracy. It consists of a federation of six states (New South Wales, Victoria, Queensland, South Australia, Western Australia and Tasmania) and two territories (Australian Capital Territory (ACT), Northern Territory). Each state has its own constitution, government, administration and judiciary. There are some 900 local government bodies at city, town, municipal and shire levels.
The federal government is located in Canberra, ACT. Federal responsibilities tend to be those with an international and national focus while state governments deal with regional issues. However, the overlap of power is considerable and companies must be prepared to deal with both levels of government.
Any amendment to the constitution must be passed by an absolute majority in each House of Parliament and must be approved in a referendum by the majority of electors in a majority of states and territories. In the past, three states (Tasmania, Queensland and Western Australia) have consistently blocked any changes to the constitution.
There is compulsory universal adult suffrage for Australian citizens, with a voting age of 18. An automatic fine of A$50 (US$35) is issued by post to those who fail to cast a vote, although this is rarely imposed through legal proceedings.

Form of state

Federal commonwealth, with the British monarch as Head of State.

The executive

The governor general represents and is appointed by the British sovereign. The role of governor general is largely ceremonial, but he has the power to dissolve parliament or the government and call new elections. He is also the commander-in-chief of the armed forces. If the governor general is ill, dies, resigns or is out of the country, an administrator is appointed to undertake the governor general's duties.
Day-to-day executive responsibility is held by the national government, which is composed of a cabinet of senior ministers formed by the party with a majority in the House of Representatives.

National legislature

The Parliament of Australia or Commonwealth Parliament has two chambers. The House of Representatives (lower house) has 150 members, elected by instant runoff voting (or alternative voting), whereby a candidate with a majority of preferential votes wins the seat. The number of seats is dependent on electoral distribution and may change at any given election. Members sit for three-year terms.
The Senate (upper house) has 76 members, 12 from each state and two for each territory, elected by proportional representation. Senators serve six-year terms with half the senators of each state standing every three years. Senate elections generally coincide with those of the lower house. Senators take up their seats on 1 July following the election and stand down on 30 June.
Under the constitution both Houses have equal standing and legislation must be passed by both chambers. Only the lower house can introduce legislation to raise taxes, therefore only the party or coalition in the majority in the lower house holds power. The prime minister and cabinet sit in the lower house.
Universal suffrage begins at age 18 years and voting is mandatory.

Legal system

The legal system is based on the constitution of 1901. The governor general and state governors appoint judges on the advice of the cabinets of federal and state governments. Each state has state courts, federal courts, family courts and a supreme court. The High Court of Australia, which has seven judges, is the ultimate court of appeal. The High Court has jurisdiction to hear and determine appeals and judgments, decrees, orders and the sentences of most lower courts, but since 1984 cases have only been referred to it if there is a difference of opinion at lower levels. The High Court's main task is to interpret the Australian Constitution.

Last elections

7 September 2013 (House of Representatives)
Results: Parliamentary: Liberal-National (LN) coalition won 89 seats (out of 150) (53.15 per cent); Australian Labor Party (ALP) 56 seats (46.85 per cent); The Greens 1 seat; Katters Australian Party 1 seat; Palmer United Party (PUP) 1 seat; independents 2 seats.
Senate (2010): 18 seats won (total 34 seats) (out of 76), ALP 15 (31), The Greens six (nine), Democratic Labor Party one (one). Senate (2007): LN coalition won 18 seats (total 37 seats), ALP won 18 seats (total 32), The Greens won three (total five).

Next elections

2017 (House of Representatives)

Political parties

Ruling party

Liberal-National (LN) coalition (from 7 Sep 2013)

Main opposition party

Australian Labor Party (ALP)
23.20 million (2013)*

Population

About 21 per cent of the total population is under 15 years of age. Sixty-three per cent of the population live in the eight major conurbations on the coast and 85 per cent of the population live in urban areas. Much of the interior is practically uninhabitable because of lack of rain, the absence of cultivable soil and the considerable distances involved in travel. There is a continuing drift to the cities from rural areas.
Last census: 8 August 2006: 20,061,646
Population density: Two inhabitants per square km (2000). Urban population 89 per cent (2010 Unicef).
Annual growth rate: 1.3 per cent, 1990–2010 (Unicef).

Ethnic make-up
The population is comprised mainly of immigrants and their descendants from over 120 countries, with Aboriginals and Torres Straits Islanders accounting for only 1.5 per cent of the population. The single largest immigrant group is from the British Isles, followed by Asians, New Zealanders, Italians, Croats, Serbs, Slovenes, Bosnians, Macedonians, Greeks, Germans, Vietnamese, Dutch, Poles and Lebanese. Over 20 per cent of the total population were born outside the country. More than half the Aboriginal population lives in urban areas.

Religions
Predominantly Christian (Anglican and Roman Catholic), although many are non-practising. There are significant Eastern Orthodox, Jewish, Muslim, Hindu and Buddhist communities in many cities.

Education
In most states, children start primary school at the age of five when they enrol in a preparatory or kindergarten year, after which primary education continues for either six or seven years followed by secondary education, available for either five or six years and may be completed by tertiary education of a student's level and choice.

State and Territory governments and the Federal government provide major financial support for primary and secondary education, delivered in public and fee-paying schools run by governments and non-government providers.

Links between the education and training sectors have been strengthened, through the introduction of the Australian National Training Authority (ANTA) national system of vocational education and training in co-operation with all levels of governments and industry. Two national communications campaigns began in late 2000 based on extensive market research into the vocational education and training needs of Australian individuals and enterprises.

Total expenditure on education is 5.3 per cent of GDP. In 2001, government expenditure on higher education totalled US$5.8 billion.

Compulsory years: 6 to 15; Tasmania: 6 to 16.

Pupils per teacher: 18 in primary schools.

Health
While health care funds direct assistance to hospitals and rebates individuals under the Medicare national health insurance system, consideration of private medical insurance is central to federal health budget funding.

Primary healthcare is provided by independent and privately owned medical practices, offering general and specialist treatment including minor surgery. Hospitals may be state, or privately run institutions.

HIV/Aids
There were an estimated 20,000 people living with HIV in 2009 (Unicef 2012)

HIV prevalence: 0.1 per cent aged 15–49 in 2009 (Unicef 2012)

Life expectancy: 82 years, 2010 (Unicef 2012)

Fertility rate/Maternal mortality rate: 1.9 births per woman, 2010 (Unicef 2012)

Child (under 5 years) mortality rate (per 1,000): 5 per 1,000 live births (WHO 2012)

Welfare
Social security payments are intended as a 'safety net' to help low income groups and anti-fraud measures are increasingly tough. In recent years, payments have been the subject of intense scrutiny to ensure that they are only distributed to those in genuine need, this has resulted in cuts in some benefits while other categories, especially disability and service pensions, have increased. Other priority groups have been defined as low-income: families with children; the long-term unemployed; and single parents.

Pensions
Australia has a forced savings 'superannuation' scheme for employees, the total value of which is approaching A$1 trillion (US$620 billion). The scheme involves compulsory contributions by employees of 9 per cent of their income. The scheme does not cover the self-employed or low-income workers. It is estimated that 94 per cent of pension schemes operate through trusts. Employees often have no choice in becoming a member and are ill-informed as to who heads the trust.

Main cities
Canberra, (national capital, estimated populations 339,106 in 2012; state capitals – Sydney (3.8 million (m)), Melbourne (3.6m), Brisbane (1.9m), Perth (1.3m), Adelaide (1.1m), Hobart (128,686), Darwin (62,513), Gold Coast (631,200).

Languages spoken
Aboriginal dialects are becoming scarce. Italian is spoken by 2.6 per cent of the population and Greek by 1.8 per cent. A wide variety of other languages are spoken, particularly from Asia, reflecting the diverse origins of Australia's population.

Official language/s
English

Media
Press
In 2007 the government relaxed the laws on media cross-ownership of press and broadcasting and allowing greater levels of foreign ownership. Around 80 per cent of all print media is owned by four newspaper publishers, News Limited, Fairfax Media Publications, APN News and Media and West Australian Newspapers Holdings. All newspapers have a home market based on the major city and state in which they are published and very few are sold elsewhere.

Dailies: The only national daily is *The Australian* (www.theaustralian.news.com.au). Major regional publications include, in NSW *The Sydney Morning Herald* (www.smh.com.au), *Sun Herald* (www.sunherald.com.au) and *The Daily Telegraph* (www.news.com.au/dailytelegraph); in VIC *The Age* (www.theage.com.au) and *Herald Sun* (www.news.com.au/heraldsun) a tabloid with the biggest circulation; in *The Canberra Times* (http://canberra.yourguide.com.au); in QLD *Courier Mail* (www.news.com.au/couriermail), *The Brisbane News* (www.brisbanenews.net); in SA *The Advertiser* (www.news.com.au/adelaidenow); in WA *The Western Australian* (www.thewest.com.au); in NT *Northern Territory News* (www.ntnews.com.au); in Tasmania *Mercury* (www.news.com.au/mercury).

Weeklies: All major dailies produce weekend editions. The are a comprehensive range of magazine catering for all interests personal and professional. APC (www.acp.com.au) publishes many of the leading magazine titles including *The Australian Womens Weekly*, *TV Week* and *Cleo* (http://aww.ninemsn.com.au). *Beat Magazine* (www.beat.com.au) is an arts and entertainment magazine. *The Chaser* (www.chaser.com.au) and *Brainsnap* (http://brainsnap.com) are satirical publications.

Business: The only national daily is the *Australian Financial Review* (www.afr.com). All daily broadsheets have business sections. Weekly publications include *Western Australian Business News* (www.wabusinessnews.com.au), which has the largest circulation, *Business Review Weekly* (www.brw.com.au), with comprehensive articles on national matters, *Lloyds List DCN (Daily Commercial News)* (www.lloydslistdcn.com.au) dealing with transport matters and *Stock & Land* (http://sl.farmonline.com.au), reporting on agriculture. Monthly publications include *Sydney Business Review*,

There are numerous commercial and trade journals, including reports from the Australian Bureau of Agricultural and Resources Economics (Abare) (www.abareconomics.com).

Periodicals: For politics and culture *Monthly* (www.themonthly.com.au) and *Quarterly Essay* (www.quarterlyessay.com).

Broadcasting

The principal public broadcaster is the Australian Broadcasting Corporation (ABC), providing national, local and Pacific regional radio, TV and Internet services.

Radio: There are hundreds of commercial radio stations which in a combined number represent the largest audiences. They broadcast local interest shows and are affiliated to major, usually city stations, with personality presenters who command significant listenership numbers.

National radio services are provided by the public services ABC (www.abc.net.au) and SBS (www20.sbs.com.au) (with programmes broadcasts in many of the immigrant community languages), and commercial radio by Austereo (www.austereo.com.au), DMG Radio (www.dmgradio.com.au) and Southern Cross Broadcasting (www.southerncrossbroadcasting.com.au). Radio Australia (www.abc.net.au/ra) is the ABC's external service.

Television: National, public TV is provided by the ABC (www.abc.net.au) and the Special Broadcasting Service (SBS), which provides multicultural programmes in over 50 languages. Both broadcast additional digital channels aimed children and world news programmes respectively. There are three, free-to-air, commercial channels, Seven (http://au.tv.yahoo.com), Nine (http://channelnine.ninemsn.com.au) and Ten (http://ten.com.au). Channels Seven and Nine regularly vie for top ratings, with domestically produced programmes and popular imports.

The conversion to digital services is expected to be completed by 2010. There are more than 250 privately owned regional TV stations that are affiliates to the metropolitan stations, the largest of which is WINTV (www.wintv.com.au).

Pay-to-view services have grown substantially since the 1990s, using terrestrial, cable and satellite platforms, including Foxtel (www.foxtel.com.au) and Optus (www.optus.com.au).

Other news agencies: AAP (Australian Associated Press): http://aap.com.au
ABC News: www.abc.net.au/news

Economy

Continent-sized Australia, with a modest-sized population, has a range of productive industries, which not only provides for its own citizens but also allows for exports. By far the most profitable sector is mining, with Australia a world leader (in quantity) in brown coal, lead, uranium and zinc. Australia is ranked second for gold, copper, bauxite, silver and industrial grade diamonds; it is third ranked in producing manganese and fourth (by weight) in producing gem quality diamonds. In 2014, petroleum production was 448,000 barrels per day; natural gas production was 55.3 billion cubic metres (a total increase of 0.9 per cent on the 2012 figure) and coal production was 269.1 million tonnes of oil equivalent (an increase of 3.6 per cent from 2013). The mining industry makes up 10 per cent of Australia's GDP. The strength of the mining industry within Australia has been significant for over a decade, with the value of exports in 2000–2010 rising by over 120 per cent. Mining currently comprises around 10 per cent of GDP.

The Australian agriculture sector, when not blighted by drought, exports grain and live animals. Australia has become a world-renowned wine producer with export sales reaching A$1.82 billion (US$1.36 billion) in 2014. Exports reached a record, by volume, of 786 million litres in 2007 (valued at A$3 billion (US$3.6 billion)). Although this figure has been on the decline, Australia is still exporting 700 million litres as of 2014. The industry employs around 30,000 people and contributes A$5.5 billion (US$5.18 billion) to the nation's economy. The UK is Australia's biggest export market by volume of 249 million litres shipped in 2014 alone.

Australia's GDP growth remained positive throughout the global economic crisis; however it fell from 4.9 per cent in 2007 to 2.2 per cent in 2008. Although it went up to 4 per cent in 2012 it fell back to 2 per cent in 2013 before rising to 2.8 per cent in 2014. The banking sector remained profitable while other countries were forced into recession. The Reserve Bank of Australia introduced wholesale funding and retail deposit guarantees to provide sufficient liquidity and helped maintain stability in the financial sector in 2009, staving off potential risk from sizable short-term wholesale funding. Commodity exports, particularly to China, began to pick up in 2009–10. The China-Australia Free Trade Agreement (ChAFTA) was signed in June 2015; the aim of which is to boost market access between the two countries.

In March 2012, Australia and China agreed to swap the equivalent of US$31 billion in each other's currencies in a measure intended to safeguard them during another global economic crisis and strengthen trade ties. Both central banks will be able to exchange each other's currency (up to the US$31 billion) without consideration to fluctuation in the money markets.

Australia was the first OECD and G20 country to lift its interest rates after the decline, with cash rates rising by 25 basis points to 3.25 per cent in 2009. The rebound in the economy was the result first of China's continued purchases of Australian raw materials and secondly the strength of the banking sector which was less exposed to toxic debts than those in the US and Europe. Exports, in 2014, account for 20.9 per cent of GDP; iron ore and coal are the highest exports by value.

External trade

Australia is a member of the South Pacific Regional Trade and Economic Co-operation Agreement (Sparteca) along with 13 regional nations, which allows products duty free access by Pacific Island Forum members to Australian and New Zealand markets (subject to the country of origin restrictions).

Export marketing organisations established under government statutes supervise and promote the export of primary income-earning commodities, and the Export Market Development Grants scheme provides taxable cash grants for developing overseas markets. Australia has an industrial base that includes: vehicle assembly, steel, aluminium and nickel smelting, textile and paper manufacturing and telecommunications and IT suppliers. There is a huge international trade in raw materials, minerals and agricultural produce supplying the Asia and Pacific region.

Australia has a free trade agreement (FTA) with the US (AUSFTA); it also signed a large FTA with the Association of Southeast Asian Nations (Asean) and New Zealand in February 2009, under which tariffs will be reduced and trade in beef, dairy products and pharmaceuticals, as well as automotives and electrical machinery, are all expected to benefit. Australia also has a FTA with Chile, India, Indonesia, Japan, Korea, Malaysia, Singapore, and Thailand. Another FTA was recently signed, in 2015, with China, which is set to increase market access for Australian beef and wine exporters while also boosting China's carmakers and electronics producers who wish to sell their goods to Australians. Total trade between the two nations totals over US$120 billion.

Imports

Principal imports are finished products such as vehicles and parts, industrial machinery, computers and office equipment, electrical goods, textiles and crude oil and petroleum products.

Main sources: China (20.6 per cent in 2014), US (11.4 per cent), Japan (7.8 per cent).

Exports

Principal exports are minerals: coal, gold, diamonds, alumina, iron ore, uranium; agricultural products: wheat, meat, wool and live animals; manufactures include vehicles, processed food, computers and telecommunications equipment.

Main destinations: China (33.9 per cent total in 2014), Japan (18.2 per cent), South Korea (7.7 per cent).

Agriculture

Farming

Agricultural output has doubled since the early 1960s; nevertheless the sector contributed just 3.7 per cent of GDP in 2014, a reduction from a high of 14 per cent. Agricultural production still accounts for around 13 per cent of exports.

Larger and more technologically enhanced farms employing fewer workers are replacing many smaller operations; the number of farms has fallen by 25 per cent since the 1980s.

The long-running drought, which was only given a short-lived respite with rains in 2007, returned with greater force in 2008 with the driest June on record and in 2015 farmers still face severe droughts with many having to sell off their land or livestock to survive. Australia's principal food growing region, the Murray-Darling basin, which produces 40 per cent of the country's fruit, vegetables and grain, was particularly hard hit. Severe cuts in water allocations also cut rice and cotton production by 90 per cent and 42 per cent respectively, with some farmers abandoning parts of their crops in the field and using the reduced water to irrigate smaller areas and maximise their returns. In 2008, the government and land users agreed to water conservation plans with the commitment of AU$3.7 billion (US$3.6 billion) in investment immediately and a further AU$9.2 billion (US$9.5 billion) to restore the river system. It has been estimated that 10,000 farming families have been forced off the land since 2002 when the drought took hold, while those farmers that remain are adopting water efficient cropping methods.

Government involvement tends to be focussed on improving infrastructure as a means of facilitating investment.

Due to the severe droughts Australia has fallen from the world's fourth-largest wheat producer to the world's seventh.

Australia is the world's sixth largest wine producing country. In 2013 Australia accounted for 4.2 per cent of all the wine produced globally, and was the fourth largest exporter of wine (after France, Italy, and Spain). The wine industry contributes AU$5.5 billion (US$5.18 billion) and is responsible for 30,000 jobs.

Fishing

Australia has the third largest fishing zone in the world and typically produces 220,000 tonnes of seafood and 13,000 tonnes of freshwater fish per annum. Rock lobsters from Western Australia account for 30 per cent of exports by value. Other species include prawns, molluscs, carp and eels. The fishing industry and aquaculture is worth over A$2 billion (US$1.85 billion) a year and employs around 11,000 people. Around 80 per cent of annual fishing production is exported. The main destinations for fish exports are Japan, Hong Kong and Taiwan, while exports to the US and Europe have benefited from the weakness of the Australian dollar.

Following the annual meeting of the Commission for the Conservation of Southern Bluefin Tuna (CCSBT), held on Cheju Island, South Korea, all members agreed to a 20 per cent cut in the roughly 17,000 tonnes in 2009 bluefin tuna catches from 2010. Scientists had warned that without a cut fish stocks could crash as numbers had become dangerously low. For Australia, which had a larger proportion of the quota for the bluefin tuna catch, the overall cut was 30 per cent.

South Australia had the world's first tuna fish farm industry. However the last tuna cannery in operation, Port Lincoln Tuna Processors in South Australia, announced in February 2010 that it would close in May 2010 due to the lack of fish caused by the 2009 tuna quota cutbacks.

Forestry

There is a substantial forestry industry in tropical Queensland, producing approximately 22 million cubic metres (cum) of timber annually. The industry contributes over AU$22 billion (US$20.7 billion) of economic turnover a year. Japan has traditionally been the sector's biggest customer, with New Zealand the second largest export market. The sector employs around 66,000 people. There are projects for new plantations to increase production by 300 per cent. More than US$350 million is generated annually in log production.

Industry and manufacturing

Australia embarked on a basic reorientation of its economy in the 1980s, and has transformed itself from an inward-looking, import-substitution economy to an internationally competitive, export-oriented economy. In the early 1990s, the sector suffered from poor investment, despite boosts to exports provided by the low exchange rate. However, having shed labour, gained more effective investment and a sharper export focus, Australian industry has become more competitive internationally with manufacturers of wood and paper products, food, beverages and tobacco becoming dominant. Industry and manufacturing make up 28.9 per cent of Australia's GDP (2014). Australia's location next to Asia makes it possible for them to import many of their required manufactured goods at a low cost.

The Liberal Party (LP)-National Party (NP) coalition government, first elected in 1995, quickly made clear its aim of transforming a traditional commodity-based economy by value-added processing of domestic raw materials into high-value consumer products for the global market. At the heart of industrial policy is a package to support innovation and improve access to venture capital for the commercial application of research and development. The government has also pledged to commit Australia to a free trade approach to the electronic market place – goods ordered and delivered electronically will remain duty free.

Tourism

Australia is a continental sized country with many of its major attractions thousands of miles apart. The tourist industry markets itself as three-centres, typically including the Great Barrier Reef (off the Queensland state coast), Uluru (Ayers Rock) in the centre of Australia and any one of its major cities. Likewise the distance Australia is from its potential markets shapes the way visitors view Australia as a place for an extended (and thus more expensive) visit. Visitor exports generated AU$42.8 billion (US$31.8 billion) (6.4 per cent of total exports) in 2014.

The direct contribution of tourism to GDP in 2014 was AU$42.8 billion (US$31.7 billion) (2.7 per cent of GDP), which was forecasted to have risen to AU$44.5 billion (US$33 billion) in 2015.

In May 2012 a major new promotional campaign began in order to attract more visitors from Asia, especially China, as the number of visitors from the US and Europe fall. This clearly had some effect, as Chinese visitors are now responsible for 17 per cent of total expenditure by foreign visitors - the biggest amount spent by any group.

The sector is managed with government backing, strong private investment and sophisticated sales and marketing, and has a network of tourist offices at federal, state and local levels to co-ordinate and target many niche markets.

In 2014 travel and tourism directly accounted for 504,500 jobs (4.4 per cent of total employment) and by 2025, Travel & Tourism is forecast to account for 549,000 jobs directly (3.9 per cent of total employment).

Investment in the industry was AU$20.4 billion (US$15.16 billion) in 2014 and was predicted to rise by 0.5 per cent in 2015.

Environment

Under the government's Eastern Australia Marine Bioregional profile, a new Coral Sea Conservation Zone, bounded by the Great Barrier Reef Marine Park, Solomon Islands, Papua New Guinea and Vanuatu was established in 2009, offering environmental protection for one million square kilometres of ocean off Australia's north eastern coast. Existing users such as fishermen, scientific research and cruise ships will be allowed to continue work at current levels; expansion will be limited. Australia, Philippines, Indonesia, Papua New Guinea and Solomon Islands are the countries with the most coral reef fish species.

In June 2012, Australia announced plans to create the world's largest marine reserve of 3.1 million square kilometres, including the Coral Sea. The reserve, incorporating over one-third of Australia's territorial waters, will restrict fishing and oil and gas exploration.

In 2009 the Bureau of Meteorology in Melbourne announced that the gigantic hole in the ozone layer over Antarctica and Australasia had begun to shrink and could be closed by 2100. News of an ozone hole in the 1980s and its significance to the welfare of the planet became the spark for awareness of the state of the planet and prompted the first worldwide action on the use of CFCs gases that were known to breakdown the ozone layer.

Mining

Mining contributed around 10 per cent of GDP in 2014 and employs around 2 per cent of the workforce. Australia has major deposits of a variety of minerals, possessing the world's biggest economic reserves of lead, uranium, silver, zinc, tantalum, mineral sands and low-cost uranium. Australia is a significant producer of gold, iron ore, bauxite, nickel, diamonds, alumina, ilmenute, zircon and rutile. Australia is the largest exporter of gold and iron ore in the world.

In March 2009 China won a bid to buy up to 17.5 per cent of the Australian mining company Fortescue Metals Group; the first in a series of bids. While cash-strapped Australian companies were looking for investment during a time of global economic downturn, China began hunting for all the vital raw materials it could secure.

The mining industry experienced a dire 12 months in 2014. For all of the major metals, such as iron ore and gold, there have been huge falls in revenue recorded off the back of historically high prices.

According to IBISWorld, while the end of 2014 and the start of 2015 will see an overall decline of 1.1 per cent in Australian mining revenues to approximately US$232 billion, the 2015/16 financial year should see growth around 7.1 per cent.

Hydrocarbons

Australia is rich in natural resources and has considerable deposits of hydrocarbons. Proven oil reserves at the end of 2014 totalled 4 billion barrels, with production at 448,000 barrels per day (bpd), which was an increase of 6.5 per cent on the 2013 production figure. However, the rate of production has been in decline since 2000, partly due to depleting reserves and the growing consumption of natural gas; nevertheless, oil consumption at 998,000 bpd in 2014 means that imports are required to make up for its shortfall. Australia's main oil fields are situated offshore in the Bass Strait and Carnarvon Basin; there are a number of smaller and younger fields becoming operational. There are also shale oil reserves in Queensland, estimated at around 30 billion barrels, but exploitation has been hampered by the cost of the technology necessary to utilise it, and environmental considerations. There is a well-developed network of oil and gas pipelines that allow transport to domestic and export outlets. Refinery capacity was 536,000bpd in 2014, primarily producing petrol (gasoline) and diesel fuel. Refining production has fallen since 2002 due to overcapacity in refining in other Asian countries and the costs of shipping crude oil to Australia, which made the end product uneconomic.

The government funds seismic and geological data from Geoscience Australia for access free of charge by hydrocarbon companies to aid exploration of its on- and off-shore sites.

There were 3.7 trillion cubic metres (cum) of proven natural gas reserves at the end of 2014; production was 55.3 billion cum, a rise of 3.6 per cent on the 2013 rate and marks a steady trend of increase from the 29.8 billion cum in 1997. Projections have shown that Australia can maintain self-sufficiency in natural gas until at least 2016. There has been a steady growth in exports of liquefied natural gas (LNG) so that by 2011 Australia was the world's third largest exporter, with exports of 25.9 billion cum, of which 19 billion cum went to Japan. Consumption of natural gas was 29.2 billion cubic metres in 2014.

The Gorgon Gas Project (GGP) is the biggest single resource project ever built in Australia. It was originally expected to begin production in late 2014, however a surge in the budget from the initial estimate of US$37 billion in 2009 has led to the schedule being slipped to late 2015. It is due to convert natural gas from the offshore Carnarvon Basin gas field (Western Australia) into liquefied natural gas (LNG) on Chevron, the US-energy company's processing plant on Barrow Island. When the 15 million tonne per annum LNG plant is in full production it will be the one of the world's largest processing plants.

Chevron will ship its first LNG cargo from the US$54 billion Gorgon project when it begins, and said the monster venture would, be 'nicely profitable' despite the drop in crude oil prices.

In May 2011, the Dutch energy company Shell announced that it would build the world's first floating LNG plant. Industry observers estimated the cost of the Prelude project could be between US$8–15 billion and is due to be completed in 2017. The custom-built ship will be moored 200km off the Australian coast and process Australian natural gas to provide 3.6 million tonnes of gas per year delivered ready to go on-stream at any Asian importer's designated port.

Proven coal reserves were 76.4 billion tonnes at the end of 2014, representing 8.9 per cent of world reserves. However the majority of reserves (39.3 billion tonnes) are lower quality coking (brown) coal, which is used almost exclusively in power stations and produces a greater quantity of carbon dioxide emissions than other primary energy sources. Production in 2014 was 280.8 million tonnes of oil equivalent (mtoe) - a rise of 4.7 per cent on the 2013 figure. Australia exports around 60 per cent of its production in both thermal and cooking coal, of which 60 per cent is destined for Japan.

Energy

Total generating capacity in Australia is just over 59.1 million KW. Around 75 per cent is produced by coal-fired power stations, most of the rest by gas and hydropower. In June 2014 Australia's biggest wind farm, near Broken Hill in New South Wales (NSW), was completed. Around 600 wind turbines will generate enough electricity to provide NSW with almost 5 per cent of its energy needs. Plans for other wind farms are under consideration; the Senate passed legislation in August setting a target of 20 per cent renewable sources of energy by 2020. Plans for a new hydroelectric power plant in Papua New Guinea (PNG) to supply electricity to northern Queensland were announced on 17 September 2010. The Australian power company Origin Energy and PNG's Energy Developments will build the power plant, with the first phase

generating 1800MW to be supplied via an undersea cable to Weipa initially and then to Townsville, by about 2020. However the project has encountered many problems and has been progressing slowly.
The Australian Energy Regulator (AER) took control of the energy market from state entities in 2006 and is responsible for the economic regulation of energy markets. It promotes investment, ensures supply security and monitors prices faced by end users.
Although Australia has a nuclear power station in southern Sydney at Lucas Heights it does not generate electrical energy.
Around 86 percent of Australia's electricity is generated from fossil fuels, with 73 percent from coal and 13 percent from natural gas. Renewable energy sources make up the remaining 14 per cent; hydropower is the largest source contributing around 60 per cent of all renewable generation and 7 per cent of total electricity.

Financial markets

Stock exchange
Australian Securities Exchange (ASX)

Banking and insurance

In 2010 the government overhauled its taxation system to allow for growth in Islamic banking, finance and insurance products.
The big 4 banks in Australia (CBA, ANZ, NAB, Westpac) service over 28 million people and are collectively worth US$318 billion.
Since the Reserve Bank began cutting interest rates in late 2011, big bank shares have delivered shareholders near 100 per cent in total returns. This is almost double that of the performance in the broader share-market. However in May 2015, the banks suffered some of their sharpest falls since the financial crisis. Shares in the top four banks dipped to 10 per cent below their peaks. A low interest rate environment and declining economic growth can drag the sector down.

Central bank
Reserve Bank of Australia

Main financial centre
Sydney

Time

There are three time zones:
Queensland, New South Wales, ACT, Victoria, Tasmania (Eastern Standard Time (EST)) – GMT +10 hours.
South Australia and Northern Territory (Central Standard Time (CST)) – GMT + 9.30 hours.
Western Australia (Western Standard Time (WST)) – GMT + 8 hours
Daylight saving, plus one hour to GMT times in all states and territories except Western Australia and Queensland, (October to March).

Geography

Australia is an island continent with the Indian Ocean to the west, the Coral Sea to the east and the Tasman Sea and Pacific Ocean to the south. Australia is the flattest of the continents, the average elevation being less than 300 metres. It has three major landform features: the western plateau, the interior lowlands and the eastern uplands. Much of the land is desert.

Hemisphere
Southern

Climate

The climate ranges from tropical to temperate. About half of Queensland and Western Australia and 80 per cent of the Northern Territory are within the tropics. The remainder of the states and territories — New South Wales, Victoria, South Australia, Tasmania and the Australian Capital Territory — are in the temperate zone. Temperatures vary greatly from warm to very hot in summer (December—February) to cool and rainy in winter (June–August). In July, the temperature in Sydney averages 17 degrees Celsius (C) and in Melbourne 14 degrees C, but in the desert centre can reach 36 degrees. Average annual temperatures can vary from 25 degrees C in the far north to 13 degrees C in the far south. For most of Australia the hottest month is January.
Much of the country receives low rainfall, but some parts of Queensland, Tasmania, Victoria and New South Wales have annual rainfall of up to 4,200mm. Tropical cyclones develop over the seas to the north-west and the north-east in summer. An average of about three cyclones hit the Queensland coast every year. The Snowy Mountains in New South Wales, a famous ski resort, receives heavy snowfalls most years.
Some 70 per cent of the continent is arid, with extremes of daytime and night-time temperatures in the interior.

Dress codes

For business a suit and tie for men; suit, dress or skirt and blouse for women.

Entry requirements

Passports
Required by all.

Visa
Required by all and must be obtained in advance and from outside Australia.
Most citizens of EU and North America can apply for an Electronic Travel Authority (ETA) which can be issued by a travel agent or airline, or can be applied for online. See www.eta.immi.gov.au for details of those eligible, and follow links to the application site. ETA-eligible business visitors may stay for up to three months without additional documentation.
Those not eligible for an ETA must apply using form 456, through the nearest embassy or mission. Business visas will require a letter of invitation from a local company or organisation, a business letter from an employer stating purpose of trip and details of employee's function, proof of sufficient funds, and a full itinerary. Further details and application form can be obtained at www.immi.gov.au/business-services/index.htm.

Currency advice/regulations
This import and export of local and foreign currencies are unstricted but amounts over A$10,000 (or foreign equivalent) must be declared.
Travellers cheques are widely accepted.

Customs
Personal effects are exempt. Duty-free shops are open to international visitors on arrival in Australia.

Prohibited imports
Strict quarantine regulations make it inadvisable to carry food, fruit, vegetables, seeds, animals or plants without prior approval. Travellers are not permitted to carry fruit, vegetables or plants into the State of Victoria. Aircraft cabins are sprayed with insecticide before disembarkation.
Importation of certain items is prohibited, including narcotic and dangerous drugs, firearms and birds. Both import and export of protected wildlife or goods derived from (ie made from skins, feathers, shell, bone, etc) is strictly prohibited.

Health (for visitors)

Mandatory precautions
Vaccination certificates are required for yellow fever if travelling from an infected area.

Advisable precautions
UK nationals can obtain free hospital treatment through a reciprocal arrangement between the two governments, but they must pay for other medical treatment. Australia provides moderately expensive, good quality medical care.
Travellers should be wary of exposure to the sun and the use of sun screening creams is advised. Australia has a high incidence of skin cancer in peoples from northern Europe. The Northern Territory has occasional outbreaks of dengue fever; prevention measures include mosquito repellents, nets and clothing that fully cover the body at dawn and dusk.

Hotels

There is a full range of hotels in all cities, they should be booked well in advance, particularly during holiday seasons. A 10 per cent tip is optional.

Credit cards
Major international credit and debit cards are accepted by virtually everyone. Some taxis also accept credit card payments, check with the driver before the journey begins.

Public holidays (national)
In addition to official public holidays observed throughout Australia, extra statutory holidays are observed in individual states and the Australian Capital Territory (ACT).

Fixed dates
1 Jan (New Year's Day), 26 Jan (Australia Day), 25 Apr (Anzac Day), 27 Sep (Queen's Official Birthday, WA only), 25 Dec (Christmas Day), 26 Dec (Boxing Day).
If Christmas Day or New Year's Day falls on a Saturday, the next Monday is given as a holiday.

Variable dates
Good Friday, Easter Monday, Queen's Official Birthday (second Mon in Jun).

Working hours

Banking
Mon–Thu: 0930–1600; Fri: 0930–1700.

Business
Mon–Fri: 0900–1700.

Government
Mon–Fri: 0900–1700.

Shops
Mon–Fri: 0900–1700; Sat: 0900–1200.
Late night shopping (to 2100) in Sydney, Perth and Darwin on Thursday, and in Melbourne, Brisbane, Hobart and Canberra on Friday.

Telecommunications
In a move that will change the structure of Australia's broadband market major telecommunications companies Telstra and Optus agreed in June 2011 to join the government's A$36 billion (US$34 billion) plan to roll-out high-speed internet across the country. The two companies will close down their infrastructure and transfer customers to the National Broadband Network Company (NBNC). Government has plans to connect 90 per cent of households to a super-fast network and although both Telstra and Optus already have extensive broadband networks government considers it will be more economical to bring the three parties together. Current broadband speeds in Australia are behind other industrialised countries.

Mobile/cell phones
GSM 3G service is available in major cities only, 900/1800 services are available in all most populated areas.

Electricity supply
220–250V AC, with 3-pin plug fittings (not UK style) and bayonet-type light sockets. Leading hotels also supply 110V outlets for razors and small appliances.

Weights and measures
Metric system

Social customs/useful tips
Australians tend to be informal, first names are quickly adopted. A handshake is normal for greetings. Business, with traditional blunt, straight-to-the-point talk, is often conducted over lunch or dinner accompanied by local wines and beers.
Australians love outdoor life and business tends to come to a standstill on weekends and public holidays, when there is a steady exodus to country areas, particularly beaches or ski-slopes depending on the season.
Visitors often complain about bureaucracy and patience is required in dealing with government departments and large corporations. There are no short-cuts and although sometimes an approach to the top official of a department might help speed up matters, this must be done with extreme caution as Australians do not tolerate queue-jumping.
Australia has strict drink-driving laws, police conduct random roadside breath tests and penalties can be severe.
From December 2012 cigarettes can only be sold in olive green packets, with graphic images warning of the consequences of smoking.

Security
Australian cities are relatively safe though care should be taken, particularly at night. Each capital city has separate emergency numbers on the inside cover of phone books. Otherwise dial 000 and the operator will direct you to the appropriate service.

Getting there

Air
National airline: Qantas Airways.
International airport/s: All states have international airports (with the exceptions of the capital territory, (which is served by NSW), and Tasmania) with connecting inter- and intra-state flights.
NSW: Kingsford Smith (SYD), 8km south of Sydney; Victoria: Tullamarine (MEL), 21km from Melbourne; Western Australia: Perth (PER), 10km from Perth, all of which have duty-free shop, bar, restaurant, bank, post office, shops; Queensland: Brisbane International (BNE), 11km north-east of city, with duty-free shop, bar, restaurant; South Australia: West Beach (ADL), 8km from Adelaide, with bar, restaurant, post office, shops; Northern Terrritory: Darwin (DRW), 8km from city with bar, money exchange and duty-free shops.
Other airport/s: Tasmania: Hobart (HBA), 17km north of city, with restaurant and bar. Queensland: Cairns (CNS), 4km north-west of Cairns, with duty-free shop, hotel reservations; Townsville (TSV), 5km from city. (More information on local airports is provided on: www.airportsaustralia.com).
Airport tax: None

Surface
Water: There are regular sea links with New Zealand. Cruiseliners call at major ports in Australia. International shipping lines that maintain contacts with Australia may provide passenger services on cargo ships.
Main port/s: There are more than 30 ports. The main ports are at Sydney, Brisbane, Melbourne, Adelaide and Fremantle. Sea transport is extensively used for internal and international freight shipment. Containerised cargo facilities are available.

Getting about

National transport
Air: Air transport is widely used and well developed. Regular services linking main centres and nearly 440 airfields are operated by Australian Airlines, East-West Airlines, Air Queensland and over 25 other operators. Charter aircraft are also available. Travellers holding international air tickets can obtain concessionary air, rail and bus fares within Australia.
Road: All cities have good arterial roads. Despite the vast distances, there are good highways and bus services between all major centres, but conditions in the interior are rugged, with road transport more limited. Seek advice from the appropriate local automobile association before travelling in remote areas, as roads may be affected by weather conditions.
Buses: Air-conditioned express coach services link main centres, including Tasmania via ferries. Buses provide good services on main town routes, but convenient cross-town transport is not always available.
Rail: Railways, mainly government-owned and operated, provide express inter-urban passenger services, electrified suburban services and long-distance freight services, using a 38,563km network of tracks. Long-distance passenger trains are air-conditioned, with dining and sleeping facilities, they are generally a slower option of transport than road or air. Advance booking is recommended.
The Ghan passenger train runs directly from Adelaide to Darwin through the centre of Australia, via Alice Springs. The refurbished, 47-hour, 2,979km transcontinental journey, began its regular services in 2004. Alice Springs is the closest base for access to the region around Uluru/Ayers Rock national park and Kings Canyon.

There are rail extensions to the Ghan from other state capital cities of Melbourne, Sydney and Perth.

Water: There is a regular passenger/vehicle ferry link between Melbourne and Hobart, Tasmania.

City transport

Taxis: Metered taxis operate in all main cities and towns from major hotels, shopping areas and signposted taxi ranks. Radio-controlled taxis are listed in local telephone directories. Tipping is not expected, but a tip of the balance of the fare rounded up to the nearest dollar is sometimes given.

Buses, trams & metro: Sydney (NSW): the rail service AirportLink connects Sydney international airport with the city centre; trains depart at 10 minute intervals, journey time 13 minutes. State Transit run extensive services of buses, trains and ferries around the city and suburbs.

Melbourne (Vic): VicTrip operate trams, buses and trains around the cityand suburbs. See www.victrip.com.au for a journey planner. Skybus links the airport to city centre; services run 24 hours, everyday with daytime departures every 15 minutes, journey time 20 minutes.

Brisbane (Qld): Buses and trains link the airport to the city centre, journey time 20 minutes, as well as to all other parts of the city and suburbs.

Ferry: In Sydney, ferries are an easy, regular and enjoyable mode of transport to the city centre and harbour suburbs. The main ferry terminal is at Circular Quay. In Brisbane there are over a dozen passenger stops along the city's river.

Car hire

Hire cars are widely available. Current overseas licences are recognised, but International Drivers Permits are recommended. The required third-party insurance is normally included in car hire charge. Use of seat belts is compulsory and speed limit in towns is generally 60km per hour. Driving is on the left. Trams have the right of way. Drink driving rules are vigorously enforced, with sizeable fines.

BUSINESS DIRECTORY

The addresses listed below are a selection only. While World of Information makes every endeavour to check these addresses, we cannot guarantee that changes have not been made, especially to telephone numbers and area codes. We would welcome any corrections.

Telephone area codes

The international direct dialling (IDD) code for Australia is +61, followed by area code and subscriber's number:

Adelaide	8	Hobart	3
Brisbane	7	Launceston	3
Cairns	7	Melbourne	3
Canberra	2	Newcastle	2
Darwin	8	Perth	8
Gold Coast	7	Sydney	2
Wollongong	2	Townsville	7

Useful telephone numbers

Emergency Services: 000.

Chambers of Commerce

ACT and Region Chamber of Commerce and Industry, 12a Thesiger Court, PO Box 192, 2600 Deakin West (tel: 6283-5200; fax: 6260-3369; e-mail: chamber@actchamber.com.au).

Australian Business Chamber, 140 Arthur Street, Locked Bag 938, North Sydney, NSW 2059 (tel: 9458-7500; fax: 9923-1166; e-mail: moreld@abol.net).

Australian Chamber of Commerce and Industry, 50 Burwood Road, PO Box E14, Kingston, ACT 2604 (tel: 6273-2311; fax: 6273-3196; e-mail: acci@acci.asn.au).

Commerce Queensland, 375 Wickham Terrace, Brisbane, QLD 4000 (tel: 3842-2244; 3832-3195; fax: 3832-3195; e-mail: qcci@qcci.com.au).

New South Wales State Chamber of Commerce, Level 12, 83 Clarence Street, GPO Box 4280, Sydney NSW 2000 (tel: 9350-8100; fax: 9350-8199; e-mail: worldtradecentre@thechamber.com.au).

Northern Territory Chamber of Commerce and Industry, 5/2 Shepherd Street, GPO Box 1825, Darwin, NT 0800 (tel: 8936-3100; fax: 8981-1405; e-mail: darwin@ntcci.com.au).

South Australian Employers Chamber of Commerce, 136 Greenhill Road, Unley, SA 5061 (tel: 8300-0000; fax: 8300-0001; e-mail: enquiries@business-sa.com).

Tasmanian Chamber of Commerce and Industry, 30 Burnett Street, PO Box 793, 7001 Hobart (tel: 6234-5933; fax: 6231-1278; e-mail: admin@tcci.org.au).

Victoria Employers Chamber of Commerce asnd Industry, 196 Flinders Street, Melbourne, VIC 3000/ PO Box 4352QQ, Melbourne, VIC 3001 (tel: 8662-5333; fax: 8662-5462; e-mail: webmaster@vecci.org.au).

Western Australia Chamber of Commerce and Industry, 180 Hay Street, East Perth, WA 6004/ PO Box, East Perth, WA 6892 (tel: 9365-7555; fax: 9365-7550; e-mail: info@cciwa.com).

Banking

Australia and New Zealand Banking Group, 100 Queen Street, Melbourne, Vic 3000 (tel: 9273-5555).

Australia & New Zealand Savings Bank Ltd, Collins Place, 55 Collins Street, Melbourne, Vic 3000 (tel: 9275-5555).

Barclays Bank Australia Ltd, Barclays House, PO Box 3357, 25 Bligh Street, Sydney, NSW 2001 (tel: 9233-6622; fax: 9221-3060).

Colonial State Bank of New South Wales, PO Box 41, Sydney, NSW 2001 (tel: 9226-8000).

Commonwealth Bank of Australia, Pitt Street and Martin Place, Sydney, NSW 2000 (tel: 9378-2000; fax: 9312-9905).

Commonwealth Savings Bank of Australia, GPO Box 2719, Pitt Street & Martin Place, Sydney, NSW 2001 (9227-7111; fax: 9232-6573, 9235-1653).

National Australia Bank, 500 Bourke Street, PO Box 84A, Melbourne, Vic 3001 (tel: 9605-3500).

Natwest Australia Bank Ltd, 41st Level, Qantas International Centre, International Square, George Street, Sydney, NSW 2000 (tel: 9250-8500; fax: 9251-2763).

Rural & Industries Bank of Western Australia, PO Box E237, 54-58 Barrack Street, Perth, WA 6001 (tel: 9320-6206; fax: 9320-6444).

State Bank of Victoria, PO Box 267D, 385 Bourke Street, Melbourne, Vic 3001 (tel: 9604-7000; fax: 9602-2150).

State Bank of New South Wales, PO Box 41, Sydney, NSW 2001 (tel: 9226-8000).

State Bank of South Australia, 97 King William Street, PO Box 399, Adelaide, SA 5001 (tel: 9210-4411; fax: 9210-4758, 9212-3056).

Westpac Banking Corporation, 60 Martin Place, PO Box 1, Sydney, NSW 2001 (tel: 9226-3311).

Australian branches

Bank of New Zealand, 333 George Street, PO Box 507, Sydney, NSW 2001 (tel: 9290-6666).

Banque Nationale de Paris, 12 Castlereagh Street, PO Box 269, Sydney, NSW 2001 (tel: 9232-8733).

Central bank

Reserve Bank of Australia, 65 Martin Place, PO Box 3947, Sydney, NSW 2001 (tel: 9551-8111; fax: 9551-8000; e-mail: rbainfo@rba.gov.au).

Stock exchange

Australian Securities Exchange (ASX), www.asx.com.au

Australian Pacific Exchange (APX), Sydney, www.apx.com.au

National Stock Exchange of Australia (NSX), www.nsxa.com.au

Travel information

Australian Capital Territory Tourist Bureau, Canberra Centre, Northbourne Avenue, Canberra City, ACT 2601 (tel: 6233-3666).

Automobile Association of the Northern Territory (AANT), 79-81 Smith Street, Darwin, NT 0800 (tel: 8981-3837).

Australian Tourist Commission, 80 William Street, PO Box 2721, Wooloomoloo, NSW 2011 (tel: 9360-1111; fax: 9361-1385; internet: www.atc.net.au).

Holiday WA Centre, 772 Hay Street, Perth, WA 6000 (tel: 9322-2999).

National Roads and Motorists Association (NRMA), 151 Clarence Street, Sydney, NSW 2000 (tel: 9260-9222).

NSW Government Travel Centre, 16 Spring Street, Sydney, NSW 2000 (tel: 9231-444).

Northern Territory Government Tourist Bureau, 31 Smith Street, Darwin NT 5750 (tel: 8981-6611/3).

Qantas Airways, Qantas Centre, QCA9, 203 Coward Street, Sydney, NSW 2020 (tel: 9691-3472; fax: 9691-4547; internet: www.qantas.com).

Queensland Government Tourist Bureau, Corner Adelaide and Edward Streets, Brisbane, QLD 4001 (tel: 3312-211; internet: www.tq.com.au).

Royal Automobile Club of Queensland (RACQ), 300 St Paul's Tce, Brisbane, QLD 4006 (tel: 3253-4444).

Royal Automobile Association of South Australia, 41 Hindmarsh Square, Adelaide, SA 5000 (tel: 8223-4555).

Royal Automobile Club of Tasmania (RACT), Corner Patrick & Murray Streets, Hobart, Tas 7001 (tel: 6382-200).

Royal Automobile Club of Victoria (RACV), 123 Queen Street, Melbourne, Vic 3174 (tel: 9790-2211).

Royal Automobile Club of Western Australia Inc (RACWA), 228 Adelaide Terrace, Perth, WA 6000 (tel: 9421-4444).

South Australian Government Travel Centre, 18 King William Street, Adelaide, SA 5000 (tel: 8212-1644).

Tasmanian Government Tourist Bureau, 80 Elizabeth Street, Hobart, Tas 7000 (tel: 6300-211).

Victoria Tourism Commission, 230 Collins Street, Melbourne, Vic 3000 (tel: 9619-9444).

VicRail Information: 619-1111 (Melbourne).

Ministry of tourism

Department of Tourism, Burns Memorial Building, 28 National Circuit, Forrest, ACT 2603 (tel: 6279-7111; fax: 6248-0734).

National tourist organisation offices

Tourism Australia, PO Box 2721, Sydney NSW 1006 (tel: 9360-1111; fax: 9331-6469; internet: www.tourism.australia.com)

Ministries

Department of Administrative Services, GPO Box 1920, Canberra, ACT 2601 (tel: 6275-3000; fax: 6275-3819).

Department of Communications and the Arts, GPO Box 2154, Canberra, ACT 2601 (tel: 6279-1000; fax: 6279-1901; internet site: http//www.dcita.gov.au).

Department of Defence, Treasury Building, Newland Street, Parkes, ACT 2600 (tel: 6265-9111; fax: 6273-3021; internet site: http://www.defence.gov.au).

Department of Employment, Education and Training, GPO Box 9880, Canberra, ACT 2601 (tel: 6240-8111).

Department of Finance, Treasury Building, Newlands Street, Parkes, ACT 2600 (tel: 6263-2222; fax: 6273-3021; internet site: http://www.dofa.gov.au).

Department of Foreign Affairs and Trade, Administrative Building, Parkes Place, Parkes, ACT 2600 (tel: 6261-9111; fax: 6261-3111; internet site: http://www://dfat/gov.au).

Department of Housing and Regional Development, GPO Box 9834, Canberra, ACT 2601 (tel: 6289-2222).

Department of Human Services and Health, GPO Box 9848, Canberra, ACT 2601.

Department of Immigration and Ethnic Affairs, PO Box 25, Belconnen, ACT 2616 (tel: 6264-1111; internet site: http://www.immi.gov.au).

Department of Industrial Relations, GPO Box 9879, Canberra, ACT 2601 (tel: 6243-7333).

Department of Industry, Science and Technology, GPO Box 9839, Canberra, ACT 2601 (tel: 6276-1000; fax: 6276-1111; internet site: http://www.industry.gov.au).

Department of National Development and Industry, Tasman House, Hobart Place, PO Box 5, Canberra, ACT 2600.

Department of Primary Industries and Energy, GPO Box 858, Canberra, ACT 2601 (tel: 6272-3933; fax: 6272-5161).

Department of the Prime Minister and Cabinet, Locked Bag 14, Queen Victoria Terrace, Parkes, ACT 2600 (tel: 6271-5111; fax: 6271-5414; internet site: http://www.dpmc.gov.au).

Department of Social Security, Box 7788, Canberra Mail Centre, ACT 2610 (tel: 6244-7788).

Department of Transport, GPO Box 594, Canberra, ACT 2601 (tel: 6274-7111; fax: 6257-2505; internet site: http://www.dot.gov.au).

Department of the Treasury, The Treasury, Parkes Place, Parkes, ACT 2600 (tel: 6263-2111; fax: 6273-2614; internet site: http://www.treasury.gov.au).

Department of Veterans' Affairs, PO Box 21, Woden, ACT 2606 (tel: 6289-1111; fax: 6281-3822; internet site: http://www.dva.gov.au).

Foreign Investment Review Board, Department of the Treasury, Parkes Place, Parkes, ACT 2600 (tel: 6263-3795; fax: 6263-2940).

Other useful addresses

ACT Department of Business, Arts, Sport and Tourism, Level 8, FAI House, 197 London Circuit, Canberra, ACT 2601 (tel: 6207-5111; fax: 6205-0577).

Attorney-General, Suite MF 21, Parliament House, Canberra, ACT 2600 (tel: 6277-7300; fax: 6273-4102; internet site: www.law.gov.au).

Australian Bureau of Agriculture and Resource Economics, MacArthur House, Lyneham, ACT 2601 (tel: 6246-9111).

Australian Bureau of Statistics, Cameron Office, Chandler Street, Belconan, ACT 2617 (tel: 6252-7911).

Australian Dairy Corporation, Dairy Industry House, St Kilda Road, Melbourne, VIC 3004 (tel: 9819-4000).

Australian Embassy (USA), 1601 Massachusetts Avenue, NW, Washington DC 20036-2273 (tel: (+1-202) 797-3000; fax (+1-202) 797-3331; e-mail: library.washington@dfat.gov.au).

Australian Industrial Development Corporation (AIDC), 212 Northbourne Avenue; PO Box 3024, Canberra, ACT 2600 (tel: 6230-1300).

Australian Mining Industry Council, 216 Northbourne Avenue, Braddon, ACT 2601 (tel: 6249-8955).

Australian Securities Commission, Corporate Affairs Commission, National Mutual Centre, 15 London Court, Canberra City, ACT 2601 (tel: 6247-5011; internet site: www.asc.gov.au).

Australian Stock Exchange Ltd, Stock Exchange Center, 530 Collins Street, PO Box 1784 Q, AU Melbourne, VIC 3001 (tel: 9617-8611; fax: 9614-0303; internet site: www.asx.com.au).

Australia Trade Commission, Austrade Centre Cnr Bary Drive and Northbourne

Ave, Canberra City, ACT 2601 (tel: 6276-5111; fax: 6276-5105).

Australian Trade Development Council, Department of Trade and Resources, Canberra, ACT 2600.

Australian Wheat Board, Ceres House, Lonsdale Street, Melbourne, VIC 3000 (tel: 9605-1555).

Australian Wool Corporation, Wool House, Royal Parade, Parkville, VIC 3000 (tel: 9341-9111).

British High Commission, Commonwealth Avenue, Yarralumia, Canberra City, ACT 2600 (tel: 6270-6666; fax: 6273-3236).

Business Council of Australia, Ethos House, 28 Ainslie Avenue, Canberra City, ACT 2601 (tel: 6247-8208).

Business Victoria, Level 13, 55 Collins Street, Melbourne, VIC 3000 (tel: 9651-9999; fax: 9651-9962).

BZW Australia Ltd, Level 22, 255 George Street, Sydney 2000 (tel: 9259-5913; fax: 9259-5477); Airports Team, GPO Box 4675, Sydney 1042 (fax: 9259-5477).

Confederation of Australian Industry, 12a The Siger Court, Deakin, ACT 2600 (tel: 282-2199); PO Box E14, Queen Victoria Terrace, Canberra, ACT 2600 (tel: 6732-311; fax: 6733-196).

International Trade Department Centre, Edgecliff Centre, 203 New South Head Road, Edgecliff, NSW 2027 (tel: 9329-297).

Major Projects Tasmania, 10/fl, 22 Elizabeth Street, Hobart, TAS 7000 (tel: 6233-5869; fax: 6233-5755).

New South Wales Department of State, Level 44, Grosvenor Place, 225 George Street, Sydney, NSW 2000 (tel: 9242-6963; fax: 9242-6970).

New South Wales Government Department of Industrial Development and Decentralisation, GPO Box 4169, Sydney, NSW 2001 (tel: 9927-2741).

Northern Department of Asian Relations, Trade and Industry, 1/fl Development House, 76 The Esplande, Darwin, NT 0800 (tel: 8999-5210; fax: 8999-5106).

Northern Territory Development Corporation, GPO Box 2245, Darwin, NT 5794 (tel: 8989-4211).

Queensland Department of Economic Development & Trade, Executive Building, 100 George Street, Brisbane QLD 4000 (tel: 3224-5970; fax: 3225-8914).

South Australia Department of Trade and Industry, Terrace towers, 178 North Towers, Adelaide SA 5000 (tel: 8303-2400; fax: 9303-2410).

Telecom Australia, 199 William Street, Melbourne, VIC 3000 (tel: 9606-5511).

US Embassy, Moonah Place, Yarralumla, ACT 2600 (tel: 6214-5600; fax: 6214-5970).

Western Australia Department of Industry and Trade, 170 St Georges Terrace, Perth, WA 6000 (tel: 9327-5666; fax: 9322-3361).

Western Australian Development Corporation, 28th Floor, City Mutual Tower, 197 St George's Terrace, Perth, WA 6000 (tel: 9322-7933).

World Trade Promotions (trade fairs and exhibitions), 291 Sussex Street, Sydney, NSW 2000 (tel: 9267-5122).

AAP (Australian Associated Press): http://aap.com.au

ABC News: www.abc.net.au/news

Internet sites

Australian Broadcasting Corporation (ABC): www.abc.net.au

Australian Capital Territory government: www.act.gov.au

Customs service: www.customs.gov.au

Department of Agriculture, Fisheries and Forestry: http://www.agriculture.gov.au/

Department of the Environment and Heritage: www.environment.gov.au

Department of Health and Aged Care: www.health.gov.au

Foreign Affairs & Trade Dept: www.dfat.gov.au

Federal Government: http://www.australia.gov.au/

Federal Parliament (Canberra): www.aph.gov.au/

General Information: www.about-australia.com

Immigration Department: www.immi.gov.au/

Invest Australia: http://www.austrade.gov.au/invest

New South Wales state government: www.nsw.gov.au

Northern Territory state government: www.nt.gov.au/

Qantas: www.qantas.com.au

Queensland state government: www.qld.gov.au/

Reserve bank: www.rba.gov.au

South Australia: www.sa.gov.au

Stock Exchange: www.asx.com.au

Statistics: www.abs.gov.au

Tasmania state government: www.tas.gov.au

Taxation office: www.ato.gov.au

Tourism: www.australia.com

Tourism: www.tourism.australia.com

Victoria state government: www.vic.gov.au

Western Australia state government: www.wa.gov.au/

White pages: www.whitepages.com.au

Yellow pages: www.Yellowpages.com.au

KEY FACTS

Official name: Republik Österreich (Republic of Austria)

Head of State: Federal President Heinz Fischer (SPÖ) (from 2004; re-elected 25 Apr 2010)

Head of government: Chancellor Werner Faymann (SPÖ) (from 2 Dec 2008, re-elected 29 Sep 2013)

Ruling party: Coalition led by Sozialdemokratische Partei Österreichs (SPÖ) (Social Democratic Party of Austria) with Österreichische Volkspartei (ÖVP) (Austrian People's Party) (from 2 Dec 2008, re-elected 29 Sep 2013)

Area: 83,855 square km

Population: 8.52 million (2014)

Capital: Vienna

Official language: German

Currency: Euro (€) = 100 cents (from 1 Jan 2002; previous currency schilling, locked at S13.76 per euro)

Exchange rate: €0.89 per US$ (Sep 2015)

GDP per capita: US$51,307 (2014)*

GDP real growth: 0.34% (2014)*

GDP: US$437.12 billion (2014)*

Labour force: 3.84 million (2014)*

Unemployment: 5.00% (2014)

Inflation: 1.46% (2014)

Balance of trade: -US$3.18 billion (2014)

* estimated figure

Austria

In the years immediately following the Second World War, in which Austria became an independent, neutral state, Austrians enjoyed not only social stability, but also remarkable economic growth rates that often bettered those of neighbouring Germany. Unemployment and inflation were both low, the trade unions rarely went on strike and for years the Austrian parliament voted unanimously on most of the legislation submitted. This social and political harmony contrasted sharply with many of Europe's other democracies.

Right turn

The twenty-first century had seen some of this comfortable social glue begin to come unstuck. This was evidenced by the steady rise in support for the far right seen in the 2015 local elections in the central state of Styria and in Burgenland in the east. The results indicated that the establishment coalition between the Sozialdemokratische Partei Österreichs (SPÖ) (Social Democratic Party of Austria) and the Österreichische Volkspartei (ÖVP) (Austrian People's Party) saw its support fall dramatically in both provinces. The coalition's loss was to the benefit of the right-wing Freiheitliche Partei Österreichs (FPÖ) (Freedom Party of Austria). Campaigning with anti-immigration slogans such as 'Foreign in your own country' the FPÖ's following had almost tripled in Styria, to over 27.00 per cent, according to initial soundings. The Styria results implied that Austrian politics were no longer a cosy two-party affair. Now there were three hats in the ring.

The two ruling coalition parties had already taken something of a drubbing in elections in the Alpine province of Vorarlberg, where the ÖVP had lost its majority as voters appeared to turn to the greens and the new Das Neue Österreich (NEOS) (New Austria Party) which secured 7 per cent of the vote. If things were bad for the ÖVP in Vorarlberg, they were worse for the SPÖ, which slumped to a mere 9 per cent of the vote. The clear winner in Vorarleberg, however, was the FPÖ, with over 23 per cent.

Europe?

Writing on the *Europe's World* website, the political commentator Alexander Klimburg observed that Austria might have been perceived as a euro-enthusiastic country, but that was no longer the case. A December 2014 *Eurobarometer* indicated that Austria is one of the European Union's (EU) most Euro-sceptic countries, despite the fact that over 66 per cent voted in 1994 in favour of joining the EU. Over one-third (36 per cent) of those polled now had a 'negative' view of the EU, more than the UK's 32 per cent and surpassed only by Greece and Cyprus. Paradoxically Austrians rank at the top (73 per cent) in terms of 'feeling European as citizens'.

According to Mr Klimburg, Austria's mainstream parties, along with the

Greens and the liberal NEOS, have traditionally depicted themselves as 'the chief line of defence towards the growing euro-scepticism.' However, the perception exists that the establishment's Grand Coalition in which the Social Democrats and the Christian Democrats had largely shared power for the previous 60 years, was 'introspective, overly preoccupied with internal factions and suffering from dwindling electoral support for both parties.' (Mr Klimburg did not mention the word 'corruption' – see below.) The ÖVP had replaced Michael Spindelegger with Reinhold Mitterlehener as leader in the autumn of 2014 and there were signs that Chancellor Werner Faymann, the SPÖ 's leader, could before long see his leadership challenged, especially if the 2015 local elections continued to go badly for the SPÖ.

In his excellent article, Mr Klimburg (a Harvard graduate who is, *inter alia*, a fellow of the Austrian Institute for International Affairs) refers to Austria's 'masterly inactivity' in Brussels, where the Vienna government often appears to have no official position, or to develop it only very late in the day. This, says Mr Klimburg, is especially true 'on issues of particular public interest for many Austrians, such as on data retention, the TTIP trans-Atlantic free trade agreement, or even smoking in public places.' The hope seems to be, says Klimburg, that the 'tough' decisions will be made in Brussels – which will then also get the blame. In short, Austrians may feel European, 'they just want more say what happens within it.'

Times change

In many superficial respects the results of the 2013 general election had suggested the 'same procedure as last time' approach to politics that had provided Austria's conservative voters the reassurance and predictability they long sought from their politicians. But for those observers who chose to interpret the results more carefully, there was just cause for concern at the gains registered by the FPÖ. The overall share of votes won by the two 'big-beast' parties fell to just above 50 per cent, way down from the 78 per cent registered in the 2002 elections. With a swing of around 30 per cent to the far right parties, principally the FPÖ with 21 per cent and the Bündnis Zukunft Österreich (BZÖ) (Alliance for Austria's Future). Team Stronach, (see World of Information – Austria 2014) polled almost 6 per cent, thereby gaining the right to enter parliament.

Look right

The FPÖ's success was to be repeated in the May 2014 European elections, revealing – not only in Austria – swelling anti-European Union sentiment – the Front National in France and UK Independence Party (UKIP) in the UK – represented widespread anti-European sentiment if not general xenophobia. In Austria's case there were sharper concerns – the FPÖ was known to have links to Neo-Nazi and fascist groups. Amazingly, at least one of the two 'big' parties has been in power since 1945, often as part of larger coalitions. Additionally, the principal parties' position of power is buttressed by a uniquely Austrian system of preferences whereby appointments to cabinet ministries are divided along party lines following a system known as *Proporz* – under which posts are neatly filled by party members in proportion to the votes won by their parties in the election.

But Austria's big-party politics has an effect beyond the government and beyond Vienna. Numerous jobs and contracts in the public sector and large state enterprises depend on party patronage. The net result is that change is often imperceptible and new ideas are hard to come by. Contentious conflicts are avoided and Austria's legislative and governmental structures risk becoming less than transparent and, often, corrupt.

Corruption continues

According to the opinion polls, in 2014 a majority of Austrians believed corruption to be a regular feature of Austrian politics. A survey conducted by the Österreichissche Gesellschaft Marketing GesmbH (OGM) found that 73 per cent of Austrians feared that the corruption, fraud and possible abuse of office revealed in their newspapers were not just odd instances of corruption, but part of a much more widespread problem. Only 22 per cent of those polled considered that the cases under investigation did not represent a trend towards political corruption.

The OGM organisation found that the BZÖ and the ÖVP were especially suspected of being involved in corrupt arrangements. Around 63 per cent of Austrians believed that the BZÖ was prone to illicit deals. Fifty-nine per cent said the same about the ÖVP which had co-operated with the BZÖ in a federal government coalition between 2005 and 2007. The FPÖ was not far behind with 54 per cent, ahead of the SPÖ (42 per cent) and the Greens (23 per cent). Overall, the Greens appeared to emerge best in the survey: as many as 55 per cent of Austrians considered that the Greens had a clean sheet, with the SPÖ in second place with 34 per cent and the FPÖ in third place with 25 per cent. Only 19 per cent gave the ÖVP a clean sheet, while 16 per cent said the same about the BZÖ.

Corruption?

The Transparency International (TI) 2014 *Corruption Perceptions Index* (CPI) placed Austria at a respectable enough 23 of the countries surveyed, not far behind the United States (19) and the United Kingdom (17) but still behind the EU

KEY INDICATORS — **Austria**

	Unit	2011	2012	2013	2014	**2015
Population	m	8.42	8.47	8.48	8.52	*8.56
Gross domestic product (GDP)	US$bn	419.20	394.68	428.46	*437.12	*380.56
GDP per capita	US$	49,809	46,620	50,500	*51,307	*44,476
GDP real growth	%	3.1	0.9	0.3	*0.3	*0.9
Inflation	%	3.6	2.6	2.1	1.5	*1.1
Unemployment	%	6.1	4.4	4.9	5.0	*5.1
Exports (fob) (goods)	US$m	169,893.0	160,148.0	165,071.0	164,320.0	–
Imports (fob) (goods)	US$m	175,433.0	163,160.0	165,185.0	167,496.0	–
Balance of trade	US$m	-5,540.0	-3,012.0	-114.0	-3,177.0	–
Current account	US$m	2,266.0	7,026.0	4,439.0	*7,967.0	*7,160.0
Total reserves minus gold	US$m	10,855.0	12,232.0	12,474.0	14,145.0	–
Foreign exchange	US$m	6,970.0	7,972.0	8,142.0	–	–
Exchange rate	per US$	0.75	0.77	0.73	0.82	–

* estimated figure ** forecast figure

benchmark country Germany at 13. However, finding himself on the political back foot, the SPÖ Chancellor Werner Faymann promised to instigate and speed up the introduction of a new law on the issue after Peter Pilz, a high profile member of the Green Party, had warned the SPÖ-ÖVP government he was prepared to press for a referendum on the issue. The OGM poll had suggested that an overwhelming 84 per cent of Austrians did not believe their politicians' pledges to ensure more transparency. A respected political scientist Fritz Plasser deplored the government's 'complete ineffectiveness', claiming that Austria's current regulations failed to meet Western European standards. The poll results were presented one day after it emerged that Austria's finance ministry had 'redacted' various documents before providing them to the parliament's anti-corruption committee – despite promising not to do so when the commission started operating in January 2012.

The economy

Austria had recovered quickly from the Great Recession of 2009, but for two years gross domestic product (GDP) has been more or less stagnating. Following a slump of 3.8 per cent in 2009, GDP rose by about 2 and 3 per cent in 2010 and 2011, respectively. But then the recovery stalled and in 2013 and 2014 GDP only rose by 0.2 to 0.3 per cent. Following the 2009 recession of 2009, Austria was one of the very few countries in which unemployment only rose marginally. However, in 2013 and 2014 the unemployment rate rose quite substantially. As a result Austria lost its position of the country with the lowest unemployment rate in the EU to Germany.

While the overall employment rate (employed persons in relation to the labour force in the age group 15 to 64) of slightly below 73 per cent (second quarter of 2014) is well above the EU average of just 65 per cent and also not far behind Germany (73.4 per cent) or Switzerland (about 80 per cent), the employment rate of people aged 55 to 64 is only 47.7 per cent, compared to 65 per cent in Germany or 71 per cent in Switzerland. In the light of a declining working-age population, the employment of older workers needs to increase in Austria if it is to reach the EU 'norm' and Austria's pension age threshold would also have to be raised.

The ÖNB View...

According to its June 2014 economic outlook, the Österreichische Nationalbank (ÖeNB) (Austrian National Bank) expected the Austrian economy to grow by 1.6 per cent in 2014. Exports would continue to be the main driver of the upswing in the second half of 2014, benefitting from the gradual recovery in the euro-zone and the moderate improvement in the global economy. Growth was expected to accelerate to 1.9 per cent and 2.1 per cent in 2015 and 2016, respectively, being increasingly supported by domestic demand. Inflation was expected to decrease to 1.8 per cent at the end of 2014 and to 1.7 per cent in 2015. According to the ÖNB forecast, inflation would also remain moderate in 2016 (1.9 per cent).

Private sector investment, which decreased in 2013, was also expected to revive on the back of necessary replacement investment, a more favourable sales outlook and improving sentiment. Amid persistent uncertainties, the growth of investment in plant and equipment would remain fairly modest. At the same time, the increase in housing investment was expected to continue as funding conditions remained benign and house prices were still rising. Lower inflation, continuously high employment growth and higher income growth on the back of the economic recovery were expected to contribute to a steady increase in real disposable household income from 2014 to 2016. As a result, real private consumption was expected to grow by 0.7 per cent in 2014, 1.0 per cent in 2015 and 1.4 per cent in 2016.

In line with developments observed in previous years in the Austrian labour market, both labour supply and employment continued to grow. Unemployment was therefore expected to remain broadly stable at 4.9 per cent to 5.0 per cent over the forecast period. This made Austria the country with the lowest unemployment rate in the EU. In the view of the ÖNB, price growth would continue to lose momentum as energy and commodity prices declined. Inflation was consequently expected to drop further, reaching 1.8 per cent in 2014 and 1.7 per cent in 2015. As the economy picked up steam, inflation was expected to edge up to 1.9 per cent in 2016.

In the view of the ÖNB, the Austrian general government budget balance was expected to deteriorate temporarily to -2.5 per cent of GDP in 2014 on account of additional bank support. In 2015 and 2016, the budget balance was likely to improve to -1.2 per cent and -0.7 per cent of GDP, respectively. The ÖNB expected that additional fiscal consolidation of some 0.25 per cent of GDP would be necessary to enable Austria to meet the structural deficit target of -0.45 per cent of GDP agreed with the EU.

... and that of the IMF

In its mid-2014 assessment of the Austrian economy, the International

Austria and owning up to the past

A shocking poll, conducted in 2013, found that 42 per cent of Austrians believed life 'wasn't all that bad under the Nazis'. And a further 39 per cent predicted a return of anti-Semitic persecution in the future.

Austria and Germany have two of the most extensive, harsh and enforceable anti-Nazi and Holocaust denial policies in the world. Indeed, Austria has banned 30 number plate combinations that could potentially allude to far-right fanaticism. The results of the polls, therefore, were especially shocking to a country that has consistently attempted to distance itself from Hitler – its most abhorrent son.

In October 1943 the Allies labelled Austria the 'first victim of Hitlerite aggression' and, in doing so, absolved it from a large part of the blame. Additionally a 1946 Austrian government investigation found that 'only a handful of traitors had collaborated with the Nazis'. By painting itself as the victim, Austria managed to remain an independent and intact state during the tumultuous post-war years. In fact, such was its victim mentality that in 1986 a former Wehrmacht recruit, Kurt Waldheim, became Austrian president despite a campaign in which his sordid past was revealed and, in turn, rebuked as just 'doing my duty'.

Since the 1990s an air of sensibility has returned to Austrian politics. Officials are increasingly willing to confront the past and offer compensation for Jewish victims and forced labourers. It is a move welcomed by those who have viewed footage of Hitler's triumphant 1938 return to Vienna – amidst Nazi salutes, fervent anti-Semitism and general euphoria – and concluded Austria's position resembled more the willing recipient, not perpetual victim. It is also what makes the polls so alarming: while political realities may have shifted, social attitudes remain stubborn.

Monetary Fund (IMF) reported that Austria had come through the global economic and financial crisis relatively well, reflecting the absence of any large pre-crisis domestic imbalances. In the run-up to the 2008–09 crisis, household and corporate debt levels had remained moderate. The household saving rate had not experienced the sharp drop of countries with a housing boom, but had in fact increased. Tax revenues did not rise rapidly, so the growth of government spending had remained modest. As a result, there were buffers to weather the crisis. The IMF noted that Austrian households could smooth consumption by letting the household saving rate decline; and Austrian firms were not under severe pressure to cut costs and could absorb demand shocks through lower profit margins and keep employment relatively stable. The government could act counter-cyclically, in contrast to 'boom-bust countries', which were forced to consolidate strongly after sharp revenue drops.

In the view of the IMF, the main impact of the crisis was on the internationally active banking system and public debt. Pre-crisis, Austrian banks had expanded rapidly in Central Europe and South East Europe (CESEE), channelling funds that they attracted in Western Europe to finance the credit boom in the region. As their funding dried up following the Lehman Brothers crash and their assets suffered from the end of the credit boom in CESEE, internationally active Austrian banks had come under pressure and needed government support. Together with the downturn, this had contributed to an increase in public debt from 60 per cent of GDP in 2007 to around 80 per cent of GDP in 2014.

The IMF also noted that after a rebound in 2010/11, a new slowdown occurred in 2012 and 2013, mainly reflecting the knock-on effect on trade and confidence from the euro-zone crisis. As with the euro-zone, in mid-2014 the economy now seemed on a more stable recovery path, creating an opportunity for resolving what the IMF termed 'crisis legacies' and 'long-standing structural issues'. In the banking sector the medium-sized banks nationalised during the financial crisis were still restructuring and internationally active large banks remained subject to risks from CESEE, most recently in Russia, Ukraine and Hungary.

The IMF also recommended 'More ambitious structural public expenditure reforms to bring down debt faster' thereby reducing the high tax burden on labour. The debt reduction proposals under current plans left debt levels above those of AAA peer levels and would not build sufficient buffers to cope with intensifying ageing cost pressures, potential further bank restructuring costs and residual risks from banks' CESEE exposure as well as other contingent liabilities. High social security contributions and income tax rates discouraged labour supply and hampered potential growth.

The IMF projected 2014 full-year inflation of 1.7 per cent, well above the euro-zone projection of 0.7 per cent for 2014 and also above the rate in Germany. This relatively high inflation was largely driven by the services sector and reflected a tight labour market. With the lowest unemployment rate in the euro-zone (in mid-2014 around 5 per cent), wage cost increases since 2008 have been amongst the highest in the euro-zone. The IMF noted that Austria's productivity per hour was 20 per cent lower than in the US and that the gap was widening. In the view of the IMF, this gap probably reflected a multitude of factors, including weaknesses in IT adaptation, education and the availability of private venture capital.

In the previous parliament (before the 2013 elections) the government had taken several structural expenditure reform steps which the IMF considered to be in the right direction, including on pensions and health care. These measures were confirmed in the new coalition agreement. However, this new agreement and the fiscal framework for 2015–18 contained no major additional structural expenditure measures, reflecting a divergence in views among coalition partners on many policy issues.

The IMF concluded by expressing concern that geopolitical developments posed risks. Two internationally active Austria-based banks (Raiffeisen Bank International AG (RBI) and Italian-owned Unicredit Bank Austria) faced problems from Ukraine and Russia. Banks also suffered idiosyncratic country risks from policy actions in Hungary. Other risk factors include the European Central Bank (ECB)'s comprehensive balance sheet assessment, which may lead to surprises on Austrian banks' CESEE asset quality; and lower-than-expected growth in emerging markets and the euro-zone that would predominantly be transmitted via exports to Germany or through strong real and financial sector ties with Italy.

Risk assessment

Politics	Fair/poor
Eonomy	Fair
Regional stability	Good

COUNTRY PROFILE

For centuries the Austrian (later Austro-Hungarian) Empire covered most of central Europe.

1918 After the Austro-Hungarian Empire was defeated in the First World War, the first Austrian Republic was declared; three-quarters of the former Empire's territory was ceded to neighbouring states.

1933 Pro-fascist Engelbert Dollfuss (elected federal chancellor in 1932) gained dictatorial powers and banned all political opposition to his Vaterländische Front (VF) (Fatherland Front). Dollfuss forged a strong relationship with fascist Italy in an attempt to preserve Austria's independence.

1934 The government put down an uprising by Socialists in February. Dollfuss was assassinated in July by Austrian Nazis, who had been conspiring to oust the government and integrate Austria with Nazi Germany.

1938 The new chancellor, Kurt von Schuschnigg, met with Adolf Hitler in an attempt to preserve Austria's independence. After refusing to meet Hitler's demands for concessions for the banned Austrian Nazi Party, von Schuschnigg resigned as chancellor and was replaced by Arthur Seyss-Inquart (leader of the Austrian Nazi Party). Austria was integrated with Nazi Germany. Austria was renamed Ostmark.

1945 After Nazi Germany was defeated in the Second World War; Austria re-emerged as an independent state but was divided into four zones of occupation by the US, UK, France and USSR. The conservative Österreichische Volkspartei (ÖVP) (Austrian People's Party) and the Sozialdemokratische Partei Österreichs (SPÖ) (Social Democratic Party of Austria) formed a coalition government.

1955 The 1955 State Treaty confirmed Austria's independence and banned re-integration with Germany. Austria joined the UN, declared its neutrality and the occupation forces withdrew.

1960 Austria joined the European Free Trade Area (EFTA).

1966 The ÖVP came to power after 20 years of a coalition.

1970-87 The SPÖ was in power until 1983, when it formed a coalition government with the Freiheitliche Partei Österreichs (FPÖ) (Freedom Party of Austria).

1986 Kurt Waldheim (independent but with ÖVP's backing) won the presidential

election. Controversy surrounded allegations of his implication in Nazi atrocities in the Balkans (1942–45), culminating in his listing as an undesirable alien by the US Department of Justice.
1987 Following an inconclusive election, the SPÖ and the ÖVP formed a coalition.
1992 Waldheim stepped down and was replaced by Thomas Klestil.
1995 Austria joined the EU. The one-year-old governing coalition collapsed over the 1996 budget.
1997 Franz Vranitsky led the government as chancellor from 1995 until his resignation in 1997, when he was replaced by Viktor Klima.
1998 Federal President Klestil was re-elected.
1999 After indecisive election results, the ÖVP-SPÖ coalition collapsed, leading to a coalition between the ÖVP and the far-right, FPÖ.
2000 The ÖVP's Wolfgang Schüssel became chancellor. The inclusion of the FPÖ in the government, with Susanne Riess-Passer (FPÖ) as vice chancellor led to EU diplomatic sanctions against Austria. Only after Joerg Haider stepped down as party leader of FPÖ were sanctions lifted.
2002 The euro replaced the Austrian schilling. After three FPÖ ministers resigned, Schüssel announced that ÖVP was withdrawing from the coalition government. The ÖVP won the snap election and Schüssel remained as Chancellor.
2003 ÖVP coalition government included the SPÖ and right-wing populist FPÖ.
2004 President Klestil died in office. Heinz Fischer (SPÖ) won the presidential elections.
2005 The FPÖ split; a breakaway faction, Bündis Zukunft Österreich (BZÖ) (Alliance for Austria's Future), was led by Joerg Haider. Austria began making payouts to those whose property had been looted during the Holocaust. Most of the victims are elderly and many resident in the US.
2006 In general elections, the SPÖ won 35.3 per cent of the vote, the ÖVP, won 34.3 per cent. Some states, led by far-right parties, introduced nationality laws for new citizens.
2007 After two months of negotiations, the SPÖ and ÖVP formed a coalition government and Alfred Gusenbauer became Chancellor. Former Austrian president and secretary general of the United Nations, Kurt Waldheim died.
2008 The ruling coalition government collapsed when the ÖVP withdrew, following disagreement over policy issues. In early elections, Chancellor Gusenbauer did not to stand for re-election. The SPÖ won 29.4 per cent of the vote the ÖVP 26 per cent and FPÖ 17.7 per cent; turnout was 76.6 per cent. Joerg Haider (BZÖ) was killed in a road accident. The SPÖ and ÖV formed a coalition in government, preventing the far-right BZÖ from forming a government. Werner Faymann (SPÖ) was sworn in as chancellor.
2009 German-based airline, Lufthansa took control of the state-owned Austrian Airlines in a privatisation deal by the government.
2010 Incumbent Heinz Fischer won the presidential elections with a decisive 78.9 per cent of the vote.
2011 In March, the European Parliament launched an investigation into the allegations that three MEPs (including one Austrian) took cash to propose amendments to draft EU legislation. Otto von Habsburg, the last heir to the throne of the long-defunct, Austro-Hungarian Empire, died on 4 July, aged 98 years.
2012 A new anti-bribery law was enacted on 21 August, following a political scandal when MEP Ernst Strasser was charged with corruption for accepting payment to propose an amendment in the European Parliament. On 25 September, a new political party, Team Stronach für Österreich (Team Stronach for Austria (Team Stronach)) was registered to participate in the next general elections. The founder, Frank Stronach, is a billionaire owner of Canada's auto-parts company Magna International and deeply sceptical of Austria's membership of the EMU. The trial of Ernst Strasser (ÖVP) began on 26 November, accused of asking for an annual payment of €100,000 (US$130,000) to influence EU legislation.
2013 Parliamentary elections were held on 29 September. The SPÖ lead the way with 26.82 per cent of the vote (52 seats out of 183), the ÖVP 23.99 per cent (47), Freiheitliche Partei Österreichs (FPÖ) (Freedom Party of Austria) 20.51 per cent (40), Die Grünen-Die Grüne Alternative (The Greens-The Green Alternative) 12.42 per cent (24), Team Stronach für Österreich (Team Stronach) 5.73 per cent (11), NEOS – Das Neue Österreich (NEOS – The New Austria 4.96 per cent (9). Team Stronach and NEOS won seats for the first time while the BZÖ-Liste Jörg Haider (BZÖ-Jörg Haider List) dropped out. A 'grand coalition' of the SPÖ and ÖVP with Werner Faymann of the SPÖ as Chancellor became the ruling coalition.
2014 The Austrian Climate Change Assessment Report 2014, published in September, notes that average temperatures in Austria have risen by almost 2C since 1880, and that the rate of increase has risen since 1980. It reports that the changes in temperature are mainly man-made and caused by 'emissions of greenhouse gases'. It goes on to warn that 'without increased efforts to adapt to climate change, Austria's vulnerability will increase', particularly in areas such as agriculture, forestry and winter tourism.
2015 The Sozialdemokratische Partei Österreichs (SPÖ) (Social Democratic Party of Austria) held on the power in municipal elections held in Vienna on 11 October, but with a reduced of margin of 39 per cent to the 31 per cent of the far right Freiheitliche Partei Österreichs (FPÖ) (Freedom Party of Austria).

Political structure

Constitution

The 1920 constitution was amended in 1929.

The state is a federal republic consisting of nine Länder (states), each with its own state Ländtag (legislature) and government. The nine states are Burgenland, Carinthia, Lower Austria, Upper Austria, Salzburg, Styria, Tyrol, Vorarlberg and Vienna. A considerable amount of political power is devolved to the state assemblies, although all matters of national interest are decided in Vienna. Each state parliament appoints its own state governor.

For some functions (for example, appointing the new president) the Nationalrat (National Council) and the Bundesrat (Federal Council) of the federal Bundesversammlung (parliament) meet in joint session, as the Nationalversammlung (National Assembly). Certain issues may be put to the popular vote in a national referendum and the people may also force a direct vote in the Nationalrat if any petition gathers more than 200,000 signatures.

Traditionally, the government has been required to work according to the principles of the *sozialpartner* (social contract). This informal organisation, comprising the Chamber of Economy, Chamber of Agriculture, Chamber of Labour and trade unions, is at the heart of the policy-making process. Such a system has served Austria well in the past as it both guarantees and feeds on national consensus and unity. However, it is becoming unworkable in a fully globalised world economy.

Form of state

Federal parliamentary democratic republic

The executive

Executive power rests with the head of the federal government, who is the chancellor appointed by the president, and usually the leader of the largest party in the Nationalrat.

The president is elected by popular vote every six years for a maximum of two terms. He has no executive powers in peace time. He has special emergency powers, as well as overseeing elections and swearing in new chancellors and governments, but in practice, he acts in accordance with the decisions of the government.

National legislature

The Nationalrat (lower house) has 183 members elected every four years by proportional representation. The seats are distributed first among 43 constituencies then among the nine states, and the remainder at federal level. The Bundesrat (upper house) has 62 members elected for between 4–6 years. Membership changes after every election of lower state assemblies. The Bundesrat may veto legislation passed by the lower chamber, although in practice such vetoes are suspensive and can be overridden by the lower chamber, except in cases of constitutional matters, rights of the Bundesrat and the jurisdiction of federal states. Although the two chambers are equal under the constitution, in practice the Nationalrat has more power. While in formal joint session both chambers constitute a third body, the Bundesversammlung (Federal Assembly).

Legal system

The legal system is divided between legislative, administrative and judicial power. There are three supreme courts Verfassungsgerichtshof (Constitutional Court), Verwaltungsgerichtshof (Administrative Court) and Oberster Gerichtshof (Judicial Court). There are around 200 local judicial courts (Bezirksgerichte), 17 provincial and district courts (Landes-und Kreisgerichte) and four higher provincial courts (Oberlandesgerichte) in Vienna, Graz, Innsbruck and Linz.

Last elections

29 September 2013 (parliamentary); 25 April 2010 (presidential)

Results: Presidential: Heinz Fischer (Sozialdemokratische Partei Österreichs (SPÖ) (Social Democratic Party)) won 78.9 per cent of the vote, Barbara Rosenkranz (FPÖ) 15.6 per cent, Rudolf Gehring (Christliche Partei Österreichs) (CPÖ) (Christian Party)) 5.4 per cent. Turnout was 49.2 per cent.

Parliamentary (2013): the SPÖ won 26.82 per cent of the vote (52 seats out of 183), the ÖVP 23.99 per cent (47), Freiheitliche Partei Österreichs (FPÖ) (Freedom Party of Austria) 20.51 per cent (40), Die Grünen-Die Grüne Alternative (The Greens-The Green Alternative) 12.42 per cent (24), Team Stronach für Österreich (Team Stronach) 5.73 per cent (11), NEOS – Das Neue Österreich (NEOS – The New Austria 4.96 per cent (9), no other party won enough votes to achieve gain a seat; turnout was 74.91 per cent.

Next elections

2016 (presidential); 29 September 2018 (parliamentary).

Political parties

Ruling party

Coalition led by Sozialdemokratische Partei Österreichs (SPÖ) (Social Democratic Party of Austria) with Österreichische Volkspartei (ÖVP) (Austrian People's Party) (from 2 Dec 2008, re-elected 29 Sep 2013)

Main opposition party

Freiheitliche Partei Österreichs (FPÖ) (Freedom Party of Austria)

As a result of negligible population growth and long life expectancy, the Austrian population is ageing significantly.

Population

8.47 million (2012)

Last census: May 2001: 8,032,926

Population density: Urban population 68 per cent (2010 Unicef).

Annual growth rate: 0.5 per cent, 1990–2010 (Unicef).

Ethnic make-up

Around 93 per cent are of German-Austrian origin. Minorities include Slovenes, Croats, Hungarians and Czechs and are mostly concentrated in the south-east. There are ethnic communities from Africa, the Middle East and Asia.

Religions

Roman Catholic (89 per cent); Protestant (6 per cent).

Education

Primary schooling lasts for four years. There are two main forms of secondary education; one academic and one geared more to technical and vocational education. The former, *Allgemeinbildende*, school may be attended for eight years or the latter, *Hauptschule*, attended for four years followed by a school offering specialised training of a technical or vocational nature. Tertiary education takes place in universities or specialist colleges including technology, music and art higher education institutions.

Compulsory years: 6 to 15

Enrolment rate: 103 per cent total primary enrolment, 99 per cent total secondary enrolment, 57 per cent tertiary enrolment; of relevant age groups (including repetition rates) World Bank.

Pupils per teacher: 12 in primary schools

Health

All Austrians have access to healthcare.

HIV/Aids

In 2009, there were an estimated 15,000 people living with HIV.

HIV prevalence: 0.3 per cent aged 15–49 in 2009 (Unicef 2012)

Life expectancy: 81 years, 2010 (Unicef 2012)

Fertility rate/Maternal mortality rate: 1.4 births per woman, 2010 (Unicef 2012)

Child (under 5 years) mortality rate (per 1,000): 4 per 1,000 live births (WHO 2012)

Welfare

Austrian social insurance is compulsory and covers health insurance, pension insurance, accident insurance and unemployment insurance. Contributions are shared by employers and employees.

Pensions

Reforms adopted in 2003, extend the years required for employee contributions from 40 to 45, before a worker can retire on a full pension with all benefits; the statutory retirement age was set at 65 for all; 10 disparate pension systems for various categories of workers were harmonised. This is expected to reverse the trend for early retirement. In 2003 the average age of retirement was 57.5, with less than 30 per cent of workers being in the 55–64 age range. With an ageing population the pension scheme will become progressively more expensive; it is expected that the new reforms wll limit spending by between 1.5–1.75 per cent of GDP a year. The government is proposing to stagger the rise in the official retirement age, while reducing state pensions by up to 30 per cent, in some cases.

Main cities

Vienna (capital, estimated population 1.7 million in 2012), Graz (261,836), Linz (188,599), Salzburg (149,218), Innsbruck (119,524), Klagenfurt (93,383), Villach (59,383), Wels (58,430), St Pölten (52,167), Dornbirn (45,474).

Languages spoken

About 94 per cent of Austrian nationals speak German, although a heavy dialect is in daily use. There are linguistic minorities of Slovenes, Croats, Hungarians, Slovaks and Czechs.

Official language/s

German

Media

Press

Almost all ownership of the print media is held by two Germany-based publishing houses, the Bertelsmann Media owns most magazine titles and Westdeutsche Allgemaine Zeitung (WAZ), through Mediaprint Group, controls most newspapers.

Dailies: In German, national newspapers include *Der Standard* (http://derstandard.at), *Die Presse* (http://diepresse.com), *Der Kurier* (www.kurier.at) a mass-circulation and *Neue Kronenzeitung* (www.krone.at), which has regional editions. Major regional newspapers include *Der Grazer* (www.grazer.at) from Graz, *Salzburger Fenster* (www.salzburger-fenster.at) from Salzburg and *Österreich*

(www.oe24.at/zeitung), published in Vienna.
Weeklies: In German, *Profil* (www.news.at/profil), *Österreich Journal* (www.oe-journal.at), and *News Magazin* (www.news.at/magazin), for news and analysis, *Die Bezirksblätter* (www.noe-anzeiger.at), for regional and local news, *Wienerin* (www.wienerin.at), for women and *Wiener Zeitung* (www.wienerzeitung.at) a semi-official publication from Vienna.
Most daily newspapers have weekend editions, which tend to be bigger and contain a large amount of advertising.
Business: In German, *Wirtschafts Blatt* (www.wirtschaftsblatt.at) is a daily, *Industrie Magazin* (www.industriemagazin.at), and *Trend* (www.news.at/trend), are weekly magazines.

Broadcasting

Österreichischer Rundfunk (ÖRF) (Austrian Broadcasting Corporation) (www.orf.at) is the national, public broadcasting network.
Radio: ÖRF broadcasts four national radio networks (including Ö1 Hit Radio and FM4), 10 regional stations and two international channels (Radio Österreich 1 International and Radio 1476). Private, commercial radio stations includes Krone Hit (www.kronehit.at) a national network and local locally Energy 104.2 (http://energy.t-online.at) and Radio Anabella (www.radioarabella.at), from Vienna, Radio Osttirol (http://radio.osttirol.net) from Lienz, and Radio Fabrik (www.radiofabrik.at) from Saltburg.
Television: ÖRF (http://tv.orf.at) has two public channels ÖRF1 and ÖRF2, broadcasting domestically produced and imported programmes. Private networks include ATV (http://atv.at) and OKTO TV (http://okto.tv) is a non-profit community TV station. There are several cable and satellite TV networks including Pulse TV (www.puls4.com), Premiere Austria (www.premiere.at) and Austria 9 TV (www.austria9.tv). There are a number of German TV affiliates throughout Austria.
Other news agencies: APA (Austria Presse Agentur): www.apa.at
Presstext Austria (in German): www.pressetext.at

Economy

Austria is a small landlocked country of less than 84,000 square kilometres and a population of less than 10 million, but it is one of the richest countries in Europe with a per capita income that reached US$51,127 in 2014. As with all post-industrial societies, the service sector is the largest component of the Austrian economy, with banking playing a major role, particularly as it is an important component of the rapidly growing Central, Eastern and South-eastern Europe (CESE) economies, into which Austrian-owned banks have expanded. Tourism is also an important sector of the economy; the country is in the top-15 countries visited worldwide, offering holiday destinations in both summer and winter.
The economy was impacted by the global economic crisis in 2009, with recessionary GDP growth of -3.8 per cent. Austria officially pulled out of recession, led by investment and exports, as global trade picked up in 2010 and by 2011 GDP growth was 3.1 per cent, falling to 0.2 per cent by 2013 before maintaining at 0.3 per cent in 2014.
The banking sector was badly hit by the economic crisis, not only within Austria but also in the CESE where the added risk of lending in foreign currencies added to Austrian banks' risks. The government had to provide special support amounting to US$148.2 million. Lending in foreign currencies by Austrian subsidiaries in the CESE was halted (although remained active in euros) and there was little withdrawal of business from CESE countries.

External trade

As a member of the European Union, Austria operates within a community-wide free trade area, with tariffs set by a central body. Internationally, the EU has free trade agreements with a number of nations and trading blocs worldwide.
Foreign trade is a vital component of the Austrian economy and accounts for over 95 per cent of GDP of which 90 per cent is attributed to the motor vehicle sector, in particular engine and transmissions production. The EU accounts for around 65 per cent of both imports and exports while Germany is Austria's major trading partner accounting for 40 per cent of trade. Total trade with the US has grown, reaching US$8.9 billion in 2009, while Austria has invested heavily in Central, Eastern and South-eastern Europe (CESE) particularly in banking and industrial sectors.

Imports

Major imports are oil and oil products, chemicals, vehicles, machinery, foodstuffs and consumer durables.
Main sources: Germany (40.7 per cent of total in 2014), Italy (6.3 per cent), Switzerland (5.3 per cent).

Exports

Major exports include machinery, vehicles and parts, paper and paperboard, chemicals (chiefly plastics and pharmaceuticals) and manufactured goods, electronic components, metal goods in ferrous and steel, textiles, foodstuffs.
Main destinations: Germany (28.7 per cent of total in 2014), Italy (6.1 per cent), USA (5.4 per cent).

Agriculture

Farming

The agricultural sector contributes 2.2 per cent to GDP and employs 6.9 per cent of the labour force. The sector is dominated by small scale farming (50 per cent of farms cover less than 10 hectares), although the trend is towards larger, more mechanised units leading to increased productivity.
About 18.2 per cent of land is crop land, 24.1 per cent permanent pasture land and 39 per cent forests and woodland. Farming is concentrated in Upper Austria, the northern part of Lower Austria, Burgenland and Styria.
Principal products are milk, beef, veal, pork, sugar beet, maize, barley, wheat and wine, but government is encouraging diversification to oilseeds, herbs, spices, hops and fast-growing timber. Quality wine, improved since a 1985 wine scandal, has become a major export product. Although output fluctuates, the country remains almost 90 per cent self-sufficient.
Fundamental reform to the Common Agricultural Policy (CAP) was introduced in 2005 in Austria. The subsidies paid on farm output, which tended to benefit large farms and encourage overproduction, were replaced by single farm payments not conditional on production. This is expected to reward farms that provide and maintain a healthy environment, food safety and animal welfare standards. The changes are also intended to encourage market conscious production and cut the cost of CAP to the EU taxpayer.
The growing of ornamental flowers and plants takes up much of Austria's horticultural land.

Fishing

The fisheries industry in Austria is based on professional lake fishing, which entails traditional breeding of trout, carp and other freshwater species. Austria promotes the EU's Common Fisheries Policy (CFP) as it benefits from the EU's structural funds for the development of aquaculture and the processing and marketing of products. Typically Austria's fishing haul is about 350 tonnes, amounting to 0.01 per cent of the EU total. Family firms run most businesses in both aquaculture and lake fishing. Despite its tradition of fish farming the sector suffers a lack of technical support.

Forestry

Forest and other wooded land occupy nearly a half of the total land area, with forest cover estimated at 3.8 million hectares (ha) in 2000. Forest cover increased an annual average of 0.20 per cent, the equivalent of 8,000ha between 1990–2000, as a result of afforestation in protected areas and natural extension onto agricultural land. Most of the forest is available for wood supply.

Forestry remains a major source of income within agriculture. Austria produces large quantities of paper and sawn wood, and is the fifth-largest exporter of sawnwood in the world with Germany, Italy and France the main export markets. The wood processing industry places an emphasis on value-added production including skis and solid wood panel manufacturing. A large proportion of raw materials including roundwood, pulp and recovered paper are imported.

Industry and manufacturing

The industrial sector contributes 31 per cent to GDP and employs 34 per cent of the labour force.

Since 1985, the industrial workforce has fallen by more than 150,000 to just over 500,000, which can be partly explained by falling productivity growth and company restructuring during the late 1990s. Since then, the industrial sector has recovered slightly, with productivity increasing by 6.7 per cent between 1998–2001.

Tourism

Austria has many cultural and historic attractions to offer its visitors, as well as a scenic terrain. As a mountainous country Austria also has two distinct holiday seasons offering either winter skiing or summer city or countryside and wildlife interests. Vienna, as the capital of the former Austro-Hungarian Empire, still boasts imperial institutions, including opera and chorale companies (Vienna Boys Choir), as well as the famous Spanish Riding School (of Lipizzaner stallions).

Travel and tourism was projected to directly contribute €15.9 billion (US$21.8 billion) to GDP in 2011 and indirectly €44.5 billion (US$61 billion).

Direct employment in the sector is around 5.3 per cent of total employment (229,000 jobs) and almost 14.5 per cent of indirect employment (622,500 jobs).

Travel and tourism is Austria's biggest foreign exchange earner, with a forecast €16.8 billion (US$23 billion) going into the economy in 2014. Investment in travel and tourism was estimated to be €3.1 billion (US$4.2 billion), 4.2 per cent of total investments in 2014.

Mining

The mining sector accounts for approximately 11 per cent of annual GDP and employs 1 per cent of the workforce.

There are deposits of various minerals, notably magnesite (of which Austria is the world's largest producer), iron, lead and zinc ores, salt, graphite, coal and gypsum. Commercial exploitation is restricted by the very small number of viable deposits and geological difficulties.

Austria's main natural resources are iron, lead and zinc ores, magnesite, salt, graphite and gypsum.

With extraction relatively expensive, oil is under-exploited and will last for little more than a decade. The main oil and gas company is Österreichische Mineralölverwaltung (ÖMV), the country's largest industrial concern. The government is the largest shareholder in ÖMV, with a 35 per cent stake.

The domestic natural gas production meets just under 20 per cent of Austria's gas requirements. The rest is imported, in particular from countries of the former Soviet bloc. Compliance with the first stage of the EU directive for liberalisation of the gas market in 2000 freed up half the market, which was largely controlled by ÖMV.

Austria produces over a million tonnes of coal per year, supplying approximately 20 per cent of domestic demand. Much of this production is low quality brown coal. The remainder of Austria's coal supplies are imported, particularly from Germany and the Czech Republic. At current production levels, Austrian coal reserves will last several decades.

Austria has deposits of various minerals, notably magnesite (of which it is the world's largest producer), iron, lead and zinc ores, salt, graphite and gypsum. However, commercial exploitation is restricted by the small number of viable deposits and by the geological difficulties facing extraction. The quality of base metals, gold and silver is very poor. Austria's largest mining product is iron, of which it typically produces over two million tonnes per annum.

Mineral raw materials such as limestone, marble, gravel and clay are widespread and are mined economically in quarries but are subject to rigorous environmental regulations. Several self-appointed protection groups have lobbied to stop the economic utilisation of the large reserves of gravel on the banks of the river Danube suitable for the civil construction industry. Privatisation of mining plants has improved production levels and has contributed to environmental protection.

Hydrocarbons

Proven oil reserves are less than 70 million barrels, but with extraction relatively expensive reserves are under-exploited and are not expected to last beyond 2015. Consumption of oil is around 270,000 barrels per day (bpd). Natural gas reserves are modest at around 535 billion cubic metres (cum), whereas total imports of gas were 10.1 billion cum, of which 5.25 billion cum came from Russia. Although Austria has reserves of coal, it is low quality brown coal and production is not commercially viable. Imported coal amounted to two million tonnes oil equivaltent (mtoe) in 2010.

Austria is poised to become an important European natural gas distribution hub with the completion of the Nabucco gas pipeline, between Turkey to Baumgarten (east Austria), in 2013, transporting gas from several central Asian producer countries.

In February 2012, the multinational, South Stream Transport group, announced the expected construction of the South Stream pipeline, to transport Russian natural gas to Western and Central Europe (and bypassing Ukraine) would begin in December 2012.

The main oil and gas company, OMV Konzern (OMV), is the country's largest industrial conglomerate; the government is its largest shareholder with a 32 per cent stake.

Energy

Austria has 15 billion gigawatts installed capacity, of which hydropower is responsible for around 75 per cent of electricity generation. The Freudenau hydroelectric power plant on the Danube is one of the world's most advanced hydroelectric power generating facilities. Austria has committed itself to a green electricity production policy under its Eco-Power Act that requires the reduction in hydrocarbon energy production in favour of sustainable sources. Biomass, and in particular wood chip, which accounts for around 10 per cent of consumed energy, is being developed for domestic heating. Austria is also one of the leading European nations in terms of solar energy utilisation.

Financial markets

Stock exchange

Wiener Börse AG (WBAG) (Vienna Stock Exchange)

Commodity exchange

EXAA Abwicklungsstelle für Energieprodukte (EXAA) (EXAA Energy Exchange Austria)

Banking and insurance

Consolidation of the Austrian banking sector began in 1997 when Bank Austria, the largest bank, took over Creditanstalt and Erste Bank took over Giro Credit. In 1998, Bank Austria merged with Germany's HypoVereinsbank. Bank Austria officially merged with Creditanstalt in 2002. During the first half of 2005 Bank Austria Creditanstalt's (BA-CA) profits rose 59 per cent, up to eur453 million.

There are around 1,000 national and local banks in Austria. Many are active in Central and Eastern Europe. Austria remains overbanked. In order to remain competitive in the new European market, significant consolidation is required.

In an effort to avoid joining the global list of non-co-operative tax havens, held by the Organisation of Economic Co-operation and Development (OECD), Austria eased its banking laws to allow the sharing of bank data that cracks down on offshore tax evasion.

Central bank

Österreichische Nationalbank (ÖeNB) (Austrian National Bank); European Central Bank (ECB).

Time

GMT plus one hour (daylight saving, late March to late October, GMT plus two hours)

Geography

Austria's land surface area is 83,855 square km. Austria is famous for its Alpine terrain, but the bulk of the country's economic activity and all of its major population centres are based on the low-lying areas around Vienna and Linz, in the north and east, and around Salzburg, on the German border.

Hemisphere

Northern

Climate

Climatic conditions vary widely across the country, with deep winter snows in the north and west, which are an essential element in the country's very important tourist economy. Seasonal variations are particularly marked: in Vienna, temperatures range from an average minus 1 degree Celsius (C) in January to 21 degrees C in July and August. Summers are often wet, with July and August recording averages of 84mm and 71mm of rainfall respectively.

Dress codes

Formality in dress is generally expected in business and for social events such as theatre and concerts. Warm clothing is essential for the winter months.

Entry requirements

Passports

Required by all, except nationals of countries which are signatories of the Schengen Accords, which includes most EU/EEA member states, who may visit on national IDs.

Visa

Visas are not required by nationals of EU and EEA countries; nationals of the US, Japan, Australia and a number of other countries do not need visas for visits of less than three months. For further exceptions contact the nearest embassy. A Schengen visa application (offered in several languages) can be downloaded from http://europa.eu/abc/travel/ see 'documents you will need'.

Currency advice/regulations

There are no restrictions on import or export of local or foreign currencies, although a permit is needed for export of over €7,000.

Customs

Personal items are duty-free. There are no duties levied on alcohol and tobacco between EU member states, providing amounts imported are for personal consumption.

Health (for visitors)

Nationals of the European Economic Area (EEA) countries and Switzerland can access reduced cost and sometimes free medical treatment using a European Health Insurance Card (EHIC) while visiting the EEA. Exceptions include nationals of the 10 countries which joined the EU in 2004 whose EHIC is not valid in Switzerland. Applications for the EHIC should be made before travelling.

Mandatory precautions

None

Advisable precautions

Vaccination for tick-borne encephalitis is recommended if visiting rural or forest regions.

Hotels

Generally of a high standard with a large selection available in most cities. Classified from five stars to one star. Rates vary according to category but are generally cheaper outside the capital.

Credit cards

Eurocard, Mastercard, Visa and, less widely, American Express and Diners Club are accepted.

Public holidays (national)

Fixed dates

1 Jan (New Year's Day), 6 Jan (Epiphany), 1 May (Labour Day), 15 Aug (Assumption Day), 26 Oct (National Day), 1 Nov (All Saints' Day), 8 Dec (Immaculate Conception), 25 Dec (Christmas Day), 26 Dec (St Stephen's Day).

Variable dates

Good Friday, Easter Monday, Ascension Day, Whit Monday, Corpus Christi.

Working hours

Banking

Mon–Wed and Fri: 0800–1500; Thu: 0800–1730.

Business

Mon–Fri: 0900–1800. Many offices do not work Friday afternoon.

Government

Mon–Fri: 0800–1230, 1300–1730. Many offices do not work Friday afternoon.

Shops

Mon–Fri: 0900–1800 (many shops close for two hours at midday); Sat: 0900–1300 or 1700. Longer opening hours exist in tourist areas.

Telecommunications

Mobile/cell phones

GSM G3 service operates in major cities only; 900 and 1800 services are available throughout the country

Electricity supply

220V AC

Social customs/useful tips

Appointments must be made in advance and punctuality is important; the usual form of address is *Herr* or *Frau*, followed by family or surname. People with an academic of professional title, eg *Doktor*, are addressed as *Herr* or *Frau Doktor*. Handshaking is universal in business and private meetings, both when arriving and leaving. Business is usually conducted in German. For restaurant meetings, dress formally, as for business meetings. Exchange pleasantries for a few minutes before getting down to business. When visiting private homes, it is usual to take flowers or confectionery for the host or hostess.

Security

There are no special problems and normal precautions apply. Vienna is possibly one of the safest cities in Europe.

Getting there

Air

National airline: Austrian Airlines

International airport/s: Vienna International (VIE), 18km south-east of city; facilities include duty-free shops, banks, bureaux de change, post office, restaurants, left luggage, conference facilities, medical facilities, tourist information, car hire. Second largest international airport is Salzburg Airport W A Mozart.

Other airport/s: Graz (GRZ), 12km from city; Salzburg (SZG), 4km from city; Innsbruck (INN), 5km from city; Klagenfurt (KLU), 4km from city; Linz (LNZ), 15km from city.

Airport tax: None

Surface

Road: There are good road links with all surrounding countries. Motorists should check advisability of routes, especially in winter, with ÖAMTC or ARBÖ (Austrian automobile clubs).

Rail: Austria participates in European rail pass schemes.

Water: Ships provide regular passenger services and cruises on the Danube, starting at Passau or Regensburg in Germany, to Vienna. There are also links with the Rhine and Main rivers and the Black Sea.

Getting about

National transport

Air: Austrian Arrows operate regular flights between main cities.

Road: There is a good road network. A toll must be paid to travel on motorways and highways – stickers (*vignettes*) to display on windscreens can be purchased from petrol stations, tobacconists and offices of Austrian automobile associations. There are additional charges for certain major routes.

Buses: Services are provided by federal and local authorities, in addition to private companies. There are more than 1,800 services in operation.

Rail: State-owned network of almost 6,000km, most of which is electrified. Also about 20 private railways covering a total 660km. There are frequent intercity services from Vienna to Salzburg, Innsbruck, Graz and Klagenfurt.

Water: There is a passenger ferry service between Vienna and the Black Sea and on upper Danube in mid-May to mid-September. Austrian Federal Railways operate passenger services on all the larger lakes.

City transport

Taxis: Widely available from stands or via radio/telephone services. The taxi journey time to the city centre from the airport is 25–30 minutes. Fares are metered but expensive, and in some areas zone charges or set charges for standard trips apply; a 10 per cent tip is usual.

Buses, trams & metro: Vienna has a very efficient, integrated system which avoids the crowded city traffic. Public transport operates between 0500 and 2400 and tickets, for all services, can be bought for 24 hour/3 day and set periods. An airport bus operates 24 hours every 20 minutes, and takes approximately 30 minutes to get to the city centre.

Trains: The OBB train service S7 operates between 0511—2216 every hour, and takes 25 minutes from the airport to the city centre.

Car hire

Self-drive and chauffeur-driven services are available at railway stations, airports and in major cities. Rates per day vary with size of car, plus additional charge per kilometre. A 'green card' (third party motor insurance) is compulsory. The speed limit is 100kph on most roads and 130kph on motorways, in built-up areas it is 50kph, unless otherwise stipulated.

EU issued driving licences are required, permitting the holders to drive in Austria for one year. Minimum driving age is 18.

BUSINESS DIRECTORY

The addresses listed below are a selection only. While World of Information makes every endeavour to check these addresses, we cannot guarantee that changes have not been made, especially to telephone numbers and area codes. We would welcome any corrections.

Telephone area codes

The international direct dialling code (IDD) for Austria is +43, followed by area code and subscriber's number:

Baden bei Wein	2252	St Pölten	2742
		Salzburg	662
Gmunden	7612	Steyr	7252
Graz	316	Vienna	1
Innsbruck	512	Villach	4242
Kitzbühel	5356	Wels	7242
Klagenfurt	463	Wien	2252
Krems an der Donau	2732	Wiener Neustadt	2622
Linz	732		

Chambers of Commerce

American Chamber of Commerce in Austria, 35 Porzellangasse, A-1090 Vienna (tel: 319-5751; fax: 319-5151; e-mail: office@amcham.or.at).

Austrian Economic Chamber, 63 Wiedner Hauptstrasse, A-1045 Vienna (tel/fax: 059-0900; e-mail: wkoe@wko.at).

Burgenland Economic Chamber, 1 Robert-Graf-Platz, A-7000 Eisenstadt (tel/fax: 059-0907; e-mail: wkgbld@wkbgld.at).

Kärnten Economic Chamber, 1 Europaplatz, A-9021 Klagenfurt (tel/fax: 059-0904; e-mail: wirtschaftskammer@wkk.or.at).

Lower Austria Economic Chamber, 10 Herrengasse, A-1014 Vienna (tel/fax: 015-3466; e-mail: wknoe@wknoe.at).

Salzburg Economic Chamber, 1 Julius-Raab-Platz, A-5027 (tel/fax: 0662-8888; e-mail: wirtschaftskammer@sbg.wk.or.at).

Steiermark Economic Chamber, 111 Körblergasse, A-8021 Graz (tel/fax: 031-6601; e-mail: office@wkstmk.at).

Tirol Economic Chamber, 14 Meinhardstrasse, A-6020 Innsbruck (te/fax: 059-0905; e-mail: office@wktirol.at).

Upper Austria Economic Chamber, 3 Hessenplatz, A-4010 Linz (tel/fax: 059-0909; e-mail: wirtschaftskammer@wkooe.at).

Vienna Economic Chamber, 8 Stubenring, A-1010 Vienna (tel/fax: 514-50; e-mail: postbox@wkw.at).

Vorarlberg Economic Chamber, 9 Wichnergasse, A-6800 Feldkirch (te/fax: 0552-2305; e-mail: praesidium@wkv.at).

Banking

Bank Austria Creditanstalt AG, Am Hof 2, A-1010 Vienna (tel: 531-240; fax: 5312-4155).

Bank für Arbeit und Wirtshaft AG (BAWAG), Seitzergasse 2 - 4, A-1010 Vienna (tel: 534-530; fax: 5345-32930).

Erste Bank, Graben 21, A1010 Vienna (tel: 531-000; fax: 5310-0625); also at Schubertring 5-7, A-1010 Vienna (tel: 711-940; fax: 713-7032).

Österreichische Postsparkasse, Georg Coch-Platz 2, A1020 Vienna (tel: 514-000; fax: 5140-01700).

Österreichische Volksbanken AG, Peregringasse 3, A-1090 Vienna (tel: 313-400; fax: 3134-03683).

Raiffeisen Zentralbank Österreich AG, Am Stadtpark 9, A-1030 Vienna (tel: 717-070).

Central bank

Österreichische Nationalbank, Otto Wagner-Platz 3, PO Box 61, A-1011 Vienna (tel: 404-20-2398; fax: 404-20-666; e-mail: oenb.info@oenb.co.at).

European Central Bank (ECB), Kaiserstrasse 29, D-60311 Frankfurt am Main, Germany (tel: (+49-69) 13-440; fax: (+49-69) 1344-6000; e-mail: info@ecb.int).

Stock exchange

Wiener Börse AG (WBAG) (Vienna Stock Exchange), * www.wienerborse.at

Commodity exchange

EXAA Abwicklungsstelle für Energieprodukte (EXAA) (EXAA Energy Exchange Austria), www.exaa.at

Travel information

ARBÕ (Auto-, Motor- und Radfahrerbund Österreichs), A-1150 Vienna, Mariahilfer Strasse 180 (tel: 891-217; fax: 891-236).

Austrian Airlines (Österreichische Luftverkehrs), PO Box 50, Fontanastrasse 1, Vienna A-1010 (tel: 683-5110; fax: 685-505).

ÖAMTC (Österreichischer Automobil-Motorrad und Touring Club), A-1010 Vienna, Schubertring 1-3 (tel: 711-990).

National tourist organisation offices

Österreich Werbung (Austrian National Tourist Office), 1 Margarethenstrasse, 1040 Vienna, (tel: 587-2000; fax: 588-6620; www.austria.info).

Ministries

Federal Chancellor's Office, Ballhausplatz 2, 1014 Vienna (tel: 531-150; fax: 535-0338).

Federal Ministry of Agriculture & Forestry, Environment and Water Resources, Stubenring 1, 1010 Vienna (tel: 711-000; fax: 715-9651).

Federal Ministry of Defence, Dampfschiffstr. 2, 1033 Vienna (tel: 515-950; fax: 515-9521).

Federal Ministry of Economic Affairs and Labour, Stubenring 1, 1010 Vienna (tel: 711-000; fax: 713-7995).

Federal Ministry of Education, Science and Culture, Minoritenplatz 5, 1014 Vienna (tel: 531-200; fax: 533-7797).

Federal Ministry of Finance, Himmelpfortgasse 8, 1015 Vienna (tel: 514-330; fax: 512-7869).

Federal Ministry of Foreign Affairs, Ballhausplatz 2, 1014 Vienna (tel: 531-150; fax: 533-2547).

Federal Ministry of the Interior, Herrengasse 7, 1010 Vienna (tel: 531-260; 531-263910).

Federal Ministry of Justice, Museumstrasse 7, 1070 Vienna (tel: 521-520; fax: 521-52727).

Federal Ministry of Public Affairs and Sport, Minoritenplatz 3, 1014 Vienna (tel: 531-150).

Federal Ministry of Social Security and Generations, Stubenring 1, 1010 Vienna (tel: 711-000; fax: 713-9311).

Federal Ministry of Transport, Innovation and Technology, Radetskystrasse 2, 1030 Vienna (tel: 711-620).

Other useful addresses

Austrian Business Agency, Opernring 3, A-1010 Vienna (tel: 202-588-5820; fax: 202-586-8659; e-mail: austrian.business@telecom.at; internet site: http://www.aba.qv.at).

Austria Presse-Agentur (APA) (Co-operative Agency of the Austrian Newspapers and Broadcasting Co), A-1199 Vienna, Gunoldstrasse 14 (tel: 36-050).

Austrian Telecommunications Regulatory Authority, Ministry of Science and Transport, Sektion IV, Kelsenstrasse 7, Vienna A-1030 (tel: 79731-4100; fax: 79731-4109; e-mail: Christian.Singer@bmv.gv.at).

Interpreters' Institute of Vienna University (tel: 347-649 ext. 298).

Österreichisches Statistisches Zentralamt (Central Statistical Office), Hintere Zollamtstrasse 2b, A-1030 Vienna (tel: 711-280; fax: 7112-87728).

Post und Telekom Austria AG, Postgasse 8, 1010 Vienna (tel: 515-510; fax: 512-8414).

US Embassy, Boltzmangasse 16, A-1090 Vienna (tel: 313-390; fax: 310-0682; e-mail: embassy@usembassy.at).

Vereinigung Österreichischer Industrieller (Association of Austrian Industrialists), A-1030 Vienna, Schwarzenbergplatz 4 (tel: 711-350).

Wiener Börse (Vienna Stock Exchange), A-1011 Vienna, Wipplingerstrasse 34 (tel: 53-499).

APA (Austria Presse Agentur): www.apa.at

Presstext Austria (in German): www.pressetext.at

Internet sites

Austrian National Tourist Office: www.austria.info

Statistics Austria: www.statistik.at/index_englisch.shtml

Azerbaijan

Azerbaijan is a complex country. And it has as neighbours an equally complex set of countries: Russia, its former Soviet overlord, Georgia – anxious to strengthen its links with the West (particularly North Atlantic Treaty Organisation (NATO) and the EU), Armenia, with which Azerbaijan has an unresolved dispute over the Nagorno Karabakh enclave, Turkey, seemingly bent on an Islamisation of sorts. And an always enigmatic Iran. Not much cause for calm relaxation in the immediate neighbourhood.

Nagorno Karabakh

For the most part, Azerbaijan has relatively good relations with its neighbouring countries. The exception is Armenia, the territory of which surrounds the enclave of Nagorno Karabakh. At the end of Soviet control with the collapse of the Soviet Union (USSR), three quarters of Nagorno-Karabakh's population were Armenian, only a quarter Azeri. Logic, if not history, dictated that the region should form part of Armenia. The almost inevitable outbreak of war between Armenia and Azerbaijan over the enclave caused significant ethnic upheaval as native Azeris departed the Armenian controlled areas and their Armenian counterparts returned to Armenian controlled regions. Despite support from Afghan, Chechen and Ukrainian mercenaries, Armenian troops turned out to be better organised and more efficient, managing to take control of territory between the enclave and Armenia itself. Following a peace agreement reached in 1994 there has been a truce of sorts. The Azeris resent the loss of land they regard as rightfully theirs, while the Armenians show no sign of willingness to give it back. In a December 2006 referendum, declared illegitimate by Azerbaijan, the region approved a new constitution. There have since been signs of life in the peace process, with occasional meetings between the Armenian and Azeri presidents. Progress was reported at talks between the leaders in May and November 2009, but the peace process then stalled and in 2010–11 there were a number of serious ceasefire violations.

In its October 2014 assessment of the Azerbaijan economy, the International Monetary Fund (IMF) noted that economic activity had been resilient to the regional turmoil thanks to the country's limited economic links with Russia. Gross

KEY FACTS

Official name: Azarbaijchan Respublikasy (Republic of Azerbaijan)

Head of State: President Ilham Aliyev (YAP) (from 2003; re-elected Oct 2008 and 2013)

Head of government: Prime Minister Artur Rasizadeh (YAP) (from 2003; re-appointed Oct 2008 and 2013)

Ruling party: Yeni Azerbaycan Partiyasi (YAP) (New Azerbaijan Party) (from 2005; re-elected 7 Nov 2010)

Area: 86,600 square km

Population: 9.38 million (2014)*

Capital: Baku

Official language: Azeri (Turkic)

Currency: new manat (M) = 100 gopik (new currency introduced 1 Jan 2006)

Exchange rate: M1.05 per US$ (Sep 2015)

GDP per capita: US$7,902 (2014)*

GDP real growth: 2.79% (2014)*

GDP: US$74.14 billion (2014)*

Labour force: 5.87 million (2010)

Unemployment: 6.05% (2014)*

Inflation: 1.35% (2014)*

Oil production: 848,000 bpd (2014)

Natural gas production: 16.90 billion cum (2014)

Balance of trade: US$18.93 billion (2014)

* estimated figure

domestic product (GDP) growth was projected by the IMF at 4 per cent in 2014 and forecast at 3.5 per cent in 2015, reflecting a modest decline in oil output and a slowdown in non-oil growth associated with greater fiscal prudence and an essential macro-prudential tightening. Inflation was projected to hover around the 3 per cent mark. The risks associated with low oil prices were fortunately mitigated in the short term by the authorities' reserve buffers.

The IMF encouraged the Azerbaijan authorities to build upon the recent progress towards fiscal sustainability by maintaining fiscal consolidation in the 2015 budget. At the time the IMF report was prepared, the Azeri budget oil price assumption of US$90 per barrel was considered prudent; however, expenditure commitments arising from international events limited the scope for fiscal manoeuvre. Presciently, the IMF judged that any further adverse oil price developments would warrant the consideration of a reduction in spending. Nevertheless, in the view of the IMF, the budget should be able to accommodate expenditure that would boost a geographical diversification of gas exports. Completion of the public expenditure and financial accountability assessment (PEFA) update should also pave the way for improving public spending efficiency.

According to the IMF, the exchange rate remained the anchor of monetary policy, supported by ample reserves. A gradual move towards exchange rate flexibility (see below) would, it was thought, foster financial market development. A further easing of growth in consumer lending, the completion of the continuing bank capitalisation and a restructuring of the International Bank of Azerbaijan would reduce financial sector vulnerabilities. The IMF stressed that improving the business climate was crucial for diversification and essential for any replacement of public investment by market-based private investment. The priorities were to tackle competition and trade barriers, as well as broadening the coverage of the anti-corruption programmes. Concluding its summary report, the IMF suggested that concerted efforts to strengthen Azerbaijan's macro-economic statistics, supported by IMF technical assistance, would help policy makers and investors to make better-informed decisions.

Devaluation

Whether or not the IMF had in mind a traditional currency devaluation, in February 2015 the Central Bank of Azerbaijan (CBA) abruptly devalued the manat against the dollar and the euro. In late February the official rate for the manat was set at 1.05 to the dollar and 1.19 to the euro. This was quite a substantial devaluation – at a stroke the manat lost 33.5 per cent and 30 per cent of its value against the US and European currencies respectively. In a statement, the CBA claimed that the devaluation was aimed at 'stimulating the diversification of Azerbaijan's economy, strengthening the international competitiveness of the economy and its export potential and guaranteeing stability in the balance of payments.'

The simple truth was that Azerbaijan had found it difficult, or impossible, to cope with the sharp, unforeseen, decline in the price of oil, Azerbaijan's main export. But the devaluation raised fears of a rapid rise in inflation, largely because it would render imports significantly more expensive. The devaluation was also expected to increase the domestic demand for dollars and euros.

The EBRD

In its 2014 *Transition Report* the European Bank for Reconstruction and Development (EBRD) noted that the fast rate of economic growth seen in 2013, fuelled by the election-related credit and public-spending boom and the stabilisation of Azerbaijan's oil output, had largely petered out in 2014. GDP growth slowed from 5.8 per cent in 2013 to a preliminary 2.5 per cent year-on-year in the first nine months of 2014. The unexpected decline in oil output at the start of 2014 held growth back. Although the non-oil sector continued to grow fast, the EBRD observed that this was at a slower pace than before. The substantial increase in fuel prices of December 2013, which was the first since 2007, did not have any permanent effect and inflation was kept in check at a manageable annual rate of one per cent in July 2014. Stable food prices were a contributory factor.

Non-oil imports continued to surge in early 2014, boosted by rising incomes and consumer credit. The balance of payments suffered accordingly. As a result, according to the EBRD, the overall current account surplus shrank from 22 per cent of GDP in 2012 to 17 per cent in 2013. The government had hoped that the ban on some used car imports that did not meet the 'Euro 4' fuel requirement that had been introduced in April 2014 might temporarily reverse this trend, a view fostered by the import data for the second quarter of 2014. Azerbaijan's external buffers seemed to be adequate, with foreign exchange reserves and oil fund assets adding up to US$49.1 billion (65 per cent of GDP) at the end of June 2014.

Although the exchange rate policy was to be seriously re-adjusted in early 2015 (see above) in mid-2014 the CBA adhered to a stable exchange rate policy. The EBRD agreed with the IMF that oil price

KEY INDICATORS **Azerbaijan**

	Unit	2011	2012	2013	2014	**2015
Population	m	*9.12	*9.23	*9.31	*9.38	*9.46
Gross domestic product (GDP)	US$bn	63.40	68.70	73.54	*74.14	*62.20
GDP per capita	US$	6,916	7,439	*7,900	*7,902	*6,576
GDP real growth	%	-1.1	2.2	5.8	*2.8	*0.6
Inflation	%	16.7	1.0	2.4	*1.4	*7.9
Unemployment	%	6.0	6.0	*6.0	*6.0	*6.0
Oil output	'000 bpd	931.0	872.0	931.0	848.0	–
Natural gas output	bn cum	14.8	15.6	16.2	16.9	–
Exports (fob) (goods)	US$m	33,996.3	31,877.0	31,781.1	28,259.7	–
Imports (fob) (goods)	US$m	9,867.9	9,964.0	11,172.9	9,332.0	–
Balance of trade	US$m	24,128.4	21,914.0	20,608.2	18,927.7	–
Current account	US$m	17,144.9	14,958.0	*12,498.0	*11,357.0	*3,308.0
Total reserves minus gold	US$m	6,984.2	11,277.0	14,400.5	14,646.6	–
Foreign exchange	US$m	6,737.0	11,040.0	14,162.9	–	–
Exchange rate	per US$	0.79	0.78	0.78	0.78	–

* estimated figure ** forecast figure

shocks and output disruptions remained the biggest short term challenges, albeit the risk was cushioned by the large foreign exchange reserves. In the view of the EBRD the government had been successful in exploiting Azerbaijan's hydrocarbon potential, thereby promoting growth and reducing poverty. However, in the post 2012 years, the limits to purely resource-led growth had become apparent. Although the dependence on hydrocarbons was diminishing, the ability of the non-oil sector to grow sustainably without periodical government stimuli was uncertain. The lack of sustained economic reforms, the absence of competition and economic transparency were all negative factors.

This mildly gloomy picture of Azerbaijan's prospects was to a degree contradicted by the World Economic Forum's *Global Competitiveness Report 2014–2015* which placed Azerbaijan 38 out of the 144 countries surveyed. This was the second-highest ranking of any former Soviet republic. The lofty ranking was attributed to Azerbaijan's stable macro-economic situation.

However satisfactory that might have been, however, the same could not be said of general ethical standards in business and politics. Despite the government's overt efforts to improve standards of governance, standards remained low, even at the top of the political tree. Following the 2013 presidential election, the *Washington Post* reported that a day before the election the authorities had inadvertently released the election 'results', before polling had actually started. The 'results' were sent from an official smart-phone run by the Central Election Commission. They showed Mr Aliyev as gaining 72.76 per cent of the votes. Azerbaijani officials later claimed that the results had been partial and a 'test run'. The BBC's headline for its story on the election was 'The Pre-determined President'.

However encouraging the World Economic Forum's ranking might have been, that of Berlin-based Transparency International's 2014 *Corruption perceptions Index* was another matter; it ranked Azerbaijan a lowly 126 out of the 175 countries surveyed. The Azeri authorities could take cold comfort that this was one better than the 127 position obtained in 2013. The other key international assessment, the World Bank's *Doing Business 2015* placed Azerbaijan 80 out of the 189 countries surveyed. Hardly likely to get international investors packing their bags or taking flights to Baku.

Despite this adverse climate, Azerbaijan placed its first sovereign Eurobond in March 2014, raising a commendable US$1.25 billion for a 10 year issue. The bond was reportedly three times over-subscribed. This success paved the way for similar arrangements, including a US$500 million 5-year Eurobond.

Energy

Azerbaijan is one of the world's oldest oil producing countries and has played a significant role in the development of today's oil industry. The world's first paraffin factory was opened there in 1823 and the world's first oil field was drilled in 1846. Azerbaijan was the site of the first offshore oil field – the Neft Dashlary – in the shallow water of the Caspian Sea, which was completed in 1951 and still produces oil today. Oil and gas production and exports are central to Azerbaijan's economy. The country's economy is heavily dependent on its energy exports, with more than 90 per cent of total exports accounted for by oil and gas exports, according to data from the International Monetary Fund. As long as the global oil price remained virtually stable, Azerbaijan's revenues from hydrocarbon exports remained virtually flat. However, the collapse of global oil prices turned what was once Azerbaijan's boom commodity from a resource into a headache. Oil production in Azerbaijan increased from 315,000 barrels per day (bpd) in 2002 to 1.0 million bpd in 2010. However, production has declined since then, falling to 932,000bpd in 2012 and 848,000bpd by 2014.

According to the United States government Energy Information Administration (EIA), Azerbaijan is an important oil and natural gas supplier particularly for European markets. Although traditionally it has been a prolific oil producer, Azerbaijan's importance as a natural gas supplier will grow in the future as field development and export infrastructure expand. The conflicting claims over the maritime and sea-bed boundaries of the Caspian Sea between Azerbaijan and Iran continue to cause uncertainty, with Iran challenging Azerbaijan's hydrocarbon exploration in offshore areas claimed by both sides.

Natural gas accounted for about 67 per cent of Azerbaijan's total domestic energy consumption in 2012. Oil accounted for 30 per cent of total energy use and hydropower contributed a marginal amount. Overall, Azerbaijan is a net energy exporter. The country swaps small volumes of natural gas with Iran – the Nakhchivan exclave receives all of its natural gas from Iran, because it is not connected to Azerbaijan's pipeline network.

Azerbaijan's total proven crude oil reserves were estimated at 7 billion barrels in December 2014, according to the Oil & Gas Journal (OGJ). The largest hydrocarbon basins are located offshore in the Caspian Sea, particularly the Azeri Chirag Guneshli (ACG) field, which accounted for almost 75 per cent of Azerbaijan's total oil output in 2013. Similar to its share of total production, ACG also holds over 70 per cent of Azerbaijan's total reserves, with about 5 billion barrels located in this field.

Almost immediately following its independence in 1991 from the Soviet Union, Azerbaijan allowed foreign participation in its oil sector and it has signed the most production-sharing agreements among all former Soviet Union countries. In general, hydrocarbons are produced under production-sharing agreements, with the share of profits dependent on the internal rate of return achieved by the project.

The State Oil Company of Azerbaijan Republic (SOCAR) produces about 20 per cent of the country's oil output. The company is responsible for exploration and production of oil and natural gas in Azerbaijan, operating the country's two refineries, running the country's pipeline system and managing the country's oil and natural gas imports and exports. Although the ministry of industry and energy handles exports as well as exploration and production agreements with foreign companies, SOCAR participates in all of the international consortia developing oil and gas projects in Azerbaijan.

The remaining 80 per cent of Azerbaijan's output comes from the ACG oil fields by the BP-operated Azerbaijan International Operating Company (AIOC) and at the BP-operated Shah Deniz field (which produces oil condensate). AIOC is a consortium of 10 petroleum companies that have signed extraction contracts with Azerbaijan. The AIOC is led by BP and includes Chevron, Inpex, Statoil, Turkiye Petrolleri, ExxonMobil, SOCAR, ITOCHU and Hess. BP and a number of other AIOC consortium members have made significant direct investments in the development of the ACG field, with some AIOC member companies also investing in the construction of the Baku-Tbilisi-Ceyhan (BTC) pipeline. BP is the largest foreign investor and has been involved in Azerbaijan since 1992. Much of Azerbaijan's oil is marketed by SOCAR's Geneva-based subsidiary Socar Trading, which has been operating since 2008. As the largest shareholder in ACG, BP is also a regular marketer of Azerbaijan's crude oil.

The industry is regulated by the ministry of industry and energy, which was established in April 2001. The ministry formulates state energy policy and regulates SOCAR. In addition, it is tasked with attracting foreign investment, setting tariffs and conducting negotiations on pipelines and production-sharing agreements.

Azerbaijan established the State Oil Fund of the Republic of Azerbaijan (SOFAZ) in 1999 to manage currency and assets from oil and gas activities. The fund had about US$36 billion in managed assets at the end of 2013, according to its annual report.

Azerbaijan exported an estimated 738,000bpd of crude oil in 2013, according the Azerbaijan's State Statistical Committee. Azerbaijan's crude oil exports peaked in 2010 when they averaged about 908,000bpd, but exports have fallen every year since then as production declines. Azerbaijan is mainly a crude oil and condensate exporter, although the country exports small volumes of refined petroleum products to its neighbours, including diesel, gasoline and jet fuel. The majority of the refined product exports go to Russia and Georgia, according to *Eastern Bloc Energy*. Azerbaijan has three export pipelines and most (about 80 per cent) of its oil is exported via the BTC, with small amounts shipped by truck and rail. The country's oil industry was transformed with the construction of the BTC, which began operations in 2006. BTC allowed for exports of lighter and sweeter crude than Russia's Urals blend from the region, but it also provided transportation capacity out of the Caspian that did not rely on using the congested Turkish Straits (including the Dardanelles and the Bosperous) or crossing Russian territory.

Natural gas

Although historically an oil producer, Azerbaijan's importance as a gas producer and exporter is growing. Most of the natural gas production comes from the Shah Deniz field, although some volumes of natural gas are produced alongside oil in the ACG field.

In 2014, Azerbaijan produced 16.9 billion cubic metres (bcm) of dry natural gas and consumed 9.2 bcm. Natural gas plays a central role domestically and it likely will gain importance in the future, particularly in the electric power sector where it now accounts for over 80 per cent of the country's power generation. Azerbaijan likely will see an increase in domestic consumption of natural gas as it continues to replace Soviet-era oil-fired power plants with new combined-cycle natural gas turbines.

Azerbaijan became a net exporter of natural gas in 2007, previously importing natural gas from Russia. In 2013, Azerbaijan exported about 240 bcf, mainly shipping it via the South Caucasus Pipeline. Volumes of natural gas are also exported to Russia via the Gazi-Magomed-Mozdok pipeline. A small volume of natural gas is shipped to Iran via the Baku-Astara pipeline. In exchange, Iran ships natural gas to Nakhchivan, Azerbaijan's exclave situated between Iran and Turkey. The exclave is wholly dependent on natural gas supplied by Iran.

Most of Azerbaijan's natural gas is destined for Turkey, but the country supplies a small volume to Greece via the Turkey-Greece inter-connector. Under a previous arrangement, Turkey was re-exporting Azerbaijani natural gas to Greece, but a new agreement allows Azerbaijan to directly export volumes to the European Union. The Shah Deniz FFD will result in increased exports to the European Union, once the needed infrastructure is completed.

Caviar diplomacy

Despite Transparency International ranking it as one of the most corrupt countries in the world, Azerbaijan has been a member of the Council of Europe since 2001 – an agency centred on the promotion of human rights. Foreign dignitaries are showered with gifts, indeed, 'in Baku a common gift is 2kg of caviar.' Such is Azerbaijan's oil wealth and strategic location on the Russian border; Western politicians have tended to shy away from outright criticism of its human rights abuses. In fact, a Downing Street poll found that 72 per cent of MPs were pleased with President Aliyev's policies and considered him a 'reliable partner of the West.'

Risk assessment

Politics	Poor
Economy	Fair/good
Regional stability	Fair

Muslims in Azerbaijan

% of population	93.4
Sunni (% of Muslims)	15
Shi'a (% of Muslims)	85

COUNTRY PROFILE

Azerbaijan has at various times been part of the Persian, Muslim Arab, Turkish Seljuk, Mongol, Ottoman and Russian empires. The modern Republic was formed from territory ceded to Russia by Iran following the second of the two Russian-Persian wars.

1848 The world's first oil well was drilled, just south of Baku.

1916 Azerbaijan joined an alliance with Armenia and Georgia.

1918–20 Azerbaijan existed as an independent republic until 1920 when it became part of the Soviet Union.

1936 The Azerbaijan Soviet Socialist Republic assumed the status of a full Soviet member.

1988–94 The Azerbaijan-Armenian war broke out as Nagorno-Karabakh (an ethnic Armenian enclave located wholly inside Azerbaijan territory) sort independence and to join neighbouring Armenia. With the assistance of Armenian troops, separatists in Nagorno-Karabakh managed to expel Azeri forces by 1994 and have since maintained *de facto* independence from Azerbaijan. The self-proclaimed breakaway Nagorno-Karabakh Republic (Artsakh in Armenian) occupies approximately 4,400 square km, to which the separatists have added through military conquest some 7,700 square km of Azerbaijan proper. The six-year war threw Azerbaijan into political turmoil.

1989 Azerbaijan became the first Soviet Republic outside the Baltic to declare its national sovereignty.

1991 Formal independence was declared, with Ayaz Mutalibov, head of the Communist Party, as president.

1992 Violent demonstrations, over repeated failures in the Nagorno-Karabakh war, forced Mutalibov to flee to Moscow. In presidential elections Abulfaz Elchibey leader of the Yeni Azerbaycan Partiyasi (YAP) (New Azerbaijan Party) came to power, declaring he would build a secular democratic system with close links to Turkey. Power was transferred from the Supreme Soviet council to a 50-person Milli Majlis.

1993 President Elchibey was forced to quit following an ultimatum issued by Colonel Suret Huseinov (Azeri commander in Nagorno-Karabakh). Elchibey invited his rival, Heidar Aliyev, a veteran politician, to become chairman of the parliament and then acting president. Suret Huseinov became prime minister. Aliyev won 98.8 per cent of the vote in presidential elections.

1994 A cease-fire agreement came into force between Azerbaijan and Armenia over Nagorno-Karabakh. The dispute had caused an estimated 35,000 deaths and created 850,000 internally displaced

persons (IDPs), mainly Azeris, between 1988–94. In a guardian *coup d'état* President Aliyev removed Huseinov.
1995 A new constitution was adopted.
1996 In National Assembly elections the Aliyev-backed YAP won a large majority. Artur Rasizade became prime minister.
1998 Opposition parties boycotted the presidential elections; Aliyev was returned to power.
2000 The ruling YAP won the general election, which was denounced as unfair by foreign observers, and leaders of five major opposition parties initiated a mass protest, calling for new elections.
2001 The government ordered that the local Azeri language should be written with a Latin, rather than Cyrillic, alphabet. Azerbaijan became a full member of the Council of Europe.
2002 US sanctions, imposed in 1992 following the outbreak of war with Armenia over the Nagorno-Karabakh enclave, were lifted after Azerbaijan agreed to participate in the US-led war on terrorism. Arkady Gukasyan was re-elected president of Nagorno-Karabakh. The Azeri constitution was amended.
2003 President Heydar Aliyev collapsed and died. His son, Ilham Aliyev, was elected president with a landslide victory. Artur Rasizade remained in post as prime minister.
2005 The Baku-Tbilisi-Ceyhan (BTC) oil pipeline was opened. The Artsakhi Demokratakan Kusaktsutyun (ADK) (Democratic Party of Artsakh) won parliamentary elections in Nagorno-Karabakh. In In Azerbaijan, the ruling YAP won the parliamentary elections. The Organisation for Security and Co-operation in Europe (OSCE) and Council of Europe observers declared that the election fell short of democratic norms. Around 15,000 people responded to opposition calls for election results to be annulled by marching in Baku. A new natural gas pipeline between Iran and Azerbaijan was inaugurated.
2006 A new manat was introduced, valued at one manat per 5,000 old manat. New parliamentary elections were held in ten constituencies, where ballots in the 2005 elections had been annulled
2007 Bako Sahakian replaced Arkadiy Gukasian as president of Nagorno-Karabakh.
2008 Fierce fighting in Nagorno-Karabakh broke out; Azerbaijan accused Armenia of inciting the fighting. In presidential elections, incumbent Ilham Aliyev won a second term in office. The main opposition party Müsavat Partiyasi (Equality Party), led by Isa Gambar, boycotted the election. International observers said the elections were neither free nor fair. Artur Rasizade remained in post as prime minister.
2009 A constitutional referendum to lift the two-term limit on the presidency was passed by 92 per cent of the vote.
2010 In Nagorno-Karabakh, Free Motherland won 46.6 per cent (14 seats out of 33), Democratic Party of Artsakh 28.6 per cent (six); Armenian Revolutionary Federation 20.3 per cent (six) in parliamentary elections. Presidents Aliyev and Medvedev (Russia) signed a treaty to agree the demarcation of the border between the two countries. Approximately 2,500 candidates, in five political parties, registered to contest the Azerbaijan parliamentary elections held; however the electoral commission allowed only 690 candidates to stand. The ruling YAP won 74 seats (out of 125); 19 women in total were elected. Observers of the European Council and the US considered the elections as peaceful and participatory; however they also noted that limitations on the media and freedom of assembly weakened political discussion.
2011 In April a number of protesters were arrested in Baku as they attempted to rally against President Aliyev's hard-line rule. In June, under the auspices of Russian President Medvedev, the presidents of Azerbaijan and Armenia discussed a settlement agreement over the disputed territory of Nagorno-Karabakh. Despite encouragement from world leaders they failed to sign it, risking future conflict and leaving some 600,000 IDPs without hope of returning to their homes with security.
2012 In presidential elections held in Nagorno-Karabakh on 19 July, incumbent Bako Sahakyan won 66.7 per cent of the vote, his rival Vitaly Balasanyan won 32.5 per cent. The first head of state after independence from the USSR, Ayaz Mutalibov, returned from exile in Russia in early July, having confirmed that he would refrain from any political activity. He had been accused of involvement in the bloody crackdown of pro-impendence demonstrators in 1990 and fled Azerbaijan in 1991. Recent legislation has granted Azerbaijan heads of state immunity from prosecution for acts committed while in office.
2013 In June President Aliyev was nominated as YAP's candidate for the October presidential election. He convincingly won the 9 October election with 84.54 per cent. Turnout was 71.62 per cent. The OSCE reported gross electoral fraud including 'clear indications of ballot box stuffing'.
2014 Skirmishes between Azerbaijani government forces and ethnic Armenians in Nagorno-Karabakh enclave flared-up in late July/early August resulting in at least 15 deaths. A spokeswoman for the Iranian foreign ministry said that Iran was concerned about skirmishes between the two sides. On 4 September US secretary of state, John Kerry, met with President Aliyev and President Sargsian of Armenia at the Nato Summit in Wales. They discussed efforts to resolve the conflict in Nagorno-Karabakh. Mr Kerry expressed his strong concern for the recent violence along the Line of Contact, marking the deadliest period in the conflict since the 1994 cease-fire took effect.
2015 Due to the European Games being hosted in Azerbaijan, its political environment has been greatly scrutinised. It has been found that there are many instances of human rights abuses. There are currently approximately 100 political detainees of which 20 are identified as 'prisoners of conscience' by Amnesty International. The state has no independent TV stations, and two of the four independent media outlets that they did have were shut down in 2015. There are 161 places in the world where it is better to be a journalist than Azerbaijan, according to the 2015 World Press Freedom Index.

Political structure

Constitution

A constitution was adopted by national referendum in November 1995, and was amended following a referendum in 2002, which made changes to the parliamentary system. The changes included replacing proportional representation in the National Assembly with the majority system (first-past-the-post), and changing the election of the president from a two-thirds to a 50 per cent majority of the votes cast. On 18 March 2009, a constitutional referendum to lift the two-term limit on the presidency was passed by 92 per cent of the vote.
The Republic of Azerbaijan is officially a democratic, secular and unitary state, with power separated among three branches: executive, legislative and judicial.
Administratively, the country is divided into 65 districts, the autonomous republic of Nakhichevan (which is separated from the main part of the country by southern Armenia), and the region of Nagorno-Karabakh (which has been occupied by Armenian forces since 1992).
Under the constitution, the autonomous republic of Nakhichevan is an autonomous state within the Republic of Azerbaijan. Executive power in Nakhichevan is implemented by the Cabinet of Ministers of Nakhichevan, which is appointed by the Nakhichevan prime minister on approval of the Milli Mejlis (National Assembly). However, presidential decrees have authority in Nakhichevan.

Independence date

18 October 1991

Form of state

Presidential republic, where despite democratic structures, there is no fair chance for the opposition.

The executive

The president is head of state. The president must be over 35-years-old and have been living permanently in the territory of Azerbaijan for over 10 years, having no previous convictions.

The president appoints a prime minister and Council of Ministers.

The president is also the supreme commander-in-chief of the armed forces and has powers to declare martial law and states of emergency.

Presidential elections are held every five years. The president is elected by a majority of half of all votes cast. If the presidential candidates fail to win a majority, a second round of elections is held between the two leading contestants. The candidate who wins the most votes in the second round is elected president.

According to the constitution, the president can only be removed from the post in cases of 'grave crimes'. In these cases the Supreme Court submits an application for removal to the Milli Mejlis (National Assembly), who must pass the application by a majority of 95 votes (over two-thirds majority).

National legislature

The unicameral Milli Mejlis (National Assembly) has 125 deputies, elected in single-seat constituencies for five-year terms.

Legislative power of the Nakhichevan Autonomous Republic is held by a 45-member Ali Mejlis (Supreme Council), which independently settles questions of taxes, budget, economic development, social policy, environmental protection, tourism, health, science and culture as enacted by the Azerbaijan national assembly. It also has powers to appoint and dismiss the prime minister and Cabinet of Ministers of Nakhichevan. However, the Ali Mejlis lacks power to 'contradict' the constitution and laws of the Republic of Azerbaijan.

Legal system

The highest judicial body is the Supreme Court, which is divided into criminal and civil sections. There is also a Constitutional Court, Economic Court, ordinary and specialised courts.

Judges of the Supreme Court are appointed by the Milli Mejlis on the recommendation of the president. It is the highest judicial body in civil, criminal, administrative and other cases directed to general and specialised courts.

The Constitutional Court consists of nine judges appointed in the same way as in the Supreme Court. It is constitutionally bound to inquire into the activities of the president, Milli Mejlis, Cabinet of Ministers, Supreme Court and Milli Mejlis of the autonomous republic of Nakhichevan. In 2002, the constitutional changes included the remit of the Constitutional Court to hear cases brought by individuals. The Economic Court is the highest court on matters of economic dispute (as envisaged by legislation) and oversees activities in the relevant specialised courts. Judicial power in the autonomous republic of Nakhichevan is exercised by the courts of Nakhichevan, although the Republic of Azerbaijan's laws apply in most cases.

Last elections

7 November 2010 (parliamentary); 22 October 2013 (presidential)

Results: Parliamentary: Yeni Azerbaycan Partiyasi (YAP) (New Azerbaijan Party) won 74 seats (out of 125), Vetendas Hemreyliyi Partiyasi (VHP) (Civic Solidarity Party) three seats, Ana Veten Partiyasi (AVP) (Motherland Party) two, independents and non-aligned 46; two other political parties did not win enough votes for any seats. Turnout 50.1 per cent.

Presidential: Ilham Aliyev (YAP) won 84.54 per cent of the vote, Jamil Hasanali (National Council of Democratic Forces) 5.53 per cent, Igbal Aghazade (Ümid Partiyasi (Party of Hope)) 2.40 per cent, seven other candidates failed to win a significant percentage of the vote; turnout was 71.62 per cent.

Next elections

2018 (presidential); November 2015 (parliamentary)

Political parties

Ruling party

Yeni Azerbaycan Partiyasi (YAP) (New Azerbaijan Party) (from 2005; re-elected 7 Nov 2010)

Main opposition party

No opposition exists in parliament as both oppostion political parties failed to win any seats in 2010 general election.

The Absheron Peninsula (which includes the capital, Baku) is the most densely populated area with some 800 people per square km.

Population

9.23 million (2012)*

Last census: January 1999: 7,953,438

Population density: 104 inhabitants per square km (2010). Urban population 52 per cent (2010 Unicef).

Annual growth rate: 1.2 per cent, 1990–2010 (Unicef).

Internally Displaced Persons (IDP)

570,000 (UNHCR 2004)

Ethnic make-up

The majority are Azeri (90 per cent). Minority groups include Dagestani (3.2 per cent), Russians (2.5 per cent) and Armenian (2.3 per cent). Almost all Armenians live in the separatist Nagorno-Karabakh region.

Religions

The main religious affiliation is Shi'ite Muslim (93.4 per cent). Others include Russian Orthodox (2.5 per cent) and Armenian Orthodox (2.3 per cent).

Education

Compulsory schooling lasts for eight years, the last two of which can be undertaken in either general secondary schools, technical schools or vocational schools. Education is free, except for higher education for which there are student grants. There are approximately 4,500 schools, including 960 primary eight-year schools, more than 2,300 secondary schools, 20 higher schools, 74 colleges and 162 technical-vocational schools. In urban areas educational services are better than in rural areas.

Literacy rate: 97 per cent of the adult population

Compulsory years: Eight to 16

Enrolment rate: 85.5 per cent net primary enrolment; 84.7 per cent, male, 86.2 per cent, female (2009)

Pupils per teacher: 20 in primary schools

Health

In conjunction with the IMF, a new health policy has been developed. The focus of government expenditure will be shifted away from input-based allocations (for example, based on the number of beds) to capital transfers based on the number and structure of local populations. Local autonomy will be increased in healthcare and the elements of a basic package are being developed, which the government will provide free of charge in all public health facilities.

Healthcare is universal and virtually free of charge but there is a chronic shortage of basic medicines and despite pay increases doctors' morale remains low.

Over 60 per cent of health expenses goes to hospitals with acute care facilities and staffed by specialised doctors rather than to preventive and basic health care. Fifty per cent of the population are severely iodine deficient.

HIV/Aids

In 2009 there were an estimated 4,000 living with HIV (Unicef 2012).

HIV prevalence: 0.1 per cent aged 15–49 in 2003 (World Bank)

Life expectancy: 71 years, 2010 (Unicef 2012)

Fertility rate/Maternal mortality rate: 2.2 births per woman, 2010 (Unicef 2012); maternal deaths 43 deaths per 100,000 live births (World Bank).

Child (under 5 years) mortality rate (per 1,000): 35 per 1,000 live births (WHO 2012); 10 per cent of children aged under five were malnourished (World Bank).

Welfare
Although it has an abundance of natural resources, Azerbaijan is classified as the poorest country in Europe with 60 per cent of the population living in poverty. The former Soviet Union developed an extensive welfare system but price liberalisation and soaring inflation have rendered pensions, unemployment benefit and money paid to single parent families virtually worthless. The government intends to initiate a participatory poverty reduction strategy, as existing social safety nets are not enough to keep the unemployed out of poverty.

Main cities
Baku (capital, estimated population in 2012, 1.2 million), Gyandzha (317,355), Sumgayit (283,549), Xirdalan (98,838), Mingechaur (98,449), Qaraçuxur (80,646), Sirvan (74,480), Nazcivan (73,922).

Languages spoken
Azeri is spoken by 95 per cent of the population. Russian (3 per cent as first language) and Armenian (2 per cent) are also spoken. English language lessons are being introduced in schools and colleges. Some Azeris speak Russian as a second language although the use of Russian is being phased out.

Official language/s
Azeri (Turkic)

Media
Freedom of speech is guaranteed under the constitution however media outlets and journalist have been in subject to sporadic harassment by the government.

Press
The circulation of all newspapers is very small. Newspapers dropped Cyrillic script in favour of Latin in 2001.

Dailies: In Azerbaijani, national newspapers, some with online editions in Russian and English, include *525 Ci* (www.525ci.com), (Tues–Sat), *Yeni Azerbaycan* (www.yeniazerbaycan.com) a broadsheet, *Echo* (www.echo-az.com), *Azadliq* (www.azadliq.az), *Uc Noqta* (www.ucnoqta.com) and *Zerkalo* (www.zerkalo.az). In Russian, *Bakinskiy Rabockiy* (www.br.az), *Yeni Musavat* (www.musavat.com), *Nash Vek* (www.nashvek.com) and *Nedelya* (www.nedelya.az). In English, *The Azeri Times* (www.theazeritimes.com), *Baku Sun* (www.bakusun.az:8101), and *Azer News* (www.azernews.net).

Weeklies: In Azerbaijani, *Ayna-Zerkalo* (Azeri language) is a tabloid issued 156 days per year. In English *Our Century* (http://ourcentury.media-az.com),

Business: In Azerbaijani, *CBN Extra* (www.cbnextra.com) is a tabloid with a business section,

Broadcasting
Radio: Azerbaijan Radio (www.aztv.az), the national public radio is government-operated with two domestic stations (AzR 1 and 2) and one international channel. The independent, Public Television and Radio Broadcasting Company (www.itv.az) broadcasts in Azerbaijani, Russian and English. Private radio stations include Burc FM (www.burc.fm), Lider Jazz FM (www.lider.fm) and Antenn FM (www.antenn.az).

Television: AzTV () is the government-controlled, national public television service. The independent, Public Television and Radio Broadcasting Company (www.itv.az). Private TV stations include Space TV (www.spacetv.az), Lider TV (www.lidertv.com) and Azad TV.

Russian and Turkish TV channels are also available.

National news agency: Azar Tac www.azertag.com

Other news agencies: Turan: www.turaninfo.com

Trend: http://news.trendaz.com

Economy
The economy has seen huge increases in GDP growth since 2005, with a world record-breaking 34.5 per cent in 2006, as the benefits of the completion of the Baku-Tbilisi-Ceyhan (BTC) oil pipeline and the South Caucasus Pipeline (SCP), which allowed an expansion in exports of Azerbaijani hydrocarbons, took effect. The BTC transports oil from the Caspian Sea to the Mediterranean, while the SCP runs parallel with the BTC, transporting natural gas from the Caspian Sea to Turkey. There were seven billion barrels of oil reserves at the end of 2014, with production of 848,000 barrels per day (bpd). Natural gas reserves were 1.2 trillion cubic metres at the end of 2014, with production of 16.9 billion cubic metres. The State Oil Company of the Republic of Azerbaijan (SOCAR) established a generation fund (State Oil Fund (Sofaz)) that will hold a proportion of the country's oil wealth in trust for future development.

In September 2014 BP began production on the Southern Gas Corridor which will link reserves in the Shah Deniz gas fields to Europe via Turkey, the project is due to be completed in 2019.

The hydrocarbon industry directly accounts for over 50 per cent of GDP, with some forecasts putting the total, direct and indirect, contribution at 90 per cent. This leaves the Azerbaijani economy fragile to external shocks and as a result the government is keen to expand the non-hydrocarbon sector. The Non-oil sectors of the economy grew by 7 per cent in 2014, mainly as a result of public investment, this figure, however, had dropped from 10 per cent in 2013.

Azerbaijan's ranking in the World Bank's *Doing Business 2014* report was 80 (out of 183) for ease of doing business yet in Transparency International's 'Corruption Perceptions Index' it ranks 126 out of 175, showing that serious reform is needed in order for Azerbaijan to attract more investment in order to expand and diversify its economy.

Since Azerbaijan's boom growth the in the middle of the last decade the GDP growth rate has slowed to more stable levels. In 2011, after the global economic crash, Azerbaijan's growth slowed to 0.1 per cent but managed to avoid negative growth and recovered adequately due to the government using Sofaz to weather the global storm and compensate for drops in revenue and rises in debt levels. GDP growth climbed again to 5.8 per cent by 2013 but then dropped slightly to 4.5 per cent in 2014.

Foreign remittances in 2013 were US$1.7 billion, rising to US$1.8 billion in 2014.

Oil companies represent most foreign direct investment (FDI); foreign interest has only recently extended to other areas of the Azeri economy. Development projects underway include a modern cement works, a thermal power plant and new infrastructure. By 2014 Azerbaijan saw an increase in foreign investment in agribusiness as the government has begun to privatise agricultural land and small to medium-sized enterprises.

The conflict with Armenia over the Nagorno-Karabakh region has the potential to destabilise the country's economic progress. Although a cease-fire was signed in 1994, no final agreement has been reached and in 2014 72 deaths were recorded as a result of the conflict, making it the bloodiest year since the ceasefire was signed. The first half of 2015 had also already seen 41 deaths.

External trade
Azerbaijan is a member of the CISFTA (free trade agreement of the CIS republics) along with Armenia, Belarus, Georgia, Moldova, Kazakhstan, Kyrgyzstan, Russia, Tajikistan, Ukraine and Uzbekistan.

International trade is vital to the economy; however hydrocarbons account for over 90 per cent of all exports and has a disproportionate influence on the economy. The second largest sector in the economy is shipbuilding; a memorandum of understanding was signed with South Korea's shipyard manufacturer STX Corporation and Azerbaijan investment interests to construct a modern port with new facilities at the new Baku Port; work began in 2009. Other export commodities include primary production and oil industry by-products. Agricultural products are also beginning to see a significant rise in export numbers.

Imports

Imports include machinery equipment, oil products, foodstuffs, metals and chemicals.

Main sources: Russian Federation (14.3 per cent of total in 2014), Turkey (14.0 per cent), UK (10.7 per cent).

Exports

Exports are primarily oil and gas (over 90 per cent), with petroleum products including plastics and chemical fertilizers; other exports are ships and marine crafts, cotton fibre, machinery, foodstuffs.

Main destinations: Russian Federation (18.4 per cent of total in 2014), Italy (17.9 per cent), Thailand (15.0 per cent).

Agriculture

Farming

Agriculture has declined by more than 50 per cent since independence, but it continued to employ 38.3 per cent of the labour force and contributes about 5.7 per cent to GDP in 2014. It is the second-largest export sector with large potential markets in the Middle East, Europe and the former Soviet Union.

Around 2 million hectares (ha) out of a total land area of 8.7 million ha is classified as arable. Some 70 per cent of the 77 per cent of land used for agricultural purposes is irrigated through an extensive canal system. Most farming takes place in the fertile lowlands surrounding the Kura and Araz rivers, in central Azerbaijan.

The whole country is well endowed with fertile land, although adversely affected by periodic drought. A wide range of crops is grown, notably cotton, tobacco, nuts, grapes, grain, tea, vegetables and citrus fruits. Cattle, sheep, pigs and poultry are reared.

Grain is the leading agricultural product, followed by raw cotton (the country's largest cash crop).

Livestock, dairy products and alcoholic beverages are also important products.

There is potential for agricultural development, greatly enhanced by the country's rich soils, wide agricultural plains and varied climatic conditions. There is scope for the cultivation of vegetables, fruits, cotton, tobacco, subtropical cultures, silkworm and sheep breeding.

However, agriculture comprises mainly smallholder farming, and is generally subsistence oriented. Despite the fact that 45 per cent of the country's population depend largely on agricultural income, the sector remains largely underdeveloped.

Fishing

Salyan on the Kura River is the main centre for processing and canning fish.

Azerbaijan once produced 10 per cent of the world's supply of caviar. The division of the Caspian Sea, which accounts for 90 per cent of world caviar production, has caused disputes between Azerbaijan and Russia. There is little effective policing of the Caspian, with smuggling and illegal fishing widespread. The Caspian is also being overfished, and combined with the threat of pollution, production levels are set to fall. International regulation of the trade in caviar was tightened in 2006 and is expected to further restrict, for the foreseeable future, Azerbaijan's caviar industry.

Forestry

Forest and other wooded land, mostly concentrated in the mountainous north, account for little more than one-tenth of its total land area.

Forests in the flood plain areas remain in poor condition and are prone to over-grazing and pollution. There is no large-scale forest industry, with most wood products imported from the Russian Federation. Commercial exploitation is limited, and production is used mostly for domestic purposes. Most forest is classified as either 'protected' or 'preserved' and is public owned.

Industry and manufacturing

The oil industry dominates the Azeri economy, providing the driving force for all other sectors.

The emphasis on heavy industry, combined with substantial primary resources, enabled the development of a major oil equipment manufacturing sector in the Soviet era. However, the disintegration of the Soviet Union meant that supplies and markets dried up, leading to the virtual collapse of most industries.

It is hoped that the development of Azerbaijan's oil and gas industry will benefit all sectors of the economy, with widespread infrastructure improvements and developments essential. The construction industry has expanded particularly rapidly on the back of Azerbaijan's oil and gas boom (by 42 per cent in 2004).

In order to stimulate growth the government has developed a medium- and long-term strategy to restructure the economy in consultation with the IMF.

Industrial production increased by 12 per cent in 2004.

Tourism

Although the service sector only constituted 33.2 per cent of GDP in 2014, the Ministry of Culture and Tourism has had long-term plans to promote Azerbaijan as an elite destination, with tourism identified as potentially the country's top income source. A major investment, in the construction of the winter ski-ing and summer holiday resort of Shahdag, in the northeast of Azerbaijan, began in 2006 as a 10,000 guest per day, tourist centre with four-star and five-star hotels as well as chalets and campsites and all necessary services to provide for visitor needs.

There are over six thousand historic sites and many more of natural beauty throughout the country, which are largely unspoiled by either the conflict in Nagorno-Karabakh or modern developments. However, Azerbaijan lacks an integrated tourist infrastructure to provide the sophisticated visitor with services to fully appreciate more than a packaged resort or the capital city, Baku.

The tourist industry grew in 2014 and directly contributed M1.4 billion (US$1.7 billion) (2.2 per cent) of total GDP, and M5.1 billion (US$6.5 billion) (8.4 per cent) in total. Investment in travel and tourism was estimated to be M388.4 million (US$498 million), constituting 2.5 per cent of total investment in the economy scheduled for 2014.

With 2.2 million visitors in 2014, resulting in direct employment in the industry of 91,500 jobs (2.0 per cent of total employment); indirect employment in travel and tourism was predicted to be 346,500 (7.6 per cent of total employment) and to rise in coming years.

Environment

Pollution comes from four main sources – agriculture, industrial plants, oil exploitation and domestic waste. It will take time and investment to clean up Azerbaijan's environment.

Mining

The mining sector accounts for 1 per cent of GDP and since independence has suffered from a lack of infrastructure investment.

The republic has abundant mineral resources, including iron, lead, zinc and copper ores, cobalt, bauxite, matrium sulphate, marl, limestone, marble, lake and rock salts, and some small amounts of gold and silver. The largest iron ore field in the Caucasus region lies within Azerbaijan.

Copper reserves are attracting foreign investors. Azerbaijan has several deposits of pure copper, the largest of which is the Karadag, in western Azerbaijan, with reserves of about 320,000 tonnes.

Hydrocarbons

Oil from the Caspian basin has dominated the economic history of Azerbaijan since the late 19th century. In 1891, half of the world's crude oil was extracted from Azerbaijan. The Caspian Sea is still the centre of oil exploration for Azerbaijan.

Proven oil reserves were 7.0 billion barrels in 2014, with production at 848,000 barrels per day (bpd), an decrease of 3.3 per cent of the 2013 figure, almost all of which was derived from the Azeri-Chirag-Guneshli (ACG) oilfield. The majority is exported to Russia, Italy, Turkey and Germany via the Baku-Tblisi-Ceyhan (BTC) pipeline, running 1,673km from Baku to the Mediterranean port of Ceyhan in Turkey via Georgia.

The government places great store on the development of an oil-driven economic boom, which, while it may have negative implications for other industries, could generate huge earnings and inward investment for years. However, as the Azeri lack the necessary financial resources and expertise to develop their fields, foreign petrochemical corporations have been encouraged to invest. In order to keep control of the industry, the resulting exploration and production projects have usually been joint ventures between the State Oil Company of the Azerbaijan Republic (Socar) and foreign companies.

Consumption of oil stood at 101,000bpd in 2014, an increase of 0.2 per cent from 2013.

Proven natural gas reserves were 1.2 trillion cubic metres (cum) in 2014, with production at 16.9 billion cum, an increase of 4.6 per cent from 2013. Around 50 per cent of the country's production comes from the offshore Bakhar oil and gas field, off the Absheron Peninsula. However, future development is likely to concentrate on the Nakhichevan, Gunashli and Shah Deniz fields, from where natural gas is being pumped through the South Caucasus Pipeline (SPC), which was financed in large part by the consortium behind the BTC. The 692km long pipeline from the Shah Deniz field to Erzurum in Turkey, via Georgia, had an initial capacity of 8.8 billion cum, which had, by the end of 2014, been increased to 14.2 billion cum.

A deal was announced by the Russian gas company Gazrom in 2009 whereby it will import 500 million cum of gas from the Shah Deniz field once it begins production. Russia and the EU have rival plans to build pipelines to export gas — Russia across the Black Sea to Europe, and the EU across the Caucasus and Turkey into Europe. The EU is concerned that Russia may be trying to corner the market in gas exports to Europe. In September 2014 BP began production on the Southern Gas Corridor which will link reserves in the Shah Deniz gas fields to Europe via Turkey, the project is due to be completed in 2019. Russia, however, are still facing problems and opposition in there plans to build the pipeline, though they have increased there efforts since their pipelines in the Ukraine have come under threat since the eruption of violence there in 2014. Russia insists that it will build a pipeline into and through Turkey, though no agreement has yet been made.

Any coal produced or used is commercially insignificant.

Energy

Total installed generating capacity is 5,5000MW, of which eight state-owned thermal power plants produce 80 per cent of all electricity generated, consuming 7.4 million tonnes of oil equivalent (mtoe) produced by natural gas and 4.5mtoe by oil. Actual production is limited to around 4,300MW due to lack of public investment and ageing and dilapidated facilities. The energy needs of the international oil and natural gas pipelines have increased demand and Azerbaijan is an importer of electricity from surrounding countries, of around 10 per cent of its needs.

The state-owned Azerenerjy company has a monopoly on power generation and the national power grid, which is divided into five regional operations, which have been liberalised to accept foreign investment via open stock companies.

Financial markets

Stock exchange

Baki Fond Birjasi (BFB), (Baku Stock Exchange) (BSE)

Banking and insurance

Azerbaijan's banking sector is underdeveloped and dominated by four Soviet-era state-owned banks. The majority of Azerbaijani banks are undercapitalised and illiquid and during the course of 2005 several had their commercial licences revoked. In May 2005 there were 46 banks operating in Azerbaijan. Banking law states that foreign ownership of any bank in Azerbaijan cannot exceed 30 per cent.

Central bank

National Bank of Azerbaijan (NBA)

Main financial centre

Baku

Time

GMT plus four hours (daylight saving, late March to late October, GMT plus five hours)

Geography

Azerbaijan is situated in eastern Transcaucasia bordering Armenia, Georgia, the Russian Federation (Daghestan Autonomous Republic), Iran and the Caspian Sea. It is the largest of the three Transcaucasian republics, covering 87,000 square km. Azerbaijan is split in two, with the Nakhichevan Autonomous Republic separated from Azerbaijan proper by southern Armenia. Approximately 20 per cent of Azeri territory is occupied by Armenia. The ethnic Armenian enclave of Nagorno-Karabakh is an area of 4,000 square km situated in the south-west of the country.

The greater part of the republic includes the lowlands of the River Kura and the lower reaches of its tributary, the Araks. The oil-rich Apsheron Peninsula, on which the capital city, Baku, is located, juts out into the Caspian Sea.

The level of the Caspian Sea, the largest salt water lake in the world, is subject to continuous change. In 1929 its surface area was larger than the Black Sea at 422,000 square km, before it started to decline reaching a record low point in 1951. Since then it has risen to about 436,000 square km. Higher water levels are causing problems along the Azeri coast.

Hemisphere

Northern.

Climate

Azerbaijan is considered to contain nine of the world's 13 climatic zones, from Alpine meadows to the subtropics. In Baku the climate is dry and Mediterranean. Due to its diversity, there are extremes of temperature in many areas – harsh winters and hot summers. Baku and other places on the Caspian Sea have mild winters. Temperatures in Baku are 0–5 degrees Celsius (C) in winter and 25–35 degrees C in summer.

Dress codes

Business dress should include a jacket and tie for men, and smart 'business-like' clothes for women.

Entry requirements

Passports

Required by all. Must be valid for at least three months after departure date.

Visa

Required by all with the exception of CIS citizens other than Armenia and Turkestan.

Application must be accompanied by an invitation from an Azerbaijani body or citizen, submitted through the Consular Department of the Ministry of Foreign Affairs of Azerbaijan in Baku. Contact the local embassy for further explanation.

Currency advice/regulations

Import/export of local currency by non-residents is prohibited.

There are no restrictions on the import of foreign currency by non-residents, although declaration on arrival is required. There are no limitations on the export of foreign currency, up to the amount declared on arrival.

US dollars, pounds sterling and euros are the preferred currencies and can be exchanged at the airport, bureaux de change, hotels, some restaurants and major banks. Hotels, exchange bureaux and restaurants will not accept US dollar bills dated before 1992 or those which are torn or in any way disfigured. Travellers are advised to take banknotes in small denominations and change small amounts of money as required. Rates offered by banks and bureaux de change are unlikely to vary significantly. Travellers'cheques are accepted only by the International Bank of Azerbaijan.

Customs

On arrival foreign currency and personal and valuable items must be declared.

Prohibited imports

Weapons, drugs, animals, anti-Azerbaijan literature and pictures, fruit and vegetables are prohibited.

Health (for visitors)

Only emergency medical treatment is available free to visitors, with small payments for medicines or hospital treatment. The level of care is limited. Private chemists in Baku stock a range of the more basic medicines. Travellers are advised to take out an insurance policy which includes emergency repatriation in case of serious illness or accident.

Mandatory precautions

None

Advisable precautions

It is advisable to be in date for the following immunisations: tetanus (within 10 years), typhoid, hepatitis A and B, tuberculosis. Anti-malarial prophylaxis are advisable. There may be some risk of meningitis, tick-borne encephalitis and leishmaniasis (cutaneous and visceral). Rabies is present.

It is advisable to take a supply of those medicines that are likely to be required (but check first that they may be legally imported). A travel kit including a disposable syringe is a reasonable precaution. Water precautions are recommended.

Hotels

Hotel space in Baku is very limited. Payment for the full stay is required in advance upon arrival at the hotel in cash (in US dollar bills which should be in good condition). VAT and service charges are included in all bills; tipping the waiters is appreciated but not compulsory.

Credit cards

Accepted in the major hotels, some restaurants and all banks in Baku. Credit cards can be used to purchase tickets at the airport.

Public holidays (national)

Fixed dates

1 Jan (New Year), 20 Jan (Day of the Martyrs), 8 Mar (Women's Day), 21 Mar (Novruz Bayramy), 9 May (Victory Day), 28 May (Republic Day), 15 Jun (Day of National Salvation), 26 June (Army and Navy Day), 18 Oct (Independence Day), 12 Nov (Constitution Day), 17 Nov (National Revival Day), 31 Dec (Solidarity Day).

Variable dates

Ramazam Bayram, Kurban Bayram.

Islamic year 1437 (15 Oct 2015–2 Oct 2016):: The Islamic year contains 354 or 355 days, with the result that Muslim feasts advance by 10–12 days against the Gregorian calendar. Dates of feasts vary according to the sighting of the new moon, so cannot be forecast exactly.

Working hours

Banking

Mon–Fri: 0900–1700.

Business

Mon–Fri: 0900–1800.

Government

Mon–Fri: 0900–1300; 1400–1800.

Shops

Mon–Fri: 0900–1900.

Telecommunications

Mobile/cell phones

There are two GSM mobile phone companies, Azercell and Bakcell.

Electricity supply

Voltage is usually 220V, 50 Hz.

Weights and measures

Metric system

Social customs/useful tips

Azeri culture blends Soviet-style courtesy with Middle Eastern informality.

The approach to business is not very well developed by Western standards, although technical knowledge and education standards are high.

Although Azeris are Muslim, they are probably the most secular of all the Muslim people of the former Soviet Union, with many considering themselves Eastern European rather than Asian. Consequently, Azerbaijan bears little relation to the Middle East with the exception of its oil and gas reserves. Business and negotiation habits are more akin to those in the rest of the former Soviet Union than with Middle Eastern practices.

The business environment has been reported to suffer from a number of ills, including very low wages for civil servants which act as an encouragement to corruption, a lack of transparency in the legal system and the inability to make decisions at lower governmental levels.

Bribery and 'gifts' were part and parcel of everyday business life in the former Soviet Union, and little has changed since 1991. However, moderate gifts and souvenirs discreetly given are usually more suitable than offers of foreign trips and shopping sprees.

Security

Crimes against foreigners are in general rare, but since late 2005 there has been an increase in violent muggings at night in the city centre (sometimes with the collusion of taxi drivers). It is advisable to arrange in advance to be transported to and from your hotel and to be vigilant in moving around on foot. Travellers should carry their passports with them at all times and ensure they travel with photocopies of their passports in case of theft.

Avoid all travel to Nagorno-Karabakh.

Getting there

Air

National airline: Azerbaijan Hava Yollari (Azal) (Azerbaijan Airlines)

International airport/s: Heydar Aliyev International (GYD), is located 25km east of Baku. Facilities include car hire, bank/bureau de change and VIP lounge.

Airport tax: None

Surface

Road: Inter-city bus routes link Baku with Tbilisi (Georgia), Derben (Dagestan) and Istanbul (Turkey).

The Regional Road Corridor Improvement Project, estimated at US$18 billion, to improve Central Asian roads, airports, railway lines and seaports and provide a vital transit route between Europe and Asia was agreed, on 3 November 2007. Six new transit corridors, between Afghanistan, Azerbaijan, China, Kazakhstan, Kyrgyzstan, Mongolia, Tajikistan and Uzbekistan, of mainly roads and rail links, will be constructed, or existing resources upgraded, by 2013. Half the costs with be provided by the Asian Development Bank and other multilateral organisations and the other half by participating countries.

Rail: There are rail connections to Tbilisi (Georgia), Derben (Dagestan) and various cities in the Russian Federation, including Moscow.

Water: Passenger ferries on the Caspian Sea link Azerbaijan with the Russian Federation, Central Asia and Iran. Ferries sail regularly to Baku from Turkmenbashy in Turkmenistan and from Bandar Anzali and Bandar Nowshar in Iran. Winter storms may disrupt services.

Main port/s: Baku.

Getting about

Travel within some regions of the country is restricted and visitors must obtain special permission from the Ministry of Interior.

National transport

Road: Azerbaijan has more than 57,770km of roads, of which over 31,000km are paved. Roads are generally in poor condition. Buses connect Baku and the main cities. The main motorway runs from Baku to Russia via the Caspian Coast.

Rail: Azerbaijan has a rail network of approximately 2,100km (1,300km electrified). The rail network is the most important form of transport, handling an estimated 75 per cent of total traffic.

City transport

Taxis: Taxis can be distinguished by a sign on top. Agree a price beforehand. Taxis are cheap, but drivers are unlikely to speak English. As the cost of a trip can vary widely, it is better to use hotel taxis or pre-arrange a car with driver.

Buses, trams & metro: Buses tend to be overcrowded. More expensive but more comfortable are *marshruts* (privately–operated minibuses), which follow the same routes. There is a metro in Baku with a total length of 28km.

Car hire

Car hire is available in Baku. An international driving licence is needed. Traffic drives on the right.

BUSINESS DIRECTORY

The addresses listed below are a selection only. While World of Information makes every endeavour to check these addresses, we cannot guarantee that changes have not been made, especially to telephone numbers and area codes. We would welcome any corrections.

Telephone area codes

The international direct dialling code (IDD) for Azerbaijan is +994, followed by area code and subscriber's number:

Baku	12	Neftechala	153
Dashkasan	216	Sumgayit	164
Nakhichevan	136		

Useful telephone numbers

Fire: 01
Police: 02
Ambulance: 03

Chambers of Commerce

American Chamber of Commerce in Azerbaijan, ISR Plaza, 340 Nizami Street, Baku 370000 tel: 971-333; fax: 971-091; e-mail: info@amchamaz.org).

Azerbaijan Chamber of Commerce and Industry, 31/33 Istiglaliyyat Street, Baku 370001 (tel: 928-912; fax: 971-997; e-mail: expo@chamber.baku.az).

Banking

Azakbank (private), 25 Xagani Street, 370070 Baku (tel: 983-109, 932-491; fax: 932-085).

Azcombank, 1 Inshaatchilar Avenue, 370073 Baku (tel: 388-323, 387-206).

AzEkoBank (joint stock bank), 11/39 Mustafa Subhi Street, Baku 370001 (tel: 929-433; fax: 980-406; e-mail: ecob@ecob.crack.azerbaijan.su; internet site: http://www.azekobank.com).

Azerbaijan Agricultural Industrial Bank, 125 Qadirli Street, Baku 370006 (tel: 389-293; fax: 389-115).

Azerbaijan Commercial Savings Bank, 71 Fizuli Street, Baku 370010 (tel: 930-561; fax: 939-489).

Azerbaijan Industrial Investment Bank, 71 Fizuli Street, 370010 Baku (tel: 931-701; fax: 931-266).

Azerbaijan National Bank, 19 Bulbul Ave, Baku 370070 (tel: 935-058; fax: 937-374).

Azerdemiryolbank, 31 Qarabagh Street, Baku 370008 (tel: 972-380, 675-321; fax: 987-936).

Azerigazbank, 37 Tbilisi Avenue, 370065 Baku (tel: 385-021; fax: 390-243).

Azerturkbank, 5 Islam Safarli Street, 370005 Baku (tel: 948-090; fax: 983-702).

Bakobank (private), 35 Yusif Safarov Street, 370025 Baku (tel: 666-549; fax: 981-927).

British Bank of the Middle East, 1 Bakihanov Street, Baku (tel: 981-234; fax: 980-817).

International Bank of Azerbaijan (IBA), 67 Nizami Street, Baku 370005 (tel: 930-091; fax: 934-091; e-mail: ibar@bar.az; internet site: http://www.ibar.az).

Most-Bank, 70 Nizami Street, Baku (tel: 971-070; fax: 972-094).

Promtekhbank (joint stock commercial bank), 69 Fizuli Street, Baku 370014 (tel: 957-874; fax: 958-360; e-mail: bank@devi.baku.az).

Rabitabank, 1 Buniat Sardarov Street, Baku 370001 (tel: 926-099; fax: 926-157).

Tajbank (commercial investment bank), 185 Azadlyg Ave, Baku 370087 (tel: 691-464; fax: 691-474).

Central bank

National Bank of Azerbaijan, 32 R. Behbudov Street, Baku (tel: 931-122; fax: 935-541; e-mail: mail@nba.az).

Stock exchange

Baki Fond Birjasi (BFB), (Baku Stock Exchange) (BSE), www.bse.az

Travel information

Azal (Azerbaijan Hava Yollari) (Azerbaijan Airlines), Prospect Azadlig 11, Baku 370000 (tel: 934-434; fax: 985-237, 651-120).

Azerbaijani Railways, Dilara Aliyeva Str 230, 370010 Baku (tel: 984-467; fax: 984-280).

Azertur Travel Agency of the State Council for Foreign Tourism (tours, hotel reservations, translation and interpreting services), 1 Azadlyg Ave, Baku 370000 (tel: 933-481; fax: 933-481).

Eur Tourism, 82 Topchubashev Str, Baku (tel: 973-444; fax: 986-810; e-mail: eurotourbaku@azeri.com).

Improtex (travel tours and conferences), 115 Azi Aslanov Str, Baku 370000 (tel: 930-896, 933-941; fax: 651-238; e-mail: toor@impro.Azerbaijan.su).

Ministries

Ministry of Agriculture and Food, 4 Shihali Kurbanov Street, Baku 370079 (tel: 935-355; fax: 943-952).

Ministry of Communications, 33 Azerbaijan Ave, Baku 370139 (tel: 930-004; fax: 984-285).

Ministry of Culture, Government House, Azadlyg Square, Baku 370016 (tel: 934-398; fax: 935-605).

Ministry of Defence, 3 Azerbaijan Ave, Azizbekov Baku 370601 (tel: 394-362; fax: 382-296).

Ministry of Economics, Government House, Azadlyg Square, Baku 370016 (tel: 936-920; fax: 932-025).

Ministry of Education, Government House, 1 Azadlyg Square, Baku 370016 (tel: 937-266; fax: 984-207).

Ministry of Finance, Sameda Vurguna Ul 6, Baku 370000 (tel: 933-012; fax: 987-969).

Ministry of Foreign Affairs, Gandjlar Meydani 3, Baku 370004 (tel: 923-401; fax: 629-756).

Ministry of Foreign Economic Relations, Lermontov Street 69, Baku 370601 (tel: 929-492; fax: 980-011).

Ministry of Grain Products, 13 Yusifzade Street, Baku 370033 (tel: 667-451; fax: 939-023).

Ministry of Health, Malaya Morskaya Street 4, Baku 370014 (tel: 932-977; fax: 988-559).

Ministry of Information and Press, 12 Ahmad Javad Street, Baku 370001 (tel: 926-357; fax: 926-747).

Ministry of Internal Affairs, 7 Gusi Hajiyev Street, Baku 370005 (tel: 986-396; fax: 923-471).

Ministry of Justice, 13 Kirov Avenue, Baku 370601 (tel: 939-785; fax: 938-367).

Ministry of Labour and Social Protection, Azadlyg Square, Baku 370016 (tel: 930-542; fax: 939-472).

Ministry of Material Resources, 83-23 Alaskar Alakbarov Street, Baku 370141 (tel: 394-296; fax: 399-176).

Ministry of National Security, 1 Azadlyg Square 1, Baku 370016 (tel: 931-000; fax: 936-296).

Ministry of Trade, Government House, Azadlyg Square 1, Baku 370016 (tel: 985-074; fax: 987-431).

Ministry of Youth and Sports, 98a Fatali Han Khoyski Avenue, Baku 370072 (tel: 981-426; fax: 643-650).

Office of the President of the Azerbaijan Republic, 19 Istiglaliyyat Street, Baku 370066 (tel: 983-113).

Other useful addresses

Azerbaijan News Service, Block 504, 1128 Street, Baku 370073 (building of the Institute of Zoology) (tel: 929-221/3; fax: 989-498).

Azerbintorg Foreign Trade Association, 14 Boyuk Gala Str, 370004 Baku (tel: 920-481, 926-492, 924-545; fax: 983-292).

Azerigaz, 23 Yusif Safarov Street, Baku 370025 (tel: 677-447; fax: 674-255).

Azerkimia, 86 Samed Vurgun Street, Baku 373200 (tel: 937-620).

Azertaj State Information Agency, Bulbul Avenue 18, 370000 Baku (tel: 935-445; fax: 938-138).

Baku General Customs Board, 62 Neftchilar Ave, Baku 370601 (tel: 939-588).

Baku Statistics Office, 10 Tabriz Street, Baku 370008 (tel: 669-327, 672-265).

Baku Telegraph Office, 41 Azerbaijan Avenue, Baku 370000 (tel: 936-142).

Baku Television, M. Husein St 1, Baku.

Board of Azerbaijan Railways, 230 Dilara Aliyeva Street, Baku 370010 (tel: 984-467).

British Embassy, 2 Izmir Street, 370065 Baku (tel: 924-813; fax: 985-558).

Caspian Shipping Company, 5 Rasulzade Street, Baku 370005 (tel: 922-058; fax: 935-339).

Central Post Office, 36 Uzeyir Hajibeyov Street, Baku 370000 (tel: 985-251).

EU Co-ordinating Unit in Azerbaijan, Government House, 8th Floor, Room 851, Baku 370016 (tel: 936-018; fax: 937-638).

Radio Baku, M Husein St 1, 370011 Baku.

Scientific Research and Test Constructive Institute of Oil Machinery of Azerbaijan Republic (Azinmash), Aras Street 4, Baku 370029 (tel: 670-888; fax: 672-888).

SME Development Agency 83, Mr Vagif G. Alikperov, S Vurguna, Azneftiechimprom Bld. 5th Floor, PO Box 114, 37000 Baku (tel: 957832; fax: 957832; e-mail: quirin@smeda.baku.az).

State Committee for Statistics, 24 Inshaatchylar Ave, Baku-136 370136 (tel: 381-171; fax: 380-577).

State Customs Committee, 2 Inshaatchilar Ave, Baku 370073 (tel: 927-545).

State Oil Company of the Azerbaijan Republic (SOCAR), 73 Neftchilar Ave, Baku 370004 (tel: 924-480, 920-745, 920-685; fax: 936-492, 923-204).

Statoil Caspian Region, 96 Nizami Street, 370010 Baku (tel: 977-340; fax: 977-944).

US Embassy, 83 Azadliq Avenue, Baku 370007 (tel: 980-335; fax: 983-755; e-mail: webbaku@pd.state.gov).

National news agency: Azar Tac www.azertag.com

Turan: www.turaninfo.com

Trend: http://news.trendaz.com

Internet sites

President of Azerbaijan: www.president.az

Bahamas

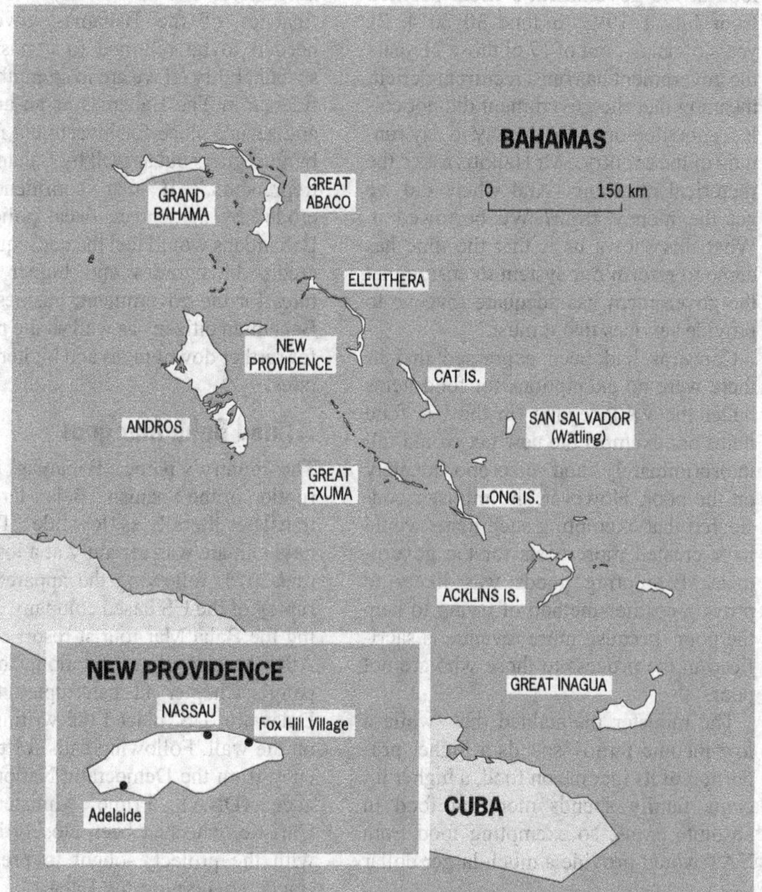

Marking his country's forty-second year of independence, in June 2015 the Bahamian Prime Minister Perry Christie presented a rather gloomy picture of twenty-first century Bahamas. As reported on the *Bahamas Weekly* website, in his address Mr Christie noted that four decades earlier Bahamians had agitated for the freedoms they now enjoyed: the freedom to vote in democratic elections, and the right to own land. Freedoms which, while fundamentally important to the country's continued growth and development, were for the most part taken for granted.

The Bahamas only gained independence in 1973. Prime Minister Christie lamented that in 2015 the Bahamas was 'a far cry from the strong independent nation that our forefathers envisioned.' Quoting Franklin Roosevelt Mr Christie observed that 'True individual freedom cannot exist without economic security and independence. People who are hungry and out of a job are the stuff of which dictatorships are made.' According to the Prime Minister, 'This could not be truer of our modern day Bahamas.' Freedom had been replaced by 'the shackles of unprecedented levels of crime and unemployment.' Instead of an educated populous, the Bahamas had to contend 'with a substandard system which continued to churn out individuals who are functionally illiterate.' The economic

KEY FACTS

Official name: Commonwealth of The Bahamas

Head of State: Queen Elizabeth II, represented by Governor General Dame Marguerite Pindling (from 8 Jul 2014)

Head of government: Prime Minister Perry Gladstone Christie (PLP) (from 8 May 2012)

Ruling party: Progressive Liberal Party (from 8 May 2012)

Area: 13,935 square km

Population: 360,000 (2014)* (353,658; 2010, census figure)

Capital: Nassau

Official language: English

Currency: Bahamian dollar (B$) = 100 cents

Exchange rate: B$1.00 per US$ Fixed

GDP per capita: US$24,034 (2014)*

GDP real growth: 1.29% (2014)*

GDP: US$8.66 billion (2014)*

Labour force: 184,000 (2009)*

Unemployment: 15.03% (2014)*

Inflation: 1.19% (2014)*

Balance of trade: -US$2.42 billion (2014)

* estimated figure

growth and stability the country's leadership had pursued for over forty years had delivered only a higher tax burden and a stagnant economy 'which threatened to choke the spirit of innovation and entrepreneurship.'

Forty years of see-saw self-governance under the Progressive Liberal Party (PLP) and the Free National Movement (FNM) had, in Mr Christie's opinion, done little to fulfil 'the dream that was once the Bahamas.' The Prime Minister alleged that the country's political leaders had used their platforms '... to further personal agendas and line the pockets of their friends, family members and party supporters, creating a nation of individuals who had become dependent on the scraps which fall from the table of the country's elite.' For forty years the country's political leaders had created policies which allowed foreign investors to become kings when Bahamians should be the property owners. The Bahamar scandal (see below) was only the latest example.

VAT arrives...

The announcement in 2014 of a value added tax (VAT) system had been expected to lead to one of the biggest changes to the economy and governance of the Bahamas in some time. As the registration process got underway in mid-2014 the 'hysteria' that had accompanied its announcement became something closer to cold reality. Initially what were described as 'Corporate services firms' alongside the 100 largest tax payers were required to register for VAT from September 2014. State Minister for Finance Michael Halkitis had noted that in the Bahamas 'Business cannot continue as usual – with an outdated tax system and a growing financial debt due to the government's inability to meet its financial obligations over the years. Fiscal reform had become critical to future national development.' Mr Halkitis went on to note that 'When we look at the government's fiscal position from July 1 1993 to June 30 2014, 21 years of data... out of 17 of those 21 years the government has run a recurrent deficit, meaning that the government did not collect enough money for the day to day running of the country.' Mr Halkitis asked the rhetorical question: 'And where did we get the money from? We borrowed it. What this shows us is that the time has come to reform our system to ensure that the government has adequate revenue to provide services that it must.'

Concerns had been expressed that as there were no exemptions for food items under the VAT regime (in the UK food items are exempt) the new tax would fall indiscriminately and disproportionately on the poor. However, the minister considered that exempting such items would have created more costs for the government. Exempting goods was likely to prove a costlier method of trying to help the poor 'because more revenue is sacrificed in the process to those who are not poor.'

The minister maintained that 'while a low income family spends a higher proportion of its income on food, a higher income family spends more on food in absolute terms, so exempting food from VAT would provide a much larger dollar benefit for a high income family than to a low income family.' The government also maintained that its Social Assistance Programme would help to reduce the impact from VAT on low income earners affected by the tax implementation.

Mr Halkitis painted a gloomy picture of the country's future were VAT not to be introduced. The hard reality was that the finances of the Bahamas government needed to be returned to a position of sustainability 'if we are to strengthen confidence in The Bahamas as an attractive and secure place for investment not only by foreigners but as well by Bahamian entrepreneurs.' If that confidence was eroded by inadequate fiscal policies, all Bahamians would feel the consequences – credit downgrades and higher interest rates for the government, businesses and Bahamian citizens as well as the potential for further downgrades and higher interest rates.

... and Baha Mar goes

The country's name, 'Bahamas' is a corruption of the Spanish, 'Baja Mar,' which translates literally as 'low tide'. The business climate was certainly at a low ebb in mid-2015, following the apparent bankruptcy of the US based company developing the Baha Mar tourist resort complex. After weeks of speculation, the company's Chapter 11 bankruptcy filing in Delaware, US, placed the writing firmly on the wall. Following calls for transparency from the Democratic National Alliance (DNA), Prime Minister Perry Christie, who had been closely involved with the project, sought to present the 'facts' concerning the Baha Mar project. The Prime Minister laid the blame for the company's failure at the feet of Baha Mar's CEO, Sarkis Izmirlian.

Bahamians could only wonder at the case's complexity: in short, China Construction America Inc (CCA), an affiliate of China State Construction Engineering Corp (CSCEC), had argued that the bankruptcy proceedings belonged in the Bahamas, not in the US. This assertion awaited the decision of a judge in Nassau to recognise – or not – the company's US bankruptcy filing.

The main contractor had argued that the bankruptcy proceedings belonged in the Bahamas. The resort and the no less than 14 (of the 15 entities involved) that had filed for bankruptcy in the US were actually located in the Bahamas. The CCA claimed that the US filing illegally permitted the current owner Sarkis Izmirlian to remain in charge and added that the

KEY INDICATORS — Bahamas

	Unit	2011	2012	2013	2014	**2015
Population	m	*0.35	0.35	0.36	*0.36	*0.36
Gross domestic product (GDP)	US$bn	8.10	8.15	8.42	*8.66	*9.19
GDP per capita	US$	23,175	23,133	23,639	*24,034	*25,221
GDP real growth	%	2.0	1.8	0.7	*1.3	*2.3
Inflation	%	2.5	2.0	0.4	*1.2	*2.3
Unemployment	%	15.9	14.0	15.8	*15.0	*14.5
Exports (fob) (goods)	US$m	834.9	984.0	909.3	848.8	–
Imports (fob) (goods)	US$m	2,965.7	3,385.5	3,126.4	3,269.5	–
Balance of trade	US$m	-2,130.7	-2,401.4	-2,217.1	-2,420.7	–
Current account	US$m	-1,090.8	-1,500.0	-1,494.0	*-1,871.0	*-1,136.0
Total reserves minus gold	US$m	1,271.2	–	807.4	874.3	–
Foreign exchange	US$m	1,078.7	–	739.2	–	–
Exchange rate	per US$	1.00	1.00	1.00	1.00	–

* estimated figure ** forecast figure

Bahamian government appeared to agree to this. Baha Mar Ltd said it would oppose the motion to dismiss, claiming that it wanted to 'achieve a consensual resolution of the issues' and was in discussions with both CCA and its lender, the Export-Import Bank of China.

The Baha Mar scandal did little to improve the Bahamas' international reputation. The apparent breakdown of funding negotiations in China would have far reaching economic implications for the government's plans for projected economic growth and would add a few thousands more Bahamians to the unemployment statistics. Opposition politicians claimed that the Christie-led government had based its entire job creation strategy on the developer's ability to open the Baha Mar resort.

The economy recovers – just about

According to the United Nations Economic Commission for Latin America and the Caribbean (ECLAC), the Bahamian economy posted a modest recovery in 2014, with growth projected to strengthen to 2.3 per cent from the 0.7 per cent seen in 2013. According to ECLAC, the improved activity was strengthened by higher value added in tourism, driven especially by a recovery in high-spending stopover visitor arrivals and buoyant construction activity. Projects financed by foreign direct investment (FDI), led by the (apparently doomed) Baha Mar resort project (see above), bolstered construction. Activity in the offshore financial services sector was buoyant. In the financial sector, private credit was subdued, amid slow gains in employment and elevated non-performing loans, which had lead to greater bank prudence in lending.

ECLAC noted that the external imbalance worsened with a widening of the current account deficit, mainly on account of the higher construction payments abroad that offset higher tourism receipts. Economic growth was projected to increase to 2.8 per cent in 2015, bolstered by a continued improvement in tourism, firm construction activity and buoyancy in the offshore financial services sector.

The main focus of policy in the near term was on structured fiscal consolidation to reduce public debt, while maintaining public investment to nurture the fledgling recovery. The central pillar of reform is the introduction of a 7.5 per cent value added tax (VAT – see above) in January 2015, which is expected to help underpin the consolidation effort. Nevertheless, the full impact will be constrained by the government's plan to increase the salaries of some public servants by 7.5 per cent in line with the VAT rate over a five-year period. The introduction of VAT was to be supported by efforts to strengthen tax efficiency and collection and to tighten procurement procedures. Reflecting initial steps towards consolidation, fiscal policy was mildly contractionary in the first 11 months of the 2013/2014 financial year (July to June). The fiscal deficit declined from 6.0 per cent of gross domestic product (GDP) in 2013 to 4.8 per cent in 2014. This improved performance stemmed from a 6.2 per cent growth in revenue that outweighed a 0.7 per cent increase in expenditure.

Revenues were boosted by a 2.6 per cent increase in tax receipts, which firmed up as a result of higher business and professional fees following the government's introduction of a more lucrative revised fee structure. Expenditure grew marginally (0.7 per cent), reflecting increased current spending linked to higher public debt and personal emoluments. The fiscal deficit was projected to decline further to 3.5 per cent of GDP in 2015 as revenues were buoyed by the new VAT and expenditure was dampened by the continued winding down of public infrastructure projects.

Public debt expanded by 9 per cent from 64 per cent of GDP in 2013 to 67 per cent year-on-year to June 2014, partly owing to a US$300 million international bond issue and loans for infrastructure projects. The Central Bank of the Bahamas maintained a neutral monetary stance in 2014, holding its policy-based discount rate at 4.5 per cent, as the modest recovery did not threaten to undermine reserves through import demand. Growth in domestic credit slowed during the first trimester of 2014 compared with 2013. Credit to the public sector contracted as government used part of the proceeds from foreign financing to retire a portion of debt owed to local banks. Credit to the private sector declined by 2.9 percentage points to 75.6 per cent of GDP in 2014, a slower rate of decline than in 2013, owing to the pickup in activity and gains in employment. Despite the build-up in liquidity, the interest rate spread widened to 10.6 per cent from 9.16 per cent in 2013.

The current account deficit was projected by ECLAC to expand from 19.4 per cent of GDP in 2013 to 22.1 per cent in 2014, reflecting a deterioration in both the goods and the services balances that offset the improvement in the income account. The trade deficit expanded by 16 per cent, owing to a rebound in imports, reflecting the rise in economic activity. Higher imports of fuel and construction material were recorded, partly reflecting ongoing construction activity. The services account surplus narrowed on account of construction-related service payments linked to hotel building, which offset growth in travel receipts due to increased visitor arrivals and spending. The income account was projected to improve in line with a reduction in other investment outflows. The surplus on the capital and financial account expanded by about 10 per cent, bolstered by a surge in FDI to US$440 million that was partly associated with the acquisition of a high-end resort. Buttressed by higher inflows, international reserves expanded year-on-year by 18 per cent to US$803 million in September 2014, covering about four months of non-oil imports.

As noted above, economic growth firmed to 2.3 per cent in 2014, compared with 0.7 per cent in 2013, propelled by the recovery in tourism, particularly high value added air arrivals, which expanded by 3.6 per cent to 984,309 visitors during the first eight months of 2014. Arrivals were boosted by promotion programmes, including the Companion Fly Free programme and increased air travel from the United States. The hotel occupancy rate also increased by 3.6 per cent to 60.2 per cent in the year to date to July, but the average daily room rate fell by 4 per cent. Construction activity picked up, led by FDI-financed hotel construction, including the Baha Mar (see above) resort and other properties in the Out Islands and infrastructure works. The opening of the Baha Mar resort had (unsurprisingly) been pushed back from December 2014 to mid-2015, which meant that it would not benefit from the lucrative winter season.

Activity in the offshore financial services sector was also buoyant, reflecting growth in trust companies and fund registrations. Growth was expected to pick up to 2.8 per cent in 2015, mainly driven by tourism and construction. With firmer demand growth, inflation in 2014 was expected to be 2.0 per cent, up from just over one per cent in 2013. The rise reflected higher prices for food and alcoholic beverages and furnishings and equipment. The introduction of VAT in 2015 is expected to push up prices further. Unemployment declined from 15.4 per cent in 2013 to 14.3 per cent in 2014, reflecting job gains among youths in the tourism and construction sectors.

Risk assessment

Economy	Fair
Politics	Poor
Regional stability	Good

COUNTRY PROFILE

1647 The Bahamas (from the Spanish *Baja Mar* – meaning low tide), originally inhabited by Arawak Indians were occupied by British settlers in 1647.
1729 A parliamentary system of government was introduced.
1783 Recognised as a colony.
1834 Britain emancipated its slaves.
1964 Internal self-government was granted.
1967 In the first elections under full universal adult suffrage, the Progressive Liberal Party (PLP), led by Lynden (later Sir Lynden) Pindling won with the support of the United Bahamian Party (UBP).
1972 The PLP won a landslide victory and began independence talks with the UK.
1973 The Bahamas gained full independence on 10 July as a member of the Commonwealth.
1992 Sir Lynden Pindling and the PLP lost power to the Free National Movement (FNM).
1997 The FNM were re-elected.
2000 Sir Lynden Pindling died. The Bahamas was removed from the Organisation for Economic Co-operation and Development (OECD) Financial Action Task Force (FATF) list of Non-Co-operative Countries and Territories (NCCT), on money laundering and terrorist financing.
2001 The US awarded the Bahamas certification as being one of 20 countries fully co-operating with anti-drug efforts. Dame Ivy Dumont became the first female governor general.
2002 The PLP won the parliamentary elections. Perry Christie became prime minister.
2004 Hurricane Frances caused widespread damage.
2005 Dame Ivy Dumont retired; Paul Adderley, became acting governor general. The Bahamas banking system was removed from the FATF list of NCCT.
2006 Arthur Dion Hanna was inaugurated as governor general.
2007 In parliamentary elections the FNM won 23 out of 41 seats, defeating the incumbent PLP, which won 18 seats. The FNM leader, Hubert Ingraham, was sworn in as prime minister.
2009 Cuba and the Bahamas signed a bilateral co-operation agreement to promote trade and investment, as well as technical information exchange and joint programmes, particularly in the education and health sectors. The Bahamas Financial Services Board (BFSB), a regulatory body, was launched.
2010 Sir Arthur Foulkes became as governor general, on the retirement of Arthur Dion Hanna.
2011 The UK-based Privy Council overturned a death penalty on a convicted killer (Maxo Tido) in June, sparking controversy concerning the sovereignty of the Bahamian justice system and the role of the Privy Council. Prime Minister Ingraham told parliament that he intended to bring forward legislation to deal with 'the question of the imposition of the death penalty in The Bahamas'. This legislation would prescribe specific categories for which the death penalty may be applied. The Bahamas Bar Association warned that abandoning the Privy Council could be 'treading in very dangerous water' and that a court of final appeal was essential to ensure justice for all. On 29 June legislation was introduced to amend the Parliamentary Elections Act, including lifting the need to re-register for voters who have not moved home for over a year and limiting the circumstances for a recount following an election. A law banning shark fishing in Bahamian waters was signed in July. It also prohibits the sale, import and export of shark products. During the Commonwealth Heads of Government summit in October, the 16 countries in which the British monarch is Head of State unanimously agreed to change the royal line of succession from that of first born son to the first born child (regardless of its gender). The change will be enacted after the succession of Prince William (currently second in line to the throne, after his father Prince Charles).
2012 Parliamentary elections were held on 7 May, in which the opposition PLP won 29 seats out of 38 and the FNM nine. Perry Gladstone Christie was sworn into office as prime minister on 8 May. On 25 September, the credit ratings agency Standard and Poor's, downgraded the Bahamas' economic outlook from 'stable' to 'negative', and could be downgraded further if the government failed to develop a credible 'medium-term plan' to deal with the country's fiscal deficit and sharp growth in debt-to-GDP. However the Bahamas' sovereign credit rating remained unchanged at BBB/A2.
2013 A two-part referendum was held on 28 January, first on whether or not to legalise 'web shops' so that citizens could gamble alongside tourist in the hotel's casinos, and secondly whether the government should create a national lottery. On a low turnout, voters rejected both proposals and after a delay the government moved to close the illegal web shops. However, within hours, an injunction prevented the government from shutting down these operations pending the outcome of all substantive matters relative to the legality of web shops. A referendum on reforming the constitution, originally set for March and later for June, was delayed until late November. By September preparations for educating the voters had still not got underway and it was suggested the referendum would be further delayed until 2014.
2014 At a Caricom meeting held in March the Bahamas endorsed plans to seek reparations for slavery from former colonisers, including Britain, France and the Netherlands. Minister of foreign affairs, Fred Mitchell, said a commission had been set up to advise on the necessity and or efficacy of any legal, political, legislative or administrative decisions that need to be taken. In April two petroleum companies, Bahamas Petroleum and Atlantic Petroleum, applied for licences to explore for oil. Prime Minister Perry Christie announced on 28 May that VAT would be reduced to 7.5 per cent 'across the board' on 1 January 2015, although there will be a number of exceptions. Dame Marguerite Pindling was sworn in as Governor General on 8 July. In September Moody's Investors Service downgraded The Bahamas' sovereign credit rating to Baa2 from Baa1. However, at the same time it changed the country's economic outlook from negative to stable, so that although the lower credit rating may make borrowing more expensive, the improved outlook will increase confidence in the economy. The main reason for the downgrade was due to the rapidly rising level of government debt – the government's debt-to-GDP ratio haing increased from 31.7 per cent in 2007 to 59.0 per cent in 2013. The Bahamas Nurses Union, the Bahamas Customs, Immigration and Allied Workers Union (BCIAWU) and the Bahamas Educators Managerial Union announced in early September that they would continue their strike despite an announcement by the government that they would seek an injunction ordering the strikers to return to work.
2015 VAT, initially at a rate of 7.5 per cent, came into effect on 1 January. Construction on the Baha Mar complex was halted n February. On 29 June the Baha Mar mega-resort announced that it had filed for chapter 11 bankruptcy in the US district of Delaware. It warned that it would have to cut jobs if it does not resolve the matter 'in the next few weeks'. The Board of Directors said the move was due to the financial consequences of the repeated delays by China State Construction Engineering Corporation (CSCEC) the general contractor (the state-owned company is the parent of China Construction America Inc (CCA), whose Bahamian subsidiary is main contractor), and the resulting loss of revenue. On the following

day Baha Mar filed a lawsuit in England against CSCEC, seeking more than US$192 million in damages. On 15 September, the Chapter 11 cases for all the Baha Mar companies based in The Bahamas were thrown out by the US Bankruptcy Court in Delaware. On 23 September Prime Minister Christie said the chairman of CSCEC had assured him that the Baha Mar resort will be completed despite the financing difficulties.

Political structure

Constitution

The 1973 constitution was enacted to validate independence. Rights of citizenship and freedom of the individual were guaranteed. The composition of parliament, with a senate and house of assembly, was mandated and the function and authority of the executive were set forth.

Voting eligibility is for citizens of the Bahamas who are 18 years or older.

Independence date

10 July 1973

Form of state

Constitutional multi-party parliamentary democracy; it is a member of the Commonwealth.

The executive

The British monarch is the nominal head of state, represented by the governor general. Executive power is exercised by the prime minister and cabinet, which advises the governor general on appointments and ratifies laws.

National legislature

The bicameral legislature consists of a House of Assembly (lower house) with 41 members elected for five-year terms in single-seat constituencies, and the Senate (upper house) with 16 members appointed by the governor general – nine members are appointed on the recommendation of the prime minister, four members are appointed on the recommendation of the leader of the opposition and three members are appointed on the recommendation of the prime minister and leader of the opposition together. The leader of the largest political party in the House of Assembly is made prime minister. The senate always reflects the political make-up of the House of Assembly.

The government may dissolve parliament at any time up to the parliament's five-year term.

Legal system

The Bahamian legal system is based on British common law with elements of former colonial legislation. Much of the business legislation enacted since independence is based on the US system. The Privy Council in London is the highest court of appeal.

Last elections

7 May 2012 (parliamentary)

Results: Parliamentary: Progressive Liberal Party (PLP) won 29 seats out of 38, the Free National Movement (FNM) nine.

Next elections

2017 (parliamentary)

Political parties

Ruling party

Progressive Liberal Party (from 8 May 2012)

Main opposition party

Free National Movement (FNM)

Political situation

The establishment of a Financial Services Authority was announced in June 2009, following the collapse in February of the insurance company CLICO Bahamas with liabilities in excess of US$9 million. This was the most tangible result of the downturn in the global economy in 2008–09. The Bahamas also had to contend with an unemployment rate of 12.1 per cent in New Providence and 14.6 per cent in Grand Bahama, with employment in the hotel and restaurant sector declining by 10 per cent and in the construction industry by 9 per cent. In May the five-star Four Seasons Resort, which had opened in December 2003, closed due to insolvency. Prime Minister, Hubert Ingraham, when he presented the 2009/10 budget, said that the economy had suffered but that the government would resume 'the path of social and economic progress temporarily interrupted by the global financial crisis' when the situation improved.

356,000 (2013)* (353,658; 2010, census figure)

Population

Approximately 32 per cent of the total population is under 15 years of age. Nearly 67 per cent of the population lives on New Providence, with 15 per cent on Grand Bahama, and the remainder on the various Family Islands.

Last census: 3 May 2010: 353,658

Population density: 30 inhabitants per square km. Urban population 84 per cent (2010 Unicef).

Annual growth rate: 1.5 per cent, 1990–2010 (Unicef).

Ethnic make-up

African (85 per cent), European and mixed race (12 per cent), other (3 per cent).

Religions

Baptist (32 per cent), Anglican (20 per cent), Roman Catholic (19 per cent), Evangelical Protestant (12 per cent), Methodist (6 per cent), Church of God (6 per cent).

Education

There is an extensive primary and secondary school system, and education is free. There are numerous options for tertiary education, including the College of the Bahamas, which is affiliated with the University of the West Indies (UWI). Local post-secondary vocational and technical training is available in mechanical, electrical and automotive engineering, television and radio, technology, computer science, electronics, construction, carpentry, secretarial services, bookkeeping, printing, photography, straw craft and dressmaking. A scholarship programme provides university training abroad in medicine, agriculture, engineering, science, education and other subjects considered necessary for national development but not available locally.

Literacy rate: 96 per cent of adults (2003)

Compulsory years: Five to 16

Enrolment rate: 98 per cent, gross primary enrolment (World Bank).

Health

There are three main hospitals in the Bahamas: Princess Margaret in Nassau and Rand Memorial in Freeport, both government owned, and the privately owned Doctors Hospital in Nassau. Lyford Cay Hospital is a smaller private establishment offering specialised treatment.

HIV/Aids

Deaths by Aids, had in the early 2000s become a leading cause of death. However through government backed health policies and education, the number of people living with HIV was reduced to an estimated 7,000 in 2009 (Unicef 2012).

HIV prevalence: 3.1 per cent aged 15–49 in 2009 (Unicef 2012)

Life expectancy: 75 years, 2010 (Unicef 2012)

Fertility rate/Maternal mortality rate: 1.9 births per woman, 2010 (Unicef 2012)

Child (under 5 years) mortality rate (per 1,000): 17 per 1,000 live births (WHO 2012)

Welfare

Welfare conditions in the Bahamas are among the best in the Caribbean and the government is working towards ensuring that economic growth is accompanied by improvements in the social sector.

The National Insurance Act of 1972 set out the law governing social security. It provides for contributions from employers and employees to be paid to the National Insurance Fund. Anyone who is employed or self-employed is insured under the act, including non-Bahamians with work permits. Benefits include sickness and maternity payments, retirement and widows' pensions and social assistance payments.

Main cities

Nassau (capital and seat of government, on New Providence Island, estimated population 255,789 in 2012) and

Freeport (on Grand Bahama Island, 45,945), West End (13,577), Coopers Town (9,948).

Languages spoken

English, Creole (among Haitian immigrants).

Official language/s

English

Media

Press

Dailies: Newspapers include the *Nassau Guardian* (www.thenassauguardian.com), *The Tribune* and the intellectual *Bahama Journal* (www.jonesbahamas.com);*Freeport News* (http://freeport.nassauguardian.net) is published on Grand Bahama.

Weeklies: Tabloid newspapers include *Punch* published twice weekly and has the largest circulation of all newspapers; *The Abaconian* is published once fortnightly, on Abaco.

Business: A quarterly magazine *The Bahamas Financial Digest* (www.bfsb-bahamas.com) is a government publication that reports on financial services and investments.

Broadcasting

The national public broadcaster is ZNS (www.znsbahamas.com), (the name is derived from its call sign: Zephyr Nassau Sunshine).

Radio: ZNS operates three commercial radio station; ZNS 1 and 2 from Nassau and ZNS3 from Freeport. There are around a dozen private stations include Splash FM (www.splash899fm.com), Radio Abaco (www.radioabaco.com) and 100 Jamz (www.100jamz.com).

Television: ZNS operates the only domestic TV station on the islands. Cable TV is available to around 96 per cent of the population offering a wide choice of imported TV programmes, sporting events and films.

Other news agencies: Caribbean Net News: www.caribbeannetnews.com

Economy

The economy is dominated by the tourism industry (43.6 per cent of GDP) and offshore financial services.

After recession in 2009 caused by the global economic crisis that cut both tourist numbers and financial activity, GDP growth had picked up to 1.5 per cent in 2010. Whilst growth remained positive thanks to slight increase in tourism, it has been shrinking since 2010 and in 2013 the Bahamas recorded growth of 0.7 per cent. Unemployment during the worst of the recession was 14.6 per cent (almost double the typical annual rate as seen in years of growth), and has grown since reaching 15.4 per cent in 2014. Workers in the tourist and construction sectors have been hit the hardest. GDP per capita fell from US$24,459 in 2008 to US$22,350 in 2010, before recovering to US$23,489 in 2013.

Although the balance of payments in 2009 was in deficit, by around 12.5 per cent of GDP, external borrowing and a one-off Special Drawing Rights (SDR) from the International Monetary Fund (IMF) of US$179 million were more than adequate to cover the shortfall before the economy recovered in 2010. However, government debt by June 2010 was around 47 per cent of GDP, which affected Bahamas' sovereign rating, which was downgraded to BBB+/stable. On 25 September 2012, the credit ratings agency Standard and Poor's, downgraded the Bahamas' economic outlook from 'stable' to 'negative', and could be downgraded further if the government failed to develop a credible 'medium-term plan' to deal with the country's fiscal deficit and sharp growth in debt-to-GDP.

In September 2014 Moody's Investors Service downgraded The Bahamas' sovereign credit rating to Baa2 from Baa1. However, at the same time it changed the country's economic outlook from 'negative' (where it had been since 2012) to 'stable', so that although the lower credit rating may make borrowing more expensive, the improved outlook will increase confidence in the economy. The main reason for the downgrade was due to the rapidly rising level of government debt – the government's debt-to-GDP ratio having increased from 31.7 per cent in 2007 to 59.0 per cent in 2013. Moody's also announced in 2015 that it would be unlikely to improve the Bahamas rating 'for the next three to five years'.

The high incidence of hurricanes hitting the islands affects the economy, although due to the islands' general preparedness, the economic impact is kept to a minimum.

The World Travel and Tourism Council estimated that tourism contributed 43.6 per cent to GDP in 2014, while attracting investment constituting 18.3 per cent of total investment. Direct employment in the industry was around 51,000 jobs (27.0 per cent of total employment) and provided total indirect employment, including jobs indirectly supported by the industry, to 51.6 per cent of the workforce (98,000 jobs). Foreign revenue from tourism was estimated to be US$2.3 billion.

In 2011, the state-owned Bahamas Petroleum Company (BPC) was seeking investors for rights to explore oil-sands deposits beneath the islands, with an offer of 25 per cent of well-head revenue returned in royalties to the government (less than the 33 per cent as contracted in the US). In June 2015 the BPC signed a license renewal allowing exploration to continue until June 2008.

VAT, initially at a rate of 7.5 per cent, came into effect on 1 January 2015.

External trade

Although the Bahamas was a founder member of the Caribbean Community (Caricom), it did not adopt the Caricom Single Market and Economy (CSME), which was ratified by 12 other member states in 2006.

Imports

Principal imports include crude oil for refining, fuel oil, machinery and transport equipment, manufactured goods, livestock and foodstuffs, and chemicals.

Main sources: US (31 per cent of total in 2014), India (30 per cent), South Korea (9.9 per cent), Colombia (6.6 per cent).

Exports

Exports include chemicals, pharmaceuticals, rum, crawfish, agricultural products, salt, aragonite, sponges, cosmetics, perfume and paintings.

Main destinations: Singapore (30 per cent of total in 2014), US (22 per cent), Poland (10 per cent), Ecuador (6.2 per cent).

Re-exports

Petroleum products

Agriculture

Farming

The agricultural and fisheries sector contributes approximately 2 per cent to annual GDP and employs about 5 per cent of the labour force.

Although only about 1 per cent of land area is cultivated, near self-sufficiency has been achieved in poultry, pork, eggs, fruit and vegetables. The expansion of export crops such as limes, pineapples, papayas, avocados, cucumbers and mangoes is being promoted.

The government has provided marketing facilities through the Product Exchange in Nassau for small-scale producers, and also supplies seed and fertilisers. There are special incentives to foreign investors in food production and processing.

The chicken industry accounts for 40 per cent of agricultural production.

Fishing

The sector employs around 9,000 Bahamians. The commercial harvesting of pearls and shells has seen a dramatic rise with the annual harvest is typically 13,000 units. The harvest of sponges averages 70,000 per annum.

Forestry

Total forest cover is estimated at 842,000 hectares, equivalent of 15 per cent of the total land area. Most forests are concentrated on the four islands of the north-western Bahamas including Ahaco, Andros, Grand Bahamas and New Providence.

Industry and manufacturing

The industrial sector is relatively small-scale, contributing around 18 per cent to annual GDP and employing 12 per cent of the labour force.

The largest contributor to the industrial sector is the crude oil transhipment terminal operated by Burmah Oil. Re-exports of crude and refined oil (mainly to the US) are estimated to account for around 16 per cent of GDP.

Other activity is centred on the production of rum, chemicals and pharmaceuticals for export. The companies manufacturing these products are largely foreign-owned and located in the Freeport trade area on Grand Bahama.

Other light industries include rum production, food processing, confectionery, garments, small boat building and furniture making.

The Bahamas Agricultural and Industrial Corporation (BAIC) is encouraging light manufacturing, furniture, toiletries, cosmetics, jewellery, linens, beachwear and the assembly of air conditioners and refrigerators.

The construction industry is also important, fuelled by the tourist trade and financial institutions requiring offices.

Tourism

The economy is dominated by the tourism industry. Tourists from the US and Canada are the greatest in number, followed by Europeans and other Caribbean residents. Visitor numbers dropped in 2011, from 1.37 million in 2010 to 1.35 million. Numbers increased in 2012 to 1.42 million before dropping to around 1.3 million in 2013. Cruise arrivals are also increasing, with growth through the expanded docks at the newly enlarged cruise-liner port on Grand Bahama. The islands also offer luxury Caribbean holidays and conference locations

The Bahamas Ministry of Tourism and Aviation (BMOTA) co-ordinates and regulates the industry. The successful 2010 'Free Companion Airfare' promotion encouraged more US citizens to either return to the Bahamas or visit for the first time. The reopening the Bimini Big Game Club resort for game-fishing, plus conference facilities and luxury resorts all added to a re-marketing of the Bahamas after the global economic crisis had cut visitor numbers dramatically.

The World Travel and Tourism Council estimated that tourism contributed 43.6 per cent to GDP in 2014, while attracting investment constituting 18.3 per cent of total investment. Direct employment in the industry was forecast to be around 51,000 jobs (27.0 per cent of total employment) and provide total indirect employment, including jobs indirectly supported by the industry, to 51.6 per cent of the workforce (98,000 jobs). Foreign revenue from tourism was expected to be US$2.3 billion.

In April 2012, the joint Spanish Baleária and US Capo Group established the first ferry service between Grand Bahama and Fort Lauderdale (US). The high-speed catamaran *Pinar del Rio* sails daily (Thursday–Tuesday) with a two and half hour journey time. The ferry accommodates 463 passengers, in either the VIP or economy lounges.

Mining

Mining contributes approximately 1 per cent to annual GDP and employs around 1 per cent of the labour force.

Crude salt is produced by solar evaporation in Great Inagua and Long Island and aragonite deposits are found near Bimini Island.

Hydrocarbons

There are no significant oil reserves; however, Bahamas is an important re-exporter of oil and transhipment earns the islands a significant amount of foreign exchange. The state-owned Bahamas Oil Refining Company (Borco) is the principal commercial entity in the petroleum market and has been involved in several joint ventures with larger international oil companies.

In 2005, the Bahamas, plus a number of other Caribbean states, signed an agreement with Venezuela to establish PetroCaribe, a multi-national oil company, owned by the participating states. PetroCaribe buys low-priced Venezuelan crude oil under long-term payment plans. However, due to the worsening state of its economy, in 2014 the Venezuelan government stated that the subsidies to the members of PetroCaribe might be reduced and in 2015 this was still under discussion.

In April 2014 two petroleum companies, Bahamas Petroleum and Atlantic Petroleum, applied for licences to explore for oil, however as of 2015 the exploration rights were still undecided. They would be joining Bahamas Petroleum Company Ltd (BPC), the only company which currently has exploratory licences, five in the south of the Bahamas, close to the border with Cuba. In June 2015, BPC renewed its licenses, allowing it to continue exploration into June 2018.

Energy

Total installed generating capacity was 493MW in 2013, producing over 1.9 billion kilowatt hours. Conventional thermal power stations produce the Bahamas' domestic energy.

Financial markets

Stock exchange

Bahamas International Securities Exchange (BISX)

Banking and insurance

Central bank

Central Bank of the Bahamas

Main financial centre

Nassau

Offshore facilities

The Bahamas is one of the largest offshore financial centres in the world. It was taken off the OECD's blacklist of countries that did not meet international requirements on taxation and transparency after it enacted new legislation which eliminated banking operations that did not have a physical presence in the Bahamas, and allowed for the exchange of tax information and the establishment of a comprehensive anti-money laundering regime. It resulted in the number of banks and trust companies licenced in the offshore sector declining.

Time

GMT minus five hours (daylight saving, April–October, minus four hours)

Geography

The Bahamas archipelago, which consists of 700 islands and nearly 2,500 small islets or cays sprawled across roughly 259,000 square km, stretches south-east from the southern coast of Florida (US). Virtually all the islands are surrounded by coral reefs and sandbanks, and nearly all are low lying.

Hemisphere

Northern.

Climate

The Bahamas is said to have one of the finest climates in the world. There are two seasons: winter (November–April), which is cool and dry, and summer (May–October), which is warm and wet. The climate is semi-tropical with temperatures ranging from 20 degrees Celsius (C) in winter to 30 degrees C in summer. Hurricanes can occur between June–November.

Dress codes

Business dress is more formal in the Bahamas than elsewhere in the Caribbean or in Florida; a business suit and tie is recommended for men and conservative business dress for women.

Visitors should bring lightweight or tropical clothing and, during the wet season, rainwear.

Entry requirements

Passports

Required by all, except nationals of the US and Canada with evidence of citizenship (all US and Canadian nationals require a passport for re-entry to their country). All passports must be valid for at least six months from the date of arrival and visitors must show proof of a return/onward ticket and sufficient funds to provide for maintenance during their stay.

Visa

Required, but nationals of various countries are exempt for periods ranging from two weeks to eight months. For details contact nearest consulate or embassy or consult www.bahamas.com.

From May 2009 EU citizens may make a short-stay visit, for up to three months, without a visa.

Currency advice/regulations

Permission is required from the Central Bank of the Bahamas to import local currency, which may be exported up to a maximum of B$70. The import and export of foreign currency is unlimited.

US dollars are accepted as legal tender. To avoid additional exchange rate charges, travellers are advised to take travellers cheques in US dollars.

Prohibited imports

Illegal drugs, firearms and other offensive weapons, animals.

Health (for visitors)

Medical facilities are on a par with the US, but can be costly and therefore medical insurance is recommended.

Mandatory precautions

A yellow fever vaccination certificate is required if arriving from an infected area.

Advisable precautions

Recommended immunisations are typhoid, diphtheria, hepatitis A and B, and tetanus. Malaria prophylaxis is recommended for Great Exuma. Tap water is safe to drink, although it can often be salty in taste. Food precautions should be observed.

Public holidays (national)

Fixed dates

1 Jan (New Year's Day), 10 Jul (Independence Day), 25 Dec (Christmas Day), 26 Dec (Boxing Day).

Holidays which fall on a Saturday or Sunday are observed on the following Monday.

Variable dates

Good Friday, Easter Monday, Whit Monday, Labour Day (first Mon in Jun), Emancipation Day (first Mon in Aug), National Heroes Day (second Mon in Oct).

Working hours

Banking

Mon–Thu: 0930–1500; Friday: 0930–1700.

Business

Mon–Fri: 0900–1700.

Government

Mon–Fri: 0900–1730.

Shops

Mon–Sat: 0900–1700. Sunday closing laws are generally strictly observed, except for some grocers open for a few hours, as well as the tourist shops on Bay Street in Nassau if cruise ships are docked.

Telecommunications

Mobile/cell phones

A GSM 1900 service is available.

Electricity supply

120V AC, 60 cycles

Social customs/useful tips

Bahamians shake hands upon meeting and business cards may be exchanged. Address first-time business acquaintances by their last names – conversations generally move to a first-name basis more slowly than in most Western countries. Appointments for business meetings should be made in advance.

Business lunches are often held. If invited to dinner at home, it is customary to take a small gift for the hostess and send a thank-you card afterwards.

Security

Visits to the Bahamas are generally trouble-free. Crime exists in the main cities of Nassau and Freeport, including incidents of murder and armed robbery. Much of this is within the local community, but tourists are often perceived as wealthy and have been the victims of robbery, particularly when alone or in isolated locations. Passports are a particular target for theft.

Visitors should take sensible precautions and be vigilant at all times. It is advisable not to carry large amounts of cash or jewellery.

The outlying Family Islands are relatively free of crime, but sensible precautions should still be taken.

Penalties for possession or trafficking of drugs are severe. Pack all luggage yourself and do not carry anything through customs for anyone else unless you are aware of the contents.

Getting there

Air

National airline: Bahamasair

International airport/s: Nassau International (NAS), 16km west of city, shop, restaurant, bank, post office, car hire; Grand Bahama International (FPO), 5km north of Freeport, shop, bar, restaurant, buffet, shops, car hire.

Other airport/s: Paradise Island (PID), 5km from Nassau; George Town (GGT), 6km from city.

Airport tax: Departure tax: US$18.

Surface

Water: All the major cruise lines operating out of Florida and liners from New York and Florida make calls in the Bahamas, either in Nassau or Freeport. In April 2012, the joint Spanish Baleária and US Capo Group established the first ferry service between Grand Bahama and Fort Lauderdale (US). The high-speed catamaran *Pinar del Rio* sails daily (Thursday–Tuesday) with a two and half hour journey time. The ferry accommodates 463 passengers, in either the VIP or economy lounges.

Main port/s: Freeport Container Port on Grand Bahama, Nassau on New Providence and Matthew Town on Inagua. There are modern berthing facilities for cruise ships at Potters Cay on New Providence, Governor's Harbour on Eleuthera, Morgan's Bluff on North Andros and George Town on Exuma.

Getting about

National transport

Air: An extensive air charter network covers the islands, serving over 50 landing sites. Local enquiries should be made for particular requirements.

Road: The main centres are well served by 1,535km of surfaced roads.

Buses: There are few conventional buses, which serve only in the main towns. Mini-buses (*jitneys*) operate in the Nassau and Freeport areas.

Rail: There is no passenger rail service.

Water: Ferry and mail-boat services are operated between the various islands in the archipelago, but for business travellers the length and frequency of journeys may prove a major drawback. Two catamarans operated by Bahamas Ferries run schedule journeys daily between the islands.

City transport

Taxis: Taxis are often metered and use a fixed-rate system, but the rate should be agreed before setting off. A 15 per cent tip is usual.

Car hire

A national or international licence valid for three months is required. Rates vary according to the season. Traffic drives on the left.

BUSINESS DIRECTORY

The addresses listed below are a selection only. While World of Information makes every endeavour to check these addresses, we cannot guarantee that changes have not been made, especially to telephone numbers and area codes. We would welcome any corrections.

Telephone area codes

The international direct dialling code (IDD) for Bahamas is +1 242, followed by subscriber's number

Chambers of Commerce

Bahamas Chamber of Commerce, Shirley Street and Collins Avenue, PO Box N-665, Nassau (tel: 322-2145; fax: 322-4649; e-mail: bahamaschamber@coralwave.com).

Grand Bahama Chamber of Commerce, The Mall and Pioneer Way, PO Box F-40808, Freeport (tel: 352-8329; e-mail: info@thegrandbahamachamberofcommerce.com).

Banking

Bahamas Development Bank, West Bay Street, PO Box N-3034, Nassau (tel: 327-5780; fax: 322-6457).

Bank of the Bahamas Ltd, PO Box N-7118, Nassau (tel: 326-2560).

Bank of Nova Scotia, PO Box N-7518, Nassau (tel: 356-1400).

Banque Privée Edmond de Rothschild Ltd, 51 Frederick Street, PO Box N-1136, Nassau (tel: 328-8121; fax: 328-8115).

Barclays Bank, PO Box N-8350, Nassau (tel: 322-4921).

British-American Bank, PO Box N-7502, Nassau (tel: 327-5170).

Canadian Imperial Bank of Commerce (CIBC), PO Box N-7125, Nassau (tel: 322-8455).

Citibank, PO Box N-8158, Nassau (tel: 322-4240).

Commonwealth Bank, PO Box SS-6263, Nassau (tel: 328-1854).

Finance Corporation of Bahamas Ltd, PO Box N-3038, Nassau (tel: 322-4822).

Handelsfinanz-CCF Bank International ltd, Maritime House, Frederick Street, PO Box N-10441, Nassau (tel: 328-8644, 328-1737; fax: 328-8600).

Inter-American Development Bank, PO Box N-3743, Nassau (tel: 393-7159).

Lloyds Bank International (Americas), PO Box N-1262, Bolam House, King and George Streets, Nassau (tel: 322-8711; fax: 322-8719).

Royal Bank of Canada, PO Box N-7537, Nassau (tel: 322-8700).

Central bank

Central Bank of the Bahamas, Frederick Street, PO Box N-4868, Nassau (tel: 322-2193; fax: 356-4307; e-mail: queries@centralbankbahamas.com).

Stock exchange

Bahamas International Securities Exchange (BISX), www.bisxbahamas.com

Travel information

Bahamasair, Windsor Field, PO Box N-4881, Nassau (tel: 327-8451; fax: 327-7409).

Bahamas Ferries, Potters Cay West, Nassau (tel: 323-2166, 394-9700; fax: 393-7451; internet: www.bahamasferries.com).

Bahamas Hotel Association, Dele West Bay Street, sub Dean's Lane, PO Box N-7799, Nassau (tel: 322-8381; fax: 326-5346).

Nassau/Cable Beach/Paradise Island Promotion Board, Dean's Lane, Fort Charlotte, PO Box N-7799, Nassau (tel: 322-8381; fax: 326-5346).

Ministry of tourism

Ministry of Tourism, PO Box N-3701, Nassau (tel: 302–2000; fax: 302–2098; e-mail: tourism@bahamas.com).

Ministries

Ministry of Agriculture and Industry, Levy Building, East Bay Street, Nassau (tel: 325-7502; fax: 322-1767).

Ministry of Economic Development, Manx Building, West Bay Street, Nassau.

Ministry of Education, Youth and Sports, Shirley Street, Nassau (tel: 322-5495; fax: 322-3267).

Ministry of Financial Services and Investment, Sir Cecil V Wallace Whitfield Centre, Cable Beach, PO Bx N-10980, Nassau (tel: 327-5826; fax: 327-5006).

Ministry of Foreign Affairs, Post Office Building, East Hill Street, Nassau (tel: 322-7624; fax: 328-8212).

Ministry of Health, Ministry of Health Building, Royal Victoria Gardens, Nassau (tel: 322-7425; fax: 322-7788).

Ministry of Housing and Social Development, Frederick House, Frederick Street, Nassau (tel: 356-0765; fax: 323-3883).

Ministry of Justice, Post Office Building, East Hill Street, Nassau.

Ministry of Labour and Immigration, Post Office Building, East Hill Street, Nassau (tel: 323-7240; fax: 326-7344).

Ministry of Public Works, John F Kennedy Drive, Nassau (tel: 323-7814; fax: 325-2016).

Ministry of Tourism, PO Box N-3701, Bolam House, George Street, Nassau (tel: 302–2000; fax: 302–2098; e-mail: tourism@bahamas.com).

Ministry of Transport, Aviation and Local Government, Pilot House Complex, Nassau (tel: 394-0451; fax: 394-5023).

Office of the Deputy Prime Minister, Churchill Building, Bay Street, Nassau (tel: 356-6792; fax: 356-6087).

Office of the Prime Minister, Cecil V Wallace Whitfield Centre, West Bay Street, Nassau (tel: 322-2805; fax: 328-8294).

Other useful addresses

Bahamas Agricultural and Industrial Corporation, PO Box N-4940, Levy Building, East Bay Street, Nassau (tel: 322-3740; fax: 322-2133).

Bahamas Economic Development Corporation, Bahamas Development Bank, Adderley Building, Bay Street/Rawson Square, PO Box N-3034, Nassau (tel: 327-5780; fax: 327-5907).

Bahamas Electricity Corporation, Big Pond and Tucker Road, PO Box N-7509, Nassau (tel: 328-7700).

Bahamas Employers' Confederation, PO Box N-166, Nassau (tel: 328-1757, 326-6644; fax: 328-1346).

Bahamas Financial Services Board, PO Box N–1764, West Bay Street, Goodman's Bay Corporate Centre, Nassau (tel: 326-7001; fax: 326–7007; e-mail: info@bfsb-bahamas.com).

Bahamas Information Services, Nassau Court, PO Box N-8172 (tel: 325-6028).

Bahamas Investment Authority, Cecil Wallace Whitfield Centre, PO Box CB-10980, Nassau (tel: 327-5970/4; fax: 327-5907; e-mail: investbahama@batelnet.bs; internet site: http://www.opm.gov.bs).

Bahamas Telecommunications Corporation, J F Kennedy Drive, PO Box N-3048, Nassau (tel: 323-4911).

Bahamas Water and Sewerage Corporation, J F Kennedy Drive, PO Box N-3905, Nassau (tel: 323-3944).

Broadcasting Corporation of The Bahamas, PO Box N-1347, Nassau (tel: 32-4623, 322-4480).

Cabinet Office, Churchill Bldg, Rawson Square, PO Box N-7147, Nassau (tel: 322-2805; fax: 328-8294).

The Comptroller of Customs, Seaban Building, Oake Field, PO Box N-155, Nassau (tel: 326-4401).

Gaming Board of the Bahamas, West Bay Street, PO Box N-4565, Nassau (tel: 327-7478).

Hotel Corporation of the Bahamas, PO Box N-9520, Nassau (tel: 327-8395; fax: 327-6978).

Port Department, East Hill Street, PO Box N-8173 Nassau (tel: 326-7354).

Securities Commission of the Bahamas, PO Box N-8347, Nassau (tel: 356-6271/2; fax: 356-7530; e-mail: secbd@batelnet.bs).

Caribbean Net News: www.caribbeannetnewss.com

Internet sites

Bahamas International Securities Exchange: www.bisxbahamas.com

Ministry of Tourism: www.bahamas.com

The Bahamas Guide: www.thebahamasguide.com

Bahrain

KEY FACTS

Official name: Al Mamlakah al Bahrayn (Kingdom of Bahrain)

Head of State: King Hamad bin Isa al Khalifa (ruler since Mar 1999; King since 14 Feb 2002)

Head of government: Prime Minister Sheikh Khalifa bin Salman al Khalifa (from 1971; re-appointed Oct 2010)

Ruling party: There is no ruling party

Area: 676 square km (35 islands)

Population: 1.20 million (2014)* (1,234,571; 2010 census figure)

Capital: Manama

Official language: Arabic

Currency: Bahraini dinar (BD) = 1,000 fils

Exchange rate: BD0.38 per US$ (fixed) (Jul 2014)

GDP per capita: US$28,272 (2014)*

GDP real growth: 4.75% (2014)

GDP: US$33.86 billion (2014)

Unemployment: 4.06% (2014)*

Inflation: 2.50% (2014)

Natural gas production: 16.90 billion cum (2014)

Balance of trade: US$7.27 billion (2013)*

* estimated figure

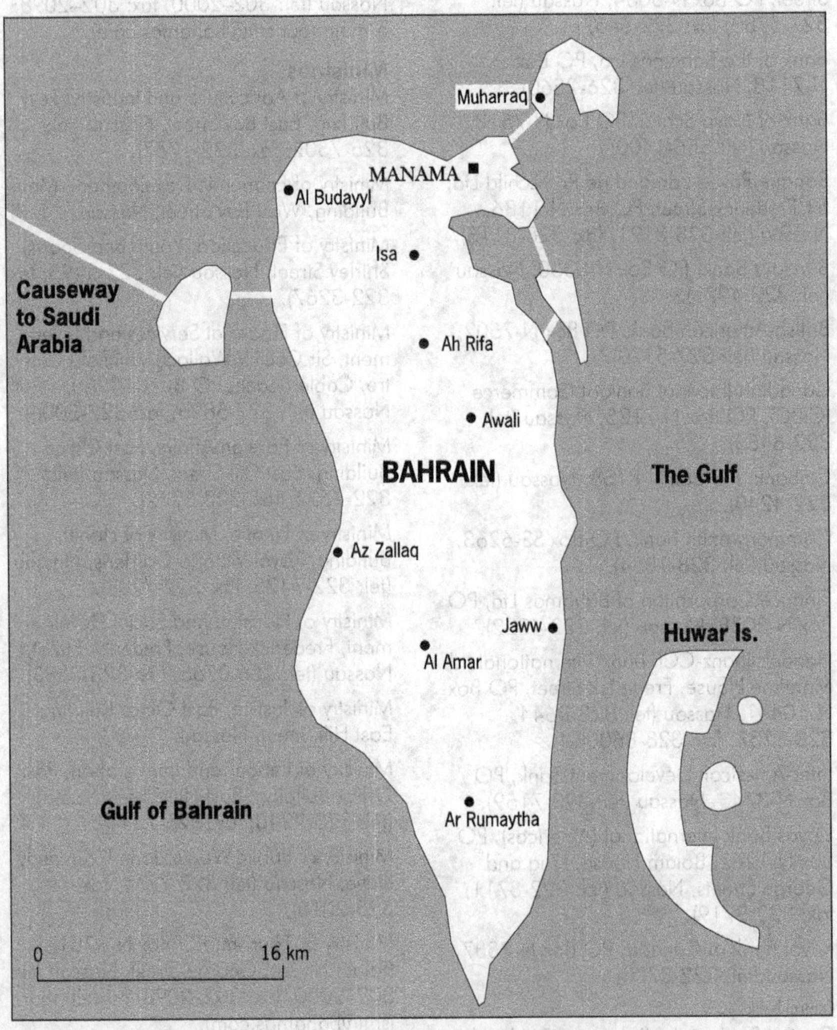

Bahrain's November 2014 elections saw a turnout of 52.6 per cent of the electorate, a figure reportedly welcomed by the authorities as 'satisfactory'. Many Bahrainis chose not to vote in what they saw as a less than democratic exercise. This was the first legislative election since the uprisings – initially considered to be related to the Arab Spring – of early 2011. The main issue surrounding the elections was the stance of the principle opposition (Shi'a) al Wefaq grouping whose 18 parliamentarians had resigned from the 40-seat lower house in the early days of the uprising in protest at the Bahraini goverment's heavy-handed response to the street protests.

What, no opposition?

Their demands ignored, the al Wefaq deputies chose to continue their boycott. This was in the face of intense government and even international pressure. Al Wefaq were not the only abstainees – three smaller opposition groupings joined them. The opposition's absence called into question the legitimacy of the election, explaining the government's relief at the turnout, although the official figure was itself challenged. The controversy inevitably meant that the actual results seemed of secondary importance.

Given the dilution of the assembly's political importance it came as no surprise that no more than four candidates from the political groupings were actually elected, the other 36 were so called independents thought to be aligned to the government. Bahrain's Sunni parties, including the al Manbar al Islami and al Asalah groupings, which represent Islamists affiliated with the Muslim Brotherhood and Salafism. Not one of the 10 al Fatih Coalition (Sunni) candidates fielded by the so-called 'Al-Fatih Coalition' obtained a seat despite their apparent pro-government popularity during and following the anti-government street protests. The apparent collapse of support for these often populist pro-government groupings came as something of a surprise.

The constitutional basis of the elections dates back to the 2002 Constitution which established a two-chamber parliament – the upper chamber appointed – effectively by the King – and an elected lower chamber. Despite this apparently democratic system, it is the King, not parliament, who appoints the prime minister. Legislation needs to be approved by both houses, giving the King a blocking right on any new legislation. The King may at any time declare marshal law.

By appointment...

According to the *Bahrain Watch* (BW) website, the directorate of Election and Referendum is responsible for conducting Bahrain's elections. It is headed by the minister of justice, who is also appointed by the King. In the November 2014 elections, requests by the Bahrain Transparency Society (BTS) to allow international monitors were rejected, although domestic monitors were permitted. BW noted that the absence of robust observation of the electoral process compounded concerns about the official results.

Also according to BW, the government had proposed to condition eligibility for government jobs and services on electoral participation and issued a statement that was interpreted as a threat to remove the right to vote for anyone who had failed to vote in this election. Those who did vote in the elections were entered into a raffle, where they could win one of twenty i-phones. According to the Bahrain centre for Human Rights, the government repressed protests and arrested over 60 people in the run-up to the elections.

Criticism?

According to Human Rights Watch (HRW), the government of Bahrain remains hyper- sensitive to any form of criticism. In early 2015 Bahrainis were given a further reminder that the Bahrain government brooked no criticism. In a statement, the Bahraini ministry of the interior cautioned against criticism of the government's decision to send eight fighter jets to take part in air-strikes in Yemen as part of the Saudi-led, US-backed coalition against Houthi forces. It warned against 'any attempt to exploit the situation through division or sedition, or issuance of statements against the approach Bahrain has taken.' The ministry 'would take appropriate steps against individuals that put the safety and security of the country at risk,' it added. This tough talk came after Bahrain's al Wahdawi political society had condemned the Gulf coalition's air strikes as a 'flagrant aggression that violated international law. Bahrain's police promptly arrested the society's secretary; Fadhel Abbas and another unnamed individual were blamed for 'exploiting the situation in Yemen to disrupt the peace and endanger security and civil order', according to the interior ministry. The justice ministry also announced that it would file a lawsuit demanding the dissolution of al Wahdawi.

The action against al Wahdawi was, according to HRW, merely the latest example of Bahrain's intolerance of speech critical of the government. During 2014 and early 2015, human rights activists and members of the political opposition have been arrested and prosecuted, often for peaceful criticism of the authorities, and the government invested itself with further powers to arbitrarily strip critics of their citizenship and the rights that attach to it.

The economy

According to the International Monetary Fund (IMF), in its May 2014 assessment of the Bahraini economy, Bahrain's gross domestic product (GDP) grew by 5.3 per cent in 2013, supported by a rebound in the hydrocarbons sector, while non-oil activity slowed to 3 per cent, largely reflecting weak investment sentiment and the delay in the 2013–14 budget approval. Within non-oil activity, transport and tourism continued to expand, reflecting buoyant activity in the service sector, particularly hotels and restaurants and social and personal services. Unemployment remained low, at 4.2 per cent at end-February 2014. Inflation picked up in late 2013 (4 per cent year on year at the end of 2013) reflecting price increases in housing, but had fallen in March to 2.3 per cent year on year. Private sector credit growth remained moderate at about 6.6 per cent at end-2013 (6.2 per cent in 2012), while deposits grew by 9 per cent for the same period (4.6 per cent in 2012).

The IMF noted that Bahrain's fiscal deficit continued on a rising trend in 2013, although by less than had been budgeted. The improved fiscal result was largely related to under-spending on the capital budget. The overall deficit (including extra-budgetary operations) was estimated at 4.3 per cent of GDP, up from 3.2 per cent of GDP in 2012 – the fiscal

KEY INDICATORS — **Bahrain**

	Unit	2011	2012	2013	2014	**2015
Population	m	*1.13	1.15	1.17	*1.20	*1.22
Gross domestic product (GDP)	US$bn	26.10	30.36	32.78	33.86	*31.32
GDP per capita	US$	23,132	26,368	27,917	*28,272	0
GDP real growth	%	1.8	3.4	5.3	4.7	*2.7
Inflation	%	1.0	2.8	3.3	2.5	*2.1
Unemployment	%	4.0	3.9	4.3	*4.1	*4.3
Natural gas output	bn cum	13.0	14.2	15.8	16.9	–
Exports (fob) (goods)	US$m	19,650.3	19,768.1	20,926.6	–	–
Imports (fob) (goods)	US$m	12,105.9	13,239.4	13,656.4	–	–
Balance of trade	US$m	7,544.4	6,528.7	7,270.2	–	–
Current account	US$m	3,247.3	2,221.0	2,560.0	1,801.0	*-646.0
Total reserves minus gold	US$m	–	5,205.0	5,347.0	6,048.5	–
Foreign exchange	US$m	–	4,898.0	5,037.8	–	–
Exchange rate	per US$	2.66	2.66	0.38	0.38	–

* estimated figure ** forecast figure

breakeven oil price increased to US$125 per barrel in 2013 from US$119 per barrel in 2012 (NB Although by the end of 2014 the price per barrel had fallen to between US$50 and US$60 per barrel). Government debt increased by eight percentage points of GDP in 2013, to 44 per cent of GDP. While the government had increased its reliance on external financing, government external debt as a share of GDP remained low, at 20 per cent of GDP. The current account remained strong with an estimated surplus of 7.8 per cent of GDP in 2013. Official reserves coverage fell marginally from about 10 months of imports in 2012 to nine in 2013.

According to the IMF, Bahrain's banking sector was in good health and the performance of the 'challenged' Islamic retail banks had improved marginally. The capitalisation of the banking system was high on average and the non-performing loans (NPLs) to gross loans ratio had continued on a downward trajectory. The Islamic retail banking segment had been tackling high NPLs due to concentrated exposures to local and regional real estate; while capital buffers for this sector declined slightly in 2013, the capital adequacy ratio remained high. After several years of posting losses, the sector's profitability has moved into positive territory, with the Islamic banking segment undergoing some consolidation in 201.

The IMF considered that Bahrain's economic outlook was characterised by moderate growth and higher public debt, with average annual inflation estimated to be subdued in 2014 and over the medium term. The most immediate policy challenges were to correct the fiscal imbalances and stabilise government debt, while balancing growth and debt sustainability considerations. Over the longer term, the challenge is to reduce fiscal dependence on oil revenues and resume robust economic growth.

Derailed?

The 2030 Economic Vision, launched by His Majesty King Hamad Bin Isa Al Khalifa in the inauspicious month of October 2008, embodied a comprehensive vision for the Kingdom of Bahrain that aimed at 'creating a clear approach to develop the kingdom's economy while focusing on the main objective which was to improve the standard of living of all Bahraini citizens.' The 'vision' had been launched after four years of discussions with a group of decision makers in the public and private sectors, including government institutions and related entities in addition to a number of think tanks and international institutions. The 2030 economic vision rather optimistically focuses on crystallising an integrated socio-economic government vision and focuses on three basic principles which are competitiveness, integrity and sustainability. The events of 2011 have clouded the government's vision somewhat.

After the launch of the vision, the Kingdom of Bahrain had begun an institutional economic reform programme that at the time was in line with the objective of the 2030 economic vision. This led to the preparation of a national economic strategy that represented a roadmap to achieve the vision. *Force majeure* after the events of 2011, the strategy has needed continuous revision to adapt to the international changes and the government's work programme.

Energy

As one of the smaller oil exporters Bahrain, alongside Oman, looked likely to face rapidly rising debt levels and negative credit ratings following the 2014 slump in oil prices. The Kingdom is, also in the company of Oman, one of only two countries bordering the Arabian Gulf that is not a member of the Organisation of the Petroleum Exporting Countries (Opec). The Bahrain Petroleum Company (BAPCO) and Bahrain National Gas Company (BANAGAS) dominate Bahrain's hydrocarbon industry.

According to the US government Energy Information Administration (EIA), Bahrain produced 48,000 barrels per day (bpd) of crude oil and lease condensate in 2013, the smallest amount of any country in the Arabian Gulf. Total petroleum production capacity at the Bahrain Field was expected to rise to 100,000bpd by 2018.

Saudi Arabia and Bahrain share production of the 300,000bpd Abu Safah offshore field in Saudi Arabia, which is connected to Bahrain's Sitra refinery via pipeline. Bahrain intends to replace the ageing pipeline system from Saudi Arabia with a new 71-mile pipeline by 2016. The planned pipeline will transport 350,000bpd of crude oil from Saudi Arabia's Abqaiq plant to Bahrain's Sitra refinery. Bahrain's refinery capacity far exceeds domestic crude oil production capacity. Bahrain has a 267,000bpd-export refinery at Sitra and plans are underway to expand the refinery's capacity to 360,000bpd by 2017.

As with oil, Bahrain is a small producer of natural gas. According to the BP Statistical Review 2015, Bahrain produced 6.4 trillion cubic feet (tcf) of natural gas in 2014. In order to meet growing natural gas needs, Bahrain plans to increase its imports of natural gas. The government plans to complete construction of a 400 million cubic feet per day (MMcf/d) LNG import facility in the beginning of 2017. Potential pipeline projects involving Iran and Qatar have been put on hold.

Bahrain had about 4 gigawatts of electricity generating capacity in 2012, almost all of which was fossil fuel fired. A 5 megawatt solar project came online at the start of 2014 and a 25 megawatt waste to energy plant is scheduled to come online by 2015. Bahrain is also taking part in the Gulf Co-operation Council's (GCC) plan to integrate the electric power grids of all GCC countries.

Jaw, but no Law

A March 2015 riot at Bahrain's notorious Jaw Prison ended up with a fierce response from the authorities and allegations of police torture. Reportedly, prisoners were subjected to tear gas, beaten up and left in a courtyard, where they were stripped to their underwear for a few hours and were left in the courtyard for three days until tents were put up. As reported by the *International Business Times* journalist Gianluca Mezzofiore, inmates were summoned one by one and apparently tortured. The reports of alleged torture and human rights violations came just after Amnesty International published a report accusing the Bahrain government of human rights abuses – with documented episodes of torture and mistreatment of detainees, continued jailing of activists and bans on protests in the capital.

The jail disturbances had started due to poor conditions and overcrowding in the prison. One of the prison buildings alone had a capacity of 456 but reportedly contained over 1,000 prisoners. A government newspaper reported that the unrest was the result of violence by prisoners after a confrontation between prison guards and three visitors. Local human rights groups claimed that the security forces had used excessive force against prisoners. The reaction of the Bahraini government was to call in riot police, mostly formed by Pakistani and Jordanian guards, who surrounded the main buildings of the prison and then broke inside. Sayed Ahmed Alwadaei, the director of Advocacy at the Bahrain Institute for Rights and Democracy told Mr Mezzofiore, saying that: 'they used tear gas and gunshots. One guy was shot at a very close range. Everyone was beaten and asked to stand down.' Bahrain's police media centre at the ministry of interior denied the torture allegations. The testimonies of the alleged violations were submitted to the UN for breaches of international human rights.

Amnesty report

After the crackdown on the Bahrain pro-democracy uprising in 2011, led by Saudi forces, Bahrain has plunged deeper into sectarian conflict between the wealthy ruling Sunni al Khalifa minority and the Shi'a majority. King Sheikh Hamad bin Isa Al Khalifa had pledged to implement the recommendations of an independent commission of inquiry but the reforms were progressing slowly and reconciliation talks had stalled.

There have for some years been allegations of torture and abuse in the Jaw prison. Well over its 1,200 prisoner capacity, it houses upwards of 2,000 prisoners by Bahrain Centre for Human Rights' estimates, many of them protesters and activists imprisoned for doing no more than exercising their free assembly, expression and association rights. One prisoner had been in solitary confinement since his detention in 2012. Tortured and abused, Mr al Taweel was on death row for a policeman's murder, for which he was coerced into confessing. Barred from contact with the outside world, in early 2015 he had handed his lawyer a suicide note.

Rather than hold its errant torturers to account, Bahrain was covering up its abuses. Rather than improve the situation, the government had allowed its deterioration, which by 2015 was if anything worse than during martial law in 2011. No one has been held accountable and there is no sign that anyone will be. The introduction of an 'Ombudsman' and a 'National Institute for Human Rights' were modest 'reforms' which the Bahrainis claimed as a success story.

Risk assessment

Economy	Fair
Politics	Poor
Regional stability	Fair

Muslims in Bahrain

% of population	81.2
Sunni (% of Muslims)	30
Shi'a (% of Muslims)	70

COUNTRY PROFILE

1816 Bahrain's first treaty with Britain was signed

1861 The second treaty made it a British protectorate.

1869 Sheikh Isa bin Ali al Khalifa was named ruler.

1913 A treaty between Britain and Turkey recognised Bahrain as an independent state, but the country remained under British administration.

1923 After more than half a century of peace and stability, Sheikh Isa bin Ali al Khalifa abdicated in favour of his son, Sheikh Hamad.

1928 Iran claimed ownership of Bahrain; the dispute was not resolved until 1970 when Iran accepted a UN report stating that the vast majority of Bahrainis wanted their complete independence.

1932 Bahrain became the first country in the Gulf to strike oil.

1942–61 Sheikh Hamad died in 1942 and his son, Sheikh Sulman bin Hamad al Khalifa ruled Bahrain until his death in 1961, when he was succeeded by Sheikh Isa bin Sulman al Khalifa.

1968 Britain announced its intention to withdraw from the Gulf by 1971.

1971 Bahrain and Qatar became independent states. Sheikh Khalifa bin Salman al Khalifa became prime minister.

1973–74 Bahrain's constitution was promulgated; it limited the Sheikh's powers and established an elected 30-member National Assembly.

1975 The National Assembly refused to ratify a bill to arrest and detain people for up to three years without trial, and was dissolved by the ruler, Sheikh Isa. The government subsequently ruled by decree.

1981 The political and economic union, Co-operation Council for the Arab States of the Gulf (CCASG) (known as Gulf Co-operation Council (GCC)) was formed by Bahrain, Kuwait, Oman, Qatar, Saudi Arabia and the United Arab Emirates (UAE).

1986 The opening of the 25km King Fahd Causeway between Bahrain and Saudi Arabia gave a boost to business and tourism.

1991 Bahrain actively supported the allied forces against Iraq in the Gulf military conflict.

1994 The majority Shi'ites staged demonstrations demanding better living conditions and the return of an elected parliament. The Sunnis, although once the majority but now in a minority, are dominant in both politics and business.

1999 Sheikh Isa bin Sulman al Khalifa, who had ruled since 1961, died and was succeeded by his son, Sheikh Hamad bin Isa al Khalifa. Sheikh Khalifa bin Salman al Khalifa continued as prime minister.

2000 For the first time, non-Muslims and women were appointed to the 40 member Majlis al-Shura (Consultative Council).

2001 A referendum on political reform was approved, under which Bahrain would become a constitutional monarchy with an elected lower chamber of parliament and an independent judiciary.

2002 Hamad bin Isa al Khalifa was declared King, and the state became a constitutional monarchy. As part of the reform process, legislation was approved to allow women to vote in elections and run for national office. In legislative elections (the first since 1973), parliament became a mix of secular and Islamic candidates. The Shi'ite opposition boycotted the election resulting in a Sunni dominated parliament.

2004 The first woman to be appointed head of a government ministry, Nada Haffadh, was made health minister. A free trade agreement was signed with the US.

2005 King Hamad called for increased global co-operation to combat international terrorism. Thousands protested in favour of a fully elected parliament.

2006 Legislative elections were held in which Sunni representatives won 22 seats (out of 40) and Shi'ites won 18.

2007 There were several days of rioting in majority Shi'a areas with protesters demanding compensation for human rights violations between 1980–90.

2008 A common market was created between Bahrain, Kuwait, Oman, Qatar, Saudi Arabia and the UAE, the six wealthiest Gulf States. Citizens of these countries are allowed to travel between and live in any of the six states, where they may find employment, buy properties and businesses and use the educational and health facilities freely.

2009 Iraqi Airways began flights to Bahrain, after a gap of 20 years. The Nation Bank of Kuwait – Kingdom of Bahrain (NBK Bahrain), posted record profits of US$88.9 million for the first two quarters of the year (an increase of 55 per cent over the same period in 2008).

2010 The authorities suspended the news network Al Jazeera's operations in Bahrain and barred its workers, following the broadcast of documentaries on the treatment of Asian labourers and poverty in Bahrain. In parliamentary elections, the Shia Al Wifaq National Islamic Society (Al Wifaq) won 18 seats (out of 40), the combined Sunni block won 22 seats, including 17 independent delegates.

2011 In March, protesters marched on the council of ministers – the authorities asked Saudi Arabia to supply 1,500 troops to help their own forces restore order. A day later, security forces used tanks to oust protestors from Pearl Square, ending its two-week occupation. Ambulances were blocked from entering the square to provide aid. Later security militia carried out a sweep of hospitals, arresting any trauma patients being treated. The UN criticised Bahraini officials for commandeering all hospitals and the arrest by various security forces of protestors receiving medical treatment. In April, the Turkish foreign minister, Ahmet Davutoglu, held talks with both the opposition group al Wifaq and King Hamad. In May, Moody's downgraded Bahrain's sovereign credit rating to 'negative'. In June, the King decreed that the state of emergency that had been imposed in March was to be lifted. Legal trials began before the Court of National Safety of 47 medical personnel arrested for treating demonstrators during the civil unrest; 20 were charged with possessing unlicensed weapons, inciting others to overthrow the monarchy, unauthorised occupation of the hospital and stealing medical equipment; 28 others were accused of spreading false news and lying about the medical condition of some patients (one accused was tried *in absentia*). In July, in a BBC interview, a doctor claimed that he had been subject to torture and coerced into making a false confession while under arrest; the families of other doctors made similar claims. National reconciliation talks began between the Sunni-led government and Shi'a opposition, al Wifaq, in which the King said that all the dialogue process would be inclusive. However, later al Wifaq withdrew from the talks, saying the national dialogue 'was not serious' and that they had been allocated too few seats. In September 20 medical staff from the Salmaniya Medical Complex, who had treated injured persons during the February and March demonstrations, were found guilty by the National Safety Court. The security court gave long jail sentences to some 80 protesters. Elections to replace 18 Al Wifaq (Shi'ite) members of parliament, who had resigned in February, were held on 24 September. The opposition boycotted the elections and voter turnout was very low with fewer than one in five voters casting ballots; four candidates were re-elected due to the lack of any opposition candidate. There were skirmishes between the security forces and opposition youths attempting to reach Pearl roundabout. In October, after international condemnation on the harshness of the sentences by international medical associations and human rights campaigners, the attorney general announced that after studying the court's judgement the 20 medical staff would be retried by the country's highest civilian court. In November, the government acknowledged that 'excessive force' had been used on pro-democracy demonstrators by security forces and 20 members of these forces were charged with abuse. An official inquiry established that there had been 'instances of excessive force and mistreatment of detainees'.

2012 A demonstration called for 14 February, the first anniversary of pro-democracy protests at the now demolished Pearl Roundabout in Manama, was thwarted by a heavy security presence. Police fired tear gas and rubber bullets at rock-throwing youths. Up to 70 people were arrested, including foreign activists. In April the government endorsed a decision to retry 21 activists, convicted by a military court in June 2011, of plotting against the state. On 14 June, an appeals court convicted nine medics that took part in the 2011 pro-democracy protests for up to five years in prison; nine other medics were acquitted. The most serious charges against all the medics were dropped from all charges. The government established Bahrain Independent Commission of Inquiry (BICI) found that the medics had been tortured while in custody. On 1 October, the sentences of nine convicted medics were upheld by the Court of Cassation (the highest appeal court). A new visa system (similar to the European Schengen agreement) allowing multiply entry for foreigners to the six Gulf Co-operation Council (GCC) countries was introduced in November.

2013 The 2013 Bahrain Grand Prix took place on 21 April after being cancelled in 2011 due to the political unrest. On 24 June parliament finally approved the 2013/14 budget. It had been delayed by several months over demands for extra spending to raise public sector salaries by 15 per cent. The measure had been opposed by the cabinet and in the end parliament passed the plan without the pay rise, but with rises in pension payments for both public and private sector retirees, and higher subsidies for food and other items. The 23rd session of the Joint Council and Ministerial Meeting of the CC and the EU was held in Manama on 30 June. Some 50 Shi'a Muslims were sentanced on 30 September for up to 15 years for forming a clandestine movement, the 14 February Coalition.

2014 Three policeman were killed in a bombing in March 2014. It occurred on the third anniversary of the start of the uprising that has seen people take to the streets to demand more democracy and an end to what they perceive as discrimination against the Shia community by the Sunni royal family.

2015 The worst attack since March 2014 occurred in July 2015 when a bombing took place outside a girls' school in the predominantly Shi'a village of Sitra. It killed two policemen and wounded six other people. Iran has since been accused of causing the continued unrest because it has deliberately stirred up tension between the Sunni population of Bahrain and the majority Shi'a population in Iran. Bahrain has recalled its ambassador from Tehran.

Political structure

Constitution

The 1973 constitution was suspended in 1975 and reinstated by royal decree, with significant amendments, in February 2002.

By a charter, agreed by referendum, Bahrain was declared a constitutional monarchy in 2002, with a bicameral parliament and independent judiciary. Women were given suffrage and although political parties remained illegal, eleven new political societies were licensed in 2001.

The King is the symbol of the country and is inviolate.

Independence date

15 August 1971

Form of state

Constitutional monarchy

The executive

Executive power rests with the King, who is Head of State, he appoints a prime minister and members of the Consultative Council, which is an advisory body that, since 2002, is empowered to make laws. The King may dissolve or extend the term of the Consultative Council. The King has the right to initiate, ratify and promulgate laws.

The King is the head of the armed forces and head of the Judiciary.

National legislature

A bicameral National Assembly consists of the Majlis an Nuwab (Chamber of Deputies (sometimes translated as 'Representatives')) (lower house) which has 40 popularly elected members and the Majlis al-Shura (Consultative Council) with 40 members appointed by the King. Membership of both houses is four years. The King may renew membership of the Council and dissolve the Chamber of Deputies by decree. Terms of both houses may be extended by the King for up to two extra years.

The King and prime minister present bills to the Chamber of Deputies for consideration before they are passed to the Consultative Council.

Legal system

The judiciary is a constitutionally independent body, whose function and organisation is regulated by law. It is a mixture, based on English common law and Sunni and Shi'a Sharia (Islamic law) traditions, where Sharia is the principal source of law.

The Supreme court is the final court of appeal for all civil, commercial and criminal matters.

Last elections

22 and 29 November 2014 (parliamentary) (first and second rounds of voting)

Results: Parliament (lower house, after two rounds): Indepedents won 37 seats (out of 40), Al Asalah 2 seats, Al-Menbar Islamic Society 1 seat. Government claims turnout was 52.5 per cent, opposition claims 30 per cent.

Next elections

2018 (parliamentary)

Political parties

Political parties in Bahrain are formally banned; MPs are members of political 'societies' of which the National Democratic Action Society (Wa'ad) represents an informal opposition.

Ruling party

There is no ruling party

Bahrain is the smallest country in the Gulf region and the only island state and has the smallest population in the region.

Population

1.15 million (2012)* (1,234,571; 2010 census figure)

Last census: 27 April 2010: 1,234,571

Population density: 966 inhabitants per square km, one of the highest in the world. Urban population 89 per cent (2010 Unicef).

Annual growth rate: 4.7 per cent, 1990–2010 (Unicef).

Ethnic make-up

Bahrain's inhabitants are mostly Arab, with a sizeable minority of Iranian descent.

Approximately 38 per cent of the population are foreign residents, mostly from South Asia and other Arab countries,

Religions

According to the constitution, Islam is the state religion. Approximately 98 per cent of the indigenous population are Muslim – two-thirds Shi'as and the remainder belonging to the Sunni branch of Islam. There is no exact figure for the number of each; the Sunnis were in the majority up until the mid-1950s but are now in a minority, although remaining in power. The government have attempted to adjust the difference by a programme of naturalising Arab and non-Arab Sunnis for work in the police and military. The remaining 2 per cent are Jewish and Christian.

About half of the foreign population are non-Muslim, including Christians, Jews, Hindus, Baha'is, Buddhists and Sikhs.

Education

Primary schooling lasts for six years between the ages of six and 12. Secondary education lasts for three years and offers students a choice of three main branches: the general, the technical or the commercial.

The government is seeking to establish Bahrain as a regional centre for human resource development. In addition to several universities, there are a number of training centres, such as the Bahrain Training Institute (BTI) and the Bahrain Institute of Training and Finance (BITF) that are designed to prepare local graduates for the modern, technology driven workforce.

There are both government-owned and private schools.

Literacy rate: 91 per cent and 82.6 per cent for males and females respectively (World Bank).

Compulsory years: 6 to 15

Enrolment rate: 105 per cent boys, 106 per cent girls total primary school enrolment of the relevant age group (including repetition rates) (World Bank).

Health

Health services in Bahrain are of a high quality and all Bahrainis receive free health care from the state. There are a mixture of government and private hospitals, with additional government health centres and maternity hospitals.

Life expectancy: 75 years, 2010 (Unicef 2012)

Fertility rate/Maternal mortality rate: 2.5 births per woman, 2010 (Unicef 2012)

Child (under 5 years) mortality rate (per 1,000): 10 per 1,000 live births (WHO 2012)

Welfare

The government provides direct financial assistance to those considered needy in addition to assistance provided by religious organisations and local charitable societies. There are seven social centres operated by the ministry of labour and social affairs (MoLSA) that provide training and assistance, especially to needy women. Public and private facilities for the elderly, handicapped and orphaned provide first class care, using the latest professional methods, approaches, and equipment. The number of needy families on government assistance lists has been growing for the past decade at double the rate of the population growth.

Family support

The social assistance programme provides approximately BD30 (US$80) per month to every family being assisted.

Main cities

Manama (capital) (estimated population 297,509 in 2012), Muharraq (176,583), Madinat Hammad (133,550), Ah Rifa (115,495), A'al (100,553), Jid Hafs (66,588), Isa (61,293).

Languages spoken

English is widely spoken. Persian (Farsi), Hindi and Urdu are also frequently used.

Official language/s

Arabic

Media

While press laws guarantee the independence of journalists, criminal penalties may be imposed for infringements, such as insulting the King; self-censorship is widespread.

Bahrain is striving to achieve a status as the primary media centre for the Middle East in competition with Dubai in United Arab Emirates.

Press

Dailies: In Arabic, *Akhbar al Khaleej* (www.akhbar-alkhaleej.com), *al Wasat* (www.alwasatnews.com), *al Ayam* (www.alayam.com), *al Meethaq* (www.almeethaq.net) and *al Waqt* (www.alwaqt.com). In English the *Bahrain Tribune* (www.bahraintribune.com) and *Gulf Daily News* (www.gulf-daily-news.com).

Weeklies: In Arabic, *Layalina* (www.layalinamag.com) and *Sada al-Usbu'*. In English, *Gulf Weekly* (www.gulfweekly.com), has general news and information.

Business: In Arabic, *Akhbar al Khaleej* (www.akhbar-alkhaleej.com) has a business section. In English, the online website *Trade Arabia* (www.tradearabia.com), has a comprehensive range of business information topics and a hard copy *Gulf Industry* in English and Arabic, concerning the petroleum industry.

Periodicals: In Arabic, *Huna al Bahrain*, published by the Ministry of Information. In English, *Bahrain This Month* (www.bahrainthismonth.com).

Broadcasting

The state-owned Bahrain Radio and Television Corporation (BRTC) (www.bahraintv.com) operates the national public broadcasting networks.

Radio: BRTC operates Radio Bahrain (www.radiobahrain.fm) over three wave lengths, in the English language, offering news and current affairs, popular music and classical music. The Radio Bahrain Second Programme broadcasts general and cultural programmes including sports events and the Qur'an in Arabic. There are other private radio stations including Voice FM (www.voicefmbahrain.com), and, via satellite, Radio Sawa Gulf (www.radiosawa.com) and Monte Carlo Doualiya (www.rmc-mo.com) broadcasting in Arabic and French.

Television: BRTC operates five channels. The private and independent Orbit Satellite Television and Radio Network (www.orbit.net) operates 48 channels in Arabic and English by subscription. Residents also have access to hundreds of regional channels broadcasting via foreign satellite or cable TV companies.

National news agency: Bahrain News Agency

Economy

Since Bahrain is the least wealthy of the six Gulf States and as its small hydrocarbon reserves are shrinking, it has had to adapt and diversify its economy to provide an income. The service sector, essentially banking and finance, constitutes 52.6 per cent of GDP. Industry and manufacturing constitutes 47.1 per cent and agriculture 0.3 per cent of GDP. Alba, one of the world's largest alumina smelting plants is state-owned in partnership with the German company, BBS Kraftfahrzeugtechnik, produces finished aluminium products for the automotive industry. There is also an automotive industry in performance car manufacturing using aluminium components. Bahrain is a major Middle Eastern banking centre and is a leading Islamic financial centre, with the largest concentration of Islamic commercial, investment and leasing banks, as well as Islamic insurance (*Takaful*) companies.

As the global economic crisis cut trade, GDP growth weakened to 3.1 per cent in 2009. In 2012 GDP growth was at 3 per cent but in 2013 there was an increase to 5.3 per cent. Growth dropped to 4.7 per cent in 2014 along with the fall in global oil prices.

Large-scale tourist resorts and projects have become a significant source of revenue, with further development designed to attract greater regional tourism. Bahrain was the first Middle East country to build a Formula One racing circuit; Abu Dhabi was the second.

Infrastructure development has included a new port and expanded airport, strengthening Bahrain's position as a regional hub. The Economic Development Board (EDB) has been active in attracting foreign investment.

The Gulf Co-operation Council (GCC) was planning to issue a common currency in 2010, but the economic crisis and the experience of the fluctuating euro on the economies of the euro-zone gave the GCC pause for thought. If the currency is introduced it may have the effect of changing the medium of oil transactions from the US dollar to the new currency.

The anti-government riots in early 2011 set back the economy. Foreign Direct Investment (FDI) dropped over the year and the banking sector stagnated but conditions are improving again with Bahrain receiving US$989 million in FDI in 2013. FDI in 2014 decreased slightly to US$957 million.

External trade

Bahrain is one of six members of the Gulf Co-operation Council (GCC) free trade agreement (FTA), a common market between Bahrain and the other five members of the GCC, which was launched in 2008. Citizens of these countries are now allowed to travel between and live in any of the six states, where they may find employment, buy properties and businesses and use the educational and health facilities freely. Bahrain is also a member of the Greater Arab free trade area, which co-ordinates shared standards and specification of Arab products, inter-custom fees and provides a platform for communication between members.

The export of goods and services accounts for around 75 per cent of GDP. In the face of falling oil reserves the government has invested in processed aluminium, which has become a major export commodity and supports many domestic downstream industries

Imports

Main imports are crude oil, machinery, raw materials, chemicals and foodstuffs.

Main sources: Saudi Arabia (24 per cent of total in 2014), Algeria (11.9 per cent), China (8.2 per cent).

Exports

Main exports are petroleum and related goods, aluminium, vehicles and automotive parts, and textiles.

Main destinations: Saudi Arabia (3.3 per cent of total in 2014), US (2.4 per cent), United Arab Emirates (2.2 per cent).

Agriculture

Farming

The agricultural sector typically accounts for 0.3 per cent of GDP and employs around 1 per cent of the workforce.

Apart from being a small island, development of agriculture is limited by labour shortages, lack of water and salinity of the soil. The major crop is alfalfa for animal fodder, although farmers produce modest amounts of crops including dates, watermelons, pomegranates, bananas, potatoes, eggplants and tomatoes for the local market.

Government agricultural plans emphasise drainage to reduce salinity, improvement of the soil and new irrigation and cultivation techniques; there have also been experiments with hydroponics.

The land tenure system, under which over 60 per cent of cultivable land is held on three-year leases, discourages the stability needed for development.

The lack of grazing inhibits livestock production. One large dairy has annual milk production of 500,000 litres. Small dairy farmers, responsible for 15 per cent of production, have established a co-operative and constructed a milk pasteurising plant.

Fishing

The waters surrounding Bahrain have traditionally been rich fishing grounds, with more than 200 varieties of fish, many of which constitute a staple of the local diet. The discovery of oil in 1935 led to a steady decline in the fishing industry, which has been unable to meet domestic demand, noticeably since the 1970s. Moreover, pollution in the Gulf, since the 1980s, has increasingly threatened fish production and the shrimp industry. Fish catches have dropped amid claims of illegal fishing, habitat destruction from land reclamation and environmental pollution that threatens overall fish stocks.

Pearl diving was once a major industry with 40 per cent of Gulf pearl exports coming from Bahrain. Diving has declined sharply since the 1930s, but Bahrain has been a leading pearl testing centre since 1990, and a new pearl and gem-testing laboratory was opened in 2008.

Industry and manufacturing

The industrial sector contributed 39.9 per cent of GDP in 2012, of which manufacturing was 15 per cent. The sector typically employs 34 per cent of the labour force.

Bahrain's most prominent non-oil industry is the Aluminium Bahrain (Alba) plant, which supplies various downstream manufacturing plants as well as the Gulf Aluminium Rolling Mill Company (Garmco). Aluminium exports are one of Bahrain's biggest earners as a result of increased world prices. Alba dominates the manufacturing sector with a production capacity of 500,000 tonnes per year. More than 50 per cent of the aluminium produced at Alba is sold on the local and regional market, while the remainder goes mainly to the Far East.

Export-oriented small- and medium-sized industries have been attracted to free industrial zones established at Mina Sulman, Ma'amir, Abu Gazal and North Sitra, which enjoy tax and duty incentives. Industries located in these areas include plastics, paper, steel-wool and wire-mesh producers, marine service industries, aluminium, asphalt, cable manufacturing, prefabricated building and furniture.

Iron and steel production is increasing. The Bahrain Ispat Company, under the control of the Indian Ispat Group (based in London), operates a plant with a capacity of 1.2 million tpy of iron briquettes produced from iron pellets.

Tourism

Bahrain as a regional destination is the key strategy for its tourist industry. Government national plans include marketing Bahrain as a 'high-quality leisure and business tourism destination' for visitors primarily from the Middle East, but also Europe and Asia. In 2014 the direct contribution of tourism in Bahrain was 4.2 per cent of total GDP (10.3 per cent of indirect GDP) and directly supported 31,000 jobs, 4.1 per cent of total

employment, and 76,500 jobs if indirect jobs are taken into account (10.0 per cent of total employment). This shows that Bahrain is recovering from the civil unrest in 2011 that had stagnated the growth of the tourism industry.
Many visitors cross the causeway from Saudi Arabia for day-trips. The government is concerned that its traditional and historic towns are an asset that could easily be damaged by unfettered development. In July 2012, the coastal and island sites on Muharraq Island, which are the traditional home of the pearling industry, were added to Unesco's World Heritage List.
Investment committed to tourism development in 2014 was BD148.9 million (US$394.9 million), 6.1 per cent of total investment. Bahrain will need a period of sustained peace and a serious promotional campaign to regain its reputation as a suitable destination.
Manama was designated as the Capital of Arab Tourism for 2013 in a move it was hoped would help restore confidence in the sector and encourage visitors.

Hydrocarbons

Proven oil reserves were 124.6 million barrels in 2015. Oil accounts for around 87 per cent of government revenue, more than 75 per cent of exports, and around 20 per cent of GDP, but the government has been diversifying the economy.
The Bahrain Petroleum Company has responsibility for all aspects of the hydrocarbon industry including exploration, production, refining and distribution in both domestic and international markets.
Bahrain had 92 billion cubic metres (cum) of natural gas in 2014 and produced 15.7 billion cum. If further gas fields are not found, current reserves are expected to be depleted over the next few years. With the imminent loss, Qatar has signed an agreement to supply Bahrain with natural gas in the future.
Bahrain does not produce or import coal.

Energy

Bahrain has 3.9GW of electricity generating capacity, almost all of which is produced from conventional thermal plants. The Kingdom has recently begun to develop solar and other renewable power. It is also taking part in the GCC's plan to integrate the electric power grids of all GCC countries.
Construction of Bahrain's largest power plant, to provide around 30 per cent of Bahrain's total output, located at Al Dour, was completed in 2012. At a total cost of US$1 billion, it will provide an additional 1,250MW of electricity and 181,680 kilolitres of desalinated water. The US electrical engineers GE Energy are contracted to provide five gas turbines, equipped with advanced emission control technologies. Further plans to increase production in other existing plants should increase generation up to a projected requirement of 3,500MW by 2020.
A Gulf Co-operation Council (GCC) project to link the six member states (Saudi Arabia, Qatar, Bahrain, Kuwait, Oman and the United Arab Emirates) to an integrated power-grid began in 2005. The first phase of the GCC power grid was completed in July 2009 at a cost of US$1,095 million, linking Saudi Arabia, Bahrain, Kuwait and Qatar through 800km of transmission lines. Kuwait and Saudi Arabia will each receive an extra 1,200MW of power capacity and later, the UAE will receive 900MW, Qatar 750MW, Bahrain 600MW and Oman 400MW. In the first phase, a 400kV overhead line links Kuwait's Al Zour power station with Doha, and a 400kV submarine line to Saudi Arabia with Bahrain. The second phase will link the UAE with Oman. The resulting two mega-grids will be joined in the final phase.

Financial markets

Bahrain has a solid reputation as an international financial hub. It remains attractive as a result of a combination of factors, including its relative political stability, open and tax-free business climate, central geographical position, low costs, excellent communications and an accommodating government. The financial sector is one of the most diverse in the region and has the largest volume of transactions in the Middle East. The International Islamic Financial Market (IIFM) has attracted a number of major financial institutions to deal specifically in Sharia compliant deals.
Bahrain Islamic International Rating Agency (IIRA) is the sole credit ratings agency set up (in 2005) to provide a ratings system of capital instruments and Islamic financial products in predominantly Islamic countries. IIRA is sponsored by several multilateral development institutions, major banks, financial institutions and ratings agencies. It operates in 11 countries in which it also has shareholders as the *Sharia* complaint board of directors maintain an independence service

Stock exchange

Bahrain Stock Exchange (BSE)

Banking and insurance

In 2008 there were some 370 offshore banking units and representative offices in Bahrain, as well as 32 Islamic commercial, investment and leasing banks. Bahrain reportedly has the largest concentration of Islamic financial institutions, including *takaful* (insurance) companies, in the Middle East.
The Central Bank of Bahrain (CBB) has full regulations for its Islamic banking community.
An agreement was reached between Saudi Arabia, Kuwait, Bahrain and Qatar to establish the Gulf Co-operation Council (GCC) Monetary Council to be established (originally in 2009), marking plans to set up a regional central bank, to be based in Riyadh (Saudi Arabia). The GCC Monetary Council will oversee the introduction of a monetary union, due to be in operation by 2013.

Central bank

Central Bank of Bahrain (CBB) replaced the Bahrain Monetary Agency on 7 September 2006. It is responsible for maintaining monetary and financial stability.

Main financial centre

Manama

Time

GMT plus three hours

Geography

Bahrain is an archipelago of 33 islands. Only three of the islands are inhabited. The main island of Bahrain contains most of the population and is linked by a causeway to the island of Muharraq. Another causeway links Bahrain to Saudi Arabia.

Hemisphere

Northern

Climate

Summer temperatures are hot and humid, reaching 49 degrees Celsius (C) in the shade, while January, the coldest winter month, has temperatures ranging from 3 degrees C to 28 degrees C. Humidity, particularly on the coast, can be extreme. Between December and the end of March the climate is temperate, with temperatures ranging between 19–25 degrees C.

Dress codes

A lightweight suit or lightweight jacket and trousers are advised. A long-sleeved shirt with a tie should be worn at business and official meetings but a jacket need not be worn. Women should dress modestly. However, bikinis may be worn on certain beaches and at international hotel swimming pools. The dress code for women is less severe than in Saudi Arabia or some other Islamic countries.

Entry requirements

Passports

Passports are required by all.

Visa

Visas are required by all except nationals of Kuwait, Oman, Qatar, Saudi Arabia and the United Arab Emirates (UAE).
For details of requirements for business and tourist visas visit: www.bahrainembassy.org/visareq.html. Tourist visas can be obtained on arrival at

Bahrain airport, business visas must be applied for in advance. Journalists must make prior arrangements with the Ministry of Information.

Women arriving in Bahrain alone and without a visa could be refused entry. Lone female travellers are advised to obtain a visa before departure.

A new visa system (similar to the European Schengen agreement) allowing multiply entry for foreigners to the six Gulf Co-operation Council (GCC) countries was introduced in November 2012.

Prohibited entry

Israeli nationals or anyone holding a passport with an Israeli visa/stamp may be denied entry.

Currency advice/regulations

Any currency, including Bahraini, may be freely imported and exported.

Customs

Personal effects are duty free. The duty free allowance is 400 cigarettes or 50 cigars and two bottles of alcoholic beverages, for non-Muslim passengers only, and 227ml of perfume for personal use. Jewellery, drugs, firearms and ammunition are subject to import permits.

Prohibited imports

Pornographic and obscene literature and pictures, cultured or undrilled pearls, and goods of Israeli origin are prohibited.

Health (for visitors)

Medical services in Bahrain are of high quality with a good general hospital in Manama and modern health centres in smaller communities. Medical insurance is advised. Consultations are offered at the American Mission Hospital, 133 Isa Al-Kabeer Avenue, Manama (tel: 17-253-447; internet: www.amh.org.bh).

Mandatory precautions

Yellow fever certificate, for visitors arriving from infected areas.

Advisable precautions

Recommended immunisations are hepatitis A and B, polio, tetanus and typhoid. There is a risk of rabies.

Hotels

There are plenty of first class hotels. A 12 per cent service charge is usual. Major hotels and most restaurants are licensed.

Credit cards

All major credit cards are accepted.

Public holidays (national)

Fixed dates

1 Jan (New Year's Day), 16–17 Dec (National Day).

Variable dates

Eid al Adha (three days), Eid al Fitr (three days), Islamic New Year, Ashura, Prophet's Birthday.

Islamic year 1437 (15 Oct 2015–2 Oct 2016):: The Islamic year has 354 or 355 days, with the result that Muslim feasts advance by 10–12 days against the Gregorian calendar each year. Dates of the Muslim feasts vary according to sightings of the new moon, so cannot be forecast exactly.

Working hours

Thursday and Friday are weekly holidays. Regular hours are subject to change during the month of Ramadan. Some banks and businesses close on Saturday.

Banking

Sat–Wed: 0730–1200; Thu: 0730–1100; some branches are open three days weekly in the afternoon; some offshore banking units close on Sunday; 1000–1330 during Ramadan.

Business

Sat–Thu: 0800–1530 or 0800–1300, 1500–1730.

Government

Sat–Tue: 0700–1415; Wed: 0700–1400. During Ramadan government offices open 0930–1430.

Shops

Sat–Thu: 0830–1230, 1530–1830; large superstores are open Sat–Thu: 0800–1900; late opening Wed and Thu: 0800–1200, 1530–2130; some are open for a few hours on Fri in the Souk.

Telecommunications

Mobile/cell phones

GSM 900/1800 services are available throughout the country.

Electricity supply

230V 50 cycles AC everywhere except Awali, which has 120V 60 cycles; various types of plug fitting, normally three-pin flat.

Weights and measures

Metric system (local measures are also used).

Social customs/useful tips

Traditionally much time is spent in exchanging small talk at business meetings; embarking on business matters before the atmosphere is favourable may cause offence. Decisions are often taken by consensus, according to the Arabian tradition, rather than exclusively on the advantages and disadvantages of the case submitted. In business, it is essential to create a mood of trust and to be persistent even when the case is apparently lost.

Always shake hands on meeting and leaving. You may find the handshake lasts longer than in the West, but this is a sign of friendship. If you have made a good impression, the handshake on departure will be longer than that on arrival.

Muslims pray five times a day although shops and offices do not close during prayer. Although alcohol is not forbidden by law, like pork, it is forbidden by Islam and should be consumed with discretion.

It is polite to avoid eating, drinking or smoking in the presence of Muslims during daylight hours in the month of Ramadan (it is illegal to do so in public).

Unless addressing members of the royal family normal Western forms of address and greeting are usual.

Everyone, including the visitor, is subject to *sharia* (Islamic law) although it is less rigorously applied than in some other Islamic countries.

Security

Visitors to Bahrain should keep in touch with developments in the Middle East as any increase in regional tension might affect travel advice.

It is advisable to avoid village areas, especially after dark. Local security precautions, religious and social sensitivities should be observed and respected.

Getting there

Air

National airline: Gulf Air (100 per cent owned by Bahrain since May 2007).

International airport/s: Bahrain International, Muharraq (BAH), 6.5km north-east of city, with bar, restaurant, buffet, bank, shops, hotel reservations.

Airport tax: International departures BD3; not applicable for transit passengers.

Surface

Road: The Saudi-Bahrain Causeway links Bahrain, Saudi Arabia and Qatar.

Water: There are passenger ferries running between Iran and Bahrain; the trip takes about 16 hours each way. There is a port tax of BD3.

Main port/s: Mina Sulman, Mina Manama and Mina Muharraq.

Getting about

National transport

Road: Bahrain's road network is fairly good. There are good tarmac roads between centres, and six-lane highways form a ring road by-pass system for Manama and Muharraq.

Buses: A national bus company provides public transport throughout the populated areas of the country.

Rail: There are no railways in Bahrain.

Water: Dhow trips are arranged most weekends to sand bars and nearby islands from the old wharf (Mina Manama) on King Faisal Road. Boat trips to neighbouring islands are frequently arranged on Friday and publicised in the local press.

City transport

It is easy to cover both Manama and Muharraq on foot, though renting a car will make it easier to get to farther-flung locations.

Taxis: Taxis (with orange side wings and black-on-yellow number plates) are plentiful and fares are regulated. Fares are by meter and only vary when coming from the airport or when travelling by night. Taxis are readily available for the 6.5km journey from Bahrain International airport to Manama, for which there is a charge in addition to the meter reading. Recommended fares from the airport are displayed outside the arrivals terminal. Shared taxis or 'pick-ups' can be hailed from any bus stop. They do not use meters. Fares vary depending on the destination, but are lower than standard taxi fares. However, they can be very cramped and uncomfortable. The 'pick-ups' have white and orange number plates, and a yellow circle with the licence number in black painted on the driver's door.

Car hire

Insurance is compulsory and international driving licences must be validated at the Ministry of Interior Traffic Headquarters before use in Bahrain. Car hire firms are listed in the local telephone directory, and it is generally recommended to compare prices. Driving is on the right. Seatbelts are compulsory for both the driver and front seat passenger, and young children must be seated in the back. Road signs are in English and Arabic. The maximum speed limit on highways is 100kph, and on inner city roads it is generally between 50–80kph. If an accident occurs, the vehicle must not be moved until traffic police get to the scene.

BUSINESS DIRECTORY

The addresses listed below are a selection only. While World of Information makes every endeavour to check these addresses, we cannot guarantee that changes have not been made, especially to telephone numbers and area codes. We would welcome any corrections.

Telephone area codes

The international direct dialling code (IDD) for Bahrain is +973 followed by subscriber's number.

Useful telephone numbers

Emergency service: 999
Directory enquiries: 181
International enquiries: 191
International bookings: 151
Operator: 100
Time in Arabic: 141
Time in English: 140
Telephone faults: 121

Chambers of Commerce

Bahrain Chamber of Commerce and Industry, Bld 122, Road 1605, Block 216, PO Box 248, Manama (tel: 17-229-555; fax 17-224-985; email: bastaki @ bahrainchamber.org.bh; internet: www.bahrainchamber.org.bh/english/index.htm)

Banking

Ahli United Bank Bahrain, 126 Government Avenue, PO Box 5941, Manama (tel: 17-221-700; fax: 17-224-322; e-mail: info@ahliunited.com).

Al Baraka Islamic Bank, PO Box 1882, Manama (tel: 17-535-300; fax: 17-533-993; e-mail: baraka@batelco.com.bh).

Arab Banking Corporation, ABC Tower, Diplomatic Area, PO Box 5698, Manama (tel: 17-543-000; fax: 17-533-163; e-mail: webmaster@arabbanking.com; internet: www.arabbanking.com).

Bahrain Development Bank, PO Box 20501, Manama (tel: 17-537-007; fax: 17-534-005).

Bahrain Islamic Bank, Al Salam Tower, Diplomatic Area, PO Box 5240, Manama (tel: 17-535-888; fax: 17-535-707; e-mail: bahisi@batelco.com.bh).

Bahraini Saudi Bank, PO Box 1159, Manama (tel: 17-211-010; fax: 17-210-989; e-mail: helpdesk@bahrainisaudibank.com).

Bank of Bahrain & Kuwait, 43 Government Avenue, PO Box 597, Manama (tel: 17-223-388; fax: 17-229-822; e-mail: bbkonline@batelco.com.bh).

First Islamic Investment Bank EC, PO Box 1406, Manama (tel: 17-218-333; fax: 17-217-555).

Gulf International Bank, PO Box 1017, Al-Dowali Building, 3 Palace Avenue, Manama (tel: 17-534-000; fax: 17-522-633; e-mail: info@gibbah.com; internet site: http://www.gibonline.com).

National Bank of Bahrain , PO Box 106, Manama (tel: 17-228-800; fax: 17-228-998; e-mail: nbb@nbbonline.com).

TAIB Bank, Sehl Centre, Diplomatic Area, PO Box 20485, Manama (tel: 17-533-334; fax: 17-533-174; e-mail: taib@taib.com).

Central bank

Central Bank of Bahrain (CBB), King Faisal Highway, Diplomatic Area, Block 317, Road 1702, Building 96, PO Box 27, Manama (tel: 17-535-535; fax: 17-533-342; web: www.cbb.gov.bh).

Stock exchange

Bahrain Stock Exchange (BSE), www.bahrainstock.com

Travel information

Bahrain International Airport, PO Box 586, Manama (tel: 17-321-151; fax: 17-324-096).

Bahrain Tourism Company, PO Box 5831, Manama (tel: 17-534-321; fax: 17-531-353; e-mail: btc@alseyaha.com).

Gulf Air, PO Box 138, Manama (tel: 17-228-820; fax: 17-224-452).

Ministry of tourism

Tourism Affairs, Ministry of Information, PO Box 26613, Manama (tel: 17-201-203; fax: 17-211-717; e-mail: btour@bahraintourism.com).

Ministries

Ministry of Cabinet Affairs, PO Box 26141, Manama (tel: 17-731-544; fax: 17-731-863).

Ministry of Commerce and Industry, PO Box 5479, Manana (tel: 17-531-531; fax: 17-530-455; email: drmansoor@commerce.gov.bh; internet: www.commerce.gov.bh).

Ministry of Defence, PO Box 245, Manama (tel: 17-653-333; fax: 17-663-923).

Ministry of Education, PO Box 43, Manama (tel: 17-680-105; fax: 17-687-866).

Ministry of Electricity and Water, PO Box 2, Manama (tel: 17-546-666; fax: 17-533-035).

Ministry of Foreign Affairs, PO Box 547, Manama (tel: 17-227-555; fax: 17-212-603).

Ministry of Health, PO Box 12, Manama (tel: 17-255-555; fax: 17-252-569).

Ministry of Housing and Public Works, PO Box 5802, Manama (tel: 17-533-000; fax: 17-536-431).

Ministry of Information, PO Box 253, Manama (tel: 17-781-888; fax: 17-682-777).

Ministry of the Interior, PO Box 13, Manama (tel: 17-272-111; fax: 17-262-169).

Ministry of Justice and Islamic Affairs, PO Box 450, Manama (tel: 17-531-333; fax: 17-531-284).

Ministry of Labour and Social Affairs, PO Box 32333. Manama (tel: 17-687-800; fax: 17-686-954).

Ministry of Municipalities and Agriculture, PO Box 53, Manama (tel: 17-226-060; fax: 17-229-666).

Ministry of Oil, PO Box 1435, Manama (tel: 17-291-511; fax: 17-293-007).

Ministry of Transport, PO Box 10325, Manama (tel: 17-534-534; fax: 17-534-041).

Prime Minister's Office, PO Box 1000, Manama (tel: 17-200-000; fax: 17-532-839).

Other useful addresses

Aluminium Bahrain (Alba), PO Box 570, Manama (tel: 17-830-000; fax: 17-830-083; e-mail: alba@alba.com.bh).

Arabian Exhibition Management, PO Box 20200, Manama (tel: 17-550-033; fax: 17-553-288; aeminfo@batelco.com.bh).

Bahrain International Exhibition Centre, PO Box 11644, Manama (tel: 17-550-111; fax: 17-553-447; e-mail: biec@batelco.com.bh).

Bahrain National Gas Company (Banagas), PO Box 29099, Manama (tel: 17-756-222; fax: 17-756-991; e-mail: bng@banagas.com.bh).

Bahrain Petroleum Company (Bapco), PO Box 25555, Awali (tel: 17-704-040; fax: 17-704-070; e-mail: info@bapco.net).

Bahrain Stock Exchange, PO Box 3203, Manama (tel: 17-261-260; fax: 17-256-362; e-mail: info@bahrainstock.com).

Central Municipal Council, PO Box 53, Manama (tel: 17-276-060; fax: 17-263-666).

Consultative Council (Majlis al-Shura), PO Box 2991 Manama (tel: 17-714-422; fax: 17-715-715).

Customs Directorate, PO Box 15, Manama (tel: 17-725-333; fax: 17-725-534).

Ports Directorate, PO Box 453, Manama (tel: 17-725-555; fax: 17-725-534).

National news agency: Bahrain News Agency, (tel: 689-044; fax: 683-825; email: news@bahrain.gov.bh; internet: www.bna.bh).

Internet sites

Arabia OnLine: www.arabia.com

Bahrain Economic Development Board: www.bahrainedb.com

Bahrain Institute of Banking and Finance: www.bibf.com

Bahrain Islamic International Rating Agency (IIRA): www.iirating.com.

Bahrain Ministry of Finance and National Economy: www.mofne.gov.bh

Bangladesh

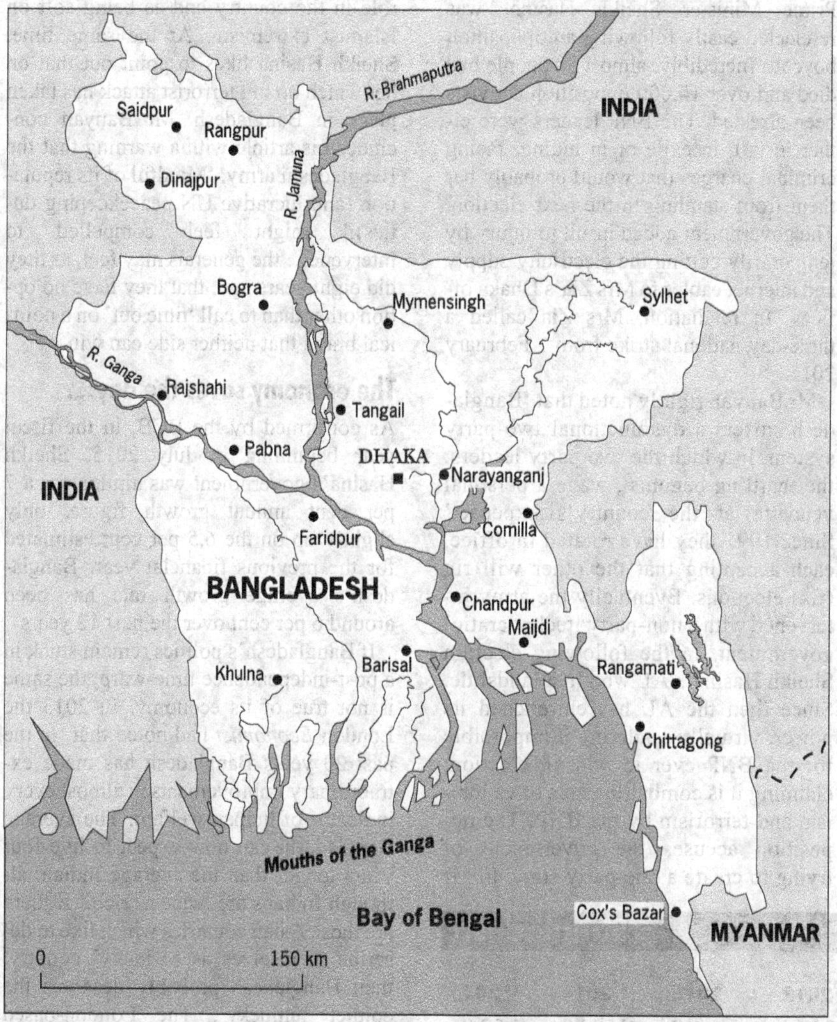

Bangladesh's political credibility wore even thinner in 2015. The country's inability to send its feuding politicians packing was a weakness that risked spreading to every level of society. An exasperated Atiur Rahman, the governor of the Bangladesh Central Bank (BCB) told Reuters that the politicians had to set aside their differences and 'focus on lifting economic growth' in the hope of rebuilding the Bangladeshi investment profile.

Bickering families

There is something Shakespearian about Bangladeshi politics: instead of Capulets and Montagues, the two families at loggerheads are those of the Prime Minister Sheikh Hasina and the opposition leader Khaleda Zia. Both women have political form, each being related to former national leaders. In a depressingly claustrophobic state of affairs, the two women have alternated as prime minister for most of the previous two decades.

Atiur Rahman also said that the Bangladeshi authorities were determined to break out of what he termed the '6 plus syndrome' (annual gross domestic growth had hovered around the 6 per cent mark for some years) and transform it into a middle income economy over the

KEY FACTS

Official name: Gana Prajatantri Bangladesh (People's Republic of Bangladesh)

Head of State: President Abdul Hamid (from 24 April 2013)

Head of government: Prime Minister Sheikh Hasina Wazed (Awami League) (from 6 Jan 2009)

Ruling party: The Mohajot (Grand Coalition) led by the Awami League (AL) (People's League) with the Jatiya Party (National Party) (since 29 Dec 2008)

Area: 143,998 square km

Population: 158.22 million (2014)*

Capital: Dhaka

Official language: Bengali (Bangla)

Currency: Taka (Tk) = 100 poisha

Exchange rate: Tk77.80 per US$ (Sep 2015)

GDP per capita: US$1,172 (2014)*

GDP real growth: 6.11% (2014)*

GDP: US$185.41 billion (2014)*

Labour force: 73.87 million (2009) (does not include extensive expatriate numbers)

Unemployment: 4.80% (2010)* (does not include underemployment)

Inflation: 7.01% (2014)

Natural gas production: 23.60 billion cum (2014)

Balance of trade: -US$10.17 billion (2014)*

* estimated figure

following six years. Mr Rahman boldly observed that 'If peace really prevails and 92 days are not lost, definitely, we will be very near to the target. Mr Rahman's mention of '92 days' was a reference to the 92 days of political unrest that had already paralysed the economy in 2015. According to Mr Rahman, the Bangladeshi garment industry, which accounted for some 80 per cent of Bangladesh's exports, has lost orders to factories in Cambodia and Vietnam; the agriculture and tourism sectors had also been badly affected. A World Bank report released in April showed that the economy lost about US$2.2 billion, or around one per cent of gross domestic product (GDP) due to the unrest. On the 2014 Transparency International *Corruption Perceptions Index*, Bangladesh could only manage a ranking of 145 out of the 175 countries surveyed. This placed Bangladesh below luminary countries such as Nigeria (136) and Uganda (142). Neighbouring Pakistan (126) and particularly India (85) returned better rankings.

Political paralysis

Anticipating Mr Rahman's comments, writing a blog on the *Economist* website in February 2015 (http://www.economist.com/blogs/economist-explains/2015/02/economist-explains-0), T J Banyan noted that the country had '(yet again) been paralysed.' At the heart of the country's political unrest was, (yet again) the often petty rivalries between the two ladies leading the country's political blocs. According to Mr Banyan, the opposition leader, Khalida Zia, had been confined to a party office in Dhaka. Her party, the Bangladesh Nationalist Party (BNP) had been staging a nationwide blockade of roads, railways and waterways. The trigger for the unrest was a banned protest to mark the 5 January anniversary of the 2015 election, in which the incumbent Awami League (AL), led by Prime Minister Sheikh Hasina, was re-elected easily following an opposition boycott. Incredibly, almost 50 people had died and over 10,000 opposition activists been arrested. The BNP leaders were either in jail, in exile or in hiding, facing criminal charges that would probably bar them from standing in the next election. The government added insult to injury by temporarily cutting the electricity supply and internet cables to Mrs Zia's Dhaka offices. In retaliation, Mrs Zia called a three-day national strike from 1 February 2015.

Mr Banyan rightly noted that 'Bangladesh suffers a dysfunctional two-party system, in which the two party leaders, the 'battling begums', wage a personal vendetta at the country's expense.' Since 1991 they have rotated in office, each accepting that the other will rig (fix) elections. Eventually the army intervened with a non-party 'technocratic' government. In the following election Sheikh Hasina's AL won in a landslide. Since then the AL has entrenched its power, virtually rendering it impossible for the BNP ever to win an election, claiming it is combatting acts of vandalism and terrorism by the BNP. The opposition accuses the government of trying to create a one-party state. In Mr Banyan's view, both sides have a point. (And so indeed, does he.)

Surprisingly, but endorsing the comments of Mr Rahman of the BCB, Bangladesh has a reasonable record of developmental success. However, India and the West distrust Mrs Zia, seeing her as both willing to allow China a greater role in the country and as being soft on Islamist extremism. At the same time, Sheikh Hasina likes to point out that on her watch no big terrorist attack has taken place in Bangladesh. Mr Banyan concludes his article with a warning that the Bangladeshi army, 'Mindful of its reputation (and lucrative UN peacekeeping duties),' might feel compelled to intervene… the generals may feel, as they did eight years ago, that they have no option other than to call 'time out' on a political brawl that neither side can win.

The economy saves the day…

As confirmed by the BCB, in the fiscal year beginning in July 2015, Sheikh Hasina's government was aiming for a 7 per cent annual growth figure, only slightly up on the 6.5 per cent estimated for the previous financial year. Bangladesh's average growth rate has been around 6 per cent over the past 12 years

If Bangladesh's politics remain stuck in a post-independence time-warp, the same is not true of its economy. In 2013 the London *Economist* had noted that 'in the past 20 years Bangladesh has made extraordinary improvements in almost every indicator of human welfare. The average Bangladeshi can now expect to live four years longer than the average Indian, although Indians are twice as rich.' If there are those Asian countries which like to describe themselves as a 'lucky' country, then Bangladesh probably deserves the epithet 'unlucky'. The London-based *Economist Intelligence Unit's* (EIU – and sister company of the magazine) strangely named annual Global Liveability Report ranked the country's capital Dhaka as the least desirable urban location in the world – hardly the stuff of inward investment promotion, behind even Lagos and Papua New Guinea's Port Moresby. The city survey took into account factors such as healthcare, transport, culture and crime. This flew pleasantly in the face of the remarks made upon independence in 1971, when US Secretary of State Henry Kissinger, describing the new state of Bangladesh, remarked dismissively 'that it was a basket case' before moving on to his next successful Asian nation-building project.

KEY INDICATORS — Bangladesh

	Unit	2011	2012	2013	2014	**2015
Population	m	142.32	154.69	156.60	*158.22	*159.86
Gross domestic product (GDP)	US$bn	113.00	122.98	161.76	*185.41	*205.33
GDP per capita	US$	678	795	1,033	*1,172	*1,284
GDP real growth	%	6.1	6.1	6.1	*6.1	*6.3
Inflation	%	10.7	6.2	7.5	7.0	*6.4
Natural gas output	bn cum	19.9	21.8	21.9	23.6	–
Exports (fob) (goods)	US$m	24,539.3	25,428.1	28,622.4	29,928.6	–
Imports (fob) (goods)	US$m	32,583.9	31,938.0	34,995.4	40,099.1	–
Balance of trade	US$m	-8,044.6	-6,509.9	-6,373.0	-10,170.6	–
Current account	US$m	-1,398.0	1,039.0	1,867.0	*-132.0	*-1,132.0
Total reserves minus gold	US$m	9,298.4	12,031.0	17,564.4	21,785.4	–
Foreign exchange	US$m	8,666.4	11,393.0	16,579.6	–	–
Exchange rate	per US$	72.67	81.00	77.68	77.91	–

* estimated figure ** forecast figure

...and the IMF is complimentary

In its September 2014 assessment of the Bangladeshi economy and as part of the fifth review under a three-year Extended Credit Facility (ECF) arrangement, the International Monetary Fund (IMF) noted that the Bangladesh authorities had made 'significant progress' in consolidating macro-economic stability under the ECF-supported programme. Despite the moderation in exports, foreign exchange reserves had continued to increase and in the view of the IMF, had reached adequate levels; inflation had also declined, the fiscal deficit was contained and public debt was on a downward path. With a calmer political environment (however, see 'Political Paralysis' above) economic activity was gaining momentum and GDP growth was expected to be around 6.25 per cent in the fiscal year to the end of June 2015. There had also been progress on structural reforms. However, the introduction of a new value added tax (VAT), a key government reform to boost development spending, was facing delays.

According to the IMF, if sustained rapid growth and poverty reduction were to be achieved in the medium term, it was necessary to preserve macro-economic stability and well-targeted social spending. Bangladesh's persistent revenue shortfalls reinforced the importance of pressing ahead with tax reforms. Implementing the new VAT was the foremost priority, as it had the potential to mobilise considerable additional resources, reduce compliance costs and boost growth.

The IMF welcomed the Bangladeshi authorities' efforts to strengthen public debt management by focusing external borrowing on projects with high social returns; to improve financial management, including improved monthly treasury cash flow forecasts; and to strengthen financial reporting by state-owned enterprises. The IMF also welcomed steps to improve the financial position of the state-owned commercial banks through enhanced supervision and corporate governance, complemented with gradual recapitalisation as required.

In the view of the IMF the Bangladeshi authorities had made good progress in improving working and safety conditions in the garment industry. Further strengthening of social safety net programmes was, however, still needed. Steps had also been taken to gradually liberalise foreign exchange regulations, helping to boost the investment climate.

The ADB view

According to the Asian Development Bank (ADB) economic growth in the 2014 fiscal year (which ended in June 2014) was provisionally estimated at 6.1 per cent, slightly improved from the 6.0 per cent of 2013. Agriculture expanded by 3.3 per cent, aided by good weather and continued government support. Industrial growth fell to 8.4 per cent from 9.6 per cent a year earlier, however, the political unrest before the parliamentary election in January 2014 had disrupted the supply of materials and undermined consumer confidence. The services sector grew by 5.8 per cent, up slightly from 5.5 per cent the year before.

On the demand side, net exports added to growth as garment exports grew briskly. A decline in remittances and weak consumer confidence ahead of the election held down growth in consumer spending. Investment rose slightly to 28.7 per cent of GDP in 2014 from 28.4 per cent in the previous year, as private investment slipped to 21.4 per cent of GDP from 21.8 per cent in 2013 while public investment rose from 6.6 per cent to 7.3 per cent. In the view of the ADB, private investment was constrained by the unsettled political environment, difficulties with infrastructure and skills deficits and procedural (bureaucratic) problems that inhibited investment. Rising public investment came as the government stepped up its implementation of election pledges. Foreign direct investment (FDI) remained low.

Annual average inflation had accelerated to 7.4 per cent from 6.8 per cent in 2013 as political unrest before the election disrupted food supplies and pushed up prices. Wage increases in both the public and the private sector and an upward adjustment to power tariffs in March 2014, contributed to inflation. By June 2014, inflation had moderated to 7.0 per cent year on year. In the first seven months of the 2015 fiscal year, to January 2015, food inflation eased and inflation for other expenditures rose slightly to converge at 6.0 per cent. Moderate demand, unchanged administered prices, a stable exchange rate and a cautious monetary policy underpinned the outcome. With ample liquidity in the banking system, the central bank raised the cash reserve requirement from 6.0 per cent to 6.5 per cent, effective in June 2014. The banks' weighted average lending rate eased to 13.1 per cent from 13.6 per cent at the end of June 2013. The deposit rate also declined, to 7.7 per cent from 8.4 per cent, widening banks' interest rate spread by 0.2 percentage points to 5.4 per cent.

The ADB pointed out that weak discipline at the state-owned commercial banks (SCBs) and specialised banks had caused non-performing loans (NPL) to proliferate in banks and the larger banking system. SCBs held about 25 per cent of banking system assets at the time and specialised banks a further 5 per cent. At the end of 2014, the ratio of NPLs to total loans stood at 9.7 per cent, up from 6.1 per cent at the end of 2013. Specialised banks had the highest ratio at 32.8 per cent and the more financially important SCBs had an extraordinarily high ratio of 22.2 per cent. Before 2012, the central bank's options were largely limited to tightening classification and provisioning requirements, but the Bank Company (Amendment) Act, in 2013, gave the central bank much more authority to supervise SCBs. To improve their performance, the central

Secular bloggers and religious extremism

Although officially a secular country, 90 per cent of Bangladesh's population is Muslim. Since the turn of the year religiously motivated attacks have increased, particularly on atheist bloggers. Four bloggers have been brutally hacked to death – the most recent murder of Niloy Chakrabart occurred on 7 August 2015.

Islamic extremism has always been a problem for Bangladesh but the recent spate of horrific killings, including the murder of a US citizen, has propelled it into the international consciousness. Remaining atheist bloggers have either fled or taken extra precaution in hiding their true identity. Bangladeshi authorities have additionally faced accusations of failing to do enough to stop the violence. It took them until May to ban hardline extremist group Ansarullah Bangla Team (ABT).

While fears abound that similar groups to ABT possess hit-lists of current bloggers and their addresses, the sheer brutality of the machete-based attacks have turned many against the extremists and political promises to crackdown have followed.

bank had undertaken a restructuring programme that set detailed requirements in memoranda of understanding that were acknowledged and signed by the board of each SCB.

According to the ADB, revenue collection by the National Board of Revenue grew by 10.4 per cent in 2014, but under-performed the budget target because of disrupted economic activity. Total domestic indirect taxes grew by 11.8 per cent, while income tax collection rose by 15.6 per cent. Revenue from taxes connected with imports was weak, however, as imports of higher-duty consumer goods slackened and the bulk of imports were low-duty items such as capital goods, industrial raw materials and food grains. As a share of GDP, revenue collection rose to 11.6 per cent in 2014 from 10.7 per cent the previous year. Meanwhile, total spending reached 16.0 per cent, limiting the budget deficit to 4.4 per cent of GDP. Domestic sources financed close to 70.0 per cent of the deficit. As part of its periodic adjustment programme, the government raised electricity tariffs for retail consumers by 6.7 per cent in March 2014. However, it did not adjust the price of furnace oil, which is used mostly to generate electricity and the last adjustment of diesel, kerosene and gasoline prices was in January 2013.

The ADB reported that exports grew by 12.0 per cent in 2014, up from 10.7 per cent growth a year earlier. Higher demand from the large traditional buyers – the European Union (EU) and the US – and from newly developed markets pushed growth in readymade garment exports to 13.8 per cent, outpacing the previous year's 12.7 per cent expansion. Import payments rose by 8.9 per cent in a marked revival from low growth of 0.8 per cent in 2013. The upturn reflected big increases in imports of petroleum products, machinery and other capital goods, industrial raw materials and food grains. A stark departure from previous patterns saw workers' remittances fall by 1.6 per cent to US$14.2 billion because of a large drop in employment abroad, especially in the Middle East. A smaller trade deficit notwithstanding, the decline in workers' remittances and the higher services deficit narrowed the current account surplus from US$2.4 billion in 2013 to US$1.3 billion, equal to 0.8 per cent of GDP. With stronger inflows into capital and financial accounts, the overall balance of payments recorded another very large surplus of US$5.5 billion in financial year (FY) 2014, slightly above the US$5.1 billion recorded in 2013. The central bank's foreign exchange reserves rose sharply by the end of June 2014 to US$21.5 billion, equal to about 5.9 months of imports.

In the view of the ADB, active management by the central bank kept the exchange rate stable for the Bangladesh taka, which appreciated by a slight 0.2 per cent against the US dollar in 2014. Because of the taka's nominal appreciation against other currencies and domestic inflation that was higher in Bangladesh than in its trading partners, the taka appreciated in real effective terms by 5.5 per cent year on year as of the end of June 2014, indicating lost export competitiveness. Key stock market indicators improved in FY2014. The Dhaka Stock Exchange broad index rose by 9.2 per cent by June 2014 and market capitalisation by 16.3 per cent. The price-to-earnings ratio rose to 16.4 in June 2014 from 14.6 a year earlier and 12 new companies were listed. Net foreign portfolio investment of US$825.0 million in 2014 – more than double the US$368.0 million in 2013 – also contributed to market vitality.

The ADB's projections for the 2015 fiscal year were based on several assumptions: first that the central bank would maintain its cautious monetary stance to contain inflation, as envisaged in its January 2015 monetary policy statement. Second, that the government would raise electricity and natural gas prices to cut subsidies and keep current spending within the budget. Third, that it would reach its targeted budget revenue and foreign financing and strengthen project implementation. Finally, that the weather would be favourable.

This being the case, the ADB projected GDP growth in 2015 at 6.1 per cent. Before the political unrest of January 2015 the economy had been expanding briskly for six months, indicating good growth prospects for 2015. Strong remittance inflows boosted consumption and private investment was rising, as indicated by higher capital equipment imports. Although exports remained subdued, they were gradually improving as export orders picked up. However, political unrest began undermining growth prospects by affecting private investment and export activity.

Continued healthy remittance inflows were nevertheless expected by the ADB to support consumer spending and sustain economic momentum. However, the ADB stressed that notwithstanding the country's resilience under domestic and external shocks, if political unrest were to continue, it would further hinder economic growth. Growth in 2016 was projected to rise to 6.4 per cent, aided by higher remittances and export growth, underpinned by the continued economic recovery in the US and (to a lesser extent) the euro-zone. Consumer and investor confidence were expected to pick up as the political situation stabilised, strengthening the growth momentum. In addition, infrastructure constraints would be likely to ease somewhat with the completion of projects already commenced, particularly the opening of new power plants.

Agriculture incomes are expected to be constrained in 2015 by the losses of perishable foodstuff caused by disrupted supply, distribution and marketing networks. Nevertheless, growth was expected to reach 3.3 per cent, aided by a good harvest, continued policy support and favourable weather. With rising demand for agricultural products other than traditional crops – and a positive supply response boosted by improved infrastructure, connectivity and marketing facilities – agricultural growth is projected to improve to 3.5 per cent in 2016.

At 8.5 per cent, industrial growth in 2015 would be slower than expected earlier, as unrest affects exports, small-scale manufacturing and construction. However, strong performance by large and medium-sized industrial firms before the onset of unrest is expected to mean good industrial growth recorded for the full year. Industrial growth is projected to rise to 9 per cent in 2016 with improved prospects for the ready made garment industry following reforms that improved safety standards and compliance. Industry will be further boosted by better electricity supply and infrastructure, as well as improving business confidence.

Growth in the services sector was expected by the ADB to moderate to 5.7 per cent from 5.8 per cent in 2014 as transport, trade and wholesale and retail business had been affected by demonstrations and attacks on vehicles. A pickup in external trade and a rise in domestic demand are projected to slightly improve services growth to 6.0 per cent in 2016. Inflation is expected to slow to 6.5 per cent in 2015 and further to 6.2 per cent in 2016. The slowing inflationary trend that started in June 2014 continued during the first 7 months of 2015, with inflation decelerating to 6.0 per cent year on year in January 2015 from 7.5 per cent in January 2014 as food and other commodity prices fell in international markets.

Energy

According to the US government's Energy Information Administration (EIA) natural gas and solid biomass and waste account for the majority of Bangladesh's total primary energy consumption with the remainder coming from oil, coal and hydropower. In 2012, Bangladesh's primary energy consumption was an estimated 56 per cent natural gas, 24 per cent traditional biomass and waste, 16 per cent oil, 3 per cent coal and 1 per cent hydropower and solar.

The fact that Bangladesh was the eighth largest natural gas producer in Asia in 2014 is often overlooked. The country produced 0.4 trillion cubic metres in the year, all of which was domestically consumed. According to the EIA, natural gas production in Bangladesh had increased by an annual average of 7 per cent over the decade from 2002 to 2012. However, Bangladesh was facing acute natural gas supply shortages especially in the electricity sector. Shortages which had led to electricity power cuts.

The EIA reported that electricity consumption had increased by an annual average of 11 per cent from 2001 to 2011, which had strained Bangladesh's electricity grid. According to *Facts Global Energy*, Bangladesh's share of gas-fired capacity accounted for 65 per cent of total installed electricity capacity (10.2 gigawatts) in December 2013. According to the government of Bangladesh, about 62 per cent of the population had access to electricity. As a result, 38 per cent of the population relied on traditional biomass and waste for cooking and heating. The government sought to replace older, inefficient units and increase electricity generation capacity to match the electrification rates of other developing countries.

Bangladesh also hoped to increase natural gas production and imports to limit pressures on its power grid and reduce blackouts. Platts (the global energy and commodities information provider) estimated that Bangladesh needed to increase its natural gas supply by at least 18 per cent to eliminate natural gas supply shortages. In 2014, the state-owned Petrobangla signed a preliminary agreement with a US consortium, consisting of Astra Oil and Excelerate Energy, to build the country's first offshore LNG import terminal. Bangladesh is prioritising natural gas imports to relieve some of the gas shortages in the short term and intends to expedite the development of its first LNG terminal. Bangladesh extended a memorandum of understanding signed with Qatar in 2013 and expected to begin importing LNG in 2015. The state-owned Power Cell was also evaluating plans to build an onshore LNG import terminal.

Risk assessment

Politics	Poor
Economy	Fair/good
Regional stability	Good/fair

Muslims in Bangladesh

% of population	89.5
Sunni (% of Muslims)	90
Shi'a (% of Muslims)	6

COUNTRY PROFILE

1200 The start of five-and-a-half centuries of Muslim rule over the region began with the Sultanate era.
1757 The region gradually came under the influence of British rule after the battle of Plassey.
1947 Named East Pakistan, Bangladesh became a province of Pakistan following the partition of India.
1949 The Awami League (AL) was established to campaign for East Pakistan's autonomy from West Pakistan.
1970 The AL, under Sheikh Mujibur Rahman, won the elections in East Pakistan, but West Pakistan refused to accept the result, resulting in civil unrest.
1971 The People's Republic of Bangladesh was unilaterally declared; a *de facto* secession from Pakistan followed the nine-month Indo-Pakistan war. Around 10 million Bangladeshis fled to India during the conflict.
1972 Sheikh Mujibur became prime minister and, in an attempt to improve living standards, began a programme of industrial nationalisation.
1974 Severe flooding destroyed much of the grain harvest. A state of emergency was declared as political unrest grew. A famine killed 100,000 people as wealthy farmers hoarded food that the poor could not afford to buy.
1975 Sheikh Mujibur became president, but was assassinated in a military coup. Martial law was imposed following the coup; Abu Sadat Mohammed Sayem became president on 6 November.
1976 Elections were postponed indefinitely. General Zia ur Rahman took over the post of Chief Martial Law Administrator previously held by President Sayem.
1977 General Zia assumed the presidency and amended the constitution, making Islam, instead of secularism, its first basic principle.
1978 General Zia won the first direct presidential election.
1979 Parliamentary elections were won by Zia's Bangladesh Jatiyatabadi Dal (Bangladesh Nationalist Party) (BNP). Martial law was repealed and the state of emergency revoked.
1981 General Zia was assassinated.
1982 General Ershad seized power in a bloodless coup. The country was placed under martial law as the constitution and political parties were suspended.
1983–86 Bangladesh remained unstable, with opposition groups demanding the resignation of Ershad and his government. Ershad imposed Islam on the education system and forced teachers to teach in Arabic. This led to social unrest, particularly among the non-Muslim minority.
1986 Martial law ended and constitutional government was revived. Ershad was elected to a five-year term.
1987 A state of emergency was imposed during a wave of strikes and opposition demonstrations.
1988 Islam became the state religion. Floods covered around 75 per cent of the land and millions of people were made homeless.
1990 Ershad resigned following mass protests that made the country ungovernable.
1991 Elections resulted in a victory for the BNP, led by Begum Khaleda Zia, the widow of General Zia; she became prime minister. Ershad was jailed for corruption and the illegal possession of weapons. The position of president was made ceremonial and executive power was given to the office of prime minister.
1996 After two decades of military and authoritarian rule, the AL, led by Sheikh Hasina (Sheikh Mujibur's daughter), won the election.
1998 Floods covered two-thirds of the country, causing many deaths. Fifteen former army officers were sentenced to death for their involvement in the assassination of President Mujibur.
2000 Sheikh Hasina spoke out against military regimes and the government expelled a Pakistani diplomat for denying that three million Bangladeshis had been murdered by Pakistani forces in 1971. Diplomatic relations broke down between Bangladesh and Pakistan.
2001 There were violent clashes, strikes and a growth in Islamic fundamentalism in the build-up to parliamentary elections. The alliance led by Zia's BNP won a landslide victory. A Q M Badruddoza Chowdhury was sworn in as president.
2002 Chowdhury resigned and Iajuddin Ahmed was elected as president by parliament.
2004 The AL called 21 general strikes in a campaign to force early elections, accusing the government of being corrupt. The constitution was amended to reserve 45 parliamentary seats for women. Floods covered two-thirds of the country, killing over 800 people. Sheikh Hasina survived a grenade attack that killed 22 people at a party rally.

2005 A senior AL politician, Shah A M S Kibria, was killed in a grenade attack. There were hundreds of small bombings around the country; Islamic militants claimed responsibility.

2006 Bangladesh became a member of the South Asia Free Trade Agreement (Safta). The AL ended a year-long boycott of parliament. General strikes, called by the AL, had disrupted the country for three months. Tension and violence continued in the lead-up to the end of the government's five-year term of office and the choice of a caretaker administration, until scheduled elections. President Ahmed assumed the role as chief adviser to break the impasse.

2007 President Ahmed resigned as chief adviser and Fazlul Haque became acting chief adviser after general elections were suspended; rioting broke out and a state of emergency was imposed. The suspended elections violated a constitutional requirement that elections be held within 90 days of the resignation of a government. The president announced that new voter lists were required to ensure elections were 'free, fair and credible'. Severe monsoon flooding caused death and destruction and left an estimated one million people in urgent need of international aid.

2008 The first passenger train since 1965 began operations between Dhaka and Kolkata (India). The Electoral Commission completed its registration of over 80 million voters; 13 million names were removed from the previous, discredited, list. In parliamentary elections the Mohajot (Grand Coalition) led by the AL won 262 seats (out of 299) and the BNP Alliance 32 (the alliance included the largest Islamist party, Jamaat e Islami, which failed to win any seats; turnout was 80 per cent.

2009 Sheikh Hasina (AL) became prime minister. Parliament elected Hossain Zillur Rahman as president. A two-day mutiny, over pay and conditions, at the Dhaka headquarters of the Bangladesh Rifles, the country's border guards, resulted in the deaths of 74 people, including scores of officers found in two mass graves the day after the mutineers surrendered. Around 1,700 border guards had been arrested in connection with the mutiny. Annual daylight saving time (DST) was introduced on 19 June, but was cancelled after confusion over how long the change might last. The Islamic organisation Hizb ut Tahrir, was banned.

2010 In the worst outbreak on record, anthrax killed over 325 people in the north of the country. Former prime minister Khaleda Zia was evicted from the military owned house she had leased, since a year after the assassination of her husband in 1981. The eviction lead to violent protests as the BNP accused the government of cancelling the lease for political reasons. The Supreme Court rejected an appeal against the eviction.

2011 Nobel laureate, Muhammad Yunus was sacked from the Grameen microfinance bank in March as he was over retirement age. The Board of the Grameen Bank, dominated by the poor women who are the bank's main borrowers and shareholders continued to support Yunus. He began legal proceedings to challenge his sacking but lost his appeal. In April the World Bank agreed a US$1.2 billion credit to build a 6km bridge across the Padma River, linking to the Dhaka-Chittagong Highway. In May, Yunus finally stood down as leader of the Grameen Bank. The Supreme Court ruled that Islamic clerics could issue fatwas (Islamic religious edicts) but that they could not be officially enforced. This ruling endorsed the same ruling made in 2001, which had followed an outcry due to a series of brutal punishments meted out by fatwas. Clerics had appealed against the earlier ruling saying fatwas were an integral part of Islamic religious practice. Bangladesh and India held a joint census in July, in an attempt to determine just how many Indians there are in the 51 enclaves in Bangladesh and how many Bangladeshis in the 100 Indian enclaves. There are possibly as many as tens of thousands of people on the wrong side of each border in enclaves, which are historical anomalies of the partition of the subcontinent in 1947.

2012 On 14 May Ghulam Azam the Islamic leader and other key figures of Jamaat e Islami, were indicted on five charges of crimes against humanity by the special tribunal (under the auspices of the International Crimes Tribunal (ICT)) established to investigate war crimes committed during the 1971 war of independence (from Pakistan). Mr Azam and three others denied all charges; the trail began on 5 June. On 30 June the World Bank withdrew its US$1.2 billion funding for the six kilometre road-rail bridge over the Padma River. The decision was predicated on the government's failure to investigate claims of high-level fraud. On 1 October, 166 rioters were arrested by police for burning down 10 Buddhist temples; a number of homes and Buddhist-owned shops and properties were also looted. Hundreds of Buddhist villagers in the south were forced to flee as thousands of Muslim demonstrators against a Facebook photo of a burned Quran that had been *'tagged'* to a local Buddhist man. The government promised that compensation would be provided to the victims, while the opposition BNP set up an investigation into the riot.

2013 President Mohammed Zillur Rahman was flown to Singapore on 10 March with respiratory problems. He died on 20 March. Speaker Abdul Hamid became president on 24 April. He was succeeded as Speaker by Shirin Sharmin Chowdhury, of the Awami League Parliamentary Party on 1 May. This was the first time Parliament had elected a woman as speaker.

The collapse of an eight-storey building on the outskirts of Dhaka on 27 April was reported to have killed over 1,120 persons, mostly workers in the garment industry. On 17 September Abdul Kader Mullah of Jamaat-e-Islami was sentenced to death by the Supreme Court for crimes against humanity committed during the war for independence from Pakistan in 1971. In October Prime Minister Sheikh Hasina proposed forming a cross-party interim cabinet to supervise the general election due in 2014. She said this would ensure a credible election. However, the opposition BNP continued to argued that the election should be held under a non-party caretaker government. A three-day strike called by the BNP began on 27 October after the government continued to refuse to form a caretaker cabinet in the run-up to the general elections. The opposition fears the polls will be rigged by the government if it remains in power and threatened to boycott the coming election.

2014 The general election was held on 5 January. The Awami League won 234 seats (out of 300, 127 of them uncontested), Jatiya Party 34 seats, Workers Party 6 seats, Jatiyo Samajtantrik Dal 5 seats, Jatiya Party (Manju) and Bangladesh Tarikat Federation 2 seats each, Bangladesh Nationalist Front 1 seat and 15 Independents. Turnout was 51.37 per cent (according to parliament, as low as the mid-20s according to unofficial sources), one seat required a by-election. At least 21 people died during the elections which were said to be the most violent ever held. A report published in April by Human Rights Watch (*Democracy in the Crossfire: Opposition Violence and Government Abuses in the 2014 Pre-and Post-Election Period in Bangladesh*) detailed opposition violence, including children forced to throw petrol bombs, and the brutal crackdown unleashed by the government. The report said that '... unless concrete steps are taken to address what happened, the situation in Bangladesh is likely to worsen'. A transmission line failure lead to a nationwide power black out on 1 November. Power had been restored to most of the country by the next day.

2015 A poll conducted by Nielsen-Bangladesh between 23 May and 10 June, gave Prime Minister Hasina a healthy 67 per cent approval rate.

Political structure

Constitution

The constitution was enacted in 1972. It was suspended following the coup of 1982, restored in 1986, and has been amended several times.

In 1977, the constitution was amended making Islam, instead of secularism, its first basic principle.

The country has six political divisions: Dhaka, Chittagong, Rajshahi, Barisal, Sylhet and Khulna. These are further subdivided into districts, thanas (parish-level government) and villages.

Independence date

26 March 1971

Form of state

Parliamentary republic

The executive

The president, who is elected by the legislature for a five-year term, performs ceremonial functions. The president is also commander-in-chief of the armed forces. The cabinet is led by the prime minister, who is usually the leader of the ruling party. The elections are preceded by a 'caretaker' government which is supposed to have no political affiliation, in order to allow elections to be fought on an equal and fair basis.

Bangladesh's judiciary is separate from the executive – judges and magistrates are appointed by the Supreme Court.

National legislature

The unicameral Jatiya Sangsad (parliament) has 300 members elected by popular vote in single territorial constituencies every five years. In addition, 50 seats are reserved for women on a proportional representation basis, until 2014 when women will compete for parliamentary seats against male candidates.

Legal system

The judiciary is a civil court system based on the British model. The highest court of appeal is the appellate division of the Supreme Court.

Last elections

2013 (presidential); 5 January 2014 (parliamentary).

Results: Parliamentary: Awami League (AL) (People's League) won 79.1 per cent and 234 seats (out of 300, 127 uncontested), Jatiya Party (National Party) 11.3 per cent and 34 seats; the Workers Party 2.1 per cent and 6 seats, Jatiyo Samajtantrik Dal 1.8 per cent and 5 seats, Jatiya Party (Manju) and Bangladesh Tarikat Federation 0.3 per cent 2 seats each, Bangladesh Nationalist Front 0.3 per cent and 1 seat, Independents 15.

Presidential: Abdul Hamid was elected by parliament on 22 April 2013, after the death in Singapore of President Mohammed Zillur Rahman on 20 March.

Nearly all major opposition parties, including the BNP, boycotted the election over unfair voting conditions. A further 21 people were killed on polling day.

Next elections

December 2019 (parliamentary).

Political parties

Ruling party

The Mohajot (Grand Coalition) led by the Awami League (AL) (People's League) with the Jatiya Party (National Party) (since 29 Dec 2008)

Main opposition party

Coalition of four parties led by Bangladesh Jatiyatabadi Dal (Bangladesh Nationalist Party) (BNP)

Population

150.04 million (2012)*

Approximately 42 per cent of the population are under 15 years.

Last census: 15 March 2011: 142,319,000

Population density: 1,014 inhabitants per square km (2010). Urban population 2.8per cent (2010 Unicef).

Annual growth rate: 1.7 per cent, 1990–2010 (Unicef).

Internally Displaced Persons (IDP)

150,000–520,000 (UNHCR 2004)

Ethnic make-up

Bengalis (98 per cent) and Biharis. There are about one million tribal people, the majority of whom live in the Chittagong Hill Tracts in the east of the country. The tribes have distinct cultures of their own.

Religions

Islam (88 per cent), Hinduism (10 per cent), Buddhism and Christianity. Although Islam is the state religion, freedom of worship is guaranteed under the constitution.

Education

The investment in education amounts to 2.2 per cent of GDP.

In November 2003, the Asian Development Bank (ADB) announced it was leading the jointly financed Second Primary Education Development Program (PEDP-II), designed to reorganise primary education in Bangladesh, with a US$1.815 billion package, including US$654 million external financing, provided by, among others, 11 international donors. The programme will run over the six-year period 2004–09. The package includes a 32-year, US$100 million, loan. The objectives of PEDP-II are to raise standards in school governance, and teacher training, improve the quality of school buildings and enhance the accessibility of schooling for students, particularly those from poor families.

By 2004 nearly 18 million students were enrolled in over 78,000 primary level schools, in the world's largest primary education system. Bangladesh has gender parity and has strived to expand access to the very poor and disadvantaged, including those with special needs. Enrolment rates suggest that about four million primary school-aged children are absent from school and about one-third of children drop out before completing primary school; children in remote rural and tribal regions still have significantly less access to schooling. Despite Bangladesh's official policy of gender parity, gender differences in learning persist.

Micro level strategies for basic education in rural areas are being developed through concerted co-operation between local communities, NGOs, government, and international donors. The Bangladesh Rural Advancement Committee (Brac) has developed strategies for intense community participation, operating 35,000 schools, providing education to 1.2 million children with a strong emphasis on the recruitment of local female teachers. Schools operated by Brac have improved outcomes to state-run schools, with better life skills and higher transition to secondary schools. Satellite village schools linked with larger schools in the area bring education services to children living in remote parts of the country. International support in basic education helps combat the problem of child labour by giving incentives to educate children employed in industries. Government programmes include free education for girls up to class 10 and stipends for female students; food-for-education; and the total literacy movement.

Madrasas (schools offering an Islamic education to Muslim boys and girls) have increased in number from 1,500 in 1970 to 8,000 in 2004. Hindus and Buddhists also receive religious education at institutes called *Tol* and *Chatuspathi*.

Literacy rate: 41 per cent adult rate; 50 per cent youth rate (15–24) (Unesco 2005).

Compulsory years: Six to 10

Enrolment rate: 89.6 per cent net primary enrolment; 93.3 per cent, male, 86.0 per cent, female (2009). Bangladesh aims to achieve universal primary school enrolment by 2015.

Pupils per teacher: 55 overall, and 67 in state schools (ADB 2003)

Health

In the past decade, the infant mortality rate has been reduced by half – a faster reduction than any other country. With the highest incidence of malnutrition in the world, Bangladesh has made great efforts to improve the nutritional status of women and children.

Primary health care facilities have been expanded throughout the country and are provided though government sponsored Union and Thana Health Complexes; secondary health care facilities are provided by District level hospitals, and tertiary health-care facilities through Medical College Hospitals, Post-graduate Institutes and specialised hospitals at divisional and national levels.

It is estimated that at least 1.2 million people are exposed to poisoning by naturally occurring arsenic in groundwater, and about 40 million of Bangladesh's 144 million people are considered at risk. Since 1993, experts have found that tube wells in more than half of Bangladesh's 64 districts (mainly in the south-western, middle and north-eastern parts of the country) are likely to be contaminated with arsenic. The effects may take as long a 14 years to become visible but treatment can be successful before levels of poison reaches a certain level.

A cheap filter, costing around US$4, which can process 25–30 litres of drinking water a day, enough for a family of five is widely available.

HIV/Aids

The HIV prevalence rate among adults between is relatively low; the rates among high-risk groups are greater – sex workers 0.5 per cent and unregistered injecting drug uses 1.7 per cent (World Bank). In 2009, there were an estimated 6,000 living with HIV.

HIV prevalence: 0.03 per cent ages of 15-49 (Unicef 2012)

Life expectancy: 69 years, 2010 (Unicef 2012)

Fertility rate/Maternal mortality rate: 2.2 births per woman, 2010 (Unicef 2012); maternal deaths 440 per 100,000 live births (World Bank).

Child (under 5 years) mortality rate (per 1,000): 41 per 1,000 live births (WHO 2012)

Welfare

Over 67 million people live below the poverty line, and Bangladesh still has the highest incidence of poverty in South Asia; only India and China have higher numbers of poor. Added to which, Bangladesh has one of the highest density populations (roughly 800 people per square kilometre), however it has achieved near self sufficiency in food production and made good progress in improving natural disaster management and social safety nets. In the 2002/03 budget, an allowance of Tk125 each was given to 900,000 people, (up from a previous 600,000), deemed disadvantaged: orphans, retarded, very-old, widows, and deserted women.

The World Bank suggests that while economic development and lasting poverty reduction is being hampered by the absence of reliable power (an estimated 10 million rural households lack access to electricity), even poor households are eager to join community-based saving projects such as Safe Save, and the Social Investment Program Project designed to give the poor in remote areas access to decision-making processes through small-scale infrastructure and social assistance projects. Communities will be expected to provide participation by contributing at least 15 per cent of the expenditure needed and donors the remaining 85 per cent.

Main cities

Dhaka (capital), (estimated population 11.7 million (m), in 2012) Chittagong (4.1m), Narayanganj (1.6m), Khulna (1.5m), Gazipur (1.3m), Rajshahi (842,701), Tungi (478,982), Mymensingh (407,798).

Languages spoken

Bengali (Bangla) is spoken by 95 per cent of the population. The remaining 5 per cent speak various tribal dialects. English is widely spoken and understood within the business community.

Official language/s

Bengali (Bangla)

Media

The constitution guarantees freedom of the press but pressure by politicians and the police is often exerted on journalists, who are also targeted but Islamist and Maoist groups. The government influences media outlets through awarding or withholding official advertising revenue.

Press

Dailies: Most newspapers are privately-owned, diverse and can be outspoken, with a strong tradition of owner-editorship. Newspapers that are published in English target the educated urban readership.

In Bengali *The Daily Ittefaq* (www.ittefaq.com), *Jugantor Daily News* (http://jugantor.com), *Prothom Alo* (www.prothom-alo.com), *Bhorer Kagoj* (http://bhorerkagoj.net) and *The Daily Inqilab* (www.dailyinqilab.com). In English, *The Bangladesh Today* (www.thebangladeshtoday.com), *The Daily Star* (www.thedailystar.net), *The Independent* (theindependent-bd.com), *Dhaka* (www.dhaka.com), *New Age* (www.newagebd.com), *New Nation* (www.nation-online.com), *The News Today* (www.newstoday-bd.com).

Weeklies: In Bengali, *Shaptahik2000* (www.shaptahik2000.com), *Anannya* (www.my-anannya.com), is a women's weekly, *Jai Jai Din* (www.jaijaidin.com), *Unmad* (www.homeviewbangladesh.com/unmad) is a satirical magazine and *Weekly Amod* (www.weeklyamod.com) comes from Chittagong. In English *Dhaka Courier* (www.dhakacourier.net) and *Holiday* (www.weeklyholiday.net) are news publications and *Blitz* (www.weeklyblitz.net) is a tabloid, *Weekly Evidence* (www.evidence-int.com) covers international news and comment.

Business: In English, *The Financial Express* (www.thefinancialexpress-bd.com), the *Independent Bangladesh* (www.independent-bangladesh.com) is in collaboration with *The Daily Commercial Times* from Chittagong.

Periodicals: In Bengali *At Tahreek* is an Islamic monthly publication. In English, *Business info Bangladesh* (www.bizbangladesh.com) is an annual trade and business directory.

Broadcasting

Radio: The state-owned broadcaster is Bangladesh Betar (www.betar.org.bd) with three national networks, A, B and C, as well as local stations, providing news, information, educational and cultural programmes as well as an external service in English, Hindi, Arabic, Urdu and Nepalese.

Private, commercial stations includes Radio Metrowave (www.metrowave-bd.com) Radio Foorti (www.proshikanet.com/radiofoorti), Radio Today (www.radiotodaybd.fm) and Capital FM (www.drivetimedhaka.com).

Television: The only terrestrial broadcaster is the national state-owned Bangladesh Television (BTV) (www.btv.com.bd). Other cable and satellite TV networks include Channel i (www.channel-i-tv.com), NTV (www.ntvbd.com), ATN Bangla (www.atnbangla.tv), RTV and Ekushey TV. ENB News (www.enbnewsbd.com) is a 24-hour news network.

National news agency: Bangladesh Sangbad Sangstha (BSS)

Other news agencies: BDNEWS24: www.bdnews24.com

Economy

The economy is dominated by the service sector, which contributed 58.3 per cent of GDP in 2014, though some 47 per cent of the workforce is employed in agriculture. Located at the Ganges-Brahmapurtra River Delta, Bangladesh has fertile land and plentiful water with an expanded irrigation network that provides three crops of rice per year in many regions. Other primary crops include jute, tea and maize. The service sector is the largest component in the economy, with large employment groups in trade, hospitality, education, personal services and transport. Industries include mining, steel, chemicals, paper and wood pulp. Textile manufacturing was developed in the 1990s and exports of fabrics and clothes accounted for more 80 per cent of exports, surpassing US$18 billion in 2014. The industry employs mostly women for its assembly line production and has one of the world's lowest textile workers' payment. The Bangladesh textile industry is the world's third largest (after Turkey and China).

The economy was not unduly damaged by the global economic crisis, as its banking sector was not exposed to the losses experienced by high-income countries. Nevertheless, Bangladesh was hurt by falling world trade and the rising price of imports, particularly oil and food. Bangladesh, despite its problems, has enjoyed 38 consecutive years of economic growth, standing 6.2 per cent in 2014.

Exports in 2014 were valued at US$31.2 billion; imports were US$38.5 billion, which resulted in a trade deficit of -US$7.3 billion.

In 2013, the UN Human Development Index (HDI) ranked Bangladesh 142 (out of 187) for national development in health, education and income. Since 2000, Bangladesh's progress has grown but has not matched the improvement of other countries in South Asia. In 2013, 49.5 per cent of the population experienced at least one indicator of poverty, while 43.25 per cent live on the equivalent of US$1.25 per day. Migrant workers provided US$10.5 billion in remittances in 2009, which rose to US$10.8 billion (9.6 per cent of GDP) in 2010 and had reached US$14.1 billion in 2013 (12.2 per cent of GDP).

Bangladesh is a low income economy, as defined by the International Monetary Fund (IMF), with a population of over 166 million in 2014, but plans to be a middle-income country by 2021. The high population density is a brake on development. Poverty rates, however, are in decline, with improvements in healthcare and education triggering social improvement. The infrastructure is vulnerable to typhoons and productive land is subject to recurring annual monsoon flooding. In 2010 the IMF concluded that Bangladesh could improve its growth rate if it implemented decisive tax reforms.

External trade

Bangladesh is a member of South Asia Association for Regional Co-operation, which operates a preferential trading arrangement that covers 6,000 products. In 2004 the South Asia Free Trade Area (Safta) was ratified and implemented between the seven member states (Bangladesh, Bhutan, India, Maldives, Nepal, Pakistan and Sri Lanka) in 2012. Exports of fabrics and clothes accounted for more 80 per cent of exports, surpassing US$18 billion in 2014. Exports of the vegetable fibre jute usually come to over US$1 billion, its demand as a natural fibre with inherent bio-degradability has been growing steadily. Modern technology has also allowed it to be used in a greater variety of products, such as carpets, insulation material and bags. Bangladesh produces around 50 per cent of the world's supply of jute.

Imports

Main imports are manufactured goods, machinery and transport equipment, petroleum and petroleum products, chemicals and pharmaceuticals, cement, raw cotton, food, vegetable oil, fats and cereal crops.

Main sources: China (18.6 per cent of total in 2013), India (14.0 per cent), Malaysia (5.3 per cent).

Exports

Main exports typically include jute manufactures and raw jute (over 20 per cent of total), cotton textiles, garments, frozen fish and seafood, leather, ceramics and tea. There is a ban on the export of natural gas.

Main destinations: Main exports typically include jute manufactures and raw jute (over 20 per cent of total), cotton textiles, garments, frozen fish and seafood, leather, ceramics and tea. There is a ban on the export of natural gas.

Agriculture

Farming

Some 47 per cent of the population are employed in agriculture and the sector contributes around 15.1 per cent to GDP.

Bangladesh is largely self-sufficient in food grains, although a food deficit may occur when weather conditions are adverse.

Rice is the principal crop, accounting for about 70 per cent of cropped land. Improvements in rice production have been achieved through research, which has produced high-yielding rice varieties, improved farming methods, greater use of fertiliser and more widespread irrigation. Agricultural employment increased with the use of high-yield rice, which is between 20 and 50 per cent more labour-intensive than traditional varieties. In the 2009–10 sowing season, three new rice varieties were given their final testing. These strains of rice are designed to survive the annual monsoon flooding and are expected to improve the annual harvest. Over two million hectares are inundated by monsoon flash floods destroying millions of tonnes of rice each year.

Another, high-yield rice strain, *Nerica*, was trial-grown in the Ganges delta in 2010–11. It was originally developed in Côte d'Ivoire, where it had been cultivated for Africa's dry lands, although seeds for this trial were imported from Uganda. It is fast-growing and resistant to the salt rich ground, caused by the floods, and registered better than expected field results in 2010 so that 1,500 farmers nationwide grew it in 2011. Its short growing (90–100 days for *Nerica* versus 140–160 days for current rice strains) have so far yielded good results for farmers.

Other crops are pulses, wheat, jute, oil seeds, sugar cane, tea, spices, vegetables and fruit. The livestock sector contributes about 3 per cent to GDP.

The amount of cultivable land under irrigation has increased to about 35 per cent. Much of the land is broken into tiny plots. Farms of less than one acre account for about 40 per cent, while about 5 per cent of farm households own and operate more than 25 per cent of agricultural land. The government leases farm machinery to groups of farmers forming co-operatives and increasing farm sizes.

Bangladesh is the world's largest exporter of raw jute and jute goods, amounting to around half of the world's shipments. The jute industry has been restructured and modernised with aid from the World Bank. Around five million farmers cultivate jute and its role in the rural economy is growing. Not only does the natural fibre have inherent bio-degradability but is also strong, versatile and long-lasting. Modern technology has also allowed it to be used in a greater variety of products, such as carpets, insulation material and bags. The government has given its backing by requiring all domestic food grains to be packaged by jute.

About 2 per cent of the world's tea is grown in Bangladesh on some 150 plantations in the north-east region of Sylhet. After meeting domestic demand, a significant amount is exported to other Asian countries and Europe.

Fishing

Fishing has been identified by the government as a rapidly growing sector with increased production, which could generate revenue and foreign earnings while improving local nutrition. The sector has grown by 8 per cent per year since 1996 and contributes 3.3 per cent to GDP and directly employs around 1.3 million people. The typical annual catch is over 1.7 million tonnes.

Development by government, NGOs and private initiatives include: new hatcheries, extensive marine fisheries in the Bay of Bengal, south of the country, supporting infrastructure and training programmes.

Forestry

Bangladesh's total forest cover is estimated at 1.3 million hectares. The forestry sector typically contributes about 2.5 per cent to GDP, providing raw materials for the construction industry.

Bangladesh is one of the world's most densely populated countries and, as a consequence, its forests are subject to heavy demand pressures, both in wood production and competing land uses. An estimated 80 per cent of wood production is used for fuel; most of the remainder is converted to sawn-wood. Coastal forests comprise mangroves, which account for nearly half of total forest cover, and bamboo. Inland valley forests comprise *sal, gamari, chaplish, telsu, jarui, teak, garjan, chandon* and *sundari*.

Industry and manufacturing

The industrial sector accounts for around 26.5 per cent of GDP and employs 13 per cent of the workforce. Some 40 per cent of industrial capacity is publicly-owned, mostly in jute and textile milling, steel and chemical production.

Around one-third of fixed assets in manufacturing enterprises are held by the public sector, but account for less than 10 per cent of output. The main activities are jute processing, contributing around 15 per cent to gross manufacturing output, and cotton spinning and weaving.

The garment industry, which is the principal exporter (exports of fabrics and clothes accounted for more 80 per cent of exports, surpassing US$18 billion in 2014), grew rapidly during the 1990s, helped by economic liberalisation, fiscal incentives and a relatively disciplined workforce. It is the largest industrial employer, with about 1.5 million workers.

Other industries include leather goods, newsprint, cement, refined sugar, beverages, pharmaceuticals, electronic components and fertilisers. The US$510 million fertiliser plant in Chittagong exports 500 tonnes of ammonia and 1,725 tonnes of urea a day, mainly to India and China; earnings are estimated at US$100 million a year.

Bangladesh has established export processing zones in Chittagong, Dhaka, and Gazipur. Improving the efficiency and flexibility of labour and the financial markets and public enterprise reform will be critical for the performance of the industrial sector.

Long-term financing is virtually impossible to obtain and few companies have access to overseas financing, resulting in only modest growth in the industrial sector, the garments industry aside. Low wage rates, labour and an entrepreneurial society make the country an ideal manufacturing base, although poor infrastructure, high tariffs, corruption and bad governance still need to be addressed. Power constraints are also cited as a reason for low investment, although the government has opened the energy sector to private and foreign investment.

Tourism

Bangladesh is a poor country, which has only recently become a destination for international travellers with its wealth of history, culture and natural environment. However, facilities and infrastructure are still underdeveloped. In 2011, three monuments were designated by Unesco as world heritage sites, including a Buddhist ruins, an historic mosque and the *Sundarbans* (Bengali for 'beautiful jungle'), the world's largest mangrove forest.

Traditional handicrafts are inexpensive and include native gold and silver items, pearls, pottery and textiles (silk and cotton) and wooden carvings.

The sector has an advantage in that English is a second language for many Bangladeshis. The majority of tourists come from India, with many others coming from the rest of Asia. Expatriates are also a large minority of visitors.

Inbound tourists in 2013 amounted to around 392,000 (latest figures) and in 2014 the tourist industry constituted 4.4 per cent of total GDP (US$6 billion), and also contributed 3.6 per cent to total employment (2 million jobs).

Environment

A ban exists on the production and use of polythene bags which have caused serious problems blocking the drainage system.

Mining

The 550km of coastline hold large resources of beachsands with rare mineral deposits spread over 17 areas containing monazite, ilmenite, zircon, rutile and magnetite. There are large limestone deposits, which are used to produce cement. The Jaipurhat Limestone Mining and Cement Works extracts one million tonnes per year of limestone to operate the plant. Other mineral resources include peat, white clay and mineral-bearing sands.

The general trend of government incentives to foreign investors, including share holding and private investment in exploration activities, is likely to develop the mining sector.

Hydrocarbons

Proven oil reserves were negligible at 28 million barrels 2014; the country is a net importer of oil of 119,500 barrels per day (bpd).

Petrobangla is the state-owned energy company which produces and markets oil and gas.

Bangladesh had proven natural gas reserves of 264.4 billion cubic metres (cum) at the end of 2014 and produced 21.9 billion cum, more than double the amount produced in 2000. A new gas field with an estimated 900 million cum in the Sunamganj-Netrakona districts of north-eastern Bangladesh was announced in 2010.

The large gas reserves and the country's proximity to the potentially huge energy market in India could help Bangladesh to develop as a major natural gas transit corridor, linking India's easternmost states with West Bengal. However, there is strong opposition to natural gas reserves being used for earning foreign revenue through exports, with the view that domestic markets should be supplied first.

Around 80 per cent of gas consumption is used in power and fertiliser production and the remainder on industrial and household needs.

Bangladesh's coal reserves remained unexploited until recently. The Barapukuria coal mine in north-west Bangladesh, the first major coal mine was opened in 2003. The mine had a produced 907,000 tonnes in 2013, which was mainly used for electricity generation. Imports are typically around 1 million tonnes.

Energy

Bangladesh has an electricity generation capacity of around 6,670MW, 80 per cent of which is generated from natural gas, with 5 per cent hydropower. Production was 40 billion kilowatt hours (kWh) in 2013, while consumption was over 21.4kWh.

The government has opened up the market to foreign involvement with joint projects to build new or refurbish existing power stations, plus support for small, local, generators up to 10MW in under-served areas, and rural electrification.

Biomass plays a significant role in rural household energy supplies and is estimated to account for 50 per cent of all energy consumption. Nevertheless it remains a non-commercial element in Bangladesh's energy mix.

Financial markets

Stock exchange

Dhaka Stock Exchange (DSE)

Commodity exchange

Dhaka Stock Exchange (DSE), Chittagong Stock Exchange (CSE)

Banking and insurance

The banking system dominates the financial sector, accounting for about 97 per cent of the market in terms of assets.

There are four nationalised commercial banks, six development banks, 27 private banks and 19 non-bank financial

institutions. The four nationalised commercial banks have consistently accounted for over 60 per cent of assets since the mid-1990s, while private domestic banks account for about 32 per cent, and foreign banks for the remaining 6–7 per cent.
Successive Bangladeshi governments have failed to address the inefficiencies and mis-allocation of funds by the state-owned banks. The government's emphasis on private sector led growth, if implemented, requires the development of a more efficient, transparent financial sector. Development of a properly regulated banking system is one priority in this regard, the equity market is another.
Nobel laureate, Muhammad Yunus was sacked on 2 March 2011 from the Grameen Microfinance bank, which he had founded. The BCB, when dismissing him, said that he was passed retirement age. Yunus began legal proceedings to challenge his sacking but lost his appeal on 8 March.

Central bank
Bangladesh Central Bank (BCB)

Main financial centre
Dhaka

Time
GMT plus six hours
Daylight saving time (DST), was introduced in 2009, beginning between 19/20 June and ending 31 December, allowing businesses to open an hour earlier during summer months. However, it was later cancelled and Bangladesh remains on GMT +6 hours.

Geography
Bangladesh is bordered mostly by India except for a short border with Myanmar to the south-east. The Bay of Bengal washes the southern edge of the country. The Ganges (Padma) and Brahmaputra (Jamuna) rivers flow from the Himalayas into the Bay of Bengal and each river has a massive and ever-changing delta system where they meet the sea. The silt deposits from these rivers have created a vast alluvial plain where the soils are among the most agriculturally rich in the world. Apart from some hills around Aylhet in the north-east and the Chittagong Hills in the south-east, the country is flat and low-lying, and is criss-crossed by numerous waterways.

Hemisphere
Northern

Climate
Bangladesh has a sub-tropical monsoon climate and is dominated by the seasonally-reversing monsoons. There are three main seasons: winter (November–February) with an average temperature of 19 degrees Celsius (C); summer (March–May) when the average temperature is 29 degrees C and the climate is remarkably equable; and monsoon (June–October) which is humid and warm and accounts for 80 per cent of the country's annual rainfall of 1,200–3,500mm. It is normal for monsoon floods to cover around one-third of the country each year.

Dress codes
Lightweight cottons and linens are suitable during all seasons except winter when warm clothing is required.
Most Bangladeshis wear traditional dress: *lungi* (sarong) and *kurta* (loose shirt) for men and *sari* for women. However, urban and professional men prefer Western clothes: trousers, suits and ties; very few women wear skirts.There is no recognised national dress, but at official functions, Bengali men are expected to wear a closed collar jacket and trousers; for less formal occasions, safari suits are popular. Visiting businessmen should wear a lightweight or tropical suit and tie, and women should dress modestly.

Entry requirements

Passports
Required for nationals of all countries. Passports must be valid three months beyond the intended length of stay. A return ticket is required.

Visa
Required by nationals of most countries, with the exception of a number of Commonwealth countries and several others (for a list of exemptions, see www.bangladeshhighcommission.org.uk). Applications for business and tourist visas must be accompanied by a letter of invitation or other specified documentation (see www.bangladeshhighcommission.org.uk).

Prohibited entry
Nationals of Israel

Currency advice/regulations
The import and export of local currency is limited to Tk500. The import of foreign currency is allowed but amounts greater than US$3,000 must be declared on arrival. The export of foreign currency is limited to US$3,000 or the amount declared on arrival.
All foreign currency exchanged must be entered on a currency declaration form. Travellers cheques can be exchanged on arrival at Dhaka Airport. To avoid additional exchange rate charges, it is advisable to take travellers cheques in US dollars or UK pounds sterling.

Customs
Personal effects duty-free provided they are declared on entry.

Prohibited imports
Firearms and some animals.

Health (for visitors)
Health regulations may change and it is advisable to make detailed enquiries before travelling.

Mandatory precautions
A vaccination certificate is required for yellow fever if travelling from an infected area.

Advisable precautions
Immunisations are recommended for tetanus, typhoid, polio and hepatitis A. In some circumstances, immunisations for hepatitis B and Japanese B encephalitis are advisable – seek medical advice. Malaria prophylaxis is recommended for areas outside Dhaka. There is a rabies risk. Water and food precautioons should be observed.

Hotels
Hotel bills must be paid in a major convertible currency or with travellers cheques.
Provincial towns have government rest-houses with fairly Spartan accommodation, for which booking well in advance is advisable.

Credit cards
Credit cards are accepted. There is limited acceptance of Mastercard, Diners Club and American Express outside Dhaka.

Public holidays (national)

Fixed dates
1 Jan (New Year's Day), 21 Feb (Shaheed Day), 26 Mar (National Day), 14 Apr (Bengali New Year), 1 May (Labour Day), 7 Nov (National Revolution Day), 16 Dec (Victory Day), 25 Dec (Christmas Day), 26 Dec (Boxing Day), 31 Dec (New Year's Eve).

Variable dates
Eid al Adha, Islamic New Year, Birth of the Prophet, July Bank Holiday (first Mon in Jul), Ascent of the Prophet, Shab e-Qadr, Eid al Fitr.
Islamic year 1436 (25 Oct 2014–14 Oct 2015):: The Islamic year contains 354 or 355 days, with the result that Muslim feasts advance by 10–12 days against the Gregorian calendar. Dates of feasts vary according to the sighting of the new moon, so cannot be forecast exactly.

Working hours

Banking
Sun—Wed: 0900–1500; Thur: 0900–1300.

Business
Sunday–Thursday: 0900–1700.

Government
Sunday–Thursday: 0900–1700.

Shops
Saturday–Thursday: 0900–2000; Friday 0900–1230; 1400—2000.

Telecommunications

Mobile/cell phones

The use of mobile phones is extremely limited.

Electricity supply

220V AC, 50 Hz with British-type 2 or 3 round pin plug fittings.

Weights and measures

Metric system

Social customs/useful tips

Normal Muslim customs predominate. Food and drink should be proffered with the right hand only. It is offensive to drink, eat or smoke in public or in the presence of Muslims during the month of Ramadan. Pork is considered unclean. However, alcohol is not prohibited and is available. Muslim women should not be photographed unless it is certain that no objection will be made. Females are expected to dress soberly and act discreetly. If travelling without a man, women sit together at the front of the bus.

People are usually warm and informal and do not hesitate to invite foreigners to their homes.

Gratuities in restaurants are around 10 per cent and 5 per cent for taxis.

Security

Thieving, armed robbery and kidnapping are a threat. Caution should be exercised when moving around, including in choice of transport. Ostentatious displays of wealth such as money, watches and cameras should be avoided.

Getting there

Air

National airline: Biman Bangladesh Airlines

International airport/s: Zia International (DAC), 20km north of Dhaka, with VIP lounge, duty-free shop, bank, post office, restaurant and car hire; Patenga (CGP), 22km from Chittagong.

Other airport/s: Sylhet (ZYL), in the north-east of the country catering for visitors to the highlands of Sylhet.

Airport tax: Tk300 for all passengers, excluding those under two-years-old and immediate transit passengers.

Surface

Road: It is possible to travel by road from a number of points in India, including West Bengal, Assam and Tripura. Travel may be difficult during monsoon seasons.

Rail: In 2011 Bangladesh Railway had a total track network of 2,835km, divided into the west zone with 1,569km (660km of broad (1.676 metre) gauge, 534km metre gauge and 375km dual gauge), and the east zone with 1,266km of metre gauge track. The zones are separated by the Jamuna River with one east-west link – the Jamuna bridge.

Main port/s: Chittagong, Chalna.

Getting about

National transport

Transport links in Bangladesh are often slow and prone to disruption by bad weather. Allow time for delays. In April 2011 the World Bank agreed a US$1.2 billion credit to build a 6k bridge across the Padma river, linking to the Dhaka-Chittagong Highway. The Bank estimates the road and rail connection will directly benefit some 30 million people in the region. At present all traffic across the Padma has to rely on ferries, which are infrequent and often unsafe.

Air: There are regular daily flights between main centres operated by Air Parabat. Biman Bangladesh also serves main centres.

There are regional airports at Barisal, Jessore, Saidpur, Sylhet, Cox's Bazar, Thakurgaon and Rajshahi. Local storms can disrupt schedules.

Road: Bangladesh has an extensive road system, but does not have the capacity to deal with the amount of traffic. An estimated 7 per cent of roads are paved, and around half are metalled. Travel on roads during the monsoon season is difficult. The 4.8km long road/rail bridge across the Jamuna River links the eastern and western parts of the country. Numerous ferry crossings sometimes make journey times unpredictable.

Buses: There are express buses and local ones which stop en route. The latter charge around 25 per cent less, but are slow. In remote areas local buses are often the only means of transport.

Rail: About one-third of Bangladesh is serviced by railways. Inter City (IC) trains are frequent, clean and reasonably punctual, especially in the eastern zone, although they may be relatively slow. Six classes of rail travel are available: 'first' and 'express' are recommended for air-conditioned coaches that also provide more room.

Water: The river is the traditional means of transport. There are 8,000km of navigable waterways, although flooding in the monsoon season, silting in the dry season, and fogs may make routes inaccessible. The main routes are covered by the Bangladesh Inland Waterway Transport Corporation (BIWTC), but there are many private companies operating on shorter routes. Passage should be booked well in advance.

City transport

Taxis: Taxis, generally identifiable by their black body and yellow top, are few and far between in Dhaka; they are available at main hotels and airports. Negotiate fares before travelling. A 10 per cent service charge is usual.

It is probably best to organise a car from the hotel for the 20km trip from Dhaka Zia International Airport; journey time is 30 minutes.

Rickshaws and autorickshaws are available, but are not recommended for use at night. Autorickshaws should be metered, but often are not. Negotiate fares in advance.

Buses, trams & metro: Buses are generally overcrowded and unreliable.

Car hire

There are a number of private car hire companies in Dhaka and other cities. The Bangladesh Parjatan Corporation (BPC), the government tourism organisation, has a fleet of air-conditioned and non air-conditioned cars, microbuses and jeeps for hire. The BPC also offers a transfer service for tourists between Dhaka airport and the city centre and main hotels. Driving is on the left. A national licence or international driving permit is required.

BUSINESS DIRECTORY

The addresses listed below are a selection only. While World of Information makes every endeavour to check these addresses, we cannot guarantee that changes have not been made, especially to telephone numbers and area codes. We would welcome any corrections.

Telephone area codes

The international direct dialling code (IDD) for Bangladesh is + 880, followed by area code and subscriber's number:

Bagerhat	401	Khulna	41
Barisal	431	Kushtia	71
Bogra	51	Moulvi Bazar	861
Chittagong	31	Mymensingh	91
Comilla	81	Narayanganj	671
Dhaka	2	Patvakhali	441
Dinajpur	531	Rajshashi	721
Jamalpur	981	Sylhet	821

Useful telephone numbers

Police: 866-551/3

Fire: 9-555-5555

Ambulance: 112

Chambers of Commerce

American Chamber of Commerce in Bangladesh, Dhaka Sheraton Hotel, 1 Minto Road, Dhaka 1000 (tel: 861-3391; fax: 831-2915; e-mail: amcham@bangla.net).

Chittagong Chamber of Commerce and Industry, Agrabad Commercial Area, Chittagong (tel: 711-355; fax: 710-183; e-mail: ccci@globalctg.net).

Dhaka Chamber of Commerce and Industry, 65 Motijheel Commercial Area, Dhaka 1000 (tel: 955-2562; fax: 956-0830; e-mail: dcci@bangla.net).

Federation of Bangladesh Chambers of Commerce and Industry, 60 Motijheel

Commercial Area, Dhaka 1000 (tel: 956-0102; fax: 861-3213; e-mail: fbcci@bol-online.com).

Foreign Investors Chamber of Commerce and Industry, 35-1 Purana Paltan Line, Inner Circular Road, Dhaka 1000 (tel: 831-9448; fax: 831-9449; e-mail: ficci@bangla.net).

Khulna Chamber of Commerce and Industry, 5 KDA Commercial Area, Khan-A-Sabur Road, Khulna (tel: 721-695; fax: 731-213).

Metropolitan Chamber of Commerce and Industry, 122 Motijheel Commercial Area, Dhaka 1000 (tel: 956-5208; fax: 956-5212; e-mail: sg@citechco.net).

Banking

Agrani Bank, Agrani Bank Building, 9D Motijheel Commercial Area, Dhaka 1000 (tel: 956-6160; fax: 956-2346).

Arab Bangladesh Bank, BCIC Bhaban, 30-31 Dilkusha Commercial Area, Dhaka 1000 (tel: 956-0312; fax 956-4122).

Bangladesh Krishi Bank (Agricultural Bank), 83-85 Motijheel Commercial Area, Dhaka 100 (tel: 956-0021; fax: 867-102).

Bangladesh Shilpa Bank (Industrial Bank), PO Box 975, 8 Rajuk Avenue, Dhaka (tel: 955-8326; fax: 956-2061).

Banque Indosuez, 47 Motijheel Commercial Area, Dhaka 1000 (tel: 956-6566; fax: 956-5707).

Citibank N A, Chamber Building, 122-124 Motijheel Commercial Area, Dhaka 1000 (tel: 955-0061; fax: 956-2236).

Dutch-Bangla Bank Limited, Sena Kalyan Bhaban, 195 Motijheel Commercial Area, Dhaka 1000 (tel: 956-8537, 956-8542-44; fax: 956-1889; e-mail: dbbl@bdmail.net).

Grameen Bank, Grameen Bank Bhaban, Mirpur, Section-2, Dhaka-1216, Bangladesh (tel: 900-5256; e-mail: grameen.bank@grameen.net).

Hongkong & Shanghai Banking Corporation, Anchor Tower, 1.1-B Sonargaon Road, Dhaka 1205 (tel: 966-0536; fax: 966-0554).

International Finance Investment and Commercial Bank, BSB Building, 8 Rajuk Avenue, Dhaka 1000.

Investment Corporation of Bangladesh, Dhaka.

Islam Bank Bangladesh, PO Box 233, Islami Bank Tower, 40 Dilkusha Commercial Area, Dhaka 1000 (tel: 956-3182; fax: 956-4532).

Janata Bank, Janata Bhadan, 110 Motijheel Commercial Area, PO Box 468, Dhaka 1000 (tel: 956-000; fax: 956-4644).

National Bank Limited, 18 Dilkusha Commercial Area, Dhaka 1000 (tel: 956-3081/5; fax: 956-3953; e-mail: nblho@citechco.net).

Pubali Bank Ltd, 26 Dikusha Commercial Area, Dhaka 1000 (tel: 956-9050; fax: 956-4009).

Rupali Bank Ltd, 34 Dilkusha Commercial Area, Dhaka 1000 (tel: 955-1624; fax: 956-4148).

Sonali Bank, Motijheel Commercial Area, PO Box 147, Dhaka 1000 (tel: 955-0426; fax: 956-1410).

Standard Chartered Bank, 18-20 Motijheel Commercial Area, Dhaka 1000 (tel: 956-1465; fax: 956-1758).

United Commercial Bank, 60 Motijheel Commercial Area, Dhaka 1000.

Uttara Bank, 90 Motijheel Commercial Area, Dhakar 1000 (tel: 955-1162; fax: 863-539).

Central bank

Bangladesh Central Bank, Motijheel Commercial Area, PO Box 325, Dhaka 1000 (tel: 956-6203; fax: 956-6212; e-mail: banglabank@bangla.net).

Stock exchange

Dhaka Stock Exchange (DSE), www.dsebd.org

Chittagong Stock Exchange (CSE), www.csebd.com

Commodity exchange

Dhaka Stock Exchange (DSE), Chittagong Stock Exchange (CSE)

Chittagong Stock Exchange (CSE)

Travel information

Automobile Association of Bangladesh, 3/B Outer Circular Road, Dhaka 17 (tel: 402-241).

Biman Bangladesh Airlines, Biman Bhaban, 100 Motijheel Commercial Area, Dhaka 1000 (tel: 240-151/90; fax: 863-005); airport (tel: 894-771/79); flight enquiries (tel: 894-350, 894-870).

Railway enquiries (tel: 409-686).

National tourist organisation offices

Bangladesh Parjatan Corporation, 233 Airport Road, Tejgaon, Dhaka 1215 (tel: 811–7855; fax: 812–6501; e-mail: bpcho@bangla.net).

Ministries

Ministry of Agriculture, Bangladesh Secretariat, Dhaka 1000 (tel: 869-277; fax: 867-040).

Ministry of Civil Aviation and Tourism, Bangladesh Secretariat, Dhaka 1000 (tel: 867-244; fax: 869-206).

Ministry of Commerce, Bangladesh Secretariat, Dhaka 1000 (tel: 869-679; fax: 865-741).

Ministry of Communications, Bangladesh Secretariat, Dhaka 1000 (tel: 864-977; fax: 866-636).

Ministry of Cultural Affairs, Bangladesh Secretariat, Dhaka 1000 (tel: 868-977; fax: 860-290).

Ministry of Defence, Ganabhaban Complex, Sher-e-Bangla Nagar, Dhaka 1207 (tel: 816-955; fax: 817-945).

Ministry of Disaster Management & Relief, Bangladesh Secretariat, Dhaka 1000 (tel: 868-744; fax: 869-623).

Ministry of Education, Bangladesh Secretariat, Dhaka 1000 (tel: 868-711; fax: 867-577).

Ministry of Energy and Mineral Resources, Bangladesh Secretariat, Dhaka 1000 (tel: 866-188; fax: 861-110).

Ministry of Environment & Forest, Bangladesh Secretariat, Dhaka 1000 (tel: 860-587; fax: 869-210).

Ministry of Finance, Finance Division, Bangladesh Secretariat, Dhaka 1000 (tel: 860-406; fax: 865-581).

Ministry of Fisheries and Livestock, Bangladesh Secretariat, Dhaka 1000 (tel: 864-700).

Ministry of Food, Bangladesh Secretariat, Dhaka 1000 (tel: 862-240; fax: 860-762).

Ministry of Foreign Affairs, Foreign Affairs Building, Segunbagicha, Dhaka 1000 (tel: 955-6020; fax: 956-2557).

Ministry of Health & Family Welfare, Bangladesh Secretariat, Dhaka 1000 (tel: 866-975; fax: 869-077).

Ministry of Home Affairs, Bangladesh Secretariat, Dhaka 1000 (tel: 864-611; fax: 869-667).

Ministry of Industries, Shilpa Bhaban, 91 Motijheel Commercial Area, Dhaka 1000 (tel: 956-3549; fax: 956-3553).

Ministry of Information, Bangladesh Secretariate, Dhaka 1000 (tel: 868-555; fax: 862-211).

Ministry of Jute, Bangladesh Secretariat, Dhaka 1000 (tel: 862-250; fax: 868-766).

Ministry of Labour and Manpower, Bangladesh Secretariat, Dhaka 1000 (tel: 862-141; fax: 868-660).

Ministry of Land, Bangladesh Secretariat, Dhaka 1000 (tel: 869-644; fax: 862-989).

Ministry of Law, Justice and Parliamentary Affairs, Bangladesh Secretariat, Dhaka 1000 (tel: 860-560; fax: 868-557).

Ministry of Local Government and Rural Development, Bangladesh Secretariat, Dhaka 1000 (tel: 869-176; fax: 864-374).

Ministry of Planning, Sher-e-Bangla Nagar, Dhaka 1207 (tel: 815-175; fax: 814-638).

Ministry of Post and Telecommunications, Bangladesh Secretariat, Dhaka 1000 (tel: 864-800; fax: 865-775).

Ministry of Primary and Mass Education, Bangladesh Secretariat, Dhaka 1000 (tel: 862-484; fax: 868-871).

Ministry of Religious Affairs, Bangladesh Secretariat, Dhaka 1000 (tel: 860-682; fax: 865-040).

Ministry of Science & Technology, Bangladesh Secretariat, Dhaka 1000 (tel: 866-144; fax: 869-606).

Ministry of Shipping, Bangladesh Secretariat, Dhaka 1000 (tel: 868-155; fax: 862-219).

Ministry of Social Welfare, Bangladesh Secretariat, Dhaka 1000 (tel: 860-452; fax: 868-969).

Ministry of Textiles, Bangladesh Secretariat, Dhaka 1000 (tel: 864-388; fax: 860-600).

Ministry of Water Resources, Bangladesh Secretariat, Dhaka 1000 (tel: 868-688; fax: 862-400).

Ministry of Women and Children Affairs, Bangladesh Secretariat, Dhaka 1000 (tel: 861-012; fax: 867-550).

Ministry of Youth and Sports, Bangladesh Secretariat, Dhaka 1000 (tel: 867-053; fax: 862-344).

President's Office, Bangabhaban, Dhaka 1000 (tel: 966-8041; fax: 946-6242).

Prime Minister's Office, Old Sangsad Bhaban, Tejgaon, Dhaka (tel: 888-160; fax: 813-244).

Other useful addresses

Asian Development Bank, Bangladesh Resident Mission, BSL Office Complex, Sheraton Hotel Annex, 1 Minto Road, Ramna, Dhaka 1000 (tel: 933-4017; fax: 933-4012; e-mail: abddrm@mail.asiandevbank.org).

Bangladesh Agricultural University, Mymensingh (tel: 4333, 4191/93).

Bangladesh Export Processing Zones Authority, 222 New Eskaton Road, Dhaka (tel: 832-553; fax: 834-963).

Bangladesh Jute Mills Corporation, Adanjee Court, Motijheel Commercial Area, Dhaka (tel: 238-182/6, 238-192/6; fax: 883-329, 883-985).

Bangladesh Small and Cottage Industries Corporation, 137-138 Motijheel Commercial Area, Dhaka (tel: 865-161).

Bangladesh Telegraph and Telephone Board, 36/1 Mymensingh Road, Dhaka (tel: 831-500; fax: 832-477).

Board of Investment, Shilpa Bhaban, 91 Motijheel Commercial Area, Dhaka (tel: 955-9378; fax: 956-2312).

Bangladesh University of Engineering & Technology, Ramna, Dhaka 2 (tel: 505-171-5).

British High Commission, United Nations Road, PO Box 6079, Baridhara, Dhaka 12 (tel: 882-705/9; fax: 883-437).

Chittagong Port Authority, Port Road, Chittagong (tel: 712-504; fax: 710-593).

Chittagong Stock Exchange, 1/F Kashfia Plaza, 923/A Sheikh Mujib Road, Chittagong (tel: 714-100; fax: 714-101).

Department of Environment, Poribesh Bhaban, Plot £16 Agargaon, Sher-e-Bangla Nagar, Dhaka (tel: 812-416).

Department of Fisheries, Matsa Bhaban Segunbagicha, Dhaka (tel: 956-9320).

Department of Immigration and Passports, 17 Segunbagicha, Dhaka (tel: 834-320; fax: 956-2787).

Department of Shipping, 8/F, 141-143, Motijheel Commercial Area, Dhaka (tel: 955-5128).

Department of Textiles, Bastra Bhaban, Kazi Nazrul Islam Avenue, Dhaka (911-6385).

Dhaka Electric Supply Authority, 1 Abdul Gani Road, Dhaka (tel: 956-3520).

Dhaka Stock Exchange, 9F Motijheel Commercial Area, Dhaka 1000 (tel: 955-1935; fax: 867-552).

Export Promotion Bureau, Chamber Building, 122-124 Motijheel Commercial Area, Dhaka 1000 (tel: 955-2245/9; fax: 956-8000; e-mail: epb.tic@pradeshta.net).

Infrastructure Development Co Ltd, c/o Economic Relations Division, Block 16, Room 3, Sher-e-Bangla Nagar, Dhaka (tel: 811-971; fax: 811-660).

Mongla Port Authority, Mongla, Bagerhat (tel: 416-2331; fax: 403-1224).

National Board of Revenue, Segunbagicha, Dhaka (tel: 838-120; fax: 836-143).

Planning Commission, G.O. Hostel, Sher-e-Bangla Nagar, Dhaka.

Power Development Board, WAPDA Building, Motijheel Commercial Area, Dhaka (tel: 956-2154; fax: 956-4765).

Privatisation Board, 14/F Joban Bima Tower, 10 Dilkusha Commercial Area, Dhaka (tel: 956-3763; fax: 956-3723).

Registrar of Joint Stock Companies and Firms, 24-25 Dilkusha Commercial Area, Dhaka (tel: 956-4005).

Securities and Exchange Commission, Jiban bima Tower, 10 Dilkusha Commercial Area, Dhaka (tel: 956-8101; fax: 956-3721).

US Embassy, Madani Avenue, Baridhara, Dhaka 1212 (tel: 882-4700; fax: 882-3744; e-mail: dhaka@pd.state.gov).

Water Sewerage Authority, 98 Kazi Nazrul Islam Avenue, Dhaka (tel: 816-792; fax: 812-109).

National news agency: Bangladesh Sangbad Sangstha (BSS)

Address: 68/2, Purana Paltan, Dhaka 1000 (tel: 955-5036; fax: 9557929; email: bssnews@bssnews.org; internet: www.bssnews.net).

BDNEWS24: www.bdnews24.com

Internet sites

Bangladesh News: www.bangladeshnews.net

Virtual Bangladesh: www.virtualbangladesh.com

Barbados

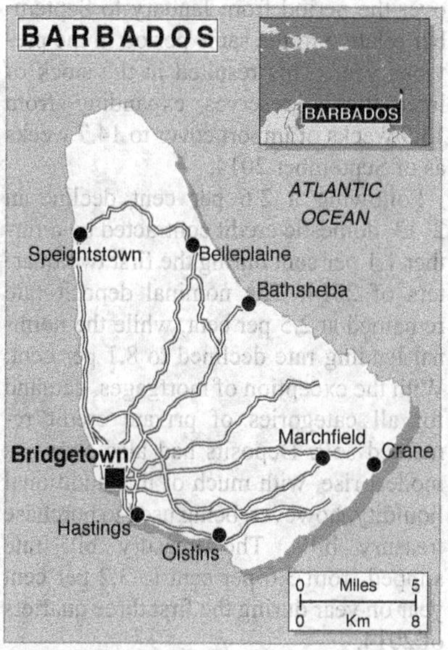

Barbados announced in 2015 that it was officially thinking of replacing the United Kingdom's Queen Elisabeth as head of state. As explained in the UK's *Guardian*, the decision, as announced by the prime minister, Freundel Stuart, was taken on the grounds that the country's head of state should no longer be a foreign white woman who only had the job because of a history of conquest and who was also head of state for 15 other countries, including most of their near neighbours. The Queen's popularity was not boosted by the fact that she had not visited Barbados since 1989. Prime Minister Stuart promised to present a bill to remove her in time for 2016's fiftieth anniversary of Barbadian independence. The bill is expected to receive parliamentary approval.

Other countries in the Commonwealth could follow Barbados. The list is long: Antigua and Barbuda, Australia, the Bahamas, Belize, Canada, Grenada, Jamaica, New Zealand, Papua New Guinea, St Christopher and Nevis, St Lucia, St Vincent and the Grenadines, the Solomon Islands and Tuvalu. Jamaica's prime minster, Portia Simpson-Miller, had vowed to change before Jamaica's own fiftieth anniversary of independence in 2012. However, the *Guardian* considered that this kind of constitutional change was often more popular than practical.

Underground moves

A July 2015 article on the *Barbados Underground* website, written by David A Comissiong – leader of the Barbados 'Clement Payne Movement' (Mr Payne was a Barbadian trades union leader and one of ten officially designated National Heroes) announced that the time had come for a recalibration of Barbados' politics. The article claimed that Barbados was suffering from 'a dearth of national political leadership' and was 'currently in a state of crisis and great peril.' However, it seemed to Mr Comissiong that there were positive signs which suggested that the 'fight-back' to save and restore Barbados had begun! Positive and hopeful signs of a national fight-back included such phenomena as the new young leaders that have come to the fore in the National Union of Public Workers (NUPW) and the Barbados Workers Union (BWU) and the renewed spirit of courage and activism that the Barbados Trade Union Movement has begun to exhibit.

Another positive indicator was the courageous and patriotic Budget reply speech that opposition leader Mia Mottley had delivered in the House of Assembly. Mr Comissiong also referred to the efforts undertaken by a number of elder patriots to propose and design a system of 'People's Initiatives' that would permit the citizens of Barbados to put forward proposals for new pieces of legislation and for changes to the Constitution. Among a number of moves towards greater honesty and business awareness, probably the most interesting was that initiated by Mr Comissiong and others 'to expose and put an end to the still existing old colonial practice of conferring outrageously privileged taxpayer-funded government contracts on a clique of elite Barbadian business-people.' This went alongside other efforts to highlight and tackle the corrupt practice of 'vote buying' that allegedly pervaded the Barbadian political class. (In fact, Barbados could be proud of its ranking on the Transparency International *Corruption Perceptions Index*,

KEY FACTS

Official name: Barbados

Head of State: Queen Elizabeth II, represented by Governor General Elliot Belgrave (from 1 Nov 2011)

Head of government: Prime Minister Freundel Stuart (DLP) (since 28 Oct 2010 on death of David Thompson; elected 21 Feb 2013)

Ruling party: Democratic Labour Party (DLP) (since 15 Jan 2008, re-elected 21 Feb 2013)

Area: 430 square km

Population: 279,000 (2014)*

Capital: Bridgetown

Official language: English

Currency: Barbados dollar (BD$) = 100 cents

Exchange rate: BD$2.00 per US$ (Sep 2015)

GDP per capita: US$15,579 (2014)*

GDP real growth: -0.70% (2013)*

GDP: US$4.35 billion (2014)*

Labour force: 145,000 (2011)*

Unemployment: 12.70% (2014)*

Inflation: 1.87% (2014)

Balance of trade: -US$1.08 billion (2010)*

* estimated figure

where it came 17 out of the 185 countries surveyed, level with the United States, Ireland and Hong Kong.) These reform initiatives had emerged in a Barbados that, according to Mr Comissiong, had been through a ten year period of 'depression, disappointment and disenchantment', thanks to a highly deficient and defective national political leadership. Mr Comissiong referred to a 'miasma of learned helplessness' that had settled over Barbados and stifled it.

The economy

According to the United Nations Economic Commission for Latin America and the Caribbean, Barbados had continued to pursue a private sector-driven growth and development strategy focused on export-led expansion, instituting regulatory reforms geared towards enhancing business facilitation. Nevertheless, this had yet to revive economic activity, which remained flat (0.0 per cent growth) during the first three quarters of 2014.

This outcome was due to continued under-performance in key segments of the economy, such as the tourism, rum and other beverages, food, sugar, other agriculture and construction sectors. Furthermore, fiscal consolidation initiatives had served to dampen aggregate domestic demand and this, coupled with declining international commodity prices, particularly for food and oil, has led to a cooling of price inflation.

ECLAC noted that Barbados had continued to run a large fiscal deficit, estimated at 12.5 per cent of gross domestic product (GDP) for the fiscal year 2013/2014. Notwithstanding this, the government's fiscal consolidation initiatives had resulted in a 16.2 per cent contraction in the deficit (year on year) for the period from April to September 2014. Fiscal adjustment measures had also succeeded in reconciling foreign-exchange supply and demand and by the end of September 2014 net international reserves were estimated to have expanded to the equivalent of 14.7 weeks' import cover.

The government's ongoing fiscal consolidation programme had also begun to yield gains. As of the end of September 2014, the fiscal deficit stood at 8 per cent of GDP, a 1.8 percentage point contraction from the previous year. However, tax revenues had remained quite flat, expanding by a mere 0.1 per cent year on year, for the period from April to September 2014. Current expenditure, on the other hand, had contracted by 5.3 per cent during the first half of fiscal 2014/2015, in comparison to the previous year. As a consequence of the retrenchment (aka early retirement or dismissal) of 3,000 public-sector workers during the first quarter of 2014, expenditure on wages and salaries fell by 8.4 per cent year on year in the second quarter. Public consumption (-1.2 per cent) and transfers and subsidies (-11.4 per cent) both contracted. Barbados had sought to finance the BD$360 million (US$180 million) fiscal deficit that had been generated as of the end of September 2014 through a combination of reductions in government deposits with the domestic commercial banking system and direct financing from the central bank and the National Insurance Scheme. Consequently, the net government debt-to-GDP ratio increased by 8.6 percentage points to 85.5 per cent in the year to September 2014, so that Barbados' debt continued to be high.

Fiscal adjustment measures had succeeded in bringing the demand for foreign exchange into line with supply during the first three quarters of 2014. Moreover, a drop in disposable incomes lowered consumption (as well as investment) and dampened import demand. More significantly, the capital and financial account experienced a 131 per cent increase in net long-term private capital flows from US$86.3 million to US$199.3 million over the period from January to September relative to the same period in the previous year. This resulted in the stock of international reserves expanding from 13.9 weeks of import cover to 14.7 weeks as of September 2014.

Following a 2.6 per cent decline in 2013, domestic credit contracted by a further 1.1 per cent during the first two quarters of 2014. The nominal deposit rate remained at 2.5 per cent, while the nominal lending rate declined to 8.1 per cent. With the exception of mortgages, demand for all categories of private credit remained soft. Deposits had also shown a modest rise, with much of this additional liquidity, however, being used to purchase treasury bills. The treasury bill rate slipped from 3.6 per cent to 3.2 per cent year on year during the first three quarters of 2014.

Year on year, the country's current account deficit remained stable at 8.8 per cent of GDP over the first three quarters of 2014, with merchandise imports remaining largely unchanged; contractions in export income from rum (10.4 per cent), other beverages (7.5 per cent), food (8.8 per cent) and sugar (19.3 per cent) were offset by increased revenues from travel (0.5 per cent), other services (5.1 per cent), chemicals (8.1 per cent), electronics (37.7 per cent) and other merchandise exports (31.3 per cent).

In the view of ECLAC, the tourism sector, which is the primary driver of economic growth, continued to under-perform during the first three quarters of 2014. The renewed growth (8 per cent) observed in arrivals from the key United Kingdom (UK) market can be attributed to the establishment of a charter service from Manchester. However, gains in this regard have been partially offset by American Airlines' cessation of direct flights from New York. Overall, tourism output expanded by a mere 0.1 per cent while the number of operational international business and financial services companies declined by 0.4 per cent relative to 2013. Other key segments of the economy, such as rum and other beverages, food, sugar, other agriculture and construction industries, also continued to perform poorly, resulting in a 1.2 per cent

KEY INDICATORS — Barbados

	Unit	2011	2012	2013	2014	**2015
Population	m	*0.28	*0.28	*0.28	*0.28	*0.28
Gross domestic product (GDP)	US$bn	4.50	4.22	4.28	*4.35	*4.44
GDP per capita	US$	16,148	15,199	*15,374	*15,579	*15,882
GDP real growth	%	0.5	–	–	*-0.3	*0.8
Inflation	%	9.4	4.5	1.8	1.9	*1.3
Unemployment	%	11.2	11.6	11.6	*12.7	*12.3
Current account	US$m	-375.0	-426.0	-396.0	*-394.0	*-225.0
Total reserves minus gold	US$m	–	840.0	681.0	632.3	–
Foreign exchange	US$m	–	744.0	585.0	–	–
Exchange rate	per US$	2.00	2.00	2.00	2.00	–

* estimated figure ** forecast figure

year-on-year contraction in output from tradable sectors. Fragile domestic demand and declining international commodity prices, particularly for food and oil, had placed downward pressures on prices. Consequently, year-on-year inflation at the end of September 2014 was down to 1.7 per cent from the 1.8 per cent registered in 2013. At the same time, unemployment averaged 12.3 per cent, a year-on-year increase of 1.7 percentage points.

Economic growth in Barbados is expected to be of the order of 0.0 per cent for 2014, with a 1.5 per cent expansion in overall output projected for 2015. The quickening recovery in major source markets, particularly the United Kingdom and the United States, coupled with the increased private investment in the tourism industry and tourism-related projects generated by the new tax incentive legislation, the Tourism Industry Relief Fund and the Enterprise Relief Fund, should provide a sustainable platform for steady economic recovery in the short- to medium-term.

Risk assessment

Economy	Poor
Politics	Fair
Regional stability	Good

COUNTRY PROFILE

Barbados was formerly a British colony and is now an independent sovereign state.

1951 Universal adult suffrage was introduced. The Barbados Labour Party (BLP) won the general election, and held office until 1961.

1955 The BLP split and a splinter group formed the Democratic Labour Party (DLP).

1961 Barbados achieved self-government. The DLP won the general elections, its leader Errol Barrow, became premier.

1966 Barbados gained independence; Errol Barrow became prime minister.

1967 Barbados joined the United Nations.

1973 Barbados, Guyana, Jamaica, and Trinidad and Tobago established the Caribbean Community and Common Market, later known just as Caribbean Community (Caricom).

1976–86 BLP retained power in elections.

1986 DLP won the general elections.

1994 The BLP won a landslide general election. Owen Arthur became prime minister.

2002 Barbados was removed from the Organisation for Economic Co-operation and Development's (OECD) blacklist of non-co-operative countries for its efforts to combat money laundering.

2003 The ruling BLP won the general elections.

2006 The opposition leader, Clyde Mascoll, resigned from the DLP and joined the ruling BLP.

2008 The opposition DLP won 52.5 per cent (20 seats out of 30) in parliamentary elections, the BLP 47.3 per cent, (10); turnout was 56.6 per cent. David Thompson (DLP) was sworn in as prime minister. The Barbados Defence Force received military aid of B$840,000 (US$1.68 million) from the Chinese Army. The donation included computers, power generators and other equipment, and military training.

2009 An amnesty and new rules concerning Caricom nationals living and working in Barbados illegally were introduced. The mandatory death penalty for murder was abolished.

2010 Barbados opened an embassy in China. David Thompson died and Freundel Stuart was sworn in as prime minister.

2011 The economy grew by 2.8 per cent in the first quarter. In June, the capital, Bridgetown, was added to the Unesco list of World Heritage Sites, as a well-preserved old town and nearby military garrison, and an outstanding example of British colonial architecture. The government announced it would invest US$100 million in the sugar industry to promote its diversification into production of bagasse, ethanol, special sugars and molasses. In July, a 16-member tourism trade-party from China, visiting to experience the Crop-Over Festival (an annual carnival). Sir Clifford Husbands retired and Elliot Belgrave took office as acting governor general in November.

2012 On 22 May Acting Governor General Belgrade was confirmed into post from 1 June. Standard and Poor's (S&P) downgraded the long-term foreign and local currency sovereign credit rating for Barbados on 17 June, from BBB-/A-3 to BB+/B ('junk' bond status). S&P considered the government's fiscal stance as weak. Prime Minister Stuart replied that he was 'not perturbed by the expression of the opinion of the rating agency'.

2013 Elections were held on 21 February. The DLP were re-elected with a narrow majority of 16 seats to the 14 of the BLP. Three ministers in the previous Cabinet, Dr Esther Byer-Suckoo, George Hutson and Patrick Todd, lost their seats in the election.

2014 The minister of finance, Christopher Sinckler, announced a comprehensive and permanent overhaul of Barbados' tourism incentive legislation in August. Mr Sinckfler said that tourism should be treated as an export industry and that legislation would set out concessions to allow for tax relief of up to 40 years on tourism inputs.

2015 The opposition Barbados Labour Party walked out on 20 January after declaring that Speaker Michael Carrington should not preside over the legislature until a court matter in which he is involved is settled. On 29 April Prime Minister Freundel Stuart signed an agreement with BHP Billiton for two offshore exploration licences in two blocks south-east of Barbados – Carlisle Bay and Bimshire. The area covered totals some 5,000 sq kilometres.

Political structure

Constitution
Promulgated on 30 November 1966.

Independence date
1966

Form of state
Parliamentary democracy, within a constitutional monarchy.

The executive
Executive power is vested in the British monarch, represented by a governor general, who is appointed by the monarch, and exercised by the prime minister and cabinet.

Freundel Stuart has vowed to replace Queen Elizabeth as head of state with a ceremonial president in time for Barbados' fiftieth year since independence in 2016.

National legislature
Legislative power is exercised through the bicameral National Assembly, comprising a 30-member House of Assembly, popularly elected in single seat constituencies, for terms of five years and a 21-member Senate of appointed members for five-year terms.

Following National Assembly elections, the leader of the majority party or coalition assumes the post of prime minister, confirmed by the governor general. The cabinet is selected by the prime minister and confirmed by the governor general.

Legal system
The legal system is based on English common law. Judges are appointed by the service commissions for the judicial and legal service. There is no judicial review of legislative acts.

Last elections
21 February 2013

Results: Parliamentary: the Democratic Labour Party (DLP) won 51.28 per cent, (16 seats out of 30), the Barbados Labour Party (BLP) 48.32 per cent (14).

Next elections
2018 (parliamentary)

Political parties

Ruling party
Democratic Labour Party (DLP) (since 15 Jan 2008, re-elected 21 Feb 2013)

Main opposition party
Barbados Labour Party (BLP)

Population
278,000 (2012)*
Last census: May 2000: 250,010
Population density: 620 inhabitants per square km. Urban population 44 per cent (2010 Unicef).
Annual growth rate: 0.3 per cent, 1990–2010 (Unicef).

Ethnic make-up
African (90 per cent), mixed race (6 per cent), European (4 per cent).

Religions
Mainly Christian, with an Anglican majority and dozens of smaller sects, plus small Jewish, Hindu and Muslim communities.
Anglican (40 per cent), Pentecostal (8 per cent), Methodist (7 per cent), Roman Catholic (4 per cent).

Education
Educational spending is around US$150 million per year. Expenditure on primary education typically fluctuates between 25–29 per cent of total public expenditure on education. The government provides assistance to all private secondary schools.
Public education at primary and secondary levels is free, although parents can opt to send their children to private schools.
Primary education begins at aged five and lasts for six years.
The secondary school programme begins at aged 11 years and last until aged 16, when students choose between academic higher education or applied further education.
The Samuel Jackman Prescod Polytechnic (SJPP), the Barbados Community College (BCC), Erdiston College and the University of the West Indies cater for higher education. Eligible students also pursue their studies in North American colleges and universities.
Compulsory years: 5 to 16
Enrolment rate: 94.7 per cent to 100 per cent, primary school enrolment of the relevant age group.
Pupils per teacher: 18 in primary schools

Health
With 16 per cent of the population aged 60 years and over, Barbados has the highest percentage of elderly population in the English speaking Caribbean.
Barbados provides high quality primary and secondary care with free treatment for young children. The Queen Elizabeth Hospital benefits from government aid.
There is universal access to improved water and sanitation facilities.

HIV/Aids
In 2009, there were an estimated 2,000 people living with HIV (Unicef 2012),
HIV prevalence: 2.0 per cent aged 15–49 in 2009 (Unicef 2012)
Life expectancy: 77 years, 2010 (Unicef 2012)
Fertility rate/Maternal mortality rate: 1.6 births per woman, 2010 (Unicef 2012)
Child (under 5 years) mortality rate (per 1,000): 18 per 1,000 live births (WHO 2012)

Welfare
The government provides an extensive welfare programme for the poor and the elderly. Assistance for the elderly comprises housing, transportation, home care and free utilities (water and utilities), assistance in kind, and food vouchers.
Financial assistance is provided to parents of underprivileged children as well as subsidies for school expenses.
Low rent housing is available to all residents; some housing is available to be purchased by low income earners.

Pensions
There is universal pension coverage from a non-contributory pension.

Main cities
Bridgetown (capital, estimated population 92,328 in 2012), Speightstown (2,192), Holetown (1,595), Bathsheba (1,521), Oistins (1,471), Bulkeley (1,070).

Languages spoken
A local Bajan dialect is spoken.

Official language/s
English

Media
Press
Dailies: There are two, *The Daily Nation* (www.nationnews.com) and the *Barbados Advocate* (www.barbadosadvocate.com).
Weeklies: Daily newspapers publish weekend editions. Others include *Eastern Caribbean News*, *Weekend Investigator* and *Caribbean Week* (published fortnightly).
Business: *The Broad Street Journal* (www.broadstreetnews.com) and *Business Monday* (www.barbadosadvocate.com), are business publications while most daily newspapers have business sections.
Periodicals: The Government Information Service (BGIS) (www.barbados.gov.bb) publishes data and research articles.

Broadcasting
The Caribbean Broadcast Corporation (CBC) (www.cbc.bb) is the nation public broadcaster.
Radio: CBC (www.cbc.bb) has three networks which cover news, cultural and sports events and all genre of music.
There are several private, commercial and religious radio stations operating including Voice of Barbados (VOB) (www.vob929.com), which competes with CBC for content, Hott FM (www.hott953.com), Mix 96.9 (www.mix969fm.com) and Gospel 97.5 (www.gospel975.com); the Barbados Broadcasting Service operates BBS 90.7 and Faith FM (www.barbadosadvocate.com).
Television: CBC (www.cbc.bb) is the only terrestrial TV network in operation, showing domestic news and current affairs, art and cultural programmes as well as imported shows. Programmes are also provided by Jump TV (www.jumptv.com), via the internet. It is the largest provider worldwide of internet programming.
National news agency: Caribbean News Agency (Cana)
Other news agencies: Caribbean Net News: www.caribbeannetnews.com

Economy
The economy is characterised by a strong service sector – contributing 82.9 per cent – that caters for the tourist industry, with related construction and retail services. The financial sector, particularly offshore services, includes call centres in insurance targeted at the east coast of the US. The global economic crisis hit hard in 2008 with the unemployment rate from within these sectors rising sharply. Per capita income fell from US$16,328 in 2007 to US$15,418 by 2010, although it jumped back to US$16,148 in 2011, as the tourist industry recovered. The country experienced a recession in 2013, as growth was -0.7 per cent and GDP per capita dropped down to US$15,373.
Overall, the economy in 2008–09 slumped as long-stay visitor numbers fell by 13.3 per cent. However, a cruise liner terminal in the capital, Bridgetown, has capacity for five ships at any one time and cruise passenger arrival numbers rose by 6.4 per cent (38,200 extra passengers) in 2009. Nevertheless, visitor revenues registered a five-year (2007–11) negative growth averaging -7.3 per cent annual loss. However, in 2014 visitor exports accounted for 36.1 per cent of total exports, and was forecast to grow by 1.8 per cent in 2015.
Since coming out of recession in 2010, Barbados has been experiencing weak growth up to 2013 that is barely in positive territory. However, in 2014, growth picked up slightly and reached 2.4 per cent, which was expected to be maintained in 2015 and 2016.
Recommendations by the IMF and World Bank after reviews conducted in 2013 were broadly in line with government policies. Encouraging new business and higher labour productivity are at the core of the Barbados growth strategy.

External trade
As a member of the Caribbean Community (Caricom), Barbados operates within

the Caricom Single Market and Economy (CSME), which became operational in 2006. It is also a member of the Organisation of American States (OAS). Barbados, as a member of the 15-country Caribbean Forum (Cariforum), has free trade agreements with the European Union (EU), Costa Rica, Dominican Republic, Colombia and Venezuela.

Barbados was the first single-crop agrarian economy to switch to the service sector provision of back office operations. Its financial sector, combined with the tourist sector, provides the greater percentage of GDP. The offshore financial centre utilises the well educated, English-speaking, workforce with its proximity to the US and Canada, as well as traditional links with the UK.

Imports

Principal imports are petroleum, consumer goods, food and beverages, construction materials, electrical components, vehicles, rubber, marine crafts and machinery.

Main sources: Nigeria (around 60 per cent of total), US (10 per cent), Trinidad and Tobago (7 per cent), Jamaica (6.2 per cent).

Exports

Principal commodity exports are refined petroleum, sugar and molasses, rum and other foods. Other exports include beverages, chemicals and electrical and electronic components.

Main destinations: Nigeria (around 30 per cent), US (15 per cent), Trinidad and Tobago (9 per cent), China (2 per cent).

Agriculture

Farming

The agricultural sector contributed 1.5 per cent to GDP in 2014 and employs around 3 per cent of the labour force.

Around three quarters of the total land area is under cultivation. In November 2013 the agriculture minister stated that research showed Barbados produced 60 to 65 per cent of the food it consumed.

Emphasis has been placed on diversifying production away from sugar and towards the farming of sea island cotton, green vegetables and market garden produce.

The EU quota of just under 50,000 tonnes per year of sugar and its guaranteed price mechanism came to an end in 2007. The pressure is on Barbados to make the sugar sector profitable, although it seems unlikely that the island will be able to compete with low-cost producers and the heavily subsidised sugar beet farmers in North America and the EU. As well as trade liberalisation, the Barbados sugar sector has had to cope with environmental degradation and the rising price of land. In October 2014, the Minister of Finance Chris Snickler, warned the government that if focus was not put on a new multipurpose sugar processing factory, the industry would die. The factory that is expected to be functional by 2016 will also be aimed at processing molasses for rum production, and renewable energy production.

Fishing

There are complaints that the small fishing industry has not been supported by the government. The government issued fish importing licences permitting processors to import fish, when the domestic catch could have provided for domestic processing needs.

Industry and manufacturing

Manufacturing employs around 9 per cent of the workforce, and construction and quarrying employs 11 per cent. Production is centred on light manufacturing and assembly of electrical and electronic goods, food processing, clothing, sugar refining, petrochemicals and beverages.

Most new foreign-owned export-oriented industries are based on the island's nine purpose-built industrial estates, which are largely managed by the Barbados Industrial Development Corporation.

Emphasis is placed on expanding the number of value-added joint venture assembly industries.

Tourism

Barbados offers a typical Caribbean experience for high-end visitors with unspoilt beaches and luxury accommodation. Sea sports (surfing and windsurfing) are very popular, along with diving and fishing.

The service sector typically constitutes 82.9 per cent of GDP of which travel and tourism contributed 36.1 per cent of GDP in 2014, this figure was forecast to rise by 1.8 per cent in 2015.

Tourist arrivals in 2012 dropped from 568,000 in 2011 to 536,000. By 2014 long stay visitor arrival numbers had increased to 519,638 visitors, 2.2 per cent up on 2013 and the first increase in two years. However, it had not returned to pre-recession levels of 2007 when visitor numbers stood at 572,937.

A cruise liner terminal in the capital, Bridgetown, has capacity for five ships at any one time. Private yachts are catered for at the Port Charles Marina and a villa complex in Speightstown.

The industry directly employed around 14,000 people in 2014, which constitutes 11.1 per cent of total employment. Indirect employment in the sector constituted 35.7 per cent of total employment at around 45,000 jobs.

Hydrocarbons

Proven oil reserves were 2.84 million barrels in 2014, located offshore, producing 1,001 barrels per day (bpd), which is exported to Trinidad and Tobago for refining and re-importing. The state-owned Barbados National Oil Company (BNOC) is responsible for domestic production, accounting for 15 per cent of the island's annual consumption in 2013 (7,980bpd).

Natural gas reserves were 141 million cubic metres (cum) in 2014.

On 29 April 2015 Prime Minister Freundel Stuart signed an agreement with BHP Billiton for the offshore exploration licences in the two blocks south-east of Barbados – Carlisle Bay and Bimshire – originally awarded to BHP in 2008. The area covered totals some 5,000 sq kilometres. Mr Stuart said that 'In addition, Barbadian nationals stand to reap early benefits on execution of the licences through the negotiated provisions for annual training, scholarships, local content, coastal and marine environment research and the acquisition of critical equipment and software.' He also noted that the existing Woodbourne Oil Field was showing signs of steady decline, producing about 700 barrels of crude oil and 1.9 million cubic feet of natural gas per day.

Any coal imports or use are commercially insignificant.

Energy

Total installed generating capacity was 239MW in 2013. Barbados relies on imported oil for most of its energy requirements. There are plans to expand solar and wind energy programmes.

Financial markets

Stock exchange

Barbados Stock Exchange (BSE)

Banking and insurance

The financial sector continues to expand.

Central bank

Central Bank of Barbados

Main financial centre

Bridgetown

Offshore facilities

Barbados is a major international business centre. It has several tax treaties in place with developed countries including Canada.

Time

GMT minus four hours

Geography

Barbados is the most easterly of the Caribbean islands, lying about 320km (200 miles) north-east of Trinidad. It is relatively flat and is one of the few coral-capped islands in the region.

Hemisphere

Northern

Climate

Generally warm but cooled by trade winds with temperature around 26–30 degrees Celsius (C) in the day and 15–18 degrees C at night. Rainy season, includes tropical storms: July–November. Humidity rises in the rainy season.

Dress codes

Business suits may be worn with jackets removed. Generally, smart casual wear is suitable in restaurants, although some restaurants may require suits and ties for men. Lightweight cottons are advised.

Entry requirements

Passports

Required by all.

Visa

Visas are not required by most European, American, Australasian and some Asian citizens. From May 2009 EU citizens may make a short-stay visit, for up to three months, without a visa. For a list of those that do, see www.barbados.org/docs.htm. All visitors must have return/onward passage.

Currency advice/regulations

No restrictions on import of local currency, but it may not be exported. Unlimited foreign currency may be imported and exported, limited to the amount declared on arrival.

Health (for visitors)

Mandatory precautions

Yellow fever vaccination certificate if arriving from an infected area.

Advisable precautions

Typhoid/polio vaccination.

Hotels

There is wide range of first-class hotels available. A 5 per cent government tax and 10 per cent service charge are generally applied.

Public holidays (national)

Fixed dates

1 Jan (New Year's Day), 21 Jan (Errol Barrow Day), 28 Apr (National Heroes' Day), 1 May (Labour Day), 30 Nov (Independence Day), 25 Dec (Christmas Day), 26 Dec (Boxing Day).

Variable dates

Good Friday, Easter Monday, Whit Monday, Emancipation/Kadooment Day (first Mon in Aug).

Working hours

Banking

Mon–Thu: 0800–1500; Fri: 0800–1700.

Business

Mon–Fri: 0800–1600/1630; Sat: 0800–1200.

Government

Mon–Fri: 0800–1600/1630.

Telecommunications

Mobile/cell phones

GSM 900/1900, 900/1800 services are available throughout most of the island.

Electricity supply

110V AC, 50Hz. American-style two-pin plugs are in use.

Social customs/useful tips

Make and confirm appointments before travelling. Many hotels do not start check-in procedures until 1500 so advise the hotel if arriving earlier. Most hotels have a business centre, although facilities vary.

Getting there

Air

International airport/s: Grantley Adams International (BGI), 13km east of Bridgetown; duty-free shops, restaurant, bank, hotel reservations, car hire.

Airport tax: Departure tax BD$25; not applicable to transit passengers.

Surface

Water: Cruise-ship passengers may conclude their journey and depart by air, normal immigration and visa control standards would apply.

Main port/s: Bridgetown Harbour.

Getting about

National transport

Road: There are over 2,000km of surfaced road. Main roads radiate from Bridgetown.

Buses: Frequent and efficient standard fare services operate throughout the island.

City transport

Taxis: Taxis are easily available. They can be hailed, ordered by telephone or found on ranks. The Tourism Board publishes a list of standard fares.

Some hotels run pick-up services.

Car hire

A local driver's permit must be obtained; they are available at police stations and the licensing authority or through car rental agencies on presentation of a national driving licence or an international driving permit. A registration fee of B$10 will be due.

Traffic drives on the left and is often heavy during the rush hours. Strict speed limits of 20mph in Bridgetown and Speightstown and 30mph elsewhere.

BUSINESS DIRECTORY

The addresses listed below are a selection only. While World of Information makes every endeavour to check these addresses, we cannot guarantee that changes have not been made, especially to telephone numbers and area codes. We would welcome any corrections.

Telephone area codes

The international direct dialling code (IDD) for Barbados is +1 246, followed by subscriber's number.

Chambers of Commerce

Barbados Chamber of Commerce and Industry, Nemwil House, Collymore Rock, St Michael (tel: 426-2056; fax: 429-2907; e-mail: bdscham@caribsurf.com).

Banking

Bank of Nova Scotia, PO Box 202, Broad St, Bridgetown (tel: 431-3000; fax: 426-0969).

Barbados Agency for Microenterprise Development Ltd (Fund Access), 30 Tudor Street, Bridgetown (tel: 228-1366; fax: 228-1343).

Barbados National Bank, PO Box 1002, Broad St, Bridgetown (tel: 431-5700; fax: 426-0969).

Barclays Bank PLC, PO Box 301, Broad St, Bridgetown (tel: 431-5151; fax: 436-7957).

Caldon Finance Merchant Bank Ltd, Hilton Hotel, 7 Shopping Arcade, St Michael (tel: 437-7550; fax: 436-4999).

Caribbean Commercial Bank, PO Box 1007C, Broad St, Bridgetown (tel: 431-2500; fax: 431-2530).

Caribbean Development Bank, PO Box 408 Wildey, St Michael, Barbados (tel: 431-1600; fax: 426-7269).

Intel Overseas Bank Inc, Suite No 7, Goding House, Spry St, Bridgetown (tel: 436-8826).

Mutual Bank of the Caribbean Inc, Triden House, Lower Broad St, Bridgetown (tel: 436-8335; fax: 429-5734).

Royal Bank of Canada, PO Box 68, Broad Street, Bridgetown (tel: 431-6700; fax: 427-8393).

Central bank

Central Bank of Barbados, Spry Street, PO Box 1016, Bridgetown (tel: 436-6870; fax: 427-3334; e-mail: cbb.libr@caribsurf.com).

Stock exchange

Barbados Stock Exchange (BSE), www.bse.com.bb

Travel information

Caribbean Airways, Terminal 1, Grantley Adams International Airport, Christ Church (tel: 428-1950; fax: 428-1652; e-mail: info@caribairways.com; internet site: www.caribairways.com).

Ministry of tourism

Ministry of Foreign Affairs, Tourism and International Transport, Tourism Division, Sherbourne Conference Centre, Two Mile Hill, St Michael (tel: 436-4830; fax: 436-4828).

National tourist organisation offices

Barbados Tourism Authority, Harbour Road, PO Box 242, Bridgetown (tel: 427-2623/4; fax: 426-4080; email: btainfo@barbados.org; internet: www.barbados.org).

Ministries

Ministry of Agriculture and Rural Development, Graeme Hall, Christ Church (tel: 428-4061; fax: 420-8444).

Ministry of Education, Youth Affairs and Culture, Jemmotts Ln, St Michael (tel: 426-5416; fax: 436-2411).

Ministry of Finance and Economic Affairs, Civil Service, Government Headquarters, Bay St, St Michael (tel: 426-3179; fax: 436-9280).

Ministry of Health and the Environment, Jemmotts Ln, St Michael (tel: 426-4669; fax: 426-5570).

Ministry of Home Affairs, Sir Frank Walcott Bldg, Culloden Rd, St Michael (tel: 431-7750; fax: 437-3794).

Ministry of Industry, Commerce and Business Development, Reef Rd, Fontabelle, St Michael (tel: 426-4452; fax: 431-0056).

Ministry of International Trade and Business, 1 Culloden Rd, St Michael (tel: 427-0427; fax: 429-6652).

Ministry of Labour, Community Development and Sports, National Insurance Bldg, Fairchild St, Bridgetown, St Michael (tel: 427-2326; fax: 426-8959).

Ministry of Public Works, Transport and Housing, The Pine, St Michael (tel: 429-3495; fax: 437-8133).

Ministry of Trade, Industry and Commerce, Savannah Lodge, Garrison, St Michael (tel: 427-270).

Prime Minister's Office, Government Headquarters, Bay St, St Michael (tel: 426-3179; fax: 436-9280).

Other useful addresses

Barbados External Telecommunications, Wildey, St Michael (tel: 427-5200; fax: 427-5808).

Barbados Investment and Development Corporation, Pelican House, Princess Alice Highway, St Michael (tel: 427-5350; fax: 426-7802; internet site: http://www.bidc.com/index.htm).

Barbados Manufacturers' Association, Prescod Blvd, Harbour Road, Bridgetown (tel: 426-4474, 427-9898; fax: 436-5182).

Barbados National Trust, 10th Avenue Relleville, St Michael (tel: 436-9033);

Barbados Tourism Investment Inc, 2nd Floor, Nemwil House, Collymore Rock, St. Michael (tel: 426-7085; fax: 426-7086; e-mail: btii@tourisminvest.com.bb; internet site: http://barbadostourisminvestment.com).

British High Commission, PO Box 676, Lower Collymore Rock, St Michael (tel: 436-6694; fax: 436-5398, 426-7916).

Caribbean Broadcasting Corporation, PO Box 900, Bridgetown (tel: 429-2041).

Caribbean Export Development Agency (Caribbean Export),

The Future Centre Trust, Edgehill Street, St Thomas (fax: 425-0075).

US Embassy, PO Box 302, Canadian Imperial Bank of Commerce Building, Broad Street, Bridgetown (tel: 436-4950; fax: 429-5246).

National news agency: Caribbean News Agency (Cana)

Address: Caribbean Media Corporation, Harbour Industrial Estate, Unit 1B, Building 6A, St Michael, BB11145 (tel: 467-1000; fax: 429-4355; email: admin@cmccaribbean.com; internet: www.cananews.net).

Caribbean Net News: www.caribbeannetnews.com

Internet sites

Barbados government portal: www.gov.bb/bigportal/big/

Barbados Nation (newspaper): http://nationnews.com

Travel and Tourism Encyclopedia: www.barbados.org

Belarus

KEY FACTS

Official name: Respublika Belarus (Republic of Belarus)

Head of State: President Aleksandr Lukashenko (from 1994; re-elected 19 Dec 2010)

Head of government: Prime Minister Andrey Kabyakow (from 27 December 2014)

Ruling party: Coalition of independent supporters of President Lukashenko, plus Kommunisticheskaya Partuya Belarusi (KPB) (Communist Party of Belarus) and Agrarnaya Partiya Belarusi (APB) (Agrarian Party of Belarus) (since 1995; re-elected 23 Sep 2012)

Area: 208,000 square km

Population: 9.47 million (2014)*

Capital: Minsk

Official language: Belarusian since 1990 and Russian since 1995 referendum.

Currency: Rouble (R)

Exchange rate: R17,822.50 per US$ (Sep 2015)

GDP per capita: US$8,042 (2014)*

GDP real growth: 1.59% (2014)*

GDP: US$76.14 billion (2014)*

Labour force: 4.66 million (2011)*

Unemployment: 0.52% (2014)* (additional large number of underemployed)

Inflation: 18.11% (2014)

Balance of trade: -US$259.84 million (2014)*

* estimated figure

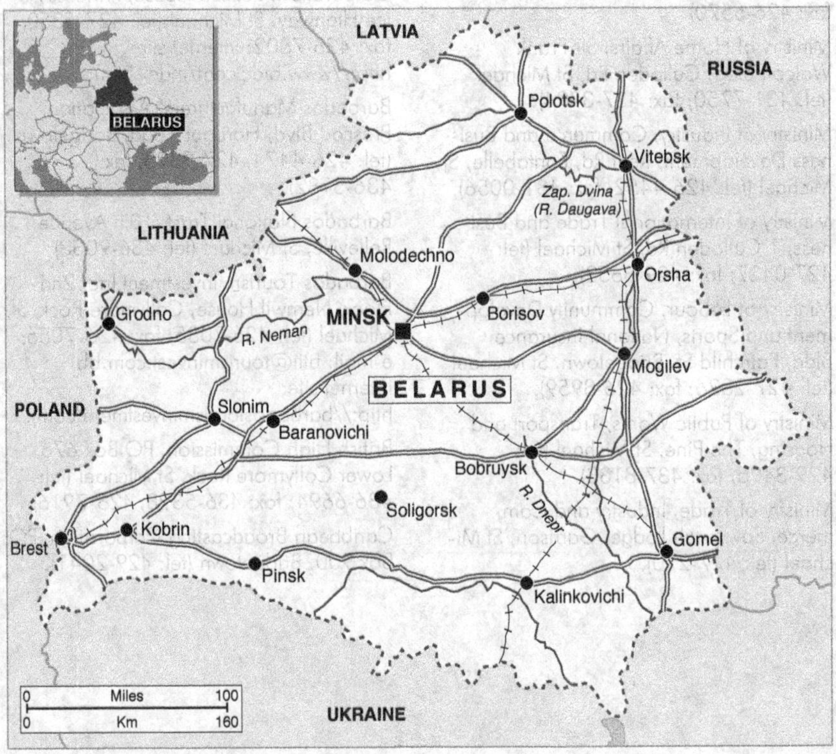

Belarusians are inevitably conscious of the fact that 2015 is an election year. Presidential elections are due to be held by November. However, the previous two elections (March 2006 and December 2010) were farcical, except for the violence that characterised election day. In 2006 protests followed the election result, with a tent city full of protestors being set up in Minsk's October square. During the run-up to the election opposition candidates were harassed and detained. If anything, the violence surrounding the 2010 election was even worse as a protest march claimed that the voting had been rigged. The presidential election in November 2015 is seen as a further extension of Alexander Lukashenko's 21-year rule. It thus becomes an endorsement of what the government describes simply as stability, others as state security. President Lukashenko wants to maintain the *status quo*. The trains run on time, the streets are swept, a lonely statue of Lenin stands on Independence Avenue. Surprisingly, the KGB has kept the name.

Puppet – on a string?

Belarus has, for decades, very much acted as a Russian puppet. However, as Russia found itself on something of an economic back foot in 2014, Belarus' motivation for acting as Russia's bagman paled somewhat. It was now the case that the political freedoms that were long discarded in Belarus also seemed to be disappearing in Russia.

Until the election of Alexander Lukashenko in 1994, Belarusians had enjoyed (according to the *Belarus Digest*) much more freedom. The press was free, opposition parties were present in Parliament and a 'cautiously pro-Western foreign policy' prevailed. Improbably, Belarus' prospects of joining the European Union (EU) were as good, if not better, than those of Romania or Bulgaria.

But this scenario did not include the ambitions of Mr Lukashenko, who skilfully took control of a number of mass media and then instigated a number of referenda to implement constitutional changes. The *Belarus Digest* narrates how he managed to eliminate the independence of the judiciary and legislature and marginalised all opposition groups using state security apparatus. In short, by the end of the 1990s, Belarus had turned from a democratic to authoritarian state with the worst human rights record in Europe. By the end of the 1990s Belarus was no social paradise. That state of affairs continued in 2015. The political spectrum is tightly controlled and economic and social freedoms, to the extent that they exist at all, cannot be taken for granted.

Big brother

The US based Freedom House, which ranks countries according to political, economic and social freedoms, describes Belarus (and Russia) as 'not free', although Russia has the better rating. There's not much to choose between the two countries when it comes to human rights; however, Russia's rating is now pretty comparable to that of Belarus. With a rising number of political prisoners and violent attacks against political opponents, the situation continues to deteriorate.

The Viasna Human Rights Centre in Minsk considers there are seven political prisoners in Belarus. The Russian organisation Memorial states there are about 45 in Russia. Of course Russia has a larger population but the number of political prisoners in Russia keeps growing, while in Belarus, ahead of the 2015 presidential campaign, it had slowly been decreasing.

The fall-out from President Putin's Ukrainian adventures in 2014 has certainly not been to the advantage of Belarus. In the first instance, Ukraine – or at least eastern Ukraine – and, of course, Crimea, has become Russia's top priority for aid and assistance – political, economic and military. Thus the once cherished position of Belarus in the proposed CIS customs union hierarchy has slipped a notch, replaced by its more strategically important neighbour to the south. An end 2013 article in the London *Financial Times*' had already pointed out that 'Belarus, with its small and centralised economy and limited geopolitical significance, is far from being the key element in Putin's reintegration projects.' This was a reference to the customs union, the regional 'common economic space' and the proposed 'Eurasian Economic Union.' The simple fact that all of these projects were little more than devices in the Kremlin's scheme to recreate a 'Greater Russia' was certainly not lost on most Belarusians. Until the advent of Russia's westward expansion, or at least its intended westward expansion, Belarus had seen itself as the blue-eyed next door neighbour, happily enjoying its relationship with its richer neighbour.

The changed priorities meant that any requests from Minsk to Moscow for aid, or even for a relaxation on the structure of oil sales to third parties might now be met with a simple refusal. The unthinkable had suddenly become the possible, as Belarus reflected on its domestic economic problems, not least a chronic current account deficit and already depleted foreign exchange reserves. In the past, Russian aid had enabled the Minsk authorities to head off any social unrest, depicting the country's economic position to be one of sweetness and light.

However, the chances were that 2014 – a pre-election year – would see the Belarusian political and social situation follow along its bland, largely aimless course. The poverty of its political leadership – or non leadership – meant that Belarus' inhabitants could hardly expect anything resembling a rebellion of revolution. Change of any consequence was simply not on the menu. There was scant chance of a political U-turn, or of improved relations with the European Union or of the West in general. On the one side there was little ability for such a change to take place and on the other there was scant interest. A number of Belarusian opposition politicians have given up the political struggle and chosen to emigrate. These include the once prominent Belarusian opposition leader who in 2011, after receiving a five year jail sentence for 'inciting mass disorder', sought exile in the United Kingdom. Mr Sannikov, a former diplomat, was Belarus's most high-profile opposition figure.

The economy

In the Soviet post-war years, Belarus had become one of the most prosperous parts of the Soviet Union (USSR), but with independence came economic decline. President Lukashenko has steadfastly opposed the privatisation of state enterprises. Private business is virtually non-existent. Foreign investors stay away. The economic situation deteriorated drastically in the summer of 2011 when a balance of payments crisis drained the country's hard-currency reserves. The government's efforts to re-peg the official exchange rate and freeze the price of staple foodstuffs failed to impress either Russia or the International Monetary Fund (IMF), to both of which Belarus appealed for assistance. But none came. In its May 2015 assessment of the Belarussian economy, the IMF noted that in late 2014, Belarus had experienced its third exchange rate crisis since 2008. According to the IMF these recurrent pressures are rooted in the persistent inability of what the IMF politely labelled its 'over-determined central-planning model' to deliver sustainable growth. Frequent bouts of expansionary macro-economic policies, in a context of deep structural rigidities, have fuelled inflation and external imbalances and left Belarus highly dependent on *ad*

KEY INDICATORS — **Belarus**

	Unit	2011	2012	2013	2014	**2015
Population	m	*9.47	9.46	9.47	*9.47	*9.42
Gross domestic product (GDP)	US$bn	55.50	63.62	71.71	*76.14	*60.53
GDP per capita	US$	5,881	6,721	7,577	*8,042	*6,425
GDP real growth	%	5.3	1.7	1.0	*1.6	*-2.3
Inflation	%	53.2	59.2	18.3	18.1	*22.1
Unemployment	%	0.7	0.6	0.5	*0.5	*0.5
Exports (fob) (goods)	US$m	40,772.5	45,574.0	36,570.8	35,735.8	–
Imports (fob) (goods)	US$m	44,374.1	45,009.0	41,110.8	38,334.2	–
Balance of trade	US$m	-3,601.6	565.4	-4,540.0	-259.8	–
Current account	US$m	-5,121.0	-1,688.0	-7,522.0	*-4,644.0	*-4,212.0
Total reserves minus gold	US$m	2,529.7	5,809.0	4,937.8	3,422.0	–
Foreign exchange	US$m	1,910.9	5,241.0	4,366.1	–	–
Exchange rate	per US$	3,017.22	8,545.00	9,540.00	11,000.00	–

* estimated figure ** forecast figure

hoc external support. Absolute poverty and income inequality are at low levels in Belarus but average life expectancy, at 72 years, remains 9 years below the Western European average. Official unemployment is steady and very low at less than one per cent of the labour force, but there is significant excess employment in state-owned enterprises reflecting a deep reluctance to restructure inefficient companies and industries. Inadequate unemployment insurance also deters labour mobility.

Selective policy tightening and a Russian loan helped navigate large external imbalances during much of 2014. Following a period of expansionary macro-economic policies and high wage increases (real wage growth outpaced productivity by a cumulative 30 per cent in 2012–14), Belarus started 2014 with a large current account deficit and a tightly-managed currency that was, on IMF estimates, substantially overvalued. The National Bank of the Republic of Belarus' (NBRB) crawling peg arrangement – which allowed the rouble to depreciate by 1–1.5 per cent per month against the US dollar – did little to address these imbalances given persistent double-digit inflation, but a moderation of wage increases and tightening control of credit helped stave off immediate pressures. This was further aided by the recovery in potash exports (after disruptions in 2013), which improved the trade balance and a US$2 billion bilateral Russian support loan that bolstered reserves. The slide of the Russian rouble in the fourth quarter triggered acute pressures.

The gradual depreciation of the Russian rouble during the second half of the year had steadily increased the overvaluation of the Belarusian currency further but this did not prompt major policy changes. In mid-December, however, when the rouble depreciation accelerated, foreign exchange (FX) demand soared abruptly, putting heavy pressure on already-low reserves. The weak rouble also prompted a surge of imports from Russia. Bond yields spiked as foreign investors reassessed risks. The initial crisis response centred on heavy-handed administrative measures. The authorities introduced a temporary 30 per cent tax on FX purchases, effectively giving rise to a dual exchange rate given the implied wedge between buy and sell rates. A number of banks offered rouble deposit instruments that were indexed to the US dollar rate, which helped stem the deposit outflow to some extent but exposed banks to significant currency risk. The NBRB's overnight credit rate was hiked from 24 to 50 per cent and foreign exchange surrender requirements for exporters were raised. The authorities also introduced a moratorium on consumer price increases that made it illegal for retailers to raise prices, causing product shortages and negatively impacting the viability of retail trade.

Eventually, a substantial adjustment of the exchange rate was allowed. The administrative measures were not sustainable and a parallel FX market quickly developed. Following a high-level reshuffle in the government and NBRB in late December, the NBRB changed course and phased out the FX tax, while devaluing the rouble by about 30 per cent against the dollar. In real effective terms, however, the devaluation only brought the rouble back to the level of the first half of 2014, owing to high inflation, the sharp depreciation of the Russian rouble and the weakening of the euro.

According to the European Bank for Reconstruction and Development (EBRD) growth had slowed to almost zero over the previous two years (0.9 per cent in 2013 and a projected 0.7 per cent in 2014), reflecting a weak external environment and insufficient export competitiveness. The continuous stimulation of domestic demand with real wage and credit increases resulted in a decline in competitiveness, wide external imbalances and recurring devaluation pressures. Partly bolstered by regulated price rises, inflation remained high between 15 and 20 per cent year-on-year during 2014.

Driven by the widening current account deficit, increased cash FX purchases and large foreign currency debt repayments, gross foreign reserves have been in steady decline to far below critical levels, posing a serious threat to external stability. As Belarus remained cut off from external markets and lacked support from the IMF, the authorities had sought funding from Russia before the sharp devaluation. After receiving a bridging loan of US$2 billion from Russia in June 2014, the international reserves improved slightly but remained low at seven weeks of import coverage. In October 2014 Belarus negotiated the right to retain all taxes on oil products it had previously been transferring to Russia. This form of subsidy may total up to US$3 billion a year and could help Belarus finance its external funding gap in 2015.

In the view of the EBRD, Belarus' existing economic model is not viable. The short-term outlook for the economy is uncertain in the light of heightened geo-political tensions in the region. The international sanctions imposed on Russia have lead to an economic slowdown and reduced Russia's ability to provide support. However, Russia's move to ban European food imports could mean an increase in demand for Belarus' agricultural exports. Uncertainty was aggravated by the forthcoming presidential elections and their implications for the country's economic policy. Belarus' persistently high external vulnerabilities, despite financial injections from Russia, meant that the risk of a sudden adjustment did not go away.

The EBRD considered that in the longer term, Belarus' economic growth is limited by the structural deficiencies of the existing economic model, which is based on full employment, for the most part in the state-controlled sector of the economy. The EBRD concluded by observing that this state of economic affairs not only constrained the re-allocation of capital and labour to new, more productive sectors of the economy, but also distorts the price system and mis-allocates resources.

Energy

Belarus remains heavily dependent on Russia to meet its own energy needs and a considerable proportion of Russian oil and gas exports to Europe pass through it. Russia's role as a major energy supplier to the rest of Europe and Belarus's position as a key transit country have come under the spotlight several times since 2006, when tensions first arose between Moscow and Minsk over the price of Russian gas and Belarus's privileged access to duty-free oil.

Relations with Russia deteriorated sharply in the summer of 2010, with disputes over energy pricing, customs union terms and the presence in Belarus of ousted Kyrgyz president Bakiyev, prompting brief speculation that Moscow might switch support from Lukashenko to another leadership candidate.

Energy remains an area in which Russia has a very strong position in Belarus. Russia dominates the nation's gas infrastructure, oversees the work of its oil refineries and has significant influence on its electrical industry.

Although the building of a nuclear power plant looks economically beneficial, Russia's control over the project, combined with Belarus' doubtful ability to repay the accompanying US$9 billion loan, raises many questions.

Currently, Russia is not using all of its energy potential to blackmail Belarus.

Kremlin has possibilities to bankrupt not only individual Belarusian enterprises, but also the entire country. The Russian energy needle will remain a significant factor in the geopolitical choice of Belarus today and even after Lukashenko's reign.

Risk assessment

Politics	Poor
Economy	Fair
Regional stability	Fair

COUNTRY PROFILE

During the thirteenth and fourteenth centuries, Belarus was part of the Grand Duchy of Lithuania.
1500s The Grand Duchy was united with Poland.
1800s The dismemberment of Poland as it then was led to Belarus becoming a part of the Russian empire.
1918 Belarus became part of the Soviet Union, following the Russo-German treaty of Brest Litovsk.
1941–44 Belarus was occupied by Nazi Germany. After the war, Belarus was returned to its status as a Soviet republic, although, uniquely, it was granted membership of the UN in its own right.
1988 The Narodni Front Belarusi (NFB) (Belarusian Popular Front) was formed.
1991 Independence was declared. Following the disintegration of the Soviet Union, the Kommunisticheskaya Partuya Belarusi (KPB) (Communist Party of Belarus) quickly established itself as the main political force. Stanislau Shushkevich (NFB), a moderate reformer, was chosen as head of the Supreme Soviet, a body dominated by old-guard communists.
1994 Shushkevich was dismissed after a vote of no-confidence. The constitution was settled. Belarus was influential in the creation of the Commonwealth of Independent States (CIS). The first free presidential elections were won by Aleksandr Lukashenko, ahead of Vyacheslav Kebich.
1996 A constitutional referendum changed the structure of government and gave the president sweeping powers. It also extended President Lukashenko's term of office until 2001.
1997 Belarus and Russia ratified the treaty establishing a Union of Russia and Belarus.
1998 Belarus and Russia agreed to begin steps to merge their currencies and taxation systems.
2000 Parliamentary elections were boycotted by the opposition. The presidents of Belarus, Kazakhstan, Kyrgyzstan, Russia and Tajikistan (formerly the Customs Five) established the Eurasian Economic Community (EEC).
2001 President Lukashenko was returned to power and began a second five-year term amid controversy over the fairness of the election. The president appointed Henadz Navitski as prime minister.
2002 The IMF refused financial assistance, on the grounds that Belarus had not made sufficient economic reforms.
2003 President Lukashenko dismissed Prime Minister Navitski; he was succeeded by Sergei Sidorski. Russia, Ukraine, Kazakhstan and Belarus signed an economic union treaty.
2004 A referendum agreed to allow Aleksandr Lukashenko to serve as president again (third time). Parliamentary elections were won by supporters of the president.
2006 President Lukashenko was re-elected with 82.6 per cent of the vote. The EU and US considered the election seriously flawed.
2007 A second amendment to the constitution was adopted. Presidential terms in office were no longer limited to two.
2008 Parliamentary elections were won by independent supporters of President Lukashenko, and the KPB and Agrarnaya Partiya Belarusi (APB) (Agrarian Party of Belarus). Protestors accused the administration of electoral fraud in anti-government demonstrations on the streets of the capital, Minsk. The Organisation for Security and Co-operation in Europe (OSCE) reported the elections as having fallen short of democratic principles of transparency and the count in 48 per cent of polling stations visited judged bad or very bad, with deliberate falsification of results observed.
2010 The on-going dispute with Russia over natural gas supplies and Belarusian payments for it resulted in Russian gas supplies to Europe, transiting Belarus, being shut down by Belarus. Agreement was finally reached, Belarus paid the outstanding debt and supplies resumed. A customs union between Belarus, Russia and Kazakhstan became fully operational. International observers declared the presidential elections held on 19 December as 'deeply flawed'. Of the 10 candidates allowed to participate, incumbent Aleksandr Lukashenko won 79.7 per cent and his closest rival Andrei Sannikov won 2.6 per cent; turnout was 90 per cent. Following announcement of the results, thousands protested. Security forces responded by arresting demonstrators and seven presidential candidates and their supporters. The president appointed Mikhail Myasnikovich as prime minister.
2011 The government closed the OSCE Minsk office in January for criticising the 2010 presidential election. Approval by the OSCE had been seen as crucial to Belarus's chances of receiving EU aid. Alexander Lukashenko was sworn in for his fourth five-year term as president in January. A number of political prisoners were released at the end of January, ahead of an EU foreign ministers' meeting to discuss re-imposing sanctions. However, both the EU and the US imposed tough sanctions and travel bans on President Lukashenko and his key political supporters, following a crackdown on the opposition. Andrei Sannikov, a former deputy foreign minister and co-founder of the Charter 97 group, went on trial on 27 April, accused of organising protests after the 2010 presidential election. In the last week of May the Central Bank lifted exchange rate restrictions, leading to a plunge in the value of the rouble that fell by 36 per cent against the US dollar. On 1 June, the government officially asked the IMF for a US$8 billion emergency loan to help it face its severe financial crisis. A team from the IMF visited Belarus on 13 June to discuss the loan but declined to provide funding until Belarus demonstrated a commitment to macroeconomic reforms. In June, Russia cut 50 per cent of its power supplies to Belarus, which admitted it owed US$54 million for the energy. In November, Russia agreed to provide natural gas at 60 per cent less than prices charged to Western Europe in exchange for the Belarussian gas pipeline company Baltranshaz. On 18 November, the presidents of Russia, Belarus and Kazakhstan signed an agreement to set targets for setting up an internal market, the Eurasian Union, by 2015.
2012 On 1 January a Eurasian Commission began overseeing Belarus' efforts to integrate its economy with its internal market partners. New restrictions on media websites were imposed in January. On 16 March two men found guilty of planting a bomb on the Minsk metro in 2011, killing at least 14 and injuring several hundred, were executed. On 16 April, two opposition activists, Andrei Sannikov and Dmitry Bondarenko, were released early from political detention. The main opposition political parties boycotted parliamentary elections held on 23 September, protesting over political detentions and the voting system, which they considered vulnerable to rigging. Political parties, including KPB and APB, won five seats between them and independents 105 seats. The official turnout was given as 74.2 per cent; however, an independent estimate placed the turnout at around 30 per cent. The OSCE concluded that not only were the elections not free and fair, but were not competitive either.
2014 President Kukashenko and Turkmenistan President Gurbanguly Berdimuhamedov held talks in early October. On 8 October, in a summing up of

the negotiations, the President said that Belarus was ready to continue taking an active part in large-scale projects to modernise the Turkmen economy, by means of supplying modern agricultural machines, automobiles, road construction machines, municipal vehicles and passenger vehicles.
2015 A presidential election is to be held in Belarus on 11 October 2015. The current president is likely to win again with the most recent opinion polls on 30 September suggesting that he will win 47 per cent of the vote. Alexander Lukashenko has been president of Belarus since 20 July 1994 and it is widely regarded that his presidency represents more of an autocracy than anything else.

Political structure

Constitution

The 1994 constitution vested legislative power in a 260-member Sejm (Supreme Council).
The first free presidential elections were held in 1994, after which differences emerged over the distribution of power between the president and the Supreme Council.
The constitutional referendum held in late 1996 and the subsequent introduction of a new constitution allowed an expansion of presidential powers and introduced a new two-chamber National Assembly, replacing the Sejm.
On 17 October 2007, the second amendment to the constitution was adopted. Presidential terms in office will no longer be limited to two.

Form of state

Authoritarian presidential republic, where political life is dominated by the president and no real opposition is allowed.

The executive

The president is directly elected for an indefinite number of five-year terms and also serves as commander-in-chief of the armed forces, appoints the cabinet and prime minister and has the power to declare a state of emergency, but not to dissolve parliament.

National legislature

The Natsionalnoye Sobranie (National Assembly) is a bicameral parliament. In the Palata Pretsaviteley (Chamber of Representatives) (lower house), 110 deputies are elected by direct election in single-seat constituencies. Members serve 4-year terms. The chamber has powers to call elections for the presidency, approve the nomination of the prime minister, draft laws and deliver a vote of no confidence in the government. The Soviet Respubliki (Council of the Republic) (upper house) has 64 members where 56 are indirectly elected by regional and Minsk city councils and eight members are appointed by the president. The council has the power to review proposed legislation, approve the nomination of top officials and consider decrees issued by the president.
All members of the national assembly serve four-year terms.

Legal system

Judicial power in the Republic of Belarus is vested in courts. The Constitutional Court adjudicates on whether law is constitutional. The prosecutor general is responsible for ensuring that all laws and presidential decrees are executed properly and uniformly across all state bodies and local Soviets.

Last elections

23 September 2012 (parliamentary); 19 December 2010 (presidential).
Results: Parliamentary: Kommunisticheskaya Partuya Belarusi (KPB) (Communist Party of Belarus) won three seats, Agrarnaya Partya (AP) (Agrarian Party) (one), Republican Party of Labour and Justice (one), independents 105 seats. Turnout was 74.2 per cent.
Aleksandr Lukashenko won 79.67 per cent, Andrei Sannikov 2.56 per cent; eight other candidates each won less than 2 per cent. Turnout was 90 per cent.

Next elections

11 October 2015 (presidential); 2016 (parliamentary)

Political parties

Ruling party

Coalition of independent supporters of President Lukashenko, plus Kommunisticheskaya Partuya Belarusi (KPB) (Communist Party of Belarus) and Agrarnaya Partiya Belarusi (APB) (Agrarian Party of Belarus) (since 1995; re-elected 23 Sep 2012)

Main opposition party

No opposition political party or individual won any seats in the last election.

Population

9.47 million (2014)*
Approximately 13 per cent of the population is aged over 65 years; this percentage is projected to increase to 13.5 per cent by 2015. The highest density of population is in the central regions of Minsk and Grodno.
Last census: March 1999: 10,045,237
Population density: Approximately 48 per square km. Urban population 75 per cent (2010 Unicef).
Annual growth rate: -0.3 per cent, 1990–2010 (Unicef).

Ethnic make-up

Belorussian (78 per cent), Russian (13 per cent), Polish (4 per cent), Ukranian (3 per cent), other (2 per cent).

Religions

Eastern Orthodox (80 per cent), Roman Catholic, Protestant, Jewish and Islam (20 per cent).

Education

School education is divided into three stages: primary from aged four; basic from aged nine; then secondary schooling, from aged 11. Secondary schooling may be taught through gymnasiums, lyceums or colleges, as well as specialised or technical schools. Gymnasiums provide secondary education at a higher level, while lyceums provide vocational education. The certificate of lyceum education gives right of admission to any higher education institution.
Specialised secondary education lasts for two to four years. Colleges are a new type of institution in Belarus and provide advanced specialist training.
Public expenditure on education is estimated at some 6 per cent of annual gross national income.
Literacy rate: 100 per cent adult rate; 100 per cent youth rate (15–24) (Unesco 2005).
Compulsory years: 4 to 9.
Enrolment rate: 94.2 per cent net primary enrolment; 77.5 per cent net secondary enrolment, of the relevant age groups (including repetition rates), in 2002 (World Bank).
Pupils per teacher: 19 in primary schools.

Health

The population declined by 0.5 per cent per annum between 1994—2000 and is projected to decline at the same rate between 1999—2015. The Ministry of Statistics and Analysis reported that the cause of the decrease is due to the number of deaths exceeding the number of births.
The dramatic fall in life expectancy since the early 1990s is caused by environmental degradation, economic distress and the ever-present radiation from Chernobyl fall-out which continues to affect health, particularly among children.
Medical care in Belarus is limited. There is a severe shortage of basic medical supplies, including anaesthetics, vaccines and antibiotics.

HIV/Aids

In 2009, there were an estimated 17,000 people living with HIV (Unicef 2012).
HIV prevalence: 0.3 per cent aged 15–49 in 2009 (Unicef 2012)
Life expectancy: 70 years, 2010 (Unicef 2012)
Fertility rate/Maternal mortality rate: 1.4 births per woman, 2010 (Unicef 2012); maternal deaths 28 per 100,000 live births (World Bank).
Child (under 5 years) mortality rate (per 1,000): 5 per 1,000 live births (WHO 2012)

Welfare

For some years now both economic and political standards have deteriorated under President Lukashenko. As long ago as 1998, a poll by the Ministry of Economy reported that almost 80 per cent of families believed their material well-being had worsened since the collapse of the Soviet Union. Although the state exercises control and mobilises funds for social care and protection, Belarus, along with other Eastern European countries, is planning to privatise its social security systems. Foreign citizens and people permanently living in Belarus have equal rights to social services.

Since independence, the number of local non-governmental organisations (NGOs) has increased dramatically in Belarus. To strengthen the NGO sector, USAID has created the Counterpart Alliance Program (CAP), which provides seed grants to social service organisations in Belarus.

There is a two tiered system of social security coverage: general employed workers and special employees (such as aviators, civil servants and certain medical personnel). Contributions are acquired from three sources: workers, 1 per cent of earnings; employer, 4.7–35 per cent of the payroll, dependent on industry or enterprise; government revenue covers the cost of social pensions and subsidies as needed.

Social security payments are made to the unemployed and those without pension rights through a general social insurance.

Pensions

Pensions are provided for old age (beginning for men at age 60 and women at age 55, with 25 or 20 years contributions, respectively), disabilities and survivors, including payments for sickness and maternity benefits.

Main cities

Minsk (capital, estimated population 1.9 million in 2012), Homel (Gomel) (489,392), Mahileu (Mogilev) (361,779), Vitsebsk (Vitebsk) (354,563), Hrodna (Grodno) (339,406), Brèst (318,709).

Names in brackets are the Russian place-names.

Minsk is the headquarters for the Commonwealth of Independent States (CIS) organisation.

Languages spoken

Ukrainian, Polish and Yiddish.

Official language/s

Belarusian since 1990 and Russian since 1995 referendum.

Media

Press freedom is severely curtailed by presidential policy, with libel laws being both civil and criminal offences, resulting in either heavy fines or imprisonment. The government denies access by the opposition to the state-owned media and can close any independent publication house without judicial review. It appoints senior editors to state-run media outlets and decides on news content, even banning musicians performing pro-opposition music from radio airtime. The state-run press distribution monopoly has refused to deliver independent newspapers around the country and internet news websites are monitored by the State Centre on Information Security. In 2006, the US Media watchdog Freedom House ranked Belarus' freedom of the press as 185 out of 194 in the world and 'not free'.

A new media law was passed in parliament that independent journalists say will restrict online reporting and private media funding ahead of the 2008 parliamentary elections.

Press

All state-owned newspapers are heavily subsidised. Newspapers in the Russian language have the major share of the Belarusian market.

Dailies: In Russian, *Sovetskaya Belorussia* (www.sb.by), is the main government organ, *Respublika* (www.respublika.info), is a Council of Ministers newspaper, other government publications include *7 Dney* (http://7days.belta.by). Private newspapers include *Beloruskaya Gazeta* (http://www.belgazeta.by) and *Narodnaya Volya*. In Belarusion *Zvyazda* (www.zvyazda.minsk.by). In English *Belarus Today* (www.belarustoday.info).

Weeklies: In Russian, *Studenckaja Dumka* (http://studumka.iatp.by) is a youth magazine. In English *The Minsk Times* (www.sb.by/minsktimes), *Belarus* (www.belarus-magazine.by) are general news and interest magazines.

Business: In Russian, *BDG Delovaya Gazeta* (www.bdg.by), *Belorussky i Rynok* (www.br.minsk.by) and *Ekonomicheskaya Gazeta* (www.neg.by). *Delo (East+West)* (www.delobelarus.com) and *Entrepreneurship in Belarus* (www.nbrb.by/bv) are monthly magazines.

Broadcasting

The national, state-run broadcaster is Teleradiocompany (TVR) (www.tvr.by).

Radio: Belarus Radio operates a network of two national stations and three local, with internet broadcasting (www.tvr.by). Programming includes of news, music, cultural and sports events. External services are broadcast in English, German, Polish and Russian. Other radio stations include Radio Roks (www.roks.com), Unistar (http://unistar.by), Alfa Radio (http://alpha.by), and Pilot FM (in Russian).

Television: TVR operates TV-First (www.tvr.by), the only national public service, it also operates the satellite service Belarus TV. The majority state-owned Nationwide TV (ONT) (www.ont.by) is operated by Russia's Channel One. Stolichnoye Televideniye (STV) (http://ctv.by) is a local Minsk broadcaster.

National news agency: Belta (Belarusian Telegraph Agency)

Other news agencies: Belapan: http://en.belapan.com

Nashe Mneniye: www.nmnby.org

Economy

The economy is largely dominated by heavy industry, which accounted for 37 per cent of GDP in 2014 (manufacturing being 26 per cent of GDP); services accounted for 55.7 per cent and agriculture 7.3 per cent. Belarus' manufacturing sector produces vehicles, particularly heavy, industrial units, motorcycles, household appliances, textiles, machine tools and fertilisers. There are mineral deposits and small reserves of oil and natural gas, all of which are exploited.

GDP growth had been strong since 2004 when it was a record 11 per cent; it remained high, reaching 10.2 per cent in 2008, but was severely disrupted by the global economic recession which cut the international trade on which Belarus relies. GDP growth was low at 1 per cent in 2013, before improving by to 1.6 per cent in 2014.

Russia is Belarus' principal trading partner; any change in their foreign relations that may inhibit imports and exports will have a direct influence on the Belarus economy. The current outlook is that Belarus is likely to have both a recession and continued external pressures. With Russia in a downturn, the Belarusian economy is projected to contract by 2.25 per cent in 2015, led by falling exports. The current account deficit is expected to remain around 7 percent of GDP. Export of goods fell from US$46 billion in 2012 to US$37.2 billion in 2013 and US$36.4 billion in 2014. Import of goods increased from US$44.8 billion in 2011 to US$46.4 billion in 2012, before falling to US$43 billion in 2013 and US$40.8 in 2014. The trade deficit was US$3 billion in 2014.

On 1 June 2011, the government officially asked the IMF for a US$8 billion emergency loan to help it face a severe financial crisis. In the last week of May 2011 the Central Bank lifted exchange rate restrictions, which resulted in a plunge in the value of the rouble of 36 per cent against the US dollar.

The World Bank, the European Commission and International Monetary Fund (IMF) have provided fiscal aid since 2007 (US$200 million, US$290 million and US$2.5 billion respectively), on condition the government reformed the economy and introduced measures to foster free-market practices. These aspects had been weakened under the rule of President Lukashenko, who had returned Belarus to Soviet-style centralised planning, where less than 10 per cent of the economy was generated by the private sector. At the start of 2009 the exchange rate for the rouble against the US dollar was devalued by 20 per cent and its pegging to the US dollar replaced by a peg to a basket of currencies including the Russian rouble, US dollar and euro. This allowed a reduction in external vulnerabilities and offered the stability necessary to maintain confidence in the economy. Selective policy tightening and a Russian loan helped Belarus to navigate large external imbalances during much of 2014. The slide of the Russian rouble in late--2014 triggered exchange market pressures in Belarus, which eventually led to a 30 per cent devaluation of the Belarus roubles against the dollar in December 2014.

It remains at 1 US dollar equalling 15,163.00 Belarusian roubles. The official exchange rate, a hangover from the soviet era and kept in place by President Lukashenko, had helped fend off intense economic fluctuations, but the resulting pressure had swiftly diminished Belarus' foreign currency reserves. Imports that were held up waiting for banking transactions to be completed sparked a steady increase in inflation as goods in the market disappeared.

External trade

Principal trading partners are Russia and CIS countries. Belarus concluded a custom union agreement with Russia and Kazakhstan in October 2010, which will improve exports to Russia. The customs union plans a single currency by 2020.

Belarus is a major exporter of tractors worldwide.

On 19 October 2011, a free trade agreement (FTA) was signed by Russia with seven of its former Soviet republics: Armenia, Belarus, Kazakhstan, Kyrgyzstan, Moldova and Tajikistan. The FTA became operational in 2012.

On 18 November 2011, the presidents of Russia, Belarus and Kazakhstan signed an agreement to set targets for setting up an internal market, the Eurasian Union, by 2015. The member states include Armenia, Belarus, Kazakhstan and Russia. Kyrgyzstan A Eurasian Commission began an overseeing role for integration on 1 January 2012.

Imports

Imports consist of petroleum and derivatives, rough diamonds, machinery and equipment, metal products, pharmaceuticals, foodstuffs, vehicles and products, chemicals and consumer goods.

Main sources: Russia (45.3 per cent of total in 2013), Germany (7.1 per cent), China (6.6 per cent).

Exports

Principal exports include machinery, vehicles and parts, mineral products, chemicals, foodstuffs, iron, steel and energy.

Main destinations: Russia (45.3 per cent of total in 2013), Ukraine (11.3 per cent), Netherlands (9 per cent).

Agriculture

Farming

About 60 per cent of arable land is used for livestock (cattle and pigs), the rest being used for cultivation of potatoes, grain, sugar beet and flax. Although agricultural lands occupy 9.4 million hectares (43.7 per cent of the total area), some of these areas are still contaminated due to the Chernobyl disaster in 1986. Particularly badly hit was the area around Gomel, where high levels of contamination are still recorded.

The sector receives heavy state support in the form of tax reductions, consumer goods, fertilisers and fuels and remains collectivised, although there are huge unpaid wage arrears on collective farms.

The climate in Belarus means that production is concentrated on hardier crops, including grains, flax, sugar beet and potatoes, of which Belarus is a leading producer.

Belarus meets its own food needs except for feed grains, sugar and vegetable oils, which the government has targeted for increased production. Agriculture is oriented towards meeting domestic market demands for food products with a trend towards animal production.

There has been a steady growth in the amount of agricultural land under private ownership, although the process is slow and obstructed by political and bureaucratic problems.

Fishing

All fishing in Belarus is derived from rivers, lakes and reservoirs, mainly with drag nets by small teams moving from location to location. There is some fish farming, owned by the state or joint stock companies with government shareholdings.

Belarus has the capacity to process up to 20,000 tonnes per year of mainly smoked and salted fish, with a total of around 300 organisations involved in the fishery industry. The main traditional products include cold smoked fish, salted, preserved and canned fish. Government programmes include increasing the level of catches, the volume and efficiency of fish processing activity by introducing new technologies.

Belarus has had an agreement with Russia since 2002, under which Belarus receives fish quotas in the Russian exclusive economic zone, Russian-Belarusian joint ventures base their fleets in Russian ports, based on the Caspian sea, and both countries co-ordinate their fisheries policies. In March 2015, the Board of Executive Directors of the World Bank approved a US$40.71 million loan to the Republic of Belarus for a new Forestry Development Project designed to enhance silvicultural management.

Forestry

Forest and other wooded land accounts for over two-fifths of the land area, with forest cover of 9.4 million hectares. About three-quarters of the forest is available for wood supply. Timber includes spruce and birch, which are generally of high quality. The state owns all forest and other wooded land. The Belavezhskaja Pusha Nature Reserve (north of Brest on the Polish border) is Europe's largest remaining area of primeval forest, totalling 1,300 square km in size.

In the period 1990–2000, re-forestation increased forest cover at an annual average rate of 3.23 per cent, the equivalent of 256,000 hectares.

The forest sector in Belarus makes an important contribution to the economy. The government has attempted to turn back the sector's deterioration in recent years by increasing exports of wood, wood processing and pulp products. It has also investigated environmentally sustainable forestry and has launched a programme of information collation, using satellite technology, to assess the best use of forestry resources.

There is abundant roundwood production, which is mainly used for sawnwood in both large state-owned and small private enterprises. A significant proportion of roundwood and nearly half of pulpwood production is exported. There is very little domestic consumption of production of sawnwood and panels, but pulp and paper production do not meet domestic demand.

Industry and manufacturing

The industrial sector accounted for 37 per cent of GDP in 2014 and employed 32.7 per cent of the workforce. It has benefited from Soviet-era industrialisation, which transformed Belarus from an agricultural economy into the region's industrial hub.

The sector is diverse and comprises heavy machine production, microelectronics, computers, chemical and mineral processing, synthetic fibre production, textiles, consumer durables and food processing. Raw materials have to be imported and manufacturing is reliant on energy imports, mainly from Russia.

One of the prime industrial sub-sectors is the automotive industry. Belarus is the world's third largest producer of tractors and also produces a large number of

lorries, motorbikes and other vehicles, which are exported mainly to Europe. The Minsk Tractor Works (MTZ) produces up to 8 per cent of the world's tractors, which are exported to more than 100 countries. Belarus' electronics sector is highly developed due to its role in supplying the Soviet military machine; it manufactures radios, televisions and electronic devices used in engineering. Furthermore, it supplies consumer goods including refrigerators and freezers to countries inside and outside the former Soviet Union.
Production of chemicals is concentrated in Soligorsk, Gomel and Grodno. The chemical sector produces potassium and nitrate fertilisers, aminophosphate, medicines, polymers and plastics, chemical and synthetic fibres, pesticides, rubber goods and building materials.

Tourism
Although the government has identified tourism as a potential important sector in the economy – Belarus has a wide range of cultural, scenic and natural sites to offer tourists – the country's tourist infrastructure is basic and lacks a pool of private capital investment to boost its assets. The range of tourist activities on offer includes eco- and agro-tourism, utilising the natural environment and rural regions, health spas and recreational tours. There are three cultural properties and one natural site included on UNESCO's list of World Heritage sites.
Travel and tourism contributed 2.6 per cent to total GDP in 2014. The industry directly employed 1.7 per cent of the workforce (74,500 jobs) in 2014, and indirectly employed 4.8 per cent (234,000 jobs). The government announced new infrastructure projects in 2010, including restoration of historic buildings and a new hotel in Minsk.
Belarus hosted the Ice Hockey World Championship in Minsk in 2014. Hotel accommodation was doubled to 10,000 beds, of which 1,000 are in four- and five-star hotels.
In November 2011 Belarus and Turkey signed a protocol for simplifying visa regulations and laws regulating tourism business and to provide technical support between each other and to run joint tourism events and projects. Plans were ratified to adopt visa-free travel between Belarus and Turkey in 2013.

Environment
One-third of the nation's agricultural land has been unusable since it was contaminated by fall-out from the 1986 Chernobyl nuclear accident.

Mining
Belarus is not rich in natural resources, except for deposits of peat, which is used in power stations and for the manufacture of chemicals. There are significant deposits of potassium, which is a major export, and rock salt. Other resources include clay, sand, iron ore, cobalt, phosphate, silver and gold. Many known mineral deposits await development, while a full survey of the country's resources has yet to be carried out.
The public joint-stock company Belaruskali is one of the largest producers and exporters of potassium fertilizers in the world. According to the International Fertilizer Industry Association, Belaruskali accounts for one-seventh of the world's output of potassium fertilizers. Belaruskali exports the merchandise to over 70 countries. The enterprise operates four mining departments and several auxiliary and service subdivisions.

Hydrocarbons
Proven oil reserves were negligible by 2012. Consumption was 175,000 barrels per day (bpd) in 2012, the majority of which came from Russia. There are two refineries in the regions of Novopolotsk Vitebsk and Gomel with a total refining capacity of 493,000bpd.
Natural gas reserves were negligible by 2012. Consumption was 7.5 billion cubic metres (cum) in 2010. Belarus is heavily reliant on Russian gas imports.
There are deposits of brown coal of little value. Coal is not produced - around six million tonnes are imported from Russia.

Energy
The public joint-stock company Belaruskali is one of the largest producers and exporters of potassium fertilizers in the world. According to the International Fertilizer Industry Association, Belaruskali accounts for one-seventh of the world's output of potassium fertilizers. Belaruskali exports the merchandise to over 70 countries. The enterprise operates four mining departments and several auxiliary and service subdivisions.

Banking and insurance
The National Bank of the Republic of Belarus (NBRB) (central bank) and the Commercial Bank for Foreign Economic Activity (CBFEA) were established in 1991. All enterprises were instructed to transfer hard currency funds from the Russian Vnesheconombank to the CBFEA. The banking system has seen an increase in state participation since President Lukashenko was first elected in 1994. Priorbank is the largest private bank and holds 8 per cent of the total assets of the banking system, making it the fifth largest in Belarus. Foreign capital participation is present in 19 banks, including two that are wholly foreign owned. Credit to the private sector amounts to 9 per cent of GDP. In January 2003, Austria's Raiffeisen Bank bought a 50 per cent stake in Priorbank for US$30.5 million, injecting competition into the sector.

Central bank
The National Bank of the Republic of Belarus

Time
GMT plus two hours, (daylight saving, late March to late October, GMT plus three hours)

Geography
Belarus is situated in north-eastern Europe. It has frontiers with Poland, in the west, Lithuania in the north-west and Latvia in the north. It has long frontiers with Russia from the north to the east, and with the Ukraine from the east to the south. The land is a plain with numerous lakes, swamps and marshes. There is a region of low lying hills north of Minsk. The highest point, Mount Dzyarzhynskaya, is only 346 metres above sea-level. The southern part of the country is an extensive flat marshland. Forests cover some 30 per cent of the territory. The main rivers are the Dnepr which flows south to the Black Sea, and the Pripyat which flows eastwards to the Dnepr through the Pripyat Marshes.

Hemisphere
Northern

Climate
Temperature ranges from minus 6 degrees Celsius (C) in January, to a high of 18 degrees C in August. The average annual rainfall is 550mm to 700mm.

Dress codes
With grey, freezing winters and wet summers, fashion takes second place to practicality in Belarus. Smart dress is required for business.

Entry requirements
Passports
Valid passport required by all and must be valid for six months after departure.
All foreign nationals must register their passports at the local police station within three days of their arrival; if staying at a hotel, reception will do this automatically.

Visa
Visas are required by almost all and must be obtained by anyone travelling through Belarus by train, including international routes Warsaw-Moscow and St Petersburg-Kiev.
Some visa exceptions include nationals of the CIS, travelling as tourists. For further details of those exempt and full requirements for visas see www.mfa.gov.by/eng/consul/3.
Business visas allow stays for up to 90 days. Applications must include an invitation, (may be originally supplied as fax) on official letterhead and should have a

signature of the head of a company as well as a corporate seal. It should also indicate the expected period of stay and a pledge by the host company to provide the invited person full support during their stay in Belarus including all possible medical expenses.

Visitors must register their stay with Belarus authorities for visits of over three days. Exit permits are required by foreigners intending to leave the country with expired visas.

Currency advice/regulations

Import and export of local currency is not permitted and all remaining money must be reconverted before departure. Import of foreign currency is unlimited; however, export of same is possible only to the amount declared on arrival. Currency exchange receipts should be retained and all transactions must be recorded on a currency declaration form, issued on arrival and surrendered on departure. The US dollar and euro currencies offer the best options for conversion. Many public services can only be paid for in hard currencies.

Traveller' cheques, in US dollars or euros, may be exchanged in large banks only, other currencies may be more problematic.

Customs

Small amounts of personal goods are duty-free. Valuable items such as jewellery, cameras, computers and musical instruments should be declared.

Health (for visitors)

Medical insurance is required by all foreign citizens visiting Belarus.

Mandatory precautions

None

Advisable precautions

Water precautions are recommended (water purification tablets may be useful). Dairy products, mushrooms and fruits of the forest (all of which may still be contaminated by radiation from the Chernobyl disaster) should be avoided. Some immunisations may be advantageous: polio, typhoid, diphtheria and tetanus, and hepatitis A for longer term visitors.

It is wise to carry adequate supplies of prescribed medicines, and have precautionary antibiotics if going outside major urban centres. A travel kit including a disposable syringe is a reasonable precaution.

Credit cards

Large hotel, restaurants and at foreign currency shops accept major credit cards. There are a few ATMs in Minsk.

Public holidays (national)

Fixed dates

1 Jan (New Year), 7 Jan (Orthodox Christmas Day), 8 Mar (Women's Day), 15 Mar (Constitution Day), 1 May (Labour Day), 9 May (Victory Day), 3 Jul (Independence Day), 2 Nov (Dzyady/Remembrance Day), 7 Nov (Day of the October Revolution), 25 Dec (Christmas Day).

Variable dates

Good Friday, Orthodox Good Friday, Easter Monday, Orthodox Easter Monday.

Working hours

Banking

Mon–Fri: 0900–1700, including Priorbank, Minsk 2 airport.

Foreign exchange outlets are open all day until late, and some open 24 hours.

Business

Mon–Fri: 0900–1800 (appointments best between 0900–1000).

Government

Mon–Fri: 0900–1300, 1400–1800.

Shops

Most food stores are now open Mon–Sat: 0900–1400 and 1500–2000. Sat: 0900–1800.

General stores open Mon to Fri: 1000–1400 and 1500–1900. Sat: 1000–1800.

There are some 24-hour food stores.

Telecommunications

Mobile/cell phones

Networks operate in urban areas and highways but do not cover rural areas. Two operators offer digital GSM, 900/1800 services, available throughout most of the country.

Electricity supply

220V AC 50Hz. European-style round two-pin plugs are in use.

Social customs/useful tips

Business is conducted formally and appointments are essential. A firm handshake is important as is negotiating an agenda at the beginning of the meeting. Smoking in meetings is very common. Ask permission before lighting a cigarette and offer cigarettes generously.

Written communications are particularly important with large bureaucracies. Address the recipient formally and keep a copy of everything. It is customary to take a small gift on a business or social visit. Offering basic food is considered insulting; offer little luxuries. It is impolite to accompany guests who are not invited to a social function. Gratuities are not obligatory but are becoming more widespread. Vodka is the national drink.

Security

Crime is still negligible and visitors should avoid political demonstrations.

It is advisable to keep away from military establishments.

Getting there

Air

National airline: Belavia

International airport/s: Minsk 2 (MSQ), 43km east of the city, facilities include banks and bureaux de change, bars, car hire, duty-free shops, post office and restaurants.

Airport tax: None

Surface

Road: Good road connections exist with Ukraine, the Baltic States, Poland and Russia. Visitors arriving by car are advised to insure their vehicle with a Belarusian insurer (eg Belingosstrakh); offices can be found at crossing sites. Note that petrol is limited and only 4-star and diesel are available. Most petrol stations only accept cash.

A fee for drivers of foreign vehicles is collected at border checkpoints and varies according to the length of stay.

Rail: There are train connections with all neighbouring countries, with express trains from most European capitals.

Getting about

National transport

Road: There is road network of over 55,000km, the majority of which is hard surfaced. Petrol is limited; only 4-star and diesel are available; and most petrol stations only accept cash. Motorways connect many of the major cities.

Rail: Total railtrack is about 5,523km broad gauge, of which approximately 875km is electrified. Train tickets and reservations can be purchased at Francyska Skaryny Prospekt No 18, Minsk.

Water: Belarus is landlocked, but there is an extensive network of inland waterways (3,800km) which mainly convey cargo goods. The Mukhavets and Pripyat rivers in south Belarus are connected by the strategic Dnepr-Buh Canal, which in turn gives access to the Baltic and Black Seas.

City transport

Taxis: Taxis are plentiful; they can be found waiting in front of hotels, at the airport, railway station and bus station. Journey time from the airport to city centre is about 40 minutes.

Buses, trams & metro: The city of Minsk has a metro that covers the central district, with two lines and 23 stations. Trains run between 0600-0100; entry to the underground is by tokens which are obtainable from stations.

There are buses from the international airport to city centre, journey time about 60 minutes.

Urban buses, trams and trolleybuses run between 0535-0055; tickets for these can be purchased at news-stands or kiosks and must be punched when boarding.

Car hire

Cars can be rented, with or without a driver. An international driving licence with international permit is required. There are numerous restrictions that apply to driving. It is illegal to drive after consuming any amount of alcohol, no matter how little. Driving is on the right. International traffic signs and regulations are in use. Speed limits are 60kph (37mph) in towns and cities and 90kph (55mph) on country lanes and speed traps are widespread.

BUSINESS DIRECTORY

The addresses listed below are a selection only. While World of Information makes every endeavour to check these addresses, we cannot guarantee that changes have not been made, especially to telephone numbers and area codes. We would welcome any corrections.

Telephone area codes

The international direct dialling (IDD) code for Belarus is +375, followed by area code and subscriber's number:

Brest	16	Minsk	17
Gomel	23	Mogilev	22
Grodno	15	Vitebsk	21

Useful telephone numbers

Emergency: 101
Mobile/cell: 011
Police: 102
Mobile/cell: 022
First aid: 103
Mobile/cell: 033
Road inquires: 104
Rail inquires: 105
Air terminal inquires: 104
Tourism inquires: 107
Pharmacies : 169
Automated services
Clock: 188
24-hour shops: 193
Weather forecast: 195

Chambers of Commerce

Belarussian Chamber of Commerce and Industry, Communisticheskaya Street, 220029 Minsk (tel: 290–7249; fax: 290–7248; e-mail: mbox@cci.by).

Brest Chamber of Commerce and Industry, 14 Kubysheva Street, 224016 Brest (tel: 223-2400; fax: 223-4854; e-mail: bo@tppbrs.belpak.brest.by).

Grodno Chamber of Commerce and Indutry, Sovetskaya Street, 20023 Grodno (tel: 224-9070; e-mail: anat@grocci.belpark.grodno.by).

Minsk Chamber of Commerce and Industry, 65 Ya Kolas Street, 220113 Minsk (tel: 266-0473; fax: 266-2604; e-mail: secret@mdbcci.belpak.minsk.by).

Vitebsk Chamber of Commerce and Industry, Kosmonavtov Street, 210001 Vitebsk (tel: 236-3052; fax: 236-4674; e-mail: vitebsk@cci.by).

Banking

Belagroprom Bank, 44 Kropotkina Street, Minsk 220002 (tel: 503-958).

Bel Vnesh Econom Bank (Belarus Bank for Foreign Economic Affairs), 10 Zaslavskaya Street, Minsk 220004 (tel: 269-757, 267-022; fax: 269-759).

Commercial Bank for Reconstruction and Development (Belbusinessbank), 6a Partizansky Ave, 220033 Minsk (tel: 298-147, 768-942; fax: 298-147, 768-504).

Central bank

The National Bank of the Republic of Belarus, 20 F Skorina Avenue, 220008 Minsk (tel: 219-2303; fax: 227-4879; e-mail: email@nbrb.by).

Travel information

Belavia (Belarusian Airlines), 14 Nemiga Street, Minsk 220004 (tel: 210-4100; fax: 220-2383; email: info@belavia.by; internet: www.belavia.by/index_en.htm).

National tourist organisation offices

Belintourist, 19 Masherov Avenue, 220004 Minsk (tel: 226-9840; fax: 223-1143: email: office@belintourist.by; internet: www.belintourist.by).

Ministries

Department of Foreign Economic Co-operation (tel: 269-169).

Department of International Relations (tel: 269-187; fax: 269-936).

Ministry of Agriculture, Dom Pravitelstva, Minsk (tel: 271-377, 271-352, 205-492).

Ministry of Finance, Dom Pravitelstva, 220010 Minsk (tel: 296-949).

Ministry of Foreign Affairs, ul. K. Mark 16, 220050 Minsk (tel: 272-011; fax: 293-383).

Ministry of Information, Prospekt Mashirova 11, Minsk (tel: 237-574).

Ministry of Statistics and Analysis of the Republic of Belarus, 12 Partizan Avenue, Minsk 220658 (tel: 491-261, 495-200; fax: 492-204).

Ministry of Trade, Kirov St. Building, Minsk 220084 (tel: 276-121).

State Committee for Foreign Economic Relations, House of Government, Minsk 220010 (tel: 296-345).

State Committee for Economic Planning, Dom Pravitelstva, Minsk (tel: 296-944).

Other useful addresses

Belarusintorg, Foreign Trade Organisation, Ulitsa Kollektornaya 10, 220048 Minsk (tel: 207-812, 209-756, 208-188; fax: 209-470, 204-763).

British Embassy, 37 Karl Marx Street, Minsk 220016 (tel: 292-303/4/5, 172105920; fax: 292-306, 172292306); Visa and Consulate Section (tel: 292-310; fax: 292-311).

Minsk Expo Exhibition Company, pr. Masherova 14, Minsk 220035 (tel: 226-9193/9890; fax: 226-9192/9936; e-mail: minskexpo@brm.minsk.by; internet site: http://www.minskexpo.com.by).

National Centre for Marketing and Price Study, 7-1117 Masherov Avenue, Minsk, PO 220004 (to reach the National Centre call for voice connection and/or fax: 266-758).

News Agency, Minsk (tel: 293-040).

Union of Enterpreneurs, 13 Internatsional'naya St, Minsk 220050 (tel: 172-587; fax: 271-596).

US Embassy, 46 Starovilenskaya Street, Minsk 220002 (tel: 210-1283; fax: 234-7853).

National news agency: Belta (Belarusian Telegraph Agency), 26 Kirov street, Minsk, 220030 (tel: 227-1991; fax: 227-1346; internet: www.belta.by).

Belapan: http://en.belapan.com

Nashe Mneniye: www.nmnby.org

Internet sites

Belarus portal: http://www.e-belarus.org

Belarusian web links: http://www.belarusian.com/links

Investment: http://www.ib.by

Chamber of Commerce: http://www.cci.by

Business information: http://www.delobelarus.com

General information: http://www.open.by

Belgium

KEY FACTS

Official name: Royaume de Belgique (French), Koninkrijk België (Dutch), Königreich Belgien (German) (Kingdom of Belgium)

Head of State: King Philippe I (crowned on 21 Jul 2013)

Head of government: Prime Minister Charles Michel (MR) (from 11 Oct 2014)

Ruling party: Coalition of Nieuw-Vlaamse Alliantie (N-VA) (New Flemish Alliance), Christen-Democratisch en Vlaams (CDV) (Christian Democratic and Flemish), Mouvement Réformateur (MR) (Reform Movement) and Vlaamse Liberalen en Democraten (VLD) (Open Flemish Liberals and Democrats).

Area: 30,518 square km

Population: 11.20 million (2014)

Capital: Brussels

Official language: Dutch (Flemish), French and German

Currency: Euro (€) = 100 cents (from 1 Jan 2002; previous currency Belgian franc, locked at Bf40.34 per euro)

Exchange rate: €0.89 per US$ (Sep 2015)

GDP per capita: US$47,722 (2014)

GDP real growth: 1.04% (2014)

GDP: US$534.67 billion (2014)

Labour force: 5.24 million (2014)*

Unemployment: 8.49% (2014)

Inflation: 0.54% (2014)

Balance of trade: -US$4.78 billion (2014)*

* estimated figure

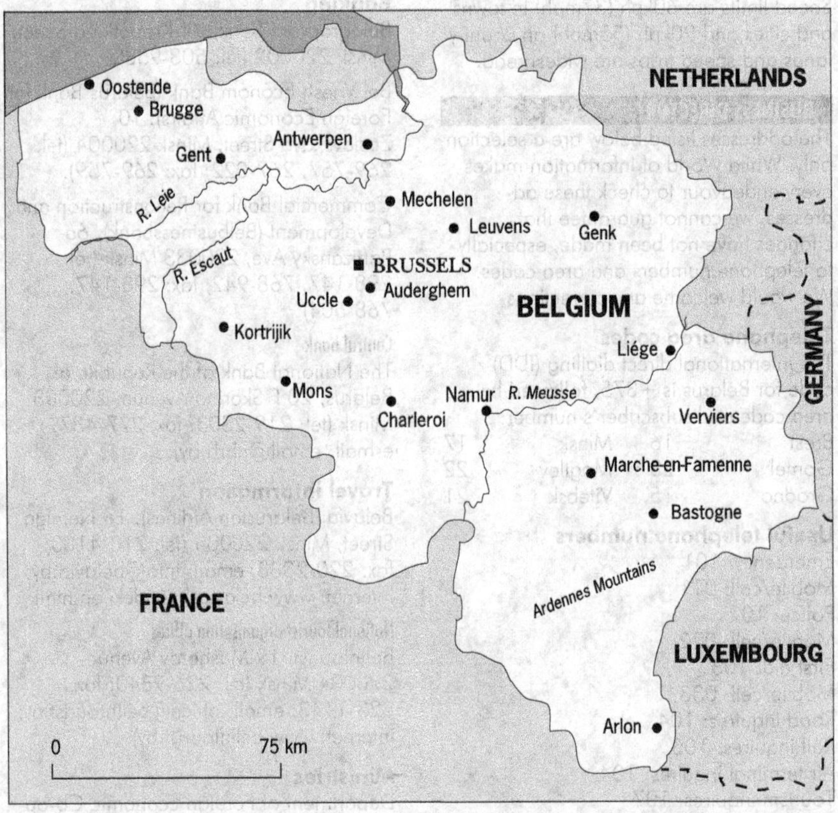

In the run up to the 2014 elections, Belgians had been preparing themselves for the worst, expecting a political upheaval. After the elections ,held on 25 May, it seemed that what they had obtained was something rather calmer and – after the 138 days of inter party negotiation as to how a government might be made up – an apparently manageable coalition, none the less called by some the 'kamikaze coalition'. The government was lead by Charles Michel, who at 38 was Belgium's youngest prime minister since 1841. A member of a traditionally strong liberal political family his Mouvement Reformateur (MR) (Reformist Movement) party was the only Francophone member of the coalition, alongside three Flemish parties. One of these was the contrarian separatist Nieuw-Vlaamse Alliantie (N-VA) (New Flemish Alliance). The others are the Christen-Democratisch en Vlaams (CD&V) (Christian Democratic and Flemish) and the Open Vlaamse Liberalen en Democraten (VLD) (Open Flemish Liberals and Democrats).

The coalition's principal concern was to embark on a further programme of economic reforms with a view to balancing the budget. Belgium's national debt was one of the highest in the European Union (EU), at around 100 per cent of GDP. The coalition government had, *inter alia*, bravely proposed to lower Belgium's levels of taxation. There were also plans to raise the pension age from 65 to 67, but not until 2030, some way behind the dates foreseen for similar measures in other European countries. Other potentially controversial measures related to immigration and asylum.

Predictably, the coalition's proposals had generated vociferous protests from Belgium's socialist parties and trade unions. The former prime minister, Elio Di

Rupo, considered that the proposals would mean that Belgians would have to 'work more to earn less'. One commentator considered that the trades unions would represent a bigger problem for the government than did the fragmented linguistic communities. Mr Michel was not playing with a strong hand. His MR party had come a modest third in the elections, with 9.3 per cent of the vote and only 20 out of the 150 parliamentary seats. The N-VA was the largest party with 20.4 per cent and 33 seats, but no Francophone party was ready to work in an administration headed by the separatists. The N-VA's leader, Bart De Wever, would remain mayor of Antwerp and not join the coalition.

The 14-strong cabinet has by law to be split evenly between French and Flemish speakers, giving MR seven ministers, with Didier Reynders continuing as foreign minister. Mr Michel was the first prime minister appointed by King Philippe. In the new prime minister's favour were his cross-cultural credentials: the Michel family's origins were in the Flemish town of Hoegaarden and his family's political base is in the border town of Jodoigne. Mr Michel became the first francophone liberal prime minister since 1938.

Needs must

However, the Belgium of late 2014 certainly looked to be a more promising prospect than that seen between 2010 and 2011 when political paralysis had prevailed and the Belgians went a record-breaking 535 days without a government. The political crisis had also fanned the flames of partition as Flemish and French speakers heaped blame on each other for their country's difficulties. In 2014, as the parliamentary, federal and European elections approached these differences had seemed to have been placed on the back burner. What was more than likely was that the outcome of the elections would determine the shape of Belgian politics for some time to come. One observer dubbed the polling day as the 'mother of all elections.'

In the run up to the elections most interest had focussed on the need to implement the remaining economic and structural reforms. Under Prime Minister Elio di Rupo, (and against a lot of odds), six reform programmes had been introduced which had included devolving power to the regions and the resolution of the linguistic tensions in the area surrounding Brussels. The leader of the N-VA, Bart de Wever, had seen fit to espouse the confederalist cause in view of the generally cool climate shown to the separatist idea. If there were electoral differences, these had seemed to turn around political programme rather than community differences.

The Royal Household

In times of austerity, it is to be expected that the expenses of any ruling entity – be it presidential or monarchical – will come under scrutiny. At the end of 2014 Belgium began to find out exactly how much its ruling Royal family, headed by King Philip, was costing the beleaguered exchequer. The total to be paid from the federal budget for the King and his family was to be €36 million (US$49.45 million), €2.7 million (US$3.03 million) less than in 2014. More than 60 per cent of this amount was to come from the various government departments that had always funded, on a daily basis, the monarchy's activities. The balance was to be paid from the so-called 'royal budget', the amount of money available to fund the activities of each member of the royal family.

Previously, Belgians seeking to establish the total cost of the royal family had to piece it together from the relevant elements of the overall federal budget, department by department. Former prime minister Elio Di Rupio had, in a previous budget, at least succeeded in grouping the expenses together under a single heading. He had gone so far as to ask the members of the royal family to make an annual declaration of their official operating expenses to the government body responsible for overseeing budget expenditure and had asked the king to pay tax on the sums he received. Previously, the public money received by the king was tax free.

In October 2014 the government passed a law under which, until 2019, the royal budget would be reduced by two per cent a year. In 2015, the former King and his son and daughter Lorenzo and Astrid, were set to see their allowance reduced. By contrast, King Phillip's allowance had been increased, from €11.6 million (US$13.03 million) to €11.8 million (US$12.3 million). The reforms had made the Belgian Royal Family one of the most transparent in Europe. The Dutch government had been the first. The Belgian family was also one of the most economical, placed sixth (out of seven) in one ranking.

If King Phillip had got off to a good start, in late 2014 – in terms of public relations – he had stumbled. The Royal Family had decided to spend Christmas in Indonesia, using a military aircraft for the journey. The question of military resources being used by the Royal Family at a time of austerity – in mid-December 2014 a general strike in protest at he austerities, had paralysed the country – had been under scrutiny, but the minister responsible avoided fanning any flames by saying that any new regulations would not take effect until 2015. But the flames were fanned by a military trades union which suggested that the king should show greater 'sobriety' and consider reimbursing the exchequer for the cost of his trip. The heir to the throne, Princess Elisabeth had travelled to Indonesia by a

KEY INDICATORS Belgium

	Unit	2011	2012	2013	2014	**2015
Population	m	10.95	11.10	11.16	11.20	*11.24
Gross domestic product (GDP)	US$bn	513.40	483.22	524.97	534.67	*463.80
GDP per capita	US$	46,878	43,554	47,033	47,722	*41,267
GDP real growth	%	1.9	-0.1	0.3	1.0	*1.3
Inflation	%	3.5	2.6	1.2	0.5	–
Unemployment	%	7.3	7.7	8.4	8.5	*8.4
Exports (fob) (goods)	US$m	324,404.0	302,371.0	321,029.0	325,986.0	–
Imports (fob) (goods)	US$m	336,121.0	311,054.0	331,171.0	330,770.0	–
Balance of trade	US$m	-11,717.0	-8,682.0	-10,142.0	-4,783.0	–
Current account	US$m	-7,294.0	-9,734.0	-1,203.0	8,710.0	*10,488.0
Total reserves minus gold	US$m	17,880.0	18,600.0	18,139.0	16,626.0	–
Foreign exchange	US$m	8,008.0	8,451.0	8,339.0	–	–
Exchange rate	per US$	0.75	0.77	0.73	0.82	–

* estimated figure ** forecast figure

commercial flight as dictated by the Belgian constitution, which forbade the King and heir to travel together.

The economy

In its March 2015 assessment of the Belgian economy, the International Monetary Fund (IMF) noted that Belgium had shown considerable resilience, but that the outlook was weighed down by weak demand in Europe. Healthy private balance sheets, integration with Germany and employment support schemes had helped sustain employment and economic activity. However, output was still well below potential and private sector job creation was insufficient. With exports accounting for about one third of domestic value added, Belgium's growth outlook (projected by the IMF at one per cent in 2015) was heavily influenced by conditions in Europe.

In the view of the IMF, the critical challenges were preserving competitiveness and addressing the looming fiscal cost of ageing. The wage policies of the previous government had reversed in part a loss in cost competitiveness compared to Belgium's three main trading partners, but the IMF considered that the economy had also been losing ground in terms of innovation and productivity growth.

The IMF noted that age-related government spending was projected to increase sizably by 2040, by as much as an annual added cost of 6 per cent of gross domestic product (GDP). This reflected the combination of demographics and early withdrawals from the labour force owing to generous access to social benefits and inadequate active labour market policies. The new federal government had announced ambitious reforms to address these challenges. Its focus was on improving competitiveness through the temporary de-indexation of wages and a modest fiscal devaluation and activating underused labour resources by tightening the eligibility to pension, pre-pension and unemployment benefits. The programme should be complemented by reforms to increase productivity growth and employment creation, by opening sheltered sectors to competition, lowering the cost of regulation, increasing labour market flexibility and improving education and professional training. Fiscal adjustment was expected by the IMF to resume after a pause in 2014. The pace of structural adjustment targeted for 2015–16 (0.7 per cent of GDP a year) was, in the view of the IMF, appropriate given debt sustainability risks and was underpinned by pro-growth expenditure measures. Co-ordination between the different levels of government still needed strengthening across a range of issues. Banks were adapting to a challenging operational environment and a more demanding regulatory framework. The IMF considered that Belgium's banking sector had fared relatively well by the ECB's comprehensive assessment, but additional efforts would be needed toward Basel III capital standards. To maintain adequate profitability, Belgium's business models needed to adapt further to the low growth and low interest rate environment.

OECD

Broadly endorsing the views of the IMF, in its 2015 *Economic Survey* of Belgium the Paris based Organisation for Economic Co-operation and Development (OECD) noted that Belgium had returned to growth and halted the deterioration in its external competitiveness, while continuing to score well on broader measures of well-being. The Belgian authorities had reduced budget deficits and substantially reformed fiscal federalism arrangements. However, in the view of the OECD, the recovery was still fragile, long-term growth was held back by low employment rates and eroded cost competitiveness and public debt remained uncomfortably high. For vulnerable groups, notably immigrants, labour market integration remained difficult and, for many, housing conditions had deteriorated.

Securing fiscal sustainability while promoting employment and competitiveness was vital. The OECD stressed that public debt was set to hover around 100 per cent of GDP if no further progress is made in fiscal consolidation. The absence of domestic multi-year expenditure ceilings made spending-based consolidation and medium-term expenditure reforms more difficult. However, the OECD believed that there was none the less considerable scope for these reforms, as public expenditure is high, reflecting public consumption and social transfers, particularly pensions. On the revenue side, taxation relied heavily on social contributions and personal income taxes, in contrast to more employment-friendly tax bases, such as consumption and environmental taxes.

Employment and competitiveness had also suffered from a wage setting process with insufficient regard to domestic productivity developments. Belgium rely heavily on its immigrant population. Immigrants already account for almost a fifth of the working-age population, but their employment rates and wages, especially among those born outside the European Union, remain very low. Immigrants are over-represented in low-skilled jobs, under-represented in white-collar jobs and generally badly affected by poor labour market performance. These disadvantages often extend to their offspring. Shortcomings in integration and training policies make it difficult for immigrants to build up human and social capital. Further, their children tend to be concentrated in disadvantaged schools, which often lacked experienced teachers. Plans to reduce grade repetition and increase the age at which students are tracked into vocational programmes should help the children of immigrants and so should more workplace training in those programmes.

According to the OECD, housing conditions in Belgium were generally good. Homeownership is widespread and benefits from long-standing public support. However, the large increase in house prices of the past decade, fuelled by

The 'Kamikaze Coalition'

The 2014 elections marked a major victory for Flemish Belgians, whose parties occupied the two greatest shares of parliament's seats. However, with the largest party only securing 33 out of 150 seats, a grand coalition has been formed. Dubbed the 'kamikaze coalition', three of its four parties are Flemish – including the separatist Nieuw-Vlaamse Alliante (N-VA). The MR party are French-Belgium's only representative in the alliance, although their leader, Charles Michel, is Prime Minister.

Added to the political turmoil, Belgium's budget is in dire straits: with debt totalling over 100 per cent of GDP, the country is one of the Eurozone's biggest borrowers. Plans to reign in public spending have been opposed by Socialist parties and unions. Marc Goblet, leader of Belgium's largest union has promised 'permanent guerrilla warfare' against the sitting government.

Michel is only the second French-speaking Prime Minister of Belgium in the last 40 years, and faces a battle simply to remain in charge.

generous tax conditions, led to overvaluation. The rental market is small, with long waiting lists for social housing and tenants in the private market spending an increasing share of their income on housing. Reflecting high transaction costs on home sales, residential mobility is mediocre, which may impede labour market flexibility, increase road congestion and raise greenhouse gas emissions from commuting.

Belgium has, considered the OECD, made progress in reviving growth and halting the deterioration in external competitiveness, while continuing to fare comparatively well on most equity indicators. Budget deficits have been reduced and fiscal governance improved by entrusting enhanced monitoring responsibilities to an independent institution and establishing a budgetary co-ordination mechanism. Fiscal federalism arrangements have been substantially redesigned with the implementation of the Sixth State Reform. The federal government which took office in October 2014 had announced a multi-year policy programme, broadly in line with OECD recommendations, to achieve a balanced budget and increase employment and competitiveness. Reforms in these areas are needed since the recovery is fragile, long-term growth held back by low employment rates and eroded cost competitiveness and public debt sustainability still not assured. Furthermore, the large foreign-born population, as already mentioned, suffers from poor employment prospects and poverty and its vulnerable groups have poor housing conditions and could face barriers to residential mobility in response to labour market opportunities.

The OECD Survey analysed various ways to address these challenges and found that:

- Pursuing fiscal consolidation was needed at all levels of government, with emphasis on savings in public consumption, in tandem with greater government efficiency and social transfers. Pension and labour market reforms to enhance employment of older workers were key to ensuring long-run debt sustainability.
- Tax bases should be broadened and rates lowered. The tax burden should be shifted from labour towards less growth-distortive taxes.
- Improving the job prospects of immigrants required developing their education and skills, in particular through a more equitable education and training system and supporting both private and public employers to integrate a diverse workforce.
- Rent allowances and support to raise the rental market supply were needed given the many tenants facing high housing costs. The growing demand for housing close to centres of economic activity and related large price increases call for a densification of urban areas.

In conclusion, the OECD noted that Belgium's economic prospects remained fragile. The Belgian economy had withstood the global financial crisis relatively well and has been growing since early 2013, but according to the OECD, the recovery remains fragile. The pick-up in domestic demand, driven by household consumption and business investment, continues to spur economic activity, with further support coming from the strengthening of exports. However, weak confidence, low competitiveness, fiscal consolidation and the economic slowdown in the euro-zone all currently weigh on growth prospects. At just above 1 per cent per annum, overall real growth is well below pre-crisis levels.

Risk assessment

Economy	Fair
Politics	Fair/good
Regional stability	Good

COUNTRY PROFILE

In the eighth and ninth centuries the area, which is now Belgium, was part of the Charlemagne Empire. It achieved independence by the tenth century. Flemish towns, with their large textile industries, enjoyed great financial and political power.

1322 The area fell under French control again.

1419 The accession of Philip of Burgundy ended a period of instability.

1477 The Low Countries (Belgium and the Netherlands) passed to the Habsburgs of Spain on the death of Philip's son, Charles the Bold.

1500–55 Under the reign of Emperor Charles V, Antwerp was a leading commercial centre and financial centre.

1555–98 Reign of Philip II, King of Spain. The Belgians and the Dutch reacted against the tyranny of Philip II. There was turmoil between Protestant and Catholic communities.

1580s The northern Netherlands managed to secede. King Philip re-conquered the south, where Catholicism was imposed. The leading traders and intellectuals migrated to the north.

1598–1621 Under Archduke Albert and Archduchess Isabella (daughter of Philip II), the southern Netherlands (Belgium excluding Liège) became semi-autonomous.

1648 The Peace of Westphalia confirmed this position.

1700–13 The War of the Spanish Succession resulted in the southern Netherlands passing to the Austrian Habsburgs. Liège remained independent within the Holy Roman Empire.

1790 The United States of Belgium was established after a local revolution inspired by the French Revolution.

1792 French troops conquered the southern Netherlands and Liège.

1793 The Austrians reoccupied the territory.

1794 The southern Netherlands and Liège were invaded by the French and the newly integrated territories were annexed to France. When Napoleon came to power, Belgium became part of the French empire.

1814–15 During the Congress of Vienna (after the defeat of Napoleon) it was agreed to unite the northern and southern Netherlands and the princedom of Liège under the rule of King William I. The Catholic Church refused to accept a protestant King, while William tried to impose Dutch rule in Flanders.

1828 The Catholics and young Liberals formed an association called Unionism and drew up a programme of demands.

1830 Revolution erupted in Brussels and the south broke away from the north. Belgium was declared independent of the Netherlands.

1831–65 Leopold I of Saxe-Coburg became the first King of Belgian.

1865–1909 King Leopold II, invested in expeditions to Africa and privately owned the Congo Free State, in which the treatment of Congolese natives by European officials was brutal. Belgian annexed the Congo Free State in 1908, shortly before the King's death.

1914 Following the outbreak of the First World War, Germany invaded Belgium and the country became a battlefield until the end of the war in 1918.

1918–39 Inter-war years saw rapid industrialisation, developing colonial wealth in Africa and the forging of regional links, leading to the Belgium-Luxembourg Economic Union (BLEU).

1940–45 Belgium was invaded and occupied by Nazi Germany.

1947 Belgium formed a customs union with Luxembourg and the Netherlands, known as Benelux.

1951 King Leopold III, who had been on the throne since 1934, abdicated in favour of his son, Baudouin (Boudewijn) I.

1958 Belgium was a founder member of the forerunner of the European Union (EU), the European Economic Community

(EEC), with Brussels becoming the favoured location for the organisation.
1960 Belgium withdrew rapidly from the Belgian Congo.
1970s There was a succession of unstable coalition governments.
1979–92 Christian Democrat Wilfried Martens was appointed prime minister twice during this period, with Mark Eyskens serving for some months in 1981.
1992 Jean-Luc Dehaene was appointed prime minister.
1993 King Baudouin I died and was succeeded by his brother, Albert II. Belgium became a federal state.
1999 Belgium was one of the first 11 countries to adopt the euro.
2001 A government reform package approved more money for schools in the French-speaking communities of the south and more political influence for the Dutch-speaking Flemish around Brussels, even though they were in a minority.
2002 The Euro currency replaced the Belgian franc.
2003 Parliamentary elections were won by the Vlaamse Liberalen en Demokraten (VLD) (Flemish Liberal and Democrats), a coalition was formed which included the Socialistische Partij Anders-Spirit (SPA-Spirit) (Socialist Party-Spirit), Parti Socialiste (PS) (Socialist Party) and Mouvement Réformateur (MR) (Reform Movement).
2004 Following conviction for racial incitement, the Vlaams Blok (VB) (Flemish Bloc) party reconstituted itself as Vlaams Belang (VB) (Flemish Interest)
2007 The VLD, SPA-Spirit, PS and MR formed a coalition government Prime Minister Guy Verhofstadt resigned; however he was re-appointed as a caretaker prime minister. His attempt at forming a coalition failed and to break the political impasse, the King asked Verhofstadt to form an interim government.
2008 After nine months of political stalemate, Yves Camille Désiré Leterme (CDV) was sworn in as prime minister leading a coalition government. The government initiated a US$2.8 billion stimulus package needed to avert a recession. Leterme resigned as prime minister following the collapse of the country's largest bank, Fortis, and a scandal over its rescue. Herman Van Rompuy took office as prime minister.
2009 Two predominantly Flemish-speaking towns of Halle and Affligem, were embroiled in controversy during EU elections, as Francophone political parties were denied advertising space on municipal billboards. Herman Van Rompuy resigned and Yves Leterme became prime minister again.
2010 Herman Van Rompuy became the EU's first permanent president. The Leterme government resigned after a coalition partner withdrew over the voting future of Brussels-Halle-Vilvoorde. The lower house of parliament passed legislation banning the wearing of the *burka* (full Islamic face veil worn by women). In parliamentary elections, the Flemish separatist party, Nieuw-Vlaamse Alliantie (N-VA) (New Flemish Alliance) won 17.4 per cent of the vote (27 seats out of 150) and the right to form a coalition government.
2011 In February, when there was still no government, Belgium achieved the dubious record of the longest time a democratic country had been without a government (249 days), as political parties from the Flemish-speaking north were unable to achieve unity with their French-speaking southern counterparts. On 16 May, Elio Di Rupo (PS) was asked to form a new government. However by 4 July he was still in coalition negotiations with others. On 14 September, caretaker prime minister, Yves Leterme, announced his resignation, to become deputy secretary-general of the OECD. On 21 November, Elio Di Rupo was unable to form a government and asked the King to relieve him of the responsibility. However, on 6 December a new government was sworn into office, with Elio Di Rupo as prime minister, following a record-breaking 541 days since the general election caused a political deadlock. The six-party agreement to form a government was probably spurred on by the downgrading of Belgium's credit rating from AA+ to AA by Standard and Poor's on 25 November.
2012 On 13 July, parliament enacted a law to spilt along linguistic lines the constituency of Brussels-Halle-Vilvoorde. The Halle-Vilvoorde was merged with Leuven electoral area to form a single constituency (of French speakers) and the Brussels electoral area became a single constituency (of Flemish speakers).
2013 Delphine Boel, said to be King Albert's daughter born out of wedlock, opened court proceedings to attempt to prove she is indeed his daughter. On 4 July King Albert II announced his abdication, stepping down in favour of his son, Crown Prince Philippe. King Albert, 79, said he was healthy enough to fulfil his duties. Philippe was sworn in as King on 21 July. On 19 December parliament adopted a number of state reforms. In future the date of the federal election will be the same as the European elections, making the date for the next election 25 May 2014. Other reforms were the abolition of the electoral constituency of Brussels-Halle-Vilvoorde in favour of each province plus the federal capital having their own constituencies (making a total of 150 seats), the Senate will no longer be directly elected and the term in office increased to five years.
2014 Federal, regional and European parliamentary elections were all held on 25 May. There was no clear federal winner, with Nieuw-Vlaamse Alliantie (N-VA) (New Flemish Alliance) winning 20.26 per cent of the vote (33 seats out of 150), Parti Socialiste (PS) (Socialist Party) 11.67 per cent (23), Christen-Democratisch en Vlaams (CDV) (Christian Democratic and Flemish) 11.61 per cent (18), Vlaamse Liberalen en Democraten (VLD) (Open Flemish Liberals and Democrats) 9.78 per cent (14), Mouvement Réformateur (MR) (Reform Movement) 9.64 per cent (20), Socialistische Partij-Anders (SP-A) (Socialist Party-Differently) 8.83 per cent (13), Groen (Green) 5.32 per cent (6); Centre Démocrate Humaniste (CDH) (Humanist Democratic Centre) 4.99 per cent (nine); PTB-GO!/PVDA (Belgian Workers' Party-Left Opening!) 3.72 per cent (2). Vlaams Belang (Flemish Interest) 3.67 per cent (3); Ecolo 3.30 per cent (6); Fédéralistes Démocrates Francophones (FDF) (Francophone Democratic Federalists) 1.80 per sent (2); Parti Populaire (People's Party) 1.51 per cent (1). Turnout was 89.45 per cent. Initially the King appointed the leader of the N-VA as *Informateur*, tasked with forming a government. However, he failed to gather enough support and with Belgium fearing another impasse, on 27 June Charles Michel, leader of the MR party, was appointed *Informateur*. A mere 135 days after the election, Mr Michel succeeded in forming a coalition of Flemish nationalists (N-VA), the Flemish Christian democrats (CDV) and the liberal parties (VLD/MR). Mr Michel will become Belgium's youngest prime minister since 1841 when he is sworn in on 11 October. The widow of King Baudouin, Queen Fabiola, died on 5 December.
2015 Counter-terrorist units foiled what was decribed as a jihadist plot to stage a major attack in eastrern Belgium on 15 January, killing two gunmen and wounding another in a shootout in the town of Verviers near the German border. The gunmen were described as an operation cell that recently returned from fighting in the war in Syria. Search operations led to finding explosives which are believed to have been part of a preparation for a terrorist attack on a grand scale.

Political structure

Constitution

A new constitution was introduced in 1994, re-defining the federal structure and introducing devolution on both a regional and language-speaking level. In 2001, a constitutional amendment

allowed greater autonomy in taxation, spending, agricultural and trade policy.
The federal state is responsible for economic, domestic, foreign, defence, legal, welfare and health policy.
The are three Régions/Gewests (Regions) of Flemish, Wallonia and Brussels. Each has its own executive and assembly, responsible for regional policies (such as transport and housing).
Overlapping the Regions are three Communautés/Gemeenschaps (Communities), representing Belgium's Flemish, French and German-speakers. They are responsible for policy on language and cultural affairs. The French and German Communities operate separate parliaments. The Flemish Region and Community (which represent the same geographical area) operate a joint assembly. Language and cultural affairs in the Brussels Region are divided between the Flemish and French Communities.
In May 2003 electoral reforms allowed changes to electoral districts for the House of Representatives, which now match the borders of the provinces, a new system of distribution of seats, an electoral threshold and Belgians abroad allowed to vote.

Independence date
21 July 1831

Form of state
Federal parliamentary democratic monarchy

The executive
The monarch has a largely ceremonial role but, as Head of State, formally appoints the head of government, although this post is always the leader of the ruling coalition. The prime minister appoints a cabinet of ministers (limited to 15 and with an equal number of French and Flemish speakers); they do not sit in parliament but must present their policies and performance before parliament for review.

National legislature
The Federale Parlement – Parlement Fédérale – Föderales Parlament (federal parliament) has two chambers. The Kamer van Volksvertegenwoordigers – Chambre de Représentants – Abgeordneten Kammer (chamber of the people's representatives) has 150 members elected by proportional representation for four-year terms. The Senaat – Sénat – Senat (senate) has 71 members in total, of which 40 are directly elected for four-year terms by proportional representation, 21 members are appointed by the lower community parliaments and 10 members are appointed by other senators – sons and daughters of the monarch are customarily senate members. Both chambers can propose and veto legislation.
Universal suffrage is at age 18; voting is mandatory, although ballot papers allow an invalid or blank vote. Voting is almost entirely undertaken by electronic means, through the use of a computerised swipe card system. Although federal elections are scheduled every four years, early elections are possible when called for by the prime minister. The federal government is typically a coalition, with ministerial posts assigned to members of political parties within the ruling coalition.
On 19 December 2013 parliament adopted a number of state reforms. In future the date of the federal election will be the same as the European elections, making the date for the next election 25 May 2014. Other reforms were the abolition of the electoral constituency of Brussels-Halle-Vilvoorde in favour of each province plus the federal capital having their own constituencies (making a total of 150 seats), the Senate will no longer be directly elected and the term in office increased to five years.

Legal system
The *Code Napoléon*, became the basis of civil law in Belgium.
The constitution guarantees the independence of the judiciary from the executive and legislative branches. Court hearings are public and trials of a serious nature are heard before a jury of civilians.
The highest court is the Cour de Cassation (Supreme Court), composed of judges appointed by the Crown. A Cour d'Arbitration rules on conflicts of authority between the many layers of federal and national government and their legal instruments.
A Consultation Committee, made up of regional and national representatives including the prime minister, is the final recourse for conflicts of interest arising from devolution. Formed with equal numbers of French and Dutch/Flemish speakers, it makes its decisions by consensus.

Last elections
25 May 2014 (parliamentary)
Results: Parliamentary: (Chamber of Representatives) Nieuw-Vlaamse Alliantie (N-VA) (New Flemish Alliance) won 20.26 per cent of the vote (33 seats out of 150), Parti Socialiste (PS) (Socialist Party) 11.67 per cent (23), Christen-Democratisch en Vlaams (CDV) (Christian Democratic and Flemish) 11.61 per cent (18), Vlaamse Liberalen en Democraten (VLD) (Open Flemish Liberals and Democrats) 9.78 per cent (14), Mouvement Réformateur (MR) (Reform Movement) 9.64 per cent (20), Socialistische Partij-Anders (SP-A) (Socialist Party-Differently) 8.83 per cent (13), Groen (Green) 5.32 per cent (6); Centre Démocrate Humaniste (CDH) (Humanist Democratic Centre) 4.99 per cent (nine); PTB-GO!/PVDA (Belgian Workers' Party-Left Opening!) 3.72 per cent (2). Vlaams Belang (Flemish Interest) 3.67 per cent (3); Ecolo 3.30 per cent (6); Fédéralistes Démocrates Francophones (FDF) (Francophone Democratic Federalists) 1.80 per sent (2); Parti Populaire (People's Party) 1.51 per cent (1). Turnout was 89.45 per cent.
Senate: No longer directly elected.

Next elections
2018 (parliament)

Political parties

Ruling party
Coalition of Nieuw-Vlaamse Alliantie (N-VA) (New Flemish Alliance), Christen-Democratisch en Vlaams (CDV) (Christian Democratic and Flemish), Mouvement Réformateur (MR) (Reform Movement) and Vlaamse Liberalen en Democraten (VLD) (Open Flemish Liberals and Democrats).

Population

11.16 million (2013)
Last census: October 2001: 10,296,350
Population density: Urban population 97 per cent (2010 Unicef).
Annual growth rate: 0.4 per cent, 1990–2010 (Unicef).

Ethnic make-up
Around 57 per cent of the population live in Dutch-speaking Flanders, 32 per cent in French-speaking Wallonia, 10 per cent in bilingual Brussels and 1 per cent in the German-speaking border region. There are also some 860,000 foreign expatriates and immigrants. The largest expatriate communities are Italian, French, Moroccan, Dutch, Turkish and Spanish. Foreigners comprise about 27 per cent of the population of Brussels.

Religions
Predominantly Roman Catholic (75 per cent). Also Protestant, Jewish and Muslim.

Education

Education budgets are set by the French, Dutch/Flemish and German language communities.
Most schools are state-run and free. Catholic and international schools are fee-paying. The Belgian education system is widely recognised as being of a very high standard. Government expenditure on education typically accounts for 3 per cent of GDP.
The teaching language is determined by the linguishic region in which a school is based: Dutch, French or German. Brussels is a bilingual region of its own, and here separate schools use the language appropriate to their pupils, drawn from the surrounding community. International schools (concentrated in Brussels and Antwerp), may teach in foreign languages and follow foreign curricula.
Belgian French and Flemish schools follow the same school cycles. However exams are particular to each language.

Primary schooling lasts from age six to 12 when students undertake exams to determine progression to one of four different schools and programmes: general, technical, artistic or vocational.
Universities and colleges offer a full range of subjects and qualifications.

Compulsory years: 6 to 18.

Enrolment rate: 103 per cent, gross primary enrolment; 146 per cent, gross secondary enrolment; of the relevant age group (including repeaters and training for the unemployed); 56 per cent teriary enrolment (World Bank).

Pupils per teacher: 12 in primary schools.

Health

Adequate healthcare is provided for all citizens. The patient pays for treatment, but the fee is reimbursed by his or her health insurance company. The reimbursement may cover almost all of the cost or very little, depending on the patient's choice of doctor. The *mutuelles* (health insurance companies) also have their own clinics where basic healthcare, optometry and dentistry can be obtained for a token fee.

HIV/Aids

There were an estimated 14,000 people living with HIV in 2009 (Unicef 2012)

HIV prevalence: 0.2 per cent aged 15–49 in 2009 (Unicef 2012)

Life expectancy: 80 years, 2010 (Unicef 2012)

Fertility rate/Maternal mortality rate: 1.8 births per woman, 2010 (Unicef 2012); maternal deaths 8 per 100,000 (World Bank)

Child (under 5 years) mortality rate (per 1,000): 4 per 1,000 live births (WHO 2012)

Welfare

A social insurance scheme covers welfare payments. Contributions are taken from all workers at 7.5 per cent of earnings and pensioners 0.5–2 per cent of pensions or pre-pensions; employers pay 8.86 per cent of the payroll and the government provides annual subsidies.
Old age pensions, disability, sickness, maternity benefits, survivors pensions are dependent on contributions to worker's insurance funds.
Workers' contributions cover around 70 per cent of social security costs. Unemployment benefits are administered by three regional offices, the Vlaamse Dienst Arbeidsbemiddeling Beroepsopleiding (VDBA) in Flanders, the Organisme de Formation et d'Emploi de la Wallonie (FOREM) in Wallonia and the Office Régional Bruxellois d'Emploi-Brusselse Gewestelijke Dienst voor Arbeidsbemiddeling (ORBEM-BGDA) in Brussels.

Pensions

The statutory age of retirement is 65 and 62 for men and women respectively; in 2009 it will be set at 65 for all.

Main cities

Brussels (Bruxelles, Brussel, Brüssel , Bruessel) (capital, estimated population 1.1 million in 2012), Antwerp (Anvers, Antwerpen) (493,920), Gent (Ghent) (248,285), Charleroi (202,981), Liège (Luik, Lüttich, Liege, Luettich, Luttich) (195,076), Brugge (Bruges) (116,342), Namur (109,686), Mons (91,200).

Languages spoken

The northern part of Belgium, Flanders, is Dutch-speaking and the southern part, Wallonia, is French-speaking. Brussels is officially bilingual, but over 80 per cent of its population are French-speakers. There is also a small German-speaking area in eastern Wallonia, which became part of Belgium after the First World War.
English, Luxembourgish, Italian, Spanish, Greek, Arabic and Turkish are also spoken.

Official language/s

Dutch (Flemish), French and German

Media

The linguistic division of Belgium society circumscribes its media.

Press

Dailies: National newspapers include, in Dutch, *The Nieuwsblad* (www.nieuwsblad.be),*Het Laatste Nieuws* (www.hln.be) is a tabloid and *De Morgen* (www.demorgen.be), *Belgisch Staatsblad* (www.ejustice.just.fgov.be) is a government gazette; in French, *La Libre Belgique* (www.lalibre.be) and *Le Soir* (www.lesoir.be); in German, *Grenz-Echo* (www.grenzecho.be).
Several regional newspapers are published by SudPress (www.lacapitale.be) including *La Capitale*, *La Meuse*, *La Gazette* and *Nord Eclair*; others include *Le Courrier Mouscron* (www.actu24.be), *Metro* (www.metrotime.be), and *Gazet van Antwerpen* (www.gva.be).

Weeklies: *Les Nouvelles du Dimanche Matin* is a Sunday newspaper. *Le 7e Soir* is a national weekly. Other weekly publications include *Knack* and *Le Vif/L'Express*.

Business: The principal daily financial newspaper is owned and published by Mediafin and in French called *L'Echo* (www.lecho.be) and in Dutch *De Tijd* (www.tijd.be). In French and Dutch, other weeklies include *Imediair* (www.imediair.be) and *Trends* (www.trends.be). *Forward* (www.vbo-feb.be) is the monthly publication of the Chamber of Commerce. In Dutch, *Impuls* (http://intersight.org/impuls) is an annual business directory.

Periodicals: Some daily newspapers publish weekend editions. In French and Dutch, *Flair* (www.flair.be), *Jet Magazine* (www.jetmagazine.be), and *Loving You* (www.lovingyou.be) are women's magazines. In English *New Europe* (www.neurope.eu), gives analysis of EU issues.In French and Dutch, monthly magazines include *Test Aankoop* (www.test-aankoop.be), a consumer magazine and *Meervoud* (www.meervoud.org) advocates Flemish sovereignty and *MM* (www.mm.be) is a magazine on marketing,

Broadcasting

National, public broadcasting is provided by Radio-Télévision Belge de la Communauté Française (RTBF) for the French-speaking community and Vlaamse Radio en Televisie (VRT) for the Dutch-speaking community.

Radio: There are two public and one commercial national networks, RTBF (www.rtbf.be/radio) has five stations and an international programme, VRT (www.vrt.be) has five stations and Belgischer Rundfunk (www.brf.be) transmitting programmes in German, has two stations. All broadcasters offer full internet access.
There are many independent, private, regional radio stations including C Dance Network (www.c-dance.be) and Topradio (www.topradio.be/); local stations include Crooze FM (www.crooze.fm) and Geel FM (www.geelfm.be) from Antwerp, Ciel Radio (www.cielradio.be) and Q Music (www.q-music.be) from Brussels and Zone 80 (www.zone80.be) from Liège.

Television: All terrestrial TV will be broadcast via digital technology by 2011. VRT is Belgium's leading broadcaster, which uses external production houses to provide domestic programmes. It has two TV channels, één (one) (www.een.be), which has a full range of programmes, Ketnet (www.ketnet.be) is for children and Canvas (www.canvas.be) is an in-depth news, alternative arts and entertainment channel. Ketnet shares its channel (0700–2000) with Canvas (2000–0100). RTBF (www.rtbf.be) operates two terrestrial, TV channels (La Une and La Deux) and a satellite network (www.rtbfsat.be). Vlaamse Televisie Maatschappij (VTM) (www.vtm.be) is the leading commercial TV network in the Dutch-speaking area, with three channels, VTM, Kanaal Twee (for children) and JIMtv.
There are many pay-to-view services provided via satellite or cable. TV Vlaanderen Digitaal (www.tvvlaanderen.be) and Liberty TV (www.libertytv.com) are satellite stations. Plug TV (www.plugtv.be) and AB3 (www.ab3.be) are cable TV services.

Belgian TV viewers can also tune into a great number of channels from Germany, France, Luxembourg, The Netherlands, Spain, Italy and the UK.

Other news agencies: Belga News Agency: www.belga.be Flandersnews (VRT news): www.deredactie.be

Economy

Belgium has used its geographic situation to develop a sophisticated transport system of roads, rail, canals and ports that is important for trade in the European Union (EU). Although it has few natural resources and has to import almost all its raw materials, with this network in place, Belgium has a diversified industrial sector, generally in the north (Flanders), based on a highly skilled, productive and multi-lingual work force.

The service sector dominates, accounting for 77.9 per cent of GDP in 2014, with industry constituting 21.3 per cent and agriculture, including fishing, 0.8 per cent (2014). Antwerp is Europe's second largest port (after Rotterdam, The Netherlands). Antwerp is also a world centre for diamond trading and processing, with imports of rough-cut diamonds, cut and polished diamonds; most of the resulting production is exported.

In 2008, when the banking crisis struck and the country had to bail-out three of its largest banks that had over-extended their assets on non-performing loans (Fortis, Dexia and KBC Groep), GDP growth fell to 1.0 per cent in 2008, (down from 2.9 per cent in 2007). The crisis caused the downfall of the government as its attempts at selling Fortis left bank shareholders litigious and many bank-workers redundant. Belgium officially entered recession in the first quarter of 2009 with annual GDP growth of -2.9 per cent. The economy went into recession again in 2012 – shrinking by 0.3 per cent – following to years of slow but positive growth. After this double-dip the economy has entered a period of moderate growth, reaching 0.3 per cent in 2013, and 1.1 per cent in 2014.

The effect of the global recession on Belgium was a drop in exports, a fall in domestic spending and a rise in unemployment. Per capita income that had been US$35,929 in 2005 jumped to US$47,756 in 2008 when the economy was buoyant, but within a year per capita income had fallen to US$44,090 in 2009 and further still to US$43,379 in 2010. However by 2014 GDP per capita had recovered to US$47,517.

When the economy is back to pre-crisis levels of growth, the government will have to tackle the imbalance of non-productive citizens and an ageing population and the resultant public expenditure in their maintenance through social welfare and pensions.

External trade

As a member of the European Union, Belgium operates within a community-wide free trade area, with tariffs set as a whole. Internationally, the EU has free trade agreements with a number of nations and trading blocs worldwide.

It has a complex and open market economy; national and multinational companies have operations that import raw materials and semi-finished items that are readied and re-exported. While 75 per cent of all exports go to other EU states, international trade has been hampered by the high value of the euro.

Belgium's hand-made, quality chocolate confectioneries are some of the world's most sought after products. The raw chocolate is typically sourced from Africa, with the finished product consumed locally and exported.

Imports

Imports consist of petroleum and derivatives, rough diamonds, machinery and equipment, metal products, pharmaceuticals, foodstuffs, vehicles and products, chemicals and consumer goods.

Main sources: The Netherlands (20.0 per cent of total in 2014), Germany (13.2 per cent), France (10.2 per cent).

Exports

Many companies export more than 80 per cent of their production. Principal exports include machinery and equipment, diamonds, steel, glass, pharmaceuticals and organic chemicals, motor vehicles, foodstuffs and carpets. A new biotechnology sector has developed.

Main destinations: Germany (16.8 per cent of total in 2014), France (15.7 per cent), The Netherlands (11.8 per cent).

Agriculture

Farming

The agriculture sector accounts for around 0.8 per cent of GDP and employs 1 per cent of the workforce. Although small-scale, cultivation is intensive, especially in Flanders, which has better soils for arable farming. Here one quarter of the organically managed land is used for arable crops. Belgium is self-sufficient in sugar, eggs, butter and meat, and is an exporter of vegetables and horticultural produce. The amount of land under cultivation (approximately 25 per cent of total land area) is falling.

Reform to the EU Common Agricultural Policy (CAP) was introduced in 2005 in Belgium, whereby subsidies paid on farm output, which tended to benefit large farms and encourage overproduction, were replaced by single farm payments not conditional on production. This rewards farms that provide and maintain a healthy environment, food safety and animal welfare standards. The changes are also intended to encourage market conscious production and cut the cost of CAP to the EU taxpayer.

Fishing

Fishing is a smaller and less important industry in Belgium than in neighbouring countries, largely because of its short coastline. The mussel- and oyster-bearing waters of the Scheldt estuary are bordered on both sides by the Netherlands. Belgium has a flotilla of small offshore trawlers, but no major deep-sea fleet.

Forestry

Forest and other wooded land cover around 22 per cent of the land area – one of the lowest ratios in Europe. The majority of timber materials imported come from Germany and France.

Industry and manufacturing

The large-scale, export-based industrial sector accounts for 21.3 per cent of GDP and employs approximately 28 per cent of the labour force.

Belgium's industrial sector is strongly regional. Flanders accounts for some 60 per cent of GDP, and has a modern industrial base. It is also more integrated into international markets than other regions, with around 85 per cent of its output going abroad and accounting for some 70 per cent of total Belgian exports. The region of Wallonia, on the other hand, accounts for 25 per cent of GDP and is burdened with declining heavy industry. The government has made considerable efforts to restructure the industrial base in Wallonia, with substantial investment incentives available.

The central government's policy is aimed at facilitating the renewal and restructuring of industry so that it can adapt to new technologies and maintain its competitive position internationally. This includes encouraging domestic and foreign investment in industry with tax incentives, particularly in advanced technology fields.

Tourism

Belgium has 10 sites registered on the Unesco World Heritage list, including pre-historic, ancient, medieval and other historical places of interest. The country has modern, well developed connections and communications with all surrounding countries, with an extensive tourism infrastructure and has a reputation for world-class chocolate and beer.

Tourism is an important component of the economy. Travel and tourism constituted around 5.9 per cent of GDP and provides employment to 6.4 per cent of the workforce. Investment in travel and tourism increased from US$1.9 billion in 2008 to US$2.8 billion in 2014 as government measures were applied to improve the prospects of the industry, investment in the tourist industry accounted for 2.4 per cent of total investment. Belgium had 7.6 million international visitors in 2013.

Mining

The mining sector accounts for approximately 0.3 per cent of GDP and employs 0.4 per cent of the workforce. There is no longer a mining industry. Only clay and sand are mined on any scale.

Hydrocarbons

There are no known oil or natural gas reserves. However it is a hub for the import and re-export of crude oil which it refines and liquefied natural gas (LNG) for which it is both a conduit and importer and blender of gas coming from The Netherlands, the UK, Norway, Germany and Russia. It imports 23.3 billion cubic metres of gas annually and 654,000 barrels per day (bpd) of oil (2013). Belgian refineries have a total capacity of 843,000 bpd.

Historically Belgium was a coal producing nation however production has been decreasing sharply and in 2010, 39 per cent of coal was imported from the US and Australia, and only accounted for 5.5 per cent of the country's energy consumption.

Energy

Installed electricity capacity is around 18.3GW. Nuclear power is the primary source of energy, accounting for around 52 per cent of electricity output; most of the rest comes from thermal sources, fired by gas, coal and oil. There are seven nuclear stations. Legislation provides for nuclear energy to be phased out by 2025, but Belgium's environmental obligations to the EU European Climate Change Programme are leading to revised considerations.

Financial markets

Stock exchange

NYSE Euronext NV

Commodity exchange

Liffe Connect

Banking and insurance

The banking sector is divided into three main groups – commercial banks, public credit institutions and private savings banks.

Belgium's efforts to meet the conditions for European Economic and Monetary Union (Emu) involved major restructuring of the financial sector.

Central bank

Banque Nationale de Belgique; European Central Bank (ECB)

Time

GMT plus one hour (daylight saving, late March to late October, GMT plus two hours)

Geography

Belgium is a small European state bordered to the north by the North Sea and The Netherlands, to the east by The Netherlands, Germany and Luxembourg, and to the south and west by France. It is flat near the coast, but hillier in the Ardennes region in the south-east.

Hemisphere

Northern

Climate

The country has a temperate climate; the proximity of the sea reduces the harshness of winter, but makes summers relatively cool.

Temperatures overall do not show great variations. The average for the hottest month, July, is 17 degrees Celsius (C) and for the coldest, January, 3 degrees C. Temperatures tend to be slightly higher along the coast and cooler in the Ardennes.

There is regular but moderate rainfall with average annual precipitation of 800mm.

Dress codes

Belgian dress codes are in general the same as those in other industrialised nations. Suit and tie for men are usual for business and formal occasions, but often a jacket and trousers are sufficient. For women, a suit, dress or skirt and blouse are suitable for most business and social occasions.

Entry requirements

Passports

Passport are required by all visitors, except EU citizens of Schengen Accord states, who require ID cards.

Visa

Required by all, except nationals of EU and Schengen area signatory countries, North America, Australasia and Japan. For further exceptions contact the nearest embassy. A Schengen visa application (offered in several languages) can be downloaded from http://europa.eu/abc/travel/see 'documents you will need'.

Currency advice/regulations

No restrictions on foreign or local currency movements.

Customs

Personal items are duty-free. There are no duties levied on alcohol and tobacco between EU member states, providing amounts imported are for personal consumption.

Health (for visitors)

Nationals of the European Economic Area (EEA) countries and Switzerland can access reduced cost and sometimes free medical treatment using a European Health Insurance Card (EHIC) while visiting the EEA. Exceptions include nationals of the 10 countries which joined the EU in 2004 whose EHIC is not valid in Switzerland. Applications for the EHIC should be made before travelling.

Mandatory precautions

There are no mandatory health precautions.

Advisable precautions

No exceptional precautions are necessary; any necessary medication should be kept with its original packaging.

Hotels

It is advisable to book hotel or pension in advance either directly or through Belgium Tourist Reservations. By law, all tariffs must be displayed. Service charges are usually included. Tipping is roughly 10 per cent. Major credit cards are accepted.

Public holidays (national)

Fixed dates

1 Jan (New Year's Day), 1 May (Labour Day), 21 Jul (Independence Day), 15 Aug (Assumption Day), 1 Nov (All Saints' Day), 2 Nov (All Souls' Day), 11 Nov (Armistice Day), 15 Nov (Dynasty Day), 25 Dec (Christmas Day), 26 Dec (St Stephen's Day). Also community public holidays: 11 Jul (Flemish community); 27 Sep (French-speaking community).

Fixed-date holidays that fall on a Sunday are observed on the following day.

Variable dates

Easter Monday, Ascension Day, Whit Monday.

Working hours

Banking

Mon–Fri: 0900–1600. Banks are open most days, although a few small banks close at lunch-time.

Business

Mon–Fri: 0830–1730; Sat: 0900–1200.

Government

Mon–Fri: 0900–1700.

Shops

Mon–Sat: 0900/1000–1800/1900. In large cities, convenience stores *(magasins de nuit/avondwinkels)* stay open either all night or until around 2200 every day, including Sundays.

Telecommunications

Mobile/cell phones

There are G3 and 900/1800 GSM services available throughout the country.

Electricity supply

220V AC

Social customs/useful tips

It can be considered impolite to use French in Dutch-speaking Flanders or Dutch in Wallonia due to historical friction between the two language groups. English is quite widely understood and has

made headway as a *lingua franca*, in Brussels in particular.
In Flanders, the names of Walloon cities are generally in Flemish and vice versa in Wallonia. There are also different names for German place names in both Belgium and Germany.
Business relations require some degree of formality and the use of the formal pronoun in French and Dutch (vous/U). It is customary to shake hands at the beginning and end of a meeting. Punctuality is valued.
Belgium has one of the highest ratios of police to population of any western European country and officers are permitted to undertake random identity checks. It is compulsory to have a passport or identity card with you at all times.
Alcohol is sold freely at any time of day or night. Smoking is banned in public places (including stations and airports).
Traffic coming from the right has priority in most situations (if the driver who has priority slows down or hesitates, he/she still has priority; a driver who has priority only loses this after having stopped and started moving again). Therefore, foreign drivers should be aware that vehicles could suddenly emerge from side-streets to their right.

Security
There is very little street crime or violence in Belgium, though the inner cities have isolated problem areas.

Getting there
Air
National airline: SN Brussels Airlines is an independent, Belgium airline.
International airport/s: Brussels Zaventem (BRU), 13km north-east of the city centre; amenities include, banks, restaurant, duty-free shops (arriving and departing), medical facilities and business centre. Antwerp International (ANR), 3km east of Antwerp; Brussels-South Charleroi (CRL), 55km south-east of Brussels; Ostend International (OST), 6km from city; Liège (LGG) 5km from the city centre.
Airport tax: Departure tax: Brussels Zaventem eur20.93; Brussels-South Charleroi: eur13.49; Antwerp and Ostend eur10; Liège eur7.
Surface
Rail: Express trains (TEE) ensure rapid connection with all French, Dutch and German cities.
Water: There are daily crossings by ferry or jetfoil to Ostend or Zeebrugge from the UK and Norway.
Main port/s: Antwerp, Ghent, Zeebrugge, Ostend, Brussels, Liège.

Getting about
National transport
Road: There is an extensive road network. Toll-free motorways serve all main towns with the exception of those in the Ardennes.
Buses: Extensive coach services operate throughout the country, particularly to rural areas, run by Société Nationale des Chemins de Fer Belges (SNCB) and Société Nationale des Chemins de Fer Vicinaux (SNCV).
Rail: First- and second-class services run between all main towns. Combined tickets allowing stop-overs in main towns offer best value. Over half the railway network is electrified.
Water: There are over 1,500km of inland waterways. Services are operated by Administration des Voies Hydrauliques. Inland canals connect with major French, Dutch and German ports.
City transport
Taxis: Readily available throughout the country. The standardised, metered fare system includes a tip in the final price. Taxis booked to call for a pick-up include a surcharge in their fare. Chauffeur-driven cars are cheaper on long journeys.
Buses, trams & metro: Flat fares are charged on tram and bus service. There are metro services in Brussels and Antwerp.
Trains: Special airport shuttle service operates from Brussels Central Station and North Station, departing every hour.
Car hire
Available at aiports and in most main towns. The minimum age of a hire car driver is 23 years. A full driving licence, valid for at least one year remaining is required. All vehicles must carry a fire extinguisher and first aid kit
Speed limit: urban roads 60kph, main roads 90kph. Maximum speed on dual carrageways and motorways 120kph, minimum speed 70kph. Drive on the right. The wearing of seat belts throughout the vehicle is compulsory. Trams have right of way on any road.

BUSINESS DIRECTORY
The addresses listed below are a selection only. While World of Information makes every endeavour to check these addresses, we cannot guarantee that changes have not been made, especially to telephone numbers and area codes. We would welcome any corrections.

Telephone area codes
The international direct dialling code (IDD) for Belgium is +32, followed by area code and subscriber's number:

Antwerp	3	Ypres	57
Arlon	63	Liège	41
Bastogne	61	La Louvière	64
Brugge	50	Libramont	61
Brussels	2	Mechelen	15
Charleroi	71	Mons	65
Chimay	60	Ostende	59
Dendermonde	52	Verviers	87
Ghent	9	Zeebrugge	50

Chambers of Commerce
American Chamber of Commerce, 50 Avenue des Arts, 1000 Brussels (tel: 513-6770; fax: 513-3590; e-mail: gch@postl.amcham.be).

Antwerp Chamber of Commerce,12 Markgravestraat, 2000 Antwerp (tel: 232-2219; fax: 233-6442; e-mail: eic@kkna.be).

British Chamber of Commerce, Egmont House, 15 Rue d'Egmont, 1000 Brussels (tel: 540-9030; fax: 512-8363; e-mail: brit.cham@britcham.be).

Bruges Chamber of Commerce and Industry, 25 Ezelstraat, 8000 Bruges (tel: 333-696; fax: 342-297; e-mail: brugge@ccibkw.be).

Brussels Chamber of Commerce and Industry, 500 Avenue Louise, 1050 Brussels (tel: 648-5002; fax: 640-9328; e-mail: inscription@ccib.irisnet.be).

Charleroi Chamber of Commerce and Industry, 1a Avenue Général Michel, 6000 Charleroi (tel: 321-160; fax: 334-218; e-mail: info@ccic.be).

Federation of Chambers of Commerce and Industry of Belgium, 1-2 Avenue des Arts, 1210 Brussels (tel: 209-1550; fax: 209-0568; e-mail: fedcci@cci.be).

Ghent Chamber of Commerce and Industry, 41 Martelaarslaan, 9000 Ghent (tel: 266-1440; fax: 266-1441; e-mail: kkngent@cci.be).

Liège Chamber of Commerce and Industry, Palais des Congrès de Liège, 2 Esplanade de l'Europe, 4020 Liège (tel: 343-9292; fax: 343-9267; e-mail: info@ccilg.be).

Banking
AXA Bank Belgium, 214 Grotesteenweg, 2600 Antwerp (tel: 286-2211; fax: 286-2407; e-mail:contact@axa.be).

Dexia, Boulevard Pachéco 44, 1000 Brussels (tel: 222-1111; fax: 222-1122; e-mail: info@dexia.be).

Fortis Banque, 20 Rue Royale, 1000 Brussels (tel: 510-5211; fax: 510-5626 e-mail: info@fortis.com).

ING Belgium., 24 Avenue Marnix, 1000 Brussels (tel: 547-2111; fax: 547-3844; e-mail: info@ing.be).

KBC Bank and Insurance, Havenlaan 2, 1080 Brussels (tel: 429-1111; fax: 429-8123; e-mail: kbc.bank@kbc.be).

Central bank

Banque Nationale de Belgique, Boulevard de Berlaimont 14, BE-1000 Brussels (tel: 221-2111; fax: 221-3100; email: info@nbb.be).

European Central Bank (ECB), Kaiserstrasse 29, D-60311, Postfach 16 03 19, Frankfurt am Main, Germany (tel: (+49-69) 13-440; fax: (+49-69) 1344-6000; email: info@ecb.int; internet: www.ecb.int).

Stock exchange

NYSE Euronext NV
Palais de la Bourse, Place de la Bourse, 1000 Brussels (tel: 509.1211; fax: 509-1212; e-mail: info@euronext.be; www.euronext.com).

Chi-X, www.chi-x.com

Commodity exchange

Liffe Connect, www.nyse.com/nyseeuronext

Travel information

Brussels International Airport Company (BIAC), Brussels Airport, B-1930 Zaventem, (tel: 2753-4200; email: info@biac.be).

Brussels International Tourism and Congress, Hôtel de Ville, Grand Place, 1000 Brussels (tel: 513-8940; fax: 513-8320; e-mail: info@brusselstourism.be).

SN Brussels Airlines, The Corporate Village, Da Vincilaan 9, 1935 Zaventem (customer service tel: 070 351-111; internet: www.flysn.be).

National tourist organisation offices

Belgian Tourist Office (Brussels and Ardennes), 61 Rue du Marché aux Herbes, 1000 Brussels (tel: 504-0390; fax: 504-0270; e-mail: info@opt.be).
Belgian Tourist Office (Tourism Flanders), 63 Rue du Marché aux Herbes, 1000 Brussels (tel: 504-0390; fax: 504-0270; e-mail: info@toerismevlaanderen.be).

Ministries

Ministry of Agriculture and Small and Medium-Sized Enterprises, 1 Rue Marie-Thérèse, 1000 Brussels (tel: 211-0611; fax: 219-6130).

Ministry of the Budget, 180 Rue Royale, 1000 Brussels (tel: 219-1911; fax: 217-3328).

Ministry for the Civil Service, Résidence Palace, 51 Rue de la Loi, 1040 Brussels (tel: 790-5800; fax: 790-5790).

Ministry of Consumer Affairs, Public Health and Environment, 7 Avenue des Arts, 1210 Brussels (tel: 220-2011; fax: 220-2067; e-mail: environment@health.fgov.be).

Ministry of Defence, 8 Rue Lambermont, 1000 Brussels (tel: 550-2811; fax: 550-2919).

Ministry of Economic Affairs and Scientific Research, 23 Square de Meeûs, 1000 Brussels (tel: 506-5111; fax: 514-4683).

Ministry of Employment, 51 Rue Belliard, 1040 Brussels (tel: 233-5111; fax: 230-1067; e-mail: info@cabmeta.fgov.be).

Ministry of Finance, 12 Rue de la Loi, 1000 Brussels (tel: 238-8111; fax: 233-8003; e-mail: contact@ckfin.minfin.be).

Ministry of Foreign Affairs, 15 Rue des Petits Carmes, 1000 Brussels (tel: 501-8211; fax: 511-6385; internet site: http://www.diplobel.fgov.be/default_em.htm).

Ministry of Interior Affairs, 60 Rue Royale, 1000 Brussels (tel: 504-8511; fax: 504-8500; e-mail: info@mibz.fgov.be).

Ministry of Justice, 115 Boulevard de Waterloo, 1000 Brussels (tel: 542-7911; fax: 538-0767; info@just.fgov.be).

Ministry of Mobility and Transport, 65 Rue de la Loi, 1040 Brussels (tel: 237-6711; fax: 230-1824).

Ministry of Social Affairs and Pensions, 62 Rue de la Loi, 1040 Brussels (tel: 238-2811; fax: 230-3895).

Ministry of Telecommunications, Public Enterprises and Participations, 7 Queteletplein, 1030 Brussels (tel: 250-0303; fax: 219-0914; e-mail: info@telcobel.be).

Prime Minister's Office, 16 Rue de la Loi, 1000 Brussels (tel: 501-0211; fax: 512-6953).

Other useful addresses

Belgian Association of International Trading Houses (ABNEI), 7 Israëlietenstraat, 2000 Antwerp (tel: 226-0712; fax: 231-9969; e-mail: tradechem@cmc.be).

Belgian Embassy (USA), 3330 Garfield Street, NW, Washington DC 20008 (tel: 202-333-6900; fax: 202-333-3079).

Belgian Foreign Trade Board, World Trade Centre, Tower 1, 30/36 Boulevard du Roi Albert II, 1000 Brussels (tel: 206-3511; fax: 203-1812; e-mail: info@obcebdbh.be).

Belgian Institute of Standardisation, 29 Avenue de la Brabançonne, 1000 Brussels (tel: 738-0111; fax: 733-4264; e-mail: info@ibn.be).

British Embassy, 85 Rue d'Arlon, 1040 Brussels (tel: 287-6211; fax: 287-6360; e-mail: info@britain.be).

Brussels Regional Development Agency, 6 Rue Gabrielle Petit, 1080 Brussels (tel: 422-5111; fax: 422-5112; info@sdrb.irisnet.be).

Ducroire/Delcredere (export credit agency), 40 Square de Meêus, 1000 Brussels (tel: 509-4211; fax: 513-5059; e-mail: ducroire@ondd.be).

Euler-Cobac (credit insurance), 15 Rue Montoyer, 1000 Brussels (tel: 289-311; fax: 289-329).

Federation of Belgian Companies (VBO-FEB), 4 Rue Ravenstein, 1000 Brussels (tel: 515-0811; fax: 515-0999; e-mail: info@vbo-feb.be).

Flemish Economic Alliance (VEV), 5 Brouwersvliet, 2000 Antwerp (tel: 202-4400; fax: 233-7660; e-mail: vev@vev.be).

Flemish Foreign Trade Board, 40 Boulevard du Régent, 1000 Brussels (tel: 504-8711; fax: 504-8899; e-mail: info@export.vlaanderen.be).

Investment Company for Flanders (GIMV), 37 Karel Oomsstraat, 2018 Antwerp (tel:290-2100; fax: 290-2105; e-mail: receptie@gimv.be).

National Institute of Statistics, 44/46 Rue de Louvain, 1000 Brussels (tel: 548-6365; fax: 548-6367; e-mail: info@statbel.mineco.fgov.be).

US Embassy, 27 Boulevard du Régent, 1000 Brussels (tel: 508-2111; fax: 511-2725; e-mail: ic@usinfo.be).

Walloon Business Union (UWE), 1-3 Chemin du Stockoy, 1300 Wavre (tel: 471-940; fax: 453-343; e-mail: info@uwe.be).
Walloon Export Agency (AWEX), 2 Place Sainctelette, 1080 Brussels (tel: 421-8211; fax: 421-8787; e-mail: mail@awex.wallonie.be).
Belga News Agency: www.belga.be
Flandersnews (VRT news): www.deredactie.be

Internet sites

Belgium Federal Information Service: http://www.belgium.be/

Belgium White Pages: www.infobel.be

Travel information: www.visitbelgium.com

Statistics: www.statbel.fgov.be

Le Soir (newspaper): www.lesoir.be

Government of Flanders: www.flanders.be

Government of Wallonia: www.wallonie.com

Belize

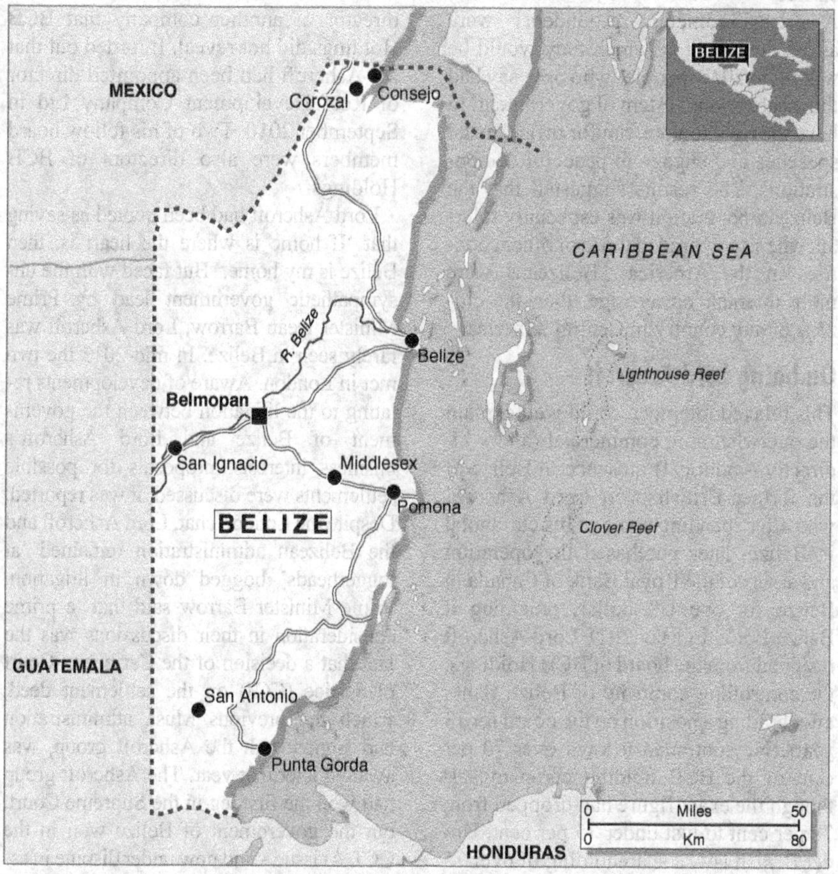

Municipal Elections were held in Belize in March 2015. The final results of the day were a huge victory for the United Democratic Party (UDP) which won 61 seats, including 8 mayorships. This was an ignominious defeat for the People's United Party (PUP), which could only muster 5 seats out a total of 67. The last time the PUP had been defeated so roundly was in 2006, when the UDP won 64 out of 67 seats. The UDP had gone on to win the 2008 general election by a landslide. A total of eight out of nine municipalities were now controlled by the UDP, including the capital, Belmopan.

PUP fades

In Belize, general elections for the House of Representatives (parliament) are held every five years. Municipal elections are held every three years throughout all the cities and towns to elect the mayors, city councillors and town councillors. In 2012, however, the incumbent government called early elections, which were not actually due until 2013. They also decided to conduct the general and municipal elections on the same day. In Belize the theory is that when the party in government chooses to call early elections, it does so out of weakness. In 2012, however, the party in government – the UDP – won 17 out of 31 seats and the PUP won 14. In the municipal elections the governing party won 44 seats and the opposition 23 seats. The next general elections in Belize are not due until 2017 but many people believe they could be called as early as next year. However, on the last occasion that early elections were called, the ruling UDP almost lost the early election and there was no guarantee that it would be

KEY FACTS

Official name: Belize

Head of State: Queen Elizabeth II (since 1952); Governor General Sir Colville Norbert Young (since 1993)

Head of government: Prime Minister Dean Oliver Barrow (UDP) (from 2008: re-elected 8 Mar 2012)

Ruling party: United Democratic Party (UDP) (from 2008: re-elected 8 Mar 2012)

Area: 22,965 square km

Population: 357,000 (2014)*

Capital: Belmopan

Official language: English

Currency: Belize dollar (Bz$) = 100 cents

Exchange rate: Bz$2.00 per US$ (Sep 2015)

GDP per capita: US$4,745 (2014)*

GDP real growth: 3.38% (2014)*

GDP: US$1.69 billion (2014)*

Unemployment: 12.93% (2014)*

Inflation: 0.93% (2014)*

Balance of trade: -US$336.85 million (2014)*

* estimated figure

able to remain as government if early elections were called before 2017.

The PUP's loss of popularity was attributed by many Belizeans to the death of its former leader, George Price. In its halcyon days many people joined the party because of Mr Price. Most of Belize's ethnic groups were members of the party. In 2015 it seemed to be controlled by a small number of families, Arab Belizeans and business people.

The general perception was that whereas the PUP used to support the poor and working class, latterly it appeared to be set on the enrichment of its leadership, allegedly benefiting from the privatisations of national assets such as the airport, ports and quarries. Meanwhile, Belizeans were left to pay the interest sums due on a bond debt of US$550 million dollars.

Belize is different

In contrast to all the other Central American countries, which are led by a president, Belize is led by a prime minister. And while Spanish is the national and official, language in most of Central America, English predominates in Belize, which as a colony was known as British Honduras. Since the arrival of the Spanish in the sixteenth century, most Central Americans have been Catholics; however, only small minorities of Belizeans are Catholics.

Traditions die hard

This is a reflection of a British colonial tradition, as is the curiously democratic nature of Belizean political culture. In the Caribbean there are many former (and continuing) British colonies. Social studies comparing Jamaica with Belize have found that Jamaican values are quite close to those found in Belize, indicating that there may be some substance to the theory that colonial heritage marks countries over the long term. In a regional survey carried out by LAPOP/AmericasBarometer respondents were asked the extent to which they would be willing to allow people 'who only say bad things about our system of government' to have the right to vote, run for office, make speeches and engage in peaceful demonstrations. The results suggested that the Belizean population was especially tolerant when compared to those of other countries in the Americas. Belizeans were more tolerant, on average, than the citizens of any country in Central America.

On being Lord Ashcroft

This relaxed tolerance could well explain the overwhelming commercial (and – indirectly – political) presence in Belize of the former British peer, Lord Ashcroft, who after spending some of his childhood in Belize, later purchased the operation and assets of the Royal Bank of Canada in Belize for one US dollar, renaming it Belize Bank. In May 2011 Lord Ashcroft resigned from the board of BCB Holdings, the controlling company of Belize Bank, after holding a position on the board for 13 years. He continued to own over 70 per cent of the BCB holding company, although the exact figure had dropped from 78 per cent to just under 75 per cent. Under British law, a shareholding of over 75 per cent constitutes a controlling interest. His post was taken over by his son Andrew. However although the BCB had declared seven existing directorships and two more where Andrew Ashcroft had sat on the board within the previous five years, public records from the Turks and Caicos Islands (TCI), where Mr Ashcroft was based, showed that he had also been a director of another company that BCB Holdings did not reveal. It turned out that Mr Ashcroft had been appointed director of Reef Development Company Ltd in September 2010. Two of his fellow board members were also directors of BCB Holdings.

Lord Ashcroft had been quoted as saying that 'If home is where the heart is, then Belize is my home.' But faced with the unsympathetic government lead by Prime Minister Dean Barrow, Lord Ashcroft was rarely seen in Belize. In mid-2013 the two met in London. Aware of developments relating to the litigation between the government of Belize and Lord Ashcroft's business interests, proposals for possible settlements were discussed, it was reported. Despite the London chat, Lord Ashcroft and the Belizean administration remained 'at loggerheads' bogged down in litigation. Prime Minister Barrow said that 'a prime consideration in their discussions was the fact that a decision of the Caribbean Court of Justice (CCJ) on the settlement deed, which the previous Musa administration had signed with the Ashcroft group, was awaited later that year. The Ashcroft group had won the first leg in the Supreme Court, but the government of Belize won in the CCJ. At issue – and now under dispute in assorted ongoing court cases – is a US$10 million transfer from Venezuela to the government of Belize that has, in effect, ended up in the coffers of Belize Bank. The Bank argues that the money it received constitutes repayment of a government-guaranteed debt; the current government says Belize Bank had no right to hang on to it and is suing to get it.

In Belize Lord Ashcroft is not an enemy to be toyed with. Such is his strength, that in 2007, when the Belize Bank faced 80 separate charges of failing to comply with anti-money-laundering laws, the case was quietly withdrawn for fear that any damage to the Bank might trigger the collapse of the Belizean economy. Lord Ashcroft has at one time or another owned, as well as the Belize Bank, the telephone company, the shipping registry, the offshore business registry and a TV company. He has also been rumoured to hold interests in citrus plants, an electricity firm and a hotel.

KEY INDICATORS — Belize

	Unit	2011	2012	2013	2014	**2015
Population	m	*0.34	0.34	0.35	*0.36	*0.36
Gross domestic product (GDP)	US$bn	1.47	1.57	1.62	*1.69	*1.76
GDP per capita	US$	4,349	4,590	4,644	*4,745	*4,834
GDP real growth	%	2.5	4.0	1.5	*3.4	*2.0
Inflation	%	1.9	1.4	0.5	*0.9	*0.5
Unemployment	%	14.9	16.1	14.1	*12.9	*12.9
Exports (fob) (goods)	US$m	603.6	628.0	608.6	588.7	–
Imports (fob) (goods)	US$m	778.2	837.0	875.9	925.5	–
Balance of trade	US$m	-174.6	-209.0	-267.3	-336.9	–
Current account	US$m	-16.0	-35.0	-72.0	*-97.0	*-0.1
Total reserves minus gold	US$m	219.1	289.0	402.8	486.9	–
Foreign exchange	US$m	180.2	252.0	365.4	–	–
Exchange rate	per US$	2.00	2.00	1.95	1.10	–

* estimated figure ** forecast figure

Lord Ashcroft has also been drawn into another rift with the government over the control of its offshore register, which has been responsible for the formation of more than 100,000 companies in the tax haven. The Belize government has also seized control of the International Business Companies Registry (IBCR) of offshore companies and the International Merchant Marine Registry of Belize (Immarbe), its register of ships. The IBCR is operated by Belize International Services Limited (BISL) which is co-owned by a Panamanian law firm and Waterloo Investment Holdings Limited (WIHL), a British Virgin Islands company in which Lord Ashcroft has a 77 per cent stake. WIHL claimed to have agreements to operate the offshore registry dating back to 1993. A deal to extend the agreement to 2020 was signed with the previous government. In addition to effectively renationalising the offshore register, Belize plans to sue BISL for unpaid of US$30 million. WIHL expressed its 'disappointment and outrage' at the decision and had launched a counter legal action to recover US$60 million in compensation from the Belize government. However, the dispute had also raised questions about just how much money Lord Ashcroft's business interests had made from helping develop Belize as a tax haven. The dispute had raised questions about whether Lord Ashcroft would distance himself even further from his adopted country. This was once unthinkable: in 2009 he wrote in his autobiography, *Dirty Politics, Dirty Times*: 'I cannot imagine my life devoid of work, politics, travel or Belize.'

Forsaking his status as a member of Britain's House of Lords, Michael (Lord) Ashcroft, long the *éminence grise* of Belize's politics continued to maintain strong links with Belize. In early 2015 Lord Ashcroft invited trade union officials in Belize to a meeting. The email sent said that 'discussions would be in areas of mutual interest and if you may have any topic of particular interest, I am sure it could be raised.' Lord Ashcroft had visited Belize during the March 2015 municipal elections and was quoted as saying that in future he planned to take greater interest in the politics of the country. 'I do intend to take quite an interest in the politics of Belize over the next period of time,' he was quoted as saying by the *Belize Guardian*.

The economy

According to the United Nations Economic Commission for Latin America and the Caribbean (ECLAC), the Belizean economy registered a fairly strong recovery in 2014, with growth projected to double to 3.4 per cent from the 1.5 per cent of 2013. ECLAC noted that growth was fuelled by strong value added in tourism, buoyant construction and an improvement in some components of agriculture, which offset a decline in oil production. The pickup in demand resulted in an increase in the rate of inflation to 1.5 per cent. Meanwhile, despite higher tax receipts and substantial inflows under the Venezuelan Petrocaribe Agreement (VPCA), the fiscal deficit was projected to expand to 1.9 per cent of GDP in 2014 from 1.1 per cent in 2013, partly reflecting wage settlements. The current account deficit was projected to widen to 6.4 per cent of GDP in 2014, owing to a larger trade deficit and increased profit repatriation and debt interest payments. Growth was expected by ECLAC to slow to 2.1 per cent in 2015, owing to a continued decline in oil production and the softness in some components of agriculture. However, tourism was expected to continue registering dynamic growth.

ECLAC considered that Belize's fiscal imbalance remained, arguably, the most important threat to macro stability, despite a debt restructuring. Belize's fiscal policy was, according to ECLAC, expansionary in 2014, with the overall deficit swelling to 1.9 per cent of GDP from 1.1 per cent in 2013. Revenue was bolstered by higher tax receipts from the general sales tax, due in part to improved collection. However, this was offset by a 10 per cent growth in spending, driven by a salary increase for public servants and increased capital expenditure. The Belizean government had used 57 per cent of the funds drawn down from the Venezuelan Petrocaribe Agreement to upgrade road and other infrastructure, especially in Belize City. The increase in spending had narrowed the window of opportunity for fiscal consolidation provided by the economic recovery in combination with the debt restructuring and VPCA inflows. A firmer effort was, in the view of ECLAC, needed to bring the debt down to a sustainable level, but this was not expected to occur in the short term. Public debt increased slightly to 75.9 per cent of GDP in 2014 due to higher external borrowing. The fiscal deficit was expected to remain stable at 1.9 per cent of GDP in 2015 as government infrastructure spending winds down and other measures are taken to contain out-goings.

In the view of ECLAC, strong liquidity in the banking system had led banks to reduce their holdings in higher interest time deposits in favour of demand and savings deposits. Belize's monetary stance had remained neutral, with the Central Bank of Belize holding its policy rate constant in the wake of the pickup in activity. Broad money (M2) was projected to expand by nearly 7 per cent, underpinned by the recovery in activity and inflows from the VPCA. A favourable development was the recovery in private-sector credit, particularly to productive activity. During the first half of 2014, the bulk of private credit had gone to agriculture, especially the sugar sub-sector. A sizeable portion of credit also went to the construction sector. With the accumulation of reserves and improved repayment by customers, banks reduced their non-performing loan ratio during 2014, although this still remained above trend.

The balance-of-payments current account deficit expanded by 2.0 percentage points to 6.4 per cent of GDP in 2014. According to ECLAC, higher economic growth fuelled increased import demand, which in the face of stagnant exports led to a widening of the trade deficit. The main imports included fuel, construction materials and pharmaceutical products. The drop in exports mainly reflected a 28.8 per cent fall in petroleum receipts to US$25.5 million and a 12.9 per cent decline in sugar exports by value to US$35.9 million in the year to June 2014. The services account surplus increased by 8.0 per cent, bolstered by growth in travel receipts on account of strong tourist arrivals and spending. Meanwhile, a surge in profit repatriations increased the deficit on the income account by 40 per cent. The capital and financial account surplus expanded by over 1.3 per cent, as a decline in the capital account surplus was offset by a surge in foreign direct investment (FDI) inflows related to greenfield investments in hotel and real estate development and higher capital grants. Growth rebounded strongly (3.4 per cent) in 2014 after having slipped to 1.5 per cent in 2013. Tourism remained an important contributor to growth, with value added in the sector projected to rise by 12.0 per cent on the back of dynamic growth in high-spending stopover visitor (12.5 per cent) and cruise passenger (36.9 per cent) arrivals in the year to June. Belize was experiencing a tourism boom, with value added in the sector increasing steadily over the previous few years and providing an opportunity for the economy to diversify, especially given the decline in oil production. Agriculture recovered in the second quarter, with an improved performance relative to 2013. Sugar cane production increased by 5.6 per cent to 1,138,818 long tons, but productivity and therefore sugar output were affected by early rain. Citrus production was stagnant, while banana production declined. Petroleum output continued a decline that had lasted for over four consecutive years, reflecting the depletion of the country's two fields. Production contracted by almost 21 per cent in the first half of 2014, dropping to an average of 1,838 barrels per day from 2,313 in 2013.

Economic growth was projected by ECLAC to slow to 2.1 per cent in 2015 as strong growth in tourism was offset by falling oil production and lower value added in some sub-sectors of agriculture. Inflation picked up to 1.5 per cent in 2014, reflecting higher prices for food, transport and electricity on the back of the rebound in activity. Unemployment fell from 11.7 per cent in 2013 to 11.1 per cent in 2014, owing to job growth in construction, tourism and other services.

Risk assessment

Politics	Fair
Economy	Good
Regional stability	Good

COUNTRY PROFILE

1802 Spain recognised British sovereignty of what became known as British Honduras, but after gaining their independence from Spain, both Mexico and Guatemala laid claim to the territory.
1970 Belmopan became the capital after Belize City was devastated by a hurricane.
1971 British Honduras joined the Caribbean Community (Caricom) as a full member.
1973 The territory was renamed Belize.
1981 Belize attained independence from the UK. However Guatemala refused to recognise Belize, citing its own territorial claims. British troops were stationed in Belize to protect it.
1984 After 30 years in power, the People's United Party (PUP) was defeated by the United Democratic Party (UDP). Manuel Esquivel became prime minister.
1989 The PUP narrowly won the general election.
1991 Guatemala recognised Belize as a sovereign state.
1993 The UDP won the general election; Esquivel became prime minister again and rejected the earlier PUP agreement with Guatemala.
1998 In elections, PUP, led by Said Musa, defeated the UDP in a landslide victory.
2000 The government began reforming the offshore banking sector following international criticism of the country's reputation as a tax haven. Hurricane Keith caused extensive damage.
2001 Hurricane Iris devastated the southern part of Belize. The UK government suspended its plan to grant Belize US$14 million of debt relief due to the government's failure to reform its financial services sector and abolish tax breaks.
2003 The ruling PUP won general elections. A referendum rejected a draft settlement, brokered by the Organisation of American States (OAS), between Belize and Guatemala
2004 The UK Privy Council dismissed an appeal by environmental protestors against the proposed construction of the Chalillo dam.
2005 Oil was discovered by Belize Natural Energy.
2007 The OAS recommended that the border dispute with Guatemala should be referred to the International Court of Justice.
2008 A new political party, the National Reform Party (NRP), was formed, led by Cornelius Dueck, a businessman from the Mennonite community. The number of deputies in the House of Representatives was increased to 31. In parliamentary elections, the UDP opposition won a landslide victory with 25 seats (out of 31). Dean Barrow (UDP) became prime minister.
2009 Unesco added the Belize Barrier Reef Reserve System (the northern hemisphere's largest coral reef) to its list of endangered heritage sites. Unesco requested more action to limit human development and the loss of mangroves. Belize Telemedia Ltd was nationalised.
2010 Belize abolished the legal link with the UK's Review Committee of the Privy Council (RCPC). At the same time Belize endorsed the Caribbean Court of Justice as its supreme court. However the RCPC continued to adjudicate on legal matters referred to it the Belize courts.
2011 In April the government signed two loan contracts with the American Development Bank (IDB), each for US$5 million, to finance the Integrated Water and Sanitation Programme and the Community Action for Public Safety (Caps), to target youth involvement in major violent crimes in Belize City and violent behaviour in schools. In June the Court of Appeal ruled that the nationalisation of Belize Telemedia was unconstitutional and the government moved to take it back into public ownership. During the Commonwealth Heads of Government summit, in October, the 16 countries in which the British monarch is Head of State unanimously agreed to change the royal line of succession from that of first born son to the first born child (regardless of its gender). The change will be enacted after the succession of Prince William (currently second in line to the throne, after his father Prince Charles).
2012 The US-oil company, Treaty Energy Corporation, announced in January that it had found oil in its first well, San Juan #2, in Stann Creek district, with an estimated 5–6 million barrels of recoverable oil in place. Prime Minister Barrow called a general election, for 8 March, in which the ruling UDP won 50.37 per cent of the vote (17 seats, out of 31) and the PUP 47.57 per cent (14). Incumbent Dean Barrow remained in office as prime minister. On 20 August, Belize missed a bond payment of US$23 million (on a loan of US$544 million); Prime Minister Barrow said that the loan needed to be restructured to enable Belize to meet repayments. However, the majority of the creditors rejected the three proposals (typically reducing the interest rate and increasing the term of repayment). On 20 September, Belize paid US$11.7 million to creditors of 2029 bonds and made an offer of further negotiation with other creditors.
2013 In September the government succeeded in re-negotiating Belize's debt obligations.
2014 Belize was among the lowest ten of all 150 countries ranked by the Inter-Parliamentary Union in Febuary 2014 for women's participation in national parliaments. Belize showed as the worst in the Americas and Caribbean and was in the bottom ten along with Iran, Lebanon, Comoros and the Marshall Islands. Three agreements between Belize and Mexico were signed on 3 October, including one on further tourism co-operation. PUP member Joseph Mahmud resigned unexpectantly on 24 November, leaving his party shocked and angry.
2015 The Cayo North bi-election held on 5 January was won back by the ruling UDP with 2,669 votes to 1,340. Turnout was 60 per cent. On 29 September Prime Minister Barrow announced a snap general election for 4 November.

Political structure

Constitution

The governor general is advised by the cabinet (led by the prime minister) which holds executive power.

Form of state

Independent state with the British monarch as head of state, represented by the governor general.

The executive

The cabinet, led by the prime minister, holds executive power.

National legislature
The bicameral National Assembly consists of the House of Representatives (lower chamber), with 31 members elected by universal adult suffrage for a five-year term in single-seat constituencies. The Senate (upper chamber) currently has 11 members appointed by the governor general, of which seven were nominated by the prime minister, three by the opposition leader and one each from the Council of Churches, Chamber of Commerce and National Trade Union Congress; each to serve for a five-year term.
Last elections
8 March 2012 (parliamentary)
Results: Parliamentary: United Democratic Party 50.37 per cent (17 seats, out of 31), the People's United Party (PUP) 47.57 per cent (14); two other political parties and four independent candidates each won less than 1 per cent and failed to win any seats. Turnout was 73.16 per cent. In a by-election held on 5 January 2015 the UDP won back a seat it had lost in 2012, giving the party a convincing lead of 18 seats to 13.
Next elections
4 November 2015 (18 months early)

Political parties
Ruling party
United Democratic Party (UDP) (from 2008: re-elected 8 Mar 2012)
Main opposition party
People's United Party (PUP)
Political situation
The government of Dean Barrow (UDP) has been trying to recover the loss of Bz$33.5 million (US$20 million) given in a promissory note by the previous administration of Said Musa (PUP) to the Belize Bank, in March 2007. The promissory note contravened laws that required any loan agreement over Bz$10 million to be sanctioned by parliament, which this note had not. In August 2008 the Central Bank required the Belize Bank to provide documentation for the authority to deposit US$10 million into the account of Universal Investment Holding (UIH) and to repay the two tranches of US$10 million, which had originally been donated to Belize by Venezuela and Taiwan for aid purposes. The Belize Bank complied and repaid US$10 million but the remaining amount was sequestered until the ruling of the High Court as to the validity of the transaction, which in May 2009 found in favour of the government, which awaits the return of the last tranche.

Population
343,000 (2012)
Belize has the smallest population in Central America.
Last census: 12 May 2010: 312,971
Population density: 11 inhabitants per square km. Urban population 52 per cent (2010 Unicef).
Annual growth rate: 2.5 per cent, 1990–2010 (Unicef).
Ethnic make-up
Mestizos (44 per cent), Creoles (30 per cent), Mayans (15 per cent), Garifunas (7 per cent), Mennonites (3 per cent). Other races: Spanish, British, Lebanese, Chinese and Eastern Indian.
Religions
Roman Catholic (62 per cent), Anglican (12 per cent), Methodist (6 per cent), Mennonite (4 per cent), Seventh-Day Adventist (3 per cent).

Education
About 22.35 per cent of the budget expenditure in 2002/03 was allocated to the education sector, of which a total of Bz$61 million (US$31 million) and Bz$16 million (US$8.1 million) were budgeted for salaries and education grants respectively. Since 1998, dozens of new school buildings have been constructed, with more than 700 new classrooms catering for additional 3,000 students. The government contributes some Bz$20 million (US$10.1 million) towards higher education student loans for the University of Belize.
Literacy rate: 77 per cent adult rate; 84 per cent youth rate (15–24) (Unesco 2005).
Enrolment rate: 123 per cent for boys, 119 per cent for girls; total primary school enrolment of the relevant age group (including repetition rates) (World Bank).

Health
The ministry of health plans to implement the National Health Insurance as part of its overall health sector reform programme, with Bz$4 million (US$2 million) from the Social Security Fund.
HIV/Aids
In 2009, there were an estimated 5,000 people living with HIV (Unicef 2012).
HIV prevalence: 2.3 per cent aged 15–49 in 2009 (Unicef 2012)
Life expectancy: 76 years, 2010 (Unicef 2012)
Fertility rate/Maternal mortality rate: 2.8 births per woman, 2010 (Unicef 2012)
Child (under 5 years) mortality rate (per 1,000): 18 per 1,000 live births (WHO 2012)

Welfare
As part of its poverty alleviation strategy, the Social Investment Fund (SIF) has sought assistance from the World Bank to spend some Bz$10.5 million (US$5.2 million) in water supply, sanitation, health, education and social services projects.
Seven per cent of a worker's weekly earning is paid into the social security fund; a ratio is determined and divided between the employer and employee. Benefits include maternity, sickness, injury and dependant's grants.
Pensions
Old age pensions are paid to those aged between 60 and 65 who have made at least 130 contributions.

Main cities
Belmopan (capital, estimated population 14,606 in 2012), Belize City (67,964), San Ignacio (17,884), San Pedro (13,381), Orange Walk (13,368), Corozal (10,271).

Languages spoken
Spanish, Creole, Garifuna and Mayan dialects are widely spoken throughout the country.
Official language/s
English

Media
Press
Weeklies: There are no daily newspaper, the most widely read weeklies include *Amandala* (www.amandala.com.bz), and *The Reporter* (www.reporter.bz), *The San Pedro Sun* (www.sanpedrosun.net) is a community newspaper published on the island of Ambergris Caye. *The Belize Times* (www.belizetimes.bz) is the newspaper that speaks for the political party People's United Party and *The Guardian* (www.guardian.bz) for the United Democratic Party.
Broadcasting
Radio: There are around 10 radio stations, all of which are private and commercial. Most broadcast either music, religious or news contents, including People's Radio, (www.belizeweb.com), see news & entertainment, also includes Integrity Radio and Positive Vibes Radio. Others stations are Love FM, (www.lovefm.com) Krem FM (www.krembz.com) and Wave Radio (http://waveradiobelize.org).
Television: All TV stations are commercial. The privately-owned, Channel 5 (www.channel5belize.com) is the leading TV channel and, along with Channel 7 (www.7newsbelize.com) and Channel 9, is a terrestrial broadcaster. Centaur Cable Network, called CTV3 (www.ctv3belizenews.com) provides a subscriber cable services, with over 60 channels, to the region of Orange Walk in the north of the country.
Other news agencies: Caribbean Net News: www.caribbeannetnews.com

Economy
The economy of Belize has more in common with the nearby Caribbean region than its Central American neighbours. A

small enterprise economy, previously dominated by the agricultural sector, but by 2014 this contributed only 13.1 per cent of GDP. The service sector, which is dominated by tourism, accounts for 63.9 per cent of GDP, attributable to the rapidly expanding cruise sector and the growth in ecotourism. The industrial sector constitutes 23.0 per cent of GDP, despite the limitations of a small domestic market and relatively high (for the region) labour costs. A number of US companies have out-sourced their operations to Belize, including petroleum, construction and garment manufacturing.

The falling tourist numbers as a result of the global economic crisis impacted on the countries of visitors lead to stagnant GDP in 2009. While revenues fell there was a corresponding increase in import commodity prices, further widening the balance of payments. However, the economy picked up as global trade increased, and by 2012 growth had reached 4.0 per cent, before dropping to 1.6 per cent in 2013. Growth was similar in 2014 and in the first quarter of 2015 had reached 7 per cent.

Belize's financial services attract foreign investors, along with onshore and offshore trust funds, Sharia compliant investment and company registration.

Damage from natural disasters has dogged the region. Belize was devastated by hurricanes in 2007 and heavy flooding in 2008, leaving the population to rebuild their lives and livelihoods.

Unemployment continues to be a problem, however, even though it has fallen from 14.4 per cent in 2013 to around 11.7 per cent in 2014.

External trade

As a member of the Caribbean Community (Caricom) and Common Market, Belize operates within the Caricom Single Market and Economy (CSME) development strategy, which became operational in 2006. Goods, services, businesses and money are free to move within CSME countries without barriers and tariffs.

Belize relies on imports of fuel and goods and services largely centred on tourism, clothing manufacture and food processing.

Imports

Main imports are machinery and transport equipment, food, beverages, tobacco, manufactured goods, fuels, chemicals and pharmaceuticals.

Main sources: US (32.1 per cent of total in 2013), Curacao (12.5 per cent), Mexico (11.4 per cent).

Exports

Principal exports are sugar, bananas, citrus, garments, fish and cultured shrimp, molasses and timber.

Main destinations: US (39.1 per cent of total in 2013), UK (21.0 per cent), Netherlands (5.6 per cent).

Agriculture

Farming

In 2012 the agriculture sector contributed 13.1 per cent of total GDP. The sector accounts for about 65 per cent of foreign exchange earnings and the banana industry is the country's largest employer. Approximately 65 per cent of the country's land mass is considered to have arable potential but only 2 per cent is used for farming; 45 per cent of the total land mass is forest, much of which is commercially exploitable.

Sugar is the main cash crop though Belize has diversified into exporting other crops, particularly banana and citrus production (mainly oranges), and fisheries. Winter vegetables, papayas, mangoes and cocoa are also grown for export, while rice, maize, roots, beans and vegetables are produced for livestock consumption.

Fishing

Fishing, mainly for lobsters, conch and shrimp, contributes significantly to the economy.

Forestry

Forestry has played an integral role in the economy of Belize but the rise of the tourism industry has reduced its importance. Almost half of the country's land mass is covered by forests, though the majority of this area has now been logged. Of the timber cut, the majority is sold in local markets including that of mahogany, soft pine, cedar, santa maria and yemeri. Chicle (a latex gum of the sapodilla tree) has also become an increasingly harvested product throughout the country.

Industry and manufacturing

Centred on agricultural processing such as sugar-milling, citrus-processing and the processing of domestic foodstuffs, the industrial sector is small-scale. Garment manufacturing previously played a prominent role in the economy of Belize but has decreased in significance since the 1990s. In all, industry contributes approximately one fifth of GDP (including a manufacturing contribution of 12.6 per cent). The industrial sector typically employs about 18 per cent of the workforce.

Tourism

Belize is home to the largest coral reef in the northern hemisphere, designated as a Unesco World Heritage Site. Its atolls and lagoons are a popular destination for marine tourism. The mainland offers ancient Mayan temples and other archaeological sites, rainforests with diverse flora and fauna and a native culture to attract visitors.

The industry has been vital to the economy since the mid-1990s when, for the first time, tourism constituted over 20 per cent of GDP; since then it has steadily assumed a greater role, so that by 2013 it constituted 36.6 per cent of GDP. Nevertheless, this represents a fall from the record high of 37.5 per cent in 2007, before the global economic crisis cut the number of visitors. Employment in the industry was likewise cut from 34.1 per cent in 2007 to 33.0 per cent in 2013. However, both GDP growth and employment were forecast to rise in 2014.

Around 250,000 tourists visit each year, either overland from other Central American countries, by air or via cruise liners, of which six major operators schedule some 19 liners to visit Belize City, mainly during the tourist season of November–June.

Environment

Scientists warned that the proposed Chalillo hydro project, which involves building a 50-metre high dam in the rainforest, would destroy rare habitat for jaguar, tapir and a sub-species of scarlet macaw. The Belize Supreme Court halted construction in 2002. However, in 2004, the Privy Council in London, ruled that work on the controversial Chalillo Dam could proceed.

Mining

Belize has insignificant mineral deposits. During the 1980s extensive drilling was undertaken in the country in a vain attempt to discover oil. Nowadays, mining mainly involves surface removal of gravel for use in the construction industry. Approximately 0.4 per cent of the workforce is employed in the mining and quarrying sector.

Hydrocarbons

Although there were oil reserves of 6.7 million barrels in 2014 they are not commercially viable. Consumption of oil was 4,980 barrels per day (bpd) in 2013, all of which was imported. In 2005, Belize, plus a number of other Caribbean states, signed an agreement with Venezuela to establish PetroCaribe, a multi-national oil company owned by the participating states. PetroCaribe buys low-priced Venezuelan crude oil under long-term payment plans. However, due to the worsening state of its economy, in 2015 the Venezuelan government lowered the subsidies to the members of PetroCaribe.

The US-oil company, Treaty Energy Corporation, announced in January 2012 that it had found oil in its first well, San Juan #2, in Stann Creek district, with an estimated 5–6 million barrels of recoverable oil in place.

Any use of natural gas or coal is commercially insignificant.

Energy

Total installed generating capacity was 178MW in 2013, producing over 450 million kilowatt hours. The privately owned Belize Electricity Limited (BEL) is the primary provider of electricity, distributing and selling electricity. It buys electricity from the Belize Electric Company Limited (Becol), which operates the Mollejon Hydroelectric facility in western Belize and the 7MW Chalillo dam, and from Hydro Maya Limited in southern Belize. It also purchases electricity from Mexico.
The national power grid is connected to that of Mexico allowing transfer of energy during periods of maximum loads.

Banking and insurance

Belize's banking sector is small, but contains both an offshore and onshore sector. The offshore sector is undergoing continued expansion owing to generous tax schemes and there are now eight banks, one insurance house and more than 22,000 international business companies. The International Financial Services Commission acts as the regulator of the offshore sector.
The onshore sector is composed of five domestic commercial banks, seven international banks and three quasi-governmental institutions, with credit unions also being prominent. Belize Banking Ltd retains a dominant market position with 45 per cent of domestic banks' assets. The Central Bank of Belize supervises banking activity and the Register of Co-operatives is the Credit union regulator.
The country's insurance sector is also small with 17 firms competing in the market; six insurance houses, nine general companies and three composites. At present there are no reinsurance firms in Belize.

Central bank
Central Bank of Belize

Main financial centre
Belize City

Offshore facilities
Belize has an important offshore banking sector. In April 2002, Belize was taken off the Organisation for Economic Co-operation and Development's (OECD) blacklist of 'un-co-operative tax havens' after the government made a commitment to greater transparency of its tax and regulatory systems and agreed to exchange information on tax matters with OECD countries from end-2005.

Time

GMT minus six hours

Geography

Belize lies on the Caribbean coast of Central America, with Mexico to the north-east and Guatemala to the south-west.
In the north the coastal area is low with fresh and sea water lagoons as well as swamps and mangroves. In the south, east and west the Maya mountain range, the Cockscomb range and the Mountain Pine Ridge, respectively, occupy around 40 per cent of the land and are dense rain forests. Close to the Guatemala border the land is relatively open. Belize possesses many small islands (Cayes) that straddle a coral reef which is the world's second largest, after the Great Barrier Reef in Australia.

Hemisphere
Northern

Climate

Sub-tropical with temperatures ranging from 10–30 degrees Celsius. Hottest months between March–September and rainy season June–October.

Entry requirements

Passports
Required by all and validity must be for at least six months longer than the intended period of stay.

Visa
Required by all, except north American, most European and Australasian citizens. For further exemptions contact the local embassy.
For a copy of the visa application visit www.un.int/belize/visappli.pdf.
All visitors should show that they have sufficient funds for the purpose and period of their stay and must be in possession of a valid return or onward ticket. Evidence in support of both funds and travel arrangements must be presented with applications for visas. Visitors are permitted to stay in Belize for up to 30 days.

Currency advice/regulations
A currency declaration form must be completed on arrival. Visitors are advised to keep a copy of the declaration form because travellers are not permitted to export more than this amount of currency.

Health (for visitors)

Mandatory precautions
Yellow fever vaccination certificate if travelling from infected area.

Advisable precautions
Typhoid, polio and rabies vaccinations. Malaria prophylaxis advisable. Water precautions should be taken.

Hotels

There are a good range of hotels. There are three charges likely to be levied locally: 8 per cent sales tax, 9 per cent hotel tax and a service charge of up to 10 per cent.

Public holidays (national)

Fixed dates
1 Jan (New Year's Day), 9 Mar (Baron Bliss Day), 1 May (Labour Day), 24 May (Commonwealth Day), 10 Sep (St George's Caye Day), 21 Sep (Independence Day), 12 Oct (Columbus Day), 19 Nov (Garifuna Settlement Day), 25–26 Dec (Christmas Holiday).

Variable dates
Good Friday, Easter Monday

Working hours

Banking
Mon–Thu: 0800–1300; Fri: 0800–1300 and 1500–1800.

Business
Mon–Fri: 0800–1200, 1300–1700.
Some businesses are open on Saturday.

Government
Mon–Fri: 0800–1200, 1300–1700; closes 1630 on Fridays.

Telecommunications

Mobile/cell phones
A GSM 1900 service operates around the capital, and north and south along the coastline.

Electricity supply

110/220/V AC, 60Hz, with US style two-pin plugs.

Getting there

Air
Intercontinental flights usually arrive via the US, other international flights are regional.
International airport/s: PSW Goldson International (BZE), 16km west of Belize City; duty-free shops, bar. Taxis to the city
Airport tax: Departure tax US$36.25, payable in cash or travellers cheques only – credit cards are not accepted.

Surface
Road: Main routes are from Melchor de Mencos (Guatemala) and Chetumal (Mexico).
Main port/s: Belize City.

Getting about

National transport
Air: Maya Airways and Tropic Air operate domestic services to main centres. The charter flight company AeroBelize flies to minor airfields.
Road: Over 1,500km of surfaced road linking the eight major towns and cities, the network in the north is in better repair than south of Belize city. Occasionally during torrential downpours all-weather roads may be flooded, especially close to ferry crossings.
A new all-weather road to Charcoal, the largest and most important archaeological site in Belize, was completed in 2004 at a cost of around US$2.5 million.

Buses: Services operate within Belize City; long-distance coach services link major centres.
Water: Regular ferry services and small boats ply to offshore cayes.

City transport

Taxis: Taxis are available in towns and resort areas, and at the airport. They are easily recognised by their green licence plates.
Fixed rates apply within Belize City (higher at night). With no meters it is advisable to agree the fare beforehand. Tipping is discretionary.

Car hire

Foreign or international licences are acceptable for 30 days. Driver must be over 18 years old. Driving on the right.

BUSINESS DIRECTORY

The addresses listed below are a selection only. While World of Information makes every endeavour to check these addresses, we cannot guarantee that changes have not been made, especially to telephone numbers and area codes. We would welcome any corrections.

Telephone area codes

The international dialling code (IDD) for Belize is +501 followed by the area code and subscriber's number:

Belize City	2	Dangriga	5
Belmopan	8	Independence	6
Corozal	4	San Ignacio	92

Useful telephone numbers

Directory enquiries: 113.
Local and regional operator-assisted calls: 114.
International operator-assisted calls: 115.
Fire and ambulance: 90.
Police: 911.

Chambers of Commerce

Belize Chamber of Commerce and Industry, 63 Regent Street, PO Box 291, Belize City (tel: 227-3148; fax: 227-4984; e-mail: bcci@btl.net).

Banking

Alliance Bank of Belize Ltd, PO Box 1988, 18 Cnr New Road & Hydes Lane, Belize City (tel: 236-783, 236-784; fax: 236-785).

Atlantic Bank Ltd, PO Box 481, Cnr Cleghorn & Freetown Road, Belize City (tel: 234-123, 277-124; fax: 233-907, 234-150).

Atlantic International Bank Ltd, PO Box 481, Cnr Freetown Road & Cleghorn Streets, Belize City (tel: 230-681; fax: 230-677).

Banca Serfin of Mexico, PO Box 1636, Cnr Eyre & Hudson Streets, Belize City (tel: 027-8179, 027-8225; fax: 027-8970).

Bank of Nova Scotia, PO Box 708, Albert Street, Belize City (tel: 027-7027/030/415/416; fax: 027-7416).

Barclays Bank PLC, PO Box 363, Albert Street, Belize City (tel: 027-7211; fax: 027-8572).

Belize Bank Ltd, PO Box 364, 60 Market Square, Belize City (tel: 277-132, 272-390; fax: 272-712, 274-519).

Development Finance Corporation, PO Box 40, Bliss Parade, Belmopan, Cayo District (tel: 082-2360, 082-2350; fax: 082-3096).

National Development Foundation of Belize, PO Box 1210, 109 Cemetery Road, Belize City (tel: 027-2139, 027-2874; fax: 027-8437).

Provident Bank & Trust of Belize Limited, PO Box 1867, 1st Floor, 35 Barrack Road, Belize City (tel: 235-698; fax: 230-368).

Central bank

Central Bank of Belize, Gabourel Lane, PO Box 852, Belize City (tel: 223-6194; fax: 223-6226; e-mail: info@centralbank.org.bz).

Travel information

AeroBelize (air charter), PSW Goldson International Airport, Ladyville (tel: 252-535).

Belize Airport Authority, PSW Goldson International Airport, Ladyville (tel: 252-045; fax: 252-439).

Belize Port Authority, Caesar Ridge Road, Belize City (tel: 272-439; fax: 273-571).

Belize Tourism Industry Association (BTIA), 99 Albert Street, PO Box 62, Belize City (tel: 275-717; fax: 271-144; e-mail: btia@btl.net).

Maya Airways (administrative office), 6 Fort St, PO Box 458, Belize City (tel: 272-312; fax: 30-585); PSW Goldson International Airport, Ladyville (tel: 252-336).

Ministry of tourism

Ministry of Tourism, 14 Constitution Drive, Belmopan (tel: 223-394; fax: 222-862).

National tourist organisation offices

Belize Tourism Board, Lower Flat, New Horizon Investment Bld, 3 1–32 Miles Northern Highway, P.O. Box 325, Belize City (tel: 223-1913; fax: 223-1943; email: info@travelbelize.org; internet: www.travelbelize.org).

Ministries

Ministry of Agriculture and Fisheries, West Block, Belmopan (tel: 222-332, 222-241; fax: 222-409).

Ministry of Budget Management, Investment and Trade, Central Bank of Belize Building, Gaol Lane, Belize City (tel: 232-128, 236-194; fax: 235-097; e-mail: chalilio@bti.net).

Ministry of Economic Development, PO Box 42, Belmopan (tel: 222-526, 222-527, 222-023, 222-672; fax: 223-111, 223-673).

Ministry of Education and Public Service, West Block, Belmopan (tel: 222-329, 222-798, 222-067; fax: 223-389, 222-206).

Ministry of Energy, Science, Technology and Transportation, Belmopan (tel: 222-435; fax: 223-317).

Ministry of Finance, Belmopan (tel: 222-169; fax: 2222-886).

Ministry of Foreign Affairs, PO Box 174, Belmopan (tel: 222-322; fax: 222-854).

Ministry of Health and Sports, Belmopan (tel: 222-325; fax: 222-942).

Ministry of Home Affairs and Labour, Belmopan (tel: 222-281; fax: 222-016).

Ministry of Housing, Urban Development and Co-operatives, Belmopan (tel: 223-339; fax: 223-298).

Ministry of Human Resources, Community and Youth Development, Culture and Women's Affairs, Belmopan (tel: 222-161; fax: 223-175).

Ministry of National Security, Belmopan (tel: 222-225; fax: 222-615).

Ministry of Natural Resources, Belmopan (tel: 222-331, 222-249; fax: 222-333).

Ministry of Statistics, Central Statistical Office, Belmopan (tel: 222-207; fax: 223-206).

Ministry of Tourism and The Environment, Belmopan (tel: 223-394; fax: 222-862).

Ministry of Trade and Industry, Belmopan (tel: 222-199; fax: 222-329).

Ministry of Works, Belmopan (tel: 222-139; fax: 223-282).

Other useful addresses

Association of National Development Agencies (ANDA), Princess Margaret Drive, Belize City (tel: 35-115; fax: 32-362).

Attorney General's Ministry, Belmopan (tel: 222-504; fax: 223-390).

Belize Electricity Board, 115 Barrack Road, Belize City (tel: 277-141; fax: 231-905).

Belize Embassy (USA), 2535 Massachusetts Avenue, NW, Washington DC 20008 (tel: 202-332-9636; fax: 202-332-6888).

Belize Export and Investment Promotion Unit (BEIPU), PO Box 291, 63 Regent Street, Belize City (tel: 273-148, 274-394, 275-108/9; fax: 274-984).

Belize Information Service, P.O. Box 60, Belmopan (tel: 222-019; fax: 223-242).

Belize Marketing Board, 117 North Front Street, PO Box 479, Belize City (tel: 272-439; fax: 273-571).

Belize Port Authority (tel: 272-439; fax: 273-571; e-mail: portbze@btl.net).

Belize Offshore Centre (tel: 234-351; fax: 233-501; e-mail: cititrust@btl.net).

Belize Telemedia Ltd. St Thomas Street, PO Box 603, Belize City (tel: 232-868; fax: 277-600; internet site: www.btl.net).

Belize Trade and Investment Development Services (BELTRAIDE) (tel: 223-737; fax: 220-595; e-mail: beltraide@belize.gov.bz).

British High Commission, PO Box 91, Belmopan (tel: 222-146; fax: 222-717).

Central Statistical Office (CSO), Ministry of Finance, Belmopan (tel: 222-207; fax: 222-206).

Citrus Control Board, 87 Commerce Bight, Melinder Road, Dangriga Town (tel: 222-145, 222-447; fax: 222-686).

Customs & Excise, PO Box 146, Fort Street, Belize City (tel: 277-405; fax: 277-091).

Export Processing Zone, Ministry of Trade and Industry, Belmopan (tel: 222-199, 222-153; fax: 222-923).

Fisheries Department, Princess Margaret Drive, Belize City (tel: 244-552, 232-623; fax: 232-983; e-mail: species@btl.net).

Forest Department, Forestry Drive, Belmopan (tel: 223-629; fax: 222-083).

Geology and Petroleum Office, Unity Boulevard, Belmopan (tel: 222-178, 222-651; fax: 223-538).

National Development Foundation of Belize, 2882 Coney Drive Coral Grove, Belize City (tel: 231-207, 231-132; fax: 231-195).

Society for the Promotion of Education & Research (SPEAR), Corner Pickstock and New Road, PO Box 1766, Belize City (tel: 231-668; fax: 232-367).

Water and Sewerage Authority, Central American Boulevard, Belize City (tel: 224-757; fax: 224-759).

Caribbean Net News: www.caribbeannetnews.com

Internet sites

Inter-American Development Bank: www.iadb.org/en/inter-american-development-bank,2837.html

Latin American Network Information Center: www.lanic.utexas.edu

Benin

KEY FACTS

Official name: République du Bénin (Republic of Benin)

Head of State: President Boni Yayi (from 2006: re-elected 13 Mar 2011)

Head of government: Prime Minister Lionel Zinsou (from 18 June 2015)

Ruling party: Forces Cauri pour un Bénin Emergent (FCBE) (Cauri Forces for an Emerging Benin) (elected 2007; re-elected 30 Apr 2011)

Area: 112,622 square km

Population: 10.59 million (2014) *(8,849,892; 2010, census figure)

Capital: Cotonou (seat of government); Porto-Novo (administrative)

Official language: French

Currency: CFA franc (CFAf) = 100 centimes (Communauté Financière Africaine (African Financial Community) franc).

Exchange rate: CFAf655.96 per US$ (Sep 2015)

GDP per capita: US$822 (2014)*

GDP real growth: 5.48% (2014)*

GDP: US$8.70 billion (2014)*

Inflation: -1.00% (2014)*

Balance of trade: -US$2,645 million (2014)*

* estimated figure

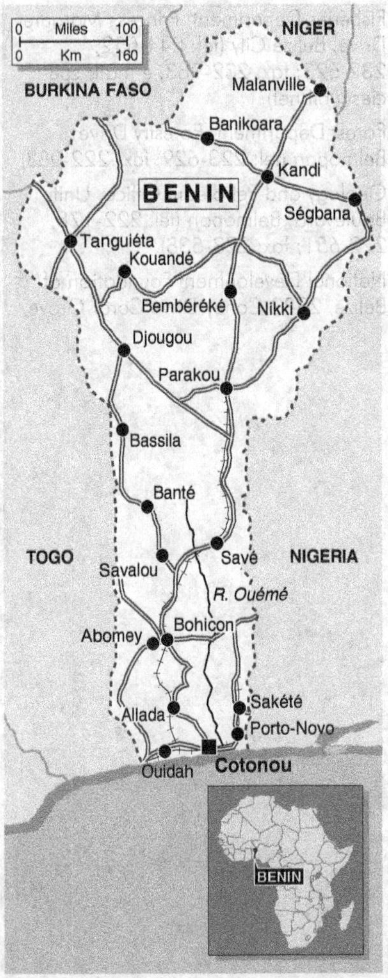

Benin, formerly known as Dahomey, is one of Africa's most stable and possibly most corrupt, democracies. It boasts a proliferation of political parties and a strong civil society. However, a Unu-Wider report by Mamoudou Gazibo points out that while procedural democracy is well established in Benin, there is still a need to deepen and widen the country's democracy. A number of issues, notably good governance, the rule of law, accountability and transparency, need to be looked at. Political parties in Benin remain weak. Second, the media and journalists display a lack of professionalism and are subject to harassment by the current administration. Third, Benin is faced with huge corruption and accountability problems which can harm the quality of democracy. Benin is one of the few countries in the world not even to feature on the Transparency International *Corruption Perceptions Index*.

According to the report, one of the key factors limiting the improvement of Benin's democracy is the state of its political parties. Liberal laws regarding the formation of parties have led to parties being created and dismantled frequently. Many parties that legally exist do not organise political activities or participate in elections. Despite the notional existence of a government majority and an opposition, no party generally presents itself as the opposition and challenges to the government are rarely based on criticisms of policy. The perception prevails that many politicians are 'bandits and thieves'.

Benin's media represents another area which needs to be strengthened if the quality of democracy is to improve. Before political liberalisation Benin had only one state television station and one radio station, there are now five independent TV stations and over ten radio stations. The media is also relatively independent of political actors. However, most journalists still do not have a degree and the sector as a whole displays a lack of professionalism. President Boni Yayi has often proved intolerant towards media accusations of corruption and authoritarian tendencies. This, combined with the lack of professionalism, has lead to a large number of journalists being sued due to the unverified and accusatory nature of most newspapers. The media is battling for a new law to penalise press offences.

Accountability and corruption are perhaps the two areas in which democracy in Benin faces the largest challenges. Benin, according to the independent watchdog, Freedom House, is one of the most corrupt of the African countries which are defined as free. According to some intelligence agencies Benin is becoming a convenient platform for Latin American drug dealers to get their merchandise into Europe and Asia. Benin has not seemed able to shake off its chronic corruption. Since 2004 a number of indicators related to the quality of democracy have declined, particularly in the area of the rule of law and corruption prevention.

Hopes had been raised in April 2006 when Benin embarked upon a new political era, as President Thomas Boni Yayi was sworn in after winning the election with 75 per cent of the vote. President Yayi's qualifications for his new job were somewhat limited – he had been manager of the Banque Ouest Africaine de Développement (BOAD) (West African Development Bank), a regional development bank established by the French west African countries (Benin, Burkina Faso, Côte d'Ivoire, Guinea Bissau, Mauritania and Togo). Five years later, after a scandal involving a pyramid investment scheme in which as many as 100,000 people may have lost money, President Yayi won a second term in office, but this time with only 53 per cent of the vote.

The economy

On the economic side, however, Benin is severely underdeveloped and corruption is rife. In its June 2014 assessment of the Benin economy, the International Monetary Fund (IMF) noted that under the IMF's Extended Credit Facility Arrangement (Benin had actually asked for a waiver of the programme's 'non-observance of a performance' criterion) there had been improved growth performance. Gross domestic product (GDP) growth was expected to reach about 5.5 per cent in 2014 for the third consecutive year. The IMF also noted that this performance had closed the gap in per capita GDP growth between Benin and the sub-Saharan African (SSA) average which was about 2 percentage points on average between 2005 and 2011. Thanks to prudent fiscal policy, macro-economic performance remained satisfactory and progress had been achieved in structural reforms. All the performance criteria were met with the exception of the ceiling on non-concessional borrowing.

The implementation of the new approach to customs reform was moving ahead well despite some delays. The government is tackling emerging issues in several areas to reduce risks to Benin's otherwise good macro-economic performance. The weak performance of domestic revenues requires a comprehensive tax administration reform, which has been initiated. While non-performing loans (NPLs) in the banking sector had risen since 2012 and might increase further due to problems in a group of companies, they did not, in the view of the IMF, constitute a systemic risk. Discussions were underway among the Banque Centrale des États de l'Afrique de l'Ouest (central bank), the government and the commercial banks on how to limit any further rise in NPLs. After some delays, the government has also initiated steps to develop a new framework for cotton management with more private sector involvement. Sound policies have created fiscal space for scaling up investment to remove growth bottlenecks, but further reforms are necessary to ensure efficiency and sustainability. To preserve the authorities' achievements under the ECF arrangement, rising investment needs to be accompanied by further progress in public financial management (PFM), suggests the IMF, and integrated into a medium-term framework anchored in debt sustainability. The authorities have requested IMF support through a new ECF arrangement. The scaling up of investment will only lead to sustainable growth if conditions for private sector development is significantly improved. Government efforts are starting to show some results, but broad-based reforms are necessary to enhance productivity. The IMF supported the Benin authorities' request for a waiver of the performance criterion on non-concessional borrowing.

Risk assessment

Politics	Fair
Economy	Fair
Regional stability	Fair

Muslims in Benin

% of population	24.4
Sunni (% of Muslims)	97
Shi'a (% of Muslims)	2

COUNTRY PROFILE

1960 Gained independence from France as the Republic of Dahomey. Hubert Maga, was elected president.

1963 Maga was overthrown by General Christophe Soglo leading a military *coup d'état*.

1965 Soglo declared himself head of state.

1967 A military coup deposed Soglo.

1969 Lieutenant Colonel Paul-Émile de Souza became president.

1970 Elections were scheduled but failed to take place due to irreconcilable differences between politicians of the north and south. Instead, a three-man presidential council was formed, with a two-year rotating presidency for each.

1972 Maga, the first president, was replaced, without incident, by Justin Ahomadegbé. Major Mathieu Kérékou led a *coup d'état*; he installed an 11-man government and declared Dahomey a Marxist-Leninist state.

1975 The Republic of Dahomey was renamed The People's Republic of Benin.

1990 With the country bankrupt and on the brink of social collapse, President Kérékou handed power to a national conference. The government abandoned Marxism-Leninism and committed itself to political and economic reform.

1991 Nicéphore Soglo became president and introduced sweeping austerity measures.

1995 Parties opposed to the president won a majority in the National Assembly in the legislative elections.

1996 Kérékou became president and Adrien Houngbédji, leader of the Parti du Renouveau Démocratique (PRD) (Party of

KEY INDICATORS — Benin

	Unit	2011	2012	2013	2014	**2015
Population	m	*9.91	*10.05	*10.32	*10.59	*10.86
Gross domestic product (GDP)	US$bn	7.30	*7.46	*8.31	*8.70	*8.33
GDP per capita	US$	802	*751	*805	*822	0
GDP real growth	%	3.1	*5.3	*5.6	*5.5	*5.5
GNP per capita	US$	0	0	0	0	*767
Inflation	%	2.8	*6.7	1.0	*-1.0	*0.7
Exports (fob) (goods)	US$m	1,250.8	1,442.6	–	–	–
Imports (fob) (goods)	US$m	1,800.4	2,002.1	–	–	–
Balance of trade	US$m	-549.5	-559.5	–	–	–
Current account	US$m	-729.0	*-596.0	*-1,321.0	*-738.0	*-967.0
Total reserves minus gold	US$m	–	713.0	694.9	726.0	–
Foreign exchange	US$m	614.8	633.0	–	–	–
Exchange rate	per US$	466.82	505.65	480.26	542.07	–

* estimated figure ** forecast figure

Democratic Renewal), assumed the role of prime minister.
1998 Houngbédji resigned, a new government was formed without a post of prime minister.
1999 After National Assembly elections, the Parti de la Renaissance du Benin (PRB) (Benin Renaissance Party), led by former president Soglo's wife, Rosine, emerged as the largest single opposition party. Adrien Houngbédji (PRD) was elected president of the new Assembly.
2001 President Kérékou was re-elected for his last five-year term.
2002 The first municipal elections were held.
2003 A large coalition of parties backing President Kérékou won the National Assembly elections.
2004 An International Development Association (IDA) credit of US$45 million was approved to assist Benin in expanding electrification and restructuring its power sector. Benin and Nigeria agreed to redefine their mutual border.
2005 The International Court of Justice (ICJ) awarded Niger most of the river islands that had been disputed along the Niger/Benin border.
2006 Boni Yayi won presidential elections. Benin assumed control of nine islands in the Niger River in accordance with the 2005 ICJ ruling settling the border dispute; Niger received the large island of Lete and several others. President Boni's coalition, Forces Cauri pour un Bénin Emergent (FCBE) (Cauri Forces for an Emerging Benin), won parliamentary elections.
2008 Unreliable voter lists delayed local elections; four million registered voters had had their names omitted. At the Community of the Sahelian-Saharan States (CEN-SAD) Executive Council meeting in Cotonou, an investment guarantee agency was launched to provide funds for infrastructure projects.
2009 The European Union banned all air carriers from Benin from flying into its airspace, due to safety fears.
2010 The World Bank agreed to fund the US$258 million refurbishment of the 998.8km West African coastal corridor road, which runs through Benin from Abidjan (Côte d'Ivoire) to Lagos (Nigeria). Benin celebrated 50 years of independence. Severe flooding killed 60 people and displaced around 120,000. Emergency relief was supplied for over 680,000 people affected by the devastation. A national census was held.
2011 The date of the presidential elections was postponed by one week, following complaints that the electoral role was not yet ready, with over one million voters still to be registered. The elections took place in March and 14 candidates took part. Incumbent Yayi Boni won 53.18 per cent and his closest rival Adrien Houngbédji 35.66 per cent. In parliamentary elections held in April, the ruling FCBE won 41 seats (out of 83), increasing its number by six seats and cutting the opposition's combined total to 42; the Union Fait la Nation (UFN) (Unite the Nation) won 30 seats and six other political parties each won two seats. In May Pascal Koupaki was named prime minister and a new government was appointed.
2012 President Yayi Boni was elected as Chairman of the African Union on 29 January. On 18 July, the agricultural minister announced that Benin would invest US$1.86 million to boost the production of palm nuts by 63 per cent (505,000 tonnes) by 2014.
2013 A cholera outbreak was reported in south Benin, with 129 confirmed cases as of 2 October. The number of cases is expected to rise.
2014 on 20 August President Yahi reshuffled his cabinet, sacking seven ministers, including from the key ministries of public security, defence and agriculture. Political commentators suggest the move is in preparation for the presidential election due in May 2016. President Yahi would not be elegible to run as the constitution stands, but he has for some time been making moves to change the constitution so that he can extend his term in office beyond the maximum two terms currently allowed.
2015 Parliamentary elections were held on 26 April. The result was a win for Forces Cauri pour un Bénin Emergent-Alliance Amana (FCBE-AA) (Cauri Forces for an Emerging Benin-Amana Alliance (CFEB-AA)) with 30.19 per cent (33 seats, out of 83), followed by L'Union fait la Nation (UN or the Union) (Union Makes the Nation (UMN)) wity 14.35 per cent (13) and Parti du Renouveau Démocratique (PRD) (Democratic Renewal Party (DRP)) with 10.57 per cent (10).

Political structure

Constitution
The 1990 constitution provides for multi-party politics and a president to be directly elected by popular vote. Presidential candidates cannot be aged over 70. No provision is made for a prime minister; the president is head of government.

Independence date
1 August 1960

Form of state
Republic

The executive
The president is directly elected by popular vote for a five-year term and has ultimate power and control.

National legislature
The directly elected Assemblée Nationale (National Assembly) has 83 members elected for a four-year term.

Legal system
The legal system is based on French civil law and customary law.

Last elections
26 April 2015 (parliamentary); 13 March 2011 (presidential)

Results: Parliamentary: Forces Cauri pour un Bénin Emergent-Alliance Amana (FCBE-AA) (Cauri Forces for an Emerging Benin-Amana Alliance (CFEB-AA)) won 30.19 per cent (33 seats, out of 83), L'Union fait la Nation (UN or the Union) (Union Makes the Nation (UMN)) 14.35 per cent (13), Parti du Renouveau Démocratique (PRD) (Democratic Renewal Party (DRP)) 10.57 per cent (10), Alliance Nationale pour le Développement et la Démocratie (AND) (National Alliance for Development and Democracy) (NADD)) 7.64 per cent (5), Parti Réveil Patriotique (PRP) (Patriotic Revival Party (PRP) 7.09 per cent (7), Alliance Soleil (AS) Sun Alliance (SA) 6.66 per cent (4), Forces Démocratiques Unies (FDU) (United Democratic Forces UDF)) 4 per cent (4), Alliance pour un Bénin Triomphant (ABT) Alliance for a Triumphant Benin (ATB) 3.70 per cent (2), Alliance Eclaireur (Scout Alliance) 3.42 per cent (2), Union pour le Bénin (Union for Benin) 2.90 per cent (2), Résoatao Party 2.16 per cent (1). Turnout was 65.92 per cent.
Presidential: Yayi Boni won 53.18 per cent of the vote, Adrien Houngbédji 35.66 per cent, Abdoulaye Bio-Tchané 6.29 per cent; 11 other candidates won less than 1 per cent each.

Next elections
2016 presidential and 2019 parliamentary

Political parties

There are over 100 registered parties in Benin, but only a handful are represented in parliament.

Ruling party
Forces Cauri pour un Bénin Emergent (FCBE) (Cauri Forces for an Emerging Benin) (elected 2007; re-elected 30 Apr 2011)

Main opposition party
Union Fait la Nation (UFN) (Unite the Nation)

Population

9.35 million (2012)*
Approximately 46 per cent of the total population is under 15 years.
Last census: 2010: 8,849,892
Population density: 51 inhabitants per square km. Urban population 42 per cent (2010 Unicef).
Annual growth rate: 3.1 per cent, 1990–2010 (Unicef).

Ethnic make-up
African (99 per cent) (42 ethnic groups, most important being Fon, Adja, Yoruba, Bariba), European (1 per cent).
Religions
Animists (70 per cent), Christians (15 per cent) and Muslims (15 per cent).

Education
Annual expenditure on education is 3–3.5 per cent of GDP of which over 55 per cent is spent on primare education.
Literacy rate: 40 per cent adult rate; 56 per cent youth rate (15–24) (Unesco 2005).
Enrolment rate: 99 per cent gross primary enrolment, of relevant age group (including repeaters); 20 per cent net secondary enrolment (UN HDR)
Pupils per teacher: 52 in primary schools.

Health
HIV/Aids
In 2005, around half of sex workers tested positive for HIV, and provided a pool of infection allowing an increase in potential cases of HIV/Aids. In 2009, there were an estimated 60,000 people living with HIV.
HIV prevalence: 1.2 per cent aged 15–49 in 2009 (Unicef 2012)
Life expectancy: 56 years, 2010 (Unicef 2012)
Fertility rate/Maternal mortality rate: 5.3 births per woman, 2010 (Unicef 2012)
Child (under 5 years) mortality rate (per 1,000): 90 per 1,000 live births (WHO 2012); 23 per cent of children aged under five were malnourished (World Bank).

Welfare
The National Social Security fund provides for general workers and farmers who have made contributions. The fund is supervised by the Ministry of Labour although its assets are autonomous and administered by trustees. Every employer must provide a contribution for each worker to cover disability and family allowances. Old age pension benefits are accrued by workers contributions to the fund.

Main cities
Cotonou (seat of government, estimated population 779,314 in 2012), Abomey-Calavi (452,811), Porto-Novo (administrative capital, 267,191), Djougou (237,040), Parakou (206,667), Bohicon (149,271), Kandi (128,172), Lokossa (106,081).

Languages spoken
French; African languages (Yoruba, Bariba and Fon) are widely used in everyday life.
Official language/s
French

Media
Benin is considered one of the most liberal media markets in Africa.
Press
Dailies: In French, *Fraternite* (www.fraternite-info.com), *Le Matinal En Ligne* (www.actubenin.com) and *Le Nation* (www.gouv.bj/presse/lanation), is a government publication.
Weeklies: In French *La Gazette du Golfe* with political debate.
Business: The *Le Magazine de l'Entreprise* (www.creationdentreprise.org), is a magazine of regional business affairs.
Periodicals: In French, a fortnightly publication includes the government information bureau's *Journal Officiel de la République du Benin*.
Broadcasting
The state-owned Office des Radiodiffusion et Télévision du Bénin (ORTB) broadcasts radio and television services.
Radio: Radio is the prime medium for public news and information and phone-in programme are popular. The ORTB broadcasts Radio Benin (www.ortb.net, site under construction), in French, English and 18 local languages. Commercial stations include Golfe FM (www.eit.to), the pan-African Radio Africa No 1 (www.africa1.com) and Radio Planete (www.planetefm.com); Radio Maranatha (www.eit.to) and Radio Immaculee Conception (www.immacolata.com/fibenafr) are religious stations.
Television: Fewer residents watch TV than listen to radio. ORTB operated Television Nationale. Internet TV is provided Espace Informatique et Telecommunications (EIT) including Canal Sat Horizons (www.eit.to), LBC (www.lbcgroup.tv) and Future Television (www.future.com.lb). Television LC2 International (www.lc2international.tv) is a satellite station.
National news agency: Agence Bénin-Presse (ABP)

Economy
The principal component of the economy is the service sector, which constitutes 54.3 per cent of GDP; of which, trade is the major constituent, followed by government services, education and healthcare. Agriculture accounts for 32.4 per cent of GDP, and is largely dominated by the production of cotton. Industry constitutes around 13.2 per cent of GDP, with textile manufacturing as the leading industry.
After suffering devastating floods in 2010, Benin has been dealing with damaged infrastructures and destroyed cash and food crops; the floods also adversely affected agriculture, trade and the informal sector. A US$50 million loan was obtained from the World Bank in 2011, and it has been providing on-going aid for an environment management project to alleviate not only the damage but also prevent future destruction.
Agriculture represents 32.4 per cent of GDP, and forestry, livestock and fisheries constitute 10 per cent of that. The single largest component of the economy is cotton and as world prices rose in 2011, the value of Benin's exports of cotton rose by 22.3 per cent. However, cotton prices have been sinking since and are forecast to hit to a five year low in 2015, which would have damaging effects on Benin's trade balance as well as increasing poverty in rural regions. Other agricultural cash crops include palm oil, coffee and cocoa. Cultivation for domestic consumption includes among other produce, wheat, yams, legumes, groundnuts and pineapples.
By 2012, the reconstruction of the agricultural sector and infrastructures had resulted in a growth rate of 5.3 per cent, which was maintained in 2013 at 5.6 per cent. Growth in 2014, which slightly dropped to an estimated 5.5 per cent, was driven by further improvements in the agricultural and services sectors, and also by the country's dynamic construction industry.
In 2014, the UN Human Development Index (HDI) ranked Benin 165 (out of 187) for national development in health, education and income. Since 2000, Benin's progress has grown overall, but has not matched the improvement of other sub-Saharan African countries. Approximately 37 per cent of the population live below the poverty line. Foreign remittances in 2012 amounted to US$180 million, a significant drop from the US$280 million in 2007, which reflects the lack of opportunity for workers overseas during the economic crisis.
Corruption and the informal sector also hamper government control of the economy. Smuggling, including of people, between Benin and Nigeria, is rife and it has been estimated that the informal sector accounts for over 45 per cent of gross national income.
Benin is a member of Union Économique et Monétaire Ouest-Aficaine (UEMOA) (West African Economic and Monetary Union (WEAMU)), and its monetary policy is set by the Banque Centrale des États de l'Afrique de l'Ouest (BCEAO) (Central Bank of West African States) using the CFA franc (Communauté Financière Africaine franc).

External trade
Benin is a member of the World Trade Organisation (WTO); through its membership of Union Économique et Monétaire Ouest-Africaine (UEMOA) (West African Economic and Monetary

Union (WEAMU)) it operates using the CFA franc (Communauté Financière Africaine franc). It has liberal trade agreements with other members, while the union has a trade agreement with the US. Benin acts as a transit country for goods from Nigeria to Togo and its landlocked neighbours Niger, Burkina Faso and Mali.

Imports

Principal imports are refined oil and petroleum products, rice, foodstuffs, tobacco and capital goods.

Main sources: China (typically over 30 per cent of total), India (over 10 per cent), U.S. (around 10 per cent).

Exports

Principal exports are cotton, palm oil, shea butter, coffee and cocoa.

Main destinations: China (typically over 20 of total), Lebanon (around 20 per cent), Nigeria (less than 10 per cent), India (less than 10 per cent).

Agriculture

Farming

Total agricultural land is 11.1 million hectares (around 33 per cent of total land mass) of which 5.0 per cent is pasture and 22 per cent arable. Agriculture constitutes 32.4 per cent of GDP.

Cotton is the principal cash crop and foreign exchange earner, farmed mainly on large industrial plantations. It is also important to the rural economy as it supports almost half of rural households. Other cash crops include palm oil, coffee, sugar, cocoa, karité nuts and tobacco. Subsistence farming (mainly collectivised) shows low productivity but the country is virtually self-sufficient in food. Livestock farming is particularly important in the north. The principal food crops are yams, cassava, sorghum, beans, millet, maize and rice.

Fishing

Fishing is confined mainly to inland waters and augments local food supplies.

Industry and manufacturing

The industrial sector is small-scale, contributing 13.2 per cent to GDP. Manufacturing activity is centred on processing primary products (palm oil, fats, sugar, beverages, cotton) for export, and the manufacture of consumer goods and construction materials for home consumption. Cement production and oil refining are the main heavy industries.

The government has encouraged foreign investment in canning, paper processing, glass manufacturing, salt processing, agribusiness, pharmaceuticals, clothing, palm oil, building materials and chemicals.

Tourism

'Land of mystery' is the epithet given to Benin by its tourism ministry. As a country, it offers traditional African culture, ancient historic monuments and artefacts, plus a wealth of wildlife to entertain visitors. The government is investing in development to improve the tourist infrastructure and market beach, cultural and eco-tourism.

The tourism industry contributed 5.9 per cent of GDP in 2014, and was predicted to rise by 5.9 per cent in 2015. The annual contribution jumped from US$540 million in 2007 to a record high of US$710 million in 2008, just before the global economic crisis cut visitor numbers. In 2013 the contribution had not fully recovered, reaching US$514 million and in 2014 it dropped to US$430 million.

Around 5.1 per cent of the working population is engaged in tourism; visitor exports in 2014 were around US$173 million.

The Fishing Road project, sited along the coast between the capital Cotonou and the historic town of Ouidah, will be the largest tourist development ever undertaken in Benin, of 10-years duration. In 2008, the UAE-based Dubai World Africa began to invest not only in the Fishing Road project, helping with the purchase of 32km of seafront and ancillary land, but also by providing specialists in wildlife management to ecology experts to evaluate Benin's national parks. Dubai World Africa is also investing in the development of an international hotel in the capital city of Porto Novo.

Mining

The mining sector accounts for 5.5 per cent of GDP and employs 3 per cent of the workforce.

Activity is mainly confined to extraction of limestone for the local cement industry, and marble. There is a limestone quarry at Onigbolo. There are known reserves of phosphate, chromite, uranium, low-grade iron ore, marble and gold. The government has awarded a number of gold exploration licences to foreign investors. Under Beninese law, all mineral resources belong to the state, which grants exclusive rights for exploration, development and mining activities.

Hydrocarbons

Proven oil reserves were 8 million barrels in 2013, and although there has been no production since 2003, Nigerian based upstream oil and gas extraction company South Atlantic Petroleum Ltd (Sapetro) has plans to produce 7,500 barrels per day in offshore fields. All petroleum products are imported to meet domestic needs, which was 34,410 barrels per day (bpd) in 2013.

Proven gas reserves were 1.1 billion cubic metres in 2013; domestic consumption is negligible. Consumption of natural gas was expected to begin following the completion of the section of the West African Gas Pipeline (WAGP) from Nigeria's Escravos gas field to Benin. However, deliveries from the pipeline have been postponed on several occasions due to leaks and irregular amounts of moisture found in the pipe, and consumption of natural gas had still not begun in 2015.

Energy

Total installed generating capacity was 61MW in 2015, producing 150 million kilowatt hours.

Only 38.4 per cent of the population has access to electricity, the majority of these located in urban areas; rural populations rely on traditional fuels such as biomass and wood. Around 30 per cent of the energy mix is provided by hydropower. The joint Benin-Togo hydroelectric power project, producing 60MW, on the river Mono has been fully operational since the building of the Nangbeto Dam. Electricity is also imported from the hydroelectric Akosombo Dam in Ghana.

Communauté Electrique de Bénin (CEB) (Electricity Community of Benin) is a joint Benin-Togo entity responsible for developing electricity infrastructure within and between each country.

The US Millennium Challenge Corporation (MCC) announced a US$370 million 'engagement' for Benin in order to aid the country with developing solar projects. These will help to bring electricity to a greater proportion of the population especially in rural areas.

Financial markets

Stock exchange

Afribourse (Bourse Régionale des Valeurs Moblières) (BRVM)

Banking and insurance

Central bank

Banque Centrale des États de l'Afrique de l'Ouest

Main financial centre

Cotonou and Parakou

Time

GMT plus one hour

Geography

Benin is a narrow stretch of territory 700km long running north/south. The country has an Atlantic coastline of about 100km, flanked by Nigeria to the east and Togo to the west. In the north it is bordered by Burkina Faso and Niger.

Hemisphere

Northern

Climate

Equatorial in the south with average daytime temperatures reaching 30–38 degrees Celsius (C). Main dry season from January–March. Rainy seasons from May–July and from September–December. Very humid in coastal areas. The north is tropical with more extreme temperatures, and single dry and rainy seasons. Length of rainy seasons varies with location but it is generally very wet from July–October.

Entry requirements

Passports

Required by all except nationals of certain African countries who have identification documents.

Visa

Required by all, except for nationals of Economic Community of West African States (Ecowas) countries. For the latest requirements and to apply, contact the local embassy or representative.

Currency advice/regulations

There are no restrictions on import of local or foreign currency, but amounts of foreign currency must be declared on arrival.
Foreign currency exports are allowed up to the equivalent of CFAf500.

Health (for visitors)

Mandatory precautions

Yellow fever and cholera vaccination certificates required.

Advisable precautions

Inoculations and boosters should be current for cholera, tetanus, polio, hepatitis A, diphtheria, typhoid and yellow fever. There may be a need for vaccinations for tuberculosis, hepatitis B and meningitis. Malaria prophylaxis, which also provides protection for hepatitis B and yellow fever, include mosquito repellents, nets and clothing that cover the body after dark. There is a risk of rabies.
Other diseases that require preventative measures, such as condoms, are HIV/Aids and hepatitis B; to avoid bilharzia, avoid exposure to fresh water and use only well-maintained, chlorinated swimming pools.
Use only bottled or boiled water for drinks, washing teeth and making ice. Eat only well cooked meals, preferably served hot; vegetables should be cooked and fruit peeled. Dairy products are unpasteurised and should be avoided. There is a shortage of routine medications, including sun-screens, and visitors should take all necessary medicines with them. A first aid kit that includes disposable syringes, is a reasonable precaution. Healthcare is not to Western standards and medical insurance, including emergency evacuation, is necessary.

Hotels

Available in all main towns. Better class accommodation is found only in and around Cotonou. Advance booking is advisable. Service charge usually included in bill, otherwise 10 per cent tip.

Credit cards

Access, Mastercard, Visa accepted on limited basis. Some banks may advance cash on Visa cards, check with card company.

Public holidays (national)

Fixed dates

1 Jan (New Year's Day), 10 Jan (Traditional Day), 1 May (Labour Day), 1 Aug (Independence Day), 15 Aug (Assumption Day), 26 Oct (Armed Forces Day), 1 Nov (All Saints' Day), 30 Nov (National Day), 25 Dec (Christmas Day).

Variable dates

Good Friday, Easter Monday, Ascension Day, Whit Monday, Eid al Adha, Eid al Fitr, Birth of the Prophet.

Islamic year 1437 (15 Oct 2015–2 Oct 2016):: The Islamic year contains 354 or 355 days, with the result that Muslim feasts advance by 10–12 days against the Gregorian calendar. Dates of feasts vary according to the sighting of the new moon, so cannot be forecast exactly.

Working hours

Banking

Mon–Fri: 0800–1100, 1500–1700.

Business

Mon–Fri: 0800–1230, 1530–1900. (Sat) 0900–1300.

Government

Mon–Fri: 0800–1230, 1500–1830.

Shops

Mon–Sat: 0830–1300, 1600–1930; (Sun) 0800–1200. Shops that open Sun mainly close Mon am.

Electricity supply

Electricity supply 220V AC 50 cycles.

Getting there

Air

International airport/s: Cotonou-Cadjehoun (COO), 6km west of city; taxi and limousine service (15–20 minutes to city centre), restaurant, business centre, 24 hours medical facility.
Airport tax: None

Surface

Road: There are routes from Burkina Faso, Togo, Nigeria and Niger.
Rail: A line linking Niger to Benin is under construction.
Water: Shipping lines from Marseille (France) and Lagos (Nigeria).
Main port/s: Porto Novo, Cotonou

Getting about

National transport

Air: Regular services between Cotonou, Parakou, Natitingou, Kandi and Djougou.
Road: Good main roads in south connecting towns to Cotonou and Porto Novo.
Mainly laterite, but the main coast road, which connects Lagos with Accra, is surfaced, and the road north from Cotonou is surfaced to Savalou.
In northern areas some roads are only passable in dry season.
Buses: Bus services link towns on these main routes.
Rail: There is only one operation railway line going north from Cotonou to Bohicon, Savé and Parakou. Facilities are limited.

City transport

Taxis: Fixed charge within towns, but advisable to negotiate fares in advance. Tipping is optional.

Car hire

Available in Cotonou. Chauffeur-driven services are recommended. Insurance/liability position should be checked. International driving licence required.

BUSINESS DIRECTORY

The addresses listed below are a selection only. While World of Information makes every endeavour to check these addresses, we cannot guarantee that changes have not been made, especially to telephone numbers and area codes. We would welcome any corrections.

Telephone area codes

The international direct dialling code (IDD) for Benin is +229, followed by subscriber's number.

Chambers of Commerce

Benin Chamber of Commerce and Industry, Avenue Général de Gaulle, PO Box 31, Cotonou (tel: 312-081; fax: 313-299; e-mail: ccib@bow.intnet.bj).

Banking

Bank of Africa Bénin (BOA), BP 08-0879, Ave Pape Jean Paul II, Cotonou (tel: 313-228; fax: 313-117).

Banque Centrale des Etats de l'Afrique de l'Ouest, BP 325, Ave Jean Paul II, Cotonou (tel: 312-466/7; fax: 312-465).

Banque Internationale du Bénin (BIBE) BP 03-2098, Carrefour des 3 Banques, Cotonou (tel: 315-549; fax: 312-365).

Continental Bank Bénin, 01 BP, Avenue Pope Jean Paul II, 2020 Cotonou (tel: 312-424, 313-393; fax: 315177).

Ecobank Bénin, BP 1280, Rue du Gouverneur Bayol, 01 Cotonou (tel: 314-023, 313-069; fax: 313-385, 313-718).

Financial Bank Bénin (FBB), BP 2700, Rue du Commandant Decoeur, Cotonou (tel: 313-100, 313-103, 313-104; fax: 313-102).

Central bank

Banque Centrale des États de l'Afrique de l'Ouest, PO Box 325, Avenue Jean Paul II, Cotonou (tel: 312-466; fax: 312-465; e-mail: webmaster@bceao.int).

Stock exchange
Afribourse (Bourse Régionale des Valeurs Moblières) (BRVM), www.brvm.org

Travel information

Transports Aériens du Bénin (tel: 314-797).

National tourist organisation offices
Office National du Tourisme et de l'Hôtellerie (ONATHO), BP 89, Contonou (tel: 315-402).

Ministries

Ministry of Public Service, Labour and Administrative Reform (tel: 313-112).

Ministry of Public Works and Transport, PO Box 16, Cotonou, Benin (tel: 313-380).

State Ministry of Government Co-ordination, Planning, Development and Employment Promotion (tel: 301-553).

Other useful addresses

Africa Rice Center (AfricaRice), 01 BP 2031, Cotonou (tel: 350 188; fax: 350 556; email: africarice@cgiar.org).

Agence Bénin-Presse, BP 120, Cotonou.

Benin Embassy (USA), 2737 Cathedral Avenue, NW, Washington DC 20008 (tel: 232-6656; fax: 265-1996).

Import/Export Alimentation de Bénin, BP 53, Cotonou.

Institut National de la Statistique et de L'Analyse Economique, BP 323, Cotonou (tel: 314-101/103).

Mission de Co-opération et d'Action Culturelle, BP 476, Cotonou (tel: 300-824).

Mission Permanente d'Aide et de Co-opération, BP 476, Cotonou (administers aid from France).

Organisation Commune Benin-Niger des Chemins de fer et des Transports (OCBN) (Benin Railways), PO Box 16, Cotonou, Benin (tel: 313-380).

Société Nationale d'Equipement, BP 2042, Cotonou (deals with capital goods).

Société Nationale de Commercialisation et d'Exportation du Bénin (Sonaceb), BP 933, Cotonou (tel: 312-822).

Société Nationale de Commercialisation des Produits Pétroliers (Sonacop), BP 245, Cotonou (tel: 312-290).

Société Nationale d'Importation du Bénin, BP 2042, Cotonou.

Syndicat National des Commerçants et Industriels Africains du Bénin, BP 367, Cotonou.

National news agency: Agence Bénin-Presse (ABP), 01 BP 72 Cotonou (tel: 2131-2655; fax: 2131-1326; internet: www.gouv.bj/presse/abp).

Internet sites

Africa Business Network: http://www.ifc.org/abn

AllAfrica.com: http://www.allafrica.com

African Development Bank: http://www.afdb.org/en/

General tourist information: http://www.africaguide.com/

Mbendi AfroPaedia (information on companies, countries, industries and stock exchanges in Africa): http://mbendi.com

Mission to the UN: http://www.un.int/benin

Bermuda

COUNTRY PROFILE

1503 A Spaniard, Juan de Bermudez, sighted the islands.
1609 Settled by the British.
1612 A charter was given by James I to the Virginia Company to include Bermuda in the dominion. The first permanent settlers arrived shortly afterwards.
1684 The islands were sold to the City of London and became the property of the Crown.
1620 Bermuda was granted limited self-government when the House of Assembly was formed.
1700s Bermuda developed links with the American colonies of North America.
1815 Hamilton was named the capital city.
1834 Slavery was abolished.
1940 An agreement between the US and Britain granted about 10 per cent of Bermuda's land to the US for military use.
1963 The first political party was formed.
1968 Bermuda was granted internal self-government. The first elections held under universal adult suffrage were won by the United Bermuda Party (UBP).
1998 The UBP lost power for the first time since 1968 when the Progressive Labour Party (PLP) won the general election under Jennifer Smith. She was the first female party leader.
2001 Regulation of the insurance sector was moved from the ministry of finance to the Monetary Authority, in order to increase the transparency of the sector.
2002 The Bermuda Companies Amendment Act simplifying the procedure for forming companies came into effect.
2003 PLP won parliamentary elections. Following an internal PLP revolt, Premier Jennifer Smith resigned and Alex Scott became premier. Hurricane Fabian, the most powerful storm since the 1950s, hit the islands and caused widespread destruction. A Constitutional amendment introduced 36 single seat constituencies within the islands (from the previous 20 dual seat constituencies).
2004 The PLP published plans for independence from the UK.
2005 Bermuda entered into a tax sharing agreement with Australia, only the second agreement signed after the US; it allows requests and information on specific tax matters under investigation or audit to be passed between states.
2006 Ewart Brown became premier, having replaced Alex Scott as leader of the PLP.
2007 Sir John Vereker retired and Sir Richard Hugh Turton Gozney became governor.
2008 The newly elected PLP government scrapped the public holiday on the Queen's official birthday, to be replaced by a National Heroes' Day (in October).
2009 The Organisation for Economic Co-operation and Development (OECD) added Bermuda to its 'white list' of countries and territories that had substantially implemented internationally agreed tax standards, after it had signed 12 tax information exchange agreements (TIEA) with various countries.
2010 Premier Brown gave his farewell speech in the last session of parliament, ahead of his retirement. Paula Cox (PLP) took office as premier. Bermuda signed a TIEA with China.
2011 Bermuda signed a TIEA with the Czech Republic in February and with Indonesia in June. A new political party, One Bermuda Alliance (OBA), was formed in May from defecting members of the UBP and BDA.
2012 On 18 May, Richard Gozney left office as governor and David B Arkley became acting governor. The Department of Tourism published figures on 31 August that showed tourism spending had declined by between US$19–25 million (January–July) 2012, as visitors cut back on most aspects of holiday personal spending. General elections were held on 17 December. The OBA won 51.7 per cent of the vote (19 seats out of 36), PLP won 46.1 per cent (17). Craig Cannonier (OBA) became prime minister on 18 December.
2013 On 1 May Bermuda, along with the British Virgin Islands, the Cayman Islands, Anguilla, Montserrat and the Turks and Caicos Islands, signed a tax sharing agreement with the tax authorities of France, Germany, Italy, Spain and the UK.

KEY FACTS

Official name: Bermuda

Head of State: Queen Elizabeth II; represented by Governor George Duncan Raukawa Fergusson (from 23 May 2012)

Head of government: Prime Minister Michael Dunkley (OBA) (from 20 May 2014)

Ruling party: One Bermuda Alliance (OBA) (from 2011; elected 18 Dec 2012)

Area: 55 square km

Population: 70,196 (2015)* (64,237; census figure 2010)

Capital: Hamilton

Official language: English

Currency: Bermudan dollar (BD$) = 100 cents

Exchange rate: BD$1.00 per US$ (fixed)

GDP per capita: US$85,700 (2013)*

GDP real growth: -2.50% (2013)*

GDP: US$519.80 million (2013)*

Inflation: 2.70% (2013)*

* estimated figure

2014 Prime Minister Craig Cannonier resigned on 19 May; his deputy, Michael Dunkley, was sworn in the following morning. Overseas Territory representatives from the British Virgin Islands, Bermuda, Montserrat, the Cayman Islands and Anguilla met with United Kingdom business networking specialists, CaribDirect International Business Network (CIBN) in May. CIBN is an agency designed to facilitate and connect entrepreneurs and business people in the UK with Caribbean government and business representatives for trade and investment.
2015 In September a little local spat developed between member of parliament, Walter Roban, who accused Prime Minister Dunkley of going into hiding when faced by a recent upsurge in crime under the OBA. A spokesperson for Mr Dunkley in turn accused Mr Roban of a classic example of '... misinforming, misrepresenting and misleading the public.'

Political structure

Constitution

1968 saw the UK government enact a constitution for Bermuda. The Queen is the ceremonial head of state, while the actual running of the country is left to the Prime Minister and his or her cabinet.

Form of state

Representative democracy; crown colony of the UK.

The executive

Bermuda has had a broad measure of internal self-government since 1968. Queen Elizabeth II is represented by a UK-appointed governor who is responsible for defence, external affairs and internal security. The governor is guided on most internal matters by a cabinet appointed from the bicameral legislature. The prime minister is chosen from the majority party and heads a cabinet of no more than 14 members of the legislature.

National legislature

The bicameral parliament comprises the House of Assembly (lower chamber), with 36-members, directly elected in single seat constituencies, for a maximum term of five years.
The Senate (upper chamber), has 11 senators, appointed by the governor, of which five are appointed on the advice of the premier, three on the advice of the leader of the opposition. The remaining three are appointed at the discretion of the governor, one of which becomes president of the senate, as voted on by the senate. The senate has the power to block constitutional changes, passed by the lower chamber, unless a two-thirds majority in senate votes in its favour.

Legal system

The legal system and Bermudian law are based on the British model. The ultimate court of appeal is the Judicial Committee of the Privy Council in the UK.

Last elections

17 December 2012 (parliamentary)
Results: Parliamentary: One Bermuda Alliance (OBA) won 51.7 per cent (19 seats out of 36), Progressive Labour Party (PLP) 46.1 per cent (17), independents 2.3 per cent (none); turnout 43.7 per cent.

Next elections

December 2017 (parliamentary)

Political parties

Ruling party

One Bermuda Alliance (OBA) (from 2011; elected 18 Dec 2012)

Main opposition party

United Bermuda Party (UBP)

Political situation

Despite its small size and negligible resource base, Bermuda has one of the highest per capita incomes in the world. The economy is based upon tourism and international business transactions, which take advantage of Bermuda's offshore banking status.
Inflation has been kept low through the policy of fixing the Bermudan dollar at parity with the US dollar. Bermuda has low levels of public debt and although borrowing has risen due to an increase in capital spending, debt remains well below the government's ceiling of 10 per cent of GDP.
The image of tax havens, such as Bermuda, suffered in 2008 as evidence of tax evasion schemes came to light. Coupled with the downturn in the global economy in 2008 and the collapse of some hedge funds, Bermuda has been forced to work harder for its share of the US$2 trillion worldwide hedge fund business, as well as offshore banking and insurance business. Some company headquarters have been moved to other less questionable destinations to bolster company images, prompting Bermuda to introduce new laws to provide greater transparency and good governance.
Following the enactment of a new regulatory framework in 2008, in June 2009 the Organisation for Economic Co-operation and Development (OECD) added Bermuda to its 'white list' of countries and territories that had substantially implemented internationally agreed tax standards. Bermuda had by then signed 12 tax information exchange agreements (TIEA) with various countries. The Bermuda Monetary Authority set up a supervisory regime to oversee Special Purpose Insurers (SPI) in October 2009. In particular, SPIs include catastrophe or cat bonds that insure against extreme events where losses are particularly high.

Population

69,080 (2011) (64,237; census figure 2010)
Last census: 20 May 2010: 64,237
Population density: 1,280 inhabitants per square km. Urban population: 100 per cent.
Annual growth rate: 0.8 per cent (2003)

Ethnic make-up

African (58 per cent), European (36 per cent). Approximately 73 per cent of the population is Bermuda-born.

Religions

Non-Anglican Protestant (39 per cent), Anglican (27 per cent), Roman Catholic (15 per cent), African Methodist Episcopal (10 per cent), Methodist (6 per cent), Seventh-Day Adventist (3 per cent).

Welfare

An insurance scheme takes contributions from the employer and employee to benefit workers during sickness or disability, for maternity leave or survivors of deceased workers, funded by contributions of a set amount, paid by both the employer and employee, each paying 50 per cent of the sum per week.

Pensions

There is an old age pension scheme funded by contributions of a set amount, paid by both the employer and employee, each paying 50 per cent of the sum per week.

Main cities

Hamilton (capital city, estimated population 1,012 in 2012), St George's (St George's Island) (1,743).

Languages spoken

English and Portuguese.

Official language/s

English

Media

Press

Dailies: The only newspaper is *The Royal Gazette* (www.royalgazette.com).
Weeklies: Magazines include the *Bermuda Sun* (www.bermudasun.bm) and the *Mid-Ocean News* published by *The Royal Gazette*. *Worker's Voice* is published by the Industrial Union.
Periodicals: Monthly magazines include *Bermudian* and *Bermudian Business*. *Preview Bermuda* (www.previewbermuda.com) is a free publication for visitors. *Bottom Line* covers business matters and is published six times annually and issued free with *The Royal Gazette*.

Broadcasting

Radio: All stations are private and commercial. The Bermuda Broadcasting Company (BBC) operates four of the most listened to stations, providing a mix of programmes including news, music and local contents, however, the top ranking station is HOTT 107.5 (www.hott1075.com). VSB operates four channels including news, religious, music and tourist information. Radio Bermuda (www.marops.bm) gives shipping weather forecasts.

Television: There are two main networks, both commercial and free-to-air. The Bermuda Broadcasting Company (BBC) and DeFontes Broadcasting (Television) Ltd) (www.vsb-bm). There is ready access to satellite and cable TV services.

Other news agencies: Caribbean Net News: www.caribbeannetnews.com

Economy

Despite its small size and negligible resource base, Bermuda has one of the highest per capita incomes in the world (US$85,700 in 2013 (latest available)). The economy is based on high-end tourism and international business transactions, which take advantage of Bermuda's offshore banking status. In 2013, GDP fell by 2.5 per cent to US$5.2 billion, 94.1 per cent of which was generated through the services sector. Foreign remittances in 2012 amounted to US$1.19 billion, which rose to US$1.22 billion in 2013. Remittances received increased slightly to US$1.3 billion in 2014.

The Bermudan dollar has parity with the US dollar. Bermuda has low levels of public debt and although borrowing has risen due to an increase in capital spending, debt remains well below the government's ceiling of 10 per cent of GDP.

Following the enactment of a new regulatory framework in 2008, the Bermuda Monetary Authority set up a supervisory regime to oversee Special Purpose Insurers (SPI) in 2009. In particular, SPIs include catastrophe or 'cat bonds' that insure against extreme events where losses can be particularly high.

External trade

The large trade deficit is offset by net invisible earnings from tourism and international business, especially insurance and shipping registration. High import duties on all items are the government's main source of income.

Imports

Principal imports include foodstuffs, tobacco, clothing, fuels, chemicals, machinery, transport equipment, and live animals.

Main sources: South Korea (56.5 per cent of total in 2014), US (17.9 per cent), Singapore (9 per cent)

Exports

Principal exports include foodstuffs, tobacco, clothing, fuels, chemicals, machinery, transport equipment, live animals, pharmaceuticals and petroleum.

Main destinations: Indonesia (8.5 per cent total in 2014) and the US (8.1 per cent).

Re-exports

Pharmaceuticals and petroleum, machinery and transport equipment.

Agriculture

Farming

Agriculture contributes less than 1 per cent to GDP annually and employs around 2 per cent of the population. Less than 6 per cent of total area is cultivated arable land, most of which is used by tenant farmers for growing fruit, vegetables and flowers. Although self-sufficient in eggs and milk, around 80 per cent of food requirements need to be imported. There is a small fishing industry.

Fishing

The typical annual fish catch is over 350 tonnes (t), plus 25t per annum other seafood.

Industry and manufacturing

Manufacturing and construction combined contribute around 7 per cent to GDP and employ less than 5 per cent of the workforce. Major activities include ship repair, small boat building and manufacture of paints, perfumes, pharmaceuticals, mineral water extracts and handicraft souvenirs. The emphasis is on encouraging light industry in the Freeport area on Ireland Island North. Bermuda has large marine engineering interests, and operates one of the world's largest flag of convenience shipping fleets.

Tourism

Tourism, formerly the mainstay of the economy, is now second to the financial sector as a source of foreign exchange. Bermuda sits in the North Atlantic Ocean, over 1,000km from the east coast of the US. It is a British Overseas Territory and retains many characteristics of the old British colony. The capital, Jamestown, is a Unesco World Heritage Site, with many historic buildings

In 2012, there were 232,000 tourist arrivals, which was largely the same as the previous three years. Most of these tourists arrived by cruise liners or yachts. Visitors from the US are the largest single group, followed by Canadians, then the UK and other Europeans. Tourism contributed 15.3 per cent of GDP in 2014. Travel and tourism provides 20.5 per cent of all jobs with US$442.7 million in visitor exports in 2014.

The Ministry of Business Development and Tourism was formed in 2010 to combine domestic and international business.

Hydrocarbons

There are no known hydrocarbon reserves. Bermuda consumed 4,600 barrels per day (bpd) of oil in 2013, all of which was imported. The government maintains a fixed price for petrol (gasoline) and Esso and Shell are the only companies allowed to sell retail petroleum products in Bermuda.

Bermuda consumes more oil and gas annually than Antigua, Dominica, Grenada, St Lucia and St Vincent combined.

There is a liquefied natural gas (LNG) terminal supplying gas in cylinders; the French-owned Rubis Gaz distributes liquefied petroleum gas (LPG) to retailers as well as propane and butane to residential and commercial customers.

Any coal used is commercially insignificant.

Energy

Total installed generating capacity was 167.4MW in 2014, producing 648.9 million kilowatt hours. The Bermuda Electric Light Company is a subsidiary of the privately owned Belco Holdings Limited. Under Belco's proposals in 2009, five large-scale renewable energy projects are under consideration, a large catchment solar photovoltaic plant, commercial wind generation, wave energy, biomass and a sealed municipal waste burning plant which in 2012 were still either under consideration or under construction. Another subsidiary, Purenergy Renewables, is offering several small-scale energy systems for private and commercial use, including micro-wind generation, solar photovoltaic and solar-thermal hot water.

Financial markets

Stock exchange

Bermuda Stock Exchange (BSX)

Banking and insurance

On 1 May 2013 Bermuda, along with the British Virgin Islands, the Cayman Islands, Anguilla, Montserrat and the Turks and Caicos Islands, signed a tax sharing agreement with the tax authorities of France, Germany, Italy, Spain and the UK.

Central bank

Bermuda Monetary Authority

Main financial centre

Hamilton

Offshore facilities

In 2000, Bermuda signed a letter of commitment with the Organisation for Economic Co-operation and Development (OECD) agreeing to exchange information with overseas authorities in criminal tax matters by 31 December 2003 and in civil tax matters by 31 December 2005.

Following the 11 September 2001 terrorist attacks on the US, a number of new reinsurance companies located on the island.

Time
GMT minus four hours (GMT minus three hours from April to October).

Geography
The Bermudas or Somers Islands are an isolated archipelago, comprising about 150 islands in the Atlantic Ocean about 917km (570 miles) off the coast of South Carolina, USA. Ten of the islands are linked by bridges and causeways to form the principal mainland.

Hemisphere

Northern

Climate
Semi-tropical with temperatures usually ranging between 16—28 degrees Celsius, from winter (Nov–Mar) to summer (Apr–Oct), with no marked rainy season. Bermuda is located more than 1,600km north of the Caribbean and is subjected to occasional hurricane-force winds between June and September.

Dress codes
There is no occasion on the island when shorts cannot be worn. For the office, tailored shorts of one colour may be worn, with long socks to the knees with at least an inch to turn over.

Entry requirements
Passports

Required by all visitors except UK, US and Canadian nationals with other documentary proof of identification. All US and Canadian nationals have required a passport for re-entry to their country.

A return/onward ticket is required by all visitors.

Visa

Visas are not required by transit passengers and most citizens of the Americas, Europe, Australasia and some Asian countries, provided their stay does not exceed six months. For further details visit www.immigration.gov.bm, or contact a UK diplomatic or consular mission locally. All visitors must have return/onward passage. Those wishing to travel to the US must have entry clearance for the country to be visited after leaving the US.

Currency advice/regulations

There is no limit to the import of local or foreign currency, provided it is declared on arrival. The export of local currency is limited to BD$250. The export of foreign currency is limited to the amount imported and declared.

Health (for visitors)
Mandatory precautions

Yellow fever vaccination certificate if travelling from an infected area.

Advisable precautions

Hepatitis, typhoid, tetanus and polio vaccinations.

Hotels
Generally expensive. Reduced rates are available in the November–March period. There is a 7.25 per cent occupancy tax payable at check-out in addition to room rates, and a 10–15 per cent tip is added unless a service charge has already been included in bill.

Credit cards
Credit cards are accepted at most hotels, restaurants and shops.

Public holidays (national)
Fixed dates

1 Jan (New Year's Day), 24 May (Bermuda Day), 11 Nov (Remembrance Day), 25–26 Dec (Christmas).

Variable dates

Good Friday, Cup Match and Somers' Day (first Thu and Fri of Aug), Labour Day (first Mon in Sep), Heroes' Day (Oct).

Working hours
Banking

Mon–Fri: 0900–1500; also 1630–1730 Fridays only.

Business

Mon–Fri: 0900–1700.

Government

Mon–Fri: 0900–1700.

Shops

Mon–Sat: 0900–1700. During summer many stores stay open until 2100.

Telecommunications
Mobile/cell phones

GSM 1900 coverage is available throughout the islands

Electricity supply
115–230V AC, 80 cycles

Getting there
Air

International airport/s: Bermuda International Airport (BDA), 16km from Hamilton; bar, restaurant, bank, shops, hotel reservations.

Airport tax: A departure tax of BD$25 is included in air tickets.

Surface

Main port/s: Hamilton, St George's. Weekly cruises link Bermuda with several east coast US ports during the summer months.

Getting about
National transport

Road: There are around 250km of well-surfaced roads.

Buses: Regularly scheduled buses operate at frequent intervals to most destinations throughout Bermuda. Passengers must have the exact fare, tokens or transport passes which provide unlimited travel by bus or ferry which can be purchased at the Central Terminal in Hamilton.

Water: Ferries to and from Hamilton, Paget, Warwick, Somerset and Dockyard.

City transport

Taxis: Metered taxis with 25 per cent surcharge between midnight and 0600; tariffs are fixed by law. Taxis displaying a small blue flag are approved by the Department of Tourism for sightseeing purposes.

Car hire

Foreign visitors are not permitted to drive cars. Motor-assisted cycles (mopeds and scooters) may be hired throughout the island and through hotel and guest-houses. Safety helmets must be worn and insurance is compulsory, although a driver's licence is not.

BUSINESS DIRECTORY
The addresses listed below are a selection only. While World of Information makes every endeavour to check these addresses, we cannot guarantee that changes have not been made, especially to telephone numbers and area codes. We would welcome any corrections.

Telephone area codes
The international direct dialling (IDD) code for +1441, followed by subscriber's number.

Chambers of Commerce
Bermuda Chamber of Commerce, 1 Point Pleasant Road, PO Box HM 655, Hamilton HM CX (tel: 295-4201; fax: 292-5779; e-mail: info@bermudacommerce.com).

Banking
Bank of Bermuda, 6 Front Street, Hamilton HM DX (tel: 295-4000, 299-5005; fax: 299-6501, 295-1386).

The Bank of N T Butterfield & Son Ltd, PO Box HM 195, 65 Front Street, Hamilton HM AX (tel: 295-1111; fax: 295-0658).

Bermuda Commercial Bank Ltd, 44 Church Street, Hamilton HM 12 (tel: 295-5678; fax: 295-8091).

Central bank

Bermuda Monetary Authority, Burnaby House, 26 Burnaby Street, Hamilton HM 11 (tel: 295-5278; fax: 292-7471; e-mail: Info@bma.bm).

Stock exchange

Bermuda Stock Exchange (BSX), www.bsx.com

Travel information
National tourist organisation offices

Department of Tourism, Global House, 43 Church Street, Hamilton HM 12 (tel: 292-0023; fax: 292-7537; internet site: http://www.bermudatourism.org).

Ministries
Ministry of Finance, Government Administration Building, 30 Parliament Street, Hamilton HM 12 (tel: 295-5151; fax: 295-5727).

Office of The Governor, Government House, 11 Langton Hill, Pembroke, Hamilton HM 13 (tel: 292-3600; fax: 292-6831; e-mail: governor@gov.bm).

Other useful addresses

Bermuda Broadcasting Company, PO Box HM 452, Hamilton HM BX (tel: 295-2828; fax: 295-4282).

Bermuda Hotel Association, 102 Reid Street, Hamilton HM 19 (tel: 295-2127; fax: 292-6671; internet site: http://www.bermudahotels.com).

Bermuda International Business Association (BIBA), Suite 203, 48 Par-la-Ville Road, Hamilton HM 11 (tel: 292-0632; fax: 292-1797).

Bermuda Insurance Management Association (BIMA), PO Box HM 1752, Hamilton HM GX (tel: 295-4864; fax: 292-7375).

Bermuda Small Business Development Corp, PO Box HM 637, Hamilton HM CX (tel: 292-5570; fax: 295-1600).

Bermuda Stock Exchange, PO Box HM 1369, 3 F Washington Mall, Church Street, Hamilton HM FX (tel: 292-7212; fax: 292-7619; e-mail: info@bsx.com; internet site: http://www.bsx.com).

Department of Civil Aviation, Bermuda International Air Terminal, 2 Kindley Field Rd, St George's GE CX (tel: 293-1640; fax: 293-2417).

Government Information Services, Global House, 43 Church Street, Hamilton HM 12 (tel: 292-6384; fax: 292-5267).

Government Statistical Department, 43 Church Street, Hamilton HM 12 (PO Box HM 3015, Hamilton HM MX) (tel: 297-7761; fax: 295-8390).

Insurance Information Office, PO Box HM 2911, Hamilton HM LX (tel: 292-9829; fax: 295-3532).

The Registrar of Companies, Government Administration Building, 30 Parliament Street, Hamilton HM 12 (tel: 295-5151; fax: 292-6640; internet site: http://www.roc.bdagov.bm).

Caribbean Net News: www.caribbeannetnews.com

Internet sites

Bermuda Sun: http://www.bermudasun.bm

Bermuda Yellow Pages: http://www.bermudayp.com

Bermuda online: http://www.bermuda-online.org

KEY FACTS

Official name: Druk-yul (The Kingdom of Bhutan)

Head of State: Druk Gyalpo (Dragon King) Jigme Kesar Namgyal Wangchuk (since 14 Dec 2006).

Head of government: Prime Minister Tshering Tobgay PDP) (from 13 Jul 2013)

Ruling party: People's Democratic Party (PDP) (from 13 Jul 2013)

Area: 47,000 square km

Population: 766,000 (2014)*

Capital: Thimphu

Official language: Dzongkha

Currency: Ngultrum (Nu) = 100 chetrums

Exchange rate: Nu66.55 per US$ (Sep 2015)

GDP per capita: US$2,730 (2014)*

GDP real growth: 6.35% (2014)*

GDP: US$2.09 billion (2014)*

Unemployment: 3.20% (2014)

Inflation: 7.70% (2014)*

Balance of trade: -US$365.80 million (2014)*

Visitor numbers: 173,300 (2009)

* estimated figure

Bhutan

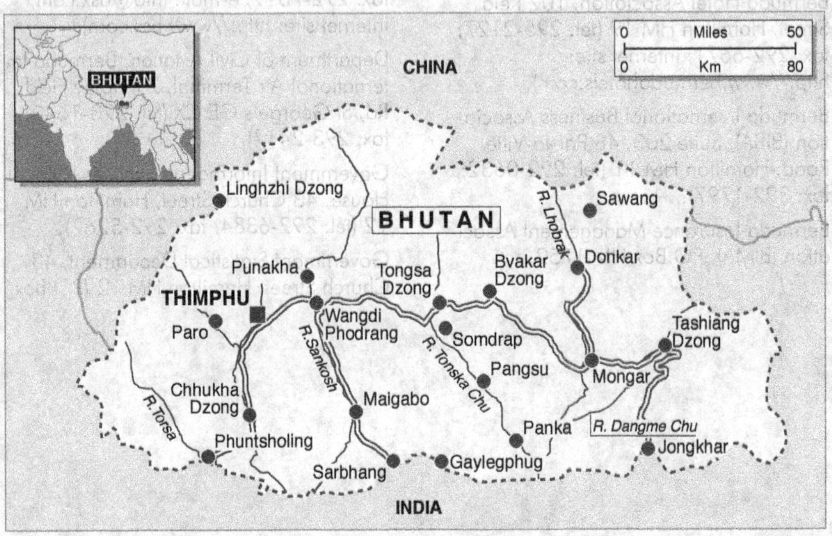

In its Overview of the Kingdom of Bhutan the Asian Development Bank (ADB) notes that the mountainous country has a large potential to produce hydropower, with only a small fraction of capacity so far exploited. Over the past few decades, it is certainly true that – starting from a low base – Bhutan has achieved strong economic growth and, between 2007 and 2012, the country's poverty levels were almost halved. However, Bhutan's growth needs to be diversified. Private sector development remains limited and growth in employment opportunity is sluggish. Hydropower is a valuable asset, but not one that automatically creates employment.

Hydropower

The commissioning of the landmark Punatsangchhu-I hydropower plant has not been without controversy. The government and other supporters of the project see it and future hydropower plants, as the only hope of lifting Bhutan out of poverty. The opponents claim that the environmental and social costs are unacceptable for what likes to be thought of as the world's 'happiest' (See The USP of GNH below) nation. Punatsangchhu-I generates 1,480 megawatts of hydroelectricity during the summer months – enough to provide light for almost every house in the country. This contrasts sharply with the situation in 1999, when less than one-quarter of Bhutanese households had an electricity supply.

By 2015 hydropower was already Bhutan's largest export; it was hoped that by 2020 hydropower would account for more than half Bhutan's gross domestic product (GDP). Bhutan is fortunate to have its customer base lined up and close-by. India which is funding the Punatsangchhu-I plant with a 40 per cent grant and 60 per cent loan (of the revised total cost of US$1.74 billion) was ready and waiting with cheque book in hand. With the direct (as financier) and indirect (as customer) support of the Indian government, Bhutan is aiming to add 10,000 MW of hydropower to its capacity by the end of the decade through the construction of 10 more projects. However, in one village, a reported 22 families lost their homes and dozens more had to abandon farmlands as Punatsangchhu-I was expected to flood the area. The government had compensated those families with cash, free electricity and new land of the same acreage as the land it proposed to flood. But villagers were not always 'happy' as it would probably take years to cultivate their new land.

The USP of GNH

When in 1972 Bhutan adopted the concept of Gross National Happiness (GNH) as a measure of national wellbeing, the initiative attracted attention from all over the world. The idea was also adopted in European and North American academic circles. A number of governments, including those of France and Canada, stated their intention to integrate GNH into their national statistics. Bhutan's (former) prime minister, the happily named Jigme Y Thinley, would pop up at international gatherings promoting the values of GNH and attracting favourable attention. In marketing terms, GNH became Bhutan's Unique Selling Point (USP), the idea that immediately identified the small mountain kingdom to the rest of the world. In 2011, the United Nations General Assembly adopted a so called 'happiness resolution', noting that the measure of GDP 'does not adequately reflect the happiness and well-being of people in a country.' The UN went further, empowering Bhutan to speak to member states about the need for happiness to be a key component of their economies. In April 2012 Prime Minister Thinley addressed a UN conference on the benefits of GNH. As Bhutan's first elected prime minister, Mr Thinley may have achieved a lot – but principally outside Bhutan.

Thinley goes

Mr Thinley's defeat in the July 2013 elections was attributed to the party's decision to challenge the concept of Gross National Happiness as being an empty slogan. This appeared to strike a chord with Bhutan's voters among whom the perception prevailed that Mr Thinley's international public relations campaign to promote GNH was being conducted at the expense of domestic exigencies.

In the final round of voting in July 2013, Bhutan's opposition People's Democratic Party (PDP) lead by Tshering Tobgay defeated Mr Thinley's Druk Phuensum Tshogpa (DPT) (Bhutan Peace and Prosperity Party). The PDP victory meant, *inter alia*, that Bhutan's ties with India would probably see a renaissance. Bhutan had been India's closest ally and supporter until the election victory of the DPT in 2008. The PDP leader Tshering Tobgay is a dedicated royalist, who believes that if anyone, it is Bhutan's King Jigme Khesar Namgyel Wangchuk who should be the ambassador for GNH in the world's forums, rather than the elected head of the government. The Harvard educated Mr Tobgay (Mr Thinley could only make Pennsylvania State) was reported as observing that 'We have experts, the foremost of whom is our king. I would like real experts to take centre-stage, leading the discourse at home and abroad. I think the Bhutanese people will be thrilled if His Majesty champions the cause.'

Bhutan's problems, as Prime Minister Tobgay pointed out in an interview with the British Broadcasting Corporation (BBC), ranged from a 'ballooning debt' that was barely sustainable, to unemployment (see The economy below) and growing corruption. Perhaps Mr Tobgay was selling his country short. On the Transparency International *Corruption Perceptions Index* for 2014, Bhutan ranked a respectable 30 out of the 175 countries surveyed, one place higher than in 2013 and ahead of Israel and Spain, both ranked 37. None the less, as a result of the perceived national problems, the BBC reported that there were those in Bhutan who referred to GNH as 'Government Needs Help'. Prime Minister Tobgay claimed to support the notion that GDP wasn't the 'be-all and end-all of development,' but, said Mr Tobgay, 'If the government spends a disproportionate amount of time talking about GNH rather than delivering basic services, then it is a distraction.' With the GNH's importance at home in question, the PDP government were also reconsidering its value as an export, too. Asked whether his government would continue promoting GNH abroad, Mr Tobgay simply repeated that: 'I believe it's not the job of the government to do that.' A report in the National Geographic magazine noted that the world's happiest places had a number of things in common, viz 'freedom from worry about getting health care and education as well as a sense of equality.' All deemed to be missing in Bhutan according to Mr Tobgay.

The economy

As Bhutan's hydropower programme began to get under way, growth increased slightly reflecting the knock-on effects for both construction and manufacturing. The government had lifted restrictions on both import and credit, relying on new monetary and fiscal policy mechanisms to manage excessive demand. The prospect in the immediate future was for rapid economic growth as more hydropower projects were built to generate electricity exports. The impact on the current account deficit will be substantial for some time, but significant capital inflows and careful demand management are expected to produce a surplus in the overall balance of payments.

According to the ADB the economy expanded in the 2014 financial year (ended 30 June 2014) at an estimated annual 4.0 per cent. This was up from 3.5 per cent a year earlier but remained below the long-term growth rate of nearly 8.0 per cent. The principal boost came from growth in industry and construction, mainly in hydropower, which comprised about one third of economic activity. Sales of cement, one of the country's few productive industries, recovered from a contraction in 2013, reflecting the stronger performance in construction as well as in manufacturing. The value of electricity output grew on higher power tariffs, despite hydropower production actually falling slightly.

KEY INDICATORS — Bhutan

	Unit	2011	2012	2013	2014	**2015
Population	m	*0.70	*0.74	*0.75	*0.77	*0.78
Gross domestic product (GDP)	US$bn	1.49	1.99	*1.99	*2.09	*2.25
GDP per capita	US$	2,121	2,671	*2,633	*2,730	*2,884
GDP real growth	%	5.9	6.5	*5.0	*6.4	*7.6
Inflation	%	8.6	10.1	8.7	*7.7	*6.3
Unemployment	%	3.1	3.2	3.2	3.2	*3.2
Exports (fob) (goods)	US$m	662.2	626.9	544.5	534.8	–
Imports (fob) (goods)	US$m	1,184.7	1,012.4	580.2	900.5	–
Balance of trade	US$m	-522.5	-385.6	-35.7	-365.8	–
Current account	US$m	-354.9	-350.0	*-439.0	*-459.0	*-591.0
Total reserves minus gold	US$m	–	954.7	991.3	1,245.1	–
Foreign exchange	US$m	–	943.2	979.8	–	–
Exchange rate	per US$	41.91	54.15	62.21	63.19	–

* estimated figure ** forecast figure

According to the ADB, the services sector grew marginally more quickly than in 2013, notwithstanding wholesale and retail trade continuing to fall from their double-digit expansion of earlier years. Although credit restrictions on housing construction and vehicles continued, output from the finance sector picked up somewhat as lending for manufacturing, tourism and personal use increased. Tourism, though a niche activity, recorded an impressive gain. Agriculture saw a marginal pickup in growth, but its share in GDP was small.

Consumer prices were highly volatile because of Bhutan's heavy dependence on imports, which supply about half of goods, both food and non-food, with most supplies coming from India. In 2014, average annual inflation accelerated to 9.6 per cent from 8.8 per cent in the previous year, due mainly to high prices for food, with price pressures coming from India as well as domestic markets. Food inflation peaked at 14.5 per cent in the fourth quarter of 2013, then receded to 5.9 per cent a year later. Inflation for other expenditures was fairly stable, averaging 7.8 per cent in 2014. The fiscal deficit in 2014 equalled 4.1 per cent of GDP, marginally lower than in the previous year but higher than the government's target of 3.0 per cent on average over the Eleventh Five-Year Plan, 2014–2018.

Preliminary estimates showed domestic revenue growing by only 3.7 per cent, much more slowly than in previous years as import restrictions cut into tax earnings. Although domestic revenue at 19.6 per cent of GDP was able to fully cover current expenditure at 17.2 per cent, the remaining balance fell short of financing the government's target of covering 15 per cent of capital expenditure. Grants picked up to equal 10 per cent of GDP but were insufficient in 2014 to cover the remainder of capital expenditure.

Money supply grew by 6.6 per cent, much less than in 2013, reflecting slower increases in net foreign assets and bank credit. Growth in credit to the private sector remained slack at 6.4 per cent, slightly less than in the previous year, as temporary credit restrictions continued in some sectors, having been imposed in 2012 to address excessive consumption and a severe shortage of Indian rupee reserves. To strengthen financial and liquidity management, the Royal Monetary Authority adopted new monetary and macro-prudential policies in the banking sector, including new risk-weighting requirements for various loans, the imposition of loan-to-value caps for housing and vehicle loans and a loan-to-income cap of 70 per cent for consumer loans. The fiscal authority also implemented demand-management policies such as revised taxes and import duties on vehicles and a new green tax on fuel.

With these new measures in place, the monetary and fiscal authorities had begun to gradually remove temporary measures, lifting in February 2014 the import and foreign exchange restrictions on furniture and alcohol and in September 2014 the remaining restrictions on credit and imports. The ADB noted that the current account deficit improved slightly from 27.3 per cent of GDP in FY2013 to 25.5 per cent in FY2014, owing to lower deficits in the trade and primary income accounts. Restrictions caused imports to fall by 5 per cent, narrowing the trade deficit. Lower interest payments in 2014 – largely reflecting the full liquidation of overdraft loans from India obtained during the rupee crises – helped reduce the primary income deficit. Financial net inflows fell but were still substantial at 13.0 per cent of GDP. With a hefty increase in investment grants from India, the capital account rose to 14.8 per cent of GDP and the overall balance remained in surplus, albeit substantially lower than in the previous year.

At the end of the 2014 financial year, the overall balance of payments surplus stood at US$98.7 million, or 5.4 per cent of GDP and gross international reserves had increased to US$997.9 million, equivalent to 13 months of imports. Of total reserves, US$829.3 million was in convertible currency. Indian rupee reserves, equivalent to US$168.6 million, were 16.9 per cent of total reserves, which was a marked improvement from the miniscule balance in 2012.

In the view of the ADB, in early 2015 economic recovery was set to continue and high growth rates were projected over the next two years. The industry sector, accounting for about 40 per cent of GDP, would continue to drive the economy, bolstered by the construction of new hydropower projects, including the Nikachhu and Kholongchhu plants and increased electricity output from the new Dagachhu plant, which opened in early 2015.

Growth in services is expected to accelerate as trade and finance activities gather pace with temporary restrictions being lifted. Expansion would not, considered the ADB, be at the rates seen during the severe rupee shortages in previous years, however, as new monetary and fiscal measures and better bank regulation were expected to help rein in excessive consumption spending. Tourism is expected to be robust with the government declaring 2015 to be 'Visit Bhutan' year. Over the first half of the 2015 financial year, tourist arrivals grew at an impressive 43.1 per cent and revenue by 18.4 per cent.

Inflation in the first half of FY2015 slowed to 7.5 per cent, as food and other prices eased from their highs in the previous year in line with lower inflation in India. Inflation was expected to ease further to an average of 7.0 per cent this year and 6.8 per cent next year. The improved inflation outlook came from price moderation in India and forecasts of declining world oil prices, which would help offset increases in domestic power tariffs.

The government plans to narrow the fiscal deficit to 2.7 per cent of GDP in 2015 with revenue-enhancing reforms such as new tax measures on fuel and telecommunication services, a revised tax and import duty on vehicles and revised export tariffs. Current expenditure was expected to grow by 13.7 per cent, mainly on planned increases in infrastructure maintenance and civil service salaries. While capital expenditure had been set much lower than in 2013, at Nu15.2 billion (US$0.23 billion), this figure might be revised when grant funding is secured during the year.

The current account deficit is projected to widen over the following two years to about 30 per cent of GDP as the trade deficit expands to accommodate large imports of goods related to hydropower investments. Although exports will also strengthen as electricity exports to India increase, adequate inflows of external funding – for the most part hydropower loans and budgetary investment grants from India – are projected to keep the overall balance of payments in surplus.

Risk assessment

Economy	Good
Politics	Fair
Regional stability	Good

COUNTRY PROFILE

1907 The first hereditary king was enthroned.

1910 The Anglo-Bhutanese Treaty was signed, granting the government of British India full control of Bhutan's foreign relations.

1949 India became independent and the 1910 treaty was re-negotiated. Bhutan became free to pursue its own foreign policy, although it agreed to seek India's advice.

1952 King Jigme Dorji Wangchuk was enthroned and established the Tsogdu (National Assembly) in 1953.
1958 The Lhotshampa population of the southern districts of Bhutan was granted Bhutanese citizenship and tenure of lands.
1965 The Lodoi Tsokde (Royal Advisory Council) was established.
1972 King Jigme Singye Wangchuk was enthroned.
1979 Bhutan supported China in preference to India at the UN, beginning a gradual reorientation of foreign policy away from India.
1987 Bhutan's Sixth Five Year Plan included a policy of 'one nation, one people'. A code of traditional *Drukpa* dress and etiquette (*Driglam Namzhag*) was introduced.
1988 A census based on ethnicity branded many domiciled Nepalis as illegal immigrants, as a new citizenship law was enforced. Tibetan-based Bhutanese culture was officially emphasised.
1989 Nepali language was banned for use in schools.
1990 Anti-government protests in southern Bhutan led to ethnic violence as Bhutan People's Party began a campaign of violence; around 80,000 ethnic Nepalis fled to Nepal.
1998 King Wangchuk handed over full executive power to a Lhengye Zhungtshog (Council of Ministers).
1993 Talks between Bhutan and Nepal attempt to resolve the refugee problem.
1999 The King granted the Tsogdu the right to dismiss a reigning monarch. The WTO Working Party on Accession for the Kingdom of Bhutan was established.
2001 A draft constitution included proposals for a democratic system of government. Further talks took place concerning refugees between Bhutan and Nepal.
2002 The Ninth Five-Year Plan was drawn up to continue Bhutan's decentralisation process and promote 'Gross National Happiness'.
2003 A new government was installed with Jigme Yozer Thinley as prime minister.
2004 Indian insurgents entered Nepal and were reported to be working with Nepalese Maoists with a view to attacking Bhutan's royal palace.
2005 A draft constitution was unveiled that aimed to transform the country's absolute monarchy into a two-party democracy. Sangey Ngedup took office as prime minister. Crown Prince Jigme Khesar Namgyel Wangchuk undertook responsibilities held by the King, to gain experience before the King's abdication.
2006 The king appointed a chief elections commissioner and other officers to prepare for the first national elections. A mock election was held to train officials in the procedure. Khandu Wangchuk took office as prime minister. King Jigme Singye Wangchuk abdicated in favour of his son, Crown Prince Jigme Kesar Namgyal.
2007 Bhutan and India signed a treaty allowing Bhutan more control of foreign policy and military purchases. India was asked to provide increased security in border regions to prevent Assam Ulfa insurgents carrying out attacks in Bhutan. Lyonpo Khandu Wangchuk resigned as prime minister and Lyonpo Kinzang Dorji took office as the acting prime minister before the formation of the interim government and the first parliamentary general elections. Elections for the National Council of Bhutan (the upper house), were held for the first time since the King dissolved his absolute monarchy. Of the 25 members, 20 independent candidates were directly elected and five appointed by the King. Elections in five constituencies were postponed for one month as the minimum two candidates per district was not achieved.
2008 In the first parliamentary elections ever held in Bhutan, the Druk Phuensum Tshogpa (DPT) (Bhutan Peace and Prosperity Party) won 67.04 per cent of the vote (winning 45 seats out of 47), the People's Democratic Party (PDP) had 32.96 per cent (two seats); turnout was 79.4 per cent. Jigme Y Thinley (DPT) became prime minister. King Jigme Khesar Namgyel Wangchuck was crowned. He became, at that time, the world's youngest monarch.
2009 Exiled Bhutanese in seven UNHCR-administered camps in Nepal launched a campaign for repatriation. An estimated 8,000 people were still awaiting a resolution of their plight; thousands more had already been offered access to third countries.
2010 Two domestic airports at Bathbalathang and Dungphu Yonphula were opened with a domestic air service.
2011 In May, King Jigme announced to parliament his intentions of marrying commoner Jetsun Pema. They were married in a Buddhist ceremony on 12 October in a monastery in the capital Thimpu. Construction of a new domestic airport in Gelephu began on 2 July.
2012 In September, four new political parties prepared to register with the Election Commission of Bhutan (ECB) as soon as the date of the 2013 elections is announced. They include, Druk Nyamrup Tshogpa (DNT), Bhutan Kuen-Ngyam Party (BKP), and Druk Chirwang Tshogpa (DCT) and Druk Me-ser Tshogpa (DMT).
2013 On 13 May voters took part in elections to determine which two out of four parties will participate in the second and decisive stage of the vote on 13 July. The opposition PDP won Bhutan's second-ever parliamentary election held on 13 July. The result was 47 seats to the PDP with the remaining 15 to the DPT. Turn out was estimated at 80 per cent.
2014 A meeting of the technical Expert Group on Bhutan-China Boundary was held in Thimphu from 9–12 October.
2015 While answering questions on an American talk programme in March Premier Tobgay described ties between India and Bhutan as a 'model relationship'. He also said that Bhutan has a 'good relations' with China, but not as deep as India.

Political structure

Constitution

A draft constitution aiming to transform the country's absolute monarchy into a two-party democracy was drawn up in April 2005. It was approved by the people in a referendum during 2007.

Independence date

8 August 1949

Form of state

Constitutional monarchy

The executive

On 20 July 1998, King Jigme Singye Wangchuk handed over full executive power to the six-member Lhengye Zhungtshog (Council of Ministers).
The King is Head of State, assisted by the 10-member Lodoi Tsokde (Royal Advisory Council), the Tsogdu (National Assembly) and the monastic head of the kingdom's Buddhist priesthood.
Since 2007, however, executive power has been exercised by the Prime Minister and his/her cabinet. Both parties support the monarchy.

National legislature

The bicameral parliament consists of the National Assembly (lower house) with between 47–55 directly elected members (dependent on the proportion of the population in each district) who serve five-year terms. The National Council (upper house) consists of 25 members (20 directly elected and five appointed by the monarch), all of which must be non-partisan; members serve five-year terms. The Druk Gyalpo (Dragon King) is also a member of the National Assembly.

Last elections

13 July 2013 (parliamentary)

Results: National Assembly (13 July 2013): the People's Democratic Party (PDP) won 32 seats, Druk Phuensum Tshogpa (DPT) (Bhutan Peace and Prosperity Party((15 seats); turnout was 80 per cent.

Next elections

2018 (parliamentary)

Political parties

Ruling party
People's Democratic Party (PDP) (from 13 Jul 2013)

Main opposition party
Druk Phuensum Tshogpa (DPT) (Bhutan Peace and Prosperity Party)

Population

743,000 (2012)*

Last census: May 2005: 634,982

In 2000 the United Nations (UN) *Statistical Yearbook* gave the population of Bhutan as 1,034,774, the CIA's *World Fact Book* had a figure of 2,005,222 and the World Bank's *World Development Report 2000/01* 782,000. Then in 2005 the Office of the Census Commission of the Royal Government of Bhutan conducted a census which gave a 2005 population count of 672,425. This figure does not include any Bhutanese refugees in camps outside Bhutan, which is put at over 100,000 by international aid agencies. There are two possible reasons for the discrepancies in these figures. Firstly that in the early 1970s the government of Bhutan gave the UN an inflated figure so that Bhutan could become a member – at the time there was a cut-off point of one million. Thereafter a normal growth rate was added each year. A second possibility is that the western and central districts inflated their numbers to ensure their dominance over the southern and eastern districts. Again, once a figure had been established, each year an estimated figure was produced by using the population growth rate.

This publication has previously used the UN *Statistical Yearbook* figures. However, it now seems more realistic to start with the 2005 census figure. We have therefore taken the census figure of 672,425 and will increase the figure each year, until the next census, using the population growth rate, although even this figure (the World Health Organisation estimates 2.6 per cent 2000–15) is debatable. The *World Economic Outlook Database* of the International Monetary Fund, published in April 2009, has similar figures, although they start with a 2005 figure of 637,000 and increase by around 1 per cent per annum.

Population density: 18 inhabitants per square km (2010). Urban population 35 per cent (2010 Unicef).

Annual growth rate: 1.3 per cent, 1990–2010 (Unicef).

Ethnic make-up
There are many ethnic groups: the Sharchhop in the east (the largest group), the Ngalong in the west, the Lhotsampas, who speak Nepali, in the south and the Bumtaps, Khengpas, Layaps, Doyas and other nomadic groups.

Religions
Mahayana Buddhism is the state religion; Hinduism. Christianity is banned.

Education

The United Nations Children's Fund (Unicef) reported that in four decades, the government established 343 primary schools and a college that offers undergraduate degrees in arts and commerce. Since education remains a national priority in the country's development process, more than 150 community schools are available from which every school-age child may choose. However, classrooms are in short supply and most schools lack basic sanitation facilities. Each teacher may have an average of 37 students but in some schools, class sizes can reach 70 pupils.

Literacy rate: 61.1 per cent and 33.6 per cent for men and women respectively; adult rates (World Bank 2002).

Enrolment rate: 88.4 per cent net primary enrolment; 89.6 per cent, male, 87.2 per cent, female (2009).

Pupils per teacher: 37 in primary schools.

Health

Although improvement in the primary healthcare system has reduced the maternal mortality rate the figure is still one of the highest in south and east Asia. The United Nations Children's Fund (Unicef) reports that about four out of five women still deliver at home, without professional help.

Bhutan conducts national and regional immunisation days annually to achieve 90 per cent coverage. Unicef estimates that 22.2 per cent of households do not have safe drinking water.

Out-reach clinics spread across rural Bhutan provide low cost health care. A network of 145 basic health units supports the clinics, with each unit serving communities of 2,000 to 5,000 people. There are 28 hospitals, which provide more advanced and referral treatment.

The Asian Development Bank (ADB) provided the government with a loan of about US$10 million covering the five years 2001–2005 to improvement of the health sector.

Unicef initiated model villages established in almost all the 202 sub-district blocks in the country have adopted a variety of health and education programmes. Its initial success has prompted Unicef to expand the model village experience into a more general community development programme.

HIV/Aids
In 2009, the desease was not a serious problem, with less than an estimated 1,000 were living with HIV.

Life expectancy: 67 years, 2010 (Unicef 2012)

Fertility rate/Maternal mortality rate: 2.4 births per woman, 2010 (Unicef 2012)

Child (under 5 years) mortality rate (per 1,000): 45 per 1,000 live births (WHO 2012); around 19 per cent of children aged under five are malnourished (World Bank).

Welfare

In October 2001, the Bhutan government and the Asian Development Bank (ADB) signed a partnership agreement aimed at poverty reduction by 2012 through income and employment generation led by the private sector. Emphasis will be put on lifting monthly average rural incomes to about Nu3,000 (about US$65) per head. In March 2002, the ADB agreed to provide a US$700,000 grant to prepare a rural electrification and network expansion project.

There is a national pension plan and provident fund plan that currently provides for government employees and members of the armed forces. Between 16 per cent and 24 per cent of monthly earnings are paid into the funds, to provide for workers and their dependents. The amounts paid are split evenly between the employer and employee. These schemes are expected to be offered to other salaried workers over the next few years.

Main cities

Thimphu (capital, estimated population 99,021 in 2012), Phuntsholing (23,915), Geylegphug (10,416), Wangdue (7,507), Somdrup Jongkhar (6,709).

Languages spoken

There are 19 dialects and languages in Bhutan. Dzongkha bears similarities to Tibetan. English (the working language), Bumthangkha, Sharchop, Nepali and other dialects also spoken.

Official language/s
Dzongkha

Media

The government regulates the freedom of the media, excluding most private broadcasters.

Press
Weeklies: Weekly newspapers include, in Dzongkha *Kuensel* (www.kuenselonline.com); in English *Bhutan Observer* (www.bhutanobserver.com) and *Bhutan Times* (www.bhutantimes.bt) is published on Sunday.

Broadcasting
The government-operated Bhutan Broadcasting Service (BBS) (www.bbs.com.bt) is the only terrestrial television broadcaster.

Radio: The only independent radio station is Kuzoo FM (www.kuzoo.net), broadcasting in Dzongkha and English.

Television: The majority of programmes on the BBS are broadcast in Dzongkha (the national language and English (the working language).While the BBS is the only broadcaster, there is cable TV with many channels on offer.

Economy

This small landlocked country has achieved good economic growth and considerable improvement in its social indicators since the mid-1990s. According to the Bhutan Living Standard Survey (BLSS), the poverty headcount ratio was 23 per cent in 2007 and by 2010 Bhutan had either met or was on track to meet its Millennium Development Goals. In 2012, the poverty headcount ratio at the national poverty line was 1.66 per cent showing large improvement. In its 2014 Human Development Index, the UN ranked Bhutan 136 out of 187, and stated 29 per cent of the population lived in multidimensional poverty. Government policy includes revitalising industry, expanding strategic infrastructure and investing in human capital (through healthcare and education). In 2011, agriculture, of which forestry is an important component, accounted for 17.7 per cent of GDP. Bhutan is almost entirely self-sufficient in the production of food and the agricultural sector employs over 60 per cent of the domestic labour force.

The service sector constituted 39.6 per cent of GDP in 2014, although it had remained at around 36 per cent since the 1980s, which reflected a closed society for so long. The move to a democracy and openness is expected to develop the economy, with the expansion of entrepreneurial businesses catering for other new and established industries. Hydroelectricity generation and construction are the principal components of the industrial sector, which accounts for 42.6 per cent of GDP. The rugged terrain has required a greater than expected investment in roads and Bhutan has relied on foreign investment to gain its modernisation.

GDP growth has considerably slowed down from the peak of 17.9 per cent in 2007, however remained positive throughout out the global economic crisis. In 2012 growth was at 6.5 per cent, and dropped down to 2.0 per cent in 2013 before recovering to 6.3 per cent in 2014. GDP per capita steadily increased from US$1,682 in 2007 to a peak of US$2,495 in 2011, before falling to US$2,379 in 2014.

Work has been carried out on tariff reform, liberalising foreign exchange and foreign direct investment (FDI) regulations, and deregulating interest rates.

Tourism has strong potential for growth, although travellers are restricted to pre-packaged holidays and arranged tours.

External trade

In 2015 Bhutan's accession to join the World Trade Organisation was still under debate. Trade is limited to small-scale agricultural production and cottage industry manufacturing, as modern industrial production is limited. Bhutan's economy is closely linked to that of India, which provides financial and technical aid and manpower.

Imports

Principal imports are fuel and petroleum products, rice, machinery parts, vehicles and textiles.

Main sources: India (78.8 per cent of total in 2012), Republic of Korea (3.1 per cent), China (2.5 per cent)

Exports

Main exports include electricity (to India), cardamom, gypsum, timber, handicrafts, cement, fruit, precious stones and spices.

Main destinations: India (93.7 per cent of total in 2012), Bangladesh (4.1 per cent), Italy (0.4 per cent)

Agriculture

Farming

Agriculture contributed around 17.7 per cent to GDP in 2014 and employed over 60 per cent of the workforce.

Approximately 15 per cent of the land area is fertile lowland arable and 72.5 per cent is forested. No trees can be cut down without a special permit.

Main crops are rice, maize, potatoes, citrus fruits, wheat, buckwheat, barley, millet, vegetables, mustard, apples and cardamom. Vegetable production is hindered by the cold climate.

Cattle, yaks, sheep, goats and pigs are reared.

The Agriculture and Forests minister Lyonpo Yeshey Dorji stated in May 2014 that Bhutan was making a united effort to rid the country of chemical fertilizers and pesticides and become the world's first fully organic country. This commitment is part of the country's Gross National Happiness programme.

Industry and manufacturing

The industrial sector contributes around 38 per cent to GDP annually. Manufacturing accounts for under 10 per cent of GDP, with cement as the principal product.

Small-scale local industries produce woodwork, fruit processing, weaving, textiles, soap, metals, handicrafts, carpets, matches and plywood manufacture. The government owns most manufacturing industries.

Industrial growth has risen mainly because of increased value of electricity exports to India (from the Chhukha hydroelectric plant). The Tala project further enhanced growth when it came on stream in 2007. There has also been significant hydropower investment in industry.

Tourism

The tourist industry is comparatively young and the government has worked hard to maintain a balance between the needs of an emerging economy and Bhutan's historic (and unspoiled) culture that could so easily be damaged by unrestricted tourism. Bhutan prides itself on having a Gross National Happiness (GNH) indicator as part of its policy making process and its application to the development of the tourist industry (referred to locally as the 'tourism resource'), has at its centre the welfare of the people.

The remoteness of Bhutan has helped regulate tourism, not only by the limited number of visitors that reach it within the Himalayas, but to travel overland or fly into the country all visitors must make arrangements through Bhutanese travel operators and obtain visas. The government sets a minimum daily package cost, which in 2014 was US$200 per night in January, February, June, July, August and December; and US$250 per night for the rest of the months. The government lifted its limit on the number of tourists that may enter the country in 2012, and in the same year there were 105,000 tourist arrivals, up from the 66,000 of 2011. There was a further increase to 116,000 in 2013, and 133,480 in 2014.

Mining

Mining contributes about 1 per cent to GDP and employs 1 per cent of the workforce.

Deposits of many minerals exist, but quarrying is restricted to limestone, dolomite, gypsum and slate due to difficulties of access. Talcum powder is the major mineral export.

Hydrocarbons

There are no known oil or gas reserves. Annual consumption was around 1,870 barrels per day of petroleum products in 2013.

Bhutan has coal reserves of 1.3 million tonnes and produces only 1,000 tonnes of coal per annum, which are used for domestic consumption. Some exploration is being carried out on the southern borders as the government encourages private sector investment in the sector.

Energy

According to the Asian Development Bank (ADB) Bhutan, the only Asian country with surplus energy available for export, has estimated hydropower output of 30,000 megawatts (MW), of which some 5 per cent has been developed. It is Bhutan's most important economic asset, constituting some 20 per cent of the economy. Primary energy consumption in 2011 was around 1.84 million tons of oil equivalent (Mtoe). All surplus is exported to India, providing the largest component of Bhutan's total exports. Bhutan's first mega hydroelectric facility, the Chhukha Hydropower Project (commissioned in 1986), is connected to the Indian electricity grid. The India-backed Tala Hydroelectric Project, producing 1,020MW was completed in 2007, including six 170MW generators, with all of its production exported to India.

The 126MW Dagachhu Hydropower Plant – which started operating in June 2014 – is Bhutan's first public-private partnership in infrastructure and provides a model for future private investments in the energy sector, particularly hydropower. As of 2015 there were several over hydroelectric power plants under construction, including the Punatsangchhu-I and Punatsangchhu-II Hydroelectric projects with joint capacity of 2,220MW.

The electrification rate has risen from 36 per cent in 2005 to 95 per cent in August 2013. As part of the US$274.5 million Dagachhu project the government has installed over 100 solar power systems generating energy for off-grid users including schools, health clinics, and other community facilities in isolated areas.

Banking and insurance

Central bank

Royal Monetary Authority (RMA)

Main financial centre

Phuntsholing

Time

GMT plus six hours

Geography

Bhutan is a landlocked country that lies in the Himalayan range of mountains, with Tibet (the People's Republic of China) to the north and India to the south.

Bhutan has three distinct regions. The high Himalayas is mountainous with little population. The tallest peak, at 7,554 metres is Kulha Gangri; there are 20 other peaks over 7,000m high.

The inner Himalayas is mostly rugged terrain, cut through with gorges and fast flowing snow-fed rivers. Mountain spurs that turn south divide the country and produce fertile, forest-lined valleys and terraced farming basins.

The southern foothills, including the Duar Plain, is only 20km wide; it is fertile flatland and home to some exotic wildlife: tigers, leopards, elephants and rhinoceros. Snow leopards, the world's rarest big cat, live at higher altitudes.

Hemisphere

Northern

Climate

There are three distinct climatic regions: the lowlands, along the border with India, are tropical with an annual monsoon, the middle band is temperate and the north is high frozen, glacial mountains. The capital Thimphu lies in the temperate zone with temperature variation ranging from: winter 12– minus 3 degrees Celsius (C) (day–night); summer 24–15 degrees C. The hottest region, in the south and Duar Plain, can range from: winter 20–11 degrees C (day–night); summer 31–23 degrees C. The monsoon usually arrives from mid-June to the end of August, with up to 4.5–5.0 metres of rain falling, although a high of 7.5 metres has been recorded.

Entry requirements

Passports

Required by all, except Indian nationals.

Visa

All visitors, except Indian nationals, require visas and these must be arranged prior to arrival.

Independent travel is not permitted, even for business purposes. Businessmen and tourists are admitted only in groups by pre-arrangement through registered tour operators in Bhutan. This can be done directly or through a travel agent abroad. A minimum daily tariff is regulated and fixed by the government. The rate includes all accommodation, meals, transport, and services.

Overseas Bhutanese embassies do not issue visas; they are issued from Thimphu. Visa applications should be made at least three months in advance. Add an extra three weeks for business visas, when a letter of introduction from a Bhutan company and an employer's guarantee, plus an itinerary should accompany applications.

The only airline servicing Bhutan is Druk-Air, which will only board travellers with visa clearance from the tourism authority. Entry is via India, Bangladesh, Nepal or Thailand.

At the point of entry, visas are stamped and a payment of US$20 is required, along with two passport photographs. The visa is required for exit from Bhutan.

If travelling overland from India a transit pass from the Indian authorities is required to permit passage through prohibited areas of the India-Bhutan border. For this, apply to the Indian Ministry of External Affairs in Delhi some months before travelling.

Enquiries can be made to the Bhutan Tourism Corporation (see travel information directory, below).

Although Bhutan has no formal diplomatic representation in Europe or the US, it has a Permanent Mission to the UN at 2 United Nations Plaza, 27th Floor, New York, NY 10017 (tel: (+1) (212) 826-1919), which has consular jurisdiction in the US. Informal contact is maintained between the Bhutanese and US Embassy in New Delhi (India).

Customs

All visitors will complete a customs declaration on arrival, when all videos, computer and personal electronic equipment must be declared,

Export of antiques and religious antiquities, plants and animal products is prohibited.

Health (for visitors)

Mandatory precautions

A vaccination certificate for yellow fever is required if arriving from an infected area.

Advisable precautions

Anti-malarial precautions are advisable. Bhutanese hospitals only provide basic care. Comprehensive medical insurance should therefore be obtained.

Hotels

All hotel bookings are made through the Bhutan Tourism Corporation. Private hotels are open only to Bhutan nationals, some Indian nationals and certain business contacts; state hotels are of adequate standard.

Credit cards

Of limited use, they may be accepted in a few shops; travellers cheques are accepted in many more places.

Public holidays (national)

Fixed dates

2 May (Third King's Birthday), 2 Jun (Coronation Day), 8 Aug (Independence Day), 11 Nov (three days, Birthday of HM Jigme Singye Wangchuck), 17 Dec (National Day).

Variable dates

Winter Solstice (Jan), Offerings Day (Jan), Losay (Lunar New Year) (two days Feb), Shabdrung Kuchoe (Apr/May), Buddha Parinirvana (May/Jun), Buddha's First Sermon (Jul/Aug), Third King's Death (Jul), Guru Rinpoche's Birthday (Jul), Blessed Rainy Day (Sep), Dashaim (Oct), Buddha Descension Day (Oct/Nov).

Bhutan uses a lunisolar calendar that follows, essentially, the Tibetan lunar calendar. There are 12 or 13 months in a year, each beginning and ending with a new moon (approximately 28 days), in a three year cycle. An extra month is added in the third year so that, on average, the calendar matches the solar year (365.25 days). Months do not have names and are referred to by their numbers. The new year begins in February and is called Losay. Buddhist festivals are declared according to local astronomical observations.

Working hours

Banking

Bank of Bhutan: 0630–0930 and 1200–1600. Other banks, Mon—Fri: 0900–1700; 0900–1300 (cash transactions); Sat: 0900–1100.

Business

Mon–Fri: 0900–1700.

Shops

Mon—Sun: 0900–2000. Closed Tuesday.

Telecommunications

Mobile/cell phones

GSM 900 service is available in major cities and towns.

Electricity supply

220 Volts, 50Hz.

Weights and measures

Metric system

Social customs/useful tips

Prior permission is required to visit some of the religious and administrative buildings (*Dzongs*) and special permits are required to visit certain areas.

Security

Most visits are trouble-free and the country is generally peaceful.

Getting there

Air

Air transport into Bhutan is by Druk-Air, which flies from India (New Delhi and Kolkata), Nepal (Kathmandu), Bangladesh and Thailand. Druk-Air bookings can only be arranged after a visa has been issued and must also be obtained from a Bhutanese tour operator.

National airline: Druk-Air (Royal Bhutan Airlines).

International airport/s: Paro (PBH), 8km south of Paro, 68km from Thimpu.

Airport tax: International departures Nu300

Surface

Road: There are two overland access routes, both from India. A new crossing between Assam and Samdrup Jongkhar in eastern Bhutan allows tours to travel on a single-lane road to the capital. The older crossing, from the Indian frontier (Jaigaon) to Phuntsholing, has the added problem for travellers of crossing the Indian state of West Bengal before reaching Bhutan. Whichever route is taken the journey is arduous.

Getting about

National transport

Air: No services exist.

Road: The road network comprises some 3,000km, largely surfaced. The mountain roads are hazardous and subject to landslides in the monsoon season. No roads exist in the northern high Himalaya regions.

Buses: Bus services are available between main centres, although local enquiries are recommended.

City transport

Taxis: The airport journey to Thimphu is 90 minutes.

Buses, trams & metro: There is a bus service to the airport from Thimphu, journey time 90 minutes.

Car hire

Certain services are available, and local enquiries are recommended. An international driving licence is needed.

Traffic drives on the left and 40kph is the average speed.

BUSINESS DIRECTORY

The addresses listed below are a selection only. While World of Information makes every endeavour to check these addresses, we cannot guarantee that changes have not been made, especially to telephone numbers and area codes. We would welcome any corrections.

Telephone area codes

The international dialling code (IDD) for Bhutan is +975, followed by area code and subscriber's number:

Jakar3Thimphu2

Chambers of Commerce

Bhutan Chamber of Commerce and Industry, PO Box 147, Doybum Lam, Thimphu (tel: 322-742; fax: 323-936; e-mail: bsdbcci@druknet.net.bt).

Banking

Bank of Bhutan, (tel: 322-621, 322-266; fax: 323-433).

Bhutan National Bank, PO Box 439, Thimphu (tel: 322-767, 323-602; fax: 323-601; e-mail: mdbnb@druknet.net.bt).

Central bank

Royal Monetary Authority of Bhutan, PO Box 154, Thimphu (tel: 323-111; fax: 322-847; e-mail: rma@rma.org.bt).

Travel information

Association of Bhutanese Tour Operators (ABTO), PO Box 938, Thimphu (tel: 322-862, 327-715; fax: 325-286; email: abto@druknet.net.bt).

Bhutan Yodsel Tours and Treks, PO Box 574, Thimphu (tel: 323-912; fax: 323-589; e-mail: dawa@druknet.net.bt).

Department of Tourism PO Box 126, Thimphu, Bhutan (tel: 232-3251, 232-3252; fax: 232-3695; email: dot@tourism.gov.bt).

SITA Travels, SITA House, Presidential Business Park, C-9, Vasant Kunj, New Delhi 110070, India (tel: (+9111) 2612-1110; fax: (9111) 2612-1125; email: info@sitaindia.com and lokeshb@sitaindia.com; internet: www.sitaspecialtours.com).

Ministry of tourism

Bhutan Tourism Corporation Ltd (BTCL), PO Box 159, Thimphu (tel: 322-045, 322-854, 322-647; fax: 323-392, 322-479; e-mail: btcl@druknet.net.bt; ynorbu@druknet.net.bt; internet site: www.kingdomofbhutan.com).

National tourist organisation offices

Tourism Authority of Bhutan (supplies lists of operators and trekking agencies), PO Box 126, Thimphu (tel: 323-251/2, 325-121/2; fax: 323-695; e-mail: tab@druknet.net.bt).

Ministries

Ministry of Agriculture, PO Box: 252, Thimphu (tel: 232-3765; fax: 232-3153; internet: www.moa.gov.bt).

Ministry of Education PO Box 112, Thimphu (tel: 232-5325; fax: 232-5183; internet: www.education.gov.bt).

Ministry of Finance, PO Box: 117, Thimphu (tel: 232-2223; fax: 232-3154; internet: www.mof.gov.bt).

Ministry of Health, PO Box: 108, Kawangsa, Thimphu (tel: 232-2602, 232-2961; fax: 232-3113, 232-4649; internet: www.health.gov.bt).

Ministry of Home and Cultural Affairs Tashichodzong, Thimphu (tel: 232-6015; fax: 232-4320).

Ministry of Information and Communications, PO Box: 278, Thimphu (tel: 232-2144, 232-4439; fax: 232-1055; internet: www.moic.gov.bt).

Ministry of Trade and Industry, PO Box 126 Thimphu (tel: 23-251; fax: 23-695; internet: www.mti.gov.bt).

Ministry of Works and Human Settlement, PO Box: 791, Thimphu (tel: 232-7998, 232-2182; fax: 232-270; internet: www.mowhs.gov.bt).

Other useful addresses

Bhutanese Embassy, India, Chandragupta Marg, Chanakyapuri, New Delhi, 110 021 India (tel: (+91-11) 2688-9230/9806/7).

State Trading Corp of Bhutan, 52 Trivoli Court, Ballygange Circular Road, Calcutta, 700019, India.

United Nations Development Programme, United Nations Building, Dremton Lam, GPO Box 162, Thimphu (tel: 322 424; fax: 322-657; e-mail: fo.btn@undp.org).

Internet sites

Bhutan government portal: www.bhutan.gov.bt

Bolivia

KEY FACTS

Official name: Estado Plurinacional de Bolivia (Plurinational State of Bolivia)

Head of State: President Juan Evo Morales Ayma (since 22 Jan 2006; re-elected in 2014)

Head of government: President Juan Evo Morales Ayma

Ruling party: Movimiento al Socialismo (MAS) (Movement towards Socialism) (from Dec 2005)

Area: 1,098,581 square km

Population: 11.25 million (2014)*

Capital: Sucre (legislative and judicial); La Paz (administrative)

Official language: Spanish

Currency: Boliviano (B) = 100 centavos

Exchange rate: B6.90 per US$ (Sep 2015)

GDP per capita: US$3,061 (2014)*

GDP real growth: 5.40% (2014)*

GDP: US$34.42 billion (2014)*

Unemployment: 4.00% (2014)* (additional widespread underemployment)

Inflation: 5.77% (2014)

Natural gas production: 21.40 billion cum (2014)

Balance of trade: US$2.21 billion (2014)

* estimated figure

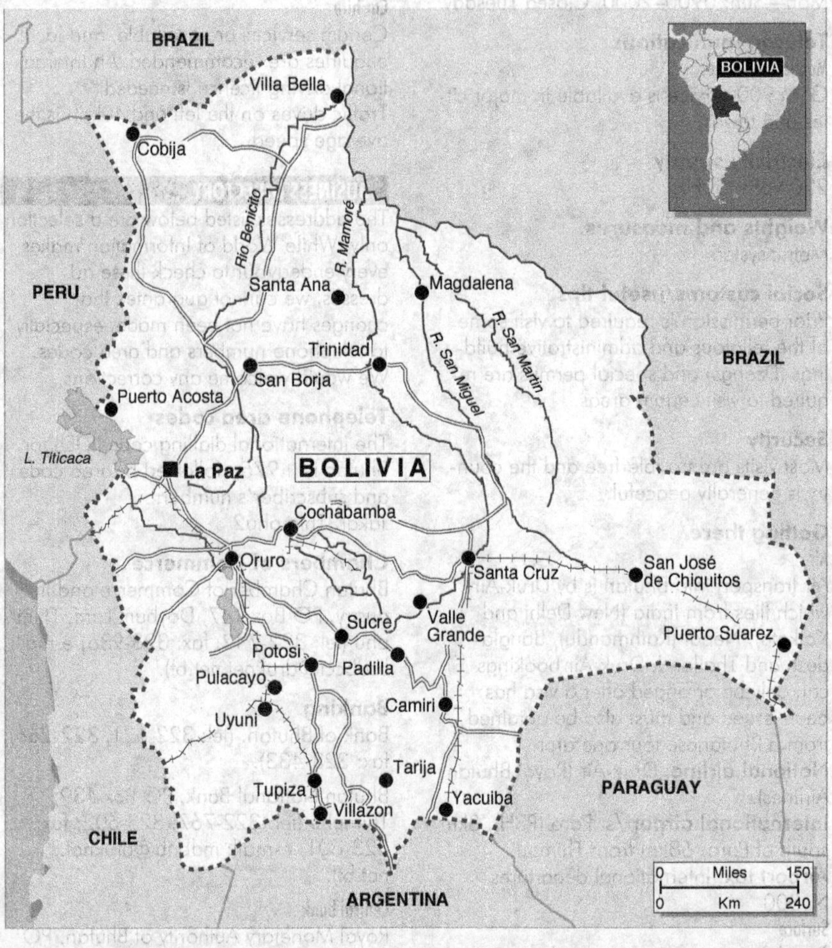

Neighbourliness has never been a central feature of Bolivia's foreign policy. In May 2015 the government submitted its case for gaining access to the Pacific to the International Court of Justice, perhaps optimistically seeking to force Chile to negotiate the granting to Bolivia a corridor of sovereign territory giving it access to the sea for its natural gas and mineral exports.

Predictably, Chile sought to have the Bolivian initiative dismissed by the court, claiming that the Court – based in The Hague – had no jurisdiction over the matter. Bolivia had lost its coastal territory following defeat by Chile in the 1880s War of the Pacific.

The Chilean representative at the Court dismissed what he described as Bolivia's 'challenge to the stability of borders and sovereign territory solemnly agreed in a peace treaty signed 111 years ago.'

Friends (?) and neighbours?

Bolivia has virtually free access to the Pacific, paying only the transport fees (but no tariffs) to export some 1.6 million tonnes of cargo through Chile's ports each year, including nickel, lead, silver and tin from Bolivia's mines. But for Bolivia this has been a matter of principle: it wanted the judges to order Chile to grant Bolivia full access, counter claiming that the 1948 Bogota Pact, to which both states are parties, gave the court's judges the authority to do so.

However, even if the Court allowed the case to proceed, it was doubtful that it would order a border revision that was not subscribed to by one of the states concerned. The hidden agenda was the need of President Evo Morales to deflect popular attention from his apparently declining popularity.

A note of tension had also entered Bolivia's relations with neighbouring Peru' following the arrest of one Martín Belaunde, a former advisor to Peru's former president, Ollanta Humala, on corruption charges. Placed under house arrest in La Paz, Mr Belaunde managed to escape, triggering the resignation of Bolivia's interior minister, Hugo Moldiz. He was replaced by the seasoned politician, Carlos Romero, regarded as a safe pair of hands within the ruling Movimiento al Socialismo (MAS) (Movement towards Socialism). Mr Romero had served as interior minister from 2012 until mid-2014.

It was alleged that Mr Belaunde, who had worked as Mr Humala's presidential campaign advisor during his failed 2006 presidential bid, was a member of a criminal network. Claiming political persecution, he had left Peru for Bolivia in 2014. President Morales placed the blame for Mr Belaunde's escape on errant police officers. In May 2015 a Bolivian court authorised Mr Belaunde's extradition to Peru, where the same corruption scandal had dented the government's popularity.

The economy

The United Nations Economic Commission for Latin America and the Caribbean (ECLAC) reported that Bolivia was among the region's countries leading the economic expansion of the region during 2015, with a 5 per cent growth of gross domestic product (GDP). Bolivia and Panama were expected to maintain up to 6 per cent GDP growth; Antigua and Barbuda 5.4 per cent; and Nicaragua and the Dominican Republic 5 per cent. The ECLAC report indicated that Bolivia would be the economy with the highest economic growth rate in South America, as well as the nation with the highest growth rate of its international reserves in Latin America

ECLAC noted, in its *Preliminary Overview of the Latin American Economies*, that the Bolivian economy slowed in 2014, but that the country still had one of the highest growth rates in the region. Slowing growth in the hydrocarbons sector had affected both economic activity and fiscal revenues (see 'Energy' below). Nevertheless, private consumption and gross fixed capital formation – supported by an ample programme of public investment – kept GDP growth at around 5.0 per cent. The easing of inflationary pressures opened space for the Banco Central de Bolivia (BCB) (central bank) to adopt a more accommodative monetary policy. Bolivia has significant savings that would enable it to implement any counter-cyclical policy that might be necessary. For 2015, ECLAC forecast that GDP would expand by 5.1 per cent on the strength of domestic demand. Bolivia's fiscal policy remained expansionary, bolstered by a high level of public investment.

In the period up to September 2014, general government expenditures were up by 21.5 per cent compared with the prior-year period, as capital expenditures surged 40.9 per cent. Current expenditures registered a smaller increase of 11.5 per cent. Expenditure for personal services and goods and services also rose, owing in part to extra-budgetary expenditures related to the so-called Patujú Plan that the government rolled out in response to the heavy flooding along the Beni River in February and March 2014. Growth in tax revenues slowed significantly, to only 8.5 per cent, compared with 21.1 per cent for the same period of 2013. This was due largely to the performance of hydrocarbon revenues, which rose just 2.0 per cent in the year (compared to 28.4 per cent for the same period in 2013) as the growth of natural gas exports slackened. The general government could post a deficit at year-end, depending on budget execution at the sub-national government level. In terms of financing, both the central government and the sub-national governments as a whole have substantial savings in the form of deposits with the central bank (estimated at 13.9 per cent and 6.8 per cent of GDP, respectively, in June 2014). In addition, ECLAC noted that the National Treasury's public debt as a percentage of GDP continued to fall in 2014, from 28.3 per cent at the end of 2013 to an estimated 26.5 per cent in September 2014.

Monetary policy ceased to be contractionary in the second half of the year. In line with cooling economic activity and lower inflation expectations, the central bank gradually adopted an accommodative policy starting in mid-year. The central bank reduced the offer of bonds in its open-market operations and increased the use of repos to provide short-term liquidity to the financial system. However, the issuance of bonds directly to individuals continued and this year the central bank will offer a 7 per cent Christmas bond. Broad money (M3) and the credit portfolio of the financial sector both continued to slow during the year. Nevertheless, business lending and housing finance saw significant growth.

The new Financial Services Law that came into force in 2014 could significantly alter the financial landscape, according to the International Monetary Fund (IMF). The law established a comprehensive legal framework for the regulation of financial services, financial institutions and financial groups. It included several good provisions that, if effectively implemented, would help

KEY INDICATORS — Bolivia

	Unit	2011	2012	2013	2014	**2015
Population	m	*10.63	*10.83	*11.04	*11.25	*11.46
Gross domestic product (GDP)	US$bn	24.60	27.23	30.82	*34.42	*35.03
GDP per capita	US$	2,315	2,514	*2,793	*3,061	*3,056
GDP real growth	%	5.1	5.2	6.8	*5.4	*4.3
Inflation	%	9.9	4.5	5.7	5.8	*5.1
Unemployment	%	5.5	6.4	*4.0	*4.0	*4.0
Natural gas output	bn cum	15.4	18.7	20.8	21.4	–
Exports (fob) (goods)	US$m	8,174.8	11,110.0	11,538.7	12,147.4	–
Imports (fob) (goods)	US$m	7,126.4	7,694.0	8,729.2	9,935.0	–
Balance of trade	US$m	1,048.5	3,416.0	2,809.5	2,212.4	–
Current account	US$m	537.2	2,127.0	1,012.0	*252.0	*-968.0
Total reserves minus gold	US$m	–	11,659.0	12,782.7	13,480.9	–
Foreign exchange	US$m	–	11,391.0	12,512.4	–	–
Exchange rate	per US$	6.96	6.91	6.91	6.91	–

* estimated figure ** forecast figure

strengthen the safety net and the integrity of the financial system. However, in the view of the IMF, the law's general thrust was to subordinate financial sector activities to social objectives with instruments that could create risks to financial stability. The main features of the law included: (i) provisions to regulate lending rates and set minimum lending quotas for the productive sector and social housing; (ii) discretion to set floors on deposit rates; and (iii) mechanisms to enhance consumer protection and financial access in rural areas.

Regarding exchange rate policy, ECLAC noted that the nominal exchange rate was maintained throughout the year. No change was anticipated in the short term owing to the exchange rate's role in anchoring inflation expectations, promoting the 'Bolivianisation' of the financial system and facilitating the purchase of capital goods abroad for investment projects.

Bolivia's external position remained strong, although the current account surplus had narrowed. Exports were up by 8.9 per cent in the third quarter of 2014, compared with the same period in 2013, driven surprisingly by sales of metallic gold, where the share of total export value rose from 2.5 per cent in 2013 to 10.8 per cent in 2014. Natural gas sales grew by only 1.3 per cent due to existing pipeline limitations and a slight reduction in price. Imports expanded by 14.6 per cent on the back of strong demand for capital goods and transport equipment in response to the increase in gross fixed capital formation in the country. According to data available for the first half of the year, the capital and financial account remained in deficit. Private-sector purchases of foreign assets rose as did portfolio investment outflows, which climbed in line with the scheduled rise in reserve requirements for foreign currency deposits. Foreign direct investment (FDI) inflows held more or less steady in net terms, with a small 1.3 per cent decrease. As a result of these trends net international reserves rose 5.2 per cent in September over the same period of the previous year, reaching US$15.3 billion or an estimated 45 per cent of GDP. This result, however, represented a significant slowdown from the double-digit growth rates registered in previous years. ECLAC noted that Bolivia's economic activity in 2014 slowed somewhat more than was expected at the beginning of the year. In the first half, GDP grew by 5.1 per cent owing to loss of momentum in the hydrocarbons sector, which expanded by 8.6 per cent compared with the first half of 2013 (20.3 per cent year-on-year in the first half of 2013). Lower growth was also seen in transport and communications, manufacturing and agriculture. On the demand side, according to ECLAC, growth was affected by a slowdown in investment, which rose just 0.5 per cent (3.5 per cent for the first half of 2013) as farm and mining sector inventories fell. Nevertheless, gross fixed capital formation alone surged 12.3 per cent (5.6 per cent for the first half of 2013). Private consumption, which accounted for about 69 per cent of GDP, slowed slightly, showing growth of 5.4 per cent compared with 5.7 per cent in the first half of 2013. The overall index of economic activity (IGAE) recorded a cumulative variation of 5.2 per cent to August, which could indicate that the economic slowdown had bottomed out. Inflationary pressures had eased significantly in the second half of 2014. After substantial increases in February, June and July because of food supply shocks, the consumer price index posted a year-on-year variation of 3.6 per cent in October – the lowest since September 2010. Among the factors behind this performance were higher food subsidies from the government through the food production support enterprise (Empresa de Apoyo a la Producción de Alimentos (EMAPA)). The easing of inflation, combined with the 10 per cent public- and private-sector wage rise decreed in May (retroactive to January) and a 20 per cent increase in the national minimum wage, served to drive real wages up.

Rankings

Worryingly for the government, on a number of key international indicators Bolivia slipped a notch or two. Its 2014 rank on the Transparency International *Corruption Perceptions Index* was an unsatisfactory 103 out of the 175 countries surveyed. On the World Bank's 2015 *Doing Business* survey, Bolivia ranked 157, down from the 151 position registered in 2014. In the World Bank's *Ease of Starting a Business* survey, Bolivia slipped 10 places from 2014 to 2015, down from 161 to 171. For its part, the US based Human Rights Watch (HRW) was hardly complimentary about Bolivia's progress. HRW identified a range of concerns, including 'restrictions on the work of human rights defenders, impunity for human rights violations, excessive pre-trial detention and limitations to children's and women's rights.' The organisation also remained concerned about a March 2013 law regulating the work of civil society groups and its regulatory decree, which gave the Bolivian authorities 'overly broad powers to interfere with these groups' activities, undermining the right to free association and the ability of human rights defenders to work independently.' According to HRW, the law's provisions authorised officials to dissolve civil society organisations on grounds that invited arbitrary, politically motivated decisions and restricted the right of organisations to freely determine their own statutes.

The Bolivian government had little choice but to accept the HRW recommendations to strengthen the capacity and the independence of the judiciary, as well as to review the legal grounds and practice of pre-trial detention. The government had recently launched a judicial reform process, which HRW hoped would contribute to strengthening judicial independence. However, in the view of HRW, outstanding key reforms included the need to ensure that criminal acts constituting serious human rights violations were not prosecuted under the military justice system and to enforce the adoption of measures to combat the widespread use of lengthy pre-trial detention, which undermined defendants' rights and also contributed to prison overcrowding.

HRW expressed its concern that Bolivia had rejected many of the recommendations made to eradicate child labour. The Code on Children and Adolescents, adopted in July 2014, had given Bolivia the unfortunate distinction of being the first country in the world to legalise employment for children as young as 10. This legislation undermined the International Labour Organisation (ILO) Convention 138 regarding the minimum age of employment, which Bolivia had ratified in 1997.

The importance of being Santa Cruz

The eastern province of Santa Cruz is often described as the 'mainspring' of the Bolivian economy. It hosts 29 per cent of national business activity and in 2013 accounted for 28.1 per cent of GDP. The province's capital city, Santa Cruz de la Sierra, is Bolivia's largest, with almost 1.5 million inhabitants, almost double the number in national capital, La Paz. The two cities are 850 kilometres apart, with a median temperature difference of 20C. La Paz is some 3,250 metres (almost two miles) above Santa Cruz. Despite the hot and humid climate of Santa Cruz, many expatriate business people find it preferable to live in Santa Cruz than regularly experiencing and recovering from, the altitude sickness (*sorochi*) of La Paz. In terms of annual growth, Santa Cruz ranks 14 among the cities of the world. For President Morales, that's about as far as the good news from Santa Cruz goes; since his inauguration in 2005, Santa Cruz and the other three departments that constitute the so-called Media Luna region have been the seat of entrenched opposition to the president. However, following the MAS victory in the referendum of 2009, in which the Media Luna area opposed the government, many opposition figures saw fit to leave the country for fear of being imprisoned.

Following the referendum victory, which saw the opposition weakened, President Morales' next objective was to gain the support of the business community, which meant winning over Santa Cruz. Fortunately for the president, who was not known to have much empathy for the business community, the business sector had reached the glum conclusion that some sort of accommodation needed to be made with the government, rather than embark on a further five years of outright opposition. In reality, the government had seen fit to simply hijack the business community's agenda and claim it as its own. One business leader was quoted as acknowledging that 'Both sides have given way. Without the backing of the business community, nothing would have happened. But it's the government that makes the rules. A stand-off would have benefited no-one. This way the country benefits.' The journalist Maggy Talavera was also quoted as saying that 'In the more radical quarters the agreement has been seen as a sell-out. I think it's a question of pragmatism. Businessmen want their business to prosper. Both sides stand to gain, even if they have had to give way here and there. But it's the government that claims not to have given way at all.'

Energy

Hydrocarbons, primarily natural gas, form a hugely important element of the Bolivian economy, accounting for 34 per cent of total public sector revenue. According to the US government Energy Information Administration (EIA) natural gas exports accounted for 49 per cent of total export revenue in 2012.

Traditional biomass is an important fuel for heating and cooking, especially for the 2.2 million Bolivians who lack access to electricity, according to the International Energy Agency's 2011 estimates. The overall electrification rate of 77.5 per cent hides large disparities between the urban and rural populations. Over 98 per cent of city dwellers have access to electricity, compared to only 38 per cent of those living in rural areas. For those who have access to electricity, natural gas-fired plants and hydropower are the dominant sources of Bolivia's electricity supply.

According to the *Oil and Gas Journal* (OGJ), Bolivia had 210 million barrels of proved crude oil reserves in January 2014, making it one of the smallest reserve-holders among the world's oil supplying nations. Reserves of crude oil remained unchanged from the previous year but had dropped significantly from 465 million barrels in 2011. Bolivia's proved reserves of natural gas had also fallen from 26.5 trillion cubic feet (tcf) in 2011 to the most recent estimate of 9.9tcf. According to the EIA, decreased investments in exploration and production because of political instability and regulatory uncertainty had contributed to this decline.

In 2013, Bolivia's petroleum and other liquids production were an estimated 65,000 barrels per day (bpd), while consumption was nearly 63,000bpd. The country has two oil refineries with a total crude oil distillation capacity of about 41,000bpd. Bolivia is a net importer of petroleum and other liquids. Bolivia exported over 8,000bpd of crude oil in 2013, with the majority sent to Argentina, the Netherlands and the United States. At the same time, Bolivia imported over 20,000bpd of petroleum products, mostly from Chile, Argentina and the United States.

Risk assessment

Economy	Good
Politics	Fair
Regional stability	Good

People to watch

David Choquehuanca, Currently serving as Bolivian foreign minister

COUNTRY PROFILE

Bolivia was inhabited by the ancient Aymará peoples, who were conquered by the Incas.

1538 The Incas were conquered by the Spanish.

1825 There were many revolts against Spanish rule; independence was finally gained under the leadership of Simón Bolívar.

1826 Bolivia's first constitution was established.

1879–83 War of the Pacific between Bolivia, Peru and Chile over disputed territory along the Pacific coast. Bolivia and Peru suffered a humiliating defeat by Chile's armed forces. A new elite, with mining interests, combined with the traditional ruling oligarchy, supported by external capitalist interests, gained power and polarised civil society into conservative and liberal factions.

1890s The exploitation of tin brought prosperity and peace after years of turbulent and unstable government. A new constitution established centralised political control and the separation of powers between the legislature, executive and judiciary. The indigenous population was disenfranchised when property and literacy were made a prerequisite.

1933–35 Defeat during the Chaco Wars with Paraguay led to a large part of the Chaco region, much of it arid and infertile, being annexed by Paraguay. The defeat discredited the ruling elite and formed the basis for a realignment of Bolivian politics with the middle-class joining the working-class and *campesinos* (peasant farmers) forming a broad revolutionary movement.

1941 Formation of the Movimiento Nacionalista Revolucionario (MNR) (Nationalist Revolutionary Movement), a broad multi-class coalition to resist the power of the traditional oligarchy and what was seen as US imperialism.

1951 A military *Junta* prevented the newly elected president, Victor Paz Estenssoro (MNR) from taking office. With the help of a militia, recruited from the national police, miners and peasants, a rebellion succeeded in installing a revolutionary council. It nationalised tin holdings and instigated land reform. Universal suffrage was extended to the indigenous population. A state-capitalist development programme was initiated, backed by the IMF and later by the US programme 'Alliance for Progress'.

1964 Vice President René Barrientos Ortuño led a *coup d'état*. The military continued to implement similar policies to the MNR's state-capitalist model.

1969 Barrientos died in a mysterious helicopter crash that many suspected was an assassination. A brief period of military populism was followed by the succession of the Bolivian left, the expulsion of the US Peace Corps and the creation of a Soviet-style People's Assembly.

1971 A violent coup led by Colonel Hugo Bánzer Suárez led to the repression of labour leaders and left-wing politicians in a period of a *Junta* known as the *Banzerato*.

1978 Strains within the ruling elite and pressure from US President Jimmy Carter forced Bánzer to call elections.

1978–1982 A period of political turbulence: seven military and two civilian governments held office for an average of six months each. Meanwhile, political parties split into different factions, resulting in 70 different parties – the MNR alone split into thirty parties – resulting in a weak civil society.
1979 The Acción Democrática Nacionalista (ADN) (Democratic Nationalist Action) was formed by Bánzer.
1982 Siles Zuazo was elected president; his rule was ineffective as he struggled to appease both the IMF and growing militant elements within the civilian population. Meanwhile, the Bolivian economy collapsed from hyperinflation and high levels of foreign debt.
1985 Siles resigned. President Paz Estenssoro (MNR) implemented austere fiscal policies and brought about economic liberalisation. He also signed a Pact for Democracy with the ADN to resolve the impasse between the executive and legislature.
1989 The new president, Paz Zamora (MIR), offered tax incentives for direct foreign investment in the mining industry.
1993 Gonzalo Sánchez de Lozada (MNR) won the presidential election.
1998 Hugo Bánzer was elected president following popular discontent with economic liberalisation measures initiated by the MNR. Bánzer's rule intensified efforts to restructure the economy prescribed by the IMF, while implementing a coca-eradication programme demanded by the US.
2001 Bánzer resigned due to ill health and was replaced by Vice President Jorge Quiroga.
2002 Hugo Bánzer died. Congress appointed Lozada (known universally by his nickname 'Goni') Gonzalo Sánchez de as president.
2003 Civil unrest throughout the year led to the resignation of President Lozada. Vice President Carlos Mesa was sworn in as president.
2004 President Mesa signed a natural gas export deal with Argentina. Opponents criticised the deal as a pre-emption of the following referendum on gas exports.
2005 President Mesa offered his resignation to Congress after 17 months in office, as a new wave of anti-government protests spread throughout Bolivia. He finally resigned in an effort to resolve the crisis over how to divide up the country's natural gas wealth. Eduardo Rodríguez was appointed president until the leftist candidate Evo Morales, leading the Movimiento al Socialismo (MAS) (Movement towards Socialism), won presidential and parliamentary elections.
2006 The oil and gas industry was nationalised. A constituent assembly was elected and opened proceedings to draft a new constitution, giving greater rights to the indigenous population.
2007 Bolivia, Brazil and Chile agreed to build a South American highway to link the Atlantic and Pacific coasts, running from Santos in Brazil, through Bolivia, to Arica and Iquique in Chile, at an estimated cost of US$600 million.
2008 Bolivia suspended operations with the US drug enforcement agency (DEA) in Bolivia.
2009 A constitutional referendum was held in which over 61 per cent of voters agreed to changes that included a separation of church and state, increased state control of the economy, (particularly natural resources) and tough laws preventing privatisation. More autonomy will be given to native peoples, including granting indigenous justice systems the same status as conventional courts (which are increasingly seen as inefficient and corrupt). The president began giving thousands of hectares of land, confiscated from large-scale owners, to indigenous farmers. A presidential agreement was signed between Bolivia and Paraguay, settling a border dispute which had led to the Chaco Wars in the 1930s. The accord leads the way to more development of oil and gas fields in the Chaco region. In national elections Evo Morales was re-elected president, and his political party, MAS, became the largest party in both chambers of parliament.
2010 French, British and Bolivian-backed power companies were nationalised by the government as part of a move to control the electricity generating sector.
2011 In March, President Morales refused to restore the operations of the US DEA in Bolivia. In June President Morales signed a new law that established state-owned companies, set up to produce seeds and fertilisers, in a national effort to enhance food security. US$500 million will be invested in the project that will emphasise indigenous crops; the scheme will also include generous financial credits for small farmers. Bolivia held the first popular election of its judiciary in October. The 1,000-strong protest march by indigenous Amazonian Indians reached La Paz on 19 October, having completed a two-month, 500km march to object to the plans for a road to be built through their rainforest reserve, El Territorio Indígena y Parque Nacional Isiboro Sécure (TIPNIS) (Isiboro Secure Indigenous Territory and National Park). President Morales scrapped the TIPNIS project in October.
2012 In January, the TIPNIS project was revived. President Morales addressed the Commission on Narcotic Drugs at the UN Office on Drugs and Crime (UNODC) on 12 March. He said that the long-standing ban on cultivation and chewing of coca leaves should be lifted and the plant should be seen as a plant with great medicinal, cultural and religious value to his people. Coca has been used for thousands of years as a mild stimulant and in sacred herbal medicine. He also said there was no data to prove the coca leaf had any adverse effect on people. In 1961 the coca leaf became a banned substance and in 1964 the UN convention on narcotic drugs stipulated that coca-chewing should be eliminated by 1988. On 1 May, President Morales ordered the military to commandeer the assets of the Spanish energy company Red Eléctica de España (REE), which owns and operates around 75 per cent of the Bolivian power grid. The president said he was expropriating the company because it had not invested sufficiently in Bolivia and that the people were fighting to regain control of their natural resources. The state-owned Transportadora de Electricidad (TDE) had been sold off in 2002 and 99.94 per cent purchased by REE, with the remainder bought by TDE employees. On 28 June, the second TIPNIS march arrived in La Paz. A census was conducted on 21 November.
2013 On 2 July France, Italy, Spain and Portugal refused to allow the plane carrying President Morales to overfly their countries, after it was reported that Edward Snowden, accused of spying by the US (and believed to be at Moscow's Sheremetyevo airport), was on board. The jet, which was flying from Moscow to La Paz, eventually landed in Vienna (Austria) where it was searched by the authorities, but Mr Snowden was not on board. A number of south American countries objected strongly, accusing the European countries of virtually 'kidnapping' the president. The French officially apologised to Bolivia, and on 24 July Mr Morales accepted the apologies of the European countries. On 8 October Luis Cutipa, head of the coca control and industrialisation agency was accused of illegally selling seized coca and arrested.
2014 In July the government lowered the legal working age to allow children to work from the age of 10 as long as they also attend school and are self-employed; 12-year-olds may be contracted to work for others. Parental authorisation is required. President Morales signed a contract to start building a new presidential palace on 1 November. The building wil replace the current colonial building, in use since the 16th Century. Mr Morales said the design was inspired by the architecture of the Tiahuanaco civilization of pre-Hispanic Bolivia.
2015 On 27 September Congress voted to amend the constitution to allow

President Evo Morales to run for re-election again in five years' time. The vote went through by a two-thirds majority after it was agreed that he had previously been elected under a different constitution.

Political structure

Constitution

The first constitution was promulgated in 1826. The 1947 constitution was revised in 1967, and again in 1994.

Bolivia is divided into nine departments, each of which elects three Senators. The prefect of each department is appointed by the president. There is obligatory universal adult suffrage.

A referendum to change the constitution was held on 25 January 2009. Over 61 per cent agreed to changes to include a separation of church and state, increased state control of the economy, particularly natural resources and tough penalties against privatisation. More autonomy will be given to native peoples, including granting indigenous justice systems the same status and conventional courts (which were increasingly seen as inefficient and corrupt).

Form of state

Presidential democratic republic

The executive

Executive power is vested in the president and his appointed cabinet.

The president is directly elected for a five-year term, but is chosen by Congress if no candidate gains a majority of the vote.

In the event of the president's death or failure to assume office, the next in line would be the vice president followed by the president of the Senate.

From 2009 presidential term limits were abandoned; all candidates that fail to win over 50 per cent of the vote and another candidate is within 10 per cent of the leader a runoff election will be held.

National legislature

The bicameral Asamblea Legislativa Plurinacional (Plurinational Legislative Assembly), consists of the Cámara de Diputados (Chamber of Deputies) (lower house) with 77 deputies directly elected in single seat constituencies, plus 53 elected by proportional representation from party lists, giving a total of 130 members. Deputies must be aged over 25 years. The Cámara de Senadores (Chamber of Senators) has 36 senators, each of the nine departments return three representatives, of which two represent the winning political party and one from the second placed party. Senators must be aged over 35 years. Both Senators and Deputies hold office for five years.

From 2009 term limits were abandoned; a runoff election will be held for all parliamentary candidates that fail to win over 50 per cent of the vote and when another candidate is within 10 per cent of the leader.

Legal system

There are five levels of jurisdiction headed by the Supreme Court.

From 1 June 2001, a criminal code was introduced which allows for public jury trials and a prosecution service independent of the police.

Last elections

12 October 2014 (presidential and parliamentary)

Results: Presidential: Evo Morales (MAS) won 61.36 per cent of the vote, Samuel Doria Medina (FUN) 24.23 per cent, Jorge Quiroga (Christian Democratic Party) 9.04 per cent, Juan del Granado (Movement without Fear) 2.71 per cent, Fernando Vargas (Green Party) 2.65 per cent

Parliamentary (Chamber of Deputies): Movimiento al Socialismo (MAS) (Movement towards Socialism) won 88 seats (out of 130), Frente de Unidad Nacional (FUN) (National Unity Front) 32, Christian Democratic Party (PDC) 10.

Senate: MAS won 25 (out of 36 seats), FUN won 9, PDC won 2

Next elections

2019 (presidential and parliamentary)

Political parties

Ruling party

Movimiento al Socialismo (MAS) (Movement towards Socialism) (from Dec 2005)

Main opposition party

Frente de Unidad Nacional (FUN) (National Unity Front)

Approximately 45 per cent of the population lives in the altiplano (highlands), 29 per cent in the highland valleys and 26 per cent in the lowlands. The most densely populated provinces are La Paz, Cochabamba and Santa Cruz, where over 68 per cent of the population live. Bolivia is the poorest country in the western hemisphere after Haiti.

Population

10.83 million (2012)*

Last census: September 2001: 8,280,184

Population density: Seven inhabitants per square km. Urban population 67 per cent (2010 Unicef).

Annual growth rate: 2.0 per cent, 1990–2010 (Unicef).

Ethnic make-up

Official figures estimate that approximately 4.2 million Bolivians (50.6 per cent of the population) are indigenous, comprising 37 different indigenous and aboriginal peoples. Of these, most live in the Andean highlands.

Religions

In 1961, the church was separated from the state and there is complete freedom of worship. The majority of the population is Roman Catholic, although Protestant denominations are expanding. Many indigenous groups mix Christian symbolism with pre-Columbian worship.

Education

Education is free of charge. Nevertheless, the average schooling completed is less than seven years.

The need to integrate education policy into broader anti-poverty strategies is exemplified by a high rate of primary school drop out among poor children. In Bolivia the wealth gap contributes to more than 90 per cent of the shortfall in primary-school completion. Education deprivation and poverty intersects with gender disparities, particularly in the case of Bolivia's indigenous population. More than half of indigenous males and two-thirds of indigenous females do not complete primary education.

Public expenditure on education is equivalent to approximately 5 per cent of annual GDP and includes subsidies to private education at the primary, secondary and tertiary levels. Bolivia has one of the lowest levels of provision in the developing world.

Literacy rate: 87 per cent adult rate; 97 per cent youth rate (15–24) (Unesco 2005).

Compulsory years: Six to 14

Enrolment rate: 114 per cent gross primary enrolment of relevant age group (including repeaters); 84 per cent gross secondary enrolment; 39 per cent gross tertiary enrolment (World Bank).

Health

Infant mortality was halved by 2010 over the previous 20 years (142 down to 63 in under five year olds and 96 down to 50 in under one year olds), however, such mortality is still the highest in Latin America. Nevertheless, mortality rates have fallen quicker than in any other Latin American country since the government introduced the Universal Mother and Child Insurance scheme (SUMI) in 2002, which provides comprehensive healthcare for the age group and a cash transfer scheme for pregnant women.

Some companies provided private medical care for their employees.

International funding has been donated to provide increased family planning and community based healthcare.

Yellow fever continues to be an important public health problem in the Americas. In 2000, Bolivia introduced the yellow fever vaccine in their child vaccination schedule, as well as the vaccination of all age groups in enzootic areas.

HIV/Aids

HIV prevalence: 0.5 per cent aged 15–49 in 2003 (World Bank)

Life expectancy: 66 years, 2010 (Unicef 2012)
Fertility rate/Maternal mortality rate: 3.3 births per woman, 2010 (Unicef 2012)
Child (under 5 years) mortality rate (per 1,000): 41 per 1,000 live births (WHO 2012); 10 per cent of children aged under five tend to be malnourished (World Bank).

Welfare

Pensions

In December 2010 parliament endorse amendments to the system, with implementation in mid-2011.
The management of the private pension system was nationalised and a state entity, the Gestora Publica de la Seguridad Social de Largú Plazo (GSS) (Long Term Social Security Agency) was established to administer the pension fund. Workers continue to contribute 12.2 per cent of their earnings into individual accounts
A 'Solidarity Fund' was established, guaranteeing a minimum level of pension for all workers, using a semi-contributory system, based on the number of contributing years (minimum 10 years personal contributions) and is intended to provide pensions for the 60 per cent of Bolivians working in the informal sector in 2010.
The statutory retirement age for males was reduced from 65 to 58 (miners may retire at 56 and others working in unhealthy conditions at 51), for women the age was reduced to 55 (with an advance of one year for each live child born, for a maximum of three years.
The new pension fund will step up benefits for low-income households, with employers paying a higher contribution for their workers.

Main cities

La Paz (administrative capital, estimated population 912,512 in 2012), Sucre (legislative and judicial capital, 338,281), Santa Cruz (1.8 million (m)), El Alto (1.1m), Cochabamba (650,038), Oruro (240,966), Tarija (234,422), Potosi (175,562), Sacaba (107,628).

Languages spoken

Approximately half the population speak Spanish as their first language. The *campesinos* (peasant farmers) often speak only Aymará or Quechua, but these languages are seldom written and are of limited commercial importance. Aymará is mainly spoken in the departments of Oruro, La Paz and Potosí. Quechua (often mixed with Spanish) is spoken in the departments of Cochabamba, Potosí and Sucre.

Official language/s

Spanish

Media

Freedom of the press is generally expressed, although journalist do not have a reputation for reporting on sensitive topics such as corruption and drug trafficking.

Press

Dailies: In Spanish, *La Prensa* (www.laprensa.com.bo), *La Razón* (www.la-razon.com) and *El Diario* (www.eldiario.net) are published in La Paz; *El Deber* (www.eldeber.com.bo), *El Mundo* (www.elmundo.com.bo) are from Santa Cruz; *Los Tiempos* (www.lostiempos.com) from Cochabamba and *Correo del Sur* (http://correodelsur.com) is from Sucre.
Weeklies: In Spanish *Pulso* (www.pulsobolivia.com), reports on current affairs, as does *Semanario* (www.semanario.8m.net) based in Tarija.
Business: The weekly *Nueva Economía* (www.elmundo.es/nuevaeconomia) and *Periódico Jornada* (www.jornadanet.com) report on economics.

Broadcasting

The government-controlled broadcasting authority is the Dirección General de Telecomunicaciones.
Radio: Low literacy levels make radio listenership, particularly in rural areas, high and important for news and information broadcasting in not only Spanish but also the Aymará and Ouechua languages.
There are over 100 mostly private owned radio stations La Paz has around 40 radio stations alone. National networks include the government owned Radio Illimani (http://abi.bo) and the Catholic-run Radio Fides (www.radiofides.com), the independent Radio Panamericana (www.panamericana.bo), commercial stations include FM La Paz (www.fmlapaz.com), Melodia FM (www.melodiafm.com) and Radio WKM (www.wkmradio.com).
Television: There are several TV networks, all of which are commercial, including the government-run Televisión Boliviana (Canal 7) privates network include Bolivisión (Canal 4) (www.redbolivision.tv), Unitel (Canal 9) (www.unitel.tv) both from Santa Cruz and ATB Red Nacional (Canal 9) (www.atb.com.bo), Red Uno from (Canal 11) (www.reduno.com.bo) and Red PAT (Canal 13) (www.red-pat.com) from La Paz. The university television service, Televisión Universitaria (www.umsa.bo), provides educational programmes.
National news agency: Agencia Boliviana de Información (ABI)
Other news agencies: Agencia de Noticias Fides (Catholic news agency): www.noticiasfides.com
Bolpress: www.bolpress.com

Economy

The economy is driven by Bolivia's primary industries, particularly natural gas extraction (there were proven reserves of 300 billion cubic metres (cum) of natural gas at the end of 2014, with annual production of 21.4 billion cum) and tin mining and, more recently, lithium (an estimated 43 per cent of the world's reserves). Construction of a pilot lithium production plant, at Salar de Uyuni, begun in 2008 and completed in 2010, and it currently extracts around 25,000 tonnes of lithium carbonate annually for export and use in batteries and high-tech equipment. Agriculture is another key component of the economy, especially the growing of coffee, soybeans, wheat, rice and potatoes.
Bolivia is also the third largest coca cultivator in the world and while the leaf of the coca plant has been a traditional chewed stimulant by locals for generations, its refinement into the illegal narcotic cocaine and its subsequent smuggling abroad continues to be a source of tension between Latin America and the US and Europe (the main markets for the product).
In a move that has angered international observers, particularly the United States, President Evo Morales has pledged to resist efforts to eradicate coca production, which he considers is part of his country's heritage.
In 2012 GDP growth was 5 per cent, reflecting the upturn in trade as the global economy recovered. Growth in 2013 reached 6.8 per cent before dropping down to an estimated 5.4 per cent in 2014.
Under President Morales, there has been greater emphasis on state participation in the economy and public investment, which since 2007 has been consistently greater than private investment (averaging around 13 per cent and 8 per cent per annum respectively). The government has plans for further expansion and industrialisation in the hydrocarbon, energy and mining sectors, including improving the infrastructure. It favours partnerships with the private sector, so as to introduce modern management, financing and technological developments.
In late-2010 parliament endorsed changes to the pension system. The plans were implemented in mid-2011 when the privately run pension system was nationalised, retirement ages were lowered and pensions were extended to include workers in the informal sector.
In 2014, the UN Human Development Index (HDI) ranked Bolivia 113 (out of 187) for national development in health, education and income, a fall from rank 108 in 2013. Since 2000, Bolivia's progress has improved but has not matched the

improvement of other countries in Latin America and the Caribbean. In 2014 20.56 per cent of the population were in multidimensional poverty.

External trade

Bolivia is a full member of the World Trade Organisation (WTO) and is an associate member of Mercosur (the South American Common Market), which allows 80 per cent of trade to pass freely to other nations within Mercosur. The country is also a beneficiary of the US's Andean Trade Preference Act. Bolivia also has Generalised System of Preferences (GSP) status with the United States, the European Union and Japan.

Imports

Manufactured goods, petroleum products, plastics, paper, aircraft and aircraft parts, machinery and vehicles, chemical products and foodstuffs.

Main sources: China (17.3 per cent of total in 2014), Brazil (15.8 per cent), United States (11.8 per cent).

Exports

Petroleum gas, precious metal scraps, mineral products and vegetable products.

Main destinations: Brazil (29.7 per cent of total in 2014), Argentina (19.7 per cent), United States (15.6 per cent).

Agriculture

Farming

Although agricultural produce remains Bolivia's main export, agriculture's share of GDP has fallen from 30 per cent in the early 1960s to around 13.0 per cent in 2014. Yet it is still economically important, employing around a third of the country's labour force. Most agricultural activities in rural areas are performed in small family units with low levels of productivity and income.

The cultivation of commercial crops is central to the advancement of Bolivia's 'agricultural frontier' and an intrinsic element of Bolivia's export-oriented development programme. This development drive has been backed by a major road-building programme and changes in land tenure laws.

In the 1990s, the Bolivian government fought a US-backed war against the production of coca leaves – the raw source of cocaine. Before the initiation of the eradication programme, coca production represented nearly 10 per cent of the country's GDP; efforts were made to replace coca production with alternative economic activities, such as commercial crops and textile manufacturing. A UN Office on Drugs and Crime (UNODC) report in September 2012 reported that the area under coca cultivation had dropped from 31,000 hectares in 2010 to 27,000 hectares in 2011, and even further to 23,000 hectares in 2013 when cultivation of coca bushes dropped by 9 per cent. Unlike the Colombian drug fiefdoms, coca production in Bolivia is largely associated with indigenous peasants who have grown the crops as a traditional medicine since pre-Colombian times and, latterly, as a cash crop to alleviate their enduring poverty. Unsurprisingly, the government's efforts to destroy coca crops damaged the rural economy and inflamed social and racial tensions. Protests by coca farmers, who rely on the crop for their income, culminated in mass unrest.

Significantly, early in his presidency, President Evo Morales underlined his opposition to the previous government's crackdown on coca production. In a hugely populist move he pledged to reverse the policy.

Fishing

Bolivia produces approximately 6,000 tons of fresh water fish per year, almost entirely for the domestic market. Bolivia's lakes, among them Lake Titicaca the world's highest navigable lake, provide the basis for this yield. However, the fishing industry does suffer from limited access to external markets, which is exacerbated by poor road transport infrastructure owing to the extreme altitude of the lakes. In addition to the domestic catch, about 7,000 tons of marine fish are imported per year.

Forestry

With a total land mass of 1.1 million sq km (424,164 sq miles), 53 per cent of which is covered by forests and woodlands, Bolivia has the potential to be one of the world's most significant forestry nations.

Sawnwood accounts for more than 90 per cent of Bolivia's total export of forest products. Brazil nuts, palm hearts and rubber are also important sources of income and are mainly derived from the Amazon forests. The export of more value-added products, such as material for doors, window frames and furniture, has increased rapidly in recent years, surpassing the levels of sawn wood, Bolivia's traditional forest export. This diversification of forest products and improvement in production processes has increased the commercial viability of Bolivian forestry.

There continue to be significant problems with the forestry sector however. Legal efforts to promote diversification and sustainability are limited and deforestation continues to out-pace forest regeneration. Forest cover decreased at an annual average rate of 0.45 per cent, the equivalent of 280,000 hectares in 1990–2010, this means that during this time period Bolivia lost 8.9 per cent of it's forest cover, around 5,599,000 hectares.

Though productivity has improved with the introduction of more sophisticated technology in the sawing and drying processes, there are still comparatively few sawmills for a country of Bolivia's forestry capacity and the industry suffers from poor transport infrastructure. The majority of the sawmills are located in the eastern region around Santa Cruz, where the standard of roads is particularly poor. Small- and medium-sized forestry companies that use old technology and outmoded production methods continue to operate with inefficient capacity and no method of producing value-added products. Valuable tree species such as mahogany, oak and cedar are dwindling in numbers. As well as contributing to the overall decline of biodiversity in the Amazon, these precious woods are now below commercial volumes. Efforts to control logging are limited as illegal colonisation of the forests and 'slash and burn' techniques continue.

Industry and manufacturing

Although it constitutes approximately 38.7 per cent to the total GDP of Bolivia, the industrial sector is considerably underdeveloped. Manufacturing in Bolivia is also capital intensive, employing only around 20 per cent of the total work force.

Production is centred on the processing of minerals (mainly tin, lead and zinc smelting) and agricultural products. Oil refining and cement production are also important activities. There is a large workshop and artisan sector of small-scale domestic industries producing textiles, clothing and food. Bolivia is a producer of natural textile fibres: cotton, alpaca wool, llama wool, merino lambswool and rabbit fur. There is no heavy industry or electronics industry.

Bolivian industry is under pressure to become more competitive. Traditionally, unprocessed or semi-processed materials have dominated Bolivian exports. The government has created new and more decentralised industries, to stimulate the development of competitive industries, particularly agro-based industries.

Tourism

There are five historic sites and one national park included in Unesco's list of World Heritage sites in Bolivia, including the pre-Colombian Tiwanaku sacred site and location of the Akapana Pyramid and Gate of the Sun steles (inscribed standing stones and lintel). Bolivia also has spectacular natural attractions, including the Andes mountain range, the world's largest salt flat Salar de Uyuni (over 10,500 square km) and the upper Amazon River basin.

Tourism is an important component of the economy and its total contribution accounted for 6.3 per cent of GDP and 5.6 of total employment in 2014. Tourism is still a relatively underdeveloped industry with tourism infrastructure secondary or an adjunct to domestic requirements. A new airport opened in Uyuni, in the south-west, in 2010, catering for tourists to the region. The state-owned Bolivian Airlines offers inexpensive flights domestically and internationally to the US and other South American countries.

Environment

On 18 September 2012 and by presidential decree, the Bolivian (freshwater) pink dolphin (*Inia boliviensis*), living in the waters of the Amazon, was given protected status under the law. The species is threatened through overfishing, plus damage to its habitat, including pollution, particularly by mercury poison due to illegal gold mining operations and erosion and logging in the Amazon forests.

Mining

Mining has long been a mainstay of the Bolivian economy and its importance to the country continues today. The mining sector contributes up to one fifth of GDP and employs 10 per cent of the labour force. Mining accounts for approximately 45 per cent of the country's total export earnings and the country's unexploited mineral potential is significant.

The industry has continued to show an improved performance especially, the mining of tin, silver and gold. Total tin reserves are estimated at 1.6 million tonnes and are mainly composed of low quality ore and accounts for approximately 17 per cent of total mining production. Bolivia is the world's fifth-largest tin producer and one of the world's leading producers of antimony and tungsten. Other minerals extracted include zinc, silver, gold, lead, copper and limestone, while large reserves of iron ore, lithium and potassium are as yet unexploited. Zinc accounts for 27 per cent of total mining production. Gold production is significant, totalling some 14 tonnes per year.

Most mining operations are small and inefficient, with many of the more promising deposits occupied by co-operatives, with little exploration being carried out.

In 2010 construction of a pilot lithium production plant at Salar de Uyuni was completed at the site of a salt-lake that is estimated to contain 43 per cent of the world's reserves of lithium. The plant now typically produces 25,000 tonnes of lithium carbonate per year.

Hydrocarbons

Proven oil reserves were 209.8 million barrels at the end of 2014, a dramatic fall from 465 million barrels in 2011. In 2009, Bolivia became a net importer of oil, following the sector's reorganisation and a subsequent decline in oil production of up to 25 per cent. In 2013 production was 63,110 barrels per day (bpd), all of which was refined domestically.

Proven natural gas reserves were 300 billion cubic metres (cum) at the end of 2014 and production was 21.4 billion cum, an increase of 14.8 per cent on the 2013 figure. Exports of natural gas were 44.9 billion cum in 2013.

Due to the extensive exploration in recent years, there have been several large discoveries holding over 10 million cubic metres of natural gas. Estimates of Bolivia's total potential gas reserves are put at approximately 1.32 trillion cubic metres. There are discussions over supplying natural gas to Argentina, Brazil, Chile, Paraguay and Uruguay. Bolivia is also considering exporting to the large markets of the US and Mexico.

In 2006 the government nationalised 12 oil and gas companies in the south-eastern region that contains the country's richest hydrocarbon fields. The state-run Yacimientos Petroliferos Fiscales Bolivianos had a 49 per cent stake in Chaco oil until January 2009 when the government seized control of 99 per cent of the BP-owned company, leaving 1 per cent in BP's hands.

Any coal production or use is commercially insignificantly.

Energy

Bolivia's capacity to generate electricity has improved markedly since the 1990s with an almost doubling of generation from a 0.8 GW to 1.4GW by 2005. Production in 2011 was an estimated 7.2 billion kilowatt hours (kWh) which was consumed domestically. The most is generated by conventional thermal plants fed by domestically supplied oil and gas. Some rural areas have unaffiliated power plants fuelled by biomass. Atypical of South America, Bolivia does not rely on hydropower, with only 460MW installed capacity, the largest being the Santa Isabel plant in Cochabamba, producing 93MW.

The three, dominant, foreign owned energy companies, Brazil's Petrobras, Spain's Repsol and France's Total were forced to pay taxes as the energy industry was progressively nationalised since 2006.

On 1 May 2012, President Morales ordered the military to commandeer the assets of the Spanish energy company Red Eléctica de España (REE), which owns and operated around 75 per cent of the Bolivian power grid. The president said he was expropriating the company because it had not invested sufficiently in Bolivia and that the people were fighting to regain control of their natural resources. The state-owned Transportadora de Electricidad (TDE) had been sold off in 2002 with 99.94 per cent purchased by REE, and the remainder by TDE employees.

Financial markets

Stock exchange

Bolsa Boliviana de Valores

Banking and insurance

Bolivia's banking system has been undergoing extensive reform since the mid-1990s. The last decade has seen the full-scale privatisation of formerly state-owned banks and significant regulatory upheaval. A high level of dollarisation has meant that approximately 90 per cent of Bolivian deposits are denominated in US dollars and the holding of deposits is highly concentrated in the country's wealthy elite. This means that the banking system is highly dependent on the financial fortunes of a select number of wealthy Bolivians. Concern has been expressed in various quarters that President Evo Morales will seek to redistribute income to the poor. Thus the banking system may feel the effects of diminished holdings by wealthy clients in future years.

Bolivia's banking system has remained largely immune from the contagious effects of financial sector turmoil that inflicted the region in the early part of the decade. This fact owes to Bolivia's comparatively low exposure to international capital markets; the majority of Bolivia's debt is with foreign states and multilateral institutions, which have worked to change the structure of the country's debt portfolio and maintain vital foreign currency reserves.

A new Bank of the South, with a headquarters in Venezuela, will be launched in 2008 to provide an alternative source of development funding for the participating countries. Assets of US$7 billion will underpin its operations.

Central bank

Banco Central de Bolivia

Main financial centre

La Paz

Time

GMT minus four hours

Geography

Bolivia straddles the Andes and is made up of mountainous areas with cold desolate plateaux and semi-tropical and fertile lowlands. It is landlocked with Chile and Peru to the west, Brazil to the north and east and Argentina to the south. The Andean range is at its widest in Bolivia, some 650km.

The Western Cordillera separating Bolivia and Chile has peaks of between 6,000 metres and 6,500 metres above sea level and a number of volcanoes along its crest. Passes across the Cordillera are at 4,000 metres. To the east of the range lies the bleak treeless Altiplano also at around 4,000 metres. The Altiplano makes up about 10 per cent of the country and is divided into basins by spurs of mountains. Around 70 per cent of the population lives on the Altiplano, particularly the northern part where most of the larger cities are located. In the south, the parched desert landscape is mostly unpopulated.

Lake Titicaca, the highest navigable lake in the world, is situated at the northern end of the Altiplano. It is 171km in length, 64km in breadth and 280 metres at its deepest point. The immense depth of water keeps the lake at an even temperature of 10 degrees Celsius and modifies extremes of winter and night temperatures on the surrounding land, thereby making the basin favourable for farming.

The Eastern Cordillera rises sharply from the Altiplano in the east and four of its peaks rise to above 6,000 metres. These north-eastern slopes are heavily forested and are indented by fertile valleys in an area known as the Yungas.

In the north and east, the Oriente has dense tropical forest and in the centre there are plains covered with rough pasture, swamp and scrub.

Hemisphere

Southern

Climate

The climate varies with the area. It is tropical in the lowlands (eastern region) with an average temperature of 25 degrees Celsius (C); temperate in the highland valley regions (middle of the country), average temperature 15 degrees C, and cooler in the Altiplano (highland) areas (western region), average temperature 10 degrees C.

La Paz is in the Altiplano where temperatures vary between three degrees C in June and 25 degrees C in November and December. In the highlands the rainy season begins in December and ends in late March.

Dress codes

For business meetings men should wear a suit and tie, women a two-piece suit, or equivalent. Warm clothing is required in the high plateau region. Lightweight clothing is needed during the day and warmer clothing for the evenings in the valleys, and very lightweight clothing for both day and night in the tropical valleys.

Entry requirements

Travellers who arrive without the correct documentation will be fined.

Passports

Passports are required by all (valid for one year beyond departure date), except holders of Cedula de Identidad issued to nationals of Argentina, Paraguay, Peru and Uruguay.

Visa

A visa is not required for tourist visits up to 90 days, by nationals of most of the Americas, Western Europe, Australasia and some Asian countries. (For further details contact the local embassy or see www.embassyofbolivia.co.uk/visas.html#2.)

The 'specific purpose visa' for non-tourist visitors requires a letter of introduction, including an itinerary and letters of guarantee by employer and host company. (See www.embassyofbolivia.co.uk/visaformfiles/specificvisaform.html for application form.).

Currency advice/regulations

There are no restrictions on the import and export of local or foreign currency; currency must be declared.

US dollar travellers' cheques are the best form of currency to take. UK sterling cheques can sometimes be exchanged, but only with difficulty.

Customs

Visitors are not required to declare valuable personal effects such as cameras and radios. Business samples are duty-free as long as they are re-exported within 90 days.

Health (for visitors)

Mandatory precautions

A yellow fever vaccination certificate is required for visitors arriving from infected areas, and for those travelling to high risk areas such as the Departments of Beni, Cochabamba, Santa Cruz and the subtropical area of La Paz Department.

Advisable precautions

Typhoid, paratyphoid, hepatitis A, tetanus and polio vaccinations. Malaria risk exists in rural areas – prophylaxis recommended. Owing to the altitude of La Paz and other places in the Altiplano region, sufferers from heart or lung complaints should seek medical advice before leaving for Bolivia. Water precautions should be taken.

Hotels

There is a wide range available. Service charge and local tax are added to the bill. Tipping 5–10 per cent.

Credit cards

Mastercard, Diners Club, Visa and American Express have limited acceptance.

Public holidays (national)

Fixed dates

1 Jan (New Year's Day), 1 May (Labour Day), 6 Aug (Independence Day), 1 Nov (All Saints' Day), 25 Dec (Christmas Day). There are other additional holidays celebrated in individual provinces and towns.

Variable dates

Carnival (Feb, seven days), Good Friday, Easter Sunday, Corpus Christi (May/Jun).

Working hours

Banking

Mon–Fri: 0830–1200, 1430–1800; Sat: 0830–1200.

Business

Mon–Fri: 0830–1200, 1430–1830.

Government

Mon–Fri: 0800–1200, 1430–1830.

Shops

Mon–Fri: 0930–1230, 1500–1930; Sat: 1000–1500.

Telecommunications

Mobile/cell phones

GSM 1900 service available.

Electricity supply

110V and 200V in La Paz and 220V in Cochabamba and most other towns; US-type flat-prong plugs.

Weights and measures

The metric system is standard, although the Imperial is sometimes used.

Social customs/useful tips

In business circles, local customs are similar to those in Europe or North America. While English is widely used in commercial and business circles, a knowledge of Spanish is a valuable asset to the visitor. Correspondence in Spanish is almost essential. On business visits, cards are presented and it is normal to shake hands when arriving or leaving. It is advisable to arrange appointments before visiting. Bolivians are informal about observing prescribed times and will often arrive 30–45 minutes late.

It is customary to address persons by their professional title, eg, doctor, engineer and *licenciado* for social science graduates. Holders of law degrees are addressed as doctor.

It is offensive to refer to rural Indians as *indios;* they are referred to as *campesinos* (peasants).

It is customary to give gratuities in a hotel or restaurant of around 5–10 per cent even if a service charge has been added to the bill. The minimum drinking age is 21 years.

Security

Since the civil disruption in 2003, road blockades can happen on all main roads at any time. Visitors should not attempt to breach road blockades and should stay away from demonstrations.

Getting there

Air

National airline: Lloyd Aéreo Boliviano (LAB).

International airport/s: La Paz-El Alto (LPB), 14km from city, duty-free shop, bar, restaurant, bank, post office, hotel reservations.

Other airport/s: Cochabamba-J Wilstermann (CBB), 4km from city..

Airport tax: US$25 for all adults, excluding 12-hour transit passengers. An additional exit tax (US$25) is levied for all visitors staying over 90 days.

Surface

Road: Road access is possible from Peru, Argentina and Chile.

Travellers who use overland routes are generally advised to check border post opening hours.

Rail: Rail services connect La Paz with Chile (Arica and Calama) and Argentina (Buenos Aires). The Expreso del Sur is a special train service from La Paz to Buenos Aires.

Water: It is possible to take the steamer on Lake Titicaca from Puno (Peru) to Guaqui.

Main port/s: Although Bolivia is landlocked, access to the sea (and in certain cases free port facilities) has been granted by Paraguay (via River Paraguay), Brazil (Belem, Santos, Corumbá, Port Velho) and Argentina (Buenos Aires, Rosario).

Getting about

National transport

Air: Air transport is the best method of travelling around the country. Lloyd Aéreo Boliviano (LAB), Aerosur, TAM (army airline) and Aero Xpress (AX) operate domestic services to main centres.

Road: Around 50,000km of road exists, but only 5.5 per cent is paved and only 20 per cent can be classed as all-weather roads. The main centres are connected by highways of reasonable standard. A toll permit system is in operation; garage and petrol services are sparse outside main centres.

Buses: *Flotas* are long-distance buses, they mostly leave in the evening and travel overnight, except on the major routes where there are some daytime departures. It is advisable to book in advance and take warm clothing.

Rail: A north-south line runs from La Paz to Oruro and Uyuni, with spurs to Cochabamba, Uncia, Potosi, Sucre and Villazón at the Argentine border. The eastern system runs from Santa Cruz to Yacuiba and to Corumbá at the Brazilian border. Sleeper and first-class services are available; advance booking is essential.

Water: Half of Bolivia's territory lies in the Amazon Basin. Transport is by cargo boats, which carry passengers, vehicles and livestock. The tributaries of the Amazon are the Ichilo, Mamoré, Beni, Madre de Dios and Guaporé rivers.

City transport

Taxis: There are *remise* (yellow cabs) which have fixed rates applicable per passenger – the cabs are frequently shared. Within La Paz, *trufis* (cabs with green flags) ply along fixed routes. Tips are not expected.

Car hire

An international driving permit is required. This may be issued in Bolivia by the Federación Interamericana de Touring y Automovil Clubes (www.fitac.org) on presentation of a national licence, but it is advisable to procure one before travelling. At the frontier, drivers must also obtain a *hoja de ruta*, a form which notes the driver's itinerary.

Traffic drives on the right.

BUSINESS DIRECTORY

The addresses listed below are a selection only. While World of Information makes every endeavour to check these addresses, we cannot guarantee that changes have not been made, especially to telephone numbers and area codes. We would welcome any corrections.

Telephone area codes

The international direct dialling code (IDD) for Bolivia is + 591, followed by area code and subscriber's number:

Beni	3465	Potosí	262
Buena Vista	3932	Saavedra	3924
Cochabamba	441	Santa Cruz	33
La Bélgica	3923	Sucre	4691
La Paz	22	Tarija	466
Montero	3922	Trinidad	346
Oruro	252	Villamontes	4672
Portachuelo	3924		

Useful telephone numbers

Police: 110

Fire: 119

Ambulance (La Paz): 118

Chambers of Commerce

American Chamber of Commerce of Bolivia, Avenida 6 de Agosto, Edificio Hilda, PO Box 8268, La Paz (tel: 244-3939; fax: 244-3972; e-mail: amgalin@caoba.entelnet.bo).

Cochabamba Chamber of Commerce, 336 Calle Sucre, Cochabamba (tel: 425-7715; fax: 425-7717; e-mail: sistema@cadeco.org).

Chuquisaca Chamber of Industry and Commerce, 64 Calle España, Sucre (tel: 645-1194; fax: 645-1850; e-mail: info@cicch.com).

National Chamber of Commerce, 1392 Avenida Mariscal Santa Cruz, La Paz (tel: 237-8606; fax: 239-1004; e-mail: cnc@boliviocomercio.org.bo).

Santa Cruz Chamber of Industry, Commerce and Services, 7 Avenida Las Américas esquina Saavedra, Santa Cruz (tel: 333-4555; fax: 334-2353; e-mail: cainco@cainco.org.bo).

Banking

Banco Bisa, Avenida 16 de Julio 1628, La Paz (tel: 359-471; fax: 316-597; e-mail: bancbisa@caoba.entelnet.bo).

Banco de Crédito de Bolivia, Calle Colón esquina Mercado 1308, La Paz (tel: 360-025; fax: 391-044).

Banco de la Nación Argentina, Avenida 16 de Julio 1486, La Paz (tel: 359-218; fax: 391-392; e-mail: bancnalp@caoba.entelnet.bo).

Banco Económico, Calle Ayacucho 166, Santa Cruz (tel: 361-177; fax: 361-184; e-mail: baneco@roble.scz.entelnet.bo).

Banco Ganadero, Calle 24 de Septiembre 110, Santa Cruz (tel: 361-616; fax: 361-617; e-mail: bangan@roble.scz.entelnet.bo).

Banco Mercantil, Calle Ayacucho esquina Mercado, La Paz (tel: 315-131; fax: 391-442; e-mail: bercant@caoba.entelnet.bo).

Banco Nacional de Bolivia, Avenida Camacho esquina Colón 1312, La Paz (tel: 318-732; fax: 359-146; e-mail: info@bnb.com.bo).

Banco Real, Avenida 16 de Julio 1642, La Paz (tel: 334-477; fax: 335-588; e-mail: real@caob.entelnet.bo).

Banco Santa Cruz, Calle Junín 154, Santa Cruz (tel: 369-911; fax: 350-114; e-mail: bancruz@mail.bsc.com.bo).

Banco Sollidario, Calle Nicolás Acosta 289, La Paz (tel: 484-242; fax: 486-468; e-mail: info@bancosol.com.bo).

Banco Unión, CalleLibertad 165, Santa Cruz (tel: 366-869; fax: 340-684; e-mail: info@bancounion.com.bo).

Interbanco, Calle Mercado No 1046, PO Box 14758, La Paz (tel: 317-707; fax: 316-787).

Central bank

Banco Central de Bolivia, PO Box 3118, Calle Mercado esquina Ayacucho, La Paz (tel: 409-090; fax: 406-598; e-mail: bancocentraldebolivia@bcb.gov.bo).

Stock exchange

Bolsa Boliviana de Valores
www.bolsa-valores-bolivia.com

Travel information

Automovil Club Boliviano, Avenida 6 de Agusto 2993, La Paz (tel: 431-132; fax: 431-139; e-mail: acblapaz@acelerate.com).

AeroSur, Calle Colón esquina Avenida Irala, Santa Cruz (tel: 364-446; fax: 365-246; e-mail: mail@aerosur.com).

Lloyd Aéreo Boliviano, Aeropuerto Jorge Wilstermann, Cochabamba (tel: 25-903; fax: 50-744; email: gergen@labairlines.com).

Ministry of tourism

Viceministerio de Turismo, Avenida Mariscal Santa Cruz, Edificio Palacio de Comunicacióónes, Piso 16, La Paz (tel: 236 7463/4; fax: 237 4630; e-mail: vturismo@mcei.gov.bo; internet: www.mcei.gov.bo).

National tourist organisation offices

Secretaría Nacional de Turismo, Calle Mercado 1328, Edificio Ballivián, La Paz (tel: 367-441; fax: 374-630).

Ministries

Ministry of Agriculture and Rural Development, Avenida Camacho 1471, La Paz (tel: 367-968; fax: 313-601).

Ministry of Defence, Avenida 20 de Octubre esquina Pedro Salazar, La Paz (tel: 431-364; fax: 433-159).

Ministry of Economic Development, Palacio de Comunicaciones, Avenida Mariscal Santa Cruz, La Paz (tel: 375-000, fax: 360-534; e-mail: contactos@desarrollo.gov.bo).

Ministry of Education, Culture and Sport, Avenida Arce 2147, La Paz (tel: 440-160; fax: 440-376).

Ministry of Finance, Palacio de Comunicaciones, Avenida Mariscal Santa Cruz, La Paz (tel: 392-220; fax: 359-955).

Ministry of Foreign Affairs, Calle Ingavi esquina Junín, La Paz (tel: 336-200; fax: 333-521; email: mreuno@rree.gov.bo).

Ministry of Foreign Trade and Investment, Palacio de Comunicaciones, Avenida Mariscal Santa Cruz, La Paz (tel: 343-519; fax: 377-451; internet site: http://www.mcei-bolivia.com).

Ministry of Government, Avenida Arce 2409 esquina Belisario Salinas, La Paz (tel: 440-114; fax: 442-589).

Ministry of Health and Social Security, Plaza del Estudiante, La Paz (tel: 371-373; fax: 391-590; e-mail: minsalud@ceibo.entelnet.bo).

Ministry of Housing, Avenida 20 de Octubre 2230, La Paz (tel: 372-241; fax: 371-335; e-mail: minviv@ceibo.entelnet.bo).

Ministry of Information, Edificio La Urbana, Avenida Camacho 1485, La Paz (339-027; fax: 391-607).

Ministry of Justice and Human Rights, Avenida 16 de Julio 1769, La Paz (tel: 361-083; fax: 392-982).

Ministry of Labour and Micro-enterprises, Yanacocha esquina Mercado, La Paz (tel: 407-740; fax: 406-867).

Ministry of Presidency, Palacio de Gobierno, Plaza Murillo, La Paz (tel: 371-082; fax: 371-388).

Ministry of Sustainable Development and Planning, Avenida Mariscal Santa Cruz 1092, La Paz (tel: 330-074; fax: 330-540).

Other useful addresses

Bolivian Embassy (USA), 3014 Massachusetts Avenue, NW, Washington DC 20008 (tel: 202-483-4410; fax: 202-3712; e-mail: embassy@bolivia-usa.org).

Bolsa Boliviana de Valores, Calle Montevideo 142, La Paz (tel: 443-232; fax: 442-308; e-mail: info@bolsa-valores-bolivia.com).

British Embassy, Avenida Arce 2732, La Paz (tel: 357-424; fax: 431-073).

Confederación de Empresarios Privados de Boliva, Avenida Mariscal Santa Cruz 1392, Edificio Camara Nacional de Comercio, La Paz (tel: 315-562: fax: 379-970; e-mail: cepbol@ceibo.entelnet.bo).

Empresa Nacional de Electricidad (ENDE), Calle Colombia 655, Cochabamba (tel: 59-500; fax: 59-509).

Eurocentro de Cooperación Empresarial de Bolivia, Calle Suárez de Figueroa 127, Santa Cruz (tel: 334-555; fax: 365-108; e-mail: eurocentro@cainco.org.bo).

US Embassy, Avenida Arce 2780 esquina Cordero, La Paz (tel: 430-120; fax: 432-051).

National news agency: Agencia Boliviana de Información (ABI), Dirección Av, Camacho 1485 Casilla, 6500 La Paz (tel: 200-373; fax: 200-246; internet: www.abi.bo).

Agencia de Noticias Fides (Catholic news agency): www.noticiasfides.com

Bolpress: www.bolpress.com

Internet sites

Bolivia Government website: boliviaweb.com/gov.htm

Bosnia and Hercegovina Republic

KEY FACTS

Official name: Republika Bosne i Hercegovine (BiH) (Republic of Bosnia and Hercegovina). BiH consists of two distinct entities: Federacija Bosne i Hercegovine (FBiH) (Federation of Bosnia and Hercegovina) and Republika Srpska (RS) (Serb Republic)

Head of State: Three-member rotating collective presidency (began with) Dragan Covic (HDZ) (elected 6 Nov 2014), Bakir Izetbegovic (SDA) (Bosniak/Muslim) (elected Oct 2010), Mladen Ivanic (SDS) (elected 6 Nov 2014)

Head of government: Prime Minister Denis Zvizdic (SDA) (from 11 Feb 2015); UN High Representative and EU Special Representative: Valentin Inzko (25 Mar 2009)

Ruling party: A three party coalition of the SDA, HDZ and DF formed after strong election results in 2014. However, since June 2015, following a series of disagreements, the DF has left the coalition.

Area: 51,129 square km

Population: 3.87 million (2014)*

Capital: Sarajevo (BiH)

Official language: Bosanski (Bosnian)

Currency: Konvertibilna marka (KM) = 100 fennings

Exchange rate: KM1.74 per US$ (Sep 2015)

GDP per capita: US$4,644 (2014)*

GDP real growth: 0.80% (2014)*

GDP: US$17.98 billion (2014)*

Labour force: 1.23 million (2011)

Unemployment: 27.50% (2014)*

Inflation: -0.09% (2014)*

Balance of trade: -US$5.49 billion (2014)*

* estimated figure

Bosnia's October 2014 elections did little more than confirm the country's deep-seated ethnic divisions. The candidates from the three principal ethnic groups won Bosnia's three-seat presidency, offering little prospect that the Balkan country was coming to terms with its recent history. The main nationalist parties represented the Bosniak, Serb and Croat communities. Mr Bakir Izetbegovic of the mainly Muslim Stranka Demokratske Akcije (SDA) (Party of Democratic Action) and Dragan Covic of the Croat Hrvatska Demokratska Zajednica Bosne i Hercegovine (HDZ BiH) (Croatian Democratic Union of Bosnia and Herzegovina) claimed to have won support in what is termed the 'collective presidency'.

The only real element of uncertainty in the elections focussed on who would win the Serb seat. Two nationalist candidates, the opposition figure Mladen Ivanic and Željka Cvijanovic, the candidate of the ruling Bosnian Serb Alliance of Independent Social Democrats (SNSD), were running level as the votes were counted. In the end the successful candidate was Mr Ivanic who along with Mr Covic took up his seat as one of the three members of the rotating collective presidency on 17 November 2014.

The presidential candidates could hardly have had less in common. Mr Izetbegovic had campaigned on the platform of a strong, unified Bosnia. Mr Covic sought the establishment of a Croat entity within Bosnia. Ms Cvijanovic is part of a Serb bloc that simply advocates Bosnia's dissolution.

In the parliamentary elections, results for the 42-seat national assembly reflected the dominance of the nationalist parties: the Muslim SDA (18.74 per cent of the vote and 10 of the 42 seats), the Serb Savez Nezavisnih Socijaldemokrata

(SNSD) (Alliance of Independent Social Democrats) (16.64 per cent, 6 seats), Srpska Demokratska Stranka (Serb Democratic Party) (SDS) (12.97 per cent 5 seats). Bosnia's complicated power-sharing arrangement is part of a political system created by the US-brokered Dayton peace accord that ended the ethnic war in which an estimated 100,000 people were killed. Sadly, the general election did little more than underscore the country's fault lines. Some 54 per cent of the 3.3 million Bosnians who were eligible to vote actually did so. The low turnout, slightly below that of the previous elections, indicated public disillusion with its political figures, structures and corruption.

Under the complex Bosnian system, voters additionally choose members of the assemblies that oversee the country's two semi-autonomous halves – one the ethnic-Serb Republika Srpska and the other the Muslim-Croat Bosnia and Herzegovenia Federation. Serbs in their semi-autonomous region were also choosing a local president (won by the incumbent, Milorad Dodik).

Sarajevo

As cities go, Sarajevo ought to be pretty exceptional. In this small Balkan capital, for centuries, different religions and ethnic groups prospered alongside each other, happily intermingling, if not often inter-marrying, for centuries. The assassination of Archduke Ferdinand a century earlier, the trigger of the First World War did little to change the city's tolerant characteristics. All that came to an end in April 1992 when, catalysed by the break up of the Yugoslavian Federation, in crudely simple terms, Bosnia became the battlefield between Serbian and Croatian warlords, each seeking to exercise control.

Permanent scars

In 2015 Sarajevo still bore the scars of wounds that will never go away or be forgotten. Bombed sites still unattended, buildings with the marks of machine-gun strafing, discreet cementeries in the corners of parks. But the more important scars are borne by the Bosnians themselves, very few of whom – according to Borka Rudic of the country's press service, are able to cast aside the past and address the future. The elephant in the Bosnian room is not so much the atrocities committed by the armies and mercenaries from outside Bosnia. It is the knowledge of what was done by Bosnians to Bosnians. Quoted by Beatriz Navarro in the Barcelona newspaper *La Vanguardia*, Boro Kontic of Mediacenter, a Sarajevo investigative reporting support group, claimed that 'All that gets reported in the press and on television is what others have done to us. Never what our peoples did to others.'

A divided press

Miss Navarro noted that Bosnian media remain clearly divided along community lines, controlled by Bosnia's political parties and different layers of government. Sadly, this divided press does not seek to highlight the positives, instances of solidarity between different religious groups during the war. 20 July 2015 marked the twentith anniversary of the Srebenica massacre (of an estimated 8,372 Bosnian Muslims), a date more likely to increase inter-ethnic tensions than to dispel them. As the date approached, there was no certainty that representatives of the Serbian community would even attend the anniversary ceremonies. Others expected to be present were the Presidents of Slovenia, Montenegro and Croatia (all once members of the former Yugoslavian Confederation), Federica Mogherini (of the European Union), Queen Noor of Jordan and possibly the former Dutch Prime Minister Wim Kok (who resigned over the massacre, recognising Holland's 'political responsibility' for the massacre – the United Nations troops who handed over the Bosnian prisoners to Serbian forces were Dutch – and former US President Bill Clinton.

One indication of the political obtuseness and pressure – was the apparent non-participation of the incumbent Serbian Bosnian President Mladen Ivanic (the Bosnian state's Presidency – not to be confused with the three 'ethnic' presidents – rotates between the communities). The announcement was made following Ivanic's meeting with the President of Bosnia's Republika Srpska (RS) Milorad Dordik. The Serbian representatives continued to insist that there should be an international enquiry to 'clarify matters'. Only 4,000 victims have been buried; Mr Dordik and the RS government had long demanded that the Serbian victims be identified.

Angry Bosnians

February 2014, had seen widespread protests over the pervasive levels of corruption and cronyism persistent in Bosnia. What began as a demonstration against lay-offs in recently privatised companies in the north-eastern city of Tuzla (the third largest – population 130,000 – in Bosnia.)

KEY FACTS

Official name: Federacija Bosne i Hercegovine (FBiH) (Federation of Bosnia-Hercegovina)

Head of State: President Marinko Cavara (Hrvatska Demokratska Zajednica Bosne i Hercegovine (HDZ BiH) (Croatian Democratic Union of Bosnia and Herzegovin) (from 9 Feb 2015)

Head of government: Prime Minister Fadil Novalic Stranka Demokratske Akcije (SDA) (Party for Democratic Action) (from Feb 2015)

Ruling party: Coalition government with 16 members chosen from the quota of nationalies. There are eight Bosniak, five Croat and three Serb cabinet ministers.

Capital: Sarajevo

Currency: Konvertibilna marka (KM) = 100 fennings (The Croatian kuna also circulates widely)

Exchange rate: KM1.74 per US$ (Sep 2015) (pegged at KM1.96 per euro)

GDP per capita: US$2,129 *

* estimated figure

KEY FACTS

Official name: Republika Srpska (RS) (Serb Republic)

Head of State: President Milorad Dodik (from 15 Nov 2010, re-elected Nov 2014)

Head of government: Prime Minister Željka Cvijanovic (SNSD (from 12 Mar 2013)

Ruling party: Stranka Nezavisnih Socijaldemokrata (SNSD) (Alliance of Independent Social Democrats) (from 3 Oct 2011)

Area: 25,053 square km

Population: 1.46 million (2011)*

Capital: Sarajevo (*de jure*); Banja Luka (*de facto*)

Currency: Konvertibilna marka (KM) = 100 fennings (pegged to the euro at KM1 per €0.51 (since 2001); the KM is the only legal tender

Exchange rate: KM1.74 per US$ (Sep 2015)

* estimated figure

Suggesting that the protestors had touched a national nerve, the protests spread rapidly, to the extent that the presidential building in Sarajevo was set on fire. A report in the London *Economist* summarised the plight of the Bosnians: 'It is not surprising that the Bosnians are angry. Eighteen years after the end of the war, the people are poor, the politicians are rich and corruption is rife.' In its 2014 *Corruption Perceptions Index* (CPI), Transparency International (TI) ranked Bosnia 80th out of the 175 countries surveyed.

TI referred to the ethnic and political divisions that had persisted long after the war in Bosnia. Both access to information and public procurement, Bosnia and Herzegovina's weak legal framework is vulnerable to corruption due to the country's public purchasing procedures and 'complicated legislation'. The lack of legal enforcement and weak sanctions create the perception that corruption pays. According to TI, the institutions responsible for implementing anti-corruption laws are either under full control of the government, or do not have the capacity or authority to implement the laws. Bosnia's audit offices have pointed out numerous irregularities in public expenditures and public contracting – but these findings have never been prosecuted by the judiciary. According to TI, 'the statistics indicate that very few cases of corruption result in criminal convictions and even fewer reach final verdicts. For example, in 2010 only two final verdicts for cases of corruption resulted in jail sentences. And 70 per cent of corruption investigations end up being dismissed.

The TI reservations were endorsed by Human Rights Watch (HRW) which opened its overview of the situation in Bosnia by noting that 'Political deadlock in Bosnia and Herzegovina (BiH) continued to impede necessary human rights reform in 2013. The Bosnian government failed to meet a European Union (EU) deadline to end discriminatory restrictions on Jews and Roma running for political office. Roma remain the most vulnerable group in the country, subject to widespread discrimination.'

HRW also noted that the Bosnian authorities failed to implement a 2009 European Court of Human Rights ruling requiring the constitution to be amended to eliminate ethnic discrimination, including in the national tri-partite presidency and House of Peoples, both currently restricted to the three main ethnic groups (Bosniaks, Serbs and Croats). An October agreement between the Bosnian political leaders failed to specify how the ruling will be implemented. The EU had announced that it would not accept the results of general elections in 2014 unless the constitution was amended.

The economy

With unemployment at around 30 per cent, the mass protests that had broken out in February 2015 were over the government's failure to fight graft and enact the reforms required for Bosnia to enter the EU. Whatever hopes there had been for a fragile recovery were dashed in mid-2014 by serious flood damage. According to the European Bank for Reconstruction and Development (EBRD) the significant brake on growth had been the weakness of domestic demand. Bosnia had suffered – albeit at one remove – from the global financial crisis that had seen the remittances received from Bosnians working abroad wither sharply – because jobs had been lost and were hard to find, or because wages had shrunk. Foreign remittances in 2014 were still below their pre-crisis levels. The 30 per cent domestic unemployment rate od 2014 was unacceptably high. There had been an improvement in export revenues in 2013, but overall gross domestic product (GDP) growth for 2014 had been modest and the floods had inflicted some €2 billion (US$2.25 billion) of damage (15 per cent of GDP) on a less than buoyant economy.

Bosnia's IMF Stand-By Arrangement (SBA) is important for guiding the country's economic reform package. The 24 month €379 million (US$426 million) SBA facility was augmented by €152 million (US$171 million) and extended by nine months in January 2014. Six months later, in June 2014, when the IMF's combined sixth and seventh reviews were completed, the amount of the SBA was increased for a second time, by €95.7 million (US$107.5 million) to help Bosnia cope with balance of payments problems arising from the flood damage. In September 2014 the IMF acccepted that the Bosnian authorities would need more time for the implementation of policies required for consideration of the 8th IMF review. Some respite was provided in mid-2014 when international donors and financial institutions pledged (which does not always mean provided) €809 million (US$909 million) to help Bosnia meet new financial liabilities arising from the floods.

None the less, the EBRD considered that it was inevitable that the disruption from the floods would hinder Bosnia's economic recovery. The efficient and prompt use of donor support was crucial in mitigating the initial damage as well as providing support for the post-flood reconstruction operation. Meanwhile, Bosnia's economic vulnerability prevailed, not only because of the problems affecting the whole region, but also – in the view of the EBRD – because of the poor investment climate and Bosnia's lack of competitiveness.

Any progress that Bosnia might have made to EU accession had long been stalled – the constitutional changes to implement the Sejdic-Finci verdict (in 2009) from the European Court of Human Rights (ECHR) had yet to be made and Bosnia had no co-ordination mechanism at national level for the negotiation of EU affairs, a sever hindrance in the accession process. In November 2014 Philip Hammond (UK foreign minister) and Frank-Walter Steinmeier (German foreign minister), sent an open letter to the people of Bosnia and Herzegovina, pledging substantive progress towards Bosnia's EU membership if Bosnia's politicians gave a written commitment to implement a package of reforms, including compliance with the Sejdic and Finci ruling of the ECHR.

In a lower key, according to the EDRB, the EU has been working with key domestic and international stakeholders on a Compact for Growth and Jobs initiative in Bosnia. The compact, which was finalised in 2014, has come up with a number of proposals, for the most part affecting improvements in Bosnia's business environment, tax reforms, anti-corruption measures and social welfare reform.

In the Republika Srpska (Serb Republic) the EBRD noted that new business registration has grown following the establishment of a one-stop business registration 'shop' in late 2013. The Republika Serbska also appeared to be leading the way with an on-line business registration procedure. In the Bosnian Federation one small step, the lowering of notary tariffs for setting up a new business appears to be as far as reforms had advanced in 2014. The federation's parliament has approved a new inspection law and amendments to the Law on Business Registration, but the draft law on companies still awaited parliamentary approval.

The impression that setting up a business in Bosnia is, in the words of the EBRD, 'problematic' is borne out by the country's ranking on the World Bank's *Doing Business 2015* report, where it came 107 out of the 189 countries surveyed, the lowest in the region.

Privatisation

A lot still remains to be achieved in transferring state-owned assets to private hands. The obvious anomalies are the two power generation companies, Elektroprivedra BiH and Elektroprivedra HZ HB. Bosnia's two telecommunications companies, BH Telecom and HT Mostar are also still state-owned. The legalities concerning the ownership of Bosnia's biggest exporter, the aluminium smelter Aluminij was sorted out in late 2013, but by late 2014 no buyers appeared to have come forward.

Encouragingly, Bosnia's banking sector was considered by the EBRD to have sound liquidity and relatively high levels of capital. Foreign banks account for 90 per cent of total assets in the financial sector, but the banking sector has not seen large credit outflows to parent banks. The only worrying aspect is the increasing number of non-performing loans, which were increasing, to 15.5 per cent of total loans in mid-2014, well up on the 2009 level of 5.9 per cent.

Draft labour market reforms were under preparation by both the Federal government and by the Republika Serbska to be submitted to their respective parliaments by the end of 2014. Undertakings had been given to the IMF that the legislation would contain a number of key features including skill related wage-setting, improving qualifications, experience and performance as well as reducing hiring disincentives. However, for the proposals to reach the statute book required trade-offs between the parties – a complicated and often fruitless bargaining process.

Risk assessment

Politics	Poor
Economy	Poor
Regional stability	Poor

Muslims in Bosnia & Herzgovinia

% of population	40
Sunni (% of Muslims)	38
Shi'a (% of Muslims)	54

COUNTRY PROFILE

1463 Bosnia and Hercegovina (BiH) became a province of the Ottoman Empire. Many of BiH's Christian Slavic population (principally Serb and Croat) were converted to Islam.

1877–78 The Congress of Berlin assigned BiH to the Austro-Hungarian Empire following the end of the Russo-Turkish War.

1914 Gavrilo Princip, a Serbian nationalist, assassinated Austrian Archduke Ferdinand in Sarajevo (capital of BiH), precipitating the First World War.

1918 The defeat of the Austro-Hungarian empire during the First World War saw the creation of the Kingdom of the Serbs, Croats and Slovenes, encompassing BiH, Croatia, parts of Dalmatia and Macedonia, Montenegro, Serbia, Slavonia and Slovenia.

1929 The Kingdom was renamed Yugoslavia.

1941 Parts of Yugoslavia were occupied by the Germans, Italians, Hungarians and Bulgarians. Most of BiH was incorporated into Croatia, which was granted independence by the Axis powers (Germany,

KEY INDICATORS — Bosnia and Hercegovina Rep

	Unit	2011	2012	2013	2014	**2015
Population	m	*3.89	3.88	*3.88	*3.87	*3.86
Gross domestic product (GDP)	US$bn	18.00	16.91	*17.85	*17.98	*16.64
GDP per capita	US$	4,618	4,353	*4,604	*4,644	*4,307
GDP real growth	%	1.7	-1.2	*2.5	*0.8	*2.3
Inflation	%	3.7	2.0	-0.1	*-0.9	*0.6
Unemployment	%	44.1	28.0	27.5	*27.5	*27.0
Exports (fob) (goods)	US$m	3,653.3	3,306.0	3,716.5	4,490.2	–
Imports (fob) (goods)	US$m	9,590.6	8,849.0	9,019.9	9,981.8	–
Balance of trade	US$m	-5,937.3	-5,543.0	-5,303.3	-5,491.6	–
Current account	US$m	-1,735.0	-1,636.0	-1,059.0	*-1,268.0	*-1,491.0
Total reserves minus gold	US$m	4,421.0	4,283.0	4,868.4	4,744.4	–
Foreign exchange	US$m	4,421.0	4,280.0	4,866.4	–	–
Exchange rate	per US$	1.39	1.51	1.43	1.62	–

* estimated figure ** forecast figure

Italy and Japan) and ruled by the country's fascist Ustasha movement. Two opposition movements, the communist Partisans led by Josip Broz Tito and the royalist Chetniks led by Draza Mihailovic and backed by the Allied powers, formed to resist Nazi rule.
1944–45 After hostilities broke out between the Chetniks and Partisans, the Allies withdrew support for the Chetniks and backed the Partisans. The Partisans then defeated the occupying forces, the Ustasha, and the Chetniks.
1945 BiH became a constituent republic of a new Yugoslav federation. Tito assumed power and adopted a Soviet-style constitution. The rest of the Yugoslav federation comprised Croatia, Macedonia, Slovenia, Montenegro, Serbia and the two autonomous regions of Vojvodina and Kosovo. In an attempt to create a Yugoslav unity, Tito imposed restrictions on religious worship, while socialism was encouraged as the country's national ideology.
1953 Constitutions adopted in 1953, 1963 and 1974 increased the autonomy of the constituent republics.
1989 Following the death of Tito in 1980 and the fall of communism elsewhere in eastern Europe, friction between the wealthier republics, Slovenia and Croatia, and the different ethnic groupings intensified.
1990 Multi-party elections in BiH brought to power a government which supported outright independence.
1992 After independence from Yugoslavia, civil war engulfed the whole of BiH.
1993 The Yugoslav dinar was replaced by the new dinar as the national currency.
1995 Hostilities were brought to an end by the Dayton Peace Agreement in late 1995. BiH was divided almost equally into two distinct entities, based along ethnic lines: the Federacija Bosne i Hercegovine (FBiH) (Federation of Bosnia and Hercegovina) (comprising the Croat and Muslim population, 51 per cent of BiH) and the RS (comprising the Serb population, 49 per cent of BiH). The disputed region of Brcko in the north-west of the country became a self-governing district within BiH. A multi-national Nato military force was deployed in BiH to enforce the military aspects of Dayton.
1996 A democratic government was elected comprising the main nationalist parties of the three ethnic communities: the Muslim Stranka Demokratski Akije (SDA) (Democratic Action Party), Hrvatska Demokratska Zajednica Bosne i Hercegovine (HDZ BiH) (Croatian Democratic Union of Bosnia and Hercegovina) and the Srpska Demokratska Stranka (SDS) (Serb Democratic Party). Alija Izetbegovic, Ante Jelavic and Zivko Radisic were elected to the three-member collective presidency.
1999 The new dinar was replaced by the Konvertibilna marka as the national currency.
2000 Nationalists did well in the general election and international hopes of multi-ethnic political co-operation declined. The Organisation for Security and Co-operation in Europe (OSCE) reported that several political parties abused the regulations during the elections.
2001 Ante Jelavic threatened to form his own government in Croat-dominated parts of the FBiH and was dismissed from the BiH presidency by UN High Representative Wolfgang Petritsch. Jozo Krizanovic became BiH president. Bozidar Matic resigned and the BiH parliament elected Zlatko Lagumdzija to replace him.
2002 Dragan Covic (Croat), Mirko Sarovic (Serb) and Sulejman Tihic (Muslim) were elected to the BiH presidency in the presidential elections. The SDA won the BiH parliamentary elections.
2003 Mirko Sarovic resigned from the BiH presidency after accusations that he had been involved with illegal arms sales to Iraq; he was replaced by Borislav Paravac.
2004 Sulejman Tihic became chairman of the presidency. UN High Representative, Paddy Ashdown, dismissed 60 top officials in the RS for failing to implement measures to catch Radovan Karadzic and General Ratko Mladic, both of whom were indicted on war-crimes charges. EU force (EUFOR) took over NATO's peace-keeping mission in Bosnia. Dragan Mikerevic, prime minister of the RS, resigned.
2005 RS parliament elected Pero Bukejlovic as prime minister. Dragan Covic was dismissed by the High Representative; Ivo Miro Jovic was appointed as the Croat member of the presidency. The EU agreed to stabilisation and association agreement talks as pre-entry measures for BiH to join the EU.
2006 The BiH rotating presidential elections were won by Haris Silajdzic, Nebojsa Radmanovic and Zeljko Komsic. In Zastupnicki dom (House of Representatives) elections the SDA won nine seats (out of 42); Stranka za Bosnu i Hercegovinu (SBiH) (Party of Bosnia and Hercegovina) won eight; Savez Nezavisnih Socijaldemokrata (SNSD) (Alliance of Independent Social Democrats) won seven; Socijaldemokratska Partija BiH (Socijaldemokrati) (Social Democratic Party of BiH) (Social Democrats) won five; HDZ BiH and SDS each won three seats and six political parties shared the remaining seven seats.
2007 Nikola Spiric became prime minister of BiH. President Milan Jelic died and Igor Radojicic (SNSD) became acting-President of RS. Spiric resigned as prime minister in protest at measures introduced by the UN High Representative to speed up decision making in the central parliament. BiH began reforms (seen as moves towards EU pre-membership) which are designed to strengthen central government and deny regional legislatures a veto on legislation. In RS presidential elections Rajko Kuzmanovic (SNSD) won with 41.8 per cent of the vote; his closest rival, Ognjen Tadic (SDP), had 35.2 per cent. Nikola Spiric was re-appointed prime minister of BiH.
2008 Haris Silajdzic became president of the BiH. BiH signed the Stabilisation and Association Agreement with the European Union. Full membership may not be achieved until 2018. The agreement was seen as a measure to bolster democratic values and counter ethnic tensions. Former Bosnian Serb leader Radovan Karadzic was arrested in Belgrade. Seven Bosnian Serbs were convicted of genocide in aiding the systematic killing of over 8,000 Bosnian Muslim men and boys during the siege of Srebrenica in 1995. All defendants had been members of either the police or army and were each given jail terms of 38–42 years. Local elections were won by nationalist political parties, which still divide communities along ethnic lines.
2009 Austrian diplomat, Valentin Inzko was appointed UN High Representative and EU Special Representative. Nedzad Brankovic resigned as prime minister of the FBiH. Former president Karadzic was charged with war crimes, genocide and crimes against humanity. The rail link between Belgrade (Serbia) and Sarajevo closed since the conflict in the 1990s, was reopened.
2010 Haris Silajdzic became chairman of the rotating presidency. The Serbian parliament offered an apology for the 1995 Srebrenica massacre. In presidential and parliamentary elections, Zeljko Komsic (SDP BiH) won 60.6 per cent of the Croat vote, for the rotating federal presidency, along with Bakir Izetbegovic (SDA) with 34.9 per cent of the Bosniaks vote and Nebojsa Radmanovic (SNSD) with 48.9 per cent of the Serb vote. Milorad Dodik was appointed president of RS. Nebojsa Radmanovic (Serb) took office as the first in the rotating BiH presidency.
2011 President Dodik (RS) appointed Aleksandar Džombic (SNSD) as prime minister of RS; he took office in February. In March, Zivko Budimir (Hrvatska Stranka Prava (HSP) (Croatian Party of Rights)) was elected president and Nermin Nikšic (Hrvatska Demokratska Zajednica (HDZ) (Democratic People's Union)) as prime minister of the Federation of BiH. The

presidency proposed Slavo Kukic as federal (BiH Republic) prime minister in June, but Serb representatives rejected his candidature and the post remained unfilled.
2012 The BiH parliament confirmed the appointment of Vjekoslav Bevanda (HDZ) as prime minister on 12 January. On 10 March, Bakir Izetbegovic became chairman of the (BiH) presidency. On 26 September, the IMF agreed a two-year, €405 million (US$522 million) standby loan to support the BiH economic programme and contain any external shocks. On 15 October, a pilot census was launched, in preparation for BiH's first full census since the 1992–05 civil war. The test run will highlight any problems likely to arise and affect the decision to hold or postpone the full census due in April 2013. On 10 November, Nebojsa Radmanovic became chairman of the presidency.
2013 Momcilo Krajisnik, who had been convicted by the International Criminal Tribunal for former Yugoslavia (ICTY) in the Hague of persecuting and forcibly expelling non-Serbs during the 1992–95 war in Bosnia, returned to his home town of Pale on 30 August. He had been released early from his prison in the UK after being called a 'model prisoner' by the authorities and said he was 'prepared to help seek reconciliation between the three peoples in Bosnia-Herzegovina.' He was welcomed home by several thousand cheering Serbs.
2014 A number of demonstrations and riots began in the northern town of Tuzla on 4 February, quickly spreading to other cities including Sarajevo. Although the disturbances had largely ended by 8 February, there were scattered outbreaks of violence until April. Presidential and parliamentary elections took place on 12 October.
2015 In February there were mass protests against the government and its inability to fight graft and enact the reforms required for Bosnia to enter the EU.

Political structure

Constitution

The effective founding constitution of modern Republika Bosne i Hercegovine (BiH) (Republic of Bosnia and Hercegovina) is the 1995 Dayton Peace Agreement. This set out the federal state, divided between the Federacija Bosne i Hercegovine (FBiH) (Federation of Bosnia and Hercegovina) and the Republika Srpska (RS) (Serb Republic). The two republics are then subdivided into cantons based on the Swiss model. A European Union pre-membership agreement in December 2007 produced parliamentary reforms to strengthen the BiH central government, whereby FBiH and RS legislatures will no long be able to block and boycott a BiH vote.
The disputed region of Brcko in the north-west of the country was placed under international arbitration in 1995. In March 1998, the Brcko Tribunal declared the Brcko municipality a separate self-governing neutral district under the sovereignty of BiH.
In 2002, the FBiH and RS governments signed an agreement to make constitutional amendments designed to give equal status to all ethnic Muslims, Croats and Serbs in BiH.
Under the terms of the Dayton Agreement, the BiH is responsible for foreign affairs, foreign trade, monetary policy and law enforcement. The FBiH and RS are primarily responsible for fiscal policy, defence and law.
Constitutional government is not yet in full operation. The UN's Office of the High Representative (OHR) is responsible for overseeing and implementing the civilian aspects of the Dayton Agreement.
Universal suffrage at 18 years of age (16 years if employed). The 2001 election law only allows voters to cast ballots for members of their own ethnic group in elections for the collective three-member presidency. Voters may only vote in constituencies where they lived prior to the 1992–95 civil war.

Form of state

Confederated parliamentary democratic republic, separated into two constituent states – Bosnia-Hercegovina Federation and Bosnia Serb Republic (RS).

The executive

BiH has a three-member collective presidency, one representative from each of the three main ethnic groups (Bosniaks, Croats and Serbs). Although this is nominally the president for the whole country, in practice, the RS appoints its own president and has frequently disregarded the authority of the three-man presidency. In 2002, the collective presidency was elected for its first four-year mandate.
The president nominates (and the Zastupnicki dom sanctions) members of the Zastupnicki dom to form the council of ministers (government). The council appoints a chairman (prime minister) as head of government; in 2005, the post of prime minister was enhanced, with power to appoint and dismiss ministers.
The UN High Representative holds *de facto* power, delegated to local politicians.

National legislature

The central legislature is the bicameral Parlementarna Skupstina BiH (National Parliament of BiH), with representatives from both of the state parliaments as members. The Predstavnicki dom (House of Representatives) (lower house) has 42 members elected by party-list proportional representation, for a four-year term – 28 members from the FBiH (14 Bosniaks and 14 Croats) and 14 from the RS. The Dom Naroda (House of the Peoples) (upper house) has 15 members appointed from the lower house and elected by the Zastupnicki dom, with equal representation of the three ethnic groups, five Bosniaks, five Croats and five Serbs.
BiH has two state parliaments (FBiH and NSRS – see below) and one central legislature.
The Federacija Bosne i Hercegovina (FBiH) (Bosniak/Croat Federation of Bosnia and Hercegovina) has a bicameral parliament with a House of Representatives (98 seats – members elected by popular vote for four-year terms); and a House of Peoples (30 Bosniak and 30 Croat seats).
The Narodna Skuptstina Republika Srpska (NSRS) (Serb Republic National Parliament) is unicameral, with 83 members elected for a four-year term by proportional representation.
The Brcko Distrikt (Brcko district), in north-east BiH, is under internationally administered supervision.

Legal system

Civil law system of former Yugoslavia. Legal infrastructure has been in disarray since the war.

Last elections

12 October 2014 (BiH presidency and parliament; state presidential and state parliaments)
Results: Since the presidential role is evenly shared between three candidates (one Bosnian, one Croat and one Serb) each has their own, respective election.
Presidential – Bosnian: Bakir Izetbegovic (SDA) won 32.87 per cent of the vote, Fahrudin Radoncic (SBB) 26.78 per cent, Emir Suljagic (DF) 15.20 per cent, Bakir Hadžiomerovic (SDP) 10.02 per cent, Sefer Halilovic 8.80 per cent (BPS), Mustafa Ceric (Independent) 4.50 per cent. Four other candidates received less than 1 per cent of the popular vote.
Presidential – Croatian: Dragan Covic (HDZ) won 52.20 per cent of the vote, Martin Raguž (HDZ 1990) 38.61 per cent, Živko Budimir (SPP) 6.27 per cent, Anto Popovic (DF) 2.93 per cent
Presidential – Serbian: Mladen Ivanic (PDP-SDS) won 48.71 per cent of the vote, Željka Cvijanovicc (SNSD-DNS-SP) 47.56 per cent, Goran Zmijanjac (FPP) 3.73 per cent
Parliamentary (House of Representatives): Stranka demokratske akcije (Party for Democratic Action) (SDA) won 18.74 per cent of the vote and 10 seats (out of 42), Savez nezavisnih socijaldemokrata (Alliance of Independent Social Democrats) (CHC) won 16.64 per cent and 6 seats,

Srpska Demokratska Stranka (Serb Democratic Party) (SDS) won 12.97 per cent and 5 seats, Demokratska fronta (Democratic Front) (DF) won 9.24 per cent and 5 seats, Savez za bolju buducnost BiH (Union for a Better Future of BiH) (SBB BiH) won 8.70 per cent and 4 seats, Hrvatska demokratska zajednica Bosne i Hercegovine (Croatian Democratic Union of Bosnia and Herzegovina) (HDZ/HSS/HKDU/HSP-AS BiH/HSP HB) won 7.54 per cent and 4 seats, Socijaldemokratska PartijaBosne i Hercegovine (Social Democratic Party of Bosnia and Herzegovina) (SDP) won 6.66 per cent and 3 seats. Five other parties won one seat each, while the other 16 parties failed to gain any.

Next elections

October 2018 (presidential and parliamentary)

Political parties

Ruling party

Seven-party coalition government (formed 9 Jan 2007)

About 21 per cent of the population is under 15 years.

The UN High Commissioner for Refugees (UNHCR) registered a year-on-year increase of almost 70 per cent in the number of BiH refugees returning to their homes in the first eight months of 2001. More than 50 per cent returned to areas not dominated by their own ethnic group. Over half of the estimated 1.5 million refugees have returned to BiH since 1995.

Population

3.88 million (2012)*

Last census: March 1991: 4,377,033

Population density: 76 inhabitants per square km. Urban population 49 per cent (2010 Unicef).

Annual growth rate: -0.7 per cent, 1990–2010 (Unicef).

Internally Displaced Persons (IDP)

330,000 (UNHCR 2004)

Ethnic make-up

Muslims (44 per cent), Serbs (31 per cent) and Croats (17 per cent). The RS is a mostly Serb enclave, while Muslims (also known as 'Bosniaks') and Croats control and inhabit the FBiH.

Religions

Islam (Muslims), Serbian Eastern Orthodoxy (Serbs), Roman Catholicism (Croats).

Education

The education system in BiH was largely destroyed by the civil war and is now influenced by politics. International aid and tax revenues are being used by the entity governments to re-build and fund the education system. In the FBiH, each canton has responsibility for education. The RS has responsibility for its own education system.

Despite the FBiH and RS signing the Declaration and Agreement on Education in BiH in 2000 to introduce much-needed reforms to the post-war education system, educational curriculums in each of the entities follow ethnic and religious lines. Segregation of students along ethnic lines is not uncommon.

BiH has universities at Banja Luka, Mostar, Sarajevo and Tuzla. Higher education is also poorly financed and most international aid has come from non-governmental organisations (NGOs).

Literacy rate: 95 per cent adult rate; 100 per cent youth rate (15–24) (Unesco 2005).

Health

The health system in BiH is poor and receives little funding from the central government, having handed down the funding responsibilities to cantonal and local government. The health system is largely dependent on aid but is also financed through employee insurance schemes.

Life expectancy: 76 years, 2010 (Unicef 2012)

Fertility rate/Maternal mortality rate: 1.1 births per woman, 2010 (Unicef 2012)

Child (under 5 years) mortality rate (per 1,000): 7 per 1,000 live births (WHO 2012)

Welfare

Higher spending on specific areas of the welfare system compared to other areas of the economy has become a major impediment to achieving economic growth in BiH. The welfare system is highly geared to supporting military veterans, war widows and their families, thus only benefiting around 230,000 people – about six per cent of the population.

According to the IMF, benefits and spending for military invalids and war widows in the FBiH and the RS account for 10–12 per cent of the country's government revenues. These payments also accounted for over 80 per cent of the annual pension fund.

The unemployment benefit system in BiH is of limited assistance to the claimant. Unemployment benefits – 30 per cent of the state average wage – in the FBiH are only available for six months – although these are available longer for those who had been in continuous employment for more than five years. Claimants need to have paid through an insurance scheme to gain unemployment benefits, while military invalids and war widows are funded by the state. As a result of the system, few register as unemployed, confusing official statistics of the unemployed in BiH (estimated at 40 per cent in 2003). About 5 per cent of those registered as unemployed actually receive state benefits.

Main cities

Sarajevo (capital, estimated population 300,855 in 2012), Banja Luka (capital of RS) (238,353), Tuzla (99,543), Zenica (93,233), Bijeljina (78,960), Mostar (the main town in Hercegovina province) (68,392), Prijedor (43,307), (64,301), Brcko (38,968), Bihac (37,511), Doboj (31,794).

Languages spoken

Bosanski (Bosnian) is one of the southern Slavonic languages and is most closely related to Serbian, Croatian and Slovene. Croatian and Serbian are also spoken. Bosnian is written in Latin script but can also be seen written in the Cyrillic alphabet.

German is a useful language for the business traveller.

English is not widely spoken, but is becoming more common as a language for business.

Official language/s

Bosanski (Bosnian)

Media

The civil war of the 1990s resulted in a highly polarised media, which the Dayton Agreement addressed by developing a media to bridge inter-communal groupings. The media is partially free although state bodies and political parties have endeavoured to bring pressure on journalists and media outlets.

Press

Dailies: From Sarajevo in Bosnian, *Dnevni Avaz* (www.avaz.ba), and the independent *Oslobodjenje* (www.oslobodjenje.ba). From Banja Luka, in Serbian, *Nezavisne Novine* (www.nezavisne.com) and the Bosnian Serb government *Glas Srpske* (www.glassrpske.com). From Mostar, in Croatian, *Dnevni List* (www.dnevni-list.ba).

Weeklies: From Sarajevo in Bosnian, *Dani* (www.bhdani.com), *Slobodna Bosna* (www.slobodna-bosna.ba), and from Banja Luka *Reporter* an independent bi-weekly.

Broadcasting

National, public broadcasting is provided by Radio Televizija Bosne i Hercegovine (BHRT) (www.bhrt.ba), by Radio Televizija BiH in the Bosniak-Croat region (RTBiH) (www.rtvfbih.ba) and in the Serb region by Radio Televizija Republik Srpske (RTRS) (www.rtrs.tv).

Radio: Public radio has the highest listening figures. There are over 200 commercial radio stations; however the number has been restricted due to the inadequate advertising market.

The BHRT (www4.bhrt.ba) broadcasts two national networks and one international.

Popular commercial stations include Bosanska Radio Mreza (Boram) (www.boram.ba), BM Radio (www.bmradio.com), Radio Stari Grad (http://rsg.software.ba), Radio M (www.radiom.net), Radio Tuzla (www.radiotuzla.com) and Big Radio 2 (www.bigradiobl.com).
Television: BHRT, RTVBiH and RTRS provide public services in all local languages. There are over 40 channels to choose from, the majority are provided by foreign cable or satellite networks. Domestic commercial channels include Balkanmedia 7 (www.balkanmedia.com), BN TV Bijelina (www.rtvbn.com) and Mreza Plus (www.mrezaplus.ba).
National news agency: FENA (Federal News Agency)
Other news agencies: SRNA (Bosnian Serb): www.srna.co.yu
Onasa (independent): www.onasa.com.ba

Economy

Structural reforms and private sector-led growth have led to a level of revitalisation since the end of the civil war in 1995. BiH has natural resources in hydropower, coal, ore and minerals, good agricultural prospects, producing wheat, fruits and livestock, timber and forest products and an industrial manufacturing base in steel, aluminium, vehicle assembly and parts, textiles, furniture, munitions, domestic appliances, aircraft repair and oil refining. The after-effects of the civil war, which left deep divisions within civil society, are still hampering development. Although the three rival federal regions have come together and agreed to strengthen central government, the divergence complicates policymaking as conflicting views impede planning and investment. Growth in tourism, particularly along the Adriatic coast, has successfully boosted the economy and provided employment.

Recovery from the global economic crash has been slow and in 2012 BiH regressed back to negative growth of -1.2 per cent as a slow, inefficient public sector, whose spending accounts for some 40 per cent of GDP, was unable to deal with economic stagnation in the region, leading to low labour force participation rates and unemployment. Since then, though growth is positive, it is still very low, reaching 0.7 per cent in 2013 and 1.1 per cent in 2014. Rampant corruption and nepotism in government and public offices, the 2014 Corruptions Perceptions Index ranked BiH 80 out of 175, had seriously hindered the nations ability to experience sustained and stable economic growth, however, more recently, extreme weather conditions have added to the lists of problems hampering BiH. The floods that hit Serbia and BiH in May 2014, the worst since records began, reportedly killed 80 people and affected the lives of well over a million people as houses, hospitals, and schools were destroyed. Although figures are sketchy, the UN and EU concluded that the floods cost BiH €1.3 billion (US$1.8 billion). The agriculture sector, was particularly affected as most the arable land in the area was destroyed. As a result, agriculture's contribution to GDP dropped from 8.5 per cent in 2013 to 7.5 per cent in 2014. The full economic and social consequences of the floods are yet t be experienced, though it is clear that they have been very costly and damaging.

Unemployment in BiH is high at 27 per cent, although unofficial data that includes the grey economy estimate a rate of 18–22 per cent. Job creation is of primary importance and the lack of jobs accounts for a high level of migration for employment. Foreign remittances have been rising slightly year on year, rising from US$1.9 billion in 2013 to US$2.1 billion in 2014.

BiH entered a Stabilisation and Association Agreement (SAA) and Interim Agreement (IA) with the EU in 2008, which created a nascent free trade area to progressively open markets in BiH and foster economic and social developments. The agreement is expected to run until 2013 with a functioning free trade area to be fully operational before membership of the EU is confirmed. However, in 2014, rioting and allegations of corruption have delayed BiH's accession into the EU.

Public dent has consistently remained high, standing at 45.5 per cent of GDP in 2014. This figure is unlikely to drop as corruption, natural disasters, and unemployment continue to plague the economy.

External trade

As of August 2015 BiH was still working towards WTO membership. It is a member of the Central European Free Trade Agreement (Cefta), along with seven other countries in the region. Cefta has an association agreement with the EU, which is its primary trading partner. A Stabilisation and Association Agreement (SAA) with the EU was signed in December 2009, with the prospect of enhanced trading links.

The EU as a whole is BiH's largest trading partner, trading in miscellaneous manufactured articles, textiles, machinery and vehicle parts and raw materials (excluding hydrocarbons).

Industrial production includes heavy industries such as steel, aluminium and mining, with vehicle and aircraft assembly and oil refining. Lighter industries include furniture and domestic appliances manufacture.

Imports

Imports consist of fuels, foodstuffs, chemicals, machinery and equipment.
Main sources: Germany (11.5 per cent of total in 2014), Croatia (11.4 per cent), Italy (10.2 per cent).

Exports

Exports consist of mainly steel, minerals, clothing and textiles, aluminium and timber products.
Main destinations: Germany (15.2 per cent of total in 2014), Italy (13.8 per cent), Croatia (11.0 per cent).

Agriculture

Farming

The legacy of war in the region has implications for BiH's agricultural policy. There is considerable uncertainty over land rights, with fragmented and small-sized farm units hindering any large-scale investment opportunities.

The varying climatic conditions in BiH offer wide possibilities both in terms of crop choice and cultivation of land farming, fruit-growing, vine-growing, vegetable-growing, forage crops and livestock production. However, the floods of spring 2014 destroyed much of the arable land in the area and since then agricultures contribution to GDP has dropped form 8.5 per cent in 2013 to 7.5 per cent in 2014. The sector employs 19 per cent of the workforce.

Agricultural activities in the Republika Srpska (RS) extend over different farming systems including mixed farming enterprises (crops and cattle) on lower flat lands that alternate with more extensive sheep grazing systems in mountainous areas.

Most of the Federation of BiH is mountainous, with farms in the south and south-east growing vegetables, fruits and rearing livestock.

The issue of land mines in rural areas complicates policies related to post-war agricultural development.

Fishing

Fishing is of little importance to BiH's agricultural sector as a whole with the fish catch totalling some 2,500 tonnes per year.

Forestry

Over half of BiH's land area is forested, covering over 2.2 million hectares (ha). Three-fifths of woodland are used for wood supply, mostly for export. Most of the woodland is state-owned. The country has a small forest sector, which produces mainly sawn-wood and wood-based panels from domestic resources.

Industry and manufacturing

The industrial sector accounted for 26.3 per cent of GDP in 2014, of which manufacturing was 13 per cent.

Since the end of the civil war, the construction industry has been the main engine of industrial growth, and since the Zenica steelworks was sold to LNM Group in 2004 steel production has boosted state industrial production based on the resurgent metals sector, as well as the civil engineering projects and Balkan regeneration.
State-owned telecommunication entities were due to be one of the first organisations offered up for privatisation. However, in 2014 the director of the privatisation agency said that there were no plans for privatisation just yet and in 2015 there were still no further steps towards it.

Tourism
Bosnia and Hercegovina projects an image of energetic tourism with plenty of water sports, winter skiing and other activities to attract the young. Its location along the Adriatic and its less commercialised resorts compared with Italy, also attracts those looking for more sedate resort holidays. There are a number of historic sites, including two sites included on the Unesco World Heritage list, for the less frenetic.
Tourism in BiH has grown quickly and solidly since 2000, with tourist numbers reaching 517,000 in 2013 (latest figures), of which international arrivals accounted for over 50 per cent. Total contribution to GDP of travel and tourism was 9.3 per cent in 2014, with total employment being 10.7 per cent (72,000 jobs) of total employment.

Mining
BiH has deposits of iron ores and good reserves of bauxite, as it used to be a major source of minerals for former Yugoslavia.

Hydrocarbons
There are no oil reserves. Consumption was over 36,000 barrels per day in 2013 (latest figures), all of which was imported, mainly from Russia.
Domestic downstream activities are limited to the Bosanski Brod oil refinery. In October 2012, the operator, Rafinerija Nafte Brod, signed a licencing agreement to upgrade BiH's refinery with US technology (Honeywell and ExxonMobil) to increase yields; the project is scheduled for completion in 2016.
Natural gas imports are supplied by Russia via the Bratsvo gas pipeline through Hungary and Serbia.
The EU and World Bank have backed plans for the Ionia-Adriatic Pipeline (IAP) to supply natural gas from the Middle East to BiH via Albania and Montenegro. Following IAP's detailed engineering phase, construction began in 2013.
BiH has deposits of coal and produces enough for its own consumption, producing 12.6 million tonnes in 2013 (latest figures). The government has included the coal industry in the programme of its Agency for Privatisation. The Visca mines, near Tuzla in the north, produce 1,000 tonnes of coal a day, used in the domestic steel industry and power generation.
In September 2012 a memorandum of co-operation was signed in Republika Srpska (RS) (Serbian Republic) to enable it to become a member of the South Stream natural gas pipeline consortium led by the Russia energy company Gazprom. However due to the crisis in the Ukraine and pressure on Russia from the West, the South Stream pipeline construction has been delayed.

Energy
Total installed generating capacity was 4,300MW in 2013 (latest figures), generating 16.5 billion kilowatt hours (kWh), which is still just short of prewar production. As BiH consumption is lower than its capacity it is a net exporter of electricity.
The state-owned Elektroprivreda Republika Srpska, operates one of the largest coal-fired power plants in BiH at Ugljevik. Plans for an additional 2,000MW are under consideration, in particular the Gacko II coal-fired power plant.
The energy market was opened up for competition for sales to commercial customers in 2008 and opened up for domestic customers in 2015. The transmission system has been unified into a single grid. Two joint stock companies have been created to undertake the operations of assets (Transco) and authorities (ISO).

Financial markets
Stock exchange
SASE (Sarajevska Berza) (Sarajevo Stock Exchange)

Banking and insurance
BiH's banking system has undergone reform since 1995. Although heavily indebted and close to bankruptcy, a number of banks underwent privatisation in the late 1990s. Foreign companies that have already invested in BiH banking have streamlined and modernised major banks. Croatia's Zagrebacka Banka has taken a major share in the banking sector, acquiring stakes in four banks. Three RS banks were granted licences from the Federation Banking Agency (FBA) and opened branches in the FBiH, assisted by the introduction of a harmonised banking code between the entities.
The central bank has responsibility as the monetary authority and currency board.

Central bank
The Centralna Banka Bosne i Hercegovine (CBBH) (Central Bank of Bosnia and Hercegovina)

Time
GMT plus one hour (daylight saving, late March to late October, GMT plus two hours)

Geography
BiH is a mountainous territory with only about 20km of coastline. Croatia forms its western border (running from north-west to south-east, along the Dinaric Alps) and its northern border. Serbia lies to the east and Montenegro to the south-east.
The ancient province of BiH lies between the Sava, Drina and Una rivers. There are fertile lowlands along the River Sava which forms the northern border.
Hemisphere
Northern

Climate
The climate in BiH is continental with warm summers and cold winters. The temperature averages one degree Celsius (C) in January and 21 degrees C in July. As the country is dominated by mountainous and hilly terrain, with central and southern BiH dominated by the Dinaric Alps, the weather can be unpredictable in valley areas in the spring and winter months.

Dress codes
During the summer, light clothing is recommended, with warmer clothes essential during the winter months.

Entry requirements
Passports
Required by all except nationals of Austria, Belgium, Finland, France, Germany, Greece, Italy, Luxembourg, The Netherlands, Norway, Portugal, Spain and Sweden, who only need a national identity card.
Visa
Not required by citizens of Europe, North America, Australasia, Kuwait, Qatar, South Korea, Malaysia and Brunei.
Currency advice/regulations
BiH has a cash economy. The Konvertibilna marka (KM) is the local currency. The dollar and euro, but not sterling, are the most acceptable foreign currencies, but it is likely that change will be supplied in KM. Credit card facilities are limited, although hotels, restaurants and shops in the major centres are beginning to accept them. Travellers cheques can be changed at only a few banks in major cities and are not recommended.
Import and export of local currency are permitted to a limit of KM200,000. There are no restrictions on import and export of foreign currencies.

Customs
A unified customs territory has been established in BiH. 200 cigarettes, 20 cigars or 200g of tobacco; one litre of wine or spirits; one bottle of perfume; and gifts up to eur76.70 are admitted duty-free.

Health (for visitors)
Medical services are not comprehensive. Visitors should carry a sufficient supply of medicines or prescription drugs.
Ensure that personal travel and health insurance covers all eventualities, including accident and evacuation.

Mandatory precautions
None.

Advisable precautions
Typhoid, tetanus and hepatitis A and B vaccinations are recommended.
Water and food precautions advisable.

Credit cards
Credit cards can be used in some shops, hotels and travel agencies (Croatia Airlines, Air Bosna) in Sarajevo and is accepted by the Privredna Banka Sarajevo for cash withdrawals.

Public holidays (national)
Fixed dates
1 Jan (New Year's Day), 7 Jan (Orthodox Christmas Day), 14 Jan (Orthodox New Year), 1 Mar (Independence Day), 1 May (Labour Day), 15 Aug (Assumption Day), 28 Aug (Orthodox Assumption Day), 8 Sep (Nativity of the Virgin Mary), 21 Sep (Orthodox Nativity of the Virgin Mary), 1 Nov (All Saints' Day), 2 Nov (All Souls' Day), 25 Nov (National Statehood Day), 25 Dec (Christmas Day).

Variable dates
Easter, Orthodox Easter, Eid al Adha, Birth of the Prophet, Eid al Fitr.

Islamic year 1437 (15 Oct 2015–2 Oct 2016):: The Islamic year contains 354 or 355 days, with the result that Muslim feasts advance by 10–12 days against the Gregorian calendar. Dates of feasts vary according to the sighting of the new moon, so cannot be forecast exactly.

Working hours
Banking
Mon–Fri: 0800–1900.

Business
Mon–Fri: 0800–1700.

Government
Mon–Fri: 0730–1530, except Wed, 0730–1730.

Shops
Mon–Fri: 0800–1200 and 1700–2000, Sat: 0800–1500, but many shops open throughout day.

Telecommunications
Mobile/cell phones
GSM 900 facilities are available throughout most of the country.

Electricity supply
220V AC

Social customs/useful tips
Punctuality depends on the region: it is important in some, more casual in others. It is customary to shake hands on meeting and taking leave.

Security
Unexploded mines are still a danger away from main centres and routes and travellers should keep to roads or paved areas. There is a threat from terrorism. Visitors are advised to keep clear of demonstrations or crowds. Beware of pickpockets in Sarajevo and tourist areas.

Getting there
Air
National airline: B&H Airlines
International airport/s: Sarajevo International Airport (SJJ), 12km south of the city centre.
Other airport/s: Mostar (OMO) and Banja Luka(BNX).
Airport tax: US$12. Transit passengers remaining in airport transport area are exempt.

Surface
BiH is included in the Pan-European Corridor 5 scheme. The project has some 3,270km of railways, linking Kiev in the Ukraine with western Europe via Italy, and 2,850 of new and upgraded roads.
Road: From Zagreb (Croatia) the border can be crossed at Zupanja/Orasje, Stara Gradiska/Bosanska Gradiska, Maljevac/Velika Kladusa and Licko Petrovo Selo/Izacic.
From Split (Croatia): Kamensko/Livno and Metkovic/Capljina.
Rail: The newly reopened Belgrade (Serbia) and Sarajevo line takes six hours by train.
Water: Bosnia has 20km of coastline on the Adriatic, but no ports.

Getting about
National transport
Air: The BiH national airline is B&H Airlines. Air Srpska operates from the RS.
Road: Night travel by road is not advised and travellers on back roads risk landmines left over from the war. Drivers should also be aware of the local population's disregard for the country's traffic laws. Speeding, particularly on dangerous valley roadways, is commonplace. Horse transport is used by substantial numbers of the local population.
Buses: Buses run between Split and Zagreb to Sarajevo. Journey times from Split vary between five hours during the summer to six in the winter. Journey times from Zagreb take eight hours in the summer and 11 in the winter.
Rail: The country's two railway services are BiH's Zeljeznice Bosne i Hercegovina (ZBH) and RS's Zeljeznice Republike Srpska (ZRS).

City transport
Taxis: Inexpensive taxi services operate in all the main cities. All taxis are metered, but there is no basic charge. A 10 per cent tip is usual.
Buses, trams & metro: Most city centres are served by trams, while buses serve the suburbs. The service is generally cheap and regular. Bus transfers operate out of Sarajevo airport.

Car hire
Avis and Hertz and other international car hire companies operate in neighbouring Croatia. Although the majority of hire cars have Croatian licence plates and are normally insured for travelling within BiH, it is advisable to check before booking.
Car rental firms mainly operate from Sarajevo airport.
Because the international Green Card is not applicable in BiH, car insurance is restricted to Third Party only. Travellers are likely to be asked for either a large deposit or to leave an open credit card voucher with the hire company.
Should travellers have an accident in BiH which is reported to the police, the hire company will impose an automatic charge fine, over and above any other hire costs; check all agreements carefully. Drivers should be 21 years with a minimum of two years' driving experience.
It is recommended that visitors who rent a car also hire a driver, especially if they intend to travel outside Sarajevo.

BUSINESS DIRECTORY
The addresses listed below are a selection only. While World of Information makes every endeavour to check these addresses, we cannot guarantee that changes have not been made, especially to telephone numbers and area codes. We would welcome any corrections.

Telephone area codes
The international direct dialling (IDD) code for BiH is +387 followed by area code and subscriber's number.

Banja Luka	51	Sarajevo	33
Mostar	36	Tuzla	35
Pale	57	Zenica	72

Useful telephone numbers
Vehicle assistance: 1282
Fire and rescue: 123/124
Police: 122
Ambulance: 124
Emergency hospital, Koldovorska Street, Sarajevo (English spoken): 611-111

Chambers of Commerce
American Chamber of Commerce in Bosnia and Hercegovina, 4 Zmaja Od Bosne, 71000 Sarajevo (tel: 269-230;

fax: 269-232; e-mail: amcham@lsinter.net).

Bosnia-Hercegovina Chamber of Foreign Trade, 10 Branislava Durdeva, 71000 Sarajevo (tel: 663-631; fax: 663-632; e-mail: cis@komorabih.com).

Federation of Bosnia-Hercegovina Chamber of Economy, 10 Branislava Durdeva, 71000 Sarajevo (tel: 217-782; fax: 217-783; e-mail: info@kfbih.com).

Sarajevo Canton Chamber of Economy, 8 La Benevolencije, 71000 Sarajevo (tel: 250-100; fax: 250-137).

Banking

Aurobanka, Mostar (tel: 444-444, 444-445, 444-456; fax: 444-400; internet site: www.aurobanka.com; e-mail: aurobanka.com).

Gospodarska Banka, International Division, Ferhadija 11/III, 71000 Sarajevo (tel: 208-907, 667-688; fax: 444-605).

Hercegovacka banka, Kneza Domagoja Street, Sarajevo (tel: 320-555; fax: 324-771; internet site: www.hercegovacka-banka.com; e-mail: herbank@hercegovacka-banka.com).

Hrvatska Banka, Kardinala Stepinca bb, 88000 Mostar (tel: 312-112; fax: 312-121).

Hrvatska Postanska Banka, Kneza Domagoja, Mostar (tel/fax: 316-020; e-mail: hpb-hb@int.tel.hr).

Investment Bank of the Federation of Bosnia and Hercegovina, Igmanska 1, 71000 Sarajevo (tel: 277-900; fax: 668-952; e-mail: info@ibf-bih.com).

Komercijalna Banka, Dzafer mahala 65/67, 75000 Tuzla (tel/fax: 259-000, 252-630; internet site: www.kombanka.com.ba; e-mail: kombanka@kombanka.com.ba).

Privredna Banka Sarajevo, Obala Vojvode Stepe 19, 71000 Sarajevo (tel: 213-144).

Universal Banka, Branilaca sarajeva 20/V, 71000 Sarajevo (tel: 664-139; fax: 668-239; internet site: www.universalbanka.ba; e-mail: uniba@bih.net.ba).

Central bank

Central Bank of Bosnia and Hercegovina, Maršala Tita 25, 71000 Sarajevo (tel: 278-100; fax: 278-299; e-mail: contact@cbbh.ba).

Stock exchange

SASE (Sarajevska Berza) (Sarajevo Stock Exchange), www.sase.ba

Banjalucka berza (Banja Luka Stock Exchange), www.blberza.com

Travel information

B&H Airlines, Kurta Schorka 36, Sarajevo(tel: 767-725; fax: 767-726; e-mail: opc@airbosna.ba).

Air Commerce, Sarajevo (tel: 663-396; fax: 663-395).

Avio Express, Sarajevo (tel/fax: 653-179).

Air Srpska, Veselina Maslese 28, 78000 Banja Luka (tel: 212-806; fax: 211-348).

Ministries

Ministry of External Trade and International Communication, 9 Musala, 71000 Sarajevo (tel: 664-831; fax: 655-060).

Ministry of Foreign Affairs of BiH, Musala 2, Sarajevo (tel: 281-100; internet site: http://www.mvp.gov.ba/Index_eng.htm).

RS Ministry of Foreign Economic Affairs, Vuka Karadzica 4, 51000 Banja Luka (tel: 331-430; fax: 331-436).

RS Ministry of Trade and Tourism, Vuka Karadzica 4, 51000 Banja Luka (tel: 331-523; fax: (331-499).

Other useful addresses

Agency for Privatisation in Federation of Bosnia and Hercegovina, Alipasina 41, Sarajevo (tel: 218-550; fax: 218-552; e-mail: apftbiro@bih.net.ba).

US Embassy of Bosnia and Hercegovina, 2109 E Street, NW, Washington DC 20037 (tel: 337-1500; fax: 337-1502; e-mail: info@bosnianembassy.org).

British Embassy, BFPO 543, 8 Tina Ujevica, Sarajevo (tel: 444-429; fax: 666-131; e-mail: britemba@bih.net.ba).

British Embassy Commercial Department, Petrakijina 22, Sarajevo (tel: 204-781, 204-782, 679-635; fax: 204-780).

Communications and Regulatory agency (CRA), Vilsonovo Setaliste 10, 71000 Sarajevo.

Directorate for Reconstruction and Development, Saravejo (tel: 650-563).

RS Directorate for Privatisation, Mladena Stojanovica 4, Banja Luka (tel: 308-311; fax: 311-245; e-mail: dip@inecco.net).

Elektrodistribucija (Power Distribution Company), Sarajevo (tel: 472-462).

Elektroprivreda BiH, Vilsonovo setaliste 20, 71000 Sarajevo (tel: 651-722; fax: 653-004).

Gras (Public Transport Company), Sarajevo (tel: 664-624).

Institute for City Development Planning, Saravejo (tel: 664-638).

Institute for City Construction, Saravejo (tel: 663-901).

Institute for Information and Statistics, Saravejo (tel: 664-450).

Office of the High Representative, Emerika Bluma 1, 71 000 Sarajevo (tel: 283-500; fax: 283-501).

Public Information Office HQ SFOR, Butmir Camp, 71 000 Sarajevo (tel: 495-149).

PTT (Post/Telegraph/Telephone), Sarajevo (tel: 664-813).

Sarajevo City Council, Reisa Dz Causevica Street No 3, Sarajevo (tel: 664-773; fax: 648-016).

Sarajevogas (Gas Company), Sarajevo (tel: 467-713).

Sarajevostan (Housing Company), Saravejo (tel: 663-522).

Sarajevski Sajam (trade fairs), Terezije bb, 71 000 Sarajevo (tel: 664-163, 201-208, 445-156; fax: 201-178, 201-208).

Telekom Srpske (e-mail: tskabinet@telekom-rs.com).

World Bank Resident Mission, Bosnia and Hercegovina, Hamdije Kresevljakovica 19, 71000 Sarajevo (tel: 440-293; fax: 440-108).

National news agency: FENA (Federal News Agency) (email: fena@fena.ba; internet: www.fena.ba).

SRNA (Bosnian Serb): www.srna.co.yu

Onasa (independent): www.onasa.com.ba

Internet sites

Republika Srpska Government: www.vladars.net/sr-SP-Cyrl/Pages/Tiles.aspx

World Bank Resident Mission: www.worldbank.org.ba

UN Office of the High Representative: www.ohr.int

Botswana

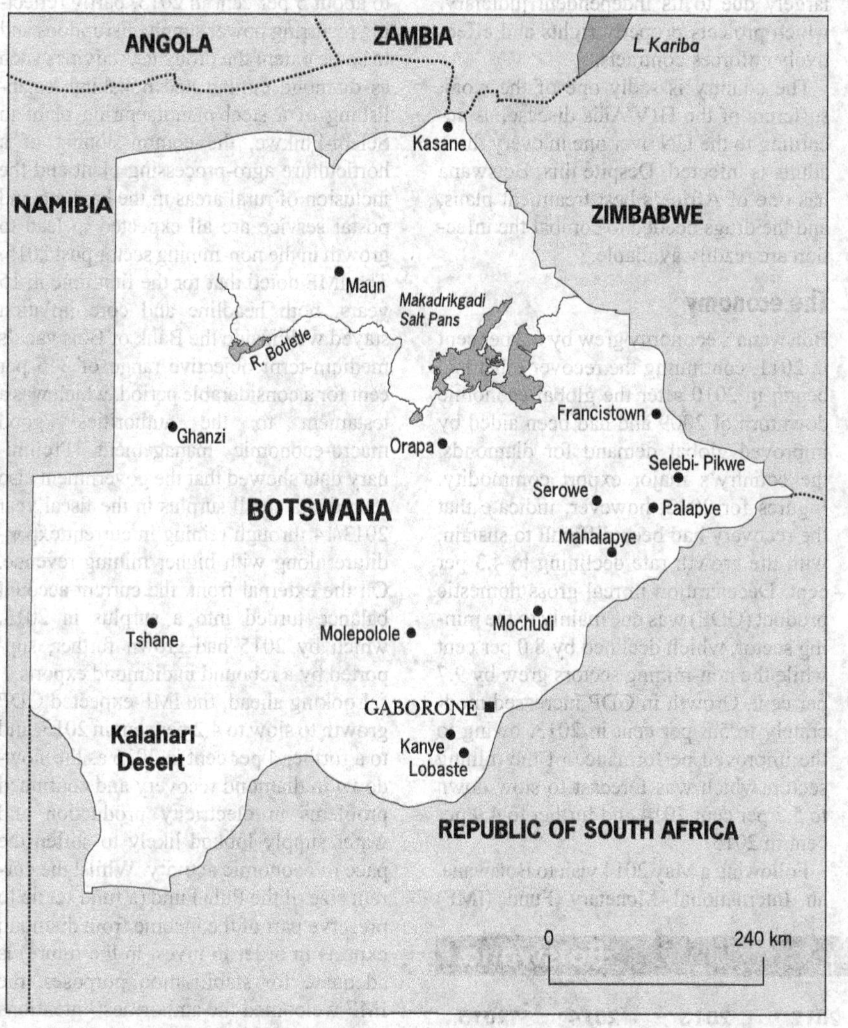

KEY FACTS

Official name: Republic of Botswana

Head of State: President Seretse Ian Khama (since 2008; re-elected 24 Oct 2014)

Head of government: President Seretse Ian Khama (since 2008; elected 24 Oct 2014)

Ruling party: Botswana Democratic Party (BDP) (since 1965; re-elected 24 Oct 2014)

Area: 582,000 square km

Population: 2.10 million (2014)* (2,038,228; 2011; census figure)

Capital: Gaborone

Official language: English (official); Setswana (national).

Currency: Pula (P) = 100 thebe

Exchange rate: P10.52 per US$ (Sep 2015)

GDP per capita: US$7,505 (2014)*

GDP real growth: 4.94% (2014)*

GDP: US$15.79 billion (2014)*

Inflation: 3.93% (2014)*

Balance of trade: US$241.30 million (2013)*

* estimated figure

Botswana, one of Africa's most stable countries, is the continent's longest continuous multi-party democracy. It is relatively free of corruption and has a good human rights record. Botswana is a parliamentary system representative democracy whereby the president of Botswana is both head of state and head of government and of a multi-party system. Executive power is exercised by the government. Legislative power is vested in both government and the parliament of Botswana. Since independence the party system has been dominated by the Botswana Democratic Party (BDP), which has won all ten elections since independence in September 1966. Refreshingly – by African standards – each of the elections since independence has been freely and fairly contested and has been held on schedule. The country's small white minority and other minorities participate freely in the political process. There are two main rival parties and a number of smaller parties. The openness of the country's political system is generally acknowledged to have been a significant element in Botswana's stability and economic growth.

In 2008, Ian Khama had assumed the presidency following the resignation of his predecessor, Festus Mogae, and in

2009 he won a full five-year term. In October 2014, after a series of controversies, President Ian Khama won his second full term. Gomolemo Motswaledi, the head of the opposition party Botswana Movement for Democracy, died in a car crash weeks before the election. Despite police saying that it was an accident members of the opposition suspected foul play. This was shortly followed by the arrest of the *Sunday Standard* newspaper editor Outsa Mokone after releasing an article claiming that the president was involved in the car crash. The arrest warrant issued by the Gaborone Magistrate Court claimed that Mr Mokone was arrested 'in connection with a seditious intention in respect of a story published by the *Sunday Standard* newspaper' at the end of August 2014. The article in question was considered by the state to be malicious and defamatory to President Khama. The contents of the article were deemed defamatory of the good name and reputation of the President in his personal and private capacity.

Following representations by the newspaper Mr Mokone was released, saying that he saw the incident as part of a 'government campaign' to intimidate the media into submission in the run-up to the general elections. The whole affair took the country by surprise. In Botswana the free press has traditionally been respected and journalists have felt able to write without censorship or interference from the government. The author of the article, one Edgar Tsimane, on hearing of Mr Mokone's arrest, fled Botswana and sought temporary asylum in South Africa following a tip-off that his life was in danger. Speculation surrounded the reasons for the President's nocturnal foray.

Botswana has been awarded the lowest corruption score in Africa by the Heritage 2015 Index of Economic Freedom, and consistently achieves some of the best results in the region on the other indexes measured by the organisation. This is largely due to its independent judiciary, which protects property rights and effectively enforces contracts.

The country is sadly one of the worst sufferers of the HIV/Aids disease, as according to the UN over one in every three adults is infected. Despite this, Botswana has one of Africa's best treatment plans, and the drugs needed to combat the infection are readily available.

The economy

Botswana's economy grew by 6.2 per cent in 2011, continuing the recovery that had begun in 2010 after the global economic downturn of 2009 and had been aided by improved global demand for diamonds, the country's major export commodity. Figures for 2012, however, indicate that the recovery had been difficult to sustain, with the growth rate declining to 4.3 per cent. Deceleration in real gross domestic product (GDP) was due mainly to the mining sector, which declined by 8.0 per cent while the non-mining sectors grew by 9.7 per cent. Growth in GDP increased moderately to 5.8 per cent in 2013, owing to the improved performance of the mining sector, which was forecast to slow down to 5.2 per cent 2014 and further to 4.9 per cent in 2015.

Following a May 2014 visit to Botswana, an International Monetary Fund (IMF) mission outlined its preliminary conclusions, saying that Botswana was undergoing a cyclical recovery in line with its major trading partners. Despite the economy experiencing higher than expected growth in 2013 due to the success of the mining industry, the non-mineral sector slowed down from about 6 per cent in 2012 to about 5 per cent in 2013, partly reflecting recurring power supply disruptions and to some extent the drought. Activities such as diamond cutting and polishing, establishing of a steel manufacturing plant in Selebi-Phikwe, the commissioning of a horticulture agro-processing plant and the inclusion of rural areas in the banking and postal service are all expected to lead to growth in the non-mining sector post 2015. The IMF noted that for the first time in 15 years, both headline and core inflation stayed well inside the Bank of Botswana's medium-term objective range of 3–6 per cent for a considerable period, which was a testament to the authorities' good macro-economic management. Preliminary data showed that the government also recorded a small surplus in the fiscal year 2013/14 through reining in current expenditure along with higher mining revenue. On the external front, the current account balance turned into a surplus in 2013, which by 2015 had grown further, supported by a rebound in diamond exports.

Looking ahead, the IMF expected GDP growth to slow to 4.2 per cent in 2015, and to a further 4 per cent in 2016 as the slowdown in diamond recovery and continued problems in electricity production and water supply looked likely to soften the pace of economic activity. Whilst the current size of the Pula Fund (a fund set up to preserve part of the income from diamond exports in order to invest in the future) is adequate for stabilisation purposes, the IMF welcomed the authorities' intentions to create additional savings from non-renewable resource revenues to transfer diamond wealth across generations. The budget's emphasis on improving the performance and finances of parastatals was also well placed. Delivering good outcomes in the implementation of the public investment programme would, however, require improving public financial management (PFM), including in the area of project management, monitoring and oversight. The IMF welcomed the initiatives that have been put in place to strengthen PFM within the government and improve the quality of the public investment programme.

The IMF also recommended that macro-prudential measures be used to

KEY INDICATORS — **Botswana**

	Unit	2011	2012	2013	2014	**2015
Population	m	2.04	*2.06	*2.08	*2.10	*2.13
Gross domestic product (GDP)	US$bn	17.60	14.43	*14.80	*15.79	*15.77
GDP per capita	US$	9,481	7,020	*7,118	*7,505	*7,407
GDP real growth	%	4.6	4.2	*5.9	*4.9	*4.2
Inflation	%	8.5	7.5	5.8	*3.9	*3.7
Exports (fob) (goods)	US$m	6,446.9	6,011.0	7,603.3	–	–
Imports (fob) (goods)	US$m	7,194.1	7,918.0	7,361.9	–	–
Balance of trade	US$m	-747.1	-1,907.0	241.3	–	–
Current account	US$m	3,910.0	-703.0	*1,536.0	*2,703.0	*2,870.0
Total reserves minus gold	US$m	–	7,628.0	7,726.1	8,322.8	–
Foreign exchange	US$m	–	7,453.0	7,453.0	–	–
Exchange rate	per US$	6.59	7.89	8.78	9.50	–

* estimated figure ** forecast figure

address Botswana's continued rapid increase in household indebtedness. In this context, the IMF welcomed the steps being taken to strengthen the capacity of the non-bank financial institutions regulatory agency. The diagnostic study on the current credit reporting system (CRS) in Botswana which was being conducted by the authorities to identify the gaps and provide recommendations on improving the current credit reporting systems was a step in the right direction. The government's emphasis on enhancing greater financial inclusion, while committing to provide adequate safeguards to preserve the stability of the financial system, was also welcome.

Returning to an era of strong growth and accelerating Botswana's convergence to higher income levels would require a set of policies to reinvigorate economy-wide productivity, including addressing the skills shortage in the economy. These would include improving the quality of public expenditure, the efficiency of the tax system and addressing the skills mismatch in the labour market. In this regard, the IMF commended the government on the skills development policies announced in the 2014/15 budget which should be seen as an integral part of a broader set of policy actions that include employment, investment and innovation policies in order to reinforce the links between the educational system and labour market outcomes. In the view of the IMF, the authorities should also continue to improve Botswana's competitiveness, including reducing further the regulatory burden on firms to create the enabling environment to facilitate the structural transformation of the economy.

Safari-based tourism is a significant source of income. It is a tightly controlled industry and mainly upmarket. The outbreak of the Ebola virus in West Africa in the summer of 2014, despite being far away from most of the wildlife parks in Africa, spread fear in tourists leading to a continent-wide drop in safari tourism. In a survey of 500 operators conducted by Safari Bookings, as of September 2014 more than half reported a 20–70 per cent decline in bookings.

Risk assessment

Politics	Fair
Economy	Fair
Regional stability	Good

COUNTRY PROFILE

1885 Britain declared the country a protectorate and called it Bechuanaland, defining its modern borders.
1966 Independence for Botswana came a year after the territory's first election, which was won by Seretse Khama and his Botswana Democratic Party (BDP).
1980 On his death, Khama was succeeded by his vice president, Quett Ketumile Masire.
1984 and 1989 The ruling BDP easily won elections but was tainted by allegations of corruption.
1994 In the elections, the opposition party, Botswana National Front (BNF), took 13 seats and unseated three ministers.
1998 President Sir Quett Ketumile Masire retired from the presidency.
1999 The legislative elections were won by the BDP. The National Assembly chose Festus Mogae as president.
2001–02 The government's policy towards the San people (formerly called the Bushmen or Basarwa) in the Central Kalahari Game Reserve has been criticised internationally for its refusal to recognise the ownership rights of the Bushmen over the land they have lived on for at least 20,000 years. The Reserve was originally created in 1961 to constitute a refuge for the marginalised San people. However, the potential for tourism and diamonds increased the value of these marginal lands, leading the government to relocate the original inhabitants.
2003 A partnership between the government, a pharmaceutical giant and the Bill and Melinda Gates Foundation began providing free anti-retroviral drugs to the country's HIV-infected population.
2004 Festus Mogae won a landslide victory when he was elected for a second (and final) five-year term.
2006 The San people won a judicial ruling that the rights to their ancestral lands in the Kalahari Desert were enduring and their eviction by the government in 2005 was illegal.
2008 Seretse Ian Khama became president, following Mogae's retirement. Khama is the son of the independence leader and former president, Sir Seretse Khama, and paramount chief of the Bamangwato tribe of Botswana. Former president Mogae won the first Mo Ibrahim prize of US$5 million for good governance in office, given as an example for other African heads of states to follow.
2009 Botswana criticised Muammar al Qadafi (of Libya) for not allowing discussion at the African Union summit, of which he was chairman, concerning the warrant issued for the arrest of Sudan's president Omar al Bashir by the International Criminal Court (ICC). Only Botswana and Chad openly stated that President Bashir should go to the ICC and clear his name.
2010 The African Development Bank granted Botswana's largest ever assistance package of US$1.5 billion, to help offset falling global diamond prices and 'fill part of the gap of the government's 2009–10 budget deficit…' In parliamentary elections the BDP won with 53.3 per cent of the vote (45 seats out of 57); the BDP re-elected Seretse Ian Khama as president.
2011 The high court ruled in January that the Basarwa Bushmen had a right to drill for water in their traditional land within the Kalahari Game Reserve. In June an eight-week strike by public workers, that closed hospitals, schools and government offices, was suspended as unions resumed talks with the government for a 16 per cent salary increase. In the end the workers settled for three per cent after the government insisted it could not afford a larger increase as the global economic crisis sapped demands for diamonds, the mainstay of the economy.
2012 De Beers began to move its diamond sorting operation from the UK to Gaborone in early August. When completed Botswana will be a major international gem capital, with around US$6 billion of diamonds being processed each year. On 31 August, the presidents of Botswana and South Africa signed a memorandum of understanding to promote trade and investment in each other's country and create opportunities in their respective industrial and manufacturing sectors. In November the Botswana People's Party (BPP), the Botswana National Front (BNF) and the Botswana Movement for Democracy launched an opposition party, the Umbrella for Democratic Change, to fight the 2014 election. Also in November the government rejected most of the electoral reforms recommended by the Independent Electoral commission. On 29 November the government announced that from January 2014 commercial hunting will be banned, due to the declining number of wildlife species.
2013 Gaborone began transforming itself from a low-rise to high-rise city as diamond-related companies began setting up factories in anticipation of the relocation of De Beers' sales business from London. In November De Beers completed the relocation of its global sales business to Botswana.
2014 A general election is scheduled for 24 October.
2015

Political structure

Constitution

The constitution came into effect on 30 September 1966. It enshrines a code of human rights.

The approval of a 15-member House of Chiefs is needed for some measures, but it cannot veto legislation.
There have been numerous constitutional amendments including a 1987 referendum whereby only those of Botswana birth or descent are eligible for the role of President and Vice President.
1997 amendments were wide-ranging and radical, instituting great change throughout Botswana. They included limiting the role of presidential office to 10 years, handing over the running of an election to an independent committee, reducing the voting age from 21 to 18 and allowing citizens who are living outside of the country to vote by proxy.

Independence date
30 Seotember 1966

Form of state
Multi-party democratic republic

The executive
The National Assembly elects a president who has executive power for a maximum of two five-year terms. He appoints a vice president and the cabinet, over which he presides. The president is an ex-officio member of the Assembly. The Vice President automatically succeeds to President after his ten years in office.

National legislature
The unicameral National Assembly has 57 directly elected members in single-seat constituencies for five-year terms. Four members are co-opted and the president and attorney general are ex-offico. A growth in population, confirmed by census, will result in an expansion of directly elected members. The assembly is responsible for passing, amending and repealing laws.
Any law relating to tribal matters of property, organisation and traditional law, plus any change to the constitution, must be referred for their opinion to the Ntlo ya Dikgosi (House of Chiefs), a 15-member advisory council of hereditary chiefs.
While the House of Chiefs has the power to summon any member of government to explain any policy or action it has no power of veto or legislation.

Legal system
Roman-Dutch law. Rural areas have customary courts.

Last elections
24 October 2014 (presidential and parliamentary)
Results: Parliamentary: BDP won 46.5 per cent of the vote (37 seats out of 57), UDC won 30 per cent of the vote (17 seats), Botswana Congress Party won 20.4 per cent of the vote (3 seats) and Independents won 3.1% but failed to gain any seats. Turnout was 83.7 per cent.
Presidential: The BDP voted Seretse Khama Ian Khama into office

Next elections
October 2019 (presidential and parliamentary)

Political parties

Ruling party
Botswana Democratic Party (BDP) (since 1965; re-elected 16 Oct 2009)

Main opposition party
The Botswana National Front (BNF) and the Botswana People's Party (BPP) formed the coalition Umbrella for Democratic Change (UDC)
Approximately 43 per cent of the total population is under 14 years.
Seventy-five per cent of the population live in the eastern 10 per cent of the country.

Population

1.88 million (2012)* (2,038,228; 2011; census figure)
Last census: 22 August 2011: 2,038,228
Population density: Three inhabitants per square km. Urban population 61 per cent (2010 Unicef).
Annual growth rate: 1.9 per cent, 1990–2010 (Unicef).

Ethnic make-up
The Batswana, of which the largest group is the Bamangwato, comprise 79 per cent of the total population. The Kalanga 11 per cent, Basarwa (the Bushmen) 3 per cent, Kgalagadi and the rest 7 per cent.

Religions
Most of the population are Christians (about 49 per cent); other religions include various traditional beliefs, including animism, mostly in rural areas (50 per cent), and a small Muslim population.

Education

Primary education is free but with a high drop-out rate. In 2001, the gender gap in primary enrolment was 25 per cent, with net enrolment among girls remaining at only 50 per cent.
Secondary schooling starts from the age of 12 and lasts till the age of 18.
The National Policy on Education (1977) and the Revised National Policy on Education (1994) have provided the policy framework for the education system in Botswana.
The United Nations International Children's Emergency Fund's (Unicef) Girls' Education Programme has focussed on the prevention of HIV/Aids, particularly among children aged 6–15. Unicef in association with the government has been formulating primary school curricula and developing four 'model' community-based pre-schools.
Literacy rate: 79 per cent adult rate; 89 per cent youth rate (15–24) (Unesco 2005).
Compulsory years: 6 to 11 years.
Enrolment rate: 84 per cent, primary school enrolment; 10 per cent for girls and 24 per cent for boys gross enrolment for secondary schools.
Pupils per teacher: 28 in primary schools.

Health

An outbreak of a polio related disease in 2006 prompted an international alert and increased vigilance in Botswana's northern border region with Namibia, Zimbabwe and Angola. Acute Flaccid Paralysis (AFP) is classed as a symptom which may lead to polio and can attack adults as well as children.

HIV/Aids
UNAids reported that Botswana was the first country to begin providing antiretroviral drugs through its public health system, courtesy of a bigger health budget and drug price reductions negotiated with pharmaceutical companies. In 2009, there were an estimated 320,000 people living with HIV.
HIV prevalence: 24.8 per cent aged 15–49 in 2009 (Unicef 2012), down from 37.3 per cent aged 15–49 in 2003, which had been one of the highest in the world.
Life expectancy: 53 years, 2010 (Unicef 2012)
Fertility rate/Maternal mortality rate: 2.8 births per woman 2010 (Unicef 2012)
Child (under 5 years) mortality rate (per 1,000): 53 per 1,000 live births (WHO 2012); 17 per cent of children under aged five are malnourished (World Bank).

Welfare

Botswana provides a non-contributory social pension for about 80,000 elderly citizens of 65 years and older, a flat-rate 151 Pula each month. This income has become an important source of revenue for families and communities and has had a significant impact on poverty reduction, as it alleviates the needs of more than just the elderly. Studies have shown that multi-generational households derive a 'safety-net' against economic hardship and these pensions support families where grandparents are fostering children of HIV/Aids parents. Pensioners are economically independent and valuable family members, this contradicts any perception that they may be a financial burden on their offspring.

Main cities

Gaborone (capital, estimated population 231,598 in 2012), Francistown (101,714), Molepolole (69,083), Mogoditshane (60,871), Maun (57,067), Selebi-Phikwe (49,777), Serowe (48,040), Kanye (45,683), Mochudi (45,162), Mahalapye (41,582).

Languages spoken
Official language/s
English (official); Setswana (national).

Media
The constitution guarantees the freedom of the press. However, since 2006 the government has been moving to enact the Mass Media Communications (MMC) bill, which journalists claim with inhibit reporting as the government-appointed press council will adjudicate complaints and recommend disciplinary sanctions where necessary.

Press
Low circulations limit newspapers to mainly urban areas.
Dailies: There are few daily newspaper, including *Daily News* (www.mcst.gov.bw/dailynews) is government-owned and the private *Mmegi* (www.mmegi.bw).
Weeklies: Most newspapers are published weekly, including the *Botswana Guardian*, *Botswana Gazette* (www.gazette.bw), *The Midweek Sun*, *Sunday Standard* (www.sundaystandard.info) and *The Voice* (www.thevoicebw.com), for news and entertainment.
Business: The government-owned *Daily Business* is an imprint of the *Daily News*.

Broadcasting
Radio: Radio is the primary medium for public news and information. In English and Setswana, the national, state-run station is Radio Botswana (www.dib.gov.bw), which also operates the commercial Botswana 2 (RB2). Commercial stations include Yarona FM (www.yaronafm.co.bw), Gabz FM (www.gabzfm.com) and Duma FM.
Television: The government-owned national, public broadcaster is Botswana TV (www.btv.gov.bw). The pay-to-view, Kenyan satellite station, Prime (www.gtv.tv) provides around a dozen channels.
National news agency: Bopa (Botswana Press Agency)

Economy
Botswana continues to depend off its large diamond reserves, the world's largest by value. In February 2014, the South African-based De Beers, the world's largest diamond mining company announced that in 2013 it had an increase of 112 per cent in it's operating profits from the 2012 figure, amounting to US$1 billion. Around two-thirds of all De Beers' diamonds came from Botswana. This was a reversal of Botswana's worst ever trade deficit of -US$753 million in 2009 (the trade balance had been US$1.6 billion in 2007). This was a result of the diamond trade being hit by the global economic crisis, leading to a fall in production from 33.6 million carats in 2007 to 17.7 million in 2009, and a subsequent decline in diamond revenue of 50 per cent. Mining and quarrying (mainly diamonds) constitutes around a third of GDP. However in 2010, the diamond trade picked up and recorded a growth in exports of 36.4 per cent (US$2.9 billion). In 2014, the diamond industry accounted for over a third of GDP, almost 80 per cent of export earnings and a third of the government's revenues.
In June 2010, the African Development Bank (AFDB) granted Botswana its largest ever assistance package of US$1.5 billion, to help offset falling global diamond prices. The government introduced a number of fiscal measures, including increasing value added tax from 10 per cent to 12 per cent, lowering public spending and raising non-mineral taxes.
GDP growth was 2.9 per cent in 2008, which dropped to -6 per cent in 2009 at the height of the global economic crisis. As world trade picked up, so did GDP growth, which grew to 7.2 per cent in 2010, before falling back to 5.9 per cent by 2013, and further to 5.2 per cent in 2014 reflecting modest overall growth in non-mining activities. The current account balance improved in 2014 to US$2.7 billion from US$1.5 billion in 2013.
Despite attempts to increase foreign involvement in non-mining sectors, through privatisation and other measures, diamonds are still the driving force of the economy, typically attracting the major share of foreign direct investment (FDI). Total inflow of FDI in 2013 was US$398 million (down from a record US$1.1 billion in 2011). FDI has since stabilised at US$393 million in 2014.
Botswana is a major tourist destination with the industry accounting for over 8.5 per cent of GDP in 2014. Agriculture, livestock, fisheries and hunting accounted for 1.9 per cent of GDP in 2014, but has fallen in importance due in large part to natural conditions (floods and droughts) and animal diseases and a lack of basic infrastructure that limits access for farmers to markets. Government backed programmes have improved and increased the productivity of commercial crops, cattle husbandry, dairy production and poultry rearing. In recent years, the government has invested heavily in communications and water technology.
The government made efforts to address the problems of not only the rise in the number of orphans of HIV/Aids victims but also those living with HIV, with the introduction of antiretroviral drugs in 2010, which has seen a decline in infection rates and longer (and more productive) lives for those in treatment. Financial aid has also been given to orphans.
In 2014, the UN Human Development Index (HDI) ranked Botswana 109 (out of 187) for national development in health, education and income. Since 2000, Botswana's progress has grown steadily and outstrips the improvements seen by other sub-Saharan African countries.
Received remittances in 2013 amounted to US$36 million, reflecting the lack of opportunity for workers overseas during the economic crisis. Received remittances increased slightly to a modest US$48.3 million in 2014.

External trade
As a member of the Southern African Customs Union (SACU) Botswana trades freely with the other members (Lesotho, Namibia, South Africa and Swaziland) and operates a common customs border with them; SACU presents a united negotiating entity to foreign traders and importers.
In 2009 international donors pledged US$1 billion to upgrade transport links across eastern and southern Africa, in an initiative to carry goods to market cheaper and faster. Not only will roads and rail links be improved, but also time-consuming official procedures will be streamlined for efficiency.

Imports
Principal imports are electricity (80 per cent of the country's requirements), vehicles and machinery, electrical and transport equipment, food products and consumer goods, chemical and rubber products, textiles and tobacco.
Main sources: South Africa (63.2 per cent of total in 2014), Namibia (12.1 per cent), Canada (10.0 per cent).

Exports
Principal exports are diamonds (typically 70–80 per cent of total) and copper-nickel ore, soda-ash, textiles, meat and meat products.
Main destinations: Belgium (25.8 per cent of total in 2014), India (14.9 per cent), South Africa (11.8 per cent).

Agriculture
Farming
Total agricultural land is 56.7 million hectares of which 45.2 per cent is pasture and 0.4 per cent arable. Agriculture makes up only 1.9 per cent of total GDP. Production is divided between small, traditional farms and around 360 large-scale commercial units (including Barolong Farms, Pandamantenga and Tuli Block).
The climate and poor soil are suitable for extensive ranching, with the result that livestock produce accounts for about 80 per cent of marketed output. In the past, rearing of livestock has been hampered by frequent outbreaks of foot-and-mouth disease – now largely controlled – and more recently by drought. However, the livestock sector has predominated due to

a lack of cultivatable land – only 5 per cent of the land is suitable for arable production – in a country that is mostly arid and contributes around 80 per cent of agriculture's share of GDP. Beef is one of the country's main exports and the Botswana Meat Commission (BMC) operates three abattoirs with a combined capacity of up to 2,000 head of cattle and smaller stock every day.

Government aims for self-sufficiency in basic foodstuffs, such as maize, millet, beans and sorghum, are far from being realised. There is potential for investment in adding value to primary products through increasing processing capacity. There is also a growing market in farm machinery, irrigation and water pumps.

Fishing

Botswana has a small freshwater fishing industry with annual average catches amounting to 2,000 tonnes.

Forestry

About 25 per cent of the total land area has forest cover. Another 20 per cent of its terrain is classified as wooded land. There are several large game reserves in the west, including the Central Kalahari Game Reserve, the largest protected area in Africa. There are no large-scale forest industries in the country. Some varieties of woods are used for fuel consumption and for the manufacture of wooden handicrafts.

Industry and manufacturing

The government's industrial strategy is geared towards export-oriented manufacture and it is keen on diversifying the industrial base away from the minerals sector.

The development of the manufacturing sector, which represents about 5 per cent of GDP, has been limited due to the small internal market and the problem of competing with South Africa where the sector is more advanced. However, Botswana continues to advance in those elements of manufacturing which give more added value to produce from the mineral and farming sectors.

The construction sector has benefitted from rapid urbanisation and the demand for low-cost housing, although expansion has been limited due to a shortage of building materials and annual growth has declined to around 4 per cent.

The Local Enterprise Agency (LEA) is used by the government to develop a business environment that is conducive to the creation of domestically owned firms in the manufacturing and services sectors.

Tourism

Botswana offers visitors some of the continent's biggest and best wildlife sanctuaries, including the Central Kalahari Game Reserve and the Okavango Delta. The cultural attractions include Tsodilo, with its ancient human rock paintings, included on the Unesco World Heritage List. Tourism is used to promote craft production and traditional foods and dance.

In an effort to diversify the economy, stimulate local commerce and create employment, in the early 2000s, tourism was identified as a major alternative industry to mining. Its role in the economy has grown from an estimated 5.5 per cent of GDP in 2001 to an estimated 8.5 per cent in 2014 and in total is responsible for 10.1 per cent of employment (69,500 jobs). Around 1.9 million people visit Botswana annually, of which around 324,000 are day visitors from neighbouring countries or visitors on holiday and based in other countries. Visitor exports in 2014 were US$956 million.

In 2009, the government recognised that Botswana was perceived as an expensive tourist destination due to the emphasis on 'low-volume, high-cost' tourism. Although it wished to defend its share of this market, while worldwide tourism was in decline it planned to market Botswana as an alternative medium-cost destination while maintaining 'sustainable tourism'. As such, capital investment in travel and tourism has increased from US$80 million in 2009 to US$180 million in 2014, 7.8 per cent of total investment.

Tourism infrastructure is being upgraded, particularly in the Chobe and Moremi Parks.

On 29 November 2012 the government announced that from January 2014 commercial hunting will be banned, due to the declining number of wildlife species.

Mining

Exploitation of rich mineral reserves, notably diamonds, provided the key to Botswana's rapid economic growth, with the mining sector accounting for up to 50 per cent of GDP and employing 7 per cent of the workforce. Botswana's diamond reserves are expected to last until 2030 at current production rates.

Diamonds, together with copper and nickel production, are the main focus of prospecting activities and account for most of the country's export revenue. Botswana is the largest producer of diamonds, and second-largest producer of gem diamonds, in the world, after Russia. All diamond mining is carried out by De Beers Botswana Mining Company (Debswana), a company jointly owned by the government and UK-based De Beers of South Africa. De Beers produces 60 per cent of the world's diamond output, a significant proportion of which comes from Botswana.

As global sales of diamonds fell two mines – Damtshaa and Orapa No 2 – operated by Debswana, a company jointly owned by the government and De Beers, were closed for 2009, to be re-opened when demand picks up.

Hydrocarbons

There are no known domestic oil or natural gas reserves; all refined petroleum products are imported from South Africa. Botswana has the largest known coal reserves in Africa – proven reserves are 17 billion tonnes, total reserves are estimated at about 50 billion tonnes, although of low quality. Coal output from the Morupule coalmine, which is mainly used in domestic power stations, is typically around one million tonnes per annum.

Energy

Total installed electricity generating capacity is 132MW (all thermal), producing around 430 million kilowatt-hours (kWh), while consumption is estimated at 3.16 billion kWh. Botswana relies on imported electricity of 2.73 billion kWh, chiefly from South Africa.

There is potential for hydroelectric generation and solar power. Half of total primary energy requirements are met by biomass, mainly fuelwood and charcoal.

Financial markets

In 2006 the African-owned, Pan African commodities and derivatives exchange (PACDEX Africa) was given the go-ahead by the African Union, the UN Conference on Trade and Development, the Pan African Commodities Platform and Botswana's finance ministry and services.

Stock exchange

Botswana Stock Exchange

Banking and insurance

Of the established commercial banks, the largest is Barclays Bank of Botswana, which was launched in 1950 and has approximately 42 branches and agencies. It has 19.6 per cent local equity with the rest held by the UK's Barclays Bank. Standard Chartered Bank of Botswana has been operating in the country since 1897 and has 14 branches and four agences.

Central bank

Bank of Botswana

Main financial centre

Gaborone

Time

GMT plus two hours

Geography

Botswana is a landlocked country in southern Africa, with South Africa to the south and east, Zimbabwe to the north-east and Namibia to the west and north. A short section of the northern frontier adjoins Zambia.

Botswana is a flat, arid country, 84 per cent of which is occupied by the Kalahari *sandveld*. The desert occupies most of the northern, central and western regions. There are some shallow valleys and low hills, notably the Tsodilo Hills, rising to 410m, located in the north-west. Other parts of the landscape, mainly along the south-eastern borders and the far north-west, are dotted with outcrops of rock and low hills.

There is little surface water outside the Okavango delta and the Chobe river areas in the north. The Okavango river rises in Angola and forms a 15,000km system of water channels, swamps, lagoons and islands, the largest inland delta in the world.

The majority of the population live in the south-eastern *hardveld*, which has a slightly higher elevation than the rest of the country. The rainfall is more reliable, but the agricultural potential remains low. The highest point in Botswana, Otse Mountain, which reaches 1,491m, is near Lobatse. 38 per cent of the country is given over to wildlife areas and national parks, including two-thirds of the Okavango delta.

Hemisphere

Southern

Climate

Sub-tropical, with hot summers and dry winters. Temperatures range from about 5–23 degrees Celsius (C) in July to 18–31 degrees C in January.

Entry requirements

Passports

Required by all. Passports should be valid for at least 12 months.

Visa

Required by all except citizens of North America, Western Europe, Australasia and Japan, plus transit passengers. All other visitors should confirm requirements from consular sections of local embassy before travelling.

A proposed tourist *univisa* (a single visa to visit all 15-member states of SADC: Angola, Botswana, DRC, Lesotho, Madagascar, Malawi, Mauritius, Mozambique, Namibia, South Africa, Seychelles, Swaziland, Tanzania, Zambia and Zimbabwe) is expected to be in use by 2013. Visitors should check with the appropriate consulates to confirm start of *univisas* and their scope before beginning a tour of southern Africa.

Business visas should be accompanied by letters of invitation.

Currency advice/regulations

Import and export of foreign currency is unlimited, provided it is declared on arrival.

Import of local currency is unlimited but export is restricted to P50.

Customs

Member of Southern African Customs Union, therefore virtually no restrictions on movement of goods from South Africa, Namibia, Lesotho and Swaziland.

Health (for visitors)

Mandatory precautions

Yellow fever vaccination certificate required for visitors arriving from infected areas.

Advisable precautions

hepatitis A and B, tetanus, polio and typhoid immunisations are advisable.

Anti-malarial prophylaxis is recommended for visitors to northern regions. Insect repellant is a necessary precaution. A medical examination is advisable within 10 days if bitten by insects while visiting game reserves, in case of sleeping sickness.

AIDS infection rates are high throughout the country but particularly in Francistown and Gaborone.

Food, water, swimming and bathing precautions should be observed.

Medical insurance is essential.

Hotels

First-class hotels available in all main towns. Generally advisable to book in advance – essential at weekends and during public holidays.

Credit cards

American Express, Access/MasterCard, Barclaycard/Visa, Diners.

Public holidays (national)

Fixed dates

1–3 Jan (New Year), 1 Jul (Sir Seretse Khama Day), 18–19 Jul (President's Day), 30 Sep–1 Oct (Botswana Day), 25–27 Dec (Christmas Holiday).

Variable dates

Good Friday, Easter Monday, Ascension Day, President's Day (third Tue and Wed in Jul).

Working hours

Banking

Mon–Fri: 0900–1530; Sat: 0815–1045.

Business

Mon–Fri, Apr–Oct: 0800–1300, 1400–1700; Mon–Fri, Oct–Apr: 0730–1630.

Government

Mon–Fri: 0730–1230, 1345–1630.

Shops

Mon–Fri: 0830–1300, 1400–1700; Sat: 0830–1300.

Telecommunications

Telephone/fax

Land lines connect the 12 main towns by microwave links. Botswana is directly connected to South Africa, Zimbabwe, Zambia and Namibia.

Mobile/cell phones

Mascom and Vista Cellular provide CSM 900 network, though coverage is limited to main towns.

Social customs/useful tips

A lightweight or tropical suit should be worn for meetings, casual clothes are acceptable at other times.

Most people rise early in the morning and nightlife is limited.

The noun for the people of Botswana is: singular, Motswana; plural, Batswana.

Getting there

Air

National airline: Air Botswana

International airport/s: The Sir Seretse Khama international airport (GBE) is 15km from Gabarone. Facilities include left luggage, bank, bar, restaurant, post office, shops and car hire.

There are no regular bus services to and from the airport but several hotels run minibuses

Taxis are available to the city centre.

Other airport/s: Francistown (FRW), 6km from city; Maun (MUB), Kasane (BBK) and Selebi-Phikwe (PKW).

Airport tax: US$20.

Surface

Road: Bitumised roads link Botswana with South Africa in the south, and Zambia and Zimbabwe in the north.

The Trans-Kalahari highway provides a shorter all-tarred road link between Namibia and South Africa's Gauteng province, crossing south-west Botswana, via Kanye and Ghanzi.

Botswanan border posts are at Ngoma Bridge and Shakawe. The road from Namibia, via Shakawe border post, is paved all the way to Maun.

Rail: There are good connections between South Africa and Zimbabwe with Botswana. Passengers are advised to take their own refreshments as the alternatives are limited. There are three classes, and sleeping compartments are available.

First-class cars have comfortable reclining seats.

Plans to extend the network include the extension of the line into Namibia, following the construction of the Limpopo line from Zimbabwe to Mozambique.

Water: A car ferry operates across the Zambezi River to Zambia.

Getting about

National transport

Air: Air travel is the best way to get around Botswana.

Regular flights operated by Air Botswana connect Gaborone, Francistown, Maun and Kasane. Air Botswana and other operators provide direct charter flights to airstrips throughout the country.

Road: There are around 20,000km of well-developed roads, of which some 5,000km are tarred, the rest being gravelled or sand tracks.

Most major towns are connected by good roads. Travellers to Okavango should note that the road to Maun is tarred, but it is impossible to travel further without use of an overland vehicle.

Buses: Bus services remain underdeveloped. Services run between Gaborone and Francistown, going on to Nata and Maun.

Rail: Botswana's railway system consists of 641km of main line plus three branch lines – between Morupule and Palapye, Selebi-Pikwe and Serule, and between Sua Pan and Francistown.

The main Cape Town (South Africa)-Bulawayo (Zimbabwe) railway runs for over 700km through Botswana, linking several towns. This section is operated by Botswana Railways, along with freight-only lines to Selebi-Pikwe and Sua Pan.

Botswana Railways has lost a great deal of freight business to road transporters. It has established the Gaborone Container Terminal (Gabcon), a dry port facility acting as a container terminal, specifically for locally based importers and exporters.

City transport

Taxis: Taxis are available in the capital. Tips are not common; if offered, 10 per cent would be acceptable.

Car hire

National driving licence (in English) or international driving licence, valid for six months, is required. Speed limits: 120kph on main roads, 60kph in built-up areas. Seat-belts must be worn. Facilities are available to hire Avis car in South Africa and deposit it in Botswana, or vice versa. Hire cars are only available for driving from Botswana to Zimbabwe or Zambia by special prior arrangement.

BUSINESS DIRECTORY

The addresses listed below are a selection only. While World of Information makes every endeavour to check these addresses, we cannot guarantee that changes have not been made, especially to telephone numbers and area codes. We would welcome any corrections.

Telephone area codes

The international direct dialling (IDD) code for Botswana is +267, followed by subscriber's number:

Francistown: 24
Gaborone: 31, 35, 36, 39
Jwaneng: 58
Kasane: 62
Lobatse: 53
Maun: 68
Selebe-Pikwe: 26

Chambers of Commerce

Botswana Chamber of Commerce and Industry, PO Box 00290, Gaborone (tel: 359-292; fax: 372-467).

Botswana Confederation of Commerce, Industry and Manpower, Boccim House, Old Lobatse Road , PO Box 432, Gaborone (tel: 353-459; fax: 373-142; e-mail: boccim@info.bw).

Francistown Chamber of Commerce and Industry, PO Box 196, Francistown (tel: 241-2149; fax: 241-2175; e-mail: boccim@info.bw).

Banking

Barclays Bank of Botswana, PO Box 478, Barclays House, Plot 8842 Khama Crescent, Gaborone (tel: 352-041; fax: 313-672).

National Development Bank, PO Box 225, Development House, Plot 1123, The Mall, Gaborone (tel: 352-801; fax: 374-446).

Standard Chartered Bank Botswana Ltd, PO Box 496, 5th Floor, Standard House, The Mall, Gaborone (tel: 360-1500, 353-111; fax: 372-933, 353-446).

Central bank

Bank of Botswana, Private Bag 154, Khama Crescent, Gaborone (tel: 360-6000; fax: 391-6000; e-mail: webmaster@bob.bw).

Stock exchange

Botswana Stock Exchange, www.bse.co.bw

Travel information

Air Botswana, Sir Seretse Khama Airport, PO Box 92, Gaborone (tel: 395-2812; fax: 397-4802; commercial@airbotswana.co.bw).

Ministry of tourism

Department of Tourism, Ministry of Environment, Wildlife and Tourism, Private Bag 0047, Gaborone (tel: 395-3024; fax: 390-8675; e-mail: botswanatourism@gov.bw).

Ministries

Ministry of Agriculture, Private Bag 003, Gaborone (tel: 350-500; fax: 356-027).

Ministry of Commerce and Industry, Private Bag 004, Gaborone (tel: 360-1200; fax: 371-539).

Ministry of External Affairs, Private Bag 00368, Gaborone (tel: 360-0700; fax: 313-366).

Ministry of Finance and Development Planning, Private Bag 008, Gaborone (tel: 350-100, 355-272; fax: 356-086).

Ministry of Mineral Resources and Water Affairs, Private Bag 0018, Gaborone (tel; 352-452; fax: 372-733).

Ministry of Works, Transport and Communications, Private Bag 007, Gaborone (tel: 358-500, 355-563, 355-303; fax: 358-500, 313-303).

Office of the President, Private Bag 001, Gaborone (tel: 350-800).

Other useful addresses

Botswana Development Corporation Ltd, Private Bag 160, Gaborone (tel: 351-790; fax: 305-375).

Botswana Diamond Company (Pty) Ltd, Debswana House, The Mall, Gaborone (tel: 351-131; fax; 356-110).

Botswana Enterprise Development Unit (promotes industrial & rural development), PO Box 0014, Gaborone.

Botswana Meat Commission, Private Bag 4, Lobatse (tel: 330-321; fax: 330-530).

Botswana Power Corporation, Motlakase House, Macheng Way, PO Box 48, Gaborone (tel: 360-300; fax: 373-563).

Botswana Telecommunications Corporation, PO Box 700, Gaborone (tel: 358-000).

Botswanan Embassy (USA), Suite 7M, 3400 International Drive, NW, Washington DC 20008 (tel: 202-244-4990; fax: 202-244-4164)

Debswana Diamond Company, Gaborone (tel: 351-131; fax: 356-110).

Department of Geological Survey, Private Bag 14, Lobatse (tel: 330-0327; fax: 332-013).

Department of Information and Broadcasting, Private Bag 0060, Gaborone (tel: 365-8000, 365-3081; fax: 357-138, 301-675; e-mail: ib.publicity@info.bw).

Department of Mines, Private Bag 0049, Gaborone (tel: 352-641; fax: 352-141).

Department of Trade and Investment Promotion (TIPA), Private Bag 004, Gaborone (tel: 351-790; fax: 305-375).

Stockbrokers Botswana Ltd, Ground Floor, Barclays House, Khama Crescent, Post Bag 00417, Gaborone (tel: 357-900; fax: 357-901).

Water Utilities Corporation, Private Bag 00276, Gaborone (tel: 352-521).

National news agency: Bopa (Botswana Press Agency)(email: dailynews@gov.bw; internet: www.gov.bw/cgi-bin/news).

Internet sites

Africa Business Network: www.ifc.org/abn

AllAfrica.com: www.allafrica.com

African Development Bank: www.afdb.org

Mbendi AfroPaedia (information on companies, countries, industries and stock exchanges in Africa): mbendi.co.za

Brazil

Poor President Rousseff; having scraped home with an uncomfortably narrow majority (three per cent of the vote) in the 2014 Presidential election, the first few months of 2015 saw things go from bad to worse. The President's approval ratings appeared to be in free fall, slumping to a lowly 13 per cent by March 2015, the lowest ever seen for a President with the exception of the subsequently impeached Fernando Collor in 1992. Dilma Rousseff's supporters could only wonder how things could possibly have gone so wrong. How had their one-time firebrand heroine gone from being the scourge of Brazil's establishment to preside over a litany of unparalleled malfeasance. The humiliating defeat of the nation's football team by Germany had come to symbolise the moral and professional distance that existed between Europe's largest economy and its Latin American counterpart.

Street-wise

In mid-March 2015 an estimated million plus protestors took to the streets in unprecedented fashion. Not only Brazil's right-wing, but also its bourgeoisie and its working classes had taken to the streets in a way unlike anything the country has seen since the return to democracy three decades earlier. The marches and rallies were not confined to Rio de Janeiro, Brasilia and São Paulo; all over the country (some reports suggested in as many as 100 cities and towns) voices of extreme discontent were raised, predictably focussing on the visible aspects of government and business corruption and the manifest effects of a stagnant economy. This was an impressive expression of discontent, particularly with President Dilma Rousseff, but also with her centre-left Partido dos Trabalhadores (PT) (Workers' Party) the

KEY FACTS

Official name: Republica Federativa do Brasil (Federative Republic of Brazil)

Head of State: President Dilma Rousseff (PT) (from 1 Jan 2011, re-elected 26 Oct 2014)

Head of government: President Dilma Rousseff (PT) (from 1 Jan 2011, re-elected 26 Oct 2014))

Ruling party: Coalition Coligação Com a Força do Povo (With the Strength of the People) with 304 out of 513 seats, led by Partido dos Trabalhadores (PT) (Workers' Party) with eight other political parties (elected 5 Oct 2014)

Area: 8,511,965 square km

Population: 202.77 million (2014) (190,755,799; 2010, census figure)

Capital: Brasília

Official language: Portuguese

Currency: Real (R$) (plural reais)

Exchange rate: R$3.80 per US$ (Sep 2015)

GDP per capita: US$11,604 (2014)

GDP real growth: 0.14% (2014)

GDP: US$2,353.03 billion (2014)

Labour force: 24.42 million (2014)

Unemployment: 4.84% (2014)*

Inflation: 6.33% (2014)

Oil production: 2.35 million bpd (2014)

Natural gas production: 20.00 billion cum (2014)

Balance of trade: -US$6.25 billion (2014)*

* estimated figure

stagnant economy and the high-profile, wide-ranging corruption scandal at the state-run oil company, Petróleo Brasileiro SA (Petrobras).

The demonstrations probably would have been impossible to organise and co-ordinate 10, even five years earlier. The acceptance and penetration of social media in Brazil makes it among the world's leading users of Facebook and Twitter. This made it much easier for the groups behind the protest such as the Free Brazil Movement and the Come to the Street activists. Some of those protesting were also calling for the President's impeachment, others for a radical clean-up of Brazilian politics and politicians. Reportedly, some protestors even sought a return to a military government. But by far the greater majority seemed to hold more moderate positions, advocating improvements in health services and education and protesting about higher bus fares, inflation and levels of taxation. The generally moderate tenor of the demonstrations was attributed in part to the increased higher involvement of its middle classes. Whatever sympathy and respect had been initially awarded the President had, by the beginning of 2015, largely evaporated.

The Petrobras Affair

The March protest showed how Ms Rousseff found herself dangerously close to impeachment. In mid-2014 Brazilian business and political circles had been rocked by detailed allegations made by Paulo Roberto Costa a jailed former director of Petrobras, that commissions, averaging three per cent, had regularly been paid by the oil giant to as many as 40 Brazilian politicians. As the affair unravelled, things got steadily worse, as it transpired that not only politicians, but also numbers of contractors had been involved. Ms Rousseff, re-elected President in December 2014, had presided over the Petrobras board of directors for some seven years after 2003 until her first term as President in 2010. In that time estimates put the scale of embezzlement as high as US$800 million, a large proportion of which ended up in the coffers of the ruling PT, headed by Ms Rousseff. As a result, some 50 members of the PT had been charged with corruption and faced criminal prosecutions. Many Brazilians found it hard to believe that Ms Rousseff had known nothing of the source of her electoral funds.

In many respects Ms Rousseff only had herself and her former boss, Luiz Inácio Lula da Silva ('Lula') to blame. Between them, they had overseen legislation that automatically granted Petrobras a 30 per cent shareholding in any new Brazilian oil field on top of sole operating rights. The underlying government motivation might have been to ensure that the country itself benefited from the predicted oil boom. According to the official slogan, the oil may have been *Nosso* (Ours). But it soon became apparent that the new legislation had meant that the proceeds and the kickbacks went to those who the PT government wished to benefit. Given the size of the fields to be developed and the ancillary activities – refining, shipbuilding, exploration equipment and so on – that went with them, the legislation had created an unwieldy industrial empire that not only owed its existence to the PT, but was also prepared to respond to PT dictats. The norm for the party 'levy' seemed to be 3 per cent of the value of all contracts . The fallout from the scandal was not merely political. Petrobras' own results had announced a massive asset write-off – some R$88 billion (US$23 billion) – which had not gone down well with its shareholders, faced with an 80 per cent drop in the value of their shares. Nor was it just the company's own management that was arraigned – managers and directors of those Petrobras contractors who had also accepted kickbacks also found themselves on the wrong side of the law – to the anger of their shareholders. Thus, the Petrobras brand had come to be synonymous with the chronic corruption from which Brazil had sought to distance itself.

In pure national balance sheet terms, the knock-on effects were quite horrendous. Two of the four refineries under construction were abandoned, at what the London *Economist* reported to be a cost of US$1 billion. Equally embarrassingly, according to the same report, a company cosily set up by Petrobras to construct and lease back the drilling rigs was also about to go bust.

Views of the economy

Following the 2008 global financial crisis, Brazil's PT leadership had proudly claimed that the country had managed to avoid the worst of the crisis. The figures seemed to support these claims, as the economy notched up growth rates around 3 per cent and unemployment hovered around the 8 per cent mark. In its mid-December 2014 report *Economic Report –Brazil's Economy* the Confederação Nacional da Indústria (CNI) (Brazilian National Confederation of Industry) noted that restoring confidence in the tattered economic policy and increasing competitiveness were decisive if Brazil was to accelerate its economic growth rate. According to a CNI forecast, the economy was set to grow by only one per cent in 2015, at least a higher figure than the

KEY INDICATORS — Brazil

	Unit	2011	2012	2013	2014	**2015
Population	m	*194.93	196.53	201.03	202.77	*204,451.00
Gross domestic product (GDP)	US$bn	2,492.90	2,247.74	2,391.03	2,353.03	*2,393.00
GDP per capita	US$	12,789	11,437	11,894	0	*9,312
GDP real growth	%	2.7	1.0	2.7	0.1	*-1.0
GNP per capita	US$	0	0	0	11,604	0
Inflation	%	6.6	5.4	6.2	6.3	*7.8
Unemployment	%	5.8	5.5	5.4	*4.8	*5.9
Oil output	'000 bpd	2,193.0	2,149.0	2,114.0	2,346.0	–
Natural gas output	bn cum	16.7	17.4	21.3	20.0	–
Coal output	mtoe	2.4	2.2	2.8	3.2	–
Exports (fob) (goods)	US$m	256,040.0	242,580.0	242,179.0	224,645.0	–
Imports (fob) (goods)	US$m	226,233.0	223,149.0	239,626.0	230,893.0	–
Balance of trade	US$m	29,807.0	19,431.0	2,553.0	-6,248.0	–
Current account	US$m	-52,480.0	-54,249.0	-81,227.0	-91,289.0	*-69,737.0
Total reserves minus gold	US$m	344,377.0	369,566.0	356,214.0	360,965.0	–
Foreign exchange	US$m	337,302.0	362,097.0	349,028.0	–	–
Exchange rate	per US$	1.62	2.06	2.40	2.66	–

* estimated figure ** forecast figure

estimated growth of 0.1 per cent for 2014. The industrial sector, which was estimated to have ended 2014 with a 1.5 per cent contraction, was forecast to expand by one per cent in 2015.

The CNI considered that levels of both consumption and investment had been adversely affected by the increased interest rate and the government's fiscal arrangements. This, in turn, suggested that in 2015 average household consumption would grow by 0.7 per cent – half the 2014 rate – and following a contraction of 6.7 per cent in 2014, investment levels would plateau. The CNI report also suggested that exports would fall; the drop in prices would outweigh any increases in volume, causing a net fall of 2 per cent, to around US$219.5 billion. Imports also looked likely to fall from their 2014 levels, to US$212 billion, resulting in a marginally positive trade balance of US$7.5 billion.

The CNI report also underlined that the focus of Brazil's economic policy in 2015 needed to be the recovery of some sort of stability. Its forecasts estimated that the government might reach its target of a 1.2 per cent primary surplus by controlling expenses and increasing revenue by the elimination of some overly generous tax exemptions. Were that to be the case, the nominal deficit might fall from 5.4 per cent to 4.2 per cent of gross domestic product (GDP). Net debt was projected to be equivalent to 37.6 per cent of GDP.

According to the CNI, interest rates would continue rising and could reach an annual 12.5 per cent by the end of 2015, not much higher than the 11.75 per cent seen in 2014. Inflation was forecast to stay around 6.2 per cent, almost reaching the upper inflation target limits, but still below the 6.4 per cent estimated figure for 2014. The CNI expected the trend of Brazil's real devaluation in relation to the dollar to be maintained in 2015. The dollar rate in December 2015, was forecast to be R$3.70, with an annual average of R$3.60.

Growth?

The CNI study noted that after the frustrating performance of the economy in 2014, Brazil had two challenges to face: restoring the macro-economic fundamentals and increasing competitiveness. The CNI recommendation was blunt: 'There is no choice between these two goals. Both are essential for the recovery of sustained growth.'

The restoration of Brazil's economic fundamentals depended on a fiscal adjustment that allowed for the generation of consistent surpluses and the control of public debt. In the view of the CNI, it was essential to respect the inflation targets, re-balance external accounts and recover the competitiveness of Brazilian products.

The Banco Central do Brasil (BCB)'s Index of Economic Activity, or IBC-Br had lowered its original growth estimate for 2014 as well as the forecast figure for 2015. The 2014 growth estimate dropped to 0.16 per cent from 0.18 per cent and the forecast for 2015 was cut from 0.73 per cent to 0.69 per cent. The GDP growth estimates were based on the IBC's weekly survey of analysts from some 100 private financial institutions on the state of the national economy.

The survey maintained its inflation estimates for 2014 and its forecasts for 2015. The expectation was that the end 2014 inflation rate would be 6.38 per cent and that for prices would rise by 6.5 per cent in 2015. The government's inflation target for 2014 had been 4.5 per cent (it was 6.3 per cent), with a 2 per cent band that allows a top rate of 6.5 per cent. In 2013 inflation had reached 5.91 per cent.

Brazil's currency, the real, fell to its lowest in almost ten years in late 2014, as the vagaries of domestic politics negated the central bank's currency-intervention programme. Investor confidence wobbled as the US dollar hit the R$2.76. The dollar rose by 4.42 per cent in December 2014 and by 13.9 per cent for the year. Affecting the exchange rate were the fall of the Russian rouble, the United States' Federal Reserve's (Fed) termination of its dollar injection plan and the steady drop of oil prices.

After the 2014 re-election of President Rousseff, the Central Bank Monetary Policy Committee (COPOM) increased basic interest rates to 11.75 per cent per year. This move was supposed to prop up the real, by widening the difference between Brazilian rates against those of the United States and consequently make Brazil more attractive to international investors. The desired result did not happen.

IMF Reservations

In its April 2015 assessment of the Brazilian economy, the International Monetary Fund (IMF) noted that in 2015, the new government has been introducing a series of measures to strengthen macro-economic policies and restore credibility. In the view of the IMF, a 'determined implementation' of these measures should help both to restore confidence and to foster a recovery in growth and investment 'in due course'. It was perhaps this open ended projection by the IMF that gave most cause for concern.

The IMF also noted that Brazil's growth had decelerated in recent years. The boost derived from decade-old reforms, expanding labour income and the favourable external conditions which boosted consumption and credit-led growth as well as underpinning a sustained reduction in poverty, had lost steam. Investment had been sluggish, reflecting the loss in competitiveness, a worsening business environment and lower commodity prices. Consumption had also moderated, despite strong wage increases, as job creation had withered and financial conditions tightened, affecting both household income and consumer confidence.

In the view of the IMF, recent years had seen Brazil's headline and core inflation approach the upper-edges of the inflation tolerance band, following sustained wage cost pressures, lingering indexation practices and, more recently, the continued drought. The longer-term inflation expectations had risen since 2011, although they had edged down since the end of 2014. The IMF welcomed the fact that modest increases in regulated energy and fuel prices had helped hold back overall inflation for some time. The scenario had changed, however, as overdue adjustments in regulated prices were underway, while inflation in market-determined prices was moderating, reflecting tighter financial conditions and subdued economic activity. The IMF also noted that new inflation pressures were emerging from the real's nominal depreciation.

The CBC had raised the monetary policy rate 375 basis points to 11 per cent between April 2013 and April 2014. This tightening was relaxed between May to September 2014. However, between October 2014 and March 2015, the rate was again increased by a cumulative 175 basis points to prevent the possible effect of currency depreciation and the anticipated increases in regulated prices.

Continuing to comment on what were a string of economic negatives, the IMF observed that despite weakening domestic demand, the current account deficit had reached 4.2 per cent of GDP in 2014, up from 2.4 per cent of GDP in 2012. The deterioration reflected the worsening terms of trade, a drop in exports to Argentina and – perhaps ironically – an increase in fuel imports triggered by the drought. The recent depreciation of the real against the US dollar, arising in some measure from the strength of the dollar, had not translated into increased competitiveness in global markets. Persistently high unit labour costs continued to erode competitiveness. Consequently, Brazil's external position was weaker than had been hoped for, with the real still effectively overvalued at end-2014.

Brazil's international reserves were high, according to the IMF and capital flows had remained stable. Direct foreign investment (FDI) financed more than 70 per cent of the current account deficit in 2014 and portfolio inflows had remained buoyant. At about US$362 billion, gross international reserves were well above the IMF's reserve benchmarks.

Reassuringly, the IMF considered that the Brazilian banking system's soundness indicators remained favourable. Although private sector leverage and past expansion of public bank lending were seen as potential sources of stress, the banks' indicators were generally encouraging, indicating adequate levels of capitalisation and provisioning.

In 2013, according to IMF figures, the non-financial public sector primary balance declined to 1.9 per cent of GDP, below its 2.3 per cent target despite one-off revenue measures. Coming on top of the tax breaks introduced over 2012–13, rapid real expenditure growth and slowing revenues reduced the primary fiscal balance of the non-financial public sector to -0.6 per cent of GDP in 2014, despite one-off measures of about 0.5 per cent of GDP. Lending to public banks also edged back up. As a result, non-financial public sector gross debt increased to 71 per cent of GDP. Declining growth and weak fiscal performance affected Brazil's sovereign credit rating in 2014. Standard & Poor's cut Brazil's credit rating to BBB- in March 2014, its first downgrade since July 2002. In September 2014, Moody's also revised Brazil's sovereign rating outlook to negative.

In January 2015, the government began introducing a series of measures to strengthen macro-economic policies and restore credibility. The lynchpin of the new strategy was an ambitious fiscal adjustment to bring the primary surplus of the non-financial public sector to 1.2 per cent of GDP in 2015 and to at least 2 per cent of GDP in 2016 and 2017.

The IMF forecast negative output growth of 1 per cent in 2015, with some drag from tighter fiscal and monetary policies and from the cuts in investment by Petrobras adding to the downward momentum in activity carried over from 2014. In the view of the IMF, the successful implementation of the fiscal adjustment strategy should strengthen confidence and help reinvigorate investment in the latter part of 2015, providing – perhaps optimistically – the basis for a return to positive growth in 2016. The IMF concluded its summary assessment by pointing out that the outlook was subject to significant downward risks, including the drought-induced rationing of energy and water, further possible fallout from the Petrobras case (See below) and a more adverse international environment

Energy

The Brazilian government had proudly in 2007 the discovery of massive offshore oil deposits that gave Brazil the prospect of becoming a major oil exporter. If ever there was a mixed blessing, the oil and gas discoveries were so on an unprecedented scale. Corruption and scandal apart, most of the calculations made in the heady atmosphere of 2007 had, by 2015, been long discarded. Whistling in the wind, the head of Brazil's National Petroleum Agency, Magda Chambriard, boldly announced that Brazil's oil production projects remained 'robust' even as international prices for crude continued to tumble. She underlined that the pre-salt projects of Brazil along its coast could resist prices as low as US$60 a barrel, saying that 'I don't know of any pre-salt project that cannot resist the US$70 or even the US$60 mark. We still have very robust projects. When we're talking of projects with investments of US$5 billion, we are also referring to projects with large scale profits. We have big lungs.' Those lungs would need to be big as Ms Chambriard, faced with a nightmare scenario of imprisoned civil servants and oil executives, abandoned refineries and price uncertainties, looked likely to be taking big breaths on a daily basis

As outlined above, Petrobras is the sole operator for the pre-salt reserves and has a guaranteed minimum participation of 30 per cent in each exploration bloc – in partnership with major foreign firms including Shell and Total and two Chinese companies. However the multi-billion dollar corruption scandal meant that Petrobras faced a funding nightmare for the projected development of the deep-water oil deposits on which so many hopes were pinned.

The deposits were conservatively estimated to hold 100 billion barrels of recoverable oil, more than double Brazil's previously identified oil reserves. It had been hoped that the find could double Petrobras' daily production to five million barrels by 2020. The only snag is that the deposits are trapped below salt formations under the ocean floor 230 kilometres off the Brazilian coast. Extracting oil from them requires cutting edge – and expensive – technologies.

Originally, Petrobras had been committed to investing no less than US$82 billion in the development of the pre-salt deposits in the period up to 2018, as part of a US$237 billion five-year investment plan. However, by the end of 2014 only one field, Lula, had reached the production phase. The rare piece of good news was that production from the Lula field costs as little as US$9.00 per barrel, according to official Brazilian estimates.

According to the United States government Energy Information Administration (EIA), preliminary statistics at the end of 2014 showed Brazil to be the 10th largest energy producer in the world in 2013. In addition, Brazil had increased its total energy production, particularly oil and ethanol. According to the governmental Empresa de Pesquisa Energética (EPE) (Energy Research Company), ethanol production represented 19 per cent of Brazil's total energy production compared to 15 per cent a decade ago. Oil remained at an average of 41 per cent of total energy production as total energy production increased 36 per cent in the past decade. Increasing domestic oil production has been a long-term goal of the Brazilian government and it was hoped – with reservations – that recent discoveries of large offshore, pre-salt oil deposits could transform Brazil into one of the largest oil producers in the world. Cynical observers would point out that Brazil has always been and possibly always will be, the country of the future.

It almost goes without saying that the state-controlled Petrobras is the dominant participant in Brazil's oil sector, holding important positions in all areas of activity. Petrobras held a monopoly on all oil-related activities in Brazil until 1997, when the government opened the sector to competition. Royal Dutch Shell was the first foreign crude oil producer in the country and it has been joined by a host of others, including Chevron (US), Repsol (Spain), BP (UK), Anadarko, El Paso (both US), Galp Energia, (Portugal) Statoil (Norway), BG Group (UK – acquired by Shell in April 2015), Sinopec (China), ONGC (India) and TNK-BP (Russia-UK). Competition in the sector is not just from foreign companies. The Brazilian oil company OGX, which is staffed largely with former Petrobras employees, started to produce oil in the Campos Basin in 2011.

The government agency responsible for regulating and monitoring the oil sector is the Agência Nacional do Petróleo, Gás Natural e Biocombustíveis (ANP), which issues exploration and production licences and ensures compliance with regulations. Recent legislation concerning pre-salt exploration and production has changed the operating environment. The EIA estimated that at the beginning of 2015, Brazil had 16.2 billion barrels of proved oil reserves. (According to ANP, Brazil had had 15.6 billion barrels of proved oil reserves at the end of 2013, the second-largest level in South America behind Venezuela.) According to the EIA, more than 94 per cent of Brazil's reserves are located offshore and 80 per cent of all its reserves are found offshore near the state of Rio de Janeiro. Offshore the state of Espirito Santo held the next largest accumulation at 9 per cent of the country's reserves.

In 2013, according to the EIA, Brazil produced 2.7 million barrels per day (bpd) of petroleum and other liquids, 2.0 million bpd of which was crude oil and 527,000bpd was biofuels. Petrobras accounted for 1.9 million bpd of domestic crude oil and natural gas liquids (NGL) production. A growing share of production came from Brazil's relatively recent discovery of oil deposits in the pre-salt layer. In 2013, crude oil production from the pre-salt layer was 303,000bpd. This accounted for 15 per cent of total production, a significant increase from 0.4 per cent of total production in 2008 when oil from the pre-salt deposits was first produced.

Increased production levels have yet to overtake consumption. According to the EIA, in 2013, Brazil's demand for liquid fuels broke the 3.0 million bpd mark, while its domestic production continued to remain relatively unchanged at about 2.7 million bpd. The EIA expects consumption will continue to be greater than production through 2015. Brazil had announced in September 2014 that it expected to produce 4.0 million bpd of crude oil by 2020–22 and export 1.5–2.0 million bpd by 2022, buoyed by the pre-salt discoveries. This figure represented a downward revision from its 2013 expectations of 5.0 million bpd of production and exports of more than 2.25 million bpd by 2021. Petrobras projects that the company will produce an average of 2.9 million bpd of oil domestically between 2013–20 and average 3.7 million bpd between 2020–30, according to its latest business and management plan.

According to the ANP, Brazil had a total of 2.2 million bpd of crude oil refining capacity at 16 refineries in 2013. Petrobras operates 13 facilities that produce 2.0 million bpd of product.7The largest facility is the 415,000bpd Replan refinery in Sao Paulo. Because Brazil's oil refineries do not have the technical capabilities to process heavier crudes, the country must export some of its heavy crude oil and import light crude oil. With domestic demand growing, Brazil's refineries are currently operating at 98 per cent capacity.

Petrobras plans to increase its Brazilian refining capacity to more than 3.2 million bpd by 2020 and by 3.9 million bpd by 2030 to meet anticipated domestic demand. Under the company's 2014–18 business and management plan, Petrobras will build four additional refineries to meet this goal. (However, since the EIA report was prepared Petrobras had decided to cocoon two of the refineries.) The Abreu e Lima, a 230,000bpd refinery, (the only functioning 'new' refinery) came into operation in December 2014. The refinery initially began as a joint-venture with Petróleos de Venezuela (PdVSA), but it moved forward without PdVSA when it was unable to provide the 40 per cent equity (US$17 billion).

According to the ANP, Brazil exported 381,000bpd of crude oil in 2013, a 31 per cent decrease from the previous year. The United States imported 110,000bpd of crude oil from Brazil in 2013, a decrease of more than 30 per cent from 2012. Because of increasing US domestic supply and growing Chinese demand, China became the largest importer of Brazil's crude oil in 2013, importing 115,000bpd. The third-largest destination of Brazil's crude oil after China and the United States is India, which imported 49,000bpd in 2013.

Biofuels...

To address Brazil's dependence on oil imports and surplus of sugar cane, the government implemented policies to encourage ethanol production and consumption as long ago as the 1960s. Impressively, Brazil is the second largest producer and consumer of ethanol in the world after the United States. According to the ANP, in 2013, Brazil produced 479,000bpd of ethanol, an 18 per cent increase from the previous year. The government raised the ethanol blend requirement in gasoline back up to 25 per cent in May 2013. It is now considering an increase to 27.5 per cent as a measure to reduce gasoline imports. In 2013, Brazil exported 50,000bpd of ethanol, 81 per cent of which was shipped to the United States, South Korea, the Netherlands and Japan. The United States imported 30,000bpd of ethanol from Brazil in 2013 and 35,000bpd in 2012, a significant increase from 12,000bpd in 2011, as US policy in 2012 removed domestic tariffs on Brazilian sugarcane. Brazil also produces biodiesel but at smaller quantities. In 2013, the country produced 50,000bpd of biodiesel. More than 80 per cent of production was concentrated in the south central region of the country.

... and pre-salt

The world's largest oil discoveries in recent years have come from Brazil's offshore, pre-salt basins. In 2005, Petrobras drilled exploratory wells near the Tupi field and discovered hydrocarbons below the salt layer. In 2007 a consortium of Petrobras, BG Group and Petrogal drilled in the Tupi field and discovered an estimated 5–8 billion barrels of oil equivalent (boe) resources in a pre-salt zone 18,000 feet below the ocean surface under a thick layer of salt. EIA defines ultra-deep drilling in the Gulf of Mexico as 5,000 feet or more. Further exploration showed that hydrocarbon deposits in the pre-salt layer extended through the Santos, Campos and Espirito Santo basins.

Pre-salt oil is generally characterised as oil reserves situated exceptionally deep under thick layers of rock and salt and requiring substantial investment to extract. The large depth and pressure involved in pre-salt production present significant technical hurdles that must be overcome. Further, the scale of the proposed expansion in production will also stretch Petrobras' financial and technical resources. Petrobras plans to develop its major pre-salt assets in three discrete phases: 1) extended well tests; 2) pilot projects; and 3) large-scale production through multiple, duplicate floating production, storage and offloading (FPSO) facilities.

Following Tupi, many pre-salt finds were announced in the Santos Basin. Pilot projects in the Lula and Sapinhoa fields began production in 2009 and 2010, respectively. In 2013, Brazil produced an average of 303,000bpd of oil from its pre-salt fields. In October 2014, Brazil produced an average of 607,000bpd of oil from the pre-salt fields. With the exception of the Libra field, all pre-salt areas currently under development were non-competitively granted to Petrobras (a decision that may be now regretted). Through the Transfer of Rights

Agreement of 2010, in exchange for US$42 billion of Petrobras shares, the government gave Petrobras rights to explore and produce 5 billion boe from six pre-salt areas in the Santos Basin: Florim, Buzios, Sul de Guara, Entorno de Lara, Sul de Lula and Nordeste de Tupi. Petrobras discovered significant reserves in addition to the original 5 billion boe. In June 2014, the government granted Petrobras the rights to produce surplus volumes estimated at 9.8–15.2 billion boe found in the Buzios, Entorno de Lara, Florim and Nordeste de Tupi areas. Petrobras expects first production from the Transfer of Rights areas by 2016 and from the surplus volumes by 2021. (It should be noted, as referred to above, that Petrobras' fortunes and its international reputation has, since 2013, suffered dramatically from the massive corruption that has been revealed within the company. This has caused an 80 per cent fall in the company's share price.)

In October 2013, Brazil concluded its first pre-salt licensing round for the Libra field, estimated to hold 8–12 billion barrels of recoverable reserves. The lone and winning bid was a consortium of Petrobras, Royal Dutch Shell, Total and Chinese national oil companies China National Petroleum Corporation (CNPC) and China National Offshore Oil Corporation (CNOOC). First production is scheduled for 2017 with peak production of 1.3 million bpd by 2030. Brazil anticipates oil production from the pre-salt layer will account for most of the projected growth from 2020–30.

A month after concluding its first pre-salt licensing round for the Libra field, Brazil's Petrobras announced its discovery of the Franco field, a pre-salt finding, which could be larger than the 8–12 billion barrels of recoverable reserves found in the Libra field. Additionally, in May 2014, Petrobras made another pre-salt finding of potentially 5 billion barrels in the Entorno de Lara block.

In its 2014–18 business and management plan, the now beleaguered Petrobras laid out plans to invest US$153.9 billion in exploration and production, representing nearly 70 per cent of Petrobras' total planned investment including downstream, distribution, international activities, etc. More than 53 per cent (US$82 billion) of the total investment will be in pre-salt exploration and production activities over the five year period. The company is shifting its focus away from downstream and international expansion to the domestic upstream sector. According to the EIA, Petrobras may have to further divest its investments into the domestic upstream sector with the addition of potentially billions of boe as a result of the surplus volumes from the Transfer of Rights areas.

China to the rescue?

In May 2015 the Chinese prime minister, Li Keqiang, paid an official visit to Brazil. Brazilian hopes were high that Beijing might come to their rescue with economic deals that had not been forthcoming from Europe or the US. Those hopes weren't disappointed when Mr Li opened his briefcase and produced a staggering 35 million dollar plus agreements, ranging from the construction of a railway line that would link Brazil to Peru's pacific coast to the construction of a steel plant in north-east Brazil. Despite the scandal that still surrounded Petrobras, Mr Li came up with proposals for collaboration with the oil giant adding up to US$6,290 million, which was interpreted as an indication of support for the beleaguered Dilma, thought by many domestic and international observers to have been aware and possibly involved, in the Petrobras affair.

Chinese funding was also to be made available for the construction of a number if ships which would carry Brazilian iron ore and soya to China. Mr Li also produced an order from China's Tianjin Airlines for 22 Embraer aircraft costing over one billion US dollars. This was the first part of a larger order for a total of 60 aircraft. Mr Li stressed that bilateral trade

Risk assessment

Economy	Fair
Politics	Fair
Regional stability	Good

COUNTRY PROFILE

1500 First sighted by Portuguese mariner, Pedro Alvares Cabral. The area was claimed by the Portuguese crown. Sugar-cane plantations were started by the Portuguese, using Indian slave labour. The Indians were decimated by disease and the survivors fled to the interior. The Portuguese turned to Africa as another source of slaves.

1807 Portuguese imperial court moved to Brazil after the invasion of Portugal by Napoleon's armies and Brazil became a kingdom within the Portuguese empire. Following Napoleon's retreat, Prince Pedro, the son of João VI, became regent of Brazil.

1822 Brazil gained independence from Portugal and Emperor Pedro became Brazil's first monarch. The immediate post-independence period was marked by minor civil wars, slave rebellions and attempts at secession, with many in the south favouring a republican form of government.

1831 Pedro I abdicated following a period of political turmoil. Under a regency, his five-year-old son, Pedro II, succeeded him.

1840 At the age of 14, Emperor Pedro II was granted full powers as monarch. Although his reign was characterised by stability and a move towards political liberalism, wealth was concentrated in the hands of a small feudal elite while the rest of the population remained illiterate and poor.

1850 Pedro II abolished the slave trade.

1864–70 Brazil, Argentina and Uruguay were at war with Paraguay, ending with Paraguay's defeat.

1888 Pedro II abolished slavery, leading to a revolt by the country's landed gentry.

1889 The monarchy was overthrown in a revolution led by Manuel Deodoro da Fonseca and the king was sent into exile. A federal republic was established, although ruled in the interest of coffee plantation owners.

1929 Turmoil caused by the Wall Street crash led to a military coup which installed a civilian politician, Gertulio Vargas, as president in 1930.

1937 Vargas assumed dictatorial powers and began a revolution in welfare provision and reformed laws governing industry.

1939-45 Brazil remained neutral in the Second World War, but received a large number of exiled Nazis after the defeat of Germany.

1945 Vargas was ousted in a military coup. Elections were held under a new caretaker government and a new constitution was promulgated.

1951 Vargas was narrowly elected president.

1954 Vargas committed suicide after the military gave him the option of resigning or being overthrown.

1956 Juscelino Kubitschek, a strong democrat, came to power after fresh elections. Construction of the new capital, Brasília, began.

1960 Brasília was declared the country's new capital city.

1964 João Goulart was elected president, but after months of hyperinflation leading to the country's virtual bankruptcy he was overthrown by the military. General Humberto Castello Branco was installed as president, overseeing a period of political repression and economic growth based on state-owned industries. Repressive military treatment of opposition led to human rights abuses and the disappearance of arrested suspects.

1974 General Ernesto Geisel became president and introduced reforms which allowed limited political activity and elections.
1982 Brazil defaulted on its foreign debt repayments, which were among the world's biggest.
1985 Tancredo Neves was elected president, but died before his inauguration. His vice-president, José Sarney, was declared president, taking over a country wracked by hyperinflation.
1986 Sarney introduced the Cruzado Plan that froze prices and wages in an effort to control inflation. However, growing public opposition led to abandoning the controls thereby maintaining hyperinflation.
1988 A new constitution was promulgated, reducing presidential powers.
1989 Fernando Collor de Mello was elected president. He introduced a radical economic reform, which involved trade liberalisation, privatisation and a controversial freeze on savings and bank accounts. However, this failed to meet expectations, inflation remained high and the country defaulted on its debt repayments.
1992 Collor resigned after being accused of corruption; he was later exonerated. Itamar Franco became president.
1994 Fernando Henrique Cardoso won the presidential election. A constitutional amendment limited presidential terms to four years.
1997 A constitutional amendment allowed presidents to run for a second term in office.
1998 President Cardoso was re-elected.
2000 Brazil's 500th anniversary celebrations were disrupted by protests by indigenous peoples on the issue of land reform and against the legacy of European colonialism, including genocide and the destruction of their cultures.
2001 Corruption scandals rocked the political establishment and a number of senior figures in government and Congress resigned.
2002 Luiz Inácio da Silva (known as Lula), leader of the Partido dos Trabalhadores (PT) (Workers' Party), was elected president.
2003 Lula was sworn in as president, heading a broad coalition government, led by the PT. The centrist Partido do Movimento Democratico Brasileiro (PMDB) (Democratic Movement Party) joined the coalition, ensuring a congressional majority able to pass social security and tax reforms.
2004 The Moviemento dos Trabalhadores Rurais Sem Terra (MST) (Landless Workers' Movement) launched its biggest campaign, known as Red April, with a wave of farm occupations to force speedier expropriation and redistribution of unused farmland. Brazil applied for a permanent seat on the UN Security Council. The country launched its first rocket into space.
2005 Allegations of corruption were made against the ruling PT. President Lula apologised to the nation, while denying any personal responsibility for illegal actions.
2006 Elections were held for federal president, vice president and legislators (deputies and one-third of the senate) and state governors, lieutenant governors and members of state unicameral legislatures. In presidential elections Lula da Silva won a second term in office with over 60 per cent of the vote.
2007 Over 1,000 people were freed from sugar-cane plantations in the Amazon by Brazil's ministry of labour's anti-slavery teams. The world's largest iron ore mine in the Carajas region, operated by Compañhía Vale do Rio Doce (CVRD), reached a record 972 million tonnes of ore processed.
2008 A previously unknown aboriginal tribe was found in the border region of Brazil and Peru.
2009 Severe floods struck in eight states across the north and north-east, killing 42 people and forcing 274,000 people to flee their homes.
2010 A controversial new, 11,000MW, Belo Monte hydroelectric dam, the world's third largest, to be built in the Amazon rainforest on the Xingu River, was given its environmental licence. When completed 500 square kilometres will be inundated and any indigenous communities within 100sq km living along the river will be displaced. In August, the Brazilian airline TAM Linhas Aereas and the Chilean airline LAN agreed to merge to form the region's largest carrier, with 115 destinations in 23 countries. The new company will be called the Latam Airlines Group, although the individual airline brand names will remain in use. Results of the national referendum recorded a population of 190,755,799. In presidential elections, Lula da Silva's chosen successor and former Marxist guerrilla, Dilma Rousseff (PT) failed to win an outright majority in the first round and was forced to contest a second round, in which she won 56.05 per cent, while her rival José Serra (PSDB) won 43.94 per cent. In parliamentary elections, Lulista (a coalition of 10 political parties led by the ruling PT won 311 seats (out of 513), the opposition centre-right coalition of six parties, led by PSDB, won a total of 136 seats; seven other political parties won 66 seats. Central bank head, Henrique Meirelles, was replaced by Alexandre Tombini. The state-owned Petrobras was ranked the third biggest energy company, based on capital value, in the world, with assets of US$228.9 billion.
2011 Dilma Rousseff took office as Brazil's first female president on 1 January. Heavy rains in early January caused flash-floods and mudslides that killed over 600 people in the mountainous regions of the state of Rio de Janeiro. Government approval for the initial work of clearing the forest for the Belo Monte dam was given in January. In March a new road, the 3,400km, US$1.3 billion, Carretera Interoceánica (Interoceanic Highway), was opened from Brazil's Atlantic coast to Peru's Pacific seaboard, bisecting the Amazon Forest and crossing the Andes Mountains. In April parliament eased the law to allow greater forest logging. New satellite pictures issued in May showed that deforestation of the Amazon rainforest had increased from 103 square kilometres in March–April 2010 to 598 square km in March–April 2011. The Mato Grosso State, the centre of soya cultivation, had the largest loss of rainforest. Despite a fall in deforestation in December 2010 with the lowest recorded loss since late-1980s, deforestation jumped by 27 per cent from August 2010–April 2011. A previously unknown aboriginal tribe of around 200 people, found in the Amazon rainforest in the Javari Valley, was identified in June. Analysis of the 2010 census showed that, for the first time, non-white people made up the majority of the population. Out of a population of 191 million, 91 million identified themselves as white, a fall from 53.7 per cent of the population in 2000 to 47.7 per cent in 2010.
2012 The leaders of the Brics countries met in Delhi on 29 March to discuss their position regarding the control the US and Europe has on the World Bank and the IMF. Indian Prime Minister Manmohan Singh said 'The Brics countries have agreed to examine in greater detail a proposal to set up a South-South development bank, funded and managed by the Brics and other developing countries.' On 25 May, President Rousseff modified and vetoed part of legislation that had been enacted in April, which among other things had required how much land farmers must preserve as forest and offered an amnesty to illegal loggers. On 16 May President Rousseff inaugurated the Comissão Nacional da Verdade (National Truth Commission), to investigate state administered human rights violations from 1946–88, focussing on the military era of 1964–85; an amnesty, however, means no-one will be held legally responsible. On 3 July the landscape of Rio de Janeiro was added to Unesco's World Heritage List. On 15 August, a federal court ordered an immediate suspension of

construction of the Belo Monte hydroelectric dam because, it adjudicated, indigenous people had not been properly consulted nor had their opinions on the project been taken into account. On 28 August work resumed on the dam as the Supreme Court overturned the lower court's ruling. However the Supreme Court undertook to study the evidence of the lower court and could reverse its ruling.
2013 In mid-June demonstrators took to the streets of Rio de Janeiro and Sao Paulo against a US$0.20 rise in public transport fares. Within a week there were more than a million people on the streets of 100 cities throughout Brazil. The rallies, and the violence that followed, coincided with Fifa's Confederation Cup football tournament, a run-up to the World Cup in 2014. Although the protests began over the cost of a bus fare, concerns over healthcare, security, rising inflation and World Cup and Olympic overspending, corruption and dissatisfaction with political leaders, who they believed did not understand the 'real people' of Brazil, became the main focus of the protestors. On 24 June Ms Rousseff promised a referendum and proposed five 'pacts' that would cover political reform, fiscal responsibility and extra spending on health, transport and education. The referendum would establish a Constituent Assembly to eventually amend the constitution. In the meantime Ms Rousseff said the government would allocate Rs50 billion (US$25 billion) to improve public transport. Pope Francis arrived in Rio de Janeiro on 22 July, his first foreign visit since becoming Pope. He attended the Roman Catholic World Youth Day festival. On 14 August Congress approved a bill that designates royalties from newly discovered oil fields to education (75 per cent) and healthcare (25 per cent). The move was one of a number of reforms proposed after protests in June after a rise in bus fares. On 23 August the central bank announced moves to prop up the real by spending US$500 million a day Monday to Thursday and US$1 billion on Fridays. The real had fallen to its lowest point for almost five years on fears of a rise in US interest rates. A row with Bolivia about the escape of an opposition politician from asylum in the Brazilian embassy in La Paz over the border to Brazil lead to the resignation of Brazil's foreign minister, Antonio Patriota, on 26 August. Mr Patriota was replaced by Luiz Alberto Figueiredo, who had been Brazil's head of mission at the UN, and himself became UN Ambassador. On 17 September President Rousseff announced the cancellation of her state visit to the US in October. The reason given was the alleged spying on herself and her aids of her cabinet by the US National Security Agency (NSA). Marina Silva, who came third in the first round of the 2010 presidential election, joined the Partido Socialista Brasileiro (PSB) (Brazilian Socialist Party) after failing to officially register her new party. On 14 October the President confirmed plans to create a secure email service to counter cyber-surveillance spying techniques. A fire in the port of Santos in October destroyed 180,000 tonnes of sugar, sending the international price of sugar to a high for the year. As the only bidder in an auction held on 21 October Petrobas, backed by Total, Shell and Chinese firms, won the rights to explore the Libra oilfield, Brazil's biggest.
2014 The Fifa Football World Cup was held successfully in June and July. Brazil made it to the semi-finals, loosing to eventual winner, Germany. Presidential candidate, Eduardo Campos, was killed in a plane crash on 13 August. His running mate, Marina Silva, stood in his stead. Mr Campos had been third in the polls, after President Rousseff and Aecio Neves. The 5 October election was won by Mrs Rousseff with 41.59 per cent of the vote, followed by Aécio Neves da Cunha (PSBD) (33.54 per cent) and Marina Silva (21.31 per cent). The run-off between the first two candidatestook place on 26 October with Marina Silva backing opposition centrist candidate Aecio Neves. Mrs Rousseff narrowly won a second term in office with 51.6 per cent of votes to the 48.4 per cent of Aecio Neves.
2015 Corruption charges were lodged against Eduardo Cunha, speaker of the Chamber of Deputies, on 20 August. He is alleged to have taken at least US$5 milion in bribes as part of a kickbacks scheme centred Petrobras.

Political structure

Constitution

The 1988 Constitution is the country's seventh charter since independence from Portugal in 1822. The federal republic consists of 26 states and one federal district (Brasília). Congress passed a Constitutional amendment in 1997 allowing Fernando Henrique Cardoso to become the first president to stand for re-election.

Form of state

Federal presidential democratic republic

The executive

Executive power is exercised by the president, aided by ministers of state who are appointed by the president. The president is elected for a four-year term.
The president is also assisted by the Council of the Republic, an advisory body consisting of the vice president of the republic, the presidents of the Chamber of Deputies and the Senate, the leaders of the majority and minority in each house, the minister of justice, and six other members (two appointed by the president of the republic, two elected by the Chamber of Deputies and two elected by the Senate). These six members have a three-year term of office. The national defence council is the president's advisory body on defence matters. It consists of the vice president of the republic, the presidents of the Chamber of Deputies and the Senate, the minister of justice, ministers of the army, navy and air force, and the ministers of foreign affairs and planning.

National legislature

The bicameral, Congresso Nacional (National Congress) consists of the Senado Federal, (federal senate) (upper house) and Câmara dos Deputados (chamber of deputies) (lower house).
The federal senate has 81 members, of which two-thirds are directly elected and one-third indirectly elected. Members are elected in rotation for eight years. The chamber of deputies has 513 members elected by proportional representation to serve for four years.
All legislation proposed by The executive must be submitted to congress. As well as fiscal and budgetary control, congress must be consulted on matters concerning payments of external debt. Congressional committees have powers of oversight on nominations to important posts proposed by the executive. The senate must approve issues of treasury bills. Constitutional amendments must be approved by a three-fifths majority of both the chambers of the national congress.

Legal system

An 11-member Supreme Federal Tribunal is Brazil's highest judicial body. Judges are appointed by the president of the republic and approved by the Senate. It gives decisions in cases involving the president, vice president, ministers of state, members of Congress, its own members and judges of other courts. It interprets the constitution, judges disputes between the federal and state authorities, between different state authorities, between federal and state authorities and foreign governments, between different levels of the judicial system, and cases involving extradition, *habeas corpus* and *habeas data*.
The Higher Tribunal of Justice is composed of at least 33 members and gives decisions in cases involving state governors. Its members are appointed by the president and approved by the Senate. Regional federal tribunals have at least seven members, who are appointed by the president. The Higher Labour Tribunal is composed of 27 members appointed by the president and approved by the Senate. The Higher Electoral Tribunal

includes at least seven judges, three from the Supreme Federal Tribunal, two elected by secret ballot from the Higher Tribunal of Justice and two appointed by the president. The labour and electoral tribunals each have regional counterparts. The Higher Military Tribunal is composed of 15 judges appointed by the president and approved by the Senate for life. Four of its judges are selected from the army, three from the navy and three from the air force. The remaining five are civilians. There is a federal court of appeal. The Federal Audit Court provides for the administrative review of national and state accounts.

Last elections

5 and 26 October 2014 (first and second round presidential); 3 October 2010 (Chamber of Deputies and Senate, partial).

Results: Presidential 2014 (first round): Dilma Rousseff (PT) won 43,267,668 votes (41.59 per cent), Aécio Neves (PSDB) 34,897,211 votes (33.55 per cent), Marina Silva (Partido Verde (PV) (Green Party) 22,176,619 votes(21.32 per cent), Luciana Genro (PSOL) 1,612,186 votes (1.55 per cent); seven other candidates won less than 1 per cent of the vote each. Turn out was 80.61 per cent. Second round: Rousseff won 54,501,119 votes (51.64 per cent), Neves 51,041,155 votes (48.36 per cent). Voting is compulsory; turnout was 78.9 per cent.

Chamber of Deputies: The nine-party pro-government coalition Coligação Com a Força do Povo (With the Strength of the People) won a total of 304 seats (out of 513) from the Partido dos Trabalhadores (PT) (Workers' Party)) 70 seats, the Partido do Movimento Democratico Brasileiro (PMDB) (Democratic Movement Party) 66, Partido da Social Democracia Brasileira (PSDB) (Party of Brazilian Social Democracy) 37, Partido Progressista (PP) (Progressive Party) 36, Partido da Republica (PR) (Republic Party) 34, Partido Republicano Brasileiro (PRB) (Brazilian Republican Party) 21, Partido Democrático Trabalhista (PDT) (Democratic Labour Party) 19, Partido Republicano da Ordem Social (PROS) (Republican Party of the Social Order) 11, Partido Comunista do Brasil (PC do B) (Communist Party of Brazil) 10. The opposition nine-party Coligação Muda Brasil (Coalition Change Brazil) won a total of 128 seats from the Partido Socialista Brasileiro (PSB) (Brazilian Socialist Party) 34 seats, Partido Popular Socialista (PPS) (Socialist People's Party) 10, Partido Humanista da Solidariedade (PHS) (Humanist Party of Solidarity) 5, Partido Republicano Progressista (PRP) (Progressive Republican Party) 3, Partido Social Liberal (PSL) (Social Liberal Party) 1.

Of the non-coalition parties the Partido Social Cristão (PSC) (Christian Social Party) won 12 seats, Partido Verde (PV) (Green Party) 8, Partido Socialismo e Liberdade (PSOL) (Socialism and Freedom Party) 5, Partido Social Democrata Cristão (PSDC) (Christian Social Democratic Party) 2, Partido Renovador Trabalhista Brasileiro (PRTB) (Brazilian Labour Renewal Party) 1.

Federal Senate (54 seats in contention): the PMDB won 16 seats the PT 11, the PSDB 5, the PP 4, PR and PSB 3 each, and the PDT, Partido Socialismo e Liberdade (PSL) (Socialism and Freedom Party), and DEM 2 each; six other political parties each won one seat.

Next elections

2018 (presidential, chamber of deputies and senate, partial)

Political parties

Ruling party

Coalition Coligação Com a Força do Povo (With the Strength of the People) with 304 out of 513 seats, led by Partido dos Trabalhadores (PT) (Workers' Party) with eight other political parties (elected 5 Oct 2014)

Main opposition party

Coligação Muda Brasil (Coalition Change Brazil) of six parties lead by Partido da Social Democracia Brasileira (PSDB) (Party of Brazilian Social Democracy).

The national census was held between 1 August and 31 October 2010; 58 million households were surveyed by 240,000 census takers. The budget for the census was US$900 million and allowed information to be given via written questionnaires or the internet.

By 2040, the population is expected to reach about 220 million and then stabilise or even fall. Approximately 22 per cent of the population live below the national poverty line.

Population

198.29 million (2013) (190,755,799; 2010, census figure)

Last census: 1 August and 31 October 2010: 190,755,799

Population density: 20 per square km. Urban population 87 per cent (2010 Unicef).

Annual growth rate: 1.3 per cent, 1990–2010 (Unicef).

Ethnic make-up

European (54 per cent), mixed race (39 per cent), black (6 per cent) and Japanese (1 per cent). The major cities in the centre-south area of the country contain substantial communities of Portuguese, Italian, Lebanese and German immigrants. There are an estimated 210 indigenous groups in Amazonia, making up only 0.2 per cent of the total population of Brazil.

Religions

Catholic (90 per cent); Protestant (5 per cent). Brazil is the largest Catholic country in the world. There is freedom of worship and many other religions are represented.

Education

The investment in education amounts to 4.2 per cent of GDP.

State education is free from pre-primary level. Primary education begins at the age of seven and lasts for eight years. Secondary education, which is not compulsory, begins at the age of 15 and lasts for four years.

Primary and secondary education suffer from scarce resources. Although the initial enrolment rate is similar between the rich and the poor, the inequality is evident at later stages. Only 15 per cent of poor children compared to 80 per cent of children from the richest households complete primary school. Inequalities in budget affect enrolment patterns between those prosperous regions and the north-east where over half of rural children receive less than four years of schooling, and one-quarter of the population has had no schooling at all.

Brazil has doubled the number of students reaching their final year in secondary school but has only places for 11 per cent of them. If the country is to compete internationally it will have to increase this amount to at least 40 per cent, to match even its neighbour Argentina.

To combat the problem of lack of opportunity for poorer students in higher education, the president introduced tax concessions, in July 2004, for private universities who reserve at least 20 per cent of their places to black or native Indian students. It is expected that these tax breaks will provided places for up to 100,000 underprivileged students.

Literacy rate: 86 per cent adult rate; 94 per cent youth rate (15–24) (Unesco 2005).

Compulsory years: 7 to 14.

Pupils per teacher: 24 in primary schools.

Health

In theory, medical, pharmaceutical and dental treatment is free. However, in practice the social health system is underfunded and cannot meet the growing needs of the population. Private health insurance and healthcare facilities are widely available for those who can afford them. The National Social Security and Assistance Institute for Medical Care (INAMPS) is responsible for healthcare.

Life expectancy: 73 years, 2010 (Unicef 2012)

Fertility rate/Maternal mortality rate: 1.8 births per woman, 2010 (Unicef 2012); maternal mortality 160 per 100,000 live births (World Bank).
Child (under 5 years) mortality rate (per 1,000): 14 per 1,000 live births (WHO 2012); 6 per cent of children aged under five are malnourished (World Bank).

Welfare

Employers pay 20 per cent of the payroll into the Social Insurance Scheme to cover payments for social benefits: pensions, invalidity pensions, sickness pay, family allowances, funeral grants, maternity grants, prisoners' family pensions, widows' pensions and special pensions for workers in dangerous jobs.
The state sets aside taxes to cover the costs of collection and administration.
Brazil shows a highly unequal distribution of income among households and individuals in both rural and urban economies.
On 14 May 2012, a range of social welfare programmes were introduced, aimed at low-income families with children. The welfare programme, targeted in the north and north-east, is intended to benefit 18 million people. Families with children under aged six and living in poverty will receive US$35 per month for each family member. Access to healthcare (with an emphasis on nutrition) will be expanded and day care facilities increased with the construction of 1,500 new day care centres.
The Instituto Nacional de Providencia Social (INPS) (National Social Security Institute), administers the scheme for all workers except military personnel, civil servants and agricultural workers, who are covered by a separate system.

Pensions

The retirement ages for those in urban areas are 70 and 65 for men and women respectively, with 35 years contributions; in rural areas 60 and 55 for men and women respectively, with 30 years contributions.

Main cities

Brasília, (capital, estimated population 2.6 million (m) in 2012), São Paulo (11.4m), Rio de Janeiro (6.4m), Salvador (2.7m), Fortaleza (2.5m), Belo Horizonte (2.4m), Manaus (1.9m), Curitiba (1.8m), Recife (1.6m), Porto Alegre (1.4m), Belém (1.4m), Goiânia (1.3m), Guarulhos (1.3), Campinas (1.1m), São Gonçalo (1.0m).

Languages spoken

Many business people and officials speak English. Spanish, Italian, French and German are also widely spoken, especially in tourist areas. There are nearly 200 indigenous languages.

Official language/s

Portuguese

Media

The constitution guarantees freedom of the press.
Brazil is the largest media market in South America and its media is dominated by a few domestically owned conglomerates of broadcasters and publishers.

Press

There are many publications for most interest groups.
Dailies: There are around 280 daily newspapers but the difficulty of distribution has limited readership to regional centres. Nevertheless, major media conglomerates supplies news and views through privately owned news agencies to local outlets.
In Portuguese, major city newspapers include *Correio Brasiliense* (www.correioweb.com.br/cbonline) and *Tribuna do Brasil* (www.tribunadobrasil.com.br) from Brasíllia, *O Dia* (http://odia.terra.com.br) and *O Globo* (http://oglobo.globo.com) from Rio de Janeiro, *Folha de São Paulo* (www.folha.uol.com.br) and *O Estado de São Paulo* (www.estado.com.br) from Sao Paulo, *Correio da Bahai* (www.correiodabahia.com.br) from Salvador, *Super Notícia* (www.supernoticia.com.br) from Belo Horizonte and *O Povo* (www.opovo.com.br) from Fortaleza.
Weeklies: In Portuguese, *Istoé* (www.terra.com.br/istoe), *Veja* (http://veja.abril.uol.com.br) and *Época (http://revistaepoca.globo.com), are general news magazines.*
In English, *Brazil Magazine* (www.brazzil.com) covers general news.
Business: In Portuguese, *Panorama Brasil* (www.panoramabrasil.com), *Prima Pagina* (www.primapagina.com.br), *Valor Economico* (www.valoronline.com.br) and *Gazeta Mercantil* (www.gazetamercantil.com.br) offer a wide range of news and information.
Magazines include the weekly *Carta Capital* (www.cartacapital.com.br) and the monthly *Amanhã* (www.amanha.com.br) and *Banco Hoje* (www.bancohoje.com.br) for banking news.
Periodicals: In Portuguese, monthly magazine include *Claudia* (http://claudia.abril.com.br) for women *Continente Multicultural* (www.continentemulticultural.com.br) for the Latin culture.
Popular magazines published in Portuguese include *Epoca*, *Isto E* and *Veja*. *Brazzil* is an English-language magazine covering the Brazilian economy, politics and culture.

Broadcasting

The responsiblity for radio and television broadcasting is overseen by the state body Empresa Brasileira de Radiodifusão (Radiobrás) (www.radiobras.gov.br).
Radio: There are over 2,000 radio stations, with an estimated 80 per cent of homes with access to a radio receiver.
The state-run public radio network Radiobrás (www.radiobras.gov.br) operates four radio stations over AM/FM. The largest commercial network is Globo Radio (http://globoradio.globo.com), others include Radio Eldorado (www.radioeldorado.com.br), Radio Bandeirantes (http://band.com.br), Radio Cultura (www.radiocultura.com.br) is a public cultural station.
Television: The conversion to digital TV began in São Paulo in 2007 and should be completed nationwide by 2016.
The state-run public TV network Radiobrás (www.radiobras.gov.br) operates four channels including news, documentaries and indigenous and cultural programmes.
Large commercial TV networks include Rede Globo (http://redeglobo.globo.com), Sistema Brasileiro de TeleviSão (SBT) (www.sbt.com.br), TV Record (www.rederecord.com.br) and TV Band (http://band.com.br).
There are many cable TV providers, although most are foreign-owned, domestic networks include Televisão Abril (www.tva.com.br) and Rede TV (www.redetv.com.br).
National news agency: Agencia Brazil (in Portuguese): www.agenciabrasil.gov.br
Other news agencies: Agencia Estado: www.ae.com.br/institucional
Agencia Globo: www.agenciaoglobo.com.br
Folha Press (business news): www.folhapress.com.br
PR Newswire (business news): www.prnewswire.com.br
Safras e Mercado (business news): www.safras.com.br

Economy

Brazil is the 'B' in BRIC, the acronym reputedly coined in a Goldman Sachs report of 2003, and in 2014 had the worlds seventh largest economy. The country has a large industrial base including manufactured aircraft, motor vehicles, armaments and refined oil products, while the agricultural sector produces a significant quantity of exports, notably coffee and soya. It has vast natural reserves, which at the end of 2014 included 16.2 billion barrels of petroleum, with production of 2.35 million barrels per day; natural gas (500 billion cubic metres (cum) with production of 20.0 billion cum), coal (6.6 billion tonnes, with production of 3.2

million tonnes of oil equivalent (mtoe), are in demand worldwide.
As global trade picked up, after the global economic crisis, the economy surged with growth of 7.5 per cent in 2010 making Brazil one of the first emerging markets to recover from the crisis. However, since then growth has slowed due to reliance on imports for raw commodities, low productivity and low investment. Brazil struggles to attract foreign investment and is a country still riddles with corruption. In 2014 Brazil ranked 120 out of 189 in the World Banks 'Ease of Doing Business' index and 69 out of 175 in Transparency International's 'Corruption Perceptions Index'. As a result of this economic growth had slowed to 2.5 per cent in 2013 and still lower to 0.3 per cent in 2014, with growth forecast to remain low in 2014. Inflation has also remained a problem for the nation, which has remained consistently relatively high at sat at 6.3 per cent in 2014.
Brazil has, however, undoubtedly many positive aspects of its economy. Unemployment has remained low for a number of years and was at only 5.5 per cent in 2014. Brazil is ranked in the top two for exports of Iron ore, beef, chicken, sugar, soybeans, orange juice, and ethanol, as well as being the worlds largest producer and exporter of coffee. On top of this its impressive hydrocarbons reserves both fuel the economy and bring in significant money from exports.
The service sector remains the the most significant component of the economy, accounting for 70.4 per cent of GDP in 2014, while industry accounted for 23.8 per cent, of which manufacturing contributed 11 per cent, and agriculture 5.8 per cent.
Poverty remains a serious problem with large income inequalities and almost a third of the country living below the poverty line. In 2013 (latest figures), the UN Human Development Index (HDI) ranked Brazil 79 (out of 187) for national development in health, education and income. In 2013, 21.4 per cent of the population lived below the national poverty line, while 6.14 per cent lived on the equivalent, or less, of US$1.25 per day. The government provides limited welfare for over 12.5 million families through a *Bolsa Familia* programme.
In June 2012 Brazil and China agreed to swap the equivalent of US$30 billion in each other's currencies. Their central banks will be able to exchange each other's currency (up to the US$30 billion) without consideration to fluctuation in the money markets and avoiding varying exchange rates when buying US dollars to make commodity purchases.

External trade

In 2008, the União das Nações Sul-Americanas (Unasul) (Union of South American Nations) (known as Unasur from the Spanish Unión de Naciones Suramericanas), modelled on the European Union (EU) was ratified by three member states (out of 10 founding members plus two associate members). Unasur intially seeked to integrate with the Andean Community of Nations and Mercosur in a single market by 2014, when tariffs on non-sensitive products are abolished with the remainder eliminated by 2019. However political tensions within the region have hampered the ongoing process.
Brazil is the world's largest producer of coffee, sugarcane and oranges and has the largest commercial cattle herd. The majority of the Amazon rain forest is located in Brazil, covering 50 per cent of the land. The government called a halt to 70 per cent of all forest clearing in 2008, which will limit to amount of new land available for cattle pastures. Many international car manufactures have assembly plants in Brazil.
Brazil is ranked in the top two for exports of Iron ore, beef, chicken, sugar, soybeans, orange juice, and ethanol.
China has now replaced the US as Brazil's largest trading partner.

Imports

Principal imports include mineral fuels and oil products, machinery and electrical equipment.
Main sources: China (16.3 per cent of total in 2014), US (15.3 per cent), Argentina (6.2 per cent).

Exports

Principal exports include vehicles and machinery, iron and steel, coffee, beef and other agricultural products, footwear and textiles.
Main destinations: China (18.0 per cent of total in 2014), US (12.0 per cent), Argentina (6.3 per cent).

Agriculture

Farming

Brazil's agricultural sector accounts for 5.8 per cent of total GDP and is responsible for 15.7 per cent of employment . This figure is no higher than that in comparable countries, but the significance of Brazil's agriculture sector lies in the fact that it has not declined as a percentage of GDP as development has gathered pace. Approximately 60 million hectares of the total land mass is used for agricultural purposes with another 90 million hectares available for cultivation. Large-scale farming is concentrated in the south and south-east of Brazil.
Brazil has shown remarkable progress in agribusiness development, which includes not just farming production but also increased investment in the sale of farm machinery and processing activities.
Brazil's agribusiness offers a diversified range of products from several regions and supplies cost-effective high quality food products. It accounts for over 40 per cent of the country's total exports.
Irrigated fruit growing in the São Francisco River and the Açu River Valleys, both located in north-eastern part of Brazil has contributed to its prosperous agribusiness sector.
Major agricultural exports include coffee (the world's largest producer and exporter), sugar cane (world's largest producer) and soya beans (world's second-largest producer after US). Orange juice (supplies 85 per cent of world market for orange juice concentrates), tobacco, cocoa, cotton, butter, maize, cattle (around 10 per cent of total world trade) and chicken are also significant.
Though agriculture has performed well in recent years, the sector's growth potential continues to be held back by poor transport infrastructure. Only 10 per cent of Brazil's roads are paved.

Fishing

Brazil has a coastline of 8,500km, 12 per cent of the world's freshwater reserves and two million hectares of flooded land. The country is yet to fulfil its vast potential for marine and freshwater fishing despite efforts by the national government to promote fish as an export commodity. Brazil's annual catch is typically in the range of 980,000 metric tonnes (mt) including 505,957mt marine fish and 117,863mt shellfish.

Forestry

Brazil has vast forest areas; some 543.9 million hectares with the humid tropical areas of the Amazon forests in the north-west of the country accounting for 95 per cent of the total forested area.
There are approximately five million hectares of forest plantations, the majority of which are pine and eucalyptus. However, vast areas of protected woodland land exist; 30 million hectares inclusive of state parks and national reserves.
In November 2009, the government reported that the annual rate of deforestation of the Amazon had fallen by 45 per cent and was the lowest level since 1988. The environmentalist campaign group, Greenpeace, claims government targets to reduce deforestation are too low, while others believe the downturn matches the global recession and will pick up when growth returns; the government plans to limit deforestation by 80 per cent by 2020.

Industry and manufacturing

Brazil's industrial sector is one of the most well developed in Latin America. Industry accounted for 23.8 per cent of GDP in 2014, of which manufacturing contributed 11 per cent to GDP, and was responsible for 13.3 per cent of employment.

and industrial goods account for up to 60 per cent of exports. Industry as a whole accounts for approximately 29 per cent of GDP and employs 20 per cent of the labour force.

Industry has relied primarily on imports of capital and intermediary goods, which are either higher quality or cheaper than domestically produced goods. This has caused balance of payments problems and depressed some sectors of industry, such as machine tools. In a drive to replace imports with domestically produced goods, the government has encouraged multinational investment in key sectors of industry. Problems arose in the pharmaceutical, biotechnology and computer industries when the government's desire for self-sufficiency caused it to ignore foreign patent rights and the payment of royalties.

Tourism

Brazil has some world-class and diverse attractions, from the primordial natural beauty of the Amazon rain forest to the street spectacle of the Rio de Janeiro Mardi Gras carnival. However, in its 2008 analysis, the Inter-American Development Bank (IADB) concluded that Brazil had the potential to be one of the world's top destination, but was hampered by its lack of general and tourist infrastructure, with tourist development largely concentrated along the coastline. Domestic tourism accounted for 5.5 times more revenue than foreign visitors in 2008 but until people can move more easily around the country a competitively structured market to attract more visitors is unlikely.

Brazil hosted the Football World Cup in 2014 and invested an estimated US$14 billion among the 12 host cities, to be used to refurbish hotels, public transport, airports and other tourism and hospitality facilities, as well as stadia. Other areas not involved in the competition were also offered US$573 million to enhance their tourism facilities as the country prepared for a surge in tourist numbers. Investments by the government, including a series of IADB loans, includes ecotourism in the Amazon region.

In 2014, over 6 million foreign visitors arrived in Brazil, with some 1.3 million arriving for the world cup. Brazil is also becoming popular with European visitors escaping a northern winter.

Travel and tourism in 2014 was forecast to directly contribute R$182.1 billion (US$82.0 billion) to GDP (3.5 per cent of total GDP) and in total, directly and indirectly, R$492.4 billion (US$221.8 billion), or 9.6 per cent of GDP. Visitor exports reached R$17.1 billion (US$7.7 billion), or 2.7 per cent of total exports. The industry was estimated to have committed R$59.6 billion (US$26.8 billion) in investment for 2014, which constitutes 6.8 per cent of total investment. Direct employment in travel and tourism was forecast to be over 3.1 million jobs, representing 3.1 per cent of total employment and 8.8 million jobs, including jobs that are indirectly supported by the industry, amounting to 8.8 per cent of total employment.

Environment

Around 20 per cent of the Amazon rain forest was felled between mid-1960s and 2007. The land cleared was given over to cattle and soya bean production. Illegal logging accounted for a proportion of this deforestation and in 2008 a presidential decree made it unlawful to trade in beef and soya produced on deforested properties.

In August 2010, the US agreed to convert US$21 million of Brazilian debt into a fund to halt deforestation and conserve the Atlantic coastal rainforest and the Cerrado and Caatinga ecosystems in Brazil. Around 90 per cent of the Atlantic coastal rainforest has been lost since Western explorers began to exploit the wealth of the region.

New satellite pictures issued in May 2011, showed that deforestation of the Amazon rainforest had increased from 103 square kilometres in March–April 2010 to 598 square km in March–April 2011. The Mato Grosso State, the centre of soya cultivation, had the largest loss of rainforest. Despite a fall in deforestation in December 2010 with the lowest recorded loss since late-1980s, deforestation jumped by 27 per cent from August 2010–April 2011.

Brazil says the rate of deforestation in the Amazon increased by 28 per cent between August 2012 and July 2013, after four years of steady decline. The contrast in the latest figures demonstrates the difficulty in obtaining accurate, consistant data.

Mining

Brazil is a major mining nation, ranking twelfth in the world gold production league (second in Latin America) with an annual output of 55 million tonnes. Forty tonnes is accounted for by formal mines and the remainder is generated by alluvial operations which are worked by prospectors.

The mineral potential of Brazil has not been fully assessed. Less than one-third of the country has been thoroughly prospected. The authorities are keen to exploit the country's raw material wealth and a comprehensive aerial survey has been completed by the government's National Mineral Resources Company (CPRM).

The centre of the mining industry is the state of Minas Gerais, named after the large number of gold and precious stone mines discovered in colonial times. Minas Gerais is also Brazil's main producer of mica, beryl, talc, marble, dolomite, graphite, zirconium, bauxite and nickel. There are also large known reserves of minerals scattered throughout the country with concentrations in the state of Rio Grande do Sul (copper, lead, zinc and wolfram), Bahia (lead, barite, quartz crystal and magnesite), Amapa (manganese) and São Paulo (lead, wolfram and zinc).

Brazil ranks as the world leader in production and reserves of niobium/colombium and as the world's top producer of tantalite (28 per cent of total world output). It is the second largest producer of iron ore, third largest producer of bauxite and fourth largest producer of tin. The Carajas mineral deposit contains most of these reserves.

Brazil has vast iron ore reserves, reportedly the world's sixth largest in volume, and is the world's second largest iron ore exporter. Iron ore is produced from the Quadrilateral area of Minas Gerais in the south-east and the Carajas region in Southern Para. The privatised Companhia Vale do Rio Doce (CVRD), which operates the Carajas deposit with 67 per cent iron metal content, is one of the world's top iron ore exporters.

Brazil is also an important gold producer. Gold production has been decentralised and the market has become more accessible. Minas Gerais is Brazil's main gold producing area, accounting for 45 per cent of the sector's total exports.

Copper has been mined from two sources, the state-owned Caraiba Metals in Bahia and a small mine in Rio Grande do Sul. Production at these two sites is uneconomic. CVRD expects to initiate production from Salobo in the Carajas complex.

Eight areas around Brazil have been found to contain uranium, although production is little more that 5,000 tonnes per annum.

Hydrocarbons

Proven oil reserves were 16.2 billion barrels at the end of 2014, with production at 2.3 million barrels per day (bpd). Consumption was 3.2 million bpd in 2014, a rise of 5.4 per cent from 2013 figure. Energy production is focussed on oil, with 48 per cent of domestic energy consumption coming from oil (including ethanol).

Brazil's refining capacity is 2.2 million bpd; work began on a joint Brazil-Venezuela oil refinery in 2007, whereby Brazil expects to increase oil refining by an additional 1.3 million bpd by 2015–20.
Oil exploration has intensified led by the state-owned entity Petrobrás, which announced in 2007, that a new offshore oil field, Tupi, could hold between 5–8 billion barrels of recoverable light oil with reserves of natural gas. Tupi alone could represent 40 per cent of the oil reserves that Brazil has ever discovered, although drilling for and extracting the gas will be challenging and costly. There are large reserves of oil shale concentrated in the south of the country, which have been exploited since 1880s.
Brazil is one of the world's largest ethanol producers, based on its sugar cane industry. It produced 6.2 trillion gallons in 2014, making Brazil the send largest producer of ethanol in the world, after the US.
Proven gas reserves were 500 billion cubic metres (cum) in 2014, despite Brazil's large gas fields located in the Campos and Santos basins. Production has grown steadily from 7.7 billion cum in 2001 to 20.0 billion cum in 2014, however consumption was 39.6 billion cum in 2014 and required imports of natural gas (from Bolivia) to make up the shortfall.
A new, 179km, natural gas pipeline was launched in 2010, capable of carrying 40 million cum per day, from the Campos and Espírito Santo basins to intersect with Brazil's principal gas terminal, Cabinúnas, in Duque de Caxias.
Proven reserves of coal were 6.6 billion tonnes in 2014, although it was sub-bituminous and lignite, used primarily in power stations. Production was 3.2 million tonnes oil equivalent (mtoe). Consumption of coal was 15.3 mtoe in 2014, a figure that has remained largely stable throughout the 2000s; imports bridged the shortfall.
At an auction held in Rio de Janeiro on 21 October 2013, a consortium of five companies won the rights to explore the Libra oilfield, reckoned to be Brazil's largest with as much as 8–12 billion barrels of recoverable oil reserves. The five companies are Petrobras (40 per cent), Total (20 per cent), Anglo-Dutch Shell (20 per cent), China National Petroleum Corporation (10 per cent) and China National Offshore Oil Corporation (10 per cent). Spain's Repsol pulled out of the auction, leaving the consortium as the only bidder. OGX, the oil and gas company controlled by the billionaire tycoon Eike Batista, filed for bankruptcy protection on 30 October 2013.

Energy

Brazil became a net exporter of energy, from sugar cane ethanol and hydroelectricity, in 2006. It has the largest hydroelectric resources in the Americas, with installed electric capacity of over 1,000MW of which hydropower provides over 80 per cent of all generation. Brazil and Paraguay jointly run one of the world's largest hydroelectric complexes, Itaipú on the Paraná River, which has a capacity of 13.3GW. Brazil financed its building, using Paraguay's resources; all excess electricity produced by Itaipú is sold to Brazil. In May 2009 a review of the contractual agreement was discussed at ministerial level as Paraguay considered the price paid by Brazil for its electricity had not increased since Itaipú became operational in 1973; Brazil considered Paraguay must consider the investment Brazil originally made. Future developments include the construction of more plants including a 4.1GW extension to Tucuruí and 37GW in other locations. Other electricity generation comes from coal and natural gas. Conventional thermal plants generate only 7.4 per cent of Brazil's total electricity. President Lula has expressed his administration's desire to expand hydroelectric power plants, leaving the future of conventional thermal generation unclear.
A controversial new hydroelectric dam, to be built in the Amazon rainforest on the Xingu River, was given its environmental licence in January 2010. When completed, at a cost of US$11 billion, the facility will produce 1.1GW of electricity. However 500 square kilometres will be inundated to provide the water catchment area and any indigenous communities within 100sq. km living along the river will be displaced.
Brazil has two nuclear power plants, both of which are operated by a subsidiary of Electrobras, Electronuclear, producing 2.5 per cent of electrical generation. The construction of the country's third nuclear facility, Angra-3 has been slowed by political disagreements and a shortfall in funds.

Financial markets

Stock exchange

Bolsa de Valores de São Paulo (Bovespa) (São Paulo Stock Exchange), La Bolsa 64, Santiago (Tel: 698-2001; fax: 697-2236

Commodity exchange

Maringá Mercantile and Futures Exchange, São Paulo

Banking and insurance

The government of President Lula da Silva, signalled its more cautious approach to bank privatisation, with the cancellation of the sale of a 17.8 per cent stake in Banco do Brasil, Latin America's largest retail bank. Less than a quarter of the banking industry in Brazil is owed by foreign institutions. The major market operators are domestic finance houses.
A new Bank of the South, with a headquarters in Venezuela, will be launched in 2008 to provide an alternative source of development funding for the participating countries. Assets of US$7 billion will underpin its operations.

Central bank

Banco Central do Brasil

Main financial centre

Rio de Janeiro and São Paulo

Time

GMT minus three hours (daylight saving GMT minus two hours): most eastern cities, São Paulo, Rio de Janeiro and Brasília
GMT minus two hours (no daylight saving): Fernando de Noronha Archipelago
GMT minus four hours (no daylight saving): Amazonas State
GMT minus five hours (no daylight saving): Acre State
Daylight saving time is determined and set locally.

Geography

Brazil borders all South American countries except Chile and Ecuador. The distance from north to south is 5,320km, and from east to west 4,328km. Brazil has a land frontier of 15,719km and an Atlantic coastline of 7,408km.
Although Brazil's topography varies greatly, it can be divided roughly into five zones: the Amazon basin, the River Plate basin, the Guiana highlands, the Brazilian highlands and the coastal strip.
The densely forested Amazon basin covers some 40 per cent of Brazil's territory but has only one inhabitant per square km. It receives heavy rainfall and floods annually.
The River Plate basin in southern Brazil is less heavily forested. The land is higher and the climate cooler. The Guiana highlands, north of the Amazon, are part forest and part scrubland. The Brazilian highlands, lying between the Amazon and the River Plate basin, form a tableland from 300 metres to 900 metres high.
There are a few mountain ranges, mostly in south-eastern Brazil.

Hemisphere

Southern

Climate

The average annual temperature increases from south to north. On the equator in the Amazon basin, average temperatures are 27 degrees Celsius (C) with no seasonal variation. From the latitude of the port of Recife to the border with Uruguay, the average temperature range is 17–19 degrees C. The two winter months in the south are June and July. Humidity is relatively high in Brazil, particularly in the Amazon basin and on the coast. The rainy seasons are January–April in the north, April–July in the north-east and November–March in the southern coastal area.

Dress codes

Suits are normally worn to business meetings, particularly in Brasília. They are also worn for formal social events and in exclusive restaurants and clubs. For other occasions smart casual clothes are suitable.

Lightweight clothing is advisable for all seasons in the north and for all but the two winter months in the south, when warmer clothing is necessary. Rainproof clothing or umbrellas are necessary during the rainy seasons.

Entry requirements

Passports

Required by all, except nationals of Argentina, Chile, Paraguay and Uruguay. Must be valid for at least six months from date of entry.

Visa

Required by all, except nationals of most EU member states, South America, Israel and some other countries. It is advisable to check online or with the nearest embassy or consulate for latest details.

Currency advice/regulations

There is no restriction on the import and export of local currency. Foreign currency import is unlimited but amounts must be declared; export of foreign currency is allowed up to US$4,000. Regulations may change at short notice. International credit cards are widely used, though cash advances are only paid in local currency.

Health (for visitors)

Mandatory precautions

A yellow fever certificate is required from travellers arriving from an infected country and any of the following countries: Angola, Bolivia, Cameroon, Colombia, Democratic Republic of Congo, Ecuador, Gabon, Gambia, Ghana, Guinea Republic, Liberia, Mali, Nigeria, Peru, Sierra Leone and Sudan.

Advisable precautions

Yellow fever vaccinations are essential for visits to infected areas within Brazil; these include Mato Grosso, Rondônia and states surrounding the Amazon.

Typhoid, tetanus and hepatitis A and B vaccinations are recommended. Malaria prophylaxis is advisable for visits to Amazon regions. There is a high risk of catching dengue fever. Rabies is also a risk. Water precautions should be taken.

Hotels

Graded from one- to five-stars. Wide range available in main towns but sometimes heavily booked (especially during Carnival) and advance booking advisable. Listings available from local tourist offices. Only five-star hotels are not price controlled.

A service charge is usually included in bill; if not, a 10 per cent tip is usual.

Credit cards

Amex, Diners, Mastercard and Visa widely accepted for purchases other than fuel.

Public holidays (national)

Fixed dates

1 Jan (New Year's Day), 21 Apr (Tiradentes Day), 1 May (Labour Day), 7 Sep (Independence Day), 12 Oct (Our Lady Aparecida, Patroness of Brazil), 2 Nov (All Souls' Day), 15 Nov (Proclamation of the Republic), 25 Dec (Christmas Day).

Variable dates

Carnival (five days, Feb), Good Friday, Easter Sunday, Corpus Christi (May/Jun).

Working hours

In Rio de Janeiro and São Paulo there is no siesta break; in Brasília there is a three-hour siesta from 1200–1500.

Banking

Mon–Fri: 1000–1600.

Business

Mon–Fri: 0900–1200; 1400–1800.

Government

Mon–Fri: 0930–1800.

Shops

Mon–Fri: 0900–1830/1900, Sat: 0900–1300. Shopping centres Mon–Sat: 0900–2200.

Telecommunications

Mobile/cell phones

GSM 900 and 1800 services available in most regions of the country.

Electricity supply

127V AC (Bahia (Salvador) and Manaus); 220V AC, 60Hz (Brasília and Recife); 110/220V AC, 60Hz (Rio de Janeiro and São Paulo).

Most hotels provide 100V and 220V outlets, transformers and adaptors.

Social customs/useful tips

There is generally a relaxed attitude towards timekeeping in Rio de Janeiro and the north-east, but people are much more punctual in São Paulo and Brasília. It is the usual practice to shake hands in greeting and on departure. When invited to someone's home for a meal, a gift of flowers for the hostess is customary.

Security

The Brazilian authorities insist on extensive personal documentation. This should be carried at all times.

Brazil's big coastal cities, particularly Rio de Janeiro and those situated in the north-east, have serious crime problems. Street robberies are common and press estimates put the number of armed assaults on bus passengers in Rio alone at about 20 per day.

First-time visitors to Rio are advised to be extremely cautious in allowing strangers to engage them in conversation, especially in areas such as the Avenida Atlantica (the Copacabana sea-front) and the western suburbs. It is inadvisable to visit the Baixada Fluminense, where a murder rate of 20 deaths per day makes the district one of the most violent areas in the world.

Getting there

Air

National airline: Varig (Viação Aérea Rio Grandense, privatised in July 2006).

International airport/s: Brasilia-International (BSB), 11km from city, with duty-free shop, bar, restaurant, buffet, bank, post office, shops, hotel reservations, car hire; Rio de Janeiro Galeão-International (GIG), 15km north of city, bank, hotel, taxi, duty-free shop, restaurant; São Paulo-Cumbica (GRU) 25km north-east of city; Recife (REC).

Other airport/s: Fortaleza (FOR), Salvador-Dois de Julho (SSA), Belem-Val de Cans (BEL), Belo Horizonte-Pampulha (BHZ).

Airport tax: US$36, but should be included in ticket price.

Surface

Road: It is possible to reach Brazil by road from Argentina, Bolivia, Paraguay and Uruguay.

In January 2011 a road from Nazca on the Peruvian coast, across the Andes cordillera to Cusco and on to Inapari on the border with Brazil was officially opened by some 30 racing drivers. The road is expected to increase trade between the two countries, especially Brazilian exports to Asia. There are, however, fears for the ecology of region as the road opens up the area to miners with heavy equipment to replace the old panners. Migration too is having an effect as miners move from the Andes to the Amazon. The 2,589km road took five years to build.

Rail: There are rail connections to Argentina and Uruguay.

Water: There are boats sailing along the Rio Paraguay between Asunción in Paraguay and Corumba. There are also boat services to Peru along the Amazon.

Getting about

When travelling between cities on public transport, visitors must carry passports as proof of identity is required.

National transport

Air: Regular domestic and charter flights to all main cities. Air is the main form of long-distance travel. Air taxis are available at most domestic airports. Advance booking is not necessary for shuttle flights between Rio de Janeiro and São Paulo (about one hour). Domestic flights are expensive, although safety and quality of service are good.

Road: All main centres are connected by surfaced highways, with particularly good roads in the north. Many of the local roads are in need of urgent repair. In total, around 1.6 million km of roads are supervised by the Departmento Nacional de Estradas de Rodagem (DNER).

Buses: Buses are the most popular means of transport with frequent inter-city bus services between main centres. Standards are variable although many routes are now served by modern high quality coaches. Sleeping berths (*leito*) are available on some routes.

Rail: State- and privately-owned railways operate limited services to most main centres throughout the country. Service is generally slower than bus and long distance travelling can be uncomfortable. Good sleeper services with restaurant cars operate between São Paulo, Rio de Janeiro and Belo Horizonte.

Water: Services on São Francisco River between Juazeiro and Pirapora and up the Amazon to Manaus. Hydrofoil service between Rio de Janeiro and Niteroi.

City transport

Taxis: Metered taxis, identified by their roof lights, are available almost everywhere in urban areas. They are inexpensive and often rudimentary. The fare is regularly adjusted according to a table posted on the inside of a rear window. In Rio de Janeiro, there are several types; these include so-called 'common' taxis (yellow with checkered stripe) and the more expensive radio taxi (white, with a red and yellow stripe). A 40 per cent surcharge operates between 2300–0600, on Sundays and public holidays. Tipping is optional.

Travellers arriving by plane are advised to use the main taxi companies which operate desks at major airports and run on a fixed-charge basis. Their cars are big and air-conditioned and although rates are more expensive than those officially charged by standard taxis, it is advisable to use them to avoid frequent exploitation of unwary travellers by individual operators.

Buses, trams & metro: Extensive services operate in all main centres. Efficient though crowded. Two types – regular and special (*fresces*).

Metro: Two-line service in Rio de Janeiro. Line one goes from Botafogo Station to Saenz Peña Station (Tijuca): Mon–Sat: 0600–2300. Line two cuts across the city's centre, from Estácio Station to the Maria de Graca Station: Mon–Sat: 0600–2000.

There is also a two-line network in São Paulo.

Integrated bus/metro tickets available.

Car hire

Car hire is expensive.

An international driving licence is advisable. Traffic is often congested in main cities. Petrol is of poor quality and expensive.

Service stations are rare on some roads and often close on Sundays.

BUSINESS DIRECTORY

The addresses listed below are a selection only. While World of Information makes every endeavour to check these addresses, we cannot guarantee that changes have not been made, especially to telephone numbers and area codes. We would welcome any corrections.

Telephone area codes

The international dialling code (IDD) for Brazil is +55 followed by the area code:

Belem	91	Porto Alegre	51
Belo Horizonte	31	Recife	81
Brasilia	61	Rio de Janeiro	21
Campinas	19	Salvador	71
Curitiba	41	Santos	132
Fortaleza	81	São Paulo	11
Manaus	92		

Chambers of Commerce

American Chamber of Commerce in Brazil (Rio de Janeiro), Praça Pio X 15, 20040-020 Rio de Janeiro (tel: 2203-2477; fax: 2223-0438; e-mail: achambr@amchamrio.com.br).

American Chamber of Commerce in Brazil (São Paulo), Rua da Paz 1431, Chácara Santo Antônio, 04713-001 São Paulo (tel: 5180-3804; fax: 5180-3777; e-mail: amhost@amcham.com.br).

Brazilian International Chamber of Commerce, 1.200 Rua Timbiras, 30140-060 Belo Horizonte (tel/fax: 3273-7021; e-mail: camint@camint.com.br).

British Chamber of Commerce in Brazil (Rio de Janeiro), Avenida Graça Aranha 1, Centro, 20030-002, Rio de Janeiro (tel: 2262-5926; fax: 2240-1058; e-mail: rio@britcham.com.br).

British Chamber of Commerce in Brazil (São Paulo), Rua Ferreira de Araújo 741, Pinheiros, 05428-002 São Paulo (tel: 3819-0265; fax: 3819-7908; e-mail: britcham@britcham.com.br).

Rio de Janeiro Chamber of Commerce and Industry, Rua da Assembléia 93, Centro, 20011-001 Rio de Janeiro (tel: 2532-0089; fax: 2532-1918; e-mail: chamber@ccirj.com).

São Paulo Associação Comercial, 51 Rua Boa Vista, Centro, 01014-911 São Paulo (tel: 3244-3322; fax: 3244-3355; e-mail: infocem@acsp.com.br).

Banking

Banco America do Sul, Alameda Ribeirão Preto 87, 7 andar, Zona postal 01331, PO Box 8075, São Paulo (tel: 287-7955; fax: 287-2762).

Banco Bandeirantes, Rua Boa Vista 162, 7 andar, Zona postal 01014-902, São Paulo (tel: 823-1122; fax: 239-5959).

Banco Boavista, Familia Paula Machado, Zona postal 20091-040, PO Box 1560, Rio de Janeiro (tel: 211-1711; fax: 253-9036).

Banco Bozano Simonsen, Av Rio Branco 138, Zona postal 20057, PO Box 3074, Rio de Janeiro (tel: 271-8232; fax: 271-8160).

Banco Brasileiro Iraquiano, Praça Pio X 54 Centro, Zona postal 20091, Rio de Janeiro (tel: 253-2020/ 2255; fax: 253-3498).

Banco Chase Manhattan, Rua Alvares Penteado 131, Zona postal 01012, São Paulo (tel: 345-751; fax: 239-0594).

Banco de Credito Nacional, Rua Boa Vista 208, Zona postal 01014-030, PO Box 4222, São Paulo (tel: 235-1079, 235-1118; fax: 356-892).

Banco de la Nación Argentina, Av Paulista 2319, Sobreloja, Zona postal 01311, PO Box 22-25, São Paulo (tel: 280-2674; fax: 881-4630).

Banco de la Provincia de Buenos Aires, Rua L Badaró 425, 26 andar, Zona postal 01009, São Paulo (tel: 258-8798; fax: 257-4557).

Banco de la República Oriental del Uruguay, Av Paulista 1776, 9 andar, Zona postal 01310, São Paulo (tel: 251-2699/ 2454; fax: 289-8245).

Banco de Montreal, Trav do Ouvidor 4, Zona postal 20149, Rio de Janeiro (tel: 270-209/ 0210; fax: 221-2706).

Banco do Estado de São Paulo, Praça Antonio Prado 06, 6 andar, Zona postal 01062-900, PO Box 35565, São Paulo (tel: 259-6622, 259-7722; fax: 348-523).

Banco Exterior de España, Av Paulista 1963, 1 andar, Zona postal 01311, PO Box 51623, São Paulo (tel: 251-4344; fax: 288-8015).

Banco Francés e Brasileiro, Av Paulista 1294, 12 andar, zona postal 01310-915, PO Box 8017, São Paulo (tel: 252-7163/64; fax: 283-0794).

Banco Geral do Comercio, Rua Funchai 160, 5 andar, Zona postal 04551-060, São Paulo (tel: 828-7322; fax: 828-7208).

Banco Mercantil de São Paulo, Av Paulista 1450, 9 andar, Zona postal

01310-917, PO Box 4077, São Paulo (tel: 252-2121/2228; fax: 284-3312).

Banco Mitsubishi Brasileiro, Rua Libero Badaró 6633/641, Zona postal 01009-904, PO Box 8449, São Paulo (tel: 239-5244; fax: 362-128, 362-060).

Banco Noroeste, Rua Alvares Penteado 216, 3 andar, Zona postal 010102, PO Box 8119, São Paulo (tel: 239-0844, 378-401; fax: 354-858).

Banco Real, Av Paulista 1347, 3 andar, Zona postal 01310-916, PO Box 5766, São Paulo (tel: 285-5645, 251-9796; fax: 251-9222).

Banco Region de Desenvolvimento do Extremo Sul, Rua Uruguai 155, Porto Alegre (tel: 228-9200; fax: 228-8283).

Banco Safra, Av Paulista 2100, Bela Vista, Zona postal 01310, PO Box 9139, São Paulo (tel: 251-7575; fax: 251-7211).

Banco Sogeral, Av Paulista 1355, 12 andar, Zona postal 01311-924, São Paulo (tel: 251-5533; fax: 283-1449).

Banco Sudameris Brasil, Av Paulista 1000, 14 andar, Zona postal 01310-100, PO Box 3481, São Paulo (tel: 283-9251/9260; fax: 283-9269).

Unibanco-União de Bancos Brasileiros, Av Euzébio Matoso 891, 4 andar, Zona postal 05423-901, PO Box 8185, São Paulo (tel: 817-4322; fax: 815-5084).

Central bank

Banco Central do Brasil, Setor Bancário Sul, Quadra 03, Bloco B, Edificio Sede, PO Box 08670, 70074-900 Brasília DF (tel: 3414-2401; fax: 3321-9453; e-mail: cap.secre@bcb.gov.br).

Stock exchange

Bolsa de Valores de São Paulo (Bovespa) (São Paulo Stock Exchange), La Bolsa 64, Santiago (Tel: 698-2001; fax: 697-2236

Alvares Peuteado 151, São Paulo (tel: 233-2147; fax: 233-2226; www.bovespa.com.br).

Bolsa de Valores do Rio de Janeiro (BVRJ), (Rio de Janeiro Stock Exchange)

Praça 15 de Novembro 20, 2010 Rio de Janeiro (tel: 271-1001; fax: 221-2151; www.bvrj.com.br).

BOVMESB (Bolsa de Valores Minas, Espírito Santo, Brasília), www.bovmesb.com.br

Maringá Mercantile and Futures Exchange, São Paulo

Brazilian Mercantile Futures Exchange (BM&F Bovespa), www.bmfbovespa.com.br

Travel information

Car Club do Brasil, Rúa Mexico 11, Rio de Janeiro 20006-900 (tel: 2533-1129; fax: 2220-2400; e-mail: viasat@carclubdobrasil.com.br).

EMBRATUR (Empresa Brasileira de Turismo), Rua Mariz e Barros 13, Rio de Janeiro 20270 (tel: 273-2212).

VARIG SA, Edif Varig, Avenida Almirante Silvio Noronha 365, 20021 Rio de Janeiro (tel: 272-5000; fax: 272-5700).

Ministry of tourism

Conselho Nacional de Turismo (CNTUR), Ministry of Infrastructure, Rua Mariz e Barros 13, 5 andar, 20270 Rio de Janeiro (tel: 273-0691).

National tourist organisation offices

Centro Brasileiro de Informação Turística (CEBITUR) (Brazilian Tourist Office), Rua Mariz e Barros 13, 6 andar, Praça da Bandeira, 20270-000 Rio de Janeiro (tel: 293-1313; fax: 273-9290).

Ministries

Ministry of Administration, Esplanada dos Ministérios, Bloco C, CEP 70046-900 Brasília-DF (tel: 224-2682; fax: 225-8927).

Ministry of Agrarian Policy, SBN Ed Palácio do Desenvolvimento, CEP 70057-900 Brasilia-DF (tel: 223-8852; fax: 226-8727).

Ministry of Agriculture, Esplanada dos Ministerios, Bloco D, 8 andar, CEO 70043-900 Brasília DF (tel: 226-5161, 226-5380; fax: 225-9046).

Ministry of the Air Force, Esplanada dos Ministérios, Bloco M, CEP 70045-900 Brasília-DF (tel: 321-5303; fax: 223-2592).

Ministry of the Armed Forces, Esplanada dos Ministérios, Bloco Q, CEP 70049-900 Brasília-DF (tel: 223-5356; fax: 321-2477).

Ministry of the Army, QG/EX, Bloco A, SMU, CEP 70630-900 Brasília-DF (tel: 315-5200, 224-2844; fax: 223-1145).

Ministry of Communications, Esplanada dos Ministerios, Bloco R, 80 andar, CEP 70040-900 Brasília DF (tel: 225-9381, 224-9723; fax: 226-3980).

Ministry of Culture, Esplanada dos Ministérios, Bloco B, CEP 70068-900 Brasília-DF (tel: 224-6064; fax: 225-9162).

Ministry of Education, Esplanada dos Ministérios, Bloco L, CEP 70047-900 Brasília-DF (tel: 321-1076; fax: 224-3618).

Ministry of Environment, Water Resources and Amazonia, Esplanada dos Ministérios, Bloco B, CEP 70068-900 Brasília-DF (tel: 322-7819; fax: 226-7101).

Ministry of External Relations, Esplanada dos Ministérios, Palácio do Itamaraty, CEP 70170-900 Brasília-DF (tel: 211-6100; fax: 223-7362).

Ministry of Finance, Esplanada dos Ministérios, Bloco P, CEP 70048-900 Brasília-DF (tel: 314-4805; fax: 322-5009).

Ministry of Health, Esplanada dos Ministérios, Bloco G, CEP 70058-900 Brasília-DF (tel: 224-5269).

Ministry of Industry, Trade and Tourism, Esplanad dos Ministerios, Bloco J, CEP 70056-900 Brasília DF (tel: 325-2001; fax: 325-2209).

Ministry of Institutional Reform, Palácio do Planalto, Praca dos Tres Poderes, CEP 70150-900 Brasília-DF (tel: 322-9619; fax: 211-1192).

Ministry of Justice, Esplanada dos Ministérios, Bloco T, Ed Sede, CEP 70064-900 Brasília-DF (tel: 226-2296; fax: 322-6817).

Ministry of Labour, Esplanada dos Ministérios, Bloco F, CEP 70056-900 Brasília-DF (tel: 226-6137; fax: 226-3577).

Ministry of Mines and Energy, Esplanada dos Ministerios, Bloco U, 70 andar, CEP 70065-900 Brasília DF (tel: 218-5447, 223-9059; fax: 225-5407).

Ministry of the Navy, Esplanada dos Ministerios, Bloco N, 20 andar, CEP 70055-900 Brasília DF (tel: 223-6858, 312-1000; fax: 312-1202).

Ministry of Planning and Budget, Esplanada dos Ministérios, Bloco K, CEP 70048-900 Brasília-DF (tel: 224-0679; fax: 225-4032).

Ministry of Science and Technology, Esplanada dos Ministérios, Bloco E, CEP 70067-900 Brasília-DF (tel: 224-4364; fax: 225-1141).

Ministry of Social Security, Esplanada dos Ministérios, Bloco F, CEP 70059-900 Brasília DF (tel: 224-5914; fax: 223-2293).

Ministry of Sport, Esplanada dos Ministérios, Bloco A, CEP 70054-900 Brasília-DF (tel: 224-5285; fax: 224-3618).

Ministry of Transport, Esplanada dos Ministerios, Bloco R, CEP 70040-900 Brasília DF (tel: 224-0185, 224-0995; fax: 226-4864).

President's Office, Palácio do Planalto, 40 andar, CEP 70150-900 Brasília-DF (tel: 211-1303, 211-1034; fax: 226-2078, 321-5804).

Other useful addresses

Associação do Comercio Exterior do Brasil (Exporters' Association), Avenida General Justo 335, Rio de Janeiro (tel: 240-5048).

British Consulate-General, Praia do Flamengo 284, 22210-030 Rio de Janeiro (tel: 553-3223; fax: 553-6850).

British Embassy, Setor de Embaixadas Sul, Quadra 801, Loto 8, Conjunto K, 70408-900 Brasília DF (tel: 225-2710, 223-5357; fax: 225-1777).

Companhia Vale do Rio Doce (CVRD – State Mining Company), Avenida Graca Aranha 26, Bairro Castelo, 20005 Rio de Janeiro (tel: 272-4477).

Companhia Vale do Rio Doce (CVRD – State Mining Company), Avenida Graça Aranha 26, Bairro Castelo, 20005 Rio de Janeiro (tel: 272-4477).

Confederação Nacional de Agricultura (CNA – National Agriculture Federation), Brasília DF (tel: 225-3150).

Confederação Nacional da Industria (CNI – National Confederation of Industry, comprising the 21 state industry federations), Edificio Roberto Simonsen, 16 andar, 70040 Brasília DF (tel: 224-1328).

Council of the States' Reform Programme, Av Borges de Medeiros, No 1501, 7 Andar, CEP 90119-900, Porte Alegre, Rio Grande do Sul (tel: 228-2708, 334-5275; fax: 226-5893, 382-4607).

Departamento Nacional de Telecomunicões (Dentel), Via N2, Anexo do Ministerio das Comunicações, Esplanada dos Ministerios, Bloco R, 70044 Brasília DC (tel: 223-3229).

Divisão de Feiras e Turismo-Departamento de Promocão Comercial (Organisers of Trade Fairs and Tourism), Ministerio das Relacões Exteriores, Esplanada dos Ministerios, 2 andar, 70170 Brasília (tel: 211-6644).

Fundacão Instituto Brasileiro de Geografia e Estatistica (IBGE – Brazil Institute of Geography and Statistics), Avenida Franklin Roosevelt 166, Castelo, 20021 Rio de Janeiro (tel: 220-6671).

National Department of Foreign Trade, Avenida Presidente Vargas 328, 11 andar, 20091 Rio de Janeiro (tel: 271-7504).

Petroleo Brasileiro-Petrobras Segen/ Gasbol (State Oil Company), Rua General Canabarro 500, CEP 20271-201, Maracana, Rio de Janeiro (tel: 566-3733; fax: 566-5723/5299).

Rede Ferroviaria Federal (SA – Federal Railway Corporation), Praça Procopio Ferreira 86, 2221 Rio de Janeiro (tel: 223-5795).

Secretaria Especial de Desenvolvimento Industrial (Industrial Development Council), Ministerio de Desenvolvimento da Industria e Comercio, Lotes 2/5-2/8, Bloco G, 8 andar, 70070 Brasília DF (tel: 225-7556).

Superintendencia da Zona Franca de Manaus (Manaus Free Zone Authority), Rua Ministro João Gonçalves de Souza, Cidade Universitaria, Distrito Industrial, 69000 Manaus (tel: 237-3288).

US Embassy, Avenida das Naçoes, Lote 3, 70403-900 Brasília DF (tel: 321-7272; fax: 225-9136).

World Trade Centre (WTC), Av das Naçoes Unidas, 12-551, Sao Paulo (tel: 893-7113; fax: 893-7101).

National news agency: Agencia Brazil (in Portuguese): www.agenciabrasil.gov.br

Agencia Estado: www.ae.com.br/institucional

Agencia Globo: www.agenciaoglobo.com.br

Folha Press (business news): www.folhapress.com.br

PR Newswire (business news): www.prnewswire.com.br

Safras e Mercado (business news): www.safras.com.br

Internet sites

Banco do Brasil: www.bancobrasil.com.br

Banco Itaú: www.itau.com.br

Brazilian Embassy in London: www.brazil.org.uk

Brazilinfo: www.brazilinfo.net

Brazil American Chamber of Commerce: www.amcham.com.br/

Brazil Statistics: www.ibge.gov.br/home/

National Industry Confederation (markets and industry information): www.cni.org.br

Discover Brazil: http://www.brazil.com/

British Virgin Islands

KEY FACTS

Official name: British Virgin Islands

Head of State: Queen Elizabeth II; represented by Governor John Duncan (from 15 Aug 2014)

Head of government: Premier Orlando Smith (from 9 Nov 2011; re-elected 8 June 2015)

Ruling party: National Democratic Party (NDP) (from 9 Nov 2011, re-elected 8 Jun 2015)

Area: 153 square km

Population: 31,148 (2011)*

Capital: Road Town

Official language: English

Currency: US dollar (US$) = 100 cents

* estimated figure

COUNTRY PROFILE

1493 The islands were sighted by Columbus.
1595 Sir Francis Drake visited the channel that runs through the islands and which now bears his name.
1648 The islands were settled by the Dutch.
1666 English settlers arrived.
1672 Tortola was taken over by the English.
1872 The islands became part of the UK colony of the Leeward Islands. The British Virgin Islands (BVI) continued to come under the authority of the governor of the Leeward Islands until 1960.
1960 An appointed administrator (renamed governor in 1971) assumed responsibility for the islands.
1967 Lavity Stoutt of the Virgin Islands Party (VIP) became the first chief minister as the islands were granted internal self-government.
1995 The VIP won the elections.
1997 The National Democratic Party (NDP) was formed.
1999 The VIP was re-elected.
2002 Islanders became British citizens under the British Overseas Territories Act.
2003 The NDP won parliamentary elections and Orlando Smith became chief minister.
2004 A review of the constitution, by the BVI Constitutional Review Commission, began.
2005 The BVI began imposing a withholding tax on EU citizens' savings. The tax is passed to the relevant EU country, although without the savers' names. The BVI government purchased the Virgin Gorda Airport for US$2.9 million, to maintain the tourist interests of the territory's second most populated island.
2006 David Pearey was sworn in as governor.
2007 A new constitution was promulgated. In parliamentary elections, the opposition Virgin Islands Party (VIP) won 10 seats out of 13, defeating the National Democratic Party (NDP) with two, and one independent; turnout was 62.3 per cent. Premier Ralph O'Neal was sworn into office.
2008 Premier O'Neal became the first locally elected leader to chair a meeting of the Executive Council.
2009 The government signed an agreement with the Organisation for Economic Co-operation and Development (OECD), removing the BVI from the list of countries that do not implement international standards for tax disclosure.
2010 Governor David Pearey retired and V Inez Archibald became acting governor until Boyd McCleary took office on 20 August. The Securities, Investment Business (and Mutual Fund) Advisory (SIBA) Committee was established to review regulations and recommend changes that govern BVI financial services.
2011 In March, the office of the Governor of US Virgin Islands official requested that BVI stopped practices that produce pollution for its neighbour, including open air rubbish burning at the BVI incineration plant on Tortola. In parliamentary elections held on 7 November, the opposition NDP won 49.4 per cent of the vote (nine seats out of 13) and the incumbent VIP won 42 per cent (four); turnout was 75 per cent. Orlando Smith took office as premier on 9 November.
2012 In January Taiwan passport holders were granted visa-free entry to BVI. A special report was published on 17 February, concerning the national health insurance scheme, planned to be rolled out in 2013. The government-run insurance plan will be compulsory for all residents, funded through a tax on a worker's wages, although the rate was not given.
2013 On 1 May the British Virgin Islands, along with Bermuda, the Cayman Islands, Anguilla, Montserrat and the Turks and Caicos Islands, signed a tax sharing agreement with the tax authorities of France, Germany, Italy, Spain and the UK.
2014 Overseas Territory representatives from the British Virgin Islands, Bermuda, Montserrat, the Cayman Islands and Anguilla met with United Kingdom business networking specialists, CaribDirect International Business Network (CIBN) in May. CIBN is an agency designed to facilitate and connect entrepreneurs and business people in the UK with Caribbean government and business representatives for trade and investment. John Duncan was sworn in as Governor on 15 August.
2015 Governor Duncan dissolved parliament on 1 May. Elections have to be held no later than 30 June. On 8 May Acting

Governor Inez Archibald announced the election would be held on 8 June. The Commonwealth election observation mission arrived on 1 June in preparation of the election. The election was won convincingly by the ruling National Democratic Party (NDP) with seven (out of nine) district constituencies, as well as the four 'at large' seats. The Virgin Islands Party (VIP) won the remaining two seats, down from the four they held after the last election.

Political structure

Constitution

BVI is a British Overseas Territory with a large degree of internal self-government, based on a new constitution which was promulgated in March 2007. A ministerial system of government is enshrined. It increases the authority of the BVI government, particularly with new powers for international affairs and internal security and direct local control of police matters. Fundamental human rights for individuals were included. The prime minister has greater influence for setting cabinet agenda and a new role of cabinet secretary has been created.

The post of premier replaced the former role of chief minister.

The British monarch appoints a governor as a representative.

Form of state

British Caribbean dependency

The executive

Executive power is exercised by the governor, appointed by the British monarch, the premier and four other ministers elected by members of the house of assembly.

National legislature

The unicameral, House of Assembly, comprises 13 members, plus an *ex-officio* attorney general and a speaker of parliament. Nine members are elected to represent each district, with the remaining four representing a territory-wide vote.

The premier nominates an executive council, which is appointed by the governor.

Legal system

The legal system is based on the English common law system with local variations. Justice is administered by the Eastern Caribbean Supreme Court. A resident puisne judge presides over the High Court, Admiralty and associated courts. There is a Court of Appeal. Final appeals go to the Privy Council in the UK.

Last elections

8 June 2015 (parliamentary)

Results: Parliamentary: National Democratic Party (NDP) won 60.2 per cent of the vote (11 seats out of 13), the Virgin Islands Party (VIP) 30.2 per cent (two).

Next elections

2019 (parliamentary)

Political parties

Ruling party

National Democratic Party (NDP) (from 9 Nov 2011)

Main opposition party

Virgin Islands Party (VIP)

Population

31,148 (2011)*

Last census: May 2001: 20,647

Population density: 121 inhabitants per square km.

Annual growth rate: 3.2 per cent (2003)

Ethnic make-up

African (83 per cent), white, Indian, Asian and mixed race.

Religions

Methodist (45 per cent), Anglican (21 per cent), Church of God (7 per cent), Seventh-Day Adventist (5 per cent), Baptist (4 per cent).

Education

The education sector will receive US$46.7 million from the 2004 Budget.

Health

Details of a national health insurance scheme was introduced in December 2011, to provide treatment for all citizens and paid for either through insurance policies or by public benefits for those that require assistance.

Welfare

A social security scheme exists for workers between the ages of 16 and 65. The scheme covers old age pensions, disability and a survivors fund. Contributions are shared between the employer and employee, each providing 3.25 per cent of salary. Self-employed workers pay the full 6.5 per cent.

Main cities

Road Town, on Tortola island (capital, estimated population 12,603 in 2012), East End-Long Look.

Languages spoken

Official language/s

English

Media

Press

There are three local weekly newspapers including *Island Sun* (http://islandsun.com), *BVI Beacon* (www.bvibeacon.com) and the *BVI Stand Point* (www.vistandpoint.com).

Broadcasting

All broadcasting is private and commercial and listeners benefit from easy access to US Virgin Island media outlets.

Radio: There are four stations located on the islands and named after their call signs. Radio ZBVI (www.zbviradio.com), Isle 95, WJKC (www.isle95.com), and ZVCR (www.zvcr1069fm.com) playing island music; Zking Radio (www.zkingradio.com) is a religious broadcaster.

Television: The Virgin Islands Television Network (VITV) is privately-owned. Orbit Satellite TV (www.orbit.net) and Innovative (www.iccvi.com) cable TV, provide many channels.

Other news agencies: Caribbean Net News: www.caribbeannetnews.com

Economy

The economy is driven by financial services and tourism. The islands have one of the highest per capita incomes of not only the Caribbean but also the world, at over US$39,015 in 2011 (most recent available). BVI's large offshore banking business is particularly successful in trust management, mutual funds and captive insurance. The financial services are fully open and connect to the North American and European banking and financial systems. The service sector was estimated to have contributed 87.2 per cent to GDP in 2013. BVI caters for wealthy tourists in high-end hotels and holiday lets and as a port of call for Caribbean cruise-liners; it is also an established charter yacht centre. Over 85 per cent of GDP was generated by the tourist sector in 2014. Apart from livestock, the agricultural sector is unable to provide sufficient food for domestic consumption and most of it has to be imported. Construction and light industry comprises just over 11 per cent of GDP, providing employment for around 40 per cent of the workforce, whilst tourism directly employed 34.5 per cent of the workforce in 2014.

Following the recession caused by the global economic crisis, GDP growth started to pick up along with tourist numbers and by 2011 it had reached 2.5 per cent. Growth was expected to have increased further in 2012 reaching an estimated 4 per cent. Inflation rate has been decreasing since the high of 7.1 per cent in 2008 caused by the crisis, and fell to 2.2 per cent in 2012 before falling even further in 2013 to 1.6 per cent.

External trade

The trade deficit is offset by tourist spending, capital inflows and by workers' remittances. BVI is an associate member of the Caribbean Community (Caricom) and the Organisation of Eastern Caribbean States (OECS).

Imports

Principal imports are special purpose ships and recreational boats, refined petroleum, foodstuffs, consumer goods, machinery and equipment, building materials and vehicles.

Main sources: US Virgin Islands, Puerto Rico, US, South Korea, Ukraine, Germany

Exports

Principal exports are recreational boats, fruit, vegetables, live animals, fish, rum, gravel and sand.

Main destinations: US Virgin Islands, Puerto Rico, US, Spain, Switzerland

Agriculture

Farming

The agricultural sector contributes just over 1 per cent to the annual GDP. About 60 per cent of the total land area is agricultural.

Production is centred on livestock farming, fishing (langoustine, prawns), food crops (mainly fruit and vegetables) and sugar cane for rum production.

Main areas of activity are Tortola, Virgin Gorda and Jost Van Dyke.

The expansion of the tourist industry has increased the dependence on imported foodstuffs, mainly from the US.

Industry and manufacturing

The industrial sector contributed 11.7 per cent to annual GDP in 2013. Industries include construction, concrete and rum production.

Tourism

Tourism is primarily based on marine activities and water sports for visitors who enjoy tropical sunshine, white beaches and the company of other tourists. With a local population of around 25,000 and annual tourist numbers of around 800,000 the industry is the principal generator of business, employment and capital investment and it is vital to the economy.

The tourism sector constituted 85.9 per cent of GDP in 2014, forecast to have risen by 1.5 per cent in 2015. This is a marked improvement on a decade low of 52.9 per cent in 2009 when visitor numbers fell by 10.7 per cent, mostly during the height of the tourist season (January–April) when 16.3 per cent fewer tourists visited. There were 41,400 fewer cruise liner passengers, despite an increase in the number of visiting ships – 408 cruise liners in 2008 and 421 liners in 2009. In 2014, tourism exports reached as high as 62.0 per cent of GDP and were forecast to have risen by 1.6 per cent in 2015. In 2014, tourism supplied employment reached over 94.5 per cent of the workforce, expected to have risen by 0.2 per cent in 2015.

In 2013, the US-based Marriott International completed construction of its new luxury spa and marina, Scuba Island Resort, development on Tortola.

Hydrocarbons

There are no known hydrocarbon reserves. Imported petroleum products meet all domestic energy needs. Consumption of oil was 1,190 barrels per day in 2013.

Any coal or natural gas products used are commercially insignificant.

Energy

Total installed generating capacity was 44MW in 2011 (most recent available), from 11 power stations. The state-owned BVI Electricity Corporation has a monopoly on electricity generation, transmission and distribution.

In June 2015, the Finnish energy company Wärtsilä announced it would be extending the Pockwood Pond Power Generating Station. After being completed in late 2016 the total capacity of the plant will be 50MW.

Banking and insurance

The business and financial services sector is the largest contributor to government income, accounting for around 60 per cent of the total. There are over 500,000 International Business Corporations (IBC) incorporated in the British Virgin Islands, regulated by the Financial Services Commission (FSC). The FSC operates as an independent regulator and is responsible for domestic and offshore finance.

The seven members of the Organisation of Eastern Caribbean States (OECS), Antigua and Barbuda, Dominica, Grenada, Montserrat, St Kitts and Nevis, St Lucia and St Vincent and the Grenadines, share a common currency (the East Caribbean dollar (EC$)) and central bank. The British Virgin Islands and Anguilla are associate members.

Under an EU tax directive, introduced in July 2005 in a number of associate and dependent EU countries, the BVI imposed a withholding tax for EU citizens. The tax is passed to the relevant EU tax department while retaining the anonymity of the saver. Withholding taxes began at 15 per cent and rose to 35 per cent in 2011. The withholding tax was abolished in January 2012 in favour of disclosure of information.

BVI has also agreed to supply information on tax fraud, for criminal or civil trials, and notify EU member states about additional malpractices.

On 1 May 2013 the British Virgin Islands, along with Bermuda, the Cayman Islands, Anguilla, Montserrat and the Turks and Caicos Islands, signed a tax sharing agreement with the tax authorities of France, Germany, Italy, Spain and the UK.

Central bank

There is no central bank.

Main financial centre

Tortola

Offshore facilities

The British Virgin Islands Financial Services Commission licenses and regulates all service providers operating within the offshore sector.

Time

GMT minus four hours

Geography

At the northern end of the Leeward Islands, in the eastern Caribbean, the British Virgin Islands consist of more than 60 islands and cays, of which only 16 are inhabited. Most of the islands are mountainous and of volcanic origin; the coralline island of Anegada is the only exception of any size. They lie about 100km to the east of Puerto Rico and adjoin the US Virgin Islands.

Hemisphere

Northern

Climate

The climate is sub-tropical, with no marked seasonal variation in temperature – generally 24–30 degrees Celsius (C) during the day and 10 degrees C cooler at night. Rainfall is generally low, although the hurricane season, occuring between July–November, can produce violent, torrential downpours.

Entry requirements

Passports

Required by all

Visa

Not required by most tourists for visits up to one month, with return/onwards tickets, pre-arranged accommodation and sufficient funds for stay. Longer stays require premission from the immigration department.

Some visitors will, and business visitors may, require a visa; see www.bvitourism.com/immigration for more details.

Currency advice/regulations

No restriction on import of foreign currency but amounts should be declared. Exports limited to the amounts declared on arrival.

Health (for visitors)

Mandatory precautions

None.

Advisable precautions

Typhoid vaccinations. Dengue fever is a viral disease transmitted by mosquitoes, which are most likely to bite two hours after sunrise and two hours before sunset. Use an effective insect repellent on all exposed skin. Take water precautions.

Hotels

Expensive, but wide range available. There is a 7 per cent government tax and hotels may impose a 10 per cent service charge usually added to the bill.

Public holidays (national)

Fixed dates

1 Jan (New Year's Day), 1 Jul (Territory Day), 21 Oct (St Ursula's Day), 25–26 Dec (Christmas).

If a holiday falls at the weekend the following Monday is taken in *lieu*.

Variable dates

H Lavity Stoutt's birthday (first Mon in Mar), Commonwealth Day (second Mon in Mar), Good Friday, Easter Monday, Whit Monday, Queen's Official Birthday (Jun), August Festival Day (first Wed in Aug).

Working hours

Banking

Mon–Fri: 0900–1500; also Fri: 1600–1700.

Business

Mon–Fri: 0800/0900–1600/1700. Sat 0800–1200

Government

Mon–Fri: 1230–2030.

Shops

Open for longer than offices and bank and are open all day Saturday.

Telecommunications

Mobile/cell phones

GSM 900/1900 coverage throughout the islands.

Electricity supply

110 volts AC, 60Hz, using US two-pin plugs.

Getting there

Air

There are no direct North American or intercontinental flights to the islands, all major air-carriers arrive via regional hubs. There are around six air charter-hire companies operating in BVI that fly to surrounding Caribbean islands.

National airline: There is no national airline.

International airport/s: Terrance B Lettsome International Airport (EIS) on Beef Island, 15km from Road Town on Tortola. Only inter-island and intra-Caribbean flights arrive at this airport, including regular flights from Puerto Rico, US Virgin Islands and Antigua.

Airport tax: Departures tax US$20, not applicable to transit passengers.

Surface

Water: There are regular, daylignt running, ferries to and from St Thomas and St John on the US Virgin Islands.

There is a US$5 departure tax when leaving by boat and US$7 for cruise passenger leaving the islands.

Main port/s: Tortola: West End, Beef Island, Road Town; Virgin Gorda: Spanish Town, Yacht Harbour.

Getting about

National transport

Air: There are around 10 domestic air charter companies that fly between the islands.

Road: The main highway from Beef Island through Road Town to West End is surfaced. There is a bridge connecting Beef Island with Tortola. There is also a surfaced road on the northern ridge from east to west. Roads on Virgin Gorda are in variable condition.

Taxis: On Tortola taxis may be chartered by agreement.

Water: Various types of boats ply between islands. Regular ferry services operate between Road Town and West End (Tortola).

City transport

Taxis: Widely available with published fixed fares. The taxi rank in Road Town is opposite the central post office, and the Taxi Association on Wickhams Cay. Tipping is optional. Taxis can be hired on an hourly or daily basis.

Car hire

Vehicles can be hired on Tortola and Virgin Gorda. Drivers must be aged at least 25 years and hold their own valid, national driving licence. A BVI driving permit must be obtained, for a fee – the rental company can issue this.

Driving is on the left and roads can be steep and unpaved.

BUSINESS DIRECTORY

The addresses listed below are a selection only. While World of Information makes every endeavour to check these addresses, we cannot guarantee that changes have not been made, especially to telephone numbers and area codes. We would welcome any corrections.

Telephone area codes

The international direct dialling (IDD) code for the British Virgin Islands is +1284, followed by subscriber's number.

Chambers of Commerce

BVI Chamber of Commerce and Hotel Association, James Frett Building, PO Box 376, Road Town, Tortola (tel: 494-3514; fax 494-6179; e-mail: bviccha@surfbvi.com).

Banking

Banco Popular de Puerto Rico, PO Box 67, Road Town, Tortola (tel: 494-2117; fax: 494-5294).

Bank of Nova Scotia, PO Box 434, Road Town, Tortola (tel: 494-2526; fax: 494-4657).

Barclays Bank International, PO Box 70, Road Town, Tortola (tel: 494-2171; fax: 494-4315).

Chase Manhattan Bank, PO Box 435, Road Town, Tortola (tel: 494-2662; fax: 494-3863).

CITCO Ban (BVI) Ltd, PO Box 662, Road Town, Tortola (tel: 494-2217; fax: 494-3917).

Crorebridge Bank, PO Box 71, Road Town, Tortola (tel: 494-2233; fax: 494-3547).

Disa Bank BVI, PO Box 985, Road Town, Tortola (tel: 494-4977; fax: 494-4980).

Guyerzeller Bank, PO Box 3162, Road Town, Tortola (tel: 494-5414; fax: 494-5417).

London International Bank and Trust Company, PO Box 3151, Road Town, Tortola (tel: 494-3045; fax: 494-3050).

Rathbone Bank, PO Box 986, Road Town, Tortola (tel: 494-6544; fax: 494-6532).

The Bank of East Asia, PO Box 901, Road Town, Tortola (tel: 495-5588; fax: 494-4513).

United Chinese Bank, PO Box 901, Road Town, Tortola (tel: 494-6775; fax: 494-8180).

VP Bank, PO Box 3463, Road Town, Tortola (tel: 494-1100; fax: 494-1199).

Travel information

Air Sunshine Inc (tel: 495-8900; email: EMail@AirSunshine.com).

Caribbean Wings (tel: 495-6000; email: carwings@yahoo.com).

Fly BVI Ltd, PO Box 3347, Roadtown (tel: 495-1747; fax: 495-1973; email: info@fly-bvi.com).

Island Birds, PO Box 993 Road Town, Tortola; Beef Island Airport (tel: 495-2002; email: info@islandbirds.com).

Island Helicopters International Ltd, PO Box 2900, East End; Beef Island Airport, Tortola (tel: 495-2538; (emergency medical transfers, tel: 499-2663); internet: info@helicoptersbvi.com; internet: www.helicoptersbvi.com).

National tourist organisation offices

BVI Tourist Board, Joshua Smith Building, PO Box 134, Road Town, Tortola (tel: 43-134; fax: 43-866; internet: www.bvitourism.com).

Ministries

Governor's Office, Government House, PO Box 702, Road Town, Tortola (tel: 494-2345, 494-2370, 494-3520; fax: 468-4490).

Other useful addresses

BVI Hotel and Commerce Association, PO Box 376, Wickhams Cay, Road Town, Tortola (tel: 43-514, 42-947; fax: 46-179).

BVI Financial Services Commission, Pasea Estate, Road Town, Tortola (tel: 494-4190; fax: 494-9399; e-mail: commissioner@bvifsc.vg; internet site: http://www.bvi.org).

BVI Offshore Financial Centre, Financial Services Department, Ministry of Finance, Pasea Estate, Road Town, Tortola (tel:

494-6430; fax: 494-5016; internet site: http://www.bvi.org).

Cable and Wireless (West Indies), PO Box 440, Road Town, Tortola (tel: 44-444; fax: 42-506).

Immigration Department, Road Town, Tortola (tel: 494-3701, 494-3471; fax: 494-4399).

Trade and Investment Promotion, Trade Department, Central Administration Complex, Road Town, Tortola (tel: 494-3701; fax: 494-5676).

VITV (Virgin Islands Television) Network, Butu Mountain, PO Box 118, Road Town, Tortola (tel: 494-8488/2257; fax: 494-5323).

ZBVI Radio, PO Box 78, Road Town, Tortola (tel: 494-2250; fax: 494-1139).

ZRODFM (radio station), PO Box 992, Road Town, Tortola (tel: 494-1037/5832; fax: 494-4564).

Caribbean Net News: www.caribbeannetnews.com

Internet sites

Caribbean Wings - BVI Airlines: www.bvi-airlines.com

The Island Sun: www.islandsun.com

Brunei

The proposed adoption of Sharia law was in response to the perception by many local Muslims that a new penal code was needed to combat a growing tide of immorality. The prospect had led to calls for Britain, for largely historical reasons Brunei's closest ally, to reconsider its close relationship with the former Protectorate, which only became independent in 1984. In 2013 the British prime minister, David Cameron, had already faced criticism for agreeing to attend a Commonwealth summit in Sri Lanka, where human rights abuses are known to be common. The prime minister now came under pressure to disavow Brunei's adoption of Sharia's medieval legal system. As reported in the *Daily Telegraph*, Phil Robertson, deputy director of the Asia division of Human Rights Watch (HRW) called for 'a major international outcry to stop this law and Great Britain should take the lead.'

The *Daily Telegraph* went on to note that 'Sultan Hassanal Bolkiah is not used to having his decisions challenged. The 67-year-old is head of state and prime minister, as well as finance and defence minister. Ruling in near feudal fashion, the Sultan does not tolerate dissent or opposition political parties.'

The Sultan's wealth 'enables him to pay for a British Army garrison of about 1,000 soldiers – mainly a battalion of Gurkhas – which informally guarantees his rule.' The Sultan's palace in Bandar Seri Begawan is patrolled by former Gurkhas, rather than local troops and the British Army retains a jungle warfare training school in Brunei.

Emergency, but not democracy

As confirmed by the human rights monitoring group, Freedom House, Brunei is anything but a modern electoral democracy. The Sultan wields broad powers under a long-standing state of emergency and no direct legislative elections have been held since 1962. Citizens convey concerns to their leaders through government-vetted councils of elected village chiefs.

The reform efforts of the Sultan have been largely superficial and have been principally designed to attract foreign investment. The unicameral Legislative Council has no political standing independent of the Sultan. However, the council's mounting oversight activity and queries aimed at the government reflect a growing demand for accountability and responsible spending. These tentative

KEY FACTS

Official name: Negara Brunei Darussalam (The Sultanate of Brunei)

Head of State: Sultan Haji Hassanal Bolkiah Mu'izzaddin Waddaulah, the Sultan and Yang Di-Pertuan of Brunei Darussalam (crowned Aug 1967)

Head of government: Sultan Haji Hassanal Bolkiah Mu'izzaddin Waddaulah, the Sultan and Yang Di-Pertuan of Brunei Darussalam

Ruling party: There is no ruling party.

Area: 5,765 square km

Population: 413,000 (2014)*

Capital: Bandar Seri Begawan

Official language: Behasa Melayu

Currency: Brunei dollar (B$) = 100 cents

Exchange rate: B$1.41 per US$ (Sep 2015)

GDP per capita: US$36,607 (2014)*

GDP real growth: -0.70% (2014)*

GDP: US$15.10 billion (2014)*

Labour force: 198,800 (2010)

Unemployment: 2.70% (2014)*

Inflation: -0.24% (2014)*

Oil production: 126,000 bpd (2014)

Natural gas production: 11.90 billion cum (2014)

Balance of trade: US$8.77 billion (2012)

* estimated figure

reforms were considered preparations for an eventual succession and the expected depletion of the country's oil and gas reserves, which account for about 90 per cent of state revenues (see 'Economy' & 'Energy' below.)

Unsurprisingly, given the context, genuine political activity in Brunei remains extremely limited. In 2007, the Registrar of Societies formally disbanded the People's Awareness Party and forced the president of the Brunei National Solidarity Party (PPKB) to resign. The PPKB was then deregistered without explanation in 2008, leaving the National Development Party as Brunei's sole remaining political party.

The government claims to have a zero-tolerance policy on corruption and its Anti-Corruption Bureau has successfully prosecuted a number of lower-level officials in recent years. The sultan's brother and former finance minister, Prince Jefri Bolkiah, has faced a number of legal challenges, including a 2008 arrest warrant, over accusations that he had misappropriated state funds. He was eventually ordered to return personal assets to the state. In 2012, Hassanal's nephew, Prince Abdul Hakeem Jefri, was also sued for a breach of agreement over shares of the Singaporean company Elektromotive Group Ltd. Brunei was ranked 46 out of 176 countries surveyed in Transparency International's 2012 *Corruption Perceptions Index.*

The economy

According to the Asian Development Bank (ADB), Brunei's gross domestic product (GDP) contracted by an estimated 1.2 per cent in 2014, a second consecutive year of decline, as oil and gas production continued to shrink. The oil and gas sector, which directly accounts for almost two-thirds of the economy, has contracted since 2012. Production of crude oil and condensate fell to 135,000 barrels per day (bpd) in the first half of 2013 from 151,000bpd a year earlier. Since 2006, daily oil output has fallen by about 40 per cent with the depletion of existing oilfields, protracted closures for maintenance of ageing equipment and government policy to manage oil production so that it lasts until other industries can generate a larger share of GDP. The production of natural gas dropped to 1,225 million cubic feet a day in the first half of 2014 from 1,248 million in the first half of 2013. (See 'Hydrocarbons' below)

The rest of the economy – mainly services, construction and manufacturing – grew by an estimated 2.6 per cent in 2014, based on data through September. The services sector, particularly those services provided by the government, contributed most of this growth. Construction and agriculture grew, but manufacturing contracted. From the demand side, private consumption recorded a modest rise. Government consumption increased, but fixed investment decelerated and net exports fell from 2013, reflecting the weakness in oil and gas production. The government rebased its 2010–2013 national accounts to 2010, which deepened the GDP contraction in 2013 to 2.1 per cent. Using the new base year, GDP grew by 0.8 per cent on average over 2011–13.

Merchandise exports comprised mainly crude oil, liquefied natural gas and methanol. In 2014, exports fell by 6.9 per cent to US$10.7 billion. Imports, which provide most of the country's food, consumer goods and capital equipment, fell by 5.1 per cent to US$3.4 billion. That narrowed the trade surplus to a still large US$7.2 billion and the current account surplus to US$4.7 billion, equal to 26.4 per cent of GDP. International reserves rose to US$3.5 billion, cover for 12.1 months of imports of goods.

Prices eased in 2014 for many consumer goods and services: food and drink, clothing and footwear, housing and utilities, household furnishings and recreation. These declines more than offset small increases in health care, transportation, communications, education and restaurant and hotels costs, so that the consumer price index fell by 0.2 per cent on average from 2013. Price controls and subsidies curtail inflation in the economy.

Income from hydrocarbons through taxes, dividends and royalties provides the government almost all of its revenue to fund a relatively large public sector and to invest in infrastructure and subsidise consumer goods and services. However, declining hydrocarbon production and plunging oil prices have reduced the government's revenue (See 'Hydrocarbons' below). In the 2013 financial year (ended 31 March 2014) revenue fell by 17.3 per cent. Government spending was virtually flat, leaving a fiscal surplus equal to 9.3 per cent of GDP. Revenue dropped by a further 21.5 per cent in the first 3 quarters of 2014, when the government reduced its spending by 8.4 per cent. The Brunei dollar, which is pegged at par to the Singapore dollar through a currency board arrangement, depreciated by 4.7 per cent against the US dollar between the end of 2013 and the end of 2014. Growth in credit slowed from 8.1 per cent in 2013 to 2.3 per cent in the third quarter of 2014.

In February 2014, the monetary authority relaxed a cap on personal loans from 30 per cent to 40 per cent of all bank loans and in October 2014 it removed a cap on interest rates on residential property loans. The launch of a real-time gross settlement system in November was part of an effort to modernise the national payment and settlement systems.

Prices eased in 2014 for many consumer goods and services: food and drink, clothing and footwear, housing and utilities, household furnishings and recreation.

KEY INDICATORS — Brunei

	Unit	2011	2012	2013	2014	**2015
Population	m	*0.42	0.40	0.41	*0.41	*0.42
Gross domestic product (GDP)	US$bn	15.50	16.95	16.11	*15.10	*11.24
GDP per capita	US$	36,584	42,402	39,659	*36,607	*26,804
GDP real growth	%	1.9	0.9	-1.8	*-0.7	*-0.5
Inflation	%	2.0	0.1	0.4	*-0.2	*0.0
Unemployment	%	2.7	2.7	*2.7	*2.7	*2.7
Oil output	'000 bpd	166.0	158.0	135.0	126.0	–
Natural gas output	bn cum	12.8	12.6	12.2	11.9	–
Exports (fob) (goods)	US$m	–	12,881.8	–	–	–
Imports (fob) (goods)	US$m	–	4,116.2	–	–	–
Balance of trade	US$m	–	8,765.7	–	–	–
Current account	US$m	5,294.0	7,947.0	5,558.0	*3,558.0	*-1,099.0
Total reserves minus gold	US$m	–	3,285.0	3,398.5	3,471.2	–
Foreign exchange	US$m	–	2,932.0	3,044.1	–	–
Exchange rate	per US$	1.28	1.22	1.27	1.33	–

* estimated figure ** forecast figure

These declines more than offset small increases in health care, transportation, communications, education and restaurant and hotel costs, so that the consumer price index fell by 0.2 per cent on average from 2013. Price controls and subsidies also curtailed inflation in the economy. Subdued production and the impact of lower global prices for hydrocarbons were expected to see GDP contract in 2015 before a slight rebound in 2016, assuming some recovery in oil and gas output.

Accurate forecasting is hampered by the uncertainty over the timing of oil and gas production from new fields and of stoppages for maintenance of wells and pipelines. Prospects for growth also depend on the timing of several large construction projects. The biggest was an oil refinery and aromatics cracker planned for Pulau Muara Besar with the capacity to produce 160,000bpd of petroleum products for domestic use and for export. Originally planned to start operating in 2017, Sheikh Rashid Salam, vice president of corporate services of petrochemical firm Hengyi Industries Sdn Bhd, told *The Brunei Times* at the end of 2014 that the project has been held back for another 12 months to make way for the installation of a coking plant and the 'construction of a single buoy mooring. The delay is in the redesigning and integration of these equipments and related processes onto the original (design) for at least 12 months.' he said.

Also in 2014, People's Republic of China (PRC) investors signed a land-lease agreement with Brunei to build a US$50 million carbon steel pipe factory. This plant was scheduled to start operating in 2017, with the capacity to produce 100,000 tons per year of welded rounding carbon steel pipes for the oil and gas and construction industries. A company from the Republic of Korea signed a non-binding agreement to build a US$107 million plant to produce 120,000 tons per year of aluminium billet casting and 48,000 tons per year of aluminium extrusions, mainly for export. Led by a company from PRC, this project was expected to involve investment over several years of more than US$2.5 billion. In January 2014, the company signed a land lease agreement with the Brunei Economic Development Board.

These projects are part of the government's strategy to diversify the economy through export-oriented manufacturing and services. The government intends to build bridges, roads and utilities for the projects. It is investing in a high-speed broadband network and hopes to revive plans to import hydropower from neighbouring Sarawak (Malaysia). However, the government had also signalled that its expenditure in 2015 would be constrained by the slide in revenue from oil and gas.

Consumer prices are forecast to decline marginally again in 2015, despite a recent increase in prices and the potential for further depreciation of the Brunei dollar against the US dollar. In 2016, prices are seen edging higher as domestic demand improves and global commodity prices turn up.

Hydrocarbons

As noted above, Brunei relies on hydrocarbon revenues for nearly two-thirds of its GDP and the vast majority of its merchandise exports and government revenues. The lower oil prices seen in 2014 and 2015 have adversely affected Brunei's export revenues. However, according to the US government Energy Information Administration (EIA), the Brunei government intends to bolster investment in its oil and gas sector and diversify the country's economic base by promoting growth in other industries over the long term.

Through its long-standing joint venture with the Royal Dutch Shell oil company, Brunei has produced oil and natural gas for several decades, primarily from two large, mature fields – Southwest Ampa and Champion – in the offshore Baram Delta. After reaching a peak of 220,000 barrels per day (bpd) in 2006, the EIA reported that Brunei's petroleum and other liquids production has declined by nearly half to an estimated 124,000bpd by 2014. Many of Brunei's oil and natural gas fields are aging and are located in shallow waters that have been explored. The Brunei government's latest energy policy in 2014 included attracting US$70-US$80 billion in foreign investment over the next 20 years to boost the country's oil and gas reserves and production levels.

Brunei has an interest in hydrocarbon development in the South China Sea and has only one claim in the hotly contested Spratly Islands – the Louisa Reef, a small island that is part of the country's exclusive economic zone and is located in the south-eastern part of the Spratly Islands. The Louisa Reef also lies within China's 'nine-dash line', a sizeable claim to the South China Sea which also encompasses all of the Spratly Islands. An offshore settlement established with Malaysia in 2010 allowed Brunei to explore untapped and formerly disputed deep-water areas in the Baram Delta and issue more production sharing contracts to help prop up oil and natural gas production and offset declines from older existing fields. Petronas of Malaysia and the Brunei National Petroleum Company (Petroleum Brunei) signed a 40-year agreement in 2010 to jointly explore these two blocks. In 2013, Petroleum Brunei and Petronas also signed several co-operation agreements for the joint development of oil and gas fields in both countries' deep-water offshore areas.

Despite the recent decline in production, the EIA notes that Brunei is the largest net exporter of total petroleum liquids in the Asia-Pacific region, given its minimal domestic consumption. In 2014, Brunei's net exports of total liquids were about 106,000bpd, primarily crude oil sent to key Asian oil consumers, including Indonesia, Japan, South Korea, China and Malaysia. Brunei plans to expand its refinery capacity; the Chinese company Zhejiang Hengyi Group (see above also) is constructing a new refinery with a capacity of 148,000bpd now scheduled to come online by 2019. This new facility could shift the dynamics of the country's oil exports in favour of consuming more crude oil and exporting more petroleum products.

Brunei produced about 440 billion cubic feet (bcf) of dry natural gas in 2013, mostly from Southwest Ampa, Champion and other fields associated with oil production. Although domestic gas demand has increased steadily in the past decade, Brunei still exports on average about three-quarters of its output. The French oil company Total made significant natural gas and condensate discoveries in Block B in 2010, which could bolster Brunei's natural gas reserve base, sustain its production levels and support LNG exports over the next decade.

Risk assessment

Politics	Poor
Economy	Good
Regional stability	Fair

Muslims in Brunei

% of population	67
Sunni (% of Muslims)	99
Shi'a (% of Muslims)	1

COUNTRY PROFILE

1839 When an English explorer, James Brooke, arrived on the island of Borneo, he helped the Sultan to suppress an uprising against the rule of the Brunei Sultanate. As a reward for the role he played in quelling the rebellion, in 1841, the Pengiran Mahkota of Brunei made Brooke the Rajah of Sarawak on the north-west

coast of Borneo (Sarawak is now the largest state in Malaysia). The British North Borneo Company began expanding its influence on the island.
1888 Brunei became a British protectorate, keeping the Sultanate out of the Malaysian confederacy. Brunei's monarch retained control over internal matters while the British took charge of external affairs.
1906 A treaty with Britain assured Brunei's status as a protectorate and the succession of the ruling dynasty. Executive power, including the right to advise the Sultan on all affairs except religion, was transferred to the British.
1929 Oil was discovered in the Seria field, ensuring the country's future prosperity.
1941–45 Brunei was occupied by the Japanese.
1959 An agreement was drawn up to allow Brunei internal self-government.
1962 In the run-up to Brunei's proposed amalgamation with Malaysia, the British pressured Sultan Omar Saifuddin into holding elections. The opposition Partai Rakyat Brunei (PRB) (Brunei People's Party) won a convincing victory, campaigning against unification, for complete independence from the UK and the creation of a constitutional monarchy. The Sultan's rejection of the result and his plans to unite with Malaysia led to an armed uprising which was quickly crushed (with British backing). A state of emergency was declared and political control was vested in the hands of the Sultan. The Sultan decided against union with Malaysia.
1970 The Sultan banned all elections, saying he would rule by decree under a state of emergency.
1979 Brunei concluded a treaty of friendship with the UK.
1984 Brunei became independent from the UK, under Sultan Haji Hassanal Bolkiah Mu'izzaddin Waddaulah, who had ruled since the abdication of his father in 1967.
1990 Sultan Bolkiah introduced his philosophy of Melaya Islam Berjaya (MIB) (Malay Islam Monarchy) which emphasises obedience and deters the questioning of authority.
1991 The sale of alcohol was forbidden. Nationals were required to wear Muslim garments.
1998 Prince al Muhtadee Billah, the Sultan's eldest son, was inaugurated as crown prince.
2000 Legal action was initiated against Prince Jefri Bolkiah, younger brother of the Sultan, for misusing US$15 billion while head of the state investment agency.
2002 Licences were awarded to two foreign consortiums, Royal Dutch/Shell and TotalFinaElf, to explore for oil deposits in Brunei's 200-mile Exclusive Economic Zone (EEZ) in the South China Sea.
2004 Parliament was reconvened for first time since 1984, with 21 appointed members.
2005 The Sultan sacked four members of his cabinet, replacing them with younger, more progressive candidates, and introduced reform measures. The constitution was changed so that the Sultan became infallible under the law. Parti Pembanguan (PP) (National Development Party) registered as a political party.
2007 Prince Jefri Bolkiah, former finance minister and brother of the Sultan, lost an appeal to the supreme court over the embezzlement of an estimated US$6 billion in public funds and was required to pay back the sum.
2008 A warrant for the arrest of Prince Jefri Bolkiah, was issued by a UK high court after he failed to attend a court summons to determine ownership of his exclusive luxury London home and to return billions of US dollars to the Brunei government.
2009 The new Sarawak legislative assembly building in Petra Jaya, was opened.
2010 A border dispute that impeded oil exploration was resolved when Brunei and Malaysia agreed to joint development of two exploration sites.
2011 In July, the US trade representative warned Brunei that it risked being placed on a US Priority Watch List of intellectual property rights violators, due to continued infringements. The statement came at the start of Brunei's first legal copyright prosecution case.
2012 The daughter of the Sultan of Brunei was married on 20 September.
2013 In a report published in October the Organisation for Economic Co-operation and Development (OECD) said that Brunei's economy was projected to grow by an average of 2.4 per cent from 2013 to 2017 as South-east Asia generally recovers from a slowdown in 2011 and 2012.
2014 In May a number of Hollywood stars boycotted the Beverly Hills Hotel after the owner, Sultan Hassanal Bolkiah, reportedly said he was going to introduce Sharia (Muslim law).
2015

Political structure

Constitution

The Sultanate of Brunei (Negara Brunei Darussalam) became a fully independent sovereign state on 1 January 1984, when a ministerial system of government was established. Previously it had been a protectorate of Britain.

The Sultan rules partly by decree, and a state of emergency has been in force since a large-scale revolt in December 1962 which resulted in the suspension of sections of the constitution.

In lieu of democracy and to act as conduits of two-way communication between government and populace, there is a system of village and rural-district consultative councils.

In addition to the cabinet or council of ministers, three other councils advise the Sultan on the running of the country. These are:
- the Religious Council, which advises on all Islamic matters. The council also gives advice on legal matters; the Islamic court falls under its jurisdiction.
- the Privy Council, which is concerned with constitutional matters such as the exercising of royal prerogative and the awarding of honorary titles.
- the Council of Succession, which is empowered to determine the succession to the throne should the need arise.

Independence date

1 January 1984

Form of state

Autocratic sultanate

The executive

The Sultan and Yang Di-Pertuan (paramount ruler) is the sovereign head of state and prime minister, retaining supreme executive authority. He is also head of the Islamic faith in Brunei and minister for defence.

A ministerial system of government was introduced following independence in 1984. The cabinet, presided over by the Sultan in his position as prime minister, consists mostly of members of the Sultan's family. Ministers are appointed to hold office at the Sultan's pleasure.

National legislature

The Legislative Council of 20 appointees was abolished at independence in 1984, ending a purely consultative role.

A General Assembly of 1,000 village chiefs from 150 villages and 35 *mukim* (village groups) took place in 1996, described as an expression of a 'grassroots political system' by the Sultanate. Chiefs were chosen by secret ballot of villagers but the Sultanate appoints the Assembly's advisers.

There is a legislative council comprised of 36 members (33 full and 3 ex officio). It works purely as a consultative body to the Sultan and all members are directly appointed by the Sultan.

Legal system

Sharia (Islamic) courts were established in 1996 to handle family and criminal law. Their emphasis on publicly shaming offenders is designed to prevent anti-social and anti-Islamic activities. In October 2013 the government announced the enforcement of a tough new Sharia law penal code. The code will apply to Muslims only and is expected to include death by

stoning for adulterers and the severing of limbs for theft.
Brunei has an independent legal system. It is a distinctive, separate branch of government, based on the English common law system. Apart from the Sharia courts, the legal system includes:
- the High Court, which hears appeals in criminal and civil matters from subordinate courts. It is presided over by the chief justice and various commissioners.
- the Court of Appeal, which hears appeals against High Court decisions. It consists of a president and two commissioners.
- subordinate courts, which have limited jurisdiction in civil and criminal cases, and are presided over by a chief magistrate.
- the Courts of Kathis, which deal with certain religious (Islamic) matters. These are marriage, divorce, inheritance and sexual crimes. The Courts of Kathis have jurisdiction over Muslims and supercede the civil law only in these matters.

Last elections
There have been no elections since 1962.

Political parties

There are three legally registered parties: Parti Perpaduan Kebangsaan Brunei (PPKB) (Brunei National Solidarity Party) (deregistered 2008), Parti Kesedaran Rakyat Brunei (PAKAR) (Brunei People's Awareness Party) (disbanded 2007 by the Registrar of Societies) and Parti Pembangunan Bangsap (NDP) (National Development Party). As members of parliament, which was re-opened in 2004, are appointed, the parties have no representation at present. The constitution has been amended to allow election of a proportion of the parliament

Ruling party
There is no ruling party.

Main opposition party
No political parties are represented in the Legislative Council.
About 46 per cent of the population are aged 20 or under. Total population figures at any given time include 25 per cent transient workers.
There is a generally high standard of living. The kingdom's population enjoys free education and a wide range of social services.
Over half of the inhabitants live in the immediate district of Brunei/Muara, close to the capital Bandar Seri Begawan.

Population

399,000 (2012)*
Last census: August 2001: 332,844 (provisional)
Population density: 72 inhabitants per square km (2010). Urban population 76 per cent (2010 Unicef).
Annual growth rate: 2.3 per cent, 1990–2010 (Unicef).

Ethnic make-up
Indigenous (predominantly Malay) (69 per cent), Chinese (18 per cent), Indian (3 per cent), other (10 per cent). There are severe obstacles to further Chinese naturalisation and their emigration to China has been encouraged. The 50,000 Chinese living in Brunei play a negligible role in the country's political life, although they are vital to its economic success. Around a third of the Chinese population is naturalised. The same is true of the non-Malay indigenous population, which remains on the fringe of society but forms a crucial part of the workforce.

Religions
Sunni Islam (official faith and religion of all Malays). Members of the Chinese community are either Buddhist, Confucianist, Taoist or Christian. There are also ancient native religions.

Education

Primary schooling includes one year of compulsory pre-school education. Secondary education is divided into junior schools, lasting for three years between the ages of 12 and 15, and upper secondary schools, for another two years. Pre-university further education lasts for up to two years.
In 1985, the government established the University of Brunei Darussalam. In addition, there are two state-run teacher training colleges and six technical schools. If a university course is not available in Brunei, the government will pay for its students to study at a foreign university.
Education for expatriate children is provided by missionary schools, the International School and Chinese schools. All are fee paying and education at the International School follows a UK curriculum, but only caters for children up to the age of 12.
Literacy rate: 91 per cent, adult rates (World Bank)
Compulsory years: Five to 12

Health

The government has used its revenues from oil to provide one of the best healthcare systems in Asia. Health services are free for Brunei citizens, although there is a nominal fee for hospital and dentist treatment.
The healthcare system is based on health clinics, which provide primary care and include mobile clinics to reach the most isolated regions, health centres and district hospitals. The central hospital in Bandar Seri Begawan (Raja Isteri Pengiran Anak Saleha) has 550 beds and provides diagnostic and therapeutic facilities for the whole country. There are also government-operated hospitals in Tutong, Temburong and Kuala Belait. A Flying Medical Service reaches areas inaccessible by road. British Shell Petroleum (BSP) has its own private facilities in Seria.
The government is committed to increase its expenditure towards health care and building more clinics. Brunei continues to rely on expatriate doctors to run its health system. Government health surveys have shown that local doctors have made up only 10 per cent, and local dentists 32 per cent, of the medical workforce in the country.
Life expectancy: 78 years, 2010 (Unicef 2012)
Fertility rate/Maternal mortality rate: 2.0 births per woman, 2010 (Unicef 2012)
Child (under 5 years) mortality rate (per 1,000): 8 per 1,000 live births (WHO 2012)

Welfare

The Employees Trust Fund or Tabung Amanah Pekerja (Tap) provides membership to a providence fund that is open to all government workers and private sector employees. The scheme requires compulsory contributions from both the employer and the employee at a contribution rate of 5 per cent each. Universal old age pensions are granted those who have been residents for 30 years.
The ministry of culture, youth and sport oversees the distribution of pensions to citizens not holding contributory pensions and also provides welfare provisions for needy families and the handicapped. The government subsidises housing and food. Under the National Housing Scheme (NHS), the state grants housing to those who have lived under Temporary Occupation Licences (TOL). The Housing Scheme for Landless Citizens also gives land title deeds to those who have been occupying land under TOL.

Main cities

Bandar Seri Begawan (capital, estimated population 34,940 in 2012), Kampong Ayer (44,687), Kuala Belait (29,682), Seria (oil field) (29,569), Tutong (22,532).

Languages spoken

The national education system is formally bilingual for all, in Malay and English. Chinese is spoken; English is the principal commercial language.

Official language/s
Behasa Melayu

Media

With media ownership in the hands of, or controlled by, the royal family or if privately owned where self-censorship for political or religious reasons is widespread press freedom is severely curtailed. Legal sanctions against journalist can be up to three years imprisonment for 'false' reporting. The US-based media watchdog, Freedom House, rated Brunei as not free, with virtual no criticism of the government allowed.

Press

Publications that provide a variety of views and information beyond anything the newspapers controlled by the Sultan's family are able to achieve are either *The Straits Times* or Chinese publications produced in Sarawak and Singapore.

Dailies: In Malay, *Media Permata* (www.brunei-online.com/mp), in English, *Borneo Bulletin* (www.brunei-online.com/bb), and the independent *The Brunei Times* (www.bt.com.bn), which reports on international news.

Weeklies: In Malay, the official government newspaper *Pelita Brunei* is published every Wednesday, and in English, the *Brunei Darussalam Newsletter* (www.information.gov.bn/bdnewsletter) is a fortnightly publication and is also produced by the government.

Broadcasting

The only broadcasting organisation is Radio Televisyen Brunei (RTB) (www.rtb.gov.bn), which is government operated, under the control of the Department of Broadcasting and Information.

Radio: RTB (www.rtb.gov.bn) operates five radio stations, including an international service. There are several private stations broadcasting in Brunei but only Kristal FM (www.dst-group.com) is a domestic station; all others originate in Malaysia.

Television: RTB (www.rtb.gov.bn) operates channels 5 and 8 as well as an RBT International, broadcast via a satellite service. Foreign cable and satellite networks provide the only alternatives to the state-run broadcaster. Viewers with access to the internet may access foreign TV.

Other news agencies: BruDirect (in English): www.brudirect.com
Brunei News (in English): www.bruneinews.net

Economy

The Brunei economy is dominated by the hydrocarbon extraction sector, which typically provides over 90 per cent of export revenue and accounts for 70 per cent of GDP. The non-hydrocarbon sector is led by government services, construction and financial services. A manufacturing sector is small, contributing some 12 per cent to GDP, with over 70 per cent of all imports being manufactured goods, vehicles and parts and machinery. Brunei is one of richest countries of the Asean community by GDP per capita, reaching an all-time high of US$42,402 in 2012, before falling back slightly in 2014 to US$41,776. GDP growth fell into negative figures in 2013, to -1.8 per cent, due to maintenance work on offshore oil and gas facilities. However the economy returned to positive growth of 5.3 per cent in 2014 as oil and gas output picked up again.

The crash in oil and gas prices in late 2014 is likely to heavily effect the economy as the government's budget for 2015/16 is likely to be US$250 million lower than the previous year, though still positive. With oil and gas prices expected to be low for a significant period it is essential for the Bruneien economy to find a way in which to diversify and become less reliant on hydrocarbons.

Brunei had total proved reserves of 1.1 billion barrels of oil at the end of 2014 and had production of 126,000 barrels per day (bpd). Brunei also had natural gas reserves of 300 billion cubic metres (cum) at the end of 2014, with production stood at 11.9 billion cum in the same year.

Key to Brunei's policy of transforming the country into an offshore financial centre and tourist destination is economic diversification and an increase in foreign investment to maintain growth and long-term viability. Brunei's ambition is to become a service hub for trade and tourism to take advantage of regional economic integration. Economic development has concentrated on infrastructure, roads, schools and numerous government buildings. In addition to promoting tourism, Brunei intends to increase the financial sector and energy-intensive industries, especially petrochemicals.

The Brunei Investment Agency (BIA) invests around 50 per cent of the hydrocarbon income in an international portfolio; the exact value of these assets is a state secret.

Major obstacles to growth include labour shortages, as many local unemployed workers are unwilling to do manual work. Complex bureaucracy and high wages are seen as deterrents to foreign investment. Brunei is a net receiver of migrant workers, although measures limit the length of their stay.

External trade

As the Association of Southeast Asian Nations (Asean) moves towards the creation of a comprehensive free trade area, it has already signed FTAs with China, Australia and New Zealand, India, Japan and South Korea. Brunei also belongs to the Asia Pacific Economic Co-operation (Apec) organisation

Most items can be imported under an open general licence. There are some restricted goods which require special licences, including used vehicles, certain listed drugs, livestock, some foodstuffs and gambling equipment (eg fruit machines).

The government is encouraging exports from the non-hydrocarbons sector, which includes small-scale manufacturing in textiles, furniture and food processing. Primary production includes timber, marine and agricultural produce. Some items are heavily subsidised by the government and their export is consequently restricted. Such goods include rice, petrol, kerosene and diesel fuels as well as cigarettes.

Imports

Brunei's limited industrial and agricultural base requires a range of principal imports including machinery, transport equipment, manufactured goods, food and chemicals.

Main sources: Malaysia (20.6 per cent of total in 2014), Singapore (20.4 per cent), China (9.9 per cent).

Exports

Crude oil (typically 50 per cent of the total exports) and liquefied natural gas (around 40 per cent) and refined products dominate the export schedule.

Main destinations: Japan (37.2 per cent of exports in 2014), Republic of Korea (11.0 per cent), India (9.1 per cent).

Agriculture

Farming

The agricultural sector plays only a minor role in Brunei's economy, typically accounting for less than 1 per cent of GDP and employs only 4.2 per cent per cent of the workforce. Brunei has to import 80 per cent of its food needs. Only around 15 per cent of the total land area is cultivated or under grazing.

Brunei's agricultural base consists mainly of small farms growing rice and vegetables. Farming is primarily a part-time occupation. The main crops are rice, vegetables, arable crops and fruits. A wide range of tropical fruit varieties are produced, but in low volumes. Vegetable production is intensive and concentrated in the fertile alluvial plain close to the urban centres. With smallholding rice production declining, the government has initiated a pilot large-scale rice mechanisation project aimed at increasing output; it is hoped that once fully mechanised, 30 per cent of Brunei's rice needs will be met by domestic production.

Government attempts to increase the importance of the sector and moves towards self-sufficiency are hampered by the population's lack of interest in outdoor, manual work. Another disincentive is that farming is perceived as less lucrative than other areas of the economy, so reducing further the likelihood of significant small-scale development. High wage costs mean that the expansion of larger-scale production depends very much on increased mechanisation rather than labour-intensive techniques, unless large scale immigrant labour can be guaranteed.

Fishing

Since 1990, the government has attempted to expand the fishing industry. The ministry of industry and primary resources granted more fishing licences to match the extension of the country's fishing boundary to 200 miles offshore. Several other sites were located for aquaculture projects. The government also improved the distribution system to ensure that the local catch reaches more remote areas of the country. The trawling industry has also been developed. The important trawling areas are Pulau Tambisan and north of Sandakan (Marchesa and Labuk Bay).

Typical annual fish production is over 1,600 tonnes (t) and other seafood over 400t.

Forestry

About 70 per cent of Brunei is covered by primary and secondary rain forest; 37 per cent of the country is designated as a national Forest Reserve. There is growing concern locally about the conservation of the forests and the environment, and exports of timber and logs are now strictly limited. Consequently timber production of logs and sawn-wood is for domestic consumption only. Some natural rubber is produced. The government hopes to develop the forestry sector as part of its diversification strategy, but investment opportunities are limited by legal restrictions. Private companies wishing to become involved in the sector must have local business participation of 51 per cent.

Industry and manufacturing

The industrial sector, including hydrocarbons, accounts for approximately 70 per cent of GDP and employs almost a quarter of the workforce. The industrial structure, long dependent on export of oil and gas, consists mainly of small-scale enterprises. Apart from the energy and construction sectors, Brunei's industrial base is limited. The small domestic market, high wage costs, bureaucracy and poor co-ordination between government departments has deterred both local and foreign investment.

Despite the government's emphasis on diversification, the industrial sector remains underdeveloped. The manufacturing sector is small and consists mainly of the production of materials for the construction sector, petroleum refining, food-processing and garment manufacture. There are also factories producing canned food, mineral water and dairy products.

Areas the government wants to develop include the manufacture of furniture, pottery, tiles, cement, chemicals, plywood and glass. As part of the industrial development programme a number of industrial estates have been established. These include a 40 hectare site near Bandar Seri Begawan and the Beribi Light Industrial Complex, which consists of four blocks including textiles, food and electrical manufacturers.

The government is eager to promote the development of a financial centre and of export-oriented, value-added industries. Investment policy is open and flexible and welcomes investors, both local and foreign, in any productive industrial activity which furthers diversification.

Tourism

Brunei has been actively marketing itself as a regional hub for stop-overs and as a destination in itself, with attractions such as national parks, cultural festivals, historic villages and extensive areas of natural beauty. Western visitors should remember that Brunei is a strict Islamic country. It is attractive to foreign visitors from other Islamic countries.

Travel and tourism constituted a total 6.8 per cent of GDP in 2014 and provided 7.6 per cent of total employment (15,500 jobs). Investment in tourism, which was 16.6 per cent of total investment in 2014 (US$426.2 million), indicates belief in growth in the sector.

Environment

Brunei is prone to occasional typhoons, earthquakes and flooding. Environmental management is overseen by the ministry of development, ministry of health and the ministry of industry and primary resources. Brunei is party to major international environmental agreements that include endangered species, ozone layer protection, ship pollution and whaling.

Mining

Brunei possesses only limited raw materials. Its principal resources are clay and silica in the form of 20 million tonnes of high quality beach sands at Tutong.

Hydrocarbons

Revenues from hydrocarbons make up over 50 per cent of GDP and 90 per cent of Brunei's exports and gives the country its international status.

The oil sector is dominated by Brunei Shell Petroleum (BSP), a 50:50 venture between Royal Dutch/Shell and the Brunei government, although a consortium formed by TotalFinaElf and Brunei-based Jasra International Petroleum has consolidated its share of production since the 1980's.

Brunei has seven offshore fields of which the largest, Champion, contains about 40 per cent of total reserves. There are believed to be significant undeveloped oil reserves in the existing fields and these will be tapped by advanced technology and modern drilling methods. Brunei, along with China, Taiwan, Malaysia, The Philippines and Vietnam, claims the potentially oil-rich Spratly Islands. In 2010, an agreement was reached between the governments of Brunei and Malaysia to share the revenue of two disputed oil blocks in territorial waters. The dispute had led to international oil companies declining to invest in exploration within the offshore waters while the countries haggled over its sovereign ownership.

Brunei had total proved reserves of 1.1 billion barrels of oil at the end of 2014 and had production of 126,000 barrels per day (bpd).

Brunei had natural gas reserves of 300 billion cubic metres (cum) at the end of 2014, with production of 11.9 billion cum in the same year.

Brunei is south-east Asia's fourth-largest liquefied natural gas (LNG) producer, the majority of which is exported to Japan and the remainder to South Korea from its Lumut LNG liquefaction plant which produced 9.5 billion cubic metres (cum) of LNG.

Energy

Total installed generating capacity was 759MW in 2013 (latest figures). All Brunei's electricity is produced in gas-fired power stations. Electricity demand is expanding by 7–10 per cent annually, making long-term electricity development a priority. A programme of electricity expansion has included the construction of a 110MW power plant in Tutong, opened in 2008, featuring new, more efficient combine cycle turbines.

Over 99 per cent of the population has access to electricity. The government agency Department of Electrical Services (DES), is responsible for generation, transmission and distribution and sets the standards for usage in public buildings and installation maintenance. The private, independent power utility Berakas Power Company (BPC) also supplies electricity to the grid, although the grid is not integrated and is divided into three networks. Metering and cable supply has been privatised in order to introduce competition and efficiencies.

Banking and insurance

The regulatory system is based on the 1906 British Banking Act, although various modifications have been made to bring it up-to-date with modern banking requirements.

The fourth pillar of the Brunei International Financial Centre (BIFC), the International Insurance and Takaful Order, was set up, designed to provide for foreign investors in the banking scene. This will enable Brunei to have a fully operational foreign offshore banking sector. The Royal Bank of Canada (RBC) became the first foreign bank to operate in the BIFC. RBC is focussing its activities on private bank services for the rich and assisting the management of Islamic funds. Three local banks dominate the domestic banking sector – the Islamic Bank of Brunei (IBB), Baiduri Bank (BB) and the Development Bank of Brunei. The IBB conducts its savings and loans operations in accordance with Islamic law. The Sultan and his family own 80 per cent of IBB's paid up capital, Japan's Daiichi Kangyo Bank holds the other 20 per cent. The three largest foreign banks in Brunei are Citibank, the Hong Kong and Shanghai Banking Corporation (HSBC) and Standard Chartered Bank. Other foreign banks include the Overseas Union Bank, Malayan Banking and the United Malayan Banking Corporation.

Central bank

Brunei has no central bank; the main duties are carried out by the Autoriti Monetari Brunei Darussalam (AMBD) (Brunei Darussalam Monetary Authority), established in January 2011.

Main financial centre

Bandar Seri Begawan

Time

GMT plus eight hours

Geography

Brunei lies 442km north of the equator on the northern coast of the island of Borneo. It consists of two wedges of land, within the Malaysian province of Sarawak and with the South China sea in the north. The country is divided into separate administrative districts: Brunei/Muara, Tutong and Seria/Belait in the western section, and Temburong, which makes up the entire eastern section of the country. Although there is a mountainous region in the eastern half of the country, Brunei mostly consists of a low-lying coastal plain. The highest peak is Bukit Pagon (1,841 metres). Brunei has four main rivers – the Belait, Tutong, Brunei and Temburong. Approximately 75 per cent of the total land area is covered by tropical rain forest.

Hemisphere

Northern

Climate

The climate is typically equatorial. Humidity averages 82 per cent, and daily temperatures range between 24 and 31 degrees Celsius (C). The rainy season lasts from September to January, although rainfall can be expected throughout the year. It can reach up to 7,500mm in the interior, but on the coast it tends to average around 2,500mm. The driest months are from January to April.

Dress codes

Lightweight clothing is suitable. In deference to the Islamic culture, Western business women should dress modestly at all times.

Entry requirements

Passports

Required by all. Must be valid for six months.

Visa

Required by all. Exceptions are granted for short stays of up to 14 or 30 days to nationals of certain countries and 90 days for US citizens (see www.mfa.gov.bn for details). Business visas require a sponsorship letter from a local company or government entity (for details see www.immigration.gov.bn/visiting.htm).

Prohibited entry

Holders of Israeli passports.

Currency advice/regulations

There are no restritions on the import of foreign and local currency, with the exception of the Singapore dollar, which is limited to B$1,000 equivalent, and Indian and Indonesian banknotes, which are prohibited. Export of local currency is restricted to B$1,000, while the export of foreign currency is limited to the amount imported. The Brunei dollar is at par with the Singapore dollar and the currencies are interchangeable in both countries.

Customs

Two litres of alcohol and 12 cans of beer; 200 cigarettes and 250g tobacco; 60ml perfume and 250ml eau de toilette allopwed duty free.

Prohibited imports

Trafficking and illegal importation of controlled drugs are very serious offences carrying the death penalty.

Health (for visitors)

Health services are not free for visitors, as it is for Brunei citizens, but there is only a very nominal charge for permanent residents and expatriate government officials and their dependants. Malaria has been eradicated in Brunei. Certificates of vaccination for both cholera and yellow fever are advisable. Normal precautions should be taken for food and drink. The authorities are becoming concerned over the growing amount of drug abuse.

Mandatory precautions

Vaccination certificates for yellow fever are required for travellers over one year of age travelling from an infected area.

Advisable precautions

Chest X-ray and blood film examination for malaria are required for the issue and renewal of labour permits as Brunei is malaria-free. Immunisations are recommended for hepatitis A, polio, tetanus, typhoid, and also advice should be sought regarding diphtheria, hepatitis A, Japanese encephalitis and TB. There is a risk of rabies.

Hotels

Rooms in major hotels have air-conditioning, telephones, TV, bathrooms and showers. A 10 per cent service charge is usual.

Credit cards

Major credit cards are accepted at some hotels and at some shops.

Public holidays (national)

Friday and Sunday are non-working days, if a holiday falls on these, then Saturday or Monday are substituted. Banks close on 30 June and 30 December.

Fixed dates

1 Jan (New Year's Day), 23 Feb (National Day), 31 May (Armed Forces Day), 15 Jul (Sultan's Birthday), 25 Dec (Christmas Day).

Variable dates

Chinese New Year (Jan–Feb), Hari Raya Aidiladha, Hari Raya Aidilfitra, Islamic New Year, Birth of the Prophet, Ascension of the Prophet, First day of Ramadan, Revelation of the Quran Anniversary.

Islamic year 1437 (15 Oct 2015–2 Oct 2016): The Islamic year contains 354 or 355 days, with the result that Muslim feasts advance by 10–12 days against the Gregorian calendar. Dates of feasts vary according to the sighting of the new moon, so cannot be forecast exactly.

Working hours

Banking

Mon–Fri: 0900–1500; Sat: 0900–1100. Many banks close during lunch hour.

Business

Mon–Thur: 0745–1215, 1330–1630; Sat: 0800–1200.

Government

Mon–Thu, Sat: 0745–1215, 1330–1630. Fasting month (Ramadan) 0800–1400.

Shops

Mon–Sat: 0800–1900/2100, 1000–2200 (most shopping centres). Post offices: Mon–Thu, Sat: 0730–1600; Fri: 0830–0930.

Telecommunications

Mobile/cell phones

There is a 900 GSM service available along with a G3 (2100) service.

Electricity supply

230V AC, with 3-pin round or 3-pin square plug fittings.

Weights and measures

Metric system.

Social customs/useful tips

The public sale and consumption of alcohol is prohibited by law. Muslims do not eat pork or drink alcohol. The right hand should be used for offering or receiving anything, from food to money. Refusal of offered refreshment is discourteous.

To point with the index finger is also considered discourteous; the thumb of the right hand should be used instead with the four fingers folded beneath it. To call a taxi or attract someone's attention, wave the whole hand with the palm facing downwards. Do not smack the fist of your right hand into your left palm; it has a different meaning in Brunei to that of Western countries. It is not customary to shake hands with members of the opposite sex. When visiting a mosque, shoes should first be removed. Do not pass in front of a person at prayer, or touch the Qur'an. Women should cover their heads, and not have their knees or arms exposed.

Security

There is no major problem with petty crime in Brunei.

Getting there

Air

National airline: Royal Brunei Airlines (RBA)

International airport/s: Brunei International Airport (BWN), 10km north of Bandar Seri Begawan, with car hire and taxi service.

Airport tax: Departures to Singapore and Malaysia B$5. All other international departures B$12.

Surface

Road: Road connections between Brunei and Sarawak (Malaysia) are good. There is a bitumen road between Miri and Kuala Belait.

Water: Most sea traffic is handled by the deep-water port at Muara, while the smaller port at Kuala Belait handles shallow-draught vessels.

Main port/s: Muara (27km from Bandar Seri Begawan), Kuala Belait, Lumut.

Getting about

National transport

Road: The total road network is around 2,500km. Brunei has 1,500km of main roads, 500km of district roads and 500km of unpaved road surface. There is no road connecting the Temburong district but a water taxi service is available. A main highway links Bandar Seri Begawan with Kuala Belait and Seria, with a road linking Muara and Tutong providing access to western districts.

Buses: There are six bus lines in Bandar Seri Begawan. Services operate betwen Bandar Seri Begawan and Kuala Belait and Seria, and also serve rural areas. Buses run from 0630–1800.

Water: The Brunei, Belait and Tutong rivers are the main inland waterways and are principally used for passenger traffic. River-going vessels use the old port at Bandar Seri Begawan. Large river taxis operate to the Temburong district; service starts at 0745 and ends at 1600. River taxi and boat services are also available to Limbang in Sarawak and Labuan in Sabah.

City transport

The City Transport Service (CTS) is the easiest way to travel in the city. Fixed fare within the CTS zone.

Taxis: From the airport to the city centre, metered taxis are in operation 0700–0030. Metered taxis are also available from hotels and shopping centres near the capital to all parts of Brunei, but are otherwise scarce. Tipping is not usual.

Buses, trams & metro: From the airport to the city centre, buses operate 0630—1800, every 15—20 minutes.

Car hire

Self-drive and chauffeur-driven cars are available from major hotels and the airport. An international driving licence is required.

BUSINESS DIRECTORY

The addresses listed below are a selection only. While World of Information makes every endeavour to check these addresses, we cannot guarantee that changes have not been made, especially to telephone numbers and area codes. We would welcome any corrections.

Telephone area codes

The international direct dialling (IDD) code for Brunei is +673, followed by subscriber's number.

Useful telephone numbers

Police: 993
Fire: 995
Ambulance: 991
Flight information: 331-747
Directory enquiries: 0213
International calls: 000

Chambers of Commerce

Brunei Darussalam International Chamber of Commerce and Industry, PO Box 2246, Bandar Seri Bagawan 1922 (tel: 2 228382; fax: 2 228389).

Brunei Malay Chamber of Commerce, PO Box 1099, Bandar Seri Begawan 8672 (tel: 2 422752; fax: 2 422753).

Chinese Chamber of Commerce, 72 Jalan Roberts, PO Box 281, Bandar Seri Begawan 8670 (tel: 2 235494; fax: 2 235492).

National Chamber of Commerce and Industry, 144 2nd Floor Jalan Pemancha, Bandar Seri Begawan BS8711 (tel: 2 243321; fax: 2 228737).

Banking

Baiduri Bank Berhad (BB), 145 Jalan Pemancha, PO Box 2220, Bandar Seri Begawan 1922 (tel: 233-233; fax: 235-722).

Citibank, 12-15 Bangunan Darussalam, Bandar Seri Begawan (tel: 243-983; fax: 225-704).

Development Bank of Brunei Bhd, 1st Floor RBA Plaza, Jalan Sultan Bandar Seri Begawan 2085 (tel: 233-430; fax: 233-429).

HSBC, cnr Jalan Sultan and Jalan Pemancha, PO Box 59, Jalan Sultan, Bandar Seri Begawan (tel: 242-305/10, 242-204; fax: 241-316).

Islamic Bank of Brunei Berhad (IBB), lot 159, Jalan Pemancha, Bandar Seri Begawan (tel: 235-686/7; fax: 235-722).

Malayan Banking Berhad, 148 Jalan Pemancha, Bandar Seri Begawan 2085 (tel: 242-494).

Overseas Union Bank (OUB), Unit G5, RBA Plaza, Jalan Sultan, Bandar Seri Begawan 2089 (tel: 225-477; fax: 240-792).

Sime Bank Berhad, Unit G 02, Kompleks Yayasan Sultan Haji Hassanal Bolkiah , Bandar Seri Begawan (tel: 222-516; fax: 237-487).

Standard Chartered Bank, 51-55 Jalan Sultan, Bandar Seri Begawan (tel: 242-386; fax: 242-390).

Central bank

Brunei Currency and Monetray Board, Simpang 295, Jalan Kebangsaan, PO Box 660, Bandar Seri Begawan BS 8670 (tel: 238-3999; fax: 238-2232; e-mail: bcb@brunet.bn).

Travel information

Brunei Travel Service, Sdn Bhd, Bandar Seri Begawan (tel: 225-664).

Department of Civil Aviation, Ministry of Communications, Brunei International Airport, 2015 (tel: 330-483, 330-142/3; fax: 331-7066).

Royal Brunei Airlines, PO Box 737, Bandar Seri Begawan 1907 (tel: 240-500, 242-222; fax: 244-737).

Tourist information (on arrival level at airport) (tel: 331-747).

Ministries

Ministry of Communications, Old Airport, Berakas, Bandar Seri Begawan 1150 (tel: 383-838; fax: 380-127).

Ministry of Culture, Youth and Sports, Jalan Residency, Bandar Seri Begawan 1200 (tel: 240-585; fax: 241-620).

Ministry of Defence, Bolkiah Garrison, Bandar Seri Begawan 1110 (tel: 230-130; fax: 230-110).

Ministry of Development, Old Airport, Berakas, Bandar Seri Begawan 1190 (tel: 241-911; fax: 240-271).

Ministry of Education, Old Airport, Berakas, Bandar Seri Begawan 1170 (tel: 244-233; fax: 240-250).

Ministry of Finance, Bandar Seri Begawan 1130 (tel: 242-405; fax: 241-829).

Ministry of Foreign Affairs, Jalan Subok, Bandar Seri Begawan 1120 (tel: 241-177; fax: 224-709).

Ministry of Health, Old Airport, Berakas, Bandar Seri Begawan 1210 (tel: 226-640; fax: 240-980).

Ministry of Home Affairs, Bandar Seri Begawan 1140 (tel: 223-225).

Ministry of Industry and Primary Resources, Old Airport, Berakas, Bandar Seri Begawan 1220 (tel: 224-822; fax: 244-811).

Ministry of Law, Jalan Tutong, Bandar Seri Begawan 1160 (tel: 244-872; fax: 223-100).

Ministry of Religious Affairs, Bandar Seri Begawan 1180 (tel: 242-565).

Other useful addresses

Asean Investment Promotion Agency, Ministry of Industry and Primary Resources, Bandar Seri Begawan 1220 (tel: 238-119; fax: 238-811).

British High Commission, 2.01, 2nd Floor, Block D, Kompleks Bangunan Yayasan Sultan Haji Hassanal Bolkiah, Jalan Pretty, PO Box 2197, Bandar Seri Begawan 8711 (tel: 222-2231; fax: 223-4315).

Brunei Darussalam Embassy (USA), 3520 International Court, NW, Washington DC 20008 (tel: (+1-202) 237-1838; fax: (+1-202) 885-0560; e-mail: info@bruneiembassy.org).

Brunei Industrial Development Authority (BINA), Km 8, Jalan Gadong, BE 1118 (tel: 444100; fax: 423300; e-mail: bruneibina@brunet.bn).

Controller of Customs and Excise, Jabatan Customs and Excise Di-Raja, Bandar Seri Begawan (tel: 222-342).

Economic Development Board, Ministry of Finance, 2nd Floor, RBA Plaza, Jalan Sultan, Bandar Seri Begawan 2085 (postal address: Locked Bag 15, Bandar Seri Begawan 1999) (tel: 229-269; fax: 241-417).

University of Brunei Darussalam, Gadong, Bandar Seri Begawan (tel: 227-001).

US Embassy, 3rd Floor, Teck Guan Plaza, cnr Jalan Sultan and Jalan MacArthur, Bandar Seri Begawan (tel: 229-670; fax: 225-293).

BruDirect (in English): www.brudirect.com

Brunei News (in English): www.bruneinews.net

Bulgaria

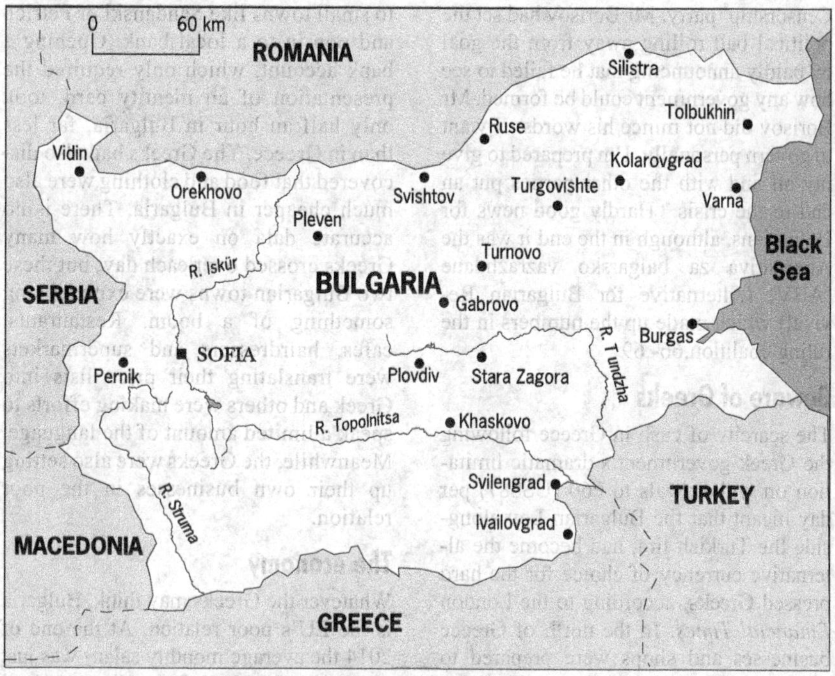

The queues to withdraw money from troubled banks and a political crisis that promised to maintain the state of chronic instability that risked paralysing the country. No, not Greece, but Bulgaria in the closing months of 2014 as internal conflicts rocked an already fragile economy.

The European Commission (EC) needed to authorise the beleaguered Bulgarian government to inject lev3,300 million (US$1,886 million) into the banking system following the arrest of various senior bankers accused of organising – with some degree of success – a conspiracy to destabilise the entire banking system. A statement from the EC reported that 'Last week it became known that various individuals had been attacking the biggest bank in the country, the First Investment Bank, recommending that customers withdraw their money. This created doubts over the liquidity of the bank in question and increased the risk that the problem affected other institutions, despite the fact that the Bulgarian banking system is well capitalised and has high levels of liquidity.'

Wobbly banks...

The customers of the First Investment Bank – Bulgaria's third largest – had withdrawn some €800 million (US$), as the bank's shares fell by 24 per cent on the Sofia stock exchange. The Bulgarian authorities had also seen fit to intervene in the affairs of the fourth largest bank, the Corporate Commercial Bank (Corpbank). Corpbank had been in a state of limbo for some time as administrators and receivers squabbled over the exact date of an earlier insolvency. The Bulgarska Narodna Banka (BNB) (Bulgarian National Bank) (central bank) had said that it would challenge a court decision setting the date of insolvency. Corpbank finally collapsed in June 2014, after a bank run triggered the biggest banking crisis in Bulgaria since the 1990s. Reuters reported that an independent audit of its books showed serious failings in the way it was run that had prompted central bank administrators at the lender to write off two thirds of its assets. The Bulgarian state was Corpbank's biggest creditor. Declaring Corpbank bankrupt in on 22 April a Bulgarian court

KEY FACTS

Official name: Republika Bulgaria (Republic of Bulgaria)

Head of State: President Rosen Plavneliev (Gerb) (from 22 Jan 2012)

Head of government: Prime Minister Boyko Borisov (GERB) (from 7 Nov 2014)

Ruling party: Coalition of Grazhdani za Evropeysko Razvitie na Balgariya (GERB) (Citizens for the European Development of Bulgaria), Reformatorski Blok (RB) (Reformist Bloc) and Alternativa za balgarsko vazrazhdane (ABV) (Alternative for Bulgarian Revival)

Area: 110,994 square km

Population: 7.20 million (2014)*

Capital: Sofia

Official language: Bulgarian

Currency: Lev (Lev) = 100 stotinki

Exchange rate: Lev1.75 per US$ (Sep 2015)

GDP per capita: US$7,753 (2014)*

GDP real growth: 1.71% (2014)*

GDP: US$55.84 billion (2014)*

Labour force: 3.29 million (2014)

Unemployment: 11.52% (2014)*

Inflation: -1.60% (2014)

Balance of trade: -US$4.56 billion (2014)

Annual FDI: US$1.80 billion (2011)

* estimated figure

had said the bank had been insolvent since November 2014. The Bulgarian police had made nine arrests related to the Corpbank case, on charges of disseminating false information about the bank's solvency on social media. Corpbank's closure left around 200,000 depositors unable to access their funds.

... wobblier government

If the banking system appeared to be on the verge of collapse, by the middle of 2014 so was the ruling coalition, headed by the Bulgarska Socialistièska Partija (BSP) (Bulgarian Socialist Party). In a period of 18 months, no less than four governments had collapsed. By August 2014 President Rosen Plevneliev had had enough, announcing the third election in five years, to take place in October 2014. The election duly took place, but did little to improve matters. This despite the fact that there was a clear electoral victor – Bulgaria's GERB party obtained just over 30 per cent of the vote, over two times as many votes as the BSP, GERB's main rival, which saw its votes diminish by some 11 per cent, to just under 16 per cent. The Turkish minority party, the Dvizhenie za Prava i Svobodi (DPS) (Movement for Rights and Freedom) came third, with around 15 per cent. All well and good, but Bulgaria's voters were not simply following the major parties script – they had managed to elect a total of eight parties to Parliament giving former prime Minister Borisov an almost impossible task. The turnout was low – barely 50 per cent of the electorate actually turned out to vote.

GERB's first choice of coalition partner was the so called Reformatorski Blok (RB) (Reformist Bloc), which had mustered around 9 per cent of the vote. Next in line on stage right were the Patriotic Front, which had garnered 7 per cent and the strangely named 'Bulgaria Without Censorship' party. Mr Borisov had set the political ball rolling away from the goal by baldly announcing that he failed to see how any government could be formed. Mr Borisov did not mince his words: 'I want to govern personally. I'm prepared to give my all and with the other parties put an end to the crisis.' Hardly good news for Bulgarians, although in the end it was the Alternativa za balgarsko vazrazhdane (ABV) (Alternative for Bulgarian Revival) which made up the numbers in the ruling coalition.66-.69

Beware of Greeks

The scarcity of cash in Greece following the Greek government's dramatic limitation on withdrawals to €60 (US$87) per day meant that the Bulgarian Lev alongside the Turkish lira, had become the alternative currency of choice for the hard pressed Greeks, according to the London *Financial Times*. In the north of Greece businesses and shops were prepared to take Bulgarian Lev in payment and a number of hoteliers and restauranteurs had resorted accepting to Lev in payment and then crossing the border to purchase essential supplies.

The irony was that the Greeks had long considered their Bulgarian neighbours as poor relations, but now they were seen more as saviours. It was estimated that some 60,000 Greeks had opened bank accounts in Bulgaria to avoid both the withdrawal and the tax impositions placed on them at home. All Greeks living near the border had to do was drive to small towns like Sandanski or Petrich and pop in to a local bank. Opening a bank account, which only required the presentation of an identity card, took only half an hour in Bulgaria, far less than in Greece. The Greeks had also discovered that food and clothing were also much cheaper in Bulgaria. There is no accurate data on exactly how many Greeks crossed over each day, but these two Bulgarian towns were experiencing something of a boom. Restaurants, cafés, hairdressers and supermarkets were translating their price lists into Greek and others were making efforts to speak a limited amount of the language. Meanwhile, the Greeks were also setting up their own businesses in the poor relation.

The economy

Whatever the Greeks may think, Bulgaria is the EU's poor relation. At the end of 2014 the average monthly salary was just over €400 (US$580). Inequality remained a problem – seven years after the country joined the EU, one-fifth of its households still lived below the poverty line. Worryingly, the growth outlook is gloomy: due to the domestic political uncertainty, poor harvest in the summer of 2014 and the crisis in Ukraine, which had hurt exports, Bulgaria's economy was expected to grow by only 1.5 per cent in 2015.

In its annual assessment of the Bulgarian economy, prepared in May 2015, the International Monetary Fund (IMF) noted that over the previous year, Bulgaria's macro-economic and financial stability had been tested by the failure of a large bank and the deterioration in the fiscal balance. Nonetheless, modest growth was achieved in 2014 and was expected by the IMF to continue in 2015, albeit at a lower rate. Consumer prices had declined by an average of 1.6 per cent in 2014, among the sharpest contractions in the EU, but were projected to turn positive late in the year.

In the view of the IMF, the banking system had shown substantial resilience to the damage to confidence resulting from the bank failure. Strong system liquidity and the liquidity support scheme introduced by the BNB and government had

KEY INDICATORS — Bulgaria

	Unit	2011	2012	2013	2014	**2015
Population	m	7.36	7.28	7.24	*7.20	*7.12
Gross domestic product (GDP)	US$bn	53.50	51.33	54.52	*55.84	*51.55
GDP per capita	US$	7,153	7,049	7,532	*7,753	*7,194
GDP real growth	%	1.7	0.6	1.1	*1.7	*1.2
Inflation	%	3.4	2.4	0.4	-1.6	*-1.0
Unemployment	%	12.0	12.4	13.0	*11.5	*10.9
Coal output	mtoe	6.1	5.4	4.7	5.2	–
Exports (fob) (goods)	US$m	28,192.2	26,707.0	29,519.6	27,895.1	–
Imports (fob) (goods)	US$m	30,918.0	31,372.0	32,641.5	32,452.3	–
Balance of trade	US$m	-3,671.4	-4,665.0	-3,121.9	-4,557.2	–
Current account	US$m	-590.6	-471.0	1,228.0	*25.0	*116.0
Total reserves minus gold	US$m	15,759.2	18,371.0	18,334.7	18,576.1	–
Foreign exchange	US$m	14,727.8	17,379.0	17,340.4	–	–
Exchange rate	per US$	1.39	1.51	1.43	1.62	–

* estimated figure ** forecast figure

helped avert system-wide knock-on effects. However, decisive actions were needed to address weaknesses exposed by the bank failure, to restore supervisory credibility and to strengthen crisis management tools.

The IMF noted that Bulgaria's fiscal deficit rose to 3.7 per cent of gross domestic product (GDP), twice the original target. The budget targeted a three per cent of GDP deficit in 2015 and a further 0.5 percentage point reduction per year in future. Measures to improve the composition and quality of expenditure and mitigate contingent liabilities arising from state-owned enterprises remained key in the opinion of the IMF. At the same time, an ageing population and emigration represented significant long-term public spending challenges.

Bulgaria's income convergence with its EU counterparts was projected to remain slow with significant age, gender and regional disparities in income. Decisive action to address long-standing concerns related to corruption also continued to be important. The government had begun to take steps to address the increasingly acute problems arising from inefficiencies in the power sector. In its 2014 *Transition Report* the European Bank for Reconstruction and Development (EBRD) the economy remained stable but 'was still struggling'.

Following a brief upturn in economic activity in 2011, growth had weakened again as GDP rose by just 0.6 per cent and 0.9 per cent in 2012 and 2013, respectively. Exports to the EU had contributed positively, but domestic consumption had a dampening effect on GDP growth in 2013. In the first half of 2014, growth picked up slightly to 1.4 per cent year-on-year (seasonally adjusted), on the back of an upturn in domestic demand. Tourism revenues might have been affected by poor weather conditions during the summer months. The combination of subdued domestic demand and a series of electricity tariff cuts (by a cumulative 13.6 per cent after the January 2014 price cut had led to a negative inflation rate, although the average inflation rate in 2013 was marginally positive at 0.4 per cent. Annual inflation had been on a downward trend since October 2012, entering negative territory (-0.7 per cent year-on-year) in August 2013 and remaining negative subsequently.

However, the EBRD thought that fiscal pressures might arise due to a potential bank bailout and the need to increase infrastructure and social spending (especially in the light of recent flooding). One piece of good news was that Bulgaria's level of public debt was still the second lowest in the EU relative to GDP. However, under the 2013 revised budget, which was first passed by parliament in July 2013 and then again in August 2013, the deficit was increased to 2 per cent of GDP, the maximum allowed under the law (the actual outcome was 1.8 per cent of GDP on a cash basis). A deficit of 1.8 per cent was budgeted again in 2014, but low revenue collection, costs associated with the resolution of Corporate Commercial Bank (see above) and spending for emergency measures as a result of the recent floods pushed the budget deficit to around or above 3 per cent of GDP.

A modest pick-up in growth was expected in 2015 by the EBRD, but a number of factors rendered the economy vulnerable to external shocks, including uncertainties surrounding the continuing crisis in Ukraine. However, the EBRD struck a positive note considering that Bulgaria's medium-term growth potential remained good. GDP per capita (adjusted for purchasing power standards) was estimated by Eurostat to be less than half the EU average, so the scope for convergence was still high, provided that structural reforms were pursued. Bulgaria had made progress under the EU's Co-operation and Verification Mechanism (CVM), but further steps were needed. The latest report from the EC on Bulgaria's progress under the CVM, published in January 2014, noted that there had been a few steps forward since the previous report, but that overall progress was fragile and insufficient. The EC made a number of recommendations for further action in the areas of judicial reform and the fight against corruption and organised crime. On the 2014 Transparency International *Corruption Perceptions Index* Bulgaria ranked low in comparison with most fellow EU members: 69th out of the 175 countries served, level with Greece, Italy and Romania.

According to the latest World Bank *Doing Business 2015* report, Bulgaria ranked 38 (out of 189 countries), scoring poorly in getting electricity and dealing with construction permits. In its June 2014 report, the European Commission recommended cutting red tape, promoting e-government and streamlining insolvency procedures.

In April 2014 parliament had adopted a number of restrictions on the purchase of agricultural land by foreign entities. A key requirement was that the purchaser, whether foreign or Bulgarian, must have lived in Bulgaria for at least five years prior to the acquisition. In January 2014 the constitutional court annulled a measure introduced in October 2013 that would have extended the moratorium on the purchase of agricultural land in the country by foreigners until 2020.

In November 2013 parliament passed a bill freezing the retirement age to 60 years and 8 months for women and to 63 years and 8 months for men. This effectively stopped the pension system reforms adopted in 2012, under which the retirement age was to be raised gradually by four months each year until it reached 63 years for women and 65 years for men. The new policy also eliminated the specified retirement age for military personnel, enabling them to retire after 27 years of service. These moves went against the advice of international institutions such as the European Commission and the World Bank, which had argued for raising the retirement age for men and women to 65 in order to help improve the sustainability of the pension system.

Energy

In August 2014 the Bulgarian interim government created an energy board that would serve as an advisory body to the government. The board would consist of all stakeholders in the sector, including the chairman of the energy regulator and was expected to invite experts from the European Commission, the World Bank and the EBRD. The overall goal of the board was to discuss imbalances in the energy sector and seek solutions to stabilise the sector. However, it was unclear whether the board had legal authority and moreover, whether the new government (after the October 2014 elections) would maintain the board's role. Major problems still needed to be resolved in the sector, including: weak social safety nets; the under-pricing of energy; high energy intensity; and lack of liquidity (that is, payment arrears) in the system. Support for renewable energy had diminished further. In December 2013 parliament approved a 20 per cent tariff on solar and wind power, however the Constitutional Court declared this fee unlawful in 2014. Parliament also voted to limit the amount of energy that can be purchased at preferential prices, which the producers of green energy estimated would reduce their income by an additional 15 to 20 per cent. These measures were part of a series of regulatory interventions that the authorities had implemented to discourage investments in renewables. Meanwhile, in a report issued in June 2014, the European Commission noted that the absence of electricity and gas exchanges and a lack of transparency in the wholesale market remained key obstacles to improving the functioning of Bulgaria's energy markets. In addition, the country's dependence on imports from a limited number of suppliers and the lack of infrastructure posed supply shock risks.

Risk assessment

Economy	Fair
Politics	Fair
Regional stability	Good/fair

COUNTRY PROFILE

The Bulgars were a Finno-Ugrian people, whose ancestors crossed the River Danube in the seventh century and merged with the Slavonic population. Bulgaria is the oldest surviving state in Europe to have retained its original name.

681 The state of Bulgaria was founded.

811–927 After defeating the Byzantine armies at the Battle of Pliska, Bulgaria expanded into the Balkans.

1014–18 The Byzantines regained control of lost territory and much of Bulgaria was again part of the Byzantine Empire.

1185–97 The Bulgarians revolted against Byzantine rule. Bulgaria re-emerged as a state and major Balkan empire.

1396 Bulgaria was conquered by Ottoman Turkey and became its European stronghold for the next 500 years.

1800s The Ottoman Empire began to fall apart as many Balkan states launched uprisings.

1878 Russia defeated Turkey and Bulgaria came into existence again as a sovereign state.

1908 German Ferdinand Saxe-Coburg-Gotha proclaimed himself King of Bulgaria.

1912 The Balkan powers of Bulgaria, Greece and Montenegro defeated the remnants of the Ottoman Empire.

1913 In the Second Balkan War, Bulgaria tried to take Macedonia from Serbia, but was defeated. Balkan states ended the war by signing the Treaty of Bucharest, which also reduced the territorial size of Bulgaria.

1915 Bulgaria invaded Serbia and Macedonia, after joining on the side of the Central Powers (Germany and Austro-Hungary).

1918 The Entente powers (Great Britain, France and Russia) defeated Bulgaria and an armistice was signed in September. The Bulgarian defeat led to the abdication of King Ferdinand I and his son, Boris, was crowned.

1923 As internal divisions intensified between the peasants, ethnic Macedonians and communists, the army overthrew the government, which was dominated by agrarian parties. Prime Minister Alexander Stambolisky was assassinated. Alexander Tsankov formed a new pro-democracy government.

1924–25 Violence from communist militants and Macedonian nationalists prevented the Tsankov government from bringing political stability to Bulgaria.

1926 An ethnic Macedonian, Andrei Liapchev, replaced Tsankov as prime minister.

1929–31 The Great Depression devastated the Bulgarian economy. Thousands of jobs were lost and a wave of strikes hit the country. In the 1931 parliamentary election, the Liapchev government was defeated by the centre-left Naroden Blok (NB) (People's Bloc), led by Alexander Malinov.

1934 A coalition of political parties, led by the Zveno Group's Kimon Georgiev and Colonel Damyan Velchev of the Voenni Sayuz (VZ) (Military Union), overthrew Malinov's government. The new government introduced one-party rule and turned Bulgaria into an authoritarian state.

1935 Disillusioned by the government's authoritarianism, King Boris III began a personal dictatorship of Bulgaria.

1939–1941 Bulgaria was neutral at the start of the Second World War, but joined the Axis powers (Germany, Italy and Japan) in 1941. Bulgaria ruled German-captured Macedonia and Western Thrace in Greece.

1943 Boris III died of a heart attack. The heir to the Bulgarian throne, Simeon II, was too young to rule. A three-man regency was established and Prime Minister Bogdan Filov became the *de facto* head of state.

1944 The Soviet Union invaded Bulgaria. The Fatherland Front, a left-wing alliance dominated by the Soviet-backed Bulgarska Komunistieska Partija (BKP) (Bulgarian Communist Party), gained power.

1946 A referendum abolished the monarchy, which had ruled Bulgaria periodically since the ninth century.

1947 All opposition parties were abolished. Political trials and executions on the Stalinist model were carried out under Vulko Chervenkov until 1953 when Todor Zhivkov became the general secretary of the BKP.

1962–88 Zhivkov cemented his position as leader of Bulgaria and the country moved politically and economically closer to the Soviet Union.

1989 Petur Mladenov was appointed Zhivkov's successor.

1990 The BCK changed its name to the Bulgarska Socialistièska Partija (BSP) (Bulgarian Socialist Party). The BSP won the first multi-party elections in Bulgaria since the inter-war period. However, growing political infighting and nationwide strikes led to its fall. An interim government was confirmed, under the leadership of Dimitur Popov.

1991 The BSP lost power in the parliamentary elections. The Sajuz na Demokratienite Sili (SDS) (Union of Democratic Forces) formed a government.

1992 The SDS's Zhelyu Zhelev became Bulgaria's first directly elected president.

1994 The BSP returned to government in the parliamentary elections.

1996 Simeon (Borisov) Sakskoburggotski (son of Boris III) returned to Bulgaria. Amid a severe economic and political crisis, Petar Stoyanov won the presidential elections.

1997 An early general election was held, resulting in a win for the SDS-led centre-right coalition, the Obedineni Demokratièni Sili (ODS) (United Democratic Forces).

2001 The Nacionale Dvisenie Simeon Tvori (NDST) (National Movement for Simeon II) won the general election. The NDST's leader (former king Simeon II (1943–44)), became prime minister and formed a coalition government. The BSP's Georgi Parvanov won the run-off presidential elections.

2003 The IMF approved of Bulgaria's efforts to improve its macroeconomic situation with a loan of US$36 million.

2004 Bulgaria joined NATO.

2005 The Koalicija za Balgarija (KzB) (Coalition for Bulgaria) (led by the BSP) won parliamentary elections, defeating the ruling NDST. Sergey Stanishev became prime minister.

2006 The European Union (EU) officially agreed to Bulgaria's membership. However, conditions were imposed, stronger than any placed on previous accession countries, to curb organised crime and corruption, plus the use of EU funding. In presidential elections Georgi Parvanov won a landslide victory with 77.3 per cent of the vote.

2007 Bulgaria joined the EU. The NDST became the Nacionalno Dvizenie za Stabilnost i Vazhod (NDSV) (National Movement for Stability and Progress).

2008 The EU judged that Bulgaria had not sufficiently tackled corruption and organised crime, as required by its entry agreement and suspended millions of euros in aid to upgrade roads and agriculture.

2009 Weeks of energy shortages were endured by Bulgarians after Ukraine, in dispute with Russia, cut Russian natural gas supplies to Bulgaria. The EU demanded the return of €33 million (US$46.3 million) in farming subsidies

that it claimed had been misappropriated. Parliamentary elections were won by Grazhdani za Evropeysko Razvitie na Balgariya (Gerb) (Citizens for European Development of Bulgaria) with 116 seats; BSP won 40 seats. Boyko Borisov (Gerb) became prime minister.
2010 Parliament approved measures to raise revenue and to further tackle the budget deficit, including by the sale of minority government holdings in companies and increased taxes on gambling and insurance premiums.
2011 In June, the EU approved Bulgaria's inclusion in the Schengen area (allowing passport-free travel of citizens and goods); however, The Netherlands vetoed the EU decision to admit Bulgaria and Romania, in view of the turmoil in the Middle East and the potential for Middle Eastern migration to the EU in 2011–12, and imposed a one-year delay. Bulgaria officially recognised the Transitional National Council (TNC) in Libya in June. Eighteen candidates took part in presidential elections held in October. Rosen Plavneliev (Gerb) won 40.11 per cent of the vote in the first round and Ivaylo Kaflin (BSP) 28.96 per cent; as none of the candidates won over 50 per cent of the votes a runoff was held on 30 October; Plavneliev won 52.58 per cent and Kaflin 47.42 per cent; turnout was 48.06 per cent.
2012 On 18 July, a suicide bomber killed five Israeli tourists, the bus driver and himself on a passenger bus at the Burgas airport. A meeting of the EU Justice and Home Affairs Council scheduled for 19–20 September, to discuss Bulgaria and Romania's admittance to the Schengen Area treaty, and The Netherland's opposition, was postponed to 25–26 October. Deputy Prime Minister Simeon Djakov said Bulgaria had 'lost patience' and that The Netherlands 'has been changing the rules of the game for election campaign reasons'. On 21 September, parliament voted to establish a six-month, cross-party investigative committee into corruption by senior officials. At the 25–26 October meeting of the EU Justice and Home Affairs Council to discuss Bulgaria and Romania's admittance to the Schengen Area treaty, it was agreed to postpone the decision until March 2013.
2013 In February, Prime Minister Boiko Borisov became the US President Obama's first European leader to visit since his re-election. Corruption, high energy costs and low living standards lead to protests in Sofia on 12 February. Borisov accepted the resignation of finance minister Simeon Djankov after a row over farm subsidides, and promised to cut power costs. However, this was not enough to pacify the protesters and the government resigned on 20 February. Early elections wrere called for 12 May. President Rosen appointed Marin Raykov as provisional prime minister and minister of foreign affairs. Results of the May election were: GERB 30.54 per cent of the vote (97 seats out of 240); BSP 26.61 per cent (84); DPS 11.31 per cent (36); Ataka (Attack) 7.3 per cent (23). Turnout was 51.33 per cent. President Plevneliev asked Borisov to form a government but he failed and the BSP were called instead. They successfully formed a coalition with the DPS and Plamen Oresharski was nominated as prime minister; he promised a technocratic cabinet and that he had always 'been skeptical towards the division between leftists and rightists. There are some situations in which the most important thing is a rational and pragmatic approach. The main criterion for the composition of the cabinet is expertise.'
2014 Mr Oresharski resigned on 23 July and was replaced by another interim prime minister, Georgy Bliznashk, on 6 August. Snap elections were held on 5 October. Grazhdani za Evropeysko Razvitie na Balgariya (GERB) (Citizens for European Development of Bulgaria) won 32.67 per cent of the vote (84 seats out of 240), followed by Bulgarska Socialistièska Partija (BSP) (Bulgarian Socialist Party) 15.40 per cent (39), Dvizhenie za Prava i Svobodi (DPS) (Movement for Rights and Freedom) 14.84 per cent (38); Reformist Bloc 8.89 per cent (23); Patriotic Front 7.28 per cent (19); Bulgaria Without Censorship 5.69 per cent (15); Ataka (Attack) 4.52 per cent (11); Alternativa za balgarsko vazrazhdane (ABV) (Alternative for Bulgarian Revival) 4.15 per cent (11) Turnout was 51.05 per cent. Former prime minister, Boiko Borisov said his party (GERB) would try to form a government and was reported as saying he 'want[s] to govern, in person'.
2015 Prime Minister Boyko Borissov paid a visit to the European Commission in January and sounded the alarm over Bulgaria's energy resources, following the freezing of the South Stream project. In particular, he warned that if Russia drags its feet over the rehabilitation of Bulgaria's two nuclear reactors, this would be a 'catastrophe' for the country.

Political structure

Constitution
A democratic constitution was passed in July 1991, defining Bulgaria as a republic with a parliamentary form of government. It has been minimally amended four times in 2003, 2005, 2006 and 2007.

Independence date
22 September 1908.

Form of state
Parliamentary democratic republic

The executive
The Council of Ministers is the supreme executive body of the government and usually consists of elected members of the National Assembly. The right to initiate new legislation is vested in the deputies and the Council of Ministers.
The head of state is the president of the Republic, elected by a direct popular vote every five years, and assisted by a vice president. The president is not allowed to initiate or veto new laws, but can bring a law back to parliament for further consideration.

National legislature
The unicameral Narodno Sabranie (National Assembly) has 240 deputies elected for four-year terms by proportional representation in multi-seat constituencies.

Legal system
The legal system is based on the 1991 constitution.
The judiciary is the third component within the political system. It is an autonomous power with an independent budget. The Supreme Legal Council has 45 members. The Constitutional Court is the supreme arbiter.

Last elections
23 and 30 October 2011 (presidential, first round and runoff); 5 October 2014 (parliamentary)
Results: Parliamentary (2014): Grazhdani za Evropeysko Razvitie na Balgariya (GERB) (Citizens for European Development of Bulgaria) won 32.67 per cent of the vote (84 seats out of 240); Bulgarska Socialistièska Partija (BSP) (Bulgarian Socialist Party) 15.40 per cent (39); Dvizhenie za Prava i Svobodi (DPS) (Movement for Rights and Freedom) 14.84 per cent (38); Reformist Bloc 8.89 per cent (23); Patriotic Front 7.28 per cent (19); Bulgaria Without Censorship 5.69 per cent (15); Ataka (Attack) 4.52 per cent (11); Alternativa za balgarsko vazrazhdane (ABV) (Alternative for Bulgarian Revival) 4.15 per cent (11) Turnout was 51.05 per cent.
Presidential (2011) (first round): Rosen Plavneliev (Gerb) won 40.11 per cent of the vote, Ivaylo Kaflin (BSP) 28.96 per cent, Meglena Kuneva (independent) 14 per cent; 15 other candidates each won less than 4 per cent of the vote. Turnout was 52.11 per cent. Runoff: Plavneliev won 52.58 per cent, Kaflin 47.42 per cent; turnout was 48.06 per cent.

Next elections
2017 (parliamentary); 2016 (presidential)

Political parties

Ruling party

Coalition of Bulgarska Socialistiéska Partija (BSP) (Bulgarian Socialist Party) and Attack (from 5 Jul 2013)

Main opposition party

Bulgarska Socialistiéska Partija (BSP) (Bulgarian Socialist Party)

Population

7.25 million (2012)

Bulgaria's birth rate, at eight per 1,000 of the population, is one of the lowest in the world.

Last census: 1 February 2011: 7,364,570

Population density: 74 inhabitants per square km. Urban population 71 per cent (2010 Unicef).

Annual growth rate: -0.8 per cent, 1990–2010 (Unicef).

Ethnic make-up

Turks, Gypsies (around one million in 2002), Russians, Armenians, Jews and Greeks.

Religions

Eastern Orthodoxy is the main religion, but Catholic, Protestant, Jewish and Muslim communities also exist.

Education

Primary education comprises basic education and pre-secondary education. Secondary school education lasts for four or five years and is provided in three types of schools – comprehensive (general secondary) schools, profile-oriented schools and vocational (technical and vocational-technical) schools. Universities, institutes and academies provide higher education. Some universities are private.

Public expenditure on education is typically equivalent to 3.2 per cent of annual gross national income.

Literacy rate: 99 per cent adult rate; 100 per cent youth rate (15–24) (Unesco 2005).

Compulsory years: 7 to 18.

Enrolment rate: 100 per cent boys and 98 per cent girls, total primary school enrolment of the relevant age group, (World Bank).

Pupils per teacher: 17 in primary schools.

Health

The National Health Insurance Fund (NHIF) is responsible for the development of the compulsory health insurance scheme in Bulgaria. Health insurance financing by the NHIF will replace funding through taxes for nearly 90 per cent of hospitals.

HIV/Aids

In 2009 there were an estimated 4,000 people living with HIV (Unicef 2012).

HIV prevalence: 0.1 per cent aged 15–49 in 2009 (Unicef 2012)

Life expectancy: 73 years, 2010 (Unicef 2012)

Fertility rate/Maternal mortality rate: 1.5 births per woman, 2010 (Unicef 2012); maternal mortality 1.5 per 1,000 live births (World Bank).

Child (under 5 years) mortality rate (per 1,000): 12 per 1,000 live births (WHO 2012)

Welfare

The Bulgarian social security system consists of a public pay-as-you-go system, a mandatory state-funded system of privately managed savings accounts and an additional voluntary private contribution. The National Social Security Institute (NSSI) administers mandatory insurance programmes for maternity, sickness, disability and old age benefits including those related to work injuries and occupational diseases. It is also responsible for the collection, control and information services for all obligatory contributions.

The current system of funding benefits was instigated in 2002. A mandatory social insurance scheme provides universal coverage for all members; contributions by individuals to a private insurance fund provide for old age pensions. These schemes are open to all employees, farmers, and artists who pay 21.75 per cent of earning for the social insurance and 0.5 per cent for the private insurance. Employers pay 8.25 per cent of payroll as a whole into these funds. The self-employed pay 31 per cent in total to the funds. The retirement is at aged 61.5 years (men) and 56.5 years (women), however the age is being increased every year until 2009 when retirement will be at age 63 (men) and 60 (women).

Main cities

Sofia (capital, estimated population 1.1 million in 2012), Plovdiv (350,718), Varna (331,540), Burgas (188,337), Ruse (155,372), Stara Zagora (143,154), Pleven (112,385), Sliven (102,141), Dobrich (101,478).

Languages spoken

Turkish (permitted since 1992), Macedonian, Romani, Gagauz, Tartar and Albanian.

Official language/s

Bulgarian

Media

The constitution guarantees freedom of the press.

Press

There are no laws regulating the print media, with publishing entirely liberated since the end of Communist control in 1989. Hybrid tabloids, which integrates elements of good journalism from the quality press with sensational stories, dominate the market.

In 2006 there were over 900 print media outlets, of which 15 were national and 10 regional, daily newspapers. All dailies have suffered from a steady drop is circulation figures and a sustainable market is dissipating.

Dailies: In Bulgarian, but with English online editions, include *Dnevnik* (http://news.dnevnik.bg), the leading quality newspaper and *Standart* (http://standartnews.com); others include *24 Chasa* (www.24chasa.bg), *Trud* (www.trud.bg), *Novinar* (www.novinar.org), and the *Monitor* (www.monitor.bg). The only English-language newspaper is *The Sofia Echo* (www.sofiaecho.com).

Weeklies: There are a variety of magazines for all interest groups. In Bulgarian, *Tema* (www.temanews.com) is a leading magazine for politics and current affairs, others include *7 din Sport* (www.7sport.net), *Novo Vreme* (www.novovreme.com) and *Kultura* (www.online.bg/kultura), which is published by the government.

Business: In Bulgarian, *Pari* (www.pari.bg) is a daily, with an English online edition; *Capital* (www.capital.bg) and the *Banker* (www.banker.bg), are both weeklies.

Broadcasting

Radio: The Bulgarian National Radio (BNR) (www.bnr.bg) has the largest market share with two national, public stations and regional services as well as an international service. There are over 100 private commercial stations, with over 30 in Sophia alone. Darik Radio (http://dariknews.bg), is a private national network. Regional stations include Radio Info (www.inforadio.bg), with news and information, from Sophia, Jazz FM (www.jazzfmbg.com) from Blagoevgrad and Radio Mixx (www.radiomixx.net), from Burgas.

Television: There are three national, commercial networks broadcasting for 24 hours. They include the public, Bulgarian National Television (www.bnt.bg) operates Kanal 1 and a satellite channel, the private bTV (www.btv.bg) with the largest audience and Nova Televisia (www.ntv.bg). There are over 180 registered cable TV operates throughout the country with digital TV services due to be fully implemented by 2015.

National news agency: Bulgarian News Agency (BTA)

Other news agencies: BGnes: www.bgnes.com

Focus: www.focus.bg

Mediapool: www.mediapool.bg

Novinite (in English): www.novinite.com

SEEnews (in English): www.seenews.com

Economy

Bulgaria has a mixed economy based on mature industries such as mining, iron and steel, construction material manufacturing, oil refining and light engineering. It has also increased its manufacturing sector in electronics, clothing, food-processing and automotive components. Tourism has grown slightly quicker than the European Union (EU) average, and, far higher than other non-EU Eastern European destinations.

Since 1994 the government has implemented conservative fiscal policies and tax reforms that have allowed the economy to grow at a steady rate. Foreign direct investment (FDI) reached a record high of US$13.2 billion in 2007, but as the global economic crisis cut world trade, investors became less inclined to part with their money, and FDI fell to US$1.8 billion in 2011; it has steadily improved to 2.03 billion in 2014.

GDP growth was 6.2 per cent in 2008, having remained at around this level since 2005. However, the economy fell into recession in 2009 with GDP growth of -5.5 per cent, which increased household debt, resulting in a rise in unemployment of 9.3 per cent. GDP growth rose to 0.4 per cent in 2010, and to 1.7 per cent in 2011 but fell to 1.1 per cent in 2013. This has since risen to 1.7 per cent in 2014.

Unemployment in 2015 is still high at 10.1 per cent. This is down from 11.6 per cent in April 2014. Accordingly with Eurostat, Euro-zone unemployment fell from 11.7 per cent in April 2014 to 11.1 per cent in 2015. Unemployment in the 28-member EU was 9.7 per cent in April 2015 (down from 10.3 per cent in April 2014). Bulgaria remains the poorest country amongst the EU members, as well as the most corrupt. The transition from communism to democracy has proved itself to be timely and often conflicted when compared to the transitions of former communist states, such as Hungary.

The annual inflation rate, which had been below 8 per cent (2001–07) jumped to 12 per cent in 2008, before falling back to 2.5–3 per cent (2009–11) and then dropping to 0.9 per cent in 2013 and -1.4 per cent in 2014.

When Bulgaria joined the EU in 2007 one specific stipulation for membership was that the government must tackle corruption and organised crime. In 2008 the European Commission (EC) declared that this had not been sufficiently robust and suspended financial aid and in 2009 requested the return of BGN 33 million (US$46.3 million) in farming subsidies that it claimed had been fraudulently misappropriated. In 2010, the newly elected government committed itself to fighting corruption (including cronyism and nepotism). However, corruption in Bulgaria broke a 15-year record in 2014, with an estimated 158,000 bribes paid out each month. A report by the European commission found that 39.4 per cent of Bulgarians aged over 18 had come under pressure to pay a bribe, and 29.3 per cent had done so.

Bulgaria's grey economy is estimated to comprise 31.2 per cent of economic activity within the state. This means that of the €41 billion that made up Bulgaria's GDP in 2013, around €13 billion was undeclared.

External trade

As a member of the European Union, Bulgaria operates within a community-wide free trade area, with tariffs set as a whole. Internationally, the EU has free trade agreements with a number of nations and trading blocs world-wide.

Refined petroleum is the biggest export of the nation, comprising 13 per cent of total exports.

Around 20 per cent of the electricity produced in Bulgaria is exported, according to data from the Electricity System Operator (ESO) for the first nine months of 2014. Bulgarian market participants are worried that the country's electricity export tariff may be more than triple which would curb exports and harm local producers, after reports the prime minister will introduce a new fee on exports. However, There are currently no plans to increase Bulgaria's electricity export tariff, according to the Bulgarian energy regulatory commission EWRC.

Imports

Principal imports include crude oil and natural gas, mining, metallurgical and petroleum equipment, raw materials, perfumes and cosmetics, vehicles, chemicals and plastics.

Main sources: Russia (15.2 per cent total in 2014), Germany (12.2 per cent), Italy (7.0 per cent).

Exports

Significant exports include energy, footwear and clothing, iron and steel, copper, machinery and equipment and fuels.

Main destinations: Germany (12.0 per cent of total in 2014), Turkey (9.4 per cent), Italy (9.0 per cent).

Agriculture

Farming

Agriculture accounted for around 4.9 per cent of GDP, in 2014, with about 6.7 per cent of Bulgaria's workforce employed in farming. Land for agricultural use covers 47.2 per cent of total land available. Principal crops are wheat, maize, barley, sugar beet; other crops include sunflowers, grapes and tobacco.

Official policy towards land reform has mainly focused on restoring property rights, which included over 99.58 per cent for agricultural land and 90 per cent for wooded areas.

With the exception of cereals, farm prices and trade have been liberalised. The outlook for wheat producers has brightened since the reduction of a 15 per cent tax on wheat export earnings to 10 per cent. According to the report, in the nine months since July 2013 Bulgaria exported 3.281 M tons of wheat, of which 2.252-M tons were exported to the EU.

There is a sizeable wine industry, which accounts for around a third of agricultural exports. In 2013 and 2014 Bulgaria's vine and wine sectors began to stabilise and show growth after years of decline. Bulgaria exports 80 per cent of its wine output, amounting to about 220,000 litres, of which 25 per cent are exported to the UK, still the biggest market for Bulgarian wine. Good yields led to 21 per cent growth in vine grapes production and a 37 per cent increase in wine output of good quality in 2013. In 2014, cool and rainy weather caused far lower yields and quality, leading to a decline of 35 per cent over the year.

Long-term development of agriculture is based on further concentration and specialisation, mechanisation, improved irrigation, increased grain production and expansion of the dairy sector. The government offers subsidised credits to farmers owning more than 10 cows. Bulgaria's 2014–2020 Fisheries Operational Program is to be approved by the European Commission at the end of 2015.

Fishing

Bulgaria's implementation of EU fisheries legislation is yet to be completed. Since progress in the compilation of standardised market data has been slow, privatisation of the processing and marketing sectors has been largely affected. Bulgaria is collaborating on a draft convention on fishing and conservation of resources in the Black Sea, which provides an abundance of fish for domestic and external markets, although it is under-utilised. The main species caught include sprats, mussels and turbot.

Forestry

Forest and other wooded land accounts for 37.2 per cent of the total land area, with 3.9 million hectares of forest cover. The proportion of forest cover has been increasing as a result of re-forestation intended chiefly for soil protection, rather than wood production. Plantations account for more than a quarter of the forest area.

Most of the forest and wooded land is available for wood supply with the main species being beech and oak. Coniferous

species include Norwegian spruce and Austrian pine. Up until 1999, all of the forests were state-owned, but in 2013 some 75 per cent were state-owned and 25 per cent were privately owned.
Local demand for sawn wood, panels, pulp and paper is generally met by using domestic wood. Large amounts of saw-logs are also exported. The forestry sector contributes 2.5 per cent to total GDP and directly employs 150,000 people.

Industry and manufacturing

The industrial sector accounts for around 31.2 per cent of GDP and employs 38 per cent of the workforce.
Economic growth in the 1990s was led by the manufacturing sector, which contributes around 18 per cent to GDP. The industrial sector is well developed, and the metal processing, machine building, chemicals, pharmaceuticals, electronics, textiles and food-processing sectors are particularly strong.
The machine building sector includes over 400 enterprises specialising in various areas including casting, machine tools, wood processing machines, machines for the mining industry, machines for the textile industry, machines for the food processing industry, agricultural machines, shipbuilding, vehicle manufacturing, fine mechanics, metal constructions and household instruments.
The Great Wall Motor Company (TGWMC) of China began car production in Bulgaria in February 2011. The plant acts as the principle source of production for the European mainland. Investment by TGWMC of US$400 million, with an initial US$114 million, will provide an annual output capacity of 1,000 units of a sport utility vehicle, with a planned sale price of less than US$15,000. The numbers of cars produced has risen to around 40,000 per year (2014). The plant is managed and operated by the Bulgarian company Litex Motors. At maximum capacity, the plant is expected to produce 50,000 mixed units with the principal market in Eastern Europe before expanding into southern Europe.
An auto component-manufacturing boom is currently underway within the European Union's poorest member. Witte Automotive, a German car part maker that supplies large companies including Ford, moved to a larger factory in 2014. Plans to double the workforce coupled with increased sales targets upwards of US$30 million has lead to total exports in the sector doubling to an estimated US$1 billion. The key markets are the in EU (particularly Germany and the Netherlands), Russia and North America.

Tourism

The main tourist attractions in Bulgaria are Black Sea resorts, including health spas, snow sports, historic sites and activity holidays in general. Bulgaria is one of the most visited countries in southeastern Europe and tourism is an important component of the economy. Romanians, Greeks and Germans are the principal visitors, accounting for over 2.5 million in 2012, out of a total of 8.9 million foreign visitors. Bulgaria has seven historical and two natural sites on the UNESCO World Heritage List.
Travel and tourism constituted 13.3 per cent of GDP in 2013, a significant fall from the 24.6 per cent in 2004. This reflects strength in other sectors of the economy rather than a weakness in the tourist industry, which registered further growth in 2014. Tourism is responsible for 12.2 per cent of employment (356,000 jobs).
The government has upgraded tourist infrastructure and private investment has improved accommodation and resort facilities. In 2013 capital investment in travel and tourism was US$743.3 million (6.6 per cent of total investment).
In May 2012 the EU granted US$192 million to restore 11 castles and other ancient monuments around Bulgaria.

Mining

The mining sector accounts for 2 per cent of GDP and employs 2 per cent of the workforce. It is forecast to grow at an annual average rate of 0.4 per cent from 2014 levels, reaching US$1.1 billion in 2019.
Bulgaria has some deposits of iron, manganese and chromium, and large reserves of zinc, lead and copper.
Apart from zinc, lead and copper, the non-ferrous ores contain some gold, silver and other precious metals. The Chala gold deposit in the area of Haskovski Mineralni Bani is one of Bulgaria's richest. The average gold content is higher than that in Madjarovo where it exceeds three grams per tonne.
Large deposits of copper ore have been discovered in the Sredna Gora Mountains.
There are deposits of marl, limestone, granite, sandstone and clay and plenty of stone that can be used in the building industry.

Hydrocarbons

Proven oil reserves were negligible in 2013 and consumption was 177,000 barrels per day (bpd) leaving Bulgaria a net importer of oil, with most of its supply coming from Russia. Known oil and natural gas deposits are of small amounts and at considerable depth. Exploration for oil and gas is concentrated in the north of the country and in the Black Sea.
The Balkan region is a major transit region for oil and gas. In 2008 Parliament ratified the US$1.2 billion pipeline deal previously agreed between Russia, Bulgaria and Greece in 2007. The pipeline will run inland from Burgas to the northern Greek town of Alexandroupolis on the Aegean Sea and carry 750,000 barrels per day. Russian oil will be transported via the 285km pipeline to the huge EU market, avoiding the busy Bosphorus exit to the Mediterranean, where oil tankers can wait for days. A Russian consortium will hold a 51 per cent stake in the deal to build and operate the pipeline and a joint Greek/Bulgarian consortium 24.5 per cent each. However in 2011 Bulgaria suspended the project due to environmental concerns.
Natural gas reserves and production were negligible in 2013 and Bulgaria is dependent on Russia for the 2.6 billion cubic metres it consumes annually. An agreement is in place, lasting up to 2018, that guarantees Russian gas supplies. Russian gas also passes through Bulgaria to other countries in Europe.
The South Stream pipeline, to transport Russian natural gas to Western and Central Europe (and bypassing Ukraine) began in December 2012. However, in 2014, due to increased tensions between Russia and the west there has been pressure on Bulgaria to halt work on the pipeline.
Proven reserves of coal were 2.4 billion tonnes at the end of 2013, of which the majority is the lesser quality brown coal, with low calorific value, which is used in power stations. Production was 4.7 million tonnes oil equivalent (toe) in 2013.

Energy

Recent published figures for 2013 showed total generating power was at 44 billion kWh, which was a fall of 6.8 per cent on the 2012 figure. Bulgaria's installed electricity capacity is approximately 1,250MW, composed of 580MW of coal-powered thermal power, 380MW of nuclear power and 290MW of hydroelectric power.
The coal-fired Maritsa Iztok complex accounts for 60 per cent of all power generated. A new thermal plant, agreed in December 2005, was constructed at Maritsa Iztok to replace capacity lost by the closure of two nuclear reactors at the Kozloduy power plant after the EU had raised safety concerns. Annual production was 3.3 million tonnes oil equivalent (mtoe). The new plant is expected to keep Bulgaria as the leading exporter of electricity in the Balkans.

Financial markets

Stock exchange

Balgarska fondova borsa (Bulgarian Stock Exchange) (BSE)

Commodity exchange

Sofia Commodity Exchange

Banking and insurance

There is a two-tier system in which an independent central bank supervises and regulates commercial banks and has exclusive rights over the issue of currency. There are approximately 33 commercial banks, with total bank credit to the private sector accounting for 14 per cent of GDP, one of the lowest rates of former Soviet countries.

Central bank

Bulgarska Narodna Banka (BNB) (Bulgarian National Bank)

Time

GMT plus two hours (daylight saving, late March to late October, GMT plus three hours)

Geography

Bulgaria lies in south-eastern Europe, on the east of the Balkan Peninsula. It is situated on the western shores of the Black Sea and shares borders with Romania to the north, Turkey to the south-east, Greece to the south, Macedonia (FYROM) to the south-west and Serbia to the north-west. The lower River Danube forms most of the border with Romania.

The Balkan Mountains dominate central Bulgaria, running from west to east and separating the Danubian plains in the north from the Thracian plains of Eastern Rumelia in the south-east. The Rhodope Mountains occupy south-west Bulgaria and separate it from Greece and Macedonia.

The Sofia depression in the west of the country is hill country which separates the Balkan Mountains from the southern mountains. It is the main centre of population and communications.

The fertile Bulgarian plateau, between the Danubian border and the Balkan Mountains, averages some 100km in width and contains several tributaries of the Danube, the major one being the Iskur. The main rivers south of the Balkan watershed are the Struma and the Maritza which run into the Aegean Sea. The broad Maritza Valley, which leads on to the Thracian plains, is one of the principal agricultural areas.

Hemisphere

Northern

Climate

Summer is hot and dry, April–September average temperature 23 degrees Celsius (C). Cold winters, average temperature minus 1 degree C, with heavy snow.

Dress codes

Dress for business is usually quite conservative but not overly formal.

Entry requirements

Passports

Passports are required by all visitors.

As from 1 January 2006, all visitors staying for longer than 24 hours must be registered with the authorities; hotels will automatically undertake this task.

Visa

Not required by citizens of Europe, North America, Australasia and some Asian countries for either 90 or 30 days. Full details and information can be found at www.bulgariatravel.org and see 'getting to Bulgaria'.

Businessmen from visa-free states may visit without a visa for up to 30 days. All other businessmen must apply for visas and include a letter of invitation from a company registered in Bulgaria endorsed by the Bulgarian Chamber of Commerce.

All visitors, tourist and business, must have travel and medical insurance to cover emergency medical expenses, repatriation, transport of mortal remains, funeral and hospitalisation. A copy of the policy, with legible policy number, company name, duration of validity and sum of coverage or a letter from the insurance company including such data, should be submitted with the application.

Currency advice/regulations

The import and export of local currency up to Lev5,000 is allowed without restrictions. Between Lev5,000–20,000 import and export is permitted if the amount was declared on arrival. The import and export of over Lev20,000 is allowed only with written permission from the central bank.

Foreign currency may be import in unlimited amounts, but must be declared on arrival; export of foreign cannot exceed the amount imported and declared.

A *bordereaux* is issued to all visitors on arrival, to record all money exchanges and must be returned to the authorities when departing. Local currency can only be exchanged on departure with the *bordereaux*. Visitors are advised to exchange money in banks and hotels.

ATMs are widespread; check with the card provider concerning terms and conditions. Travellers cheques are accepted in major hotels and establishments; US dollars and pound sterling attract less additional rate charges.

Customs

Small quantities of spirits, wines and beverages are allowed in duty-free. Valuable personal effects should be declared verbally to Customs on entry. There are no restrictions on goods bought for foreign exchange in duty free shops at ports of entry.

Health (for visitors)

Foreign travellers must present valid evidence of health insurance to the Bulgarian border authorities in order to be admitted into the country.

Mandatory precautions

None

Advisable precautions

Recommended immunisations: hepatitis A, polio, tetanus and typhoid.

Hotels

Deluxe, first- and second-class ratings system. Hotels have been upgraded to attract business people. Radisson, Sheraton and Hilton groups have hotels in Sofia.

Credit cards

Main international credit cards are accepted in larger hotels and stores in larger cities, and in some restaurants in Sofia.

Public holidays (national)

Fixed dates

1 Jan (New Year's Day), 3 Mar (National Day), 1 May (Labour Day), 6 May (St George's Day), 24 May (St Cyril and Methodius Day/Culture Day), 6 Sep (Unification Day), 22 Sep (Independence Day), 24–26 Dec (Christmas).

Variable dates

Orthodox Good Friday, Orthodox Easter Monday.

Working hours

Banking

Mon–Fri: 0800–1230, 1330–1530; Sat: 0830–1130.

Business

Mon–Fri: 0800 (0900)–1730 (1800).

Government

Mon–Fri: 0800 (0900)–1730 (1800).

Shops

Mon–Fri: 1000–2000; Sat: 0800–1400.

Telecommunications

Mobile/cell phones

There is good GSM coverage of 3G, with nationwide coverage of GSM 900 and 1800.

Electricity supply

220–240V AC/50 HZ

Social customs/useful tips

A nod of the head means 'No', a shake of the head means 'Yes'. Shaking hands is the traditional form of greeting. It is usual to invite your host to a good restaurant.

Security

By Western standards, the streets of Sofia and other towns and cities are generally safe. Street crime is slowly rising and the usual precautions should be taken.

Getting there

Air

National airline: Bulgaria Air

Hemus Air connects Sofia to some European and Middle Eastern destinations.

International airport/s: Sofia (SOF) airport, 10km east of the city centre. Facilities include banks, post office, duty-free shops, restaurant and car hire.

By day, buses run every 10 minutes to the city, at night they run every 20 minutes between 2100–0030. Taxis are available, if the metre is not in use, a fare may have to be negotiated before travelling.

Other airport/s: Varna (VAR), 9km from city; Burgas (BOJ), 13km from city.

Airport tax: None, except US nationals who are charged US$20.

Surface

Road: The pan-European corridor, which is being built or existing roads upgraded, links Bulgaria to the European motorway network. Border crossings exist from all surrounding countries; new roads and border controls are planned with Turkey, Greece and Serbia. The Trans-European Motorway (TEM), includes routes connecting Budapest with Athens via Sofia and with Istanbul via eastern Bulgaria. In July 2006 the proposal for a north-south road tunnel under Shipka Mountain estimated at US$120 million, was still under consideration.

Rail: There are no direct rail services between Bulgaria and Western Europe. Links exist to Serbia, Turkey, Romania and Greece.

Water: Ships provide regular passenger service and cruises on the Danube, starting at Passau in Germany, to Vienna, passing through Slovakia, Hungary and Serbia. There are also links with the Rhine, Black Sea and Main.

Main port/s: Burgas, Varna.

Getting about

National transport

Air: Bulgaria Air operates a domestic flight from Sofia to Varna. Hemus Air connects Sofia to the Black Sea cities of Varna and Bourgas.

Road: The overall quality of the 13,000km of roads linking the major cities is good but some roads are in poor repair and full of potholes. International road signs are used and traffic drives on the right.

Rail: Approximately 6,500km of track connect all main towns. First-class travel is recommended. It is necessary to make reservations.

City transport

Taxis: Taxis are plentiful and cheap. Official taxis have meters, although some privately operated ones may not. A 5–10 per cent tip in local currency is usual.

Taxis to Sofia airport have a journey time of 15 minutes. Fares should be agreed before departure.

Buses, trams & metro: Efficient and cheap tram and bus services operate in Sofia. Flat rate fares are charged.

Trolleybus services are available in Plovdiv and Varna.

Buses to the city centre from the airport run every 10 minutes during the day and every 20 minutes between 2100–0030, and take 25 minutes.

Car hire

An international driving permit is required. A green card (international car insurance) is compulsory. Most car hire accounts are transacted in hard currency. Drivers are normally given special petrol coupons, which can be used throughout the country. Speed limits: out of town 90kph and 120kph on motorways, in town 50kph. Drinking and driving is strictly prohibited. There are tolls on motorways and other major roads.

BUSINESS DIRECTORY

The addresses listed below are a selection only. While World of Information makes every endeavour to check these addresses, we cannot guarantee that changes have not been made, especially to telephone numbers and area codes. We would welcome any corrections.

Telephone area codes

The international direct dialling (IDD) code for Bulgaria is +359, followed by area code and subscriber's number:

Blagoevgrad	73	Rousse	82
Burgas	56	Smoliyan	301
Dobritch	58	Sofia	2
Gabrovo	66	Stara Zagora	42
Lovech	68	Varna	52
Plovdiv	32	Veliko Tûrnovo	62

Useful telephone numbers

Ambulance: 150

Fire brigade: 160

Police: 166

Operator: 121 (inland); 123 (international)

Directory enquiries: 144 (business); 145 (domestic lines)

Traffic police: 165

Road service: 91-146

Chambers of Commerce

British Bulgarian Chamber of Commerce, 8 Charles Darwin Street, 1113 Sofia (tel: 971-4756; fax: 738-331; e-mail: info@bbcc.bg).

Bulgarian Chamber of Commerce and Industry, 42 Parchevich Street, 1058 Sofia (tel: 987-2631; fax: 987-3209; e-mail: bcci@bcci.bg).

Burgas Chamber of Commerce and Industry, 12B L Karavelov Street, PO Box 644, 8000 Sofia (tel: 812-007; fax: 810-130; e-mail: bscci@bcci.bg).

Dobritch Chamber of Commerce and Industry, 14 Nezavisimost Street, PO Box 182, 9300 Dobritch (tel: 601-433; fax:601-434; e-mail: dbcci@bcci.bg).

Gabrovo Chamber of Commerce and Industry, 1Vazrazhdane Square, PO Box 217, 5300 Gabrovo (tel: 288-39; fax: 341-83; e-mail: gbcci@mbox.eda.bg).

Plovdiv Chamber of Commerce and Industry, 7 Samara Street, 4003 Plovdiv (tel: 652-645; fax: 652-647; e-mail: pcci@plovdiv-chamber.org).

Sousse Chamber of Commerce and Industry, 3 A Ferdinand Boulevard, PO Box 484, 7000 Rousse (tel: 825-884; fax: 825-873; e-mail: info@chamber.rousse.bg).

Stara Zagora Chamber of Commerce and Industry, 66 GS Rakovski Street, 6000 Stara Zagora (tel: 461-94; fax: 260-33; e-mail: office@chambersz.com).

Varna Chamber of Commerce and Industry, 135 Primorsky Boulevard, 9000 Varna (tel: 615-140; fax: 612-146; e-mail: office@vcci.bg).

Banking

Biochim Bank, 1 Ivan Vazov Street, 1040 Sofia (tel: 926-9210; fax: 981-9151; e-mail: info@biochim.com).

BulBank Ltd, 7 Sveta Nedelya Square, 1000 Sofia (tel: 984-1111; fax: 988-4636, 988-5370; e-mail: infor@sof.bulbank.bg).

Bulgarian Post Bank, 1 Bulgaria Square, 1414 Sofia (tel: 963-2104/5; e-mail: iap@postbank.bg).

DSK Bank, 19 Moskovska Street, 1040 Sofia (tel: 939-1220; fax: 980-6477).

Central bank

Bulgarska Narodna Banka, 1 Alexander Battenberg Square, 1000 Sofia (tel: 91-459 fax: 980-2425).

Stock exchange

Balgarska fondova borsa (Bulgarian Stock Exchange) (BSE), www.bse-sofia.bg

Commodity exchange

Sofia Commodity Exchange, Sofia (tel: 952 6212, 952 6225, 952 6203; fax: 952 6232; e-mail: sce@sce-bg.com; www.sce-bg.com).

Travel information

Bulgaria Air, 1 Brussels blvd, Sofia Airport Sofia 1540 (tel: 402-0306; fax: 937-3254; email: office@air.bg; internet: www.air.bg/en/).

Balkantourist, 2 Enos Street, 1408 Sofia (tel: 981-9806; fax: 988-4177; email: sofia.agency@balkantourist.bg; internet: www.balkantourist.bg).

Central Railway Station, Maria Luisa Boulevard, Sofia (tel: 31-111; internet: www.sofia.com/transport).

Sofia Airport (email: public@sofia-airport.bg; internet: www.sofia-airport.bg/En).

National tourist organisation offices

Bulgarian Tourism Authority, 1 Sveta Nedelia Square, 1000 Sofia (tel: 987-9778; fax: 989-6939; email: webmaster@bulgariatravel.org; internet: www.bulgariatravel.org).

Ministries

Ministry of Agriculture and Forests, 55 Hristo Botev Boulevard, 1000 Sofia (tel: 981-1546; fax: 885-557).

Ministry of Culture, 17 Alexander Stamboliiski Boulevard., 1000 Sofia (tel: 980-5384; fax: 981-8145).

Ministry of Defence, 3 Vassil Levsky Street, 1000 Sofia (tel: 862-4135; fax: 873-626).

Ministry of Economy, 12 Kniaz Alexander Batenberg Street, 1000 Sofia (tel: 981-9965, 987-9778; fax: 981-2515, 981-5039).

Ministry of Education and Science, 2a Doundukov Boulevard, 1000 Sofia (tel: 84-81; fax: 987-1289).

Ministry of Environment and Waters, 67 Gladstone Street, 1000 Sofia (tel: 814-269; fax: 521-634).

Ministry of Finance, 102 Georgi Rakovski Street, 1000 Sofia (tel: 869-1870; fax: 980-6863); external department (tel: 869-223; fax: 876-008).

Ministry of Foreign Affairs, 2 Alexander Jendov Street, 1000 Sofia (tel: 714-3507; fax: 736-069).

Ministry of Health, 5 Sveta Nedelya Square, 1000 Sofia (tel: 86-31; fax: 875-040).

Ministry of the Interior, 23 Gurko Street, 1000 Sofia (tel: 877-511; fax: 824-047).

Ministry of Justice, 1 Slavianska Street, 1000 Sofia (tel: 86-01; fax: 876-3226).

Ministry of Labour and Social Policy, 2 Triaditza Street, 1000 Sofia (tel: 981-1717; fax: 800-609).

Ministry of Regional and Urban Development, 17 Kiril & Methodius Street, 1000 Sofia (tel: 83-841; fax: 872-517).

Ministry of Transport, 9 Levski Street, 1000 Sofia (tel: 872-862; fax: 885-094).

Council of Ministers, 1 Dondoukov Blvd., 1000 Sofia (tel: 8501; fax: 884-252).

Other useful addresses

Agency for Economic Co-ordination and Development, 1 Vassil Levsky Street, 1000 Sofia (tel: 543-386; fax: 833-323).

Agency for Privatisation, 29 Aksakov St, 1000 Sofia (tel: 873-188; fax: 882-938, 885-395).

Board of Customs Houses at the Ministry of Finance, 1 Aksakov Street, Sofia 1000 (tel: 869-528; fax: 884-909).

Bulgarian Academy of Sciences, 1 7-mi Noemvri Street, 1000 Sofia (tel: 841-41; fax: 803-023).

Bulgarian Embassy (USA), 1621 22nd Street, NW, Washington DC 20008 (tel: (+1-202) 387-0174; fax: (+1-202) 234-7973; e-mail: office@bulgaria-embassy.org).

Bulgarian Foreign Investment Agency, 3 Sveta Sofia Street, 1000 Sofia (tel: 980-0918; fax: 980-1320; e-mail: fia@geobiz.com; internet site: www.bfia.org).

Bulgarian Industrial Association (BISA), 14 Alabin Street, 1000 Sofia (tel: 879-611, 872-960; fax: 872-604).

Bulgarian National Television, 29 San Stefano Str, 1504 Sofia (tel: 446-329; fax: 662-388).

Bulgarian News Agency (BTA), 49 Tzarigradsko Chaussee Blvd, 1024 Sofia (tel: 877-363, 877-739; fax: 802-488).

Bulgarian Telecommunication Company (BTC), 8 Totleben Blvd (tel: 870-143; fax: 875-885).

Bulgarian Telegraph Agency, Trakija Boulevard 49, Sofia (tel: 8461).

Bulgarian Translators' Union, 16 Graf Ignatiev Street, 1000 Sofia (tel: 661-602, 662-564; fax: 510-845, 661-233).

Bulgarreklama (trade show agency), 147 Tsarigradsko Chaussee Blvd, 1784 Sofia 1784 (tel: 965-5220; fax: 965-5230; email: bul-reklama@bulgarreklama.com; internet: www.bulgarreklama.com).

Central Co-operative Union, 99 Rakovski Street, 1000 Sofia (tel: 84-41; fax: 878-157).

Committee for Energy, 8 Triaditsa Street, 1000 Sofia (tel: 861-91; fax: 876-279).

Committee for Forests, 17 Antim I Street, 1000 Sofia (tel: 861-71; fax: 873-235).

Committee for Geology and Mineral Resources, 22 Maria Louisa Blvd, 1000 Sofia (tel: 832-767; fax: 833-976).

Committee for Posts and Telecommunications, 6 Gourko Street, 1000 Sofia (tel: 889-646, 871-837; fax: 814-512, 800-044).

Committee for Television, 29 San Stefano Street, 1504 Sofia (tel: 43-481).

Committee for Standardisation and Metrology, 21 6-ti Septemvri Street, 1000 Sofia (tel: 85-91; fax: 801-402).

EU Energy Centre (Thermie), 51 James Boucher Blvd, 1407 Sofia (tel: 681-461, 683-542; fax: 681-461).

Euro Information Centre, Network/Correspondence Centre, 54 Dr GM Dimitrov Blv, 1125 Sofia (tel: 738-448; fax: 730-435).

First Bulgarian Stock Exchange, 1 Macedonia Square, 1040 Sofia (tel: 815-711; fax: 875-566; internet site: www.bse-sofia.bg).

Foreign Aid Agency, 1 Vrabcha Street, 1000 Sofia (tel: 881-951; fax: 885-039).

Intercommerce (import, export, re-export and transit operations, compensation deals and foreign trade transactions), 21 Aksakov Str, 1000 Sofia (tel: 879-364; fax: 873-753).

International Fair – Plovdiv, G. Dimitrov Boulevard 37 (tel: 553-191, 553-146, 26-129, 26-139).

International Road Transport (SO MAT), Gorublyane, 1738 Sofia (tel: 712-121, 758-015; fax: 758-015).

Interpred World Trade Centre (representation of foreign companies), 36 Dragan Tzankov Boulevard, 1040 Sofia (tel: 7146-4646; fax: 700-006, 706-401).

Law Offices for Foreign Legal Matters (tel: 877-782).

Scientific Institute for International Co-operation and Foreign Economic Activities, 3A 165 Street, Zh K Izgreva, 1113 Sofia (tel: 708-336; fax: 705-154, 700-131).

Small and Medium-Sized Enterprises (SME) Development Programme, Agency for Privatisation, 29 Aksakov Str, 1046 Sofia (tel: 871-913; fax: 871-912).

Sofia Press Agency, 113 Tsarigradsko Shosse Blvd. (tel: 878-428; fax: 883-455).

Sofia Customs Office, 1 Aksakov Street, 1000 Sofia (tel: 800-402; fax: 884-909).

Union for Private Economic Enterprise, 2a Suborna Street, 1000 Sofia (tel: 659-371; fax: 659-411).

National news agency: Bulgarian News Agency (BTA), 49 Tsarigradsko Chaussee Blvd, 1124 Sofia, (tel: 9262-279, 9262-205; email: dnews@bta.bg; internet: www.bta.bg).

BGnes: www.bgnes.com

Focus: www.focus.bg

Mediapool: www.mediapool.bg

Novinite (in English): www.novinite.com

SEEnews (in English): www.seenews.com

Internet sites

Bulgaria financial and business newspaper: http://www.capital.bg/

Burkina Faso

KEY FACTS

Official name: République Démocratique Populaire de Burkina Faso (Popular Democratic Republic of Burkina Faso)

Head of State: Interim President Michel Kafando (since 1 November 2014) following the resignation of Blaise Compaore on 31 October 2014 after efforts to amend the constitution to enable him to run for another term led to violent protests

Head of government: Prime Minister Lt Col Yacouba Issac Zida (since 19 November 2014) (named by the army). Zida was briefly removed from office by the Regiment of Presidential Security in a September 2015 coup, but he was restored as Prime Minister within a week.

Ruling party: There is no ruling party, Zida was named as head of the transitional government on 1 November 2014 by the military. On 14 November, military and opposition party leaders agreed to a charter returning the government to civilian rule and holding elections in late 2015.

Area: 274,000 square km

Population: 17.43 million (2014)*

Capital: Ouagadougou

Official language: French

Currency: CFA franc (CFAf) = 100 centimes (Communauté Financière Africaine (African Financial Community) franc).

Exchange rate: CFAf586.44 per US$ (Sep 2015); CFAf655.95 per euro (pegged from Jan 1999)

GDP per capita: US$717 (2014)*

GDP real growth: 4.02% (2014)*

GDP: US$12.50 billion (2014)*

Labour force: 6.67 million (2007) (excludes seasonal, expatriate numbers)

Inflation: -0.26% (2014)*

Balance of trade: -US$132.40 million (2010)

* estimated figure

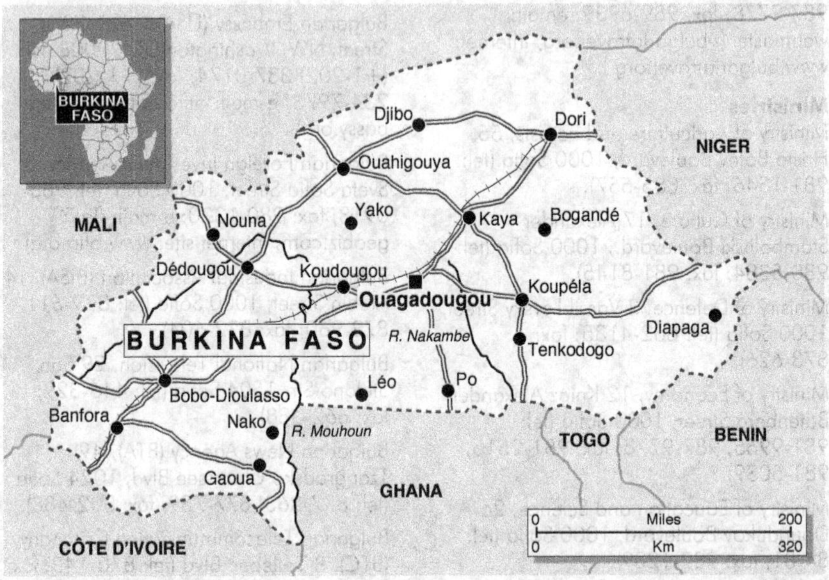

Burkina Faso is a poor country, even when compared to the standards of West Africa. However the country is rich in minerals, and the government's main challenge is using the country's revenues from mining to create more inclusive growth and combat the high rate of poverty. The government is also planning on creating regional growth centres, concentrated mainly in the capital, in order to stimulate development and improve land usage.

After 27 years of power, Burkina Faso's President Blaise Compaoré was removed from his position by a violent popular uprising in October 2014. Mr Compaoré was one of Africa's longest serving heads of state, having been president since a *coup* in 1987 in which he elbowed his way to leadership by organising the assassination of the former president, Thomas Sankara. Mr Compaoré announced his resignation as thousands of people took to the streets to protest his attempt to change the constitution to allow himself to extend his term in office. Following the resignation, General Honoré Traoré declared himself in charge of the country, however, a commander of the presidential guard, Lieutenant Colonel Isaac Zida claimed Traoré's claim obsolete and announced himself president. After reports of gunfire near the presidential palace as a result of this dispute, an agreement of sorts was met and on 1 November 2014 the Military of Burkina Faso declared Zida to be head of state of Burkina Faso in a statement signed by army chiefs including Traoré. On 18 November 2014 the former Permanent Representative of Burkina Faso to the United Nations, Michel Kafando, assumed office as interim president on to lead a transition government in the lead up to the elections in October 2015.

The economy

The combination of the political crisis, lower gold and cotton prices and the outbreak of the Ebola epidemic in West Africa lead to significant effects on Burkina Faso's economy in 2014. Despite this, the real GDP growth still reached 5.0 per cent in 2014, decreasing from 6.6 per cent in 2013. The continued infrastructure investment has lead to a positive economic outlook for the years 2015 and 2016, with projected growth of 5.5 per cent and 7 per cent respectively.

Despite Mr Compaoré's reputed left-wing leanings, on becoming president he soon embarked on a programme of privatisation and austerity measures sponsored by the International Monetary Fund (IMF). In July 2014, the Executive Board of the IMF completed the first review of Burkina Faso's economic performance under a three-year programme supported by the IMF's Extended Credit Facility (ECF) arrangement. The completion of the first review enabled the immediate release of an amount equivalent to SDR2.55 million (about US$3.9 million), bringing total disbursements under the arrangement to an amount equivalent to SDR5.1 million (about US$7.9 million).

In completing its first review, the IMF also approved the authorities' requests for a waiver for non-observance of the end-December 2013 performance criterion on net domestic financing and for the modification of the continuous performance criterion on non-concessional external debt and modification of the performance criterion on net domestic financing for the end-June and end-December 2014 periods. The 36-month ECF arrangement of SDR27.09 million (about US$37.97 million, or 45 per cent of Burkina Faso's quota at the IMF) was approved by the Executive Board in December 2013. In June 2015 the second and third reviews for Burkina Faso were completed, enabling the immediate release of SDR23.03 million (US$32.28 million) which brought total disbursements to SDR28.13 million (US$39.42 million).

In the view of the IMF, Burkina Faso has a long track record of strong macro-economic policy management, supported by IMF programmes. Structural reforms to improve productivity and resilience in agriculture and increased spending for poverty reduction and food security have resulted in robust growth rates and progress toward the Millennium Development Goals.

The IMF also noted that Burkina Faso's performance under the new ECF-supported programme have been satisfactory, with all structural reforms implemented and most quantitative targets reached. Growth has remained robust and the fiscal deficit has been contained. While the outlook for growth remains strong, there are challenges arising from unfavourable terms of trade in the near term. However, fiscal deficits look likely to remain contained at around 3 per cent of gross domestic product (GDP), due to spending adjustments and increased grants. As gold prices recover over the medium term, external balances also ought to improve. The risk of debt distress remains classified as 'moderate'.

The IMF also noted that the Burkina Faso authorities had reaffirmed their strong commitment to the programme against the backdrop of a more challenging policy environment. Three macro-economic challenges have been identified to set the foundation for progress over the longer term. First, ensuring that the quality and composition of spending allows for scaling up critical investment, both in infrastructure and people, needed to support private sector-led growth. Second, accelerating investments for increased and more reliable electricity supplies to meet growing demand, while putting the energy sector on a more financially sustainable footing and scaling down untargeted subsidies. Finally, updating the mining code to harness natural resource revenues and creating mechanisms, such as a fiscal rule, to direct them toward growth-enhancing spending over a multi-year horizon.

In order to support the transitional government leading up to the October 2015 elections – which had to deal with the severe challenges of political upheaval, spill overs from the Ebola crisis and unfavourable trading conditions – the authorities decided to continue with the ECF arrangements.

Due to the slower growth and reduction in food prices, inflation turned negative in 2014, reducing by 0.3 per cent. Despite the reduction of investment leading to a narrowed current account deficit, a large external imbalance still remains and the country's imputed international reserves have sharply declined.

The economic outlook

In its 2015 *Economic Outlook* for Burkina Faso the African Development Bank (AfDB) observes that Burkina Faso is vulnerable to old, cotton and oil prices. The major concerns remain to be a high level of poverty in a young population and disparities between regions. Although there has been good progress in education, better access to clean water and a strong fight against HIV/Aids, not all the Millennium Development Goals (MDG) will be reached in 2015. Most of the developed economic infrastructure is concentrated in the capital, Ouagadougou, while little development has taken place in the countryside in which 77.3 per cent of population lives. In order to over come this challenge government policy is to implement regional growth centres that are based on the potential of each particular area.

In the 2015 edition of the World Bank's *Doing Business Report* Burkina Faso was 167 out of the 189 countries surveyed, a fall from 154 in 2014. The most challenging areas include infrastructure, health, primary education, higher education and training and business sophistication. The underlying challenges are those of the poorly skilled labour force, a lack of business sophistication and credit constraints.

Risk assessment

Politics	Poor
Economy	Fair
Regional stability	Fair

Muslims in Burkina Faso

% of population	50
Sunni (% of Muslims)	99
Shi'a (% of Muslims)	1

COUNTRY PROFILE

1958 The country was given self-government.
1960 Granted full independence from France as Upper Volta. Maurice Yameogo became first president.

KEY INDICATORS — Burkina Faso

	Unit	2011	2012	2013	2014	**2015
Population	m	*15.03	*16.50	*16.97	*17.43	*17.93
Gross domestic product (GDP)	US$bn	10.10	11.03	*12.20	*12.50	*11.32
GDP per capita	US$	600	668	*720	*717	*631
GDP real growth	%	5.6	9.0	*6.6	*4.0	*5.0
Inflation	%	2.8	3.8	0.5	*-0.3	*0.7
Current account	US$m	-115.0	-471.0	*-807.0	*-767.0	*-914.0
Total reserves minus gold	US$m	–	1,025.0	628.5	297.1	–
Foreign exchange	US$m	–	939.0	542.7	–	–
Exchange rate	per US$	466.82	497.16	480.26	542.07	–

* estimated figure ** forecast figure

1966 Yameogo was ousted in a military coup by Colonel Sangoule Lamizama.
1970 A new constitution was agreed by a referendum, it detailed the introduction of an elected president and civilian administration by 1975.
1974 Lamizama suspended the constitution and assumed the presidency.
1978 Multiparty elections for president and the National Assembly were held. Lamizama and his followers won and he retained the presidency.
1980 Yameogo, was overthrown in a coup by Colonel Saye Zerbo.
1982 Major Jean-Baptiste Ouédraogo overthrew Zerbo.
1983 Captain Thomas Sankara led a coup and took over as president.
1984 Upper Volta's name was changed to the Popular Democratic Republic of Burkina Faso.
1987 Sankara was assassinated. Captain Blaise Compaoré seized power backed by the Organisation pour la Démocratie Populaire-Mouvement du Travail (ODP-MT) (Organization for People's Democracy-Workers' Movement).
1991 A new constitution established a semi-presidential government. Compaoré was elected president, following the withdrawal of opposition candidates.
1992 The ODP-MT won a convincing victory in the national legislature elections.
1996 The ODP-MT merged with the Parti pour la Démocratie et le Progrès (Party for Democracy and Progress) to become the Congrès pour la Démocratie et le Progrès (CDP) (Congress for Democracy and Progress).
1998 Compaoré won the presidential election, which was boycotted by opposition parties.
1999 Prime Minister Ouédraogo and his cabinet resigned, but he and his cabinet were reinstated by presidential decree.
2000 The constitution was amended so that presidential terms were limited to two and a limit of five years per term was imposed. A UN report accused the president of not only allowing Burkina Faso to be involved in sanctions busting of UN embargoes on Angola but also of being in personal receipt of payments for diamond smuggling activities undertaken through his country by Unita rebels.
2001 International donors agreed to fund a US$85 million programme to combat Burkina Faso's HIV/Aids epidemic.
2002 The Chambre des Représentants (House of Representatives) was abolished. The CDP retained its majority in National Assembly elections.
2005 Opposition parties objected to President Compaoré's third time running for office saying it defied the constitution. The Constitutional Court ruled that since the constitution was changed after his first term in office his candidacy was acceptable. Blaise Compaoré was re-elected president with 80.3 per cent of the votes, while Bénéwendé Stanislas Sankara won 4.9 per cent. Turnout was 57.5 per cent.
2007 In the general elections the ruling CDP won 73 seats (out of 111). Tertius Zongo became prime minister following Paramanga Ernest Yonli's resignation.
2009 A national 'free birth certificate' programme began, which started the process of enfranchising all citizens. Other documentation and services such as passports and access to education will flow from the scheme and should cut, not only the ease with which trafficked children are exploited, but also deter child marriages. The ruins of Loropéni were added to Unesco's prestigious list of world heritage sites. Situated close to the border of Côte d'Ivoire, the stone enclosure is an historic site that is a tangible link with the past trans-Saharan gold trade.
2010 Heavy rains caused two dams in the east to brake and over 20,000 people were made homeless. Seven candidates took part in presidential elections. As expected incumbent President Blaise Compaoré won, with 81 per cent of the vote, his nearest rival, Hama Arba Diallo, won 8 per cent. Turnout was reported to be so low that the president turned to the media to encourage people to vote. The official declaration was a turnout of 53 per cent.
2011 Prime Minister Zongo and his government resigned in January. He was reappointed immediately and chose a new (but almost unchanged) cabinet. The conflict in Côte d'Ivoire disrupted supplies to land-locked Burkina Faso and also pushed up prices for processed foods such as dried milk, sugar and vegetable oil. In April gunfire was heard in Ouagadougou, at an elite barracks of the presidential guard, as members rampaged through the city protesting at unpaid housing allowances. The mutiny lasted until a curfew was finally imposed on 16 April. A day later the government of Prime Minister Tertius Zongo was dissolved. Luc-Adolphe Tiao was appointed prime minister; the unrest had spread to the north as people demonstrated against the high cost of food. The mutiny spread to a fourth city. On 21 April Compaoré appointed himself minister of defence in a cabinet reshuffle. In July the World Bank announced a grant of US$23 million to enhance the information communication technology infrastructure in Burkina Faso.
2012 The head of the customs service, Ousmane Guiro, was sacked following the seizure of almost US$4 million in currency found in two suitcases traced back to Guiro. On 12 June, parliament granted amnesty and immunity from prosecution to President Compaoré and all previous heads of state in Burkina Faso. On 27 July, there were an estimated 100,000 Malian refugees in Burkina Faso and the UNHCR warned that there was a funding shortfall with a food supply limited to September. Parliamentary elections took place on 2 December, of which 127 seats were elected by proportional representation (PR) and 16 seats through party lists. The party list results were published first: CDP won 48.66 per cent (eight seats, out of 16), ADF-RDA 11.24 per cent (two), Union pour le Progrès et la Réforme (UPR) (Union for Progress and Reform) 11.09 per cent (two); four other political parties each won one seat, 67 other parties failed to win any seats. The PR seats were mostly won by CDP with 62 (total 70 seats).
2014 In July, 15 years after a peace accord called for its creation, Burundi finally set up a Peace and Reconciliation Commission (PRC) to examine crimes committed since 1962. However, controversies and disagreements between the parties still continued, mostly over who would be chosen to select members of the commission. On 30 October Blaise Compaoré resigned as president after several days of protests over the his attempts to change the constitution to allow him to run in the 2015 presidential election (under the 2012 constitution the president may only stand for re-election once). Although under the constitution the president of the Senate should take over after the national president resigns, on 1 November the army named Lieutenant Colonel Isaac Zida as leader of a transitional government. There were further demonstrations, against the army takeover, followed by a statement from the army announcing that 'a transition body... with all the components to be adopted by a broad consensus' would be put in place. 'Power does not interest us, only the greater interest of the nation', said the military spokesman. The African Union (AU) says the army acted unconstitutionally when it took over after President Blaise Compaore was forced to resign. On 3 November the AU gave the military two weeks to hand power to a civilian ruler or face sanctions. Lt Col Isaac Zida promised to comply with the deadline. The presidents of Ghana, Nigeria and Senegal mediated talks held in Ouagadougou on 5 November. Agreement was reached for a year of political transition, followed by elections in November 2015, but not on who would head the transitional government. On 8 November, Lt Col Isaac Zida said the two week deadline imposed by the AU was impossible to meet; the AU replied that the threat of sanctions stood. Michel Kafando was chosen as interim president

and inaugurated on 18 November. On 19 November he appointed Zida as prime minister.

2015 In April eight supporters of former president Blaise Compaoré, including three ex-ministers, were arrested. On 7 April the interim parliament passed a bill banning allies of Mr Compaoré from standing in the coming (planned for October) presidential election. CDP, the former ruling party, opposed the move. On 17 September President Michel Kafando and Prime Minister Isaac Zida were detained by members of the elite Régiment de la Sécurité Présidentielle (RSP) (Regiment of Presidential Security), lead by General Gilbert Diendere, supporting former president Compaoré. (A commission had earlier recommended the disbanding of the RSP.) On 20 September military chiefs demanded General Diendere stand down; the army marched on Ouagadougou, reaching the capital the next day, shortly after the General said he was prepared to hand back power under certain conditions. By the end of the month the interim government said it had retaken the presidential guard barracks; the whereabouts of General Diendere were not known.

Political structure

Constitution

Constitutional changes were adopted in January 1997. These included the abolition of the limit of two seven-year terms for the president, and an increase in the number of seats in the legislature from 107 to 111.

In October 2014, President Blaise Compaoré attempted to change the country's democratic constitution, which would have allowed him to remain in power for another term. Compaoré came to power nearly three decades ago in a military coup d'état in 1987. He failed because tens of thousands of people in Burkina Faso took to the streets of their capital, Ouagadougou to protest it. The clashes soon became violent as security forces tried to prevent the protests. Protestors stormed parliament and torched other state buildings, the security forces responded by shooting dead three and wounding scores of others.

Form of state

Unitary and secular state

The executive

Executive power is vested in the Head of State (the president), who is elected by universal suffrage for a five-year term (eligible for a second). The Council of Ministers is appointed by the president on the recommendation of the prime minister who is also appointed by the president, with the consent of the legislature.

National legislature

The unicameral Transitional National Council is an interim legislative body with 90 seats of which members serve a nominal one-year term.

Last elections

21 November 2010 (presidential); 2 December 2012 (parliamentary)

Results: Presidential: Blaise Compaoré won 81 per cent of the vote, Hama Arba Diallo 8 per cent, Bénéwendé Stanislas Sankara 5.5 per cent; turnout was 53 per cent.

Parliamentary: Congrès pour la Démocratie et le Progrès (CDP) (Congress for Democracy and Progress) won 48.7 per cent (70 seats out of 127), Alliance pour la Démocratie et la Fédération–Rassemblement Démocratique Africain (ADF-RDA) (Alliance for Democracy and Federation–African Democratic Rally) 11.2 per cent (19), Union pour le Progrès et la Réforme (UPR) (Union for Progress and Reform) 11.1 per cent (19), Union pour la Renaissance-Mouvement Sankariste (UpR-MR) (Union for Rebirth-Sankarist Movement) 4.4 per cent (four), Union pour la République (UR) (Union for the Republic) 3.1 per cent (four); eight other political parties each won less than 3 per cent and shared the remaining 11 seats. Turnout was 79.9 per cent.

Next elections

22 November 2015 (presidential and parliamentary)

Political parties

Ruling party

There is no ruling party, Zida was named as head of the transitional government on 1 November 2014 by the military. On 14 November, military and opposition party leaders agreed to a charter returning the government to civilian rule and holding elections in late 2015.

Main opposition party

Currently every party within Burkina Faso opposes the interim military government Approximately 46 per cent of the population are under 15 years. An estimated two million Burkinabes live in neighbouring Côte d'Ivoire.

Population

17.43 million (2014)*

Last census: 9 December 2006: 14,017,262

Population density: 39 inhabitants per square km. Urban population 26 per cent (2010 Unicef).

Annual growth rate: 2.8 per cent, 1990–2010 (Unicef).

Ethnic make-up

There are a number of ethnic groups, the most numerous of whom are the Mossi in the north (49 per cent), the Gourma in the east and the Bobo in the south-west. Other sizeable groups include the Fulani, the Hausa, the nomadic Tuareg with their Bella domestic serfs in the north-west and the Lobi in the south.

Religions

Animist (55 per cent), Muslim (40 per cent), Catholic (5 per cent).

Education

Only two in five children are able to attend school, due to the chronic lack of places.

Burkina Faso secured financial aid from the international donor community in 2002, in the form of a three-year package aimed at building capacity in education. The agreement encompassed the Education For All Fast Track Initiative (EFA-FTI) with the goal of providing every child with primary school education by 2015. The first phase of financing is aimed at the 1.2 million children currently unable to attend primary school. The initial financing will also be used to train new teachers, pay teachers' salaries, build new schools, help education systems, respond to HIV/Aids, and put in place other steps to ensure a quality primary education for all children.

French is the language used in schools, although most children will not have heard any spoken at home. School fees are charged although payment can be deferred until after harvest. About 10 per cent of schools are run outside the state system.

Literacy rate: 13 per cent adult rate; 19 per cent youth rate (15–24) (Unesco 2005).

Pupils per teacher: 47 in primary schools.

Health

A CFA6 billion, 10 year (2006–15) plan to make contraceptives available throughout the country is supported by the USAID and the UN Population Fund. The government believes that increasing the use of contraception will help reduce the maternal mortality rate, which at 484 per 100,000 births is one of the highest in West Africa.

HIV/Aids

In 2009, there were an estimated 110,000 people living with HIV (Unicef 2012).

HIV prevalence: 1.2 per cent aged 15–49 in 2009 (Unicef 2012)

Life expectancy: 55 years, 2010 (Unicef 2012)

Fertility rate/Maternal mortality rate: 5.9 births per woman, 2010 (Unicef 2012)

Child (under 5 years) mortality rate (per 1,000): 102 per 1,000 live births (WHO 2012); 34 per cent of children aged under five are malnourished (World Bank).

Welfare
The Social Insurance Scheme provides benefits for old age pensions, disability and a survivior's fund. The fund is open to workers who contribute 4.5 per cent of the wages and this is matched by their employer.

The government announced a national 'free birth certificate' programme in May 2009, which will begin the process of enfranchisement for all. Other documentation and services such as passports and access to education will flow from the scheme. It should also cut not only the ease with which trafficked children are exploited but also deter child marriages.

Main cities
Ouagadougou (capital, estimated population 1.6 million in 2012), Bobo Dioulasso (537,728), Banfora (93,750), Koudougou (91,981), Ouahigouya (86,569), Pouytenga (84,156).

Languages spoken
African languages include More, Dioula, Gourmantche and Peul. French is the universal medium for documentation.

Official language/s
French

Media
The government regulates the media through the Ministry of Communications and Culture.

Press
Dailies: In French, *Sidwaya* (www.sidwaya.bf), is the official government newspaper, other private publications include *Le Pays* (www.lepays.bf) and *L'Observateur Paalga* (www.lobservateur.bf).

Weeklies: In French, magazines or weekend editions of daily newspapers include *L'Observateur Dimanche* (www.lobservateur.bf), *Bendré* (www.journalbendre.net), *Indépendent* (www.independant.bf), *L'Opinion* (www.zedcom.bf), *Journal du Jeudi* (www.journaldujeudi.com), is a satirical magazine. *L'Evénement* (www.evenement-bf.net), is published fortnightly.

Broadcasting
The national, public broadcaster is Radio Télévision du Burkina (RTB) (www.tnb.bf).

Radio: For most of the population radio is the primary means of accessing news and information. There are many private and community stations in operation.

Radio Burkina (RTB) (www.radio.bf) has a national network with regional services, broadcasting in French and 13 local languages. Private stations include Savane FM (www.savanefm.bf), Africa No 1 (www.africa1.com), Radios Gambidi, Pulsar and Horizon FM and Radio Maria Burkina Faso (www.radiomaria.org) run by the Catholic Church.

Television: The public TV service is La Télévision du Burkina (RTB) (www.tnb.bf), which transmits programmes in French and local languages. Alternatively Canal 3 (www.tvcanal3.com), is a private, commercial TV station. There is satellite TV, primarily from French sources but with other international services available.

National news agency: Agence d'Information du Burkina

Economy
Burkina Faso is one of the poorest countries in the world, with an estimated per capita income of US$729 in 2013, which was an increase on 2012's value of US$668. The majority of the population work in agriculture, typically in subsistence farming, which constitutes about 35.3 per cent of GDP including livestock (goats and cattle).

Cotton was the principle export revenue earner until 2010 when exports of gold provided the major source of foreign exchange; gold exports by volume were 32 tonnes in 2013, which were forecast to have risen to 35 tonnes in 2014. Industry, particularly gold mining, and manufacturing constitutes 26.2 per cent of GDP, while the service sector, including transport and communications, construction and government services constitutes around 38.5 per cent of GDP. However, unemployment is very high, estimated at around 77 per cent in 2004 (latest available), which encourages migration.

Economic recovery following the global economic crisis was strong and GDP growth had reached 9.5 per cent by 2012. However, political crisis, falling gold and cotton prices and the Ebola epidemic lead to significant adverse effects on Burkina Faso's economy. In 2013 growth had slowed down to 6.6 per cent, and decreased even further to an estimated 5.0 per cent in 2014.

The economy, despite positive developments, remains fragile and vulnerable to weather conditions and world commodity prices, specifically gold, cotton and oil. The growing strength of the economy is encouraging foreign support for poverty reduction and reform; foreign loans and grants account for approximately 70 per cent of revenues.

In 2014, the UN Human Development Index (HDI) ranked Burkina Faso 181 (out of 187) for national development in health, education and income. Since 2005 (beginning of the earliest records for the HDI), Burkina Faso's progress has shown overall growth in development factors, but they are markedly below the improvement of other sub-Saharan African countries. In 2010 (latest available), 64.9 per cent of the population experienced at least one indicator of poverty. Remittances were around US$120 million in 2010, around 1.3 per cent of GDP that year.

In January 2010 the government implemented a poverty reduction social expenditure programme, focussing on education and health, committing 25.4 per cent of all government expenditure (6.4 per cent of GDP) to this programme.

In June 2015 the European Union (EU) increased its aid for the transitional government's poverty reduction strategy by signing a US$134 million budget support agreement.

The civil unrest and ensuing instability in neighbouring Côte d'Ivoire added to Burkina Faso's problems at the time. Resources had to be diverted for humanitarian assistance; over one million refugees sought shelter and extra security measures were implemented. The export of cotton via rail through Côte d'Ivoire to the coast was curtailed for a time but by 2015 had mostly recovered.

External trade
As a member of the Economic Community of West African States (Ecowas), Burkina Faso is also a member of the West African Economic and Monetary Union (WAEMU) using the common currency: the CFA franc. Remittances from seasonal workers add to the balance of trade.

Imports
Main imports are chemical products, machinery, foodstuffs, fuel and energy and capital goods.

Main sources: Main import sources are Côte d'Ivoire (17 per cent of total), Ghana (16 per cent), France (14 per cent), Togo (7 per cent).

Exports
Main exports include raw cotton, gold, vegetable products, live animals, hides and skins.

Main destinations: Turkey (30 per cent of total), China (29 per cent), Belgium (6.2 per cent), Côte d'Ivoire (4 per cent).

Agriculture
Farming
Total agricultural land is 27.4 million hectares of which 21.9 per cent is pasture and 21.6 per cent arable.

It typically accounts for around 65 per cent of export earnings. Over 80 per cent of the population is engaged in subsistence farming and nomadic stock raising. Burkina Faso is prone to drought and has poor soil. Only 10 per cent of the total land area is cultivated. There are plans to mechanise farming and open up new areas for development. Government figures released in June 2011 warned that deforestation was occurring by 110,550 hectares (ha) every year (4 per cent of wooded area). The chief cause is agricultural encroachment. The eastern region of Kompienga was the worst hit with the loss of over 100,000ha each year. Other factors in the loss of forests include the demand for firewood, decreased rainfall and bush fires. An increase in the population has also placed an added burden on food production. To combat deforestation, Burkina Faso received a US$30 million grant from the Forest Investment Programme in July 2013.

Principal food crops are sorghum, millet, yams, maize, rice and beans.

Cotton was the main cash crop and was the country's principal foreign exchange earner until 2010; others are sheanuts, sesame and sugar cane.

Livestock production is concentrated in the north, mainly for export to Côte d'Ivoire (which has severely restricted its Burkinabè beef imports in recent years) and Ghana.

Industry and manufacturing

The industrial sector as a whole contributes just over 26.2 per cent to GDP and employs under 10 per cent of the workforce; manufacturing also contributes about 10 per cent.

Production is centred on the processing of agricultural commodities (flour milling, sugar refining, manufacture of cotton yarn and textiles) and production of consumer goods, including moped/bicycle assembly, footwear and soap manufacture.

Foreign investment is minimal and development remains handicapped by the chronic shortages of raw materials and spares.

Tourism

The level of tourism has grown, as have the facilities to provide for visitors. The capital, Ouagadougou, boasts a range of hotels from five-star to modest *pensions*. The city and its region is the base of many cultural festivals that attract not only tourists but also business conferences. There are four national parks with extensive wildlife and which provide specific holidays tailored for individual enthusiasts.

The travel and tourism sector constituted 3.3 per cent of GDP and 2.9 per cent of total employment in 2014. European visitors represent the largest group – around 30 per cent of all tourists are French. Although nomadic people in the north welcome visitors, foreign governments warn their nationals not to travel to this area due to episodes of kidnapping by Islamic terrorists affiliated to al Qaeda. In 2014, visitor exports reached 5.7 per cent of total exports.

International aid has helped this poor country to develop its infrastructure to provide facilities for tourists in order to bring in foreign earnings. The growth of internet bookings is a sign of the country using modern techniques to market itself.

Environment

In June 2010 the African Union backed a proposal to build the 'Great Green Wall' project, of a 15km wide, 7,775km long, continuous belt of trees from Senegal in the west to Djibouti in the east (traversing 11 countries) in an effort to halt the advance of the Sahara Desert. The trees to be used would be drought-adapted, preferably native to the area from a list of 37 possible species, and should help to slow soil erosion and filter rain water.

Mining

The sector typically contributes around 7 per cent to GDP and employs 2 per cent of the workforce.

Activity is confined to extraction of gold-bearing quartz at Poura (reserves estimated at 30 tonnes), marble and antimony.

There are viable deposits of zinc and silver at Perkoa, and some 15 million tonnes of manganese deposits at Tambao, as well as known reserves of limestone, bauxite, nickel, phosphates and lead.

Exploitation of resources is hindered by weak infrastructure.

Burkina Faso has a geological structure similar to that of the world's richest gold producing areas, and is Africa's fourth biggest producer of gold.

Hydrocarbons

There are no known reserves of hydrocarbons and Burkina Faso relies entirely on imports of refined oil (10,250 barrels per day in 2013, mainly gasoline and distillate). Nigeria has used trade deals of oil with Burkina Faso as a way of improving relations.

Energy

Total installed generating capacity was 252MW in 2013, of which over 80 per cent is supplied by thermal power. Electricity distribution is overseen by the Société Nationale Burkinabe d'Electricité (Sonabel). Only 13.1 per cent of the country, mainly the urban areas, has access to electricity and there is no national electricity grid. There are several dams producing hydropower, all publicly owned and accounting for 32MW, with an additional 75MW planned. Private energy generation is only used for private purposes. The country also generates 42MW of solar power, including 20MW from the Zagtouli Solar Power Station, which was completed in 2015.

Some electricity is imported from Côte d'Ivoire. Electricity is regarded as crucial to the country's development and the government is keen to extend transmission lines and improve supply to meet growing demand. The rural population relies on biomass, typically wood fuel, for cooking, lighting and power, which is leading to deforestation and desertification in some areas.

Financial markets

Burkina Faso has no stock exchange.

Stock exchange

Afribourse (Bourse Régionale des Valeurs Moblières) (BRVM)

Banking and insurance

The banking sector has undergone liberalisation in recent years, with the government restricting its involvement to around a quarter of the sector.

Central bank

Banque Centrale des Etats de l'Afrique de l'Ouest (central banking authority for the members of the West African Monetary Union)

Main financial centre

Ouagadougou

Time

GMT

Geography

Burkina Faso is a landlocked country in West Africa, bordered by Mali to the west and north, by Niger to the east, and by Benin, Togo, Ghana and Côte d'Ivoire to the south.

Burkina Faso is a generally flat country. The north lies in the Sahel region, the semi-arid fringes of the Sahara desert. To the south-west there are hills. The highest point in the country, Ténakourou, which rises to 749m, is in this region. Rainfall is negligible in the Sahel area, but is heavier to south, supporting areas of wooded savannah, rice-growing and large plantations.

The main rivers, which flow southwards into Lake Volta in Ghana, are the Mahoun, Nakambé and Nazinon (formerly known as the Black, White and Red Volta rivers respectively). Other rivers include tributaries of the Niger. Only the Mahoun flows throughout the year, the rest being seasonal. There are many lakes.

Hemisphere

Northern

Climate

The climate is tropical. The dry season runs from November–March, when the Harmattan wind blows, keeping the humidity low. Temperatures in Ouagadougou range from 14 degrees Celsius (C) at night to over 35 degrees C during the day. The main rainy season is from June–October. The highest rainfall is in the south, lowest in the far north where an arid desert climate prevails.

Entry requirements

Passports

Required by all, except holders of national identity cards issued to nationals of Ecowas countries.

Passports must have at least six months validity.

Visa

Required by all, except nationals of Ecowas countries and transit travellers. Applications for tourist and business visas should include itineraries and vaccination certificates against yellow fever. Business visas require a company letter of introduction.

An onward or return ticket is also required.

Currency advice/regulations

There are no restrictions on the import/export of foreign currency or local currency.

Health (for visitors)

Mandatory precautions

Yellow fever vaccination certificate.

Advisable precautions

Typhoid, tetanus, hepatitis A and polio vaccinations are recommended. Malaria prophylaxis should be taken as risk exists throughout the country. Water precautions are also advisable. There is a risk of rabies. Visitors should seek advice with regard to vaccinations for diphtheria, hepatitis B, meningitis and tuberculosis.

Hotels

Hotels are available in Ouagadougou and Bobo Dioulasso with limited availability elsewhere. It is advisable to book in advance. Service is included in bills and gratuities are customary for taxis and porters.

Public holidays (national)

Fixed dates

1 Jan (New Year's Day), 3 Jan (Anniversary of the 1966 Coup d'État), 8 Mar (Women's Day), 1 May (Labour Day), 4 Aug (Revolution Day), 5 Aug (Independence Day), 15 Aug (Assumption Day), 15 Oct (Anniversary of the 1987 Coup d'État), 1 Nov (All Saints' Day), 11 Dec (Proclamation of the Republic), 25 Dec (Christmas Day).

Variable dates

Easter Monday, Ascension Day, Eid al Adha, Eid al Fitr, Islamic New Year, Birth of the Prophet.

Islamic year 1437 (15 Oct 2015–2 Oct 2016):: The Islamic year contains 354 or 355 days, with the result that Muslim feasts advance by 10–12 days against the Gregorian calendar. Dates of feasts vary according to the sighting of the new moon, so cannot be forecast accurately.

Working hours

Banking

Mon–Thur: 0730–1130 and 1500–1600; Fri: open to 1700.

Business

Mon–Fri: 0730–1230 and 1500–1730.

Government

Mon–Fri: 0730–1230 and 1500–1730.

Shops

(Mon–Sat) 0800–1300 and 1500–1900; (Sun) 0800–1200.

Telecommunications

The telephone company ONATEL was privatised in 2009.

Electricity supply

220/380 V AC, 50 cycles.

Getting there

Air

National airline: Air Burkina

International airport/s: Ouagadougou (OUA), 8km from city, banks, shops, post office, restaurants, car hire.

Other airport/s: Bobo Dioulasso (BOY), 16km from city.

Surface

Road: Most practical during dry seasons – from Mali (Bamako), Côte d'Ivoire (Abidjan) and Niger (Niamey), when buses operate on these routes. Land journeys are also possible from Ghana, Benin and Togo. Skirmishing between rival political factions makes it advisable to check conditions locally before departure.

Rail: Ouagadougou is linked to Abidjan (Côte d'Ivoire) by an express service, which operates up to three times a week. Sleeping and dining cars.

Getting about

National transport

Air: Air Burkina serves Ouagadougou, Bobo Dioulasso and other main centres. Bobo Dioulasso is the main domestic airport.

Road: Conditions vary; some roads are only passable in dry season, although international roads are all-weather.

Buses: Services between Ouagadougou and main towns. Advance booking advisable.

Rail: Daily service runs Ouagadougou-Bobo Dioulasso and on to Côte d'Ivoire; two classes; some trains have restaurant cars, sleeping accommodation and air-conditioning. Service can become overcrowded.

City transport

Taxis: Unmetered and available in main centres. A 10 per cent tip is usually given.

Buses, trams & metro: Frequent in Ouagadougou and Bobo Dioulasso.

Car hire

National licence plus permit or international driving licence required. Use of chauffeur-driven cars advised.

BUSINESS DIRECTORY

The addresses listed below are a selection only. While World of Information makes every endeavour to check these addresses, we cannot guarantee that changes have not been made, especially to telephone numbers and area codes. We would welcome any corrections.

Telephone area codes

The international direct dialling code (IDD) for Burkina Faso is +226, followed by subscriber's number.

Useful telephone numbers

Police: 17

Fire: 18

Ambulance: 3066-43/44/45

Chambers of Commerce

Burkina Faso Chamber of Commerce, Industry and Handicrafts , 118/220 Rue 3.119, 01 PO Box 502, Ouagadougou (tel: 306-114; fax: 306-116; e-mail: ccia-bf@ccia.bf).

Banking

Banque Internationale du Burkina, BP 1336, Av Nelson Mandela 800, Ouagadougou 01 (tel: 307-888, 307-878; fax: 310628).

Banque Internationale du Burkina SA, BP 362, Rue de la Chance, Ouagadougou 01 (tel: 306-170, 306-171; fax: 300-171, 310-094).

Banque Internationale pour le Commerce, l'Industrie et l'Agriculture du Burkina SA, BP 8, Avenue Dr Kwamé N'Krumah 479, Ouagadougou 01 (tel: 306-226/8, 306-227; fax: 311-955).

Caisse Nationale de Crédit Agricole du Burkina (CNCAB), BP 1644, Avenue Gamal Abdel Naser 2, Ouagadougou 01 (tel: 333-333).

Ecobank-Burkina, BP 145, Rue Maurice Bishop 633, Espace Fadima, Ouagadougou 01 (tel: 318-975, 318-980; fax: 318-981, 318-982).

Société Générale de Banque au Burkina (SGBB), BP 585, Rue du Marché 4, Ouagadougou 01 (tel: 323-232; fax: 310-561).

Central bank

Banque Centrale des Etats de l'Afrique de l'Ouest, Avenue Gamal Abdel Nasser, PO Box 356, Ouagadougou (tel: 306-015; fax: 310-122).

Stock exchange

Afribourse (Bourse Régionale des Valeurs Mobilières) (BRVM), www.brvm.org

Travel information

Air Burkina, Avenue de la Nation, BP 1459, Ouagadougou 016 (tel: 5030-7676; fax: 5031-4517).

Direction du Tourisme et de l'Hôtellerie, BP 624, Ouagadougou 01(tel: 306-399; fax: 311-904).

Ministry of tourism
Ministry of Culture, Arts and Tourism, 03 BP 7007, Ouagadougou 03 (tel: 5033-0963; fax: 5033-0964; e-mail:webmestre–mcat@mcc.gov.bp).

National tourist organisation offices
Office Nationale du Tourisme Burkinabè, BP 1311, Avenue Frobénius, Ouagadougou 01 (tel: 311-959; fax: 314-434).

Ministries

Ministry of Agriculture, 03 BP 7005, Ouagadougou 03 (tel: 324-114).

Ministry of Administration, 03 BP 7034, Ouagadougou 03 (tel: 324-833).

Ministry of Commerce and Industry, 01 BP 365 Ouagadougou 01 (tel: 324-786).

Ministry of Communications, 03 BP 7045, Ouagadougou 03 (tel: 324-833).

Ministry of Defence, 01 BP 496, Ouagadougou 01 (tel: 307-214).

Ministry of Education, 03 BP 7032, Ouagadougou 03 (tel: 324-870).

Ministry of Employment and Social Security, 03 BP 7016, Ouga 03 (tel: 310-960).

Ministry of Energy and Mines, 01 BP 3922 Ouagadougou 01 (tel: 324-786).

Ministry of the Environment and Water, 03 BP 7044 Ouagadougou 01 (tel: 324-074).

Ministry of the Family, 01 BP 515, Ouagadougou 01 (tel: 310-960).

Ministry of Finance and Economy, 03 BP 7012, Ouagadougou 03 (tel: 306-995).

Ministry of Foreign Affairs, 03 BP 7038, Ouagadougou 03 (tel: 324-733; fax: 308-792; internet: www.mae.gov.bf/).

Ministry of Health, 03 P 7009 Ouagadougou (tel: 324-158).

Ministry of Higher Education and Scientific Research, 03 BP 7047, Ouagadougou 03 (tel: 324-567).

Ministry of Integration and African Affairs, 01 BP 6943, Ouagadougou 01 (tel: 324-833).

Ministry of the Interior, 03 BP 7011, Ouagadougou 03 (tel: 324-905).

Ministry of Justice, 01 BP 526, Ouagadougou 01 (tel: 324-833).

Ministry of Public Relations and Modernisation of Administration, 03 BP 7006, Ouagadougou 03 (tel: 306-995).

Ministry of Youth and Sports, 03 BP 7035, Ouagadougou 03 (tel: 324-786).

Other useful addresses

Burkina Faso Embassy (USA), 2340 Massachusetts Avenue, NW, Washington DC 20008 (tel: 202-332-5577; fax: 202-667-1882; e-mail: ambawdc@rcn.com).

Groupement des Petits Commerçants, BP 952, Ouagadougou.

Institut de la Statistique et de la Démographie, BP 374, Ouagadougou (tel: 335-537).

Office National de Commerce Extérieur, BP 389, Ouagadougou (tel: 336-225).

Société de Commercialisation, BP 531, Ouagadougou (tel: 333-007); BP 375, Bobo-Dioulasso (tel: 390-423).

Syndicat des Entrepreneurs et Industriels, BP 446, Ouagadougou.

Télévision Nationale du Burkina, BP 7029, Ouagadougou (tel: 336-801).

West African Economic Community, BP 643, Ouagadougou.

National news agency: Agence d'Information du Burkina 01 BP 2507 Ouagadougou 01 (tel: 50 324-640; fax: 50 337-316; email: infos@aib.bf; internet: www.aib.bf).

Internet sites

Air Burnina : www.air-burkina.com

AllAfrica.com: www.allafrica.com

African Development Bank: www.afdb.org

Mbendi AfroPaedia (information on companies, countries, industries and stock exchanges in Africa): mbendi.co.za

KEY FACTS

Official name: Republika y'Uburundi (Republic of Burundi)

Head of State: President Pierre Nkurunziza (Hutu) (from 2005 (appointed by Parliament); elected 28 Jun 2010; re-elected 21 July 2015)

Head of government: President Pierre Nkurunziza

Ruling party: Conseil National Pour la Défense de la Démocratie–Forces pour la Défense de la Démocratie (NCDD–FDD) (National Council for the Defence of Democracy–Forces for the Defence of Democracy) (from 2005; re-elected 23 Jul 2010 and 21 Jul 2015)

Area: 27,834 square km

Population: 9.20 million (2014)*

Capital: Bujumbura (plans to build a new capital nearer to the centre of the country were announced in 2007)

Official language: Kirundi and French

Currency: Burundi franc (Buf) = 100 centimes

Exchange rate: Buf1,559.15 per US$ (Sep 2015)

GDP per capita: US$336 (2014)*

GDP real growth: 4.74% (2014)*

GDP: US$3.09 billion (2014)*

Inflation: 4.42% (2014)*

Balance of trade: -US$531.00 million (2014)*

* estimated figure

Burundi

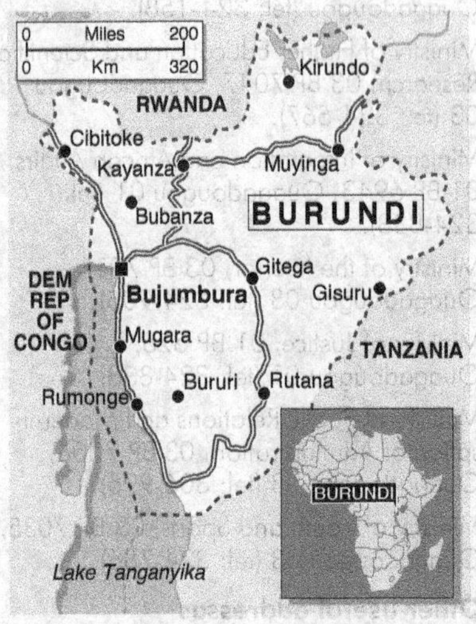

Burundi's mid-May 2015 attempted – and failed – *coup d'état* risked tipping Burundi over into a complex conflagration between President Pierre Nkurunziza's supporters and those who opposed his decision to serve an unprecedented (and unconstitutional) third term as president. The *coup*, led by Major General Godefroid Niyombare, was timed to coincide with the President's absence at a conference in Tanzania. Given the febrile political state of the nation, it was certainly unwise of the President to leave his country, tantamount to an invitation to general Niyombare and his co-plotters. Perhaps the only positive aspect of the stand-off was that the opposing parties appeared not to be divided along the tribal, Hutu-Tutsi division that had triggered a seven year long civil war in 1993 during which an estimated 300,000 people died. The peace accord signed between the warring factions in 2000 was followed by the 2005 Constitution, which clearly stated that Burundi's presidents were limited to two terms of office.

The President and his supporters had resorted to a degree of sophistry in defending a third term, claiming that in 2005 the President was not elected by popular suffrage, but by parliament. His opponents countered that in appointing the president at the time, parliament was reflecting the will of the people, which according to the constitution, was sovereign.

Fragility

Quite why their president wanted to stay in power was unclear to most Burundians, whether they were from the majority Hutus or the minority (around 10 per cent) Tutsis. Following the President's return to Bujumbura, Major General Niyombare, who had been in charge of Burundi's intelligence services, had (perhaps wisely) disappeared. To show his displeasure and re-establish his authority, President Nkurunziza promptly sacked his defence and foreign ministers. No reason was given for the dismissals. The extent to which they reflected cabinet splits was also unclear. Reuters posited that the President might be running out of truly loyal appointees. Those considered to be behind the *coup* were immediately jailed, prompting further rounds of protests in the streets of Bujumbura.

Plus ca change...

Depressingly, for most Burundians, in early May 2015 the Congressional Court had approved President Pierre Nkurunziza's bid for a third term in power. This despite often fatal protests and the blunt refusal of he court's deputy president to sign the ruling. In a ruling characterised by waffle the judges decided, against all common sense and reason, that the President's transparent ambition to secure for himself a third term did not, in fact, contradict the country's constitution. Such was the opposition to the ruling that it looked likely to usher in a further period of uncertainty and instability, the last thing needed by its 10 million inhabitants. Such was the fear of further strife that an estimated 30,000 Burundians had already packed their bags, seeking refuge in neighbouring countries, for the most part, in Rwanda.

The imposition of their President for a further term of office was the icing – or rather the vinegar – on the top of a very sour tasting cake for most Burundians. Not that the densely populated country was unfamiliar with corruption. By the end of 2014, Burundi's population was approximately double the figure of a year earlier according to the United Nations Development Programme (UNDP). The population growth rate is 2.5 per cent per year, more than twice the average global pace and the average Burundian woman has 6.3 children, nearly triple the international fertility rate. The flow of refugees out of Burundi was more than matched by the estimated half a million refugees who had left during the 1993–2005 civil war (and even as a result of earlier ethnic violence) and had come back as of late 2014. A further 7,000 were expected to arrive in 2015.

For the most part Burundians rely on subsistence farming for a living, but the fast growing population has, according to the US based Woodrow Wilson International Center for Scholars, resulted in the average farm size shrinking from around 10 acres to little more than one. In the 2013 Global Hunger Index, Burundi had the severest hunger and malnourishment rates of all the 120 countries ranked. According to the United Nations, around 85 per cent of the disputes pending in Burundian courts pertain to land. Most returning refugees are Hutu, but the land they left behind has often been purchased by Tutsis. Thus the land issue is delicately positioned over the ethnic divide. The Institute for Security Studies, a South African-based think tank, has warned that 'attempts to politicise land management… risks reigniting ethnic tensions' perhaps even surfacing before the mid-2015 elections.

The economy

According to the International Monetary Fund (IMF) in its 2015 assessment of Burundi's economy, gross domestic product (GDP) growth reached an estimated 4.7 per cent in 2014, underpinned by the rebound in coffee production, strong momentum in the construction sector and the implementation of major infrastructure projects, including fibre optics, hydropower and roads. Inflation decreased from an average of 9 per cent in 2013 to 4.5 per cent in 2014, helped by falling international oil prices. The IMF noted that the current account deficit (including grants) narrowed slightly in 2014. Lower oil prices resulted in improved terms of trade. The ratio of imports of goods and services to GDP fell by about 2 percentage points, while exports increased by 1 percentage point as coffee exports rebounded. The deficit was financed by foreign direct investment (FDI), project grants and concessional loans. The official foreign exchange reserves remained stable at the equivalent of 3.5 months of imports.

The corrective revenue measures adopted by the government in July 2014 were instrumental in keeping the economy on track. Together with the receipts from telecom licences, these measures helped reverse the revenue shortfall registered in the first half of the year and the end-year revenue target was attained. Expenditures were broadly in line with programmed levels, with the wage bill falling from 7 per cent in 2013 to about 6.6 per cent of GDP; however, the budget deficit at end-December exceeded the level originally projected in the programme by 1.7 per cent of GDP, mainly due to a shortfall in the disbursement of budgetary grants. Domestic public debt increased from 13.1 per cent of GDP at the end of 2013 to 14.1 per cent of GDP by the end of 2014. The financing shortfall was filled by the Banque de la République du Burundi (central bank). The Treasury situation will be regularised in the first quarter of 2015, upon the disbursement of budgetary grants from the African Development Bank (AfDB) and World Bank. The drop in international fuel prices allowed restoring the petroleum pricing mechanism and eliminating fuel subsidies.

According to the AfDB, Burundi's growth accelerated to an estimated 4.6 per cent in 2013, up from 4.2 per cent in 2012, thanks to increased activity in the secondary and tertiary sectors. In 2014, the World Bank estimated Burundi's GDP growth rate at 4.0 per cent, below the average of 4.5 per cent for countries in sub-Saharan Africa. The Bank expected this gap to widen in 2015, with Burundi's growth rate declining to 3.7 per cent and the region's climbing slightly. In 2013 government finances improved, but Burundi was still faced with major constraints due to the poor mobilisation of domestic resources and the volatility of external aid; meanwhile, political tensions (see above) had grown in the run-up to 2015 elections.

Given the uncertainty surrounding foreign aid over the next few years, the government aims to focus on mobilising domestic revenue by pursuing its taxation reforms. The measures it planned included simplifying procedures, introducing a flexible tax system, broadening the tax base, decentralising and modernising collection structures and harmonising the tax system with the regulations of the East African Community (EAC).

Land and the seeds of strife

Historically, agriculture has been an economic mainstay in Burundi. Traditionally over the centuries Burundi's farmers cultivated the country's arable hilltops; the low-lying swamplands went largely unclaimed. An aristocratic class, known as the Ganwa, technically owned the land, but farmers' access was administered at the local level by a network of 'land chiefs,' many of whom were Hutu. The chiefs also resolved land conflicts.

Under Belgian rule, which lasted from 1916 to 1962, things had begun to change. The King, the head of the Ganwa, kept control of the highlands. But the state assumed ownership of the lowlands and began to encourage their cultivation. The colonial government also concentrated political power among the Tutsi minority, which then comprised about 14 per cent of the population, giving the group a near

KEY INDICATORS — Burundi

	Unit	2011	2012	2013	2014	**2015
Population	m	*8.44	*8.78	*8.98	*9.20	*9.42
Gross domestic product (GDP)	US$bn	2.36	2.51	*2.72	*3.09	*3.39
GDP per capita	US$	279	286	*303	*336	*360
GDP real growth	%	4.2	4.0	*4.5	*4.7	*4.8
Inflation	%	14.9	12.0	*7.9	*4.4	*5.0
Exports (fob) (goods)	US$m	124.0	135.0	90.9	–	–
Imports (fob) (goods)	US$m	552.5	711.0	675.6	–	–
Balance of trade	US$m	-428.5	-576.0	-584.7	–	–
Current account	US$m	-323.0	-433.0	*-502.0	*-544.0	*-450.0
Total reserves minus gold	US$m	342.6	307.0	328.1	316.0	–
Foreign exchange	US$m	204.9	177.0	200.8	–	–
Exchange rate	per US$	1,236.86	1,505.60	1,552.00	1,556.00	–

* estimated figure ** forecast figure

monopoly on Burundi's government, military and economy. Among other actions, this consolidation involved gradually stripping the Hutu land chiefs of their authority. More broadly, too, it sowed the seeds of ethnic divisions.

Under colonialism, official land deeds and titles were few and far between, which meant that Burundians often could not prove that they owned acreage. In the early 1960s, as independence loomed, the government began offering land registration to parties that requested it, which, for the most part, were foreign businesses such as hotels. Families also had the option to register their land, but because the centralised system was inaccessible for most farmers and required a huge tax payment, few did. So land plots quickly fell into two categories: those with boundaries recognised by the state and those with borders determined by custom, or traditional natural borders.

The government has, in the past, set up commissions (in 1977 and 1991), to resolve land disputes, but they proved to be largely ineffective. Ethnic tensions had continued to mount, coming to a head in 1993. That October, Tutsi extremists assassinated Burundi's first democratically elected Hutu president, Melchior Ndadaye and civil war erupted as Hutu peasants responded by murdering Tutsis. In just the first year of conflict, tens of thousands of people were killed; by the time the war ended more than a decade later, some 300,000 Burundians, most of them civilians, had died. The war also produced a new wave of refugees. The pressure on agricultural resources has given the land question a higher profile.

In the twenty-first century, dozens of scenarios have emerged under which Burundians are able to claim land and the same plot can often be the subject of competing claims. According to the International Crisis Group, some 95 per cent of Burundian land still falls under customary law: a family says it purchased its farm from neighbours before the war, but holds no formal deed, while another claims village elders approved the purchase of a few acres after the war and so on. A centralised registration system does exist and according to the country's land code (which was revised in 2011 for the first time since 1986), any person who owns property must hold a land certificate. The bureaucratic system, however, is complicated and the government has done little in terms of enforcement. The land problem is infinitely complex, with roots that run deep into Burundi's history.

Risk assessment

Economy	Fair
Politics	Poor
Regional stability	Fair

COUNTRY PROFILE

1899 Burundi and its neighbour, Rwanda, were incorporated into German East Africa.

1916 Belgium occupied the area.

1923 Re-named Ruanda-Urundi, Belgium continued its administration.

1959 Many Tutsi refugees from Rwanda sought shelter from ethnic violence.

1962 On 1 July the Kingdom of Burundi became independent from Belgium under a Tutsi King, Mwambutsa IV.

1963 Many Hutus fled into Rwanda due to ethnic violence.

1965 Hutu candidates won a majority in parliamentary elections. However, Mwambutsa refused to appoint a Hutu prime minister. A Hutu coup led by Michel Micombero failed and the Hutu elite were massacred in retaliation.

1966 Mwambutsa was deposed by his son Ntare V. Micombero led a successful *coup d'état* overthrowing the monarchy.

1972 Ntare was killed, supposedly by Hutus, sparking violence that led to the killing of 150,000 Hutus.

1976–87 Micombero was deposed by Tutsi Colonel Jean-Baptiste Bagaza. Bagaza's dictatorship was notorious for its violations of human rights.

1987 Bagaza was overthrown by Tutsi Major Pierre Buyoya.

1988 Thousands of Hutu were killed and many more fled into Rwanda

1992 A new constitution endorsed multi-party elections.

1993 Melchior Ndadaye, who was committed to reforming the Tutsi-dominated army, won the elections and became the first Hutu president. Ndadaye was assassinated by pro-Bagazza paratroopers. More massacres followed.

1994 Cyprien Ntaryamira, a Hutu, was appointed president by the National Assembly. He and the Hutu president of Rwanda were killed in a plane crash. Sylvestre Ntibantuganya, a Hutu, became president.

1995 A coalition government was formed under Antoine Nduwayu, a Tutsi. Ethnic violence continued.

1996 Major Pierre Buyoya seized power and suspended the constitution.

1998 Buyoya came to an agreement with parliament under a transitional constitution and was formally sworn in as president.

1999 Tutsi and Hutu factions agreed to talks brokered by former Tanzanian president Julius Nyerere.

2000 President Buyoya and 13 political parties signed the Arusha peace accord but two important Hutu groups refused to sign.

2001 In talks chaired by former South Africa president Nelson Mandela, it was agreed that Buyoya, a Tutsi, should remain president for 18 months of a new three-year transitional government, when a Hutu vice president would become president.

2002 The Burundi franc was devalued by 20 per cent to the US dollar. Violence between government forces and Hutu rebel groups continued.

2003 Vice President Domitien Ndayizeye was sworn in as president in accordance with the power-sharing agreement. The president and Pierre Nkurunziza, the leader of the main opposition group Conseil National Pour la Défense de la Démocratie–Forces pour la Défense de la Démocratie (CNDD–FDD) (National Council for the Defence of Democracy–Forces for the Defence of Democracy), signed an agreement to end the civil war.

2004 A South African-style truth and reconciliation commission was set up. A new constitution was deferred until the transitional government was replaced with a fully elected Assembly.

2005 A referendum approved a new power-sharing constitution. The main former rebel Hutu group, CNDD-FDD, won the parliamentary elections. Pierre Nkurunziza was sworn in as president. Martin Nduwimana (Tutsi) and Alice Nzomukunda (Hutu) were appointed vice presidents.

2006 The 34-year old midnight-to-dawn curfew was lifted. A cease-fire between the government and the longest-established Hutu rebel group, the Forces Nationales de Libération (FNL) (National Liberation Forces), the armed wing of the Parti Pour la Liberation du Peuple Hutu (Palipe Hutu) (Hutu People's Liberation Party), was agreed. Burundi was admitted to membership of the East African Community (EAC).

2007 The Communauté Economique des Pays des Grands Lacs (CEPGL) (Great Lakes Countries Economic Community) was re-launched by Burundi, Democratic Republic of Congo and Rwanda. CEPGL promotes regional economic co-operation and integration. Fighting between rival FNL factions resulted in 100 deaths; 40,000 civilians fled the fighting. Burundi joined the African Union (AU) peacekeeping force in Somalia.

2008 The UN assessment mission to implement the peace agreement was postponed due to fighting between government forces and the FNL.

2009 Agathon Rwasa, the leader of the FNL formally surrendered to AU troops in a ceremonial end to hostilities. They were the last rebel group to lay down their arms. The FNL became a political party – FNL under the leadership of Alain Mugabarabona Icanzo.

2010 Five candidates, including Agathon Rwasa, withdrew from the presidential election following criticism by the opposition of the electoral commission. When the presidential election took place, incumbent Pierre Nkurunziza was the only candidate; he won 91 per cent of the vote (turnout was 76.9 per cent). All opposition parties boycotted the parliamentary elections; the NCDD–FDD won 81 seats (out of 106), Union pour le Progrès National (Uprona) (Union for National Progress) (predominately Tutsi) 17; turnout was 67 per cent. The global anti-corruption watchdog organisation, Transparency International, stated that Burundi was considered the most corrupt state in Eastern Africa and that its neighbour, Rwandan was by far the least corrupt.

2011 In June, the African Development Bank (AfDB) approved a US$67.23 million grant from the AfDB's Fragile States Facility (FSF) to fund phase two of the Gitega-Nyangungu-Ngozi road project. An attack in September on a crowded bar in Bujumbura by over a dozen unidentified gunmen killed 36 people. Although the government blamed 'bandits' there were reports that the attackers wore army uniforms and had come from the DRC; the more likely notion was that it had been carried out by former FNL fighters in revenge for the killing of FNL personnel since 2009.

2012 In a Unicef report published in September, Burundi was ranked as first for its strides in education, by providing free, compulsory education, with school enrolment rising from 59 per cent in 2005 to 96 per cent in 2011. On 25 September the India government provided US$120 million in credit for two projects; US$80 million to help fund the Kabu hydroelectric plant and US$40 for a farm mechanisation and food processing project. Burundi and India also signed memorandums of understanding concerning rural development, education, health and medicine and to strengthen bilateral trade and investment. On 27 September the US State Department announced that Burundi had declared itself free of land mines.

2013 The Tanzanian government announced on 25 July that all 'illegal aliens' had to leave the country by 11 August 2013. As a result over 19,000 Burundians fled across the border to Burundi in the 15 days before the deadline.

2014 A single cross-border tourist visa for Burundi, Kenya and Uganda was launched on 20 February. The visa costs US$100 and is valid for 90 days. Tanzania and Rwanda are expected to join in the future. An Amnesty International report published in July accused Burundi's ruling party of waging a 'relentless campaign of intimidation' against its critics ahead of presidential elections in June 2015. Although under the constitution president's are limited to two terms in office, President Pierre Nkurunziza was rumoured to be intending to stand again for a third term.

2015 On 25 April the ruling CNDD-FDD nominated President Nkurunziza as their candidate in the presidential election scheduled for June. In the run up to the party conference security had been increased and demonstrations banned as the opposition called for the President not to stand again, in contravention of the terms of the constitution. Despite this police clashed with protesters, who had set up barricades around Bujumbura, even though the government had deployed the army and shut down the main independent radio station; a number of people were killed. In early May the constitutional court confirmed that since President Nkurunziza had been appointed by parliament and not elected by the people, his first term in office did not count, so that should he win the June election, this would be his second not third term in office. On 11 May, although both the AU and EU had called for a postponement of the election, President Nkurunziza confirmed it would take place on schedule in June. The election was won convincingly by the incumbant with 69.41 per cent of the vote, ahead of Agathon Rwasa with 18.99 per cent; turn out was reported to be 30 per cent. Pierre Nkurunziza was sworn in for his third term on 20 August.

Political structure

Constitution

The Constitution endorses multi-party elections by universal suffrage.

The 2005 referendum approved a new power-sharing Constitution, under which Burundi's president has a deputy from each of the ethnic groups while 60 per cent of the cabinet is Hutu and 40 per cent Tutsi.

Representation in the National Assembly is apportioned on a 60/40 basis between the Hutu and Tutsi with three seats reserved for the Twas ethnic group. In the Senate (upper house), seats are split 50-50 between Hutus and Tutsis. Two members are elected from each of Burundi's 17 provinces (one Hutu and one Tutsi), plus three from the Twas ethnic group. Women must account for at least 30 per cent. Four former presidents were also co-opted as senators in July 2005. The army and the police service are staffed equally along ethnic lines.

Independence date

I July 1962

Form of state

Republic

The executive

Executive power is vested directly in the elected president, with one Hutu and Tutsi vice president each.

National legislature

The bicameral parliament consists of the Assemblée Nationale (National Assembly) and Senate. The National Assembly has 100 deputies which are elected by proportional representation from party lists in 17 multi-seat constituencies. In addition, there are 18–21 co-opted members. The Senate has no fewer than 37 and no more that 54 members. 34 members are indirectly elected by a college of provincial councils using a two-thirds majority vote and 20 seats are reserved for former heads of state. All members of parliament serve for five-year terms.

Legal system

Burundi law is based on Belgian and German law. The legal system is composed of a Supreme Court, Constitutional Court and a Courts of Appeal.

Last elections

29 July 2015 (parliamentary); 21 July 2015 (presidential)

Results: Parliamentary: Conseil National Pour la Défense de la Démocratie–Forces pour la Défense de la Démocratie (NCDD–FDD) (National Council for the Defense of Democracy–Forces for the Defense of Democracy) won 77 seats (out of 121), Burundians' Hope Independent won 21 seats and the Union pour le Progrès national (Uprona) (Union for National Progress) won 2 seats. Co-opted members won 18 seats while three were reserved for Twas. The remaining thirteen parties all received under two per cent of the vote.The turnout was 74.3 per cent. Presidential: Pierre Nkurunziza won 69.41 per cent of the vote, Agathon Rwasa won 18.99 per cent of the vote, Gerard Nduwayo won 2.14 per cent of the vote. The remaining presidential candidates each won less than two percent of the vote.The turnout was 73.44 percent.

Next elections

2020 (parliamentary); 2020 (presidential).

Political parties

Ruling party

Conseil National Pour la Défense de la Démocratie–Forces pour la Défense de la Démocratie (NCDD–FDD) (National Council for the Defence of Democracy–Forces for the Defence of Democracy) (from 2005; re-elected 23 Jul 2010 and 21 Jul 2015)

Main opposition party
Burundians' Hope Independent Party.

Population
9.20 million (2014)*
Approximately 46 per cent of the total population is under 15 years.
Last census: September 1990: 5,139,073
Population density: 250 inhabitants per square km. Urban population 11 per cent (2010 Unicef).
Annual growth rate: 2.0 per cent, 1990–2010 (Unicef).

Internally Displaced Persons (IDP)
381,000 (UNHCR 2004)

Ethnic make-up
The Hutu people are believed to comprise 85 per cent of the population, the Tutsi 14 per cent and the Twa 1 per cent, but there have never been any census statistics on ethnic groups.

Religions
Christianity (over 60 per cent), 32 per cent traditional beliefs.
A bill was passed by the lower house of parliament in July 2014 in an attempt to curb the 'proliferation of churches' in the country. A government survey in 2013 reported there were 557 denominations in the country, most of whom had come about during the civil war which had ended in 2005. Under the new legislation churches will have to have at least 500 members and to have a building. Foreign churches can only register if they can show they have at least 1,000 followers.

Education
In a Unicef report published in September 2012, Burundi was ranked as first for its strides in education, by providing free, compulsory education, with school enrolment rising from 59 per cent in 2005 to 96 per cent in 2011
Secondary education is divided into two: academic and technical. Academic secondary education is available for four years between ages 12 and 16, then a national test determines access to higher education. Technical secondary education lasts from ages 12–19.
Kirundi is the language of instruction in primary schools and French in secondary schools.
Higher education is mainly provided by the Université du Burundi, which is largely financed by the government.
Literacy rate: 50 per cent adult rate; 66 per cent youth rate (15–24) (Unesco 2005).
Compulsory years: Six to 12.
Enrolment rate: 55 per cent boys and 46 per cent girls, total primary school enrolment for the relevant age groups (including repetition rates) (World Bank).
Pupils per teacher: 42 in primary schools.

Health
Burundi's infant mortality rate is relatively high compared to the other African countries. Although women have a higher life expectancy, it is still less than the other East African countries. Immunisation campaigns have resulted in high levels of vaccinations against measles, TB, polio and other childhood deseases.

HIV/Aids
In 2009 there were an estimated 180,000 adults living with HIV.
HIV prevalence: 3.3 per cent aged 15–49 in 2009 (Unicef 2012)
Life expectancy: 50 years, 2010 (Unicef 2012)
Fertility rate/Maternal mortality rate: 4.3 births per woman, 2010 (Unicef 2012)
Child (under 5 years) mortality rate (per 1,000): 104 per 1,000 live births (WHO 2012)

Welfare
Burundi has 800,000 internally displaced people, while another 250,000 refugees fled to Tanzania.
The National Social Security Institute administers the old age, disability and survivor's pension insurance fund. It is a scheme funded by workers who contribute 2.6 per cent of their wages (3.8 per cent if working an arduous job), and employers contribute 3.9 per cent of the payroll (5.7 for arduous occupations). Old age pensions are paid at aged 60 (45 for arduous work).

Main cities
Bujumbura (capital, estimated population 392,863 in 2012), Muyinga (100,715), Ruyigi (44,220), Makamba (26,644), Ngozi (24,932), Rutana (23,654), Gitega (22,989).

Languages spoken
French is the administrative language; KiSwahili is used commercially. English is a compulsory subject in secondary academic education.

Official language/s
Kirundi and French

Media
Press
There is a low readership for newspapers.
Dailies: In French, *Le Renouveau du Burundi* is a government-run newspaper that has had Unesco investment to allow it to publish every day and increase readership.
Weeklies: In French, *Arc-en-Ciel* and in Kirundi (local language) *Ubumwe* is government-run and the fortnightly *Ndongosi* is a Catholic publication and *Intahe* published by the Tutsi dominated political party, Union pour le Progrès national (Uprona) (National Progress Union).

Broadcasting
The government-controlled, Radiodiffusion et Télévision Nationale du Burundi is the national public broadcaster.
Radio: With low levels of literacy radio is the primary source of news and information. Radio Burundi (RTNB) broadcasts in Kirundi and Swahili as well as French and English. It also broadcasts an educational network. Radio Culture is funded partly by the health ministry. Private radio stations include Radio Isanganiro (www.isanganiro.org) and Radio CCIB+ is operated by the Chamber of Commerce. Bonesha FM (www.boneshafm.org) and Studio Ijambo (www.studioijambo.org) are funded by international organisations.
Television: The only TV station operating is the state-owned RTNB.
National news agency: Agence Burundaise de Presse: www.cbinf.com
Other news agencies: Burundi Information (in French): www.burundi-info.com
Burundi Quotidien (in French): www.burundi-quotidien.com
Iteka (in French and English): www.ligue-iteka.africa-web.org
Net press (L'Agence Burundaise d'Information): www.netpress.bi

Economy
Agriculture, forestry, fishing and hunting, but particularly subsistence farming, are still the main area of economic activity. Contributing 45 per cent of GDP in 2009 it had however dropped to 40.3 per cent by 2014, yet still is responsible for 90 per cent of employment. Regeneration is driving the economy, through revitalisation of food and export (cash) crops, development of livestock production (by rebuilding the national herd and improving cattle, pig and goat breeds), development of bee-keeping and fisheries and the revival of fish farming. Traditional crops of tea and coffee account for around 90 per cent of all foreign earnings.
GDP growth was 5 per cent in 2008, which weakened to 3.5 per cent in 2009, due to lower private transfers and less foreign direct investment (FDI); it grew modestly to 3.8 per cent in 2010; by 2014 it had steadily grown back to an estimated 4.7 per cent. As prices for imported oil and foods fell, headline inflation fell from 26 per cent to 4.5 per cent between 2008–10. However inflation jumped to 14.9 per cent in 2011, due partly to the rising prices of food and fuel imports. By 2014 inflation had dropped to an estimated 6.7 per cent.
Burundi is one of the poorest countries in the world. Sporadic fighting between

ethnic groups has continued since the civil war ended in 2003, disrupting the social and economic fabric. The per capita income during the period of the civil war fell by 33 per cent – in 2007 it was still only US$169 but had risen to, a still low, US$295.1 in 2014.

In 2013, the UN Human Development Index (HDI) ranked Burundi 180 (out of 187) for national development in health, education and income. Since 2000, Burundi's progress has grown overall (it has dropped 5 rankings since 2011) but still lags behind the improvement of other sub-Saharan African countries. In 2013, 81.8 per cent of the population experienced multidimensional poverty and about 81.3 per cent of the population lived on less than the equivalent of US$1.25 per day. This may go some way in explaining why Burundi was ranked as top for the 'most bribery prone country in East Africa' in 2011 by Transparency International. In 2014, though no longer the most corrupt nation in Africa, Transparency International ranked Burundi 159 (out of 177 countries) in the Corruptions Perception Index.

Remittances in 2013 amounted to US$48.6 million, up from the US$46.4 million of 2012.

To assist agricultural development the government, with the help of international aid and financial institutions, is investing in infrastructure projects, such as inter-province link roads. A feasibility study has been undertaken to determine the possibility of linking such roads to the Tanzanian railway system. Deregulations of the coffee, tea and cotton industries initiated in 2009, have improved the prospects of coffee and cotton farmers whose industries had been in decline.

Despite the improving outlook for Burundi, it still has much to do to make a significant impact on poverty and development. The mining industry is underdeveloped although there are, among other minerals, deposits of petroleum, nickel, gold, copper, uranium, platinum and rare earth oxides. The manufacturing sector is small and caters for local needs.

External trade

As a founding member of the Common Market of Eastern and Southern Africa (Comesa), and the Economic Community of Central African States (ECCAS). Burundi operates a free trade zone to 13 of the 19 Comesa member states.

Burundi is a member of the East African Community (EAC) (with Kenya, Rwanda, Tanzania and Uganda). The East African Community Common Market Protocol (EACMP) was launched on 1 July 2010, which will lead to the free movement of labour, capital, goods and services between member states as well as employment opportunities and easier flow of investment capital. The signed protocol now requires that legislation in all states must be harmonised to conform to its jurisdiction.

Imports

Principal imports include refined petroleum, soybeans, packaged medicaments, oil seed flower and cereal flours.

Main sources: India (11.2 per cent of total in 2014), Saudi Arabia (10.9 per cent), China (10.8 per cent).

Exports

Principal exports are coffee (normally 75 per cent of total), tea, sugar, cotton and hides.

Main destinations: Democratic Republic of the Congo (20.1 per cent of total in 2014), United Arab Emirates (17.6 per cent), Switzerland (16.6 per cent).

Agriculture

Farming

Total agricultural land is 2.6 million hectares of which pasture and arable both account for 35 per cent and 13.6 per cent given over to permanent crops.

The agriculture sector has up until recent years been the mainstay of the economy (the services sector now dominates), although there was a sharp drop in agricultural output due to disruptions caused by the civil war. The sector has to contend with a damaged infrastructure, broken market networks and poor productivity. Internally displaced persons (IDP) caught up in the civil war were lead to over-exploitation of land causing ecological damage.

Burundi is potentially self-sufficient in food. Food products account for around 13 per cent of all imports.

The main cash crop is coffee, which accounts for up to three-quarters of the country's exports. More than 90 per cent of coffee production is arabica, which is being encouraged for its higher producer prices. The Burundian brand of coffee has won international best quality prizes.

Other cash crops include tea, cotton, palm oil and tobacco.

Agriculture traditionally employs around 90 per cent of the population and contributed around 40 per cent of GDP in 2014. Most land under cultivation is devoted to subsistence crops – mainly cassava, bananas, sweet potatoes, pulses, maize and sorghum

Cattle rearing is also an important source of food, as is fishing on Lake Tanganyika.

Fishing

Lake Tanganyika is a rich source of fish.

Forestry

Almost 4 per cent of the land area, around 95,000 hectares, is forest. Around 8.7 million cubic metres of wood is felled each year, of which 8 million cubic metres is used for firewood.

Industry and manufacturing

The industrial sector, which is centred almost entirely in Bujumbura, is based on import substitution and accounted for around 17.1 per cent of GDP in 2014. Production includes beer, soft drinks, cigarettes, glass, textiles, insecticides, cement, oxygen and coffee processing.

The civil war had discouraged foreign investment and high import costs hampered development of industrial capital; with strengthening peace these trends are reversing.

Tourism

Tourism, particularly ecotourism, could be Burundi's principal revenue earner if security in the country can be improved. Infrastructure, both tourist and generally, is under-developed. Although the country has a wealth of natural beauty to offer the visitor, warnings by several governments to their citizens to avoid certain areas and restrict travel to others to daylight hours, due to threats from terrorists and lawlessness, deter visitors.

Travel and tourism accounted for 4.3 per cent of GDP in 2014, which has been largely the same since 2011. Employment in the sector was 3.7 per cent of total employment (71,000), a fall from 3.9 per cent in 2013. Capital investment in travel and tourism rose by 11.5 per cent in 2010, but fell by 4.4 per cent in 2011, although it remained at 0.8-0.9 per cent of total capital investment through to 2013. 149,000 tourists visited the country in 2013.

Foreign interest in the Eastern Lowland Gorillas, found in the border region with Rwanda and Uganda, have the potential of bringing in significant foreign exchange.

Burundi is expected to join the single cross-border tourist visa for Rwanda, Kenya and Uganda, which was launched on 20 February 2014. The visa costs US$100 and is valid for 90 days.

Mining

Gold and tungsten are mined.

Substantial nickel reserves (up to 5 per cent of world total) have been found, but low world prices and an inadequate infrastructure mean extraction is not economically viable. Deposits of vanadium and uranium are being surveyed.

Phosphates and limestone are used for cement production.

Hydrocarbons

There are no known deposits of hydrocarbons, making Burundi reliant on imported petroleum products, which represent 10 per cent of the country's energy needs, 15 per cent of all imports and cost up to 30 per cent of all foreign exchange earnings. Over 90 per cent of Burundi's energy requirements are met by burning wood, charcoal or peat.

In 2009 the East African Community discussed oil and gas exploration and future exploitation including petroleum exploration in Burundi in the Ruzizi and Tanganyika basins, which have, as of 2015, yielded no commercial discoveries.

A feasibility study on the extension of an oil pipeline from Uganda to Bujumbura, was announced in 2009. The proposed pipeline will connect with one under construction between Kenya and Uganda. However the pipeline is not expected to be complete until 2020.

Energy

Total installed generating capacity was 52MW in 2013, generating 150 million kilowatt hours; virtually all electricity is generated by hydropower. Burundi is considered to be one of the world's poorest countries; only Bujumbura and Gitega have a municipal electricity service. The majority of the population relies on non-commercial biomass, mostly fuel wood and peat for cooking, lighting and power; only around 10 per cent of the population has access to electricity.

There are two private companies in operation, the Régie de Production et Distribution d'Eau et d'Electricité (Régideso), which operates all thermal power stations and is responsible for urban distribution as well as some small hydro units in rural areas; and the Société Internationale des Pays des Grand Lacs (Sinelac) (a joint Burundi, Rwanda and Democratic Republic of Congo entity) which develops and maintains international power projects, including the major Ruzizi hydroelectric power plant, which in 2015 was under consideration for an upgrade and extension.

Banking and insurance

Central bank

Banque de la République du Burundi

Main financial centre

Bujumbura

Time

GMT plus two hours

Geography

Burundi is a landlocked country lying on the eastern shore of Lake Tanganyika, in central Africa, just south of the Equator. It borders Rwanda to the north, Tanzania to the south and east, and the Democratic Republic of Congo to the west.

Plains rise from Lake Tanganyika in the west to a central sloping plateau; hills and valleys have cultivated fields and pastures. In the east the region in mostly savanna. The southern tributary of the Nile begins its 6,650km journey to the Mediterranean in the south. The highest peak is Karonje at 2,760 metre.

Hemisphere

Southern

Climate

Around Lake Tanganyika (including Bujumbura), equatorial with hot, humid temperatures 23–33 degrees Celsius (C), and frequent winds. Elsewhere is temperate with average temperatures of 20 degrees C. The rainy season is from October–May (except brief dry period December–January); the long dry season is from June–September.

Entry requirements

Passports

Required by all, with at least six months validity remaining at time of departure.

Visa

Required by all. Applications for tourist and business visas should include itineraries and vaccination certificates against yellow fever and cholera. Business visas require a company letter of introduction from the employer and a local host company.

Currency advice/regulations

Import and export of the local currency is limited to Buf2,000.

Import and export of foreign currency is unlimited but subject to declaration on entry. All currency exchanges must be made through the main banks in Bujumbura or Gitega.

Travellers cheques have a limited market and commissions can be high; to avoid extra exchange rate charges cheques are best in US dollars or euros.

Health (for visitors)

Mandatory precautions

Cholera vaccination certificates are required by all visitors. Visitors arriving from countries where yellow fever is endemic are required to have meningitis and yellow fever vaccination certificates.

Advisable precautions

Yellow fever and cholera vaccinations are considered essential. Occasionally a certificate for meningococcal meningitis is required when arriving. Vaccinations for hepatitis A, polio, tetanus and typhoid are recommended. Malaria prophylaxis should be taken as risk exists throughout the country. Hepatitis B is endemic; visitors should seek advice on diphtheria, dysentery and tuberculosis vaccinations. There is a rabies risk.

To avoid the risk of Bilharzia use only well-maintained swimming pools. Drinking water precautions are essential and water must first be boiled or otherwise sterilised for drinking, brushing teeth or making ice. Eat only well-cooked meat and fish, preferably served hot; vegetables should be cooked and fruit peeled. Pork, salad and mayonnaise and most dairy products, made from unboiled milk, may carry an inherent risk. Avoid food from street vendors.

HIV/Aids is widespread, with 15 per cent HIV positive among adults in Bujumbura. A travel kit including a disposable syringe is a reasonable precaution; all personal medications should be carried, along with their original packaging. Medical insurance, including repatriation is essential.

Hotels

Advisable to book in advance. Very little accommodation available outside Bujumbura. A 10 per cent tip is usual.

Public holidays (national)

Fixed dates

1 Jan (New Year's Day), 5 Feb (Unity Day), 12 Mar (Labour Day), 1 Jul (Independence Day), 15 Aug (Assumption), 13 Oct (Anniversary of Rwagasore's Assassination), 21 Oct (Anniversary President Ndadaye's Assassination), 1 Nov (All Saints' Day), 25 Dec (Christmas Day).

Variable dates

Easter (Mar/Apr), Ascension (May), Eid al Fitr.

Working hours

Banking

Mon–Fri: 0800–1130; 1500–1600.

Business

Mon–Fri: 0730–1200, 1400–1730.

Government

Mon–Fri: 0730–1200, 1400–1730.

Shops

Mon–Fri: 0830–1200, 1500–1800. Sat: 0830–1230.

Telecommunications

Mobile/cell phones

Several GSM 900 services operate in major areas of population in the north, west and south of the country.

Electricity supply

220V AC

Security

It is not recommended driving to and from Rwanda, unless travelling as part of a UN convoy; militia from rival political factions are likely to ambushed lone travellers.

Getting there

Air

The only direct intercontinental flights are from Europe.

National airline: Air Burundi (not approved by IATA)

International airport/s: Bujumbura (code: BJM), 11km north of city; café, currency exchange and post office.

Airport tax: Departure tax: US$20.

Surface

Road: All border crossings can be closed at very short notice depending on prevailing political conditions. There are reasonably passable roads from the Democratic Republic of Congo, either north or south, however the roads from Tanzania are generally in poor condition. The road from Kigali in Rwanda may be passable.

Water: There are connections across Lake Tanganyika, with ferries operating from Kigoma, (Tanzania), Kalenjie (DCR) and Mpulungu (Zambia).

Dar es Salam (Tanzania) is the closest sea port.

Main port/s: Bujumbura, Nyanza-Lac

Getting about

National transport

Air: There are no scheduled internal flights operating.

Road: Most of the roads leading to provincial towns are surfaced. Unsurfaced roads elsewhere can be difficult in the rainy season. Surfaced routes are being extended and local advice should be sought. Major roads are often closed after 1600 for security reasons. Driving outside the cities can be dangerous, particularly in border areas.

Buses: Very little public transport is available and buses are not recommended.

Water: Local boats are available on Lake Tanganyika, they can be slow depending on their cargo.

City transport

Taxis: Available in Bujumbura.

Car hire

Local firms only. International driving licence is required.

BUSINESS DIRECTORY

The addresses listed below are a selection only. While World of Information makes every endeavour to check these addresses, we cannot guarantee that changes have not been made, especially to telephone numbers and area codes. We would welcome any corrections.

Telephone area codes

The international direct dialling (IDD) code for Burundi is +257, followed by area code and subscriber's number:

Bubanza	42	Gitega	40
Bujumbura	2	Muramvya	43
Bururi	50	Ngozi	30
Cibitoke	41		

Useful telephone numbers

Police: 18, 19.

Chambers of Commerce

Burundi Chamber of Commerce, Industry, Agriculture and Handicrafts, Avenue du 18 Septembre, PO Box 313, Bujumbura (tel: 222-280; fax: 227-895; e-mail: ccib@cbinf.com).

Banking

Banque Commerciale du Burundi, PO Box 990, Libere Ndabakwaje; 84 Chaussée Prince Louise Rwagasore, Bujumbura (tel: 222-317; fax: 221-018).

Banque de Crédit de Bujumbura, PO Box 300, Avenue Patrice Emery Lumumba, Bujumbura (tel: 222-091; fax: 223-007; email: bcb@bi-network.com).

Interbank Burundi SA, PO Box 2970; 15 Rue de l'Industrie, Bujumbura (tel: 220-629; fax: 220-461; email: interb@cbinf.com).

Central bank

Banque de la République du Burundi, PO Box 705, Avenue du Gouvernement, Bujumbura, Burundi (tel: 225-142 fax: 223-128).

Travel information

Air Burundi, BP 2460, Avenue du Commerce, Bujumbura (tel: 223-460; fax: 223-452).

Bujumbura International Airport, PO Box 694, Bujumbura (tel: 223-707; 223-797; fax: 223-428).

Tourist office (for accommodation) 7 place de L'Indépendence, Bujumbura, BP 1402, (tel: 222-321, 220-704; email: nitra@cbinf.com).

National tourist organisation offices

Office National du Tourisme, 2 Avenue des Euphorbes, BP 902, Bujumbura (tel: 222-202/023; fax: 222-390; email: ontbur@cbinf.com); internet (in French): www.burundi.gov.bi).

Ministries

Ministry of Agriculture, Bujumbura (tel: 210-342; fax: 222-873).

Ministry of Commerce, Industry and Tourism, Bujumbura (tel: 217-775; fax: 225-595).

Ministry of Communication with the Government, Bujumbura (tel: 212-601; fax: 216-318).

Ministry of Community Development, Bujumbura (tel: 213-098; fax: 224-678).

Ministry of Defence, Bujumbura (tel: 219-994; fax: 225-686).

Ministry of Education, Bujumbura (tel: 217-776; fax: 226-839).

Ministry of Energy and Mines, Bujumbura (tel: 218-586; fax: 223-337).

Ministry of the Environment, Bujumbura (tel: 221-649; fax: 228-902).

Ministry of Finance, Bujumbura (tel: 217-918; fax: 223-827).

Ministry of Foreign Affairs and Co-operation, Bujumbura (tel: 217-595; fax: 226-313).

Ministry of Health, Bujumbura (tel: 218-200; fax: 229-916).

Ministry of Human Rights, Law Reforms and Relations with the National Assembly, Bujumbura (tel: 217-365; fax: 213-847).

Ministry of the Interior, Bujumbura (tel: 212-480; fax: 223-904).

Ministry of Justice, Bujumbura (tel: 210-595; fax: 222-148).

Ministry of Labour, Public Office and Professional Education, Bujumbura (tel: 217-928; fax: 224-079).

Ministry of Peace Process, Bujumbura (tel: 219-457; fax: 219-459).

Ministry of Planning, Development and Reconstruction, Bujumbura (tel: 219-079; fax: 224-193).

Ministry of Public Works and Equipment, Bujumbura (tel: 219-646; fax: 226-840).

Ministry of Repatriation of Displaced Persons, Bujumbura (tel: 218-184; fax: 218-201).

Ministry of Social Action and Promotion of Women, Bujumbura (tel: 210-376; fax: 216-102).

Ministry of Transport, Post and Telecommunications, Bujumbura (tel: 210-462; fax: 226-900).

Ministry of Youth Sport and Culture, Bujumbura (tel: 216-729; fax: 226-231).

Office of the President, Bujumbura (tel: 217-806; fax: 226-424).

Other useful addresses

APEE (export promotion) BP 3535, Bujumbura (tel: 225-997; fax: 222-767).

BCC (Burundi Coffee Co) BP 780, Bujumbura.

Burundi Embassy (USA), Suite 212, 2233 Wisconsin Avenue, NW, Washington DC 20007 (tel: (+1-202) 342-2574; fax: (+1-202) 342-2578).

Burundi Mining Co. BP468 Bujumbura (tel: 223-229).

CIGERCO (Cotton growers), BP 2571, Bujumbura (tel: 222-208).

National news agency: Agence Burundaise de Presse: www.cbinf.com

Burundi Information (in French): www.burundi-info.com

Burundi Quotidien (in French): www.burundi-quotidien.com

Iteka (in French and English): www.ligue-iteka.africa-web.org

Net press (L'Agence Burundaise d'Information): www.netpress.bi

Internet sites

Africa Business Network: http://www.ifc.org

AllAfrica.com: http://www.allafrica.com

African Development Bank: http://www.afdb.org

Cabo Verde

KEY FACTS

Official name: República de Cabo Verde (Republic of Cape Verde)

Head of State: President Jorge Carlos Fonseca (MpD) (9 Sept 2011)

Head of government: Prime Minister José Maria Neves (PAICV) (since 2001; re-elected 6 Feb 2011)

Ruling party: Partido Africano da Independência de Cabo Verde (PAICV) (African Party of Independence of Cape Verde) (since 2001; re-elected 6 Feb 2011)

Area: 4,033 square km (nine islands and 10 islets)

Population: 518,000 (2014)* (491,575; 2010, census figure)

Capital: Praia

Official language: Portuguese and Creole (national language)

Currency: Cape Verde escudo (CVE) = 100 centavos

Exchange rate: CVE99.05 per US$ (Sep 2015)

GDP per capita: US$3,663 (2014)*

GDP real growth: 1.00% (2014)*

GDP: US$1.90 billion (2014)*

Unemployment: 12.00% (2014)*

Inflation: -0.24% (2014)

Balance of trade: -US$609.13 million (2014)*

Annual FDI: US$92.94 million (2011)

* estimated figure

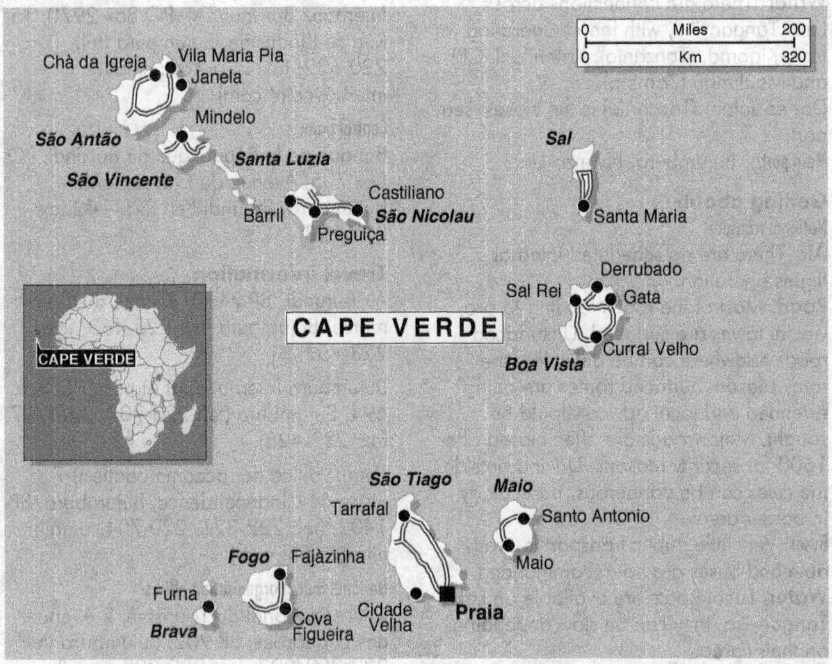

Cabo Verde (Cape Verde up until October 2013) continued to be one of Africa's most stable democratic governments in 2015. Political openness has become central to Cabo Verde's economic and social progress. Since the adoption of a multi-party system in 1991, there have been four national elections and two orderly changes in government. Cabo Verde is one of the freest and most democratic nations in Africa: it rated 7.94 on the *Economist Intelligence Unit's Democracy Index* – which placed it in the 'flawed democracy' category: this was, however, a better rating than Greece, Italy, France, Israel or Brazil. A free press further supported the building of an open society.

Macroeconomic policies in Cabo Verde have strengthened significantly over recent years, enabling the country to correct the severe macro-economic imbalances that emerged in 2000 in the run-up to parliamentary and presidential elections. Since then external and domestic debt has declined, international reserves have been built up. There has been progress on structural reforms to support investment and improve the business climate. Real growth averaged around 6 per cent in between 2000–10 and inflation remained low; however since 2010 economic growth has been subdued averaging at around 2 per cent.

Cabo Verde's *diaspora* population is greater than its domestic one and while the money that is sent home by the expatriates brings in much needed foreign currency, it will continue to underpin the economy. One worrying development has been the allegations that Cabo Verde is a trans-shipment point for illicit drugs moving from Latin America and Asia destined for Western Europe. It is only the lack of a well-developed financial system that has, at least to a degree, limited the country's usefulness as a money-laundering centre. On the Transparency International 2014 *Corruption Perceptions Index* Cabo Verde ranked a respectable 42 out of the 175 countries surveyed.

The biggest eruption in decades of Cabo Verde volcano, Pico de Fogo, forced 1,500 people to abandon their homes in November 2014. The devastating eruption destroyed two villages and ended the whole local economy.

The economy

In its September 2014 assessment of Cabo Verde's economy, the International Monetary Fund (IMF) was full of praise, noting that over the last two decades, good governance and sound macro-economic management had delivered remarkable economic and social progress. In the latter half of 2014, however, growth was subdued due to external factors such as the prolonged downturn in Europe – on which Cabo Verde's economy relies heavily – and the country also underwent a sharp deterioration in the *Economist Intelligence Unit's Democracy Index* of domestic confidence. A longer-term decline in the contribution of productivity to growth may also have played a role. Financial stability risks have increased with the rise in non-performing loans and fall in bank profitability. Cabo Verde remains vulnerable to external shocks, given its dependence on tourism, remittances and concessional financing. Over the longer term, Cabo Verde's challenge as a 'new' middle-income country is to bolster productivity and diversify the sources of growth. In the view of the IMF, fiscal consolidation remains critical to safeguard macro-economic and debt sustainability.

In the March 2015 statement at the conclusion of the IMF mission to Cabo Verde, it was reported that growth had picked up slightly due to a weak recovery in Europe, dampened by the fact that tourism had declined for the first time in many years due to the outbreak of the Ebola virus in West Africa, despite Cabo Verde being free of the infection. On the other hand, exports of goods consisting mainly of fish increased considerably. However the country is still heavily reliant on external means of powering its economy- – remittances remained stable and foreign direct investment (FDI) resumed in the latter half of 2014. The report also noted that 'credit to the private sector stagnated as excess liquidity is weakening the transmission of monetary policy, and banks are burdened by high non-performing loans from the recent economic downturn'.

Moderately accelerated growth is predicted for 2015, due to the improving situation in Europe, a rebound in tourism, a reduction in oil prices and a rise in FDI. Also due to the economy's progress in dealing with the debt overhang, there could potentially be a restart of bank lending to the private sector.

Budgetary plans for 2015 and the medium term entail rising public debt and are subject to downside risks to revenue. The national authorities have decided on a package of expenditure containment measures for 2014–17. However, given the high, albeit sustainable, level of public debt, further measures are needed to put public debt on a more robust downward path. Bolstering domestic revenue mobilisation, increasing the efficiency of public investment and managing existing infrastructure better are also, in the view of the IMF, central to sound public finances. International reserves have recovered, which provides room to ease monetary policy in support of the recovery. In the absence of imminent pressures on the balance of payments or on prices and with private sector credit growth having stalled, Banco de Cabo Verde (central bank) cut the base rate. At the same time, in view of the pressures on the banking system, continued vigilance regarding risks to financial stability is warranted. Structural reforms hold the key to bolstering competitiveness, creating jobs and delivering inclusive growth.

Increasing labour market efficiency and reducing skill mis-matches would be particularly constructive. Enhancing the efficiency of state-owned enterprises is also essential to improve the delivery of infrastructure services. The IMF drew the authorities' attention to some shortcomings in the preparation of national accounts. Although, in the view of the IMF, the data supplied was adequate for surveillance purposes, national accounts data were released with a long delay. This complicated the formulation of macro-economic policies.

In its 2015 *Economic Outlook*, the African Development Bank (AfDB) observed that since 2012, Cabo Verde's economy had been hit by the weak international economic situation. GDP growth dropped from 4 per cent in 2011 to 0.7 per cent in 2013. Business and consumer confidence indicators had deteriorated while FDI flows had pursued their declining trend in the balance of payments. However, public sector demand continued to provide support to the economy. Growth picked up modestly to 2.0 per cent in 2014, largely due to the construction sector according to the AfDB. The slowdown in tourism revenue persisted, however, and the industry had a negative contribution to GDP in 2014. Economic growth is forecast to break 3 per cent in 2015 and continue growing in 2016 – mainly due to the success of the tourist industry, as the Ebola scare dies away, the resumption of private credit growth, product diversification to increase export of goods and better performance in Europe.

As a result of the increase in the public sector's borrowing requirements to finance large investments in infrastructure, the total nominal government debt had increased from 57 per cent of GDP in 2008 to an estimated 107 per cent at the end of 2014. In 2014, the government focused on medium-term fiscal consolidation to rebuild policy buffers and lower debt related risks, but some temporary fiscal and monetary easing might be considered in line with the economic cycle if weakness persists. In this context, it would be critical to accelerate the reforms in the business environment to improve

KEY INDICATORS **Cabo Verde**

	Unit	2011	2012	2013	2014	**2015
Population	m	*0.52	*0.49	0.51	*0.52	*525.00
Gross domestic product (GDP)	US$bn	1.96	1.79	*1.86	*1.90	*1.80
GDP per capita	US$	3,676	3,630	*3,632	*3,663	*3,433
GDP real growth	%	5.0	1.0	*0.5	*1.0	*3.0
Inflation	%	2.0	2.5	1.5	-0.2	*1.5
Unemployment	%	10.0	16.8	16.4	*12.0	*10.0
Exports (fob) (goods)	US$m	196.5	173.0	184.2	253.0	–
Imports (fob) (goods)	US$m	1,039.7	879.0	804.5	862.1	–
Balance of trade	US$m	-843.2	-706.0	-620.3	-609.1	–
Current account	US$m	-287.8	-201.0	-74.0	*-173.0	*-173.0
Total reserves minus gold	US$m	317.1	376.0	475.3	510.9	–
Foreign exchange	US$m	307.7	371.0	471.9	–	–
Exchange rate	per US$	78.47	85.00	79.42	90.05	–

* estimated figure ** forecast figure

competitiveness, particularly in the labour market. In parallel, returns to the impressive investments in infrastructure would need to be raised by strengthening the management of the public capital stock. In the financial sector, credit to the economy was likely to remain limited, as banks grow increasingly cautious given the high levels of non-performing loans and the need to build provisions, limiting the potential for growth.

The AfDB attaches some importance to 'global value chains', which it saw operating in the services sector, mainly through tourism and people working abroad. The tourism sector was engaged in global value chains, having become an important engine of growth in the Cabo Verdean economy since 2005. The export of sea products, which are mostly canned and frozen seafood, also connected the country to value chains abroad, and were a significant contributor to the subdued growth of 2014. Cabo Verde is seeking strategies that can position the country at higher-value stages in the global value chains by stimulating new exports of goods and services and expanding existing ones, especially around the creative sector.

Despite having made economic progress over the 2011–15 period, there are still exclusion zones within the islands that have not enjoyed the same growth. These pockets are largely due to strong flows of emigration to the two islands of São Vicente and Sal where most of the 500,000 residents of the islands live. The Cabo Verde development strategy is therefore a national vision aimed at spreading the success of the country to the entire populace and especially to the islands that deal with high levels of poverty.

Risk assessment

Politics	Fair/good
Economy	Good
Regional stability	Good

COUNTRY PROFILE

1462 The previously uninhabited islands were colonised by the Portuguese and became one of the most important slaving stations in West Africa.

1961 The movement for independence gathered strength, adopting guerrilla tactics against the Portuguese.

1975 Cape Verde gained independence after the fall of the dictatorship in Portugal.

1975–80 Moves to unite Cape Verde and Guinea-Bissau were made, but came to nothing following the overthrow of President Luiz Cabral in Guinea-Bissau.

1980 The constitution was adopted.

1981 A revision to the constitution was passed.

1990 A multi-party system was introduced.

1991 Cape Verde's first free multi-party elections were won by the Movimento para a Democracia (MpD) (Movement for Democracy) and a government under Carlos Veiga was formed.

1992 A new constitution was adopted.

1995 The MpD secured an absolute majority in the elections to the National Assembly.

1996 President Antonio Mascarenhas Monteiro (MpD) was re-elected; no other parties put up candidates.

1999 The constitution was amended.

2001 Pedro Pires was elected president.

2003 The IMF approved a three-year programme for US$11.5 million under the Poverty Reduction and Growth Facility (PRGF).

2004 Poor rainfall and locust damage resulted in reduced harvests and a larger than usual food deficit.

2006 PAICV won the general elections. Pedro Pires was re-elected president.

2007 Cape Verde withdrew its support for Polisario, the separatist movement in Western Sahara, and allied itself to Morocco. The WTO approved Cape Verde's membership.

2008 Cape Verde announced its backing of the Moroccan Sahara autonomy plan, which allowed Morocco and the Polisario to discuss the future of Western Sahara without pre-conditions.

2009 Cidada Velha, located west of the capital Praia, became Cape Verde's first addition to the prestigious list of Unesco world heritage sites.

2010 An Economic Partnership Agreement with the EU was finalised, to provide new funding and favourable export conditions. Tourist numbers increased after a reduction in prices offered by the Cape Verdean tourist industry encouraged more visitors during the European winter.

2011 The ruling PAICV won parliamentary elections held in February, with 50.9 per cent of the vote (37 seats out of 72); the MPD remained as the second party in the national legislature with 41.9 per cent (33 seats). The new PAICV government took office in March; José Maria Neves remained in office as prime minister. Four candidates took part in the first round of presidential elections; but only Jorge Carlos Fonseca (MpD), who won 37.3 per cent of the vote, and Manuel Inocêncio Sousa (PAICV), with 32 per cent, went forward to the runoff election in August. Fonseca won 54.1 per cent, Sousa 45.9 per cent in the runoff; turnout was 59.7 per cent. President Jorge Carlos Fonseca took office in September. Former president, Pedro Verona Pires was awarded the US$5 million Mo Ibrahim prize for good governance (and those who have voluntarily left office) in Africa, in October. On 17 December, Cesaria Evora died. She was considered one of the world's greatest exponents of *Morna*, a national musical style of Cape Verde, similar to the US-blues.

2012 Electricity cuts that lasted for hours and were experienced throughout the islands in early October lead to street protests as customers complained at the lack of explanation for the outages. Electra, the supply company cited technical problems and generator maintenance as the cause of the cuts. However, with the imposition of rationing many consider it a lack of fuel as the most likely cause and question the public investment in renewable energy that should have responded to the current need.

2013 President Fonseca paid an official visit to Angola in November as part of an effort to develop trade ties. On 25 October an official note was sent to the United Nations requesting the official name of the country be changed from Cape Verde to Cabo Verde.

2014 On 25 May the Executive Board of the International Monetary Fund (IMF) concluded the 2014 Article IV consultation with Cabo Verde.

2015

Political structure

Cape Verde has a mixed presidential/parliamentary form of government.

Constitution

A new constitution was adopted in 1992, this transformed the country from a one party state to a multiparty democracy. It was substantially amended in 1999. There are 17 *municipios* (administrative districts).

Form of state

Unitary republic

The executive

Executive power rests with the prime minister and the Council of Ministers, proposed by the prime minister and appointed by the president. The prime minister is appointed by the president, in consultation with the National Assembly. The president is elected by universal suffrage by electors registered in the electoral census in the national territory and abroad, for a five-year term. The presidential candidate must be a Capeverdean citizen by origin, thirty-five or more years of age on the date of his candidature, and, in the three years immediately preceding that date, have had permanent residence in the national territory.

National legislature

The unicameral Assembléia Nacional (National Assembly) has 72 members, of which 66 are elected by proportional representation, and six deputies are elected by Cape Verdeans living abroad (two each for Africa, the Americas and the rest of the world). All serve for five-year terms.

Legal system

The legal system is derived from that of Portugal.

Last elections

6 February 2011 (parliamentary); 7 and 21 August 2011 (presidential)

Results: Parliamentary: the Partido Africano da Independência de Cabo Verde (PAICV) (African Party of Independence of Cape Verde) won 50.9 per cent of the vote (37 seats out of 72), Movimento para a Democracia (MpD) (Movement for Democracy) 41.9 per cent (33), União Caboverdiana Independente e Democrática) (UCID) (Democratic and Independent Cape Verdean Union) 4.9 per cent; two other political parties each won less than 1 per cent of the vote and failed to win any seats. Turnout was 75.5 per cent.

Presidential (first round): Jorge Carlos Fonseca (MpD) won 37.3 per cent of the vote, Manuel Inocêncio Sousa (PAICV) 32.0 per cent, Aristides Lima (independent) 27.4 per cent and Joaquim Jaime Monteiro (independent) 2.0 per cent.

Runoff: Fonseca 54.2 per cent, Sousa 45.8 per cent.

Next elections

2016 (presidential and parliamentary)

Political parties

There are six registered political parties.

Ruling party

Partido Africano da Independência de Cabo Verde (PAICV) (African Party of Independence of Cape Verde) (since 2001; re-elected 6 Feb 2011)

Main opposition party

Movimento para a Democracia (MPD) (Movement for Democracy)

Population

527,000 (2012)*

It is estimated that 53 per cent of the population live in the country's three main cities, exerting great pressure on social services. Beside the Cape Verdians resident on the islands, there are some 500,000 living abroad, many in the US.

Last census: 16 June 2010: 491,575

Population density: 237 inhabitants per square km. Urban population 61 per cent (2010 Unicef).

Annual growth rate: 1.8 per cent, 1990–2010 (Unicef).

Ethnic make-up

Creole (71 per cent), African (28 per cent), European (1 per cent).

Religions

Constitutional separation of church and state allows for freedom of religion. Christian (97 per cent Roman Catholic).

Education

The National Development Plan of 2002–06 aims to increase vocational training and job creation and reduce illiteracy in an effort to generate foreign investment and therefore increase employment.

Literacy rate: 74 per cent adult population.

Enrolment rate: 100 per cent of children age six to 11 will enrol for school in 2015, Oxfam estimate.

Health

HIV/Aids

The government had a National Aids programme in place for the period 2001–04, financed by the World Bank.

Life expectancy: 74 years, 2010 (Unicef 2012)

Fertility rate/Maternal mortality rate: 2.4 births per woman, 2010 (Unicef 2012)

Child (under 5 years) mortality rate (per 1,000): 22 per 1,000 live births (WHO 2012)

Welfare

Around a third of the population live under the poverty line with around 14 per cent living in absolute poverty. Unemployment is estimated at 25 per cent, while underemployment is far higher. Poverty is worse in rural areas where employment opportunities are poor and incomes are declining. As a result, there is a steady migration to urban areas, creating pockets of extreme poverty within cities and towns.

Main cities

Praia, on Santiago Island (capital, estimated population 134,900 in 2012); Mindelo, on São Vicente (commercial centre, 71,952), Santa Maria (26,550).

Languages spoken

Official language/s

Portuguese and Creole (national language)

Media

Press

The only daily is the government-run *Jornal Horizonte*, the only other local publications are *Expresso das Ilhas* (www.expressodasilhas.cv) and *A Semana* (www.asemana.cv). *Terra Nova* is a weekly based on São Vicente. Government publications include *Novo Jornal Cabo Verde* published twice a week and the periodical *Boletim Informativo*.

Broadcasting

The state-run broadcaster is Radio e televisão de Cabo Verde (RTC).

Radio: The state-run radio RTC (www.rtc.cv) has one station that has programmes relayed throughout the islands on a variety of frequencies. Private commercial stations include Praia FM (www.praiafm.biz), Mosteiros FM (www.mosteiros.com), Rádio Nova (www.radionovaonline.com) and Crioula FM (www.crioulafm.cv). Several foreign broadcasts, from Portugal and France, are readily available.

Television: RTC (www.rtc.cv) operates the country's only television station.

National news agency: Inforpress (Agência de Notícias de Cabo Verde)

Other news agencies: Voz di Povo: www.vozdipovo-online.com

APA: www.apanews.net

Panapress: www.panapress.com

Economy

Cabo Verde has limited natural resources and much of the economy is dominated by the service sector, which constitutes 74.9 per cent of GDP, of which trade, transport and government services account for around 55 per cent. Agriculture of any significant level is only possible on four of the 10 main islands as the rugged volcanic nature of the landscape is subject to erosion and persistent periods of severe drought; around 90 per cent of all food is imported.

Due to its problematic external environment, growth in gross domestic product (GDP) in 2013 had dropped to 0.7 per cent having been 4.0 per cent in 2011. This poor performance was a result of a decline in remittances and foreign direct investment (FDI) from Europe, and also a reduction in official development assistance. Despite a negative contribution from tourism, growth moderately picked up in 2014, reaching 2.0 per cent largely due to the construction sector. The tourism sector is expected to pick up in 2015/16, contributing to an expected growth rate of 3 per cent. Resumption of private credit growth, increased investment in agriculture, increase in productivity and a modest improvement of the economic situation in Europe are also expected to drive performance.

Cape Verde reduced its poverty rate and graduated from UN least developed country (LDC) status in 2008. In 2014, the UN Human Development Index (HDI) ranked Cape Verde 123 (out of 187) for national development in health, education and income. Since 2011, Cape Verde has progressed 10 places in the rankings. Remittances were estimated to have reached US$189 million in 2014, a 7.4 per cent increase on the previous year. There is a high level of unskilled workers (30–40 per cent of the population) and foreign investors are able to take advantage of low wage rates.

Tourism, which typically attracts over 50 per cent of total foreign direct investment (FDI), is of growing importance to the economy. Total FDI was US$211.3

million in 2008, falling to US$111.7 million in 2010, and even further to US$38.7 million by 2013, which was only 2.2 per cent. The industry was hit by external shocks in 2008–09 with the record price of fuel and the weakness of foreign economies cutting tourist numbers so that the industry declined by -16.2 per cent, down from a record growth of 23 per cent in 2007. As the global economy has recovered so has the tourist numbers, and in 2013 there were 511,000 visitors, up from under 300,000 in 2009. In 2014, the industry accounted for 40.0 per cent of GDP.

External trade

Cape Verde is a member of the Economic Community of West African States (Ecowas) and has indicated that it is interested in joining the West African Monetary Zone (WAMZ). Cape Verde became a member of the World Trade Organisation (WTO) in 2008.

There are free-trade zones (known as Foreign Trade Zones), which specialise in duty-free goods storage and raw materials for either re-export or manufacturing into goods for overseas markets.

Imports

Principal imports include mineral products (mainly refined petroleum), machinery, transportation vehicles and foodstuffs such as: rice, wheat and maize, cooking oil and milk.

Main sources: Main import origins are Portugal (typically 48 per cent of total), The Netherlands (12 per cent), US (8.8 per cent) and Spain (8.4 per cent).

Exports

Principal exports are fuel, fish, hides, salt and *entrepôt* trade.

Main destinations: Main export destinations are Spain (typically 64 per cent of total), Portugal (11 per cent), US (4.3 per cent) and El Salvador (4.1 per cent).

Re-exports

Petroleum, fish and crustaceans, clothing and shoes.

Agriculture

Farming

Total agricultural land is 403,000 hectares of which 6.2 per cent is pasture and 14.9 per cent arable (mostly on the island of São Tiago). Almost 17 per cent of the population is engaged in subsistence farming.

Recurrent drought, interrupted by torrential rains and floods, soil erosion, disease and a weak infrastructure have reduced agricultural production considerably, but there are schemes for water conservation and irrigation.

Beans and maize are the staple foodstuffs. Maize covers 25–80 per cent of cultivated land according to rainfall. Only 10 per cent of food is produced locally.

Other crops include bananas, sweet potatoes, yams, manioc, pumpkins, sugar cane, coffee and groundnuts. About 90 per cent of food requirements are met by imports, largely in the form of food aid.

Fishing

Tuna and lobster are the main catches of the fishing industry, however, being underexploited the industry lacks growth.

Industry and manufacturing

The industrial sector accounts for around 17 per cent of GDP and employs around 15 per cent of the workforce.

Industries include ship repair and fuelling, construction, fish processing and canning, flour milling, soft drinks, cigar manufacture and garment making. Construction, which has been one of the main drivers of performance in 2014, and civil engineering contribute about 10 per cent of GDP and are primarily related to the development of the tourism sector.

Two zones have been set up with industrial parks: Lazareto on São Vicente and Achada Grande Tras in Praia.

Tourism

Located off the coast of West Africa at the northern limit of the tropics, Cape Verde can offer European visitors a break from cold, cloudy winters with warmth and sunshine, for a relatively short flight with economic package tours. The islands offer modern beach resorts, diving and fishing and tours of the islands.

Travel and tourism is vital to the economy as it contributed 40.0 per cent of GDP (in 2014) and provided employment for 35.8 per cent of the workforce (around 79,500 jobs). In 2013 there were 511,000 visitors to the islands.

Environment

Cape Verde faces serious environmental problems, particularly concerning water management. Serious drought caused by global warming and the country's geographical location has undermined agriculture as well as plant cover. The government has drawn upon the Global Environment Facility (GEF) to help protect biodiversity and is supported by the UN's Food and Agriculture Organisation (FAO) in a forestry action plan.

Mining

The mining sector employs about 1 per cent of the workforce.

Activity is largely confined to exploitation of pozzolana (volcanic derivative) at São Antão, gypsum at Maio and production of salt on Sal and in Mindelo by evaporation method.

Hydrocarbons

There are no known oil or natural gas reserves. Consumption of oil was 2,780 barrels per day (bpd) in 2013, all of which was imported, mainly from Portugal and West African countries. The downstream industry is regulated by Direcão Geral da Energia (Directorate General for Energy) and distribution is by Shell Capo Verde and Enacol.

Any use of natural gas or coal is commercially insignificant.

Energy

Total installed generating capacity was 89.8MW in 2013. Although the majority of power is generated by conventional thermal power stations, there are six 300kW wind turbines in operation.

The state-owned Empresa Pública de Electricidade e Água (Electra) is responsible for generation, transmission, distribution and sales of electricity.

Financial markets

Stock exchange

Bolsa de Valores de Cabo Verde (BVC) (Cape Verde Stock Exchange)

Banking and insurance

Central bank

Banco de Cabo Verde

Main financial centre

Praia

Time

GMT minus one hour

Geography

Cape Verde is an archipelago of 10 islands and five islets in the North Atlantic Ocean, about 500km (300 miles) west of Dakar, Senegal.

Hemisphere

Northern

Climate

Hot with very little rainfall. Temperatures range from around 20 degrees Celsius (C) at night to 32 degrees C during the day. Hottest months are July, August and September and rain most likely from August–September.

Entry requirements

Passports

Required by all. Passport must be valid for six months.

Visa

Required by all, except nationals of Ecowas countries, former Cape Verde nationals (with proof of origin) and transit passengers.

Currency advice/regulations

Import and export of local currency prohibited. No restriction on import of foreign currency, but amounts must be declared on arrival. Export of foreign currency is limited to equivalent of CVEsc1,000,000 or the amount declared on arrival if higher.

Health (for visitors)

Mandatory precautions

Yellow fever certificates if arriving from countries having notified cases in the last six years.

Advisable precautions

Typhoid, tetanus, hepatitis A and polio vaccinations. Malaria limited risk exists September to November in São Tiago Island. Water precautions should be taken. There is a rabies risk. There is a slight risk of cholera. Milk is unpasteurised and should be boiled. Dairy products should be avoided.

Hotels

Accommodation is available in all islands but the best establishments are situated in Fogo, Sal, Santiago, São Vicente.

Credit cards

Credit cards are only accepted in the bigger hotels.

Public holidays (national)

Fixed dates

1 Jan (New Year's Day), 20 Jan (Heroes' Day), 1 May (Labour Day), 5 Jul (Independence Day), 15 Aug (Assumption Day), 12 Sep (National Day), 1 Nov (All Saints' Day), 25 Dec (Christmas).

Variable dates

Carnival (Feb), Ash Wednesday, Good Friday.

Working hours

Banking

Mon–Fri: 0800–1400.

Business

Mon–Fri: 0800–1230, 1430–1800.

Shops

Mon–Fri: 0800–2000; Sat: 0900–1700.

Electricity supply

220V AC, 50Hz

Weights and measures

Metric system

Getting there

Air

TAAG of Angola flies weekly from São Tomé and Príncipe. South African Airlines, TAP Air Portugal and Tower Airlines also service Cape Verde.

National airline: Transportes Aéreos de Cabo Verde (TACV) guarantees daily inter-island flights and weekly flights.

International airport/s: Amilcar Cabral International (SID), 2km south of Espargos on Sal island; Praia International (RAI) on Santiago island.

Airport tax: None.

Surface

Water: A high-speed ferry service between Cape Verde and São Tomé is planned by the ferry company Expresso LDA with a one-way journey taking five days. The ferry will have 400 berths and a capacity of 800 passengers. The service was still not operational in July 2011.

Getting about

National transport

Air: Transportes Aéreos de Cabo Verde (TACV) flies daily to all islands except Brava and Santo Antâo. Discounted trips among the islands are available with the Cape Verde Airpass, which can be purchased when booking international flights with TACV. A charter service is provided by Cape Verde Express.

Buses: Buses available on main islands.

Water: Boats ply between the islands.

City transport

Taxis: Available on main islands. Taxis are available from Amilcar Cabral International Airport to city centre.

BUSINESS DIRECTORY

The addresses listed below are a selection only. While World of Information makes every endeavour to check these addresses, we cannot guarantee that changes have not been made, especially to telephone numbers and area codes. We would welcome any corrections.

Telephone area codes

The international dialling code (IDD) for Cape Verde is +238 followed by subscriber's number.

NB From 3 July 2004, standard and cellular numbers have seven digits: add '2' to the beginning of the existing standard number; add '9' to the beginning of the existing cellular number.

Useful telephone numbers

Praia, Santiago
Airport docks: 2615-821, 2615-646
Electricity Board: 2611-909
Fire brigade: 2612-727
Ambulance: 2612-462
Police: 2613-637

Chambers of Commerce

Barlavento Cámara de Comércio, Indústria, Agricultura e Serviços, Rua de Luz 31, PO Box 728, Mindelo, Saõ Vicente (tel: 2328-495; fax: 2328-496; e-mail: camera.com @mail.cvtelecom.cv).

Sotavento Cámara de Comércio, Indústria e Serviços, Rua Andrade Corvo, PO Box 105, Praia, Santiago (tel: 2617-234; fax: 2617-235; e-mail: cciss@mail,cvtelecom.cv).

Banking

Banco Insular (IFI), PO Box 556, Conjunto Residencial Comunidades, Lote Oito- Bloco D Fracção Oitava, Achada Santo Antonio-Praia (e-mail: bancoinsular@mail.cvtelecom.cv).

Banco Comercial do Atlantico, PO Box 474, Avenida Amílcar Cabral, Praia (tel: 2614-953; fax: 2613-235).

Banco Interatlântico, Avenida Cidade de Lisboa 131-A, Praia (tel: 2614-008, 2613-829, 2614-425; fax: 2614-712, 2614-752).

Caixa Económica de Cabo Verde SARL, PO Box 199, Avenida Cidade de Lisboa, Praia (tel: 2615-561; fax: 2615-560).

Central bank

Banco de Cabo Verde, Avenida Amilcar Cabral, PO Box 101, Praia (tel: 2615-526; fax: 2611-914; e-mail: drs@bcv.cv).

Stock exchange

Bolsa de Valores de Cabo Verde (BVC) (Cape Verde Stock Exchange), www.bvc.cv

Travel information

Agencia Cabetur, Viagens e Turismo, Rua Guerra Mendes 4, Praia (tel: 2615-551; fax: 2615-553).

Intertur SARL, Av Cidade de Lisboa, 2 Esq Fazenda, Praia (tel: 614-643; fax: 614-644); Rua 5 de Julho Espargos, Sal (tel: 2411-580/590).

Orbitur, Rua Roberto Duarte Silva, CP 161, Praia (tel: 2615-737; fax: 2613-888).

Praiatur, 100 Av Amilcar Cabral, CP 470, Praia (tel: 2615-746/7; fax: 2614-500).

Sal Amilcar Cabral International Airport, ASA-Empresa Nacional de Aeroportos E Seguranca Aerea-EP, PB 50, Ilha do Sal (tel: 2411-135, 2411-394, 2411-468; fax: 2411-570, 2411-323; e-mail: asacv@milton.cvtelecom.cv).

Transportes Aéreos de Cabo Verde (TACV), Av Amilcar Cabral, CP 1, Praia (tel: 2615-813; fax: 2615-905).

Ministries

Ministry of Agriculture, Alimentation and Environment, Praia (tel: 2615-716; fax: 2614-717).

Ministry of Defence, Praia (tel: 2610-372; fax: 2611-286).

Ministry of Economic Co-ordination, Avenue Amilcar Cabral, Praia (tel: 2613-210; fax: 2611-922).

Ministry of Education, Science and Culture, Praia (tel: 2610-507; fax: 2612-764).

Ministry of Foreign Affairs, Praia (tel: 2614-773; fax: 2611-960).

Ministry of Health and Social Promotion, Praia (tel: 2615-721; fax: 2613-991).

Ministry of Justice and Internal Administration, Praia (tel: 2615-687; fax: 2611-396).

Ministry of Sea, Praia (tel: 2616-662; fax: 2611-770).

Ministry of Transport and Infrastructure, Praia (tel: 2615-709; fax: 2614-822).

Prime Minister's Office, Palacio do Governo, Praia (tel: 2610-513; fax: 2612-288).

Other useful addresses

Associação Commercial e Agricola de Sotavento de Cabo Verde, CP 78, Praia (tel: 2612-991).

Associação Comercial Barlavento, CP 62, Mindelo, S Vicente (tel: 2313-281).

Cabo Verde Motors, CP 51-B, Praia (tel: 2612-345; fax: 2612-612).

Ceris, Sociedade Caboverdiana de Cerveja e Refrigerantes (beer and refrigeration), CP 320, Praia (tel: 2615-575; fax: 2614-488).

Direcção-Geral das Alfandegas (customs body), CP 98, Praia (tel: 2613-835, 2613-026).

Direcção-Geral do Comércio (trade body), CP 105, Praia (tel: 2614-159).

Direcção-Geral de Estatistica (Statistics Department of the Ministry of Economic Co-ordination), Avenida Amilcar Cabral, Praia (fax: 2611-922).

Direcção-Geral das Pescas (national fisheries authority), Praia (tel: 2612-976).

Direcção-Geral do Plano (Planning Department of the Ministry of Economic Co-ordination), Avenida Amilcar Cabral, Praia (fax: 2611-922).

Embassy of Portugal, Achada de S António, Praia (tel: 2615-602).

Empresa Nacional de Aeroportos e Segurança Aérea, Aeroporto Amilcar Cabral, Ilha do Sal (tel: 2411-394).

Empresa Nacional de Combustiveis (national combustibles corporation), CP 1, Mindelo, S Vicente (tel: 2313-659).

Garantia (insurance company) (tel: 2615-661, 2615-662; fax: 2313-221, 2313-470).

Promex (Centro de Promoção Turística, do Investimento e das Exportações), CP89c, Praia (tel: 2622-736; fax: 2622-657; e-mail: promex@cvtelecom.cv).

Radio Nacional de Cabo Verde, CP 26, Praia (tel: 2613-729).

Shell Cabo Verde, CP 4, S Vicente (tel: 2314-470; fax: 2314-755).

US Embassy, R Abilio Macedo, Praia (tel: 2615-616).

National news agency: Inforpress (Agência de Notícias de Cabo Verde)

Address: A Largo de Marconi, Achada de Santo António, Cabo Verde CP 40 (tel/fax: 262-2554; email: inforpress@mail.cvtelecom.cv; internet: www.inforpress.cv).

Voz di Povo: www.vozdipovo-online.com

APA: www.apanews.net

Panapress: www.panapress.com

Internet sites

Africa Business Network: http://www.ifc.org

African Development Bank: http://www.afdb.org/en/

Allafrica.com: http://allafrica.com

Mbendi AfroPaedia (information on companies, countries, industries and stock exchanges in Africa): http://mbendi.co.za

Cambodia

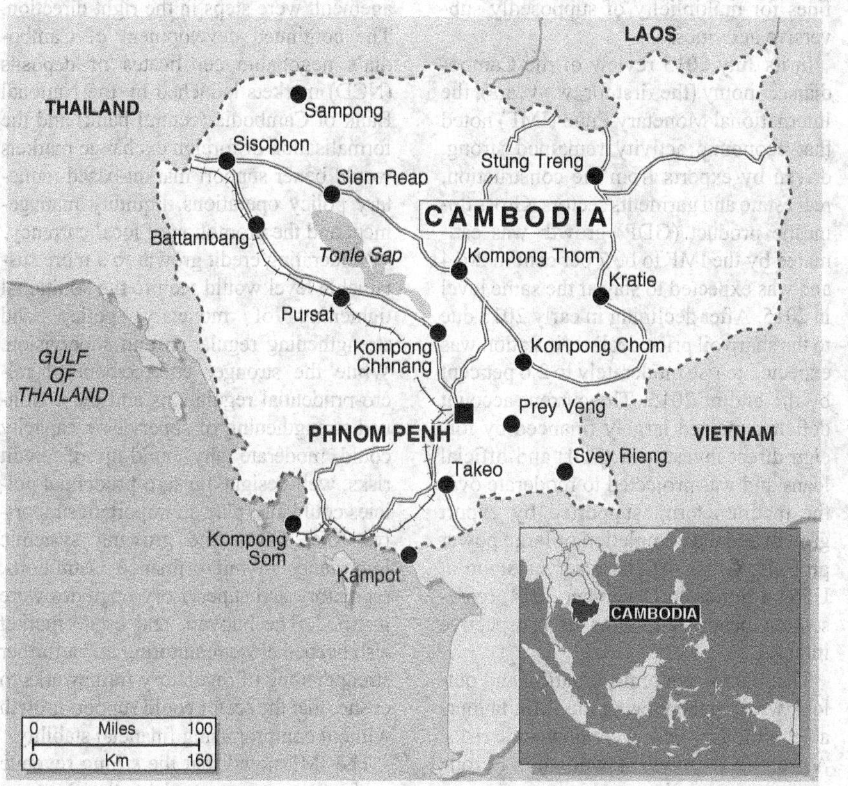

KEY FACTS

Official name: Preah Réachéanachâkr Kâmpuchéa (The Kingdom of Cambodia)

Head of State: King Norodom Sihamoni (crowned 2004)

Head of government: Prime Minister Hun Sen (KPK) (since 1985; re-elected Jul 2013)

Ruling party: Kanakpak Pracheachon Kâmpuchéa (KPK) (Cambodian People's Party) (re-elected 28 Jul 2013)

Area: 181,035 square km

Population: 15.31 million (2014)*

Capital: Phnom Penh

Official language: Khmer

Currency: Riel (R) = 100 sen

Exchange rate: R4,115.00 per US$ (Sep 2015)

GDP per capita: US$1,081 (2014)*

GDP real growth: 6.97% (2014)*

GDP: US$16.55 billion (2014)*

Labour force: 8.80 million (2010)

Inflation: 3.85% (2014)*

Balance of trade: -US$2.96 billion (2013)

* estimated figure

In October 2015 a Cambodian court jailed 11 opposition party members for between seven and twenty years on charges of 'insurrection' after violence broke out during a 2014 anti-government protest. The verdict put at risk the so-called truce between the ruling Kanakpak Pracheachon Kâmpuchéa (KPK) (Cambodian People's Party) and the opposition Cambodia National Rescue Party (CNRP). The 'crime' allegedly committed by the demonstrators had been an attempt to open the locked gates of Phnom Penh's only specifically designated protest area, which had become known as 'Freedom Park'.

Hun Sen – thirty years on

The park had been 'temporarily' closed as protests against the ruling CPP became more commonplace following the disputed 2013 election in which veteran politician Hun Sen once again emerged as prime minister. The election result meant that Hun Sen was celebrating his 30 years as Cambodia's prime minister. During that time he has constantly been accused of corruption and human rights abuses. But Hun Sen's political formation took place in the days of the Khmer Rouge; he is no political softy. The non-governmental organisation Human Rights Watch (HRW) marked the anniversary by accusing Hun Sen of a long list of more serious offences. This itemised extra-judicial killings, torture, arbitrary arrests, summary trials, censorship, bans on assembly and association and maintaining an espionage apparatus, enabling him to keep a tight grip on the Cambodian population.

Since first taking up the job at age 33, becoming the world's youngest premier in the process, Hun Sen has consolidated power with violence and intimidation of opponents that continues to draw criticism. But he could also take some credit for bringing modest economic growth and stability in a country devastated by the communist Khmer Rouge's regime in the 1970s, a movement Hun Sen abandoned as they left some 1.7 million people dead from starvation, disease and executions.

Party changes

Following their arrest the CNRP activists had been granted bail as part of a peace agreement between the two parties that ended the CNRP's parliamentary boycott. Reuters reported that Cambodia's political commentators had been doubtful about how permanent the so-called 'culture of dialogue' would turn out to be. There has been a long, troubled history in the relations, such as they were, between the party leaderships. The newly formed CNRP, a grouping based on a former opposition party, surprised the CPP in the 2013 election by drawing support from the urban middle classes, disaffected workers and farmers angered by the compulsory purchase or appropriation of land. Cambodia's next elections are in 2018, when it is assumed that Hun Sen would be seeking to extend his lengthy hold on power.

The economy

For most of Cambodia's twentieth and twenty-first century history, human rights have taken something of a back seat. Political in-fighting and plotting was far more important. Thus in the first months of 2015, it came as no surprise to Cambodia's tentative trade unions that their power – such as they were – would be curtailed even further. Draft legislation meant that a union could only be established in a workplace if a minimum of at least 20 per cent of the workforce had signed up as members. The draft law would also grant the government the right to punish or wind up unions that had co-operated with any groups thought to have committed what was described as 'economic sabotage' or engaged in activities that might be considered 'damaging' to Cambodia's interests. The catch-all law also stipulated disproportionately large fines for multiplicity of supposedly subversive activities.

In its July 2015 review of the Cambodian economy (the first for two years), the International Monetary Fund (IMF) noted that economic activity remained strong, driven by exports from the construction, real estate and garments sectors. Gross domestic product (GDP) growth was estimated by the IMF to be 7 per cent in 2014 and was expected to stay at the same level in 2015. After declining in early 2015 due to the sharp oil price decline, inflation was expected to rise moderately to 2.6 per cent by the end of 2015. The current account deficit remained largely financed by foreign direct investment (FDI) and official loans and was projected to moderate over the medium term, supported by export growth and the completion of large power projects. Gross official reserves stood at US$4.4 billion in December 2014, representing nearly 4 months of prospective imports.

The macro-economic situation and outlook were, in the view of the IMF, favourable, although there were downside risks. A protracted growth slowdown in Europe or a stronger dollar would constrain garment exports. Weaker-than-expected growth in China would have an effect on the FDI, banking and tourism sectors. On the domestic front, rapid credit growth, particularly to the buoyant real estate and construction sector, had intensified financial stability risks. Any erosion of competitiveness could, said the IMF, adversely affect exports and investment.

Cambodia's expansion of reserve requirements to cover foreign borrowing and the enhanced focus on liquidity risk management, were steps in the right direction. The continued development of Cambodia's negotiable certificates of deposits (NCD) markets launched by the National Bank of Cambodia (central bank) and the formalisation of foreign exchange markets would better support market-based monetary policy operations, liquidity management and the promotion of local currency.

Moderating credit growth to a more sustainable level would require the additional tightening of monetary policy and strengthening regulation and supervision. While the stronger enforcement of micro-prudential regulations and the continued strengthening of supervision capacity could moderate any build-up of credit risks, well-designed macro-prudential policies could also play an important supportive role. Given the growing systemic importance of micro-finance institutions, regulatory and supervisory upgrades were justified. The buoyant real estate market also needed close monitoring and a further strengthening of regulatory frameworks to ensure that the sector could support growth without compromising financial stability.

The IMF noted that the strong revenue performance, supported by the Revenue Mobilisation Strategy (RMS) and solid growth, had eased immediate fiscal pressures and improved fiscal buffers by replenishing government deposits. The fiscal deficit narrowed (including grants) to 1.3 per cent of GDP in 2014, primarily driven by stronger revenues. The IMF stressed that further wage increases should be contingent on projected fiscal performance (such as meeting revenue targets and maintaining an adequate fiscal buffer). Continued focus on upgrading the quality of public services by improved civil service reform and by linking the budget to policy measures through the Public Financial Management reform programmes was needed to better support the momentum of fiscal consolidation over the medium term, reported the IMF. Although debt remained sustainable with a low risk of distress, a closer monitoring of fiscal risks from contingent liabilities and the further strengthening of capacity to analyse these risks would help safeguard the fiscal space.

KEY INDICATORS — Cambodia

	Unit	2011	2012	2013	2014	**2015
Population	m	*15.10	*15.25	*15.09	*15.31	*15.54
Gross domestic product (GDP)	US$bn	12.90	14.12	15.36	*16.55	*17.81
GDP per capita	US$	852	926	*1,018	*1,081	*1,146
GDP real growth	%	6.1	7.3	7.4	*7.0	*7.2
Inflation	%	5.5	2.9	3.0	*3.9	*-0.3
Exports (fob) (goods)	US$m	5,034.6	6,016.0	6,530.2	–	–
Imports (fob) (goods)	US$m	6,937.3	7,965.0	9,488.6	–	–
Balance of trade	US$m	-1,902.7	-1,949.0	-2,958.4	–	–
Current account	US$m	-1,040.0	-1,233.0	-1,880.0	*-1,987.0	*-1,786.0
Total reserves minus gold	US$m	3,430.1	4,267.0	4,516.3	5,626.0	–
Foreign exchange	US$m	3,320.6	4,162.0	4,411.0	–	–
Exchange rate	per US$	4,040.33	4,007.00	3,971.00	4,069.95	–

* estimated figure ** forecast figure

In summary, the IMF considered that the continued regional transformation offered a unique opportunity for Cambodia to diversity its production base and move up the value chain. Improving competitiveness and human capital would make growth more sustainable and inclusive. To take better advantage of regional opportunities and Cambodia's own demographic dividend, the continued improvement in skills and vocational training, energy and logistics and of the business climate, were critical.

For its part, the Asian Development Bank (ADB) took the view that the solid growth seen in 2014 – estimated at 7.0 per cent – had slightly under-performed the 7.3 per cent average attained in the previous three years. According to the ADB, industry and services were the drivers as agriculture lagged. Prolonged expansion had lifted Cambodia's gross national income per capita toward the US$1,045 threshold for entry into lower-middle-income status.

The knock-on effects of political tensions and, in the garment industry, labour unrest, spilled from 2013 into 2014 to temporarily dampen investment and disrupt garment manufacturing and tourism. These headwinds eased as the year progressed. Exports of garments and footwear, based on customs data, reached US$6.0 billion in 2014, rising by 10.7 per cent but decelerating from the previous year. Shipments to the European Union (EU) increased by 22 per cent to US$2.4 billion, but those to the US fell by 5.4 per cent to US$2.0 billion. Construction continued to expand, funded by inflows of FDI and a 34.3 per cent rise in bank credit for the sector. Industry as a whole grew by an estimated 9.8 per cent.

Growth in wholesale and retail trading, tourism and real estate contributed to an estimated 7.9 per cent expansion in services. Tourist arrivals increased by 7.0 per cent to 4.5 million, although this was slower than in 2013 because of the political tensions early in the year and a decline in tourism to neighbouring Thailand and, consequently, side trips to Cambodia.

Flooding and drought hurt agriculture, curbing its growth to an estimated 1.8 per cent. Preliminary estimates showed rice production falling by 2 per cent to 9.2 million tons. Output of maize and soybeans also declined, but cassava production jumped by 41 per cent, mainly to meet rising demand from the People's Republic of China.

The political and labour uncertainties also appeared to dent foreign investor sentiment, opined the ADB, causing net FDI inflows to fall by 9.9 per cent to US$1.6 billion in 2014. Inflation accelerated through the first half of 2014, mainly on higher meat prices, before easing in the second half of the year. Lower global oil prices brought inflation down to 1.1 per cent year on year in December. For 2014 as a whole, inflation averaged 3.9 per cent. Fiscal estimates suggested an improvement in 2014. Robust domestic demand and stronger tax collection lifted revenue to an estimated 15.7 per cent of GDP, while expenditure as a ratio to GDP declined slightly to 19.8 per cent, narrowing the fiscal deficit excluding grants to an estimated 4.1 per cent of GDP. Foreign loans and grants funded the fiscal deficit. The government replenished its deposits in the banking system to the equivalent of 7.0 per cent of GDP, approaching the 7.8 per cent maintained in 2008, before the global financial crisis.

According to the ADB, credit to the private sector grew by a rapid 31.3 per cent and M2 money supply, excluding foreign currency outside the banking system, by 29.9 per cent. The Cambodian riel depreciated by a slight 0.3 per cent against the US dollar over the year. Dollarisation remained high, with foreign currency deposits accounting for more than 80 per cent of liquidity. External accounts strengthened in 2014. Merchandise exports – mainly garments, footwear and milled rice – rose by an estimated 13.4 per cent to US$7.4 billion. Merchandise imports rose by 10.1 per cent to US$10.7 billion. The current account deficit excluding official transfers shrank to an estimated 12.5 per cent of GDP. This gap was fully financed by FDI and official loans and grants. Gross international reserves rose to US$4.4 billion, cover for 4.2 months of imports of goods and services.

The ADB considered that the outlook was for economic growth to pick up in the light of an anticipated stronger performance in trade partners – the US and Thailand and, to a lesser extent, the EU – coupled with a calmer domestic political environment and lower fuel costs. GDP was projected to increase by 7.3 per cent in 2015 and 7.5 per cent in 2016. Over the medium term, growth would be stimulated by gradual diversification into light manufacturing and further integration into regional and global supply chains.

Garments and footwear were expected to benefit in 2015 from an improved demand in major markets. Industry as a whole was seen growing by 9.7 per cent as services growth accelerated slightly to 8.1 per cent. Wholesale and retail trade would gain from rising incomes. The Fiscal estimates suggested an improvement in 2014. Robust domestic demand and stronger tax collection lifted revenue to an estimated 15.7 per cent of GDP, while expenditure as a ratio to GDP declined slightly to 19.8 per cent, narrowing the fiscal deficit – excluding grants – to an estimated 4.1 per cent of GDP. Foreign loans and grants funded the fiscal deficit. The government replenished its deposits in the banking system to the equivalent of 7.0 per cent of GDP, approaching the 7.8 per cent maintained in 2008, before the global financial crisis.

Credit to the private sector grew by a rapid 31.3 per cent and M2 money supply, excluding foreign currency outside the banking system, by 29.9 per cent. The Cambodian riel depreciated by a slight 0.3 per cent against the US dollar over the year. Dollarisation remained high, with foreign currency deposits accounting for more than 80 per cent of liquidity.

External accounts strengthened in 2014. Merchandise exports – mainly garments, footwear and milled rice – rose by an estimated 13.4 per cent to US$7.4 billion. Merchandise imports rose by 10.1 per cent to US$10.7 billion. The current account deficit excluding official transfers shrank to an estimated 12.5 per cent of GDP. This gap was fully financed by FDI and official loans and grants. Gross international reserves rose to US$4.4 billion, cover for 4.2 months of imports of goods and services.

The ADB considered that the outlook was for economic growth to pick up in the light of an anticipated stronger performance from trade partners – the US and Thailand and, to a lesser extent, the European Union – coupled with a calmer domestic political environment and lower fuel costs. GDP was projected to increase by 7.3 per cent in 2015 and 7.5 per cent in 2016. Over the medium term, growth would be stimulated by gradual diversification into light manufacturing and further integration into regional and global supply chains.

Garments and footwear would benefit in 2015 from improved demand in major markets. Industry as a whole was seen growing by 9.7 per cent as services growth accelerated slightly to 8.1 per cent. Wholesale and retail trade were expected to gain from rising incomes. The improved political environment in both Cambodia and Thailand should pave the way for tourism to pick up.

Real estate activity was supported by FDI inflows and moderately accommodative fiscal and monetary conditions. Agriculture was expected to grow by 2.5 per cent in 2015, assuming better weather conditions than in 2014. Inflation was seen edging up to 3.0 per cent by the end of 2015, but the year's average rate was expected to be a low 1.6 per cent. The 2015 budget targeted a 10.1 per cent increase in government spending and a budget deficit of 4.8 per cent of GDP excluding grants. The target for domestic revenue was 12.1 per cent higher than for 2014.

Risk assessment

Economy	Good
Politics	Fair
Regional stability	Fair

COUNTRY PROFILE

1863 Cambodia was made a French Protectorate.
1941 Prince Norodom Sihanouk became King. Cambodia was occupied by the Japanese during the Second World War.
1945 Japanese occupation ended.
1946 France re-imposed its protectorate. A new constitution permitted Cambodians to form political parties. Communist guerrillas began an insurgency against French rule.
1953 Cambodia became independent with King Sihanouk as head of state.
1955 Sihanouk abdicated to pursue a political career as prime minister. His father, Norodom Suramarit, became King.
1960 King Suramarit died and Sihanouk became head of state.
1965 Sihanouk cut off relations with the US and gave support to North Vietnamese guerrillas fighting the US-backed regime in South Vietnam.
1969 The US began bombing Cambodia.
1970 Sihanouk was overthrown in a US-backed coup. General Lon Nol became president, proclaimed the Khmer Republic and began fighting the North Vietnamese in Cambodia. Sihanouk formed a guerrilla movement, known as the Khmer Rouge, while in exile in China.
1970–75 Civil war and intensive American bombing caused widespread destruction.
1975 Lon Nol was overthrown by the Khmer Rouge, led by Pol Pot. Sihanouk briefly served as head of state.
1975–79 Under the Khmer Rouge regime, around 1.7 million people were killed and towns and industry destroyed. The cities were emptied and people were forced into the countryside to become agricultural workers.
1976 Sihanouk was replaced by Khieu Samphan as head of state and Pol Pot as prime minister.
1979 The Khmer Rouge was ejected by a Vietnamese invasion and the regime's policies were reversed.
1981 The pro-Vietnamese Kampuchean People's Revolutionary Party (KPRP) won the elections to the National Assembly, but the international community, led by the US, refused to recognise the new government. Instead, Cambodia was represented in the UN by the Khmer Rouge.
1985 Hun Sen became prime minister.
1989 Vietnam claimed to have withdrawn its remaining troops from the country. Hun Sen abandoned his socialist programme in an effort to appease the US and gain international recognition.
1991 The signing of a peace agreement brought to an end 13 years of civil war. A UN transitional authority was established to share power between the country's various factions. Sihanouk returned and became head of state.
1993 The UN organised elections. The Cambodian National Unity Party (Khmer Rouge) guerrilla group boycotted the poll. The two main parties, United National Front for an Independent, Neutral, Peaceful and Co-operative Cambodia (Funcinpec) and Kanakpak Pracheachon Kâmpuchéa (KPK) (Cambodian People's Party), agreed on a joint government under which they would share power. A constitutional monarchy was established and, in May, the country was renamed the Kingdom of Cambodia. The government-in-exile lost its seat in the UN.
1994 Thousands of Khmer Rouge fighters surrendered after the government called an amnesty.
1997 Second Prime Minister Hun Sen (KPK) seized power, removing First Prime Minister Prince Norodom Ranariddh (Funcinpec) from office, in a move condemned by the international community.
1998 The Khmer Rouge founder, Pol Pot, died. The KPK won the elections, but the opposition parties objected saying the election was fraudulent. A coalition government was formed with Funcinpec. Hun Sen became prime minister and Ranariddh became president of the National Assembly.
1999 Two Khmer Rouge leaders were arrested and charged with genocide.
2001 Parliament approved a law to create a special tribunal to bring genocide charges against Khmer Rouge leaders.
2002 The KPK scored an overwhelming victory in the country's first multi-party local elections, giving it control of over 98 per cent of the country's communes.
2003 Anti-Thai riots were set off by Thai claims that Angkor Wat belonged to Thailand and not to Cambodia. The KPK was re-elected in parliamentary elections, but failed to secure the two-thirds majority required under the constitution to govern alone.
2004 Two main political parties, KPK and Funcinpec, agreed to form a coalition government with Hun Sen remaining as prime minister, ending a government crisis that had crippled the kingdom for almost a year. Cambodia became a member of the WTO. Sihanouk went into self-imposed exile, first in Pyongyang, North Korea, and later to Beijing. He abdicated on 7 October. The Council of the Throne chose Prince Norodom Sihamoni as the new King.
2005 The UN agreed to the funding of a tribunal to try the leaders of the Khmer Rouge for genocide. Cambodia concluded a border agreement with Vietnam. The opposition leader, Sam Rainsy, was convicted *in absentia* for defaming prime minister Hun Sen.
2006 In the first senate elections, the ruling KPK won a majority. Sam Rainsy was given a royal pardon and returned from exile. The royalist political party, Funcinpec, dismissed Prince Norodom Ranariddh as leader.
2007 Prince Ranariddh was sentenced *in absentia* to 18 months in prison, for selling the headquarters of Funcinpec, for an alleged US$3.6 million. The most senior surviving member of the Khmer Rouge, Nuon Chea (Brother Number Two) was arrested and charged with crimes against humanity. The Khmer Rouge genocide tribunal began its first public hearings.
2008 The ruling KPK won a landslide victory and became the sole party in power. Hun Sen was re-elected prime minister unanimously (the opposition had boycotted the session).
2009 Opposition parties Pak Sam Rainsy (Sam Rainsy Party) (SRP) and Human Rights Party (HRP) created an alliance (Democratic Movement for Change) and agreed not to field candidates in competition with one another. Former Khmer Rouge leader, Kaing Guek Eav (known as Duch), was tried for murder and the torture of at least 15,000 inmates while in command of the notorious S-21 prison. Twenty ethnic Uighur asylum seekers were repatriated to China, just days before deals worth some US$1.2 billion were signed with the Chinese government. A new national carrier Cambodia Angkor Air (CAA) was launched with international flights to Vietnam.
2010 Kaing Guek Eav was found guilty and sentenced to 35 years in prison (reduced to 16 years, due to time served). He was the first Khmer Rouge official to be convicted of the 1975–79 genocide. A major stretch of the Pan-Asean railway project between Phnom Penh and Touk

Meas near the Vietnam border was opened for freight transport. Further construction should connect Phnom Penh with the port city of Sihanoukville and the borders of Thailand and Vietnam by 2013. US$141.6 million in funding was provided by the central government, the ADB, the Opec Fund for International Development and the Australian and Malaysian governments. Celebrants of the Water Festival, crossing the overcrowded Diamond Island Bridge in Phnom Penh, suddenly stampeded which resulted in the deaths of 351 people and injury of more than 700.

2011 A decision by the four-country Mekong River Commission to implement plans to build the controversial Mekong Xayaburi dam in Laos was due to be taken in April, but following ecologically and socially adverse reports the decision was postponed. The Mekong River is a food source for millions of people along its length; the dam would reduce food production in favour of electricity generation. Construction of a new bridge across the Tonle Bassac River, close to Phnom Penh began in July. Funded by China, the bridge will connect national highways one and two. The World Bank halted lending in August after villages were destroyed and thousands forcibly evicted from an area in the centre of Phnom Penh which had been given over to a property developer to build luxury flats. Cambodia has become a major recipient of investment from China and may not be too concerned by the suspension of loans from the World Bank. In November, three of the last remaining leaders of the Khmer Rouge were put on trial for genocide, war crimes and crimes against humanity. They are blamed for the deaths of up to 2.2 million people killed between 1975–79.

2012 On 26 April, Chut Wutty, a prominent environmentalist was shot dead by military police while attempting to document illegal logging and land seizures. The government suspended the leasing of land for development by private companies in May, in an attempt to curb illegal logging. In June the Norodom Ranariddh Party (NRP) and Funcinpec failed to agree to a merger as proposed by Prince Norodom Ranariddh. On 10 August Prince Norodom Ranariddh resigned from his role in politics and leadership of the NRP, which on 13 August changed its name to the Nationalist Party (NP). On 16 October, former-King Norodom Sihanouk died.

2013 Opposition leader Sam Rainsy returned to Cambodia on 19 July, having been granted a royal pardon on 12 July (he had been tried and sentenced *in absentia* in 2010 on what he said were trumped up politically motivated charges). However, he was not permitted to stand in the 28 July election. Initial results showed the ruling KPK ahead with 68 seats and the opposition CNRP with 55. The opposition Cambodia National Rescue Party (CNRP) said it could not accept the results of the election since there were a number of irregularities in the voting. On 12 August the National Election Committee announced the results, confirming KPK had won a majority of the votes – 3.2 millon votes to the opposition's 2.9 million votes. However, the number of seats won by each party has yet to be confirmed. The number of seats was announced on 8 September as 68 for the KPK and 55 for the CNRP. On 23 September parliament approved a new five-year term as prime minister for Hun Sen; he was sworn in on 24 September. The opposition CNRP under Sam Rainsy accused the ruling CPP of widespread election fraud.

2014 In July the principal opposition group, Mr Rainsy's CNRP, struck a deal with the CPP. The bare bones of the proposed agreement were that the CNRP would end their boycott of the parliament in exchange for an important bit of electoral reform. Seven deputies who had been jailed following the protests and a CNRP supporter were all released.

2015 Chea Sim, president of the ruling Cambodian People's Party (CPP), died on 8 June. He was considered the second-most-powerful figure in government. His state funeral, however, drew no more than a few thousand mourners, despite the fact that Prime Minister Hun Sen declared a national holiday.

Political structure

July 2013

Constitution

The 1993 Constitution provides for a pluralistic, liberal democratic political system and for a limited monarchy.

To govern alone, a political party is required to have a two-thirds majority.

Independence date

9 November 1953

Form of state

Multiparty liberal democracy under a constitutional monarchy established in 1993.

The executive

Executive power is vested in the Council of Ministers led by the prime minister. The King appoints the prime minister from the representatives of the largest party in parliament on the recommendation of the president of the National Assembly.

National legislature

The bicameral parliament consists of the Radhsphea ney Preah Recheanachakr Kampuchea (National Assembly of Cambodia) with 123 members, elected by proportional representation for five-year terms, and the Sénat (Senate).

In 2006 the first elections for the Senate took place, whereby National Assembly members and councillors of subordinate assemblies voted for 54 members to represent their constituents and serve as Senators for six-year terms. The Senate consists of 61 seats, of that 57 are indirectly elected by parliamentary councils, while two are appointed by the monarch and two are appointed by the National Assembly. The Senate, led by a 12-person cabinet, advises on all matters determined by law and the constitution.

Legal system

The judiciary is granted independence under the constitution. The Supreme Council of the Magistracy, chaired by the King, has the right to discipline any judge who breaks the law, but judges cannot be dismissed. The King has sole authority to appoint judges on the advice of the Supreme Council of the Magistracy.

Last elections

28 July 2013

Results: 28 July 2013 (National Assembly): Kanakpak Pracheachon Kâmpuchéa (KPK) (Cambodian People's Party) 68 seats (3.2 million votes), Cambodia National Rescue Party (CNRP) 55 (2.9 million votes). Confirmation of the result was delayed until 8 September after the opposition leader, Sam Rainsy, had challenged the result.

Next elections

2018 (National Assembly); 2018 (Senate)

Political parties

Ruling party

Kanakpak Pracheachon Kâmpuchéa (KPK) (Cambodian People's Party) (re-elected 28 Jul 2013)

Main opposition party

Cambodia National Rescue Party (the result of a 2012 merger between the Pak Sam Rainsy (Sam Rainsy Party) (SRP) and the Human Rights Party or (Kanakpak Sethi Manus) (founded in 2007)).

Population

15.25 million (2012)* Approximately 28 per cent of the population live below the poverty line. About 60 per cent of the population is under 20 years of age.

Last census: 3 March 2008: 13,388,910 (provisional)

Population density: 79 inhabitants per square km (2010). Urban population 20 per cent (2010 Unicef).

Annual growth rate: 2.0 per cent, 1990–2010 (Unicef).

Religions

Theravada Buddhism, Christianity (Roman Catholicism).

Education

Primary school lasts between the ages of six and 12.

Secondary education is divided into lower secondary and upper secondary lasting for three years each. All students follow the same curriculum through the six years. Nearly 40 per cent of total expenditure in primary schools is paid through household contributions. Public expenditure on education typically amounts to around 3 per cent of annual gross national income.
Literacy rate: 69 per cent adult rate; 80 per cent youth rate (15–24) (Unesco 2005).
Enrolment rate: 123 per cent and 104 per cent for boys and girls respectively, total primary school enrolment of the relevant age group (including repetition rates) (World Bank).
Pupils per teacher: 44 in primary schools.

Health

In 2009 international research showed that there was an emergence of drug-resistant malaria in western Cambodia. The disease kills millions of people worldwide each year and with so few effective drugs the appearance of this new strain represents a global health catastrophe.
In 2010 the ministry of rural development said it aimed to provide one-third of two million rural households with access to proper sanitation facilities by 2015. The lack of facilities has led to one of the highest rates of under-five mortality rates in Asia. The NGO, International Development Enterprises (IDE) will provide assistance and work with rural communities to educate and provide facilities for sanitation and safe drinking water. Rural households will contribute to the construction of a latrine.

HIV/Aids

In 2009, there were an estimated 63,000 people living with HIV (Unicef 2012).
HIV prevalence: 0.3 per cent aged 15–49 in 2009 (Unicef 2012)
Life expectancy: 63 years, 2010 (Unicef 2012)
Fertility rate/Maternal mortality rate: 2.6 births per woman, 2010 (Unicef 2012); maternal mortality ratio 470 deaths per 100,000 live births (World Bank).
Child (under 5 years) mortality rate (per 1,000): 40 per 1,000 live births (WHO 2012); 47 per cent of children under aged five are malnourished (World Bank).

Welfare

Five Cambodian government ministries and their departments directly or indirectly offer social welfare support for the general population, including people with disabilities. There is provision for pensions of disabled veterans. There are no universal social security benefit entitlements in Cambodia.

Main cities

Phnom Penh (capital, estimated population 1.4 million in 2012), Ta Khmau (205,756), Bat Dâmbâng (196,709), Sisophon (190,349), Siem Réab (189,292), Kâmpóng Saôm (118,699), Preah Sihanouk (110,856).

Languages spoken

French is spoken. English is becoming the most commonly used business language, superseding French.

Official language/s

Khmer

Media

Press freedom, while not guaranteed, is practiced with the support of Prime Minister Hun Sen.

Press

Dailies: In Khmer, *Kaoh Santepheap* (www.kohsantepheapdaily.com.kh), *Reaksmei Kampuchea* and *Rasmei Angkor*. In Chinese, *Jian Hua Daily Cambodic and Con Rhuong Pao*. In English, *Cambodian Daily* (www.cambodiadaily.com).
Weeklies: In Khmer, the pro-communist *Trung Lap* and *Pracheachon* (Communist Party) published twice weekly. In English, *The Cambodian Magazine* (www.cambodianscene.com) and *Phnom Penh Post* (www.phnompenhpost.com) is published every Friday.
Business: In Chinese *The Commercial News* (www.thecommercialnews.com), has various news and economy articles.

Broadcasting

The unregulated ownership of satellite dishes allows full access to domestic and foreign broadcasts.
Radio: The National Radio of Cambodia (NRC) operates three stations, relayed nationwide and NRC International in English, French, Thai, Lao and Vietnamese. There are several other private commercial stations, including Radio 103 FM, Radio 97 FM, Radio 95 FM, Beehive 105 FM (www.sbk.com.kh), Bayon Radio is part of the Bayon TV network.
Television: The National Television of Cambodia (TVK) (www.tvk.gov.kh) is the state broadcaster. Other, private and commercial stations include TV3 (based in Phnom Penh), TV5 (www.ch5cambodia.com), CTN (www.ctncambodia.com), CTV9 (www.tv9.com.kh), Bayon TV (www.bayontv.com.kh) and Apsara TV. All TV stations provide satellite coverage, to which three other foreign channels are available.
National news agency: AKP (Agence Kampuchea Presse)

Economy

Cambodia is, for the most part a rural, developing country, which despite extensive reforms and massive donor support, has an economy that remains weak. Agriculture accounted for 32.7 per cent of GDP in 2014, and is characteristically subsistence farming. The service sector accounted for 41.8 per cent of GDP, concentrated in trading activities, and industrial production was 25.5 per cent of GDP, of which around 15 per cent was manufacturing.
Cambodia has experienced strong economic growth since 2000, averaging 8 per cent over the 2000–10 period, mainly generated by increases in the tourism sector and clothing manufacturing. Cambodia avoided recession following the global economic crisis, however, growth slowed to 0.1 per cent in 2009. Since then strong growth has returned, reaching 7.3 per cent in 2012, which was maintained in 2013 and at 7.0 per cent in 2014. The US dollar has become integrated into the economy and is interchangeable with the domestic currency (riel).
Sustainable development is not possible without greater private sector commitment coupled with social programmes. The government is in the process of improving its trade policy machinery in expectation of improving the prospects of its nascent market economy. Economic growth has been driven by increases in clothing production (around 80 per cent of which is exported to the US), tourism with over two million visitors annually (over one million people visit Angkor Wat, Cambodia's main tourist attraction) and agriculture and construction activity. The infrastructure is weak and cannot provide the base for sustained growth in all sectors.
In 2014, the UN Human Development Index (HDI) ranked Cambodia 136 (out of 187) for national development in health, education and income. Since 2000, Cambodia's progress has grown but has not matched the improvement of most countries in South Asia. In 2014, 46.8 per cent of the population lived in multidimensional poverty, while 18.6 per cent lived on less than the equivalent of US$1.25 per day. As one of the least developed countries in the world, per capita income was US$703 in 2009, which was estimated to have risen to US$1,090.1 in 2014. Cambodia's received remittances rose from US$172 million in 2012, to US$175 million in 2013 and US$304 million in 2014.
Despite the weakness of the economy, the International Monetary Fund (IMF) has advised that further investment should be applied to infrastructure development and high-impact social programmes. The major economic challenge for Cambodia over the medium term will be to encourage private sector growth that can create enough jobs for its young population,

while improving the living standards of the population as a whole.

External trade

Cambodia is one of the world's least developed countries and its export market is dominated by the textile industry.

Cambodia is a member of Asean and is negotiating free trade arrangements with the other regional members.

Imports

Main imports are petroleum products, vehicles and machinery, construction materials, energy, pharmaceutical products, cigarettes, gold, artificial textiles and cotton yarns and textiles.

Main sources: Thailand (28.1 per cent of total in 2014), China (20.6 per cent), Vietnam (16.8 per cent)

Exports

Major exports are clothing and footwear, timber and rubber, precious gems, rice, fish and tobacco.

Main destinations: US (24.1 per cent of total in 2014), UK (8.7 per cent), Germany (8.1 per cent)

Agriculture

Farming

Agriculture accounted for 32.7 per cent of GDP and employed around 50 per cent of the workforce in 2014. Agriculture is hampered by poor soil fertility and irrigation and unclear land-ownership rights.

The principal crop is rice (both hill and lowland types), which is grown on 70 per cent of the cultivated land. Rice output accounts for around 17 per cent of GDP.

Only 16 per cent of rice lands are irrigated and there have been no large-scale projects since the 1960s.

Other crops include rubber (a major export), maize, cassava and fruit and vegetables. The smuggling of rubber to neighbouring countries, to get a better price, is a problem. Cambodia also produces jute and sawn timber products.

Cattle stocks are improving, but fish represents the only animal protein for most people.

Fishing

The Tonle Sap (Great Lake) floods during the monsoon and is the breeding ground for many fish. It is one of the world's most productive inland fisheries; it provides around 75 per cent of the annual inland fish catch and 60 per cent of Cambodia's protein intake.

Industry and manufacturing

The industrial sector accounts for 29 per cent of GDP and employs around 20 per cent of the workforce.

Most of what little industry Cambodia possessed was wrecked during the 1970s under the Khmer Rouge, particularly by the virtual closure of the towns in the drive to force people back to the land.

Development has been hampered by the absence of adequate transport and other infrastructure. The manufacturing sector is beset by shortages of power and raw materials and by poor quality products. A number of state factories have been leased to the private sector since 1990 and joint ventures established in enterprises such as hotels, rattan, mineral water, wood processing, a tannery, plywood, tyres and textiles.

Industrial expansion has been led by the growth in the garment-manufacturing sector, but the level of growth might be affected by the ending of garment quotas by the WTO in 2005. In order to offset this, the government will need to create a more investor-friendly environment.

In June 2009 the US removed Cambodia from its economic black list and opened up opportunities for bilateral trade.

Tourism

With its world renowned historic and Unesco World Heritage Listed sites of Angkor Wat and the Preah Vihear, Cambodia offers culture and ecotourism to visitors. Travel and tourism attracted 15.6 per cent of total capital investment in 2014, focussed mainly on the tourist destination of Sihanoukville on the Gulf of Thailand. The resort has beaches, new hotels, a shopping centre and casino to attract a high volume of international visitors.

The majority of visitors come from Vietnam (over 18 per cent), South Korea (over 10 per cent), and China (over 7 per cent).

Travel and tourism began to contribute a significant share of GDP when it jumped from 9.8 per cent in 1999 to 14.2 per cent in 2000. Since then the number of tourists has risen steadily (466,365 visitors in 2000), so that by 2007 the tourist sector constituted a record 24.6 per cent of GDP (two million visitors). However, since the global economic crisis caused a slowdown in 2009, the share had fallen to 19.7 per cent by 2011, despite overall numbers of visitors reaching 2.5 million in 2010. By 2014 the travel and tourism industry's total contribution to GDP had reached 29.9 per cent, and supplied employment to 26.4 per cent of the workforce (2,221,500 jobs). Visitor exports in 2014 grew to US$3.2 billion along with number of foreign tourist arrivals, which reached 4.5 million.

A project begun in the 1960s to reconstruct the Baphuon monument which was finally completed and re-opened in July 2011. The 11th-Century, intricately-carved three-tier tower, part of the Angkor temple complex, had been on the brink of collapse by the 1950s. A French team of archaeologists dismantled the tower, numbering each of the 300,000 sandstone blocks as they went. Work was interrupted by the civil war and the master plan to re-build the tower was destroyed. With the ending of the civil war in the mid-1990s, work began to solve the puzzle of putting the blocks back together.

Angkor attracts some two million tourists each year.

Environment

The UN designated Tonle Sap (Great Lake) as an ecological hotspot and designated it a Unesco biosphere in 1997.

Between 2000–2005 it is estimated that logging of forests amounted to 140,500 hectares (ha) per year or 1.9 per cent annual deforestation. Primary forest cover has fallen from 766,000ha in 1999 to 322,000ha in 2005. Cambodia has 775 species of wildlife, of with 60 are under threat; it has 862 native tree species with 13 endangered and 10 critically endangered. Illegal logging, within the country and along Cambodia's borders, threatens not only the forests but also the communities that depend on these local resources.

Mining

The mining sector typically contributes under 10 per cent to GDP and employs 1 per cent of the workforce.

There are deposits of iron ore, copper, manganese, gold and bauxite, but exploitation is hindered by the absence of transport facilities. Phosphates are the only economically viable mineral and are mined for use in the local fertiliser industries. Gemstones are also mined.

In 2014 the mining industry was attracting some investor interest as the government was promoting opportunities in the extraction of bauxite, gold, iron and gems.

Hydrocarbons

There are no known oil or natural gas reserves. Cambodia is dependent on imports from Thailand, which were 47,490 bpd in 2013.

Exploration is being undertaken particularly in offshore areas, where reserves of oil and gas are likely to be.

There are indications of small coal reserves.

Energy

Total installed generating capacity was around 949MW in 2013, producing 1.77 billion kilowatt hours (kWh); consumption was 3.55 billion kWh and imports of 2.28 billion kWh came from Vietnam and Thailand.

About 30 per cent of the population have access to electricity, but largely only in Phnom Penh and provincial towns; consumption is growing. Current generation is small-scale and inefficient, mostly from oil-fired power stations with some hydropower. There is no national power

grid and rural consumers as well as industries frequently use costly generators to ensure an uninterrupted supply.
Cambodia's largest ever hydropower plant became operational in January 2015. The Chinese-built 338MW Russey Chrum Krom plant was built in the south-western Koh Kong province. There are other hydro-projects currently planned such as the Lower Sesan 2 hydroelectric dam which was approved by the Cambodian government in November 2012, due to be completed by 2018.
The Asian Development Bank (ADB) has been involved in promoting the Greater Mekong Sub-region (GMS) electricity market to form a regional electricity grid, which incorporates the uneven load demands and different resource bases.

Financial markets

Stock exchange
Cambodian Securities Exchange

Banking and insurance

The banking system is underdeveloped. The economy is highly dollarised, with foreign currency making up 70 per cent of the total money supply. This hinders the central bank's ability to implement an effective monetary policy.
Since 2000, Cambodia has been reforming the banking sector, introducing a minimum capitalisation requirement of US$11 million. This led to the closure of 11 banks by 2002.

Central bank
National Bank of Cambodia

Time

GMT plus seven hours

Geography

Cambodia occupies part of the Indochinese peninsula in south-east Asia. It is bordered by Thailand and Laos to the north, by Vietnam to the east and by the Gulf of Thailand to the south.
Around 60 per cent of Cambodia is rain forest, of which 3 per cent is primary forest with extensive bio-diversity. The Tonle Sap (Great Lake) is the largest freshwater lake in south-east Asia, at 2,700 square km but only about one metre deep for most of the year. During the monsoon the lake grows by another 16,000 square km and its depth increases by nine metres. The lake flows out into the Mekong River. The highlands are located in the north-east and there are numerous islands along the south-west coast.

Hemisphere
Northern

Climate

Generally hot and very humid, with a rainy season from June to October/November. Likely temperatures in Phnom Penh are 22–30 degrees Celsius (C) from November–December and 24–34 degrees C in April.

Entry requirements

Passports
Required by all. Must be valid for six months from departure date.

Visa
Visas are required by all, with a few exceptions; to find a list and download a tourist one-month e-visa, see http://evisa.mfaic.gov.kh. An e-visa can only be used at Pochentong (Phnom Penh) and Siem Reap airports. Tourists can also get a visa on arrival at the Pochentong and Siem Reap airports, as well as the Poi Pet international checkpoint, overland from Thailand. If planning to arrive by boat from Vietnam, or overland at checkpoints other than Poi Pet, a visa must be obtained prior to arrival; the place of entry must be specified.
A business visa should be applied for before departure, contact the closest Cambodian consulate for further details.

Currency advice/regulations
Import and export of local currency is prohibited. Import of foreign currency must be declared on arrival; export of foreign currency can only be up to amount declared.

Health (for visitors)

Mandatory precautions
Vaccination certificates for yellow fever if travelling from an infected area.

Advisable precautions
Vaccinations recommended for diphtheria, tuberculosis, hepatitis A and B, Japanese B encephalitis. Anti-malarial precautions should be taken. There is risk of rabies.

Credit cards

Credit cards are only accepted in large hotels and shops.

Public holidays (national)

Fixed dates
1 Jan (New Year's Day), 7 Jan (Victory Day), 8 Mar (Women's Day), 14–16 Apr (Traditional Cambodia New Year), 1 May (Labour Day), 13–15 May (King's Birthday), 16 May (Royal Ploughing day), 18 Jun (Queen's Birthday), 24 Sep (Constitution Day), 29 Oct (Coronation Day), 31 Oct (last King's Birthday), 9 Nov (Independence Day), 10 Dec (International Human Rights Day).

Variable dates
Birth of Buddha Day (Visaka Buja Day) (May); Royal Ploughing Ceremony (Visakha Bochea Day) (May); three-day spirit festival (Pchum Ben festival) (Sep/Oct); three day Water Festival (Bonn Om Touk) (Nov).
The religious festivals are determined by the Buddhist lunar calendar.
Any public holiday that falls at the weekend is carried over to the next working day.

Working hours

Banking
Mon–Fri: 0800–1500.

Business
Mon–Fri: 0800–1200 and 1400–1700.

Government
Mon–Fri: 0800–1200 and 1400–1700.

Shops
0700–1800.

Telecommunications

Mobile/cell phones
There are 900 and 1800 GSM services available around main towns and cities only.

Social customs/useful tips

Business cards are essential and are usually exchanged during introductions; offering and receiving business cards with both hands is considered particularly polite.
Punctuality is important and visitors should allow plenty of time for travelling. It is acceptable to shake hands with both men and women.
In conversation speak clearly using a moderate pace and complete sentences. Always give time for your host to answer and maintain courtesies.
Even during difficult negotiations remain calm as anger will give a poor impression.
Criticism of the Royal Family and Buddhism should be avoided.
Learning some Cambodian greetings will both surprise and impress your host.
Photography is permitted although it is polite to ask permission before photographing Cambodian people, particularly monks.
Gratuities are welcome in restaurants and hotels.
The minimum drinking age is 18 years.

Security

The government has taken action to reduce crime but visitors are still advised not to walk alone at night in many areas of the city. Most hotels can arrange cars with drivers.
When visiting the temples at Angkor Wat, travel by air to Siem Reap airport, remain within the main temple complex and do not attempt to travel to Banteay Srei or to other outlying temples.

Getting there

Air
National airline: Cambodia Angkor Air (CAA) (only international destination is Vietnam).
Mostly foreign carriers provide international services and usually only from neighbouring countries.

International airport/s: Pochentong International (PNH), 8km from Phnom Penh.
Airport tax: International departures from Pochentong and Siem Reap airports US$25; from all other airports US$20.

Surface

Not all crossings are open to foreign visitors, check with local authorities before travelling. Some crossings will issue visas, but to avoid disappointment organise all visas before arriving at a crossing.
Road: Overland access is via Thailand, Vietnam and Laos.
Rail: The government is rehabilitating the railways to build links to Thailand by the Phnom Penh–Poipet line, and constructing a new line linking Phnom Penh and Ho Chi Minh City. These projects are part of the Asian Development Bank's (ADB) Greater Mekong sub-regional co-operation scheme. The Phnom Penh–Ho Chi Minh City link is part of the Trans-Asia railway aimed at linking Singapore to Kunming in Yunnan province of China.
Water: There are ferry services, via the Mekong River, from Vietnam and Laos. A sea-ferry runs from Thailand.
Main port/s: The Mekong river port of Phnom Penh, the seaport of Sihanoukville.

Getting about

National transport

Air: Domestic flights connect all major cities.
Road: There are 13,500km of roads. Only 12 per cent of national highways are paved, meaning that many communities are cut off during the rainy season.
The Phnom Penh–Ho Chi Minh City (HCMC) Highway refurbishment project is expected to be completed by 2012.
Buses: Some bus or passenger truck services are available.
Rail: There are 612km of track. Rail services operate between Phnom Penh–Aranyaprathet, and Phnom Penh–Kompong Som. There is a critical need to improve infrastructure over the medium-term.
Water: Ferries operate along the Mekong River.

City transport

The most convenient way to travel around the capital is by *cyclo* (tricycle) or *motodops* (motorcycles).
Taxis: There are ranks of cars with taxi signs at the airport and can be hired in all the main cities, but cruising taxis are not the norm.
Buses, trams & metro: Buses link all of Phnom Penh's suburbs.

Car hire

It is advisable to hire a car with driver as local conditions can overwhelm foreign visitors; most hotels can arrange the services of a car and driver.

BUSINESS DIRECTORY

The addresses listed below are a selection only. While World of Information makes every endeavour to check these addresses, we cannot guarantee that changes have not been made, especially to telephone numbers and area codes. We would welcome any corrections.

Telephone area codes

The international direct dialling (IDD) code for Cambodia is +855, followed by area code and subscriber's number.

Battambang	53	Pusat	52
Kampong Som	62	Stung Treng	74
Phnom Penh	23	Siem Riep	63

Useful telephone numbers

Police: 722-353
Fire: 723-555
Ambulance: 723-173
Local directory assistance: 1213

Chambers of Commerce

Phnom Penh Chamber of Commerce, 7B Street 81 corner Street 109, Sangkat Beung Raing, Daun Penh District, Phnom Penh (tel: 212-265; fax: 212-270; e-mail: ppcc@camnet.com.kh).

Banking

Acleda Bank Plc, P O Box 1149, #61, Preah Monivong Blvd., Sangkat Srah Chork, Khan Daun Penh, Phnom Penh (tel: 998-777; fax: 23 998-666).

Cambodia Mekong Bank Public Ltd, 1 Kramuon Sar Street, Khan Daun Penh, Phnom Penh (tel: 217-112; fax: 217-122).

Cambodian Commercial Bank Limited, 26 Monivong Road, Sangkat Phsar Thmei 2, Khan Daun Penh, Phnom Penh (tel: 426-145, 426-639, 213-601, 213-602, 426-638; fax: 426-116).

Cambodian Public Bank Ltd, Villa No. 23, Street 114, Vithei Kramounsar, Phnom Penh (tel: 426-067; fax:426-068).

Canada Bank Ltd, 265-269 Prash Ang Doung Street, Sangkath Wattphnom, Khan Daun Penh, Phnom Penh (tel:-266-046, 725-548).

Crédit Agricole Indosuez, 70 Blvd Norodom, Phnom Penh (tel: 427-233).

First Commercial Bank, 263 Ang Duong St, Phnom Penh (tel: 210-026; fax: 210-029).

Foreign Trade Bank of Cambodia, 24/26 Preah Norodom Boulevard, Phnom Penh (tel: 724-466, 723-866, 722-466, 723-466).

National Bank of Cambodia, PO Box 25, 22-24 Preah Norodom Blvd, Phnom Penh (tel: 428-105, 722-563; fax: 426-117).

Singapore Banking Corporation Ltd, 68 Samdech Pan Street (St. 214), Sangkat Beung Raing, Khan Daun Penh, Phnom Penh (tel: 217-771).

Singapore Commercial Bank Ltd, 316 Preah Monivong Boulevard, Sangkat Chak To Mok, Khan Daun Penh, Phnom Penh (tel: 427-471).

Union Commercial Bank Plc, UCB Bldg, No. 61, 130 Road, Psa Chas Quater, Khan Daun Penh, Phnom Penh (tel: 724-831, fax: 427-997).

Central bank

National Bank of Cambodia, 22-24 Preah Boulevard Norodom, Phnom Penh (tel/fax: 426-117).

Stock exchange

Cambodian Securities Exchange

Travel information

Cambodia Angkor Air (CAA), No 206A, Preah Norodom Blvd. Tonle Bassac, Chamkarmorn Phnom Penh (tel: 6666 786–9, 212 564; fax: 224 164; internet: http://cambodiaangkorair.com)

Canby Publications, PO Box 2349, Phnom Penh 3; House #23A, Street 55, Sangkat Chaktomuk, Khan Duan Penh, Phnom Penh (tel: 16-779-900; fax: 23-216-754; email: cambodia@canbypublications.com; internet: www.canbypublications.com).

Ministry of tourism

Ministry of Tourism, 3 Monivong Bld, Phnom Penh 12258 (tel: 211-593, 222-409; internet: www.mot.gov.kh).

National tourist organisation offices

Tourism of Cambodia, 262 Monivong Blvd, Khan Daun Penh, Phnom Penh (tel: 216-666; fax: 213-331; e-mail: info@tourismcambodia.com; internet: http://www.tourismcambodia.com).

Ministries

Ministry of Agriculture, 200 Norodom Blvd, Phnom Penh (tel: 723-689, 722-127).

Ministry of Commerce, Norodom Blvd, Phnom Penh (tel: 723-263; fax: 426-396).

Ministry of Culture, Monivong Blvd, Red Cross Street, Phnom Penh (tel: 724-769).

Ministry of Defence, Pochentong Blvd, Phnom Penh (tel: 725-697).

Ministry of Education, Youth and Sport, 80 Blvd Norodom, Phnom Penh (tel: 362-338; fax: 426-791).

Ministry of Finance, 60 St 92, Phnom Penh (tel: 426-841).

Ministry of Foreign Affairs and International Co-operation, Sisowath Quay, St 240, Phnom Penh (tel: 426-146, 724-441; fax: 26-144).

Ministry of Health, 153-153 Blvd Kampuchea Krom, Phnom Penh (tel: 725-833, 724-573).

Ministry of Industry, 45 Norodom Bld, St 45, Phnom Penh (tel: 723-477; fax: 427-840).

Ministry of Information, 62 Monivong Bld, Phnom Penh (tel: 723-369, 722-869).

Ministry of the Interior, 275 Norodom Blvd, Phnom Penh (tel: 426-494).

Ministry of Justice, Sothearos Blvd, Phnom Penh (tel: 724-543, 360-329).

Ministry of Planning, 386 Monivong Blvd, Phnom Penh (tel: 725-143, 724-543).

Ministry of Posts and Telecommunications, Street 13, Street 102, Phnom Penh (tel: 723-911, 426-817; fax: 426-786).

Ministry of Public Works and Transport, Norodom Blvd, Mahaksatriyani St, Phnom Penh (tel: 427-862; fax: 427-862).

Ministry of Religious Affairs, Sothearos Blvd, St 240, Phnom Penh (tel: 725-699).

Ministry of Rural Development, Pochentong Blvd, Phnom Penh (tel: 426-814).

Ministry of Social Welfare, 68 Norodom Blvd, Phnom Penh (tel: 725-191, 427-322).

Prime Minister's Office, 22 Street 214, Phnom Penh (tel:426-053 and 426-025).

Other useful addresses

ASEAN Investment Promotion Agency, Cambodian Investment Board, Government Palace, Sisowath Quay, Wat Phnom, Phnom Penh (tel: 50-428; fax: 61-616, 60-606).

ASEAN Secretariat, 70 A J1 Sisingamangaraja, Jakarta 12110, Indonesia (tel: 62(21)726-2991, 724-3372; fax: 724-3504, 739-8234).

Asian Development Bank, Cambodia Resident Mission, 93 Preah Norodom Boulevard, Phnom Penh (tel: 725-805; fax: 725-807).

British Embassy, 27-29 Street 75, Phnom Penh (tel: 427-124; fax: 427-124/5).

Cambodian Development Council (CDC), Phnom Penh.

Cambodian Embassy (USA), 4530 16th Street, NW, Washington DC 20011 (tel: (+1-202)- 726-7742; fax: (+1-202)-726-8381; e-mail: cambodia@embassy.org).

Cambodia Mine Action Centre, 22 Street 122, Phnom Penh (tel: 913-506).

Chemins de Fer du Cambodge, Moha Vithei Pracheathippatay, Phnom Penh (tel: 25-156).

Department of Civil Aviation, 62 Boulevard Norodom, Phnom Penh (tel: 427-141; fax: 26-169).

Global, Business Centre, 378 EO Sivutha Street, Group 1, Sangkat Olympic, Khan Chamcarmon, Phnom Penh (tel: 27-124; fax: 27-125).

Phnom Penh Port Authority (tel: 23-369).

National news agency: AKP (Agence Kampuchea Presse)

Address: 62 Monivong Blvd, Phnom Penh (tel: 430-564; fax: 427-945; email: akp@camnet.com.kh; internet: www.camnet.com.kh).

Internet sites

Asian Development Bank: http://www.adb.org/countries/cambodia/contacts

Cambodia web sites: http://mekong.net/cambodia/links.htm

UN Food and Aid administration: http://www.fao.org/waicent/search/default.asp

Cameroon

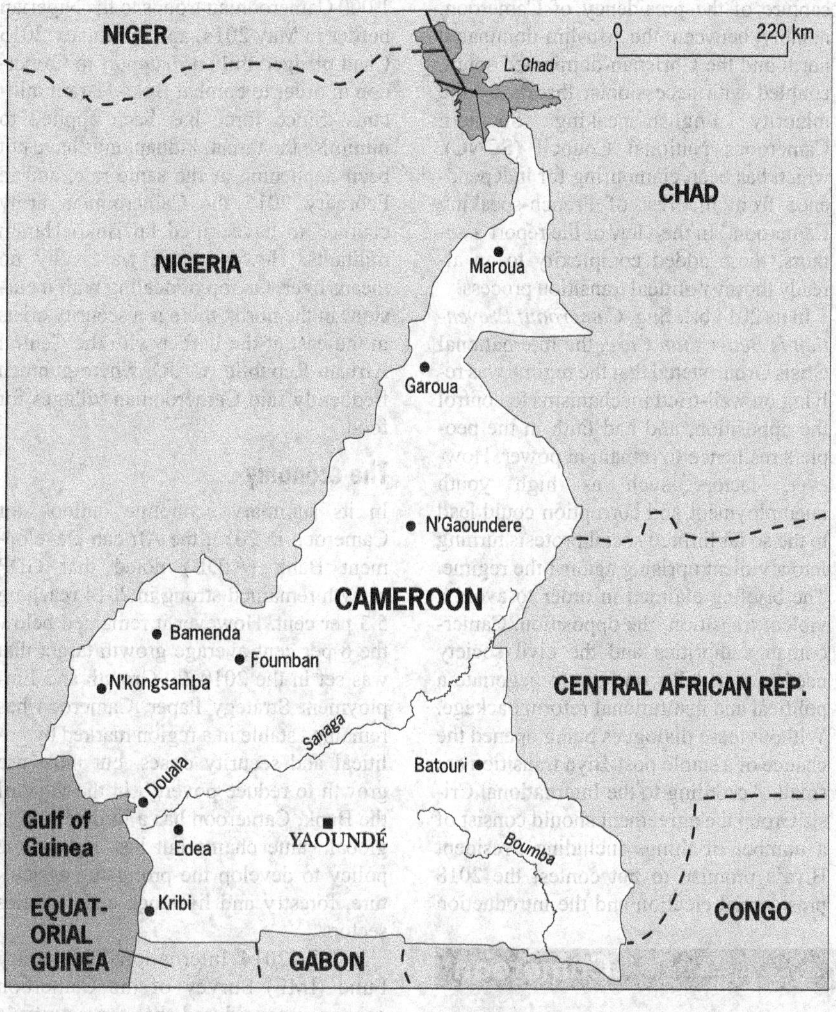

President Paul Biya has held office as Cameroon's president for over 30 years, making him one of Africa's longest serving heads of state. President Biya virtually became president in 1980 when the incumbent, President Ahidjo was thought to be terminally ill, handed over the presidency to Paul Biya who at the time was prime minister. The scare over the president's health turned out to have been a false alarm – however Mr Biya wasn't in favour of returning leadership, resulting in a deadlock between the two former colleagues, this time ending with Mr Ahidjo leaving the country in 1983. Mr Biya set about eliminating every trace of the former president and removing from their posts all the Ahidjo cabinet appointees. Despite Mr Biya's efforts to solidify his position, in 1984 evidence of plans to mount a military *coup* emerged, supposedly the work of Mr Ahidjo. This time, Mr Biya sentenced the former President to death *in absentia* and banished him from Cameroon. Mr Ahidjo finally gave up, ending his life in exile in Sénegal in 1989. In 1984 the country's name was formally changed from the 'United Republic of Cameroon' to the simpler 'Republic of Cameroon', suggesting that the unification was complete.

KEY FACTS

Official name: République du Cameroun (Republic of Cameroon)

Head of State: President Paul Biya (from 1982; re-elected 9 Oct 2011)

Head of government: Prime Minister Philémon Yang (appointed 30 Jun 2009)

Ruling party: Rassemblement Démocratique du Peuple Camerounais (RDPC) (Cameroon People's Democratic Movement) (since 1992; re-elected July 2007 and September 2013)

Area: 475,442 square km

Population: 22.54 million (2014)*

Capital: Yaoundé

Official language: French, English

Currency: CFA franc (CFAf) = 100 centimes (Communauté Financière Africaine (African Financial Community) franc)

Exchange rate: CFAf586.44 per US$ (Sep 2015)

GDP per capita: US$1,405 (2014)*

GDP real growth: 5.14% (2014)*

GDP: US$31.67 billion (2014)*

Labour force: 7.84 million (2010)*

Inflation: 1.85% (2014)*

Oil production: 61,990 bpd (2011)

Balance of trade: -US$2,401.00 million (2014)*

* estimated figure

Unification may have been completed, but the people of Cameroon did not seem to be a great deal happier for it. This was especially the case with the Anglophone part of the population, who had actually voted to join forces with their Francophone neighbours. Corruption has been a persistent feature of the Biya presidency – on the 2014 Transparency International *Corruption Perceptions Index* Cameroon ranked 136 out of the 175 countries surveyed. One US survey ranked President Biya among the 20 worst dictators in the world.

A 2012 report for the Brookings Institution by Messrs Julius Agbor and John Mukum notes that: 'In spite of his various public pronouncements that he would democratise Cameroon's politics, Biya has twice (in 1996 and 2008) manipulated the constitution to allow him to prolong his term in office. Also, although Cameroon officially became a multi-party state in 1992, under Biya's leadership the country has not conducted a presidential election in which the opposition has had a fair chance of defeating the incumbent. While the opposition bears some blame for its ineffectiveness, there is no question that Biya has used the power of incumbency as well as his control of various institutions such as the national media, the Supreme Court and the National Assembly to ensure his success at the polls. Thus, many observers believe that political transition in Cameroon is likely to result only when Biya dies or is removed from office by a military *coup d'état.* Each of these options, unfortunately, has extremely destabilising consequences for Cameroon and the sub-region.' Thus the prospects for a smooth constitutional change in power seem very unlikely. Proper political education and formation is lacking, rivalries are more important than co-operation and corruption is unlikely to simply fade away.

The Brookings report also referred to Cameroon's 'ethno-linguistic and regional tensions', mentioning what it described as 'present latent struggles' for capture of the presidency of Cameroon, notably between the Muslim-dominated north and the Christian-dominated south, coupled with secessionist threats by the minority English-speaking Southern Cameroons National Council (SCNC), which has been clamouring for independence from the rest of French-speaking Cameroon.' In the view of the report's authors, these added complexity to an already thorny political transition process.

In its 2014 briefing, *Cameroon: Prevention Is Better than Cure*, the International Crisis Group stated that the regime was relying on well-tried mechanisms to control the opposition, and had faith in the people's resilience to remain in power. However, factors such as high youth unemployment and corruption could lead to the so far limited social protests turning into a violent uprising against the regime. The briefing claimed in order to avoid a violent transition, the opposition, Cameroonian authorities and the civil society need to start talks on how to negotiate a political and institutional reform package. Without these dialogues being opened the chance of a stable post-Biya transition are small. According to the International Crisis Group the agreement should consist of a number of things including President Biya's promise to not contest the 2018 presidential election and the introduction of age quotas to inject new blood into leadership structures and political parties.

Northern Cameroon has been dealing with the threat from the extremist Islamic organisation Boko Haram since February 2013 when a French family of seven were kidnapped near the Nigerian border. The rising threat of incursions and kidnappings lead to the deployment of 1,000 Cameroonian troops to the Nigerian border in May 2014, and in January 2015 Chad pledged military support to Cameroon in order to combat Boko Haram militants. Since force has been applied to minimise the threat, kidnappings have not been happening at the same rate, and in February 2015 the Cameroonian army claimed to have killed 86 Boko Haram militants. However, the war is by no means over. On top of dealing with incursions in the north, there is a security crisis in the east at the border with the Central African Republic (CAR), where gunmen frequently raid Cameroonian villages for food.

The economy

In its summary economic outlook for Cameroon in 2015, the African Development Bank (AfDB) noted that GDP growth remained strong in 2014 reaching 5.3 per cent. However it remained below the 6 per cent average growth target that was set in the 2010–20 Growth and Employment Strategy Paper. Cameroon has remained stable in a region marked by political and security crises, but must use growth to reduce poverty. In the view of the Bank, Cameroon has a limited role in global value chains but has a proactive policy to develop the promising agriculture, forestry and livestock and fisheries sectors.

A July 2014 International Monetary Fund (IMF) Survey of the Cameroon economy considered that the country's steady economic growth was driven by an ambitious public investment programme which was expected to expand both electricity supply and transport infrastructure. But, the IMF had also said in its regular review of the Central African nation's economy, that recurrent budget deficits left a fragile fiscal situation, and oil revenue could dip due to rising production costs.

The IMF predicted 2015 growth at 5 per cent, and to remain unchanged in 2016. Agriculture, which provides a livelihood to most of the poor, has not expanded enough to reduce poverty and inequality, the report said. Poverty stands close to 40 per cent of the population, and social

KEY INDICATORS — Cameroon

	Unit	2011	2012	2013	2014	**2015
Population	m	*20.93	*21.46	*21.99	*22.54	*23.11
Gross domestic product (GDP)	US$bn	25.80	*25.34	29.58	*31.67	*28.83
GDP per capita	US$	1,230	*1,181	*1,345	*1,405	*1,247
GDP real growth	%	4.1	*4.6	5.6	*5.1	*5.0
Inflation	%	2.9	2.4	2.0	*1.9	*2.0
Exports (fob) (goods)	US$m	5,219.5	5,752.7	6,079.8	–	–
Imports (fob) (goods)	US$m	6,709.5	6,031.2	6,174.4	–	–
Balance of trade	US$m	-1,490.1	-278.5	-94.6	–	–
Current account	US$m	-1,053.0	*-1,017.0	-1,119.0	*-1,333.0	*-1,398.0
Total reserves minus gold	US$m	–	3,381.0	–	3,168.2	–
Exchange rate	per US$	466.82	505.65	480.26	542.10	–

* estimated figure ** forecast figure

indicators such as life expectancy, infant mortality, and youth literacy, are all weak. Annual inflation, at 2.2 per cent in 2014, was also steady at relatively low levels thanks to stable food prices supported by an ample supply of foodstuffs. But retail fuel prices stayed frozen at their 2009 levels, reflecting substantial fuel subsidies that crowded out more 'pro-poor' spending in the budget, where public spending on health and education is low.

Among the main recommendations in the IMF report were policies to:

- promote higher and more inclusive growth through a shift toward social spending, a friendlier business climate, and deeper regional integration;
- reprioritise public spending by gradually reducing fuel subsidies while providing targeted compensation to the most vulnerable; and
- improve non-oil revenue by broadening the tax base and streamlining tax exemptions.

Cameroon's fiscal challenge, according to the IMF report, is to reorganise its tax base and develop alternative forms of taxation. Positive impacts expected from an economic partnership agreement signed with the European Union (EU) include a widening of the tax base, as incomes rise. The long-term effect would ultimately depend on the authorities' capacity to offset a reduction in customs revenue with receipts from other sources, such as the value-added tax, excise taxes, and reductions in tax exemptions.

In an accompanying report on Cameroon's economy, the IMF also noted that the country's infrastructure indicators trail those of regional peers. In spite of a slight improvement in the overall quality of infrastructure in 2013, indicators were low by sub-Saharan African standards, especially for roads, air transportation, and electricity. Closing the infrastructure gap is essential to achieve Cameroon's development objective of attaining emerging market status by 2035, the report said.

The report also noted that Cameroon's government had launched a ten-year development plan that gave priority to infrastructure development. A massive public investment programme covered various large infrastructure projects, including roads, a deep-sea port in Kribi, a bridge, and thermal and hydroelectric power plants. These major infrastructure projects will be beneficial to regional development and planning. However, they will lead to transfers in the ownership of productive capital in rural areas and place great pressure on arable land.

In the view of the IMF, Cameroon's authorities could make judicious (if optimistic) use of public-private partnerships (PPPs) to boost private sector participation in large infrastructure projects, but risks need to be properly addressed. Such partnerships would feature in transportation through roads, railways, tramways, and a deep-sea port; in energy through wind farms and hydroelectric plants; and also in urban development and the agro-food industry.

PPPs could offer efficiency gains from private sector management and innovation, while transferring some responsibilities and risks to the private sector, the report observed. While this option can be attractive when governments' borrowing constraints are tight, the report noted the associated risk of weak institutional capacity and contingent liabilities for the government.

However, for public-PPPs to offer better value for money than traditional public procurement, efficiency gains needed to offset PPPs' typically higher borrowing and transaction costs. Moreover, public-private partnerships usually involve long-term contracts with the private sector, reducing flexibility for governments when public policy priorities change.

Cameroon is sub-Saharan Africa's tenth-largest crude oil producer and, although oil is a relatively small share of overall economic activity, it plays an important role in exports and government revenues. Cameroon is also a mature oil producer, where the oil sector is more than 65 years old and production peaked in 1987. However, the drop in oil prices in the second half of 2014 has weakened the trading balance, which has weighed heavily on the fiscal accounts.

Yet the authorities believe there are significant prospects for discovering new oil fields both off- and on-shore. In addition, technological progress in drilling and extraction techniques has made it possible for previously unprofitable discoveries to become commercially viable.

Risk assessment

Politics	Poor
Economy	Fair
Regional stability	Fair

Muslims in Cameroon

% of population	20
Sunni (% of Muslims)	100
Shi'a (% of Muslims)	0

COUNTRY PROFILE

1470s Portuguese mariners arrived and gave Cameroon its name. Having found what they thought to be shrimps (*camaroes*) in the main river, they named it *Rio dos Camaroes*.

1884 Germany established the protectorate of Kamerun.

1916 The German administration was ousted by Allied forces in the First World War.

1919 A post-war League of Nations mandate gave some four-fifths of the territory to France, and the remainder, bordering Nigeria, to Britain.

1960 French East Cameroon gained its independence.

1961 British West Cameroon gained its independence.

1972 A unified state was formed, with the Union Nationale Camerounaise (UNC) (Cameroonian National Union) dominating both the executive and legislative branches.

1982 Prime Minister Paul Biya became president after the resignation of President Ahidjo.

1985 Biya renamed the ruling party the Rassemblement Démocratique du Peuple Camerounais (RDPC) (Cameroon People's Democratic Rally), and introduced a number of political reforms which were largely viewed as cosmetic.

1990 A multi-party political system was legalised. Although this change marked the gradual opening of the Cameroonian political system, subsequent elections were marred by irregularities and accusations of electoral fraud.

1996 In response to pressure from the Anglophone regional groups the constitution was amended to include a federal system with the addition of a senate in the National Assembly. Presidential terms in office will in future last seven years.

1997 President Paul Biya was re-elected. The elections were boycotted by the three main opposition parties after their complaints about the handling of voter registration were ignored.

1999 English-speaking secessionists, led by the Southern Cameroon National Council (SCNC), announced a breakaway Federal Republic of Southern Cameroon.

2001 Demonstrations calling for decentralisation of power were banned and several southern Cameroon separatists were killed.

2002 The ruling RDPC increased its number of seats in the legislative elections. The International Court of Justice gave Cameroon sovereignty of the potentially oil-rich Bakassi Peninsula, claimed by Cameroon and Nigeria.

2003 The communications minister ordered the closure of an English-speaking private radio station, Magic FM, for

running programmes critical of the government.
2004 Presidential Biya was re-elected. Ephraïm Inoni was appointed prime minister. Nigeria failed to withdraw troops from the Bakassi Peninsula.
2005 Presidents Obasanjo and Biya and UN Secretary General Kofi Annan failed to resolve the dispute concerning Bakassi Peninsula, thought to hold about 10 per cent of the world's oil and gas reserves.
2006 Nigeria ceded the Bakassi peninsula to Cameroon, in accordance with a 2002 International Court of Justice ruling.
2007 In the general elections, the ruling RDPC won 152 seats (out of 180) and the opposition SDF won 21.
2008 Parliament overwhelmingly voted to amend the constitution. The amendments included presidential immunity from prosecution for acts undertaken as president and an unlimited number of presidential terms in office. Nigeria finally surrendered sovereignty of the oil-rich Bakassi Peninsula.
2009 President Biya dismissed Ephraim Inoni as prime minister and appointed Philémon Yang as his replacement.
2010 The parliamentary opposition claimed the figure of 19,406,100 million inhabitants as presented in the 2005 census was inaccurate and had been manipulated. Researchers agreed there could be inaccuracies as all figures presented were projections. Critics claim the projections for the English-speaking coastal region were 'exceptionally low', given overall growth rates. The national voter registration began, prior to the 2011 presidential elections.
2011 In July, the government enacted a right for Cameroon's diaspora to vote in the presidential election, which was held in October. Of the 23 candidates that took part, only two candidates won over 10 per cent of the vote. Incumbent Paul Biya won 77.99 per cent and John Fru Ndi 10.71 per cent; turnout was 65.8 per cent. The supreme court endorsed the result, however both France and the US denounced the election process as having 'many failures' and 'irregularities at all levels'. President Biya took office, for his sixth term, on 3 November.
2012 In April a law extending the mandate of members of parliament was adopted. The result was the postponing of the 2012 elections by a year. On 2 October, the UK energy company Bowleven announced that oil production from its offshore Etinde project was postponed from 2013 to 2015. On 4 October, Nigerian President Jonathan ordered a review of the ICJ ruling concerning the Bakassi Peninsula, which had been awarded to Cameroon in 2008, with a view to challenging the decision.
2013 Parliamentary elections were finally held on 30 September, after being postponed in February and July. The Rassemblement Démocratique du Peuple Camerounais (RDPC) (Cameroon People's Democratic Rally) won 148 seats (out of 180), followed by the Front Social-Démocratique (FSD) (Social Democratic Front) with 18. In August President Biya was accused of using the military to shut down Pentecostal churches after they were critical of his government. Mr Biya said the churches were threatening Cameroon's security and ordered nearly 100 Christian churches in Yaoundé and Bamenda, the North West Regional capital, be permanently shut down.
2014 In October 27 people including 10 Chinese workers held for months by suspected Boko Haram militants arrived in Yaoundé from the far northern region. They had been freed on 11 October having been taken hostage in May and June. The hostages included the wife of Cameroon's vice prime minister, Amadou Ali.
2015

Political structure

Constitution

The Constitution was promulgated in 1972 and revised in 1975 and 1996, when pressure from Anglophone regional groups resulted in Constitution amendments, whereby a federal system of government would be introduced and a senate in the National Assembly instigated; neither of these provisions were implemented. However an increase in the presidential term in office extension to seven years was applied.
In April 2008 parliament overwhelmingly voted to amend the constitution, to include presidential immunity from prosecution for acts undertaken as president and an unlimited number of presidential terms in office.

Form of state

Unitary republic; multiparty presidential regime.

The executive

Executive power is vested in the president, who appoints a cabinet. The president serves a seven-year term. A prime minister, who acts as Head of government, is appointed by the president. The president names and dismisses cabinet members and judges, ratifies treaties, heads the armed forces, controls legislation and can rule by decree.

National legislature

The bicameral Parliament consists of the Senate made up of 100 seats of which 70 members are indirectly elected by regional councils and 30 appointed by the president. The National Assembly is made up of 180 seats, members are directly elected in multi-seat constituencies by simple majority vote. The Senate was formed at the time of the 2013 Parliamentary elections. All members serve five year terms.

Legal system

Cameroon's legal system is based on French civil law with common law influences. The country has a Supreme Court, the judges of which are appointed by the president. Provisions in the 1996 constitution for judicial independence have not been put into force. Cameroon does not accept the compulsory jurisdiction of the International Court of Justice, but does belong to the International Court of Arbitration of the International Chamber of Commerce.

Last elections

30 September 2013 (parliamentary); 9 October 2011 (presidential)
Results: Parliamentary: The ruling RDPC won 148 seats (out of 180); SDF 18; Union Nationale pour la Démocratie et le Progrès (UNDP) (National Union for Democracy and Progress) 5; Union Démocratique du Cameroun (UDC) (Democratic Union of Cameroon) 4; Union des Populations du Cameroun (UPC) (Union of the Peoples of Cameroon) 3; Mouvement pour la Renaissance du Cameroun (MRC) (Cameroon Renaissance Movement) 1; Mouvement pour la Défense de la République (MDR) (Movement for the Defence of the Republic) 1. Turnout was 76.3 per cent.
Presidential: Paul Biya (RDPC) won 77.99 per cent, John Fru Ndi (SFD) 10.71 per cent, Garga Haman Adji (ADD) 3.21 per cent, Adamou Ndam Njoya (UDC) 1.73 per cent, Paul Abine Ayah (PAP) 1.26 per cent; 18 other candidates each won less than 1 per cent. Turnout was 68.2 per cent.

Next elections

February 2018 (parliamentary); 2018 (presidential)

Political parties

Ruling party

Rassemblement Démocratique du Peuple Camerounais (RDPC) (Cameroon People's Democratic Movement) (since 1992; re-elected July 2007 and September 2013)

Main opposition party

Front Social-Démocratique (SDF) (Social Democratic Front)

Population

22.54 million (2014)*
Last census: April 1987: 10,493,655
Population density: 29 inhabitants per square km. Urban population 58 per cent (2010 Unicef).
Annual growth rate: 2.4 per cent, 1990–2010 (Unicef).

Ethnic make-up

Cameroon has a highly diversified population comprising some 200 ethnic groups, including Cameroon Highlanders (31 per cent), Equatorial Bantu (19 per cent) and Kirdi (11 per cent). There are about 200,000 Europeans in the country, mainly French speakers.

Religions

Indigenous beliefs are practiced by 40 per cent of the population, another 40 per cent are Christian, and 20 per cent are Muslim.

Education

Literacy rate: 68 per cent adult rate (Unesco 2005)

Enrolment rate: 107 per cent gross primary enrolment, 33 per cent gross secondary enrolment; of relevant age groups (including repeaters) (World Bank).

Pupils per teacher: 44 in primary schools.

Health

HIV/Aids

In 2009 there were an estimated 160,000 adults living with HIV.

HIV prevalence: 5.3 per cent aged 15–49 in 2009 (Unicef 2012)

Life expectancy: 51 years, 2010 (Unicef 2012)

Fertility rate/Maternal mortality rate: 4.5 births per woman, 2010 (Unicef 2012)

Birth rate/Death rate: 34.7 births and 15.4 deaths per 1,000 population (2005)

Child (under 5 years) mortality rate (per 1,000): 95 per 1,000 live births (WHO 2012); 22 per cent of children aged under five are malnourished (World Bank).

Head of population per physician: 0.19 physician per 1,000 people, 2004 (WHO 2006)

Welfare

Cameroon's social insurance system provides cover for old-age pension, disability pension, sickness and maternity benefits, work injuries and family allowances.

Main cities

Douala (commercial centre, estimated population 2.4 million (m) in 2012), Yaoundé (capital, 2.4m), Bamenda (348,766), Bafoussam (301,894), Garoua (296,870), Maroua (239,026), Ngaoundéré (195,603), Kumba (173,049).

Languages spoken

24 major African language groups including Bamileke, Ewondo, Bassa and Bamoun are spoken. Around 80 per cent of the population speak French as a second language (francophone Cameroon) and 20 per cent speak English as a second language (anglophone – formerly British West Cameroon).

Official language/s

French, English

Media

The government maintains a tight control of media outlets with official restrictions and stringent libel laws that have regularly imprisoned journalists and led to self-censorship.

Press

Dailies: In French, the *Cameroon Tribune* is the official state-owned newspaper, with an English edition, published twice weekly, *La Nouvelle Expression* (www.lanouvelleexpression.net), is published three-times weekly. In English, *The Post* (www.postnewsline.com).

Weeklies: In French, private publications include *Le Messager* (www.lemessager.net), and in English *Postwatch* (www.postwatchmagazine.com).

Business: In French, *La Dépêche Economique* is a bi-weekly publication.

Periodicals: In French, monthly publications include *La Voix du paysan* a farmer's magazine, *Dikalo* (http://www.dikalo.biz) and *Le Météo* an independent magazine.

Broadcasting

The national broadcaster is Cameroon Radio and Television (CRTV).

Radio: CRTV (www.crtv.cm) operates one national and several provincial services in French, English and local languages. Other commercial stations include Nostalgie (www.cameroun-plus.com), Sky One (www.skyonecameroun.com) and the pan-African Radio Africa No 1 (www.africa1.com).

English-speaking separatists in the south of the country have used pirate-radio for propaganda.

Television: CRTV (www.crtv.cm) is the national public TV station. There are two private stations Canal 2 and STV (www.stvgroup.com) with two channels, which broadcast via satellite.

Other news agencies: Africa News Agency: www.africanewsagency.co.uk

APA: www.apanews.net

Panapress: www.panapress.com

Economy

Cameroon has a wealth of natural resources that underpin the economy, including mining, agriculture, forestry and oil and natural gas. Although the service sector constitutes around 50 per cent of GDP, industry 30 per cent (of which manufacturing is around 16 per cent), and agriculture 20 per cent, oil exports provide the largest export revenue. Other industries include aluminium smelting (from imported bauxite), hydroelectric power generation, rubber production and timber felling. Manufacturing includes use of these raw materials for finished items. Agricultural produce includes cotton, coffee, cocoa and palm oil.

GDP growth was 2.0 per cent in 2009, which increased to 2.9 per cent in 2010, and was estimated to have grown to 4.1 per cent in 2011.

Cameroon has a reputation for widespread corruption and has consistently ranked low in the World Bank's poll of ease of doing business, which in 2011 was 165 out of 183 countries, with enforcing a contract as the single most difficult element of the poll (174 out of 183). The benefits gained through its natural resources, industry and commodity trading have not spread through the population. In 2011, the UN Human Development Index (HDI) ranked Cameroon 150 (out of 187) for national development in health, education and income. Since 2000, Cameroon's progress has improved and it has matched the average growth of other countries in sub-Saharan Africa. In 2010, 53.9 per cent of the population experienced at least one indicator of poverty, while 9.6 per cent lived on less than the equivalent of US$1.25 per day. Migrant workers provided US$192 million in remittances in 2009, which fell to US$115 million (0.9 per cent of GDP) in 2010 and was estimated to have reached US$121 million in 2011.

The government implemented its Growth and Employment Strategy Paper (GESP) in late 2009, which was designed to boost growth and create employment in the formal sector to reduce poverty from 2010–20. Unemployment, currently estimated at around 76 per cent, is an ongoing problem with the government looking to reduce it to less than 50 per cent over the period. A reduction of the poverty rate from 39.9 per cent in 2007 to 28.7 per cent by 2020 is also a priority. The government will also increase its efforts in expanding the non-oil sectors to reduce the economy's vulnerability to external volatility.

External trade

As a member of the Communauté Économique des États d'Afrique Centrale (Economic Community of Central African States (ECCAS) Cameroon uses the CFA franc (Communauté Financière Africaine franc), issued by the Banque des États de l'Afrique Centrale (BEAC) (Bank of Central African States). ECCAS operates a customs and economic union with a common external tariff between its six members, with free movement of capital, people and goods and services.

Imports

Imports consist principally of crude oil, pharmaceuticals, transport equipment, vehicles, machinery, electrical equipment, grain and foodstuffs.

Main sources: China (26.2 per cent of total in 2014), Nigeria (12 per cent), France (11,8 per cent), Belgium (4.9 per cent) and the US (4.2 per cent).

Exports

Principal exports include crude oil and petroleum products, timber and finished wood items, rubber, coffee, cotton, cocoa beans, aluminium and tobacco.

Main destinations: Spain (13.9 per cent of total in 2014), China (12 per cent), India (10.1 per cent), Italy (8.1 per cent) and the Netherlands (8 per cent).

Re-exports

Light crude oil for refining.

Agriculture

Farming

Total agricultural land is 47.3 million hectares of which 4.2 per cent is pasture and 12.6 per cent arable.

In order to broaden the country's economic base and increase the value added to domestic production, the government is encouraging development of its full agricultural potential. Some 40 per cent of Cameroon's labour force is employed in the agricultural sector, although only 3 per cent of Cameroon's land area is used for permanent crops. Principal crops include cocoa, coffee, bananas, cotton and oil palms. Virtually all food requirements are met by local production. Most agricultural production is in the hands of smallholders, with the exception of rubber and palm, which are run under the plantation system.

Mayuka, located in the northern region of Cameroon, is the centre of the cocoa industry, where business made sweeping profits as prices soared following the political crisis in Côte d'Ivoire. As demand for cocoa rose, the government aimed to double the amount of production.

Fishing

As a consequence of its short coastline and the intrusion on its territorial waters of Bioko Island, which belongs to Equatorial Guinea, Cameroon's fishing industry is underdeveloped. Offshore waters are not well stocked, as the currents which provide richer fishing grounds off Nigeria and other parts of West Africa do not flow close to Cameroon's coastline. Nevertheless, catches of both freshwater and marine fish have been steadily increasing in recent years.

Fisheries legislation in Cameroon contains specific clauses dealing with the aquaculture sector, covering issues related to registration and licensing, and the export/import of fish species. It aims to improve artisnal fishing methods, preservation and processing of fishery products.

Forestry

While the country is well forested, with more than 40 per cent forest cover and an additional 30 per cent of other wooded land, unsustainable deforestation led to the loss of 222,000 hectares between 1990–2000. Nevertheless Cameroon has the second-largest area of tropical rainforest in Africa after the Democratic Republic of Congo (DRC). It is one of Africa's leading producers and exporters of tropical logs and sawn timber; smaller quantities of veneer and plywood are also exported. Important non-wood forest products include medicinal plants, nuts, wild fruits, rattan and bushmeat. Three-quarters of Cameroon's forestry exports consist of industrial roundwood, with sawnwood accounting for another 18 per cent. Forestry imports to Cameroon are composed almost exclusively of paper and paperboard, totalling 96.5 per cent of forestry imports.

Industry and manufacturing

The industrial sector accounts for around a fifth of GDP, a proportion which has been in steady decline since the late 1980s, contracting by an average of 3 per cent per year since 1990. However, the agro-industrial sub-sector has been growing, gradually substituting imports with domestically produced goods. The sector employs around 10 per cent of the workforce. Industrial output accounts for 25 per cent of Cameroon's exports.

The government is a major participant in the industrial sector, mainly through the Société Nationale d'Investissement (SNI) (National Investment Agency). The emphasis of policy is on reducing the sector's dependence on imports, decentralisation away from Yaoundé and Douala, increased local participation in small- and medium-sized enterprises (SMEs) and privatisation. The Technical Commission for the Rehabilitation of Public Enterprises oversees privatisation and restructuring of all state-owned companies.

Tourism

Cameroon has rain forests with lakes and waterfalls, ocean shorelines, cities and the western highlands, home to several endangered primates, including gorillas, the common chimpanzee and monkeys. Although tourism is still an undeveloped industry, it is growing and the government is enthusiastic about promoting Eco-tourism that combines revenue from tourism with conservation. The Dja Faunal Reserve is one of the best-protected rainforests in Africa, with 90 per cent of its area (5,260 square km) left undisturbed, according the UNESCO, which has included it on its World Heritage List since 1987. The capital, Yaoundé is home to several museums and national monuments and the second (but largest) city, Douala, is a major port and commercial capital, and is the main destination for most business travellers.

Travel and tourism accounts for around 5.5 per cent of GDP, and typically provides over US$1 billion in total contribution to GDP. The sector also provides around 4.5 per cent of total employment, at around 200,000 jobs. Travel and tourism was affected by the global economic crisis and visitor numbers fell from 2007. Despite a significant fall in visitor revenue in 2008 – US$167 million, down from US$254 million in 2007 (a fall of 41.8 per cent) – since then visitor numbers have recovered and have continued to grow so that by 2011 the estimated visitor revenue was US$290 million.

The biggest challenge for the government is to provide the infrastructure, particularly in the east and south, to allow tourism to grow in these areas.

Environment

Cameroon's tropical forest is the largest in-tact rainforest in the world but it is being exploited at a faster rate than is sustainable threatening the habitat of numerous species and the long-term existence of elephants and gorillas.

As the forests have become more accessible, poachers are shooting antelope, chimpanzees and gorillas, for commercial purposes. In June 2006, as part of its commitment to debt relief, the French government agreed to invest in the conservation of Cameroon's natural resources, to include better management of protected areas, wildlife and forest production.

In October 2005 a UN inspection team warned that a natural dam in the north-west province was in imminent danger of collapsing and flooding the Nyos Valley. The cost to repair the dam is estimated at US$15 million.

Mining

The mining sector accounts for around 10 per cent of GDP and employs 2 per cent of the workforce. Bauxite deposits of some 1,100 million tonnes at Adamaoua Province have been identified but they remain un-exploited, although an upturn in world aluminium prices encouraged Société des Bauxitese de Cameroun (SBC) to begin mining operations. There are deposits of iron ore at Kribi (reserves estimated at 197 million tonnes), and potential reserves of gold, diamonds, uranium, rutile, industrial clays and low-grade nickel and cobalt. Tin is mined on a very small scale. Investment by large mining companies is needed to exploit underground riches.

Hydrocarbons

Proven oil reserves were 200 million barrels in 2008, located offshore in the Niger

Delta in Rio del Rey Basin. With production at 81,330 barrels per day (bpd) and consumption at 26,000bpd, Cameroon is a net exporter of oil. Stocks have been declining since the 1980s and without finding further oil fields it could become a net importer by 2020.
The state-owned Société Nationale des Hydrocarbures (SNH) is responsible for exploration and production of Cameroon's oil assets and has undertaken joint exploration projects with international oil companies.
Cameroon and Chad jointly operate the 1,080km Chad-Cameroon pipeline project (CCPP), with a capacity of 225,000bpd, transporting Chadian oil to the Cameroon Kribi port terminal. There is one refinery in Limbe with a capacity of 42,000bpd with plans to upgrade the facility and refine crude oil from regional oil producers. A contract, to revamp much of the Limbe refinery and upgrade to include a power generator and related facilities, was let in June 2010.
Proven natural gas reserves were 110 billion cubic metres (cum) in 2008, with production at 28 million cum which are entirely consumed domestically. Constructions of the Logbaba gas and condensate facilities near Douala are almost complete and the UK-based Victoria Oil and Gas company expects commercial production to begin by January 2012. Initial production is set for 226.4 million cubic metres (cum) of gas per day, rising to 1.24 billion cum by 2014; at full capacity the plant will produce 1.69 billion cum.
The industry is still in its early stage of development and should take off dramatically since the territorial dispute with Nigeria over the Bakassi Peninsula was resolved in Cameroon's favour in 2007. Some analysts estimate that the Bakassi Peninsula holds some 10 per cent of the world's oil and gas reserves. The government also believes there is considerable potential in two largely unexplored areas – the Logone Birni and Douala basins – and is also hoping for the discovery of big offshore finds. However, the coastline is limited and the country's maritime area is small.
Commercial quantities of coal are neither produced nor imported.

Energy

Total generation capacity was 875MW in 2007, nearly 90 per cent of which is hydroelectric. Although Cameroon has the second largest hydroelectric power potential in Africa (after the Democratic Republic of Congo), its hydro plants are old, having been built mainly in the 1950s, and operate well below capacity. Therefore, gas may have a more immediate influence on power generation as an alternative source of power, especially in the dry season. Cameroon expects its demand for power to double in the course of the next decade. There are four operational hydroelectric power stations including Edéa, Lagdo, Song-Loulou and Memve'ele.
The utility Société Nationale d'Electricité du Cameroun (AES-Sonel) is 51 per cent owned by the US's AES Corporation. AES-Sonel managed generation and distribution to over 500,000 customers, which is around 2 per cent of the population, who have access to electricity supplies; only 9 per cent of the capital's potential consumers use electricity. The remainder of the population relies on wood fuel as their primary source of energy.
To comply with a World Bank loan to develop the electricity sector emphasis on sustainable energy has increased. The Export-Import Bank of India agreed to lend Cameroon US$251.5 million, which resulted in a contract whereby the Indian engineering firm Angelique International will build two hydropower stations and drinking water and sanitation projects.

Financial markets

Stock exchange

Doula Stock Exchange (DSX)

Banking and insurance

Cameroon's banking sector has become significantly stronger as the result of IMF-led restructuring, but is still poorly developed. The last state-owned bank in Cameroon was bought by a French banking company in 1999. Cameroon's largest bank is the Société Générale de Banques au Cameroun (SGBC). The commercial banking sector is made up of nine commercial banks with 60 branches, but suffers from a lack of available capital, an unwillingness to take risks and outdated products.

Central bank

Banque des Etats de l'Afrique Centrale (BEAC) (Bank of the Central African States)

Main financial centre

Douala

Time

GMT plus one hour

Geography

Cameroon lies on the Gulf of Guinea. Nigeria is to the west, Chad and the Central African Republic to the north-east and east, and the Republic of Congo, Gabon and Equatorial Guinea to the south.
The country can be divided into four main regions. The coastal plain is tropical but tempered by the effects of the sea. The tropical plateau in the south is heavily forested and cut through by a number of rivers flowing west into the Bight of Biafra or south-east to join the River Congo. The Adamawa and Bamenda highlands rise to 2,500 metres and are drier and cooler than the forest areas. The highlands are volcanic in origin, and include Mount Cameroon (4,070 metres). The savannah grasslands to the north lie between Nigeria and Chad, and stretch northwards to Lake Chad.

Hemisphere

Northern

Climate

In the north the single wet season is between April and September, and there is a dry season during the rest of the year.
It is tropical in the south with fairly constant average temperatures throughout the year, ranging between 18 degrees Celsius (C) at night and 30–32 degrees C during the day. In the south rainfall is distributed throughout the year with two wet seasons and two dry seasons.

Dress codes

Tropical clothes are advised, with warmer clothes required for the higher altitudes. Lightweight raincoats are recommended for the rainy season.

Entry requirements

Passports

Passports are required by all and should be valid for at least six months from date of arrival.

Visa

Required by all, except nationals of Central African Republic, Chad, Mali and Nigeria. Nationals of countries without Cameroonian diplomatic representation may be issued with a visa on arrival. A business visa requires a letter from applicant's company outlining purpose of visit and a letter from business partners in Cameroon (endorsed by the local police), plus a full itinerary.
An onward/return ticket and proof of sufficient funds are required.

Currency advice/regulations

There are no restrictions on the import or export of foreign currency.
Local currency import is limited to CFAf20,000 (approximately US$35) and export is limited to CFAf20,000 for tourists and CFAf45,000 (approximately US$80) for business purposes. Travellers cheques are accepted, but cash is advised.

Prohibited imports

Pornographic materials, illegal drugs, weapons and ammunitions may not be brought into Cameroon. Alcohol and other spirits (maximum 30 bottles) should be sent separately.
An invoice must accompany all furniture and electrical appliances to prove that they are more than six months old. Newer items are subject to customs duties and

taxes. Home computers do not qualify as personal effects, and are subject to customs duties and taxes.

Health (for visitors)

Mandatory precautions

An international certificate of vaccination against yellow fever.

Advisable precautions

The principal health hazards are cholera, malaria and HIV. Vaccination against tetanus, typhoid, polio, meningitis, and hepatitis A and B are all advisable. Rabies and bilharzia also occur, and necessary precautions should be taken. Avoid swimming in fresh water; well-chlorinated swimming pools should be safe. Bottled water is readily available. Milk is unpasteurised and should be boiled; meat and vegetables should be cooked and fruit peeled.

Medical care is adequate, but can be expensive.

Hotels

Good hotel accommodation is available in main centres. Service charges usually added to bill.

Credit cards

There is limited acceptance of the major credit cards only.

Public holidays (national)

Fixed dates

1 Jan (New Year's Day), 11 Feb (Youth Day), 1 May (Labour Day), 20 May (National Day), 21 May (Sheep Festival), 15 Aug (Assumption Day), 1 Oct (Unification Day), 25 Dec (Christmas Day).

Variable dates

Good Friday, Easter Monday, Ascension Day, Eid al Adha, Eid al Fitr, Birth of the Prophet.

Islamic year 1437 (15 Oct 2015–2 Oct 2016):: The Islamic year contains 354 or 355 days, with the result that Muslim feasts advance by 10–12 days against the Gregorian calendar. Dates of feasts vary according to the sighting of the new moon, so cannot be forecast exactly.

Working hours

Different hours are kept in the French-speaking (including Yaoundé and Douala) and English-speaking areas (south-west and north-west frontier areas) of Cameroon.

Banking

French-speaking areas: Mon—Fri: 0800—1200 and 1515—1630.

English-speaking areas: Mon—Fri: 0800—1330.

Business

French-speaking areas: Mon—Fri: 0730—1200 and 1430—1800.

English-speaking areas: Mon—Fri: 0730—1500; Sat: 0730—1200.

Government

French-speaking areas: Mon—Fri: 0730—1200 and 1430—1800.

English-speaking areas: Mon—Fri: 0730—1500; Sat: 0730—1200.

Shops

French-speaking areas: Mon—Sat: 0700/0800—1230 and 1430/1500—1830/1900.

English-speaking areas: Mon—Sat: 0700/0800—1200 and 1430/1530—1830—1900.

Post offices:

French-speaking areas: Mon—Fri: 0800—1200 and 1400—1700; Sat: 0800—1200.

English-speaking areas: Mon—Fri: 0800—1200 and 1430—1700.

Telecommunications

Mobile/cell phones

Cellular telephones services are available.

Electricity supply

220V AC, 50 cycles; plugs are of the two-pin round type.

Social customs/useful tips

Handshaking is the customary form of greeting. Business is conducted primarily in English or French.

Care should be taken to respect Islamic and other local religious practices and conventions, and visitors should be aware of restrictions on food and drink in Muslim areas, particularly during the Islamic fasting period of Ramadan.

Visitors should take care when photographing. It is considered polite to ask permission to photograph traditional dances, and it is advisable not to take pictures of official buildings or military installations.

Security

Muggings and petty crime have increased in recent years, mainly in the large cities. It is unwise to carry valuables or large amounts of cash in the street and thieves should not be resisted. Armed bandit attacks are a serious problem throughout the country. Journeys should be carefully planned and travelling in convoy is recommended. At the international airports, to avoid luggage being stolen, care should be taken to employ only the official porters.

Getting there

Air

National airline: Cameroon Airlines

International airport/s: Douala International (DLA), 10km from the city; duty-free shop, bars, restaurants, bank, post office and shops.

Other airport/s: Yaoundé-Nsimalen (YAO), 20km from the city; Garoua International (GOU), 6km from the city, also accept international flights.

Airport tax: Approximately US$18.

Surface

Road: Road access is possible from Nigeria, Chad, Gabon, Equatorial Guinea and the Central African Republic. These routes are rough and may become impassable during rainy seasons. Bush taxis and minibuses are available. Armed banditry is a problem in the area bordering the Central African Republic and in other parts of Cameroon.

Rail: Rail access is available from N'Gaoundal and Belabo in the Central African Republic.

Water: There are two boats a day from Calabar (Nigeria) across the Cross River to Oron, and from Ikang (Nigeria) there are speedboats to Ekondo Titi.

Douala offers more freight links with Europe than other Central African ports. Cameroon Shipping Lines (Camshiplines) maintains an office in Paris.

Main port/s: Douala. Other ports are at Limbe, Kribi and Garoua (on the River Bénoué), which handle river trade during the dry season.

Getting about

National transport

Air: Cameroon Airlines operates domestic services between the main cities, including several daily flights between Yaoundé and Douala. Early arrival at the airport terminal is advisable, as overbookings are common. However, air services are generally efficient and certainly the fastest means of travelling within Cameroon.

Road: Cameroon's road network totals 31,800km of roads. Surfaced roads run between main centres although there are no tarmac road links between Yaoundé and Ngaoundéré. Major routes are from Douala to Limbé, Buea, Bafoussam, Sangmelima, Bamenda and Yaoundé (all-weather road). Most other roads are unsurfaced and are often impassable during rainy season.

Buses: There are coach services between the main centres. Connections to rural areas are unreliable, dangerous and subject to suspension in the rainy season.

Rail: The track network extends 1,168km. Cameroon Railways (Camrail) links Kumba, Douala, Yaoundé and Ngaoundéré. An overnight service runs from Yaoundé to Ngaoundéré (12 hours). Second-class travel is cheap but uncomfortable. Sleeping facilities are available on some trains. There is an express three-hour service between Yaoundé and Douala with good facilities.

City transport

Taxis: Taxis are not metered but have a minimum fare and fixed prices. Long journeys and daily hire should be negotiated. A 10 per cent tip is optional. There are taxis from the airport to Douala city centre.

Car hire

Chauffeur- or self-driven cars are available in Yaoundé and Douala, but can be expensive. An international driving licence is required.

BUSINESS DIRECTORY

The addresses listed below are a selection only. While World of Information makes every endeavour to check these addresses, we cannot guarantee that changes have not been made, especially to telephone numbers and area codes. We would welcome any corrections.

Telephone area codes

The international direct dialling code (IDD) for Cameroon is +237 followed by the subscriber's number.

Useful telephone numbers

Police:17
Fire:18
Ambulance:23-40-20

Chambers of Commerce

Cameroon Chamber of Commerce, Industry and Mines, Rue de Chambre de Commerce, PO Box 4011, Douala (tel:342-6855; fax: 342-5596; e-mail: cride-g77@camnet.cm).

Banking

Banque Internationale pour le Commerce et l'Industrie du Cameroun (BICIC), PO Box 1925, Avenue du Général-de-Gaulle, Douala (tel: 428-431, 420-001; fax: 424-184, 424-116).

Commercial Bank of Cameroon, PO Box 4004, Douala (tel: 420-202; fax: 433-802).

International Bank of Africa-Cameroon, PO Box 3300, Douala (tel: 428-422; fax: 428-423).

Société Générale de Banques au Cameroun, PO Box 4042, 78 Rue Joss, Douala (tel: 427-010, 427-004; fax: 430-353) .

Standard Chartered Bank Cameroon, PO Box 1784, Boulevard de la Liberté, Douala (tel: 424-191; fax: 422-789).

Central bank

Banque des États de l'Afrique Centrale, Direction Nationale, PO Box 83, Yaoundé (tel: 223-0511; fax: 223-3380; e-mail: beacyde@beac.int).

Stock exchange

Doula Stock Exchange (DSX), www.douala-stock-exchange.com

Travel information

Cameroon Airlines, Littoral BP 4092, 3 Avenue General de Gaulle, Douala (tel: 422-525, 424-949; fax: 422-487, 423-459).

Douala International Airport, BP 3131, Douala (tel: 423-630, 423-577; fax: 423-758).

Ministry of tourism

Ministry of Tourism, Yaoundé (tel: 223-353, 235-258; fax: 221-295).

National tourist organisation offices

Société Camerounaise de Tourisme (Socatour), BP 7138, Yaoundé (tel: 233-219).

Ministries

Ministry of Agriculture, Yaoundé (tel: 234-085, 225-166, 231-190).

Ministry of Communications, Yaoundé (tel: 234-075; 223-155, 233-974).

Ministry of External relations, Yaoundé (tel: 220-133).

Ministry of Economy and Finance, BP 18, Yaoundé (tel: 234-000, 232-299).

Ministry of Environment and Forestry, BP 14276, Yaoundé (tel: 229-483, 221-225).

Ministry of Industrial and Commercial Development, Yaoundé (tel: 234-040, 225-085).

Ministry of Culture, Yaoundé (tel: 223-155, 233-974).

Ministry of Livestock, Fisheries and Animal Industries, Yaoundé (tel: 223-311, 220-443).

Ministry of Mines, Water and Energy, Yaoundé (tel: 233-404).

Ministry of Post and Telecommunications, Yaoundé (tel: 234-016; fax: 223-497).

Ministry of Public Works and Transport, Yaoundé (tel: 232-236).

Other useful addresses

Cameroon Development Corporation (CDC), BP 28, Bota, Limbe (tel: 332-251).

Cameroon Embassy (USA), 2349 Massachusetts Avenue, NW, Washington DC 20008 (tel: 202-265-8790; fax: 202-387-3826; e-mail: info@ambacam-usa.org).

Cameroon Telecommunications, BP 1571, Yaoundé (tel: 234-065; fax: 230-303).

Commission Technique de la Mission de Réhabilitation des Entreprises due Secteur Public et Parapublic, SNI Building, 9th Floor, Yaoundé (tel: 239-750; fax: 235-108).

Centre National d'Assistance aux Petites et Moyennes Entreprises, BP 1377, Douala (tel: 425-858).

Centre National du Commerce Exterieur (CNCE), BP 2461, Douala (tel: 421-685).

Department of Statistics, BP 25, Yaoundé (tel: 220-788).

National Tenders Board, Mballa II, 4th Floor, PO Box 6604, Yaoundé (tel: 201-803; fax: 206-042; e-mail: DGTC@GCNET.CM).

Office National du Café et du Cacao (ONCC), BP 378, Douala (tel: 426-776, 425-088) – sole marketing agency for cocoa, coffee, cotton, groundnuts, palm kernels.

Office de Radiodiffusion-Télévision Camerounaise (CRTV), BP 1634, Yaoundé (tel: 234-088).

Regifercam, BP 304, Douala (tel: 407-159; fax: 423-205).

Société Camerounaise des Depots Petroliers, Siège Social BP 2271, Douala (tel: 405-445; fax: 404-796).

Société de Développement du Cacao SODECAO), BP 1651, Yaoundé (tel: 220-991).

Société de Développement du Coton, Headquarters, BP 302, Garoua (tel: 271-556; fax: 272-068).

Société Nationale des Eaux du Cameroun, BP 157 Douala (tel: 433-066, 430-067; fax: 422-945).

Société Nationale de Raffinage, Cape Limboh, PO Box 365, Limbe (tel: 423-815, 423-817; fax: 423-444, 424-199).

Société Nationale d'Investissement, BP 423, Place de la Poste, Yaoundé (tel: 224-499, 224-422).

Société de Recouvrement des Créances du Cameroun, BP 11991, Yaoundé (tel: 223-739, 220-911; fax: 233-833).

Syndicate of Wood Producers and Exporters (SPEBC), BP 2064, Douala (tel/fax: 428-617).

Syndicat des Commerçants, Importateurs et Exportateurs du Cameroun (SCIEC), BP 562, Douala (tel: 420-304).

Syndicat des Industriels du Cameroun, BP 1516, Yaoundé (tel: 222-468; BP 673, Douala (tel: 423-058).

Technical Committee for Privatisation and Liquidations, SNI Building, 9th Floor, Yaoundé (tel: 239-750; fax: 235-108).

Africa News Agency: www.africanewsagency.co.uk

APA: www.apanews.net

Panapress: www.panapress.com

Internet sites

AllAfrica.com: allafrica.com

African Development Bank: www.afdb.org

Canada

KEY FACTS

Official name: Canada

Head of State: Queen Elizabeth II (since 1952), represented by Governor General David Johnston (from 1 Oct 2010) (since 27 Sep 2005)

Head of government: Prime Minister Stephen Harper (from 2006; re-elected 2 May 2011)

Ruling party: Conservative Party of Canada (CPC) (from 2006; re-elected 2 May 2011)

Area: 9,976,139 square km

Population: 35.49 million (2014)*

Capital: Ottawa

Official language: English, French

Currency: Canadian dollar (C$) = 100 cents

Exchange rate: C$1.32 per US$ (Sep 2015)

GDP per capita: US$50,398 (2014)*

GDP real growth: 2.53% (2014)

GDP: US$1,788.72 billion (2014)

Labour force: 19.03 million (2014)

Unemployment: 6.92% (2014)

Inflation: 1.90% (2014)

Oil production: 4.29 million bpd (2014)

Natural gas production: 162.00 billion cum (2014)

Balance of trade: US$4.56 billion (2014)

* estimated figure

Nota

The general election of 19 October was convincingly won by the Liberal Party of Canada; leader Justin Trudeau was sworn in as prime minister on 4 November 2015.

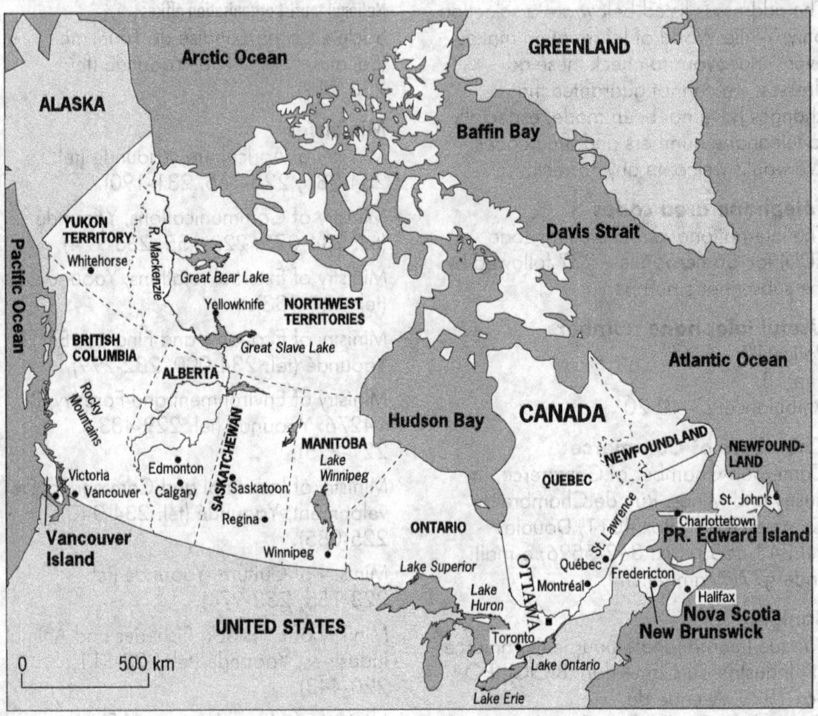

Stephen Harper, Canada's conservative prime minister has twice been re-elected – in 2006 and again in 2010. In the elections scheduled for October 2015, he would be seeking his fourth term of office, placing him alongside Canada's five longest serving prime ministers. Should he be re-elected, he would be the first leader to win a fourth consecutive term of office in Canadian history.

Safer Canada/stronger economy

Canada is generally considered to be a safe, attractive, prosperous country – but boring. Which means that when an election comes along it almost combines the excitement of Australia's Melbourne Cup and the UK's Grand National in a single day – well, almost. For most of 2014 Canadians probably expected the next election to be a shoe-in for Mr Harper. At the time, Mr Harper's popularity was formal rather than enthusiastic. But as the economy faltered, the polls suggested that the election might be a close run thing between Mr Harper's Conservative Party of Canada (CPC) and the left-wing New Democratic Party (NDP), lead by Thomas Mulcair. The NDP had won a number of state elections, but never a general election. If, as the opinion polls suggested, over 60 per cent of Canadians would like to see a change from Mr Harper, the NDP appeared to have usurped the position of party once seen as the 'natural' opposition. The Liberal Party, lead by Justin Trudeau, had at one time seemed the obvious opposition – but Mr Mulcair was now the opposition's front runner by some distance.

The contrast between Mr Mulcair and Mr Harper could hardly be greater, both in terms of personality as well as politics. As the election approached, Canadian voters could certainly see what sort of a politician Mr Mulcair was; whether, come the day, they will be prepared to vote for him is another matter. One group of supporters the NDP can count on is the disaffected French-speaking Québécois. Many have deserted what they now see as the lost cause of independence, preferring to vote for the federalist NDP.

Shifting (tar) sands

On Mr Harper's already long watch, there have been a number of far reaching changes in the very nature of Canada as a body politic. The once welfare state, the country of consensus has been replaced by a country that preferred to focus on its links with Asia rather than with Europe. Canada's hydrocarbons boom (see Energy below) have increased the importance of its western provinces, at the perceived expense of Ontario and French speaking Quebec. If the swing towards Asia from Europe was half completed, the Canadians could certainly see a much greater rapprochement with the US – a country with which Canadians already share a close cultural identity – than had been the case.

With all the enthusiasm of a recent convert, at the age of 19 the Ontario-born Mr Harper had moved to Alberta to work in the petroleum industry. When appointed prime minister in 2006 he was considered by many as a doppelganger for the US' George Bush, advocating economic and social policies that were far to the right of those of the traditional Liberal Party. By 2014 he could rightly claim to be – alongside Germany's Angela Merkel – the longest serving (and the most conservative) head of government in the powerful G7 group of countries. The very fact that Canada is even a member of the G7 speaks volumes. Its geographical extension is the second largest in the world (after Russia) but its population of only 37 million (little more than a tenth of the US's population) makes it the smallest G7 country by population.

The economy – whistling in the wind?

In mid-2015 both Mr Harper and his finance minister, Joe Oliver, were putting a brave face on sets of statistics that did more than just suggest that all was not well with the economy. In the first quarter of 2015 the Canadian economy didn't just creep forward, it actually went backwards, contracting at an annual rate of 0.6 per cent. Before the second quarter figures were published, forecasters were whispering that the economy was technically in recession – which implied that it had contracted during the year's second quarter.

Claiming the high ground on economic performance had been Mr Harper's trump card in winning the previous two elections. Whether by luck or sound management, Canada had managed to avoid the seriously adverse effects of the 2008 financial crash. Helped on by the post-crash boom in commodity prices, the Canadian economy surged encouragingly, with Mr Harper happily taking the credit.

Taking a cautious view in July 2015, the Paris-based Organisation for Economic Co-operation and Development (OECD) expected Canada's growth to slow to around 1.5 per cent in 2015 before rebounding in 2016. The OECD agreed with other commentators that the fall in oil prices had resulted in falls in investment and gross domestic product (GDP). However, the OECD subscribed to the view that a shift towards non-energy exports was underway, supported by the currency depreciation and stronger foreign-market growth. The OECD expected non-oil related business investment to strengthen eventually. The OECD appeared to have bought in to the government's 'blame it on the weather' policy, suggesting that 'following recent weather-related weakness, consumption growth should pick up'. The OECD projection considered that 'with economic slack fully absorbed, inflation is projected to return to the 2 per cent mid-point of the inflation target range by mid-2016.' The OECD agreed with the International Monetary Fund (IMF) (see below) that high household debt and house prices posed financial-stability risks and further macro-prudential measures might be required should these risks increase. According to the OECD, Canadian business investment in 2015 was above its pre-recession level. This partly reflected the expansion of the oil and gas sector; however, the OECD warned that investment plans had been pared back with the fall in oil prices. Nevertheless, in the OECD's view, financial conditions remained supportive for investment overall and the higher demand for non-energy exports and related capacity requirements should support investment in the medium term.

In a February 2015 'Economic Health Check' on the Canadian economy, the IMF noted that Canada's economic performance had been 'solid', for the most part due to the stronger than anticipated US recovery. However, the IMF expected growth to 'ease slightly this year', although the IMF avoided using the more emotive possibilities of 'contraction' or 'shrinkage'. The slowdown, according to the IMF, would reflect globally lower oil prices and enable the Canadian economy to 'become more balanced with a cooling housing market.'

A report in the London *Economist* offered a more blunt analysis, suggesting that Canada could move from being 'leader, to laggard'. The writer pointed out that although the consensus forecast was for a 2015 growth rate of 2 per cent in 2015 – roughly around the average G7 growth rate – a fall in commodity prices (notably that of oil) (see Hydrocarbons below) meant that Canada's growth forecasts would need to be adjusted downwards. Of the G7 member countries, only France and Italy, said The *Economist*, had higher unemployment rates. According to Statistics Canada, the unemployment rate was 6.80 per cent (and rising) in July

KEY INDICATORS — Canada

	Unit	2011	2012	2013	2014	**2015
Population	m	34.44	34.70	35.10	*35.49	35.88
Gross domestic product (GDP)	US$bn	1,736.90	1,821.44	1,838.96	1,788.72	1,615.47
GDP per capita	US$	50,436	52,489	52,393	*50,398	*45,029
GDP real growth	%	2.5	1.7	2.0	2.5	*2.2
Inflation	%	2.9	1.5	1.0	1.9	*0.9
Unemployment	%	8.1	7.3	*7.1	6.9	*7.0
Oil output	'000 bpd	3,522.0	3,741.0	3,948.0	4,292.0	–
Natural gas output	bn cum	160.5	156.5	154.8	162.0	–
Coal output	mtoe	35.6	35.2	36.8	36.7	–
Exports (fob) (goods)	US$m	462,905.0	462,883.0	465,498.0	478,351.0	–
Imports (fob) (goods)	US$m	460,739.0	474,911.0	472,525.0	473,789.0	–
Balance of trade	US$m	2,166.0	-12,028.0	-7,028.0	4,561.0	–
Current account	US$m	-52,846.0	-62,266.0	-54,627.0	-39,372.0	*-42,015.0
Total reserves minus gold	US$m	63,060.0	68,365.0	71,821.0	74,584.0	–
Exchange rate	per US$	0.94	0.99	1.06	1.16	–

* estimated figure ** forecast figure

2015. Canada's unemployment rate had averaged 7.73 per cent from 1966 to 2015, reaching an all time high of 13.10 per cent in December 1982 and a record low of 2.90 per cent in June 1966.

IMF figures showed the economy expanding at an 'above-potential rate since' 2013, with a growth rate of 2.4 per cent in 2014. The awaited pickup in exports, driven by a stronger US recovery and a depreciating Canadian dollar, was, according to the IMF, encouraging. However, the *Economist* reported that 'economist's expected that a weaker Canadian dollar would boost demand for manufactured goods, especially from the US.' But, according to the *Economist*, that had not happened. It reported that ' Exports to Canada's southern neighbour, including oil, were 6.5 per cent lower in May 2015 than in the same month in 2014.'

In 2015, the oil and gas industries, which have traditionally accounted for a large proportion of Canadian exports, had been hit hard by the dramatic fall in the price per barrel, which had on occasion fallen to almost US$50. Business plans had to be re-visited and, as a result investment plans either cancelled, revised downwards or simply forgotten.

The recent strength of the Canadian economy meant that the scope for improving productivity and efficiency was limited. This meant that the government could not look to the private sector for salvation. Mr Harper had little option but to turn to the public sector: there were obvious possibilities for infrastructure projects. In the good years, Canada had reduced its levels of debt, making it the least indebted of all the G7 countries. This provided scope for borrowing, even if such a Keynesian solution was anathema to the low tax, low expenditure philosophy of the Harper government. Despite the economy's apparent downturn, finance minister Oliver had firmly stuck to the C$5.8 billion (US$4.4 billion) allocated for infrastructure expenditure in November 2014. In an effort to jump start the faltering economy, in January 2015 the Bank of Canada (central bank) had cut interest rates to 0.75 per cent.

Meanwhile, the rebalancing of the economy – away from private consumption and housing – remained incomplete. January 2015's interest rate cut didn't help finance minister Oliver much: quite the opposite as the lower cost of mortgages risked increasing the demand for houses, which in turn risked pushing house prices upwards. The prospect of shifting away from an obsession with rising house prices towards stimulating exports and investment just did not seem to be happening in mid-2015.

In February 2015 the IMF appeared to consider the worst to be over, reporting that ' In terms of key domestic risks, household debt has stabilised, but is still high.' In the first few months of 2015 housing markets certainly remained strong, with estimated house price overvaluation ranging between 7–20 per cent, but – the IMF pointed out – with large differences across regions and markets.

The IMF was among those forecasters who had expected GDP growth to edge down slightly in 2015 – to 2.3 per cent – mainly because of the significant drop in oil prices, which hurts investment in the oil sector, but will be offset in part by the weaker Canadian dollar (aka the 'loonie') and stronger US growth. The IMF was certainly prescient when it reported that 'Risks to the outlook have increased, given sluggish global growth, still-unfolding effects from lower oil prices and housing market risks.'

Canada's public finances, according to the IMF, had continued improving in 2014 and in the (February 2015) view of the IMF, the federal government was on track to achieve its balanced budget target in the 2015 fiscal year, despite lower oil prices. The IMF 'saw scope for shifting the fiscal stance into neutral at the federal level and encouraged the government to use the available fiscal resources for growth-friendly measures.'

In February 2015, the IMF considered Canada's housing markets to remain overvalued. The IMF noted that Canadian banks were well capitalised and profitable. The financial stability risks posed by the housing market and the household sector as well as those from lower oil prices, appeared to be contained, given the extensive government-guaranteed mortgage insurance system and Canadian banks' limited exposure to the energy sector.

Hydrocarbons

Canada is a net energy exporter; the energy sector plays an important role in the economy, accounting for some 10 per cent of GDP, a quarter of exports and as much as 25 per cent of non-housing private investment. Any persistent and large drop in oil prices was expected to dampen Canada's growth, both through weaker investment in the energy sector and the resultant lack of job creation. Mr Harper's hope was that the impact on oil production might be mitigated given Canada's existing capacity and its growing market share in the United States.

More positively, lower oil prices were expected to benefit consumers and the non-hydrocarbon sectors of the economy, especially (another hope) in the context of a weaker currency and stronger US growth. Lower oil prices would, it was also hoped, contribute to the rebalancing of the economy through the cooling impact on the most overheated housing markets. However, there were those who expected the drop in interest rates to do just the opposite. With the main engine of Canada's recent growth – the energy sector – taking the biggest hit, the economy's ability to overcome longer-standing weaknesses in the non-energy sector by boosting its productivity would be increasingly important.

Canada is not just an exporter of oil and gas, but of most energy commodities and is also a major producer of unconventional oil and hydroelectricity. Above all, it is the largest foreign supplier of energy to the US. The relationship works well for both countries. Just as the United States depends on Canada for much of its energy needs, so does Canada rely on the United States as an export market. However, wider economic and political considerations have lead Canada to explore the diversification of its trading partners, particularly in Asia.

Canada ranks among the five largest energy producers in the world, behind only China, the US, Russia and Saudi Arabia. It is the world's fifth-largest oil producer and virtually all of its crude oil exports are directed to US refineries. Canada is a major onshore and offshore producer of crude oil and the recent growth in its liquid fuels production has been driven by bitumen and upgraded synthetic crude oil produced from the oil sands of Alberta. According to the US government Energy Information Administration (EIA), most of Canada's reserves and the expected future growth in Canada's liquid fuels production, will be derived from these resources.

According to the Oil & Gas Journal (OGJ), Canada had 173 billion barrels of proved oil reserves at the end of 2014. The Alberta Energy Regulator placed Canada's reserves at 169 billion barrels of proved oil reserves at the end of 2013. Canada controls the third-largest amount of proved reserves in the world, after Venezuela and Saudi Arabia. Among the top ten reserve holders, the only state other than Canada that is not a member of the Organisation of the Petroleum

Exporting Countries (OPEC) is Russia. Canada's proved oil reserve levels from 1980 to 2002 were well below 10 billion barrels. In 2003, they rose to 180 billion barrels after oil sands resources were deemed to be technically and economically recoverable. The oil sands now account for approximately 167 billion barrels, nearly all of Canada's current proved oil reserves.

The EIA notes that many Canadian firms have a presence in the upstream oil and gas industry, from large-scale active or planned commercial projects to smaller pilot projects that serve as test beds for new technologies. The participation of international oil companies (IOCs), both private and state-owned, in Canada's oil sector has risen rapidly. Aside from economic and political motivations, investments in the oil sands enable foreign companies to gain technological expertise that can be applied to unconventional resources elsewhere. Chinese companies, including PetroChina and its China National Petroleum Corporation (CNPC) parent company, the China National Offshore Oil Corporation (CNOOC) and Sinopec, have invested heavily in the oil sands and other parts of Canada's energy sector.

Canada produced more than 4.3 million barrels per day (bpd) of petroleum and other liquid fuels in 2013 according to the *BP Statistical Review of World Energy* of June 2015 (BP15); this represented an increase of more than 930,000bpd from the levels seen a decade earlier. Of this production, 3.3 million bpd was crude oil and a small amount of lease condensate. Oil production in Canada comes from three principal sources: the oil sands, the resources in the broader Western Canada Sedimentary Basin (WCSB) and the offshore oil fields in the Atlantic Ocean. Production from the oil sands accounted for more than half of Canadian oil output in 2013, a proportion that has steadily increased in the past decade. In total, Alberta was responsible for 78 per cent of Canadian oil production in 2013.

Canada is expected to be one of the largest sources of growth in global liquid fuel supply, in both the near term and long term. The EIA forecast that Canada's production would grow by an annual average of 180,000bpd in 2015. Looking forward, the EIA projected that Canadian production could grow to 6.7 million bpd by 2040 as a result of the growing expansion of the oil sands.

Almost 97 per cent of Canadian oil exports went to the United States in 2013. It was the largest supplier of foreign oil to the United States, accounting for one-third of US crude oil imports in 2013. In the same year, the United States imported 3.1 million bpd of oil and petroleum products from Canada, of which 2.6 million bpd were crude oil.

While overall US imports of crude oil are declining, Canada is one of the few countries from where US crude oil imports are increasing. From a decade ago, US imports of Canadian crude have increased 59 per cent, while imports from the other major suppliers have decreased. Although the United States is a large net crude oil importer from Canada, at 2.6 million bpd in 2013, the cross-border oil trade flows in both directions. With existing legal restrictions, Canada was the only country to import US crude oil (133,000bpd in 2013). The United States exported 415,000bpd of total petroleum products to Canada in 2013.

Despite holding a relatively smaller share of the world's proved natural gas reserves, Canada ranks fifth in dry natural gas production. It is the fourth-largest exporter of natural gas, behind Russia, Qatar and Norway. Although Canada has plans to export liquefied natural gas (LNG), all of Canada's current natural gas exports are sent to US markets via pipeline. The BP2015 estimated that Canada's proved natural gas reserves were 71.7 trillion cubic feet (tcf) at end of year 2014. Most of Canada's natural gas reserves are traditional resources in the WSCB, including those associated with the region's oil fields. Other areas with significant concentrations of natural gas reserves include offshore fields near the eastern shore of Canada, principally around Newfoundland and Nova Scotia, the Arctic region and the Pacific coast. Vast deposits of unconventional natural gas reside in the WCSB in the form of coal bed methane (CBM), shale gas and tight gas, although they have not been developed as extensively as similar formations in the United States. Canada has an estimated 573tcf of technically recoverable shale gas resources, according to the EIA.

Risk assessment

Economy	Fair/good
Politics	Good
Regional stability	Good

COUNTRY PROFILE

1497 John Cabot claimed Newfoundland for Henry VII of England.

1534 Jacques Cartier explored Newfoundland and charted the Gulf of St Lawrence as far as what is now Québec city and Montréal. He claimed this land for France.

1600 King Henry IV of France granted fur trading rights in the Gulf of St Lawrence to a group of French merchants. The French settled in Acadia – the Canadian maritime provinces of what are now New Brunswick, Nova Scotia and Prince Edward Island.

1608 Founding of Québec as France's first colony by Samuel Champlain.

1629 Québec city was captured by the English fleet.

1632 Québec was returned to France by the treaty of St Germain-en-Laye.

1642 Founding of Ville Marie, which later became Montréal.

1660 The English Navigation Act prohibited foreigners from trading with English colonies.

1663 Louis XIV assumed personal control of the French settlements that included Québec, Montréal, Nova Scotia, New Brunswick and the area around the Gulf of St Lawrence and called this *Nouvelle France* (New France). Québec became a royal province.

1665 Jean Talon came from France to administer colonial affairs and brought about a significant expansion of the colony, encouraging agriculture, arts and business, stimulating immigration. By this time, the English, fighting for territorial dominance, controlled 10 colonies on the Atlantic coast and exceeded New France in terms of population and self-sufficiency.

1670 In competition with the French, the English established the Hudson Bay Company, giving themselves a monopoly on the fur trade in the Hudson Bay area.

1702 Queen Anne's War broke out between the English and the French. This led to the capture of Port Royal (capital of Acadia) by the English.

1713 Peace was established under the Treaty of Utrecht. This required France to surrender the Hudson Bay Area, Newfoundland and Acadia to Britain. France was permitted to keep Cape Breton Island and her inland colonies.

1754 The French and Indian War began in North America; it became the Seven Years War when fighting spread to Europe.

1755–56 The British attacked Québec, the nerve-centre of the French empire. Québec came under British rule.

1759 Montréal, cut off from reinforcements and supplies from France, fell to the British.

1774 Britain passed the Québec Act, which officially recognised French civil law and granted religious freedom to Roman Catholics. Britain assumed full control of

the North Atlantic provinces of Canada, Nova Scotia, New Brunswick, Prince Edward Island and Newfoundland.
1858 British Columbia became a Crown Colony.
1862 The British withdrew troops from Canada.
1867 Ontario, Québec, Nova Scotia and New Brunswick joined together under the terms of the British North America Act to become the Dominion of Canada. These four territories became provinces with their own governments, law making bodies and lieutenant governors.
1870 Manitoba joined the Dominion, followed by British Columbia and Prince Edward Island. Hudson Bay became part of Canada and was renamed the Northwest Territories.
1898 The territory of Yukon was carved out of the Northwest Territories and entered the Dominion. The Territories, unlike the provinces that existed within their own right, were subject to federal legislative power. The federal government had the right to intrude in administrative and social affairs.
1905 Alberta and Saskatchewan became provinces of Canada.
1914–18 Canada joined the allies in the First World War.
1931 The Statute of Westminster was passed by the British parliament, granting dominion parliaments the right to reject the laws of the British parliament and allowing British dominions, including Canada, complete autonomy. Canada became a free associate of the British Commonwealth of Nations, but had to swear allegiance to the British Crown.
1939–45 Canada joined the allies against Nazi Germany, Italy and Japan in the Second World War.
1949 Newfoundland became Canada's tenth province.
1969 Canada recognised English and French as its two official languages.
1977 Following an amendment to the Citizenship Act, Canadians ceased to be British subjects.
1980 A referendum to make Québec a separate country was rejected by the people of Québec.
1982 The Constitution Act stated that Canada no longer required British approval for new laws.
1995 The Canadian parliament passed a resolution recognising Québec as a distinct society within Canada. A referendum in Québec produced another 'no' vote for independence.
1999 Nunavut, created out of part of the Northwest Territories, became Canada's third territory.
2000 Jean Chrétien called snap elections, in which the Liberal Party of Canada (LPC) took 40.8 per cent of the vote, winning 172 seats.
2001 Québec's premier, Lucien Bouchard, resigned. Bernard Landry took over the post. Canada became the first country to legalise cannabis for people suffering from chronic medical conditions and terminal illnesses.
2002 Jean Chrétien announced he would resign in 2004.
2003 Toronto was seriously hit by an outbreak of the flu-like Sars virus. A power blackout – the biggest in North American history – hit Toronto, Ottawa and other parts of Ontario, as well as cities in the north-eastern US. Paul Martin took over as prime minister after Jean Chrétien's retirement.
2004 The ruling LPC won the parliamentary elections, but lost its majority.
2005 Haitian-born Michaëlle Jean was appointed as Governor General (GG).
2006 The Conservative Party of Canada (CPC) won elections but without an overall majority. Parliament approved the recognition of Quebec as a nation within a united Canada.
2007 Increased melting ice in Arctic waters opened the Northwest Passage between the Pacific and Atlantic Oceans, which become navigable during summer months. Canada asserted its territorial rights to manage the waterway ahead of any international recognition of its control.
2008 Prime Minister Harper dissolved parliament and called early parliamentary elections. The ruling CPC increased its share of the vote and its number of seats with 37.63 per cent and 143 seats (out of 308). However the total was less than the 155 seats necessary to achieve a majority. Stephen Harper remained in post as prime minister of a minority government.
2009 Canada imposed visa controls on visitors from Czech Republic and Mexico; there had been a disproportionate rise in asylum requests from the two countries. Parliament was prorogued for two months, conveniently while the winter Olympic Games took place in Vancouver. This was the second time Prime Minister Harper had employed this device to avoid critical parliamentary motions; this closure stalled attempts by parliament to force the government to release uncensored documents concerning torture of Afghan detainees.
2010 Parliament reopened. A ruling by the Speaker of the House of Commons declared that the documents concerning Afghan detainees must be released or the government risked contempt of parliament. A parliamentary committee was formed and having taken an oath of confidentiality was allowed to review uncensored documents, to determine which, without threatening national security, would go forward for possible public release. David Johnston took up his appointment as the governor general.
2011 In March, Canada joined in a five-country coalition (France, Italy, the UK and the US) to impose a no-fly zone over Libya. Three opposition parties rejected the budget. The minority government of Steven Harper fell on 25 March following a parliamentary vote of no confidence. New, early elections took place in May. The Conservatives won a decisive majority with 39.62 per cent of the vote (167 seats out of 308) giving Prime Minister Harper a clear majority. The New Democratic Party (Nouveau Parti Démocratique) (NDP) boosted their standing by winning 102 seats (up from 36 seats in 2008). The leaders of the Liberal Party, Michael Ignatieff and Bloc Québécois, Gilles Duceppe, quit their chairmanships following their defeat in the polls. Canada began to withdraw its combat troops from Afghanistan in July. On 25 July the leader of the NDP, Jack Layton, announced he was stepping down to receive treatment for cancer; he died on 22 August. During the Commonwealth Heads of Government summit, in October, the 16 countries in which the British monarch is Head of State unanimously agreed to change the royal line of succession from that of first born son to the first born child (regardless of its gender). The change will be enacted after the succession of Prince William (currently second in line to the throne, after his father Prince Charles).
2012 Minting of the Canadian penny (one cent piece) was stopped as part of the government's March budget as the cost of producing them was greater than their face value. The budget recommended that cash transactions be rounded up to the nearest five cents although card transactions were to remain specific. On 19 June Canada was invited by US President Obama to join the negotions for the Trans-Pacific Partnership (TPP) (of nine existing member countries), a free trade market of over 500 million people in Asia, Oceania and Americas.
2013 On 7 October Prime Minister Harper confirmed that he would not be attending the Commonwealth Heads of Government meeting in Sri Lanka in protest over alleged human rights abuses. He also said that Canada would be reviewing the financial support it gives the Commonwealth. Canada and the EU agreed a free trade agreement on 19 October. The deal is designed to lower tariffs, streamline regulation and cut red tape and is imed at boosting growth and employment.
2015 Canada was one of the 12 Pacific-Rim countries to agree the

Trans-Pacific Partnership (TPP) on 5 October. The agreement with seek to lower trade barriers such as tariffs, establish a common framework for intellectual property, enforce standards for labour law and environmental law, and establish an investor-state dispute settlement mechanism. The general election of 19 October was convincingly won by the Liberal Party of Canada, lead by Justin Trudeau, with 184 seats (out of 338); the Conservative Party of Canada came in second with 99 seats, followed by the New Democratic Party of Canada (44 seats). Bloc Québécois (10) and the Green Party of Canada (1). Justin Trudeau became prime minister designate. As part of his election campaign, Mr Trudeau had pledged to bring home the Canadian CF-18 fighter jets that were deployed to the Middle East until March 2016 where they were involved in air strikes against Islamic State. Within hours of being elected he confirmed his decision to US President Obama.

Political structure

Constitution

Although Canada is formally a constitutional monarchy with the British monarch as the nominal head of state, for all practical purposes the country is a sovereign state. The governor general is the Queen's representative in Canada.

The Canadian government has a federal structure, with 10 provincial governments plus the three northern territories of the Northwest Territories, Yukon and Nunavut on the lower tier and a national government on the upper tier.

The constitution is contained in the Constitution Act of 1982, although the province of Québec did not agree to this legislation. The division of power between the national and provincial governments is set out in the constitution which also contains a Charter of Rights and Freedoms. The federal government has authority over areas of national interest, while provincial governments have specific authority over local matters, including education, hospitals and public lands (including natural resources). The provinces exercise considerable autonomy over their affairs. Each province has an elected legislature together with an executive led by a provincial premier.

All Canadian citizens aged 18 years and over have the right to vote.

Form of state

Constitutional monarchy

The executive

The executive comprises the prime minister, appointed by the governor general, and his cabinet. The prime minister is the leader of the majority party in the House of Commons; the cabinet is also drawn from the ruling party's ranks.

National legislature

The House of Commons (lower legislature) does not have a fixed number of members, seats are apportioned based on the constitution. Seats are distributed among the provinces and reflect their population, however the provinces are also entitled to as many lower house seats as they have in the Senate and are entitle to as many seats as they had in 1976 or 1985, thus the current house has 308 sitting members. Members of the House of Commons sit for a maximum of five years and may be re-elected any number of times.

The Senate is a chamber of appointed members representing different political parties. The Governor General appoints members for a life-term, based on the recommendation of the prime minister. Seats are allocated to provide each province with equal representation. Over 50 per cent of membership is allocated to less-populated parts of the country to provide a balance of views. Senate tenure is guaranteed until aged 75. The Senate is a chamber of review whereby all legislatures must be passed before it for enactment. Legislature may be proposed by the Senate as long as it does not incur revenue collection.

Legal system

Based on English common law, except in Québec, where a French civil law system prevails.

The prime minister, through the governor general, appoints all judges to the federal courts, but not those to the provincial courts. Apart from this, the judiciary is independent of the executive. The Supreme Court of Canada is the highest court of appeal in both civil and criminal cases. Each province has its own court structure, headed by a provincial Supreme Court.

Last elections

19 October 2015 (parliamentary)

Results: Parliamentary: Liberal Party (LP) 54 per cent of the vote (184 seats out of 338), Conservative Party (Conservatives) 29 per cent (99 seats out of 308), New Democratic Party (NDP) 13 per cent (44), Bloc Québécois 3 per cent (10), Green Party 1 per cent (1); Turnout was estimated at 68 per cent.

Next elections

2020 (parliamentary)

Political parties

Ruling party

Conservative Party of Canada (CPC) (from 2006; re-elected 2 May 2011)

Main opposition party

New Democratic Party (Nouveau Parti Démocratique) (NDP)

Population

34.83 million (2012)

Last census: 16 May 2006: 31,612,897

Population density: Three inhabitants per square km. Urban population 81 per cent (2010 Unicef).

Annual growth rate: 1.0 per cent, 1990–2010 (Unicef).

Ethnic make-up

British and Irish origin (28 per cent), French origin (23 per cent), other European origin (15 per cent), indigenous (2 per cent), other (including Asian, African, Arab) (6 per cent), mixed background (26 per cent).

In 2002, about 52 per cent of immigrants settled in Toronto, 15 per cent in Vancouver and 11 per cent in Montréal; the populations of many rural areas are declining.

Religions

Christianity is the prevailing religion in Canada. Approximately 45 per cent of the population belong to the Roman Catholic Church. The leading Protestant churches are the Anglican Church of Canada and the United Church of Canada. Orthodox Churches are also represented. Jews make up 1.2 per cent of the population and Muslims just under 1 per cent.

Education

Public investment in education amounts to 5.5 per cent of GDP. Universal primary education and gender parity, at this level and in secondary schools, have been achieved. Although methods of funding higher education vary from province to province, the federal and provincial governments fund approximately 85 per cent of the expenditure. Total government spending on education in 2002/03 amounted to C$25 billion (US$39 billion). Canada has strong initiatives to monitor and detect inequities in schooling across the provinces. There is stiff entrance exams for teaching courses and extensive in-service training for qualified teachers, which affords them high status in the community.

Each province is responsible for its own education system. In general, education is provided free of charge to the end of the secondary level. The number of private schools is small, except in the province of Québec. Levels of educational attainment continue to rise, with record numbers attending university. However, enrolments at elementary and secondary schools have steadily declined since the late 1960s, reflecting the decline in both the birth rate and the number of new immigrants.

The proportion of young people attending full-time university and college courses continues to expand, while part-time higher education courses for mature students are becoming increasingly popular.

Canada has over 80 universities and 160 community and technical colleges, as well as 35 colleges of religious study.

Education services for indigenous students are an area of responsibility that is not clearly defined between provincial, territorial and federal government, who along with various local authorities have come up with different plans. There has been a rapid development of non-formal educational programmes, provided by non-governmental organisations. Citizenship education is a subject of renewed interest in the education curriculum.

Enrolment rate: 100 per cent total gross primary enrolment; 107 per cent boys, 106 per cent girls, gross secondary enrolment of relevant age groups (including repeaters) (Unesco).

Pupils per teacher: 16 in primary schools.

Health

Private expenditure averages 29 per cent of GDP, 39 per cent of which is funded by prepaid health plans and 52 per cent in out-of-pockets expenses.

Nationwide state-sponsored health insurance is achieved through a series of interlocking provincial plans, with the federal government providing substantial financial support through national Hospital Insurance and Medical Care Programmes. The insurance programmes are designed to ensure that all residents have access to medical services as needed. Most hospitals are run by non-profit, non-governmental, corporations.

HIV/Aids

In 2009 there were an estimated 68,000 adults living with HIV.

HIV prevalence: 0.3 per cent aged 15–49 in 2009 (Unicef 2012)

Life expectancy: 81 years, 2010 (Unicef 2012)

Fertility rate/Maternal mortality rate: 1.7 births per woman, 2010 (Unicef 2012)

Child (under 5 years) mortality rate (per 1,000): 5 per 1,000 live births (WHO 2012)

Head of population per physician: 2.14 physicians per 1,000 people, 2003 (WHO 2006)

Welfare

Canada has a comprehensive welfare system, which is administered at both federal and provincial levels of government. The system provides for social assistance, old age pensions, family allowances and unemployment insurance. Family allowances are credited for dependent children up to the age of 18.

Social assistance or welfare is the income programme of last resort in Canada. It helps people in need who are not eligible for other benefits. Benefit payments help pay for food, shelter and other health services.

The federal government provides monthly payments to parents or guardians on behalf of children under the age of 18, through a programme called the Child Tax Benefit. The amount is different according to family income, number of children and their ages. Successive federal governments have moved to target their financial support to families at the lower end of the income spectrum.

Pensions

In March 2012, it was announced that the age at which citizens would be eligible for the old age security (OAS) benefit on retirement would increase by one year to aged 67 years, from 2023. However those Canadians who were above the age of 54 year in March 2012 would not be affected by the new ruling and retirement remained at 66.

There are essentially two social security programmes aimed at providing income for the elderly in Canada.

The OAS pension is given to people aged 66 and over, who meet residence requirements. Those who have little or no other income are eligible for the Guaranteed Income Supplement (GIS). People who have lived in Canada for less than 40 years receive a reduced pension.

The Canada and Québec Pension Plans are a form of insurance into which people must contribute during their working years to receive monthly payments starting at age 66. These plans also include survivor's pensions for the spouses of deceased pensioners, disability pensions and children's and death benefits.

Main cities

Ottawa (capital, estimated population 945,438 in 2012), Toronto (5.2 million (m)), Montréal (3.4m), Vancouver (2.2m), Calgary (1.1m), Edmonton (979,504), Québec (703,415), Winnipeg (676,399), Hamilton (674,915).

Languages spoken

English is spoken by 61 per cent of the population, French by 26 per cent and both languages by 13 per cent. French predominates in the province of Québec (Montréal is the second largest French-speaking city in the world). A wide variety of other languages are spoken, reflecting the diverse origins of Canada's population.

Official language/s

English, French

Media

Press

Nearly all cities have at least one daily newspaper, and there is likely to be a tabloid if there is more than one on offer. The bilingual cities of Montreal and Ottawa offer newspapers in both English and French.

Dailies: The only national newspapers are the *National Post* (www.nationalpost.com) and *Globe and Mail* (www.theglobeandmail.com). The newspapers with the highest circulation include *Toronto Star* (www.thestar.com), *The Toronto Sun* (www.torontosun.com) a tabloid, *Vancouver Sun* (www.canada.com) and *The Gazette* (www.canada.com) from Montreal, and in French *Le Journal de Montréal* (www.canoe.com), and *La Presse* (www.cyberpresse.ca).

Weeklies: There are numerous local and community newspapers with dailies publishing weekend editions.

Business: National publications include *Canadian Business* (www.canadianbusiness.com), *The Northern Miner* (www.northernminer.com), Black Press has over 100 publications. Regional publications include *Business in Calgary* (www.businessincalgary.com) and *Business Edge* (www.businessedge.ca), from Alberta, *Business Examiner* (from Black Press), *Toronto Business Times* (www.torontobusinesstimes.com) and *Ottawa Business Journal* (www.ottawabusinessjournal.com) from Ontario and, in French, *Businest* (www.hebdosquebecor.com) and *Regard Économique* (http://www.linfonet.com) from Québec.

Periodicals: There are a range of magazines published by central and regional government, including *Government Executive* (www.networkedgovernment.ca), *Municipal World* (www.municipalworld.com), and *The Hill Times* (www.thehilltimes.ca). News and current affairs are covered by *Inroads* (www.inroadsjournal.ca) published in November and May, *L'Actualité* (www.lactualite.com), published 20-times a year and *This Magazine* (www.thismagazine.ca) a bi-monthly with alternative political views. Monthly magazines include women's titles *Chatelaine* (http://en.chatelaine.com) in English and French and *Flare* (www.flare.com), others include *Our Times* (www.ourtimes.ca), and *Yourthink Magazine* (www.youthink.ca) for the young.

Broadcasting

The Canadian Broadcasting Corporation (CBC) is the national, public broadcaster with programmes in English and French that can be accessed by internet.

Radio: There are over 2,000 private, commercial radio stations providing entertainment, news and information for most tastes. CBC (www.cbc.ca/radio) operates four networks, including Radio One, Two, Radio Canada International and a radio station for indigenous communities with broadcasting news, cultural and speech-based programmes. Newcap (www.ncc.ca) has a network of 76 radio stations, and Rogers Broadcasting Limited (www.rogers.com) operates a pay-to-listen network, throughout the country. Local radio stations are found in all urban and many rural areas.

Television: Analogue TV is due to be replaced by digital TV by 31 August 2011. Until then all pay-to-view cable TV companies must supply a proportion of their output in analogue form until it has a digital subscription rate of 85 per cent.

CBC Television has three channels, CBCtelevision, CBCnews and CountryCanada with some domestic programmes broadcast in English and French.

CTV (www.ctv.ca) is the largest, English-language, privately-owned network, broadcasting mainly high rating US shows, as well as its own productions. The Global Television Network (Global TV) (www.globaltv.com) is the second English-language, privately-owned network, which relies on foreign programmes for its contents.

There are several French-language TV stations mainly based in Province of Quebec, including Télé-Québec (www.telequebec.tv) and CJNT-TV (www.cjntmontreal.ca) from Montreal.

The national, Aboriginal People's Television Network (www.aptn.ca) is based in Winnepeg.

There are many cable and satellite channels in English and French, available throughout the country offering all varieties of entertainments, news and educational programmes.

Other news agencies: CBCNews: www.cbc.ca/news
CNW Group (in English and French): www.newswire.ca
The Canadian Press: www.thecanadianpress.com

Economy

Canada has vast natural resources of natural gas, timber, minerals and abundant fresh water and agricultural land that is used to produce beef, wheat, dairy products and fish, most of which is used in export trade. Its manufacturing sector is dominated by vehicle and aircraft construction, plus processing its natural resources.

When the global economic crisis began to weaken the economy, GDP growth fell to 0.7 per cent in 2008, the economy slipped into recession in 2009 with negative growth of -2.8 per cent, due to lower commodity prices and less exports in general. By 2010 GDP growth had picked up by 3.2 per cent as global trade increased; but by 2013 it had fallen to 2 per cent. In 2014 growth began to recover and reached 2.5 per cent.

The Canadian banking system did not suffer the disastrous losses encountered elsewhere during the global economic crisis. This was due to the conservative nature of the sector, coupled with sound financial regulations and an economy that was already underpinned by high global commodity prices, historically low unemployment and low corporate and bank leverage rates that allowed the sector to ride out the downturn. Nevertheless, the impact on not only the volume of commodities exported but also profits from exports did reduce government revenue from US$242 billion in 2007/08 to US$234 billion in 2008/09 but by 2014 it had recovered and increased to US$271.7 billion. As a result the country's current account balance, which fell from US$9.6 billion in 2008 to -US$38.4 billion in 2009 and further still to -US$56.6 billion in 2010 and in 2012 it was at -US$59.9 billion. By 2014 the deficit had reduced and the current account was at -US$39.3 billion.

The federal government instigated measures, along with other countries, to stimulate the economy back into growth following the oil shock-driven slump, including injections of public funds into money markets and guarantees for financial institutions.

As global trade picked up Canada's prospects improved. Nevertheless, it is the health of the US economy that has the greatest influence on Canada's economy, as the two countries are comprehensively linked by trade, with millions of jobs on both sides of their border relying on how well each other fares. Each is the other's largest export market; around 76.8 per cent of Canada's exports and 54.3 per cent of imports are with the US. China, which is buying up a large proportion of Canada's natural resources each year, has become Canada's second largest export market.

The unemployment rate in Canada reached a peak of 8.7 per cent in 2009, however, it has been decreasing since and dropped from 7.1 per cent in 2013 to 6.6 per cent in 2014. This drop correlates with the improving performance of the export market.

External trade

Canada's largest trading partner by far is the US and the country is now the leading export market for 35 separate US states. The North American Free Trade Agreement (Nafta), under which Canada has tri-lateral trade agreements with Mexico and the US, has been in operation since 1994. Canada's other top trading partners are China and the UK.

In 2014 export commodities by rank were oil, motor vehicles, machines, engines and pumps, precious metals including gold, electronic equipment, plastics, wood, larger aircraft and spacecraft, aluminium and cereals. However, among the above product groups exported only export sales of electronic equipment and aluminium declined over the five-year period ending in 2014, falling by 6.8 per cent and 0.6 per cent respectively. Cereals posted the highest increase of 57.3 per cent, followed by wood and oil, growing 49.4 per cent and 39.9 per cent respectively.

Canada is the world's largest source of nickel, zinc and uranium and has large reserves of hydrocarbons, exported mainly to the US.

Imports

Main imports are machinery and equipment, vehicles and parts, industrial materials, crude oil, consumer goods, foodstuffs, durable consumer goods and construction materials.

Main sources: US (54.3 per cent of total in 2014), China (11.5 per cent), Mexico (5.6 per cent)

Exports

Major exports include oil, motor vehicles, machines, engines and pumps, precious metals including gold, electronic equipment, plastics, wood, larger aircraft and spacecraft, aluminium and cereals.

Main destinations: US (76.8 per cent of total in 2014), China (3.7 per cent), UK (2.9 per cent)

Agriculture

Farming

The agricultural industry is of considerable importance to the country's economy. Canada has somewhere in the region of 280,000 farms and is the world's second-largest wheat exporter, with its high-quality spring wheat commanding a premium price on world markets. The country is also a sizeable producer of other grains, notably barley, rapeseed (canola) and oats. Livestock rearing is as important a source of income as field crops. Agriculture contributes 1.9 per cent to total GDP and is responsible for 2 per cent of total employment.

Despite the relative importance of agriculture in the Canadian economy compared with other industrialised nations, the federal government tends to argue that it cannot afford to match the plentiful subsidies and other aid offered to farmers in the EU and US. However, delays in co-ordinated elimination of the world's farm subsidies through the WTO are focussing the government's attention on support programmes for Canadian farmers.

Fishing

In 2014 Canada was the seventh-largest exporter of fish in the world with 3.6 per cent of the world total. Approximately half of the country's sizeable annual fish catch is processed for export. Aggressive fishing has depleted Canada's stocks, causing the closure of Canada's Atlantic fisheries in 1992, which led to a bitter salmon war with the US when wild salmon stocks dipped to perilously low levels. Such were the tensions, annually renewed during the salmon spawning season, that Canada encouraged the capture of fish bound for rivers in Washington and Oregon, in retaliation for rising US catches of Canadian-origin salmon.

Criticism has been raised that Canada has not protected its wild salmon population of fish. Three of the world's largest salmon farming companies operate in British Columbia and overall there are some 17 companies managing around 100 salmon farms. The fear is that Canada is raising non-native species of salmon and feeding them fish protein that creates risks for other species of wild fish. The resulting intermingling of populations risks the spread of disease, a competition for habitat and the alteration of the wild salmon gene pool. A salmon enhancement programme has been set up to enable the annual catch to reach 150,000 tonnes instead of the current average 70,000 tonnes.

In July 2015, it was announced that the University of Moncton would receive US$23.2 million from the Canada Foundation for Innovation (CFI) for salmon farming research. The investment, which is part of a group of infrastructure research products across the country, is aimed at reducing stress among fish and therefore producing healthier salmon with lower costs.

Canada has imposed a moratorium on commercial cod fishing and has a 320km exclusion zone off its eastern coast, patrolled by an increased number of coast guard vessels.

Forestry

Of Canada's total landmass some 53.8 per cent is covered with forests and woodland, around 400 million hectares. The country accounts for approximately 10 per cent of the world's forests and is worth C$26 billion (US$24.4 billion) in exports of forest products.

There is enormous variation in forest types across this vast country, including temperate softwood rainforests in coastal British Columbia, mixed boreal shield forests in central Canada, the maritime forests of New Brunswick and Nova Scotia on the Atlantic seaboard, and the sparse and slow-growing forests found at the Arctic tree line.

Québec, Ontario and British Columbia have the largest forest resources. Most forest and other wooded land is publicly owned, with 71 per cent under provincial jurisdiction and a further 23 per cent under the wing of the federal and territorial governments. Just 6 per cent is privately owned, and is generally located in the more productive regions. Large areas of forest land are under legislative protection, including the almost 8 per cent protected from harvesting.

Canada is the world's largest exporter of market pulp (almost 30 per cent of world total) and newsprint (near 40 per cent), with most production located in British Columbia, Ontario and Québec.

Non-wood forest products in Canada include maple syrup, berries, mushrooms, medicinal plants and game.

Industry and manufacturing

For the Canadian economy the industrial sector contributes approximately 32 per cent to total GDP. The sector also accounts for around 1.7 million jobs.

Canada's traditional manufacturing sectors include petroleum refining, pulp and paper mills, motor vehicles, steel, sawmills and planing mills, the dairy products industry, motor vehicle spare parts and accessories, metal stamping and pressing, smelting and refining, industrial chemicals, food processing, commercial printing, communications equipment, feed industries, plastics fabricating industries and aircraft and aircraft parts. Notable new sectors are in advanced telecommunications and network technology.

Production of primary metals and transport equipment has grown in recent years, reflecting exceptional growth in the automotive industry. The vast majority of automobile production is exported to the US.

Tourism

Canada has huge wilderness areas situated within or close to the Arctic Circle; it also has impressive mountain ranges, wide prairies and many rivers and lakes, enough to keep even the most avid activity-tourist fully occupied. Those less keen on the great outdoors can visit Canada's major cities for cultural and historic interests.

In 2014 Canada received 17.1 million international visitors, an increase of 3 per cent on 2013; however Canada's domestic tourist trade out-performs all international business by spending. Domestic expenditure in 2012 was C$66 billion (US$66.7 billion) and expenditure by foreign visitors was C$15.4 billion (US$15.6 billion). Citizens from the UK and France were the next largest group of visitors. The majority of trips by US citizens were for the purpose of leisure, while for those travelling from UK and France it was evenly split between leisure and visiting family and friends.

Travel and tourism in 2014 contributed C$23.1 billion (US$17.7 billion) directly to total GDP, 1.2 per cent of total GDP, and indirectly C$88.6 billion (US$67.9 billion), or 4.5 per cent of total GDP. The industry also directly employed some 462,000 workers (2.6 per cent of total employment), the majority of which are employed in small to medium sized enterprises (SMEs), often family owned; employment including related jobs was expected to be 6.0 per cent of the total workforce (1,075,000 jobs).

The industry was estimated to have had C$11.7 billion (US$8.9 billion) investment committed for 2014, or 2.5 per cent of total investment in the economy.

Environment

The Northwest Passage between the Pacific and Atlantic Oceans opened up in 2007 as a result of record ice melting in the Arctic. The ice shelf had retreated further than at any time in recorded history.

Mining

Canada remains a significant producer of gold and achieved the record output in 2014 of 160 tonnes, a 29 per cent increase on the 2013. Other base metal and metal stocks have declined, but Canada remains a major producer of nickel, copper, zinc, lead, iron ore and diamonds.

Most of Canada's exploration is focused on diamonds, mainly in Northwest Territories, Alberta, Québec and Saskatchewan. The country's first diamond mine opened in 1998.

Hydrocarbons

Canada's proven oil reserves at the end of 2014 stood at 172.9 billion barrels. The country is the world's fourth largest oil producer, outputting 4.3 million barrels per day (bpd). Canada is among the top ten places in the world consumption league, consuming 2.4 million bpd (as at end 2014).

The majority of oil is extracted from the west of the country, particularly Alberta which typically produces 55 per cent of Canada's total oil production. While oil production is steadily declining in the west, it is rising in the east, where production costs are higher and reserves are smaller. The US is the largest supplier of refined oil products to Canada. Bitumen production from Canada's oilsands is due to expand over the next decade with several large investment projects being developed. Currently this form of production is reliant on natural gas, however due to the high prices of natural gas this industry is seeking alternative methods of production. Until it becomes economically viable

the development of this industry could be slow.
There are two major pipeline networks. The Enbridge Pipelines cover 14,000km, delivering oil from Edmonton, Alberta, to Montréal, Québec, eastern Canada and refineries in the US Great Lakes region. The Trans-Mountain Pipeline (TMPL) delivers oil from Alberta to Vancouver and British Columbia as well as the US state of Washington.
Canada had 2.0 trillion cubic metres (cum) of natural gas reserves and produced 162.0 billion cum in 2014, making it the world's fifth-largest gas producer after Russia, the US, Qatar and Iran, and the second-largest gas exporter after Russia. Canada's gas exports are exclusively destined for the US. Domestic gas consumption is rising due to an increase in demand from the electricity generating sector.
The 3,000km Alliance Pipeline, opened in 2000, carries 36.8 million cum of gas per day from western Canada to the Chicago area in the US. The Millennium Pipeline is planned to connect Canadian gas fields to New York and Pennsylvania in the US. In mid-2003, the pipeline was in its initial planning stages but by December 2003 the planning permission was in abeyance as developers and local conservation authorities in the US argued about the best course for the pipeline. However in 2007 the Federal Energy Regulatory Commission authorised the commencement of the project and in December 2008 it officially went into service.
The proposed Keystone XL pipeline that would carry 830,000 barrels per day (bpd) of oil from the oil sands in Alberta, Canada to Steele City, Nebraska, was vetoed by President Barack Obama in February 2015 despite being approved by congress. The building of the pipeline would supposedly create 42,000 jobs over the two-year period of its construction.
Canada's coal reserves amounted to around 6.6 billion tonnes at the end of 2014. Estimated coal production (as at end 2014) totalled 36.7 million tonnes oil equivalent (toe). Canadian coal consumption of around 20.3 million toe is primarily used for electricity generation with the remainder used for steel production.
In May 2015, Teck Resources Ltd., the world's second largest exporter of coal used in steel making announced that as a result of a four-year slump in prices and demand it would be idling six of its Canadian operations in the third quarter of the year.

Energy

Canada currently has one of the world's most diversified electricity generation bases. The country has hydroelectricity, natural gas, oil, coal and nuclear power sources, which combined produce enough electricity to meet all domestic demand. The energy industry accounts for around 10 per cent of national GDP. At around 20 per cent of all export value, energy exports totalled C$128 billion (US$97.7 billion) in 2014, 92 per cent of which was sent to the US. Canada was the world's second largest exporter of electricity in 2014.
In 2013 total installed electric generating capacity was around 8.1 billion kilowatts. Electricity generation and pricing are determined and controlled by each province with federal control exercised only for international and inter-provincial movement of energy. Environmental assessments of energy projects and the development of policies and regulations are also under federal control.
Hydroelectric power plants provide over 60 per cent of electricity generation; there are plans to increase this total through further expansion of power plants. Natural gas provides around half the electricity of hydropower, and nuclear production half as much again. Natural gas alone provides 25 per cent of all domestic energy needs, supplied either directly to homes or in the production of electricity. There are 20 nuclear power reactors located in five sites, of which two were closed in 2011 and another in 2012. However despite the decline in short-term energy production there has been a resurgence of interest in nuclear power generation.
Sustainable energy production has increased with the growth in the use of wind turbines and in 2014 wind power accounted for almost 2 per cent of total electricity production.

Financial markets

Stock exchange
Toronto Stock Exchange (TSX)
Commodity exchange
Bourse de Montréal (Montreal Exchange)

Banking and insurance

Toronto Dominion Bank is Canada's largest banking and financial services institution, in terms of both its retail network and overall personal deposits and lending, having merged with Canada Trust in 2000.
Financial legislation, (Bill C–8) allows foreign and local banks to increase stakes in Canadian banks and to encourage global competitiveness and economic growth. The legislation allows a single shareholder to hold up to 20 per cent of the voting shares of a big Canadian bank, and opened the way to strategic alliances with foreign banks.
Central bank
Bank of Canada
Main financial centre
Toronto

Time

Canada has six time zones:
Newfoundland – GMT minus 3.5 hours;
Atlantic standard time (Maritimes and Labrador) – GMT minus four hours;
Eastern zone (Québec and most of Ontario) – GMT minus five hours;
Central zone (Manitoba, north-west Ontario and eastern Saskatchewan) – GMT minus six hours;
Mountain zone (west Saskatchewan, Alberta and north-east Columbia) – GMT minus seven hours;
Pacific zone (Yukon and the bulk of British Columbia) – GMT minus eight hours;
Daylight saving operates, in all states except Saskatchewan, from early March to late October – local time plus one hour.

Geography

Canada is the second-largest country in the world (Russia is the largest) and it stretches from the Atlantic Ocean to the Pacific. Apart from the border with Alaska in the north-west, Canada's frontier with the US follows the upper St Lawrence Seaway and the Great Lakes, extending westwards along latitude 49 degrees N.
There are six principal geographical regions. The south-east corner is the most densely populated part of the country and comprises the Atlantic Provinces and the lowland area to the north of the Great Lakes and the St Lawrence Seaway. To the north and west of this region lies the Canadian Shield, which is covered by forests, bare rock and lakes. Further to the west are the Interior Plains which are largely prairies, while the coastal area along the Pacific is dominated by the Rocky Mountains. The Northwest Territories extend into the Arctic with a barren landscape and sparse population density.
Hemisphere
Northern

Climate

The climate is extreme, especially inland. Winter temperatures drop well below freezing, but summers are usually warm. There are often heavy snowfalls in winter, making travel difficult.

Dress codes

Canadians are generally casual about dress. It is best to ask about dress codes if you are unsure.

Entry requirements

Passports
Required by all, except permanently resident US citizens with photo-ID; (all US nationals require a passport for re-entry to the US from January 2007).

Visa
Are required by all, except citizens of EU, the Commonwealth and US. For further information see www.cic.gc.ca/english/index.html and choose 'to visit'.
Business travellers should seek further information from a Canadian consulate or see
http://canadainternational.gc.ca/dbc/Business-travel-entering-canada-en.aspx.
Business visitors from exempted countries do not need to fulfil extra entry criteria, as long as their permanent employment is typically outside Canada, however work may not be undertaken beyond that allowed.

Currency advice/regulations
There are no restrictions on the import and export of currency.

Customs
Personal effects are allowed duty-free. Certain items, such as plants, meat, cereals, dairy products and live animals are subject to import licensing.

Prohibited imports
Include illegal drugs, marijuana, firearms, mace, pepper spray, switchblades (flick-knives) and fireworks. Vegetable matter including, apples, pears, stoned fruit, potatoes, fresh corn and firewood.

Health (for visitors)

Advisable precautions
No vaccinations or certificates are required. Comprehensive travel and medical insurance is essential though, as medical treatment can be very expensive.

Hotels

Many international hotel chains operate in most cities. However, it is advisable to book rooms in advance.
A goods and services tax of 7 per cent applies to all hotel bills, although visitors may be able to apply for a refund (for details and procedure see: www.nationaltaxrefund.com/eng/demarch.htm). Some states and provinces apply their own taxes.
Most large hotels have facilities for small displays or exhibitions, and smaller rooms may be rented as sample rooms. Most hotels impose a substantial surcharge on telephone calls.
For visitors travelling by car, good quality motels are available around all major towns and cities where rates are considerably less than those charged by city-centre hotels.

Credit cards

Credit cards are widely used.

Public holidays (national)

Fixed dates
1 Jan (New Year's Day), 1 Jul (Canada Day), 11 Nov (Remembrance Day), 25–26 Dec (Christmas).
When Canada Day falls on a Sunday, the next day is considered a holiday.
When Christmas Day or Boxing Day fall at a weekend, an extra day is given in lieu.
Additional holidays are observed by individual provinces and territories.

Variable dates
Good Friday, Easter Monday, Victoria Day (Mon preceding 24 May), Labour Day (first Mon in Sep), Thanksgiving Day (second Mon in Oct).

Working hours

Working hours vary throughout the country and government departments may work variable or flexible hours, especially during the summer months.

Banking
Mon–Wed: 1000–1500; Thu: 1000–2000; Fri: 1000–1600. Opening hours depend on the region and institution.

Business
Mon–Fri: 0830–1700.

Government
Mon–Fri: 0830–1700. Post offices Mon–Fri 0800–1745.

Shops
There is a five-day working week, but most retail stores in cities open on Saturday and a few on Sunday as well. Late shopping (to 2100) on Thursday or Friday is common in large cities; in suburban shopping centres, supermarkets often stay open until 2100 or 2200 Mon–Fri. Some convenience stores and supermarkets remain open 24 hours, especially in heavily populated areas.

Telecommunications

Mobile/cell phones
GSM 850/1900 services available in highly populated areas.

Electricity supply

120–240V (mostly 120V) 60 cycles AC, with two-pin flat-prong plug fittings (or three-pin with one round and two flat prongs) and screw-type lamp sockets. Adapters and transformers are available for appliances using other voltages.

Weights and measures

Metric system (Imperial and US systems also still in use).

Social customs/useful tips

When making introductions, the hand shake is considered rather formal unless you are meeting someone for the first time. To Canadians, eye contact is very important in conversation as it shows that you are paying attention.
It is best to avoid touching people unless you know someone fairly well. Touching someone of the opposite sex may well be considered harassment but touching the arm of your conversation partner is acceptable.
Tipping is expected and tends to be more generous in Canada than in other countries. 10 or 12 per cent would be considered frugal.

Getting there

Air

National airline: Air Canada
International airport/s: Ottawa (YOW) (www.ottawa-airport.ca), 13km south of the capital city. All major airports have full banking and catering facilities, duty-free shops and car hire. Airport-to-city bus and taxi services and, in some cases, rail links, are available.
Toronto Pearson International (YYZ) (www.gtaa.com), 27km north-west of Toronto, is Canada's busiest airport. It has three terminals catering for domestic and international flights; the latest was opened in April 2004 and handles Air Canada's domestic and international passengers.
Other airport/s: Calgary (YYC) (www.calgaryairport.com), 8km north of city. Edmonton (YEG) (www.edmontonairports.com), 28km south of city. Montréal Dorval (YUL) (www.admtl.com), 25km west of Montréal. Vancouver (YVR) (www.yvr.ca), 15km south-west of city. Winnipeg (YWG), 10km north-west of city.
Airport tax: There are two taxes that may or may not be included in the price of the ticket.
Both levies vary depending on destination, the Airport Improvement Fee (AIF) is C$5 for intrastate, C$10 interstate and US, and C$15 for all other international flights; the Air Travellers Security Charge is C$12 for intrastate and C$24 for interstate and all international flights. Travel agents and airport information can provide last minute details.

Surface

Road: Numerous border crossings from the US link directly with the Canadian highway system. Avoid crossings during peak times at weekends during the summer months when there are long delays.
Rail: Via Rail Canada Inc provides links with the US. Routes include:
Montréal-New York; Toronto-New York; Toronto-Chicago; Toronto-Cleveland/Detroit.
Water: Ferries connect the east coast of the US with Canada across the great lakes. Hudson Bay ports are subject to closure during winter months.

Main port/s: On the Atlantic Ocean: Halifax (Nova Scotia), St John (New Brunswick) and St John's (Newfoundland). Montréal and Québec have ports on the St Lawrence Seaway (linking the Atlantic with the Great Lakes). Toronto's port is on the north-western shore of Lake Ontario. Montréal is the only port for passenger liners from Europe.

On the Pacific Ocean: Vancouver (British Columbia).

Getting about

National transport

Air: There are frequent and extensive air services connecting all towns and cities of importance with 68 major airports and over 700 smaller ones lacking control tower facilities. Privatised Air Canada serves the main routes, and several regional carriers operate as well. Air travel is the most widely recommended form of travel between major cities, except between Toronto, Montréal and Ottawa, where train service is comfortable, reasonably priced and usually punctual.

Road: There are about 392,000km of roads, about 84 per cent surfaced. Motorways connect some large industrial centres and most large cities have a motorway network. The trans-Canada highway at 7,821km is the longest national highway worldwide. It runs from Victoria in British Colombia in the west to St Johns in Newfoundland in the east. The speed limit on motorways is 100kmph, 80kmph on rural highways and 50kmph on urban roads. Seatbelts are compulsory for all passengers.

Buses: Long-distance coach services link all major centres. They are very well air-conditioned, and it is often recommended that travellers keep a sweater handy.

Rail: There is an extensive rail network that comprises around 100,000km of track. The Canadian National Railway (CN) and Canadian Pacific Rail are the two main railway services, but passenger services are operated by Via Rail Canada (Canrail), a government agency. Air-conditioning, refreshment facilities and sleeping accommodation are available on long-distance passenger services. The Transcontinental, runs a northern route through Saskatoon, Edmonton and Jasper, three times a week. It is advisable to book seats/sleepers as early as possible. Canrail passes give unlimited travel for certain areas and routes.

The southern route through Regina, Calgary and Banff was cut when government subsidies were stopped.

Water: The St Lawrence Seaway provides deep-water passage from the Atlantic to the Great Lakes; there are 3,017km of canals, mainly used for leisure.

City transport

Taxis: Good taxi services operate in all major cities; rates vary between cities.

Buses, trams & metro: Toronto, Montréal, Vancouver and Edmonton have efficient, safe and clean underground systems. Most cities have reliable and extensive bus services.

Car hire

Car hire is widely available. Overseas driving licences may be used for the first three months of a visitor's stay (six months in British Columbia). Driving is on the right-hand side of the road.

BUSINESS DIRECTORY

The addresses listed below are a selection only. While World of Information makes every endeavour to check these addresses, we cannot guarantee that changes have not been made, especially to telephone numbers and area codes. We would welcome any corrections.

Telephone area codes

The international direct dialling (IDD) code for Canada is +1, followed by area code and subscriber's number:

Calgary	403	Québec	514
Edmonton	780	Saskatoon	306
Fredericton	506	St John	506
Halifax	902	St John's	709
Kingston	613	Toronto	416
London	519	Vancouver	604
Montréal	514	Windsor	519
Niagara Falls	905	Winnipeg	204
Ottawa	613		

Chambers of Commerce

American Chamber of Commerce in Canada, 260 Adelaide Street, PO Box 160, Toronto, Ontario, M5A 1N1 (tel: 777-8512; fax: 738-7714; e-mail: info@amchamcanada.ca).

British Canadian Chamber of Trade and Commerce, PO Box 1358, Station 'K', Toronto, Ontario, M4P 3J4 (tel: 502-0847; fax: 502-9319; e-mail: central@bcctc.ca).

Canadian Chamber of Commerce, Delta Office Towers, 350 Sparks Street, Ottawa, Ontario, K1R 7S8 (tel: 238-4000; fax: 238-7643; e-mail: info@chamber.ca).

British Columbia Chamber of Commerce, 750 West Pender Street, Vancouver, British Columbia, V6C 2T8 (tel: 683-0700; fax: 683-0416; e-mail: bccc@bcchamber.org).

Halifax Chamber of Commerce, 7 Spectacle Lake Drive, Dartmouth, Nova Scotia (tel: 468-7111; fax: 468-7333;e-mail: info@halifaxchamber.com).

Kingston Chamber of Commerce, 67 Brock Street, Kingston, Ontario, K7K 1R7 (tel: 5448-4453; fax: 548-4743; e-mail: info@kingstonchamber.on.ca).

Manitoba Chamber of Commerce, 227 Portage Avenue, Winnipeg, Manitoba, R3B 2A6 (tel: 948-0100; fax: 948-0110; e-mail: mbchamber@mbchamber.mb.ca).

Montréal Board of Trade, 380 St Antoine Street West, Montréal, Québec, H2Y 3X7 (tel: 871-4000; fax: 871-1255; e-mail: info@ccmm.qc.ca).

North Vancouver Chamber of Commerce, 124 West 1st Street, North Vancouver, British Columbia, V7M 3N3 (tel: 987-4488; fax: 987-8272; e-mail: info@nvchamber.bc.ca).

Ontario Chamber of Commerce, 180 Dundas Street West, Toronto, Ontario M5G 1Z8 (tel: 482-5222; fax: 482-5879; e-mail: info@occ.on.ca).

Ottowa Chamber of Commerce, 1701 Woodward Drive, Ottowa, Ontario, K2C 0R4 (tel: 236-3630; fax: 236-7498; info@greaterottowachamber.com).

Québec Federation of Chambers of Commerce, 500 Place d'Armes, Montréal, Québec, H2Y 2W2 (tel: 844-9571; fax: 844-0226; e-mail: info@ccq.ca).

Toronto Board of Trade, 1 First Canadian Place, PO Box 60, Toronto, Ontario, M5X 1C1 (tel: 366-6811; fax: 366-8406; e-mail: info@bot.com).

Vancouver Board of Trade, World Trade Centre, 999 Canada Place, Vancouver, British Columbia, V6C 3E1 (tel: 681-2111; fax: 681-0437; e-mail: contactus@boardoftrade.com).

Winnipeg Chamber of Commerce, 259 Portage Avenue, Winnipeg, Manitoba, R3B 2A9 (tel: 944-8484; fax: 944-8492; e-mail: info@winnipeg-chamber.com).

Banking

Bank of Montréal, First Canadian Place, Concourse Level, PO Box 3, Toronto, Ontario M5X 1A1 (tel: 867-7662).

Bank of Nova Scotia, 44 King Street West, Toronto, Ontario M5H 1H1 (tel: 866-6161).

Business Development Bank of Canada, 3rd Floor, 5 Place Ville Marie, Montréal, Québec H4Z 1L4 (tel: 283-5904; fax: 496-8036).

Canadian Imperial Bank of Commerce (CIBC), Commerce Court, Toronto, Ontario M5L 1G9 (tel: 980-2211).

National Bank of Canada, 50 O'Connor Street, Suite 1224, Ottawa, Ontario K1P 6C2 (tel: 238-8383).

Royal Bank of Canada, 200 Bay Street, Royal Bank Plaza, Toronto, Ontario M5J 2J5 (tel: 974-5151; internet site: www.royalbank.com).

Toronto Dominion Bank, PO Box 1, Toronto Dominion Centre, 55 King Street, Toronto, Ontario M5K 1A2 (tel: 982-7730).

Central bank

Bank of Canada, 234 Wellington Street, Ottawa, Ontario, K1A 0G9 (tel: 782-8111; fax: 782-7713; e-mail: paffairs@bankofcanada.ca).

Stock exchange

Toronto Stock Exchange (TSX), www.tsx.com

CNQ (Canadian National Stock Exchange), Toronto, www.cnq.ca

Nasdaq Canada, www.nasdaq- canada.com

Commodity exchange

Bourse de Montréal (Montreal Exchange), www.m-x.ca

ICE Futures Canada (Winnipeg Commodity Exchange), www.theice.com

Travel information

Tourism Industry Association of Canada, 130 Albert Street, Suite 1016, Ottawa K1P 5G4 (tel: 238-3883).

Air Transport Association of Canada, 99 Bank St, Suite 747, Ottawa, ON, K1P 6B9 (tel: 233-7727; fax: 230-8648).

Ministry of tourism

Tourism Canada, Federal Department of Industry, Science and Technology, 235 Queen Street, 4th Floor East, Ottawa K1A 0H6 (tel: 954-3851).

Ministries

Ministry of Agriculture and Agri-Food, Sir John Carling Building, 930 Carling Avenue, Ottawa, Ontario, K1A OC5 (tel: 995-8963).

Ministry of Foreign Affairs and International Trade, Lester B Pearson Building, 125 Sussex Drive, Ottawa, Ontario, K1A OG2 (tel: 996-9134; fax: 952-3904).

Ministry of Industry, CD Howe Building, 235 Queen Street, Ottawa, Ontario, K1A OH5 (tel: 952-4782).

Ministry of Natural Resources, 580 Booth Street, Ottawa, Ontario, K1A OE4 (tel: 995-0947; fax: 992-6424/5230).

Ministry of Public Works and Government Services, Sir Charles Tupper Building, Confederation Heights, Ottawa, Ontario, K1A OM2 (tel: 736-2027; fax: 736-23440).

Other useful addresses

Advertising Standards Canada, 350 Bloor Street, Suite 402, Toronto ON M4W 1H5 (tel: 961-6311; fax: 961-7904; email: info@adstandards.com; internet: www.adstandards.com).

Alberta Stock Exchange, 10th Floor, 300 Fifth Avenue SW, Calgary T2P 3C4 (tel: 974-7400; fax: 237-0450).

Bourse de Montréal (Stock Exchange), Tour de la Bourse, CP 61, 800 Square Victoria, Montréal H4Z 1A9 (tel: 871-2424; fax: 871-3553; e-mail: info@me.org).

British High Commission, 80 Elgin Street, Ottawa, Ontario, K1P 5K7 (tel: 237-1530; fax: 237-7980).

Canadian Broadcasting Corporation, 1500 Bronson Avenue, PO Box 8478, Ottawa, Ontario K1G 3J5 (tel: 724-1200; fax: 738-6843).

Canadian Embassy (USA), 501 Pennsylvania Avenue, NW, Washington DC 20001 (tel: 202-682-1740; fax: 202-682-7701; e-mail: webmaster@canadianembassy.org).

Canadian Importers' Association, 210 Dundas St West, Suite 700, Toronto, Ontario, M5G 2E8 (tel: 595-5333; fax: 595-8226).

Canadian Manufacturers' Association, One Yonge St, Toronto, Ontario, M5E 1J9 (tel: 363-7261; fax: 363-3779).

CTV Television Network, 42 Charles St East, Toronto, Ontario, M4Y 1T5 (tel: 928-6000; fax: 928-0907).

Department of Energy, Mines and Resources, 580 Booth St, Ottawa, Ontario, K1A 0E4 (tel: 995-3065; fax: 996-9094).

Department of Finance, 140 O'Connor St, Ottawa, Ontario, K1A 0G5 (tel: 992-1575; fax: 996-2690).

Department of Labour, Labour Canada, Ottawa, Ontario, K1A 0J2 (tel: 997-2617; fax: 953-0176).

Department of Regional Industrial Expansion, 235 Queen St, Ottawa, Ontario, K1A 0H5 (tel: 995-9001).

Economic Council of Canada, PO Box 527, Ottawa, Ontario, K1P 5V6 (tel: 993-1253; fax: 991-4904).

Investment Canada, PO Box 2800, Station 'D', Ottawa, Ontario, K1P 6A5 (tel: 996-2515; fax: 995-0465).

Ontario International Trade Corporation, 5th Floor, Hearst Block, 900 Bay Street, Toronto, Ontario, M7A 2E1 (tel: 325-6514; fax: 325-6509).

Retail Council of Canada, 210 Dundas St West, Suite 600, Toronto, Ontario, M5G 2E8 (tel: 598-4684; fax: 598-3707).

Statistics Canada, Statistical Reference Centre, Ottawa, Ontario, K1A OT6 (tel: 951-8116; internet site: www.statcan.ca/start.html).

Toronto Stock Exchange, The Exchange Tower, 2 First Canadian Place, Toronto, Ontario, M5X 1J2 (tel: 947-4700, 947-9301; fax: 947-4662).

Vancouver Stock Exchange, Stock Exchange Tower, 609 Granville Street, PO Box 10333, Vancouver, BC V7Y 1H1 (tel: 689-3334; fax: 688-6051).

Winnipeg Stock Exchange, 620 One Lombard Place, Winnipeg, Manitoba R3B 0X3 (tel: 987-7070; fax: 987-7079).

CBCNews: www.cbc.ca/news

CNW Group (in English and French): www.newswire.ca

The Canadian Press: www.thecanadianpress.com

Internet sites

Air Canada: www.aircanada.com

Canada Online: http://www.ic.gc.ca/Intro.html

Canadian Airlines: www.cdnair.ca

Canadian Automobile Association: www.caa.ca

Canadian Energy: www.centreforenergy.com/AboutEnergy/

Canadian International Development Agency (CIDA): http://www.international.gc.ca/

Canadian Parliament: www.parl.gc.ca

Government of Canada (all dept): http://www.canada.ca/en/index.html

Government of Alberta: http://alberta.ca/

Government of Ontario: http://www.ontario.ca/

Government of Québec: http://www.gouv.qc.ca/portail/quebec/pgs/commun/

Inuit and Artic news: http://www.nunatsiaqonline.ca/

North American Free Trade Agreement: https://www.nafta-sec-alena.org/Default.aspx

Trans-Canadian highway: www.transcanadahighway.com

Cayman Islands

Elections were held on 22 May 2013 with the result a win for the People's Progressive Movement (Progressives) with nine seats (out of 18), followed by the UDP and Coalition for Cayman (C4C) with three seats each. The PNA won one seat (former interim prime minister, Juliana O'Connor-Connolly) and the two incumbent independents were also re-elected. Progressive leader Alden McLaughlin formed a new government.

According to the World Bank, the Cayman Islanders have the third highest per capita gross domestic product (GDP) (after Bermuda and the US) in the Americas and the Caribbean (US$46,500 in 2010), and they pay no income tax. However, in 2012 the government was discussing levying a 10 per cent tax (rather oddly called a 'community enhancement fee'), although only on expatriates. The reason for this appears to be that the government has been spending too much on itself and needs bailing out.

Insiders point out that these same expatriates could up-sticks and move to another zero or low tax island, such as other Caribbean islands of Bermuda or Bahamas. And this would leave the government in even more trouble. The economy grew by 1.6 per cent 2012, slightly up on the the 1.3 per cent 2011.

Risk assessment

Politics	Poor
Economy	Poor
Regional stability	Good

COUNTRY PROFILE

1503 Little Cayman and Cayman Brac were sighted by Christopher Columbus during his fourth and final voyage to the New World. The islands were first named Las Tortugas (turtles); the name was later changed to Lagartos (alligator or large lizard).
1540 The name Caymanas was given to the islands, derived from the Carib word for marine crocodile.
1585–86 Sir Frances Drake visited the islands.
During the sixteenth, seventeenth and eighteenth centuries, Dutch, English, Spanish and French ships used the islands for watering and provisioning.
1655 The islands came under British control when Jamaica was captured from the Spanish.
1670 In the Treaty of Madrid, Spain recognised UK sovereignty over Jamaica and the Cayman Islands. The early settlers were ex-soldiers from Oliver Cromwell's army, with other settlers from Jamaica, together with shipwrecked or marooned sailors.
1773 Grand Cayman's population reached 400.
1831 It was agreed that representatives should be appointed for the five different districts of Grand Cayman for the purpose of forming local laws for better government. After elections in the five districts, the legislative assembly met in George Town.
1833 Cayman Brac and Little Cayman were settled permanently.
1835 The proclamation declaring the emancipation of all slaves throughout the colonies was read.
1962 When Jamaica became independent, Caymanians retained direct links with the Crown and the Cayman Islands became a separate British Crown Colony.
1971 The first governor was appointed.
1972 A new constitution was adopted giving greater autonomy and making the islands a British Overseas Territory.
1994 A constitutional amendment introduced a ministerial form of government.
2000 Only independent candidates were elected to parliament.
2001 The United Democratic Party (UDP) was formed. Its leader, W McKeeva Bush, became the leader of government business.
2002 The People's Progressive Movement (PPM) was formed.
2003 The previously informal title for the government's chief minister, the Leader of Government Business, was formally recognised by the UK government.
2004 The worst hurricane since 1918, Hurricane Ivan, struck the islands, causing severe flooding and infrastructure damage.
2005 The PPM won the parliamentary elections; Kurt Tibbetts became Leader of Government Business.
2007 Public discussion in the Phase one of the Constitutional Modernisation Initiative began.

KEY FACTS

Official name: Cayman Islands

Head of State: Queen Elizabeth II; represented by Governor Helen Kilpatrick (from 6 Sep 2013)

Head of government: People's Progressive Movement (Progressives) (from 22 May 2013)

Ruling party: People's Progressive Movement (Progressives) (from 22 May 2013)

Area: 259 square km

Population: 54,914 (2014)* (55,456; 2010, census figure)

Capital: George Town (Grand Cayman)

Official language: English

Currency: Cayman Islands dollar (CI$) = 100 cents

Exchange rate: CI$0.82 per US$ (Sep 2015)

Labour force: 35,267 (2011; including 19,000 foreign workers)

Unemployment: 6.70% (2010)

Visitor numbers: 288,000 (2010)

* estimated figure

2009 Governor Stuart Jack stepped down. The opposition UDP won parliamentary elections. A referendum agreed, by 63 per cent of votes, to overhaul the constitution. W McKeeva Bush (UDP) became Leader of Government Business. The Cayman Islands agreed to adopt measures to allow the Organisation for Economic Co-operation and Development (OECD) to remove it from the OECD list of countries that do not implement international standards for tax disclosure. The new constitution was inaugurated; changes included the head of government becoming a premier, with a limit of two terms in office, and a bill of rights to be introduced in November 2012. Donovan Ebanks became acting governor.
2010 Duncan Taylor took office as governor. Legislation was introduced establishing bilateral agreements for exchanging tax information. A census was undertaken.
2011 Preliminary results from the census, published in March, indicated that the population was fewer, at an estimated 54,878, than the 2008 forecast of 57,000. In June a National Energy Policy Committee (NEPC) was convened for the first time to plan Cayman Islands' response to rising fossil fuel prices and future energy needs.
2012 Full results of the census were published on 23 April and the total population was recorded at 55,036, however there were an additional 420 'institutionalised' individuals. On 28 September, at the meeting of the EU's Overseas Countries and Territories Association (OCTA) in Greenland, Premier McKeeva Bush voiced his opposition to Article 70 of the draft Overseas Association Decision (OAD), which calls for a convergence of financial services regimes with EU legislation. He considered that such a merging of legislation would seriously damage the financial services industry of not only the Cayman Islands but other overseas territories as well. The OAD is at an advanced stage of negotiation and without revision is scheduled to come into effect in January 2014. The Cayman Islands trust that the support promised by the UK government will limit any damage to its financial sector. Premier McKeeva Bush was arrested on 11 December on suspicion of corruption, including the misuse of government credit cards and importing explosive materials. As a result the government fell on a vote of no confidence and an interim government lead by Juliana O'Connor-Connolly as prime minister took over until elections could be held. Ms Juliana O'Connor-Connolly headed the People's National Alliance (PNA), consistiting of former members of the UDP.
2013 On 1 May the Cayman Islands, along with Bermuda, the British Virgin Islands, Anguilla, Montserrat and the Turks and Caicos Islands, signed a tax sharing agreement with the tax authorities of France, Germany, Italy, Spain and the UK. Elections were held on 21 May and were won by the People's Progressive Movement (Progressives) with nine seats (out of 18), followed by the UDP and Coalition for Cayman (C4C) with three seats each. Ms O'Connor-Connolly was the only PNA member to retain a seat, as did the two independents. Alden McLaughlin of the Progressives became prime minister. The government signed an agreement with the US for automatic exchange of tax information under the US Foreign Account Tax Compliance Act (FATCA) on 29 November. At the same time a new tax information exchange agreement (TIEA) was signed, replacing the earlier TIEA of 2001.
2014 Overseas Territory representatives from the British Virgin Islands, Bermuda, Montserrat, the Cayman Islands and Anguilla met with United Kingdom business networking specialists, CaribDirect International Business Network (CIBN) in May. CIBN is an agency designed to facilitate and connect entrepreneurs and business people in the UK with Caribbean government and business representatives for trade and investment.
2015 Governor Helen Kilpatrick announced in January the appointment of the Electoral Boundaries Commission 2015 (EBC). The prime task of the Commission is to make recommendations for the creation of single-member electoral districts and to submit a report in time for the changes to come into force in time for the May 2017 general election. US Securities and Exchange Commission (SEC) filed a lawsuit against the Caledonian Bank and four other companies in early February; four days later the Cayman Islands Monetary Authority (CIMA) placed Caledonian Bank and its brokerage arm into controllership. On 18 February Caledonian Bank filed for bankruptcy protection in the US Bankruptcy Court of the Southern District of New York in order to prevent a feared run on the bank's liquid assets.

Political structure

Constitution

The constitution of 1972, revised in 1994, created ministers and ministries and provided for a system of government headed by a governor, an Executive Council (ExCo) and Legislative Assembly. Unlike other Caribbean Overseas Territories, there is no chief minister, but a leader of government business. The appointed governor retains responsibility for the civil service, defence, external affairs and internal security.

On 6 November 2009, a new constitution was inaugurated; the head of government became a premier, with a limit of two terms in office. A bill of rights came into force on 6 November 2012.

In January 2015 Governor Helen Kilpatrick announced the appointment of the Electoral Boundaries Commission 2015 (EBC). The prime task of the Commission was to make recommendations for the creation of single-member electoral districts and to submit a report in time for the changes to come into force in time for the May 2017 general election.

Form of state

Self-governing British Crown Colony

The executive

The British monarch is Head of State and is represented by the governor. Government is exercised by the Executive Council (ExCo) presided over by the governor, consisting of three official members appointed by the governor and five members drawn from the elected members of the Legislative Assembly. As ministers, the five elected members of the ExCo have direct responsibility for government portfolios.

National legislature

The Legislative Assembly has 18 members (from six electoral districts), 15 elected members (MLAs) for a four-year term in two-seat constituencies, and three *ex-officio* members. In January 2015 the Electoral Boundaries Commission 2015 (EBC) was tasked with making recommendations for the creation of single-member electoral districts and to submit a report in time for the changes to come into force in time for the May 2017 general election.

Legal system

The legal system is based on English common law with local changes. Courts: Juvenile Court, Summary Court Grand Court and the Cayman Islands Court of Appeal. Final appeals go to the Privy Council in the UK.

Last elections

22 May 2013 (parliamentary)

Results: People's Progressive Movement (Progressives) won 36.1 per cent and 9 seats (out of 18), United Democratic Party (UDP) 27.8 per cent and 3 seats, Coalition for Cayman (C4C) 18.6 per cent 3 seats, People's National Alliance (PNA) 5.7 per cent and 1 seat, independents won the remaining 2 seats. Turnout was 79.82 per cent.

Next elections

May 2017 (parliamentary)

Political parties

Ruling party

People's Progressive Movement (Progressives) (from 22 May 2013)

Main opposition party

People's Progressive Movement (Progressives) (from 22 May 2013)

Political situation

The Cayman Islands has the highest standard of living of any other Caribbean country and it relies heavily on its offshore banking to maintain this and must judge the balance between offering a discrete, and no-questions-asked, banking service against the potential retaliatory action of foreign governments keen to stem the flow of revenue from their coffers.

Population

51,384 (2011)*

Ninety per cent of the population live on Grand Cayman; Little Cayman is virtually uninhabited.

Last census: 10 October 2010: 55,036

Population density: 150 inhabitants per square km.

Annual growth rate: 4.4 per cent (2003)

Ethnic make-up

Mixed race (40 per cent), white (20 per cent), black (20 per cent). Thirty-four per cent of the population are foreign residents, of whom 10 per cent are British or American.

Religions

Mainly Presbyterian with Anglican, Roman Catholic, Seventh-Day Adventists, Pilgrims, Pilgrim Holiness Church of God, Jehovah's Witnesses and Baha'i minorities on Grand Cayman. Baptists on Cayman Brac.

Health

The Cayman Islands have a variety of modern medical facilities. There are government-operated hospitals on Grand Cayman and Cayman Brac. The George Town Hospital on Grand Cayman is affiliated with the Baptist Hospital of Miami, USA, for patient referrals involving advanced care or treatment.

Life expectancy: 80 years (estimate)

Fertility rate/Maternal mortality rate: Two births per woman (2003)

Birth rate/Death rate: 13 births per 1,000 population; five deaths per 1,000 population (2003).

Child (under 5 years) mortality rate (per 1,000): Nine per 1,000 live births (2003)

Main cities

George Town, on Grand Cayman (capital, estimated population 29,175 in 2012); West Bay (11,885), Bodden Town (11,376).

Languages spoken

Spoken English has a distinctive 'brogue'. The Jamaican patois and a stronger accent is also common. Spanish, particularly regional dialects of Central America and Cuba, is also spoken.

Official language/s

English

Media

Press

The private publisher Cayman Free Press (CFP) (www.caymanfreepress.com) has a variety of publications.

Dailies: There are two newspapers, *The Caymanian Compass* (www.caycompass.com) published by CFP and *Cayman Net News* (www.caymannetnews.com).

Weeklies: The *New Caymanian* newspaper is published on Friday. There are two TV guide publications.

Business: The *Cayman Observer* (www.caymanobserver.com) is a weekly publication. The *Cayman Islands Yearbook and Business Directory* is published yearly.

Periodicals: A free-issue tourist magazine *Key to Cayman* is a quarterly, *Inside Out* is a bi-annual home and lifestyle magazine, *The Journal* is a monthly general interest broadsheet; these are published by CFP. *Newstar* is a tourist publication.

Broadcasting

Radio: The public broadcaster is Radio Cayman (www.radiocayman.gov.ky), which has two networks, One (for news, information and music) and Two (for popular music). Private, commercial radio stations include Vibe FM (www.vibefm-cayman.com), Z99FM (www.z99.ky), Hot 106.1 (www.hot1041fm.ky), Kiss FM (www.kiss1061fm.ky) and X107.1 (www.x1071.ky).

Television: There are four commercial, free-to-air TV stations, Cayman International Television Network (CITN), called Channel 27 (www.cayman27.com.ky), transmits local, Caribbean and International news and entertainment, Cayman Television Service (CTS) with Island 24, which has evolved into a tourism information channel. There are two religious channels, CCTV and CATN.

There are four pay-to-view platforms. Digital cable providers include WestTel (www.weststartv.com) with 120 channels and CITN with 35-channels showing imported programmes. Satellite stations include Dish Direct TV with over 200 channels and Island TV.

Other news agencies: Caribbean Net News: www.caribbeannetnews.com

Economy

The Cayman Islands has no direct taxation and has therefore proven to be a booming financial centre with over 93,000 companies registered there, though the Islands have a population of some 53,000 people.

In 2014 the service sector accounted for 73.2 per cent of GDP, dominating the economy, especially in offshore financial services and tourism, which provide virtually the sole sources of export earnings. The land is not productive enough to feed the population and the islands are dependent on imports for the bulk of its consumption and investment requirements.

The economy is vulnerable to external shocks, such as the global economic crisis, which caused a downturn in trade and investment. As with other Caribbean countries, the Cayman Islands are susceptible to devastating hurricanes that injure people and damage property.

The first Islamic compliant bond (*Sukuk*) issuance programme to be listed on the London Stock Exchange in 2007 was issued by the Cayman Islands, valued at US$5 billion. The Cayman Islands have a growing reputation as a leader in Islamic finance.

The government has implemented measures to retain and enhance international business as well as identifying assets to be sold. The premier announced in 2010 that residency may be purchased by financial workers for a one-off payment of US$1 million.

The Cayman Islands felt the full effect of the global economic crisis as it is heavily reliant on imports for its needs, around 90 per cent of the islands consumer goods and food are imported, and the real estate and financial services were also hit heavily, along with construction. The Caymans experienced some years of negative growth but in 2012, as the economic climate improve, they registered positive growth again at 1.6 per cent. Though this figure dropped slightly to 1.2 per cent in 2012, it grew to 1.7 per cent in 2014. Despite the fact growth is still low, it is showing a gradual recovery.

Over 50 per cent of the workforce are expatriates with most working in the financial industry. The Cayman Islands keep abreast of international compliance measures for money laundering.

In 2009 the Cayman Islands government was in need of a US$61 million loan to cover the shortfall in domestic spending; the UK, which is responsible for Cayman Islands' external affairs, provided security for the loan so long as fiscal reforms were implemented. In particular the UK wanted a commitment to cutting expenditure and an independent assessment of direct taxation to broaden the tax base.

In November 2011, the UK government submitted a framework for fiscal responsibility (FFR), to the government for review, discussion and eventual signing. The FFR had four central tenets and was intended to provide a clearly defined and understood framework of working practices. They were that the government should first undertake effective medium-term planning to ensure that the full impact of fiscal

decisions was understood; second put value for money considerations at the heart of decision-making process; thirdly demonstrate effective management of risk; and lastly drive the delivery of improved accountability in all public sector operations.
Premier Bush (who was arrested in December 2012 for corruption allegations) considered the FFR to have the potential to impact not only on the government's fiscal policy making, but also the broader economic status of the Cayman Islands.
The 2012/13 budget became the first within a four-year frame, agreed with the UK under the FFR, to put the Cayman Islands government's financials on a stable and sustainable footing.
Aside from financial enterprises the Caribbean nation also has a thriving tourist industry that serves mainly visitors from North America. In 2014 tourism contributed a total of 28.1 per cent to GDP and employed, including jobs indirectly supported by the industry, a total of 30 per cent of the workforce (10,000 jobs). Investment in travel and tourism accounted for 26.1 per cent of total investment (US$207.3 million).

External trade
The economy is heavily dependant on the financial services sector and tourism. A substantial deficit is traditionally run on the merchandise trade account, which is usually covered by invisible earnings and capital inflows from tourism and financial services. Trade is limited to small-scale agricultural and marine production and manufactured consumer goods.

Imports
Principal imports are foodstuffs, petroleum and derivatives, consumer goods, machinery and transport equipment, tourist-related goods.
Main sources: US, UK, The Netherlands Antilles, Japan

Exports
Principal exports are aquaculture products including turtles and crustacean livestock and manufactured consumer goods.
Main destinations: US, Canada and other Caribbean islands.

Agriculture
Farming
Poor soil conditions and scarcity of land make agriculture uneconomic. Only about 8 per cent of the total land area is farmed and the industry only contributes 0.3 per cent to GDP and employs only 1.9 per cent of the workforce. The Cayman Islands do not produce enough food to meet local demand and are reliant on imports. A National Tree Crop Husbandry Programme has increased the output of mangoes, citrus fruit and bananas. Government policies focus on sustainable development and using new technologies.

Fishing
The typical annual fish catch is 125 tonnes (t). All spawning areas for groupers were closed for fishing for a period of eight years from 2003, in a move aimed at preserving stocks for future generations. Groupers take eight years to mature.

Industry and manufacturing
The industrial sector contributed 28.4 per cent to GDP in 2014. Diversification is hampered by factors such as high labour costs and a shortage of labour. Activity is centred on building materials (concrete blocks and tiles) and tourist-related industries such as jewellery, printing and food processing.

Tourism
The Cayman Islands offer typical Caribbean holidays based around its beaches. In 2014 the World Travel Awards named the Cayman Islands as the Worlds Leading Dive Destination. The *Brides Magazine* also ranked the Cayman Islands as among the top 20 honeymoon destinations. Industry planning identified *niche* marketing based on 'sun, sand and surf' as the future of tourism in the Cayman Islands.
The industry contributed over US$1 billion to the economy in 2014, which accounted for 28.1 per cent of GDP. Real growth in tourism has been recovering since 2004 when a devastating hurricane inflicted so much damage on the islands that in 2005 tourism was in negative growth of -37.8 per cent. Since then contribution to GDP has grown from some US$600 million to its former pre-hurricane levels. The tourist industry provided employment to 30 per cent of the working population in 2014, which was the equivalent of 10,000 jobs. Investment in travel and tourism accounted for 26.1 per cent of total investment (US$207.3 million).

Hydrocarbons
There are no known hydrocarbons reserves and all domestic needs are met by oil imports, which were 3,360 barrels per day (bpd) in 2013 (latest figures).
Any use of natural gas or coal is commercially insignificant.

Energy
Total installed generating capacity was 151MW in 2013 (latest figures), generating around 600 million kilowatt hours. The Caribbean Utilities Company (CUC) is responsible for generation, distribution and supply of electricity; it has 18 generating units, including 16 diesel turbines. Solar-photovoltaic panels have been installed in community centres such as hospitals but the uptake by households was, in 2013, low. According to CUC this was due to a lack of clear sell-back regulations which made it difficult for individuals to upload excess power to CUC, thus making the proposition of investing in the technology less attractive.

Financial markets
Stock exchange
Cayman Islands Stock Exchange (CSX)

Banking and insurance
Under an EU tax directive introduced in July 2005 in dependent EU countries, the Cayman Islands now informs all EU citizens' tax departments about the amount of money in savings accounts to allow tax to be levied from the home country while retaining a saver's anonymity.
The Cayman Islands has also agreed to supply information on tax fraud, for criminal or civil trials, and notify EU member states about additional malpractices.
On 1 May 2013 the Cayman Islands, along with Bermuda, the British Virgin Islands, Anguilla, Montserrat and the Turks and Caicos Islands, signed a tax sharing agreement with the tax authorities of France, Germany, Italy, Spain and the UK. However, the banks in the Cayman Islands still have a notorious reputation for being less vigorous in adhering to international banking regulations.

Central bank
The Cayman Islands Monetary Authority (CIMA) was established in January 1997.

Main financial centre
George Town, Grand Cayman

Time
GMT minus five hours

Geography
The Cayman Islands are located in the western Caribbean, south of Cuba and north-west of Jamaica.
The three islands of Grand Cayman, Cayman Brac and Little Cayman are limestone outcroppings, the tops of a submarine mountain range called the Cayman Ridge, which extends west-south-west from the Sierra Maestra range of the south-east part of Cuba to the Misteriosa Bank near Belize. There are no rivers or streams because of the porous nature of the limestone rock. All three islands are surrounded by healthy coral reefs.

Hemisphere
Northern

Climate
Prevailing north-east trade winds; moderate, otherwise hot climate. Average temperatures 24–29 degrees Celsius. The rainy season is May–Oct, but annual rainfall is low.

Dress codes
Neat, casual, tropical attire is appropriate. Public nudity and topless bathing are strictly prohibited by law.

Entry requirements

Passports

Required by all except citizens of the UK, US and Canada with proof of citizenship (authenticated birth certificate and photographic identity document) and a return ticket (all US and Canadian nationals require a passport for re-entry to their country from January 2007).

The pink immigration slip given upon arrival should be kept with travel documents and presented when departing.

Visa

Not required by transit passengers or nationals of the EU, North America, Australasia or Japan, provided their stay does not exceed 30 days. For further exceptions see http://cayman.com.ky/visiting/reqs.htm.

Salespeople planning to solicit business and take orders require a temporary work permit, applications should be obtained in advance from the Department of Immigration.

Currency advice/regulations

There is no restriction on import of foreign or local currency, apart from import of Jamaican dollars, which are restricted to J$20.

Customs

It is advised not to export products made from wild green sea turtles as they are illegal in most countries; farmed sea turtles may be allowed by a visitor's home country, however, the US prohibits its transshipment and will confiscate any such material.

Prohibited imports

Illegal drugs, including marijuana. Permits are necessary for firearms of any kind, including spearguns (or pole spears or Hawaiian slings), live plants and plant cuttings, raw meat and raw fruits and vegetables.

Health (for visitors)

Modern medical facilities are available, particularly on Grand Cayman and Cayman Brac. The George Town Hospital is well equipped for any diving accidents.

Mandatory precautions

None

Advisable precautions

Immunisation against typhoid, and less so TB, diphtheria and hepatitis B and C. Outbreaks of dengue fever and dengue haemorrhagic fever can occur. Hepatitis A has been reported in the northern Caribbean generally.

Tap water is safe to drink.

Hotels

There is a wide choice of hotels throughout the islands, mainly on the beach. There is a government room tax of 10 per cent and an automatic gratuity of 10 per cent of the room rate. Restaurants often add a 15 per cent gratuity to their bills.

Credit cards

Major credit cards are widely accepted.

Public holidays (national)

Fixed dates

1–2 Jan (New Year's holiday), 23 Jan (Heroes' Day), 15 May (Discovery Day), 12 Jun (Queen's Birthday), 3 Jul (Constitution Day), 31 Nov (Remembrance Day), 25–26 Dec (Christmas).

Some bank, legal and public holidays that fall on days other than Monday are moved to the following Monday. The above dates take this into account.

Variable dates

Feb/Mar (Ash Wednesday), Mar/Apr (Easter, three days).

Working hours

Banking

Mon–Thu: 0900–1600; Fri: 0900–1630.

Business

Mon–Fri: 0830–1700.

Government

Mon–Fri: 0800–1700

Post offices: Mon–Fri 0830–1530; Sat 0830–1200.

Shops

Mon–Sat: 0900–1700.

Telecommunications

Mobile/cell phones

There are 850/1900 and 900/1800 GSM services available throughout the islands.

Electricity supply

110V AC, 60Hz. American-style (flat) two-pin plugs are standard.

Getting there

Air

National airline: Cayman Airways.

International airport/s: Owen Roberts International (GCM), 3km from the centre of George Town, duty-free shop, bar, restaurant, buffet, money exchange, shops.

Other airport/s: Gerrard Smith (CYB) on Cayman Brac. Little Cayman is served by inter-island flights arriving at the Edward Bodden Airstrip.

Airport tax: Departure tax US$25

Getting about

National transport

Air: Cayman Airways operates a service from Grand Cayman to Cayman Brac. Island Air offers a four-times-a-day service between Grand Cayman and both Cayman Brac and Little Cayman.

Road: There are over 175km of road, mostly surfaced. Speed limits of 50, 40, 30, 25mph are strictly enforced. Most hotels have bicycles available for complimentary guest use.

Buses: Daily bus services start at 0600. There are regular bus services between West Bay and George Town, and between the latter and Bodden Town and East End. Mini-buses are operated by licensed operators.

City transport

Taxis: Taxis are readily available at hotels and airport. Fares are based on a fixed place-to-place tariff. Tipping optional.

Car hire

An international licence is recommended. A local permit is obtainable on production of a national licence. Traffic drives on the left. Wearing seat belts is mandatory.

BUSINESS DIRECTORY

The addresses listed below are a selection only. While World of Information makes every endeavour to check these addresses, we cannot guarantee that changes have not been made, especially to telephone numbers and area codes. We would welcome any corrections.

Telephone area codes

The international direct dialling code (IDD) for the Cayman Islands is + 1 345, followed by subscriber's number.

Useful telephone numbers

Emergency service (island-wide): 911.

Chambers of Commerce

Cayman Islands Chamber of Commerce, Harbour Centre, PO Box 1000, George Town, Grand Cayman (tel: 949-8090; fax: 949-0220; e-mail: info@caymanchamber.ky).

Banking

The Bank of Nova Scotia, PO Box 689, Grand Cayman (tel: 949-7666; fax: 949-0020).

Bank of Butterfield International (Cayman) Ltd, PO Box 705 G, Grand Cayman (tel: 949-7055; fax: 949-7761).

Barclays Bank International, PO Box 68 G, Grand Cayman (tel: 949-7300; fax: 949-7179).

Canadian Imperial Bank of Commerce and Trust Co (Cayman), PO Box 694 G, Grand Cayman (tel: 949-8666; fax: 949-7904).

The Cayman Islands Bankers' Association, PO Box 1321, Grand Cayman (tel: 949-0330).

Cayman National Bank and Trust Co, PO Box 1097, Grand Cayman (tel: 949-4655; fax: 949-7506); Galleria Branch, PO Box 1097, Grand Cayman (tel: 949-7137; fax: 949-7506).

First Home Banking, PO Box 914, Grand Cayman (tel: 949-7822; fax: 949-6064).

The Royal Bank of Canada, PO Box 245 G, Grand Cayman (tel: 949-4600; fax: 949-7396).

Swiss Bank and Trust Corporation Ltd, PO Box 852 G, Grand Cayman (tel: 949-7344; fax: 949-7308).

Central bank
Cayman Islands Monetary Authority, PO Box 10052 APO, Elizabethan Square, 80e Shedden Road, Grand Cayman (tel: 949-7089; fax: 949-2532; e-mail: cima@cimoney.com.ky).

Stock exchange
Cayman Islands Stock Exchange (CSX), www.csx.com.ky

Travel information

Cayman Airways, PO Box 1101, George Town, Grand Cayman (tel: 949-2311/8272; fax: 949-7607).

Ministry of tourism
Ministry of Tourism, Aviation and Commerce, Government Administration Building, Grand Cayman (tel: 949-7900; fax: 949-1746).

National tourist organisation offices
Cayman Islands Department of Tourism, PO Box 67, The Pavilion, Cricket Square, George Town, Grand Cayman (tel: 949-0623; fax: 949-4053; fax: 949-4053; internet sites: http://www.caymanislands.ky; http://www.divecayman.ky).

Ministries

Governor's Office, 4th Floor, Government Administration Building, Elgin Avenue, George Town, Grand Cayman (tel: 949-7900; fax: 945-4131).

Ministry of Agriculture, Environment, Communications and Works, Government Administration Building, Grand Cayman (tel: 949-7900; fax: 949-2922).

Ministry of Community Development, Sports, Women's and Youth Affairs, Government Administration Building, Grand Cayman (tel: 949-7900; fax: 949-0726).

Ministry of Education and Planning, Government Administration Building, Grand Cayman (tel: 949-7900; fax: 949-9343).

Ministry of Health, Drug Abuse, Prevention and Rehabilitation, Government Administration Building, Grand Cayman (tel: 949-7900; fax: 949-7544).

Ministry of Internal and External Affairs, Government Administration Building, Grand Cayman (tel: 949-7900; fax: 949-7544).

Ministry of Finance and Development, Government Administration Building, Grand Cayman (tel: 949-7900; fax: 949-9838).

Ministry of Legal Affairs, Government Administration Building, Grand Cayman (tel: 949-7900; fax: 949-1746).

Sports Office, Ministry of Community Development, Sports, Women's and Youth Affairs, Third Floor, Tower Building, Grand Cayman (tel: 914-3480; fax: 949-8487).

Other useful addresses

Cable and Wireless (West Indies) Ltd, PO Box 293, George Town (tel: 949-7800; fax: 949-5472).

Cayman Islands Port Authority, PO Box 1358, Georgetown, Grand Cayman (tel: 949-2055; fax: 949-5820; e-mail: info@caymanport.com).

Cayman Islands Stock Exchange, Fourth Floor, Elizabethan Square, P.O Box 2408GT, Grand Cayman (tel: 945-6060; fax: 945-6061; e-mail: csx@csx.com.ky; internet site: http://www.csx.com.ky).

Civil Aviation Authority, PO Box 278, George Town, Grand Cayman (tel: 949-7811).

Customs Department, PO Box 898GT, Grand Cayman (tel: 949-2473; fax: 945-1573).

Government Information Services, Broadcasting House, Grand Cayman (tel: 949-8092; fax: 949-5936).

Immigration Department (tel: 949-8344; fax: 949-8486).

Radio Cayman, PO Box 1110, George Town, Grand Cayman (tel: 949-7799).

Registrar of Companies, Ground Floor, Tower Building, Grand Cayman (tel: 949-7999; fax: 949-0969).

Caribbean Net News: www.caribbeannetnews.com

Internet sites

Cayman Islands information: http://www.cayman.com.ky/cayman.htm

Central African Republic

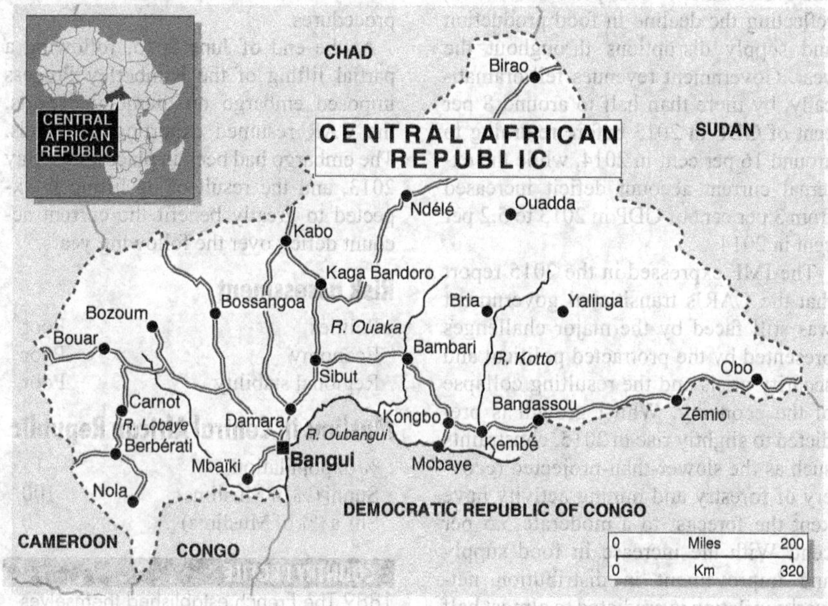

The Central African Republic's (CAR) economic development has long been hampered by the country's land-locked position, a poor transport system, a largely unskilled workforce and a legacy of misdirected economic policies. The CAR is in significant arrears to several multinational creditors, including the International Development Agency (IDA). The government has also had poor revenue collection and budget outcomes and is behind in military and civilian payrolls. The country thus remains poor despite the economic potential of the CAR's natural resources (diamonds, gold, uranium and timber) and favourable farming conditions. In fact, the CAR's considerable agricultural potential means that in an ideal world it would be capable of feeding itself. The majority of the population still lives off the land on subsistence plots. Vast areas of land, however, are covered by forest (a rich resource in itself), which probably deters organised, industrial scale agriculture.

However, in late 2013 the economy was not the largest of CAR's concerns. In March 2013 a mainly Muslim rebel group calling themselves Séléka – a coalition of five major rebel units – managed to depose the president François Bouzizé and replace him with their own man, Michel Djotodia, who announced that he was the CAR's 'interim president'. President Bozizé had been accustomed to rebel opposition – insurgents had continually challenged his rule during his decade in office. So this opposition did not come as a surprise: Bozizé was not democratically elected but came to power after a 2003 military *coup*, which too followed on from a history of political unrest. His administration was clearly corrupt, but despite his unpopularity Bozizé was able to keep rebel forces at bay for a decade until his deposition, essentially by keeping the military – the traditional source of *coups d'état* – underfunded and unmotivated.

After a period of uncertainty, during which it appeared that a large proportion of the population were opposed to Séléka, to the extent that before long the interim president himself turned against the rebels that had put him in place. The rebellion had created an estimated 400,000 refugees, causing the UN Secretary General Ban Ki-moon to announce that he wished to send as many as 9,000 peacekeepers to the CAR pending a Security Council resolution. The UN leader also announced that if there were to be any deterioration in the situation he would detail peacekeepers

KEY FACTS

Official name: République Centrafricaine (Central African Republic)

Head of State: Interim President Catherine Samba-Panza (sworn in 23 Jan 2014)

Head of government: Acting Prime Minister Mahamat Kamoun (from 10 Aug 2014)

Area: 622,984 square km

Population: 4.70 million (2014)*

Capital: Bangui

Official language: French

Currency: CFA franc (CFAf) = 100 centimes (Communauté Financière Africaine (African Financial Community) franc)

Exchange rate: CFAf586.44 per US$ (Sep 2015)

GDP per capita: US$380 (2014)*

GDP real growth: 101.00% (2014)*

GDP: US$1.79 billion (2014)*

Inflation: 14.96% (2014)

Balance of trade: -US$81 million (2014)*

Annual FDI: US$109.18 million (2011)

* estimated figure

from other UN missions in Africa to go to the CAR. Regional peacekeeping efforts from both the African Union and the Economic Community of Central African States (ECCAS) failed to address the country's problems. The rebels' random attacks on civilians had triggered counter attacks by Christian militia calling themselves Anti-Balaka.

However, politically things looked up with the appointment of Catherine Samba-Panza as her country's interim president in January 2014, to lead the country out of months of sectarian killings. Mrs Samba-Panza is a French-trained lawyer who had served as the mayor of the capital Bangui. By the time of her appointment by parliament the rebel bands had resulted in the number of refugees rising to an estimated one million. Hopes for some sort of a solution were pinned on the new president – Africa's third female head of state – and a year after she took her oath some improvements had been made. Mainly due to the deployment of international troops there have been advances in security, yet many challenges still remain and there are still regular outbreaks of violence. Catherine Samba-Panza's transitional government is to serve until the presidential elections in October 2015.

The economy

In June 2015 the CAR reached agreement with the International Monetary Fund (IMF) on financial assistance under its Rapid Credit Facility. In its assessment the IMF noted that 'The political and security crises that the CAR has faced since December 2012 have led to a collapse of economic activity, paralysed the government and caused an unprecedented humanitarian crisis, with nearly a quarter of the population displaced'. Gross domestic product (GDP) had contracted sharply (by approximately 36 per cent) in 2013, as all sectors of economic activity experienced downturns. In 2014 growth was expected to have returned to positive at 1 per cent. Inflation had accelerated to 6.6 per cent in 2013, compared with 5.9 per cent in 2012, and even further to 11.2 per cent in 2014, reflecting the decline in food production and supply disruptions throughout the year. Government revenues fell dramatically, by more than half to around 8 per cent of GDP in 2013 before returning to around 16 per cent in 2014, while the external current account deficit increased from 3 per cent of GDP in 2013 to 5.2 per cent in 2014.

The IMF expressed in the 2015 report that the CAR's transitional government was still faced by the major challenges presented by the protracted political and security crisis and the resulting collapse of the economy. Whilst growth is predicted to slightly rise in 2015, constraints such as the slower-than-projected recovery of forestry and mining activity have kept the forecast to a moderate 5.5 per cent. With the increase in food supply and improvement in distribution networks inflation is predicted to almost half to 5.7 per cent – a decent amendment, although still above the Central African Economic and Monetary Community convergence criterion of 3 per cent. Rising investment related imports are expected to increase the current account deficit to 11.8 per cent of GDP.

The IMF also considered that as far as the budget went, the priority was to progressively restore public finances through the improved mobilisation of tax revenues and more effective control of spending with a view to limiting the domestic primary balance to 7.6 per cent of GDP. The interim government (Transition Authorities) and the IMF had agreed on measures to resume and strengthen public financial management by restoring revenue mobilisation capacity, rationalising and enhancing the monitoring of cash flow management, cleaning up the database for civil servants and payroll and resuming swiftly normal expenditure execution procedures.

At the end of June 2015, following a partial lifting of the Kimberley Process imposed embargo on diamond exports, the CAR resumed exporting diamonds. The embargo had been in place since May 2013, and the result of its lifting is expected to greatly benefit the current account deficit over the following years.

Risk assessment

Politics	Poor
Economy	Poor
Regional stability	Poor

Muslims in Central African Republic

% of population	15
Sunni (% of Muslims)	100
Shi'a (% of Muslims)	0

KEY INDICATORS — Central African Republic

	Unit	2011	2012	2013	2014	**2015
Population	m	*4.74	*4.52	*4.61	*4.70	*4.79
Gross domestic product (GDP)	US$bn	2.17	2.17	*1.54	*1.79	*1.80
GDP per capita	US$	489	480	*335	*380	*376
GDP real growth	%	3.3	4.1	*-36.0	*1.0	*5.7
Inflation	%	1.9	5.9	7.0	15.0	*5.2
Current account	US$m	-167.0	-122.0	-46.0	*-110.0	*-201.0
Total reserves minus gold	US$m	–	158.0		259.6	–
Foreign exchange	US$m	–	153.0		–	–
Exchange rate	per US$	466.82	505.65	480.26	542.10	

* estimated figure ** forecast figure

COUNTRY PROFILE

1889 The French established themselves at Bangui.
1907 The colony of Oubangi-Shari (named after two main rivers) was founded.
1958 The country was proclaimed a republic.
1960 David Dacko became the president of the independent and newly named country
1966 Dacko's cousin, Jean-Bedel Bokassa, an army commander, seized power, declaring himself life-president in 1972.
1977 Bokassa crowned himself emperor – the coronation consumed about one quarter of the country's annual income.
1979 Bokassa's repressive regime ended when French troops reinstated David Dacko.
1981 Dacko was ousted by the army chief of staff, General André Kolingba.
1986 Kolingba established a one-party state.
1990 Opposition groups united and forced the government to adopt a multi-party system.
1992 Elections were held but the results were nullified after several groups boycotted the poll.
1993 Ange-Félix Patassé became president in the first multi-party elections.
1995 A democratic constitution was adopted.

1996 Army mutinies erupted, the last of which degenerated into ethnic violence and was suppressed by French troops in January 1997.
1997 Patassé appointed Michel Gbezera-Bira at the head of an 11-party coalition government.
1998 Parliamentary elections were indecisive.
1999 A number of deputies defected to Patassé's Mouvement de Libération du Peuple Centrafricain (MLPC) (Movement for the Liberation of the Central African People), giving it a slight majority. Presidential elections confirmed support for Patassé. France withdrew its troops.
2001 Libya sent troops to protect Patassé.
2002 Rebels seized part of Bangui; they were fought off by the army, aided by Libyan warplanes.
2003 General François Bozizé led a military coup that captured Bangui while President Patassé was abroad. Bozizé proclaimed himself president, suspended the constitution and dissolved the National Assembly.
2004 The National Transitional Council created an independent commission to oversee elections. A new constitution was approved.
2005 The Convergence Nationale-Kwa Na Kwa (CN-KNK) (National Convergence-Kwa Na Kwa) coalition won parliamentary elections and incumbent François Bozizé was elected president. Elie Doté was named as prime minister.
2006 President Bozizé ruled by decree for three months. Rebel activity continued throughout the year, causing the president to seek French military assistance.
2007 An agreement was signed between Sudan, Chad and the Central African Republic whereby no shelter would be given to rebel movements between these countries.
2008 Élie Doté resigned and the president appointed Faustin-Archange Touadéra as prime minister. Jean-Pierre Bemba was arrested (in Belgium) on charges that his troops allegedly committed atrocities in the Central African Republic in 2002. He faced charges at the International Criminal Court (ICC). Peace agreements with three rebel groups were signed allowing disarmament and the demobilisation of rebel fighters.
2009 Prime Minister Touadéra and his cabinet were dismissed; the president re-appointed him as head of a national unity cabinet, which included two senior members of two rebel groups and two opposition parliamentary members. The International Monetary Fund (IMF) approved the immediate payment of US$18.46 million for poverty reduction programmes, following CAR's successful economic performance under the Poverty Reduction and Growth Facility (PRGF).
2010 Presidential and parliamentary elections were postponed from April to 2011. Troops of the Lord's Resistance Army (LRA), a brutal and indiscriminate rebel force from Uganda, began attacking villagers in CAR. The reputation of former president Jean-Bedel Bokassa was formally rehabilitated by presidential decree. Although he was accused of great cruelty during his reign, President Bozizé said that Bokassa had 'built the country but we have destroyed what he built'. His widow was awarded a state medal of honour.
2011 In January, in presidential elections, incumbent François Bozizé (Kwa Na Kwa) won 66.08 per cent of the vote, his closest rival Ange-Félix Patassé (independent) won 20.1 per cent. After the second round of parliamentary elections held on 27 March, Kwa Na Kwa won a majority of 61 seats. All opposition parties, including 18 independent candidates, alleged that there had been election fraud. However, the electoral commission confirmed President Bozizé's re-election on 26 January. The government signed a ceasefire agreement with the rebel group, Convention des Patriotes pour la Justice et la Paix (Convention of Patriotes for Justice and Peace (CPJP)), in June.
2012 On 7 June two northern rebel groups, the L'Armée Populaire pour la Restauration de la République et la Démocratie (APRD) (Popular Army for the Restoration of Democracy) and the Union des Forces Républicaines (UFR) (Republican Forces Union), were disbanded after a decade long insurgency. They agreed to join the disarmament, demobilisation and reintegration (DDR) programme.
2013 President Bozizé fled Bangui ahead of rebels of the Seleka Coalition who took the capital on 24 March. On 25 March Michel Djotodia declared that he would rule by decree. In early August UN Secretary General Ban Ki-moon said the CAR had suffered a 'total breakdown of law and order' since rebels seized power in March. He urged the UN Security Council (UNSC) to consider sanctions or to set up a panel of experts to monitor the situation. The UNSC also warned that the CAR posed a 'serious threat' to regional stability. On 18 August Michel Am-Nondokro Djotodia was sworn in as president. On 9 September a large scale force of supporters of former President Bozizé launched an attack on forces loyal to President Djotodia. Reports said that there had been at least 60 deaths. The army chief was sacked. Seleka Coalition rebels were reported to be looting and killing civilians. As a result a decree was issued from the President's office dissolving the Seleka Coalition 'over the length and breadth of the Central African Republic's territory.' In October Medecins Sans Frontieres (MSF) reported that there had been 'appauling' levels of violence since rebels took over in March. In October the UN approved a force of 250 to protect UN workers in CAR. A UN official reported that a worrying new religious dimension to the violence was developing, with armed groups inciting Christian and Muslim communities against each other. Despite the President's decree, Muslim Seleka fighters continued to attack Christian communities, who formed 'anti-balaka' (machete) self defence forces. As the situation deteriorated it became unclear who was leading the various groups of fighters. The violence escalated further as a force of militia, reportedly supporters of former president, Francois Bozize, launched an attack in Bangui on 5 December. There were as many as a hundred deaths. The UNSC voted on the same day to allow French troops to join African peacekeepers. President Hollande said that the troops already there would be 'doubled within a few days, if not a few hours'. The African-led Mission Internationale de Soutien à la Centrafrique sous conduite Africaine (MISCA) (International Support Mission to the Central African Republic) was established by UNSC resolution 2127. The force, backed by France and lead by the AU, deployed on 19 December.
2014 Prime Minister Nicolas Tiangaye resigned on 23 January and was succeeded by André Nzapayeké as acting prime minister on 25 January. Interim President Catherine Samba-Panza was sworn in on 23 January. By February fighting between Christians and Muslims had become so severe that Human Rights Watch emergency director Peter Bouckaert was reported as saying that the entire Muslim population (some 15 per cent of the population) could be forced to flee. On 26 March Gen Jean-Marie Michel Mokoko, commander of the AU peacekeeping force, announced that the anti-balaka Christian militia group would in future be treated as enemy combatants. Mr Nzapayeké lasted until 10 August when he was succeeded by Mahamat Kamoun, also as acting prime minister, on the same day.
2015 Sports minister, Armel Sayo, was abducted by a militia group demanding the release of its detained commander, Rodrigue Nagibona, on 25 January. Mr Nagibona had earlier been arrested by UN troops on charges of alleged murder and rape in connection with attacks on minority Muslims in December 2013, as well as on charges over rebellion and looting. On 27 September there were clashes between Christians and Muslims

in Bangui after a Muslim motorbike taxi driver was killed. At least 20 people were killed and the UN peace-keeping force was accused of not taking firm enough action.

Political structure

Constitution

A new Constitution was approved in December 2004. The transitional parliament has begun work on a new constitution which citizens should be able to assess in 2015.

Form of state

Republic

The executive

Under the new Constitution, approved in December 2004, the presidential term has been reduced from six to five years. Presidents can only serve a maximum of two terms in office.

National legislature

The unicameral, National Assembly has 105 members elected in single-seat constituencies using a two-round voting method if required. All members serve for five-year terms.

Last elections

23 January 2011 (presidential and first round parliamentary); 27 March 2011 (second round parliamentary).

Results: Presidential: François Bozizé (Kwa Na Kwa) won 66.08 per cent of the vote, Ange-Félix Patassé (independent) 20.1 per cent, Martin Ziguélé (MLPC) 6.46 per cent, Emile Gros Raymond Nakombo (RDC) 4.64 per cent, Jean-Jacques Démafouth (APRD) 2.72 per cent; turnout was 54.01 per cent.

Parliamentary: Convergence Nationale 'Kwa Na Kwa' (KNK) (National Convergence) won a total of 61 seats (out of 105), independent candidates 26, Majorité Présidentielle (MP) (Parliamentary Majority) 11, Mouvement de Libération du Peuple Centrafricain (MLPC) (Movement for the Liberation of the Central African People) one, Rassemblement Démocratique Centrafricain (RDC) one. Five other seats were unaccounted for.

Next elections

Presidential elections on 18 October 2015 and parliamentary elections on 22 November 2015.

Political parties

Main opposition party

Collectif des Forces du Changement (CFC) (Combined Forces for Change)

Population

4.61 million (2013)*

Approximately 43 per cent of the total population is under 15 years.

It is estimated that 63 per cent of the total population and 75 per cent of the rural population lives below the poverty line.

Last census: 8 December 2003: 3,151,072

Population density: Five inhabitants per square km. Urban population 39 per cent (2010 Unicef).

Annual growth rate: 2.0 per cent, 1990–2010 (Unicef).

Internally Displaced Persons (IDP)

200,000 (UNHCR 2004)

Ethnic make-up

Bayas (34 per cent), Bandas (27 per cent), Manzas (21 per cent), Saras (10 per cent), Mbums (4 per cent), Mbakas (4 per cent)

Religions

About 24 per cent of the population hold traditional beliefs; 25 per cent Protestants; 25 per cent Catholics; 15 per cent Muslims.

Education

Only 60 per cent of eligible children receive education. Basic education lasts for 10 years divided into six years' basic first stage and four years' basic second stage. General secondary school lasts for three years, which gives access to higher education. Only 10 per cent of secondary school-aged children are enrolled due to limited resources. Technical education at the secondary level is offered at two levels. School instruction is mainly in French, but the government has sought to promote Sango literacy and encourages its use in schools.

Higher education is offered at the Université de Bangui, which also has a teacher training college.

Literacy rate: 49 per cent adult rate; 59 per cent youth rate (15–24) (Unesco 2005).

Compulsory years: Six to 14

Health

Modern healthcare facilities exist only in Bangui (with one major hospital) and a few other towns.

In 2004, CAR launched a 10-year programme to reduce maternal deaths and infant mortality rates.

HIV/Aids

In 2009 there were an estimated 130,000 adults living with HIV.

HIV prevalence: 4.7 per cent aged 15–49 in 2009 (Unicef 2012)

Life expectancy: 48 years, 2010 (Unicef 2012)

Fertility rate/Maternal mortality rate: 4.6 births per woman, 2010 (Unicef 2012); maternal mortality 1,100 per 100,000 live births (World Bank).

Child (under 5 years) mortality rate (per 1,000): 129 per 1,000 live births (WHO 2012); 23 per cent of children under aged five are malnourished (World Bank).

Welfare

The country is in deep poverty, with two out of three people earning less than US$1 a day. All social security programmes are administered by the Central African Social Security Office.

Main cities

Bangui (capital, estimated population 734,350 in 2012), Bimbo (250,195), Berbérati (105,155), Carnot (54,551), Bria (43,322), Bambari (41,486), Nola (41,462).

Languages spoken

Sango, Banda, Baye and Zanda are widely spoken.

Official language/s

French

Media

Despite the repeal of press laws the resulted in criminal prosecution, journalist are still subject to harassment and imprisonment by government ministers.

Press

The press does not have a great influence due to the relatively costliness of newspapers and high levels of illiteracy.

Dailies: In the Sango-language *E Le Songo* is state-owned. In French, *Le Confident* (www.leconfident.net), is a private publication as are *Le Citoyen*, *L'Hirondelle Le Démocrate* and *L'Evenementiel*.

Weeklies: In French, *Centrafrique Presse* (www.centrafrique-presse.com) is a published newsletter, twice a week. There are several private newspapers including, *Les Collines de l'Oubangui*, *Temps Nouveaux*, and *Le Centrafricain*,

Periodicals: In French, *Journal Officiel de la République Centrafricaine* is a government publication.

Broadcasting

Radio: The state-owned Radio Centrafrique (www.radiocentrafrique.org) does not provide independent news, alternatively, Radio Ndeke Luka (www.radiondekeluka.org), a UN-sponsored station provides a balanced output and international rebroadcasts from France, UK and US.

Other radio stations and signals are provided by international organisations, including the pan-African, Radio Africa No 1 (www.africa1.com), the French Radio Nostalgie and the Roman Catholic Radio Notre Dame.

Television: Television Centrafricaine is state-run and the private, Tropic RTV, is the only other broadcaster.

National news agency: Centrafrique Presse

Other news agencies: Africa News Agency: www.africanewsagency.co.uk

APA: www.apanews.net

Panapress: www.panapress.com

Economy

The Central African Republic (CAR) is one of the poorest and least developed countries in the world. Its economy is dominated by subsistence agriculture, forestry and fishing, which constituted 54.3 per cent of GDP in 2014. Forestry is a major export revenue earner and it is the single largest employer in the CAR, drawing on over 27 million hectares of exploitable forests. Major crops include, cotton, food crops (such as maize, cassava and yams), coffee and tobacco. However, the sector is vulnerable to drought and regional political strife. The service sector led by government services and transport, comprised less than 32.0 per cent of GDP and industry less than 13.7 per cent of GDP.

Mining is largely underdeveloped, but there are deposits of gold, uranium and other minerals. Diamond mining is the second largest export earner, but it has been estimated that 30 per cent of all diamond production is illegally smuggled abroad.

In 2013 the Central African Republic recorded a record fall in production, with a growth in gross domestic product (GDP) of -36.0 per cent. There was a slight recovery in 2014 as the country recorded growth of 1.0 per cent, however the main contributor to GDP – the agricultural sector – continues to lose ground. There is progression in returning the main road corridor from Bangui to Douala to a state of security, the route that carries most of external trade. Commercial and transport activities are therefore being facilitated, and are expected to help accelerate growth in 2015 to a projected 5.4 per cent and to 4.0 per cent in 2016.

According to the African Development Bank (AfDB), the installation of a new transitional government – the election of Catherina Samba-Panza as head of state and the appointment of a new prime minister – have been favourably received and have strengthened the mobilisation of the international community. Despite these factors stabilising the country, social and humanitarian conditions are difficult and security remains in a worrying state.

In 2014 the UN Human Development Report ranked CAR at 185 out of 187, for national development in health, education and income. CAR's progress has shrunk since 2011 when the country was ranked at 179. According to the UN report 76.3 per cent of the population were in multidimensional poverty. Poverty is a hindering development, as the workforce is largely unskilled with only half of the population over 15 years of age literate.

External trade

The Central African Republic is a member of the Communauté Économique et Monétaire de l'Afrique Centrale (Cemac) (Economic and Monetary Community of Central Africa), which operates a customs union with import taxes and capital flowing freely among member states. Import duties, levied on third parties, are pooled and shared between members. The CAR is also a member of the World Trade Organisation (WTO).

International trade is largely based on the export of timber, (around 50 per cent of export earnings) and diamonds. There is a potential for a great deal more in mineral exports but a poor investment record and weak infrastructure hampers progress.

Imports

Principal imports are refined petroleum, chemicals, pharmaceuticals, foodstuffs, textiles, machinery, vehicles and electrical equipment.

Main sources: Norway (14 per cent of total in 2014), France (7.7 per cent), US (7.6 per cent).

Exports

Principal exports are diamonds, timber, raw cotton, gold, coffee, natural rubber, tobacco and leather.

Main destinations: China (29.2 per cent of total in 2014), Indonesia (15.1 per cent), Democratic Republic of the Congo (15 per cent), Norway (7 per cent), Morocco (5.9 per cent), Saudi Arabia (4.4 per cent) and France (4 per cent).

Agriculture

Farming

Agriculture and forestry are the mainstays of the economy. Total agricultural land is 62.3 million hectares of which 5.1 per cent is pasture and 3.1 per cent arable; much of the rest is savannah. The sector employs 54.3 per cent of the workforce. The sector consists mainly of subsistence farming and animal husbandry. The main crops are maize, cassava, sorghum, groundnuts, sesame and rice. Cotton and tobacco are also cultivated. The main export crop is coffee. Soil erosion, widespread drought and underdeveloped marketing and infrastructure, as well as poor internal security and mass migration hamper production.

Forestry

Forest covers 50 per cent of the country. There is significant forestry potential, including over 60 species of commercially viable trees, but it is under-exploited because of poor transport infrastructure.

Industry and manufacturing

The industrial sector accounted for around 13.7 per cent of GDP in 2014, and employs around 10 per cent of the workforce. Manufacturing accounted for around 6 per cent of GDP in 2014. Manufacturing is relatively small-scale and is concentrated in the brewing, tanning, food processing, soap manufacture and textile sectors. There are also import substitution industries such as motorcycle and bicycle assembly.

The main industrial centre is the Bangui district.

Tourism

Although the Central African Republic (CAR) has many natural sights to offer visitors, its unstable political situation has lead to warnings by foreign governments to their citizens not to visit CAR due to the lawlessness of insurgents and foreign militia. At the moment CAR cannot look to tourism to improve its economy. Visitors mainly arrive for business purposes. Nevertheless, there is potential for the industry when security improves, and eco-tourism in the national parks can expand. The Manovo-Gounda St Floris National Park, of savannah and northern floodplains, contains a wide variety of African wildlife and is included on the UNESCO's World Heritage List. A new website is in operation that provides information about CAR (www.centrafricaine.info).

Travel and tourism constituted 5.0 per cent of GDP in 2014, and provided employment for around 35,000 or 4.2 per cent of the total workforce.

CAR needs major investment in infrastructure before it can hope to expand and capitalise on its potential in tourism. But without the security necessary to protect not only its own people but visitors as well, prospects are limited.

Mining

The CAR has many natural mineral resources, including copper, graphite, and iron ore however the only minerals produced are gold and diamond, which are large contributors to its GDP.

The mining sector officially accounts for around 4 per cent of GDP, employs 3 per cent of the workforce and generates 40 per cent of the country's export earnings. Smuggling is endemic and production and trade is likely to be far higher than official estimates.

Around 80,000 autonomous artisanal miners are engaged in mining production, mostly of diamonds and gold. Diamond output is typically around 400,000 carats per year, over half of which are gem quality. Other mineral deposits include uranium, limestone, iron ore, copper and manganese.

The Bozizé government withdrew mining licences and seized mines belonging to foreigners and figures associated with the government of former president Patassé. The measures were taken as part of an anti-corruption campaign, which targeted divested interests associated with vital revenue-generating sectors. An embargo was placed on the diamond industry in May

2013 following the overthrowing of Bozizé. However, due to higher taxes on diamonds in CAR than neighbouring countries, even before the ban 30 per cent of output was smuggled out of the country.

Hydrocarbons

There are no known exploitable oil or gas reserves, but exploration is being undertaken in regions where the geology gives rise to high expectations of deposits, typically crossing international borders.
Domestic consumption was 2,910 barrels per day in 2013, all of which was imported. The Central African Republic does not have any oil refining capacity.
There are no known reserves of natural gas; coal reserves are negligible and any amounts being imported or consumed are not recorded.

Energy

Total installed generating capacity is around 44MW, producing 175 million kilowatt hours (kWh), little of which is provided to the general population. The state-owned Energie Centrafricaine (Enerca) is responsible for electricity generation and operates the Boali, M'Bali and Gamboula hydroelectric dams, which between them provide 56.8 per cent of total capacity (29MW); an additional 137MW is planned through a mixture of upgrading and expansion or existing plants, and by new ones. There are small-scale, isolated diesel generators providing the majority of the country's community needs. The majority of the population relies on non-commercial biomass, mostly fuel wood for cooking, lighting and power.
Power lines cross the border into the Democratic Republic of Congo (DRC) from where power is accessed

Financial markets

Stock exchange
Afribourse (Bourse Régionale des Valeurs Moblières) (BRVM)

Banking and insurance

Central bank
Banque des Etats de l'Afrique Centrale (BEAC) (Bank of the Central African States)
Main financial centre
Bangui

Time

GMT plus one hour

Geography

The Central African Republic is a landlocked country in the heart of equatorial Africa. It is bounded by Chad to the north, and Sudan to the east, by the Republic of Congo and the Democratic Republic of Congo to the south and Cameroon to the west.
Most of the land is rolling or flat plateau, apart from the rising land in the west. Around 36 per cent of the country is covered in tropical forest particularly in the south-west. Desertification in the north-east has resulted in scrubland. The Chari River runs through the centre from the east.
Hemisphere
Northern

Climate

Hot all year with temperatures up to 36 degrees Celsius. The dry season runs from November–February with cooler nights. The rainy season runs from May–October.

Entry requirements

Passports
Required by all
Visa
Visas are required by all except citizens of surrounding countries, Israel and Switzerland. Visas can be issued in neighbouring countries, generally within 24 hours but are expensive. Visas can be obtained in advance from the Central African Republic Embassy in Paris, 30 rue des Perchamps, 75116 Paris.
A business letter and itinerary must accompany the application for a business visa.
Proof of onward/return passage is required.
Currency advice/regulations
No restrictions on import of foreign currency, but amounts must be declared; export up to declared amount allowed.
Unlimited import of local currency; export limited to CFAf75,000.

Health (for visitors)

Mandatory precautions
Yellow fever vaccination certificate required by all.
Advisable precautions
Typhoid, tetanus, hepatitis A and polio vaccinations are recommended. Malaria prophylaxis should be taken as risk exists throughout country. There is a rabies risk. Water precautions are necessary – bilharzia risk in some areas. AIDS risk.

Hotels

Good standard hotels are available in Bangui – limited accommodation elsewhere. Where service charge is not included in bill a 10 per cent tip is usual.

Public holidays (national)

Fixed dates
1 Jan (New Year's Day), 29 Mar (President Boganda's Remembrance Day), 1 May (Labour Day), 30 Jun (Prayer Day), 13 Aug (Independence Day), 15 Aug (Assumption Day), 1 Nov (All Saints' Day), 1 Dec (National Day), 25 Dec (Christmas Day).
Variable dates
Easter Monday

Working hours

Banking
Mon–Fri: 0730–1230.
Business
Mon–Fri: 0730–1530.
Government
Mon–Fri: 0700–1200, 1430–1700; Sat: 0700–1200.
Shops
(Mon–Sat) 0800–1200; 1600–1900.

Telecommunications

Mobile/cell phones
A GSM 900 service is available in limited areas.

Electricity supply

220/380V AC, 50 cycles

Weights and measures

Metric system

Security

Full civil control following the 2003 coup has yet to be restored. Visitors are recommended not to travel to the Central African Republic unless it is absolutely necessary. When travelling outside the capital extra precautions should be taken and advice sort from local authorities and diplomatic missions.

Getting there

Air
National airline: Air France and Sudan Airways serve CAR.
International airport/s: Bangui-M'Poko (Code: BGF), 4km from city, restaurant, post office, shops, car hire.

Getting about

National transport
Air: Small light aircraft can be chartered.
Road: Eight main roads run from Bangui to the main towns and those that are surfaced are toll roads. The Trans-African Lagos-Mombasa highway passes through the Central African Republic. Most other roads can become impassable during rainy season. NB Spare parts and petrol stations tend to be rare outside Bangui.
Buses: Limited coach service operates between Bangui and Bangassou.
Water: Large volume of freight is carried on rivers. The principal trading route is on the Oubangui River south of the capital Bangui which runs into the River Congo, connecting Bangui to the Democratic Republic of Congo and the Congo Republic (including Brazzaville, from where railway runs to Pointe-Noire). Also services from Salo on the Sangha River.
City transport
Taxis: Available in Bangui; fares by negotiation.

Car hire
Self- or chauffeur-driven cars available. International driving licence required.

BUSINESS DIRECTORY

The addresses listed below are a selection only. While World of Information makes every endeavour to check these addresses, we cannot guarantee that changes have not been made, especially to telephone numbers and area codes. We would welcome any corrections.

Telephone area codes

Dialling code for Central African Republic: IDD access code +236 followed by subscriber's number.

Chambers of Commerce

Chambre de Commerce, d'Industrie, des Mines et d'Artisinat de Centrafrique, PO Box 252/ 813, Bangui (tel: 611.668; fax: 613-561; e-mail: ccima@intnet.cf).

Chambre de d'Agriculture, d'Elevage, des Eaux, Forêts, Chasses, Pêches et du Tourisme, PO Box 850, Bangui (tel:/fax: 619-052; e-mail: denissio@intnet.cf).

Banking

Banque de Crédit Agricole et de Développement, BP 801, Place de la République, Bangui (tel: 613-200).

Banque Internationale pour le Centrafrique, BP 910, Place de la République, Bangui (tel: 610-042; fax: 616-136, 613-438).

Banque Populaire Maroco-Centrafricaine, BP 844, Rue Guerlliot, Bangui (tel: 613-190, 611-290; fax: 616-230).

Caisse Nationale d'Epargne, BP 839, Siège social, Bangui (tel: 612-296).

Commercial Bank Centrafrique SA, BP 839, Rue de Brazza, Bangui (tel: 612-990; fax: 613-454).

Central bank
Banque des États de l'Afrique Centrale, Direction Nationale, PO Box 851, Bangui (tel: 612-405; fax: 611-995; e-mail: beacbgf@beac.int).

Stock exchange
Afribourse (Bourse Régionale des Valeurs Moblières) (BRVM), www.brvm.org

Travel information

Central African Republic Government (with tourism information): www.centrafricaine.info

Inter-RCA, BP 1413, Bangui.

Ministry of Water, Forests, Wildlife, Fisheries and Tourism, Bangui.

Office Centrafricain de Tourisme (OCATOUR), BP 655, Bangui (tel: 614-566).

Ministries

Central African Republic Government: www.centrafricaine.info

Ministry of Economy and Finance, Planning and International Co-operation, Bangui (tel: 610-811).

Ministry of Energy, Mines, Geology and Water Resources, Bangui.

Ministry of Posts and Telecommunications, Bangui (tel: 612-946).

Ministry of Rural Development, Bangui (tel: 612-800).

Ministry of Trade, Industry and Small- and Medium-scale Enterprises, Bangui (tel: 614-488).

Ministry of Transport and Civil Aviation, Bangui (tel: 612-307).

Other useful addresses

Central African Republic Embassy (USA), 1618 22nd Street, NW, Washington DC 20008 (tel: 202-483-7800; fax: 202-332-9893).

European Development Fund, BP 1298, Bangui (tel: 613-053, 610-113).

Office of the President, Palais de la Renaissance, Bangui (tel: 610-323).

Société Centrafricaine de Développement Agricole (SOCADA), ave David Dacko, BP 997, Bangui (tel: 613-033).

National news agency: Centrafrique Presse, (email: info@centrafrique-presse.com; internet: www.centrafrique-presse.com).

Africa News Agency: www.africanewsagency.co.uk

APA: www.apanews.net

Panapress: www.panapress.com

Internet sites

Africa Business Network: www.ifc.org

AllAfrica.com: http://allafrica.com

African Development Bank: www.afdb.org

Mbendi AfroPaedia (information on companies, countries, industries and stock exchanges in Africa): http://mbendi.co.za

Central African Republic Government: www.centrafricaine.info

Chad

KEY FACTS

Official name: République du Tchad (Republic of Chad)

Head of State: President Colonel Idriss Déby Itno (MPS) (from 1996; re-elected 25 Apr 2011)

Head of government: Prime Minister Kalzeube Pahimi Deubet (since 21 November 2013)

Ruling party: Mouvement Patriotique du Salut (MPS) (Patriotic Movement for Salvation) (since 1997; re-elected 20 Feb 2011)

Area: 1,284,000 square km

Population: 11.28 million (2014)*

Capital: N'Djamena

Official language: French and Arabic

Currency: CFA franc (CFAf) = 100 centimes (Communauté Financière Africaine (African Financial Community) franc)

Exchange rate: CFAf586.44 per US$ (Sep 2015)

GDP per capita: US$1,236 (2014)*

GDP real growth: 6.89% (2014)*

GDP: US$13.95 billion (2014)*

Inflation: 1.68% (2014)*

Oil production: 78,000 bpd (2014)

Balance of trade: US$171.30 million (2009)*

Annual FDI: US$781.40 million (2010)

* estimated figure

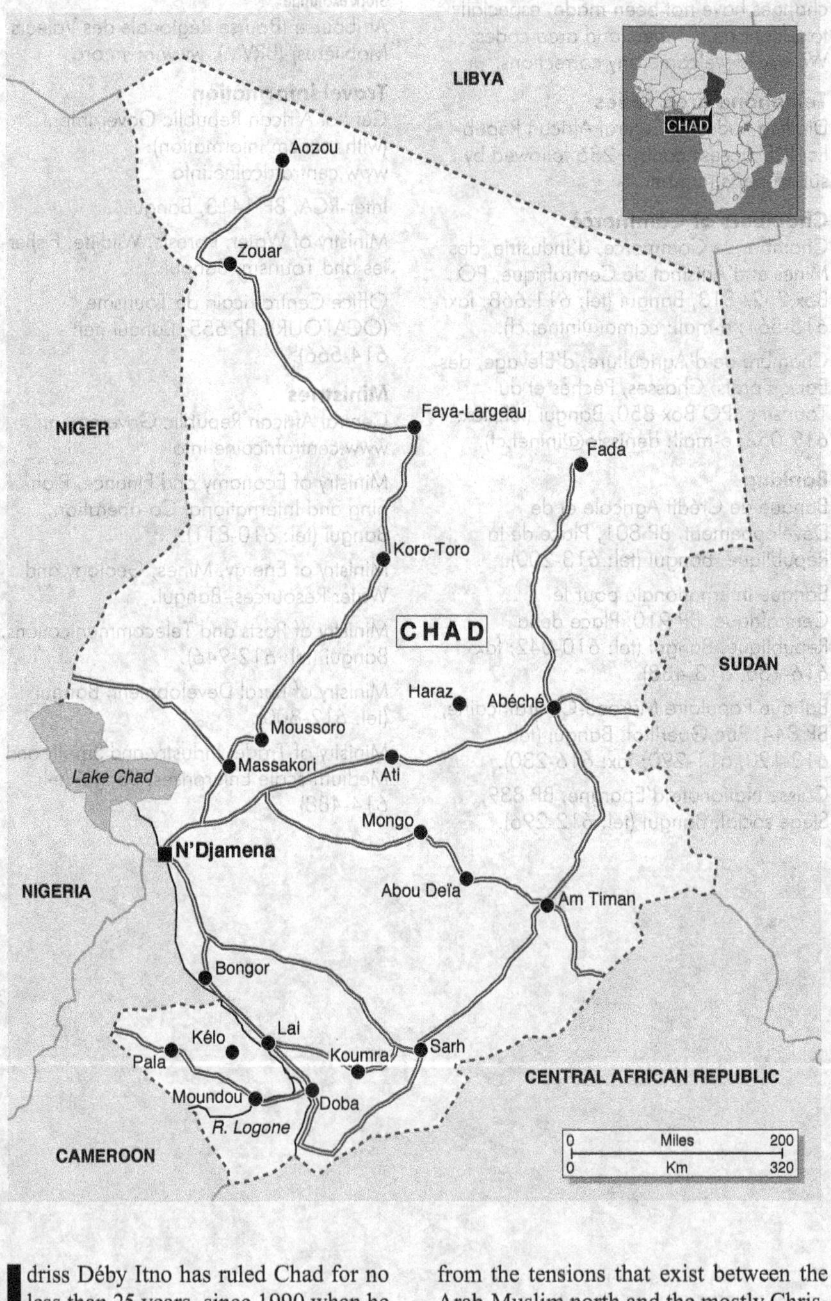

Idriss Déby Itno has ruled Chad for no less than 25 years, since 1990 when he ousted former president, Hissène Habré in a *coup*. This makes him one of Africa's longest serving heads of state. Africa's fifth largest nation, since independence from French rule (in 1960) has been characterised by chronic instability and violence emanating for the most part from the tensions that exist between the Arab-Muslim north and the mostly Christian and animist south.

Wars and coups

In 1969 matters came to a head when Muslim dissatisfaction with the first president, Christian southerner Ngarta Tombalbaye, broke out and developed into a guerrilla war. This, combined with a severe drought, destroyed Mr Tombalbaye's presidency and in 1975 he was killed in a *coup* led, ironically, by another southerner, Felix Malloum.

Mr Malloum didn't have much success in ending the north-south tensions; in 1979 he was replaced by Goukouki Oueddei, a northerner with Libyan support. The next time round, however, it was French support that won the day for the presidential contender, Hissène Habré. In 1982 forces loyal to Mr Habré had captured N'Djamena. Not to be removed in this way, Mr Oueddi repaired to the north, where he formed an alternative government. The stand-off ended in 1990, when Mr Habré was removed, by the Libyan-backed Idriss Déby. It was not until 1996 that Mr Déby was confirmed president in what was Chad's first election.

Unrest continued – in 1998 an armed insurgency threatened from the north, led by President Déby's former defence chief, Youssouf Togoimi. Libyan attempts to negotiate a peace settlement failed to calm things down and the Libyan brokered peace deal in 2002 failed to put an end to the fighting. Over the years thousands of Chad nationals have fled the violence between ethnic Arab and ethnic African Chadians.

Chad is host to a great number of refugees – in 2003, unrest in neighbouring country Sudan spilled across the border along with people seeking a new home. Since late 2013 the fighting in another neighbour, the Central African Republic (CAR), has led to tens of thousands of refugees fleeing to Chad.

Chad is positioned in the area that is plagued with the threat from Boko Haram, and has been aiding other countries in combatting the Islamist insurgency. In 2015 Chad pledged military support to Cameroon, an act that Boko Haram responded to by attacking the Chadian shore of Lake Chad. This raised fears that the insurgency would spread east, and in July 2015 the first attacks on the capital N'Djamena happened as two suicide bombers blew themselves up targeting the police headquarters.

The economy

In a summary economic outlook on the Chad economy, the African Development Bank (AfDB) observed that after a slow-down in 2013, the economy surged to a 7.2 per cent increase in gross domestic product (GDP) in 2014, mostly thanks to new oilfields coming into production. However, in the view of the AfDB, since Chad is highly exposed to oil price fluctuations it needs to step up its efforts of budgetary consolidation. On top of this, the country has major social challenges involving security crises and preparation of the electoral process. The report also recommended the introduction of more efficient and profitable global value chains and their extension to sectors with high potential, in order to contribute to more inclusive growth and sustainable development. In order to achieve economic emergence by 2030, the AfDB suggests that Chad must implement policies of spatial inclusion and structural transformation and says this must be done to develop its natural resources properly.

In its April 2014 assessment of the Chad economy, the IMF noted that Chad continued to be a fragile country with weak institutional and policy capacity, facing already declining oil revenues (barring those from new oil discoveries – see 'Hydrocarbons' below) and vulnerable to oil price and regional security shocks. None the less, in April 2015, in combination with the World Bank the IMF announced US$1.1 billion in debt relief for Chad. This debt relief was awarded as a result of both the institutions agreeing that the country had made sufficient progress in meeting the requirements to reach the completion point under the Heavily Indebted Poor Countries (HIPC) Initiative. On the positive side in 2015 Chad had been enjoying its longest period of domestic political stability since independence and had, against all the odds, become a beacon of stability in a very volatile region, actively contributing to international efforts to restore order in Mali and the CAR. Macro-economic policy over the previous few years had achieved a gradual tightening of the underlying fiscal policy stance, despite a sizeable increase in public investment.

The economic outlook was, in the view of the IMF, relatively positive – driven by a projected temporary upturn in oil production, with a high risk of debt distress. Growth is expected to have increased even further in 2015 to 7.6 per cent before dropping to a projected 4.9 per cent in 2016. The main sources of risk to the outlook stemmed from the volatility of fiscal oil revenue and the still difficult regional security situation. Negative oil price and production shocks could well force downward adjustments to public investment plans and reduce the availability of foreign exchange. Regional security instability could require continued elevated levels of security spending and could well damage investor confidence. The IMF recommended that fiscal policy remain anchored on a sustained reduction of the non-oil primary deficit, supported by public financial management reforms (to enhance fiscal control and the quality of spending) and sizable increases in non-oil revenue collection to offset the projected eventual exhaustion of oil revenue (through enhancements in both tax policy design and revenue and customs administrations). The IMF concluded by noting that a more diversified and competitive economy over the medium- and long-terms would require increased efforts to improve the business environment for the private sector, promote agricultural activities and expand access to basic and financial services.

Hydrocarbons

Chad became an oil-producing nation in 2003 with the completion of a US$4

KEY INDICATORS **Chad**

	Unit	2011	2012	2013	2014	+2015
Population	m	*10.48	*10.74	*11.01	*11.28	*11.57
Gross domestic product (GDP)	US$bn	9.50	12.89	12.95	*13.95	*12.02
GDP per capita	US$	823	1,201	*1,176	*1,236	*1,039
GDP real growth	%	3.1	8.9	5.7	*6.9	*7.6
Inflation	%	2.6	7.7	0.2	*1.7	*3.2
Oil output	'000 bpd	114.0	101.0	94.0	78.0	–
Current account	US$m	-102.0	-1,076.0	*-1,169.0	*-1,219.0	*-1,259.0
Total reserves minus gold	US$m	881.7	1,156.0	–	–	–
Foreign exchange	US$m	876.9	1,151.0	–	–	–
Exchange rate	per US$	466.82	505.65	480.26	542.10	–

* estimated figure ** forecast figure

billion pipeline linking its oilfields to terminals in Cameroon on the Atlantic coast. The government has moved to relax a law controlling the use of oil money, which the World Bank had made a condition of its US$39 million loan. According to the British Petroleum (BP) Statistical Review of World Energy 2015 Chad ranks as the tenth-largest oil reserve holder among African countries, with 1.5 billion barrels of proven reserves at the end of 2014. Crude oil production in Chad was an estimated 115,000 barrels per day (bpd) in 2011 but had steadily fallen to 94,000bpd in 2013 and maintained at the same rate through to 2015. Almost all of this was exported via the Chad-Cameroon Pipeline.

The China National Petroleum Corporation (CNPC) and the Chadian government jointly constructed the 20,000bpd N'Djamena refinery, which began supplying the local market with petroleum products in 2011. However, operations have occasionally been temporarily suspended due to price disputes and operational issues. Petroleum is the only hydrocarbon that Chad consumes. Traditional wood fuel is the primary source of total energy consumption in the country. Very few households in Chad have access to electricity. The country has installed electric generation capacity of 31 megawatts that is thermal-powered using refined oil products. In March 2015 the Sustainable Energy Fund for Africa (SEFA) approved a US$780,000 preparation grant for the development of a 40MW Solar Photovoltaic (PV) Plant near N'Djamena. The plant is expected to generate around 64GWh of electricity and supply electricity to around 17,000 households in the N'Djamena area as well as to the industrial and public sectors.

Risk assessment

Politics	Poor
Economy	Fair
Regional stability	Poor

Muslims in Chad

% of population	53.1
Sunni (% of Muslims)	92
Shi'a (% of Muslims)	1

COUNTRY PROFILE

1900s France defeated the local ruler, Rabeh Zubeit, at a battle in Kousseri in 1916, and the territory of Chad was formed.

1929 A northern, Saharan, segment was added.

1946 Chad was granted status as a French overseas territory with its own regional assembly.

1960 Chad was granted independence. A one-party regime was imposed under President Francois Tombalbaye. A series of rebellions against Tombalbaye's rule were repressed.

1975 Tombalbaye was killed in a coup and replaced by Colonel Félix Malloum. Malloum agreed to share power with rebel leader, Hissène Habré.

1979 Habré forced Malloum out of N'Djamena after a violent power struggle.

1980 A new alliance was formed between Habré and Goukouni Oueddei, which lasted until 1980 when Libya sided with Goukouni and Habré fled. Libyan troops and Chadian factions defeated Habré, at which point France intervened and the invading force was driven back from N'Djamena, leaving Habré in nominal control of the country.

1987 After several years of stalemate, President Mitterand of France and Colonel al Qadafi of Libya attempted to resolve the conflict, with both agreeing to withdraw their forces from Chad. The French troops withdrew but those of Libya did not. The French returned and pushed Libya back across the Chad-Libya border.

1989–90 A rebellion was launched by Idriss Déby, an army commander. Habré fled to Senegal and Déby proclaimed himself president.

1996 A new constitution was introduced, based on the French model. In Chad's first multi-party presidential elections, Idriss Déby was elected president.

1997 Legislative elections were won by the Mouvement Patriotique du Salut (MPS) (Patriotic Movement for Salvation).

2001 President Déby was re-elected. A peace agreement was signed in Libya between the Chadian government and the northern rebel movement, Mouvement pour la Démocratie et la Justice au Tchad (MDJT) (Movement for Democracy and Justice in Chad).

2002 The ruling MPS won the parliamentary elections. Haroun Kabadi was appointed prime minister by the president after the resignation of Nagoum Yamassoum.

2003 In January, Chad and the Central African Republic began peace talks. Moussa Faki became prime minister. Chad became an oil exporter, with the opening of a pipeline from its oil fields to Cameroon.

2004 Thousands of Sudanese refugees fleeing the unrest in the Darfur region of western Sudan arrived. Fighting between Chadian troops and pro-Sudanese government militias (Janjaweed) spilled across the border.

2005 Prime Minister Moussa Faki resigned and was replaced by Pascal Yoadimnadji. A referendum amended the constitutional with a 65.75 per cent approval vote, which removed the limit of terms in office for presidents; the senate to be replaced by a Cultural, Economic and Social Council.

2006 The World Bank suspended all loans to Chad as the government announced its intentions of steering oil revenue, originally destined for healthcare and education, to the military. Chad broke-off diplomatic relations with Sudan, following attacks on Chadian towns by Chad rebels based in the Darfur region of Sudan. An agreement was reached with the World Bank to resume loans and release oil revenue from an escrow account in return for an portion of petroleum profits being set aside for programmes for the poor. The presidential election, which was boycotted by the main opposition parties, was won by the incumbent Idriss Déby, giving him his third five-year term in office.

2007 An agreement was signed between Sudan, Chad and the Central African Republic, whereby no shelter would be given to rebel movements from each other's countries. Prime Minister Pascal Yoadimnadji died; Adoum Younousmi became interim prime minister. Germany-based Transparency International declared Chad to be one of the most corrupt regimes in the world.

2008 A state of emergency was declared after a coup attempt. The rebels were defeated after two days and driven back towards the border with Sudan. The president dismissed Koumakoye and appointed Youssouf Saleh Abbas as prime minister. Former president, Hissène Habré, living in exile in neighbouring Senegal, was convicted of planning to overthrow the government and sentenced to death *in absentia*.

2009 A new rebel alliance, Union des Forces de Résistance (UFR) (Union of Resistance Forces) was established by eight local dissident groups. A UN peace-keeping force (Minurcat) took over from EU troops in eastern Chad.

2010 Chad and Sudan signed a peace agreement. Youssouf Saleh Abbas resigned as prime minister and was replaced by Emmanuel Nadingar. At the request of Chad the UN agreed to withdraw its troops by the end of the year. According to the UNHCR, two million people were in need of food aid due to poor harvests in 2009–10. The worst rains since the 1970s caused flooding that left thousands homeless and destroyed entire villages and cultivated land.

2011 Postponed parliamentary elections took place on 13 and 20 February. The ruling MPS won 83 seats (out of 188) and, with the support of allies in parliament, retained power. On 25 April the presidential election was contested by three candidates, with a further three boycotting the vote claiming it would be an 'historic fraud' and that electoral reforms and issuance of new voter identification cards had failed. Incumbent Idriss Déby (MPS) won 88.66 per cent of the vote; turnout was 64.22 per cent. By the end of April around 54,200 refugees had crossed the Sahara Desert to escape the conflict in Libya and were given refuge in camps in Chad. Senegal's foreign minister Madicke Niang announced in July that Senegal was suspending the repatriation of Hissène Habré on the grounds that he might be tortured in Chad. President Déby took office again in August and immediately reappointed Emmanuel Nadingar as prime minister.

2012 On 2 May President Déby called for, as a matter of urgency, the creation of a regional force to counter the threat of the Islamic extremist group Boko Haram in northern Nigeria. Nigeria estimated that the number of deaths as a result of bombs and other acts of violence was, by 2012, 900. A number of West African governments had become concerned by the spread, and increased frequency, of attacks attributed to Boko Haram, and its possible connection with Al Qaeda senior leadership, most likely through the lands of the Islamic Maghreb. On 20 July, the International Court of Justice (ICJ) ruled that Senegal must either begin legal proceedings against Habré 'without delay' or extradite him to face trial in Belgium, for murder and torturing his opponents in Chad. On 22 July Senegal and the African Union agreed to establish a special court to try Habre, using the existing Senegalese legal and court structure.

2013 Several people, including two army generals, a ruling coalition MP and an opposition MP, were arrested in Djamena on 1 May after the government reported that 'A small group of ill-intentioned individuals attempted to carry out a destabilisation plot against the institutions of the republic.' A number of deaths were also reported. In mid-August the government suspended the operations of a China National Petroleum Corporation (CNPC) run company after an oil spill. CNPC also owns 60 per cent of one of Chad's oil refineries.

2014 A bill which threatens to impose heavy fines and jail sentences of up to 20 years for people found guilty of same sex activity went before parliament in October. Amnesty International stated that should the bill become law, President Déby would be 'blatantly disregarding the country's international and regional human rights obligations.'

2015 In an effort to curtail the activities of Boko Haram in Chad and Niger the two countries launched a ground and air offensive against the militant group in north-eastern Nigeria on 8 March. Former president, Hissene Habré, went on trial in Dakar, Senegal, on 21 July, accused of sanctioning killings and widespread torture during the 1980s. Ten members of Boko Haram were executed on 29 August after being found guilty of terrorist activities the previous day.

Political structure

Constitution

A new Constitution was introduced in 1996, based on the French model with a strong executive branch and a legal system based on French civil law and Chadian customary law. However it has little *de facto* authority to provide civil liberties. Amendments agreed by referendum in 2005 removed the limit on terms in office for presidents; the justice system was subordinated to the executive branch; the senate was replaced by a Cultural, Economic and Social Council and the Constitutional amendment process was moved to the president (rule by prerogative).

Form of state

Republic

The executive

The executive branch consists of the president who is Head of State, and the prime minister and cabinet. The president is elected by popular vote to serve a five-year term; the prime minister is appointed by the president.

National legislature

The legislative branch consists of a unicameral National Assembly made up of 188 seats of which 118 are directly elected in multi-seat constituencies using the proportional representation vote. The remaining 70 seats are directly elected in single-seat constituencies by absolute majority vote with a second round if required. Members serve four-year terms.

Legal system

Based on the French civil law system and customary law.

Last elections

13 and 20 February 2011 (parliamentary); 25 April 2011 (presidential)

Results: Parliamentary: Mouvement Patriotique du Salut (MPS) (Patriotic Movement for Salvation) won 83 seats (out of 188), Union Nationale pour la Démocratie et le Rénouveau (UNDR) (National Union for Democracy and Renewal) eleven, Union pour le Rénouveau et la Démocratie (URD) (Union for Renewal and Democracy) eight, Rassemblement National pour la Démocratie au Tchad (RNDT) (National Rally for Democracy in Chad) six; 21 other political parties shared the remaining 81 seats but none won more than four seats. Out of the two-fifths of the population that were registered to vote (4.8 million citizens), turnout was just 56.6 per cent.

Presidential: Idriss Déby (MPS) won 88.66 per cent of the vote, Albert Pahimi Padacké (RNDT-le Réveil) 6.03 per cent, Nadji Madou (ASRI) 5.32 per cent; turnout was 64.22 per cent.

Next elections

2016 (Presidential), 2016 (Parliamentary).

Political parties

Ruling party

Mouvement Patriotique du Salut (MPS) (Patriotic Movement for Salvation) (since 1997; re-elected 20 Feb 2011)

Main opposition party

Union nationale pour la démocratie et le renouveau (National Union for Democracy and Renewal) led by Saleh Kebzabo.

Population

11.28 million (2014)* Approximately 43 per cent of the total population are under 15 years.

Last census: April 1993: 6,279,931

Population density: Six inhabitants per square km. Urban population 28 per cent (2010 Unicef).

Annual growth rate: 3.1 per cent, 1990–2010 (Unicef).

Ethnic make-up

There are 200 distinct groups of Chadeans. In the north and centre: Arabs, Gorane (Toubou, Daza, Kreda), Zaghawa, Kanembou, Ouaddai, Baguirmi, Hadjerai, Fulbe, Kotoko, Hausa, Boulala, and Maba, most of whom are Muslim; in the south: Sara (Ngambaye, Mbaye, Goulaye), Moundang, Moussei, Massa, most of whom are Christian or animist. About 1,000 French citizens live in Chad. Of the population, 48 per cent of over 15s can read and write.

Religions

Muslim (44 per cent), traditional beliefs, Christians (33 per cent).

Education

As reform in the education sector has been slow following from the period of disturbances, local communities continue to play a greater role in financing and operating their schools. To rebuild the education system, the government of Chad developed an Education-Training-Employment strategy for 1990—2000 with the help of the International Labour Organisation, and other UN development agencies.

Five national programmes were developed including basic, secondary, higher education and research, vocational training and literacy. Estimates show that the programme has trained some 2,400 teachers and 1,000 classrooms have been built.

French is the primary language of instruction in most higher education institutions. The University of N'Djamena is the country's main university, with three faculties.
Literacy rate: 46 per cent adult rate; 70 per cent youth rate (15–24) (Unesco 2005).
Enrolment rate: 73 per cent gross primary enrolment, 12 per cent gross secondary enrolments; of relevant age groups, inlcuding repeaters (World Bank).
Pupils per teacher: 67 in primary schools.

Health

As one of the poorest countries in the world, Chad has the largest proportion of external resources committed to health at 62.9 per cent of all spending on healthcare.
Unicef and the Public Health Ministry began a campaign to inoculate nearly 90,000 children – half of them Sudanese refugees – against measles in the most remote areas, in 2004; their target was children aged between six months and 15 years. As well as the inoculations, staff distributed Vitamin A to children to reinforce their immune systems and protect them from blindness.

HIV/Aids

In 2009 there were an estimated 210,000 adults living with HIV.
HIV prevalence: 3.4 per cent aged 15–49 in 2009 (Unicef 2012)
Life expectancy: 49 years, 2010 (Unicef 2012)
Fertility rate/Maternal mortality rate: 6.0 births per woman, 2010 (Unicef)
Child (under 5 years) mortality rate (per 1,000): 150 per 1,000 live births (WHO 2012)

Welfare

An old age pension is paid at age 55 to workers with full contributions who pay 2 per cent of their wages. An employer pays 10 per cent of a worker's wage overall, for old age, disability and survivors' pensions. The government does not pay social security benefits. Roughly half the workforce has no jobs.
While Chad remains a traditional society, the role of women is expected to remain unchanged. Female Genital Mutilation (FGM) is practiced on 60 per cent of females, prior to puberty; and girls as young as 11 may be forced into an arranged marriage. Wives are subservient to their husbands and domestic violence is not uncommon. In 2003 a law was passed prohibiting FGM.

Main cities

N'Djamena (capital – formerly Fort Lamy – estimated population 1.1 million in 2012), Moundou (137,929), Sarh (103,269), Abéché (76,492), Faya (48,090), Koumra (47,782), Kélo (45,224).

Languages spoken

The language group in Chad is Afro-Asiatic; Arabic is spoken by most of the population and there are more than 50 African dialects.

Official language/s

French and Arabic

Media

Press

Newspapers are generally considered to be independent; however they have small circulations and are not distributed much beyond urban areas.
In French, daily newspapers include *Le Progres* and *Tchadien* (www.tchadien.com), other, weekly, private newspapers includes *N'Djamena Hebdo* (http://www.chez.com/ndjamenahebdo), and *Le Temps*, *Le Contact* is a bi-weekly.

Broadcasting

Radio: With high levels of illiteracy, radio services are the main medium of mass communication and sources of news and information.
The government-owned, Radiodiffusion Nationale Tchadienne, operates a national and three regional stations. Private radio stations include FM Liberté, owned by international human rights groups, Dja FM and Al Nassr are privately owned and La Voix du Paysan and Radio Arc-en-ciel are Roman Catholic stations.
Television: In Arabic and French, the only television station is the state-owned Téléchad, which favours the government.
Other news agencies: Afrik (French based): www.afrik.com/tchad
Africa News Agency: www.africanewsagency.co.uk
APA: www.apanews.net
Panapress: www.panapress.com

Economy

Chad is one of the poorest countries in the world, with much of its economy dependent on subsistence farming and foreign aid. In 2011, the UN Human Development Index (HDI) ranked Chad 183 (out of 187) for national development in health, education and income. Since 2000, Chad's progress has improved but it has not matched the growth of other sub-Saharan countries in Africa. In 2010, 54.7 per cent of the population experienced at least one indicator of poverty and the headcount poverty rate was 62.9 per cent of the population (2000–10).
The formal sector of GDP is officially made up of around 50 per cent industry, with services at less than 40 per cent and the remainder by agriculture (23.4 per cent in 2011); a larger, more vibrant informal sector also operates. Exports include, cotton, cattle and gum Arabic, as well as some minerals including petroleum, gold, bauxite, natron and iron ore. Manufacturing production includes meatpacking, beer brewing and soft drinks bottling and construction materials.
GDP growth was 14.6 per cent in 2008, which dropped to -1.2 per cent in 2009 due to poor rainfall and a reduced harvest that cut agricultural production and a fall in oil production. It climbed to an estimated 13 per cent in 2010 as world trade picked up, however, its growth has since settled to approximately 7.2 per cent in 2014.
Development investment, in one of Africa's smallest oil fields, began in 2001 and oil production began in 2003, with the completion of the Doba oil pipeline (allowing Chad to export its oil via Cameroon). Proven oil reserves at the end of 2011 were 1.5 billion barrels of oil, with production of 114,000 barrels per day (bpd). Despite a production forecast to peak at 225,000bpd, the country will remain dependent on imports of refined petroleum products, as there are no refineries. Investment by the government in the project was only possible through support by the World Bank, which agreed to loans on the proviso that a proportion of dividend payments from the oil production should be invested in socio-economic growth to enhance the living standards of the population. However, the World Bank judged that Chad had failed to undertake the necessary measures and withdrew from the agreement, demanding repayment of its loans; Chad complied in 2009.
Foreign direct investment (FDI) rose from US$233.6 million in 2008 to US$781.4 million in 2010, to be invested almost exclusively in the petroleum extraction industry and its supporting services. The latest value for its FDI was $538.4 million in 2013.
The economy has been undergoing a programme of liberalisation under the auspices of the IMF's Poverty Reduction and Growth Facility (PRGF). This has been coupled with debt service relief under an enhanced Heavily Indebted Poor Countries (HIPC) initiative. The government has privatised public enterprises, aimed at securing macroeconomic stability and strengthening its fiscal position.

External trade

Chad is a member of the Communauté Économique et Monétaire de l'Afrique Centrale (Cemac) (Economic and Monetary Community of Central Africa), which operates a customs union with import taxes and capital flowing freely among member states; import duties, levied on third parties, are pooled and shared between members.

Imports

Principal imports are machinery and transport equipment, industrial goods, petroleum products, foodstuffs and textiles.

Main sources: Algeria (54.6 per cent of total in 2014), China (11.2 per cent), Italy (6.2 per cent) and France (5.4 per cent).

Exports

Principal exports are petroleum, raw cotton, fish, meat and cattle, hides, sodium carbonate (natron), ground nuts, gum Arabic and resins.

Main destinations: US (77.6 per cent of total in 2014) and Japan (10.2 per cent).

Agriculture

Farming

The agricultural sector forms the mainstay of the economy, total agricultural land is 125.9 million hectares of which 35.7 per cent is pasture and 3.4 per cent arable and most of this is in the southern flood plains of the Logone and Chari rivers. The sector employs 65 per cent of the workforce.

Rice is produced on the irrigated land along the banks of the Oubangi River north of Lake Chad. Subsistence farming and livestock predominate in the north.

The country's main food crops are sorghum, millet, dry beans, sesame, potatoes, rice and maize. Cash crops include oil seeds (groundnuts and sesame), sugar cane and tobacco. Cotton is the most important agricultural product.

Cattle's farming involves nearly 40 per cent of the population. It contributes 39 per cent to total agricultural production and 20 per cent to Chad's GDP. About 90 per cent of beef production is exported to Nigeria.

Industry and manufacturing

The industrial sector contributes around 15 per cent of GDP and employs 10 per cent of the workforce.

The sector is small-scale and underdeveloped. Activity is centred in N'Djamena, Moundou and Sarh and is based on agriculture, particularly food processing, textiles, brewing, tobacco processing, leather and construction materials.

Tourism

Chad has recently achieved peace and security from external and internal disruption and has, since 2010, been able to market desert and travel adventure holidays in the north, as well as visits to the Zakouma National Park, with an area of 3,000 square km, in the south. Although Chad is benefiting from its oil industry, its general infrastructure remains underdeveloped and needs more capital investment to provide the level of facilities to attract more than just intrepid travellers. In July 2012, the Lakes of Ounianga, in the arid region of Ennedi, were added to UNESCO's World Heritage List.

Travel and tourism constituted a static 1 per cent of direct contribution to GDP from 2006–11 with around 2.8 per cent of total contribution to GDP, despite an overall increase in revenue. Total contribution of travel and tourism to the economy was US$175 million in 2006, rising to an estimated US$211 million in 2011, which reflects a strengthening in other sectors of the economy rather that a weakening in the tourism sector. Around 20,000 people are directly employed in the industry and over 55,000 people indirectly, with growth dependent on visitor numbers.

Several international hotel chains have invested in Chad, but targeting business travel, particularly to N'djamena; elsewhere accommodation is limited.

In May 2011, Chad joined the Africa Travel Association (ATA), to provide greater exposure to professional tourism industry instruments to increase its potential for international tourism.

Environment

In June 2010 the African Union backed a proposal to build the 'Great Green Wall' project, of a 15km wide, 7,775km long, continuous belt of trees from Senegal in the west to Djibouti in the east (traversing 11 countries) in an effort to halt the advance of the Sahara Desert. The trees to be used would be drought-adapted, preferably native to the area from a list of 37 possible species, and should help to slow soil erosion and filter rain water.

Mining

Mining contributes less than 3 per cent to GDP. The only minerals extracted in any quantities are soda and rock salt (which are exported mainly to Nigeria) and natron from Lake Chad (used in preservation of meat and in tanning).

Known deposits of chromium, tungsten, titanium, iron, wolfram, gold, uranium and tin remain under exploited.

Other mineral deposits are thought to lie in the disputed Aouzou Strip along the Libyan border.

Hydrocarbons

At the end of 2011, Chad had proven oil reserves of 1.5 billion barrels, most of which is located in the Doba basin (production of 114,000 barrels per day (bpd). As a landlocked country, oil is exported via the Chad-Cameroon oil pipeline, opened in 2003. There are no downstream facilities for refining and all exports are crude oil. Nigeria and Cameroon provide refined oil to Chad, which imports around 143,000bpd. There are plans to build a small refinery in N'djamena to process the oil from Sedigi in the Lake Chad Basin. Industry experts consider Chad to have more undiscovered oil reserves; West Africa is one of the world's fastest growing oil regions.

An agreement signed in 2009 between the government of Chad and Exxon that allows the government in the form of the Société des Hydrocarbures du Tchad to market the government's share of output (20,000bpd), finally came into force in 2012.

The upstream oil industry is regulated by the Ministère des Mines, de l'Energie et du Pétrole (MMEP) (ministry of mines, energy and oil). The China National Petroleum Corporation (CNPC) and the government signed a memorandum of understanding in August 2009 to operate an oil refinery north of N'djamena. The refinery is 60 per cent owned by CNPC and 40 per cent by the government.

CNPC also began construction of a 300km-oil pipeline from the Koudalwa oil field to the refinery in October 2009. It was scheduled to be completed in 2013; however, in August 2013 the government suspended operations, after an oil spill caused by a CNPC run company that was drilling for oil.

Chad is not known to have either natural gas or coal reserves and nor does it import either in commercial quantities.

Energy

Chad had an installed electricity generation capacity of 30MW in 2007, which generated 90 million-kilowatt hours. Only 2 per cent of the population have access to electricity with the rest relying on bio-fuel for domestic use. The electricity supply is provided by two power stations in N'djamena and plants in Moundou, Sarh and Abéché. Imports from Nigeria and Cameroon provide most of Chad's power requirements. The World Bank has identified the necessity for an even distribution of regional energy, including electricity and gas, and in 2008 it was prepared to find funding for a detailed assessment of the feasibility of such a programme for provision of infrastructure. The Société Tchadienne d'Eau et d'Électricité (STEE) is the company responsible for electricity generation and supply in Chad.

Banking and insurance

The banking sector was fully privatised in 1999. The two main banks in Chad are the Banque Internationale de l'Afrique au Tchad (BIAT) and the Société Générale de Banque Tchadienne (SGBT).

Central bank

Banque des Etats de l'Afrique Centrale (BEAC) (Bank of the Central African States)

Main financial centre
N'Djamena

Time
GMT plus one hour

Geography
Chad is a landlocked country in north and central Africa, bordered in the north by Libya, the east by Sudan, the south by the Central African Republic, the south-west by Cameroon, to the west by Nigeria and the north-west by Niger.

Lake Chad is a large body of freshwater that forms part of the border in the south-west and is fed largely by the Chari River.

There are tropical forests in the south and the Sahara desert stretches across the north, which includes Ennedi and Tibesti volcanic mountain ranges.

Hemisphere
Northern

Climate
Hot and arid in northern desert regions, and wet and tropical in the south. Southern rainy season from May to October, central rainy season from June to September with temperatures ranging from 20 degrees Celsius (C) at night to as high as 40 degrees C during the day. Dry season throughout the rest of the year, lower evening temperatures.

Entry requirements
Passports
Required by all except nationals of certain African countries. Passports must be valid for six months after date of visit.

Visa
Required by all, except a number of nationals of West and Central Africa.

Ordinary visas are issued for both business and tourist purposes, valid for one month. Apply at either a Chadian consulate or a French consulate.

All visitors must register with authorities on arrival. Exit permits must also be obtained if leaving via Niger or Sudan.

Currency advice/regulations
The import and export of CFA francs from outside the African Financial Community is limited to CFAf10,000; import of CFA francs from inside the community is unlimited. There is unlimited import of foreign currency but it must be declared on arrival; export of foreign currency is limited to declared amount.

To avoid extra exchange fees US dollars or euros are preferred.

Health (for visitors)
Mandatory precautions
Yellow fever vaccination certificate required if arriving from an infected area.

Advisable precautions
Hepatitis A, tetanus, typhoid and polio vaccinations. Malaria prophylaxis recommended as risk exists throughout the country. There is a rabies risk. Water precautions necessary outside the capital.

Hotels
Reservations should be made well in advance of visit. If service charge is not included in bill a 10 per cent tip is usual. Limited availability outside of N'Djamena.

Public holidays (national)
Fixed dates
1 Jan (New Year's Day), 13 Apr (National Day), 1 May (Labour Day), 25 May (Africa Day), 11 Aug (Independence Day), 1 Nov (All Saints' Day), 28 Nov (Proclamation of the Republic), 1 Dec (Day of Liberty and Democracy), 25 Dec (Christmas Day).

Variable dates
Easter Monday, Eid al Adha, Eid al Fitr.

Islamic year 1437 (15 Oct 2015–2 Oct 2016):: The Islamic year contains 354 or 355 days, with the result that Muslim feasts advance by 10–12 days against the Gregorian calendar. Dates of feasts vary according to the sighting of the new moon, so cannot be forecast exactly.

Working hours
Banking
Mon–Thu and Sat: 0700–1300; Fri: 0700–1030.

Business
Mon–Sat: 0900–1230, 1600–1930.

Government
Mon–Thu and Sat: 0700–1400; Fri: 0700–1200. Specific times vary within this period.

Shops
Tue–Sat: 0900–1200; 1600–1930.

Telecommunications
Mobile/cell phones
GSM 900 services are available in populated areas only.

Electricity supply
220V AC, 50 cycles

Getting there
Air
National airline: Government owned Air Tchad provides only domestic flights. International flights are best provided by Air France.

International airport/s: N'Djamena (NDJ), 4km from city. Facilities include a post office, refreshments, bar, duty-free and car hire.

Airport tax: CFAf5,000 (tourist tax) and CFAf3,000 (security tax), except transit passengers continuing their journey within 24 hours.

Surface
Road: Access is possible via Sarh (Central African Republic), Bongor and Maroua (Cameroon). There is a paved road through the province of Kanem to Ngiugmi in Niger – the road runs to the Nigerian border.

Road conditions are variable and access can be very difficult, especially in the rainy season; driving is best undertaken between November and May.

It is dangerous to drive in the border region of Chad and Sudan, due to the situation in Darfur, Sudan.

Water: The main overland points of entry by ferry are via the Logone River (Cameroon) and Lake Chad (Nigeria).

Getting about
National transport
Air: Restricted domestic service operated by Air Tchad. Scheduled services occasionally commandeered by armed forces.

Road: Permits and four-wheel drive vehicles are required for all travel outside N'Djamena. Conditions are arduous, there are no emergency services; rest houses and petrol stations are not widely available. The government restricts travel in the central and northern territories. It is advisable to travel in convoy.

There are surfaced roads around N'Djamena; most other roads are not in good condition and are often impassable during rainy season (Jun–Oct).

City transport
Taxis: Available in N'Djamena and the principal towns – Sarh and Moundou; set-fare system in operation; 10 per cent tip is usual; can be hired on a time basis or by the day.

Car hire
Availablity is limited to N'Djaména only. French or international driving licence is required as well as a *autorisation de circuler*.

BUSINESS DIRECTORY
The addresses listed below are a selection only. While World of Information makes every endeavour to check these addresses, we cannot guarantee that changes have not been made, especially to telephone numbers and area codes. We would welcome any corrections.

Telephone area codes
The international dialling code (IDD) for Chad is + 235 followed by subscriber's number.

Chambers of Commerce
Chad Chamber of Commerce, Industry, Agriculture, Mines and Handicrafts, PO Box 458, N'Djamena (tel: 525-264; fax: 521-452; e-mail: cciamat@hotmail.com).

Banking
Banque Agricole du Soudan au Tchad, BP 1727, 1727 N'Djamena (tel: 519-041, 519-042; fax: 519-040).

Banque Commerciale du Chari Tchad, BP 757, N'Djamena (tel: 515-958, 515-231; fax: 516-249).

Banque de Développement du Tchad, BP 19, N'Djamena (tel: 522-829, 523-284; fax: 523-318).

Banque Internationale pour l'Afrique au Tchad, BP 87, Ave Charles de Gaulle, N'Djamena (tel: 525-684, 524-321; fax: 523-053, 522-345).

Banque Tchadienne de Crédit et de Dépôts, BP 461, N'Djamena (tel: 524-203, 522-801, 524-195; fax: 523-713).

Financial Bank, BP 804, N'Djamena (tel: 523-389, 522-660; fax: 522-905).

Central bank

Banque des États de l'Afrique Centrale, Direction Nationale, PO Box 50, N'Djamena (tel: 525-014; fax: 524-487; e-mail: beacndj@beac.int).

Banque des États de l'Afrique Centrale, (headquarters), 736 Ave Monseigneur Vogt, 1917 Yaoundé, Cameroon (tel: +237 223-4030/4060; fax: (+237) 223-3329/3350; email: beac@beac.int

Travel information

Air Tchad, 27 Avenue du Président Tombalbaye, BP 168, N'Djamena (tel: 515-090, 513-581, 514-564).

Direction du Tourisme, BP 86, N'Djamena (tel: 515-032, 512-303, 512-305).

Ethiopian Airlines, BP 989, N'Djamena (tel: 513-027, 513-143).

Sudan Airways, BP 167, N'Djamena (tel: 515-148).

National tourist organisation offices

Direction du Tourisme, BP 86, N'Dajmena (tel: 524-416; fax: 524 419).

Other useful addresses

Chad Embassy (USA), 2002 R Street, NW, Washington DC 20009 (tel: 202-462-4009; fax: 202-265-1937; e-mail: info@chadembassy.org; internet: www.chadembassy.org).

Chambre Consulaire du Tchad, BP 458, N'Djamena (tel: 515-264).

Commission for Trade and Industry, BP 453, N'Djamena (tel: 515-656).

European Development Fund, BP 532, N'Djamena (tel: 515-977, 512-276).

Office National des Céréales (ONC), BP 21, N'Djamena (tel: 513-731, 574-014).

Afrik (French based): www.afrik.com/tchad

Africa News Agency: www.africanewsagency.co.uk

APA: www.apanews.net

Panapress: www.panapress.com

Internet sites

Africa Business Network: http://www.ifc.org/abn

AllAfrica.com: http://allafrica.com

African Development Bank: http://www.afdb.org

Africa Online: http://www.africaonline.com

Chad: http://www.tchadrepertoire.com

Mbendi AfroPaedia (information on companies, countries, industries and stock exchanges in Africa): http://mbendi.co.za

Chile

KEY FACTS

Official name: República de Chile (Republic of Chile)

Head of State: President Michelle Bachelet (elected 16 Dec 2013, sworn in 11 Feb 2014)

Head of government: President Michelle Bachelet (from 11 Mar 2014)

Ruling party: A centre-left coalition of 7 parties known as Nueva Mayoría (New Majority), led by Partido Socialista de Chile (PS) (Socialist Party of Chile)

Area: 756,626 square km

Population: 17.82 million (2014)* (16,572,475; 31 August 2012, census preliminary result)

Capital: Santiago

Official language: Spanish

Currency: Chilean peso (CH$) = 100 centavos

Exchange rate: CH$689.04 per US$ (Sep 2015)

GDP per capita: US$14,477 (2014)*

GDP real growth: 1.84% (2014)*

GDP: US$257.97 billion (2014)*

Labour force: 8.20 million (2012)*

Unemployment: 6.39% (2014)*

Inflation: 4.93% (2014)

Balance of trade: US$7.77 billion (2014)

* estimated figure

The positive image that Chile had generated in the post Pinochet years had begun to look a little tarnished in 2015. In simple terms, the country was going through a crisis and a crisis that was more than simply economic. What was once a *luna de miel* had become something of a *luna de vinagre*. President Michelle Bachelet, who had inspired high hopes on her return to power in 2013, had seen her popularity ratings slump to around the 30 per cent mark. The rating for the President's coalition, the centre-left Nueva Mayoría (New Majority) grouping, had fallen similarly. The President's reputation for probity had been severely dented by the corruption scandals levelled at her son, Sebastian. These included influence peddling and using insider information for personal gain. The President also had to cope with accusations that her daughter-in-law had benefited from preferential access to a bank loan. This was not a loan to finance an extra bedroom or a swimming pool; it was a loan for US$10 million.

Time for change?

In Chile, disasters rarely come singly. In March 2015 Chileans had to deal with an erupting volcano, forest fires, a worsening drought and, to cap it all, extensive flooding in the north in which 23 people died. Natural disasters had always been happening in Chile and Chileans had learned to live with them. However, the economic difficulties that had begun to confront Chile in 2014 were something of a novelty, at least for some decades. But the fundamental lesson seemed to be that Chile's economic model, that had done it proud for so long, had been overtaken by events. Chile's economic vulnerability lay in the fact that however successful the macro-economic development had been, the prosperity it generated was by no means evenly distributed. In the eyes of many Chileans, this inequality ran parallel to rising signs of political corruption. Nowhere was this more apparent than in the way in which Chile's political parties were financed. In June 2015 – the former minister of the interior in the Nueva Mayoría administration, Rodrigo Peñailillo, was questioned as a suspect in one of the corruption cases being investigated by the Chilean judiciary. Mr Peñailillo's interrogation hinged on a payment of US$26,000 to a company called Asesorías y Negocios SpA, belonging to a Mr Giorgio Martelli. The latter, known to be a fund-raiser for the Bachelet coalition, was also under investigation for a number of alleged offences relating to the funding of political campaigns. Mr Peñailillo, once considered the 'dauphin' of Mrs Bachelet, had been minister of the interior until early May 2015 when the Bachelet government purged its ministerial team in an effort to regain popular confidence following the corruption revelations. It had emerged that a number of companies controlled by political figures, were engaged in funding political campaigns, disguising the payments received as being in respect of services provided, services which in fact had never been rendered.

In response to the mounting allegations, President Bachelet whose first term as president began in 2006, had proposed a constitutional reform which would set aside the current constitution, which had been in force since 1980 with hardly any changes. Its architect had been none other than President Pinochet, who had ruled from 1973 to 1990. Bachelet sought to set stricter rules for the financing of political parties, to regulate labour conflicts of interest and end the insidious custom of electing public officials for indefinite periods. This much was public knowledge; what was less clear was the nature of the social reforms that the President sought to encompass with the new constitution. These, too, would need to be approved by Congress in a process that President Bachelet envisaged getting under way in September 2015.

The proposed changes were received with some reserve by many Chileans, not least because the government's track record with its existing reform programme has been less than brilliant. June 2015 had seen students and trades' union members take to the streets in protest at the government's new legislation. The demonstrations focussed on a range of reforms, large parts of which – those affecting the teaching profession, private pensions and the new fishing law – were viewed as inadequate. The demonstrators took particular exception to much of the fishing legislation (which was originally conceived under the Piñera administration). Organised by the fishing trade union, the Unión Portuaria de Chile, demonstrators claimed that 'the authorities are forcing us to take direct action because we are not being listened to. The only people they do listen to are the corrupt people who fund their election campaigns.' The demonstrations were not limited to Santiago; similar manifestations took place in Valparaíso, La Serena, Concepción, Curanilahue and Temuco.

The economy

Chile is the only South American member of the Paris based Organisation for Economic Co-operation and Development (OECD). In its 2013 assessment of the Chilean economy, the OECD was largely complimentary of Chile's economic management, saying that: 'Sound macro-economic policies and a commodity price boom have yielded an enviably long phase of economic growth and job creation. The banking system is healthy and the strong government financial position has been rewarded by low sovereign spreads and credit rating upgrades. The economy is projected to continue growing at a healthy pace. Historically-low unemployment has resulted in some labour-market tightness, but inflation remains contained. Strong domestic demand and weakening foreign markets have pushed the current account balance into deficit, which has been financed mostly through foreign direct investment (FDI), thus limiting the risk of capital flow reversals. Downside risks to growth might, in the view of the OECD, '... emerge mainly from a sharper fall in the price of copper. Inflationary pressures could also be reignited by the tight labour market. Monetary and fiscal policies are well positioned to address these short-term risks, with the help of the floating exchange rate.'

The OECD also noted that Chile's economic growth and recent policy reforms had managed to increase employment, reduce poverty and lower income inequality, although (significantly) it drew attention to the fact that social inequality 'remained high'. Although women and young people have entered the labour force in greater numbers, the OECD noted that their participation rates remain surprisingly low when compared to most Latin American countries. Engrained attitudes towards women's work and child care commitments, as well as regulations regarding childcare provision continue, in the view of the OECD, to pose a barrier to

KEY INDICATORS **Chile**

	Unit	2011	2012	2013	2014	**2015
Population	m	*17.40	*17.40	*17.63	*17.82	*18.01
Gross domestic product (GDP)	US$bn	248.40	266.27	276.59	*257.97	*250.47
GDP per capita	US$	14,278	15,300	*15,687	*14,477	*13,910
GDP real growth	%	5.9	5.5	4.3	*1.8	*2.7
Inflation	%	3.3	3.0	1.9	4.9	*3.0
Unemployment	%	7.3	6.4	5.9	*6.4	*7.2
Exports (fob) (goods)	US$m	20,034.0	78,277.0	76,684.3	75,674.8	–
Imports (fob) (goods)	US$m	15,679.0	74,855.0	74,567.8	67,907.8	–
Balance of trade	US$m	4,355.0	3,422.0	2,116.5	7,767.1	–
Current account	US$m	-3,284.0	-9,081.0	-10,127.0	*-2,993.0	*-2,889.0
Total reserves minus gold	US$m	34,846.2	41,636.0	41,083.7	40,437.9	–
Foreign exchange	US$m	33,108.2	39,733.0	39,296.2	–	–
Exchange rate	per US$	473.76	477.69	529.10	605.66	–

* estimated figure ** forecast figure

female employment, though progress (a possible reference to new proposed legislation) was underway. Overall education quality and access to higher education were considered by the OECD to have improved, but the early stages of compulsory schooling remain a priority. Among low-skilled workers, a high minimum wage and strong employment protection paradoxically hampered access to the job market and Chile's public employment services and training systems continued to be underdeveloped.

Growth has been driven largely by parallel increases in the essential components of the economy: labour, capital, land and entrepreneurship. There had been the occasional glitch, but in 2013 there were signs that productivity growth had picked up. However, the OECD also noted that business research and development (R&D) intensity was low, innovative outputs had been weak and technological progress had suffered from a shortage of qualified graduates. The 'Start-up Chile' innovation had attracted international attention as a way to foster entrepreneurship. In general, Chilean firms have become more innovative, including in traditional sectors centred on comparative advantages and natural resources. Still, there was scope to further expand the innovation system, improve existing programmes and strengthen institutional coherence. Chile's strong economic growth with its heavy reliance on natural resources had, in the view of the OECD, come at a cost for the environment, notably in air quality and – in some areas – water availability. In Chile the use of renewable energy sources is high, but this is limited primarily to hydropower and energy needs are still met to a significant degree by imported fossil fuels.

The IMF – a note of caution

Introducing a note of caution, in its June 2014 assessment of the Chilean economy, the International Monetary Fund (IMF) noted that Chile was confronting a challenging macro-economic environment. After several years of strong economic performance, investment in Chile had weakened and growth had slowed markedly, due in part to a weaker copper price perspective, as the economy's performance fell below par. At the same time, according to the IMF, the depreciation of the peso had generated higher inflation, but Chile's medium-term expectations remained anchored around the Banco Central de Chile (central bank)'s target. The current account deficit had narrowed rapidly to 3.1 per cent of GDP in the first quarter of 2014, but gross external financing needs, though smaller than in 2013, remain high at 17 per cent of GDP. The labour market – albeit still tight – has softened.

In mid-2014 monetary policy had eased and the Chilean government's fiscal policy had stayed broadly neutral. The central bank reduced its base interest rate from 5 to 4 per cent between October 2013 and April 2014, reflecting the weakening economic outlook and inflation levels that were below target. The reductions had worked through to interbank and lending rates and had contributed to peso depreciation. Nonetheless, credit growth had moderated for all types of credit, except for mortgage credit, which remained brisk. The 2013 structural deficit was estimated by IMF staff at 0.8 per cent of GDP. The fall in copper revenue pushed the balance to a deficit of 0.6 per cent of GDP from a surplus of similar proportions in 2012. However, central government net assets remained at a surplus of 6.7 per cent of GDP.

GDP growth was expected by the IMF to have bottomed out in 2014 and gradually return to trend. Growth reached 1.8 per cent in 2014 and looked set to recover to its potential level by 2016, supported by monetary easing, the peso depreciation and a recovery in the global economy. Key risks to this outlook arose from the potential of further declines in copper prices and a return of global financial volatility. Although there were signs that investment was stabilising and could pick up later in 2014, consumption of durable goods had declined and a further weakening could not be ruled out. Net exports looked set to continue to provide a boost to the recovery.

The Chilean government had launched an ambitious policy agenda to bolster long-term growth and reduce inequality. This included important reforms in taxation, education, productivity and energy. The authorities' tax reforms aimed to create a more progressive tax structure and raise 3 per cent of GDP in revenue to fund greater spending on education and health, while raising public savings. The education reform focussed on early childhood education and fostering equal access and improving quality and accountability in education. The energy agenda aimed to promote investment and efficiency and facilitate the use of clean technologies. The authorities' plans to bolster competitiveness included improving infrastructure, promoting research and development and job training and providing new services for small- and medium-sized enterprises.

The IMF noted that the Chilean financial sector was large, but that risks were contained. Financial system assets exceeded 200 per cent of GDP. Bank capitalisation appeared adequate, profitability remained comfortable and non-performing loans were low and fully provisioned. The investment returns of the private pension system had declined and the government had appointed a commission to propose parametric changes to ensure adequate replacement rates. The authorities have sent to congress legislation that established risk-based insurance supervision and a comprehensive credit registry and strengthened the legal framework of the Securities and Insurance Supervisor and the Financial Stability Council.

ECLAC notes a slackening

In its December 2014 review of the Chilean economy the United Nations Economic Commission for Latin America and the Caribbean (ECLAC/CEPAL) notes that Chile's GDP grew by 1.8 per cent during 2014, down from 4.1 per cent the year before. The slowdown was contributed to by slackening domestic demand, especially consumption (the main driver of growth in previous years) and a fall in construction and machinery investment. Both factors reflected the lower expectations that began in the first quarter of 2013 as a result of rising uncertainty about future growth in the world economy and, in particular, the demand for Chilean exports, given lower growth forecasts in key markets such as China and Europe. The weak performance of the euro-zone economy and slower economic expansion seen in China over the previous two years confirmed the forecasts, which foreshadowed the end of a period of steadily rising copper prices and growth in investments in new mining projects. ECLAC reported that Chilean firms had been behaving more cautiously since early 2013, reducing investments in machinery, equipment and construction activity. Inventories were run down sharply during 2014. The drop in demand had also resulted in lower job creation in 2014. This had weakened the basis for consumption, which had underpinned growth until then.

Annual inflation had averaged 4.5 per cent in the first ten month of 2014, compared to 1.9 per cent in 2013.The unemployment rate was 6.4 per cent (6 per cent in 2013) while the balance of payments current account deficit fell from 3.4 per cent of GDP in 2013 to 1.3 per cent in the first three quarters of 2014. The economic policy implemented by the new Nueva Mayoría government in March 2014 had similar features to those applied by previous executives. The main new developments in the current approach focussed on tax reforms, where the core provision was increased taxation of income from capital and proposals for structural reform in education.

ECLAC reported that Chile's fiscal policy had continued to be guided by the goal of structural balance in the medium term. In October 2014, total central government revenue was down by 0.2 per cent in real terms on the same period the year before, attributed to the sharp drop in mining receipts from both the state and private sectors. The tax take from private-sector mining fell by 10.3 per cent in real terms, while revenues from the National Copper Corporation of Chile (Codelco) were down by 15.7 per cent in real terms. Current expenditure grew by 6.4 per cent in real terms in this period, while investment grew slowly (by 1.2 per cent) and capital transfers shrank by 1.7 per cent.

ECLAC forecast a deficit of 1.8 per cent of GDP in 2014, as against 0.6 per cent in 2013. In view of the economic slowdown, a budget containing counter-cyclical measures to boost activity and particularly investment, had been passed for 2015. Public spending was projected to increase by 9.8 per cent, including public investment growth of some 28 per cent, while a deficit of 1.9 per cent of GDP is forecast. Monetary policy continued to target an annual inflation rate of 3 per cent over a two-year horizon. Having held the nominal interest rate at 5 per cent since January 2012, the central bank began to lower the rate in October 2013 in the face of signs of slackening of activity, bringing it down to 3 per cent by October 2014.

From May 2013, demand for foreign financial assets increased; the Chilean peso began to depreciate, with – according to ECLAC – a cumulative 12 month decline of 17.8 per cent by October 2014. As a result of the contraction in domestic demand, ECLAC noted that the current account deficit narrowed over the first three quarters of 2014. The value of goods and services exports fell by 0.7 per cent during the period reflecting lower demand which resulted in lower revenues that could not be offset by higher export volumes. At the same time, the value of imports fell by some 7.6 per cent.

Net FDI in 2014 remained at levels comparable to the previous year. However, lower net portfolio returns alongside outflows of capital meant that international reserves only increased by US$317 million by November 2014. The slowdown in GDP growth in 2014 was mainly accounted for by the reduced contribution of non-tradable sectors, which continued on the downward trend of the previous two years, compounded by the low contribution of manufacturing in general. The determining factor in both cases was the behaviour of domestic demand (consumption and investment) described earlier. Natural resource sectors (agriculture, forestry, fisheries and mining) continued to make a positive contribution, albeit one that weakened over the year owing to the sluggishness of external demand. Inflation increased gradually from September 2013, so that by the end of 2014 the annual rate was close to 5 per cent. Owing to the moderation of domestic demand, non-tradable goods prices rose steadily at a rate of between 4 per cent and 5 per cent, while tradable goods inflation accelerated strongly from the start of the year owing to the depreciation of the currency. The labour force expanded, according to ECLAC, at an average annual rate of 2.1 per cent up to September 2014 (the figure for 2013 was 1.6 per cent). The number of people in work grew at an annual rate of 1.5 per cent in the first nine months of 2014, down on the 2.1 per cent seen in 2013. The unemployment rate rose from 5.9 per cent in 2013, to an average of 6.4 per cent in 2014.

Energy

Chile is, according to the US government's Energy Information Administration (EIA), the fifth-largest consumer of energy on the continent, but unlike most other large economies in the region, it is only a minor producer of fossil fuels. This makes Chile heavily dependent on energy imports. In 2013 Chile imported over 300,000 barrels per day (bpd) of oil, which was, according to the EIA, evenly split between refined petroleum products and crude oil. Imported crude oil, as well as a small amount of domestically produced crude, is processed in three refineries owned by the state-owned Empresa Nacional del Petróleo (ENAP), with a total capacity of 227,000bpd.

Most of Chile's crude oil imports originate in other South American countries, particularly Ecuador, Brazil, Colombia and Argentina. However, the United States remains Chile's leading source of refined petroleum product imports. In 2013, the United States supplied 143,000bpd, mostly in the form of distillate fuel oil. In 2013, Chile imported 140 billion cubic feet (bcf) of natural gas. Most of Chile's natural gas imports arrive as liquefied natural gas (LNG) from Trinidad and Tobago, Qatar and Yemen. Chile has two regasification terminals: Mejillones, in the north and Quintero, near the large urban centres of Valparaíso and Santiago. Chile also imports natural gas from Argentina by various pipelines that were constructed in the late 1990s. Imports from Argentina grew dramatically in the decade that followed, but Chile expedited its efforts to develop LNG import capabilities after policy changes and production declines curtailed Argentina's natural gas exports. More recently, the Canadian methane-producing company, Methanex Corporation, closed down a part of its large methanol production in southern Chile, reportedly because of inadequate supplies of natural gas from Argentina. Methanex reportedly had plans to relocate two of its Chilean plants to the US.

According to the energy ministry, Chile plans to meet more of its domestic demands through increased natural gas supplies. The expansion of the Panama Canal widened Chile's import options, including LNG from the United States and other South American countries. According to the EIA, Chile has also been exploring in its Magallanes shale basin to boost domestic production.

Risk assessment

Economy	Good
Politics	Fair
Regional stability	Good

COUNTRY PROFILE

Inca rule barely touched Chile, with Aymara and Atacameno farmers and herders pre-dating the Incas. Chango Indians fished along the coastal areas while Diaguitas farmed the interior of Coquimbo. Beyond the central valley, Araucanian or Mapuche Indians resisted Inca aggression.

1535 Indigenous Araucaria people successfully resisted the first Spanish invasion of Chile.

1540 Santiago was founded by Pedro de Valdivia, who began the Spanish conquest of Chile.

1553 Araucarias captured and executed Valdivia.

1553–58 Indigenous people staged an uprising against Spanish colonialism; however most of the country was eventually subdued, although the Mapuche

managed to hold onto their remaining territory for almost three centuries.
1578 Sir Francis Drake, an English adventurer, led a raid on the port of Valparaíso, which was repulsed by the Spanish armies.
1700 For most of the eighteenth century it was ruled by a small oligarchy of landowners.
1759 Chile began reforms under the auspices of the Bourbon monarchs, who succeeded the Habsburg dynasty in Spain.
1788 Irish-born Ambrosio O'Higgins y Ballenary began his tenure as governor of Chile. He outlawed slavery and forced labour, strengthened production and administration and bolstered the power of the military. Chile was granted more autonomy than most other Latin American colonies.
1807 Napoleon Bonaparte's invasion of Spain fuelled the independence movement in Chile.
1810 Independence leader Bernardo O'Higgins Riquelme, son of Ambrosio O'Higgins, led a revolt against José Miguel Carrera Verdugo, the Chilean leader who had brought more autonomy to the country.
1814 Spanish troops re-conquered Chile.
1818 Bernado O'Higgins joined forces with José de San Martín in Argentina and led successful battles against the Spanish that resulted in Chile's independence from Spain. Bernado O'Higgins became Chile's first post-independence leader.
1823 O'Higgins was forced to resign. Civil war between liberal federalists and conservative centralists ensued, lasting for seven years.
1830 The Conservatives won the civil war.
1851–61 President Manuel Montt liberalised the constitution, reducing the power of landowners and the Roman Catholic Church.
1879–84 Chile's victory in the War of the Pacific against Peru and Bolivia increased its territory by one-third.
1880s–90s The pacification of the Araucarias led to increased European immigration. Mining of nitrates and copper began.
1891 A civil war over a constitutional dispute between the president and congress led to a congressional victory, with the role of the president reduced to a figurehead.
1925 A new constitution saw the disestablishment of the church.
1927 General Carlos Ibañez del Campo seized power in a military coup and established a dictatorship.
1938–46 A Popular Front coalition was formed by communists, socialists and radicals.
1948–58 The Communist Party was banned.
1952 Carlos Ibañez was elected president, promising to strengthen law and order.
1964 Eduardo Frei Montalva was elected president, pledging to introduce limited social reform.
1970 Salvador Allende Gossens was elected president and imposed an extensive programme of nationalisation.
1973 The government failed to win a congressional majority in the elections as opposition to its policies mounted and the country faced ever-increasing economic problems. Food shortages followed high inflation and fighting broke out between pro- and anti-government activists. Backed by the CIA, the armed forces intervened. President Allende died during the military takeover.
1974 General Augusto Pinochet Ugarte became president, remaining in power for 16 years.
1988 Chilean voters rejected Pinochet's bid to extend his power until 1997.
1989 The Concertación de Partidos por la Democracia (*Concertación*) (Coalition of Pro-Democracy Parties) was formed to contest the general elections. Patricio Aylwin (*Concertación*) defeated both Pinochet's protégé and a right-wing independent candidate in the presidential election.
1990 The *Concertación* won the general elections with 49.3 per cent of the vote in the Chamber of Deputies and 50.5 per cent in the Senate.
1993 Eduardo Frei Ruíz-Tagle won the presidential election. He began reducing the military's influence in government.
1998 Pinochet retired from the army and was made senator-for-life. He was arrested in the UK on a warrant issued by a Spanish magistrate on murder charges related to his 'caravan of death' in the 1970s.
2000 Ricardo Lagos Escobar (*Concertación*) won the elections and became Chile's first socialist president since 1973. The UK government declared Pinochet unfit for extradition to Spain and the former dictator was returned to Chile. A Chilean judge subsequently charged Pinochet with kidnap.
2001 Chile's appeal court ruled that Pinochet was mentally unfit to stand trial on human rights violation charges. The ruling centre-left *Concertación* held on to its majority in Congress.
2002 All charges against Pinochet were dropped after the Supreme Court upheld a verdict finding him mentally unfit to stand trial for human rights crimes. Pinochet resigned from his post as a lifelong senator.
2004 The right to divorce became law. Chile's court lifted Pinochet's immunity from prosecution, opening the way to possible trials of the octogenarian general on charges of human rights abuses during his 17-year rule.
2006 Michelle Bachelet (Partido Socialista de Chile (PS) (Socialist Party of Chile)) took office as Chile's first female president, after she won 53.5 per cent in the presidential election runoff; Sebastián Piñera, a moderate conservative won 46.5 per cent of the votes. Augusto Pinochet, former Head of State (1973–90), died. The controversy surrounding his rule denied him a state funeral. All senate membership became by direct election, replacing the system of appointments.
2007 Bolivia, Brazil and Chile agreed to build a South American highway to link the Atlantic and Pacific coasts, running from Santos in Brazil, through Bolivia, to Arica and Iquique in Chile, at an estimated cost of US$600 million.
2008 Chile recalled its ambassador from Peru, after Peru had asked the International Court of Justice (ICJ) to make a ruling over the disputed maritime border between them. The sea is a rich fishing ground. The Chaiten volcano in Patagonia erupted.
2009 Chile agreed with the Organisation for Economic Co-operation and Development (OECD) to implement international tax information exchange standards. In elections for the Chamber of Deputies, the Coalición por el Cambio (CC) (Coalition for Change) (alliance of five parties) won 43.44 per cent of the vote (58 seats out of 120), the ruling *Concertación*-Juntos Podemos won 44.36 per cent (57). In the Senate, where 18 seats were up for election (out of a total of 38), CC won nine seats, *Concertación*-Juntos Podemos nine, while Chile Limpio lost its only seat.
2010 Following two rounds of presidential elections, Miguel Juan Sebastián Piñera Echenique (Sebastián Piñera) (CC) won the run-off, with 51.6 per cent of the vote. A massive earthquake of 8.8 magnitude struck offshore near Chile's second city, Concepción. Over 800 people were killed and many buildings were destroyed. The Brazilian airline TAM Linhas Aereas and the Chilean airline LAN agreed to merge to form the region's largest carrier, with 115 destinations in 23 countries. The company became the Latam Airlines Group, although individual airline brand names remain in use.
2011 In March the new 3,400km, US$1.3 billion, Carretera Interoceánica (Interoceanic Highway), was opened from Brazil's Atlantic coast to Peru's Pacific seaboard, bisecting the Amazon forest

and crossing the Andes Mountains into Chile. In March, Bolivia threatened to lodge a complaint against Chile in the ICJ for return of land won during the 1879–83 War of the Pacific. Since Chile annexed land from Peru and Bolivia following the war, Bolivia has been landlocked. Despite several attempts to resolve the issue, including the offer of free access to ports designated specifically for Bolivian trade, a peace deal has remained out of reach. Miners working for the world's largest copper mining company, Codelco, began a strike in July, protesting plans to restructure the industry. President Piñera reshuffled his cabinet, in an effort to boost his popularity rating, which had fallen to 30 per cent. He also reassured miners that there were no plans to nationalise Codelco. On 21 December, parliament changed the voting system and dropped compulsory and automatic enrolment to a wholly voluntary voting system.

2012 On 11 September, following an exhumation in 2011 and at the end of an investigation, an appeal court upheld an earlier court's conclusion that president Salvador Allende had committed suicide and had not been shot by forces of General Pinochet during a *coup d'état* in 1973. A census was undertaken on 31 August; the preliminary result was 16,572,475 people.

2013 Despite winning the primary elections, on 17 July conservative presidential candidate, Pablo Longueira, withdrew from the election campaign. He was said by his son to be suffering from depression. Polls suggest that former left wing president Michelle Bachelet is favourite to win the 17 November election. Labour minister Evelyn Matthei replaced Mr Longueira as presidential candidate for the conservative alliance. On 7 August the government announced it had been advised to annul the 2012 census since it had failed to count as many as a million people. A 24 hour strike in Chile's largest copper mine, the Escondida mine, was held on 14 August. In the presidential election held on 17 November, left-wing candidate Michelle Bachelet won the first round with 47 per cent, just short of the 50 per cent needed to avoid a second round of voting. Her main rival, Evelyn Matthei, a former Labour minister in the centre-right government of Sebastian Pinera, took 47 per cent. The run-off will be held on 15 December. The general election was also held 17 November. Mrs Bachelet's New Majority Coalition, lead by the Christian Democratic Party, won a majority in the Chamber of Deputies with 67 seats (out of 120). The Alliance coalition, lead by the Independent Democratic Union, won 49 seats; the Liberal Party won one seat and there three successful independents. In the Senate the New Majority coalition won 12 of the 20 seats contested, giving the coalition a total of 21 (of 38) seats. The Alliance won seven seats (total 16) and there was one independent. The presidential run-off on 15 December was won convincingly by Mrs Bachelet with 62 per cent to Ms Matthei's 38 per cent; turn out was 42 per cent.

2014 Michelle Bachelet was sworn in as President on 11 February.

2015

Political structure

Constitution

The constitution dates from 1980, when it was accepted by two-thirds of voters in a plebiscite organised by the military government. Following a further plebiscite in 1989, 54 reforms passed into law. They included increasing the number of directly elected members in the Senate, abolishing Article 8 (which outlawed Marxist groups) and balancing the number of civilian and military representatives on the powerful Council of National Security. Further changes to the constitution require a two-thirds majority in both houses of the Congreso Nacional (National Congress). Voting age is 18 for all citizens and foreigners who have been legally living in Chile for over 5 years.

Form of state

Presidential democratic republic

The executive

Executive power is held by the president and cabinet. The president is head of state and commander-in-chief of the armed forces. Elected for a fixed term of six years, the president cannot be re-elected for the following period.

The relationship between the executive and the armed forces is enshrined in the constitution. The president should take note of discussions within the Council of National Security. This consists of eight members, four military and four civilian. The four military members are the heads of the army, navy, air force and police. The four civilian members are the president of the republic, president of the Senate, president of the Supreme Court and the comptroller general of the republic. According to the constitution, the Council of National Security provides a forum within which it is possible to present, at the highest level, the military's opinion. The armed forces see the council as having the function of letting civilian governments know of potential conflicts between military and civilian interests, thereby acting to prevent future military intervention in government.

National legislature

The bicameral Congreso Nacional (National Congress), is composed of the Cámara de Diputados (Chamber of Deputies) (lower house) with 120 deputies directly elected in 60 two-member electoral districts, serving for four-year terms. The Senado de la República (senate) (upper house) has 38 directly elected members, serving for eight-year terms; around one-third of the membership is elected every four years.

Laws can originate in either of the chambers or be proposed by the president.

Legal system

The main tribunals of the independent judiciary system are the Supreme Court, 16 regional courts of appeal and the lower courts. The Supreme Court consists of 16 members appointed for life by the president from a list of five names proposed by the Supreme Court as vacancies arise. Members of the courts of appeal are appointed in the same way as those of the Supreme Court. Judges in lower courts are appointed in a similar manner, but from lists submitted by the court of appeal of the district in which the vacancies arise.

Last elections

17 November 2013 (parliamentary and first round of presidential); 15 December 2013 (presidential run-off)

Results: Parliamentary (Chamber of Deputies): Nueva Mayoria won 47.74 per cent of the vote and 67 seats (out of 120), Allianza 36.18 per cent and 49 seats, Independents 3.32 per cent and 3 seats, Si tú quieres, Chile cambia 5.45 per cent and 1 seat. The other parties and alliances failed to gain any seats.

Parliamentary (Senate): Nueva Mayoria won 50.64 per cent of the vote and 21 seats (out of 38), Allianza 42.10 per cent and 16 seats, Independents won 1.52 per cent and 1 seat. The other parties and alliances failed to gain any seats.

Presidential (first round): Michelle Bachelet (PS/Nueva Mayoria) won 46.70 per cent, Evelyn Matthei (UDI/Allianza) 25.03 per cent, Marco Enríquez-Ominami (PRO) 10.98 per cent, Franco Parisi (Independent) 10.11 per cent. The five other candidates polled less than 3 per cent.

Presidential (second round): Michelle Bachelet won 62.16 per cent and Evelyn Matthei 37.83 per cent

Next elections

2017 (presidential, national congress and senate (half the membership))

Political parties

Ruling party

A centre-left coalition of 7 parties known as Nueva Mayoria (New Majority), led by Partido Socialista de Chile (PS) (Socialist Party of Chile)

Main opposition party

A right-wing coalition called Alianza (Alliance), led by Unión Demócrata

Independiente (Independent Democratic Union) (UDI)

Population

17.56 million (2013)* About 29 per cent of the population is under 15 years of age.

Last census: 31 August 2012: 16,572,475 (preliminary result)

Population density: 20 inhabitants per square km. Urban population 89 per cent (2010 Unicef).

Annual growth rate: 1.3 per cent, 1990–2010 (Unicef).

Ethnic make-up

Mixed European and indigenous peoples (mestizos) account for approximately 75 per cent of the population, with a further 23 per cent of European descent and 2 per cent Indians, mainly Mapuches, in the south.

Religions

Approximately 85 per cent Roman Catholic, 10 per cent Protestant, with small minorities of Jews, Muslims and other religions.

Education

The investment in education amounts to 4.0 per cent of GDP. This figure has doubled since the early 1990s. Chile has achieved gender parity in both primary and secondary education and has extended the school year by around 15 per cent.

Education is free and compulsory for the first eight years, beginning at the age of five or six.

All other education institutions charge fees, either partly or in full. The subsidies system applies equally to municipal and private education but has been directed mostly to basic education. The role of the ministry of education is now limited to licensing private education and carrying out school inspections.

Over 80 per cent of children complete secondary education, which begins at the age of 13 or 14 years and is divided into a humanities/science programme or a technical/vocational programme. Higher education consists of universities, professional and technical institutes.

Literacy rate: 96 per cent adult rate; 99 per cent youth rate (15–24) (Unesco 2005).

Compulsory years: Five or six to 13 or 14 (eight years in total)

Enrolment rate: 103 per cent boys, 100 per cent girls, total primary school enrolment of the relevant age group (including repetition rates), (World Bank).

Pupils per teacher: 30 in primary schools

Health

Healthcare is distributed between the ministry of health and social security institutions as well as private funds and the public sector. Health and social security have increasingly come into the hands of pension fund administration companies (AFPs). Since 1999, over a quarter of Chileans had taken out private health insurance. The state is responsible for the financing of health promotion, protection and prevention through the National Health Fund. The decentralised national health service is able to provide healthcare at different levels. The most basic care is in the hands of regional health authorities, responsible for preventive medical services which are part of the health promotion and protection programmes.

Care for pregnant women, children under six and members of indigent and low income families is free. More specialised medical consultation and care is given at hospitals and maternity units. For patients who voluntarily choose the state system, a contribution of 25 to 30 per cent of the cost is required (depending on income). People under any social security scheme are entitled to preventive medical services (periodical health examinations) and in the case of illness, are granted full-paid sick leave. Occupational accidents or disease are covered by a special fund.

HIV/Aids

In 2009 there were an estimated 40,000 adults living with HIV.

HIV prevalence: 0.4 per cent aged 15–49 in 2009 (Unicef 2012)

Life expectancy: 79 years, 2009 (Unicef 2012)

Fertility rate/Maternal mortality rate: 1.9 births per woman, 2010 (Unicef 2012)

Child (under 5 years) mortality rate (per 1,000): 9 per 1,000 live births (WHO 2012)

Welfare

The statutory age of retirement is 65 years for men and 60 years for women. The system requires 13 per cent of a worker's wage to be deducted and accumulated in one of seven independently managed mutual-fund companies selected by the worker, with a small part of the contribution going towards disability insurance. Neither employers nor the government contribute to the individual accounts. The contributions remain under the workers' control, if they change jobs, and are deferred from any tax.

However, critics of the Chilean pension model argue that given the country's poverty rate, some workers would never be able to save enough toward retirement. Besides, 42 per cent of the workforce, in the informal economy, are not covered by any pension system, according to government statistics. Although they can make voluntary contributions to the system, most workers' incomes are very low. Hence, the government guarantees a minimum pension to anyone who has worked as a regular employee for 20 years.

Monetary subsidies apply to those outside any social security scheme include a special family allowance for both pregnant women and children under 15, in extreme poverty, and a special pension allowance for people over 65, or the handicapped without economic resources.

The system allows up to 20 per cent foreign investment in pension funds and it is likely to push that limit to 35 per cent with new legislation.

Main cities

Santiago (capital, estimated population 5.3 million in 2012), Puente Alto (886,132), Antofagasta (369,855), San Bernardo (325,241), Viña del Mar (285,513), Valparaíso (267,213), Temuco (257,819), Iquique (245,299), Talca (236,774).

Languages spoken

English is the main second language.

Official language/s

Spanish

Media

Press

Dailies: In Spanish, national newspapers include the state-owned *La Nación* (www.lanacion.cl) and privately owned *El Mercurio* (http://diario.elmercurio.com) a long established publication *La Tercera* (www.latercera.cl) is its rival. Tabloids include *Las Ultimas Noticias* (www.lun.com) and *La Cuarta* (www.lacuarta.cl), which is written in Chilean vernacular. *La Segunda* (www.lasegunda.com) is an evening newspaper.

In Spanish, regional newspapers include from Santiago *La Hora* (www.lahora.cl) and *Publimetro* (www.publimetro.cl), which are free newspapers. From Los Angeles *La Tribuna* (www.diariolatribuna.cl), from Punta Arenas *La Prensa Austral* (www.laprensaaustral.cl), and from Antofagasta *La Estrella del Norte* (www.estrellanorte.cl). *Prensa Al Día* (www.prensaaldia.cl) carries a compilation of daily reported news. In English, the *Santiago Times* (www.tcgnews.com/santiagotimes) provides news and general information about Chile and Santiago.

Weeklies: Some daily newspapers have weekend edition and there are many magazines for all tastes and ages. Fortnightly publications include, in Spanish, *La Firme* (www.lafirme.cl), a analytical political magazine, *The Clinic* (www.theclinic.cl), a satirical magazine and *Ercilla* (www.ercilla.cl) for general information. Women's magazines include

Cosas (http://www.cosas.cl) and *Vanidades* (www.vanidades.cl); *Conozca Más* (www.conozcamas.cl) for men and *Condorito* (www.condorito.com) is a humourus publication.
In German *Condor* (http://www.condor.cl), is a general news weekly.
Business: In Spanish, dailies include *Estrategía* (www.estrategia.cl) and *Diario Financiero* (www.diariofinanciero.cl), is an influential newspaper. Monthlies include *América Economía* (www.americaeconomia.com), was the first business magazine published, *Datos Sur* (www.datossur.cl) and *Estrategia* (www.capital.cl). *Punto Final* (www.puntofinal.cl) for fortnightly general business news. For Latin American news, *Business News Americas* (www.bnamericas.com) with an English daily on-line digest.

Broadcasting

The Ministerio de Transportes y Telecommunicaciones (www.mtt.cl) has overall authority for broadcasting.
The geography of Chile has resulted in more nationwide coverage of radio than TV signals.
Radio: There are over 300 radio stations, most of which are private, local and commercial. Several national networks include the private, Radio Cooperativa (www.cooperativa.cl) with news based programmes, Radio Agricultura (www.radioagricultura.cl), Bío Bío La Radio (www.radiobiobio.cl) and Radio Infinita (www.infinita.cl). Local stations in Santiago include Radio Tiempo (http://fmtiempo.cl), Radio Oasis (www.radiooasis.cl) and Radio Integral (www.radiointegral.cl).
Television: The national public, commercial broadcaster is Televisión Nacional de Chile (TVN) (www.tvn.cl). There are several other private TV networks, including Chilevisión (www.chilevision.cl), Megavisión (www.megavision.cl), Red TV (www.redtv.cl) and Canal 13 (www.canal13.cl).
There are many foreign and domestic channels available via satellite or cable.
National news agency: Agencia Chile Noticias

Economy

Chile is the world's leading supplier of copper at around 30 per cent of global production. Copper provides over 20 per cent of national GDP and 19 per cent of government revenue. Industry and manufacturing in 2014 constituted 23 per cent of GDP, of which manufacturing was 12 per cent and the service sector contributed 61.1 per cent, of which financial services represented almost 16 per cent of GDP.
Chile has a strong trade based economy and, for this reason, was hit especially hard by the global economic crash in 2008 and registered negative growth of -1 per cent in 2009. Since then, however, Chile has had strong growth due to a favourable domestic investment climate, Chile ranks 41 in the World Banks ease of doing business index, making it one of the leading South American countries in this area. On top of this, the growth in the mining industry helped lift Chile out of recession.
Since then Chile has experienced strong positive growth, sitting at 5-6 per cent, but in 2014 growth dropped to 1.8 per cent due to a fall in the price of commodities affected Chile's exports.
A severe earthquake struck the central region, near the city of Concepción, in 2010, killing 708 people, causing US$30 billion in damage to vital infrastructure and housing and disrupting energy production and copper mining. The necessary reconstruction led to an economic surge in GDP growth of 4.6 per cent in April alone.
Over the last two decades Chile has experienced a strong push towards privatisation and now few enterprises remain in state hands. However, Chile's largest company, the Chilean National Copper Corporation (CODELCO), remains state owned.
High unemployment has been a persistent trend at around 7 per cent for much of the 2000s. As the economic crisis deepened year-on-year unemployment reached 9.9 per cent in May 2009; employment growth became negative, at around -1.0 per cent. However, since then, Chile has managed to tackle the problem, albeit only slightly, and in 2014 unemployment stood at 6.4 per cent.
In 2014, in order to make good on her electoral promise of tackling inequality in the country and provide more widely spread education and healthcare, President Michelle Bachelet introduced further tax reforms. The reforms were mainly aimed at an increase in corporate tax and are expected to increase tax revenues to the equivalent of 3 per cent of GDP.

External trade

Chile has 25 preferential trade agreements in place.
Chile is an associate member of Mercusur, a member of the Organisation of American States (OAS) and has a free trade agreement with the European Union (EU) as well as other individual countries in Asia. It is also an associate member of the Unión de Naciones Suramericanas (Unasur) (Union of South American Nations), modelled on the European Union (EU), which seeks to integrate with the Andean Community of Nations and Mercosur in a single market by 2014, when tariffs on non-sensitive products are to be abolished with the remainder eliminated by 2019. However political tensions within the region have hampered the ongoing process.
Chile has recently also been pushing trade agreements with the Asia-Pacific region and now has strong agreements with South Korea, India and China. Chile has also, since 2010, joined 11 other countries, including the US, in negotiating the Trans-Pacific Partnership (TPP) trade agreement. The negotiating process has been long has contentious issues have been hotly debated. The details of the agreement and negotiations have as yet not been made public. The final round of negotiations were set to take place in July 2015, however, negotiations stumbled and finalisations still look to be postponed. Due to the lack of public information the exact details and areas of the partnership are not known.
Chile is the world's largest source of copper.

Imports

Main imports include petroleum and petroleum products, natural gas, chemicals, electrical and telecommunications equipment, industrial machinery and vehicles.
Main sources: US (20.4 per cent of total in 2014), China (20.0 per cent), Brazil (8.7 per cent).

Exports

Major exports include copper, fruit and processed foods including wine and fish products, timber, paper and pulp.
Main destinations: China (24.6 per cent of total in 2014), US (11.8 per cent), Japan (10.5 per cent).

Agriculture

Farming

The contribution of the agricultural sector to the Chilean economy is significant, employing 13.2 per cent of the total workforce and generating 3.5 per cent of GDP in 2014. Approximately 8 per cent of the total land mass is cultivated. The country's soil is fertile and well irrigated, particularly in the central area and main river valleys.
Dependence on imported foodstuffs has been reduced by improved wheat, sugar and vegetable oil production. Other important crops are oats, barley, rice, beans, lentils, maize and chickpeas. Important cash/export crops are maize, beans, asparagus, onions and garlic.
The production and export of a variety of fruit have all recorded impressive figures, given Chile's favourable growing conditions and good soil, relatively cost-effective labour and protection from disease. Table grapes, citrus fruits, avocados, pears, nectarines, peaches, kiwis, plums and nuts have done well. Chilean wine is

growing in importance as a value-added agricultural product and a highly important export.
Livestock farming is concentrated in the south of the country.

Fishing

The Fishing industry in Chile is one of the economy's most important export industries. Chile is second only to Norway as a producer of fresh, frozen and prepared salmon, with annual exports totalling more than US$800 million. The productivity of the fishing industry is largely attributable to the large number of salmon farms in the south of the country.
Fishing and fish processing have become a diversified industry. Pilchards have traditionally been the main species of fish landed (75 per cent), with jack mackerel second. Abalone is exported to Japan, algae to Taiwan, hake to Spain, fresh salmon to the US and canned pilchards to the UK. Such diversification has been fuelled by substantial and continued increases in investment.
The typical annual fish catch is 4.3 million tonnes, including 3.6 million tonnes marine fish and 164,477 tonnes shellfish.

Forestry

Chile has a significant amount of forested land, approximately 15.5 million hectares (ha), equating to 23 per cent of the total land area. Since 2000, Chile forest area has lost an average of 0.32 per cent per year, or 48,400ha. Forestry is an important sector suitable for commercial exploitation. Up to 80 per cent of Chile's rainforests to have already been destroyed.
Chile has abundant softwood plantations used for the manufacture of forest products. The forestry industry is primarily located in the south, stretching from the Seventh to the Tenth region, with the main concentration in the Eighth Region around Concepción. The three ports of the area (San Vicente, Lirquén and Talcahuano) handle up to 95 per cent of all forestry exports.
The sawn wood sector is characterised by a wide variety of producers, ranging from small portable sawmills to large highly automated mills. The larger sawmills tend to specialise in *pinus radiata*. Sawnwood production is largely a seasonal industry, with the highest activity occurring between spring and autumn (September to April).
In the global market, Chile is the third-largest exporter of woodchips while nearly 50 per cent of its sawn timber, panels and softwood pulp production are exported.
Japan is the single most important purchaser of Chilean wood cellulose. Paper production has a large domestic market. The government has promoted private sector investment in forestry with land tax exemptions, rebates and subsidies.

Industry and manufacturing

Chile's manufacturing sector employs approximately one quarter of the country's total workforce. The sector also contributes around a third of Chilean GDP. Financial conglomerates control a substantial section of denationalised industries, although small firms with less than 10 employees still dominate.
Export-based industries include petrochemicals, pulp and paper, base metals, plastics, rubber and food processing (particularly fish and malted barley). Domestic market industries include textiles, footwear, cement, food processing, beverages and machinery.

Tourism

Chile has a rich variety of terrain, from glacier-fed fjords of Patagonia in the south to the fertile central coastal region in the western shadow of the Andes and the rocky, salt and sandy Atacama Desert which begins in the north and runs south, east of the Andes. There are five historic sites included on Unesco's World Heritage List (four on the mainland and one on Easter Island). According to official statistics, Santiago, the vineyards of the central valleys and the Chilean Antarctic are the most popular tourist destinations. Many cruise ships with Antarctic destinations begin their voyages from Punta Arenas.
Travel and tourism directly contributed around 3.2 per cent of GDP and 9.6 per cent in total in 2014. Over 3.2 per cent of total employment (253,000 jobs) is directly supported by the industry and a total, including jobs indirectly supported by the industry, of 9.1 per cent of employment (721,000). Chile saw 3.8 million visitors in 2014, up slightly from 3.6 million in 2013, and
Visitor exports have increased from US$1.9 billion in 2006 to an estimated US$3.2 billion in 2014 (3.5 per cent of total exports), which matches the rise in capital investment over the same period, from US$1.3 billion in 2006 to an estimated US$5.8 billion in 2014 (10 per cent of total investment).

Environment

Santiago suffers from a serious smog problem, which is at its worst May–September and is aggravated when the winter weather is interrupted by spells of milder temperatures.

Mining

The mining sector is of great importance to the Chilean economy, contributing 9 per cent to GDP and providing employment for 6 per cent of the workforce. It is the main export earner and a major focus of foreign investment in the country.
Activity is concentrated in copper, of which Chile is the world's leading producer and holds around 30 per cent of the world's proven reserves. The state-owned copper enterprise, Corporación Nacional del Cobre de Chile (Codelco), holds 70 per cent of national reserves and administers the four largest mines: Chuquicamata, El Teniente, Andina and El Salvador. Copper is also extracted from the Escondida mine, the biggest proven deposit in the world.
Mining of silver, gold (the El Indio mine ranks among the highest grade mines in the world), iron ore, manganese and lead is also undertaken. Other mining sub-sectors include natural nitrates, mercury, marble, coal, sulphur and limestone
Proven and probable reserves at the Fachinal mine in southern Chile (Coeur d'Alene Mines Corporation) are estimated at 317,915 ounces of gold and 14.6 million ounces of silver.

Hydrocarbons

The country is a net importer of energy, with less than 10 per cent of its needs fulfilled by domestic hydrocarbon production. Domestic oil production, mainly from offshore fields at the Straits of Magellan and onshore at Tierra del Fuego and the southern mainland, provides less than 6 per cent of domestic consumption. Chile's oil reserves were a mere 150 million barrels in 2014 and are no longer significant to its energy mix. Oil consumption was 355,000 barrels per day in 2014 which was imported either as refined products or crude oil to be process in the three oil refineries opertated by the state-owned Empresa Nacional del Petróleo (ENAP), which controls the energy sector.
Chile has less than 98 billion cubic metres of proven natural gas reserves, with production limited to the urban markets of central Chile, particularly Santiago, standing at around 947 million cubic metres (cum). However nationally, gas consumption has risen from 3.1 billion cum in 2009 to 4.8 billion cum in 2014, despite a government push for conservation since consumption in 2004 was a record 8.7 billion cum.
Imported liquid natural gas (LNG) has increased, to become Chile primary source of energy. In 2014 LNG accounted for 3.8 billion cum, while piped natural gas from Argentina only amounted to 340 million cum.
There are two LNG terminals, one in Quintero on the central coast, the other in Mejillones in the north, centred on Chile's copperbelt.

Chile's coal resources come mainly from Lota/Coronel and the extreme south of Tierra del Fuego. All domestic coal production goes to power generation. Chile has total recoverable coal reserves of 1.3 million tonnes; production has fallen to around 40,000 tonnes a year.

Energy

Generation, transmission and distribution are entirely privately run entities. The sector is regulated by the Ministerio de Economía y Energía (MEE) (ministry of economy and energy) as a function of Comisión Nacional de Energía (CNE) (national energy commission).

Chile generated a total of 16.2 billion kW of electricity in 2013 (latest figures), of which 60 per cent was generated by thermal and 40 per cent by hydroelectric power stations. Whenever possible, hydropower is used as the lead source of energy but climatic conditions, particularly the lack of rainfall, have an impact on the need to use and ability to generate power.

Financial markets

Stock exchange

Bolsa de Comercio de Santiago (Santiago Stock Exchange) (SSE)

Banking and insurance

Chile's banking and insurance sector was once an exclusive enclave of the economy where only the rich were able to access financial services. However, the 1990s saw an expansion of the banking sector throughout the country. Today Chile has one of Latin America's most developed and sophisticated banking sectors and Chilean banks have shown relative strength in a weak economic environment. The authorities do not allow new banks to enter the Chilean market, except via the purchase of an existing bank. Restrictions remain on the range of activities a bank can undertake, with pension fund management reserved for private pension fund companies.

Competitive pressures have increased with domestic banks facing increased competition from Spanish banks. Following Banco Santander Central Hispano's (BSCH) takeover of Banco Santiago and Santander Chile – two of Chile's largest banks – BSCH has a market share of just under 30 per cent.

Central bank

Banco Central de Chile

Main financial centre

Santiago

Time

GMT minus four hours (daylight saving, mid-October to mid-March, GMT minus three hours)

Geography

Chile occupies a thin strip of land, rarely more than 200km wide, which stretches 4,640km down the west coast of Latin America from north of the tropic of Capricorn to Cape Horn. Geography and climate range from hot deserts in the north to icy Andean peaks at almost 7,000 metres high in the east and thousands of rainswept islets in the south. Chile is bordered by the Pacific to the west, by Argentina to the east, by Bolivia in the north-east and Peru to the north. Several Pacific islands, including the Juan Fernandez archipelago and Easter Island, are Chilean.

There are three main geographical belts running from north to south – the Andes, the central valley, and the narrow coastal range. The Andes are characterised not only by their great height but also by being a broad mass, generally over 80km wide, and making a superb natural border with Argentina. West of the Andes, the central valley has a varied form. In the north, it is a high desert basin, characterised by inward drainage and near complete aridity. Further south it disappears, until re-emerging near Santiago. From Santiago to Puerto Montt, it constitutes the agricultural heart of Chile, until it disappears under the sea at Puerto Montt. The coastal range, significantly lower than the Andes and generally under 3,000 metres, forms a barrier between the populated central valley and the coast, except for certain gaps made by powerful rivers, as at Concepción in the south. Of the mainland area, 2.2 per cent is suitable for crops, 17.1 per cent for livestock and 10.8 per cent for forestry. The remaining 69.9 per cent is considered unproductive and is mostly covered by deserts or mountains.

Hemisphere

Southern

Climate

Generally hot and dry in north, Mediterranean in central region (cool nights) and wet and cold in the south. Temperatures in Santiago range from 10–33 degrees Celsius (C) in summer (December–March) and 2–20 degrees C in winter (June–September). The rainy season in the Santiago area is from May to September.

Dress codes

Relatively formal. A suit or a jacket and tie for men and skirts for women are usual for business.

Entry requirements

Passports

Required by all, with the exception of tourists travelling direct to Chile from Argentina, Brazil, Colombia, Paraguay and Uruguay, for whom national identity cards are sufficient. Entry will be permitted only with proof of return/onward passage and sufficient funds for stay.

Visa

Visas are not required by citizens of neighbouring countries or most EU states. For further details contact the local embassy. Business visas are not required by those citizens who do not need a tourist visa, all others, including those who do not normally require them but who are visiting on short-term contracts or receive fees from a local company, do need a visa.

On arrival a 'tourist card' is issued and must be returned when leaving.

Currency advice/regulations

No restrictions on import and export of foreign or domestic currency. International credit cards are widely accepted. Receipts for money changed on entry should be retained. Travellers cheques are readily acceptable in cities only.

Health (for visitors)

Mandatory precautions

None

Advisable precautions

Typhoid, polio, hepatitis A and tetanus vaccinations are useful.

Water precautions should be taken (avoid tap water) and eating unpeeled fruit or uncooked vegetables is not advised. Foreigners may get free primary health care from the state-run health service's hospitals, but for more serious cases they are required to pay the costs. Travel health insurance is advised if not already covered by one's own national health insurance.

Hotels

Numerous luxury and first-class hotels as well as good hotels in lower price range. The Stars Classification System is used. Bookings may be made at the Sernatur information office at Pudahuel Airport. An 19 per cent hotel tax is added to bill, unless paid for with foreign currency. Service charge is usually included, but an extra 5–10 per cent tip is usual.

Public holidays (national)

Fixed dates

1 Jan (New Year's Day), 1 May (Labour Day), 21 May (Navy Day), 26 Jun (St Peter and St Paul Day), 15 Aug (Assumption Day), 18 Sep (Independence Day), 19 Sep (Army Day), 12 Oct (Columbus Day), 1 Nov (All Saints' Day), 8 Dec (Immaculate Conception), 25–26 Dec (Christmas).

Variable dates

Mar/Apr (Good Friday, Holy Saturday), May/Jun (Corpus Christi), first Mon in Sep (Reconciliation Day).

Working hours

Banking

Mon–Fri: 0900–1400.

Business

Mon–Fri: 0900–1800.

Business visits are best made outside the summer month of February when the great majority of people are on holiday.

Government
Mon–Fri: 0830–1730.

Shops
Mon–Sat: 0900–2000. Supermarkets and many shopping centres are open continuously until 2100, including Sundays and public holidays.

Telecommunications

Mobile/cell phones
GSM 1900 services exist throughout most of the country.

Electricity supply

220V AC, with two-pin plugs.

Social customs/useful tips

People are expected to be punctual for business appointments. However, for social appointments, being 30 or 40 minutes late is quite usual. Chileans are very hospitable and do not necessarily expect reciprocity. Entertaining at home is common practice and a small gift of thanks is acceptable.

In Latin American Spanish it is acceptable to address others in a familiar form *tu*, or in a polite form *usted*. The latter is more appropriate for business although the familiar form is often rapidly adopted. Chileans are quite easy about smoking habits, but it is banned in cinemas, theatres, churches and public transport.

It is necessary to carry car documents when driving.

Security

Santiago is generally regarded as a safe city with low incidences of assault and mugging compared with other Latin American capitals. However, pickpocketing is common in the city centre and on buses.

Getting there

Air

National airline: LAN-Chile (Línea Aérea Nacional de Chile).

International airport/s: Santiago-Comodoro Arturo Merino Benítez (often known as 'Pudahuel') (SCL), 21km west of city; bar, restaurant, bank, post office, shops, tourist office, car hire. A bus service to the city runs 24 hours.

Other airport/s: Arica-Chacalluta (ARI), 18km from city; bar, restaurant, buffet, shops, car hire.

Airport tax: Departure tax: US$18

Surface

Road: The road system is dominated by the 3,455km Pan-American Highway, which links the Peruvian frontier to Puerto Montt in the south. Between Santiago and Puerto Montt, the Pan-American follows the course of the central valley. A trans-Andean highway links Valparaíso with the Argentine city of Mendoza. This is frequently closed during winter due to snow, when more southerly and lower passes have to be used.

Rail: Five lines to neighbouring Argentina, Bolivia and Peru are operated by the government-owned Ferrocarriles del Estado.

Water: Empremar (Valparaíso) is the principal port with developed passenger routes mainly to Argentina. Chile has around 60 ports.

Getting about

National transport

Air: Línea Aérea del Cobre (Ladeco) provides most domestic services. Lanexpress operates frequent flights to major centres only. Air taxi services also operate. The south of the country relies heavily on air links and seats must be booked well in advance.

Road: There are 80,000km of good roads including the Pan-American Highway running north-south and qualified as first-class. It is only possible to reach Punta Arenas by land from Rio Gallengos (Argentina).

Buses: Express coaches link main centres and are generally recommended (eg Santiago-Arica, typically one departure daily; Santiago-Valparaíso, approx hourly service).

Rail: A fast diesel-electric train service is available. The main line runs from Santiago to Puerto Montt (includes sleeper service, restaurant cars, air-conditioning, typical total journey time around 18 hours); Japanese-built train links between Santiago and Concepción (first-class service and a journey time around nine hours including bus service from Chillián to Concepción).

City transport

Taxis: From Santiago's Arturo Merino Benitez airport, there are metered taxis into town.

Taxis are cheap and widely available in main towns. An initial charge (*Bajada de Bandera*) is displayed on front windscreen. Large blue taxis do not have meters. Tipping is not customary. Radio taxis charge higher fares.

Within Santiago and Chile's main towns black and yellow taxis can be hailed but are scarce at rush hour. These taxis are mostly metered but for long journeys fares should be negotiated in advance. There are extra charges at night and on holidays.

Taxis operating from the airport require a special permit, and it is advised that visitors check a taxi's authenticity before boarding. The journey to central Santiago takes about 30 minutes. However, any taxi can go to the airport and the fare is often cheaper than from the airport.

Buses, trams & metro: Frequent inner city bus service. Shuttle service – mini-buses for several passengers – from airport to city centre.

Fast, frequent, clean and safe metro system in Santiago consisting of two main lines: line 1 San Pablo-Escuela Militar line; line 2 Lo Ovalle-Cal y Canto line which has 13 stations. Trains run 0700–2245.

Car hire
A national or international licence is accepted. Car hire can be arranged at the airport and in most major towns. A large deposit may be required. All car drivers require a 'Carnet de Passages et Douanes' issued by the Automobile Club. Traffic drives on the right.

BUSINESS DIRECTORY

The addresses listed below are a selection only. While World of Information makes every endeavour to check these addresses, we cannot guarantee that changes have not been made, especially to telephone numbers and area codes. We would welcome any corrections.

Telephone area codes

The international dialling code (IDD) for Chile is +56, followed by area code and subscriber's number:

Antofagasta	55	Linares	73
Arica	58	Punta Arenas	61
Chillán	42	Santiago	2
Concepción	41	Temuco	45
Coquimbo	51	Valparaíso	32
Iquique	57	Vina del Mar	32
La Serena	51		

Chambers of Commerce

Antofagasta Cámara de Comercio, Servicios y Turismo, Latorre 2580, Antofagasta (tel: 225-175; fax: 55-222-053; e-mail: info@comercioantofagusta.cl).

Arica Cámara de Comercio, Industria, Servicios y Turismo, Rafael Sotomayor 252, Arica (tel: 224-643; fax: 253-718; e-mail: comercio@camaracomercioarica.cl).

Iquique Cámara de Comercio, Industria, Servicios y Turismo, San Martín 225, Iquique (tel: 412-942; fax: 414-090; e-mail: info@iquiquenegocios.cl).

Talca Cámara de Comercio, Servicios y Turismo, 2 Sur 1061, Talca (tel/fax: 233-569; e-mail: contact@camaradecomerciotalca.cl).

Temuco Cámara de Comercio, Servicios y Turismo, Vicuña Mackenna 396, Temuco (tel: 210-556; fax: 237-047; e-mail: camcotem@entelchile.cl).

Valparaíso Cámara Regional del Comercio y la Produccion, Pasaje Ross

149, Valparaiso (tel: 253-065; fax: 212-770).

Banking

Banco de A Edwards, Huérfanos 740, Santiago (tel: 388-3000; fax: 388-4100; e-mail: marketing@baenet.cl).

Banco de Chile, Ahumada 251, Santiago (tel: 637-1111; fax: 637-3434)

Banco de Crédito e Inversiones, Huérfanos 1134, Santiago (tel: 692-7000; fax: 699-0729; e-mail: consulta@bcl.cl).

Banco del Estado de Chile, Avenida Libertador Bernardo O'Higgins 1111, Santiago (tel: 670-7000; fax: 670-5478; e-mail: msoto9@bech.cl).

Central bank

Banco Central de Chile, PO Box 967, 1180 Agustinas, Santiago 8340454 (Tel: 670-2000; fax: 670-2099; e-mail: bcch@bcentral.cl).

Stock exchange

Bolsa de Comercio de Santiago (Santiago Stock Exchange) (SSE), www. bolsadesantiago.com

Bovalpo (Valparaíso Stock Exchange), www.bovalpo.com

Bolsa Electrónica de Chile (Santiago Electronic Stock Exchange), www.bolchile.cl

Travel information

LADECO (Línea Aérea del Cobre), Avenida Américo Vespucio 901, Santiago (tel: 661-3131; fax: 639-5757; e-mail: josecotd@cmbchile.cl).

LAN-Chile (Línea Aérea Nacional de Chile), Avenida Américo Vespucio 901, Santiago (tel: 687-2525; fax: 687-2483; e-mail:sdelpino@lanchile.cl; internet: www.lan.com).

National tourist organisation offices

Servicio Nacional de Turismo (SERNATUR), (National Tourist Service) Avenida Providencia 1550, Santiago (tel: 236-1416; fax: 251-8469; internet: www.visit-chile.org; e-mail: sernatur@ctc-mundo.net or info@ sernatur.cl).

Ministries

Ministry of Agriculture, Teatinos 40, Santiago (tel: 393-5000; fax:672-5654; e-mail: xbarrera@minagri.gob.cl).

Ministry of Defence, Edificio Diego Portales, Villavicencio 364, Santiago (tel: 222-1202; fax: 634-5339; e-mail: dn@defensa.cl).

Ministry of Economy, Mining and Energy, Teatinos 120, Santiago (tel: 672-5522; fax: 672-6040; e-mail:economia@minecon.cl).

Ministry of Education, Avenida Libertado Bernardo O'Higgins 1371, Santiago (tel: 390-4000; fax: 380-0317; e-mail: ineduc@chilnet.cl).

Ministry of the Government, Palacio de la Moneda, Santiago (tel: 671-4103; fax: 699-1657).

Ministry of Housing, Avenida Libertado Bernardo O'Higgins 924, Santiago (tel: 638-0801; fax: 633-3892; e-mail: martinez@minvu.cl).

Ministry of the Interior, Palacio de la Moneda, Santiago (tel: 690-4000; fax: 699-2165; e-mail: alopez@interior.gov.cl).

Ministry of Justice, Morandé 107, Santiago (tel: 696-8151; fax: 696-6952).

Ministry of Labour and Social Security, Huérfanos 1273, Santiago (tel: 695-5133; fax: 671-6539).

Ministry of Mining, Teatinos 120, Santiago (tel: 671-4373; fax: 698-9262; e-mail: chileminero@mixmail.com).

Ministry of National Properties, Pdte. Juan Antonio Rios 6, Santiago (tel: 633-9305; fax: 633-6521; e-mail: aleonp@mbienes).

Ministry of Planning and Co-operation, Ahumada 48, Santiago (tel: 675-1400; fax: 672-1879; e-mail: misoto@mideplan.cl).

Ministry of the Presidency, Palacio de la Moneda, Santiago (tel: 690-4000; fax: 698-4656).

Ministry of Public Health, Enrique Mac-Iver 541, Santiago (tel: 639-4001; fax: 633-5875; e-mail: info@minsal.cl).

Ministry of Public Works, Morandé 59, Santiago (tel/fax: 361-2700; e-mail: mop.doh@chilnet.cl).

Ministry of Transport and Telecommunications, Amunategui 139 Santiago (tel: 672-6503; fax: 699-5138).

Ministry of Women's Affairs, Teatinos 950, Santiago (tel: 549-6100; fax: 549-6247; e-mail:sernam@ entelchile.net).

Other useful addresses

Asociación de Exportadores de Manufacturas (ASEXMA Chile), Nueva Tajamar, Santiago (tel: 203-6699; fax: 203-6730; e-mail: asexma@ asexmachile.cl).

Bolsa de Comercio de Santiago, La Bolsa 64, Santiago (Tel: 698-2001; fax: 697-2236; e-mail: fledermann@ comercio.bolsantiago.cl).

Chilean Embassy (USA), 1732 Massachusetts Avenue, NW, Washington DC 20036 (tel: 202-785-1746; fax: 202-887-557; e-mail: embassy@embassyofchile.org).

Comisión Chilena del Cobre (Cochilco), Agustinas 1161, Santiago (tel: 382-8100; fax: 382-8300; e-mail: cochilco@cochilco.cl).

Comité de Inversiones Extranjeras, Teatinos 120, Santiago (tel: 698-4254; fax: 698-9476; e-mail: investment@cinver.cl).

Corporación de Fomento de la Producción (CORFO) (Development Corporation), Moneda 921, Santiago (tel: 631-8692; fax: 631-8686; e-mail: drmetro@corfo.cl).

Corporación Nacional de Cobre (CODELCO), Huérfanos 1270, Santiago (tel: 690-3000; fax: 690-3059; e-mail: comunica@stgo.codelco.cl).

Empresa Nacional de Minería (ENAMI), MacIver 459, Santiago (tel: 664-7244; fax: 637-5436;e-mail: ghormaza@enami.cl).

Empresa Nacional de Petróleo (ENAP), Vitacura 2736, Santiago (tel: 280-3000; fax: 280-3199).

Instituto de Promoción de Exportaciones (ProChile), Avenida Libertador Bernardo O'Higgins 1315, Santiago (tel: 565-9000; fax: 696-0639; e-mail: info@prochile.cl).

Instituto Nacional de Estadísticas (INE), Avenida Presidente Bulnes 418, Santiago (tel: 366-7777; fax: 671-2169; e-mail: inecedoc@terra.cl).

Sociedad de Formento Fabril (SOFOFA)(Chilean Federation of Industry), Avenida Andrés Bello 2777, Santiago (tel: 391-3100; fax: 391-3200; e-mail: sofofa@sofofa.cl).

US Embassy, Avenida Andrés Bello 2800, Santiago (tel: 232-2600; fax: 330-3710).

National news agency: Agencia Chile Noticias, Carlos Antúnez 1884, Office 104, Comuna de Providencia, Santiago (tel/fax: 223-0205; email: prensa@ chilenoticias.cl; internet: www. chilenoticias.cl).

Internet sites

Chile Business Directory: http://www.chilnet.cl/

Chile Trade Commission: http://www.prochile.cl

Government of Chile: http://www.gobiernodechile.cl

Latin World: http://www.latinworld.com

China

KEY FACTS

Official name: Zhonghua Renmin Gongheguo (Zhongguo) (People's Republic of China)

Head of State: President Xi Jinping (from 14 March 2013)

Head of government: Premier of the State Council Li Keqiang (from 15 March 2013)

Ruling party: Zhongguo Gongchangdang (Chinese Communist Party) (CCP)

Area: 9,596,961 square km

Population: 1.37 billion (2014) (1,337,400,000; 2010, census figure)

Capital: Beijing (Peking)

Official language: Putonghua (Mandarin Chinese – Beijing dialect).

Currency: Yuan (Renminbi) (Rmb) = 100 fen

Exchange rate: Rmb6.37 per US$ (Sep 2015)

GDP per capita: US$7,589 (2014)*

GDP real growth: 7.36% (2014)*

GDP: US$10,380.38 billion (2014)*

Labour force: 779.95 million (2009)

Unemployment: 4.09% (2014)

Inflation: 1.99% (2014)

Oil production: 4.25 million bpd (2014)

Natural gas production: 134.50 billion cum (2014)

Balance of trade: US$384.32 billion (2014)*

* estimated figure

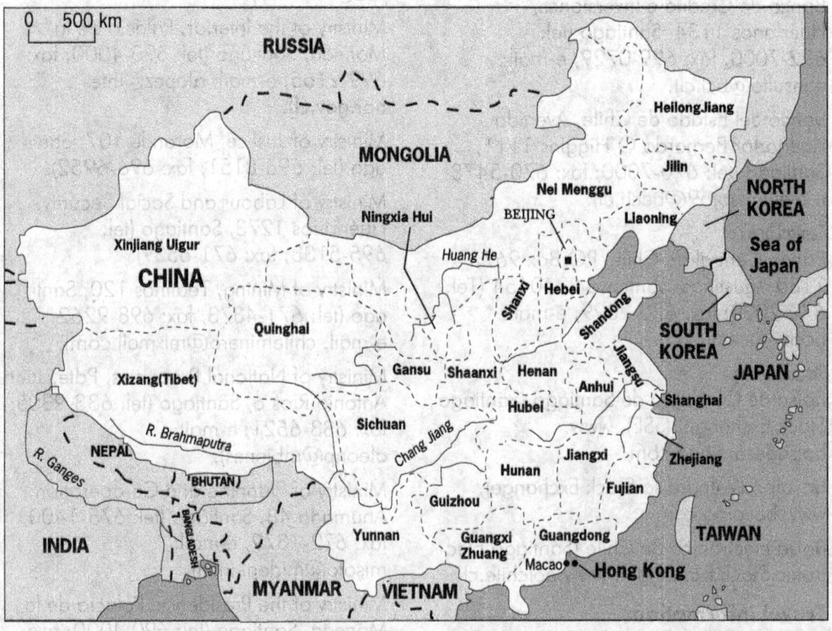

As President of China and the General Secretary of the Chinese Communist party, it could certainly be argued that Xi Jinping is the most powerful man on earth. His credentials are sound – not least because as a youth he had spent a decade dodging the perils of the Cultural Revolution. An excellent article 'Born Red' by Evan Osnos and published in the *New Yorker* magazine noted that as President he held authority 'over every general, judge, editor and state-company CEO'.

New Broom...

According to Mr Osnos, after little over two years in the job, Mr Xi had emerged as 'the most authoritarian leader since Chairman Mao'. However powerful, on the most important of the challenges he sought to address – that of corruption – things didn't quite seem to be going to plan. China's ranking on the Transparency International *Corruption Perceptions Index* was a lowly 100 out of the 175 countries surveyed. In 2013 and 2014 the ranking had been twenty points higher, at 80. Those defending the President's effectiveness dismissed the ranking by claiming that it reflected Mr Xi's success in investigating, reportedly, 'tens of thousands' on various charges of corruption, espionage and even 'inciting the overthrow of the state'. The government had called on officials to 'slay tigers and swat flies'. However, corruption has for decades been an integral part of the Chinese system, dating back to the days of Deng Xiaoping's rule in the 1990s. The Deng economic liberalisation had allowed party members and their associates to get rich, and quickly. An article in the Tokyo *Diplomat* in 2014 had estimated the wealth of the 50 richest members of China's National Assembly at no less than 94.7 billion dollars. By comparison, the richest 50 members of the American Congress could only muster US$1.6 billion dollars.

A June 2015 article by Bao Tong (an adviser to former Prime Minister Zhao Ziyang) in the *New York Times* noted that 'the legions of corrupt officials exposed may only be the tip of the iceberg, but these revelations have already eclipsed other reported instances of corruption in China or abroad'. In the same article, Mr Bao noted, however, that exposing corruption remained a government monopoly. '... if independent citizens – members of civil society – take up the cause, it is a crime.' Often those who had succeeded in exposing corruption found themselves arraigned, put on trial or just simply put in jail. There seemed a long way to go.

... Old Brush

None the less, high profile names were falling in face of an anti-corruption *tsunami*. In 2014 Zhou Yongkang a former security chief appeared – alongside his associates, friends and family – to have 'disappeared'. Mr Zhou was the highest ranking Chinese leader to fall on his sword since 1989. He had controlled the police and judiciary, as well as China's burgeoning intelligence services. According to Chinese state media his crimes included abusing power, leaking party and state secrets and... committing adultery. Zhou was certainly the biggest 'tiger' caught in the crackdown. The former security chief was arrested and expelled from the party in December 2014. The *People's Daily*, had branded him as a traitor.

Mr Zhou's disappearance came shortly after the arrest of general Xu Caihou, once the most powerful officer in the People's Liberation Army, he was accused of accepting payments for promotions. He was also the highest-profile military leader to face prosecution. State media said that the 71-year-old former general had accepted 'huge bribes personally and through his family and... sought profits for others in exchange for bribes'. Press reports said it had taken 14 trucks to carry away the cash and treasures from his luxury villa – including a solid gold statue of Mao Zedong and 20 crates of expensive liquor. While these two cases were relatively straightforward, that of Bo Xilai, the former Chonqging party chief was much messier, reading more like a cheap novel than a case of corruption. All three, however, had one thing in common – each represented a potential threat to President Xi.

The economy

It has to be remembered that China is the world's most populous country, with 1.37 billion people in 2014. The Chinese government's decision to lower its growth target to around 7 per cent for 2015 from around 7.5 per cent in 2014 was seen by many analysts as a positive move, underlining the Chinese administration's continuing commitment to achieving a more sustainable but still high rate of expansion. The lower growth rate would avoid endangering macro-economic stability; China's gross domestic product (GDP) growth rate in 2014 was the country's lowest in 24 years, but still one of the strongest among emerging market economies.

China mitigated the effects of the 2008 global financial crisis with a massive stimulus package spread over two years, that helped bolster China's investments and industrial demand. Economic growth has slowed since 2012 as industrial production and exports decreased and as the government attempted to curb high debt levels and excessive investment in certain markets. In response to the rapidly slowing economy and deflationary trend in 2014, the government eased its monetary policy through interest rate cuts, providing medium-term loans to Chinese banks and reducing the reserve requirements by banks. These measures have been followed by the government's announcement of a smaller, more strategic fiscal stimulus targeting infrastructure projects in 2015.

IMF approval

In its May 2015 review of the Chinese economy, the International Monetary Fund (IMF), noted that China was 'transitioning' to what the IMF described as 'a new normal', aimed at safer and higher quality – even if a bit slower – growth. In the view of the IMF this was a transition that was both challenging and necessary. The IMF could not ignore the fact that as one of the world's largest economies, 'China's success was of vital importance for its own future and that of the global economy'.

The IMF considered that growth in China was moderating, a slowdown that was not a goal in itself, but a by-product of moving the economy away from the unsustainable growth pattern of the past decade. The IMF projected that China would grow at 6.8 per cent in 2015, consistent with the Chinese authorities' growth target of around 7 per cent and well within the 6.5–7 per cent range that the IMF considered appropriate for the year. The labour market had remained resilient despite slower growth, which, in turn, had supported household consumption. Inflation was expected to end the year at around 1.5 per cent.

Since the global financial crisis, according to the IMF, growth had relied on an unsustainable mix of credit and investment that had resulted in rising vulnerabilities. The Chinese authorities had moved on several fronts to address these vulnerabilities, as seen by the decline in total social financing (TSF) growth, tighter oversight of shadow banking, moderating investment growth and the slowdown in real estate construction. Nevertheless, vulnerabilities in these areas remained large and continued; determined efforts were needed to address them, said the IMF.

The IMF took the view that China's macro-policy stance was broadly

KEY INDICATORS **China**

	Unit	2011	2012	2013	2014	**2015
Population	m	1,348.12	1,354.04	1,360.72	1,367.82	*1,374.96
Gross domestic product (GDP)	US$bn	7,298.10	8,229.38	9,469.13	*10,380.38	*11,211.93
GDP per capita	US$	5,414	6,078	6,959	*7,589	*8,154
GDP real growth	%	9.2	7.7	7.8	*7.4	*6.8
Inflation	%	5.4	2.6	2.6	2.0	*1.2
Unemployment	%	4.1	4.1	4.0	4.1	*4.1
Oil output	'000 bpd	4,090.0	4,155.0	4,180.0	4,246.0	–
Natural gas output	bn cum	102.5	107.2	117.1	134.5	–
Coal output	mtoe	1,956.0	1,825.0	1,840.0	1,844.6	–
Exports (fob) (goods)	US$m	1,812,319	1,970,945	2,147,529	–	–
Imports (fob) (goods)	US$m	1,569,850	1,653,347	1,795,763	–	–
Balance of trade	US$m	242,469	317,598	351,766	–	–
Current account	US$m	201,714	193,139	182,807	209,819	*356,340
Total reserves minus gold	US$m	3,219,760	3,331,120	3,839,548	3,859,168	–
Foreign exchange	US$m	3,197,491	3,311,589	3,821,315	–	–
Exchange rate	per US$	6.56	6.30	6.05	6.21	–

* estimated figure ** forecast figure

appropriate and consistent with the annual growth and inflation outlook. The impact of recent developments (the IMF Review was prepared before the stock market slump) such as appreciation of the real exchange rate, lower oil prices, adjustments in reserve requirements and interest rates and implementation of the new budget law – were still reverberating through the economy. If incoming data suggested that growth was likely to exceed 7 per cent, the authorities would be advised to take advantage of the opportunity to reduce vulnerabilities faster. If, however, instead growth looked set to dip below 6.5 per cent, then fiscal policy should be eased. Fiscal stimulus, if needed, should be on-budget and rely on measures that protected the vulnerable, supported rebalancing and were consistent with the reform agenda. All goals that could best be achieved through fiscal policy.

The IMF stressed that in 2016 'policies should continue to address vulnerabilities, even if that required allowing growth to slow into the range of 6–6.5 per cent'. The IMF forecast of 6.25 per cent growth in 2016 assumed such progress. The IMF also noted that slower growth was not a goal unto itself, but a by-product of efforts to move the economy to a safer and higher-quality growth path. China had a comprehensive plan, the ambitious *Third Plenum Blueprint*, to enable this transformation to be achieved. Now, the key was to press ahead with timely implementation, including financial, fiscal, state-owned enterprise and external sector reforms. Successful implementation would reduce excess savings, lower investment while making it more productive, boost consumption and allow China to continue its convergence towards high-income status.

In the view of the IMF, moving to a market-based financial system was essential for boosting productivity growth. With deposit insurance now in place, the time had come to complete the liberalisation of deposit rates. Doing so would, said the IMF, facilitate the move toward using interest rates as the primary tool of monetary policy. This, in turn, involved establishing a policy interest rate and using it as the main tool to adjust monetary conditions and signal changes in policy. Another priority was to break the web of implicit guarantees, which were still prevalent throughout the financial system. This could not be done overnight, but the process needed to start and would involve a greater acceptance of defaults and bankruptcies.

'Levelling the playing field between the private and public sectors was', said the IMF, 'a key goal of the Blueprint and rightly so'. Progress with SOE reform, however, had been too slow. Important reforms would include increasing the dividends to the budget, eliminating direct or indirect subsidies of factor costs, strengthening governance and introducing a greater tolerance of SOE bankruptcy and exit. Successful SOE reforms had the potential significantly to boost productivity growth and create millions of new jobs.

The implementation of the new budget law would create a much-needed new framework for local government borrowing, improve transparency and strengthen medium-term fiscal planning. While implementation was complex and might take some time, it was important for the authorities to announce a clear and comprehensive transition plan for local government financing as soon as possible. Finding a long-term solution to the imbalance between local government spending responsibilities and revenue assignments remained a priority.

As far as external trade was concerned, in the view of the IMF China had made good progress in recent years in reducing the very large current account surplus and accumulation of foreign exchange reserves. Nevertheless, the IMF's projections for 2015 suggested that China's external position was still moderately stronger than that consistent with medium-term fundamentals and desirable policies. There were several factors influencing a country's external position, the exchange rate being one of them. While under-valuation of the renminbi was a major factor causing the large imbalances in the past, the IMF assessment was that the substantial real effective appreciation over the previous year had brought the exchange rate to a level that was no longer under-valued. However, the still-too-strong external position highlighted the need for other policy reforms – which were part of the authorities' agenda – to reduce excess savings and achieve sustained external balance. This would also require that, going forward, the exchange rate adjusted with changes in fundamentals and, for example, appreciated in line with faster productivity growth in China (relative to its trading partners). On the exchange rate question, the IMF urged the Chinese authorities to make rapid progress toward greater exchange rate flexibility, a key requirement for a large economy like China's that strove for market-based pricing and was integrating rapidly in global financial markets. Greater flexibility, with intervention limited to avoiding disorderly market conditions or excessive volatility, would also be key to preventing the exchange rate from moving away from equilibrium in the future. The IMF believed that China should aim to achieve an effectively floating exchange rate within 2–3 years.

Concluding its review, the IMF considered that 'In recent years, China had played an increasingly important role in driving global growth, contributing to global economic and financial stability and helping to improve the international monetary system.' As part of the review of the Special Drawing Rights (SDR) basket at the IMF, the Chinese authorities had stated publicly their interest in including the renminbi in the SDR basket. The IMF welcomed and shared this objective and would work closely with the Chinese authorities in this regard. Christine Lagarde, the Managing Director of the IMF had stated that 'Renminbi inclusion was not a matter of 'if' but 'when'.'

Dangerous days

However, even the IMF could not have foreseen the events of mid-2015. After a

No longer lonely?

A statement from the Community Party's Central Committee carried by the official Xinhua News Agency on 29 October confirmed the end of China's 'one-child policy'. The policy had been relaxed in 2013 to allow couples where either parent is an only child to have two children, but there had been fewer applications than expected and the birth rate had not increased appreciatively. The new move is hoped to address the ageing population problem by encouraging families to have two children.

However, a survey conducted by state-run *China Youth Daily* among 3,000 people (over 50 per cent of them women) showed less than half (46 per cent) were enthusiastic about the change. Indeed, 52 per cent said they were concerned that having one more child would reduce the standard of living they now enjoy.

period of eight months in which the Shanghai Composite index (the Chinese market's benchmark index) managed to revalue itself by an unprecedented 100 per cent, June 2015 saw the party come to an end, when the index fell back by 30 per cent. Steady growth was replaced by equally unprecedented volatility. In thinly disguised panic, the regulatory authorities took the step of limiting the level of falls to ten per cent in a single day. To the question: 'What caused the plunge?' came the simple answer: 'Nothing'. This was simply a lemming-like rush to nowhere.

As noted above, the Chinese economy's growth rate in 2014 and 2015 was the lowest in a quarter of a century. A contributing factor to the moderation was the shift to a more sustainable business model. This gradual process, initiated in 2013, coincided with ever rising share prices. The coincidence was no more than that. China's economic fundamentals did not appear to have a lot to do with market behaviour. That 'behaviour' was attributed to the actions of China's millions of small private investors, most of whom had little market experience basing their investment decisions on rumours, press reports and past performance.

According to the official figures, in 2015 more than 40 million Chinese had opened investment accounts in the previous 12 month period – double the total number when the market opened in 1990. The US business analysts and publishers Bloomberg reported in 2015 that the total number of active investors on the Chinese stock markets (over 90 million) outnumbered the membership of the Communist Party. That so many Chinese were active investors was not in itself a problem. What was a problem was that an estimated two thirds of the new investors only had the most basic education. The same estimates, prepared by the China Household Finance Survey, put at 30 per cent the number who had left school at the age of 12 or earlier.

A simplification of this state of affairs joked that in China there had emerged a new type of business advisor, the country's taxi drivers, waiters and even its cleaners. But the mini-crash of 2015 often showed the advice to be pure hearsay. This oracle had run its course and in 2015 had lost the respect of its clientele. In turn that clientele, many of whom had borrowed to invest, saw its investment appetite shrink together with its available funds. Word of mouth had fuelled the dizzy share-price rise as the new investors, for the most part 'mobile savvy' watched their investments soar, not because of any intrinsic business factors, but because the same 'advisors' had imparted their wisdom to more and more amateur investors.

Fashion was, therefore, an important factor.

Of equal importance, was the need to identify a better rate of return for savings. The traditional savings investment model worked on a rate of return set by the People's Bank of China (PBC) (central bank). In mid-2015 the interest rate was set at an annual 2.4 per cent. Chinese public debt carried an interest rate of 2.3 per cent. It was therefore predictable that with inflation hovering around the 1.5 per cent mark, alternative investments would be sought. The Chinese property market had long been the goose that laid the golden egg, but as the property market slumped, or even collapsed, equity investments, publicly quoted shares, became an attractive opportunity.

For the most part, the rookie Chinese investors did not take into account fundamentals such as the country's growth possibility, or even the annual reports of the companies whose shares they were buying. They had sadly taken greater heed of government inspired articles affirming that the stock market was 'set for a long period of steady growth'. However, in response to regulatory measures limiting an individual's ability to borrow to buy shares and require higher levels of guarantees from brokers, the same investors take fright and flee.

When the opposite happens and transaction costs are reduced, or credit is freed, the same investors were expected to flood back to the market.

But the 'shock' of 2015 had probably introduced an element of caution that had not existed before. The three week share 'crisis' of 2015 had shown many investors that the fundamentals of their hasty investments were less than clear. What was clear was that China risked a share debt 'bubble'. Large domestic debt levels had been built up on the back of share deals which had in the space of days turned 'red'. Almost half the shares quoted were suspended and, rather dramatically, a police investigation was under way to bring to brook excessive speculation.

All's well that ends... Well?

After the crash, Chinese shares managed to regain some momentum as a result of the government's anti-sell measures, although millions of Chinese people had made significant losses. China's Shanghai Composite index, which had been climbing for months, had plummeted by 31.5 per cent from its peak of around 5,000.00 to 3,500.00.

This steep descent, which started quite suddenly on 25 June, saw around US$3 trillion of Chinese equity lost. In response, the government's China Securities Regulatory Commission (CSRC), ruled that major stakeholders who held more than 5 per cent of a company's shares would not be allowed to sell their shares for six months. Although the measures did have the desired effect and the index had soon recovered to 3,900.00, analysts and economists criticised the fact that the Chinese stock market was hemmed in by the regulations.

The seriousness of the situation was confirmed by the relentless introduction of new measures by the Chinese authorities (the CSRC and the PBC) between 27 June and 8 July to encourage the rise of the Shanghai Composite. The importance of the Composite lay in the unnerving fact that millions of Chinese citizens had invested large proportions of their savings in shares on the stock market. The giant losses hit many small investors the hardest, wiping out personal capital in many cases.

Desert(ed) islands

Continued disagreements by the countries bordering the South China Sea, including ownership of the Spratly and Paracel Islands, have hindered efforts for the joint exploration of hydrocarbon resources in the area. Members of the Association of Southeast Asian Nations (Asean) had signed a Declaration of Conduct in 2002 that encouraged countries to use restraint and co-operate in the South China Sea, but no regulations were established. Increasing demand for both oil and natural gas have exacerbated tensions, pitting China against the Philippines and Vietnam (both members of Asean). CNOOC's June 2012 tender for nine offshore blocks in the disputed area overlapped several fields located within Vietnam's 200-nautical mile exclusive economic zone. China's deployment of an oil rig in disputed waters near the Paracel islands for two months in 2014 did little to calm matters. Quite the contrary – there were clashes with Vietnamese vessels. Despite the climate of tension, China's stated policy is to enter partnerships with the region's countries to develop maritime hydrocarbon resources.

In late May 2015 the Chinese ministry of defence published its White Paper spelling out its new (or expanded) military strategy. A notable feature of the document was a less than amicable warning to the United States about its naval operations in the South China Sea. An analysis of the document was published by the Washington based Council on Foreign Relations. The US authors did not mince their words: 'The new strategy leaves little doubt that the Chinese ambition is to transform its navy into a modern force capable of challenging the US'.

Speaking at a Singapore conference, the US secretary for defence, Ashton Carter, bluntly stated that: 'This has to come to a lasting stop.' Mr Carter was obliged to accept that other countries in the region – Japan, Malaysia, the Philippines and Taiwan – had established bases in the region, but 'no-one had gone so far, so quickly, as the Chinese. According to the Chinese White Paper, Peking had 'created' around 1,000 hectares of terrain in the previous 18 months. According to Mr Carter 'It is unclear just how far Beijing wishes to go, which is why the creation of man-made islands has become a source of tension and headline news throughout the world'. Satellite images showed that China had placed two heavy artillery units on one of the reefs to establish its primacy. The reef in question was thought to be an oil and gas rich enclave. (See: Energy below).

Mr Carter sought to assuage the fears of its allies by reaffirming that US aircraft and ships would continue to patrol any part of the region's seas where international law made it legal to do so. Patrolling was one thing; putting a stop to, or ending China's concerted construction activity on the disputed reefs of the South China Sea, was quite another. Alarm bells were sounding across the Pacific, raising fears that Beijing was 'putting steel in the ground' to back up its contentious claims. China had been busy transforming underwater reefs hundreds of miles from its coastline into artificial islands. Dredging vessels had been taking out sand to create land where none had been before. China was building new installations on the islands, including possibly airstrips, barracks and radar sites.

Surveillance photos published by the Asia Maritime Transparency Initiative, a branch of the United States Centre for Strategic and International Studies, showed flurries of construction activity on half a dozen islands. The construction activity was another chapter in a long-running conflict over the South China Sea that had set China against most of its maritime neighbours and had brought it into direct conflict with the United States and Japan. China had nominally claimed sovereignty over swathes of the South China Sea since the end of the Chinese Civil War in the late 1940s – ironically based on a map drawn up by the communists' Nationalist opponents – but under the rule of President Xi Jinping, Beijing had hardened its bid for outright control. Actions, such as the deployment of an oil-drilling rig and a dozen escort vessels to Vietnamese waters in 2014, triggered diplomatic disputes and skirmishing. And now the reef-building frenzy is getting China's neighbours nervous, including the Philippines, Indonesia, Malaysia and Vietnam.

Washington and Tokyo have become alarmed at the prospect of Beijing being able to position air and naval forces in the middle of a key shipping lane that carries about US$5 trillion worth of commercial traffic a year. 'Talking softly, but carrying a big stick', the US response was phased; there were reports that Washington was considering stationing warships in Australia, in addition to the possibility of several new warships being deployed to Singapore in 2017.

Meanwhile, the Japanese prime minister, Shinzo Abe, was advocating a departure from Japan's post-World War II pacifism towards a more interventionist military role. Japan had said that it was considering expanding its maritime patrols to the South China Sea.

That looks even more likely after China said that it had made a 'large-scale' natural gas discovery in the South China Sea. (See 'Energy' below).

Energy – overview

China was a net oil exporter until the early 1990s and became the world's second-largest net importer of crude oil and petroleum products in 2009. The US Energy Information Administration (EIA) reported that China surpassed the United States at the end of 2013 as the world's largest net importer of petroleum and other liquids. China's oil consumption growth accounted for about 43 per cent of the world's oil consumption growth in 2014. Despite China's slower oil consumption growth in the past few years, the EIA projected that China would account for more than one-fourth of the global oil consumption growth in 2015.

Natural gas use in China had also increased rapidly over the previous decade and China had sought to raise natural gas imports via pipeline and as liquefied natural gas (LNG). China is the world's top coal producer, consumer and importer and accounts for almost half of global coal consumption, an important factor in world energy-related carbon dioxide emissions. China's rising coal production was the key driver behind the country becoming the world's largest energy producer by 2009. China's sizeable industrialisation and swiftly modernising economy helped the country became the world's largest power generator in 2011.

Energy – coal

Coal supplied the majority (nearly 66 per cent) of China's total energy consumption in 2012. The second-largest source was petroleum and other liquids, accounting for nearly 20 per cent of the country's total energy consumption. Although China has made an effort to diversify its energy supplies, hydroelectric sources (8 per cent), natural gas (5 per cent), nuclear power (nearly 1 per cent) and other renewables (more than 1 per cent) account for relatively small shares of China's energy consumption. The Chinese government plans to limit coal use to 62 per cent of total primary energy consumption by 2020 in an effort to reduce the heavy air pollution that has afflicted a number of areas. China's National Energy Agency claimed that coal use dropped to 64.2 per cent of energy consumption in 2014. The Chinese government has set a target to raise non-fossil fuel energy consumption to 15 per cent of the energy mix by 2020 and to 20 per cent by 2030 in an effort to ease the country's dependence on coal. In addition, China is increasing its use of natural gas to replace some coal and oil as a cleaner burning fossil fuel and plans to use natural gas for 10 per cent of its energy consumption by 2020. Even though absolute coal consumption is expected to increase over the long term as total energy consumption rises, higher energy efficiency and China's goal to increase environmental sustainability are likely to lead to a decrease in coal's share.

As a result of high coal consumption, China was also the world's leading energy-related CO_2 emitter, releasing 8,106 million metric tons of CO_2 in 2012. The government had planned to reduce carbon intensity (carbon emissions per unit of GDP) by 17 per cent between 2010 and 2015 and energy intensity (energy use per unit of GDP) by 16 per cent during the same period, according to the country's 12th Five-Year Plan (2011–15).

Energy – oil

The United States government EIA noted that according to an article in the *Oil & Gas*

Journal (OGJ), published in January 2015, China held 24.6 billion barrels of proved oil reserves, up almost 0.3 billion barrels from the 2014 level and the highest in the Asia-Pacific region (excluding Russia). The EIA also reported that China's total petroleum and other production, the fourth-largest in the world, had risen about 50 per cent over the previous two decades and served only its domestic market. However, production growth had not kept pace with demand growth during this period. In 2014, China produced nearly 4.6 million barrels per day (bpd) of petroleum and other liquids, of which 92 per cent was crude oil and the remainder was non-refining liquids and refining gain. The EIA forecasts indicated that China's oil production would increase slightly to higher than 4.6 million bpd by the end of 2016. In the medium and long term, the EIA predicted that China's oil production would grow incrementally to 5.1 million bpd by 2020, 5.5 million bpd by 2030 and 5.7 million bpd by 2040, based on the organisation's *International Energy Outlook 2014*. The industry's long-term growth would require continued success in enhancing recovery at mature crude oil fields, greater investment to access more technically challenging initiatives such as shale oil, tight oil and deep-water fields and growth in non-petroleum liquids such as gas-to-liquids, coal-to-liquids and biofuels.

China's annual growth in oil consumption had eased after a recent high of 11 per cent in 2010, reflecting the effects of the most recent global financial and economic downturn as well as China's policies to reduce excessive investment and capacity overbuilding. Despite the slower growth, China still accounted for more than one-third of global oil demand growth in 2014, according to EIA estimates. China consumed an estimated 10.7 million bpd of oil in 2014, up 370,000bpd, or almost 4 per cent, from 2013. Notably, China became the largest global net importer of oil in the first quarter of 2014, surpassing the United States. Average net total oil imports reached 6.1 million bpd in 2014. Significant US oil production from shale oil developments and rapid Chinese oil demand growth occurring simultaneously over the past few years pushed China ahead of the United States as the largest importer. The EIA forecasts indicated that China's oil consumption would continue growing through 2016 at a moderate pace to approximately 11.3 million bpd. China's oil consumption growth was forecast to rise by about 2.6 per cent annually up to 2040, reaching 13.1 million bpd in 2020, 16.9 million bpd in 2030 and 20.0 million bpd in 2040. The EIA expected China's oil consumption to exceed that of the United States by 2034.

In the 1980s, China established three major national oil companies (NOC) – China National Petroleum Corporation (CNPC), the China Petroleum and Chemical Corporation (Sinopec) and China National Offshore Oil Corporation (CNOOC) – to serve in various areas of the oil sector. According to the EIA, CNPC was put in charge of most of the country's onshore upstream assets and Sinopec was given responsibility for the downstream activities such as refining, distribution and petrochemicals. In the late 1990s, a reorganisation created separate operating companies or publicly-listed arms of each of the NOCs. Additionally, in 1998, the government restructured CNPC and Sinopec, with CNPC taking some downstream assets and Sinopec acquiring some fields for exploration and production. CNPC accounts for an estimated 54 per cent and 77 per cent of China's crude oil and natural gas output, respectively, according to FACTS Global Energy (FGE).

According to the EIA, China experienced more moderate oil production growth after 2010, having boosted its domestic oil output by over 7 per cent in the year, after incremental growth in the previous two decades. Petroleum and total liquids production in 2014 reached nearly 4.6 million bpd, 50 per cent higher than the level two decades earlier. In 2014 approximately 80 per cent of Chinese current crude oil production capacity is located onshore and 20 per cent was from shallow offshore reserves. New offshore production, the use of enhanced oil recovery (EOR) in older onshore fields and small discoveries in existing basins are the main contributors to incremental production increases.

In the view of the EIA, China's recent energy policy aimed to improve domestic production by developing new oil fields. Meeting this goal would probably require significant investment. The recent low-price oil environment, after oil prices plunged by about 50 per cent sin

Risk assessment

Economy	Good
Politics	Poor
Regional stability	Poor

Muslims in China

% of population	1.5
Sunni (% of Muslims)	99
Shi'a (% of Muslims)	1

COUNTRY PROFILE

China has one of the world oldest civilisations. Imperial China dates from 221 BC – 1271 AD, with the beginning of the Mongol rule, during which Beijing was established as the capital of a united country. In 1368 the Ming Dynasty ousted the Mongols and created a strong centralised bureaucracy and military, underpinned by a sophisticated agricultural economy.

From the nineteenth century onwards, the ruling Manchu Qing Dynasty (1644–1911) came under pressure from an increasing population and economic imbalances internally, and incursions from Western powers externally. Following defeat at the hands of the Japanese (1895) and escalating concessions to Western powers after the Boxer Uprising (1901), the centuries-old system of promotion to the civil service via examinations ended in 1905 and dynastic rule collapsed in 1911. Yuan Shikai failed to become emperor and a chaotic period of rule by 'warlords', regional power-brokers with military resources, ensued.

1920s The Zhongguo Gongchangdang (Chinese Communist Party) (CCP) was formed and declared the southern province of Jiangxi an autonomous 'soviet' in 1927. The Communists were brutally suppressed by the rival Kuomintang (Nationalist Party).

1935 Mao Zedong took control of the CCP during the 'Long March', begun in 1934, in which thousands of Communist fighters fled Jiangxi for the northern Shanxi province.

1937–45 The Japanese occupied increasingly large areas of China. The government of Chiang Kai-shek and the Kuomintang retreated to Sichuan province in the west of China.

1949 The People's Republic of China was established in October following the victory of Communist guerrilla forces led by Mao Zedong over the Kuomintang government, which fled to the island province of Formosa (now Taiwan).

1950 Tibet (Xizang), an independent region of western China, was occupied by the Chinese People's Liberation Army (PLA).

1958–60 In Mao's Great Leap Forward to collectivise agriculture and a socialist economic system, some 40 million people died from hunger.

1965 Tibet became an autonomous region of China, but has not enjoyed any real political or cultural autonomy.

1966 Chairman Mao launched the Great Proletarian Cultural Revolution. Some 800,000 died in the cities, but the wider effects of enforced rural re-education were widespread psychological trauma and the breakdown of industry and educational institutions.

1980–97 China's elder statesman, Deng Xiaoping ran the CCP, which had political control, through over 40 million members; he initiated gradualist economic reform designed to create a socialist market economy.
1986 The CCP Central Committee adopted a resolution redefining the general ideology of the CCP to provide a theoretical basis for the programme of modernisation and the open door policy of economic reform. An anti-corruption campaign was launched and there was significant liberalisation in the field of culture and the arts. However, student demonstrations in major cities were regarded by China's leaders as excessive 'bourgeois liberalisation'.
1987 In the ensuing clampdown of the 1986 demonstrations Hu Yaobang unexpectedly resigned as CCP general secretary, accused of 'mistakes on major issues of political principles'. The 'reformist' faction within the Chinese leadership emphasised the need for further reform and the extension of an open door policy. Li Peng became premier of the state council.
1989 The death of Hu Yaobang served as a catalyst for the most serious student demonstrations ever seen in China. The protests were against alleged corruption and nepotism within the government and sought a limited degree of Soviet-style *glasnost* in public life. A state of martial law was declared in Beijing. With the government fearing for its security, the army attacked protesters in and around Tiananmen Square, causing an unknown number of deaths. All over China, similar demonstrations were put down using force. The reformist Zhao Ziyang, CCP general secretary, was confined under house arrest. Deng brought in Jiang Zemin as general secretary to replace him. Jiang was also made chairman of the Central Military Commission (CMC) (head of the PLA).
1990 Martial law was lifted.
1992 The World Bank ranked China's economy the third largest in the world after the US and Japan.
1993 Deng retired from his civilian offices, but continued to exert influence over the 'third generation' of leaders, including Jiang, who was elected state president.
1997 China regained sovereignty over Hong Kong, which had been in British control since a treaty signed in 1842.
1998 The NPC re-elected Jiang Zemin as president and approved major changes in the leadership, bringing in a new cabinet of younger technocrats.
2000 China signed bilateral trade deals with the EU and the US in preparation for its eventual accession to the World Trade Organisation (WTO) and consequent deeper integration within the global trading system.
2001 Tajikistan, China, Russia, Kazakhstan, Kyrgyzstan and Uzbekistan formed the Shanghai Co-operation Organisation (SCO). President Jiang Zemin offered China's support to the US for military action against terrorist activities following the 11 September attacks in the US. China was formally admitted to the WTO.
2003 The NPC elected Hu as state president and Zeng Qinghong as vice president; Wen Jiabao was appointed premier. China became the third country to put a man in space.
2004 Jiang Zemin resigned early as chairman of the CMC and President Hu Jintao assumed supreme authority. A landmark free-trade agreement was signed with the 10-member Association of Southeast Asian Nations (Asean).
2005 China threatened Taiwan with military force in the event of Taiwan's formal independence. Lien Chan was the first Taiwanese leader to visit China since 1949. China led the opposition to the proposal that Japan should become a permanent member of the UN Security Council citing Japan's failure to acknowledge its aggression during the 1930–40s. China scrapped its decade-old currency peg with the US dollar and sanctioned a 2.1 per cent revaluation of the renminbi against the dollar. Yao Wenyuan, last of the 'Gang of Four', died.
2006 China's Africa Policy, setting out its objectives for its relations with Africa, which promised investment and technical aid in return for African natural resources, was published. A China-Africa summit attracted 41 African heads of state and 48 heads of government to Beijing to meet hundreds of Chinese trade negotiators and business people. China's global annual trade surplus reached a record US$177 billion, an increase of 74 per cent.
2007 Vice Premier Huang Ju died. The Dalai Lama (Tibetan spiritual leader), announced that he was considering breaking a long tradition by naming his own successor, in an attempt to reduce the influence of CCP on his succession. China had taken into custody the chosen Panchen Lama, the second-highest spiritual leader in Tibetan Buddhism, Gedhun Choekyi Nyima, in 1995 and replaced him with its own, Gyancain Norbu, considered loyal to the communist party. The Panchen Lama chooses the succeeding Dalai Lama. Tibetan Buddhists fear that China will subvert their religion and culture by appointing its own Dalai Lama after the death of the reigning Dalai Lama.
2008 Hu Jintao and Wen Jiabao were re-elected president and prime minister respectively. A devastating earthquake of 7.9 magnitude struck the south-west province of Sichuan. A recorded 55,239 people died, 24,949 people were missing and 281,006 were injured by the earthquake. Over 5.46 million buildings collapsed and the authorities asked for 3.3 million tents from international aid to help house the 5.47 million people who were left homeless. China was given permission by the Convention on International Trade in Endangered Species (CITES) to import ivory. The government spent US$586 billion in a stimulus package to counter the effects of the worst of the global economic crisis.
2009 China and Russia signed a US$25 billion agreement, guaranteeing Russian oil to China until 2029. Ethnic violence in Xinjiang region erupted as young Islamic Uighurs demonstrated against discrimination. There were riots and attacks on the Han community; scores of people were killed and hundreds injured. Shanghai relaxed the one-child policy to encourage a second child to counter the social and economic effects of its aging population. The CCP celebrated 60 years in power with a huge parade involving 200,000 people along Beijing's Avenue of Eternal Peace. The populace had been told to view the spectacle on television and only the ruling elite were able to watch in person.
2010 China and Nepal agreed the height of Mount Everest to be 8,848m, the snow height, rather than the rock height as proposed by China. The economy grew by 11.9 per cent in the first quarter and overtook Germany as the world's second largest economy.
2011 On 1 May a smoking ban in public places was enforced, although smoking will still be permissible in workplaces. China had its first quarterly trade deficit (US$1.02 billion) in seven years in the first quarter although there was a trade surplus of US$140 million in March. The government increased the cost of electricity for industrial, agricultural and commercial users in a number of provinces from 1 June. The first ever audit of China's local government showed that at the end of 2010 there was a total debt of US$1.6 trillion. China's foreign exchange in the first quarter reached US$197 billion and in the second quarter US$153 billion. The world's longest road bridge (42.4km), spanning the coastal waters between the city of Qingdao and the suburb of Huangdao in Jiaozhou Bay, was opened on 7 July. In March, the Tibetan Dalai Lama announced that he was devolving power to his parliament-in-exile (in Dharamsala, India). Amendments to the Tibetan constitution (for the nation in exile), included an elected leader. The

Dalai Lama retired from politics (aged 75), on 18 March. It was announced on 27 April that Lobsang Sangay would take over from the Dalai Lama as Kalon Tripa (prime minister) of the Tibetan government-in-exile. Sangay had won 55 per cent of the vote, beating two other candidates. Dr Sangay, a US university professor, was born in exile in India and has never visited Tibet. He was sworn in as the Tibetan premier on 8 August. On 24 July, 39 people were killed and almost 200 people injured when a high-speed train collided with another and derailed. There were accusations of design flaws in the signalling system and official corruption during construction. Tibet: On 7 November, the Dalai Lama answered Chinese criticism about a wave of self-immolation among monks and nuns (protesting about Chinese occupation of Tibet) saying that it was caused by Chinese 'cultural genocide' and that uncompromising officials had created a 'desperate' situation for Tibetans. In 2011, nine monks and two nuns committed public suicide in protest at what they saw as Chinese repression. A decision, by the four-country Mekong River Commission, to implement plans to build the controversial Mekong Xayaburi dam in Laos was due in April, but following ecologically and socially adverse reports the decision was postponed twice. The Mekong River is a food source for millions of people along its length; the dam would reduce food production in favour of electricity generation.

2012 The number of urban dwellers outnumbered the rural population for the first time. The leaders of the Bric countries met in Delhi on 29 March to discuss their position regarding the control the US and Europe has on the World Bank and the IMF. Prime Minister Manmohan Singh (India) said 'The Brics countries have agreed to examine in greater detail a proposal to set up a South-South development bank, funded and managed by the Brics and other developing countries.' China closed the border of Tibet to foreign visitors at the height of the tourist season, due to the increase in protesting Tibetans killing themselves through public immolation. China's first female astronaut was sent into space on 16 June, in a mission to dock with China's own orbiting space module. On 16 April the Yuan Renminbi foreign exchange rate was allowed to fluctuate by up to 1 per cent against the US dollar (an increase of 0.5 per cent on the previous limit). On 14 November, during the last day of the seven-day CCP congress, President Hu Jintao stepped down from office. On 15 November, Xi Jinping was officially confirmed into the post of General Secretary of the CCP and president of China; six other CCP leaders were voted on to the Politburo Standing Committee and constitute the new ruling administration.

2013 Growth in the second quarter of 2013 slowed to 7.5 per cent from 7.7 per cent for the same period in 2012. On 19 July the government annouced that banks would in future be allowed to set their own lending rates. Previously they were not allowed to lend at rates below a certain level set by the People's Bank of China. On 25 July Bo Xilai was charged by prosecuters in Jinan with bribery and abuse of power. Mr Bo had been Communist Party chief of Chongqing until becoming part of one of China's biggest scandals when his wife was convicted of murdering a British business partner and Bo was exposed for being involved in corruption. He was stripped of his party membership. Bo Xilai's trial began on 22 August. He denies the charges of bribery. Although foreign journalists were not allowed in the court, the Jinan Intermediate People's Court itself posted testimony on its official blog, including details of Mr Bo's 'spirited' defence. The trial ended on 25 August with the prosecutor saying that there 'should be no leniency shown'. Although the Japanese government has said it would like talks with China on the future of the disputed East China Sea islands, deputy foreign minister Li Baodong has said that China is not in favour of a meeting at the G20 meeting in early September. On 22 September the Intermediate People's Court in Jinan, Shandong province, found Bo Xilai guilty of bribery, embezzlement and abuse of power. He was sentanced to life imprisonment but has the right to appeal. Mr Bo's appeal was rejected on 24 October.

2014 China's economy grew by 7.4 per cent in the first quarter of 2014, down on the 7.7 per cent of the last quarter of 2013, but better than had been expected.

2015 The China's National People's Congress (NPC), the country's top legislative body, began its 2015 gathering on 5 March. At the end of the NPC on 15 March, Li Keqiang, China's number two leader, said that China could be in for some tough years, starting with a growth target for 2015 of 7 per cent, down from 7.5 per cent for 2014. He said that achieving this slower growth would be like 'taking a knife to one's own flesh' and would not be just a 'nail-clipping'. On 11 August the central bank announced it had devalued the yuan by 1.9 per cent, setting the mid-point at Rmb6.2298 to the US$1.0. Exports fell by 1.1 per cent in September while imports registered a higher than expected fall of 17.7 per cent; the trade suplus was US$59.4 billion. A statement from the Central Commiittee on 29 October confirmed the lifting of the 'one child policy' to allow couples to have two children.

Political structure

Constitution

The current constitution came into effect in 1982 and mandates complete CCP rule of the country. China's constitution emphasises strict ideological homogeneity and forbids acts that endanger the state security. It states that the Chinese people must adhere to Marxism-Leninism and Mao Zedong Thought.

The People's Republic of China, a unitary state consisting of 22 provinces, four special municipalities under central government control and five autonomous regions, was established in October 1949. The provinces, special municipalities and autonomous regions elect local people's congresses and are administered by people's governments.

Minor amendments in 2004 addressed the issues of private property and human rights.

Form of state

People's republic

The executive

The executive is the 15-member State Council which is elected by the National People's Congress (NPC). State Council members, including the premier of the State Council, who is appointed by the president, may not serve more than two consecutive five-year terms. The NPC also elects the 155 members of the Standing Committee which convenes annually when the NPC is not in session.

Effective political control is in the hands of the CCP which has over 40 million members. All ministers are party members. The party's central committee of 175 full members meets irregularly for plenary sessions. A National Congress is usually held every five years when a new central committee is elected.

The political bureau (politburo) of the CCP sets policy and controls all administrative, legal and executive appointments; the nine-man politburo standing committee is the focus of power.

CCP committees are the key decision-making bodies in the provinces, cities and regions into which China is divided.

The president, who plays no formal role in administration, and vice president, are elected for a maximum of two consecutive five-year terms by the NPC.

Real power is in the hands of the General Secretary, who, in recent years, has also taken on the post of President – effectively, Xi Jinping holds executive power in China as of August 2015.

National legislature

The unicameral Quanguo Renmin Daibiao Dahui (National People's

Congress) (NCP) can have up to 3,500 members (currently 2,268 in 2012), elected for five-year terms. Candidates are directly elected by voters of a local people's congress (village council) and raised to successive levels through a multi-tiered electoral system from provinces, municipalities, autonomous regions (including Hong Kong, Macao and Taiwan) and the armed forces to reach, eventually, the NCP.

The People's Political Consultative Conference (PPCC), with members drawn from a broader background coupled with the NCP make up the Lianghui (Two Meetings) to agree national political decisions.

Legal system

The Chinese legal system is an opaque mix of custom and statute. The judiciary and the government are closely connected. Much of the legal system remains at a partial stage of development.

The hierarchy of people's courts, ranging from Local People's Courts through Intermediate and then Higher People's Courts to the Supreme People's Court, is headed by the Ministry of Justice. The ministry was re-established in 1979 (it had been abolished in 1959 during Mao's 'Great Leap Forward'). Before 1979, arrests and sentences had to be approved by Communist Party committees. Although this practice was abolished in 1979, criminal law is still largely applied by the government as a form of public education, with periodic campaigns of mass arrests and executions used to frighten law-breakers.

People's courts, at all levels, deal with criminal, civic and economic matters in separate tribunals. Local people's mediation committees supplement the work of the courts by dealing with minor criminal offences and civil disputes, as well as helping implement government policy (such as the one-child per couple policy) at street level.

There is a similar hierarchy of people's procurates, re-established in 1978 after their abolition in the cultural revolution, extending from the localities to the Supreme People's Procurate. These monitor the work of state officials in the courts and the public security organs to ensure that they are observing the constitution and the law.

Supreme People's Court judges are appointed by the National People's Congress (NPC).

Last elections

October 2007 until February 2008 (NCP and PPCC); 15 March 2008 (presidential, indirect)

Results: Parliamentary: the CCP and the eight 'democratic' parties – all members of the China People's Political Consultative Conference – are allowed to stand in elections. The CCP forms the government.

Next elections

2018 (NCP and People's Political Consultative Conference (PPCC)); 2018 (presidential, indirect)

Political parties

Ruling party

Zhongguo Gongchangdang (Chinese Communist Party) (CCP)

Main opposition party

Opposition parties are strictly controlled and do not offer alternative policies.

Population

1.36 billion (2013) The one-child family planning programme was introduced in 1980. Under the programme urban families were restricted to one child, and rural families to two children. In 2012 the government was reported to be considering revising the one-child rule and in 2015 it was relaxed to allow two children. The national statistics office had reported, in 2010, that gender imbalance was becoming a serious demographic problem as couples choose in favour of a male offspring; by 2020, 24 million Chinese men will be unable to find a partner. the lifting of the one-child policy is expected to address this imbalance.

Millions of rural dwellers are moving to the major cities in search of a steady income and a better way of life.

The 2010 census revealed that the population grew to 1.34 billion (in 1953 the population was 594 million, less than half the current number) with 49.7 per cent of the population living in cities. People over aged 60 accounted for 13.26 per cent of the population, a growth of 2.93 per cent since 2000, while the number of people aged up to 14 years has fallen by 6.29 per cent since 2000, to 16.6 per cent

Last census: November 2010: 1.34 million

Population density: 140 inhabitants per square km (2010). Urban population 47 per cent (2010 Unicef).

Annual growth rate: 0.8 per cent, 1990–2010 (Unicef).

Ethnic make-up

The largest ethnic group is the Han, constituting 93.3 per cent of the population, which is largely concentrated around the basins of the main rivers (the Yellow River, the Yangtse and the Pearl River) and along the coast. Of the 55 other ethnic groups, 15 number over a million people each, including the Zhuang (Guangxi province), Hui (Muslims), Uygurs (in Xinjiang), Manchus, Tibetans, Mongolians and Koreans. The rest vary in size from several hundred thousand down to a few hundred.

Religions

China is officially atheist, but religion is tolerated to the extent that it does not challenge the state. Buddhism, Taoism, Islam, Catholicism and Protestantism all have followings. The formerly dominant belief system, Confucianism, continues to influence habits throughout society. Old temples, mosques and churches are being reopened and new ones built, but numbers are still far short of pre-revolutionary days. The Falun Gong religious movement is one of the religions considered to be subversive and its members have been arrested and imprisoned.

Education

The Ministry of Education in China estimates that 99 per cent of school-age children enter primary education, the length of which is six years. The retention rate in primary education for the whole country is 93 per cent.

Secondary education extends over six years, divided into general secondary education and vocational/technical secondary education. Both include two stages, junior secondary and senior secondary, of three years each. There are specialised schools and skilled workers' schools which cater for vocational training. The Ministry of Education estimated that 94 per cent of pupils finishing primary education enter secondary schools. It also says that half of pupils finishing junior secondary schools enter senior high education.

The Ministry of Education has encouraged the establishment of community colleges in major cities across China. Public expenditure on education was equivalent to less than 3 per cent of annual GDP in 2001 and included subsidies to private education at the primary, secondary and tertiary levels.

Literacy rate: 91 per cent adult rate; 99 per cent youth rate (15–24) (Unesco 2005).

Compulsory years: 7 to 16.

Pupils per teacher: 24 in primary schools.

Health

Employers pay for the medical care of most Chinese city-dwellers, while the rural population is in theory covered by local insurance schemes, village collectives or rural factories. The state and collective entities, such as factories or villages, run all large hospitals. There are a large number of private practitioners and privately run clinics.

It is estimated that more than one in five Chinese will be 60 years or older by 2030, which is likely to increase state expenses towards old age health care.

World Bank estimates show that 68 per cent and 24 per cent respectively in urban and rural areas have access to improved sanitation. Safe water facilities are available to 94 per cent of the urban population and 66 per cent of the rural population. Around 90 per cent of women use contraceptives, mainly due to the government's drive to keep down the birth rate.

Chinese consumption of tobacco products is popular and estimates say two-thirds of men smoke by the age of 25, with the vast majority maintaining the habit for many years. It is estimated that one third of Chinese men will die from smoking-related diseases, with the annual death toll reaching three million by 2050.

Hospitals rely on drug sales for 70 per cent of their budgets; in 2004 the Chinese government ordered price cuts for antibiotics, which account for 35 per cent of the Rmb49.6 billion (US$6 billion) pharmaceutical market. This measure is expected to have repercussions as it decreases hospital sales. Analysts say antibiotics are prescribed unnecessarily and the government is concerned about incentives, legal and illegal, that have resulted in hospital doctors prescribing them to about 80 per cent of in-patients.

In 2008, it was announced that a basic healthcare programme would be introduced for every citizen of China. Healthy China 2020 will provide universal health services to replace the patchy service that disadvantaged poorer patients, particularly the rural poor. The service will also monitor disease control and evaluate public health hazards.

The government announced that it was planning to invest an initial US$120 billion in healthcare reforms over the period 2009–11. Improving health insurance to include more people with basic cover and raising standards in public hospitals are priorities. The old state system was dismantled in the 1990s, during economic reforms, and since then there has been a growing disaffection among China's population, as around 50 per cent of all costs are met by the patient. Rural healthcare collapsed with secondary healthcare services provided only in towns and cities.

With changes to the diet and a more Western lifestyle, which have led to Western afflictions such as heart disease and strokes, plus an ageing population, the health system is facing long-term challenges and a demand for more medical services, including screening and preventative measures.

Research in 2009 revealed that under the one-child policy selective abortion has left a marked imbalance between the sexes in China, with 32 million more males than females. Any measures, which may be introduced to re-dress the gender balance, will take many years to accomplish.

HIV/Aids

In 2009 there were an estimated 740,000 adults living with HIV (Unicef 2012). The virus is present in at least 31 regions and has exploited distinct risk groups. The prevalence of HIV infection among injecting drug users ranges from 35–80 per cent in Xinjiang, and 20 per cent of the population in Guangdong. Some rural communities in Anhui, Henan and Shandong have been hit by infection levels of 10–20 per cent, and as much as 60 per cent in the worst hit areas, where locals sold their blood plasma to supplement their poor incomes. Death rates in these areas are high, although not yet significant enough to affect national statistics.

In 2009 government officials said that HIV/Aids was the leading cause of infectious death, at almost 7,000 by September 2008; tuberculosis and rabies fell to second and third causes of infectious deaths. Official statistics have become more reliable recently and there is a willingness by health officials to recognise HIV as a public health crisis; there had been reports of concerns of under-reporting by provincial and local officials. The disease has moved from high-risk groups into the mainstream population and officials are concerned that with growing industrialisation and with millions of migrant workers moving away from home the possibility of containing the disease has already been lost. Education programmes have been initiated.

HIV prevalence: 0.1 per cent aged 15–49 in 2009 (Unicef 2012)

Life expectancy: 73 years, 2009 (Unicef 2012)

Fertility rate/Maternal mortality rate: 1.6 births per woman, 2010 (Unicef); maternal mortality 55 per 100,000 live births (World Bank).

Birth rate/Death rate: 7 deaths and 16 births per 1,000 people

Child (under 5 years) mortality rate (per 1,000): 14 per 1,000 live births (WHO 2012)

Head of population per physician: 1.6 physicians per 1,000 people, 2001 (WHO 2006)

Welfare

China's economic development is uneven, with a wide gap between cities and the countryside and between regions.

China's social security expenses are typically equivalent to around 10 per cent of GDP.

The social insurance system includes provision for old age pensions, unemployment, medical care and industrial injury. Social insurance is implemented in accordance with state laws. The current focus of reform is on old age pension and unemployment insurance systems for urban enterprises. Social security entitlements have been allocated on a geographical footing with the working population being divided into urban and rural residents with the latter receiving far less in terms of benefits. Moreover, the urban population has been further split up into various layers depending on the size and importance of the employing enterprise or work unit. Therefore, a key state-owned enterprise (SOE) would offer better pension rights, wages and medical benefits than a smaller SOE or a township collective enterprise (COE).

The government increased the availability of the social security fund to more beneficiaries in 2003. The pension system is available to 150 million people, up from 130 million; the unemployment insurance system benefits approximately 110 million up from 100 million; and the medicare insurance system treats 100 million, an increase of 10 million people.

Another safety net beneath these systems is the minimum livelihood guarantee (MLG), which is administered by the Ministry of Civil Affairs (MCA). There are unemployment insurance schemes and some regions have started reforms of the basic medical insurance system.

Pensions

There is a partially funded pension scheme, which was launched in 1997, with two mandatory elements, a pay-as-you-go state pension administered by provinces, and individual pension accounts. There are also voluntary company pensions and for those most disadvantaged a social security fund. The pay-as-you-go system is based on contributions from employers and employees with the funds being pooled into a general account. In case of any shortfall, it is the responsibility of the local government to ensure funds are available to pay basic pension allowances. Government statistics indicate that SOEs contribute the majority of cash to pension funds.

In general, the contribution of the employer does not exceed 20 per cent of the overall wage bill of an enterprise. Employee contributions are between 4 and 8 per cent with employees in more developed areas paying the higher rate. The lower tier pension, known as the basic pension, is calculated at 20 per cent of the average wage of employees in the town or city.

As yet, China does not have a national policy for pension provision. Nevertheless the government is aware that with an ageing population and falling fertility rate China's dependency ratio – the numbers in work supporting the numbers in retirement – is projected to drop from 9:1 to 2.6:1 by 2045.

In August 2005 the government awarded operating licenses to 15 investment managers to operate China's new corporate pension scheme. Of the 15, four are foreign financial services ING, Fortis, Deutsche Bank and Bank of Montreal which are required to be in joint Chinese partnership. The new scheme will hold pension contributions in a legally distinct fund governed by trust law.

Main cities

Beijing (capital, estimated population 10.2 million (m) in 2012), Shanghai (21.2m), Xian (4.9m), Tianjin (4.6m), Chongqing (4.6), Wuhan (4.0m), Chengdu (3.8m), Shenyang (3.7m), Harbin (3.7m), Nanjing (3.7m), Changchun (2.9m), Guangzhou (Canton, 2.9m), Taiyuan (2.8m).

Languages spoken

There are seven main Chinese dialects, but the written language is the same for all dialects. Other languages include Tibetan, Uygur (a Turkic language) and Mongolian.

English is not widely spoken, especially outside the main cities, although there will usually be someone who can speak a little in hotels, restaurants and taxi stations.

Official language/s

Putonghua (Mandarin Chinese – Beijing dialect).

Media

All forms of media are tightly controlled by the authorities and recent labialisation has only been extended to distributions and advertising and not to editorial content.

The growth of the internet has resulted in 'the most extensive and effective legal and technological systems for internet censorship and surveillance in the world' according to an academic report of 2005. China regularly blocks websites for groups it considers dissenting. Internet service providers and news organisations have agreed to Chinese censorship as part of their business contracts with China, which then allows access to its vast market.

Press

Dailies: The primary government-owned, Communist party, national newspaper, published in seven languages is *Renmin Ri Bao* (*People's Daily*) (www.people.com.cn), which has ten other separate newspapers. All cities have their own newspaper, typically published by the Communist party and therefore lacking much criticism of it. Corruption and inefficiency is reported but only after approval by Communist party officials. News outlets that have flouted this convention are subject to censure or swift closure.

In Chinese, *Zhongguo Qingnian Bao* (*China Youth Daily*) (www.cyol.net) aimed at Communist Young League, *Jie Fang Ri Bao* (*JF Daily*) (www.jfdaily.com) from Shanghai, *Dongnan Kuai Bao* (*Southeast Express*) (www.dnkb.com.cn), from Fujian, and *Guangzhou Metro Daily* (http://ycdtb.dayoo.com).

From Shanghai, in English, *Shanghai Daily* (www.shanghaidaily.com), *East Day* (http://english.eastday.com), includes business news, *The Shanghai News* (www.theshanghainews.net), *Shanghalist* (http://shanghaiist.com).

From Lassa, in Tibetan, *Bod Kyi Dus Bob* (*Tibet Times*) (www.tibettimes.net), in Chinese *Lasa Wan Bao* and online *China Tibet News* (www.chinatibetnews.com).

Weeklies: In Chinese, *Sanlian Shenghuo Zhoukan* (*Life Week*) (www.lifeweek.com.cn) a weekly of general interest, *Feng Hua Yuan* (*Chinese News & Culture Magazine*) (www.fhy.net), *Hau Xia Wen Zhai* (www.cnd.org) are bi-weeklies news magazines. *Trends* (www.trendsmag.com.cn) for women. In English, *Beijing Review* (www.bjreview.com.cn), is a national weekly news magazine and *Beijing Scene* (www.beijingscene.com), is a popular lifestyle magazine.

Business: There are several daily business newspapers, printed in Chinese, and some with English online editions, including *Jingii Ri Bao* (*Economic Daily*) (http://paper.ce.cn), *Jingii Guancha Bao* (*The Economic Observer*) (www.eeo.com.cn), *Guo Ji Shang Bao* (http://ibdaily.mofcom.gov.cn), *Qihuo Ri Bao* (www.qhrb.com.cn), *Zhongguo Gongshang Bao* (*China Industry & Commerce News*) (www.cicn.com.cn), *Zhongguo Jingji Shibao* (*China Economic Times*) (www.jjxww.com) and *Zhongguo Jinggii Bao* (*China Business*), which specifically focusses on steel (www.chinaccm.com/0n). Other, major, regional cities have their own editions of the *Economic Daily*.

Magazines include a bi-weekly *Caijing* (*Business and Financial Review*) (www.caijing.com.cn).

Periodicals: In English, *Beijing This Month* is a semi-tourist magazine.

Broadcasting

All broadcasting is overseen by the Ministry of Radio, Film and Television.

Broadcast media, for most people, is limited to government-run organs, as foreign short wave radio signals are regularly jammed and the use of satellite receivers restricted. There are more than one billion television views and TV is a popular source of news and information.

Pay-to-view TV is a growing market and is expected to have around 130 million customers by 2010.

Yahoo closed its email service in August 2013, and its news and community services in September. Users were redirected to a site run by Alibaba.

Radio: The government-run China National Radio has four national networks, plus China Radio International (CRI) (www.cri.cn) with services in 45 languages and a service devoted to Taiwan. Domestic radio services broadcast in the country's major languages and dialects. There are over 500 government-owned local radios stations, including the Beijing People's Broadcasting Station (BPBS), which has several services including a Special Educational Service, and Economic, Traffic and Literary stations.

The first foreign language radio station, in Beijing, Radio 774 (http://am774.bjradio.com.cn), was set up in 2004 by the Chinese government, specifically for foreign residents.

Television: The national state-run, China Central Television (CCTV) (http://english.cctv.com), has over 2,000 channels available for its viewers through a network of regional and municipal stations.

Non-domestic programmes are limited, with a few foreign TV companies providing services via either cable or satellite dishes.

National news agency: Xinhua (New China News Agency)

Economy

China has natural resources that provide most of the basics for an advanced economy, including almost above all else a huge labour force (an estimated 801.6 million in 2014). However, around 33 per cent of this workforce is a peasant class engaged in agriculture. The industry may use technology to maintain intensive cultivation techniques, but in many remote areas farming is still dependent on manual labour. China's arable land is only 75 per cent that of the US total, but it produces around 30 per cent more than the US, partly due to efficient governmental policies and investment. China is the world's largest producer of rice and a significant producer of wheat, tea, pork and fish. Agriculture provides China with a high level of self-sufficiency in food; nevertheless agriculture's share of GDP fell from 27 per cent in 1990 to 9.2 per cent in 2014 as the industrial-manufacturing sector expanded. China's primary industries include coal mining, with reserves of 114.5 trillion tonnes and production of 1,845 million tonnes of oil equivalent (mtoe) in 2014. What it doesn't grow or produce it imports to power its manufacturing base, which has turned China into the world's factory.

China is the 'C' in Bric but unlike the other Bric countries, it has a putative Communist, authoritarian government that has been able to plan and follow a

strategy for a centralised economy based on set objectives. This means, for example, imports of natural materials are purchased on a national basis to be distributed and supplied at wholesale prices among its industrial bases. Single item factory towns have been built, providing cheap labour for factories geared up for mass production, wholly for export sales. The industry and manufacturing sector constituted 42.6 per cent of GDP while exports in 2014 produced a trade balance of US$219.7 billion. China has built up the largest surplus current account of any country in the world. Since becoming a member of the WTO in 2001, trade has grown so much that by 2010 China had overtaken Germany, Japan and the US to become the world's largest exporter.
GDP growth in 2007 was at a record 14.2 per cent, falling markedly to 9.6 per cent in 2008 as global oil prices rose, due in large part to demand by China reaching around 10 per cent of total world use (only the US at around 20 per cent was higher). As the global economic crisis weakened the economies of trading partners, so exports fell. GDP growth in 2009 was 9.2 per cent and as global trade picked up in 2010, growth rose to 10.4 per cent. However, the European economic crisis caused a drop in growth to 9.3 per cent in 2011. Growth had fallen further by 2013 reaching the lowest it had it several years at 7.7 per cent and agin to 7.4 per cent in 2014. The fall in China's economic growth rate can be accredited to the slow recovery of China's trading partners, as well as industrial over capacity, inefficient allocation of capital by the state, and overhanging debt.
Although China didn't slip into recession in 2008–09 it did worry that rising unemployment could trigger social unrest and as a result social security was improved. Around 10 million (rural) migrant workers had lost their jobs by 2009. In 2010 migrant workers not only went on strike to demand better wages and working condition, but also formed an independent and effective trade union. Since then China has seen a number of strikes and protests by its workers demanding better working conditions, better wages and better rights to protect them.
In 2013 (latest survey), the UN Human Development Index (HDI) ranked China 101 (out of 187) for national development in health, education and income. Since 2000, China's progress has grown to match the average world improvement rate. In 2013 (latest survey), 44.9 per cent of the population experienced at least one indicator of poverty, while 13.1 per cent lived on less than the equivalent of US$1.25 per day; the headcount poverty rate was 12.5 per cent of the population (2000–13).
Remittances from migrant workers amounted to US$39 billion (0.4 per cent of GDP).
Inflation rose to a 28-month high of 5.1 per cent in November 2010, although annual inflation was only 3.3 per cent, rising to an estimated 5.4 per cent in 2011. Inflation in July 2011 was 6.5 per cent and the government instigated measures to promote an economic slowdown and reduce inflation and by 2013 inflation had steadied to 3.0 per cent and further still to 2.0 per cent by 2014.
September 2011, the average minimum wage had risen by over 21.7 per cent, and rose another 14.1 per cent in 2015. Increased production costs is threatening China's pre-eminence as one of the world's cheapest manufacturing centres.
Despite being a regime that espouses Communist principals China has picked up some of the worst malpractice excesses of the West, from petty provincial officials misappropriating land and government funds, to capitalists manipulating China's only stock exchange through insider trading. However, when Chinese authorities move to punish such felons, it is swift and harsh, including capital punishment.
The People's Bank of China (PBOC) (the central bank) de-linked the renminbi from the US dollar in 2005, and kept it within a 3 per cent margin of the US dollar. However it was re-linked in 2008 as the economic crisis cut Chinese exports leaving the renminbi undervalued and drawing criticism0 from the US and India. In June 2010 the central bank announced an incremental revaluation of the currency, of 0.43 per cent, which raised the value of the yuan while not threatening export sales. The IMF noted that the yuan was still 'undervalued', although this was an improvement on the 'substantially undervalued' earlier comment and in 2014 it was Rmb6.21 to the US$1. In August 2015 the PBOC shocked global markets by devaluating the Renminbi three days in a row in order to boost export figures and to try and push domestic economic reforms that the government hopes will lead to the Renminbi to become one of the reserve currencies of the IMF's Special Drawing Rights (SDR) group. After the three days of devaluation the renminbi dropped by three per cent against the dollar to 0.16 USD to the renmindi.
The property bubble also contends to become a major problem in China. In 2014 the ratio number of unsold property to annual sales reached 51.5 per cent, up from 24.7 in 2011. In the first two moths of 2014 home sales fell by some 18 per cent.
In December 2011, China and Japan signed an agreement to exchange up to US$339 billion in each of their currencies in a measure intended to safeguard them during another global economic crisis and strengthen trade ties. In March and June 2012 China signed similar agreements with Australia (US$31 billion) and Brazil (US$30 billion). These measures are seen as China's intention to position its currency as a reserve currency alongside the US dollar. On 25 June 2012, Qatar applied for a licence to invest in China's capital market. The investment of US$5 billion is five times greater than the quota allowed under China's Qualified Foreign Institutional Investor (QFII) programme. Within days, China announced that it was searching for ways to ease the entry rules for foreign investors. Some of the intended investment comes from China's purchase of Qatar's liquefied natural gas (LNG).

External trade

Since becoming a member of the WTO trade has grown so much that by 2015 China had become the largest exporter in the world.
Its agricultural, manufacturing and industrial sectors export a huge range of items from seeds to hi-tech electronic equipment, from mass-produced garments to custom-built oil tankers; its service sector is not as well developed.
In 2009 China pledged US$10 billion in concessionary loans (2010–13) to Africa, this was in addition to 50 previous co-operation agreements and US$5 billion to encourage Chinese firms to invest in Africa.
China and Taiwan signed a direct trade agreement in 2008, enhancing trade links by increasing the number of flights between the countries, allowing many more passengers to visit. Tax free, direct cargo shipments are allowed between designated ports. Direct postal services have been improved and expanded.
In March 2012, the US, Japan and EU filed a case with the WTO against China, for restricting the export of rare earth (minerals), and so breaking WTO rules. China contains 95 per cent of the world's deposits of rare earths, which are critical to making high-tech products, and its restriction on exports has pushed up the price of manufactured goods elsewhere. The Ruling sided against China and stated that the restrictions on the exports of the rare earths breached WTO rules and the restrictions on exports were lifted.

Imports

Main categories are petroleum, energy, light industrial and metal products, machinery and equipment, plastics, optical

and medical equipment, organic chemicals, timber, iron and steel.
Main sources: South Korea (9.7 per cent of total in 2014), Japan (8.3 per cent), US (7.8 per cent).

Exports

Principal exports include machinery and equipment, plastics, clothing, optical and medical equipment, finished goods, vehicles and parts, iron and steel.
Main destinations: US (16.9 per cent of total in 2014), Hong Kong (SAR of China) (15.5 per cent), Japan (6.4 per cent).

Agriculture

Farming

China's economy was traditionally based on agriculture, but since collectivisation and the Mao-era requirement for self-sufficiency in food was replaced with co-operatives in 1976, farming has experienced the progressively hard realities of the market place with large unprofitable state farms closing down and workers made redundant. Around 34 per cent of China's workforce is employed in agriculture, using technology to maintain intensive cultivation techniques, so that by 2010 China became the world's largest consumer of fertilisers. China's arable land is only 75 per cent that of the US total, yet it produces around 30 per cent more than the US. China is the world's largest producer of rice and a significant producer of wheat, tea, pork and fish. Agriculture provides China with a high level of self-sufficiency in food; nevertheless agriculture's share of GDP fell from 28 per cent in 1978 to 9.2 per cent in 2014 as the industrial-manufacturing sector expanded. With a burgeoning industrial base, China is experiencing rapid urbanisation and rural workers, looking for better wages and a share of China's increasing standard of living, have joined the factory line. A land reform law enabled farm collectives and members to sell their land; the government's ultimate aim is land privatisation. About 5 per cent of farmland, or 6.7 million hectares (ha), have been lost to mainly industrial development since 1997 and pressure on resources, such as water, is, in some areas, becoming critical. Land use and erosion have resulted in pollution and flooding, which prompted the government to modify the land reforms, including delisting 70 per cent of development zones, thus saving over 24,000 square kilometres of farmland.
Although all land is officially owned by the state, land ownership comes in the form of 'land use rights', which give the title-owner rights for between 30–70 years. Forty million farmers have lost the rights to their land since 1984 and rural communities are protesting at the manner of the purchase and sale of farmland.
Re-designated land use has also been initiated by the government with 5.4 million ha of arable land given over to forestry, while cotton growing has dropped by over 7 per cent. Both of these measures, and the reinforced embankment of the middle and lower reaches of the Yangtze and Yellow rivers, are measures designed to stem the disastrous flooding seen increasingly since the early 1990s.
Government policy, incorporating the changes that entry to the WTO have imposed, is mostly concerned with food security. The government's traditional agricultural policy has been to encourage farmers to increase production to meet the needs of the cities, while keeping prices low. This has involved guaranteeing farmers a price for a proportion of their crop and offering it at a subsidised price in the towns.
The government is attempting to increase farm incomes – which are markedly below those in the cities – in the hope that the sector can provide the impetus for growth of consumer products. The government is considering changing agricultural policy to focus more on grain quality rather than quantity in order to cope with external competition. There is likely to be increased rural poverty and unemployment in the medium-term as cheaper imports bite. The conundrum remains of how to increase rural incomes and provide food for a huge population without significant state intervention and, by extension, state distortion of the market.
From 2005, a policy that limits foreign producers of genetically modified (GM) seed crops from accessing the Chinese market runs concurrently with the country's own research and development to produce GM crops in cotton and rice. The government's problematic position is hampered by its appreciation of the sales potential for unmodified crops in overseas markets that are reluctant to take GM crops, against the need for higher domestic yields and the possibility for sales of Chinese patented GM seed crops abroad.
According to the Centre for Chinese Agricultural Policy, China will need to produce more than 1.5 times the 1999 level of grain output to feed a population of 1.6 billion by 2030. The demand for livestock and aquatic products is forecast to double in the same period. By 2014 China was increasingly using GM products in order to feed it's growing population.

Fishing

With its extensive river network and long coastline, China is the largest producer and exporter of fish in the world. The total marine fishing ground area is about 818,000 square nautical miles and China has a total of 150 commercially exploitable marine species in its waters. The main species are silver carp, bighead carp, grass carp and tilapia.
China's marine fishing production is made up of small-scale fisheries and the state-owned enterprises (SOEs). The small scale fisheries produce an estimated 90 per cent of the total seafood supply. The reform of SOEs has improved productivity in large-scale fishing operations. In common with other fishing grounds, stocks in the South and East China Seas are becoming depleted. Inland fishing is showing an increase, following a period of decline caused by the depletion of inland freshwater habitats due to dam-building, industrial pollution and land reclamation for agriculture.

Forestry

China has around 23 per cent forest cover, almost evenly divided between coniferous and broadleaved forests. Southern forests are mainly lowland rain forests and monsoon forests. In the north, the majority of forests are mixed coniferous.
The government has embarked on a policy of reforestation. Deforestation was partially blamed for the disastrous extent of the 1998–99 floods which killed thousands and swamped cities, agricultural land and industrial enterprises. Huge coniferous forests have been planted and it is hoped that slower-growing deciduous trees will augment them in the reforested areas.
The State Forestry Administration, has set ambitious targets for China to raise afforestation by 26 per cent by 2050.
China is one of the world's five largest wood-producing countries, although the majority of production is burned as fuel. It is a net exporter of wood products and also produces a large amount of non-wood forest products such as resins, tung oil, essential oils, bamboo poles and bamboo shoots, nuts, mushrooms, honey and medicinal plants.

Industry and manufacturing

China's industrial base is highly diversified and ranges from the production of metals and oil refining to light industry such as textiles and computer hardware. The Industrial sector accounts for around 42.6 per cent of GDP and employs 30.3 per cent of the labour force. The major industries are mechanics, electronics, metallurgy, chemicals, building materials, furniture, woodwork, textiles, clothing, food, petroleum and coal processing. The government has been focussing on restructuring the industrial sector and introducing advanced technology. The government hopes to phase out small scale production and encourage foreign participation, particularly in the chemicals industry. The development of effective, low-cost chemicals for agricultural use is a top priority.

China has become a production centre for a multitude of labour-intensive assembly industries. China produces around 75 per cent of the global supply of textiles. There is considerable foreign investment coming from Hong Kong (SAR) (which accounts for most of new funding in the Shenzhen Special Economic Zone), Japan and the US. China has the ability to exploit vertical economic linkages from its impressive natural resources to heavy industy and the manufacturing of white goods, which has shown impressive growth since the early 1990s.

China is a net exporter of aluminium and is the world's largest aluminium producer, accounting for 46 per cent of global output. It is also a major exporter of magnesium, although competitors have complained that China has driven down global magnesium prices through price dumping on commodity markets. China is the world's largest steel producer.

Vehicle production is an important growth sector and in 2014 China was the largest producer of motor vehicles in the world. China's attraction as a foreign investment destination has increased since it became a WTO member, since low production costs and cheap labour have encouraged many foreign businesses to transfer their operations to the mainland. The main concern is that increased competition will have a devastating effect on state-owned industries. More joint-venture companies are likely to evolve over time, leading to mixed-ownership control in the industrial sector.

Chinese industry is faced with an increasing domestic oversupply problem. At the same time, domestic demand has fallen as state-owned enterprises lay off workers as part of the government's restructuring programme. This has increased competition within Chinese industry, causing deflation and putting pressure on factory gate prices. The problems facing the industrial sector have led to concerns that Chinese companies, stimulated by the government's fiscal pump-priming of the economy, have been investing too much in increasing capacity.

Problems facing China's industrial sector are the lack of workable bankruptcy laws and the corruption of local officials, who are keeping failing industries afloat. State-owned banks are forced to carry the burden of the industrial sector's debt, a burden that is unsustainable. An eventual clamp-down on non-performing loans within the banking sector will affect the industrial sector. The government is encouraging investment in privately-owned industrial firms, with the possibility of opening up the sector to further foreign investment.

In 2014, industrial output rose by 7 per cent from 2013. The rising production costs, caused mainly by the workers demand for higher wages, could weaken China's pre-eminence as one of the world's cheapest manufacturing centres.

Tourism

China has a wealth of history, varied culture and an internationally acclaimed cuisine to offer visitors and hosts 48 UNESCO world heritage sites, second only to Italy globally. Popular tourist destinations include from the Great Wall of China, the Dragon King's Tomb, performances of Chinese opera and circuses, old and new cities and a variety of landscapes. However, with the great distances between centres of interest tourists are faced with remaining fairly static or undertaking some internal travelling. As a by-product of China's immense industrialisation it has been in the process of expanding its infrastructure, which has benefited tourists. A train can now carry passengers into Nepal, up into the Himalayas, and a new high-speed train between Beijing and Shanghai, opened on in 2011, has reduced the 1,318km journey to five hours.

Travel and tourism is a relatively novel pastime for many Chinese but the increase in disposable income plus a relaxation in travel permits in recent years means that many more are visiting the outside world. Tourism contributes 9.4 per cent of GDP (2014), with around 8.6 per cent of the workforce engaged in the industry, including jobs indirectly related to the industry (66.1 million jobs). China received 61.5 million international visitors in 2014.

Environment

China is a land of contrast. While a project of land reclamation has been in operation since 2001 in the north- western Ningxia Hui autonomous region, where willows and grass are helping to beat back the desert, for many regions around China the prospects are not so good. The Yellow River typically runs dry before it reaches the sea due to the overuse of water for irrigation. Desertification is accelerating and threatens one-third of the country and 400 million people. The national policy of self-sufficiency in food in the past resulted in the cultivation of unsuitable grain crops in desert areas and, coupled with logging and over-exploitation exacerbated by a natural lack of water and rainfall, has led to rapid soil erosion. The beginnings of a forest have been planted in Yanchi in an effort to avert the spring sandstorms that sweep through Beijing each spring.

In contrast, the central and southern regions are hit every summer by severe floods. The worst affected areas are the middle and upper reaches of the Yangtze River, where the Three Gorges Dam is expected to bring some relief when it is completed. As it neared its completion, the risk to the environmental and ecology, wich included landslides and loss of drinking water, prompted officials to plan to relocate over four million people to the city of Chongqing from the immediate vicinity of the Three Gorges Dam between 2007–22.

In 2005 an explosion in a state-run chemical plant caused an 80km toxic benzene slick that flowed down the Songhua River endangering over nine million inhabitants who depend on the river for their supply. Many residents of the city of Harbin joined an exodus to avoid the danger when authorities halted river-water supplies and handed out thousands of bottles of water while the slick passed.

In 2008, China was reported to be the biggest carbon polluter in the world. The figures in the report came from provincial-level data from China's own Environmental Protection Agency. Nevertheless, the US per capita emission is still 5–6 times higher than China and any pressure to cap emissions in either country will require overcoming their no-harm-to-economic-growth stance.

The government declared a drought emergency in February 2009 in eight northern and central provinces. Around four million people lacked drinking water and half of the country's winter crops of wheat and rapeseed were threatened. Irrigation in the effected areas traditionally relies on rainwater; the drought is the worst since 1951.

Mining

China's mining industry ranks as one of the largest in the world, although production statistics are sketchy. Most of China's mineral production is consumed locally by state-owned enterprises (SOEs). There are around 80,000 SOEs and 200,000 collectively-owned mines. China is an important producer of copper, tungsten, antimony, lithium and molybdenum, and also produces significant quantities of zinc, lead, manganese, tin, mercury and rare earths. China ranks among the top five countries for its reserves of antimony, barite, graphite, magnesite, fluorite, molybdenum, tin and tungsten. China imports alumina, chromite, cobalt, copper, iron ore, manganese and other platinum-group metals. China is an extremely important market for the global minerals industry and is one of the largest mineral exporters, importers and producers in the world.

China is becoming increasingly important in the molybdenum market and has substantially more deposits of rare earth elements than the rest of the world, 95 per cent of them in the Bayan Obo iron ore mined in Inner Mongolia. In March 2012, the US, Japan and EU filed a case with the WTO against China, for restricting the export of rare earth (minerals), and so breaking WTO rules. These metals are critical to making high-tech products, and its restriction on exports has pushed up the price of manufactured goods elsewhere. The Ruling sided against China and stated that the restrictions on the exports of the rare earths breached WTO rules and the restrictions on exports were lifted.

A Chinese-owned mining company won a tender to develop one of the world's largest copper mines sited in Logar Province in Afghanistan. It is estimated that the site has 13 million tonnes of copper. Australia, Canada, China and Russia all contested the tender, ultimately won by Metallurgical Group with an investment of US$3 billion.

Hydrocarbons

Proven oil reserves were 18.5 billion barrels at the end of 2014, with production at 4.2 million barrels per day (bpd), an increase of 0.7 per cent on the 2013 figure. However with consumption at 11.1 million bpd in 2013 China relies on imported oil to meet its domestic needs and since the early 1990s has rapidly moved from being a net exporter of oil to the world's third largest net importer (after the US and Japan). It also has the second largest refining capacity in the world after the US, at 14.1 million bpd in 2014.

Around 85 per cent of Chinese oil production is located onshore, in the ageing Daqing and Shengli fields in north-eastern and east China respectively. Exploration is concentrated in new offshore sites in the north-eastern Bohai Sea and the southern Pearl River Delta. Oil production is currently controlled by two state-owned oil firms, the China National Petroleum Corporations (CNPC) and the China Petroleum and Chemical Corporations (Sinopec), which combined dominate the upstream and downstream oil markets. CNPC, with a publicly listed subsidiary, PetroChina, concentrates on exploration and output, while Sinopec focuses on refining and distribution.

A US$25 billion deal was signed in 2009, whereby China is supplied with Siberian oil in exchange for Chinese loans to Russian companies. The Chinese Development Bank loaned Rosneft and Transneft, the Russian state oil company and pipeline company, US$15 billion and US$10 billion respectively. Some 300,000 barrels a day of oil annually began flowing through the pipeline in January 2011. China considers the agreement to be strategically vital as it diversifies its hydrocarbon supplies away from the Middle East. The inauguration of a new oil refinery in Guangxi Province took place in 2010. PetroChina, the owner/operator invested US$2.2 billion for the 200,000 barrels of oil capacity plant, located near the border with Vietnam, in the city port of Qinzhou. In February 2012, Sinopec announced that it had plans to invest US$8.41 billion and dramatically expand its oil refining plant in the Xinjigang region and double its refined oil output to 200,000bpd by 2015.

China, along with Vietnam, Taiwan, Brunei, Malaysia and The Philippines, claims the potentially oil-rich Spratly Islands.

Proven natural gas reserves were of 3.5 trillion cubic metres (cum) in 2014, the majority of which are located in the south-western Sichuan Province, and the north-western region Xinjiang Uyghur Autonomous region. The latest discovery, the Puguang field in Sichuan Province, has proven reserves of 356 billion cum that could reach a total of 500–550 billion cum. Production in 2014 was 134.5 billion cum, which was an increase of 7.7 per cent on its 2013 levels. In 2007 China imported 3.3 billion cum of liquefied natural gas, which by 2014 had risen to 27.1 billion cum and total imports of natural gas were 31.3 billion cum. Indonesia and Australia are the source of the greatest proportion of LNG imports.

China plans to replace coal with natural gas as the main source of power generation in homes in its major cities and the 4,000km west-east pipeline extending across the country to the urban coastal areas could eventually be extended to tap the large gas reserves of Central Asia. The Sichuan-Shanghai natural gas pipeline became operational in 2010. The US$9.2 billion pipeline is designed to transport 12 billion cubic metres of natural gas per year. China's consumption of natural gas was 5.4 per cent of total world gas consumption in 2014 standing at 185.5 billion cum.

Coal is China's primary source of energy; there were proven reserves of 114.5 billion tonnes at the end of 2014, of which around 62 billion is thermal anthracite and 52 billion the lesser coking (brown) coal used in power stations. Production was 1,844 million tonnes of oil equivalent (mtoe), a fall of 2.6 per cent on the 2013 levels. The main export destinations for Chinese coal are South Korea and Japan. China is becoming more open to foreign investment in its coal industry, in a bid to modernise the industry.

Energy

China's total installed generating capacity exceeded 1.5 trillion kWh by 2014, of which around 70 per cent was produced by low quality and polluting coking coal, as a result there are plans to increase the number of natural gas electricity power stations. The giant Three Gorges dam was completed in 2006, with 26 generators capable of producing 98.8 million kilowatt hours (kWh) through hydropower, making it the biggest hydropower source in the world.

Another large hydroelectric project will involve a series of dams on the Yellow River, with 25 generating stations with a combined installed capacity of 158 million kW. The government is also expanding nuclear power generating capacity, with the construction of eight new nuclear power plants in joint ventures with Russian, French and Canadian firms.

The government hopes eventually to unify electricity distribution into one national power grid with power generators selling their electricity at rates determined by a free market.

Financial markets

In 1986, the stock market in Shanghai, the largest in East Asia before 1949, reopened to trade shares and bonds. China has since opened securities exchanges in 44 cities, including the capital Beijing, but trading so far has been thin. Shanghai and the Shenzhen Stock Exchange (formally opened in 1991) remain the two major markets for both domestic and foreign investors. Both markets list 'A' shares (for domestic investors) and 'B' shares (for foreign investors) as well as bonds and warrants. As a result of further planned privatisation, Shanghai's total market capitalisation is expected to increase from US$600 billion in 2002 to US$2 trillion by 2010, although there are uncertainties surrounding the government's commitment to the privatisation programme. The market, driven by millions of retail investors, is thought to be overvalued and subject to illegal manipulations.

An equity market for small- and medium-sized companies (similar to the Alternative Investment Market in London) was established on the Shenzhen stock market in 2009. Called the Growth Enterprise Board it was expected to start operations in October.

Stock exchange

Shanghai Stock Exchange (SSE)

Commodity exchange

Dalian Commodity Exchange (DCE)

Banking and insurance

China's accession to the WTO in late 2001lead to reforms in the country's banking sector to permit domestic banks to compete with foreign-owned banks in the future. This meant eliminating corruption at the highest levels of management. Under the WTO agreement, foreign banks were allowed to offer renminbi banking services to Chinese corporations from 2004, and to offer services to Chinese individuals from 2007.

In 2003, the country was dominated by four large banks, the Bank of China, the Agricultural Bank of China, China Construction Bank and Industrial and Commercial Bank of China, which between them controlled 80 per cent of banking services. WTO membership gave foreign banks the right to compete with domestic ones and all restrictions on the setting up, operation and licensing of foreign banks were eliminated by 2005. In addition, state-owned banks could provide foreign currency services. In December 2001, HSBC became the first foreign bank to obtain equity in mainland China when it acquired 8 per cent in the Bank of Shanghai.

On 19 July 2013 the government annouced that banks would in future be allowed to set their own lending rates. Previously they were not allowed to lend at rates below a certain level set by the People's Bank of China.

Central bank

People's Bank of China. The central bank became an autonomous financial institution in 1995.

Time

GMT plus eight hours

Despite its size, China works to one time zone only.

Geography

China is the third-largest country in the world after Russia and Canada. Its 28,000km land boundary touches North Korea, Russia, Mongolia, Afghanistan, Pakistan, India, Nepal, Bhutan, Myanmar, Laos and Vietnam.

China is bounded by the Yellow and East China Seas to the east and by the South China Sea to the south.

Deserts and semi-arid grasslands make up much of the western and northern parts of the country. Central and eastern China are the most heavily populated parts of the country. The plains of north and north-east China are flat and fertile, but frequently suffer from prolonged drought.

Mountain ranges occupy 33 per cent of China's area. Most of China's main rivers run west to east. The longest is the Yangtze River, followed by the Yellow River. The Yangtze River is known as Chiangjiang (long river) in China.

Much of China was once covered by forest, but due to dense settlement and intensive agriculture, most forests have disappeared.

There are 23 provinces including Henan, Guangdong, Shandong, Sichuan, Jiangsu, Hebei, Hunan, Anhui, Hubei and Zhejiang; four municipalities – Beijing (Northern Capital), Chongqing (Double Celebration), Shanghai (Above the Sea) and Tianjin (Heaven's Crossing); five autonomous regions – Guangxi (Western Expanse), Neimengu (Inner Mongolia), Ningxia (Peaceful China), Xinjiang Uygur (New Frontier) and Xizang (Tibet) (Western Buddhists) and two special administrative regions – Hong Kong and Macau.

Hemisphere

Northern

Climate

China, with its extensive land mass, has a diverse climate with five temperature zones: cold-temperate, mid-temperate and warm-temperate, subtropical and tropical zone, as well as a plateau climate zone in Tibet.

Weather patterns for most of China are influenced by the monsoon periods that strike in different parts from April to October. Not only is there a series of monsoons drawn from the Pacific Ocean that dominate in turn, the south-east, eastern then northern regions but also one that is drawn from the Indian Ocean that strikes southern mainland China.

The average temperature in summer in Beijing is 28 degrees Celsius (C); Shanghai 16 degrees C and Guangzhou 32 degrees C.

Dress codes

Foreign businessmen generally wear suits and ties to negotiating sessions with Chinese counterparts, who have abandoned the Mao suit for Western dress. Less formal attire is acceptable outside the main cities.

Fashion-consciousness is growing among younger urban Chinese.

Entry requirements

Passports

All visitors need to hold a passport with validity of a minimum of six months. Passports should have at least a few blank pages for visas and entry and exit stamps.

Visa

Required by all, except transit passengers. Business visits can only be made with an invitation fom a Chinese organisation such as a ministry or commercial institution. Foreign firms may request such invitations from a trading corporation. An invitation in the form of a fax is usually sufficient for the visa application which should also include a business letter and itinerary. For up-to-date information concerning visas contact the nearest consulate.

It is possible for individuals to organise their own itinerary and when this has been confirmed by the authorities, the visitor must finance the cost of accommodation and the tour by depositing the amount, through a home bank, with China International Travel Service.

If arriving from Mongolia, airlines in Ulaanbaatar require holders of foreign passports to have a Chinese visa in order to board the aircraft for flights to Beijing. This requirement applies regardless of the length of time in transit at Beijing.

Currency advice/regulations

Export and import of local currency is limited to Rmb20,000; all exports of renminbi must be accompanied by a foreign currency conversion receipt, issued by domestic banks. Renminbi may be converted overseas within six months from any Bank of China operation but only with a foreign currency conversion receipt.

Import and export of foreign currency is unlimited but any amount over the equivalent of US$5,000 being exported must be declared.

Travellers cheques, preferably in US dollars, are accepted in major cities, in banks and four and five star hotels.

Customs

Certain items produced in China before 1949, such as embroidery, silks, porcelain, scrolls and *objets d'art*, may be subject to export restrictions. When arriving, listing electonic equipment and camera gear etc is compulsory on customs forms; if these items are not with the traveller on departure, the traveller is liable to pay duty on them. Receipts for any major purchases, especially paintings and antiques, should be kept.

Prohibited imports

Printed material, films, tapes that are viewed to be adverse to China's politics, economy, culture and ethics.

Health (for visitors)

Mandatory precautions

Vaccination certificates are required for yellow fever if travelling from an infected area.

Advisable precautions

Take precautions against HIV/Aids and malaria (generally confined to the southern part of China near the border with Myanmar and Vietnam, although in the summer months the Yangtze River basin is also affected). Rabies is endemic and bilharzia is present in southern and eastern parts of the country. Vaccinations should be taken against hepatitis A and B, diphtheria, tuberculosis, Japanese A encephalitis, polio, tetanus and typhoid. Drink only bottled water, avoid unpeeled fruit and salads and try to ensure all food has been thoroughly cooked. It is advisable to have emergency medical insurance; in Beijing two companies – Asia Emergency

Assistance (AEA) and International SOS Assistance – offer evacuation services.

Hotels

There is no shortage of accommodation in peak seasons. The main hotels in major cities are of a reasonable standard, but many hotels are frugal, often with fixed-time, fixed-menu meals and even cold water only during certain hours in the evening and morning. There are new hotels built, with foreign assistance, in Nanjing, Guangzhou, Beijing and Zhjanjiang and international-standard joint-venture hotels in Tianjin, Hainan, Xiamen, Fujian, Hangzhou and Shenzen. Charges for government guest houses, which are used to accommodate hotel overflows, are high.

Reservations for business visitors are made by their host organisations. Joint venture hotels are able to accept bookings from outside China. Hotel reservations for over 70 Chinese cities are being computerised.

Tipping is officially forbidden in China, although small tips are occasionally 'expected' by porters in larger hotels. The custom is uneven, and tips will often be refused.

Credit cards

Credit cards are accepted at tourist hotels and tourist shops in major cities. Use of cash or traveller's cheques is more usual. Cash withdrawals from banks are possible with major cards, but are not encouraged and frequently entail long delays.

Public holidays (national)

Fixed dates

1–2 Jan (New Year's Holiday), 1–3 May (May Day), 1–3 Oct (National Day).

Variable dates

Chinese New Year (Jan/Feb)

Working hours

Banking

Mon–Fri: 0900–1200, 1400–1700.

Business

Mon–Fri: 0800–1130, 1300–1700.

Government

Mon–Fri: 0800–1200, 1300–1700.

Shops

Mon–Sun: 0900–1900.

Telecommunications

Telephone/fax

Telephone directories may not be readily available, visitors should keep a note of important telephone numbers.

Mobile/cell phones

GSM 900 service available in eastern provinces.

Electricity supply

220/240V AC, 50Hz. Two-pin sockets and some three-pin sockets used. Mostly flat plug fittings, with two-pin round as well in some hotels, and generally, screw-type light bulb fittings.

Weights and measures

Metric system (with Chinese units in use).

Social customs/useful tips

A ban on smoking in public places came into force on 1 May 2011. The new rules prohibit smoking in restaurants, hotels, railway stations and theatres, but not at the office. It is estimated that up to a third of all smokers in the world are Chinese, and that there are some million smoking-related diseases diagnosed every year. The new rules have been criticised because they do not include punishments for those who choose to ignore them.

Doing business needs patience; punctuality is vital, being especially valued on the part of the visitor. It is customary to present a business card. The full title of the People's Republic of China should be used for formal communications.

If working towards a major contract, ir is a good idea to read the government's five-year plan (currently the 12th, 2011–15) so that you can relate your company or project to the overall picture of China's development. It is always advisable to have a local partner or representative, although personal meetings are important.

Bureaucratic procedures are many and the frustrations of grappling with the Chinese bureaucracy are considerable. The visitor should assume that virtually all negotiations are going to take far longer than expected.

It is advisable to have a destination written in Chinese characters.

Eating can be a tricky business but there are a few important things to remember to save embarrassment on the part of the foreigner. When dining with the Chinese, and certainly with professionals, you should wait until your seat is 'allocated' by a nod or a subtle indication by the host. The Chinese have great respect for authority and title and this determines where a person will be seated at a table. One should not begin eating until indicated to do so. Take care not to 'upset' the presentation of the food as this is considered very offensive. When eating with chopsticks do not position them upright in your ricebowl. The gesture is symbolic of death and should be avoided.

The Chinese are highly 'face' conscious and try to avoid self-embarrassment at all costs. It is important that foreigners endeavour not to mock, satirise or embarrass their Chinese counterparts in any way as this will definitely ruin any developing relationship.

Unofficial contact between foreigners and local Chinese was effectively banned until reforms gathered momentum in the 1980s and 1990s. The borderline of what is permissible remains unclear, and contact by Chinese with some categories of foreigners such as journalists may still attract adverse attention.

Taiwan (Formosa) is considered a province of China, and should not be referred to as a country. It is quite acceptable now adays to discuss Taiwan.

Security

China's cities probably rate among the world's safest after dark, although some, such as Shenzhen and Wuhan have a worse reputation. Thefts are relatively rare, perhaps because the authorities investigate and punish crimes against foreigners with special vigour. The usual precautions should be taken with valuables.

Organised gangs, some of them Hong Kong-based, are reported to operate in the southern city of Guangzhou (formerly Canton). Their methods include drugging and robbing businessmen.

Chinese criminal law is much harsher than in most Western countries, and Chinese society is still very puritanical in sexual matters.

Getting there

Air

An agreement was signed with Taiwan on 13 June 2008 to allow 36 direct flights (18 each) a week to start on 4 July. A further agreement will allow 3,000 tourists per day into each country from 18 July.

National airline: Air China.

International airport/s: Capital, Beijing (PEK), 26km north of the city, with duty-free shop.

Hongqiao (SHA), 12km from Shanghai, with restaurant, shops; Pudong International, 30km from Shanghai, 60 minutes by car. There are special buses; services to and from the city run from 0600–1900. Facilities include internet cafés and short-stay hotel rooms for passengers.

Baiyun International (CAN) 12km north of Guangzhou.

All airports have duty-free shops, banks, restaurants, post offices and business facilities.

Other airport/s: Include: Chengdu; Guilin; Haikou; Kunming and Tianjin.

Airport tax: Departure tax: domestic Rmb50; international Rmb90, to be paid in local currency only, excluding 24-hour transit passengers.

Surface

Road: Motorways have been built between Guangzhou and Shenzhen and Guangzhou and Zhuhai. These roads link the cities of Dongguan, Zhongshan, Foshan, Jiangmen, Huizhou and Shunde to Hong Kong and Macau. Motorway links to major cities from neighbouring countries are few, partly reflecting the fact that most of China's neighbours, including Laos and North Korea, are poorer than China itself.

The Regional Road Corridor Improvement Project, estimated at US$18 billion, to improve Central Asian roads, airports, railway lines and seaports and provide a vital transit route between Europe and Asia was agreed, on 3 November 2007. Six new transit corridors, between Afghanistan, Azerbaijan, China, Kazakhstan, Kyrgyzstan, Mongolia, Tajikistan and Uzbekistan, of mainly roads and rail links, will be constructed, or existing resources upgraded, by 2013. Half the costs with be provided by the Asian Development Bank and other multilateral organisations and the other half by participating countries.

Rail: The Kowloon-Canton Railway Corporation (KCRC) has express trains serving Kowloon-Guangzhou and an indirect Kowloon-Lowu service.

The Trans-Siberian Express operates two weekly services between Beijing and Moscow, one via Ulaanbaatar in Mongolia and a second via Harbin in northern China.

Nanning, in Guangxi province, is linked by rail to Hanoi, Vietnam. A second cross-border track runs from Kunming, the capital of China's south-western province of Yunnan, via Lao Cai, to Hanoi.

Water: Ferry services operate between Weihai and Inchon in South Korea, and between Shanghai and Osaka in Japan.

Getting about

National transport

Air: Air travel is the quickest way of getting around the country. There are several airlines including China Eastern, China Northern, China Southern and Yunnan Airlines. These provide regular services between the major cities, with first-class service on some routes. Flights are frequently overbooked and seats should be confirmed as a matter of course. Independent regional airlines also operate. Tickets not booked through an official guide/travel service should be booked and collected well in advance. Allow plenty of time for inevitable and often prolonged delays in services. Airport announcements are not multilingual.

Road: There are over 1.18 million km of internal roads, around 250,000km are paved, but most are narrow and poorly surfaced making long-distance travel time-consuming. A superhighway links Beijing and Tianjin, and a 138km four-lane toll highway links Hangzhou and the port of Ningbo in Zhejiang Province. These are linked into a network of 12 major highways across the country.

Buses: Extensive, long distance services are available, it is advisable to book seats in advance.

Rail: The rail network in 2011 was around 91,000km of track. Although many lines are electrified, many locomotives are steam-powered. Beijing is the hub of the rail network with lines radiating throughout the country. There are two major railway stations, the Beijing Railway Station and Beijing West Railway Station, which between them run various services to Guangdong, Shanghai, Heilongjiang, Shanxi, Hebei and Kowloon.

In April 2011 Sheng Guangzu, railway minister, confirmed that the government would be spending US$428.8 billion on railway construction over the period to 2015. This was less than previously announced, but will still mean an expansion to 120,000km by 2015.

Operating speeds on bullet train lines was reduced from 350km per hour to 300km in April 2011. The Beijing–Shanghai line, scheduled to open in 2011, will also be reduced to 300km, from the planned 380km.

On 1 July 2006 the 1,930km passenger service between Quighai and Tibet, at elevations of 4,000–4,800 metres, began operating.

Rail services operate between main cities. Deluxe rail services, with opulent German-made sleeping cars and private dining coaches, are available. Generally, rail travel is comfortable and safe, but time-consuming because of the long distances involved.

The 2007/08 budget has set aside US$175bn for railway investment. The China Railway Construction floated on the Shanghai Stock Exchange in February 2008, raising Rmb22.25bn (US$3.1bn). The China Railway Group had previously raised US$5.5bn in December 2007.

Water: Hydrofoil and ferry services operate between Hong Kong and Guangzhou, and also serve Shekou, Shenzhen and Zhuhai. Inland waterways and coastal shipping services are an important form of transport.

City transport

Taxis: Taxi service is available in all major cities, from railway stations, hotels and shopping districts. Not all taxis are metered, but a standard rate per kilometre is regulation check before starting a journey. Taxis may be hailed in the street. Destinations may need to be written down in Chinese characters, as not many drivers speak a foreign language. It may be best to retain a taxi until returning to the hotel and paying the driver a small waiting fee during appointments or meals. Tipping is not practised.

Buses, trams & metro: Beijing has a serious transport problem with heavy congestion during the day and the risk of grid-lock during rush-hours. It has a metro system, with over 60 stations, with an upgrade and new lines, including the Olympic branch line, under construction, most of which are expected to be completed for the 2008 Olympic Games. However for the size of the city and population it is a small operation. The *yikatong* transport card is the only ticket that allows travel on most lines; individual lines have their own, non-transferable tickets. There are also buses, trams and trolleybuses but these are unsuitable for visitors without a working knowledge of Chinese.

There are metro systems in Chongqing, Guangzhou, Nanjing, Shanghai, Shenzhen, Tianjin and Wuhan.

There are extensive local bus services in all main cities, generally inexpensive but crowded and without timetables.

Trains: There are six main, metropolitan railway station that handle traffic from surrounding suburbs and districts.

Car hire

Most rental companies require the driver's passport as deposit, making car rental impractical. Cars with a driver can be hired for a day or week.

Bicycle hire is available in some towns, but it is advisable to carry proof of identity when riding.

BUSINESS DIRECTORY

The addresses listed below are a selection only. While World of Information makes every endeavour to check these addresses, we cannot guarantee that changes have not been made, especially to telephone numbers and area codes. We would welcome any corrections.

Telephone area codes

The International direct dialling (IDD) code for China is +86, followed by the area code:

Beijing	10	Qingdao	532
Chengdu	28	Shanghai	21
Dalian	411	Shenyang	24
Fuzhou	591	Shenzen	755
Guangzhou	20	Tianjin	22
Harbin	451	Wenzhou	577
Jinan	531	Wuhan	27
Lhasa	891	Xi'an	29
Nanjing	25		

Useful telephone numbers

Beijing

Police: 110

International calls, English-language: 337-431, 553-536

Local, long-distance enquiries: 116

Cable and telex information: 664-900

Taxis: 557-671

Airport-flight enquiries: 552-515, 555-531, ext 382

Shanghai

Ambulance: 120

Police: 110

Fire: 119

Taxis for disabled: 6215-5555

Chambers of Commerce

American Chamber of Commerce PRC, 1903 China Resources Building, 8 Jianguomenbai Dajie, Beijing 100005 (tel: 8519-1920; fax: 8519-1910; e-mail: amcham@amcham-china.org.cn).

British Chamber of Commerce in China, China Life Tower, 16 Chaoyangmenwai Avenue, Beijing 100020 (tel: 8525-1111; fax: 8525-1100; email: director@pek.britcham.org).

Banking

China Banking Regulatory Commission, Jia No 15 Financial Street, Xicheng District, Beijing 100140 (tel: 6627-9113; web: www.cbrc.gov.cn)

Agricultural Bank of China, Jia 23 Fu Xing Road, Beijing 100036 (tel: 6847-5321; fax: 6829-7160).

Bank of China, 410 Fuchengmen Nei Dajie, Beijing 100818 (tel: 6601-6688; fax: 6601-6869).

Beijing City Commercial Bank Corp Ltd, 2nd Floor, Tower B Beijing International Financial Building, 156 Fuxingmennei Street, Beijing 100031 (tel: 6642-6928; fax: 6642-6691/9).

Bank of Communications, 18 Xianxia Lu, Shanghai 200335 (tel: 6275-1234; fax: 6275-6784).

China Construction Bank, No 25 Finance Street, Beijing 100032 (tel: 6759-8050; fax: 6759-7353).

China Minsheng Banking Corporation Ltd, 4 Zheng Yi Lu, Dong Cheng District, Beijing 100006 (tel: 6526-9578).

Hua Xia Bank, Xidan International Mansion, No. 111 Xidan North Avenue, Xicheng District, Beijing 100032 (tel: 6615-1199, 6612-9139; fax: 6618-8484).

Central bank

People's Bank of China, 32 Chengfang Street, Xi Cheng District, Beijing 100800 (tel: 6619-4114; fax: 6601-5346; e-mail: webbox@pbc.gov.cn; internet: www.pbc.gov.cn/english).

Stock exchange

Shanghai Stock Exchange (SSE), www.sse.com.cn

Shenzhen Stock Exchange, www.szse.cn

Commodity exchange

Dalian Commodity Exchange (DCE), www.dce.com.cn

Zhengzhou Commodity Exchange (ZCE), http://english.czce.com.cn

Travel information

Air China, Beijing Capital Airport, Beijing 100621 (tel: 6456-3201; fax: 6456-3831; e-mail: webmaster@airchina.com.cn).

Beijing Capital Airport, Beijing 100621(tel: 6456-4247; fax: 6457-0487).

China Eastern Airlines, 2550 Hingqiaolu, Shanghai 200335 (tel: 6268-6268; fax: 6268-6116; e-mail: webmaster@ce-air.com).

China International Travel Service (CITS), 103 Fuxingmennei Dajie, Beijing 100800 (tel: 6601-1122; fax: 6601-2021; e-mail: webmaster@cits.net).

China Southern Airlines, Baiyun International Airport, Guangzhou 510405 (tel: 8612-4738; fax: 8665-9040; e-mail: webmaster@cs-air.com).

Shanghai Hongqiao Airport, Shanghai 200335 (tel: 6269-0029; fax: 6269-0027).

National tourist organisation offices

National Tourism Administration of the People's Republic of China (CNTA), 9A Jianguomennei Avenue, Beijing 100740 (tel: 6520-1114; fax: 6512-2096; internet site: http://www.cnta.gov.cn/lyen/index.asp).

Ministries

Ministry of Agriculture, 11 Nonzhanguan Nanli, Beijing 100026 (tel: 6419-1114; fax: 64192468).

Ministry of Civil Affairs, 147 Beiheyan Dajie, Beijing 100721 (tel: 6523-5511; fax: 6513-5332).

Ministry of Communications, 11 Jianguomennei Dajie, Beijing 100736 (tel: 6529-2114; fax: 6529-2345).

Ministry of Construction, Baiwanzhuang, Haidian District, Beijing 100835 (tel: 6839-3970; fax: 6839-3333).

Ministry of Culture, A83 Dong'anmen Beijie, Beijing 100722 (tel: 6401-2255; fax: 6403: 1266).

Ministry of Defence, 20 Jinshanquianjie, Beijing 100009 (tel: 6673-0000).

Ministry of Education, 37 Damucang Hutong, Xidian, Beijing 100820 (tel: 6609-6114; fax: 6601-1049).

Ministry of Foreign Affairs, 2 Chaonei Dajie, Dongcheng Districti, Beijing 100701 (tel: 8596-1114).

Ministry of Health, 44 Beiheyan, Xicheng District, Beijing 100725 (tel: 6403-4433; fax: 6401-2369).

Ministry of Information Industry, 13 Xichang'anjie, Beijing 10084 (tel: 6601-4249; fax: 6201-6362).

Ministry of Justice, 10 Chaoyangmen Nandajie, Beijing 100020 (tel: 6520-5254).

Ministry of Labour and Social Security, 12 Hepingli Zhongjie, Dongcheng District, Beijing 100716 (tel: 6421-3240).

Ministry of Land and Natural Resources, 64 Funeidajie, Xicheng District, Beijing 100812 (tel: 6616-5566; e-mail: master@mail.mlr.gov.cn).

Ministry of Personnel, 12 Hepingli Zongjie, Beijing 100716 (tel: 6421-3240).

Ministry of Public Security, 14 Dongchang'anjie, Beijing 100741 (tel: 6512-1967).

Ministry of Railways, 10 Fuxinglu, Haidian District, Beijing 100844 (tel: 6324-0114; fax: 6324-2150).

Ministry of Science and Technology, 15 Fuxinglu, Haidian District, Beijing 100038 (tel: 6851-5544; fax: 6851-5004).

Ministry of State Security, 14 Dongchang'anjie, Beijing 100741 (tel: 6524-4702).

Ministry of Supervision, 4 Zaojunmiao, Haidian District, Beijing 100081 (tel: 6225-4129).

Ministry of Water Resources, 2 Ertiao, Baiguanglu, Xuanwu District, Beijing 100053 (tel: 6320-2114; fax: 6320-2650).

Other useful addresses

China International Trust and Investment Corporation (Citic), Capital Mansion, 6 Xinuan Nanlu, Beijing (tel: 6466-0088; fax: 6466-1186; e-mail: g-office@citic.com.cn).

China National Chemicals Import & Export Corporation (Sinochem), A2 Fuxingmenwai Dajie, Beijing 100046 (tel: 6856-8888; fax: 6856-8890).

China National Instruments Import & Export Corporation, Erligou, Xijiao, Beijing 100044 (tel: 6831-7393; fax: 6831-59251).

China National Light Industrial Products Import & Export Corporation (Chinalight), 910 Jinsongjiu Qu, Beijing 100747 (tel: 6776-6688; fax: 6774-7245).

China National Machinery Import & Export Corporation, PO Box 49, Erligou, Xijiao, Beijing (tel: 6849-4851; fax: 6831-4143).

China National Metals & Minerals Import & Export Corporation, Building 15, Block 4, Anhui Li, Chaoyang District, Beijing 100101 (tel: 6491-6666; fax: 6491-7031).

China National Offshore Oil Corporation, PO Box 4705, 6 Dongzhimenwai Xioajie, Beijing 100027 (tel: 8452-1010; fax: 8452-1044; e-mail: webmaster@cnooc.com.cn).

China National Petroleum Corporation, 6 Liupukang Jie, Xicheng District, Beijing 100724 (tel: 6422-2946; fax:

6426-6302; e-mail: webmaster@hq.cnpc.com.cn).

China National Technical Import and Export Corporation (CNTIC), Jiuling Building, 21 Xisanhuan Bei Lu, Beijing 100081 (tel: 6840-4106; fax: 6841-4877).

China Ocean Shipping Agency (PENAVICO), Tower Crest Plaza, 3 Maizidian Road West, Chaoyang District, Beijing (tel: 6461-1188; fax: 6467-3118; e-mail: general@penavico.com.cn).

Chinese Embassy (US), 2300 Connecticut Avenue, NW, Washington DC 20008 (tel: (+1-202) 238-5000; fax: (+1-202) 588-0032; e-mail: chinaembassy_us@fmprc.gov.cn).

Chinese Export Commodities Fair, 117 Liuhua Road, Guangzhou (tel: 8666-1664; fax: 8333-5880; e-mail: info@cecf-info.com).

General Administration of Customs, 6 Jiannei Dajie, Beijing 100730 (tel: 6519-4114; fax: 6519-4004).

Shanghai Advertising Corporation, 117 Xianggang Road, Shanghai 200002 (tel: 6321-7599; 6329-0068).

State Administration for Industry and Commerce, 8 Sanlihe Donglu, Xicheng District, Beijing 100820 (tel: 6803-2233; fax: 6857-0848).

State Administration of Entry-Exit Inspection and Quarantine, A10 Chaowai Dajie, Chaoyang District, Beijing 100020 (tel: 6599-4600; fax: 6599-4306).

National news agency: Xinhua (New China News Agency), Head Office, 20F Dacheng Plaza, 127 Xhuanwumen St (W), Beijing 100031 (email: xxp69@xinhuanet.com; internet: www.xinhuanet.com).

Internet sites

Archive of Chinese news digest, also contains links to other Chinese sites: www.cnd.org.

China Business Pages: www.chinapages.com.

China Web (investment data, Shanghai city information, stock prices, travel arrangements and a searchable directory of key figures in commerce, industry and government): www.comnex.com

China Window information on country, government and business activities: http://china-window.com

Official Chinese Olympic website: http://en.beijing2008.com

Shanghai business: www.sh.com

Colombia

KEY FACTS

Official name: República de Colombia (Republic of Colombia)

Head of State: President Juan Manuel Santos (PSUN) (from 7 Aug 2010; re-elected 15 May 2014)

Head of government: President Juan Manuel Santos

Ruling party: Coalition led by Partido Social de Unidad Nacional (PSUN) (Social National Unity Party), with Partido Liberal Colombiano (PLC) (Colombian Liberal Party) and Cambio Radical (CR) (Radical Change)

Area: 1,138,914 square km

Population: 47.66 million (2014)*

Capital: Santa Fé de Bogotá

Official language: Spanish

Currency: Colombian peso (Col$) = 100 centavos

Exchange rate: Col$3,148.30 per US$ (Sep 2015)

GDP per capita: US$8,076 (2014)*

GDP real growth: 4.55% (2014)*

GDP: US$384.90 billion (2014)*

Labour force: 23.23 million (2012)*

Unemployment: 9.11% (2014)

Inflation: 2.90% (2014)

Oil production: 990,000 bpd (2014)

Natural gas production: 11.80 billion cum (2014)

Balance of trade: -US$4.69 billion (2014)

* estimated figure

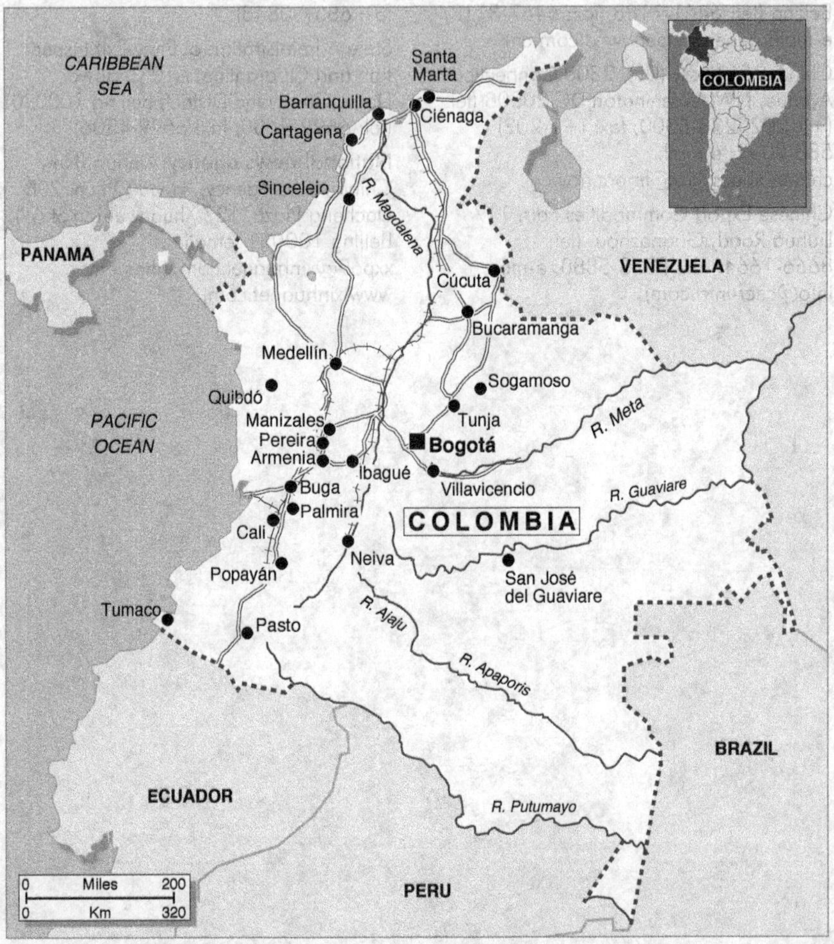

As 2015 began, there were muted hopes in Colombia that the decades long conflict with the Fuerzas Armadas Revolucionarias de Colombia-Ejército del Pueblo (Farc) guerrillas was approaching its end. The new year, it was hoped, promised to be a make or break year in resolving the final differences of what has been a lengthy period of negotiation. Quite apart from the casualties on both sides, the guerrilla warfare created an estimated 5 million internal refugees, fleeing their homes to escape either attacks or retribution. There remained Colombians, with former President Alvaro Uribe at their head, who are opposed to any negotiated peace, but they are almost certainly in a minority.

The Farc negotiations – almost there? Not quite…

The so called Havana 'peace process' between the Colombian government and the Farc had taken a new turn in May 2014 with the announcement of an agreement on the thorny issue of the Farc 's narco-traffic and illegal drugs trade. The narco-agreement was the third deal achieved in the negotiations (the first two had been on the agrarian question and on the guerrillas' eventual participation in the political process) which had been taking place in Cuba since November 2012 and ended five months of negotiation, arriving only one week before the first round of Colombia's presidential elections in May 2014. Additionally, a side agreement was announced between the Farc and its companions in arms, the lesser guerrilla movement, the Ejército de la Liberación (ELN) (Liberation Army).

The agreement on drug trafficking was a major achievement since Colombia's guerrilla movements had traditionally denied any involvement in the activity. The Farc's position had always been that it received an agricultural production levy, a *gramaje* and that it was up to the farmer what he chose to grow. Given the economic attractiveness of marijuana production, it was an inevitably popular crop.

The May 2014 agreement left three areas to be resolved in what had been a lengthy process: reparations, disarmament and agreement on the way in which the Havana agreements would be put to the Colombian electorate for its approval. The totality of the Havana discussions was not to be revealed until final agreement was reached, on the principle that nothing was agreed until everything was agreed. The May Agreement came at a critical moment for President Santos' re-election campaign. The incumbent President's principle election platform was that on his watch the guerrilla activity that had blighted Colombia for some 50 years had been brought to an end. A codicil to the May Agreement was the announcement by both the Farc and the ELN of a week's cease-fire. The announcement came at a moment when polls had showed the Santos campaign stalling. Significantly, the cease-fire announcement was signed by the two leaders of the guerrilla movements, Tímoleon Jiménez (Timochenko) for the Farc and Nicolás Gabino (Gabino) for the ELN. The two leaders also expressed the hope that their initiative would see a corresponding gesture from the government, something that President Santos had simply ruled out. Interviewed by Andrés Oppenheimer for the Spanish daily, *El País* President Santos had claimed that the satisfactory conclusion of the Farc negotiations would see Colombia's gross domestic product (GDP) growth rise to around seven per cent.

Half a truce

In late December 2014 the representatives of the Farc, aka Ejército del Pueblo (EP) (People's Army) initiated a unilateral truce. So far, so good; however, in April 2015 the slaughter of ten soldiers by Farc operatives in the province of Cauca caused indignation among Colombians. Opinion was divided as to whether the government of President Santos should continue with its efforts to establish a bi-lateral truce (which it had been hoped might be concluded in 2016) or whether to abandon its faltering attempts to seek a peaceful end to the guerrilla war.

Thus the May 2015 Farc announcement that it was ending the December 2014 truce hardly came as a surprise to Colombians. Many considered that there had never actually been a truce, inasmuch as the Farc had continued to mount attacks across the country. Alejandro Ordoñez, Colombia's procurador general (attorney general) described the Farc's behaviour as a 'caricature which is simply not being adhered to in practice.' Mr Ordoñez added that he still thought that the peace process should be continued. 'If they don't accept peace, if they don't want peace, they will end up in body bags for waging war against the rights of Colombians.' The government's view was that the Colombian army could not renounce its constitutional responsibilities.

Neither side in the peace negotiations was prepared to accept – publicly at least – that the breaking point had been reached and that the re-integration into society of thousands of Farc officers and soldiers needed, finally, to be addressed. Sooner or later the government need to confront the Farc negotiators with this unpleasantly bald fact and the Farc negotiators would have to accept that a substantial number of their army would have to accept prison sentences. This process, known in the Havana talks as 'transitional justice', was described by President Santos as the most difficult point in ending any conflict.

Government proposals hinged on granting an amnesty for the Farc foot soldiers, but not for Farc officers deemed responsible for war crimes. However, these officers would be tried by specially appointed tribunals. If found guilty they would receive light sentences in specially built prisons. It was thought that the Farc might go along with this as long as there was a reciprocal procedure for those army officers found guilty of similar crimes.

President Santos knew that a complete amnesty was politically unacceptable and that the idea of sending army officers to jail for simply doing their job was anathema to the Colombian military. Whatever was contained in the agreement on this issue would be unsatisfactory for someone or other. But without it no agreement would be forthcoming.

Stopping smoking?

The agreement signed in Cuba on drug trafficking in May 2014 was a major achievement, since Colombia's guerrilla movements had traditionally denied any involvement in the activity. The document signed suggested that once the conflict had been ended, the Colombian authorities would concentrate on encouraging voluntary crop substitution, abandoning the fumigation programme that

KEY INDICATORS Colombia

	Unit	2011	2012	2013	2014	**2015
Population	m	*46.05	*46.60	*47.12	*47.66	*48.21
Gross domestic product (GDP)	US$bn	328.40	369.79	378.42	*384.90	*332.38
GDP per capita	US$	7,132	7,936	*8,031	*8,076	*6,895
GDP real growth	%	5.9	4.2	4.9	*4.6	*3.4
Inflation	%	11.6	3.2	2.0	2.9	*3.4
Unemployment	%	10.8	10.4	9.7	9.1	*9.0
Oil output	'000 bpd	930.0	944.0	1,004.0	990.0	–
Natural gas output	bn cum	11.0	12.0	12.6	11.8	–
Coal output	mtoe	55.8	58.0	55.6	57.6	–
Exports (fob) (goods)	US$m	12,800.0	61,506.0	59,815.1	56,982.1	–
Imports (fob) (goods)	US$m	11,649.0	56,635.0	57,123.9	61,676.1	–
Balance of trade	US$m	1,150.0	4,872.0	2,691.2	-4,694.0	–
Current account	US$m	-9,955.0	-11,846.0	-12,828.0	*-19,291.0	*-19,128.0
Total reserves minus gold	US$m	31,283.0	36,444.0	42,758.0	46,408.0	–
Foreign exchange	US$m	29,750.0	34,920.0	41,196.0	–	–
Exchange rate	per US$	1,827.57	1,806.00	1,938.15	2,376.50	–

* estimated figure ** forecast figure

had for long been the order of the day. A codicil added that in the event of non-co-operation from Farc, the government reserved the right to resume fumigation.

The May 2015 announcement that the Consejo Nacional de Estupefacientes de Colombia (CNE) (National Drug Council) was to cease its fumigation programme was reportedly as requested by President Santos. 'Adjusting the anti-drug policy to reflect reality' had been implicit in remarks made by the President for some time. References to the 'manual elimination of coca' were seen as forerunners of the May announcement, which chimed with the Farc statement that when a full agreement was signed, it would break off all connections with the illicit drug industry.

Land Mines

Despite the shaky climate surrounding the implementation of the December 2014 agreement, in March 2015 the Colombian government and the Farc announced an agreement to clear the landmines sown by the Farc over the guerrilla war's long duration. The International Campaign to Ban Landmines had described the Farc as 'the most prolific' user of the mines in the world. According to the London *Economist*, over 11,000 Colombians have been killed or wounded by land mines, the second highest toll in the world, after Afghanistan. There was a degree of whistling in the wind by the government over the importance of the agreement. The Farc may have proffered assistance in identifying the exact location of mines, they had not given any undertakings to stop laying them.

False positives: murdered Colombians

The peace process was also endangered by the extensive revelations published in late June 2015 by Human Rights Watch (HRW). The US-based organisation had uncovered previously unpublished evidence that implicated a number of Colombian army generals and colonels in a series of 'extrajudicial' killings of civilians between 2002 and 2008. Entitled *On Their Watch: Evidence of Senior Army Officers' Responsibility for False Positive Killings in Colombia*, the 95 page report presented evidence strongly suggesting that numerous generals and colonels knew or should have known about 'false positive' killings and may have ordered or otherwise actively furthered them. The confusing term 'False Positive' killings was used to describe scenarios where members of the military arranged for marginalised and often mentally impaired civilians to be taken to remote parts Colombia with offers of work, murdered and subsequently presented to the authorities as Farc *guerrilleros* killed in battle, thereby inflating body counts and receiving promotions or other benefits. One report suggested that those responsible were paid US$500 per body. Colombian prosecutors were allegedly investigating some 3,000 of these cases, in which troops under pressure to boost body counts killed civilians and reported them as combat fatalities. According to HRW, hundreds of lower-ranking soldiers have been convicted, but just a handful of colonels and no generals.

According to HRW, 'False positive killings amount to one of the worst episodes of mass atrocity in the Western Hemisphere in recent years and there is mounting evidence that many senior army officers bear responsibility. Yet the army officials in charge at the time of the killings have escaped justice and even ascended to the top of the military command, including the current heads of the army and armed forces.' The HRW analysis of official Colombia data indicated that Colombia prosecutors had identified more than 180 battalions and other units that allegedly committed extrajudicial killings between 2002 and 2008. Human Rights Watch also obtained recordings and transcriptions of testimony to prosecutors from military personnel who reported that their superiors, including generals and colonels, allegedly knew of, or planned, ordered, or otherwise facilitated the crimes. HRW claimed that a number of the army officers who commanded the 11 brigades allegedly involved, were later promoted.

Transparent judiciary?

Despite its aspirations to become a member of the Organisation for Economic Co-operation and Development (OECD) Colombia had a rather wretched ranking on the Transparency International *Corruption Perceptions Index*, where it came 94 out of the 175 countries surveyed. This was below such beacons on transparency such as Zambia and Burkina Faso (both of which ranked 85) and Benin (80). Colombia's image was not helped by the 2014 strike by workers in the judiciary, which lasted three months, nor by the allegations that the president of the Constitutional Court had accepted a bribe of 500 million pesos (US$210,000) to issue a ruling in favour of an oil company. Opinion polls suggested that around two-thirds of Colombians mistrusted their high courts. An issue in the closing stages of the Peace Process had been the extent to which Farc members might – or might not – be subsequently prosecuted. The judiciary's state of array was heaven-sent for the Farc negotiators, who announced that they would not be judged by 'this corrupt judicial system'.

The economy

According to the United Nations Economic Commission for Latin America and the Caribbean (ECLAC/CEPAL) in 2014 the Colombian economy continued on a favourable growth trend. It was estimated that growth in gross domestic product (GDP) would out-perform 2013 and expand by 4.8 per cent in 2014. The buoyant economy was evident in soaring domestic demand (especially through investment), which cushioned the affect of the adverse international scenario. The re-election of the incumbent President Santos ensured the continuity of investment programmes, especially for housing and roads. And the peace negotiations taking place in Havana had boosted investor confidence, as had Colombia's commitment to carry out the reforms needed for accession to the OECD.

ECLAC noted that this sound economic performance was not without its problems, owing to both external and internal factors. First, the recovery of international demand was still perceived to be uncertain and the falling prices of oil and other export products had adversely affected Colombia's terms of trade while the country's external deficit had expanded. In the view of ECLAC there had been little progress in terms of productivity; industrial performance had been lacklustre. ECLAC projected economic growth of 4.3 per cent for 2015.

Colombia's fiscal performance for 2014 was in line with the fiscal rule. The consolidated public sector deficit was likely to be equal to 1.6 per cent of GDP – up 0.5 percentage points over 2013. The reason was a central government deficit that, at 2.4 per cent of GDP, was similar to the figure posted for 2013, combined with a decentralised sector surplus that fell to 0.9 per cent of GDP over the same period. Central government tax revenue for 2014 totalled 14.8 per cent of GDP, which was 0.5 percentage points higher than in 2013. Income tax (7.2 per cent of GDP) accounted for some 50 per cent of that revenue, thanks to the equality income tax (CREE) initiative approved under the

2012 tax reform. Government spending grew by 8.8 per cent in 2014 to stand at 19.5 per cent of GDP. Investment spending was down, without affecting the amount equivalent to 1.6 per cent of GDP allocated to infrastructure and housing programmes. The decentralised sector posted a smaller surplus as Colombia local authorities, whose term of office was due to end 2015, sped up the pace of expenditure execution. The tax reforms proposed by the administration in October 2014 were expected to yield the additional resources needed to step up investment in 2015. The reform bill called for a new wealth tax, an equality income tax surcharge and the possibility of coming into compliance with tax obligations by paying a fee equal to 10 per cent of assets not reported on previous tax returns; this was significantly lower than the applicable fine. The bill also proposed making it a crime to omit assets from tax returns when large amounts of capital were involved. Signs of inflationary pressures that began to appear in the first few months of the year had led the Colombian authorities to change their monetary policy stance in April 2014, when they began to scale back monetary stimulus. The positive economic growth underpinned by domestic demand, falling unemployment, rising household incomes and growth in bank lending, fuelled a larger than expected rise in prices, leading the monetary authority to progressively raise the bank intervention rate by 1.25 percentage points between April and September 2014. The contractionary policy was transmitted to lending and borrowing rates; bank loan portfolio growth thus slowed somewhat to post an annual increase of 13 per cent by September (3.1 percentage points lower than in September 2013).

ECLAC noted that JP Morgan's announcement that it would gradually increase the weighting of Colombia's debt in two of its bond indexes boosted the flow of dollars into the country and set off further gains in the value of the peso starting in March. During the first half of 2014, the Colombian peso appreciated in nominal terms against the dollar (2.2 per cent) but depreciated by 7.8 per cent compared with the first half of 2013. In 2014 the Banco de la República (central bank) maintained and reinforced its policy of building up reserves, which stood at US$47 billion in November. In the second half of the year, this measure, combined with declining foreign exchange inflows (due to falling oil prices and the expected hike in the United States Federal Reserve's intervention rate as growth takes hold there) steepened the peso's devaluation.

Colombia's falling exports and rising balance-of-payments current account deficit were, in the view of ECLAC, a warning sign that reflected weak international demand and declining international prices for oil and other export products. By late in the first half of 2014, the balance of goods had turned negative; this had not happened since 2007. Along with the decline in mining and energy product prices, their export volume had dropped as well, owing to production and transport problems. Moreover, the temporary closure of the Cartagena refinery made it necessary to step up imports of fuels and derivatives, which increased the negative balance between exports and imports. The 15.3 per cent cumulative growth of agricultural exports (especially coffee, bananas and flowers) from January to August 2014 did not offset the slump in mining and energy export value. The service balance deficit widened by 5.6 per cent owing above all to growth in spending on travel; the transfer surplus (mainly remittances) narrowed by 11.8 per cent. The net factor income balance decreased by 6.2 per cent during the first half of 2014 as remittances of profits and dividends on foreign investment in Colombia declined. By November foreign direct investment (FDI) flows stood at US$13.376 billion, 6.2 per cent below the figure for the same month of 2013 but still enough to cover the increase in the current account deficit. The high GDP growth seen in the first quarter of 2014 (6.5 per cent) moderated in the second quarter (4.3 per cent). During the first six months of the year, the Colombian economy grew by 5.4 per cent over the same period in 2013. The fastest-growing sectors were construction (14.2 per cent), financial, insurance, real estate and business services (6.1 per cent) and social, community and personal services (6.1 per cent). During the same period, industrial activity grew by only 0.9 per cent, held back by the appreciation of the peso and the decline in traditional exports. Mining, too, posted weak growth (1.7 per cent) owing to oil exploitation and production issues and low crude oil prices. On the demand side, economic growth was driven by the expansion of private investment (17.1 per cent) and final consumption expenditure (8.9 per cent). In October, the year-on-year variation in prices reached 3.3 per cent, which was within the inflation target range of 2–4 per cent. But a rise in prices expected in late 2014 would push inflation above the long term goal set by the monetary authority (3 per cent). This increase in inflation stems from high food prices owing to weather events and depreciation of the local currency.

The labour market continued to improve in 2014. The average national participation rate between January and September was 63.8 per cent (unchanged from the previous year); the national unemployment rate fell from 10.1 per cent to 9.4 per cent thanks to the rising level of employment. Economic growth and the job formalisation strategy, especially in the fastest-growing sectors, pushed wage employment up by 4.2 per cent between January and October. Lastly, the incidence of monetary poverty dropped 2.9 percentage points during the rolling year between July 2013 and June 2014 as household incomes rose thanks to labour improvements and subsidies targeting the poorest households.

Energy

According to the United States government's Energy Information Administration (EIA), in recent years Colombia has increased its importance as an energy producer in the Western Hemisphere. Colombia is currently the third-largest oil producer in Latin America and is the seventh-largest crude exporter to the United States. It is also the largest coal producer in South America. A series of regulatory reforms to make the oil and natural gas sector more attractive to foreign investors led to an increase in Colombian production. The government implemented a partial privatisation of the state oil company, Ecopetrol, (formerly known as Empresa Colombiana de Petróleos SA) in an attempt to revive its upstream oil industry. However, after nearly a half-decade of relatively secure operations, guerrilla attacks on oil and natural gas pipelines appeared to have increased and disruptions to oil supply averaged about 45,000 barrels per day (bpd) in 2014.

According to the *Oil and Gas Journal* (OGJ), Colombia had more than 2.4 billion barrels of proved crude oil reserves in January 2015. Although exploration continues and discoveries are announced, Colombian officials estimate that, at current reserve levels, the current oil reserves will only last about seven years. Much of Colombia's crude oil production occurs in the Andes foothills and in the eastern Amazonian jungles. Meta department, in central Colombia, is also an important production area, predominately of heavy crude oil. The area's Llanos basin contains the Rubiales oilfield, the largest producing oil field in the country.

According to the EIA, Colombia produced one million bpd of petroleum and other liquids in 2014, which included crude oil, condensate, natural gas plant liquids, other liquids and refinery processing gain. Colombia's oil production has increased by an annual average of almost 10 per cent since 2008, but in recent years growth has slowed leaving any growth in production relatively flat from 2013 to 2014. Colombia consumed 290,000bpd in 2014, allowing it to export most of its oil production. Before 2008, Colombia's oil production had been largely flat for many years, following a period of steady decline that started in 1999 when oil production peaked at 830,000bpd. The principal causes of the fall in oil production were natural declines at existing oil fields and a lack of new reserve discoveries. However, the changes made to the regulatory framework led to higher levels of investment in the country by international oil companies. As a result of these improvements, Colombia experienced rapid growth in oil production between 2008 and 2013. However, increased rebel attacks on oil infrastructure and a lower world oil price led to a levelling off of production in 2014. In the May 2015 edition of its *Short Term Energy Outlook*, the EIA projected that Colombian oil production would remain steady over the following two years, averaging one million bpd in 2015 and 2016.

In 2014, according to the EIA, the United States was Colombia's top oil export destination, followed by China, Panama and India. In that year, Colombia exported 294,000bpd of crude oil to the United States. Crude oil exports to the United States have fallen more than 100,000bpd since 2012 because of strong crude production growth in the US itself. China has expressed an interest in financing new infrastructure projects in Colombia to facilitate the transport of oil to the Pacific coast for export. In May 2012, agreements were made for the China Development Bank to finance a 600,000bpd pipeline to transport Colombian and Venezuelan oil to the south Colombian Pacific coast starting in 2016.

Natural gas

Colombia had proved natural gas reserves of 6.4 trillion cubic feet (tcf) in January 2015. The bulk of Colombia's natural gas reserves are located in the Llanos basin, although the Guajira basin accounts for most current production. Natural gas production, like oil production, has risen substantially in the past few years, because of increasing international investment in exploration and development. Colombia produced 360 billion cubic feet (bcf) of dry natural gas in 2013 and consumed 269bcf. Of the country's total gross natural gas production, about half was reinjected to aid in enhanced oil recovery. In 2007, natural gas production had begun to exceed consumption, allowing for exports.

Three companies – Ecopetrol, Equión Energía (a partnership between Ecopetrol and Talisman Energy) and Chevron – account for most of Colombia's natural gas production. Ecopetrol operates the Cupiagua and Cupiagua Sur fields in the large Llanos Basin in eastern Colombia. Equion Energia, formed after Ecopetrol and Talisman Energy acquired BP's Colombian assets in 2010, operates the Cusiana, Cusiana Norte and Cupiagua Liria fields, also in the Llanos Basin. Chevron, in partnership with Ecopetrol, operates the Caribbean Chuchupa offshore field in the Guajira basin, the largest non-associated natural gas field in the country. The company also operates the nearby onshore Ballena and Riohacha fields.

The Colombian government published a decree in March 2011 outlining plans to increase domestic natural gas production, including production from shale or coalbed methane gas fields. Policies aimed at increasing domestic natural gas consumption and exports, combined with increased demand from the power sector as a result of weather-related hydroelectric shortages, have made expanding natural gas production a priority for the government.

Coal

Colombia was the fifth-largest coal exporter in the world in 2013. According to the BP Statistical Review of World Energy 2015 Colombia had 6,746 million short tons (MMst) of probable coal reserves (mostly bituminous coal) in 2014, the largest in South America. These deposits are concentrated in the Guajira peninsula bordering the Caribbean and in the Andean foothills. Most of Colombia's coal production and export infrastructure is located on the Caribbean coast. Colombia's coal is relatively clean-burning, with a sulphur content of less than 1 per cent. Colombia exports most of its coal production and was the fifth-largest coal exporter in the world in 2012 after Indonesia, Australia, Russia and the United States.

Colombia produced 94.2MMst of coal in 2014, while only consuming 7.4MMst. Colombian coal production is exclusively carried out by private companies and according to the EIA, has doubled since 2002. The largest coal producer in Colombia is the Carbones del Cerrejón (Cerrejón) consortium, composed of Anglo-American, BHP Billiton and Xstrata. The consortium operates the Cerrejón Zona Norte (CZN) project, the largest coal mine in Latin America and among the largest open-pit coal mines in the world. CZN is an integrated system connecting the mine, railroad and a Caribbean coast export terminal. US-based Drummond Company, the second-largest coal producer in Colombia, operates two mines near La Loma, in the Cesar Basin. In June 2011, Drummond entered into an 80 per cent/20 per cent partnership with Japan's Itochu Corporation known as Drummond International, which now owns and operates its Colombia interests. Itochu's initial investment of US$1.5 billion enabled the expansion and construction of a new export facility, increasing Drummond's export capacity to 60MMst per year. The partnership aims to increase coal exports to Japan and other Asian countries.

Risk assessment

Politics	Fair
Economy	Good
Regional stability	Good

COUNTRY PROFILE

1820 Colombia became independent from Spain.

1800s Outbreaks of fighting erupted sporadically throughout the nineteenth century, often between anti-clerical Liberals and pro-church Conservatives.

1899–1903 The (Civil) War of 1,000 Days in which some 100,000 people were killed. Panama separated from Colombia during the war and became an independent state.

1930 A Liberal president was elected, leading to social reform.

1948–57 The two major parties, the Partido Social Conservador (PSC) (Social Conservative Party) and the Partido Liberal (PL) (Liberal Party) became more extreme – the Conservatives veering towards fascism and the Liberals towards left-wing populism. Civil war broke out, resulting in up to 300,000 deaths.

1957 The civil war ended when the PSC and PL agreed on a power-sharing pact with the presidency going alternately to a PL then PSC member, with seats in cabinet and Congress to be split equally.

1965 The Ejército de Liberación Nacional (ELN) (National Liberation Army) and the

Maoist People's Liberation Army were founded.
1966 Another and largest rebel group, the Fuerzas Armadas Revolucionarias de Colombia-Ejército del Pueblo (Farc) (Revolutionary Armed Forces of Colombia-Peoples' Army), was formed.
1971 After disputed elections, elements of the defeated Alianza Nacional Popular (Anapo) formed an armed movement (M-19) to fight the PSC government. They were joined by dissident members of the Farc.
1970s Guerrilla violence increased, at the same time as an increase in cocaine production.
1982 President Belisario Betancur granted guerrillas an amnesty and freed political prisoners.
1984 The assassination of the justice minister led to a step-up in the government war on drug traffickers.
1985 M-19 guerrillas stormed the Palace of Justice, killing 11 judges and 90 other people. The Andean volcano, Nevado del Ruiz, erupted and killed around 23,000 people in four surrounding towns.
1986 Virgolio Barco Vargas (PL) won an overwhelming victory in the presidential election. Violence became endemic as right-wing paramilitaries targeted PL politicians, left-wing groups carried out insurgency actions and death squads were controlled and sent out by drug cartels.
1989 A peace agreement between the government and M-19 allowed it to become a legal political party; other guerrilla groups remained active. PL and Unión Patriótica (UP) Patriotic Union (founded by Farc) presidential candidates were killed on the hustings, allegedly by drug cartels.
1991 A new constitution legalised divorce and gave indigenous people democratic rights.
1993 The infamous Medellin drugs lord, Pablo Escobar, was shot dead while trying to evade police arrest.
1994 Ernesto Samper won the presidential election.
1998 Andrés Pastrana Arango won the presidential election, bringing the Partido Conservador Colombiano (PCC) (Colombian Conservative Party) to power and ending 12 years of rule by the PL. In a move to allow peace talks to continue uninterrupted, the government agreed on a demilitarised area where military action against rebel groups would be suspended.
1999 President Pastrana began formal peace talks with the Farc in an attempt to end the region's longest-running civil war; after only two weeks the talks stalled. The two rebel movements, the Farc and the ELN, were estimated to control 40 per cent of Colombia. The president's *Plan Colombia* won US$1 billion in US support through the anti-drug trafficking and insurgency plan. The peace talks broke down with recrimination on both sides.
2000 President Pastrana issued 11 emergency decrees to increase the armed forces from 10,000 to 42,000, with further increases to 52,000 by end-2001. The demilitarised area order was revoked.
2001 Pastrana agreed to extend the life of the demilitarised areas for a further eight months; Farc released 359 police and military in exchange for 14 rebel prisoners. An agreement to negotiate a cease-fire was signed.
2002 After three years of complex peace talks Pastrana broke off negotiations with Farc and ordered rebels out of the demilitarised area and stepped up a government crackdown. Threats from Farc and the Autodefensas Unidas de Colombia (AUC) (United Self-Defence Forces of Colombia) hindered electoral campaigning in rural areas, despite a security operation involving 150,000 troops and police; only 48 per cent of the population voted. The political party linked to the Farc, Unión Patriótica (UP) (Political Union), failed to present any candidates for the election and lost its legal standing. Presidential candidate Ingrid Betancourt was kidnapped by Farc while campaigning. The PCC and the PL remained the largest groups in the legislature. Álvaro Uribe won the presidential election.
2003 Uribe's legislation raised tax revenues and boosted funding for the state pension system. Certain regional factions of the AUC disarmed.
2004 Farc guerrilla leader Ricardo Palmera was sentenced to 35 years imprisonment. The right-wing AUC movement and the government began peace talks.
2005 An international confrontation erupted when a leading Farc guerrilla commander was captured in Venezuela. The Presidents of both countries held a summit to resolve the matter. The national government passed new legislation, reducing jail terms for members of paramilitary groups who surrendered and disarmed. Tentative peace talks began, in Cuba, between the government and ELN, the second-largest rebel group.
2006 A disarmament agreement with right-wing paramilitaries led to a reported 20,000 fighters surrendering their weapons and being pardoned and retrained for civilian life. Colombia and the US signed a free-trade agreement. President Álvaro Uribe won re-election and the Partido Social de Unidad Nacional (PSUN) (Social National Unity Party) formed a coalition government in support of the president.
2008 Ecuador cut diplomatic relations with Colombia after Colombia took pre-emptive strikes against terrorists of Farc hiding out in Ecuador, killing senior Farc leader Raul Reyes. The founder and leader of Farc, Manuel Marulanda, died. Ingrid Betancourt, captured by Farc in 2002, was freed by government troops.
2009 Farc continued to release foreign and high profile hostages. The president offered a cease-fire with Farc in return for a cessation in criminal activities.
2010 In parliamentary elections, over 2,500 candidates contested seats in both houses. The ruling PSUN coalition won 101 seats (out of 166) in the chamber of representatives and 58 seats (out of 102) in the senate. Following two rounds of presidential elections , Juan Manuel Santos (PSUN) won with 69.1 per cent of the vote, Antanas Mockus (PV), his nearest rival, was runner-up with 27.5 per cent. President Chavez of Venezuela severed diplomatic ties with Colombia, objecting to claims by Colombia that Venezuela was harbouring Farc guerrillas.
2011 In the latest army tactic of combatting Farc by targeting high-ranking members, the Farc security chief was killed by the army in June. In response Farc formed an elite unit (called Teófilo Forero) to engage in hit-and-run attacks on villages and military posts and kidnapping for extortion. The UN reported in June that annual cultivation of coca had fallen by 15 per cent in 2010, a drop for the third year running, as acres of coca crops fell from 182,500 in 2009 to 155,000 acres in 2010. The on-going result was credited to *Plan Colombia*, in which billions of US dollars in aid funds efforts for countering drug trafficking. A trade agreement with the US was agreed by both houses of the US congress in October. A military operation which targeted a Farc encampment resulted in the death of Farc's leader (since 2008), Alfonso Cano (real name Guillermo Leon Saenz), in November.
2012 In February, Farc announced that it would stop its campaign of kidnapping for ransom and that it was prepared to release six military and police hostages currently being held. President Santos welcomed the news confirming that halting kidnapping was an 'important and necessary step in the right direction, but it's not enough.' Civilian hostages of Farc were not mentioned in its announcement. On 28 August, President Santo announced that secret meetings with Farc had resulted in the planned resumption of peace negotiations. On 19 October, talks got underway, with representatives from Norway and Venezuela acting as 'honest brokers'. On 2 December President Santos set a deadline of November 2013 for reaching an agreement with Farc. On 19 November, the International Court of Justice (ICJ) rejected Nicaragua's claim to

ownership of a group of seven disputed islets in the Caribbean and awarded them and the seabed around them to Colombia. The maritime border was redrawn and more sea territory (including fishing grounds) was awarded to Nicaragua. However, President Santos rejected this aspect of the court's decision, despite the ICJ ruling being binding. On 28 November the government announced that it was withdrawing Colombia's recognition of the jurisdiction of the ICJ.

2013 The Farc linked UP party regained its legal standing, lost in 2002 when it refused to put forward candidates for the election. President Santos announced on 16 July that the ELN, the second largest armed group after the Farc, had laid down their arms. Although not part of the peace talks with the Farc they have expressed an interest in joining the negotiations. The government has insisted that they must first release their hostages. On 19 August farm workers went on strike, blocking roads and leaving the central province of Boyaca cut off. The farmers were striking for subsidies on farm products and cheaper fuel. Within a week there were concerns that Bogota could face shortages of basics such as milk and potatoes. The President met with strikers on 26 August and later said that ministers would work with strike leaders to settle the dispute. Colombia was beaten into second place by Peru as the world's largest producer of coca leaves in 2013. By 6 November the government and Farc had agreed on a political future should talks, being held in Cuba, lead to a peace deal.

2014 Parliamentary elections wre held on 14 March. The main party winners were: PSUN with 16.05 per cent (48 seats, out of 166), PLC 14.13 per cent (37), PCC 13.17 per cent (27), PCR 7.74 per cent (16), CD 9.47 per cent (12), PV 3.35 per cent (six), OC 3.26 per cent (six), PDA 2.89 per cent (four). The first round of the presidential election were held on 25 May. Óscar Iván Zuluaga (CD) headed the list with 29.25 per cent of the vote, followed by Juan Manuel Santos (PSUN) 25.69 per cent, Marta Lucía Ramírez (PCC) 15.52 per cent, Clara López Obregón (PDA) 15.23 per cent and Enrique Peñalosa (PV) 8.28 per cent. Turnout was 40.07 per cent. Since no candidate won more than 50 per cent a second round was held on 15 June and was won by the incumbent Santos with 50.95 per cent of the vote, followed by Zuluaga 45.00 per cent. Turnout was 47.89 per cent. Talks being held in Cuba, that had begun in 2012, between government officials and the Farc were joined by a group of some 60 victims for the first time in August. Navi Pillay, UN High Commissioner for Human Rights praised the move, calling it unprecedented. The main points at issue are land reform, political participation, illicit drugs, rights of the victims, disarmament and peace deal implementation. On 17 December Farc rebels declared a unilateral ceasefire for an indefinite period, starting 20 December. President Santos did not immediately agree to suspend military action, saying the rebels would use a bilateral truce to rearm and regroup.

2015 A unilateral cease-fire declared by Farc began. President Santos, said that the government will de-escalate its attacks on the guerrillas. On 6 October the public prosecutor called for an investigation into whether former president Alvaro Uribe was linked to a massacre carried out by paramilitaries in 1997.

Political structure

Constitution

The current constitution dates from 6 July 1991. Colombia has a representative democracy composed of an executive, legislative and a judicial branch.

Administratively, the country is divided into 32 departments ruled by governors, representing the executive branch, and a Departmental Assembly representing the legislative branch. Cities are governed by a mayor and a municipal council. All are elected by democratic vote.

In 2005, sitting president Álvaro Uribe amended the constitution to allow for the re-election of a president in successive periods. One year later, Uribe became the first president to utilise this change and served his second term from 2006-2010.

Colombian citizens aged 18 and over are eligible to vote.

Form of state

Presidential democratic republic

The executive

Executive power is vested in the president, elected by universal adult suffrage for four years but not for consecutive terms. The president appoints a cabinet.

National legislature

The bicameral Congreso de la República (Congress of the Republic) (lower house) is composed of the Cámara de Representantes (Chamber of Representatives), with 166-members. The Chamber may examine the budget and treasury audit, review government actions and impeach senior national office holders. The Senado de la República (Senate of the Republic) (upper house) has 102 members. Among other things the Senate may approve or reject the resignation of the executive and military promotions and authorise the government to declare a war. All Congress members are elected for four-year terms by proportional representation from party lists.

Legal system

The judicial system maintains formal independence but has experienced problems operating normally in circumstances that have extended to massed attacks using heavy firepower on major court institutions.

Last elections

9 March 2014 (parliamentary); 25 May and 15 June 2014 (presidential, first and second round)

Results: Chamber of Representatives (9 March 2014): Partido Social de Unidad Nacional (PSUN) (Social National Unity Party) 16.05 per cent (48 seats out of 166), Partido Liberal Colombiano (PLC) (Colombian Liberal Party) 14.13 per cent (37), Partido Conservador Colombiano (PCC) (Colombian Conservative Party) 13.17 per cent (27), Partido Cambio Radical (PCR) (Radical Change Party) 7.74 per cent (16), Centro Democrático (CD) (Democratic Center) 9.47 per cent (12), Partido Verde (PV) (Green Party) 3.35 per cent (six), Opción Ciudadana (OC) (Civic Option) 3.26 per cent (6), Polo Democrático Alternativo (PDA) (Alternative Democratic Pole) 2.89 per cent (four), Movimiento Independiente de Renovación Absoluta (Independent Movement of Absolute Renovation) 2.87 per cent (three), Por un Huila Mejor (For a Better Huila) 0.51 per cent (one), Fundacion Ebano de Colombia (Ebony Foundation of Colombia) 0.41 per cent (one), Movimiento de Inclusión y Oportunidades (Inclusion and Opportunities Movement) 0.13 per cent (one), Autoridades Indígenas de Colombia (Indigenous Authorities of Colombia) 0.19 per cent (one). Turnout was 43.57 per cent.

Senate: PSUN won 15.58 per cent of the vote (21 seats out of 102), CD 14.29 per cent (19), PCC 13.58 per cent (19), PLC 12.22 per cent (17), PCR 6.96 per cent (nine), PV 3.94 per cent (five), PDA 3.78 per cent (five), OC 3.68 per cent (five), Movimiento Alternativo Indigena y Social (Indigenous and Alternative Social Movement) 0.32 per cent (one), Alianza Social Independiente (Indigenous Social Alliance) 0.21 per cent (one). Turnout was 43.58 per cent.

Presidential first round (25 May 2014): Juan Manuel Santos (PSUN) 25.69 per cent of the vote, Óscar Iván Zuluaga (CD) 29.25 per cent, Marta Lucía Ramírez (PCC) 15.52 per cent, Clara López Obregón (PDA) 15.23 per cent, Enrique Peñalosa (PV) 8.28 per cent. Turnout was 40.07 per cent. Second round (15 June 2014): Santos won 50.95 per cent of the vote, Zuluaga 27.5 per cent. Turnout was 47.89 per cent.

Next elections

2018 (presidential and parliamentary)

Political parties

Ruling party

Coalition led by Partido Social de Unidad Nacional (PSUN) (Social National Unity Party), with Partido Liberal Colombiano (PLC) (Colombian Liberal Party) and Cambio Radical (CR) (Radical Change)

Main opposition party

Centro Democratico (CD) (Democratic Centre)

Population

47.15 million (2013)*

The population is projected to reach 52.6 million by 2015. About 34 per cent of the total population is under the age of 15 years.

22 May 2005: 41,468,384

Population density: 39 inhabitants per square km. Urban population 75 per cent (2010 Unicef).

Annual growth rate: 1.7 per cent, 1990–2010 (Unicef).

Internally Displaced Persons (IDP)

*3.1 million (UNHCR 2004)

*estimate

Ethnic make-up

Mestizo 57 per cent, white 20 per cent, mulatto 14 per cent, Indian 1 per cent, and others 8 per cent.

Religions

Roman Catholicism is the official religion and the vast majority of Colombians consider themselves Catholic. There is freedom of worship.

Education

Financing for the education sector is decentralised and municipalities are required to use 30 per cent of the resources transferred to them from central government for education purposes.

Although the illiteracy rate averages 8 per cent among adults over 15 years of age, drop-out rates are increasing on an annual basis; Oxfam estimates that one in every four children drops out before completing primary education and girls' enrolment rates, estimated at 65 per cent, are at least 30 per cent lower than boys' enrolment rates. Primary education has also suffered due to cuts in government budget, while per capita spending is 12 times higher in the tertiary sector.

The New School Programme, known as the *Escuela Nueva*, was begun in the mid-1970s and governs the principles of the Colombian education system. It emphasises flexible school schedules and an appropriate curriculum catering to the needs of the poor rural areas.

Literacy rate: 92 per cent adult rate; 97 per cent youth rate (15–24) (Unesco 2005).

Compulsory years: Nine years in urban areas

Five years in rural areas

Enrolment rate: 113 per cent in primary; 67 per cent in secondary, of relevant age groups (including repitition rates) (World Bank).

Pupils per teacher: 25 in primary schools

Health

HIV/Aids

HIV prevalence: 0.7 per cent aged 15–49 in 2003 (World Bank)

Life expectancy: 73 years, 2010 (Unicef 2012)

Fertility rate/Maternal mortality rate: 2.4 births per woman, 2010 (FAO 2012); maternal mortality 80 per 100,000 live births (World Bank).

Child (under 5 years) mortality rate (per 1,000): 18 per 1,000 live births (WHO 2012); 7 per cent of children aged under five were malnourished (World Bank).

Head of population per physician: 1.35 physicians per 1,000 people, 2002 (WHO 2006)

Welfare

UN agency World Food Programme (WPF) stated that in 2003 there were two million internally displaced persons (IDP) who had fled their homes due to conflict and violence; 80 per cent of the two million lacked access to food production.

Food aid is being provided for over 300,000 people, particularly in the northern states. International medical aid provides primary care, prenatal treatment and vaccinations for victims of the internal conflict, and the rural and urban disadvantaged.

Pensions

Colombia undertook major reforms in its pension system in the 1990s by shifting its priorities from government-run pay-as-you-go systems to multi-tier systems characterised by a privately run and fully-funded scheme. New workers have the choice of a pay-as-you-go defined-benefit as the primary system, if they prefer. An individual can only be a member of one scheme. In addition, there is a redistributive scheme for the elderly poor who are not entitled to a social insurance pension. Estimates show that only 30 per cent of individuals above the age of 60, or 2 per cent of the population, receive a pension. Consequently, compared to other industrial countries, the average pension remains very high and is estimated at about twice the GDP per capita.

Main cities

Bogotá (capital, estimated population 7.5 million (m) in 2012, 2,640 metres above sea-level), Medellín (2.4m), Cali (2.3m), Barranquilla (1.1m), Cartagena (943,163), Cucuta (617,932), Bucaramanga (526,923), Ibagué (513,671), Santa Marta (464,771), Villavicencio (436,978). More than 40 cities have populations of over 100,000.

Languages spoken

Some 200 Indian dialects are spoken. English is spoken in the business community.

Official language/s

Spanish

Media

Colombia is one of the most dangerous countries in the world for journalists to work in, with intimidation coming from drug runners, guerrillas, paramilitary groups and corrupt politicians.

Press

Dailies: There are many newspapers, in Spanish, including *El Espectador* (www.elespectador.com), *El Tiempo* (www.eltiempo.com) and *El Nuevo Siglo* (www.elnuevosiglo.com.co) are owned by political parties, *Vanguardia Liberal* (www.vanguardia.com) and *El Espacia* (www.elespacio.com.co) is an evening edition. Other provincial dailies include *El Colombiano* (www.elcolombiano.com) and *El Mundo* (www.elmundo.com) from Medellín, *Diario Occidente* (www.diariooccidente.com.co), from Cali and *El Heraldo* (www.elheraldo.com.co) from Barranquilla.

Weeklies: In Spanish, *Semana* (www.semana.com) is a news magazine with several specialist imprints. *Reviste Gatopardo* (www.gatopardo.com) and *Revista Diner* (www.revistadiners.com.co).

Business: In Spanish, dailies include *La Republica* (www.la-republica.com.co) is an authoritative newspaper, *Portafolio* (www.portafolio.com.co), *La Nota Económica* (www.lanota.com), also publishes special supplements. *Deporte y Negocios (Sports & Business)* (www.deporteynegocios.com) is a monthly magazine.

Broadcasting

The Comisión de Regulación de Telecommunicaciones is responsible for all broadcasting regulations. The national broadcaster is the Radio Televisíon Nacional de Colombia (RTVC) (www.rtvc.gov.co).

Broadcasting is closely controlled by the government although most programmes are produced by commercial companies.

Radio: RTCV operates Radio Nacional de Colombia (www.radionacionaldecolombia.gov.co) with music and cultural programmes for news. Radio Continental de Noticias (RCN) (www.rcn.com.co) operates a national network of 27 stations across the frequencies offering programmes of news, music and culture, for all audiences including the young and international listeners.

There are many local and regional commercial stations including La Z (www.laz92.com), Radio Activa (www.radioactiva.com.co) and Caracol Cadena Basica (www.caracol.com.co) with news programmes, from Bogata and Tropicana Estereo (www.tropicanafm.com) from Cartagena.
Television: There are over 30 TV stations broadcasting a wide variety of channels and programmes via cable and satellite facilities providing local, regional and national services. Most people gather their news from television.
RTCV operates Señal Colombia (www.senalcolombia.tv) with cultural and information programmes. Other national networks include Caracol TV (www.canalcaracol.com) and RCN Television (www.rcntv.com), showing domestically produced news, cultural, entertainment and sports programmes
Other news agencies: Prensa Latina: www.plenglish.com

Economy

The wealth of Colombia lies in its natural resources, which constitutes the majority of its exports. At the end of 2014 oil reserves were 2.4 billion barrels with production at 990,000 barrels per day (bpd), a reduction of 1.4 per cent on the 2013 production levels. In 2014, natural gas reserves were 200 billion cubic metres (cum), with production of 11.8 billion cum; coal reserves were 6.7 billion tonnes with production at 57.6 million tonnes of oil equivalent (mtoe). Oil exports in 2014 totalled 4099 barrels per day. The net energy export percentage of GDP was equivalent to 8.4 in the same year. In 2014, Colombia attracted US$16,053,845,090 FDI. Agricultural products for export include coffee, bananas and cut flowers.
GDP growth in 2014 was 4.6 per cent, a decrease of 0.3 per cent from the previous year. Long-term unemployment is a problem, with a rate in double digits for all of the 2000s, with the national rate year-on-year of 12.1 per cent in May 2010. Unemployment was measured at 9.2 per cent in 2014. Some regional cities have fared worse than others with the highest unemployment rate of 21.3 per cent recorded in Pereira and 18 per cent in Armenia. Remittances were at a record high in 2008, of US$4.9 billion (2 per cent of GDP), which fell steadily to US$4.1 billion (1.5 per cent of GDP) in 2010. However remittances were estimated to have risen to US$4.2 billion in 2011. This figure has not changed too significantly since, with remittances recorder at US$4.166 billion in 2014.
The illegal production and export of cocaine underpins some of the economy; in 2009 smuggled cocaine was estimated to be valued up to US$13 billion and with no of signs of reduction. Recent figures for the illicit trade estimated that the industry earns around 5–10 per cent of Colombia's GDP. Drug trafficking not only undermines the rule of law but denies the national treasury revenue that would otherwise come to it if the work undertaken was legitimate. It has promoted paramilitary organisations in isolated regions of the country to usurp legitimate governance through violence, intimidation, bribery and political corruption. It has greatly weakened the political system in the whole of Colombia as a result.

External trade

Colombia belongs to the Unión de Naciones Suramericanas (Unasur) (Union of South American Nations) – formerly known as the South American Community of Nations (CSN), modelled on the European Union (EU), which seeks to integrate with the Andean Community of Nations and Mercosur in a single market by 2019. Political tensions within the region have hampered the ongoing process.
Coffee and petroleum, both commodities that react to world prices, are the main export products while Colombia is the world's second largest exporter of cut flowers (after The Netherlands).
Colombia is the world's largest exporter of illegal cocaine. A US Office of National Drug Control Policy estimated that Colombia's potential cocaine production is at 245 metric tonnes. On 15 May 2012 the US-Colombia Free Trade Agreement (FTA) came into effect. In 2014, The UN reported that coca acreage had risen from 48,000 hectares to 69,000 hectares.

Imports

Principal imports include industrial equipment, vehicles and transport equipment, consumer goods, chemicals, paper products, fuels, electricity, plastics and natural rubber products.
Main sources: US (28.5 per cent of total in 2014), China (18.4 per cent), Mexico (8.2 per cent).

Exports

Principal exports are petroleum, emeralds, coffee, coal, clothing, bananas, nickel and cut flowers.
Main destinations: US (26.3 per cent of total in 2014), China (10.5 per cent), Panama (6.6 per cent), Spain (5.8 per cent) and India (5.1 per cent).

Agriculture

Farming

The agricultural sector has traditionally played a prominent role in the Colombian economy and it continues to contribute a sizable amount to total GDP. A wide variety of crops are grown throughout Colombia, depending on the altitude in a given region, but coffee is by far the most lucrative crop farmed.
Agricultural exports, primarily coffee, earn US$2 billion or more annually, and when prices have been high, have generated over half of the country's US dollar income. Colombia is the world's second largest producer of coffee after Brazil. Other important cash-export crops include bananas, exotic fruits, cut flowers, tobacco, cotton, sugar cane and cocoa. The illegal export of cocaine, and to a lesser extent marijuana, has been estimated to earn the country between US$500 million and US$1 billion per year.
The government has been successful in promoting the diversification of agricultural export crops and lessening the economy's dependence on coffee revenues. Projects included drainage and irrigation schemes to bring more land under cultivation, cheaper credit for farmers, the improvement of road networks and taking electricity to isolated areas. Basic food subsidies in favour of urban consumers were revised to increase incentives for farmers.
Colombia's flower industry began in 1970 and the country is now the world's second-largest exporter of cut flowers after The Netherlands. The US is the main destination for this product. Climatic conditions are ideal, with no special heating or cooling conditions required. Colombia produces over 3.5 billion flowers a year, mostly on the plains near Bogotá. Shipments of fresh and processed tropical fruit are also increasing.
Meat production was hit by guerrilla violence in ranching zones. The government has launched emergency development programmes in low-income farming districts as part of its plans to boost agricultural output and to pacify politically turbulent regions.

Fishing

Despite a substantial coastline of 2,880km and recent modest successes in developing the shrimp and shellfish industries, the fishing industry as a whole remains underdeveloped. As a member state of the Andean Community Colombia has benefited form special duty-free status and is increasing its shipments of canned tuna to the EU. Exports of artificially reared shrimps are rising as the sector gathers strength.
The typical annual catch is 190,000mt, inclusive of 91,420mt marine fish and 20,580mt shellfish.

Forestry

Approximately half of Colombia's total landmass is forested. There are 49.6 million hectares (ha) of forests in the country. Most of the forests are located in the

southeast of the country and form part of the Amazon jungle. Around 20 per cent of forested land is protected, with 40 national parks and reserves.
Despite its extensive forest resources, Colombia has a very modest production of industrial round timber. Sawn timber and panels have a large domestic market. Import of paper meets nearly one-third of the country's demand.

Industry and manufacturing
Manufacturing accounted for 13 per cent of Colombia's total GDP in 2014, having employed around 46 per cent of the workforce. Products include textiles and garments, chemicals, metal products, cement, cardboard containers, plastic resins and manufactures, beverages, wood products, pharmaceuticals, machinery and electrical equipment.
The industrial sector accounted for around 37 per cent of GDP in 2014.
Food processing, beverages and textiles are the largest industries, followed by chemicals, leather goods, shoes and clothing, capital goods industries and motor vehicles. Metals, tobacco, cement, electrical engineering and paper are also important.

Tourism
The tourist industry has been severely impeded by the political situation and poor security resulting in the kidnapping of foreigners by the Farc terrorist group. Colombia's government is currently engaged in ongoing peace negotiations with the main guerilla group (FARC). As security has improved since the late 2000s the government has promoted Colombia as a tourist destination. It has five ancient and historic cultural sites as well as two natural sites on the UNESCO World Heritage List. It is also a destination for those that wish to see a wide variety of birds and butterflies.
Travel and tourism only directly contributed to 1.9 per cent of total GDP in 2014. However, this is forecasted to rise by 3.4 per cent in 2015. The total contribution to employment was 6.1 per cent of total employment, which totals 1,287,000 jobs.
The government has made a commitment to the industry and foreign direct investment (FDI) has been attracted, particularly Bogota for luxury business trips. As a result capital investment in travel and tourism rose from US$1.8 billion in 2006 to an estimated US$2.5 billion in 2014.

Mining
Mining in Colombia is concentrated on gold and other precious metals, iron ore, nickel and coal. In a typical year the mining industry contributes 4 per cent to the country's total GDP and employs 5 per cent of the total workforce. The industry is Colombia's main legal source of foreign exchange. Mining production grew on average by 6.2 per cent over the decade 2004--2014.
In recent years foreign investors have become fully aware of Colombia's potential for coal mining. With 20,000 tonnes of proven and inferred reserves the country's coal resource base is extensive and the quality of Colombian coal is high. Colombia is the second largest exporter of coal to Europe and the largest exporter to the US.
Colombia is one of the largest gold producers in the world, the fifth largest in Latin America after Peru, Brazil, Chile and Argentina. About 70 per cent of Colombian gold originates from the mines of Buritaca in Antioquia, using small-scale and primitive methods. Other precious minerals include silver and platinum (fourth largest producer of platinum in South America), which are found in Choco Province along the pacific coast.
Colombia is the world's top producer of high-grade emeralds, accounting for over 90 per cent of world output. The Muzo mine in the Eastern Andes near Bogotá is the world's largest emerald mine. Estimates put total emerald exports at US$250 million, of which a little more than 15 per cent is exported legally, for the most part (90 per cent) to Japan.
Worker supervision in many of the emerald mines is minimal, fuelling the problems of smuggling.
Reserves of 100 million tonnes of iron ore assure Colombia of self-sufficiency until 2050. The known reserves are owned by Colombia's only steel company, Acerías Paz del Rio. The reserves are on the whole deep, expensive to extract and of low quality with a high sulphur content. A large part of the industry is located northeast of Bogotá, including the fully integrated steel works of Acerías Paz del Río.
Colombia has a high output of nickel supplying around 12 per cent of world demand. The country also mines copper, lime, sulphur, manganese, phosphates and salt.

Hydrocarbons
Colombia has one of the largest proven crude oil reserves in South America. At the end of 2014 proven oil reserves were 2.4 billion barrels, however, reserves have fallen from 2.6 billion barrels since 1997.
Annual production of oil was 990,000 barrels per day (bpd), a decrease of 1.4 per cent over the 2013 production. Colombia has managed to contain its consumption of oil, an average 310,000bpd (2014), mainly by switching to other energy supplies.
Crude oil remains Colombia's largest export earner. It is a key source for foreign exchange earnings and it is a major contributor to fiscal revenues. Expansion and exploration have therefore been at the forefront of the activities of the state owned entity, Ecopetrol. Geological features that match existing oil fields in Colombia suggest further hydrocarbon-rich territories.
With responsibility for all aspects of oil exploration, production, refining, transporting and trade in oil and gas, Ecopetrol is one of the world's top forty largest oil companies. There are five major oil pipelines, four of which link Colombia's largest oil field in the Cusiana/Cupiagua complex to ports in the Caribbean. But the ongoing civil conflict has resulted in attacks on its pipelines and sabotage of its installations by insurgent groups.
Colombia had proven reserves of 200 billion cubic metres (cum) of natural gas at the end of 2014, with production at 11.4-billion cum. Government policy through the *Plan de Masificación de Gas Natural* is to increase domestic consumption of natural gas.
There are plans to establish Columbia as an Andean regional gas hub with over 3,200km of gas pipelines providing national domestic supplies already. A 230km pipeline for gas from Colombia to Venezuela transports a minimum of 5.7 million cum per day.
Colombia had 6.7 billion tonnes of proven coal reserves at the end 2014. Production was 11.8 billions cum of, which represented a 6.3 per cent decrease on the 2013 production figure.
The country has the largest coal reserves in Latin America of high-quality and profitable bituminous coal most of which is exported. Sixty per cent of Colombia's coal reserves lie in the interior around Bogotá, where the giant El Cerrejón Norte mine is located. New development is centred on an open-cast mine in Guajira.
Coal is Colombia's third most important export after oil and coffee.

Energy
Total electricity capacity in 2012 was over 15 million kilowatt (KW). Total electricity net generation decreased from 59 billion kilowatt hours (KWH) in 2011 to 58 billion KWH in 2012. Consumption in the same year was 49 billion KWH. This surplus allows Colombia to be a net exporter of energy to neighbouring countries, particularly Ecuador. Around three-quarters of the energy produced came from hydropower, with conventional thermal and renewable sources constituting the remainder. Colombia has been self-sufficient in energy since 1984.

The energy sector has been deregulated since the 1990s and it is composed of a mixture of private and publicly owned operators.

Financial markets

Stock exchange

Bolsa de Valores de Colombia (BVC), (Colombian Stock Exchange), Bogotá

Banking and insurance

Both Bancolombia and BBVA Colombia, two of the country's largest banking houses, have enjoyed significant profitability in recent years. Bancolombia, one of the oldest banks in Latin America, recorded pre tax profits of US$339 million in 2004, an increase of 53 per cent on the previous year's total. BBVA Colombia reported an earnings increase of 80 per cent in 2004. Both banks have indicated the likelihood of continued robust growth in 2005.

Following several years of a difficult economic and financial environment in the Colombia, the country's banking sector is now considered to be one of the leading markets in Latin America.

A boom in foreign direct investment (FDI) between 2010 and 2013 has come to an end as the government announces an expected drop in foreign investment for both 2014 and 2015. Despite this, Risks are mainly on the downside, including higher interest rates and financial volatility.

Central bank

Banco de la República

Main financial centre

Bogotá

Time

GMT minus five hours

Geography

Colombia, covering 1.14 million square km, is split between a coastal plain, high Andean peaks rising to more than 5,000 metres and a tropical Amazonian lowland. The only nation in South America with both Pacific and Caribbean coastlines, Colombia is bordered by Venezuela and Brazil to the east, Peru and Ecuador to the south and Panama to the north.

Colombia owns the Isla de Malpelo in the Pacific and several Caribbean islands – including the San Andrés y Providencia islands. Its territorial waters border those of nations as distant as Honduras and Haiti.

Around 80 per cent of the population is concentrated in the Andean region, which covers around a quarter of the country's area. The Andes fan out northwards from the Ecuadorian border into three high *cordilleras* (parallel ranges) separated by deep valleys. Many of the peaks are volcanic. Colombia's highest mountain, the Pico Cristobal Colón, reaches 5,800 metres; it is 50km from the Caribbean coast in the Sierra de Santa Marta, which is isolated from the three main *cordilleras*.

Just over half of the country lies east of the Andes. Known as Los Llanos, most of this region is virtually unexplored and sparsely populated jungle. A low plain fringes most of the coast in the west and the north. About a fifth of the population lives in this area, which is also about a fifth of the total land area.

Hemisphere

Northern

Climate

The equator runs across the south of Colombia. The low coastal plain and the jungle regions east of the Andes have a tropical climate, with frequent rains and temperatures between 24–28 degrees Celsius (C). Temperatures fall with the higher altitudes. In Bogotá, at 2,650 metres, temperatures average around 14 degrees C.

Dress codes

Dress codes in Colombia are partly determined by formality but mostly by climate. In the capital, Bogotá, at 2,650 metres, suits for men and skirts for women are usual for business. Residents recommend a light coat for the evenings. In low-lying cities such as Cali in the south or Cartagena on the Caribbean coast, informal lightweight clothing is common.

Entry requirements

Passports

Required by all with few exceptions (eg certain nationals of Ecuador and certain tourist visitors from Trinidad and Tobago).

Visa

Required for all business visits and must be obtained before arrival. A letter, issued by the traveller's company, giving name and position of applicant, a detailed summary of intended purpose of trip, an itinerary, and the acceptance of full responsibility for any expenses incurred during the term of stay must be submitted with the application, (an original and copy, to be translated into Spanish), which will be notarised by the Colombian embassy.

Tourist visas are not required by citizens of North America, most EU and West European and most South American countries for stays up to 90 days. For further details and confirmation, contact the nearest embassy.

Currency advice/regulations

There are no limitations on the import of foreign and local currency. The export of foreign currency is limited to US$25,000. Travellers' cheques are recommended. Banks are generally the only reliable location for changing travellers' cheques or cash.

Prohibited imports

Illegal drugs, food products, vegetables and plant material are prohibited. Permits are required for the import of firearms and ammunition.

Health (for visitors)

Mandatory precautions

None, although vaccination against yellow fever is essential for visitors travelling to certain parts of the country, notably the central valley of the Magdalena River, the inland border areas (with Ecuador, Peru, Brazil and Venezuela), Uraba district, the south-eastern part of the Sierra Nevada de Santa Marta and the forest area along the Guaviare River. A certificate of inoculation may be required by immigration officials.

Advisable precautions

Precautions should be taken against cholera, malaria, hepatitis; typhoid immunisation should be current. There are risks of dengue fever, TB, measles and rabies. Tap water is not considered safe to drink, boiled or bottled water should be used at all times. Milk is unpasteurised and should therefore be boiled or avoided. Meat and fish should be thoroughly cooked and preferably eaten hot. It is advised to avoid uncooked vegetables and dairy products made from local milk. Fruit should be peeled. Visitors to Bogotá should take it easy for a few days to get used to the altitude, which may induce drowsiness, dizziness or altitude sickness. Health insurance including medical evacuation is strongly recommended.

Hotels

Hotels are graded from one- to five-star by the Colombian Hotel Organisation. There are two seasonal tourist tariffs, low season is May–Nov and high season is Dec–Apr. A 5 per cent tax is imposed on all hotel bills. It is advisable to book well in advance. Service charge is normally added to bill, otherwise a 10 per cent tip is expected.

Credit cards

American Express, Diners, Visa and Master Card are widely used.

Public holidays (national)

Fixed dates

1 Jan (New Year's Day), *6 Jan (Epiphany), *19 Mar (St Joseph's Day), 1 May (Labour Day), *17 Jun (Corpus Christi/Thanksgiving Day), *29 Jun (St Peter and St Paul Day), 20 Jul (Independence Day), 7 Aug (Battle of Boyacá), *21 Aug (Assumption Day), *16 Oct (Columbus Day), *6 Nov (All Saints' Day), 8 Dec (Immaculate Conception), 25 Dec (Christmas Day).

Variable dates

Maundy Thursday, Good Friday, *Ascension Day, *Corpus Christi (May/Jun).

* Holidays that do not fall on Monday are taken on the following Monday.

Working hours

Banking

In Bogotá: Mon–Fri: 0900–1500.
Other cities: 0800–1130 and 1400–1630.
On the last working day of the month, banks open up to 1200 only.

Business

Mon–Fri: 0800–1230, 1400–1800.

Shops

Mon–Fri: 0900–1900 or 2000.

Telecommunications

Mobile/cell phones

Some GSM 850 and 1900 services available in limited areas.

Electricity supply

110V AC 60 cycles; two-pin flat blade plugs.

Social customs/useful tips

It is customary to tip porters but not maids or clerks in hotels.

Security

With a virtual war being fought between the government, drug barons and Farc insurgents, realistic security measures must be carried out as kidnapping, armed robbery and bomb explosions are frequent hazards. Visitors should exert due care and vigilance at all times. It is advisable that embassy officials be informed of their national's presence in Colombia and itinerary, particularly if travelling to the north of the country.
Colombia has the highest murder rate in the Americas and one of the worst reputations, in South America, for street crime, which is common during daylight hours in main cities. Visitors are advised not to display jewellery and to carry as little cash and documentation as possible; watches and briefcases are prime targets. It is advisable to keep a copy of all documents in an hotel safe in case of mishap. Much crime is drug-related and visitors should be wary of any unwarranted attention from strangers.

Getting there

Air

National airline: Avianca (Aerovías Nacionales de Colombia).
International airport/s: Bogotá-El Dorado (BOG), 12km from city, duty-free shop, restaurant, post office, bank, shops, hotel reservations, car hire.
Other airport/s: Regional international flights also arrive at Barranquilla-Ernesto Cortissos (BAQ), 10km from city, car hire; Cali-Palmaseca (CLO), 19km from city, restaurant; Cartagena-Crespo (CTG), 2km north-east of city; Medellín-Rionegro (MDE), 15 minutes' flight by scheduled and frequent helicopter service to city, (36km south-east of Medellín).
Airport tax: International departures US$25–29 in cash, not applicable to transit passengers. An exit tax of US$19 is charged to travellers whose stay exceeds two months.

Surface

Road: Access is possible by road from Ecuador via Tulean to Ipiales and Venezuela from Christóbal to Cucuta.
Water: The rivers Meta, between Venezuela, Putumayo and a section of the upper Amazon in Peru, and the Orinoco between Brazil and Colombia, all act as borders. They are used by small boats.
Main port/s: Caribbean: Santa Marta, Barranquilla, and Cartagena. Pacific: Buenaventura and Tumaco. Upper Amazon: Leticia.

Getting about

National transport

Air: Domestic air travel is the most practical way of getting around the country. There are frequent and cheap air services between Bogotá and all main centres. Major international air carriers operate internal flights as well as smaller companies that operate domestic services.
Road: Travelling by road can be arduous and potenially dangerous. There are paramilitary groups in rural areas.
Fifty per cent of the main roads wind through steep *cordilleras*, with bridges and tunnels in constant need of repair. Only 4,600km of the country's 120,000km road network are considered to be in good condition and less than 13,000km are paved.
There are highway links for Bogotá-Cali; for other journeys local enquiries are advisable.
Buses: There are many bus companies providing services between coastal towns and cities. Bogotá-Medellín inter-city service is fairly reliable and comfortable.
Rail: There is no longer an intercity passenger rail service.
Water: Cargo boats that travel along the Magdalena, Guaviare, Caqueta, and Meta river systems offer passage to passengers; the is a slow means of travel. There are 10,000km of navigable rivers between the three main Andean ranges.

City transport

Taxis: Within Bogotá, taxis are usually metered with minimum charge and extra at night, holidays, Sundays and for out-of-town journeys. Tourist taxis (green and cream) are likely to have drivers able to speak English and can be hired by the hour/day from major hotels. Typical taxis can be hailed in the street and tipping is not usual. For unmetered, taxis fares should be agreed in advance of journey.
Shared taxis, *colectivos*, operate within cities and suburbs.
Buses, trams & metro: Bogotá has a trolleybus system, buses and minibuses with flat rate fares.

Car hire

It is not recommended for foreign drivers as local conditions are so poor. Nevertheless, major car hire companies exist. Urban speed limits are 45–60kph while the rural speed limit is 80kph. An international driving licence (in Spanish) is required. Traffic drives on the right and during the working day is heavily congested in main towns.

BUSINESS DIRECTORY

The addresses listed below are a selection only. While World of Information makes every endeavour to check these addresses, we cannot guarantee that changes have not been made, especially to telephone numbers and area codes. We would welcome any corrections.

Telephone area codes

The international dialling code (IDD) for Colombia is +57 followed by the area code:

Armenia	67	Cartagena	5
Baranquilla	5	Cucuta	70
Bogotá	1	Manizales	69
Bucaramanga	73	Medellín	4
Cali	2		

Chambers of Commerce

American-Colombian Chamber of Commerce, 22-64 Calle 98, Bogotá (tel: 623-7088; fax: 621-6838; e-mail: info@amchamcolombia.com.co).

Barranquilla Chamber of Commerce, 36-135 Via 40, Barranquilla (tel: 330-3701; fax: 330-3750;e-mail: info@camarabaq.org.co).

Bogotá Chamber of Commerce, 16-21 Carrera 9, Bogotá (tel: 2381-0270; fax: 284-7735; e-mail: ccbcentro@ccb.org.co).

British-Colombian Chamber of Commerce, 77A-52 Carrera 12A, Bogotá (tel: 321-7077; fax: 321-7964; e-mail: britanica@cable.net.co).

Bucaramanga Chamber of Commerce, 36-20 Carrera 19, Bucaramanga (tel: 652-7000; fax: 633-4062).

Cali Chamber of Commerce, 3-14 Calle 8, Cali (tel: 886-1300; fax: 886-1399; e-mail: contacto@ccc.org.co).

Cartagena Chamber of Commerce, 32-41 Calle Santa Teresa, Cartagena (tel: 660-0795; fax: 660-0802; e-mail: camaradecomercio@cccartagena.org.co).

Colombian Confederation of Chambers of Commerce, 27-47 Carrera 13, Oficina 502, Bogotá (tel: 346-7055; fax:

346-7026; e-mail: confecamaras@confecamaras.org.co).

Cucuta Chamber of Commerce, 4-38 Calle 10, Cucuta (tel: 571-5922; fax: 571-2502; e-mail: cccuc02@col1.telecom.com.co).

Manizales Chamber of Commerce, 26-60 Carrera 23, Manizales (tel: 884-1840; fax: 884-0919; e-mail: ccm@ccm.org.co).

Medellín Chamber of Commerce, 52-82 Avenida Oriental, Medellín (tel: 511-6111; fax: 513-7757; e-mail: subcontramed@camaramed.org.co).

Pereira Chamber of Commerce, 23-09 Carrera 8, Local 10, Risaralda, Pereira (tel: 252-587; fax: 250-957; e-mail: camarap@pereira.multi.net.co).

Banking

Banco Andino, Carrera 7a No 14-23, Piso 3, Apdo Postal 6826, Bogotá (tel: 284-8800; fax: 286-7919).

Banco Anglo Colombiano (associated to Lloyds Bank plc), Cra 8 No 15-46/60, Zonal postal 1, Bogotá (tel: 334-5088; fax: 286-1383).

Banco Cafetero, Calle 28 No 13 A-15, Apdo Postal 240332, Bogotá (tel: 282-7742; fax: 284-5430).

Banco Caldas, Calle 72 No 7-64, Apdo Postal 240332, Bogotá (tel: 282-7742; fax: 284-5430).

Banco Central Hipotecario, Carrera 6a No 15-32, Zona Postal 1, Bogotá (tel: 283-7100; fax: 283-2802).

Banco Colombo Americano, Carrera 7a No 16-36, Piso 10, Apdo Postal 12327, Bogotá (tel: 334-5530; fax: 283-2939).

Banco Colpatria, Calle 13, No 7-90, Piso 2, Apdo Postal 30241, Bogotá (tel: 283-1567; fax: 286-3914).

Banco Co-operativo de Colombia (Bancoop), Calle 98 No 14-41, Apdo Postal 12242, Bogotá (tel: 257-7411; fax: 218-1601).

Banco de Antioquia (Bancoquia), Calle 12 No 746, Bogotá (tel: 334-9040).

Banco de Bogotá, PO Box 3436, Calle 36 No 7-47, Bogotá (tel: 332-0032 fax: 338-3302).

Banco de Colombia, Calle 30A No 6-38, Zona Postal 1, Apdo Postal 6836, Bogotá (tel: 285-6767; fax: 287-0595).

Banco de Cio Exterior de Colombia (Bancoldex) (Foreign Trade Bank of Colombia), Calle 28 No 13A-15, Apdo Postal 240-092, Bogotá (tel: 341-0677; fax: 282-5071).

Banco de Crédito, Calle 27 No 6-48, Zona Postal 1, Bogotá (tel: 286-8400; fax: 282-7256).

Banco del Occidente, Carrera 5a No 12-42, Apdo Postal 7607, Cali, Valle (tel: 824-081; fax: 822-705).

Banco del Estado, Carrera 10 No 18-15, Apdo Postal 8711, Bogotá (tel: 282-8471; fax: 284-9775).

Banco Extebandes de Colombia, Calle 74 No 6-65, Zona postal 2, Bogotá (tel: 217-7200; fax: 212-5786).

Banco Ganadero, Carrera 9A No 72-21, Apdo Postal 53851/9, Bogotá (tel: 217-0100; fax: 255-2457).

Banco Industrial Colombiano, Carrera 52 No 50-20, Apdo Postal 768, Medellín, Antioquia (tel: 251-5216; fax: 251-4716).

Banco Latino de Colombia, Calle 72 No 10-07, Apdo Postal 056397, Bogotá (tel: 210-999; fax: 284-0056).

Banco Mercantil Colombia, Carrera 9A No 99-02, Zona Postal 8, Bogotá (tel: 618-2249; fax: 618-2111).

Banco Popular, Calle 17 No 7-35, Zona Postal 1, Bogotá (tel: 334-9640; fax: 282-4246).

Banco Real de Colombia, Carrera 7a No 33-80, Apdo Postal 034262, Bogotá (tel: 269-8523; fax: 287-0507).

Banco Sudameris Colombia, Carrera 8a No 15-42, Zona Postal 1, Bogotá (tel: 283-8700; fax: 281-6191).

Banco Superior, Carrera 10a No 64-28, Bogotá (tel: 217-3888; fax: 235-4352).

Banco Tequendama, Diagonal 27 No 6-70, Apdo Postal 29799, Bogotá (tel: 285-9900; fax: 287-7020).

Banco Uconal, Calle 72 No 8-56, Bogotá (tel: 310-5155; fax: 212-2094).

Banco Unión Colombiano, Piso 2, Carrera 7 N°71-52, Bogotá (tel: 3120411 fax: 3120843).

Caja de Crédito Agrario Industrial y Minero, Carrera 8a No 15-43, Zona Postal 1, Bogotá (tel: 334-9066; fax: 286-5824).

Caja Social, Calle 72 No 10-71, Apdo Postal 58175, Bogotá (tel: 310-0099; fax: 211-6036).

Citibank, Carrera 9a No 99-02, Bogotá (tel: 618-4455; fax: 618-2515).

Central bank

Banco de la República, Carrera 7, No 14-78, Bogotá (tel: 342-1111; fax: 286-1686; e-mail: wbanco@banrep.gov.co).

Stock exchange

Bolsa de Valores de Colombia (BVC), (Colombian Stock Exchange), Bogatá

www.bvc.com.co

Travel information

American Express, TMA, Cra.10 No 27-91, Offices 1-26, Bogotá (tel: 283-2955).

Avianca (Aerovías Nacionales de Colombia), Avenida, Eldorado 93-30, Piso 4, Bloque 1, Bogotá (tel: 413-9511; fax: 413-8325).

Colombian Hotel Organisation, Carrera 7, No 60–92 Bogotá (tel: 130-3640; internet: www.cotelco.org).

Fondo de Promoción Turistica de Colombia, Carrera 16A No 78-55 Of. 604, Bogotá (tel: 611-4330, 611-4185; fax: 236-3640; e-mail: turismocolombia@andinet.com; internet site: http://www.turismocolombia.com).

National tourist organisation offices

National Tourist Office, Calle 28 No. 13A-15 P 17 Y 18, Bogotá (tel: 283-9466; fax: 283-8945).

Ministries

Ministry of Agriculture and Rural Development, Avenida Jiménez No. 7-65, Santafé de Bogotá (tel: 334-1199; fax: 284-1775).

Ministry of Communications, Edificio Murillo Toro, Carrera 7 y 8 Calle 12 y 13, Santafé de Bogotá (tel: 286-6911; fax: 286-1185).

Ministry of Culture, Calle 8 No 6-67, Santafé de Bogotá (tel: 282-0854; fax: 282-0666).

Ministry of Economic Development, Carrera 13 No. 28-01, Apartado Aéreo 99412, Santafé de Bogotá (tel: 320-0077; fax: 287-6025).

Ministry of the Environment, Calle 38 No 8-61, Santafé de Bogotá (tel:288-6010; fax: 243-3004).

Ministry of Finance and Public Credit, Carrera 7a No. 6-45, Santafé de Bogotá (tel: 284-5400; fax: 284-5396).

Ministry for Foreign Affairs, Palacio de San Carlos, Calle 10 No. 5-51, Santafé de Bogotá (tel: 282-7811, 287-6800; fax: 341-6777).

Ministry of Foreign Trade, Calle 28 No. 13A-15 P 5,6,7,9, Santafé de Bogotá (tel: 286-9111; fax: 284-9537, 334-9908).

Ministry of Health, Carrera 13 No. 32-76, Santafé de Bogotá (tel: 336-5066; fax: 336-0116, 336-0296).

Ministry of the Interior, Palacio Echeverry, Carrera 8a No. 8-09, Santafé de Bogotá (tel: 283-0676, 283-6853; fax: 281-5884, 286-8025).

Ministry of Justice and Law, Avenida Jiménez No. 8-89, Santafé de Bogotá (tel: 286-0211, 286-5888, 286-9711; fax: 281-6384, 283-2761).

Ministry of Labour and Social Security, Carrera 7a No. 34-50, Santafé de Bogotá (tel: 287-3434/5045, 285-7092/7098, 285-8362/7361; fax: 285-7091, 287-3861/8342).

Ministry of Mines and Energy CAN, Santafé de Bogotá (tel: 222-4555, 2068, 222-0179; fax: 222-3651).

Ministry of National Defence, Avenida El Dorado Cra 52 CAN, Santafé de Bogatá (tel: 220-4999; fax: 222-1874).

Ministry of National Education, CAN, Santafé de Bogotá (tel: 222-2800; fax: 222-0324).

Ministry of Transport, CAN, Santafé de Bogotá (tel: 222-4411, 222-7577, 7966; fax: 222-1647, 222-1121).

Other useful addresses

Asociación Nacional de Industriales (ANDI), Carrera 13 No 26-45, Bogotá (tel: 334-6673, 281-0600).

Bolsa de Bogotá (Stock Exchange), Carrera 8a, No 13-82, Apartado Aéreo 3584, Bogotá (tel: 243-6501, 243-8471; fax: 281-3170).

Bolsa de Medellín S.A. (Stock Exchange), Carrera 50 No 50-48 Piso 2, Medellín (tel: 260-3000; fax: 251-1981).

British Embassy, Apartado Aéreo 4508, Torre Propaganda Sancho, Calle 98, No 9-03, Piso 4, Bogotá (tel: 218-5111; fax: 218-2330, 218-2460).

Caja de Crédito Agrario Industrial y Minero, Carrera 8 No 15-43, Bogotá (tel: 284-4600).

Carbones de Colombia (CARBOCOL), Carrera 7, No 31-10, Pisos 5-18, Bogotá (tel: 287-3100).

Colombian Embassy (USA), 2118 Leroy Place, NW, Washington DC 20008 (tel: 202-387-8338; fax: 202-232-8643; e-mail: emwash@colombiaemb.org).

Colombian Government Trade Bureau (Proexport Colombia) Calle 28 No. 13 A - 15 Piso 35, Santafé de Bogotá, (tel: 341-2066; fax: 282-8130, 282-8230).

Departamento Administrativo de Aeronáutica Civil (DAAC), Aeropuerto Internacional El Dorado, Bogotá (tel: 266-2237).

Departamento Administrativo Nacional de Estadísticas (DANE), Oficina 222, CAN-Avenida Eldorado, Bogotá.

Departamento Nacional de Planeación, Calle 26 No 13-19, Bogotá (tel: 282-4055; fax: 281-3348).

Empresa Colombiana de Mina (ECOMINAS), Calle 32, No 13-07, Apartado Aéreo 17878, Bogotá (tel: 287-7136; fax: 287-4606).

Empresa Colombiana de Petróleos (ECOPETROL), Carrera 13 No 36-24, Bogotá (tel: 285-6400).

Empresa Nacional de Telecomunicaciones (TELECOM), Calle 23 No 13-49, Bogotá (tel: 286-0077, 282-8280).

Federación Nacional de Cafeteros de Colombia, Calle 73 No 8-13, Apartado Aéreo 57534, Bogotá DE (tel: 217-0600).

Instituto Colombiana de Comercio Exterior (INCOMEX), Edifico Centro Comercio Internacional, Calle 28 No 13A-15, Bogotá (tel: 281-2200).

Instituto de Fomento Industrial (IFI), Calle 16, No 6-66, Pisos 7-15, Bogotá (tel: 282-2055).

Instituto Nacional de Investigaciones Geológico-Mineras (INGEOMINAS), Diagonal 53, No 34-53, Apartado Aéreo 4865, Bogotá (tel: 222-1811; fax: 222-3597).

Instituto Nacional de Radio y Televisión, Via del Aeropuerto Eldorado, Bogotá (tel: 222-0700; fax: 222-0080).

Invertir Corporation of Colombia (COINVERTIR), Cra 7 no 71-52 Torre A, Oficina 702, Bogotá (tel: 312-0312; fax: 312-0318).

US Embassy, Calle 38, No 8-61, Bogotá (tel: 285-1300; fax: 288-5687).

Prensa Latina: www.plenglish.com

Internet sites

Business News, Latin Trade online: http://www.latintrade.com

Organisation of American States: http://www.oas.org

President of the Republic (in Spanish): http://www.presidencia.gov.co/webpresi/

Colombia Trade: http://www.coltrade.org/

Comoros

KEY FACTS

Official name: Udzima wa Komori (L'Union des Comores) (The Union of the Comoros) (from Jan 2002)

Head of State: President Ikiliou Dhoinine (from 26 May 2011)

Head of government: President Ikiliou Dhoinine (from 26 May 2011)

Ruling party: Únion-Presidential Movement (MP-Union) (Presidential Movement-Union) (from 24 Dec 2009)

Area: 2,171 square km

Population: 776,000 (2014)*

Capital: Moroni

Official language: Arabic and French

Currency: Comoros franc (Cf) = 100 centimes

Exchange rate: Cf439.83 per US$ (Sep 2015)

GDP per capita: US$923 (2014)*

GDP real growth: 3.35% (2014)*

GDP: US$717.00 million (2014)*

Inflation: 2.85% (2014)*

Balance of trade: -US$198.30 million (2012)

* estimated figure

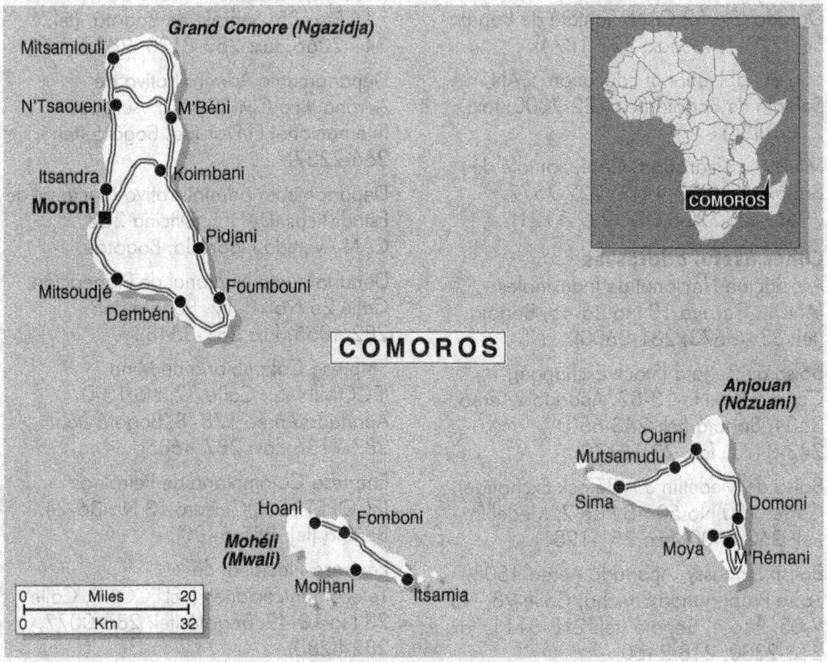

With an overall population density of around 150 per square kilometre, there has for decades been little prospect for many Comorians except emigration, with any luck to France. Many settled for less and went to Madagascar but were expelled *en masse* in the late 1970s. The return of some 14,000 refugees coincided with the eruption of Mount Kartalla, which left 20,000 people homeless. Before independence from France, French aid had allowed the islands to run a budget deficit and to leave what little development of the infrastructure there was to the French. A beneficial by-product of independence was aid from elsewhere. Agreements were signed with Saudi Arabia, China and the United Arab Emirates as well as with the Arab Bank for Economic Development (ABEDA). The islands have no known mineral resources and fishing is poor due to the absence of a continental shelf.

Political benefits

There has also been significant political progress in the Comoros. On the three small islands inhabited by less than 800,000 people political infighting and *coups* have been regular occurrences (over 20 *coups d'état* or at least attempted *coups* at the last count) since independence from France in 1975, but national reconciliation has advanced, helped by domestic leadership as well as by concerted international support. The African Union, the United Nations Development Programme (UNDP) and regional partners in the Southern African Development Community (SADC) have played critical roles. Progress on the political front has also benefited economic performance. The central government has been at pains to consolidate political stability in the face of tensions and threats of secession from what are in most respects semi-autonomous islands. This history of political violence left the Comoros impoverished and often dangerously close to disintegration as a body politic.

Immediately after independence, President Ahmed Abdallah was ousted in a *coup* master-minded by the French mercenary Colonel Bob Denard. For some years, Colonel Denard's reputation hovered between that of the

Comoros' *éminence grise* and its *bête noire*. The islands of Anjouan and Moheli declared unilateral independence after a violent confrontation in 1997. In what many saw as open appeasement, Moheli, Anjouan and the largest island, Grande Comore, were subsequently granted greater autonomy under the 2001 constitution. The Union of the Comoros retained control of security and financial matters.

The economy

In its December 2013 assessment of the Comoros economy, the International Monetary Fund (IMF) noted that the country was in the last year of a multi-year economic and structural adjustment programme and had made significant progress in stabilising the economy. Further progress had also been made on the structural front. The programme has, and continues, to receive the support of a broad range of stakeholders. Economic growth was expected to strengthen to 3.5 per cent of GDP in 2013 and average inflation was expected to be less than 3 per cent. While official transfers and remittances remained strong, international reserve holdings were expected by the IMF to decline somewhat, mainly due to strong imports that more than offset the sizeable increase in exports. Performance under the Extended Credit Facility (ECF) supported programme was broadly satisfactory. All but one of the performance criteria and all indicative targets for the end of June were met. Most structural benchmarks were also met. However, fiscal performance weakened in the third quarter of 2013. Increases in capital spending, mainly on road construction in anticipation of receipts that did not materialise, caused the end- September indicative targets on net credit to the government and the domestic primary balance to be missed. However, additional fiscal measures taken subsequently were expected to allow stabilisation gains to be broadly preserved. The authorities had requested a waiver for the non-observance of the performance criterion on net credit to the government at the end of June 2013.

Largely endorsing the IMF observations, the African Development Bank (AfDB) in its Economic Outlook noted that the Comoros had recorded positive growth since 2011. Growth was estimated at 3.6 per cent in 2013, driven mainly by agriculture (representing almost half of GDP), retail, tourism, construction (above 4.0 per cent) and banking and other services (around 8.0 per cent).

The return to growth was aided by an expansionary fiscal policy thanks to major multilateral external financing and especially bilateral financing from Arab countries. The Comoros has thus been able to run fiscal surpluses since 2011, increasing the surplus each year. A 5.6 per cent surplus was projected for 2014 thanks to ongoing grants and programmes in the pipeline with the AfDB, the World Bank and the European Union (EU). Nevertheless, the Comoros' economic impetus since 2011 has not led to structural changes in the economy. It remains dominated by the agricultural sector (agriculture, forestry and fisheries), which represented almost half of GDP. The secondary sector, including construction, has grown slightly since 2010, remaining above 12 per cent of GDP. The services sector, meanwhile, has declined since 2008 and by 2013 accounted for less than 40 per cent of GDP.

The telecommunications sector remains a state monopoly. With support from the World Bank, the authorities are expected to sell a second licence in the near future and to open up the capital of the state monopoly Comores Télécom to create a competitive environment.

With the country's population growing at a rate of 2.1 per cent a year, in the view of the AfDB the level of economic growth was too low to increase real per capita income and reduce poverty and youth unemployment. Poverty remains high, estimated at 45.6 per cent in 2012, well above the Millennium Development Goal (MDG) target of 31.5 per cent by 2015. The economic growth referred to above has done little to create jobs, with unemployment estimated at 14.3 per cent and youth unemployment (under 25s) at 44.5 per cent.

As part of the Stratégie de Croissance Accélérée et de Développement Durable (SCA2D) (Strategy for Accelerated Growth and Sustainable Development) currently being drawn up for the period 2015–19, the government has set a growth objective of 6 per cent, which will be driven by the development of basic infrastructure, improvements to the business climate and private-sector financial support.

Risk assessment

Politics	Fair
Economy	Fair
Regional stability	Fair

Muslims in Comoros

% of population	98
Sunni (% of Muslims)	99
Shi'a (% of Muslims)	1

COUNTRY PROFILE

1843 The Comoros was ceded to France by Portugal.
1886 The islands became a French protectorate.
1912 The islands became a French colony; they were administered from Madagascar.
1947 The Comoros became a separate French Overseas Territory and given representation in the French parliament.
1961 It achieved internal self-government.
1972 Elections produced a large majority for parties advocating independence and Ahmed Abdallah Abderrahman became president of the government council.
1973 Abderrahman was restyled president of the government.
1974 Mayotte voted to retain links with France while Grand Comore, Anjouan, Mohéli voted for independence.
1975 The Federal Islamic Republic of the Comoros claimed independence from

KEY INDICATORS — Comoros

	Unit	2011	2012	2013	2014	**2015
Population	m	*0.68	*0.69	*0.75	*0.78	*0.80
Gross domestic product (GDP)	US$bn	0.61	0.60	0.66	*0.72	*0.68
GDP per capita	US$	903	859	*873	*923	*847
GDP real growth	%	2.2	3.0	3.5	*3.3	*3.5
Inflation	%	6.8	6.3	1.6	*2.9	*2.5
Current account	US$m	-55.0	-23.0	-96.0	*-76.0	*-96.0
Total reserves minus gold	US$m	165.5	194.0	173.4	170.5	–
Foreign exchange	US$m	146.6	176.0	150.2	–	–
Exchange rate	per US$	350.11	379.24	360.19	439.00	–

* estimated figure ** forecast figure

France, Mayotte was the only island in the archipelago that voted to retain links with France.
1978 A constitution was approved by referendum.
1982 Constitutional amendments increased the president's power by reducing those of each island's governor.
1989 Abderrahman was assassinated.
1990 In Comoros' first democratic elections, Said Mohamed Djohar was elected president.
1992 A new constitution was approved that included the new post of prime minister.
1995 An abortive coup to topple Djohar was foiled by French troops.
1996 Mohammed Taki Abdoul-Karim won the presidential election. Constitutional changes adopted *sharia* as law.
1997 The islands of Anjouan (Ndzuani) and Mohéli (Mwali) declared their independence from the Comoros. Economic depression was given as the reason for their wish to reintegrate with France.
1998 President Taki Abdoul-Karim died. Tajidine ben Said Massonde became president.
1999 Colonel Azali Assoumani seized power in a bloodless coup and became president. In legislative elections on Anjouan, hardline secessionists won every seat.
2001 A military, unionist force on Anjouan took control in August. Attempts to wrest control from it failed and in December the Comoran government, by amending the constitution, implemented a change to unify the country in a loose federation as a decentralised Comoran Union of three autonomous islands: Anjouan, Mohéli and Grand Comoros.
2002 The country's name was changed to L'Union des Comores (The Union of the Comoros). In May, Assoumani was declared president of The Union. Mohamed Bacar was elected president of Anjouan. Mohamed Said Fazul was elected president in Mohéli, and Abdou Soule Elbak was elected president of Grande Comore.
2003 Power-sharing agreements were signed to allow national elections to take place and the presidency to rotate between the islands.
2004 Parliamentary elections took place for the Union. Opposition candidates to the Union president (Assoumani) formed an alliance: Camp des Îles Autonomes (CIA) (Autonomous Islands Party) and won 27 seats against six for the president's party. The first federal government was sworn in.
2005 Mount Karthala, a volcano on Grande Comore, erupted twice.
2006 Presidential elections for the Union took place. In the first round, held on Anjouan, 10 of the 13 candidates were eliminated. In the nation-wide second round, Ahmed Abdallah Mohamed Sambi won 58.02 per cent of the vote, Ibrahim Halidi Djaanffari 28.32 per cent and Mohamed Djaanfari 13.65 per cent. President Sambi took office.
2007 President Becar (of Anjouan) refused to give up his office, as according to the constitution he was required to do before scheduled elections. His forces clashed with the national army sent to enforce the constitution; the African Union (AU) also sent troops to support the constitution. Dhoihirou Halidi was appointed interim president of Anjouan. The constitutional court dismissed the president of Mohéli and Mohamed Ali Said was sworn in as its president.
2008 Forces of the AU overthrew the renegade president of Anjouan, Mohamed Bacar, and Moussa Toybou took office as president. Comoros was given full membership of the Islamic Development Bank (IDB).
2009 A referendum held in Mayotte (sponsored by the interior ministry of France), voted by 95 per cent to become an integral region of France. The government in Comoros claimed Mayotte as part of its territory and considered the referendum as provocative. The constitution was changed, extending the presidential term of office from four years to five. In parliamentary elections held in December the Únion-Presidential Movement (MP-Union) (Presidential Movement-Union) won 20 out of 24 seats.
2010 The International Monetary Fund (IMF) considered Comoros had undertaken enough political and economic reforms to warrant debt relief under the Heavily Indebted Poor Countries (HIPC) initiative. After two rounds in the presidential elections Ikililou Dhoinine won with 61.12 per cent of the vote, Mohamed Said Fazul 32.65 per cent and Abdou Djabir 6.23 per cent; turnout was 50.96 per cent respectively.
2011 In January, the IMF agreed to the disbursement of US$2.42 million following the second review under its Extended Credit Facility (ECF) that registered the government's commitment to continued macroeconomic and structural reform, bringing the total amount disbursed to US$11.41 million. President Sambi's term of office expired in April. On 23 May, Mouigni Baraka Said Soilihi took office as governor of Grande Comore and Anissi Chamsidine became governor of Anjouan. On 26 May Ikiliou Dhoinine, former vice president and Sambi supporter, took office as president of Comoros.
2012 On 28 March Comoros awarded its first ever, oil exploration and production licence to the Kenya-based Bahari Resources oil company, to undertake exploration offshore in its territorial waters in the Indian Ocean.
2013 President and Prime Minister Ikililou Dhoinine reshuffled his government team on 15 July. It included six new ministers, including one woman.
2014 In February the European Union sent two experts to help the government prepare for the elections due in November. Hayley Ibrahim, minister of the interior, was reported in the *La Gazette des Comores* as wanting the elections to be 'free, democratic, transparent and clear'.
2015 Parliamentary elections were held on 25 January (first round) and 22 February (second round). The main winners were the Union pour le Développement des Comoros (UPDC) (Union for the Development of the Comoros) with eight seats (out of 24) and the Parti Juwa (PJ) (Juwa Party) with seven seats.

Political structure

Constitution

The national constitution which was ratified by referendum in December 2001 created a federation – The Union of the Comoros – with each of the three islands having its own legislature, constitution and budget. Foreign relations, defence and currency were the responsibility of the Union. This inevitably caused some confusion with different election dates, different levels of authority on the islands and a mix of political parties holding power.
In an effort to sort out some these inconsistancies, constitutional changes were adopted on 17 May 2009 following a referendum in which 93.8 per cent of voters agreed to the changes; turnout was 52.7 per cent. Under these amendments, the island presidents were renamed governors, with the federal president assuming overall authority. President Ahmed Abdallah Mohamed Sambi's term of office was extended by one year so that the next presidential election (in 2011) coincides with that of the island governors. More powers were transferred to the president, such as replacing the federal rotating presidency with a permanently elected office and allowing the president to declare a state religion.

Form of state

Federal republic

The executive

The presidency of the Union of the Comoros rotates between the islands of Grand Comore, Anjouan, and Moheli every four years according to the 2001 power-sharing constitution.
First round presidential elections are held on the island that will hold the next presidency; the top three candidates become the only candidates that the whole union votes on in the second round.

National legislature
The 33-member Assemblée de l'Union (federal parliament) has 15 members appointed by the three island legislatures (five each) and 18 elected through direct universal suffrage. Each island has its own assembly.

Legal system
French Nepolean Code and *Sharia* (Islamic) law in a new consolidated code.

Last elections
7 November and 26 December 2010 (presidential, first round on Mohéli and second round nationwide); 14/ 21 March 2004 (autonomous islands' assemblies); 25 January and 22 February 2015 (legislative first and second rounds).

Results: Federal parliament: Union pour le Développement des Comoros (UPDC) (Union for the Development of the Comoros) won 8 seats (out of 24), Parti Juwa (PJ) (Juwa Party) 7 seats, Rassemblement Démocratique des Comoros (RDC) (Democratic Rally of the Comoros) 2 seats, Convention pour le Renouveau des Comores (CRC) (Convention for the Renewal of the Comoros) 2 seats, Rassemblement pour une Alternative de Développement Harmonieux et Intégré (RADHI) (Rally for an Alternative of Harmonious and Integrated Development) 1 seat, Parti pour l'Entente Comorienne (PEC) (Party for the Comorian Agreement) 1 seat, the remaining 3 seats were won by independents. Turnout was 71.35 per cent.

Autonomous Islands' Assemblies:

Grande Comore: supporters of the island president won 13 seats out of 20 and supporters of the Union president (Assoumani), seven.

Anjouan: supporters of the island president won 23 seats out of 25 and supporters of the Union president (Assoumani), two.

Mohéli: supporters of the island president won nine seats out of 10 and supporters of the Union president (Assoumani), one.

The opposition candidates to the Union president (Assoumani) formed an alliance: Camp des Îles Autonomes (CIA) (Autonomous Islands Party).

Presidential (first round (Mohéli primary)): Ikililou Dhoinine won 28.19 per cent of the vote, Mohamed Said Fazul 22.94 per cent, Abdou Djabir 9.88 per cent, Bianrifi Tarmidhi 9.31 per cent; six other candidates each won less than 9 per cent of the vote. Second round: Dhoinine won 61.12 per cent of the vote, Fazul 32.65 per cent, Djabir 6.23 per cent. Turnout was 67.1 per cent and 50.96 per cent respectively.

Next elections
2020 (federal parliament); 2016 (presidential)

Political parties
Comoros does not have a tradition of strong ideological political parties and political movements tend to support certain leaders. The only major issue of divergence is between those who favour a strong federal government and those who support autonomous island governments.

Ruling party
Únion-Presidential Movement (MP-Union) (Presidential Movement-Union) (from 24 Dec 2009)

Main opposition party
Convention pour le Renouveau des Comores (CRC) (Convention for the Renewal of Comoros)

Population
694,000 (2012)*

Approximately 48 per cent of the population are under 15 years of age.

Anjouan is overpopulated, with 650 inhabitants per square km, while Mohéli (Mwali) has a population density of 100 per square km.

Last census: 1 September 2003: 575,660

Population density: 244 per square km. Urban population 28 per cent (2010 Unicef).

Annual growth rate: 2.6 per cent, 1990–2010 (Unicef).

Ethnic make-up
Antalote, Cafre, Makao, Oimatsaha, Sakalava.

The descendants of Arab traders, Malay immigrants and African peoples contribute to the islands' complex ethnic mix.

Religions
Sunni Muslim 86 per cent (official religion), Roman Catholic 14 per cent.

Education
Unicef concluded that school enrolment dropped due to insufficient classrooms and qualified teachers, among other infrastructural inadequacies. Education also suffers from poor performance and quality. A Unicef-sponsored humanitarian action plan in 2002 provided US$122,000 towards basic education.

Literacy rate: 59 per cent; adult rates (World Bank 2002).

Enrolment rate: 60 per cent (Unicef).

Health
The World Health Organisation (WHO), in 2003, funded health projects aimed at reducing mortality from common diseases and encouraging better use of existing health facilities, while improving the quality of healthcare overall. It also organised mosquito control activities to reduce the incidence of malaria.

HIV/Aids
Although prostitution is relatively rare, over 60 per cent of sex workers in Moroni tested HIV positive.

HIV prevalence: 0.12 per cent aged 15–49 in 2000

Life expectancy: 64 years, 2004 (WHO 2006)

Fertility rate/Maternal mortality rate: 4.9 births per woman, 2010 (Unicef); maternal mortality five per 1,000 live births (World Bank).

Child (under 5 years) mortality rate (per 1,000): 78 per 1,000 live births (WHO 2012); 26 per cent of children aged under five years are malnourished (World Bank).

Head of population per physician: 0.15 physicians per 1,000 people, 2004 (WHO 2006)

Welfare
There is no minimum wage, there are no laws prohibiting bonded or forced labour and no protection for anti-union practices by employers. The labour code allows for one day off per week and one month of paid leave per year, although the government generally does not enforce the law due to a lack of provision.

The World Bank reported, in October 2003, that 47 per cent of households were living in poverty and 42 per cent of the population were malnourished. It stated that the government were poor in implementing, even in partnership, basic social infrastructure, and health and educational services tended to be of low quality and poorly utilised. Local communities were found to be keen to undertake projects in partnership with a World Bank poverty reduction plan, the 'Social Fund Project,' to creat small, income-generating activities. In future, proposed projects will rely mainly on village committees, community groups, NGOs and private firms.

Main cities
Moroni (on Grand Comore (Ngazidja) (capital, estimated population 50,721 in 2012), Mutsamudu (on Anjouan (Ndzuani), (26,469), Fomboni (on Mohéli (Mwali) (18,277), Domoni (16,279), Tsémbehou (12,962), Ongodjou (12,405).

Languages spoken
Shikomor and numerous African languages are spoken. English is rarely spoken.

Official language/s
Arabic and French

Media
The government maintains tight control of the media, with newspapers and radio stations suspended and journalists risk arrest following items deemed disrespectful to its interests. Consequently self-censorship is prevalent.

Press

There are few commercial publications due to a small advertising market and a poor distribution network

In French, weeklies include *Al Watwan* (www.alwatwan.net) and *La Gazette de Comores* are official publications. Independent newspapers include *KashKazi* (www.kashkazi.com) (weekly), and *L'Archipel* (monthly).

Broadcasting

The national, state broadcaster is Office Radio et Télévision des Comores (ORTC) (www.radiocomores.km).

Radio: With high levels of illiteracy and poverty the radio is the principal medium for news and information.

ORTC operates Radio Comoros which broadcasts in Arabic, French, Comoran and Swahili. Two regional governments run their own stations, including Radio Television Anjouanaise (RTA) (www.rtanjouan.org) on Anjouan, and Radio Ngazidja on Grand Comore. Other stations include Radio Ocean Indien (www.radioceanindien.km) and Radio Dziyalandze (www.radiodziyalandze.com). Radio France International (RFI) (www.rfi.fr) has news programmes in French.

Television: ORTC operates the national, Television Nationale Comorienne (TNC). Other TV stations include RTA (www.rtanjouan.org) on Anjouan, TV Ulezi is a private provider while Mtsangani Television (MTV) broadcasts educational and cultural programmes. There are satellite services from Arabnet.

TV and radio services can be received from Mayotte.

Other news agencies: APA (African Press Agency): www.apanews.net

The Comoran Press: www.comores-online.com

Panapress: www.panapress.com

Economy

The islands of Comoros are largely formed from volcanic rock, making it unsuitable for agriculture, so that what production is possible remains at the level of subsistence farming. Nevertheless, the economy is dominated by agriculture, at 46.3 per cent of GDP in 2014 (up slightly from 43.9 per cent in 2011), industry at 12.1 per cent, of which manufacturing was 4.3 per cent, and services 41.6 per cent of GDP. Around 30 per cent of the workforce is employed in agriculture (2010 figure; latest available), where hunting, fishing and forest products supplement meagre crops.

Comoros has been experiencing steady gross domestic product (GDP) growth of around 3 per cent annually since 2011, but much needed major structural transformations have not occurred yet. However, this stable growth has allowed the country to reduce its poverty and unemployment rates, especially among the young – an age group (16-25) 50 per cent of who in 2014 were unemployed. Growth in 2014 was 3.5 per cent, and was forecast to maintain at 3.6 per cent in 2015 and 2016.

A change in the political system in 2001 resulted in centralised, national planning which has achieved a somewhat more effective economic policy. There is an increasing number of young people in the population that require education and social services before they can become productive members of the workforce.

Comoros must rely on international aid, either through remittances, which typically provide over US$110 million per annum, paid directly into households and allowing private consumption, or disbursements from financial institutions. The Paris Club of creditors agreed to debt restructuring in 2009, which was predicated on continued fiscal reforms. The World Bank and the International Monetary Fund (IMF) supports Comoros through a Heavily Indebted Poor Countries (HIPC) Initiative, which has resulted in enhanced growth, poverty reduction and debt sustainability. In December 2012, the IMF and World Bank's International Development Association decided to support Comoros with US$176 million in debt relief.

In its 2014 Human Development Index, the UN ranked Comoros 159 out of 187 countries with 61.2 per cent of the population living on less that US$2 a day.

External trade

Comoros is a member of the Common Market for Eastern and Southern Africa (Comesa), and operates within a free trade zone with 13 of the 19 member states. It is also a member of the Communauté Financière d'Afrique (CFA) (Financial Community of Africa), so that its currency is pegged to the French franc (pre-euro). Comoros runs annual deficits on its trade account, largely due to its limited export base.

Imports

Principal imports are rice and other foodstuffs, consumer goods, chemical products, petroleum products, cement and transport equipment.

Main sources: France (typically 51 per cent of total), China (7.5 per cent), Pakistan (5.9 per cent), India (3.8 per cent).

Exports

Principal exports consist principally of agricultural plantation products, including cloves (40 per cent of total), essence of ylang-ylang (a major component of perfume) and vanilla – of which Comoros is a leading world producer – and other foodstuffs.

Main destinations: Singapore (typically 17 per cent of total), Spain (15 per cent), Turkey (14 per cent) and France (13 per cent).

Agriculture

Farming

The agriculture sector is the principal source of export earnings. Total agricultural land is 186,000 hectares of which 8.1 per cent is pasture and 43 per cent arable. The agricultural sector remains underdeveloped (due to poor soil, adverse weather conditions and inadequate facilities) and over 50 per cent of the country's food requirements (notably rice) have to be imported. The sector employs around 30 per cent of the workforce.

Major food crops grown are cassava, sweet potatoes, rice and bananas; yams and coconuts are also produced, while main cash crops are cocoa, ylang-ylang (perfumes), vanilla and cloves (which make 40 per cent of total exports).

Comoros produces around 1,700 tonnes of vanilla a year but its cultivation has suffered a drop in value due to overseas competition from new plantations and synthetic vanilla.

Fishing

Fishing is underexploited, with tuna being the main catch. The fishing sector has received considerable aid from Japan and the EU.

Forestry

Deforestation, caused by clearing for the cultivation of the ylang-ylang crop, is an increasing ecological problem.

Industry and manufacturing

The industrial sector contributed 13.7 per cent to GDP in 2014 and employs 5 per cent of the workforce; manufacturing contributes 4.3 per cent. The sector is underdeveloped, with activity confined to distillation of essences and perfumes (particularly from ylang-ylang), vanilla processing, soft drinks, plastics and woodwork.

Tourism

The islands of Comoros offer a pristine marine environment with tropical coral reefs, an active volcano and unique flora and fauna. However its low population has also resulted in a lack of tourism infrastructure and no direct flights from Europe (Comoros' primary market).

Tourism had constituted 13.1 per cent of GDP in 2000, but had fallen to 7.5 per cent by 2009, due, not only to the political instability in the islands, but also by the global economic crisis (2007–09), which cut visitor numbers. By 2014, the contribution to GDP had dropped even further to 6.6 per cent. Likewise, visitor exports were cut from US$20 million in 2008 (an amount deemed half the value

of visitor exports in 2000), to US$10 million in 2009. By 2014, visitor exports had returned to around US$16 million. Total employment in travel and tourism was 9.8 per cent in 2000, which had fallen to 6.5 per cent in 2009, and dropped even further to 5.8 per cent by 2014; the equivalent of 9,000 jobs.
By 2007, the government had identified tourism as a key sector for potential growth of the economy. It has largely been foreign investment, particularly by the Gulf Co-operation Council (GCC) countries, that has driven the market in the latter half of the decade. Travel and tourism constituted 3.8 per cent of total investment in 2014, which was forecast to rise by 7.0 per cent in 2015.

Mining
There is no mining activity.

Hydrocarbons
There are no known hydrocarbon reserves. Consumption of oil was 1,080 barrels per day (bpd) in 2013, all of which was imported. The state-owned Société Comorienne des Hydrocarbures (SCH) was responsible for sourcing foreign oil through the French oil company, Total.
Any consumption of natural gas or coal is commercially insignificant.

Energy
Total installed generating capacity was 6MW in 2013, generating 40 million kilowatt hours. Electricity is provided by the parastatal utility Electricite et Eaux des Comores (EEDC).
The electricity infrastructure is poor and there are frequent blackouts, partly due to generator breakdowns and partly due to a lack of fuel. Small and rural communities use solar-photovoltaic installations.

Banking and insurance
The Banking sector is composed of the Banque Centrale des Comores (BCC), the central bank, the Banque de Développement des Comores (BDC), which focusses on development lending, and the Banque pour l'Industrie et le Commerce des Comores (BIC). The BDC stopped lending in 1997 due to liquidity problems, but still exists and is scheduled for restructuring some time in the future. The BIC is linked to France's BNP-Paribas and provides full international trade finance as well as local personal and business banking services.

Central bank
Banque Centrale des Comores (BCC)

Main financial centre
Moroni

Time
GMT plus three hours

Geography
The Comoros is an archipelago in the Mozambique Channel, between the island of Madagascar and the east coast of the African mainland. The group comprises four main islands (Grand Comore, Anjouan, Mohéli and Mayotte), and numerous islets and coral reefs. Mayotte, although geographically part of the Comoros group of islands, elected to remain as a French overseas territory, in 1975, and is politically separate from the Comoros.

Hemisphere
Southern

Climate
Tropical. Dry season May to October with average temperature 24 degrees Celsius (C). Rainy season from November to April with temperature 27–35 degrees C. Very hot and humid on coasts, cooler on inner highlands.

Entry requirements
Passports
Required by all.

Visa
Required by all.
Tourist visas obtained at the port of entry, are valid for 14 days. Visas valid for up to 90 days can be obtained in advance of travelling. Proof of return/onward passage is needed.
For business visas, information can be obtained from the Comoran Embassy 20 Rue Marbeau, 75116 Paris France (tel: (+33) 140-679-054; fax: (+33) 140-677-296).

Currency advice/regulations
There are no restrictions on the import of domestic or foreign currencies.
There are limited banking facilities for foreign travellers, credit cards are not universally accepted and travellers cheques can only be cashed in the Banque Internationale des Comores, in the capital. To avoid additional fees travellers cheques should be in euros. Foreign currency is exchanged in city and provincial banks.

Prohibited imports
Firearms, ammunition and radio transmission equipment, plants and soil.

Health (for visitors)
Mandatory precautions
Yellow fever vaccination certificates requested from visitors arriving from infected areas.

Advisable precautions
Typhoid, hepatitis A, tetanus and polio vaccinations recommended. Malaria prophylaxis advisable as risk exists throughout the country. Water precautions should be taken. There is a rabies risk. Seek further advice with regard to vaccinations for diphtheria, hepatitis B, meningitis and tuberculosis.

Hotels
Advisable to book in advance. Limited first-class accommodation available on Grande Comore, Anjouan and Mayotte (Maore), but several high-quality resort hotels have been built.

Public holidays (national)
Fixed dates
18 Mar (Death of Said Mohamed Cheikh Day), 25 May (Africa Day), 29 May (Death of President Ali Soilih Day), 6 Jul (Independence Day), 26 Nov (Death of President Ahmed Abdallah Day), 25 Dec (Christmas Day).

Variable dates
Eid al Adha, El am Hejir (Islamic New Year), Ashura, Eid al Fitr.

Islamic year 1436 (25 Oct 2014–14 Oct 2015): The Islamic year contains 354 or 355 days, with the result that Muslim feasts advance by 10–12 days against the Gregorian calendar. Dates of feasts vary according to the sighting of the new moon, so cannot be forecast exactly.

Working hours
Banking
Mon–Thu: 0730–1300; Fri: 0730–1100.

Business
Mon–Thu: 0730–1430; Fri: 0730–1130, Sat: 0730–1200.

Government
Mon–Thu: 0730–1200 and 1500–1730, Fri: 0730–1100, Sat: 0730–1200.

Shops
Closed daily between 1200–1500.

Telecommunications
Mobile/cell phones
A GSM 900 service is in operation.

Electricity supply
220V AC

Social customs/useful tips
Few people speak English, business is usually conducted in French or Arabic.

Getting there
Air
Regional flights from Africa are supplemented by scheduled flights from Paris, France and Dubai. Air Mohéli was set up in 2011 to fly the Moroni–Dubai route.
National airline: Air Comores International
International airport/s: Moroni International Prince Said Ibrahim (Code: HAH), 25km north of Moroni, on Ngazidja. Facilities include refreshments and a post office. There are no money changing facilities. Taxis, with fixed prices are available.
Airport tax: None

Surface

Water: Cargo ships that carry passengers provide an irregular service from East Africa, Réunion, Madagascar and Mauritius.

Main port/s: Moroni (Grand Comore) and Fomboni (Anjouan): both have offshore anchorage for larger vessels.

Getting about

National transport

Air: Each island is served by Air Comores. There are regular flights between the islands.

Road: Surfaced roads on Grande Comore and Anjouan; other islands' roads can be difficult in rainy season. Mohéli has only very basic tracks.

Water: Small boats, which can be hired, ply between the islands.

City transport

Taxis: Service is provided by *taxi-brousse* (bush taxis) on each island. The journey from the International Airport to the city centre takes 30 minutes.

Car hire

International driving licence required.

BUSINESS DIRECTORY

The addresses listed below are a selection only. While World of Information makes every endeavour to check these addresses, we cannot guarantee that changes have not been made, especially to telephone numbers and area codes. We would welcome any corrections.

Telephone area codes

The international direct dialling code (IDD) for Comoros is +269, followed by the area code and subscriber's number:

Anjouan	71	Moroni	73
Mohali	72		

Useful telephone numbers

Emergency services: 744-890

Chambers of Commerce

Chambre de Commerce, d'Industries et d'Agriculture, PO Box 763, Moroni (tel: 730-958;fax: 731-983; e-mail: pride@snpt.km).

Banking

Banque de Développement des Comores, Place de France, BP-298 Moroni (tel: 730-154, 730-818; fax: 730-397, e-mail: bdc@snpt.km).

Banque pour l'Industrie et le Commerce - Comores, BP 175, Place de France, Moroni (tel: 730-243, 730-225, 730-289; fax: 731-229).

Central bank

Banque Centrale des Comores, BP 405, Place de France, Moroni (tel: 73-1002/1814; fax: 73-0349).

Travel information

Comorian Association of Tourism (ACT) (tel: 732-847, 731-942; fax: 732-846).

Société Comorienne de Tourisme et d'Hotellerie (COMOTEL), Itsandra Hotel, Ngazidja (tel: 732-365).

International Prince Said Ibrahim Airport, BP 1003, Moroni (tel: 731-593, 732-452, 732-135; fax: 731-468).

Ministry of tourism

Ministry of Transport, Tourism, Post and Telecommunications, BP 97 Moroni (tel: 744-242; fax: 744-241).

Ministries

Ministry of Culture, Youth and Sports, Moroni (tel: 744-044).

Ministry of the Economy, Commerce, Handicrafts and Investment, BP 474 Moroni (tel: 744-232; fax: 730-144).

Ministry of Education, Professional Formation and Human Rights, BP 73 Moroni (tel: 744-185; 744-180).

Ministry of Equipment, Energy and Urbanism, Moroni (tel: 744-500).

Ministry of Finance, Budget and Privatisation, BP 324 Moroni (tel: 744-141; fax: 744-140).

Ministry of Foreign Affairs and Co-operation, BP 428 Moroni (tel: 744-100; fax: 744-111).

Ministry of Health, Population and Women's Affairs, Moroni (tel: 744-070).

Ministry of the Interior and Decentralisation, BP 686 Moroni (tel: 744-666; fax: 744-688).

Ministry of Justice and Islamic Affairs, Moroni (tel: 744-200).

Ministry of Production and the Environment, BP41 Moroni (tel: 744-630; fax: 744-632).

Ministry of Public Service, Employment and Labour, Moroni (tel: 744-540).

Other useful addresses

British Honorary Consulate, BP 986, Moroni (tel/fax: 733-182).

Comoros Embassy (France) 20 Rue Marbeau, 75016 Paris, France (tel: (+33) 1-4067-9054; fax: (+33) 1-4845-1365).

Comoros Mission to UN (US), 866 United Nations Plaza, Suite 418, New York, NY 10017 (tel: (+1-212) 750-1637; e-mail: comun@undp.org; internet: www.un.int/comoros).

Société Internationale des Comores, BP 175, Moroni (tel: 730-243).

APA (African Press Agency): www.apanews.net

The Comoran Press: www.comores-online.com

Panapress: www.panapress.com

Internet sites

Africa Business Network: www.ifc.org/abn

AllAfrica.com: http://allafrica.com

African Development Bank: www.afdb.org

Africa Online: www.africaonline.com

Mbendi AfroPaedia (information on companies, countries, industries and stock exchanges in Africa): http://mbendi.co.za

Congo

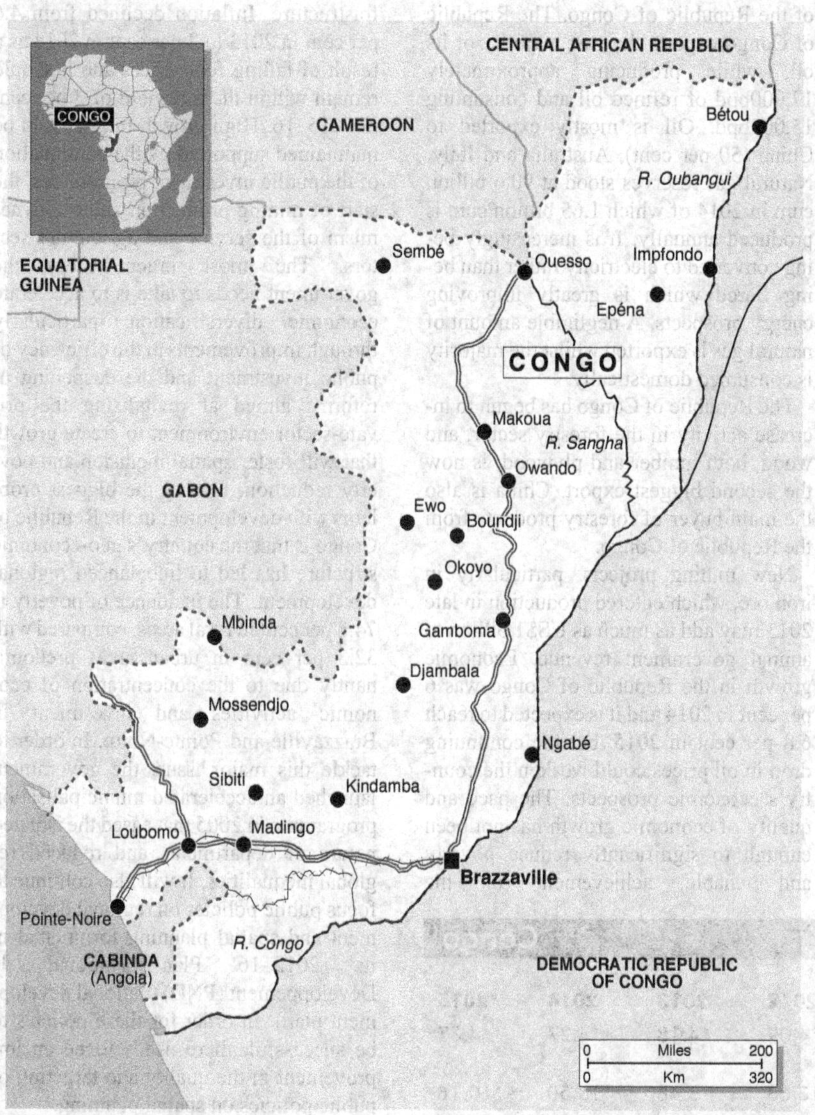

Upon independence in 1960, the former French region of Middle Congo became the Republic of Congo, with a catholic priest, Abbé Fulbert Youlou, as president. Subsequently, the political system became Marxist for 30 years with the Parti Congolais du Travail (PCT) (Congolese Workers' Party) the only legal political party. In 1979 Colonel Denis Sassou-Nguesso appeared for the first time when he took over the PCT until Marxism was abandoned in 1990 and a democratically elected government under the Union Panafricaine pour la Démocratie Sociale (UPADS) (Pan-African Union for Social Development), led by Pascal Lissouba, defeated Sassou-Nguesso and took office in 1992.

Ethnic and political tensions exploded into a full-scale civil war in 1997, fuelled in part by the prize of the country's offshore oil wealth, which motivated many of the warlords. The army split along ethnic lines, with most northern officers joining President Sassou-Nguesso's side, and most southerners backing the rebels. The

KEY FACTS

Official name: République du Congo (Republic of Congo)

Head of State: President Denis Sassou Nguesso (from 1997; re-elected 12 Jul 2009)

Head of government: President Denis Sassou Nguesso (from 2009)

Ruling party: Parti Congolais du Travail (PCT) (Congolese Labour Party) (from 1997; re-elected 5 August 2012)

Area: 342,000 square km

Population: 4.27 million (2014)*

Capital: Brazzaville (political); Pointe-Noire (business)

Official language: French

Currency: CFA franc (CFAf) = 100 centimes (Communauté Financière Africaine (African Financial Community) franc)

Exchange rate: CFAf586.44 per US$ (Sep 2015)

GDP per capita: US$3,159 (2014)*

GDP real growth: 6.02% (2014)*

GDP: US$13.50 billion (2014)*

Inflation: 0.91% (2014)*

Oil production: 296,000 bpd (2012)

Balance of trade: US$2.08 billion (2013)*

* estimated figure

rebels were supporters of the former president, Pascal Lissouba, and his prime minister, Bernard Kolelas, who had been deposed by Sassou-Nguesso in 1997. By the end of 1999 the rebels had lost all their key positions to government forces, who were backed by Angolan troops. Subsequently, the rebels agreed to a ceasefire. Southern-based rebels agreed to a final peace accord in March 2003, however, remnants of the civil war militias, known as Ninjas, are still active in the southern Pool region. Most of them have not disarmed yet and a lot of them have turned to banditry. President Sassou-Nguesso remains as head of state and head of government in the Republic of Congo as of 2015. The last presidential elections were held on 12 July 2009 in which Sassou-Nguesso won 79 per cent of the vote with his main opposition, Joseph Mboungou having won a mere 7.5 per cent.

President Sassou-Nguesso has said he will run in the 2016 presidential elections despite the fact that according to the 2002 Constitution he is over age and is banned from seeking a third term as president. Despite several demonstrations in Brazzaville in September 2015, a referendum to change the constitution to allow Sassou-Nguesso to run is scheduled for 25 October.

The economy

The economy is a mixture of subsistence farming and hunting, an industrial sector based largely on oil and support services, and government spending. Oil and the forestry industry represent the mainstay of the economy, providing a major share of government revenues and exports. Proven reserves of oil were 1.6 billion barrels at the beginning of 2015 with production at 281,000 barrels per day (bpd) in 2014. It has the seventh largest reserve of oil in Africa, and is the sixth largest producer of oil. Oil, therefore, plays an important role in both the economic and political sphere of the Republic of Congo. The Republic of Congo exports the vast majority of its oil, while producing approximately 17,000bpd of refined oil and consuming 15,000bpd. Oil is mostly exported to China (50 per cent), Australia and Italy. Natural gas reserves stood at 90.6 billion cum in 2014 of which 1.65 billion cum is produced annually. It is increasingly being converted to electricity rather than being flared which is greatly improving energy prospects. A negligible amount of natural gas is exported whilst the majority is consumed domestically.

The Republic of Congo has begun to increase activity in the forestry sector, and wood, both lumber and plywood, is now the second biggest export. China is also the main buyer of forestry products from the Republic of Congo.

New mining projects, particularly in iron ore, which entered production in late 2013 may add as much as US$1 billion to annual government revenue. Economic growth in the Republic of Congo was 6 per cent in 2014 and it is expected to reach 6.8 per cent in 2015, but the continuing drop in oil prices could weaken the country's economic prospects. The pace and quality of economic growth has not been enough to significantly reduce poverty and enable achievement of the Millennium Development Goals. Forty-three per cent of the population remained in multi-dimensional poverty in 2014 and 54 per cent of the population lived on under US$1.25 a day. The country's centralised economic structure results in weak spatial inclusion, despite advances due to recent investments in infrastructure. Inflation declined from 4.6 per cent in 2013 to 3 per cent in 2014 as a result of falling food prices and it should remain within the threshold of 3 per cent in 2015–16. High growth rates should be maintained supported by the continuation of the public investment programmes, the start of mining production and the dynamism of the service and agriculture sectors. The most urgent steps the government needs to take is to accelerate economic diversification, particularly through improvements in the efficiency of public investment and the deepening of reforms aimed at revitalising the private-sector environment to create growth that will foster spatial inclusion and poverty reduction. One of the biggest problems with development in the Republic of Congo is that the country's geo-economic structure has led to imbalanced regional development. The incidence of poverty is 74.8 per cent in rural areas, compared with 32.3 per cent in urban areas predominantly due to the concentration of economic activities and investment in Brazzaville and Pointe-Noire. In order to tackle this major issue, the government launched an accelerated municipalisation programme in 2005 that eased the isolated nature of departments and reduced regional inequalities. It will also continue to focus public policies on regional development and spatial planning formulated in its 2012–16 Plan National de Développement (PND) (national development plan). In order for these policies to be successful, there needs to be an improvement in the quality and targeting of public policies on spatial planning.

KEY INDICATORS **Congo**

	Unit	2011	2012	2013	2014	**2015
Population	m	*3.98	*4.09	*4.18	*4.27	*4.37
Gross domestic product (GDP)	US$bn	15.60	13.68	13.48	*13.50	*10.18
GDP per capita	US$	3,485	3,343	*3,223	*3,159	*2,329
GDP real growth	%	3.4	3.8	3.3	*6.0	*5.2
Inflation	%	10.7	5.0	4.6	*0.9	*3.0
Oil output	'000 bpd	295.0	296.0	281.0	–	–
Exports (fob) (goods)	US$m	1,221.0		–	–	–
Imports (fob) (goods)	US$m	507.7		–	–	–
Balance of trade	US$m	713.3		–	–	–
Current account	US$m	103.0	-177.0	*-653.0	*-839.0	*-1,145.0
Total reserves minus gold	US$m	5,715.9	163.0	–	4,926.1	–
Foreign exchange	US$m	5,602.8	1,091.0	–	–	–
Exchange rate	per US$	466.82	497.99	480.26	542.10	–

* estimated figure ** forecast figure

Global value chains

Apart from oil, sugar and forestry products, Congo has not been very active in the area of developing global value chains (GVC). GVCs have, of late, become something of a developmental 'buzz-word'. In 2013, the United Nations Commission for Trade and Development (UNCTAD) published two reports on GVCs and their contribution to development. These concluded that GVCs made a significant contribution to international development. Value-added trade contributed about 30 per cent to the GDP of developing countries, significantly more than it does in developed countries (18 per cent). Furthermore, the level of participation in GVCs is associated with stronger levels of GDP per capita growth. GVCs thus have a direct impact on the economy, employment and income and create opportunities for development. They can also be an important mechanism for developing countries to enhance productive capacity, by increasing the rate of adoption of technology and through workforce skill development, thus building the foundations for long-term industrial upgrading. The Congo's main activity in GVCs has been mostly confined to exporting primary inputs. Finished goods, mainly refined oil products, account for no more than 5 per cent of total exports. With respect to forestry, where there is an undoubted comparative advantage, the share of timber production with high added value stands at just 3 per cent. Congo's integration into GVCs runs up against failing infrastructure in terms of decent transport and availability of energy; the lack of a qualified workforce; the lagging technological and productive capacity of small and medium-sized enterprises (SMEs) and an uncongenial business climate. To remove these obstacles the NDP 2012–16 stresses:

- Increasing infrastructure investment and skills acquisition
- Improving the business climate
- Improving access to credit for SMEs
- Setting up special economic zones (SEZs)
- Strengthening regional integration

Congo is similar to most African countries in its need to balance the interests of its different ethnic groups if it is to achieve any sort of political homogeneity. As is the case with many African nations, the government has found it difficult to attach priorities or agree on specific objectives – be they economic, social or administrative. There's a lot of competition for development dollars and increasingly Africa-wise monetary funds, international banks and donor nations will neither give nor lend unless the important social restructure has reasonable priority. This has to be succeeded with continued transparency – not a favourite of the government. In the Transparency International 2014 *Corruption Perceptions Index* Congo could only rank 152 out of the 175 countries surveyed, a slightly better ranking than the 154 placement it had in 2013.

Congo also has extensive hydropower potential, but most of it remains untapped. Despite Congo's rich energy resources, the electrification rate is low, especially in rural areas, mainly because of a lack of electricity infrastructure. According to the latest (2012) estimate from the World Bank, 42 per cent of the country has access to electricity, leaving 2.6 million people without access. The Congolese civil war (1997–99) left much of the country's transmission and distribution infrastructure damaged, especially in southern Brazzaville (the capital city) and in the Pool, Bouenza and Niari regions, which have not yet been restored. Wood fuel will remain the dominant fuel, particularly in rural areas, until the government introduces effective change. The US government's Energy Information Administration (EIA) estimates that more than 80 per cent of Congo's primary energy consumption is from traditional biomass and waste (typically consisting of wood, charcoal, manure and crop residues). This high share represents the use of biomass and waste to meet off-grid heating and cooking needs, mainly in rural areas.

Risk assessment

Politics	Fair
Economy	Fair
Regional stability	Fair

COUNTRY PROFILE

From the fifteenth century, the Bakongo, Bateke and Sanga began settling in what is now the Republic of Congo.
1482 Portuguese explorer Diogo Cao mapped the coastline.
1880s The colonisation of what is now the Republic of Congo began in the late nineteenth century after the French explorer Pierre Savorgnan de Brazza signed a treaty with the Chief of the Batekes to establish a French protectorate over the north bank of the Congo river.
1910 Middle Congo, as the country was then known, became a colony of French Equatorial Africa.
1928 Africans revolted over forced labour that had been used to build the Congo railway. More than 17,000 Africans died in the revolt.
1946 Congo was granted a territorial assembly by the French and representation in the French parliament.
1960 Congo became independent with a catholic priest, Abbé Fulbert Youlou, as president.
1963 Alfonse Massamba-Debat became president and Pascal Lissouba became prime minister. The country became a one-party socialist state.
1969 Captain Marien Ngouabi led a coup against Massamba-Debat and became president. The Parti Congolais du Travail (PCT) (Congolese Workers' Party) was declared the only legal political party.
1970 Ngouabi proclaimed Congo a Marxist state.
1977 Ngouabi was assassinated by forces loyal to Massamba-Debat, who in turn was executed for treason. Joachim Yhombi-Opango of the Comité Militaire du Parti (CMP) (Party of the Military Committee) became president.
1979 Colonel Denis Sassou-Nguesso took over the PCT, and remained in power under one-party PCT rule until 1992.
1990 The PCT abandoned Marxism.
1992 A new constitution was approved by a referendum. Multi-party legislative elections were won by the Union Panafricaine pour la Démocratie Sociale (UPADS) (Pan-African Union for Social Development), led by Pascal Lissouba. Lissouba was elected president, defeating Sassou-Nguesso.
1993 Political unrest forced new elections, which were won by UPADS.
1994 A peace agreement saw members of the opposition join the government. The currency was devalued.
1997 The government attempted to disarm rebel militia loyal to Sassou-Nguesso, resulting in a civil war. Thousands of people were killed and tens of thousands forced to flee their homes. After several months of fighting the Angolan Army invaded and sided with Sassou-Nguesso who succeeded in overthrowing the government of Pascal Lissouba.
Sassou-Nguesso assumed the presidency at the head of the Conseil National de Transition (CNT) (National Transitional Council).
1999 The warring factions signed a peace accord with the government. However, armed conflict continued.
2001 A peace conference proposed a new constitution and 15,000 militia were given financial incentives to demobilise. Lissouba was convicted *in absentia* of treason and corruption and sentenced to 30 years' hard labour. Congo signed a treaty establishing the Gulf of Guinea Commission.
2002 The new constitution, which strengthened the powers of the president, was endorsed by 80 per cent of the electorate. Sassou-Nguesso was elected president with almost 90 per cent of the vote after his rivals were either banned from running or withdrew. The legislative election for the new bicameral parliament led to the creation of a pro-Sessou-Nguesso coalition consisting of the PCT, the Forces Démocratiques Unies (FDU) (United Democratic Forces) and a number of independents. Electoral disputes between government forces and rebels in the south loyal to former prime minister Bernard

Kolelas led to intense fighting, which reached Brazzaville. An agreement on power-sharing was reached between the government and two main rebel groups, but fighting continued in the east.
2003 All parties signed a peace agreement ending the civil war. A new constitution was adopted paving the way for elections.
2004 The Congo, which was held responsible for large-scale diamond smuggling from the Democratic Republic of Congo (DRC), was expelled from the Kimberley Process Certification Scheme (for diamonds), when it was unable to explain why its exports outstripped its production. The move severely limited the Congo's exports of diamonds.
2005 The president appointed his close ally, Isidore Mvouba, as prime minister and caused a wave of criticism, as the constitution does not allow for presidential appointees. Bernard Kolelas was given an amnesty and allowed to return home after eight years in exile.
2006 Congo was chosen to hold the year's presidency of the African Union, after Sudan withdrew its candidacy amid diplomatic concern about its human rights record.
2007 Former Ninja rebels, who had been led by Pastor (Frederic) Ntoumi in support of Lissouba in the 1997–99 civil war, symbolically burned their weapons to demonstrate their commitment to peace. Around 40 political parties boycotted parliamentary elections. The ruling PCT won 88 seats (out of 137). The London Club (a group of private sector creditors) cancelled 80 per cent of Congo's debt.
2008 A government programme to demobilise, disarm and re-integrate ex-combatants of Paster Ntoumi, was launched.
2009 President Denis Sassou Nguesso was re-elected. The position of prime minister was abolished and all cabinet responsibility reverted to the president.
2010 The World Bank and International Monetary Fund (IMF) announced a package of debt relief amounting to US$255.2 million, which allowed a total debt savings of US$1.9 billion. The president announced one of Africa's toughest child protection legal frameworks. Transparency International successfully appealed against a Paris court's ruling of 2009 that it could not act against foreign heads of state. France's highest appeals court gave the judiciary permission to proceed with investigations into assets held in France by President Denis Sassou-Nguesso, as well as by Teodoro Obiang Nguema of Equatorial Guinea and the late Omar Bongo, former president of Gabon.
2011 An ecology summit of heads of state, ministers and representatives of 35 rainforest countries was held in Brazzaville at the beginning of June. The meeting, to strengthen co-operation, issued a call for international funding for equatorial forest conservation (forests are deemed to provide an international service in carbon capture and provision of livelihood to an estimated 1.5 billion people worldwide). However, they failed to agree a formal structure of co-ordinated forestry policies. Later in June the government announced that four economic zones would be established in 2012, in a move to diversify the economy from hydrocarbons to manufacturing and service industries. The zones will provide tax breaks and other incentives for participating companies. The Singapore Co-operation Enterprise signed a memorandum of understanding (MOU) for help to develop the zones. Several companies from various countries expressed an interest in the zones.
2012 On 4 March a military munitions depot exploded in a suburb of Brazzaville and killed almost 300 people, injured around 2,300 and left 17,000 people homeless. Parliamentary elections were held on 20 July and 5 August, in which the ruling PCT won an overwhelming majority with 89 seats out of 139, plus a further 21 seats of allies, which will allow the government to change the constitution to allow President Denis Sassou Nguesso to run in the 2016 presidential elections. The opposition UPDS declared the result marred by fraud and irregularities. In September, Charles Zacharie Bowao was sacked as defence minister, having been held responsible for the explosion in March, which he had referred to as a 'minor incident without significant damage'.
2013 In September six people were found guilty of being involved in the March 2012 munitions dump explosion. The heaviest sentence went to an army colonel, who received 15 years of forced labour for arson. Another colonel was sentenced to five years for embezzling funds which were supposed to be used to build proper containers for the munitions.
2014 In May it was reported that a vast peat bog had been located in northern Congo. The swamp is is thought to contain billions of tonnes of peat dating back 10,000 years. Studies of this carbon-rich material could reveal how the environment has changed over millennia in central Africa.
2015 Demonstrations were held in Brazzaville on 22 September against a planned referendum that would remove the two-term limit on the presidency and lift the age limit. Although there is as yet no date for the referendum, were it to be successful it would allow President Sassou Nguesso to run in the 2016 election. The referendum was held on 25 October. Exit polls suggested the result would be heavily in favour of allowing Sassou Nguesso to stand for the presidency again.

Political structure

Constitution

President Sassou Nguesso suspended the 2000 constitution in 2002 in favour of an older version in which presidential the term in office is seven years.

Form of state

Republic

The executive

Executive authority is vested in the directly elected president, who serves a seven-year term.

National legislature

The bicameral Parliament consists of the Assemblée Nationale (national assembly), with 153 members, elected in single seat constituencies for five-year terms. The Sénat (senate) has 72 members, elected by local, district and regional councils (six representatives for each of the 12 regions), to serve for six years.

Legal system

Based on the French inquisitorial system, where questions of criminal process is undertaken by a *juge d'instruction* (examining judge), who investigates and conducts serious and complex enquires. Membership of the judiciary ensures independence from the executive. Traditional, customary law sometimes applies.

Last elections

12 July 2009 (presidential); 20 July and 5 August 2012 (parliamentary)

Results: Presidential: Denis Sassou Nguesso won 78.6 per cent of the vote, Joseph Kignoumbi Kia Mboungou (independent) 7.46 per cent; turnout 66.42 per cent (official figure).

Parliamentary: Parti Congolais du Travail (PCT) (Congolese Labour Party) won 89 seats out of 139, Mouvement Congólais pour la Démocratie et le Développement Integral (MCDDI) (Congolese Movement for Democracy and Integral Development) seven, Union Panafricaine pour la Démocratie Sociale (UPDS) (Pan-African Union for Social Development) seven, independents allied to PCT 12, other parties allied to PCT nine, others 12. *Three seats remained vacant*

Next elections

2016 (presidential); 2017 (parliamentary)

Political parties

Ruling party

Parti Congolais du Travail (PCT) (Congolese Labour Party) (from 1997; re-elected 5 August 2012)

Main opposition party

The Union Panafricaine pour la Démocratie Sociale (UPDS) (Pan-African Union for Social Development)

Population
4.09 million (2012)* Seventy per cent of the population lived below the national poverty line in 1995–2001.
Two-thirds live within 510km of the Congo–Océan Railway, which links Pointe-Noire on the Atlantic coast with Brazzaville, the national capital, in the interior. The government is anxious to discourage the present urban drift.
Last census: June 1996: 2,600,000 (provisional)
Population density: 7.6 inhabitants per square km. Urban population 62 per cent (2010 Unicef).
Annual growth rate: 2.6 per cent, 1990–2010 (Unicef).
Internally Displaced Persons (IDP)
100,000 (UNHCR 2004)
Ethnic make-up
Kongo (48 per cent), Sangha (17 per cent), Teke (17 per cent).
Religions
Traditional beliefs (over 50 per cent), Christianity (about 40 per cent, mainly Roman Catholic, some Protestant).

Education
Primary education is followed by seven years of secondary school which is divided into a four-year first cycle (ages 12 to 16) and a three-year second cycle (ages 16 to 19). In the second cycle, students can opt between general or technical education.
Higher education is provided by the Université Marien-Ngouabi, which is largely state subsidised. It has a yearly enrolment of about 12,000 students.
Public expenditure on education typically amounts to 6 per cent of annual gross national income.
Literacy rate: 83 per cent adult rate; 98 per cent youth rate (15–24) (Unesco 2005).
Compulsory years: Six to 12
Enrolment rate: 120 per cent for boys, 109 per cent for girls, total primary school enrolment of the relevant age group (including repetition rates) (World Bank)
Pupils per teacher: 70 in primary schools.

Health
In 2004 a measles epidemics broke out in remote regions of northern Congo due to 'weak vaccination coverage' in earlier programmes and it was expected that, without a thorough immunisation campaign, measles would continue to return in two- to three-year cycles.
Pneumonic plague broke out in February 2005 in the north-east killing over 60 people and prompted control teams to be sent by international medical agencies to treat the victims. Many locals had fled the area and raised the fear of the infection spreading.

HIV/Aids
HIV prevalence: 4.9 per cent aged 15–49 in 2003 (World Bank)
Life expectancy: 54 years, 2004 (WHO 2006)
Fertility rate/Maternal mortality rate: 4.5 births per woman, 2010 (Unicef)
Child (under 5 years) mortality rate (per 1,000): 96 per 1,000 live births (WHO 2012); 16 per cent of children aged under five were malnourished (World Bank).
Head of population per physician: 0.2 physicians per 1,000 people, 2004 (WHO 2006)

Main cities
Brazzaville (political capital, estimated population 1.6 million in 2012), Pointe-Noire (economic capital, 822,850), Loubomo (86,433), Nkayi (76,491), Kindamba (61,304), Impfondo (40,654), Ouesso (31,062).

Languages spoken
French is used for all business documentation. Other major languages are Lingala, Kikongo and Munukutuba. English is not much spoken.
Official language/s
French

Media
Despite the repeal of repressive press laws in 2000 the international human rights watchdog, Freedom House, described the Republic of Congo in 2006 as only partially free, as the government monopolised the broadcast media, which has a much larger share of the potential media audience.
Press
While there are many, small, independent newspapers published in Brazzaville few have a sustainable market outside the capital.
In French, the principal newspapers include the government-owned *Les Dépêches de Brazzaville* (www.brazzaville-adiac.com), the independent *Le Choc* (www.lechoc.info), and the Catholic publication *Semaine Africaine* (www.lasemaineafricaine.com).
Broadcasting
Radiodiffusion-Télévision Nationale Congolaise (RTN) is the state-run broadcaster.
Radio: RTN operates Radio Congo which broadcasts programmes in French, Lingala and Kikongo. The capital's own station, Radio Brazzaville, is also state-run and canal FM is a community station for the city. Radio Liberte is a private station. Foreign radio stations include Reveil FM, from Kinshasa (Democratic Republic Congo) and Radio France International (RFI) (www.rfi.fr) with news programmes in French.
Television: RTN operates the only locally broadcasting TV station, while satellite reception is available.
National news agency: Les Dépêches de Brazzaville
Other news agencies: APA (African Press Agency): www.apanews.net
Congopage (in French): www.congopage.com
Mwinda Press (in French): www.mwinda.org
Panapress: www.panapress.com

Economy
The economy is dominated by petroleum extraction, which accounts for most government spending. Foreign direct investment (FDI), which amounted to US$2 billion in 2013 (latest figures), is typically limited to petroleum extraction and forestry - the prime industry before oil was found. Between them the two industries account for 80 per cent of GDP. However, these sectors are dependent on external markets and global commodity prices which fluctuate. Agriculture accounts for only around 3.3 per cent of GDP in 2014, which is typically subsistence farming and is the country's largest employer. About half the area of forest is exploitable for commercial logging, while only 5 per cent remains protected from development. The service sector, both government and private are also largely supportive of the primary industries and constitutes almost 22.3 per cent of GDP.
Eco-tourism is a fledgling industry and in 2008 and 2009 measures were undertaken to preserve the environment of isolated regions and the Congo Basin for the indigenous pigmy (BaAka) tribes, gorillas, rainforests and bio-diversity in general.
GDP growth was 3.3 per cent in 2013, rising to 6 per cent in 2014, mainly due to an increase in oil production as well as other industries which saw a growth in productivity with help from public investment.
Before the international creditors, led by the Paris Club, agreed to reschedule the Republic of Congo's debts, the government had to demonstrate that it was implementing macroeconomic reforms. In 2008 US$643 million of debt was cancelled and in 2010 a further US$2.4 billion was cancelled, which amounts to all bilateral debts. The debt-to-GDP ratio of 198.7 per cent of GDP at the end of 2004 was reduced to 55.6 per cent of GDP at the end of 2008. With the cancellation of its debts the International Monetary Fund (IMF) expected the ratio to move into surplus of 2.5 per cent of GDP in 2010. In 2012 the IMF reported that net external debt in 2011 had turned negative and assets exceeded debt by 30 per cent of GDP, where it remained in 2014.

World Bank donors pledged up to US$3.9 billion for sub-Saharan Africa in 2006, with around three-quarters of this sum being invested in the regional transportation system. The Trans-African Highway 3 (from Tripoli to Windhoek) passes through the Republic of Congo, but there are still gaps in the highway to both north and south, preventing most through traffic. Improvements to the roads and mass transit could further encourage foreign investment. For its own benefit the government will have to broaden the tax base and improve revenue collection.

In 2013, the UN Human Development Index (HDI) ranked Congo 140 (out of 187) for national development in health, education and income. Since 2000, Congo's progress has grown beyond the average improvement of other sub-Saharan countries in Africa. In 2013, 43.0 per cent of the population experienced multidimensional poverty, while 54.1 per cent lived on less than the equivalent of US$1.25 per day.

The Congo's economic and development prospects have recently been hampered due to the global drop in oil prices in 2014.

External trade

As a member of the Communauté Économique des États d'Afrique Centrale (Economic Community of Central African States (ECCAS) Republic of Congo uses the CFA franc (Communauté Financière Africaine franc), issued by the Banque des États de l'Afrique Centrale (BEAC) (Bank of Central African States). ECCAS operates a customs and economic union with a common external tariff between its six members, with free movement of capital, people and goods and services.

There is a regular large trade surplus from oil export earnings, but invisibles and debt payments keep the current account in deficit.

Imports

Principal imports are manufacturing equipment, vehicles and machinery, construction materials and foodstuffs.

Main sources: China (19.0 per cent of total in 2013 (latest figures)), France (18.7 per cent), Italy (6.2 per cent).

Exports

Principal exports are petroleum, timber, plywood, sugar, cocoa, coffee and diamonds.

Main destinations: China (53.8 per cent of total in 2013 (latest figures)), US (11.1 per cent), Australia (9.4 per cent).

Agriculture

Farming

The agricultural sector employs 30 per cent of the workforce. Agriculture has been overshadowed by development of the petroleum industry.

Total agricultural land is 34.2 million hectares of which 29.3 per cent is pasture and 1.5 per cent arable (mainly in the alluvial Niari Valley).

Farming is small-scale with output concentrated on subsistence crops such as plantains, cassava, yams, groundnuts, manioc, potatoes, wheat, maize, beans and paddy rice. Despite some growth in food production, Congo relies heavily on food imports.

The main cash crops are coffee, cocoa, tobacco and sugar. Attempts to expand production of other cash crops include the rehabilitation of oil palm estates and a major new cocoa project.

Fishing

Fishing is underdeveloped but is practised commercially on a small scale.

Forestry

The main agricultural export is timber, mostly Okoumé logs (of which Congo is a major world supplier). About half the total timber output is used for wood processing. Approximately 60 per cent of the country is covered by woodlands and forests, much of it unsuitable for commercial exploitation. There are large eucalyptus (fast growing) plantations near Pointe-Noire.

Industry and manufacturing

The industrial sector contributes over 10 per cent to GDP and employs a fifth of the workforce. The manufacturing sector is largely underdeveloped, contributing less than 5 per cent to GDP. Construction contributes a further 5 per cent, although this figure could grow rapidly, particularly in the repair of the damaged infrastructure, if political stability remains calm and reconstruction efforts are sustained.

Most manufacturing enterprises operate in the Brazzaville and Pointe-Noire districts and in the Niari Valley. Activity is centred on agri-food and timber processing, textiles and oil refining.

There are also a few small-scale import substitution industries (footwear, soft drinks, metal working, chemicals) and a cement plant.

Structure and ownership of parastatals is being reformed and the privatisation programme is expected to be renewed after years of delay. Emphasis is on joint-venture enterprises, particularly in pulp/paper and light manufacturing.

Tourism

Apart from business arrivals generated by the growing oil industry, tourism is underdeveloped and is in need of foreign investment to improve facilities. Around 80 per cent of the country is covered in dense rainforest, with the population located mainly in the south-east around the capital. The remainder of the country is sparsely populated. Not only are the domestic roads and rail system in a poor state but incentives for the government and foreign investors to upgrade and extend them are only now emerging.

One of the Congo's potentially biggest tourist attractions is gorilla watching. The western lowland gorilla, which is designated as a critically endangered mammal by the International Union for Conservation of Nature (IUCN), and the forest elephant, are found in the Odzala National Park. The Park includes the northern swamp forest and a neighbouring Marantaceae (dryland) forest.

The travel and tourist industry accounted for only 1.5 per cent of GDP in 2014, despite an increase in annual contribution from US$90 million in 2006 to an estimated US$500 million in 2014. Direct employment in the industry in 2014 was 12,500 jobs (1.4 per cent of total employment) and a total contribution to employment, including jobs indirectly supported by the industry, of 32,500 jobs (3.7 per cent of total employment).

Eco-tourism offers great potential, but Congo has only just begun to fund and attract investment in the tourist sector and it will take time before the returns benefit the country as a whole.

The Congo only hosted just over 250,000 international visitors in 2014.

Mining

Congo has significant deposits of magnesium, gold, diamonds, cement, potash and salt. Much of commercial exploitation of these deposits were damaged by the civil war or had been held taken over by warlords. Now much over the mineral deposits have been reclaimed by more legitimate sources and production is in the up again and 112 out of 155 mines have passed the new validation process as 'clean'.

Gold production has been stable for a number of years now, standing at 150kg in 2012 (latest figures). Diamond production, on the other hand, has seen a slight decline, dropping from 76,548 carats in 2011 to 51,588 carats in 2012 (latest figures). Though the Congo has great potential in the non-hydrocarbon extraction industry, many of the mines are run by small artisans and companies. Investment in the mines is desperately needed but the the business climate is not ripe to attract foreign investors, in the 2014 World Bank's Doing Business Indicator the Congo ranked 178 out of 189 countries.

Hydrocarbons

Proven oil reserves were 1.6 billion barrels in 2013 (latest figures), with production at 265,000 barrels per day (bpd), which was a fall of -5.4 per cent on the 2012 figure.

French oil company Total E&F (Elf and Fino) has the dominant role in Congo's oil sector although it has lost its monopoly status as other foreign companies, especially Italy's Agip, are also investing in the country's petroleum industry. Italy's Eni and Total E&F have said that they would invest in production of Congo's tar sands field. Total E&F began production of the Moho Bilondo deep-water oil field in 2008, with an estimated 230 million barrels of recoverable oil. It has also invested in the only oil terminal in Congo, processing 250,000bpd from all domestic oil fields and able to handle one tanker every four days, loading from offshore buoys.
In 2012 the Congo and Angola signed an agreement to undertake a joint exploration and development of deep sea oil reserves in a Joint Development Zone (JDZ). In 2013 the two nations boosted exploration and production is expected to begin in late 2015.
Oil refining capacity was 21,000bpd, which is more than adequate for domestic consumption of over 13,000bpd.
Proven natural gas reserves were 90.6 billion cubic metres in 2012 (latest figures), most of which was oil-associated. A lack of infrastructure and investment means that most gas is vented or flared.
The French energy company Total announced, in early 2011, the discovery of two new hydrocarbon reserves, situated 70km offshore of Congo in deep waters.
The 25MW gas plant in Djeno utilises gas for electricity production for supply to the Pointe Noire area.
Any use of imported coal is commercially negligible.

Energy
Total installed generating capacity was 559MW in 2013 (latest figures), although generating potential is estimated at 3,000MW, from unexploited hydropower. Around 25 per cent of the country's electricity requirements are imported from the Democratic Republic of Congo (DRC).
The state-owned Société Nationale d'Électricité (SNE) is responsible for generating and distribution of energy but transmission is severely limited so that consumption is low and most rural inhabitants rely on wood fuel as a primary source of power.

Banking and insurance
In 2004 the banking system was considered fragile by the IMF, with credit growth limited by the lack of viable projects and a reluctance by banks to make loans as loan recovery is problematic. Of the four domestic banks two have been classified as in good condition and two in either a fragile or critical condition and in need of restructuring.

Central bank
Banque des Etats de l'Afrique Centrale (BEAC) (Bank of the Central African States)

Main financial centre
Brazzaville

Time
GMT plus one hour

Geography
The Republic of Congo is an equatorial country on the west coast of Africa. A flat, treeless plane stretches down from the highlands to the coast. The coastline stretches about 170km along the Atlantic Ocean. The rain-forested highlands extends northward to Cameroon and the Central African Republic. Congo is bordered by Gabon in the west, and with the Democratic Republic of Congo to the east. In the south there is a short frontier with the Cabinda enclave of Angola.

Hemisphere
Straddles the equator.

Climate
Equatorial or sub-equatorial. Main dry season from June–September with average temperatures ranging from 15 degrees Celsius (C) at night to 32 degrees C during the day. Rainy season from October–May with higher average temperatures and high humidity. Generally hotter and more humid in Congo Basin, drier and cooler in highlands.

Entry requirements
Passports
Required by all, valid for at least six months.

Visa
Required by all. Tourists must provide evidence of accommodation arrangements in Congo and of sufficient funds. If on business, a letter, issued by the traveller's company, giving a detailed summary of intended purpose of trip, a full itinerary including intended contacts with host company, and the acceptance of full responsibility for any expenses incurred during the term of stay, and repatriation expenses in case of emergency, must be submitted with the application to the local embassy.

Currency advice/regulations
There is no limit to the amount of foreign currency which can be imported, but amounts above US$335 must be declared; export of foreign currency is limited to the amount declared on arrival. The import and export of local currency is prohibited, except between countries in the CFAf zone.

Health (for visitors)
Medical and dental facilities are inadequate.

Mandatory precautions
A yellow fever vaccination certificate is required by all.

Advisable precautions
Typhoid, hepatitis A and B, polio and tetanus vaccinations are recommended. Malaria prophylaxis should be taken, as a risk exists throughout the country. Water precautions should be taken. Visitors should avoid uncooked fruit and vegetables. There is an Aids risk and a risk of rabies.

Hotels
Good hotels are available in Brazzaville, Pointe-Noire and Loubomo; there are few elsewhere. It is advisable to book well in advance. A 10 per cent tip is usual.

Credit cards
Two hotels in Brazzaville and several in Pointe Noire accept major credit cards.

Public holidays (national)
Fixed dates
1 Jan (New Year's Day), 5 Feb (President's Day), 8 Mar (Women's Day), 18 Mar (Marien Ngouabi Day), 1 May (Labour Day), 22 Jun (Army Day), 31 Jul (Revolution Day), 13–15 Aug (Independence celebrations), 25 Dec (Christmas Day), 31 Dec (Republic Day).

Variable dates
Easter Monday; Ascension Day.

Working hours
Banking
Mon–Fri: 0630–1300. Counters close at 1130.

Business
Mon–Fri: 0800–1200 and 1430–1730, Sat: 0800–1200.

Government
Mon–Fri: 0700–1400, Sat: 0700–1200.

Shops
Mon–Fri: 0800–1200 and 1530–1800. Sat: 0800–1200 and 1530–1800/1900. Some shops close on Mon afternoons; a few open Sun mornings.

Telecommunications
Telephone/fax
Telephone services are inadequate. Major hotel may provide fax and Internet services.

Mobile/cell phones
There there are two GSM 900 networks operating: CelTel Congo and Libertis Telecom; however, coverage is generally restricted to Brazzaville and Pointe Noire.

Electricity supply
220V AC 50 cycles; the voltage varies erratically.

Weights and measures
The metric system is used.

Getting there
Air
National airline: Lina Congo

International airport/s: Brazzaville-Maya Maya Airport (BZV), 4km from city; restaurant, car hire.

Other airport/s: Pointe-Noire Airport (PNR), 6km from city.

Airport tax: CFAf500.

Surface

Road: There is a road from Lambaréné, in Gabon, to Loubomo and Brazzaville; this is not surfaced all the way. Entry from Cameroon is only practicable in the dry season. There is a surfaced road from the Cabinda enclave of Angola.

Water: A ferry service across the River Congo is operational daily from 0800–1200 and 1400–1700 between Kinshasa (Democratic Republic of Congo) and Brazzaville. Cars can be carried. The ferry takes about half an hour. There is also a *vedette* service for passengers only, which takes 15 minutes. Both services are liable to short-notice cancellation or delay.

Main port/s: Pointe-Noire. Brazzaville is the inland river port.

Getting about

National transport

Air: Internal air service operated by Lina Congo from Brazzaville to Pointe-Noire and the main provincial towns.

Road: There are 1200km of tarred roads; other routes are mainly tracks which can be impassable in wet weather.

There are very few metalled roads outside Brazzaville and Pointe-Noire, while the roads within the towns are generally poor. The main route from Pointe-Noire, through Brazzaville to Ouesso, is not uniform in quality; the section from Loubomo to Pointe-Noire is liable to become impassable in the rainy season.

Rail: The Congo-Océan railway runs from Pointe-Noire to Brazzaville, a distance of around 500km. The service has been improved, but the journey is slow. The only other line is the 280km Comilog railway from Mbinda on the Congo/Gabon border which links to the Congo-Océan railway and is used mainly for the carriage of manganese ore produced by Comilog. The railways suffer from lack of maintenance and general upkeep.

Water: The ferries on the rivers Congo and Oubangui are a principal form of transport.

City transport

Taxis: Freely available in Brazzaville and Pointe-Noire; tipping is not usual. Can be hired by the hour or day. Fares should be negotiated in advance of journey.

Car hire

Available from main hotels in Brazzaville and Pointe-Noire. International or national driving licence accepted. Traffic drives on the right.

BUSINESS DIRECTORY

The addresses listed below are a selection only. While World of Information makes every endeavour to check these addresses, we cannot guarantee that changes have not been made, especially to telephone numbers and area codes. We would welcome any corrections.

Telephone area codes

The international direct dialling code (IDD) for Congo is + 242, followed by subscriber's number.

Useful telephone numbers

Fire: 18.

Police: 17.

Ambulance: 822-365/368.

Chambers of Commerce

Congo National Chamber of Commerce, Industry and Agriculture, PO Box 1119, Brazzaville (tel: 832-956).

Brazzaville Chamber of Commerce, Industry, Agriculture and Crafts, Avenue Amilcar Cabral, PO Box 92, Brazzaville (tel/fax: 811-608; e-mail: cciam_brazza@hotmail.com).

Dolisie Regional Chamber of Commerce, Industry and Agriculture, PO Box 78, Dolisie (Tel: 910-017).

La Sangha Regional Chamber of Commerce, Industrie and Agriculture, PO Box 122, Ouessa (tel: 983-200).

Pointe-Noire Chamber of Commerce, Agriculture, Industry and Crafts, PO Box 665, Pointe-Noire (tel: 941-280; fax: 943-467; e-mail: cciampnr@cg.celtelplus.com).

Banking

Banque de Développement des Etats de l'Afrique Centrale, PO Box 1177, Brazzaville (tel: 811-885, 811-761; fax: 811-880).

Banque des États de l'Afrique Centrale, PO Box 126, Brazzaville (tel: 832-814/5, 833-626, 833-362; fax: 836-342).

Banque Internationale du Congo, PO Box 33, Avenue Amilcar Cabral, Brazzaville (tel: 830-308, 831-411; fax: 815-092, 835-382).

Crédit pour l'Agriculture, l'Industrie et le Commerce (CAIC), PO Box 2889, Brazzaville (tel: 810-978, 814-050; fax: 810-977, 835-352).

Mutuelle Congolaise d'Epargne et de Crédit, PO Box 13237, Brazzaville (tel: 837-001; fax: 837-930).

Union Congolaise de Banques; PO Box 147, Avenue Amilcar Cabral, Brazzaville (tel: 833-000; fax: 836-845).

Central bank

Banque des États de l'Afrique Centrale, Direction Nationale, PO Box 126, Brazzaville (tel: 813-684; fax: 811-094; e-mail: beacbzv@beac.int).

Travel information

Direction Générale du Tourisme et de Hotellerie, BP 2480, Brazzaville (tel: 814-030; fax: 815-549; e-mail:mcatcongo@yahoo.fr).

Ministries

Ministry of Construction and Urban Development, BP 1218, Brazzaville.

Ministry of Decentralisation and Regional Development, BP 630, Brazzaville.

Ministry of Defence, BP 1219, Brazzaville.

Ministry of the Economy, BP 2120, Brazzaville.

Ministry of Finance and the Budget, BP 64, Brazzaville (tel: 411-266; fax: 814-145).

Ministry of Foreign Affairs, BP 2070, Brazzaville.

Ministry of Industry, Fisheries and Crafts, Palais du Peuple, Brazzaville (tel: 835-130).

Ministry of the Interior and of Security, BP 64, Brazzaville.

Ministry of Trade and Small- and Medium-sized Enterprises, Brazzaville (tel: 831-827).

Ministry of Transport and Civil Aviation, BP 2146, Brazzaville.

Other useful addresses

Agence Congolaise d'Information (ACI), BP 2144, Brazzaville

Bureau pour le Développement de la Production Agricole, BP 2222, Brazzaville.

Direction de la Statistique, BP 2031, Brazzaville (tel: 834-324).

Institut de Développement Economique de la République Populaire du Congo, c/o The Presidency, Brazzaville.

Office du Café et du Cacao (OCC), BP 2488, Brazzaville (tel: 831-902).

Office Congolais des Bois (OCB), BP 1229, Pointe-Noire (tel: 948-248).

Office Congolais de l'Entretien Routier (OCER), BP 2073, Brazzaville.

Office National du Commerce (ONC), BP 2305, Brazzaville (tel: 834-399).

Republic of Congo Embassy (USA), 4891 Colorado Avenue, NW, Washington DC 20011 (tel: 726-5500; fax: 726-1860; e-mail: info@embassyofcongo.org).

Société Nationale de Recherche et d'Exploitation Pétrolières (Hydro Congo), BP 2008, Brazzaville (tel: 833-560).

Syndicat des Commerçants, Importateurs et Exportateurs de l'Afrique Equatoriale (Sycomimpex), BP 84, Brazzaville.

National news agency: Les Dépêches de Brazzaville, Les Manguiers, 76 Ave Paul Doumer, Brazzaville (tel: 532-0109; fax: 532-0110; email: belie@congonet.cg; internet: www.brazzaville-adiac.com).

APA (African Press Agency): www.apanews.net

Congopage (in French): www.congopage.com

Mwinda Press (in French): www.mwinda.org

Panapress: www.panapress.com

Internet sites

Africa Business Network: http://www.ifc.org/abn

AllAfrica.com: http://allafrica.com

African Development Bank: http://www.afdb.org

Africa Online: http://www.africaonline.com

Congo-Brazzaville (French only, Actualité dossier): http://www.solcongolais.net/

Mbendi AfroPaedia (information on companies, countries, industries and stock exchanges in Africa): http://mbendi.co.za

Democratic Republic of Congo

KEY FACTS

Official name: République Démocratique du Congo (Democratic Republic of Congo) (DRC)

Head of State: President Joseph Kabila Kabange (elected 2006; re-elected 28 Nov 2011)

Head of government: Prime Minister Augustin Matata Ponyo (from 19 Apr 2012)

Ruling party: Caretaker-coalition led by Parti du Peuple pour la Reconstruction et la Démocratie (PPRD) (People's Party of Reconstruction and Democracy) with Parti Lumumbiste Unifié (PLU) (United Lumumbist Party) and Union des Démocrates Mobutistes (UDM) (Union of Mobutist Democrats) (elected 2006; re-elected 28 Nov 2011)

Area: 2,345,409 square km

Population: 79.30 million (2014)*

Capital: Kinshasa

Official language: French

Currency: Congolese franc (Cf)

Exchange rate: Cf925.00 per US$ Nov 2015)

GDP per capita: US$437 (2014)*

GDP real growth: 9.09% (2014)*

GDP: US$34.68 billion (2014)*

Inflation: 1.00% (2014)

Oil production: 281,000 bpd (2014)

Balance of trade: US$1.00 billion (2014)

* estimated figure

In 2015 the Democratic Republic of Congo (DRC) joined the increasing number of African countries who are changing their constitutions to accommodate presidents with a taste for the trappings of power. On 17 January 2015 it was announced that electoral laws were being changed to allow the forty-four year old President Joseph Kabila to stay in office beyond his mandated two-term limit. This move by Kabila, president since 2001, was not entirely well received by the population and led to demonstrators from the University of Kinshasa taking to the streets. According to the NGO Human Rights Watch (HRW), 36 people died at the protests as a result of DRC's security forces using unlawful and excessive force to crack down. Of these, 21 were fatally shot by the security forces on 19 January, and additionally at least four were killed in protests in Goma on the 22 January.

Equivalent in size to Western Europe and with immense economic resources, the DRC is at the centre of Africa's potentially most serious region of conflict. Its position in the heartland of Africa gives it inevitable strategic importance. A five-year civil war pitted government forces, supported by Angola, Namibia and Zimbabwe, against rebels backed by Uganda and Rwanda. Despite a 2003 peace deal and the formation of a transition government, the threat of more conflict remains. The fighting is fuelled by the country's vast mineral wealth, with all sides taking advantage of the anarchy to plunder its natural resources.

The history of the DRC has been one of civil war and corruption. After independence in 1960, the country immediately faced an army mutiny and an attempt at secession by its mineral-rich province of Katanga. A year later, its prime minister, Patrice Lumumba, was seized and killed by troops loyal to army chief Joseph Mobutu. In 1965 Mobutu seized power, later renaming the country Zaïre and himself Mobutu Sese Seko. He turned Zaïre into a springboard for operations against Soviet-backed Angola and thereby ensured US backing. But he also made the country synonymous with corruption. That situation continues: on the 2014 Transparency International *Corruption Perceptions Index* the DRC ranked 154 out of the 175 countries surveyed, just below neighbouring Republic of Congo (152).

The backdrop

After the Cold War, the then Zaïre ceased to be of interest to the US. In 1997 anti-Mobutu rebels quickly captured the capital, Kinshasa, installed Laurent Kabila as president and renamed the country. A rift between Kabila and his former allies backed by Rwanda and Uganda sparked a new rebellion. Angola, Namibia and Zimbabwe took Kabila's side and the country became a vast battleground. The United Nations has maintained more than 14,000 peacekeepers in the region since 1999. Laurent Kabila was assassinated in 2001 to be succeeded by his son, Joseph, who in 2015 had ruled for 14 years. The death of Laurent Kabila was not attributed to any international conspiracy, nor to the Congolese rebels who controlled much of the eastern part of the Democratic Republic of Congo. In a scenario worthy of Shakespeare, he was assassinated by his own *kadogos* (Swahili for child soldiers) who believed him to have betrayed them. Laurent Kabila had naively believed that the *kadogos* who had served him loyally since his rebellion in 1997 against ex-president Mobutu were completely loyal. He was quoted as saying: 'They will never do anything against me. They have been with me since the beginning. They are my children.'

Since the accession of Joseph Kabila in 2001, the DRC has experienced a significant turnaround under difficult circumstances, but the figures do not tell the full story. In some instances, overall economic objectives have been met, but the composition of expenditure has not improved as envisaged. Low levels of spending on public investment and social sectors have been offset by overspending on security and political institutions. Militias, rebel and other armed groups remain active in the illegal exploitation of minerals in the east. The Kinshasa government has no control over large parts of the country and tension remains high in the east.

President Joseph Kabila's victory in the 2011 election was fragile and contested. His swearing-in ceremony coincided with a 'parallel' ceremony in which the 'opposition' leader Etienne Tshisekedi, 79, was to be sworn in as president 'by the people' at a mass rally in Kinshasa's Martyrs' stadium. Mr Tshisekedi was the leader of the Union for Democracy and Social Progress (UDPS), an important political movement. Alarmingly, for a period it was uncertain who exactly was running the show in this vast country. The stark truth is that the international community has minimal leverage over President Kabila; DR Congo is so resource rich that it is able to call the shots.

The economy

In its 2015 African Economic Outlook on DRC, the African Development Bank (AfDB) mentioned that strong growth of 9 per cent in 2014 was driven by the extractive and manufacturing industries, agriculture, commerce and construction, and benefited from fairly good external demand and moderately high raw material prices. The business climate has also improved in DRC and the infrastructure deficit has also reduced. The outlook given by AfDB was that growth should remain strong in 2015 and 2016 if the domestic political and security situation stays calm and if external conditions remain good. The extractive and agro-food industries attract the most large-scale investment and will boost growth.

The rate of investment in the private sector has been growing steadily for the last five years, however the sector is still small. Its prospects have improved since the environment has been developed, including abolition of some taxes, simplified procedures for setting up businesses and importing goods, upgrading of infrastructure and membership of the Organisation for the Harmonisation of Business Law Africa.

The AfDB stated that despite higher world prices for food and oil products in the first half of the year, the macroeconomic situation remained under control in 2014 and inflation was below expected at 1.2 per cent. The exchange rate between the Congolese franc and the US dollar remained largely unchanged. The report claimed these results were due to a cautious macroeconomic policy and revival of export revenue.

The outlook stated the DRC had not done enough to reach its 2015 Millennium Development Goals (MDGs), as economic performances have only had a limited affect on overall living standards. There aren't enough jobs, especially for the youth, and population growth hampers the effectiveness of the government's steps to eliminate hunger. Support has been pledged to small farmers and there are plans for agro-industrial parks, however, the quality and quantity of education and health services need to be improved further.

The AfDB finished the outlook report by attributing the sharp social and economic inequalities among provinces and the rural-urban divide to the country's geographical isolation, being almost landlocked and having poor infrastructure. Since 2007, the government has made efforts at decentralisation, however, they have been slow to come into action.

KEY INDICATORS — Democratic Republic of Congo

	Unit	2011	2012	2013	2014	**2015
Population	m	*72.57	*74.75	*76.99	*79.30	*81.68
Gross domestic product (GDP)	US$bn	15.70	17.70	*31.62	*34.68	*39.06
GDP per capita	US$	216	236	*411	*437	*476
GDP real growth	%	6.9	7.1	*8.5	*9.1	*9.2
Inflation	%	15.5	9.3	0.8	1.0	*2.4
Exports (fob) (goods)	US$m	9,417.9	8,534.2	11,613.0	12,981.9	–
Imports (fob) (goods)	US$m	8,915.6	8,355.7	10,808.4	11,980.1	–
Balance of trade	US$m	556.3	178.5	804.5	1,001.8	–
Current account	US$m	-1,814.0	-2,192.0	-3,513.0	*-3,312.0	*-4,179.0
Total reserves minus gold	US$m	1,948.9	–	1,678.5	1,557.0	–
Foreign exchange	US$m	1,384.7	–	1,136.1	–	–
Exchange rate	per US$	922.80	917.27	917.00	928.72	–

* estimated figure ** forecast figure

Risk assessment

Politics	Poor
Economy	Fair
Regional stability	Poor

COUNTRY PROFILE

During the sixteenth and seventeenth centuries, the British, Dutch, Portuguese and French bought slaves from the Kongo Empire.

1870 King Leopold II of Belgium set up a private venture to exploit the riches of the Kongo Empire.

1879–87 British explorer, Henry Stanley was commissioned to established Belgian authority over the Congo basin.

1884–85 European governments recognised Leopold's claim to the Congo basin.

1885 Leopold established the Congo Free State, which he headed.

1891–92 Belgium conquered Katanga.

1892–94 Belgium conquered eastern Congo, which was controlled by Arab and east African merchants.

1908 The Belgian state annexed Congo following atrocities carried out by Leopold's officials.

1959 A nationalist uprising based in Leopoldville (now Kinshasa) began the disintegration of Belgian colonial authority.

1960 Congo gained independence. Joseph Kasavuba became president. The Belgian community fled and too few professionals were left to run the government. Chaos ensued as the diamond and copper mining province of Katanga attempted to secede under the leadership of Joseph Tshombe.

1961 Prime Minister Patrice Lumumba was deposed and murdered, allegedly by Katangan separatists. Marshal Joseph Mobutu was appointed prime minister. UN soldiers began disarming the Katangese soldiers on behalf of the Kasavuba government.

1963 Tshombe agreed to end the Katangan separatist war.

1964 President Kasavuba dismissed Mobutu and appointed Tshombe as prime minister.

1965 Mobutu seized power after a coup.

1971 Congo was renamed Zaïre. Mobutu renamed himself Mobutu Sese Seko.

1973–74 Mobutu nationalised foreign firms and forced foreign investors out of the country.

1977 French, Belgian and Moroccan troops fought an attack on Katanga by Angolan-based rebels.

1989 Zaïre defaulted on its debt servicing to Belgium; the economy began to deteriorate as development programmes were suspended.

1990 Mobutu appointed a transitional government and lifted the ban on multi-party politics.

1991 A series of short-lived coalition governments were presided over by President Mobutu, who retained control of security and key ministries.

1993 Rival pro- and anti-Mobutu governments were formed

1996 Tutsi rebels, in eastern Zaire, captured much of the eastern border area

1997 Mobutu fled to Togo when the Alliance des Forces Démocratiques pour la Libération (AFDL) (Alliance of Democratic Forces for Liberation), led by Laurent-Désiré Kabila, seized Kinshasa, after a seven-month campaign. Kabila had been backed by Tutsi rebels and the Rwandan government. Zaïre was renamed the Democratic Republic of Congo (DRC). Kabila became president. All government institutions were dissolved and a new constitution drafted. Mobutu Sese Seko died in Morocco.

1998 The Rassemblement Congolais pour la Démocratie-Goma (RCD-Goma) (Congolese Democratic Coalition) was formed, supported by Rwanda, Burundi and Uganda, and aimed at overthrowing Kabila, who was backed by Zimbabwe, Namibia and Angola. A full-scale civil war broke out. Peace talks began in Zambia but were ultimately unsuccessful.

1999 A split developed between the Mouvement pour la Libération Congolaise (MLC) (Movement for Congolese Liberation) backed by Uganda and the RCD-Goma supported by Rwanda. The six countries involved in the war signed a cease-fire, and the RCD-Goma and MLC signed later.

2000 The UN authorised a 5,500-strong force to monitor the supposed cease-fire; fighting continued between government and rebel forces and Rwandan and Ugandan forces.

2001 President Kabila was assassinated. His son, Major General Joseph Kabila became president. A peace agreement between DRC, Uganda and Rwanda allowed foreign troops to withdraw. An estimated 2.5 million people had died in the conflict; the UN reported that the warring parties had continued the fighting to mask plundering of DCR's rich mineral assets.

2002 Goma was devastated by the eruption of Mount Nyiragongo. Rwanda and the DRC signed a peace deal whereby Rwanda withdrew troops and DRC disarmed and arrested Rwandan Hutu militia held responsible for the genocide in Rwanda in 1994. The DRC government signed a peace deal with the two main rebel groups. UN sponsored power-sharing talks were undertaken in South Africa.

2003 A transitional constitution sanctioned an interim government pending democratic elections to be held within two years. Leaders of the principal former rebel groups were sworn in as vice presidents.

2004 The massacre of 160 mostly Tutsi DRC refugees in Burundi prompted renewed warnings of war, and the Tutsi-led RCD-Goma, the former main rebel group during the DRC's civil war, suspended its participation in the power-sharing government.

2005 Nine UN peacekeepers were killed in the north-east; UN troops retaliated, killing over 50 militia members. The national assembly adopted a draft constitution, which had been agreed by former rebel groups. A referendum on the new constitution was gave resounding approval for the changes, with 84.31 per cent voting 'yes'. The result paved the way for presidential and parliamentary elections.

2006 Etienne Tshisekedi, leader of the opposition Union pour la Démocratie et le Progrès Social (UDPS) (Union for Democracy and Social Progress) withdrew his call for a boycott of the general elections. In the first free democratic elections since the 1960s over 9,700 candidates contested 500 seats in the national assembly. In presidential elections, incumbent Joseph Kabila won 58.05 per cent of the vote and Vice President Jean-Pierre Bemba 41.95 per cent; turnout was over 70 per cent. Antoine Gizenga of the Parti Lumumbiste Unifié (Palu) (United Lumumbist Party) was appointed prime minister.

2007 In senate elections Kabila's Alliance pour la Majorité Présidentielle (AMP) (Alliance for a Presidential Majority) won 58 seats (out of 108). The Union pour la Nation Congolese (UNC) (Congolese National Party) coalition won 21 (including a seat for Jean Pierre Bemba, its leader). The Communaute Economique des Pays des Grands Lacs (CEPGL) (Great Lakes Countries Economic Community) was re-launched by Burundi, DRC and Rwanda. CEPGL is intended to promote regional economic co-operation and integration. Rebel leader, Laurent Nkunda, fighting in the eastern provinces of North and South Kivu, declared that the ceasefire with government forces had ended. Fighting displaced over 300,000 people from the area to UNHCR camps near the city of Goma, while many more fled into rebel held territory and out of reach of international aid. Renegade leader Kasereka Kabamba was forced to surrender to government forces in North Kivu province.

2008 Jean-Pierre Bemba was arrested (in Belgium) to face charges of war crimes at the International Criminal Court (ICC). Bemba had been in exile since being

accused of high treason in DRC for refusing to disarm his militia, following his defeat in 2006 presidential elections. The president appointed Adolphe Muzito (Palu) as prime minister.
2009 Rwandan troops crossed into DRC in a joint military operation to eliminate Rwandan Hutu militia, exiled in DRC since 1994 and causing widespread mayhem in DRC's eastern province, destabilising the region. Former general and Tutsi rebel leader Laurent Nkunda (Conseil National pour la Défense du Peuple (CNDP) (National Council for the Defence of the People) was arrested in Rwanda, having fled from his stronghold in Bunagana. Another, Hema, militia leader, Thomas Lubanga, caught in 2005, went on trial before the ICC, charged with the use of child soldiers and the killing of rival militia of the Lendu tribe in Ituri Province. A Swiss court ruled that the assets of former president Mobutu Sese Seko, held in Swiss banks, must be returned to his family. It rejected the appeal that the money (over US$6 million) should be returned to DRC, because the legal claim to the money took too long to be brought before the court.
2010 The Paris Club of creditors agreed to forego almost half DRC debts in an agreement. Of the US$3 billion covered by the agreement, around US$1.3 will be cancelled and the remainder rescheduled and debt service payments deferred until 1 July 2012. The UN agreed to withdraw its peacekeeping troops, at the request of the government. A US$12 billion debt relief package was agreed by the International Monetary Fund (IMF); the country would no longer have to carry its heavy debt service burden on its revenue and foreign exchange reserves. Army commander Sadoke Kokunda Mayele was arrested on charges of encouraging the gang rape of more than 300 persons; he was handed over by his fellow rebels. The trial began of former vice president, Jean-Pierre Bemba, at the ICC in The Hague (The Netherlands). He was charged with crimes against humanity and war crimes while leading his military forces in the Central African Republic in 2002–03; the abuses included murder, rape and pillage, which were alleged to have been 'widespread and systematic'.
2011 Constitutional amendments were adopted in January, when among other amendments, electoral changes were introduced that stopped the presidential run-off process. There were rumours of an attempted coup against the president on 27 February. The ban on mining in the east of the country that had been imposed in 2010 was lifted in March. Oil exploration in DRC's old Virunga national park, which is also a Unesco World Heritage Site and important habitat for mountain gorillas, was suspended following worldwide outcries from environmental groups. A project to refurbish DRC's railway network by 2015 was announced in May. The 3,000km, US$600 million programme of works is backed by the World Bank and Chinese investors. Railway tracks will be replaced and new rolling stock purchased, while personnel of the existing rail company, who have not been paid for over four years, will be either retired with a pension or re-employed. Parliamentary and presidential elections took place in November. Of the 11 candidates that took part in the presidential elections, Joseph Kabila won 48.95 per cent of the vote and Etienne Tshisekedi 32.33 per cent; the remainder won less than 8 per cent each. International observers of the elections considered the results 'lacked credibility' with numerous examples of problems with vote counting. Supporters of unsuccessful candidates took to the streets to voice their complaints. The UNC announced it would challenge the presidential election result in the supreme court. Joseph Kabila was sworn into office on 20 December. Parliamentary results were not due for publication until 13 January 2012.
2012 On 6 March, Prime Minister Muzito resigned and Louis Koyagialo was appointed as acting prime minister. Fly Congo announced that from April old and unsafe airplanes it owned and operated were going to be destroyed and new planes bought to replace them. The decision followed the blacklisting in July 2011 by the EU of Hewa Bora Airways, Fly Congo's previous identity, and the bad reputation that Congolese airlines had in general. On 19 April the President promoted finance minister Augustin Ponyo to prime minister. On 28 May, the UN revealed evidence that Rwanda was supporting the March 23 Movement (M23) rebels in the eastern region of DRC through the training of troops in Rwanda and supplying some recruits (a number of which were deemed under-aged) to the insurgency. M23 are largely former members of CNDP who had formed the group in April, following an army mutiny, complaining that they had not been given the army posts they had been promised after the 2009 peace deal). On 2 July, three new, higher denomination, bank notes were issued in a bid to counter the growing trend of 'dollarisation' in the economy – in June 2012, 89 per cent of all financial transactions in DRC were conducted in US dollars. The new notes are Cf1,000 (US$1.07), Cf5,000 (US$5.36) and Cf10,000 (US$10.73). On 10 July, Thomas Lubanga was convicted of war crimes and human rights violations and recruiting and using child soldiers in his militia over 2002–03 (the first ever defendant to be condemned by the ICC) and sentenced to 14 years in jail. On 15 July the AU brokered an agreement between DRC and Rwanda to allow a neutral, international force to patrol their mutual border and tackle the militia forces active in the region. An outbreak of the deadly disease Ebola was reported in north-east DRC on 18 August. Medical authorities said this strain of the Ebola virus was not the same strain as the Ebola outbreak recorded in neighbouring Uganda in July 2012. On 20 November rebels of the M23 rebels entered the eastern city of Goma. Forces of M23 withdrew from Goma on 1 December, following a regionally negotiated agreement.
2013 A raid by the Allied Democratic Forces (a group of Ugandan rebels based in eastern DRC) on the border town of Kamango on 11 July led to some 30,000 (according to the UNHCR) fleeing. The unexpected move caused constenation in Uganda where there was a shortage of accommodation, food and sanitation for the refugees. On 1 August he conservation group WWF called on UK-based company Soco International to abandon its plans to explore for oil in the Virunga National Park, Africa's oldest national park. After 18 months of intermittent skirmishes in North Kivu, peace talks between the M23 and government restarted in September after pressure from regional leaders. Martin Kobler, UN special envoy to the DRC, reported in October that the M23 was 'all but finished as a military threat' after it abandoned nearly all it's military positions in the east and was reduced to a small triangle close to the Rwandan border. Within hours of the government declaring a military victory, the M23 rebel group said it was ending its insurgency and its leader surrendered in Uganda on 7 November. However, on 12 November minister of information, Lambert Mende, said the deal could not be signed, not because of its content, but because of the title. He reported it should be called a 'declaration' not an 'accord' since that gave too much credibility to the rebels.
2014 President Joseph Kabila announced the formation of a new government on 6 December. Augustin Matata Ponyo remained prime minister. Three vice prime ministers were also named, including Thomas Luhaka, secretary general of the Movement for the Liberation of Congo (MLC), who was later expelled from his party for accepting the position. Also named as a vice prime minister was Evariste Boshab, leader of the ruling People's Party for Reconstruction and Democracy. The 47 ministers and vice ministers

include a number of supporters who may be prepared to vote for a constitutional change to allow the president to run for a third term in the 2016 election.
2015 Fighting broke out in Kinshasa after the House of Representatives approved plans on 17 January for a census to be held (the last one had been conducted in 1984 and showed just under 30 million). The opposition suggested that since a census would take at least three years to organise and conduct, the move would in effect extend the President Kabila's time in office by two years since elections due in 2016 could not take place before the census was completed. Under the constitution Mr Kabila cannot stand for a third term.

Political structure

Constitution

A draft of a new constitution was approved by the national assembly in May 2005, and by a majority (84.31 per cent) of the people in a referendum held in December. It was officially adopted on 18 February 2006. The new constitution increases the number of provinces from 10 to 26, allows greater autonomy for some of the mineral-rich regions and lowers the minimum age for presidents from 35 to 33, thereby allowing 33-year-old Joseph Kabila, who has been president since the death of Laurent Kabila (his father) in 2001, to stand for the presidency in the 2006 elections. The president, who is limited to two five-year terms, names the prime minister from the largest party.
The flag is blue, to symbolise peace, crossed by a red line (the blood of the four million people who died in the civil war) and hedged by two yellow lines (the vast mining deposits of the country).

Independence date

30 June 1960

Form of state

Presidential republic

The executive

Under an accord signed in 2002 by the government, rebel groups and the civilian opposition, President Joseph Kabila was expected to remain in office until election in 2004, however elections have been postponed to 2006. The president is assisted by four vice presidents, each representing the government, two armed rebel groups and the civilian opposition.

National legislature

The bicameral parliament consists of the Assemblée Nationale (national assembly; lower chamber) with 500 members, of which 61 are elected in single-seat constituencies and the remainder in multi-seat constituencies from an open list of candidates; the Senat (senate, upper chamber) has 120 members elected by representatives of subordinate assemblies.

Legal system

The civil code is based on the Belgian system, including the structure of the Supreme Court. Legal issues at the local level are usually dealt with according to tribal law.

Last elections

28 November 2011 (presidential and parliamentary); 19 January 2007 (senate)
Results: Presidential: Joseph Kabila won 48.95 per cent of the vote, Etienne Tshisekedi 32.33 per cent, Vital Kamerhe 7.74 per cent, Leon Kengo 4.95 per cent; seven other candidates each won less than 2 per cent. Turnout was 58.81 per cent.
Parliamentary: *interim results scheduled for publication on 13 January 2012*
Senate: the Alliance pour la Majorité Présidentielle (AMP) (Alliance for a presidential majority) won 58 seats (out of 108, of which PPRD won 22), the Union pour la Nation Congolese (UNC) (Congolese National Party) coalition won 21 (of which MLC won 14, including a seat for Jean Pierre Bemba, its leader).

Next elections

June 2016 (presidential and parliamentary); June 2013 (senate)

Political parties

Ruling party

Caretaker-coalition led by Parti du Peuple pour la Reconstruction et la Démocratie (PPRD) (People's Party of Reconstruction and Democracy) with Parti Lumumbiste Unifié (PLU) (United Lumumbist Party) and Union des Démocrates Mobutistes (UDM) (Union of Mobutist Democrats) (elected 2006; re-elected 28 Nov 2011)

Main opposition party

Mouvement pour la Liberation du Congo (MLC) (Movement for the Liberation of Congo)

Population

74.75 million (2012)* At the end of 2012 there were some 40,000 Angolan refugees still in DRC. Most have had their refugee status withdrawn, yet are unwilling to return to Angola.
Last census: July 1984: 29,916,800
Population density: 20 inhabitants per square km. Urban population 35 per cent (2010 Unicef).
Annual growth rate: 3.0 per cent, 1990–2010 (Unicef).

Internally Displaced Persons (IDP)

3.4 million (UNHCR 2004)

Ethnic make-up

There are over 200 ethnic groups in DRC. The largest is the Kongo, which predominates in Bandundu province. The Mongo are mainly found in the heavily forested north and north-west. The Luba predominate in the two Kasai provinces and the Shabans and Bemba live mainly in Katanga (formerly Shaba) province. Other large ethnic groups include the Zande, the Bwaka, the Lulua and the Songe. There are a large number of people of Nilotic origin, mainly concentrated in the eastern North Kivu province.

Religions

Some 50 per cent of the population adhere to animist beliefs. The remainder are mostly Christian, of which a majority are Roman Catholic. Muslims make up some 10 per cent of the population, residing mainly in North Kivu province.

Education

Estimates by major non-government organisations show that at least four out of every 10 children of primary school age are denied the basic right to education in the DRC. Several obstacles towards accessing basic education include the inability of parents to pay school fees, massive displacement of population and destruction of school buildings during the civil war. Between 1997 and 2003, millions of children had no access to schools, leading to an increase in the dropout rate from 49 per cent to 75 per cent during the period.
The UN Children's Fund (UNICEF) has helped in the rehabilitation of seven schools and four health centres in Kisangani (damaged in 2000), which cater for 20,000 children. Unicef will also provide financial assistance towards training teachers and for various educational materials.
Literacy rate: 72 per cent men and 49 per cent women, adult rates (World Bank).
Compulsory years: Six to 12.
Pupils per teacher: 45 in primary schools.

Health

The Mobutu government had placed a low priority on standards of health and welfare, and continuing civil war inhibited improvement. From this low base, expenditure has slowly risen from the 1.5 per cent in 2000.
Only one-third of the population, mostly those in the larger cities, have access to local healthcare. There are more than 900 hospitals with a total capacity of over 75,000 beds, but many of these are not operating due to a lack of resources and loss of unpaid staff. There are an estimated 1,900 physicians working in the DRC, for a population of 58 million. Tuberculosis incidence is about 260 per 100,000 population.
Unicef in association with the DRC government started a major measles immunisation campaign in October 2002, targetting some 15 million children initially.
Forty five per cent of the population have access to an improved water sources.

There were cases of polio reported to the World Health Organisation – Global Polio Eradication Initiative in 2006; the country had previously been free of the disease and its re-emergence was due to infected travellers.
The border between Angola and the Democratic Republic of Congo (DRC) was closed on 6 January 2009 due to an outbreak of Ebola in the Luande Norte province of DRC.

HIV/Aids

One million people were HIV positive in 2003, of which 570,000 were women, plus there were 110,000 children infected and 770,000 orphans (aged 0–17) created. Deaths from Aids amounted to 100,000 in 2003.
An HIV infection rate of 12 per cent has been characteristic for women who were caught up in civil war atrocities, or attacked by exiled Hutu Militia, and been raped. Such militia erroneously believe that raping a woman will be protection from HIV infection.

HIV prevalence: 4.2 per cent aged 15–49 in 2003 (World Bank)

Life expectancy: 44 years, 2004 (WHO 2006)

Fertility rate/Maternal mortality rate: 5.8 births per woman, 2010 (Unicef); maternal mortality 9.4 per 1,000 (World Bank)

Birth rate/Death rate: 15 deaths to 45 births per 1,000 people (World Bank 2001).

Child (under 5 years) mortality rate (per 1,000): 146 per 1,000 live births (WHO 2012); 34 per cent of children aged under five were malnourished (World Bank 2004).

Head of population per physician: 0.11 physicians per 1,000 people, 2004 (WHO 2006)

Welfare

While several UN agencies and non-governmental organisations, through a diverse range of activities, manage the welfare situation in the DRC, there have been setbacks when humanitarian teams were withdrawn for safety reasons. The western provinces of the country have remained stable, but the eastern provinces, featuring unrivalled poverty and insecurity, are gripped by a humanitarian emergency. Over 3.3 million people are estimated to have been killed or died as a result of the war, to overthrow the DRC government, which started in 1998.
The UN estimates that there are 3.4 million internally displaced persons (IDPs), and the UN World Food Programme (WFP) estimates that 16 million people (including refugees from Angola), are in need of emergency food aid, or have been cut off from traditional means of subsistence. In early 2004, two million people benefited from WFP's programmes, at a total cost of US$196 million.
The UN reported that during 2002–03, there were 'unprecedented levels of violence by armed factions in eastern DRC, including cannibalism, systematic killings, rape and lootings,' despite some political stability following the installation of a government of transition in mid-2003. While there are no precise rape figures, records show over 40,000 cases were reported since the civil war of 1998 began, and exiled Hutu militia (from Rwanda) began attacking villagers in eastern DRC.

Main cities

Kinshasa (capital, estimated population 9.5 million (m) in 2012), Lubumbashi (1.8m), Mbuji-Mayi (1.7m), Kananga (1.1m), Kinsangani (535,977), Bukavu (806,940), Tshikapa (587,548), Kolwezi (453,147).

Languages spoken

Among the many African languages spoken, Lingala, KiSwahili, Tshiluba and Kikongo are the most prominent in DRC.

Official language/s

French

Media

Press

Dailies: There are several dailies, all published in French, the majority of which are located in Kinshasa, including *La Potentiel* (www.lepotentiel.com), the independent, *La Référence Plus* (http://groupelareference.afrikart.net), *L'Avenir* (www.groupelavenir.net), *L'Observateur* (www.lobservateur.cd), *La Conscience* (www.laconscience.com), *La Phare* (www.lepharerdc.com), *La Prospérité* (www.laprosperiteonline.net), and *La République* (www.la-republique.com).

Weeklies: In French, *Le Soft* (www.lesoftonline.net), covers political matters.

Periodicals: In French, *Observatoire de l'Afrique Centrale* (www.obsac.com), a quarterly magazine with reviews of the news in Central Africa and the bi-monthly *C Retro Actuel* (http://c-retro-actuel.net), covering current affairs, politics, the economy and culture.

Broadcasting

The national, public broadcaster is Radio Télévision Nationale Congolaise (RTNC).

Radio: Radio services are the main medium of mass communication and sources of news and information.
RTNC operates La Voix du Congo (The Voice of Congo), which broadcasts programmes in French, Swahili, Lingala, Tshiluba and Kikongo. Private radio stations include the UN-backed Radio Okapi (www.radiookapi.net), Top Congo FM (www.topcongo.com) and Mangembo FM (www.mangembo-fm.com). There are also several stations broadcasting religious content. International transmissions from Radio France International (RFI) (www.rfi.fr) and the BBC World Service (www.bbc.co.uk/worldservice) (92.7 FM) are available through satellite and internet or relayed via local radio stations. There are many more private radio stations broadcasting in small localities throughout the country.

Television: Television coverage is almost nationwide, with four channels available including the government-owned RTNC. Commercial stations include RTGA (www.groupelavenir.net), Canal Tropical TV and Raga TV. There are many more private TV stations broadcasting in small localities throughout the country.

National news agency: ACP (Agence Congolaise de Presse)

Economy

The Democratic Republic of Congo (DRC) has much potential, with huge mineral wealth of cobalt, copper, gold, diamonds and uranium, its rivers with abundant hydroelectric potential, fertile farmland and its virgin forests. It experienced exploitation during colonial times and civil war, and mismanagement during corrupt regimes following independence and is slowly beginning to develop its riches for itself, using foreign investment. There are still worrying risks of widespread violence in north-western and eastern provinces, coming from domestic insurgents, Rwandan Hutu militia, and more brutal attacks from the Ugandan Lord's Resistance Army. Such attacks cause deaths and maiming and displace communities and disrupt farming and commercial life.
The majority of the population is engaged in subsistence farming, which remains a primary industry and the principal component of GDP, at 42.5 per cent in 2014. 62 per cent of the men and 84 per cent of the women are employed in the industry. Since 2011, the DRC has been ranked first on the Global Hunger Index, whilst agricultural production has fallen 40 per cent since 1990. Average daily food consumption is below the minimum required for an individual to maintain good health.
The service sector contributed 34 per cent and industry 23.5 per cent, of which manufacturing was 8 per cent of total GDP.
Although rich in so many ways, DRC is nevertheless one of the poorest countries in the world with per capita income of US$475 in 2014. In 2014, the UN Human Development Index (HDI) ranked the DRC as 186 (out of 187 countries) for improvement in health, education and

income and indicated that DRC had had a consistently below average improvement rate compared to other sub-Saharan African countries since 1980. The poverty rate (those living on less than US$1.25 a day) was recorded as 87.7 per cent, and 53.7 per cent of households experienced at least three indicators of poverty.

GDP growth was 6.2 per cent in 2008, which fell to 2.8 per cent in 2009 as the global economic slowdown led to mine closures by multinational mining companies as they scaled back their operations. As a result almost overnight around 300,000 miners in Katanga Province lost their jobs. However, by 2013 GDP growth had picked up again to 9 per cent. Inflation, which had been 18 per cent in 2008 jumped to 46.2 per cent in 2009, before falling back to an estimated 26.2 per cent in 2010 and by 2013 had returned to single digits, being at 1 per cent. GDP growth reached 9.1 per cent for 2014, whilst inflation recorded the same level of 1 per cent for 2014.

External debt was US$6.09 billion at the end of 2012 and US$6.96 billion at the end of 2014.

Corruption is a major problem, especially in dealings in natural resources. The government has implemented reforms necessary to restore macroeconomic stability, cut corruption and apply measures of good governance. However, with a country so large (the second largest in Africa, behind Algeria) and a world market willing to accept dubious provenance, despite international sanctions, the authorities have a hard task securing the country's assets and borders. Diplomatic tension and militia fighting in the border region with Burundi has isolated the area from total government control and the smuggling of gold, diamonds and other minerals is rife.

The infrastructure is poor and in need of major investment, either foreign or domestic. DRC could become a powerhouse for Africa, supplying raw materials and surplus energy, if given time to develop a stable civil society.

External trade

(Comesa), although in 2014 it was still not a member of the free trade area, as operated by 13 other member states, nor are there plans to join the customs union. It is also a member of the Economic Community of Central African States (ECCAS) and the Southern African Development Community (SADC).

DRC was a leading producer of industrial diamonds before its civil war and they remain dominant in the economy, although production figures are sketchy.

The narrow export base is concentrated mainly on minerals, with some agricultural cash crops. The DRC's balance of trade is therefore susceptible to the vagaries of world commodity markets. Under-investment and regular strikes have further weakened the mining industry. The mining sector accounts for around 75 per cent of all exports.

Imports

Principal imports are foodstuffs, mining and other machinery, transport equipment and fuels.

Main sources: South Africa (12.5 per cent of total in 2013), China (15.1 per cent), Zambia (12.1 per cent)

Exports

Principal exports are diamonds, copper, palm oil, cobalt, crude oil, rubber, cotton and coffee.

Main destinations: China (44 per cent of total in 2013), Zambia (21.3 per cent), Italy (11.1 per cent)

Agriculture

Farming

Total agricultural land is 226.7 million hectares of which 6.6 per cent is pasture and 3.0 per cent arable; forestry accounts for over 50 per cent. Over 60 per cent of the workforce is active in subsistence farming.

Despite enormous agricultural potential, the sector has been handicapped by transport problems, occasional drought, smuggling and inflexible pricing policies. Farmers in the eastern provinces have also had to contend with the deadly Hutu militia, exiled from Rwanda, who target isolated farms and villages for supplies while often committing atrocities.

The government is developing the forestry sector with multilateral financial assistance.

Main food crops are cassava, maize, rice and plantain. Production is insufficient to meet demand, and poor transport restricts supplies to the urban areas. Main cash and export crops are plantation-grown coffee, cocoa, oil palm, rubber, tea, cotton, sugar and tobacco.

Fishing

Although the DRC has only a narrow coastline, the fisheries sector is evenly based between inland and coastal resources. Around 150,000 artisanal fisherman operate in the DRC, providing 90 per cent of the total national catch. Excluding subsistence production, inland fishing in the many rivers and lakes produces around 150,000 tonnes, comparable with the 160,000 for seafood production. The country is a substantial net importer of seafood and freshwater fish.

Forestry

DRC has 86 million hectares (ha) of tropical forest, roughly half the timber resources of the central African region. The first industrial exploitation started in 1930 at Mayumbe. The sector is vastly under-exploited and holds out much potential, particularly in terms of export revenue. From 1970 onwards, the focus of activity shifted from Mayumbe to the Cuvette region. The DRC produces large quantities of sawnwood, as well as plywood and veneer. Tropical hardwood logs and sawnwood are the principal exports. However the principal use of timber is as domestic firewood.

According to Greenpeace, an estimated US$12 million per annum is lost through tax avoidance by international logging companies.

Industry and manufacturing

The industrial sector contributes around 23.5 per cent to GDP. Approximately three-quarters of production is centred around Kinshasa or in the Katanga province, owing to the availability of electricity and adequate transport facilities in these areas.

The country holds almost half of the world's cobalt reserves and in 2012 cobalt produced in the DRC covered 55 per cent of global production according to the same report. Economic growth in 2014 was driven by the extractive and manufacturing industries, agriculture, commerce and construction, and benefited from fairly good external demand and quite high raw material prices.

In an environment of political instability, endemic corruption and poor regulation, few manufacturing industries have developed. The few that remain have also been hindered by a lack of technical and management expertise, the comparatively poor transport infrastructure and a chronic decline in domestic purchasing power eroded by inflation and lack of foreign exchange to purchase essential manufacturing inputs.

Output is geared towards the domestic market and is mainly concentrated on brewing, food processing, textiles, consumer goods, construction industry inputs and transport equipment.

Mismanagement and shortages of spare parts and materials have led to cut-backs in production with most firms operating at below half capacity. The government is attempting to increase production by encouraging foreign investment and offering substantial tax incentives.

Tourism

After a long and bloody civil war, DCR has a tourist infrastructure in poor condition, coupled with continued internal disorder in the eastern region, which makes it a destination for business visitors and hardy travellers only. In November 2011, tourist arrivals were boosted by visitors who wished to view the eruption of the

Nyamulagira volcano, located in Africa's oldest national park, Virunga, which is one of four national parks and one wildlife reserve included on Unesco's World Heritage List. A new tourist lodge opened in January 2012 in Virunga to cater for the growing numbers to the park.
Tourists also visit to see the endangered lowland gorilla and the rare bonobo chimpanzees and okapi (of the giraffe family). The Bembenga (pygmy) people still live in their dense forest homes.
Travel and tourism directly contributes around 1.1 per cent of GDP in 2014, and 2.2 per cent indirectly, and it employs 1.9 per cent of the workforce (300,000 jobs).
Capital investment in the tourist industry was US$148 million in 2014, 2.7 per cent of total investment.

Environment

In February 2008 the governments of DRC, Rwanda and Uganda agreed to joint measures to protect the mountain gorillas found within their shared border regions. Tourists visiting the area to view the endangered great apes raise a combined US$5 million for the countries concerned. However, poaching and civil strife have dropped the numbers of gorillas to critically endangered levels, so that a 10-year conservation project which focuses of security and encouraging local people to preserve the animals and habitat is seen as the only hope for the gorilla's survival.

Mining

The country is rich in mineral resources and is potentially one of Africa's richest countries. DRC's copper reserves are estimated at 75 million tonnes with iron at one billion tonnes, 240 million carats of diamonds and over 600 tonnes of gold.
In the past, mining contributed around a third of GDP and employed 5 per cent of the workforce. With around half of DRC's foreign exchange earnings gained from diamond exports, the industry watchdog called for stricter application of existing laws to reduce smuggling and exploitative practices that lead to less revenue for DRC than was possible.
Moves towards peace should lead to a resumption of investment in the mining sector, backed by planned new mining and investment codes. Mining is likely to be the driving force of the economy over the medium-term.
Diamonds are mined on a commercial scale by the Société Minière de Bakwanga (Miba) at Bakwanga in Kasai Oriental, but artisanal diggers account for almost three-quarters of total output.
There is tin mining and small-scale mining of cadmium, cassiterite and wolframite.
Activity is concentrated in the copper-rich Katanga (formerly Shaba) province.
Twangiza gold deposits are estimated at 4.1 million tonnes of ore. With the exception of diamonds, these minerals have been hit by weak world demand.
Katanga Province is part of the Central African Copperbelt, which extends from Angola through the DRC into Zambia.
The state-run Gécamines has holdings containing the biggest concentrations of copper and cobalt in the world.
Gécamines' troubles are rooted in long-term problems of corruption and mismanagement. Its misfortune is exacerbated by the civil war, which has led to foreign partners scaling down or pulling out of joint ventures.
Australia's Anvil Mining has production of the Dikulushi copper and silver mine.
In March 2011, the ban on mining gold, tin and coltan was lifted in three provinces of eastern DRC. Following successful military action in the area to rout militia operations, the mining ministry dispatched officials to oversee legitimate shipments of ore from the region.
International companies such as Glencore Xstrata through Katanga Mining, Randgold Resources, AngloGold Ashanti, Lundin Mining and Freeport McMoRanall, have all invested in concessions in the DRC, often in partnership with state-owned mining firm Gécamines.
DRC's ranking of 154 on the Corruptions Perception Index (2014) needs improvement in order to provide greater investment security in the future.

Hydrocarbons

Proven oil reserves totalled 180 million barrels in 2014, most of which are located off the Atlantic coastline and in the Congo River estuary. Oil production was 20,000 barrels per day (bpd) with consumption at around 12,000bpd. There is no domestic refinery and all crude oil must be exported, via the Moanda Oil Terminal.
Total natural gas reserves stood at 1.3 billion cubic metres in 2013, most of which is located beneath Lake Kivu, however the cost of exploiting this reserve has made production non-viable.
Coal reserves stood at 88 million tonnes, typical production is 10 million tonnes per annum. Mines are located at Luena and Kalemie.

Energy

Total installed generating capacity was 2,500MW in 2013; however the DRC has the potential to produce 419,210MW of economically feasible electricity, a figure, which is greater than Africa's current total generating capacity, if it were able to harness the power of its rivers. The Inga Dam near the port of Matadi at the mouth of the Congo River produces 1,700MW supplying not only the capital but also the copper mines in Katanga. Inga provides DRC with its biggest foreign exchanger earner. Only 6 per cent of the population have access to the power grid; energy in rural areas is mainly derived from charcoal and wood.
DRC is a member of the Southern African Power Pool (SAPP); set up to provide reliable and economical energy supplies to all members in twelve countries. However, DRC is unable to receive electricity from Namibia due to a lack of high voltage lines in Angola.
Congo provides less than 3 per cent of its hydropower potential, according to the World Bank in 2012. Because of mismanagement, only about half of that energy is available and most of the population of 70 million has no electricity.
The DRC will be ready to build the 4,800 megawatt Inga III hydroelectric plant by 2015, after two failed attempts to kick-start the US$12 billion project.
Inga III is the next step in the creation of a 40,000 megawatt Grand Inga complex, which would be the largest hydropower project in the world.
The parastatal utility company Société Nationale d'Electricité (SNEL) is responsible for production, transmission, distribution and sales of electricity, through subsidiary agencies.

Banking and insurance

The banking system is virtually non-existent as persistent hyperinflation has led to the collapse of all the country's banks.

Central bank
Banque Centrale du Congo (BCC)

Main financial centre
Kinshasa

Time

Kinshasa and the western provinces – GMT plus one hour
Elsewhere – GMT plus two hours

Geography

The country is bordered by the Republic of Congo in the west, by the Central African Republic in the north, by Sudan in the north-east, by Uganda, Rwanda and Burundi in the northeast to east, by Tanzania in the east to south-east, Zambia in the south and Angola in the south to south-west. Lake Tanganiyka forms most of the border with Tanzania.
DRC is the second largest country in Africa (after Sudan), it is over two million square kilometres in area, encompassing a huge central basin of tropical rain forest, with mountains that rise in the east and the continent's second longest river (after the Nile) running through its northern and western regions. It has a tiny 37km coastline where the River Congo drains into the eastern South Atlantic seaboard. In its eastern range of mountains

live the endangered mountain gorilla whose habitat is under threat from illegal logging and deforestation. Pic Marguerite on Mont Ngaliema (Mount Stanley) at 5,110 metres is the tallest peak. Close to the city of Goma are Africa's two most active volcanoes, Nyamuragira and Nyiragongo – which has the world's fastest flowing lava. The southern part of the country is savannah grassland.

Most of the population is concentrated in areas with the best communications, near Kinshasa in the far west, along the Congo River and other main rivers, and in the southern and eastern border regions.

Hemisphere

Straddles the equator, although most of the country is situated in the southern hemisphere.

Climate

The climate varies widely owing to the size of the country. The lowlands in the western region are hot and humid, including Kinshasa, where rain is concentrated in the period from November to March and temperatures reach 32 degrees Celsius (C) in the hottest month, January, with 26 degrees C in the coolest month, June. On the central plateau, the likely temperature range is 18–20 degrees C. In the south and the eastern province of Kivu the climate is a Mediterranean type and is slightly cooler, particularly in the winter months.

Dress codes

Business clothes may be casual and lightweight clothing is essential, especially if visiting during the rainy season.

Entry requirements

Visitors are advised to contact embassy representatives in advance to ascertain current entry requirements. Visitors are also advised to register their presence in DRC with their local embassy representative.

Passports

Required by all. All passports must be valid for six months from the date of departure. Proof of return/onward passage is also necessary.

Visa

Required by all. A proposed tourist *univisa* (a single visa to visit all 15-member states of SADC: Angola, Botswana, DRC, Lesotho, Madagascar, Malawi, Mauritius, Mozambique, Namibia, South Africa, Seychelles, Swaziland, Tanzania, Zambia and Zimbabwe) is expected to be in use by 2013. Visitors should check with the appropriate consulates to confirm start of *univisas* and their scope before beginning a tour of southern Africa.

Applications for a business visa requires a letter from a tour company stating the trip has been paid in full, or from an employer accepting responsibility for any expenses incurred; proof of status and a letter of finance giving proof of sufficient funds and a full itinerary. An official letter of invitation endorsed by the DRC authorities must also accompany the application. Travel regulations should be studied carefully before a visit as restrictions apply.

Prohibited entry

Those with visas/entry/exit stamps for Rwanda, Burundi or Uganda are likely to be refused entry.

Currency advice/regulations

The import or export of local currency is prohibited. Foreign currency import is limited to US$10,000 and must be declared. Currency declaration forms must be kept and all currency exchanges should be recorded.

Customs

Visitors are advised not to take in any equipment which may arouse suspicion, such as cameras, binoculars, maps or any kind of tools or military equipment.

Health (for visitors)

Mandatory precautions

Yellow fever vaccination certificate is required if arriving from an infected area.

Advisable precautions

Visitors should take precautions against all tropical diseases. Vaccinations for diphtheria, tetanus, hepatitis A, polio and typhoid are recommended. Other vaccinations that may be recommended are cholera, tuberculosis, hepatitis B and meningitis. There is a risk of rabies.

Anti-malaria tablets are essential, and HIV/Aids is widespread among both men and women. Dysentery, typhoid and typhus are prevalent, especially outside Kinshasa. Bubonic plague exists in the Bunia region.

Tap water must be treated as unsafe unless boiled and filtered (bottled water is available in the main cities). Outside Kinshasa and Lubumbashi, eat only hot, cooked food and avoid raw salad, fruit, vegetables and ice cubes. Dairy products are unpasteurised and should be avoided.

A first aid kit that includes disposable syringes, is a reasonable precaution. Medical insurance is essential, including emergency evacuation, and an adequate supply of personal medicines is necessary.

Hotels

Several major hotels in Kinshasa and other cities. Most tend to be expensive and are often heavily booked. A service charge is usually added to bill and further tipping is optional.

Public holidays (national)

Fixed dates

1 Jan (New Year's Day), 4 Jan (Commemoration of the Martyrs of Independence), 17 Jan (National Heroes' Day), 1 May (Labour Day), 17 May (National Liberation Day), 30 Jun (Independence Day), 1 Aug (Parents' Day), 17 Nov (Army Day), 25 Dec (Christmas Day).

Working hours

Banking

Mon–Fri: 0800–1130.

Business

Mon–Fri: 0730–1200, 1430–1700; Sat: 0730–1200.

Government

Mon–Fri: 0730–1500; Sat: 0730–1200. It is normal practice for ministers and senior officials to work Mon–Fri: 0830–1300 and from 1600–2000.

Shops

Mon–Fri: 0800–1200, 1500–1700; Sat: 0800–1200.

Telecommunications

Mobile/cell phones

There are 900 and 1800 GSM services operating in highly populated areas.

Electricity supply

220V AC

Social customs/useful tips

With its vast range of ethnic groups and huge land area, there are many different traditions, according to the locality.

As in most French-speaking African countries, business etiquette when visiting government and (to a lesser degree) private commercial offices is more formal than in English-speaking Africa.

Do not openly criticise the government or attempt to photograph public buildings. Military installations are also best avoided if possible.

Security

The insecurity and lawlessness in eastern and northern DRC makes travelling to these areas dangerous. Visitors should consider whether their journey is vital before travelling in the rest of DRC.

Street crime is rife, especially in Kinshasa. Visitors are advised not to wear expensive jewellery or watches or to carry cameras conspicuously. To achieve anything expect to pay *katamulomo* tips, especially to soldiers (both genuine and fake), who are seldom paid and who man the roadblocks. Visitors should beware of unofficial 'porters' at N'djili airport. Those visiting for the first time should try to arrange for a local business associate or friend to meet them at the airport. Visitors are advised to stay in their hotels after dark. They should avoid public transport altogether and use hire cars rather than taxis whenever possible.

The DRC is undergoing profound political change which means that any official efforts which may be made to protect foreign visitors are unlikely to be effective outside Kinshasa. The best advice is to contact embassy representatives in advance in order to check the safety of the region to which you wish to travel.

Getting there

Air

National airline: Hewa Bora Airways

International airport/s: Kinshasa-N'djili International airport (FIH) is 25km from central Kinshasa. As N'djili is located a long way from the city, it is advisable to pre-arrange transport either with a hotel or local car hire firm such as Hertz (office within the shopping gallery at the Inter-Continental Hotel) or to arrange for a business or social contact to meet first-time visitors to the country at the airport.

Other airport/s: There are almost 60 airports and airfields around DRC.

Airport tax: Departure tax: Cf500

Surface

Road: There are 2,400km of poorly maintained asphalted roads leading to neighbouring countries. However, most borders are closed and the roads leading to them are considered very dangerous.

Rail: The three main lines into DRC are the Voie Nationale running from Matadi port to Kinshasa (366km); the eastern route entering from Tanzania at Kalemie and the northern route entering from the Sudan at Mungbere. There are also links to southern African states via Zambia. An end to Angola's civil war would allow reconstruction of the Benguela line from Shaba to Lobito port in Angola, but this could take several years.

Water: From Kinshasa there is a regular ferry service to Brazzaville, although it is subject to distruption.

Main port/s: The main port is Matadi, about 150km inland on the Congo River. Kinshasa is the main inland river port and the ferry crossing point from Brazzaville.

Getting about

National transport

Air: There are connections from Kinshasa-N'djili to over 40 local destinations. Charter facilities are available.

Road: There are indefinite restrictions on travel throughout the country. A permit from the interior ministry is required for travel outside Kinshasa.

The 240,000km road network is in poor condition outside main population centres and some parts have become impassable through lack of maintenance. Bridges should be checked before crossing and banditry is common.

Buses: Very irregular, crowded and infrequent service.

Rail: A network of over 5,000km is operated by Société Nationale des Chemins de Fer Zaïroise (SNCZ), but some parts are inoperable while others subject to disruption. Of the four classes – 'deluxe' and first-class are advisable.

A project to refurbish DRC's railway network by 2015 was announced on 12 May 2011. The 3,000km, US$600 million programme of works including railway tracks to be replaced and new rolling stock purchased, will be backed by the World Bank and Chinese investors.

Water: Inland navigation is important, particularly for freight on the Congo River between Kinshasa and Kisangani and the Kasai River from Ilebo to the Congo River north of Kinshasa. However, all routes around Kisangani have been disrupted by the civil war. When available, passenger services run on all major rivers and lakes. It is advisable to travel luxury or first class.

City transport

Shared taxis provide the best form of transport and are widely available. There is little or no public transport outside Kinshasa.

Taxis: Volatile inflation rates and political instability mean it is virtually impossible to keep track of taxi fares in local currency. If resorting to a local taxi, it is absolutely essential to negotiate a fixed fare before starting the journey.

Car hire

Self-drive cars are available in Kinshasa and at the airport. A deposit is required unless an acceptable credit card can be produced. International driving licence required. Traffic drives on the right.

BUSINESS DIRECTORY

The addresses listed below are a selection only. While World of Information makes every endeavour to check these addresses, we cannot guarantee that changes have not been made, especially to telephone numbers and area codes. We would welcome any corrections.

Telephone area codes

The international direct dialling (IDD) code for DRC is +243, followed by the area code and subscriber's number. In late 2006 the landline telephone system was not functioning. To call a mobile number (beginning with 8 or 9) dial +243 and then the number.

Kinshasa	12	Lubumbashi	2
Cellular network	8		

Chambers of Commerce

Fédération des Entreprises du Congo, 10 Avenue des Aviateurs, PO Box 7247, Kinshasa (tel: 880-7297; fax: 780-0660; e-mail: feccongo@hotmail.com).

Franco-Congolaise Chambre de Commerce et d'Industrie, 407 Avenue Roi Baudouin, PO Box 8.211, Kinshasa 1 (tel: 780-5871; fax: 880-7158).

Banking

Banque Commerciale du Congo SARL, BP 2798, Boulevard du 30 Juin, Kinshasa-Gombe (tel: 217-73, 217-76; fax: 221-770).

Banque Continentale Africaine (Zaire) SARL, 4 Avenue de la Justice, Kinshasa-Gombe (tel: 28-006, 28-537; fax: 25-243).

Banque Internationale de Crédit SARL, 191 Ave de l'Equateur, Kinshasa-Gombe (tel: 882-0404, 884-1940/5631, 884-3159/3790, 880-1487; fax: 880-1125, 377-97900/34).

Citibank NA Congo, BP 9999, Citibank Building, Coin des Avenues Colonel Lukusa et Ngongo Lutete, Kinshasa-Gombe 1 (tel: 20555/57; fax: 40015).

Fransabank (Congo) SARL, BP 9497, Avenue du Port, 14/16 Immeuble Zaïre-Shell, Kin. 1, Kinshasa-Gombe (tel: 20121/2/3/4; fax: 12-27864).

Nouvelle Banque de Kinshasa, 1 Place du Marché, Kinshasa-Gombe 1 (tel: 12-20562-5, 12-0459-60, 12-3461-63; fax: 12-581-4961 80043).

Stanbic Bank Congo SARL, 12 Avenue de la Mongala, Kinshasa-Gombe (tel: 88-48445, 88-41984, 88-43453, 88-43419, 88- 04512; fax: 88-46216).

Union de Banques SARL, BP 197, Coin des Avenues de la Nation et des Aviateurs, Kinshasa-Gombe (tel: 88-4133, 88-43620, 88-44887; fax: 88-46628).

Central bank

Banque Centrale du Congo, 563 Boulevard Colonel Tshashi, PO Box 2697, Kinshasa-Gombe (tel: 20-704; fax: 880-5152; e-mail: cabgouv@bcc.cd).

Travel information

Air Zaïre, BP 10120, Airport de N'Djili, Kinshasa (tel: 20-939; fax: 20-940).

N'Djili International Airport, BP 10124, Kinshasa 24 (tel: 23-570).

SNCZ Railways, BP 597, Kinshasa.

Ministry of tourism

Ministry of Tourism, BP12.348, 15 Avenue Papa Ileo (ex des Cliniques), Kinshasa 1 (tel: 34-390, 88-02-394; fax: 88-44-987).

National tourist organisation offices

Office National du Tourisme de la République Démocratique du Congo, BP 9502, Kinshasa-Gombe 1 (tel: 89-32-2238, 815-091-627, 99-31-939; fax: 33-781; e-mail: ont-rdc@raga.net).

Ministries

Civil Service Ministry, Avenue des Ambassadeurs, BP 3, Kinshasa-Gombe.

Ministry of Agriculture, Boulevard du 30 Juin, Building Sozacom, 3e Etage, BP 8722 KIN I, Kinshasa-Gombe.

Ministry of Economy, Industry and Commerce, Boulevard du 30 Juin, Building Onatra, BP 8500 KIN I, Kinshasa-Gombe.

Ministry of Energy, 239 Avenue de la Justice, Building SNEL, BP 5137 KIN I, Kinshasa-Gombe.

Ministry of Environment and Tourism, 15 Avenue des Cliniques, BP 12348 KIN I, Kinshasa-Gombe.

Ministry of Finance, Boulevard du 30 Juin, BP 12998 KIN I, Kinshasa-Gombe.

Ministry of Foreign Affairs and International Co-operation, Place de l'Indépendance, BP 7100, Kinshasa-Gombe 14 (tel: 32-450, 30-248, 32-239, 30-996, 32-735, 33-325; fax: 88-02-368; internet site: www.minaffeci-rdcongo.net/).

Ministry of Health, Boulevard du 30 Juin, BP 3088 KIN I, Kinshasa-Gombe.

Ministry of Home Affairs, Kinshasa-Gombe.

Ministry of Information and Cultural Affairs, Avenue du 24 Novembre, BP 3171 KIN I, Kinshasa-Kabinda.

Ministry of International Co-Operation, Avenue de la Justice, Enceinte SNEL, Kinshasa-Gombe.

Ministry of Justice, 228 Avenue des 3 Z, Kinshasa-Gombe.

Ministry of Mines, 239 Avenue de la Justice, Building SNEL, BP 5137 KIN I, Kinshasa-Gombe.

Ministry of National Education, Enceinte de l'Institut de la Gombe, BP 3163, Kinshasa-Gombe.

Ministry of Planning and Development, 4155 Avenue des Coteaux, BP 9378 KIN I, Kinshasa-Gombe.

Ministry of Post and Telecommunications, 4484 Avenue des Huiles, Building Kilou, BP 800 KIN I, Kinshasa-Gombe.

Ministry of Public Works, Building Travaux Publics, Kinshasa-Gombe.

Ministry of Reconstruction, Boulevard Colonel Tshatshi, Building Travaux Publics, BP 26, Kinshasa-Gombe.

Ministry of Transport, Boulevard du 30 Juin, Building Onatra, BP 3304, Kinshasa-Gombe.

Ministry of Youth and Sports, 77 Avenue de la Justice, BP 8541 KIN I, Kinshasa-Gombe.

Other useful addresses

Democratic Republic of Congo Embassy (USA), 1800 New Hampshire Avenue, NW, Washington DC 20009 (tel: (+1-202) 234-7690; fax: (+1-202) 237-0748).

Democratic Republic of Congo Permanent mission the UN, 866 United Nations Plaza, Suite 511, New York (tel: (+1-212) 319-8061; fax: (+1-212) 319-8232; email: drcongo@un.int).

National news agency: ACP (Agence Congolaise de Presse), 44-48 Avenue Tombalbaye, BP 1595, Kinshasa (internet: www.un.int/drcongo).

Internet sites

Africa Business Network: www.ifc.org/abn

AllAfrica.com: http://allafrica.com

African Development Bank: www.afdb.org

Africa Online: www.africaonline.com

Congoplantet (gateway site): www.congoplantet.com

Democratic Republic of Congo (French only): www.congonline.com

Mbendi AfroPaedia (information on companies, countries, industries and stock exchanges in Africa): http://mbendi.co.za

Cook Islands

The Cook Islands went to the polls on 9 July 2014 to elect the 24 members of the 14th Cook Islands Parliament. The election was called over a year earlier than necessary after Prime Minister Henry Puna said a new parliament should be installed before the Islands' fiftieth anniversary of the Constitution on 4 August 2015 (elections would normally have taken place in November 2015). The opposition accused Mr Puna of calling the election early to avoid a vote of no-confidence after education and tourism minster, Teina Bishop, had 'destabilised' the government. Mr Bishop resigned the day after the election was announced and formed the One Cook Islands party.

The results were another win for the Cook Islands Party (CIP) with a total of 13 seats to the Democratic Party's eight. The One Cook Islands party won two seats. One seat (Mitiaro) was tied at 50 votes each, with a by-election to be held before 28 November.

Speaking to regional participants at a regional summit on climate change and relocation in May 2013. Prime Minister Henry Puna told delegates he had had first-hand experience on communities affected by climatic conditions. He said Cyclone Martin in 1997 had had a tremendous impact on the lives of the people of his home island, Manihiki, which is just 4 metres (13 feet) above sea level at its highest point.

'As a resident in Manihiki, I have a deep appreciation of how serious the implications of forced human mobility can be,' Puna said. 'Traumatised and devastated by this disaster, our people – including the children – required counselling as well as relief assistance.'

Puna said devastation caused by Cyclone Martin – including wind and sea surge damage – forced many islanders to relocate and move to other islands within the group. Many families left the Cook Islands entirely, relocating to New Zealand or Australia. He told the Nansen Initiative-Secretariat Pacific Regional Consultation on Human Mobility, Natural Disasters and Climate Change that 'The internal displacement had a profound effect and impact upon the island and the population numbers have not recovered to this day.'

The Manihiki experience was one of the issues highlighted at the meeting, held in Rarotonga. It was supported by the Secretariat of the Pacific Regional Environment Programme and was the first in a series of international summits organised by the Nansen Initiative, a joint effort of the Norwegian and Swiss governments.

About 50 ministers, permanent secretaries and technical experts from the region attended the four-day event. Puna said that Pacific countries faced several threats – sea surges, coral degradation, *tsunami* and strengthened cyclones.

'We need to strengthen the collective Pacific voice in the area of cross-border displacement, climate change and natural disasters,' Puna said. He added that 'This is the first step towards global dialogue.'

Puna said the issue of relocation of any community needed serious attention and all stakeholders – including donors, leaders and communities – had a collective responsibility to address the issues.

The economy

Public spending on infrastructure and a stronger tourism sector contributed to a jump in gross domestic product (GDP) for financial year (FY) 2012 to 3.3 per cent from 1.0 per cent in 2011. As infrastructure construction slows with the completion of projects and public spending declines, so growth in FY2013 is expected to slow to 3.0 per cent. However, growth in Australia and New Zealand is expected to improve in 2014, which in turn will impact positively on the Cook Islands.

Tourist arrivals have increased by an average of 8 per cent over the last two years – to maintain this growth, the sector will need to expand facilities. Inflation, thanks to declining food and fuel prices, is expected to remain relatively low at 3 per cent for 2013. Higher tax collections and grant inflows in FY2013 are expected to cover increases in personnel and capital expenditures, keeping the fiscal deficit within government targets at 2.3 per cent of GDP.

Inflation rose to 2.8 per cent for FY2012, a sharp increase over 0.6 per cent

KEY FACTS

Official name: Cook Islands

Head of State: Head of State Queen Elizabeth II; represented by HM the Queen's Representative in the Cook Islands, Tom Marsters (from 27 July 2013); High Commissioner Linda Te Puni (from 10 Mar 2010)

Head of government: Prime Minister Henry Puna (CIP) (from 18 Nov 2010)

Ruling party: Cook Islands Party (CIP) (from 18 Nov 2010, re-elected 9 July 2014)

Area: 234 square km (15 islands); Rarotonga (67 square km)

Population: 17,791 (2011; census figure)

Capital: Avarua, on the island of Rarotonga

Official language: English and Cook Islands Māori

Currency: New Zealand dollar (NZ$) = 100 cents; Cook Islands' own currency is defunct

Exchange rate: NZ$1.58 per US$ (Sep 2015)

GDP per capita: US$20,452 (2010)

GDP real growth: 3.30% (2012)

GDP: US$241.30 million (2010)

Inflation: 0.60% (2011)*

Balance of trade: -US$105.00 million (2012)*

Visitor numbers: 99,500 (2009–10)

* estimated figure

in FY2011, largely due to higher transport and utility costs. By the end of the year, however, inflation began to drop as international food and fuel costs fell. For FY2013, thanks to the continuing decline in food and fuel prices, inflation is expected to remain relatively low at 3 per cent. Higher tax collections and grant inflows in FY2013 are expected to cover increases in personnel and capital expenditures, keeping the fiscal deficit within government targets at 2.3 per cent of GDP.

Risk assessment

Politics	Fair
Economy	Fair
Regional stability	Good

COUNTRY PROFILE

1200 The islands were believed to have been settled by neighbouring Tahitians.
1596 The Spaniard, Alvaro de Mendana, was thought to be the first European to sight the islands.
1733 The islands were named in honour of Captain James Cook.
1789 Rarotonga, the main island, was sighted by the Bounty mutineers.
1888 The islands became a British protectorate.
1901 New Zealand became colonial administrators of the Cook Islands.
1945 The island of Pukapuka (55km north-west of Nassau island) was bought by the Cook Islands Administration for UK£200 and then sold to the Island Councillors and Chiefs of Pukapuka six years later for the same price.
1965 The islands became self-governing, as a New Zealand dependency. Albert Henry of the Cook Islands Party (CIP) became prime minister.
1978 The Democratic Party (DP) won the election and Tom Davis became prime minister.
1994 The CIP won the general elections with 20 seats in the 25-seat parliament – the greatest margin of victory in 30 years. Geoffrey Henry became prime minister.
1997 The DP experienced internal conflict and a majority of party members broke away to become the Democratic Alliance Party (DAP). A faction of the DP became the New Alliance (NA) Party, led by Norman George.
1999 The CIP lost the general election and Terepai Maoate of the DAP formed a government with the NA.
2001 The Cook Islands was placed on the international money laundering blacklist of the Organisation for Economic Co-operation and Development (OECD).
2002 Maoate was ousted as prime minister in a vote of no-confidence. Robert Woonton (DAP) formed an all-party coalition.
2003 The DAP and the NA merged and reverted to their original name, Democratic Party (DP). Cook Islands Mäori became an official language.
2004 Jim Marurai, leader of DP was elected prime minister.
2005 After a dispute with his party, Marurai, remained prime minister with the support of the CIP. The Cook Islands was removed from the OECD international money laundering blacklist. Marurai's alliance with the CIP broke down and he returned to the DP for support, but not the party leadership.
2006 A by-election tipped the balance of power in parliament. The DP won snap elections, called by Prime Minister Marurai. A census was held in which 19,569 people were recorded, including tourists.
2008 Brian Donnelly became high commissioner but was forced to resign because of ill-health; he later died in New Zealand. Sophia Vickers became acting high commissioner until Tia Barrett was appointed acting high commissioner.
2009 The OECD published a list of countries that had not implemented international tax information exchange standards, of which Cook Islands was one, despite signing a co-operation agreement in 2002. High Commissioner Tia Barrett died suddenly.
2010 Linda Te Puni became high commissioner. Sir Frederick Goodwin was re-appointed as the Queen's Representative, for the third time. In a referendum, to reduce the number of parliamentary members, 76 per cent of the votes approved the motion; however as less than two-thirds of the voting population participated the proposed change was unsuccessful. In parliamentary elections the opposition CIP won 16 seats (out of 24). Henry Puna became the prime minister.
2011 In July the first direct flight from Sydney (Australia) landed at Rarotonga International Airport. A population census was held on 1 December, and recorded 17,791 people, which included tourists and other visitors. The majority of people were on the island of Rarotonga; the gender split was almost 50/50 per cent.
2012 Initial results of the population census showed that although there had been a 30-year decline in population numbers, since 2006 the population had increased by over 10 per cent on three major islands and that nearly 50 per cent of the population was aged 15–44. The first Ui Ariki Day (the day of Chiefs) holiday was held on 6 July. On 29 August, the leaders of seven Pacific island countries signed a maritime boundary agreement (MBA) that agreed to an official, legal and accurate boundary position of several overlapping jurisdictions among neighbouring islands. The new MBA should provide improved governance, protection, conservation and management of resources within the territories.
2013 Prime Minister Henry Puna visited the US, France and Belgium in July. He returned with some US$6.5 million of funding to develop energy from renewable sources.
2014 Parliamentary elections were held on 9 July. The Cook Islands Party retained its majority with 13 seats (out of 24) (42.3 per cent of the vote) to the Democratic Party's 8 seats (46.1per cent) and the newly-formed One Cook Island Party with 2 seats (9.6 per cent). There will be a by-election for the seat in Mitiaro after it was tied (50 votes each) in the gneral election. The by-election to be held before 28 November.
2015 The Cook Islands celebrated 50 years of self government on 4 August.

Political structure

Constitution
Under the 1965 constitution, New Zealand has responsibility for defence and foreign affairs and the Cook Islands is self-governing with full responsibility for internal affairs. Local affairs are handled by island councils and village committees in the outer islands.

Independence date
The Cook Islands became a self-governing territory in free association with New Zealand on 4 August 1965 when the Constitution of the Cook Islands took effect.

Form of state
Self-governing state in free association with New Zealand.

The executive
Executive power is excised by the prime minister and cabinet, through the High Commissioner (Queen's Representative).

National legislature
The unicameral parliament comprises 25 members (10 representing the main island of Rarotonga, 14 representing constituencies on other islands, and one representing expatriate Cook Islanders), elected by universal suffrage for a five-year term. Parliament chooses a prime minister from among its members, who then appoints a cabinet.
The House of Ariki is a 15-member chamber of hereditary chiefs, which advises on matters of land and issues of tradition.

Last elections
9 July 2014

Results: Parliamentary: Cook Islands Party (CIP) won 13 seats (out of 24) (42.3 per cent of the vote), Democratic Party (DP) eight seats (46.1 per cent), One Cook Islands 2 seats (9.6 per cent). The

result for Mitiaro was tied (50 votes each) and will be re-run in November. Turn-out was 80.47 per cent.
Referendum: 76 per cent of the votes approved the motion to reduce the number of members of parliament (MPs); however as a two-thirds majority of the voting population did not participate the referendum was unsuccessful.

Next elections
2019 (parliamentary)

Political parties

Ruling party
Cook Islands Party (CIP) (from 18 Nov 2010, re-elected 9 July 2014)

Main opposition party
Democratic Party (DP)

Political situation
In October 2009 the government of the Cook Islands adopted an economic support programme. The government hoped the programme would give a lift to the economy by supporting infrastructure expenditure, which would create employment; the programme would also target vulnerable groups in society by giving extra support.
There was an increase in tourist arrivals in 2009, largely as a result of an increase in tourism marketing overseas and a number of special events. The government has agreed to extend airline subsidies, especially on the Los Angeles–Rarotonga route, and the new direct air link to Sydney.
The Asian Development Bank (ADB) has provided a loan for some 15 projects totalling US$55 million, of which infrastructure and information and communication technology (ICT) accounted for US$20.91 million, by December 2009.
Economic growth in 2011 was estimated at 3.4 per cent.

Population

17,791.
Last census: 1 December 2011: 17,791.
The 2011 population census recorded 17,791 people, which included tourists and other visitors and registered a gender split of almost 50/50 per cent. The majority of people located were on the island of Rarotonga at 73.6 per cent of total numbers.
Initial results of the population census showed that although there has been a 30-year decline in population numbers, since 2006 the population has increased by over 10 per cent on three major islands and that nearly 50 per cent of the population was aged 15–44.
Population density: 97 inhabitants per square km (2010). Urban population 75 per cent (2010 Unicef).
Annual growth rate: 0.7 per cent, 1990–2010 (Unicef).

Ethnic make-up
Polynesian (81 per cent), Polynesian and European mixed (8 per cent), Polynesian and non-European mixed (8 per cent), European 2 per cent.

Religions
The majority are Cook Islands Christian Church (70 per cent), although Roman Catholics, Latter Day Saints, Seventh-Day Adventists and Assembly of God are also represented.

Health

The National Health Service in the Cook Islands is of a good standard relative to the needs of the country, managed by the ministry of health. There is a 90 bed central hospital on Rarotonga, seven outer island hospitals, 13 outpatient clinics, five healthcare centres and 58 maternity-child clinics. Difficult clinical cases are referred to New Zealand for specialised treatment. There is a comprehensive and compulsory immunisation programme for all new-born children. There are no dangerous animals, no poisonous insects and no lethal viruses such as malaria indigenous to the Cook Islands.

HIV/Aids
The first case of HIV infection by a resident of the Cook Islands was reported in December 2010.
Life expectancy: 72 years, 2004 (WHO 2006)
Fertility rate/Maternal mortality rate: 2.6 births per woman, 2004 (WHO 2006)
Child (under 5 years) mortality rate (per 1,000): 11 per 1,000 live births (WHO 2012)
Head of population per physician: 0.78 physicians per 1,000 people, 2001 (WHO 2006)

Main cities

Avarua, on the island of Rarotonga (capital, estimated population 13,509 in 2012), Amuri (334), Mangaia (258).

Languages spoken

Rarotongan is spoken on Rarotonga; Pukapuka and Nassau both have their own quite different languages, while other islands have differing versions of Cook Islands Māori. Most of the islanders also speak English.

Official language/s
English and Cook Islands Māori

Media

Elijah Communications (EC) owns and operates radio and television stations and publishes a newspaper.

Press
Dailies: EC publishes the *Herald* (www.ciherald.co.ck), while the *News* (www.cookislandsnews.com) is another independent newspaper; both are weeklies.

Broadcasting
Radio: There are two radio stations with services that are broadcast in English and Māori. The EC-owned Radio Cook Islands has a network that includes AM, FM and Internet streaming for coverage throughout the islands. It also operates HITZ 101.1 aimed at a young audience. Radio Ikurangi is also a private station.
Television: The EC-owned Cook Islands Television broadcasts for up to 18 hours per day. Services are provided via satellite and include not only domestic programmes but also some broadcast from New Zealand.
Other news agencies: ABC Pacific Beat: www.radioaustralia.net.au/pacbeat
Pacific Magazine: www.pacificmagazine.net
Pacific Islands News Association (Pina): www.pina.com.fj

Economy

Tourism and some offshore financial services are the principal components of the economy. Subsistence agriculture and fishing, particularly for pearls, continue as important activities for the population. Remittances from migrant workers, aid from New Zealand and Australia, sales of postage stamps and export of agricultural produce also play a role. The pearl industry, based on the islands of Manihiki and Penrhyn, has become a significant export sector and the government has invested in the industry's future through quality control and marketing. There has been a shift to paid labour and small businesses on the southern atolls, although many still work their own plantations. A significant offshore banking business has developed; regulations have been revised and a Financial Supervisory Commission established, allowing for further improvements to be implemented. The sale of fishing licences to foreign fleets is a key revenue earner.
Major infrastructure projects include expansion of the electricity system, installation of photovoltaic units in the Northern Group Islands, and improvements to telecommunications and the harbour and shipping services.
The long term prospects for the Cook Islands economy is not particularly bright. The economy had been in recession, averaging -2.4 per cent over 2007–09, before growth picked up in 2010 at 0.2 per cent, increasing to 3.4 per cent in 2011. Growth dropped to around 2.5 per cent in 2012, which fell to -1.7 per cent in 2013. This improved, though not significantly, to -1.2 per cent in 2014 and is forecast to rise to 2.1 per cent in 2015 as the economy recovers. GDP per capita reached US$14917.7 in 2012.

Visitor arrivals in the Cook Islands are expected to stabilise in 2015 and 2016 after years of steady increase. Arrivals from New Zealand and Australia, the key source markets, began to soften in late 2014. Capacity constraints loom in Rarotonga, the capital island, as the accommodation occupancy rate reached 75 per cent in 2014. Tourism remains steady; the industry catered for 99,500 visitors in 2009–10 and over 101,000 in 2010–11. By 2012 the number of visitors had increased to 117,000 and 121,458 by 2014.

The economy remains heavily reliant on tourism; 60 per cent of revenues are generated through tourist receipts. Officially being residents of New Zealand, Cook Islanders are free to move to either New Zealand or Australia, which has led to a decline in the population and workforce. The government has problems in maintaining basic health and education services on the outer islands, due to continued migration of skilled workers to New Zealand. The local population is not only aging but also in decline as migration takes the younger, productive workforce overseas. Although the subsequent remittances sustain elderly family members, who are no longer productive, the goods and services provided are increasingly based on their needs and are not necessarily used in capital investment.

External trade

The Cook Islands is a member of the South Pacific Regional Trade and Economic Co-operation Agreement (Sparteca) along with 12 other regional nations. This allows products duty free access by Pacific Island Forum (PIF) members (which includes the Cook Islands) to Australian and New Zealand markets (subject to the country of origin restrictions).

The Cook Islands suffer from an adverse balance of trade, particularly with New Zealand, with which it maintains a free trade agreement and free movement of workers.

Imports

Principal imports are manufactured goods, foodstuffs, textiles, fuels, timber, capital goods and live animals.

Main sources: New Zealand (69.2 per cent of total in 2012 (latest available figures in 2015)), Australia (5.1 per cent), US (2 per cent).

Exports

Principal exports are predominantly black pearls, copra, papayas, fresh and canned citrus fruit, fish, and pearl shells and clothing manufacture.

Main destinations: Japan (65.1 per cent of total in 2012 (latest available figures in 2015)), New Zealand (2.4 per cent), US (1.6 per cent).

Agriculture

Farming

The rich volcanic soil on the southern islands helps subsistence farming cater for local consumption. The agriculture sector accounts for around 5 per cent of GDP.

Fishing

Long-line catches of tuna and billfish are most often exported to either American Samoa or Japan. The various problems of the Cook Islands' huge fishery exclusive economic zone includes the continued attraction of illegal operators, too little data on migratory fish stock and the high cost of its operation. In order to develop the domestic fishing industry, the government introduced exemption on levies for fuel, bait and equipment, but labour shortages are a constant constraint.

In January 2012 the government issued fishing licences to 17 Taiwanese vessels. They will be allowed to fish for tuna and swordfish until 2015. However, local fishermen see competition from these vessels as potentially devastating and called on the international environmental campaign group, Greenpeace, to provide support for their cause in reversing the decision. By mid-2013 there was concern that the vessels were looking to sell catch locally, thereby hitting local businesses.

Pearl farming used to be the second-largest income earner, after tourism. Commercial fishing generates three times as much export income as pearl production. The bases for pearl fishing are the northern group atolls Manihiki, Penrhyn and Rakahanga.

The Cook Islands enforces a strict ban on shark finning. The Luen Thai Fishing Venture, a multinational fishing company licensed to fish in Cook Islands waters with 14 vessels, has been fined US$120,000 and stripped of its fishing licence for Marshall Islands waters since being found with shark fins on board their vessels. There is a 1.9 million square kilometre shark sanctuary, established in 2012, in Cook Islands waters.

Industry and manufacturing

The Cook Islands economy earns around US$4.5 million per annum from its pearl industry. The other main secondary industries include agricultural exports, clothing manufacture, fruit canning/processing, electronic component assembly and handicrafts.

Industry accounts for around 13 per cent of GDP.

Tourism

Cook Islands' palm fringed, largely white beaches and azure seas fulfil most visitor's idea of a tropical paradise and the sector offers visitors as much of the local Polynesian culture as any could wish. The sector constituted around 75 per cent of GDP in 2013, which is higher than the regional average. There are direct, daily international flights from New Zealand and Australia, to the upgraded and expanded Rarotonga International Airport, opened in June 2010.

The government policy is to redirect the sector from a reliance on 'sea and surf' holidays to value-added geo-tourism, 'that sustains or enhances the geographical character of a place – its environment, culture, aesthetics, heritage, and wellbeing of its residents.

Mining

The Japanese government's Metal Mining Agency has discovered significant reserves of manganese in nodules on the seabed in Cook Islands territorial waters. New techniques are being developed to exploit this resource.

The Cook Islands hopes to transform itself into one of the world's richest countries within a decade by sending robots to the sea floor to collect minerals that it believes are worth tens of billions of dollars. It is estimated that the Cook Islands could supply 10 per cent of the global cobalt reserve.

Hydrocarbons

There are no known hydrocarbon reserves. Consumption of oil was 1,050 barrels per day (bpd) in 2013, all of which was imported.

The country aims to have eliminated its carbon footprint as early as 2020.

Energy

In 2012 nearly 99 per cent of households on Rarotonga and Aitutaki were connected to the grid; some 8 per cent have solar photovoltaic home systems (SHS) and 3 per cent used diesel generators. On the smaller islands 43 per cent had a SHS and 60 per cent were connected to the grid.

Total installed generating capacity was 11.75MW in 2012. The Rarotonga Electricity Authority is responsible for electricity supply to Rarotonga only.

In May 2015, the Government of New Zealand announced the completion of a project that brought solar arrays to Rakahanga, Pukapuka, Nassau, and Palmerston, and to the northern Cook islands of Penrhyn and Manihiki, where the solar panels are expected to provide over 95 per cent of the electricity needs for the villages and deliver power to more than 230 homes and public buildings. The $20.5 million project began in 2013.

Banking and insurance

Legislation to enable Cook Islands' development as an offshore financial centre and tax haven was enacted in 1981/82. Since 2001, when the Cook Islands was among nine countries listed by the OECD Financial Action Task Force (FATF) as havens for money laundering, offshore banking regulations have been revised and the Financial Supervisory Commission established in 2003 to license and regulate all trustee companies both domestic and international.
In February 2005, the Cook Islands came off the list of non-co-operative countries and territories of the OECD FATF.
There have been limited attempts to consolidate the banking sector, with 16 licensed banks in operation.

Central bank
The Cook Islands do not have a central bank.

Main financial centre
Avarua (on Rarotonga).

Offshore facilities
The offshore financial industry provides 8 per cent of GDP.

Time

GMT minus ten hours.

Geography

The Cook Islands comprise 13 inhabited and two uninhabited islands located in the southern Pacific Ocean, between American Samoa to the west and French Polynesia to the east. The islands are spread over about two million square km (more than 750,000 square miles) of ocean, and form two groups – the Northern Group of the six atolls of Nassau, Pukapuka, Rakahanga, Penrhyn, Suwarrow and Manihiki, and the more populous Southern Group which includes Rarotonga, Aitutaki, Mangaia, Palmerston and Takutea, all volcanic islands.
Rising sea levels as a result of global climate change are a potential threat to the low-lying islands. Heights above sea level range from Te Manga, Rarotonga at 652m (2,139ft) to Manihiki at 4m (13ft) above sea level at its highest point.

Hemisphere
Southern

Climate

Damp and tropical, mild from Apr–Nov but Dec–Mar hot and humid, with likelihood of hurricanes. The mean temperature is 24 degrees Celsius, with average yearly rainfall over 2,000mm; heaviest on the forested volcanic slopes of the southern islands.

Entry requirements

Passports
Required by all, valid for six months beyond initial visa-free 31 days.
Proof of onward passage, adequate funds and suitable booked accommodation are also required.

Visa
For tourist purposes, visas are not required for stays of up to 31 days. Monthly extensions can be arranged up to a maximum of five months.

Currency advice/regulations
No restrictions on import of local and foreign currency. Export of local currency is limited to NZ$250 and of foreign currency to amount declared on arrival.

Customs
Incoming passengers are permitted to bring in a maximum of 200 cigarettes, 1kg of tobacco or 50 cigars and two litres of wine or spirits or 4.5 litres of beer.

Health (for visitors)

There are no dangerous animals, no poisonous insects and no lethal viruses such as malaria indigenous to the Cook Islands.

Mandatory precautions
None.

Advisable precautions
Vaccinations for diphtheria, tuberculosis, hepatitis A and B, polio, tetanus and typhoid are recommended.
The World Health Organisation has warned of a high risk of catching dengue fever.

Hotels

A 10 per cent Government Turnover Tax applies. Tipping is not customary.

Credit cards

Visa and Mastercard are accepted.

Public holidays (national)

Fixed dates
1 Jan (New Year's Day), 25 Apr (Anzac Day), 6 July (Ui Ariki Day (Day of Chiefs)) 25 Jul (Gospel Day, Rarotonga), 4 Aug (Constitution Day), 27 Oct (Gospel Day), 25 Dec (Christmas Day), 26 Dec (Boxing Day).

Variable dates
Good Friday, Easter Monday, Queen's Official Birthday (first Mon in Jun).

Working hours

Banking
Mon–Thur: 0900–1500; Fri: 0900–1100.

Business
Mon–Fri: 0800–1600.

Government
Mon–Fri: 0800–1600.

Shops
Mon–Fri: 0900–1600; Sat: 0900–1200.

Telecommunications

Telephone/fax
There are automatic telephone exchanges in Rarotonga and Aitutaki. International telecommunications are via Cable and Wireless and Peacesat satellite links.

Mobile/cell phones
Mobile phone services have been available since the end of 2003 and are provided by Telecom Cook Islands (TCI) using the GSM900 network and 2.5G Edge technology for data. Local mobiles can be hired in Rarotonga from the Telecom office near Cook Islands Tourist Corporation.

Electricity supply

240V DC/50 cycle. Mostly diesel generators; supply is continuous on Rarotonga, Aitutaki and Mauke, but may be 12 hours per day elsewhere. Plugs are the same as Australia and New Zealand i e three prongs set at an angle.

Social customs/useful tips

Bargaining is discouraged. Gratuities are not customary, as tradition requires that something is then given in return.
Dress: Brief attire (eg bikinis) should not be worn in towns or villages. Nude or topless sunbathing will cause offence.
Homosexuality is generally accepted, although officially illegal (for men, not women). Public displays of affection would be considered offensive though. Same sex marriage is not permitted and civil unions aren't recognised.
'Kia orana' is the usual greeting; it means 'May you live long'.

Getting there

Air
There are direct, daily international flights from New Zealand and Australia.
International airport/s: Rarotonga (RAR), three kilometres west of Avarua. Restaraunts, duty-free shop, shops, car rental. Hotel coaches meet each flight and taxis and buses are also available.
Airport tax: Included in air fares. From 2013 it is NZ$65 and applies only to internation travel.

Surface
Water: Inter-island shipping services are provided by major passenger carrying cargo lines, operators include Express Cook Islands Line Shipping Ltd and Hawaii-Pacific Maritime Ltd.
Main port/s: Avatiu (on Rarotonga), and Aitutaki. Penrhyn Island (northern Cook Islands) is also a Port of Entry.

Getting about

National transport
Air: Air Rarotonga operates inter-island services. Airstrips for small planes on Aitutaki, Penryhn, Rakahanga, Mitiaro, Atiu, Mauke, Mangala and Manitiki. Services do not operate on Sunday.
Road: The Ara Tapu surfaced road runs 32km around Rarotonga coast. There is also an older inland road, which winds cross-country.

Buses: *The Island Bus* (yellow buses) – a round-the-island service in both directions (Mon–Fri 0700–1600; Sat 0800–1300).

Taxis: Taxi service is available on Rarotonga.

Water: There are harbours on Aitutaki, Atiu, Penrhyn and Suwarrow.

Car hire

Car, scooter and bicycle hire are available on Rarotonga and Aitutaki. Driving is on the left.

A local licence is required; they can be obtained from the police station on Avarua, on presentation of an international or Commonwealth national driving licence. In 2013 the cost was NZ$20 (US$15.50).

BUSINESS DIRECTORY

The addresses listed below are a selection only. While World of Information makes every endeavour to check these addresses, we cannot guarantee that changes have not been made, especially to telephone numbers and area codes. We would welcome any corrections.

Telephone area codes

The international direct dialling (IDD) for Cook Islands is +682 followed by subscriber's number.

Useful telephone numbers

Police: 999
Fire: 996
Ambulance: 998

Chambers of Commerce

Cook Islands Chamber of Commerce PO Box 242, Avarua, Rarotonga (tel: 20-925; fax: 20-969).

Banking

Bank of the Cook Islands, PO Box 113, Rarotonga (tel: 29-341; fax: 29-343).

Wall Street Banking Corporation Ltd, PO Box 3012, CITC House, Avarua (tel: 23-445; fax: 23-446; e-mail: info@wallbank.co.ck).

Westpac Banking Corporation, PO Box 42, Rarotonga (tel: 22-014; fax: 20-014).

Travel information

Air Rarotonga (tel: 22-888; e-mail: bookings@airraro.co.ck; internet site: http://www.airraro.com).

Flight information (24 hours) (tel: 25-890).

Government Information Office, PO Box 106 (tel: 29-304; fax: 20-856).

Principal Immigration Officer, Ministry of Foreign Affairs and Immigration, PO Box 105, Rarotonga (tel: 29-347; fax: 21-247).

Rarotonga International Airport, PO Box 90, Rarotonga (tel: 25-890; fax: 21-890; e-mail: aaci@airport.gov.ck).

National tourist organisation offices

Cook Islands Tourism Corporation, PO Box 14, Avarua, Rarotonga (tel: 29-435; fax: 21-435; e-mail: headoffice@cook-islands.com).

Other useful addresses

Asian Development Bank (ADB), South Pacific Regional Mission, La Casa di Andrea, Fr. Dr. W. H. Lini Highway; PO Box 127, Port Vila (tel: +678 2 23-300; fax: +678 2 23-183; email: adbsprm@adb.org; internet: http://www.adb.org/SPRM).

Cook Islands Development Investment Board, Rarotonga (tel: 24-296; fax: 24-298; e-mail: cidib@oyster.net.ck; internet site: http://www.cookislands-invest.com).

Cook Islands Investment Corporation, Rarotonga (tel: 29-391; fax: 29-381; e-mail: ciic@oyster.net.ck).

Cook Islands News, PO Box 15, Rarotonga (tel: 22-999; fax: 25-303; e-mail: editor@cookislandsnews.com; internet site: http:/www.cinews.co.ck).

ABC Pacific Beat: www.radioaustralia.net.au/pacbeat

Pacific Magazine: www.pacificmagazine.net

Pacific Islands News Association (Pina): www.pina.com.fj

Internet sites

Cook Islands government: www.cook-islands.gov.ck

Cook Islands News: www.cinews.co.ck

Cook Islands shipping movements: www.ck/shipping.htm

Cook Islands website: http://www.cookislands.org.uk/

Costa Rica

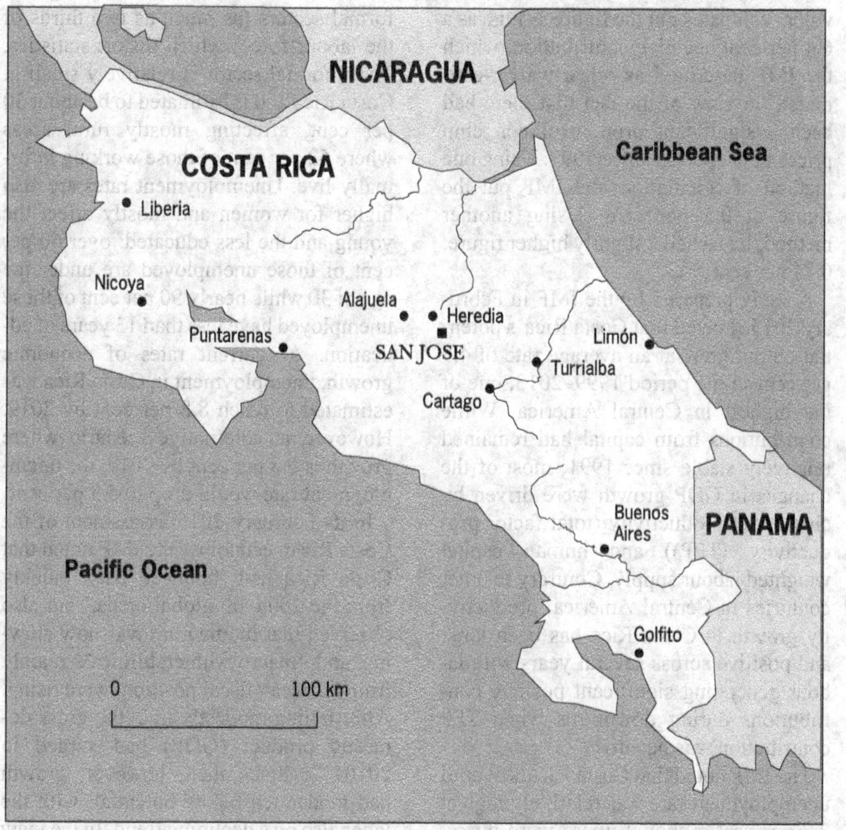

KEY FACTS

Official name: República de Costa Rica (Republic of Costa Rica)

Head of State: President Luis Guillermo Solís (PAC) (since 8 May 2014)

Head of government: President Luis Guillermo Solís (PAC) (since 8 May 2014)

Ruling party: (Partido Acción Ciudadana (PAC) (Citizen Action Party) (took office 1 May 2014)

Area: 51,060 square km

Population: 4.78 million (2014)* (4,301,712; 2011 census figure)

Capital: San José

Official language: Spanish

Currency: Colón (CC) = 100 céntimos

Exchange rate: CC536.50 per US$ (Sep 2015)

GDP per capita: US$10,083 (2014)*

GDP real growth: 3.50% (2014)*

GDP: US$48.14 billion (2014)*

Labour force: 2.12 million (2009)

Unemployment: 8.20% (2014)*

Inflation: 3.19% (2014)*

Balance of trade: -US$5.68 billion (2014)*

Annual FDI: US$2.80 billion (2011)

* estimated figure

For the newly elected Costa Rican President Luis Guillermo Solis, 2014 was not the best of years for business in Costa Rica. Two high profile companies, Bank of America (BoA) and Intel, closed down a large part of their operations in the country, laying off a total of some 2,000 workers. Quite apart from the damage to the Costa Rican economy, the closures sent out all the wrong signals about Costa Rica's willingness and ability to see foreign businesses set up shop in the country. Before the two big companies announced their decision, the US call centre operator CustomerSpeak had laid off some 500 employees. The CustomerSpeak decision was also likely to create knock-on consequences as the call-centre business was a sector Costa Rica had identified – with some success – as of particular interest. The lay-offs happened shortly before the outgoing president, Laura Chinchilla, relinquished the Presidency. A worried president elect, Luis Guillermo Solis, had met with Intel executives who, it was announced, had assured him that the decision to downscale had nothing to do with the election of his new government. Foreign direct investment (FDI) had been seen as the El Dorado of many Central American governments. The competing administrations had never seen FDI as a matter of 'Easy Come'; but Costa Rica had not factored in the 'Easy Go' that transpired when distant global companies took decisions that were solely in the interest of their shareholders.

Intel, Customerspeak and the BoA

Not that Intel's decision was a complete surprise. The closure of the company's assembly and test operation had been under discussion for almost a year; it was the result of the company's apparent failure to respond to the mobile computing of the smartphone. The closure of the site, which had been a significant contributor to Costa Rica's exports since 1997was simply part of a larger plan to cut spending as it endeavoured to get to grips with the mobile market. Intel planned to move its assembly and testing operations from its site in Heredia, to existing sites in China, Malaysia and Vietnam. Intel as a company was experiencing the same problems as Nokia had some three years earlier. In Finland Nokia laid off 12,000 workers and managers in 2012. Intel was laying off 5 per cent of its employees worldwide. The case of Bank of America may have had different origins, but the result was the same. The bank was going through a general downsizing that not only affected Costa Rica, but also nearby Mexico. The *Wall Street Journal* had reported that as many as 45,000 employees had been laid off worldwide since 2010.

While reassuring the Costa Rican government that the decision to downsize had nothing to do with the election, Intel pointed out that it would continue to have over 1,000 employees in Costa Rica and would continue to carry out some research and development activities there. The company also announced that it expected to recruit another 200 staff later in 2015.

A major reason for Costa Rica's attractiveness as a business and manufacturing centre was its relatively high levels of education. About 60 per cent of Costa Rica's labour force has at least secondary education, compared to the Latin America and Caribbean (LAC) average of 40 per cent. Nearly one quarter of Costa Rica's labour force has tertiary education, making it the only country in the region which exceeds the LAC average of 20 per cent.

The economy – mixed blessings

While Costa Rica's economists attempted to assess the cost to the economy of the Intel closure, the International Monetary Fund (IMF) suggested that the bottom line cost had been greatly over-estimated. The wilder estimates put the figure as high as a 6.4 per cent negative contribution, which the IMF described as 'clearly over-estimated' in view of the fact that there had been a significant drop in silicon chip prices in the period since 1997. Using one method of calculation, the IMF put the figure at 0.5 per cent. Using another method, it reached a slightly higher figure, 0.74 per cent.

A study prepared by the IMF in February 2015 showed that Costa Rica's potential output grew at an average rate of 4.5 per cent in the period 1999–2013, one of the highest in Central America. While contributions from capital had remained relatively stable since 1991, most of the changes in GDP growth were driven by changes in productivity (total factor productivity (TFP)) and human capital weighted labour supply. Contrary to other countries in Central America, productivity growth in Costa Rica has been large and positive across several years with labour generating significant positive contributions during downturns when TFP contribution was negative.

The IMF noted that Costa Rica's overall unemployment rate was relatively high at 7.7 per cent, although there were differences across gender and age. The trend was stable – the national unemployment rate averaged 9.6 per cent for the first three quarters of 2014, unchanged on the same period in 2013. Costa Rica had the third highest unemployment rate in the region after the Dominican Republic (14.7 per cent) and Nicaragua (8.0 per cent). However, countries like El Salvador, Guatemala and Honduras have large informal sectors (as much as two thirds of the labour force) which distort statistics. The informal sector is relatively small in Costa Rica and is estimated to be about 30 per cent, affecting mostly rural areas where 62 per cent of those working informally live. Unemployment rates are also higher for women and mostly affect the young and the less educated: over 60 per cent of those unemployed are under the age of 30 while nearly 90 per cent of those unemployed have less than 13 years of education. At current rates of economic growth, unemployment in Costa Rica was estimated to reach 8.8 per cent by 2019. However, an alternative scenario where growth is 6.3 per cent by 2019, the unemployment rate would drop to 5.3 per cent.

In its February 2015 assessment of the Costa Rican economy, the IMF noted that Costa Rica had 'bounced back quickly from the 2008–09 global crisis,' but also observed that momentum was now slowing and 'macro vulnerabilities', mainly from the weak fiscal position, were rising. After falling modestly in 2009, gross domestic product (GDP) had surged in 2010–12. Since then, however, growth had moderated below potential, with the latter also on a declining trend. In the view of the IMF, structural impediments needed to be removed to maintain sustained rates of economic expansion. The counter-cyclical budgetary stimulus initiated in 2009 pushed the deficit above 5 per cent of GDP in 2010 (mainly through a rise in wages and transfers). The deficit has been creeping up further since then, placing the public-debt-to-GDP ratio on an unsustainable upward trajectory, which was fast approaching levels shown to increase risks of disorderly adjustment for emerging economies.

According to IMF figures, after expanding by about 5 per cent in 2012, economic activity rose by 3.5 per cent in 2013, largely on account of weaker domestic consumption and net exports, the latter mirroring slower growth in the US – Costa Rica's major export market. Growth was expected by the IMF to have stayed the same in 2014, as activity was to some extent dampened by the closure of Intel manufacturing, announced in April (see

KEY INDICATORS — Costa Rica

	Unit	2011	2012	2013	2014	**2015
Population	m	4.30	*4.65	*4.71	*4.78	*4.84
Gross domestic product (GDP)	US$bn	40.90	45.38	49.24	*48.14	*52.80
GDP per capita	US$	8,877	9,753	*10,447	*10,083	*10,916
GDP real growth	%	4.2	5.1	3.4	*3.5	*3.8
Inflation	%	4.9	4.5	5.2	*3.2	*4.6
Unemployment	%	7.7	7.8	8.5	*8.2	*8.3
Exports (fob) (goods)	US$m	4,932.3	5,314.0	5,125.2	9,138.6	–
Imports (fob) (goods)	US$m	11,867.7	12,741.0	13,161.1	14,813.9	–
Balance of trade	US$m	-6,935.4	-7,427.0	-8,036.0	-5,675.4	–
Current account	US$m	-2,195.5	-2,382.0	-2,486.0	–	*-1,922.0
Total reserves minus gold	US$m	4,806.6	6,857.0	7,330.9	7,211.4	–
Foreign exchange	US$m	4,562.6	6,622.0	7,096.0	–	–
Exchange rate	per US$	502.38	499.15	501.41	539.42	–

* estimated figure ** forecast figure

above). With growth below the trend rate of 4.25 per cent, output had now fallen short of potential. As already noted, the unemployment rate had been elevated since the global crisis and increased further in early 2014, reflecting new and returning entrants into the labour force.

Inflation remained within the target range in 2013, but rose sharply and breached its new upper limit in 2014. Inflation at end-2013 was 3.7 per cent. To signal commitment to lower inflation, the Banco Central de Costa Rica (BCCR) (central bank) lowered its target range from 4–6 per cent to 3–5 per cent in early 2014. However, owing mainly to the pass-through to domestic prices from exchange rate depreciation and the inflation expectations, which persisted above the target range, inflation reached 5.7 per cent in October 2014 and was estimated to have finished 2014 above the upper limit of the target range.

The private capital inflows of 2012 had gone into reverse and the exchange rate had depreciated markedly in early 2014. The current account deficit declined slightly to 5 per cent of GDP in 2013 and was expected to remain broadly stable in 2014. In the wake of US monetary policy normalisation, the national currency, the colón, lost 10 per cent of its value between January and March 2014, as private inflows and government use of its foreign exchange deposits ceased. However, according to the IMF it had subsequently recovered with year-to-date depreciation standing at 7 per cent in mid-November 2014.

ECLAC concurs

The United Nations Economic Commission for Latin America and the Caribbean (ECLAC) in its annual *Preliminary Overview of the Economies of Latin America and the Caribbean* expected the Costa Rican economy to have expanded by 3.6 per cent in 2014, a 0.1-percentage-point increase on the 2013 growth rate. The current account deficit was forecast to reach 5.3 per cent of GDP, up 0.2 percentage points on the 2013 figure, while overall public sector debt amounted to 56.1 per cent of GDP in August 2014, 3.5 percentage points higher than in August 2013. Year-on-year variation in the consumer price index stood at 5.7 per cent in October 2014, while the average unemployment rate remained at 9.6 per cent for the first three quarters of the year. The economy was projected by ECLAC to grow by 3.2 per cent in 2015.

The central government fiscal deficit widened to 4.4 per cent of GDP in October 2014, up 0.3 percentage points on the same period the previous year. Central government tax revenues posted 7.3 per cent nominal year-on-year growth in October 2014, as incomes rose. General sales tax receipts were up by 8.9 per cent on the strength of higher revenues from customs duties (up 14.4 per cent) and, to a lesser extent, domestic goods and services (4.3 per cent). Tax proceeds from the consumption of imported goods and services jumped 10.1 per cent and corporate and personal income tax revenues also rose by 6.3 per cent.

Capital expenditure surged by 24.3 per cent in October 2014 (10.2 per cent in October 2013), owing primarily to a rise in capital transfers to the public sector. Greater borrowing requirements pushed up debt levels, with total overall public sector debt reaching 56.1 per cent of GDP in August 2014, up 3.5 percentage points on the August 2013 figure. External debt contributed 4.0 points to this increase, partially offset by a 0.5 point drop in domestic debt. In April 2014 the ministry of finance issued US$1 billion in 30-year bonds on the international market, with an interest rate of 7 per cent. In September 2014, the credit rating agency Moody's announced that it had downgraded Costa Rica's government bond rating from Baa3 (negative outlook) to Ba1 (stable outlook), with the consequent loss of investment grade status. The downgrade was prompted by the deterioration of the central government's financial position, which had accelerated in the previous six years.

The balance-of-payments current account deficit was projected to be 5.3 per cent of GDP at the end of 2014 (compared with 5.1 per cent at year-end 2013). This worsening position reflected an expected widening of the goods balance deficit by 0.6 percentage points of GDP and of the income account deficit by 0.5 points, partly offset by a 0.9-percentage-point improvement in the services balance. Meanwhile, FDI was forecast to reach US$2.2 billion at the end of 2014 (4.4 per cent of GDP, compared with 5.5 per cent of GDP in 2013). Aggregate demand was projected to post slower growth of 1.1 per cent by the end of 2014, (compared with 3.1 per cent in 2013), owing to the weaker expansion of domestic demand (3.1 per cent at year-end 2014, compared with 3.7 per cent in 2013) and falling exports of goods and services (down 2.3 per cent in 2014, compared with 3.6 per cent growth in 2013). The domestic demand trend in turn reflected slower growth in gross fixed investment (5.1 per cent in 2014, compared with 11.8 per cent in 2013), partially counterbalanced by faster growth in consumption (3.6 per cent in 2014, against 3.2 per cent the previous year). The sectors projected to maintain the strongest growth in 2014 included financial and insurance services (6.0 per cent), transport, storage and communications (5.6 per cent), agriculture and fisheries (4.0 per cent) and commerce (3.8 per cent). Robust activity in the financial and insurance services sector reflected brisk lending and deposit-taking and an increase in foreign-exchange commissions.

Transport, storage and communications posted steady growth on the strength of mobile telephony and Internet services and cargo and passenger transport. The strong performance of the agriculture sector was driven by an improvement in pineapple, banana, melon and watermelon crops, while commercial activity was mainly fuelled by retail sales of electrical and household appliances, mobile telephones and televisions.

Abundant energy?

Compared to other countries in the region, Costa Rica has a relatively well performing electricity system. According to the IMF, the service quality is high (nearly complete coverage, limited interruptions, low technical losses), prices are relatively competitive (industrial tariffs are the lowest in the region) and Costa Rica has an adequate regulatory and policy framework. Electricity generation in Costa Rica is the greenest in the region, with 66 per cent coming from hydro, 12 per cent from geothermal and wind and the rest coming from thermal energy. Although Costa Rica's hydro potential remains significant, it is estimated that, by 2040, its growth potential will be severely limited. There is, of course, an immense potential for solar energy, which currently remains untapped in part owing to its significant variability.

The Instituto Costarricense de Electricidad (ICE) (Costa Rican Electricity Institute), a state-owned enterprise, largely controls generation, transmission and distribution. ICE has a monopoly on electricity transmission and controls 79 per cent of distribution, with co-operatives and other small state-owned companies distributing the rest. Until 1990, ICE also had a monopoly in generation. Since then, the share of private sector participation in generation has been growing; private sector generation now stands at around 17 per cent and is expected to continue increasing as ICE faces capacity expansion constraints. The President has also declared that he is open to higher private sector participation if it leads to lower tariffs. Costa Rica's electricity had been steady over the previous decade. However, an increase of over 30 per cent in 2013 (after 3 years with no increases) generated an outcry over electricity prices.

Risk assessment

Politics	Good
Economy	Good
Regional stability	Good

COUNTRY PROFILE

1502 Christopher Columbus visited the region, naming it Costa Rica (Rich Coast).
1561 Colonisation of Costa Rica began. The country became a dependency of Nicaragua within the kingdom of Guatemala in the vice-royalty of Mexico, then known as Nuevo España (New Spain).
1808 Coffee was introduced into Costa Rica and became the country's main crop.
1821 The Central American provinces (Costa Rica, Guatemala, Honduras, Nicaragua and El Salvador) declared independence from Spain.
1822 Central American confederation annexed itself to the Mexican Empire, under General Agustín de Iturbde, later Emperor Agustín I.
1823 Agustín I was overthrown and Mexico became a republic. The Central American states formed the United Provinces of Central America.
1825 Costa Rica, Guatemala, Honduras, Nicaragua and El Salvador formed the Central American Federation (CAF).
1838 The CAF was dissolved and Costa Rica became a fully independent republic.
1849 Under the leadership of Juan Rafael Mora, Costa Rica helped organise Central American resistance against William Walker, the US bucaneer who took over Nicaragua.
1859 A *coup d'état* saw Mora lose power.
1870 Costa Rican leader, Tomás Guardía, began a process of development, encouraging foreign investment in the rail system.
1874 The United Fruit Company began operations in Costa Rica.
1889 The country embraced democracy and Bernardo Soto was elected as the country's first president.
1940 President Rafael Angel Calderón Guardía, founder of the Partido Unidad Social Christiana (PUSC) (Social Christian Unity Party), introduced social reforms, including labour rights and a minimum wage.
1948 The result of the presidential election was annulled after the government's candidate, Rafael Calderón, who came second, refused to accept defeat. An opposition leader, José Figueres Ferrer, led a revolt in favour of the winning candidate, Otilio Ulate. An interim regime was set up, the constitution was changed, the army was abolished and Otilio Ulate became president.
1953 José Figueres Ferrer, a democratic socialist and leader of the Partido Liberación Nacional (PLN) (National Liberation Party), won the election. He began social reforms with the help of the reformist bishop of San José and a communist union leader, remaining president until 1958.
1982 Luis Alberto Monge (PLN) was elected president. He introduced a programme of austerity measures designed to stabilise the deteriorating economy.
1986 Oscar Arías Sánchez (PLN) was elected president and began brokering a peace plan with the leaders of Nicaragua, El Salvador, Guatemala and Honduras to end regional political turbulence and civil war.
1987 Arías won the Nobel Peace Prize for securing a regional peace deal.
1990 Rafael Angel Calderón Fournier of the PUSC was elected president and enacted a series of austerity measures.
1994 José María Figueres (PLN) won the presidential election.
1998 Miguel Angel Rodríguez of the PUSC was elected president.
2000 Costa Rica and Nicaragua reached an agreement to end a dispute over navigation along the San Juan river, which serves as the border between the two countries.
2001 Privatisation of Costa Rica's Pacific ports began.
2002 The PUSC defeated the PLN in the parliamentary elections. Abel Pacheco de la Espriella (PUSC) won the run-off election and became president.
2003 Strikes were held by energy and telecommunications workers over President Pacheco's privatisation plans for the sector and by primary and secondary school teachers over problems in paying their salaries. The strikes led to the resignations of three ministers.
2004 Three former presidents – José María Figueres, Miguel Angel Rodríguez and Rafael Angel Calderón – were investigated over allegations of corruption.
2005 A national state of emergency was declared after days of heavy rainfall resulted in severe flooding along the Caribbean coast.
2006 Oscar Arías Sánchez and the PLN won presidential and parliamentary elections.
2007 Costa Rica cut diplomatic ties with Taiwan; President Arias said his country needed to attract more investment from China. The Central American Free Trade Agreement (Cafta) with the US was narrowly approved by referendum.
2009 President Arías renewed diplomatic ties with Cuba. At the G20 summit the leaders agreed to sanctions against Costa Rica, which the Organisation for Economic Co-Operation and Development (OECD) had labelled a secretive tax haven. Honduran President Manuel Zelaya was exiled to Costa Rica.
2010 In parliamentary elections, incumbent PLN won 37.16 per cent of the votes (23 seats out of 57); in presidential elections, Laura Chinchilla (PLN) won 46.76 per cent of the vote; her closest rival Ottón Solís (PAC) won 25.17 per cent.. Nicaraguan troops crossed into a disputed border area and planted a Nicaraguan flag on Costa Rica's Calero Island, claiming that Google Earth (the internet atlas) showed the island as Nicaraguan. Costa Rica lodged a complaint with the International Court of Justice (ICJ) immediately.
2011 In March, the ICJ ordered both sides to withdraw all personnel while judgement was pending. Both sides welcomed the ruling. In April, Google Earth admitted that it had incorrectly marked the border between Costa Rica and Nicaragua. It blamed the US State Department for supplying incorrect data and began updating its map. A population and housing census was held between May–June. In July, Costa Rica was removed from the OECD black-list of non-compliant tax havens, having introduced laws and practices, providing tax information to other OECD members.
2012 Preliminary census results published on 2 February showed there was a total of 4,301,712 residents and 1.36 million households in Costa Rica. On 12 May, the US-based electronics company IBM, opened its new call centre in the America Free Zone (industrial park) in Heredia, providing customer services. IBM plans to invest US$300 million (2012–22) and employ up to 1,000 people by 2014. On 12 October a powerful earthquake of 5.1 magnitude struck near Parrita, in Puntarenas. Early indications were that it had affected very few people.
2014 Parliamentary and the first round of presidential elections were held on 2 February. In the parliamentary election Partido Liberación Nacional (PLN) (National Liberation Party) won 25.54 per cent of the votes (18 seats out of 57); Partido Acción Ciudadana (PAC) (Citizen Action Party) 23.84 per cent (13); Frente Amplio (FA) (Broad Front) 13.09 per cent (9), Partido de Unidad Socialcristiana (PUS) (Social Christian Unity Party) 10.01 per cent (eight), Partido Movimiento

Libertario (PML) (Libertarian Movement) 7.92 per cent (4), Partido Restauración Nacional (PRN) (National Restoration Party) 4.11 per cent (1), Partido Renovación Costarricense (PRC) (Costa Rican Renovation Party) 3.97 per cent (2), Partido Accesibilidad sin Exclusión (PASE) (Accessibility without Exclusion) 3.95 per cent (1) and Alianza Demócrata Cristiana (ADC) (Christian Democratic Alliance) 1.14 per cent (1), 12 other political parties won too few votes to gain any seats. Turnout was 69.08 per cent. The first round of the presidential election was won by Luis Guillermo Solís (Partido Acción Ciudadana (PAC) (Citizen Action Party)) won 30.64 per cent, with Johnny Araya Monge (Partido Liberación Nacional (PLN) (National Liberation Party)) 29.71 per cent, José María Villalta Florez-Estrada (Frente Amplio (FA) (Broad Front)) 17.25 per cent, Otto Guevara (Partido Movimiento Libertario (PML) (Libertarian Movement)) 11.34 per cent and Rodolfo Piza (Partido de Unidad Socialcristiana) (Social Christian Unity Party)) 6.02 per cent. Turnout was 68.19 per cent. The second round was held on 7 April. The result was a win for Luis Guillermo Solís (PAC) with 77.81 per cent of the vote, Johnny Araya Monge (PLN) 22.19 per cent. Turnout was 56.63 per cent. In September the Sea Shepherd Conservation Society of Costa Rica and Latin American Sea Turtles (LAST) Association launched Operation Pacuare, an anti-poaching campaign to protect sea turtles on Pacuare Beach in Costa Rica's Limón province. September is the time of greatest egg laying.
2015

Political structure

Constitution

Under the November 1949 Constitution, government consists of three branches: legislative, executive and judicial.
In April 2003, the Constitutional court annulled a constitutional reform enacted by the Legislative Assembly in 1969, barring presidents from running for re-election; the law reverts to the 1949 constitution, which states that presidents may run for re-election after being out of office for two presidential terms – eight years.
In 2005 an amendment declaring Costa-Rica a multicultural, multi-ethnic country is pending final Legislative Assembly approval in 2015.
Voting: compulsory over 18 years.

Form of state

Presidential democratic republic

The executive

Executive power is held by the president, elected by modified majority popular vote for one four-year term — if a 40 per cent vote for any candidate is not obtained, a second ballot is held. The president is also Head of government. The president appoints and is assisted by a 15-member cabinet.

National legislature

The unicameral Asamblea Legislativa (Legislative Assembly) has 57-members directly elected by proportional representation in multi-seat constituencies corresponding to the country's seven provinces. Members serve for four-year terms. Although serving successive terms as a deputy is prohibited, a deputy may serve in a subsequent assembly after sitting out a term.

Legal system

The legal system is based on the Spanish civil law system. There are judicial reviews of legislative acts in the Supreme Court. Justices are elected for renewable eight-year terms by the Legislative Assembly. Costa Rica has not accepted compulsory International Court of Justice (ICJ) jurisdiction.

Last elections

2 February 2014 (first round presidential and parliamentary), 6 April (second round presidential)
Results: Parliamentary 2 February 2014: Partido Liberación Nacional (PLN) (National Liberation Party) won 25.54 per cent of the votes (18 seats out of 57); Partido Acción Ciudadana (PAC) (Citizen Action Party) 23.84 per cent (thirteen); Frente Amplio (FA) (Broad Front) 13.09 per cent (nine), Partido de Unidad Socialcristiana (PUS) (Social Christian Unity Party) 10.01 per cent (eight), Partido Movimiento Libertario (PML) (Libertarian Movement) 7.92 per cent (four), Partido Restauración Nacional (PRN) (National Restoration Party) 4.11 per cent (one), Partido Renovación Costarricense (PRC) (Costa Rican Renovation Party) 3.97 per cent (two), Partido Accesibilidad sin Exclusión (PASE) (Accessibility without Exclusion) 3.95 per cent (one), Alianza Demócrata Cristiana (ADC) (Christian Democratic Alliance) 1.14 per cent (one), 12 other political parties won too few votes to gain any seats. Turnout was 69.08 per cent.
Presidential: 17 February first round: Luis Guillermo Solís (Partido Acción Ciudadana (PAC) (Citizen Action Party)) won 30.64 per cent, Johnny Araya Monge (Partido Liberación Nacional (PLN) (National Liberation Party)) 29.71 per cent, José María Villalta Florez-Estrada (Frente Amplio (FA) (Broad Front)) 17.25 per cent, Otto Guevara (Partido Movimiento Libertario (PML) (Libertarian Movement)) 11.34 per cent, Rodolfo Piza (Partido de Unidad Socialcristiana) (Social Christian Unity Party)) 6.02 per cent. Turnout was 68.19 per cent.
7 April second round: Luis Guillermo Solís (PAC) won 77.81 per cent of the vote, Johnny Araya Monge (PLN) 22.19 per cent. Turnout was 56.63 per cent.

Next elections

2018 (presidential and parliamentary)

Political parties

Ruling party

(Partido Acción Ciudadana (PAC) (Citizen Action Party) (took office 1 May 2014)

Main opposition party

Partido Acción Ciudadana (PAC) (Citizens' Action Party)

Population

4.78 million (2014)* (4,301,712; 2011 census figure)
Last census: 3 June 2011: 4,301,712
Population density: 70 inhabitants per square km. Urban population 64 per cent (2010 Unicef).
Annual growth rate: 2.1 per cent, 1990–2010 (Unicef).

Ethnic make-up

The majority of the population, 98 per cent, is white or racially mixed, except in Limón province on the Caribbean coast, where an estimated 70,000 blacks and 5,000 Indians live. The Northern Guanacaste province also has a sizeable Indian population.

Religions

Roman Catholic (approximately 2.33 million followers); Methodist (estimated 6,000 followers); Baptist and Episcopalian.

Education

Education is compulsory at the elementary level, between the ages of six and 13, and is free at both elementary and secondary level. State-owned and private primary and secondary schools are of a high standard and the country has one of the highest literacy rates in Latin America. The adult illiteracy rate is estimated at 4.4 per cent and 4.3 per cent for men and women respectively. World Bank estimates show that the total primary school enrolment of the relevant age group typically stood at 104 per cent for boys and 103 per cent for girls (including repetition rates) between 1994 and 2000.
Costa Ricans are very proud of their education system, with about 12,000 university graduates joining the workforce each year. Costa Rica has 250,000 graduates from higher education per annum and 630,000 graduates from secondary academic schools and around 50,000 graduates of vocational schools.
Public expenditure on education typically amounts to 5–6 per cent of annual gross national income according to UN surveys.
Literacy rate: 96 per cent adult rate; 98 per cent youth rate (15–24) (Unesco 2005).

Pupils per teacher: 29 in primary schools.

Health

It is estimated that 10 per cent of all deaths are caused by prenatal or infectious diseases. Immunisation programmes against measles, diphtheria, polio and tetanus are very successful with between 85 and 95 per cent of all relevant ages being immunised.

Improved water sources and sanitation facilities are available to 98 per cent and 96 per cent of the population, respectively.

The Ministry of Health units operate a preventive health programme in all parts of the country. Most of Costa Rica's health services are supplied by the Caja Costarricense del Seguro Social (CCSS) (Costa Rican Social Security Agency), an independent state institution which operates a national insurance fund.

HIV/Aids

HIV prevalence: 0.6 per cent aged 15–49 in 2003 (World Bank)

Life expectancy: 77 years, 2004 (WHO 2006)

Fertility rate/Maternal mortality rate: 1.8 births per woman, 2010 (Unicef); maternal mortality 29 per 100,000 live births (World Bank).

Child (under 5 years) mortality rate (per 1,000): 10 per 1,000 live births (WHO 2012); 5 per cent of children aged under five are malnourished (World Bank).

Welfare

The state-owned National Insurance Institute (INS) administers all social security insurance. Wage-earners and their dependants enjoy disability and retirement pensions, workers' compensation and family assistance. A pay-as-you-go system operates alongside voluntary individual accounts which provide second-tier benefits. The pay-as-you-go benefit, financed by employee, employer, and government contributions, is equal to a proportion of adjusted average monthly earnings.

Main cities

San José (capital, estimated population 291,135 in 2012), San Francisco (80,505), Liberia (62,995), Limón (58,522), Paradise (50,751), Alajuela (47,873).

Languages spoken

Business is conducted in Spanish, but many executives speak English. French, German and Italian are also spoken.

Official language/s

Spanish

Media

Press

Granma is the official publication of the central committee of the Communist Party of Cuba.

Dailies: In Spanish, major newspapers include *La Nación* (www.nacion.com), *La República* (www.larepublica.net), *Al Día* (www.aldia.co.cr), *Diario La Extra* (www.diarioextra.com) and *La Prensa Libre* (www.prensalibre.co.cr), which is an evening publication.

Weeklies: In English, *Tico Times* is an independent publication.

Business: In Spanish, *El Financiero* (www.elfinancierocr.com) is a daily, while *Actualidad Económica* (www.actualidad-e.com) and *EKA* (www.ekaenlinea.com), with an online version in English, are monthly magazines.

Broadcasting

Radio: There are over 100 commercial radio stations. Radio Nacional (www.sinart.go.cr) is the state broadcaster with cultural, news, information and music programmes. Other national networks include Radio Reloj (www.radioreloj.co.cr) and Radio Colombia (www.columbia.co.cr).

Television: Canal 13 (www.sinart.go.cr) is the national, public TV network. There are another seven national private TV stations offering a wide range of domestic and foreign programmes, including Repretel (www.repretel.com) with channels 4, 6 and 11 and Teletica (www.teletica.com) with channel 7. There has been a strong growth in cable and satellite TV with over a dozen companies offering international programming.

Economy

The economy grew by 4.56 per cent in 2010 and at an estimated 4.2 per cent in 2011, making Costa Rica one of the strongest performers in the region, according to the IMF. Inflation fell below 10 per cent in 2009 and in 2011 it stood at 4.9 per cent. The last 20 years have seen a marked reduction in the level of poverty – halved since 1990 – as the standard of living has improved and purchasing power parity (PPP) per capita has grown steadily to an estimated US$12,100 by 2011. Although poverty has been reduced, distribution of income has remained unequal.

The Costa Rican economy relies predominantly on a combination of tourism, with services accounting for some 62 per cent, industry 29 per cent, of which manufacturing such as electronic components is 21 per cent and agriculture at 8 per cent of the economy.

Foreign investment has led the industrial development, initially from the free trade zone operating in Costa Rica since the 1990s, where companies invested in plant and people within the zone to take advantage of favourable tax rates. The country has a well-educated population and it is situated within easy reach of the eastern Atlantic and western Pacific ports of the US. It has attracted investment by top US companies operating manufacturing plants, administrative centres and warehousing facilities. The opening of an Intel Corporation plant in 1997 was a major boost to the economy, and electrical components soon overtook both bananas and coffee as the country's largest export product. In 2012 Intel Corporation itself was Costa Rica's largest exporter, contributing 6 per cent of GDP.

The tourist industry accounts for around 13 per cent of total GDP and is Costa Rica's second largest sector. Eco-tourism has expanded as visitors have experienced Costa Rica's well-preserved rain forests; 25 per cent of land is dedicated national parks and reserves. According to the Costa Rican Tourism Board there were more than two million tourists/visitors in 2011.

Costa Rica has signed the US-Central America-Dominican Republic Free Trade Agreement (CAFTA-DR), which aims to facilitate trade and investment and further regional integration by eliminating tariffs, opening markets, reducing barriers to services, and promoting transparency. The United States is Costa Rica's most important trading partner accounting for almost half of Costa Rica's exports, imports, and tourism, and over half of its foreign direct investment (FDI). US exports to Costa Rica include machinery, oil, agricultural products, plastic, and semiconductors. US imports from Costa Rica include computer accessories, semiconductors, medical instruments, pineapples and bananas, and coffee.

External trade

As an overseas commonwealth territory of the United States, the US has authority over interstate trade, commerce and customs administration. Costa Rica is part of the North American Free Trade Agreement (Nafta).

Since Nafta was signed, the level of exported manufactured goods has fallen as Mexico, with its lower unit costs, has become a major supplier to the US and Canada. However, while low paid jobs were lost to Mexico there was an increase in pharmaceutical and hi-tech manufacturing in Costa Rica.

The US accounts for over 38 per cent of both imports and exports. Most trade is intra-company shipments, as parts from US companies are imported and finished goods are exported in return. This flow of materials and products creates profits for private companies and jobs for workers in Costa Rica and the US.

Imports

Principal imports include petroleum and derivatives, chemicals, capital machinery, electronic components, textiles and yarns, processed foodstuff, building materials, raw materials and consumer goods.

Main sources: US (44.4 per cent of total in 2014), China (10 per cent), Mexico (6.7 per cent).

Exports

Principal exports include bananas, pineapples, coffee, melons, ornamental plants, sugar, beef, seafood, electronic components and medical equipment.

Main destinations: US (38.4 per cent of total in 2014), The Netherlands (6.2 per cent), Panama (5.3 per cent), Nicaragua (4.4 per cent) and Guatemala (4.1 per cent).

Agriculture

Farming

Costa Rica's agricultural sector is an important contributor to the country's GDP. The sector represents approximately17 per cent of total GDP and employs a fifth of the workforce.

The most important cash crops are coffee, bananas and sugar. A considerable amount of meat, mostly beef, is also exported. The share of traditional agricultural exports declined from 95 per cent of total exports in 1990 to less than 30 per cent by 2004. Bananas account for just over a fifth of Costa Rica's exports. Costa Rica is the world's second-largest banana exporter, representing 12 per cent of the world's banana trade.

Around 10 per cent of the total land is cultivated arable land and 25 per cent is pasture.

Production of cash crops has risen in recent years, but increased exports have tended to be offset by falling prices.

Staple food crops including rice, maize and beans are grown, although Costa Rica is not self-sufficient in these.

Non-traditional products include tropical fruits, ornamental plants and cut flowers.

Fishing

The industry has the potential for positive growth. However, the industry has suffered from a lack of organisation and infrastructure over the years.

The majority of the fishing industry is concentrated on the pacific coastline. Shrimp fishing has decreased due to over fishing, but the potential for tuna, shark and sardine fishing has remained largely untapped due to a lack of investment in modern canning factories.

In a typical year the annual fish catch is 35,003mt, including 19,838mt marine fish and 6,341mt shellfish.

Forestry

Approximately 25 per cent of Costa Rica's total landmass is forested. Significant variations in elevation and topography have led to the development of a wide array of vegetative zones ranging from coastal mangroves to sub-alpine paramó. The predominant forests of Costa Rica can be broadly classified according to elevation and precipitation. The most extensive are lowland humid tropical forests in the southeast of the country and on the Peninsula de Osa. Common species are guacimo colorado (*Luehea seemanii*) and laurel (*Cordia alliodora*). Dry tropical forests are characteristic of the Guanacaste province in the northwest. The most extensive montane forests occur in the Cordillera de Talamanca mountain range in the south. Quercus are the most common trees at higher elevations. Costa Rica has an extensive network of protected areas with more than 25 per cent of the country's land area protected as forest reserves, national parks, and reservations for indigenous peoples.

Costa Rica produces a moderate amount of roundwood, three-quarters of which is used as fuel. The majority of industrial roundwood is used for sawn timber, but Costa Rica also has small wood-based panels and paper industries. Most pulp and paper is imported.

Industry and manufacturing

Unlike other Central American countries, the industrial sector rather than agricultural production dominates the economy, contributing around 23 per cent to annual GDP and employing 24 per cent of the workforce. The manufacturing sector alone contributes 18 per cent to GDP and is concentrated on export-oriented processing of agricultural products. Costa Rica's manufacturing sector is divided into small-to-medium companies producing amongst other things, shoes, packing materials, glass and leather goods, and larger companies involved in producing beer, cement, paper, textiles and palm oil. There is also a growing number of companies involved in the processing of fish, fruit and meat. Other important industries are petroleum refining and pulp/paper processing.

Manufacturing output fell by 3.1 per cent in 2000, largely as a consequence of reduced demand for computer-related products in Costa Rica's principal export markets.

The government's promotion of the manufacturing sector with investment incentives and tax holidays has largely been curtailed in the name of fiscal discipline. There are industrial free zones (Zonas Francas), where incentives apply, at Puerto Limón, Puntarenas and Cartago. Costa Rica has one of the lowest unit costs among developing countries for the creation of new jobs.

Tourism

Costa Rica has coastlines on both the Pacific Ocean and the Caribbean Sea with dedicated holiday resorts offering a wide variety of accommodation and entertainment including water sports. Eco-tourism is an expanding market that takes advantage of stunning natural wonders in a number of UNESCO World Heritage sites. These include the Guanacaste Reserve and the Tortuguero Range-La Amistad National Park with its nesting Leartherback sea turtles. The Cocos Island National Park, a marine sanctuary for many pelagic species, particularly sharks, is also on the list. Tourist facilities include forest canopy tours and aerial trams.

The success of Costa Rican tourism is heavily dependent on the economic prospects of the US, with over 50 per cent of all visitors. The downturn in the US economy affected arrivals and resulted in a fall of 8 per cent in the sector's contribution to GDP 2008–10. Travel and tourism contributed a total of 16.6 per cent (US$4.4 billion) of GDP in 2007 but by 2011 this had fallen to an estimated 12.8 per cent (US$4.7 billion), which followed two years of decline. The fall in tourism's share of GDP is more of a reflection of a strengthening in other areas of the service sector than a decrease in visitor numbers.

Environment

Since the 1960s and 1970s, the Costa Rican authorities have been increasingly anxious to protect the environment.

By 2001, over a quarter of the total land area was protected. There has also been a great deal of success in protecting valuable natural resources in a sustainable way, while at the same time promoting a growing eco-tourism sector.

Mining

The mining sector in Costa Rica is not a substantial contributor to the total GDP. However, Costa Rica does have substantial deposits of various precious metals and the industry is notable for the activity of Canadian firms in the country. In October 2005 two of the largest Canadian corporations operating in Costa Rica announced positive news. Glencairn announced that the Bellavista mine, which it operates, was nearing completion, while Vannessa Ventures Ltd announced the go-ahead of its Las Crucitas Project. Gold and silver are mined in the western part of Costa Rica. Deposits of manganese, nickel, mercury and sulphur are largely unused. Petroleum deposits are found in the south, but not exploited. Salt is produced from seawater. Large gold deposits in Costa Rica are found near the border with Nicaragua, although estimates vary wildly on the level of reserves. The government is reluctant to explore other reserves found in national parks in the Peninsula de Osa region, due to the environmental impact.

Deposits of manganese, bauxite, aluminium, zinc, copper and sulphur exists in Costa Rica, although their quantity and potential for commercial mining is unknown. Discovery of a valuable bauxite deposit in Boruca area prompted large-scale investment in an aluminium smelting plant. Commercial deposits of iron ore may also be present.

Hydrocarbons

Although Costa Rica is thought to possess considerable oil reserves none has been proven. Consumption of oil was 45,000 barrels per day (bpd) in 2008, all of which was imported. Over 50 per cent of crude oil imports were refined domestically; refinery capacity is 24,000bpd. The president re-iterated Costa Rica's 2002 ban of onshore and offshore oil exploration in March 2009.

Any use of natural gas is commercially insignificant.

Coal imports were over 70,000 tonnes in 2008, all used in power generation.

Energy

Total installed generating capacity was 1,962MW in 2007, producing 8.52 billion-kilowatt hours. Hydroelectricity is responsible for 90 per cent of all power generated; the potential for more is considered very high. The government is backing investment in renewable energy sources including solar, wind, geothermal and biomass. The government plans to build 29 new hydroelectric power plants by 2020.

The state-owned Instituto Costarricense de Electricidad (ICE) (Light and Power Company) has exclusive rights to generate, distribute, transmit and sell electricity until 2040.

Financial markets

The main stock exchange in Costa Rica, the Bolsa Nacional de Valores (BNV), was established in 1976. Most transactions are in finance ministry debt and central bank monetary stabilisation bonds. The stock market index is the ALDESA and all shares are traded electronically. There is another exchange, the Bolsa Electrónica de Valores de Costa Rica (BEVCR), which trades in the same amount of paper and shares. The agricultural commodities exchange was set up in 1990 and trades in coffee, maize, potatoes and timber.

Stock exchange

Bolsa Nacional de Valores (Costa Rica Stock Exchange)

Banking and insurance

Costa Rica's financial services sector is composed of the Central Bank, three state-owned commercial banking houses, nineteen private commercial banks (including one jointly owned state bank), one workers' bank, one state-owned mortgage bank and four mutual house-building companies. There are also 15 private finance companies, 27 savings and loans co-operatives and 30 investment and retirement funds/trusts.

Both local and international companies have looked to raise capital abroad because of the poor service and high costs offered by the state banks in Costa Rica. Some of the larger private banks have capitalised on this by offering a wide range of international services and financing in dollars through offshore banks affiliated to them. However, reforms introduced under the administration of Manuel Angel Rodríguez (1998–2002) introduced regulations for the interbank market and for offshore banking operations and made the banking sector more flexible.

By opening up the financial sector to both domestic and foreign investors, Costa Rica is going down the same path as other Latin American countries which have secured economic stability by having a foreign presence in the financial sector. The last few years have seen a number of joint ventures and takeovers by both domestic and foreign banking groups. The banks with the most presence in Costa Rica's banking system include Citibank, Banco de la Industria, Bancrecén, Banco de San José, Banco del Pacifico, Banca Promérica and Scotiabank.

There is also a sizable offshore banking service with the financial services sector.

In recent years the Costa Rican authorities have co-operated with international agencies in order to guard against money laundering.

Central bank

Banco Central de Costa Rica

Main financial centre

San José

Time

GMT minus six hours

Geography

Costa Rica is the second smallest country in Central America after El Salvador. The country lies between Nicaragua and Panama and has coastlines on the Caribbean Sea and the Pacific Ocean. A low, thin line of hills between Lake Nicaragua and the Pacific extends into northern Costa Rica, broadening and rising into high and rugged mountains in the centre and south. The capital city, San José, lies in the Meseta central basin set in these highlands.

Both coasts have lowland areas. The sparsely inhabited east coast has a narrow swamp strip and tropical forests as the terrain rises inland. The Pacific coast has two peninsulas: the mountainous Nicoya peninsula in the north and the lowland Osa peninsula in the south. A rich lowland savannah patched by deciduous forests stretches along the Pacific coast between the two peninsulas.

Hemisphere

Northern

Climate

Costa Rica's weather is influenced by altitude. The Pacific coast is drier while the Caribbean coast has the most rainfall – about 300 days a year. It is hot and humid in lowland coastal areas; temperate and warm in central highlands. The dry season is December–May; the rainy season runs from June–November. The temperature in San José ranges from a high of 24–27 degrees Celsius (C) to a low of 14–16 degrees C. The hottest months are March and April.

Dress codes

Formal dress is required for business engagements. Shorts, especially for women, are for the beach and should not be worn in restaurants or at parties. Women can wear trousers. Strapless dresses are only acceptable for evening events.

Entry requirements

Passports

Passports are required by all, and must be carried at all times. Passports must be valid for at least six months.

Visa

Required by all, except nationals of the Americas, Europe, Australasia and some Asian countries visiting either as tourists or for business purposes, for up to 30 or 90 days. For confirmation and further details contact the nearest consulate or email: miginfor@racsa.co.cr. Business visitors should carry a company letter stating that they represent a foreign company on legitimate business.

Those staying up to 90 days must obtain an exit visa from the Immigration Department in San José at least three days before leaving. Those whose stay is less than 30 days need only their disembarkation card (issued on arrival).

Prohibited entry

Entry is refused to persons of unkempt appearance or without sufficient funds (minimum US$200), who will be deported immediately.

Currency advice/regulations

No restrictions on import of foreign or local currency. Foreign currency should be changed only at banks and authorised bureaux. Street-corner foreign exchange transactions are illegal. Visitors may change excess local currency back to US dollars, but only at main offices of state commercial banks and on production of an onward airline ticket and passport.

Customs

It is prohibited to import arms and drugs. Import tariffs range from 1 to 20 per cent except for vehicles, textiles, shoes, clothing (which are higher). Food products and medicines require registration.

Health (for visitors)

Mandatory precautions

There are no compulsory vaccinations.

Advisable precautions

Typhoid, tetanus and hepatitis A vaccinations are advised.

There is a malaria risk in some low-lying areas – prophylaxis is advisable if visiting the provinces of Limón, Guanacaste, Alajuela and Heredia. Dengue fever mosquitoes are present throughout the country.

Water precautions should be taken outside of San José. There is a risk of rabies.

Hotels

It is advisable to book well in advance. A 3 per cent tourism tax, 10 per cent sales tax and 10 per cent service charge will be added to the bill. Gratuities of around 5–10 per cent are also expected.

Public holidays (national)

Fixed dates

1 Jan (New Year's Day), 19 Mar (Feast of San José (San José only)), 11 Apr (Anniversary of the Battle of Rivas), 1 May (Labour Day), 29 Jun (St Peter and St Paul Day), 25 Jul (Guanacaste Annexation), 2 Aug (Our Lady of the Angels), 15 Aug (Assumption/Mothers' Day), 15 Sep (Independence Day), 12 Oct (Columbus Day), 8 Dec (Immaculate Conception), 24 Dec (Christmas Eve), 25 Dec (Christmas Day), 31 Dec (New Year's Eve).

Most businesses close for Holy Week and between Christmas and New Year.

Variable dates

Maundy Thursday, Good Friday, Corpus Christi (Mon/Jun).

Working hours

Banking

Mon–Fri: 0900–1500.

Business

Mon–Fri: 0800–1200; 1400–1600.

Government

Mon–Fri: 0800–1600.

Shops

Mon–Sat: 0900–1800/1900.

Telecommunications

Mobile/cell phones

GSM 1800 service available.

Electricity supply

110/220V AC, 60Hz. Two-pin plugs are standard.

Social customs/useful tips

Appointments should be made in advance. It is customary to shake hands on meeting and taking leave. The usual form of address is Don for a man, and Doña for a woman, followed by the first name. Business cards to indicate academic/professional titles are exchanged after introduction.

Costa Ricans are not very punctual for social activities, except for football matches, the cinema and weddings, but are more formal with their business appointments. Mothers are regarded as the leading family figures; grandparents and elders are highly respected.

The national pastimes are football and politics. The people have a strong sense of democracy.

Costa Ricans are called Ticos for short. Although a service charge is added to restaurant and hotel bills, gratuities of 5–10 per cent are also expected.

Security

Petty crime is frequent. Thefts, especially in urban areas, and car break-ins are common. Thefts take place on the street and from cars. The loss or theft of a passport should be reported immediately to the local police and the relevant embassy. Some remote trails in national parks have been closed because of the low number of visitors and reported robberies of hikers in the area. Tourists should check with forest rangers for current park conditions. There are pickpockets in downtown San José. Beware of mugging in the national parks at night and of theft at beaches and ports.

Getting there

Air

National airline: Taca International Airlines

International airport/s: Juan Santamaría International (SJO), 22km from San José; duty-free shop, bar, restaurant, buffet, bank, post office, shops, car hire.

Airport tax: US$26; also payable in local currency or combination of both currencies.

Surface

Road: It is possible to travel overland from North or Central America. The nearest US town is Brownsville, Texas, on the Mexican border. From there it is about 4,000km by road on the Inter-American Highway to San José, crossing Mexico and going through Guatemala, Honduras, Nicaragua and into Costa Rica. There is one major crossing point between Nicaragua and Costa Rica at Peñas Blancas, which is not a town, so there is nowhere to stay. There are two border crossings between Panama and Costa Rica.

Rail: There is no rail link with neighbouring countries.

Water: Cruise ships stop at Limón, Punterenas and Caldera. Freighters may accept a small number of passengers and private yachts cruise down the Pacific coast from North America.

Main port/s: Limón (Caribbean coast), Puntarenas and Caldera (Pacific coast).

Getting about

National transport

Air: SANSA is the main domestic carrier and operates cheap regular flights from San José to provincial towns. Travelair also provides domestic services. It is advisable to book in advance. A number of smaller airlines provide internal flights. There are over 200 small airfields throughout the country.

Road: Total network of some 30,000km of all-weather roads. Main routes are the Pan-American Highway; San José-Caldera; San José-Guapiles; and San José-Puerto Limón. Tolls are paid on all four-lane highways entering San José. Taxis are a form of public transport outside urban areas and can be hired by the hour, half-day or the day. Arrange the fare beforehand.

Buses: There are bus services around the country, but both the quality of services and prices vary considerably. Major tourist areas are better provided with short-distance bus services.

Rail: There is a short commuter train which links San José with Heredia and one which links Puerto Limón with the Río Estrella area. There is also a 'banana train' which travels on a section of track in the banana plantations around Guápiles.

Water: There are passenger and car ferries in operation.

City transport

Taxis: Taxis are red, except those serving Juan Santamaría International airport which are orange. Taxis are usually metered, but where there are no meters, it is advisable to agree a price before setting off. Taxis connecting to the airport or distant destinations charge a flat, official rate, but negotiation is possible.

Car hire

A temporary permit must be obtained from local traffic authorities on production of a national licence. Always carry a driving licence. There are tough drink-drive laws – the penalty includes having your driving licence impounded for a minimum of three years.

BUSINESS DIRECTORY

The addresses listed below are a selection only. While World of Information makes every endeavour to check these addresses, we cannot guarantee that changes have not been made, especially to telephone numbers and area codes. We would welcome any corrections.

Telephone area codes

The international direct dialling (IDD) code for Costa Rica is +506 followed by the subscriber's number.

Useful telephone numbers

Emergencies: 911
Ambulance: 128
Fire: 118
Police: 222-1365, 221-5337
Highway police: 222-9330, 222-8245

Chambers of Commerce

American-Costa Rican Chamber of Commerce, PO Box 4946-1000, San José (tel: 220-2200; fax: 220-2300; e-Mail: chamber@amcham.co.cr).

Costa Rica Cámara de Comercio, PO Box 1114-1000, San José (tel: 221-0005; fax: 233-7091; e-mail: servicos@camara-comercio.com).

Costa Rica Cámara de Industrias, PO Box 10003-1000, San José (tel: 281-0006; fax: 234-6163; e-mail: cicr@cicr.com).

Franco-Costa Rican Chambre de Commerce et d'Industrie, PO Box 912-1007 Centro Colon, San José (tel: 257-1138; fax: 257-1345; e-mail: cfcci@camarafranco-cr.org).

German-Costa Rican Cámara de Comercio, PO Box 2139-1000, San José (tel: 222-4789; fax: 221-1219; e-mail: cacoral@racsa.co.cr).

Unión Costarricense de Cámaras y Asociaciones de la Empresa Privada, PO Box 539-1002 Paseo de los Estudiantes, San José (tel: 290-5594; fax: 290-5596; e-mail: uccaep@uccaep.or.cr).

Banking

Banco Banex, Apdo 7983, 1000 San José (tel: 233-4855; fax: 223-7192).

Banco BCT, Apdo 7698, 1000 San José (tel: 233-6611; fax: 233-6833).

Banco Continental, Apdo 7969, 1000 San José (tel: 257-1155; fax: 255-3983).

Banco Co-operativo Costarricense, Apdo 8593, 1000 San José (tel: 233-5044; fax: 233-9661).

Banco Crédito Agrícola de Cartago, Apdo 5572, 1000 San José (tel: 251-3011; fax: 252-0364).

Banco de Costa Rica, Apdo 10035, 1000 San José (tel: 255-1100; fax: 255-0911).

Banco del Comercio SA, Apdo 1106, 1000 San José (tel: 233-6011; fax: 222-3706).

Banco de Fomento Agrícola, Apdo 6531, 1000 San José (tel: 231-4444; fax: 232-7476).

Banco de la Construcción, Apdo 5099, 1000 San José (tel: 221-5811; fax: 222-6567).

Banco de la Industria, Apdo 4254, 1000 San José (tel: 221-3355; fax: 233-8383).

Banco de San José, Apdo 5445, 1000 San José (tel: 221-9911; fax: 222-8208).

Banco Federado de Co-operativas de Ahorro y Crédito, Apdo 4748, 1000 San José (tel: 222-3323; fax: 257-1724).

Banco Fincomer, Apdo 57, Cartago (tel: 251-1351, 233-7822; fax: 222-0405).

Banco Germano Centroamericano, Apartado 2559, 1000 San José (tel: 233-8022; fax: 222-2648).

Banco Interfín, Apdo 6899, 1000 San José (tel: 221-8022; fax: 233-4823).

Banco Internacional de Costa Rica, Apdo 6116, 1000 San José (tel: 223-6522; fax: 233-6572).

Banco Lyon, Apdo 10184, 1000 San José (tel: 221-2611; fax: 221-6795).

Banco Mercantil de Costa Rica, Apdo 32101, 1000 San José (tel: 231-0724, 255-3636; fax: 255-3076).

Banco Metropolitano, Apdo 3932, 1000 San José (tel: 233-8111; fax: 222-8840).

Banco Nacional de Costa Rica, Apdo 10015, 1000 San José (tel: 223-2166; fax: 255-2436).

Corporación Costarricense de Financiamiento Industrial, Apdo 10507, 1000 San José (tel & fax: 221-2212).

Central bank

Banco Central de Costa Rica, Avenida Central y Primera, Calles 2 y 4, Apdo 10058, San José (tel: 243-3333; fax: 243-3011; internet: www.bccr.fi.cr).

Stock exchange

Bolsa Nacional de Valores (Costa Rica Stock Exchange), Central Street, 1st Avenue, PO Box 1736-1000, San José (tel: 221-8011; fax: 255-0131: www.bolsacr.com).

Travel information

American Airlines, Calle 26 & 28, Paseo Colón, San José (tel: 257-1266; fax: 222-5213).

British Airways, Calle 32, paseo Colón and Avenida 2, San José (tel: 223-5648; fax: 223-4863).

SANSA (Servicios Aéreos Nacionales), Apdo 999-1007, Centro Colón, San José (tel: 233-2714, 233-1673; fax: 255-2176).

Tourist Information Office, Plaza de la Cultura, Calle 5, Avenida 0-2, San José (tel: 223-1733 Ext 277; fax: 222-1090).

National tourist organisation offices

Instituto Costarricense de Turismo (ICT), Edificio Genaro Valverde, Calles 5 y 7, Avenida 4, PO Box 777, 1000 San José (tel: 223-8423; fax: 223-5452).

Ministries

Ministry of Agriculture and Livestock, Science and Technology, Apdo 10094, 1000 San José (tel: 232-4496; fax: 232-2103).

Ministry of Culture, Apdo 10227, 1000 San José (tel: 223-1658; fax: 233-7066).

Ministry of Economy, Industry and Commerce, Foreign Commerce, Apdo 10216-1000, San José (tel: 222-1016; fax: 222-2305).

Ministry of Environment and Energy, Apdo 10104 1000 San José (tel: 257-1417; fax: 257-0697).

Ministry of Finance, Apdo 5016, San José (tel: 222-2481; fax: 255-4874).

Ministry of Foreign Affairs, Apdo 10027-1000, San José (tel: 223-7555; fax: 223-9328).

Ministry of Foreign Trade, Apdo 96-2050 Mtes de Oca, San José (tel: 222-5910; fax: 233-5090).

Ministry of Health, Apdo 10123, 1000 San José (tel: 233-0683; fax: 255-4997).

Ministry of Housing, Apdo 222-1002 Paseo de Los Estudiantes, San José (tel: 233-3665; fax: 255-1976).

Ministry of Information, PO Box 520-2010, Zapote (tel: 225-9936/9797; fax: 253-6984).

Ministry of the Interior, Police and Public Security, Apdo 10006, 1000 San José (tel: 223-8354; fax: 222-7726).

Ministry of Justice, Apdo 5685, 1000 San José (tel: 223-9739; fax: 223-3879).

Ministry of Labour and Social Security, Apdo 10133, 1000 San José (tel: 221-0238; fax: 222-8085).

Ministry of the Presidency and Planning, Apdo 520 Zapote, San José (tel: 224-4092; fax: 253-6984).

Ministry of Public Education, Apdo 10087, 1000 San José (tel: 222-0229; fax: 255-2868).

Ministry of Public Security, Apdo 55-4874, San José (tel: 226-0093; fax: 226-6581).

Ministry of Public Works and Transport, Apdo 10176, 1000 San José (tel: 226-7311; fax: 227-1434).

Ministry of Science And Technology, Apdo 5589-1000, San José (tel: 253-7446; fax: 224-8295).

Other useful addresses

Bolsa Nacional De Valores S.A. (Stock Exchange), Central Street, 1st Avenue, PO Box 1736-1000, San José (tel: 221-8011; fax: 255-0131).

British Embassy, Apdo 815, 11th Floor, Edificio Centro Colón, 1007 San José (tel: 221-5566, 255-2937; fax: 233-9938).

Centro de Promoción de Exportaciones e Inversiones (CENPRO) (Costa Rican Export & Investment Promotion Centre), PO Box 5418 San José (tel: 221-7166; fax: 223-5722).

Costa Rican Investment Promotion Agency (CINDE), Plaza Roble Los Balcones, 4th Floor, Escazu, San Jose (tel: 2201-2800

Costa Rican Electricity Institute (ICE), PO Box 10032, 10 San José (tel: 220-7720; fax: 220-1555).

Costa Rican Embassy (USA), 2114 S Street, NW, Washington DC 20008 (tel: (+1-202)-234-2945; fax: (+1-202)-265-4795; e-mail: embassy@costarica-embassy.com).

Costa Rican Institute of Pacific Ports (INCOP), Calle 36, Avenida 3, San José (tel: 223-7111).

Costa Rican Investment and Development Corporation (CINDE), P.O. Box 7170-100 San José (tel: 220-0366, 220-4755; fax: 220-4750, 220-4754).

Costa Rican Investment Promotion Programme (CINDE-EUROPE), Eisenhowerlaan 128, 22517 KM Den Haag, The Netherlands (tel: (31-70)512-1212, 515-010).

Costa Rican Oil Refinery (RECOPE), Apdo 43351, 1000 San José (tel: 223-9611; fax: 255-2049).

Costa Rican Stock Exchange (BNVSA), Apartado 1736-1000, San José (tel: 222-8011; fax: 255-0131).

Ferias Internacionales SA (FERCORI), Apartado 1843, 1000 San Jose (tel: 233-6990; fax: 233-5791).

Free Zones Export Corporation, Apdo 96, 2020 Montes de Oca (tel: 222-5855).

Grupo Centro, PO Box 6133, 1000 San José (tel: 235-4509; fax: 240-7591).

National Association for Economic Development (ANFE), Apartado 3577-1000, San José (tel: 253-4497).

Red Nacional de Televisión, PO Box 7-1980, 1000 San José (tel: 231-333; fax: 231-6604).

Sistema Nacional de Radio y Televisión Cultural (SINART), PO Box 27941, Administración Central, 1000 San Jose (tel: 231-6474; fax: 231-6604).

Televisora de Costa Rica, PO Box 3786, 1000 San Jose (tel: 232-2222; fax: 231-7545).

TNT Correos de Costa Rica, Calle 34-36, Avenida 1RA, San Jose (tel: 233-4993; fax: 221-5046).

Union Pack de Costa Rica (UPS), Aveida 3, Calle 30 & 32, San Jose (tel: 257-7447; fax: 257-5343).

US Embassy, Pavas Frente Centre Comercial, Apdo 920-1200, San José (tel: 220-3939; fax: 220-2305).

Internet sites
Information about the country, investment and the Stock Exchange: http://incostarica.net

Côte d'Ivoire

KEY FACTS

Official name: République de Côte d'Ivoire (Republic of Côte d'Ivoire)

Head of State: President Alassane Ouattara (since 4 December 2010, re-elected 25 Oct 2015)

Head of government: Prime Minister Daniel Kablan Duncan (from 14 Nov 2012)

Ruling party: Rassemblement des Républicains (RDR) (Republican Party)

Area: 322,630 square km

Population: 22.72 million (2014)*

Capital: Yamoussoukro (administrative capital); Abidjan (economic and diplomatic centre)

Official language: French

Currency: CFA franc (CFAf) = 100 centimes (Communauté Financière Africaine (African Financial Community) franc). New notes have been issued; old notes cease to be legal tender from Jan 2005.

Exchange rate: CFAf586.44 per US$ (Sep 2015)

GDP per capita: US$1,495 (2014)*

GDP real growth: 7.48% (2014)*

GDP: US$33.96 billion (2014)*

Inflation: 0.45% (2014)

Balance of trade: US$2.99 billion (2014)

* estimated figure

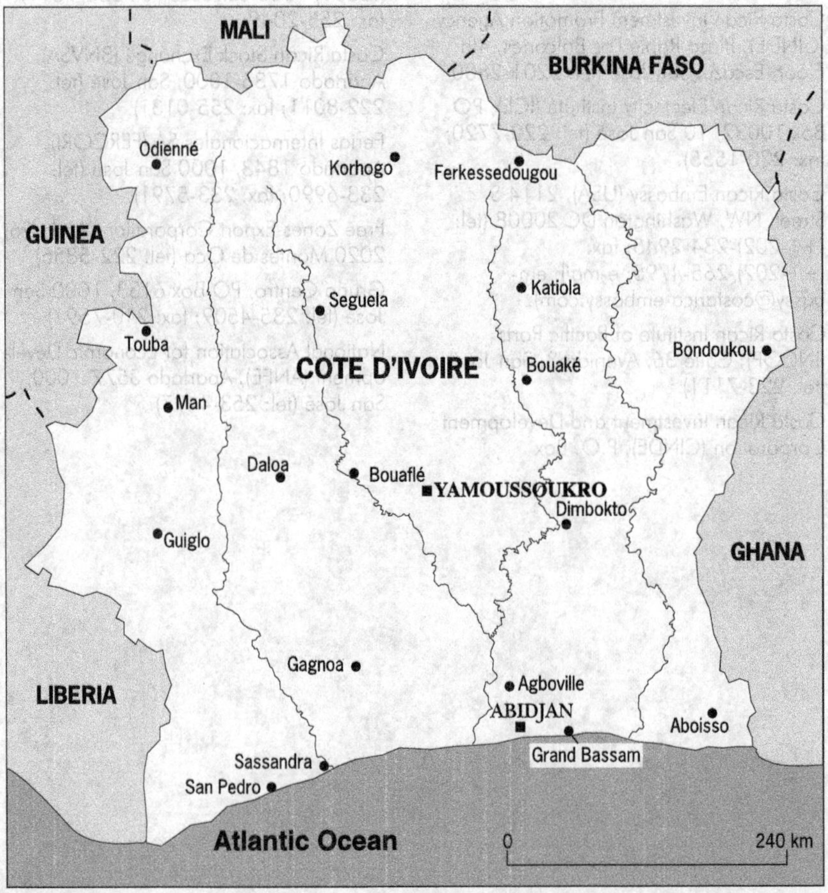

Close ties to France following independence in 1960, the development of cocoa production for export, and significant foreign investment joined to make Côte d'Ivoire one of the more prosperous of the West African states. However, this success did not protect it from political turmoil. The first military coup in the history of the Côte d'Ivoire occurred in 1999 which overthrew the government of Henri Konan-Bédié. Subsequently, the military leader, Robert Gueï seized the presidency and banned Alassane Ouattara, the northern Muslim leader, from standing in the forthcoming presidential election. Laurent Gbagbo declared himself president following controversial elections and Gueï fled the country.

Ivorian dissidents and dissatisfied members of the military launched a failed coup attempt in September 2002 that developed into a rebellion and then a civil war. The war ended in 2003 with a ceasefire that left the country divided between rebels holding the north, the government holding the south, and peacekeeping forces forming a buffer zone between the two. In March 2007, President Gbagbo and former New Forces rebel leader Guillaume Soro signed an agreement in which Soro joined the president's government as prime minister and the two agreed to reunite the country by dismantling the buffer zone, integrating rebel forces into the national armed forces, and holding elections. Difficulties in preparing electoral registers delayed the ballot until November 2010.

The election resulted in Alassane Ouattara winning the presidential election over Gbagbo but he refused to hand over power resulting in a five-month standoff. In April 2011, following widespread fighting, Gbagbo was formally forced out of office by armed Ouattara supporters with the help of UN and French forces. Several thousand UN peacekeepers and several hundred French troops remain in Côte d'Ivoire to support the transition process. Ouattara is focused on rebuilding the country's economy and infrastructure while revitalising the security forces. Laurent Gbagbo is in The Hague awaiting trial (set for November 2015) for crimes against humanity.

The Côte d'Ivoire held presidential elections on 25 October 2015. Alassane Ouattara won a second term in a landslide victory over his closest rival Pascal N'Guessan. Ouattara won 83.7 per cent of the vote whilst Pascal N'Guessan won a mere 9.3 per cent. According to the 2000 Constitution, presidential candidates are limited to two consecutive terms and, therefore, Ouattara should be due for his final consecutive term in office. The opposition party, Ivorian Popular Front (FPI), called for a boycott of the elections in protest against the trial of former President Laurent Gbagbo by the International Criminal Court supported by Pascal N'Guessan, however, it clearly had no effect. The much improved political situation is still held back by insufficient dialogue amongst the political forces. It took a long time before the opposition parties finally joined the independent electoral commission. The government took further steps to calm the political climate including the release of pro-Gbagbo prisoners, allowing the return of high-level political refugees and unfreezing their bank accounts. The justice system, however, is still viewed as biased by a portion of the population.

In 2012 a government appointed commission reached the conclusion that both sides of Côte d'Ivoire's civil war had committed atrocities. Although the incumbent president, Mr Ouattara, was 'freely and fairly' elected, he would not have made it to the presidency without the support of once rebellious warlords who, for the most part, were loyal not to Mr Ouattara, but to Guillaume Soro who managed to segue smoothly from rebel commander to becoming the speaker in the national assembly. In return for the loyalty of former rebels, Mr Ouattara was happy to turn a blind eye to the extensive and highly profitable, smuggling activities of the former rebels in the north

Côte d'Ivoire's economy is heavily dependent on agriculture and related activities, which engage roughly two-thirds of the population. It is the world's largest producer and exporter of cocoa beans and a significant producer and exporter of coffee and palm oil. Côte d'Ivoire was also one of West Africa's major cotton exporters, with an annual output of 400,000 tonnes, prior to the 2002 civil war. Its cotton industry is beginning to bounce back with production forecast at 484,000 tonnes in the 2015/16 season and a target of 600,000 tonnes before 2020. Due to the Côte d'Ivoire's heavy dependence on exporting primary products, the economy is highly sensitive to the fluctuations in international prices for these products. The country also mines gold, it produced 17.6 tonnes in 2014 (up from 15.5 tonnes in 2013) which makes it a significant player in the gold market (the eleventh largest producer in Africa).

Following the end of the civil war in in 2011, Côte d'Ivoire has experienced a boom in foreign investment and economic growth. It recorded growth rates of 10.7 per cent in 2012 before falling to 8.7 per cent in 2013 and 8.3 per cent in 2014. Foreign direct investment (FDI) was US$371 million in 2013. One of the biggest challenges to making this growth inclusive is to strengthen the role of local authorities in new projects that have a structuring impact and speed up public access to modern services that will enable more productivity and efficiency. Côte d'Ivoire needs to mobilise its internal and external funding of development better and it needs to ensure social and political stability before it can achieve its goal of becoming an emerging nation by 2020. Economic growth is driven by internal and external demand. Public and private infrastructure investment and household consumption accounted for most internal demand, while external demand boosted commodity exports thanks to higher world prices. The government also created a national development plan which aimed to improve the business climate and speed up structural reform, this has significantly contributed to improved economic growth since the country has become more attractive, especially for FDI. As part of a programme conducted with the International Monetary Fund (IMF), the budgetary situation became much healthier in 2014 due to better tax collection and control of spending, which was lower than expected. The effects of this programme have lowered the budget deficit slightly to 2.2 per cent of GDP from 2.3 per cent in 2013.

The challenge of spatial inclusion – common amongst developing African nations – will be to sustain growth in the long run and increase its impact in rural areas and city suburbs. Jobs are being created but not enough for the large number of unemployed young people. Women, long the main victims of conflict, have a long way to go to revive their activities, involving strengthening local government and their managerial ability to launch projects that have a structuring impact and to speed up local access to good public services. Côte d'Ivoire has significant regional advantages compared to most other African countries including a denser road network, several kinds of farmland and a climate that enables the development of a

KEY INDICATORS — Côte d'Ivoire

	Unit	2011	2012	2013	2014	**2015
Population	m	*22.69	*23.37	*22.14	*22.72	*23,308.00
Gross domestic product (GDP)	US$bn	24.10	24.69	*31.07	*33.96	*31.75
GDP per capita	US$	1,062	1,057	*1,403	*1,495	*1,362
GDP real growth	%	-4.7	9.8	*8.7	*7.5	*7.7
Inflation	%	4.9	1.3	2.6	0.4	*1.2
Exports (fob) (goods)	US$m	–	–	12,049.3	–	–
Imports (fob) (goods)	US$m	–	–	9,055.2	–	–
Balance of trade	US$m	–	–	2,994.1	–	–
Current account	US$m	3,117.0	-310.0	*-1,528.0	*-1,113.0	*-715.0
Total reserves minus gold	US$m	3,750.6	3,928.0	4,242.7	4,478.5	–
Foreign exchange	US$m	3,317.5	3,507.0	3,821.0	–	–
Exchange rate	per US$	466.82	505.65	480.26	538.70	–

* estimated figure ** forecast figure

range of agro-industrial and food products that are in big demand worldwide.

Following the visit of a team from the IMF in late September and early October 2014 the IMF issued a statement saying that in its view macro-economic performance in the first half of 2014 was solid, with continued strong economic activity, particularly in the construction, public work and service sectors. Inflation remained subdued. Budget execution was also satisfactory with stronger-than-expected revenue performance and expenditures contained to budgeted amounts. As a result, the basic primary balance recorded a small surplus compared to the deficit projected under the programme.

The IMF noted that Côte d'Ivoire successfully issued in July 2014 a Eurobond, raising US$750 million to help finance the budget, extend average debt maturities and repay some domestic debt. In the view of the IMF, macro-economic prospects for 2015 were encouraging. GDP growth was expected to reach about 8 per cent in 2014 and 2015. The draft 2015 budget aimed at supporting near and medium-term growth through a further expansion of public investment.

Progress has been made in accelerating public procurement processes with a view to reducing sole-source contracting. The IMF welcomed the authorities' plans to set up a single Treasury account and further restructure public banks. It also welcomed the authorities' intentions to reinforce the financial position of the energy sector and clear the stock of domestic arrears.

Risk assessment

Politics	Fair
Economy	Fair/good
Regional stability	Good

Muslims in Côte d'Ivoire

% of population	38.6
Sunni (% of Muslims)	96
Shi'a (% of Muslims)	1

COUNTRY PROFILE

1960 Côte d'Ivoire gained independence from France. Felix Houphouet-Boigny was selected to be the first president of Côte d'Ivoire by French colonial rulers as the most promising successor to their rule. Politicians, after independence, were drawn from oligarchs who had gained power through government positions or ran state-owned companies or gained positions in the ruling party, the Parti Démocratique de la Côte d'Ivoire (PDCI) (Democratic Party of Côte d'Ivoire).

1970s–1980s Economic decline increased pressure for political reform. Laurent Gbagbo, a lecturer and long-term dissident, emerged as the main opposition leader. He went into exile in 1982.

1988 Gbagbo returned from exile and founded the Front Populaire d'Ivoirie (FPI) (Ivorian Popular Front) to campaign for multi-party democracy.

1990 Houphouet-Boigny was forced to call elections, which were won by the PDCI. Houphouet-Boigny was re-elected president; Alassane Dramane Ouattara became prime minister.

1993 President Felix Houphouet-Boigny died after 30 years in power. Henri Konan-Bédié became president.

1995 Legislative and presidential elections were convincingly won by Konan-Bédié and the PDCI party.

1999 President Bédié was toppled in a military coup and General Robert Gueï seized the presidency. Tension between the Muslim north and Christian south was aggravated when Gueï banned Alassane Ouattara, the northern Muslim leader, from standing in the forthcoming presidential election.

2000 Laurent Gbagbo declared himself president following controversial elections. Gueï fled the country and supporters of Ouattara were killed after he called for new elections.

2002 An uprising split the country. The rebel Force Nouvelle (FN) (New Force) took control of the north and about 60 per cent of the country. Alassane Ouattara, leader of the Rassemblement des Républicains (RdR) (Republican Party) and head of FN, was granted citizenship, resolving his status for future elections. A cease-fire was negotiated and a French-manned buffer zone imposed between north and south. Former president Gueï was shot dead in Abidjan.

2004 UN peacekeepers were deployed, led by French troops. Rebels appointed ministers to join a coalition Government of National Reconciliation, but the PDCI pulled out amid on-going violence. Abidjan was bombarded by rebel forces. When the Ivorian Air Force targeted Bouake, the northern stronghold of the FN, it killed nine French soldiers in the air raid. The French Air Force retaliated by destroying the Ivorian Air Force. Pro-government demonstrators rioted on the capital's streets, looting and threatening foreign, particularly French, targets.

2005 A UN report accused both rebel and government forces of atrocities including torture, systematic rape and mass execution. The government, FN and opposition leaders signed a deal to end the civil war. The Government of National Reconciliation was revived to take over until the next elections. Presidential elections were cancelled and President Gbagbo carried on as de facto president from his powerbase in the south. Presidents Obasanjo and Mbeki of Nigeria and South Africa respectively named Charles Konan Banny as interim prime minister. Banny was given powers to run an interim government (planned to end in 2006) and organise presidential elections; for this all militias had to be disarmed and voter registration undertaken.

2006 Banny faced his first test when international mediators called for the dissolution of parliament, which backed President Gbagbo. As a result, the ruling FPI briefly withdrew from the transitional government, accusing the mediators of a 'constitutional coup d'etat'. In the first meeting since 2000, the four main Ivorian leaders, Gbagbo (FPI), Bédié (PDCI), Ouattara (RdR) and Guillaume Soro (Mouvement Patriotique de Côte d'Ivoire (MPCI) (Patriotic Movement of Côte d'Ivoire)), attended a meeting with the prime minister to discuss plans for future elections and government. Militia loyal to Gbagbo failed to disarm as scheduled. Public identity hearings began to determine who could claim Ivorian citizenship and vote in the upcoming elections. The hearings were suspended following violent clashes between supporters of Gbagbo and Soro. Negotiators failed to agree terms for disarmament and voter registration. Presidential elections were postponed. The UN Security Council voted to extend the mandates for President Gbagbo and Prime Minister Konan Banny for another year.

2007 A peace agreement was reached between President Gbagbo and Guillaume Soro (MPCI). A plan to integrate some members of the FN rebel militia with the regular army was mandated by presidential decree. Soro became prime minister. President Gbagbo visited the former rebel-held north and watched as weapons were destroyed at a peace party attended by five other African heads of state. The introduction of identity papers for all citizens sparked fears that large numbers would be fraudulently given to foreigners. A number of former northern rebels were absorbed into the regular army, the remainder were offered a three-month stipend to return to civilian life. Presidential and general elections were postponed.

2008 A public sector strike was settled when ministers cut their own wages by 50 per cent to help cover the cost of reintroducing subsidised fuel. Presidential and general elections were postponed.

2009 Presidential and general elections, delayed since 2005, were rescheduled; but were later postponed.

2010 Prime Minister Soro announced a new government, following the dismissal of his previous administration by the President, who had also dismissed the electoral commission. Voter registration was suspended after allegations of fraud as the lists were being drawn up. After six postponements, presidential elections were finally held on 31 October; Laurent Gbagbo won 38 per cent of the vote and Alassane Ouattara (Rassemblement des Républicains (RDR) (Republican Party) 32 per cent. However the opposition immediately lodged a formal challenge to the result in the constitution court, which failed. International observers stated the elections were 'credible' despite some organisational deficiencies. As no candidate reached a necessary 50 per cent of the vote a run-off election was held. The run-off led to an immediate deadlock as supporters of Gbagbo accused the northern rebels of trying to steal the election on behalf of Ouattara and stopped an official of the electoral commission from reading out the results on national TV. Of the electoral regions nationwide, both candidates accepted the results from 13, but in the remaining seven under dispute, four were districts loyal to Ouattara, election commissioners loyal to Gbagbo prevented publication of the results. An attack on the offices of Ouattara, in which four supporters were killed by automatic gunfire, followed the failure of results being published within the 72-hour deadline. The chief electoral commissioner declared that Ouattara had won 54.1 per cent and Gbagbo 45.9 per cent. Gbagbo's campaign team claimed that as the results had not been announced in time they were invalid and that Ouattara was in effect mounting a *coup d'état*. The Constitutional Council annulled the electoral commission's results, and the votes from the seven disputed regions cancelled, stating that Gbagbo had won with 51.5 per cent of the vote, against 48.5 per cent for Ouattara. Foreign media were denied access as the country's borders were closed. Although the UN called on both sides to respect the outcome of the election Gbagbo was sworn into office on 4 December. On the same day Prime Minister Soro resigned, saying he recognised Ouattara as president-elect. President Gbagbo appointed Gilbert Marie N'gbo Aké as prime minister. The AU suspended Côte d'Ivoire's membership until a 'democratically elected president effectively assumes state power'. Ouattara also took his official oath of office as president and appointed Soro as his prime minister. Parliamentary elections were postponed indefinitely. The UN, US, EU, AU and Ecowas all recognised Ouattara as the legitimate president of Côte d'Ivoire.

2011 In January Laurent Gbagbo rejected the Ecowas and AU-sponsored talks, which had offered him legal amnesty and residence in exile if he agreed to stand down as president. Financial assets of Gbagbo were seized by Swiss banks in January. Henri Dacoury-Tabley, governor of the central bank and a Gbagbo appointee, refused to accept Gbagbo's signature for funds and resigned in January, following international pressure. Gbagbo ordered the assets of all local branches of the Central Bank of West African States (BCEAO) to be seized. In February, major foreign banks, Paribas, Citibank and Standard Chartered, had suspended operations in Côte d'Ivoire due to 'security concerns'. Four domestic banks had also closed, as depositors queued to withdraw their money. Gbagbo's administration took control of those foreign banks that had suspended operations. Ecowas asked the UN in March if it would adopt a mandate to use military intervention as a 'last resort'. By the end of March an estimated one million people had fled their homes due to the on-going political violence. At the request of the UN peacekeepers, French troops and tanks surrounded the presidential palace. Laurent Gbagbo was captured by French special forces, in April; he was taken to the headquarters of Mr Ouattara. International sanctions began to be lifted after Gbagbo was deposed, but without a functioning banking system trade in cocoa was severely hampered. In mid-April the World Bank said it was ready to offer help, including reactivating programmes worth some US$100 million. The most notorious warlord, Ibrahim (IB) Coulibaly was killed by pro-Ouattara forces in Abidjan in April. He had been a supporter of President Ouattara, but had refused to disarm after the capture of Gbagbo. The banks reopened, leading to a rush to withdraw cash and receive delayed salaries. In May, President Quattara announced the setting up of a Dialogue, Truth and Reconciliation Commission (DTRC) headed by former prime minister, Charles Konan Banny. Switzerland moved to freeze assets (which had already been seized in January) of Gbagbo. The funds could to be blocked for up to three years, pending a request from Côte d'Ivoire for legal assistance to ensure the return of the funds. Alassane Ouattara took the oath of office on 6 May, with the inauguration ceremony held on 22 May, attended by French President Nicolas Sarkozy and the UN Secretary General Ban Ki-moon and several African heads of state. Amnesty International said in a report published in May that both sides in the recent conflict had committed war crimes. It also said that all those who had committed human rights violations should be prosecuted. In July, the economic and finance minister reported that Côte d'Ivoire had been in default of its international debts since January and that it was unable to service its external debt in 2011, but would resume its payments to bondholders in 2012 following a deal agreed with the IMF. In July, officials from the National Museum of Abidjan reported to Interpol the loss of around 80 historic and culturally precious gold pieces stolen during the battle for Abidjan between the rival forces of Gbagbo and Ouattara. The stolen items included the best gold jewellery, masks and statues in the museum's collection, valued at an estimated US$6 million, which suggested insider knowledge and help given to the thieves. Michel Gbagbo (son of former president, Laurent Gbagbo) was arrested on 10 August and charged with post-election violence. Later in August, Laurent Gbagbo was charged with economic crimes, including looting, embezzlement and armed robbery. A Truth, Reconciliation and Dialogue Commission was inaugurated in September to consider the widespread violence following the presidential elections in 2010. Former president Gbagbo was flown to the ICC in The Hague on 30 November, to stand trial for crimes against humanity committed between 16 December 2010–12 April 2011. Elections held on 11 December were won by the Rassemblement des Républicains (RDR) Rally of the Republicans) with 42.1 per cent of the vote (122 seats out of 255), followed by Parti Démocratique de la Côte d'Ivoire – Rassemblement Démocratique Africain (PDCI-RDA) (Democratic Party of Côte d'Ivoire – African Democratic Rally) with 28.6 per cent (76). Turnout was a low 36.6 per cent, but the elections went off relatively calmly.

2012 On 24 February the ICC extended its investigation back to 2002 and a decade of political turmoil leading to atrocities in Côte d'Ivoire.on 12 March former prime minister Guillaume Soro won a unanimous vote electing him speaker of parliament. The post makes him the country's second in command, in accordance with the constitution. On 15 May the EU and Côte d'Ivoire ratified the International Cocoa Agreement (2010), which was implemented in October. The agreement ensures certain standards of production (such as the prohibition of child labour) while guaranteeing the integrity of the product. A report published by the UN Operation in Côte d'Ivoire (UNOCI) in June said that tens of thousands of combatants who had fought in the 2010–11 post-election conflict were still armed and

potentially dangerous. The report called for a disarmament, demobilisation and reintegration (DDR) programme to be set up urgently. On 2 November, the International Criminal Court ICC) ruled that Laurent Gbagbo was fit to stand trial for crimes against humanity, including murder, rape and violence following the disputed presidential elections in 2010. On 14 November the president dismissed the government of Prime Minister Ahoussou-Kouadio and appointed Daniel Kablan Duncan as prime minister.
2013 In September ministers voted to try Simone Gbagbo (wife of the former president) in local courts, and not send her to the ICC. She will face charges of alleged crimes against humanity following the 2010 presidential election.
2014 Charles Blé Goudé (the 'street general'), was flown to The Hague on 22 March, to be charged at the ICC, alongside his patron, former president, Laurent Gbagbo, with four counts of crimes against humanity. On 12 June the ICC confirmed that Gbagbo would be charged with murder, rape and other forms of sexual violence. The African Development Bank (AfDB) returned to its head quarters in Abidjan in September.
2015 On 9 March Simone Gbagbo, the wife of former president. Laurent Gbagbo, was sentenced to 20 years in jail for her role in the violence that followed the 2010 elections. Mr Gbagbo himself is awaiting trial at the ICC. In May AfDB held its first annual meeting since returning to its head office in Abidjan in 2014. Presidential elections were held on 25 October with Alassane Ouattara winning a second five-year term with ease – 84 per cent to the 9 per cent of his nearest rival, Pascal Affi N'Guessan. Turnout was low at 55 per cent (compared to 80 per cent in 2010). Although several candidates had withdrawn, US election observers said the election was credible.

Political structure

Constitution

A multi-party system is enshrined in the Constitution, but in practice no party other than Parti Démocratique de la Côte d'Ivoire (PDCI) (Democratic Party of Côte d'Ivoire) was allowed to operate until May 1990 when the government legalised party political activity.
A 1990 Constitutional amendment allowed for the appointment of a prime minister, with the speaker of the National Assembly empowered to assume the office of president of the republic prior to a presidential election in the event of a sudden presidential vacancy.
The constitution was suspended following a military takeover in December 1999. In 2000, the constitution was revised, stipulating that presidential candidates must be of Ivorian origin, born of parents who are not naturalised Ivorians, should not have dual nationality and must have lived in Côte d'Ivoire for a minimum and uninterrupted period of five years. Those with at least 21 years of Ivorian citizenship are eligible to vote.
According to the terms of the electoral legislation as laid down by the constitution and the electoral code, the material organisation of elections is the responsibility of the Commission Electorale Indépendante (CEI) (Independent Electoral Commission) (Article 59 of the new electoral code), whose role it is to collect and announce the provisional results of the election. The same article provides that the commission should send a copy of the election report to the Constitutional Council, which, on the basis of Article 94 of the constitution, is responsible for announcing the final results.

Form of state

Republic

The executive

Executive power rests with the president (elected by universal suffrage for a five-year term) who appoints the cabinet. The president can veto legislation, but his veto can in theory be overridden by a two-thirds vote of the National Assembly.

National legislature

The unicameral National Assembly consists of 225 seats, members are directly elected in single constituencies by simple majority vote. Members serve five-year terms. Internal political crisis and the civil war hampered parliamentary democracy.

Legal system

All civil, criminal, commercial and administrative cases come under the jurisdiction of the tribunaux de première instance (magistrates' courts), the assize courts and the court of appeal.

Last elections

11 December 2011 (parliamentary)
Results: Presidential (first round): Alassane Ouattara (Rassemblement des Républicains (RDR) (Republican Party) 84 per cent, Pascal Affi N'Guessan 9 per cent; turnout was 55 per cent. Runoff: since Mr Ouattara won over 50 per cent a second vote was unnecessary.
Parliamentary: Rassemblement des Républicains (RDR) (Republican Party) won 42.1 per cent of the vote (122 seats out of 255), Parti Démocratique de la Côte d'Ivoire-Rassemblement Démocratique Africain (PDCI-RDA) (Democratic Party of Côte d'Ivoire–African Democracy Party) 28.6 per cent (76), Union pour la Démocratie et la Paix en Côte d'Ivoire (UDPCI) (Union for Democracy and Peace in Côte d'Ivoire) 3.1 per cent (six), Rassemblement des Houphouetistes pour la Démocratie et la Paix (RHDP) (Rally of Houphouetists for Democracy and Peace) 1.7 per cent (four); 35 independents and two political parties won the remaining 35 seats. Turnout was 36.6 per cent.

Next elections

25 Oct 2015 (presidential); 2016 (parliamentary)

Political parties

Ruling party

Rassemblement des Républicains (RDR) (Republican Party)

Main opposition party

Parti Démocratique de la Côte d'Ivoire-Rassemblement Démocratique Africain (PDCI-RDA) (Democratic Party of Côte d'Ivoire–African Democracy Rally)

Population

22.72 million (2014)* More than a quarter of the population is under the age of 20; 18 per cent is under nine and only 2 per cent over the age of 60.
Last census: November 1998:15,366,672
Population density: 44 inhabitants per square km. Urban population 51 per cent (2010 Unicef).
Annual growth rate: 2.3 per cent, 1990–2010 (Unicef).

Internally Displaced Persons (IDP)

500,000–800,000 (UNHCR 2004)

Ethnic make-up

Akan (the Baoule subgroup accounts for 23 per cent of the population), Kru (the Bete subgroup accounts for 18 per cent), Senoufo 15 per cent, Malinke 11 per cent, Agni, Mande. There are nearly 3 million foreign Africans (mainly from Burkina Faso and Mali) and an estimated 130,000–330,000 non-Africans (French 30,000 and Lebanese 100,000–300,000).

Religions

Islam (60 per cent), Christianity (mainly Roman Catholic) (22 per cent), traditional animist beliefs (18 per cent) (some of these are also numbered among the Christians and Muslims).

Education

Education is provided free of charge. Primary education lasts for six years from the age of six. Secondary education lasts for up to seven years from the age of 13. There are universities at Abidjan and Yamoussoukro, but many students attend French universities.
Only 50 per cent of girls attend primary school.
Literacy rate: 60 per cent, youth rate (15–24) (Unesco 2005)
Pupils per teacher: 41 in primary schools.

Health

HIV/Aids

Aids-related costs typically absorb 11 per cent of the total public health budget.

HIV prevalence: 7.0 per cent aged 15–49 in 2003 (World Bank)
Life expectancy: 44 years, 2004 (WHO 2006)
Fertility rate/Maternal mortality rate: 4.4 births per woman, 2010 (Unicef); maternal mortality six per 1,000 live births (World Bank).
Child (under 5 years) mortality rate (per 1,000): 108 per 1,000 live births (WHO 2012); 24 per cent of children under aged five are malnourished (World Bank).
Head of population per physician: 0.12 physicians per 1,000 people, 2004 (WHO 2006)

Welfare

An employer must declare each worker employed to the Caisse National de Prevoyance Sociale (CNPS), the national social security fund, and is responsible for deducting social security contributions paid by the worker. Large firms are also expected to provide in-house medical care.
Social security is divided into three areas: family allowances, retirement pensions, medical care and compensation payments in case of accident at work. There are no payments for illness unconnected to work. Contributions are paid every quarter by firms employing fewer than 20, and each month for those employing over 20, people. The CNPS funds are ring-fenced from the government's main budget.
The social security system does not cover unemployment, which is paid monthly through labour exchanges and financed by a national solidarity contribution of 1 per cent of salary, which is levied on each employee's wages.
Child labour is used in domestic service, farming, mining and factory work as well as casual labour in street markets. Law restricting the age of employment is enforced in large enterprises but is more lax in small industries and the informal sector. Local opinion concerning child labour is equivocal; while rural children are needed for subsistence farming, and urban street children can avoid destitution through work, the need for change would seem to be moot.

Main cities

Abidjan (economic and diplomatic centre, estimated population 4.4 million in 2012), Yamoussoukro (political capital since 1983, 259,373), Bouaké (649,841), Daloa (261,789), Korhogo (225,547), Man (172,867), San Pédro (171,906), Gagnoa (153,935), Divo (147,379).

Languages spoken

Approximately 60 local African languages are spoken, including Djoula, Baoule, Akan, Kru and Bete.

Official language/s

French

Media

According to the France-based media watchdog Reporters Without Borders, Côte d'Ivoire is one of the Africa's most dangerous places for journalists to carry out their work.

Press

Dailies: In French, national newspapers includes the government-owned, *Fraternité Matin* (www.fratmat.info) and *Notre Voie* (www.notrevoie.com) and *Le Patriote* (www.lepatriote.net), which are owned by the political parties PCT and UDR-Mwinda respectively. Other, national, private newspapers include *Le Nouveau Reveil,24 Heures* (www.24heuresci.com), *Le Front* and *Soir Info* (www.soirinfo.com). Newspapers with the same internet address (http://news.abidjan.net), include *L'Inter* and *Le Jour* and *Fraternité Matin*. Newspapers published in Abidjan include *Le Courrier d'Abidjan* (www.lecourrierdabidjan.info), *Le Matin d'Abidjan* (www.lematindabidjan.com) and *Nord-Sud* (www.nordsudmedia.info).

Broadcasting

For most of the population, radio is the principal medium for news and information. Radiodiffusion Télévision Ivoirienne (RTI) (www.rti.ci) is the national, public broadcaster funded through a license fee, advertising revenue and grants.
Radio: There are many private radio stations with a limited area of broadcasting around cities and other urban regions. RTI relays its two channels, RTI Frequence 2 (www.frequence2.ci) and La Nationale (www.lanationale.ci), with entertainment, news, education, information and cultural programmes, through a network of numerous, local stations. Other private stations include Nostalgie (www.nostalgie.ci) from Abidjan and Radio Jam (www.radiojam.ci), from Yamoussoukro. Religious stations include the Catholic Radio Paix Sanwi (www.radiopaixsanwi.net) and the Islamic Radio al Bayane (http://radio-albayane.com).
Television: The government controls the only terrestrial TV station although private, pay-to-view cable and satellite services are available through the French-owned Canal Satellite Horizons (www.canalhorizons.com).
RTI (www.rti.ci) operates La Premiere, a national channel and TV2, which for viewers of terrestrial TV can only be received within a radius of 150km of Abidjan. RTI also have dedicated sports and music channels. RTI services can be received throughout the country and also into some neighbouring countries via satellite services.
National news agency: AIP (Agence Ivoirienne de Presse)
Other news agencies: APA (African Press Agency): www.apanews.net
Panapress: www.panapress.com

Economy

The wealth of Côte d'Ivoire comes from its natural resources. It has small reserves of petroleum and natural gas and the country operates an oil refinery and hydroelectric power stations, which results in Côte d'Ivoire being a significant energy exporter in the region. Agriculture accounted for around 25.9 per cent of GDP in 2014, with the industrial sector constituting 21.9 per cent (of which the manufacturing sector accounts for 13 per cent of GDP), and the service sector amounting to 52.1 per cent of GDP. Agricultural exports of cocoa (Côte d'Ivoire is the world's leading producer, providing around 40 per cent of total), coffee, bananas, rubber, palm oil and pineapples, along with tuna and timber constitute over 50 per cent of both export revenue and GDP.
The country has a good and extensive infrastructure, including a large, modern port, which allows for rapid transport of goods and people.
The global economic crisis did not cause Côte d'Ivoire's economy to fall into recession; its own political crisis in late 2010 lead to a contraction of an estimated -4.7 per cent in GDP growth in 2011. As the situation was resolved GDP growth shot up, reaching 10.7 per cent in 2012 and slowing slightly to, a still strong, 8.7 per cent in 2013 and 7.5 per cent in 2014.
In 2012 the IMF, together with The World Bank, announced a US$4.4 billion debt relief package under the Highly Indebted Poor Countries Initiative. The initiative was put in place in order to try and tackle the inequalities and poverty that plague the west African nation and helped lower the budget deficit slightly from 2.3 per cent in 2012 to 2.2 per cent in 2013.
In 2013 (latest survey), the UN Human Development Index (HDI) ranked Côte d'Ivoire 171 (out of 187) for national development in health, education and income. Since 2000, Côte d'Ivoire's progress has scarcely grown and has not matched the improvement of other sub-Saharan countries in Africa. In 2013, 59.3 per cent of the population were in multidimensional poverty, while 23.8 per cent lived on less than the equivalent of US$1.25 per day. Remittances were US$373 million in 2010 (latest figures) (1.5 per cent of GDP).

The country has the potential for solid growth, with a history of foreign direct investment (US$371 million in 2013) providing 40–45 per cent of total capital in domestic businesses, typically from French firms.

External trade

As a member of the Economic Community of West African States (Ecowas). Côte d'Ivoire is also a member of the West African Economic and Monetary Union (WAEMU) with a common external tariff and using the common currency, the CFA franc.

The northern region is the primary area for growing cocoa, the country's major export commodity, while the principal port for international trade is in the south. The country is a hub for international trade in West Africa and transhipment is an important element of the economy.

The UN banned the export of rough diamonds after it was found they were used in the purchase of weapons during the civil war. Since the peace accord was signed in 2007, calls for a relaxation in the ban have grown and the introduction of a state-run buying house to regulate and promote legitimate diamond sales.

Imports

Principal imports include fuel, capital equipment and foodstuffs.

Main sources: Nigeria (23.1 per cent of total in 2013 (latest figures)), Bahamas (11.7 per cent), China (11.4 per cent).

Exports

Principal exports include cocoa, coffee, timber, fuel, cotton, bananas, pineapples, palm oil, fish and diamonds (currently banned).

Main destinations: Ghana (15.3 per cent of total in 2013 (latest figures)), The Netherlands (8.0 per cent), Nigeria (7.1 per cent).

Agriculture

Farming

The agricultural sector is the mainstay of the economy. Total agricultural land is 31.8 million hectares of which 41.5 per cent is pasture and 8.8 per cent arable. The sector employs some 68 per cent of the workforce and accounts for 25.9 per cent of GDP. The climate in some parts of the north is suitable for the production of wheat to support an estimated local consumption of about 200,000 tonnes a year.

However, the principal cash crops are cocoa and coffee. Côte d'Ivoire accounts for around 40 per cent of total world cocoa production. The cocoa and coffee sectors have undergone liberalisation and institutional reform since 1995. This has included transferring some responsibility for price stabilisation to the private sector, making operations more transparent, and reducing customs duties on cocoa and abolishing them for coffee. Price liberalisation was achieved for coffee in 1998 and cocoa in 1999, when Caistab, the price stabilisation fund, was disbanded and replaced by a private-sector operation. Privatisation of the coffee and cocoa sectors was highly controversial among farmer.

The Fonds de Regulation et de Controle (FRC), is the national cocoa and coffee marketing institution, which is owned by farmers (45 per cent), banks (20 per cent), insurance companies (20 per cent) and the government (15 per cent). The FRC determines minimum guaranteed farm-gate prices and bears the cost of implementing the price stabilisation mechanism, which cushions farmers' exposure to volatile international markets. Coffee and cocoa production is regulated by the Autorité de Regulation du Café et Cacao (ARCC), which determines export quotas. The cocoa harvest was a record crop and warehouses in the south of Côte d'Ivoire were stocked ready for export before a disputed presidential election in 2010. However, the EU, Côte d'Ivoire's single largest market, rejected any purchases of cocoa from Côte d'Ivoire until the post-presidential election political crisis was resolved. In March 2011, Laurent Gbagbo (who lost the election but was refusing to stand down as president) ordered his government to take control of all cocoa production and exports. His rival, Alassane Ouattara had called for a temporary ban on exports in an effort to deny Gbagbo the funds. Following the resolution of the political turmoil cocoa exports returned to pre-election levels.

Fishing

Côte d'Ivoire is the second largest exporter of canned tuna in the world. The port of Abidjan handles more than 400,000 tonnes of fish a year. The government has launched a series of initiatives to modernise local fishing and assist local fishermen to benefit from the country's 150,000 hectares of lagoon and 350,000 hectares of lakes and rivers. The EU and Côte d'Ivoire run a fisheries agreement which provides EU fishermen with fishing rights in Côte d'Ivoire waters in return for the funding of research and training programmes.

Forestry

Côte d'Ivoire has 17 per cent forest cover and an additional 25 per cent of other wooded land. Ten per cent of forests are inside protected reserves, including the Parc National de Tai which has the largest tract of primary rainforest in West Africa. The southern half of the country, which was once covered by tropical forest, has suffered extensive deforestation for logging and agriculture. The northern half contains savannah woodland. Forestry is important and Côte d'Ivoire has been Africa's leading exporter of sawn timber. Wood is also an important source of domestic fuel.

Industry and manufacturing

The industrial sector contributed around 21.9 per cent to GDP in 2014, a level that has been maintained within the economy for the last decade.

The industrial and manufacturing sectors have expanded rapidly since independence in 1960 but suffered some setbacks in the late 1980s as a result of increased foreign competition and a decline in consumer purchasing power. In addition, the industrial plant is ageing and has often not been renewed on account of the low level of private investment.

The industrial sector is mainly confined to the processing of agricultural produce but recently has also been pushed towards other natural resources. Recent exploration into offshore oil reserves has made the ation set a goal of producing 200,000 barrels per day (bpd) by 2020, more than triple the current rate of 60,000bpd.

During the 1990s, privatisation reduced the state's custodial role in industry and manufacturing. Consequently, policy has focussed upon encouraging private sector involvement in the hydrocarbons sector which it is hoped will encourage the expansion of the industrial and manufacturing sectors.

Tourism

Côte d'Ivoire offers visitors a variety of forests with wildlife, lagoons and shoreline, cities and African culture. There are two national parks and a nature reserve included on Unesco's World Heritage List. In July 2012, the historic colonial town of Grand-Bassam was added to Unesco's World Heritage List.

With the improvement in the political situation in 2011, tourism has enjoyed a boost and in 2014 contributed a total of 4.4 per cent of GDP and accounted for 3.8 per cent of total employment (89,500 jobs). However, foreign governments still warn their citizens about personal security and the potential for civil unrest, which deters some from visiting Côte d'Ivoire. Investment in the industry amounted to US$89 million in 2014, 1.6 per cent of total investment in the country.

Environment

In July 2010 the Anglo-Dutch shipping company Trafigura was fined €1 million (US$1.3 million) by a court in The Netherlands after it had been found guilty of exporting and dumping toxic waste to Abidjan in 2006. In 2007 Trafigura had paid the government US$160 million without admitting liability and US$50 million shared among individuals harmed by the waste. Trafigura continues to deny responsibility for the spill.

Mining

The mining sector holds considerable potential and could become the second mainstay of the economy. It contributes around 3.7 per cent to GDP annually and employs 1 per cent of the workforce. A state company, Société pour le Développement Minier Ivorien (Sodemi) carries out exploration and production, in some cases in joint ventures with foreign companies. Gold is found in three main reserves: Issia, Lobo and Ity.

Diamonds have traditionally been mined by small independent prospectors, but the incidence of diamond smuggling and consequent loss of revenue prompted the Ministry of Mines to introduce licences for prospectors and diamond purchasing offices in 2000. Diamonds are produced at Séguéla and Tortiya. Reserves at Séguéla are estimated at 150,000 carats, and at Tortiya 450,000 carats.

Grand-Lehou produces 90,000 to 100,000 tonnes of manganese per year. A deposit, estimated at 1.2 million tonnes (47 per cent manganese), was discovered at Ziemougoula, near Odienne.

A large iron ore deposit at Monogaga-Victory has estimated reserves of 140 million tonnes. Further reserves, estimated at three billion tonnes, are located on the border with Guinea at Mount Nyumba and Mount Kalayo.

Hydrocarbons

Proven oil reserves were 100,000 million barrels in 2013 (latest figures), with production at 60,000 barrels per day (bpd). The majority of oil reserves are located offshore in the shallow water Espoir field and the deep-water Baobab field. Domestic consumption is around 26,000bpd with the remainder exported, representing almost 30 per cent of foreign revenue, surpassing traditional export commodities of cocoa and coffee.

The state-run Société Nationale d'Operations Pétrolières de la Côte d'Ivoire (Petroci) is responsible for the hydrocarbons industry through its four subsidiaries. Petroci Holding manages the oil sector; Petroci Exploration-Production is responsible for upstream hydrocarbon activities; Petroci-Gaz deals with the natural gas sector; Petroci Industries-Services manages all other related services.

There is one operational oil refinery, with a capacity of 65,200bpd, sufficient to supply domestic requirements, as well as some export volumes for neighbouring countries. The refinery is connected to the Lion and Panther fields by pipelines and receives crude oil from Nigeria for processing. Construction of another refinery began in 2008, with a capacity of 60,000bpd. Both facilities are located in Abidjan.

Recent explorations have led to discoveries of extension potential oil reserves. Though not yet proven, the Ivorians have set a goal of producing 200,000bpd by 2020.

Proven natural gas reserves were 28.3 billion cubic metres (cum), with production over 1.3 billion cum, primarily consumed in domestic power stations.

Any coal produced or imported is commercially insignificant.

Energy

Installed electricity generating capacity was 1,222 MW in 2013 (latest figures). Around 70 per cent of annual production is generated by gas-powered plants, with a declining contribution from hydroelectric sources. Côte d'Ivoire is an exporter of electricity, supplying Ghana, Benin, Togo, Mali and Burkina Faso, through the West African Power Pool (Wapp). The state-owned Société d'Opération Ivoirienne d'Electricité (Sopie) is responsible for strategic planning and implementation of national standards in electricity provision.

The 288MW Azito power station provides around 30 per cent of the country's power and is located in Abidjan. A government sponsored rural electrification programme has extended access to electricity to the distribution system for around 50 per cent of the rural population. Investment in the programme is ongoing.

Financial markets

Stock exchange

Afribourse (Bourse Régionale des Valeurs Moblières) (BRVM)

Banking and insurance

Abidjan is traditionally a major regional banking centre. There is no clear distinction between commercial, merchant and development banks since they may all accept deposits and engage in long- and short-term financing. Local banks generally handle retail banking and export-crop financing as well as funding small- and medium-sized businesses and housing. Some specialise in development of industry, agriculture and small businesses.

Côte d'Ivoire has a liberal policy towards foreign banks, but entry has become more difficult in recent years because of the large number of banks already present. A minimum capital is required for a new bank to start operating, but Ivorian participation is not obligatory.

Political instability has undermined the Ivorian banking sector, with the African Development Bank (AfDB) tranferring its head-quarters from Côte d'Ivoire to Tunisia in early 2003.

Central bank

Banque Centrale des Etats de l'Afrique de l'Ouest

Main financial centre

Abidjan

Time

GMT

Geography

Côte d'Ivoire is in West Africa on the Atlantic coast, bordered by Liberia and Guinea to the west, Mali and Burkina Faso to the north, and Ghana to the east. To the south is a 470 kilometre coastline on the Gulf of Guinea, the eastern part of which is inset with lagoons.

The terrain rises from the coastal plains to a plateau, 300 metres high for most of its length, rising to 1,200 metres near the country's western border.

The three main geographical areas are the equatorial zone along the coast, the tropical rain forests of the south and the drier savannah belt in the north.

There are four main rivers, the Bandama, Comoe, Sassandra and Cavally, but they are not navigable for long distances due to rapids.

Hemisphere

Northern

Climate

There are four distinct seasons in the centre and south of the country. Here the climate is tropical, with a long dry season running from December–April, followed by the rainy season from May–July. From August–September a dry spell is followed in October–November by a short rainy spell.

Average temperatures on the southern coastal plains are 21–34 degrees Celsius (C). Humidity is 80–90 per cent. Annual rainfall can be as heavy as 2.5 metres spread over about 140 days. In the central region temperature ranges are 14–39 degrees C. Annual rainfall varies from 1–2.5 metres.

In the northern savannah the climate is more extreme, but less humid with temperatures between 21–40 degrees C. Rainfall averages 1.4 metres a year. There are two seasons, rains from July–November and the dry season from December–June.

Dress codes

When calling on senior personnel, businessmen should wear suits, even though this may be uncomfortable in Abidjan's hot and humid climate. The capital, Yamoussoukro, is less humid and at an altitude of 220 metres is cooler. In general loose-fitting, tropical lightweight clothing is advisable.

Women may wear sleeveless cotton dresses or lightweight skirts and blouses, and this mode of dress is adequate for business calls.

Entry requirements

Passports

Required by all except particular document holders of certain African countries.

Visa

Required by all except citizens of other Ecowas countries, and nationals of Andorra, Chad, Monaco, Morocco, Seychelles, Tunisia and Vatican City, for stays of up to three months. Applications for business visas require a letter from the visitor's company accepting responsibility for any expenses incurred, and a letter of invitation (can be faxed copy) from host company in Côte d'Ivoire.

Currency advice/regulations

The import of CFA francs is unlimited; export is limited to CFAf10,000. The import of euros is unlimited, all other currencies must be declared. Export of all foreign currencies is limited to CFAf25,000, or the amount declared on arrival.

Travellers cheques are accepted in banks and hotels.

Health (for visitors)

Mandatory precautions

Yellow fever vaccination certificate.

Advisable precautions

Cholera, hepatitis A and E and typhoid vaccinations are strongly recommended and polio immunisation is a benefit. Malaria prophylaxis should be taken as risk exists throughout the country all year. Avoid tap water and drink only bottled beverages (including water) or beverages made with boiled water; cooked food is advisable and all fruit should be peeled. Bilharzia is present, use only well chlorinated swimming pools. Rabies and sleeping sickness are a risk. It is advisable to pack a sterilised syringe kit.

Hotels

Abidjan and Yamoussoukro have several five-star hotels. There are a wide range of other hotels in the other main centres. Tipping usually 10–15 per cent.

Credit cards

American Express and Mastercard are widely accepted; charge cards are of limited use.

Public holidays (national)

Fixed dates

1 Jan (New Year's Day), 1 May (Labour Day), 7 Aug (Independence Day), 15 Aug (Assumption Day), 1 Nov (All Saints' Day), 9 Nov (Day of Mourning), 15 Nov (Peace Day), 7 Dec (Félix Houphouët-Boigny Remembrance Day), 25 Dec (Christmas Day).

Variable dates

Easter Monday, Ascension Day, Whit Monday, Eid al Adha, Eid al Fitr, Birth of the Prophet, Ascent of the Prophet.

Some companies allow an informal one-day holiday before or after a Sunday holiday

Islamic year 1437 (15 Oct 2015–2 Oct 2016):: The Islamic year contains 354 or 355 days, with the result that Muslim feast advance by 10–12 dars against the Gregorain calendar. Dates of feasts vary according to the sighting of the new moon, so cannot be forecast exactly.

Working hours

Banking

Mon–Fri: 0800–1130 and 1430–1630.

Business

Mon–Fri: 0800–1200 and 1430–1700.

Government

Mon–Fri: 0730/0800–1200 and 1430–1730.

Shops

Mon–Fri: 0800–1200 and 1530–1830/1900, Sat: 0800–1200 and 1430–1730.

Telecommunications

Mobile/cell phones

There are several 900 and a 1800 GSM services operating in main urban areas.

Electricity supply

220V AC, 50 cycles

Social customs/useful tips

Ivorians like to shake hands and exchange greetings and other pleasantries before getting down to business.

It is considered polite to arrive punctually to social occasions when kissing on the cheek and hugging are reserved only for old friends.

Security

There are ongoing security problems in the country in general and increased trouble in the west – visitors are advised not to travel to the area. Foreign visitors should register their presence with their diplomatic missions on arrival, although many suspended their representation in 2005. Visitors must take added precaution for their own safety and take note of local warnings.

Getting there

Air

National airline: Air Ivoire: flies to France, South Africa and Dubai.

International airport/s: Abidjan-Félix Houphouet-Boigny (ABJ), is the country's airport hub accepting all intercontinental flights. It is 16km from city; duty-free shop, restaurant, bank, post office, pharmacy, car hire.

Yamoussoukro (ASK) accepts regional flights .

Airport tax: Departure tax: continental, CFAf3,000; intercontinental: CFAf5,000.

Surface

Road: There are good links from Ghana, Burkina Faso, Guinea and Liberia.

Rail: Travellers should check information concerning regular services from Burkina Faso, connecting Ouagadougou with Abidjan. Sleeping and restaurant facilities are available for these long journeys.

Getting about

National transport

Air: Air Ivoire no longer operates internal flights. Contact local airports for information on charter flights.

Departure tax: CFAf800.

Road: Extensive network of roads stretching from south to north with transverse roads interconnecting.

Buses: The once extensive service has been curtailed by the civil war. Contact local operators concerning services.

Taxis: Bush taxis run to all parts of the country.

Rail: A 1,145km network from Abidjan to Ouagadougou passes through Agboville, Dimbokra, Bouaké, Katiola and Ferkessedougou.

City transport

Taxis: In Abidjan, red taxis with meters can be hailed or ordered by telephone in main centres. Two tariffs operate: one from 0600–2400, the other 2400–0600. The early morning tariff is double that for the day and evening. Do not hesitate to haggle over the fare, especially if the meter is not running, or if arriving at the airport.

Buses, trams & metro: Buses usually run from 0600–2100 or 2200, operated in Abidjan by state-run Sotra.

Most hotels have their own airport buses. Check at hotel booths near the terminal exit.

Car hire

Self-drive and chauffeur-driven cars can be hired in Abidjan, Bouaké, Daloa, Gagnoa, Man and Sassandra.

An international driving licence is required (not less than 12 months old). Drivers must be at least 21-years-old. Seat-belts must be worn in front seats. Traffic drives on the right.

BUSINESS DIRECTORY

The addresses listed below are a selection only. While World of Information makes every endeavour to check these addresses, we cannot guarantee that changes have not been made, especially to telephone numbers and area codes. We would welcome any corrections.

Telephone area codes

The international direct dialling (IDD) code for Côte d'Ivoire is +225, followed by subscriber's number.

Useful telephone numbers
Ambulance (SAMU): 185, 2044-3445, 2044-5353.
Police (emergency): 111, 170.
International telephone enquiries: 160.
National telephone enquiries: 120.

Chambers of Commerce
American Chamber of Commerce, 01 PO Box 3394, Abidjan 01 (tel: 2021-4616; fax: 2022-2437; email: amcham@AfricaOnline.co.ci).

Côte d'Ivoire Chambre de Commerce et Industrie, 6 Avenue Joseph Anoma, PO Box 1399, Abidjan 01 (tel: 2033-1600; fax: 2032-3942; email: mail@ccici.org).

French Chambre de Commerce et d'Industrie, 141 Boulevard de Marseille, Immeuble Jean Lefebvre, 01 PO Box 189, Abidjan 18 (tel: 2025-8206; fax: 2024-1000; email: ccifci@ccif.ci).

Banking
Bank of Africa Côte d'Ivoire, BP 4132, 11 Ave Joseph Anoma, Abidjan 01 (tel: 2033-1536; fax: 2033-2398, 2032-8993).

Banque Atlantique (Côte d'Ivoire SA); BP 04, Immeuble Atlantique, Avenue Nogues, 1036 Abidjan 04 (tel: 2031-5950; fax: 2021-6852).

Banque de l'Habitat de Côte d'Ivoire, BP 2325, 22 Ave Joseph Anoma, Abidjan 01 (tel: 2022-6000; fax: 2022-5818).

Banque Internationale pour le Commerce et l'Industrie de la Côte d'Ivoire SA; Avenue Franchet d'Espérey, 01 BP 1298 Abidjan 01 (tel: 2020-1600, 2020-1700; fax: 2020-1700) .

Banque Paribas Côte d'Ivoire; BP 09, 17 Avenue Terrasson de Fougères, Abidjan 17 (tel: 2021-8686, 2021-3032; fax: 2021-8823).

BIAO-Côte d'Ivoire; BP 1274, 8/10 Avenue Joseph Anoma, Abidjan 01 (tel: 2020-0720, 2020-0722; fax: 2020-0700).

Caisse Autonome d'Amortissement Société d'Etat, BP 670, Immeuble SCIAM, Ave Marchant, Abidjan 01 (tel: 2021-0611, 2032-8575; fax: 2021-3578).

Cofipa Investment Bank Côte d'Ivoire, BP 411, Rue Botreau Roussel/ Ave Delafosse, Abidjan 04 (tel: 2021-8452; fax: 2021-8599).

Compagnie Bancaire de l'Atlantique en Côte d'Ivoire, 01 BP, Immeuble Atlantique, Avenue Nogues, 522 Abidjan 01 (tel: 2021-2804, 2030-1520; fax: 2021-0798).

Compagnie Financière de la Côte d'Ivoire; BP 1566, Tour BICICI 01, Rue Gourgas 15e étage, Abidjan 01 (tel: 2021-2732; fax: 2021-2643, 2020-1700).

Ecobank Côte d'Ivoire SA, BP 4107, Immeuble Alliance, 1 Av Terrasson de Fougères, Abidjan 01 (tel: 2031-9200, 2021-1041; fax: 2021-8816).

Société Générale de Banques en Côte d'Ivoire SA; BP 1355, 5 & 7 Avenue Joseph Anoma, Abidjan 01 (tel: 2020-1234, 2020-1111; fax: 2020-1482, 2020-1486).

Société Générale de Financement et de Participation en Côte d'Ivoire (SOGEFINANCE); BP 3904, 5-7 Avenue Joseph Anoma, Abidjan 01 (tel: 2022-5530, 2022-1234; fax: 2032-6760, 2020-1492).

Société Ivoirienne de Banque, BP 1300, Immeuble Alpha 2000, 34 Boulevard de la Republique, Abidjan 01 (tel: 2020-0000; fax: 2021-9741).

Central bank
Banque Centrale des Etats de l'Afrique de l'Ouest, Direction National, Angle Boulevard Botreau-Roussel et Avenue Delafosse, PO Box 1769, Abidjan (tel: 208-500; fax: 222-852).

Stock exchange
Afribourse (Bourse Régionale des Valeurs Moblières) (BRVM), www.brvm.org

Travel information
Air Ivoire, 2 Avenue du Général de Gaulle, PO Box 7782, Abidjan 01 (tel: 2021-3429; internt: www.airivoire.com).

Félix Houphouet-Boigny International Airport (tel: 2027-7322, 2023-4000).

Wagonlits (Railway Information), Boulevard de Marseille, Abidjan (tel: 2021-2066, 2021-3910).

Ministry of tourism
Ministry of Tourism, BP V184, Abidjan (tel: 2044-5500, 2044-5129, 2044-6474, 2044-6953; fax: 2044-5580).

National tourist organisation offices
Office Ivoirien du Tourisme et de l'Hôtellerie (OITH), Place de la République, BP 8538, Abidjan 01 (tel: 2020-2516; fax: 2020-3388; email: oith@tourismeci.org; internet: www.tourismeci.org).

Ministries
Ministry of Agriculture and Animal Resources, Immeuble de la Caisse de Stabilisation, BP V84, Abidjan (tel: 2021-3858; fax: 2021-4618; e-mail: minagra@cimail.net).

Ministry of Communication and Information Technology, Tour C, Tours Administratives, BP V138, Abidjan (tel: 2021-1116; fax: 2021-8495).

Ministry of Construction and Urbanism, Tour D, Tours Administratives, 20 BP 650, Abidjan (tel: 2021-8235; fax: 2021-3568).

Ministry of Defence and Civil Protection, Immeuble EECI, BP V 241, Abidjan (tel: 2021-2682; fax: 2022-4175).

Ministry of Economic Infrastructures, Immeuble Postel 2001, 18 BP 2203, Abidjan (tel: 2034-4273; fax: 2034-7322).

Ministry of Economy and Finance, Immeuble SCIAM, BP V163, Abidjan (tel: 2020-0842; fax: 2021-3208).

Ministry of Education, Tour D, Tours Administratives, BP V 120, Abidjan (tel: 2022-7406; fax: 2022-9322).

Ministry of Family, Women and Children, Tour E, Tours Administratives, BP 200, Abidjan (tel: 2021-7626; fax: 2021-4461).

Ministry of Foreign Affairs, Bloc Ministériel, Boulevard Angoulvand, BP V109, Abidjan (tel: 2022-7150; fax: 2033-2308).

Ministry of Health, Tour C, Tours Administratives, 01 BP V 04, Abidjan (tel: 2021-0871; fax: 2021-5240).

Ministry of Higher Education and Scientific Research, Tour C, Tours Administratives, BP V 151, Abidjan (tel: 2021-3316;

fax: 2021-2225).

Ministry of the Interior and Decentralisation, Bloc Ministériel, Boulevard Angoulvand, BP V 121, Abidjan (tel: 2022-3816; fax: 2022-3648).

Ministry of Justice and Public Freedom, Bloc Ministériel, Boulevard Angoulvand, BP V 107, Abidjan (tel: 2021-1727; fax: 2033-1259).

Ministry of Labour, Civil Service and Administrative Reform, Immeuble Fonction Publique, Boulevard Angoulvand, BP V 93, Abidjan (tel: 2021-4290; fax: 2021-1286).

Ministry of Mines and Energy, Immeuble Postel 2001, BP V 40, Abidjan (tel: 2034-4851; fax: 2021-3730).

Ministry of Trade, Immeuble CCIA, Rue Jean-Paul II, BP V65, Abidjan (tel: 2021-6473; fax: 2021-6474).

Ministry of Transport, Immeuble Postel 2001, BP V 06, Abidjan (tel: 2034-7315; fax: 2021-3730).

Other useful addresses
Agence des Télécommunications de Côte d'Ivoire (ATCI), BP 2203, Immeuble Postel 2001, Rue le Coeur, Abidjan 18 (tel: 2034-4255; fax: 2034-4254).

Association of Businessmen and Industry of Côte d'Ivoire, Imm Lefébre, Bd de Marseille, 01 BP 464, Abidjan 01.

Association of Exporters of Coffee-Cocoa, Imm CCIA, 01 BP 1399, Abidjan 01 (tel: 2022-5446/5).

Association of Fishing Industry, Port de Pêche, 01 BP 14, Abidjan 01 (tel: 2025-7998; fax: 2025-2065).

Association of Import and Export Traders, Imm Résidence du Front Lagunaire 2 étage, 01 BP 3792, Abidjan 01 (tel: 2032-5427; fax: 2032-5652).

Association of West African Home Grown Product Dealers, Imm CCIA 7 étage, O & BP 5407, Abidjan 01 (tel: 2022-5795).

Bourse des Valeurs Abidjan, Ave Marchand 10, BP 1878, 01 Abidjan (tel: 2021-5783, 215742; fax: 2022-1657).

British Embassy, 3rd Floor, Immeuble Les Harmonies, Angle Boulevard Carde et Avenue Dr Jamot, BP 2581, Plateau, 01 Abidjan (tel: 2022-6850/2, 2032-8209; fax: 2022-3221).

Bureau National d'Etudes Techniques et de Dévéloppement (BNETD) (National Office for Technical and Development Studies), BP 945, 04 Abidjan (tel: 2044-2805, 2044-5877; fax: 2044-5666; email: nzoro@ bnetd.sita.net; internet site: http://www.bnetd.sita.net.).

Caisse de Stabilisation (CAISTAB), BP V132, Abidjan (tel: 2020-2700; fax: 2021-8994).

Centre de Commerce Internationale d'Abidjan (conference bookings), Abidjan (tel: 2022-4070).

Centre de Promotion des Investissements en Côte d'Ivoire (CEPICI), CCIA-WTR 5th Floor, BP V152, Abidjan 01 (tel: 2021-4070; fax: 2021-4071).

Committee of Insurers, Imm Les Arcades, 01 BP 3873, Abidjan 01 (tel: 2022-5437; fax: 2021-1835).

Committee of Privatisation, 6 Boulevard de l'Indénié, Abidjan-Plateau, BP 1141, Abidjan 01 (tel: 2022-2231/2232/2236; fax: 2022-2235).

Compagnie Ivoirienne pour le Développement des Textiles, BP 622, Bouaké (tel: 2063-3113, 2063-3013; fax: 2063-4167).

Conseil Economique et Social, 04 BP 301, Abidjan (tel: 2021-2060).

Côte d'Ivoire Embassy (USA), 3421 Massachusetts Avenue, NW, Washington DC 20007 (tel: (+1-202) 797-0300; fax: 20(+1-202) 265-2454).

The Customs Department, Boulevard de la République, BP V 25, Abidjan (tel: 2021-5223).

Direction et Controle des Grands Travaux, Département Industrie et Energie, Boulevard de la Corniche, Cocody, 04 BP 945, Abidjan 04 (tel: 2044-2118; fax: 2044-5866).

Energie Electrique de la Côte d'Ivoire, BP 1345, 1 place de la République, Abidjan (tel: 2020-6000; fax: 2032-7477).

French Embassy; BP 175, Rue Lecoueur 17, Abidjan 17 (tel: 2020-0404; fax: 2020-0447).

General Surveillance Co (Responsible for Import Controls), PO Box 795, Abidjan (tel: 2021-1290).

Côte d'Ivoire Investment Promotion Centre (CEPECI), PO Box V 152, Abidjan 01 (tel: 2021-4070; fax: 2021-4071; internet site: http://www.cepici.go.ci).

National Enterprise Assistance and Promotion Centre (CAPEN), Immeuble La Pyramide, 9th floor, 08 BP 868, Abidjan 08 (tel: 2032-0145).

Organisation Centrale pour la Commercialisation de l'Ananas et la Banane (OCAB), Imm Corniche, 16 BP 1908, Abidjan 16 (tel: 2032-5882; fax: 2032-1060).

Port Autonome d'Abidjan, BP V85, Abidjan (tel: 2024-0866, 2024-2640; fax: 2024-2328).

Professional Association of the Oil Industry, 13 Impasse Paris Village, 01 BP 1777, Abidjan 01 (tel: 2021-7320; fax: 2022-2858).

Société des Mines d'Ity, BP 872, Abidjan 08 (tel: 2044-6363; fax: 2044-4100).

Société Ivoirienne de la Poste et de L'Epargne, BP 105, Abidjan 17 (tel: 2034-7004; fax: 2034-7107).

Société Ivoirienne de Raffinage (SIR), Boulevard de Petit-Bassam, BP 1269, Abidjan 01 (tel: 2027-0427, 2027-0160; fax: 2027-1798, 2027-3217).

Société Nationale d'Opérations Petrolières de la Côte d'Ivoire, BP V194, Abidjan (tel: 2021-4058).

Société pour le Développement Minier de la Côte d'Ivoire, BP 2816, Abidjan (tel: 2021-2994).

SODEMI (State Company for Mineral Development), BP 2816, 31 Boulevard Latrille, Abidjan Cocody-Nord, Abidjan 01 (tel: 2044-0994; fax: 2044-0821).

US Embassy, 5 rue Jesse Owens, 01 BP 171, Abidjan 01 (tel: 2021-0979).

World Trade Centre, PO Box V 68, Abidjan (tel: 2021-6189, 2022-4072/3; fax: 2022-7112).

National news agency: AIP (Agence Ivoirienne de Presse), 04 Avenue Chardy, BP 312, Adidjan 04 (tel: 20-22-64-13; fax: 20-21-57-12; internet: www.aip.ci).

APA (African Press Agency): www. apanews.net

Panapress: www.panapress.com

Internet sites

Africa Business Network: www.ifc.org/abn

AllAfrica.com: allafrica.com

African Development Bank: www.afdb.org

Africa Online: www.africaonline.com

Mbendi AfroPaedia (information on companies, countries, industries and stock exchanges in Africa): mbendi.co.za

Croatia

Since the beginning of 2009 Croatia has been in a state of constant recession. Hopes were raised in 2011 when there were two non-recessionary quarters, but the hope didn't last. At the end of 2014 unemployment was stuck at over 20 per cent, one of the highest in the European Union (EU) which Croatia joined in 2013.

It's the economy – let's meet

Elected with the narrowest of margins in the 28 December 2014 presidential election – 50.74 per cent of the votes (to Ivo Josipovic's 49.26 per cent) – Croatia's photogenic new president Kolinda Grabar-Kitarovic of the Hrvatska Demokratska Zajednica (HDZ) (Croatian Democratic Union Party), indicated that she saw the economy as her country's biggest problem. The new President has form – a seasoned politician she had been foreign minister and Ambassador to the US, as well as deputy secretary general of the North Atlantic Treaty Organisation (NATO). Her election victory meant that an HDZ president was installed for the first time since the death of the party's almost iconic leader Franjo Tudman in 1999. Quite how she was going to impose her priorities on the Socijaldemokratska Partija Hrvatske (SPH) (Social Democratic Party) government whose candidate, the incumbent Ivo Josipovic, she had so narrowly edged out of the presidency, was not altogether clear. Mr Josipovic had been seeking a second five-year term with the backing of his coalition allies, and had probably considered victory to be his having won the first round of the election in December, albeit by a narrow margin. Mrs Grabar-Kitarovic obviously proposes to hold the SPH-led government to account over the economy, the government's weakest point. Prime Minister Zoran

KEY FACTS

Official name: Republika Hrvatska (Republic of Croatia)

Head of State: President Kolinda Grabar-Kitarovic (since 19 February 2015)

Head of government: Prime Minister Zoran Milanovic (SPH) (since 23 December 2011)

Ruling party: Kukuriku coalition, led by Socijaldemokratska Partija Hrvatske (SPH) (Social Democratic Party of Croatia), with Hrvatska Narodna Stranka-Liberalni Demokrati (HNS-LD) (Croatian People's Party- Liberal Democrats), Istarski Demokratski Sabor (IDS) (Istrian Democratic Assembly) and Hrvatska Stranka Umirovljenika (Croatian Pensioner's Party) (from 4 Dec 2011)

Area: 56,538 square km

Population: 4.24 million (2014)* (4,290,612; 2011; census figure)

Capital: Zagreb

Official language: Croatian

Currency: Kuna (K) = 100 lipas

Exchange rate: K6.76 per US$ (Sep 2015)

GDP per capita: US$13,494 (2014)*

GDP real growth: -0.40% (2014)

GDP: US$57.16 billion (2014)

Labour force: 1.90 million (2014)

Unemployment: 17.10% (2014)*

Inflation: -0.21% (2014)

Balance of trade: -US$8.35 billion (2013)*

* estimated figure

Milanovic of the SPH could look forward to a year of fractious relations with his country's new president. The election of an HDZ president in Croatia had also gone down badly in neighbouring Serbia, where Mrs Grabar-Kitarovic was described as a 'fascist' in Serbia's left-wing press.

However, Croatia's presidency does not normally carry much political clout. While Mrs Grabar-Kitarovic will be able to intervene in questions of foreign affairs and even defence, she has no right to veto legislation. The fact that the president has the right to seek and attend special cabinet meetings was, in early 2015, still unclear. Mr Milanovic had rejected her original proposal to attend a cabinet meeting, claiming that there was no precedent for such interventions. However, given the SPH-led government's poor economic record, to refuse the President's request would not necessarily be a vote-winning move.

If Mrs Grabar-Kitarovic's election victory was seen as a breath of fresh air by most Croatians, she nevertheless managed to inject some stale air into Croatia's foreign relations in mid-2015. This was on an official visit to Austria to lay a wreath in memory of the Croats who had served the pro-Nazi Ustasha regime. The President's critics called this an insult to the memory of al the people, including Jews and Serbs, who were killed by the Croat Ustasha.

Immigrants

In the summer of 2015 Europe saw an unprecedented wave of refugees, many of them from Syria, sweeping cross the continent towards Germany, which had offered to accommodate as many as 80,000. For many of the refugees this meant crossing Croatia, where the infrastructure – and the economy – simply did not have the resources or the money to look them properly. The government soon recognised the problem and announced that instead of registering them and providing them with accommodation as stipulated by the European Union (EU), it would be happy to pack them in buses or place them on board trains and move them on to countries better able to look after them adequately. As Hungary decided to close its borders with Serbia (from where most of the refugees were crossing), so did Croatia.

Mr Milanovic acknowledged that Croatia was not up to the task, telling journalists that he could not risk Croatia becoming a 'migrant hotspot', whatever that was. Rather than actually closing its borders, Croatia was prepared to redirect refugees through to Hungary and Slovenia.

Milanovic said Croatia cannot and will not close its borders, but will redirect people towards Hungary and Slovenia, from where they could make plans to reach whatever was their final European destination. This plan of action did not go down a storm in Hungary, which accused Croatia of encouraging the refugees to cross the border between the two countries illegally.

Elections

One of the Presidential tasks that Mrs Grabar-Kitarovic probably did relish in early October 2015 was that of calling for Croatia's next parliamentary elections to take place in early November 2015. The President's obvious aspiration was to see Croatia's electorate repeat their choice for the presidential election and vote for an HZD lead government. Mr Milanovic obviously wanted his SPH lead coalition to be re-elected as the governing group.

'Llet's go to the November elections and form the future of our country' said the President. 'It's time to leave behind us the ashes of the past and return to building with the cement of a better future.' The current parliament had been elected in December 2011 for a four year period. The electoral polls suggested that the election would be a close-run thing between the HDZ, lead in parliament by Tomislav Karamarko.

The economy: cautious IMF optimism

In its July 2015 assessment of the Croatian economy, the International Monetary Fund (IMF) struck a faintly optimistic note, reporting that 'robust retail sales, value added tax (VAT) receipts and better consumer confidence' suggested that private consumption had bottomed out. Employment had stabilised and corporate profits were recovering. The beneficial effect of the favourable external environment had, according to the IMF, also helped, notably through lower energy prices, stronger euro-zone growth and ample domestic and external liquidity enabling debt servicing costs to be contained. The IMF also noted that better exports, industrial production and foreign direct investment (FDI) also suggest that the economy's shift from inward orientation towards what it described as the 'the tradable sector' was making progress.

However, in the view of the IMF, the Croatian economy was not yet out of the woods. Corporate investment was still contracting, as companies struggled with high debt levels; and an end to this process was not yet in sight. State-owned enterprises (SOEs) continued to tie up a disproportionate part of Croatia's economic resources. Together with a chronically weak business environment and wages that remained relatively high compared to peers (ie, other new EU member states), this increased the costs of operation for private corporations, complicating the strengthening of competitiveness and the re-orientation toward markets with growth potential. Uncertainties over future government policies – heightened by the forthcoming December 2015 elections – did not help.

Following the long lasting recession, large fiscal vulnerabilities had built up.

KEY INDICATORS — **Croatia**

	Unit	2011	2012	2013	2014	**2015
Population	m	4.29	4.28	4.26	*4.24	*4.24
Gross domestic product (GDP)	US$bn	36.80	56.16	57.85	57.16	*48.87
GDP per capita	US$	14,457	13,119	13,592	*13,494	*11,538
GDP real growth	%	-0.1	-1.9	-0.9	-0.4	*0.5
Inflation	%	2.3	3.4	2.2	-0.2	*-0.9
Unemployment	%	14.3	16.1	16.9	*17.1	*17.3
Exports (fob) (goods)	US$m	13,463.6	12,449.0	12,073.2	–	–
Imports (fob) (goods)	US$m	22,432.9	20,311.0	20,425.0	–	–
Balance of trade	US$m	-8,969.4	-7,862.0	-8,351.9	–	–
Current account	US$m	-466.3	-17.0	*453.0	*380.0	*1,080.0
Total reserves minus gold	US$m	16,049.4	14,807.0	17,766.8	15,423.6	–
Foreign exchange	US$m	15,564.2	14,339.0	17,296.8	–	–
Exchange rate	per US$	5.26	5.80	5.58	6.33	–

* estimated figure ** forecast figure

Public debt had increased from 35 per cent of gross domestic product (GDP) in 2008 to 85 per cent at the end of 2014, reflecting fiscal deficits averaging almost 6.5 per cent of GDP since 2009 – due in part, according to the IMF, to the assumption of debts from state-owned enterprises – and the economic contraction. At around 20 per cent of GDP, public annual gross financing needs are large.

None the less, the IMF considered that Croatia's macro-economic and financial risks appeared contained. Whatever optimism there had been was conditioned by the fact that in the first half of 2014 most economic indicators were still in negative territory. However, in the second half of the year, the IMF noted that exports, tax revenue, retail sales and industrial production all showed signs of recovery. Despite this, figures for the entire year showed that the economy had contracted by 0.4 per cent (annual average).

Private investment seemed to be the main brake on activity, while exports contributed positively to growth. The economy maintained positive momentum in the early months of 2015, with real growth in the first quarter estimated at an annual 0.5 per cent. Monthly CPI inflation had dropped into negative territory in late 2013 and had remained there for much of 2014, reflecting mostly lower prices for imported food and energy. With non-food, non-energy inflation stable and nominal wages growing slightly, in the view of the IMF there appeared to be limited deflationary knock-on.

EBRD – caution

In the view of the European Bank for Reconstruction and Development (EBRD) at the end of 2014 Croatia's economy remained stalled in recession. Croatia had been in recession for the previous five years, during which period, its GDP had contracted by a cumulative 12 per cent. In 2013 GDP had fallen by 0.9 per cent on the back of continued declines in household consumption and investment, as well as a drop in exports. GDP dropped a further 0.6 per cent year-on-year in the first quarter of 2014 and 0.8 per cent in the second quarter. Although Croatia suffered from deep structural problems, progress with reforms remained hesitant. When upward pressures on prices faded for over a year, Croatia experienced three months of deflation at the beginning of 2014. However, prices rose again by 0.4 per cent year-on-year in May 2014. Pressure on the kuna in 2014 had led the Hrvatska Narodna Banka (HNB) (Croatian National Bank) to intervene several times on foreign exchange markets to support the currency.

The EBRD noted that the economic difficulties of the previous five years had taken a toll on public finances. In January 2014 Croatia entered the EU's excessive deficit procedure due to persistent government deficits of above 3 per cent of GDP and a rising level of consolidated general government debt that had reached almost 70 per cent of GDP by mid-2014. This implied that the authorities had committed to a gradual fiscal consolidation, including further austerity measures in line with EU requirements. The government had undertaken measures both on the revenue side of the budget (raising the intermediate value added tax rate from 10 per cent to 13 per cent and abolishing certain tax reliefs) and on certain spending reductions. In addition, the government was planning to introduce taxes on savings and real estate and to increase the residence tax for tourists. The weakening fiscal position also resulted in the downgrade of Croatia's sovereign debt rating to non-investment grade by all three main credit agencies.

In the view of the EBRD, the outlook for Croatia in 2015 was uncertain. The economy continued to face long-standing problems of weak competitiveness, an over- large public sector and difficulties in the business environment. GDP fell moderately in 2014 (to -0.4 per cent) – the sixth consecutive year of contraction for the Croatian economy – returning to mild growth only in 2015. Over the medium term, Croatia's economy might see a boost from improved regional and global conditions, as well as from the efficient use of EU cohesion funds, but growth prospects would, in the view of the EBRD, depend on the extent to which long-awaited reforms to public administration and economic governance were implemented.

The EBRD noted that Croatia's privatisation programme had achieved mixed success in the previous year. The government successfully sold the country's largest insurance company, Croatia Osiguranje, to the local Adris Group, which is listed on the Zagreb Stock Exchange. Also, there had been substantial investor interest in Kupari – a hotel resort ruined and abandoned in the 1990s – for which the privatisation process was under way. However, the government received no bids for the purchase of 49 per cent of Croatia Airlines in November 2013. In March 2014 the government's attempts to sell a stake of 25 per cent plus one share in the fertiliser producer, Petrokemija also failed to attract any binding offers, even though several foreign companies had expressed an interest. Furthermore, in December 2013 the government rejected a bid by Erste Bank for a 99.1 per cent stake in the state-owned postal bank, Hrvatska Postanska Banka (HPB), because the offer, including the proposed price, was considered unacceptable. Erste Bank was the only bidder as OTP Banka, which had participated in the first round of tendering, subsequently dropped out. Meanwhile, the government was working on its 2015 privatisation agenda, which would probably again include Croatia Airlines, as well as the HPB, Croatian Railways Cargo and ACI, a chain of national marinas. In the World Bank's *Doing Business 2015* report, Croatia's score for ease of doing business remains relatively low in comparison with other EU countries. Out of 189 countries in the index, Croatia ranked 65. Following the enactment of the Hydrocarbons Exploration and Exploitation Act in July 2013, the Croatian authorities opened the first offshore bidding round in April 2014 for 29 exploration blocks in the Adriatic Sea, with bids to be awarded in 2015. The tender attracted considerable interest, with more than 30 oil and gas companies reportedly present at the launch.

In October 2013 the ministry of transport had launched an international tender to monetise operating motorways, which were under the management of two state-owned companies, HAC and ARZ. Five bidders came forward and financial closure was envisaged for 2015. In addition, performance-based maintenance contracts were introduced in April 2014 by Croatian Roads, the company responsible for local and regional roads. In December 2013 the French Zagreb Airport International Company (ZAIC) signed a 30-year concession deal for Zagreb Airport. Under the terms of the contract, ZAIC will invest around €300 million (US$337 million) in the construction of a new terminal. In the railways sector, two new cargo operators entered the market – the local Adria Transport and Rail Cargo Carrier from Hungary. There were no new operators in passenger services. The planned sale of a 75 per cent stake in Croatian Railways Cargo had been abandoned following the collapse of negotiations with Romania's Grampet Group in January 2014. Croatia's banking system was, in the view of the EBRD, well developed by regional standards, with one of the highest capital adequacy ratios in

Europe, at 20.8 per cent in June 2014. Croatia's banking sector is highly 'euroised' with over 70 per cent of loans and deposits denominated or indexed to foreign currency. However, monthly year-on-year private sector credit growth had been negative since mid-2012. In addition, the level of non-performing loans had been rising steadily, reaching 16.6 per cent by June 2014.

Risk assessment

Economy	Poor
Politics	Good
Regional stability	Fair/good

COUNTRY PROFILE

The Croats formed an independent kingdom during the tenth century.
1089 Inner Croatia came under the control of Hungary and then the Habsburg Empire, remaining that way for eight centuries.
1529 After Hungary's defeat by the Ottoman Turks, a militarised border was formed between Croatia and Bosnia-Hercegovina.
1918 The defeat of the Austro-Hungarian Empire during the First World War saw the creation of the Kingdom of the Serbs, Croats and Slovenes, encompassing Bosnia and Hercegovina (BiH), Croatia, parts of Dalmatia and Macedonia, Montenegro, Serbia, Slavonia and Slovenia.
1921 Prince Alexander, Regent of Serbia, became King.
1929 Following disputes between Serbs and Croats, King Alexander assumed dictatorial powers and the country was renamed Yugoslavia.
1934 King Alexander of Yugoslavia was assassinated in France by Croatian extremists. Power passed to Prince Paul, acting as Regent to 11-year-old King Peter II. He ruled with the support of the armed forces.
1939 Croatia was granted internal autonomy.
1941 A coup by air force officers replaced Prince Paul and the pro-Nazi Germany government with the 17-year-old King Peter II and established a pro-Allied government. In response, German and Italian forces invaded Yugoslavia, forcing the royal family and government into exile. The fascist Ustasha movement, led by Ante Pavelic, created the Nezavisna Drzava Hrvatska (NDH) (Independent State of Croatia).
1943 Civil war ensued between two rival groups, the communist partisans, led by General Josip Broz Tito, and the Royalist Chetniks. The partisans proclaimed their own government in liberated areas.
1944 King Peter II was deposed.
1945 The Federal People's Republic of Yugoslavia was proclaimed, with Tito as prime minister – a Croat opposed to expressions of Croat (or any other) nationalism. Croatia became a constituent republic of the federation. The other republics were: BiH, Macedonia, Slovenia, Montenegro, Serbia and the two autonomous regions of Vojvodina and Kosovo.
1953 Constitutions were adopted and Tito became president of Yugoslavia. Increased autonomy for the constituent republics was extended in 1963 and 1974.
1971 A mass movement in favour of Croatian nationalist revival was crushed by Tito.
1980 Tito died. A system of a collective (rotating) presidency was adopted.
1989 Differences and friction between the wealthier republics, Slovenia and Croatia, and the different ethnic groups intensified.
1990 Following Slovenia's secession from Yugoslavia, Croatia held its own free elections which were won by the nationalist Hrvatska Demokratska Zajednica (HDZ) (Croatian Democratic Community). Franjo Tudjman became the first president of the Republic of Croatia. In August, Croatian Serbs held their own referendum, which favoured maintaining their cultural autonomy. Rebel Serbs took control of the Krajina and two other regions in Croatia – Eastern and Western Slavonia. The secession of Croatia, Slovenia and BiH led to invasions of these republics by the Jugoslovenska Narodna Armija (JNA) (Yugoslav National Army).
1991 Independence from Yugoslavia was unilaterally declared.
1992–94 Croatia was recognised as an independent state by the then European Community (EC) on 15 January and became a member of the UN. Franjo Tudjman was re-elected president. The declaration of independence was followed by several months of war, first against the JNA and then against local rebel ethnic Serbs. JNA units had been incorporated into the ethnic Serb armies in the Krajina region. The Croatian government began to finance and support Bosnian Croat attempts to separate from BiH. This exacerbated the civil war in BiH between the Muslim and Bosnian Croats, until a cease-fire was achieved and the Muslim-Croat Federation was established in 1994.
1995 After nearly four years of Serb control, western Slavonia and Krajina were recaptured by the Croatian army. Tudjman's ruling nationalist HDZ won the parliamentary elections and Zlatko Matesa became prime minister. President Tudjman of Croatia, along with President Slobodan Milosevic of Yugoslavia and President Alija Izetbegovic of BiH, agreed to end the Bosnian civil war.
1996 Yugoslavia (by now consisting of Serbia and Montenegro and the two autonomous regions of Kosovo and Vojvodina) and Croatia signed an agreement on mutual recognition, formally ending five years of hostility.
1997 The HDZ won a majority in the upper house of the Sabor and President Franjo Tudjman was re-elected.
1998 Eastern Slavonia (some 5 per cent of Croatia's total territory) was handed back to Croatia by the UN Transition Authority for Eastern Slavonia (UNTAES).
1999 Franjo Tudjman died; Vlatko Pavletic became acting president.
2000 The Socialdemokratska Partija (SDP) (Social Democratic Party) won the general election. A centre-left coalition government was formed, led by the SDP, with Ivica Racan (SDP) as prime minister. Stjepan 'Stripe' Mesic of the Hrvatska Narodna Stranka (HNS) (Croatian People's Party) and regarded as an ally of the SDP, was sworn in as president.
2001 A constitutional amendment abolished of the upper house of parliament. Croatia agreed to extradite several suspected war criminals to the International Criminal Tribunal for former Yugoslavia (ICTY) at The Hague (The Netherlands). War veteran groups protested strongly at the government's co-operation.
2002 Ivica Racan resigned as prime minister, but was re-appointed and formed a new centre-left coalition government, comprising the SDP, HNS, Hrvatska Seljacka Stranka (HSS) (Croatian Peasant Party), Liberalna Stranka (LS) (Liberal Party) and Libra.
2003 Croatia submitted its formal application for EU membership. The nationalist HDZ, won parliamentary elections defeating pro-Western parties. Ivo Sanader (HDZ) became prime minister of a coalition government led by the HDZ with Hrvatska Socialna Liberalna Stranka, Demokratski Centar (HSLS, DC) (Croatian Social Liberal Party, Democratic Centre).
2004 Milan Babic, a Croatian Serb, was jailed for 13 years by the ICTY Tribunal in The Hague for war crimes during his leadership, in the early 1990s, of the self-proclaimed Krajina Serb republic.
2005 Stjepan 'Stripe' Mesic won the run-off presidential election. The EU began accession talks with Croatia; they had been stalled because Croatia was deemed unco-operative in handing over suspected war criminals. The fugitive, General Ante Gotovina was arrested in the Canary Islands and sent to the war crimes tribunal in The Hague.
2006 Croatia membership talks with the EU were caught up in internal discord about enlargement when the EU decided to wait until at least 2010 before offering Croatia membership. Talks with Croatia

continued with the EU, separately from Turkey, which had applied for membership at the same time.
2007 A coalition government between the HDZ and the Hrvatska Seljacka Stranka-Hrvatska Socijalno Liberalna Stranka (HSS-HSLS) (Croatian Peasant's Party-Croatian Social Liberal Party) was formed following parliamentary elections.
2008 An accession protocol with Croatia was signed by NATO ambassadors in Brussels.
2009 A border dispute with Slovenia that began in 1991 with the collapse of Yugoslavia impeded Croatia's efforts to join the EU. With such a short coastline (46km) Slovenia was intent on using the small Bay of Piran on the Adriatic Sea to give it access to international waters. Croatia wanted the border to be halfway through the bay and submitted maps and documents showing this to EU negotiators. Slovenia vetoed Croatia's first accession attempt and without an agreement by April Croatia was unable to join the EU in 2009. Croatia joined NATO. Ivo Sanader resigned and Jadranka Kosor became prime minister. Ivo Josipovic (Socijaldemokratska Partija Hrvatske (SPH) (Social Democratic Party of Croatia) won the first round of presidential elections.
2010 Josipovic won the run-off presidential elections, with 60.3 per cent of the vote, Milan Bandic (independent) 39.7 per cent; turnout was 50.2 per cent. In a tit-for-tat move Serbia began legal action against Croatia at the ICJ for genocide committed in the early 1990s. The alleged genocide was said to have occurred during clashes between the two countries as Croatia fought for independence. The action was in retaliation for Croatia's refusal to drop a similar suit before the ICJ for atrocities by Yugoslav and Serbian forces against Croats in 1999. A referendum held in Slovenia voted in favour of allowing international arbitrators to resolve the border dispute concerning the Bay of Piran. A five-person panel, including one Slovene and one Croat, will settle the matter. Sretko Kalinic, the assassin of Serbia's first democratically elected prime minister (Zoran Djindjic) in 2001, was extradited to Serbia to serve a 30-year prison sentence; a Serbian court had found him guilty *in absentia*. Croatia signed a protocol to jointly found a new company, Cargo 10, with Macedonia, Serbia and Slovenia to incorporate their railway companies; later joined by Bosnia Herzegovina. Former prime minister, Ivo Sanader, left the country, just hours before parliament voted to lift his immunity from prosecution. An international arrest warrant was issued and he was arrested in Austria on charges of bribery and corruption.
2011 A census, carried out on 31 March, recorded a population of 4,290,612 people residing in the country, of which 792,875 were in Zagreb. In May, Croatia and Slovenia submitted their maritime border arbitration agreement to the UN. Extradition papers for Ivo Sanader's return to Croatia were signed in Austria in July. Parliamentary elections took place on 4 December, in which the four-party Kukuriku coalition (led by SPH) won 40 per cent of the vote and replaced the incumbent coalition led by HDZ, which won 23.5 per cent (47). The HDZ coalition had been blamed for the poor state of the economy, rising unemployment and a number of corruption scandals, which marred the election campaign. The Kukuriku leader, Zoran Milanovic (SPH) had warned that he would introduce an austerity budget to avoid a credit agency downgrading and that he would approach the IMF for financial aid if necessary.
2012 On 22 January, a referendum on European Union membership was held, in which 66.27 per cent of the vote was in favour of joining. The EU accession treaty was ratified by parliament on 9 March; Croatia's date of accession is scheduled for 1 July 2013. On 5 September, the ratings agency Fitch gave an unexpected fillip by upgrading Croatia's outlook from negative to stable and reaffirming its rating of BBB. This followed the government's progress in developing a medium-term plan of addressing fiscal challenges, improving tax compliance and fighting tax avoidance.
2013 Croatia became a member of the European Union (EU) on 1 July. Despite only just becoming a member of the EU, in late August Croatia refused to implement a European Arrest Warrant requested by Germany for the killing of a Croatian dissident in 1983. Croatia had passed a law to prevent arrests for crimes committed before August 2002. Signs in Serbian Cyrillic script put up in the town of Vukovar were torn down by protestors on 2 September. The law states that where a minority reaches one third of the population signs must be bilingual. Serbs, according to the 2011 census, make up 34.8 per cent of the population.
2014 The first round of the presidential election was held on 28 December. The result was a win for Kolinda Grabar-Kitarovic (HDZ) (Croatian Democratic Union) with 37.22 per cent of the vote, followed by Ivo Jospovic (independent) 38.46 per cent, Ivan Sincic (Zivi zid) (Human Wall) 16.42 per cent and Milan Kujundzic (Savez za Hrvatsku) (Alliance for Croatia) 6.3 per cent. Turnout was 47.12 per cent. As no candidate won the required 50 per cent a second round was scheduled for January.
2015 In the second round of the presidential election held on 11 January Kolinda Grabar-Kitarovic (HDZ) won a majority of 50.74 per cent while Ivo Josipovic won 49.26 per cent. Turnout was 59.06 per cent. Ms Grabar-Kitarovic assumed office on 19 February.

Political structure

Constitution

The written Constitution was first adopted in December 1990, with amendments in 2000 and 2001 that cut back presidential powers and abolish the upper house of parliament.
Under the Constitution there is a principle of the separation of power into legislative, executive and judicial branches, which are limited by the right to local and regional self-government.
The laws of Croatia must conform to the constitution
The electoral law gives the vote to all Croatians over the age of 18, including those living abroad. Ethnic minorities are equal with ethnic Croats according to the constitution. However, in recent years the international community has raised strong objections to laws that *de facto* discriminate against other groups – specifically returning Serb refugees. Until these problems are solved, Croatia is unlikely to be recognised as a fully democratic state.
The administration of Croatia is divided into 21 *zupanije* (counties). There are also two *kotari*, or special districts, at Glina and Knin, which are under direct Serb control.
The Constitution was last amended in 2013 with a referendum that was supported by a 66.28 per cent majority. It stated that marriage is a matrimony between a woman and a man, thereby creating a constitutional prohibition against same-sex marriage.

Independence date

25 June 1991

Form of state

Parliamentary democracy.

The executive

Executive power is vested in the president who is Head of State and supreme commander of the armed forces and is directly elected for five years and a maximum of two terms.
The president appoints the prime minister and, by recommendation of the prime minister, other members of the government. These appointments are subject to confirmation by the House of Representatives.

National legislature

The unicameral Hrvatski Sabor (Parliament of Croatia) (known as Sabor) consists of 151 seats; members are directly elected in multi-seat constituencies (up to a maximum of six), by party-list proportional representation vote using the D'Hondt method with a 5 per cent threshold, to serve for four-year terms. Of the total number, eight seats are reserved for minority communities and three for expatriates.

Legal system

All civil and criminal cases are dealt with by basic and higher courts. The Supreme Court is the highest authority for civil and criminal law, charged with ensuring uniform application of laws and equality of citizens. All judges and other judicial officials are appointed by the Judicial Council, an elected body that is answerable to the parliament. The Judicial Council also acts as the Constitutional Court to determine the conformity of national legislation with the Constitution.

All prosecutions are the responsibility of the Office of the Public Prosecutor. There is also a Public Attorney. The Justice Ministry is the administrative authority of the Croatian judiciary. Its major instrument is the Croatian police, which falls under the jurisdiction of the interior minister.

Last elections

4 December 2011 (parliamentary); 28 December 2014 (presidential); 22 January 2012 (EU referendum)

Results: Parliamentary: Kukuriku coalition (of four political parties, led by Socijaldemokratska Partija Hrvatske (SPH) (Social Democratic Party of Croatia) won 40 per cent of the vote (80 seats, out of 151), the HDZ coalition (of three parties, led by Hrvatska Demokratska Zajednica (HDZ) (Croatian Democratic Union) 23.5 per cent (47), Hrvatski Laburisti-Stranka Rada (HL-SR) (Worker's Party-Labour Party) 5.1 per cent (six), Hrvatski Demokratski Sabor Slavonije i Baranje (HDSSB) (Croatian Democratic Assembly of Slovonija and Banranja) 2.9 per cent (six); four other political parties (two with seats reserved for ethnic minorities and other independent and community representatives) won the remaining 12 seats. Turnout was 61.77 per cent.

Presidential 1st round: Kolinda Grabar-Kitarovic (HDZ) (Croatian Democratic Union) won 37.22 per cent of the vote, Ivo Jospovic (independent) won 38.46 per cent, Ivan Sincic (Zivi zid) (Human Wall) won 16.42 per cent and Milan Kujundzic (Savez za Hrvatsku) (Alliance for Croatia) won 6.3 per cent. Turnout was 47.12 per cent.

Presidential 2nd round: Kolinda Grabar-Kitarovic (HDZ) won a majority of 50.74 per cent while Ivo Josipovic won 49.26 per cent. Turnout was 59.06 per cent.

Referendum: 66.27 per cent of votes (1.3 million) were in favour of the motion to approve membership of the European Union, 33.13 per cent (650,000) disagreed; turnout was 43.51 per cent.

Next elections

On or before 2016 (parliamentary); 2019-20 (presidential)

Political parties

Ruling party

Kukuriku coalition, led by Socijaldemokratska Partija Hrvatske (SPH) (Social Democratic Party of Croatia), with Hrvatska Narodna Stranka-Liberalni Demokrati (HNS-LD) (Croatian People's Party- Liberal Democrats), Istarski Demokratski Sabor (IDS) (Istrian Democratic Assembly) and Hrvatska Stranka Umirovljenika (Croatian Pensioner's Party) (from 4 Dec 2011)

Main opposition party

HDZ coalition (led by Hrvatska Demokratska Zajednica (HDZ) (Croatian Democratic Union), with Hrvatska Gradanska Stranka (HGS) (Croation Citizens Party) and Demokratski Centar (DC) (Democratic Centre)

Population

4.24 million (2014)* (4,290,612; 2011; census figure)

Last census: 31 March 2011: 4,290,612

Population density: 79.8 inhabitants per square km. Urban population 58 per cent (2010 Unicef).

Annual growth rate: -0.1 per cent, 1990–2010 (Unicef).

Internally Displaced Persons (IDP)

11,000 (UNHCR 2004)

Ethnic make-up

Croats (90 per cent of the population), plus Serbs, Hungarians and Gypsies. The April 2001 census, the first since the 1991—95 war, indicated that Serbs made up 4.5 per cent of the population (the figure was 12 per cent in the early 1990s).

Religions

Predominantly Roman Catholic, with Christian Orthodox, Muslim and Jewish minorities, living mostly in Zagreb.

Education

Primary education is compulsory and free of charge. Secondary education is between the ages of 14–18. Vocational schools offer courses lasting for three or four years, including a period of practical instruction. There are four universities offering courses in science, engineering and medicine that meet international standards.

Public expenditure on education typically amounts to 5 per cent of annual gross national income.

Literacy rate: 98 per cent adult rate; 100 per cent youth rate (15–24) (Unesco 2005).

Compulsory years: Six to 14

Enrolment rate: 99 per cent; gross primary enrolment, of the relevant age group (including repetition rates), (World Bank).

Pupils per teacher: 19 in primary schools

Health

The healthcare system has recovered since the internal conflict ended in 1995, but national coverage remains patchy, notably in the Krajina and Eastern Slavonia regions.

HIV/Aids

HIV prevalence: 0.1 per cent aged 15–49 in 2003 (World Bank)

Life expectancy: 75 years, 2004 (WHO 2006)

Fertility rate/Maternal mortality rate: 1.5 births per woman, 2010 (Unicef); maternal mortality 6 per 100,000 live births (World Bank).

Child (under 5 years) mortality rate (per 1,000): 5 per 1,000 live births (WHO 2012); 1 per cent of children under five years are malnourished (World Bank).

Head of population per physician: 2.44 physicians per 1,000 people, 2003 (WHO 2006)

Welfare

The government faces a huge fiscal burden with an ageing population and a legacy of insufficient funds to pay retirees, particularly those who retired early following reforms of the late 90s. In 2002 the government introduced a dual social insurance and mandatory, privately managed, compulsory pension schemes, for all workers, with contributions that vary depending on the class of old age pension. Regular pensions require contributions of 10.75 per cent and 8.75 per cent (of payroll), from employee and employer respectively. Basic pensions require contributions of 8.75 per cent and 5.75 per cent (of payroll), from employee and employer respectively. Insurance contributions cover among other benefits, medical, disability and survivor's pensions. By 2020 projected pension fund assets should reach 25–30 per cent of GDP. In 2003 it was estimated there were over 50,000 Croatian refugees, of which 27,700 were internally displaced persons (IDP).

Main cities

Zagreb (capital, estimated population 685,799 in 2012), Split (165,013), Rijeka (126,013), Osijek (82,830), Zadar (70,775), Pula (57,053), Sesvete (55,458), Slavonski Brod (52,978), Karlovac (46,588), Varazdin (38,487).

Languages spoken

Croatian is written using the Latin alphabet. German and English are commonly used as second languages and business people are fluent in English. Bosnian and Serbian are also spoken and, near the Adriatic coast, Italian is spoken.

Official language/s

Croatian

Media

The constitution guarantees press freedom and bans censorship.

Press

Dailies: Most popular newspapers have a tabloid format with commercialised stories.

In Croatian, national newspapers include *Jutarnji List* (www.jutarnji.hr), *Vecernji List* (www.vecernji.hr), and *Vjesnik* (www.vjesnik.com). Regional newspapers include *Slobodna Dalmacija* (www.slobodnadalmacija.hr) from Split, *Novi List* (www.novilist.hr) from Rijeka, *24 Sata* (www.24sata.hr) from Zagreb and Glas Istre (www.glasistre.hr) from Pula.

Weeklies: In Croatian, the most influential news magazine *Globus* (www.globus.com.hr) has reported on corruption and organised crime that have been avoided by more mainstream publications. Another independent political magazine is *Nacional* (www.nacional.hr). *Gloria* (www.gloria.com.hr) is the most popular women's magazine and *Nogometni Magazin* (www.nogometni-magazin.com) is a sports publication.

Business: In Croatian, *Business.hr* (http://business.hr) and *Privredni Vjesnik* (www.privredni-vjesnik.hr with an English online edition) are both weekly newspapers.

Broadcasting

Television is the medium of choice for news and information for most people. Hrvatska Radiotelevizija (HRT) (www.hrt.hr) is the national, public broadcaster, which is funded through license fees and advertising revenue.

Radio: RTH operates three stations RTH1, 2 and 3, with a network provides by regional linking stations. There are numerous private stations centred on cities and regional centres, including Radio Samobor (www.radiosamobor.hr) with news and music, from Zagreb, Radio Mrežnica (www.radio-mreznica.hr) from the Central region, Radio Laus (www.radio-laus.hr) from Dubrovnik, Radio Istra (www.radioistra.hr) from Istria and Gradski Radio (www.eter.hr) from Slavonia.

Television: There are three national, commercial, networks including the government-owned HRT (www.hrt.hr) TV, which has two channels providing domestically produced news and entertainment programmes and foreign imports. The private TV channels include RTL Televizija (www.rtl.hr) and Nova TV (http://dnevnik.hr). The Croatian media company OIV (www.oiv.hr) provides a comprehensive cable TV service, with 21 channels, to Croatia and neighbouring countries.

The conversion of terrestrial signals to digital is scheduled to be completed by 2010 and will provide the opportunity for transmission of many more channels.

Other news agencies: HIC (Croatian Information Centre): www.hic.hr

Hina (Croatian News Agency): http://websrv2.hina.hr

Economy

Croatia has a free-market, service sector led, economy, with its industrial sector, particularly shipbuilding, underpinning its international trade. Shipbuilding accounts for around 10 per cent of all exported goods and with manufacturing represents around 30 per cent of the structure of the economy. Farming includes crops for both a processed food industry and organic crops for export to other EU countries. The service sector represented 69.0 per cent of GDP in 2014, with tourism as its principal sector and the country's major foreign exchange earner.

The economy of Croatia is dependent on exports and tourism; GDP growth began to fall early in 2008 as the global economic crisis took hold and trade weakened and tourist numbers fell. Growth dropped from 5.1 per cent in 2007 to 2.2 per cent in 2008, before falling into recession in 2009 with GDP of -6.0 per cent. Recovery was slow and remained in negative growth of -1.2 per cent in 2010, and again at -0.3 per cent in 2011. Croatia's economy has not stopped shrinking following this, reaching a low of -2.2 per cent in 2012, speeding up slightly along with increasing tourist arrivals to -0.4 per cent by 2014 when there was 12.9 million visitors (4.6 per cent increase on 2013).

Unemployment in Croatia follows an annual cycle, peaking during the winter months and minimising in the summer tourist season. Unemployment has been typically high at 12.7–8.7 per cent over 2005–08, but it rose sharply after this period reaching 23.6 per cent in the winter of 2014. However, 2015 has shown a decreasing trend in unemployment, at 20.4 per cent in the winter and a 5-year low of 15.9 per cent in July.

The International Monetary Fund (IMF) considered that Croatia had benefited from global growth before 2008 but had not used the large-scale foreign direct investment (FDI) to improve either its overall competitiveness through structural reforms, or benefits founded in the tourist sector (which accounts for around 50 per cent of export earnings and services). In 2008, FDI amounted to a record US$6 billion, which halved to US$3.3 billion in 2009 before plunging to US$426 million in 2010. However, FDI increased in 2011 to US$1.5 billion. In 2013 the net inflow of FDI in Croatia was –US$769 million.

The World Bank ranked Croatia overall as 65 (out of 189), on its *Doing Business* list in 2014, which was a rise of 14 from its ranking in 2012. From 2011, Croatia adopted a World Bank backed model for a new range of civil procedures and enforcement of judgements in credit laws. This propelled Croatia higher up the ranking for getting credit and enforcing contracts. On 5 September 2012, the ratings agency Fitch gave an unexpected fillip by upgrading Croatia's outlook from negative to stable and reaffirming its rating of BBB. This followed the government's progress in developing a medium-term plan of addressing fiscal challenges, improving tax compliance and fighting tax avoidance.

External trade

As a member of the European Union (EU), Croatia operates within a community-wide free trade area, with tariffs set as a whole. Internationally, the EU has free trade agreements with a number of nations and trading blocs worldwide.

International trade plays an important role in the economy. Shipbuilding is the major manufacturing industry, with ferrous steel and aluminium products also important. Electronics, including military applications, are part of the new technology industries, with pharmaceutical products and energy production. Traditional industries provide agricultural products such as timber, textiles, organic crops (prized in the EU) and processed food.

Imports

Principal imports are vehicles, machinery and electrical equipment, chemicals and foodstuffs, natural gas, electricity and petroleum products.

Main sources: Germany (15.1 per cent of total in 2014), Italy (14.2 per cent), Slovenia (10.8 per cent).

Exports

Principal exports are ships, transport equipment, electronic equipment, textiles, chemicals, foodstuffs and energy.

Main destinations: Italy (13.9 per cent of total in 2014), Bosnia and Hercegovina (11.9 per cent), Slovenia (11.3 per cent)

Agriculture

Farming

Almost half of the population lives in rural areas where agriculture continues to be the traditional source of income. Of a total of 3.2 million hectares (ha) of arable land, 63 per cent is cultivated and the rest is pastureland. Only around 68 per cent of agricultural land is privately owned. Agriculture contributed 4.8 per cent to GDP in 2014; it employed around 15 per cent of the workforce.

Family farms with an average holding of 2.8ha per farm, contribute to the overall animal and horticultural production. Crop production is especially well developed, covering the needs for cereals, while cattle breeding accounts for almost 50 per cent of agriculture-generated GDP. The warm weather and mild winters suit grape-growing.

The government is committed to initiating agricultural market reform and promoting private farming. Reform in the agrarian production sector is accompanied by rising food imports, mostly from the EU. Agriculture within the country meets the domestic demand for wine, wheat, corn, eggs and poultry. Croatia's oil and sugar processing facilities are big enough to provide exports. However, with high production costs and a series of free trade agreements, farm products cannot compete internationally.

Fishing

There are rich marine resources concentrated on the Dalmatian Adriatic coast.

Forestry

Of a total of 1.7 million hectares (ha) of forest cover, nearly four-fifths of the forest is owned by the state, and the rest is in private hands.

Croatia has a well-developed wood processing industry. Although a large amount of wood is reserved for domestic fuel consumption, the country manages to export industrial roundwood and sawnwood mainly to Slovenia and Italy respectively. Small volumes of wood pulp and panels are also exported, but paper is largely imported.

Industry and manufacturing

The industrial sector contributes around 30 per cent to GDP and typically employs around 30 per cent of the workforce. Manufacturing accounted for around 20 per cent of GDP.

State owned enterprises (SOE) are due to be restructured, in preparation for the expected competition within the EU.

Privatisation of SOE has begun, although progress is slow. In 2005 government commitment to fiscal constraints, necessary for staff cuts, is still needed as SOE incur significant losses, particularly in the shipbuilding industry and the railway system.

Private enterprise in retail and wholesale businesses and manufacturing, as a whole typically attracts 24 per cent of FDI.

Tourism

Croatia is a destination for the visitor attracted to beach resorts. Tourism within the country is limited and underdeveloped, with the exception of Zagreb. There are six historic sites included on Unesco's World Heritage List as well as the Plitvice Lakes National Park, which has a record 70 mammal and 126 bird European species (including brown bear, wolf, eagle owl and capercaille).

Travel and tourism has grown steadily in importance to the economy, as from 16.2 per cent of GDP in 2000 and 28.3 per cent by 2014. Likewise, employment in the industry has grown from 21.2 per cent (219,100 jobs) in 2000 to 30.2 per cent (310,500 jobs) in 2014. However, the sector was affected by the global economic crisis – tourism contributed a record 29.1 per cent in 2008, before dropping to 25.3 per cent in 2009 as visitor numbers slumped, and more importantly foreign receipts fell from US$11.7 billion to US$9.3 billion in 2008 and 2009. In 2009 there were 8.7 million visitors, which grew to 12.9 million visitors in 2014.

Hydrocarbons

Proven oil reserves in 2014 were 71 million barrels located in three regions: Slavonia, offshore in the Adriatic, near the Dalmatia coast and the Croatian region of the Pannonian Basin, where an estimated 1.2 million barrels per day (bpd) remains to be discovered. Consumption of oil was 84,000 barrels per day (bpd) in 2014 but is rising each year.

The Croatian state oil company INA is 45 per cent government-owned, with the majority share holder being Hungarian company MOL. INA has also invested US$500 million in exploration and drilling in the Middle East and Africa.

The 400,000bpd capacity Croatian Adriatic Oil (Adria) Pipeline, run by Jadranski Naftovod (JANAF) of Croatia, takes oil that arrives by tanker at the Croatian Adriatic port of Omisalj into the interior of Croatia. However there are plans to redirect the flow of oil, picking up Russian oil for delivery to the Adriatic for onward transportation. The negotiations, involving six countries, had not been concluded by 2015, but when agreement is reached an estimated 100 million barrels of crude oil, rising to 300 million barrels will be exported.

In 2014, natural gas reserves stood at 24.9 billion cubic metres (cum), with an annual production of 1.9 billion cum. An estimate of undiscovered gas in the Pannonian Basin, to be shared with Hungary, is 210 billion cum but is likely to be from hard to reach sites. Imports in 2014 totalled 1.1 billion cum, with consumption rising to around 3.2 billion cum annually. Imported gas comes primarily from Russia and Slovenia via pipeline.

In February 2012, the multinational, South Stream Transport group, announced the expected construction of the South Stream pipeline, to transport Russian natural gas to Western and Central Europe (and bypassing Ukraine) would begin in December 2012, however, in mid-2015 this was not the case.

Croatia has extensive coal reserves but production runs at less than 100,000 tonnes per annum, mostly for consumption by domestic power plants.

Energy

Croatia has 4,132MW of electricity generation capacity, of which almost 2,100MW is produced by hydropower, over 1,400MW by thermal power, 300MW by nuclear power plants and the remainder by alternative sources. Imports of electricity account for around 10 per cent of total energy consumption. Demand for electricity is increasing by around 5 per cent per year, creating an urgent need to increase generating capacity in Croatia. Hydroelectric plants are mainly located along the Adriatic coastline (Obrovac, Senj, Zakucac). Croatia does not operate a nuclear power plant but has joint ownership and responsibility for the plant in Krsko (Slovenia).

There is a geothermal resource in the north which could provide an estimated 839MW if harnessed, but which is currently used for heating spaces and swimming pools and balneology.

Financial markets

Stock exchange

Zagrebacka Burza (Zagreb Stock Exchange)

Banking and insurance

The central bank has general supervisory powers, endorsed by law, of the banking system. Legislation, since 2001, permits foreign investment in banks and since 2004 foreign banks may open branches in Croatia, although the EU is unimpressed about some of the restrictive stipulation necessary for this. Foreign exchange laws permit individuals opening foreign exchange accounts abroad and local banks offering foreign currency denominated loans.

There will be an amount of merging of supervisory authorities of the insurance, securities, investment funds and pensions into a financial services authority in line with EU requirements, before accession.

Central bank

Hrvatska Narodna Banka (HNB) (Croatian National Bank)

Main financial centre

Zagreb

Time
GMT plus one hour (daylight saving, late March to late October, GMT plus two hours)

Geography
Croatia is bounded by Slovenia to the north-west, Hungary to the north-east and the Serbian province of Vojvodina to the east. Bosnia and Hercegovina (BiH) takes a bite out of Croatia causing a rough horse shoe shape in the middle of the country from the east to the south-west. There is a very short border with Montenegro at the southern tip of the narrowing stretch of Croatia, near Dubrovnik. In the Adriatic Sea, Croatia also has maritime boundaries with Slovenia, Italy and Montenegro. There are 1,185 islands and islets along the 1,778km Croatian coast. At 56,538km square, the country consists of two principal parts: the Slavonian or Danubian plains of the north and east, through which the River Sava flows, and the extended Mediterranean coastal region of the Istrian peninsula and Dalmatia to the south-west and south-east. The hinterlands of this coastal region are the Dinaric Alps, which also extend into BiH. To the south-west of Zagreb, a narrow neck of territory connects the two elongated parts of the country.

Hemisphere
Northern

Climate
In northern Croatia, the climate is continental, on the Adriatic it is Mediterranean, while in the mountainous regions, it is alpine. The coastal hinterlands have a colder climate with heavy snow in winter, but they can be very hot in summer. Temperatures inland average around 10 degrees Celsius (C), while average temperatures on the coastal areas are around 15 degrees C. During the summer months, temperatures along the coast are often in excess of 30 degrees C. Precipitation is fairly constant country-wide throughout the year. The summer is the wettest season in the north, where the average annual rainfall in Zagreb is 890 millimetres. During the winter months, violent wind storms, known locally as the *Bora*, are common along the coast. A subsidiary sea of the Mediterranean, the Adriatic exercises a major influence on Croatia's climate, moderating the excesses of the continental climates of the north and east.

Dress codes
Business dress is formal, particularly in Zagreb.

Entry requirements
Passports
Required by all, except citizens of the EU, Switzerland, Norway and BiH who only need valid, official photographic identification.

Visa
Required by all, except nationals travelling as tourists from North America, Europe, Australasia, and some Asian countries, for stays of up to 90 days. Visitors are issued border passes on arrival, these must be kept until departure. For further details and exemptions see www.mfa.hr – visa requirements overview.
Nationals who do not require a tourist visa may visit for business purposes without a visa. All others business persons must apply for a business visa. Business visas require an official letter of invitation from a registered Croatian company or entity, on a formal declaration form that can be downloaded from www.hgk.hr. For further information contact the Croatian Chamber of Commerce e-mail: hgk@hgk.hr.

Currency advice/regulations
The import and export of local currency is limited to K15,000 in total, of which K500 is the maximum in banknotes. The import and export of foreign currency is unlimited. Amounts over K40,000 equivalent should be declared. Foreign currency can be exchanged in banks, by authorised dealers and post offices. Automated teller machines (ATMs) are common.
Travellers cheques in US dollars, pounds sterling or euros avoid extra exchange fees.

Customs
Goods for personal use up to the value of K300 can be imported free of duty.
Export of objects historic, cultural or scientific value must have a licence from the appropriate authorities.
A foreign national can be exempt from paying customs duties on equipment imported on the basis of a foreign investment contract. Appeals for exemption from duty should be submitted to the Ministry of Finance.

Prohibited imports
Illegal drugs. Firearms and ammunition must have the relevant Croatian permits.

Health (for visitors)
Nationals of the European Economic Area (EEA) countries and Switzerland can access reduced cost and sometimes free medical treatment using a European Health Insurance Card (EHIC) while visiting the EEA. Exceptions include nationals of the 10 countries which joined the EU in 2005 whose EHIC is not valid in Switzerland. Applications for the EHIC should be made before travelling.

Mandatory precautions
None

Credit cards
American Express, Diners' Club, Mastercard and Visa are accepted.

Public holidays (national)
Fixed dates
1 Jan (New Year's Day), 6 Jan (Epiphany), 1 May (Labour Day), 22 Jun (Anti-Fascism Day), *25 Jun (National Day), 5 Aug (Thanksgiving Day), 15 Aug (Assumption Day), *2 Oct (Independence Day), 1 Nov (All Saints' Day), 25–26 Dec (Christmas).
* Some companies allow an informal one-day holiday before or after a Sunday holiday.

Variable dates
Mar/Apr Easter Monday, Jun Corpus Cristi

Working hours
Banking
Mon–Fri: 0700–1900; Sat: 0700–1300.

Business
Mon–Fri: 0800–1600.

Government
Mon–Fri: 0830–1630.

Shops
Food shops: Mon–Fri: 0700–2000, Sat: 0700–1500.
Non-food shops: Mon–Fri: 0800–1200, 1700–2000; Sat: 0800–1500.

Telecommunications
Mobile/cell phones
There are GSM roaming facilities available in the 900 band width, the 1800 is planned. Coverage is virtually throughout the country.

Electricity supply
220V AC, 50 Hz

Weights and measures
Metric system

Social customs/useful tips
Although Croats are a rather gregarious people, there is a growing tendency to reserved formality in business contexts. The formality extends to the exchange of business cards that state professional and acedemic status.
On balance, foreigners should avoid informality with their business and other hosts and should observe western business standards. Foreigners are advised to avoid discussions of a political nature in Croatia.
Trade fairs are part of the regular business life in Croatia and are a useful way to meet potential partners and gain entry to the market. The principal venue is Zagreb, although Rijeka, Split and Osijek also host fairs.

Security
There is some street crime in Zagreb and other major cities.

Getting there
Air
National airline: Croatia Airlines
International airport/s: Zagreb-Pleso International Airport (ZAG), 17km from the

capital; business centre, bank, post office, restaurants, bars, duty-free shopping and car hire. Buses to the city run between 0700–2000. Taxis are available; travelling time 25 minutes.
Other airport/s: Dubrovnik International (DBV), 18km south-east of the city. Flights are inter-Euopean only. Facilites include money-changing offices, duty-free shopping, post office and car hire.
Airport tax: None

Surface

Croatia is included in the Pan-European Corridor 5 scheme. The project has some 3,270km of railways, linking Kiev in the Ukraine with western Europe via Italy, and 2,850 of new and upgraded roads.
Road: International buses connect Croatia with Austria, Italy, Hungary, France, Germany, Slovak Republic, Bosnia and Hercegovina.
Rail: There are international rail routes to Zagreb from Munich, Vienna, Venice, Budapest and Graz.
Water: Ferry services connect Rijeka and Pula with Durres and Vlora (Albania).

Getting about

National transport

Air: There are regular routes from Zagreb-Rijeka, Zagreb-Split and Zagreb-Ljubljana (Slovenia).
The main domestic airports are Rijeka (RJK), 25km from Rijeka and Split (SPU), 24km from Split.
Road: The government plans construction of 700km of new roads by 2011, making a total of 1,220km of highways and superhighways. The last 33km of the 380km Dalmatian Motorway, joining Zagreb and Split was opened on 26 June 2005.
Buses: Intercity bus services are available across the country.
Rail: Major rail links run from Zagreb to Rijeka and Varazdin.
Water: Split and Rijeka are connected by a daily sea-ferry service, but domestic sea connections with Dubrovnik are less frequent.

City transport

Taxis: Good taxi services operate in all main cities. All taxis are metered with a basic charge. A 10 per cent tip is usual.
Buses, trams & metro: Trams in Zagreb and Osijek only; buses in other cities and towns. Services are generally cheap and regular.

Car hire

A national driving licence is usually acceptable, although there have been instances where hire companies also requested an international driver's licence.
Traffic drives on the right. Speed limits are 130kph (81mph) on motorways, 100kph (62mph) on dual carriageways, 50kph (31mph) in built-up areas and 80kph (50mph) outside built-up areas. Right turns on red lights are strictly forbidden unless an additional green light (in the shape of an arrow) allows it. Right of way is always to the vehicle entering from the right.
Drink-driving is banned and subject to heavy penalties. The police also crack down on speeding and other road traffic offences. Croatia has a poor road safety record.

BUSINESS DIRECTORY

The addresses listed below are a selection only. While World of Information makes every endeavour to check these addresses, we cannot guarantee that changes have not been made, especially to telephone numbers and area codes. We would welcome any corrections.

Telephone area codes

The international direct dialling code (IDD) for Croatia is +385, followed by area code and subscriber's number:

Zagreb	1	Split	21
Dubrovnik	20	Rijeka	51

Useful telephone numbers

Emergency road help and information (Croatian Automobile Association (HAK), English speakers): 987
Police:92
Ambulance:94

Chambers of Commerce

American Chamber of Commerce in Croatia, 1 Krsnjavoga, 10000 Zagreb (tel: 483-6777; fax: 483-6776; e-mail: info@amcham.hr).

Croatian Chamber of Economy, 2 Rooseveltov trg, PO Box 630, 10000 Zagreb (tel: 456-1555; fax: 482-8380; e-mail: hgk@hgk.hr).

Dubrovnik County Chamber, 6 Pera Cingrije, 20000 Dubrovnik (tel: 411-376; fax: 412-044; e-mail: hgkdu@hgk.hr).

Rijeka County Chamber, 23 Bulevar Oslobodjenja, 51000 Rijeka (tel: 209-111; fax: 216-033; e-mail: hgkri@hgk.hr).

Split County Chamber, 4 Obala A Trumbica, 21000 Split (tel: 321-100; fax: 346-956; e-mail: hgkst@hgk.hr).

Zagreb County Chamber, 45 Draskoviceva, 10000 Zagreb (tel: 460-6777; fax: 460-6803; e-mail: hgkzg@hgk.hr).

Banking

Croatian Bank for Reconstruction and Development, Trg J J Strossmayera 9, 10 000 Zagreb (tel: 459-1620; fax: 459-1721).

Privredna Banka Zagreb, Corporate Finance Division, Capital Markets, Rackoga 6, Zagreb (tel: 472-3124; e-mail: capital.markets@pbz.hr; internet site: http://www.pbz.hr).

Central bank

Hrvatska Narodna Banka (Croatian National Bank), PO Box 603, Trg hrvatskih velikana 3, Zagreb 10002 (tel: 456-4555; fax: 461-0551; e-mail: info@hnb.hr).

Stock exchange

Zagrebacka Burza (Zagreb Stock Exchange), www.zse.hr

Travel information

Croatian Chamber of the Economy, Director of Tourism, Rosseveltov Trg 2, 10000 Zagreb (tel: 456-1570; fax: 448-618).

Croatia Airlines, Savska 4A, 41000 Zagreb (tel: 616-0066; fax: 530-475).

Croatian Railways (HZ-Hrvatske Zeljeznice), Mihanoviceva 12, Zagreb (fax: 457-7597).

Tourist Community of Zagreb, Kaptol 5, 41000 Zagreb (tel: 426-411; fax: 272-628).

Tourist Information Centre, Trg bana Jelacicá 11, 41000 Zagreb (tel: 278-855; fax: 274-083).

Ministry of tourism

Ministry of Tourism, International Relations Department, Ulica grada Vukovara 78, 10000 Zagreb (tel: 610-6300; fax: 610-9300).

National tourist organisation offices

Hrvatska Turisticka Zajednica (Croatian Tourist Board), Gunduliceva 3, 41000 Zagreb (tel: 424-637, 431-015; fax: 428-674).

Ministries

Government of the Republic of Croatia, Trg Svetog Marka 2, 10000 Zagreb (tel: 456—9222; fax: 630-3023).

Ministry of Administration, Republike Austrije 16, Zagreb 10000 (tel: 378-2111; fax: 378-2192).

Ministry of Agriculture and Forestry, Ulica grada Vukovara 78, 10000 Zagreb (tel: 610-6111; fax: 610-9200).

Ministry of Culture, Trg Burze 6, 1 000 Zagreb (tel: 461-0477, 456-9022; fax: 461-0489).

Ministry of Defence, Trg Kralja Petra Kresimira 4 br 1, 10000 Zagreb (tel: 456-7111; fax: 455-1105).

Ministry of Development and Reconstruction, Nazorova 61, 10000 Zagreb (tel: 378-4500; fax: 378-4551).

Ministry of Economic Affairs, Ulica grada Vukovara 78, 10000 Zagreb (tel: 610-6111; fax: 610-9120).

Ministry of Education and Sports, Trg Burze 6, 10000 Zagreb (tel: 456-9000; fax: 456-9087).

Ministry of Environmental Protection and Zoning, Ul Republike Austrije 20, 10000 Zagreb (tel: 378-2444; fax: 377-2822).

Ministry of European Integration, Ul grada Vukovara 62, 10000 Zagreb (tel: 456-9335, 456-9336; fax: 469-8310).

Ministry of Finance, Kataneiaeva 5, 10000 Zagreb (tel: 459-1333; fax: 492-2583).

Ministry of Foreign Affairs, Trg Nikole Subica Zrinskog 7–8, 10000 Zagreb (tel: 456-9964; fax: 456-9988, 455-1795; internet: www.mfa.hr).

Ministry of Health, Ulica baruna Trenka 6, 10000 Zagreb (tel: 459-1333, 460-7555; fax: 467-7076).

Ministry of Homeland War Veterans, Park Stara Tresnjevka 4, 10000 Zagreb (tel: 365-7888; fax: 365-7852).

Ministry of Immigration, Savska cesta 41/12, 10000 Zagreb (tel: 617-6011; fax: 617-6161).

Ministry of Internal Affairs, Savska 39, 10000 Zagreb (tel: 612-2111; fax: 612-2036, 612-2452).

Ministry of Justice, Administration and Local Self-Government, Ul Republike Austrije 14, 10000 Zagreb (tel: 371-0666; fax: 371-0772).

Ministry of Labour and Social Care, Prisavlje 14, 10000 Zagreb (tel: 616-9111; fax: 616-9200).

Ministry of Maritime Affairs, Transportation and Communication, Prisavlje 14, 10000 Zagreb (tel: 616-9111; fax: 615-6292, 619-6473).

Ministry of Physical Planning, Building Construction and Housing, Ulica Republike Austrije 20, Zagreb (tel: 378-2444; fax: 377-2555).

Ministry of Privatisation and Property Management, Gajeva 30a, 10 000 Zagreb (tel: 456-9103; fax: 456-9133).

Ministry of Public Works, Reconstruction and Construction, Ul Vladimira Nazora 61, 10000 Zagreb (tel: 378-4500; fax: 378-4598).

Ministry of Science and Technology, Trg J J Strossmayera 4, 10000 Zagreb (tel: 459-4444; fax: 459-4469; e-mail: office@science.hr; internet site: www.mzt.hr).

Ministry of Trades and Small and Medium Businesses, Ksaver 200, 10000 Zagreb (tel: 469-8300; fax: 469-8310).

Parliament of the Republic of Croatia, Trg Sv Marka 6 i 7, 10000 Zagreb (tel: 456-9222; fax: 492-0384).

Other useful addresses

Association of Croatian Hoteliers, Hotel Kvarner, Park 1 maja 4, 51410 Opatija (tel: 711-415; fax: 711-415).

British Embassy, Commercial Section, Vlaska 121 (3rd Floor), PO Box 454, 10000 Zagreb (tel: 455-5310; fax: 455-1685; email: commercial.section@zg.htnet.hr).

Croatian Parliament, Trg SV, Marka 6, 10000 Zagreb (tel: 456-9222, 630-3222; fax: 630-3018; email: sabor@sabor.hr).

Croatian Embassy (USA), 2343 Massachusetts Avenue, NW, Washington DC 20008 (tel: (+1-202) 588-5899; fax: (+1-202) 588-8936; e-mail: webmaster@croatiaemb.org).

Croatian Guarantee Agency, Ilica 49, 10000 Zagreb (tel: 484-6622; fax: 484-6612).

Croatian Investment Promotion agency, World Trade Centre Building, Avenija Dubrovnik 15, 10000 Zagreb (tel: 655-4558; fax; 655-4563).

Croatian Privatisation Fund, Lueiaeeva 6, 10000 Zagreb (tel: 456-9119, 459-6377; fax: 456-9140, 611-5568; e-mail: croatia.eoi@hfp.hr; internet site: www.hfp.hr).

Croatian Securities Exchange Commission, Bogovieeva 3, 10000 Zagreb (tel: 481-1407; fax: 481-1507).

Croatian Shipbuilding Co Ltd (Hrvatska brodogradnja-Jadranbrod), Av V Holjevca 20, 10020 Zagreb (fax: 652-8420).

Economic Development Corporations – see Ministry of Development and Reconstruction.

Information Department, Ilica 1a, 10000 Zagreb (tel: 455-6455; fax: 455-7827; internet site: www.hic.hr/english/index.htm).

Luka Ploce (second largest Croatian Port), Trg Kralja Tomislava 21, 20340 Ploce (tel: 067-9601; fax: 067-9836; email: luka-ploce@du.tel.hr).

State Agency for Deposit Insurance and Bank Rehabilitation, Jurisiceva 1, 10000 Zagreb (fax: 481-3222: fax: 481-1907; e-mail: dragbank@zg.tel.hr).

State Bureau of Standards and Measures, Ul grada Vukovara 78, 10000 Zagreb (tel: 610-6111; 610-9324; e-mail: pisarnica@dznm.hr).

State Bureau of Statistics, Ilica 3, 10000 Zagreb (tel: 480-6111; fax: 481-7666; e-mail: ured@agram.dzs.hr).

Zagrebacki Velesajem (Zagreb fairs, exhibitions and conferences), Dubrovacka Avenija 2, Zagreb (fax: 520-6430).

Zagreb Stock Exchange, Ksaver 208, 41000 Zagreb (tel: 455-1866; fax: 455-1118; internet site: www.zse.hr).

HIC (Croatian Information Centre): www.hic.hr

Hina (Croatian News Agency): http://websrv2.hina.hr

Internet sites

Croatia homepage: www.hr/english

Croatian Business Pages: www.hrvatska.com

Croatian Government: www.vlada.hr/english/contents.html

HINA, Croatian News Agency: www.hina.hr/nws-bin/ehot.cgi

Croatian Heritage Foundation: www.matis.hr/english/index.php

Hrvatska Radio Televizija: www.hrt.hr

Hrvatski Telekom: www.ht.hr

Cuba

KEY FACTS

Official name: República de Cuba (Republic of Cuba)

Head of State: President of the Council of State Raul Castro Ruz (since 24 Feb 2008, re-elected Feb 2013)

Head of government: President of the Council of State Raul Castro (since 24 Feb 2008, re-elected Feb 2013)

Ruling party: Partido Comunista de Cuba (PCC) (Cuban Communist Party)

Area: 110,860 square km

Population: 11.08 million (2011)*

Capital: Havana

Official language: Spanish

Currency: Cuban Convertible peso and Cuban peso (Cu$) (CUC) both = 100 centavos (NB From 2004, the US dollar was only to be used to convert to CUC)

Exchange rate: CUC1.00 per US$ (Sep 2015)

GDP per capita: US$5,410 (2011)*

GDP real growth: 2.70% (2011)*

GDP: US$60.80 billion (2011)*

Unemployment: 1.60% (2009)

Inflation: 4.70% (2011)*

* estimated figure

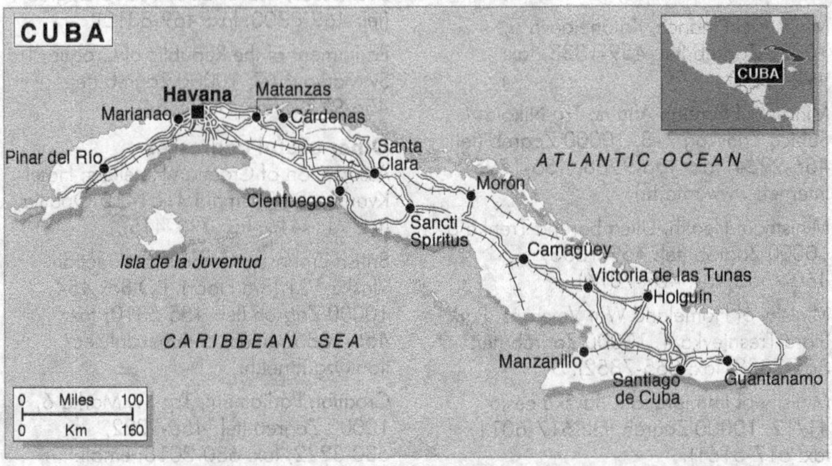

In the heyday of the Cuban revolution, Fidel Castro once famously remarked that if the United States of America did not like having a communist country only 90 miles from its shore, 'They could move.' (*Que se muden*). Times change – and so it was with a handshake and an hour's conversation there ended, in mid-April 2015, one of the world's strangest 'non-relationships' of the previous half century. The first meeting of Cuba's Head of State, Raúl Castro with his US counterpart, Barak Obama, saw Cuba welcome as 'fair' a US decision to remove it from a list of state sponsors of terrorism, by saying it should never have been on the list in the first place.

Thanks for the memory

President Raúl Castro (Fidel's brother) and his government colleagues were certainly not prone to dismiss the past easily. In his speech at the Panama summit of the Organisation of American States (OAS), Raúl Castro launched into a long list of grievances, recounting several attempts by the US to overthrow and destabilise the Communist government in Cuba. An additional statement by Josefina Vidal, Cuba's senior diplomat responsible for handling US affairs said that: 'The Cuban government recognised the fair decision made by the president of the United States to eliminate Cuba from a list that it never should have been included on, especially considering our country has been the victim of hundreds of acts of terrorism that have cost 3,478 lives and maimed 2,099 citizens. Cuba had first been placed on the state department list for what the US called efforts 'to promote armed revolution by organisations that used terrorism'. The US believed that Cuba had for some time provided a safe haven for members of the Basque separatist group ETA and for Colombia's Farc guerrilla group, according to the 2013 *Report on Terrorism*. Not long before their meeting, Raúl Castro had strongly criticised President Obama for declaring Cuba's ailing ally Venezuela, to be a threat to national security.

None the less, at the end of May 2015 Cuba's name had finally been removed from the list on which it had featured since 1982. The State Department spokesman, Jeff Rathke stated that the decision was: 'a reflection of our evaluation that Cuba fulfils the legal criteria for this reassessment. In Miami's 'Little Havana', the heartland of Cuban exiles, the decision was greeted less warmly, described as 'Illogical', 'painful' and 'distressing'. The fervently anti-Castro John Boehner, Speaker in the House of Representatives, claimed that President Obama 'had granted the Castro regime an important political victory in return for nothing.'

The announcement in June 2015 that each country was to re-open its embassy was at first calmly noted rather than frenziedly welcomed. In terms of public fervour, it ranked level with the June 2015 reappearance of 78 year old Fidel Castro in public. Improbably enough, this was at a meeting of Cuban cheesemakers, whom Castro addressed for no less than 4 hours. Where Castro had his innocuous cheesemakers, the Washington administration had a tougher bunch to win over, its Cuban exiles. This community, for the most part based in Florida, had for fifty years exerted a powerful conservative force on US politics, not only in its home state, but occasionally on the whole nation. In 2000 the presidential election outcome – in favour of George Bush – was probably decided by Florida's largely Republican (Cuban exiles) voters.

Embassy milestones

In mid-July 2015 the next visible sign of the 'Cuban thaw' appeared, when the two countries re-opened their embassies after a gap of over half a century. The US Secretary of State John Kerry welcomed what he called a 'new beginning' following the relatively low key ceremony marking the Washington embassy's reopening. The Cuban flag flew in the US capital for the first time in 54 years – a symbolic milestone as the two former Cold War foes began to rebuild diplomatic ties. The next – possibly the most emotive – sign of the rapprochement was the opening of the US embassy in Havana, a ceremony attended by Mr Kerry. The Secretary of State had hosted Cuban Foreign Minister Bruno Rodriguez – a Cuban minister's first official visit to Washington since the 1959 Cuban Revolution. At the Washington ceremony, Mr Kerry had noted that 'Today, with the opening of our embassies and the visit of the foreign minister, we are taking an historic and long overdue step in the right direction,' adding that the business of fully restoring relations would be 'Long and complex.'

Guantánamo

One issue which remained unresolved in mid-2015 was the future of the US military base in Guantánamo Bay, Cuba, which at the Washington embassy ceremony, the Cuban foreign minister had highlighted in his remarks. The relevance, symbolism and importance of the 1959 Cuban Revolution had always been greater for the United States than for the countries of Latin America. Cuban efforts to 'export' the revolution southwards had failed hopelessly. The trade embargo imposed on Cuba under President Eisenhower had certainly affected Cuba, but possibly not so much as its alignment with the (then) Soviet Union (USSR) headed by Russia.

In 2015 it was only the history books that remembered that towards the end of his second term as President, in 1809 Thomas Jefferson had offered to buy the entire island from the Spanish. This followed lengthy consideration by the US of annexing Cuba for commercial, political and strategic reasons. In 1805 Jefferson had sent secret agents to Cuba to negotiate with the Spanish Governor Someruelos.

Following the catastrophic defeat of Spain by the US in 1898, the island became a *de facto* colony, playground and criminal hideaway for the US. Following the 1959 revolution, the Guantánamo base became an anachronistic symbol of the relationship between the two countries. Under the terms of the lease, the US would have the use of 116 square kilometres paid for by a rental fee of US$4,085 per month – which the Cuban government had never deigned to collect. In the 2015 rapprochement, the future of Guantánamo was specifically referred to by Cuba's foreign minister following the independence ceremony and anticipating his meeting with Secretary of State Kerry. Mr Rodriguez bluntly stated that 'The historic events we are living today will only make sense with the removal of the economic, commercial and financial blockade, which causes so much deprivation and damage to our people, the return of occupied territory in Guantánamo and respect for the sovereignty of Cuba.'

Guantánamo had been leased in perpetuity to the US under a 1901 agreement imposed while Cuba was still under US military occupation. Later, the Platt amendment set out conditions for a withdrawal of US troops, but gave Washington the right to intervene in Cuba whenever it felt its interests to be threatened. In 2015, over a century later, the agreement limped on. But since 2002, thanks to the Bush administration, the name had become synonymous with illegal detention and torture, the measures taken against those suspected of Islamist activities.

The US base is an island within an island. The 28 kilometre long frontier is maintained by a three metre high fence and closely patrolled. Amazingly, apart from the two or three Cuban asylum seekers who manage to swim in each month there has not been a Cuban-US incident. Guantánamo has been an exemplary military co-operation between enemies. The US commander has a monthly meeting with his Cuban frontier commander counterpart and since 2008 the two sides have held joint emergency exercises. In April 2015, the base's spokeswoman, Kelly Wirfel told visiting journalists that 'Nothing has changed for us.' In the negotiations between Cuba and the US, in mid-2015 it appeared that Guantánamo had not been on the agenda. The Cuban government continued to insist on the territory's return, but the US side had simply put it to one side.

Political support

Despite the fierce opposition from the embargo supporters in the US Congress, a growing Republican-Democrat grouping in both Congress and the Senate had pronounced in favour of the restoration of relations and had formulated draft legislation covering the ban on travel to Cuba, increased trade and investment in Cuba's telecommunication companies. However, there remained those Republicans – among them two of the republican presidential candidates, Senators Marco Rubio and Ted Cruz (both Cuban Americans), who agreed with Mr Boehner that President Obama had conceded too much. In fact, however symbolic the opening of embassies, the changes agreed upon had been incremental rather than sweeping. Writing in the *New York Times*, the former US Secretary of Commerce in the Bush Administration, Carlos M Gutiérrez noted that 'Contrary to popular belief, President Obama's executive actions do not allow for free and open commerce with Cuba, nor do they open the doors for Americans to visit the island as tourists… the embargo prohibits most American companies from undertaking transactions with Cuba and travel remains restricted. Rather, the reforms have allowed some American companies and individuals to engage in limited additional activities in Cuba.'

Banking

One such 'additional activity' began when the Stonegate Bank of Florida signed the first agreement between a US banking enterprise and a Cuban counterpart in July 2015. The correspondent banking agreement was signed with the Banco Internacional de Comercio (BICSA) one day after the establishment of diplomatic representation.

Once up and running, the banking agreement would enable payments to be effected between each bank and its branches. Announcing the agreement, the President of the Stonegate Bank, David Seleski, added that the ability to manage payments and other transactions directly between the two countries would facilitate trade and benefit those US companies anxious to do business with Cuba. In reality, the agreement did nothing more than place the incipient commercial relations between the two countries on a par with those that had long existed between Canada and most of Europe with Cuba. The Stonegate Bank has 21 branches in Florida where many of the companies eventually hoping to do business with Cuba are located.

The economy

According to the United Nations Economic Commission for Latin America and the Caribbean (ECLAC) Cuba's gross domestic product (GDP) grew by 1.3 per cent in 2014 (compared to 2.7 per cent in 2013). While the agricultural and construction sectors continued to do well, activity in manufacturing (except for the sugar industry) and mining and quarrying was down. Nickel production declined, owing in part to maintenance work on the Che Guevara plant. The sugar industry grew less than the government had planned, because of low yields, bad weather and logistical issues. The lack of financing for the necessary investments in technology upgrades – and the economic, financial and trade embargo, still in place in spite of the recent announcement restoring diplomatic relations between the United States and Cuba – exacerbated the external constraints on expansion and acted as structural factors that kept the Cuban economy from reaching its growth potential. ECLAC noted that in the second half of 2014 the new Foreign Investment Act came into force. In order to attract foreign capital, the act made a portfolio of 246 investment projects amounting to US$8.700 billion available to foreign investors. In keeping with the economic and social policy guidelines aimed at increasing the non-State owned sector's share of total employment, 314 non-farm co-operatives were operating in September 2014. Most of them were concentrated in the commerce, hotel and restaurant sectors and in the repair of personal effects. Non-state sector jobs account for 26 per cent of total employment. The process of rationalising public expenditure, supporting enterprise capitalisation and separating business-related and state-related functions within ministries continued.

The draft budget for 2014 had been, according to ECLAC, based on GDP growth of 2.2 per cent and a fiscal deficit of 4.7 per cent of GDP, 70 per cent funded by secondary issues and 30 per cent funded by primary issues (both in 2.5 per cent 20-year bonds) purchased by commercial banks and the central bank, respectively. Slower economic growth brought revenue shortfalls and non-execution of some expenses, leading to an estimated fiscal deficit of around 3 per cent of GDP in 2014. Budget priorities included supporting agricultural activity (including the sugar sector) and cutting back the spending earmarked for budgetary units.

As a result, the subsidy to ensure local availability of food (rice, beans, pork, milk and sugar, among others) increased by 24.6 per cent between 2013 and 2014. Meanwhile, spending on budgetary units decreased by 1.6 per cent compared with the figure for 2013, although it might be somewhat higher due to pay rises in the public health sector. The decentralisation process seeking financial autonomy for Cuba's local governments continued. To this end, in 2015 the property tax for local development began to apply to all Cuba's municipalities (in 2014 it had only applied to three). ECLAC expected the self-employment tax and the tax on non-agricultural co-operatives to increase in 2015, to 11 per cent of gross income.

Following the October 2013 announcement of currency unification, the composition of individual savings had been shifting from convertible pesos (CUC) to Cuban pesos (CUP). One of the government's monetary policy objectives was to increase participation in the formal banking system. The number of current accounts increased in both CUC and CUP because own-account worker and non-farm co-operative accounts operated with cheques and cards. At the end of September 2014, 378,011 loans amounting to 3.231 billion pesos had been granted; 63 per cent of these loans were for housing construction work.

In October 2014, Cuba acquired a degree of financial respectability when the International Financial Action Task Force announced that the country was no longer subject to its monitoring process. This was in recognition of the country's efforts to prevent money laundering and terrorist financing. External debt servicing and the fact that Cuba was not a member of international financial institutions had held its current account balance to GDP ratio at about one per cent in recent years. In addition, tourist arrivals were dynamic, posting a growth rate of 5.3 per cent in 2014. Exports of medical and biotechnological services continued to grow (in 2014 revenue from services was expected to total about US$12.000 billion) and progress continued to be made in diversifying destination markets. Exports of goods were set to reach US$5.500 billion. Food imports, which accounted for about 20 per cent of total imports, stood at US$2.057 billion.

ECLAC noted that in 2014 Cuba continued to look for a realistic solution for its external obligations to its creditors and managed to restructure its short-term debt with the Netherlands insurer Atradius, some Japanese companies and other trade creditors. This was a continuation of restructuring efforts in previous years involving cross-obligations with the Russian Federation, official short-term secured debt with Japan and private entrepreneurs, as well as with Mexico (which pardoned a substantial portion) and China (Cuba's second-ranking trading partner and its main source of funding). Negotiations for an agreement on short-term secured debt with other European insurers were thought to be nearing completion.

Growth in the agricultural sector (which employs about 20 per cent of the population) and construction was not enough to offset declines in manufacturing, quarrying and mining activity. While investment continued to show positive growth rates, its share of GDP was still low (14 per cent). The agricultural sector received special attention, for reasons of food security and import substitution. In 2014 more than US$2.000 billion dollars was spent on importing food. According to official figures, in the first half of the year the agricultural production volume index (which excluded sugar cane and small home and lot gardens) was 17.6 per cent higher than in the same period in 2013. Crops such as corn, beans, rice, meats, vegetables and tubers and roots were up by between 15 per cent and 17 per cent. Milk production held steady, but production of tomatoes, onions, peppers and citrus declined – onions and tomatoes by more than 10 per cent in the first half of the year. Agricultural sector growth during the second half of the year was not as robust as in the first half, because the planting season began in September.

Cuba's unemployment rate is set to remain between 3.3 per cent and 3.5 per cent for 2014 (in 2013 it was 3.3 per cent). The number of own-account workers continued to rise and totalled 476,197 at the end of September 2014 (50,000 more than in 2013). Prices were rising as subsidised items are removed from the ration book system, triggering adjustments in supply and demand (especially for agricultural products). Prices were expected to stabilise in the short term, so inflation was forecast to be close to 3 per cent at the end of 2014.

Risk assessment

Economy	Poor
Politics	Poor
Regional stability	Good

COUNTRY PROFILE

1492 Christopher Columbus landed in Cuba and claimed the island for Spain.
1511 Diego Columbus, son of Christopher, settled the island. Spanish settlers established sugar plantations and exploited slaves from West Africa.
1514 The city of Havana was founded.
1607 Havana was named the capital of Cuba.
1762–64 Havana was captured by the British but was returned to Spain under the Treaty of Paris.
1868–78 The first war of independence ended in a truce after Spain promised reforms and greater autonomy – which were never fulfilled.
1886 Slavery was abolished.
1895–98 José Martí led a second war of independence; the US declared war on Spain.
1898 Spain was defeated and gave up all claims to Cuba, ceding it to the US.
1901 The constitution of the Republic of Cuba, modelled on the US constitution, was adopted.
1902 Cuba was officially granted independence from the US. Tomas Estrada Palma became its first president. However the US retained the right to intervene in Cuban domestic affairs.
1925 The Partido Comunista de Cuba (PCC) (Cuban Communist Party) was founded.
1933 Fulgencio Batista took power in a *coup d'état*.
1934 The US abandoned its right to intervene in Cuban internal affairs.
1940 A new constitution was promulgated.
1944 Batista retired from office.
1952 Batista seized power again, backed by the US government. His regime was oppressive and corrupt.
1953 On 26 July Fidel and Raul Castro lead an attack on the Moncada barracks. This is reckoned to be the first battle of the Cuban revolution
1956 Fidel Castro began a guerrilla war against Batista's dictatorship.
1958 US backing for Batista was withdrawn.
1959 The Cuban revolution concluded when Castro's revolutionaries defeated the Cuban army and assumed power, founding a socialist state.
1960 All US owned businesses in Cuba were nationalised without compensation; the US broke off diplomatic relations.
1961 The US sponsored an unsuccessful military invasion, by Cuban exiles, at the Bay of Pigs. Cuba was declared a Communist state and Castro allied it to the USSR.
1962 Castro's fear of US aggression resulted in the Cuban missile crisis when he agreed to deploy USSR nuclear missiles on Cuba. The US blockaded Cuba, published evidence of the missiles and US President Kennedy gave an ultimatum that they be removed or the US would bomb Cuba. The crisis was resolved when the USSR agreed and withdrew the missiles, and in return the US closed its missile sites in Turkey. The US imposed a full trade embargo on Cuba and rationing was introduced on certain essentials.
1976 A new constitution created a National Assembly, which held its first session and elected Fidel Castro as president.
1982 Cuba was designated a state sponsor of terrorism by the United States. As a result restrictions are imposed on arms-related exports, dual-use exports, economic assistance and a number of financial restrictions.
1989 The USSR began to disintegrate and the trade in Cuban sugar for subsidised oil collapsed.
1991 Soviet troops left Cuba. The economy fell into depression.
1993 To ameliorate the economy some market reforms were adopted and the US dollar was made an official currency alongside the Cuban peso.
1998 US restrictions on remittances were eased.
2000 US approves the sale of food and medicines to Cuba.
2001 The first shipment in 40 years of US exported food arrived.
2002 The UN criticised Cuba for its poor civil rights. It was announced that at least 71 of Cuba's 156 sugar refineries were to be scrapped.
2003 A crackdown on dissidents resulted in international condemnation, as 75 people were imprisoned. The EU broke off diplomatic contacts.
2004 The official exchange rate of Cu$1 per US$ replaced the convertible rate of Cu$21 per US$. The US tightened restrictions on visits and money remittances to Cuba; the US dollar ceased to be legal tender and a 10 per cent commission for converting dollars to pesos was imposed.
2005 EU diplomatic relations with Cuba were re-established. President Hugo Chávez of Venezuela and Fidel Castro signed a co-operation agreement; Cuba supplied doctors and medical treatment to Venezuela in exchange for crude oil at a preferential price.
2006 The Non-Aligned Movement held its 14th meeting in Havana under Cuban chairmanship. Fidel Castro, amid rumours and speculation about his health, did not attend delayed celebrations of his 80th birthday or the 50th anniversary parade of his return to Cuba.
2007 A letter by Castro was read out on national television saying he would not hold on to power indefinitely.
2008 In parliamentary elections 614 candidates, including Fidel Castro, contested the 614 seats; turnout was 95 per cent. Fidel Castro announced he would not return to the presidency due to ill health. Raúl Castro was voted in unopposed as president. The Marxist ideologically driven system of equal pay for all was abandoned. The EU lifted sanctions imposed in 2003. Talks on mutual co-operation resumed between the European Commission and Cuba.
2009 The US Congress voted to remove restrictions on family members travelling to Cuba, once a year, and sending remittances; trade in medicines and food was also eased. Costa Rica opened an embassy in Havana. The Organisation of American States (OAS) voted to lift Cuba's suspension of its membership.
2010 Political prisoner Orlando Zapata Tamayo died after an 85-day hunger strike. Zapata was one of 75 dissidents jailed in 2003, and was serving a 25-year prison sentence for political activities against the regime. El Salvador, the last Central American nation withholding diplomatic relations, opened an embassy in Havana. For the first time since 2006, Fidel Castro publicly addressed the National Assembly, appearing fully recovered from his illness.
2011 In January, the US further eased travel restrictions, allowing religious groups and students to visit Cuba. It also allowed the payment of remittances of up to US$500 per quarter to non-family members for private economic activity, and greater amounts for religious institutions in Cuba. In 14 March, in an effort to stimulate the flagging economy by boosting exports and domestic production, the hard-currency convertible peso was devalued to match the US dollar, losing around 8 per cent in value. The devaluation increased the value of remittances from relatives in the US as well as the spending power of tourists. However, the convertible dollar remains worth 24 domestic pesos, so the cost of imports will rise for most Cubans. In April, during the first congress of the ruling PCC since 1997, President Raúl Castro said that top political jobs should be limited to two five-year terms in office and that the PCC leadership was in need of renewal and should be open to critical self-analysis. President

Castro was elected first secretary of the PCC. In April, the government announced that people would be allowed to buy and sell their homes for the first time since the communist revolution in 1959. The law was passed in November and included the selling of cars. In December, an amnesty released 2,500 prisoners, some political convicts, ahead of the planned papal visit.
2012 Pope Benedict XVI began a three-day visit to Cuba on 27 March. In a speech on 29 March he criticised the 50-year old US embargo imposed on Cuba, saying that the economic measures 'unfairly burden' the Cuban people. On 31 March, the government declared that Good Friday (central day of Christian Easter celebrations) would become a public holiday, following an appeal by Pope Benedict. In June import duties on food carried in by visitors was reintroduced, to curb resale in Cuba. On 6 July the Council of State announced that general elections would begin on 21 October. On 19 October, it was announced that the exit fee levied on Cubans travelling aboard will be removed on 14 January 2013. Hurricane Sandy, which struck the eastern province of Santiago on 25 October, caused extensive damage to buildings and the sugar cane crop in the region.
2013 On 4 Feb 86-year old Fidel Castro was shown on television voting in the parliamentary elections. Raúl Castro was re-elected president on 24 February. Five members of the powerful Central Committee were removed by President Castro on 2 July, including Ricardo Alarcón, a close ally of ex-leader Fidel Castro. President Castro pointed out that the moves were a normal course of events. In a speech celebrating the 26 July 1953 start of the revolution Raúl Castro said power in Cuba was being gradually transferred to a new generation who would keep socialist ideals alive. In a long article published in *Granma* the day after his 87th birthday on 13 August, Fidel Castro said that when he handed power to his brother in 2006 he had not expected to live another 7 years. In September the council of ministers approved measures to allow Cuban athletes to keep more of their overseas earnings. Cubans earning large salaries in the US will not benefit since US sanctions prevent funds being remitted to the Cuban government. On 9 October the Politburo replaced the editors of *Granma* and *Juventud Rebelde*. On 22 October *Granma* reported that the council of ministers had approved a timetable for implementing 'measures that will lead to monetary and exchange unification' between the lower-value CUP and the more valuable convertible peso (CUC) which is pegged to the US dollar. Reuters reported that the conversion could take 18 months.
2014 The Cuban parliament unanimously passed a new foreign investment law on 29 March. The new law was described as an important move towards building a prosperous and sustainable socialist system. Thomas Donohue, president of the Chamber of Commerce of the United States, visited Cuba in May. In a lecture given at the University of Havana he said that the moment had come for the two countries to move towards more normal relations. He also had a meeting with President Raúl Castro. In July the Russian State Duma (lower chamber of parliament) ratified an agreement to write off 90 per cent of Cuba's US$35. 2 billion debt to the former Soviet Union. The remaining US$3.52 will be repaid over 10 years, ending in October 2014. On 11 July Russian President Putin announced on a visit to Havana that Russia had plans to expand co-operation with Cuba through a number of projects in key areas such as energy and health. It was also reported by Russian business daily *Kommersant* that following Mr Putin's visit Russia's signals intelligence base in Lourdes, used mostly to spy on the US, would be reopened. However, within days ITAR-TASS reported that President Putin denied the report. In 17 December Cuba and the US announced a number of moves to improve relations between the two, including the release by Cuba of US contractor Alan Gross and three Cubans held in the US. The 'rigid and outdated policy' of isolating Cuba, in place since the time of President Kennedy, had clearly failed, said President Obama. Lifting the trade embargo, however, will have to be agreed by the US Congress. In early December Cuba was invited by the government of Panama to attend the Summit of the Americas in April 2015. This will be the first time Panama has attended the Summit, which is being hosted by Panama.
2015 The US government confirmed on 12 January that the 53 political prisoners to be released as a part of the deal signed in December had been released. Talks with the United States were held 21 and 22 January. The second round of talks towards restoring diplomatic relations between Cuba and the US began in late February. On 14 April President Obama submitted a statute to the US Congress indicating the administration's intent to rescind Cuba's designation as a state sponsor of terrorism. Mr Obama had instructed the Department of State to undertake a review of Cuba's designation as a state sponsor of terrorism in December 2014. Cuba had been designated a state sponsor of terrorism in 1982. Former president Fidel Castro exercised his right to vote in the municipal elections held on 20 April. On 15 April US President Obama shook hands with President Castro at a Summit of the Americas meeting in Panama. On 1 July Cuba and the US agreed in an exchange of letters to restore diplomatic relations on 20 July. The return the naval base at Guantanamo Bay, which the US has leased since 1903, as sovereign Cuban territory, and the lifting of the economic embargo remain the two major items to be agreed before normal relations can be fully resumed. On 21 July Cuba once again had an embassy in the US with the raising of the Cuban flag on their 16th Street building in Washington. On the same day the US embassy in Cuba opened in Havana. US President Obama met Raul Castro in New York on 29 September.

Political structure

Constitution

The 1979 constitution gives all legislative power to the Asamblea Nacional de Poder Popular (National Assembly of People's Power) which runs local and central government. An amendment in 2002 made the Partido Comunista de Cuba (PCC) (Cuban Communist Party) the permanent party of government.

Form of state

Socialist republic.

The executive

The president and the Consejo de Estado (Council of State) and council of ministers are appointed by the national assembly and drawn from the state (communist) party.
The council of state is the highest-ranking executive institution and is made up of a president, first vice president, and five vice presidents and 30 members. It has legislative powers when the national assembly is in recess. The council runs foreign trade and foreign relations, draws up the draft budget and is responsible for the general organisation of the revolutionary armed forces.

National legislature

The unicameral, Asamblea Nacional del Poder Popular (National Assembly of People's Power) has 609 members, elected for a five-year term from a closed list of PCC members. Its chief role is to approve laws put forward by the council of state. According to the constitution the national assembly is the 'supreme organ of state power and represents and expresses the sovereign will of all the working people'. Its role includes approving laws, discussing and approving the state budget and supervising other official bodies.

Legal system

While the constitution provides for independent courts it explicitly subordinates the courts to state control. The national assembly chooses all judges. The People's Supreme Court is the highest judicial body; it oversees a system of regional tribunals and is accountable to the national assembly.

Last elections

January 2013 (presidential, elected by national assembly); 4 February 2013 (parliamentary)

Results: Parliamentary: 612 pro-government candidates stood for exactly the same number of seats in the National Assembly and were elected unopposed. Voter turnout was 90.88 per cent.

Next elections

2018 (presidential, elected by national assembly); 2018 (parliamentary)

Political parties

Ruling party

Partido Comunista de Cuba (PCC) (Cuban Communist Party)

Main opposition party

There is no opposition party.

Population

11.08 million (2011)*

Last census: September 2002: 11,177,743

Population density: Population density: 102 inhabitants per square km. Urban population 75 per cent (2010 Unicef).

Annual growth rate: 0.3 per cent, 1990–2010 (Unicef).

Ethnic make-up

The Cuban population is a product of the mix of four cultural groups: the indigenous people, Spaniards, Africans and Asians.

Mulatto (51 per cent), white (37 per cent), black (11 per cent), Chinese (1 per cent).

Religions

Many Cubans are agnostic or atheist, while unofficial estimates are of 75,000–100,000 practising Catholics. There is a smaller Protestant community. Practices based on African religions are reported to be increasing in popularity.

Education

Public expenditure on education amounts to 8.7 per cent of GDP. There is sustained investment in education with incentive rewards for excellence in pupils, teachers and schools. The education system promotes inclusively for learning outcomes and curriculum development between teachers and students.

Education is free at all levels. It is based on the Communist principle of combining learning with manual labour. Day nurseries and pre-school centres are available to all children after just six weeks. Primary schools are compulsory for six years until aged 12. Secondary schools are for 13- to 18-year-olds. State subsidies are available for workers returning to education to complete university courses.

Literacy rate: 97 per cent adult rate; 100 per cent youth rate (15–24) (Unesco 2005).

Compulsory years: 6 to 12.

Enrolment rate: 106 per cent gross primary enrolment, of the relevant age group (including re-enrolment); 81 per cent gross secondary enrolment, of the relevant age group (World Bank).

Pupils per teacher: 12 in primary schools.

Health

There are approximately 260 hospitals and over 400 clinics that provide full and free medical services in all regions of the country. However, current US economic embargoes limit access to internationally purchased branded medical supplies.

In 2005 US$100 million was allocated to invest in the pharmaceutical industry. Generic medicines have become a major export item.

HIV/Aids

HIV prevalence: 0.1 per cent aged 15–49 in 2003 (World Bank)

Life expectancy: 77.6 years, 2004 (MEDICC 2007)

Fertility rate/Maternal mortality rate: 1.5 births per woman, 2010 (Unicef); maternal mortality 52.2 per 100,000 live births (MEDICC 2007).

Birth rate/Death rate: 10.7 births per 1,000 population; seven deaths per 1,000 population (2003).

Child (under 5 years) mortality rate (per 1,000): 6 per 1,000 live births (WHO 2012)

Head of population per physician: 6.2 physicians per 1,000 people (MEDICC 2007)

Welfare

In a 2005 economist reported to Castro that the minimum monthly income to survive in Cuba was Cu$300 (US$14.4). The minimum monthly wage was increased to Cu$225 (US$10.8), and monthly pension payments to CU$150 (US$7.2) benefiting 54 per cent of state employees. Wages in other sectors grew in line with these increases. Pensions and social assistance were also increased by 50 pesos a month.

The 1976 constitution guarantees all Cubans the right and duty to have a job, while the state provides basic support for the aged, the disabled and others unable to work. Although the principle of full employment stands unchanged, the government has admitted that unemployment does indeed exist.

Main cities

Havana (estimated population 2.1 million in 2012), Santiago de Cuba (444,383), Camagüey (315,386), Holguín (303,068), Santa Clara (219,660), Guantánamo (223,145), Las Tunas (171,957), Bayamo (167,073), Cienfuegos (164,924), Pinar del Río (154,107).

Languages spoken

The Spanish in use in Cuba is more Latin American than Castillian and many words are quite different from the Spanish used in Spain. Quite often the endings of words are dropped, shortened nouns are used and slang is prevalent. The further south in Cuba, the more pronounced the accent.

English is quite widely spoken, as it is the main foreign language taught in schools.

Official language/s

Spanish

Media

The constitution prohibits private ownership of electronic media and there are punitive laws which suppress journalists in a country where the media is tightly controlled and independent media and journalists are targeted for intimidation. The government strictly regulates Internet access.

Juventud Rebelde is Cuba's youth paper. The Cuban Communist party sees the media as an important tool for reinforcing socialist ideals within the scope of entertainment and education.

In December 2010 Cuba launched a Spanish language online encyclopaedia (www.ecured.cu) similar to Wikipedia. 'Its philosophy is the accumulation and development of knowledge, with a democratising, not profitable, objective, from a decoloniser point of view.'

Press

There are several news agencies publishing newspapers in six major languages.

Dailies: In Spanish, regional and local newspapers include *Cubahora* (www.cubahora.co.cu), *Periódico 26* (www.periodico26.cu) from Las Tunas, *Guerrillero* (www.guerrillero.co.cu) form Pinar del Rio, *Venceremos* (www.venceremos.co.cu) from Gauntanamo, with an English online edition, *Sierra Maestra* (www.sierramaestra.cu) from Santiago de Cuba, and *Vanguardia* (www.vanguardia.co.cu) from Villa Santa.

Weeklies: In Spanish, national publications include the government-run *Trabajadores* (www.trabajadores.cubaweb.cu), and Communist party-run *Granma* (www.granma.co.cu), *Cinco de Septiembre* (www.5septiembre.cu) from Cienfuegos, with an English online edition. Alternative magazines include *Bohemia* (www.bohemia.cubaweb.cu) an illustrated and *Dedete*

(www.dedete.cubaweb.cu) is a humorous publication.
Business: In Spanish, *El Economista de Cuba* (www.eleconomista.cubaweb.cu), *Opiones* (www.opciones.cu), a weekly publication by the tourist industry and *Negocios en Cuba* (www.prensa-latina.cu) published by Prensa Latina.

Broadcasting

Services controlled by the Ministerio de la Informática y las Comunicaciones (Ministry of Information and Communications).
Radio: There are over 40 radio stations throughout Cuba, most local and catering for their captive audiences. National transmissions run parallel to international services provided via satellite and the Internet. Radio Cubana (www.radiocubana.cu) (with access to local radio streaming), Radio Havana Cuba (www.radiohc.cu) and Radio Rebelde (www.radiorebelde.com.cu) are the principal organs of state for news and propaganda.
Television: The national, state-run Cubavisión (Sistema Informativo de la Televisión Cubana), (www.cubavision.cubaweb.cu) shows domestic programmes ranging from soap operas to university education and a wide range of imported material. There is also an international channel, Cubavision Internaciónal via satellite.
Cuba also joined Venezuela, Argentina and Uruguay – and later Bolivia, Ecuador and Nicaragua – to form a pan-American public news channel, Telsur (www.telesurtv.net) to broadcast programmes to offset what they saw as the overwhelming influence of popular, privately-run channels such as the US-run CNN en Español.
The only officially approved domestic satellite TV service is available to resident foreigners, tourist and approved Communist party officials. Illegal satellite provisions, using the US-based, anti-Castro TV Marti, have resulted in criminal convictions.
National news agency: Agencia de Información Nacional (Cuban News Agency)
Other news agencies: Prensa Latina: www.plenglish.com.mx

Economy

Although 95 per cent of the economy is state-controlled, it is diverse and includes primary industries, such as agriculture and mining, secondary industries such as pharmaceuticals, and the famous cigar manufacturing (in 2013 international sales of cigars rose eight per cent to US$447 million) and tertiary industries such as healthcare and tourism. The US embargo on the Cuban economy since the 1950s has been both a constraint, by limiting growth and innovation, and a spur to seek out alternative markets, technologies and inventiveness. Cuba has managed to survive with a 'make-do and mend' regime during the economic siege.
More normal diplomatic relations between the United States and Cuba were announced in 2014. Fewer restrictions will be in place on travel, business and banking on the island. Cuba's famous export of cigars still faces obstacles in increasing its share of the market within the U.S; removing the embargo on Cuban imports would require an act of congress.
The economic landscape has undergone a sharp change since 2008 when three hurricanes caused over US$10 billion of damage. A recovery began in 2010, with growth of 2.4 per cent rising to 2.8 per cent in 2011. Growth reached 3.0 per cent in 2012 before dropping down to an estimated 2.7 per cent in 2013 and 1.3 per cent in 2014.
While the economy did not fall into recession, Cuba is faced with more hurdles to recovery than experienced generally by other trading nations. The US is Cuba's biggest source of food and although food is not part of the long-standing embargo, the US requires that all imports be paid for before delivery. Cuba's cash-flow problems forced it to cut its imports in 2009 by 26 per cent, as it was faced with unpaid debts to foreign creditors. Cuba looked to other sources, such as Vietnam, for cheaper food and better terms of business.
An embargo on remittances from Cuban exiles (mainly in Miami, USA), which were estimated to bring the island over US$1 billion a year, was lifted in March 2009. The Cuban authorities require that any such remittances are used in special dollar stores where commodities are priced at a higher mark-up than elsewhere.
There are two currencies in Cuba: all local people use the Cuban peso (Cu$) whilst international trade by foreign visitors is conducted through a convertible peso (CUC).
The government maintains the price of certain basics for its citizens but all products outside this system must be paid for in CUC, which has led to a flourishing black market, estimated to be as much as 40 per cent of the economy.
The Marxist ideologically driven system of equal pay for all was abandoned in 2008 when the government announced that workers and managers would begin to earn performance bonuses. Workers earn a minimum 5 per cent bonus if targets are met and managers can earn up to 30 per cent when increased production can be demonstrated. Self-employment figures rose from 157,000 in 2010 to 295,000 in 2011 and by May 2015 this figure had risen to 504,613.
In 2010 rationing of potatoes and tobacco was eliminated and subsidised worker's canteens were phased out in several ministries. Although there were plans in 2011, to remove comprehensive food rationing, in 2013 rice, chicken, sugar, milk, eggs, cooking oil were still included on a list of subsidised food.
Most Cubans depend on monthly rations of rice, beans, coffee and a few other staple foods for their sustenance. There is also a thriving black market for food, supplying the wealthy and the foreigners with gourmet items like blue cheese and smoked salmon smuggled in by suitcase.
The new relations with the U.S. may mean that changes will eventually occur in the food industry, however, huge numbers of issues are embedded in the complex trade relationship between the two countries. In April 2011, the government announced that it would allow people to buy and sell their homes for the first time since the communist revolution in 1959. A law was passed in November 2011, to allow the buying and selling of private property and cars.
According to the World Bank, Cuba is an upper-middle income country, based on social criteria of life expectancy and education as well as water and sanitation infrastructure. However, without a fully functioning commercial economy, with entrepreneurial businesses and a free labour market Cuba is still a hybrid society with benefits of one system outweighing what could be the benefits of another.
In March 2011, in an effort to stimulate the flagging economy by boosting exports and domestic production, the hard-currency convertible peso was devalued to match the US dollar, losing around 8 per cent in value. Not only did the devaluation increase the value of remittances from relatives in the US but it also gave an increase in spending power for tourists. However the convertible dollar was still worth 24 domestic pesos, so the cost of imports rose for most Cubans. On 22 October 2013 *Granma* reported that the council of ministers had approved a timetable for implementing 'measures that will lead to monetary and exchange unification' between the lower-value CUP and the more valuable CUC which is pegged to the US dollar. Reuters reported that the conversion could take 18 months.
The Cuban parliament unanimously passed a new foreign investment law on 29 March 2014. The new law offers guarantees to investors, including the free transfer abroad of profits in convertible currency, exemption from taxes on income from net profits and other benefits authorised for reinvestment.

In July 2014 the Russian State Duma (lower chamber of parliament) ratified an agreement to write off 90 per cent of Cuba's US$35. 2 billion debt to the former Soviet Union. The remaining US$3.52 will be repaid over 10 years, ending in October 2014.

External trade

The balance of payments is reliant on foreign currency earnings from tourism, remittances, nickel and cobalt. Sugar has fallen in importance as an export commodity and nickel and cobalt has expanded to take advantage of increasing world prices.

The US trade embargo continues to have a negative effect on trade, although Venezuela has been supporting Cuba with preferential oil imports in exchange for Cuban goods and services (as part of PetroCaribe). China and Russia have both entered agreements for investment in Cuba.

Cuba has a trade co-operation protocol with the 15-member Caribbean Community (Caricom).

Imports

Domestic companies require a licence to import certain goods, and the withdrawal of these licences a means for the government to control imports and its trade deficit, although the mechanism is regarded as heavy-handed.

Imports comprise petroleum, machinery and equipment, food, chemicals.

Main sources: Venezuela (36.8 per cent of total in 2013 (latest available figures in 2015)), China (12 per cent), Spain (9.2 per cent)

Exports

Principal exports include, nickel, cobalt, sugar tobacco, fish, bio-technical medical products, citrus and coffee. Healthcare professionals are hired as a team to visit overseas countries (typically in South America and the Caribbean) to treat patients chosen by the host government.

Main destinations: Canada (16.4 per cent of total in 2013 (latest available figures in 2015)), China (15.6 per cent), Venezuela (14.5 per cent)

Agriculture

Farming

In 2013 agriculture contributed 3.8 per cent of GDP and employed around 18 per cent of the population.

Sugar is Cuba's most important export crop, however since its collapse as a top cash crop, there has been a concerted effort to diversify. The sugar industry has undergone restructuring to make the production more efficient and identify new markets. Over 70 of the 156 sugar refineries in Cuba have been decommissioned with some 100,000 workers laid off. Half of Cuba's 3.5 million hectares (ha) of sugar cane fields have been re-utilised to produce other crops, particularly foodstuffs for domestic consumption and reduce the need for imports.

Two new cocoa processing plants with a capacity of 45,000 tonnes are planned to provide exports of high quality cocoa butter.

Approximately 95 per cent of Cuba's coffee plantations are the highly prized arabica bean. Coffee exports should be enhanced by the refurbishment of seven processing mills. The international cost of coffee rose by 69 per cent 2010–11 and forced the authorities to reintroduce the practice of mixing roast peas with roast beans for sale and local consumption. In 2010 domestic consumption of coffee was 18,000 tonnes (t), whereas production was only 12,000t and imports costs rose to US$50 million. Since then the cost of Arabica coffee has fallen from a peak of US$6.617 per kilogram in 2011 to US$3.405 per kilogram in 2014.

Cuba has begun developing organic farming, and there are over 100,000 small-to medium-sized organic farms reflecting the government's commitment to the 'greening of Cuba'.

In November 2011, the government relaxed its rules allowing farmers to sell their produce directly to hotels, restaurants and the public and to make a profit. The new rules led to the cutting out of official middlemen, transportation costs and improve productivity.

However, agriculture in Cuba remains in crisis. The Cuban agricultural sector remains highly de-capitalised. Although the reform in agriculture has gone further than in many other sections of economic life, it may still be too early to gauge the effects.

Fishing

Catches have fallen since the mid-1980s. The contraction of finfish catches by the deep-sea fleet, partly as a result of changes in fishing agreements, has been largely responsible. Cuba is investing considerable resources in shrimp farming, but production has not been commercially significant.

Forestry

Forests cover around 2.3 million hectares (ha), around 15 per cent of the total land area. Since 1990 forest cover has increased by an average of 1.27 per cent per annum or 28,000ha. In 2012 the government announced plans to increase the forest cover to 29.3 per cent of the total land area by 2015.

Industry and manufacturing

Industrial development in Cuba formed part of the effort to diversify the economy away from sugar while at the same time raising sugar output. Major sectors targeted as potential sources of export earnings have been the machine and electronics industries, light industry, pharmaceutical, biotechnology, sugar cane by-products and tourism. The government is keen to target chemicals and electronic components industries for import substitution. Cuba produces a wide range of industrial goods for domestic use, including televisions and refrigerators.

Industry, dominated by sugar and other food processing, is the biggest sector of the economy, accounting for almost half of GDP. Sugar processing normally accounts for about 14 per cent of industrial production while other food processing accounts for about a fifth. The Hola processing plant in Havana toasts and grinds coffee beans for export to the UK, Ukraine, Bulgaria, the Bahamas and Spain.

Industry established before the 1959 revolution, including sugar processing plants, is based on technology from non-communist countries. The need to earn hard currency to buy spare parts and new machinery is behind the push for exports. Technical supplies have been lacking since the demise of the Soviet Union, and poor harvests have meant difficulty in securing credits needed to invest in fertiliser, herbicide and equipment.

Tourism

The importance of tourism to Cuba has grown since it has had to deal with external and internal pressures that require not only hard currencies to buy commodities but also to maintain growth in its centralised economy. The US embargo on trade with Cuba has hindered development and all capital investment in the industry has been either government backed or in partnership with sympathetic foreign sources.

The sector has experienced a downturn as the share of direct contribution to GDP began to fall from 3.6 per cent in 2005 to 3.1 in 2006 to its lowest of 2.6 per cent in both 2009–10. By 2014 this figure had dropped even further to 2.6 per cent, whilst total contribution to GDP was 10.4 per cent. Total contribution to employment was 9.6 per cent in the same year, which was the equivalent of 494,500 jobs. Visitor exports generated 15.9 per cent of total exports in 2014.

In January 2015, President Obama expanded the categories of authorised travel to Cuba. U.S. citizens can legally travel to Cuba if they are engaging in activities such as professional research, participating in an athletic event, performing in a concert, working on a humanitarian project or taking part in educational activities. Americans are as yet still not allowed to visit Cuba as tourists.

In 2010, Cuba was a country unspoiled by mass tourism, but at the expense of a people held back from a potentially good living through tourism. Some of the current, quaint sights that enchant visitors, such as vintage cars left over from the days before the revolution, which have been lovingly conserved not for their good looks but because they were the only vehicles available, are likely to be lost (either snapped up by collectors or exchanged for a modern vehicle) in any headlong rush to modernise. It will require skilled management to move from an old Soviet style economy to a modern, open market where tourism provides a realistic living for workers and does not exploit them based on traditional poorer wages or overwhelm or monopolise local resources. The number of tourists visiting Cuba since 1 January 2015 reached the two million mark by 10 July, over a month faster than in 2014.

Environment

Incessant rain, following tropical storm Noel, falling from 11 October to 5 November 2007, caused the worst floods in forty years, destroying tens of thousands of homes, leaving roads impassable and damaging crops of sugar and coffee. The drought that began in 2009 had by 2011 become the worst since the 1960s, as water levels in reservoirs fell to a fifth of normal amounts and tens of thousands of families became reliant on water lorries for their essential supplies. Even if the rainy season, in May–June, brings relief, normal rainfall will be insufficient to compensate for the deficit.

Mining

Mining contributes around 6 per cent to GDP. The island's extensive nickel and cobalt ore reserves, among the largest in the world, offer attractive large-scale mining opportunities. Cuba's rich mineral resources are open to foreign exploration and development.

Exploration for gold, silver and base metals is carried out by more than a dozen foreign firms in concession areas covering nearly a third of Cuba's national territory. Cuba has updated its mining legislation, bringing it into line with most other Latin American countries.

Nickel production has been boosted by the injection of Canadian capital and technology. Since 2000 Cuba has supplied over half the nickel China uses in the production of stainless steel, and to maintain supplies China agreed, in November 2004, to invest US$500 million in the nickel industry.

China and Cuba signed an array of 29 cooperation agreements to support the Caribbean country's development and enhance bilateral ties as President Xi Jinping paid his first-ever state visit to Cuba in 2014.

Cuba intends to modernise its processing plants and continue exploration for other base and precious metals. More than half the production comes from the Comandante Pedro Sotto Alba processing plant at Moa Bay, jointly operated since 1994 by Sherritt (Canada) and a Cuban company, Compania General de Niquel (General Nickel Company). Cuba's two other operating nickel plants are being modernised with the help of export-linked revolving credits from Dutch, German and other foreign banks and trade houses.

Hydrocarbons

Cuban oil has a high sulphur content, which requires adaptations to refineries. Some local crude has been used experimentally to provide fuel for a cement plant and in power stations, while refining capacity has reached 300,000 barrels per day (bpd). Cuba has also opened up to inward investment from the US since the first Cuban-US trade fair in 2000.

The state-run Cupet is responsible for exploration, production and supply of all oil in Cuba, either solely or in partnership with international oil companies. Exploration has been located mainly onshore in the northern Matanzas Province. However, offshore exploration is expected to find larger deposits in the future; some analysts have predicted amounts up to 5.0 billion barrels, but most finds are likely to be in deep water which is difficult and expensive to exploit. Drilling offshore began in 2009. In January 2014 Cuban officials announced plans to continue off shore oil drilling in deep waters, some of the areas targeted are as close as 80km to the Florida close – causing Floridians to worry about their states beaches and sea wildlife. The Chinese engineering company Yantai Raffles built a semi-submersible rig, completed by the engineering company Saipem Singapore. The rig's first well was drilled in the North Cuba Basin and began at the beginning of 2012. In May 2012, the Spanish oil company, Repsol announced that it and Cuba's first attempt at oil exploration (50km off the north coast) had failed and the site abandoned.

Gas production is expected to increase in the coming years as the government proceeds with its plan to utilise Cuba's gas resources, which exist mainly in heavy oil deposits.

Under the current embargo, Cuba cannot access US oilfield equipment for both drilling and environmental protection. The embargo prohibits the exporting and re-exporting of items that contain more than 10 per cent American components.

The most positive area for oil in Cuba is the North Cuba Basin. It is located in the Gulf of Mexico, along the north shore of the island.

Energy

Total installed generating capacity was 6.05 million KW in 2013 (latest available figures in 2015), producing over 19.14 billion KWh, the majority of which is produced by oil-fired power stations. Cuba has a system of distributed generation (DG), whereby small-scale plants are located around the country and closer to their end users. This has allowed Cuba to recover from Caribbean hurricanes, which strike annually, much more rapidly than countries which adopted more centralised power generation plants. Around 40 per cent of all electricity is provided by DG, most generators being powered by diesel but also by renewable sources such as photovoltaic panels and wind turbines.

The government programme Energy Revolution, introduced in 2008 encourages energy awareness along with the installation of over 700 small generators (producing up to 1,700MW).

Hydropower was first introduced in the 1930s and in 2012 the installed hydroelectric capacity was 65MW. Other renewable energy sources include bagasse (residue of sugar cane, burned to produce energy) as an oil substitute, and wave power.

Banking and insurance

The Cuban banking sector has been transformed from a closed and highly centralised Soviet-style model to a diversified two-tier banking system.

In a bilateral agreement signed in 2005 Cuba opened a subsidiary of the Foreign Bank of Cuba in Caracas, Venezuela, while a subsidiary of the Industrial Bank of Venezuela has been approved to open in Cuba.

Central bank

Banco Central de Cuba (BCC)

Time

GMT minus four hours in summer, GMT minus five hours in winter (October – March).

Geography

Cuba is the largest island in the Caribbean, lying 150km south of Florida. Together with offshore islands and an archipelago of about 1,600 coral cays surrounding the main island, the country has an area of 110,860 square km. The largest offshore island is the Isla de la Juventud, formerly known as the Isla de Piños, which covers 2,200 square km. Most of the long, thin main island consists of plains and low ranges of hills. The highest mountains are in the Sierra Maestra in the extreme south-east, where the Pico Real de Turquina rises to 1,974 metres.

Hemisphere

Northern.

Climate

Subtropical, with an annual mean temperature of 26 degrees Celsius (C) the average summer shade temperatures can rise to 30 degrees C and higher. November–April is the cooler, dry season with maximum temperatures peaking at around 26 degrees C. Trade winds and sea breezes cool the air; there are sudden, short showers in summer. The months of June, September and October–November usually bring hurricanes.
The north is wetter than the south and the south, in particularly Santiago Province, is much hotter than the north.
There is rainfall of up to 250mm a year in the mountains.
It can be humid between May and October with some heavy rain. Humidity averages 62 per cent. However, during September and October, humidity can reach 95 per cent.

Dress codes

Dress since the 1959 revolution has been casual. Cubans wear lightweight and loose-fitting clothes, and formal dress, such as a tie, is an extremely rare sight.

Entry requirements

Passports

Required by all. Passports of nationals of countries without diplomatic relations with Cuba must be valid for two months beyond date of arrival.

Visa

Required by all, except nationals of countries who have reciprocal visa-free agreements.
Business visas, valid for 90 days from issue, are only obtained through sponsorship by an appropriate Cuban government organisation. For sponsorship contact the relevant State Trading Organisation or the commercial office of a Cuban embassy. Without a sponsor a visa will not be issued and a tourist card does not provide local firms with the opportunity to trade with business visitors.
Tourist cards are provided by airlines and tour operators who are registered with Cubatur. Exit visas are required for visitors staying more than 90 days.

Currency advice/regulations

The import and export of local currency is forbidden. There are no restrictions on the import of foreign currency, subject to declaration of amounts over US$5,000. Currency can be exchanged at the airport or hotel for 'convertible pesos'. When departing, they can be converted back again.
Hard currency is generally required from visitors for most transactions, although the US dollar is no longer legal tender. Visitors arriving with US currency must change it into 'convertible pesos', for which a 10 per cent commission is charged.

Health (for visitors)

Mandatory precautions

A yellow fever vaccination certificate is required if arriving from an infected area.

Advisable precautions

Vaccinations are recommended for typhoid, hepatitis A, tetanus and polio, as well as malaria prophylaxis – mosquitoes are a problem outside Havana.
The water supply in most upmarket hotels is excellent but elsewhere water precautions should be taken. Bottled water is readily available.
Medical services are good and free to visitors in an emergency. Insurance is advisable in case repatriation is required.
Resorts and major cities have international clinics for tourists but the US embargo often means branded medicines may not be available. An adequate supply of regularly administered medication should be carried.
A visitor admitted to hospital is likely to be tested for HIV/Aids and will be deported if found to be a carrier.

Hotels

The best hotels can be found in Havana and Varadero beach. Foreign currencies should be exchanged at official Cadeca outlets.
The practice of tipping is growing – restaurants 5–10 per cent.

Credit cards

Only credit cards which are not issued in the US (Visa, Eurocard, MasterCard, Access) are accepted, generally only at tourist sites.

Public holidays (national)

Fixed dates

1 Jan (Liberation Day), 1 May (Labour Day), 25 Jul (Rebellion anniversary, three days), 10 Oct (Anniversary of the War of Independence), 25 Dec (Christmas Day).

Variable dates

Carnival: Havana (Feb); Varadero (late Jan/Feb); Trinidad and Santiago de Cuba (Jun).

Working hours

Banking

Mon–Fri: 0830–1200, 1330–1500; Sat: 0830–1030.
Banks in resorts tend to stay open longer.
Banks and post offices do not accept Eurocheques or American Express travellers cheques.

Business

Mon–Fri: 0830–1230 and 1330–1630; some offices open alternate Saturdays between 0800–1700.

Government

Mon–Fri: 0830–1230, 1330–1730.

Shops

Mon-Fri: 0900-1700; Sat: 0900-1200.
Shops are normally closed on Sunday, except those in tourist areas. Resort shops and supermarkets often open seven days a week and their hours vary according to demand.
Pharmacies are open daily 0800–2000; those with *turno permanente* signs are open 24 hours.

Telecommunications

Postal services

Cuba suspended mail deliveries to the US in January 2011. The move was thought to be in retaliation for the return of mail by the US as part of stricter security measures introduced after the attempt to mail explosives from the Yemen in 2010. President Obama had allowed the resumption of mail services, via third countries, in 2009; services had been suspended since 1969.
Cuba has very few official mail collection boxes, so visitors are advised to post mail in a hotel, or at the airport.

Mobile/cell phones

GSM 900 service available in main tourist areas and cities only.
In March 2008 reforms were announced which gave Cubans unlimited access to mobile phones. Until then Cubans could only own them through a third party, which meant that mobile phone usage in Cuba was one of the lowest in Latin America. However, payment has to be made in foreign currency.

Internet/e-mail

An under-sea fibre-optic cable from Venezuela improved internet down-load speed by some 3,000 times from early 2011. It also reduced international telephone costs. The 1,600km cable was paid for by the Bolivarian Alliance for the Peoples of Our America (Alba) – a left-wing regional grouping founded by President Hugo Chavez of Venezuela.

Electricity supply

110V AC, 60 cycles
Most plugs in hotels are two-pin, flat-pin type, although some are the two-pin, round-pin variety.
Some electric shaver points can be 220/240V.
Lighting is usually of the screw in, rather than bayonet, type.

Social customs/useful tips

Foreign residents say there are few restrictions on foreign visitors, however, they

advise against vociferous public criticism of the government.
Cuba has placed great emphasis on sports; baseball, originally imported from the US, is the national sport with boxing vying as the most popular spectator sport.
Cubans address each other, and often foreign visitors, as *compañero* or *compañera*, and the informal *tu* form is often used when speaking Spanish.
Photographing airports and sensitive sites is forbidden and permission should be sought before photographing public or religious buildings.

Security
Although Cuba is considered to be a generally safe country, the usual precautions should be followed.
Keep to the main busy areas in the cities. Keep valuables and money belt out of sight. Avoid going out alone if possible, especially at night.

Getting there
Air
National airline: Cubana de Aviación.
International airport/s: Havana-José Marti International (HAV), 25km from city, with duty-free shops, bank, tourist information, hotel reservation and car hire; Varadero-Juan Gómez International (VRA), 12km from Cuba's main beach resort.
Other airport/s: Santiago-Antonio Macea (SCU).
Airport tax: 25 convertible Cuban pesos, except transit passengers.
Surface
Water: There is no scheduled passenger traffic due to the US blockade. Some cruise vessels and private yachts visit Cuba.
Main port/s: Antilla, Cienfuegos, Guayabal, Havana, Mariel, Matanzas, Nuevitas, Santiago de Cuba.

Getting about
National transport
Air: Cubana operates limited domestic services to main centres. Internal flights by visitors are generally arranged through Cubatur.
Road: The Central Highway (Autopista Nacional) runs for over 1,100km, virtually from end to end of the island and gives access to a network of local roads. Total road system exceeds 30,000km, at least 40 per cent surfaced although some roads/tracks may not be passable in wet weather.
Buses: Cross-country buses are cheap and fairly reliable, but can be overcrowded. Coaches link main centres. An air-conditioned service operated by Viazul offers more comfortable travel around the island; payment in convertible pesos is required.
Rail: Cuba's rail capacity is not as extensive as it once was, due to natural disasters and lack of investment. There was 4,226km of public service track in 2003, an increase on the previous year. The main line connects Havana and Santiago de Cuba; some services on this route offer refreshments and air-conditioning. Other lines include between Havana-Cienfuegos and Cardenas-Jaguey. Railway stations in Cuba are immaculately clean, but timetables are often unreliable.
Water: Hydrofoils run twice daily from the southern port of Surgidero de Batananó to the Isla de la Juventud. There are also slower boats sailing three times a week, but a day trip is not possible using these.
City transport
Taxis: There are state and private taxi services, usually ordered through a hotel. Official taxis are metered and less expensive and more comfortable than private taxis, with which prior agreement on the fare is advisable. Turistaxis, the official taxi service for tourists, has stands at tourist centres and can also be flagged down in the street. Taxis can also be hired for the day; for travel outside Havana, taxis or cars with drivers are cheap but scarce.
Buses, trams & metro: Services in towns are generally considered erratic, inexpensive but invariably crowded. Cubanacan buses are available for tours of cities.
Car hire
Car hire is the most reliable form of transport for covering larger distances. Modern cars are available and can be booked in advance via the Internet through Cubatur (www.cubatur.cu). Hired locally, the price may rise sharply outside airport, city or tourist areas. Chauffeur-driven vehicles are also available.
A valid driver's licence is necessary. Traffic drives on the right; seat belts are not compulsory and the blood alcohol limit is 80mg/100ml.
Speed limits: autopista 100kph; paved roads 90kph; dirt roads 60kph; urban roads 50kph (40kph near schools).
Petrol is relatively easy to obtain and comes in two grades: *especial* and regular. Both are leaded and as a rule only the dearer *especial* is available to tourists. It is sold at 24-hour Servi-Cupet and Oro Negro petrol stations.

BUSINESS DIRECTORY
The addresses listed below are a selection only. While World of Information makes every endeavour to check these addresses, we cannot guarantee that changes have not been made, especially to telephone numbers and area codes. We would welcome any corrections.

Telephone area codes
The international direct dialling code (IDD) for Cuba is +53, followed by the area code and subscriber's number:

Camaguey	32	Manzanillo	23
Ciego de Avila	33	Matanzas	45
Cienfuegos	43	Pinar del Rio	82
Florencia	33	Santiago de Cuba	226
Havana	7	Villa Clara	42

Useful telephone numbers
There is an efficient, almost omnipresent, police service, but officers are unlikely to speak English.
Police: 116 can be dialled from any call box.
Havanautos (24-hour breakdown service): 338176 or 338177.

Chambers of Commerce
Cámara de Comercio de la República de Cuba, Calle 21, esq. A No 661, Vedado, Havana (tel: 551-321; fax: 333-042; e-mail: bic@camara.com.cu).

Banking
Banco de Inversiones SA, 5ta Ave No 6802 e/ 68 y 70, Miramar, Havana (tel: 243-374/5; fax: 243-373; e-mail: bdi@bdi.colombus.cu).

Banco Exterior de España, Línea esq a 2, El Vedado, Havana (tel: 334-560; fax: 334-559).

Banco Financiero Internacional SA, Línea No 1, Vedado, PO Box 4068, Havana 4 (tel: 333-003, 333-148; fax: 333-006).

Banco Internacional de Comercio SA, 20 de Mayo y Ayestarán, Apartado 6113, Plaza de la Revolución, Havana 6 (tel: 335-482/5484; fax: 335-112; e-mail: bicsa@bicsa.columbus.cu).

Banco Metropolitano SA, (successor of the international branch of the Banco Nacional de Cuba), Línea No 63 esq a M, Vedado, Plaza, Havana (tel: 553-116/7; fax: 334-241; e-mail: banmet@nbbm.columbus.cu).

Casas de Cambio SA (CADECA), Calle Aguiar No 411, e/ Obrapia y Lamparilla, Habana Vieja, Havana (tel: 335-673; fax: 335-673; e-mail: cadeca@cadeca.columbus.cu).

Grupo Nueva Banca SA (NB), Calle 1ra, No 1406 e/ 14 y 16, Miramar, Havana (tel: 247-564/67; fax: 245-674; e-mail: nbanca@nbanca.columbus.cu).

The Netherlands Caribbean Banking, 5ta Avenida No 6407 esq a 76, Miramar, Havana (tel: 240-419/21; fax: 240-472).

Central bank
Banco Central de Cuba, PO Box 746, Cuba 402, Habana Vieja, Havana (tel: 866-8003; fax: 866-6601; e-mail: webmaster@bc.gov.cu).

Travel information

Cubamar, Paseo 306 esq a 15, Vedado, Havana (tel: 662-523.4; fax: 333-111; e-mail: cubamar@cubamar.mit.cma.net).

Cubana, Calle 23, No 64 esq Infanta, Vedado, Havana (tel: 334-949/50; fax: 333-323; e-mail: eca@iacc.3.get.cma.net).

Havanatur/Infotur, Calle Obispo 358, (e/ Habana y Compostella), Old Havana (tel: 614-881); Plaza de Martí, Santiago de Cuba (tel: 23-302).

Ministry of tourism

Ministerio de Turismo Calle 19, No 710, Entre Paseo y A, Vedado, Havana (tel: 334 087; 334 318/9; fax: 334 086: Internet: www.cubatravel.cu; www.cubaweb.cu; www.ceniai.inf.cu).

National tourist organisation offices

Cubatur (Empresa de Turismo Nacional e Internacional), Calle F No 157 el Calzada y Novena, Vedado, Havana (tel: 835-4155; fax: 836-3170; e-mail: casamatriz@cubatur.cu).

Ministries

Ministry of Agriculture, Avenida Independencia, entre Cornill y Sta Ana, Havana (tel: 845-770; fax: 335-086).

Ministry of Basic Industries, Avenida Salvador Allende 666, Havana (tel: 707-711; fax: 333-845).

Ministry of Communications, Plaza De la Revolución José Martí, CP 10600, Havana (tel: 817-654).

Ministry of Construction, Avenida Carlos M de Cespedes y Calle 35, Havana (tel: 818-385; fax: 335-585).

Ministry of Construction Materials Industry, Calle 17, esq 0, Vevado, Havana (tel: 322-541; fax: 333-176).

Ministry of Culture, Calle 2, No 258, entre 11y 13, Vedado, Havana (tel: 399-945).

Ministry of Economy and Planning, 20 de Mayo y Ayestaran, Plaza de la Revolucion, Havana (tel: 816-444).

Ministry of Education, Obispo 160, Havana (tel: 614-888).

Ministry of Finance and Prices, Obispo 211, esq Cuba, Havana (tel: 604-111; fax: 620-252).

Ministry of the Fishing Industry, Avenida 5 y 248 Jaimenitas, Santa Fé, Havana (tel: 297-034).

Ministry of the Food Industry, Calle 41, No 4455, Playa, Havana (tel: 726-801).

Ministry of Foreign Affairs, Calzada 360, Vedado, Havana (tel: 324-074).

Ministry of Foreign Investment and Economic Co-operation, Calle 1, No 201, Vedado, Havana (tel: 736-661).

Ministry of Foreign Trade, Infanta 16, Vedado, Havana (tel: 786-230; fax: 786-234).

Ministry of Health, Calle 23, No 301, Vedado, Havana (tel: 322-561).

Ministry of Higher Education, Calle 23, No 565, esq aF, Vedado, Havana (tel: 552-314).

Ministry of the Interior, Plaza de la Revolucion, Havana (fax: 733-5261).

Ministry of Internal Trade, Calle Habana 258, Havana (tel: 625-790).

Ministry of Iron and Steel, Metallurgical and Electronic Industries, Avenida Rancho Boyeros y Calle 100, Havana (tel: 204-861).

Ministry of Justice, Calle 0, No 216, entre 23 y Humboldt, Vedado, Havana (tel: 326-319).

Ministry of Labour and Social Security, Calle 23, esq Calle P, Vedado, Havana (tel: 704-571).

Ministry of Light Industry, Empedrado 302, Havana (tel: 624-041).

Ministry of the Revolutionary Armed Forces, Plaza de la Revolución, Havana.

Ministry of Sugar, Calle 23, No 117, Vedado, Havana (tel: 305-061).

Ministry of Transport, Avenida Independencia y Tulipán, Havana (tel: 812-076).

Other useful addresses

British Embassy, Calle 34, No 702/4, Miramar, Havana (tel: 24-1049; fax: 24-9214).

CariFin (financial services Cuba), 311 and 313 22nd Street, Between 3rd and 5th Avanues, Mirimar, Havana (tel: 244-468/70; fax: 244-140; e-mail: havana@cdc.com.cu).

Compañía Fiduciaria SA (investments), Calle 36A No 121 apto, 2 e/ 1ra y 3ra, Miramar Playa, Havana (tel: 247-434/5; fax: 249-745; e-mail: nbfid@nbfid.columbus.cu).

Cuban Investment Company, PO Box 30003, North Vancouver, B.C. Canada V7H 2Y8 (tel: 00(1-604)929-9694; fax: 00(1-604)929-3694; e-mail: cubaninvestments@idmail.com).

Etecsa (Empresa de Telecomunicaciones de Cuba SA), Havana (tel: 452-221, 451-221; fax: 578-036).

Financiera Nacional SA (FINSA) (non-banking activities), Calle G No 301, esq a 13, Vedado, Havana (tel: 553-177, 338-863; fax: 662-232; e-mail: finsa@finsa.columbus.cu).

TIPS (Technological and Commercial Information Promotion System), National Office, No 302, Calle 30, Miramar, Havana (tel: 331-797/798; fax: 331-799).

National news agency: Agencia de Información Nacional (Cuban News Agency), Calle 23, 358 Vedado (tel: 662-049; fax: 325-541; internet: www.cubanews.ain.cu).

Prensa Latina: www.plenglish.com.mx

Internet sites

Cubana de Aviación airline: www.cubana.cu

Granma International (daily update in English, French, Spanish and Portuguese, with a summary in German): www.granma.cu

Viazul Bus Transportation: www.viazul.com

Curaçao

KEY FACTS

Official name: Curaçao (Kòrsou in *Papiamentu*)

Head of State: King William-Alexander of The Netherlands, represented by Governor Lucille George-Wout (4 Nov 2013)

Head of government: Prime Minister Ben Whitemen (Pueblo Soberano) (Sovereign People)) (from 1 September 2015, resigned 10 November 2015)

Ruling party: Coalition of Pueblo Soberano (PS) (Sovereign People), with Partido pa Adelanto I Inovashon Soshal (PAIS), Partido Nashonal di Pueblo (PNP) (National People's Party) and Partido Antiá Restrukturá (PAR) (Party for the Restructured Antilles), plus an independent (from 22 Nov 2015)

Area: 444 square kilometres

Population: 149,679 (2011; census figure)

Capital: Willemstad

Official language: Dutch and Papiamentu (official)

Currency: US dollar (US$) = 100 cents

Exchange rate: US$1.00 per US$ (Feb 2014)

GDP real growth: 0.10% (2011)

Unemployment: 10.50% (2011)

Inflation: 3.10% (2011)*

Balance of trade: -US$1.27 billion (2013)

* estimated figure

COUNTRY PROFILE

The islands of the Netherlands Antilles were first inhabited by Carib and Arawak Indians.

1493 Christopher Columbus was the first European to sight the islands.

1499 The Spanish explorer, Alonso de Ojedo, visited Curaçao but left without establishing a settlement.

1527 The islands were settled, mainly by Spanish and Portuguese Jews escaping persecution.

1634 The Dutch East India Company took over the islands, 'persuading' the settlers to depart, first from St Maarten and later from Aruba.

1642–46 Peter Stuyvesant was governor.

1816 After a number of changes of possession, the islands – Curaçao, Aruba and Bonaire (known as the Leeward Islands), St Eustatius, Saba and Sint Maarten (half of which is the French territory of St Martin) (known as the Windward Islands) – were confirmed as Dutch territory.

1863 Slavery was abolished.

1916 The first oil refinery was opened in Curaçao.

1954 Internal autonomy was granted as associated states within a federacy.

1986 Aruba separated from the other islands and became a self-governing member of the Kingdom of The Netherlands. The remaining islands became the Antilles of Five.

1998 The general election resulted in a six-party coalition government under Prime Minister Suzanne Camelia-Römer.

1999 The Partido Laboral Krusado Popular (PLKP) (Labour Party People's Crusade) left the coalition, to be replaced by the Partido Antiá Restrukturá (PAR) (Party for the Restructured Antilles), with Miguel Pourier becoming prime minister.

2000 In a referendum, St Maarten voted in favour of separate status within the Kingdom of The Netherlands and relinquishing membership of The Netherlands Antilles government.

2002 The ruling coalition was returned to power in the elections.

2004 The coalition government avoided collapse, caused by a corruption crisis, when support was offered by the Democratische Partij (DP) (Democratic Party) of Bonaire. The government finally collapsed when the National People's Party (PNP) withdrew, citing its unwillingness to work with Justice Minster Ben Komproe. Prime Minister Louisa-Godett resigned and Etienne Ys became prime minister.

2005 The islanders of Curaçao voted to become an autonomous state within the Kingdom of The Netherlands and break with The Netherlands Antilles. The tiny neighbouring island, Sint Eustatius, decided to remain within the Antilles. The Movishon Antia Nobo (New Antilles Movement) was renamed Partido MAN.

2006 Emily de Jongh-Elhage became prime minister, following parliamentary elections. The islands of Curaçao and St Maarten signed an agreement of independence to become autonomous territories within the Kingdom of the Netherlands. At the same time Bonaire, Saba and St Eustatius agreed to become city-states of the Kingdom of the Netherlands. When these changes are enacted the Netherlands Antilles will cease to exist. A new terminal in the Curaçao International Airport was opened, designed to accommodate around 1.6 million passengers per year. The growth in tourism on the island and in the region is seen as a major industry and a phase two expansion is planned for when arrivals are expected to reach 2.5 million in 2031.

2007 Negotiations for a change in their status began between Bonaire, Saba and St Eustatius and The Netherlands.

2008 The Netherlands Antilles failed to have its name removed from the blacklist of tax havens by the Tax Directorate of the European Commission, despite being named a co-operative country by the Organisation for Economic Co-operation and Development (OECD) and the IMF.

2009 A national census was undertaken, which recorded 141,766 people.

2010 Early general elections in Curaçao were automatically triggered when parliament failed to pass a new constitution. In the resulting parliamentary elections no single political party won outright power and a coalition was formed led by Movementu Futuro Korsou (MFK) (Movement for the Future of Curaçao), with Pueblo Soberano (PS) (Sovereign People) and Partido MAN (MAN Party). On 10 October the Netherlands Antilles ceased to exist and Curacao and St Maarten became semi-autonomous countries within the Kingdom of The Netherlands. Bonaire,

St Eustatius and Saba (the BES islands) became Bijzondere Gemeenten (special municipalities). Gerrit Schotte became prime minister.

2011 A new airline InselAir, began a non-stop service between Caracas and Hato in July.

2012 On 3 August Gerrit Schotte resigned as prime minister following the collapse of his coalition government. On 13 September, parliament convened and sacked nine members of the caretaker government. On 29 September Stanley Betrain was appointed as interim prime minister. Weeks of ill-tempered negotiations resulted in an interim government elected by parliament. Parliamentary elections were finally held on 19 October. On 26 October, The PS and MFK won five seats each and agreed to form a coalition with MAN to form a government, with Ivar Asjes as prime minister. However on 30 October MFK officials withdrew from the coalition agreement when its leader, former prime minister Schotte, objected to the process of choosing ministers, which included a full screening for probity. A coalition agreement formed a government of PS, PAIS, PNP and an independent with Stanley Betrian as prime minister. On 19 November Glenn Camelia was named *formateur* (head of coalition government). On 24 November, Governor Frits Goedgedrag resigned due to prolonged illness and his deputy, Adèle Van der Pluijim-Vrede, became acting governor. New airport fees were introduced on 1 December, with various charges depending on destination. Daniel Hodge was sworn in as prime minister on 31 December.

2013 An economic survey was conducted by the Central Bureau of Statistics in June. Preliminary results showed that confidence in the economy had improved somewhat in the opinion of entrepreneurs. Fewer entrepreneurs, 49 per cent, indicated that confidence in the economy in the past six months had deteriorated, compared to 56 per cent in December 2012. Ivar Onno Odwin Asjes (Pueblo Soberano) became prime minister on 7 June 2013.

2014 In June the committee for the division of properties and debts (set up to formulate a balanced division of the properties and debts of the former Netherlands Antilles) announced that it would be able to present its findings in August. The chaiman announced that they still awaited reports from the Stichting Overheidsaccountantsbureau (SOAB) (the original accounting agency for the governments of the Netherlands Antilles and Curaçao) and accountants KPMG. Once these are received the final formula dividing the properties and debts between Curaçao, St Maarten and the BES islands will be presented to the governments of Curaçao, St Maarten and the minister of Kingdom relations in The Netherlands. The one sticking point appeared to have been the Saba Bank Resources Inc, which had been set up in the 1980s to exploit any potential oil found in the Saba Bank (in Saba territorial waters). Chairman Faroe Metry said that although no oil has so far been found, it is possible that with new techniques and 'some luck' it may be in the future, and in which case the islands should benefit. A report published by the Central Bureau of Statistics in July noted that economic development in Curacao fell by 0.8 per cent in July 2013. In October Venezuela national oil company PdVSA announced it was sending a shipment of crude oil from Russia to the Isla oil refinery. The oil had been purchased from Petrochina and would break the UN sanctions against Russia if the oil arrives. A parliamentary motion was filed in October (by Gerrit Schotte) to get rid of the Netherlands-appointed governor, who must by law approve ministerial appointments. This would allow the appointment of ministers without first being screened for integrity. The motion is a response to the intervention by Dutch interior and kingdom relations minister, Ronald Plasterk, in St Maarten when the Council of Ministers in The Hague told the island governor to postpone the appointment of the new cabinet until incoming prime minister, Theo Heyliger, and his team of ministers had been screened under Dutch rules.

2015 A decision was reached between the governments of The Netherlands, Aruba, Curaçao and St Maarten on 9 January whereby the four should work to agree a mechanism whereby future disagreements between the countries of the kingdom can be resolved. The result should be a proceedure to be followed to avoid disputes such as that between Aruba and the Netherlands over instructions as to its budget and St Maarten over problems with the reliability of politicians as candidates for ministerial posts.

Political structure

Constitution

A new constitution was adopted in September 2010.

Form of state

Parliamentary democratic monarchy. Curaçao became a semi-autonomous country within the Kingdom of the Netherlands on 10 October 2010. The Netherlands government remains responsible for defence and foreign policy, and has oversight over Curacao's finances under a debt relief agreement.

The executive

The Governor of Curacao is the representative of the King in Curacao. He defends the general interests of the state and is head of the government in Curacao. The governor has no political responsibilities and is not part of the Cabinet of Curacao.

.

National legislature

The staten (legislature) has 21 members, directly elected to serve four-year terms.

Legal system

The legal system is based on Dutch civil law, with some English common law. Judges are appointed by the monarch. Rights of appeal exist from The Netherlands Antilles Court of Appeals to the Supreme Court of The Netherlands, in The Hague.

Last elections

19 October 2012 (parliamentary)

Results: Parliamentary: Pueblo Soberano (Sovereign People) won 22.6 per cent of the vote (five seats out of 21), Movementu Futuro Korsou (MFK) (Movement for the Future of Curaçao) 21.2 per cent, (five), Partido Antiá Restrukturá (PAR) (Party for the Restructured Antilles) 19.7 per cent, (four), Partido pa Adelanto I Inovashon Soshal (PAIS) (Party for Advancement and Social Innovation) 17.7 per cent (four), Movishon Anita Nobo (MAN) (MAN Party) 9.5 per cent (two), Partido Nashonal di Pueblo (PNP) (National People's Party) 5.9 per cent, (one); two other political parties failed to win any seats. Turnout was 74.5 per cent.

Next elections

Next elections 2016 (parliamentary)

Political parties

Ruling party

Coalition of Pueblo Soberano (PS) (Sovereign People), with Partido pa Adelanto I Inovashon Soshal (PAIS) and Partido Nashonal di Pueblo (PNP) (National People's Party), plus an independent (from 19 Nov 2012)

Main opposition party

Movementu Futuro Kòrsou (MFK)

Political situation

Curaçao came into being on 10 October 2010, after the Netherlands Antilles ceased to exist and Curaçao and St Maarten became semi-autonomous countries within the Kingdom of The Netherlands. Bonaire, St Eustatius and Saba became Bijzondere Gemeenten (special municipalities) of the Netherlands. An early general election in Curaçao had been automatically triggered when parliament failed to pass the new constitution in June 2010. On 27 August no single political party won outright power in parliamentary elections and a coalition was formed led by Movementu Futuro Korsou (MFK) (Movement for the Future of

Curaçao), with Pueblo Soberano (Sovereign People) and Partido MAN (MAN Party). Gerrit Schotte became prime minister on 10 October.

Population

149,679*

Last census: 149,679 (2011)

Ethnic make-up

African and mixed race (85 per cent), Carib Amerindian, white, East Asian.

Religions

Baptist, Roman Catholic, Protestant, Jewish, Seventh-Day Adventist and others.

Education

Primary schooling lasts for six years (from age six to 12) and junior secondary school lasts four years (age 12 to 16). Following primary education, students have a choice of attending technical or vocational colleges in place of secondary school.

Higher education is provided by the Universiteit van de Nederlandse Antillen (University of the Netherlands Antilles). There is also a nursing school and a teacher training college in Curaçao.

Health

Curaçao has two general hospitals and one surgical hospital and receives patients from the other islands of The Netherlands Antilles. Most health professionals receive training in The Netherlands.

It is estimated that around 30 per cent of the population of the Netherlands Antilles suffer from hypertension; psychological problems are also highly prevalent among adults. The general standard of health among the Antilleans is poor, with poor nutrition and little or no exercise undertaken by the adult population. The Dutch government has assigned priority to encouraging the population to develop healthier lifestyles.

HIV/Aids

There is a national strategic action plan to halt the rapid spread of the disease. The drugs problem could prove to be a potent source of transmission.

Life expectancy: 76.3 years (estimate 2003)

Fertility rate/Maternal mortality rate: 2.1 births per woman (World Bank)

Birth rate/Death rate: 16 births per 1,000 population; 6.4 deaths per 1,000 population (2003).

Child (under 5 years) mortality rate (per 1,000): 11 per 1,000 live births (2003)

Welfare

A public insurance programme covers 100 per cent of health care costs for blue-collar workers. There is also an insurance fund for retired workers. Private companies also provide insurance plans for their employees. A social security fund covers employees of small private establishments.

Main cities

Willemstad (capital, estimated population 103,119 in 2012), Sint Michiel (5,429), Montana Abou (4,477), Tera Cora (3,873), Montana Rey (3,773), Souax (3,691).

Languages spoken

Papiamentu is a local patois mixture of Portuguese, Spanish, Dutch, English and French.

Spanish is widely understood and spoken.

Official language/s

Dutch and Papiamentu (official)

Media

Press

Dailies: The only regional daily newspaper is *Amigoe* (www.amigoe.com) with *Vigilante* (http://vigilante.nl) from Curacao as the local island publication

Business: Business publications include in English *Business Curaçao Directory* (www.businesscuracao.com) and the annual Trade Statistics by Central Bureau of Statistics (www.cbs.an).

Broadcasting

There are several radio stations with the three based in Curacao, Radio Hoyer (www.radiohoyer.com), Easy FM and Dolfijn FM (www.dolfijnfm.com). There are two commercial television channels operating and TeleCuracao is government owned.

Economy

The Curaçao economy is dominated by petroleum refining. The Venezuelan state-owned oil company Petróleos de Venezuela (PdVSA) operates several oil refineries in Curaçao, including Isla refinery, which produces of 335,000 barrels per day destined mainly for America, Central America and the Caribbean. However, these refineries are old and becoming increasingly unproductive so that tourism is becoming progressively more important to Curaçao's future development. Agriculture only accounts for less than 1 per cent of GDP, producing aloes, sorghum, vegetables and tropical fruit. Dutch aid remains important to the economy.

Following recession in 2009 due to global crisis, growth picked up as a result of global trade and tourists returning to Curaçao and in 2010 GDP grew by 0.4 per cent. This was expected to have dropped in 2011 to 0.1 per cent, before increasing in 2012 at 3.6 per cent.

The unemployment rate remains high – in 2013 it rose from around 9.8 per cent to 13 per cent of the population. The islands have a higher per capita income and a well-developed infrastructure compared with other countries in the region.

The commercial enterprise, Space Experience Curaçao (SXC), and Curaçao Airport Partners (CAP) signed a letter of intent in January 2011 to develop a spaceport and SXC committed US$75 million to the project. In February 2011 a government-backed financial feasibility study began into the proposed building of a spaceport and relevant activities on Curaçao. However, in 2015, the facility was still a concept.

A report published by the Central Bureau of Statistics in 2014 noted that economic development in Curacao fell by 0.8 per cent in July 2013.

External trade

Trade is dominated by crude oil imports and the export of refined oil products.

Imports

Main imports include refined and crude petroleum, vehicles, food and manufactures.

Main sources: Venezuela (typically 50 per cent of total), US (21 per cent), Italy (5 per cent).

Exports

Main exports include petroleum products, food and gold.

Main destinations: US (typically 26 per cent of total), Aruba (23), Netherlands (17 per cent), St Maarten (10 per cent).

Agriculture

Farming

The agricultural sector contributes less than 1 per cent to GDP and employs 5 per cent of the workforce.

About 8 per cent of total area is cultivated arable land. Soil is generally poor and rainfall inadequate for most crops.

Small amounts of fruit and vegetables are grown for local consumption

Industry and manufacturing

The industrial sector contributes 15.5 per cent to GDP and employs 20 per cent of the workforce. Petroleum refining and transshipment dominate the sector.

Manufacturing is concentrated on food processing and import substitution (paints, paper, soap, beer, chemicals).

The emphasis is on diversification into light export-based industries such as electronics and pharmaceuticals.

Tourism

The island of Curaçao offers a typical Caribbean experience of sun, sea and surf; it also has a historic capital town centre that is included in the list of Unesco World Heritage sites. It hosts an annual jazz festival in March, as well as other more sporting events, in particular diving among the coral reefs. The Curaçao-based airline InselAir has flights to a number of American destinations while Air Canada and Continental Airlines have expanded their services since independence in 2010 to include non-stop flights from Toronto-Pearson and Newark, respectively. As a one-year old state in 2011, statistics for tourism in Curaçao were presented within the statistics of the defunct Netherland Antilles until 2012. In general, travel and tourism was estimated to have contributed 34 per cent of GDP in the former Netherland Antilles, and provided a total of 36.9 per cent of all jobs. In 2014 there were around 444,000 stay over visitors, and around 48,000 day-trippers – a slight increase on the numbers of 2013. Visitors from the Netherlands are the single largest group followed by Venezuelan visitors wishing to stay close to home; it is also a popular destination for the slightly older US traveller, who can find pleasure in peaceful surroundings.

Hydrocarbons

There are no known hydrocarbon resources. The 1914 discovery of oil in Venezuela was the impetus for the island of Curaçao's choice as the location of what was then the largest oil refinery in the world, which currently has a capacity of 335,000 barrels per day (bpd). Crude oil is imported mainly from Venezuela and Mexico under the San José Pact. Some of this is consumed domestically but the majority is refined and exported.

Any imported natural gas or coal used is commercially insignificant.

Banking and insurance

Under an EU tax directive introduced in 2005 in a number of associate and dependent EU countries, impose a withholding tax to be passed to the relevant EU country but typically retains the anonymity of the saver. Withholding taxes began at 15 per cent and will rise to 35 per cent by 2011.

The Netherlands Antillies has also agreed to supply information on tax fraud, for criminal or civil trials, and notify EU member states about additional malpractice.

Central bank

Centrale Bank van Curaçao en Sint Maarten (Central Bank of Curaçao and St Maarten)

Main financial centre

Willemstad

Time

GMT minus five hours (minus six hours during summer daylignt saving).

Geography

Curaçao is located in the Caribbean Sea, 70km off the coast of northern South America, in the Netherlands Windward islands and consists of low hills.

Hemisphere

Northern

Climate

There are low levels of humidity and rainfall on Curaçao where temperatures average 29 degrees Celsus (C). Average annual rainfall is 550mm. There are higher levels of rainfall from May–December.

Entry requirements

Passports

Required by all and must be valid for at least three months from date of departure.

Visa

Not required by nationals of countries which are signatories of the Schengen Accords, which includes most EU/EEA member states; North America and Australasia for visits up to three months. Lists of nationals that do and do not require a visa can be found on the website of the Dutch Ministry of Foreign affairs: www.mfa.nl/lon-en/homepage under visas.

All visitors must provide evidence of sufficient funds for their stay and a return/onward ticket.

Currency advice/regulations

There are no restrictions regarding the import and export of local or foreign currencies.

Travellers cheques are widely accepted; US dollar cheques will avoid additional exchange charges.

Health (for visitors)

Mandatory precautions

Yellow fever vaccination certificate required if arriving from an infected area.

Advisable precautions

Inoculations and boosters should be current for tetanus and hepatitis A. There may be a need for vaccinations for diphtheria, typhoid, tuberculosis and hepatitis B.

Hotels

There are numerous tourist hotels. Government tax of 5 per cent and 10–15 per cent service charge is added to the bill.

Credit cards

All major credit and charge cards accepted. ATMs are available in major centres.

Public holidays (national)

Fixed dates

1 Jan (New Year's Day), 30 Apr (Queen's Birthday), 1 May (Labour Day), 2 Jul Curaçao Flag Day, 25–26 Dec (Christmas).

Variable dates

Carnival (Jan/Feb), Easter Monday (Mar/Apr) Ascension Day (Aug).

Working hours

Banking

Mon–Fri: 0830–1200, 1330–1630.

Business

Mon–Fri: 0800–1200, 1330–1630.

Government

Mon–Fri: 0800–1200, 1330–1630.

Shops

Mon–Sat: 0800–1200, 1400–1800. Gift shops open on Sundays and public holidays when cruise ships call.

Telecommunications

Mobile/cell phones

There are several 900, 900/1800 GSM services covering the island.

Electricity supply

Variable: 120/127/220V AC at 50 cycles or 60 cycles.

Getting there

Air

Regional airline InselAir is based in Curaçao.

National airline: Windward Island Airways (Winair) (short haul flights only)

International airport/s: Curaçao (CUR), 12km north of Willemstad; with duty-free shops, bar, restaurant, hotel reservations and car hire. Taxis are available, fares are standard and should be agreed in advance.

Airport tax: Passenger facility charge (PFC), from 1 December 2012: destination Bonaire US$10; destination Aruba and Sint Maarten US$20; destination elsewhere US$39; transfer passengers US$5.

Surface

Water: There is a weekly ferry to Curaçao from Venezuela.

Getting about

National transport

Road: There is an all-weather network on the island.

City transport

Taxis: Taxis are usually identified by TX before the licence plate. Fares are standard and should be agreed before travelling. Tipping is discretionary.

Car hire

Car hire is widely available. An international licence is required.

BUSINESS DIRECTORY

Telephone area codes

The international dialling code (IDD) for Curaçao is + 599, followed by area code and subscriber's number:

Willemstad9

Chambers of Commerce

Curaçao Chamber of Commerce and Industry, 1 Kaya Junior Salas, PO Box 10, Willemstad (tel: 9461-3918; fax: 9461-5652; e-mail: businessinfo@curacao-chamber.an).

Banking

Banco di Caribe, Schottegatweg Oost 205, PO Box 3785, Willemstad, Curaçao (tel: 9432-3410; internet: www.bancodicaribe.com).

Banco Industrial de Venezuela CA, Handelskade 12, PO Box 701, Willemstad, Curaçao (tel: 9461-1621; fax: 9461-6534).

Banco Mercantil Venezolano NV, A Mendez Chumaceiro Bvd; PO Box 565, Curaçao (tel: 9461-1566, 9461-2117; fax: 9461-1974; internet: www.bancomercantilcu.com).

Citco Bank Antilles NV, Schottegatweg Oost 44, Willemstad, Curaçao (tel: 9732-2322; fax: 9732-2330; email: curacao-bank@citco.com).

FirstCaribbean International Bank (Curacao) NV, De Ruyterkade 61, PO Box 3144, Willemstad (tel: 9433-8338; fax: 9433-8198; email: www.firstcaribbeanbank.an).

MCB Maduro & Curiel's Bank NV, Plaza Jojo Correa 2-4, PO Box 305, Willemstad, Curaçao (tel: 9466-1100; fax: 9466-1444; email: infor@mcb-bank.com).

MCB Maduro & Curiel's Bank, Schottegatweg Oost 130, Saliña, Curaçao (tel: 9466-1100; fax: 9466-1444; internet: mcb-bank.com).

Orco Bank N V, Dr H Fergusonweg 10, PO Box 3987, Curaçao (tel: 9737-2000; fax: 9737-6741).

Central bank

Centrale Bank van Curaçao en Sint Maarten (Central Bank of Curaçao and St. Maarten) (CBCS), Simon Bolivar Plein 1, Willemstad (tel: 434-5500; fax: 461-5004; email: info@centralbank.an).

Travel information

InselAir (tel: +599 9 737 0444).

National tourist organisation offices

Curaçao Tourist Board, PO Box 3266; Pietermaai 19, Curaçao (tel: 9434-8200; fax: 9461-5017: internet: www.curacao-tourism.com).

Ministries

Ministry of Finance, Pietermaai 4–4A, Willemstad, Curaçao (tel: 9461-2052).

Office of the Minister Plenipotentiary of the Netherlands Antilles, Badhuisweg 175, 2597 JP The Hague, The Netherlands (tel: (+31-70) 351-2811; fax: (+31-70) 351-2722).

Other useful addresses

British Consulate, PO Box 3803, Brombadiersweg z/n, Willemstad, Curaçao (tel: 9436-9366; fax: 9436-9533).

Curaçao Inc (for business information), International Trade Centre Bldg, Piscaderabay, PO Box 6112, Curaçao (tel: 9463-6250; fax: 9463-6485).

Curaçao Industry and International Trade Development Co (CURINDE), Emancipatie Boulevard 7, Curaçao (tel: 9437-6000; fax: 9437-1336).

Foreign Investment Agency Curaçao, Scharlooweg 174 Willemstad, Curaçao (tel: 9465-7044; fax: 9461-5788).

International Trade Centre, PO Box 6005, International Trade Centre Building, Piscadera Bay, Curaçao (tel: 9462-4433, 9463-6250; fax: 9462-4408, 9463-6485).

Island Government of Curaçao, Department of Economic Affairs, Hoogstraat 18, Curaçao (tel: 9462-4066; fax: 9462-6596).

Cyprus

Time was – in the 1970s – when Cyprus styled itself as the 'New Beirut', aiming to replace the civil war smitten Lebanese capital as the new regional business hub. The best laid plans faltered as Nicosia – with an unusable airport – turned out to lack both the infrastructure and the experience needed to become an international business centre. For predictable reasons, the Greek business philosophy rather than the Anglo Saxon, prevailed. Instead, following its accession to the European Union (EU), Cyprus became not so much an offshore banking centre, as a backwater centre, where illegal Russian funds could quietly be stashed and not many questions asked. Northern Cyprus, controlled by Turkey since 1974, became a haven of an even more doubtful nature. The absence of extradition legislation made it a natural choice for those – the highest profile was the failed UK businessman Asil Nadir – who had managed to evade justice elsewhere.

Ironically, Cyprus had become beholden to the two – long standing enemy – countries that had throughout history controlled the fortunes of the Eastern Mediterranean. Greece, with which most Cypriots shared cultural and emotional ties, and Turkey, controlling much of Northern Cyprus. A further irony was that it had been the Greek Cypriot government that was dragging its feet on the question of unification. Both Greece and Cyprus are members of the EU. Turkey under Erdogan has cooled off the prospect of EU membership, but Turkish Cypriots could see at close quarters how their part of the island could benefit.

The economy

By mid-2014 Cyprus' banking and political circles had seen greater changes than they could possibly have imagined at the beginning of 2013. Gradually and painfully, Cyprus was getting to grips with its daunting financial legacy. The small island's offshore and regional financial services were beginning to show signs of life and – perhaps surprisingly – new business registrations were increasing. None the less, the banking sector was estimated to have shrunk by half. Many Cypriots considered that to be a positive sign – they had seen too many of their compatriots generating substantial incomes from what few considered to be the 'real' economy. The worrying thing for the small country's government and financial authorities was that despite the substantial financial shocks of 2013, the island's business model had not changed that much.

What had changed was the perception of and attitude towards, the EU. The Brussels organisation had gone from

KEY FACTS

Official name: Kypriaki Dimokratia-Kibris Cumhuriyeti (Republic of Cyprus)

Head of State: President Nicos Anastasiades (DISY) (from 28 Feb 2013)

Head of government: President Nicos Anastasiades (DISY) (from 28 Feb 2013)

Ruling party: Coaltion led by Dimokratikos Sinagermos (DS) (Democratic Rally), with Anorthotikon Komma Ergazomenou Laou (AKEL) (Progressive Party for Working People) (from Jun 2011)

Area: 9,251 square km (including the north)

Population: 891,000 (2014)*

Capital: Lefkosia (Nicosia); Greek spellings in use since 1995

Official language: Greek and Turkish

Currency: Euro (€) = 100 cents (from 1 Jan 2008; previous currency Cypriot pound, locked at C£0.58 per euro)

Exchange rate: €0.89 per US$ (Sep 2015)

GDP per capita: US$26,115 (2014)

GDP real growth: -2.26% (2014)

GDP: US$23.27 billion (2014)

Labour force: 404,000 (2010)

Unemployment: 16.17% (2014)

Inflation: -0.03% (2014)

Balance of trade: -US$3.54 billion (2014)

* estimated figure

being perceived as Lady Bountiful to the organisation that in 2013 had sought to impose a levy on even the smallest Cypriot saver. The decision to deprive Cypriots of their savings had, rather theatrically, caused even Vladimir Putin to describe the measure as 'unfair, unprofessional and dangerous.'

Thus Cyprus in the second decade of the twenty-first century had almost become a failed time warp, its economy bailed out by the Troika of the EU, the European Central Bank (ECB) and the International Monetary Fund (IMF). In its October 2014 assessment of the Cyprus economy, the IMF noted that the large imbalances accumulated prior to the global financial crisis had culminated in the collapse of Cyprus's banking system in early 2013. In response, the Cypriot authorities had taken unprecedented measures to resolve and recapitalise weak systemic banks at no fiscal cost and adopted a three-year economic-adjustment programme aimed at securing financial stability and fiscal sustainability.

The programme was supported by international financial assistance of about €10 billion (US$11.24 billion), of which about €1 billion (US$1.12 billion) is provided by the IMF under an Extended Fund Facility arrangement and €9 billion (US$10,1 billion) by the European Stability Mechanism (ESM). By October 2014 about €5.75 billion (US$6.46 billion) had already been disbursed under the programme by the IMF and the ESM.

In the view of the IMF, Cyprus had made considerable progress in addressing the crisis. In the context of their adjustment programme, the Cyprus authorities had restructured and recapitalised the financial sector while preserving fiscal sustainability, removed domestic payment restrictions imposed at the height of the crisis, consolidated the public finances and initiated structural reforms. These achievements had helped Cyprus re-access international capital markets in the course of 2014.

However, the IMF noted that overcoming the legacies of the crisis was still a challenge and the outlook remained difficult. The economy had contracted sharply in 2013 and unemployment was still very high in early 2015. Output was expected to decline in 2014 by a further 3.2 per cent before recovering modestly in 2015. Both the private and public sectors were heavily indebted. The banking sector remained vulnerable given the high and rising level of non-performing loans and the tight funding conditions, with external payment restrictions still needed to protect financial stability. Achieving a durable economic recovery would depend critically on maintaining the reform momentum, which required overcoming recent delays in programme implementation.

For its part the European Bank for Reconstruction and Development (EBRD) considered that the Cypriot economy was beginning to show positive signs. This despite the severe recession it had experienced following the crisis in the banking sector and the introduction of severe austerity measures. In 2013 Cyprus' gross domestic product (GDP) had fallen by 5.4 per cent, this on top of the 2.4 per cent fall already registered in 2012. According to the EBRD unemployment continued climb, reaching 16 per cent in 2013, well up on the 11.9 per cent of 2012 and the 6.3 per cent of 2010. Some – perverse – solace could be sought in the fact that wages were adjusting, as pay levels continued to fall. It was a sign of just how bad things had become that the fall in GDP of 2.4 per cent in the second quarter of 2014 was greeted as the best news since the financial crisis had begun. Fiscally, there were also glimmerings: the government deficit was hacked back from 6.4 per cent in 2012 to 4.9 per cent in 2013. Public expenditure cuts had combined with increased rates of taxation to show signs of stronger economic management. But there was a long way to go – Cyprus' general government debt was, according to the EBRD, over 110 per cent of GDP in 2013, a massive increase from the 50 per cent or less seen in 2008. And the worst was still to come, with estimates putting the peak figure at some 124 per cent in 2015. The decline in import levels had combined with buoyant tourism to keep the current account deficit in check. This had enabled the government to report that the current account was approximately in balance.

Some degree of international respectability had been regained in mid-2014 when Cyprus successfully issued a five-year €750 million (US$843 million) bond. In late 2014 Standard & Poor's upgraded Cyprus' credit rating from B to B+. But Cyprus was by no means out of the woods; 2014 promised further recession with GDP expected to fall by 3.5 per cent. However, 2015 was expected to bring some respite and even some possible growth. But Cyprus could easily be adversely affected by regional instability, with the uncertain situation in Greece continuing to throw a shadow over the Cypriot economy.

According to the EBRD, Cyprus ranked 64 out of the 189 countries surveyed in the World Bank's *Doing Business 2015* report, among the lowest in the EU. The low ranking reflected the difficulties encountered in securing basic business necessities such as obtaining electricity supplies, arranging construction permits, registering property and enforcing contracts. Cyprus' laws on solvency and their implementation had, according to the World Bank, proved inadequate in dealing with the legacy of non-performing loans – these had reached a staggering 48 per cent of total loans at the end of August 2014. In September 2014 the government had passed a law on foreclosure designed to

KEY INDICATORS — Cyprus

	Unit	2011	2012	2013	2014	**2015
Population	m	0.84	0.87	0.88	0.89	*0.90
Gross domestic product (GDP)	US$bn	24.90	23.00	24.07	23.27	*19.81
GDP per capita	US$	30,571	26,377	27,300	26,115	*22,007
GDP real growth	%	0.5	-2.4	-5.4	-2.3	*0.2
Inflation	%	3.5	3.1	0.4	–	*-1.0
Unemployment	%	8.1	11.9	15.9	16.2	*15.9
Exports (fob) (goods)	US$m	2,748.0	2,602.0	2,523.0	4,198.0	–
Imports (fob) (goods)	US$m	2,241.0	6,755.0	5,859.0	7,743.0	–
Balance of trade	US$m	-1,664.0	-4,153.0	-3,337.0	-3,545.0	–
Current account	US$m	-2,581.0	-1,565.0	-412.0	-432.0	*-381.0
Total reserves minus gold	US$m	564.1	449.0	379.1	354.8	–
Foreign exchange	US$m	238.1	143.0	75.9	–	–
Exchange rate	per US$	0.75	0.77	9.73	0.82	–

* estimated figure ** forecast figure

reduce the time needed to foreclosure on business loans and mortgages. However, some of the accompanying legislation caused creditors to raise an eyebrow or two.

The Turkish Conundrum

The faint hopes that existed that a solution to Cyprus' four decades long division between the Turkish north and the Greek south were bolstered in late April 2015 by Northern Cyprus' presidential elections. Turkish Cypriots, it seemed, had simply had enough of being treated as second-class citizens. The presidential election gave them the opportunity to deliver a clear message advocating reunification. In the election, the left-wing candidate Mustafa Akinci (with 60 per cent of the votes) defeated the right wing incumbent Dervis Eroglu, who had essentially continued engrained Turkish policies. If the election result represented a step towards reunification, by definition it represented increased tensions with Ankara.

Writing for the *Al Monitor* website, Turkish journalist Fehim Tastekin of the newspaper *Radikal* noted that the tensions were swiftly confirmed when then president elect Akinci described the old relationship between Northern Cyprus and Turkey as one perceived by Ankara to be that between a 'motherland' and a 'baby motherland'. In a remark certain to irritate the nationalist President Erdogan, Mr Akinci indicated his preference of 'a relationship between brothers'. A live television interview with Mr Akinci on Turkish television was, according to Mr Tastekin, cut short and replaced with a presidential press conference. President Erdogan took advantage of the limelight to respond to Mr Akinci: 'working together even as brothers has its prerequisites. This country (viz Turkey) has paid a price for Northern Cyprus. We've sacrificed martyrs and we are continuing to pay a price. We spend about US$1 billion annually.' In his article, Mr Tastekin noted that when the CNN Turk interview with Mr Akinci was resumed, he said that he had 'difficulties in understanding his annoyance. Doesn't Turkey want the baby to grow up?'

Times change. Mr Tastekin noted that when he was prime minister, Mr Erdogan had lent his support to the Northern Cyprus opposition leader Mehmet Ali Talat of the pro-settlement Cumhuriyetçi Türk Partisi (CTP) (Republican Turkish Party), 'both in the 2004 referendum on the failed Annan Plan and in the 2005 presidential elections.' Now President and adopting a worryingly nationalist approach, Erdogan hedges his responses, to the irritation of many Turkish Cypriots. If President Erdogan doesn't mince his words, nor does Mr Akinci. According to Mr Tastekin he 'has been the most vocal critic of Turkish military commanders, ambassadors or special envoys bossing the Kuzey Kýbrýs Türk Cumhuriyeti (KKTC) (Turkish Republic of Northern Cyprus) (TRNC) (aka Northern Cyprus) about.

In the 2004 referendum, Turkish Cypriots voted massively in favour of reunification. The problem was that the Greek Cypriot government had joined the EU. The Turkish Cypriots had cause for anger, as the EU failed to keep its promises to the Turkish Cypriots. The 2015 elections, marked a return to the pre-2004 spirit. The voting was not a straightforward matter. In the first round on April 19, incumbent President Eroglu got 28.15 per cent of the vote, with the Akinci coalition (he had the support of the Communal Democracy Party and the United Cyprus Party) came second with 26.94 per cent. In the second round, however, Mr Akinci secured the Republican Turkish Party's support and romped home.

Old enemies

Mr Tastekin concluded by noting that the frostiness between Messsrs Akinci and Erdogan dated back to 2003, when the two crossed swords at a conference in Spain. Mr Akinci warned that the 2003 elections in Northern Cyprus had to allow the Turkish Cypriots the opportunity of joining the EU alongside the Greek Cypriots. In 2015, the Greek Cypriots, who had failed to vote for the Annan Reunification Plan in 2004, faced growing economic woes, with the EU no longer seen as the answer. In any discussions, President Akinci's opposite number in the negotiations would be Nicos Anastasiades, who had backed the Annan Plan. Hopes run high that with two proponents of the plan facing each other, prospects could only improve.

Energy

The discovery of commercially viable oil and gas deposits in Cyprus waters has changed – or reinforced – Cyprus' strategic position in the region. In short, this is because Cyprus and Israel share significant natural gas reserves. The same companies that own Israel's Leviathan and Tamar gas fields – Noble Energy, Delek Drilling and Avner Oil & Gas Exploration – also own Aphrodite, a 4.5 trillion cubic feet field that lies off the coast of Cyprus. Cyprus has already signed a

KEY FACTS

Official name: Kuzey Kýbrýs Türk Cumhuriyeti (KKTC) (Turkish Republic of Northern Cyprus)

Head of State: President Mustafa Akinci (independent) (since 30 April 2015)

Head of government: Prime Minister Omer Soyer Kalyoncu (since 16 July 2015)

Ruling party: Cumhuriyetçi Türk Partisi (CTP) (Republican Turkish Party) (from 28 Jul 2013)

Area: 3,355 square km

Population: 302,000 (2013)*

Capital: Lefkosa (Lefkota) (Nicosia)

Official language: Turkish

Currency: Yeni Turk Lirasi (YTL) = 100 kurus

Exchange rate: YTL3.02 per US$ (Sep 2015)

GDP per capita: US$13,253 (2013)

GDP real growth: 6.10% (2013)

GDP: US$3.32 million (2013)

Balance of trade: -US$1.17 million (2013)

* estimated figure

memorandum of understanding to supply gas to Egypt but, like Israel, it has yet to work out the mechanics of converting reserves into dollars. Particularly after the 2014 slump in oil prices. An obvious option is for Cyprus to join Israel in developing energy resources and to jointly undertake the implementation of a regional energy development plan.

The US government Energy Information Administration (EIA) notes that in March 2014, Cyprus had no proved reserves of oil or natural gas. However, according to the EIA, an offshore discovery of natural gas resources, with additional exploration on the horizon, has the potential to alter radically Cyprus' energy sector. Cyprus has substantial offshore acreage in the Levant Basin, estimated by the US Geological Survey to contain mean recoverable resources of 1.7 billion barrels of oil and 122 trillion cubic feet (tcf) of natural gas.

In 2011, the US company, Noble Energy, discovered the Aphrodite field in Block 12 of Cyprus' offshore territory and estimates indicate that the field contains 5tcf of recoverable natural gas resources. A bidding round for the country's offshore blocks concluded in late 2012 and further exploration could begin in the near future. Recent seismic exploration by Noble Energy in the Eastern Mediterranean has discovered what it believes to be evidence of oil resources in the offshore area between Cyprus and Israel and estimates are that the formations could contain as much as three billion barrels of ultimately recoverable oil.

Cyprus consumed 60,000 barrels per day (bbl/d) of petroleum in 2012. Cyprus' only oil refinery closed in 2004, ending any ability to produce refined petroleum products for the domestic market. Cyprus now imports all of its petroleum products – primarily from fellow European Union member countries – to meet internal demand, with residual fuel oil and distillate fuel oil comprising approximately 65 per cent of all petroleum imports in 2010. In 2014 construction was underway on a new oil trans-shipment terminal at Vasilikos on the country's southern coast, with the first phase of development scheduled to

Northern Cyprus

Northern Cyprus, or the Turkish Republic of Cyprus, is a self declared state that occupies around a third of the island's territory. The area has been an issue for international tension and is only officially recognised as an independent state by Turkey, which has maintained a large military force on the island since the invasion in retaliation to a Greek backed *coup d'état* in 1974.

The July 1974 *coup* saw President Makorios III ousted by the Cypriot National Guard and the Greek Military Junta and replaced with the more nationalist and pro-Enosis (union with Greece) Nikos Sampson as a dictator. This attempt to annex the island to Greece sparked an invasion by Turkish forces later that year who took control of the northern part of the island in order to protect the Turkish Cypriots who now felt threatened under the new regime. Sampson's military government eventually collapsed and the Turkish continued to divide Cyprus along what has become known as the Green Line. Since then Northern Cyprus has become a *de facto* government which officially announced their independence from the Republic of Cyprus in November 1983, though they are still only recognised as a state by Turkey.

Northern Cyprus is heavily dependent on Turkey for political, economic, and military support due to its lack of legitimacy on the international stage. Hope for a push to a solution has grown recently, however, as Northern Cypriots have grown discontented with the isolation and dependence on Turkey that their situation has generated. The April 2015 presidential elections saw the hardline, nationalistic president, Dervis Eroglu, who was in line with traditional Turkish policies, replaced by the political rookie and independent candidate Mustafa Akinci. This shift in the dynamic of power signalled a slight anti-Turkish sentiment that had spread through the Northern Cypriot population. The new President has backed calls for the retraction of Turkish forces from parts of the territory and has reached agreements with the officially recognised Greek Cypriot government to open international shipping lanes and to permit direct flights to the North. This will open up tourism for the North and will hopefully allow further steps towards reunification and peace on the Island.

Economy

Due to Northern Cyprus not being recognised as a sovereign state and instead being seen as a part of the world that is partially under occupation, statistics and information on the economy can be hard to come by.

Northern Cyprus's economy is led by the service sector which made up 58.7 per cent gross domestic production (GDP) in 2012, compared to 35.1 per cent for industry and only 6.2 per cent for agriculture. GDP growth rate has been slow and steady in the last years, falling slightly from 2.8 per cent in 2013 to 2.3 per cent in 2014. Unemployment is still a slight problem which, according to official government statistics, stood at 9.5 per cent in 2013. Relatively slow growth and the problems of unemployment are hopefully on the mend as public opinion and official policy of the territory shift towards more co-operative and reunification-orientated goals. The election of Mustafa Akinci opened up possibilities for investment and cash flow as shipping lanes and airspace were reopened to allow increased trade and a more extensive and supportive tourism sector. The tensions that have plagued the island have previously hindered the Northern territory from expanding its tourist industry adequately and on an island where the total contribution of tourist industry accounted for some 21.3 per cent of GDP and 12.3 per cent of total investment this is a vital lifeline that the economy needs to exploit.

Mustafa Akinci

Since Turkey's invasion 40 years ago and seizure of Cyprus' northern third, which led to 200,000 Greek Cypriots fleeing south, ethnic tensions between the two groups have been constantly near breaking point.

Thrice mayor of Nicosia – Cyprus' capital and largest city – Mustafa Akinci has devoted his political career to unifying Greek and Turkish Cypriots. Now new leader of the Turkish side of Cyprus, Akinci has embarked on a revolutionary peace programme, not seen in years. In his first four weeks in power, Akinci oversaw the removal of visa requirements for Greek Cypriots wanting to visit Northern Cyprus and, in a highly symbolic act, walked arm-in-arm with his Greek presidential counterpart across the demilitarised buffer zone.

conclude in 2015. This is part of a broader effort to develop Cyprus into a regional energy hub, a plan that includes the construction of a liquefied natural gas (LNG) facility (also at Vasilikos) that will be supplied with natural gas from Cyprus' own offshore fields. If completed, the LNG facility could also incorporate natural gas from elsewhere in the eastern Mediterranean, but agreements have been slow to materialise. Turkey might well become the most important route of natural gas shipments from Eastern Mediterranean reserves. Additional volumes from Cyprus' offshore areas or from fields elsewhere in the Levant Basin may be required to make an LNG terminal in Vasilikos economically viable. As a result of the high import costs of petroleum products, consumers in Cyprus pay some of the highest prices for electricity in the European Union.

Risk assessment

Economy	Poor
Politics	Fair
Regional stability	Fair

Muslims in Cyprus

% of population	18
Sunni (% of Muslims)	99
Shi'a (% of Muslims)	1

COUNTRY PROFILE

1925 Cyprus became a British crown colony.
1955 The Greek Cypriots of the Ethniki Organosis Kipriakou Agonos (Eoka) (National Organisation of Cypriot Combatants) launched a guerrilla war against British authority. The Eoka wanted Cyprus to unify with mainland Greece.
1960 President Makarios oversaw Cyprus' independence, which followed a compromise agreement between Greek and Turkish Cypriots, with Britain retaining sovereignty over two military bases.
1961 Cyprus joined the IMF and World Bank.
1963 Makarios upset the Turkish Cypriots when he proposed constitutional change, which would abrogate power-sharing arrangements. Inter-communal fighting erupted and the Turkish Cypriot community withdrew from the central government.
1964 A UN peace-keeping force was sent to the island.
1968–74 Talks on constitutional reform were inconclusive, as Turkish Cypriots sought separate municipalities in the five main towns.
1974 A brief Greek junta sponsored coup by supporters of a union with Greece toppled President Makarios who fled the island. On 20 July Turkey launched an invasion on northern Cyprus and Greek Cypriots fled their homes in the north; 37 per cent of the island came under Turkish control, enforcing partition between north and south. The border between the two became known as the Green Line. The coup failed and Glafcos Clerides took over as the Greek Cypriot president, until Makarios returned at the end of the year.
1975 Northern Cyprus declared the formation of the 'Turkish Federated State of Cyprus' with Rauf Denktash as president and with the aim of eventually gaining independence.
1977 President Makarios died and was succeeded by Spyros Kyprianou.
1980 UN-sponsored peace talks resumed.
1983 Rauf Denktash suspended talks and northern Cyprus officially seceded as the Kuzey Kýbrýs Türk Cumhuriyeti (KKTC) (Turkish Republic of Northern Cyprus (TRNC)) introducing its own government and legal system. The international community rejected the secessionist move and only Turkey recognised it as a state.
1988 Georgios Vassiliou was elected Greek Cypriot president.
1992–93 Additional UN-sponsored talks with Rauf Denktash failed when the UN Security Council rejected Turkish demands for the recognition of separate sovereignty for the KKTC, including a right to secession.
1993 Glafcos Clerides defeated George Vassiliou in the presidential election.
1994 The European Court of Justice ruled that all direct trade between northern Cyprus and the EU was illegal.
1994–95 Talks continued between north and south with little progress. The Greek Cypriots and the UN pushed for a federal system, but this was rejected by the KKTC.
1996 Tension between the two sides increased and there was violence along the Green Line.
1997 UN-mediated talks between Clerides and Denktash failed.
1998 Clerides was narrowly re-elected for a second term. The EU listed Cyprus as a potential member.
1999 Further peace talks in the US failed to find a solution to Cyprus' division.
2000 Rauf Denktash was elected for a fourth five-year term as the KKTC president.
2001 The leaders of the two Cypriot communities held their first direct talks in four years and agreed to restart peace talks to pave the way for EU membership.
2002 A UN-sponsored plan for reunification as a federation with a rotating presidency was rejected by the KKTC, which insisted on international recognition. The EU invited Cyprus to join, however if the two estranged communities could not agree to reunification then only the Greek Cypriot part of the island would become a member.
2003 Tassos Papadopoulos of the Dimokratikon Komma (DIKO) (Democratic Party) won the presidency. A coalition led by the leftist, Anorthotikon Komma Ergazemenou Laou (Akel) (Progressive Party of the Working People) with Kinima Sosialdimokraton (Kisos) (Social Democrats Movement) won parliamentary elections. The UN deadline for agreement on reunification passed without agreement. Crossing points between the two zones were temporarily opened and the government lifted 20-year-old trade sanctions against the KKTC, thus allowing farmers in the north to sell produce in the south and export to the EU, and permitting Turkish Cypriots to work in the south.
2004 Twin referenda on the UN reunification plan and united EU entry saw Greek Cypriots voting against unification with the north by 76 per cent, while in the north, 65 per cent voted in favour of the proposal. The Republic of Cyprus joined the EU. Turkey agreed that it would recognise Cyprus as an EU member.
2005 Turkey agreed to extend a free trade accord with the EU, including Cyprus. Mehmet Ali Talat became president of KKTC. In Cyprus' worst ever air accident, 121 people on board a Helios Airways plane were killed in a crash as it approached Athens' airport.
2006 The ruling coalition won the parliamentary elections with a combined vote of 49 per cent.
2007 EU officials formally invited Cyprus to join the third stage of the European Monetary Union (EMU). The ruling coalition was dissolved as Akel nominated its own candidate for the 2008 presidential election. Ministerial posts were filled by technocrats. Cyprus became a member of the European Union Schengen area whereby all travellers may cross borders without a passport or visa.
2008 Cyprus adopted the euro as its official currency. Demetris Christofias became president. Ledra Street, which runs through the UN buffer zone in Lefkosia, was reopened; it had been closed since 1964.
2009 In KKTC elections the ruling CTP lost power to the Ulusal Birlik Partisi (UBP) (National Unity Party) and Dervis Eroglu (UBP), became prime minister; he is expected to adopt a more hard-line stance in talks with the government of the Republic of Cyprus. Cyprus blocked progress of Turkey's accession (to the EU) talks when it refused to allow the start of talks in five policy areas unless Turkey changed its position on the Cyprus dispute.
2010 In KKTC presidential elections, Dervis Eroglu (UBP) won 50.4 per cent of the vote and incumbent Mehmet Ali Talat

42.9 per cent. The president of KKTC appointed Irsen Kucuk as prime minister of KKTC. Cyprus and Romania signed a Memorandum of Understanding (MoU), covering technical and entrepreneurial development in renewable energy sources. UN-mediated talks on the future of northern Cyprus were held.

2011 In parliamentary elections held in May, the opposition, centre-right, Dimokratikos Sinagermos (DS) (Democratic Rally) won 34.28 per cent of the vote (20 seats out of 56), while the ruling Anorthotikon Komma Ergazomenou Laou (AKEL) (Progressive Party for Working People) won 32.67 per cent (19 seats). Without enough seats for a majority in parliament, DS formed a coalition government with AKEL. An explosion in July, in the arms depot of the Evangelos Florakis Naval Base on the south coast, killed 12 people and destroyed Cyprus' largest power plant. Total damage was estimated at US$2.8 billion; repairing just the power station, which had produced about half of the island's electricity, could cost US$1.4 billion. The governor of the central bank, Athanasios Orphanides, warned that as a result of the explosion the country faced a 'state of emergency' and that Cyprus could become the next southern eurozone member to look for a bail-out from the EU. He recommended a harsher programme of austerity measures. Cyprus began drilling for oil in the eastern Mediterranean in September; Turkey has said it will also start drilling, risking an escalation in tension between the two countries.

2012 Former president of North Cyprus, Rauf Denktas died on 13 January. He was the founder and first president of the breakaway KKTC. In April, Turkey began drilling for oil and natural gas offshore in Cypriot waters. On 27 April, talks between the governments of Cyprus and KKTC chaired by the UN were cancelled. On 13 June 2012, the credit ratings agency, Moody's, cut Cyprus's rating from Ba1 to Ba3 (two notches), a rate considered as 'junk' and effectively worthless. Fitch, another ratings agency, stated that Cyprus's debt level was likely to climb to over 100 per cent of GDP in 2012. On 4 October 2012, the government announced that it intended to apply for €11.5 billion (US$15 billion) in financial assistance from the European Financial Stability Facility (EFSF), to shore up its failing banks, which were exposed to Greek debt.

2013 Presidential elections were held in Cyprus on 17 February with the run-off held on 24 February. The first round was won by Nicos Anastasiades (DISY) with 45.46 per cent, followed by Stavros Malas (AKEL) 26.91 per cent and Giorgos Lillikas (EDEK) 24.93 per cent; turnout was 83.13 per cent. The run-off was won by Mr Anastasiades (57.48 per cent) ahead of Mr Malas (42.52 per cent); turnout was 81.58 per cent.

2015 Presidential elections were held in the north on 26 April 2015. The winner was Mustafa Akinci, an Independent, with 60.3 per cent. The result raised hopes for a resolution of the over forty years of dispute with the south.

Political structure

The government of southern Cyprus is internationally recognised as the sole administration of the Republic of Cyprus. Occupied by Turkish troops since 1974, northern Cyprus has its own government and calls itself the Kuzey Kýbrýs Türk Cumhuriyeti (KKTC) (Turkish Republic of Northern Cyprus (TRNC)). It is only recognised by Turkey.

Constitution

The constitution was promulgated in 1960.

The voting age was extended to include all citizens above the age of 18 for the 1998 presidential election.

Northern Cyprus introduced its own consitution after declaring unilateral independence in 1983.

Independence date

1960

Form of state

Presidential republic

The executive

Executive power is held by the president who is directly elected for a five-year term by universal suffrage. A council of ministers is appointed by the president, who convenes and presides over its meetings. Ministers may not sit in the house of representatives, but may introduce bills.

National legislature

The unicameral Vouli Antiprosópon (House of Representatives) has 59 members elected for a five-year term, of which 56 members are elected by proportional representation; three members are observers representing the Maronite, Latin and Armenian communities and 24 seats are allocated to the Turkish Cypriot community but have not been filled since 1963.

In 1983, northern Cyprus introduced its own parliament, the 50-member Temsilciler Meclisi (House of Representatives).

Legal system

The Republic of Cyprus' legal system is embodied in the 1960 constitution and is based on British common law. The legal system in northern Cyprus is based on Turkish law.

Last elections

22 May 2011 (parliamentary); 17 and 24 February 2013 (presidential, first and second rounds); 19 April 2009 (KKTC parliamentary), 18 April 2010 (KKTC presidential).

Results: Parliamentary: Dimokratikos Sinagermos (DS) (Democratic Rally) won 34.28 per cent of the vote (20 seats out of 56), Anorthotikon Komma Ergazomenou Laou (AKEL) (Progressive Party for Working People) 32.67 per cent (19), Dimokratikon Komma (DK) (Democratic Party), 15.76 per cent (nine), Kinima Sosialdimokraton (KSD) (Movement for Social Democracy) 8.93 per cent (five), Evropaiko Komma (EK) (European Party) 3.88 per cent (two), Kinima Oikologon Perivallontiston (KOP) (Ecological and Environmental Movement) 2.21 per cent (one); four political parties and independents failed to win enough votes to win seats. Turnout was 78.7 per cent.

Presidential: 17 and 24 February 2014 The first round was won by Nicos Anastasiades (DISY) with 45.46 per cent, followed by Stavros Malas (AKEL) 26.91 per cent and Giorgos Lillikas (EDEK) 24.93 per cent; turnout was 83.13 per cent. The run-off was won by Mr Anastasiades (57.48 per cent) ahead of Mr Malas (42.52 per cent); turnout was 81.58 per cent.

KKTC parliamentary: Ulusal Birlik Partisi (UBP) (National Unity Party) won 44.07 per cent; 26 seats (out of 50), Cumhuriyetçi Türk Partisi (CTP) (Republican Turkish Party) 29.15 per cent (15), Demokrat Partisi (Democratic Party) (Democrats) 10.65 per cent (five), Toplumcu Demokrasi Partisi (TDP) (Communal Democracy Party) 6.87 per cent (two), Özgürlük ve Reform Partisi (ÖRP) (Freedom and Reform Party) 6.2 per cent (two); two other parties failed to win enough votes to reach the threshold for gaining a seat. Turnout was 81.42 per cent.

KKTC presidential: Dervis Eroglu (UBP) won 50.4 per cent of the vote, Mehmet Ali Talat (CTP) 42.9 per cent.

European parliament (June 2009): turn out was 59.4 per cent, compared to 72.5 per cent in 2004.

Next elections

2018 (presidential); 2016 (parliamentary).

Political parties

Ruling party

Coaltion led by Dimokratikos Sinagermos (DS) (Democratic Rally), with Anorthotikon Komma Ergazomenou Laou (AKEL) (Progressive Party for Working People) (from Jun 2011)

Main opposition party

Dimokratikos Sinagermos (Disi) (Democratic Coalition); KKTC parliament: Cumhuriyetçi Türk Partisi (CTP) (Republican Turkish Party)

Population
881,000 (2013)*
Last census: 1 October 2011: 638,897 (excluding Northern Cyprus)
Population density: 82 inhabitants per square km. Urban population 70 per cent (2010 Unicef).
Annual growth rate: 1.8 per cent, 1990–2010 (Unicef).

Ethnic make-up
Greeks (84.1 per cent), Turks (11.8 per cent), Maronites (0.6 per cent), Armenians (0.3 per cent), Latins (0.1per cent), foreign residents (mainly British and Greek) (3.1 per cent).

Religions
Christian Orthodox (77 per cent), Muslim (18 per cent).

Education
Primary schooling lasts for six years between the ages of six and 12. Public general secondary education extends over six years. Almost 20,000 students, mostly from Turkey, Eastern Europe and the Middle East, attend six private universities in northern Cyprus.
Literacy rate: 97 per cent, adult rate (World Bank)
Compulsory years: Six to 15.
Enrolment rate: 100 per cent gross primary enrolment of the relevant age group (including repeaters) (World Bank)

Health
The government is looking for ways to persuade Greek-Cypriot medical specialists to return from overseas and offer high-quality healthcare services at a considerably lower cost than in Western Europe.
Life expectancy: 79 years, 2004 (WHO 2006)
Fertility rate/Maternal mortality rate: 1.5 births per woman, 2010 (Unicef)
Birth rate/Death rate: 8 deaths and 17 births per 1,000 people (World Bank)
Child (under 5 years) mortality rate (per 1,000): 3 per 1,000 live births (WHO 2012)
Head of population per physician: 2.34 physicians per 1,000 people, 2002 (WHO 2006)

Welfare
Cyprus offers a statutory social insurance scheme securing decent pensions and allows pensioners to continue working without affecting their pensions. The Social Insurance Scheme provides insurance for all employees who contribute 16.6 per cent on the insured income. The employer deducts 6.3 per cent of the employees' income and contributes 6.3 per cent, while the remaining 4 per cent is paid by the state. There is provision for a non-contributory social pension for elderly people who are not entitled to a pension from any other source. There is also a complementary public assistance scheme for people whose resources are not sufficient to meet their basic and special needs. There is provision for unemployment and disability benefits. The National Social Security System allows women a paid 16-week maternity leave and a substantial birth allowance. Cyprus also offers crime victims a financial compensation programme.

Main cities
Lefkosia (commonly known as Nicosia) (capital, estimated population 237,854 in 2012), Lemesos (Limassol) (179,450), Larnaka (Larnaca) (58,007), Pafos (Paphos) (32,700), Aradippou (14,229). In Turkish-occupied northern Cyprus, Lefkosa (the part of Lefkosia under Turkish control, estimated population 57,269 in 2012), Gazimagusa (35,912), Girne (34,362), Gonyeli (14,229).

Languages spoken
English is widely spoken in tourist regions.

Official language/s
Greek and Turkish

Media
Media services have outlets in each zone operating under their own regulations.

Press
Dailies: In Greek, the most popular newspapers are all independents, including *Phileleftheros* (www.philenews.com), *Simerini (Today)* (www.simerini.com.cy), *Politis (Citizen)* (www.politis-news.com) and *Haravgi* (www.haravgi.com.cy). In Turkish important newspapers include *Kibris Gazetesi* (www.kibrisgazetesi.com) and *Halkin Sesi (Voice of the People)* (www.halkinsesi.org), both independents and *Yeni Kibris* (www.ykp.org.cy) published by the unification, YKP (New Cyprus Party), with Greek and English online versions. In English, *The Cyprus Mail*, (www.cyprus-mail.com).
Weeklies: In Greek, the SSP Media Group publishes several titles for women, men and lifestyle magazines (www.sppmedia.com). *To Periodiko* (www.toperiodiko.com) for current affairs, The Cyprus Government Gazette (www.cygazette.com) is a comprehensive weekly publication. In English, *The Cyprus Weekly* (www.cyprusweekly.com.cy) has the largest circulation, followed by the *Cyprus Observer* (www.observercyprus.com).
Business: Two publications that are closely linked are the *Financial Mirror* (www.financialmirror.com), published in English, with a Greek version *Xpress Economiki*.
In Greek, *Euro Kerdos (Euro Profit)* (www.eurokerdos.com) a financial and *Chrimatistiriaki* a stock exchange, monthly magazines.
Periodicals: Monthlies include, in Greek, *Flash* (www.flashcy.com) for young people, as is, in English, *Scoop* (www.scoop-magazine.com) and *Sports in the City* (www.sportsinthecitynews.com), *In Touch* (www.intouchcyprus.com) for lifestyle articles.

Broadcasting
Cyprus Broadcasting Corporation (CyBC) (www.cybc.com.cy) is state broadcaster for the Republic of Cyprus.
Bayrak Radio and Television Corporation (BRT) (www.brtk.cc) operates in Northern Cyprus.
Radio: CyBC operates three radio stations: the First Programme, International Programme, Third Programme and Fourth Programme, offering a range of news, talk, education, entertainment and music programmes, also in English, Armenian and Turkish.
BRT (www.brtk.cc) has five stations including Bayrak Radio, Bayrak FM, Baryrak International, Bayrak Classic FM and Bayrak Turkish Music, all broadcasting from Famagusta.
Private commercial radio stations include Radio Astra (www.astra.com.cy) Radio 91.4 FM (www.91.4coastfm.com) and Mix FM (www.mixfmradio.com).
Television: CyBC (www.cybc.com.cy) is the national public TV station, which operates two terrestrial channels, Pik 1, with news and factual programmes and Pik 2, with entertainment programmes and one satellite television channel (Pik TV).
BRT (www.brtk.cc) operates two TV channels Bayrak TV 1 and 2.
There are several other satellite and pay-to-view TV stations including Sigma (www.sigma.com.cy), Music Box TV (www.musicbox.com.cy) and Lumiere TV (www.lumieretv.com).
National news agency: Cyprus News Agency (CNA)
Other news agencies: TAK (Arca Haber Ajansi) (in Turkish): www.arcaajans.com

Economy
The service sector, in particular tourism, but also financial services and real estate, constitutes 78.3 per cent of GDP (2014), and employs over 80.1 per cent of the workforce (2013). In 2014, 2.44 million tourists visited the island and typically over 50 per cent of visitors come from the UK. Industry and manufacturing enterprises in ship repair and construction materials, pharmaceutical and clothing contribute 19.6 per cent of GDP, while agriculture comprises around 2.1 per cent, providing potatoes, grapes, oranges, olives and wine for export.
Cyprus formally joined the Economic Monetary Union (Emu) of the EU in 2008 and adopted the euro as its currency, not only to enhance its prospects of trading

within the EU but also, ironically as the eurozone crisis worsened in 2011, to gain a degree of safety from external shocks. However as tourist numbers fell during the global economic crisis so Cyprus' fortunes also weakened. GDP growth in 2007 was a strong 5.1 per cent, falling to 3.6 per cent in 2008, before dropping into recession in early 2009, with -1.9 per cent growth as tourism, the real estate market and local construction contracted sharply. Domestic demand fell as unemployment rose.

The government introduced measures to ease the economy and aid its recovery by allowing increased public debt. This increased its budget deficit to above 8 per cent of GDP, a figure that, in 2009, the European Central Bank (ECB) required to be lowered to 3 per cent by 2012. Measures to achieve this included reducing the size of public employment. However by 2012, the budget deficit was 6.4 per cent of GDP and therefore had not met the ECB's requirement.

Recovery began slowly, so that by the third quarter of 2010, GDP growth year-on-year was 1.7 per cent; the annual figure was 1.1 per cent. In 2013 the budget deficit, which was still above the ECB's target amount, was at 5.4 per cent of GDP. The growth of the country's GDP fell to a low of -5.0 per cent in the same year, whilst unemployment was at a high of 16.0 per cent. The banking sector also suffered a due to the global crisis as the two largest Cypriot banks were among the chief holders of Greek bonds and as their credit ratings began to fall Cypriot banks were excluded form international capital markets in may 2011. On 13 June 2012, the credit ratings agency Moody's cut Cyprus's rating from Ba1 to Ba3 (two notches), a rate considered as 'junk' and effectively worthless. The government began seeking a €5 billion (US$6.3 billion) bailout from the eurozone and IMF. On 24 June 2012, the government announced that it intended to become the fifth country to apply for financial assistance from the European Financial Stability Facility (EFSF) in the sum of €1.8 billion (US$2.3 billion), to shore up its failing banks, which were exposed to Greek debt. In 2013 Cyprus was still experiencing negative growth at -5.4 per cent, this has improved slightly by 2014, though the crisis still kept growth negative as -2.8 per cent growth as Cyprus tries desperately to recover from the global crisis.

In october 2013 and US-Israeli team finished searching for hydrocarbon deposits on the island after they found 141.6 billion cubic metres (CUM) of natural gas, though drilling has not yet commenced.

Northern Cyprus, which uses the Turkish lira as its currency, suffers from high inflation – estimated at 8 per cent in 2013. Financial aid from Turkey and remittances from the more than 200,000 Turkish Cypriots living abroad are vital sources of revenue. Tourism is the principal economic activity, although all visitors have to access the northern sector via Turkey.

External trade

As a member of the European Union, Cyprus operates within a community-wide free trade area, with tariffs set as a whole. Internationally, the EU has free trade agreements with a number of nations and trading blocs worldwide.

Cyprus' name is directly derived from the Greek word for 'copper' due to the fact the island was so rich in the metal which is one of the world's most valuable and traded commodities. Historically, the country was a hub for copper trade; however mining has become more of a niche in recent years and manufactured products dominate exports now.

Imports

Cyprus has a large trade deficit as most goods must be imported, including crude oil, raw materials and machinery for manufacturing, and all transport vehicles.

Main sources: Greece (23.5 per cent of total in 2014), Israel (9.5 per cent), UK (7.3 per cent).

Exports

Export of manufactured goods, including electric and electronic equipment, processed food, chemicals, paper, textiles and refined oil represent the largest portion of foreign earnings; important agricultural exports include potatoes, grapes, wine and citrus. Minerals exported include copper, pyrites, chrome, asbestos, and gypsum.

Main destinations: Greece (15.2 per cent of total in 2014), UK (9.4 per cent), Israel (5.4 per cent).

Re-exports

Refined oil accounts for a significant share of total annual exports.

Agriculture

Farming

The agriculture sector contributed just 2.1 per cent to GDP in 2014. Major crops are potatoes, grapes, citrus fruits and barley. Cattle, sheep and goats, swine and poultry are raised. Fresh pork, poultry meat and eggs satisfy local demand. Local production of beef, veal, mutton and lamb is supplemented by imports. Agriculture typically employs around 3.5 per cent of the workforce.

The implementation of modern irrigation technologies has helped to address the sector's water shortage. A large-scale water development programme culminated in the Southern Conveyor Project that carries surplus water from the south-western part of the island to the central and eastern areas in an effort to broaden and boost agricultural production and alleviate water shortages.

Now a member of the EU, Cyprus has been eligible for full EU agricultural subsidies and rural development aid through the Common Agricultural Policy (CAP) from 2013.

Fishing

The fishing industry largely consists of inshore and trawl fishing, as well as aquaculture. Annual fish production typically totals 4,300 tonnes.

Forestry

Forest and other wooded land accounts for less than a third of the land area. Industrial wood and paper products are largely imported.

Industry and manufacturing

The industrial sector contributed around 19.6 per cent to GDP in 2014 and accounts for around 16 per cent of the workforce.

Major growth industries, which are mainly export-based, include cement, food and drink, footwear and clothing. Chemical and pharmaceutical products, plastics and publishing are also expanding areas. Foreign investment is encouraged. Industrial activity in northern Cyprus is limited to food and textiles.

Tourism

Cyprus markets itself as an island of ancient myth and culture. However, its political turmoil has cut the island in two and left relations fractious with not only its own Turkish community but also Turkey as its closest mainland neighbour. Tourists from the UK constitute the largest visitor group (approximately 50 per cent), followed by those from Russia.

In 2014, the contribution of tourism and travel was 21.3 per cent, and was predicted to rise by 5.5 per cent in 2015. The industry provided jobs to 82,500 people which was 22.6 per cent of the total workforce and is also accounts for 12.3 per cent of total investment.

An open sky policy for more budget airlines to land, plus a new terminal at Larnaca Airport, opened in 2009, capable of processing 7.5 million passengers annually, should enhance the experience of travellers to Cyprus. There are marina projects being constructed around the south and west coasts to attract yachting enthusiasts. A cruise liner terminal, with facilities and berths for six ships, is planned.

Environment

The problems of water shortages, sewage disposal, industrial and agricultural pollution and waste disposal are acute. The

government has introduced a programme of legislation incorporating the principle that the polluter pays. By July 2008, Cyprus had had no substantial winter rainfall since 2004 and water reservoirs were at their lowest since 1908 so that potable water had to be imported from the Greek mainland; contamination fears condemned a shipment of 40,000 cubic metres of water, which had to be discarded and pumped into the ground. Cyprus will import eight million cubic metres of water, costing US$70 million, by November 2008.
Northern Cyprus is particularly badly affected by water shortages, a problem accentuated by the Turkish soldiers stationed on the island. Shortages have caused many to stop cultivating the land as low rainfalls mean water reserves are used faster than they are replenished. The Turkish government has proposed building a water pipeline to northern Cyprus, capable of carrying 70–100 million cubic metres a year to the island. Since the 1990s, giant plastic 'sacks' of water have been pulled across the Mediterranean from Turkey to northern Cyprus; there is a concern about a long-term shortage of water.

Mining
Cyprus was once famous for its enormous copper reserves. It has a 3,000 year tradition of copper mining, which was the biggest source of the nation's revenue. However after the 1974 Turkish invasion copper mining stopped.
Continued expansion in the construction industry has led to a boom in quarrying of construction materials and non-metallic minerals. Other quarried materials include marble, bentonite, umber, sienna, ochra and limonite.

Hydrocarbons
Although oil reserves are thought to be present in waters surrounding Cyprus and exploration has been undertaken, no commercial drilling is in operation. Oil exploration licences for the entire Cypriot territorial waters were issued to foreign oil companies from 2006 and evoked opposition from Northern Cyprus and Turkey which considered that any benefits from oil and gas finds would be garnered by the Republic of Cyprus. Cyprus began exploratory drilling for oil in the eastern Mediterranean in September 2011.
The Turkish oil company, TPAO began exploration drilling for oil and natural gas in Northern Cyprus in April 2012. The Cyprus government was swift in condemning the work saying 'Turkey and the Turkish Cypriot leadership are violating the law by going ahead with drilling in the occupied area of Famagusta'.
Cyprus does not produce natural gas, although Cyprus has 141.1 billion cubic metres (cum) of reserves, and any imports of liquefied natural gas (LNG) are negligible.
There are reserves of coal but production is not commercially recorded.

Energy
Total installed generating capacity was 1,527MW in 2013, producing 4.57 billion kilowatt hours.
The Electricity Authority of Cyprus (EAC) operates three power stations, two of which use heavy fuel oil. Valilikos Power Station, the third, and latest, plant, uses a combination of heavy fuel and gas and has a capacity of 840MW.
Cyprus is well suited to solar power with over 300 days of sunshine per annum. The government subsidises the installation of solar technology to a maximum 55 per cent of the cost, and has now started to subsidise wind power.
Cyprus began drilling for oil in the eastern Mediterranean in September 2011; Turkey has said it will also start drilling, risking an escalation in tension between the two countries.

Financial markets
The Cyprus Stock Exchange (CSE) was transformed in 1996 from an over-the-counter market to an official stock exchange. The CSE became a fully computerised trading system in 1999. The overall supervision of the stock exchange is assigned to the minister of finance and is exercised by the minister through the Securities and Exchange Commission.

Stock exchange
Cyprus Stock Exchange (CSE)

Banking and insurance
The Bank of Cyprus, which was founded in 1899, leads the Cypriot banking sector. The Central Bank of Cyprus (CBC) oversees monetary policy. There are nine commercial banks. The abolition of the interest rate ceiling was part of a drive to reform banking practices in line with those of the EU. The banking sector also suffered a due to the global crisis as the two largest Cypriot banks were among the chief holders of Greek bonds and as their credit ratings began to fall Cypriot banks were excluded form international capital markets in may 2011. Cyprus's credit rating is still meagre as the country still attempts to recover from the global economic crisis.

Central bank
Central Bank of Cyprus

Time
GMT plus two hours (daylight saving, late March to late October, GMT plus three hours)

Geography
Cyprus is an island in the eastern Mediterranean Sea, about 100km south of Turkey. The landscape varies between rugged coastlines, sandy beaches, rocky hills and forest-covered mountains. The Troodos Mountains in the centre of the island rise to almost 1,950 metres.

Hemisphere
Northern

Climate
Mediterranean. Summers are long and dry. Winters are changeable with occasional rain. Temperatures range from 0–27 degrees Celsius (C) (in the mountains), 5–40 degrees C (inland) and 9–35 degrees C (on the coast). Hottest months are July and August; coldest are January and February. Average annual rainfall is 500mm.

Entry requirements
Passports
Required by all except citizens of EU, Switzerland, Iceland and Norway travelling with official national ID cards. Passports must have at least three months validity from the date of departure from Cyprus.

Visa
Required by all except citizens of most European countries, America and Japan. Contact the local embassy or High Commission for a full list of exceptions and application, see consular and protocol information in: www02.mfa.gov.cy. A Schengen visa application (offered in several languages) can be downloaded from http://europa.eu/abc/travel/ see 'documents you will need'.
For a business visa, applications should include an introductory letter from the employer, which gives details and the nature of business to be conducted.

Prohibited entry
Cypriot authorities do not recognise any ports of entry other than those in the Republic of Cyprus. Visitors with passports stamped in the Turkish Republic of Northern Cyprus must have their visa stamps cancelled by the Republic of Cyprus immigration authorities.

Currency advice/regulations
Local currency may be imported without restriction but must be declared; foreign currency over US$1,000 (or the equivalent) must be declared. The export of foreign and local currency is limited to the amount declared on arrival. Export of local currency withdrawn from Cypriot banks is permitted, provided a holding certificate is obtained.
To avoid extra exchange fees travellers cheques in UK pounds sterling or Cyprus pounds are advised.

Customs
Personal items are duty-free. There are no duties levied on alcohol and tobacco

between EU member states, providing amounts imported are for personal consumption.
Unauthorised export of antiquities is prohibited; permission of the Cyprus Museum is required.

Health (for visitors)
Nationals of the European Economic Area (EEA) countries and Switzerland can access reduced cost and sometimes free medical treatment using a European Health Insurance Card (EHIC) while visiting the EEA. Exceptions include nationals of the 10 countries which joined the EU in 2004 whose EHIC is not valid in Switzerland. Applications for the EHIC should be made before travelling.

Mandatory precautions
None

Advisable precautions
Recommended immunisations include tetanus and polio, while long-term visitors are advised to consider a hepatitis A immunisation.
Tap water is safe to drink, but fruit, especially soft fruit, should be washed.

Hotels
There are over 500 hotels (from deluxe to one star). Visitors should book well in advance, especially during the peak holiday season (April–October). Cyprus Tourism Organisation (CTO) operates a rating system, both for hotels and any other licensed tourist accommodation. Tipping is not obligatory. A 15 per cent valued added tax (VAT) is charge on all bills.

Credit cards
Most leading cards are accepted in the main hotels, restaurants and shops.

Public holidays (national)

Fixed dates
1 Jan (New Year's Day), 6 Jan (Epiphany), 25 Mar (Greek National Day), 1 Apr (Greek Cypriot National Day), 1 May (Labour Day), 15 Aug (Assumption Day), 1 Oct (Cyprus Independence Day), 28 Oct (Greek National Day/Ochi Day), 24–26 Dec (Christmas Holiday).

Variable dates
Green Monday (Feb/Mar), Greek Orthodox Easter (Mar/Apr, four days Thu–Mon); Pentecost (Festival of the Flood (Jun)).

Working hours

Banking
Mon–Fri: 0815–1230; Mon (only) 1515–1645, (year around).
In summer (Jun–Aug), in central districts, some banks have extended hours Tue–Fri: 1515–1645.

Business
Mon–Fri: 0800–1300 and 1500–1800 (winter), 0730–1300 and 1600–1830 (summer); Wed and Sat half-day (year round).

Government
Mon–Fri: 0730–1430; in winter Sept–June, Thu: 1500–1800.

Shops
Mon–Fri: 0800–1300 and 1430–1800 (winter), 0730–1300 and 1600–1830 (summer); Wed and Sat half-day 0800–1400.

Telecommunications

Telephone/fax
GSM 900/1800 and G3 services are available in Greek Cypriot areas

Electricity supply
240V AC. Sockets are the UK flat three-pin style.

Weights and measures
The metric system is used.

Social customs/useful tips
It is considered impolite to refuse drinks offered at a first meeting. Cypriots customarily offer fruit preserves to guests. Between 1300–1600 hours is siesta time in the summer (May–September).
There are restrictions on photographing military installations in both south and north Cyprus.

Getting there

Air
International airport/s: Larnaka International (LCA), 8km from Larnaka (49km from Lefkosia); Pafos International (PFO), 10km east of Pafos (146km from Lefkosia).
Both airports offer tourist information, foreign exchange, hotel reservations and duty free shops.
Other airport/s: Northern Cyprus has an airport at Ercan with flights to and from Turkey. Flights are provided by a number of Turkish airlines and the northern Cypriot airline, Kibris Türk Hava Yollari (KYHY) (Cyprus Turkish Airlines). Visitors planning to arrive via Turkey are not allowed into southern Cyprus.
Airport tax: None

Surface
Water: Access by ship from Greece, Syria, Israel, Italy, Lebanon and Egypt.
Main port/s: Lemesos (Limassol)

Getting about

National transport
Buses: An efficient *intra-cud* (inter-town) bus service is available. All buses run from the central bus depots, connecting towns and villages. A rural bus operation is limited to once or twice a day, usually to the local market.

City transport
Taxis: An efficient service is operated throughout the island by metered taxis. The transurban service-taxis are shared taxis connecting all main towns. Prices are regulated. Between 2300–0600 an additional 15 per cent is charged. Tipping is standard practice.
Buses, trams & metro: Urban buses operate frequently during the day. In certain tourist areas during the summer, buses extend their operations until midnight.

Car hire
Car hire is available in all parts of the island, particularly from airports and commercial centres. Rates vary depending on the size of the car and are also subject to seasonal variations. For a higher price, a prestige service is also available. Cheap rates are available for hire periods of more than one week. Visitors should book cars well in advance during the period June–September. A national or international driving licence is required. Driving is on the left. Road signs are in both Greek and English.

BUSINESS DIRECTORY

The addresses listed below are a selection only. While World of Information makes every endeavour to check these addresses, we cannot guarantee that changes have not been made, especially to telephone numbers and area codes. We would welcome any corrections.

Telephone area codes
The international direct dialling codes (IDD) for Cyprus is +357, followed by area code and subscriber's number:

Larnaka	24	Lemasos	25
Lefkosia	22	Pafos	26

North Cyprus numbers are preceded by +90-392, in place of +357. Area code for Famagusta 366, Kyrenia 815.

Useful telephone numbers
Emergencies112

Chambers of Commerce
Cyprus Chamber of Commerce and Industry, Chamber Building, 38 Grivas Dighenis Ave and 3 Deligiorgis Street, PO Box 21455, 1509 Lefkosia (tel: 889-600; fax: 667-433).

Famagusta Chamber of Commerce and Industry, 339 Ayiou Andreou Street, Andrea Chamber Bldg, PO Box 3124, Limassol (tel: 370-165, 370-167; fax: 370-291).

Larnaka Chamber of Commerce and Industry, 12 12 Gregoriou Afxentiou Str, Skourou Bldg, 4th Floor, PO Box 287, Larnaka (tel: 655-051; fax: 628-281).

Lefkosia Chamber of Commerce and Industry, 38 Grivas Dighenis Ave and 3 Deligioris Str, Chamber Building, PO Box 1455, Lefkosia (tel: 449-500; fax: 367-433).

Limassol Chamber of Commerce and Industry, PO Box 347, 25 Spyrou Araouzou Street, Verengaria Building, PO Box 347, Limassol (tel: 362-556; fax: 371-655).

Pafos Chamber of Commerce and Industry, 32 Grivas Dighenis Avenue, Demetra Court, 2nd Floor, Flat 22, Pafos (tel:235-115; fax: 244-602).

Banking

Alpha Bank Ltd, Yiorkion Bldg, 1 Prodromou Street, 1095 Lefkosia (tel: 77-3799, 88-8888; fax: 77-3744).

Bank of Cyprus Ltd, Box 1472, 86-90 Phaneromeni Street, Lefkosia (tel: 46-4064; fax: 46-4340).

Cyprus Development Bank, PO Box 1415, Alpha House, 50 Archbishop Makarios III Avenue, Lefkosia (tel: 45-7575; fax: 46-4322).

Cyprus Investment and Securities Corporation, 60 Digenis Akritas Avenue, PO Box 597, Lefkosia (tel: 45-1535; fax: 44-5481).

Cyprus Popular Bank Ltd, PO Box 2032, 39 Archbishop Makarios III Avenue, Lefkosia (tel: 45-0000; fax: 44-9169).

Federal Bank of the Middle East Ltd, J & P Building, 90 Archbishop Makarios III Avenue, 1077 Lefkosia (tel: 88-8444; fax: 88-8555).

Hellenic Bank Ltd, Corner 92 Dhigenis Akritas Ave & Cretes Str, 1061 Lefkosia (tel: 86-0000; fax: 76-507).

Sociéte Générale Cyprus Ltd, PO Box 25400, 7-9 Grivas Dighenis Ave, 1309 Lefkosia (tel: 81-7777; fax: 76-4471).

Central bank

Central Bank of Cyprus, 80 Kennedy Avenue, PO Box 25529, 1395 Lefkosia (tel: 714-100; fax: 378-153; internet: www.centralbank.gov.cy).

Stock exchange

Cyprus Stock Exchange (CSE), www.cse.com.cy

Travel information

Cyprus Airways, PO Box 1903, 21 Alkeou Street, Lefkosia (tel: 44-3054, 2246-1800; fax: 44-3167, 2236-0075; e-mail: marketing@cyprusair.com.cy; internet site: www.cyprusairways.com.cy).

Cyprus Hotel Association, PO Box 24772, Lefkosia (tel: 37-4251; fax: 36-5460).

Ministry of tourism

Ministry of Commerce, Industry and Tourism, 1421 Lefkosia (fax: 375-120).

National tourist organisation offices

Cyprus Tourism Organisation (main office, for postal enquiries only), 19 Limassol Ave, PO Box 4535, Lefkosia (tel: 315-715; fax: 313-022); (for personal and telephone enquiries only, open every morning except Sun, and on Mon and Thurs afternoons) Laiki Yitonia, East of Eleftheria Sq, Lefkosia (tel: 444-264); (24-hour service) Larnaka International Airport (tel: 654-389).

Ministries

Ministry of Agriculture, Natural Resources and Environment, Loukis Akritas Avenue, Lefkosia (tel: 30-0807; fax: 78-1156).

Ministry of Commerce, Industry and Tourism, 2 A Araouzos Street, Lefkosia (fax: 35-7120).

Ministry of Communication and Works, 28 Acheon Street, Lefkosia CY-1101 (tel: 30-2830; fax: 77-6272, 46-5462, 36-0578).

Ministry of Defence, 4 Emmanuel Roides Street, Lefkosia (tel: 80-7528; fax: 36-6225).

Ministry of Education and Culture, Gr Afxentiou Street, Lefkosia (tel: 30-5188; fax: 42-7559).

Ministry of Finance, Ex Secretariat Compound, Lefkosia (tel: 80-3530; fax: 36-6080).

Ministry of Foreign Affairs, Dem Severis Avenue, Government House No. 18-19, Lefkosia (tel: 30-0600; fax: 45-1881).

Ministry of Health, Ex Secretarial Offices, Lefkosia (tel: 30-9526; fax: 36-8883).

Ministry of Interior, Dem Severis Avenue, Ex Secretariat Offices, Lefkosia (tel: 51-0222; fax: 45-3465, 36-6709).

Ministry of Justice and Public Order, 12 Helioupoleos, Lefkosia (tel: 30-2355; fax: 76-1427).

Ministry of Labour and Social Insurance, Byron Avenue, Lefkosia (tel: 30-3481; fax: 45-0993).

Presidential Palace, Lefkosia (tel: 45-1333; fax: 44-5016).

Other useful addresses

British High Commission, Alexander Pallis St, PO Box 1978, Lefkosia (tel: 47-3131/7; fax: 36-7198).

Central Post Office, Eleftheria Square, Lefkosia (tel: 30-3219).

Cyprus Broadcasting Corporation, PO Box 4824, Lefkosia (tel: 42-2231; fax: 31-4050).

Cyprus Employers' and Industrialists' Federation, 30 Grivas Dhigenis Avenue, PO Box 1657, Lefkosia (tel: 44-5102; fax: 45-9459).

Cyprus News Agency, 7 Kastorias St, PO Box 3947, Lefkosia (tel: 31-9009; fax: 31-9006).

Cyprus Petroleum Refinery Ltd, PO Box 40275, 6302 Larnaka (fax: 2464-1401; e-mail: lambroug@cprl.com.cy).

Cyprus Telecommunications Authority, PO Box 4929, Lefkosia (tel: 31-3111).

Department of Customs & Excise, Customs Headquarters, 29 Katsonis Street, Ay Omoloyitae, Lefkosia (tel: 30-5404, 30-5737; fax: 35-5050).

Department of Statistics and Research, Ministry of Finance, 13 Andreas Araouzos Street, 1444 Lefkosia (tel: 30-9305, 30-3208; fax: 37-4830, 45-6712).

Embassy of the United States of America, Therissos St & Dositheos St, Lefkosia (fax: 45-9571).

Press and Information Office, Apellis Street, Ay Omoloyitae, 1456 Lefkosia (tel: 80-1155/1164/1177; fax: 36-6123; email: communications@pio.moi.gov.cy).

National news agency: Cyprus News Agency (CNA), 7 Kastorias Street, 2002 Strovolos, Lefkosia (tel: 556-009; fax: 556-103; email: news@cna.org.cy; internet: www.cna.org.cy).

TAK (Arca Haber Ajansi) (in Turkish): www.arcaajans.com

Internet sites

Bridge to Greece and Cyprus: www.greekvillage.com/bridge/bridge.htm

Cyprus News: www.cyprusnews.com

Cyprus Telecommunications Authority: www.cytanet.com.cy

Cyprus Tourism Organisation: www.cyprustourism.org

Official Cyprus homepage: www.pio.gov.cy

Czech Republic

KEY FACTS

Official name: Ceská Republika (Czech Republic)

Head of State: President Miloš Zeman (Strana Práv Obcanu-Zemanovci (SPOZ) (Party of Civic Rights-Zeman's people) (elected 26 January 2013, inaugurated 8 March 2013).

Head of government: Prime Minister Bohuslav Sobotka (CSSD) (since 17 January 2014).

Ruling party: Coalition of Ceská Strana Sociálne Demokratická (CSSD) (Czech Social Democratic Party), Akce Nespokojených Obcanu (ANO) (Action of Dissatisfied Citizens) and Krestanská a Demokratická Unie–Ceskoslovenská Strana Lidová (KDU–CSL) (Christian and Democratic Union–Czechoslovak People's Party) (from Jan 2014)

Area: 78,864 square km

Population: 10.51 million (2014)*

Capital: Prague

Official language: Czech

Currency: Czech koruna (Kc) = 100 hellers

Exchange rate: Kc24.19 per US$ (Sep 2015)

GDP per capita: US$19,563 (2014)*

GDP real growth: 2.02% (2014)*

GDP: US$205.66 billion (2014)

Labour force: 5.43 million (2011)

Unemployment: 6.10% (2014)*

Inflation: 0.35% (2014)

Balance of trade: US$11.63 billion (2014)

* estimated figure

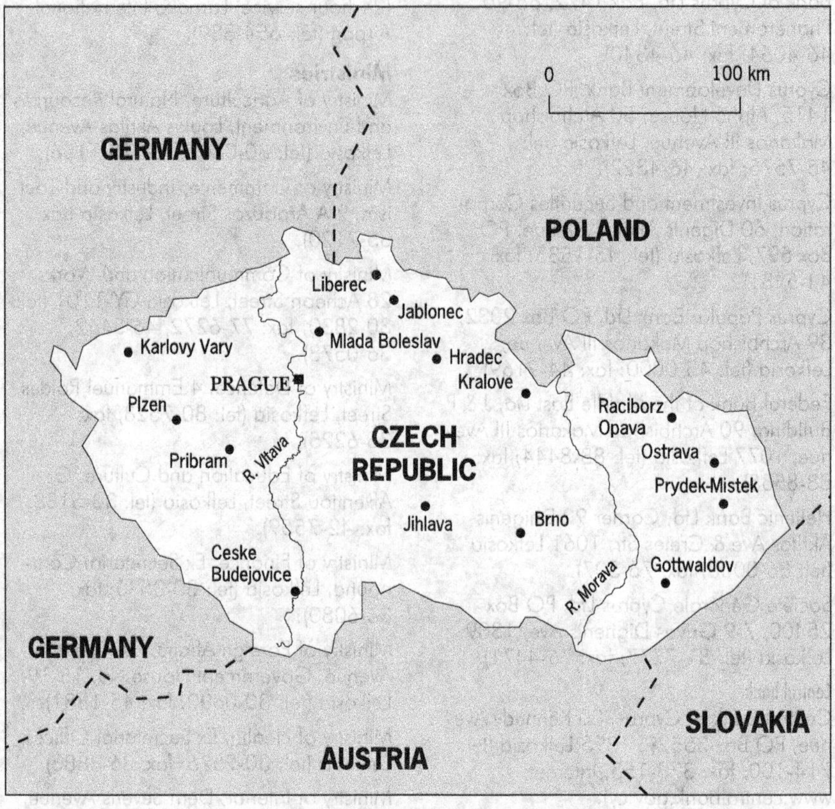

In an interesting paper entitled *Flaws in the Czech political culture*, prepared for the Reuters Institute at the University of Oxford, the author Jiri Zatloukal attributes a number of the problems afflicting Czech politics to the days of communism. Czech society, according to Mr Zatloukal, was undermined by 'the gradual erosion of all moral standards, the breakdown of all criteria of decency and the widespread destruction of confidence in the meaning of values such as truth, adherence to principles, sincerity, altruism, dignity and honour.'

Flying start?

When, following the collapse of communism in 1989 the states in Central and Eastern Europe had to be re-built, Mr Zatloukal considers that the Czech Republic started well. There were relatively functional administrative and fiscal legacies (the lowest level of public debt compared to other post-communist states), low inequality and relatively high socio-economic development. In the early 2000s, the Czech lands were described as 'a nearly consolidated democratic state.' The 1993 division of Czechoslovakia into two states (the Czech Republic and Slovakia) may have proceeded more smoothly than many had feared, but it reflected a shift in Czech politics. In the 1992 elections, the right-wing Obcanská Demokratická Strana (ODS) (Civic Democratic Party) lead by Václav Klaus had won the elections, confirming a duopoly in the Czech political landscape, with Messrs Havel and Klaus as emblematic rivals.

The privatisation of what were national assets that was embarked upon in the 1990s was seriously mis-handled (as it was elsewhere) creating a financial free for all and providing ample scope for financial misconduct. In the 1997 elections the Ceská

Strana Sociálne Demokratická (CSSD) (Czech Social Democratic Party) won, but not only did they not have an overall majority, nor were they able to form a coalition government. After some time they came to a rather dodgy agreement with Mr Klaus and the ODS, who in principle were the opposition. The agreement meant that after almost ten years of proper parliamentary rule, the Czech Republic had returned to one-party politics. The joint government happily appointed its cronies to run large state-owned companies and public institutions.

Mr Zatloukal noted that the 'opposition' ODS happily participated in this process because their politicians were under suspicion and being investigated in corruption cases. According to the Confederation of Industry of the Czech Republic, the amount of money stolen in this period reached tens of billions of crown a year. The two politicians running the show at the time were Václav Klaus and Miloš Zeman. Both later became presidents of the Czech Republic. According to a recent study quoted by Mr Zatloukal, one third of the funders of Czech political parties are linked to public procurements. Between 2006 and 2013, these sponsors gained public procurement contracts worth Kc390 billion (US$16.00 billion). Many of their owners were based in 'tax havens' or simply preferred not to disclose their identity. However, party donors included companies with no employees and also state-owned enterprises (which is illegal.) Mr Zatloukal claims that the law had been violated by all the major Czech political parties: the CSSD, the ODS, the Christian democratic Krestanská a Demokratická Unie–Ceskoslovenská Strana Lidová (KDU–CSL) (Christian and Democratic Union–Czechoslovak People's Party) and the Komunistická Strana Cech a Morava (KSCM) (Communist Party of Bohemia and Moravia).

Allegedly, every tenth public contract since 2006 had involved a company which sponsors one of the political parties at the same time. The results also showed that companies donating to parties obtained between 40 to 60 per cent more contracts than firms that didn't. It was hardly surprising, therefore, that the Czech political scene had been so turbulent in recent years. The once stable political landscape had fallen completely apart in the 2010 Chamber of Deputies' elections when a new political party – Veci Verejné (VV) (Public Affairs) – entered parliament. Originally a local Prague party, it obtained 10.88 per cent of votes, campaigning on a populist anti-corruption platform. It also sought the replacement of what it considered to be the Czech Republic's 'political dinosaurs'. To general surprise, the Public Affairs Party became a member of the government coalition, where it remained in 2015 despite some speculation concerning the leadership of the party.

Doctor Who?

In July 2015 Czech electors could perhaps regain some of the confidence they had lost in their politics and their politicians. The high profile arrest of Dr David Rath, a member of parliament and a former health minister and subsequent sentencing to eight and a half years in jail for accepting bribes of US$652,000 for projects which involved European Union (EU) subsidies, was a breakthrough. In what was a rare success, police had caught Dr Rath with a wine box stuffed with seven million crowns (US$290,000) in bank-notes. The court had also ordered the confiscation of a total of nearly 22 million crowns (US$910,000), including money uncovered during a search of Dr Rath's house and in a bank account.

The government's anti-corruption campaign had for some time struggled to secure convictions, to the extent that one prime minister, Peter Necas, had resigned over its perceived failure. The former Civic Democrat prime minister had stepped down in 2013 after a scandal involving police investigation of abuse of power, an investigation, however, that had not led to any convictions of senior officials or politicians.

Corruption in the Czech Republic was not limited to any particular party. Both the CSSD and the centre-right ODS, who between them had ruled for more than half of the period since the split with Slovakia, had been marked by scandals. On the transparency International 2014 *Corruption Perceptions Index*, the Czech Republic ranked 53 out of the 175 countries surveyed. Slovakia ranked one place behind, at 54.

The economy

Surprisingly, following the 2008–09 financial crisis, the Czech economy had remained weak for longer than many other comparable countries. In the early days of independence from Soviet rule, there were heady hopes that the Czech Republic would become the 'new Netherlands' its well educated and confident younger generation driving it forward. In 2015, after a few wilderness years, a hesitant export-led recovery was beginning to get under way. However, there remained a long way to go. The income convergence process with the euro-zone has stalled, reflecting both the effects of the prolonged recession and a worrying decline in perceived growth opportunities, arising from diminished levels of investment and lower productivity.

Despite this depressed scenario, in its July 2015 overview of the Czech economy, the International Monetary Fund (IMF) reported that the Czech economy was growing strongly due to improving

KEY INDICATORS — Czech Republic

	Unit	2011	2012	2013	2014	**2015
Population	m	*10.53	10.51	10.52	*10.51	*10.53
Gross domestic product (GDP)	US$bn	215.30	196.45	208.80	205.66	*180.79
GDP per capita	US$	20,444	18,699	19,855	*19,563	*17,171
GDP real growth	%	1.7	-1.0	-0.7	2.0	*2.5
Inflation	%	1.9	3.3	1.4	0.4	*-0.1
Unemployment	%	9.5	7.0	7.0	*6.1	*6.1
Coal output	mtoe	21.6	20.7	18.0	17.3	–
Exports (fob) (goods)	US$m	131,415.6	125,179.0	129,677.9	146,797.0	–
Imports (fob) (goods)	US$m	126,987.3	119,049.0	120,668.0	135,168.1	–
Balance of trade	US$m	4,218.0	6,129.0	9,009.9	11,629.0	–
Current account	US$m	-6,348.8	-4,727.0	-1,106.0	*1,266.0	*2,887.0
Total reserves minus gold	US$m	42,564.0	44,625.0	55,798.0	54,085.0	–
Foreign exchange	US$m	40,730.0	42,412.0	53,893.0	–	–
Exchange rate	per US$	17.32	19.41	20.14	22.91	–

* estimated figure ** forecast figure

domestic demand and robust exports. According to the IMF, growth accelerated in the first quarter of 2015 and a number of indicators, including retail sales, production and consumer confidence appeared to suggest that the growth momentum had continued through the year. The IMF also noted that the labour market had also been recovering fast and the unemployment rate had fallen to its lowest level since 2009. Led by the improving trade balance that reflected more positive terms-of-trade developments, the current account turned into a surplus. And in the face of a drop in energy and food prices, headline inflation had decelerated sharply in 2014 and by July was hovering just above zero, while core inflation remained stable.

Following substantial pro-cyclical fiscal tightening in 2011–13, Czech fiscal policy had been supportive of the economic recovery. Specifically, the general government deficit increased from 1.2 per cent of GDP in 2013 to 2.0 per cent in 2014, implying a one percentage point easing in the fiscal stance. The relaxation was mainly due to a negative surprise in excise collections and an increase in capital spending.

The IMF noted that Czech monetary policy had remained accommodative. In November 2013, constrained by the zero lower band and facing deflationary pressures, the Ceska Národni Banka (CNB) (Czech National Bank) (central bank) had decided to use the exchange rate as an additional instrument for inflation targeting and announced its commitment 'to prevent excessive appreciation of the koruna below Kc27 per € by intervening in the foreign exchange market.' The exchange rate had been hovering above that level without any official intervention in the foreign exchange market since November 2013.

The Czech banking sector was stable and credit growth showed signs of a recovery. Czech banks were self-financed with a low system-wide loan-to-deposit ratio and strong capital and liquidity buffers. Despite a slight increase in the non-performing loan ratio to 5.6 per cent in 2014, the ratio remained low. Credit growth was slowly recovering, driven by demand from the corporate sector. Recent lending surveys pointed to easing lending standards and gradually rising demand for credit. Funding costs had declined further.

In the view of the IMF, the outlook was for strong growth and low inflation. Growth was projected to accelerate to 3 per cent in 2015, mainly on account of higher investment and improving household consumption. Inflation looked likely to remain very low in 2015, before rising gradually toward the central bank's target in 2016, as base effects from the oil price shock fade and declining economic slack starts to pull inflation up. Over the medium term, output growth looks set to stabilise at around 2.25 per cent, but a period of faster growth is possible, driven by the strong pipeline of foreign direct investment (FDI) coming into effect.

Looking at the factors underlying the changes in the Czech economy and their effects, the Paris-based Organisation for Economic Co-operation and Development (OECD) noted that the continuing structural changes occurring in the economy had lead to major changes in labour demand, in turn requiring a reallocation of available labour resources as well as workers with new and different skills. However, in the view of the OECD, the Czech education system had not kept up sufficiently, with the exception of a quantum increase in graduates with tertiary degrees. Students leaving the educational system without a degree were experiencing difficulties in finding a job, while many of those with vocational training found that either there was little demand for their particular skills or that those skills were not suitable to modern work practises. The large expansion of tertiary education for the most part reflected a higher intake in the public system, but also the emergence of many private institutions. The public education system had not had a corresponding increase in resources, which might lead to bottlenecks and had raised concerns about how to secure quality that is able to compete internationally. The gender wage gap was also high and the labour participation of women with young children was relatively low, accentuating the labour shortages created by an ageing Czech society.

Risk assessment

Economy	Fair
Politics	Fair
Regional stability	Good

COUNTRY PROFILE

1918 Czechoslovakia's independence was established. Before this, Moravia and Bohemia had been ruled by Austria, while Slovakia had been governed by Hungary.
1938 Czechoslovakia ceded its German-speaking areas of Sudetenland to Germany.
1939–45 The country fell under German control until the end of the Second World War.
1946 The Czechoslovak Communist Party (CPCz) formed a power-sharing government following national elections.
1948 After mass protests and strikes orchestrated by the Communists, a government crisis left the CPCz with a majority in government. Czechoslovakia became a People's Republic, adopting a Soviet-style system.
1949–67 Stalinist-style rule, complete with party purges.
1968 Alexander Dubcek, the CPCz leader, introduced the policy of *socialism with a human face* – a period known as the 'Prague Spring' – which ended with the crushing of the reformist movement by the Soviet army.
1969–88 There were on-going protests at occupation by the Soviet troops. Václav Havel and a group of dissidents called for the restoration of civil and political rights. Mass demonstrations in 1988 marked the anniversary of the 1968 invasion.
1989 The new spirit of *glasnost* was met with scepticism as the government initially resisted political and economic change. However, large public demonstrations in the major cities, the 'Velvet Revolution', led to the resignation of the Communist Party leadership. Václav Havel was elected president and a pluralistic political system and market economy were introduced.
1990 The country was renamed the Czech and Slovak Federative Republic. The first free elections since 1946 resulted in a coalition government involving all major parties, with the exception of the CPCz, and Havel was re-elected president.
1991 The Soviet forces completed their withdrawal.
1992 In elections, the Czech voters backed the centre-right, while the Slovaks supported Slovak separatists and left-wing parties. Vladimir Meciar (a supporter of Slovak separatism) became Slovak prime minister. He opposed the rapid privatisation of the public sector proposed by the Czech prime minister, Václav Klaus. Neither was prepared to compromise and agreed to the separation of Slovakia, despite President Havel's objections.
1993 Czechoslovakia divided into two independent countries, the Czech Republic (comprising the regions of Bohemia, Moravia and Silesia) and the Slovak Republic (Slovakia). Václav Havel was elected president of the Czech Republic and Václav Klaus continued as prime minister.
1996 Klaus was reappointed prime minister in a minority coalition government, following the Czech Republic's first parliamentary election.

1997 The Klaus government resigned following the collapse of its coalition over disagreements on the economic reform programme and allegations of financial corruption.
1998 Milos Zeman, leader of the Ceská Strana Sociálne Demokratická (CSSD) (Czech Social Democratic Party), became prime minister and Václav Havel was re-elected president.
1999 The Czech Republic joined NATO.
2000 In elections, a coalition of four small liberal parties, the '4Koalice', became the strongest force in the upper house.
2002 Areas of Prague were flooded when the river Vltava rose to its highest level since 1890. The CSSD won parliamentary elections. President Václav Havel appointed Vladimír Spidla as prime minister.
2003 Parliament elected Václav Klaus as president. In a referendum to join the European Union (EU) 77.3 per cent voted in favour; turnout was 55 per cent.
2004 The Czech Republic became a member of the EU. The government resigned and Stanislav Gross formed a government.
2005 Gross resigned and Jirí Paroubek became prime minister; the new cabinet, unchanged in the key posts, was endorsed on the same day.
2006 Parliamentary (Chamber of Deputies) elections resulted in a stalemate, with both CSSD and Obcanská Demokratická Strana (ODS) (Civic Democratic Party) coalitions winning 100 seats in the lower house. After an initial rejection by parliament, the president appointed Mirek Topolánek as prime minister, who went on to form a government.
2007 The Czech Republic became a member of the European Union Schengen area whereby all travellers may cross borders within the area without a passport or visa.
2008 Incumbent Václav Klaus was re-elected president after two sets of three-rounds of voting. Visa-free visits by Czech nationals to the US was signed.
2009 The minority government lost a vote of no confidence, following an accusation that government advisors had attempted to stifle a critical television programme. Prime Minister Topolanek resigned. An interim government, with Jan Fischer as caretaker prime minister, was formed.
2010 Constitutional and legal wrangling set back the date of parliamentary elections several times (postponed from 2009); they were eventually held on 28 and 29 May. Three new political parties contested the Chamber of Deputies elections, but only two of them won enough votes to gain seats (Tradice Odpovednost Prosperita 09 (TOP 09) (Tradition Responsibility Prosperity 09) and Veci Verejné (VV) (Public Affairs)). The CSSD won 22.08 per cent of the vote (56 seats out of 200) and had the right to form a coalition government. However when the CSSD proved unable to form a government, Petr Necas (ODS) became prime minister as the head of a three party coalition (ODS, TOP 09 and VV). In senate elections, one-third of total seats (27) were in contention. The CSSD won 12 seats to take its senate number up to a total of 41, while the ODS lost 11 seats but retained eight for a total of 25 seats. The opposition CSSD began disrupting the government's austerity programme.
2011 Václav Havel, the first post-Communist president of Czechoslovakia (1989–1993; 1993–2003 Czech Republic only) died on 18 December. He oversaw the transition to democracy of Czechoslovakia and its division when the Czech Republic and Slovakia were created.
2012 On 21 April an estimated 120,000 anti-government protestors rallied in Prague to complain about the government's austerity measures and corruption. On 30 May, the European Central Bank (ECB) announced that none of the eight countries (including the Czech Republic), which are scheduled to join the European single currency (euro) are ready. In September 16 people were killed and 22 injured by 'bootleg' alcohol that had been distilled from industrial methanol. Two rounds of senate elections were held, on 12–13 and 19–20 October, in which one-third of seats were in contention. However by 20 November the results had still to be published.
2013 The first round of the presidential election was held on 11–12 January. There were nine candidates: Miloš Zeman (Strana Práv Obcanu-Zemanovci (SPOZ) (Party of Civic Rights-Zeman's people)) won 24.21 per cent, Karel Schwarzenberg (TOP 9) 23.4 per cent, Jan Fischer (Independent) 16.36 per cent, Jirí Dienstbier Jr 16.12 per cent; the remaining five candidates all polled under 10 per cent. Since no candidate won a majority, a second round was held on 25–26 January which was won by Miloš Zeman with 54.8 per cent, followed by Karel Schwarzenberg with 45.19 per cent. Miloš Zeman was inaugurated on 8 March, the day after Václav Klaus stepped down at the end of his second (and maximum allowed) term. Prime Minister Petr Necas resigned on 17 June. Although nicknamed 'Mr Clean' when he became prime minister, he resigned in an effort to end political turmoil over a corruption inquiry involving his chief of staff, Jana Nagyova, a close aid of Mr Necas for ten years. President Zeman asked Mr Necas to stay on as caretaker prime minister until a new administration is named. Mr Necas denied all accusations. On 25 June President Zeman appointed Jiri Rusnok prime minister. He was to form a caretaker cabinet and seek a parliamentary vote of confidence within 30 days. In the event, a technocratic 'government of experts' was sworn in on 10 July, but the vote of confidence held on 7 August was lost by 93 votes to 100. It is likely that an election will have to be called before the end of the year. Mr Rusnok will continue in a caretaker capacity until either a new prime minister is appointed (by the President) or elections are held. Elections were held on 26 October. The result was inclusive with the Ceská Strana Sociálne Demokratická (CSSD) (Czech Social Democratic Party) winning 20.45 per cent of the vote (50 seats out of 200), Akce Nespokojených Obcanu (ANO) (Action of Dissatisfied Citizens) 18.65 per cent (47), Komunistická Strana Cech a Morava (KSCM) (Communist Party of Bohemia and Moravia) 14.91 per cent (33), Tradice Odpovednost Prosperita 09 (TOP 09) (Tradition Responsibility Prosperity 09) 11.99 per cent (26) and no other party with more than 10 per cent.
2014 A centre-left coalition government was finally agreed by 6 January, lead by the CSSD under Bohuslav Sobotka and including the new party ANO and Krestanská a Demokratická Unie–Ceskoslovenská Strana Lidová (KDU–CSL) (Christian and Democratic Union–Czechoslovak People's Party). The agreement gave the coalition a majority of 111 seats. Mr Sobotka became prime minister on 29 January, pledging 'a change for the better, support for economic growth and employment.'
2015 In November police announced that in the first ten months of the year they had detained 7,697 migrants, mostly Syrians, but also Ukrainians, Afghans, Kuwaitis and Iraqis. This was almost double the number for the same period in 2014.

Political structure

Constitution

The Constitution came into force on 1 January 1993. A majority of three-fifths of the members of parliament is required to change the Constitution.

All citizens over the age of 18 are eligible to vote.

Independence date

1 January 1993

Form of state

Unitary parliamentary democratic republic.

The executive

The highest organ of executive power is the Council of Ministers, composed of the prime minister, the deputy prime ministers

and ministers. It is answerable to the Chamber of Representatives.
The two legislative bodies together elect the president of the republic for not more than two five-year terms. The president's post is largely ceremonial but the president is the commander-in-chief of the armed forces. The president appoints the prime minister, and on the prime minister's recommendation, appoints the remaining members of the Council of Ministers.

National legislature

The bicameral Parlament (Parliament) is comprised of the Poslanecká Snìmovna (Chamber of Deputies) (lower house), with 200 members directly elected from multi-seat constituencies by proportional representation from party lists to serve for four-year terms. The Senát (Senate) (upper house), with 81 (possibly non-partisan) members. Every two years one third of the membership (27) is elected under an absolute majority vote of two-rounds if needed in single-seat constituencies. Senators serve a six-year term.

Legal system

The civil law system is based on Austro-Hungarian codes. Judicial power is exercised by independent courts.

Last elections

11–12 and 25–26 January 2013 (presidential, first and second rounds)
25 and 26 October 2013 (Chamber of Deputies and Senat, brought forward from 2014 after government lost a vote of no-confidence in June 2013)
Results: Presidential 11–12 January 2013 (first round): Miloš Zeman (Strana Práv Obcanu-Zemanovci (SPOZ) (Party of Civic Rights-Zeman's people)) 24.21 per cent, Karel Schwarzenberg (TOP 09) 23.4 per cent, Jan Fischer (Independent) 16.35 per cent), Jirí Dienstbier Jr (CSSD) 16.12 per cent, Vladimir Franz (Independent) 6.84 per cent, Zuzana Roithová (KDU-CSL) 4.95 per cent, Tána Fischerová (Key Movement) 3.23 per cent, Premysl Sobotka (ODS) 2.46 per cent, Jana Bobošíková 2.39 per cent. Turnout was 61.31 per cent.
Presidential 25–26 January 2013 (second round): Miloš Zeman 54.8 per cent; Karel Schwarzenberg 45.19 per cent. Turnout was 59.11 per cent.
Senate: Ceská Strana Sociálne Demokratická (CSSD) (Czech Social Democratic Party) won 20.45 per cent of the vote (50 seats out of 200), Akce Nespokojených Obcanu (ANO) (Action of Dissatisfied Citizens) 18.65 per cent (47), Komunistická Strana Cech a Morava (KSCM) (Communist Party of Bohemia and Moravia) 14.91 per cent (33), Tradice Odpovednost Prosperita 09 (TOP 09) (Tradition Responsibility Prosperity 09) 11.99 per cent (26), Obcanská Demokratická Strana (ODS) (Civic Democratic Party) 7.72 per cent (16), Úsvit prímé demokracie (UPD) (Dawn of Direct Democracy) 6.88 per cent (14) and Krestanská a Demokratická Unie–Ceskoslovenská Strana Lidová (KDU–CSL) (Christian and Democratic Union–Czechoslovak People's Party) 6.78 per cent (14). Turnout was 59.48 per cent.

Next elections

2018 (presidential); in or before 2017 (parliamentary)

Political parties

Ruling party

Coalition of Ceská Strana Sociálne Demokratická (CSSD) (Czech Social Democratic Party), Akce Nespokojených Obcanu (ANO) (Action of Dissatisfied Citizens) and Krestanská a Demokratická Unie–Ceskoslovenská Strana Lidová (KDU–CSL) (Christian and Democratic Union–Czechoslovak People's Party) (from Jan 2014)

Main opposition party

Ceská Strana Sociálne Demokratická (CSSD) (Czech Social Democratic Party)

Population

10.51 million (2014)*
Last census: March 2001: 10,230,060
Population density: Urban population 74 per cent (2010 Unicef).
Annual growth rate: -0.1 per cent 1994–2004 (WHO 2006)

Ethnic make-up

The chief minorities are Slovaks (3 per cent of the population), Poles (0.6 per cent), Germans (0.5 per cent) and Silesians, Roma, Hungarians and Ukrainians.

Religions

Christianity is the principal religion, although 40 per cent of the population define themselves as atheist. Roman Catholicism is the main denomination (39 per cent of the population), followed by Protestant (5 per cent), Orthodox (3 per cent). There is a very small Jewish community, mainly in Prague.
The state and the church are linked, but there is growing pressure for their separation and the state no longer exercises control over church affairs.

Education

Compulsory education is free. Basic schooling is divided into two cycles with primary lasting for five years from aged six to 11; the second cycle lasts for four years until aged 15. Secondary schooling is offered in one of three designated institutions, a secondary general, technical or vocational school. Technical school programmes last up to six years, vocational courses last between three and four years and general secondary education last for four years and leads to higher education.
There are three universities, Prague's Charles' University (the oldest in Central Europe, founded in 1348), Masarykova University in Brno and Palacky University in Olomouc.
Public expenditure on education typically amounts to 5.1 per cent of annual gross national income.
Literacy rate: Virtually universal.
Compulsory years: Six to 15
Enrolment rate: 104 per cent gross primary school enrolment; 95 per cent gross secondary enrolment, of the relevant age group (including repetition rates) (World Bank).
Pupils per teacher: 18 in primary schools.

Health

Since a market economy replaced the previously planned centralised economy healthcare has become more reative to local requirements, there are more clinics, many operated by foreign medical companies. Recently instituted heath insurance companies took in US$5.3 billion in 2004. The Czech constitution guarantees free health care for all citizens and sponsors health insurance through the General Health Insurance Company. Pure supplementary health care insurance is scarce and simply covers those items outside the mandatory state insurance. Some private companies cover four supplementary areas such as surgery, hospitalisation in the event of illness or accident, permanent disability and accidental death.

HIV/Aids

HIV prevalence: 0.1 per cent aged 15–49 in 2003 (World Bank)
Life expectancy: 76 years, 2004 (WHO 2006)
Fertility rate/Maternal mortality rate: 1.5 births per woman, 2010 (Unicef); maternal mortality 9 per 100,000 live births (World Bank).
Child (under 5 years) mortality rate (per 1,000): 4 per 1,000 live births (WHO 2012)
Head of population per physician: 3.51 physicians per 1,000 people, 2003 (WHO 2006)

Welfare

The social security scheme provides old age pension insurance, sickness insurance, state social support benefits, and social care. Those registered in contracted employment, as self-employed (including farming personnel), and informal employment (employed for household duties), pay insurance premiums.

Pensions

In 1999, the Czech government encouraged domestic savings through gradual reforms and development of a

supplemental pension insurance programme. The amended law assured both employers and employees of significant tax relief. An employer who assists his employees to pay for supplementary pension insurance saves money both on tax payments for social and health insurance (to which supplementary pension insurance is not subject) and income taxes.
A contribution not exceeding 3 per cent of the gross pay is regarded as a tax-deductible expense. The pension scheme significantly altered the conditions for retirement savings. The minimum retirement age for both men and women gradually increases to 63 years by 2012 and the government is proposing stricter criteria for early retirement.
The Czech Republic has a challenge ahead. The current pay-as-you-go system, where employees pay the pensions of those already retired, is poorly suited to cope with a negative population growth. It has been estimated that the system, by 2020, will have debts amounting to Kc1.5 trillion (US$50 billion), with insufficient assets or income to fund pensions.
Proposals for private pension funds that rely on market equities to pay pensions also have their critics; market growth and volatility could fluctuate and disadvantage many. However, economic growth would be strengthened, and the government would only need to fund retirement for the poorest citizens.

Main cities

Prague (capital, estimated population 1.3 million in 2012); Brno (main city of Moravia) (316,614), Ostrava (Moravia) (133,568), Plzen (Pilsen) (133,164), Liberec (104,585), Olomouc (102,356), Hradec Králové (94,661).

Languages spoken

The Czech and Slovak languages are mutually comprehensible. A large proportion of the population, particularly those engaged in industry and foreign trade, speak German. Hungarian, Romani and Polish are also spoken.

Official language/s

Czech

Media

Press

Dailies: In Czech, by popularity *Mladá fronta Dnes* (www.mfdnes.cz), (known as MF Dnes), *Právo* (http://pravo.novinky.cz) and *Lidové Noviny* (www.lidovky.cz).
Other national newspapers include the tabloid, *Blesk* (www.blesk.cz), *ZN Zemské Noviny*, *Hospodárské Noviny* and *Haló Noviny* (www.halonoviny.cz) which publishes political news.
Weeklies: Regional publications include weekly newsmagazine and special interest publications. One of the largest regional media groups, Vktava-Labe-Press (VLP) (www.vlp.cz) publishes daily newspapers in all major cities and regions under the *Deník* (daily) (www.denik.cz) suffix, such as *Brunenský Deník* (http://brnensky.denik.cz) from Brno.
In Czech, *Respekt* (www.respekt.cz), reports on political and economic issues, *Týden* (www.tyden.cz) is a newsmagazine *Mladý Svet*, takes a humorous view of the news. Some of the dailies publish weekend or supplementary weekly magazines. *Spy* (www.ispy.cz) is a tabloid
Business: In Czech, the daily *Hospodárske Noviny* (www.ihned.cz) is an authoritative newspaper. Magazines include *Ekonom* (http://ekonom.ihned.cz) and *Profit* (www.profit.cz). In English, *Czech Business Weekly* (www.cbw.cz) and the *The Prague Tribune* (www.prague-tribune.cz) have comprehensive coverage of news and the markets. The magazine *Finance New Europe* (www.financeneweurope.com) that began publication in 2006, was the first to focus on business matter within the new EU members; it is published every two months.
Periodicals: In Czech, *Sedmá Generace* (www.sedmagenerace.cz), is an environmentalist publication. The monthly *Awrot* (*The Return*) (www.zwrot.cz) is the largest Polish circulation.

Broadcasting

Radio: The national pubic radio station is Ceský Rozhlas (www.rozhlas.cz) operated several national services including Radio 1, Radiozurnal for news and information, Radio 2, Praha (www.radio.cz), for family audiences, Radio 3 Vltava, for culture, Radio 6 is a magazine style programme and Radio 7 (through Praha) is an international, multilingual service. There are also 12 regional stations.
There are numerous private stations broadcasting on FM and AM frequencies, including Evropa 2 (www.evropa2.cz) and Radio City (www.radiocity.cz), both from Prague, Kiss Hády (www.kisshady.cz) and Radio Petrov (www.radiopetrov.com) from Brno, and Radio Cas (www.casradio.cz) from Ostrava. Radio Blanik (www.radioblanik.cz) broadcasts in the western regions.
Television: All analogue TV is scheduled to be replaced by digital signals in 2012 as the TV services market share provided via satellite and cable grows.
Ceská Televize (CT) (www.ceskatelevize.cz), is the national, public broadcaster, operating channels CT1 and CT2, CT24 (www.ct24.cz), the 24-hour news channel and CTSport.
Other private TV stations include TV Nova (www.nova.cz) and Prima (www.iprima.cz).
National news agency: CTK (Czech News Agency)

Economy

With an open market economy, based on manufacturing and engineering, the Czech Republic relies on its export trade (83.6 per cent of GDP in 2014) to provide its economic growth. Main industries include vehicle assembly, typically in partnership with foreign vehicle manufacturers, with output destined for overseas markets (Škoda, which has been wholly owned by Volkswagen of Germany since 2010, is the country's single largest employer and exporter), iron and steel production, metalworking, electronics, pharmaceuticals, textiles, brewing and traditional expertise in glass and crystal ware and ceramics. Cars and electrical appliances are manufactured by foreign-owned companies and specifically target export markets. Main agricultural produce includes sugar beet, potatoes, wheat and hops.
GDP growth in 2008 was 3.1 per cent, down from 5.7 per cent in 2007. The economy had avoided damage during the first wave of the global economic crisis (2007/08) due to its sound banking system, but as global trade weakened and exports were cut GDP growth by 2009 had fallen into recession at -4.3 per cent and by 2013, although still negative, had improved to only -0.7 per cent before jumping to 2.0 per cent in 2014. Since 2005 the trade balance has remained in credit, despite exports falling from US$145.7 billion in 2008 to US$108.9 billion in 2009 (rising back to US$172 billion by 2014). Domestic demand matched the trend with imports falling from US$139.3 billion in 2008 to US$103.1 billion in 2009, but rose back to US$158 billion by 2014.
The Czech Republic decided in 2006 to postpone entry to the European Monetary Union (EMU) and adopting the euro as its currency. In 2009 it became increasingly leery of joining the EMU, when the euro came under pressure and was stressed by the state of some weaker economies among its membership. In 2010 then Prime Minister Necas said that he would not commit his country to a target date for joining the EMU, as adopting the euro risked fuelling inflation while the economy generally would benefit from a flexible exchange rate. In 2013 the ministry of finance stated that the Czech republic would not adopt the euro before 2019.
Germany is the Czech Republic's single largest trading partner and, in the medium-to long-term, economic growth is as much dependent on the economic strength and growth of Germany as it is on the global recovery in trade.

External trade

As a member of the European Union (EU), the Czech Republic operates within a community-wide free trade area, with tariffs set as a whole. Internationally, the EU has free trade agreements with a number of nations and trading blocs worldwide.

The Czech Republic has several renowned exported products including beer (Pilsner beer is named after the Bohemian town in Czech Republic) and Bohemian crystal and porcelain. Vehicle manufacturing, led by Škoda, is typically in partnership with foreign car manufactures, with output destined for overseas markets.

Imports

The main classes of imports are machinery and transport equipment, typically around 45 per cent, raw materials and fuels, chemicals.

Main sources: Germany (26.2 per cent of total in 2014), China (11.3 per cent), Poland (7.7 per cent)

Exports

Main exports are vehicles and machinery (over 50 per cent), chemicals, raw materials and fuel.

Main destinations: Germany (32.0 per cent of total in 2014), Slovakia (8.4 per cent), Poland (6.0 per cent)

Agriculture

Farming

The agricultural sector accounts for around 2.4 per cent of GDP and around 3 per cent of employment. Approximately 41 per cent of the country is arable land, 11 per cent permanent pasture and 2 per cent permanent crops. The most important crops are sugar beet, wheat, potatoes, maize, barley, rye and hops. The livestock industry is well developed with cattle, pigs, chickens and dairy products supplying the food processing industry.

Agriculture was collectivised during the communist period. Although production increased with the creation of large farms, soil erosion and the heavy use of machinery and chemicals have had a long-term detrimental effect on the landscape and environment. In 1991, parliament passed a law on land restitution, under which all land taken by the state after February 1948 was returned to its original owner or, if such a return was not possible, provided for the owner to be compensated. Large-scale operations still dominate the sector, with many of the same problems experienced during the communist era.

Agriculture remains labour intensive, relying on inefficient techniques, outdated technology and a poor distribution system. EU membership should eventually help the sector to modernise and redevelop.

Fishing

The Czech Republic has a long tradition in freshwater fishing and aquaculture, owing to the thousands of man-made fishponds dating from the middle ages. The principal catch is the common carp. The Czech Republic produces around 25,000 tonnes of freshwater fish per annum, of which around 13,000 tonnes are exported. Being landlocked, the country also imports over 200,000 tonnes of seafood per year. There are 12 processing plants.

Forestry

Forests cover around 2.6 million hectares (ha), about one-third of the total land area, with the growing stock volume per hectare considered among the highest in Europe. Coniferous species make up more than four-fifths of the stock volume. There is no other wooded land.

Three-quarters of forest land is publicly-controlled, mainly at national level; the remainder is privately-owned. Forest output is moderate and the industry depends largely on processing of domestic raw materials. Austria and Germany are important export markets for roundwood and sawn wood respectively.

The domestic wood industry satisfies the majority of industrial needs for newsprint, plywood, furniture and traditional woodworking.

Industry and manufacturing

The industrial sector was among the most advanced in the world before the Second World War, with national GDP per capita the seventh highest in the world in 1938. The Communist takeover in 1948 led to the nationalisation of all enterprises and a concentration on heavy industry. Under communism there was insufficient capital investment, while a lack of management, marketing and financial skills handicapped the development of the sector. In common with its counterparts in other communist countries, Czech industry became characterised by outdated and inefficient technology, over-staffing and poor quality.

Since 1989, the Czech economy has diversified away from its heavy industrial base. Between 1986–98, industry's share of GDP fell from 60 per cent to 39 per cent as a flourishing services sector began to establish itself. In 2004, industry's share of GDP was 39.4 per cent, a drop from a high of around 40 per cent in 2001. The slowdown matched the global trend with manufacturing jobs increasingly being sourced in Asia.

Engineering is beginning to dominate the industrial sector. Automotive engineering accounted for 15.8 per cent of manufacturing exports in 2004.

Tourism

The Czech Republic has become one of Europe's top destinations for short city breaks and extended health and wellness holidays. Domestic tourists have given the industry a boost following its downturn when the global economic crisis cut visitor numbers in 2009. There are 12 sites included on Unesco's World Heritage sites: 11 are historic, of which one is described as a cultural landscape, and one of modernist architecture.

Travel and tourism experienced four years of decline over 2007–10 (except in 2008), including its share of GDP, employment, visitor numbers and capital investment. The share of GDP fell from 10.1 per cent in 2007 (US$17.7 billion) to 7.8 per cent (US$15.3 billion) in 2010 and has been maintained at this level since, at 8.0 per cent in 2014. Likewise employment in the industry fell from 12.2 per cent of total employment (605,300 jobs) to 9.3 per cent (457,800 jobs) over the same period, jumping up to 10.0 per cent in 2014 (498,500 jobs). Visitor spending was 5.1 per cent of total export revenue in 2007 (US$7.2 billion) falling to 4.4 per cent in 2014. Capital investment in the industry remained steady at 4.2–4.1 per cent of total investment, except when it spiked at 4.7 per cent in 2008 (which may have been related to the visa free agreements with the EU and US introduced in 2007–08). Electrical capacity is predominantly from thermal sources, with the remainder from hydroelectric and nuclear stations. The Czech Republic is a net exporter of electricity to Germany, Austria, Poland and Slovakia.

Ceské Energetické Závody (CEZ) is the dominant power company in the Czech Republic, supplying over 70 per cent of the Republic's power, which was around 90 billion kilowatt hours (kWh) in 2014. Consumption was around 70 billion kWh. CEZ operates two nuclear power stations, at Dukovany and Temelin, as well as thermal and hydroelectric power plants. Electricity exports, particularly from the Temelín nuclear power station, are an important source of foreign earnings.

Construction of the controversial Temelín nuclear power station began in the 1980s. The first reactor became operational in 2000, but was shut down several times due to technical problems. A second reactor became operational in 2003, allowing Temelín to generate an extra 2,000MW of power. However expansion plans were scrapped in 2014 due to EU pressure on environmental issues.

In 2009, the Federated State of Micronesia (FSM) challenged Czech Republic government plans to expand its coal-fired Prunerov Two power plant, Europe's second-largest. Low-lying FSM is threatened by submersion as global warming adds to rising sea levels. It feels this expansion, and its resulting increase in carbon dioxide output could exacerbate its problems.

FSM used a legal instrument of the UN Convention on Environmental Impact Assessment in a Transboundary Context (known as the EIA convention) in Czech Republic. Although the court found in favour of the FSM, polluting activity has not halted. . The Czech government was successful in passing the expansions despite clear evidence of the environmental damage it would cause. The approval of the expansion caused the Green party to withdraw two of it's members from the government.

Environment

One of the most lasting legacies of the communist era is pollution, with the Czech Republic one of the most despoiled corners of Europe. Not only is air pollution a major problem, water supplies have become infected and raw sewage has reportedly been dumped in waterways by individuals as well as factories. Although environmental awareness has grown since 1989, the government and the majority of the population have focussed on economic transformation and improving living standards rather than on the environment.

Hydrocarbons

Proven oil reserves were some 15 million barrels in 2014, with production at around 7,000 barrels per day (bpd). Consumption was 187,800bpd meaning the Czech Republic currently imports oil from both Russia and Italy. International oil companies are still interested in the region and currently the Western Carpathians are being explored, although two wells have been found to be non-commercial. There are three oil refineries with a total capacity of 183,000bpd, with the Ceská Rafinérská being the largest.

Proven natural gas reserves were 4.3 billion cubic metres (cum) in 2014, while production was 252 million cum. However, consumption is around 8.5 billion cum per annum, the balance of which is imported, mainly from Russia, Germany and Norway.

Reserves of coal were around 1.05 billion tonnes at the end of 2014, with production at 17.3 million tonnes oil equivalent (mtoe), down 3.5 per cent from the 2013 figure.

Energy

Electrical capacity is predominantly from thermal sources, with the remainder from hydroelectric and nuclear stations. The Czech Republic is a net exporter of electricity to Germany, Austria, Poland and Slovakia.

Ceské Energetické Závody (CEZ) is the dominant power company in the Czech Republic, supplying over 70 per cent of the Republic's power which was 81.7 billion kilowatt hours (kWh) in 2007. Consumption was over 60 billion kWh. CEZ operates two nuclear power stations, at Dukovany and Temelin, as well as thermal and hydroelectric power plants. Electricity exports, particularly from the Temelín nuclear power station, are an important source of foreign earnings.

Construction of the controversial Temelín nuclear power station began in the 1980s. The first reactor became operational in 2000, but was shut down several times due to technical problems. A second reactor became operational in 2003, allowing Temelín to generate an extra 2,000MW of power. However expansion plans were scrapped in 2014 due to EU pressure on environmental issues.

In 2009, the Federated State of Micronesia (FSM) challenged Czech Republic government plans to expand its coal-fired Prunerov Two power plant, Europe's second-largest. Low-lying FSM is threatened by submersion as global warming adds to rising sea levels. It feels this expansion, and its resulting increase in carbon dioxide output could exacerbate its problems.

FSM used a legal instrument of the UN Convention on Environmental Impact Assessment in a Transboundary Context (known as the EIA convention) in Czech Republic. Although the court found in favour of the FSM, polluting activity has not halted. . The Czech government was successful in passing the expansions despite clear evidence of the environmental damage it would cause. The approval of the expansion caused the Green party to withdraw two of it's members from the government.

Financial markets

Stock exchange

Burza Cennych Papíru Praha (Prague Stock Exchange) (PSE)

Banking and insurance

The country is suffering from high levels of public debt, approximately 18.8 per cent of GDP. Most of this debt can be attributed to government bail-outs in the banking sector. The IMF has estimated that continued bank restructuring will take up a large percentage of the Czech Republic's GDP.

Much of the bank restructuring has been as a result of the government attempting to ensure that there is compatibility between Czech and EU laws, following EU membership in 2004. This also includes continued privatisation, not least in the banking sector, where state-owned stakes in banks will gradually be eliminated.

The Foreign Exchange Act introduced partial liberalisation for capital account and full convertibility for current account transactions in Czech koruna. It also cleared the way for Czech membership of the Organisation for Economic Co-operation and Development (OECD), enabled companies to accept credit from non-resident banks and eased restrictions on direct investment.

The accumulation of bad domestic and international debt and non-performing loans, particularly to Russia, has reduced the attraction of Czech banking corporations to foreign investors. However, with the introduction of more stringent financial regulations and an improvement in accounting standards, bank privatisation will likely gain momentum.

Central bank

Ceska Národnì Banka (CNB) (Czech National Bank).

Time

GMT plus one hour (daylight saving, late March to late October, GMT plus two hours)

Geography

The Czech Republic is a landlocked country in central Europe, bordering Germany to the west, Poland to the north, Slovakia to the east, and Austria to the south. The landscape varies greatly from lowlands to Alpine-type mountains. It has numerous rivers (the Elbe (Labe), and its largest tributary, the Vltava, provide important links to sea ports).

With a total area of 78,864km square the Czech Republic is slightly smaller than Austria and one-third the size of the UK. The country is split into two principal regions, Bohemia in the west and Moravia to the east. Surrounded by low mountains Bohemia is a plateau forming a basin drained by the Elbe and the Vltava – on which Prague is situated. The lowlands of Moravia are drained by the Morava River which flows into the Danube and by the Oder (Odra) eventually flows into the Baltic Sea.

Hemisphere

Northern

Climate

The climate is continental with warm, showery summers and cold, snowy winters. June is the hottest month and January the coldest. February and March are the driest months and June, July and August the wettest. The average temperature in winter is minus 5 degrees Celsius (C) and in the summer around 20 degrees C.

Dress codes

Most people wear standard casual clothes. They do, however, dress up when eating out or going to the theatre or a concert. Some more exclusive restaurants do not admit people in casual wear and it is useful to enquire beforehand. For business, a suit and tie is advisable for men and a suit or dress for women.

Entry requirements

Passports

Passport required by all, except nationals of EU/EEA and Switzerland, with valid national ID cards.

Visa

Required by all, except nationals of EU and Schengen area signatory countries, North America, Australasia and Japan. For further exceptions contact the nearest embassy. A Schengen visa application (offered in several languages) can be downloaded from http://europa.eu/abc/travel/ see 'documents you will need'.

See http://czech.embassyhomepage.com for a full list of exceptions to visa controls.

Business visas for nationals requiring visas require evidence of invitation from a local company and business letter of intention from employer.

Currency advice/regulations

The import and export of local currency is limited to Kc200,000, while there are no restrictions on the import of export of foreign currency.

Travellers cheques are readily accepted but euros, US dollars, or UK pounds avoid extra exchange fees. ATMs are found in most banks.

Customs

Personal items are duty-free. There are no duties levied on alcohol and tobacco between EU member states, providing amounts imported are for personal consumption.

Health (for visitors)

Nationals of the European Economic Area (EEA) countries and Switzerland can access reduced cost and sometimes free medical treatment using a European Health Insurance Card (EHIC) while visiting the EEA. Exceptions include nationals of the 10 countries which joined the EU in 2004 whose EHIC is not valid in Switzerland. Applications for the EHIC should be made before travelling.

Mandatory precautions

None

Advisable precautions

Immunisation for hepatitis A and B may be useful.

Hotels

Prague has a wide range of hotels. Business travellers are advised to book rooms well in advance.

Credit cards

All major credit and charge cards are accepted.

Public holidays (national)

Fixed dates

1 Jan (New Year's Day), 1 May (Labour Day), 8 May (Liberation Day), 5 Jul (St Cyril and St Methodius Day), 6 Jul (Jan Hus Day), 28 Sep (Czech Statehood Day), 28 Oct (National Day), 17 Nov (Freedom and Democracy Day), 24–26 Dec (Christmas).

Variable dates

Easter Monday

Working hours

Banking

Mon–Fri: 0800–1800; some banks close early on Fri.

Bureau de Change in main city centres operate seven days a week until 1900.

Business

Mon–Fri: 0800–1700.

Government

Mon–Fri: usually 0800–1600, but may vary.

Shops

Mon–Fri: 0800–1800; Sat: 0900–1200; some shops remain open late on Thursday evening.

Telecommunications

Mobile/cell phones

GSM 900/1800 services are available throughout the country.

Electricity supply

Domestic: 220V, 50 cycles AC is almost universal, with two-pin continental plugs.

Weights and measures

The metric system is in use. In addition, the following measures are used: quintal or metric hundredweight = 100kg. Food is usually purchased by the decagram and kilogram.

Social customs/useful tips

A handshake is a traditional accompaniment to a greeting. Using a person's title is customary. Managing directors should be addressed as *reditel* and the chairman as *predseda*.

When visiting private homes it is customary to take flowers for the hosts. Visitors also generally leave their shoes in the hallway, partly as a mark of respect and partly because of pollution in the streets.

The difference between a Slovak and a Czech may be difficult to spot; however mistaking one for the other can cause offence.

Tipping is appreciated in any restaurant, usually 5 to 10 per cent.

Drinking and driving is strictly forbidden. Illegally parked cars tend to be towed away by the police and it is advisable to park at attended car parks where the cost is relatively low.

Security

Street crime, especially in the centre of Prague, has increased since the 1989 revolution, as the police tend to keep a low profile. It is advisable to carry as little as possible in the way of valuables and cash. Car vandalism and theft have also increased.

Report any robberies in central Prague to the Central Police Office, Jungmannova 9, Prague 1 (tel: 6145-1760), where interpreters are available.

Getting there

Air

National airline: CSA Czech Airlines

International airport/s: Vaclav Havel Airport Prague (PRG), 20km north-west of the city. Facilities include duty free shopping, post office, money exhange, restaurants and car hire. An airport bus service runs every 30 minutes between 0600–2100, with a journey time of 30 minutes to the city centre. Taxis are available 24 hours.

Airport tax: Departure tax, from Prague only: Kc700

Surface

Road: Entry is possible from Germany, Poland, Slovak Republic and Austria.

Rail: As part of the European intercity network there are convenient routes to the Czech Republic from Western Europe including the cities of Berlin, Frankfurt, Munich, Zurich and Vienna. The most famous and fastest trains include the Kafka, Goethe and the Einstein, which are operated by the formerly state-owned České Dráhy (CD) (Czech Railways). The Vindobona Express operates daily from Vienna to Prague and on to Berlin. For more rail information call (tel: 2422-4200).

Water: There are ferries along the Vltava River from Germany.

Getting about

National transport

Air: CSA Czech Airlines operates extensive low-cost domestic network.

There are regular daily flights from Prague to Brno, Ostrava, Presov, Holesov, Kosice, Piestany, Bystrica, Karlovy Vary and Poprad.

The approximate travel time from Prague to Brno is 45 minutes, one hour to Karlovy and 30 minutes to Karlovy Vary.

Road: There are several major highways linking Prague with the main towns (usually marked with an E). Motorways run from Prague to Plzen and Podebrady to Bratislava (Slovak Republic) via Brno. Users of the Czech motorways are required to purchase a *vignette* (season ticket) for each year.

Buses: The services of the national bus company, CAD, are faster and more comfortable than the train for many routes. Tickets can be bought in advance from larger stations.

Rail: The rail service is efficient and coverage is comprehensive, composed of approximately 9,365km of track. It is advisable to book seats in advance on the main routes. Fares are low, although supplements may be charged for travel on express trains.

Water: There are many navigable waterways in the Czech Republic. The main river ports are located at Prague, Usti nad Labem and Decin.

City transport

Taxis: Taxis travelling to and from the airport are allowed to charge higher rates. Within the city, it is advisable to either negotiate a price before travelling or agree the use of the meter. Higher charges are usually levied for night services.

Buses, trams & metro: The bus network is extensive, covering many areas not visited by rail. In addition to a flat-fare service, the buses are reliable and comfortable.

In Prague, tickets can be bought in advance from tabak shops and other shops displaying the sign *Predprodej Jizdenek*. On boarding the buses, insert your ticket into the top of the machines attached to the poles, then pull the handle towards you. Passes do not need to be punched. City buses operate predominantly on the outskirts of towns. City bus 119 leaves daily every five to seven minutes (peak times) or every 15 minutes (off-peak) for round trips from Dejvicka metro station to the airport. From the metro, follow the exit signs for Ruzyne Airport. An ordinary city transport ticket or pass is required before boarding. The CSA Czech Airline bus service operates every 30 minutes from its terminal, off Revolucni near the river, to the airport. It also stops at Dejvicka metro station. Look for the sign that says Ruzyne. For more city transport information see: www.dp-praha.cz/en/index.htm

Trams cover all the major streets and intersect with metro lines. There are tram services in Prague, Brno, Ostrava, Plzen and several other towns. Services usually operate between 0430–2400. After midnight, night trams run approximately every 40 minutes. Blue badges on tram and bus stops denote an all night service. Tram 91, the 'historic tram', stops at most of the city's top sights, except for the castle. These trams run Saturdays, Sundays and during holidays, making hourly stops during the summer. Tickets should be punched in the appropriate machine on entering the tram. Note that a separate ticket is required when changing tram routes.

Car hire

Many of the international car hire companies, including Avis, Eurodollar and Hertz, operate in the Czech Republic. Speed limits are 60kph in towns and villages, 90kph on the main roads and 110kph on motorways. The speed limit is reduced to 80kph on motorways in built-up areas. It is advisable to avoid driving in the city centre as illegal parking will result in the use of car clamps.

Traffic drives on the right. Seat belts are compulsory and drink driving is strictly prohibited. An emergency road rescue service is available by calling 154. A valid national driving licence is required.

BUSINESS DIRECTORY

The addresses listed below are a selection only. While World of Information makes every endeavour to check these addresses, we cannot guarantee that changes have not been made, especially to telephone numbers and area codes. We would welcome any corrections.

Telephone area codes

The international dialling code (IDD) for the Czech Republic is + 420, followed by area code and subscriber's number:

Breclav	51	Ostrava	59
Brno	54	Plzen	37
Havirov	6994	Prague	2

Useful telephone numbers

Emergency calls: 158
Ambulance service: 112/155
Police: 158, 2121-1111
Traffic accidents: 154, 2121-3747
Emergency Medical Aid: 298-341 (24-hours: doctors speak English and German):290-651
Fire: 150
Directory enquiries: (Prague only): 120
International enquiries: 0135
Breakdown assistance: 154, 123, 777-521
Car repair service (24-hours): 733-351/3
Lost property office: 235-8887
Car repair service (24-hours): 733-351/3
Lost property office: 235-8887

Chambers of Commerce

American Chamber of Commerce, 10 Dusni, 11000 Prague 1 (tel: 2232-9430; fax: 2232-9433; email: amcham@amcham.cz).

Breclav Chamber of Commerce, 10 namisti TG Masaryka, 69002 Breclav (tel: 932-6116; fax: 937-4126; email: ohk@breclav.net).

British Chamber of Commerce, 3 Pobrezni, 18600 Prague 8 (tel: 2483-5161; fax: 2483-5162; email: britcham@britcham.cz).

Czech Chamber of Commerce, Freyova 27, 19000 Prague 9, (tel: 9664-6111; email: office@komora; internet: www.komora.cz).

Ostrava Regional Economic Chamber, 2224/8 Vystavni, 70900 Ostrava-Marianske Hory (tel: 747-9328; fax: 747-9324; email: info@rhko.cz).

Banking

ABN AMRO Bank NV, Amsterdam, Revolucni 1, 110 15 Prague 1 (tel: 2481-5141; fax: 2481-5100, 22481-5139).

Agrobanka Praha A S (largest private bank), Hybernska 18, 110 00 Prague 1 (tel: 2444-1111; fax: 2444-6199, 22444-1500).

Bankovni Asociace (Banking Association), Vodickova ulice 30, 110 00 Prague 1 (tel: 2422-5926; fax: 2422-5957).

BNP - Dresdner Bank, Vitezna 1, 150 000 Prague 5 (tel: 5700-6111).

Ceska Sporitelna A S (Czech Savings Bank), Na Prikope 29, 113 98 Prague 1 (tel: 2422-9268; fax: 2421-3455).

Ceskomoravska Stavebni, Ruzova 15, 110 00 Prague 1 (tel: 2407-2024; fax: 2407-2225).

Ceskomoravska Zarucni a Rozvojova Banks A S, Jeruzalemska 4, 115 20 Prague 1 (tel: 2423-0734).

Ceskoslovenska Obchodni Banka A S (CSOB), Na Prikope 14, 115 20 Prague 1 (tel: 2411-1111; internet: www.csob.cz).

Chase Manhattan, Karlova 27, 110 01 Prague 1 (tel: 2423-4313).

Citibank A S, Evropska 178, 166 40 Prague 6 (tel: 2430-4243).

Commerzbank AG Frankfurt/Main, Pobocka Praha, Masarykovo Nabrezi 30, 110 00 Prague 1 (tel: 2491-5077, 22491-5329; fax: 2491-5850).

Credit Lyonnais Bank Praha, Ovocny trh 8-Myslbek Building, Prague 1 (tel: 2433-3543).

Creditanstalt A S Praha, Siroka 5, 110 01 Prague 1 (tel: 2110-2111; fax: 2481-2185).

Deutsche Bank AG, Pobocka Praha, Jungmannova 34, 110 00 Prague 1 (tel: 2421-2857; fax: 2422-5727).

Evropabanka A S, Strosmayerovo nam 1, 170 01 Prague 7 (tel: 6671-2134).

GiroCredit Banka Praha A S, Vaclavske nam 56, PO Box 749, 111 21 Prague 1 (tel: 2403-3333).

HVB Czech Republic, Prague (tel: 2111-2111; internet: www.hvb.cz).

Interbanka A S Praha, Vaclavske nam. 40, 110 00 Prague 1 (tel: 2440-6111).

Komercni Banka A S, Na Prikop 33, 114 07 Prague 1 (tel: 2402-1111; fax: 2424-3020).

Podnikatelska banka A S, Rohacova 79, 130 79 Prague 3 (tel: 6121-6089; fax: 6121-6085).

Raiffeisenbank A S Praha, Vodickova 38, 110 00 Prague 1 (tel: 2423-1270; fax: 2423-1278).

Realitbanka A S, Antala Staska 32, 146 20 Prague 4 (tel: 6104-5439).

Royal banka CS A S, Krocinova 1, 110 00 Prague 1 (tel: 2422-8582; fax: 2422-4833).

Wustenrot - Stavebni Sporitelna A S, Jugoslavska 29, 120 00 Prague 2 (tel: 2400-7200; fax: 2400-7204).

Zivnostenka Banka A S, Na Prikope 20, 113 80 Prague 1 (tel: 2412-1111; fax: 2412-5555).

Central bank

Czech National Bank, Na Prikope 28, 110 03 Prague 1 (tel: 2441-1111; fax: 2441-2404; e-mail: info@cnb.cz).

Stock exchange

Burza Cennych Papíru Praha (Prague Stock Exchange) (PSE), www.pse.cz

Travel information

Cedok (travel and hotel corporation), Na Prikope 18, 111 35 Prague 1-Nove Mesto (tel: 2419-7642; internet www.cedok.com).

Ceske Drahy (CD), Nábrezi Ludvíka Svobody 1222/12 110 15 Praha 1 (tel: 97-224-1881 reservations for inter-city trains only; internet: www.cd.cz/static/eng/).

Cestovni Kancelar, (national rail travel agency), V Celnici 6 110 00 Praha 1 (tel: 2423-9464; email: CKPHApob692@dop.pha.cd.cz; internet: www.czech-travel-guide.com).

CSA Czech Airlines, Airport Praha, Ruzyne 16008 (tel: 2480-6111; fax: 2481-5183; internet: www.czechairlines.com/en/; City Service Centre, V Ceinici 5, 110 00 Prague 1 (underground line B, station Namesti Republiky) (tel: 2010-4111); sales and ticket reservations (tel: 2010-4310).

National tourist organisation offices

Czech Tourism, PO Box 46, Vinohradska 12041 Praha 2 (tel: 2158-0111; fax: 2424-7516; internet: www.czechtourism.com); tourist information (tel: 2011-3229, between 0800 and 2000 hours; 2011-4512, 24 hours a day).

Ministries

Ministry of Agriculture, Tisnov 17, 117 05 Prague 1 (tel: 2181-2111; fax: 2481-0478).

Ministry of Culture, Milady Horakove 220, 160 41 Prague 6 (tel: 5708-5111; fax: 2431-8156; email: minkult@mkcr.cz).

Ministry of Defence, Tychonova 1, 160 01 Prague 6 (tel: 2021-0255; fax: 2021-0257; email: otevrenalinka@army.cz).

Ministry of Education, Youth and Sport, Karmelitska 8, 118 12 Prague 1 (tel: 5719-3111; fax: 5719-3790).

Ministry of the Environment, Vrsovicka 65, 100 10 Prague 10 (tel: 6712-1111; fax: 6731-0308: internet: www.env.cz).

Ministry of Foreign Affairs, Loretanske Namisti 5, 125 10 Prague 1 (tel: 2418-1111; fax: 2431-0017; email: info@mzv.cz; internet: www.czech.cz/).

Ministry of Health, Palackeho nam 4, 128 01 Prague 2 (tel: 2497-1111; fax: 2497 2111; email: mzcr@mzcr.cz).

Ministry of the Interior, Nad Stolou 3, 170 34 Prague 7 (tel: 6142-1115; email: dotazy@mvcr.cz; internet: www.mvcr.cz).

Ministry of Justice, Vysehradska 16, 128 10 Prague 2 (tel: 2199-7111; fax: 2491-9927; email: msp@msp.justice.cz: internet: www.justice.cz).

Ministry of Labour and Social Affairs, Na Poøienim Pravu 1, 128 01Prague 2 (tel: 2491-8391; fax: 2192-2664).

Ministry of Regional Development, Staromestske Namisti 6, 110 15 Prague 1 (tel: 2486-1111; fax: 2486-1333).

Ministry of Transport and Communications, Naboei Ludvika Svobody 12, 110 15 Prague 1 (tel: 5143-1111; fax: 2481-0596; email: utv0001@mdcr.cz).

Office of the Prime Minister, Naboei Eduarda Benese 4, 118 01 Prague 1 (tel: 2400-2111; fax: 2481-0231).

Office of the President, Prague Castle, 119 08 Prague 1 (tel: 2437-1111; fax: 2437-3300).

Other useful addresses

Asociace Investicnich Fondu (Association of Investment Companies and Funds), Tynska 21, 110 00 Prague 1 (tel: 2481-0063; fax: 2481-0063).

Asociace Obchodnich Spolecnosti a Podnikatelu CR (Association of Trading Companies and Businessmen), Skretova 6, 120 59 Prague 2 (tel: 2421-5371/81; fax: 2423-0570).

Association of Czech Entrepreneurs, Skretova 6, 12059 Prague 2 (tel and fax: 2423-0580).

BBC (Radio), Na Porící 12, Prague 1 CZ-110 00 (tel: 2487-2545; fax: 2487-2546).

Board of Legislation and Public Administration, Vladislavova 4, PO Box 596, 117 15 Prague 1 (tel: 2419-1111; fax: 2421-5060).

British Embassy, Commercial Section, Palac Myslbek Na Prikope 21, 11719 Prague 1 (tel: 2224-0021/22/33; fax: 2224-3625).

Centrum Vnejsich Ekonomickych Vztahu (Centre For Foreign Economic Relation), Politickych Veznu 20, PO Box 791, 111 21 Prague 1 (tel: 2422-1586,22406-2421; fax: 2422-1575).

Cesky Statisticky Urad (Czech Statistical Office), Sokolovska 142, 180 00 Prague 8 (tel: 6604-2414).

Confederation of Industry of the Czech Republic, Mikulandska 7, 11361 Prague 7 (tel: 2499-5679).

CzechInvest (Czech Agency for Foreign Investment), Stepanska 15, 120 00 Prague 2 (tel: 9634-2500; fax: 9634-2502; e-mail: marketing@czechinvest.org; internet site: http://www.czechinvest.org).

Czech Republic Embassy (USA), 3900 Spring of Freedom Street, NW, Washington DC 20008 (tel: (+1-202) 274-9100; fax: (+1-202) 966-8540; e-mail: amb_pol_washington@embassy.mzv.cz).

Czech Television (CTV) - Public Corporation, Kavcí Hory, Prague 4 CZ-140 70 (tel: 6113-1111).

Euro Information Centre, Network/Correspondence Centre, NIS Havelkova 22, 130 00 Prague 3 (fax: 2423-1114).

Fond Narodniho Majetku (National Property Fund), Rasinovo Nabrezi 42, 120 00 Prague 2 (tel: 2491-1111; fax: 206-618).

Nejvyssi Soud CR (Czech Supreme Court), Buresova 20, 657 37 Brno (tel: 4132-1237; fax: 4121-3493).

National Information Centre of the Czech Republic (NIS), Havelkova 22, 130 00 Prague 3 (tel: 2421-5808–15, 2422-2026–9; fax: 322-1484, 2422-3177).

Prazska Informacni Sluzba (Prague Information Service), Senovazne Namesti 23, 110 00 Prague 1 (tel: 544-444; fax: 421-1989).

Sdruzeni Soukromych Zemedelcu Cech, Moravy a Slezska (Association of Private Farmers of Bohemia, Moravia and Silesia), Tesnov 17, 117 05 Prague 1 (tel: 491-3606; fax: 491-0162).

Svaz Prumyslu a Dopravy CR (Confederation of Industry of the Czech Republic), Mikulandska 7, 113 61 Prague 1 (tel: 2491-5253).

UNIDO (Federation of Czech Industries), Mikulandska 7, 113 61 Prague 1 (tel: 2491-5679; fax: 2491-5253).

Ustavni Soud CR (Czech Constitutional Court), Jostova 8, 660 83 Brno 2 (tel: 4216-1111).

National news agency: CTK (Czech News Agency), 5/7 Opletalova, 111 14

Prague 1 (tel: 2209-8111; internet: www.ctk.cz).

Internet sites

Atlas (the national coach company) http://jizdnirady.atlas.cz/

Brno Trade Fairs and Exhibitions Co Ltd (press information): www.bvv.cz/bvv

Ceské Dráhy, (national rail information) www.cd.cz/static/eng/

Czech business directory: www.muselik.com/czech/cbd.html

Czech directory: www.inform.cz/def.asp

Czech Embassy in Washington DC: www.mzv.cz/washington

Czech Ministry of Finance: www.mfcr.cz

Czech Ministry of Industry and Trade: www.mpo.cz

Czech Office for Protection of Competition: http://compet.cz

Czech Republic (provides links to information about the country): www.muselik.com/czech/toc.html

Czech Telecommunications Office: www.ctu.cz

Czech Trade Promotion Agency: www.czechtrade.cz/

Czech Trade Promotion Agency (in English): www.czechtradeoffices.com/Global

Hotels and history: www.abaka.com/Czech/

IPB (Investicni A Postovni banka as): www.ipb.cz

Office of Czech Republic: http://vlada.cz

Prague city transport www.dp-praha.cz/en/index.htm

Denmark

KEY FACTS

Official name: Kongeriget Danmark (The Kingdom of Denmark)

Head of State: Queen Margrethe II (since 1972)

Head of government: Prime Minister Lars Løkke Rasmussen (Venstre) (since 28 June 2015)

Ruling party: Venstre (Liberal Party)

Area: 43,080 square km

Population: 5.63 million (2014)

Capital: Copenhagen

Official language: Danish

Currency: Danish krone (Kr) = 100 ore

Exchange rate: Kr6.67 per US$ (Sep 2015)

GDP per capita: US$60,564 (2014)*

GDP real growth: 0.99% (2014)*

GDP: US$340.81 billion (2014)*

Labour force: 2.85 million (2014)

Unemployment: 6.53% (2014)

Inflation: 0.56% (2014)

Oil production: 167,000 bpd (2014)

Natural gas production: 4.60 billion cum (2014)

Balance of trade: US$10.13 billion (2014)*

* estimated figure

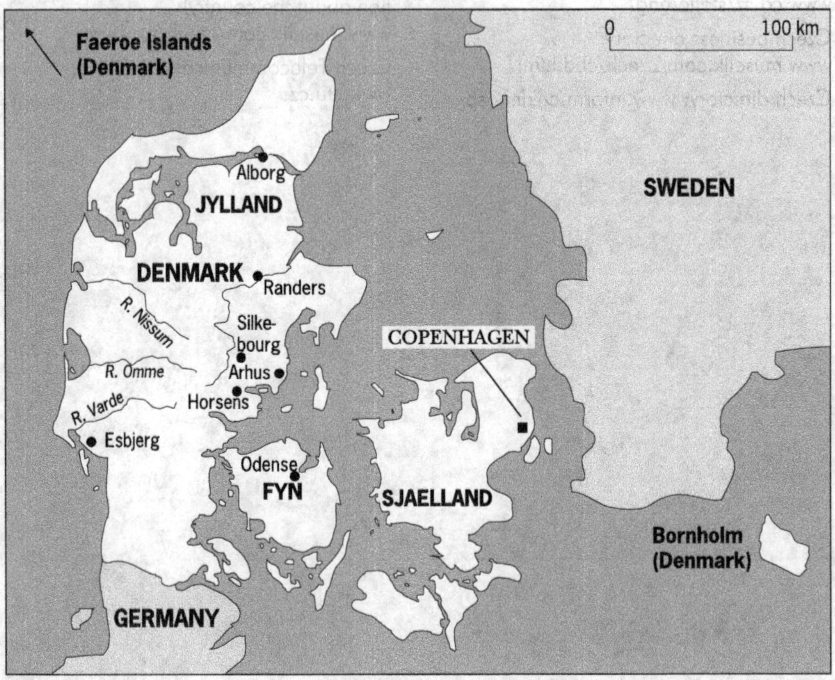

As if the mandarins of Brussels did not already have enough irritations, the success of the Dansk Folkepartei (DF) (Danish People's Party) in the June 2015 election, was one they could have done without. Denmark's post-election political picture was as confusing as it was ironic. The irony was that although the ruling Socialdemokraterne (SDP) (Social Democrats) had increased its vote to 26.3 per cent and gained more seats than its rivals, the incumbent prime minister, Helle Thorning Schmidt, had resigned.

High turnout – low prospects

The election turnout was high, estimated at around 90 per cent. The DF had come second with 21.5 per cent and the Danmarks Liberale Parti (DLP or Venstre) (Liberal Party), lead by Lars Løkke Rasmussen third, with 19.5 per cent. The DF, led by Kristian Thulesen Dahl and known for its anti-European and anti-immigration policies had, if achievement and surprise were factored in, won the elections. Its election platform also included a referendum on Denmark's relationship with the European Union (EU). Founded by Pia Kjaersgaard two decades earlier, the DF had also campaigned for improved welfare services, especially for the elderly. Denmark's membership of the European free movement Schengen agreement had also been called into question by the DF. Mr Dahl had promised to support the UK's calls for EU reform. The DF's vice chairman, Morten Messerschmidt, announced that it was the party's objective 'to make Denmark into Cameron [the UK prime minister]'s biggest ally.' The SDP, which despite a patchy record, had increased its share of the vote, was not only forced to select a new leader, but also to seek new coalition partners as its centre-left alliance was five seats less than the right-wing bloc of the former liberal prime minister Lars Løkke Rasmussen. Mr Rasmussen shared a number of the more moderate views expressed by DF members, especially those relating to immigration.

However, the saving grace for the incumbent SDP was the improvement in Denmark's economic performance. Had it not been for the forecast of gross domestic product (GDP) growth of 1.7 per cent for 2015, the ruling SDP would certainly not have fared so well in the elections. A flat economy would have worked well for Mr Rasmussen. Denmark's Social democrats had long favoured a Denmark open to immigrants, especially those fleeing conflict-ridden countries. Mr Rasmussen claimed that Denmark's generously subsidised welfare state meant that there was little incentive in working. Ms Thorning-Schmidt countered with the slogan 'If you come to Denmark, you have to work.'

Denmark's first female prime minister had impressed by her handling of a terrorist attack on a café where a meeting in support of free speech was being held. The prime minister had also managed to raise the Danish profile internationally, notably in Brussels where the small Scandinavian country punched above its weight, but also outside Europe. A 'selfie' photo taken by the smiling prime minister sitting alongside President Obama and the UK's David Cameron may have raised her game, but it also attracted criticism for insensitivity. In Denmark's pre-election television debates Ms Thorning-Scmidt had also attracted criticism for her expensive clothes, earning her the nickname 'Gucci Helle'.

At first blanche, therefore, it looked as though Mr Rasmussen would be the politician invited to form a government, despite his party's dismal performance. The task of forming a government, however, was no simple matter. Kristian Thulesen Dahl of the DF had already indicated that he was not interested in becoming prime minister or indeed in joining a coalition government. He had said that 'It is not necessarily within government that the DF can achieve maximum influence. Should the new government have to seek our approval for its every move seems more attractive.'

In or out of government, the DF votes might well turn out to be decisive in approving parliamentary legislation. Outside government, the Eurosceptics would enjoy a free hand, able to distance themselves from some of the government's more difficult decisions. Denmark has long been seen as one of the more Eurosceptic EU members. In 1992 it triggered a small crisis when it rejected the Maastricht Treaty. In 2000 a popular referendum voted against joining the euro, despite the government's wishes.

The economy

Denmark, probably embarrassed by the moniker of being 'Europe's happiest country'' has scored highly on many interpretations of 'well-being'. Despite this, according to the Paris-based Organisation for Economic Co-operation and Development (OECD) in a 2014 survey of the Danish economy, weak productivity growth over the previous two decades had contributed to a widening of the income gap when compared to the leading OECD economies. Generating stronger productivity growth over the longer run has been a critical challenge for Denmark, calling for persistent structural reform efforts.

In the view of the OECD, the economy is set to recover gradually as world trade regains momentum and confidence improves. However, household debt remains high and there remain fragilities in the financial sector, which in turn entails risks for private consumption and public finance. Denmark's financial sector is disproportionately large, with seven systemically important financial institutions, and the sector's share of deferred-amortisation mortgage loans had become 'too high for comfort.' On the fiscal side, the framework has been strengthened in recent years, public finances are in a relatively good shape and automatic stabilisers are large, which helped buffer adverse shocks. Past and recent structural reforms would, in the view of the OECD, help to raise labour market participation and to control public expenditure. However, the tax burden on upper labour incomes remain elevated and are probably detrimental to economic growth.

Denmark suffers from weak competition in some sectors and shortcomings in the innovation policy framework have held back productivity growth, notwithstanding the often high levels of spending on research and development (R&D). This could hinder participation in global value chains, which is one potential channel for achieving productivity gains. The OECD noted that regulatory hurdles impede competition in the services sector. Ownership, zoning and size regulations, as well as national standards that differ from international ones restrict entry in several sectors. With public spending in relation to GDP among the highest in the OECD, intensifying competition in the public sector could also raise productivity. In addition, there is room to enhance the efficiency of innovation policies. In particular, it is important to make sure that some schemes provide efficient support to young and dynamic innovative companies.

The OECD noted that Denmark's free and broad access to education, its long tradition of active labour market policies and its well-developed adult learning system mean that skills are relatively good, although some groups lack basic skills. The continuing reforms of compulsory education and of the vocational education and training system were expected by the OECD to raise youth skills and improve transitions to the labour market. While the flexibility of the Danish labour market helped achieve an efficient allocation of skills within the economy, the share of high-skilled workers in the private sector is relatively low, which can partly be

KEY INDICATORS — Denmark

	Unit	2011	2012	2013	2014	**2015
Population	m	5.56	5.58	5.60	5.63	*5.63
Gross domestic product (GDP)	US$bn	333.20	315.16	355.88	*340.81	*297.36
GDP per capita	US$	59,928	56,476	59,950	*60,564	*52,822
GDP real growth	%	1.1	-0.4	-0.5	*1.0	*1.6
Inflation	%	2.8	2.4	0.8	0.6	*0.8
Unemployment	%	4.6	7.5	7.0	6.5	*6.2
Oil output	'000 bpd	224.0	207.0	178.0	167.0	–
Natural gas output	bn cum	7.1	6.4	4.8	4.6	–
Exports (fob) (goods)	US$m	111,693.0	105,084.0	109,744.0	111,449.0	–
Imports (fob) (goods)	US$m	102,502.0	96,833.0	101,509.0	101,321.0	–
Balance of trade	US$m	9,192.0	8,251.0	8,236.0	10,128.0	–
Current account	US$m	21,568.0	18,846.0	24,207.0	21,319.0	*18,097.0
Total reserves minus gold	US$m	85,190.0	86,138.0	86,099.0	72,812.0	–
Foreign exchange	US$m	81,766.0	82,368.0	82,417.0	–	–
Exchange rate	per US$	5.31	5.75	5.46	6.15	–

* estimated figure ** forecast figure

explained by weak incentives to undertake tertiary education and to choose demanding jobs. Employment rates are high, but those outside the labour market face low financial incentives to take a job. The recent reform of the 'flexjob' and disability programmes should help to better activate skills if adequately implemented.

In its December 2014 assessment of the Danish economy, the International Monetary Fund (IMF) noted that the Danish economy was recovering slowly and unevenly. The economy had contracted slightly – by 0.1 per cent – in 2013, but in the view of the IMF it had looked likely to accelerate modestly in 2014. Growth was held back by the persistent decline in North Sea oil and gas production as well as of exports to euro-area partners. At the same time, private domestic demand and non-oil exports were supporting growth. Employment had increased and unemployment had been drifting downward slightly over the past year. Inflation and interest rates also remained low. Domestic inflation was at about 1.5 per cent, although lower inflation in imports held down the broader indices. Wage growth was also moderate.

The IMF also reported that Denmark's fiscal policy had turned slightly supportive in 2014 after a substantial consolidation in 2013. While the 2013 consolidation was sufficient to exit from the Excessive Deficit Procedure, the headline deficit was expected to have expanded in 2014 and was projected to widen further in 2015.

Denmark's financial system profitability was also still low, in line with weak credit growth, but in general capitalisation had improved. For commercial banks as a whole, already-high capital ratios had risen even further and liquid assets as a share of total assets had also increased. At mortgage credit institutions, capital ratios were also high. However, the IMF warned that the weaknesses in some non-systemic banks warranted close monitoring, and might require intervention.

The IMF considered that Denmark's recovery was likely to continue, but remained fragile. Annual growth was estimated at 0.7 per cent in 2014, projected to increase to 1.4 per cent in 2015, and to rise to slightly above 2 per cent thereafter. Domestic demand and exports to non euro-area countries should support the recovery. As the recovery continues at a modest pace, the output gap is expected to close by 2018.

However, in the view of the IMF, risks remained 'on the downside.' Surges in global financial markets volatility (disorderly exit from unconventional monetary policy or other causes) that lead to a rise in market interest rates could readily depress consumption as households' cash flow is diverted to higher debt service on adjustable rate mortgages. A protracted period of low euro-area interest rates as the Danish economy recoveres could create overheating pressures and overvalued asset prices. And a drop in confidence in Danish covered bonds could depress consumption through higher debt service on adjustable rate mortgages. Last but not least, the Nordic-Baltic financial system is tightly integrated, which means that problems elsewhere in the region might spill over into Denmark and outward spill-overs from Denmark could well propagate through the financial system channel.

The IMF's Executive Directors, in conclusion, welcomed the rebound in economic activity, the steady decline in unemployment, and the improved housing market. They confirmed that Denmark's growth prospects were favourable, underpinned by a strong track record of prudent macroeconomic policies and financial system stability, while the exchange rate peg continued to serve the economy well.

A windy day

On 9 July 2015, Denmark's wind farms produced 140 per cent of the country's energy needs. The remaining 40 per cent surplus was exported to Norway, Germany and Sweden. While much of this was down to a particularly windy Danish day, it does highlight the possibility of a future Denmark sustained solely on ecologically friendly energy.

Critics have pointed to the 'unusually windy day', rather than the marketability of wind farms, for Denmark's renewable energy surge. However – whilst it is true that 140 per cent is well over their usual production – it is always a windy day somewhere in the world. Led by Denmark's example, energy surplus and deficits can be made up in trade, all within a renewable, and ecologically friendly framework.

Risk assessment

Economy	Fair
Politics	Fair
Regional stability	Good

COUNTRY PROFILE

Denmark is an ancient kingdom situated on an archipelago, which has historically served as a bridge between continental Europe and the Scandinavian Peninsula. During the Napoleonic era, the Danes sided with the French and, as a result of their defeat, lost their dominance in Scandinavia.

1397 The Union of Kalmar united Denmark, Sweden and Norway under a single monarch with Denmark the leading power.
1523 Denmark recognised Swedish independence.
1729 Greenland became a Danish province.
1814 Denmark ceded Norway to Sweden.
1849 Denmark became a constitutional monarchy with a bicameral parliament.
1903 Iceland was granted home rule from Denmark.
1918 Iceland became a sovereign state in union with Denmark.
1914–18 Denmark was neutral during the First World War.
1918 Denmark's transition to parliamentary government with universal suffrage was fully established after the First World War and has been suspended only during the Nazi occupation of the Second World War.
1939 Denmark signed a non-aggression pact with Nazi Germany.
1940 Germany invaded Denmark.
1945 The German occupation ended. Denmark recognised the independence of Iceland.
1948 The Faroe Islands were granted self-government within the Kingdom.
1949 Denmark was one of the founder members of NATO.
1953 A revision of the constitution allowed for female succession to the throne, abolition of the upper house of parliament and the introduction of proportional representation. Greenland became an integral part of Denmark.
1959 Denmark joined the European Free Trade Association (EFTA).
1972 Queen Margrethe ascended the throne.
1973 Denmark joined the European Economic Community (EEC).
1979 Greenland was granted home rule; Denmark retained control over Greenland's foreign affairs and defence.
1985 Parliament passed legislation to ban the construction of nuclear power plants.
1992 In a referendum, voters rejected the Maastricht Treaty on further European integration.
1993 Poul Schlüter, prime minister since 1982, resigned after a judicial enquiry criticised him for misleading parliament in 1989 over the Tamil visa scandal. A four-party coalition government was formed by Poul Nyrup Rasmussen.
1994 Rasmussen was returned to power after a general election.

2000 In a referendum, Denmark voted against joining Europe's single currency.
2001 The Venstre (Liberal Party), led by Anders Fogh Rasmussen, formed a minority government, in coalition with the Konservative Folkeparti (Konservative) (Conservative People's Party), relying on support from the far right Dansk Folkeparti (DF) (Danish People's Party).
2004 Crown Prince Frederik married Australian-born Mary Donaldson, (their first son was born on 15 October 2005). Denmark and US agreed a deal to modernise the US Thule airbase in Greenland, over the objections of many local people.
2005 A dispute with Canada over the ownership of the Hans Islands, halfway between Greenland and Canada, erupted. The dispute was settled with a draft protocol to manage their dealings concerning the island.
2006 Cartoons of Mohammed which had appeared in *Jyllands Posten* newspaper provoked protests and boycotts of Danish exports in Middle Eastern countries.
2007 Crown Princess Mary gave birth to a daughter. Danish troops were withdrawn from Iraq. Prime Minister Rasmussen called a snap parliamentary election 15 months earlier than was necessary. The ruling Venstre won 26.3 per cent of the votes (46 seats out of 175) and with their coalition parties secured another term in office. Prime Minister Rasmussen remained in office.
2008 Ny Alliance (New Alliance) was renamed Liberal Alliance. Denmark approved more autonomy for Greenland in which Greenlanders are recognised as a separate people under international law and the local government has more control of resources, including a bigger share of oil revenues, and control of internal security.
2009 Anders Fogh Rasmussen resigned as prime minister, to become Secretary General of NATO; Lars Løkke Rasmussen (no relation) became prime minister. Denmark hosted the UN Climate Change Conference in Copenhagen. Delegates from around the world, including 115 heads of state and governments, discussed measures necessary to halt global warming. The outcome was thought to be less than successful as, although a temperature rise of no more than 2 degrees centigrade was an agreed limit, no limit was agreed on the emission of greenhouse gases.
2011 In February, a Somali refugee was convicted of attempting to kill Kurt Westergaard, the cartoonist whose cartoon of the Prophet Mohammed in 2006 had sparked Islamic protests across the Middle East. Despite its participation in the visa-free Schengen agreement, in July Denmark introduced border controls by instituting spot checks to prevent criminals and illegal immigrants entering the country (via Germany and Sweden). In parliamentary elections, held in September, Venstre won 26.7 per cent of the mainland vote (47 of 175 mainland seats), and Socialdemokraterne 24.9 per cent (44). These two parties lead opposing coalitions (known as the Blue Alliance and the Red Alliance, respectively) and their total share of the vote was Red Alliance 50.2 per cent (89 seats), Blue Alliance 49.8 per cent (86). Greenland returned two, and Faroe Islands returned one, candidates supporting the Red Alliance, giving it a total of 92 seats. Faroe Islands also returned one supporting the Blue Alliance. Total turnout was 87.2 per cent. On 16 September Prime Minister Lars Løkke Rasmussen (Venstre) resigned. Helle Thorning-Schmidt (Socialdemokraterne) became prime minister on 4 October. The world's largest container-shipping line, Maersk made an operating loss of US$5 billion (down from a profit of US$7 billion in 2010) and in December announced an alliance with other shipping companies to allow a cut in costs.
2012 On 3 January, Maersk was fined US$31.9 million by the US government for overcharging for shipments to its military forces in Iraq and Afghanistan over the past decade. In March the national news agency Ritzau became a limited company and purchased Newspaq (the financial news service).
2013 The World Happiness Report 2013 compiled by the UN Sustainable Development Solutions Network (SDSN) and published in September put Denmark top of the 156 countries surveyed.
2014 The Socialistisk Folkeparti (SF) (Socialist People's Party) resigned from the government on 30 January.
2015 On 9 July, Denmark's wind farms produced 140 per cent of the country's energy needs. The remaining 40 per cent surplus was exported to Norway, Germany and Sweden.

Political structure

Constitution

Denmark has a written constitution – *The Constitution Act* – a revised constitution was adopted on 5 June 1953. It set out the rights and requirements of the monarchy, state, church, government, judiciary and the individual. It legalised female succession to the throne, abolished the upper house of parliament and introduced proportional representation.
The monarchy is governed by the *Succession to the Throne Act*, adopted 27 March 1953, whereby royal power is inherited.
The Faroe Islands are a Danish external territory, electing two members to the Danish parliament, which maintains responsibility for constitutional, foreign and defence matters. A High Commissioner represents the Danish government and advises on joint affairs.
Greenland is a special cultural community in the Kingdom of Denmark. Only foreign policy, defence, police and monetary policy are Danish state affairs. Greenland elects two members to the Danish parliament.

Form of state

Constitutional monarchy

The executive

Executive power is vested in the monarch, and legislative power vested jointly in the monarch and parliament. The King appoints the prime minister and cabinet, who form the Council of State; they are responsible to the Folketing (parliament). All legislation is subject to the constitution.

National legislature

The unicameral Folketing has 179 members, of which 135 are elected by proportional representation in 17 districts, plus 40 seats that are allocated to balance the difference between the district and national vote. All members serve four-year terms unless early elections are called by the prime minister. Two representatives each from the Faroe Islands and Greenland are elected separately.

Legal system

Denmark's highest court is the Supreme Court in Copenhagen, made up of 15 judges. It hears appeals from two superior courts in Copenhagen and Viborg. These courts deal with appeals from the 84 tribunals, or lowest courts of justice, around the country. They can also deal initially with cases of greater consequence.

Last elections

18 June 2015 (parliamentary)
Results: Parliamentary: Socialdemokraterne (Social Democrats) won 26.3 per cent of the vote and 47 seats (out of 179), Dansk Folkeparti (DF) (Danish People's Party) 21.1 per cent and 37 seats, Venstre (Liberal Party) 19.5 per cent and 34 seats, Enhedslisten – De Rød-Grønne (Enhl., Ø) (Red-Green Alliance) 7.8 per cent and 14 seats, Liberal Alliance (LA) 7.5 per cent and 13 seats, Alternativet (The Alternative) 4.8 per cent and 9 seats, Radikale Venstre (RV) (Danish Social Liberal Party) 4.6 per cent and 8 seats, Socialistisk Folkeparti (SF) (Socialist People's Party) 4.2 per cent and 7 seats, Det Konservative Folkeparti (DKF) (Conservative People's Party) 3.4 per cent and 6 seats.
Although the ruling Social Democrats actually increased their vote share from the 2011 election, their left-leaning 'Red Bloc' lost parliamentary majority to the right-leaning 'Blue Bloc'. Lars Løkke Rasmussen's Venstre party – despite losing 13 seats – attempted to form a coalition with

other Blue Bloc members. However, due to political differences, this never materialised. On 28 June 2015, Rasmussen formed a minority government with a cabinet comprised solely of Venstre members.

Next elections

2019 (parliamentary)

Political parties

Ruling party

Venstre (Liberal Party)

Main opposition party

Red Alliance, led by Social Democrats

Population

5.59 million (2013)

Denmark has an ageing population, with those aged over 65 growing by an annual 0.3 per cent, while the population below the age of 14 declines each year by 0.7 per cent.

Last census: January 2001: 5,349,212

Population density: 120 inhabitants per square km. Urban population 87 per cent (2010 Unicef).

Annual growth rate: 0.4 per cent, 1990–2010 (Unicef).

Ethnic make-up

Danes make up the majority of the population, along with some 9,000 Greenlanders and around 12,000 Faroese. The largest immigrant groups from outside the kingdom are Turkish, British and Norwegian. There is a small German minority in southern Jutland.

Religions

The majority of the population (90 per cent) belong to the Lutheran Church although there are small groups of other Christian denominations.

Education

There are 10 years of compulsory schooling, although the average student attends school for 15 years.

The participation rate at primary and secondary levels is close to 100 per cent of the relevant age groups. Forty-six per cent of the relevant age group attend education at a tertiary level. The cost of university or post-high school further education is financed by a system of student grants supplemented by bank loans carrying a state guarantee.

Compulsory years: Seven to 16.

Pupils per teacher: 10 in primary schools.

Health

Hospitalisation and treatment by general practitioners is free of charge, but there are part-charges for medicine prescribed by GPs. Treatment by dentists and opticians is subsidised but not free. Since 1988, several small private hospitals have opened, the fees for which can be covered by insurance schemes.

HIV/Aids

HIV prevalence: 0.2 per cent aged 15–49 in 2003 (World Bank).

Life expectancy: 78 years, 2004 (WHO 2006)

Fertility rate/Maternal mortality rate: 1.9 births per woman, 2010 (Unicef); maternal mortality 0.1 per 1,000 live births: (World Bank)

Child (under 5 years) mortality rate (per 1,000): 4 per 1,000 live births (WHO 2012)

Head of population per physician: 2.93 physicians per 1,000 people, 2002 (WHO 2006)

Welfare

There is an extensive cradle-to-the-grave social security system, however the size of the welfare system has gradually been reduced since the 1990s. In 2005, the system came under close scrutiny and a government commissioned appraisal recommended that the pension aged should be raised and early retirement phased out, and charges set for some healthcare and educational services.

Currently welfare benefits include unemployment benefits, supplementary benefits and rent and heating grants.

Social security and welfare spending as a share of GDP is approximately 5.8 per cent.

Pensions

Denmark was the first country to introduce old age pensions in 1895, funded by two general taxes. To sustain the current pensions, there is a three pillar approach to provision. Pillar one is a basic, mandatory, publically administered scheme, maintained to provide for the poor in old age and may be supplemented by other allowances. Pillar two are mandatory, privately administered schemes and workplace pensions, which are devised to attract contributions as high as 16 per cent of wages. Pillar three are privately administered schemes with individual and voluntary contributions. Other schemes exist and fall within the rules of the three pillars.

Main cities

Copenhagen (capital, estimated population 1.2 million in 2012), Aarhus (256,292), Odense (168,906), Aalborg (104,771), Esbjerg (71,686), Randers (61,078).

Languages spoken

English and German are widely spoken in business and administration.

Official language/s

Danish

Media

Press freedom is guaranteed by law, as demonstrated in 2006 by the international furores following the publication of images of the Prophet Mohammad by a Danish newspaper, which was un-censured.

Press

Most publications are privately owned and tend to have fairly strong political leanings.

Dailies: There are around 50 daily newspapers, with Sunday readership particularly high. The leading newspapers are *Morgenavisen Jyllands Posten* (http://jp.dk) *Ekstra Bladet* (http://ekstrabladet.dk) a tabloid, BT (www.bt.dk), Politiken (http://politiken.dk) and *Berlingske Tidende* (www.berlingske.dk).

Weeklies: Most daily newspapers publish weekend editions. In Danish, a variety of political magazines include *LO* (www.lo.dk), *Solidaritet* (www.solidaritet.dk), and *Danske Regioner* (www.regioner.dk). For general news *Weekend Avisen* (www.weekendavisen.dk), and *Grønland* (www.groenlandselskab.dk) for news from Greenland. In English, *The Copenhagen Post* (www.cphpost.dk).

In Danish, women's magazines include *Ingelise* (www.ingelise.dk), and *Alt for Damerne* (www.altfordamerne.dk); *Euroman* (www.euroman.dk) is for men. *Udfordringen* (*Showtime*) (www.udfordringen.dk) covers music and performing arts.

Business: In Danish, national dailies include *Net Posten* (www.netposten.dk) and *Scandinavia Now* (www.scandinavianow.com), national magazines include *Berlingske Nyhedsmagasin* (www.business.dk) and *Pengte & Privatøkonomi* (www.penge.dk). Regional newspapers from Copenhagen include *Børsen* (http://borsen.dk), *Erhvervs Bladet* (www.erhvervsbladet.dk), and *Okonomisk Ugebrev* (www.ugebrev.dk). *Ase Nyt* is a commercial quarterly.

Periodicals: Periodicals on general interest, life-style, consumer and commercial interest include *Blender*, *En Skør Skør Verden* and *Social Demokraten*.

Broadcasting

The national public broadcaster is DR (www.dr.dk).

Radio: DR (www.dr.dk/drdkradio) operates two national stations (P1 and P2), plus a regional station (P3) and a DAB, digital radio (P4), providing a comprehensive mix of all music genre, talk radio and information. A DR station also broadcasts in Nyheder (an Indonesian and Malaysian language).

There are many privately operated commercial radio stations and most located within relatively small areas or population centres. Regional and national networks include The Voice (www.thevoice.dk),

Radio Mojn (www.mojn.dk) and Hit FM (www.hitfm.nu).
Television: Analogue transmissions will begin to be closed down by late 2009, with High Definition TV transmissions begun in January 2008.
DR (www.dr.dk) operates two national channels DR1 and DR2.
Other commercial TV services are provided by either cable or satellite, of which TV 2 (http://tv2.dk) the government-owned network is a multi-channel service. Foreign-owned services, include the Swedish, MTG (www.mtg.se), SBS (www.sbsbroadcasting.com) and US Disney Channel, which provide a wide variety of programmes.

Economy

Although the economy is balanced, with a well-developed, export-based manufacturing sector and an important agricultural sector, like all post-industrial societies services account for the largest share of GDP, at 76.2 per cent in 2014. Agriculture and food industries combined are Denmark's largest industry, employing around 150,000 people, with annual sales of over €15 billion (over US$20 billion); it is also a net exporter of food. Even so agriculture accounts for only 1.3 per cent of GDP, while industry and manufacturing account for around 22 per cent. Denmark is a net exporter of energy and has oil reserves of 0.6 thousand million barrels producing 167,000 barrels per day (in 2014).
Following the global recession, the economy recovered in 2010 with GDP growth of 1.3 per cent; growth in 2011 was 1.2 per cent. The economy dipped in the subsequent two years before returning to a growth of 1.1 per cent in 2014. Unemployment that had averaged 2.7 per cent (2007–09) jumped to 5.9 per cent in 2010 as the economy reacted to the market forces. It has since risen to 7 per cent in 2014.
Weak productivity growth over the past two decades has lead to an increasing income gap within the country. The economy is set to recover gradually as world trade improves and business confidence returns. Inflation has remained stable around 0.5 per cent.
Denmark provides revenue to the governments of Greenland and the Faroe Islands (59 per cent and 6 per cent of each country's GDP, respectively).

External trade

As a member of the European Union (EU), Denmark operates within a community-wide free trade area, with tariffs sets as a whole. Internationally, the EU has free trade agreements with a number of nations and trading blocs worldwide.
Denmark's heavy industrial base is limited by a lack of natural resources. However it has sophisticated hi-tech, pharmaceutical and bio-technical industries, an aircraft manufacturing base and is a net exporter of food and energy. It is also the home of the world-famous Lego, toy building blocks, designed in the 1930s.
Denmark is a world leader in export of pork and manufactured wind turbines.

Imports

Principal imports are machinery and equipment, raw materials and semi-manufactures for industry, chemicals, grain and foodstuffs and consumer goods.
Main sources: Germany (20.5 per cent of total in 2014), Sweden (12.3 per cent), The Netherlands (7.7 per cent)

Exports

Principal export commodities include machinery and instruments, pork and meat products, dairy products, fish, chemicals and pharmaceuticals, furniture, ships.
Main destinations: Germany (18.1 per cent of total in 2014), Sweden (11.7 per cent), UK (7.8 per cent)

Agriculture

Farming

The agricultural sector typically contributes around 1.3 per cent of GDP and employs 3 per cent of the labour force. The sector is organised into local co-operatives that are united in national federations.
Agriculture benefits from the Common Agricultural Policy (CAP), which imposes import duties on products entering the EU from other countries in order to equalise the price of imported commodities with those produced within the union. Efforts to reform the CAP could have a significant impact on future production.
The government primarily acts as a regulator in the agricultural sector. It sets veterinary standards and lays down the rules for farm mergers and ownership. The government does not set production or export and import targets, and as a member of the EU, agriculture is subject to the EU agricultural production quota regime.
Intensive farming is concentrated on livestock production, mainly pig-meat, beef, veal, poultry and dairy produce.
Denmark has large world market shares in products such as pig-meat, dairy products, seeds, mink pelts and fish products.

Fishing

Typical seafood catches total around 1.7 million tonnes per annum (tpy), yielding over 140,000 tpy of fish oils.
Denmark ranks fourth among the world's leading seafood exporters. It continues to export significant quantities of processed seafood, fish oil and meal mainly processed from imported raw material. Decreased Danish cod catches are putting pressure on prices and import substitutes. Cod and other fish imports from other countries have considerably increased.

Forestry

Forest and other wooded land accounts for only one-eighth of the land area, with forest cover estimated at 455,000 hectares (ha). Plantations constitute about 75 per cent of the forest area, with the remainder classed as semi-natural. Less than 25 per cent of the forest is under public ownership, with the rest shared between individuals and private institutions.
Demand for forest products is high and is mostly met by imports. Most of the softwood logs are processed locally while high quality hardwood logs are increasingly imported. The furniture industry depends on imported raw materials and exports most of its production.

Industry and manufacturing

Denmark has a highly developed and diversified industrial sector, which is almost wholly under private ownership. The industrial sector contributes around a quarter of GDP (22 per cent) and employs a quarter of the labour force.
As a country with a market economy and free external trade, government industrial policy plays a relatively minor role, especially as there is no significant state ownership in the industrial sector. With close to 800,000 employees, the state sector plays a significant role in the economy.
Government support for industry is largely confined to export credit arrangements and funds for research and development.
The engineering, food processing and wood-paper industries are the economy's three biggest production areas.

Tourism

Denmark offers a full range of tourist destinations, including modern cities, historic sites, a multitude of islands and galleries and museums specific to its culture heritage. It is home to the famous Lego plastic building block, which has a themed amusement park in Billund. There are three cultural sites on Unesco's World Heritage List (a medieval site in Jutland, the renaissance Kronburg Castle and the gothic Roskilde Cathedral).
The contribution of tourism to GDP was 6.8 per cent of the total in 2014. The total contribution to employment was 7.8 per cent in the same year (205,500 jobs). Visitor exports were 4 per cent of total exports in the same year.
The number of arrivals reached 8.5 million in 2014.

Mining

The mining sector contributes under 1 per cent to Denmark's GDP. Denmark has no exploitable raw materials other than sand and gravel for construction.

In Greenland, there are substantial deposits of coal, iron ore, uranium, gold and diamonds, none of which are currently being exploited.

Hydrocarbons

Denmark is Western Europe's third-biggest oil and gas producer. Denmark has neither coal nor hydroelectricity resources, but has found oil and gas in the Danish sector of the North Sea. The introduction of new technology in the Dansk Underground Consortium (DUC) fields in the North Sea has enabled the extraction of hitherto inaccessible reserves.

Denmark is Western Europe's third-biggest producer of oil and gas, which are obtained from off-shore fields in the North Sea. No commercially viable finds have been made in coastal waters or on land. Denmark is self-sufficient in oil and gas and a net exporter of both products. Surplus gas is exported to Sweden and Germany, while oil is mainly sold on the spot market.

Proven oil reserves amount to around 600 million barrels at the end of 2014, with production of 167,000 barrels per day. Proven reserves of natural gas are around 1.2 trillion cubic feet, with production of 171 billion cubic feet in 2014, 37 per cent of which is exported. The introduction of new technology in the Dansk Undergrunds Consortium (DUC) fields in the North Sea has enabled the extraction of hitherto inaccessible reserves.

Denmark does not produce coal but consumed 4625 thousand short tons in 2012.

Energy

Total electricity capacity amounts to around 12,969MW, in thermal power stations fuelled primarily by coal, followed by gas, wind, oil and biomass.

15.7 billion kWH of energy was produced in 2013 from renewable sources. Wind power generation peaked on a day on July 2015, with 140 per cent of Denmark's electricity demands met. A surge in wind-farm installations means Denmark could be producing half of its electricity from renewable sources well before a target date of 2020.

In 2014 Denmark had 5,252 wind turbines in operation, with an installed wind capacity of 4.855 megawatts (MW). It includes the largest wind farm in the EU at Nysted, with a trend for fewer but larger turbine wind power plants. Wind power accounted for 19.7 per cent of domestic electricity supplies; the target is to reach 50 per cent of capacity by 2030. Around three-quarters of Denmark's wind capacity comes from onshore windfarms, which have strong government backing.

Financial markets

Stock exchange

The Københavns Fondsbørs (Copenhagen Stock Exchange) (CSE)

Banking and insurance

Denmark has a healthy banking sector which is open to foreign competition. There are around 100 commercial banks in operation, although the two largest account for 60 per cent of total bank assets.

Central bank

Danmarks Nationalbank

Main financial centre

Copenhagen

Time

GMT plus one hour (daylight saving, late March to late October, GMT plus two hours)

Geography

Denmark is a low-lying country in northern Europe. Its only land frontier is with Germany and totals 67.7km, while the coastline exceeds 7,300km. Nowhere is more than 52km from the sea. Norway lies to the north of Denmark, across the Skagerrak – a gulf in the North Sea. Sweden lies to the north-east, its most southerly region being separated from Zealand by a narrow strait.

Outlying territories of Denmark are Greenland and the Faroe Islands in the North Atlantic Ocean.

The mainland consists of the peninsula of Jutland, the islands of Zealand, Funen, Lolland, Falster and Bornholm and 401 smaller islands. The average elevation of land above sea level is 30 metres and its highest point is only 173 metres above sea level. Denmark lies between the North Sea to the west and the Baltic Sea to the east.

Hemisphere

Northern

Climate

Predominantly western winds bring warm, moist air from the West Atlantic, tempering the climatic influences from the east. In winter these can take the form of long periods of frost with ice-bound waters and, in summer, occasional high temperatures and drought. The average temperature in Denmark is 7.5 degrees Celsius (C); the temperature varies from minus 0.1 degrees C in the coldest months to 16 degrees C in July. The average rainfall amounts to 664mm and is distributed fairly evenly over the year, with August normally being the wettest.

Dress codes

Danes are generally informal about clothing. Businessmen usually wear jackets and ties at meetings and only adopt a dinner jacket (or long dresses for women) on very formal occasions.

Entry requirements

Passports

Required by all, except EU visitors travelling on national ID cards.

Visa

Required by all except nationals of EU, North America, Australasia or Japan. For further exceptions contact the nearest consulate. Denmark is a member of the Schengen visa accord and all visitors that require a visa must apply to a Danish consulate; when a visa has been issued a visitor may travel to any other Schengen zone without further visas.

Business trips can be undertaken on a Schengen visa, nevertheless, an original invitation from a business contact in Denmark is necessary when applying. A Schengen visa application (offered in several languages) can be downloaded from http://europa.eu/abc/travel/ see 'documents you will need'.

Currency advice/regulations

There are no restrictions on import and export of local or foreign currency, however sums over eur15,000 should be declared on arrival. Some banks refuse to change large denomination foreign notes. ATMs are plentiful. Travellers cheques in US dollars, pound sterling and euros save additional exchange fees.

Customs

Personal items are duty-free. There are no duties levied on alcohol and tobacco between EU member states, providing amounts imported are for personal consumption.

Health (for visitors)

Nationals of the European Economic Area (EEA) countries and Switzerland can access reduced cost and sometimes free medical treatment using a European Health Insurance Card (EHIC) while visiting the EEA. Exceptions include nationals of the 10 countries which joined the EU in 2004 whose EHIC is not valid in Switzerland. Applications for the EHIC should be made before travelling.

Mandatory precautions

None.

Hotels

There is no official rating system. Tarrifs include 15 per cent service charge. It is advisable to book accommodation in Copenhagen in advance, especially during summer.

Credit cards

All the usual credit and charge cards are accepted.

Public holidays (national)

Fixed dates

1 Jan (New Year's Day), 5 Jun (Constitution Day), 24–26 Dec (Christmas).

Variable dates
Maundy Thursday, Good Friday and Easter Monday, Great Prayer Day, Ascension Day, Whit Monday.
Public holidays that fall on the weekend are not carried over to a weekday.

Working hours

Banking
Mon–Fri: 0930–1600; Thu: 0930–1800.

Business
Mon–Fri: 0800/0900–1600/1700; offices frequently close early before the weekend or on the eve of public holidays.

Government
Mon–Fri: generally 0900–1700.

Shops
Mon–Thu: 0900–1730; Fri: 0900–1900/2000; Sat: 0900–1300/1400. First Saturday in each month most shops open: 0900–1600/1700.

Telecommunications

Mobile/cell phones
The GSM 1800 and 900 networks operate throughout the country.

Electricity supply

220/380V AC.

Social customs/useful tips

Shaking hands is the acceptable way to greet and depart from both business contacts and friends. Punctuality is expected on all occasions.
Service is normally included on bills and further tipping is not necessary in hotels, restaurants or taxis.

Security

Apart from the occasional pickpocket, the streets of Copenhagen are generally safe.

Getting there

Air
National airline: Scandinavian Airline System (SAS) – jointly owned with Sweden and Norway.
International airport/s: Copenhagen (CPH) at Kastrup, 8km south-east of capital. Business/conference centre, Internet access, duty-free shops, bars, restaurants, bank, post office, transfer hotel (maximum stay 18hrs), shower and sauna facilities. Car hire available. A new rail link between the airport and main railway station in Copenhagen takes 12 minutes. There are also regular bus services from the airport departing every 10–20 minutes taking 20 minutes.
Other airport/s: Aalborg (AAL), 6km north-west of city; Aarhus (Tirstrup) (AAR), 44km north-east of city; Billund (BLL), 2km east of city, Esbjerg (EBJ), 8km from city.
Airport tax: None

Surface
Road: The 18km Great Belt bridge and tunnel, linking Copenhagen to the island of Funen (Fyn), provides the first seamless surface connection from mainland Europe to Copenhagen. It includes a 6.5km long suspension bridge, the world's second longest. A second bridge and tunnel, the Øresund connection, links Copenhagen with Malmø in Sweden consisting of an 8km bridge and an 8km tunnel connected by an artificial island. Tolls are applicable on both bridges.
Rail: High-speed Intercity trains via Copenhagan airport connect to Funen (1 hour) and Jutland (2 hours) with additional connections to Malmø (Sweden) on a 30-minute journey via the Øresund link. Access from other European countries is via Germany.
Water: Regular ferry services from UK, Norway, Sweden, Poland, Iceland, the Faroe Islands and Germany.

Getting about

National transport
Air: The network of scheduled services radiates from Copenhagen. Domestic airports are generally situated between two or more cities which are within easy reach of each other. Domestic flights are usually of no more than 30 minutes duration.
Road: About 70,000km of roads including 593km of motorway. The road system in the Danish archipelago makes frequent use of ferries. Motorways are not subject to toll duty.
Buses: There are few private long-distance coaches.
Rail: Approximately 2,500km of railways are operated by Danish State Railway (DSB) and a few private companies, providing a very efficient service linked to the ferry services. Country bus network operates where there are no railways.
Water: Ferry services connect the islands of Zealand, Funen and Lolland and Jutland peninsula, operated by DSB.

City transport
Taxis: There is a good service in all major towns. Taxis can be hailed in the street when they display their green 'Fri' sign, or by telephone or at ranks. Fare includes a tip.
Buses, trams & metro: Good bus service in Copenhagen, including night buses until 0230. Frequent, efficient services in other main towns. Flat-rate fares are usual.

Car hire
Hire cars are available throughout the country at main DSB stations and all airports. They can be booked in advance through stations, international car hire firms and travel agents. A valid driving licence is required, which must be carried when driving. Most firms stipulate a minimum age between 20–25. The speed limits are 130kmph on motorways, 80kmph on highways, and 50kmph in urban areas; speed traps are commonplace. Even for minor speed limit offences, drivers are liable to pay heavy on-the-spot fines; if payment cannot be made, the car may be detained. Avoid drinking and driving, as the laws of misuse are tough. Seatbelts, throughout a vehicle, are compulsory.

BUSINESS DIRECTORY

The addresses listed below are a selection only. While World of Information makes every endeavour to check these addresses, we cannot guarantee that changes have not been made, especially to telephone numbers and area codes. We would welcome any corrections.

Telephone area codes

The international direct dialling code (IDD) for Denmark is +45, followed by subscriber's number.

Useful telephone numbers

Fire, police, ambulance 112
Emergency dental treatment 3138-0251
24-hour chemist 3314-8266

Chambers of Commerce

American Chamber of Commerce in Denmark, 28 Christians Brygge, 1559 Copenhagen V (tel: 3393-2932; fax: 3313-0507; e-mail: mail@amcham.dk).

Danish Chamber of Commerce, Børsen, 1217 Copenhagen K (tel: 7013-1200; fax: 7013-1201; e-mail: hts@hts.dk).

Banking

BG Bank, 68 Nørre Voldgard, 1390 Copenhagen K (tel: 7011-9999; fax: 3914-4899; internet: www.bgbank.dk).

Den Danske Bank AS (commercial bank), Holmens Kanal 2-12, DK-1092 Copenhagen K (tel: 3344-0000; fax: 3118-5873; internet: www.danskebank.com).

Finansrådet (bankers' association), Bankernes Hus, Amaliegade 7, DK-1256 Copenhagen (tel: 3312-0200; fax: 3393-0260; internet: www.finansraadet.dk).

Jyske Bank (Bank of Jutland, private bank), Vestergade 8-16, DK-8600 Silkeborg (tel: 8922-2222; fax: 8922-2499; internet: www.jbpb.com).

Spar Nord Bank AS, 15 Skelagervij, PO Box 162, 9100 Aalborg (tel: 9634-4000; email: ine@sparnord.dk; internet: www.sparnordbank.com).

Sydbank, PO Box 169, 4 Peberlyk, DK-6200 Aabenraa (tel: 7463-1111; fax: 7463-1320; email: info@sydbank.dk; internet: www.sydbank.dk).

Nordea Bank AS, PO Box 850, Christiansbro Strandgade 3, DK-0900 Copenhagen C (tel: 3333-3333; email:

hotline@nordea.dk; internet: www.nordea.dk).

Central bank

Danmarks Nationalbank, Havnegade 5, DK-1093 Copenhagen (tel: 3363-6363; fax: 3363-7103; e-mail: info@nationalbanken.dk).

Stock exchange

The Københavns Fondsbørs (Copenhagen Stock Exchange) (CSE), www.omxnordicexchange.com

Travel information

Copenhagen Airport, PO Box 74, Lufthavnsboulevarden 6 DK-2770, Kastrup (tel: 3231-3231; fax: 3231-3132; email: cphweb@cph.dk; internet: www.cph.dk).

Copenhagen Airtaxi, Copenhagen Airport Roskilde, DK-4000 Roskilde (tel: 391-114).

DSB (Danish State Railways), 1349 Sølgade 40, 1349 Copenhagen (tel: 3314-0400).

Forenede Danske Motorejere (FDM) (the Danish motoring organisation), Blegdamsvej 124, DK-2100 Copenhagen Ø (tel: 7013-3040; fax: 4527-0993).

Scandinavian Airlines System (SAS), Frosundaviks Alle 1, Stockholm S-16187, Sweden (tel: (+46-8) 7970-000; fax: (+46-8) 858-741).

National tourist organisation offices

Danmarks Turistrad (tourist board), Vesterbrogade 6 D, 1620 Cogenhagen V (tel: 3311-1415; fax: 3393-1416).

Ministries

Ministry of Agriculture, Fisheries and Food, Holbergsgade 2, 1057 Copenhagen K (tel: 3392-3301; fax: 3314-5042; e-mail: fvm@fvm.dk).

Ministry of Business and Industry, Slotsholmsgade 10-12, 1216 Copenhagen K (tel: 3392-3350; fax: 3312-3778; e-mail: em@em.dk).

Ministry of Business and Industry, Invest in Denmark, Slotsholmsgade 10-12, Copenhagen K, DK-1216 (tel: 3392-3350; fax: 3312-3778; e-mail: Investdk@em.dk; internet site: www.investindk.com).

Ministry of Culture, Nybrogade 2, 1203 Copenhagen K (tel: 3392-3370; fax: 3391-3388; e-mail: kum@kum.dk).

Ministry of Defence, Holmens Kanal 42, 1060 Copenhagen K (tel: 3392-3320; fax: 3332-0655; e-mail: fmn@fmn.dk).

Ministry of Economic Affairs, Ved Stranden 8, 1061 Copenhagen K (tel: 3392-3222; fax: 3393-6020; e-mail: oem@oem.dk).

Ministry of Education, Fredriksholms Kanal 21-25, 1220 Copenhagen K (tel: 3392-5000; fax: 3392-5547; e-mail: uvm@uvm.dk).

Ministry of Employment, Holmens Kanal 20, 1060 Copenhagen K (tel: 3392-5900; fax: 3312-1378; e-mail: am@am.dk).

Ministry of the Environment and Energy, Hojbro Plads 4, 1200 Copenhagen K (tel: 3392-7600; fax: 3332-2227; e-mail: mem@mem.dk).

Ministry of Finance, Christiansborg Slotsplads 1, 1218 Copenhagen K (tel: 3392-3333; fax: 3332-8030; e-mail: fm@fm.dk).

Ministry of Foreign Affairs, 2 Asiatisk Plads, 1448 Copenhagen K (tel: 3392-0000; fax: 3254-0533; e-mail: um@um.dk; internet site: www.um.dk/english).

Ministry of Health, Holbergsgade 6, 1057 Copenhagen K (tel: 3392-3360; fax: 3393-1563; e-mail: sum@sum.dk).

Ministry of Housing and Urban Affairs, Slotsholmgade 1, 3, 1216 Copenhagen K (tel: 3392-6100; fax: 3392-6104; e-mail: bm@bm.dk).

Ministry of the Interior, Christiansborg Slotsplads 1, 1218 Copenhagen K (tel: 3392-3380; fax: 3311-1239; e-mail: inm@inm.dk).

Ministry of Justice, Slotsholmsgade 10, 1216 Copenhagen K (tel: 3392-3340; fax: 3393-3510; e-mail: jm@jm.dk).

Ministry of Research, Bredgade 43, 1260 Copenhagen K (tel: 3392-9700; fax: 3332-3501; e-mail: fsk@fsk.dk).

Ministry of Social Affairs, Holmens Kanal 22, 1060 Copenhagen K (tel: 3392-9300; fax: 3393-2518; e-mail: sm@sm.dk).

Ministry of Taxation, Slotsholmsgade 12, 1216 Copenhagen K (tel: 3392-3392; fax: 3314-9105; e-mail: skm@skm.dk).

Ministry of Transport, Fredriksholms Kanal 27, 1220 Copenhagen K (tel: 3392-3355; fax 3312-3893; e-mail: trm@trm.dk).

Parliament, Christiansborg, 1240 Copenhagen K (tel: 3337-5500; fax: 3332-8536).

Prime Minister's Office, Christiansborg, Prins Jorgens Gard 11, 1218 Copenhagen K (tel: 3392-3300; fax: 3311-1665; e-mail: stm@stm.dk).

Other useful addresses

American Embassy, Dag Hammarskjolds Alle 24, DK-2100 Copenhagen Ø (tel: 423-144; fax: 430-223).

British Embassy, Kastelsvej 36, DK-2100 Copenhagen Ø (tel: 264-600; fax: 381-012, 431-400).

Central Telegraph Office, Købmagergade 37, DK-1150 Copenhagen K (tel: 3312-0903).

Copenhagen Stock Exchange, Nikolaj Plads 6, DK-1067 Copenhagen K (tel: 3393-3366).

Danish Convention Bureau, 27 Skindergade, 1159 Copenhagen K (tel: 3332-8601; fax: 3332-8803).

Danmarks Agentforening (association of commercial agents of Denmark), Børsen, DK-1217 Copenhagen K (tel: 3314-4941).

Danmarks Statistik, Sejrøgade 11, DK-2100 Copenhagen Ø (tel: 3917-3917; fax: 3118-4801).

Dansk Arbejdsgiverforening (employers' confederation), Vester Voldgade 113, DK-1503 Copenhagen V (tel: 3393-4000; fax: 3312-2976).

Det Okonomiske Rad (economic council), Kampmannsgade, DK-1604 Copenhagen V (tel: 3313-5128).

Grosserer Societetet, Børsen (royal exchange), DK-1217 Copenhagen (tel: 3391-2323).

Industriraadet (Confederation of Danish Industries), H C Andersen's Boulevard 18, DK-1790 Copenhagen V (tel: 3377-3377; fax: 3377-3410).

IPC (International Press Centre), Snaregade 14, DK-1205 Copenhagen K (tel: 131-615; fax: 911-613).

Regional Development Organisation (Copenhagen Capacity), Kongens Nytorv 6, 4, sal DK-1050 Copenhagen K (tel: 3333-0300; fax: 3333-7333).

Ritzaus Bureau 1/S (news agency), Mikkel Bryggersgade 3, DK-1460 Copenhagen K.

Royal Danish Embassy (USA), 3200 Whitehaven Street, NW, Washington DC 20008 (tel: (+1-202) 234-4300; fax: (+1-202) 238-1470; e-mail: wasamb@um.dk).

Teknisk Forlag AS (technical press-publishing house), Skelbaekgade 4, DK-1717 Copenhagen V.

Thomson Communications (Scandinavia) AS, Hestemøllestrede 6, Postboks 2181, DK-1017 Copenhagen K.

Internet sites

Danish web index: www.web-index.dk

Interactive travel site: www.visitdenmark.com

Statistical Office: www.dst.dk

Trade directory for Denmark: http://uhk.dk

Yellow pages: www.yellowpages.dk

Djibouti

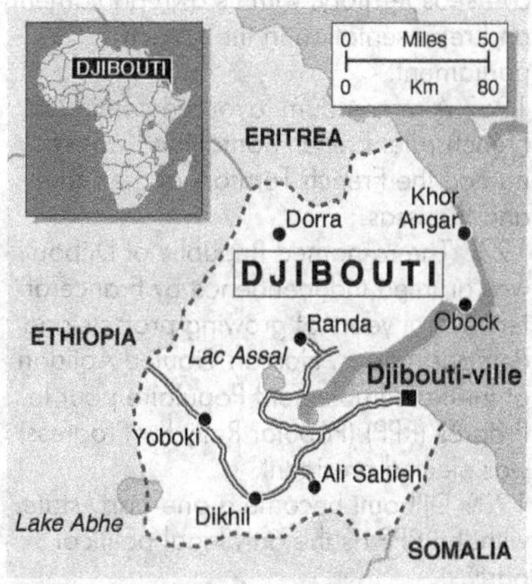

Djibouti sits on Africa's picturesque eastern coastline and acts as an access point to the Gulf of Aden. Its geographical location has ensured that it has experienced a steady flow of foreign assistance. During the Gulf War, Djibouti acted as a base of operations for the French Military and, to this date, there remains a strong French presence across the nation. Djibouti's government once favoured close ties with France, but for a period it developed increasingly stronger ties with the United States, which was allowed to set-up what is the only US military base in sub-Saharan Africa. This made Djibouti a front-line state both in the US' global war on terrorism and on activities to counter the maritime piracy that had become endemic in the Indian Ocean.

Traditionally, but no longer, Djibouti was dependent on its two neighbours and their relations with the country's two main ethnic groups. The Issas were linked to the Somalis and the Afars more inclined towards the Ethiopians. Roughly 60 per cent of the population are Issas. However, in the years before independence in 1977, and to the annoyance of Somalia, the French authorities systematically bolstered the position of the minority Afars.

Djibouti's location on the Horn of Africa is the main political and economic asset of a country that is mostly barren. It is strategically located at the mouth of the Red Sea, close to the world's busiest shipping lanes and the Arabian oilfields. It is the terminus of rail traffic into Ethiopia and clearly serves as an important trans-shipment location for goods entering and leaving the east African highlands. The transport infrastructure enables several landlocked African countries to fly in their goods for re-export. This earns Djibouti much needed transit taxes and harbour fees.

The economy

The International Monetary Fund (IMF) in its recent report (February 2015) stated that Djibouti is undergoing an investment boom. Aggregate investment is expected to increase from 26 per cent of GDP in 2010–13 to 52 per cent in 2014–16. GDP growth is also forecast to increase from 5.9 per cent in 2014 to 7 per cent in 2015–19. Inflation should rise by 0.3 per cent over the same period, as demand for housing and services increases. This acceleration of economic growth is important in combating the fundamental development changes that still remain in Djibouti. Widespread poverty and unemployment still pervade much of the barren landscape of the nation. 42 per cent of the population remain in extreme poverty, whilst 48 per cent of the labour force remain unemployed. The African Economic Outlook, published by the African Development Bank (AfDB) in 2014, argued that diversification is required in order to reduce the high levels of poverty. Djibouti's economy is dominated by the services sector.

In recent years, Djibouti has experienced vast improvements in macroeconomic stability with sustainable GDP growth experienced since 2003. This comes after a period of low and negative growth, predominantly due to the civil war of 1991–94. According to data from the World Bank, Djibouti has averaged a population growth of 1.5 per cent in recent years. This growth contributes more to the poverty statistics of the country.

There is little information about Djibouti's current account; yet the IMF has reported that high debt-financed public investment spending is exerting various and considerable fiscal debt pressures. The report argues that the fiscal deficit rose from 5.9 per cent in 2013 to an estimated 12 per

KEY FACTS

Official name: République de Djibouti/Jumhouriyya Djibouti (Republic of Djibouti)

Head of State: President Ismail Omar Guelleh (from 1999; re-elected 8 Apr 2011)

Head of government: Prime Minister Abdoulkader Kamil Mohamed (from 1 Apr 2013)

Ruling party: Union pour la Majorité Présidentielle (UMP) (Union for a Presidential Majority) (since 22 Feb 2013)

Area: 23,200 square km

Population: 939,000 (2014)* (818,159; 2009 census figure)

Capital: Djibouti-ville

Official language: French/Arabic (Somali/Afar are the national languages)

Currency: Djibouti franc (Df) = 100 centimes

Exchange rate: Df177.72 per US$ (Sep 2015)

GDP per capita: US$1,692 (2014)*

GDP real growth: 6.00% (2014)

GDP: US$1.59 billion (2014)

Inflation: 2.94% (2014)

Balance of trade: -US$606.70 million (2013)

* estimated figure

cent in 2014. It is forecast to rise to 13.8 per cent in 2015. The current account deficit is estimated to widen from 23.3 per cent of GDP in 2013 to 28 per cent in 2014–15. This is predominantly due to foreign direct investment (FDI). Djibouti operates a fixed exchange rate regime, which has generally served the country well. It has safeguarded the stability of the currency through good levels of reserves.

It is imperative that structural reforms take place within Djibouti to ensure a greater competitiveness and diversified growth. This should help in diminishing the large problems of poverty and unemployment, which the country faces. Over 80 per cent of GDP is dedicated to the services sector (as of 2014). The hostile environment means that there is a disparate production of crops, resulting in a heavy dedication to imported foods. It is important for the government to co-ordinate and manage public investment projects as well as encouraging FDI. The debt needs to be controlled and reforms need to occur in improving electricity and water within the country.

Political stability

In recent years, Djibouti has offered a relatively stable political environment as a result of a peace agreement signed in 2001 between the government and an armed opposition, which became part of the opposition members participating in a coalition. In 2010, the parliament amended the constitution to enable President Guelleh to run for a third time. In April 2011; the President defeated an independent candidate to win his third five year term. An ongoing dispute with Eritrea remains a potential source of instability in the north.

Corruption

Corruption in Djibouti could become an obstacle to FDI. It is by no means the most corrupt in the African continent; but it still ranks 107 out of 175 on the 2014 transparency *Corruption Perception Index*. Privatisation of ports and custom operations continue to substantially increase transparency in the most important sectors of the economy. Recent major foreign investors have reported that they have operated free of government interference or corruption, and the government of Djibouti has pledged to protect as well as welcome new investment. However, there have been reports in the past of government officials applying pressure on smaller investors to become their 'partners' or to obtain sub-contracts.

Risk assessment

Politics	Fair
Economy	Fair
Regional stability	Fair

Muslims in Djibouti

% of population	94
Sunni (% of Muslims)	100
Shi'a (% of Muslims)	0

COUNTRY PROFILE

1862 France reached agreements with local leaders which gave the French the right to settle in Djibouti. They also acquired the port of Obock. The country was called French Somaliland.
1888 Construction of Djibouti-ville began on the southern shore of Tadjoura Bay. At the end of the century, France signed an agreement with the Emperor of Ethiopia designating French Somaliland as the 'official outlet of Ethiopian commerce'. The agreement led to the construction of the vital Addis Ababa-Djibouti railway.
1892 Djibouti-ville became the capital of French Somaliland.
1917 The Addis Ababa-Djibouti railway was completed.
1946 French Somaliland was made an overseas territory, with its own parliament and representation in the French parliament.
1967 A referendum favoured continued French rule. French Somaliland was renamed the French Territory of the Afars and the Issas.
1977 The re-named Republic of Djibouti was granted independence by France after several years of growing protests and demonstrations. Hassan Gouled Aptidon of the Rassemblement Populaire pour le Progrès (RPP) (Popular Rally for Progress) was elected president.
1981 Djibouti became a one-party state, with the RPP as the only legal political party.
1991 The Front pour la Restauration de l'Unité et de la Démocratie (FRUD) (Front for the Restoration of Unity and Democracy) launched a civil war in northern Djibouti. The ethnic Afar organisation called for multi-party elections.
1992 Following several months of fighting, Aptidon agreed to a referendum, which led to a limited, multi-party constitution. In the elections to the Chamber of Deputies only four parties are allowed to take part; the RPP won 72 per cent of the vote while a newly formed alliance led by the Parti du Renouveau Démocratique (PRD) (Party of Democratic Renewal) won the remainder.
1993 President Aptidon was re-elected for a fourth term.
1994 Despite the new constitution, FRUD did not end its armed struggle until December, when the government and FRUD signed a peace accord confirming the constitutional and electoral reforms of 1992.
1997 President Aptidon was re-elected for a fifth term. FRUD joined RPP in a coalition government.
1999 The 83-year-old president resigned after 22 consecutive years in power. Ismael Omar Guelleh was elected president.
2001 Dileita Mohamed Dileita replaced Barkat Gourad Hamadou as prime minister.
2002 The law limiting four parties to contest elections, passed in 1992, expired. US led coalition troops arrived, in preparation for military action in Afghanistan and against al Qaeda targets in the region.

KEY INDICATORS — Djibouti

	Unit	2011	2012	2013	2014	**2015
Population	m	*0.84	*0.89	*0.91	*0.94	*0.97
Gross domestic product (GDP)	US$bn	1.24	1.35	1.46	1.59	*1.74
GDP per capita	US$	1,467	1,523	*1,593	*1,692	*1,805
GDP real growth	%	4.5	4.8	5.0	6.0	*6.5
Inflation	%	5.1	3.7	2.4	2.9	*3.0
Exports (fob) (goods)	US$m	85.0	111.4	112.7	–	–
Imports (fob) (goods)	US$m	510.6	538.1	719.4	–	–
Balance of trade	US$m	-425.6	-426.8	-606.7	–	–
Current account	US$m	-171.8	-166.0	-339.0	-436.0	*0.0
Total reserves minus gold	US$m	–	249.0	425.0	393.1	–
Foreign exchange	US$m	–	234.0	410.5	–	–
Exchange rate	per US$	177.72	177.72	175.05	178.00	–

* estimated figure ** forecast figure

2003 The first fully multi-party elections held since independence, were won by parties supporting President Guelleh. Large numbers of illegal immigrants – estimated at 15 per cent of the population – were deported.
2005 In presidential elections, Ismail Omar Guelleh, the only candidate, was re-elected with 100 per cent of the vote.
2008 The opposition boycotted the parliamentary elections, won by the UMP coalition (consisting of five political parties, all supporters of President Ismail Omar Guelleh). Border clashes in the Mount Gabla area – also known as Ras Doumeira – that killed nine Djibouti troops and injured many more – were blamed, by the US, on 'military aggression' by Eritrea. The US and France called for a cease-fire and troop withdrawals on both sides and for negotiations to begin.
2009 Eritrea denied it had troops in Djibouti, contrary to a UN Security Council announcement that Eritrea had failed to withdraw.
2010 Parliament amended the constitution; a president may now serve for more than two terms although the mandate was reduced to five years in office and an upper age limit of 75 years was set. The amendment meant that President Guelleh would be allowed to run for office in 2011.
2011 The largest anti-government demonstration since independence was held in February in Djibouti-ville. Around 30,000 people called on President Guelleh to quit office. Security forces used teargas and rubber bullets to disperse the crowds. in March opposition groups decided to boycott the upcoming presidential election and called on voters to do likewise. The opposition warned that voting would not be free and fair and would most likely be rigged. Security forces arrested four opposition political leaders, as they planned to head a demonstration against Guelleh. In March, international observers (funded by the US) quit Djibouti, after they were declared 'illegal' by the foreign minister, Mahmoud Ali Youssouf, and accused of failing to maintain neutrality. In April, parliament voted to allow unlimited terms in office for a president. The presidential election took place on 8 April, incumbent President Guelleh won 80.58 per cent of the vote and Mohamed Warsama Ragueh 19.42 per cent; turnout was 69.68 per cent. Parliamentary elections that had been due to take place at the same time as the presidential election were postponed until 2013. In July, the UN issued an emergency appeal for US$136.3 in funds to provide aid for thousands of malnourished people caught up in the drought in the Horn of Africa.
2012 In February, the IMF approved a US$14 million loan to support the economy. In June, the year-on-year inflation rate reached 4.2 per cent. On 18 October, the United Arab Emirates agreed to provide financial assistance of US$7 million to support the budget. On 21 October, a new 128-bed hospital in Arta, built with Chinese investment, was inaugurated by the president and the Chinese Ambassador.
2013 Parliamentary elections were held on 22 February. The ruling Union pour la Majorité Présidentielle (UMP) (Union for a Presidential Majority) won 61.5 per cent of the votes (43 seats out of 65); Union pour le Salut National (USN) (Union for National Salvation) 35.6 per cent (21). Turnout was 69.2 per cent. The USN (who had boycotted the last election in 2008) contested the result for Djibouti City; their figures would have given them 25 seats and the ruling UMP 40. Abdoulkader Kamil Mohamed replaced Dileita Mohamed Dileita as prime minister on 1 April
2014 On 9 July the government cancelled DP World's concession at the Doraleh Container Terminal. It said that there was evidence the Dubai-based company had paid bribes to Abdourahman Boreh, who was chairman of Djibouti Ports and Free Zones Authority, while he was negotiating the concession agreement. The allegations were denied.
2015

Political structure

Constitution

The constitution was amended in April 2010 so that a president may now serve for more than two terms, although the mandate was reduce to five years in office and an upper age limit of 75 years was set.

The executive

Executive power is vested in the president as Head of State, who is directly elected by absolute majority vote, is typically leader of the largest political party in parliament. The president appoints a prime minister as head of government and leader of the council of ministers, both of which are responsible to the president. There is no term limit on the presidency, although there is an upper age limit of 75 years. The term in office is five years.

National legislature

The unicameral Assemblée Nationale (National Assembly) has 65 members elected in multi-seat constituencies for five-year terms. Membership includes 30 representatives of Somali groups (of which 21 are Issa) and 32 Afar peoples.

Last elections

8 April 2011 (presidential); 2013 (parliamentary);

Results: Parliamentary (2013): Union pour la Majorité Présidentielle (UMP) (Union for a Presidential Majority) won 61.5 per cent of the votes (43 seats out of 65); Union pour le Salut National (USN) (Union for National Salvation) 35.6 per cent (21). Turnout was 69.2 per cent. The USN contested the result for Djibouti City; their figures would have given them 25 seats and the ruling UMP 40.
Presidential: Ismail Omar Guelleh won 80.58 per cent of the vote, Mohamed Warsama Ragueh 19.42 per cent; turnout was 69.68 per cent.

Next elections

2016 (presidential); 2018 (parliamentary)

Political parties

Ruling party

Union pour la Majorité Présidentielle (UMP) (Union for a Presidential Majority) (since 22 Feb 2013)

Main opposition party

Union pour le Salut National (USN) (Union for National Salvation)

Population

914,000 (2013)*
Last census: 818,159 (2009) (December 1960 81,200).
According to the 2009 census, 70.6 per cent of the population live in urban areas, with 58.1 per cent of the population resident in the city of Djibouti, especially in the Balbala and Boulaos neighbourhoods. The rest of the population is spread across the different regions: Dikhil (10.9 per cent), Ali Sabieh (10.6 per cent), Tadjourah (10.6 per cent), Arta (5.2 per cent) and Obock (4.6 per cent). There are 161,132 nomadic people, accounting for 19.7 per cent, while the sedentary rural population accounts for 9.7 per cent of the total. Of the total poulation 53.8 per cent are male and 46.2 per cent female and 60.7 per cent of the population are aged between 15 and 59 years old.
Population density: 28 inhabitants per square km. Urban population 76 per cent (2010 Unicef).
Annual growth rate: 2.3 per cent, 1990–2010 (Unicef).

Ethnic make-up

About 60 per cent of the national total are Issas, of Somali origin and about 35 per cent are Afars who have links with Ethiopia; there are about 5 per cent European residents.
The population also includes refugees from the Ogaden and Eritrean wars in Somalia and Ethiopia.
The nomadic population (principally Afars) totals around 100,000.

Religions

Islam (94 per cent), Christianity (6 per cent)

Education

Literacy rate: 75.6 per cent men, 54.4 per cent women; adult rates (World Bank).

Enrolment rate: 45 per cent boys, 33 per cent girls, total primary school enrolment of the relevant age group (including repetition rates) (World Bank).

Health

The results of this spending appear limited, due mainly to poor management and the high costs of foreign staff and medicines.

HIV/Aids

This percentage is high enough to pose a significant threat to the country's future prosperity. Under a funding agreement in June 2004, US$12 million from the Global Fund to fight Aids, tuberculosis (TB) and malaria, will be spent on antiretroviral drugs to be supplied to Aids suffers until 2007. From an initial 200 patients it is expected that 4,000 patients will be treated, however the estimate of HIV positive cases in Djibouti is 9,000, with only 1,000 people registered – gaining them access to free treatment – though there has been an improvement in the numbers of people being tested.

HIV prevalence: 2.9 per cent aged 15–49 in 2003 (World Bank)

Life expectancy: 56 years, 2004 (WHO 2006)

Fertility rate/Maternal mortality rate: 3.8 births per woman, 2010 (Unicef)

Child (under 5 years) mortality rate (per 1,000): 81 per 1,000 live births (WHO 2012); 18 per cent of children aged under five are malnourished (World Bank).

Head of population per physician: 0.18 physicians per 1,000 people, 2004 (WHO 2006)

Welfare

A new national poverty survey in 2012 showed living conditions had worsened, with 79 per cent of Djiboutians living in relative poverty (74 per cent in 2002). Unemployment affects 48 per cent of the working population.

Main cities

Djibouti-ville (capital, estimated population 513,669 in 2012), Ali Sabieh (24,456), Dikhil (20,908), Tadjourah (13,138), Arta (11,934), Obock (10,734).

Languages spoken

English is understood by the larger trading houses. Cushitic languages, as well as Somali and Saho-Afar are widely spoken.

Official language/s

French/Arabic (Somali/Afar are the national languages)

Media

Although the constitution provides for a free press, in practice the government maintains tight control of media outlets and circulation of information is highly restricted. Journalists generally have to avoid sensitive issues covering human rights, the army, and the government, relations with Ethiopia and foreign financial aid. A law prohibits the dissemination of false information and regulates the publication of newspapers, which has led to journalists exercising self-censorship. Journalists are largely untrained and poorly paid.

Press

In French, the main locally published newspaper *La Nation* (www.lanation.dj) is government owned. Political parties, Parti National Démocratique publishes *La Republique*, and Union pour l'Alternance Démocratique publishes *Le Renouveau*.

Broadcasting

The government owns the only radio and television stations allowed within the country with news programmes uncritical of the government or government policy. External services are available.

Radio: Radio Télévision Djibouti (RTD) (www.rtd.dj) provides a national network for news, information, religious and musical programmes. External services via AM and local FM relays provide foreign broadcasts.

Television: RTD (www.rtd.dj) has a monopoly in broadcasting, providing a few hours TV per day.

National news agency: ADI (Agence Djiboutienne d'Information) (internet: (in French): www.adi.dj).

Other news agencies: Presidential Press Office: www.spp.dj

Economy

Djibouti's location on the Horn of Africa is the main economic asset of a country that is mostly barren. It is strategically located at the mouth of the Red Sea, close to the world's busiest shipping lanes and the Arabian oilfields; it is the terminus of freight traffic to Dire Dawa (Ethiopia).

Djibouti's economy is reliant on services, as it constitutes an estimated 79.3 per cent of GDP. The agricultural sector is small at round 3.8 per cent, whilst industry constitutes only 16.9 per cent of GDP, of which manufacturing is less than 5 per cent. GDP growth is forecasted to increase from 5.9 per cent in 2014 to 7 per cent in 2015–19. The port and adjacent free zone is of paramount importance in relation to the economic activity of Djibouti. The trans-shipment of goods from the port to Ethiopia, in particular, and other hinterlands is the primary activity for the port. The authorities are planning to develop the port into a shipping hub; however the prevalence of Somali pirates in the region may have an adverse effect on this strategy.

The US has contributed to a military presence alongside the already large French constituency.

Djibouti is predominantly utilised as a military base for activities in the region, whilst the port is used for patrolling the busy and vulnerable shipping lanes that lead to the Suez Canal.

The International Monetary Fund (IMF) reported in February 2015 that Djibouti is undergoing an investment boom. Aggregate investment is expected to increase from 26 per cent of GDP in 2010–13 to 52 per cent in 2014–16. GDP growth is also forecast to increase from 5.9 per cent in 2014 to 7 per cent in 2015–19. Inflation should rise by 0.3 per cent over the same period, as demand for housing and services increases. Foreign Direct Investment (FDI) inflow was a record US$286,004,468 in 2014, a huge increase from the dramatic drop to US$36,501,033 in 2010. GDP per capita remained fairly constant, averaging US$1,784.4 in 2014.

In 2013, the UN Human Development Index (HDI) ranked Djibouti 170 (out of 187) for national development in health, education and income. In 2013, around 40 per cent of the population were living in extreme poverty. Remittances were US$33 million in 2010 (2.9 per cent of GDP), and have stayed largely the same up to 2013.

External trade

Djibouti is a member of the Common Market for Eastern and Southern Africa (Comesa), and operates within a free trade zone with 13 of the 19 member states. The country has few assets with an unskilled labour force, limited natural resources and little scope for agriculture with poor, unproductive soil. The majority of foreign earnings come from its strategic function as a trans-shipment corridor for goods transported to and from the Port of Djibouti and Ethiopia. The presidents of the Djibouti Ports and Free Zones Authority (DPFZA) and the Chinese state-owned group, China Merchants Holdings (CMH), signed an agreement on 24 March for the expansion of the Djibouti Free Trade Zone (FTZ). The agreement includes the construction of a shipyard, a highway and the expansion of the Doraleh Container Terminal, which is to occur over the next decade at a cost of US$7 billion. This will provide a significant boost for the Djiboutian economy, which is projected to grow by seven per cent in 2015. When complete, the Djibouti FTZ will cover an area of 48.2 km2, making it the largest free trade area in Africa.

There is a free trade zone near the port of Djibouti.

Imports

Principal imports are fresh fruits and vegetables (from Ethiopia), foods, beverages, clothing, transport equipment, construction material, chemicals and petroleum products.

Main sources: China (29.3 per cent of total in 2014), Saudi Arabia (16.3 per cent), Indonesia (8 per cent), India (7.7 per cent).

Exports

Principal exports transiting Djibouti are scrap metal, live animals, cotton, sugar, cereals, salt, skins, leather and coffee.

Main destinations: Somalia (82.9 per cent of total in 2014), Yemen (5.0 per cent), UAE (4.4 per cent).

Agriculture

Farming

Total agricultural land is 2.3 million hectares of which 73.3 per cent is pasture and 0.1 per cent arable. The underdeveloped agricultural sector employs approximately 70 per cent of the workforce.

Due to poor terrain (mostly desert), most agricultural producers are nomads engaged in herding goats, sheep and camels. Drought has severely affected the livelihoods of the herd owners. Around 95 per cent of food requirements are imported. Projects under consideration include increasing the amount of arable land by irrigation schemes and rehabilitation of water dams and wells.

Industry and manufacturing

The industrial sector is limited to construction, agricultural processing and shipping. Small-scale concerns such as mineral water bottling, tanning, dairy and animal food plants also comprise some of the contributions in the sector. New industries in Djibouti include cement, tiles, paints and meat processing. Foreign investment is being encouraged and should be aided by renewed political stability in the region. Industry contributed to 16.6 per cent to GDP in 2014.

Tourism

The sector is small and underdeveloped and any visitor will need to be experienced in self-sufficiency to enjoy anything on offer outside the capital of Djibouti-ville. There are sites of natural wonder, such as active volcanoes, the bay of black lava, turned dark green near the western end of the Gulf of Tadjoura and the rare trees being conserved in the Day Forest National Park on Mount Goda.

Environment

In June 2010 the African Union backed a proposal to build the 'Great Green Wall' project, of a 15km wide, 7,775km long, continuous belt of trees from Senegal in the west to Djibouti in the east (traversing 11 countries) in an effort to halt the advance of the Sahara Desert. The trees to be used would be drought-adapted, preferably native to the area from a list of 37 possible species, and should help to slow soil erosion and filter rain water.

Mining

Surveys have indicated the presence of minerals such as copper, gypsum and sulphur. No minerals are mined commercially. Salt is extracted and exported.

Hydrocarbons

There are no proved oil reserves; consumption of oil was 11,680 barrels per day in 2013, all of which were imported. Djibouti relies entirely on oil to generate electricity; it opened the Doraleh oil terminal, in 2006, which can manage and store up to 240,000 tonnes of oil.

Any import and use of either natural gas or coal is commercially insignificant.

Energy

Total installed generating capacity was 130MW in 2013, producing over 330 million kilowatt hours. Djibouti is constrained in its energy generation by having no natural resources to exploit, it is without oil, natural gas and hydroelectric potential.

The state-owned Electricité du Djibouti is responsible for generation, transmission and distribution of electricity, which is only available in cities and a few small towns, plus those villages that have financed their own diesel-powered generators. In urban areas that are supplied with electricity around 99 per cent of the population use it for lighting only; kerosene is commonly used for other domestic purposes such as cooking and heating.

Djibouti has been recognised as a country with a high potential for renewable power generation from solar, wind and geothermal sources. The government is keen to exploit its renewable energy capacity in order to reduce dependence on imported power from Ethiopia (in 2013 some 65 per cent).

The government signed an agreement with the Reykjavik Energy Invest (REI) of Iceland in 2008 to initially build a 50MW geothermal power plant in the Rift Valley, which, along with an additional seven other geothermal plants, will produce a total of 900MW. As a result the country's geothermal capacity in 2014 is expected to double by 2016.

Banking and insurance

Central bank

National Bank of Djibouti

Main financial centre

Djiboutiville

Time

GMT plus three hours

Geography

Djibouti is in the Horn of Africa, at the southern entrance to the Red Sea. It is bounded on the north, west and south-west by Ethiopia, and on the south-east by Somalia. The land is volcanic desert.

Hemisphere

Northern

Climate

Very hot and arid from April–August; average temperature 32 degrees Celsius (C) and can reach 45 degrees C. Slightly cooler from October–March, with occasional light rain.

Dress codes

Djibouti has a large Muslim population so visitors should dress modestly, especially in the city. However, it is far less strict than other Islamic countries.

Entry requirements

Passports

Required by all. Must be valid for six months beyond date of departure.

Visa

Required by all, except French nationals. For business visits, a letter of invitation from a company in Djibouti is necessary.

Currency advice/regulations

No restrictions on import/export of local or foreign currency.

Health (for visitors)

Mandatory precautions

Yellow fever vaccination certificate if arriving from an infected area.

Advisable precautions

Yellow fever, typhoid, tetanus, hepatitis A and polio vaccinations. Malaria prophylaxis recommended as risk exists throughout the country. There is a rabies risk. Water precautions should be taken. Eat only well cooked meals, preferably served hot. Pork, salad and mayonnaise may carry increased risk. Vegetables should be cooked and fruit peeled.

Hotels

Available in Djibouti-ville – limited elsewhere. Service charge is normally included. Tipping is not usual.

Credit cards

Generally not accepted, except by airlines and Sheraton Hotel.

Public holidays (national)

Fixed dates

1 Jan (New Year's Day), 1 May (Labour Day), 27 Jun (Independence Day), 25 Dec (Christmas Day).

Variable dates

Eid al Adha, Eid al Fitr, Islamic New Year, Birth of the Prophet.

Islamic year 1437 (15 Oct 2015–2 Oct 2016):: The Islamic year contains 354 or 355 days, with the result that Muslim feasts advance by 10-12 days against the Gregorian calender. Dates of feasts vary according to the sighting of the new moon, so cannot be forecast exactly.

Working hours

Banking

Sat–Thu: 0715–1145.

Business

Sat–Thu: 0630–1300.

Government

Sat–Thu: 0630–1300.

Shops

0730–1200, 1600–1900; closed Fri.

Telecommunications

Telephone/fax

A 100 per cent automatic service; outside Djibouti-ville there are very few telephones.

Electricity supply

220V AC, 50 cycles.

Getting there

Air

National airline: DAALLO Airlines

International airport/s: Djibouti-Ambouli (JIB), 5km south of city; restaraunts, duty free shops, bureau de change, car hire.

Airport tax: US$20

Surface

Road: There is a surfaced road from Addis Ababa (Ethiopia). Local advice should be taken as to when to travel by road as it can be difficult, with problems caused by the political situation.

Rail: There is a rail link with Ethiopia with a daily service, but it is not reliable or safe.

Main port/s: Djibouti-ville.

Getting about

National transport

Air: Djibouti Airlines operates a daily domestic service to Obock and Tadjoura from Djibouti. Dikhil and Ali-Sabieh can be reached by chartered aircraft.

Road: There are surfaced roads to the Ethiopian border and to Arta, and from Djibouti-ville to Tadjoura; most roads are in need of repair. Take local advice when planning to travel by road.

Rail: Some towns are served on the Djibouti– Addis Ababa railway.

Water: Ferry service links Djibouti-ville with Tadjoura and Obock.

City transport

Taxis: They are available in main towns. Tipping is not usual as fares include gratuities; there is an official tariff, but it is usual for visitors to be charged 50 per cent more; there is a similar increase at night.

The journey from the airport to the centre of Djibouti-ville takes 10 minutes.

Car hire

Available in Djibouti-ville and at the airport. Valid international driving licence recommended. A temporary licence can be obtained on presentation of national licence. Traffic drives on right.

BUSINESS DIRECTORY

The addresses listed below are a selection only. While World of Information makes every endeavour to check these addresses, we cannot guarantee that changes have not been made, especially to telephone numbers and area codes. We would welcome any corrections.

Telephone area codes

The international dialling code (IDD) for Djibouti is + 253 followed by subscriber's number.

Useful telephone numbers

Police: 17

Fire: 18

Chambers of Commerce

Djibouti International Chamber of Commerce et Industry, Place de LaGuarde, PO Box 84, Djibouti (tel: 351-070; fax: 350-096; e-mail: cicid@intnet.dj).

Banking

Banque de Développement de Djibouti; PO Box 520, Angle Ave Georges Clémenceau et rue Pierre Curie, Djibouti-ville (tel: 353-391; fax: 355-022).

Banque Indosuez Mer Rouge; PO Box 88, 10 Place Lagarde, Djibouti-ville (tel: 353-016; fax: 351-638).

Banque pour le Commerce et l'Industrie-Mer Rouge; PO Box 2122, Place Lagarde, Djibouti-ville (tel: 350-857; fax: 354-260).

Central bank

Banque Centrale de Djibouti, Avenue Saint Laurent du Var, PO Box 2118, Djibouti-ville (tel: 352-751 fax: 356-288; e-mail: bndj@intnet.dj).

Travel information

DAALLO Airlines (Airline of Horn of Africa), PO Box 1954, Djibouti-ville (tel: 353-401, 356-660; fax: 351-765).

Djibouti Airlines, Place Lagarde, PO Box 2240, Djibouti-ville (tel: 351-006; fax: 352-429).

Djibouti Airport, BP 204, Djibouti-ville (tel: 340-101 ext 300, 382-322; fax: 340-723).

Puntavia Airline de Djibouti, CP 2240, Djibouti-ville (tel: 351-036, 351-006; fax: 353-429, 356-660).

National tourist organisation offices

Office National du Tourisme de Djibouti, BP 1938, place du 27 Juin, Djibouti-ville (tel: 353-790; fax: 356-322; e-mail: onta@intnet.dj).

Ministries

Ministry of Agriculture and Rural Development, BP 453, Djibouti-ville (tel: 351-297).

Ministry of Commerce, Transport and Tourism, BP 121, Djibouti-ville (tel: 352-540).

Ministry of Foreign Affairs and Co-operation, BP 1863, Djibouti-ville (tel: 353-342).

Ministry of Industry and Industrial Development, BP 175, Djibouti-ville (tel: 350-340).

Other useful addresses

British Consulate, BP 81, Gellatly Hankey et Cie, Djibouti-ville (tel: 355-718; fax: 353-294); c/o Inchcape Shipping Office, Djibouti-ville (tel: 353-836/844).

Compagnie du Chemin de Fer Djibouti-Ethiopien, BP 2116, Djibouti-ville (tel: 350-353).

Djibouti Embassy (USA), 1156 15th Street, NW, Washington DC 20005 (tel: (+1-202)-331-0270; fax (+1-202)-331-0302).

Office National d'Approvisionnement et de Commercialisation (ONAC), BP 75, Djibouti-ville (tel: 350-327).

Office of the Prime Minister, BP 2086, Djibouti-ville (tel: 351-494; fax: 355-049).

Radiodiffusion Télévision de Djibouti (RTD), BP 97, Djibouti-ville (tel: 352-294).

Service de Statistique et de Documentation, BP 1846, Djibouti-ville (tel: 353-331).

US Embassy, BP 185, Villa Plateau du Serpent, Boulevard Maréchal Joffré, Djibouti-ville (tel: 353-995).

National news agency: ADI (Agence Djiboutienne d'Information)

(internet: (in French): www.adi.dj).

Presidential Press Office: www.spp.dj

Internet sites

Africa Business Network: http://www.ifc.org/abn

AllAfrica.com: http://allafrica.com

African Development Bank: http://www.afdb.org

Africa Online: http://www.africaonline.com

Information on Horn of Africa: http://www.djibouti.com

Local online newspaper: http://www.djiboutipost.com

Dominica

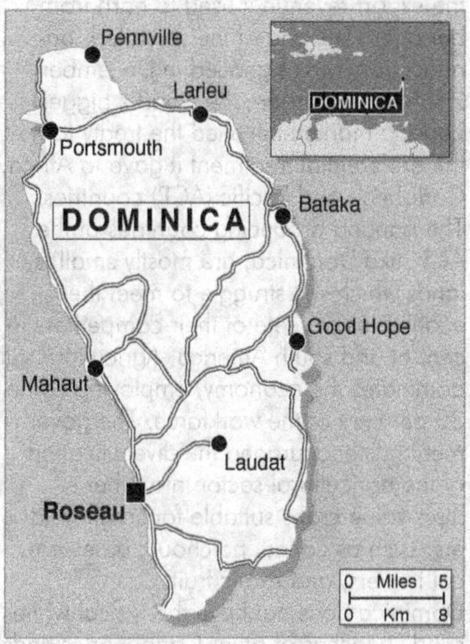

COUNTRY PROFILE

1493 Christopher Colombus visited the island and named it Dominica (Sunday Island).
1627 Despite attempts by the Earl of Carlisle, who was put in charge of Dominica by England, initial attempts at colonisation are fiercely resisted by the indigenous Carib community.
1635 France claimed Dominica. Resistance by the Carib Indians continued.
1763 Britain won possession of Dominica in accordance with the Treaty of Paris, which had ended the Seven Years' War between France and Britain. Britain established a legislative assembly, representing only the minority white population.
1831 Britain conferred political and social rights on free non-whites.
1834 Slavery was abolished.
1838 Dominica become the first British colony in the Caribbean to have a black-controlled legislature.
1865 Britain replaced the elected assembly with one consisting of one-half elected members and one-half appointed.
1896 Dominica became a crown colony again.
1940 The administration of Dominica was transferred to the Windward Islands.
1951 Universal adult suffrage was established.
1958 Dominica became part of the UK-sponsored West Indies Federation.
1960 Dominica was granted self-government by the UK.
1961 Edward leBlanc (Dominica Labour Party) (DLP) became chief minister.
1974 LeBlanc retired and was replaced by Patrick John (DLP).
1967 Full autonomy of its internal affairs was gained.
1978 Dominica became an independence republic and a member of the Commonwealth. Patrick John (DLP) became prime minister.
1980 The Dominica Freedom Party (DFP) won a convincing victory and Eugenia Charles become prime minister – the first female prime minister in the Caribbean.
1981 Two attempted coups failed and the Dominican Defence Force was disbanded.
1995 The United Workers' Party (UWP), led by Edison James, won the general election, defeating the ruling DFP.
2000 The UWP lost the election to a coalition composed of the Dominica Labour Party (DLP) and the DFP. Prime Minister Roosevelt Douglas died suddenly and Pierre Charles was appointed as his successor. Under legislation, the National Commercial Bank was permitted to engage in offshore financial services.
2002 Dominica ended the sale of passports under its economic citizenship programme.
2003 Dr Nicholas Liverpool became president, elected by parliament despite an opposition boycott of the sitting.
2004 Prime Minister Pierre Charles died; Roosevelt Skerrit was sworn in as his successor. Diplomatic relations with Taiwan was cut in favour of China, which agreed to provide aid of US$100 million over five years. An earthquake damaged buildings in the north of the island and cost millions of dollars in repairs.
2005 Roosevelt Skerrit's DLP won the parliamentary elections; the DFP, the junior partner in the former coalition government, lost both of its seats – the first time in 35 years that the DFP did not win a seat.
2006 A section of the fibre optic cable, which when completed will traverse the entire Eastern Caribbean (around 1900km in length), reached Dominica.
2007 Hurricane Dean ruined around 99 per cent of the banana crop, severely damaging the country's principal industry.

KEY FACTS

Official name: The Commonwealth of Dominica

Head of State: President Charles Savarin (from 2 Oct 2013)

Head of government: Prime Minister Roosevelt Skerrit (DLP) (from 2004; re-elected 18 Dec 2009 and 8 Dec 2014)

Ruling party: Dominica Labour Party (DLP) (since 2000; re-elected 18 Dec 2009 and 8 Dec 2014)

Area: 750 square km

Population: 71,000 (2014)*

Capital: Roseau

Official language: English

Currency: East Caribbean dollar (EC$) = 100 cents

Exchange rate: EC$2.70 per US$ (fixed)

GDP per capita: US$7,436 (2014)*

GDP real growth: 1.10% (2014)*

GDP: US$526.00 million (2014)*

Inflation: 0.69% (2014)*

Balance of trade: -US$137.60 million (2013)

* estimated figure

However, the tourist infrastructure remained largely untouched.
2008 President Liverpool agreed to serve another term in office.
2009 Dominica formally applied for US$5 million from the IMF Rapid-Access Component of the Exogenous Shock Facility (ESF). The ESF is intended to assist small islands respond to adverse external economic conditions, brought about by the global financial crisis. The ruling DLP won parliamentary elections; Roosevelt Skerrit remained in office as prime minister.
2010 Dominica celebrated 40 years of membership in *La Francophonie*, the international organisation of French speaking countries.
2011 An agreement to jointly fund a project to drill exploratory geothermal wells was signed in April between the government, Agence Francaise de Development (French Development Agency) and the EU, with work beginning at the end of July. A new ferry service *L'Express Des Iles* was launch, carrying up to 350 passengers between Dominica, St Lucia and other neighbouring French-speaking islands. Former ambassador Irwin LaRacque was appointed as Secretary General of the Caribbean Community. In August citizens of the Organisation of Eastern Caribbean States (OECS) – Antigua and Barbuda, Dominica, Grenada, St Kitts and Nevis, St Lucia and St Vincent and the Grenadines – were granted freedom of movement, allowing them to reside, work, establish businesses and provide services throughout the organisation.
2012 On 16 March, Panama and Dominica agreed to establish diplomatic and ambassador level relations with one another. President Liverpool resigned on 17 September due to ill health and Eliud Williams was elected by parliament, despite a boycott by the opposition UWP, which declared the procedure was unconstitutional.
2013 The 2013–14 National Budget Presentation took place on 24 July. Prime Minister Roosevelt Skerrit said a slight growth in Dominica's economy was expected, although there would be no new taxes. Anhui Shui An Construction Group from China visited the island in December to discuss the constuction on an international airport on Crompton Point.
2014 Dominica announced on 2 July that it intends severing ties with the London Privy Council and will adopt the Trinidad-based Caribbean Court of Justice (CCJ) as its final court. Parliament passed the bill to approve the move on 1 July. On 12 September Prime Minister Skerrit said that he would call an election shortly. In October Lennox Linton, leader of the opposition United Workers Party (UWP), accused Prime Minister Roosevelt Skerrit and the Dominica Labour Party (DLP) of using state resources for vote buying in their political campaign for the next national election, which are scheduled for late 2014. The general election held on 8 December was again won by the DLP, this time with 15 seats, two fewer than in 2009; the UWP won the remain six seats. Mr Skerritt continued as prime minister.
2015 A short-stay visa waiver agreement signed between the EU and a number of ACP countries on 28 May will allow citizens of Dominica to travel visa free to the Schengen area.

Political structure

Independence date
1978

The executive
Executive power rests with the prime minister who acts on the advice of the cabinet.
The role of the president, as Head of State, is largely ceremonial. The president is nominated by the prime minister, in consultation with the leader of the opposition, and is then elected by the House of Assembly for five years, renewable once.

National legislature
The unicameral House of Assembly has 32 members, of which 21 (representatives) are directly elected in single seat constituencies for five-year terms. Senators are elected (by votes of Assembly representatives) or may be appointed (a maximum of five senators by the president on the advice of the prime minister and four on the advice of the leader of the opposition). There is also an *ex officio* member with the remaining seat is held by the speaker of the Assembly.
The assembly appoints the president, who is a ceremonial head of state. The prime minister is the leader of the majority in the House of Assembly and the leader of the opposition is appointed by the president as leader of the main grouping outside the government.

Legal system
The legal system is based on English common law. There are three local levels of judiciary courts. The Eastern Caribbean Supreme Court, located in St Lucia, hears appeals. The Privy Council in the UK is the highest court of appeal.

Last elections
8 December 2014 (parliamentary)
Results: Parliamentary: Dominica Labour Party won 56.99 per cent and 15 seats (out of 21), United Worker's Party won 42.92 per cent and 6 seats. Turnout was 57 per cent.

Next elections
2019 (parliamentary)

Political parties

Ruling party
Dominica Labour Party (DLP) (since 2000; re-elected 18 Dec 2009 and 8 Dec 2014)

Main opposition party
United Workers' Party (UWP)

Political situation
Dominica has been struggling to replace the export revenue it used to earn from bananas. The end of the so called 'banana wars' was signalled in December 2009 when Europe, the world's biggest banana market, initialled the treaty to halt the preferential treatment it gave to Africa, Caribbean and Pacific (ACP) countries. The banana producing countries of the ACP, like Dominica, are mostly small islands which will struggle to meet the economies of scale of their competitors in central and south America. Agriculture still dominates the economy, employing some 30 per cent of the workforce. The government has encouraged the diversification of the agricultural sector into other high-value crops suitable for small-holders, such as coffee, patchouli, aloe vera, cut flowers, and exotic fruits.
Dominica does not have the typical white sandy beaches of other Caribbean islands and missed out on the first wave of tourist destinations. It has, however, managed to promote its landscape of mountains, hot-springs and fresh water lakes to a more adventurous holiday maker. Cruise ship stop-overs have also increased since the construction of a new dock with waterfront facilities in Roseau.
Dominica is still one of the poorest countries in the Caribbean and receives aid from both the IMF Rapid-Access Component of the Exogenous Shock Facility (ESF) and the joint Caricom and Caribbean Development bank, Caribbean Catastrophic Risk Insurance Facility (CCRIF) when necessary.
In the last elections, held in December 2009, the Dominica Labour Party was re-elected and Roosevelt Skerrit continued as prime minister. The president is elected by the prime minister in consultation with the leader of the opposition.

Population
71,000 (2013)*
Last census: 14 May 2011: 71,293
Population density: 97 inhabitants per square km. Urban population 67 per cent (2010 Unicef).
Annual growth rate: -0.2 per cent, 1990–2010 (Unicef).

Ethnic make-up
Black, mixed black and European, European, Syrian, Carib.

Religions
Roman Catholic (77 per cent), Methodist (5 per cent), Pentecostal (3 per cent),

Seventh-Day Adventist (3 per cent), Baptist (2 per cent).

Education

Literacy rate: 94 per cent, adult rate (2003)
Compulsory years: Five to 16

Health

The country has experienced notable improvements with a decline in infant and maternal mortality and communicable diseases and an increase in life expectancy; chronic and other non-communicable diseases are now the leading causes of death and ill-health, even as new problems such as HIV/Aids present themselves.
Life expectancy: 74 years, 2004 (WHO 2006)
Fertility rate/Maternal mortality rate: 2.0 births per woman, 2004 (WHO 2006)
Birth rate/Death rate: 17 births per 1,000 population; seven deaths per 1,000 population (2003).
Child (under 5 years) mortality rate (per 1,000): 13 per 1,000 live births (WHO 2012)

Welfare

Dominica has a national insurance system in which employee contributions are 3 per cent of salary and employer contributions are 7 per cent.

Main cities

Roseau (capital, estimated population 13,067 in 2012), Canefield (3,596), Portsmouth (3,335), Salisbury (2,699), Marigot (2,665), Atkinson (2,212).

Languages spoken

English and French-Creole.
Official language/s
English

Media

Press
There are no daily newspapers. Weekly publications include *The Chronicle* (www.dachronicle.com) *The Times*, *The Sun* and *The Tropical Star*.
Online news is carried by Dominica News (www.dominicanewsonline.com), Dominican Weekly (www.dominica-weekly.com) News-Dominica (www.newsdominica.com) and Cakafete (www.sakafete.com).
Broadcasting
Radio: DBS (Dominica Broadcasting Services) (www.dbcradio.net) is the government-operated radio service. Commercial stations include Q95 FM (www.wiceqfm.com), Kairi FM (http://kairifmonline.com) and Voice of Life Radio (www.voiceoflife.com) plays religious programmes
Television: There is no national TV service although a Marpin Telecoms (www.marpin.dm) provides a cable service with 52 channels.
Other news agencies: Caribbean Net News: www.caribbeannetnews.com

Economy

The economy is still largely dependent on primary industries, particularly agriculture, with around 40 per cent of the workforce employed in farming, fishing and forestry. Mining of minerals, such as pumice and gravel, for the construction industry is also important. Manufacturing is dependent on agriculture as it uses domestic produce to make foodstuffs, such as fruit juice and alcohol, and soap from coconuts. The service sector, in particular tourism, has grown to be the largest component of GDP.
Dominica is subject to extreme weather conditions – hurricanes, especially, have caused widespread devastation. The island has one of the highest rainfalls in the Caribbean (averaging 150cm–370cm on the coast, 635cm in the highlands), and following the commercialisation of its water resource since 2009, has benefited from the export of fresh water.
Dominica went into recession in 2012, recording a growth of -1.1 per cent. This came after a period of slow, but positive growth from 2010–11. In 2013 the country left recession and reached a growth rate of 0.8 per cent, rising further to 1.4 per cent in 2014.
Around 5.5 million expatriate workers sent US$23.5 million (4.6 per cent of GDP) in remittances in 2012 (latest figures), a figure which had remained largely the same since 2009, with money flowing directly into family budgets. Private enterprise is still considered to be the long-term solution to high unemployment and poverty. GDP per capita rose US$7,034 in 2013 US$7,434 in 2014.
In July 2010 the European Investment Bank provided credit of US$10 million to support small – and medium – sized enterprises (SME) and projects for renewable energy in Dominica. The EU has also provided assistance in the development of the government's tourism development plan, which seeks to promote Dominica's ecotourism as well as help to develop geothermal energy resources.

External trade

Dominica is a member of the Caribbean Community (Caricom) and operates within the single market (Caribbean Single Market and Economy (CSME)), which became operational in 2006. As a member of the Eastern Caribbean Currency Union (ECCU), Dominica uses the common Eastern Caribbean Dollar.
Light manufacturing has become more important to Dominica's export trade as banana exports to the EU were cut in the mid-2000s. Post 2010, bananas are still an export commodity, despite their fall in production and pre-eminence.
Imports
Principal imports include manufactured goods, machinery and equipment, food and chemicals.
Main sources: Japan (35.5 per cent of total in 2013), Trinidad and Tobago (18.4 per cent), US (16.3 per cent).
Exports
Principal exports include, soap, bay oil, vegetables and citrus fruit, foodstuffs and fresh water.
Main destinations: Japan (43.5 per cent of total in 2013), Jamaica (9.8 per cent), Antigua and Barbuda (9.0 per cent).

Agriculture

Farming
Agricultural production accounted for 14.8 per cent of total GDP in 2014, with an overall decrease in the sector of some 1 per cent on 2013. All of the major sub-sectors have been experiencing positive growth apart from livestock. Forestry has recorded an average growth of 0.5 per cent annually since 2011.
Fishing
The typical annual fish catch is over 1,100 tonnes (t), plus 4t of other seafood.
Forestry
Forestry potential is not exploited.

Industry and manufacturing

Industry accounted for 14.1 per cent of GDP in 2014. The manufacturing sector is small-scale and centred on soap production, construction, agricultural processing (mainly coconut oil and copra), canned fruit juices, cigarettes, cigars and rum. Water bottling for export is also important.

Tourism

In 2014, the travel and tourism industry accounted for 32.0 per cent of GDP (US$200 million) and employed 29.1 per cent of the workforce (10,000 jobs). Total number of visitor arrivals in 2013 (latest figures) reached 78,000. The number of cruise calls and passengers is estimated to have decreased significantly, due mainly to a very inactive off-season during which there were no cruise calls. However, noticeable increases in the average daily expenditure and average length of stay have compensated for the shortfall in numbers. Total visitor exports reached US$100 million in 2014.

Hydrocarbons

There are no known hydrocarbon reserves. Import of oil was 960 barrels per day in 2013 (latest figures). In 2005, Dominica, plus a number of other Caribbean states, signed an agreement with Venezuela to establish PetroCaribe, a multi-national oil company, owned by the

participating states. PetroCaribe buys low-priced Venezuelan crude oil under long-term payment plans. However, due the weakening state of it's economy in 2014, Venezuela said there was a chance that the subsidies to the PetroCaribe members may be reduced, which would have adverse affects on the Dominican balance of trade.
Any use of natural gas or coal is commercially insignificant.

Energy
Total installed generating capacity was 97MW in 2013 (latest figures). The Dominica Electricity Services (Domlec) has exclusive rights until 2025 to provide generation, distribution, transmission and sale of electricity. Both hydro and conventional thermal plants generate power.
Plans for the commercial development of a geothermal-fuelled power plant, developed by the Eastern Caribbean Geothermal Development Project (ECGDP) (or Geo-Caraïbes), were dropped by EDF in 2013 due to the project not promising the required profit. However, in 2014, a French consortium of CDC Infrastructure, GDF Suez and NGE Group declared an interest in reviving the project, which is estimated will provide 60–130MW overall.

Financial markets
Stock exchange
Eastern Caribbean Securities Exchange (ECSE)

Banking and insurance
The seven members of the Organisation of Eastern Caribbean States (OECS), Antigua and Barbuda, Dominica, Grenada, Montserrat, St Kitts and Nevis, St Lucia and St Vincent and the Grenadines, share a common currency (the East Caribbean dollar (EC$) and central bank. The British Virgin Islands and Anguilla are associate members.
Central bank
Eastern Caribbean Central Bank, St Kitts and Nevis.
Offshore facilities
The offshore financial sector makes a significant contribution to Dominican GDP and it is an area that the government would like to see progress. The government introduced anti-money laundering legislation and in 2003 Dominica was removed from the OECD blacklist of non-compliant countries.

Time
GMT minus four hours

Geography
Dominica is situated in the Windward Islands group of the West Indies, lying between Guadeloupe to the north and Martinique to the south.
The island has a rugged mountainous interior. It has volcanic activity, with the second largest boiling lake in the world (after Rotorua, New Zealand), where a waterfall feeds water onto a crater that is thought to have a magma chamber below. Morne Diablatins is the highest peak at 1,447 metres.
Much of the island is virgin rain forest with steep rivers flowing down to the shore of either black volcanic or golden sands.
Hemisphere
Northern

Climate
Sub-tropical with year-round tradewinds moderating the heat. Daytime temperatures range from 24–32 degrees Celsius; coolest from December–March. It is driest from January–May. The hurricane season, when storms can be very violent, is from June–October; rainfall is much higher in mountain areas. Annual rainfall in Roseau is 125–200cm and much higher inland.

Dress codes
Formal business attire.

Entry requirements
Passports
Required by all except, Canadian citizens travelling with proof of citizenship with photo ID and French nationals using their national *Carte identite*. Proof of onward/return passage is also required. Canadian nationals require a passport for re-entry to their country from January 2007).
Visa
Tourist visas up to 21 days are valid for all visitors who can show proof of a return/onward ticket and sufficient funds for the duration of the stay. Longer visa-free stays are only granted to designated nationals of the Americas, Europe and Australasia. Business visas will be issued to visitors who represent foreign companies, who must present proof of employment.
Contact the nearest High Commission or embassy for further information and application form.
Currency advice/regulations
The import of local and foreign currency is unlimited but must be declared, export is limited to the amount imported.
Travellers cheques are accepted but to avoid extra exchange fees US dollar denominations are recommended. ATMs are available.

Health (for visitors)
Mandatory precautions
Yellow fever vaccination certificate required if arriving from infected area.
Advisable precautions
Immunisation for hepititis A is useful. Other lesser risks include typhoid, bacillary and amoebic dysentery and occasional outbreaks of dengue fever as well as haemorrhagic dengue fever. Water precautions should be taken in rural areas. As visitors are required to pay up-front for treatment, it is strongly recommended to take out full medical insurance.

Hotels
Most hotels are family-run and situated around the capital. Hotel bills include a 10 per cent service charge.

Credit cards
All major cards are accepted.

Public holidays (national)
Fixed dates
1 Jan (New Year's Day), 3 Nov (Independence Day), 4 Nov (Community Service Day), 25–26 Dec (Christmas).
Variable dates
Carnival (Feb), Good Friday, Easter Monday (Mar/April), May Day (first Mon in May), Whit Monday (last Mon in May), August Monday (first Mon in Aug).

Working hours
Banking
Mon–Thu: 0800–1500; Fri: 0800–1700.
Business
Mon–Fri: 0800–1600. Sat: 0800–1300.
Government
Mon: 0800–1300, 1400–1700; Tue–Fri: 0800–1300, 1400–1600.

Telecommunications
In December 2006, a section of the fibre optic cable, traversing the entire Eastern Caribbean (around 1900km in length), was landed in Dominica. The cable begins in Puerto Rico and ends in Trinidad, connecting 12 islands. The cable delivers internet and telephony services.
Mobile/cell phones
GSM 850 and 900/1900 services available throughout most of the islands.

Electricity supply
220/240V AC, 50 cycles, with European three pin plugs.

Social customs/useful tips
Dominica's national dish is made from a large land frog, the *crapaud* or mountain chicken. In 2004, a ban was placed on hunting the amphibians, which are facing extinction.

Getting there
Air
National airline: None
International airport/s: Melville Hall (DOM), 64km north-east of Roseau; Canefield (DCF), 5km north of Roseau. Both of these airports are too small for international jets; access by air is via Antigua, Barbados, Costa Rica, Martinique or Guadeloupe.
Airport tax: Departure tax: EC$55, for a stay of more than 24 hours.

Surface

Water: There are ferries to surrounding islands.

Main port/s: Roseau (Woodbridge Bay) and Portsmouth (Prince Rupert's Bay).

Getting about

National transport

Air: Regional airline Carib Express based in Barbados.

Road: The network is over 750km, most of which is classified as first class.

City transport

Taxis: Available at airports and through hotels. Fixed rate system.

Car hire

A temporary local driver's permit is required, priced EC$30, and can be obtained on production of an national driving licence. Drivers must be aged between 25–65 years with at least two years experience.

The speed limit is generally 20mph.

BUSINESS DIRECTORY

The addresses listed below are a selection only. While World of Information makes every endeavour to check these addresses, we cannot guarantee that changes have not been made, especially to telephone numbers and area codes. We would welcome any corrections.

Telephone area codes

The international direct dialling code (IDD) for Dominica is +1 767, followed by subscriber's number.

Chambers of Commerce

Dominica Association of Industry and Commerce, 6 Cross Street, PO Box 85, Roseau (tel:448-2874; fax: 448-6868; e-mail: daic@marpin.dm).

Banking

Agricultural, Industrial & Development Bank (AID Bank), Charles Avenue, Goodwill (tel: 448-2853).

Bank of Nova Scotia, 28 Hillsborough Street, PO Box 520, Roseau (tel: 448-8580).

Banque Française Commerciale Antilles Guiyane, Queen Mary Street, PO Box 166, Roseau (tel: 448-4040).

Barclays Bank, 2 Old Street, PO Box 4, Roseau (tel: 448-2571).

Dominica Co-operative Credit Union, Great Marlborough Street, Roseau (tel: 82-191).

National Commercial Bank of Dominica, 64 Hillsborough Street, PO Box 271, Roseau (tel: 448-4401).

Royal Bank of Canada, Bay Front, PO Box 19, Roseau (tel: 448-2771).

Central bank

Eastern Caribbean Central Bank, Agency Office, PO Box 23, Dorsett House, Corner Old Street and Hodges Lane, Roseau (tel: 448-8001; fax: 448-8002).

Stock exchange

Eastern Caribbean Securities Exchange (ECSE), www.ecseonline.com

Travel information

Cardinal Airlines, 26 King George V Street, PO Box 661, Roseau (tel: 449-8922; fax: 449-8923).

Ministry of tourism

Ministry of Tourism, Port and Employment, Government Headquarters, Kennedy Avenue, Roseau (tel: 82-401).

National tourist organisation offices

Dominica Tourist Board, National Development Corporation, PO Box 293, Roseau (tel: 82-045; fax: 85-840).

Division of Tourism (National Development Corporation), PO Box 73, Valley Road, Roseau (tel: 82-186, 82-351; fax: 85-840).

Ministries

Ministry of Agriculture and the Environment, Government Headquarters, Kennedy Avenue, Roseau (tel: 82-401; fax: 87-999).

Ministry of Communications, Works and Housing, Government Headquarters, Kennedy Avenue, Roseau (tel: 82-401; fax: 84-807).

Ministry of Community Development and Women's Affairs, Kennedy Avenue, Roseau (tel: 82-401; fax: 98-220).

Ministry of Education, Sports and Youth Affairs, Government Headquarters, Kennedy Avenue, Roseau (tel: 82-401; fax: 80-080).

Ministry of External Affairs, Legal Affairs and Labour, Government Headquarters, Kennedy Avenue, Roseau (tel: 82-401; fax: 85-200).

Ministry of Finance, Industry and Planning (The Economic Development Unit), Government Headquarters, Kennedy Avenue, Roseau (tel: 82-401; fax: 80-054).

Ministry of Health and Social Security, Government Headquarters, Kennedy Avenue, Roseau (tel: 82-401; fax: 86-086).

Ministry of Privatisation and Foreign Investment (National Development Corporation), PO Box 293, Valley Road, Roseau (tel: 82-045).

Ministry of Trade and Marketing, Government Headquarters, Kennedy Avenue, Roseau (tel: 82-401; fax: 86-103).

Office of the Prime Minister, Government Headquarters, Kennedy Ave, Roseau (tel: 82-406).

Other useful addresses

Co-operative Citrus Growers' Association, 21 Hanover St, Roseau (tel: 82-062).

Dominica Banana Marketing Corp (DBMC), Corner of Queen Mary St and Turkey Lane, Roseau (82-671).

Dominica Broadcasting Corporation, Victoria Street, Roseau (tel: 83-283; fax: 82-918).

Dominica Embassy in US, 3216 New Mexico Ave, NW Washington DC 20016 (tel: (+1-202) 364-6781).

Dominica Export-Import Agency (Dexia), PO Box 173, Roseau (tel: 82-780; fax: 86-308).

Dominica Hotel Association, PO Box 270, Roseau (tel: 84-436).

Dominica National Development Corporation (NDC), PO Box 293, Valley Road, Bath Estate, Roseau (tel: 82-045; fax: 85-840; internet site: http://ndcdominica.dm/index.htm).

International Business Unit, Ministry of Finance, Government Headquarters, Kennedy Avenue, Roseau (tel: 82-401; fax: 80-406; e-mail: ibu@cwdom.dm).

Caribbean Net News: www.caribbeannetnews.com

Internet sites

Tourist website: www.avirtualdominica.com

Dominican Republic

KEY FACTS

Official name: República Dominicana (Dominican Republic)

Head of State: President Danilo Medina (PLD) (elected 20 May 2012, sworn in 16 August)

Head of government: President Danilo Medina (PLD)

Ruling party: Partido de la Liberación Dominicana (PLD) (Dominican Liberation Party) (from 2010)

Area: 48,400 square km

Population: 10.60 million (2014)*

Capital: Santo Domingo de Guzmán

Official language: Spanish

Currency: Dominican Republic peso (RD$) = 100 centavos

Exchange rate: RD$45.10 per US$ (Sep 2015)

GDP per capita: US$6,044 (2014)*

GDP real growth: 7.30% (2014)*

GDP: US$64.08 billion (2014)*

Unemployment: 6.40% (2014)

Inflation: 4.80% (2013)

Balance of trade: -US$7.31 billion (2013)

Visitor numbers: 4.12 million * (2010, excludes cruise passengers)

* estimated figure

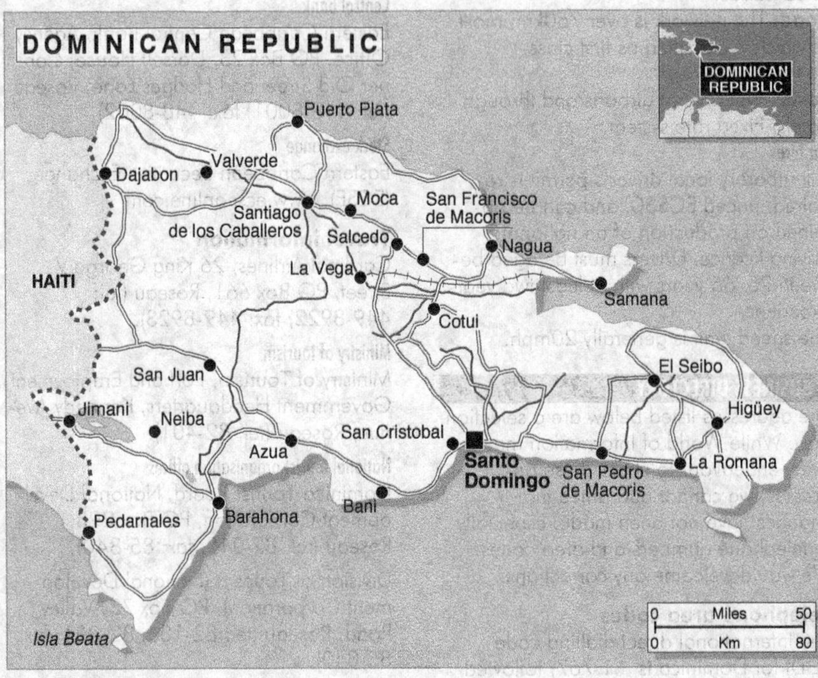

Tensions between the Dominican Republic and French-speaking Haiti, its neighbour on the island of Hispaniola, rose in October 2013 following the decision of the Dominican Republic's Constitutional Court that an existing policy, under which those born in the country were only granted citizenship if at least one of their parents was a legal resident, should somehow apply retroactively – i.e. to people born before the law was introduced in 2004. Whatever the doubtful legality of the new law, according to some human-rights groups (including the UN refugee agency – UNHCR), the change would render over 200,000 people of Haitian descent simply stateless. Unsurprisingly, Haiti saw fit to complain about the move, even though those involved had effectively turned their backs on their mother country.

Good – or just anti-Haitian – housekeeping?

The government of President Danilo Medina claimed that the changes clarified what had been an ambiguous situation. In November 2013 Medina, decreed that all undocumented foreigners had an 18 month period to legalise their presence in the Dominican Republic, during which they could not be deported. Applicants who could demonstrate what were described as 'unquestionable' ties to the country would be eligible for residency. These included studying or working in the Dominican Republic, a command of Spanish, having native relatives or owning property in the Dominican Republic. The government planned to introduce a naturalisation law, which it promised would offer a fast track to citizenship.

The government refuted its critics by announcing that the effect of the legislation had been exaggerated. It claimed that its audit of the birth register found exactly 24,392 people whose citizenship was now invalid. However, human rights campaigners challenged the soundness of the audit, which apparently had been carried out in only eight days, a phenomenal work rate. Some put the figure at ten times higher as unknown thousands of those affected did not even have birth certificates.

The Constitutional Court's decision did little to improve Haitian-Dominican relations. In a speech Haiti's President Michel Martelly, quoting a Dominican journalist, complained of 'civil genocide,' causing Dominican officials to cancel a meeting with their Haitian counterparts set up to discuss the issue. It soon looked as though the Dominican Republic had made a legal error with wider consequences than ever envisaged. The United States, while accepting that the court's decision held sway, diplomatically recommended that the Dominican government do more to protect human rights. However, other Caribbean countries – where mostly black populations sympathised with the Haitian-descended Dominican community as simple victims of racism – lost no time in voicing their criticism.

Where the consequences of the legal changes were most acutely felt were with Caribbean Community and Common Market (Caricom), the regional political grouping that the Dominican Republic had been trying to join since 2005. In early 2014 the membership application was abruptly suspended. More was to come: Ralph Gonsalves, prime minister of the tiny St Vincent and the Grenadines, demanded that the Dominican Republic be ejected from Cariforum, the body that represented the region in talks with the European Union (EU), as well as from Petrocaribe, Venezuela's subsidised-oil programme.

Let's reconsider

The pressure and the international reactions brought about change. In May 2014 the Dominican Congress passed a law that would regularise the children of 'illegal' migrants who have birth certificates; the law also enabled the descendants of irregular migrants who had never possessed papers to naturalise. Thus, the embarrassing legal stalemate that had lasted some eight months ended. It had failed to take into account the flimsy international validity of the October ruling, nor had it anticipated the high profile regional opposition and criticism that had seriously impinged on the Dominican Republic's international standing.

In May 2012, the candidate of the governing Partido de la Liberación Dominicana, (PLD) (Dominican Liberation Party), Danilo Medina, had defeated former President Hipólito Mejía of the Partido Revolucionario Dominicano (PRD) (Dominican Revolutionary Party) in the Dominican Republic's closely-contested presidential election. The 62 year-old Mr Medina brought with him extensive political baggage, having once been an activist for the PRD, which he left to join the PLD in 1973. The party, initially to the left of the Revolutionary Party, moved steadily to the centre in the 1990s. Mr Medina had served as chief of staff to the PLD leader Leonel Fernández during his presidential terms in the 1990s and again in 2004–06. He had also stood as PLD candidate in the 2000 presidential election, losing to Hipólito Mejía. After internal differences and squabbles, in 2006 he fell out with President Fernández when the latter defeated him in the PLD primaries for the presidential election of 2008. Mr Medina eventually secured the PLD nomination for the 2012 election. His narrow win over Mr Mejía consolidated the PLD's domination. It already controlled both houses of Congress.

In the run up to the election it had seemed quite likely that the result would hinge on whether Dominicans were more frustrated with their current government, or more apprehensive of electing a former president whose first (and only) term in office had ended with a serious economic crisis. In 2012 disenchantment with the government, had focused on the high cost of living. Mr Medina had promised to improve upon, but not make any major changes to, the policies of the outgoing president. Both presidential candidates had proposed to increase spending on education and to do what they can to create jobs in a country of 10 million people that is largely dependent on tourism and where unemployment was officially about 14 per cent, although the vast majority of workers are in the poorly paid informal sector. The typical salary for those who do have regular jobs averaged around US$260 per month.

The economy

In the midst of these deep seated economic imbalances, according to the United Nations Economic Commission for Latin America and the Caribbean (ECLAC-CEPAL) the Dominican Republic was expected to post economic growth of around 6 per cent in 2014 (pretty much the same as the 6.8 per cent of 2013), driven by agriculture, mining and quarries, construction and financial services. On the demand side, less government consumption during the first half of the year contributed to the economic slowdown. Inflation looked likely to close 5 per cent, up from 4.8 per cent in 2013 but still within the target range set by the monetary authorities. On the strength of fiscal consolidation efforts, the consolidated public sector deficit was expected to come in at around 4.3 per cent at the end of 2013, well down from 7.8 per cent in 2012.

ECLAC noted that the tax reform legislation (Law 253-12) introduced in late 2012 raised the transaction tax on industrialised goods and services (ITBIS) from 16 per cent to 18 per cent, with a lower tax (8 per cent) for goods that had previously been exempt. This boosted central government revenue, which was up 12.4 per cent in September, while total central government expenditures fell by 13.4 per cent reflecting falling fixed investment down by 59.6 per cent) and capital transfers (down by 49 per cent). This fiscal consolidation effort was expected to bring down

KEY INDICATORS — Dominican Republic

	Unit	2011	2012	2013	2014	**2015
Population	m	*10.06	10.23	10.41	*10.60	*10.79
Gross domestic product (GDP)	US$bn	56.70	58.98	61.29	*64.08	*66.20
GDP per capita	US$	5,639	5,765	5,885	*6,044	*6,134
GDP real growth	%	4.5	3.9	4.8	*7.3	*5.1
Inflation	%	8.5	3.7	4.8	3.0	*1.6
Unemployment	%	14.6	6.4	7.0	6.4	*5.8
Exports (fob) (goods)	US$m	8,535.9	8,935.5	9,503.7	–	–
Imports (fob) (goods)	US$m	17,422.7	17,673.3	16,809.6	–	–
Balance of trade	US$m	-8,886.8	-8,737.8	-7,305.9	–	–
Current account	US$m	-4,499.0	-4,012.0	-2,493.0	*-2,002.0	*-1,613.0
Total reserves minus gold	US$m	3,468.8	3,549.0	4,678.6	4,839.7	–
Foreign exchange	US$m	3,437.2	3,528.0	4,676.5	–	–
Exchange rate	per US$	37.91	38.80	42.55	44.13	–

* estimated figure ** forecast figure

the consolidated deficit to the equivalent of 4.3 per cent of gross domestic product (GDP) at year-end. As a result, external debt had fallen to 22.3 per cent of GDP in September, down from 23.6 per cent of GDP at end-2012.

The strong contraction generated by fiscal policy and lower inflation was, in the view of ECLAC, behind the decision by the Banco Central de la República Dominicana (central bank) to ease monetary policy. In May 2013 the central bank cut its reference rate by 75 basis points to 4.25 per cent, while relaxing reserve requirements by the equivalent of US$500 million, in a bid to incentivise production and housing credit. Against this backdrop, the financial system's total assets were up in September by 12.3 per cent over the previous year (9.3 per cent in September 2012). However, the increase in liquidity in a low-reserve environment, as a result of weaker exports, generated pressure on the exchange rate, such that on 26 August the Monetary Board reversed its policy stance, raising the interest rate from 4.25 per cent to 6.25 per cent to prevent exchange rate volatility from driving up inflation.

ECLAC noted that as a result of the weak growth in employment in the United States and rising unemployment in Europe, family remittances climbed by only just 0.8 per cent year-on-year in September, although they continue to contribute over 5 per cent to GDP. Tourism performed strongly between January and September, growing by 6.6 per cent over the previous year, compared with growth of 4.1 per cent in the same period in 2012. Foreign direct investment (FDI) plummeted by about 50 per cent with the completion in 2012 of the Pueblo Viejo mining project, which was now in operation. 2013 also saw the purchase of the brewery Cervecería Nacional Dominicana by a transnational company. In 2013, the top sectors receiving FDI were energy, commerce, real estate and tourism, which together accounted for 66.7 per cent of the total.

Risk assessment

Politics	Fair
Economy	Fair
Regional stability	Fair

COUNTRY PROFILE

1492 The island was visited by Christopher Columbus. He named it Hispaniola (Little Spain).
1496 Colombus' brother, Bartolomeo, founded the city of Santo Domingo and his son, Diego was the first governor of the Spanish colony.
1697 Western part of island (Haiti) given to France under Treaty of Ryswick.
1795 Remainder of island (Santo Domingo) ceded to France.
1808 Santo Domingo regained by Spain, after revolt by Spanish creoles.
1821 Independence gained following uprising against Spanish rule.
1822 Annexed by Haiti under Jean-Pierre Boyer.
1844 Boyer was overthrown and the eastern part of the island became independent as the Dominican Republic.
1861–63 President Santana returns republic to Spanish rule.
1864 Spain annuls its annexation of the Dominican Republic after a popular revolt.
1865 Second Dominican Republic declared.
1906 US and Dominican Republic sign 50-year Treaty of Accord.
1916–24 US armed forces occupied the island, following internal disorder.
1930–1961 General Rafael Trujillo leads *coup d'état*, overthrowing President Horacio Vázquez and becoming a dictator.
1961 Trujillo was assassinated.
1962 Democratic election of Juan Bosch, in the first free elections in 38 years.
1963 Bosch deposed by military.
1965 Civil revolt resulted in another intervention by US armed troops.
1966 Joaquín Balaguer (protégé of Trujillo) won the presidential election, leading the Partido Reformista Social Cristiana (PRSC) (Social Christian Reform Party). He was re-elected in 1970 and 1974, and survived several coup attempts.
1978 Sivestre Antonio Guzmán, (Partido Revolucionario Dominicano (PRD) (Dominican Revolutionary Party)) defeated Balaguer in presidential elections.
1979 The economy deteriorated following two hurricanes that caused US$1 billion in damage and left 200,000 people homeless; fuel prices rose and sugar prices fell.
1994 The constitution was established, setting out the power of the executive.
1996 Leonel Fernández Rayana of the Partido de la Liberación Dominicana (PLD) (Dominican Liberation Party) narrowly won the presidency.
1998 PLD won a majority in both chambers of parliament.
2000 Rafael Hopólito Mejía Domínguez (PRD) won the presidential election.
2002 The PRD won legislative elections. Former president Joaquín Balaguer died.
2004 A two-day general strike was held in protest at the sharp devaluation of the peso. The Dominican Republic joined the Central American Parliament.
2007 The Central American Free Trade Agreement (Cafta) with the US was ratified.
2008 Incumbent Leonel Fernández Rayana (PLD) won the presidential elections.
2010 Following a severe earthquake in Haiti, the Dominican Republic became a focal point for summit meetings and conferences concerning relief efforts for its neighbour. A 49 per cent stake in the state-owned Refidomsa oil refinery (near Haina Occidental port) was sold to the Venezuelan PdVSA, for US$130 million. In legislative elections, the ruling PLD won 54.61 per cent of the vote (105 deputies and 31 senators), the PRD 41.9 per cent (75 deputies); turnout was 54.15 per cent.
2011 An agreement was signed in January, whereby the Organisation of American States (OAS) provides technical assistance in reforming Dominican Republic's electoral law to provide a more transparent system. In July the Inter-American Development Bank (IDB) announced that it will disburse US$324 million over the year, of which US$200 million will be used by the government for budgetary support, and in line with macroeconomic stability as stipulated by the IMF in February. This brings the total loans to the Dominican Republic by the IDB up to US$1.9 billion.
2012 Presidential elections were held on 20 May, in which six candidates took part. Danilo Medina (PLD) won 51.21 per cent of the vote and former president, Hipólito Mejía (PRD) won 46.95 per cent; no other candidate won more than 1.5 per cent of the vote. President Danilo Medina was sworn in to office on 16 August.
2013 On 2 October Glencore Xstrata announced it was temporarily closing its mine (Falcondo), leaving about 1,000 workers out of a job. President Medina met with Darren Bowden of Glencore on 4 October. Mr Bowden said his company had been in the country for 40 years and would do everything possible to re-open the mine.
2014 On 22 October the Comisión Interamericana de Derechos Humanos (CIDH) (Inter-American Court of Human Rights) convicted the Dominican Republic for violation of various rights in deportations carried out from 1999 to 2000, reported the Spanish news agency, EFE. Dominican Republic was guilty of violating rights to identity, equality before the law, personal freedom, fair trial, judicial and family protection, dignity and a ban on the collective expulsion of aliens. The incidents took place when Dominican authorities stopped and arbitrarily expelled 27 people, 22 of whom were Dominican and

five Haitians, among them children who lived in Dominican Republic.
2015 The government redeemed US$4 billion in outstanding debt accumulated under the PetroCaribe agreement from 2005–14 in February. The deal reduced the country's public debt burden, lowered interest costs and extended average maturity. The significant discount led to a decrease of 3.3 per cent of GDP in public debt and reduced annual debt servicing costs by US$100 million.

Political structure

In addition to their unicameral national parliaments, El Salvador, Guatemala, Honduras, Nicaragua, Panama and Dominican Republic also return directly-elected deputies to the supranational Central American Parliament.

Constitution

The 1994 Constitution prevents the re-election of an individual as president for consecutive periods.
However, on 19 April 2015, the ruling PLD party amended the constitution to allow a president to be re-elected once. This has allowed incumbent Danilo Medina to stand again in 2016.

The executive

Executive power rests with the president, who is also head of government and commander-in-chief of the armed forces. The president is directly elected for a four-year term and may stand once again immediately. The cabinet is appointed and presided over by the president. The president, by constitutional decree, names the provincial governors, who are his representatives in each province.

National legislature

The bicameral Congress of the Republic is comprised of a Chamber of Deputies, with 183 deputies, elected for four-year terms by preferential vote and block votes by provinces with one representative per 50,000 citizens, with a minimum of two per province. The 32-member Senate is elected for a four-year term, one member for each province plus one for the Distrito Nacional. The Senate elects the members of the judiciary.

Last elections

16 May 2010 (parliamentary); 20 May 2012 (presidential)
Results: Parliamentary (Chamber of Deputies): Partido de la Liberación Dominicana (PLD) (Dominican Liberation Party) coalition won 54.6 per cent of the vote (105 seats out of 183), the Partido Revolucionario Dominicano (PRD) (Dominican Revolutionary Party) coalition 41.9 per cent (75), Partido Reformista Social Cristiana (PRSC) (Social Christian Reform Party) 1.46 per cent (3); eight other political parties did not win enough votes to gain any seats. Senate: the PLD won 31 seats out of 32, the PRSC 1. Turnout was around 54.1 per cent.
Presidential: Danilo Medina (PLD) won 51.21 per cent of the vote, Hipólito Mejía (PRD) won 46.95 per cent; four other candidates each won less than 1.5 per cent of the vote.

Next elections

15 May 2016 (presidential and parliamentary)

Political parties

Ruling party

Partido de la Liberación Dominicana (PLD) (Dominican Liberation Party) (from 2010)

Main opposition party

Gran Alianza Nacional coalition led by Partido Revolucionario Dominicano (PRD) (Dominican Revolutionary Party)

Population

10.24 million (2012)* About 34 per cent of the total population is under 15 years of age (2003).
Last census: 1 December 2010: 9,378,819
Population density: 168 inhabitants per square km. Urban population 69 per cent (2010 Unicef).
Annual growth rate: 0.6 per cent, 1990–2010 (Unicef).

Ethnic make-up

Mixed race (73 per cent), white (16 per cent), black (11 per cent).

Religions

Roman Catholic (95 per cent). There is also a small Protestant community.

Education

Primary education lasts for six years and is free of charge. There are two systems of secondary education in operation, the traditional has six years of study divided into two-year then four-year cycles. The reform system has two cycles of three years. The emphasis of the former is academic and the latter scientific/technical. Both systems allow for specialised studies.
Secondary schooling is subsidised in private schools.
Literacy rate: 84 per cent adult rate; 92 per cent youth rate (15–24) (Unesco 2005).
Compulsory years: Seven to 17
Pupils per teacher: 28 in primary schools.

Health

Seventy-nine per cent of the population have access to an improved water source.

HIV/Aids

The HIV/Aids infection rates is one of the largest in the Caribbean.
HIV prevalence: 1.7 per cent aged 15–49 in 2003 (World Bank)
Life expectancy: 67 years, 2004 (WHO 2006)
Fertility rate/Maternal mortality rate: 2.6 births per woman, 2010 (Unicef)
Birth rate/Death rate: 24 births per 1,000 population; seven deaths per 1,000 population (2003).
Child (under 5 years) mortality rate (per 1,000): 27 per 1,000 live births (WHO 2012)

Main cities

Santo Domingo de Guzmán (capital, estimated population 2.7 million in 2012), Santiago de los Caballeros (696,206), San Pedro de Macoris (293,659), La Romana (260,266), Higuey (188,875), Puerto Plata (140,378), San Francisco de Macoris (132,396), The Vega (111,025).

Languages spoken

English is widely spoken.

Official language/s

Spanish

Media

Press freedom is guaranteed by law although some contentious matters are generally avoided, such as the army and Roman Catholic Church.

Press

Dailies: In Spanish, there are several national and regional newspapers including *El Caribe* (www.elcaribecdn.com), *Hoy* (www.hoy.com.do), *Listín Diario* (www.listin.com.do), *Diario Libre* (www3.diariolibre.com) *La Información* (www.lainformacionrd.net), *El Día* (www.eldia.com.do), *Nuevo elDiario* (www.elnuevodiario.com.do) and *El Observador Cibaeño* (www.observador.tk) from Santiago de los Caballeros. An evening newspaper is *El Nacional* (www.elnacional.com.do).
In English, from the northern coast, *Dominican Today* (www.dominicantoday.com), *Gringo News* (www.gringo-times.com) is a humorous publication and *The Adscene* (www.theadscene.com) is also in Spanish and German.
Weeklies: In Spanish *(A)Hora* (www.ahora.com.do), covers general interest news.
Periodicals: In English the monthly *The Puerto Plata Report* (www.popreport.com), is a regional magazine from the northern coast.

Broadcasting

The national government-owned broadcaster is Corporación Estatal de Radio y Televisión (CERTV).
Commercial broadcasting companies are generally owned by a few either economically or politically powerful entities.
Radio: There are over 200 FM radio stations. CERTV (www.certvdominicana.com) operates three stations, Dominicana FM, Quisqueya FM and 620 AM. Commercial stations include LA91 FM

(www.la91fm.com), Super Mix (CDN) (www.elcaribecdn.com.do), La Nueva 106.9 FM (www.lanueva106fm.com) and Radio Moca (http://cima100fm.com).
Television: The national public broadcaster is CERTV (www.certvdominicana.com), which operates Canal 4. There are many cable and satellite services including the government-run, commercial Antena Latina (http://antenalatina.antena-sin.com) Canal 7. Private stations include Hola Gente (www.holagente.com.do), Color Visión (www.colorvision.com.do), Telemicro (www.telemicro.com.do), Cadena de Noticias (CDN) (www.elcaribecdn.com) news TV, Aster TV (www.aster.com.do) for children, Telesistema (www.telesistema11.tv) and Teleantilles (www.tele-antillas.tv).
Other news agencies: Caribbean Net News: www.caribbeannetnews.com
Prensa Latina: www.prensalatina.com.mx

Economy

The Dominican Republic has become an upper-middle income country, as ranked by the World Bank, with a national income per capita of US$5,834. The economy has moved from a typically agrarian to a service based, open market system, following the opening up of the economy to foreign investment and domestic macroeconomic reforms. The manufacturing sector is centred on foreign owned operations, based in a number of free-trade zones, and involved in assembly or light manufacturing. Other, service orientated companies, such as customer service call centres, also operate from these zones.
Tourism is the single, principal industry and leading employer, while mining of ferronickel, gold and silver are the major export commodities, along with agricultural products such as sugar, coffee, tobacco, cocoa, meats and consumer goods.
Growth fell from a high of 8.3 per cent in 2010 to 2.8 per cent in 2011, which remained largely the same in 2012 at 2.6 per cent. The economy's expansion accelerated to 4.8 per cent in 2013 and further to 7.3 per cent in 2014 as the economy rebounded from the global economic crisis and the fiscal situation improved.
Remittances from expatriate workers make an essential contribution to the economy; 1.5 million live abroad, mostly in the US but increasingly in Europe and in 2013 US$4.5 billion (7.4 per cent of GDP) was injected into the economy (particularly into family economies) – a 5.2 per cent increase on 2012. Remittances have increased even further to US$4.7 billion in 2014.
The government redeemed US$4 billion in outstanding debt accumulated under the PetroCaribe agreement from 2005–14 in February 2015. The deal reduced the country's public debt burden, lowered interest costs and extended average maturity. This significant discount led to a decrease of 3.3 per cent of GDP in public debt and reduced annual debt servicing costs by US$100 million.

External trade

The Dominican Republic is the only Caribbean member of the Central America Free Trade Agreement (DR-Cafta), which includes Costa Rica, El Salvador, Guatemala, Honduras and the US; it is also a member of the Caribbean Community (Caricom), along with 15 other members.
There are a number of free trade zones (FTZ), which manufacture clothes and footwear, leather goods and jewellery, electronic and medical products, pharmaceuticals and tobacco for export.

Imports

Principal imports are foodstuffs, petroleum, industrial raw materials, cotton and fabrics, chemicals and pharmaceuticals, consumer goods and foodstuffs.
Main sources: US (41.0 per cent of total in 2014), China (11.6 per cent), Mexico (6.0 per cent)

Exports

Principal exports are ferro-nickel, sugar, gold, silver, coffee, cocoa, tobacco, meats and consumer goods.
Main destinations: US (49.1 per cent of total in 2014), Haiti (14.3 per cent), Canada (9.2 per cent)

Agriculture

Farming

The principal commercial crop is sugar cane, production of which has fluctuated due to vagaries of weather, falling export demand and labour shortages.
The main agricultural exports – sugar, coffee, cocoa and tobacco – account for just under a half of the country's export earnings. Rice, vegetables and citrus fruits are grown for home consumption.
Cattle-raising has expanded considerably and commercial fishing is being developed.
Estimates of cultivated arable land vary between 18–25 per cent; pasture 17–30 per cent; woodland/forest 25–40 per cent. Soil is generally fertile and rainfall/water availability is adequate.
Agriculture is becoming more commercialised. The country benefits from agreements that provide it with duty free access to the US markets. These include the Generalised System of Preferences and the US Caribbean Basin Initiative.

Fishing

Despite the abundance of fish in the surrounding waters, the fishing industry is largely underdeveloped.

Industry and manufacturing

The industrial sector contributed around 29.1 of GDP in 2013 and employed just under 20 per cent of the workforce.
Activity is centred on sugar refining (which is the dominant industry), cement production, the processing of foodstuffs, tobacco, beverages and textiles. The country is the largest exporter in the Caribbean region of apparel to the US. Some of the best-known labels are manufactured in the Dominican Republic. The Caribbean Basin Initiative allows the country's textiles duty-free entry to the US market. However, with China now a member of the WTO this trade is threatened.
Other light industries include plastics, rubber, chemicals and paper.
The emphasis is on encouraging joint ventures that utilise a high percentage of local materials, expanding facilities at the main industrial free zones (La Ramona, San Pedro de Macoris, Santiago) and overcoming the serious supply/energy problems. The free trade zone programme is the country's leading earner of foreign exchange.

Tourism

The Dominican Republic offers typical Caribbean holidays, with white-sanded beaches and a diverse marine life. The government supports the growing industry, spending 5.1 per cent of total investment in 2014. The country accommodated 5.1 million visitors in the same year (an increase of 7.8 per cent on 2013), with total visitor exports reaching US$5.67 billion – the equivalent of 35.1 per cent of total exports. The industry's total contribution to GDP was US$9.7 billion, or 16.0 per cent of GDP. Just over 624,000 workers' jobs were directly or indirectly related to travel and tourism, which was equal to 14.7 per cent of total employment.
The newly developed US$85 million Amber Cove port started receiving six of Carnival Corporation's nine brands of cruise liners in October 2015. Over 250,000 cruise passengers are expected in its first year of operation; it is also expected that the project will provide some 430 local jobs. Carnival Corporation is said to be the world's largest travel and leisure company.

Mining

The mining sector as a whole typically accounts for 2 per cent of GDP and employs 3 per cent of the workforce.
Gold, silver and ferro-nickel are all mined in significant quantities. Gypsum, limestone and marble are mined for the domestic market. Deposits of copper, iron, titanium and platinum also exist.
The country's largest mining facility is operated by Falconbridge, a Canadian

company, which exports 33,000 tonnes of nickel per year.
Some industry analysts believe that large deposits of nickel, copper and gold have yet to be discovered.

Hydrocarbons

There are no known hydrocarbon reserves. Consumption was 123,450 barrels per day (bpd) in 2013, almost all of which was imported. In 2005, the Dominican Republic, plus a number of other Caribbean states, signed an agreement with Venezuela to establish PetroCaribe, a multi-national oil company, owned by the participating states. PetroCaribe buys low-priced Venezuelan crude oil under long-term payment plans. In June 2009 is was agreed that a 49 per cent stake in the state-owned refinery would be sold to Venezuela for US$130 million in exchange for oil supplied via PetroCaribe.
In March 2015, due to falling oil prices, Venezuela cut its subsidies to PetroCaribe member countries.
There are no known reserves of natural gas but total imports were 1.28 billion cubic metres in 2012. There is a regasification terminal that feeds two gas-fired power plants with liquefied natural gas (LNG) imported from Trinidad and Tobago.
Around 582,000 tonnes of coal were consumed in energy production in 2012.

Energy

Total installed generating capacity was 5,701MW in 2013, producing over 13 billion kilowatt hours. The energy market has been deregulated and the US-AES Corporation is the single largest private energy provider, owning seven power plants with a total capacity of 988MW, including a regasification terminal that feeds liquefied natural gas to two separate gas-fired power plants with a total capacity of 555MW and a coal-fired power station at Itabo with a capacity of 295MW. Hydropower accounts for over 400MW of all electricity produced and there are plans to double capacity.
In June 2014 the Inter-American Development Bank (IADB) approved a US$78 million loan to support a modernisation programme of the electrical grid and to reduce electricity waste.

Financial markets

Stock exchange
Bolsa de Valores de la República Dominicana (Dominican Republic Stock Exchange)

Banking and insurance

The foreign investment law of 1997 permits overseas banks to operate banks in the Dominican Republic.
The banking sector hit a crisis in 2003 when the Banco Intercontinental (Baninter) collapsed as a result of massive fraud.
The Women's Development bank (Banmujer) began operations in 2001, lending small loans of around US$1,000 to women for entrepreneurial ventures.

Central bank
Banco Central de la República Dominicana.

Main financial centre
Santo Domingo.

Time

GMT minus four hours

Geography

The Caribbean island of Hispaniola is divided north/south into the Dominican Republic in the east, occupying around 65 per cent of the land, and Haiti in the west. The closest other islands are Jamaica in the south-west, Cuba in the west, the Turks and Caicos in the north and Puerto Rico in the east.
In the centre of the island the *Cordillera Central* is the tallest mountain range with peaks over 3,000 metres. Lake Enriquillo, the largest lake and lowest spot, is located in the south-west.

Hemisphere
Northern

Climate

Tropical with temperatures ranging from 27 degrees Celsius (C) during the dry season (November–April) to 37 degrees C from June–October when humidity is highest.

Entry requirements

Passports
Required by all. The exception is nationals of US and Canada, who may travel with proof of citizenship including photo ID, birth certificate or driving licence and after purchasing a tourist card (US$10). All US and Canadian nationals require a passport for re-entry to their country from January 2007.
All passports must have twice as much time left of validity as the length of stay in the Dominican Republic.

Visa
Required by all. Some exceptions can be found at www.dr1.com/travel/prepare/documentation.shtml; a list of nationals that may enter with a tourist card is also given.
Business visitors and visitors from countries that may not use a tourist card should contact the nearest Dominican Republic consulate.

Currency advice/regulations
The import and export of local currency is prohibited. Only a limited number of foreign currencies may be exchanged in the Dominican Republic. While the accepted currencies include the euro, the Canadian dollar, and pound sterling, the US offers the maximum exchange rate. On departure up to 30 per cent of exchanged currency can be reconverted, in US dollars only, on presentation of official exchange reciepts.
Import of foreign currency must be declared and export cannot exceed the imported amount. Travellers cheques, in US dollars, are accepted in most locations.
ATMs, dispensing the Dominican Republic peso only, are found in city and tourist centres.

Prohibited imports
Illegal drugs, weapons, plants and vegetables and pornographic material.

Health (for visitors)

Mandatory precautions
Yellow fever certificate if travelling from an infected area.

Advisable precautions
Vaccinations for meningitis, typhoid, diphtheria polio and TB; other lesser risks include hepatitis A and B and dengue fever.
Bilharzia is endemic; use only well chlorinated and maintained swimming pools.
Malaria precautions are recommended.
Rabies is a risk.
Water precautions are essential; use only bottled or boiled water. Eat only well cooked meals, preferably served hot.
Pork, salad and mayonnaise may carry increased risk. Vegetables should be cooked and fruit peeled.
Health insurance (to include emergency medical repatriation) is strongly recommended, as medical care is limited and variable in quality. All personal medication should be carried, with their prescription.

Hotels

Following intensive tourist development, there are a full range of hotels available. Tourist locations charge more than city hotels and in general hotels are considerably more expensive during the winter.
Bills usually include 12 per cent government tax and 10 per cent service charge.

Public holidays (national)

Fixed dates
1 Jan (New Year's Day), 6 Jan (Epiphany), 21 Jan (Our Lady of Altagracia), 26 Jan (Duarte's Birthday), 27 Feb (Independence Day), 1 May (Labour Day), 16 Jul (Restoration Day), *24 Sep (Our Lady of las Mercedes), 6 Nov (Constitution Day), 25 Dec (Christmas Day).
* Businesses may take Mondays *in lieu*.

Variable dates
Good Friday (Mar/Apr), Corpus Christi (May/Jun).

Working hours

Banking
Mon–Fri: 0830–1700.

Business
Mon–Fri: 0800–1200, 1400–1800.
Government
Mon–Fri: 0800–1500.

Telecommunications
Mobile/cell phones
There are 1800/1900 GSM services available in most urban areas.

Electricity supply
110–120V AC, 60 cycles.

Weights and measures
The metric system has been adopted. However, certain other units are still in use, eg ounces and pounds are used in weighing solids, petrol and motor oils are measured in imperial gallons, cooking oil is retailed in pounds and fabrics are measured by the yard. Land surfaces in rural areas are generally measured by tarea – equal to 624 square metres.

Getting there
Air
International airport/s: Santo Domingo-Las Américas (SDQ), 30km east of city, duty-free shop, bar, restaurant, bank, post office, shops, hotel reservations, car hire; Gregorio Luperon International Puerto Plata (POP), 18km from city, bank, duty-free shop, restaurant, bar, car hire.
Airport tax: International departures US$10, excluding transit passengers.
Surface
Road: The main route runs from Haiti via Elias Pina.
Main port/s: There are 14 ports, including Santo Domingo (the largest) and Haina.

Getting about
National transport
Air: There are flights between Santo Domingo, Santiago, Samana, Punta Cana and Puerto Plata. These are provided by Bavaro Sun Flight, Aerolineas Santo Domingo and Dorado Air.
Road: There are about 17,120km of roads. Highways link Santo Domingo-Hinguey, Montecristo, Dajabon, San Juan, Elias Pina. There is a direct route from Santo Domingo to Port-au-Prince in Haiti.
Buses: There are bus stations in all towns. Fairly numerous services from Santo Domingo to Puerto Plata, La Romana – journey times vary. Also to Barahona and Samana.
Rail: There are a number of freight-only railways.
City transport
Taxis: In Santo Domingo taxis are freely available in the main business districts. These are not metered and it is advisable to agree the price with the driver before setting out. Taxis which travel off these routes may be difficult to find, especially at night. No tip is expected.
Buses, trams & metro: Buses in Santo Domingo are cheap, though crowded.
Car hire
National or international licence required. Chauffeur-driven cars can be negotiated with taxi drivers outside main hotels. Car hire facilities are good, but fairly expensive.

BUSINESS DIRECTORY
The addresses listed below are a selection only. While World of Information makes every endeavour to check these addresses, we cannot guarantee that changes have not been made, especially to telephone numbers and area codes. We would welcome any corrections.

Telephone area codes
This international direct dialling code (IDD) for the Dominican Republic is +1 809 followed by subscriber's number.

Useful telephone numbers
Santo Domingo
Emergency (Ambulance, Police): 911
Police: 682-3151
Police (radio patrol): 533-1074
Centro Médico Nacional (hospital): 682-0171
Fire Department: 682-2000
Red Cross: 682-4545

Chambers of Commerce
American Chamber of Commerce of the Dominican Republic, Avenida Sarasota 20, Torre Empresarial, PO Box 95-2, Santo Domingo (Tel: 381-0777; fax: 381-0286; e-mail: amcham@codetel.net.do).
British Chamber of Commerce of the Dominican Republic, Avenida San Martin 253, Edificio Santanita, PO Box 718-2, Santo Domingo (tel: 616-2335; fax: 616-2336; e-mail: britcham@tricom.net).

Santiago Cámara de Comercio y Producción, Avenida Las Carreras 7, Edificio Empresarial, Santiago (tel: 582-2856; fax: 241-4546; e-mail: csantiago@camarasantiago.com).

Santo Domingo Cámara de Comercio y Producción, Calle Arzobispo Nouel 206, PO Box 815, Santo Domingo (tel: 682-2688; fax: 685-2228; e-mail: camara.sto.dgo@codetel.net.do).

Banking
Banco BHD, Ave 27 de Febrero esq, Winston Churchill, Santo Domingo DN (tel: 243-3232; fax: 541-4949).

Banco del Exterior Dominicano, Ave Abraham Lincoln No. 756, Piantini, Santo Domingo (tel: 565-5540; fax: 565-5547).

Banco de los Trabajadores De La República Dominicana, Av México Esq Calle Altagracia, Santo Domingo (tel: 682-0171; fax: 685-6536).

Banco de Reservas de la República Dominica, Isabel La Catolica No. 72, Santo Domingo (tel: 688-2241; fax: 685-0602).

Banco Dominicano del Progreso, Ave John F Kennedy No. 3, Miraflores, Santo Domingo (tel: 563-3233; fax: 563-2451).

Banco Gerencial y Fiduciario Dominicano, Ave 27 de Febrero No 50, El Vergel, Santo Domingo (tel: 541-9400; fax: 567-6747).

Banco Latinoamericano, Gustavo Mejía Ricart Esq Agustín Lara, Ens Piantini, Santo Domingo (tel: 562-2662; fax: 562-1915).

Banco Mercantil, Ave Bolivar No. 308 Esq Jose Joaquín Pérez Gazcue, Santo Domingo (tel: 221-7151; 688-0608).

Banco Metropolitano, Ave Lope de Vega Esq Gustavo Mejía Ricart, Edif. Goico Castro, Ens Naco, Santo Domingo (tel: 562-4242; fax: 540-1566).

Banco Nacional de Crédito, John F Kennedy Esq Tiradentes, Ens Naco, Santo Domingo (tel: 540-4441; fax: 567-4698).

Banco Popular Dominicano, Av. John F Kennedy No 20 Esq Máximo Gómez, Torre Popular, 11 Avo. Piso, Santo Domingo (tel: 544-5900; fax: 544-5999).

Bank of Nova Scotia, Ave. John F Kennedy Esq Lope de Vega, Ens Naco, Santo Domingo (tel: 544-1700; fax: 542-6302).

Citibank, Ave John F Kennedy No 1 Esq San Martín, Santo Domingo (tel: 566-5611; fax: 567-2255).

Central bank
Banco Central de la República Dominicana, PO Box: 1347, Calle Pedro Henríquez Ureña, Esq Leopoldo Navarro, Santo Domingo (tel: 221-9111; fax: 686-7488; e-mail: info@bancentral.gov.do).

Stock exchange
Bolsa de Valores de la República Dominicana (Dominican Republic Stock Exchange), www.bolsard.com

Travel information
Aerolíneas Argo, Avenida 27 de Febrero 409, Santo Domingo (tel: 566-1844).

Dominicana de Aviación, Leopoldo Navarre, Edificio San Rafael, PO Box 1415, Santo Domingo (tel: 687-7111).

Santo Domingo-Las Américas International Airport, Santo Domingo (tel: 549-0450/0480).

Ministry of tourism

Secretaría de Estado de Turismo, PO Apdo 497, Avenida México esp, 30 de Marzo, Ofiinas Gubernanentales Bloque B, Santo Domingo (tel: 221-4660; e-mail: dominicantourism@globalserve.net).

Other useful addresses

Asociación Dominicana de Empresas de Inversión Extranjera (ASIEX), Av Independencia Santo Domingo, RD (tel: 535-6165; fax: 535-1744).

Asociación Dominicana de Exportadores (ADOEXPO), Av W Churchill 5, Santo Domingo (tel: 532-6779; fax: 533-9734).

Asociación Dominicana de Zonas Francas (ADOZONA), Gustavo Mejía Ricart 72, Santo Domingo, RD (tel: 566-0230, 566-0437).

British Embassy, Floor 7, Edificio Corominas Pepín, Avenida 27 de Febrero No. 233, Santo Domingo (tel: 472-7111; fax: 427-7574).

Centro Dominicano de Promoción de Exportaciones (CEDOPEX), Av 27 de Febrero, Plaza de la Independencia, Santo Domingo, RD (tel: 530-5549; fax: 530-8208).

Consejo Nacional de Zonas Francas de Exportación, Leopoldo Navarro 61, Edif San Rafael 5ta Planta, Santo Domingo (tel: 686-8077; fax: 686-8079).

Corporación de Fomento Industrial, Av 27 de Febrero, Plaza de la Independencia, Santo Domingo, RD (tel: 530-1686; fax: 530-1303).

ITT-America Cables and Radio Inc, Julio Verne 21, Santo Domingo (tel: 682-3115).

Public Enterprise Reform Committee, Gustavo Mejía Ricart No 73, Santo Domingo (tel: 683-3591; fax: 683-3964).

RCA Global Communications Inc, Edificio Diez, Calle Conde 203, Santo Domingo (tel: 682-3722).

Secretariat of State for Finance, Avda México, Santo Domingo, DN.

Secretariat of State for Industry and Commerce, Edif. de Oficinas Gubernamentales 7, Avda México, Santo Domingo, DN (tel: 685-171).

Caribbean Net News: www.caribbeannetnews.com

Prensa Latina: www.prensalatina.com.mx

Internet sites

Dominican Republic One: http://www.dr1.com/

Export promotion (in Spanish): http://www.cedopex.gov.do/

Easter Island

KEY FACTS

Official name: Isla de Pascua (Easter Island) (Rapa Nui)

Head of State: President of Chile: Michelle Bachelet (from 11 Mar 2014); represented by *Intendenta* (provincial governor) Carmen Cardinali Paoa (from 13 Aug 2010)

Head of government: Mayor Pedro Pablo Edmunds Paoa (since Dec 2012)

Area: 180 square km

Population: 5,806 (2012, census)

Capital: Hanga Roa (only inhabited township)

Official language: Spanish

Currency: Chilean peso (CH$) = 100 centavos

Exchange rate: CH$689.04 per US$ (Sept 2015)

Visitor numbers: 40,000 (annually)*

* estimated figure

COUNTRY PROFILE

1680 Work on the *moai* (the large stone statues for which Easter Island is famous) ceased due to tribal wars induced by overpopulation and famine.
1722 The Dutch navigator, Jacob Roggeveen, came to the island on Easter Sunday, hence its name.
1770 Spaniards came from Peru and named the island San Carlos.
1774 Captain Cook visited the island.
1862–63 More than 1,000 islanders were kidnapped and despatched to Peru to work on the guano islands and plantations. Only 15 survived to be repatriated, but some were carrying infectious diseases that quickly decimated the population.
1866 Catholic missionaries converted the remaining population to Christianity.
1871 Conflict between the missionaries and a French settler, who had established a sheep farm, forced the missionaries to leave with around 100 followers. Around 110 natives remained on the island.
1888 The island was annexed by Chile.
1966 The international airport opened and Chile declared the island a province.
1986 The airport runway was extended for use as an emergency landing strip for the US Nasa space shuttle.
1996 Easter Island was declared a World Heritage Site by Unesco.
2002 The first outbreak of dengue fever in Chile occurred on Easter Island.
2003 Unesco awarded a German company a contract for US$11.5 million to restore the stone *moai*. Work was completed in 2005.
2006 Melania Carolina Hotu Hey was appointed as *Intendenta* (provincial governor).
2008 A Finnish visitor was arrested for damaging an ancient monument when he chipped off a piece of a *moai*, while wishing to find how hard the stone was. He was later forced to make a public apology, pay a fine of US$17,000 and was banned from the island until 2011.
2009 In a referendum, residents voted by up to 90 per cent in favour of legislation to curb the number of migrants from Chile allowed to live and work on the island. As tourism developed, hundreds of Chileans from the mainland migrated to work in bars, hotels and as taxi drivers. Luz Zasso Paoa became mayor. In August the Rapa Nui blocked the airport for two days, demanding the length of time tourists can stay be restricted.
2010 Pedro Edmunds Paoa (a pro-independence politician) was appointed provincial governor of Easter Island. Around 70 people, who had been squatting on public land in Hanga Roa were evicted; the squatters claimed the land was ancestral and therefore theirs. Pedro Edmunds resigned and Carmen Cardinali was appointed to the post of *Intendenta*. Clashes between native islanders of the Rapu Nui group and Chilean police occurred, after the group refused to leave buildings occupied earlier in 2010; they claimed the buildings had been 'illegally taken' from their ancestors. Security forces used pellet guns and rubber bullets, injuring around 19 demonstrators, one of whom was air-lifted to Chile for emergency medical treatment; arrests were made and reinforcements travelled to the island.
2011 Police evicted a group of native Rapa Nui from a luxury hotel in February. The indigenous Hitorangi clan had occupied the Hangaroa Village and Spa since 2010, protesting that their ancestors had been cheated out of ownership of the hotel land. They were also protesting at plans to develop Easter Island.
2012 A census was undertaken on 31 August; the preliminary result was 5,806 people recorded. A new hospital was opened by the Chilean government.
2013 The Rapa Nui continued to remonstrate with the government in Santiago to restrict the number of tourists allowed to visit the island, and for tighter controls on the number of mainland Chileans taking the few jobs available on the island. They have requested more money for healthcare and education and threatened to lodge a complaint against the government at the International Court of Justice in the Hague.
2014 Some 80,000 tourists visited Easter Island mid-2013–mid-2014.
2015 The Easter Island Statue Project went public on the digging work they have been doing round a number the 'head' statues since 2012. It turns out that the heads have bodies too. Many of the <I>moai<W0> are on the slope of a volcano and were buried up to their necks after one particulary severe eruption.

Political structure
Easter Island is administered as a province of Chile (part of the Valparaíso region), with a governor and locally elected council.
Elections are held every four years for six councillors, who then elect the mayor.
A Council of Elders was formed in 1983 to represent the interests of the native *Rapa Nuis* (Easter Islanders).

Form of state
Province of Chile

Political parties
Island politicians belong to a number of national political parties including Partido Demócrata Cristiano (PDC) (Christian Democratic Party), Partido Humanista (PH) (Humanist Party), Unión Demócrata Independiente (UDI) (Independent Democratic Union) and the Partido por la Democracia (PLD) (Democratic Party)

Political situation
The pro-independent movement in Isla de Pascua (Easter Island) (Rapa Nui) was given tacit support by the former governor Pedro Edmunds Proa when, in 2010 he allowed islanders to squat on government land close to the centre of Hanga Roa. Despite claims that it was ancestral land and denials that they were trespassing the central government in Chile moved quickly to diffuse the situation by replacing Governor Pedro Edmunds Proa with another islander politician Carmen Cardinali, on 13 August. Governor Cardinali authorised the eviction of the protestors and demolition of their temporary structures.
The Rapa Nui continued to remonstrate with the government in Santiago to restrict the number of tourists allowed to visit the island, and for tighter controls on the number of mainland Chileans who the Rapa Nui say are taking over their jobs, their land and, ultimately, control of the economy . They have requested more money for healthcare and education and in 2013 threatened to lodge a complaint against the government at the International Court of Justice in the Hague. Rapa Nui Assembly leader, Leviante Araki, reportedly said that the island could ask to become part of Polynesia, which is closer than Chile.

Population
5,806 (2012, census). There is a high level of migration and emigration.
Population density: 35 persons per square km.
Last census: 5,806 (31 August 2012)
Annual growth rate: 0.0 per cent (2003)

Religions
Christianity

Main cities
Hanga Roa is the only inhabited township.

Languages spoken
Rapa Nui, an Eastern Polynesian language, is spoken. English is not used.

Official language/s
Spanish

Media
Press
News publications are pamphlets and internet connections, such as *Te Rapa Nui* (www.rapanui.co.cl). Newspapers from the mainland have to be flown in and may be days old. The bi-annual (May and October) *Rapa Nui Journal* (www.islandheritage.org) is an academic publication. *El Correo del Moai* is an on-line newspaper.

Broadcasting
Radio: There are several radio stations, broadcasting in Spanish, including the (Chilean) government-run Radio Cooperativa (www.cooperativa.cl), the private Radio Activa (www.radioactiva.cl) from Santiago, ADN Radio (www.adnradio.cl) and Armada de Chile broadcasts to military personnel. Radio Manukena is a community radio station broadcasting in the local language.
Television: Satellite television is broadcast from Chile (TV Chile: www.tvchile.cl) with reception available on the island.

Economy
Tourism is the principal industry, which offers employment to a significant proportion of the population. There are a number of hotels and guesthouses catering for visitors interested in archaeological and activity pursuits. The Rapa Nui National Park and open museum encompasses almost the entire island and is run by the inhabitants. Flights link the island with Santiago, Chile, and French Polynesia.
Population estimates by explorers in the eighteenth and nineteenth century ranged from 1000--3000. However, severe depopulation occurred in the late nineteenth century as smallpox, kidnappings and relocation ravaged the already small population. In 1981, there were around 1,900 inhabitants upon the island. Tourism is the principal industry, which offers employment to a significant proportion of the population. There are a number of hotels and guesthouses catering for visitors interested in archaeological and activity pursuits. The Rapa Nui National Park and open museum encompasses almost the entire island and is run by the inhabitants. Flights link the island with Santiago, Chile, and French Polynesia.
Population estimates by explorers in the eighteenth and nineteenth century ranged from 1000--3000. However, severe depopulation occurred in the late nineteenth century as smallpox, kidnappings and relocation ravaged the already small population. In 1981, there were around 1,900 inhabitants upon the island.
Fishing and commerce also provide income.
Problems facing the tiny island in recent times include dengue fever, lack of sanitation, over-fishing and damage to the *moai*, the giant stone statues that have made the island famous. In 2014, a new hospital and recycling plant has led to improvements regarding the quality of life on the island. However many problems still pervade the island. 20 tonnes of rubbish are produced a day, and, whilst the recycling plant is aiding in processing some of it, much of the islands garbage cannot be disposed off quickly enough.
In short, Easter Island cannot maintain the amount of visitors that contribute towards the vast amount of waste. A tax may be imposed in the future, similar to that of the Galapagos Islands, to ensure protected areas are free from rubbish.

External trade
As a province of Chile, all international trade agreements are negotiated by the government in Santiago.

Imports
Main imports are food, fuel, construction materials and machinery from Chile.

Exports
Main exports are tuna, avocados and pineapples to Chile.

Agriculture
Farming
Traditional subsistence farming is carried out.
Although the island is predominantly grassland, pine, eucalyptus and fruit trees have been planted.
The island's main crops are bananas, pineapples, sweet potatoes, yams, sugar cane, maize, potatoes, tomatoes, castor beans, melons, grapes and avocados.
Sheep farming has declined rapidly since the mid-twentieth century due to soil erosion. There are wild horses in addition to those used as draught animals and for riding. Poultry bred on the island includes pigeons, quail and ducks.

Fishing
Lobster, tuna and king fish are an important local source of protein.

Industry and manufacturing
There is a small manufacturing sector, based on the production of local handicrafts.

Tourism
Easter Island is famous for its giant stone heads, called *moai* (statues), of which nearly a thousand of these ancient sculptures are strewn along the coastline and

extinct volcano. Easter Island was awarded Unesco status as a world heritage site in 1995 and in 2005, the *moai* were restored by Unesco. Easter Island is visited by over 65,000 tourists each year not only to see the *moai* but they are also attracted in early February by the Tapati Festival. Many visitors arrive either by airplane or cruise ships, which because the island lacks a deep-water harbour must land passengers and crew by tenders. There are over a dozen hotels and a number of hostels catering for visitors. There are also opportunities for hiking, horse-riding, cycling and swimming. Mass tourism is opposed by the Rapa Nui, considering that it endangers the fragile ecosystem.

Hydrocarbons

There are no known oil reserves; all domestic needs are met by imports from Chile.

Energy

The former state-owned and now limited company, Sociedad Agricola y Servicios Isla de Pascua (Sasipa) manages the supply of electricity on the island. In 2007 a 15-year contract began to develop and plan the provision of a comprehensive electrical service, including the investment needed to cope with projected growth.

Banking and insurance

Central bank

Banco del Estado de Chile

Time

GMT minus 11 hours

Geography

Easter Island is a small volcanic rock, measuring 166 sq km, in the southern Pacific Ocean. It lies about 3,500km off the coast of Chile, the closest land mass. The nearest inhabited island (Pitcairn) is about 1,600km to the west. The island is roughly triangular in shape, with a rugged coastline and few beaches. Inland are low rolling hills and grasslands. There is no flowing water; volcanic craters round the edge of the island hold standing water.

Hemisphere

Southern

Climate

Subtropical, cooled by constant winds. Average rainfall is 1,250mm falling mainly in June–July; average temperature ranges from 16–27 degrees Celsius.

Entry requirements

Passports

Required by all, with the exception of tourists travelling from Argentina, Brazil, Colombia, Paraguay and Uruguay, for whom national identity cards are sufficient. Entry will be permitted only with proof of return/onward passage and sufficient funds for stay.

Visa

As a province of Chile, the requirements are the same. Citizens of neighbouring countries or most EU states do not need visas. For further details contact the local embassy. Business visas are not required by those citizens who do not need a tourist visa; all others, including those who do not normally require them but who are visiting on short-term contracts or receive fees from a local company, do need a visa.

On arrival a 'tourist card' is issued and must be returned when leaving. Proof of onward/return passage is necessary.

Health (for visitors)

Mandatory precautions

Vaccination certificates are required for yellow fever if travelling from an infected area.

Advisable precautions

Vaccinations for diphtheria, tuberculosis, hepatitis A and B, polio, tetanus and typhoid are recommended. There is a risk of rabies.

Telecommunications

Telephone/fax

There is a limited telephone service available. There is no direct international dialling, although satellite links enable calls to be made through the international operator in Chile.

Internet/e-mail

There are internet bars in Hanga Roa.

Getting there

Air

National airline: Lan (part of the Latam Airlines Group)

International airport/s: Mataveri International (IPC), 1.6km south of Hanga Roa.

Surface

Main port/s: Hanga Roa.

Getting about

National transport

There are few surfaced roads. Four-wheel drive vehicles, motor cycles and horses are the main means of transportation. Minibuses are used by tourists.

Car hire

Make local enquiries regarding availability of car hire.

BUSINESS DIRECTORY

The addresses listed below are a selection only. While World of Information makes every endeavour to check these addresses, we cannot guarantee that changes have not been made, especially to telephone numbers and area codes. We would welcome any corrections.

Telephone area codes

The international direct dialling (IDD) code for Easter Island is +56 (Chile) followed area code 32 and Easter Island number 100 + subscriber's number.

Other useful addresses

Gobernación Provincial, Isla de Pascua (tel: 100-254)

Internet sites

Easter Island Foundation: www.netaxs.com/~trance/rapanui.html

Ecuador

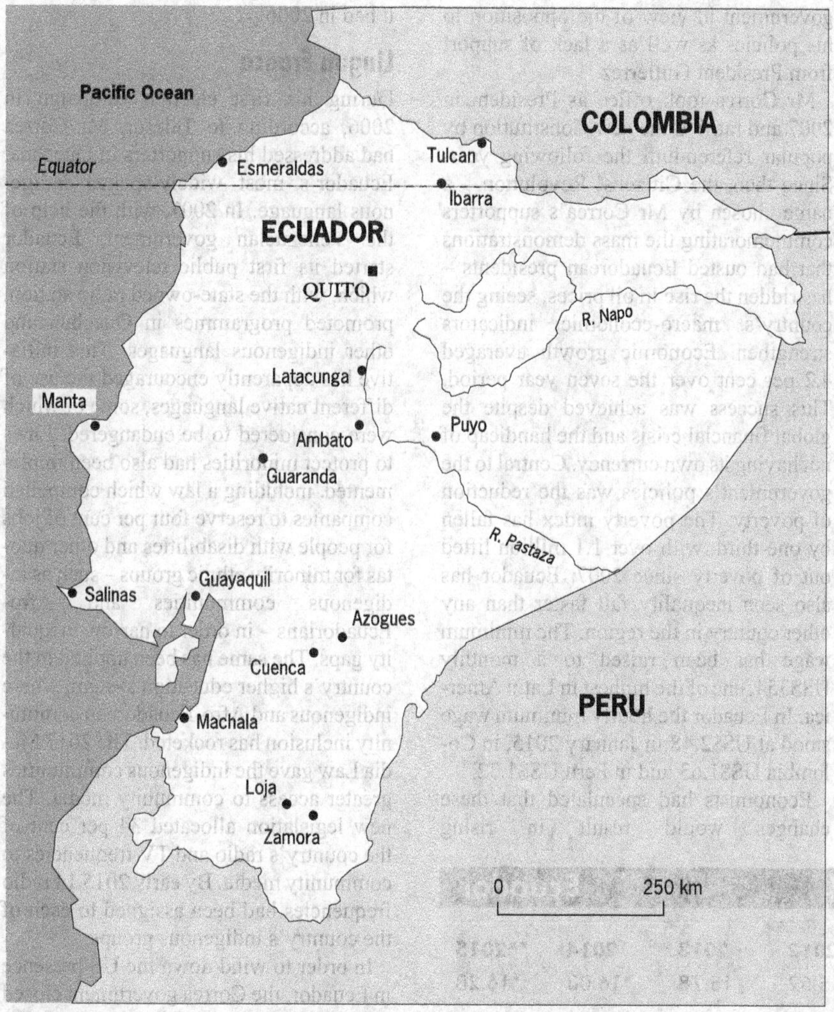

KEY FACTS

Official name: República del Ecuador (Republic of Ecuador)

Head of State: President Rafael Vicente Correa Delgado (from 2007; re-elected 26 Apr 2009 and 17 February 2013)

Head of government: President Rafael Correa (since 15 January 2007).

Ruling party: Movimiento PAIS (Patria Altiva i Soberana) (Proud and Sovereign Fatherland Movement)

Area: 270,670 square km

Population: 16.03 million (2014)*

Capital: Quito

Official language: Spanish

Currency: US dollar (US$) = 100 cents

Exchange rate: US$25,000.00 per US$ (Sep 2015)

GDP per capita: US$6,286 (2014)*

GDP real growth: 3.64% (2014)*

GDP: US$100.76 billion (2014)*

Labour force: 4.48 million (2010)

Unemployment: 5.00% (2014)

Inflation: 3.59% (2014)

Oil production: 556,000 bpd (2014)

Balance of trade: -US$637.80 million (2013)

Annual FDI: US$567.77 million (2011)

* estimated figure

In May 2015 President Rafael Correa presented his lengthy annual report to the nation, in which he detailed the economic issues affecting the country, as well as the achievements of his government during 2014 and over the 8 years of his presidency, which he preferred to refer to as the Citizens Revolution. However broad the President's smile, in mid-2015 the Quito rumour mill was busily bubbling away. An anonymous recording circulating on social media implied that some members of the military hierarchy had withdrawn their support from the Correa government. The men in the hot seat were Ecuador's defence ministe,r Fernando Cordero, and the chief of the Armed Forces Joint Command, Luis Garzón, both of whom were quick to deny the rumours. For some time there had been right wing demonstrations on the streets of Quito and Guayaquil, in protest at increased taxes for Ecuador's wealthier citizens. The demonstrators had called for the President's resignation. There was also a sense of déjà vu about the rumour mill: the Ecuadorean military had long played a significant role in Ecuadorian politics.

Transformation?

Summarising the government's overview in a television interview, the secretary of planning and development, Pabel Muñoz, singled out the fall in rates of income poverty by 15 percentage points, and in what was described as 'consumption poverty' by 12.5 per cent; 'basic needs' poverty was also down by 16 percentage points. May 2015 marked two years of Mr Correa's third term as president of Ecuador. Since 2007, he has led the transformation of Ecuador. After decades of being one of the poorest countries in the region, the government has endeavoured to introduce reforms that have, in principle, benefited Ecuador's 'excluded' majorities.

As reported by Telesur (www.telesurtv.net/english) in adopting these measures, Ecuador had joined Bolivia and Venezuela in rejecting what it descried as the 'extreme free-market policies' advocated by the International Monetary Fund (IMF) and similar institutions. In 2014, President Correa had announced that 'People must prevail over capital.' He went on to ask just who it was that governments serve: 'Elites or the majority? Capital or humankind? The market or society? Policies and programmes depend on who holds the balance of power.'

Before his election as President, Mr Correa had served as the economy minister during the interim government of Alfredo Palacio, who had succeeded the ousted President Lucio Gutiérrez. Gutiérrez was the seventh president to be forced out of office in less than a decade. Ecuador had experienced severe political instability following the economy's collapse triggered by the banking crisis of 1999, which in turn lead to the adoption of the US dollar as the national currency in 2000. High unemployment had lead to almost 10 per cent of Ecuadoreans emigrating. As economy minister, Mr Correa had expressed his opposition to Palacio's plans of signing a free trade agreement with the United States and ultimately resigned after the World Bank placed an important loan on hold. Mr Correa left the government in view of the opposition to his policies as well as a lack of support from President Gutiérrez.

Mr Correa took office as President in 2007 and ratified the new Constitution by popular referendum the following year. Since then, the Citizens' Revolution – a name chosen by Mr Correa's supporters commemorating the mass demonstrations that had ousted Ecuadorean presidents – has ridden the rise in oil prices, seeing the country's macro-economic indicators strengthen. Economic growth averaged 4.2 per cent over the seven year period. This success was achieved despite the global financial crisis and the handicap of not having its own currency. Central to the government's policies was the reduction of poverty. The poverty index has fallen by one-third, with over 1.1 million lifted out of poverty since 2007. Ecuador has also seen inequality fall faster than any other country in the region. The minimum wage has been raised to a monthly US$354, one of the highest in Latin America. In Ecuador the hourly minimum wage stood at US$2.48 in January 2015, in Colombia US$1.63 and in Peru US$1.32.

Economists had speculated that these changes would result in rising unemployment, the contrary seemed to be the case. By 2015 Ecuador had the lowest unemployment rate in its history at 4.9 per cent. It also had the second highest level of public investment in higher education in the world. Tax evasion had been addressed, a problem which had been draining public revenues. By 2014 Ecuador was raising three times more in taxes than it had in 2006.

Lingua Franca

During his first election campaign in 2006, according to Telesur, Mr Correa had addressed his supporters in Quechua, Ecuador's most widely-spoken indigenous language. In 2007, with the help of the Venezuelan government, Ecuador started its first public television station which, with the state-owned radio station, promoted programmes in Quechua and other indigenous languages. This initiative has apparently encouraged the use of different native languages, some of which were considered to be endangered. Laws to protect minorities had also been implemented, including a law which compelled companies to reserve four per cent of jobs for people with disabilities and other quotas for minority ethnic groups – such as indigenous communities and Afro-Ecuadorians – in order to narrow inequality gaps. The same has been applied in the country's higher education system, where indigenous and Afro-Ecuadorean community inclusion has rocketed. The 2013 Media Law gave the indigenous communities greater access to community media. The new legislation allocated 34 per cent of the country's radio and TV frequencies to community media. By early 2015 14 radio frequencies had been assigned to each of the country's indigenous groups.

In order to wind down the US presence in Ecuador, the Correa government closed the US military base in Manta, as well as taking control of the country's oil and other natural resources. Moves to cancel Ecuador's significant debt payments resulted in the 2010 attempted *coup d'état* against President Correa.

The economy – The IMF

In July 2014, the IMF presented its annual assessment of the Ecuadorian economy, noting that Ecuador had made significant economic and social progress over the previous decade. Economic growth had averaged about 4.5 per cent since 2001 and inflation had gradually declined to around 3 per cent a year. The financial stability that had been achieved with dollarisation, had in the view of the IMF,

KEY INDICATORS — Ecuador

	Unit	2011	2012	2013	2014	**2015
Population	m	*15.01	*15.52	15.78	*16.03	*16.28
Gross domestic product (GDP)	US$bn	66.40	87.50	94.47	*100.76	*102.66
GDP per capita	US$	4,424	5,638	5,989	*6,286	*6,307
GDP real growth	%	7.8	5.1	4.6	*3.6	*1.9
Inflation	%	4.5	5.1	2.7	3.6	*3.2
Unemployment	%	6.0	4.9	4.3	5.0	*5.0
Oil output	'000 bpd	509.0	505.0	527.0	556.0	–
Exports (fob) (goods)	US$m	23,099.7	24,647.6	25,687.2	–	–
Imports (fob) (goods)	US$m	23,233.0	24,578.7	26,325.0	–	–
Balance of trade	US$m	-133.3	68.9	-637.8	–	–
Current account	US$m	-259.3	-279.0	-983.0	*-840.0	*-3,387.0
Total reserves minus gold	US$m	2,605.0	1,080.0	3,328.0	3,484.1	–
Foreign exchange	US$m	2,552.5	1,012.0	3,256.2	–	–
Exchange rate	per US$	25,000.00	25,000.00	25,000.00	25,000.00	–

* estimated figure ** forecast figure

together with low inflation, sustained growth and higher social spending, helped reduce poverty and improve Ecuador's social indicators. The high oil prices in the previous few years had generated a windfall income that supported the balance of payments and fiscal accounts, facilitating higher public spending.

After rebounding strongly from the impact of the global financial crisis, the IMF reported that growth had moderated somewhat over the previous two years. Gross domestic product (GDP) growth had levelled out at an annual 4.5 per cent in 2013, down from 5 per cent in 2012, reflecting less buoyant domestic demand, but remained slightly above potential. Inflation fell to 2.7 per cent in 2013, from 4.2 per cent in 2012, owing to the unwinding of supply side shocks. The unemployment rate fell to a historic low while real wages continued to rise. However, a fiscal deficit had re-emerged despite buoyant tax revenue collection. Higher capital spending widened the fiscal deficit to 4.7 per cent of GDP, financed mainly by loans from China. Ecuador's gross public debt stood at 24.4 per cent of GDP at the end of 2013, which was low by regional standards. The current account deficit widened to 1.3 per cent of GDP in 2013 from 0.4 per cent in 2011–12. Credit to the private sector and banks' profitability declined but the financial system remained healthy.

According to the IMF, the economy was expected to grow at 4 per cent in 2014-15 but the outlook was less favourable than in the past, as oil prices were expected to fall and interest rates in the US were expected to rise over the medium-term. Risks to the outlook were broadly balanced. However, the ability to respond to these risks was limited given the absence of monetary policy in Ecuador's fully dollarised economy and the limited ability to react on the fiscal side. On the downside, further rises in US dollar interest rates (and additional strengthening of the dollar) might jeopardise growth prospects and competitiveness. On the upside, geopolitical tensions might well increase oil prices, which would support growth and improve the fiscal position.

While the public sector had been an important engine of growth over the previous several years, the private sector needed a larger role to avoid potential fiscal and external imbalances. The emergence of sizeable fiscal deficits called for restraint in public spending plans and a moderation in current spending was necessary to accommodate the growth of the public sector investment programme (PSIP). The fundamental objective of the PSIP is to reverse the expected decline in oil revenues, not only by increasing oil production (see 'Energy' below), but also by replacing fuel imports and diversifying energy resources. In the financial system, it would be important for new banking legislation and regulation to support growth prospects.

The economy – ECLAC concurs

According to the United Nations Economic Commission for Latin America and the Caribbean (ECLAC), the slowdown in economic activity in Ecuador continued in 2014, with GDP expanding by 4 per cent (as against 4.5 per cent in 2013 and 5.2 per cent in 2012) as a result of more muted growth in investment and private consumption as well as a slackening in public consumption. This trend was offset by higher export volumes on the back of increases in oil production and, to a greater extent, rising output of bananas, cocoa and shrimp. For 2015, for general State budgetary purposes, the Ecuadorian authorities forecast inflation of 3.9 per cent and an average oil price of US$79.7 per barrel. ECLAC estimated that GDP will expand by some 3.8 per cent in 2015.

ECLAC noted that in 2014 monetary policy had been less expansionary than in previous years. According to available data, central government expenditure between January and July 2014 was up by 4 per cent compared with the same period of 2013, which had seen public expenditure soar by 17.1 per cent in respect of the same period of 2012. This more modest growth in spending reflected the smaller rise in current expenditure (3.1 per cent) and a cooling off in capital expenditure on fixed investment (-0.2 per cent). Current revenue, meanwhile, rose by 0.4 per cent in the same period, reflecting the continuing slump in oil revenues and a slowdown in non-oil income. The overall central government deficit thus widened from US$846.6 million in the period from January to July 2013 to US$1.315 billion in the same period of 2014. In the first half of the year current revenue in the non-financial public sector was up by 7.9 per cent on the same period of 2013, chiefly as a result of the greater operating surpluses run by non-financial public enterprises (53.3 per cent). Total spending rose by 5.6 per cent, boosted by the rise in expenditure on gross fixed capital formation, given that current expenditure grew by only 1.1 per cent.

According to ECLAC, in 2014 public debt continued its upward trend as financing requirements increased. It stood at 27.7 per cent of GDP in September 2014 (up from 24.2 per cent in December 2013), owing to growth in both domestic debt (which rose from 10.5 per cent of GDP in December 2013 to 11.2 per cent of GDP in September 2014) and external debt (which grew from 13.7 per cent of GDP to 16.5 per cent of GDP in the same period). Most of the rise in domestic public debt in 2014 was in the form of long-term bond issues, while external public debt expanded as a result of growth in debt to Chinese institutions (especially in late 2013 and early 2014) and a US$2 billion sovereign bond offering in the international market in June 2014. Readily available international reserves peaked at US$6.689 billion in September 2014 and stood at US$5.7 billion in November. China remained Ecuador's largest foreign public creditor, holding around 30 per cent of its external public debt. In April 2014 the Banco Central del Ecuador (central bank) changed benchmark interest rates, which had remained constant throughout 2012 and 2013. The deposit rate was increased from 4.53 per cent to 5.11 per cent and the lending rate was lowered from 8.7 per cent to 7.64 per cent. The maximum conventional reference rate remained the same. Both the lending and deposit rates have since been changed. In November 2014 the lending rate stood at 5.07 per cent, while the deposit rate was 8.13 per cent. Individual credit segments also saw changes. Between January and September 2014 total lending by the private financial system bounced back, surging by 10.1 per cent on figures from the same period of 2013; growth in public sector lending tailed off, expanding 3.3 per cent on the year-earlier period.

ECLAC reported that Ecuador's negotiations with the European Union (EU) continued in 2014, culminating in an agreement (which had to be ratified by the relevant national parliaments before it can fully enter into force) to replace the current agreement under the preferential tariffs system which expired on 31 December 2014. In September the Basic Monetary and Financial Code was adopted, which lays down provisions for, among other things, the use of electronic money.

Between January and September 2014, exports expanded by 7.5 per cent in respect of the same period of 2013, driven by booming exports of shrimp (57.5 per cent) and cocoa and processed cocoa products (43.5 per cent), despite stagnant oil exports (-0.1 per cent), mainly as a result of a precipitous drop in exports of petroleum derivatives (59.7 per cent), while exports of crude oil rose by 2.9 per cent. Goods imports contracted by 0.4 per cent compared to the same period of 2013. Except for imports of fuels and fuel derivatives (which were up 6.3 per cent), most other imports were down: consumer goods imports fell by 0.7 per cent, raw materials by 0.2 per cent and capital goods by 5.8 per cent. There was therefore a balance of trade surplus of US$502.3 million, compared with a deficit of US$987.9 million for the same period of 2013.

According to ECLAC, Ecuador's external debt stood at 22.8 per cent of GDP in September 2014, compared to 19.9 per cent in December 2013. This deterioration was primarily attributable to rising external public debt, given that external private debt was practically unchanged on December 2013 levels (6.3 per cent of GDP as opposed to 6.2 per cent of GDP in December 2013). GDP grew by 4 per cent in the first half of 2014, as a result of a sharp slowdown in both public consumption, which crept up by 0.2 per cent in respect of the first half of 2013 (after growth of 8.1 per cent on the year-earlier period in the first half of 2013) and investment, which increased by 2.9 per cent (as opposed to growth of 14.4 per cent in the first half of 2013 on the same period of 2012). Exports of goods and services, meanwhile, expanded by 7.4 per cent in real terms in the same period. Imports of goods and services were up 1.5 per cent (compared with 8.5 per cent in the first half of 2013) as domestic demand cooled. Overall figures for the principal sectors of economic activity, compared with the first half of 2013, showed an improved performance in agriculture and aquaculture, oil, tourism and business services and downturns in government services, the postal service and communications. Construction remained one of the most dynamic sectors. National crude oil production was up 7 per cent between January and August 2014 compared with the same period of 2013, boosted by growth (11.5 per cent) in production by state-owned enterprises while production by private companies fell again (by 5.6 per cent).

The cumulative 12-month rate of inflation to September 2014 was 4.2 per cent, up from the year-on-year rate of 1.7 per cent in the same period of 2013, on the back of an increase in food prices (5.7 per cent). The average urban unemployment rate between January and September 2014 stood at 5.3 per cent, an increase on the figure of 4.7 per cent recorded in the same period of 2013. In January 2014, the standard minimum monthly wage was raised from US$318 to US$340. As a monthly average, it increased by 3.2 per cent in real terms on the same period of 2013, down from an average growth of 6.1 per cent in 2013.

Energy

According to the US government Energy Information Administration (EIA), Ecuador's oil sector traditionally accounts for more than half of the country's export earnings and approximately two-fifths of public sector revenues. Resource nationalism and debates about the economic, strategic and environmental implications of oil sector development have been prominent issues in the politics of Ecuador since your correspondent first visited the country in 1967. Ecuador is the smallest producer in the Organisation of the Petroleum Exporting Countries (Opec producing 556,000 barrels per day (bpd) of petroleum and other liquids in 2014, of which crude oil production was 555,000bpd. A lack of sufficient domestic refining capacity to meet local demand has forced Ecuador to import refined products, limiting net oil revenue. In January 2015, the EIA reported that Ecuador had 8.8 billion barrels of proved crude oil reserves, which was a year-on-year increase of 7 per cent. Ecuador has the third-largest oil reserves in South America, after Venezuela and Brazil. Most of Ecuador's oil reserves are in the Oriente Basin, which is located physically under the Amazon.

In 1992, Ecuador left Opec owing an unpaid debt of more than US$5 billion. Ecuador re-joined the organisation after a 15-year hiatus in 2007. The EIA notes that Ecuador has a 'challenging' investment climate triggered by government initiatives to increase the share of crude oil revenue for the state, an initiative which has contributed to near-stagnant oil production level for over 10 years. The energy mix is largely dependent on oil, which represented 79 per cent of the country's total energy consumption in 2013. Hydroelectric power was the second-largest energy source. Natural gas and non-hydro renewable fuels are also important.

The national oil companies (NOCs) Petroecuador, Petroamazonas and Operaciones Rio Napo, a joint venture between Petroecuador and Petróleos de Venezuela, account for most of the oil production in Ecuador. The remaining production is attributed to fields operated by international oil companies, Repsol (Spain), Eni (Italy), Tecpetrol (Argentina's state-owned company) and Andes Petroleum, which is a consortium of the China National Petroleum Corporation (CNPC, 55 per cent share) and the China Petrochemical Corporation (Sinopec, 45 per cent share).

In 2006, Petroecuador took over the production assets of Occidental Petroleum after contracts expired. In 2009, following a tax dispute, the government also expropriated two blocks assigned to Perenco. Chevron's lengthy legal battle with Ecuadorean plaintiffs also raised questions about the potential costs of investing in Ecuador. In February 2011, a US$18 billion judgment – later reduced to US$9.5 billion was made against Chevron by a court in Lago Agrio, Ecuador, for alleged contamination resulting from crude oil production in the region by Texaco's operations in Ecuador between 1964 and 1990 (Texaco was later acquired by Chevron). On 4 March 2014, a New York District Court ruled that the US$9.5 billion Ecuadorian judgment was the product of fraud and racketeering activity, finding it unenforceable. Since 2009, Ecuador has shifted its energy reliance from the US to China, signing multiple oil-for-loan deals that explicitly guarantee oil exports to China in exchange for loans.

Ecuador exports roughly 70 per cent of the crude oil it produces and it is a leading source of crude oil imports to the US West Coast. In 2014, the United States imported 210,000bpd of Ecuadorean crude oil. Other leading destinations for Ecuadorean crude are Chile, Peru and Panama. Ecuador was the third-largest source of foreign oil for the US West Coast which was the destination of most Ecuadorean oil exports to the United States. To diversify, Ecuador began exporting crude oil to China in 2012. In 2013, the United States received roughly 63 per cent of all Ecuadorean crude oil exports and remained the largest importer of Ecuadorean crude oil in 2014. Chile, Peru, Panama and India were also among the top five importers of Ecuadorean crude oil in 2014.

As of January 2015, Ecuador had an estimated 212 billion cubic feet (bcf) of proved natural gas reserves. The country's gross natural gas production was 54bcf in 2013, of which 37bcf was marketed and the remaining amount was flared and vented. Dry natural gas production (occurring when associated liquid hydrocarbons are removed) was 18bcf, of which all was domestically consumed. Ecuador's low natural gas utilisation rates are mainly the result of a lack of infrastructure needed to capture and market natural gas. Located in the Gulf of Guayaquil, the Amistad field is Ecuador's primary natural gas project. The field is operated by Petroamazonas and produced an estimated 48 million cubic feet per day (MMcf/d) between January 2014 and September 2014. Amistad's natural gas production flows to the Machala facility, a 130-megawatt (MW) onshore, gas-fired power plant that supplies electricity to the Guayaquil region. Exploration activities are done mostly by Petroamazonas, although Andes Petroleum, ENAP (Chile) and PdVSA (Venezuela) also participate in exploration.

Risk assessment

Economy	Fair
Politics	Fair
Regional stability	Good

COUNTRY PROFILE

1530 Ecuador formed part of the Inca Empire until its conquest by Francisco Pizarro of Spain who landed on the Ecuadoran coast en route to Peru and defeat the Incas.

1822 Antonio José de Sucre Alcalá defeated the monarchist forces of Spain at the battle of Pichincha. Ecuador gained its independence as part of the federation of Gran Colombia.

1930 Ecuador seceded from Gran Colombia and became an independent republic.

1941 Peru invaded the mineral-rich province of El Oro.

1942 Ecuador lost about 200,000 square kilometres of the disputed land to Peru.

1960s and 1970s A series of elected and appointed presidents (usually by the armed forces) ruled Ecuador. Few saw out their full terms of office.

1967 A new constitution was came into law.

1968 Jose Maria Velasco was elected president for the fifth time. As support declined he had assumed dictatorial powers by 1970.

1972 Ecuador became a significant oil producer. General Guillermo Rodriguez Lara became president after overthrowing Jose Maria Velasco

1978 A new constitution was approved, providing for presidential elections.

1979 Jaime Roldós became president. Democratisation was encouraged and supported by US policy.

1981 Roldós was killed. Oswaldo Hurtado became president.

1984 President Febres Cordero introduced free-market economy measures. An earthquake destroyed a long section of Ecuador's only oil pipeline.

1992 Sixto Durán Ballén became president. Ecuador resigned its membership of the Organisation of Petroleum Exporting Countries (Opec) in order to increase production.

1997 President Abdala Bucarem was removed from office; he was accused of corruption and mental incompetence. Fabian Alarcón, became interim president. Popular protests called for a national assembly and new constitution.

1998 A new constitution was inaugurated. Jamil Mahuad Witt became president.

2000 With the economy in recession and inflation running at almost 60 per cent, the US dollar was adopted, by presidential decree, as Ecuador's currency. The rate for changing the sucre was set at 25,000 sucre per US$1. Mahuad was ousted during widespread protests. Vice President Gustavo Noboa assumed the presidency.

2002 Colonel Lucio Gutiérrez became president. Indigenous peoples protested against the oil companies, bringing production to a halt and demanding that more revenue be spent on their communities.

2003 Former president Noboa escaped to Dominican Republic to avoid corruption charges.

2004 The Congress dismissed and replaced most members of the Supreme Court. Gutiérrez accused the former court of bias in favour of the opposition.

2005 Congress voted (60–2) to remove President Gutiérrez; Vice President Alfredo Palacio became interim president. Former president Gutiérrez was arrested on conspiracy charges following his return from exile in Colombia.

2006 The Partido Renovador Institucional de Acción Nacional (Prian) (Institutional Renewal Party of National Action) won parliamentary elections, but Rafael Correa (PAIS Alianza) won the presidency.

2007 The president called for a Constituent Assembly to reform Congress. Although most members boycotted the session the Congress agreed to a referendum on the proposal. Congress later withdrew its support, claiming the president had changed the agreed text. An electoral tribunal was empowered to conduct the referendum, despite members being threatened with impeachment by Congress. The supreme electoral court dismissed 57 Congress members for attempting to obstruct the referendum; 21 substitute Congress members were sworn in, achieving the 50-plus quorum. The referendum was passed when 81.72 per cent voted in favour of the proposition to re-write the constitution and form a Constituent Assembly (turnout 71 per cent). Elections to the new Constituent Assembly were won by the president's political party PAIS Alianza. Having dissolved Congress, the Constituent Assembly was given a mandate to draft a new constitution to replace the congress. All visitors were required to buy a permit to land on the Galápagos Islands. As a conservation measure, the Tarjeta de Control de Transito (TCT) (transit control card) limits the number of people who may visit the islands at any one time.

2008 Ecuador cut diplomatic relations with Colombia for three months, following pre-emptive strikes by Colombia against its domestic terrorists, Fuerzas Armadas Revolucionarias de Colombia-Ejército del Pueblo (Farc) (Revolutionary Armed Forces of Colombia-Peoples' Army) hiding out in Ecuador and Venezuela. Over a dozen Farc members including the senior Farc leader Raul Reyes were killed. The new draft constitution was agreed by a majority of the Constituent Assembly and put to a national referendum. The new constitution was approved by 64 per cent of the vote. President Correa declared that Ecuador would default on billions of US dollars of foreign debt, which he described as 'illegitimate'.

2009 In early presidential elections, incumbent Rafael Correa won 51.99 per cent of the vote, his closest rival, former president Lucio Gutiérrez, won 28.24 per cent. In parliamentary elections for the new National Congress, Movimiento PAIS (PAIS Movement) won 45.78 per cent of the vote (59 seats out of 124) and Partido Sociedad Patriótica 21 de Enero (PSP) (January 21 Patriotic Society Party) 14.9 per cent (19).

2010 The UN withdrew the Galápagos Islands from its list of endangered world heritage sites, after the government improved its protection of the natural environment and unique biodiversity. The government signed a US$3.6 billion trust fund deal with the UN not to develop and exploit the Yasuni National Park, which contains an estimated one billion barrels of oil and thousands of species of trees, endangered mammals such as jaguars, monkeys and otters, as well as hundreds of bird species. The rich Amazon rainforest is also home to rarely seen indigenous aboriginal tribes. The UN Development Programme (UNDP) will administer the money raised from governments, organisations and individuals to pay for the trust fund. A 48-hour state of emergency was imposed as President Correa was held by protesting police for 10 hours in a hospital until rescued by the army. The Police had been protesting against civil service reforms that would have cut their benefits. President Correa described the attack as an attempted coup. A national census was held.

2011 In March, scientists launched a campaign to catch and kill thousands of invasive rats that threaten indigenous animals on the Galápagos Islands.

Year-on-year GDP growth for the first quarter was 8.6 per cent compared to the same period in 2010, according to the Central Bank of Ecuador and was the highest growth in ten-years. Preliminary results of the 2010 census, published on 11 July, recorded a population of 14.3 million inhabitants recorded.

2012 On 19 June, Julian Assange (founder of Wikileaks) asked for political asylum in Ecuador's London embassy. On 25 July, the Inter-American Court of Human Rights ruled that the government had ignored the rights of the residents of Sarayaku to be consulted before it granted permission for an energy project to the Argentine Campañía General de Combustibles (CGC). On 16 August the UK's Foreign Office warned that it could lift the embassy's diplomatic status and arrest Assange (to be extradited to Sweden). On 18 August, President Correa granted Assange asylum until the UK and Sweden guaranteed that he would not be extradited to a third country (the US). On 10 November, President Correa confirmed that he would stand for election as president for a third time in February 2013.

2013 Presidental and parliamentary elections were held on 17 February. Mr Correa was re-elected with 57.17 per cent of the vote, with Guillermo Lasso runner up with 22.68 per cent. Turnout was 81.09 per cent.

2014 On 18 August Julian Assange, the WikiLeaks founder, said he intends to leave the Ecuadorean embassy in London 'soon'. He has been in the Embassy building for over two years after being granted political asylum as part of his long-running bid to avoid extradition on sex crime allegations.

2015 In June protesters marched against bills that would greatly increase taxes on inheritances and capital gains.

Political structure

Constitution

28 September 2008, A new constitution was approved by 64 per cent of the vote. Among the 144 articles, the president may now hold office for two consecutive four-year terms; the president may dissolve congress within three years of its four-year term; control of strategic industries has been tightened and monopolies reduced; some foreign national loans were declared illegitimate; farm land that remains inactive may be expropriated and redistributed; free health care for elderly citizens will be provided by the state and civil marriage for single-sex partners is now allowed.

The 1979 constitution was amended in 1998 to strengthen the executive branch of government and abolish mid-term congressional elections and restrict the power of congress to dismiss cabinet ministers.

Ecuador comprises 24 provinces, including the Galapagos Islands, each is administered by an appointed governor.

Form of state

Presidential democratic republic

The executive

Executive power rests with the president, elected by direct vote for a four-year term. The president appoints and presides over a cabinet.

National legislature

The former unicameral Congreso Nacional (National Congress) consisted of 100 members elected from party-lists by proportional representation, for four-year terms. Each of the country's 24 provinces returns a minimum of two deputies, plus an additional member for every 200,000 inhabitants. The 137-member unicameral Asamblea Constituyente (National Assembly) dissolved the National Congress on 29 November 2008. Of the 137 seats, 116 members are directly elected in single-seat constituencies by simple majority vote, 15 members are directly elected in a single nationwide constituency by proportional representation vote, and 6 directly elected in multi-seat constituencies for Ecuadorians living abroad by simple majority vote. Members serve four-year terms.

Legal system

The Supreme Court heads the judiciary. Its judges are appointed by Congress for four-year, renewable terms.

Last elections

19 February 2013 (presidential, parliamentary and Andean Parliament)

Results: Presidential (2013): Rafael Correa won 57.17 per cent of the vote, Guillermo Lasso 22.68 per cent, Lucio Gutiérrez 6.73 per cent, Mauricio Rodas 3.90 per cent, Álvaro Noboa 3.72 per cent and Alberto Acosta 3.26. No other candidate won over 2 per cent. Turnout was 81.09 per cent.

Parliamentary: Movimiento PAIS (PAIS Movement) won 52.3 per cent of the vote (86 seats out of 116 constituency seats, 8 out of 15 PR seats and 6 seats from abroad, total 100 out of 137 seats), Creando Oportunidades (CREO) (Creating Opportunities) (a new party) 11.42 per cent (9 plus 2, 11 seats in total), Partido Social Cristiano (PSC) (Social Christian Party) 13.58 per cent (5 + 1, total 6), Partido Sociedad Patriótica 21 de Enero (PSP) (January 21 Patriotic Society Party) 5.64 per cent (4 + 1, total 5), Unidad Plurinacional de las Izquierdas (Pluinational Unity of the Lefts) 4.72 per cent (1 + 4, total 5), Partido Avanza (Forward Party) 2.92 per cent (5 constituency seats). There were 3 independents, but no other parties won any constituency seats. Turnout was 80.89 per cent.

Next elections

2017 (presidential, parliamentary)

Political parties

Ruling party

Movimiento PAIS (Patria Altiva i Soberana) (Proud and Sovereign Fatherland Movement)

Main opposition party

Creando Oportunidades (CREO) (Creating Opportunities).

Political situation

In the 15 October 2006 parliamentary elections the Partido Renovador Institucional de Acción Nacional (PRIAN) (Institutional Renewal Party of National Action) won 28 of the 100 seats in the national congress, the Partido Sociedad Patriótica 21 de Enero (PSP) (January 21 Patriotic Society Party) won 23, the Partido Social Cristiano (PSC) (Social Christian Party) won 13, and the Partido Roldosista Ecuatoriano (PRE) (Ecuadorian Roldosist Party) won six. No candidates stood for the Alianza Patria Altiva y Soberana (PAIS Alianza) (Proud and Sovereign Fatherland Alliance)). In the first round of the presidential election, Álvaro Noboa (PRIAN) won 26.8 per cent of the vote, Rafael Correa (PAIS Alianza) 22.8 per cent, Gilmar Gutiérrez 17.5 per cent, León Roldós Aguilera 14.8 per cent and Cynthia Viteri 9.6 per cent. The run-off took place on 26 November; Correa won 57 per cent of the vote against Noboa with 43 per cent. Noboa called for a recount, claiming vote rigging by his opponent; the electoral commission confirmed the result on 28 November.

In the 30 September 2007 Asamblea Constituyente (Constituent Assembly) the PAIS Alliance won 74 seats (out of 130)..

Population

16.03 million (2014)* Approximately 60 per cent of the population is aged between 15 and 64 years

Last census: 28 November 2010: 14,306,876

Population density: 42 inhabitants per square km. Urban population 67 per cent (2010 Unicef).

Annual growth rate: 1.7 per cent, 1990–2010 (Unicef).

Ethnic make-up

Mestizo (mixed Indian and white) (65 per cent), Indian (25 per cent), white and others (7 per cent), black (3 per cent). The indigenous Indian population is composed of eight main groups, five in the Oriente and three on the coast, each with their own language. One of the Oriente groups, the Quechua, also live in the highlands (sierra).

Religions

Over 95 per cent of the population is nominally Roman Catholic, although Protestant churches have made inroads in recent years. There is freedom of worship.

Education

The education sector in Ecuador needs increased funding and technology.

Enrolment in primary schools has been increasing at an annual rate of 4.4 per cent per year, although many children drop out before the age of 15.

Public universities have an open admissions policy. The number of people entering university, however, has increased and this is putting a strain on resources, contributing to a decline in academic standards.

Literacy rate: 91 per cent adult rate; 96 per cent youth rate (15–24) (Unesco 2005).

Compulsory years: Six to 15

Enrolment rate: 117 per cent gross primary enrolment (including repeaters); 59 per cent gross secondary enrolment (World Bank).

Pupils per teacher: 25 in primary schools

Health

Improved water sources and sanitation facilities are available to 71 per cent and 59 per cent of the population, respectively.

HIV/Aids

HIV prevalence: 0.3 per cent aged 15–49 in 2003 (World Bank)

Life expectancy: 72 years, 2004 (WHO 2006)

Fertility rate/Maternal mortality rate: 2.5 births per woman, 2010 (Unicef); maternal mortality 160 per 100,000 live births (World Bank).

Child (under 5 years) mortality rate (per 1,000): 23 per 1,000 live births (WHO 2012); 14 per cent of children, aged under five, are malnourished (World Bank).

Welfare

The Ecuadorian Social Security Institute operates under the ministry of social welfare and offers old-age benefits, sickness and maternity coverage, work, injury and unemployment benefits. The system covers only around 30 per cent of the working population. Coverage is particularly poor in rural areas.

Main cities

Quito (capital, estimated population 1.8 million (m) in 2012), Guayaquil (2.4m), Basin (340,164), Santo Domingo (269,404), Machala (237,177), Blanket (216,324), Eloy Alfaro (209,738), Portoviejo (201,159), Ambato (180,664).

Languages spoken

Quechua and Jarvo are spoken. There is pressure from indigenous groups for Quechua to be made an official language.

English, taught to all schoolchildren, is also widely spoken.

Official language/s

Spanish

Media

Freedom of the press is guaranteed but foreign investment in the media is prohibited. Journalists operate a form of self-censorship particularly concerning perceived sensitive issues and defamation is a criminal offence and liable to up to three years in prison.

A change to the electoral law called 'vital' by President Correa came into effect on 4 February 2012, ahead of the 2013 elections. The new article prohibits the media from 'either directly or indirectly promoting any given candidate, proposal, options, electoral preferences or political thesis, through articles, specials or any other form of message.'

Press

Dailies: In Spanish, national newspapers include *El Comercio* (www2.elcomercio.com) and *El Universo* (www.eluniverso.com). Regional publications include *El Telégrafo* (www.telegrafo.com.ec) and *Expreso* (www.expreso.ec) from Guayaquil, *La Hora* (www.lahora.com.ec) and *Hoy* (www.hoy.com.ec) from Quito, *Correo* (www.diariocorreo.com.ec) from Machala and La Prensa (www.laprensa.com.ec) from Chimborazo.

Business: In Spanish, *El Financiero* (www.elfinanciero.com) is published weekly.

Broadcasting

The government seized TC Television in Quito and Guayaquil and Gamavision in Quito in July 2008, in a dispute lnked to the collapse of banks in the late 1990s. The Deposit Guarantee Agency (AGD) seeks to recover funds from banks that closed or went bankrupt in the financial crisis.

Radio: Radio is the most popular medium for entertainment, news and information and there are hundreds of stations, some in rural areas broadcasting in indigenous languages. Private, national commercial radio stations include Radio Sucre (www.radiosucre.com.ec), JC Radio (www.jcradio.com.ec) and Radio Caravana (http://radiocaravana.com); from Quito Radio Megaestacion (www.radiomegaestacion.com) and Radio i99 (www.i99.com.ec); from Guayaquil Radio America (www.americaestereo.com) and Radio Latina (www.radiolatina.com.ec). There are several religious radio stations.

Television: There are several national, commercial broadcasters, programming mostly consists of Latin American soap opera shows and US imports, but domestic productions are growing. News, sports and music are also featured. Ecuavisa (www.ecuavisa.com), ETV Telerama (www.etvtelerama.com), Teleamazonas (www.teleamazonas.com), Telesistema (www.rts.com.ec) and Gamavision (www.gamavision.com).

The satellite TV station RTU (www.rtu.com.ec), which began transmitting in 2005, offers news and current affairs programmes.

Other news agencies: Prensa Latina: www.prensalatina.com.mx

Economy

The economy is heavily dependent on the oil industry, manufacturing for the domestic market, commerce and agriculture. Exports are dominated by petroleum, but Ecuador is also a leading exporter of bananas and plantains as well as a major exporter of shrimp (prawns) and, to a lesser extent, fresh flowers, canned fish and vehicles. The mining industry is in need of further development, but produces gold and copper. A wide range of cash and subsistence crops are produced, including coffee, cacao (cocoa beans), sugar, tropical fruits rice and livestock

GDP growth was 7.2 per cent in 2008, as oil, copper and gold prices reached record high prices, but as the global economic crisis cut trade, particularly in commodities, the economy fell to 0.4 per cent in 2009. The economy rebounded with GDP growth of 3.6 per cent in 2010, which grew steadily to an estimated 7.8 per cent in 2011. Growth has been slowing down since but still remains positive, as the economy grew my 3.6 per cent in 2014. At the height of the 2008 boom inflation peaked at 8.4 per cent as a result of corresponding high prices of imports; it settled down to an average 4.4 per cent (2009–11) as domestic spending weakened, and decreased even further by 2013 at 2.7 per cent before jumping to 3.6 per cent in 2014.

The political influence of President Correa has re-focussed the economy. He championed investment in public services, education and health, which resulted in increased income tax. Ecuador's poverty index decreased from 37.6 per cent in December 2006 to 33 per cent in June 2010. Remittances in 2010 were US$2.3 billion (4.1 per cent of GDP) and were estimated to have risen to US$2.5 billion in 2011, which was largely maintained into 2013 at US$2.6 billion.

In 2008 Ecuador officially defaulted on US$10 billion of its foreign debts, which it considered 'illegitimate'. Around 20 per cent of GDP was used in foreign debt repayments. The president claimed that some of the debt was contracted illegally by previous administrations and that the debt will be restructured. According to the Alternate Governor of the Bank of Ecuador, Katiuska King Mantilla, foreign debt was 13.8 per cent of GDP in August 2010 and the total service for this debt (public and private) was reduced to 9.6 per cent of GDP. Public debt has been rising since 2010 (reaching 29.8 per cent of GDP at the end of 2014) as a result of the government seeking out external funding to finance its investments in various development projects, owing mainly to China.

Chinese company Sinohydro pledged foreign direct investment (FDI) of US$1.682 billion in 2010 for the future construction of Ecuador's largest hydroelectric project. FDI recorded in 2010 by the World Bank was US$167 million, a significant fall from FDI in 2008 of US$1 billion. FDI had recovered by 2013, however not to 2008 standards, reaching US$725 million.

External trade

Ecuador belongs to the South American Community of Nations (SACN) (which combines the Andean Community of Nations and Southern Common Market (Mercosur)) in the creation of an economic and legislative union.

Imports

Principal imports are vehicles, pharmaceuticals and medical products, telecommunications equipment and electricity.

Main sources: US (28.0 per cent of total in 2014), China (16.7 per cent), Colombia (7.5 per cent)

Exports

Principal exports are petroleum, bananas, fresh flowers, shrimp, canned fish and vehicles.

Main destinations: US (43.9 per cent of total in 2014), Chile (8.9 per cent), Peru (6.1 per cent)

Agriculture

Farming

Prior to the rise in significance of the oil industry, and other related economic activities, the agricultural sector was Ecuador's most prominent economic activity. In recent years output from the sector has fluctuated due to the adverse effects of the *El Niño* weather phenomena in the 1990s and shifts in world cocoa and banana prices.

Virtually the whole of the country is suitable for some form of agricultural exploitation. However, the sector has suffered from low levels of mechanisation and irrigation, and lack of financial incentives.

In coastal regions the main crops are bananas, cocoa, coffee, oil palms, sugar cane, cotton, rice and maize, while the sierra produces legumes, maize, wheat, potatoes, rye and barley. Ecuador is the world's largest producer of bananas.

Cattle are mainly reared in the highlands. There is small-scale poultry farming in Manabi province.

Rose growing and cut-flower production started in the early 1980s and the country has a number of rose growing enterprises. The potential for rose exports from Ecuador is enormous since all-year-round production is possible with no heating or cooling costs.

Temperate crops include blackberries, tamarillos (tree tomatoes), lemons, limes and avocados. In warmer regions, mangoes, pineapple, passion fruit, papaya, pepper, heart-of-palm and orito (kind of banana) thrive. In colder and temperate areas, broccoli, strawberry, asparagus, artichoke and peppers are grown. In addition, cucumbers, okra and melons are cultivated. The majority of the annual pineapple harvest is sold to the US and to Europe.

Fishing

Over recent years the fishing industry has increased in importance. Both sea and shrimp fishing have become more economically significant, with shrimp now being the second most important foreign exchange earner in the agricultural sector, after bananas.

Government policy has concentrated on the development of sea food, including tuna, fish oil and fishmeal for export.

The fisheries union in Ecuador has pressed for immediate reforms within the sector, asking for modernised management. The country's fishing legislation lacks organisation with poorly defined fishing rights.

In a typical year the annual fish catch is over 550,000mt, including around 5,000mt freshwater fish and 60,000mt shellfish.

Forestry

Over 40 per cent of Ecuador's total land mass is forested; approximately 10.5 million hectares (ha).

Forests are mostly concentrated in the eastern Amazonian region characterised by lowland humid tropical rainforests. Forest plantations are mainly eucalyptus.

Large quantities of sawn timber and wood based panels are produced, although exports remain limited. Production of hardwoods and balsa wood is dependent on the Andean market. Most of the paper and pulp demand is met by imports.

According to some critics, there will be no forests left in Ecuador by 2030 and the government has been supporting a project which aimed to re-forest 500,000 hectares by the end of 2005, both for commercial and ecological reasons, with an emphasis on profitable exotic species.

Industry and manufacturing

Approximately 20 per cent of Ecuador's total GDP is generated by activity in the industrial sector, which is geographically concentrated in Quito and Guayaquil.

The sector accounts for 15 per cent of the entire labour force in a typical year.

A free trade zone (FTZ), offering incentives for the manufacture of export products, was established at Esmeraldas.

Tourism

The tourist industry specialises in niche holidays. As such the industry has benefitted from growth at a time when many competitors have seen a decline. The tourist board identified the top reasons given for visiting Ecuador as eco-tourism and nature, cultural tourism, sports and adventure and business trips, which between them account for over 70 per cent of all visits. The Galapagos Islands are at the top of the eco-tourist's list of places to see, closely followed by the Sangay National Park, which includes 10 eco-systems of the Andean-Amazon region. Both of which are included in Unesco's World Heritage List, along with the City of Quito and the historic centre of Santa Ana de los Ríos de Cuenca. Luxury holidays have also grown, with all-inclusive hotels and travel plans.

Travel and tourism constituted 4.9 per cent (US$2.1 billion) of GDP in 2006, which increased steadily for two years to 5.7 per cent (US$3.2 billion) in 2008, before falling back for two years to 5.2 per cent (US$3.1 billion) in 2010. This contribution has largely been constant, reaching 5.5 per cent in 2014. The estimated growth for 2015 was 1.0 per cent. Employment in the tourist industry is 5.0 per cent (369,500 jobs) of total employment.

Environment

All visitors are required to buy a permit to land on the Galápagos Islands. As a conservation measure, a Tarjeta de Control de Transito (TCT) (transit control card) was instituted in 2007 to limit the number of people who may visit the islands at any one time.

Mining

Mining concessions can be found over approximately 5.6 million hectares of Ecuador's total land mass. Approximately 36,000 miners make their living in the informal sector, which represents about 1 per cent of the country's labour force.

Despite a growing foreign presence, Ecuador's mining industry is very much in its infancy, although it could become one of the economy's most dynamic sectors. The government is keen to make mining a high priority in view of its enormous production potential and the opportunity it offers to diversify the country's export base as an alternative to oil.

The most important mineral is gold, which is mined on a small-scale basis, although a number of foreign and local companies are negotiating with miners to take over their operations and introduce more technical expertise. Interest has been shown in gold, with a joint government and private mining venture in the Nambija region.

There are also major deposits of limestone, clay, plaster, barytine, feldspar, silica, phosphate, bentonite and pumice stone (Ecuador has one of the biggest reserves of pumice stone in the world). Kaolin, marble, puzzolan and gypsum are mined.

Hydrocarbons

Total oil reserves were 8.0 billion barrels in 2014, with production at 556,000 barrels per day (bpd). Consumption was 259,000bpd, which allowed the remainder to be exported. As Ecuador is one of South America's largest oil exporters the sector dominates the economy and provides around 50 per cent of total export earnings and 33 per cent of tax revenues. However, Ecuador does not possess sufficient refining capacity, just 176,000bpd from three refineries, so it relies on imported refined oil for domestic purposes. In 2011 the South Korean KS Engineering began work to refurbish and upgrade the largest refinery, Esmeraldas, which was still on-going throughout 2015.

Although the state-owned Petroecuador is responsible for exploration, production and transport of all hydrocarbons it typically works in partnership with foreign oil and gas companies and only produces around 50 per cent of crude oil. In 2007 the government began to transform contracts with foreign oil companies into service agreements, whereby oil companies act as government agents in producing oil and are given a fee in compensation for production. In 2009, the largest foreign oil producer, the Argentinean company, Repsol-YPF, agreed to the new contract structure.

Petroecuador utilises the older Sistema Oleducto Trans-Ecuatoriano (Sote), to transport oil to the Balao oil terminal on the Pacific coast, for export. The latest pipeline, which parallels Sote, the Oleducto de Crudos Pesados (OCP), has allowed private oil companies to double output.

Total natural gas reserves were 6.0 billion cubic metres (cum) in 2014, however domestic demand is negligible and the infrastructure to increase use is limited. All natural gas output is used in energy generation. The oil industry produces 3.3 billion cum, but all of it is lost due to the lack of infrastructure for its capture.

Although, there are small reserves of recoverable coal (lignite and sub-bituminous) estimated at 23.5 million tonnes, any consumption is commercially insignificant.

Energy

Total installed electricity capacity was 5,243MW in 2013, producing 22.9 billion kilowatt hours (kWh), which was more than sufficient to provide for consumption of 19.4 billion kWh. The majority of energy is provided by hydropower and the remainder by conventional thermal power stations. Although there is a net electricity surplus, supplies are often affected during the dry season of October-March when hydroelectric output declines. Ecuador imports electricity from Colombia during periods of shortfall.

The state regulator of energy is Consejo Nacional de Electricidad (Conelec) (National Electricity Council), under the mandate of the Ministerio de Energía y Minas (MEM) (Ministry of Energy and Mining). It has responsibilities for policy, planning and regulation of the independent utility companies.

Ecuador's largest power plant is the massive Paute River hydroelectric dam in Azuay Province, producing over 50 per cent of all domestic energy needs. In 2008 a new hydroelectric dam in San Francisco, Quito, which was inaugurated in 2007 and supplied 12 per cent of the country's electricity, became the focus of international disagreement between the government and its Brazilian backers and builders, Odebrecht. In June 2008 it was shut down by the government for claimed structural defects that had interrupted power supplies. Four contracts totalling US$800 million with Odebrecht were annulled by presidential decree, while Ecuador demanded repairs and recompense, while loans of US$243 million to the National Economic and Social Development Bank of Brazil (BNDES) were withheld. Other, smaller, hydropower projects are under construction.

The worst drought since the 1960s forced the government to introduce electricity rationing in November 2009, aimed at reducing consumption by 5–10 per cent. Water levels in the Paute River hydroelectric dam were at an historic low, with water flowing at 20–30 cubic metres (cum) per second instead of the average 70–80cum expected.

Financial markets

Stock exchange

Bolsa de Valores de Quito (BVQ) (Quito Stock Exchange)

Banking and insurance

A new Bank of the South, with a headquarters in Venezuela, will be launched in 2008 to provide an alternative source of development funding for the participating countries. Assets of US$7 billion will underpin its operations.

Central bank

Banco Central del Ecuador

Main financial centre

Guayaquil and Quito

Time

Mainland Ecuador: GMT minus five hours
Galapagos Islands: GMT minus six hours

Geography

Ecuador has three main regions – a low coastal strip, a high Andean *cordillera* with peaks rising to more than 6,000 metres, and a tropical lowland in the Amazon basin. The Andes, which here comprise two parallel ranges running north to south, form a barrier between 100 and 120km wide.

Chimborazo, an extinct volcano, is the highest mountain, at 6,310 metres, and there are several active volcanoes. Quito itself, which lies at 2,850 metres above sea level, is the second highest capital in South America, and visitors are advised to take things easy for a few days after arrival to avoid altitude sickness.

To the north, Ecuador is bordered by Colombia and to the east and south by Peru. To the west lies the Pacific Ocean. Of the Spanish-speaking nations of South America, only Uruguay is smaller in area.

Hemisphere

Straddles the Equator

Climate

Although the equator crosses the north of the country (and gives it its name), only the eastern lowlands (the Oriente) and the northern coastal region have a typically tropical climate, with abundant rains, high humidity and little seasonal change in temperature, which averages around 25 degrees Celsius (C). The port city of Guayaquil is in the tropical zone and has most rain between January and April. In the Andes, the climate varies from the cold of the high glaciers to the temperate zone of the central valley around Quito, where the mean annual temperature is between 13 degrees C and 19 degrees C. Days are warm and nights are cool all year round. The rainy season in the valley lasts from November–May.

Dress codes

In government offices and private businesses in Quito, dress is relatively formal. Women usually wear skirts, while the men wear suits or jacket and tie. Dress is generally less formal in Guayaquil, the largest city and Ecuador's major port.

Entry requirements

Passports

Passports are required by all. Passports must be valid for six months.

Visa

Nationals of most countries do not need a visa for stays up to three months, but travellers should contact the local embassy for confirmation.

Currency advice/regulations

No restrictions on import or export of foreign or local currency.

International credit cards are generally accepted in Quito and Guayaquil. Travellers cheques can be difficult to exchange outside main towns. US dollar travellers cheques are the most easily negotiable.

Prohibited imports

Firearms, ammunition, illegal drugs, fresh or dry meat and meat products, plants and vegetables are prohibited/restricted unless prior permission is obtained.

Health (for visitors)

Mandatory precautions

A yellow fever certificate is required if arriving from infected areas and for those intending to visit Pastaza province in the east.

Advisable precautions

Typhoid, tetanus and hepatitis A and B vaccinations are recommended. Malaria prophylaxis is advisable; the malaria risk is high and widespread all the year. Yellow fever vaccinations are recommended for most areas east of the Andes. There is a rabies risk.

Tap water is not safe to drink. Bottled mineral water is widely available.

Hotels

Wide range available in Quito and Guayaquil. A government tax of 5 per cent and a service charge of 10 per cent payable on all rates.

Credit cards

Major credit cards are generally accepted.

Public holidays (national)

Fixed dates

1 Jan (New Year's Day), 1 May (Labour Day), 24 May (Battle of Pichincha Day), 10 Aug (Independence Day), 12 Oct (Columbus Day), 2 Nov (All Souls' Day), 25 Dec (Christmas Day), 31 Dec (New Year's Eve).

If New Year's Day falls on a Sunday, 2 Jan becomes a holiday instead. Holidays falling on a Tuesday are observed on the preceding Monday, while those falling on Wednesday and Thursday are moved to Friday. The exceptions to the latter rule are 1 Jan, 1 May, 2 Nov and 25 Dec.

Variable dates

Carnival (two days), Maundy Thursday, Good Friday.

Carnival is celebrated on Shrove Tuesday and Ash Wednesday (six weeks before Good Friday).

Working hours

Banking

Mon–Fri: 0900–1330, 1430—1030; Sat: 0900–1800.

Business

Mon–Fri: 0800–1630.

Government

Mon–Fri: 0830–1630.

Shops

Mon–Fri: 0900–1300, 1500–1900. Sat: 1000–2000. (Shopping centres, Mon–Sat: 1030–2030; Sun: 1030–1830.)

Telecommunications

Mobile/cell phones

GSM 850 service available in cities and large towns.

Electricity supply

110/120V AC, 60 cycles

Weights and measures

The metric system is in use.

Social customs/useful tips

Speak Spanish; if not, ensure that promotional material is in Spanish or has Spanish inserts.

Ecuadoreans prefer to deal with people they have spent time getting to know; lunches/business meetings can last from 1330 to 1800, dinners from 2000 onwards. Meetings often start late.

Ecuadoreans are polite and formal. Do not be discouraged by lack of enthusiasm; they like to be convinced. The use of the title Doctor, Engineer or Economist is common.

Security

Guayaquil has a serious street crime problem. Crime in Quito is on the increase, especially in the colonial centre of town, and police advise visitors to be wary of thieves and pickpockets and to watch luggage at all times.

Getting there

Air

National airline: TAME (Línea Aérea del Ecuador); Lan Ecuador.

International airport/s: Quito-Mariscal Sucre (UIO), 8km from city centre, duty-free shop, bar, restaurant, buffet, bank, post office, shops, car hire, tourist information. Guayaquil-Simón Bolivar (GYE), 5km north of city centre, duty-free shop, restaurant, buffet, currency exchange, post office, shops, car hire, tourist information;

Airport tax: US$25.

Surface

Access is possible from Colombia and Peru, although the quality of roads may vary.

Road: Buses run between Colombia and Ecuador via Tulcán, and between Peru and Ecuador via either Huaquillas or Macará.

Water: All visitors are required to buy a permit to land on the Galápagos Islands. As a conservation measure, a Tarjeta de Control de Transito (TCT) (transit control card) was instituted in 2007 to limit the number of people who may visit the islands at any one time.

Main port/s: Guayaquil, Manta and Esmeraldas.

Getting about

Passport checks are frequently made by the police, especially near the borders.

National transport

Air: Air transport is the usual mode of travel between cities. TAME, the commercial wing of the Ecuadorian Air Force, and several other airlines operate domestic services to main centres. Air-taxi and charter services are available from Guayaquil and Quito.

With the exception of flying to the Galápagos Islands, internal flights are cheap. All visitors are required to buy a permit to land on the Galápagos Islands.

Road: Most parts of the country are accessible by surfaced or all-weather roads. Major routes run north-south in the coastal lowlands and the sierra. The Pan-American Highway runs from Tulcan via Ibarra, Quito, Riobamaba, Cuenca, Loja to Macara. Good roads link the sierra to the coastal ports.

Buses: Bus services link main towns, including Quito-Esmeraldas, Quito-Manta, Guayaquil-Manta and Quito-Guayaquil. Most towns have a *terminal terrestre* (central bus terminal). Reservations in advance should be made for long-distance services. Timetables are changed frequently and not always adhered to.

Rail: Routes include Quito-Riobamba, Guayaquil-Bucay, Alausi-Huigra, Sibambe-Cuenca and Ibarra-San Lorenzo. Rail travel is generally uncomfortable and unreliable.

Water: Boats are a frequent mode of travel, particularly in the Oriente region, and on the north-west coast.

City transport

Taxis: Taxis are cheap. They can be hailed or found on ranks. It is best to ask the fare beforehand. At weekends and at night, fares are 25–50 per cent higher. Journey time from airport to city centre 20–30 minutes. Tips are not expected.

Car hire

Major companies operate from Quito and Guayaquil. An international permit is required. Traffic drives on the right. Police checks are common.

BUSINESS DIRECTORY

The addresses listed below are a selection only. While World of Information makes every endeavour to check these addresses, we cannot guarantee that changes have not been made, especially to telephone numbers and area codes. We would welcome any corrections.

Telephone area codes

The international direct dialling code for Ecuador is +593, followed by area code:
Ambato3Machala7
Cuenca7Manta4
Esmeraldas6Portoviejo4
Guayaquil4Quito2

Useful telephone numbers

Police:101
Fire:102
Ambulance (Quito):131

Chambers of Commerce

American-Ecuadorian Chamber of Commerce, Avenida 6 de Diciembre y La Niña, Edificio Multicentro, Quito (tel: 250-7450; fax: 250-4571; e-mail: info@ecamcham.com).
British-Ecuadorean Chamber of Industry and Commerce, Avenida El Tiempo 464 y El Telegrafo, Quito (tel: 244-9239; fax: 225-7433; e-mail: info@egbcc.org).
Guayaquil Cámara de Comercio, Avenida Francisco de Orellana y Miguel H Alcivar, Centro Empresarial Las Cámaras, Guayaquil (tel: 268-2771; fax: 268-2725; e-mail: info@lacamara.org).
Quito Cámara de Comercio, Avenida Amazonas y República, Edificio Las Cámaras, Quito (tel: 244-3787; fax: 243-5862; e-mail: ccq@ccq.org.ec).

Banking

Banco Bolivariano, Junín 200 y Panamá, Guayaquil (tel: 562-777; fax: 565-025).
Banco de Guayaquil, Pichincha 105 y P Icaza, Guayaquil (tel: 514-209; fax: 512-427; e-mail: glasso@bankguay.com).
Banco del Pacífico, P Icaza 200 y Pedro Carbo, Guayaquil (tel: 566-010; fax: 564-636; e-mail: webadmin@bp.fin.ec).
Banco del Pichincha, Avenida Amazonas 4560 y Pereira, Quito (tel: 980-980; fax: 981-280).
Banco la Previsora, Avenida 9 de Octubre 100, Guayaquil (tel: 561-656; fax: 566-665; e-mail: blp@bprevisora.fin.ec).
BancoUnion, Cordova 916 y VM Rendon, Guayaquil (tel: 566-555; fax: 313-295; e-mail: info@banunion.com).
Filanbanco, Avenida 9 de Octubre 203 y Pichincha, Guayaquil (tel: 322-780; fax: 326-916).
Superintendencia de Bancos (Banking Supervisory Agency), Avenida 12 de Octubre 24-185, Quito (tel: 554-422).

Central bank

Banco Central del Ecuador, Avenida 10 de Agosto y Briceño, Plaza Bolivar, Quito (tel: 257 2523).

Stock exchange

Bolsa de Valores de Quito (BVQ) (Quito Stock Exchange), www.ccbvq.com

Bolsa de Volores de Guayaquil (BVG) (Guayaquil Stock Exchange), www.mundobvg.com

Travel information

Ecuatoriana Airlines, Reina Victoria y Colón, Edificio Torres de Almagro, Quito (tel: 563-003; fax: 563-920).

SAETA Airlines, Avenida Carlos Julio Arosemena Km 2.5, Guayaquil (fax: 201-153; e-mail: ehbuzon@saeta.com.ec).

TAME Airlines, Avenida Amazonas 13-54 y Colón, Quito (tel: 509-392; fax: 509-594).

Ministry of tourism

Ministry of Tourism, Av Eloy Alfaro N32-300 y Carlos Tobar, Quito (tel: 228-303, 507-560; fax: 507-564, 229-330; e-mail: mtur1@ec_gov.net).

National tourist organisation offices

Asociación Ecuatoriana de Agencias de Viajes y Turismo (ASECUT), Avenida Amazonas 2468, Quito (tel: 552-617; fax: 552-916).

Corporación Ecuatoriana de Turismo (CETUR), Reina Victoria 514 y Roca, Quito (tel: 527-002; fax: 568-198).

Ministries

Ministry of Agriculture, Avenida Amazonas y Eloy Alfaro, Quito (tel: 504-433; fax: 504-922).

Ministry of Defence, Exposición 208, Quito (tel: 512-803; fax: 569-386).

Ministry of Education, San Gregorio y Juan Murillo, Quito (tel: 583-337; fax: 580-116).

Ministry of Energy and Mines, Santa Prisca 223, Quito (tel: 552-533; fax: 502-092).
Ministry of the Environment, Avenida Eloy Alfaro y Amazonas, Quito (tel: 540-920; fax: 255-172).
Ministry of Finance and Public Credit, Avenida 10 de Agosto 1661 y Jorge Washington, Quito (tel: 503-328; fax: 500-702).
Ministry of Foreign Affairs, Avenida 10 de Agosto y Carrión, Quito (tel: 503-093; fax: 227-025; e-mail: dgproeco@mmrree.gov.ec).
Ministry of Foreign Trade, Avenida Amazonas y Eloy Alfaro, Quito (tel: 529-076; fax: 507-549).

Ministry of Government, Espejo y Benalcázar, Quito (tel: 584-919; fax: 580-067).

Ministry of Housing and Urban Development, Avenida 10 de Agosto 2270 y Cordero, Quito (tel: 238-060; fax: 566-785).

Ministry of Labour, Luis Felipe Borja y C Ponce, Quito (tel: 566-148; fax: 503-122).

Ministry of Public Health, Juan Larrea 445, Quito (tel: 529-163; fax: 569-092).

Ministry of Public Works, Avenida Orellana y Juan León Mera, Quito (tel: 222-749; fax: 223-077).

Ministry of Social Welfare, Robles 850 y Páez, Quito (tel: 227-975; fax: 563-469).

Other useful addresses

Corporación Financiera Nacional, Juan León Mera 130 y Patria, Quito (tel: 564-900; fax: 223-823).

Ecuadorian Embassy (USA), 2535 15th Street, NW, Washington DC 20009 (tel: (202) 234-7200; fax: (202) 667-3482; e-mail: embassy@ecuador.org).

Empresa Estatel de Telecomunicaciones (EMETEL), Avenida 6 de Diciembre y Colón, Edificio Partenon, Quito (tel: 200-700; fax: 568-000).

National Bureau of Mines (DINAMI), Baquedano E7-13 y Reina Victoria, Edificio Araucaria, Quito (tel: 554-110; fax: 554-110; e-mail: dinami@accessinter.net).

Petroecuador, Avenida 6 de Diciembre y Paul Rivet, Edificio El Pinar, Quito (tel: 561-250; fax: 524-766).

Superintendencia de Compañías del Ecuador (Companies Supervisory Authority), Roca 660 y Avenida Amazonas, Quito (tel: 529-960; fax: 565-685).

US Embassy, Avenida 12 de Octubre y Patria, Quito (tel: 562-890; fax: 502-052).

Prensa Latina: www.prensalatina.com.mx

Internet sites

Economic Commission for Latin America (gateway site): http://www.eclac.cl/index1.html

Inter-American Development Bank: http://www.iadb.org

Latin Trade Online: http://www.latintrade.com

Organisation of American States: http://www.oas.org

Egypt

KEY FACTS

Official name: Jumhuriyat Misr al Arabiya (Arab Republic of Egypt)

Head of State: President Abdel Fattah el Sisi (Independent) (sworn in 9 June 2014)

Head of government: Acting Prime Minister Ibrahim Mahlab (from 1 Mar 2014)

Ruling party: No ruling party as such

Area: 1,001,499 square km

Population: 86.70 million (2014)

Capital: Cairo

Official language: Arabic

Currency: Egyptian pound (LE) = 100 piastres

Exchange rate: LE7.83 per US$ (Sep 2015)

GDP per capita: US$3,304 (2014)

GDP real growth: 2.16% (2014)

GDP: US$286.44 billion (2014)

Labour force: 26.19 million (2011)*

Unemployment: 13.37% (2014)

Inflation: 10.10% (2014)

Oil production: 717,000 bpd (2014)

Natural gas production: 48.70 billion cum (2014)

Balance of trade: -US$30.83 billion (2014)

* estimated figure

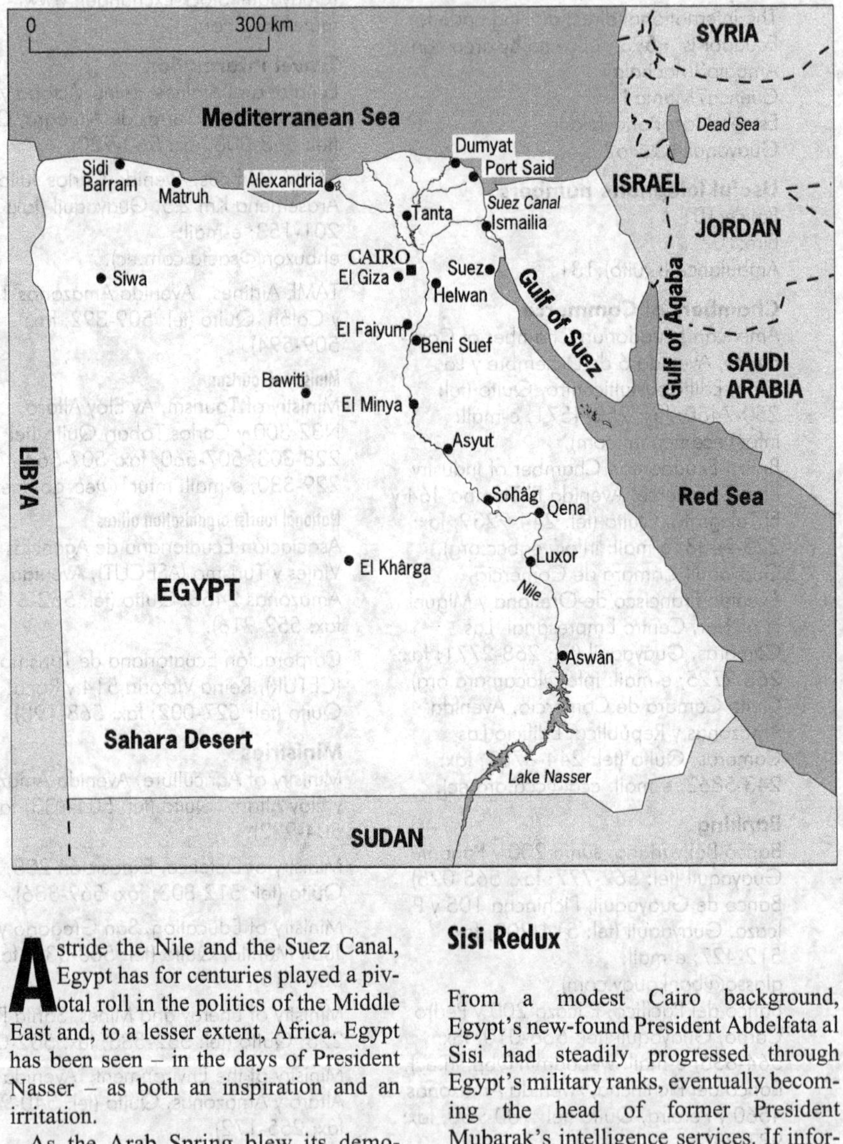

Astride the Nile and the Suez Canal, Egypt has for centuries played a pivotal roll in the politics of the Middle East and, to a lesser extent, Africa. Egypt has been seen – in the days of President Nasser – as both an inspiration and an irritation.

As the Arab Spring blew its democratic breezes through the region in 2011, for a short while, Egypt had been looked to for guidance and encouragement. However, the political temperature fell as quickly as it had risen. The brief interlude of democracy and the election of the Muslim Brotherhood came to an end; Mubarak, a military man, was eventually replaced by Abdel Fattah el Sisi, another military man. President Mohammed Morsi soon became a memory, albeit an imprisoned but still powerful memory.

Sisi Redux

From a modest Cairo background, Egypt's new-found President Abdelfata al Sisi had steadily progressed through Egypt's military ranks, eventually becoming the head of former President Mubarak's intelligence services. If information was the key to power, then al Sisi was certainly well placed. One of the new President's peculiar abilities seems to be that of being all things to all men, happily merging with the surroundings and the personalities of the day. This stance was, however, deceptive. His military career had certainly trained him well, but it had not dulled a fierce determination to mould Egypt as he wished and – quite literally – to eliminate those who chose to stand in his way. No-one was better able to testify to this than the deposed President

Mohammed Morsi of the Muslim Brotherhood, who, on becoming President. had made a number of fatal misjudgements regarding General al Sisi. The first miscalculation was to appoint al Sisi minister of defence, thereby giving him effective control of Egypt's army. The second was to trust al Sisi. The third was to underrate the general's determination to restore order to the country by resorting to an authoritarianism far more severe than that seen under Mubarak.

Well trained...

A brief study of al Sisi's recent history is an excellent pointer to the President's qualifications as President. In 2015 an impoverished Egypt, facing civil unrest and increasing poverty, had a disproportionate dependency on its principal ally – the United States. US military aid to Egypt each year is a massive US$1.5 billion. Quite how this money is spent is determined, with some secrecy, by the Egyptian military. But the Egypt-US connection is fundamental and sacrosanct in Egyptian military thinking. So it was no coincidence that general al Sisi spent a year at the US Army War College in Pennsylvania where he appears to have been something of a model pupil. Ironically enough, al Sisi's end of year project was the production of a paper entitled *Democracy in the Middle East.* Following the presidential election in which he managed to gain 93.3 per cent of the votes cast, some of his critics suggested that he might benefit from reading his own paper. Central to his paper was that there should be a Third Way between the notion of Western democracy and Islamism.

... well trusted?

Whatever the Third Way amounted to, in the Egyptian scenario it clearly did not have any room for, or trust in, the Muslim Brotherhood. While still minister of defence, al Sisi went on record as saying that 'No-one is going to depose anybody and no-one should entertain the idea that the army holds the answer to Egypt's problems.' Al Sisi's apparent conversion, or re-conversion, to the discredited idea of a military dictatorship (albeit in the guise of an elected democracy) ran counter to the false perception seemingly accepted by the Muslim Brotherhood. In May 2015 ex-President Morsi had cause to reflect on how wide of the mark his trust in al Sisi had been, as he languished in jail, cooped up with over a hundred of his supporters, all of whom had been sentenced to death. In sharp contrast, ex-President Mubarak had been pardoned and was due to be released from jail.

The US concerns

The US-based non-governmental organisation (NGO), Human Rights Watch (HRW), noted that Egypt has had no lower house of parliament since the body was dissolved by court order in 2012. In its absence, President al Sisi has issued no less than some 175 laws and decrees since taking office in mid-2014. Not bad for a busy military man, but the government has repeatedly postponed elections for a new parliament. By law, any new parliament would have only 15 days after its first session to review and amend all the legislation passed in its absence before that legislation becomes final.

President al Sisi's time at the Pennsylvania War College did not seem to cut much ice with the US administration. A 2015 report submitted to Congress concluded that Egypt was 'moving away from democracy, stifling freedom of expression, arresting thousands for political dissent and failing to hold the security services to account for arbitrary or unlawful killings.' The US administration was clearly over a geo-political barrel when dealing with Egypt. HRW observed that Europe and Washington had gone back into business with a government that celebrates rather than investigates what may have been the worst single-day killing of protesters in modern history. The argument deployed by the US and Egypt's European allies was that this was an internal matter, rather than a matter for external involvement. There appeared to be a consensus that at a time of heightened volatility in the Middle East it was a question of national security to restore their relationships with Egypt. An unmentioned item for a number of countries, notably the US, France and the UK was their lucrative arms sales to Egypt.

NGOs such as HRW were not the only critics of the al Sisi régime. Despite the US government's rapprochement with the Egyptian régime, the administration report didn't pull its punches, observing that 'the overall trajectory for rights and democracy has been negative.' Nor could the administration see much improvement on the horizon: 'A series of executive initiatives, new laws and judicial actions severely restrict freedom of the press, freedom of association, freedom of peaceful assembly and due process and they undermine prospects for democratic governance.'

One particularly sensitive area of repression was that of the universities. On entering university premises students faced police checks and body searches, as well as the insidious presence of the Falcon private security agency, known for its often brutal methods. The tight control of the universities was not confined to Islamist establishments. Outside the University of Cairo were parked as many as ten police trucks manned by anti-riot details. Over 200 students at this one university alone were detained at the beginning of term, mostly following demonstrations

KEY INDICATORS — Egypt

	Unit	2011	2012	2013	2014	**2015
Population	m	*79.36	*82.50	*84.15	86.70	*88.43
Gross domestic product (GDP)	US$bn	235.70	262.26	271.43	286.44	–
GDP per capita	US$	2,970	3,179	*3,226	3,304	0
GDP real growth	%	1.8	2.2	2.1	2.2	*4.0
Inflation	%	11.1	8.6	6.9	10.1	*10.3
Unemployment	%	8.9	12.3	13.0	13.4	*13.1
Oil output	'000 bpd	735.0	728.0	714.0	717.0	–
Natural gas output	bn cum	61.3	60.9	56.1	48.7	–
Exports (fob) (goods)	US$m	27,913.4	26,835.0	–	25,203.7	–
Imports (fob) (goods)	US$m	47,311.5	52,350.0		56,034.6	–
Balance of trade	US$m	-19,398.1	-25,516.0		-30,830.9	–
Current account	US$m	-5,483.9	-10,146.0	-5,582.0	-2,356.0	–
Total reserves minus gold	US$m	28,309.8	11,628.0	13,608.0	11,995.0	–
Foreign exchange	US$m	27,208.6	10,368.0	12,343.0	–	–
Exchange rate	per US$	5.91	6.31	6.96	7.15	–

* estimated figure ** forecast figure

dispersed by the police with tear gas. Some were arrested in dawn raids at their homes. The government appeared to fear a repetition of events in 2013, when the universities became the focal points for demonstrations and protests.

Quoted in the *New York Times*, Mohamed Lotfy a human rights advocate said that 'The US was making the same mistake as it did when supporting Hosni Mubarak. Sisi is creating a new generation of terrorists and exporting them to Iraq and Syria.' He added that the US had been 'contradicting its values – or at least the values that it tries to export in its speeches'. A veiled reference to President Obama's much vaunted 'New Beginning' speech in Cairo in 2009.

The report made specific reference to the massacre of some 1,000 Islamist demonstrators in August 2013, an affair which, two years on, had not been investigated and for which no accountability had been traced. The fact that the report was made public, rather than treated as classified information underlined the impossible dilemma facing the administration. The report was discreetly submitted to Congress with no public announcement.

The economy

As a result of lower oil prices and their impact on government fiscal balances, external current accounts and economic growth the economy had at least stabilised. Lower oil prices would be credit positive for the Middle East and North Africa (MENA) region's five oil-importing and sub-investment-grade 'sovereigns', especially Egypt. Financial assistance from the Gulf States had enabled the beleaguered Egyptian government to rebalance its reserves, easing pressure on the Egyptian pound. The government had also managed to launch two fiscal stimulus packages each of 1.6 per cent of gross domestic product (GDP). What was discreetly referred to as political 'stabilisation' (aka 'military rule') had certainly improved macro-economic conditions. GDP growth had reached 2.1 per cent in the 2012/13 financial year, rising to an annual 2.5 per cent largely driven by increased government consumption and investment, as well as a rise in private consumption. Exports had failed to keep pace, however, and growth would have to pick up significantly if it was to bring about any reduction in the unemployment rate, which still remained high at 13.4 per cent in the third quarter of the 2013/14 fiscal year. The European Bank for Reconstruction and Development (EBRD) noted that Egypt's fiscal deficit had reached an estimated 12 per cent of GDP (excluding grants) in the 2013/14 fiscal year. This was largely due to higher interest payments and increases in public sector wages, along with the worrying shortfall in tax revenues. The government had been forced to rely heavily on domestic borrowing at a high cost, increasing Egyptian banks' exposure to sovereign credit risk and significantly crowding out private sector credit. Meanwhile, Egypt's balance of payments had improved thanks to foreign grants. Egypt's current account deficit had narrowed in the first three quarters of the 2013/14 fiscal year, thanks to official grants. According to the EBRD, however, this had masked the obstinate weakness of exports and tourism. Fortunately further outflows were cushioned by the strength of remittances and Suez Canal receipts. Net foreign direct investment (FDI) inflows had improved, but were dominated by investments in the oil sector rather than the non-oil economy.

The Egyptian government had been planning to attract FDI of the order of US$8–10 billion in the 2014/15 fiscal year, mainly in the oil sector, power stations and the Suez Canal. This was to be driven by a new law introduced to overcome the obstacles and difficulties that investors had been facing with the current legislation, which required investors to go to as many as 78 different ministries and committees in order to obtain the necessary licences to launch their projects. A new 'investment-window' system had been created to allow the investment committee to have authorised delegates capable of taking decisions within ministries. A new entity, called the Higher Investment Council, had been created to oversee policies and plans and their implementation; the General Investment Committee remained in place.

Meanwhile, foreign exchange reserves had remained steady, covering more than three months of imports. The Central Bank of Egypt had unexpectedly raised interest rates by 100 basis points in July 2014.This was seen as a pre-emptive move to anchor inflationary expectations in the light of increases in fuel and electricity prices. Before this move, the Central Bank had eased its monetary policy through three cuts to its interest rates in the previous year, in an effort to stimulate a degree of economic growth. While the move might have helped limit a generalised increase in inflation, there existed the risk that higher rates would have a negative effect on levels of investment and growth.

There was indeed some hope that the economy was gradually recovering. Economic growth was expected to reach 3.2 per cent in the 2014/15 fiscal year, up from the 2.2 per cent seen in the previous year. Growth would not only be supported by the implementation of the government's fiscal stimulus programmes, but would also rely on continued strong domestic demand. In addition, the expected increase in FDI was expected by the EBRD to be largely driven by an increase in investments from the Gulf States. But the general outlook was prone to the downside risks likely to result from any deterioration in the security situation or a further flare-up in internal and regional turmoil, with inevitably adverse effects on tourism and investor confidence.

The Egyptian government had announced an overhaul of energy subsidies in July 2014. The authorities had embarked on a broad restructuring plan to bring energy prices closer to cost recovery levels, which would mean raising the prices of gasoline, diesel and natural gas for consumers and selected industries. In addition, electricity prices had been raised both for commercial and residential use under a plan to eliminate power subsidies by 2018. The price reforms were designed to ease the drain on the central budget – estimated at around 7 per cent – and reduce market distortions. Nevertheless, in the view of the EBRD, the impact on the most vulnerable groups in Egyptian society would depend on the extent to which an adequate social safety net could be put in position.

The EBRD noted that fiscal consolidation measures had been introduced to reduce budgetary imbalances. A reduced budget containing a series of revenue enhancement measures had been approved for the 2014-15 fiscal year. The budget sought to lower the fiscal deficit to 10 per cent of GDP by implementing a wide ranging number of tax increases in the new fiscal year. According to the EBRD, progress on reforms to the business environment had been limited. Egypt ranked 112th out of 189 countries in the World Bank Doing Business 2015 report. In the Transparency International 2014 'Corruption Perceptions Index' Egypt ranked 94th, a low position but nevertheless 10 places better than its ranking in 2013. Egypt's business environment was perceived to be hindered primarily by weak contract enforcement and the labyrinthine bureaucratic process that resulted in substantial delays for most types of transactions. Apart from the failure to introduce significant regulatory changes on competition policy, foreign companies wishing to operate in Egypt also faced numerous other hurdles.

Energy

According to the US government's Energy Information Administration (EIA) Egypt is the largest oil producer in Africa that is not a member of the Organisation of the Petroleum Exporting Countries (OPEC). Egypt is also the second-largest natural gas producer on the continent, after Algeria. Egypt plays a vital role in international energy markets through the operation of the Suez Canal and the Suez-Mediterranean (SUMED) Pipeline.

The Canal is an important transit route for oil and liquefied natural gas (LNG) shipments travelling north-bound from the Arabian Gulf to Europe and to North America and shipments travelling south-bound from North Africa and countries along the Mediterranean to Asia. The SUMED Pipeline is the only alternative route nearby the Suez Canal to transport crude oil from the Red Sea to the Mediterranean if ships are unable to navigate through the Suez Canal. Fees collected from the operation of these two transit points are significant sources of revenue for the Egyptian government. However, the high cost of energy subsidies in Egypt has contributed to the country's high budget deficit and the inability of the Egyptian General Petroleum Corporation (EGPC), the country's national oil company, to pay off its debt to foreign operators. EGPC owes foreign oil and natural gas operators billions of dollars, which has led foreign operators to delay their investments in existing and new oil and natural gas projects.

Egypt's total primary energy consumption was 813,000 barrels per day (bpd) of oil in 2014, according to the BP 2015 Statistical Review of World Energy. Natural gas (consumption 48 billion cubic metres) and oil are the primary fuels used to meet Egypt's energy needs, accounting for 94 per cent of the country's total energy consumption in 2014. Oil is mostly used in the transportation sector, while natural gas is used in the power sector and transportation sector in the form of compressed natural gas (CNG) in vehicles.

Egypt is the largest oil and natural gas consumer in Africa, accounting for about 20 per cent of petroleum and other liquids consumption and 40 per cent of dry natural gas consumption in Africa in 2013. The rapid growth of oil and natural gas consumption over the past few decades has been driven by increased industrial output, economic growth, energy-intensive natural gas and oil extraction projects, population growth, an increase in private and commercial vehicle sales and energy subsidies.

According to the *Oil & Gas Journal* (OGJ), Egypt held 4.4 billion barrels of proved oil reserves at the beginning of 2015. Other estimates placed Egypt's official oil reserves estimate slightly lower, at just 4 billion barrels, of which 2.8 billion barrels is crude oil and 1.2 billion barrels is condensate. New oil discoveries have boosted Egypt's reserve estimate over the past few years. In 2013, 86 discoveries, mostly of oil, were made, according to the EGPC. About half of Egypt's oil production comes from the Western Desert. Most of Egypt's production is derived from relatively small fields that are connected to larger regional production systems.

Egypt's oil production has declined for more than a decade after reaching a peak of more than 900,000bpd in the mid-1990s. In 2008, increased output from the Western Desert and offshore areas helped to increase production over the next few years, but production then started to decline again. The use of enhanced oil recovery (EOR) techniques at mature fields has eased production declines. Natural gas plant liquids production has increased over the past decade as a result of expanding natural gas production, partially offsetting declines in crude oil production. One of Egypt's main challenges is to satisfy increasing domestic oil demand amid falling production. Total oil consumption grew by an annual average of 3 per cent over the past 10 years, reaching 813,000bpd in 2014. According to the EIA, Egypt's oil consumption currently outpaces its oil production.

According to OGJ estimates, in January 2015, Egypt held 77 trillion cubic feet (tcf) of proved natural gas reserves, an increase from the 2010 estimate of almost 59tcf and the fourth-largest amount in Africa, after Nigeria, Algeria and Mozambique. New discoveries have been made almost every year, particularly in the deep-water Mediterranean, the Nile Delta and the Western Desert.

Despite new discoveries, Egypt's dry natural gas production has declined by 5 per cent from 2012 to 2013. Egypt produced 2.0tcf of dry natural gas in 2013, of which almost 1.9tcf was domestically consumed and more than 0.1tcf was exported. Egypt had been diverting natural gas supply away from exports to the domestic market to meet demand. As a result, Egypt's total natural gas exports has declined substantially by an annual average of almost 30 per cent from 2010 to 2013 as rising domestic demand, particularly in the electricity sector, competed with exports.

Egypt began importing LNG in 2015 to satisfy its natural gas consumption, which increased by an annual average of 7 per cent over the previous decade (2004 to 2013). In May 2014, Egyptian Natural Gas Holding Company (EGAS), the country's national gas company, signed a letter of intent with Hoegh LNG of Norway to use one of its Floating Storage and Regasification Units (FSRUs) for five years to allow Egypt to import LNG.

Risk assessment

Economy	Fair/poor
Politics	Poor
Regional stability	Poor

Muslims in Egypt

% of population	90
Sunni (% of Muslims)	100
Shi'a (% of Muslims)	0

COUNTRY PROFILE

1571 Egypt became part of the Ottoman Empire. Mohammed Ali assumed the rule of Egypt. His descendants ruled until 1952.

1859–69 The Suez Canal was built.

1882 Britain occupied Egypt and although it remained under Ottoman suzerainty, it became *de facto* a British colony.

1914 Britain eliminated the Ottoman suzerainty and the country became a British protectorate – the Egyptian Sultanate.

1922 Following the revolution of Saad Zaghloul in 1919, Britain granted partial independence to Egypt, but retained the right to defend the Suez Canal and Egypt itself. Egypt was renamed Kingdom of Egypt.

1928 Muslim Brotherhood founded by Hasan al Banna.

1936 Signing of the Anglo-Egyptian Treaty, which restricted British military presence to the Suez Canal Zone.

1947–49 Egypt contributed to a pan-Arab military force that failed to occupy the newly-created state of Israel.

1952 The 23 July Revolution, led by the army, ousted King Fu'ad, who had just succeeded his father, King Faruq.

1953–56 Egypt was declared a republic under President Mohammed Neguib in 1953. Neguib relinquished power in 1954 to Colonel Gamal Abdel Nasser, who was officially elected in 1956.

1956 Nasser nationalised the Suez Canal to fund the construction of the Aswan High Dam to regulate the annual flooding

of the Nile River. Egypt blockaded the Israeli Red Sea port of Eilat; Israeli forces attacked and occupied the Sinai Peninsula, later being joined by Britain and France seeking to regain control of the Canal Zone. In the face of strong international opposition, particularly from the US, all three withdrew their forces.
1958 Egypt and Syria formed the United Arab Republic (UAR) in the first step towards their aim for Arab unity.
1961 Syria withdrew from the union with Egypt but Egypt remained known as the UAR.
1967 Egypt again blockaded Eilat; Israel launched and won the Six Day War against Egypt, Jordan and Syria, taking control of the Sinai Peninsula and the Gaza Strip, which had been Egyptian territory. Crucially, they also took control of the Golan Heights, overlooking Syria. The Suez Canal was closed.
1968–70 The War of Attrition was a limited war fought between Egypt and Israel, initiated by Egypt as a way to recapture the Sinai Peninsula from Israel; the war ended without changes to the frontiers.
1970–73 Anwar al Sadat was elected president following the death of Nasser. He renamed the country the Arab Republic of Egypt and ruled it as a one-party state. The Aswan High Dam was inaugurated by the President. In the 6 October War (also known as the Yom Kippur War), Egypt and Syria invaded Israel to reclaim some of the land lost in the Six Day War, but despite early strategic gains for Egypt and Syria, Israel counter-attacked and repelled the invasion, re-conquering the Golan Heights from Syria.
1975 The Suez Canal reopened, having been closed since the 1967 war.
1977 Sadat visited Jerusalem, which led to the Camp David Peace Accords, the signing of the Egyptian-Israeli Peace Treaty in 1979 and the eventual Israeli withdrawal from the Sinai Peninsula in 1982.
1981 President Sadat was assassinated by Islamic extremists. A national referendum approved Hosni Mubarak as president and also allowed political opposition parties for the first time. A State of Emergency (SoE) (known locally as emergency laws) was declared, extending police powers, suspending constitutional rights, legalising censorship, and curtailing political activity and street protests.
1979 Egypt was expelled from the Arab League.
1989 Egypt re-joined the Arab League.
1991–94 Egypt contributed to the US-led military campaign against Iraq. Egypt was a party to peace agreements between Israel and the Palestinians, which began negotiations on the status of the former Egyptian territory of Gaza.
1996–2000 The Al Hizb al Watani al Dimuqrati (National Democratic Party) (NDP) was re-elected in the 1996 and 2000 elections. Mubarak was re-elected president for a fourth term.
2003 Emergency powers established when Sadat was assassinated in 1981 were extended for another three years.
2004 Ahmed Nazif became prime minister. The funeral of Palestinian leader, Yasser Arafat, was held in Cairo.
2005 Egypt hosted the Sharm El Sheik summit, at which Palestinian President Abbas and Israeli Prime Minister Sharon signed a truce; Israel was to withdraw from Gaza and the Palestinian authorities curb the violence of militant groups opposed to Israel. Egypt resumed diplomatic ties with Israel. A constitutional amendment allowed multiple candidates in the presidential elections, which was won by incumbent Mubarak, for a fifth consecutive term.
2006 Emergency laws, which gave broad powers of arrest and detention to the security forces, were extended by two years.
2007 A referendum amended 34 articles in the constitution, including items aimed at banning political activities and the establishment of political parties based on race, religion and ethnicity; it also increased the power of the president and adopted an anti-terrorism law to replace emergency laws.
2008 Hamas militants breached several sections of the Egypt-Gaza Rafah border crossing allowing thousands of Palestinians to cross into Egypt, many to stock up on food and other necessities. Israel demanded that the border be closed to prevent the restocking of Hamas armouries. While foreign-led negotiations failed to provide a permanent solution, Hamas and Egyptian officials reached their own agreement.
2009 Egyptian forces closed the last breach along the Gaza border. In a crackdown on Islamist militants 25 leading members of Hizb al Wasat (Muslim Brotherhood) were jailed. Liberal democrat and opposition politician Ayman Nour (El Ghad) was released from jail on health grounds. Egypt sponsored talks between Palestinian rivals, Fatah and Hamas, over a proposed unity government.
2010 Mohammed Badi was named as leader (*general guide*) of Egypt's outlawed opposition Islamist movement, the Muslim Brotherhood. Analysts consider him a conservative who would likely steer the Brotherhood away from political activism and focus on religious and social work. The World Bank approved a US$280 million loan for a second terminal at Cairo's international airport. Sheikh Mohammed Sayed Tantawi, Grand Imam of the al Azhar mosque and head of the al Azhar University, died in Saudi Arabia, aged 81. President Mubarak issued a decree renewing the country's emergency laws for a further two years. Egypt signed an agreement with Ethiopia, Uganda, Tanzania and Rwanda to redistribute their relative share of Nile waters; negotiations had begun in 1997. In elections for the Majlis al Shura, the ruling NDP won 80 seats in total (out of 132). All opposition parties withdrew from further involvement in the general elections, following results that showed the NDP had won 209 out of 221 seats. The ruling NDP won an overwhelming majority of 420 seats (out of 518). The opposition, which had quit the election after the first round, cited extensive electoral fraud.
2011 Following mass-protests in Cairo's Tahrir Square at the leadership of President Mubarak, which began in January, Mubarak dismissed his government and appointed Ahmed Shafiq as prime minister in an attempt to pacify the protestors. However, the protests continued and in February, Mubarak resigned and control of Egypt was taken over by the Supreme Council of the Armed Forces (SCAF)), led by Field Marshall Mohamed Hussein Tantawi (defence minister); Ahmed Shafiq remained as prime minister. The SCAF refused to lift the emergency laws. Mr Mubarak and his family retreated to their residence in Sharm el Sheikh, the Red Sea resort. By 11 February there had been 384 confirmed deaths related to the demonstrations; of which 232 deaths were in Cairo. All prisoners arrested since January were released and an investigation into officials responsible for violence towards demonstrators was begun.
A constitutional referendum was held in March, in which 77.27 per cent of voters agreed to constitutional changes that included limiting the presidential term to four years and a two-term limit. SCAF announced that Mubarak and his family had been placed under house arrest. Essam Abdel-Aziz Sharaf became prime minister. The former ruling-NDP was dissolved in April and its assets, including its headquarters and other buildings, were seized and handed over to the government treasury. The prosecutor general ordered the arrest of Mubarak and his sons, Alaa and Gamal, on charges of corruption.
In April the Muslim Brotherhood announced it was setting up a new political party, the Hizb al Hurriya wa al'Adala (Freedom and Justice Party) (FJP). It said it would be a civil, not a theocratic, group and would contest up to half the seats in the September election. It was officially recognised as a political party in June. Nabil al Arabi became secretary general of the Arab League.

In May the Egyptian government relaxed restrictions at the Rafah border crossing into Gaza, allowing women, children and men over 40 to pass freely. Men aged between 18 and 40 will still require a permit, and trade is prohibited.
In July, thousands of protestors gathered in Tahrir Square, Suez and Alexandria, as part of the 'Friday of Determination' demanding immediate reforms and a quicker prosecution of former government officials. Prime Minister Essam Sharaf reshuffled his cabinet in mid-July, after protesters complained about the slow rate of reform. Too many of the ministers, especially foreign minister Mohamed Orabi, were said to have been close to former President Mubarak, resulting in Orabi's resignation. The news agency Mena stated that Hosni Mubarak was 'depressed and refusing food' in hospital. In August Mubarak was put on trial for corruption and complicity in the deaths of protestors, during the Arab Spring uprising. The judge at Mubarak's trial announced that it would be merged with that of former interior minister, Habib al Adly, who was also accused of ordering the killing of protesters. The trial was adjourned until September and the live televising of the trial was halted.
In September the Israeli embassy was attacked by demonstrators in Cairo.
Changes to the issuance of visas were announced it September, including halting the facility whereby US and many European citizens could obtain a visa on arrival. The move was expected to have an adverse effect on tourism, although the government denied this.
An amendment to the election law was granted by the Supreme Council of the Armed Forces, in October to allow one-third of parliamentary seats that had been set aside for political parties to be contested by independent candidates.
There were clashes between Copts and security forces in October. The clashes led to the resignation of finance minister, Hazem el Beblawi, who objected to the way the government handled the protest.
In November, a government-sponsored set of guidelines for drafting the constitution were published and caused controversy with plans to exempt the military and its budget from civilian scrutiny and by giving the military a veto over legislation dealing with its affairs, as well as limiting the power of parliament to select a panel to write the constitution. In November, the Higher Administrative Court ruled that former members of the NDP (former-president Mubarak's political party) were allowed to stand for parliament as independent candidates. Prime Minister Sharaf and his government resigned on 21 November, following three days of violence as demonstrators again occupied Tahrir Square in Cairo, protesting at the military's entrenchment of its power in the political life of Egypt. By 22 November, 26 people had been killed and many more maimed and wounded; Field Marshal Tantawi declared that scheduled parliamentary elections would take place and presidential elections would be held in July 2012 (brought forward from late-2012 or 2013). However, protestors continued to call for the military rulers to step aside. There were protests and injuries in other cities as well. On 24 November, the ruling (SCAF appointed Kamal Ganzouri as prime minister.
Parliamentary elections for the lower chamber began on 28 November, and were held in three rounds (the second on 5/6 December and the third on 14/15 December) to allow judicial supervision of each round. Over 40 political parties fielded a combined total of around 6,000 candidates to contest the 498-seat lower house, of which two-thirds will be chosen by proportional representation using party lists; the remaining one-third are open to all who are nominated regardless of affiliations – of these half must be 'professional' and the other half 'workers' or 'farmers'.
2012 The final results of three rounds of elections were posted on 13 January. The combined results were: Democratic Alliance for Egypt (DAE) (a coalition of five political parties, led by the FJP, plus independents) (Islamic, Muslim Brotherhood) won 127 seats by proportional representation (PR) and 108 seats by first-past-the-post (FPTP) for a total of 235 seats; the Islamic Bloc (a coalition of three political parties, led by the Al Nour Party) 96 PR, 27 FPTP, total 123 seats; New Wafd Party 36 PR, two FPTP, total 38 seats; Egyptian Bloc (a coalition of three political parties, led by the Social Democratic Party), 33 PR, one FPTP, total 34 seats; Al Wasat Party 10 PR, total 10 seats; Reform and Development Party eight PR, one FPTP, total nine seats; the Revolution Continues Alliance (a coalition of five political parties, led by the Socialist Popular Alliance Party) seven PR, two FPTP, total nine seats; eight other political parties and 21 independent candidates won the remaining 40 seats. Although the DAE will have overall legislative powers the military council retains presidential powers until a new president is elected later in the year.
The rules of the first post-Mubarak presidential elections were announced on 31 January. All candidates must be born Egyptian to Egyptian parents, not be of dual nationality nor married to a foreigner. All candidates must be endorsed by at least 30 members of parliament or 30,000 eligible voters.
The new parliament was sworn in on 23 January. In an interview on 19 February, the electoral commissioner declined to set a date for presidential elections, which were expected for June. Instead he expressed a hope that the organisational process necessary before the elections take place could be completed by May. The delay was due to problems of organising the expatriate vote and the foreign minister had asked for more time.
On 1 March, the presidential election was announced for 23–24 May; a runoff was scheduled for 16–17 June if necessary.
Coptic Pope Shenouda III died on 17 March at the age of 88.
On 24 March, the liberal block of members of parliament (MPs) walked out during a vote to elect members of a panel that will draft a new constitution, due to what they said were Islamists trying to monopolise the process. One of the first topics to be discussed for the new constitution will be how heavily it would be based on *sharia* (Islamic law).
On 29 March, senior members of the Sunni Islamic faith withdrew from the talks for the draft constitution saying it was under-represented in the constitutional assembly. This was followed by the Coptic Orthodox (Christian) Church on 2 April, which announced that it was withdrawing from the talks saying its participation was 'pointless' as the process was dominated by Islamists.
The SCAF expunged two court convictions against the new presidential candidate of the Muslim Brotherhood, Khairat al Shater. He had been convicted by the military in 1995 of reviving the Muslim Brotherhood (then a banned political party) and in 2007 of supplying weapons and giving training to university students.
On 10 April the Administrative Court in Cairo suspended the constitutional assembly (formed to draft the new constitution), saying the legitimacy of parliament to select members of the assembly and allocate 50 seats (out of 100) to sitting MPs did not reflect the diversity of Egyptian society. The choices were repeating the poor representation of women, minority communities and young people. Nobel peace prize winner and former Director General of the International Atomic Energy Agency (IAEA), Mohamed El Baradei, launched a new political party on 28 April, called the Constitution Party. The launch came too late to field a candidate in the presidential election.
In the first round of the presidential election, held on 23–24 May, 13 candidates took part. Mohamed Morsi (FJP, (Muslim Brotherhood)) won 24.78 per cent of the vote, Ahmed Shafiq (independent but

allied to military government of Mubarak) 23.66 per cent and Hamdeen Sabahi (independent) 20.72 per cent. On 1 June, the 31-year state of emergency (SoE) was lifted.

On 2 June Hosni Mubarak was sentenced to life imprisonment, along with former interior minister, Habib al Adly, for complicity in the killings of protestors in Tahrir Square in early 2011. Four other high ranking officials were acquitted; Mubarak's sons were also acquitted of corruption. Following the announcement crowds gathered in Tahrir Square protesting that the sentences were either too lenient or improper.

On 8 June, an agreement was reached between 22 political parties and the head of SCAF on selection of the 100-member constitutional assembly. On 14 June, the justice minister granted military police and intelligence officers the right to investigate and arrest civilians for offences related to national security and public order. The authorisation caused disquiet among civil liberty groups that warned that the move reintroduced powers cancelled when the SoE ended.

On 14 June the Supreme Court overturned the results of the December 2011 parliamentary elections saying the results were unconstitutional and ordered fresh elections; the decision effectively returned power to the SCAF. The biggest winners of the last elections, the FJP, warned that fragile democratic gains were under threat and Egypt was on course for 'very difficult days that might be more dangerous than the last days of Mubarak's rule'. It also said that all 'democratic gains could be overturned with the handing of power to one of the symbols of the pervious era.' FJP presidential candidate Mohammed Morsi accepted but was dissatisfied with the court ruling.

The presidential election run-off was held on 16–17 June. On 18 June, the SCAF granted itself extensive powers, including near total autonomy in military matters and the ability to exercise a veto over the drafting of the new constitution. On 19 June Hosni Mubarak was taken to hospital following a stroke and remained in a 'critical' condition for several days. The result of the runoff president elections was due to be announced on 21 June, however on 20 June the electoral commission said it was delaying the announcement because it needed more time to consider complaints made by the candidates. Both candidates by this time had claimed victory and the delay caused tension within their respective supporter groups. On 24 June, the election commission announced that Mohammed Morsi had won the run-off and he was inaugurated as president on 30 June.

On 9 July President Morsi ordered parliament to reconvene until new elections could be held. The edict countermanded the dissolution ordered by the SCAF, which held emergency talks to formulate a response. On 10 July the Supreme Constitutional Court overturned President Morsi's decree to reopen parliament, leading to the gathering of thousands of protestors in Tahrir Square.

On 16 July former president Mubarak was ordered to return to prison, having survived his medical emergency. On 24 July, President Morsi appointed an independent politician, Hesham Qandil as prime minister (he took office on 2 August). On 12 August, President Morsi ordered Field Marshall Tantawi and the military Chief of Staff, Sami Annan, to retire 'for the benefit of this nation'. President Morsi also said that the constitutional declaration aimed at curbing presidential powers, introduced in June by SCAF had been cancelled. On 7 August, 16 soldiers were killed in Sinai, close to the border with Gaza, which resulted in a military operation to counter 'criminal elements' in September; 32 'non-Egyptians' were killed and 38 arrested. On 23 October, the Cairo Administrative Court requested the Supreme Court to make a ruling on the constitutionality of allowing the MPs to decide who was chosen to draw up the new constitution. On 4 November, Bishop Tawadros was chosen in a ceremony to become Pope Theodoros II of Alexandria, leader of the Coptic Church; he took office on 18 November. On 22 November, President Morsi assumed extensive powers banning any challenges to his presidential decrees, laws and decisions, including a bar on legal rulings that might dissolve parliament and the constitutional assembly. The president also sacked the chief prosecutor and ordered retrials of top officials under former president Mubarak who were alleged to have ordered the attack on protestors during the 2011 political demonstrations. On 3 December senior judiciary announced that they would refuse to oversee the referendum on the new constitution, due to be held on 15 December.

2013 Mubarak appealed his sentence, citing 'procedural failings', and a retrial was ordered. Mubarak's retrial began on 13 April but Judge Mustafa Hassan Abdullah immediately withdrew citing 'unease' over reviewing the case. A court ruled on 15 April that he could nolonger be held on charges related to the killing of protesters, although corruption charges remained. On 17 April he was ordered back to prison from military hospital. The retrial began on 11 May, presided over by Judge Mahmud al-Rashidi. President Morsi gave a long (two hours) speech on 26 June, marking his first year in office, in which he acknowledged making 'mistakes' and offering opponents a say in amending the new constitution. There were demonstrations by opponents of Mr Morsi. On 1 July the army warned that unless the two sides could settle their disagreements by 3 July the army would intervene, although what they actually meant by this was unclear. On 3 July President Morsi was put under house arrest and the head of Egypt's constitutional court, Adli Mansour, was sworn in as head of state on 4 July. Protesters for and against Mr Morsi gathered in Tahrir Square (against) and around the Rabaa al-Adawiya mosque (for). On 5 July the African Union suspended Egypt's membership. On 8 July at least 51 people – mostly pro-Morsi supporters from the Muslim Brotherhood – were killed by the army outside the Presidential Guard headquarters where Mr Morsi was believed to be held. Mr Mansour put forward a proposal for a timetable for a panel to be formed within 15 days to review the constitution with amendments to be finalised and put to a referendum in four months; parliamentary elections would be held by early 2014 with a presidential election to be called once the new parliament convenes. The proposal was rejected by the Muslim Brotherhood as talks of any sort became more and more difficult. The Salafist Nour party, the second largest Islamist force, pulled out of negotiations over a new caretaker prime minister and cabinet.

Rumours started that pro-reform leader Mohamed El Baradei would be appointed as interim prime minister after he had met with Mr Mansour. However on 8 July Mr Mansour named ex-finance minister Hazem el Beblawi as prime minister and el Baradei as vice president. Talks on forming a cabinet began on 10 July. Mr Beblawi said that he would offer positions to Brotherhood's FJP and the ultraconservative Salafist Nour party, even though both had refused to take part in the talks.

On 9 July Saudi Arabia and the United Arab Emirates announced aid packages for Egypt – US$8 billion and US$3 billion respectively. The aid will be a mix of cash, central bank deposits and oil products.

An interim government was sworn in on 16 July. Army chief General Abdel Fattah al Sisi, who led the ousting of Morsi, became deputy prime minister. The US announced on 24 July that they would be delaying the delivery of four F-16 fighter jets. Riots and demonstrations in Cairo and Alexandria by groups both for and against deposed president Morsi lead to a number of deaths in late July. The Muslim Brotherhood accused the army of opening fire on them. EU foreign policy chief,

Baroness Catherine Ashton, had two hours of 'in-depth' discussions with Mr Morsi on 29 July. Although she was taken to see him, reportedly by helicoptor, she says she does not know where he is being held. She said he was well and able to follow developments through television and newspapersin early August US senators John McCain and Lindsey Graham joined top diplomats in Cairo to help find a peaceful solution to Egypt's political stalemate. On 7 August the interim government said foreign mediation had failed. The US and the EU called on all sides to end 'a dangerous stalemate'. The army-backed government was reported as saying it will break up sit-ins in Cairo being held by supporters of ousted President Morsi. Although the government said they would be dispersing the two sit-ins supporting Mr Morsi, on 12 August they postponed their plans. In the early hours of 14 August armoured troops moved on the demonstrators's camps. Initial reports were of hundreds killed. A state of emergency was declared on 14 August and Mohamed El Baradei resigned as vice president. There was widespread international condemnation. The US still refrained from calling the army take over (on 3 July) as a 'coup' since under US law this would mean withdrawing all aid (US$1.15 billion), nearly all in the form of military aid. The number of persons killed was finally recorded as 638 and those injured over 3,500. On 16 August the Muslim Brotherhood called for a 'day of anger' protest in Ramses Square. Over 170 were said to have died. On 17 August the army laid seige to al-Fath mosque and eventually cleared away the demonstrators. Reports circulated that interim Prime Minister Beblawi had proposed dissolving the Muslim Brotherhood. Army chief, General Abdul Fattah al Sisi, said in a speech on 18 August that 'We will not stand idle in face of the destruction and torching of the country, the terrorising of the people and the sending of a wrong image to the Western media that there is fighting in the streets'. In an apparent move to address the adverse international reaction his comments followed those of a presidential advisor who accused Western media of ignoring attacks on police and the destruction of churches blamed on Islamists. On 19 August it was reported that 36 members of the Muslim Brotherhood died while being transported to prison. Muslim Brotherhood leader, Mohammed Badie, was arrested on 18 August; his deputy, Mahmoud Ezzat, temporarily replaced his as 'general guide'. Hosni Mubarak was released from the Tora jail on 22 August, ostensibly because he had served the maximum amount of pre-trial detention. Initially taken to a military hospital, he will remain under house arrest until he can be tried on charges of corruption and being involved in the killing of demonstrators during the 2011 protests. The interim government relaxed the curfew on 25 August. Mr Mubarak and his two sons appeared in court on 25 August. On 1 September the state prosecutor referred ex-president Morsi for trial on charges of inciting the murder of protesters. Four TV stations, including Ahrar 25 (run by the Muslim Brotherhood) and Al Jazeera, were ordered to close by the government on 3 September. This follows a crackdown on media said to be in support of Mr Morsi. Supporters of Mr Morsi were convicted of attacking the army and given long prison sentences by a military court on 3 September. The government denied on 6 September reports in the media that the Muslim Brotherhood would be banned. The state of emergency was extended by another two months on 23 September. A media black out was imposed by Judge Mahmoud el Rachidi for the Mubarek re-trial sessions to be held on 19–21 October. The Cairo Court for Urgent Matters ruled on 23 September that all Muslim Brotherhood activities should be banned. The ruling included the Islamist movement, its non-governmental organisation and any affiliated groups. The Court also ordered the seizure of all Brotherhood funds. On 7 October the US announced it was suspending the delivery of large-scale military systems and withholding cash support. The trial of Mr Morsi was set to begin on 4 November. The charges are of inciting murder and violence. The trial of Muslim Brotherhood leader Mohammed Badie and his two aides was halted on 29 October after the three presiding judges retired for 'reasons of conscience'. The trial of Mr Morsi was adjourned until 8 January after he told the judge the trial was illigitimate as he was still president. A high level Russian delegation visited Cairo in November to hold talks which are reported to include the sale of arms. The state of emergency was lifted on 12 November.

2014 The cabinet resigned *en masse* on 24 February. Ibrahim Mahlab was appointed Acting Prime Minister on 1 March. On 26 March Field Marshall Abdul Fattah al Sisi announced his decision to run for president in the next presidential election. He resigned as defence minister the following day and was succeeded by Sedki Sobhi who was sworn in as armed forces chief and defence minister the same day. Presidential elections were held on 26–28 May between Abdul Fattah al Sisi and Hamdeen Sabahi (voting was extended for a third day). Al Sisi won convincingly with 23.78 million votes (96.91 per cent). Turnout was 47.5 per cent. Muslim Brotherhood leader Mohammed Badie and 36 other Islamists were sentenced to life in jail on 5 July. The *al-Masry al-Youm* newspaper reported on 8 July that President al Sisi had said he wished that the three al Jazeera journalists who had been tried for of aiding the banned Muslim Brotherhood group had never been put on trial. The journalists had been found guilty of 'supporting the Muslim Brotherhood' and in July were sentenced to seven years (Peter Greste and Mohamed Fahmy) and ten years (Baher Mohamed) in prison. The charges against Mubarak over killings during the uprisings in 2011 were dropped by the court on 29 November. Police used tear gas to disperse protesters. Mubarak will continue to serve a separate three-year sentence for embezzlement of public funds.

2015 On 13 January the convictions for embezzlement of Hosni Mubarak and his two sons (Alaa and Gamal Mubarak) were overturned by the Court of Cassation which had found that legal procedures had not been followed properly. A retrial was ordered. Also in January the convictions of the three al Jazeera journalists were overturned a retrial was ordered. Alaa and Gamal Mubarak were released from prison on 26 January although their father remained in Cairo military hospital. On 29 January at least 26 people were killed in the Sinai Peninsula Islamist militant attacks. Al Jazeera journalist Peter Greste, was freed from jail on 1 February and returned to Australia. On 7 March Mahmoud Ramadan, a supporter of deposed president Morsi, became the first to be hung after being convicted of taking part in the violent uprisings of March 2013. Housing minister, Mostafa Madbouly, announced plans on 13 March to build a new capital to the east of Cairo. Costing US$45 billion the project would take five to seven years to complete and would help ease congestion and overpopulation in Cairo over the next 40 years. On 20 April Mr Morsi was sentenced to 20 years in jail for ordering the arrest and torture of protesters during his rule. He is expected to appeal the verdict. The Egyptian public prosecutor, Hisham Barakat, was killed by a car bomb on 29 June. The perpetrators were thought to be Sinai Province, which was known as Ansar Beit al-Maqdis until it pledged allegiance to Islamic State in November. Two days later a group of militants, also thought to be Sinai Province, launched several attacks in the Sinai Peninsula. The Egyptian military responded with heavy weapons and reported that '100 members of the terrorist elements' had been killed, and 'large numbers' injured in fighting in

North Sinai. It also said 17 soldiers had been killed. On 1 July nine members of the Muslim Brotherhood were killed in a police raid on a flat in Cairo, including leader Nasser al-Houfi. The AU agreed to lift the freeze on Egypt's membership in June; President Sisi planned

Political structure

Constitution

Under the 1971 constitution, amended in 1980, Egypt is an Arab Republic with a democratic socialist system. The constitution states that there should be no discrimination on the grounds of race or religion. The country is divided into 26 governorates, with governors appointed by the president. There is universal suffrage with a voting age of 18.

On 20 March 2011, in a constitutional referendum, 77.27 per cent of voters agreed to constitutional changes that included limiting the presidential term to four years and to a two-term limit. Other changes included the appointment, by the president, of a vice president within 60 days of taking office; the power of the president to declare a state of emergency to be circumscribed by a parliamentary majority; presidential candidates to be aged over 40 years and not of dual-nationality, nor married to a non-Egyptian; the judiciary to be responsible for monitoring the electoral process; the Supreme Court to have the power to adjudicate electoral challenges and disputes; civilians to no-longer be tried by military courts and the newly elected parliament must write a new constitution within 60 day of its election in 2011.

A controversial 2012 constitution passed into law by similarly controversial president Mohamed Morsi was recently superseded by a military-backed 2014 version. The current constitution outlines the role of president and parliament and bequeaths parliament the power of impeachment. It also stipulates that political parties are forbidden to be based 'religion, race, gender or geography', while guaranteeing freedom of expression, freedom of religion (although Islam remains the state religion) and equality between the sexes. However, it has been criticised in some quarters as continuing the Egyptian military's historic stranglehold on political power, as they retain the ability to appoint the Minister of Defence for the next 8 years. It was passed with a 98.13 per cent majority; turnout was 38.59 per cent.

Independence date

1922 (Britain supervised until 1946)

Form of state

Republic

The executive

Executive power rests with the president, who is elected by universal suffrage for a six-year term (and may be re-elected), having been nominated by at least one-third of the People's Assembly and approved by at least two-thirds. The president may choose one or more vice presidents, and appoints, and may dismiss, the prime minister and cabinet.

The president may take emergency measures, but these must be approved by a referendum within 60 days; he may also dissolve the People's Assembly (the legislative body) prematurely, but a referendum and elections must be held within 60 days.

The president is supreme commander of the armed forces and head of the police.

National legislature

The bicameral parliament consists of the Majlis al Shaab (People's Assembly, lower house), with 454 members directly elected by universal suffrage and 10 members appointed by the president. All members serve for a five-year term. The Majlis al Shura (Advisory Council, upper house) has 264 members of which 174 are directly elected and the remainder appointed by the president, to serve for six-year terms. Every three years elections for an alternate half the membership takes place. Legislative powers of the Advisory Council are limited; the People's Assembly has ultimate power.

Legal system

The legal system is based on the constitution of 1971. Officially, Egyptian law is based on *Sharia* (Islamic law), although in practice it is based on English common law and the French Napoleonic code. Christians and Jews are subject to their own jurisprudence in personal status affairs. The Court of Cassation, consisting of five judges, is the highest court of appeal. Courts of appeal (three judges) sit in Cairo and four other cities. Assize courts (three judges) deal with serious crimes. Central tribunals (three judges) handle ordinary civil and commercial cases. Summary tribunals (one judge) deal with both civil and criminal cases and have the power to impose fines and decree three-year prison terms.

Last elections

28–29 November, 5–6 and 14–15 December 2011 (parliamentary (lower house)); 26–28 May 2014 (presidential).

Results: Parliamentary (combined total after three rounds): Democratic Alliance for Egypt (a coalition of seven political parties, led by the Freedom and Justice Party (Islamic, Muslim Brotherhood) plus independents) won 127 seats by proportional representation (PR) and 108 seats by first-past-the-post (FPTP) for a total of 235 seats (out of 498); the Islamic Bloc (a coalition of three political parties, led by the Al Nour Party) 96 PR, 27 FPTP, total 123 seats; New Wafd Party 36 PR, two FPTP, total 38 seats; Egyptian Bloc (a coalition of three political parties, led by the Social Democratic Party) 33 PR, one FPTP, total 34 seats; Al Wasat Party 10 PR, total 10 seats; Reform and Development Party eight PR, one FPTP, total nine seats; The Revolution Continues Alliance (a coalition of five political parties, led by the Socialist Popular Alliance Party) seven PR, total seven seats; eight other political parties and 21 independent candidates won the remaining 40 seats. 10 seats are reserved for executive appointees, typically from the military.

Presidential: Abdel Fattah el Sisi 23.78 million votes (96.91 per cent), Hamdeen Sabahi (Egyptian Popular Curren) 757,511 votes (3.09 per cent). Turnout was 47.5 per cent.

Next elections

2018 (presidential); 2016–17 (parliamentary, lower house);

Political parties

Ruling party

No ruling party as such

Main opposition party

While the Islamic Bloc (a coalition of three political parties, led by the Al Nour Party) won the second largest number of seats in parliament it is ideologically closer to the ruling Islamic Brotherhood coalition, whereas the Egyptian Bloc (a coalition of three political parties, led by the Social Democratic Party) are more opposed to both parties' political position. The Freedom and Justice Party has since been banned, but continues operations underground.

Population

82.50 million (2012)* The birth rate is projected to fall by 0.2 per cent per annum in the period 1997–2010, while the population aged over 15 years will grow by 2.5 per cent per annum. Approximately 37 per cent of the population is under 14 years.

An estimated 99 per cent of the total population is based on or around the river Nile.

Last census: 11 November 2006: 72,798,013

Population density: 63 inhabitants per square km. Urban population 43 per cent (2010 Unicef).

Annual growth rate: 1.4 per cent, 1990–2010 (Unicef).

Ethnic make-up

Eastern Hamitic (99 per cent); the remaining 1 per cent comprises minorities including Armenian, Italian and Greek.

Religions

Muslim (mostly Sunni, but including between six and seven million Sufis) (92 per cent); Coptic Christian and others (8 per cent).

Education

Primary education is compulsory and free; followed by three years of intermediate school and two years of secondary school, which are also free, but not compulsory. University graduates have long been guaranteed employment by the state, and this has contributed to the growth of a bloated and overstaffed state bureaucracy. The desire by graduates for office-based professional employment has led to a shortage of skilled technical labour. The government is encouraging more students to go into technical education.

Literacy rate: 56 per cent adult rate; 73 per cent youth rate (15–24) (Unesco 2005).

Compulsory years: 6 to 12

Enrolment rate: 101 per cent, total primary school enrolment of the relevant age group (including repetition rates); 78 per cent, total enrolment of the relevant age group, in intermediate and secondary schools, (World Bank).

Pupils per teacher: 23 in primary schools

Health

Healthcare in the private sector has become increasingly popular in recent years, especially in Cairo, with the construction of a number of private hospitals that provide an alternative to the severely over-stretched public health service. However the general decline in living standards has placed many private sector healthcare institutions in financial difficulties.

Family planning is widely available and officially encouraged, although many religious leaders continue to preach that it is against Islam. The population continues to grow and the government expects it to double to 110 million over the next 30 years, even if the target of halving the average family size is achieved.

Improved water sources and sanitation facilities are available to 95 per cent and 94 per cent of the population, respectively.

HIV/Aids

HIV prevalence: 0.1 per cent aged 15–49 in 2003 (World Bank)

Life expectancy: 68 years, 2004 (WHO 2006)

Fertility rate/Maternal mortality rate: 2.7 births per woman, 2010 (Unicef); maternal mortality 170 per 100,000 live births (World Bank).

Child (under 5 years) mortality rate (per 1,000): 21 per 1,000 live births (WHO 2012); 4 per cent of children aged under five were malnourished (World Bank).

Head of population per physician: 0.54 physicians per 1,000 people, 2003 (WHO 2006)

Welfare

Social security provisions include sickness benefits, pensions, health insurance, training and subsidies on basic goods, including pharmaceuticals. The government places particular stress on the improvement of rural living standards and has established rural social units to provide health, education and agricultural services. Social services include care for mothers and children, the aged, the handicapped and prisoners, family planning, cultural education and literacy courses. The government, employers and employees contribute to a national insurance scheme that covers pensions and sickness benefit. A social development fund provides retraining, unemployment insurance and assistance to people who lose their jobs as a result of reforms and the privatisation of public enterprises.

Main cities

Cairo (capital, estimated population 8.3 million (m) in 2012); Greater Cairo, 10.6m, is the largest city in Africa. Other cities include Alexandria (4.5m), Giza (6.6m), Shubra al Khaymah (1.1m), Port Said (625,958), Suez (565,716), Luxor (506,588), El Mansura (495,630), El Mahalla el Kubra (465,278), Tanta (445,560).

Languages spoken

French and English are widely spoken, especially in business circles.

Official language/s

Arabic

Media

Egypt is the centre for pan-Arab electronic broadcasting having been the first with its own satellite (Nilesat 101) (www.nilesat.com.eg), it has the largest production facilities for Arabic films and TV shows and is the most influential news broadcasting and publishing centre in the Middle East.

While libelling the president, state institution and foreign heads of state may carry a penality of imprisonment, criticism of the regime in unexceptional.

On 23 August 2012, President Mursi banned pre-trail detention of journalists.

Press

Dailies: In Arabic, *Al Ahram* (www.ahram.org.eg) the oldest Arabic newspaper anywhere and the government-owned *Al Jumhuriyah* (www.algomhuria.net.eg), and the semi-state owned *Al Akhbar* (www.elakhbar.org.eg). Party political newspapers include and *Al Messa* (www.almessa.net.eg), *Almasry Alyoum* (www.almasry-alyoum.com), and *Al Ahali* (www.al-ahaly.com). Other private newspapers include *Al Wafd* (www.alwafd.org), *El Akhbar* (www.elakhbar.org.eg) and *El Fagr* (www.elfagr.org).

In English, the state-owned *The Egyptian Gazette* (www.algomhuria.net.eg/gazette) and *Daily News Egypt* (www.dailystaregypt.com).

In French, in government-owned *Al-Ahram Hebdo* (http://hebdo.ahram.org.eg) and *Le Progrès Egyptien* (www.progres.net.eg).

Weeklies: Some daily newspapers have weekend editions. In Arabic, the political magazine *Al Watan al Arabi* (www.alwatanalarabi.alqanat.com) covers regional news, *Akidaty* for general interest and *Horreyati* (www.horreyati.net.eg) for entertainment. Women's magazines include *Nisf el Dunia* with social and women's issues, *Hawwa* covers home and family issues and *Kolenas* is distributed internationally.

In English, the *Middle East Times* (www.metimes.com) provides general interest and commercial and financial news, *Watani* (www.wataninet.com), and *Al-Ahram* (http://weekly.ahram.org.eg).

Business: Most daily newspapers have sections on business matters. The only dedicated newspaper is the *Business Today Egypt* (www.businesstodayegypt.com), in English, which has a section called *In the Black* specifically covering commercial and corporate news.

In Arabic the weekly *Al Ahram Iktisadi* covers analysis of Egyptian business.

Periodicals: Monthly publications in Arabic includes the influential *Sabah el Kheir* (www.rosaonline.net/sabah) which covers general interest features. The quarterly *Al Siassa al Dawlya* covers domestin and international politics.

IBA Media is Egypt's leading English-language publisher with *Egypt Today* (www.egypttoday.com), published six times per year.

Broadcasting

The national, public broadcaster is the Egypt Radio Television Union (ERTU) (www.ertu.org).

Radio: ERTU provides cultural, news, entertainment, youth and sports programmes through a network of eight national radio stations with two external services. Private, commerical stations include El Gouna Radio (www.romolo.com) and Nile FM (http://nilefmonline.com), both playing western music.

Television: ERTU operates two national and local channels. There are numerous satellite TV stations available, led by the ERTU Nile Channel, (www.nilesat.com.eg), Dream TV and Al Mihwar (www.elmehwar.tv) are privately owned.

Egyptian broadcasters transmit over 80 channels throughout the Middle East and the Mediterranean region.
National news agency: MENA (Middle East News Agency)

Economy

Despite natural resources of petroleum, natural gas, phosphates, gold and iron ore, plus agricultural produce of wheat and cotton, and a major tourist industry, manufacturing in pharmaceuticals, vehicles and parts, the economy could only provide a per capita income of US$2,808 in 2010, however, economic improvements and prosperity within the country have ensured that this figure has risen to US$3,436 in 2014.

Egypt is Africa's second most populous country (after Nigeria), with over 80 million citizens, and Cairo is the continent's largest city. In 2014, the UN Human Development Index (HDI) ranked Egypt 110 (out of 187) for national development in health, education and income. Since the mid-1990s, Egypt's progress has grown to match other Arab states in the region. Even so, in 2014, the UN reported that 8.93 per cent of the population were in some form of multidimensional poverty.

The global economic crisis had little effect on the Egyptian economy, as its banking sector is not heavily integrated into world financial markets, and there is relatively low private credit. Banking regulations over 2004–07 increased bank asset requirements, which proved to be a major buffer to the weakness suffered by foreign banks in Western markets. In fact at no time did the economy slip into recession and the 4.7 per cent growth in 2009 grew to 5.1 per cent in 2010. Since then, growth has stabilised to 2.2 per cent in 2014.

The crisis that toppled the regime of Hosni Mubarak in 2011 was estimated to have cost the country over US$301 million per day. Economic growth was also affected as the tourist industry collapsed, followed by a significant decrease in investment and trade. The political turmoil resulted in an estimated fall in growth rate to 1.8 per cent. Inflation, which has been a long-term problem with an annual average of 11 per cent, peaked at 16.2 per cent in 2009. It has since reduced to 10 per cent in 2014.

The economy is also sustained by Suez Canal tolls and remittances from expatriate workers. However, both recorded declines as global trade slowed and employment became scarce in 2008. Suez Canal tolls fell from a high of US$5.2 billion in 2007/08 to US$4.7 billion in 2008/09; but by 2012/13 revenues were up to US$5 billion. Remittances averaged US$7.2 billion over 2006–09, surging to US$12.5 billion in 2010 – which the World Bank speculated could have been sparked by falling domestic house prices which encouraged expatriate Egyptian's to invest in their home country. Remittances stood at US$20 billion in 2013.

Egypt inaugurated a major extension of the Suez Canal in 2015, which President Sisi hopes will power an economic turnaround in the Arab world's most populous country. Egypt expects the economic zone to eventually make up about a third of the country's economy, according to the investment minister in March 2015.

The industrial sector constituted 39.9 per cent of GDP in 2014, of which manufacturing accounted for 15 per cent. The service sector remained dominant at 45.6 per cent and agriculture registered 14.5 per cent of GDP.

The hydrocarbon sector is the mainstay of the economy. Oil reserves at the end of 2014 stood at 4.4 billion barrels and production was 667,000 barrels per day (bpd). Natural gas reserves stood at 2.2 trillion cubic metres (cum) at the end of 2013 and production was 61.2 billion cum.

Agriculture is largely in private hands, although certain commodities deemed strategic to the economy such as cotton, sugar and rice, are still regulated by the government.

Textile and garment manufacturing is a major sector in the economy, not only as a large employer but also as an earner of foreign exchange. Around 25 per cent of non-hydrocarbon exports are made up of finished clothes and fabrics. Egypt has the continent's largest garment industry.

The Islamic Development Bank (IDB) and the World Bank announced in 2010, that they were setting up a regional initiative of up to US$1 billion to help close the infrastructure gap in the Middle East and North Africa (Mena) and help boost economic growth. The World Bank considered that the Mena region required US$75–100 billion per year to sustain the growth of recent years and boost economic competitiveness. However private sector investment is limited and the new initiative should address the shortfall in investment, through Sharia-compliant and conventional investment. The initiative will benefit Egypt, Morocco, Jordan and Tunisia in particular.

According to the IMF, the political turmoil of 2011 triggered a sharp capital account reversal and left growth depressed. For the last four years, growth has been only 2 percent on average, and the unemployment rate has risen to over 13 per cent. Fiscal deficits have been above 10 per cent of GDP since 2011, and have been largely financed domestically, thereby contributing to the relatively high level of inflation; general government debt reached 90.5 per cent of GDP in mid-2014.

On 23 August 2012 Egypt applied to the IMF for a US$4.8 billion loan at the same time as Qatar paid US$500 million in financial support to Egypt, the first instalment of US$2 billion, with payment in full in September. Central bank reserves had fallen from US$36 billion at the end of 2010 to US$14.6 billion in August 2012 and there was a risk that Egypt could not maintain imports of basic commodities (such as wheat and fuel) and could default on its international loans. The IMF stated that Egypt needed a reform programme to deal with its economic crisis. However, The Egyptian government believed many of these reforms could be politically risky and so in 2013 postponed plans to accept the IMF loan.

External trade

Egypt, as a member of the Common Market for Eastern and Southern Africa (Comesa), operates within a free trade zone (FTZ) with 13 of the 19 member states. It has also signed the Agadir Agreement which proposes to set up a FTZ between Egypt, Jordan, Tunisia and Morocco. In 2005 the Greater Arab Free Trade Area (Gafta) was ratified by 17 members, including Egypt, creating an Arab economic bloc. A customs union was established whereby tariffs within Gafta are reduced by one per cent each year, until none remain.

The EU-Egypt Association Agreement, in force since 2004, establishes a free-trade area with the elimination of tariffs on industrial products and significant concessions on agricultural products. In addition, an ambitious agreement on agricultural, processed agricultural and fisheries products entered into force in June 2010.

Imports

Principal imports are machinery and equipment, foodstuffs, chemicals, wood products and fuels.
Main sources: China (11.3 per cent of total in 2014), Germany (7.8 per cent), United States (7.3 per cent)

Exports

Principal exports are crude oil and petroleum products, cotton, textiles, metal products and chemicals. Other exports include refined sugar cane, raw cotton, potatoes, rice and oranges.
Main destinations: Italy (9.2 per cent of total in 2014), Saudi Arabia (7.4 per cent), India (7.2 per cent).

Agriculture

Farming

Total agricultural land is 3.3 million hectares, 3.7 per cent of total land, and the agriculture sector employs around 29 per

cent of the workforce. Its importance is declining in relation both to industry and to population growth.
Irrigation is supplied by the River Nile and the government is looking at ways to improve the efficiency of water use through the construction of lined canals and pipes. Problems surrounding the ecological effects of the Aswan High Dam persist. The construction of the Aswan High Dam and the subsequent filling of Lake Nasser in the 1970s initially improved crop yields by providing a constant source of water for irrigation. However, the dam had a damaging long-term effect on agriculture. It has permanently raised the water table, causing serious drainage problems and high salinity as well as depriving the Nile valley of annual silt, a natural fertiliser, previously brought down by the river during the flood season. The silt has had to be replaced by costly chemical fertilisers.
Fertile land is found in the Nile Valley and Delta – the cultivatable area accounts for only 2.4 per cent of the total land area at around 3.1 million hectares.
Virtually all water in Egypt comes from the River Nile, from which Egypt is allowed to take 55.5 billion cubic metres of water a year, under its agreement with nine other Nile basin countries. This imposes strict limitations on the expansion of agriculture.
A number of major irrigation schemes are under way. These are along the coast north-west of Alexandria, the Nile border with Sudan, East Oweinat in the desert and the largest project of them all, the Southern Valley Scheme. The cost of the Southern Valley Scheme is projected to reach US$85 billion by 2017.
Agricultural production in Egypt is highly labour-intensive. Output suffers from crop infestation, price controls, fragmented land tenure, increased soil salinity and consumer preference for imported foods.
Major subsistence crops include maize, sorghum, rice, wheat, beans and vegetables. Egypt's wheat consumption far outstrips local production, with Egyptian wheat crops supplying just 40 per cent of annual domestic demand. Some 65 per cent of food requirements are imported, making Egypt's annual food import bill around US$5.5 billion.
Cotton is a major export crop; however, WTO agreements, which came into force in 2005, removed tariffs and trade and have put enormous pressure on the industry as it attempts to compete with Asia and its lower production costs and lower prices. Egypt produces high-quality long staple cotton that has been traditionally exported to Europe, the US and Japan. It is like that the industry will have to shed jobs as it carves out a niche market in quality cotton rather than competing for the mass market. In 2011 the land area used for cotton cultivation had decreased to less than a quarter of what it was in 1990.

Fishing

There are active fishing industries in the Mediterranean and the Red Sea, as well as more limited freshwater fishing on the Nile and Lake Nasser. Egypt typically produces over 300,000 tonnes of seafood and 190,000 tonnes of freshwater fish per annum. Virtually all of this is used for domestic consumption. The rate of catching freshwater fish has declined in recent years due to overfishing, lack of investment and pollution.

Forestry

Forests cover less than 1 per cent of Egypt's land area.

Industry and manufacturing

Industrial production, with a growth rate of 1.4 per cent in 2014, is an important component of the economy, providing 45.6 per cent of GDP, including manufacturing which provides 15 per cent of total GDP. However, individually they were both outperformed by the total services industry that provided 47.9 per cent of GDP in 2014, of which tourism represented the lion's share.
The government places emphasis on: industrial diversification and import substitution, the development of downstream chemicals, and of heavy industry such as the Helwan Iron and Steel Company, the Nag Hammadi aluminium plant and El Dikheila integrated steel works. Industry and manufacturing has been dominated by state-owned companies although there is a renewed interest by the government in selling off enterprises, including metallurgical, food, wood pulp, and chemical processing, and various smelting works.
A number of cotton concerns are also on the privatisation list, although these companies are at risk, not from the shift in economic rationalisation, but rather by global trading dynamics. World Trade Organisation (WTO) rulings that came into practice on 1 January 2005 removed all global tariffs and subsidies on processed cotton. Egypt, as a major manufacture of cotton thread and cloths, could lose thousands of jobs and millions of dollars in export sales, the amount of land cultivated for cotton in 2011 was less than a quarter of what it was in 1990. However, a niche market is being formed, supplying cotton apparel to the US under the Qualified Industrial Zones (QIZ) protocol, whereby manufactured goods from nominated QIZ, which must contain 11.7 per cent Israeli input, will be given free access to US markets.
The petrochemical sector is a leading contributor to GDP and employs around 7,600 people.
Egypt has a growing automotive industry, supplying both vehicles and components. There are 18 vehicle manufacturers operating under joint trade agreements with foreign companies, including BMW which opened in May 2004. There are plans to invest a further US$25 million in more facilities. Nissan opened a new assembly plant in 2007, geared to produce 3,800 cars a year. During the political unrest in 2011 Nissan closed down the plant but it was reopened in February 2014.
With unemployment at 13.4 per cent in 2014, Egypt needs to find around 800,000 new jobs each year in order to sustain its growth.

Tourism

Egypt has a wealth of archaeological and historic sites, coastal resorts and is the outlet for the longest river in Africa, the Nile, which is a major waterway, offering tourists cruise trips down to Aswan. It is close enough to its target market of Europe to be recognisable and exotic enough to provide interest for those looking for more stimulation than a beach holiday.
According to the World Travel and Tourism Council (WTTC), tourism has provided steady income for Egypt, with tourist numbers averaging 11 million visitors annually. Tourism's total contribution to the economy was US$32 billion in 2014. Visitor exports provided US$7.6 in 2014.
The tourist industry was badly affected by the civil unrest of the Arab Spring at the beginning of 2011. Foreign governments initially advised their citizens not to visit Egypt and both tour operators and individuals cancelled their bookings. However, since the political situation has eased, the sector has returned to normal, following a short burst of promotion.
Changes to the issuance of visas were announced it September 2012, including halting the facility whereby US and many European citizens could be able obtain a visa on arrival. The move is expected to have an adverse affect on tourism, although the government denied this. By December 2011, annual hotel occupancy had fallen by 15 per cent as the tourist sector became the worst affected by the overthrow of the Mubarak regime.
Revenues from ancient Egyptian monuments such as the pyramids have fallen by 95 per cent since Egypt's 2011 revolution, the country's antiquities minister has said. Revenues have been reported to fall from US$390.29 million in 2010 to US$16.4 million in 2014. Only 9.5 million tourists stayed in Egypt's hotels in 2013, compared to 14.7 million in 2010.

In the first quarter of 2012, 2.5 million tourists visited Egypt, a year-on-year increase of 32 per cent on 2011, but still a fall of 27.8 per cent on the same period in 2010. However in the first quarter of 2014, Egypt saw a 28 per cent drop in visitors from the same time in the previous year. Egypt's tourism industry cannot stabilise until the country does.

Mining

Government policy aims to encourage foreign and local companies to explore for and exploit raw materials. Agreements have been reached for exploration and production of sulphur, phosphate and gold. The government is keen to extend franchises for other minerals, especially titanium and silver. Among non-oil raw materials, only iron ore, phosphate rock and limestone is produced on a significant scale. Other minerals produced include baryte, clay, feldspar, fluorspar, gypsum, kaolin, quartz, salt, silica sand and talc. Manganese and chrome deposits have also been exploited, while commercial deposits of zinc, tin, lead and copper have been discovered in Sinai.
A contract to mine sulphur in Sinai is held by Freeport Egyptian Sulphur Company, a wholly owned subsidiary of US firm Freeport McMoran. The annual production capacity is thought to be around 250,000 tonnes per year (tpy). Egypt also has deposits of uranium.
Although Egypt has no bauxite, it has developed a significant aluminium industry based on electric power from the Aswan High Dam. Production was initially used for basic consumer goods but Egypt now exports a wide range of basic aluminium products.
Interest has been shown in the southeast of Egypt where numerous ancient gold workings exist in banded iron formations. Three active foreign companies in Egypt include AngloGold Ashanti, Canadian-listed Alexander Nubia International and Australian firm Centamin Egypt. Centamin has progressed its Sukari Gold Mine to production in 2009 with a projected annual gold output of 250,000 oz.

Hydrocarbons

Proven oil reserves were 4.4 billion barrels in 2015, with production of 667,000 barrels per day (bpd). Mature oil fields are declining in production and have been supplemented by new fields. The discovery of a new oil field in 2009, Ak Zahraa, in East Ras Qattara (ERQ), has an estimated flow rate of 2,615bpd.
Egyptian General Petroleum Corporation (EGPC) is responsible for oil exploration. Its subsidiary Petrobel is a joint venture with the Italian Agip and is exploring for and operating wells in Badr el Din, near the Gulf of Suez.
Egypt has Africa's largest oil refinery sector with nine refineries; total annual production is 726,000bpd. EGPC operates the largest refinery of El Nasr at Suez. The government has plans to upgrade facilities to increase production of value-added petroleum products.
Proven natural gas reserves were 1.8 trillion cubic metres (cum) in 2014, with production at 58 billion cum. Reserves are expected to last until the 2040s given current levels of production. Domestic consumption in 2013 was 51.4 billion cum.
Under a 20-year agreement signed in 2008 Egypt exports gas to Israel (constituting 40 per cent of Israel's requirements); Natural gas began flowing to the Lebanese Beddawi gas-fired power plant in 2009. On 6 March 2012, the main natural gas pipeline in the northern Sinai desert running to Jordan and Israel was damaged by two large explosions. The security service said there had been at least a dozen previous attacks on pipelines since the overthrow of President Mubarak in 2011.
Coal reserves total some 27 million tonnes, but there is no commercial production.

Energy

Total installed generating capacity in 2013 was 27 million kilowatts (kW), producing 155 billion kilowatt hours. Generation is achieved through use of gas-fired turbines.
Saudi investment built the largest wind farm in the world (six times bigger than Singapore), which reached full production in 2010 and employs 25,000 people permanently, as well as additional seasonal labour.
The Aswan High Dam, in Upper Egypt, provides 12 per cent of the country's electricity. Renewable energy schemes include photovoltaic panels (solar energy) which accounts for 45MW and installed wind energy accounting for 230MW.
When at full capacity around 850,000cum of natural gas will operate two turbines.
Siemens AG received an order in 2015 to build gas and wind power plants in Egypt valued at US$9 billion, which the German company describe as the largest single order in its history. It is estimated that the plants will have a total capacity of 14.4 gigawatts and will enter the early stages of operation in 2017.

Financial markets

On 27 January 2010 the stock exchange was closed while political unrest was ongoing; it re-opened in March following consultations with the new prime minister. The Egyptian stock exchange (EGX) had, until its closure, been one of the most dynamic in the Middle East, but it had lost 16 per cent in value of the benchmark EGX 30 Index in the two days before closure. The stock exchange authorities set up new rules to avoid further slumps, including suspending trading for 30 minutes if stocks move by up to 5 per cent and cutting, by one hour, trading hours.

Stock exchange

Cairo and Alexandria Stock Exchange (EGX)

Banking and insurance

The banking sector is dominated by four public-sector commercial banks – Banque Misr, Bank of Alexandria, Banque du Caire and the National Bank of Egypt – which hold about 60 per cent of deposits, 70 per cent of assets and 65 per cent of loans, and are the main conduit for public-sector trade, savings and financing.
In February 2004, Egypt was removed from the OECD list of non-co-operative countries on money laundering after reforms had been implemented.
The Central Bank of Egypt (CBE) strengthened the monetary policy framework over 2004 which should aid it as it manages and limits inflationary pressures while stimulating market driven interest rates. The IMF in a 2005 report stressed that the CBE independence from political interference should be maintained.
As a whole, strong current account trading enabled banks to strengthen their net foreign assets in 2004 and 2005 and the CBE also took advantage of market conditions to build up its reserves. Total external debt remained stable at about US$29 billion (31 per cent of GDP) by the end of 2004.
As part of the privatisation programme under way by the government two state banks are in the process of being sold off to the commercial sector. In October 2006, bids for the Bank of Alexandria valued the bank at US$1.6 billion – a figure over five times greater than the government's own valuation. Proceeds of the sale will go to re-capitalising other state-owned banks and a reduction in Egypt's public debt.

Central bank

Central Bank of Egypt

Main financial centre

Cairo

Time

GMT plus two hours (GMT plus three hours from May to September).

Geography

Most of Egypt is located in the north-east corner of Africa between the Mediterranean Sea, the Red Sea, Sudan and Libya. The Sinai peninsula, separated from the African continent by the Suez Canal and the Red Sea, borders Israel. The peninsula also faces Jordan and Saudi Arabia across the Gulf of Aqaba.

The world's longest river, the Nile, flows through deep gorges from mountains in the south, before ending its journey in the Nile delta on Egypt's northern coast, with outlets into the Mediterranean Sea. Its influence on Egypt has been profound as over thousands of years the river has been the lifeblood of the country, its flood plains have provided fertile agricultural land and the necessary freshwater for life in an arid landscape. About 95 per cent of Egypt is uninhabitable desert and over 90 per cent of the population lives within 20km of the Nile.

The Awan Dam, completed in 1970, created Lake Nasser, the world's third largest reservoir. Its hydroelectric power station produces about half of Egypt's electricity and maintains a steady flow of water downstream.

Hemisphere

Northern

Climate

The climate is dry with very little rainfall, hot in summer and cool in winter. Temperatures in Cairo in the north vary from 43 degrees Celsius (C) maximum in summer to 18 degrees C maximum in winter. Sandstorms (the *khamsin* or *simoon* winds) can disrupt air traffic between March and May.

Rainfall is largely confined to the Mediterranean coast, with around 200 millimetres a year in Alexandria. Egypt is dependent on the Nile for nearly all its water needs. The government is pressing ahead with desert reclamation schemes, but these are also dependent on limited Nile waters as reserves of water under the desert have so far proved relatively insignificant.

Dress codes

Lightweight clothing is necessary for the hot summer months (May to September). Business dress is formal – suits are worn for all occasions. Men should not wear shorts, except at the beach and women should wear modest clothing in public, covering their arms and legs.

Entry requirements

Passports

Required by all. Some exceptions are allowed for a few nationals of the Middle East. Contact the nearest Egyptian Consulate for more information.

Passports must be valid for six months beyond the intended length of stay.

Visa

Required by all, except citizens of some adjacent countries, for full list of exceptions contact the local embassy or visit http://egypt.embassyhomepage.com.

Business and tourist visas, valid for three months, available for most Europeans and North Americans, were obtainable at the point of entry until September 2011 when it was announced that visas would have to be required before arrival. There are a number of exceptions to this ruling (including tourist groups, family groups through travel agencts) and it is advisable to check with an Egyptian embassy before travelling.

All visitors, except those Europeans and US nationals on tourist visas, must register at the Office of Foreigners and Nationality within seven days of arrival. Hotels will normally undertake this on the visitor's behalf.

Currency advice/regulations

The Import of local currency is unlimited, however its export is prohibited. The import and export of foreign currency is unrestricted.

Customs

It is permitted to import one bottle of alcohol and 200 cigarettes. Camera, video equipment and computers should be declared at customs.

Prohibited imports

Illegal drugs, firearms and cotton. Export of any antiquity older than 100 years must have a clearance from the Ministry of Cultural Affairs.

Health (for visitors)

Mandatory precautions

A vaccination certificate against yellow fever is required if travelling from an infected area.

Advisable precautions

Typhoid, hepatitis A, tetanus vaccinations are recommended. Malaria exists from June–October in the El Faiyum area. There is also a rabies risk. Polio was eradicated in 2005.

Avoid drinking tap water and use bottled water instead; water used for brushing teeth or making ice should be boiled first or otherwise sterilised. All fruit should be peeled and only well-cooked meat, vegetables and fish, served hot, should be eaten. Salad and mayonnaise may carry increased risk, except in top-class restaurants. Avoid food sold on the streets.

Hotels

There is a wide range available. Bills are quoted in US dollars and may be settled in Egyptian currency. A 20 per cent tax and service charge should be added to all prices.

Credit cards

Most credit cards are widely accepted. Excepting airline tickets, the free market exchange rate is used in calculating credit card transactions.

Public holidays (national)

Fixed dates

*7 Jan (Coptic Christmas Day), 25 Apr (Sinai Liberation Day), 1 May (Labour Day), 23 Jul (Revolution Day), 6 Oct (Armed Forces' Day), 24 Oct (Suez Victory Day).

Variable dates

*Coptic Easter Monday, Eid al Adha, Eid al Fitr, Islamic New Year, Birth of the Prophet.

* Followers of the Coptic faith observe this holiday.

Islamic year 1437 (15 Oct 2015–2 Oct 2016):: The Islamic year contains 354 or 355 days, with the result that Muslim feasts advance by 10–12 days against the Gregorian calendar. Dates of feasts vary according to the sightings of the new moon, so cannot be forecast exactly.

Islamic year 1433 (26 Nov 2011–14 Nov 2012)

Working hours

As a Muslim country the official weekend begins on Friday. Embassies and the offices of some foreign companies also close on Saturday and Sunday. Some companies treat Thursday as a half day. Hours may also vary between winter and summer.

Banking

Sun–Thu: 0830–1400. Money exchanges in city centres also 1700–1900 or 1800–2000.

Business

Sat–Thu: 0900–1700.

Government

Sun–Thur: 0900–1500.

Shops

Sat–Thur: 0900—1300 and 1600—2000 (summer); 1000—1800 (winter). During Ramadan Sat–Thur: 0930—1530 and 2000—2200.

Department stores offer extended hours and local shops may vary their hours to suit.

Telecommunications

Mobile/cell phones

There are GSM 900 services operating in all popluated areas.

Electricity supply

220–440V AC in most areas; in some rural districts 110–380V AC is still found.

Weights and measures

Metric system (local units also in use).

Social customs/useful tips

Hospitality is considered a prime virtue and it would be rude for visitors not to accept a token drink or other invitation. Many hosts will not allow a guest to pay for anything during his or her stay. Guests should therefore not squabble over paying at a restaurant, for example. In address, use the first name with the appropriate

title (for instance Mr, Madame, Doctor, Engineer). Business cards in Arabic are appreciated.
In June 2010 authorities in Alexandria began enforcing a smoking ban in government buildings. The ban will extend to cafes in 2012 with the plan to make Alexandria the first non-smoking city in Egypt. Egyptians smoke some 19 billion cigarettes annually, including the traditional shisha water pipes which are found in many coffee shops.

Security

Violent crime against foreigners is rare. However, thieves operate in busy tourist areas such as Giza and Luxor. In these areas it is best to avoid wearing flashy or expensive jewellery.
Given its strategic position in the Middle East, Egypt is particularly sensitive regarding national security. Photographing bridges, railway stations and military installations is forbidden. Carrying a video camera can cause problems with the Egyptian authorities.

Getting there

Air
National airline: Egyptair
International airport/s: Cairo International (CAI), 24km from city, facilities include incoming/outgoing duty-free shops, banks, post office, restaurants and car hire. Borg el Arab-Alexandria International (HBE), 60km from city, including business centre, bank, post office, restaurant, shops, pharmacy and car hire. Luxor Airport (LXR) 5.5km from the city.
Taxis and bus services run to all.
Airport tax: None
Surface
Road: There are road links from Libya and Israel.
A new road from Aswan to Port Sudan was under construction in 2003 but has yet to be completed. Until then no roads to Sudan are recommended.
Water: There are ferry services to Port Said and Alexandria from many destinations across the Mediterranean, run by Menatours. There are ferries between Aqaba in Jordan and Nuweiba on the Sinai peninsular and to Suez from Jeddah in Saudi Arabia. There are steamer services across Lake Nasser from Sudan, although these are suspended during periods of instability in Sudan.
Main port/s: Alexandria, Al Ghardaqah, Aswan, Bur Safajah, Damietta, Marsa Matruh, Port Said and Suez.

Getting about

National transport
Air: Egyptair operates domestic services from Cairo to Luxor, Aswan, Hurghada, Abu Simbel and Alexandria. Air Sinai operates services to North and South Sinai. If planning to fly south, book well in advance. Travel to certain areas of the Nile Delta is restricted.
Road: There is a 31,000km surfaced network which includes good roads linking Cairo-Alexandria, Cairo-Port Said, Ismailia-Suez-Sinai, Cairo-El Faiyum-Luxor-Aswan.
Buses: There are four intercity bus companies: luxury service Superjet, West Delta Bus Company, East Delta Bus Company, and Upper Egypt Bus Company. There are fast and comfortable services between most towns and cities, although they tend to be crowded, and tickets should be booked in advance where possible.
Rail: There are train services to all main cities and towns in Egypt, including express and through trains from Cairo to Alexandria, Luxor and Aswan. Four classes available; certain routes have air-conditioned sleeping cars and buffet service. Tickets must be reserved, sometimes up to two days in advance.
Water: Traditional sailboats (*felucca*) offer rides along the Nile river.
City transport
Taxis: Metered and unmetered taxis are readily available, but meters where fitted are often not used. Fares should be agreed in advance.
Air-conditioned limousines are available at airports and main hotels. Chauffeured taxis from Cairo airport to the city centre are recommended. Hotels have their own shuttle services. Hotel taxis or chauffeured hire cars are more efficient and can be hired by the day, subject to negotiation. Fares are usually listed in the major hotels.
City centre taxis are cheap, although often uncomfortable and never have air-conditioning. If you are travelling beyond the city centre, it is a good idea to carry a map to guide the taxi driver. The journey time from Cairo International Airport to the city is about 40–60 minutes. Tipping is usually 10 per cent.
Buses, trams & metro: Local buses are numerous, cheap and crowded, as are the few trams still in existence. The Cairo metro is fast, inexpensive and not too crowded, it has 43 stations, five of which run through central Cairo.
Ferry: Several routes run north and south of the city plied by waterbuses.
Car hire
An international driving licence and third-party insurance are needed. Hire charges should be negotiated in advance. The maximum speed limit on main roads is 90kph, rising to 100kph on the Cairo-Alexandria desert road; fines for speeding are substantial. Traffic in Cairo is heavily congested.

BUSINESS DIRECTORY

The addresses listed below are a selection only. While World of Information makes every endeavour to check these addresses, we cannot guarantee that changes have not been made, especially to telephone numbers and area codes. We would welcome any corrections.

Telephone area codes

The international direct dialling code (IDD) for Egypt is +20, followed by area code and subscriber's number:

Alexandria	3	Ismailiya	64
Ashara Ramadan	15	Kafr El Sheik	47
Aswan	97	Luxor	95
Asyut	88	Maeria	3
Benha	13	Mahalla	43
Beni Suef	82	Mansoura	50
Cairo	2	Marsa Matruh	3
Damanhur	45	Port Said	66
Damietta	57	Pyramids	2
El Arish	68	Sacheia	16
El Minya	86	Sohag	93
Fayoum	84	Suez	62
Giza	2	Tanta	40
Heliopolis	2	Zagazig	55

Useful telephone numbers

Cairo
Police: 122
Fire: 125
Ambulance: 123
Aswan
Police: 22147
Alexandria
Police: 960-151-122
Suez
Police: 23-929

Chambers of Commerce

Alexandria Chamber of Commerce, 31 El-Ghorfa El-Togaria Street, Alexandria (tel: 809-339; fax: 808-993).

American Chamber of Commerce in Egypt, 33 Soliman Abaza Street, Doki-Giza, Cairo (tel: 338 1050; fax: 338-1060; e-mail: info@amcham.org.eg).

Aswan Chamber of Commerce, Abtal El-Tahreer Street, Aswan (tel: 323-084).

Cairo Chamber of Commerce, 4 Midan El-Falaki, Cairo (tel: 354-2943; fax: 355-7940).

Damietta Chamber of Commerce, Saad Zaghloul Street, Damietta (tel: 322-799; fax: 320-632).

Egyptian-British Chamber of Commerce, PO Box 4EG, 299 Oxford Street, London W1A 4EG (tel: 020-7499-3100; fax: 020-7499-1070; e-mail: info@theebcc.com).

Fayoum Chamber of Commerce, El-Nadi El-Reyadi Street, El Fayoum (tel: 322-148).

Federation of Egyptian Chambers of Commerce, 4 Midan El-Falaky, Cairo (tel: 795-1136; fax: 795-1164; e-mail: fedcoc@menanet.net).

Ismailia Chamber of Commerce, 163 Saad Zaghloul Street, Ismailia (tel: 221-663; fax: 322-515).

Port Said Chamber of Commerce, Benayet Souk El Goumla, Port Said (tel: 222-733; fax: 236-141).

Red Sea Chamber of Commerce, Old City Council Building, Hurghada (tel: 440-761).

Suez and South Sinai Chamber of Commerce, 47 Salah Eldin Elayoubi Street, Suez (tel: 227-783).

Banking

Alexandria Commercial and Maritime Bank, PO Box 2376, 85 El Horreya Avenue, 21519 Alexandria (tel: 392-1237, 392-1556, 392-9203; fax: 391-3706).

Arab African International Bank, 5 Midan Al-Saray Al Koubra, Garden City, Cairo (tel: 794-5094/5/6; fax: 795-8493).

Arab International Bank, 35 Abdel Khalek Sarwat Street, Cairo (tel: 391-8794, 391-6391; fax: 391-6233).

Bank of Alexandria, 49 Kasr El Nil Street, Cairo (tel: 393-6262, 391-1203; fax: 391-0481, 391-980).

Bank of Commerce & Development, 'Al Tegaryoon', PO Box 1373, 13 26th July Street, Sphinx Square, Mohandessin, Cairo (tel: 302-8156, 302-1623; fax: 302-3963).

Cairo Barclays Bank, PO Box 110, Maglis El Shaab, 12 Midan El Sheikh Youssef, Garden City, Cairo (tel: 366-2600; fax: 366-2810/11).

Cairo Far East Bank, PO Box 757, 104 El Nil Street, Dokki, Cairo (tel: 336-2516/18; fax: 348-3818).

Crédit International d'Egypte, 46 El Batal Ahmed Abdel Aziz Street, Mohandessin, Cairo (tel: 336-1897, 336-1898; fax: 360-8673).

Delta International Bank, PO Box 1159, 1113 Corniche El Nil Street, Cairo (tel: 575-3492; fax: 574-3403).

Egyptian American Bank, PO Box 1825, 4 & 6 Hassan Sabri Street, Zamalek, Cairo (tel: 738-0126, 738-0136, 738-2661; fax: 738-0609, 738-0450).

Misr Exterior Bank; Cairo Plaza Building, Cornish El Nil, Boulaque, Cairo (tel: 778-701, 778-619, 766-381, 766-360; fax: 762-806, 578-0238).

Misr International Bank, PO Box 218, Embaba, 54 El Batal Ahmed Abdel Aziz Street, Mohandessin, Cairo (tel: 749-4424, 749-7091; fax: 700-928).

National Bank for Development (NBD), PO Box 647, 5(A) El Borsa El Gedida Street, 11511 Cairo (tel: 392-3245; fax: 390-5681).

National Bank of Egypt, PO Box 11611, National Bank of Egypt Tower, 1187 Corniche El Nil, Cairo (tel: 574-9101; fax: 576-2672).

Nile Bank, PO Box 2741, 35 Ramses Street, Abdel Moneim Riyad Sq, Cairo (tel: 574-1417, 574-3502, 575-1105; fax: 575-6296, 575-3640).

Suez Canal Bank, PO Box 2620, 11 Mohamed Sabri Abu Alam St, Cairo (tel: 393-1066, 393-1048, 393-1215; fax: 391-3522).

Central bank

Central Bank of Egypt, 31 Kasr el Nil Street, Cairo (tel: 392-6211; fax: 391-7168; email: info@cbe.org.eg).

Stock exchange

Cairo and Alexandria Stock Exchange (EGX), www.egyptse.com

Travel information

Cairo Airport, Airport Road, Heliopolis, 11776 Cairo (tel: 265-4611; fax: 263-7132; internet: www.cairo-airport.com).

Egyptair, New Administrative Complex, Airport Road, Cairo (tel: 267-4700–4709; fax: 418-3715; internet: www.egyptair.com).

Ministry of tourism

Ministry of Tourism, Misr Tourist Tower, Abbassiya Square, Abbassiya (tel: 284-1707; fax: 285-9551; email: mot@idsc.gov.eg).

National tourist organisation offices

Egyptian Tourist Authority, Misr Travel Tower, Abbassia Square, Cairo (tel: 286-4509, 284-1970; fax: 285-4363; internet: www.touregypt.net).

Ministries

Ministry of Agriculture, Animal and Fish Wealth and Land Reclamation, Nadi El Seid Street, Dokki, Giza (tel: 702-677; fax: 703-889; email: capi@idsc.gov.eg)..

Ministry of Cabinet Affairs and Administrative Development, 1 Magles El Shaab Street, Cairo (tel: 354-1722; fax: 355-6306; email: cabinet1@idsc.gov.eg).

Ministry of Culture, 2 Shagaret El Dor St, Zamalek Cairo 03 (tel: 341-5568; fax: 340-6449; email: mculture@idsc.gov.eg).

Ministry of Defence and Military Production, 5 Ismail Abaza Street, Cairo (tel: 355-3063; fax: 354-8739; email: mod@idsc.gov.eg).

Ministry of Economy and International Co-operation, 8 Adly St, Cairo (tel: 390-6796; fax: 390-3029; email: mineco@idscl.gov.eg; internet site: www.sis.gov.eg).

Ministry of Education, 4 Ibrahim Naguib St, Garden City, Cairo (tel: 355-7952; fax: 356-2952; Email: moe@idsc.gov.eg).

Ministry of Electricity and Energy, Ramses Street, Abbassia, Nasr City Cairo (tel: 261-6514; fax: 261-6302; email: mee@idsc.gov.eg).

Ministry of Finance, Lazoughly Square, Justice and Finance Building, Cairo (tel: 354-1055; fax: 354-5433; email: mofinance@idsc1.gov.eg).

Ministry of Foreign Affairs, Maspero, Cairo (tel: 574-9820; fax: 574-9533).

Ministry of Information Maspero, Corniche El Nil, Cairo 02 (tel: 574-8986; fax: 574-8781; email: minexter@idsc1.gov.eg; internet: www.mfa.gov.eg).

Ministry of Health and Population, Magles El Shaab St, Cairo (tel: 354-1076; fax: 355-3966; email: moh@idsc.gov.eg).

Ministry of Higher Education, 4 Ibrahim Naguib Street, Garden City, Cairo (tel: 355-7952; fax: 356-2952; email: mheducat@idsc1.gov.eg, info@sti.sci.eg).

Ministry of Housing, Reconstruction and New Urban Communities, 1 Ismail Abaza St, Cairo (tel: 355-3320; fax: 355-7836; email: mhuuc@idsc1.gov.eg).

Ministry of Industry and Mineral Wealth, 2 Latin America Street, Garden City (tel: 355-7034; fax: 354-8362; email: moimw@idsc.gov.eg).

Ministry of Information, Maspero, Corniche El Nil, Cairo (tel: 747-193; fax: 757-144; email: rtu2@idsc.gov.eg).

Ministry of Insurance & Social Affairs, El Sheikh Rihan Street, Bab El-Louq, Cairo (tel: 337-0039; fax: 337-5390; email: msi@idsc.gov.eg).

Ministry of Interior, El Sheikh Rihan St, Cairo (tel: 355-7500; fax: 355-7792; email: moi1@idsc.gov.eg).

Ministry of Justice, Justice and Finance Building, Lazoughli Sq, Cairo 15 (tel: 355-1176; fax: 355-8103; email: mojeb@idsc1.gov.eg).

Ministry of Land Reclamation, Nadi El Seid St, Cairo 10 (tel: 703-011).

Ministry of Local Administration, Kasr El Aini St, Cairo 04 (tel: 355-3566).

Ministry of Manpower and Immmigration, 3 Youssef Abbas St, Nasr City, Cai (tel: 260-9363; fax: 260-9891; email: mwlabor@idsc1.gov.eg).

Ministry of Petroleum, 16 El Mokhayyam El Da'em Street, Nasr City (tel:

262-2268; fax: 263-6060; email: mopm@idsc1.gov.eg).

Ministry of Planning, Salah Salem Road, Nasr City (tel: 602-935; fax: 263-4747).

Ministry of Public Enterprises, Magles El Shaab Street, Cairo (tel: 355-8026; fax: 355-3606); PEO, 2 Latin America Street, Garden City, Cairo (tel: 794-3484; fax: 795-9233).

Ministry of Public Works and Water Resources, El Nil St, Embaba, Cairo 04 (tel: 354-5884; fax: 355-8008; email: mpwwr@idsc.gov.eg).

Ministry of Rural Development, 4 Shooting Club Street, Dokki, Cairo (tel: 349-7470; fax: 349-7785).

Ministry of Shipping, 7 Abdel Khalek Sarwat St, Cairo, 01 (tel: 764-343).

Ministry of Social Affairs and Insurance, El Sheikh Rihan St, Bab El Louk, Cairo 06 (tel: 354-2900; fax: 917-799).

Ministry of State for Administrative Development and Environment and Ministry of the Public Enterprise, 1 Magles El Shaab Street, Lazoughli Square, CAI 06 (tel: 355-8026; fax: 355-5882; email: mops3@idsc.gov.eg).

Ministry of State for the Affairs of the People's Assembly and the Shoura Council, Magles El Shaab St, Cairo 04 (tel: 355-7750; fax: 355-7681; email: parli@idsc.gov.eg).

Ministry of State for Environmental Affairs, Helwan Road, Cairo (tel: 375-7306; fax: 378-4285; email: eeaa@idsc.gov.eg).

Ministry of State for Military Production, 23 Kobri Al Kubba St, Cairo 36 (tel: 257-8697/2915).

Ministry of State for Planning and International Co-operation, Salah Salem Street, Nasr City (tel: 401-4615; fax: 401-4733; email: miceu@idsx.gov.eg).

Ministry of State for Scientific Research Affairs, 101 Kasr El Aini St, Cairo 04 (tel: 355-7952).

Ministry of Trade and Supply, 99 Kasr El Aini St, Cairo 04 (tel: 355-0360; fax: 354-4973; email: msit@idsx.gov.eg).

Ministry of Transport, Communications and Civil Aviation, 105 Kasr El Aini Street, Cairo (tel: 354-3623; fax: 355-5564; email: garb@idsc.gov.eg).

Ministry of Waqfs, 5 Sabry Abou Alam Street, Bab El-Louq, Cairo (tel: 392-6163; fax: 392-6305; email: mawkaf@idsc1.gov.eg)

Prime Minister's Office, 1 Magles El Shaab St, Lazoughli Square, Cairo 04 (tel: 354-7376; fax: 355-8048).

President's Office, Abdin palace, CAI 06 (tel: 391-0130).

Other useful addresses

Arab League, The Arab League Building, Corniche El Nil, Cairo (tel: 393-4499; fax: 775-626).

Arab Organisation for Industrialisation, 2D Abassiya Square, PO Box 770 (tel: 823-377; fax: 826-010).

Arab Republic of Egypt National Telecommunications Organisation (ARENTO), 26 Ramses Street (tel: 760-333; fax: 771-306).

British Embassy, 7 Ahmed Ragheb St, Garden City, Cairo (tel: 354-0852; fax: 354-0859).

Cabinet Office, 1 Maglis El Shaab Street, Lazoughli Square, CAI 04 (tel: 354-7376; fax: 355-8048).

Cairo Regional Center for International Commercial Arbitration, 3 Aboul Feda Street, Zamalek, Cairo (tel: 340-1330; fax: 340-1336).

Cairo Stock Exchange, 4 Sharia esh-Sherifein, Cairo (tel: 392-1402; fax: 392-8526).

Capital Market Authority, 20 Emad El Din Street, Sixth Floor, Downtown (tel: 777-774; fax: 755-339).

Central Agency for Public Mobilisation and Statistics (CAPMAS), Saleh Salem Street, Nasr City, Cairo (tel: 603-717; fax: 604-099).

Central Post Office, Ataba Square, Cairo.

Commercial International Investment Company (CIIC), 66-68 Mohie El-Din Abou El-Ezz St, Dokki, Cairo (tel: 335-8035, 335-7093, 337-6251; fax: 335-7095).

Commercial Representation Office, 96 Ahmed Orabi Street, Mohandiseen (tel: 347-1892; fax: 345-1840).

Commission of the European Communities Delegation in Egypt, 6 Ibn Zenki Street, Zamalek, Cairo (tel: 340-8388; fax: 340-0385).

Customs Information Centre, 4 El Tayaran Street, Nasr City (tel: 260-5711; fax: 261-2672).

Egyptian Electricity Authority, Abassia, Cairo (tel: 261-6537; fax: 261-6512, 401-1630).

Egyptian Embassy (USA), 3521 International Court, NW, Washington DC 20008 (tel: (+1-202) 895-5400; fax: (+1-202) 244-5131).

Egyptian General Petroleum Corporation (EGPCC), 4 Palestine Street, Fourth Sector, new Maadi (tel: 353-1438; fax: 353-1457).

Egyptian Radio and Television Corporation (ERTC), Radio and TV Building, Sharia Maspiro, Corniche el Nil, PO Box 504, Cairo (tel: 749-508; fax: 746-989).

Faud Nemah (Interpreter Service), 40 Kasr El Nil Street, Cairo (tel: 746-394).

General Authority for Control of Imports and Exports, Atlas Building El Sheikh Maarouf and Ramses Streets (tel: 574-2830; fax: 766-971).

General Authority for Investment and Free Zones, 8 Sharia Adly, PO Box 1007, Cairo (tel: 390-6804).

General Organisation for Industrialisation (GOFI) 6 Khali Agha Street, Garden City (tel: 355-7005; fax: 354-4984).

General Organisation for International Exhibitions and Fairs (GOIEF), Exhibition Ground, Nasr City, Cairo (tel: 260-7811; fax: 260-7845, 260-7848).

International Finance Corp (IFC), 5 El Fallah Street, Mohandessin, Cairo (tel: 347-8081; fax: 347-3738).

Internatinal Monetary Fund (IMF), 31 Kasr El Nil Street, Central Bank, Cairo (tel: 392-4257; fax: 351-7137).

Local Governorates, El-Islah El-Zerai Building, 10th Floor, 4 Nadi El-Seid Street, Dokki (tel: 349-4770; fax: 349-7788).

Sales Tax Authority, 4 El Tayaran Street, Nasr City (tel: 260-7500; fax: 260-7501).

Social Fund for Development (SFD), Hussein Hegazy and El Aini Streets, Cairo (tel: 354-8339; fax: 355-0628).

Taxation Authority, 5 Hussein Hegazi Street (tel: 355-7784; fax: 355-5438).

US Embassy, 5 Sharia Latin America, Garden City, Cairo (tel: 355-7371).

National news agency: MENA (Middle East News Agency); MENA Head Office, PO Box 1165, 17 Hoda Sharawi Street, Cairo (tel: 393-3000; internet: www.mena.org.eg).

Internet sites

Africa Online: www.africaonline.com

AllAfrica.com: http://allafrica.com

American Chamber of Commerce in Egypt: www.amcham.org.eg

Arab Bank: www.arabbank.com

Egypt Business Directory: www.telefax.com.eg/default.htm

Egypt corporate information: www.corporateinformation.com/egcorp.html

Egypt economic indicators: www.economic.idsc.gov.eg/

Egypt www index: http://ce.eng.usf.edu/pharos/

El Salvador

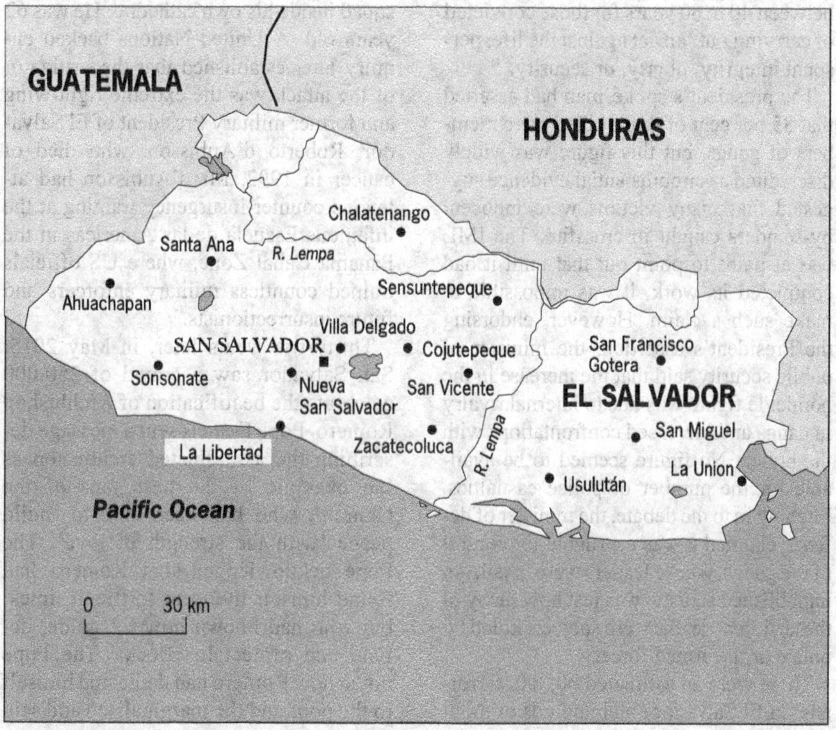

In 2016 the US Salvadorans will probably pass the Cubans as the third-largest Latin American community in the United States, behind the Mexicans and Puerto Ricans. There are an estimated two million Salvadorans in the US – almost a third of the entire population of El Salvador itself (6.4 million), Central America's smallest country. Many were born in the US, but most are migrants. An exodus on this scale suggests to many observers that not all is well with El Salvador.

Ironically, when compared to neighbours like Honduras – which in 2014 had the world's highest murder rate – at first glance El Salvador looks relatively stable. It is a country where democratic institutions appeared to be working. But by 2016 the murder rate in El Salvador could well be higher than that in Honduras. It has a dark side: the notorious gang culture that prevails appears to be beyond control.

The gangs

In 2015 the violence between El Salvador's street gangs continued its deadly increase. El Salvador's Instituto de Medicina Legal (IML) (National Forensics Institute) announced that there were 911 homicides in August 2015 – a daily average of almost 30 – the deadliest month in 25 years. On one single day in August there were 52 murders, making it the bloodiest day of the year. From January to August 2015, El Salvador recorded a total of 4,246 homicides, an average of 17.5 a day and up by 67 per cent on the same period in 2014. Violence had risen steadily in El Salvador since a 2012 truce between the country's two main gangs, the Mara Salvatrucha (MS-13) (the most prominent gang) and its rival Barrio 18, had begun to fail in 2014. While it lasted, the truce had helped reduce the murder rate in mid-2013 to around five a day, a 10-year low. In June 2014, the US authorities named half a dozen of the MS-13 hierarchy as leaders of an international criminal organisation. Although the MS-13 membership is mostly Salvadorian, the gang was originally formed in Los Angeles in the 1990s. In

KEY FACTS

Official name: República de El Salvador (Republic of El Salvador)

Head of State: President Salvador Sánchez Cerén (Frente Farabundo Martí para la Liberación Nacional (FMLN) (since 9 Mar 2014) (sworn in 1 Jun 2014)

Head of government: President Salvador Sánchez Cerén (Frente Farabundo Martí para la Liberación Nacional (FMLN) (since 9 Mar 2014) (sworn in 1 Jun 2014)

Ruling party: Alianza Republicana Nacionalista (Arena) (Nationalist Republican Alliance).

Area: 21,400 square km

Population: 6.35 million (2014)*

Capital: San Salvador

Official language: Spanish

Currency: US dollar (US$) (from 1 Jan 2001; previous currency colón locked at C8.75 per US dollar)

Exchange rate: US$8.75 per US$ (Sep 2015)

GDP per capita: US$3,988 (2014)*

GDP real growth: 2.00% (2014)*

GDP: US$25.33 billion (2014)*

Unemployment: 5.54% (2014)* (plus additional underemployment)

Inflation: 1.14% (2014)*

Balance of trade: -US$5.21 billion (2014)

* estimated figure

2013 MS-13 was thought to have around 10,000 gang members in the US, with several thousand more in Central American republics, of which El Salvador was the most prominent. Although the MS-13 membership is mostly Salvadorian, the gang was originally formed in Los Angeles in the 1990s. MS-13's principal rival, Barrio 18, has cells operating from Central America to the US and Canada, with thousands of members and interests in a number of illicit activities. Barrio 18 first emerged as a small-time street gang, also in Los Angeles; originally, the group's cells, known as *cliques*, came from Mexican immigrants in Southern California. As it grew, Barrio 18 began to recruit members from a variety of Central American nationalities.

El Salvador's police had estimated that 80 per cent of the country's homicides were related to purges and score-settling between various gangs. In simple terms, El Salvador is almost 20 times deadlier than the US and 90 times deadlier than the UK. The statistics produced by the national IML and quoted in the excellent *Tim's Salvador Blog* made chilling reading: the victims were overwhelmingly male – 92.3 per cent and young, 53.4 per cent between ages 15–30, more than 76 per cent younger than 40, over 10 per cent of the victims were aged between 15–17. Most of the murders were by firearms. Predictably, the highest total number of murders was in San Salvador – 311. But the departments *with the highest rates were Cuscatlan and Usulatan. The IML complained that in times of austerity it was running out of body-bags*

A desperate El Salvador government invoked anti-terrorism laws to prosecute alleged gang members, triggering a debate over definitions of crime and terrorism. Under terrorism charges, gang members could receive between eight and 12 years in prison, while gang leaders could be sent down for 10 to 15 years. The anti-terrorism law also spelled out prison terms of between 40 to 60 years for those convicted of carrying out 'an act against the life, personal integrity, liberty, or security. '

The president's spokesman had asserted that 85 per cent of those killed were members of gangs, but this figure was widely discredited as circumstantial evidence suggested that many victims were innocent by-standers caught in crossfire. The IML was at pains to point out that until it had completed its work, it was impossible to make such a claim. However, endorsing the President's assertion, the minister of public security said that the increase in the homicide figure was due to internal rivalry in gangs and increased confrontations with the police. No figure seemed to be available for the number of police casualties. Pitching in to the debate, the minister of defence claimed it was a struggle for control of the gangs, whose leaders were in jail. An unpublished statistic was just how many of these violent deaths were subjects killed by police or the armed forces.

There were an estimated 60,000 'terrorists' in El Salvador and hundreds of thousands more collaborators. Human rights activists were concerned that defining the anti-gang campaign as a war against terrorism risked sanctioning arbitrary, police and military abuse, for the most part against young men already living in marginalised communities.

The Death of an Archbishop

On 24 March 1980 San Salvador's Catholic Archbishop Monsignor Arnulfo Romero became one of the highest profile victims of Central America's 'dirty wars' when he was gunned down by a death squad inside his own cathedral. He was 62 years old. A United Nations backed enquiry later established that the instigator of the attack was the extreme right-wing and former military President of El Salvador, Roberto d'Aubisson, who died of cancer in 1992. Mr d'Aubisson had attended counter-insurgency training at the infamous Escuela de las Americas in the Panama Canal Zone, where US officials trained countless military enforcers and future insurrectionists.

Thirty-five years later, in May 2015, San Salvador saw a crowd of 250,000 celebrate the beatification of Archbishop Romero. Pope Francis sent a message describing the assassinated archbishop as 'an example of the best sons of the Church', who had been able to 'build peace 'with the strength of love'. The Pope acknowledged that Romero had found himself living in 'difficult times' but who had known how to 'guide, defend and protect his flock'. The Pope noted how Romero had dedicated himself to the poor and the marginalised and said that he had prayed that Romero's example 'might inspire the Catholic Church of today.'

Despite the Pope's words, the sad fact was that it had taken the Catholic Church decades to reach its decision. For much of that time there had been strong opposition to Romero's beatification among leading Latin American prelates and even within the Vatican fearing that to beatify the Archbishop might imply a belated approval of the once prevalent liberation theologies or even a blessing on those priests who approved of the revolutionary movements of the time. Times change – the Cold War had ended – it was hoped – and by 2015 there was a Latin American Pope. Theological sophistry had apparently also come into play: the definition of martyrdom had advanced. This was no ISIS murder, but one carried out by Salvadorans, baptised in the church where they had also taken their first communion. A precedent had been set in Italy by the beatification of an Italian Priest, Pino Puglisi, murdered by the Mafia. Next on the list for Salvadorans was the Jesuit Rutilio Grande, Archbishop Romero's

KEY INDICATORS — **El Salvador**

	Unit	2011	2012	2013	2014	**2015
Population	m	*5.90	*6.30	*6.33	*6.35	*6.38
Gross domestic product (GDP)	US$bn	22.80	23.86	24.26	*25.33	*26.15
GDP per capita	US$	3,855	3,788	*3,835	*3,988	*4,101
GDP real growth	%	1.4	1.9	1.7	*2.0	*2.5
Inflation	%	3.6	1.7	0.8	*1.1	*-0.8
Unemployment	%	5.6	5.6	*5.7	*5.5	*5.3
Exports (fob) (goods)	US$m	4,242.6	9,175.0	43,334.2	4,255.4	–
Imports (fob) (goods)	US$m	9,014.8	4,236.0	9,629.1	9,463.1	–
Balance of trade	US$m	-4,772.2	-4,939.0	-5,294.9	-5,207.7	–
Current account	US$m	-1,070.1	-1,284.0	-1,576.0	*-1,272.0	*-1,132.0
Total reserves minus gold	US$m	2,516.7	2,806.0	2,476.2	2,430.3	–
Foreign exchange	US$m	2,254.7	2,554.0	2,221.2	–	–
Exchange rate	per US$	–	8.75	8.75	8.75	8.75

* estimated figure ** forecast figure

mentor, also murdered by unknown gunmen in El Salvador.

Economic and political stability

The even split that had characterised the 2014 presidential election continued to be the case in the 2015 parliamentary election voting. In the election for the National Assembly, Alianza Republicana Nacionalista (ARENA) (Nationalist Republican Alliance) had 38.77 per cent of the vote and the Frente Farabundo Martí para la Liberación Nacional (FMLN) (Farabundo Martí National Liberation Front) had 37.28 per cent. This gave ARENA and its allies 42 seats, the same number as the FMLN and its ally Gran Alianza por la Unidad Nacional (GANA) (Grand Alliance for National Unity). In the election for the regional Central American Parliament, ARENA and the FMLN each won 8 seats with the minor parties dividing up the remaining four seats. The electoral stand-off created a form of stability, which for a country where civil war memories still persisted, was important.

In an interview following his 2014 election as President, Salvador Sánchez Cerén made the obvious observation that it was remittances from the huge Salvadoran population in the US that kept the Salvadoran economy afloat. He might well have added, 'Thank goodness' as one of the major challenges of his presidency looked likely to be the revitalisation of an economy that had grown at an average annual rate of just 1.8 per cent from 2010 to 2013, was expected to have expanded by 2.2 per cent in 2014 and was forecast to grow at 2.5 per cent in 2015, according to projections drawn up by the United Nations Economic Commission for Latin America and the Caribbean (ECLAC). A further challenge was to reduce the large deficits in the public finances and the current account, which official forecasts for 2014 had put at levels slightly lower than the 4 per cent and 6.5 per cent of GDP, respectively, posted in 2013.

As had been the case for several years, El Salvador's fiscal policy in 2014 was, in the view of ECLAC, preoccupied with striking a balance between the need for spending and investment, principally associated with social policy, and the sustainability of the public finances. It was against this backdrop that a wide range of tax reforms were adopted in August 2014, including the introduction of the financial transaction debit tax and the tax on non-productive luxury properties, a change to the minimum income tax contribution, the removal of an income tax exemption for owners of print works and various amendments to the tax code. According to official estimates, the tax burden would rise by around 0.8 per cent of GDP in 2015 on the back of the reform, so that it should yield more than the 0.60 per cent of GDP raised by the reforms of 2010 and 2011.

Reversing the growth trend observed since 2010, income in the non-financial public sector (NFPS) expanded by only 0.1 per cent in real terms in the first nine months of 2014 compared to the same period in 2013. This was attributable to a contraction of 1.1 per cent in tax revenues, which had been equivalent to 15.4 per cent of GDP at the end of 2013, since growth of just 0.5 per cent in income tax receipts was too little to offset a fall of 1.7 per cent in value added tax revenue resulting from a slowdown in consumption from the third quarter onwards.

The austerity measures imposed on public spending were considered by ECLAC to be a contributing factor in the slight contraction (-0.1 per cent) in current spending and the fall of 16 per cent in capital expenditure. Consequently, spending by the NFPS was down by 2.4 per cent in real terms up to the third quarter, in contrast to the 7.3 per cent expansion in the same period of 2013. As a result, the NFPS deficit narrowed by almost 25 per cent in real terms to September. Official projections put the fiscal deficit, including the cost of pensions and trust funds, at 3.9 per cent of GDP, slightly below the 4 per cent recorded in 2013.

By contrast with 2013, when the budget shortfall was chiefly financed by selling short-term bonds on the domestic market, in 2014 debt accrued by issuing Treasury bills was replaced by a 12-year global bond worth US$800 million with a yield of 6.4 per cent, half a percentage point above that of a similar bond sold in late 2012. Bank lending to the private sector, which had grown by 5.7 per cent in real terms to September 2013, rose by 6.4 per cent over the same period of 2014.

Exports of goods contracted by 4.6 per cent up to the third quarter of 2014 – reversing the growth of 3.9 per cent seen in the same period of 2013 – this was due to a fall in exports of coffee, since production had yet to recover from the impact of coffee-leaf rust. This was compounded by a drop of 7.9 per cent in *maquila*exports, partly representing a fall-off from the particularly high values seen in 2013, when exports grew by 8.7 per cent to the third quarter and partly resulting from lower demand for textiles from the United States, which could be a symptom of a loss of competitiveness vis-à-vis exports from other Central American producers. Imports of goods, meanwhile, were down 2.9 per cent in nominal terms, a far cry from the growth of 5.7 per cent posted during the same period of 2013. The fall in imports by value is chiefly attributable to the effect of lower hydrocarbon prices on the oil bill, which contracted by 13.6 per cent to the third quarter of 2014. The overall result was a nominal reduction of 1 per cent in the trade deficit. Remittance flows expanded by 8 per cent in nominal terms to September, which compares favourably with the muted growth of 1.3 per cent in the same period of 2013.

El Salvador's economy grew at a rate of 2 per cent in the first half of 2014, half a percentage point higher than in the same period of 2013. This slight acceleration was driven by growth of 1.7 per cent in agriculture and 2.6 per cent in commercial activity, the latter spurred by buoyant remittance receipts. The recovery in agriculture, however, was principally a reflection of the weakness of the previous year's results, since coffee production remained affected by coffee-leaf rust and that of basic grains by drought.

According to ECLAC, monthly indicators of economic activity pointed to a slowdown in the third quarter of 2014, attributable to a continuing contraction in construction together with a loss of momentum in manufacturing and commerce. Given the growth of remittances, this slower pace of activity might have reflected more cautious behaviour by households in the wake of the rising violence between gangs. Nonetheless, the authorities were projecting growth of 2.2 per cent for 2014 as a whole in view of the launch of a number of investment projects, particularly those associated with the second phase of the Millennium Fund (FOMILENIO II) project, financed out of United States co-operation resources intended for the development of the country's coastal marine area.

Cumulative 2014 inflation to October was 1.8 per cent, more than one percentage point higher than in the same period the previous year. This increase occurred primarily because food prices were pushed up by the relative scarcity of basic grains owing to the drought, something lower fuel prices were insufficient to offset. The official projection for December-to-December inflation in 2014 was 1.9 per cent. Data on contributors to the Salvadoran Social Security Institute pointed to a slowdown in formal job creation, with growth to September averaging 2.7 per cent , well below the 4.5 per cent seen in the same period of 2013. The greatest fall-off in new job growth was in manufacturing and, to a lesser extent, commerce.

Risk assessment

Economy	Fair
Politics	Fair/good
Regional stability	Good
Crime	Appalling

COUNTRY PROFILE

1821 The Central American provinces (Costa Rica, Guatemala, Honduras, Nicaragua and El Salvador) declared independence from Spain.
1825 Costa Rica, Guatemala, Honduras, Nicaragua and El Salvador formed the Central American Federation (CAF).
1838 The CAF was dissolved and El Salvador became an independent republic. By the twentieth century, the majority of the indigenous population had been reduced to poverty and discontent, having been pushed off their land, which had been turned over to crops for export. Most of El Salvador's income came from coffee exports.
1929 Coffee prices plummeted following the US stock market crash.
1932 During the uprising of peasants and Indians an estimated 30,000 people were killed by the military, referred to as *La Matanza* (the massacre).
1961 The right-wing Partido de Conciliación Nacional (PCN) (National Reconciliation Party) came to power following a military coup.
1969 Honduras and El Salvador fought what became known as the 'soccer war', which was prompted by land disputes and El Salvador's win in the World Cup play-offs between the two countries; over 3,000 people died.
1970s There were demonstrations, civil disobedience and strikes. The *esquadrones de muerte* (death squads) were formed. Thousands of Salvadorians were kidnapped, tortured and murdered.
1977 General Carlos Romero was elected president.
1979 Romero was ousted by reformist military officers, although this failed to stem the number of deaths at the hands of military-backed death squads.
1980 Archbishop Oscar Romero was assassinated on 25 March while celebrating Mass. In December Napoleón Duarte became El Salvador's first civilian president since 1931.
1980s Civil war between the US-backed right-wing government and a leftist guerrilla group, Frente Farabundo Martí para la Liberación Nacional (FMLN) (Front for National Liberation), was based largely in the countryside. Right-wing groups carried out indiscriminate street killings of 'subversives'. Some rural communities were targeted by the security forces for eradication.
1982 The far-right Alianza Republicana Nacionalista (Arena) (Nationalist Republican Alliance) came to power following violent parliamentary elections.
1984 Duarte won the presidential election and began to negotiate a settlement with the FMLN.
1989 Arena's Alfredo Cristiani was elected president.
1992 A formal cease-fire, under UN auspices, came into effect. An estimated 75,000 people had been killed in the 12-year civil war.
1994 Political killings and threats continued right up to the elections. Arena's Armando Calderón Sol was elected president.
1997 Arena won the Assembly elections.
1998 Hurrican Mitch devastated large swathes of the country, destroying coffee and banana crops.
1999 Francisco Flores (Arena) won the presidential election.
2000 The FMLN become the largest party in the National Assembly. Arena formed a coalition government with the PCN, giving the right-wing block a majority in the Assembly.
2001 The US dollar was adopted as the official currency. Around 1,500 people were killed in the worst earthquakes for more than a decade and 1.5 million were made homeless.
2003 A free trade agreement (FTA) with Panama came into effect.
2004 Antonio Saca (Arena) won the presidential elections. El Salvador, along with the Dominican Republic, Costa Rica, Guatemala, Honduras and Nicaragua, agreed to a proposed Central American Free Trade Agreement (Cafta) with the US.
2005 The OAS human rights court voted to re-open an investigation into the El Mozote massacre in 1981. Thousands of people fled the area surrounding the Ilamatepec volcano after it erupted and a tropical storm caused many deaths and damaged the surrounding area.
2006 Arena won 34 seats in the national assembly elections; the FMLN won 32 seats. The newly defined border between Honduras and El Salvador was inaugurated.
2007 Three members of Arena were murdered in Guatemala. After eight years of conflict, the International Court of Justice (ICJ) ruled on a new maritime boundary between Honduras and Nicaragua. The result gives both countries equal access to the rich fishing grounds and oil and gas exploration waters in the area.
2009 In parliamentary elections, the opposition and former revolutionary guerrilla group, FMLN won 42.6 per cent, (35 seats out of 84), the ruling Arena 38.6 per cent (32). In the presidential election, opposition leader, Mauricio Funes (FMLN) won 51.3 per cent, Rodrigo Avila (Arena) 48.7 per cent. Mauricio Funes and his government took office and diplomatic ties with Cuba were restored after a break of 50 years.
2011 In April the Supreme Court disbanded the Christian Democratic Party (CDP) and the National Conciliation Party (NCP), as neither conservative party had won the minimum level of votes (of 3 per cent) required in the 2004 presidential election. The parties will cease to exist once the terms of office of their mayors and legislators have ended. A draft bill set before parliament in July for a new wealth and estate tax came in for criticism. It was considered that a levy on investment and entrepreneurial achievement could lead to de-capitalisation in El Salvador.
2012 Parliamentary elections were held on 10 March, in which the opposition Arena won 33 seats (out of 84) narrowly beating the ruling FMLN (31 seats) into second place. On 12 October, the US treasury called the violent criminal gang MS-13 (organised by El Salvador immigrants) as a 'transnational criminal organisation'. The US authorities are now allowed to seize profits of the gang, from drug-trafficking and other criminal activities and estimated in millions of US dollars, much of which is repatriated to El Salvador. MS-13 is estimated to have thousands of members living in North America.
2013 El Salvador has banned gold mining (and all other metal mining since 2008) in an effort to protect its clean water supplies. In 2013 the two main parties were split into anti-mining FMLN and the Arena opposition which is pro-mining, a poll in 2012 showed that nearly two-thirds of the population were in favour of a complete ban.
2014 The first round of the presidential election held on 2 February was won by Mr Salvador Sánchez Cerén with 48.9 per cent of the votes, just short of the 50 per cent necessary to win outright. The right-wing Arena party candidate, Norman Quijano, came second with 38.95 per cent. Former president Antonio Saca (2004-09) came third with 11.4 per cent. The run-off between the two leaders was held on 9 March. The result was a narrow victory (0.22 per cent or just 6,384 votes) for Sánchez Cerén over Norman Quijano with 50.11 per cent to 49.89 per cent. Turn-out was 60 per cent.

2015 In mid-2015 the NGO Centro de Intercambio y Solidaridad (CIS), began distributing free cans of the pepper spray Kuros! to women as a means of defence against sexual attacks.

Political structure

In addition to their unicameral national parliaments, El Salvador, Guatemala, Honduras, Nicaragua, Panama and Dominican Republic also return directly-elected deputies to the supranational Central American Parliament.

Constitution

The Constitution came into effect in December 1983. It delineated the three arms of government – legislative, executive and judicial – granting them official autonomy. Executive power is held by the president who serves a non-renewable five-year term of office. Legislative power, formed of members elected on three-year terms is held by the unicameral National Assembly – which also holds the power to appoint a president if no candidate gains an absolute majority in the elections. In 1991 constitutional reforms strengthened the judicial and electoral systems. There are 14 *departamentos* (administrative divisions) which each have a governor and an elected local council headed by a mayor. On the 12 June 2014, the constitution was amended to recognize indigenous communities.

Form of state

Presidential democratic republic

The executive

Executive power is vested in the president (who is elected every five years in March), assisted by the vice president and council of ministers. A second round of elections must be held within 30 days of the declaration of the result of the first round if no candidate secures an absolute majority (51 per cent) at the first attempt.
The presidential term begins on 1 June. The president is both the Head of State and Head of government.

National legislature

The unicameral Asamblea Legislativa (Legislative Assembly), has 84 members directly elected in multi-seat constituencies for three years by proportional representation, of which 64 are elected in 14 multi-seat constituencies relating to the 14 departments (returning between 3–16 deputies each, depending on population sizes) and 20 deputies selected in a single national constituency. Deputies may serve successive terms.

Legal system

Since 1993, El Salvador has undergone a full-scale review of its judicial structure. In order to achieve a basic level of judicial independence, judicial appointments are the responsibility of the Legislative Assembly, and funding for the courts has been ensured. In 1998, the Legislative Assembly replaced the 1860 criminal code and code of criminal procedure with more efficient procedures. With a US$22.2 million loan from the Inter-American Development Bank (IDB), approved in 1996, El Salvador began a programme of judicial training, the renovation and expansion of efforts to educate juvenile offenders, and projects to strengthen administration and planning. The process of reform is continuing and is more autonomous and professional than at any time in El Salvador's history.

Last elections

9 March 2014 (presidential); 1 March 2015 (parliamentary)
Results: Presidential (2014): First round: Salvador Sánchez Cerén (Frente Farabundo Martí para la Liberación Nacional (FMLN)) 48.9 per cent, Norman Quijano (Alianza Republicana Nacionalista (Arena)) 48.9 per cent. Run-off: Sánchez Cerén 50.11 per cent, Norman Quijano 49.89 per cent. Turn-out was 60 per cent.
Parliamentary: Alianza Republicana Nacionalista (Arena) (Nationalist Republican Alliance) won 38.77 per cent of the vote (32 seats, out of 84), Frente Farabundo Martí para la Liberación Nacional (FMLN) (Farabundo Martí National Liberation Front) 37.28 per cent (31), Alianza por la Unidad Nacional (AUN) (Grand Alliance for National Unity) 9.26 per cent (11), Concertación Nacional (CN) (National Coalition) 6.77 per cent (four), ARENA-PCN 1.67 per cent (three), Partido Demócrata Cristiano (Christian Democratic Party) 2.47 per cent (one), PCN-PDC 0.3 per cent (one) and PCN-DS, 0.2 per cent (one). The remaining three parties and the independents failed to win any seats.

Next elections

2019 (presidential); 2018 (parliamentary)

Political parties

Ruling party

Alianza Republicana Nacionalista (Arena) (Nationalist Republican Alliance).

Main opposition party

Farabundo Martí National Liberation Front (FMLN).

Population

6.35 million (2014)* Population density is particularly high in the capital, San Salvador, where population density is more than twice the national average.
Last census: 12 May 2007: 5,744,113
Population density: Around 280 inhabitants per square km. Urban population 64 per cent (2010 Unicef).
Annual growth rate: 0.7 per cent, 1990–2010 (Unicef).

Ethnic make-up

Approximately 94 per cent of the population are *mestizo*, 5 per cent Amerindian and 1 per cent white.

Religions

Predominantly Roman Catholic (75 per cent); most of the remaining 25 per cent belong to a number of Protestant churches.

Education

Low levels of literacy and educational skills are regarded by the government as a major impediment to foreign investment.
Literacy rate: 80 per cent adult rate; 89 per cent youth rate (15–24) (Unesco 2005).
Enrolment rate: 112 per cent gross primary enrolment of relevant age group, including repeaters; 56 per cent gross secondary enrolment; 17 per cent gross tertiary enrolment (World Bank).
Pupils per teacher: 33 in primary schools

Health

Approximately 55 per cent of the population has access to safe water.

HIV/Aids

HIV prevalence: 0.7 per cent aged 15–49 in 2003 (World Bank)
Life expectancy: 71 years, 2004 (WHO 2006)
Fertility rate/Maternal mortality rate: 2.3 births per woman, 2010 (Unicef); maternal mortality 1.2 per 1,000 live births (World Bank).
Child (under 5 years) mortality rate (per 1,000): 16 per 1,000 live births (WHO 2012); 11 per cent of children aged under five are malnourished (World Bank).
Head of population per physician: 1.24 physicians per 1,000 people, 2002 (WHO 2006)

Welfare

El Salvador operates a mandatory private insurance system, introduced into law in 1996 and implemented in 1998 as part of the government's privatisation strategy. The law ensured state provision for those aged over 36-years in 1996 but was closed to new entrants. The new private system is funded through a mixture of contributions made by workers and employers.
The state also operates a welfare system for benefits covering sickness, maternity and work injury. These are based on contributions by the employer and worker and subsidised by the state, but exclude casual workers and those involved in domestic work. Agricultural workers are denied sickness and maternity pay and teachers are excluded from work injury benefits.

Pensions

Old-age pensions are available to men aged over 60 and women over 55 with 25 years of contributions. There is no minimum age requirement for those with more than 30 years' contributions. The 1996 pension reform created five private pensions funds, but in September 2000 three of these were merged into a new fund – AFP Crecer, run by Spanish bank BBVA – which in 2002 controlled around 60 per cent of the country's pensions market.

Main cities

San Salvador (capital, estimated population 561,327 in 2012), Soyapango (420,916), Santa Ana (197,552), San Miguel (183,733), Mejicanos (167,389), Apopa (143,185), New San Salvador (135,895).

Languages spoken

Nahua is spoken by some Amerindians. English is widely spoken in business circles.

Official language/s

Spanish

Media

Press freedom is guaranteed by constitution.

Press

Dailies: In Spanish, Most newspapers include sections on business and economic matters.

National newspapers include *El Diario de Hoy* (www.elsalvador.com) and *La Prensa Gráfica* (ultra-conservative) (www.laprensagrafica.com) and *El Mundo* (www.elmundo.com.sv), an evening newspaper. Local newspapers include *Diario Co Latino* (www.diariocolatino.com) from San Salvador and *El Pais* (www.elpais.com.sv) from Santa Ana. *El Faro* (www.elfaro.com.sv) is a weekly publication.

Broadcasting

Radio: There are over 80 commercial radio stations. Radio El Salvador (www.radioelsalvador.com.sv) is the state-run network with local stations providing nationwide coverage. Most stations provide services for a localised area and the majority are located around San Salvador.

Television: There are 17 TV channels provided by around five networks. One of the largest private, commercial network is Telecorporacion Salvadorena (TCS), with ESMI TV (www.esmitv.com), which has five channels, covering news, sport, music and drama and entertainment. Agape TV (www.agapetv8.com) has both commercial and religious programmes. Iglesia del Camino (www.delcamino.org.sv) is run by the Catholic Church. The government runs a cultural and educational channel (canal 10).

There are many pay-to-view digital, cable and satellite services available.

Other news agencies: Prensa Latina: www.prensalatina.com.mx

Economy

The service sector constitutes over 62.2 per cent of the economy, employing around 50 per cent of the total labour force; the industry sector comprises a total of 27.0 per cent of GDP, of which manufacturing accounts for around 20 per cent, and agriculture around 10 per cent.

There are free trade zones where companies (*maquila*) import materials duty free, add value and re-export the goods. Industries that have been encouraged include textile and garment manufacturing, as well as customer service industries such as offshore call centres. The number of workers employed is estimated at around 70,000. As to the general economy retail, financial services and ancillary service businesses have grown as the economy has expanded. Agriculture produce includes coffee, sugar, and livestock for export, along with manufactured goods in iron and steel, paper, pharmaceuticals and foodstuffs.

GDP growth was 1.3 per cent in 2008. The economy fell into recession in 2009 with negative growth of -3.1 per cent. However, by 2010 it had recovered and growth was 1.4 per cent with and slow growth has been maintained since, reaching 2.0 per cent by 2014.

The economy is steadily strengthening, although there are risks from external shocks, such as natural disasters (a devastating earthquake struck in 2001 and hurricanes are an almost annual occurrence). It also felt the downturn in foreign economies during the global economic crisis in 2008. The government is committed to reducing the public debt-to-GDP ratio and has implemented measures to maximise tax revenue, including modernising the tax administration, reducing tax avoidance, increasing co-ordination between the tax and customs agencies, as well as providing an audit division with increased resources to function independently. These measures had by 2011 met the government's fiscal targets at a time of higher spending on subsidies.

High levels of unemployment and under-employment persist and remain a government priority, however unemployment has been decreasing since 2010, when the rate was 7.3 per cent, to 5.9 per cent in 2014. The ability to earn foreign exchange is hampered by El Salvador's comparative disadvantage in terms of productivity, due to low levels of capital investment.

Worker remittances in 2014 were US$4.2 billion (16.8 per cent of GDP), rising from US$4.0 billion in 2013, delivering funds directly into typically poorer family budgets.

External trade

El Salvador is a member of the Central American Free Trade Agreement (Cafta) along with the US, Costa Rica, Guatemala, Honduras and Dominica Republic.

The *maquila* sector dominates trade with manufactured goods (in particular garments) exported, typically, to the US. Other such enterprises include light manufacturing and offshore call centres.

Agricultural produce for export includes coffee, sugar and livestock. There has also been an increase in non-traditional exports such as shrimps, sesame seeds, nuts, fruits and honey.

Imports

Principal imports include raw materials, consumer goods, capital goods, fuels, foodstuffs, petroleum and electricity.

Main sources: US (41.0 per cent of total in 2014), Guatemala (9.5 per cent), China (7.3 per cent)

Exports

Principal exports include offshore assembly exports, coffee, sugar, shrimp, textiles, handcrafts, chemicals and electricity.

Main destinations: US (46.5 per cent of total in 2014), Honduras (14.2 per cent), Guatemala (13.4 per cent)

Agriculture

Farming

The agricultural sector of El Salvador's economy employs approximately a third of the country's total workforce. The sector contributed 10.8 per cent to total GDP in 2014. Approximately 34 per cent of total land is arable; 30 per cent permanent pastures.

Coffee is the most important crop. Other major crops are cotton, sugar cane, maize, beans and rice. There has been some diversification within the sector, with non-traditional exports such as sesame seeds, nuts, vegetables, fruits, honey and, above all, shrimps, taking an increasing share.

Fishing

The Gulf of Fonseca is regarded as one of Central America's greatest natural resources with rich fisheries and diverse marine life, which is shared by Honduras, Nicaragua and El Salvador. Typically, the annual catch is over 18,000mt per year.

Forestry

The forestry industry in El Salvador is relatively small.

Industry and manufacturing

Contributing approximately 28 per cent to total GDP and employing around a fifth of the total workforce, the industrial sector

is a significant part of El Salvador's economy.
The national government has made efforts to shift the industrial sector towards manufacturing for export through the development of the *maquila* (in-bond manufacturing) sector and the creation of free zones. *Maquila* exports have accounted for the bulk of growth in the export sector since 1992. Investment incentives in the free zones include a 10-year income tax exemption, import duty exemptions or reduced exposure to taxes on equity or assets for 10 years.

Tourism

El Salvador has a variety of tourist attractions, including Pacific Ocean and Caribbean Sea coastlines, nature parks, cities and culture. The pre-Colombian archaeological site of Joya de Cerén, with the remains of a Maya farming community buried beneath the Laguna Caldera Volcano (AD600), is included on Unesco's World Heritage List. However, El Salvador also has a problem with internal lawlessness and foreign nationals are urged by their governments to exercise extra personal security.
Travel and Tourism accounted for around 10 per cent (US$2.2 billion) of GDP until 2008, but the global economic crisis cut visitor numbers, particularly from the US, from where a high proportion of visitors originate, so that by 2010 tourism only contributed 6.3 per cent (US$1.4 billion) of GDP. Likewise, employment in tourism and related industries accounted for 8.9 per cent (211,500 jobs) in 2008, falling to 5.7 per cent (137,600 jobs) in 2010. However, by 2014 the tourism industry had returned to its pre-crisis standards, contributing 10.1 per cent of GDP (US$2.5 billion) and providing employment to 9.1 per cent of the population (237,000 jobs).

Mining

Mining has been a stable sector of the El Salvadorian economy for several years. Gold, silver, sea salt and limestone are mined or quarried and there are deposits of copper, iron ore, sulphur, mercury, lead, zinc and perlite. There are two gold mines, one at San Cristobal and the other near San Salvador which also mines silver. However, the mining sector is small and underdeveloped, contributing only 0.1 per cent to GDP. There are two cement works, the 240,000 tonnes per year (tpy) Cemento Mayan at Canton Tecomapa and the 684,000tpy Cemento de El Salvador at El Ronco.

Hydrocarbons

There are no known hydrocarbon reserves, although oil exploration is ongoing. The country is totally reliant on imported products, of which oil imports are typically around 20,000 barrels per day (bpd), with consumption at around 50,000bpd; refinery capacity is 22,000bpd, at the Acajutla Port site.
In 2006 an association of 20 municipal mayors signed an agreement with Venezuelan to buy oil on preferential terms. In 2009 a presidential scheme began, to take over the purchase of oil from Venezuela for national distribution and have El Salvador considered for membership of the Petrocaribe programme, through which Venezuela provides oil at below market prices to participating Caribbean countries. However, as of 2014 El Salvador was still not a member of Petrocaribe.
The first ethanol producing plant was opened in 2006 at Acajutla Port, processing 227,000 kilolitres per year. In 2008 the US Southridge Enterprises arranged with major domestic sugar cane growers to use their crops for ethanol production of up to 75,700 kilolitres per year. All ethanol is exported to the US.
Any natural gas or coal imports are commercially insignificant.

Energy

Total installed generating capacity was around 1.5GW in 2014, producing around 6 billion kilowatt hours. The energy market is open to competition but subject to the autonomous regulatory body of the Superintendencia General de Elécticidad y Telecomunicaciones (Siget) (Superintendent General of Electricity and Telecommuncations).
El Salvador is the largest producer of geothermal electricity in Central America. The privately owned LaGeo operates the Ahuachapán and Berlin geothermal power plants. Hydroelectric installations include Guajoyo, Cerrán Grande, 5 de Novembre and 15 de Septembre.

Financial markets

Stock exchange
Bolsa de Valores de El Salvador (BVES) (El Salvador Stock Exchange)

Banking and insurance

The banking system of El Salvador remained under state ownership until 1991. Thereafter the government implemented market reforms that handed control to private investors. Interest rates are determined by the market.
Central bank
Banco Central de Reserva de El Salvador

Time

GMT minus six hours

Geography

El Salvador lies on the Pacific coast of Central America. Guatemala is to the west and Honduras to the north and east. The basins in the centre of the country rise to little more than 600 metres at San Salvador. Across this upland and surmounting it, run two more or less parallel rows of volcanoes, 14 of which are over 900 metres. Lowlands lie to the north and south of the high backbone. The ash and lava from the volcanoes have produced an ideal soil in which to grow coffee.
Hemisphere
Northern.

Climate

The climate is semi-tropical. The dry season is from November–April; temperatures range from 15–23 degrees Celsius (C); the rainy season runs from May–October, when the average temperature is 28 degrees C. Generally, the temperature depends on the altitude; coastal areas are hotter and more humid than upland areas.
The driest month is February with just 5mm average rainfall. The wettest month is June with 328mm. The coldest month is December when the average daily temperature varies between 16 and 32 degrees C. In May, the hottest month, the variation is only slightly different, ranging between 19 and 33 degrees C.

Dress codes

Light cotton suits and ties are the generally accepted form of dress for businessmen, although some Salvadoreans will dress less formally in *guyaberas* (styled cotton shirts worn outside the trousers), particularly in the warmest months. Businesswomen should wear a light suit or equivalent. Dress as for business if invited to a social occasion unless suggested otherwise.
A sweater or light jacket will be required for evenings and for the highlands.

Entry requirements

Passports
Required by all. Passports must be valid for six months from date of departure.
Visa
Required by all, except citizens of most Central American, EU and some Asian countries (for a full list visit www.elsalvador.org or contact the local embassy). Business visas require, in Spanish, a letter of invitation from an El Salvadorian company and a letter from the foreign company being represented.
Currency advice/regulations
There are no restrictions on the import or export of local or foreign currencies. In the case of foreign currencies, the quantity being imported, especially if sizeable, should be declared, as there is a restriction on export of larger amounts to the level imported.
Prohibited imports
Fruit, vegetables, plants and animals.

Health (for visitors)
Mandatory precautions
A yellow fever vaccination certificate is required if arriving from an infected area.
Advisable precautions
Typhoid, polio, hepatitis A and tetanus vaccinations. Dengue fever cases have risen, visitors should avoid exposing their skin during early morning and evening when the risk of being bitten by mosquitoes is highest. Malaria is not a virulent strain but prophylaxis should be taken as there is some risk in the Santa Anna province and rural locations. There is a high rabies risk. Water precautions are essential and only well-cooked food should be eaten. Milk is unpasteurised and should be boiled.

Hotels
The best hotels can be found in the capital. A 10 per cent tip is usual.

Public holidays (national)
Fixed dates
1 Jan (New Year's Day), 1 May (Labour Day), 4 Aug (Transfiguration Bank Holiday), 15 Sep (Independence Day), 12 Oct (Columbus Day), 2 Nov (All Souls' Day), 24 Dec (Christmas Eve), 25 Dec (Christmas Day), 31 Dec (New Year's Eve).
Variable dates
Holy Wednesday, Maundy Thursday, Good Friday.

Working hours
Banking
Mon–Fri: 0900–1700. Sat: 0900–1300.
Business
Mon–Fri: 0900–1800.
Government
Mon–Fri: 0800–1730.
Shops
Mon–Sat: 0900–1200, 1400–1800. Supermarkets Mon–Sat: 0800–2200. The main shopping centres are open on Sunday.

Electricity supply
110V AC, 60Hz

Social customs/useful tips
Appointments should be made in advance. Salvadorans have a distinctly Latin sense of time and can be among the least punctual people in Central America, although many businessmen and bankers, particularly those with export experience, keep *horas inglesas* (punctual time).
Business relationships and meetings tend to be formal in early stages. Use proper titles such as Licenciado (college graduate), Ingeniero (engineering graduate) and Doctor (physicians and lawyers), followed by the person's surname. Handshaking before and after meetings is important. First names should not be used until a business relationship has been consolidated. Upon introduction it is important to exchange cards; a supply of Spanish-printed cards is advisable.
Business is conducted in Spanish although some executives speak English. Some knowledge of spoken Spanish is much better than none.
Meetings over meals, including breakfast, are becoming common. Working lunches and dinners can be lengthy. Gratuities in restaurants and hotels are around 10 per cent.

Security
El Salvador has a poor personal security environment, with a homicide rate twice that of Los Angeles. Kidnappings, carjackings, and robbery are common and can occur anywhere. There is a risk of murder for those robbed, even if they do not resist. Downtown San Salvador should be avoided at all times, as should roads outside the city after dark. Reports indicate the border with Guatemala has been a site for attacks on vehicles. Jewellery or large amounts of cash should not be carried.
Business travellers should arrange to be met at the airport and be accompanied by a local representative, as this has been shown to reduce problems.

Getting there
Air
National airline: TACA Airlines.
International airport/s: El Salvador International (SAL), 35km south of San Salvador; bank, car hire, restaurants, shops. The airport and the highway that runs to it are the most modern and developed in the region. It is expanding its services in order to become an international cargo warehousing and distribution centre.
Airport tax: US$27.15.
Surface
Road: Roads run from Guatemala and Honduras. Duty is paid at the border when entering or leaving the country by land. It is advisable to carry small denomination notes to pay the border duties.
Rail: Lines run through El Salvador from Guatemala to Honduras.
Main port/s: Acajutla, La Unión/Cutuco, La Libertad (fishing only). Major ports on the Pacific are Puerto Barrios and Santo Tomás de Castilla.

Getting about
National transport
Air: Scheduled internal services from San Salvador to San Miguel, La Unión and Usulután. Charter flights are available.
Road: There is a network of 9,800km of paved roads. The Pan-American Highway (over 300km) runs through the country linking San Salvador with Santa Ana in the west and San Miguel in the east; Carretera Litoral runs south of the Pan-American Highway linking the capital with Sonsonate, Zacatecoluca and Usulatan. Many roads have fallen into considerable disrepair as a result of the war and cuts in government spending.
Buses: The bus system is excellent, with services between major towns. The buses are often crowded and run frequently.
Rail: There are 602km of railway, including 429km of line from Guatemala to Honduras. A narrow gauge line links the western town of Ahuachpan and the port of Acajutla with San Salvador, which is in turn connected to La Unión in the east. The railway is used largely for freight traffic.
City transport
Taxis: Taxis are bright yellow. The regular taxi line is Taxi Acacya. Taxis can be hailed or ordered by telephone. The fixed rate system is not rigidly followed – check before proceeding. No taxis have meters. Tipping is unusual but 10 per cent of fare is appreciated. Taxi from airport to city centre journey time is 25 minutes.
Car hire
A national or international permit valid for 30 days is required. Traffic drives on the right.

BUSINESS DIRECTORY
The addresses listed below are a selection only. While World of Information makes every endeavour to check these addresses, we cannot guarantee that changes have not been made, especially to telephone numbers and area codes. We would welcome any corrections.

Telephone area codes
Dialling code for El Salvador: IDD access code +503 followed by subscriber's number.

Useful telephone numbers
Emergency:121
Information:114
International enquiries/calls (operator): 119, 120
For collect calls (US only):190
Migration Office:222-7328
Foreign Office:222-6611

Chambers of Commerce
American Chamber of Commerce of El Salvador, Paseo General Escalón 5432, San Salvador (tel: 264-7609; fax: 263-3237; e-mail: contact@amchamsal.com).

El Salvador Cámara de Comercio e Industria, 9a Avenida Norte y 5a Calle Poniente, PO Box 1640, 1118 San Salvador (tel: 244-2000; fax: 271-4461; e-mail: camara@camarasal.com).

Banking
Ahorromet Scotiabank, Avenida Olímpica 129, Edificio Torre Ahorromet

Scotiabank, San Salvador (tel: 245-1211; fax: 245-2884).

BANCASA (Banco de Construcción y Ahorro), 75 Avenida Sur 709, Colonia Escalon, San Salvador (tel: 263-5508; fax: 263-5506).

Banco Agrícola Comercial, Paseo General Escalón 3635, Colonia Escalón, San Salvador (tel: 224-0283; fax: 224-3948).

Banco de Comercio de El Salvador, 25 Avenida Norte y 23 Calle Poniente, San Salvador (tel: 226-4577; fax: 225-7767; e-mail: webmaster@banco.com.sv).

Banco Creditomatic, 55 Avenida Sur y Alameda Roosevelt, Centro Roosevelt, San Salvador (tel: 298-1855; fax: 224-4138).

Banco Cuscatlán, Km 10 Carretera a Santa Tecla, Edificio Pirámide Cuscatlán La Libertad (tel: 228-7777; fax: 228-9999).

Banco Hipotecario, Pje. Senda Florida Sur, Paseo General Escalón, San Salvador (tel: 223-3753; fax: 298-0447).

Banco Salvadoreño, Alameda Dr Manuel Enrique Araujo 3550, San Salvador (tel: 298-4444; fax 298-0102).

Grupo Capital, Alameda Dr Manuel Enrique Araujo, Edificio Century Plaza, San Salvador (tel: 245-6000; fax: 224-3303).

Unibanco, Alameda Roosevelt 2511, San Salvador (tel: 245-0651; fax: 298-5261).

Central bank

Banco Central de Reserva, Alameda Juan Pablo, entre 15 y 17 Avenida Norte, PO Box 106, San Salvador (tel: 281-8000; fax: 281-8013; e-mail: comunicaciones@bcr.gob.sv).

Stock exchange

Bolsa de Valores de El Salvador (BVES) (El Salvador Stock Exchange), www.bves.com.sv

Travel information

Corporación Salvadoreña de Turismo (CORSATUR), Boulevard del Hipódromo 508, San Benito, San Salvador (tel: 243-7835; fax: 243-0427).

TACA International Airlines, Edificio Caribe, San Salvador (tel: 298-5055; fax:279-4345).

National tourist organisation offices

Instituto Salvadoreño de Turismo (ISTU) (El Salvador Tourist Board), Calle Rubén Darío 619, San Salvador (tel: 228-000, 222-8699, 222-8144, 222-9366; fax: 221-208).

Ministries

Ministry of Agriculture and Livestock, Final 1a Avenida Norte 13 Calle Oriente y Avenida Manuel Gallardo 704, San Salvador (tel: 279-1579; fax: 224-2944).

Ministry of Defence, Alameda Manuel Enrique Araujo, Carretera a Santa Tecla, San Salvador (tel: 223-0233; fax: 298-2005).

Ministry of Economy, Alameda Juan Pablo II Calle Guadalupe, Centro de Gobierno, San Salvador (tel: 281-7134; fax: 221-2797).

Ministry of Education, Alameda Juan Pablo II Calle Guadalupe, Centro de Gobierno, San Salvador (tel: 281-0256; fax: 281-0257).

Ministry of Environment, Alameda Roosevelt y 55 Avenida Norte, Torre El Salvador, San Salvador (tel: 260-8876; fax: 260-3092).

Ministry of Finance, Edificio Las Tres Torres, Avenida Alvarado, San Salvador (tel: 225-6500; fax: 225-7491).

Ministry of Foreign Affairs, Alameda Manuel Enrique Araujo 5500, San Salvador (tel: 243-3805; fax: 243-3710).

Ministry of Health, Calle Arce 827, San Salvador (tel: 271-0008; fax: 221-0985).

Ministry of Interior, Centro de Gobierno, San Salvador (tel: 221-8582; fax: 281-5959).

Ministry of Justice and Public Security, 6a Calle Oriente 42, Antiguo Local Policia Nacional, San Salvador (tel: 271-2655; fax: 245-2650).

Ministry of Labour, Paseo General Escalón 4122, San Salvador (tel: 263-5423; fax: 263-5272).

Ministry of Public Works, 1a Avenida Sur 603, San Salvador (tel: 293-6603; fax: 271-0163).

Other useful addresses

Asociación Nacional de la Empresa Privada (ANEP), 1a Calle Poniente y 71a Avenida Norte 204, Colonia Escalón, San Salvador (tel: 224-1236; fax: 223-8932; e-mail: anep@telesal.net).

Asociación Salvadoreña de Industriales (ASI), Calles Roma y Liverpool, Colonia Roma, San Salvador (tel: 279-2488; fax: 279-2070; e-mail: unatias@sv.cciglobal.net).

Bolsa de Valores de El Salvador, Alameda Roosevelt 3107, Edificio La Centroamericana, San Salvador (tel: 298-4244; fax: 223-2898; e-mail: webmaster@bves.com.sv).

British Embassy, Paseo General Escalón 4828, Edificio Inter-Inversiones, San Salvador (tel: 263-6527; fax: 263-6516; e-mail: britemb@sal.gbm.net).

Corporación de Exportadores de El Salvador (COEXPORT), Condominios del Mediterráneo A-23, Colonia Jardínes de Guadalupe, San Salvador (tel: 243-3110; fax: 243-3159; e-mail: service@coexport.com).

El Salvador Embassy (USA), 2308 California Street, NW, Washington DC 20008 (tel: (202) 2265-9671; fax: (202) 234-3834; e-mail: correo@elsalvador.org).

Fundación Salvadoreña para el Desarrollo Económica y Social (FUSADES), Urbanización y Boulevard Santa Elena, Edificio FUSADES, Antiguo Cuscatlán, La Libertad (tel: 278-3366; fax: 278-3369; e-mail: fusades@fusades.com.sv).

Superintendencia del Sistema Financiero, 7a Avenida Norte 240, San Salvador (tel: 281-24444).

Unión de Dirigentes de Empresas Salvadoreñas (UDES), Condominios del Mediterráneo C-22, Colonia Jardines de Guadalupe, San Salvador (tel: 243-2746; fax: 243-3145).

US Embassy, Boulevard Santa Elena Final, Antiguo Cuscatlán, La Libertad (tel: 278-4444; fax: 278-6011).

Prensa Latina: www.prensalatina.com.mx

Internet sites

Bolsa de El Salvador (Stock Exchange) (Spanish): http://www.bolsavalores.com.sv/

El Salvador trade and investment: http://www.elsalvadortrade.com.sv/

Fundación Salvadoreña para el Desarrollo Económico e Social (Salvadorean Foundation for Social and Economic Development) (Spanish): http://www.fusades.com.sv/

Equatorial Guinea

KEY FACTS

Official name: República de Guinea Ecuatorial (Republic of Equatorial Guinea)

Head of State: President Teodoro Obiang Nguema Mbasogo (PDGE) (since 1979)

Head of government: Prime Minister Vicente Ehate Tomi (from 21 May 2012)

Ruling party: Partido Democrático de Guinea Ecuatorial (PDGE) (Democratic Party of Equatorial Guinea) (from 1993; re-elected 4 May 2008)

Area: 28,051 square km

Population: 778,000 (2014)*

Capital: Malabo

Official language: Spanish and French

Currency: CFA franc (CFAf) = 100 centimes (Communauté Financière Africaine (African Financial Community) franc)

Exchange rate: CFAf586.44 per US$ (Sep 2015)

GDP per capita: US$18,389 (2014)*

GDP real growth: -3.11% (2014)*

GDP: US$14.31 billion (2014)*

Inflation: 3.00% (2014)*

Oil production: 281,000 bpd (2014)

Balance of trade: -US$5.94 billion (2010)*

* estimated figure

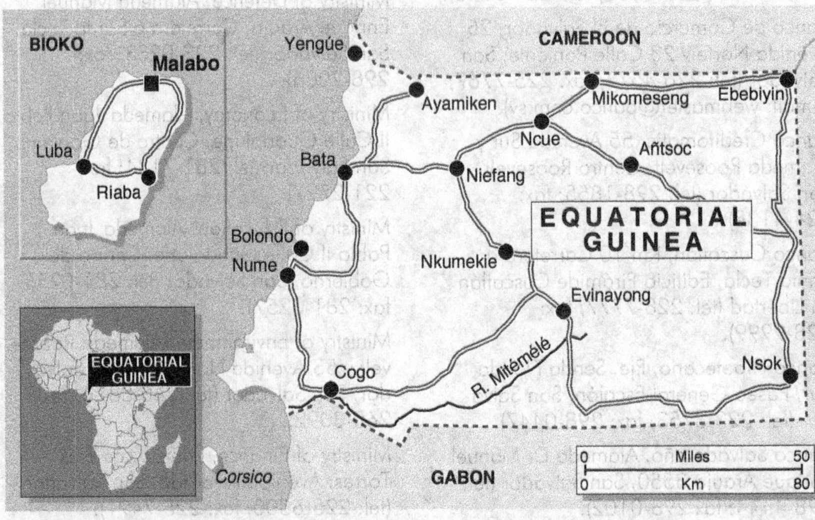

In 2014, according to the African Development Bank (AfDB), Equatorial Guinea failed to recover from the 2013 recession caused by cheaper oil prices and lower oil and gas production. To maintain its budgetary balance, the country had to draw on the reserves it had stowed away in offshore banks and in Banque des Etats de l'Afrique Central (BEAC) (Bank of Central African States).

The IMF sums it up

In its July 2015 annual assessment of the Equatorial Guinea economy, the International Monetary Fund (IMF) concluded that the decade-long hydrocarbon boom had led to a fast rise of average incomes and spurred a large scaling up of investment spending on infrastructure, although progress on social indicators had been slow. In general, economic prospects were dominated by the weakening hydrocarbon sector. In sharp contrast to the boom years, in 2015 Equatorial Guinea's economic performance has been weak, notwithstanding the high quality infrastructure that has been built. Overall gross domestic product (GDP) growth had averaged about 0.5 per cent from 2010–14, mainly driven by the trend decline in hydrocarbon production. Until recently, growth in the non-resource sector, led by the large infrastructure spending programme, had largely compensated for the declining hydrocarbon sector. The fiscal position had come under strain, as overruns on capital investment translated into larger-than-expected overall deficits financed through a draw-down of accumulated government savings. The current account deficit had progressively increased to around 10 per cent of GDP by 2014 as a result of lower exports from maturing hydrocarbon fields combined with high import levels associated with the public infrastructure programme, although there was considerable uncertainty about this figure given very weak external sector statistics. Consumer price inflation (CPI) had averaged about 4 per cent in recent years, above the 3 per cent regional convergence ceiling set by the Communauté Economique et Monétaire de l'Afrique Centrale (CEMAC) (Economic and Monetary Community of Central Africa).

The IMF considered Equatorial Guinea's growth outlook to pose very significant challenges, with prospects dominated by falling production volumes and very weak oil prices, as hydrocarbons accounted for around 80 per cent of the economy. With limited fiscal buffers to cushion the drop in government revenues, fiscal retrenchment appeared unavoidable and would contribute to an economic contraction of 9.5 per cent in 2015. Growth was expected by the IMF to remain in low negative figures through the medium term. In the view of the IMF, the gradual decline in oil output looked likely to continue in the coming years, but might be mitigated by the introduction of new extraction technologies and further exploration.

By some measures Equatorial Guinea can be classed as Africa's wealthiest state. But the reality differs from the appearance: sadly, the country's wealth appears to be diverted away from the long-suffering population and into the pockets of the family of President Teodoro Obiang Nguema Mbasogo, who *inter alia* have extensive property interest in Malibu California and elsewhere in the US. On human development indexes Equatorial Guinea ranks low for virtually every indicator although in theory it is as rich per capita as Italy. One budget transparency indicator gave the country a record zero ranking.

Hydrocarbons

Equatorial Guinea's economy is heavily reliant on its oil and natural gas industry, which accounts for almost 95 per cent of its gross domestic product (GDP) and 99 per cent of its export earnings, according to the latest estimates from the IMF. Equatorial Guinea's declining oil and natural gas production, coupled with a decline in global oil prices, is adversely affecting its economy and has resulted in lower and at times negative, GDP growth. Emphasis on the oil and natural gas industries has also led to the lack of development in non-hydrocarbon sectors.

Equatorial Guinea held 1.1 billion barrels of proved crude oil reserves in January 2015, according to *BP Statistical Review of World Energy* of June 2015 (BP15), making the country the eighth largest crude oil reserve holder in Sub-Saharan Africa. Proved natural gas reserves were 1.3 trillion cubic feet (tcf) as of January 2015, the tenth-largest in the region. Most of the reserves and operating fields are located offshore, near the Bioko Island. In 2014, total oil production averaged almost 281,000 barrels per day (bpd), well below Equatorial Guinea's peak production of 369,000bpd in 2007.

The Zafiro field, operated by ExxonMobil, is the country's most prolific oil field, but its current output has more than halved since its peak, leaving the country eager to start production from new fields. Despite the recent start of the Alen field, which produces natural gas condensate, new production is not enough to offset natural declines. Equatorial Guinea does not have any refining capacity. The country consumed 2,100bpd of petroleum in 2014, all of which was imported. The government has announced plans to open a 20,000bpd refinery in Mbini, but the project has been slow to develop.

Equatorial Guinea exports crude oil to markets in Asia, Europe and the Americas. China is the largest destination for Equatorial Guinean crude oil. The United States used to be one of the top importers, but US crude oil imports from the country have decreased from an average of 41,000bpd in 2012 to 4,000bpd in 2014

Risk assessment

Economy	Fair
Politics	Poor
Regional stability	Fair

COUNTRY PROFILE

1470 The island of Anobon was first visited by the Portuguese, who subsequently settled it and the other islands in the Gulf of Guinea, including Bioko.
1477 Portugal ceded Bioko to Spain. Bioko became an important slave-trading base for several European nations up to the nineteenth century.
1844 Spanish began settling the mainland region of Río Muni.
1904 Río Muni and Bioko became the West African Territories, later named Spanish Guinea.
1968 Spanish Guinea was granted independence from Spain and renamed the Republic of Equatorial Guinea. Macias Nguema became president.
1972 Nguema became 'President for Life' and his presidency degenerated as democratic institutions and practices were dismissed. The regime used terror to maintain power and up to one third of the population fled the country as the economy collapsed.
1979 Teodoro Obiang Nguema Mbasogo (the president's nephew) seized power in a *coup d'état*. Macias Nguema was executed. Even though a ruling Supreme Military Council (SMC) was established Obiang retained all effective power.
1982 A new constitution was drafted with the help of the UN Commission on Human Rights. It came into effect on August 15 and the SMC was abolished
1984 and 1989 President Obiang was re-elected unopposed.
1992 The president dismissed the government as a prelude to the introduction of multi-partyism.
1993 The first multi-party elections were won by the president's Partido Democrático de Guinea Ecuatorial (PDGE) (Democratic Party of Equatorial Guinea); the main opposition parties boycotted the election.
1995 Zafiro, the country's largest oil field was discovered off Bioko Island.
1996 President Obiang won the presidential elections, which were described as 'a farce' by international observers.
1999 PDGE won 75 seats in the first fully contested parliamentary elections. Opposition parties alleged fraud and boycotted parliament.
2000 Equatorial Guinea and Nigeria signed a treaty agreeing to the demarcation of their maritime border.
2002 Opposition members accused the government of mass human rights abuse. President Obiang was re-elected.
2004 The ruling and allied parties won the 25 April parliamentary elections; foreign observers criticised both the poll and the results. Perpetrators of an alleged coup were arrested in Harare, Zimbabwe, when their plane landed for refuelling. Nineteen mercenaries accused of the

KEY INDICATORS — Equatorial Guinea

	Unit	2011	2012	2013	2014	**2015
Population	m	*1.35	*0.74	*0.76	*0.78	*0.80
Gross domestic product (GDP)	US$bn	19.79	16.49	15.58	*14.31	*8.51
GDP per capita	US$	27,478	22,391	*20,581	*18,389	*10,641
GDP real growth	%	7.1	3.2	-4.8	*-3.1	*-15.4
Inflation	%	21.4	3.4	3.2	*3.0	*3.0
Oil output	'000 bpd	252.0	283.0	311.0	281.0	–
Current account	US$m	-1,799.0	-752.0	-1,879.0	*-1,878.0	*-2,764.0
Total reserves minus gold	US$m	2,629.1	4,396.1		2,906.8	–
Foreign exchange	US$m	2,587.9	4,356.9		–	–
Exchange rate	per US$	466.82	505.65	480.26	542.10	–

* estimated figure ** forecast figure

planned overthrow were convicted, including opposition leader, Severo Moto, who was sentenced to 63 years in prison

2005 Sir Mark Thatcher, son of the former UK prime minister, Margaret Thatcher, was arrested in South Africa and pleaded guilty to financing the helicopter used in the 2004 attempted coup; he was fined US$500,000 and given a suspended gaol sentence. Spain overturned the asylum status of opposition leader, Severo Moto, after receiving evidence he had been involved in a number of coup attempts.

2006 The government resigned following accusations by the president of corruption and incompetence.

2008 President Obiang announced that presidential elections would take place in 2010. Opposition leader, Severo Moto, was arrested in Spain and charged with trafficking weapons into Equatorial Guinea. He had been given political asylum by Spain in 1986; political asylum had been revoked in 2005 after he was accused of attempting to promote a *coup d'etat* from Spain, but it was re-instated in 2008. In parliamentary elections, the ruling PDGE, allied to the Front of Democratic Opposition (FOD), won 99 seats out of 100, the Convergencia para la Democracia Social (CPDS) (Convergence for Social Democracy) won one seat. The government of Prime Minister Nfubea resigned; Ignacio Milam Tang was appointed in his stead. British national Simon Mann was sentenced to more than 34 years in jail over a 2004 coup plot in Equatorial Guinea but was later given a presidential pardon and deported.

2009 Gunmen attacked the presidential palace in the capital Malabo, but were repelled by security guards. The thirty-year anniversary of President Obiang's coup was celebrated. Obiang Nguema won the presidential elections with 95.8 per cent of the vote. Opposition and human rights organisations claim the voting was neither free nor fair.

2010 The parliament of Economic Community of Central African States (ECCAS), Communauté Économique des États d'Afrique Centrale (EEAC, French), Comunidade Económica dos Estados da África Central (CEEAC, Portuguese) was opened in Malabo. An agreement to export two million barrels of oil a year to Ghana was announced. Transparency International successfully appealed against a French court's ruling in 2009 that it could not act against foreign heads of state and France's highest appeals court gave permission to proceed with investigations into corruption and the assets held in France by President Teodoro Obiang Nguema, as well as by Denis Sassou-Nguesso of Congo and the late Omar Bongo, former president of Gabon.

2011 In January, President Mbasogo became the 2011 chairman of the African Union (AU). He described criticism of his chairmanship by human rights groups as 'un-African'. The AU lost credibility when President Mbasogo offered AU support for the regime of Colonel Qadafi, while other African leaders supported the Libyan rebels. A referendum was held on 13 November to vote on whether to limit the number of presidential terms in office to two, to establish the post of vice president, to add a arrangement that the serving president can choose a successor, and to remove the existing clause on a president's age limit. The proposals were accepted by 97.73 per cent of the vote. Opposition leaders called the referendum a 'sham' and reported there was evidence of 'ballot stuffing'; human rights campaigners said the changes 'will strengthen the near-absolute powers of President Teodoro Obiang Nguema Mbasogo and further deprive citizens of their civil and political rights'. The post of vice president was considered an opportunity for Mbasogo's eldest son Teodoro to be groomed to succeed his father.

2012 On 18 May, Prime Minister Tang resigned and on 21 May, Ehate Tomi was appointed as prime minister. Teodoro 'Teodorin' Nguema Obiang Mangue was inaugurated as vice president on 22 May. On 13 July, French authorities issued an international arrest warrant for Vice President 'Teodorin' Obiang for failing to attend an investigation into money laundering; at the same time his Paris mansion was seized. On 26 September, Equatorial Guinea authorities called on the International Court of Justice (ICJ) to order France to end its corruption case against 'Teodorin' Obiang. The ICJ confirmed the appeal but stated France would have to agree to abide by its ruling, which was unlikely.

2013 The Africa-South America summit took place in Malabo in February. Sixty-six countries attended the meeting, which, although primarily a political gathering, covered a number of investment projects throughout Africa as well.

2014 Equatorial Guinea offered to hold the 2015 Africa Cup of Nations after Morocco pulled out over fears of the Ebola virus.

2015 The first match in the 2015 Africa Cup of Nations was held on 21 January.

Political structure

Constitution

A new constitution designed to usher in multi-party politics was adopted on 16 November 1991. It provided for the separation of powers between the president and prime minister and gave the president protection from impeachment, prosecution and *subpoena* before, during and after his term of office. However, in reality this has failed to materialise.

In 2011, in the midst of the Arab Spring, President Obiang passed a referendum (with 99 per cent support) that limited presidents to two terms. Critics have derided the amedment as a constitutional way to keep him in power for a further 14 years, given it would not count his consecutive terms since 1979.

Form of state

Republic

The executive

The president is elected for a seven-year term by universal suffrage. The prime minister is appointed by the president.

National legislature

The unicameral Cámara de Representantes del Pueblo (House of People's Representatives) has 100 members directly elected by proportional representation from party lists, who serve five-year terms.

Legal system

Judges are appointed, transferred and dismissed for political reasons, even though the constitution provides for judicial independence. The judicial system does not appear to operate independently, thus undermining basic rights.

Last elections

26 May 2013 (parliamentary); 29 November 2009 (presidential)

Results: Parliamentary: Partido Democrático de Guinea Ecuatorial (PDGE) (Democratic Party of Equatorial Guinea), allied to the Front of Democratic Opposition (FOD), won 99 seats out of 100, the Convergencia para la Democracia Social (CPDS) (Convergence for Social Democracy) won one.

Presidential: Teodoro Obiang Nguema Mbasogo (PDGE) won 95.8 per cent of the vote, Plácido Micó Abogo (CPDS) 3.6 per cent; turnout was 93.5 per cent.

Next elections

2016 (presidential); 2018 (parliamentary)

Political parties

Ruling party

Partido Democrático de Guinea Ecuatorial (PDGE) (Democratic Party of Equatorial Guinea) (from 1993; re-elected 4 May 2008)

Main opposition party

Convergencia para la Democracia Social (CPDS) (Convergence for Social Democracy).

Population

744,000 (2012)*

Last census: 1 February 2002: 1,014,999

Population density: 16 inhabitants per square km. Urban population 40 per cent (2010 Unicef).
Annual growth rate: 3.1 per cent, 1990–2010 (Unicef).
Ethnic make-up
The mainland region of Rio Muni is occupied by 75 per cent of the population, 90 per cent of whom belong to the Fang ethnic group. The island province of Bioko consists of Bubis, Fangs and Creoles.
Religions
Christianity (98 per cent, mostly Roman Catholic), traditional beliefs (2 per cent).

Education

Public expenditure on education typically amounted to 2.3 per cent of annual gross national income between 1994–1997 according to World Bank estimates.
Literacy rate: 83.2 per cent adult rate; 92.5 per cent male rate (Unesco).
Enrolment rate: 126 per cent gross primary enrolment of relevant age group (including repeaters); 115 per cent gross secondary enrolment.
Pupils per teacher: 41 in primary schools.

Health

Approximately 43 per cent of the total population is under 15 years. World Bank surveys show that 43 per cent of the population have access to improved water sources.
HIV/Aids
The government has failed in its commitments to eradicate the continuing epidemics of malaria and yellow fever, while allowing HIV prevalence to increase. There are an estimated 1,100 people living with HIV/Aids – most sufferers are over the age of 15.
Life expectancy: 43 years, 2004 (WHO 2006)
Fertility rate/Maternal mortality rate: 5.2 births per woman, 2010 (Unicef)
Child (under 5 years) mortality rate (per 1,000): 100 per 1,000 live births (WHO 2012)
Head of population per physician: 0.3 physicians per 1,000 people, 2004 (WHO 2006)

Welfare

Welfare conditions in the country are virtually non-existent, with limited access to primary healthcare, education and job opportunities.
In 2003 the Government introduced a two-tier system that created a separate wage system for private sector workers inside and outside of the oil sector. The minimum monthly wage for all private sector workers was set at CFAf77,000 (approximately US$154), and an additional differential payment is made dependent on a worker's skills. However the minimum wage law does not apply to public sector workers who are generally paid much less than their counterparts in the private sector.
Under-age youths perform both family farm work and street vending. The government does not enforce the legal minimum age for child employment.
Equatorial Guinea is also a destination and transit point for the trafficking in children (as unpaid workers) and women (for prostitution).
Human rights conditions in the country are considered, by Amnesty International, as 'alarming' as the security forces continue to harass civilians and political dissidents; imprisonment, torture and extrajudicial killings have been cited in all parts of the country.

Main cities

Malabo (capital, on island of Bioko, estimated population 187,302 in 2012), Bata (Rio Muni) (250,770), Ebebiyin (36,565), Anisoc (16,626), Aconibe (16,543).

Languages spoken

Fang, Bubi Ibo and Creole (pidgin English) are spoken.
Official language/s
Spanish and French

Media

In 2006 Equatorial Guinea was ranked 137 out of 168 for press freedom by the French-based, Reporters without Borders. Despite a constitutional guarantee of freedom of the press, rights to freedom of opinion, expression, the sharing and publication of information are severely restricted, with the government using military courts, repressive laws and arbitrary arrests and prosecutions to restrict political freedom and civil rights.
Press
There are few newspapers available. In Spanish, *Ebano* is state-owned and *La Nacion* and *La Opinion* (a weekly), are privately owned. *La Gaceta (de Guinea Ecuatorial)* (www.lagacetadeguinea.com) is published monthly.
Periodicals: In Spanish, *La Diaspora* (Spanish) is published overseas every other month.
Broadcasting
Radio: There are two radio stations broadcasting in Spanish and local African languages Radio Nacional de Guinea Ecuatorial is state-run and the commercial, Radio Asonga, is run by Teodorino Obiang Nguema (the president's son). The French-based RF1 and several foreign Christian radio stations broadcast into the country.
Television: There is a limited service provided by the state-run Television Nacional.
Other news agencies: AFP (Agence France-Presse): www.afp.com
AllAfrica: www.allafrica.com
APA (African Press Agency): www.apanews.net
Panapress: www.panapress.com

Economy

Oil is transforming the economy; however it has yet to achieve a fully developed, economically diverse, open market. Following rapid economic growth in the early 2000's spurred by a discovery of oil, the country's GDP has increased almost fifty-fold (1995–2014), which has allowed the government to embark on an ambitious infrastructure programme; completion of the first phase of the Horizon 2020 development plan, which emphasises infrastructure construction, is near. Better roads and ports have provided the region with greater opportunities. The government announced plans in 2014 to improve the ease of doing business within the country by creating a one-stop-shop for investors and a co-investment fund of US$1 billion. However, pervasive corruption and inefficient bureaucracy undermines the investment climate in Equatorial Guinea (EG). EG was ranked 169 out of 189 in the 2015 World Bank's Ease of doing business report, whilst it was rated 145 out of 174 on Transparency's 2014 Corruption Perceptions Index.
EG is endowed with abundant oil and natural gas resources, which account for over US$12 billion in U.S. investment. Growth has slowed in recent years as the oil fields have matured. In 2014, Equatorial Guinea failed to recover from the 2013 recession caused by cheaper oil prices and lower oil and gas production. GDP growth increased slightly from -4.8 per cent in 2013 to -3.1 per cent in 2014.
The government is attempting to reduce the predominance of hydrocarbons in the economy. However balancing an economy that is prone to distortion by one overarching sector is proving difficult. Much of the remainder of the economy is underdeveloped even though Equatorial Guinea is rich in timber, fishing and agricultural land. There are also undeveloped mineral resources of titanium, iron ore, manganese, uranium, and alluvial gold. The cocoa industry has suffered from falling world prices, a higher foreign exchange rate than competitor countries and stagnation due to a loss of immigrant farm labourers and farmers leaving the land to seek higher wages in the oil and related sectors.
The majority of the working population is engaged in subsistence farming and while the GDP per capita is estimated at over US$32,000, inequality within society is

widespread, with capital expenditure on social programmes between 2004–07 remaining static at around 18 per cent and reaching just over 20 per cent in 2014. Equatorial Guinea was ranked 144 out of 187 countries in the 2014 UN Human Development Index (HDI) list. There has been an improvement in Equatorial Guinea's HDI compared to other sub-Saharan countries since 2005 - less favourable when compared to world trends.
High unemployment rates, averaging around 12 per cent between 1983–2008, indicate a segmented employment pattern with the majority of the population dependent on primary industries and too few employed in value-added secondary or tertiary industries. However unemployment dropped to around 22 per cent of total employment in 2009. Youth unemployment remains high for the region at 12.5 per cent in 2014.

External trade

As a member of the Communauté Économique des États d'Afrique Centrale (Economic Community of Central African States (ECCAS)) Equatorial Guinea uses the CFA franc (Communauté Financière Africaine franc), issued by the Banque des États de l'Afrique Centrale (BEAC) (Bank of Central African States). ECCAS operates a customs and economic union with a common external tariff between its six members, with free movement of capital, people and goods and services.
As a primary producer over 90 per cent of exports are unprocessed petroleum, timber, coffee and cocoa.

Imports

Principal imports are petroleum sector equipment, general equipment, vehicles and construction materials.
Main sources: US (23.5 per cent of total in 2014), Spain (17.3 per cent), China (13.6 per cent), France (5.7 per cent).

Exports

Principal exports are petroleum, methanol, timber and cocoa.
Main destinations: China (26.7 per cent of total in 2014), UK (16.0 per cent), Brazil (10.0 per cent), France (8.3 per cent), Japan (7.0 per cent).

Agriculture

Farming

Total agricultural land is 2.8 million hectares of which 3.7 per cent is pasture and 4.7 per cent arable; the sector employs around 64 per cent of the workforce. The main cash crop, cocoa is grown on Bioko and Rio Muni, which also produces timber and coffee for export. Main food crops are cassava, sweet potatoes, bananas, palm oil and kernels.

Fishing

The fishing sector is a developing, and potentially lucrative, sector of the economy. The industry has been partially restored, since the 1970s when former President Nguema had banned fishing and destroyed the entire fishing fleet. Nevertheless, the industry is held back by low levels of investment and President Obiang's reluctance to permit a potential conduit that might allow access into the country by those opposed to his regime.
The government is developing the 314,000 square kilometre exclusive maritime economic zone surrounding the island of Anobon, off the mainland territory coastline, which is one of the Atlantic's richest fishing fields.
An EU-Equatorial Guinea fisheries agreement gives EU trawlers the right to capture 5,500 tonnes of fish per year. Under the deal, the EU pays Equatorial Guinea ?412,500 (US$458,000) per year, much of which goes into expanding and improving local fishing production.

Forestry

Equatorial Guinea has 63 per cent forest cover and logging is an important economic sector. Timber is one of the main export products.

Industry and manufacturing

The industrial sector contributed 87.3 per cent of GDP in 2013. The sector used to account for an even higher share but since the boom in oil exports reliance on industry and manufacturing has been reducing. Most production is related to the oil sector although as of 2013 there is no refining capacity. The manufacturing sector is very small, contributing less than 2 per cent of GDP. The non-oil industrial sector is underdeveloped, with activity centred on very small-scale food and timber processing. The traditional industries of cocoa and coffee suffer from a lack of investment.

Tourism

The political situation in Equatorial Guinea has an inhibiting effect on tourism and the industry is localised and underdeveloped. The country's natural beauty and rich bio-diversity is secondary to business travel, related to the oil industry. However, investment from the latter is being redistributed into the former, with infrastructure projects to provide roads and tourist resorts for future growth. The total contribution to GDP was 4.4 per cent in 2014 and total contribution to employment was 3.5 per cent of total employment. Investment was 0.7 per cent of total investment

Mining

Industrial production is underdeveloped and activity is limited to artisan exploitation of alluvial gold. There are reserves of copper, iron ore, uranium, tantalum and manganese.

Hydrocarbons

Production of oil in Equatorial Guinea has experienced a sharp rise over the last two decades, from 5,000 barrels per day (bpd) in 1995, to 311,000bpd in 2013 from offshore in the Alba and Zafiro oilo fields of the Gulf of Guinea. However domestic consumption has remained negligible, reaching a peak of around 5,000bpd in 2010, but had fallen to 2,290bpd by 2013. Sale of the surplus has allowed Equatorial Guinea's GDP to grow in step with the new industry. As sub-Saharan Africa's third largest exporter of oil (after Nigeria and Angola) oil exports account for over 90 per cent of all foreign earnings.
The national oil company of Equatorial Guinea, GEPetrol, is responsible for safeguarding the interests of the government in all aspects of production sharing agreements (PSAs) and joint ventures with foreign oil companies, which undertake upstream activities in the country. Legislation ensures that GEPetrol has a minimum 35 per cent stake or share allotted to it, of all investment in the hydrocarbon sector, to guarantee local participation.
Downstream activities are limited, as a monopoly exists on distribution. The country is without refining facilities and the infrastructure to deliver petroleum products beyond the cities is rudimentary. Although a 20,000bpd refinery is planned for Mbini, it is still to be constructed.
Most of the proven natural gas reserves are associated natural gas from offshore Bioko Island, where there is a liquefied natural gas (LNG) facility. Natural gas reserves are estimated to be around 36.81 billion cubic metres (cum) in 2014. Natural gas production has risen sharply since 2005, from 100 million cum to 6.9 billion cum in 2013; with growth expected as the policy to end gas flaring is implemented.
A second LNG facility is planned, to process surplus natural gas from Nigeria and Cameroon; production is expected to begin by 2016.
The state-owned Sociedad Nacional de Gas de Guinea Ecuatorial (Sonagas) manages all assets and the development of an industrial and residential natural gas market. It is also responsible for the exploration, production, distribution and marketing of natural gas reserves. Legislation ensures that Sonagas has a minimum 35 per cent stake or share allotted to it, of all investment in the hydrocarbon sector, to guarantee local participation.
Any coal production or imports are of insignificant amounts.

Energy

Total installed generating capacity was 38MW in 2013 produced by conventional thermal and hydroelectric plants. However capacity is well below the potential of

11,000MW that could be produced through hydro-power alone. Ageing equipment limits output from the natural gas fired power station on Bioko Island to 28MW. There are plans to expand the network; in the meantime small diesel powered generators are widely used during the frequent power outages.
The government has been unsuccessful in its attempt to privatise the state-owned Sociedad de Electricidad de Guinea Ecuatorial (Segesa), due to lack of interest by foreign investors.

Banking and insurance

Central bank
Banque des Etats de l'Afrique Centrale (BEAC) (Bank of the Central African States)
Main financial centre
Malabo

Time

GMT plus one hour

Geography

Equatorial Guinea is situated on the west coast of Africa. The country comprises the island of Bioko (formerly Fernando Po), 40km off the coast of Cameroon; the mainland territory of Río Muni, 250km south of Bioko; and the islands of Annobón, Corisco, Great Elobey and Small Elobey. The Río Muni enclave is bounded to the north by Cameroon and to the east and south by Gabon.
The islands, in the Gulf of Guinea, are volcanic and mountainous with beaches. Malabo, the capital, is located on Bioko, which covers 2,000 square km. Annobón (17 square km), together with the other smaller islands, are close to the mainland and are all part of Río Muni region.
The mainland is heavily forested with some mountains. There is a coastal plain, which supports plantations. The south of the region is fairly inaccessible.
Hemisphere
Northern

Climate

Equatorial with heavy rainfall for most of the year except for slightly drier period from December–February. The mainland Rio Muni is drier and cooler than Bioko. Average temperature is 26 degrees Celsius throughout the year, and generally very humid.

Entry requirements

Passports
Required by all, valid for six months beyond date of departure.
Visa
Required by all, except US nationals. Business visas require a letter of invitation from a local company and proof of visitor's status and a letter of finance giving proof of sufficient funds for length of stay and a full itinerary.
Currency advice/regulations
Import of local and foreign currencies is unrestricted, provided that amounts in excess of CFAf50,000 (approximately US$90) are declared on arrival. Export of currencies is limited to the amount declared. Failure to declare excess currency risks forfeiture of any amount over the CFAf50,000 limit when departing.
Equatorial Guinea is a cash economy and CFA francs is the only form of payment accepted. Foreign currency should be exchanged at banks, which are few in number.

Health (for visitors)

Mandatory precautions
A yellow fever vaccination certificate is required if arriving from an infected area.
Advisable precautions
Vaccinations against hepatitis A and B, tetanus, diphtheria, polio, typhoid and meningitis are strongly recommended. Malaria prophylaxis is advisable as risk exists throughout the country. There is a rabies risk. Water precautions should be taken.
Medical facilities are limited so it is advisable to pack any personal medications required.

Hotels

Accommodation is very limited but there are hotels in Malabo and Bata. It is essential to book a hotel before travelling, preferably through local business contacts.
Food is rarely available at the Bata Hotel and, in Malabo, air-conditioning is available only in some rooms in the Apartotel Impala.
When there is no service charge, gratuities are around 10 to 15 per cent.

Public holidays (national)

Fixed dates
1 Jan (New Year), 8 Mar (Women's Day), 1 May (Labour Day), 25 May (Africa Day), 5 Jun (President's Day), 3 Aug (Armed Forces Day), 15 Aug (Constitution Day), 12 October (Independence Day), 10 Dec (Human Rights' Day), 25 Dec (Christmas Day).
Variable dates
Good Friday, Corpus Christi (May/Jun), Human Rights Day (Dec).

Working hours

Banking
Mon–Sat: 0800–1200.
Business
Mon–Fri: 0800–1500.
Government
Mon–Fri: 0830–1500; Sat: 0830–1200, (alternate Sat) 1000–1200.
Shops
(Mon–Sat) 0800–1300 and 1600–1900.

Electricity supply

220 V AC, 50 cycles

Social customs/useful tips

Corruption is endemic. Special permits from the Ministry of Information and Tourism are required for most photography, including the presidential palace and its environs, military installations, government buildings, airports, harbours and other areas.

Getting there

Air
Several European airlines link Malabo with Madrid, London, Paris, Amsterdam and Zurich.
International airport/s: Malabo Airport (SSG), 7km from the capital city on the island of Malabo.
Bata Airport (FGBT), 6km from city, on the mainland of Equatorial Guinea.
Surface
Road: There is access by semi-surfaced road from Gabon to Mbini and Bata, although this route is not generally recommended.
Main port/s: Malabo, Bata, Luba, Mbini and Kogo.

Getting about

National transport
Air: There are a number of small airlines serving domestic routes, especially Ecuato Guineana, which operates between Bata and Malabo. They do not meet international standards and most of them have been grounded.
Road: On Bioko a surfaced road links major towns in the north. On mainland Río Muni a surfaced road links Bata with Mbini and a partly surfaced road links Bata with Ebebiyin (near Gabon border). Other roads are unsurfaced and can be difficult.
Water: There is a boat service between Malabo and Bata.

BUSINESS DIRECTORY

The addresses listed below are a selection only. While World of Information makes every endeavour to check these addresses, we cannot guarantee that changes have not been made, especially to telephone numbers and area codes. We would welcome any corrections.

Telephone area codes

The international direct dialling code (IDD) for Equatorial Guinea is +240 followed by area code and subscriber's number:

Bata	8	Malabo	9

Chambers of Commerce

Camara Oficiel de Comercio, Agricola y Forestal, 43 Avenida de la Indepencia, PO Box 51, Malabo (tel: 923-43; fax: 932-66).

Banking

Banco de Crédito y Desarrollo (credit and development bank), 1 Avenida de la Libertad, PO Box 39, Malabo (tel: 2146).

Banco Exterior de Guinea Ecuatorial, Carretera de Aeropuerto, Malabo (tel: 2001).

Banque Internationale pour l'Afrique Occidentale, Calle de Argelia No 6, PO Box 686, Malabo (tel: 2367, 2887).

Caisse Commune d'Epargne et d'Investissement en Guinée Equatoriale (CCEI-GE); PO Box 428, Malabo (tel: 2003, 2910; fax: 3311).

Société Générale de Banque GE; PO Box 686, Calle Argelia, Malabo (tel: 3337; fax: 2743).

Central bank

Banque des Etats de l'Afrique Centrale, Direction Nationale, PO Box 501, Malabo (tel: 20-10; fax: 20-06; e-mail: beacmal@beac.int).

Other useful addresses

Comite Sindical de Cacao (cocoa growers' organisation), Bioko.

Dirección General de Correos y Telecomunicaciones, Malabo.

Empresa Estatal de Comercio Interior y Exterior, Malabo.

Empresa General de Industria y Comercio (EGISCA), Malabo.

Empresa Guineano-Española de Petróleos (Gepsa), Malabo.

AFP (Agence France-Presse): www.afp.com

AllAfrica: www.allafrica.com

APA (African Press Agency): www.apanews.net

Panapress: www.panapress.com

Internet sites

Equatorial Guinea oil: http://www.equatorialoil.com/

Africa Business Network: http://www.ifc.org/abn

AllAfrica.com: http://allafrica.com

African Development Bank: http://www.afdb.org

Africa Online: http://www.africaonline.com

Mbendi AfroPaedia (information on companies, countries, industries and stock exchanges in Africa): http://mbendi.co.za

Official site (in Spanish): http://www.guineaecuatorial.net/ms/main.asp

Eritrea

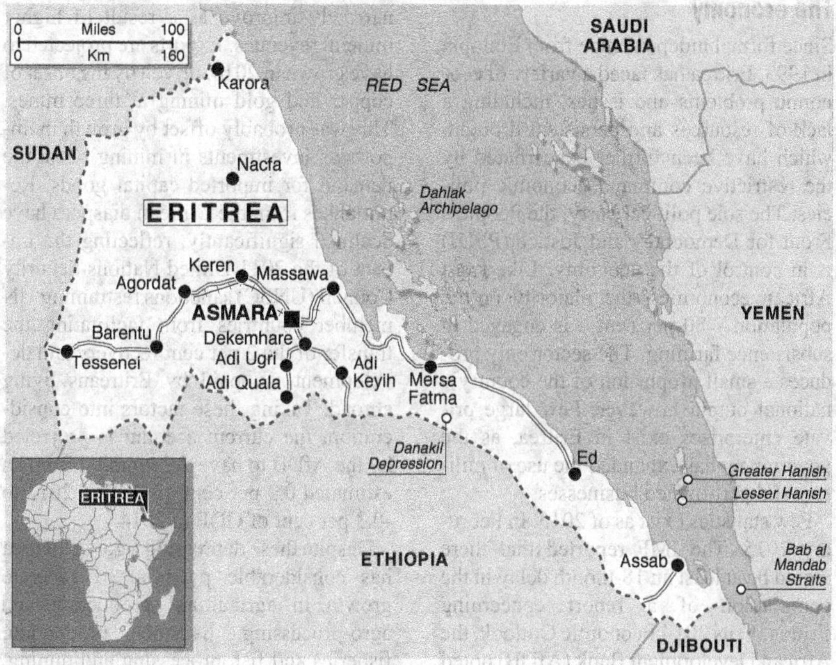

Eritrea was part of the first Ethiopian kingdom of Aksum until the eighth century. It then became part of the Ottoman Empire in the sixteenth century and later of the Egyptians. The Italians captured the coastal areas in 1885, with sovereignty over parts of Eritrea granted a couple of years later in 1889. The Italians named their colony *Mare Erythraeum* – after the Latin for the Red Sea. Eritrea became the base of Benito Mussolini's conquest of Abyssinia in 1933. British forces captured and occupied the country in 1941 after the Italians joined the Second World War. It was later administered as a UN Trust Territory, which the United Nations established as an autonomous region within Ethiopia as a compromise between Ethiopian claims for sovereignty and Eritrean aspirations for independence. Despite this, the Ethiopian emperor, Haile Selassie, decided to annex it 10 years later. This then triggered a 32-year armed struggle. After Selassie's successor, the Communist government of Mengistu Hailemariam, was overthrown in 1991, Eritrea declared its independence, a move that was eventually recognised in 1993. The rebel forces, the Eritrean People's Liberation Front (EPLF), was renamed the People's Front for Democracy and Justice (PFDJ) in 1994, took power and installed a Marxist regime under President Issaias Afewerki. President Issaias was once hailed as an African liberation hero but his government has proven incapable of gaining legitimacy. According to US-based NGO Human Rights Watch, Eritrea has no constitution, no functioning legislature, independent judiciary or independent press. A 2015 report by the UN Commission of Inquiry on Human Rights in Eritrea cites the violations against humanity as of a scope and scale seldom witnessed anywhere else. All power is vested in the office of the longstanding president, Issaias Afewerki.

The optimistic days after Eritrea's separation from Ethiopia in 1991 and its formal incorporation as an independent state in 1993 seemed to many to be distant aspirations by 2015. Eritrea had been under the rule of the EPLF until the referendum of 1993 endorsed its independence with over 1.1 million votes in favour and only 1,800 against. Such was the cordial

KEY FACTS

Official name: Hagere Ertra (State of Eritrea)

Head of State: President Issaias Afewerki (since 1991; elected president 1993)

Head of government: President Issaias Afewerki

Ruling party: dem

Area: 125,000 square km

Population: 6.36 million (2014)*

Capital: Asmara

Official language: There is no official language but the working languages are Tigrinya, Arabic and English.

Currency: Nakfa (Nk) = 100 cents

Exchange rate: Nk15.00 per US$ fixed (pegged from 1 Jan 2005)

GDP per capita: US$590 (2014)*

GDP real growth: 1.70% (2014)*

GDP: US$3.86 billion (2014)*

Inflation: 12.26% (2014)*

* estimated figure

climate between Ethiopia and Eritrea that agreement was rapidly reached on Eritrea's continued use of Massawa and Assab ports. Full freedom of movement between the two countries was also agreed.

Human Rights

Due to Eritrea's dismal human rights situation, which is exacerbated by indefinite military conscription, thousands of Eritreans flee their country every month. The widespread abuses faced by many in the Horn of Africa nation have prompted many to seek asylum in Europe. According to the UN report and estimates produced by Italian authorities, 32,000 Eritreans were rescued in 2014 as they attempted to cross the Mediterranean. The UN refugee agency numbers 357,400 Eritreans outside of the country that fall within its reach of concern. More than 5,000 Eritreans crossed into Ethiopia in October 2014 alone. However, despite escaping from domestic tyrannies and abuse, many of the refugees have experienced further abuses en route to Israel and Europe, whilst others have been detained in deplorable conditions within nations such as Libya.

The UN report details numerous incidences in which Eritrea's initial promise of democracy following its independence has been removed and destroyed by the government under a pretext of defence. Terror is pervasive across the country; torture, forced labour, national service, mass surveillance and severe curtailing of rights and freedoms demonstrate the tyrannical and oppressive nature of the de facto leader – and government of – Isaias Afewerki. In early 2014, President Afewerki confirmed his lack of interest in an open and free society, stating: 'If there is anyone who thinks there will be democracy or a multiparty system in this country... then that person can think of such things in another world.' The UN report concluded that because the use of torture is so widespread, it must follow that it is a policy of the government to encourage its use for individuals perceived to be opponents of its rule. Arbitrary detention is featured across Eritrea to install fear and acquire confessions from those who rebel against President Afewerki.

The economy

Since formal independence from Ethiopia in 1993, Eritrea has faced a variety of economic problems and issues, including a lack of resources and persistent drought, which have been further exacerbated by the restrictive command economic policies. The sole political party, the People's Front for Democracy and Justice (PFDJ) is in control of the economy. Like most African economies, the majority or the population – 80 per cent – is engaged in subsistence farming. The sector only produces a small proportion of the country's national output however. Few large private enterprises exist in Eritrea, as the government has expanded the use of military and part-owned businesses.

Few statistics exist as of 2015. In February 2015, The IMF reported that there would be at least an 18-month delay in the compilation of a report concerning Eritrea. In its 2014 Economic Outlook, the African Development Bank (AfDB) noted that Eritrea had faced considerable challenges over the years, including variable climatic conditions. This has been compounded by restrictive economic policies, political isolation, a significant decline in remittances and scarcity of foreign exchange. Reflecting these factors, estimated real gross domestic product (GDP) growth for 2013 fell sharply to 1.1 per cent from 7 per cent the previous year and was projected to increase marginally to 1.9 per cent in 2014. This growth would be driven by a number of factors, including copper production at the Bisha mine, the start of gold production at the Zara mining project in 2014 and continued exploration activity and investment in the mining sector. In the medium term, Eritrea, rather optimistically, sees further prospects in oil production, fisheries and tourism.

The budget deficit improved to an estimated 10.3 per cent of GDP in 2013 from 15.5 per cent in 2010, and is projected to narrowly improve as a result of higher mineral revenues. Exports are projected to have grown in 2014, driven by the onset of copper and gold mining at three mines. This was probably offset by growth in imports as investments in mining boost the demand for imported capital goods. Remittances from the Eritrean diaspora have declined significantly, reflecting the impact of the 2011 United Nations Security Council (UNSC) sanctions restraining UN member countries from facilitating the transfer of the 2 per cent recovery and development tax paid by Eritreans living abroad. Taking these factors into consideration, the current account is projected by the AfDB to have deteriorated from an estimated 0.3 per cent of GDP in 2013 to -0.3 per cent of GDP in 2014.

Despite these depressing figures, Eritrea has considerable potential to generate growth in agricultural production and agro-processing, livestock production, fisheries and fish processing and mining, as well as through the development of small and medium-sized enterprises, tourism and related hospitality services and infrastructure. The country is currently focusing on developing both its tourism industry around the Red Sea port of Massawa as well as the export potential of its mineral reserves.

KEY INDICATORS — Eritrea

	Unit	2011	2012	2013	2014	**2015
Population	m	*5.49	*6.13	*6.33	*6.36	*6.75
Gross domestic product (GDP)	US$bn	2.61	3.09	*3.44	*3.86	*4.25
GDP per capita	US$	475	505	*544	*590	*563
GDP real growth	%	8.7	7.0	*1.3	*1.7	*0.2
Inflation	%	13.3	12.3	*12.3	*12.3	*12.3
Current account	US$m	14.0	72.0	*12.0	*-8.0	*-69.0
Exchange rate	per US$	15.38	15.38	14.85	10.47	–

* estimated figure ** forecast figure

Risk assessment

Politics	Poor
Economy	Poor
Regional stability	Fair

Muslims in Eritrea

% of population	44
Sunni (% of Muslims)	99
Shi'a (% of Muslims)	1

COUNTRY PROFILE

1889–1941 Under Italian rule. Eritrea first emerged as a political entity following the Italian occupation of the Red Sea port of Massawa and other coastal enclaves in the 1880s. In 1889, Italy signed the Treaty of Ucciali with the Ethiopian Emperor, Menelik, and in 1890, named the country Eritrea.

1941 The UK defeated Italy during the Second World War and Eritrea became a British protectorate.

1952 UN-sanctioned federation with Ethiopia.
1962 Eritrea was annexed to Ethiopia as a province under Emperor Haile Selassie.
1991 The Eritrean People's Liberation Front (EPLF) overthrew Ethiopian Colonel Mengistu's forces and liberated the territory; Issaias Afewerki assumed power.
1993 A vote resulted in a virtually 100 per cent acceptance of independence.
1994 Eritrea achieved nationhood and Afewerki was elected president by the National Assembly. In February the EPLF was renamed the People's Front for Democracy and Justice (PFDJ).
1998 Eritrea and Ethiopia resumed border warfare. The Permanent Court of Arbitration in the Hague ruled that Yemen should have the Red Sea island of Greater Hanish, fought over in 1995 by Eritrea and Yemen, and it was announced that Eritrea would return it to Yemen. The nakfa was introduced as Eritrea's national currency, to be used alongside the Ethiopian birr.
2000 UN peacekeepers opened a 1,000km cease-fire land corridor between Ethiopia and Eritrea and the two countries signed a peace deal in Algiers, ending the two-year war.
2001 The UN established a buffer zone along the border between Ethiopia and Eritrea.
2002 Eritrea and Ethiopia accepted a ruling on the border dispute, made by the Boundary Commission at the Permanent Court of Arbitration of The Hague. A new 1,000km boundary was established between the two countries.
2003 The UN Mission in Ethiopia and Eritrea (UNMEE) mandate was extended.
2004 Eritrea suffered a harsh drought, resulting in severe drinking-water problems both for humans and animals. Implementation of the peace process that was to resolve the border conflict between Ethiopia and Eritrea remained stalled.
2005 New Bank of Eritrea regulations required all transactions to be conducted in the national currency, the nakfa. The new currency was pegged against the US dollar at Nk15 per US$. Eritrea restricted the movement of UNMEE peacekeepers along the Eritrea/Ethiopia border, leading to fears that the war would flare up again. The independent commission at the Permanent Court of Arbitration in The Hague, set up as part of the peace deal signed in Algiers in 2000 between Eritrea and Ethiopia, ruled that Eritrea had launched unlawful attacks against Ethiopia in 1998, thereby triggering the border war between the two countries.
2006 Tensions continued in the border dispute with Ethiopia. Eritrea rebuffed international attempts to mediate. Eritrea was accused of arming Islamist opponents of the Somali transitional government, which was supported by Ethiopia.
2007 Talks, set by the Ethiopia-Eritrea Border Commission, to confirm the demarcation between Ethiopia and Eritrea, failed to reach an agreement on time. The Commission considered the border it drew in 2006 to be binding in the face of the impasse. While Ethiopia and Eritrea accepted the ruling neither attempted to implement its recommendations and 1,700 UN peace-keeping troops remained in the area in a notionally demilitarised zone.
2008 United Nation's troops along the disputed border began what was described as a 'temporary relocation' out of Eritrea, after the government cut off fuel supplies. Border clashes in the Mount Gabla area – also known as Ras Doumeira – that killed nine Djibouti troops and injured many more was blamed by the US on 'military aggression' by Eritrea. The US and France called for a cease-fire, troop withdrawals on both sides and for negotiations to begin. The Security Council terminated the UNMEE.
2009 The Eritrean national football team refused to return to Eritrea after playing in the Senior Challenge Cup in Nairobi and applied for, and eventually found, asylum in Australia. Eritrea denied it had troops in Djibouti, contrary to UN Security Council announcement that it had failed to withdraw. The UN imposed arms and travel sanctions and froze assets on top politicians and military personnel from Eritrea due to their support of insurgents in Somalia.
2010 President Afewerki invited foreign and domestic journalists to visit military installations in an attempt to influence the UN to lift sanctions against Eritrea. Qatar mediated an agreement between Eritrea and Djibouti over their border dispute. However despite Eritrea's step towards 'constructive engagement' with Djibouti, the UN refused to lift sanctions, saying that President Afewerki's regime still supported armed opposition groups destabilising the region as well as non-compliance with the agreement to withdraw troops from Djibouti.
2011 In June the Nabro volcano erupted (for the first time in recorded history), and forced airline flights in East Africa to be curtailed. In July, 13 top Eritrean football players refused to return to Eritrea after playing in an East African tournament and applied for asylum in Tanzania. In December, the UN Security Council imposed tougher sanctions against Eritrea, accusing it of giving sanctuary to militant Islamist groups (particularly Al Shabab) that have attacked neighbouring countries. Foreign mining companies are required to maintain more control over their funding of the industry, including foreign investment; remittances were also affected by the sanctions.
2012 On 17 January, five European tourists were killed, two seriously injured and four kidnapped in Ethiopia's Afar region (close to the border with Eritrea). Ethiopia held Eritrea responsible for the attack as the kidnap victims were taken into Eritrea. On 15 March Ethiopia attacked three military bases in Eritrea where they believed militants were being trained. On 17 March, minister of information, Ali Abdu, announced that Eritrea would not retaliate for the cross-border incursion On 2 May, Eritrea was listed as the most censored country in the world (followed by North Korea, Syria and Iran), according to the US-based, Committee to Protect Journalists (CPJ), for barring international media and for dictatorial controls on domestic media.
2013 There was a failed coup attempt on 21 January when soldiers stormed the ministry of information and took over the state-run television service.
2014 In May 18 members of the Eritrean soccer team arrived in the small town of Gorinchem in the Netherlands. The team had initially disappeared while playing in an international tournament in Uganda in 2012. They sought shelter in the compound of the United Nations High Commissioner for Refugees in Kampala and after six months were sent to an emergency transit camp, a clearinghouse for high-risk refugees, in Timisoara, western Romania. From there they travelled to the Netherlands.
2015 A report published by the UN in June painted a damaging picture of human rights in Eritrea. The report detailed the government's systematic use of extrajudicial killing, torture, rape, indefinite national service and forced labour.

Political structure

Constitution

A new constitution was adopted in May 1997, but has not been implemented.
A 150-member National Transitional Council was set up, with 75 seats allocated to the People's Front for Democracy and Justice (PFDJ), 60 to the Constitutional Assembly and 15 to overseas Eritreans.
There are six administrative regions, each with regional, sub-regional (55) and village administrations (651). The regions enjoy a degree of autonomy.

Independence date

24 May 1993

The executive

The president holds supreme executive power and governs with the help of his 24-member Consultative Council. The

Consultative Council is composed of ministers and regional governors.

National legislature

The unicameral Hagerawi Baito (National Assembly) has 150 members, of which 75 were appointed by the ruling PFDJ and 75 were elected. Eritrea is effectively a one-party state as no opposition parties are legally recognised.

The original intention, in 1991, was for 399 elected members to represent regional constituencies but in 2001 it was decided that no elections would take place until all of the territory claimed by Eritrea was under its control. Regional and local assemblies are in operation with attendant elections.

Last elections

24 May 1993 (presidential)

Results: Presidential: Issaias Afwerki was elected by the National Assembly with 95 per cent of the vote.

Next elections

No information available

Political parties

Ruling party

People's Front for Democracy and Justice (PFDJ) (formerly the Eritrean People's Liberation Front (EPLF))

Main opposition party

Opposition parties are not allowed.

Population

5.66 million (2012)* Approximately 44 per cent of the total population is under 15 years; 53 per cent 15–64; 3 per cent over 65.

Last census: May 1984: 2,748,304

Population density: 32 inhabitants per square km. Urban population 22 per cent (2010 Unicef).

Annual growth rate: 2.5 per cent, 1990–2010 (Unicef).

Internally Displaced Persons (IDP)

59,000 (UNHCR 2004)

Ethnic make-up

There are nine ethno-linguistic groups.

Religions

Tigrigna-speaking Christians (mainly Orthodox), are the traditional inhabitants of the highlands, with some Protestant and Roman Catholic communities (49 per cent); Muslim communities of the western lowlands, northern highlands and east coast are 49 per cent. A small number of the population adhere to traditional beliefs.

Education

There are approximately 260 primary schools and over 50 secondary schools. It has been estimated by Oxfam that 93 per cent of children age 6–11 will enrol for school in 2015.

Literacy rate: 67 per cent men, 36 per cent woman; adult rates (World Bank 2002).

Enrolment rate: 53 per cent gross enrolment, of relevant age group, in primary education (World Bank 2001).

Pupils per teacher: 44 in primary schools.

Health

Access to an improved water source is available to 46 per cent of the population.

HIV/Aids

A survey published in 2001 revealed that 4.6 per cent of soldiers were HIV-positive and 22.8 per cent of female bar workers were affected as well. By 2002, more than 13,000 people had been registered as infected with HIV/Aids. The main incidences are in Asmara, the capital, and Assab, the sea port, where prostitution is rife. Up to 30 per cent of prostitutes are HIV positive.

HIV prevalence: 2.7 per cent aged 15–49 in 2003 (World Bank)

Life expectancy: 60 years, 2004 (WHO 2006)

Fertility rate/Maternal mortality rate: 4.5 births per woman, 2010 (Unicef); maternal mortality 10 per 1,000 per live births (World Bank).

Child (under 5 years) mortality rate (per 1,000): 52 per 1,000 live births (WHO 2012); 44 per cent of children aged under five were malnourished (World Bank).

Head of population per physician: 0.05 physicians per 1,000 people, 2004 (WHO 2006)

Welfare

A post-war rehabilitation project, implemented by the UN Development Programme (UNDP), has put metal roofs, doors and windows back on houses that were deserted and ransacked during the border war with Ethiopia. An estimated 60,000 children were left crippled by the war, and another 45,000 orphaned. A large proportion of the population is dependent on food aid. UNICEF appeals in 2002 for refugee welfare raised a total of US$10.3 million, a large part of which was spent on establishing and rehabilitating water supplies in settlement areas, as well as setting up basic health and sanitation facilities.

Main cities

Asmara (capital, estimated population 697,013 in 2012), Asseb (101,284), Keren (82,198), Massawa (Mitsiwa) (53,090), Addi Ugri (25,332), Barentu (18,778), Addi K'eyih (16,758).

Languages spoken

The principal language group in Eritrea is Afro-Asiatic; Arabic, Afar, Bilen, Hedareb, Kunama, Nara, Saho, Tigray and Tigrinya are spoken. English is rapidly becoming the language of business and is the medium of instruction at secondary schools and at university.

Official language/s

There is no official language but the working languages are Tigrinya, Arabic and English.

Media

On 2 May 2012, Eritrea was listed as the most censored country in the world (followed by North Korea, Syria and Iran), according to the US-based, Committee to Protect Journalists (CPJ), for barring international media and for dictatorial controls on domestic media.

Press

There are no daily newspapers, all publications are government-owned, including in Tigrinya and Arabic *Hadas Eritrea* (*New Eritrea*), *Tirigta* (owned by the PFDJ political party) and *Geled* for a youth readership and in English *Eritrea Profile*.

Broadcasting

Radio: Two radio stations exist, Radio Zara and Dimtsi Hafash Radio (Voice of the Broad Masses of Eritrea) operates two networks that broadcast in Arabic and local languages. Services can also be received via Arabsat satellite.

Television: The government-owned ERI-TV broadcasts in Arabic, and local languages although transmissions are limited to Asmara and surrounding areas.

Other news agencies: Erina (Eritrean News Agency): www.dehai.org/erina

Economy

Subsistence farming is the mainstay of the economy, sustaining around 80 per cent of the population, despite only 10 per cent of arable land being cultivated. Agricultural products include grains and potatoes, cotton and flax, fruit and vegetables, dairy products and meat. Agriculture constituted 11.6 per cent of GDP in 2014, characterised as subsistence farming; the service sector represented 60.2 per cent of GDP in the same year and industry 28.1 per cent, of which manufacturing constituted around 7 per cent. Agriculture directly employs under 20 per cent of the workforce (although far more are active in production for household needs), the service sector employs around 60 per cent and industry over 20 per cent. Industrial production is centred on mining – of gold, copper, iron ore, potash and petroleum. Manufacturing production includes food processing (using local produce), drinks (including alcoholic beverages), leather goods and textiles, construction materials, chemicals and salt, paper and matches. The service sector provides resources for most of agriculture and industry. Eritrea's command economy means that government services provide most paid employment in Eritrea.

With this old-style, Communist, centrally planned economy, Eritrea has to deal with problems inherent to the system (lack of investment, suppressed entrepreneurial enterprise, limited diversity, lack of swift change due to changing circumstances). In addition, Eritrea has faced considerable challenges over the years, including variable climatic conditions. This has been compounded by restrictive economic policies, political isolation, a significant decline in remittances and scarcity of foreign exchange. There is an inadequate and still war-ravaged infrastructure, a lack of hard currency to pay for imports, a weak tax collection system and unproductive subsistence agriculture, which is subject to harsh climate changes. A severe drought in 2008 resulted in a 25 per cent loss in agricultural productivity for that year, forcing the government to import food, just at a time when world food prices had risen sharply. Another harsh drought occurred in 2012, with the UN estimating that more than 320,000 people were food insecure in Eritrea. The drought was only one reason for low productivity – manpower shortages and unexploded ordnance (UXO) (landmines) continue to be problems. The global recession meant Eritrea was hit by a reduction in remittances from overseas workers. Private transfers from abroad and remittances typically account for over 30 per cent of GDP.
GDP growth was 1.1 per cent in 2013, falling from 7 per cent the previous year, 2 per cent in 2014 with predictions of 2.1 per cent in 2015.

A number of factors, including copper and gold production, have caused this drive behind the growth. Prospects for GDP growth include oil production, tourism and fisheries.
The country's economic future depends on the government adopting an open market economy, which it has claimed it is committed to introduce, and its ability to eradicate the widespread illiteracy and unemployment. In 2011, Eritrea was included in the UN Human Development Index (HDI) for the first time and in 2013 was ranked 182 (out of 187) for national development in health, education and income. The border between Ethiopia and Eritrea, implemented after a UN Boundary Commission ruling in 2002, ought to have encouraged stability and allowed Eritrea to focus on these problems, but relations between the two countries remain fractious and continuing tensions are likely to deter investment until a lasting accord is reached.
In the long term, Eritrea may benefit from the development of offshore oil as well as fishing and a growing tourism industry.

External trade

Eritrea is a member of the Common Market of Eastern and Southern Africa (Comesa), however due to its command economy and tightly controlled import/export policies it does not have plans to join the customs union and free trade area as agreed by other member states.

Imports

Principal non-petroleum imports include machinery, food and manufactured goods.
Main sources: Germany (typically over 20 per cent of total), Italy (20 per cent), France (15 per cent).

Exports

Principal exports include livestock, sorghum, textiles, food, small manufactures, gold and other minerals.
Main destinations: Italy (typically over 35 per cent of total), US (15 per cent), Belarus (5 per cent).

Agriculture

Farming

Total agricultural land is 10.1 million hectares of which 68.3 per cent is pasture and 6.8 per cent arable, farming directly employs under 20 per cent of the population, however far more are involved in subsistence farming, typically in cattle husbandry.
Land has been nationalised but leases to use the land are available.
Serious environmental degradation has been caused directly and indirectly by the war. Careful water management and conservation are essential. Eritrea's main crops are millet, sesame, maize, beans, wheat, sorghum, barley, vegetables, pulses, cotton, fruit, and some coffee.

Fishing

Fishing for sardines, anchovies, tuna, shark and mackerel is practised in the Red Sea on a very small scale. There are over 1,000 different species of fish off Eritrea's shores, with the stocks virtually untouched since the 1950s. The government believes there is potential for exporting 80,000 tonnes of fish annually. The sector has been badly affected by the closure of its market in Yemen as a result of a territorial dispute.

Forestry

The majority of timber harvested is used for domestic purposes.

Industry and manufacturing

The industrial sector contributes 28.1 per cent of GDP and employs around 10 per cent of the workforce.
The industrial base is traditionally centred on the production of glass, cement, footwear and canned goods, but most industrial enterprises have been badly damaged by war. All state-owned distribution and import/export enterprises established by the former (Ethiopian) government have been dissolved.
Major problems include outdated machinery and techniques, supply of energy, and the need for imports throughout the sector. With a lack of foreign currency and investment, industry is suffering from outdated machinery and intermediary goods, which need to be imported.

Tourism

The government designated the entire coastline as an environmentally protected zone in 2006. Other attractions include active volcanoes and the Afar Triance or Danakil Depression where three tectonic plates, the Arabian and two African plates, are pulling away from each other. The resulting split can be seen in the East African Rift Zone. There are also traditional dwellings and a few remaining native wildlife areas.

Environment

In June 2010 the African Union backed a proposal to build the 'Great Green Wall' project, of a 15km wide, 7,775km long, continuous belt of trees from Senegal in the west to Djibouti in the east (traversing 11 countries) in an effort to halt the advance of the Sahara Desert. The trees to be used would be drought-adapted, preferably native to the area from a list of 37 possible species, and should help to slow soil erosion and filter rain water.

Mining

Fighting along the border regions disrupted mining activities, although exploration continued elsewhere in Eritrea. The Phelps Dodge Exploration Corporation conducted exploration on the Debarwa copper-zinc deposits and identified up to four million tonnes of reserves, including at least two million tonnes of mineable high-grade copper and a large amount of gold.
Gold-bearing seams exist in highland areas. There are over 15 gold mines and a large number of prospects close to Asmara. The potential for new discoveries in the area is good. Substantial gold reserves have also been identified at Adi Nefas by LaSource Development SAS.
Artisanal mining production is estimated to produce around 550kg per year.
Despite Eritrea's mining potential, salt and marble remain the country's main exported minerals.

Hydrocarbons

In December 2008 Iran deployed military personnel in Eritrea in return for refurbishing the defunct refinery at the Red Sea port of Assab, which had a crude oil capacity of 18,000bpd before it was closed down in 1997. Following several oil exploration projects it was determined that there are no exploitable oil and gas

reserves in Eritrea; it is dependent on imports at around 4,810 barrels per day (bpd) of oil to meet its requirements.
The Red Sea Afar Democratic Organisation (RSADO) rebel group accused the Australian South Boulder Mines Ltd, in 2015, of partnering with the Eritrean government to illegally exploit resources of the Afar's region of Danakil, stressing it caused environmental damage on their traditional homeland. The rebel group warned the company to stop its economic partnerships with the Eritrean government and leave the Afar Region (Dankalia) immediately. Otherwise, the group threatened to launch retaliation attacks against the foreign company.

Energy

Total installed electricity generating capacity was 140.8MW in 2013, powered mainly by diesel-fired generators. Until an upgrade in the dated power grid, which was completed in 2009, became operational the electricity supply remained available only in mainly large urban areas, leaving the majority of the population without access. However, still only 32 per cent of the population have access.
Some villages provide themselves with electricity from community diesel generators for water pumps, while photovoltaic electricity generation of around 2KW are used to a limited extent in health centres and schools to power operating theatres, refrigerators and lighting.

Banking and insurance

Central bank

Bank of Eritrea

Time

GMT plus three hours

Geography

Eritrea extends inland from the Red Sea coast of eastern Africa. To the south, the country has a long frontier with Ethiopia, and a short frontier with Djibouti. Sudan lies to the north and west.
The coastal area is a desert plain, around 50km wide in the south, and one of the driest places in the world. Inland, the terrain becomes hillier, rising to 2,000m, in the north-west, while further south it turns to rolling plains.The highlands are cool and receive up to 60cm of rainfall annually; fertile valleys support agricultural activity.

Hemisphere

Northern

Climate

Coastal and lowland regions very hot and dry throughout the year. On the plateau, which includes Asmara, the dry season runs from October–May with temperatures ranging from as low as 6 degrees Celsius (C) in December to 26 degrees C in March (light rain from February–April). Temperatures can fall sharply at night during the dry season.
The rainy season runs from June–September with average temperature 21 degrees C. Rainfall is less than 500mm per year in lowland areas, increasing to 1,000mm in the highlands. The temperature gradient is similarly steep: average annual temperatures range from 17 degrees C in the highlands to 30 degrees C in Massawa.
The Danakil depression in the south-east, which is more than 130 metres below sea-level in places, experiences some of the highest temperatures recorded, frequently exceeding 50 degrees C.

Entry requirements

Passports

Required by all, valid for three months beyond intended length of stay.

Visa

Required by all except nationals of Kenya and Uganda. Business visas are valid for one month, but can be extended on application to the Eritrean Foreign Ministry. A business letter giving proof of sufficient funds for length of stay, a full itinerary and copy of return/onward ticket, should accompany application.

Currency advice/regulations

There are no restrictions on import or export of local and foreign currency. From January 2005, all transactions have been conducted in the national currency, the nakfa.

Health (for visitors)

Mandatory precautions

A yellow fever vaccination certificate is required if travelling from or via an infected area.

Advisable precautions

Inoculations and booster should be current for diphtheria, polio, tetanus, hepatitis A, and typhoid. There may be a need for vaccinations for, tuberculosis, hepatitis B and meningitis. Use malaria prophylaxis if travelling in areas below 2000 metres. Malaria and hepatitis B are caused by mosquitoes, precautions including mosquito repellents, nets and clothing covering the body after dark should be used. There is a risk of rabies in rural areas. There is a shortage of routine medications and visitors should take all necessary medicines with them. A first aid kit that includes disposable syringes, is a reasonable precaution. Use only bottled or boiled water for drinks, washing teeth and making ice. Eat only well cooked meals, preferably served hot; vegetables should be cooked and fruit peeled. Dairy products are unpasteurised and should be avoided, unless cooked.
Healthcare is not to Western standards and medical insurance, including emergency evacuation, is necessary.

Hotels

Both Asmara and Massawa suffer from a severe shortage of hotel space; booking is advisable. Standards are low but are being improved. Service charge of 10 per cent and a small tip is usual in addition to service charge. Visitors are expected to pay bills at government-run hotels in US dollars or denominated traveller's cheques.

Credit cards

Credit cards are only accepted at a few outlets in Asmara.

Public holidays (national)

Fixed dates

1 Jan (New Year's Day), 8 Mar (Women's Day), 24 May (Independence Day), 20 Jun (Martyrs' Day), 1 Sep (Start of the Armed Struggle), 25 Dec (Christmas Day).

Variable dates

Eid al-Fitr, Eid al-Adha, Prophet's Anniversary, Easter.

Islamic year 1437 (15 Oct 2015–2 Oct 2016):: The Islamic year contains 354 or 355 days, with the result that Muslim feasts advance by 10–12 days against the Gregorian calendar. Dates of feasts vary according to the sighting of the new moon, so cannot be forecast exactly.

Working hours

Banking

(Mon–Fri) 0800–1200, 1400–1700; (Sat) 0800–1200.

Business

Mon–Thu: 0700–1200, 1400–1800; Fri: 0700–1130, 1400–1800.

Shops

Mon–Fri: 0830–1300, 1430–2030.

Electricity supply

220V AC, 50 cycles.

Weights and measures

The metric system is in force.

Security

Street crime such as theft and robbery is rare in most cities. However, it is advisable not to walk around alone late at night in any town, particularly Asmara and Massawa. Valuables, especially cameras and including passports, should be kept out of sight.

Getting there

Air

National airline: Eritrean Airlines
International airport/s: Asmara (ASM), 6km from city, restaurant, currency exchange, post office, duty-free.
Airport tax: International departures: US$20; domestic departures Nk15.

Surface

Road: There are no roads considered safe to enter the country. The 300km road from Kassala in Sudan, to Tessenai, is largely unsurfaced.

Main port/s: Massawa and Assab.
Assab's cargo levels are very low. The port had previously relied on Ethiopia for 90 per cent of its trade.

Getting about

National transport

Road: The extensive road network is undergoing major rehabilitation with US$27m allocated by the government to road reconstruction.
There are 622km of asphalt roads. The Massawa-Asmara main route (107km) is open. Other main routes (largely unsurfaced) are Asmara-Keren to Afabet-Nacfa in the north, and Asmara-Tessenai to the west.
In many parts of the country, roads are difficult or impassable during the rainy season. There are extensive mine fields in Eritrea, especially near the border with Ethiopia. Travelling on main roads outside of the border areas is generally safe, but it is advisable not to drive off-road or travel after dark in rural areas.

Buses: Some bus services available, including one service to Addis Ababa.

Taxis: Taxis are available for trips outside the city, but the fares are higher.

Rail: The link from Asmara to the coast is functioning.

City transport

Taxis: The journey time by taxi from the Asmara International Airport to the city is 15 minutes. Taxi drivers do not expect a tip.

BUSINESS DIRECTORY

The addresses listed below are a selection only. While World of Information makes every endeavour to check these addresses, we cannot guarantee that changes have not been made, especially to telephone numbers and area codes. We would welcome any corrections.

Telephone area codes

The international dialling code (IDD) for Eritrea is +291 followed by 1 and subscriber's number.

Chambers of Commerce

Eritrean National Chamber of Commerce, 46 Aboit Avenue, PO Box 856, Asmara (tel: 121-589; fax: 120-138; e-mail: encc@eol.com.er).

Banking

Commercial Bank of Eritrea; PO Box 291, 212 Liberty Avenue, Asmara (tel: 116-005, 121-844/48; fax: 124-8871, 121-849).

Eritrean Development & Investment Bank; PO Box 1266, 29 Atse Yohannes Street, Asmara (tel: 123-787, 114-520, 126-777).

Housing & Commerce Bank of Eritrea; PO Box 235, Bahti Meskerem Square, Asmara (tel: 120-350; fax: 120-401).

Central bank

National Bank of Eritrea, Zeraai Derres Square, PO Box 849, Asmara (tel: 123-033; fax: 122-091; e-mail: tekieb@eol.com.er).

Travel information

Ministry of tourism

Ministry of Tourism, PO Box 1010, Asmara (tel: 126-997).

Ministries

Ministry of Agriculture, PO Box 124, Asmara (tel: 181-499; fax: 181-415).

Ministry of Defence, PO Box 629, Asmara (tel: 113-349; fax: 114-920).

Ministry of Education, PO Box 5610, Asmara (tel: 113-044; fax: 113-866).

Ministry of Energy and Mines, PO Box 5285, Asmara (tel: 116-872; fax: 127-652); Department of Energy (fax: 112-339); Department of Mines (fax: 112-994).

Ministry of Finance and Development, PO Box 896, Asmara (tel: 113-633; fax: 117-947).

Ministry of Fisheries, PO Box 923, Asmara (tel: 114-271; fax: 112-185).

Ministry of Foreign Affairs, PO Box 190, Asmara (tel: 113-811; fax: 123-788).

Ministry of Health, PO Box 212, Asmara (tel: 112-877; fax: 112-899).

Ministry of Information, PO Box 242, Asmara (tel: 115-171; fax: 119-847).

Ministry of Justice, PO Box 241, Asmara (tel: 111-822).

Ministry of Local Government, PO Box 225, Asmara (tel: 113-006).

Ministry of Public Works, PO Box 841, Asmara (tel: 119-077).

Ministry of Trade and Industry, PO Box 1844, Asmara (tel: 118-386, 113-910; fax: 120-586).

Ministry of Transport and Communications, PO Box 204, Asmara (tel: 110-444; fax: 127-048).

Other useful addresses

African Minerals Inc (AMI), PO Box 3508, Asmara (tel: 120-280, 120-030; fax: 120-332).

British Consulate, 27 Lorenzo Tazaz Street, PO Box 997, Asmara (tel: 123-415; fax: 127-230).

Communications and Postal Authority, PO Box 234, Asmara (tel: 112-900; fax: 110-938).

Eritrean Association in London, UK (tel: (0)181-748-0547).

Eritrean Business Licence Office, PO Box 3045, Asmara (tel: 114-809, 114-752; fax: 126-694).

Eritrean Shipping Lines, PO Box 1110, Asmara (tel: 120-308/359/257; fax: 120-331).

Grain Board of Eritrea, PO Box 1234, Asmara (tel: 115-624; fax: 120-586).

Investment Promotion Centre, Asmara (tel: 118-822, 118-124; fax: 124-293).

Prima Eritrea Oil Company, Asmara (tel: 120-050; fax: 120-099).

Red Sea Trading Corporation (import/export services operated by the PFDJ), 29/31 Ras Alula Street, PO Box 332, Asmara (tel: 127-846; fax: 124-353).

US Embassy, PO Box 211, Asmara (tel: 120-004, 120-009; fax: 127-584).

Voice of the Broad Masses of Eritrea (Dimtsi Hafash), Ministry of Information, Radio Division, PO Box 872, Asmara.

Erina (Eritrean News Agency): www.dehai.org/erina

Internet sites

Eritrean news: http://www.messelna.com

Africa Business Network: http://www.ifc.org/abn

AllAfrica.com: http://www.allafrica.com

African Development Bank: http://www.afdb.org

Africa Online: http://www.africaonline.com

Mbendi AfroPaedia (information on companies, countries, industries and stock exchanges in Africa): http://mbendi.co.za

Estonia

KEY FACTS

Official name: Eesti Vabariik (The Republic of Estonia)

Head of State: President Toomas Hendrik Ilves (since 2006; re-elected 29 Aug 2011)

Head of government: Prime Minister Taavi Roivas (since 26 March 2014)

Ruling party: Coalition: Reformierakond (RE) (Reform Party), Sotsiaaldemokraatlik (SDE) (Social Democratic Party) and Isamaa ja Res Publica Liit (IRL) (Pro Patria and Res publica Union). (Elected Mar 2015, coalition agreement signed 8 Apr)

Area: 45,227 square km

Population: 1.32 million (2014)* (1,294,236; 2011; census figure)

Capital: Tallinn

Official language: Estonian

Currency: Euro (€) = 100 cents (from 1 Jan 2011; previous currency kroon, locked at EEK15.6466 per euro)

Exchange rate: €1.37 per US$ (Sep 2015)

GDP per capita: US$19,671 (2014)*

GDP real growth: 2.08% (2014)*

GDP: US$25.95 billion (2014)*

Labour force: 673,000 (2014)*

Unemployment: 7.01% (2014)*

Inflation: 0.50% (2014)*

Balance of trade: -US$1.34 billion (2014)

* estimated figure

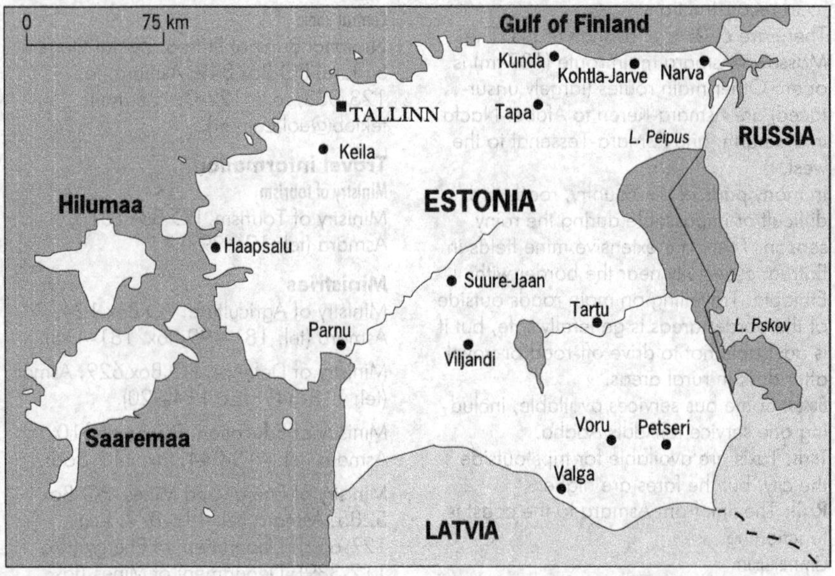

On Tallinn's Old Town Rataskaevu Street, two restaurants face each other, vying for visiting customers. Outside one, the Hermitage, a Russian registered car is casually parked at a 45 degree angle to the kerb seemingly unaware of any parking protocol or restrictions. At the Hermitage, the staff appear to be Russian speakers and the formal atmosphere is maintained by ultra-correct waitresses who hesitate to enjoin conversation. Opposite, is the Old House restaurant – most famous customer Hillary Clinton – where the waitresses are laid back, the décor is quirky and the food unorthodox. Between them, life goes past, goes on. The two coexisting restaurants unwittingly sum up the structure of Estonia's population – 25 per cent are Russian speakers – and its politics – the leading opposition party, headed by Tallinn's mayor, has close ties to Vladimir Putin's Yedinaya Rossiya (YR) (United Russia) party.

From Russia with…

Estonia first came into existence as an independent body politic in 1918 at the end of the First World War. However, for 51 of the intervening years it was a Russian fiefdom, a reluctant member of the USSR. In 2015 roughly one quarter of the population are Russian speakers. Those who have either failed the state's Estonian language test, or couldn't be bothered to take the exam, hold second class Alien's passports. Estonia's total population is only 1.35 million, but as in the Ukraine, its Russian speakers tend to be concentrated in particular townships. One such grouping is in Narva (see below) close to the Russian border where ninety per cent of the population are Russian speakers. Tallinn was once a member of the hugely successful Hanseatic League free trading area from 1285, when it was known as Reval. At the time, Reval was a Danish territory. Since that time there has always been a Russian community in Tallinn, often rivalling the German merchant community in importance.

In the twenty-first century, many of Estonia's Russian speakers are the descendants of the Russians who were transported here in Soviet schemes to dilute the country's Estonian identity. The same process saw thousands of Estonians – mostly rural dwellers, then called 'kulaks' – transported to Russia, or more precisely to Siberia, in most cases never to be seen again. Estonia's history has always been marked by the boots of conquerors as

Germans, Danes, Poles, Swedes and Russians held sway. It was Russia's relationship with Estonia that in 2015 was its major preoccupation. The post Second World War annexation of Estonia into the Soviet Union was never recognised by many countries. In the UK and the US, fully credited diplomatic missions recognising the former government existed into the 1980s.

Reservists to the rescue

The military exercises that took place in Estonia in May 2015 were no longer considered exceptional by Estonians. They were the third such set of exercises since November 2013. No less than 13,000 troops, based around the eastern city of Läsna participated in the exercises, for the most part Estonian reservists and units from other North Atlantic Treaty Organisation (NATO) member countries. The exercises pitted Estonia's reservists and NATO allies against a hypothetical enemy – named Aslavia – that sought to invade the Baltic country.

The reservist contingents were essential to any realistic military resistance of the imaginary invasion. Estonia's regular army establishment consists of barely 3,000 troops, a similar number to the armies of its Baltic neighbours, Latvia and Lithuania. The location and nature, of the military exercises left nothing to the imagination: Läsna is on the road from Tallin to the border city of Narva, where Russian – language, culture, society – predominates. Russian military aircraft had entered Estonian airspace eight times in 2014, the highest number of such intrusions experienced by any NATO state. As a result. NATO's aircraft patrols over the Baltics were increased in 2015.

The parallels with Eastern Ukraine are too close for comfort for the Estonian government. Although the opinion polls show a majority of Estonia's Russian community preferring democracy and European Union membership to the prospect of annexation by Russia, the doubts persist. Not all the Russian community have received equal treatment with their Estonian neighbours and with immigrants from other countries. Around 15 per cent of Estonia's Russians still hold Alien's passports rather than the full Estonian passports granted to immigrants who have managed to pass the Estonian state's language test (no mean feat in itself: the Estonian language has 14 declensions). In addition to its standing army of 3,000, (some of which have seen service in Afghanistan), Estonia still has military service which provides some 3,000 conscripts each year. There are a total of 20,000 reservists and a further 20,000 members of the Defence League, a cross between Britain's home guard and the US National Guard.

Narva, never

The once industrial city of Narva has a population of 60,000 – 96 per cent are Russian-speakers. Geographically, Narva is nearer to St Petersburg than it is to Tallin. Although the Estonian government could take some comfort from the regular military exercises, it can not ignore the training exercises of the Russian army on the other side of the border. However, most Estonians, including most of the country's Russian community, discount the idea of a Russian invasion or attempt at sequestration. Nevertheless, the Estonian minister of defence, Sven Mikse, is on record as saying that the Ukrainian crisis 'was a reminder that Russia is an expansionist and aggressive power.' Estonia had gone so far as to request a permanent NATO presence in the country, but the organisation's hierarchy considered that this would be viewed by Russia as provocative and counter to the spirit of the post-Soviet agreements signed with Russia.

In Narva, the most obvious effect of the Ukrainian crisis and the sanctions placed on Russia by the EU and the US, has been the absence of Russian tourists. Of concern to the government in Tallinn has been the virtual disappearance of prospective Russian investors, who have also faded away. Another concern is the brain-washing effect of propagandist Russian television on Russian speaking Estonians; the government decided to counter this effect by launching its own Russian language service, something the Russian community had long requested. However neglected they may feel, few – if any – of Narva's citizens nurse a wish to re-locate to Ivangorod, the Russian town over the border.

In one newspaper report, the rector of Narva's respected university, Jaanus Villiko, also sought to reject the idea of a Russian invasion, pointing out that the parallels didn't really exist: 'The Ukrainian government did little to integrate the two communities. We do a lot. We respect the Russian Orthodox religion and we help them to study in Estonian in the university.' Other Estonians have a simpler explanation: 'It's all about cash; here unemployment is around 4 per cent and salaries are three or four times higher than in Ukraine.'

Elections

Estonia's March 2015 election saw the incumbent governing Eesti Reformierakond (ER) Reform Party), lead by Taavi Roivas (Europe's youngest prime minister) win 30 seats, again positioning it to form a coalition government. The sighs of relief that followed the election result in Brussels, London and Washington were attributed to the failure of the pro-Russian Eesti Keskerakond (Keskerakond) (Estonian Centre Party – reportedly linked to Vladimir Putin's Yedinaya Rossiya (YR) (United Russia) party) to win more seats; none the less, it managed a respectable 28 seats, one more than in the previous election

KEY INDICATORS **Estonia**

	Unit	2011	2012	2013	2014	**2015
Population	m	1.29	*1.29	1.32	*1.32	*1.32
Gross domestic product (GDP)	US$bn	22.20	22.39	24.89	*25.95	*23.11
GDP per capita	US$	16,583	17,295	18,852	*19,671	*17,562
GDP real growth	%	7.6	3.9	1.6	*2.1	*2.5
Inflation	%	5.1	4.2	3.2	*0.5	*0.4
Unemployment	%	14.4	10.0	8.6	*7.0	*7.0
Exports (fob) (goods)	US$m	3,633.8	14,479.5	15,218.1	15,119.3	–
Imports (fob) (goods)	US$m	3,811.5	15,680.9	16,520.2	16,461.4	–
Balance of trade	US$m	-177.7	-1,201.4	-1,302.0	-1,342.0	–
Current account	US$m	472.0	-399.0	-281.0	*-14.0	*-91.0
Total reserves minus gold	US$m	234.7	287.4	304.8	427.2	–
Foreign exchange	US$m	135.5	179.4	188.9	–	–
Exchange rate	per US$	0.75	0.77	0.73	0.82	–

* estimated figure ** forecast figure

Mr Roivas' party saw its share of the vote fall slightly, to 27.7 per cent, down from 28.6 per cent in the previous – 2011 – parliamentary elections. The Sotsiaaldemokraatlik Erakond (SDE) (Social Democrats) which had been the Reform party's coalition partner, now held 15 seats having lost four, while the Isamaa ja Res Publica Liit (IRL) (Union of Pro Patria and Res Publica) lost nine seats to take them down to 14. Mr Roivas had upped the electoral ante by suggesting that Russia might seek to destabilise the Baltic states. In sharp contrast, the Centre Party leader, Edgar Saavisar, adopted a much more sympathetic attitude to Moscow, going so far as to suggest that Russia's annexation of Crimea could be legitimate.

In the aftermath of the election, reality dawned when, at the invitation of the ER, the IRL, the SDE and a newcomer to parliament, the Eesti Vabaerakond (Estonian Free Party) convened for discussions about forming a coalition. The centre-right ER remained the largest party in the Riigikogu (the Estonian Parliament), as it has been since 2007. The Free Party withdrew from coalition talks and the remaining three signed an ageement on 8 April. The resulting coalition had 59 out of the 101 seats in parliament. The leading opposition party remained the EK, with 27 seats.

The economy

According to the European Bank for Reconstruction and Development (EBRD) in its 2014 Transition Report, following the moderate expansion of 4.7 per cent seen in 2012, gross domestic product (GDP) growth in 2013 amounted to 1.6 per cent only (according to ESA 2010), as a number of public investment projects came to an end and the slow-down in key export markets such as Finland, Russia and Sweden showed its effects in the second half of 2013. Estonia then experienced an even sharper slowdown in the first quarter of 2014. This was largely attributed to adverse trends in the domestic services sector and lower trans-shipment of goods from and to Russia through Estonian ports. While export volumes recovered slightly, amid a strong recovery in industrial production, in annual terms exports fell by 4.5 per cent in the first half of the year. The negative impact on GDP was, however, offset by positive trends in private consumption and investment.

According to the EBRD, real wages in Estonia had been rising since November 2011, with the first half of 2014 showing a 6 per cent increase in annual terms, even though GDP growth had stalled during the first quarter. In 2013 real wages increased by 4.9 per cent, against the background of persistent skills mis-matches, a rising number of job vacancies and rises in the minimum wage. The Estonian authorities plan to increase the minimum wage further in 2015. The unemployment rate continued to decline and reached 7.3 per cent in June 2014, the lowest level registered since the end of the financial crisis.

The EBRD noted that the small fiscal deficit might widen slightly reflecting the economic slow-down. After registering a surplus in 2010 and 2011, the government balance showed a small deficit of 0.2 per cent of GDP in 2013, while Estonia's level of public debt remained the lowest in the European Union (EU) at only 10 per cent of GDP. The 2014 budget law included a structural surplus target that should help to prevent increases in unsustainable expenditure during upturns. A new fiscal council, established in March 2014, was expected to keep a tight grip on general government finances. This council will serve as an independent advisory body to assess economic forecasts as a base for fiscal policy, in line with the EU's Fiscal Compact.

The EBRD also noted that Estonian inflation had remained on a downward trend since 2010. Following a 4.2 per cent increase in average consumer prices in 2012, inflation had slowed to 3.2 per cent in 2013. Despite a strong rise in energy prices (see Energy below) in the first half of 2013, prompted by the electricity market liberalisation of January 2013, consumer prices had been following euro-zone deflationary trends, with the annual inflation rate falling to zero per cent in July 2014

The Estonian Parliament has approved Estonia's Entrepreneurship Growth Strategy for 2014–20. The main objective of the new programme, Estonia's third R&D and innovation strategy, was to make Estonia the most attractive country for major corporations' development centres in Europe. The state would focus mainly on areas where co-operation between businesses and researchers had the greatest potential to create added value (so-called 'smart specialisation'), with the goal of increasing the average productivity per employee from 69.4 per cent of the EU average in 2013 to 80 per cent by 2020. The areas with the biggest growth potential are information and communication technology, health technology and services, the more effective use of resources (such as health food products, material technology, smart housing and shale oil production).

Exports of smart manufacturing goods continued to rise. The share of high-tech exports amounted to 14.8 per cent of total exports in 2013, which was slightly below the EU average of 15.3 per cent. However, Estonia outperformed its two Baltic neighbours, Latvia and Lithuania, where high-tech exports averaged around 6.9 per cent of total exports. However, according to the EBRD, Estonia still remained below the EU average in innovation performance on the Innovation Union Scoreboard for 2014, although it had been rising at a steady pace since 2007. The new growth strategy adopted by parliament should underpin these developments. It also appeared that the informal economy had been further reined in. According to the Shadow Economy Index for the Baltic Countries, Estonia, together with Lithuania, had continued its long-term trend of reducing the size of its shadow economy from 20.2 per cent of GDP in 2009 to less than 16 per cent in 2013. Undeclared business revenues and wages made up the bulk of the shadow economy in the three Baltic states, with the construction sector showing the highest level of shadow activity.

In March 2014 the EstLink 2 power cable connection with Finland was completed. The undersea power cable, which links Estonia and Finland, was built by the Finnish national electricity grid operator, Fingrid, and its Estonian counterpart, Elering. The new connection of 650MW, together with the existing EstLink 1, raised the capacity of the interconnection between Estonia and Finland to 1GW. This was expected to boost the electricity flow between the Baltic States and Nordic countries, reinforcing the regional electricity market, underpinned by the existing Nordic trading system. The new power connection has increased competition in the local electricity market, which in turn has lead to a modest fall in electricity prices in the first half of the year. This was a notable change in the trend after the sharp rise – of about 30 per cent – in 2013, when the energy market was deregulated and the period of free CO2 quotas for internal electricity consumption came to an end. Regional gas linkages were also advancing. The European Commission (EC) had agreed to co-finance 75 per cent of the construction costs (estimated at about €200 million) of the Baltic Connector pipeline between Estonia and Finland. The project, which was meant to be completed in 2019, would allow Estonia and

Finland to share gas imports. In addition, the two countries had agreed to construct their own liquid nitrogen gas (LNG) terminals, although the EC had initially rejected this proposal. The project, together with the LNG terminal currently under construction in Klaipeda, aimed to diversify energy sources (a polite way of describing a reduced dependence on Russian supplies) and enhance competition in the Baltic region's gas market.

Risk assessment

Economy	Fair/good
Politics	Good
Regional stability	Good/fair

COUNTRY PROFILE

Around 3,000 BC the Finno-Ugric peoples began to migrate from Eastern Europe to the north-east coast of the Baltic Sea.
1219 Valdemar II of Denmark and the German Sword Brethren, a crusading order, conquered Estonia.
1346 The Danes sold their share of Estonian territory to the Livonian Order of Teutonic Knights (an alliance of the Sword Brethren and the German Order of Teutonic Knights).
1524–39 The State of Teutonic Knights, including Estonia, renounced religious allegiance to Rome and converted to Lutheranism.
1561 In the secularisation and partition of the State of Teutonic Knights, Estonia (now northern Estonia) became part of Sweden. Livonia (now Latvia and southern Estonia) was placed under Polish rule.
1721–1917 Estonia became a Baltic province of Russia.
1918–40 Estonia was an independent republic.
1940–88 Estonia was a constituent republic of the USSR.
1988 Estonia declared its sovereignty.
1989 Economic autonomy was granted.
1990 Independence from the USSR was declared. The break-up of the Soviet Union led to a sharp decline in industrial and commercial output.
1991 Independence was reaffirmed.
1992 Following the country's first free elections since independence, a coalition of various right-wing conservative parties, operating under the name Isamaa Pro Patria, was the heart of the government coalition, headed by Mart Laar as prime minister. Lennart Meri became president. A new constitution was adopted based on the 1938 model that provided the legal continuity to the Republic of Estonia prior to the Soviet occupation. Inflation soared to nearly 1,000 per cent as the Soviet energy and food supply system crumbled and hard currency was required for imports. A new currency, the kroon, was introduced and pegged to the Deutsche mark under a currency board system of a ratio of eight to one.
1994 GDP growth was registered for the first time since independence. Estonia joined the NATO Partnership for Peace programme (PfP). Laar lost a vote of no-confidence and Andres Tarand became caretaker prime minister until elections could be held.
1995 The governing coalition parties lost ground in the parliamentary elections. A centre-left government was formed under Tiit Vähi as prime minister. Estonia applied to join the EU. The government collapsed when the Eesti Keskerakond (EK) (Estonian Centre Party) left the government.
1996–97 The re-formed coalition collapsed when six ministers resigned and the resulting minority government also collapsed after Vähi's resignation. The ECP leader, Mart Siimann, became prime minister and formed a minority government with the Estonian Rural Union (EM) and independents.
1999 The EK became the largest party in parliament; Mart Laar remained in office as prime minister. Estonia joined the World Trade Organisation (WTO).
2000 The economy recovered from the 1998 Russian crisis and foreign investment picked up.
2001 Arnold Rüütel was elected president by the electoral college.
2003 Juhan Parts formed a coalition government comprising Uhendus Vabariigi Eest-Res Publica (ResP) (Union for the Republic-Res Publica), the Reformierakond (RE) (Reform Party) and Eestimaa Rahvaliit (ER) (Estonian People's Union). Estonians voted to join the EU.
2004 Estonia joined NATO and the EU.
2005 The failure to pursue a controversial tough anti-corruption plan led to the demise of the government. Andrus Ansip (RE) was appointed prime minister of a new, three-party coalition government of RE, Keskerakond and ER.
2006 Parliament voted for Toomas Hendrik Ilves, to replace the incumbent president, Arnold Rüütel.
2007 In parliamentary elections the ruling RE-ER-Keskerakond coalition won with an increased majority of 66 seats (out of 101). Estonia became a member of the European Union Schengen area whereby all travellers may cross borders without a passport or visa.
2008 An agreement allowing visa-free visits of citizens to the US was signed.
2009 The international ratings agency Standard and Poor's cut Estonia's long-term sovereign foreign currency credit rating from A to A-, due to Estonia's dependence on external financing.
2010 The Organisation for Economic Co-operation and Development (OECD) voted unanimously to admit Estonia as a member. The new threat of concerted cyber-attacks attracted almost 40 countries to a conference in Tallinn to discuss possible counter-measures. The Estonian government, banks and other institutions had collectively been one of the first to experience an all-out attack on their computers in 2007; the perpetrators were never caught, despite suspicion falling on Russia.
2011 Estonia adopted the euro as its currency on 1 January, at an exchange rate of 15.6466 kroon to the euro. From February–March the census was continued for those recording their details by paper documentation. In parliamentary elections held in March, the ruling RE won 28.6 per cent of the vote and increased its seats to 33 (out of 101). A coalition government was agreed between the RE and the Isamaa ja Res Publica Liit (IRL) (Union of Pro Patria and Res Publica (Party of National Affairs)); Prime Minister Ansip (RE) remained as prime minister. The preliminary result of the census was published in May, showing a total of 1,294,236 permanent residents. Trade figures released in July showed a year-on-year increase in exports of 53 per cent and a decrease in the deficit. In August, parliament re-elected Toomas Hendrik Ilves as president. The eleventh population and housing census was conducted, 31 December–1 February 2012, in which permanent residents could complete their details via the internet.
2012 On 1 October a national strike by healthcare workers and medics began, calling for pay increases of up to 40 per cent. The strike ended on 26 October following a preliminary agreement on the main conditions for the stoppage.
2013 In August, Swedbank forecast Estonia would grow by 1.9 per cent in 2013 and 3.9 per cent in 2014. It also reported that inflation in 2013 would be 3 per cent and in 2014 will show a slight fall to 2.8 per cent.
2015 The 1 March parliamentary elections were won by Alianza Republicana Nacionalista (Arena) (Nationalist Republican Alliance) with 38.77 per cent of the vote (32 seats, out of 84), hotly followed by Frente Farabundo Martí para la Liberación Nacional (FMLN) (Farabundo Martí National Liberation Front) wth 37.28 per cent (31 seats).

Political structure

Constitution

The Constitution was adopted on 28 June 1992. It is based on the 1938 model, that provides legal continuity to the Republic of Estonia prior to Soviet occupation.

The Constitution defines the areas of responsibility of the government as: to implement domestic and foreign policies; to direct and co-ordinate the work of government institutions; to organise and implement legislation, the resolutions of the Riigikogu (parliament) and edicts of the president; to submit draft laws and foreign treaties to the parliament; to prepare drafts of the state budget and to implement and report on the budget and to organise relations with foreign states.
Only Estonian citizens are allowed to vote, leaving the 38 per cent non-Estonian population largely disenfranchised. The constitution can only be amended by referendum and two successful passages through the Riigikogu.
Estonia is divided into 15 counties and six towns (the other 27 towns form part of the counties). The counties are divided into 193 parishes.
There is universal suffrage – for Estonian citizens only – from age 18.

Form of state
Democratic republic

The executive
Executive power is vested in the president who is indirectly elected for a five-year term by Parliament consisting of 101 parliamentary deputies and 266 local government representatives. The winning candidate has to secure a majority within three rounds of voting otherwise the election returns to parliament and they choose between the two candidates with the highest number of votes.
The president nominates the prime minister who then forms a government. In case of the failure of the president's candidate(s) to form a government (the constitution permits the president two nominations), the parliament will name a prime minister to form a government. The prime minister alone nominates the ministers of his cabinet, who are formally appointed by the president and swear an oath before the parliament. Members of the government need not have any political party affiliation nor be members of the parliament.

National legislature
The unicameral Riigikogu (parliament) has 101 representatives elected in multi-seat constituencies by proportional representation for four-year terms. Its prime constitutional function is legislation, but it also has constitutional duties to review the activities of The executive and directly represent voters.

Legal system
Estonia's legal system is similar to that of continental Europe. The Civil Code underwent large-scale reforms in 2002, the most notable being the implementation of the Law of Obligations Act, which overhauled old contract laws that dated back to the Soviet era.
The Supreme Court has seventeen justices, of which the chief justice is appointed by the parliament after nomination by the president; the rest are appointed by the parliament after nomination by the chief justice. Justices are appointed for life. The Supreme Court can hear appeals, either in full session, or by means of a special *ad hoc* panel.
There are town and county courts where cases are heard by a judge and assistant judges, elected by popular vote.

Last elections
1 March 2015 (parliamentary); 29 August 2011 (presidential, indirect)
Results: Parliamentary: the Reformierakond (RE) (Reform Party) won 27.7 per cent of the vote (30 seats out of 101), Eesti Keskerakond (Keskerakond) (Estonian Centre Party) 24.8 per cent (27), Sotsiaaldemokraatlik Erakond (SDE) (Social Democratic Party) 15.2 per cent (15), the Isamaa ja Res Publica Liit (IRL) (Union of Pro Patria and Res Publica) 13.7 per cent (14), Eesti Vabaerakond (Estonian Free Party) 8.7 per cent (eight), Eesti Konservatiivne Rahvaerakond (EKRE) (Conservative People's Party of Estonia 8.1 per cent (seven); four other political parties and all independent candidates each won less than one per cent and failed to gain any seats. Turnout was 64.2 per cent.
Presidential: Toomas Hendrik Ilves won 73 votes (out of 101).

Next elections
2016 (presidential, indirect); 2019 (parliamentary)

Political parties

Ruling party
Coalition: Reformierakond (RE) (Reform Party), Sotsiaaldemokraatlik (SDE) (Social Democratic Party) and Isamaa ja Res Publica Liit (IRL) (Pro Patria and Res publica Union). (Elected Mar 2015, coalition agreement signed 8 Apr)

Main opposition party
Eesti Keskerakond (Keskerakond) (Estonian Centre Party)

Population

1.32 million (2014)*
Last census: 31 March 2012: 1,294,236
Population density: 33.2 inhabitants per square km. Urban population 69 per cent (2010 Unicef).
Annual growth rate: -0.8 per cent, 1990–2010 (Unicef).

Ethnic make-up
Estonians make up the majority of the population (62 per cent), followed by Russians (30 per cent), Ukrainians (3 per cent) and Belarussians (2 per cent). Russians are in the majority in many towns.

Religions
The main religious denominations are Lutheran, Russian Orthodox and Baptist, with Lutherans in the majority.

Education

Schools may be private, municipal or state run. The backbone of the education system is general comprehensive schooling, which caters for children of all ages and abilities. Pre-school attendance is high but is not a prerequisite for primary schooling. This is part of basic school education, lasting for nine years, starting from the age of seven.
On completion of basic education (aged around 16 – a student may choose to extend or abbreviate their study), a student may continue in an upper secondary or vocational school. The majority of schools offer a general curriculum. Some specialise in a branch of the humanities or sciences.
The oldest university is Tartu University, founded in 1632. Since 1999, some selected post-secondary vocational schools have been given the right to offer vocational higher education. There are six public universities, nine private universities and seven state vocational education institutions. The usual duration of studies is three to four years.
Literacy rate: 100 per cent adult rate; 100 per cent youth rate (15–24) (Unesco 2005).
Compulsory years: 7 to 17
Enrolment rate: 95 per cent boys, 93 per cent girls, total primary school enrolment of the relevant age group (including repetition rates) (World Bank).
Pupils per teacher: 17 in primary schools.

Health

Private healthcare provision is negligible. Overall indices show an improvement in health in the general population.

HIV/Aids
HIV prevalence: 1.1 per cent aged 15–49 in 2003 (World Bank)
Life expectancy: 72 years, 2004 (WHO 2006)
Fertility rate/Maternal mortality rate: 1.7 births per woman, 2010 (Unicef); maternal mortality 50 per 100,000 live births (World Bank).
Child (under 5 years) mortality rate (per 1,000): 4 per 1,000 live births (WHO 2012)

Welfare

The guiding principle behind the government's social welfare development policy is the complete dismantling of the state-centred Soviet system. Government priorities include the establishment of an adequate social security system, funded

by contributions from employers and employees.
Estonia is moving away from the pay-as-you-go pension system to a three-tier partially state-funded pension scheme. The first tier is financed by a 33 per cent social tax, 20 per cent of which is kept for pensions. The fully funded second pillar came into effect in 2002. The scheme offers additional pension coverage and it is suggested it be mandatory only for people currently under the age of 18. The third tier consists of voluntary contributions administered by private pension funds and insurance companies.
In 2002, the retirement age was 63 years for men and 58 years for women, which is likely to increase gradually to 63 years by 2016.

Main cities

Tallinn (capital, estimated population 390,107 in 2012), Tartu (102,495), Narva (64,904), Kohtla-Järve (43,572), Pärnu (42,677), Viljandi (19,807).

Languages spoken

Estonian belongs to the Baltic-Finnic group of the Finno-Ugric languages, which also includes Hungarian and Finnish. The Latin alphabet is used. Various other languages spoken include Latvian, Lithuanian, Ukrainian, Belarusian, Russian, Finnish, Yiddish and German. English has replaced Russian as the primary business language.
By law, all transactions, contracts and company returns have to be in Estonian. Notarised transactions in English often accompany these.

Official language/s

Estonian

Media

Press

Dailies: There are 11 daily newspapers, of which six are distributed nationally. In Estonian the highest circulating newspapers are *Postimees* (www.postimees.ee), *Eesti Päevaleht* (www.epl.ee), *Maaleht* (www.maaleht.ee), *SL Õhtuleht* (www.sloleht.ee) is an evening tabloid. In Russian, *Vesti Dnya* (www.vesti.ee) *Sillamyaesky Vestnik* (www.vestnik.ee) and *Narva* (www.narvaleht.ee).
Weeklies: In Estonian *Kesknädal* (www.kesknadal.ee), for general interest, *Eesti Loodus* (www.eestinaine.ee) for cultural items, *Kroonika* (www.kroonika.ee) is a tabloid and *Sirp* (www.sirp.ee) another popular publication. In English, the *Baltic Independent* and *Baltic Times* (www.baltictimes.com).
Business: In Estonian, *Aripäev* (www.ap3.ee) is published daily, with online English and Russia editions.

Broadcasting

Eesti Rahvusringhääling (ERR) (Estonian Public Broadcasting) (www.err.ee) replaced Eesti Televisioon (Estonian Television) and incorporated Eesti Raadio (Radio Estonia), as the combined national, public broadcasting service, in June 2007.
Radio: Eesti Raadio (Radio Estonia) (www.er.ee) operates five stations catering for all domestic demographics and foreign listeners. The private, national, commercial radio network, U-Pop (www.u-pop.ee) has five stations including Radio Elmar (Estonia music), Radio Uuno and Radio Kuku. There are many local commercial radio stations broadcasting throughout Estonia.
Television: ERR has one TV channel. There are several private TV stations, some of which are foreign and broadcast through cable or satellite channels. Domestic TV includes Kanal 2 (www.kanal2.ee) and TV3 (www.tv3.ee), showing foreign imports, Seitse (www.seitse.tv) and Alo TV, based in Tartu.
Other news agencies: BNS (Baltic News Service): www.bns.ee
Delfi (in Estonian): www.delfi.ee

Economy

Although the economy is structured around the service sector, which contributes 67.2 per cent of GDP, including telecommunications and information technology, business services, retail, construction and real estate, the industrial sector contributes 29.2 per cent to GDP, in particular, engineering, electronic components, as well as the more traditional manufacturing of textiles, foodstuffs and timber and paper products linked to Estonia's forestry wealth. Agriculture accounts for 3.6 per cent of GDP, providing dairy, cereals, potatoes and livestock. Export commodities include minerals, electricity, manufactured goods and agricultural products.
GDP growth was 6.7 per cent in 2007, but because Estonia had restructured and opened up its economy, adopting Western banking business practices, when the global economic crisis struck in 2008–09 it was quickly caught-up in the international recession, which exposed its underlying weaknesses. GDP growth was -5.3 per cent in 2008, falling further to -14.7 per cent in 2009, before recovering in 2010 with growth of 2.5 per cent. The economy has recovered strongly since, with growth of 8.3 per cent in 2011, before slowing down to 2.1 per cent and by 2014 due to weak EU and Russian growth.
The International Monetary Fund (IMF) determined that Estonia's problems going into the recession included weak competitiveness and salaries that exceeded productivity, unsustainable public expenditure as job losses cut tax revenue and private sector indebtedness which had grown beyond assets and income. This resulted in a sudden halt in domestic demand as well as a severe fall in export demand; output declined by over 15 per cent in 2008–09, and wages fell by 6.5 per cent by the end of 2009. Inflation that had been rising in 2007 jumped from 6.6 per cent to 10.4 per cent in 2008, before crashing to -0.1 per cent in 2009. Many companies shed staff to remain in business and the unemployment rate, which had fallen to 5.9 per cent in 2006 (down from a high of 13.6 in 2000) rose swiftly to around 20 per cent by 2010.
Since the crisis inflation has been maintained at a more steady rate, averaging 3.5 per cent in between 2010–13, dropping into negative in 2014 at -0.1 per cent. Unemployment has also been improving, falling to 6.5 per cent by mid-2015.
Despite the improvements in unemployment, Estonia is still challenged by a shortage of labour including both skilled and unskilled workers. The government has made changes to its immigration policies in order to allow highly skilled foreign labour to be more easily hired.
In order to join the European Monetary Union (EMU) (in 2011), Estonia had to undertake policies to maintain macroeconomic stability and support its currency. As a member Estonia would be required to maintain a fiscal deficit limit of 3 per cent of GDP. Estonia managed to achieve this by halting benefit and wage increases and increasing its competitiveness. Estonia adopted the euro as its currency on 1 January 2011, at an exchange rate of 15.65 kroon to the euro.

External trade

As a member of the European Union, Estonia operates within a community-wide free trade union, with tariffs determined centrally and as a whole. Internationally, the EU has free trade agreements with a number of nations and trading blocs worldwide.

Imports

Principal imports are machinery and equipment, chemical products, textiles, foodstuffs and vehicle equipment.
Main sources: Russia (10.8 per cent of total in 2014), Finland (10.3 per cent), Germany (10.2 per cent)

Exports

Main exports include electrical and electronic equipment, wood, charcoal and paper, textiles, food products, metals, chemical products and vehicle parts.

Main destinations: Sweden (16.4 per cent of total in 2014), Russia (14.1 per cent), Finland (14.0 per cent)

Agriculture

Farming

The agricultural reform programme has produced mixed results. Most large state-run farms have been dismantled but some co-operatives and state-owned farms persist.

Government agricultural policy is designed to provide affordable food for Estonians while balancing farm income and guaranteeing farm workers equivalent earnings to industrial workers.

Estonia is eligible for EU subsidies and rural development funds through the Common Agricultural Policy (CAP). However, like the other new EU member countries, it only got the full amount in 2013. The EU decided to introduce CAP support funds gradually over a 10-year period. During its transitional entry stage Estonia has decided to implement the reform of the CAP in 2009. The reform was introduced throughout most of the EU on 1 January 2005, when subsidies on farm output, which tended to benefit large farms and encourage overproduction, were replaced by single farm payments, not conditional on production. The change is expected to reward farms that provide and maintain a healthy environment, food safety and animal welfare standards. The changes are also intended to encourage market conscious production and cut the cost of CAP to the EU taxpayer.

Fishing

Some 130,000 tonnes of fish are caught per annum. The total catch has fallen dramatically as disputes with Latvia over territorial waters and falling investment have contributed to lower catches. Estonia has been a net fish importer since independence, although the value of exports has increased.

Forestry

Forest makes up around 50 per cent of available land in Estonia. As with all sectors the forestry industry suffers from out-dated machinery, equipment and a lack of finance and investment, yet despite this, total timber production has increased.

The government has established special credits for the forestry industry to develop technology. Traditionally most Estonian timber exports were of logs and for paper. A further increase in the overall value of timber exports is anticipated as paper related exports decline and the export of finished timber products increases.

The timber-processing industry has developed quickly, and the export potential for Estonian timber products is good, principally in Scandinavia, but also in Russia and Ukraine.

Industry and manufacturing

Industry contributed 29.2 per cent to GDP in 2014, with around half of that figure contribution from the manufacturing sector.

During the Soviet-era, the Estonian industrial sector was characterised by a high degree of concentration (20 per cent of enterprises produced two-thirds of industrial output), dependence on imports from the Soviet Union (80 per cent of all imports) and a reliance on the markets of the Soviet Union (90 per cent of exports). The collapse of the Soviet Union forced massive structural changes on Estonian industry. As Soviet markets closed, markets in the West had to be found, new sources of raw materials exploited and new management techniques developed.

Industry and manufacturing is now dominated by the food industry, high-tech electronics and wood processing. Estonia's relatively cheap labour, energy and raw materials are the main reasons for the country's industrial competitiveness. These advantages are being constantly eroded as living standards rise in Eastern Europe.

Tourism

Estonia has become an attractive destination for other European nationals. A concession in the tax rate, granted by the government (2009–11), meant visitors only paid tax on purchases up to EEK600, with purchases over that tax free. This measure, along with the competitive prices offered by tourist companies, increased visitor numbers from other Baltic states. The leading European budget airline Ryanair began flying into Estonia in 2010, boosting visitor numbers at a time when the market was at its lowest. In 2014 there were 3.1 million overnight visitors to Estonia, a 3.6 per cent increase on 2013, reaching a record for the fifth consecutive year.

The historic centre of Tallinn is included on Unesco's World Heritage List. Tallinn was the European Capital of Culture in 2011, which gave a direct boost to tourism, with foreign visits recording a year-on-year increase (to October) of 15.6 per cent with an average of 17.2 nights per visitor, the third highest recorded in the EU.

Travel and tourism accounted for 14.2 per cent of GDP in 2014, which was forecast to fall by 1.1 per cent in 2015. Employment in the sector fell from 14.7 per cent of total (95,300 jobs), in 2006 to 13.1 per cent (77,000 jobs) in 2010, and despite not making a full comeback had recovered to 13.9 per cent by 2014 (87,000 jobs).

Mining

Estonia has a limited range of mineral resources, principally for use in the construction industry. Mining and quarrying activities contribute less than 1 per cent of GDP. In 2013 the annual turnover from the mining industry was EUR474.1 million (US$644 million).

Hydrocarbons

There are no proven crude oil reserves; however there is a substantial amount of oil shale in the north-east, exploited by Eesti Põlevkivi (Estonian Oil Shale), run by Eesti Energia, the state-owned energy company. Since Estonia joined the EU oil shale production has been significantly cut back as the country has tried to meet EU environmental regulations. Oil consumption in 2013 was 29,550 barrels per day (bpd).

The Estonian port of Tallinn remains ice-free during winter and is an important transit point for Russian oil into the EU.

National gas consumption was 678 million cubic metres (cum) in 2013, all of which was imported, primarily through a 250-mile pipeline from Russia. There are no coal reserves and Estonia relies entirely on imports.

Energy

Total installed generating capacity is over 2,750MW and Estonia is a net exporter of electricity, mainly to Latvia and north-west Russia. The Narva thermal power plants produce over 90 per cent of all the electricity generated. It is divided into two major, shale oil fired stations, the Balti power plant and the Eesti power plant. Investments in new technology have reduced some of the environmentally damaging emissions derived from burning shale oil. EU environmental regulations have challenged the country to find alternative, cleaner energy sources.

The Estlink project, connecting an underwater cable linking the Baltic States with the Scandinavian and Nordic power grids, is sponsored by Estonia and Finland and partly funded by the EU; it became operational in 2007.

Natural gas, petroleum and by-products are all imported, mainly from Russia. The Connectbaltic project is a plan to build a natural gas pipeline between Finland and Estonia, laid across the Baltic seabed, supplying 2 billion cubic metres of gas per annum. The environmental impact assessment was completed in 2008 and in 2013 the seabed studies began. The project has an estimated cost of EUR110 million (US$122.5 million).

Financial markets

Stock exchange

Tallinn Stock Exchange (TSE)

Banking and insurance
The commercial banking sector is licensed by the central bank. Foreign-owned banks are permitted to operate and bank shares are freely traded.

Central bank
Eesti Pank (Bank of Estonia)

Main financial centre
Tallinn

Time
GMT plus two hours (daylight saving, late March to late October, GMT plus three hours)

Geography
Estonia is situated in north-east Europe, the northernmost of the three Baltic States, bordering the Russian Federation to the east and Latvia to the south. Its northern coastline is on the Gulf of Finland and its western coastline in the Gulf of Riga and the Baltic Sea. From north to south the country measures 240km, from east to west 360km. With a total land area of 45,227 square km, Estonia is the smallest of the Baltic states and about the same size as Denmark.
The terrain is flat and heavily wooded; there are numerous lakes, rivers and bogs. Offshore, there are around 1,500 islands.

Hemisphere
Northern

Climate
The mildest areas are along the Baltic coast. Summer is short, with sunshine lasting up to nine hours a day, and an average temperature of 15 degrees Celsius (C). Winters are cold, with slush, ice and repeated light coverings of snow (average minus 4 degrees C). Spring and autumn are very short.

Dress codes
Warm clothes are required during winter, with a raincoat and umbrella necessary during the summer. Business dress is conservative but relatively informal, with a jacket and tie expected for meetings.

Entry requirements
Passports
Required by all, except nationals of EU/EEA countries and Switzerland

Visa
Required by all, except nationals of EU and Schengen area signatory countries, North America, Australasia and Japan. For further exceptions contact the nearest embassy or see full list can be found at www.vm.ee. A Schengen visa application (offered in several languages) can be downloaded from http://europa.eu/abc/travel/ see 'documents you will need'.

Currency advice/regulations
There are no restrictions on the import and export of local or foreign currency.

Customs
Personal items are duty-free. There are no duties levied on alcohol and tobacco between EU member states, providing amounts imported are for personal consumption.

Health (for visitors)
Nationals of the European Economic Area (EEA) countries and Switzerland can access reduced cost and sometimes free medical treatment using a European Health Insurance Card (EHIC) while visiting the EEA. Exceptions include nationals of the 10 countries which joined the EU in 2004 whose EHIC is not valid in Switzerland. Applications for the EHIC should be made before travelling.

Mandatory precautions
No specific requirements.

Advisable precautions
Vaccinations may be advised for hepatitis A and diphtheria.
Take mosquito lotion if travelling outside the towns. There is a risk of rabies.

Hotels
There are numerous good quality western style hotels in Tallinn. It is advisable to book a hotel before travelling.
For the peak period of June and July, the Estonian Tourist Board suggests the traveller books in January.
Bills must be paid in Estonian kroons if credit cards are not accepted.

Credit cards
Most major hotels and restaurants and a few shops accept American Express, Visa, Eurocard and Diners' Club.

Public holidays (national)
Fixed dates
1 Jan (New Year's Day), 24 Feb (Independence Day), 1 May (Spring Day), 23 Jun (Victory Day), 25 Jun (St John's Day, Midsummer), 20 Aug (Restoration of Independence Day), 24 Dec (Christmas Eve), 25 Dec (Christmas Day), 26 Dec (St Stephen's Day).

Variable dates
Good Friday.

Working hours
Banking
Mon–Fri: 0900–1600.

Business
Mon–Fri: 0830–1830. Lunch around 1300. Some offices stop work at 1630.

Government
Mon–Fri: 0900–1700.

Shops
Mon–Fri: 0930–1900, Sat: 0930–1600.

Telecommunications
Mobile/cell phones
Estonia has three mobile service providers, operating on a GSM system.

Social customs/useful tips
Estonians can be quite reserved and are not particularly talkative. Shaking hands is the normal form of greeting. Flowers are generally acceptable as a gift.
There is a service charge of 10 to 15 per cent, but a small tip in addition is appreciated.
Saunas are popular in Estonia, usually followed by a substantial meal washed down with liberal quantities of beer and vodka.
Until you are sure of the ethnic background of your host avoid talking about Russians and the communist past. Many Estonians have relatives who were sent to Siberia, which has left strong feelings when it comes to Russia. Also avoid asking what your host did during the Soviet occupation – it may sound as if you are asking if they were a member of the Communist Party or even if they were sent to Siberia.
There is a strong sense of national pride and identity among Estonians and they do not appreciate being lumped together with Latvia and Lithuania as 'the Baltic states', or even being described as part of eastern Europe.

Security
Estonia is a safe place to visit compared to some of the other former Soviet republics, although muggings do occur in urban areas, especially at night. Car theft is also a problem.

Getting there
Air
National airline: Estonian Air
International airport/s: Tallinn (TLL) airport, 5km north-west of city. Includes a business centre, bank, post office, restaurant, bar, shops and car rental. Conference facilities also available. Bus no 2 runs between the city and the airport, taking 15 minutes. A shuttle bus to the main hotels and the city centre meets all flights.
Airport tax: There is no airport tax.

Surface
Road: Foreign cars are flagged down at borders to examine the documents in an attempt to block the flow of stolen foreign cars. Check insurance before travelling and do not buy cheap insurance at the frontier. There are direct routes along the Baltic coast connecting Latvia and Lithuania and also the Russian Federation.
Rail: International lines run from surrounding countries, although rail travel between Estonia, Latvia and Lithuania is time-consuming.
Water: Ferry services run between Stockholm and Tallinn, Helsinki and Tallinn

and Rostock (Germany) and Tallinn via Helsinki.

Main port/s: Muuga is Tallinn's port and is the most modern in the country.

Getting about

National transport

Air: There is limited domestic air travel with Baltic Aeroservis, which serves the islands of Kuressaare and Kärdla. Charter flights to other destinations can also be booked.

Road: Estonia has a high density of roads although there are few major highways. Signs are not illuminated and fairly small, so driving at night is best avoided. In winter roads can be icy and ungritted.

The high level of car crime in the Baltic States means that border crossings can be very lengthy processes and insurance can be difficult to find.

Buses: Estonia has a very extensive bus network linking every area of the country. Tickets should be booked in advance.

Rail: The majority of major cities are covered. Tallinn and Tartu are connected by an express service.

City transport

Taxis: Taxis in Tallinn are relatively cheap. There is a good taxi service from Tallinn International Airport to the city centre, with a journey time of 10 minutes. Private services should display the name of the company and its number on the roof. Fares should be agreed upon beforehand. There are also minibuses called *Marshrut-taxis*, which operate on set routes, stopping at fixed destinations and seating up to 10 people.

Buses, trams & metro: All parts of the city can also be reached by bus, trolley-bus and tram. Tickets can be bought from stalls in the main shopping areas.

Car hire

Car hire can be arranged at the airport. Never drink and drive – no level of alcohol is permitted. Speed limit is 50km per hour in built-up areas, 90km per hour in the country and 110km per hour on motorways. In towns there are parking permits, fines and wheel clamps. Driving is on the right. EU nationals should be in possession of a national driving licence. The international car hire firms Avis, Hertz and Europcar all have bureaux in Estonia. Roads, although deteriorating, are of a reasonably good standard but can be dangerous in winter due to ice.

BUSINESS DIRECTORY

The addresses listed below are a selection only. While World of Information makes every endeavour to check these addresses, we cannot guarantee that changes have not been made, especially to telephone numbers and area codes. We would welcome any corrections.

Telephone area codes

The international direct dialling code (IDD) for Estonia is +372, followed by area code and subscriber's number:

Haapsalu	47	Rapla	48
Jögeva	77	Tallinn	none
Narva	35	Valga	76
Pärnu	44	Viljandi	43
Polva	79	Voru	78

Useful telephone numbers

Fire brigade: 01

Police: 02

Ambulance: 03

Gas: 04

NB Numbers 01–04 cannot be dialled from mobile telephones; 112 should be dialled instead.

Chambers of Commerce

American Chamber of Commerce Estonia, Tallinn Business Centre, 6 Harju, 10130 Tallinn (tel: 631-0522; fax: 631-0521; e-mail: acce@acce.ee).

British-Estonian Chamber of Commerce, 21 Suur-Karja, 10148 Tallinn (tel: 640-5872; fax: 640-5873; e-mail: info@becc.ec).

Estonian Chamber of Commerce and Industry, 17 Toom-Kooli, 10130 Tallinn (tel: 646-0244; fax: 646-0245; e-mail: koda@koda.ee).

Banking

Eesti Forekspank (Estonian Forexbank), Narva mnt 9a, Tallinn (tel: 630-2100; fax: 630-2200; e-mail: bank@forex.ee); international settlements (tel: 640-6400).

Eesti Hoiupank (Estonian Savings Bank), Kinga 1, Tallinn (tel: 630-2600; fax: 630-2602; e-mail: mailbob@esb.ee).

Eesti Investeerimispank (Estonian Investment Bank), PO Box 26, Narva mnt 7, Tallinn (tel: 620-0800; fax: 620-0812/0801; e-mail: info@estib.ee); international settlements (tel: 620-0828).

Eesti Krediidipank (Estonian Credit Bank), Narva mnt 4, Tallinn (tel: 640-5000; fax: 631-3533; e-mail: krediidipank@ekp.ee).

Eesti Maapank (Land Bank of Estonia), Tallinna 12, Rakvere (tel: 43-821; fax: 43-617); in Tallinn (tel: 646-6295; fax: 646-6649/6313-720); international settlements (tel: 640-8321).

Eesti Pangaliit (Estonian Association of Banks), Pärnu mnt 19, Tallinn (tel: 245-5400; fax: 245-5401; e-mail: panagaliit@teleport.ee).

Eesti Uhispank (Union Bank of Estonia), Tartu mnt 13, Tallinn (tel: 610-4300, 631-2728; fax: 610-4302); international settlements (tel: 640-3516, 640-3519).

Hansapank, Liivalaia 8, EE0001 Tallinn (tel: 631-0311/310; fax: 631-0410; e-mail: webmaster@hansa.ee).

Merita Bank Ltd (foreign bank's branch), Harju 6, Tallinn (tel: 631-4040; fax: 631-4153; e-mail: merita@estpak.ee).

Tallinna Aripanga Aktsiaselts (Tallinn Business Bank), Estonia pst 3/5, Tallinn (tel: 245-5349; fax: 242-3322; e-mail: tbb@torn.ee).

Tallinna Pank, Parnu mnt 10, Tallinn (tel: 631-0100/0102, 640-5880; fax: 631-0111; e-mail: info@tp.ee); international settlements (tel: 640-5829).

Central bank

Eesti Pank (Bank of Estonia), Estonia Boulevard 13, Tallinn 15095 (tel: 668-0719; fax: 668-0836; e-mail: info@epbe.ee).

Stock exchange

Tallinn Stock Exchange (TSE) www.omxnordicexchange.com

Travel information

Baltic Tours, Vene 23B, Tallinn (tel: 244-6331; fax: 244-0760).

Estonian Air, Vabaduse, Valjak 10, Tallinn (tel: 244-6383, 244-0295; fax: 631-2740).

Estonian Association of Travel Agents, Pikk 71, Tallinn (tel: 260-1705; fax: 242-5594).

Estonian Railways, 36 Pikk Str, Tallinn (tel: 240-1610; fax: 240-1710).

Finest Hotel Group, Parnu mnt 22, Tallinn (tel: 245-1510; fax: 244-6029).

Lufthansa Airport Office (tel: 638-8077; fax: 638-8077); Lufthansa city centre, Pärnu mnt 10, Tallinn (tel: 631-4444).

National tourist organisation offices

Estonian Tourist Board, Liivalaia 13/15, Tallinn (tel: 627-9770; fax: 627-9777; e-mail: tourism@eas.ee).

Ministries

Ministry of Agriculture, Lai 39/41, Tallinn (tel: 244-1166; fax: 244-0601).

Ministry of Citizenship and Immigration, Ministry of the Interior, Pikk 61, Tallinn (tel: 244-5080; fax: 260-2785).

Ministry of Culture and Education, Suur Karja 23, Tallinn (tel: 244-5077; fax: 244-0963).

Ministry of Defence, Pikk 57, Tallinn (tel: 239-9160/50; fax: 239-9165).

Ministry of Economic Affairs, Harju 11, Tallinn (tel: 244-0577; fax: 244-6860).

Ministry of Energy, Ministry of Economy, Kiriku 6, Tallinn (tel: 244-3941; fax: 244-8091).

Ministry of Environment, Toompuiestee 24, Tallinn (tel: 245-2507; fax: 245-3310).

Ministry of Finance, Suur Ameerika 1, Tallinn (tel: 268-3445; fax: 268-2097).

Ministry of Finance (Foreign Affairs Dept), Kohtu 8, Tallinn (fax: 245-2992).

Ministry of Foreign Affairs, Ravala 9, Tallinn (tel: 231-7091; fax: 277-1677, 231-7099; internet site: http://www.vm.ee).

Ministry of Industry and Energy, Gonsiori Str 29, Tallinn (tel: 242-3550; fax: 242-1133); Foreign Relations Dept (fax: 242-5468).

Ministry of the Interior, Pikk 61, Tallinn (tel: 266-3611; fax: 260-2785, 244-1112).

Ministry of Justice, Suur Karja 19, Tallinn (tel: 244-5120; fax: 224-6235).

Ministry of Reform, State Chancellery, Lossi Plats 1a, Tallinn (tel: 231-6730; fax: 244-0372).

Ministry of Social Affairs, Gonsiori 29, Tallinn (tel: 242-3434; fax: 242-1862).

Ministry of Trade and Commerce, Kiriku Tn 6, Tallinn (tel: 244-3941, 244-5921); Foreign Relations Dept (fax: 244-8091).

Ministry of Transport and Communication, Viru 9, Tallinn (tel: 239-7613; fax: 239-7606); Foreign Relations Department (fax: 244-9206).

Prime Minister's Office, Losi Plats 1a, Tallinn (tel: 231-6701; fax: 244-0372).

Other useful addresses

A/S Seesam Insurance, Kreutzwali 2/Narva mnt 24, Tallinn (tel: 243-3518; fax: 242-4886).

A/S Central (shipping agents), Hospidali 6, Parnu (tel: 244-0707).

Asker (building advice), Roosikrantsi 12, Tallinn (tel: 244-2165, 277-1304/124; fax: 277-1189).

Association of Construction Materials Producers of Estonia, Jaama 1A, Tallinn (tel: 251-2230; fax: 650-6178).

Baltic Insurance Co, Olevimagi 12, Tallinn (tel: 260-1384; fax: 260-1790).

Baltic Trade Company (commercial service organising exhibitions, seminars, joint ventures), Ravala Str 27, Tallinn (tel: 245-5089; fax: 244-5768).

Baltlink, Tartu mnt 13, Tallinn (tel: 242-1003; fax: 245-0893).

British Embassy, Kentmanni 20, 20001 Tallinn (tel: 631-3461/2; fax: 631-3354); commercial section (fax: 631-3463).

Business Advisory Services Centre, Lei 9, Tallinn (tel: 260-9675; fax: 631-3523).

Confederation of Estonian Industry, Gonsiori 29, Tallinn (tel: 242-2235; fax: 242-4962).

Department for Foreign Economic Relations, Suur Ameerika 1, Tallinn (tel: 268-3559; fax: 268-3622).

Department of Statistics, Endla 15, Tallinn (tel: 245-3889; fax: 245-3923; internet site: http://stat.vil.ee/K.E.S-ENGL.htm).

Eesti-Estline, Sadama 29, Tallinn (tel: 244-9051; fax: 242-5352).

Estonian Association of Construction Entrepreneurs, Ravala 8, Tallinn (tel/fax: 243-3213).

Estonian Business Advisory Services, Tallinn BAS Centre, Lai 0, Tallinn (tel: 260-9795; fax: 631-3523).

Estonian Embassy (USA), 1730 M Street, NW, Washington DC 20036 (tel: 202-588-0101; fax: 202-588-0108; e-mail: info@estemb.org).

Estonian Export Council, Kiriku 2/4, Tallinn (tel: 244-4703; fax: 244-3615).

Estonian Foreign Trade Association, Uus 32/34, Tallinn (tel: 260-1462; fax: 260-2184).

Estonian Institute for Market Research, Vaike-Karja 1, Tallinn (tel: 244-8605; fax: 244-1378, 277-1675).

Estonian Institute (information service), PO Box 3469, Tonismagi 8, Tallinn (tel: 244-0513; fax: 268-2057; e-mail: einst@einst.ee; internet site: http://www.einst.ee).

Estonian Investment Agency (EIA), Ravala Str 6 (room 602B), Tallinn (tel: 641-0166; fax: 641-0312).

Estonian Maritime Industry, Sadama 17, Tallinn (tel: 260-1723; fax: 244-4808).

Estonian Shipping Co, 3/5 Estonian Blvd, Tallinn (tel: 244-3802; fax: 242-4958, 243-1228).

Estonian State Energy Department, 29 Gonsiori Str, Tallinn (tel: 242-1579; fax: 242-5468, 242-1908); external department (tel: 242-1480).

Estonian Trade Council, Kiriku Str 2/4, Tallinn (tel: 244-4703; fax: 244-4615).

Hanson Insurance, Narva mnt 24, Tallinn (tel: 261-2440; fax: 242-5977).

Loksa Shipyard, Tallinn (tel: 257-5241; fax: 263-91230).

Municipality of Tallinn, Vabaduse Valjak 7, Tallinn (tel: 266-6146; fax: 244-1230).

National Customs Board, Ravala pst 9, Tallinn (tel: 231-7722; fax: 231-7727).

Port of Tallinn Authority, Sadama 25, Tallinn (tel: 242-7009; fax: 242-2950).

Radio Estonia – Foreign Service, Gonsiori 21, Tallinn (tel: 243-4282; fax: 243-4139).

Reklaam/Television Ltd, Tonismagi 2, Tallinn (tel: 243-4606; fax: 231-1077).

Ookean State Stock Corporation (Estonian Fishing Company), Paljassaare Str 28, Tallinn (tel: 247-1421, 249-7212; fax: 249-8190).

State Department of Foreign Trade, Komsomoli 1, Tallinn (tel: 268-3559; fax: 268-3097).

State Chancellery, Lossi Plats 1a, Tallinn (tel: 231-6730; fax: 244-0372).

Swiss Baltic Re-Advisers, Lai 27, Tallinn (tel: 244-8949; fax: 274-6469).

Tallink, PO Box 3495, Tallinn (tel: 244-0770; fax: 244-5224).

Tallinn New Port, Maardu tee 57, Tallinn (tel: 223-6500, 223-4313; fax: 223-8805).

Tallinn Stock Exchange, Tallinn (tel: 244-1920; fax: 244-9382).

BNS (Baltic News Service): www.bns.ee

Delfi (in Estonian): www.delfi.ee

Internet sites

Estonia Business: http://www.ee/www/Business/welcome.html

Estonia Country Guide: http://www.ciesin.ee/estcg/

Estonia Investment: http://www.investinestonia.com

Ethiopia

KEY FACTS

Official name: Ityopia (Federal Democratic Republic of Ethiopia)

Head of State: President Mulatu Teshome (elected by parliament 7 Oct 2013)

Head of government: Prime Minister Hailemariam Desalegn (from 22 Aug 2012)

Ruling party: Coalition Ethiopian People's Revolutionary Democratic Front (EPRDF), an alliance of the Tigray People's Liberation Front (TPLF), the South Ethiopian Peoples' Democratic Movement (SEPDM), the Amhara National Democratic Movement (ANDM), and Oromo People's Democratic Organization (OPDO) (from 1991, elected 1995, re-elected 2015)

Area: 1,251,282 square km

Population: 90.98 million (2014)*

Capital: Addis Ababa

Official language: Amharic

Currency: Birr (Birr) = 100 cents

Exchange rate: Birr20.87 per US$ (Sep 2015)

GDP per capita: US$575 (2014)*

GDP real growth: 10.35% (2014)

GDP: US$52.34 billion (2014)

Inflation: 7.38% (2014)

Balance of trade: -US$7.29 billion (2012)

* estimated figure

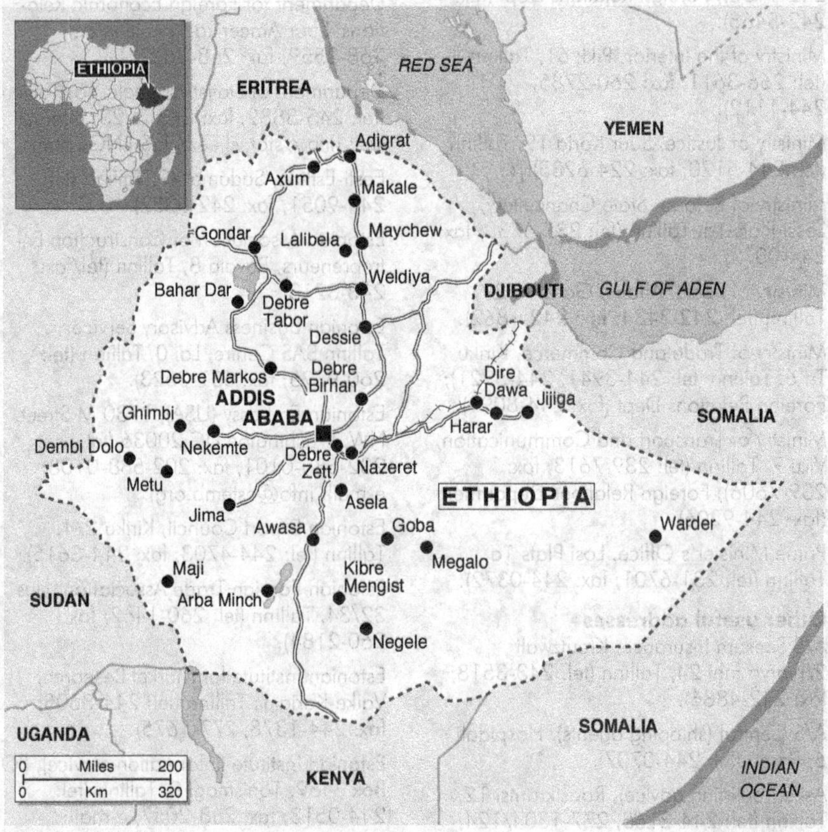

The ruling party, Ethiopian People's Revolutionary Democratic Front (EPRDF) and its allies achieved an overwhelming victory in the May 2015 general election, winning all 546 parliamentary seats. Prime Minister Hailemariam Desalegn's landslide victory stripped the opposition of the one seat it held in the outgoing chamber according to the chairman of the electoral board.

The EPRDF has been in power in Africa's second-most populous country for over two decades, however, some critics dismissed the most recent results. Taye Negussie, a sociology professor at Addis Ababa University claimed 'This result was completely expected, there is no multi-party system in Ethiopia. It's just fake'. Following the death of former Prime Minister Meles Zenawi in 2012, his successor Hailemariam claimed he was committed to opening up the country's political system to allow more space for other parties. Despite this, rights groups continually criticise the EPRDF of silencing opposition supporters and journalists, as well as manipulating anti-terrorism laws to incarcerate critics. The European Union (EU) has said that true democracy has yet to take root in Ethiopia. The US has also stated that it was 'deeply concerned by continued restrictions on civil society, media, opposition parties, and independent voices and views'. However, in late July 2015, President Barack Obama became the first sitting US president to visit Ethiopia, where he praised the country's role in fighting Al-Shabab militants in Somalia.

Since 1984, when the country's famine triggered a worldwide fundraising effort, Ethiopia has been experiencing near double-digit economic growth as well as large investments in infrastructure, establishing it as one of Africa's top-performing economies and a prime destination for foreign investment. Just over thirty years later the UN confirmed that the failure of the rains in 2015 were as severe as the failure of the rains in 1984. However the government in late 2015 was in a much stronger position than it was in the earlier drought, and it wasn't fighting a war to stop Eritrea from breaking away, a war that was draining the country's coffers. The aid agencies warned in November that emergency food supplies would be needed before the end of the year.

The names of the Oromo Liberation Front and Ginbot 7 are hardly internationally familiar – but in Ethiopia the names mean a lot. According to an article in the London *Economist*, the first is a rebel organisation that is pushing for a better political deal for Ethiopia's Oromo, an ethnic group that also inhabit northern Kenya and parts of Somalia. With some 30 million members, they constitute the single largest ethnic grouping in Ethiopia, accounting for some 35 per cent of the population according to the 2007 census. The Ginbot 7 website describes itself as a movement for Justice, Freedom and Democracy that 'envisions the creation of a nation wherein each and every Ethiopian enjoys the full respect of its democratic and human rights, achieves economic prosperity and social justice, and the respect of the citizen's life, safety and human dignity.' The organisation's 'primary mission' is 'the realisation of a national political system in which government power and political authority is assumed through peaceful and democratic process based on the free will and choice of citizens of the country.'

Since April 2014 Ethiopia has held on trial ten journalists and bloggers, accused of contravening the country's all encompassing anti-terrorism legislation. The *Economist* reported that those accused had links to one or both of the rebel groups. One of those arrested was, again according to the *Economist*, Andargachew Tsigie, the exiled secretary general of Ginbot 7. Mr Tsigie had already been sentenced to death (twice) by the Ethiopian courts. Following the April arrests, the Ethiopian authorities widened their net, issuing new charges against a newspaper and five magazines as well as their publishers. The *Economist* report attributed the government's nervousness to the advent of Ethiopia's 2015 general election.

Ethiopia is the second most populous country in sub-Saharan Africa. One of the world's oldest continuous civilizations, it is also one of the world's poorest – the annual per capita gross domestic product (GDP) of less than US$200 is only about a fifth of the sub-Saharan average, although even this comparison is distorted by the more developed countries in the region, such as South Africa. Ethiopia's poverty-stricken economy is based on agriculture, which accounts for nearly half of GDP, 60 per cent of exports, and 80 per cent of total employment. The agricultural sector suffers from frequent droughts and poor cultivation practices. Coffee is critical to the Ethiopian economy, but historically low prices have seen many farmers switching to qat (a mildly narcotic leaf) to supplement their income.

The economy

The International Monetary Fund ranks Ethiopia as one of the world's five fastest growing economies. In 2014, following a decade of growth averaging 10.8 per cent annually, the economy expanded by 10.3 per cent. In its African Economic Outlook (AEO) report, the African Development Bank (AfDB) stated that every major sector performed well in the 2013/14 fiscal year. Agriculture grew by 5.4 per cent, industry grew by 21.2 per cent and services rose by 11.9 per cent. The AfDB expects this trend to continue over the following two years, however, it notes that private sector development constraints could decelerate the momentum.

The slowdown in global commodity prices, the government's use of a tight monetary policy and using base money as a nominal anchor helped to bring the inflation rate down from 39.2 per cent in 2011 to 7.1 per cent by the end of 2014. According to the AfDB, fiscal policy has been focused on strengthening domestic resource mobilisation, and reducing domestic borrowing with the goal of maintaining macroeconomic stability. The fiscal deficit was contained to 2.6 per cent of GDP in 2013/14, thanks to a strong fiscal stance.

The AEO report went on the state merchandise exports expanded in value by 5.6 per cent in 2013/14 and reached US$3.25 billion, despite dropping in GDP share from 6.5 to 5.9 per cent year-on-year. Imports are mainly sourced from Europe and Asia, and grew to 19.1 per cent to US$13.7 billion in 2014, which worsened the trade deficit (from US$8.4 billion to US$10.5 billion). A good performance on other accounts, including non-factor services, private transfers and a surplus in the capital account, has however contained the effect on the overall balance of payments.

The AfDB concluded the report by mentioning that despite debt as a percentage of GDP increasing in 2014, the country presents a low risk of debt distress. However, the country is challenged with rebuilding its foreign exchange reserves, as they have fallen to less than two months' import cover.

Risk assessment

Politics	Fair
Economy	Good
Regional stability	Fair

COUNTRY PROFILE

100 BC A kingdom including part of modern-day Ethiopia existed around Axum.
450 AD The kingdom converted to Christianity and the Ethiopian church became part of the Coptic community.
1896 Italy tried to seize Ethiopia but lost the Battle of Adwa. The Italians held on to Eritrea on the Red Sea coast.
1916 Ras Tafari, later known as Emperor Haile Selassie, gained power over local lords but his appeal to the League of

KEY INDICATORS — Ethiopia

	Unit	2011	2012	2013	2014	**2015
Population	m	*86.83	*86.77	*88.85	*90.98	*92.98
Gross domestic product (GDP)	US$bn	31.30	42.52	46.64	52.34	*57.56
GDP per capita	US$	360	490	*525	*575	*619
GDP real growth	%	7.5	8.5	9.8	10.3	*8.6
Inflation	%	18.1	24.1	8.1	7.4	*6.8
Exports (fob) (goods)	US$m	3,029.0	3,258.0	–	–	–
Imports (fob) (goods)	US$m	8,328.9	10,547.3	–	–	–
Balance of trade	US$m	-5,299.8	-7,289.3	–	–	–
Current account	US$m	201.0	-2,757.0	-2,821.0	*-4,704.0	*-3,781.0
Exchange rate	per US$	16.75	18.08	19.16	20.20	–

* estimated figure ** forecast figure

Nations for help against the occupying Italians went unheeded.
1936 Benito Mussolini's Fascist Italian army invaded Ethiopia, which became part of Italian East Africa. Haile Selassie went into exile in Bath, England.
1941 British and Commonwealth troops along with the *Arbegnoch* (patriots), Ethiopian resistance fighters battled the Italian occupiers. Emperor Haile Selassie returned to Addis Ababa on 5 May 1941.
1962 Eritrea was annexed by Ethiopia.
1974 Haile Selassie was deposed in coup led by Teferi Benti.
1975 Haile Selassie died in custody.
1977 Benti was killed and replaced by Colonel Mengistu Haile Mariam, who led a brutal regime known as the Dergue. At least 100,000 opponents or critics were killed.
1977 Somalia tried to annex part of Ethiopia's Ogaden region, where most people are ethnic Somalis. Cuban and Soviet troops and tanks assisted Ethiopia in repelling the Somali invasion.
1984 Drought led to a famine in which as many as one million people may have died.
1987 A Soviet-style constitution was adopted and the People's Democratic Republic of Ethiopia was formed. The regime was supported by the Soviet Union.
1991 Rebellions in Eritrea, led by the leftist Eritrean People's Liberation Front (EPLF) and, in Tigray province, by the Tigray People's Liberation Front (TPLF) ensued. Mengistu fled to Zimbabwe as the EPLF took control of Eritrea and a TPLF-led coalition, the Ethiopian People's Revolutionary Democratic Front (EPRDF), led by Meles Zenawi, who became president in a transitional government.
1995 A general election was won by the EPRDF. The country was officially renamed the Federal Democratic Republic of Ethiopia. Negaso Gidada became titular president; Meles Zenawi took up the post of prime minister.
1998 Border disputes resulted in Eritrea and Ethiopia resuming full-scale fighting in mid-year and sporadic clashes thereafter.
1999 Eritrea refused to withdraw from the disputed Badme area and armed conflict ensued.
2000 Former head of state, Haile Selassie was buried in Trinity Cathedral, Addis Ababa. The EPRDF parties won the legislative elections. UN Mission in Ethiopia and Eritrea (UNMEE) peacekeepers opened a 1,000km cease-fire buffer zone between Ethiopia and Eritrea after the two countries signed a peace deal in Algiers, ending the two-year war.
2001 President Gidada quit the ruling coalition but finished his term in office. Girma Wolde Giorgise was elected, by parliament, to the largely ceremonial position of president.
2002 Eritrea and Ethiopia accepted a ruling by the international Boundary Commission in The Hague on their border dispute and a new 1,000km frontier was established. Ethiopia, ravaged by drought, requested food aid for nearly six million people.
2004 A resettlement programme started to move over two million people away from parched, over-worked highlands to the pastoral, but disease rife plains of south-west Ethiopia. Long-term drought in Afar region resulted in over 350,000 people needing food aid, when livestock deaths became widespread.
2005 The ruling EPRDF and its allies won disputed parliamentary elections; Meles Zenawi was elected prime minister. The independent commission at the Permanent Court of Arbitration in The Hague, set up as part of the peace deal signed in Algiers in 2000 between Eritrea and Ethiopia, ruled that Eritrea had launched unlawful attacks against Ethiopia in 1998, thereby triggering the border war between the two countries. The Ethiopian government said that it would lodge a claim for compensation. Donors put on hold US$375 million of budget support because of a government crackdown on opposition supporters.
2006 A new Alliance for Freedom and Democracy was formed by several opposition parties and rebel groups. Ethiopian troops intervened in Somalia to support the transitional government against Islamist militia forces. Ethiopia, together with Eritrea, rejected international proposals to settle their continuing border dispute.
2007 A limited census was undertaken; it did not include populations in Afar and Somali which were due to be recorded separately at a later date. Ethiopia, which uses the Coptic calendar of 13 months and is seven years later than the Gregorian calendar, celebrated its millennium. Parliament re-elected President Giorgise. Talks on an Ethiopia and Eritrea border agreement reached an impasse. The Ethiopia-Eritrea Border Commission duly considered the border it drew in 2006 to be binding. While Ethiopia and Eritrea accepted the ruling neither attempted to implement its recommendation; the 1,700 United Nations Mission in Ethiopia and Eritrea (UNMEE) peace-keeping troops remained in the area in a notional demilitarised zone.
2008 Ethiopia severed diplomatic ties with Qatar because of 'its hostility to Ethiopia' and the *Al Jazeera* media coverage of Ethiopian affairs. The UN Security Council terminated the UNMEE mandate. A new national coffee exchange was established in Addis Ababa. Ethiopia is Africa's largest coffee producer. Ethiopia consolidated its coffee collection and sales to increase quality and pay farmers a better return on their crop.
2009 Ethiopia began withdrawing its troops from Somalia.
2010 Israel restarted the immigration scheme for Ethiopians of Jewish descent after halting it in 2008. Members of the Falash Mura community, who had been pressurised into converting to Christianity in the nineteenth century and the last remaining Jewish community in Ethiopia, trace their roots back to King Solomon. Some 20,000 Ethiopians had been admitted in 2003. In parliamentary elections held on 23 May the EPRDF won 59.8 per cent of the vote (327 seats out of 547), which, coupled with seats won by its allies, gave the ruling party 499 seats out of 547; opposition parties won only two seats. The opposition rejected the results as 'completely fraudulent'. International observers claimed that government intimidation of voters for a period of months before the election had influenced the outcome, although voting on the day remained 'peaceful and calm' and the AU declared that the elections were 'free and fair' and had met all AU election standards. Opposition leader, Birtukan Mideksa, was released after serving five years of a life sentence.
2011 In February the UN World Food Programme (WFP) appealed for US$226.5 million in relief funds as the worst drought for over 50 years, resulting in ruined crops and the death of herds, and threatening 1.3 million southern Ethiopians with severe hunger. In May, the consumer price index (CPI) for food increased by over 40 per cent. In June, the UN estimated that 10 million people in the Horn of Africa were affected by severe food insecurity. In July the WFP increased its appeal for US$477 million to cope with the developing disaster as food aid was scaled up. Refugees for Somalia added to Ethiopia's food supply problems as thousands crossed the border to find relief from the famine.
2012 On 17 January, five European tourists were killed, two seriously injured and four kidnapped in Ethiopia's Afar region (close to the border with Eritrea). Ethiopia held Eritrea responsible for the attack as the kidnap victims were taken into Eritrea. On 15 March, Ethiopian military forces crossed into Eritrea in retaliation for earlier border incursions. Ethiopia said that it had attacked three military bases where militants were being trained. Eritrean minister of information, Ali Abdu, announced that Eritrea would not retaliate for the cross-border incursion. Prime Minister Meles Zenawi died in hospital in Belgium

on 18 July, having received treatment for a stomach ailment. Hailemariam Desalegn became acting prime minister on 20 August and then confirmed into the post on 21 September.
2013 The government stopped a demonstration taking place by opposition party Semayawi (Blue). The party leader, Yilekal Getachew, said that several hundred protestors had been arrested, and some beaten severely. Mulatu Teshome was elected president on 7 October. The vote was unanimous. On 24 October the state-run Erta news agency announced the government was banning travel overseas for work. As many as 23,000 Ethiopians without current work permits are said to have surrendered to the authorities in Saudi Arabia.
2014 Drought was again threatening food supplies in Ethiopia in mid-2014. The UN estimated that some 10 million people were at risk and in need of emergency supplies.
2015 Parliamentary elections wete held on 24 May. The result was a win for the Ethiopian People's Revolutionary Democratic Front (EPRDF) (coalition of four political parties) 500 seats (out of 547). The Somali People's Democratic Party (SPDP) 24 seats, were runners up. An urban commuter rail service was launched in Addis Ababa on 20 September 2015. It cost US$470 million and is said to be the first fully electrified rail system in Africa south of the Sahara.

Political structure

Constitution

A constitution was adopted 8 December 1994 which established a federal system of government. The constitution formally came into force in August 1995 when the Federal Democratic Republic of Ethiopia was proclaimed.
Ethiopia comprises 11 semi-autonomous administrative regions organised loosely along major ethnic lines.

Form of state

Federal democratic republic

The executive

The role of president is largely a figurehead position. The prime minister, who is elected by parliament for a five-year term, holds executive power.
The president is elected by a joint session of the upper house and lower house of parliament for a six-year term.

National legislature

The bicameral Federal Parliamentary Assembly consists of the Yehizbtewekayoch Mekir Bet (Council of People's Representatives) with 547 members, elected for a five-year term in single-seat constituencies, of which 22 are reserved for representatives of minority peoples, and the Yefedereshn Mekir Bet (Council of the Federation) with 117 members, elected by subordinate assemblies, of which 22 represent each of the designates minority nationalities and the remainder representatives of the professional sector and any other interests so designated.

Last elections

24 May 2015 (parliamentary); 7 October 2013 (presidential)
Results: Presidential: Mulatu Teshome was elected unanimously by parliament on 7 October 2013.
Parliamentary: the Ethiopian People's Revolutionary Democratic Front (EPRDF) (coalition of four political parties) 500 seats (out of 547), The Somali People's Democratic Party (SPDP) 24 seats, The Bensishangul Gamuz People's Democratic Party (BGPDP) 9 seats, The Afar National Democratic Party (ANDP), The Gambela People's Unity Democratic Movement (GPUDM), The Harari National League (HNL) 1 seat, The Argoba People Democratic Organization (APDO) 1 seat

Next elections

2020 (parliamentary); 2019 (presidential)

Political parties

Ruling party

Coalition Ethiopian People's Revolutionary Democratic Front (EPRDF), an alliance of the Tigray People's Liberation Front (TPLF), the South Ethiopian Peoples' Democratic Front (SEPDF), the Amhara National Democratic Movement (ANDM), and Oromo People's Democratic Movement (OPDM) (from 1991, elected 1995, re-elected 2010)

Main opposition party

No effective opposition party exists in parliament, the last remaining seat held by an opposition party was lost in the 2015 election.

Population

88.85 million (2013)* Ethiopia is the third most populous country in Africa. About 46 per cent of the population is under 14 years; 51 per cent 15–64; 3 per cent over 65.
Last census: 28 May 2007: 73,918,505. The country's third national census was taken over a nine-day period and cost US$45.7 million.
Population density: 49.9 inhabitants per square km. Urban population 17 per cent (2010 Unicef).
Annual growth rate: 2.7 per cent, 1990–2010 (Unicef).

Internally Displaced Persons (IDP)

132,000 (UNHCR 2004)

Ethnic make-up

Oromo (40 per cent), Amhara and Tigrayan (32 per cent), Sidamo (9 per cent), Shankella (6 per cent), Somali (6 per cent), Afar (4 per cent), Gurage (2 per cent).

Religions

The Ethiopian Coptic Church is influential, particularly in the north. There is a large Muslim community in the south, made up mainly of Arabs, Somalis and Oromos. Ethiopian Orthodox (40 per cent), Muslim (40 per cent), animist and other (20 per cent).

Education

Ethiopia has one of the world's lowest school enrolment rates. The government aims to enrol 5.3 million children in primary schools by 2005. The pattern of enrolment shows large gender gaps with girls being more likely to drop out in the early stages. Oxfam estimates that fewer than one-third of boys and one-tenth of girls aged 6—11 start school and one quarter of these drop out during the first two grades. Female literacy rates are only 32 per cent and girls of primary school age work 14—16 hours a day on a variety of tasks, either helping out at home or earning an income. In regions where tuition fees have been abolished, school enrolment has increased by up to 20 per cent.
In secondary schools, English has replaced Amharic as the medium of instruction, although several local languages are also used.
Literacy rate: 42 per cent adult rate; 57 per cent youth rate (15–24) (Unesco 2005).
Pupils per teacher: 43 in primary schools.

Health

The government aimed at reorganising health services through a twenty-year health development strategy, with a series of five-year investment programmes; the second phase began in 2003. The system provides access to health services for only about half of the population, mainly in the urban areas. Estimates suggests that 24 per cent and 15 per cent of the population respectively had access to improved water and sanitation facilities.
In 2005 the World Health Organisation – Global Polio Eradication Initiative (WHO – Polio Eradication) launched an Africa-wide mass polio immunisation programme, this coincided with the first case of the desease reported in Ethiopia in four years; its re-emergence was due to infected travellers. In a synchronised campaign with Somalia and Kenya, inoculation began for under fives by WHO – Polio Eradication and the country's health authorities in 2006.

HIV/Aids

There were 1.4 million people HIV positive in 2003, of which 770,000 were women, plus 120,000 children were HIV positive and 720,000 children were made

orphans. There were 120,000 deaths due to aids in 2003.
The loss in annual GDP growth per capita was projected to be 0.6 per cent between 2002–10 due to the impact of the disease.
In Addis Ababa the prevalence rate of HIV/Aids has been falling from a high of 24 per cent in 1995 to 11 per cent in 2004.
HIV prevalence: 4.4 per cent aged 15–49 in 2003 (World Bank)
Life expectancy: 50 years, 2004 (WHO 2006)
Fertility rate/Maternal mortality rate: 4.2 births per woman, 2010 (Unicef); maternal mortality 18 per 1,000 live births (World Bank).
Child (under 5 years) mortality rate (per 1,000): 68 per 1,000 live births (WHO 2012); 47 per cent of children aged under five were malnourished (World Bank).
Head of population per physician: 0.03 physicians per 1,000 people, 2003 (WHO 2006)

Welfare
Ethiopia is one of the poorest countries in the world, with annual income per capita below US$100. Following the end of the border conflict with Eritrea in 2000, the government of Ethiopia started to implement an ambitious adjustment and reform programme and renewed its commitment to poverty reduction.

Main cities
Addis Ababa (capital, estimated population 3.5 million in 2012), Dire Dawa (355,641), Nazret (299,621), Gondar (252,537), Mek'ele (219,818), Desé (219,423), Bahir Dar (218,429), Jimma (207,573), Debre Zeyit (171,115).

Languages spoken
Oromigna and Tigrigna are widely spoken. English is taught in schools; as well as Arabic, French and Italian, it is used in business circles and understood in most hotels and major towns. Over 80 local languages are also spoken.

Official language/s
Amharic

Media
Press
Newspaper circulation is limited to the urban literate. The government maintains a strict control over journalists and many are in exile.
Dailies: In Amharic, *Addis Zemen* (www.ethpress.gov.et) is a state-owned, *Addis Admass* (www.addisadmass.com) is privately owned. In English, the *Ethiopian Herald* (www.ethpress.gov.et) is a state-owned, *The Africa Monitor (with The Daily Monitor, as an imprint) (www.theafricamonitor.com) is privately owned.*
Weeklies: There are a few magazines published in Amharic and English, including *Ethiopian Weekly Press Digest* and *The Sun*. There are many more online publications.
Business: In English, weekly publications include *Capital* (www.capitalethiopia.com) and *Addis Fortune* (www.addisfortune.com), both provide business news and features.

Broadcasting
The national broadcaster is the Ethiopian Radio and Television Agency (ERTA) (www.erta.gov.et).
Radio: Radio services are the main medium of mass communication and sources of news and information.
The government-owned Radio Ethiopia (www.angelfire.com/biz/radioethiopia) operates nationally over several AM frequencies in 11 languages including Amharic, Arabic, English, French and local languages.
The are just a few private, independent radio stations, including Radio Fanaa (www.radiofanaa.com) and Radio Jigjiga (www.radiojigjiga.com). External services include Voice of America (VOA). Ethiopia admitted jamming the Amharic broadcasts of VOA in March 2010.
Television: The state-controlled Ethiopian Television (www.erta.gov.et) is a monopoly, which broadcasts to most of the country via a microwave link-up. Foreign satellite services are available from Jump TV (www.jumptv.com).
Erta news agency, state-run
National news agency: Ethiopain News Agency
Other news agencies: AllAfrica: www.allafrica.com
The Reporter: http://en.ethiopianreporter.com
Walta Information Centre (WIC): www.waltainfo.com

Economy
The World Bank rates Ethiopia as a low-income economy, with agriculture as the principal component of the economy, constituting 47.7 per cent of GDP in 2014, and characterised as subsistence farming. Nevertheless, agriculture provides over 85 per cent of exports with its coffee and teas considered some of the best in the world. Ethiopia also exports spices, fruit, vegetables and flowers to Europe and other African countries. Ethiopia is one of the top ranked in Africa for livestock, with herds of mainly cattle, goats and sheep growing from 54.5 million in 1996 to over 103.5 million in 2013, with an average annual increment of 3.4 million. Ethiopia is Africa's largest coffee producer and it established a national coffee exchange in 2008, to consolidate its coffee collection and sales to increase quality and pay farmers a better return on the value of their crop. In 2014, coffee exports amounted to US$839 million.
The industrial sector, which constituted 10.4 per cent of GDP in 2014, is dominated by mining, with mineral reserves in iron ore, gold, platinum and copper that have yet to be fully exploited. Gold accounts for almost 100 per cent of mining exports.
The service sector accounts for 41.9 per cent of GDP, of which the greater part is government services. The tourist sector is still dependent on intrepid, self-reliant travellers who can provide for themselves, visiting world-renowned archaeological sites (the cradle of Mankind) and wildlife and game reserves. The private sector is mostly small-scale, informal and service-orientated.
The International Monetary Fund (IMF) has ranked Ethiopia as one of the five fastest growing economies in the world. The economy grew consecutively for ten years leading up to 2013, averaging an expansion in GDP of 10.8 per cent. In 2014 this rapid growth continued, posting a growth of 10.3 per cent. Each of the main sectors performed well in the fiscal year ending in July 2014; agriculture grew by 5.4 per cent, industry grew by 21.2 per cent and services expanded by 11.9 per cent.
Inflation has been a long-term problem, however, the government was able to achieve a drop in consumer price inflation from 39.2 per cent in 2011 down to a low of 5.4 per cent in October 2014, aided by the slowdown in global commodity prices. Despite these efforts, since the low in October 2014, inflation has been increasing and reached 11.6 per cent in August 2015.
Despite the success of its economy over the last decade, Ethiopia's performance and ranking according to the UN Human Development Index (HDI) over the same period did not move appreciably. In 2014 Ethiopia was ranked 173rd out of 186 countries for national development in health, education and income, and 88.3 per cent of the population experienced multidimensional poverty.
The Export and Import Bank of China has agreed to fund part of a massively ambitious 5,000km rail network starting out from Addis Ababa. Currently the only rail link is between Dire Dawa and Djibouti. The project involves two phases, the first the construction of five lines. It is estimated that the cost will be some US$336 million annually for five years, and will provide around 300,000 jobs.
The project was launched in 2010 by the Ethiopian Railway Corporation (ERC). The

railway is part of a five-year infrastructure expansion plan, coupled with a boost of 10,000MW of electricity to the current 2,000MW, to enhance Ethiopia's ability to gain growth from its productive potential. In 2015 the project was still on-going.

Remittances from migrant workers amounted to US$345 million (0.9 per cent of GDP) in 2010, which jumped to US$513 million in 2011 and even further to US$624 million in 2012 (1.4 per cent of GDP).

In August 2012, Ethiopia's long-serving leader, Prime Minister Meles Zenawi died and left a country with a strong GDP growth, but no obvious successor. However, the Deputy Prime Minister and Minister of Foreign Affairs under Zenawi - Hailemariam Desalegn – assumed the role in the same month.

External trade

Ethiopia is a member of the Common Market of Eastern and Southern Africa (Comesa), which in 2009 launched a customs union between all 19 member states. In 2009, Ethiopia became a member of the Comprehensive Africa Agriculture Development Programme (CAADP), which under the auspices of the African Union (AU) promotes economic growth through agricultural-led development, designed to eliminate hunger, reduce poverty and food insecurity and enable expansion of exports.

Ethiopia is the origin of the coffee plant, and coffee beans are still a major export product providing over 30 per cent of the country's foreign earnings (a fall from over 60 per cent in the mid-1990s due to a slump in world prices).Ethiopia is a member of the Common Market of Eastern and Southern Africa (Comesa), which in 2009 launched a customs union between all 19 member states. In 2009, Ethiopia became a member of the Comprehensive Africa Agriculture Development Programme (CAADP), which under the auspices of the African Union (AU) promotes economic growth through agricultural-led development, designed to eliminate hunger, reduce poverty and food insecurity and enable expansion of exports.

Ethiopia is the origin of the coffee plant, and coffee beans are still a major export product providing over 30 per cent of the country's foreign earnings (a fall from over 60 per cent in the mid-1990s due to a slump in world prices).

Imports

Principal imports are food and live animals, petroleum and petroleum products, chemicals, machinery, motor vehicles, cereals, textiles, semi-manufactured goods and fertilisers.

Main sources: China (19.2 per cent of total in 2014), United States (11.4 per cent), Saudi Arabia (6.7 per cent) and India (5 per cent).

Exports

Principal exports are coffee, khat, gold, leather products, live animals, oilseeds, marble and other minerals.

Main destinations: China (17.1 per cent of total in 2014), Germany (7.6 per cent), United States (7.2 per cent), Belgium (6.8 per cent) and Saudi Arabia (6.7 per cent).

Agriculture

Farming

The agricultural sector is the mainstay of the economy. Total agricultural land is 100 million hectares of which 20 per cent is pasture and 13.9 per cent arable and employs 77 per cent of the workforce.

Large parts of the country are affected by soil erosion. Intensive subsistence agriculture has depleted the soil and Ethiopia can no longer feed its population, even when the weather is good. Very little of the cultivated area is irrigated.

Ethiopia, as Africa's largest coffee producer, has benefited from rising coffee prices and the establishment of a national coffee exchange opened in 2008. It will consolidate coffee collection and sales to increase quality and pay farmers a better return on the value of their crop.

Other cash crops include cotton and sugar, as well as the mildly narcotic plant khat, which has a traditional market in the Middle East. The main food crops are maize, sorghum, wheat, barley, millet and teff.

Despite the insecurity and harassing from bandits, a booming trade in livestock has thrived for more than two decades along the borders between Somalia, Ethiopia and Kenya.

Forestry

Only 4 per cent of Ethiopia's land area is forested. Since the mid-1970s, there has been extensive deforestation with up to 75 per cent of forest cover cleared or degraded, according to the UN's Food and Agriculture Organisation (FAO). The overwhelming majority of timber production is used as domestic fuel. Ethiopia is also a world leading exporter of natural gum.

Industry and manufacturing

The industrial sector contributes 12.4 per cent of GDP and employs about 7 per cent of the workforce. Manufacturing of small handicrafts and other small industry sub-sectors make up around 7 per cent of GDP.

Industry is primarily based on the processing of agricultural raw materials. Principal among these is food processing, but textiles, handicrafts, and leather production are also significant.

Growth is constrained by a lack of raw materials, outdated machinery and techniques and the need for imports throughout the sector.

Tourism

The ancient culture of Ethiopia offers any visitor a variety of experiences, including natural sites such as the Simien National Park with its spectacular landscapes and rare animals. Historic and cultural sites include the classical ruins of Aksum, the fortress city of Fasil Ghebbi, the medieval monolithic cave churches of Lalibela and the archaeological site of Tiya. These and more are included on Unesco's World Heritage List.

The tourist sector had been left undeveloped during the 1970–80s with the lack of hotels and poor quality of roads hampering growth. From a low start, the contribution of travel and tourism to GDP almost doubled from 5.9 per cent (US$736 million) in 2005 to 10.5 per cent (US$1.6 billion) in 2006. Since then, the contribution remained above 10 per cent until 2014 when it dropped to 9.3 per cent (US$4.4 billion). Employment in the sector reflects the growth of tourism, with 9.1 per cent of the workforce (1.9 million jobs) in 2006, rising to 9.2 per cent (2.2 million jobs) in 2010 and dropping to 8.5 per cent by 2014 (2.3 million jobs).

A new Tourism Development Policy has been implemented to integrate policy and strategies for the key sectors. The national carrier, Ethiopian Airlines, Africa's most profitable airline, introduced new destinations within Africa while also expanding its European, North American and China services, using newly commissioned long-haul aircraft.

Not only is eco-tourism becoming a popular activity for visitors there has also been a growth in business and conference tourism. The new headquarters of the African Union was opened in Addis Ababa in January 2012.

Environment

In June 2010 the African Union backed a proposal to build the 'Great Green Wall' project, of a 15km wide, 7,775km long, continuous belt of trees from Senegal in the west to Djibouti in the east (traversing 11 countries) in an effort to halt the advance of the Sahara Desert. The trees to be used would be drought-adapted, preferably native to the area from a list of 37 possible species, and should help to slow soil erosion and filter rain water.

Mining

The mining sector accounts for around 5 per cent of GDP.

The government says there are at least 500 tonnes of proven gold reserves in the

country. Activity is limited to small-scale gold mining.
The country has substantial reserves of iron ore and untapped reserves of platinum, tantalum (used in the electronics industry), nickel, phosphate, diatomite, copper, zinc, soda ash and potash. Tantalum reserves are estimated at 25,000 tonnes at one site alone.
The output of non-metallic minerals such as limestone and marble has increased significantly.
A number of foreign mining companies have been awarded exploration concessions.

Hydrocarbons

Ethiopia does not produce oil, but there is considered to be commercial potential and foreign interest and investment in the sector is high. An exploration deal between the Ethiopian government and White Nile (UK) was signed in 2008, one of many inward investments into the oil industry. Ethiopia relies on imports of refined oil to meet energy requirements, which was 56,940 barrels per day (bpd) in 2013. Sudan became an important source of supplies, as shipment by tanker truck along a new road began.
A memorandum of understanding (MOU) was signed between South Sudan and Ethiopia on 10 February 2012, to build a new oil pipeline, taking South Sudanese oil through Ethiopia to the Ports of Lamu (Kenya) and Djibouti. Industry analysts consider that such a pipeline, of 1,000km through rugged terrain, with roving band of militia, could take up to three years to build at a cost of US$4 billion. On 2 March construction began on the US$23 billion port and oil refinery project in Lamu District, southern Kenya. The presidents of Kenya, South Sudan and Ethiopia were at the launching ceremony, amid tight security in an area close to the border with war-torn Somalia. The project, known as the Lamu Port South Sudan Ethiopia Transit Corridor (Lapsset), is due to be completed by 2016, with initial investment from all three countries, with plans to attract international investment. Lapsset will be one of Africa's largest civil engineering projects.
Natural gas reserves were 24.9 billion cubic metres in 2014.
Coal is not imported and any produced or used is commercially insignificant.

Energy

Ethiopia has 2,061MW installed electricity-generating capacity, of which 85 per cent is produced by hydropower. Full hydroelectricity potential is estimated at 45,000MW but the Ethiopian Electric Power Corporation (EEPCO), which is responsible for generating, distributing and sales of electricity, has only twelve hydropower stations. There are, nationally, 22 stations in total, mostly small diesel powered plants and one geothermal plant at Aluto Langano. Around 27 per cent of the population has access to electricity and EEPCO has electrified almost 2,000 towns and the programme is on going.
The joint Ethiopian-UAE, Grand Millennium Dam hydroelectric project, designed to regulate the flow of the Nile River and produce 5,000MW for export to neighbours, will not reduce the flow of water to Egypt, according to the Minister of Industry Tadesse Haile, in July 2011. The US$4.5 billion project, under construction since April 2011, should have a strong influence on Ethiopia's future economic prospects.

Financial markets

Commodity exchange

Ethiopia Commodity Exchange (ECX)

Banking and insurance

Central bank

National Bank of Ethiopia

Main financial centre

Addis Ababa

Time

GMT plus three hours
The Ethiopian day officially begins at 0600 (midnight elsewhere).

Geography

Ethiopia extends inland from the Red Sea coast of eastern Africa. The country has a long frontier with Somalia near the Horn of Africa. Sudan lies to the west, Djibouti to the east, Eritrea to the north and Kenya to the south.
The country is a high central plateau, at 1,800–3,000 metres above sea level which is dissected by the Great Rift Valley that runs diagonally across the country. The tallest peak is Mount Ras Dashen, at 4,620 metres in the Simien Mountains, in the rugged north. In the north-west the Blue Nile rises in Lake Tana. The landscape in the south is flatter and more suited to agriculture.

Climate

Dependent on altitude. Lowland regions are very hot and dry throughout the year. On the plateau (including Addis Ababa) dry season from October–May with temperature range from as low as 6 degrees Celsius (C) in December to 26 degrees C in March (light rain from February–April). Temperatures can fall sharply at night during the dry season. Rainy season from June–September with average temperature 21 degrees C.

Entry requirements

Passports

Required by all. Must be valid for at least six months.

Visa

Required by all. For business visas, an application should be accompanied by a letter from a sponsoring organisation or company. For those self-employed, a letter from a solicitor, accountant or business registration authority should suffice. Visas are usually issued for a one month period; heavy penalties may be imposed for unauthorised extensions. If necessary, contact the Immigration Office for an Alien's Registration Card and an exit visa. Visa application forms can be downloaded from a number of Ethiopian embassy websites (www.mfa.gov.et/Consular_Affair_Diplomatic/Consular_Affair.php).
An international certificate of vaccination against yellow fever is required when applying.
Foreign nationals are advised to register their arrival with the consular representative of their embassy.

Currency advice/regulations

Up to Birr100 can be imported, if a visitor has a re-entry permit Birr100 may be exported, or else local currency export is prohibited.
Unlimited foreign currency may be imported but it must be declared on arrival. Export of foreign currency is allowed up to the amount declared.
Travellers cheque are accepted and are best taken as either US dollars or pound sterling.

Customs

Skins, hides and any antique articles require an export certificate. Laptop computers must be declared upon arrival and departure. Tape recorders require special customs permits.

Health (for visitors)

Health facilities are extremely limited in Addis Ababa and inadequate outside the city. Travellers should bring their own prescription drugs and a doctor's note describing the medication. If the quantity of drugs exceeds that expected for personal use, a permit from the ministry of health is required.
The altitude in Addis Ababa may cause health problems.

Mandatory precautions

A yellow fever inoculation certificate.

Advisable precautions

Visitors should be in date for the following vaccinations: yellow fever, polio, typhoid, tetanus, hepatitis A and B, meningitis.
There is a rabies risk.
Malaria prophylaxis recommended before visiting the lowlands. There is no malaria risk in Addis Ababa.
Tap water must be treated as unsafe unless boiled and filtered (bottled water is available in the main cities). Eat only well cooked meals, preferably served hot;

vegetables should be cooked and fruit peeled. Dairy products are unpasteurised and should be avoided
A first aid kit that includes disposable syringes, is a reasonable precaution. Medical insurance is essential, including emergency evacuation, and an adequate supply of personal medicines is necessary.

Hotels

Hotels are available in Addis Ababa and other main centres. A service charge of 10 per cent and a tax of 2 per cent are added to bills but a small tip is usual in addition to the service charge. Payment is generally required in foreign currency.

Credit cards

Credit cards are accepted by airlines and the larger hotels only.

Public holidays (national)

Fixed dates

*7 Jan (Genna/Ethiopian Christmas Day), *19 Jan (Timket/Epiphany), 2 Mar (Victory of Adwa Day), 28 May (Downfall of the Dergue), *11 Sep (Enkutatash/New Year's Day), *26 Sep (Meskel/Finding of the True Cross).

Variable dates

*Ethiopian Good Friday, *Ethiopian Easter Day, Eid al Adha, Birth of the Prophet, Eid al Fitr.
* Coptic Christian feasts only.
Ethiopia follows the Julian calendar, instead of the Gregorian calendar, used in most other parts of the world. The Ethiopian calendar year is divided into 13 months: 12 months of 30 days each and one month of five days (six in a leap year). The Ethiopian year commences on 11 September and runs seven years and eight months behind the Gregorian calendar.
Islamic year 1437 (15 Oct 2015–2 Oct 2016):: The Islamic year contains 354 or 355 days, with the result that Muslim feasts advance by 10–12 days against the Gregorian calendar. Dates of feasts vary according to the sighting of the new moon, so cannot be forecast exactly.

Working hours

Banking

Mon–Thu: 0800–1500; Fri: 0800–1100, 1330–1500; Sat: 0830–1100.

Business

Mon–Thu: 0830–1230, 1330–1730; Fri: 0830–1130, 1330–1730. Most private businesses also work on Saturdays.

Government

Mon–Thu: 0830–1230, 1330–1730. Fri: 0830–1130, 1330–1730.

Shops

Mon–Sat: 0800–1300, 1400–2000. Local variations.

Telecommunications

Mobile/cell phones

A GSM 900 service is available in large cities and towns only.

Electricity supply

220V, 50 cycles AC. Plugs are of the two-pin variety.

Social customs/useful tips

Handshaking is the usual mode of greeting. The first name is followed by that of the father – there are no family names. The words Ato, Woizero and Woizrity are the equivalents of Mr, Mrs and Miss respectively, and should be used when addressing people.
Smoking is not popular among traditional people, or in front of priests. Dress should be modest. Shoes are removed on entering churches/mosques. Private formal entertaining is common in Addis Ababa, and cocktail parties are not uncommon.
Ethiopian law strictly prohibits the photographing of military installations, police/military personnel, industrial facilities, government buildings and infrastructure.

Security

Crime is an increasing problem in Addis Ababa. Normal precautions should be taken.
Exercise caution if travelling to the northern Tigray and Afar regions (within 50km of the Ethiopian/Eritrean border) because of landmines and unsettled conditions in the border area. Travel to the Ogaden Region is considered very dangerous and should not be attempted. Limit road travel outside major towns to daylight hours only.

Getting there

Air

National airline: Ethiopian Airlines
International airport/s: Addis Ababa-Bole International (ADD), 8km from city, bar, restaurant, bank, post office, shops, car hire.
Airport tax: International departures US$20 in cash and exact amount, excluding transit passengers.

Surface

Road: Entry by land into Ethiopia is possible, if difficult, via Dewale and Galafi (Ethiopia-Djibouti), Moyale (Ethiopia-Kenya), Humera and Metema (Ethiopia-Sudan), Jijiga (Ethiopia-Somalia). The road linking Nairobi and Addis Ababa forms part of the Trans-East African Highway.
Rail: The rail route from Djibouti to Addis Ababa is subject to disruption.
Water: Ethiopia has been landlocked since Eritrea gained independence.
Main port/s: Until the outbreak of hostilities with Eritrea in 1998, Ethiopia relied heavily on the Eritrean ports of Assab and Massawa. Djibouti has subsequently become Ethiopia's principal trading gateway.

Getting about

National transport

Air: Ethiopian Airlines operates domestic service to main towns.
Road: An all-weather road network connects principal towns. The road system is undergoing expansion.
There are border posts at Moyale on the Kenyan border, Adwa and Adigrat near the border with Eritrea, and Dewelle for Djibouti.
Roads are impassable to Lalibela from June to September.
Drivers bringing their own vehicles to Ethiopia will require a *carnet de passage*.
Buses: Coach services (liable to suspension) Addis Ababa-Gondar.
Rail: A line runs from Addis Ababa to Dire Dawa (and on to Djibouti). However, visitors are advised not to use this line for security reasons.

City transport

Taxis: In Addis Ababa, the National Tour Operations (NTO) provides taxis at the main hotels and the airport, although independent and communal cabs are available. It is advisable to check the fare and the destination before entering the cab. The most reliable taxis are available from the office of the Hilton Hotel. The taxi journey from the airport to the city centre takes about 30 minutes. Tipping is not usual.
Buses, trams & metro: Journey time from airport to city centre 30 minutes.
An urban commuter rail service was launched in Addis Ababa on 20 September 2015. It cost US$470 million and is said to be the first fully electrified rail system in Africa south of the Sahara.

Car hire

Car hire (with or without driver) is available in the main centres. A valid international driving licence is required. Traffic drives on the right.
Payment for car rental is generally required in foreign currency.

BUSINESS DIRECTORY

The addresses listed below are a selection only. While World of Information makes every endeavour to check these addresses, we cannot guarantee that changes have not been made, especially to telephone numbers and area codes. We would welcome any corrections.

Telephone area codes

The international dialling code (IDD) for Ethiopia is +251 followed by area code and subscriber's number.

Addis Ababa	11	Gondar	58
Awassa	46	Jimma	47
Bahir Dar	58	Mekelle	4
Dire Dawa	25	Nazareth	22

Chambers of Commerce

Addis Ababa Chamber of Commerce, PO Box 2458, Addis Ababa (tel: 515-055; fax: 511-479; e-mail: aachamber1@telecom.net.et).

Awassa Chamber of Commerce, PO Box 167, Awassa (tel: 200-375; fax: 205-197).

Bahir Dar Chamber of Commerce, PO Box 48, Bahir Dar (tel: 200-481; fax: 201-787).

Dire Dawa Chamber of Commerce, PO Box 198, Dire Dawa (tel: 113-082; fax 112-468; e-mail: luiji@telecom.net.et).

Ethiopian Chamber of Commerce, PO Box 517, Addis Ababa (tel: 518-240; fax: 517-699; e-mail: ethcham@telecom.net.et).

Gondar Chamber of Commerce, PO Box 50, Gondar (tel: 110-320; fax: 115-656).

Mekelle Chamber of Commerce, PO Box 503, Mekelle (tel: 402-529; fax: 408-914).

Nazareth Chamber of Commerce, PO Box 36, Nazareth (tel: 112-083; fax: 122-699).

Banking

Awash International Bank SC; PO Box 12638, Bole Road, Addis Ababa (tel: 614-482/83, 612-919; fax: 614-477).

Bank of Abyssinia SC; PO Box 12947, Addis Ababa (tel: 514-130, 514-752; fax: 511-575).

Commercial Bank of Ethiopia; PO Box 255, Unity Square, Addis Ababa (tel: 511-271, 515-004; fax: 514-522, 512-166).

Construction and Business Bank, PO Box 3480, Addis Ababa (tel: 512-300; fax: 515-103).

Dashen Bank SC; PO Box 12752, Garad Building, Debre Zeit Road, Addis Ababa (tel: 661-380, 655-525; fax: 661-640, 653-037).

Development Bank of Ethiopia, PO Box 1900, Josep Broz Tito, Addis Ababa (tel: 511-188; fax: 511-606).

Wegagen Bank SC; PO Box 1018, Addis Ababa (tel: 655-015; fax: 653-330).

Central bank

National Bank of Ethiopia, PO Box 5550, Addis Ababa, Ethiopia (tel: 517-430; fax: 514-588; email: nbe.excd@telecom.net.et; internet: www.nbe.gov.et).

Commodity exchange

Ethiopia Commodity Exchange (ECX), www.ecx.com.et

Travel information

Addis Ababa-Bole Airport, PO Box 978, Addis Ababa (tel: 180-455; fax: 612-533).

Antiquities Authority, National Museum of Ethiopia, PO Box 76, Addis Ababa (tel: 117-150; fax: 553-188).

Ethiopian Airlines, PO Box 1755, Bole International Airport, Addis Ababa (tel: 612-222; fax: 611-474); town office (tel: 517-000; fax: 611-474; internet: www.flyethiopian.com).

National Tour Operations (NTO), PO Box 5709, Addis Ababa (tel: 512-955; fax: 517-688).

National tourist organisation offices

Ethiopian Tourism Commission, PO Box 2183, Addis Ababa (tel: 517-470, 150-609, 513-962; fax: 513-899; internet: www.visitethiopia.com).

Other useful addresses

African Union, PO Box 3243, Addis Ababa (tel: 557-700; fax: 511-299).

British Embassy, Commercial Section, Fikre Mariam Abatechan Street, Addis Ababa (tel: 612-354; fax: 610-588).

Central Statistical Office, PO Box 1143, Addis Ababa (tel: 113-010).

Department of Immigration and Refugee Affairs, PO Box 5741, Addis Ababa (tel: 553-899).

Djibouti–Ethiopian Railway Corporation, PO Box 1051, Addis Ababa (tel: 517-250; fax: 513-533).

Ethiopian Customs Office, PO Box 3248, Addis Ababa (tel: 513-100; fax: 518-355).

Ethiopian Embassy (USA), 3506 International Drive, NW, Washington DC 20008 (tel: 202-364-1200; fax: 202-686-9551; e-mail: ethiopia@ethiopianembassy.org).

Ethiopian Investment Authority, PO Box 2313, Addis Ababa (tel: 510-033; 514-396).

Ethiopian Privatisation Agency, PO Box 11835, Ethiopian Investment Authority Building, Bole Road, Addis Ababa (tel: 521-833; fax: 513-955).

Ethiopian Private Industries' Association, PO Box 8739, Addis Ababa (tel: 512-384; fax: 552-633).

Ethiopian Television, PO Box 5554, Addis Ababa.

Ethiopian Tourist Trading Enterprise, PO Box 8640, Addis Ababa (tel: 612-277; fax: 610-500).

Maritime and Transit Services, PO Box 1186, Addis Ababa (tel: 510-666; fax: 514-097).

Ministry of Culture and Information, PO Box 1364, Addis Ababa (tel: 551-011; fax: 551-609).

Ministry of Economic Development & Co-operation, PO Box 2428, Addis Ababa (tel: 519-684; fax: 517-988).

Ministry of Foreign Affairs, PO Box 393, Addis Ababa (tel: 517-345; fax: 514-300).

Ministry of Trade and Industry, PO Box 2559, Addis Ababa (tel: 518-200; fax: 514-288).

Voice of Ethiopia, PO Box 1020, Addis Ababa.

Wildlife Conservation Department, PO Box 386, Addis Ababa (tel: 510-455; fax: 510-168).

National news agency: Ethiopain News Agency, PO Box 530 Addis Ababa (tel: 155-0011; fax: 155-1609; internet: www.ena.gov.et).

AllAfrica: www.allafrica.com

The Reporter: http://en.ethiopianreporter.com

Walta Information Centre (WIC): www.waltainfo.com

Internet sites

Africa Business Network: http://www.ifc.org/abn

AllAfrica.com: http://www.allafrica.com

African Development Bank: http://www.afdb.org

ENA - Ethiopian News Agency: http://www.telecom.net.et/~ena

Ethiopian Mission to the UN: http://www.undp.org/missions/ethiopia

Ethiopian Privatisation Agency: http://www.undp.org/missions/ethiopia

Mbendi AfroPaedia (information on companies, countries, industries and stock exchanges): http://mbendi.co.za

Falkland Islands/Islas Malvinas

In its annual report the Falkland Islands government stated that the gross domestic product (GDP), which is currently about £100 million (US$160 million) annually, enables the Falklands to be economically self sufficient in all areas but defence. The cost of defending the Islands is currently met by the British government and is estimated to amount to 0.177 per cent of the total UK defence budget annually. Beyond the cost of defence, the Falkland Islands do not receive any further financial assistance from the United Kingdom. Through the revenues received, the Falkland Islands government (FIG) maintains a balanced budget and provides a high standard of public services. Estimated Operating Expenditure for the 2011/12 Financial Year was £43 million (US$68.8 million), while it is estimated government Revenue for the same period was £46.5 million. The FIG reserves currently stand at some £200 million (US$3.2 million).

Defence

In early 2015 two Chinook helicopters were deployed by the UK government to the Falkland Islands to deter an increasingly belligerent government in Buenos Aires. Speaking in the House of Commons, the UK Defence Secretary, Michael Fallon, announced that the two transport aircraft would help bolster the defence of the islands amid Argentine rumblings of a second invasion. Mr Fallon said that the helicopters would enable the Islands' garrison to mount a 'swift and decisive response' to any 'incidents' and that the UK government was proceeding with an enhanced communications system at the military headquarters on Mount Pleasant as well as preparing plans to replace the Rapier air defence missiles when they are decommissioned in 2020. The Falkland Islands patrol ship, *HMS Clyde*, was also to be maintained. Mr Fallon closed by saying that 'We will continue to defend the right of the islanders and to maintain their way of life against whatever threats may arise.' The reported cost of the military enhancements amounted to some £180 million (roughly US$288 million) over a ten year period.

Febrile thinking?

The occasionally febrile Argentinian political thinking that had pervaded the Casa Rosada in late 2014 and the first few months of 2015 had one other consequence. The political conflict between Argentina and Great Britain over the future of the Falkland Islands was back at the top of the agenda, 33 years after the beginning of the war that saw 649 casualties and 1,300 wounded. Argentina's latest move was a legal attempt to prevent five oil companies, three of them British, from exploring for oil some 200 kilometres from the Falklands' shores. The legal move coincided with what turned out to be an unofficial visit to London by the Argentine Minister for Falklands' Affairs, Daniel Filmus. Stressing that Argentina had been a democracy since 1983 (in no small measure thanks to the Falklands defeat), Mr Filmus announced that the purpose of his visit was to gain British public support for Argentina – something of a lost cause since the Falklands continue to strike a very patriotic chord with most of the UK's population. Mr Filmus also referred to the revelations by the US analyst Edward Snowdon (who had taken refuge in Moscow) that the UK was spying on the Argentine government. This revelation hardly came as a surprise to British military analysts who since the 1982 invasion would have expected the UK to prefer low cost anticipation rather than expensive reaction as a military strategy.

Argentine concerns were inevitably heightened by the fact that the three British companies involved, Premier Oil, Falkland Oil and Gas and Rockhopper had chosen the anniversary of the 1982 Argentine invasion to announce that they had struck oil (See 'Energy' below). For her part, Argentine's President Kirchner speaking in the southerly port of Ushaia at a memorial service for Argentina's war dead, promised to seek legal redress and to raise the matter of 'British aggression' in international fora. This prompted the British government to summon the Argentine ambassador to the Foreign Office for an explanation.

KEY FACTS

Official name: Falkland Islands

Head of State: Queen Elizabeth II, represented by Governor Colin Roberts, CVO (from 29 Apr 2014)

Head of government: Chief Executive Keith Padgett (since 1 Feb 2012)

Area: 12,173 square km (including East and West Falkland and adjacent islands)

Population: 3,140 (2010)* (2,563; census figure 15 Apr 2012)

Capital: Stanley

Official language: English

Currency: Falkland pound (FI£) = 100 pence

Exchange rate: FI£0.65 per US$ (Sep 2015)

* estimated figure

The legal arguments

The legal arguments on both sides were set out on the US (Miami) based *PanamPostNews* website. Listing the points in favour of the Argentine case, the Argentine lawyer Eloisa Raya de Vera claimed numerous – if in some cases tenuous – grounds for the support of Argentina's sovereignty over the Falklands, the first of which were the original 'methods' of the acquisition of territory. This argument runs that the allocation of land in the Americas was originally conducted by the Papacy, which assigned to Spain title to all the new lands west of the meridian passing 100 leagues west of the Cape Verde Islands. This was done through papal bulls – *Inter caetera* and *Dudum siquidem* – in the fifteenth and sixteenth centuries. Following the Treaty of Tordesillas between Spain and Portugal, the dividing line was arbitrarily moved to the west.

According to Ms Raya de Vera, acquisition in international law outranks mere discovery and requires both settlement and permanent control. This line of thinking has it that although the first effective settlement was French (in 1764), facing claims from Spain, France returned the islands to Spain and the Spanish kingdom immediately sent a governor and built dwellings and a chapel. All the published documents of that time, according to the Argentine lawyer, provide evidence that the islands were discovered by Spanish sailors.

In something of a *non-sequitur*, Ms Raya de Vera asserts that 'derivative methods of territorial acquisition' are also part of the legal arguments that support Argentina's sovereignty over the Malvinas. This resorts to a feature of Roman law that has it that states that 'as you possess under law', is the underlying argument to define the borders of the independent states that succeeded the Spanish Empire. In the case of the Malvinas, it mysteriously justifies Argentina's as the successor of Spanish rule in the region. This claim is backed up (or not) under the terms of the Treaties of Versailles and the Pinckney Treaty, which also – rather absurdly – prohibited the British to sail in the South Atlantic.

In a further *non sequitur*, the author points out that as was clearly expressed in Argentina's 1964 Ruda Allegation, all of these arguments determine that the occupation conducted by Great Britain in 1833 in the Malvinas was: (1) illegal, because it violated the treaties and general principles of international law (2) resisted, first by Spain and then by Argentina making international protests (3) late, since it happened after the French and Spanish and (4) partial, as occupation was limited to the British settlement at Port Egmont. Argentina also resorts to what it calls the 'factual arguments' that the Malvinas are embedded in 'our' continental shelf and 'twinned' with its weather and geography. This rather haphazardly summarises Argentina's opposition to 'the illegitimate British occupation and its fallacious arguments – such as the right of the kelpers (the name used for the island's long term residents), to self-determination.'

Also in *PanamPost*, Rosario (Argentina) based academic Guillermina Sutter Schneider points out that the dispute over the Falkland Islands has lasted far longer than most people think. Ms Sutter notes that the issue has been manipulated very adeptly by contemporary Argentine politicians in order to hide the country's most important issues, such as poverty, inflation, corruption and the country's calamitous financial, economic and institutional situation. Ms Sutter goes back to the sixteenth century, when Amerigo Vespucci, at the service of Portugal, was the first to arrive in the islands. He was later followed by French, Spanish, British, German and Dutch explorers.

In 1833, Britain took possession of the archipelago, at the time notionally possessed by Argentina. Five years later, Juan Manuel de Rosas, through Manuel Moreno – who served as foreign minister in London – proposed the cancellation of a loan agreement with the British government, in exchange for conferring sovereignty over the islands.

Ms Sutter then takes something of a leap forward, to what she describes as the 'irresponsibility' of Argentina's military government, which caused the Falklands War to break out in 1982. One of the military *troika* ruling Argentina, General Galtieri embarked on a military adventure that had no objective other than to distract the population from Argentina's severe internal problems. The principal aim was one of distraction, the invasion was designed to arouse the xenophobic passions of the Argentine people. Little more than three months later, in June 1982, Argentine troops surrendered to the British. The final toll of the war was atrocious. Hundreds of soldiers from both sides lost their lives, many of them young Argentine conscripts.

The question can be asked: 'can sovereignty be reclaimed over something that was already lost?' Can Argentina's surrender to British troops be erased? Even if they were able to do this, it would be detrimental for the kelpers, most of whom support the archipelago remaining under British jurisdiction and many of whom remember the days of the invasion.

In a referendum held on the islands in 2013, with the presence of international observers, 1,513 people voted (in a turnout of over 90 per cent) to remain part of the United Kingdom – in contrast to just three votes against. Miss Sutter closes her piece by observing that 'Surely the desire of the individuals and the community to self-determination should prevail over the will of the state?'

Energy

As described above, the three oil companies had discovered a richer reservoir after drilling for some nine months. The operator of the project, Premier Oil, had had to lower its sights when it found finding a partner for the project difficult and at the same time, global oil prices had plummeted. It remains to be seen whether the new oil discoveries will turn out to be commercially viable. Refuting Argentine claims the FIG also said the Argentines had no case. 'We have the right to develop our economy, including the hydrocarbons industry and we are exercising that right,' said a spokesman, adding that 'It is worth remembering that it was the government of Argentina who walked away from working with the Falkland Islands on the development of a hydrocarbons industry some years ago.'

Risk assessment

Politics	Good
Economy	Good
Regional stability	Poor

COUNTRY PROFILE

1592 First sighted by English mariners (Captain John Davis in ship *Desire* – the motto of the islands became Desire the Right).

1690 The first landing was by British Captain John Strong in the ship, *Welfare*. The Falkland Islands were named after the then Treasurer of the Navy, Viscount Falkland.

1764 French settlement was recorded. The islands were named Les Malouines after the French town of St Malo, hence the Argentine name of Malvinas for the islands.

1765 Captain John Byron (British) took formal possession of the islands at Port Egmont.

1767 The French settlement was sold to Spain and named Puerto de la Soledad.
1770 The Spanish ousted the British from Port Egmont.
1771 The British garrison was re-established.
1774 The garrison was withdrawn, leaving a plaque 'as a mark of possession' and a flag 'left flying'.
1820 The flag of the United Provinces of La Plata (Spanish) was hoisted at Puerto de la Soledad.
1823 The governor of the islands was nominated by the United Provinces Government (but did not visit).
1824 A German merchant, Louis Vernet, was given land by grant of the Buenos Aires government and a settlement of mixed nationalities, over the next few years, was established at Puerto de la Soledad.
1828 Vernet was appointed governor by the United Provinces. He attempted to stop sealing operations by other nations.
1831 The US protested about these actions and sent *USS Lexington* to sack Puerto de la Soledad (with the US president's approval). The islands were again unpopulated.
1833 Port Louis (Puerto de la Soledad) was taken over by the British, asserting full rights under naval superintendents until 1842.
1842 The first British governor, Richard C Moody, took up residence.
1981 The Falkland Islands and its dependencies were designated as British Dependent Territories.
1982 Argentina invaded the Falkland Islands. The UK despatched a military force, composed of naval ships and troops. The UK recaptured the islands.
1983 The British Nationality (Falkland Islands) Act gave islanders full British citizenship.
1990s The UK and Argentina resumed diplomatic relations. Both sides agreed to a formula to protect their respective positions on sovereignty and maritime jurisdiction, while discussing other matters. The UN committee on decolonisation urged the UK and Argentina to negotiate an ending to the dispute. The UK remained adamant that the self-determination of Falkland Islanders was paramount. Argentina adopted a constitutional amendment asserting its sovereignty over the islands.
1999 In an effort to improve relations, Argentine nationals were allowed to visit the islands for the first time since 1982.
2001 The UK agreed to allow Argentinean private aircraft and shipping to visit the islands.
2002 The Falkland Islands and its dependencies were designated as a self-governing British Overseas Territories (BOT).
2003 The 33rd General Assembly of the Organisation of American States (OAS) passed a statement of support for Argentina's claim to the Falkland Islands. The OAS called on Britain and Argentina to resume negotiations over the South Atlantic archipelago as soon as possible.
2004 Relations between Argentina and the UK deteriorated as Argentina banned charter flights to and from the Falklands crossing its airspace, and an Argentinean ice breaker, the *Almirante Irizar*, began 'policing' a Falklands conservation zone by challenging fishing vessels, demanding details of their permits. Argentina also gave permission for Aerolineas Argentinas to begin direct flights to the Falkland Islands, without regard for any UK agreement.
2006 The BBC ceased its broadcasts to the Falklands Islands, after 62 years. Alan Huckle became governor.
2007 Argentina terminated a 1995 agreement with the UK on oil exploration in the vicinity of the Falkland Islands. An agreement with BHP Billiton for at least two exploration wells to be drilled by 2010 was signed.
2008 Dr Tim Thorogood became chief executive of the Falkland Islands. Following an Anglo-Argentine feasibility study, it was estimated that there were 20,000 unexploded ordinances (UXO) that had yet to be disarmed, and which 'would present significant technical challenges and risks'.
2009 Argentina laid claim to 1.7 million square kilometres of ocean, including the Falklands Islands and other island chains governed by the UK. Argentina passed the Falkland Islands, South Georgia and the South Sandwich Islands and the British law, which defined the southern-most Argentine province as Tierra del Fuego, Antarctica and the Southern Atlantic Islands, including the Falkland Islands and part of Antarctica. The law means Argentine local government could try and collect royalties from oil companies with offshore operations that had previously been levied by the Argentine federal government.
2010 Rockhopper Exploration announced that it had made a 'significant oil discovery'. In retaliation for the drilling, the Argentine government decreed that all vessels sailing to and from Argentina, the Falklands, South Georgia and South Sandwich Islands were first to request authorisation from the Argentine government. The UK responded with a note to Argentina's chargé d'affairs in London, pointing out that the UK considers that Argentine Presidential Decree 256/2010 and Disposition 14/2010 'are not complaint with International Law including the UN Convention on the Law of the Sea'. The note also reaffirmed British sovereignty over the Falklands and South Atlantic Islands, and stated it has 'no doubt that the surrounding maritime areas of the Falkland Islands, and South Georgia and the South Sandwich Islands are not Argentine jurisdictional waters'. The island government released its Economic Development Strategy for public consultation, in July. It aims for a sustainable financial future of the islands, ensuring employment, maximising income and facilitating growth, using private and public interests. Uruguay denied entry to *HMS Gloucester*, the frigate charged with guarding the Falklands. The frigate was en route to the Falklands and the captain had requested permission to take on fuel and provisions in Montevideo. Nigel Haywood was sworn in as governor. In his annual Christmas message Prime Minister Cameron assured the Falkland Islanders that there were '... no doubts whatsoever about the United Kingdom's sovereignty over the Falkland Islands; and there can and will be no negotiations on the sovereignty of the Islands unless you, the Falkland Islanders, want them.'
2011 The points system in the immigration policy for a permanent resident's permit was deemed to be too difficult to achieve and members of the legislative assembly (MLA) agreed to review and discuss altering the criteria used. In December, the Latin American trading bloc Mercosur approved a proposal by Argentina to deny access to members' ports of any ship flying the Falklands Islands' flag.
2012 On 18 January the UK's Prime Minister David Cameron accused Argentina of 'colonialism' when claiming continued sovereignty of the Falklands, and its demand for renewed talks on the future of the islands. The UK announced the deployment of *HMS Dauntless*, one of its new advanced Type-45 destroyers, to the South Atlantic region of the Falkland Islands on 31 January. On 1 February Keith Padgett became the Chief Executive. On 4 February Prince William (second in line to the UK throne) arrived in the Falklands Islands for a six-week rotation as a RAF search-and-rescue pilot. His arrival, and the warship's deployment, drew criticism from Argentina, which regarded them as acts of provocation by the UK as the 30th anniversary of the Falkland's war drew near. On 10 February Argentina submitted an official protest to the UN for what it called the UK's 'militarisation' of the seas around the islands. The UN General Secretary called on both parties to avoid 'escalation' in tensions. On 12 June, President Fernandez de Kirchner (Argentina) demanded that the UK enter negotiations over the sovereignty of the Falkland Islands (Las Malvinas), while addressing the UN Committee on

Decolonisation. Prime Minister Cameron (UK) responded on 13 June by saying there would be 'absolutely no negotiation' on sovereignty rights. Meanwhile the Falkland Islanders decided to conduct a referendum on their 'political status' in 2013. On 2 August Buenos Aires province, in a largely symbolic move, banned all British merchant ships passing to or from the Islands from using its ports. The move is to prevent Falklands' ships flying the British Red Ensign (instead of the Falklands' flag) from using the ports. On 19 October, Rockhopper Exploration announced a £600 million (US$965 million) co-operative deal with Premier Oil to undertake drilling in the Sea Lion prospect, with oil expected to flow by 2017. Sir Rex Hunt, the former governor of the Falklands Islands in post during the Argentine occupation, died on 12 November. On 22 December the appointment of Mr Colin Roberts CVO was announced as the next Governor of the Falkland Islands. He will take up his appointment in April 2014.

2013 A referendum held on 10 and 11 March on whether the Falklands should remain as a British Overseas Territory (BOT) was overwhelmingly won with 92 per cent voting to remain a BOT. Turnout was 99.7 per cent. In July the Falkland Islands were allocated US$5.2 million from the 10th Round of the European Development Fund to support economic development priorities. The funds will enable FIG to further develop its tourism and rural strategies. Also in July the Executive Council published its Hydrocarbon Development Policy Statement. At the core of the policy are robust regulations, supply chain support and the insurance of long-term benefits for Islanders. On 8 August Argentine President Fernandez restated Argentina's demand for sovereignty of the Falkland Islands when speaking at a UN Security Council (UNSC) meeting in New York. Argentina had became a non-permanent member of the UNSC in January. She reiterated her demand that UN Resolution 2065 should be observed and that both parties should 'sit down and discuss' the issue. The UK says there is nothing to discuss since the Islands had voted overwhelmingly in a referendum in March to remain British. Admiral Sir Sandy Woodward who commanded Britain's task force sent by then prime minister, Margaret Thatcher, to retake the Falklands in 1982, died on 5 August. In December the European Commission announced an allocation of €5.9million (US$7.9 million) to support economic development activities over 2014–20.

2014 A poll carried out by *The Telegraph*, a London daily, in early January appeared to show a majority in favour of Argentine rule for the Falklands (74 per cent of the total 26,434 votes cast to 24 per cent for the UK). Analysis of the voters, however, showed that some 66 per cent of the votes came from Argentina after a social media campaign and of these 97 per cent voted for Argentine rule. Of the votes cast in the UK 93 per cent voted in favour of UK rule. In the Falkland Islands themselves 21of the 22 votes were in favour of remaining British. Mr Colin Roberts, CVO was sworn in as Governor on 29 April. The postal service was privatised on 1 August when Falklands Post Service Ltd took over the running of both the Post Office and the Philatelic Bureau.

2015 In March the British government announced it would 'beef up' the defences of the Falkland Islands after reports of an increased risk of invasion by Argentina.

Political structure

Constitution

The original constitution, which dated from 1985, with amendments in 1997 and 1998, was replaced by a new constitution in January 2009. The islander's rights to self-determination are prescribed. The operations of the Governor and Executive and Legislative Councils are mandated under the constitution. The first chapter enshrines the Falkland Islanders's right to self-determination in accordance with the United Nations Charter, although Argentina has never accepted the principle as applying to the Falkland Islands. Defence and foreign affairs are the responsibility of the UK government.

Form of state

Overseas territory of the United Kingdom

The executive

Supreme authority is vested in the British monarch and exercised by the governor with the advice and assistance of the Executive and Legislative Councils.

The governor presides over a five-member Executive Council (three elected and two *ex-officio* members). The governor is obliged to consult the Executive Council, except for defence and security issues (when the Commander of the British Forces in the islands advises and directs). If the governor opposes the Executive Council an immediate report must be presented to the UK government in explanation. The governor is responsible for external affairs and the public service.

National legislature

The Legislative Council is composed of eight members (three from Camp (countryside) constituency and five from the Stanley constituency) elected by universal adult suffrage and two *ex-officio* members – the chief executive and the financial secretary. The council has a substantial measure of responsibility for the island's affairs.

Legal system

English common law

Last elections

7 November 2013 (legislative council); 10 and 11 March 2013 referendum on whether the Falklands should remain as a British Overseas Territory (BOT).

Results: Legislative council: eight out of the ten seats were filled by election of non-partisan candidates, the remaining places being filled by ex-officio members. Referendum (2013) 92 per cent voted to remain a BOT. Turnout was 99.7 per cent.

Next elections

November 2017 (legislative council)

Political parties

Ruling party

Members of the Legislative Assembly are elected as independents.

Main opposition party

There is no formal opposition.

Political situation

Along with all other British Overseas Territories, a new constitution, proposed by the UK government, was agreed by the Falkland Islanders in 2008. The UK government was keen to see all of its territories take more responsibility for themselves, while maintaining implacable support for Falkland Islands' self-determination in the face of Argentina's adamant refusal to give up any part of its claim on the Falkland Islands.

The islands are prospering with the growth in tourism, a low unemployment rate and the continued quartering of military staff. In 2010, oil and gas exploration was underway and in May Rockhopper Exploration announced that it had made a 'significant oil discovery' offshore. On 9 July, the island government released its *Economic Development Strategy*, for public consultation. It set out the aims for the economic and sustainable financial future of the islands, ensuring employment, maximising income and facilitating growth, using private and public interests.

Population

3,140 (2010)*

Last census: (2,563; census figure 15 Apr 2012)

Population density: 4.8 inhabitants per square km.

Annual growth rate: 1.1 per cent (2003)

Ethnic make-up

White, almost exclusively of British descent. Workers from St Helena make up about 10 per cent of the population.

Religions

Anglican, Roman Catholic, United Free Church, Evangelist Church, Jehovah's Witnesses, Lutheran, Seventh-Day Adventist.

Main cities

Stanley (capital, estimated population 2,279 in 2012); Goose Green (68), Port Howard (34), Grytviken (20).

Languages spoken

Official language/s

English

Media

Press

The two weekly newspapers are *Teaberry Express* (www.falklandnews.com) and *Penguin News* (www.penguin-news.com). Official announcements and government directives are published in periodic publications of *The Falkland Islands Gazette*. The Falkland Islands News Area Network (www.falklandnews.com) provides a news agency service covering local headlines and from other regional newspapers such as *SAFIN Magazine*, *St Helena News*, *The Islander Newspaper* and the *Antarctic Sentinel*.

Broadcasting

Radio: The Falkland Islands Broadcasting Service and British Forces Broadcasting Service operate a local radio station and provide 24 hours/day listening on FM and MW. Satellite radio services are also available.

Television: Apart from the BFBS which provides satellite and cable TV services primarily for the military personnel stationed on the islands, KTV (www.ktv.co.fk) also operates a satellite service which distributes nine channels including BBC, CNN, TNT and HBO. Falkland Islands Television Limited (FITV) was set up in 2010 to broadcast locally produced news programmes.

Economy

The Falkland Islands are self-financing with an economy largely dependent on tourism and agriculture, of which fisheries are the main sector. The sale of fishing licences to foreign trawlers typically generates over £40 million (around US$70 million) and tourism around £5 million (US$8.8 million) annually. The most lucrative seafood is the *Illex argentinus* (Argentine shortfin squid). Around 74 per cent of all exports are destined for Spain, and the same percentage of imports come from the UK.

The Falkland Islands Development Corporation (FIDC) is keen to enhance the island's development prospects through a National Aquaculture Strategy. After fishing, wool is the largest component of farming income. High quality wool is exported to the UK while FIDC is attempting to increase value added features. Other developments include an abattoir designed to meet EU standards in order to exploit the islands' certification as a country producing organic food. Exports go to Denmark, Sweden and Spain as well as the UK.

Over 40,000 tourists typically visit each year, most arriving by cruise ship. Land based tourism generates over £3 million (around US$4.8 million), encouraged by the new inter-island ferry service. Improved hotel accommodation and access have been included in development plans. There are regular, scheduled flights from Chile, and the UK, via the RAF military airbase at Brize Norton in Oxfordshire. Although the RAF and Falkland Islands Tourist Board are committed to providing a comprehensive service for travellers, the route and distance still places a limitation on the numbers visiting by air.

In July 2013 the Falkland Islands were allocated US$5.2 million from the 10th Round of the European Development Fund to support economic development priorities. The funds will enable the Falkland Islands Government (FIG) to further develop its tourism and rural strategies.

In December 2013 the European Commission announced an allocation of EU€5.9 million (US$7.9 million) to support economic development activities over 2014–20.

In March 2013 the referendum on the political status of the Falkland Islands was held in order to ask the residents whether or not they supported the continuation of their status as an overseas territory to the United Kingdom. The votes on the referendum, held as a result of Argentina's call for negotiations on the islands sovereignty, turned out to be 99.8 per cent in favour of remaining part of the UK, with only three voters disagreeing.

External trade

As a UK Overseas Territory the Falkland Islands is a part of the European Union's Association of Overseas Countries and Territories (OCT Association), and some EU laws apply, specifically animal slaughter and commercial food hygiene regulations.

There are several rural associations that market local meat, wool, hides and fish. Around 74 per cent of all exports are destined for Spain.

Imports

Principal imports include fuel, food and drink, building materials and clothing.

Main sources: UK (typically 74 per cent of total), Greece (13 per cent), The Netherlands (7.6 per cent) and the US.

Exports

Wool, sheepskins and hides were virtually the only exports until the arrival of the fishing industry, which has grown to dominate commodity exports. Finfish, including hake, and *Dissostichus eleginoides* (Patagonian toothfish, also known as Chilean sea bass), plus *Illex argentinus* (Argentine shortfin squid) are, together with wool, the main exports.

Main destinations: Spain (typically 74 per cent of total), US (6 per cent), Croatia (3.8 per cent), and the UK.

Agriculture

Farming

Soil quality is generally poor – peat over clay (peat is used as fuel). Virtually all the available land has been used for sheep farming although small areas of arable land are cultivated (eg potatoes, hay crops, vegetable crops grown by individual households).

A hydroponic garden facility constructed in Stanley yields good quality vegetable crops for local and shipping consumption. There is an indigenous tussock (or tussac) grass (*Poa Flabellata*, which will grow to a height of 3–4 metres) but because of its palatability for livestock, it has been over-grazed in most places.

Constant strong winds affect the suitability of all flora, and only the hardiest will survive. Indigenous grass covering large areas is known locally as 'whitegrass' (*Cortaderia Pilosa*) and a heather-like plant 'diddle-dee' (*Empetrum Rubrum*) is common.

There are around 90 farms. The average size is 10,000ha, with an average of 6,400 sheep. Sheep stocks are a Corriedale/Polwarth mixture with small admixture of other breeds, eg Romney. The average clip per sheep is over 3.55kg. There are around 500,000 sheep on the islands, which is about 167 sheep for each permanent resident.

Certain sheep diseases found elsewhere (eg foot rot, skin complaints/parasites) are either absent or not considered a problem on the islands.

Mutton is the principal source of protein and is supplemented during winter by beef. A dairy farm on East Falkland provided an important proportion of the islands' milk until it was closed in July 2009. The pasture is improved by nitrogen fertiliser in quantities that would be uneconomic over a larger area.

Fishing

The Interim Conservation and Management Zone inaugurated by the British government in 1986 was substantially revised in 2005. The revised law regulates the new system of transferable fishing rights. The Falklands have managed and policed a fish reserve and generated significant revenues through the annual award of fishing licences. These go to support the islands' health, education and welfare system. They have dropped to around £15 million (US$30 million) in recent years as a result of drop in Illex (squid) catches.

Squid accounts for around three quarters of the fish taken.

The Fisheries Department monitors marine activity daily and restrictions have been imposed on seismic fleets, especially during the fishing season.

The Falkland Islands Fishing Companies Association (FIFCA) was formed in 2007 to represent the fishing industry.

In July 2015, Argentina's Secretary for the Malvinas Islands claimed that the explanation for the Falkland Islands' recent economic success was due to the fact that the islands sea trawlers were stealing Argentinian sea life. The claim that the government had been giving local fishers illegal licences was immediately disregarded by a member of the Legislative Assembly, Phyl Rendell, who stated: 'It represents yet another example of efforts to damage the Falklands economy.'

Industry and manufacturing

Small industrial units serve both onshore and offshore commitments. Hand-knitted local garments are produced for sale to visitors.

The Falkland Islands' largest private company, Falkland Islands Holdings plc, is quoted on the London Stock Exchange where it began trading in 1998. Activities are mainly retail trading and provision of services to the Falkland Islands. It controls about 80 per cent of retail sales, is the agent for Land Rover, the most popular vehicle, owns the Darwin Shipping Line and operates the port in Stanley.

Tourism

Tourists to the islands typically have to display determination to visit the islands down in the South Atlantic, 500km from South America and 770km from South Africa. Arriving by air requires either a flight on an RAF aeroplane from the UK (Brize Norton), which involves an 18-hour flight with two refuelling stops or a once weekly LAN scheduled connecting flight from Punta Arenas, Chile, to Mount Pleasant International airport.

The islands have little in the way of tourist infrastructure, but the islanders are welcoming and can provide accommodation, typically on a bed-and-breakfast basis. Wildlife tourism is popular, as is visiting the battlegrounds of the 1982 military conflict.

Mining

There is speculation that the great blanket bogs which obscure much of the inland geology of the islands may hide some diamond-bearing kimberlites and exploration is under way. There has been some evidence of gold.

Hydrocarbons

Although there is potential in the oil sector in the Falkland Islands, currently no oil is being produced and the islands rely on the import of petroleum products. Coal and gas is neither produced nor imported. Oil consumption is under 1,000 barrels per day.

Exploration for oil began in 1996 and in 2002 Falkland Oil and Gas Ltd (FOGL) was formed to manage exploration and operations of any potential oil field finds. Geological mapping has included most offshore regions surrounding the islands, and Premier Oil and Noble Energy will be leading a six well drilling campaign off the remote islands in late 2015 in which over 1.4 million barrels of oil equivalent (boe) are being targeted. The first drilling of an exploratory well was in 2009.

An announcement on 27 June 2011 by the UK-based, Rockhopper Exploration confirmed that commercially viable oil and natural gas deposits offshore, in the North Falkland Basin, in a field known as Sea Lion had been recorded. The independent British oil company, Premier Oil is expected to develop the oil field that contains an estimated 400 million barrels of recoverable oil.

The US-based Noble Energy Company announced on 8 August 2012 that it had an agreement to take over the operations of much of FOGL's prospectus and its potential hydrocarbons finds in the south and east Falklands basins in the South Atlantic for the investment of US$180–230 million (2012–15). Later in 2013 Noble Energy also acquired a 35 per cent stake in FOGL's offshore licence in the northern areas (excluding two already allocated).

In July 2013 the Executive Council published its Hydrocarbon Development Policy Statement. At the core of the policy is robust regulation, supply chain support and ensuring long-term benefits for Islanders.

Energy

The majority of households use oil for heating. Stanley has a power station that generates 9MW of electricity. Outside Stanley, settlements generate their own power on an individual basis. There is a plentiful supply of peat (turf), although few houses have peat stoves.

The Sand Bay Wind Farm has three turbines, installed in 2007, producing 300,000 units of electricity, and around 25 per cent of all electricity consumed in Stanley, saving the island 20–25 per cent of annual oil imports as the existing diesel generators are used less. Another three wind turbines were installed in 2010.

The total installed generating capacity of the islands is above 10MW.

Time

GMT minus four hours (GMT minus three hours April–September)

Geography

The Falklands Islands, comprising two large islands and about 700 smaller ones, are in the south-western Atlantic Ocean, about 770km (480 miles) north-east of Cape Horn, South America. They are 500km (300 miles) from the South American mainland.

The coastlines are marked by rocky headlands and sandy beaches. Vegetation comprises low grasses, ferns and shrubs. There are many small lakes and peaty pools and three rivers: the San Carlos on East Falkland and the Warrah and Chartres on West Falkland. There are hill ranges on both main islands, the highest points being Mount Usborne on East Falkland (705m) and Mount Adam on West Falkland (700m).

Hemisphere

Southern

Climate

Temperatures range from minus 6–21 degrees Celsius (C) with occasional lows of minus 10 degrees C and highs of 25 degrees C. Rainfall is around 700mm per year. Strong to gale-force winds are frequent during spring and early summer.

Entry requirements

Passports

Valid passports required by all, valid for three months.

Visa

Not required by nationals of EU/EEA countries, North America, Australasia and other commonwealth countries, Argentina, Chile, Brazil, Uruguay, Japan, Hong Kong, South Korea, Israel, Andorra, Liechtenstein, San Marino and Vatican City. For further confirmation and exceptions contact the Travel Co-ordinator in London (+44-(0)207-222-2542). Booking forms for the flight from the UK include details and purpose of visit and are required to be completed before or on arrival. All visitors are required to have a return ticket, accommodation and sufficient funds.

Currency advice/regulations

There are no restrictions on the import and export of local or foreign currency. The Falkland Islands has its own currency which is equivalent to UK sterling. The notes and coins cannot easily be exchanged for sterling or other currencies outside the Islands. Sterling is freely used on the islands and dollars are accepted.

Customs

200 cigarettes, 50 cigars, 100 cigarillos or 250 grams of tobacco; one litre of alcohol, two litres of wine; and 10 litres of beer or cider.

Import licences are required for plants, foodstuffs and firearms.

Prohibited imports
Uncooked or cured meat and plants are only allowed in under licence. Livestock is allowed on any in-coming aircraft.

Health (for visitors)

Mandatory precautions
None

Advisable precautions
Yellow fever vaccination in case of any stopover in Africa en route.
Radiation alerts are issued with local weather forecasts when the ozone hole stretches over the islands. Precautions against skin cancer should be taken with high factor suncream and clothing protection.

Credit cards

Credit cards are generally accepted at hotels and retail outlets.

Public holidays (national)

Fixed dates
1 Jan (New Year's Day), 21 Apr (Queen's Birthday), 14 Jun (Liberation Day), 8 Aug (Battle Day), 25 Dec (Christmas Day), 26 Dec (Boxing Day), 28–29 Dec (Stanley Races).

Variable dates
Good Friday, Peat Cutting Day (first Mon in Oct).

Working hours

Business
Mon- Fri: 0800-1200. 1300-1700.

Government
Mon–Fri: 0800–1200, 1300-1630.

Shops
Mon-Fri: 0900-1200, 1300-2000.

Telecommunications

Telephone/fax
Direct satellite telephone and telefax links are in operation throughout the Islands.

Postal services
The post code for the islands, issued through the Universal Postal Union, is FIQQ 1ZZ. The postal service was privatised on 1 August 2014 when Falklands Post Service Ltd took over the running of both the Post Office and the Philatelic Bureau.

Internet/e-mail
E-mail use is widespread and there is an Internet cafe in Stanley.

Electricity supply

Voltage and plugs for electrical appliances are the same as in the UK, 240V 50Hz.

Getting there

Air
Flights to the Falkland Islands depart from RAF Brize Norton, Oxfordshire, UK, six or seven times per month. For information, contact a travel agent or the Falklands Islands Government office in London (tel: +44 (0)207-222-2542). LanChile operate weekly flights from Santiago via Puerto Montt and Punta Arenas. Details from any travel agent or from International Tours and Travel in Stanley (tel +500-22041; fax +500-22042).
Air Seychelles are contracted by the brokers to run the Brize Norton flights from 24 January–30 September 2010.
International airport/s: Mount Pleasant International Airport (MPN); 56km from Stanley.
Other airport/s: Stanley Airport
Airport tax: Embarkation tax of £22 per passenger (applicable departure flights only).

Surface
Water: Cruise ships stop in at Stanley.
Main port/s: Stanley.

Getting about

National transport
Air: Depending on bookings and weather conditions, the Falkland Islands Government Air Service (FIGAS) operates daily services to the majority of settlements with a fleet of eight-passenger Britten-Norman Islander aircraft.
Road: There is a limited amount of surfaced road mainly around Stanley and Mount Pleasant. Gravel roads are a common feature.
Water: There is an inter-island ferry service between East and West Falkland.

City transport
Taxis: There is a limited taxi service in Stanley and at the airport, provided by Stanley and Lowes Taxis (tel: (+500) 21381) and Cindy Cars (tel: (+500) 22123).
Buses, trams & metro: There is a bus service from the airport to Stanley, operated by Falkland Islands Tours & Travel (+500-21775).

Car hire
4X4 vehicles can be rented from Falkland Islands Company Ltd, Crozier Place, Stanley (tel: (+500) 27678).

BUSINESS DIRECTORY

The addresses listed below are a selection only. While World of Information makes every endeavour to check these addresses, we cannot guarantee that changes have not been made, especially to telephone numbers and area codes. We would welcome any corrections.

Telephone area codes

The international dialling code (IDD) for the Falkland Islands is +500 followed by subscriber's number.

Chambers of Commerce

Falkland Islands Chamber of Commerce, PO Box 378, West Hillside, Stanley (tel: 22-264; fax: 22-265; e-mail: commerce@horizon.co.fk).

Banking

Standard Chartered Bank, Box 166, Ross Road, Stanley (tel: 27-220; fax: 27-219); UK contact (tel: +44(0) 20-7280-7500).

Travel information

Falkland Islands Company Travel Services, Stanley (tel: 27-633; fax: 27-603).

Falkland Islands Government Air Service (FIGAS), c/o Falkland Islands Government, Stanley Airport (tel: 27-219; fax: 27-309; e-mail: figas@horizon.co.fk).

Falkland Islands Tourist Board, London, UK (e-mail: manager@tourism.org.fk) issues an accommodation guide.

Falkland Islands Tours & Travel (tel: 21-775; e-mail: astewart@horizon.co.fk).

RAF Brize Norton, Oxfordshire, UK (tel: +44 (0)1993-897-366).

Travel Co-ordinator, Falkland Islands Government Office, Falkland House, 14 Broadway, Westminister, London SW1H 0BH, UK (tel: (+44 -20) 7222-2542; fax: (+44-20) 7222-2375; e-mail: travel@figo.u-net.com).

National tourist organisation offices
Falkland Islands Tourist Board (FITB), Shackleton House, Stanley (tel: 22-215; fax: 22-619; e-mail: jettycentre@horizon.co.fk; internet site: www.falklandislands.com).

Ministries

Chief Executive, Thatcher Drive, Stanley (tel: 27-110; fax: 27-109).

Department of Agriculture and Mineral Resources, Stanley (tel: 27-355; fax: 27-352).

Department of Civil Aviation, Stanley Airport (tel: 27-300; fax: 27-302).

Department of Education, 23 Ross Road, Stanley (tel/fax: 27-292).

Department of Fisheries, PO Box 598, Stanley (tel: 27-260; fax: 27-265).

Department of Oil, Ross Road, Stanley (tel: 27-322; fax: 27-321).

Department of Public Works, Stanley (tel: 27-193; fax: 27-191).

Governor's Office, Government House, Stanley (tel: 27-433; e-mail: gov.house@horizon.co.fk).

Treasury, Falkland Islands Government, Thatcher Drive, Stanley (tel: 27-143; fax: 27-144).

UK Government Office, Falkland House, 14 Broadway, Westminster, London SW1H 0BH, UK (tel: +44 (0)20-7222-2542; fax: +44 0)20-7222-2375; e-mail: rep@figo.u-net.com).

Other useful addresses

Attorney General, PO Box 143, Stanley (tel: 27-273/4; fax: 27-276).

British Geological Survey, Petroleum Geology Group, Murchison House, West Mains Rd, Edinburgh, EH9 3LA (tel: +44(0)131 667-1000; fax: +44 (0)131 668-4930).

Cable & Wireless, Stanley (tel: 20-800; fax 22-206).

Customs & Immigration, Stanley (tel: 27-340; fax: 27-342).

Falkland Islands Development Corporation, Stanley (tel: 27-211; fax: 27-210).

Falklands Islands Co Ltd (FIC), Crozier Place, Stanley (tel: 27-600; fax: 27-603).

Medical Services/King Edward VII Memorial Hospital, Stanley (tel: 27-415; fax: 27-416).

Meteorological Office, RAF Mount Pleasant (tel: 73-557).

Overseas Territories Department, Foreign & Commonwealth Office, King Charles St, London SW1A 2AH (tel: +44(0)20-7270-3000; fax: (0)20-7270-2086).

The United Kingdom Falkland Islands Trust (administers the Shackleton Scholarship fund), c/o 14 Broadway, Westminster, London SW1H 0BH, UK (tel: +44 (0)20-7222-2542; fax: +44 (0)20-7222-2375).

Internet sites

Falkland Islands Government: http://www.falklands.gov.fk

Falkland Islands information: http://www.falklands-malvinas.com/

Falkland Islands web portal: http:/www.falklandislands.com

Falkland Islands News Network: http://www.sartma.com

United Kingdom Falkland Islands Trust: www.ukfit.org.uk

Faroe Islands

COUNTRY PROFILE

The first Norse settlers arrived in the Faroes from neighbouring Denmark and the Orkneys in the ninth century.
1380 Early administration was undertaken by a parliamentary body known as the Alting. The end of parliamentary procedures saw the Alting renamed the Løgting and becoming a royal court.
1397 The Faroes become a Danish province, with the political merger of Norway and Denmark into the Kalmar Union.
1849 The first Danish constitution included the Faroe Islands, administered under the Danish county Roskilde.
1939–45 The Faroe Islands were occupied by the British during the Second World War, although they remained largely self-governing. With continuous war work the economy improved steadily and was sustained.
1946 The Faroe Islands returned to Danish control. In a referendum, a very small majority voted in favour of becoming an independent state. Negotiations and diplomacy led to a home rule arrangement instead.
1948 The Home Rule Act made the Faroes security, foreign and economic affairs the responsibility of Denmark.
1998 Anfinn Kallsberg replaced Edmund Joensen as prime minister. Offshore oil prospecting began.
2001 A referendum to be held for approval of legislative amendments to enable a gradual winding-down of Denmark's authority on the islands was shelved after Denmark's Prime Minister Poul Nyrup Rasmussen said that subsidies would stop after four years if the islanders voted for independence.
2004 Jóannes Eidesgaard (JF) became prime minister, leading a coalition of the SF, the Javnaðarflokkurin (JF) (Social Democrats) and the Fólkaflokkurin (FF) (People's Party).
2006 A trust fund agreement was signed with the World Bank, whereby the Faroe Islands provides development collaboration with the Pacific island of Palau. Iceland and the Faroe Islands signed a special economic treaty granting many free trade arrangements for goods, services, capital and workers.
2007 The parliamentary membership was amended and a fixed number of representatives at 33 persons, was introduced.
2008 In parliamentary elections, the Tjóðveldisflokkurin (TF) (Republican Party) won 23.3 per cent of the vote (8 seats out of 33), the Sambandsflokkurin (SF) (Union Party) 21 per cent (seven), the FF 20.1 per cent (seven), the JF 19.4 per cent (six), the Mioflokkurin (MF) (Centre Party) 8.4 per cent (three), and the Sjálvstýrisflokkurin (Home Rule Party) 7.2 per cent (two). Turnout was 89.2 per cent. Jóannes Eidesgaard remained as prime minister until the coalition collapsed and Kaj Leo Johannesen (SF) took over.
2009 Plans for an Arctic military force were announced by Denmark, with a base in the Faroe Islands, to protect Danish activities as the ice cap melts and opens up access to the polar region.
2010 An association of five interested parties (including Faroe Petroleum) began deep sea oil prospecting in the Atlantic margin offshore, in Faroe Islands' territorial waters.
2011 A new licensing open-door policy was introduced by the government that allows any prospector to search for oil and gas without a pre-arranged contract under license. Parliamentary elections were held in October, three-months earlier than scheduled. The balance of power within the ruling coalition switched as the SF won 24.7 per cent of the vote and the erstwhile leading FF won 22.5 per cent. Kaj Leo Johannesen (SF) remained in office as prime minister.
2012 On 20 September, the European parliament backed proposals for sanctions against the Faroe Islands and Iceland due to a dispute over fishing rights. Scotland and Ireland argued that increased fishing quotas for mackerel favouring these countries could be unsustainable as an increasingly larger share of mackerel is being caught in regional waters.
2013 The EU voted on 31 July to ban the import of herring and mackerel from the end of August. This followed concern over the Faroese government's decision to set its own catch limits.
2014 On 3 September the German shipping giant Hapag Lloyd, which operates luxury cruises that dock in the Faroe Islands, issued an open letter to Prime Minister Kaj Leo Johannesen, calling for an end to the controversial 'grindadrap' or 'grind' when pilot whales are hunted and

KEY FACTS

Official name: Føroyar (Faroe Islands)

Head of State: Queen Margrethe II of Denmark, represented by the High Commissioner Dan M Knudsen (from 1 Jan 2008)

Head of government: Prime Minister Aksel V. Johannesen (from 15 September 2015)

Ruling party: Coalition led by Javnaðarflokkurin (JF)

Area: 1,399 square km (18 islands)

Population: 48,863 (2011)

Capital: Tórshavn

Official language: Faroese, Danish

Currency: Faroese krone (FKr) (same value as Danish krone)

Exchange rate: FKr6.67 per US$ (Sep 2015)

GDP per capita: US$45,206 (2009)

GDP real growth: 2.90% (2010)

Unemployment: 570.00% (2010)

Inflation: 2.30% (2010)

slaughtered. Later the same month three volunteer members of Sea Shepherd, the marine conservation charity committed to ending the destruction of habitat and slaughter of wildlife across the world's oceans, were arrested by the Danish Navy for protecting a large pod of hundreds of Atlantic white-sided dolphins, preventing them from approaching the dangerous killing shores of the Faroe Islands.
2015 2015 Election of 2 seats to the Danish Parliament was held on 18 June. The JF and Tjóðveldi won 1 seat each. The general election held on 1 September was won by Javnaðarflokkurin (JF) (Social Democratic Party) with 25.1 per cent and 8 seats (out of 33), followed by Tjóðveldi (Republic) 20.7 per cent and 7 seats, Hin føroyski fólkaflokkurin – radikalt sjálvstýri (HFF-RS) (Faroese People's Party – Radical Self-Government) 18.9 per cent and 6 seats and Sambandsflokkurin (Union Party) 18.7 and 6 seats.

Political structure

Constitution

The Faroe Islands were administered as a Danish county until they achieved home rule in 1948. The Faroe Islands are a Danish external territory, electing two members to the Danish parliament, which maintains responsibility for constitutional, foreign and defence matters. A High Commissioner represents the Danish government and advises on joint affairs.

Form of state

Parliamentary democratic dependency

National legislature

Internal affairs are under the legislative control of the Løgting (parliament) which has 33 members. New elections laws were introduced in 2008 under which the Faroe Islands is comprised of one constituency with a fixed number of members, elected for up to four years. Universal suffrage is 18 years.
The Landsstyri (a government of nine members) is formed, based on the strength of the parties in the Løgting. The Løgmadur (prime minister) has to ratify all Løgting laws.
All Danish legislation must be submitted to the Landsstyri before becoming law.

Last elections

1 September 2015 (parliamentary); 18 June 2015 election of 2 seats to the Danish Parliament.
Results: Parliamentary: Javnaðarflokkurin (JF) (Social Democratic Party) won 25.1 per cent and 8 seats (out of 33), Tjóðveldi (Republic) 20.7 per cent and 7 seats, Hin føroyski fólkaflokkurin – radikalt sjálvstýri (HFF-RS) (Faroese People's Party – Radical Self-Government) 18.9 per cent and 6 seats, Sambandsflokkurin (Union Party) 18.7 and 6 seats, Framsókn (Progress) 7.0 per cent and 2 seats, Miðflokkurin (Centre Party) 5.5 per cent and 2 seats, Sjálvstýrisflokkurin (Self-Government Party) 4.2 per cent and the remaing 2 seats. Turnout was 88.8 per cent.

Next elections

2019 (parliamentary)

Political parties

Ruling party

Coalition led by Javnaðarflokkurin (JF)

Main opposition party

Tjóðveldi (Republic)

Political situation

The rise in importance of oil exploration has grown in the 2000s. The independent energy company, Faroe Petroleum, was awarded rights to explore for oil and gas in regions between Scotland and the Faroe Islands, and subsequently found oil. In 2010 it bought a significant stake in the North Sea oilfield, for over US$100 million, as well as exploration sites elsewhere. Oil was also discovered by Cairn Energy in Faroe waters in 2010.
In July 2009, the Danish government announced plans to set up a permanent military presence in the Arctic and establish a regional joint service command in the Faroe Islands. Untapped natural oil and gas reserves under the melting Arctic ice could spark a scramble by all countries with a claim to the region.

Population

48,863 (2011). More than one-third of the total population lives on the island of Streymoy.
Last census: July 2002: 47,350
Population density: 33 inhabitants per sq km (2000).
Annual growth rate: 1.2 per cent (2003)

Ethnic make-up

Scandinavian

Religions

Evangelical Lutheran Church of Denmark (85 per cent). The Faroe Islands are a diocese under the Danish national church. Of the various smaller religious communities the largest is the Plymouth Brethren.

Health

Life expectancy: 79 years (estimate 2003)
Fertility rate/Maternal mortality rate: Two births per woman (2003)
Birth rate/Death rate: 14 births per 1,000 population; nine deaths per 1,000 population (2003).
Child (under 5 years) mortality rate (per 1,000): Seven per 1,000 live births (2003)

Main cities

Tórshavn (Thorshavn), on the island of Streymoy (capital, estimated population 12,324 in 2012), Klaksvík (4,562), Hoyvik (3,658), Argir (2,105).

Languages spoken

Faroese (derived from Old Norse) and Danish. Icelandic, English, Norwegian and Swedish are also widely spoken and understood.

Official language/s

Faroese, Danish

Media

Press

In Faroese, the only newspapers are published daily, including *Sosialurin* (www.sosialurin.fo), *Dimmalætting* (www.dimma.fo) and *Vikublaðið* (www.vikublad.fo).

Broadcasting

The national, public broadcasting company is Kringvarp Føroya (www.uf.fo).
Radio: The public network Útvarp Føroya (ÚF) and three other stations broadcast on several frequencies to provide national radio coverage. Rás (www.ras2.fo), Linden Kristligt Kringvarp (www.lindin.fo) a Christian broadcast, and Sundfelli broadcast in Faroese.
Television: The public network Sjónvarp Føroya (Svf) (www.svf.fo) provides between eight hours (weekdays) up to 15 hours (weekend) with local news and information and imported, dubbed, foreign entertainment programmes.

Economy

The economy is heavily dependent on fishing and processed fish and is sensitive to the international market in fish and fish stocks. As a result the sector can fluctuate significantly, in turn affecting the rest of the economy. The sector normally accounts for 95 per cent of the total exports and around 50 per cent of GDP. The industry employs around 15 per cent of the workforce. Employment in public administration and services accounts for 35 per cent of the workforce, while other service sector employment accounts for another 33 per cent. Unemployment in mid-2008 was less than 1.5 per cent; however the rate had grown to 4.4 per cent by the third quarter of 2009, due in large part to a fall in global trading. By 2012 the unemployment rate had reached 5.5 per cent. A total of 1,214 people remain unemployed as of 2014, and the unemployment rate decreased to 3.9 in July 2014. GDP growth was 0.0 per cent in 2008, falling to about -3.3 per cent in 2009, before reviving in 2010 to around 3 per cent. These results followed two years of high GDP growth, which were due to an increase in credit-finance, private consumption and investment growth; all of which were cut by the global economic crisis in 2008. GDP growth was 2.5 per cent in 2011, and was estimated to have stayed the same in 2012, and reached 3.6 per cent in 2013.

The Faroe Islands, being an autonomous region of Denmark, receive annual subsidies and transfers from the Danish government that usually equal approximately 3 per cent of the islands GDP.

Oil business activities have also improved the economic situation. In 2010, deep sea oil prospecting began in the Atlantic offshore the Faroe Islands' territorial waters, by an association of five parties (including Faroe Petroleum). Drilling of eight exploration wells began in 2012 and continued into 2013, although by 2014 there had been no viable finds.

In December 2014, the Faroe Islands and Turkey concluded a free trade agreement, the result of a 15-year process. The agreement provides the Faroe Islands with duty-free access to the significant market of Turkey, whilst also raises export competitiveness with other seafood exporting countries such as Iceland and Scotland.

The tourism industry is small and not only dependent on external factors but subject to the domestic infrastructure schemes necessary to provide service-based tourism.

In August 2013, the EU banned imports of herring and mackerel from the Faroe Islands as a result of the islands trebling their herring quota, a move deemed detrimental to fish stocks. However, the EU in August 2014 lifted the trade sanctions against the Faroe Islands. Furthermore, a 5-year agreement on mackerel quotas has been concluded with the other North Atlantic coastal countries.

External trade

As an autonomous overseas territory of Denmark the Faroe Islands negotiates it own bilateral trade agreements. It has executive and legislative powers over marine resources and trade relations. It is also a separate customs territory from Denmark and the EU.

Foreign trade is mainly with other EU countries, which provides almost 70 per cent of imports, mainly consumer goods and raw materials. However the single largest import product is petroleum and its derivatives. Around 95 per cent of exports are destined for the EU. Of total exports over 95 per cent are fish and their products, of which Atlantic salmon accounts for the bulk at around 23 per cent, followed by cod at around 17 per cent and saithe (coalfish) at around 14 per cent. Processed fish is typically frozen for export, but also includes traditional salted and smoked fish, destined specifically for Danish and other Scandinavian markets.

The Faroe Islands run a small balance of payments deficit, with exports totalling 6,085 KR million (US$894 million) in 2013, whilst imports totalled 6,271 KR million (US$921 million).

Imports

Principal imports are petroleum, machinery and vehicles, consumer goods, raw materials and semi-manufactures, foodstuffs and agricultural products.

Main sources: Denmark (typically 32 per cent of total), Norway (21 per cent), Germany (8 per cent).

Exports

Principal exports are fish and fish products (95 per cent), postage stamps and fishing vessels.

Main destinations: UK (typically 20 per cent of total), Norway (16 per cent), Denmark (12 per cent).

Agriculture

Farming

Sheep rearing is an important activity on the Faroe Islands. There are 70,000 sheep ranging free on the islands, providing meat and wool for the use of the inhabitants. Cattle are also kept for milk and meat. The islands have to import meat and other agricultural products, but have become self-sufficient in milk. Increasing co-operation among agricultural organisations has been fostered to make the islands as self-sufficient as possible. Potatoes are grown and also hay for the cows reared for milk production.

Fishing

Fishing is the dominant economic activity, accounting for 95 per cent of exports. The main fish stocks are salmon, cod, haddock and coalfish. Annual fish catches in excess of 600,000 tonnes have been the basis of sustained growth. The rising global price of fish has also contributed to the industry's profits as well as the investment in salmon and trout sea farming. Nevertheless, the business is highly vulnerable to fluctuations in not only world prices but also in amounts caught.

The fishing fleet consists of around 240 vessels and a further 1,000 smaller craft.

Industry and manufacturing

Most industrial activities are connected to the fishing sector. They include processing plants and shipyards, as well as the making of nets, ropes, etc. Small industries include breweries, building components, fibreglass boats, computer software, food and milk products, tinned fish and spun and woollen goods.

The fishing sector is still a source of major uncertainty. All Faroese fishing licences will, in principle, be revoked in 2018 and may then be politically reallocated. This makes it less attractive to invest since quota access after 2018 is uncertain.

Tourism

The isolation of the islands limits the potential for tourism. Even so tourism still contributes a large portion to the economy, and has developed since the 1990s.

Greenland, Iceland and Faroe Islands have combined in an initiative to promote new tourism activities, with short and long-term stays at selected destinations combined with conferences, cruises and themed holidays.

Hydrocarbons

In 2010, deep sea oil prospecting began in the Atlantic offshore the Faroe Islands' territorial waters, by an association of five parties (including Faroe Petroleum). Exploratory drilling began in 2012; as of 2015, no commercially viable finds are yet to occur, however expectations of financial gains from oil are still high.

The Faroe Islands relies on imported petroleum products. It does not currently produce or import gas and coal. Consumption of oil in 2013 was 4,900 barrels per day (bpd).

Energy

Installed generating capacity was 100MW in 2011, of which imported oil and petrol accounted for 90 per cent of energy demand. The total energy production mix is 30–40 per cent hydro- and wind-power and the remainder through diesel generation.

SEV, the Faroese electricity company, joined in partnership with Voith Siemens to produce a new SeWave, 1MW electricity generator, fuelled by wave power, which began operation in 2007 in Nípan on Vágar; it supplies 1 million kilowatt hour per annum. The installation site of another SeWave has been identified at Søltuvík on Sandoy.

Banking and insurance

Monetary policy and administration is headed by the Danish central bank (Danmarks Nationalbank).

When the banking crisis began in 1992, there were two big banks, one small private bank and savings banks in the Faroe Islands. One of the big banks was owned by Den Danske Bank. By the end of the crisis, the small bank had gone into bankruptcy, the two big banks had merged and were taken over by the Home Rule authorities and the savings banks were still in business. The savings banks and the merged bank function as banks under the same law.

Central bank

Danmarks Nationalbank

Time

GMT (daylight saving, end-March to end-September, GMT plus one hour).

Geography

The Faroe Islands are a group of 18 islands (of which 17 are inhabited) in the North Atlantic Ocean, south-east of Iceland and north-west of the north coast of Scotland. The main island is Streymoy and nowhere on the archipelago is over 3km from the sea. The islands are rocky with little opportunity for growing crops or forestry, although grass is plentiful.

Hemisphere

Northern

Climate

Mild winters and cool summers; usually overcast; can be foggy and windy.

Entry requirements

Passports

Required by all.

Visa

Even though a Danish territory, visas for Denmark are not valid for the Faroe Islands unless specified on the permit. For a business visa, an original letter of invitation from a local company or organisation, giving details about purpose of visit and duration of stay must accompany an application, along with evidence of hotel reservations.

Health (for visitors)

As for Denmark.

Advisable precautions

Without appropriate clothing for the climate hypothermia is a hazard.

Public holidays (national)

Fixed dates

1 Jan (New Year's Day), Apr 25 (Flag Day, afternoon only), 5 Jun (Constitution Day), 28 Jul (St Olav's Eve, afternoon only), 29 Jul (St Olav's Day), 24–26 Dec (Christmas Holiday), 31 Dec (New Year's Eve).

Variable dates

Maundy Thursday, Good Friday, Easter Monday, Prayer Day (Apr/May), Ascension Day, Whit Monday.

Working hours

Banking

Mon–Fri: 0930–1600 (Thu 0930–1800).

Business

Mon–Fri: 0800–1600 or 0830–1630.

Government

Mon–Fri: generally 0900–1700.

Shops

Mon–Fri: 0800–1700 or 0900–1730, Sat: close at 1300 or 1400.

Telecommunications

Mobile/cell phones

GSM 900 services cover virtually the entire territories.

Getting there

Air

National airline: Atlantic Airways has regular flights to Denmark, Norway, Iceland, Scotland, England and Greenland.

International airport/s: Vágar Airport (FAE) on the island of Vágar, located near the town of Sørvágur, a ferry links the island to Streymoy. Facilities include bank, restaurant, bar and shops.

BUSINESS DIRECTORY

The addresses listed below are a selection only. While World of Information makes every endeavour to check these addresses, we cannot guarantee that changes have not been made, especially to telephone numbers and area codes. We would welcome any corrections.

Telephone area codes

The international direct dialling (IDD) for the Faroe Islands is +298. There are no area codes.

Useful telephone numbers

Emergency services 000

Chambers of Commerce

Faroe Islands Trade Council, 12 Bryggjubakki, PO Box 259, Tórshavn 110 (tel: 353-100; fax: 353-101; e-mail: trade@trade.fo).

Banking

Central bank

Landsbanki Føroya, Müllers hús, í Gongini, PO Box 229, Tórshavn 110 (tel: 318-305; fax: 318-537; e-mail: landsbank@landsbank.fo).

Danmarks Nationalbank, Havnegade 5, DK-1093 Copenhagen (tel: (+45) 3363-6363; fax: (+45) 3363-7103; e-mail: info@nationalbanken.dk).

Travel information

Atlantic Airways, Vagar Airport, FR-380 (tel: 333-700; fax: 333-380).

Maersk Air, Aarvegur 6, PO Box 3225, FO-110 Tórshavn (tel: 333-700; fax: 318-670; e-mail: ff@olivant.fo).

Smyril Line, Jonas Broncksgota 37, PO Box 370, FO-110 Tórshavn (tel: 315-900; fax: 315-707; e-mail: office@smyril-line.fo).

Air Iceland, Vagar Airport, FO-380 Sorvagur (tel: 332-755; fax: 332-280).

The Faroe Islands Tourist Board Copenhagen, Hovedvagtsgade 8, 2, DK-1103 Copenhagen K, Denmark (tel: (+45) 3314-8383; fax: (+45) 3393-8575).

Faroe Travel, PO Box 1199, FO-110 Tórshavn (tel: 312-600; fax: 319-200).

National tourist organisation offices

Faroe Islands Tourist Board, Undir Bryggjubakka 17, PO Box 118, FO-110 Torshaven, (tel: 355-800; fax: 355-801; email: tourist@tourist.fo; internet site; www.tourist.fo).

Other useful addresses

British Consulate, Yviri vid Strond 19, PO Box 19, FR-3800 Tórshavn (tel: 313-510).

The Faroese Government, PO Box 64, FR-110 Tórshavn (fax: 314-942).

Faroese Press Agency, P/f Salvará, Tjarnardeild 12, Tórshavn.

Sjónvarp Føroya (television broadcasting), PO Box 21, FR-3800 Tórshavn (tel: 317-780).

Útvarp Føroya (general broadcasting), PO Box 328, FR-3800 Tórshavn (tel: 316-566).

Internet sites

Danish embassy with useful information on the Faroes:
http://www.denmarkemb.org

Faroe business news: www.news.fo

Faroe Islands general site:
www.faroe.com

Faroe Islands tourist site:
www.faroeislands.com

Fiji

This apparently idyllic island, where the birthday of the UK's Queen Elisabeth is still celebrated as a national holiday has seen three *coups d'état* since its independence in 1970. However, in 2014, Fiji was preparing for a return to democratically-elected government. The apparent progress towards the elections had contributed to increasing confidence in the economy. Supported also by increased disposable income and credit expansion, gross domestic product (GDP) growth was forecast to accelerate to an annual 3.8 per cent in 2014, well above the average growth rate over the past decade. Inflation had remained low partly due to low import prices but pervasive price controls cloud inflation assessment. While good progress has been made in recent years, structural reforms need to continue for the country to achieve sustainably high growth and increase resilience to external shocks.

Election continuity

In September 2014 Fiji First, the party of Fiji's military ruler Voreqe Bainimarama managed to win an outright majority in parliament, winning 32 of 50 seats. Voter turn-out was just under 84 per cent. This was the first time voters in the ethnically divided nation had gone to the polls since Mr Bainimarama, popularly known as 'Frank', took control in a 2006 *coup d'état.* The opposition Social Democratic Liberal Party (Sodelpa) won 15 seats and the National Federation Party (NFP) three seats.

The international observers present announced that they had seen no evidence of fraud. The Multinational Observer Group's preliminary findings were that the 'election was enthusiastically embraced by the voters of Fiji who were keen to participate in the democratic process. The election was conducted in an atmosphere of calm, with an absence of electoral misconduct or evident intimidation.' The Fijian government could heave a sigh of relief at this endorsement, which meant that international sanctions might be dropped and Fiji regain its position as a full member of the Commonwealth. The election result saw 'Frank' Bainimarama returned to power as prime minister eight years after he led the revolt that deposed Fiji's last elected government.

Political backdrop

Fijian politics had long been determined by the ethnic fault line that in 2013 continued to divide the island nation. In simple terms, this is the ethnic division between the country's native Fijian population and the Indian population which owes its presence in Fiji to the British. Under colonial rule indentured Indian labour was introduced to Fiji to work on the sugar plantations. By the twenty first century the Indians had become a majority, a position which creates understandable unease on the part of the Fijians, matched by resentment on the part of the Indians that they have been unable to play a full part in the country's government. The Bose Levu Vakaturaga (Great Council of Chiefs) is the assembly of traditional chiefs of Fiji that meets annually to discuss matters of concern to the Fijian people (but not necessarily the Indian people). The Council appoints the President of Fiji – a power embodied in the 1997 constitution and seen by most Indians as excluding them indefinitely from fair representation.

Bainimarama and the Constitution

Subtlety has not been a feature of the rule of Fiji's leaders since 2006, when Commodore Voreqe 'Frank' Bainimarama took over. In March 2013, according to an article in the London *Economist*, the Commodore announced that he was doing away with plans for a constituent assembly that was supposed to be considering his new constitution. At the turn of the year he had scrapped a draft constitution drawn up by a commission he himself had appointed. It seemed that the draft was not to his liking.

The economy

In the view of the International Monetary Fund (IMF), there were both domestic and external risks to the outlook. Domestic risks were focused on the complex political situation. On the upside, successful elections and a smooth transition to reform-oriented democratic government could result in stronger confidence in the economy and higher capital inflows. On the external risks, Australia

KEY FACTS

Official name: Republic of the Fiji Islands

Head of State: President Ratu Epeli Nailatikau (from 2009; reappointed 12 Nov 2012)

Head of government: Prime Minister Commodore Voreqe 'Frank' Bainimarama (from 17 Sept 2014)

Ruling party: Fiji First (from 17 Sept 2014)

Area: 18,333 square km (about 332 islands, 110 inhabited)

Population: 885,000 (2014)*

Capital: Suva (on Viti Levu)

Official language: English, Fijian and Hindi

Currency: Fijian dollar (F$) = 100 cents

Exchange rate: F$2.19 per US$ (Sep 2015)

GDP per capita: US$4,757 (2014)*

GDP real growth: 4.08% (2014)*

GDP: US$4.21 billion (2014)*

Unemployment: 8.75% (2014)*

Inflation: 0.53% (2014)*

Balance of trade: -US$1.33 billion (2013)*

Foreign debt: US$537.00 million (2012)*

Visitor numbers: 675,050 (2011)

* estimated figure

and New Zealand, the two most important tourism markets for Fiji, might be adversely affected by lower commodity demand from China and elsewhere.

According to the Asian Development Bank (ADB), the Fijian economy was estimated to have grown by 4.6 per cent in 2013 and 4.2 per cent in 2014. The economic expansion that began in 2010 had been one of the longest sustained periods of growth since independence. Greater government capital expenditure, higher remittance income and improved business confidence in the run-up to the 2014 elections saw new lending for consumption increase by 72.8 per cent and for investment by 11.3 per cent. These trends had contributed to record growth in private sector investment, which was expected to reach 13.5 per cent of GDP in 2014.

The ADB noted that growth had been broad based, with investments in finance, construction and transport leading the trend. The increase in construction saw demand for domestic cement increase by 17.6 per cent. Despite high growth, inflation slowed to 0.5 per cent in 2014, reflecting the steep fall in global oil prices, which led the Fiji Commerce Commission to reduce its retail price of gasoline and diesel by nearly 8 per cent. The Fiji Revenue and Customs Authority reported that its collections in 2014 totalled US$1.12 billion, exceeding their original forecast of US$1.08 billion. The rising revenues were an improvement of 13.7 per cent over 2013 collections. This solid performance came on the back of strong growth in revenues from income tax by 12.5 per cent and value-added tax by 5.7 per cent. Planned asset sales fell below expectations, however, leaving a fiscal deficit in 2014 equal to 2.0 per cent of GDP. This was larger than anticipated, even as a planned large increase in government expenditure was scaled back.

According to the ADB, Fiji's macro-economic policies continued to support growth. An expansionary fiscal policy had boosted growth through substantial spending on infrastructure, mainly for transport, as well as higher spending on education aimed at implementing a policy of providing free primary and secondary education to all school-aged children. While a moderately expansionary fiscal policy had been appropriate, new programmes were expected to be financed in large part by the disappointing asset sales. Over the medium term, faster growth and higher revenue collection were needed to support public programmes and allow the government to meet its objective of ensuring that debt, currently 49.7 per cent of GDP, remained manageable. Monetary policy was able to support higher economic growth by stimulating domestic demand because the outlook for inflation was soft.

Bank lending rates remained low and commercial banks enjoyed comfortable liquidity. Foreign reserves at the end of 2014 were estimated at 4.7 months of import cover. With the exception of fishing and mining, all productive sectors of the economy were estimated to have grown in 2014. Earnings from tourism continued to grow, with a record-breaking 692,630 tourist arrivals in 2014, which was 5.3 per cent higher than in the previous year. Tourist arrivals from Fiji's two largest markets maintained solid growth in 2014, as the number of visitors from Australia rose by 2.7 per cent and New Zealand by 14.5 per cent. Arrivals from the People's Republic of China were up 13.4 per cent during the year, further boosting Fiji's strong tourism performance.

Fiji's production of sugar, its primary agricultural commodity, exceeded expectations in 2014 as output grew by 13.7 per cent year on year. Investment to improve milling efficiency and introduce higher-yielding varieties of sugarcane contributed to higher output. Data from the Fiji Bureau of Statistics indicated that the value of sugar exports increased by about 22 per cent in 2014. This reversed the fall in export returns seen in 2013. Gold production fell modestly in 2014 and by year's end output was 1.8 per cent lower year on year. The fall was partly attributed to the declining quality of the ore extracted and partly to the sharp downtrend in the price of gold, which began in 2013. The value of gold exports continued to decline dramatically, plunging by 72.7 per cent in the year to November 2014.

Exports of fish and garments also fell in 2014, but this was offset by strong exports of sugar and mineral water to generate 0.3 per cent growth in exports net of re-exports. Fiji recorded a current account deficit equal to 8.9 per cent of GDP in 2014, improving on the previous year's deficit of 14.9 per cent, which included Fiji Airways' purchases of new aircraft. Excluding aircraft purchases, however, the trade deficit widened on rising imports of machinery and mechanical and electrical appliances in 2014. Tourism receipts and remittances from abroad grew by 13 per cent year on year, which helped to narrow the current account deficit.

According to the ADB, indicators suggested that growth would moderate slightly in 2015 to 4.0 per cent as the economy navigated a transition in its growth drivers. Tourism was expected to continue to grow at a steady pace, but current sugar and gold prices would make it hard to maintain growth in these industries in the coming year. In an effort to maintain the previous year's growth momentum, the 2015 budget increases public expenditure on infrastructure for transport, energy and water supply and sanitation. This was expected to directly boost construction and indirectly spur growth in other sectors.

KEY INDICATORS — Fiji

	Unit	2011	2012	2013	2014	**2015
Population	m	*0.89	0.87	0.88	*0.89	*0.89
Gross domestic product (GDP)	US$bn	3.50	3.85	4.03	*4.21	*4.41
GDP per capita	US$	3,965	4,415	4,578	*4,757	*4,959
GDP real growth	%	2.0	1.7	4.6	*4.1	*3.3
Inflation	%	8.6	3.4	2.9	*0.5	*1.5
Unemployment	%	7.0	8.6	*8.7	*8.8	*8.8
Exports (fob) (goods)	US$m	770.6	1,213.3	1,047.5	–	–
Imports (fob) (goods)	US$m	1,543.2	1,976.2	2,379.7	–	–
Balance of trade	US$m	-772.6	-762.9	-1,332.2	–	–
Current account	US$m	-360.3	-56.0	-835.0	*-369.0	*-355.0
Total reserves minus gold	US$m	923.9	920.0	940.9	915.2	–
Foreign exchange	US$m	816.1	816.2	836.7	–	–
Exchange rate	per US$	1.79	1.78	1.90	1.99	–

* estimated figure ** forecast figure

Risk assessment

Economy	Good
Politics	Good
Regional stability	Good

COUNTRY PROFILE

1643 The islands were first sighted by a European.
1874 Fiji became a British crown colony.
1879–1916 Over 60,000 Indian indentured labourers were imported to work on sugar plantations. The government in India stopped the recruitment of labourers.
1920 All indenture labour agreements were ended.
1963 General elections were held with the first majority Indian-led political party standing. The great council of chiefs signed the Wakaya Letter that asserted Fijian paramountcy.
1966 The Fijian Alliance Party was formed.
1968 Ratu Sir Kamisese Mara, Fiji's first prime minister was given the first instruments of independence. The Fijian Alliance Party won elections by appealing to both Indians and Fijians.
1970 On 10 October Fiji became independent and introduced a British-style political system with a new constitution. The British monarch remained Head of State, a bicameral parliament was introduced and a separate electoral roll for each ethnic group was provided.
1972 The first independent general elections were won by Ratu Mara's Fijian Alliance Party.
1977 Internal dispute between the leaders of the (ethnic Indian) National Federation Party (NFP), which had won a majority in the lower house of parliament elections resulted in a failure to form a government and Ratu Mara was recalled to power. The Fijian Alliance Party had won a majority in the upper house of parliament.
1981 The ethnic Fijian Western United Front political party was formed.
1985 The Fijian Labour Party (FLP) was formed, led by Timoci Bavadra.
1987 The NFP-FLP won the general elections and formed the first Indian-dominated government, led by Timoci Bavadra. The Alliance Party became defunct. Lieutenant Colonel Sitiveni Rabuka led two coups that overthrew the government as a republic was declared and all ties to the British monarch severed. Fiji was expelled from the Commonwealth and overseas aid was suspended.
1990 A new constitution was promulgated and considered by foreign observers as racist, as it enshrined the supremacy of ethnic Fijians by allocating 37 seats to Fijians, 27 seats to Indians and 6 to others in the lower house of parliament.
1992 The Soqosoqo Duavata ni Lewenivanua (SDL) (Fijian People's Party), led by Rabuka won general elections. Rabuka became prime minister.
1994 The great council of chiefs appointed Ratu Sir Kamisese Mara as president.
1995 The president appointed a team to review the 1990 constitution.
1997 After three years of discussion a new non-discriminatory constitution was enacted. Fiji was re-admitted to the Commonwealth.
1999 The FLP won general elections and formed a coalition government with the Christian Democratic Alliance, Party of National Unity and the Fijian Association Party. Mahendra Chaudhry, the first Fijian of Indian descent, became prime minister. President Ratu Sir Kamisese Mara was sworn in for a five-year term.
2000 In a coup, led by George Speight, Chaudhry and his cabinet were held captive by an armed group seeking more power for ethnic Fijians and forced to resign from office. The great council of chiefs ordered President Mara to sack the government. Supporters of Speight rioted in Suva while he called for the 1997 constitution to be scrapped. The Commonwealth suspended Fiji's membership. All the hostages were freed as Commodore Frank Bainimarama seized power and restored order. President Mara retired from office and the great council of chiefs appointed the father-in-law of Speight, Josefa Iloilovatu Uluivuda (commonly known as Ratu Josefa Iloilo) as president. Laisenia Qarase was appointed prime minister of an all-Fijian interim government. The High Court ruled that the deposed government of Mahendra Chaudhry should be reinstated.
2001 The Court of Appeal ruled that the interim government was illegal, and stated that the 1997 multi-racial constitution should remain in place. President Iloilo was re-appointed by the great council of chiefs for a five-year term; he re-appointed Laisenia Qarase as caretaker prime minister. In a general election, observed by the Commonwealth, Qarase's SDL won, but since it failed to secure an outright majority, it joined with the Matanitu Vanua (MV) (Conservative Alliance Party) in a coalition government. Qarase was sworn in as prime minister; his cabinet barred all ethnic Indians.
2002 Samisoni Speight Tikonasau, the brother of George Speight, was elected to parliament, reflecting the extent of George Speight's support among the voting public.
2003 The High Court ruled that the FLP should be allowed its seats in the cabinet.
2004 Ratu Sir Kamisese Mara died. The FLP declined a government role in favour of official opposition duties.
2006 Prime Minister Qarase agreed to review the Reconciliation, Tolerance and Unity Bill. President Ratu Uluivuda was re-appointed. The MV agreed to dissolve as a party and its members to merge with the ruling SDL, after it changed its stance on working to free its party members convicted of coup related offences. The ruling SDL won 36 out of 71 seats in the general elections and the FLP won 31 seats. The FLP entered into coalition with the SDL. In a bloodless, military coup d'état led by Commodore 'Frank' Josaia Voreqe Bainimarama, the president and government were dismissed. Bainimarama assumed the presidency and Jona Senilagakali Baravilala was appointed as the interim prime minister. Fiji was suspended from the Commonwealth.
2007 Under pressure from the great council of chiefs, Bainimarama reinstated Ratu Josefa Iloilo Uluivuda (Ratu Josefa Iloilo) as president and Bainimarama became interim prime minister. Bainimarama announced that parliamentary elections would be held in 2010. Bainimarama dismissed the great council of chiefs, which refused to endorse his government and proposed his own vice president. A six-month long state of emergency was finally lifted following two failed coup attempts; public gatherings and restrictions on the media were not lifted.
2008 Bainimarama convened a great council of chiefs with himself as chairman. Fiji withdrew its participation in the Pacific Islands Forum – Joint Working Group on Fiji, leading to fears that the parliamentary elections would not go ahead. Bainimarama delayed democratic elections until reforms to what he considered 'racist' election laws are undertaken.
2009 Growing opposition to the government of Bainimarama came from leaders of the Pacific Islands Forum, who said that he must hold general elections as promised. The Samoa prime minister, Tuilaepa Sailele Malielegaoi, accused Bainimarama of lying to the Pacific Forum about Fiji's political future and its return to democracy and urged Fijians to reclaim their government. In reply Bainimarama said Sailele had 'acted unprofessionally and unbecomingly' by criticising another country's leader. Bainimarama rejected demands for general elections, which followed the Commonwealth's threat to suspend Fiji's membership if elections were not held. Leaders of two opposition parties were denied invitations to the crucial agenda-setting meeting, to discuss the course back to parliamentary democracy. Details of the 2007 census were released, which showed the percentage of Indo-Fijians had fallen from 51 per cent in 1966 to 37.5 per cent and was expected to fall further due to a steady stream of emigration. The Court of Appeal found the interim government of Commodore Frank Bainimarama, appointed after the military coup d'état in 2006, to be illegal. President Ratu Josefa

Iloilo repealed the 1997 constitution, became Head of State and sacked the judiciary and postponed elections until 2014. The four major political parties were excluded from the political process. The former military government was re-installed, with Bainimarama as prime minister. The UN Security Council condemned the repeal of the constitution and called for an early general election. Fiji was suspended from the Pacific Islands Forum. The EU suspended financial assistance. The high court was re-opened after six weeks closure following the coup. A presidential decree de-registered all legal practitioners who had to apply to the chief registrar, a former military lawyer, for a new licence. In a national address, Prime Minister Bianimarama announced that before parliamentary elections can be held in 2014, political reforms must be undertaken. He also called on donor countries to be understanding and offer financial help over the period. Fiji's membership of the Commonwealth was suspended including all technical assistance. Ratu Epeli Nailatikau became president.

2010 The government announced that any politician who had engaged in national politics since 1987 would be banned from contesting the proposed 2014 parliamentary elections, effectively preventing any current politician from standing for re-election. Eight men accused of attempting to kill Mr Bainimarama in 2007 were found guilty and jailed.

2011 Former president Ratu Josefa Iloilo died in February, aged 92 years. In March, the government proposed a new system of electoral campaigning, changing from targeted ethnic groups to open-list proportional representation. Of the 71 seats in the lower house of parliament, 45 will be open to any candidate of any ethnic group. In March, Ratu Inoke Takiveikata was convicted of inciting a military mutiny at the Queen Elizabeth Barracks in 2000. The nobleman was sentenced to life in prison. Lieutenant Colonel Ratu Tevita Mara left Fiji by devious means in May, ending up in Tonga, with the help of the Tongan navy that claimed it had 'rescued' Mara at sea. Mara issued a condemnation of Bainimarima's regime and called for tougher sanctions to be applied. Mara was subsequently charged with mutiny by the Fijian government. Fiji also officially demanded that Tonga extradite Mara to stand trial in Fiji, but a decision was deferred. In June Ratu Tevita Mara was granted permission to address the Fijian democratic movement in Canberra (Australia). He reiterated his belief that Bainimarima had no intention of holding parliamentary elections in 2014 as promised. In June, Fiji called on Australia to extradite Tevita, but Australia also deferred its decision to comply with its bilateral extradition agreement. Solomon Islands' Prime Minister Danny Philip said he was reluctant to grant entry to Tevita and risk upsetting relations with Fiji.

2012 On 7 January, the public emergency regulations were lifted. However, on 6 January, new public order decrees were issued to limit political opposition and continue detention for up to 14 days as directed by the commissioner of police. In addition a media council was created, with powers to ensure the government's control over what is published. On 7 February the State Proceedings Amendment Decree came into effect, in which government ministers were given immunity from prosecution, in the form of parliamentary privilege, for anything they said in the lead-up to the 2014 general elections. The government said the decree offered the media the opportunity of reporting political statements for open discussion. The decree is expected to lapse in 2014. Opposition leader, Mahendra Chaudhry, criticised the decree, saying it was unfair and ridiculous to give parliamentary privilege to ministers in a country that did not have a parliament. The government announced on 9 March that a new constitution would be introduced ahead of democratic elections. Consultations on the new constitution will take place between constitutional commissioners (CC) and citizens from July–September. From October–December, the CC will draft a constitution based on collected submissions and guiding principles. (The draft constitution will be submitted for review to the constituent assemble, which will include representatives of civil society groups and Fiji-registered organisations in January 2013. When the draft has been approved (scheduled for the end of February) the text will be presented to the president for ratification.) In a news broadcast on 13 March Interim Prime Minister Bainimarama, announced that the Great Council of Chiefs had been abolished, because, he said, it perpetuated elitism and created divisive politics. He also announced that that the term 'Fijian' would apply to everyone, while indigenous people would also still be known as i-Taukei. On 30 July, Australia and New Zealand agreed to restore full diplomatic relations with Fiji. On 3 August, former prime minister Qarase was jailed for one year, having been convicted of corruption. On 2 November, the minimum wage was increased by 10.4 per cent (F$2 (US$1.1) per hour). On 12 November, President Ratu Epeli Nailatikau was reappointed for another three-year term in office. The decision by the Reserve Bank of Fiji in November to replace the image of Queen Elizabeth with Fijian flora and fauna on the currency was met with indignation by traditional chiefs, who said that the British royals had been given the aristocratic title of Tui Viti and that Queen Elizabeth was the monarch of Fiji and loved by Fijians. In November the EU named eight countries, including Fiji and Vanuatu, as possible non-cooperating third countries to it's fight against Illegal, Unreported and Unregulated (IUU) fishing. The EU has accused Fiji of having weak laws to tackle illegal fishing, which could lead to the banning of fish imports into the EU. Fiji earns some US$200 million in foreign exchange from fish exports annually.

2013 In May Prime Minister Bainimarama told New Zealand's Radio Taran that he hopes to have a new constitution by June. He said that with public consultations completed, submissions were being compiled. Three political parties had already registered for the 2014 elections, he said. The National Federation Party (NFP) and the Fiji Labour Party (FLP) had been re-registered, and the Social Democratic Liberal Party (Sodelpa), which was formed out of the old SDL, had been registered. In July Radio Australia reported that the FLP had been suspended for not paying for newspaper advertisements detailing its assets and liabilities, as required under law. Although upset by the law, both the NFP and Sodelpa paid. Until it pays the bill, Labour will not be permitted to operate as a party, and if it has still not paid at the end of its suspension, it will be deregistered. The new constitution was signed into law by President Epeli Nailatikau on 18 September. The constitution abolishes race-based electoral rolls, race-based seat quotas, district-based representation, the unelected upper chamber and the role of the hereditary Council of Chiefs.

2014 Elections were held on 17 September. The result was a clear win for Fiji First, the party of Frank Bainimarama, with 32 seats out of a total of 50. The Social Democratic Liberal Party (Sodelpa) won 15 seats and the National Federation Party (NFP) three seats. Turnout was 84 per cent. Fiji was reinstated as a member of the Commonwealth on 26 September. Australian foreign minister, Julie Bishop, announced at the end of October that Australia would immediately lift all sanctions against Fiji.

2015 After a meeting in October to dicuss climate change, the Pacific islands of Fiji, Kiribati, Tuvalu and Tokelau issued a joint statement in which they asked for help in funding the cost of raising buildings above predicted sea level increases and to safeguard water supplies from saltwater intrusion. The low-lying nations said that moving people because of rising sea levels, storms and ruined agriculture was a last resort, but the 'calamity' of climate change required industrialised countries to devise a plan.

Political structure

Constitution

President Ratu Epeli Nailatikau gave his assent to Fiji's fourth constitution on 18 September 2013. The new constitution vests sole legislative authority in a single-chamber, 50-seat, at-large Parliament, to be first convened following general elections in 2014. The voting age is 18. Voting is by the open list form of party-list proportional representation using the D'Hondt method in one nationwide constituency consisting of 50 seats. There is a threshold of 5 per cent of the vote for a list to gain representation.

Independence date

10 October 1970

The executive

While the President is commander-in-chief of the armed forces, his actual role is largely ceremonial. Elected for three year terms by the sitting parliament, the president is constitutionally granted 'reserve powers' but rarely is this right exercised. Executive power instead rests with the cabinet and Prime Minister.

National legislature

Fiji's parliament is unicameral as of September 2013. The fifty-strong house is elected for four year terms via proportional representation. The Prime Minister is usually the leader of the largest party and picks his/her own cabinet.

The *Bose Levu Vakaturaga* (Great Council of Chiefs) (GCC) comprises the highest-ranking members of the traditional chief system. The composition of the GCC was changed from 24 August 2007, when the number of members was reduced from 55 to 52, made up of 42 members representing chiefs from the 14 provinces, six co-opted members, three representatives of the chiefs of Rotuma and the Fijian affairs minister. The president, vice president and prime minister are no longer members, and commoners are excluded.

Legal system

Based on the British legal system.

Last elections

17 September 2014 (parliamentary)

Results: Fiji First 59.20 per cent (32 seats, out of 50), Social Democratic Liberal Party (SDLP) 28.20 per cent (15), National Federation Party (NFP) 5.50 per cent (3). No other parties reached the 5 per cent necessary to be allocated seats. Turnout was 83.97 per cent.

Next elections

2018 (parliamentary)

Political parties

Ruling party

Fiji First (from 17 Sept 2014)

Main opposition party

Soqosoqo Duavata ni Lewenivanua (SDL) (United Fiji Party)

Population

877,000 (2013)* Approximately 32 per cent of the population is under 15 years of age (2003).

Almost 70 per cent of the population live on the island of Viti Levu. There has been a population explosion in squatter settlements in Suva, due to the expiration of more than 4,000 land leases – there are 182 squatter settlements housing more than 80,000 people.

Last census: September 2007: 837,271

Population density: 46 inhabitants per square km (2010). Urban population 52 per cent (2010 Unicef).

Annual growth rate: 0.8 per cent, 1990–2010 (Unicef).

Ethnic make-up

Ethnic Fijians represent about 51 per cent of the population. Indians comprise about 44 per cent. There are also some Europeans, other Pacific islanders and Chinese.

Religions

Methodist (37 per cent), Roman Catholic (9 per cent), Hindu (38 per cent), Muslim (8 per cent).

Education

Fiji showed remarkable progress in access to basic education in the years following 1996. Basic education was boosted with the introduction of tuition assistance for primary schools in 1994. Totalling about F$4.8 million (US$2.3 million) annually, this assistance enabled primary schools to meet their annual development costs.

Primary schooling lasts for eight years; secondary education lasts for a possible seven years, with intermediate stages of four-year junior secondary, two-year senior secondary and one-year seventh form schooling. Progression through all stages culminates in examinations. Lessons are taught mainly in English but may also be taught in Fijian and Hindi.

The University of the South Pacific, which serves 10 English-speaking territories in the South Pacific, is the main provider of higher education.

Government expenditure on education increased through the 1990s and typically amounts to 16.21 per cent of the national budget.

The EU funded a US$44 million programme aimed at improving the quality of education in Fiji, by assisting more than 70 per cent of primary schools and 50 per cent of secondary schools.

Literacy rate: 93 per cent adult rate; 99 per cent youth rate (15–24) (Unesco 2005).

Compulsory years: 6 to 14.

Enrolment rate: 110.45 per cent gross enrolment in primary education (including repitition rates).

Health

In October 2010, the health minister declared that Fiji was free of typhoid, a disease that had been a constant threat across the region. On 30 November 2011, the Asia Pacific Observatory on Health Systems and Policies (APOHSP) reported that life expectancy in Fiji had fallen from 72.9 years to 67.8 over from 2000–05. The drop in expectancy was attributed to several factors, in particular political and economic pressures and including social and cultural changes.

Health care facilities in Fiji are barely adequate for routine medical problems. Two major hospitals, the Lautoka Hospital and the Colonial War Memorial Hospital in Suva, provide emergency and outpatient services. Other hospitals and clinics provide only a limited range of health services.

Access to clean water is available to 47 per cent of the total population.

HIV/Aids

HIV prevalence: 0.1 per cent aged 15–49 in 2003 (World Bank)

Life expectancy: 67.8 years (APOHSP 2011)

Fertility rate/Maternal mortality rate: 2.7 births per woman, 2010 (Unicef); 31.1 deaths per 1,000 live births (Ministry of Health, 2008).

Birth rate/Death rate: 20.7 births per 1,000 population; 7.1 deaths per 1,000 population (2007).

Child (under 5 years) mortality rate (per 1,000): 22 per 1,000 live births (WHO 2012)

Head of population per physician: 3.26 physicians per 100,000 people, 2007 (Fiji Statistics 2008)

Welfare

Analysis in 2010, by economist Professor Waden Narsey, of the Fiji Islands Bureau of Statistics *Household Income and Expenditure Survey for 2008–2009*, concluded that almost one-third of citizens will be living in poverty by 2011.

Main cities

Suva (capital, on Viti Levu, estimated population 85,345 in 2012), Nasinu (89,522), Nausori (on Viti Levu) (62,073), Lautoka (on Viti Levu) (56,892), Nadi (on Viti Levu) (49,930), Labasa (on Vanua Levu) (28,934).

Languages spoken

English is widely used in business circles. Fijian dialects are spoken by the indigenous Fijians (Bauan is the most spoken). The Indian community speaks Fiji-Hindi. Cantonese is also spoken.

Since 2003, compulsory classes teaching the Fijian and Hindi languages have been introduced in some primary and secondary schools in order to avert the threat of losing the ethnic languages of the country.

Official language/s

English, Fijian and Hindi

Media

In 2010 the government introduced new media laws (a code of standards and ethics and practice) to control the content of news reports and provide punishments of prison terms and heavy fines for any illegality. Foreign media ownership was severely curtailed and all media outlets must pledge allegiance to Fiji. Officials of the Fiji based, Pacific Islands New Association (Pina) have called for the organisation to be moved to another member state to avoid the growing censorship in Fiji.

Press

Journalistic standards are generally regarded as vigorous.

Dailies: In English, newspapers include *Fiji Daily Post* (www.fijidailypost.com), with its Fijian *The Fiji Times* (www.fijitimes.com) has business news and *Fiji Sun* (www.sun.com.fj), which is a tabloid.

According to new media laws that came into effect on 28 June 2010, which required all directors and 90 per cent of all shareholders of media organisations to be either Fijian or permanent Fijian residents, the *Fiji Times* had until 28 September 2010 to find new owners or be closed down. The *Fiji Times* was owned by News Limited (owned by media tycoon Rupert Murdoch) and a strong critic of the military government. The Fiji-based Motibhai Group took over control of News Limited's *Fiji Times* just before the September deadline.

Weeklies: In Fijian *Nai Lalakai* takes stories from *The Fiji Times* (www.fijitimes.com/nailalakai.aspx) and *Na Volasiga*, covering current affairs. Two Hindi language publications include *Sartaj* and *Shanti Dut* which features national and international news. The Pacific University Journalism publishes *USP Bulletin* and online news (www.usp.ac.fj/journ/).

A new, news magazine *Republika* began publishing in September 2012, concentrating on politics and investigative journalism.

Business: In English *Fiji Islands Business* (www.islandsbusiness.com) and *Island Business* are twin publications with varing domestic or international markets.

Periodicals: In English, the monthly *Pacific* (www.pacificmagazine.net) has regional news articles.

Broadcasting

Radio: Radio is the most popular medium for entertainment, news and information, particularly on remote islands.

The Fiji Broadcasting Corporation (FBCL) (www.radiofiji.com.fj) network has five stations providing a range of programmes based on the Fijian-, English or Hindi-languages. The Communications Fiji Ltd (www.cfl.com.fj) has a commercial network of five stations broadcasting to difference audiences including Radio Navtarang, in Hindi and Viti FM, in Fijian and FM96 for the under 25 years age group. Another commercial station, in English, is Radio Fiji Gold (www.radiofiji.com.fj).

The UK-based BBC World Service, the French Radio Internationale and Radio Australia are broadcast through local FM relay stations.

Television: The national public TV station is Fiji TV (www.fijitv.com.fj), which also has a satellite, pay-to-view service, provided by Sky Fiji, with over 20 channels. Local programmes are provided in Fijian, Hindi and English. Services are also transmitted to other Pacific territories, for a fee. A new free-to-air station, operated by FBC TV, began operations in October with full programming by December 2011.

Other news agencies: ABC Pacific Beat: www.radioaustralia.net.au/pacbeat

Pacific Magazine: www.pacificmagazine.net

Pacific Islands News Association (Pina): www.pina.com.fj

Economy

The service sector constituted 69.1 per cent of the economy in 2014, with industry accounting for 18.2 per cent, of which manufacturing accounted for around 15 per cent, and agriculture 12.7 per cent.

Tourism is the principal sector of the economy – in 2014 there were over 689,000 visitors, bringing in a total of US$984.8 million in visitor exports. The industrial sector is dominated by the mining of gold, silver and limestone, all contributing to Fijian exports. In 2011, a Chinese company began mining for bauxite after a mining licence was awarded to it in January 2010. If sugar production falls further, mining may become the second largest component of the economy by 2015.

Remittances from expatriates are also an important source of foreign exchange, which in 2013 were around US$200 million (5.0 per cent of GDP), rising from US$160 million in 2011.

GDP growth in 2006 was 1.9 per cent, but following the coup led by Commodore Bainimarama the economy went into recession as two corresponding international pressures compounded Fiji's situation. In 2006, the World Trade Organisation required the US and the EU to stop preferential imports from Fiji of textiles and sugar respectively. Both of these industries went into decline. The EU had agreed to provide financial aid to allow reinvestment in agriculture, but since the 2006 coup it set a proviso of democratic reforms and an improvement in human rights in Fiji. In the face of concerted opposition by international bodies and governments the Fijian military government rejected all calls to evolve a democratically inclusive regime. This meant that financial aid that might have been forthcoming has been restricted and has had a direct effect on the economy.

Average growth in the 2007-10 period, following global economic crisis was -0.7 per cent, impeded by drop in tourist numbers, floods and reduction in the value of sugar exports. GDP growth in 2011 reached 2.0 per cent, spurred on by reconstruction and a return of tourist numbers. By 2013, growth had grown to 3.0 per cent after having dropped to 1.7 per cent in 2012. Strong performance in 2014 lead to a growth of 4.2 per cent.

In the first four months of 2015, number of visitor arrivals increased by 7.5 per cent on the same period in 2014. Arrivals from New Zealand and the US increased the most, and arrivals from the main source, Australia, increased steadily. Arrivals from Asia increased by 30 per cent year-on-year and now contribute 10 per cent of all tourists. Visitor exports in 2014 increased by 6.6 per cent contributing the equivalent of 18.0 per cent of GDP. Arrivals are expected to be boosted by the leasing of two new aircraft by Fiji Airways in 2015, and another in 2017.

Gold production in Fiji, following years of decline, increased by 18.3 per cent in the first four months of 2015. Despite facing lower global prices, the sugar industry is still a major foreign exchange earner and accounted for 20.0 per cent of merchandise exports in 2014. Sugar production is forecast to rise by 8.5 per cent in 2015, reaching 245,500.

External trade

Fiji is a member of the South Pacific Regional Trade and Economic Co-operation Agreement (Sparteca) along with 12 other regional nations, which allows products duty free access by Pacific Island Forum members to Australian and New Zealand markets (subject to the country of origin restrictions). It is also a member of the Melanesian Spearhead Group (with Papua New Guinea, Solomon Islands and Vanuatu) as a sub-regional trade group, whereby customs tariffs have been harmonised under the Melanesian free trade agreement (MFTA).

Imports
Principal imports include manufactured goods, petroleum products, chemicals, machinery and transport equipment and food.
Main sources: Singapore (25.6 per cent of total in 2014), Australia (14.0 per cent), New Zealand (14.0 per cent), China (13.6 per cent).

Exports
Principal exports are sugar, garments and shoes, gold, timber, fish, molasses and coconut oil.
Main destinations: US (12.4 per cent of total in 2014), Australia (11.6 per cent), UK (7.7 per cent), China (5.9 per cent).

Agriculture
Farming
The agricultural sector accounted for around 12.7 per cent of GDP in 2014 and employs around 28 per cent of the workforce.
Historically, 85 per cent of land is granted to Fijian clans *(Mataqali)* and by law cannot be sold. This has led to underutilisation of some land. The soil is generally fertile and easily worked.
Sugar normally accounts for half agricultural output, but has declined both in quality and quantity. The sugar industry supports about 25 per cent of the working population, consumes around 12 per cent of all goods and services and earns more than 40 per cent of export income. The Fiji Sugar Corporation aims to diversify into ethanol and to encourage other uses for spare land, especially rice (50 per cent of which is imported).
The European Union announced in May 2009 that it would no longer pay a subsidised price for Fiji's sugar crop, worth over US$30 million annually. This was the second year in a row where Fiji missed out on business with the EU due to its unwillingness to adhere to democratic principles, which breach the Cotonou Agreement, and the EU's opposition to Bainimarama's military government and its refusal to hold democratic elections before 2014. However, in January 2015 the EU earmarked US$33.12 million in funding support over the next five years to assist Fiji's steady development, particularly directed at the sustainable expansion of the sugar industry.

Fishing
Fishing for local consumption includes skipjack, yellowfin and commercial species. Prawns and oysters are raised in fish farms. Bêche-de-Mer, shark-fins, trochus, mother-of-pearl and turtle shells are collected and sold.
The typical annual fish catch is over 44,700 tonnes (t) with over 14,000t of other seafood. One million pieces of coral are harvested annually as well as 160,000 units of pearls and shells.
The prawn industry was given an investment boost in July 2011, with the introduction of a species of giant freshwater prawn, which has a better survival rate than the local species. The new species, to be farmed, should boost employment and the economy.

Forestry
In addition to natural rain forest, large new plantations of pine and hardwood were established in the late 1970s. There are exports of pine chips to Japan and sawn pine to Australia. The clearing of forests has caused soil erosion.

Industry and manufacturing
The industrial sector as a whole accounted for 18.2 per cent of GDP in 2014 and employs about 15 per cent of the workforce. The manufacturing industry accounts for around 15 per cent of GDP and sugar accounts for one-third of industrial output. The industrial sector is dominated by the mining of gold, silver and limestone.

Tourism
Fiji can offer the quintessential tropical holiday, with white sandy beaches and azure lagoons with colourful coral gardens just offshore. Although Unesco has yet to award the status of World Heritage Site to any of the four sites proposed, they are nevertheless highlights of a trip to Fiji. The sites include a range of natural sights and the traditional township of Levuka, Ovalau. The tourist industry is geared up to cater for visitors arriving by air for packaged holidays and offers eco-tourist activities in its lush forests, water sports and traditional cultural encounters.
Australians are overwhelmingly the largest group of tourists, followed by tourists from New Zealand and the US.
Although the political turmoil has taken its toll on the economy and Fiji has had international sanctions imposed in 2000 and 2006, the tourism sector maintained its level of significance for the economy. In 2005, travel and tourism constituted a then record high of 36.9 per cent of GDP; however since then it has steadily fallen as the world economic downturn lead to a cut in the number of visitors and by 2011 its share of GDP was 27.7 per cent, a figure similar to that of 2000. Likewise, 30 per cent of total employment was typically found in travel and tourism, but fell to 25 per cent in 2010. However, the industry had picked up again by 2014, as travel and tourism contributed 37.0 per cent of GDP and supplied employment to 33.4 per cent of the working population – the equivalent of 112,500 jobs.
In the first four months of 2015, number of visitor arrivals increased by 7.5 per cent on the same period in 2014. Arrivals from New Zealand and the US increased the most, and arrivals from the main source, Australia, increased steadily. Arrivals from Asia increased by 30 per cent year-on-year and now contribute 10 per cent of all tourists. Visitor exports in 2014 increased by 6.6 per cent contributing the equivalent of 18.0 per cent of GDP. Arrivals are expected to be boosted by the leasing of two new aircraft by Fiji Airways in 2015, and another in 2017.

Environment
An Asian Development Bank (ADB) study published in November 2013 reported that Fiji's losses from the impacts of climate change could reach 4 per cent of its annual GDP by 2100, as higher temperatures and more extreme weather events hit agriculture and the broader economy.

Mining
The mining sector accounts for around 3 per cent of GDP and employs 2 per cent of the workforce.
Gold is Fiji's second largest export. Production is centred on one large mine, Vatukoula, owned by Emperor Gold Mines, which produces 120,000–160,000 ounces per annum and has 4.1 million ounces of mineral resources and 750,000 ounces of reserves. Accessible ore is expected to be exhausted within 10 years. Another smaller mine at Mount Kasai is operated by Pacific Island Gold and was reopened in 1997 following a 50-year closure.

Hydrocarbons
Fiji has no proven hydrocarbons reserves and relies on imports, which amounted to 11,380 barrels per day in 2013.
Oil exploration has been undertaken but the government curtailed all further development as the cost of extraction outweighed the return on investment, as well as environmental reasons.
No gas is produced or imported. Fiji stopped importing and consuming oil in 2005.

Energy
The Fiji Electricity Authority (FEA) is responsible for providing and maintaining national power, as well as regulating the market. The FEA is encouraging the use of renewable energy sources to reduce the country's dependence on imported diesel. A mini-hydroelectric scheme in Vanua Levu supplies electricity to 40 villages and other processing industries. Total installed generating capacity was 245,100 in 2013 whilst annual electricity generation was around 840 million kilowatt hours (kWh).

A financing system helps domestic and community users to purchase photovoltaic (solar) panels. Community projects will be able to lease the solar panels, which will be installed and maintained as part of the contract. The World Bank and the Australian-based ANZ bank provided initial investment to start the renewable energy project.

Financial markets

Stock exchange

South Pacific Stock Exchange (SPSE)

Banking and insurance

Central bank

Reserve Bank of Fiji (RBF)

Time

GMT plus 12 hours

Geography

Fiji comprises more than 800 islands, of which 100 are inhabited, situated about 3,100km north-east of Australia and 5,000km south-west of Hawaii, in the Pacific Ocean. The four main islands are Viti Levu, Vanua Levu, Tavenui and Kadavu. Plains and valleys, including flood plains, and low mountains provide agricultural land. High mountains are rugged and volcanic.

Hemisphere

Southern

Climate

Hot and damp, tempered by cool winds from May–October. Maximum temperature during summer (December–April) 32 degrees Celsius (C), when hurricanes and cyclonic storms sometimes occur; rarely falls below 18 degrees C during the rest of the year.

Entry requirements

Passports

Required by all. Passports must be valid for three months beyond the the date of departure and visitors must possess sufficient funds and return/onward passage.

Visa

Visitor's visa (for stays up to four months) are issued on arrival to many foreign nationals from the Americas, Europe, Australasia and some Asian countries.

Business visas, by representatives of overseas companies, from countries that do not require a visa may visit without further documentation.

Contact the nearest Fiji Consulate for further information.

Currency advice/regulations

There is no restriction on the import of local or foreign currency although it must be declared. Export of all currencies can only be up to the amount declared on entry.

Travellers cheques are accepted and are recommended in Australian dollars or pound sterling, to avoid added exchange fees.

In a review of currency designs in 2005 it was decided to retain the image of the head of the British monarch on the currency, even though Fiji has been a republic since 1987.

Customs

Personal effects allowed duty-free. Strict animal and plant quarantine regulations; fruit or plant material should not be brought in. Many agricultural and manufactured items subject to import embargoes and licensing and the list is subject to alteration. Details available from the Ministry of Commerce and Industry in Suva.

Prohibited imports

Strict animal and plant quarantine regulations apply; fruit or plant material are prohibited. Many agricultural and manufactured items are subject to import embargoes and licensing; a list and details are available from the Ministry of Commerce and Industry in Suva.

Health (for visitors)

Mandatory precautions

Vaccination certificates are required for yellow fever if travelling from an infected area.

Advisable precautions

Vaccination for diphtheria, tuberculosis, hepatitis A and B, polio, tetanus, typhoid and dengue fever. There is a rabies risk.

In rural areas water should be boiled before drinking.

Hotels

There are many tourist hotels of all standards and types, frequently in scenic locations around the islands.

Tipping is not encouraged but visitors may give a gratuity for excellent service.

Credit cards

Most major credit cards accepted at hotels, restaurants, shops and rental car agencies, tours, cruises and travel agencies. American Express, Diners Club, Visa, JCB and Master Card have representatives in Suva.

Public holidays (national)

Fixed dates

1 Jan (New Year's Day), 25–26 Dec (Christmas Holiday).

Variable dates

Good Friday, Easter Monday, National Youth Day (first Fri in May), Ratu Sir Lala Sukuna Day (last Mon in May), Queen's Official Birthday (Jun/Jul), Fiji Day (Oct), Diwali (Oct/Nov), Birth of the Prophet Mohammed.

Muslim and Hindu festivals are timed according to local sightings of various phases of the moon.

Working hours

Banking

Mon–Thu: 0930–1500; Fri: 0930–1600. Foreign exchanges Mon–Fri 0830–1700; Sat: 0830–1200.

Business

Mon–Fri: 0830–1630/1700 (some business close early on Fri).

Government

Mon–Thu: 0800–1300, 1400–1630; Fri: 1400–1600.

Shops

Mon–Fri: 0800–1700; Sat: 0800–1300.

Telecommunications

Mobile/cell phones

A GSM 900 service is available throughout most of the islands.

Electricity supply

240/415V AC, with flat three-pin plug fittings. Larger hotels have 110V conversion units for electric shavers.

Social customs/useful tips

Lightweight suit and tie for men and lightweight suit or equivalent for women. It is customary to shake hands on meeting and taking leave. On social occasions punctuality is appreciated, and dress should be formal.

An invitation to a traditional village is regarded as an important occation. When visiting a *bure* (a native thatched cottage) shoes must be removed and head lowered when entering. Hats must be removed and an invitation to drink kava should be accepted to avoid insult.

Clothing may be casual, but should be modest: swimsuits are not acceptable anywhere except on beaches and around hotel pools.

Getting there

Air

National airline: Air Pacific

International airport/s: Nadi International (NAN), 8km north of Nadi, 200km from Suva; duty-free shop, restaurant, bank, post office, car hire.

Other airport/s: Nausori (SUV), 21km from Suva.

Airport tax: Departure tax: F$150; not applicable to 24 hour transit passengers.

Surface

Water: Regular ferries operate between Kiribati, Nauru, Samoa and Tuvalu.

Main port/s: Labasa, Lautoka, Levuka, Savusavu and Suva.

Getting about

National transport

Air: Air Pacific operates the main route between Nadi and Suva. Sunflower Airlines and Turtle Island Airways operate on parts of Viti Levu and are available for charter. Helicopters can be chartered from Pacific Crown Aviation, Suva.

Road: There is a 3,300km road network, about one-third of which is metalled. On Viti Levu, a 500km coastal highway links main centres. A trans-insular road on Vanua Levu connects Labasa with Savusavu.

Buses: Air-conditioned buses operate daily between Suva, Nadi and Lautoka; fares are cheap. Air-conditioned coaches for longer distances.

Water: Small inter-island vessels operate from Suva and Lautoka. A regular ferry service connects Suva and Labasa, Ovalau and Koro Island. Ferries also connect the majority of the major coastal areas of Viti Levu and Vanua Levu with all the major islands. It is also possible to charter boats.

City transport

Taxis: Metered taxis are available in main centres. It is advisable to negotiate fares for long journeys, in advance. Journey time for a taxi from the airport to the city centre is around 10 minutes.

Buses, trams & metro: Journey time from airport to city centre 20 minutes; buses operate 0700–1830.

Car hire

Chauffeur-driven and self-drive car hire available. Current overseas or international licence acceptable for six months. Driving is on the left-hand side of the road, speed limits are 50kph in towns and villages, 80kph on highways.

BUSINESS DIRECTORY

The addresses listed below are a selection only. While World of Information makes every endeavour to check these addresses, we cannot guarantee that changes have not been made, especially to telephone numbers and area codes. We would welcome any corrections.

Telephone area codes

The international dialling code (IDD) for Fiji is +679 followed by the customer number.

Useful telephone numbers

Police, fire and ambulance: 000

Chambers of Commerce

Suva Chamber of Commerce, 7th Floor, Honson Building, Thomson Street, PO Box 337, Suva (tel: 331-3505).

Banking

Australia & New Zealand Banking Group Ltd, PO Box 179, ANZ House, 25 Victoria Parade, Suva (tel: 321-3000; fax: 330-0267).

National Bank of Fiji, 107 Victoria Parade, PO Box 1166, Suva (tel: 331-4400; fax: 330-2190, 330-2032).

Westpac Banking Corporation, 6th Floor, Civic House, Town Hall Road, Suva (tel: 330-0666; fax: 330-0718).

Central bank

Reserve Bank of Fiji, Private Mail Bag,Viti Levu Island, Suva (tel: 331-3611; fax: 330-1688; email: rbf@reservebank.gov.fj).

Stock exchange

South Pacific Stock Exchange (SPSE), www.spse.com.fj

Travel information

Air Fiji, 185 Victoria Parade, Suva (tel: 331-5055, 331-4495; fax: 330-0771, 337-0693).

Flight information (24 hours) (tel: 672-2599).

Hotel reservations (available 24 hours on arrival concourse) (tel: 672-2433).

Nadi International Airport, Civil Aviation Authority of Fiji, Private Mail Bag (tel: 672-2500, 672-1555; fax: 652-1500, 672-3795).

Tourist information (0800–1700 hours) (tel: 672-2433).

National tourist organisation offices

Fiji Visitors' Bureau, Thomson Street, PO Box 92, Suva (tel: 330-2433; fax: 330-0970, 330-2751; e-mail: infodesk@fijifvb.gov.fj; internet site: http://www.bulafiji.com).

Ministries

Ministry of Primary Industries and Co-operatives, PO Box 358, Rodwell Road, Suva (tel: 331-1233).

Prime Minister's Office (tel: 321-1201; fax: 330-6034).

Other useful addresses

Asian Development Bank (ADB), South Pacific Regional Mission, La Casa di Andrea, Fr. Dr. W. H. Lini Highway; PO Box 127, Port Vila (tel: +678 2 23-300; fax: +678 2 23-183; email: adbsprm@adb.org; internet: www.adb.org/SPRM).

Bureau of Statistics, PO Box 2221, Government Buildings, Suva (tel: 331-5144, 331-5822; fax: 330-3656).

Commonwealth Development Corporation, 371 Victoria Parade, Suva (tel: 330-2577).

Department of Information, PO Box 2225, Government Buildings, Suva (tel: 321-1250/1; fax: 330-0776).

Fiji Posts and Telecommunications Ltd, PO Box 40, Suva (tel: 321-0329; fax: 330-5591; internet site: www.TelecomFiji.com.fj).

Fiji Trade and Investment Board, PO Box 2303, Government Buildings, Suva (tel: 331-5988; fax: 331-5783).

Forum Secretariat, Ratu Sukuna Road, Suva (fax: 330-3069).

National Marketing Authority of Fiji, PO Box 5085, Raiwaqa, Suva (tel: 338-5888).

Pacific Islands News Association Secretariat (PINS), Private Mail Bag, Level II, Damodar Centre, 46 Gordon Street, Suva (tel: 330-3623; fax: 330-3943).

ABC Pacific Beat: www.radioaustralia.net.au/pacbeat

Pacific Magazine: www.pacificmagazine.net

Pacific Islands News Association (Pina): www.pina.com.fj

Internet sites

Fiji government: www.fiji.gov.fj

Fiji information: www.fijiatoz.com

Fiji Statistics: www.statsfiji.gov.fj

Tourism Council of the South Pacific: www.tcsp.com/destinations/fiji

Finland

KEY FACTS

Official name: Suomen Tasavalta: Republiken Finland (Republic of Finland)

Head of State: Presidential Sauli Niinistö (from 1 Mar 2012)

Head of government: Prime Minister Juha Petri Sipila (Suomen Keskusta, Kesk) (from 29 May 2015)

Ruling party: Coalition led by Juha Sipila (Suomen Keskusta) (Kesk) (Centre Party of Finland), with Timo Soini (Perussuomalaiset) (PS) (Finns Party) and Alexander Stubb (Kansallinen Kokoomus) (Kok) (National Coalition Party).

Area: 338,144 square km

Population: 5.48 million (2014)*

Capital: Helsinki

Official language: Finnish and Swedish

Currency: Euro (€) = 100 cents (from 1 Jan 2002; previous currency markka, locked at M5.95 per euro)

Exchange rate: €0.89 per US$ (Sep 2015)

GDP per capita: US$49,497 (2014)*

GDP real growth: -0.11% (2014)

GDP: US$271.17 billion (2014)

Labour force: 2.64 million (2014)*

Unemployment: 8.64% (2014)*

Inflation: 1.21% (2014)

Balance of trade: US$4.80 billion (2013)*

* estimated figure

Finland is featured regularly in the world suicide rankings top 20 countries. However, the *Independent* newspaper pointed out that according to a recent UN World Happiness Report, it appears to be the second 'happiest' country in the world (only Denmark ranked higher), based not simply on wealth, but on political freedom, strong social networks and the absence of corruption. In the latter case, Finland ranked second in the world on the 2013 Transparency International *Corruption Perceptions Index*, alongside Denmark and behind New Zealand. The United Kingdom (UK) ranked 16 out of the 174 countries surveyed, the United States (US) ranked 24.

Happy? Or suicidal?

However, it's not just a matter of 'happiness'. The *Independent* noted that academically Finland's students are also just about the best in the West, obtaining impressively high scores in a survey conducted for the Organisation for Economic Co-operation and Development (OECD). Anu Partanen, a Finnish journalist writing in *The Atlantic* made a surprising, but certainly true, observation: 'Decades ago, when the Finnish school system was badly in need of reform, the goal of the programme that Finland instituted, resulting in so much success today, was never excellence. It was equity.' Surprisingly, Finland has no nationally standardised tests, inspections or league tables, no private schools or private universities and no fees. Competition is actually discouraged, co-operation encouraged.

Surprised? The *Independent* noted that Finland could boast of exceptional equality in many social spheres. In 1906 it was the first country in the world to give women the vote, 12 years before the UK and 14 before the US. In 2009, Finland was the first country to enshrine broadband as a fundamental human right, when the government promised every Finnish citizen access to a 100mbps connection by 2015.

Paying for their pensions

September 2014 saw the Finnish government and representatives of its employers and trades unions reach agreement on proposed reforms to the country's pensions system, the most significant of which was the raising to 65 (from 63) the age at which pensions would become payable. The changes had become an essential element of government efforts to restore the balance of Finland's public finances.

The agreement, reached after three weeks of tough negotiations, was approved by all those attending the meetings, with the exception of Akateemisesti Koulutettujen Ammatillinen Keskusjärjestö (Akava) (Confederation of Trades Unions for Professional Workers and Management) which represents half a million professionally qualified employees. The revised pensions system would exclude from the higher age qualification those whose work might involve 'a high level of physical or mental effort' who would still be able to take full retirement benefits from the age of 63 as long as they had paid into the system for a minimum of 38 years. An additional reform was a new method of calculating pensions, based on the amounts paid in during the recipient's working life from age 17 to age 65. Those employed would need to pay in 1.5 per cent of their income during their entire working life and the pension to be received would depend upon the total amount paid in, with the net effect being that the longer a person worked, the higher would be the pension receivable.

Under the existing arrangement, the amount paid out as a pension was proportional to the amount paid in principally over the age of 53, making that of workers receiving higher salaries in their final 10–12 years of employment better off. According to preliminary government estimates, the reform would allow public expenditure on pensions to be contained and increase the amounts received by way of contributions, which it was estimated would save around one per cent of gross national product (GNP).

In 2013 the Finnish government spent some €27 billion (US$37 billion) on pensions, roughly corresponding to 43 per cent of its total expenditure on social services. The reforms, which needed to be properly drafted and then submitted for parliamentary approval, would not take effect until 2017 and in effect would only fully affect employees born after 1962.

Although agreement in principle had been reached on the pension reforms, it seemed that the ink had still to dry. The reforms had proved to be a difficult subject for many policy-makers. Akava representatives claimed that a number of parliamentarians had contacted them to express their concerns over the settlement. One representative considered that 'The pension settlement will surely become an issue in the parliamentary elections next spring (in 2015). What was certainly the case was that while the current administration lead by Prime Minister Alexander Stubb (KOK) would draw up the necessary legislative changes, it would be the responsibility of the next government to implement them.

The economy

In its May 2014 assessment of the Finnish economy, the International Monetary Fund (IMF) noted that of late Finland's strong economic record 'had stalled'. The economy had been in recession for three of the previous five years and unemployment was now more than 8 per cent, with more people without work for longer. The shortfall in growth, coming at a time when Finland's peer economies had seen gross domestic product (GDP) improve and unemployment fall, pointed to deeper, structural problems. Exports had suffered from the continued decline of the information and communications technology industry and falling demand for paper and pulp, but also because Finnish wage costs had increased at a time when labour productivity had deteriorated. Longer-term factors such as a rapidly ageing workforce added to the headwinds. Inflation, while still above the euro-zone average, had recently been decelerating. Against this background, government debt had been rising towards 60 per cent of GDP.

In the view of the IMF, the outlook was for a slow and fragile recovery. Weaker external demand could easily derail any upturn – for example, because of the negative effects from an escalation of geopolitical tensions. Domestically, the growth outcome could change with the timing and composition of fiscal adjustment. While the Finnish banking system remains strong, it is highly concentrated with the majority of assets controlled by subsidiaries of foreign Nordic banks, exposing it to the risk of short-term funding shortfalls and financial-sector spill-overs. And Finland's still rising levels of household debt could make consumers more cautious to spend if interest rates normalised faster than expected.

KEY INDICATORS — Finland

	Unit	2011	2012	2013	2014	**2015
Population	m	*5.40	5.43	5.45	*5.48	*5.51
Gross domestic product (GDP)	US$bn	266.60	247.28	268.28	271.17	*235.28
GDP per capita	US$	49,350	45,568	49,214	*49,497	*42,733
GDP real growth	%	2.9	-1.0	-1.3	-0.1	*0.8
Inflation	%	3.3	3.2	2.2	1.2	*0.6
Unemployment	%	7.8	7.7	8.1	*8.6	*8.7
Exports (fob) (goods)	US$m	82,390.0	76,457.0	78,559.0	–	–
Imports (fob) (goods)	US$m	79,264.0	72,128.0	73,759.0	–	–
Balance of trade	US$m	3,125.0	4,329.0	4,799.0	–	–
Current account	US$m	-4,245.0	-4,113.0	-2,466.0	*-1,555.0	*-623.0
Total reserves minus gold	US$m	8,397.0	8,453.2	9,369.2	8,773.8	–
Foreign exchange	US$m	5,778.2	5,697.2	6,685.9	–	–
Exchange rate	per US$	0.75	0.77	0.73	0.82	–

* estimated figure ** forecast figure

Reforms are under way to support growth and address risks. Finland remains a high-capacity economy with a skilled labour force and favourable business climate and there are plans to boost public sector productivity by consolidating the local administration of health and social services and lengthen working careers (see above). However, there is ample scope for additional reforms to address obstacles to longer-term growth, such as the shrinking workforce and the slowdown in private sector productivity growth. In the short- to medium-term, Finland's newly set expenditure ceilings should help strengthen the public finances, but the path of the recovery depends critically on the implementation. Additionally, draft legislation to strengthen macro-prudential policy and the reform of financial regulation at the European level promises to help guard against domestic and regional financial stability risks.

In an additional paper on some of the specific issues confronting Finland, the IMF looked at possible economic improvements, noting that Finland which has an economy known for its dynamic performance after the crisis of the early 1990s, is struggling to recover from the effects of the global financial crisis, indicating that deeper, structural issues might be holding back growth. The question was asked whether Finland's growth potential had actually changed? Based on a selection of approaches to estimate potential output, the paper considered that Finland's potential output growth had either slowed or was contracting, indicating the need for structural reforms able to boost overall growth in view of the fact that the economy had 'failed to return to trend growth' as had been the case in the 1990s recovery. Furthermore, the role of the preponderant telecommunications giant Nokia in the Finnish economy had implications for so-called steady-state growth and the need for an examination of Finland's research and development policies. Finally, any estimation of economic potential for Finland is particularly difficult given the high degree of variability affecting economic estimates suggesting that policies relying on these estimates should proceed with appropriate discretion. GDP levels had dropped markedly after the crisis in the early 1990s. However, on the back of strong structural reforms and a telecommunications sector dynamically expanding around Nokia, the Finnish economy had quickly resumed its pre-crisis pace. In contrast, the drop in GDP after the more recent financial crisis and recession of 2007–09, had turned out to be more persistent. This raised the question whether GDP growth would resume its pre-crisis trend.

Risk assessment

Politics	Good
Economy	Fair
Regional stability	Good

COUNTRY PROFILE

Before independence in 1917, Finland was controlled by Sweden and later Russia. Prior to Sweden's conquest of Finland in the 1150s, the country had been a feudal and tribal society.

1150–1293 Sweden was in control of Finland.

1362 Finland was granted the full rights of a Swedish province.

1523 Treaty gave Russia part of Karelia (area between Finland and Russia).

1721 Russia took control of the whole of Karelia.

1809 Finland was conquered by Russia.

1905–06 Strikes were held by the population demanding rights and liberties. Parliamentary government and universal suffrage were established; in 1906, Finland became the first European country to give votes to women.

1917 Collapse of the Russian Empire. A Finnish declaration of independence was followed by a brief civil war.

1919 Establishment of a republic; Kaarlo Ståhlberg became Finland's first president. In the following 70 years, more than 60 governments, mainly minority coalitions, held power.

1939–41 The Soviet Union invaded Finland and after the bitter conflict of the 1939–40 'Winter War', Finland entered the Second World War on the side of Nazi Germany. In December 1940, German troops were invited by the Finnish government to occupy parts of the country and Finland joined Germany's invasion of the Soviet Union in 1941.

1944 Finland signed a peace treaty with the Soviet Union and its troops withdrew from Soviet territory. Finnish troops were then engaged in the 'Lapland War' in northern Finland against withdrawing German soldiers.

1945 Following the end of the Second World War, punitive reparations and the cession of Southern Karelia and its only Arctic port, Petsamo, were forced on Finland by the Soviet Union.

1948 The Treaty of Friendship, Co-operation and Mutual Assistance was signed by Finland and the Soviet Union. It lasted until 1992 after the Soviet Union's break-up.

1956–82 The powers of the strong executive presidency allowed for in the constitution were further enhanced by President Urho Kekkonen. He was succeeded by President Mauno Koivisto in 1982.

1987 The Suomen Keskusta (KESK) (Centre Party of Finland) was replaced after 50 years in government. Conservatives were in the coalition government for the first time in 21 years. Harri Holkeri was appointed Finland's first conservative prime minister since 1946.

1994 Martii Ahtisaari was elected as president. The Suomen Kristillinen Liitto (SKL) (Christian League of Finland), which opposed EU membership, withdrew from the coalition after Finland completed negotiations on joining the EU.

1995 Finland joined the EU. The Suomen Sosialidemokraatinen Puolue (SDP) (Social Democratic Party) won the parliamentary elections and formed a coalition government, with the SDP's Paavo Lipponen as prime minister.

1999 The SDP was again returned as the strongest party in the parliamentary elections; a five-party government coalition was formed. Lipponen was re-elected as prime minister.

2000 Tarja Halonen was elected as president – Finland's first female president. The powers of the president were reduced, following the introduction of a new constitution.

2001 Finland joined other EU states to support the US's military action in Afghanistan, following the 11 September terrorist attacks.

2002 The Vitireä Liitto (VIHR) (Green League) left the coalition government after parliament voted to proceed with plans to build Finland's fifth nuclear reactor.

2003 Anneli Jäätteenmäki became Finland's first female prime minister, heading a coalition of her own KESK, which won the March parliamentary elections, the SDP and the SFP/RKP. Jäätteenmäki was forced to resigned as prime minister; she was unable to form a working coalition as she was seen as untrustworthy following her revelations of secret international undertakings by the former prime minister, during the election campaign. Parliament elected the defence minister, Matti Vanhanen, as prime minister.

2004 Former prime minister Jäätteenmäki was acquitted of charges of illegally obtaining secret documents about the Iraq War while she was opposition leader.

2005 Former prime minister, Paavo Lipponen, stepped down as party leader of the SDP; Eero Heinäluoma replaced him. The popularity of the EU fell, in line with a number of other EU member states that had rejected the new EU constitution in referenda, as a poll conducted in showed that 49 per cent of Finns would

vote 'no' to EU membership if given a choice at that time.
2006 The incumbent president, Tarja Halonen, won another term in office.
2007 In parliamentary elections the ruling KESK won 23.1 per cent of the vote (51 seats out of 200), only one seat more than its rival, the Kansallinen Kokoomuspuolue (KOK) (National Coalition Party). Prime Minister Matti Vanhanen (KESK) began talks with other parties immediately to form a coalition government.
2008 Former president Martii Ahtisaari was awarded the Nobel Peace Prize.
2009 GDP declined by 7.6 per cent in the first quarter. The start-up date for the Olkiluoto nuclear power plant (OL3) was postponed until 2012.
2010 Prime Minister Vanhanen resigned and Mari Kiviniemi became prime minister. Permits for two new nuclear reactors were granted in a measure to cut Finland's dependency on Russian oil and natural gas. The decision sparked protests, including a 10-hour blockade of the Olkiluoto nuclear power plant.
2011 Parliamentary elections were held in April, amid controversy concerning Finland's contribution to the economic bail-out of other, collapsing euro economies. The ruling SDP and NCP coalition approved the European Monetary Union's (EMU) efforts, but called for modifications in the procedures. The nationalist, PerusS opposed any Finish economic help. The NCP won 20.4 per cent of the vote (44 seats out of 200) and the SDP 19.1 per cent (42). Notably, the share of votes for PerusS jumped from 4.1 per cent in 2007 to 19.1 per cent and its parliamentary seats increased from five to 39; it became the leading opposition party. A coalition government was formed with Jyrki Katainen (NCP) as prime minister; it took office in June.
2012 Following two rounds of presidential elections, held on 22 January and 5 February, the ruling NCP's candidate, Sauli Niinistö won 62.6 per cent, while his rival, Pekka Haavisto (VIHR) won 37.4 per cent; turnout was 66 per cent. President Niinistö took office on 1 March. On 14 October, Prime Minister Katainen said that he had reservations about a proposed centralised euro-zone budget as backed by Germany and France.
2014 In April Prime Minister Jyrki Katainen announced he would be stepping down to take up an international position. On 24 June Cai-Göran Alexander Stubb became prime minister after first being elected chairman of the NCP. He formed a five-party coalition government, although the Vihreä Liitto (Green League) withdrew after a majority of the cabinet voted to approve a new decision-in-principle for the Fennovoima nuclear project in September.
2015 Elections were held on 19 April. The main winners were Suomen Keskusta (Centre Party of Finland) with 21.1 per cent of the vote (49 seats, out of 200), Perussuomalaiset (Finns Party) 17.65 per cent (38), Kansallinen Kokoomus (National Coalition Party) 18.2 per cent (37), Suomen Sosialidemokraattinen Puolue (SDP) (Social Democratic Party) 16.51 per cent (34) and Vihrea litto (Vihr) (Green League) 8.53 per cent (15). A coalition was formed, led by Juha Sipilä (Suomen Keskusta) (Kesk) (Centre Party of Finland), with Timo Soini (Perussuomalaiset) (PS) (Finns Party) and Alexander Stubb (Kansallinen Kokoomus) (Kok) (National Coalition Party).

Political structure

Constitution

Finland's republican Constitution, approved in 1919, was based on the principle of a unicameral parliament and a strong executive president.

In 2000, a new Constitution reduced the president's powers, and increased the role of the government – consisting of a prime minister and cabinet – who exercise power in conjunction with the president.

Independence date

17 June 1919, Declaration of independence

Form of state

Constitutional republic

The executive

The president is Head of State and is directly elected, by universal vote, for a six-year term, and is allowed to stand for office for two further consecutive terms.

The president and government exercise executive power over matters of foreign policy and national security. The president is expected to approve or reject all measures adopted by the Eduskunta (parliament) within a period of three months, and if no decision is reached, a bill lapses.

National legislature

The unicameral Parliament or Eduskunta has 200 seats of which 199 members are elected in single – and multi-seat constituencies by proportional representation and one member in the province of Aland elected by simple majority vote; members serve 4 year terms.

The parliament appoints the prime minister and the 17–18 members of the Valtioneuvosto (Council of State/cabinet). Most of its members are drawn from within the parliament, but a few may come from outside. It is responsible to parliament for the general administration of the country. Because Finland has a loose, multi-party system, the cabinet always contains a coalition of parties and may be re-formed frequently. The president is empowered to order elections, but the parliament decides when, typically the third Sunday in March.

Legal system

The legal system is based on Swedish civil law and is codified. The judicial system is divided between ordinary civil and criminal jurisdiction and special courts of litigation.

The president appoints a chancellor of justice who is not a cabinet member. His function is to oversee the Council of State and to submit an annual report on its legal conduct.

The Court of the Realm is supreme constitutional court, six of whose 13 members are elected by parliament for a term of four years. The final court for civil and criminal cases is the Korkein Oikeus (supreme court), whose president and 21 members are appointed directly by the state president; the supreme administrative court is the Korkein Hallinto-Oikeus. Composed of 21 presidentially-appointed judges, it is the highest tribunal of administrative appeal.

Last elections

19 April 2015 (parliamentary); 22 January/5 February 2012 (presidential, first round and runoff)

Results: Parliamentary: Suomen Keskusta (Centre Party of Finland) won 21.1 per cent of the vote (49), Perussuomalaiset (Finns Party) 17.65 per cent (38), Kansallinen Kokoomus (National Coalition Party) 18.2 per cent (37), Suomen Sosialidemokraattinen Puolue (SDP) (Social Democratic Party) 16.51 per cent (34), Vihrea litto (Vihr) (Green League) 8.53 per cent (15), Vasemmistolitto (VAS) (Left Alliance) 7.13 per cent (12), Svenska folkpartiet I Finland (SFP) (Swedish People's Party of Finland) 4.88 per cent (nine), Kristillisdemokraatit (KD) (Christian Democrats) 3.54 per cent (five), Alandsk Samling (Aland Coalition) 0.4 per cent (one); the remaining nine parties including the independents all received less than one percent of the vote and failed to gain any seats. Turnout was 70.1 per cent.

Presidential (first round): Sauli Niinistö (NCP) won 37 per cent of the vote, Pekka Haavisto (VIHR) 18.8 per cent, Paavo Väyrynen (KESK) 17.5 per cent, Timo Soini (PerusS) 9.4 per cent, Paavo Lipponen (SDP) 6.7 per cent, and Paavo Arhinmäki (VAS) 5.5 per cent. Turnout is 69.7 per cent. Runoff: Niinistö won 62.6 per cent, Haavisto 37.4 per cent; turnout was 66 per cent.

Next elections

March 2019 (parliamentary); January 2018 (presidential)

Political parties

Ruling party

Coalition led by Juha Sipila (Suomen Keskusta) (Kesk) (Centre Party of Finland), with Timo Soini (Perussuomalaiset) (PS) (Finns Party) and Alexander Stubb (Kansallinen Kokoomus) (Kok) (National Coalition Party).

Main opposition party

Perussuomalaiset (PS) (Finns Party).

Population

5.48 million. Finland is one of the most sparsely populated countries of the world. The industrial southern third of the country has a density of only 46.8 persons per square km, compared with a European average of 170 per square km; the north has barely nine persons per square km.

Last census: 5.48 million (2014)*
December 2000: 5,181,115

Population density: 17 inhabitants per square km. Urban population 85 per cent (2010 Unicef).

Annual growth rate: 0.4 per cent, 1990–2010 (Unicef).

Ethnic make-up

Virtually all the population is of Finnish origin, apart from a small foreign population of around 20,000, a small number of Romany Gypsies, a Sámi (Lapp) minority in the north and a significant Swedish-speaking minority in the west.

The Estonians are close cultural relatives of the Finns. There are some small ethnic groups related to the Finns living in Russia.

Religions

Nearly 90 per cent of the Finnish population belongs to the Evangelical Lutheran Church. The Orthodox Church accounts for most of the remainder; there are Catholic, Jewish and Pentecostal minorities.

Education

Unesco reported, in 2004, that Finland achieved the highest overall scores in international tests for educational quality. Public expenditure on education amounts to 5.7 per cent of GDP. Universal primary education and gender parity, at this level and in secondary schools, have been achieved.

A sustained investment in education has resulted in high standards with the most rapid rise seen among those achieving a tertiary level qualification. The younger age groups are now more highly educated than their elders with about 83 per cent of people aged 25–34 having at least an upper secondary qualification in 1997, as against only 23 per cent of the population over the age of 65 achieving the same.

The education system consists of comprehensive secondary schools, post-comprehensive general and vocational education, higher education and adult education each lasting for three years. Vocational institutions provide initial apprenticeship training, in nearly all fields. A three-year vocational qualification gives access to all forms of higher education. The Finnish higher education system comprises polytechnics and universities. The polytechnic system is founded on a nationwide network of 29 regional polytechnics. There are 20 universities, all of which are in the public sector. In addition to degree programmes, universities also provide adult education and various research and consultant services.

Compulsory years: 7 to 16

Enrolment rate: 99 per cent, for both boys and girls, total primary enrolment of the relevant age group. Enrolment in secondary and tertiary levels of the relevant age group was 118 per cent and 74 per cent respectively (World Bank).

Pupils per teacher: 18 in primary schools.

Health

The national healthcare system is excellent and few take out private health insurance. Employers pay towards national health insurance through social security contributions. Health services have traditionally been free, but the 1990s saw changes and nominal charges introduced on a range of basic services.

HIV/Aids

HIV prevalence: 0.1 per cent aged 15–49 in 2003 (World Bank)

Life expectancy: 79 years, 2004 (WHO 2006)

Fertility rate/Maternal mortality rate: 1.9 births per woman, 2010 (Unicef); maternal mortality 0.06 per 1,000 live births (World Bank).

Birth rate/Death rate: 10 deaths and 11 births per 1,000 people (World Bank).

Child (under 5 years) mortality rate (per 1,000): 3 per 1,000 live births (WHO 2012)

Head of population per physician: 3.16 physicians per 1,000 people, 2002 (WHO 2006)

Welfare

Finland has a well-developed system of social welfare, and the high level of support has proved to be a stabilising factor in social terms. However, the government has been forced by a steadily rising budget deficit to seek ways of cutting its social spending. Welfare spending, despite cuts, typically totals over 50 per cent of GDP. Finland has an ageing population; those aged over 65 are expected to constitute over a quarter of the population by 2030, one of the highest proportions in the world. Pension regulations have permitted earlier retirement than in many other countries. These factors, combined with high life Most Finns receive health insurance, unemployment benefit, pension and family allowances.

Main cities

Helsinki (capital, estimated population 583,331 in 2012), Esbo (251,896), Tampere (216,486) Vantaa (202,125), Åbo (175,965), Oulu (136,292), Lahti (100,530), Koupio (92,093).

Languages spoken

Finnish belongs to the Baltic-Finnic group of the Finno-Ugric languages, which also includes Estonian and Hungarian and is also related to Sámi, the language of the indeginous people of northern Scandinavia.

English is widely understood in business circles; German and Russian are also spoken.

Official language/s

Finnish and Swedish

Media

Press

The constitution guarantees the freedom of the press.

Dailies: There are over 50 newspapers published daily, of which 10 are national. In Finnish, morning newspapers include *Helsingin Sanomat* (www.hs.fi), which has the largest subscription circulation and *Aamulehti* (www.aamulehti.fi) with the second highest, *Borgåbladet* (www.bbl.fi), *Turun Sanomat* (www.turunsanomat.fi). The largest circulation newspaper in Swedish is *Hufvudstadsbladet* (www.hbl.fi). Evening newspapers are tabloid including *Ilta-Sanomat* (www.iltasanomat.fi) and *Ilalehti* (www.iltalehti.fi) which has the third largest circulation in Finland. There are also a number of newspapers sponsored by political parties.

Weeklies: Most daily newspapers publish a weekend edition. There are a full range of magazines for all interests, *Katso* (www.katso.fi) features popular entertainment, *Urheilulehti* (www.urheilulehti.fi) is a sports magazine and *Äpy* (www.apy.fi) is the country's oldest humorous magazine.

Business: Prominent publications include *Kauppalehti* (www.kauppalehti.fi), *Talous Sanomat* (www.taloussanomat.fi), and *Talouselämä* (www.talouselama.fi), which is a economic journal.

Periodicals: There are over 3,000 magazines on offer, most popular are of general interest.

Broadcasting

The national, public broadcaster is YLE (Yleisradio Oy) (www.yle.fi), which is funded by a licence fee. It typically attracts 44 per cent of TV viewers and over 50 per cent of radio listeners.

All analogue services were switched to digital in September 2007, allowing a mix of free-to-air and pay-TV services.

Radio: YLE operates seven radio stations through either digital or FM/MW/SW frequencies, which cater for all genres including cultural, music, talk, news, entertainment and education, in Finnish, Swedish and the Sámi-language. Radio Finland provides external services, including worldwide news in Latin.

There are many private national and local radio stations including Radio Nova (www.radionova.fi), Groove FM (www.groovefm.fi) from Helsinki, Radio 957 (www.radio957.fi) from Tampere and Radio Iskelmä (www.iskelma.net) from Lahti.

Television: There are over 20 TV stations of which the public broadcaster YLE (www.yle.fi) has six channels showing a full range of programmes. MTV3 (www.mtv3.fi) is the most popular commercial station, Nelonen (www.nelonen.fi) has 50 per cent foreign and domestic programming, Sub TV (www.subtv.fi) is aimed at the young.

National news agency: STT (Finnish News Agency)

Economy

The economy is strong, open and export-led, with paper and card, telecommunications equipment and engineering foremost. Finland is a world leader in innovation, by investing heavily in research and development (3.5 per cent of GDP) and has a highly-educated workforce. Its industrial base is mineral extraction of gold, silver, copper, limestone, lead, zinc, chromium and iron ore. Around 70 per cent of the country is forested and the timber it produces is used in quality products such as furniture and veneer boards as well as general products such as paper and wood pulp. However, the service sector is the largest component of the economy, constituting over 65 per cent of GDP and employing the majority of the workforce in public services, financial and banking services and the private sector.

GDP growth was 5.3 per cent in 2007, which fell to 0.9 per cent in 2008 as the economy began to weaken as the global economic crisis cut trade and imports of petroleum in particular were at a record high. By 2009 Finland was in recession with GDP growth of -8.0 per cent, the worst fall of any country within the euro-area. In 2010 a modest growth was recorded, with GDP growth of 1.2 per cent. The unemployment rate, which had been at 6.5 per cent in 2008 rose to 8.2 per cent by 2009 as domestic and foreign demand slumped. The government backed programmes of temporary employment, however it is anticipated that unemployment will remain at around 8 per cent until the economy is fully restored.

Nokia is a leading world brand of mobile (cell) phones and had a global market share of 38 per cent in 2009. Exports have been falling as other, typically US, manufacturers have introduced more popular models, such as Apple iPhones. Year-on-year Nokia global sales in 2008–09 fell by 7 per cent and it made a net loss of US$1.4 billion in the third quarter of 2009.

The banking sector was not unduly damaged by the global turmoil as Finland's strong regulatory and supervisory environment helped shield the financial sector. Any weakness exposed in 2008 was fully recovered by 2009. However, the future growth of the economy is largely dependent on the wellbeing of the global economy and when exports pick up.

External trade

As a member of the European Union (EU), Finland operates within a community-wide free trade area, with tariffs determined centrally and as a whole. Internationally, the EU has free trade agreements with a number of nations and trading blocs worldwide. Its economy is export-oriented, with over 40 per cent of production being shipped abroad and export trade representing 70 per cent of GDP.

Timber, wood pulp and paper constitute Finland's core export base.

Imports

Main imports are foodstuffs, including grain, fuel and petroleum products, chemicals, transport equipment, machinery, textile yarn and fabrics, and industrial raw materials such as iron and steel.

Main sources: Russia (15.4 per cent of total in 2012), Sweden (14.6 per cent), Germany (13.4 per cent).

Exports

Main exports are forestry products (Finland is the world's second largest forestry exporter, after Canada), mobile phones and wireless network technology, vehicles, machinery and equipment, bio-technology, chemicals.

Main destinations: Sweden (10.3 per cent of total in 2012), Russia (9.7 per cent), Germany (8.4 per cent).

Agriculture

Farming

The opening up of Finland's agricultural sector was a major issue in the negotiations for EU membership.

Finnish agriculture is based on small family farms, with the average agricultural area of a farm about 25 hectares (ha). Forests are an integral part of the country's farms, and the average forest area of farms is 43ha. About 43 per cent of the farms produce food crops. Wheat and rye are cultivated on about 10 per cent of the arable land, and about 9 per cent is used for growing other crops including potatoes and sugar beets.

Agriculture typically contributes 1.1 per cent of GDP, although active farms employ 5 per cent of the workforce. On average, only about half of the income of farm families is obtained from agriculture, while farm forestry usually provides 10 to 15 per cent of the income.

Production is based on livestock, and about 80 per cent of the agricultural area is used as pasture or for arable fodder cropping. About 33 per cent of the farms are dairy farms. Finland is 85 per cent self-supporting in food grains, dairy products and root crops.

The EU's Fundamental reform to the Common Agricultural Policy (CAP) was introduced in Finland in 2005. The subsidies paid on farm output, which tended to benefit large farms and encourage overproduction, were replaced by single farm payments not conditional on production.

Fishing

Fishing, aquaculture and fish processing are a traditional part of Finnish industries. The food fishing industry is managed in accordance with the EU's Common Fisheries Policy (CFP), which covers resource, market and structural policies including inland waters and sea fishing as a monitoring system.

Fish farming is carried out both in the sea and in inland waters. The most important economic fish for sea fishing are Baltic herring and salmon. Although employment in the sector has dropped considerably, the catch remains stable due to the adoption of more efficient fishing techniques. The total catch is around 120,000 tonnes, of which less than a third is used for human consumption.

The annual production of farmed fish is around 17,500 tonnes consisting mainly of large rainbow trout.

Forestry

Nearly three-quarters of the country is covered by forest, estimated at 21.9 million hectares (ha). Forest resources have been increasing steadily, as annual growth exceeds felling and natural losses. About two-thirds of the forest area is privately-owned, mainly by small-scale farmers. Timber products account for nearly one third of export products and nearly one third of manufacturing output. There is a high level of product specialisation, aided by the fact that the transport and machinery sectors tend to cater for the forest industry. The most common species of tree growing are Scots pine, spruce and birch.

Industry and manufacturing

Industry in Finland is concentrated in three areas: paper and pulp production; machinery and other metal products; and

hi-tech electronics (particularly mobile phone production). The metals, engineering and electronics sector account for over 50 per cent of the country's work force and exports. Finnish exports have underpinned its strong economy and only a severe global downturn could leave the country vulnerable, not only to industry-specific shocks affecting its three principal sectors, but also performance in its key markets.
Research and development (R&D) investment in Finland is one of the highest in the world.
In the first quarter of 2012, Nokia lost its place as the world's largest seller of mobile phones when the South Korean company, Samsung, announced sales of 93 million units, compared to Nokia's sales of 83 million units.

Tourism

Finland's natural environment is the backdrop to its tourist industry. It has vast forests and many lakes that offer a variety of activity holidays, which combined with a winter setting provides extended holiday seasons. Trips to visit Lapland and the home of Santa Claus are popular for families. The tradition of the sauna is part of holidays geared to health (particularly for the old traveller) and outdoor activities.
There are ancient and historic cultural sites to visit, a number of which are included on Unesco's World Heritage List.
Travel and tourism accounted for 6.6 per cent of GDP in 2010 (US$15.7 billion), a fall from the high of 7.7 per cent in 2007 (US$18.9 billion) recorded before the global economic crisis cut visitor numbers. Real growth in tourism had shown three years of decline by 2010, but by 2011 growth was 1.8 per cent with a small improvement in revenue.

Mining

The sector accounts for only 0.3 per cent of GDP.
There are around a dozen ore mines, producing mainly chromium, mercury, zinc, silver, copper and nickel.
Deposits are small. Prospecting is being intensified to curb imports; refining technology is a major focus of development work. Outokumpu, the mining and metals group, has modernised the production facilities at its Harjavalta plant through an investment programme. The programme includes the copper smelter and nickel production line located at Harjavalta and the copper refinery located at Pori, both towns in western Finland.

Hydrocarbons

There are no known oil resources and there are no current exploration plans. All demand for oil is met by imports amounting to around 220,000 barrels per day (bpd). There are two refineries in Finland with a joint capacity of 252,000bpd; both are located on the southern coastline.
There are no gas resources although consumption is typically around 4.4 billion cubic metres (cum), with imports mainly from Russia. In February 2009 Finland was still considering joining the consortium responsible for building a natural gas pipeline between Russia's Siberian natural gas fields to the energy hungry German, French and Dutch markets, via the Baltic Sea.
There are no coal reserves and the country's needs are met by imports from Poland, Russia and the US amounting to 3.4mtoe in 2008.

Energy

Finland has a sophisticated energy mix, which include oil, natural gas, hydro, nuclear, geothermal, solar, wind and biomass, including wood, coal and peat-fired power stations. Total installed generating capacity is around 18.6GW, with consumption of over 80 billion kilowatt hours (kWh) per annum.
Owing to the high proportion of energy-intensive industry, long distances between population centres and geographic situation with a cold climate, Finland's per capita energy consumption is one of the highest among International Energy Agency (IEA) countries.
There are four nuclear reactors – two Russian and two Swedish-built. Expansion of nuclear power has reduced dependence on imported coal and oil. Around 33 per cent of the energy mix is met by nuclear energy. The fifth nuclear power plant, in Olkiluoto on the west coast, began construction in 2005, but construction problems have delayed completion and commercial electricity production of 1,600MW is not expected until 2012. The Finnish electricity company, Teollisuuden Voima Oy (TVO), oversees construction. Approval for two new nuclear reactors was given in July 2010; this should make Finland self-sufficient in electricity by 2020.
Natural gas fulfils around 11 per cent of Finland's energy needs and wood fuels around 10 per cent of electricity generation and 15 per cent of the total energy requirement, which is one of the highest rates among industrialised nations.

Financial markets

Stock exchange

Helsingin Pörssi (Helsinki Stock Exchange)

Banking and insurance

There are around 341 banks in Finland. Nordea, the largest bank in the Nordic region is Finnish. Other major banks in Finland include Oko Bank, Sampo Bank and Sweden's Svenska Handelsbanken AB.

Central bank

Suomen Pankki (Bank of Finland); European Central Bank (ECB).

Time

GMT plus two hours (daylight saving, late-March to late-September, GMT plus three hours).

Geography

Finland is the fifth-largest country in Europe, but is one of the most sparsely populated. The land frontier with Sweden to the north-west is 586km long, while the far northern border with Norway runs for 716km and the eastern border with Russia for 1,269km. Finland's western and southern shores are washed by the Baltic Sea.
The coastal regions consist of flat clay plains, where most agriculture is undertaken. The lake district, which is estimated to contain over 55,000 lakes and is densely wooded forests, occupies much of the south-east. Northern Finland is within the arctic circle and is mostly scrubland.

Hemisphere

Northern

Climate

Finland's climate varies widely across the country, with exceptionally strong differences between the summer and the winter norms. Temperatures average 5 degrees Celsius (C) in Helsinki and minus 0.4 degrees C in the north. January is the coldest of the long winter months, with an average minus 9 degrees C. Peak average temperatures in Helsinki are reached in July (18 degrees C).
Average annual rainfall in Helsinki is 675mm. Spring months are relatively dry, declining to 36mm in March, but higher rainfall starts in July, reaching a peak of around 70mm in the August–October period. Finland's snow season usually runs from November to April (although it runs up to May further north).

Dress codes

Formal dress, including dark-coloured suits for men, is normal for business purposes. In winter, heavy, warm clothing is essential for outdoor wear. A fur cap and winter boots or overshoes are also strongly recommended.

Entry requirements

Passports

Passports are required by all and must be valid for up to six months beyond the date of stay. Nationals of countries which are signatories of the Schengen Accord may visit on national IDs.

Visa

Visas are required by all except nationals of Schengen Accord countries, North America, Australasia and some Asian countries, for up to three months. All visas

issued will adhere to Schengen Accord requirements. For business visas a letter of invitation from a local business contact, stating nature and duration of stay, plus proof of return/onward ticket and travel insurance, with a minimum coverage of US$25,000, or other medical insurance that covers Finland, must accompany the application.
For further information see http://formin.finland.fi/doc/eng/services/entry/main.html or contact the consular section of the nearest embassy. A Schengen visa application (offered in several languages) can be downloaded from http://europa.eu/abc/travel/ see 'documents you will need'.

Currency advice/regulations
There is unrestricted import of local and foreign currency.
Travellers cheques are widely accepted.

Customs
Personal items are duty-free. There are no duties levied on alcohol and tobacco between EU member states, providing amounts imported are for personal consumption. Visitors aged less than 22 years may not import alcohol over 22 per cent proof.

Prohibited imports
Alcohol drinks over 60 per cent by volume are prohibited. Certain plant material and food, firearms and works of art are subject to restrictions and formalities. The Finnish tourist board can provide further advice.

Health (for visitors)
Nationals of the European Economic Area (EEA) countries and Switzerland can access reduced cost and sometimes free medical treatment using a European Health Insurance Card (EHIC) while visiting the EEA. Exceptions include nationals of the 10 countries which joined the EU in 2004 whose EHIC is not valid in Switzerland. Applications for the EHIC should be made before travelling.

Mandatory precautions
No special requirements are necessary.

Advisable precautions
All imported medication that are narcotics must be accompanied by a doctor's letter. Mosquito repellent is advised for visits to the north in summer.

Hotels
In Helsinki and the surrounding area, hotels are classified into five price categories. Generally of a high standard. Rates vary depending on location, facilities and season. Accommodation should be booked well in advance, especially during summer. If accommodation is unobtainable, a place may be found through *Hotellikeskus* (accommodation clearing-house) at the Central Railway Station in Helsinki. Gratuities are not expected, with the exception of porters. Service is included in restaurant bills, although a little extra can be added.

Credit cards
All major international credit cards are accepted.

Public holidays (national)
Fixed dates
1 Jan (New Year's Day), 6 Jan (Epiphany), 1 May (May Day), 6 Dec (Independence Day), 24–26 Dec (Christmas Holiday).

Variable dates
Good Friday, Easter Monday, Ascension Day, Midsummer's Eve, All Saints' Day.

Working hours
Finns tend to take fairly frequent holidays during the summer months. As a result, business visits between mid-June and mid-August should be undertaken only after making sure that the other party will be available. September to May is the favoured time for business visits. Some businesses and shops close from midday on the day before public holidays.

Banking
Mon–Fri: 0915–1615. Post offices may close later than commercial, savings and co-operative banks.

Business
Mon–Fri: 0800–1600; in summer businesses frequently close at 1530.

Government
Mon–Fri: 0800–1600.

Shops
Mon–Fri: 0900–1700; Sat: 0900–1300. Large department stores and supermarkets open Mon–Fri: 0900–2000; Sat: 0900–1800.

Telecommunications
Mobile/cell phones
There are extensive GSM 900/1800 and G3 services available.

Electricity supply
220V AC, 50Hz. Continental two-pin plugs are standard.

Social customs/useful tips
Finns appreciate punctuality. A gift of flowers is usual when visiting a business partner's home for the first time. Guests should not start drinking before their hosts have proposed their health.
Tips are small, except for unusually good service.
Think twice before refusing to go to a sauna with a host, since such an invitation is seen as a gesture of confidence and friendship by your host. Business meetings are sometimes conducted in saunas.
There are strict laws on drinking and driving.

Security
Street crime is a relative rarity in Finland; normal precautions apply.

Getting there
Air
National airline: Finnair
International airport/s: Helsinki-Vantaa (HEL), 19km north of capital; facilities include banks/bureaux de change, duty-free shops, car hire, hotel reservations, VIP lounge, conference rooms and restaurants.
Other airport/s: Jyväskylä (JYV), 21km from city; Kemi (KEM), 6km from city; Kokkola (KOK), 22km from city; Oulu (OUL), 15km south-west of city; Rovaniemi (RRVN), 10km from city; Tampere (TMP), 15km from city; Turku (TKU), 7km from city; Vaasa (VAA), 12km from city.
Airport tax: None

Surface
Road: The majority of road routes include sea ferry links from Sweden or Germany. There is a land link via Norway or Sweden to Finnish Lapland, involving travel through the Arctic Circle.
Rail: There are rail/sea links from Hamburg, Copenhagen and Stockholm to Helsinki or Turku. A rail connection to Stockholm is available from Haparanda/Tornio in the north. There are daily trains to Moscow and St Petersburg.
Water: Daily ferry services from Sweden, twice weekly from Germany and Poland. Reservations should be made in advance as these tend to be heavily booked, especially during summer and at weekends. Also regular services to Estonia and St Petersburg (Russia).
Main port/s: Helsinki, Kotka, Hamina, Mariehamn, Vaasa, Turku, Pori, Sköldvik, Rauma and Oulu.

Getting about
National transport
Air: Finland has one of the densest internal networks in Europe. Finnair provides connections between Helsinki and Ivalo, Joensuu, Jyväskylä, Kajaani, Kemi, Kittilä, Kokkola, Kuopio, Kuusamo, Lappeenranta, Mariehamn, Mikkeli, Oulu, Pietarsaari, Pori, Rovaniemi, Saonlinna, Tampere, Turku, Vaasa and Varkaus.
Road: Finland's 77,000km network of public roads include 12,000km of high-grade national highway and 30,000km of secondary routes, but there is only just over 600km of motorways. Traffic is light but distances are great, the roads remain passable at all times of the year, although weight restrictions are imposed during April and May in southern Finland and May to June in northern Finland.
Buses: Efficient coach services cover the entire country, and are the main form of transport in Lapland.

Rail: Network of around 6,000km (including 1,600km electrified), operated by state railway company, Valtionrautatiet (VR). Relatively inexpensive and there are several passes available allowing travel over a set period. Seat reservation is obligatory on special express trains. Tickets are valid for one month. Sleeper services are available on the main connections.

Water: Important method of transport, owing to large number of lakes (187,888), which cover 31,500 square km.

City transport

Taxis: Taxis have a yellow *taksi* sign, which is lit when the taxi is vacant. They can be hired at taxi ranks or signalled from the street. Fares are more expensive at night. Taxi drivers are not tipped.

Buses, trams & metro: An efficient and integrated bus, metro and tramway service, suburban rail lines and ferry services to Suomenlinna Islands, operates in Helsinki. A common fares system applies to all the modes (including the ferries) with a zonal flat fare and free transfer between services. Multi-trip tickets are sold in advance, as are various passes.

Regular bus services, including Finnair City Bus, operate from the airport to the city, taking 35 minutes. Some Helsinki hotels run courtesy coaches.

Car hire

Available in most major towns. Rates include maintenance and insurance. The minimum age varies (usually 20–25) and at least one year's driving experience is a requirement for all drivers. The speed limits are 50kph in built-up areas, 80kph on normal roads and 120kph on motorways. The wearing of seat belts is compulsory. The use of headlights at all times is obligatory. Traffic drives on the right. A national driving licence or International Driving Permit is required. Driving around Helsinki is not recommended due to the lack of parking spaces. Any accident involving elk or raindeer must be report to the police.

BUSINESS DIRECTORY

The addresses listed below are a selection only. While World of Information makes every endeavour to check these addresses, we cannot guarantee that changes have not been made, especially to telephone numbers and area codes. We would welcome any corrections.

Telephone area codes

The international direct dialling (IDD) code for Finland is +358, followed by area code and subscriber's number:

Hämeenlinna	3	Mikkeli	15
Helsinki	9	Oulu	8
Imatra	5	Pori	2
Joensuu	13	Rovaniemi	16
Jyväskylä	14	Tampere	3
Kotka	5	Tornio	16
Kuopio	17	Turku	2
Lahti	3	Vaasa	6

Useful telephone numbers

Emergencies 114

Chambers of Commerce

Central Chamber of Commerce of Finland, 17 Aleksanterinkalu, PO Box 1000, Helsinki 00101 (tel: 696-969; fax:650-303; e-mail: keskuskauppakamari@wtc.fi).

Central Finland Chamber of Commerce, 4 Sepänkatu, Jyväskylä 40100 (tel: 652-400; fax: 652-411; e-mail: info@centralfinlandchamber,fi).

Helsinki Chamber of Commerce, 12 Kalevakatu, Helsinki 00100 (tel: 228-601; fax: 2286-0228; e-mail: kauppakamari@helsinki.chamber.fi).

Kuopio Chamber of Commerce, 2 Kasarmikatu, Kuopio 70110 (tel: 282-0291; fax: 282-3304; e-mail: kauppakamari@kuopiochamber.fi).

Lapland Chamber of Commerce, 29 Maakuntakatu, Rovaniemi 96200 (tel: 318-877; fax: 318-885; e-mail: kauppakamari@lapland.chamber.fi).

Turku Chamber of Commerce, 1 Puolankatu, Turku 20100 (tel: 274-3400; fax: 274-3440; e-mail: kauppakamari@turku.chamber.fi).

Banking

Nordea Bank Finland, Aleksanterinkatu 36 B, Helsinki, Fin-00020 Helsinki (tel: 1651; fax: 1654-2838).

Nordic Investment Bank, Fabianinkatu 34, PO Box 249, Fin-00171 Helsinki (tel: 18-001; fax: 180-0210).

Oko Bank, PO Box 308, Fin-00101 Helsinki (tel: 4041).

Sampo Plc, Unioninkatu 22, Fin-00075 Helsinki (tel: 105-1515).

Suomen Pankkiyhdistys r y (Finnish Bankers' Association), Museokatu 8 A, Box 1009, Fin-00101 Helsinki (tel: 405-6120; fax: 4056-1291).

Suomen Säästöpankkiliitto (Savings Bank Association), Pohjoisesplanadi 35A, 00101 Helsinki 10 (tel: 13-341).

Central bank

Suomen Pankki (Bank of Finland), Rauhankatu 16, PO Box 160, FI-00101 Helsinki (tel: 108-311; fax: 174-872; e-mail: info@bof.fi); European Central Bank (ECB), Kaiserstrasse 29, D-60311 Frankfurt am Main, Germany (tel: (+49-69) 13-440; fax: (+49-69) 1344-6000).

Stock exchange

Helsingin Pörssi (Helsinki Stock Exchange), www.omxnordicexchange.com

Travel information

Finland Travel Bureau Ltd, Mail Department, PB319, 00101 Helsinki 10 (poste restante service).

Finnair, Tietotie 11A, Helsinki-Vantaa Airport (tel: 81-881; fax: 818-4401; internet site: http://www.finnair.com).

Finnish State Railways (internet site: http://www.vr.fi/e-index.htm).

Helsinki-Vantaa Airport (tel: 82-771).

Helsinki Tourist Office, Pohjoiiesesplanadi 19, Helsinki.

National tourist organisation offices

Finnish Tourist Board (Matkailun Edistamiskeskus), Töölönkatu 11, PO Box 625, SF-00100 Helsinki (tel: 4030-1211; fax: 4030-1301/1333; e-mail: mek@mek.fi; internet site: http://www.mek.fi).

Ministries

FINNIDA (Finnish International Development Agency), c/o Ministry for Foreign Affairs, Merikasarmi, Laivastokatu 22, 00160 Helsinki (tel: 134-151; fax: 629-840).

Ministry of Agriculture and Forestry, Hallituskatu 3 A, PO Box 232, 00171 Helsinki (tel: 1601 (exchange); fax: 160-2190).

Ministry of Defence, Et. Makasiinikatu 8 A, PO Box 31, 00131 Helsinki (tel: 16-161; fax: 653-254).

Ministry of Education, Meritullinkatu 10, PO Box 293, 00171 Helsinki (tel: 134-171; fax: 135-9335).

Ministry of the Environment, Kasarmikatu 25, PO Box 380, 00131 Helsinki (tel: 19-911; fax: 1991-9545).

Ministry of Finance, Aleksanterinkatu 3, PO Box 286, 00171 Helsinki (tel: 1601 (exchange); fax: 160-3120).

Ministry for Foreign Affairs, Merikasarmi, Laivastokatu 22, PO Box 176, 00161 Helsinki (tel: 134-151; fax: 1341-5070).

Ministry of the Interior, Kirkkokatu 12, 001070 Helsinki (tel: 1601; fax: 160-2927).

Ministry of Justice, Eteläesplanadi 10, PO Box 1, 00131 Helsinki (tel: 18-251; fax: 1825-7730).

Ministry of Labour, Eteläesplanadi 4, PO Box 524, 00101 Helsinki (tel: 18-561; fax: 1856-7950).

Ministry of Social Affairs and Health, Snellmaninkatu 4-6, PO Box 267, 00171 Helsinki (tel: 1601 (exchange); fax: 160-4716).

Ministry of Trade and Industry, Aleksanterinkatu 4, PO Box 230, 00171 Helsinki (tel: 1601; fax: 160-3666).

Ministry of Transport and Communications, Eteläesplanadi 16, 00130 Helsinki (tel: 1601 (exchange); fax: 160-2596).

Prime Minister's Office, Snellmaninkatu 1 A, Fin-00170 Helsinki (tel: 3589-1601).

Other useful addresses

American Embassy, Itäinen Puistotie 14B, 00140 Helsinki (tel: 171-931; fax: 635-332).

British Embassy, Itäinen Puistotie 17, 00140 Helsinki (tel: 2286-5100; fax: 2286-5262).

Confederation of Finnish Industries, Eteläranta 10, SF 00130, Helsinki 13 (tel: 661-665).

Council of State, Aleksanterinkatu 3 D, 00170 Helsinki (tel: 1601 (exchange); fax: 160-2163).

Finnish Embassy (USA), 3301 Massachusetts Avenue, NW, Washington DC 20008 (tel: 202-298-5800; fax: 202-298-6030; e-mail: info@finland.org).

Finnish Foreign Trade Association, Arkadiankatu 2, PO Box 908, 001001 Helsinki (tel: 69-591; fax: 694-0028).

Helsinki Stock Exchange, Fabianinkatu 14, 00100 Helsinki 10 (tel: 624-161).

Invest in Finland Bureau, Aleksanterinkatu 17, 00100 Helsinki (tel: 696-9125; fax: 6969-2530; internet site: http://www.investinfinland.fi).

Liiketyönantajain (Confederation of Commerce Employers), Eteläranta 10, 00130 Helsinki 13 (tel: 19-281).

Main Post Office, Mannerheimintie 11, 00100 Helsinki 10.

Meilahti Hospital Haartmanink 3, Helsinki (tel: 4711).

Nesté (largest industrial corporation), Keilaniemi, 02150 Espoo, Helsinki (tel: 4501).

Oy Suomen Tietotoimisto (news agency), Lönnrotinkatu 5, 00120 Helsinki 12 (tel: 646-224).

Statistics Finland, Työpajankatu 13, PO Box FI-00022, Helsinki (tel: 17-341; fax: 1734-2279; internet site: http://tilastokeskus.fi/index_en.html).

Suomen Työnantajain Keskusliitto (Finish Employers' Confederation) Eteläranta 10, Helsinki 13 (tel: 17-281).

Tullihallitus (Board of Customs), Erottajankatu 2, 00120 Helsinki (tel: 6141).

Ulkomaankaupan Agenttiliitto (Finnish Foreign Trade Agents' Federation) Mannerheimintie 42A 00260 Helsinki 26 (tel: 446-768).

National news agency: STT (Finnish News Agency), Albertinkatu 33, 00180 Helsinki (tel: 695-811; fax: 695-81203 internet: www.stt.fi).

Internet sites

Virtual Finland: http://virtual.finland.fi
Finnish company information (top 100 Finnish companies): http://www.nedecon.fi

France

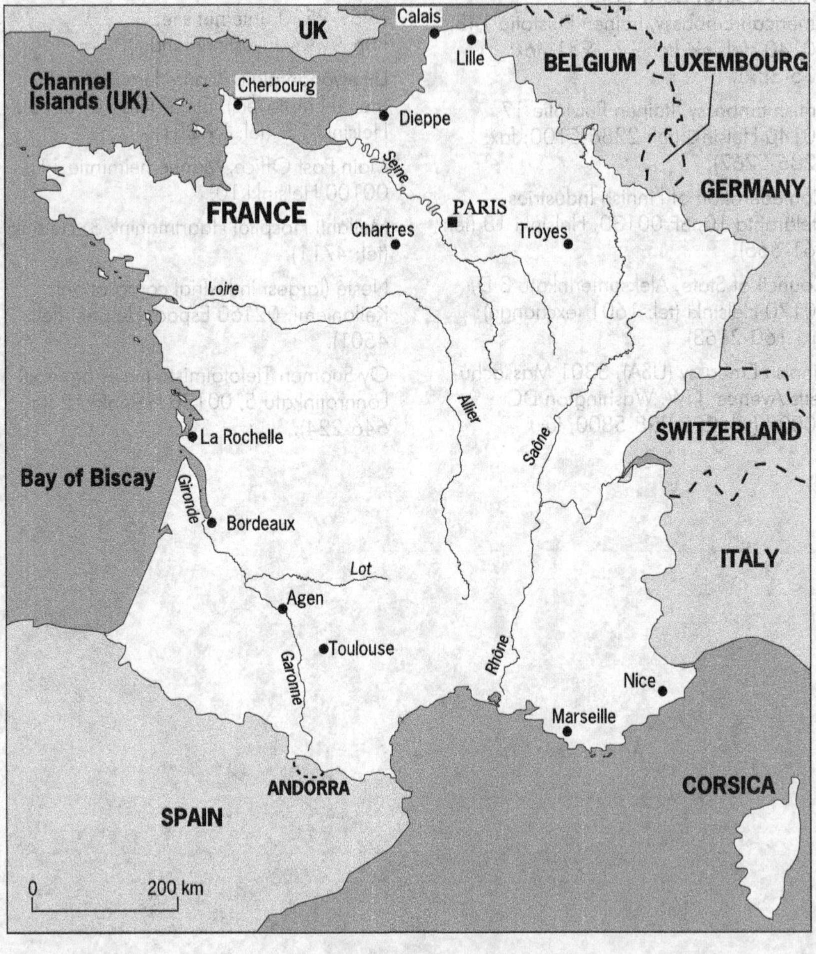

KEY FACTS

Official name: La République Française (The French Republic)

Head of State: President François Hollande (PS) (from 15 May 2012)

Head of government: Prime Minister Manuel Valls (PS) (from 31 March 2014, following the resignation of Jean-Marc Ayrault).

Ruling party: Coalition, Majorité présidentielle (presidential majority), led by Parti Socialiste (PS) (Socialist Party), with Divers Gauche (DVG) (Miscellaneous Leftist), Europe Écologie-Les Verts (EELV) (Europe Ecology-The Greens) and Parti Radical de Gauche (PRG) (Radical Party of the Left) (from 17 Jun 2012)

Area: 543,965 square km

Population: 63.92 million (2014)

Capital: Paris

Official language: French

Currency: Euro (€) = 100 cents (from 1 Jan 2002; previous currency French franc, locked at Ff6.56 per euro)

Exchange rate: €0.89 per US$ (Sep 2015)

GDP per capita: US$44,538 (2014)

GDP real growth: 0.36% (2014)

GDP: US$2,846.89 billion (2014)

Labour force: 28.27 million (2009)

Unemployment: 10.20% (2014)

Inflation: 0.62% (2014)

Balance of trade: -US$48.43 million (2014)

Nota

On Friday 13 November France suffered its worst terrorist attack when a number of persons thought to be members of IS shot and killed as many as 129 persons at the Bataclan concert hall and pavement cafes and restaurants. An attack by two suicide bombers on the Stade de France where France was due to play Germany in a friendly football match was foiled.

France has always been a country proud of its image, protective of its *amour propre*. In 2015 there was cause for concern. The world's sixth largest economy (France had been the fifth largest at the beginning of the year) was lagging behind in the race to recover from the effects of the global financial crisis. Germany, which had traditionally been seen as France's principal competitor, was distancing itself steadily each month. Under former President Sarkozy, France had tried to position itself as the pre-eminent ally of the US in Europe; in 2015 it emerged that the US had been listening in on the conversations of three French Presidents, Messrs Chirac, Sarkozy and Hollande.

The Anglo-French 2011 intervention in Libya to rid it of Muammar Qadafi had ended in the disastrous tribal division of that country. Worse, it had given *carte blanche* to the so-called Islamic State to establish a foothold in North Africa as well as aggravating an already horrendous refugee problem. But France's most embarrassing problems were home grown: two iconic French companies had passed into foreign ownership. The engineering giant, Alstom had been bought by General Electric of the US and Alcatel-Lucent by Finland's Nokia. In contrast to more open economies such as the UK, France has doggedly maintained both control and state ownership of its energy sector, with the monolithic Electricité de France (EDF) at the helm. Ironically, EDF itself has not been slow to invest in foreign energy companies.

Charlie Hebdo

The cold-blooded execution of 10 journalists and free-lancers working for the satirical magazine *Charlie Hebdo*, as well as of two policemen, in January 2015, shocked France. The further attack at a Jewish supermarket in Paris only reinforced the national resolve. The official response was surprisingly quick and effective, although perhaps inadvertently it encouraged French citizens to see the attack as a clash of civilisations or religions, rather than a one-off attack by a group of sadly deranged individuals. For years *Charlie Hebdo* had poked fun at the world's great and the good. No-one was spared – from politicians to Popes, from Britain's Queen Elisabeth to sundry fanatics. Slowly it dawned on the French that the magazine, more than most symbols of French values, represented everything that France was supposed to stand for. President François Hollande discussed the events with his predecessor, Nicolas Sarkozy, with the leader of the (anti-Islamic) National Front and with representatives of the Muslim community.

Sadly, the resolve to present a united front against the attack lasted little more than 24 hours when bickering among the political parties started over the possible presence of Marine Le Pen, leader of the FN, at the memorial service. But what mattered was that France's 'chattering classes' in the media and in politics, for the most part sought the positives to be cherished. 'Je suis Charlie' became a nationally respected slogan.

Nevertheless, underlying the January events was the knowledge, at all levels of society, that France's secular constitution and the society that created and followed it, was ill suited to deal with the problems confronting some of its Muslim population. The complex relations with the Muslim community, especially those with Algerian roots, go back over 50 years to the days of a fierce and bloody war of independence in which France suffered a *de facto* defeat. In 2015 France had over 3,000 troops deployed across five countries in Africa – Mali, Mauritania, Burkina Faso, Niger and Chad – as part of Operation Burkhane. Based in Chad, this operation is designed to disrupt any potential militant threat across the Sahel region of the continent. But at the same time, it brings France into the firing-line at home. France has joined countries such as the UK as a 'little Satan'.

France's attitude towards immigrants has, since the race-riots of 2008, looked to be in need of recalibration. It's employment laws appear to work against those seeking work, in favour of those already in employment. The global financial crisis may have exacerbated matters, but youth unemployment levels have been unacceptably high, especially among immigrant communities, for decades.

Straws in the wind

The April 2015 local elections may not have carried the level of gravitas seen in national elections, but they did give a clear idea of the way in which French politics were moving. The opinion polls had suggested that the populist Front National (FN) (National Front) would continue to gain ground and the Socialists would continue to lose it. The first round of voting saw the UMP (see below) gain around 29 per cent of the votes, with the FN only just behind, on 25 per cent. The Socialist Party managed to avoid a catastrophic beating, but the 21.5 per cent obtained was well down on previous results and augured badly for the party's prospects in the November 2015 elections. The advent of the FN as a serious political threat produced a knee-jerk negativity on the part of the Socialists – where Prime Minister Manuel Valls encouraged voters to cast their vote for any party except the National Front. Nicolas Sarkozy in his latter day Union pour un Mouvement Populaire (UMP) (Union for a Popular Movement) role (see below) went a stage further, encouraging voters to abstain rather than vote for a Parti Socialiste (PS) (Socialist Party) or FN candidate. The FN's prospects seemed to be highest in Southern France, according to one report in the London *Financial Times*, which noted that 'The FN has achieved some of its highest scores in southern France by exploiting anxiety over immigration and an unemployment rate that exceeds the national average of 12 per cent.'

Sarkozy Redux

In May 2015 it seemed that former President Nicolas Sarkozy had managed to regain the political centre ground, under a new name – The Republicans – which may have owed something to Mr Sarkozy's fondness for things American. Mr Sarkozy's objective was to ready himself and his supporters for the 2017 elections. Sarkozy's initiative took his rivals by surprise, opening up a debate on the very nature of French politics.

Sarkozy's move came at a time when the Socialist party, led by President Hollande and his prime minister, Manuel Valls, was on the back foot, unable to find an acceptable solution to France's dire economic problems. However weak the PS government was perceived to be, the party that had long been the political centre's flag carrier, the UMP, once led by Mr Sarkozy, had been unable to gain any political advantage. France's opinion polls suggested that voters were deserting the political centre, instead opting for the

KEY INDICATORS — France

	Unit	2011	2012	2013	2014	**2015
Population	m	63.09	63.38	63.65	63.92	*64.21
Gross domestic product (GDP)	US$bn	2,776.30	2,612.67	2,807.31	2,846.89	*2,469.53
GDP per capita	US$	44,008	41,223	44,104	44,538	*38,459
GDP real growth	%	1.7	*0.0	0.3	0.4	*1.2
Inflation	%	2.3	2.2	1.0	0.6	*0.1
Unemployment	%	9.2	10.2	10.3	10.2	*10.1
Coal output	mtoe	0.1	0.1	–	0.1	–
Exports (fob) (goods)	US$m	593,510.0	56,735.0	580,840.0	581.7	–
Imports (fob) (goods)	US$m	681,620.0	46,343.0	637,300.0	630.1	–
Balance of trade	US$m	-88,110.0	-7,607.0	-56,450.0	-48.4	–
Current account	US$m	-54,169.0	-57,114.0	-40,207.0	-29,907.0	*-2,679.0
Total reserves minus gold	US$m	59,530.0	54,231.0	50,849.0	49,547.0	–
Foreign exchange	US$m	37,206.0	30,350.0	27,414.0	–	–
Exchange rate	per US$	0.75	0.77	0.73	0.82	–

* estimated figure ** forecast figure

more peripheral parties, particularly the extreme right wing FN lead by Marine Le Pen (see below). Mr Sarkozy appeared to believe that he could reverse this trend, hijacking the centre ground traditionally held by the UMP and its ancestors.

The UMP hierarchy, Messrs Fillon, Juppé and Le Maire, considered the Sarkozy scheme to be little more than a distraction, an exercise in self-aggrandisement. Mr Sarkozy's riposte was to insist that what was needed was the re-integration 'of those who are fed up with seeing the steady decline of the French Republic and want to end it once and for all.' Sarkozy insisted that 80 per cent of party militants and 70 per cent of all French citizens shared his opinions. However, Sarkozy's major challenge was, quite simply, that of recovering the voters lost to Marine Le Pen. This required him to adopt positions to the right of his natural political inclinations. He will have to wait until the December 2015 regional elections to put his views to the test. In the event that his position is indeed shared by a wider electorate, he would be both vindicated and strengthened. On the other hand, by shifting to the right, however moderately, he might find himself weakened. His shift to the right has been openly tactical, rather than subtly strategic.

Meanwhile, as a post Sarkozy legacy, the weakened UMP continued to face allegations that it had 'systematically' falsified its accounts to allow Sarkozy's electoral campaign team to exceed the legal limit on electoral spending in 2012. As might be expected, Mr Sarkozy denied all knowledge of the accounting legerdemain. Distancing themselves from the UMP, his supporters suggested that the cash was possibly embezzled by rogue party officials. Nonetheless Sarkozy's enemies within the UMP (and they are numerous) hoped that these revelations would, once and for all, end the diminutive former president's chances of returning to the political centre stage.

Ironically, in the lead up to the April elections, Mr Sarkozy had seen fit to sport his UMP colours, enabling him to bask in the limited glory of the UMP's rather limited success. Sarkozy may have been successful in the polls, but he was doing less well in his battle with the judges. The enquiries that were being made into his 2012 electoral expenditure had resulted in the former president not only having to repay €153,000 (US$172,000), but also pay a fine of €363,000 (US$408,000). The UMP, blissfully unaware of Sarkozy's plans – to be announced a matter of weeks later – to abandon the UMP and chance his luck with the new Republicans Party, appealed to all its members to contribute to the Sarkozy rescue fund, in what became known as a Sarkothon. The appeal exceeded expectations, gathering a reported €11 million (US$12.4 million). Although Mr Sarkozy had not been formally charged with breaking the electoral law, he was clearly sailing close to the wind; by April 2015 seven of the UMP hierarchy had been accused of complicity in the affair.

Le Pen – en Famille

In 2015 the meteoric rise of Marine Le Pen in the French electoral hierarchy risked being prejudiced by her increasingly unpleasant feud with her father, Jean-Marie Le Pen. Le Pen père was the co-founder of the party in 1972, which then presented an openly racist, anti-immigrant, anti-semitic and anti-coloureds platform. Mr Le Pen was arrested on a number of occasions for allegedly offensive speeches. Jean Marie Le Pen ran in the French presidential elections in 1974, 1988, 1995, 2002 and 2007. His moment of glory came in the presidential elections of 2002,when he obtained over 16 per cent of the votes in the first round. The weak performance of the Socialist candidate Lionel Jospin enabled Le Pen to proceed to the second, final round. This was a headline grabbing moment; however in the final round Le Pen was comfortably defeated by the incumbent president Jacques Chirac, who obtained a record breaking 82 per cent of the votes. In 2015 his remarks continued to hit the headlines, not least when he described prime Minister Valls as 'an immigrant'.

Aiming to bring the FN on to the centre stage of French politics, Marine Le Pen – who took over from her father in 2011 – successfully managed to play down the party's more extremist views, at the same time riding the wave of anti-European Union (EU) and anti-immigration sentiment that had begun to take hold throughout Europe. Part of the process of establishing the party – which had performed exceptionally well in the 2014 European elections – involved marginalising Jean-Marie Le Pen, reportedly (in the *New York Times*) accused by his daughter of falling back on a strategy 'somewhere between scorched earth and political suicide.'

Hollande flounders

To acquire the accolade of the 'worst president of the Fifth Republic' is no mean achievement. It was one of many given to Francois Hollande, none of them complimentary. According to *Le Parisien Dimanche* in May 2014 to the question 'Who is the best president of the Fifth Republic?' only 0.5 per cent opted for Mr Hollande, placing him last, six per cent behind his nearest rival and way behind the poll's leader, General de Gaulle, president from 1959 to 1969. The PS Francois Mitterand, Mr Hollande's mentor, president from 1981 to 1995, came second with 27 per cent. Nicolas Sarkozy (see 'getting the UMP' below), whom Mr Hollande defeated in the 2012 election came third with a surprising 10 per cent, in front of Valéry Giscard d'Estaing (1974–81) with 8 per cent, level with Jacques Chirac (1995–2007). Georges Pompidou (1969–74) came fifth with 7 per cent. Even among PS voters, Hollande could only manage penultimate place, in front of his predecessor, Sarkozy. Among right-wing voters, De Gaulle won 48 per cent of the votes, Hollande came a predictable last. Another poll, in the *Journal du Dimanche* indicated that only 18 per cent of the electorate were satisfied with Hollande.

The art of unpopularity

An article in the London *Independent* noted that French presidents generally appear to suffer from two types of political unpopularity. The first derives from a need to take mid-term 'difficult' decisions'. Electors on the receiving end of budget cuts and tax increases are prone to express their dissatisfaction in polls and mid-term elections. The second type of unpopularity, according to the *Independent*, derives from leaders who are simply incoherent, their half-hearted reforms simply to range the electorate against them and their government. Mr Hollande's problem was that having failed to impose his authority, he found that virtually any new measure he proposed – from eco-taxes to the retro-active tax proposed on life insurance policies – attracted a wave of discontent, forcing the government on to the back foot and eventually to the rejection of the new measures. As many as 100 deputies on the party's left-wing had threatened to block proposed spending cuts. Even those few who remained well-disposed to Mr Hollande had found plans to merge the 22 French regional governments into just 14 over a two year period a bridge too far.

Thus, to the impression of incompetence is added that of weakness. Within Mr Hollande's PS party there ran numerous, contradictory, currents. Ministers argued in public, making it impossible to discern any clear policy direction. Mr Hollande found himself paying the price of an election victory won with the assistance of a programme described by Gunther Nonnenmacher writing in the *Frankfurter Allgemeine Zeitung* as 'completely Utopian', a programme that envisaged France overcoming the after-effects of the global financial crisis without any sacrifices on the part of the electorate or any serious reforms. All this was to be financed by the simplistic ploy of taxing the rich. The reality was, however, that the middle classes found their taxes increasing. By mid-2014 the French economy was showing barely visible signs of growth. France's socio-economic future was at best unknown. The French future was about fear rather than certainty. After a cabinet re-shuffle in the spring of 2014, President Hollande had pinned all his and many of his country's hopes on the arrival – to the rescue cavalry style – of France's new, right of centre- Prime Minister, Manuel Valls

Arriba Areva?

In 2015 the state-owned nuclear energy company AREVA was thought to be close to bankruptcy. Its accounts for 2014 showed a loss of €4,830 million (US$5,428 million). This, in a country that derives around 75 per cent of its electricity from nuclear generation was quite something. Just as surprising, was the fact that the company was in effect the sole supplier of nuclear weapons to the French government. The commissioning of its showcase generator, the third generation EPR (a pressurised water reactor (PWR) designed and developed for the most part by a company called Framatome (which later became known as Areva NP) and EDF), was seven years behind schedule. In Europe the new reactor design was called the European Pressurised Reactor, but elsewhere the name Evolutionary Power Reactor was preferred. In either case, it became the EPR and was projected to enter service in 2018. In 2015 it had already cost €9,000 million (US$10,100 million), three times the original forecast. The first EPR order was for Finland and two more had been ordered by China.

The French Autorité de Sureté Nucléaire (ASN) (Nuclear Security Authority) had added to Areva's woes by reporting that the core of the EPR reactor risked fissures due to the enormous pressures involved. This meant that the core, made of steel and nickel, weighing some 425 tonnes, needed to be replaced. More bad news followed when it emerged that in 2006 and 2007 Areva had purchased expensive uranium and nickel mines which it had yet to exploit. The French government had little choice but to 'sell' Areva to EDF for a few thousand millions of euros and the appropriate accounting legerdemain. It was hoped that a Chinese company might be interested in investing, as had been the case with the airports of Nice and Lyon. Not that this would do much for French self-esteem.

The OECD – the view from Paris

In the view of the Paris-based Organisation for Economic Co-operation and Development (OECD) in its 2015 Economic Survey 'France has an enviable standard of living due to its high levels of productivity' and well educated labour force. France's levels of inequality were considered to be low and the OECD thought that France had emerged from the global financial crisis relatively unscathed. The government's borrowing costs were low and the banking sector appeared to be sound. Surprisingly, the cost of credit did not, in the eyes of the OECD, seem to be a constraining factor, even for small- to medium-size enterprises. The OECD, in what was a rather vague generalisation, stated that 'France also stands out in terms of work-life balance, health status, social connections and environmental quality.'

That was the good news. The OECD went on to note that 'France's fundamental problem is a lack of growth.' In the view of the OECD 'growth had been sluggish for about a generation.' Supply-side weaknesses had led to 'a gradual deterioration on the competitiveness if its enterprises, manifest in a weakening in foreign trade performance since 2002.'

The IMF- the view from Washington

In its May 2015 assessment of the French economy, the International Monetary Fund (IMF) (headed by former French minister of economic affairs, Christine Lagarde) noted that the French economy was recovering, but that – echoing the view of the OECD – its growth potential still appeared to be much weaker than was the case before the global financial crisis. After almost four years of near-stagnation, the IMF projected gross domestic product (GDP) growth to rise to 1.2 per cent in 2015, a figure that was higher than the government's forecast. The economy's recovery was, in the view of the IMF, supported by the highly accommodative external environment, in particular sharply lower oil prices, a depreciated euro and interest rates that were at historic lows. An initial surge in growth had been driven by increased household consumption; exports also looked set to pick up. However, according to the IMF, investment had not yet responded, unemployment remained stubbornly high and public debt continued to rise. Moreover, there existed the possibility that the positive external environment might dissipate, leaving France's structural rigidities continuing to weigh on its growth potential – projected by the IMF at an average of just 1.25 per cent over the following five years.

In the view of the IMF, high and rising government spending has been at the heart of France's fiscal problems for decades. Driven by local governments, social security and the wage bill, general government expenditure reached a record high of 57.5 per cent of GDP in 2014, 11 per cent of GDP above the euro-zone average. While the growth of central government and health care spending had been contained, local government spending had continued to expand and France's social spending was the highest among OECD members. These persistent spending pressures had pushed up not only public debt but also the tax burden on the private sector, to very high levels. After years of significant fiscal adjustment through higher revenues, the IMF considered that France's switch to spending-based consolidation was the right strategy and needed to be maintained.

The IMF projected that the fiscal deficit would be brought to below 3 per cent of GDP in 2017, but it acknowledged that there was a risk that this target would be missed in the event of adverse shocks. The macro-economic assumptions underlying the government's April 2015 *Programme de Stabilité* were prudent, but the expenditure measures needed to implement the programme were not yet fully specified. Moreover, the planned pace of adjustment provided little margin should growth and inflation fail to meet targets or new spending needs arise. Keeping expenditure flat in real terms would deliver a structural fiscal adjustment of about 0.5 per cent of GDP per year and build larger buffers to achieve the medium-term deficit objectives, including a structural balance by 2020. Crucially, it would help ensure that public debt was on a firm downward trajectory by 2017.

In the view of the IMF, the fact remained that high unemployment and stagnant job creation remained the defining challenge for the French government.

Important steps had been taken to address these issues, in particular through a reduction of the tax take on lower salaries specified in the *Pacte de Responsibilité* and the Crédit d'impôt pour la compétitivité et l'emploi (CICE) tax credit) introduced in 2013 to enhance the competitiveness of businesses in France. The CICE was to be used to boost investment, research, innovation, training, employment and the exploration of new markets and to help firms recover their working capital. Other 2013 agreements had been designed to enhance flexibility at the enterprise level and those set out under the so-called *Loi Macron* were designed to reduce judicial uncertainties over dismissal issues through a reform of the *prud'homme* system (The French Employment Tribunal system handling employment issues such as dismissal, salary disputes, contractual differences, holiday allowances etc. A *prud'homme* tribunal consists of non professional judges drawn from both employers and employees in equal numbers. However, the IMF considered that without further structural reforms, France's unemployment rate was only likely to decline at a slow rate.

The decline in competitiveness over the previous decade continued, according to the IMF, to weigh on exports and investment. It was hoped that the *Loi Macron* would liberalise the legal professions, the retail and public transport sectors while enhancing the Competition Authority's mandate. The efforts led by France's Business Simplification Council should help reduce red tape. The disincentives for smaller companies to grow above certain employee thresholds should be reduced, including by easing labour-related regulations as envisaged under the draft *loi Rebsamen* (named after the incumbent minister of labour), but also other legal requirements such as accounting, tax and profit sharing. The functioning of the housing sector should said the IMF, also be reviewed, with a view to removing constraints on the supply of affordable housing.

In conclusion, the IMF took the view that France's financial sector still had further to go to adapt to the changing economic and regulatory environment. The 2014 Comprehensive Assessment by the European Central bank (ECB) did not result in any banks needing to raise additional capital and bank lending was gradually picking up. However, the decline in interest rates to historic lows was putting pressure on margins for both banks and insurance companies, while the prospects of a continued tightening of regulatory standards might further weigh on their profitability. To ensure the efficient functioning of the financial sector, the IMF recommended a reduction in the guaranteed interest rates under the regulated savings schemes, which it was thought hampered the efficient transmission of the ECB's monetary policy.

The CGT –The view from the streets

Parisian protestors are adept at taking to the streets, whether for political, economic or social reasons; demonstrations are well organised and policed. In April 2015 it was the Conféderation Général du Travail (CGT) (General Labour Confederation) that organised an anti-austerity protest that brought an estimated 300,000 demonstrators to the streets of the capital and other major cities. In Paris an estimated 120,000 demonstrators walked from the Place de l'Italie to Les Invalides, a distance of some 5 kilometres. The demonstrations came one day after the government had announced the continuation of its labour reform programme. The CGT focussed mainly on wage rises for the public sector and on a tighter adherence to the 35 hour working week, as proscribed by French law.

Also on the agenda was the perception that the government was doing more to help investors and businesses than those who worked in them. The General Secretary of the CGT since January 2015, Philippe Martínez, flatly advocated a 32 hour week. The CGT, however, could not count on total support from French wage-earners. The more moderate Confédération Française Démocratique du Travail (CFDT) (French Democratic Confederation of Labour) had chosen not to join the CGT on the streets. It's take on events in France was more supportive of the government: the CFDT's leader, Laurent Berger, going as far as to say that 'In France there is no austerity, especially when compared to Spain, Portugal and Greece.'

The economy – the ministerial view

The French minister of labour, François Rebsamen, noted that the purchasing power of the French had at no time stopped increasing, growing at a rate of 1.1 per cent in 2014. Public expenditure (which at 56 per cent of GDP is one of the world's highest) had also continued to rise, although in 2015 the government planned to reduce it to 55.4 per cent and to 54.7 per cent in 2016. Mr Rebsamen's rosy view was challenged by the CGT secretary general, who claimed that 'the policies of the Socialist government are not appropriate for a left-wing party, they are austerity policies.'

Risk assessment

Politics	Fair
Economy	Poor
Regional stability	Good

Muslims in France

% of population	7.5
Sunni (% of Muslims)	97
Shi'a (% of Muslims)	3

People to watch

Manual Valls, the son of Spanish immigrants from Barcelona appointed Prime Minister by President Hollande.

COUNTRY PROFILE

1337–1453 The Hundred Years' War took place between the English and the French. The English were defeated in 1453 and driven out of Aquitaine in southern France.

1789 The lack of representation for the increasingly powerful middle class, opposition to France's absolute monarchy and economic problems led to the French Revolution and the overthrow of Louis XVI.

1792 The First Republic was declared.

1804 Napoléon Bonaparte declared himself emperor and launched a military campaign in Europe.

1815 Napoléon's defeat at Waterloo by the British, Belgians, Dutch and Prussians saw the end of his reign. Louis XVIII became King of France.

1848 An uprising led by students and workers, although quickly crushed, again led to the overthrow of the monarchy. Louis Napoléon (nephew of the first Napoléon) was elected president.

1852 Louis Napoléon declared himself emperor.

1871 France's defeat in the Franco-Prussian War resulted in the annexation of Alsace-Lorraine by the Germans.

1914 France was invaded by Germany.

1918 Following the end of the First World War and Germany's defeat, France regained Alsace-Lorraine.

1939 After Germany's invasion of Poland, France and the UK entered the Second World War by declaring war on Germany.

1940 France signed an armistice after Germany had invaded the country. The Germans installed a puppet government, the Vichy, led by Henri-Philippe Pétain. A Free French resistance built up in the UK under the leadership of General Charles de Gaulle.

1944 Following the liberation of France by the Allied powers, a provisional

government took office under General de Gaulle.
1945 After the war in Europe General de Gaulle retired from public office. The Fourth Republic was created with a constitution giving ultimate power to the Assemblé Nationale (National Assembly).
1946–1958 France had 26 different governments, many including large communist elements.
1958 The Fifth Republic was created after the introduction of a new constitution, which allowed for the creation of a powerful presidency. General de Gaulle was elected president. France became a founder member of the forerunner of the EU, the European Economic Community (EEC), along with Belgium, Italy, Luxembourg, The Netherlands and West Germany.
1962 Algeria, which had been a *département* of France since 1948, gained its independence, following a brutal insurgency.
1968 Discontent with low wages, lack of social reform and poor education policies led to a revolt by students and workers. The general strike was settled by the granting of generous wage rises and the student revolt collapsed, although De Gaulle's political position was fatally weakened.
1969 De Gaulle resigned from the presidency after losing a referendum on his programme for strengthening regional governments. He was succeeded by Georges Pompidou (1969–74) who was followed by Valéry Giscard d'Estaing (1974–81).
1970 Former president Charles de Gaulle died.
1981 François Mitterrand became the first socialist president since 1958 following Giscard d'Estaing's electoral defeat, governing with the first left-wing cabinet for 23 years.
1995 Jacques Chirac succeeded François Mitterrand as president. Pacific and Oceania countries condemned French nuclear testing in French Polynesia.
2002 The euro replaced the franc as France's currency. President Chirac defeated Jean-Marie Le Pen in elections. Prime Minister Lionel Jospin resigned and Chirac appointed Jean-Pierre Raffarin (UMP) in his place. After legislative elections, a coalition government was formed, led by the Union pour un Mouvement Populaire (UMP) (Popular Movement Party), with Union pour la Démocratie Française (UDF) (French Democracy Party), the Démocratie Libérale (DL) (Liberal Democracy) and allies.
2003 France was crippled by a series of public sector strikes over pension reform.
2004 Voting in regional elections showed national discontent with the government, as the left-wing opposition carried 21 out of the country's 22 mainland regions. Prime Minister Raffarin resigned, but was immediately re-instated.
2005 France held a referendum on the European Constitution in which almost 55 per cent voted No, with 45 per cent in favour; turnout was about 70 per cent. Prime Minister Raffarin resigned the next day; Dominique de Villepin was appointed prime minister. Rioting in disadvantaged and disaffected immigrant communities broke out, first in the Paris suburb of Clichy-sous-Bois, then elsewhere in the capital and in other towns and cities. Final figures reported by the French police were 8,973 vehicles burnt and 2,888 arrests forcing the government to declare a state of emergency for several weeks.
2006 France provided 1,700 troops for UN peace-keeping duties in the Lebanon. France and Germany combined to apply pressure on the EU demanding tougher conditions for Turkey's proposed membership.
2007 Nicolas Sarkozy (Rassemblement pour la République (RPR) (Party of the Republic)), won the presidential elections, defeating Ségolène Royal (Parti Socialiste (PS) Socialist Party)). François Fillon (UMP) was appointed prime minister.
2008 Société Générale, one of France's largest banks, lost US$7.1 billion through fraud by a rogue trader. President Sarkozy married Carla Bruni at the Elysée Palace. Parliament scraped the 35-hour working week, 10 years after it was introduced, so that companies could organise working patterns based on agreements with their workforces.
2009 An economic stimulus package of US$33.1 billion was launched. The Natixis corporate and investment bank declared it had 'toxic assets' of US$44 billion and losses of US$2.8 billion in the first quarter of the year.
2010 The burka (full Islamic face veil worn by women) was banned in France. The penalties for wearing a burka or forcing a female to wear a burka include fines and imprisonment. Over three million French protestors took part in marches and widespread strikes, called to object to government plans to increase the age of retirement from 60 to 62 years by 2018.
2011 In March, France became the first country to formally recognise the Libyan Transitional National Council (TNC) as the legitimate government of Libya. It joined a five-country coalition (with Canada, Italy, the UK and the US) to impose a no-fly zone over Libya. In March a referendum was held in Mayotte to decide whether it should become a French Département d'Outre-Mer (DOM) (Overseas Department). The result was 95.24 per cent of votes in favour. The island of Mayotte became France's fifth DOM. Comoros, which claimed the territory, protested the action of France. In June, the French finance minister, Christine Lagarde was appointed as managing director of the International Monetary Fund (IMF), and took up her post in July. In June a supply of weapons (including assault rifles, machine guns and rocket launchers) was parachuted into rebel held territory of Libya by the French military. The African Union condemned the move saying it puts the whole region at risk. The French stated that this was a one-off decision to re-arm a town cut off from supplies from its allies. In an unannounced visit to Afghanistan in July President Sarkozy announced that 1,000 French troops would be withdrawn by the end of 2012. In indirect elections held in September the left wing Socialist Party and its Communist and Green allies won enough seats to win control of the upper house (Senate). The conservatives had held power in the Senate since the formation of the Fifth Republic in 1958. 200 French troops that were part of a 4,000 military contingent stationed in the district of Surobi and the neighbouring Kapisa Province, were withdrawn from active service in the NATO mission in Afghanistan in October. In November, France announced that it would no longer buy Iranian oil, typically amounting to 49,000 barrels per day, on a 'national basis'. The French ban was in response to Iran's continued nuclear programme. France also joined its EU partners in joint sanctions.
2012 On February 15 President Sarkozy formally declared he would stand for re-election in the presidential polls. The first round was held on 22 April, in which 10 candidates took part. Incumbent Nicolas Sarkozy (UMP) won 27.18 per cent of the vote but his chief rival François Hollande (PS) won 28.63 per cent. The runoff was held on 6 May, in which the socialist candidate, François Hollande won 51.63 per cent of the vote and Nicolas Sarkozy 48.37 per cent; turnout was 80.35 per cent. On 16 May President Hollande appointed Jean-Marc Ayrault as prime minister; Ayrault immediately appointed his cabinet. On 10 July, 200 NATO troops began the phased withdrawal of French forces from Afghanistan; with completion scheduled for December. After two rounds of parliamentary elections, held on 10 and 17 June, the socialist coalition of four parties supporting President Hollande, led by PS, won a total of 57.7 per cent of the vote (331 seats out of 577). The opposition Droite parlementaire (Parliamentary Right) coalition of five parties, led by UMP, won 39.7 per cent (229). On 25 June the socialist

government restored the official age of retirement to 60 years. On 28 August, a murder inquiry into the death of Palestine and Fatah leader, Yasser Arafat, was opened by French investigators. Arafat had died in a French military hospital and his family claimed the poison polonium-210 had been used to kill him. On 17 October, President Hollande acknowledged that Algerians had been massacred by the police force during and Algerian independence rally in Paris in 1961; saying 'I pay homage to (the) victims fifty-one years later'. On 16 November the credit ratings agency Moody's downgraded France from an AAA rating to AA1; Moody's also retained the negative outlook, which was a warning that France could be downgraded again.

2013 On 2 September Prime Minister Ayrault presented a report to parliament which reported that the chemical attack in the outskirts of Damascus on 21 August 'could not have been ordered and carried out by anyone but the Syrian government' and that it involved a 'massive use of chemical agents'. Standard and Poor's cut France's credit rating from AA+ to AA on 8 November.

2014 Prime Minister Jean-Marc Ayrault resigned on 24 February, after the poor showing of the PS in the local elections. On 31 February President Hollande named Manuel Valls as the new prime minister. In a cabinet reshuffle anounced by Mr Valls on 2 April President Hollande's former partner, Segolene Royal, was named as the new minister for environment, sustainable development and energy. Prime Minister Manuel Valls announced the resignation of the entire cabinet on 25 August. On 26 August President Hollande asked Mr Valls to form a new cabinet. The resignation had been caused by a dispute between the prime minister and economy minister, Arnaud Montebourg, Former president, Nicolas Sarkozy, was elected leader of the UMP on 29 November. It was seen as a move towards standing in the presidential election due in 2017.

2015 On 13 November France was rocked by a number of suicide bombs and shootings that left over 130 dead. The so-called Islamic State (IS) claimed responsibility. A state of emergency was declared and three days of mourning announced.

Political structure

Constitution

The 25 September 1958 Constitution of the Fifth Republic maintained the original French republican ideals of liberty, fraternity and equality. It was designed to end post-war political deadlock by granting greater powers to the president. It guarantees the unity and indivisibility of the French state.

Since 1982 much administrative and financial power, traditionally held by the state, has been devolved to the 22 *régions* (regions) and 96 *départements* (departments) of metropolitan France. In March 2003, parliament approved Constitutional amendments which allow all of the regions and departments a greater amount of autonomy.

In mid-2000, legislation was passed granting semi-autonomy to the island of Corsica as a single administrative unit, replacing its previous status as two standard *départements*. France's overseas territories are either classed as Département d'Outre-Mer (DOM) (Overseas Department) or Térritoire d'Outre-Mer (TOM) (Overseas Territory), depending on the level of autonomy.

Independence date

14 July 1789.

Form of state

Semi-presidential democratic republic.

The executive

Executive power is held by the president, elected by universal adult suffrage for a five-year term which can be renewed only once. A two-round voting system operates for presidential elections, with the second round a run-off between the two highest polling candidates from the first round. The president appoints the prime minister and other members of the government, can dissolve the Assemblée Nationale and can also veto laws. In practice, the president traditionally accepts as prime minister the leader of the largest party in the National Assembly, and approves the prime minister's choice of government ministers.

The presidential term of office was reduced from seven years to five with effect from the 2002 presidential elections.

National legislature

The bicameral Parlement (Parliament) consists of the Assemblée Nationale (National Assembly) with 577 deputés (deputies) directly elected in single seat constituencies, for five-year terms. The Sénat (Senate) has 348 seats in total, of which members are indirectly elected for six-year terms by an electoral college of elected representatives from each department; the remainder are elected by overseas regions, departments, collectivities and territories.

Legal system

The country has no supreme court but this role is filled by a nine-member Conseil Constitutionel (Constitutional Council). Its task is to ensure that law treaties and regulations are in keeping with the constitution and that elections are conducted in a regular manner. The highest court of appeal is the Cour de Cassation, which can overrule decisions in all lower courts, but not government legislation. Since the signing of the Single European Act in 1986, the European Court of Justice (ECJ) has been the highest authority in certain areas of French law. France also accepts International Court of Justice (ICJ) jurisdiction.

Last elections

10 and 17 June 2012 (parliamentary); 22 April and 6 May 2012 (presidential first round and runoff)

Results: Parliamentary: Majorité présidentielle (Presidential Majority) coalition of four parties led by Parti Socialiste (PS) (Socialist Party), won a total of 57.7 per cent of the vote (331 seats, out of 577), Droite parlementaire (Parliamentary Right) coalition of five parties, led by Union pour un Mouvement Populaire (UMP) (Union for a Popular Movement) won 39.7 per cent (229), five other political parties won the remaining 17 seats. Turnout was 55.4 per cent.

In March 2014, following major losses to centre-right and extreme-right political parties in French municipal elections, President Francois Hollande appointed Manuel Valls to the post of Prime Minister. He replaced Jean-Marc Ayrault who had resigned earlier that day. The Valls Cabinet consists of 16 members from the Socialist Party and one minister from the Radical Party of the Left.

Presidential (first round): François Hollande (PS) won 28.63 per cent of the vote, Nicolas Sarkozy (UMP) 27.18 per cent, Marine Le Pen (Front National (FN) (National Front)) 17.9 per cent, Jean-Luc Mélenchon (Front de Gauche (FG) (Left Front)) 11.1 per cent, François Bayrou (Mouvement Démocrate (MD) (Democratic Movement)) 9.13 per cent; five other candidates each won less than 3 per cent of the vote. Turnout was 79.5 per cent. Runoff: Hollande won 51.63 per cent of the vote, Sarkozy 48.37 per cent; turnout was 80.35 per cent.

Next elections

June 2016 (parliamentary); April/May 2017 (presidential)

Political parties

Ruling party

Coalition, Majorité présidentielle (presidential majority), led by Parti Socialiste (PS) (Socialist Party), with Divers Gauche (DVG) (Miscellaneous Leftist), Europe Écologie-Les Verts (EELV) (Europe Ecology-The Greens) and Parti Radical de Gauche (PRG) (Radical Party of the Left) (from 17 Jun 2012)

Main opposition party

Droite parlementaire (parliamentary right) coalition of five parties, led by Union pour un Mouvement Populaire (UMP) (Union for a Popular Movement)

Population
63.92 million (2014)
Last census: 1 January 2006: 61,399,541
Population density: 107 inhabitants per square km. Urban population 85 per cent (2010 Unicef).
Annual growth rate: 0.5 per cent, 1990–2010 (Unicef).

Ethnic make-up
The population is predominantly Western European. North Africans form the principal ethnic minority, with smaller communities from former French colonies in Asia and sub-Saharan Africa.

Religions
There is no state religion, but Roman Catholicism predominates (90 per cent of population), with a significant Protestant minority concentrated in southern France (2 per cent) and Muslim and Jewish communities in major urban areas (1 per cent each).

Education
Compulsory education is provided for free. Primary schooling lasts to the age of 11, after which all pupils transfer to a four-year course in secondary school. At the age of 15 there are two options: either a three-year course leading to the *baccalauréate* examination or a two-year vocational course. An average of 80 per cent of schoolchildren are expected to achieve the *baccalauréate*, which is the minimum entry qualification to university. Educational expenditure is typically equivalent to 6 per cent of gross national income.
Compulsory years: Six to 16
Pupils per teacher: 19 in primary schools

Health
France's liberal state-subsidised medical system allows doctors and dentists to establish private practices. Patients, who are free to choose their own providers, are reimbursed by the state for up to 85 per cent of medical costs. The government makes full provision for people who are unable to make any contributions, by treating them as private patients covered by insurance.
Proposed reforms to reduce the cost of the health system have met with vociferous opposition from doctors, nurses and health professionals. Fraud is estimated to cost the system more than US$980 million per year, and ease of access to prescription drugs is thought to be the principal reason for the fact that French consumption of drugs and medicine is more than three times the European average.

HIV/Aids
HIV prevalence: 0.4 per cent aged 15–49 in 2003 (World Bank)
Life expectancy: 80 years, 2004 (WHO 2006)
Fertility rate/Maternal mortality rate: 2.0 births per woman, 2010 (Unicef); maternal mortality 0.1 per 1,000 live births (World Bank).
Child (under 5 years) mortality rate (per 1,000): 4 per 1,000 live births (WHO 2012)
Head of population per physician: 3.37 physicians per 1,000 people, 2004 (WHO 2006)

Welfare
France's extensive social security system, including health insurance, family allowances and retirement insurance, covers 99.2 per cent of the population. In common with other industrialised nations, France's ageing population is an increasing concern.
In June 2012, the new government announced plans to reverse the previous government's controversial introduction of a raised retirement age from 60 to 62 years, the proposal should benefit around 110,000 public servants.

Pensions
In June 2010, pension reforms were introduced, to be implemented by 2012, including raising the retirement age from 60 to 62, with workers having worked for a minimum of 41.5 years. France's pension deficit for 2010 was estimated at US$39.5 billion and could treble by 2050 if measures to stem the costs are not employed.

Main cities
Paris (capital, estimated population 2.2 million in 2012), Marseille (795,600), Lyon (495,840), Toulouse (469,854), Nice (329,311), Nantes (283,226), Strasbourg (282,496), Lille (273,168), Montpellier (266,645), Bordeaux (229,500).

Languages spoken
Breton is spoken in Brittany and Euskera (Basque) is spoken in the south-west, while in Alsace and Lorraine, in the east, German is widely spoken.
English is spoken in the business community, but an understanding of French is considered essential for visitors.
Flemish, Catalán, Occitan, Corsu, Arabic, Kabyle and Antillean are also spoken.

Official language/s
French

Media
Press
French newspapers are editorially free from government control and censorship, and cover the full political spectrum.
There are 85 daily newspapers published, of which 24 are nationals. There are around 870 newspapers and 6,000 magazines published reaching over 45 per cent of adults. Regional newspapers have a larger readership than national titles.
Dailies: In French, major newspapers include *Le Monde* (www.lemonde.fr), *Le Figaro* (www.lefigaro.fr) is a conservative newspaper, *Libération* (www.liberation.fr) a left-wing newspaper, *Ouest France* (www.ouest-france.fr) has the largest circulation, *Le Parisien* (www.leparisien.fr) a centrist newspaper and *La Croix* (www.la-croix.com) a Catholic newspaper.
Weeklies: In French, the *Courrier Intenational* (www.courrierinternational.com), *L'Express* (www.lexpress.fr) and *Le Point* (www.lepoint.fr) report on news and current affairs, *Le Journal du Dimanche* (www.lejdd.fr) is a popular Sunday newspaper. Special interest publications include *Maghreb Hebdo* concerning north African news and *La Marseillaise* a communist publication and two humourist magazines are *Le Canard Enchaîné* and *Le Herisson*. In English *The Riviera Times* (www.rivieratimes.com).
Business: In French, daily newspapers include *Les Echos* (www.lesechos.fr), *La Tribune* (www.latribune.fr) and *Investir* (www.investir.fr). Monthly publications include the popular economics magazine *Capital* (www.capital.fr), *L'Expansion* (www.lexpansion.com) and *Valeurs Actuelles* (www.valeursactuelles.com) a weekly and *Le Revenu* (www.lerevenu.com) a bi-weekly magazine. *Jeune Afrique Economie* is an Africa-oriented bi-weekly.
Periodicals: In French, monthly publications include *Le Monde Dipomatique* (www.monde-diplomatique.fr) a left-wing magazine, *Entrevue* (www.entrevue.fr) a tabloid entertainment magazine, *Lire* (www.lire.fr) a cultural magazine and *Le Nouvel Afrique Asie* a left-wing third world-orientated monthly magazine. Influential women's magazines include *Vogue* (www.vogue.fr) and *Marie Claire* (www.marieclaire.fr).

Broadcasting
France is a world leader in broadcasting, providing international news and entertainment services to most continents, via radio, satellite, pay-to-view digital services and internet links.
Radio: The national public radio service is Radio France (www.radiofrance.fr) with seven stations offering a range of genre including classical, news, sport, information, culture and modern music. Radio France Internationale (RFI) (www.rfi.fr) is funded wholly by the French ministry of foreign affairs; it broadcasts worldwide in 19 languages, other than French.
Nationally, there are 17 commercial radio stations including Europe 1 (www.europe1.fr), Fun Radio (www.funradio.fr), RTL (www.rtl.fr) a major

news and entertainment network, Sud Radio (www.sudradio.fr), NRJ (www.nrj.fr), a leading music network and Alouette (www.alouette.fr).

Apart from private local and regional radio stations, many are affiliates of national networks.

Television: The national public broadcaster is France Télévisions (www.francetelevisions.fr) with five networks. Some channels carry advertising. Channels are designated France 2, 3, 4, 5 and RFO (www.rfo.fr) for overseas territories. Combined, France Télévisions typically has 40 per cent of the audience share and 30 per cent of revenues.

TF1 (www.tf1.fr) is the leading commercial TV channel with typically 35 per cent audience share and almost 50 per cent of advertising revenues. Programmes include locally made and foreign imports. TFI operates a national 24-hour news channel, La Chaine Info (http://tf1.lci.fr), as well as a major digital and internet TV service, France 24 (www.france24.com), with a wide range of international news and current affairs in French, English and Arabic. All analogue services will be switched to digital services by 2011.

National news agency: Agence France Presse

Other news agencies: Reuters: http://fr.reuters.com
Focus: www.focusinfo.eu

Economy

The French economy, following on after Germany and the UK, is Europe and the EU's most productive economy. It manufactures some of the biggest global brands of automobiles and luxury goods, space technology and heavy machinery, pharmaceuticals and construction materials, foodstuffs and cultural items. It is a major exporter of energy, particularly electricity from its network of nuclear power stations and in 2014 it had two of the world's top-ten largest banks, operating worldwide.

As a result of the global economic crisis, France started a period of slow growth; the trade deficit in 2008 was 37 per cent higher than in 2007, at US$71.4 billion, due to record high petroleum prices coupled with weakened export trade. The financial sector was caught up in the US mortgage-based toxic debt, which caused the economy to fall further to -2.2 per cent in 2009, so that France officially fell into recession in the first quarter of 2009. The government was forced to bail out six of the country's banks at the cost of US$14 billion to its taxpayers. At the same time as the global banking system was going into meltdown a trader working for Société Générale lost US$7.2 billion of the bank's money by speculating on the stock market through bogus transactions. It was the largest loss in France's corporate history and resulted in the bank being downgraded by two international credit ratings agencies. On 16 November 2012 the credit ratings agency Moody's downgraded France from an AAA rating to AA1; Moody's also retained the negative outlook, which was a warning that France could be downgraded again. The loss of the triple rating was due to 'persistent structural economic challenges', economic growth that had stalled, the weakness in the euro-zone caused by the Greek economy and France's obligation in bailing out other economies. In September 2014 when queried about a review of the rating, Moody's announced its decision to maintain the negative outlook on France's economy.

Some much-needed reforms, notably in pensions, were begun in June 2010. They included raising the retirement age from 60 to 62, implemented in 2011; workers will also have to have worked for a minimum of 43 years as of a 2013 reform. France's pension deficit is estimated to reach US$26.2 billion by 2020 and could almost treble by 2050 if measures to stem the costs are not employed. Another major priority for the government continues to be unemployment, which remained at around 10 per cent at the start of 2015, and, more worryingly, with disproportionately high youth unemployment.

Annual GDP growth in France hasn't fully recovered from the blows of the global economic crisis, and remains slow. In 2012, growth dropped to 0.2 per cent after reaching 2.1 per cent in 2011. 2013 growth showed the country moderately improving by 0.7 per cent before returning to the stagnant growth of 0.2 per cent in 2014.

External trade

As a member of the European Union (EU), France operates within a community-wide free trade area, with tariffs set as a whole. Internationally, the EU has free trade agreements with a number of nations and trading blocs worldwide. France has several overseas *départements* which are treated as *de jure* mainland France with fully implemented treaties with the EU.

France is a leading world trader; it is a major exporter of agricultural produce and processed food, its industrial base includes vehicles, aerospace and high-speed trains, telecommunications, weapons and consumer goods.

Imports

Principal imports are machinery and equipment, vehicles, crude oil, aircraft, plastics and chemicals.

Main sources: Germany (19.4 per cent of total in 2014), Belgium (11.1 per cent), Italy (7.6 per cent).

Exports

Principal exports include machinery and vehicles, trains and other rail equipment, aircraft, plastics, chemicals and pharmaceuticals, iron and steel, food and beverages.

Main destinations: Germany (16.4 per cent of total in 2014), Belgium (7.3 per cent), Italy (7.1 per cent).

Agriculture

Farming

France is a major European food producer with self-sufficiency in dairy produce and is a substantial exporter of livestock produce, wine, fruit and vegetables. Agriculture contributed around 1.8 per cent to GDP in 2014 and employed 3 per cent of the labour force.

The EU's fundamental reform to the Common Agricultural Policy (CAP) was introduced in France in 2005. The subsidies paid on farm output, which tended to benefit large farms and encourage overproduction, were replaced by single farm payments not conditional on production.

The global demand for Champagne has shrunk overall since the global economic crisis, and has fallen from a record of 339 million bottles in 2007. However the 308 million bottles sold in 2014 were an improvement on 2013, and as a result the government extended the growing region, officially allowing vintners within the newly expanded area to designate their sparkling wine as Champagne. An area of 33,500 hectares in north-eastern France is the only place worldwide allowed to use the coveted Appellation d'Origine Controlee (AOC) and to label its wine Champagne. The last expansion of the Champagne region was in 1927; the latest enlargement began in 2009, with the new AOC Champagne expected to be ready for sale by 2019. In 2014 France beat Spain and Italy to be the world's largest wine producer, producing around 47 million hectolitres of wine.

Fishing

Although oyster farming remains highly vulnerable to the risk of disease, France is the top European producer of oysters and among the first three producers of mussels (from both fishing and aquaculture). France is also the top European producer of fresh water trout and has remained competitive with European regions with more favourable environmental conditions. Sea bass and sea bream represent the majority of marine farm production with turbot farming expanding. Only part of the production is for domestic consumption, the remainder being exported.

Forestry

Forestry is France's richest natural resource with over a quarter (15 million hectares) of metropolitan France covered by forest, giving it the largest tree-covered area in the EU. The Office National des Forêts (ONF) (National Forestry Office) manages over a quarter of this area. Forestry is concentrated in the east, south and south-west of the country, with the largest area being the Landes, coastal forests south of Bordeaux. Deciduous forests account for 61 per cent of the total, while 38 per cent are coniferous or mixed.

About 8 per cent of the wooded area is brushwood.

Although it is a net importer of sawn softwoods and pulp for its paper industry, France remains the largest producer of sawn hardwood in Europe.

The forestry industry supplies raw materials to several industries. About 60 per cent of French wood production is used in the construction industry.

Industry and manufacturing

France has a broad industrial base incorporating a large capital-intensive state-owned sector, composed mainly of small- and medium-sized manufacturing enterprises, which together contribute around 25 per cent to GDP and employ 27 per cent of the labour force.

Industrial policy is generally aimed at developing the domestic market, promotion of 'new technology' sectors and internationalisation of state-owned companies.

Government protection of industry is an important economic issue and one which threatens both to retard the efficiency of domestic markets and alienate France's European partners.

Leading sectors include agri-foodstuffs, telecommunications, aerospace, motor industry, metallurgy, chemicals, parachemicals and pharmaceuticals, textiles and clothing.

Tourism

France has a reputation for haute cuisine, couture and culture, as offered in world class restaurants, cities and museums and galleries; it has historical sites that stretch back to the Roman Empire and others that have an importance to the modern world, it produces outstanding wine and cheeses. It was the birthplace of sun-worshipping holidays along its Mediterranean coast and any number of winter skiing resorts.

France is the number one tourist destination in the world, attracting over 83.7 million visitors in 2014.

Travel and tourism in 2014 directly contributed 3.6 per cent of GDP, and 8.9 per cent through total indirect contribution.

Direct employment in the sector was predicted to be 4.1 per cent of total (1.13 million jobs) and 9.9 per cent of indirect employment (2.71 million jobs). The industry had direct investment of EU€31.0 billion (US$43.1 billion), 6.7 per cent of total investment committed for 2014.

Mining

The mining sector typically contributes 7 per cent to annual GDP and employs less than 1 per cent of the workforce. France is a significant producer of iron ore, bauxite and potash. Société Le Nickel is the world's third-largest nickel producer. In an effort to reduce dependence on imported minerals, exploration for lead, zinc, barium and tungsten has been intensified.

Domestic uranium mining operations were finally closed in mid-2001 after exhaustion of commercial reserves. Total production of uranium was estimated at 156 tonnes in the same year.

In 2001, French steel production was 19.3 million tonnes but by 2013 this figure had decreased to 15.7 million tonnes, while production of aluminium was 713,000 tonnes in 2007 and had decreased to 349,000 in 2013.

In September 2014, the world's leading steel and mining company, ArcelorMittal, announced that it was creating 700 new jobs across its French sites. The company is the largest steel producer in the country with a workforce of over 20,000.

Hydrocarbons

Proven oil reserves were 90 million barrels in 2013. Crude oil production was 72,300 barrels per day (bpd), France is a heavy consumer of oil, amounting to 1.6 million bpd, most of which is imported from Norway, Russia and Saudi Arabia.

Although France has a lack of crude oil supplies the French oil company TotalFinaElf is one of the world's largest and most active international oil producers.

On 6 July 2011, parliament voted to ban hydraulic fracturing of shale oil and gas development. France was the first country to ban the technique (commonly referred to as fracking), that releases hydrocarbons from shale after being bombarded by high-pressure water, but has also been blamed for causing substrata instability.

Proven natural gas reserves were 10 million cubic metres (cum) in 2013, and production was 620 million cum. However, with consumption is typically over 42.8 billion cum imports are required to make up the shortfall. Gaz de France (GdF), the majority government-owned utility, dominates gas activities and since energy markets inside the EU were opened to competition, around 30 per cent of GdF customers live outside France. The majority of gas pipelines are operated by GdF, including intra-European links.

Negotiations began in October 2009 between the majority state-owned energy company EDF and Russia to invest in the South Stream gas pipeline between Russia and Bulgaria in exchange for a long-term contract. EDF aimed to acquire 15 per cent of gas volume sales in France, Germany, Italy and the UK by 2015. Tensions between Russia and Western Europe over the crisis in Ukraine has meant that in 2014 construction of the pipeline was suspended and was still halted as of 2015.

The coal-mining industry ended with the closure of the last mine in 2004, but some coal is imported for the remaining coal-fired power stations and the steel industry.

Energy

France is one of the world's largest nuclear power producers and is Europe's largest electricity net exporter. Total electricity generation capacity was 124 gigawatts (GW) in 2013, producing 532 billion kilowatt hours (kWh). Over 80 per cent of French electricity is generated by its 58 nuclear power stations, comprising 34 reactors of 900MW, 20 reactors of 1.3GW and 4 reactors of 1.45GW. In 2012 France consumed over 499 billion kWh. The government plans to expand the sector with the construction of a new generation of reactors as well as upgrading existing assets.

In July 2015, France's National Assembly gave final approval of a new energy transition bill. Nuclear power currently accounts for 75 per cent of all energy generated in the country; the new legislation seeks to limit this figure to 50 per cent by 2025.

The leading electricity entity is EDF (Electricité de France), which is a limited-liability corporation, with 85/15 per cent government/private ownership, responsible for producing electricity, supplying around 95 per cent of all electricity in the country and delivering it nationally.

Overseas, EDF has partnerships with electricity companies in North and South America, Africa, Asia and Europe.

Financial markets

Stock exchange

Euronext Paris

Commodity exchange

Liffe Connect

Banking and insurance

Central bank

Banque de France; European Central Bank (ECB)

Time

GMT plus one hour (daylight saving, late March to late October, GMT plus two hours)

Geography

France is bordered to the north by the English Channel (La Manche), and to the

north-east, east and south-east by Belgium, Luxembourg, Germany, Switzerland and Italy, respectively. The Mediterranean Sea forms the southern boundary, and Spain the south-western, while the west coast faces the Atlantic Ocean.
France, the largest country in the west of Europe, has lush farming land, extensive forest and a large alluvial salt mash that makes up much of the province of the Camargue. The overall impression is of a rolling landscape from the south-west to north-east and mountainous regions for the rest of the country. There are four major river systems (the Seine, Loire, Rhone and Marne) that drain into either the Atlantic Ocean, English Channel or the Mediterranean Sea. The highest mountain, Mont Blanc (4,810 metres), is situated in the French Alps in the south-east.

Hemisphere
Northern

Climate
France has a moderate maritime climate in the north with a small temperature range and abundant rainfall. By contrast, southern France has a Mediterranean climate, with hot dry summers and mild, moist winters. Eastern France has a continental climate, with thunderstorms prevalent in summer. The average temperature in Paris in January is three degrees Celsius (C) and in July 18 degrees C. Annual rainfall in Paris is 573mm.

Dress codes
Western dress is the norm.

Entry requirements
Passports
Passports are required by all, expect nationals of EU countries with national ID cards. Passports must be valid for three months beyond the length of stay.

Visa
Required by all, except citizens of EU countries, North America, Australasia and Japan, for stays up to three months; this includes business trips by representatives of foreign entities with an invitation from a local company or organisation. Proof of adequate funds for stay, an itinerary, a guarantee of repatriation if necessary and return/onward ticket are also required. For further exceptions, full details and a copy of the application form visit www.diplomatie.gouv.fr/thema/dossier.gb.asp and follow the path (entering France) to the database. A Schengen visa application (offered in several languages) can be downloaded from http://europa.eu/abc/travel/ see 'documents you will need'.

Currency advice/regulations
There are no limits to the amount of local or foreign currency imported or exported, although amounts exceeding eur7,600 must be declared.

Customs
Personal items are duty-free. There are no duties levied on alcohol and tobacco between EU member states, providing amounts imported are for personal consumption.
Plant material, meat products from Africa and valuable art or antique objects must be declared.

Health (for visitors)
Nationals of the European Economic Area (EEA) countries and Switzerland can access reduced cost and sometimes free medical treatment using a European Health Insurance Card (EHIC) while visiting the EEA. Exceptions include nationals of the 10 countries which joined the EU in 2004 whose EHIC is not valid in Switzerland. Applications for the EHIC should be made before travelling.

Mandatory precautions
None

Advisable precautions
There are no particular health hazards in France, although rabies is a problem in some rural areas.
Medical insurance is advisable for visitors of non-EEA countries as healthcare costs can be high. Only medication for personal use may be bought into France.

Hotels
Classified into deluxe and one- to four-star. Reservations (either direct or through centralised booking offices) should be made in advance during holiday seasons. Single rooms are rare and rates are usually quoted for double rooms. A tip of around 12–15 per cent of the bill is usual, provided no service charge has already been added.

Credit cards
All major credit cards are accepted.

Public holidays (national)
Fixed dates
1 Jan (New Year's Day), 1 May (Labour Day), 8 May (Victory Day), 14 Jul (Bastille Day), 15 Aug (Assumption Day), 1 Nov (All Saints' Day), 11 Nov (Armistice Day) and 25 Dec (Christmas Day).
The months of July and August are traditionally when the French take their holidays.

Variable dates
Easter Monday, Ascension Day, Whit Monday.

Working hours
Anyone intending to visit France for business purposes should avoid the traditional holiday month of August, when most businesses and government departments have only a skeleton staff at work.

Banking
Mon–Fri: 0900–1200 and 1400–1600. Some banks close on Mondays and all close early on the day before a Bank Holiday.

Business
Mon–Fri: 0900–1200 and 1400–1800.

Government
Mon–Fri: 0830–1800.

Shops
Mon–Fri: 0900–1830 (most shops are closed between 1200–1430). Some shops open on Sundays and some close on Mondays.

Telecommunications
Postal services
The main Paris post office, at Louvre metro station, is open 24 hours, all year round.

Mobile/cell phones
There are 900/1800 and 3G GSM services available throughout all of the country.

Electricity supply
220V AC

Social customs/useful tips
In France, strangers and acquaintances shake hands at the beginning and end of a meeting.
Most offices traditionally have a long lunch hour, lasting from 1200 until at least 1400. Lunchtime remains a popular time for doing business, with a number of restaurants in big cities catering expressly for business clients.
French nationals must carry identification at all times. Visitors should carry their passports. Spot identity checks are not uncommon and it is illegal to be without identification.

Security
Serious crimes represent only a tiny percentage of the total number reported, while there has been a big rise in delinquency, vandalism and petty theft. Pickpockets operate particularly in train stations and subways.
France has one of the highest road accident rates in Europe.

Getting there
Air
France has a number of airports located in the various regions receiving international flights.
National airline: Air France
International airport/s: Paris-Charles de Gaulle Airport (CDG), 23km north-east of Paris. Facilities include a business centre, bank, post office, restaurants, bars, duty-free shopping, medical centre and pharmacy. Car hire is available.
Lyon–Saint Exupéry Airport.
Other airport/s: Orly (ORY), 14km south of Paris; Bordeaux (BOD), 12km from

city; Lille (LIL), 15km from city; Lyon (LYS), 24km east of Lyon; Marseille (MRS), 24km north of city; Nice (NCE), 6km west of Nice; Toulouse (TLS), 10km from city; Biarritz (BIQ); Nantes (NTE); Perpignan (PGF) and Strasbourg (SXB).
Airport tax: None

Surface

France has good rail, road and sea connections with all surrounding countries.
Rail: The Eurostar service is provided by Belgium, UK and French railways, operating high speed rail connections between London, Paris and Brussels. Road vehicles are transported through the tunnel in Le Shuttle trains.
Water: There are regular cross channel ferries from the UK and Mediterrean ferries to Corsica, Spain (Balearic Islands) and North Africa.
Main port/s: Marseille (Europe's third-largest port), Boulogne, Nice, Calais, Dieppe, Dunkirk, Cherbourg, Le Havre, Rouen.

Getting about

National transport

Air: Paris is the most important business destination in France and is served by the two main airports, at Orly and Charles de Gaulle. Major cities are linked by Air France. Some services operate only during summer.
Road: France has the densest road network in the world. There are 806,000km of roads, including 7,100km of motorways, most of which are *autoroutes à péage* (toll roads).
Buses: There are good local bus services and some long-distance coach services.
Rail: French transport policy favours the railways. The Société Nationale des Chemins de Fer Français (SNCF) (French National Railroad Company) operates a nationwide network reaching to almost every part of the country. The most important rail lines radiate from Paris. Three high-speed train (TGV) lines link northern and southern France. These trains are modern and comfortable; seats can be booked in advance.
Water: There are approximately 9,000km of inland navigable waterways. Major canal areas are situated in the north and north-east of Paris, where the majority of the navigable rivers, including the Seine, the Rhine, the Midi, Brittany and the Loire are connected with canals.

City transport

Paris has one of the best urban transport networks in the world. A *Carte Orange Hebdomadaire* allows unlimited travel for one week on most forms of public transport.
Taxis: From Charles de Gaulle and Orly airports to the city centre, limousines and taxis are available. Taxis are only available from *stations de taxi* (taxi ranks). Day and night rates should be displayed inside the vehicle. Note that extra charges are usually levied for journeys to racecourses, stations and airports. Tipping is usually 10–15 per cent.
Buses, trams & metro: In Paris, the same tickets may be used on buses and the metro; a carnet of 10 tickets is cheaper. Buses operate between 0600–2100; some exceptional routes operate until 0030.

Car hire

All major international hire companies have offices in Paris and other main towns. Drivers must carry at all times: a passport or national ID card, a valid driving licence, car ownership papers and proof of insurance.
Traffic drives on the right. *Priorité à droite* applies, particularly in built-up areas – cars coming out of a side turning on the right have priority, unless suspended where a sign indicates. Speed limits: 130kph on toll motorways, 110kph on dual carriageways, 90kph on other roads and 60kph in towns. Note that these limits are reduced when wet. Speed limits for drivers who have held their licence for less than two years are 110kph on motorways, 100kph on dual carriageways and 80kph on other roads.
Wearing of seat belts is compulsory in front seats.

BUSINESS DIRECTORY

The addresses listed below are a selection only. While World of Information makes every endeavour to check these addresses, we cannot guarantee that changes have not been made, especially to telephone numbers and area codes. We would welcome any corrections.

Telephone area codes

The International direct dialling (IDD) code for France is +33, followed by area code and subscriber's number:

Paris	1
North-west (Nantes, Rouen, etc)	2
North-east (Lille, Strasbourg etc)	3
South-east and Corsica (Lyon, Marseilles, etc)	4
South-west (Bordeaux, Toulouse, etc)	5

Useful telephone numbers

Police: 17
Fire: 18
Medical emergency and ambulance: 15

Chambers of Commerce

American Chamber of Commerce in France, 156 Boulevard Haussmann, 75008 Paris (tel: 5643-4567; fax: 5643-4560; e-mail: amchamfrance@amchamfrance.org)

Assemblée des Chambres Françaises de Commerce et d'Industrie, 45 Avenue d'Iéna, PO Box 3003, 75773 Paris Cedex 16 (tel: 4069-3700; fax: 4720-6128; e-mail: contactdie@acfci.cci.fr).

Boulogne-sur-Mer Chambre de Commerce et d'Industrie, 98 Quai Gambetta, 62204 Boulogne-sur-Mer (tel: 2199-6200; fax: 2199-6201; e-mail: ccibco@boulogne-sur-mer.cci.fr).

Bordeaux Chambre de Commerce et d'Industrie, 12 Place de la Bourse, 33076 Bordeaux (tel: 5679-5000; fax: 5569-5265; e-mail: bourse@bordeaux.cci.fr).

British-French Chamber of Commerce and Industry, 31 Rue Boissy d'Anglas, 75008 Paris (tel: 5330-8130; fax: 5330-8135; e-mail: information@francobritishchamber.com).

Calais Chambre de Commerce et d'Industrie, 24 Boulevard des Alliés, PO Box 199, 62104 Calais Cedex (tel: 2146-0000; fax: 2146-0099; e-mail: ccic@calais.cci.fr).

Grenoble Chambre de Commerce et d'Industrie, 1 Place André Malraux, PO Box 297, 38016 Grenoble Cedex 1 (tel: 7628-2828; fax: 7628-2747; e-mail: ccig@grenoble.cci.fr).

Loiret Chambre de Commerce et d'Industrie, 23 Place du Martroi, 45044 Orléans Cedex 1 (tel: 3877-7777; fax: 3853-0978; e-mail: direction@loiret.cci.fr).

Lorraine Chambre de Commerce et d'Industrie, 10 Viaduc J-F Kennedy, CS 4231, 54042 Nancy Cedex (tel: 8390-1313; fax: 8328-8833; e-mail: crci@lorraine.cci.fr).

Lyon Chambre de Commerce et d'Industrie, Palais du Commerce, Place de la Bourse, 69289 Lyon Cedex 2 (tel: 7240-5858; fax: 7837-5346; e-mail: info@lyon.cci.fr).

Nantes Chambre de Commerce et d'Industrie, 16 Quai Ernest Renaud, PO Box 90517, 44105 Nantes Cedex 4 (tel: 4044-6060; fax: 4044-6090; e-mail: administrator@nantes.cci.fr).

Nice Chambre de Commerce et d'Industrie, 20 Boulevard Carabaçel, PO Box 1259, 06005 Nice Cedex 1 (tel: 0820-422-222; fax: 9313-7399; e-mail: mde.nice.carabacel@cote-azur.cci.fr).

Rennes Chambre de Commerce et d'Industrie, 2 Avenue de la Préfecture, CS 64204, 35042 Rennes Cedex (tel: 9933-6666; fax: 9333-2428; e-mail: info@rennes.cci.fr).

Rouen Chambre de Commerce et d'Industrie, Palais des Consuls, Quai de la Bourse, PO Box 641, 76007 Rouen

Cedex 1 (tel: 3414-3737; fax: 3514-3838; e-mail: ccir@rouen.cci.fr).

Strasbourg Chambre de Commerce et d'Industrie, 10 Place Gutenburg, 67081 Strasbourg Cedex (tel: 0388-752-525; fax: 0388-223-120; e-mail: direction@strasbourg.cci.fr).

Banking

Association Française de Banques, 18 Rue la Fayette, 75009 Paris (tel: 4246-9259).

Banque Française du Commerce Extérieur (BFCE), 21 Boulevard Haussmann, 75009 Paris (tel: 4800-4800; fax: 4800-3970).

Banque Indosuez, 96 Boulevard Haussmann, 75008 Paris (tel: 4420-2020; fax: 4420-1522).

Banque Nationale de Paris SA, 16 Boulevard des Italiens, 75009 Paris (tel: 4014-4546; fax: 4014-5599).

Banque Paribas, 3 Rue d'Antin, 75078 Paris Cedex 02 (tel: 4298-1234; fax: 4298-0433).

Caisse Centrale des Banques Populaires, 10-12 avenue Winston Churchill, 94677 Charenton Le Pont Cedex (tel: 4039-0000; fax: 4039-3940).

Caisse d'Epargne, 19 Rue du Louvre, 75001 Paris (tel: 4041-3031; fax: 4233-4518).

Compagnie Bancaire, 5 Avenue Kléber, 75798 Paris Cedex 16 (tel: 4525-2525; fax: 4501-7805).

Compagnie Financière de Crédit Industriel et Commercial (CIC Group), Rue de la Victoire 66, 75009 Paris (tel: 4280-8080).

Crédit Agricole, Boulevard Pasteur 91-93, 75015 Paris (tel: 4323-5202).

Crédit Commercial de France (CCF), 103 Avenue des Champs-Elysées, 75008 Paris (tel: 4070-7040; fax: 4070-7353).

Crédit Foncier de France, SA, 19 Rue des Capucines, 75001 Paris (tel: 4244-8000; fax: 4244-7822).

Crédit Local de France, 7-11 Quai André Citroen, 75015 Paris (tel: 4392-7777; fax: 4592-7672).

Crédit Lyonnais SA, Boulevard des Italiens 19, 75002 Paris (tel: 4295-7000).

Crédit Mutuel, 88 Rue Cardinet, 75017 Paris (tel: 4401-1010; fax: 4401-1227).

Société Générale, Boulevard Haussmann 29, 75009 Paris (tel: 4298-2000).

Union Européenne de CIC (CIC Group), 4 Rue Gaillon, 75107 Paris Cedex 02 (tel: 4266-7000; fax: 4266-7878).

Central bank

Banque de France, 31 Rue Croix des Petits Champs, 75001 Paris (tel: 4292-4292; fax: 4292-3940; e-mail: infos@banque-france.fr).

European Central Bank, Kaiserstrasse 29, D-60311 Frankfurt am Main, Germany (tel: (+49-69) 13-440; fax: (+49-69) 1344-6000; e-mail: info@ecb.int).

Stock exchange

Euronext Paris, www.euronext.com

Chi-X, www.chi-x.com

Commodity exchange

Liffe Connect, www.nyse.com/nyseeuronext

Travel information

Air France (head office), 1 Place Max-Hymans, Paris 75757 Cedex 15 (tel: 4323-8181; internet site: http://www.airfrance.fr).

Airport office: 45 Rue de Paris, Roissy Charles de Gaulle, Paris 95747 (tel: 4156-7800).

Maison de la France (tourist office), 8 Avenue de l'Opéra, Paris 75001 (tel: 4296-1023; fax: 4286-8052).

Roissy Charles de Gaulle and Le Bourget airports, BP 20101, 95711 Roissy Charles de Gaulle Cedex (tel: 4862-1212, 4864-6807) (24 hours).

Ministries

Ministry of Agriculture, Fisheries and Food, 78 Rue de Varenne, 75700 Paris (tel: 4955-4955; fax: 4955-4039).

Ministry of Capital Works, Housing, and Transport, 246 Blvd Saint-Germain, 75007 Paris (tel: 4081-2122; fax: 4081-3099).

Ministry of the Civil Service, Administrative Reform and Decentralisation, 72 Rue de Varenne, 75700 Paris (tel: 4275-8000; fax: 4275-8970).

Ministry of Culture and Communication, 3 Rue de Valois, 75042 Paris (tel: 4015-8000; fax: 4261-3577).

Ministry of Defence, 14 Rue Saint-Dominique, 75700 Paris (tel: 4219-3011; fax: 4505-4091).

Ministry for the Economy, Finance and Industry, 139 Rue de Bercy, 75572 Paris Cedex 12 (tel: 5318-4000; fax: 5318-9701; internet site: www.minefi.gouv.fr).

Ministry of Employment, Rue de Grenelle, 75700 Paris (tel: 4438-3838; fax: 4438-2010).

Ministry of the Environment, 20 Avenue de Segur, 75302 Paris 07 SP (tel: 4219-2021; fax: 4219-1120).

Ministry of Foreign Affairs, 37 Quai d'Orsay, 75700 Paris (tel: 4317-5353; fax: 4551-6012).

Ministry of Industry, the Post Office and Telecommunications, 101 Rue de Grenelle, 75700 Paris 9 (tel: 4319-3636; fax: 4319-3052).

Ministry of the Interior, Place Beauvau, 75800 Paris (tel: 4927-4927; fax: 4266-1280).

Ministry of Justice, 13 Place Vendome, 75042 Paris (tel: 4477-6060; fax: 4477-6000).

Ministry of Labour and Social Affairs, 127 Rue de Grenelle, 75700 Paris (tel: 4438-3838; fax: 4056-6710).

Ministry of National Education, Higher Education and Research, 110 Rue de Grenelle, 75700 Paris (tel: 4955-1010; fax: 4955-1556).

Ministry for Relations with Parliament, 69 Rue de Varenne, 75700 Paris (tel: 4275-8000; fax: 4081-7300).

Ministry of Small- and Medium-Sized Enterprises, Trade and Artisan Activities, 80 Rue de Lille, 75700 Paris (tel: 4319-2424; fax: 4319-3767).

Ministry of Town and Country Planning, Urban Affairs and Integration, 35 Rue Saint-Dominique, 75700 Paris (tel: 4275-8000; fax: 4275-7755).

Ministry of Youth and Sport, Rue Olivier de Serres, 75015 Paris (tel: 5369-3000; fax: 5369-4370).

Prime Minister's Office, 57 Rue de Varenne, 75700 Paris (tel: 4275-8000; fax: 4544-1572).

Other useful addresses

Agence France Presse (news agency), 11–15 Place de la Bourse, 75002 Paris (tel: 4041-4646; fax: 4041-4632).

ANIT (public information service), 8 Avenue de l'Opéra, 75001 Paris (tel: 4260-3738).

La Bourse de Paris (Stock Exchange), 39 Rue Cambon, 75001 Paris (tel: 4927-7000; fax: 4289-7868).

Bureau International des Expositions (International Exhibition Bureau), 56 Avenue Victor-Hugo, 75116 Paris (tel: 4500-3863; fax: 4500-9615).

Caisse Centrale de Co-opération Economique (CCCE), 233 Boulevard Saint-Germain, Paris (tel: 4550-3220).

Centre Française du Commerce Extérieur, 10 Avenue d'léna, 75116 Paris (tel: 4505-3000).

Direction Générale des Impôts, Centre des Non-Résidents, 9 Rue d'Uzés, 75094 Paris.

France Télécom, 6 Place d'Alleray, 75505 Paris Cedex 15.

French Embassy (USA), 4101 Reservoir Road, NW, Washington DC 20007 (tel: (+1-202)-944-6000; fax: (+1-202)-944-6166).

Institut National de la Statistique et des Etudes Economiques (INSEE), 18 Boulevard Adolphe Pinard, 75675 Paris Cedex 14 (tel: 4117-5050; fax: 4117-6666; internet site: http://www.insee.fr).

Invest in France Network/DATAR, 1 Avenue Charles Floquet, 75343 Paris Cedex 07 (tel: 4065-1006; fax: 4065-1240).

Service de la Répression des Fraudes et du Contrôle de la Qualité, 44 Boulevard de Grenelle, 75732 Paris.

Post Office, 52 rue du Louvre, Paris (tel: 4028-2000).

National news agency: Agence France Presse, 11–15 Place de la Bourse, 75002 Paris (tel: 4041-4646; fax: 4041-4632; www.afp.com).

Reuters: http://fr.reuters.com

Focus: www.focusinfo.eu

Internet sites

France Bottin (provides market information on France's main companies): www.bottin.fr

French electronic phonebook (searches can be conducted by name or by regions): www.epita.fr:5000/11/english.html

Tourist information: www.francetourism.com/

French Guiana

KEY FACTS

Official name: Guyane Française (French Guiana)

Head of State: President of France François Hollande (PS) (from 15 May 2012), represented by *Préfet* Eric Spitz (from 10 Jun 2013)

Head of government: President of the Regional Council, Rodolphe Alexandre (from 26 Mar 2010); President of the General Council, Alain Tien-Liong (since Mar 2008)

Ruling party: Parti Socialiste Guyanais (PSG) (Socialist Party) (since 2000; re-elected 2004)

Area: 91,000 square km

Population: 250,109 (2013)*

Capital: Cayenne

Official language: French

Currency: Euro (€) = 100 cents (from 1 Jan 2002; previous currency French franc, locked at Ff6.56 per euro)

Exchange rate: €0.89 per US$ (Sep 2015)

* estimated figure

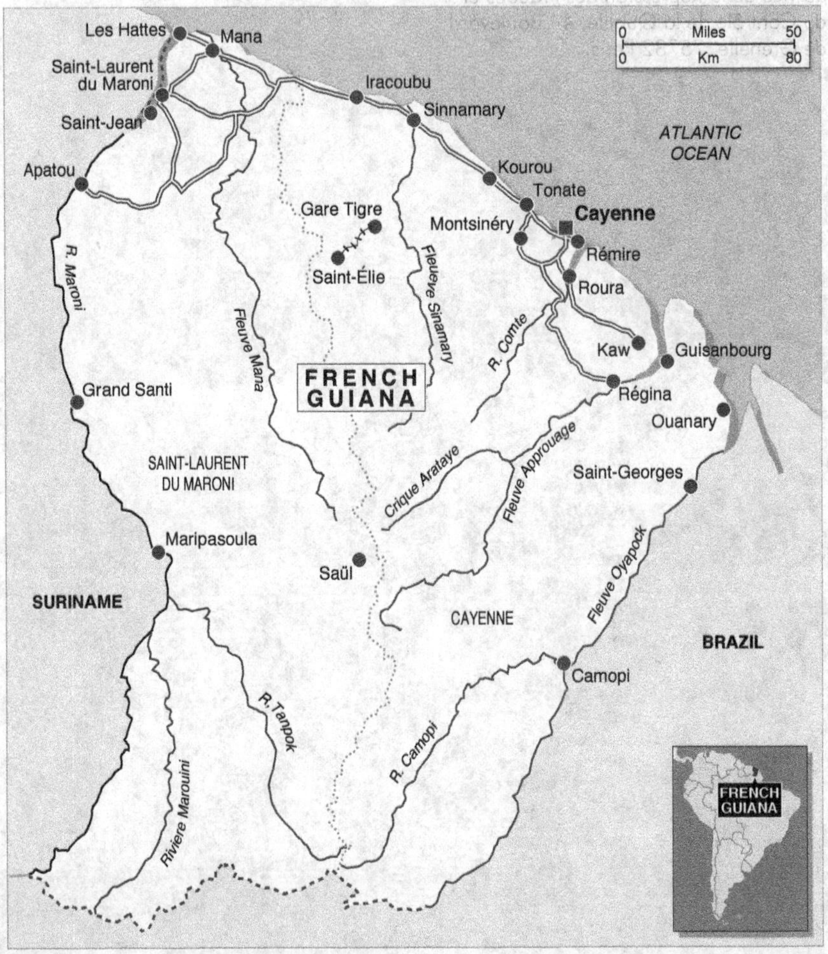

COUNTRY PROFILE

Carib and Arawak Indians were the original inhabitants of French Guiana.

1496 First reported European sighting.

1604 The French established their first settlement on French Guiana.

1654–1915 There were numerous changes in control between the French, British, Dutch, Brazilian and Portuguese, as well as border disputes. During this period the economy of the region came close to collapse, particularly after the abolition of slavery in 1848. Black African slaves had previously worked on French Guiana's sugar plantations.

1946 French Guiana became a French Département d'Outre-Mer (DOM) (Overseas Department).

1953 Closure of penal colony on Devil's Island.

1964 The Kourou Space Centre was established.

1974 French Guiana was further incorporated into the French political system and granted the status of region of France.

1983 French Guiana was granted devolution. A Regional Council was established under the French decentralisation policy.

1998 The Parti Socialiste Guyanais (PSG) remained the single largest party in the Regional Council after the elections.

2000 There were pro-independence demonstrations and French Guiana sought to alter its relationship as a DOM.

2002 French Guiana adopted the euro as its official currency. Arianespace launched Intelsat 904 into orbit from Kourou. The satellite provides Internet, telecommunications and television services for Europe, Africa, Central Asia and Australia.
2003 A revision to the constitution began a process of change to the political and administrative organisation with the Regional Council assuming more influence.
2004 Early elections for the Regional Council were won by the PSG with 17 seats.
2005 Arianespace and the Russian Space Agency signed an agreement for construction of the Soyuz launch pad.
2007 Nicolas Sarkozy became head of state and president of the French Republic. Under a deal with the European Space Agency (ESA), the l'Ensemble de Lancement Soyouz (ELS) (Launch Pad for Soyouz) began construction
2009 Daniel Ferey became *Préfet*. The largest telecommunication satellite ever built, TerreStar-1, was launched from the Space Centre.
2010 The first flight of a medium-lift space launcher, which had been planned for 2009, took off from Kourou. Voters rejected the option of increased autonomy in a referendum. Rodolphe Alexandre was elected president of the Regional Council.
2011 In April, Denis Labbé became *Préfet*. In July, the EU agreed to allow French Guiana to impose import tariffs from 1 July 2014 to protect 46 locally produced items, including food and manufactured goods. The target date for completion of the ELS for the Russian-built Soyuz-2 space rocket was postponed. In September, an exploration consortium of Tullow Oil, Shell and Total announced that they had discovered an oilfield 150km off the coast of French Guiana that was described as 'significant'. As planned, in October, the ESA launched two satellites as part of Europe's development of its own global positioning system (GPS). To undertake this task not only was the completed ELS used for the first time, but the Russian giant Soyuz rocket was employed for the first time in French Guiana.
2012 The first round of the French presidential elections was held on 21 April (in the Americas), in which 10 candidates took part. Incumbent Nicolas Sarkozy (UMP) won 27.18 per cent of the vote but his chief rival François Hollande (Parti Socialiste (PS) (Socialist Party)) won 28.63 per cent. The runoff was held on 5 May (in the Americas), in which the socialist candidate, François Hollande won 51.63 per cent of the vote and Nicolas Sarkozy 48.37 per cent; turnout was 80.35 per cent. On 15 May François Hollande took office as president and head of state. On 4 June, two French soldiers were killed by illegal gold miners.
2013 On 25 July Arianespace launched Europe's largest telecommunications satellite ever as well as a meteorological spacecraft for India from Kourou. The Alphasat satellite will provide voice and data transmission services for Europe, Africa and the Middle East. Eric Spitz became Préfect on 10 June. President Hollande paid a brief visit in December.
2014 Following on the visit of French President Hollande to Guyana in December 2013 a meeting was held in Paris in May between French officials and Rodolphe Alexandre, President of the Regional Council, to further discuss the formation of a mining company to boost the economic mining sector in Guyana. The company would be a potential source of jobs and resources for the development of the area.
2015 In January the three French Caribbean countries (French Guiana, Guadeloupe and Martinique) began discussions on becoming associate members of Caricom.

Political structure

Constitution

28 September 1958 (French Fifth Republic)

Under the 1946 constitution of the French Fourth Republic, French Guiana became a Département d'Outre-Mer (DOM) (Overseas Department) of France. In 1974, it was granted additional status as a region of France.

The president of France is represented by a préfet, appointed by the government in Paris. French Guiana is represented in the French National Assembly and in the French Senate by two deputies and one senator.

Since 1983, following the French government's policy of decentralisation, regional councils have been elected with powers similar to those of the regions.

The local government comprises a Conseil Régional (Regional Council) of 31-members and a 19-member Conseil Général (General Council), both directly elected for six-year terms. Since a revision to the constitution in March 2003 the political and administrative organisation has been in a state of change; the Regional Council is assuming more influence.

Form of state

Département d'Outre-Mer (DOM) (Overseas Department) of France, with additional status as a région (region) of France.

The executive

Executive power is vested in the president of France, represented by a Préfet (Commissioner), appointed by the president on the advice of the French Ministry of Interior.

National legislature

Local administration is provided by two unicameral councils with divergent powers. The Conseil Régional (Regional Council) has 31 members, elected in single seat constituencies, for four-year terms. The Conseil Général (General Council) (for department administration) has 19 members elected in single seat constituencies, for six-year terms. Presidents of the General and Regional Councils are appointed by the members of individual councils.

Three representatives of French Guiana are elected to the parliament of France: two deputies are elected to the French National Assembly and one senator to the French Senate.

Legal system

French legal system

Last elections

14 and 21 March 2010 (regional council); March 2006 (general council)

Results: Regional Council: Comité de Liaison de la Majorité Présidentielle (Liaison Committee for the Presidential Majority) (Presidential Majority) won 40.61 per cent of votes (21 seats), Parti Radical de Gauche (Radical Party of the Left) (Radical Left) 23.02 per cent 10; eight other parties each won less than 10 per cent of the vote and no seats. Turnout was 49 per cent.

Next elections

2016 (general council)

Political parties

Ruling party

Parti Socialiste Guyanais (PSG) (Socialist Party) (since 2000; re-elected 2004)

Main opposition party

Union pour un Mouvement Populaire (UMP) (Union for the Popular Movement), Walwari Committee (aligned with the PRG in France)

Population

250,109 (2013)*

Last census: 1 January 2006: 205,954

Population density: Two inhabitants per square km.

Annual growth rate: 4.6 per cent (2003)

Ethnic make-up

Black or mixed race (66 per cent), white (12 per cent), East Indian, Chinese or Amerindian (12 per cent).

There are settlements of Hmong farmers from Laos. The troubles in neighbouring Suriname encouraged thousands of Surinamese to cross the border illegally and settle. The space centre has brought in thousands of scientists who live in a community of their own.

The minimum wage has attracted not only Surinamese but also Brazilians. These *clandestines* (illegal immigrants) are marginalised and forced to live in the poorest areas of the country, often without work.

Religions

Roman Catholic

Education

Schooling is compulsory and French Guiana has both public and private elementary schools, a high school, and two vocational schools. The condition of schools is, however, very poor, leading students to strike.

Literacy rate: 84 per cent, male; 82 per cent, female; adult rates (World Bank).

Health

Government health planning is seriously affected by the high prevalence of sexually transmitted diseases and an endemic level of dengue fever.

Health insurance is provided by the state-sponsored social security system, financed with compulsory contributions from salaries. People are usually reimbursed on the basis of rates negotiated between care providers and the social security.

Life expectancy: 77 years (estimate 2003)

Fertility rate/Maternal mortality rate: Three births per woman (2003)

Birth rate/Death rate: 21 births per 1,000 population; five deaths per 1,000 population (2003).

Child (under 5 years) mortality rate (per 1,000): 13 per 1,000 live births (2003)

Welfare

The official unemployment rate is 22 per cent with higher rates among young people. Jobs connected with satellite launching, combined with orderly French rule and an annual financial contribution amounting to US$500 million from Paris, have provided benefits such as good roads, decent health care, and a generous social security system.

Main cities

Cayenne (capital, estimated population 77,231 in 2012), Matoury (40,766), St Laurent-du-Maroni (81,898), Kourou (main town around the space centre) (31,143), Rémire-Montjoly (23,946), Macouria (16,506), Maripasoula (10,506).

Languages spoken

French and French-Creole. Some business executives speak English, although business is generally conducted in French.

Official language/s

French

Media

Press

Daily papers are *Guyane-Matin*, *France-Guyane* and *La Presse de Guyane*. There are no English-language newspapers. US and metropolitan French papers are available. Several periodicals are in circulation but there are no trade publications.

Broadcasting

Radio-Télévision Française d'Outre-mer (RFO) broadcast in French. There are two independent radio stations: Cayenne FM and Radio Tout Mount.

Economy

The overall economy remains underdeveloped. The poor soil limits the agriculture and so the main activities are fishing (particularly for shellfish), which accounts for 75 per cent of exports, and forestry, which is under exploited due to poor infrastructure. An expanding sawmill industry has increased the exports of hardwood logs from managed plantations. Gold is mined and is the single largest contributor to exports. Eco-tourism is beginning to grow in importance – although French Guiana has large tracts of unspoilt rain forests, it still has few facilities to cater for all but the hardiest of visitors.

A major contributor to the economy, accounting for 25 per cent of GDP and half of tax revenues, is the Centre Spatial Guyanais (Guiana Space Centre) at Kourou, which launches commercial and government funded rockets, using either the European Ariane 5 or Russian Soyuz launchers. An estimated 24 per cent of the population work directly or indirectly in jobs connected with the space industry. French Guiana is otherwise dependent on aid, technical assistance and imports from France. As a department of France, it receives the same benefits as mainland France: a minimum wage, free education and health care, and a large, well-paid civil service.

External trade

As a département d'outre-mer (DOM) of France, French Guiana is integrated as an outermost region of the European Union, which includes all EU trade agreements. There is heavy dependence on France for financial aid. The balance of trade deficit is mainly due to high imports of food and fuels, and undeveloped export potential.

Imports

Principal imports are food (grains, processed meat), machinery and transport equipment, fuels and chemicals.

Main sources: France (typically over 60 per cent), US, Trinidad and Tobago, Italy.

Exports

Principal exports are gold, shrimp, timber and rosewood essence, rum and clothing.

Main destinations: France (over 60 per cent total), Switzerland (7 per cent), US (2 per cent)

Agriculture

Farming

Cultivation is limited to the coastal area. Less than 1 per cent of the total land area is cultivated and crops are primarily farmed for domestic consumption. Such crops include rice, maize, bananas, cassava and cabbages, while sugar cane is grown for rum production. Most exports are grown on large estates and are destined for metropolitan France.

A small number of cattle farms have also been established.

Fishing

The typical total annual fish catch is over 5,000 tonnes (mt). Shellfish, molluscs and cephalopods account for another 2,700mt per annum.

Forestry

The rainforest covers around 90 per cent of the land area. Poor infrastructure means the vast timber resources have not been fully exploited. Exports consist of some 50,000 cubic metres of raw hardwood while imports are mostly processed sawn wood and wood panels used in construction.

Industry and manufacturing

The sector includes construction, shrimp processing, forestry products, rum and gold mining. Manufacturing is virtually non-existent, except for small factories processing agricultural or seafood products and a few sawmills. A tile and brick-making plant, based on important fields of red clay, operates in the Cayenne neighbourhood. Production of rum from sugar cane has declined. Industrial activity is limited to the area around the Kourou space centre.

Tourism

Although French Guiana has a wealth of flora and fauna in its rainforests, including nine national parks, one of which contains part of the Amazon forest, and a long Caribbean coastline, the tourist industry is under-developed. Eco-tourism is beginning to grow in importance – although French Guiana has large tracts of unspoilt rain forests, it still has few facilities to cater for all but the hardiest of visitors.

Mining

Bauxite deposits of 42 million tonnes and kaolin deposits of 40 million tonnes have been found, but extraction is not economically viable, although kaolin mining has begun in the Mana area. There are also reserves of silica, niobium and tantalite. Gold is mined, both legally and illicitly, the latter activity on a large scale and causing serious environmental damage. Significant exploitation of the mineral resources will come about only with further improvements in infrastructure.

Mineral exploitation is of little importance, and French Guiana must import fossil fuels and metallic minerals.

Hydrocarbons

French Guiana does not produce oil, gas or coal. It is heavily dependent on imports of petroleum products to meet its energy needs, importing around 6,870 barrels per day (bpd) in 2013. Gas and coal are not imported.

Energy

Total installed generating capacity was around 140MW in 2013, produced by thermal power stations. French Guiana relies on petroleum imports from France to fuel its power stations.

Banking and insurance

The Banque Nationale de Paris Guyane Sa (BNP Guyane) is a major commercial bank offering a wide range of services. There are branches in Cayenne, Kourou and Rémire-Montjoly.

Central bank

European Central Bank

Time

GMT minus three hours

Geography

French Guiana lies on the north coast of South America, with Suriname to the west and Brazil to the south and east. The country is largely low lying with hills no higher that 600 metres and covered in dense Amazonian rainforest that grows down to the mangrove fringed coastline.

Hemisphere

Northern

Climate

The climate is tropical. It is generally hot and humid with heavy rain. The dry season is August–December with an average temperature of 28 degrees Celsius (C). The rainy season is January–June with a temperature range of 22–32 degrees C.

Dress codes

For business meetings men should wear a lightweight or tropical suit and tie and women a lightweight suit or the equivalent.

Entry requirements

Passports

Passports are required by all except nationals of France and some francophone countries holding national identity cards. Passports should be valid for three months from the date of departure.

Visa

Required by all, except citizens of EU, North America, Australasia and Japan, for stays up to one month; this includes business trips by representatives of foreign entities with an invitation from a local company or organisation. Proof of adequate funds for stay, an itinerary, a guarantee of repatriation if necessary and return/onward ticket are also required. For further exceptions, full details and a copy of the application form visit www.diplomatie.gouv.fr/thema/dossier.gb.asp and follow the path (entering France) to the database.

Currency advice/regulations

There are no limits to the amount of local or foreign currency imported or exported, although amounts exceeding eur7,600 should be declared.

Travellers cheques are accepted; to avoid extra exchange fees, it is recommended that they be in euros, US dollars or pound sterling.

Health (for visitors)

Mandatory precautions

A yellow fever certificate.

Advisable precautions

Hepatitis A, B and D, typhoid and polio immunisations are recommended. Dengue fever is endemic. Malaria prophylaxis is advisable if travelling outside Cayenne. Water precautions should be taken, although tap water in Cayenne is safe. There is a rabies risk.

Hotels

There is a good standard of accommodation available in Cayenne, Kourou and St Laurent. Rates normally include service and taxes; if not, a 10 per cent tip is usual.

Public holidays (national)

Fixed dates

1 Jan (New Year's Day), 1 May (Labour Day), 8 May (Victory Day), 10 Jun (Abolition Day), 14 Jul (Bastille Day), 15 Aug (Assumption Day), 1 Nov (All Saints' Day), 11 Nov (Armistice Day), 25 Dec (Christmas Day).

Variable dates

Ash Wednesday (Carnival – Feb/Mar), Easter Monday (Mar/Apr), Ascension Day (Thur – May/June).

Working hours

Banking

Mon–Fri: 0730–1230, 1430–1730.

Business

Mon–Fri: 0800–1300, 1500–1800.

Government

Mon–Fri: 0730–1300, 1430–1830 (closed Wed and Fri afternoons).

Electricity supply

220V AC, 50 cycles

Social customs/useful tips

Appointments should be made in advance. It is customary to shake hands on meeting and taking leave. Business cards are exchanged after introduction.

Getting there

Air

International airport/s: Cayenne-Rochambeau (CAY), 15km from city; bar, post office, shops, hotel reservations, car hire.

Airport tax: None

Surface

Road: There is a coastal road to Suriname but there is no road access to Brazil.

Water: Ferries run regularly to Suriname, and from St George to Oiapoque (Brazil).

Getting about

National transport

Air: Air Guyane, Guyane Aero Service and Heli-Inter Service serve main centres and the interior of the country. (Bookings can be made through Air France.)

Road: There are 356km of national routes and 366km of departmental roads. Cayenne district is served by a good road system, but the streets of Cayenne itself are inferior. The only major road runs from Cayenne, via Kourou, to St Laurent on Suriname border.

Buses: Scheduled services on Cayenne to St Laurent route.

Water: Major form of travel. Motor boat serves some coastal towns. River boats and small planes link interior centres with coast. 400km rivers are navigable by small ocean-going vessels and river and coastal steamers but interior connections are made by local craft.

City transport

Taxis: Taxis are available in main towns. Fares include gratuities.

Car hire

Car hire is available in Cayenne and at the airport. An international licence required.

BUSINESS DIRECTORY

The addresses listed below are a selection only. While World of Information makes every endeavour to check these addresses, we cannot guarantee that changes have not been made, especially to telephone numbers and area codes. We would welcome any corrections.

Telephone area codes

The international direct dialling (IDD) code for French Guiana is +594 followed by another 594 and the subscriber's (six digit) number.

Useful telephone numbers

Talking clock: 3699
Times of tides: 378-300
Radio taxi: 307-305, 305-225
Bus service: 314-554
Fire: 18
Police: 17

Chambers of Commerce

Guyane Chambre de Commerce et d'Industrie, PO Box 49, Hôtel Consulaire, Place de l'Esplinade, 97321 Cayenne (tel: 299-600; fax: 299-634; e-mail: contact@guyane.cci.fr).

Banking

Banque Française Commerciale, 8 Place des Palmistes, 97300 Cayenne (tel: 291-111; fax: 301-312).

Banque de la Guyane, PO Box 35, 2 Place Victor-Schloelcher, Cayenne (tel: 310-515).

Banque Nationale de Paris Guyane, 2 Place Victor-Schoelcher, Cayenne (tel: 396-300; fax: 302-308).

Crédit Agricole, Angle av L Héder et rue Damas, 97300 Cayenne (tel: 318-000; fax: 317-524).

Crédit Martiniquais, 76 Av Gal de Gaulle, 97300 Cayenne (tel: 315-700; fax: 314-801).

Crédit Populairé Caisse Crédit Mutuel, 93 rue Lalouette, 97300 Cayenne (tel: 301-523; fax: 301-765).

Central bank

Banque de France, 31 Rue Croix des Petits Champs, 75001 Paris (tel: 4292-4292, 6480-2020; fax: 4292-3940; email: infos@banque-france.fr).

European Central Bank, Kaiserstrasse 29, D-60311 Frankfurt am Main, Germany (tel: (+49-69) 13-440; fax: (+49-69) 1344-6000; email: info@ecb.int).

Travel information

Air France, Cayenne (tel: 379-899).

Air Guyane, Aéroport de Rochambeau, 97351 Matoury (tel: 356-555; fax: 356-506).

AOM French Airlines (tel: 353-934).

Guyane Aero Services, Aéroport de Rochambeau, 97351 Matoury (tel: 356-162; fax: 358-450).

Héli-Inter Service Guyane, Aéroport de Rochambeau, 97351 Matoury (tel: 356-231; fax: 358-256).

Rochambeau International Airport, Cayenne (tel: 299-700).

Surinam Airways, c/o Atlas Voyages, 15 Rue Louis Blanc, 97300 Cayenne (tel: 317-298; fax: 305-786).

Syndicat Autonome des Hoteliers Restaurateurs et Cafétiers de Guyane, PK 9,2 Route de Rémire, 97354 Rémire Montjoly (tel: 354-100; fax: 354-405).

Syndicats d'Initiative Office du Tourisme, 7 Av du Président Monnerville, Cayenne 97300 (tel: 312-919).

TABA, PK 2,5 Route de Baduel, 97300 Cayenne (tel: 312-147; fax: 312-154).

National tourist organisation offices

French Guiana Tourist Board, 12, Rue Lallouette; BP 801; 97338 Cayenne (tel: 296-500; fax: 296-501; internet: www.tourisme-guyane.com/en).

Other useful addresses

Agence Régionale pour le Développement de l'Industrie Minière (Ardim), 111 rue Christophe Colomb, 973000 Cayenne (tel: 294-575).

British Consulate, 16 Ave G. Monnerville, B.P. 211, 97324 Cayenne (tel: 311-034; fax: 304-094).

Centre Spatial Guyanais, Korou (tel: 326-123).

Direction Régionale de l'Industrie, de la Recherche et de l'Environnement, pointe Buzaré, PO Box 7001, 97307 Cayenne (tel: 297-530; fax: 290-734).

Ligue pour la Protection des Oiseaux (LPO), Fonds Mondial pour la Nature (WWF), Cayenne (tel: 309-189).

Radio-Télévision Française d'Outre-mer(RFO), 43 bis Rue du Dr Devèze, BP 336, 97305 Cayenne (tel: 311-500).

Internet sites

Latin world, commercial directory: http://www.latinworld.com

Centre Français du commerce exterieur (site in French): http://www.cfce.fr

French Guiana Consular Information: http://travel.state.gov/french_guiana.html

French Polynesia

French Polynesia is a sprawling group of islands in the Pacific Ocean, made up of 118 volcanic and coral islands and atolls. There are five island groups – the Society Islands (including Tahiti), the Tuamotu archipelago, the Gambier Islands, the Marquesas Islands and the Tubuai Islands.

In 2004 they were designated as an overseas country (*pays d'outre-mer*) of France, which had been planned as the official designation for France's Pacific dependencies. However the status was never created and French Polynesia falls into the category of overseas collectivity. It sends two deputies to the French National Assembly and two senators to the Senate.

The islands have two main calls to fame – the post-impressionist French artist Paul Gauguin spent his most interesting and famous period there from the 1890s, and for a number of years from 1966 until forced by international pressure to switch to underground tests, France used the Mururoa atoll and neighbouring Fangataufa on which to conduct their nuclear atmospheric tests.

French Polynesians had a change of government in 2013 when the second round of the elections held on 5 May was convincingly won by the Tahoera'a Huiraatira party with 45.11 per cent (38 of the 57 seats in the Assembly). Former leader, Oscar Tamaru, was out of the country at the time, although that probably wasn't the reason for the defeat.

Back on decolonisation list

However, on 17 May 2013 the United Nations General Assembly (UNGA) voted to place French Polynesia back on the UN list of territories that should be decolonised. And it has requested the French Government to 'facilitate rapid progress… towards a self-determination process.'

Adopting a consensus resolution tabled by Nauru, Tuvalu and Solomon Islands, the UNGA affirmed 'the inalienable right of the people of French Polynesia to self-determination and independence' under the UN Charter, and declared that 'an obligation exists… on the part of the Government of France, as the administering power of the territory, to transmit information on French Polynesia.' The UNGA's action places French Polynesia back on the UN list of non-self governing territories, bringing the number of inscriptions to 17. Meanwhile, President Gaston Flosse has denounced the UNGA decision to reinscribe French Polynesia on the UN list of territories to be decolonised, describing it as dictatorial and vowing that he won't ever let the UN flag fly on his palace.

The vote in New York, which was boycotted by France, came in the dying hours of the presidency of Oscar Temaru, for whom it was a last minute political win after a personal campaign of more than 30 years.

Tourism is an important money-earner with visitors mostly favouring Tahiti and Bora Bora. Although the islands are prone to typhoons, there is a year-round warm climate, volcanic peaks and tranquil lagoons, to attract the visitor.

Although there is a high standard of living, wealth is unevenly distributed and unemployment is high.

COUNTRY PROFILE

French Polynesia consists of 118 islands and was settled by Polynesians between 300 and 800 AD. From these islands, Hawaii, the Cook Islands and New Zealand were colonised.
1843 Tahiti, the largest island, and Moorea became French protectorates.
1880 Tahiti became a French colony. The other islands were annexed under the name Comptoirs Français de l'Océanie.
1957 The group of islands became the Territoire d'Outre-Mer (TOM, overseas territory) of French Polynesia, administered by a governor in Papeete on Tahiti.
1960 An international airport opened at Faa'a on Tahiti.
1963 French nuclear tests were conducted for the first time at Mururoa Atoll.
1977 Increased powers for the council of ministers were approved by the French government.
1984 New powers for the government, particularly in commerce, were approved by the French government.
1983 Despite strong local protests, French authorities insisted that nuclear

KEY FACTS

Official name: Territoire de la Polynésie Française (Territory of French Polynesia)

Head of State: President of France François Hollande (PS) (from 15 May 2012), represented by High Commissioner Lionel Beffre (from 13 Sep 2013)

Head of government: President of the Territorial Government Édouard Fritch (from 12 Sep 2014)

Ruling party: Tahoera'a Huiraatira (from 5 May 2013)

Area: 3,600 square km (35 islands and 83 atolls)

Population: 274,512 (2012)*

Capital: Papeete (on Tahiti)

Official language: French and Reo Maohi (Tahitian)

Currency: Change Franc Pacifique (CFPf) = 100 centimes

Exchange rate: CFPf106.11 per US$ (Sep 2015); (pegged CFPf119.33 per euro)

Inflation: 1.80% (2011)*

* estimated figure

tests would continue for 'as long as necessary'.

1984 Jurisdiction over certain local affairs (local budget, health services, primary education, culture, social welfare, public works, agriculture and sports) was conferred on the council of ministers. Gaston Flosse became president of the governing council.

1986 The Tahoeraa Huiraatira-Rassemblement pour la République (TH-RPR) (People's Servant-Rally for the Republic) won the Territorial Assembly elections.

1987 Following accusations of misappropriation of public funds, Flosse resigned as president.

1990 Amendments to the constitution augmented presidential and Territorial Assembly powers.

1996 Gaston Flosse was re-elected president. France ended nuclear testing. The French government relinquished control of all affairs except for defence, law enforcement, the judiciary and the local currency.

2002 An appeal court in Paris dismissed fraud accusations against President Flosse.

2004 France's President Chirac dissolved the Territorial Assembly and changed French Polynesia's status to Pays d'Outre-Mer (overseas country) (POM). Oscar Temaru (pro-independence, Tavini Huira'atira (People's Servant) (PS) was elected president of the new Assemblée de la Polynésie Française (APF) (Assembly of French Polynesia). Temaru was ousted by Gaston Flosse (TH-RPR).

2005 Oscar Temaru (PS), leader of the pro-independence movement and supported by the ADN, was elected president.

2006 President Temaru (PS) was ousted and Gaston Tong Sang (Tahoera'a Huiraatira (TH) (Popular Rally) was elected president, by the APF.

2007 In the first round of the postponed presidential elections for the APF, the incumbent, Gaston Tong Sang received the least votes and was eliminated. In the runoff, Oscar Temaru (PS) won 27 votes and Édouard Fritch (TH) 17. A group of Tong Sang supporters broke away from the ruling TH and formed a new party, the O Porinetia To Tatou Ai'a (OPTTA). The French National Assembly approved a new parliamentary voting system of proportional representation and a minimum electoral threshold in a bid to bring a measure of stability to the islands' politics.

2008 The cabinet of President Oscar Temaru resigned. After two rounds in the general elections, the To Tatou Ai'a (Our Home) coalition (led by Temaru) won a total of 45.2 per cent of the vote (27 seats out of 57), the UPLD (led by Tong Sang) won 37.2 per cent (20) and the TH (led by Flosse) 17.2 per cent (10). Turnout was 76.9 per cent. A coalition of opposites, Our Home and TH, voted Flosse into the presidency, but he lost a vote of no confidence and was replaced by Tong Sang, with support from minor parties.

2009 President Tong Sang resigned. Oscar Temaru became president for the fourth time in 13 years. Former president, Gaston Flosse, was convicted of corruption and complicity to destroy evidence and abuse of public funds. He was stripped of all public offices and given a one-year suspended jail sentence, while further legal action was considered. President Temaru lost a vote of no confidence in parliament (29 votes to 24) and was replaced by Gaston Tong Sang.

2010 A general strike called in protest at the cut in over 9,000 government jobs carried out by the government in an effort to limit its budget deficit, lasted for five days and resulted in grounded air flights and paralysed public services. Central government officials in Paris summoned political leaders from French Polynesia to discuss not only the instability of the government in the islands, following six years when the leadership changed nine times, but also the on-going financial crisis. Following an inconclusive end to the talks, Paris declared that without political reform economic support would be limited. The central government had sent a delegation in 2009 to audit the work of the French Polynesian government and recommended a reduced civil administration. However, this was rejected by President Tong Sang and the central government (in Paris) cut financial aid. Foreign borrowing by the French Polynesian government was found to be prohibitively expensive. The government in Paris said it would require a commitment to change, backed by a referendum on economic development and French Polynesia's status as a DOM, before it extended credit to the islands. The French minister for overseas territories, Marie Luce Penchard, on a visit to French Polynesia, proposed an electoral reform plan that would reduce the number of representatives in the APF and the proportion of seats set aside for remote island communities. In effect French Polynesia would be spilt into two parts for administrative purposes: the remote outer islands and the populated inner islands. Leaders of all political parties initially rejected the proposals; which were nevertheless enacted.

2011 Richard Didier took up his post of *Préfet* in January. In April, Gaston Tong Sang lost a vote of no-confidence in parliament (57:29) and his long-time opponent Oscar Temaru replaced him as president. This was the fifth time that Temaru had been voted into the presidential office. By the beginning of June electoral reform laws (introduced from Paris) were passed, whereby votes of no-confidence will be limited; in future, a ratio of three to five in favour of a parliamentary motion will be required before a call will be allowed. President Temaru announced severe cuts to public spending of up to 50 per cent. Gaston Flosse called for early elections to give voters an opportunity to decide on these policies. His critics opined that he wanted to return to parliament before a legal judgement banned him for up to five years. In July President Sarkozy said he would veto any Polynesian plan to hold early parliamentary elections, saying that new laws of governance precluded elections at any interval except the prescribed time (due 2013). In October, former president Gaston was sentenced by a criminal court to four years in jail for abuse of public funds. In November, an appeal court in Paris annulled Gaston Flosse's ban on holding public office, although his one-year suspended sentence was confirmed. Tahitipress news agency was closed down in December following cost-cutting measures recommended by the French government to balance the large government deficit.

2012 The first round of the French presidential elections was held on 22 April, in which 10 candidates took part. Incumbent Nicolas Sarkozy (UMP) won 27.18 per cent of the vote but his chief rival François Hollande (Parti Socialiste (PS) (Socialist Party)) won 28.63 per cent. The runoff was held on 6 May, in which the socialist candidate, François Hollande won 51.63 per cent of the vote and Nicolas Sarkozy 48.37 per cent; turnout was 80.35 per cent. On 15 May François Hollande took office as president and head of state. On 3 September, Jean-Pierre Laflaquière took office as *Préfet* (high commissioner); Richard Didier was promoted into another post. In October, France appointed Rear Admiral Anne Cullère, the first woman, to hold the posts of Joint Commander Armed Forces in French Polynesia and commander of the French Maritime Forces in the Pacific.

2013 Former president Gaston Flosse was convicted in January on corruption charges involving French Polynesia's OPT telecommunications company; he was given a five-year prison sentence and fined US$110,000. He immediately appealed the conviction. A new political group, the A Tia Porinetia, was formed in February, incorporating the To Tatou Aia and leaders of several small parties. Legislative elections were held on 21 April and 5 May. The result of the second round was a solid win for the Tahoera'a Huiraatira party with 45.11 per cent (38 of the 57 seats in the Assembly). The

Union for Democracy won 29.26 per cent (11 seats) and the new party, the A Tia Porinetia, 25.63 per cent (8 seats). Turn out was 72.79 per cent. On 17 May the assembly elected Gaston Flosse as territorial president by a margin of 38 votes to 19. This was the fifth time he has become president and may be a short spell since he awaits the results of an appeal against his conviction for corruption. Also on 17 June the UN General Assembly adopted a resolution sponsored by Nauru, Solomon Islands and Tuvalu with support from Vanuatu, Samoa and Timor-Leste to reinscribe French Polynesia on the UN list of non-self-governing territories. In June the government warned that the financial situation was so bad that payments were being delayed from the usual 35 days to more than 50. Government debt had grown to just under US$1 billion. In July the government called for France to change its constitution to allow MPs to conduct debates in the Tahitian language. The request came after the French government had rejected two proposed laws because the debate took place in Tahitian, rather than French. On a visit to France in July Gaston Flosse said he would be raising the assembly's wish to hold an independence referendum as soon as possible.

2014 Municipal workers went on strike in March, after French reforms were feared to be leading to job losses. The strike was called off on 23 March after the French high commission agreed to a timetable to discuss their grievances. The strike had been interrupted by the first round of the municipal elections, held on 24 March. None of the major parties made significant gains or losses in the elections. Former president and current opposition leader, Oscar Temaru, was re-elected mayor in Faa'a, a position he has held for some 30 years. Gaston Flosse was forced to resign after being convicted of corruption, and failing to secure a pardon from French President Francois Hollande. He was succeeded by his deputy, Edouard Fritch, on 12 September

2015 Edouard Fritch is number two in the ruling party, Tahoeraa Huiraatira, which Mr Flosse still heads. In February the two leaders held their first meeting in five months in a bid to heal an unprecedented rift within the ruling party on whether or not to support an oposition motion to sue France for compensation for damage caused by its nuclear weapons tests, which had continued until 1996.

Political structure

Constitution

In 1996, the French government relinquished control over all the territory's affairs except for defence, foreign affairs, law enforcement, the justice system and the local currency. France is represented by a high commissioner who has a supervisory role. The territory is represented in the French Parliament by two deputies and two senators.

The local government has control over the territory's more than three million square kilometres of sea, as well as shipping, civil aviation, work permits, mineral exploration, foreign investment and local economic affairs. Under the Statute of Autonomy, it has full control over its Exclusive Economic Zone.

French Polynesia became a Pays d'Outre-Mer (POM) (overseas country) of France in 2004 with the implementation of the Assemblée de la Polynésie française (Assembly of French Polynesia) statute. It has 57 members in the assembly representing six constituencies.

Under the autonomy law, the electoral list gaining the most votes in general elections wins a bonus of extra seats, amounting to a third of the seats in the local parliament.

Form of state

Autonomous Pays d'Outre-Mer (POM) (overseas country) of France

National legislature

The unicameral Assemblée de la Polynésie Française (Assembly of French Polynesia) has 57 members elected for a five-year term, either directly or by proportional representation, in six multi-seat constituencies. The assembly elects the president of the territorial government

In 2007, the French National Assembly approved an amendment to the parliamentary voting system in an attempt to streamline the chaotic nature of politics in French Polynesia. The new proportional representation system has two rounds of voting; to reach the second round any candidate must have at least 12.5 per cent of the vote from the first round and their party much achieve a minimum electoral threshold 5 per cent.

Last elections

21 April and 5 May 2013 (first and second rounds of national assembly)

Results: In the first round the Tahoera'a Huiraatira (Popular Rally) won 40.16 per cent, the Union for Democracy alliance (of Aia Api, Here Ai'a, Tavini Huiraatira, Tapura Amui No Raromatai and Tapura Amui No Te Faatereraa Manahune-Tuhaa Pae) 24.09 per cent and the A Tia Porinetia 19.92 per cent. Six other parties won less than the 12.5 per cent threshold to proceed to the second round. Second round results were: Tahoera'a Huiraatira 45.11 per cent (38 seats), the Union for Democracy 29.26 per cent (11 seats) and the A Tia Porinetia 19.92 per cent (8 seats). Turn out was 72.79 per cent.

Next elections

2018 (national assembly)

Political parties

Ruling party

Tahoera'a Huiraatira (from 5 May 2013)

Main opposition party

Union for Democracy

Political situation

In August 2010, central government officials in Paris summoned political leaders from French Polynesia to discuss not only the instability of the government in the islands, following six years when the leadership changed nine times, but also the ongoing financial crisis. Following an inconclusive end to the talks, Paris declared that without political reform economic support would be limited. The central government had sent a delegation in 2009 to audit the work of the French Polynesian government and recommended a reduced civil administration. However, this was rejected by President Tong Sang and the central government (in Paris) cut financial aid. Foreign borrowing by the French Polynesian government was found to be prohibitively expensive. The government in Paris has said it will require a commitment to change, backed by a referendum on economic development and French Polynesia's status as a DOM, before it will extend credit to the islands. In October the French minister for the overseas territories, Marie Luce Penchard, on a visit to French Polynesia, proposed an electoral reform plan that would reduce the number of representatives in the assembly and the proportion of seats set aside for remote island communities. In effect French Polynesia would be spilt into two parts for administrative purposes: the remote outer islands and the populated inner islands. Leaders of all political parties initially rejected the proposals.

Population

274,512 (2012)*

Approximately 34 per cent of the population is under 15 years.

The growing population is gradually converging on Tahiti and the capital, Papeete, as conditions elsewhere become more difficult.

Last census: 20 August 2007: 259,596

Population density: 63 inhabitants per sq km. Urban population: 53 per cent (1995–2001).

Annual growth rate: 2.5 per cent (2003)

Ethnic make-up

Polynesian (78 per cent), Chinese (12 per cent), local French (6 per cent), metropolitan French (4 per cent).

Religions

Protestant (54 per cent), Roman Catholic (30 per cent), other (16 per cent).

Education

Enrolment rate: 116 per cent gross primary enrolment, of relevant age groups, (including repeaters) (World Bank).

Health

Life expectancy: 73 years (men) 77 years (women), 2007

Fertility rate/Maternal mortality rate: 2.04 births per woman

Birth rate/Death rate: 16.93 births per 1,000 population; 4.63 deaths per 1,000 population.

Child (under 5 years) mortality rate (per 1,000): 8.44 deaths per 1,000 live births

Main cities

Papeete (capital, on Tahiti, estimated population 25,852 in 2012), Faa'a (on Tahiti, 31,326), Punaauia (27,506), Mahina (15,537), Parae (14,467), Paea (12,134), Papara (11,889).

Languages spoken

English is spoken, especially in tourist and business circles.

In 2010, the French ministry for the overseas territories continued to reject the promotion of Tahitian as an official language of French Polynesia. Currently only French may be used in conducting government business; any decisions made in another language can and have been challenged. An appeal to the European Court of Human Rights in 2006 failed to get Tahitian recognised as an official language..

Official language/s

French and Reo Maohi (Tahitian)

Media

Press

Dailies: There are two newspapers available, in French, *La Dépêche de Tahiti* (Tahiti's largest newspaper) and *Les Nouvelles de Tahiti*.

Weeklies: In French *La Tribune Polynesienne* has general interest news. In English the *Tahiti Sun Press*, is a free-issue publication for tourists.

Periodicals: In French, monthly magazines include *L'Hebdo Maohi* (www.hebdo.pf) and the *Tahiti-Pacifique* (www.tahiti-pacifique.com) both covering current affairs.

Broadcasting

Radio: In addition to the government-operated RFO Polynésie (www.rfo.fr/polynesie.php) service, there are a number of private radio stations operating mostly on larger, inhabited islands, including Radio Bleue, Radio Tefana Te Reo, Radio Maohi and Radio Te Vevo, which all broadcast in Tahitian.

Television: The French overseas broadcaster RFO (http://polynesie.rfo.fr) provides all local produced news and imported French programmes, as well as internet TV services.

L'Agence Tahitienne de Presse (Tahitipress) was closed down in December 2011 following cost-cutting measures recommended by the French government to balance the large government deficit.

Economy

Around 10.2 million black cultured pearls, are exported annually (almost 70 per cent of all exports) – French Polynesia is the Pacific region's second-largest source of loose pearls (after the Australian production of yellow pearls). Co-operatives and private producers farm quality cultured black pearls under strict guidelines introduced to maintain a healthy crop of oysters. The fisheries sector is growing with deep-sea resources (particularly tuna) fished, mainly by Asian fleets under licence. French Polynesia has the Pacific region's largest exclusive economic zone. Agriculture consists of smallholders growing fruit and vegetables, while plantations provide copra and coconut oil for export. However, the single largest component of the economy is the tourist sector. The global economic crisis in 2008–09 cut the number of visitors to French Polynesia by 6.2 per cent in 2009 to 160,000; the biggest drop was in visitors from North America and Europe. By 2012 visitor numbers had recovered slightly to 169,000, before reducing to 164,000 in 2013.

Another major source of revenue is financial transfers from France, which represent around 30 per cent of GDP; expatriate remittances, which dropped from US$756 million in 2011 to US$669 million in 2012 before recovering to US$689 in 2013, are also an important source of revenue and foreign exchange.

There is a long-term and serious problem of unemployment, especially since France ceased its nuclear testing and withdrew most military personnel in 1996. France agreed to contribute funds as compensation for a limited period, although it has since been agreed that these payments will last for an indefinite period. In November 2014, the ruling anti-independence party requested nearly US$1 billion in compensation from Paris for damage caused by the nuclear tests carried out by France from 1966–96.

Development of the remote archipelagos (Marquesas, Australs, Tuamotu and Gambiers) has begun with the construction of more airstrips and roads to improve port facilities and public services. Capital development throughout the territory has helped create new businesses, while strengthening social services. Standard of living is high on the islands however wealth is very unevenly distributed.

External trade

French Polynesian exports are dominated by pearls, which account for 68 per cent of total exports and have a value of approximately US$156 million. Being an overseas-territory of France, the islands are reliant on French imports, which account for around a quarter of al imports.

Imports

Principal imports include refined petroleum, medical goods, foodstuffs, consumer goods, capital goods, vehicles, machinery and equipment.

Main sources: France (24 per cent of total in 2014), South Korea (10 per cent), China (9.6 per cent), US (9.3 per cent).

Exports

Principal exports include pearls, non-fillet fresh fish, coconut and its derivatives (flesh, oil and copra), other processed fruit and nuts, beer, and vanilla.

Main destinations: Japan (35 per cent of total in 2014), US (24 per cent), Hong Kong (17 per cent), France (9.1 per cent).

Agriculture

Farming

The agriculture sector accounts for around 3 per cent of GDP and employs 3 per cent of the workforce. Its development is a central plank of government policy. Primary products are pearls, copra, vanilla, and taro.

Weather permitting, local production supplies over 60 per cent of overall demand for some vegetables.

Local production supplies about 28 per cent of demand for dairy products and 83–87 per cent of demand for pork. Fruit is produced for export, for fruit juice factories, and for the local market.

Fishing

Green mussels, prawns, live bait and freshwater shrimp aquaculture are under development. The fishing industry, in particular tuna, is growing. Typically, the annual catch is over 500,000 tonnes including both fish and other seafood.

The government aims to increase its commercial tuna-fishing fleet to around 150 vessels, which are to be built locally and overseas.

Pearl farming is the second most important economic activity, after tourism, accounting for 68 per cent of total exports. Black pearls are the main merchandise export. They are mainly shipped to Japan and US.

Forestry

Although 70 per cent of the islands' land area is covered in forest, conditions limit exploitation to random felling, and almost all timber is imported. Plantations will yield productive forest of 11,250 hectares (ha) of Caribbean pine by 2025.

Industry and manufacturing

The small industrial sector primarily processes agricultural products. It accounts for approximately 20 per cent of GDP and employs 8 per cent of the workforce. The oil mill, Huilerie de Tahiti, purchases all copra produced and processes it into coconut oil and meal (for animal feed), soap-making and monoi (scented coconut oil). Other industries include breweries, soft drinks and fruit juice factories and a power station. Several small concerns produce textiles and handicrafts.

Tourism

While French Polynesia is not the best-known destination for a Pacific holiday, Tahiti, the largest of the French Polynesian archipelago, certainly is. Tourism is the most important economic activity, being the main constituent of the service sector which accounts for around 77 per cent of GDP, and is the primary earner of foreign income. The islands have all of the natural sights of a tropical island with a surviving cultural tradition. The Paul Gauguin Museum, in the capital Papeete, is dedicated to the works and life of the French artist who painted images of Polynesians in the late nineteenth century. There are several airlines with scheduled flights to Tahiti; an increase in cruise ship passengers has contributed to the improvement and the authorities are actively encouraging cruise visits.

Mining

Reserves of phosphate are present but not exploited.

Hydrocarbons

No oil, natural gas or coal is produced. Imported petroleum products amounted to 7,430 barrels of oil per day in 2013.

Energy

The government-owned monopoly, Électricité de Tahiti, is responsible for power production, supply and sales in French Polynesia. The total installed generating capacity in 2013 was 187MW, producing 830 gigawatt hours (GWh), of which hydropower accounted for around a third. Around 95 per cent of the population has access to mains electricity. On remote islands electricity is supplied by small hydro, solar and wind generated installations.

Banking and insurance

Although banking facilities in the principal urban centres are good, and include ATMs, financial service providers are scarce on some of the outlying islands.

Central bank

The Paris-based Institut d'Emission d'Outre-Mer (IEOM) provides all central banking services except foreign exchange reserves.

Time

GMT minus 10 hours

Geography

French Polynesia comprises several scattered groups of islands (120 islands in total) in the south Pacific Ocean, lying about halfway between South America and Australia.The Cook Islands are to the west and the Line Islands (part of Kiribati) to the north-west. The island groups in French Polynesia include the Iles du Vent (including the islands of Tahiti and Moorea) and the Iles Sous le Vent (about 160km north-west of Tahiti), which together constitute the Society Archipelago (the most populous); the Tuamotu Archipelago which comprises 78 islands scattered east of the Society Archipelago in a line stretching north-west to south-east for about 1,500km; the Gambier Islands located 1,600km south-east of Tahiti; the Austral Islands lying 640km south of Tahiti; and the Marquesas Archipelago, 1,450km north-east of Tahiti.

Most islands are mountainous (volcanic) and ringed with coral reefs; the Tuamotu and Gambier groups are mainly low-lying atolls.

Hemisphere

Southern

Climate

French Polynesia is located in the tropical zone of the southern hemisphere. It has two seasons: warm and moist (Dec–Feb) average temperature 27 degrees Celsius (C); cool and dry (Mar–Nov), average temperature 21 degrees C. Rainfall varies, depending on relief of island and exposure to prevailing winds, but heaviest Nov–Mar.

Entry requirements

Passports

Required by all, valid for six months after date of departure.

Visa

Required by all, except nationals of EU, other European countries and Australia for stays up to three months and nationals of the US, Canada, New Zealand, Japan, South Korea and most Latin American countries for stays up to one month.

Customs

Visitors are allowed to bring 200 cigarettes, 100 cigarillos, 50 cigars or 200 grams of tobacco; one or two litres of spirits depending on strength; 50g perfume and 250ml eau de toilette; and goods to the value of CPFf5,000 duty free.

All baggage coming in from Fiji and Samoa, except hand luggage, is fumigated. Travellers should carry clothing and toilet articles for an overnight stay in their hand luggage and arrange for their hotel to collect other baggage from the airport after fumigation.

Prohibited imports

Import of foodstuffs, weapons and illegal drugs.

Health (for visitors)

Mandatory precautions

Vaccination certificate for yellow fever if travelling from an infected area.

Advisable precautions

Vaccination for diphtheria, tuberculosis, hepatitis A and B, polio, tetanus, typhoid are recommended. There is a rabies risk.

Hotels

Most of the major international hotel chains are represented. Hotels are expensive and tend to be clustered in resorts. Cheaper, but off the beaten track, are *pensions* (bed-and-breakfast type accommodation).

Credit cards

American Express, Diners' Club, Master Card and Visa accepted throughout Tahiti.

Public holidays (national)

Fixed dates

1 Jan (New Year's Day), 5 Mar (Missionary Day), 1 May (Labour Day), 8 May (Victory Day), 14 Jul (Bastille Day), 15 Aug (Assumption Day), 8 Sep (Autonomy Day), 1 Nov (All Saints' Day), 11 Nov (Armistice Day), 25 Dec (Christmas Day).

Variable dates

Good Friday, Easter Monday, Ascension Day, Whit Monday.

Working hours

Banking

Mon–Fri: 0800–1530.

Business

Mon–Fri: 0800–1200, 1330–1730; Sat: 0800–1200.

Government

Mon–Fri: 0800–1200, 1330–1730; Sat: 0800–1200.

Shops

Mon–Fri: 0730–1130, 1400–1700; Sat: 0730–1130.

Telecommunications

Telephone/fax

Tahiti has an automatic telephone network.

Electricity supply

220V AC, 60 cycles (check with hotel before using appliances).

Weights and measures

Metric system

Social customs/useful tips

Tipping is not customary, and is contrary to traditional Tahitian hospitality.

Getting there

Air

National airline: Air Tahiti Nui

International airport/s: Tahiti-Faa'a International Airport (PPT), 6km from Papeete; restaurant, bank and car hire.
Airport tax: None.

Surface

Main port/s: Papeete.

Getting about

National transport

Air: There are over 25 airfields in addition to Tahiti-Faa'a International Airport. Air Tahiti operates scheduled flights to Moorea, Huahine, Raiatea, Bora-Bora, Maupiti, Rangiroa, Manihi, Takapoto, Tubuai, Nuku-Hiva (Marquesas), Ua Huka, Hiva Oa, Ua Pou, Anaa, Makemo, Hao, Rurutu and Mangareva (Gambiers) and several other atolls. Air Moorea operates daily services between Tahiti and Moorea. Both airlines also offer air taxi services, charters, circle island flights and transportation to other islands. Other air operators include Tahiti Conquest Airlines and Pacific Helicopter Tours.
Road: There are approximately 200km of road on Tahiti, including a circular 120km asphalt road around the main part of the island, and 100km of road on Moorea.
Buses: *Le truck* runs an unscheduled transport service between Papeete and outlying districts, leaving approximately every half hour for nearby areas and daily for distant points. The system also operates on Moorea, Bora Bora and some other islands.
Water: There is a scheduled boat service between Papeete and Moorea.

City transport

Taxis: Fares are controlled and should be displayed in each cab. In Tahiti, fares double between 2300 and 0500. Information on fares is available at GIE Tahiti Tourisme at the airport and in Papeete.
The journey time from the airport to the city centre is 10 minutes.
Buses, trams & metro: Airport to city centre bus service operates 0400–2359 hours, every 15 minutes.

Car hire

There are numerous car hire establishments; rates include insurance. Drivers must hold a licence valid for at least one year and must be at least 21-years-old. Driving is on the right-hand side of the road.

BUSINESS DIRECTORY

The addresses listed below are a selection only. While World of Information makes every endeavour to check these addresses, we cannot guarantee that changes have not been made, especially to telephone numbers and area codes. We would welcome any corrections.

Telephone area codes

The international dialling code (IDD) for French Polynesia is + 689 followed by subscriber's number.

Useful telephone numbers

Police: 17
Fire: 18

Chambers of Commerce

French Polynesia Chamber of Commerce and Industry, PO Box 118, Rue Docteur Cassiau, 98713 Papeete (tel: 540-700; fax: 540-701).

Banking

Banque de Polynésie SA, PO Box 530, 355 Boulevard Pomare, Papeete (tel: 466-666; fax: 466-664).

Banque de Tahiti SA, PO Box 1602, Rue Cardella, Papeete (tel: 417-000; fax: 423-376).

Banque Socredo, PO Box 130, 115 rue Dumont d'Urville, Papeete (tel: 415-123; fax 433-661).

Central bank

Institut d'Emission d'Outre-Mer (IEOM), 5 rue Roland Barthes, 75012 Paris, France (tel : +33 1 5344-4141; fax : +33 1 4347-5134; e-mail: contact@ieom.fr).

Travel information

Air Moorea, BP 6019, Faa'a International Airport (tel: 864-141; fax: 864-299).

Air Tahiti Nui, Immeuble Dexter, Pont de l'Est, BP 1673, Papeete (tel: 460-303; fax: 460-222).

National tourist organisation offices

Tahiti Tourisme, Immeuble Paofai, Bvd Pomaré, BP 65 Papeete (tel: 505-700; fax: 436-619; e-mail: tahiti-tourisme@mail.pf; internet site: http://www.tahiti-tourisme.com).

Other useful addresses

Institut Territorial de la Statistique, BP 395, Papeete, Tahiti (tel: 437-196; fax: 427-252).

Service des Affaires Economiques, BP 82, Papeete, Tahiti.

Syndicat des Importateurs et des Négociants, PO Box 1607, Papeete, Tahiti.

Syndicat d'Initiative de la Polynésie Française, BP 326, Papeete.

Internet sites

Tourism Council of the South Pacific: http://www.infocentre.com/spt.

Enterprise and development agency (in French): http://www.creation-entreprises.pf/

Gabon

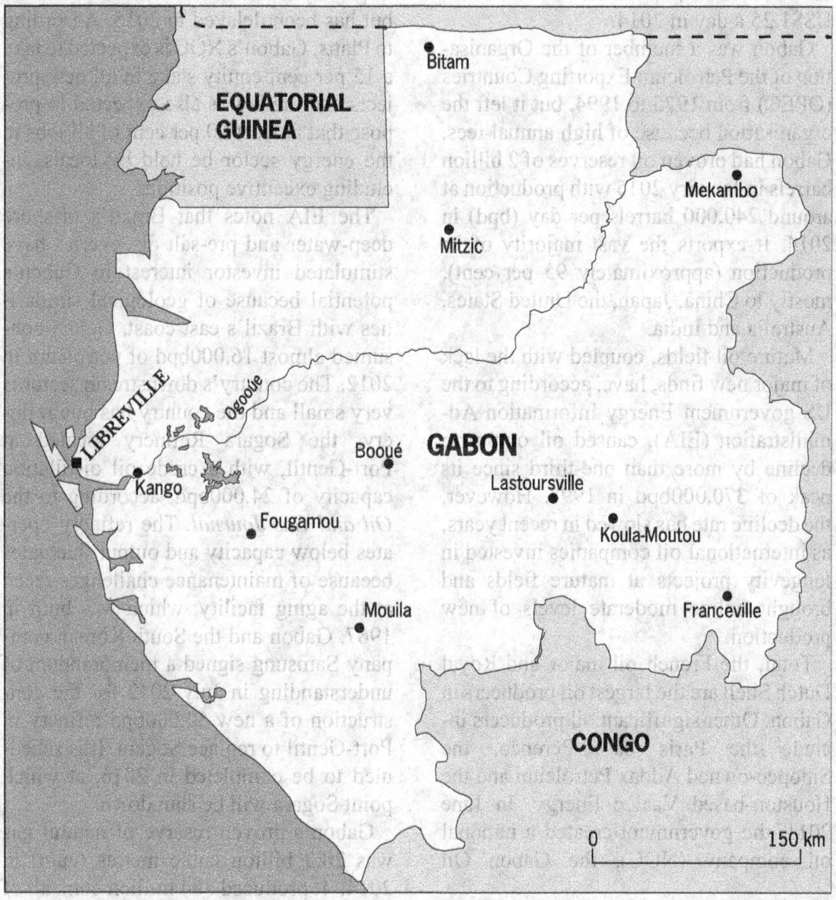

KEY FACTS

Official name: République Gabonaise (Gabonese Republic)

Head of State: President Ali Ben Bongo Ondimba (from 16 Oct 2009)

Head of government: Prime Minister Daniel Ona Ondo (PDG) (from 27 Jan 2014)

Ruling party: Parti Démocratique Gabonais (PDG) (Gabonese Democratic Party) (since 1960; re-elected 17 Dec 2011)

Area: 267,667 square km

Population: 1.59 million (2014)*

Capital: Libreville

Official language: English (from Oct 2012)

Currency: CFA franc (CFAf) = 100 centimes (Communauté Financière Africaine (African Financial Community) franc)

Exchange rate: CFAf586.44 per US$ (Sep 2015)

GDP per capita: US$10,836 (2014)*

GDP real growth: 5.08% (2014)*

GDP: US$17.18 billion (2014)*

Inflation: 4.51% (2014)

Oil production: 236,000 bpd (2014)

Balance of trade: US$5.21 billion (2011)

* estimated figure

Gabon's head of state, President Bongo, is one of the longest serving leaders in the world, he has dominated the country's political scene for four decades (1967–2009) following independence from France in 1960. President Bongo introduced a multi-party system and a new constitution in the early 1990s, however, allegations of electoral fraud during local elections in 2002 and the presidential election in 2005 exposed the weaknesses of formal political structures in Gabon. Following Bongo's death in 2009, a new election brought his son, Ali Bongo Ondimba to power which highlights the corrupt nature of Gabon's political system. Gabon's small population, abundant natural resources, and considerable foreign support have helped it make it one of the more stable African countries.

Gabon enjoys a per capita income four times higher than that of most sub-Saharan African nations – US$22,900 in 2014. Despite high per capita income, high income inequality has kept a large proportion of the population in poverty. Gabon's economy depended on timber and manganese until oil was discovered offshore in the early 1970s. Currently, the economy is heavily reliant on oil which constitutes approximately 50 per cent of GDP, 70 per cent of government revenues, and 87 per cent of goods exports. Some oil fields in Gabon have passed their peak production and, subsequently, declining production has hampered Gabon from fulfilling potential gains. Oil prices that had remained high from 1999 to 2013 significantly helped growth, but, conversely, the sharp decline in oil prices since June 2014 has slowed growth. Economic growth fell from 5.6 per cent in 2013 to 5.1 per cent in 2014 and it is predicted to decrease to 4.6 per cent in 2015. Gabon's dependence on oil, timber and manganese exports means that it is highly vulnerable to the volatile global market. Despite the abundance of wealth from its natural resources, poor fiscal management has stifled the economy. In light of this problem, President Bongo has made efforts to increase transparency and is taking steps to make Gabon a more attractive investment destination to diversify the economy. Bongo has attempted to boost growth by increasing government investment in human resources and infrastructure.

The drop in oil revenue has meant that the 2015 budget had to be cut by 11.4 per cent. These cuts have hit small= and medium-sized enterprises through delayed payments from their main customer, the government. The cuts have led to repeated strikes by civil servants and by the main oil and gas sector trade union which caused significant disruption. Inflation was 6 per cent in 2014, twice the limit set by the Central African Economic and Monetary Community (CEMAC). The government presented a new human investment strategy at the beginning of 2015 in an effort to ease social pressures. Furthermore, the government's ambitious spatial development scheme, Plan Stratégique Gabon Emergent (PSGE) (Strategic Plan for an Emerging Gabon), is based on setting up ten 'clusters' of economic activity around the country to make best use of national potential as a way of diversifying the economy, and will require major investment in infrastructure and social services. Despite President Bongo's efforts to improve the economy, Gabon's low social indicators will prevent it from achieving most of the 2015 Millennium Development Goals. Of the total population, 16.7 per cent of remained in multi-dimensional poverty and 4.8 per cent of the population lived under US$1.25 a day in 2014.

Gabon was a member of the Organisation of the Petroleum Exporting Countries (OPEC) from 1975 to 1994, but it left the organisation because of high annual fees. Gabon had proven oil reserves of 2 billion barrels in January 2015 with production at around 240,000 barrels per day (bpd) in 2014. It exports the vast majority of its production (approximately 95 per cent), mostly to China, Japan, the United States, Australia and India.

Mature oil fields, coupled with the lack of major new finds, have, according to the US government Energy Information Administration (EIA), caused oil output to decline by more than one-third since its peak of 370,000bpd in 1997. However, the decline rate has slowed in recent years, as international oil companies invested in longevity projects at mature fields and brought online moderate levels of new production.

Total, the French oil major and Royal Dutch Shell are the largest oil producers in Gabon. Other significant oil producers include the Paris based-Perenco, the Sinopec-owned Addax Petroleum and the Houston-based Vaalco Energy. In June 2011, the government created a national oil company (NOC), the Gabon Oil Company, to increase the government's involvement in oil production by taking equity stakes in future exploration. Gabon did not have a NOC for more than two decades after the previous one, the Société Nationale Petroliére Gabonaise, was disbanded in 1987. The government is working on a new petroleum law. It was originally scheduled to be enacted in 2014 but has been delayed to 2015. According to Platts, Gabon's NOC is expected to take a 15 per cent equity stake in all new projects and the law is also expected to propose that at least 90 per cent of all jobs in the energy sector be held by locals, including executive positions.

The EIA notes that Brazil's offshore deep-water and pre-salt discoveries have stimulated investor interest in Gabon's potential because of geological similarities with Brazil's east coast. Gabon consumed almost 16,000bpd of petroleum in 2012. The country's downstream sector is very small and the country has one refinery, the Sogara Refinery located at Port-Gentil, with a crude oil distillation capacity of 24,000bpd, according to the *Oil and Gas Journal*. The refinery operates below capacity and output fluctuates because of maintenance challenges faced at the aging facility, which was built in 1967. Gabon and the South Korean company Samsung signed a memorandum of understanding in July 2012 for the construction of a new 50,000bpd refinery in Port-Gentil to replace Sogara. It is scheduled to be completed in 2016, at which point Sogara will be shut down.

Gabon's proven reserve of natural gas was 28.3 billion cubic metres (cum) in 2014. It produced 384 million cum, all of which is consumed domestically. Gabon does not import or export any natural gas. More than 90 per cent of the natural gas produced in Gabon is either flared and vented or re-injected into oil wells to aid oil recovery. There has recently been some progress in building pipelines to connect some associated gas fields to onshore power plants, but there are no firm project commitments to continue expanding infrastructure and commercialising additional natural gas output.

According to the latest (2012) estimates from the World Bank, 89 per cent of Gabon's population has access to electricity. Much of Gabon's rural population still relies on traditional biomass and waste (typically consisting of wood, charcoal, manure and crop residues) to meet household cooking and heating needs. Gabon has an estimated 5,000 to 6,000MW of undeveloped hydropower potential,

KEY INDICATORS Gabon

	Unit	2011	2012	2013	2014	**2015
Population	m	*1.52	*1.54	*1.56	*1.59	*1.61
Gross domestic product (GDP)	US$bn	17.10	17.86	17.14	*17.18	*15.03
GDP per capita	US$	11,114	11,595	*10,966	*10,836	*9,343
GDP real growth	%	4.8	5.5	5.6	*5.1	*4.4
Inflation	%	17.4	2.7	0.5	4.5	*2.5
Oil output	'000 bpd	245.0	245.0	237.0	236.0	–
Exports (fob) (goods)	US$m	8,071.0	–	–	–	–
Imports (fob) (goods)	US$m	2,861.0	–	–	–	–
Balance of trade	US$m	5,210.0	–	–	–	–
Current account	US$m	2,676.0	2,506.0	*2,566.0	*1,933.0	*-352.0
Total reserves minus gold	US$m	2,149.3	2,351.6	–	2,478.5	–
Foreign exchange	US$m	1,937.1	2,146.4	–	–	–
Exchange rate	per US$	466.82	505.65	480.26	542.10	

* estimated figure ** forecast figure

according to IHS Cera, which if exploited, could substantially increase the country's electrification rate. However, the country's main business hubs have suffered from blackouts in the past because of low levels of rainfall.

Gabon recently launched a plan to expand the hydroelectricity sector by constructing new power plants and extending transmission lines to satisfy rising demand from industrial consumers, according to IHS World Markets Energy. The first project to come online was the 160-Megawatt Grand Poubara hydroelectric dam on the Ogooué River, which in May 2013 had four hydro turbines in operation. The project was built in 56 months under an engineering-procurement-construction (EPC) basis by PowerChina subsidiary Sinohydro Corporation.

Risk assessment

Politics	Fair
Economy	Fair
Regional stability	Good

COUNTRY PROFILE

1472 Portuguese navigators arrived in the Ogooué estuary and Gabon soon became an important centre for slave trading for the Portuguese, Dutch, British and French.

1839 Having gained a dominant position in the area and despite Fang resistance, Gabon became part of the French Congo. The French began work to abolish the slave trade.

1910 Gabon became part of French Equatorial Africa.

1939–1945 Gabon was held by the Free French.

1946 Gabon became a province of French Equatorial Africa. In gratitude for the support of the local population for the Free French, President Charles de Gaulle of France granted French citizenship to all the territory's people.

1957 Gabon gained internal autonomy.

1958 It achieved self-government within the French community.

1960 Gained full independence from France, under President Léon M'Ba. The Parti Démocratique Gabonais (PDG) (Gabonese Democratic Party) assumed power.

1964 French forces restored M'Ba to the presidency after an abortive military *coup d'état*.

1967 President M'Ba died. Vice President Albert-Bernard Bongo became president.

1973 Bongo was re-elected and converted to Islam, adopting the forename Omar.

1981–89 Political unrest grew as people called for more democracy.

1990 After demonstrations by students and strikes by workers, President Bongo legalised opposition parties.

1991 A new constitution was introduced that formalised the multi-party system.

1993 Bongo narrowly won the presidential election, although the opposition claimed massive electoral fraud.

1996 Parliamentary elections gave the PDG an overwhelming majority.

1998 President Bongo won another seven years in power with more than two-thirds of the vote.

1999 The country was plunged into a deep recession due to the fall in the world price of oil.

2001 The PDG won the parliamentary elections.

2002 The PDG formed a coalition with the opposition to form the government.

2003 Constitutional changes made in July allow presidents to run for office for unlimited terms. The president modified his name to El Hadj Omar Bongo Ondimba.

2004 Gabon signed separate agreements to export around one billion tonnes of iron ore as well as oil to China.

2005 In presidential elections incumbent El Hadj Omar Bongo Ondimba won 79.2 per cent of the presidential vote; Pierre Mamboundou 13.6 per cent and Zacharie Myboto 6.6 per cent. Turnout was 63.3 per cent.

2006 Omar Bongo Ondimba was sworn in as president for a third seven-year term. Jean Eyeghe Ndong (PDG) was appointed prime minister. In parliamentary elections the ruling PDG won 82 out of the 120 seats, allied parties won 17, opposition 17 and independents four seats.

2008 Former foreign minister Jean Ping was elected chairman of the African Union Commission.

2009 The ruling PDG won senate elections. President Omar Bongo Ondimba had his assets in France frozen by the authorities and a French court ordered him to return a payment made to him for the release of a French businessman, jailed in Gabon. The president was thought to have around US$4 million held in French bank accounts; he claimed the money received was for the sale of a business and not for the release. The president suspended his functions as head of state and was reported to be seriously ill. He died in Spain and his body was flown back to Gabon for burial. Senate leader Rose Francine Rogombé became interim president. Ali Ben Bongo Ondimba (son of the late president Bongo) (PDG) won presidential elections. The Constitutional Court rejected opposition challenges to the official election results. Paul Biyoghé became prime minister.

2010 The government signed contracts, expected to generate up to US$4.5 billion in investment, with three Asian companies in a move designed to diversify the economy as oil reserves begin to dwindle. The contracts included the setting up of a special economic zone in Nkok (27km east of Libreville) with a capacity to process one million cubic metres of timber annually; improving the infrastructure, which would create around 50,000 jobs; developing a palm oil plantation of up to 300,000 hectares, and a palm oil refinery, with a possible new port for exports in the south east of Gabon. 5,000 low-cost homes are also included in the plans. Transparency International successfully appealed against a Paris court's ruling in 2009 that it could not act against foreign heads of state. France's highest appeal court gave investigative judges permission to proceed with investigations into assets held in France by the late president, Omar Bongo and his family, as well as Teodoro Obiang Nguema of Equatorial Guinea and Denis Sassou-Nguesso of Congo. The Singaporean multinational, Olam International, agreed to invest US$1.7 billion in Gabon, including the construction of a fertiliser plant and palm oil plantations.

2011 In April, members of the oil workers union, the National Organisation of Oil Employees, went on strike for four days, shutting down Total and Royal Dutch Shell operations, in protest at the employment of foreign workers rather than local workers. The cost to the government and companies was estimated at US$131 million. In May, the opposition leader André Mba Obame was stripped of his parliamentary immunity as the government prepared to charge him with treason, following his TV broadcast in January, when he had declared himself the winner of the 2009 presidential election. Parliamentary elections were held on 17 December; however, since the government rejected the suggestion of biometric voter registration to prevent fraud, the opposition and other community and civic groups called on voters to boycott the elections, declaring that they could not be free and fair and would be rigged in favour of the President's PDG. Of the five political parties that contested the elections all-but-one supported the presidency of Ali Bongo Ondimba. The PDG won 74.2 per cent of the vote (115 seats out of 121) and the RPG 4.3 per cent (three). Three other political parties (including the only opposition party, Union pour la nouvelle République (UPNR) (Union for a New Republic) each won one seat; turnout was 34.8 per cent.

2012 On 13 February, Paul Biyoghé Mba resigned; Raymond Ndong Sima (PDG) was appointed as prime minister on 27 February. On 7 September the credit

ratings agency, Standard and Poor's revised Gabon's rating upward from BB- to B with a stable outlook. On 19 October, over 300 Nigerian fishermen and their families were removed from three small islands in Akanda National Park (north of Libreville) and relocated either to another island outside the park or back to Nigeria. The families had originally fled during the war in Biafra in 1967.
2013 Gabon withdrew the right of Addax Petroleum, a subsidiary of Chinese oil giant Sinopec, to exploit the south-western Obangue oilfield, transfering it to state-run Gabon Oil Company (GOC). The Chinese company was accused of failing to meet 'contractual obligations'.
2014 In September The L'Union des forces pour l'alternance (UFA) (Union of Forces for Alternance) called for a constitutional amendment to limit the mandate of the President of the Republic to two terms.
2015 Teachers went on strike in early February, followed by public service workers in March.

Political structure

Constitution
In 1991 a new constitution was introduced which restored multi-party elections and protected civil liberties. The constitution maintained a strong presidential role but allowed for a more influential prime minister.
In July 2003, the constitution was changed to allow presidents to run for office for unlimited number of times, and the number of presidential election rounds was reduced from two to one.

Independence date
17 August 1960.

Form of state
Presidential democracy

The executive
Executive power is divided between the president, elected by universal suffrage every seven years, and the prime minister and Council of Ministers (Cabinet) who are appointed by the president.
Government members must be more than 35 years of age and have at least seven years' professional experience.
The president is head of state, head of administration and chief of the armed forces.

National legislature
The bicameral parliament consists of the Assemblée Nationale (national assembly) with 120 members, of which 111 are elected in single seat constituencies and nine are appointed by the president, all to serve for five-year terms, and the Sénat (senate) with 91 members elected in single seat constituencies by representatives of subordinate assemblies, to serve for six-year terms.

Legal system
The legal system is based on the French civil law system and customary law. There is judicial review of legislative acts in the Constitutional Chamber of the Supreme Court.

Last elections
17 December 2011 (parliamentary); 30 August 2009 (presidential)
Results: Parliamentary: Parti Démocratique Gabonais (PDG) (Gabonese Democratic Party) won 74.2 per cent of the vote (115 seats out of 121), Rassemblement pour le Gabon (RPG) (Rally for Gabon) 4.3 per cent (three); three other political parties each won one seat. Turnout was 34.8 per cent.
Presidential: Ali Ben Bongo Ondimba (PDG) won 41.73 per cent of the vote, André Mba Obame (indendent) 25.88 per cent, Pierre Mamboundou (Union du Peuple Gabonais (UPG) (Union of the Gabonese People)) 25.22 per cent; 15 other candidates each won less than 4 per cent.

Next elections
November 2016 (presidential); 2016 (national assembly)

Political parties

Ruling party
Parti Démocratique Gabonais (PDG) (Gabonese Democratic Party) (since 1960; re-elected 17 Dec 2011)

Main opposition party
With only one parliamentary seat the Union pour la nouvelle République (UPNR) (Union for a New Republic) has little opportunity of providing any effective opposition..
The rural population is lightly spread over a large area.
Although the Gabonese enjoy one of the highest per capita incomes in sub-Saharan Africa, income distribution is unequal.

Population

1.54 million (2012)* The rural population is lightly spread over a large area.
Although the Gabonese enjoy one of the highest per capita incomes in sub-Saharan Africa, income distribution is unequal.
Last census: 1 December 2003: 1,269,000 (provisional)
Population density: Five inhabitants per square km. Urban population 86 per cent (2010 Unicef).
Annual growth rate: 2.4 per cent, 1990–2010 (Unicef).

Ethnic make-up
There are some 40 different ethnic groups, of which the Fangs are the largest (40 per cent of the total); the Bapounous (20 per cent) are also highly significant. There are some 25,000 Europeans, mainly of French nationality.

Religions
Christianity (59 per cent), mostly Roman Catholic; indigenous animist beliefs (40 per cent). There is a small Muslim community (less than 1 per cent).

Education

School is compulsory and free for all children up to the age of 16 years. Secondary education covers seven years, divided into a lower cycle lasting four years and an upper cycle lasting three years. On completion of the upper cycle, pupils take the examinations for the *Baccalauréat* for advancement to university. On completion of the lower cycle, pupils may opt to take a 'short' or a 'long' course of technical secondary education. The former leads to the *Brevet de Technicien* and the latter to the *Baccalauréat technique*.
Two universities – Omar Bongo University and the University of Science and Technology of Masuku (USTM at Franceville) – as well as various independent institutions provide higher education. Universities enjoy a certain degree of autonomy, even though higher education is financed exclusively by public funds.
Public expenditure on education typically amounts to 2.5 per cent of annual GDP.
Literacy rate: 79.8 per cent, male; 62.2 per cent, female; adult rates (World Bank).
Enrolment rate: 62 per cent total primary school enrolment of the relevant age group (World Bank).
Pupils per teacher: 56 in primary schools.

Health

Gabon is plagued by poor health conditions, which are aggravated by the hot and humid climate and is the country worst affected by malaria in sub-Saharan Africa.
Gabon faces a growing crisis of male impotence affecting 25 per cent of all adult men, blamed on high levels of alcohol and tobacco use.

HIV/Aids
HIV/Aids is a rapidly growing crisis the World Health Organisation (WHO) estimates that 30,000 people in Gabon are being infected with HIV each year and Gabon is beginning to experience the serious effects of the African pandemic. Around 8,600 children have been orphaned by the disease. The main concentration of HIV/Aids cases is in the capital, Libreville. The government has launched a campaign to prevent the disease spreading further.
HIV prevalence: 8.1 per cent aged 15–49 in 2003 (World Bank)
Life expectancy: 57 years, 2004 (WHO 2006)
Fertility rate/Maternal mortality rate: 3.3 births per woman, 2010 (Unicef);

maternal mortality 600 per 100,000 live births (World Bank).
Birth rate/Death rate: 16 deaths to 36 births per 1,000 population,
Child (under 5 years) mortality rate (per 1,000): 62 per 1,000 live births (WHO 2012)
Head of population per physician: 0.29 physicians per 1,000 people, 2004 (WHO 2006)

Welfare
Gabon's social welfare system, while deeply flawed, is one of the best in sub-Saharan Africa. It operates a social insurance system and healthcare system through separate funds administered by the National Social Security Fund (CNSS) and National Social Guarantee Fund (CNGS) for self-employed and state workers under contract through a pay-as-you-go system. As these funds have experienced financial difficulties and the government has undertaken to restructure them with a view to their long-term viability. Inadequate contributions have been blamed for the over-spending.
The social insurance system covers benefits including old age, disability, sickness, maternity and work injuries with provision for certain categories of self-employed workers. Old age pensions are available to men aged 55 with 20 years of insurance and 120 months of contribution during the last 10 years. It is set at a minimum of 40 per cent of average earnings during the last three or five years of pay. There is also provision for old-age settlement with a lump sum equal to 50 per cent of average monthly earnings for every six months of contribution, if the person is ineligible for pension.
Medical services are provided by hospitals and dispensaries operated by the CNSS, and by other establishments. Free maternity care is payable up to six weeks before, and eight weeks after, confinement. A family allowance law also offers benefits to employees with one or more children under the age of 16 years. Family Allowance Benefits provide a month income for each child and a year school allowances for primary, secondary and technical school students.

Main cities
Libreville (capital, estimated population 797,003 in 2012), Port-Gentil (150,484), Masuku (59,231), Oyem (42,556), Moanda (41,564), Mouila (30,974).

Languages spoken
French is used for all documentation. The main native language is Fang, with a number of other Bantu dialects spoken. It is essential that business visitors should be able to conduct business in French. Interpreters can be hired locally.

Official language/s
English (from Oct 2012)

Media
The constitution guarantees freedom of speech and of the press, however, these are not always respected and this has led to self-censorship by local journalists.

Press
The national press is heavily influenced by government which owns the majority of newspapers used to discredit opposition political parties and independent media. While all newspapers may be critical of the government and political leaders, none are critical of the president. The government has shown itself to be quick to use libel laws, which can be both criminal and civil matters, and to suspend publications it deems unacceptable in their reporting.
Foreign newspapers and magazines are readily available in Libreville.
Dailies: The only newspaper is the government-owned *L'Union*, published in French.
Weeklies: In French, privately-owned newspapers include *Le Temps* which has a satirical tenor, *Le Temoin* covers general news and information, *La Lowe*, *La Relance* and the fortnightly *Le Journal*.
Business: In French, a monthly journal *Business Gabon* (www.gaboneco.com/busnessgabon/Business_Gabon.pdf) has business articles and information.
Periodicals: *L'Union* also publishes a monthly magazine, with a similar circulation. *M'Bolo* has three issues on holiday and travel.

Broadcasting
Gabon is developing as the centre of Francophone broadcasting for Central and West Africa, being the base of the radio service Africa No 1 and for the African operations of France's Canal Plus. The state has taken a financial interest in these broadcasting media, as well as in the main newspaper, directly and through parastatal groups. It therefore retains a high degree of control.
The government-owned, national, public broadcasting service, Radiodiffusion-Télévision Gabonaise (RTG), operates radio stations and a network of provincial stations.
Radio: RTG operates two national radio stations, based in Libreville, and a network of six regional stations broadcasting in French and local languages.
A major international station, Africa No 1, is 60 per cent government owned, with the rest owned by private Gabonese shareholders. It is in partnership with the French-owned Radio France Internationale (RFI), broadcasting throughout Africa.
Other, commercial stations include Black FM and Radio Emergence.
Television: RTG operates a network of provincial TV stations, which broadcast in French and local languages. RTG 1 is a national service, broadcast in Libreville and Franceville; while RTG 2 can be received only in the Libreville and the coastal area.
Téléafrica, is a private commercial channel that broadcasts 24 hours a day. Subscription TV is available through the French, Canal Horizons (Gabon), a channel designed to serve the whole of Francophone Central Africa.
National news agency: Agence Gabonaise de Presse (AGP)
Other news agencies: Gabonews: www.gabonews.ga
Internet Gabon: www.internetgabon.com

Economy
Gabon has sub-Saharan Africa's fourth-largest oil reserve – oil exports account for over 65 per cent of government revenue. The dominance of oil in the economy has resulted in undue bias, not only in a weak non-oil sector but also a wide gap in pay levels. Although GNI per capita in 2014 was US$16,500 (by purchasing power parity), income is distributed extremely unevenly with 90 per cent of the wealth held by 5 per cent of the population. It has been estimated that over 30 per cent of the population lives below the poverty line of which most of them live in rural areas.
The 2005 criticism by the International Monetary Fund (IMF) of the Gabonese economy that it faced a 'lack of economic diversification and weak non-oil growth' has become increasingly addressed in recent years. Real GDP growth has averaged about 6 per cent in the last 4 years as increased capital spending by authorities has occurred to implement the strategy plan Stratègique Gabon Emergent (PSGE), which aims at promoting economic diversification and inclusive growth. Inflation has remained low. In March 2014, the World Bank approved funds of US$18 million to Gabon in order to help diversify the economy.
Timber exports are an important source of foreign exchange, although coupled with farming, agriculture only accounted for 3.7 per cent of GDP in 2014. The service sector accounted for 34.6 per cent of GDP, which typically provides support for the extractive industry. Industry accounted for 61.7 per cent of GDP. GDP growth reached 5.1 per cent in 2014 - a fall of 0.5 per cent from the previous year.
Public sector employment and wages are considered a drag on entrepreneurial enterprises, while domestic growth in non-oil

activities has been modest and dominated by foreign companies.

External trade

Gabon is a member of the Economic and Monetary Community of Central Africa (Cemac), the Economic Community of Central African States (ECCAS) and the Bank of Central African States, using the CFA franc. There is a common external tariff (CET) within Cemac.

Imports

Principal imports are machinery and equipment, metals, chemicals and construction materials and foodstuffs.

Main sources: France (20 per cent of total in 2014), Côte d'Ivoire (15.3 per cent), China (9.6 per cent), United States (9.3 per cent), Algeria (5.1 per cent) and Belgium (4.5 per cent).

Exports

Principal exports are crude oil (84 per cent of total), timber, manganese and uranium.

Main destinations: China (15.8 per cent of total in 2014), Japan (14.6 per cent), Australia (11 per cent), United States (7.9 per cent), India (7.8 per cent) and South Korea (6.3 per cent).

Agriculture

Farming

Total agricultural land is 25.8 million hectares of which 18.1 per cent is pasture and 1.3 per cent arable and employs 26 per cent of the workforce.

The agricultural sector in Gabon has been neglected, forcing the importation of a large percentage of the country's food needs. A shortage of cultivated lands has been the major problem facing the agricultural sector, which, mostly through subsistence farming, supports a large portion of the population.

Principal cash crops are palm oil, cocoa and refined sugar, while subsistence crops are cassava, maize and plantains. Cocoa is grown mainly in Woleu Ntem province and coffee mainly in Ogooué-Ivindo, Ogooué-Lolo and Haut Ogooué provinces. Sugar cane is grown and refined by the Société Sucrérie du Haut-Ogooué (Sosuho). Annual sugar output is around 30,000 tonnes. Agrogabon set up three cattle ranches in the 1980s, importing tsetse fly-resistant cattle. They are located at Lekabi, Nyanga and N'Gounie. The only industrial-scale poultry farm is run by the Société Industrielle d'Agriculture et d'Elevage de Boumango (SIAEB).

Fishing

Gabon has well-stocked fishing grounds, which are only partially exploited. Domestic demand is estimated at around 36,000 tonnes. The typical annual catch is over 40,000 tonnes. Traditional fishing accounts for two-thirds of national fishing output. There are about a dozen fleets, most of which are foreign, engaged in industrial fishing in Gabonese waters.

Forestry

Exports of forest products amount to around US$320 million annually and timber is a source of employment for nearly a third of the working population outside the public sector. Forests cover almost 85 per cent of the land area, estimated at 21.8 million hectares (ha). Deforestation typically accounts for 0.05 per cent annual average decrease, or the equivalent of 10,000ha of forest cover.

The forestry industry is one of the largest industries in the country. Gabon commercially exploits and exports both soft and hard woods, but cultivation and processing of timber comprises the main portion of forestry activities. The country produces sawn timber, veneers and plywood. Tropical hardwood logs constitute the bulk of its round wood exports. The potential commercial volume of live trees is estimated at 400 million cubic metres, 130 million of which is the much-celebrated Gaboon (black) ebony wood.

Gabon is the fifth-largest world producer of timber, behind Finland, Canada, Sweden and New Zealand.

The forest is divided into three administrative zones. The coastal area is already fairly well exploited. The zone around Ngounie, Nyanga and Haut-Ogooué has the bulk of current activity. The Booue-Lastourville axis of the Transgabon railway is largely undeveloped. Seven large companies dominate okoume production. The largest is the majority state-owned Compagnie Forestière du Gabon (CFG).

Okoume, designated as the most important commercial timber, is selectively logged in a significant proportion of the country's forests. Exploitable forest potential is more than 300 million cubic metres. One-third of this is okoume, which is particularly suited to the production of plywood.

Industry and manufacturing

A fair proportion of the very modest industrial sector has been based on a policy of import substitution. This is now being abandoned as part of structural adjustment measures. The outlook for industry is therefore bleak but there are plans to develop a regional export market within the Union Douanière des Etats de l'Afrique Centrale (UDEAC) (Central African Customs and Economic Union) countries. In theory, this larger potential market would allow industry to develop economies of scale that the small domestic markets do not justify. In practice, however, high labour costs are likely to frustrate efforts to promote the regional market. Gabon's labour costs are high on account of the well-established social security system, most of the cost of which is borne by employers, offering benefits that are not found in many other West and Central African countries.

The main industrial activities are oil refining and timber processing, although these activities are treated separately from other industries in the national accounts. The main manufacturing sectors, apart from these, are food processing, drinks and tobacco, metal transformation (mainly connected with shipyard activities and supplying the oil and wood industries) and building materials. Small sub sectors include textiles and chemicals (lubricants, paints, varnishes and detergents).

In an effort to stimulate the non-oil sector, the government is developing an export processing zone (EPZ) on the island of Mandji, which will be primarily geared towards petroleum services and wood processing industries.

Tourism

The tourism sector is still in its infancy, but since the global economic crisis cut trade in Gabon's principal export earners, timber and oil (a declining resource), the government has given tourism a higher profile in its long-term plans, not only to stimulate the economy but also to encourage diversification. Gabon can offer tourists sights of spectacular natural wonder, traditional cultures, history and treasures. The number of arrivals in 2008 was 358,000, which by 2013 had grown to 524,000.

The National Infrastructure Master Plan 2011 to 2016 is worth over US$11 billion and comprises of 21 major projects. Its aim is to develop a new infrastructure to support the socio-economic growth of Gabon. This includes new roads, railways, ports and other transport infrastructure. Under the Gabonese Master Plan, over US$85 million will be spent in the development of tourism.

The travel and tourism industry contributed 2.4 per cent in total to GDP in 2014, and supplied employment to 2.1 per cent of the workforce, the equivalent of 8,500 jobs.

Gabon's vast forests with their abundant flora and fauna, are becoming important centres for eco-tourism. Unesco designated the ecosystem and prehistoric landscape of Lopé-Okanda as a World Heritage site in 2007. A Gorilla sanctuary was established in 2001, on the island of Evangué-Ezango just north of the Loango National Park, to promote practical and sustainable tourism while curbing the trade in 'bush-meat' that threatens the survival of gorillas, which have been identified as a potentially lucrative source of foreign exchange.

Mining
Mining and hydrocarbons together contribute around 50 per cent of GDP while employing 10 per cent of the workforce. Gabon is one of the world's leading producers of manganese and uranium. Other areas of interest are gold and iron ore. Activity is concentrated on extraction and export of manganese ore (reserves of 200 million tonnes) and uranium (reserves of 35,000 tonnes). Both are crudely refined before export, the manganese as a 51 per cent concentrate and the uranium as 74 per cent pure yellow cake. Manganese goes mainly to Europe, but also to the US and the Far East. Uranium goes mainly to France (about 10 per cent of France's requirements), the rest to Belgium and Japan. Manganese and uranium account for 10 per cent of merchandise exports. Manganese production is declining, while large deposits of iron ore, barytes (used in paint-making) and niobium - discovered during construction of the Transgabon railway, have yet to be exploited.
There are 50 million tonnes of phosphate reserves.

Hydrocarbons
Gabon is sub-Saharan Africa's fifth-largest oil producer, after Nigeria, Angola, the Republic of Congo and Equatorial Guinea. With income from oil exports representing around 50 per cent of GDP and 80 per cent of export revenue, Gabon's economy is highly dependent on this one commodity. The exports go primarily to Western Europe, although China also imports Gabonese crude oil.
Proven oil reserves were 2 billion barrels at the end of 2013, with production at 237,000 barrels per day (bpd), down by 3.3 per cent on the 2012 figure. Production has fallen from the high of 364,000bpd in 1997. The country's downstream industry consists of the Sogara refinery, which was expanded in 2010, to a total capacity of 24,000bpd. The government has consistently maintained a market-oriented policy towards its sizeable oil reserves and has one of the most attractive hydrocarbons codes in Africa. Under this law, the state has a minimum 25 per cent holding in all oil-producing companies. Oil exploration permits are awarded under production-sharing agreements, which are individually negotiated.
In July 2012, Gabon signed a memorandum of understanding with the South Korean company Samsung for the construction of a new 50,000bpd refinery. The new refinery at Port-Gentil, expected to be completed by 2016, will replace the current one at Sogara.
Natural gas reserves totalled 28.3 billion cubic metres (cum) in 2013. All gas produced in Gabon is used for electricity or refinery fuel.
Any coal produced or imported is commercially insignificant.

Energy
In 2013, Gabon had a total installed generating capacity of 415MW. Electricity generated from hydroelectric plants equated to 41 per cent in 2011. In 2000 around 60 per cent of all energy was generated by conventional thermal power stations and the remainder by hydroelectricity. More recently the energy mix has changed as hydroelectric power stations provide around 80 per cent of all energy while solar panels are being installed in remote villages. Around 90 per cent of urban households have access to electricity and 35 per cent of rural households.
The largest hydroelectric dams are Tchimbele (69MW) and Kinguele (58MW), on the M'Bei River. There is around 6,000MW of undeveloped hydroelectric potential and the government plans to increase the role of hydropower while diminishing the role of thermal power, with commitments to upgrade and develop existing dams, power stations and the distribution network.
While the Société d'Energie et d'Eau du Gabon (SEEG) has a monopoly on electricity sales, production and distribution of electricity is open to commercial competition.

Banking and insurance
Central bank
Banque des Etats de l'Afrique Centrale (BEAC) (Bank of the Central African States)
Main financial centre
Libreville

Time
GMT plus one hour

Geography
Gabon is an equatorial country on the west coast of Africa, with Equatorial Guinea and Cameroon to the north, and the Republic of Congo to the south and east.
The eastern boundary lies along the watershed of the Democratic Republic of Congo (DRC), so that all rivers flow broadly west through Gabon into the sea. The sandy coastal strip consists of palm-fringed bays, lagoons and estuaries. The uplands are heavily eroded by river action, and there is a wide coastal plain, which is largely alluvial in nature. The natural vegetation is dense rain forest.
Hemisphere
Straddles the equator; Liberville, the capital, is in the north.

Climate
The climate is equatorial with an annual mean temperature of 28 degrees Celsius and high levels of humidity. The rainy seasons are between October and mid-December, and between mid-January and May. The dry season is from June to September.

Dress codes
Lightweight or tropical clothing is suitable, with rainwear for the monsoon season. Businessmen should wear a lightweight or tropical suit and women a lightweight suit or equivalent.

Entry requirements
Passports
Required by all. Passports must be valid for more than six months after the date of departure.
Proof of return/onward passage is necessary.
Visa
Required by all and to be applied for before travelling. Applications for business visas require a letter from the representative's company accepting responsibility for any expenses incurred, a full itinerary and a letter of invitation from a host company in Gabon.
Currency advice/regulations
There are no limits on the import of foreign or domestic currency, although any sum should be declared on arrival. Export of local currency, to countries outside the CFA franc zone, is limited of CFAf200,000.
Visitors are advised to carry travellers cheques in euros to avoid extra exchange fees.

Health (for visitors)
Mandatory precautions
A yellow fever vaccination certificate is required.
Advisable precautions
Immunisations are advisable for yellow fever, hepatitis A, tetanus and typhoid. There is a rabies risk.
Malaria and HIV/Aids are prevalent and standard measures should be taken to avoid these diseases.
Water which is used for drinking, brushing teeth or making ice should first be boiled. Dysentery can be caught from contaminated raw fruit and vegetables and unboiled water. Dairy products made from local milk should be avoided. Meat and fish should be well cooked and eaten hot.

Hotels
Available in Libreville, Port Gentil, Lambaréné and other main centres. Service charge is usually included in bill, if not a tip of 10–15 per cent is usual.

Credit cards
Credit cards are not widely accepted.

Public holidays (national)

Fixed dates

1 Jan (New Year's Day), 1 May (Labour Day), 16 Aug (Assumption Day), 16–18 Aug (Independence Day celebrations), 1 Nov (All Saints' Day), 25 Dec (Christmas Day).

Variable dates

Easter Monday, Whit Monday, Eid al Adha, Eid al Fitr.

Islamic year 1437 (15 Oct 2015–2 Oct 2016):: The Islamic year contains 354 or 355 days, with the result that Muslim feasts advance by 10–12 days against the Gregorian calendar. Dates of feasts vary according to the sighting of the new moon, so cannot be forecast exactly.

Working hours

Banking

Mon–Fri: 0730–1130, 1430–1630.

Business

Mon–Fri: 0730–1200, 1430–1800.

Government

Mon–Fri: 0730–1530 (30 minute lunch break); Sat: 0800–1300.

Shops

Mon–Sat: 0800–1200, 1500–1900.

Telecommunications

Mobile/cell phones

GSM 900 services are available in the most populated areas.

Electricity supply

220-30V AC, 50 cycles. Round two-pin plugs are standard.

Social customs/useful tips

Business is conducted in French. Appointments should be made in advance. It is customary to shake hands when meeting and taking leave. Business cards are exchanged after introduction.

Gratuities are between 10–15 per cent if no service charge is included.

The lifestyles of the middle classes in Libreville, Port-Gentil and Franceville have been heavily influenced by the French, and French etiquette has been largely adopted.

As elsewhere in Africa, it is extremely unwise to attempt to photograph any military installations or troop movements, security checkpoints, etc.

Security

Crime is increasingly a problem with incidents of robbery and armed attacks, particularly around Libreville and Port-Gentil. Avoid carrying valuables or wearing jewellery in public and walking alone at night.

Avoid travelling at night and always comply with the frequent police roadblocks.

Getting there

Air

National airline: Air Gabon (Compagnie Nationale Air Gabon).

International airport/s: Libreville-Léon M'Ba (LBV), 12km from city; restaurant, currency exchange; Port Gentil (POG), 4km from city.

Other airport/s: Franceville-Mvengue (MVB) has air charters. There are 65 other public and 50 private airfields linked mostly with the forestry and petroleum industries.

Airport tax: None

Surface

Road: The major routes are from the Republic of Congo, Cameroon or Equatorial Guinea. These are semi-surfaced but generally are in good condition and well maintained.

Water: There is a boat to and from São Tomé every five days.

Main port/s: The principal deep-water ports are Port Gentil, Owendo (Libreville). Mayumba and Nyanga are used for shipping timber. There is a fishing port in Libreville.

Getting about

National transport

Air: Air Gabon operates scheduled and charter flights to all main centres.

Road: There are an estimated 8,590km of roads, including 3,290km of main roads and 1,950km of secondary roads. Except for the routes Libreville-Ndende, Booué-Bitam, roads can be difficult in the rainy season. Travel by bush taxis and truck can be dangerous, especially in the rainy season.

Buses: Regular coach and minibus services link Libreville with Lambaréné, Oyem, Mouila and Bitam. Some services are subject to rainy season conditions.

Rail: Regular services operate on the Transgabon railway linking Libreville with Booué, Ndjolé and Franceville. There are two classes. The railcars are air-conditioned for some services but no refreshment or sleeping accommodation is scheduled. The rolling stock is generally new.

Water: The principal river is the Ogooué, navigable from Port-Gentil to Ndjole (310km), and serving the towns of Lambaréné, Ndjolé and Sindara.

A ferry service (taking two hours) operates between Libreville and Port-Gentil.

City transport

Taxis: Unmetered 'collective' and private taxis are available in main towns; tipping is not usual; rates vary according to the time of day. The journey from the airport to the Libreville city centre takes 10 minutes.

Car hire

Available in main towns, at airports and through hotels. International driving licence required. Charges are high.

BUSINESS DIRECTORY

The addresses listed below are a selection only. While World of Information makes every endeavour to check these addresses, we cannot guarantee that changes have not been made, especially to telephone numbers and area codes. We would welcome any corrections.

Telephone area codes

The international dialling code (IDD) for Gabon is + 241 followed by subscriber's number.

Useful telephone numbers

Police:732-036761-044
760-950720-951
Fire:18 761-520
Ambulance:732-771 762-344

Chambers of Commerce

Gabon Chamber of Commerce, Agriculture, Industry and Mines, PO Box 2234, Libreville (tel: 722-064; fax: 746-477).

Banking

Banque Gabonaise de Développement; PO Box 5, Rue Alfred Marche, Libreville (tel: 762-429, 762-489; fax: 742-699).

Banque Gabonaise et Française Internationale (BGFI), PO Box 2253, Blvd de l'Indépendance, Libreville (tel: 732-326, 764-035; fax: 740-894, 744-456).

Banque Internationale pour le Commerce et l'Industrie du Gabon SA, PO Box 2241, Avenue du Colonel Parant, Libreville (tel: 762-613, 763-811; fax: 746-410).

Banque Nationale du Crédit Rural, PO Box 1120, Avenue Bouët, Libreville (tel: 724-742, 766-144, 763-045; fax: 740-507).

Banque Populaire du Gabon, PO Box 6663, Blvd de l'Indépendance, Libreville (tel: 724-719; fax: 728-691).

Caisse Nationale d'Epargne, Siège Social, Libreville (tel: 766-509).

Centre de Chéques Postaux, Siége Social, Libreville (tel: 766-509).

Union Gabonaise de Banque SA, PO Box 315 & 2238, Avenue du Colonel Parant, Libreville (tel: 777-000; fax: 764-616).

Central bank

Banque des Etats de l'Afrique Centrale, Direction Nationale; PO Box 112, Libreville (tel: 761-352; fax: 744-563; e-mail: beaclbv@beac.int).

Travel information

ADL (Aeroport de Libreville), BP 363, Libreville (tel: 736-128).

Air Gabon (Compagnie Nationale Air Gabon), BP 2206, Aeroport International Léon M'ba, Libreville (tel: 730-027; fax: 731-156).

Eurafrique Voyages, BP 4026, Libreville (tel: 762-787; fax: 761-897).

Libreville Léon M'Ba International Airport, BP 363, Libreville (tel: 736-244/246/247; fax: 736-128).

Ministry of tourism

Ministry of Transport, Tourism and National Parks, BP 3974, Libreville (tel: 763-240).

Ministries

Ministry of Agriculture and Rural Development, BP 551, Libreville (tel: 721-579).

Ministry of the Arts, Culture and People Education, BP 1007, Libreville (tel: 724-028).

Ministry of Defence, Security and Immigration, BP 13493, Libreville (tel: 760-835).

Ministry of Economy, Finance, Budget and Privatisation, BP 9672, Libreville (tel: 721-571, 760-580; fax: 761-518).).

Ministry of Foreign Affairs and Co-operation, BP 2245, Libreville (tel: 762-251).

Ministry of Forestry and Environment, BP 199, Libreville (tel: 733-191).

Ministry of Higher Education, BP 3919, Libreville (tel: 763-252).

Ministry of Home (in charge of Local Collectivities and Mobile Security), BP 2110, Libreville (tel: 762-181).

Ministry of Housing, Land Registry and Town Planning, BP 512, Libreville (tel: 740-461).

Ministry of Justice, BP 547, Libreville (tel: 720-160).

Ministry of Labour and Human Resources, BP 2256, Libreville (tel: 732-739).

Ministry of Mining, Energy and Hydraulic Resources, BP 4041, Libreville (tel: 762-863).

Ministry of National Education and Professional Training, BP 6, Libreville (tel: 721-741).

Ministry of Public Health, BP 50, Libreville (tel: 762-522).

Ministry of Public Service and Administrative Reform, BP 496, Libreville (tel: 762-150).

Ministry of Shipping, BP 803, Libreville (tel: 733-210).

Ministry of Small and Medium Businesses, BP 4120, Libreville (tel: 720-636).

Ministry of Social Affairs, Family and Solidarity, BP 5684, Libreville (tel: 761-700).

Ministry of State Control, Decentralisation, Administration of Territory and Regional Integration, BP 178, Libreville (tel: 763-550).

Ministry of Trade Industry, BP 3906, Libreville (tel: 722-887).

Ministry of Youth and Sport, BP 3904, Libreville (tel: 763-576).

Other useful addresses

Compagnie Minière de l'Ogoué (Comilog), BP 578, Libreville (tel: 722-474).

Conseil Economique et Sociale de la République Gabonais, BP 1075, Libreville (tel: 762-668).

European Development Fund, BP 321, Libreville (tel: 732-250).

Gabonese Embassy (US), 2034 20th Street, NW, Washington DC 20009 (tel: (+1-202) 797-1000; fax: (+1-202) 332-0668).

Société de Développement de l'Agriculture au Gabon (Agrogabon), BP 2248, Libreville (tel: 764-082).

Société Equatoriale de Travaux Pétroliers Maritimes, BP 493, Libreville (tel: 753-509).

Société Gabonaise de Financement et d'Expansion, BP 2151, Libreville.

Société Gabonaise de Participation et de Développement, BP 1624, Libreville.

Société Gabonaise de Raffinage, BP 530, Libreville (tel: 752-365).

Société Nationale de Transports Maritimes (Sonatram), BP 3841, Libreville (tel: 740-632; fax: 745-967).

US Embassy, Boulevard de la Mer, BP 4000, Libreville (tel: 762-002).

National news agency: Agence Gabonaise de Presse (AGP), BP 168, Libreville (tel: 443507; fax: 443509; internet: www.agpgabon.ga).

Gabonews: www.gabonews.ga

Internet Gabon: www.internetgabon.com

Internet sites

Africa Business Network: http://www.ifc.org/abn

AllAfrica.com: http://allafrica.com

African Development Bank: http://www.afdb.org

Africa Online: http://www.africaonline.com

Mbendi AfroPaedia (information on companies, countries, industries and stock exchanges in Africa): http://www.mbendi.co.za

The Gambia

KEY FACTS

Official name: The Gambia

Head of State: President Sheikh Professor Alhaji Dr Yahya AJJ Jammeh Babili Mansa (APRC) (since 1994; re-elected 24 Nov 2011)

Head of government: President Yahya Jammeh

Ruling party: Alliance for Patriotic Reorientation and Construction (APRC) (since 1996; re-elected 29 Mar 2012)

Area: 11,295 square km

Population: 1.93 million (2014)*

Capital: Banjul

Official language: English

Currency: Dalasi (D) = 100 butut

Exchange rate: D39.63 per US$ (Sep 2015)

GDP per capita: US$428 (2014)*

GDP real growth: -0.22% (2014)*

GDP: US$825.00 million (2014)*

Inflation: 6.27% (2014)*

Balance of trade: -US$176.38 million (2012)

* estimated figure

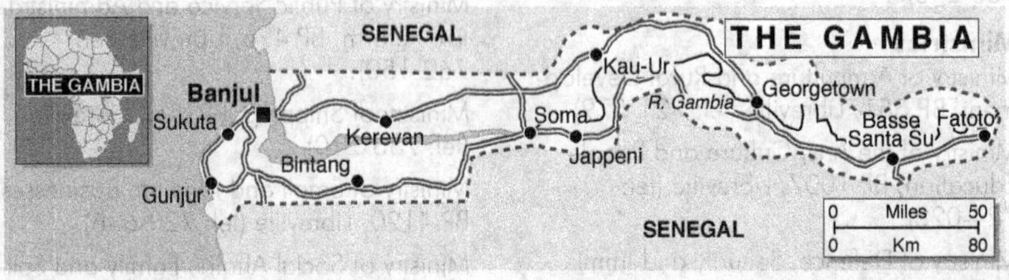

The Gambia is one of Africa's smallest and poorest nations with a ranking of 165 out of 187 countries in the United Nations Development Programme's 2014 Human Development Index. Poverty is widespread, but predominantly rural. A measure of acute poverty, the Multi-dimensional Poverty Index in 2014 determined that more than 60 per cent of overall population are poor, 19 per cent of the population are vulnerable to further poverty and, in rural areas, 82 per cent live in poverty. This is vast when compared to the 32 per cent in urban areas. Rapid population growth and urbanisation has increased spatial inequality in the nation.

The economy

The African Economic Outlook (AEO) in 2014 reported that local and physical development policies are central to The Gambia's development agenda. However, these policies have not been fully implemented which has resulted in poor service delivery and significant rural-urban imbalance. The International Monetary Fund (IMF) reported in its 2015 report that the economy experienced a variety of exogenous shocks in 2014, on top of the persistent policy slippages. The nation suffered at the hands of the Ebola outbreak in 2015, with estimates of the cut to tourism for the 2014/2015 season expected to be more than half. The AEO reports that hotel cancellation rates reached 60 per cent in the 2014–2015 winter season. Delayed rains in 2014 also led to a 15 per cent decline in the year's crop, a result with dire implications for the food security of the nation.

This is particularly relevant to The Gambia as it is one of the most densely populated countries in the African continent – in 2015 there are 173.6 persons per square kilometre. This exerts vast pressure on the resources and social services of the nation. The drought and the ebola crisis of 2015 arrived at an unwelcome time after extended periods of weak policy implementation, thereby putting pressure upon current account and fiscal deficits. Real gross domestic product (GDP) contracted by about 0.25 per cent in 2014, with inflation up to 7 per cent at the end of 2014 from the previous year's rate of 5.5 per cent. In order to support The Gambian economy, the IMF disbursed US$8–10 million in April 2015. The IMF is also monitoring the government's efforts and implementations of corrective policies aimed at enhancing the nation's fiscal sustainability.

However, significant spending pressures have emerged since April 2015. Faced with pressures from foreign exchange receipts, the authorities issued a directive fixing of the exchange rate at more than 20 per cent of the market value compared to the market rate in May 2015. International reserves had been under pressure in 2014 from a massive injection of liquidity. The spending pressures are proving detrimental to the government's domestic borrowing, thereby threatening both the fiscal sustainability and the social progress of the nation.

Completely enveloped by its giant neighbour, Sénégal, and lying on the fringes of a steadily encroaching Sahara desert, The Gambia – one of the most northerly of West African countries – has often been hard hit by the droughts which have adversely affected the economies of so many sub-Saharan countries. The Gambia's economic performance continues to be uneven owing to exogenous shocks, macro-economic and structural policy slippage, poor governance and weak institutions. Expansionary policies have increased the government's recourse to domestic bank financing, which, in turn, has raised real interest rates, increased the domestic debt burden and tended to crowd out private investment.

President Yahya Jammeh (full title President Sheikh Professor Alhaji Dr Yahya A J J Jammeh Babili Mansa) announced as long ago as 2004 that large reserves of oil had been discovered, but there has been no subsequent announcement of any 'new' oil-based future for The Gambia. This vulnerability to drought limits the scope for economic growth. The IMF recommended heavy investment in water management schemes in order to protect the country from future occurrences. The government of The Gambia has received financing from the African Development Bank (AfDB) in various currencies towards the cost of *The Gambia Rural Water Supply and Sanitation Project*. Bidding for the contracts took place on 30 July 2015.

Popularity?

Taking a page out of the North Korean book, posters display a happy nation wherein children sing the president's praises, lithe women dance in his honour and males visibly hold him in the greatest respect. The publicity devoted to 'His Excellency Sheikh Professor Alhaji Dr. Yahya Abdul-Azziz Jemus Junkung Jammeh Babili Mansa' every day makes life difficult for The Gambia's ineffectual opposition. A report by the British Broadcasting Corporation (BBC) pointed out that like elsewhere on the African continent, The Gambia's opposition parties have a host of other problems besides that of being out of power. The Gambia has known only two political régimes since independence from the UK in 1965, and this seems to have resulted in a less than functioning, fractured opposition, more concerned with inter party rivalries than with the job of bringing their wayward president to rights. This has allowed the president's authoritarian presence to hold firm sway over a country bogged down with appalling poverty. There are no less than five parties competing for opposition pre-eminence; and a divided opposition means that the ruling Alliance for Patriotic Reorientation and Construction (APRC) can pretty well do as it pleases. The most substantial opposition party is the United Democratic Party (UDP), banned by the government from even holding public rallies. The UDP managed to come second in the 2006 election, theoretically making it the official opposition.

Another presidential election took place in November 2011. Due to the low literacy rate of the country (51.1 per cent), voting took place which involved marbles being dropped into coloured containers each containing a gong. President Yayha Jammeh secured an extension of his 17-year rule by winning his fourth term in office in the election. The Economic Community of West Africa States (Ecowas) criticised the electoral environment as not conducive to free and fair elections and refused to send observers. The government continues to intimidate and persecute journalists, the political opposition, and civil society groups throughout the year.

Yahya Jammeh and homosexuality

'If you [practice homosexuality in the Gambia] I will slit your throat – if you are a man and want to marry another man in this country and we catch you, no one will ever set eyes on you again, and no white person can do anything about it.' So said Yahya Jammeh, Gambian dictator in all but name in May 2015. It is the latest in a line of abhorrent anti-gay rhetoric. Having previously compared homosexuals to vermin and promised to behead any he came across, Jammeh has scapegoated the LGBT community in an attempt to maintain power.

The EU has since cut US$14.5 million worth of aid in response to growing concerns over Gambian human rights abuses. Jammeh, however, has managed to convice the large proportion of his 95 per cent Muslim population that this is, once again, the fault of homosexuals as without them there would be no need for an aid reduction. In fact, the 'white person' is reference to foreign economic sanctions and widespread international outrage at his medieval policies.

Political corruption

President Jammeh has drawn criticism for his erratic statements and behaviour. Between 2007 and 2009 he claimed that he could personally cure HIV/Aids using traditional herbs, threatened decapitation for any homosexuals who remained in the country, and warned against causing instability through human rights activism. Jammeh threatened to withhold government services to voters who failed to support him in the 2011 presidential election, while declaring that neither coups nor elections could remove him from power as he had been installed in office by God.

President Yahya Jammeh was once known as Lieutenant Jammeh. After gaining independence from Britain in 1965, The Gambia functioned for almost 30 years as an electoral democracy under President Dawda Jawara and his People's Progressive Party. Lieutenant Yahya Jammeh deposed Jawara in a 1994 military coup. In a closely controlled referendum in 1996, a new constitution was adopted. This allowed Jammeh to transform his military dictatorship into a nominal civilian administration.

The government announced in March 2006 that it had foiled an attempted coup, leading to the arrest of dozens of people, including several prominent journalists and officials. Ten military officers were sentenced to lengthy prison terms in April 2007. Eight individuals, most of whom belonged to the military, were arrested in

KEY INDICATORS — **The Gambia**

	Unit	2011	2012	2013	2014	**2015
Population	m	*1.80	*1.83	*1.88	*1.93	*1.98
Gross domestic product (GDP)	US$bn	0.98	0.91	*0.90	*0.82	*0.78
GDP per capita	US$	543	497	*479	*428	*395
GDP real growth	%	3.3	5.3	*4.8	*-0.2	*5.1
Inflation	%	4.8	4.6	5.2	*6.3	*6.2
Exports (fob) (goods)	US$m	162.1	182.5	–	–	–
Imports (fob) (goods)	US$m	295.6	358.8	–	–	–
Balance of trade	US$m	-133.5	-176.4	–	–	–
Current account	US$m	-138.0	-154.0	*-96.0	*-105.0	*-92.0
Total reserves minus gold	US$m	207.9	236.2	210.6	159.3	–
Foreign exchange	US$m	166.4	169.4	172.2	–	–
Exchange rate	per US$	29.11	33.69	38.10	43.20	–

* estimated figure ** forecast figure

late 2009 on suspicion of planning another coup to overthrow Jammeh. In July 2010, all of the accused were found guilty of treason and conspiracy and received death sentences.

A lack of respect for the freedom of the press pervades much of Jammeh's legislation. Journalists are subject to arrests and violence. The whereabouts of *Daily Observer* journalist, Ebrima Manneh, remain unknown since his 2006 arrest for publishing a critical report of Jammeh. In the run-up to the 2011 election, journalists practiced self-censorship, and the National Intelligence Agency (NIA) shut down community and independent radio stations. Notably, in August, it ordered Teranga FM, the only independent radio station in the country that had continued to broadcast news, off the air.

In 2013, President Jammeh announced The Gambia's departure from the Commonwealth, dismissing it as a 'neo-colonial' institution. Critics said the move was motivated by anger at foreign criticism of the country's human rights record. A group of Gambian expatriates calling themselves the Gambian Freedom Fighters attempted to overthrow the government whilst Jammell was out of the country on 30 December 2014. It was the eighth such attempt during his 20 years in office. In the same month, Gambia was dropped from the African Growth and Opportunity Act, a trade incentive programme established during the Clinton administration in 2000 to provide duty-free access for African goods to the US.

Risk assessment

Politics	Poor
Economy	Fair
Regional stability	Fair/Good

Muslims in The Gambia

% of population	95
Sunni (% of Muslims)	96
Shi'a (% of Muslims)	1

COUNTRY PROFILE

When independence came to The Gambia in 1965, there were many who doubted that Africa's newest state would hold on to its status for any appreciable length of time. The oldest and most northerly of Britain's former West African possessions, The Gambia is surrounded, except on the Atlantic seaboard, by the bigger and more populous Senegal. It is said that but for the river the country would not have existed.

1455 The Portuguese established trading stations along the River Gambia.

1889 The boundaries of The Gambia were agreed by the British and French.

1894 The Gambia became a British protectorate.

1965 Following independence, Dawda Jawara, as the head of the People's Progressive Party (PPP), became prime minister, with the British monarch as head of state.

1970 Following a referendum, The Gambia became a republic. Dawda Jawara was elected president.

1981 Around 500 people were killed when Senegalese troops intervened in support of Jawara and suppressed a coup.

1982 Senegal and The Gambia formed a confederation called Senegambia intended to integrate military, economic and political institutions.

1989 The Gambia, the subordinate partner, withdrew from Senegambia and the confederation collapsed.

1991 The Gambia and Senegal signed a treaty of friendship.

1994 President Jawara was deposed by a military coup led by Lieutenant Yahya Jammeh. The 1970 constitution was suspended and all political parties banned.

1996 A new constitution was approved giving multi-party democracy. The Alliance for Patriotic Reorientation and Construction (APRC) were formed to support Yahya Jammeh in the presidential election. Three political parties were prohibited from taking part in the elections. Jammeh and the APRC were elected to the presidency and legislature, in what observers said were neither free nor fair elections.

2001 President Jammeh lifted the ban on opposition political parties. He was re-elected president.

2002 The centrist United Democratic Party (UDP) boycotted parliamentary elections, leaving the ruling APRC to win most seats unopposed in the parliamentary elections.

2005 Border tensions rose when Gambia doubled the price of ferry crossings across the river Gambia and Senegalese haulage firms, in protest, blockaded access routes. Senegal was effectively split in two as goods were hauled around Gambia on roads that were not all-weather and were unsuitable for heavy loads. Gambia experienced a shortage of goods in the marketplace due to the loss of revenue and blockaded imports. Nigeria, representing the Economic Community of West African States (Ecowas), mediated between the protagonists.

2006 Thousands of refugees found sanctuary in The Gambia during fighting between the Senegalese army and Casamance separatists in southern Senegal. President Jammeh was re-elected.

2007 The APRC won 42 out of 48 seats in the national assembly. The UDP won four seats and the National Alliance for Democracy and Development (NADD) one seat and an independent one seat. The government expelled a senior UN official, Fadzai Gwaradzimba, after she criticised the president for his widely publicised herbal cure for HIV/Aids, which he claimed could cure the disease within days.

2009 Hundreds of villagers were rounded up and tested for activities in witchcraft, as ordered by President Jammeh.

2010 A trial began following the arrests of 12 foreign nationals in possession of two tons (1.8 tonnes) of cocaine bound for Europe, with a street value of US$1 billion. The Gambia has grown as a distribution point for Latin American drugs cartels that take advantage of the region's ties to Europe, the weak security and judicial systems and the poverty that provides a ready workforce. The government ordered the withdrawal of all Iranian government representatives. No reasons were given but the move was thought to be related to an illegal shipment of arms, supposedly destined for Gambia, found by Nigerian customs officials in October. There was speculation that the arms were to be sent on to the Casamance region of Senegal. In an interview with the Kenyan newspaper *The Nation* President Jammeh vowed not to seek another term in office.

2011 Presidential elections were postponed from early in the year but were finally held in November, contested by three candidates. Despite his statement in 2010 that he would not stand again, incumbent Yahya Jammeh (APRC) won with 71.5 per cent of the vote, Ousainou Darboe (UDP) 17.4 per cent and Hamat Bah (NADD) (five-party coalition) 11.1 per cent, with a turnout of 83 per cent. Ecowas condemned the elections an 'lacking legitimacy' and declared before the elections that the elections would not be free and fair because of high levels of ruling party intimidation.

2012 Former information minister, Amadou Jenneh, and three others were arrested for distributing T-shirts printed with a slogan 'Coalition for Change the Gambia (sic), End Dictatorship Now'. Jenneh was sentenced to life imprisonment, one died in custody in July and the other two were sentenced to three years. All three were released later in the year. Six opposition political parties boycotted the parliamentary elections held on 29 March, claiming the ruling APRC was abusing the system to favour itself in the polls. Only 23 out of 48 constituencies held ballots, as candidates of APRC in the remaining 25 constituencies were elected unopposed. Fatou Bensouda took up the post of the International Criminal Court (ICC)'s chief prosecutor on 15 June.

2013 On 2 October the government announced on state TV that The Gambia was withdrawing from the Commonwealth. It said it was nolonger prepared to be a member of a 'neo-colonial institution'. On 14 November Gambia announced that it has cut diplomatic ties with Taiwan. President Jammeh's office said the move was for reasons of 'national strategic interest'.

2014 A Bill with a proposed amendment to the Criminal Code which introduces the criminal offence of 'aggravated homosexuality', with a sentence on conviction of life imprisonment, was passed by parliament on 25 August. The Bill will be reviewed by the President before becoming law.

2015 A small group of mostly expatriate Gambians staged an attempted coup on 30 December. The plot had supposedly been planned in the US and the group had expected local support, which did not materialise. Papa Faal, a former US army sergeant with dual American and Gambian nationality, pleaded guilty to involvement in the failed coup attempt after he was arrested on returning to the US. On 16 June the Office of the President announced that with effect from 17 June, the President should be addressed as: His Excellency Sheikh Professor Alhaji Dr Yahya A J J Jammeh Babili Mansa. The addition of 'Babili Mansa', which means 'bridge builder', had been used before, but dropped after four months.

Political structure

Constitution

The constitution was enacted in 1970, amended in 1982 and 1996. The constitution was suspended in 1994 following the coup d'état, with the amended version coming into law in 1997.

Form of state

Democratic republic

The executive

Power rests with the president, who is elected by universal suffrage every five years. The president is both the head of state and head of government and appoints the cabinet.

National legislature

The unicameral National Assembly has 53 members, of which 40 belong to the rank of chieftain and each constitutes a constituency; three are elected to represent the capital and five to represent Kanifing Municipality. The remaining five are nominated by the president, to include the Assembly speaker and deputy. All serve for five-year terms.

The Assembly legislates, ratifies treaties and forms committees to review the work of the government.

Last elections

24 November 2011 (presidential); 29 March 2012 (parliamentary)

Results: Presidential: Yahya Jammeh (APRC) won 71.5 per cent of the vote, Ousainou Darboe (UDP) 17.4 per cent and Hamat Bah (National Alliance for Democracy and Development (NADD) (five-party coalition)) 11.1 per cent; turnout was 83 per cent.

Parliamentary: Alliance for Patriotic Reorientation and Construction (APRC) 51.8 per cent of the vote (43 seats out of 48), National Reconciliation Party (NRP) 9.4 per cent (one), independents 38.6 per cent (four). Turnout was 38.7 per cent.

Next elections

2016 (presidential); 2017 (parliamentary)

Political parties

Ruling party

Alliance for Patriotic Reorientation and Construction (APRC) (since 1996; re-elected 29 Mar 2012)

Main opposition party

The United Democratic Party (UDP)

Population

1.88 million (2013)* Approximately 41 per cent of the total population is under 14 years.

Last census: 15 April 2003: 1,364,507 (provisional)

Population density: 105 habitants per square km. Urban population 58 per cent (2010 Unicef).

Annual growth rate: 2.9 per cent, 1990–2010 (Unicef).

Ethnic make-up

Three major ethnic groups: Mandinka (42 per cent), Fula (18 per cent), Wolof (16 per cent). Other substantial ethnic groups: Jola, Serahule, Serere, Manjago, Bambara, Creole/Aku.

Religions

Muslim (90 per cent), Christian (9 per cent), animist beliefs (1 per cent).

Education

Primary schooling begins at aged seven and is free of charge and non-selective until aged 15. Secondary education is either vocational or academic. Basic vocational schools offer two-year courses and vocational secondary schools provide four-year courses. General secondary schools offer a three-year course leading to higher education provided by the University of The Gambia. The Gambia College offers vocational courses in agriculture, education, nursing, midwifery, and public health.

Literacy rate: Adult rates: 38.9 per cent, male; 31.9 per cent, female (World Bank).

Compulsory years: None

Enrolment rate: 77 per cent gross primary enrolment; 25 per cent gross secondary enrolment, of relevant age groups (including repeaters) (World Bank).

Pupils per teacher: 30 in primary schools.

Health

Improved water sources are available to 62 per cent of the population. Around 90 per cent of children are immunised against measles.

HIV/Aids

The Gambia has so far escaped much of the African pandemic. However, with 14 per cent of sex workers testing positive, there is a chance that the infection will spread.

HIV prevalence: 1.2 per cent aged 15–49 in 2003 (World Bank)

Life expectancy: 57 years, 2004 (WHO 2006)

Fertility rate/Maternal mortality rate: 4.9 births per woman, 2010 (Unicef); maternal mortality 1,100 per 100,000 live births (World Bank).

Child (under 5 years) mortality rate (per 1,000): 73 per 1,000 live births (WHO 2012)

Head of population per physician: 0.11 physicians per 1,000 people, 2003 (WHO 2006)

Welfare

The Gambia has two important funds, the social security fund and the housing finance fund, that receive contributions from employers and employees either directly or indirectly. The Department of Social Welfare in Banjul has been restructured with four major units covering child care, adult, elderly and disabled services. The Gambia government and the Social Security and Housing Finance Corporation (SSHFC) initiated mass housing projects including a rural electrification programme covering all major towns and villages.

Main cities

Banjul (capital, estimated population 31,834 in 2012), Serekunda (415,962), Brikama (101,119), Bakau (72,039), Lamin (39,112), Nama Kunku (31,834), Brufut (31,692).

Languages spoken

Mandinka, Wolof and Fula are local languages. French is taught in some secondary and high schools. German, Italian, Dutch and the Scandinavian languages are also spoken by tourism staff.

Official language/s

English

Media

Press

Dailies: In English. *Daily Observer* (www.observer.gm) and *The Gambia Daily News* (www.gambia.dk). Several

online news outlets exist include Gambia News (www.gambianow.com), The Gambia Times (http://afrikanpath.com) which was launched on 5 July 2007 with local and regional news and Freedom Newspaper (www.freedomnewspaper.com).
Weeklies: The *Gambia News & Report* magazine, the Foroyaa (www.foroyaa.gm) is published bi-weekly and *The Point Newspaper* (www.thepoint.gm) thrice weekly; all are privately-owned.

Broadcasting

The state-owned Gambia Radio and Television Services (GRTS) provides a national network.
Radio: GRTS is non-commercial and broadcast in English and local languages. Other commercial stations, Radio 1 FM, West Coast Radio and City Limits Radio are privately owned.
Television: GRTS provides the only national service with a single channel which covers 60 per cent of the country. There are other private satellite, subscription channels, the most popular includes GAMTV and Premium TV Network which broadcasts throughout the coastal area.

Economy

The Gambia is one of the poorest countries in the world; in 2014 the GDP per capita was US$419, down from US$477 in 2013. The tourism industry is the single largest foreign earnings sector, while only providing direct paid employment for 4.2 per cent of the workforce. Subsistence farming employs around 70 per cent of the workforce, which is reflected in per capita income, in the form of peanuts, oil and cattle cake, and which account for 50 per cent of goods exported, while forestry and fisheries remain important sectors of agriculture. Major capital investment projects of infrastructure improvements, including a new terminal at the capital's Banjul International Airport and improved port facilities, have aided exports. The port in Banjul brings in foreign earnings as well as trans-shipment costs for goods travelling between north and south Senegal.
In 2012 The Gambia's economy jumped out of recession, recording an expansion in GDP of 5.9 per cent. However, since this peak growth has been decelerating, falling to 4.3 per cent in 2013 and back into recession in 2014 with a contraction of -0.7 per cent. The main causes for the dip in economic performance were tourism-related industries being hampered by the outbreak of the Ebola virus, reduced agricultural output due to the delayed rains in 2014 and the continued macro-economic policy changes being implemented. The country still faces a heavy debt burden (estimated at 100 per cent of GDP in 2014), particularly interest on domestic debt, which consumes a large portion of government revenues, thereby reducing spending on social programmes. Received remittances are extremely important to the economy, contributing some 20 per cent to GDP.
In 2014 the UN Human Development Index (HDI) ranked The Gambia 172 out of 187 countries for lack of national development in health, education and income. The UN also reported that in 2014 61 per cent of the population was living in multi-dimensional poverty. With such deprivation The Gambia has grown as a distribution point for Latin American drug cartels that take advantage of the region's ties to Europe, the weak security and judicial system and the poverty that provides a ready workforce. A trial began in June 2010 following the arrests in May of 12 foreign nationals in possession of two tons (1.8 tonnes) of cocaine from Latin America, bound for Europe, with a street value estimated at US$1 billion. The trial was still on going in mid–2015. The government has introduced capital punishment in an attempt to curb the growing problem.
President Jammeh has said that he wants to lessen the country's dependence on the export of peanuts, and turn the Gambia in to an oil-producing state, despite no crude oil having been found as of 2014. In January 2014, three exploration licences were cancelled due to the licensees (African Petroleum and Oranto Petroleum) holding the concessions for speculative purposes. The Gambian government said that this was against the country's petroleum law.

External trade

The Gambia is a member of the Economic Community of West African States (Ecowas), which was set up to promote economic integration among members. It is also a member of the Anglophone West African Monetary Zone (WAMZ), which will introduce a common currency in due time. WAMZ will eventually be merged with the Francophone-members' currency (Communauté Financière d'Afrique (CFA) (Financial Community of Africa), CFA franc) to produce a single currency (the eco) for the region. In the meantime The Gambia continues to use dalasi as its currency.
With few natural resources, foreign exchange is dependent on remittances, tourism and the export of groundnuts (both raw and processed). Geographically, The Gambia is a long wedge separating the north and south of Senegal and as a result haulage firms must cross The Gambia to avoid the long and arduous route around it. Re-exports are estimated at over 30 per cent of total imports, which supply significant foreign exchange for the Gambian economy.

Imports

Principal imports are foodstuffs, manufactured items, fuel, machinery and transport equipment that support the transit trade.
Main sources: Côte d'Ivoire (20.6 per cent of total in 2014), Brazil (11.0 per cent), China (8.3 per cent)

Exports

Principal exports are groundnuts (peanuts), fish, cotton lint, palm kernels and re-exports.
Main destinations: Mali (37.9 per cent total of total in 2014), Guinea (24.7 per cent), Senegal (16.0 per cent).

Agriculture

Farming

Agriculture remains important to the economy, contributing 22.8 per cent of GDP in 2014. Total agricultural land is one million hectares of which 26 per cent is pasture and 40 per cent arable; the sector employs around 70 per cent of the workforce.
Groundnuts are cultivated on about 60 per cent of the planted area, and provide 85 per cent of official export earnings. The Gambia is the second-largest producer of groundnuts in the world, after Senegal. Production of food crops (rice, maize, millet, sorghum, cassava) is insufficient to meet local needs, but receives a great deal of official encouragement. Small-scale fruit and cotton farming are also important while some livestock is exported to neighbouring countries for breeding.
The government, backed by international development agencies and donors, is attempting to increase agricultural production. The on-going US$2.5 million Lowlands Agricultural Development Project (LADEP) is aimed at developing 6,000 hectares for cultivation and the rehabilitation of 1,500 hectares in various lowland ecologies. US$2 million has been allocated to assist women's groups engaged in sheep, goat and poultry production while US$1.5 million is dedicated to an integrated rural development scheme.

Fishing

Total annual fish production is around 50,000 tonnes. The government, with assistance from the UN Development Programme (UNDP), is encouraging improved methods and modernisation of boats. Illegal fishing by foreign trawler fleets remains a problem.

Industry and manufacturing

The industrial sector contributes around 12.9 per cent to GDP and employs under 5 per cent of the workforce.
The manufacturing sector is small-scale and underdeveloped.

The main activities (most of which are centred around Banjul, particularly in the Kanifing Industrial Estate) include groundnut and fish processing, brewing, footwear, perfume, cement and brick production.

Tourism

The Gambia is a popular destination for visitors from Western Europe who wish to avoid a cold winter season. It offers affordable resorts and activities focussed on its wildlife (bird-watching is of particular interest) sand and surf sports along its Atlantic coast, traditional culture and general sports, such as golfing and fishing.
The government has backed expansion of the travel and tourism sector by financing tourism campaigns in major media outlets. Niche tourist products include marine eco-tourism along the shoreline, the Kiang West National Park and a rich mix of ethnic groups and deep-rooted traditions and beliefs. Cultural sites are also promoted including the slave island, Kunta Kinteh, and the Stone Circles of Senegambia, a prehistoric burial site; both are included on Unesco's World Heritage List.
Travel and tourism accounted for a record high of 21.8 per cent (US$180 million) of GDP in 2007, which has been falling since the global economic crisis cut visitor numbers and began a two-year decline in the industry. By 2014, the sector contributed 13.8 per cent of GDP. Employment in the industry has also fallen from 2007 when a record 100,900 were employed in travel and tourism and related industries, to 81,500 jobs related to tourism in 2014 (11.8 per cent of total eomplyment). Within a decade (2000–10) capital investment rose from 2.5 per cent to 9.9 per cent of total investment and in 2014 was 10.7 per cent.
The Gambia has high rates of youth unemployment, of prostitution, drugs peddling and begging. The government has become concerned by the impact of an influx of relatively rich foreigners and the growing trade in 'sex tourism', prostitution and drugs. There are agencies and measures to combat child sex exploitation working in co-operation with international organisations.

Environment

Concerns are mounting over the ecological effects of tourism on the local environment, particularly shore erosion and the depletion of water resources.

Mining

Most mining activity is centred on the production of industrial minerals for local consumption. The Australian Carnegie Corporation is investigating the Brufut deposits located along the coast and around 11,000 tonnes of zircon has been found. There are known deposits of kaolin, tin, ilmenite and rutile, mostly unexploited.

Hydrocarbons

There are no proved hydrocarbon reserves and all domestic energy needs are met by imports. Consumption of petroleum products was 3,350 barrels per day in 2013.
Exploration for oil offshore in deepwater is underway. Legislation exists to harness any revenue if oil is discovered; downstream the market is unregulated.
In January 2014, three exploration licences were cancelled due to the licensees (African Petroleum and Oranto Petroleum) holding the concessions for speculative purposes. The Gambian government said that this was against the country's petroleum law.
Any use of natural gas or coal is commercially insignificant.

Energy

Total installed generating capacity was 62MW, producing around 200 million kilowatt hours in 2013. Power generation is typically from thermal power plants.
The Gambia is poorly resourced and has little potential for hydropower. However it is a partner in the West African Power Pool (Wapp), which is a regional integration project to improve power supply within the Economic Community of West African States (Ecowas) area, with affordable electricity as the goal for all. Four countries, Guinea, Senegal, Guinea Bissau and The Gambia, have agreed to build two hydroelectric power stations on the River Gambia at Kaleta in Guinea and Sambanglou in Senegal.

Banking and insurance

The banking sector is underdeveloped, but is growing as a result of increased economic activity and macroeconomic stability. The sector has seen consolidation, with two large mergers and privatisations.
It was announced in March 2005 that the introduction of the shared currency, the Eco, in The Gambia, Ghana, Guinea, Nigeria and Sierra Leone, which was due in July 2005, would be postponed. The currency was proposed to facilitate trade and growth with an ultimate plan to merge it with the CFA franc.

Central bank

Central Bank of The Gambia

Main financial centre

Banjul

Time

GMT

Geography

At its widest part The Gambia is only 48km wide as it straddles the River Gambia over its last 470km down to the Atlantic Ocean, where the country has a short coastline. The Gambia is the smallest country in Africa, and lies on both banks of the river, completely surrounded by Senegal. The land is low-lying, with mangroves towards the river mouth, and open savannah plains for most of the remaining land, with a maximum elevation of only 73 metres at the higher reaches of the river, in the east. During the dry season, when water levels drop, the river's width, at the capital Banjul, is only 5km across and tidal saltwater washes along its length for almost 250km turning the water brackish.

Hemisphere

Northern

Climate

Sub-tropical with distinct seasons. Dry season from November–May with temperatures around 21–27 degrees Celsius (C). The dry *harmattan* wind keeps the humidity low, but can obscure the sun and severely limit vision for days. Rainy season from June–October has high humidity and temperatures around 26–32 degrees C.

Entry requirements

Passports

Required by all. Passports must be valid for three months from date of departure.

Visa

Required by all, except citizens of countries with reciprocating visa-free entry for both tourism and business, (UK 30 days, others 90 days). See www.thegambia.net/visa.htm for initial details and contact the nearest embassy for confirmation All visitors must have onward/return tickets.

Currency advice/regulations

There is no restriction on the import or export of local currency – although exchanging local currency abroad may be difficult. The import of currency from Algeria, Ghana, Guinea, Mali, Morocco, Nigeria, Sierra Leone and Tunisia is prohibited. The import of all other currencies is unrestricted but must be declared; export is unlimited up to the amount declared.
Travellers cheques are accepted.

Health (for visitors)

Mandatory precautions

Yellow fever vaccination certificate required only if travelling from an infected area.

Advisable precautions

Inoculations and boosters should be current for cholera, tetanus, polio, hepatitis A, diphtheria, typhoid and yellow fever. There may be a need for vaccinations for tuberculosis, hepatitis B and meningitis. Use malaria prophylaxis (that also provide protection for hepatitis B and yellow fever)

including mosquito repellents, nets and clothing that cover the body after dark.
There is a risk of rabies.
HIV/Aids is prevalent. To avoid bilharzia, do not bath in fresh water lakes or rivers, use only well-maintained, chlorinated swimming pools.
Use only bottled or boiled water for drinks, washing teeth and making ice. Eat only well cooked meals, preferably served hot; vegetables should be cooked and fruit peeled. Dairy products are unpasteurised and should be avoided, unless cooked. There is a shortage of routine medications, including sun-screens, and visitors should take all necessary medicines with them. A first aid kit that includes disposable syringes, is a reasonable precaution.
Healthcare is not to Western standards and medical insurance, including emergency evacuation, is necessary.

Hotels

Book well in advance, especially if arriving during tourist season (Nov–May). Many Gambian hotels are geared to package holidays. 10 per cent tip is usual.

Credit cards

International credit cards are accepted; arrangements for hotel payment by credit cards should be arranged at the beginning of a stay. ATM exist in large towns but may be unreliable.

Public holidays (national)

Fixed dates

1 Jan (New Year's Day), 18 Feb (Independence Day), 1 May (Labour Day), 22 Jul (Revolution Day), 25 Dec (Christmas Day).

Variable dates

Eid al Adha, Good Friday and Easter Monday (Mar/April, Birth of the Prophet, Eid al Fitr.

Islamic year 1437 (15 Oct 2015–2 Oct 2016):: The Islamic year contains 354 or 355 days, with the result that Muslim feasts advance by 10–12 days against the Gregorian calendar. Dates of feasts vary according to the sighting of the new moon, so cannot be forecast exactly.

Working hours

Banking

Mon–Thu: 0800–1330; Fri: 0800–1100 in Banjul; Mon–Fri: 0800–1200, 1600–1800 elsewhere.

Business

Mon–Thu: 0800–1600; Fri: 0800–1230.

Government

Mon–Fri: 0800–1800 (from 1 Feb 2013)

Shops

Mon–Thu: 0800–1700; Fri–Sat: 0800–1300.

Electricity supply

220V AC, 50 cycles, with a mix of round and flat, three pin plugs.

Social customs/useful tips

In business, the personal approach is important; handshaking is widely used and the traditional greeting is *salam alaikum*. Jackets and ties should be worn at meetings; women may wear trousers.
Many Gambians are Muslim and their religious customs and beliefs should be respected. There are prohibitions concerning smoking and eating in public during Ramadan.

Getting there

Air

National airline: Gambia International Airlines (GIA)
International airport/s: Banjul International (BJL), 24km from city; bar, bank, restaurant, post office, shop and business lounge including internet connections. Taxis are available to the city.
Airport tax: Arrival tax at Banjul International (BJL) airport: either US$10, UK £5 or eur10.

Surface

Road: Road access to Banjul is possible from Dakar (Senegal), by the Trans-Gambia Highway which crosses the River Gambia by ferry between Farafenni and Mansa Konko. There is an alternative car ferry crossing between Barra and Banjul.
Water: Regular ferry services run between Banjul and Dakar (Senegal).

Getting about

National transport

Road: There are over 3,000km of roads, of which 450km are paved, particularly around Banjul; unsealed roads often become impassable in the rainy season. Highways run along each bank of the River Gambia; the Trans-Gambia highway runs north to south, crossing the river at Farafenni-Mansa Konko (car ferry).
Buses: The Gambia Public Transport Corporation (GPTC) operates cheap and reliable services linking Banjul with the coastal hotel area and other main centres.
There are several commercial bus services, such as Amdalaye and Transgambia services.
Water: There are around a dozen ferry crossing points where people, livestock and vehicles cross the river between the north and south shores. The Banjul-Barra ferry runs every 90 minutes (journey time 20—30 minutes) and there are small wooden ferries up-country which carry only three or four vehicles at a time.
A boat travels the length of the River Gambia, from Banjul to Basse, once a week. The journey takes about three days. It is possible to return overland by coach.

City transport

Taxis: Green (tourist) taxis have a diamond sign and a serial number on the side. They are licensed by the Gambia Tourism Authority and dedicated to serving tourists and other visitors. They are normally parked outside the hotels in the resort areas. The journey from the international airport to the city centre takes 30–40 minutes.
Yellow and Green taxis are mainly four-passenger saloon cars which run a shared taxi service between short distances or park by the roadside for individual hire.
The most common way of travelling is by collective *bush* taxis. These are mainly seven-passenger saloon cars, vans, minibuses and buses. They do not have a single colour and they operate a shared service between both short and long distances. It is advisable to agree the fare in advance when hiring collective taxis.
A 10 per cent tip is usual.

Car hire

International driving licence accepted for a period of three months. National licence can be used for a short visit. Traffic drives on the right.
Car hire facilities are somewhat limited and local enquiries through the tourist office are advised. Take care, there is a lack of adequate traffic signs.

BUSINESS DIRECTORY

The addresses listed below are a selection only. While World of Information makes every endeavour to check these addresses, we cannot guarantee that changes have not been made, especially to telephone numbers and area codes. We would welcome any corrections.

Telephone area codes

The international dialling code (IDD) for The Gambia is + 220 followed by subscriber's number.

Useful telephone numbers

Police17
Fire18
Ambulance (Banjul)16

Chambers of Commerce

Gambia Chamber of Commerce & Industry, 1-3 Ecowas Avenue, PO Box 333, Banjul (tel: 4227-765; fax: 4229-671; email: gcci@qanet.gm).

Banking

Arab Gambian Islamic Bank Ltd, 7 Ecowas Avenue, Banjul (tel: 4223-773; fax: 4223-770).

First International Bank Ltd, PO Box 1997, 6 OAU Boulevard, Banjul (tel: 4202-000/5; fax: 4202-001, 4202-000).

International Bank for Commerce (Gambia) Ltd, PO Box 211, 11a Liberation Avenue, Banjul (tel: 4228-144, 4228-145; fax: 4229-312).

Standard Chartered Bank Gambia Ltd, PO Box 259, 8 Ecowas Avenue, Banjul (tel: 4228-681/4; fax: 4227-714).

Trust Bank Limited (TBL), PO Box 1018, 3-4 Ecowas Avenue, Banjul (tel: 4225-777, 4225-778/9; fax: 4225-781).

Central bank

Central Bank of The Gambia, 1-2 Ecowas Avenue, Banjul (tel: 4227-786; fax: 4226-969).

Travel information

Banjul (Yundum) International Airport, PO Box 285, Banjul (tel: 4473-000; fax: 4472-190).

Gambia International Airlines, Satellite House, PO Box 268, 68-69 Wellington Street, Banjul (tel: 4223-702, 4223-706; internet: www.gia.gm).

Gambia River Excursions, Lamin Lodge, Jangjangbureh Camp, PO Box 664 Banjul (tel: 4497-603; fax: 4495-526; internet: www.gambiariver.com).

West African Tours, PO Box 222, Serrekunda, (tel: 4495-258, 4495-532; fax: 4496-118; internet: www.westafricatours.gm).

Ministry of tourism

Department of State for Tourism and Culture, The Quadrangle, Banjul (tel: 4229-563, 4223-210).

National tourist organisation offices

Gambia Tourism Authority, Kololi, KMC, PO Box 4085, Bakau (tel: 4462-491–4; fax: 4462-487; email: info@gta.gm; internet: www.visitthegambia.gm).

Ministries

Ministry of Agriculture and Natural Resources (MANR), The Quadrangle, Banjul (tel: 4472-888; fax: 4237-034).

Ministry of Finance and Economic Affairs, The Quadrangle, Banjul (tel: 4227-221).

Other useful addresses

British High Commission, 48 Atlantic Road; PO Box 507, Fajara, Banjul, (tel: 4495-133–4; fax: 4496-134; email: bhcbanjul@gamtel.gm).

Central Statistics Office, Central Bank Building, Buckle Street, Banjul (tel: 4228-105).

Gambia Embassy (USA), Suite 905, 1156 15th Street, NW, Washington DC 20005 (tel: (+1-202) 785-1399; fax: (+1-202) 785-1425).

Gambia Hotel Association, c/o The Bungalow Beach Hotel, PO Box 2637, Serrekunda (tel: 4465-288; fax: 4466-180).

Gambia Investment Promotion and Free Zones Agency (GIPFZA), 5 Nelson Mandela Street, PO Box 757, Banjul (tel: 4222-4412, 4222-836; fax: 4222-829; e-mail: dipm.gipfza@qanet.gm; ceo.gipfza@qanet.gm).

National Investment Promotion Authority (NIPA), Independence Drive, Banjul (tel: 4228-332; fax: 4229-220).

US Embassy, 92 Kairaba Ave; PO Box 19, Fajara, Banjul (tel: 4392-856, 4392-858; fax: 4392-475; email: ambanjul@gamtel.gm).

Internet sites

Africa Business Network: www.ifc.org/abn

AllAfrica.com: allafrica.com

African Development Bank: www.afdb.org

Africa Online: www.africaonline.com

Gateway site: gambiagateway.tripod.com

Mbendi AfroPaedia (information on companies, countries, industries and stock exchanges in Africa): mbendi.co.za

The Gambia Tourism Authority: www.visitthegambia.gm

The Gambia website: www.gambia.net

Georgia

KEY FACTS

Official name: Sak'art'velos Respublika (Republic of Georgia)

Head of State: President Giorgi Margvelashvili (Georgian Dream) (elected 27 Oct 2013, assumed office 17 Nov 1013)

Head of government: Prime Minister Irakli Garibashvili (KO-DS) (from 20 Nov 2013)

Ruling party: Kartuli Otsneba (Georgian Dream) (coalition of six political parties led by Kartuli Otsneba–Demokratiuli Sakartvelo (KO-DS) (Georgian Dream-Democratic Georgia) (from 25 Oct 2012)

Area: 69,700 square km

Population: 4.47 million (2014)*

Capital: Tbilisi

Official language: Georgian

Currency: Lari (L) = 100 tetri

Exchange rate: L2.38 per US$ (Sep 2015)

GDP per capita: US$3,699 (2014)*

GDP real growth: 4.73% (2014)*

GDP: US$16.54 billion (2014)*

Unemployment: 14.58% (2012)*

Inflation: 3.07% (2014)

Balance of trade: -US$4.24 billion (2014)

* estimated figure

For Georgia's Prime Minister, Irakli Garibashvili, the June 2015 floods that hit the capital city region were a disaster, an embarrassment and a warning. That 20 or so Tbilisi citizens should die in the floods was, of course, a disaster. That a number of animals, including a tiger, should end up prowling around the city's streets was both disaster and embarrassment. That a penguin should make its way to neighbouring Azerbaijan, some 50 kilometres away was both surprising and amusing. A Tbilisi television channel reportedly advised the city's residents to 'Run towards it shouting and screaming.' 'Should you do that for a tiger or a bear?' asked one viewer.

The Russian bear

The flash floods had shown up the government's weakness at dealing with a crisis. To have wild animals roaming around the streets was, however, preferable to finding that the Russian bear had arrived in their midst. For the Georgian government Russia's activities in the Crimea and eastern Ukraine could only be taken as a warning. As Russian forces consolidated their territorial gains and Ukraine's government sweated, memories of Russia's *de facto* annexation of South Ossetia (with which Russia was on the point of signing a Treaty of Alliance and Integration) and Abkhazia (with which it was also preparing a similar treaty) Georgia found itself once gain sitting astride a global fault line. Russian revanchism was keeping Georgia's diplomats and officials very much awake.

Georgia has long styled itself a solidly pro Euro-Atlantic partner and has more reasons than most to declare itself an opponent of Russian military expansion. After all, Georgians had seen Russia and its proxies walk off with 20 per cent of their territory and corral around 300,000 of their compatriots. However, in Tblisi Russia could not easily be ignored, causing occasionally vocal protest groups to ask if their country's pro-Western stance was the answer. Increasingly, a number of Georgians seemed to be questioning the policy.

The groups could be seen protesting in Tbilisi streets, preaching in Georgian churches and organising apparently well-funded rallies. Russian influence in Georgia appeared to be growing stronger. Conversely, Washington and Brussels, Paris, Bonn and London all appeared to be in denial, downplaying the possibility of Georgia 'switching'. Opinion polls from the US-funded International Republican Institute (IRI) and the National Democratic Institute (NDI) had consistently shown Georgia's support for Euro-Atlantic integration at between 60 and 70 per cent of the population. Georgia's politicians had relied on these soundings to justify their pro-Western policies.

However, according to one NDI poll in 2014 Georgia's relations with Europe and the US was not at the top of their worry-list. More mundane issues prevailed with concerns about jobs (63 per cent) and poverty (32 per cent) eclipsing other issues (See Economy below). North Atlantic Treaty Organisation (Nato) and EU integration came low on the list, at 10 and 17, respectively. And of 21 issues polled, Georgians picked Nato and EU membership as the top issues the government spent too much time discussing.

Look East

At the same time, the survey detected growing support for joining the Moscow alternative, the almost laughable Eurasian Union (membership – 3: Belarus, Kazakhstan and… Russia. Total population size 183 million (EU population: 508 million). An estimated 20 per cent of the population were in favour of membership. The percentage had risen from 11 per cent in late 2013 to 16 per cent by mid-2014. Georgia's pro-Russian groups avoided calling themselves 'Russian' in any way, preferring titles such as the 'Eurasian Institute', or the 'Eurasian Choice'. Reports from both sides of Georgia's political divide suggested that these groupings received funding from Russia, more specifically from the Kremlin. Populist in their approach, they tend to dwell on Georgia's economic weaknesses and blame virtually every government deficiency on its would-be relationship with the West and the desire for closer affiliation with the EU and Nato.

In 2014 and early 2015, the existence of the pro-Russian organisations, coupled with the manifestly anti-Western attitude stance of the Georgian orthodox church, was beginning to impact on the Georgian parliament. Pro-Russian politicians had initially appeared on the margins of Georgian politics, gradually morphing into something resembling a political force.

Formerly a pro-Western politician, Nino Burjanadze had stitched together a pro-Russian coalition aimed at breaking the Euro-Atlantic consensus. In the 2013 presidential and the 2014 local elections, Ms Burjanadze's Democratic Movement-United Georgia party which favoured closer ties with Russia (and, rather perversely, the European Union), obtained about 10 per cent of the vote. Another pro-Russian group, the Alliance of Patriots – a populist party with anti-Western leanings – won almost 5 per cent in June 2014. The parliamentary elections in 2016 promise to provide a more accurate insight into Georgians' political inclinations. It remains to be seen whether the vote will produce a differently oriented Georgian government. A number of smaller parties have left the ruling Georgian Dream coalition's ranks.

The economy

In its February–March 2015 assessment of the Georgian economy, the International Monetary Fund (IMF) noted that Georgia's economy had been hit by a number of external shocks: the Russia-Ukraine crisis, the deepening recession in Russia (both of which had created knock-on effects throughout the region) and the currency devaluations seen in a number of trading partners. Due to these shocks, Georgia's exports were 30 per cent lower than a year earlier and remittances from Georgian workers abroad were down by 25 per cent.

As a result, according to the IMF, the economy was slowing. In January 2015, output had grown by only 0.5 per cent compared to the previous year. While growth in 2015 might reach 2 per cent, the IMF stressed that the projection was subject to risks. The economies of many of Georgia's main trading partners were slowing down by even more and the depreciation of their exchange rates was hurting Georgia's competitiveness.

The lower exports, remittances and tourism receipts had increased the current account deficit in 2014 to around 9.5 per cent of gross domestic product (GDP). Because foreign earnings were lower, the lari had depreciated by more than 20 per cent against the US dollar since January 2014. Although this depreciation was large, it was in line with the depreciation experienced by many other countries, given the strength of the US dollar. Indeed, the IMF noted, most of the region's currencies had depreciated by even more. The lari's depreciation against the US dollar would also increase costs for foreign currency borrowings, which would slow down economic growth.

Because of the depreciation, inflation was expected by the IMF to pick up somewhat in the short term, moving towards the National Bank of Georgia's (NBG) inflation target of 5 per cent. But this increase in inflation would take place from a low starting point: inflation in February 2015 was only 1.3 per cent, in part because of lower oil prices. Lower import prices were also expected to contain inflation.

The IMF considered that the government deserved credit for keeping the budget deficit to 3 per cent of GDP in 2014. However, in 2015, lower growth means that tax revenues will be less than projected in the budget. The government will therefore need to take measures to keep the budget deficit under control, by limiting employee bonuses and by taking efforts to contain administrative spending. The government needed to pass amendments to the budget that included specific tax increases and spending cuts to limit the increase in the budget deficit. However, the IMF recommended that spending on the social safety net should be maintained and targeting improved to protect the vulnerable and the poor.

KEY INDICATORS **Georgia**

	Unit	2011	2012	2013	2014	**2015
Population	m	*4.47	4.50	4.48	*4.47	*4.46
Gross domestic product (GDP)	US$bn	14.30	15.85	16.14	*16.54	*13.76
GDP per capita	US$	3,210	3,543	3,600	*3,699	*3,087
GDP real growth	%	7.0	6.2	3.3	*4.7	*2.0
Inflation	%	8.5	-0.9	-0.5	3.1	*3.0
Unemployment	%	15.1	15.0	14.6	–	–
Exports (fob) (goods)	US$m	3,223.0	3,457.6	4,191.0	3,995.1	–
Imports (fob) (goods)	US$m	6,643.8	7,681.6	7,697.0	8,235.3	–
Balance of trade	US$m	-3,420.9	-4,224.0	-4,226.1	-4,240.1	–
Current account	US$m	-1,905.8	-1,854.0	-926.0	*-1,593.0	*-1,579.0
Total reserves minus gold	US$m	2,781.6	2,872.9	2,823.4	2,699.2	–
Foreign exchange	US$m	2,544.2	2,651.7	2,601.5	–	–
Exchange rate	per US$	2.70	1.66	1.73	1.88	–

* estimated figure ** forecast figure

The IMF supported the NBG's policy to refrain from intervening in the foreign exchange market and to allow the lari to float. The main objective of the NBG was to ensure price stability: achieving this goal depended on having a floating exchange rate. In addition, the floating rate allows the exchange rate to absorb external shocks. Intervening to resist shocks that could well be long-lasting would only waste Georgia's foreign currency reserves and slow the reduction of Georgia's trade deficit with the rest of the world.

The IMF looked forward to seeing plans to accelerate the reforms needed to make Georgia a more attractive place for doing business and for investing, for creating jobs and for boosting growth in the future. (Georgia ranked 50 out of the 175 countries surveyed on the Transparency International *Corruption Perceptions Index*, behind Hungary, but ahead of the Czech Republic.)

For its part, the European Bank for Reconstruction and Development (EBRD) estimated that Georgia's GDP expanded by 4.7 per cent in 2014, up from 3.3 per cent in 2013. Data issued through the third quarter of 2014 indicated that the recovery reflected mainly gains of 8.5 per cent in industry, particularly in construction and 5.4 per cent in services, in particular for financial intermediation and tourism. In the same period, agriculture expanded by only 1.3 per cent. On the demand side, growth came from a 5.5 per cent expansion in consumption and, in particular, a 21.2 per cent rise in investment, mainly in the private sector. However, a major slowdown began in the fourth quarter and continued into 2015 as the drop in oil prices and the impact of economic sanctions on the Russian Federation triggered recession there and much slower growth in other key trading partners. As a consequence, their imports from and remittances to Georgia plunged.

Declining prices for ferroalloys, which represent some 10 per cent of Georgia's exports, also reduced export earnings. The decline in foreign exchange inflows put downward pressure on the Georgian lari, which depreciated by about 6 per cent against the US dollar from October 2014 to the end of the year and a further 15 per cent by March 2015. Reversing reported deflation in 2013, annual average inflation reached 3.1 per cent in 2014, driven by increases of 5.5 per cent for health care, 5.2 per cent for food, 4.3 per cent for utilities and 3.5 per cent for services. Overall inflation slowed to 2.0 per cent in 2014 from 2.4 per cent a year earlier.

The fiscal deficit amounted to an estimated 3.0 per cent of GDP, which was less than budgeted because revenue exceeded the budget projection by 1.1 per cent while expenditure reached only 95 per cent of planned outlays. Revenue and grants together amounted to 28.0 per cent of GDP, while expenditure equalled 31.0 per cent. Total revenue rose by 8.3 per cent and tax revenue by 8.7 per cent on higher receipts from excise tax on tobacco and value-added tax. Public expenditure rose by 9.8 per cent, reflecting a 14.5 per cent increase in current expenditure, in particular a 13.1 per cent rise for goods and services and 9.1 per cent from higher compensation for government employees. Public debt was estimated at 35.0 per cent of GDP at the end of 2014.

Monetary policy remained accommodative, the policy rate unchanged at 4.0 per cent until February 2015, when it was raised to 4.5 per cent in response to exogenous shocks. Credit expansion accelerated to 25.4 per cent from 21.2 per cent in 2013, mainly reflecting higher consumer and mortgage lending in line with increased consumption and output. Loans denominated in US dollars grew by 20.4 per cent but decreased as a percentage of all loans to 60.8 per cent from 62.4 per cent at the end of 2013.

Georgia's banks remained well capitalised, their capital adequacy ratio at 18.0 per cent and liquidity ratio at 39.1 per cent. Non-performing loans stayed modest at 3.6 per cent of all loans with the timely restructuring or writing off of problem loans. However, the depreciation of the lari against the US dollar helped foreign currency deposits rise to 57.1 per cent of all deposits.

To reduce dollarisation and improve the monetary transmission mechanism, the National Bank of Georgia started accepting for its refinancing facility a wider range of securities in local currency and promoted loans in local currency with variable interest rates. Average lending rates in lari fell by 1.4 percentage points to 17.5 per cent, while average rates on loans denominated in foreign exchange fell by 1.2 percentage points to 10.5 per cent. Excess bank liquidity helped reduce deposit interest rates by 0.9 percentage points to 5.3 per cent.

The current account deficit widened to an estimated 9.5 per cent of GDP from 5.7 per cent in 2013. Higher growth fuelled a 7.1 per cent rise in imports, while exports declined by 1.6 per cent, reflecting a 3.5 per cent drop in the fourth quarter that erased increases in the two previous quarters. Steep currency depreciation in its main trading partners eroded Georgia's competitiveness despite lari depreciation against the US dollar. In addition, Azerbaijan's adoption of Euro 4 automobile standards in April 2014 cut Georgia's exports of second hand vehicles. The fourth quarter drop in exports – followed by the 30.0 per cent decline year on year recorded in January 2015 – also reflected the weakening in the economy of the Russian Federation, which by 2014 had become Georgia's third-largest export destination, taking nearly 10.0 per cent of all exports. Tourism receipts declined and remittances fell by 2.5 per cent, with a notable drop of 16.3 per cent in the fourth quarter and an even heftier decline of 22.5 per cent in January and February 2015 compared with the same period a year earlier. Higher remittance inflows from southern Europe did not offset the drop from the Russian Federation, where remittances to Georgia plunged by 30.1 per cent in the fourth quarter.

Despite the slow recovery in Europe, foreign direct investment (FDI) performed well, exceeding US$1.2 billion by official estimates. Gross international reserves rose at the end of 2014, to US$2.7 billion, down only slightly from US$2.8 billion in 2013 and equivalent to 3 months of imports. External debt totalled an estimated 64.0 per cent of GDP, excluding inter-company loans equivalent to about 20 per cent of GDP. In July 2014, Georgia had entered into a 3-year standby arrangement with the IMF that provided a US$155 million cushion against external shocks and set a framework to discipline macro-fiscal policies. Growth was expected by the EBRD to slow to 2.0 per cent in 2015 in tandem with slowdowns in the European Union and neighbouring Azerbaijan and a projected recession in the Russian Federation. Some recovery in growth, to 2.5 per cent, is forecast in 2016 as manufacturing strengthens and services pick up. The European Union Association Agreement with Georgia includes provisions for a Deep and Comprehensive Free Trade Area that, along with an expected improvement in the global environment, should support exports and remittances during 2016 while boosting FDI from Europe. Higher public spending and a stable political situation following peaceful parliamentary elections in 2016 would support growth by strengthening consumer and investor confidence.

Despite projected reductions in international prices, domestic food price inflation could worsen if demand increases for Georgian food exports, especially from the Russian Federation. Inflation is forecast to reach 5.0 per cent in 2015 and 2016, in part because of further lari depreciation.

The base interest rate might well be raised further in 2015 and 2016 if the authorities decided to limit currency depreciation, particularly if US interest rates rose from mid-2015. The fiscal deficit was likely to expand to at least 4.0 per cent of GDP in 2015 as slowing growth squeezed revenue. The 2016 deficit would depend on the macro-economic environment and the trade off between promoting growth and containing the current account deficit. The government had an ambitious reform agenda to improve its management of revenue, expenditure, debt and fiscal risk. After a 44 per cent rise in social spending from 2012 to 2014, social benefits might level off in 2015. Public debt was projected to climb to 40.0 per cent of GDP at the end of 2015 before subsiding to 38.5 per cent at the end of 2016.

After widening in 2014, the current account deficit was projected to expand further to 12.0 per cent of GDP in 2015 before narrowing to 10.5 per cent in 2016. Merchandise exports were projected to decrease by 15.0 per cent in 2015, reflecting the slowdown that began in late 2014, before recovering by 5.0 per cent in 2016 as the external environment improves and the positive effects of the free trade area with the European Union are increasingly felt. Imports are projected to show a fall of 3.0 per cent in 2015, reflecting the slowdown in growth and remittances, and to increase by 3.0 per cent in 2016 with some improvement in growth. Remittances are expected to decline in 2015 with the sharp deterioration in regional economies before recovering in 2016 as the external environment improves. Gross international reserves are projected to remain low at US$2.5 billion at the end of 2015, equivalent to about 3 months of imports, before increasing to US$2.6 billion in 2016. External debt excluding inter-company loans are projected to reach 75.0 per cent of GDP in 2015 and 74.0 per cent in 2016.

The growth forecast is subject to multiple downside risks: lower exports and remittances from slower European growth or a recession in the Russian Federation that exceeded expectations, stress on exports or tourism from tensions involving Ukraine and other countries in the region and the impact of further lari depreciation on debt service burdens and household disposable income, as about 68 per cent of mortgages are denominated in US dollars.

Risk assessment

Economy	Fair
Politics	Fair
Regional stability	Poor

COUNTRY PROFILE

1801–04 Most of what is now Georgia became part of the Russian Empire.
1917 Georgia joined an alliance with Armenia and Azerbaijan to become the Transcaucasian Federation.
1918 The Federation was dissolved and Georgia became an independent state.
1918–21 There was a brief spell of independence until the Russian Red Army invaded in 1921.
1922 Georgia was incorporated into the Soviet Union first as a Soviet Republic, and then as a member of the Transcaucasian Soviet Federative Republic (TSFR) along with Armenia and Azerbaijan.
1936 The TSFR was dissolved and the three states became republics of the Soviet Union.
1940–45 An estimated 10 per cent of the population perished in the Stalin purges.
1989 The killing of 20 people by Soviet troops during a national demonstration in Tbilisi triggered the final disillusionment with communism.
1990 Following a referendum which called for independence from the Soviet Union, Zviad Gamsakhurdia was elected the first president in July. Racist policies caused problems.
1991 Independence from Russia was declared. Prime Minister Teniz Sigua resigned.
1992 Gamsakhurdia was overthrown in a coup and Eduard Shevardnadze assumed power. Parliamentary elections were held, in which Shevardnadze was elected Chairman of the State Security Council. Shevardnadze re-appointed Teniz Sigua as prime minister. After Georgian independence the northern region of Abkhazia declared itself independent of the new state. The subsequent war killed an estimated 10,000 and created 300,000 internally displaced persons (IDP).
1994 A cease-fire was signed.
1995 After surviving a car bomb assassination attempt, Shevardnadze was elected by popular vote, and the Sak'art'velos Mokalaketa Kavshiri (SMK) (Union of Georgian Citizens) secured a majority vote in the parliamentary elections. A constitution was adopted. The Abkhaz parliament rejected the proposed status of autonomous republic within Georgia.
1996 In accordance with the constitution, a National Security Council was established.
1997 A Civil Code, second only to the constitution in importance, was adopted. Capital punishment was abolished.
1998 Shevardnadze survived a second assassination attempt.
1999 Georgia became a member of the Council of Europe.
2000 President Shevardnadze won the presidential elections. He said that he would not stand for a third term.
2001 Fighting erupted between Georgian security forces and Abkhazia separatists, despite the signing of a peace agreement. Mass demonstrations followed a raid by security forces on an independent television station, which had criticised the government for corruption.
2002 US special forces arrived to help train and equip Georgian forces for counter-terrorist operations. Russia accused Georgia of harbouring Chechen militants in South Ossetia and the Pankisi Gorge. Russian President Putin warned of military action if Georgia failed to deal with them.
2003 Work began laying the Georgian section of the 1,760km Baku-Tbilisi-Ceyhan (BTC) oil pipeline. Rigged elections resulted in mass protests and the storming of the parliament. President Shevardnadze was forced to resign; Nino Burdzhanadze became acting president. The Supreme Court later annulled the election results.
2004 Mikhail Saakashvili was sworn in as president and he nominated Zurab Zhvania for the re-introduced post of prime minister. A bloc led by the President's party won all the seats in the parliamentary elections.
2005 Prime Minister Zurab Zhvania died and Zurab Noghaideli became prime minister. The BTC oil pipeline, capable of carrying one million barrels per day of Caspian oil to Western markets, opened.
2006 Relations with Russia deteriorated as energy supplies to Georgia were interrupted and Georgia demanded withdrawal of Russian troops from South Ossetia and Abkhazia. Russia imposed embargoes on Georgian produce, transport and postal links, before and after Georgia arrested four Russians in Tbilisi on spying charges. In a referendum, over 90 per cent of South Ossetians voted for independence.
2007 A 15-day state of emergency was declared as opposition protesters accused the president of corruption and demanded new elections. Only state-television was allowed to report on the news, while Imedi TV, which had broadcast the views of opposition leaders, was suspended. The president acceded to protesters' demands and called for fresh elections. President Saakashvili replaced Zurab Noghaideli with Lado Gurgenidze as prime minister.

2008 Mikhail Saakashvili was re-elected president. The opposition challenged the result. International observers claimed the election had been democratic and that 'the outcome should be respected'. Within a month of his defeat in the presidential elections, Badri Patarkatsishvili died in exile in the UK, of natural causes. In parliamentary elections, the Natshhionakhuri Modzraoba (ENM) (United National Movement) won a majority of seats. After days of fighting in South Ossetia (which wishes to cede from Georgia), the government sent in troops to restore order. Fierce fighting in the South Ossetia capital, Tskhinvali, resulted in the Georgian air force bombing surrounding areas. The Russian region of North Ossetia sent forces via the Roki tunnel in the Caucasus Mountains to aid South Ossetia. Georgia mobilised its army. Russia officially launched a 'peace enforcement' programme in support of South Ossetia. The Russian air force bombed the Georgian town of Gori as a convoy of Russian tanks and armoured vehicles arrived in the area. Russian troops engaged Georgian troops inside Georgia as thousands of refugees fled the area. Russia forced Georgian forces out of South Ossetia and adopted defensive positions within Georgia. Russia refused to withdraw completely and left a contingent to maintain a 'security buffer zone' of seven kilometres on either side of the South Ossetian border. The Russian government formally recognised the breakaway regions of South Ossetia and Abkhazia as independent states. President Saakashvili sacked Prime Minister Lado Gurgenidze and appointed Grigol Mgaloblishvili as prime minister. Aslanbek Bulatsev became prime minister of South Ossetia.

2009 Prime Minister Mgaloblishvili resigned and Nikoloz (Nika) Gilauri became prime minister. Parliamentary elections were held in Russian-backed South Ossetia, in which political parties committed to links with Russia won most votes. The elections were condemned by the EU and NATO as unauthorised by the sovereign state of Georgia. Georgia sent an initial 125 troops (later increased to 500) to join the NATO-led forces in Afghanistan, thereby strengthening its ties with NATO. Georgia will also allow NATO to use its territory as an alternative land bridge to Afghanistan. Russia vetoed the mandate of the UN Observer Mission in Georgia (Unomig) and obliged its withdrawal. Russian Prime Minister Putin announced that Russia would spend US$500 million in reinforcing its military base in Abkhazia. Russia claimed to have found evidence that Ukrainian troops and volunteers had fought alongside Georgians in the dispute over South Ossetia. Abkhazi President Bagapsh was re-elected for a second term in office.

2010 The Verkhny Lars-Kazbegi border checkpoint between Georgia and Russia, which had been closed in 2006, was reopened. Russia deployed a S-300 missile system in Abkhazia; the system was already deployed in South Ossetia. Parliament approved, by 112 votes to 5, an amendment to the constitution. The amendment moves primary political power from the president to the prime minister by introducing a number of checks and balances.

2011 A new Russian language TV news station, Kanal Pik, began broadcasting from Tbilisi in January. It has a mandate to provide Georgian views on cross-border matters and to counter negative Russian reports concerning Georgia. President of Abkhazia, Sergey Bagapsh, died in May; his deputy, Aleksandr Ankvab became acting president. In the presidential election held in Abkhazia in August, Aleksandr Ankvab won 54.9 per cent of the vote, Sergey Shamba 21 per cent, Raul Khadjimba 19.8 per cent; turnout was 71.9 per cent. In South Ossetia President Eduard Kokoyty resigned in December; Prime Minister Vadim Brovtsev became acting president. The Georgian citizenship of billionaire Bidzina Ivanishvili was revoked in October, on the grounds that he was already a Russian citizen and was in receipt of a French passport. However Ivanishvili claimed it was part of a campaign of dirty tricks following after he formed a new political party (Kartuli Otsneba–Demokratiuli Sakartvelo (KO-DS) (Georgian Dream-Democratic Georgia)) to contest the next parliamentary elections.

2012 In presidential elections that took place in South Ossetia on 25 March, Leonid Tibilov won most votes, 42.5 per cent, but was unable to reach the 50.1 per cent necessary to win outright. In a runoff with David Sanakoyev, who had won 24.6 per cent in the first round, Tibilov won 55.4 per cent and Sanakoyev 43.6 per cent; turnout was 71.3 per cent. Leonid Tibilov took office as president of South Ossetia on 19 April. On 15 May Rostislav Khugayev was confirmed into office as prime minister of South Ossetia. On 30 June, President Saakashvili named Ivane 'Vano' Merabishvili as prime minister. Parliamentary elections took place on 1 October in which the KO-DS led a coalition of six parties under its name and won 85 seats out of 150, the ruling ENM was the only other party to win any seats (65). Bidzina Ivanishvili became prime minister on 25 October.

2013 At the beginning of 2013 Russian troops were still stationed in 20 per cent of Georgian territory, after the August 2010 five-day war which had ended with Moscow and Tbilisi breaking off diplomatic relations. In May Prime Minister Ivanishvili launched an inquiry into the conduct of the war. However in 2013, the government, which ousted President Saakashvili's party from power in October 2012, said that it wants to re-establish trade and business links with Moscow. Political overtures from Tbilisi have already persuaded Moscow to scrap its ban on sales of Georgian wine and mineral waters in Russia. Although there was concern in the West that Georgia would follow Ukraine back into a Russian orbit, in fact Ivanishvili has made it clear that Georgia's main foreign policy objective remains Nato and EU membership. In the presidential elections held on 29 October Giorgi Margvelashvili (Georgian Dream-Democratic Georgia) was elected President with 62.12 per cent of the vote. Davit Bakradze (United National Movement) polled 21.72 per cent and Nino Burjanadze (Democratic Movement – United Georgia) 10.19 per cent. None of the 20 other candidates polled over 3 per cent; turn out was 46.95 per cent. Mr Irakli Garibashvili was nominated as prime minister on the resignation of Bidzina Ivanishvili on 20 November.

2014 Russian moves to formalise its ties with Abkhazia and South Ossetia in late 2014 lead to fears in Georgia that Moscow was seeking to annex the two statelets.

2015 Over 15 people died in flash floods in June that also flooded Mziuri Park zoo leading to the escape of a number of animals, including a 16-year-old hippo.

Political structure

Constitution

The 1995 constitution provides for a presidential republic with federal elements. The country is divided into nine districts and 64 regions.

Independence date

26 May 1918

Form of state

Presidential democratic republic

The executive

The president, who is head of state and head of government, is directly elected for five years and can serve no more than two terms. The head of state holds supreme executive power, together with the cabinet of ministers.

National legislature

The unicameral Sak'art'velos Parlamenti (Georgian Parliament) (also known as Umagheisi Sabcho (Supreme Council)) has 235 members elected by proportional representation, of which 150 are elected in multi-seat constituencies by party lists and 75 in single-seat constituencies; 10

members represent displaced citizens in the separatist region of Abkhazia.

Legal system

The legal system is based on the civil law system.

Last elections

27 October 2013 (presidential); 1 October 2012 (parliamentary)

Results: Presidential (2013): Giorgi Margvelashvili 61.12 per cent, Davit Bakradze 21.72 per cent, Nino Burjanadze 10.19 per cent. No other candidate won more than 2 per cent. Turnout was 46.95. A run-off election was not necessary.

Parliamentary (2012): Kartuli Otsneba (Georgian Dream) (coalition of six political parties led by Kartuli Otsneba-Demokratiuli Sakartvelo (KO-DS) (Georgian Dream-Democratic Georgia) won 54.97 per cent of the vote (85 seats out of 150), Ertiani Natshhionakhuri Modzraoba (ENM) (United National Movement) 40.34 per cent (65); 15 other political parties failed to win any seats. Turnout was 59.76 per cent.

Next elections

2018 (presidential); 2016 (parliamentary)

Political parties

Ruling party

Kartuli Otsneba (Georgian Dream) (coalition of six political parties led by Kartuli Otsneba–Demokratiuli Sakartvelo (KO-DS) (Georgian Dream-Democratic Georgia) (from 25 Oct 2012)

Main opposition party

Ertiani Natshhionakhuri Modzraoba (ENM) (United National Movement)

Living standards in Georgia, once among the highest of the former Soviet republics, plummeted after several years of ethnic and civil strife and economic collapse.

Population

4.48 million (2013)

Last census: January 2002: 4,371,535

Population density: 64 inhabitants per square km (2010).Urban population 53 per cent (2010 Unicef).

Annual growth rate: -1.1 per cent, 1990–2010 (Unicef).

Internally Displaced Persons (IDP)

260,000 (UNHCR 2004)

Ethnic make-up

There are over 100 different ethnic groups in the country, including Georgian (70 per cent), Armenian (8 per cent), Russian (6 per cent) and Azeri (6 per cent). Other significant ethnic groups include Abkhazians and Ossetians.

Religions

The Georgian Orthodox Church is the main religion (supported by some 80 per cent of the population, although only some 15–25 per cent attend regularly). There are also Shi'ite and Sunni Muslims, Jehovah Witnesses, Jews, Armenian Gregorians, Catholics and Baptists. There is inter-communal strife between the Christian Georgians and the Ossetian and Abkhazian ethnic Muslim minorities.

Education

Elementary schooling lasts for six years followed by two years of basic education. Secondary school education lasts for three years. Technical and vocational upper secondary education takes another two to four years.

There are 26 public higher education institutions in Georgia including eight universities and 14 technical and specialised institutes. In addition, 209 private higher education institutions have been established.

Public expenditure on education typically amounts to 5.2 per cent of annual gross national income (World Bank). Loans of US$60 million from the World Bank helped reform Georgia's secondary education.

Compulsory years: 6 to 14.

Enrolment rate: 89 per cent boys; 88 per cent girls, total primary school enrolment of the relevant age group (including repetition rates) (World Bank).

Pupils per teacher: 18 in primary schools.

Health

The population has 76 per cent and 99 per cent access to improved water and sanitation facilities, respectively.

HIV/Aids

HIV prevalence: 0.1 per cent aged 15–49 in 2003 (World Bank)

Life expectancy: 74 years, 2004 (WHO 2006)

Fertility rate/Maternal mortality rate: 1.6 births per woman, 2010 (Unicef); maternal mortality rate 70 per 100,000 live births (World Bank).

Child (under 5 years) mortality rate (per 1,000): 20 per 1,000 live births (WHO 2012); 3 per cent of children aged under five are malnourished (World Bank).

Head of population per physician: 4.09 physicians per 1,000 people, 2003 (WHO 2006)

Welfare

Georgia has to cope not only with 58.5 per cent of its people living below the official poverty line but also an increased influx of refugees in the Pankisi Valley, 150km north of Tbilisi, inhabited largely by ethnic Chechens, known as Kists. The US Agency for International Development (USAID) has funded Georgia to implement community level activities, which benefit refugees, internally displaced people and others affected by ethnic violence and the deterioration of the social welfare system.

The benefits system includes pensions, unemployment benefits and family allowance, all paid at flat rates. The government provides 100 per cent electricity tariff discounts for war veterans and 50 per cent discounts for tax, customs, defence and security personnel.

Increased poverty in the urban areas leads to high incidence of wage and social transfer arrears. UN reports suggest that the average minimum wage is still insufficient to ensure an adequate standard of living for large parts of the Georgian population.

Main cities

Tbilisi (population 1.1 million in 2012), Kutaisi (200,611); Rustavi (121,696), Batumi (120,568), Zugdidi (95,541).

Languages spoken

Russian and English are spoken and in the territory of Abkhazia, Abkhazian is sometimes spoken.

Official language/s

Georgian

Media

The constitution guarantees freedom of speech and of the press. However political turmoil during the 2008 presidential election saw intimidation of journalists by political leaders of on all sides of the debate.

Press

There are around 200 newspapers but most are small, local and without influence. Newspapers are typically subsidized by patrons, in business and politics, and editorial independence is correspondingly compromised.

Dailies: In Georgian *Sakartvelos Respublika (Republic of Georgia)* (www.opentext.org.ge/sakartvelos-respublika), was the official government newspaper. Other private publications include *24 Saati (24 Hours)* (www.24saati.ge), *Rezonansi (Resonance)*. In Russian *Svobodnaya Gruzia (Free Georgia)* (www.svobodnaya-gruzia.com). In English *The Messenger* (www.messenger.com.ge).

Weeklies: In English, *The Georgian Times* (www.geotimes.ge) and *Georgia Today* (www.georgiatoday.ge).

Business: The EU-funded *Georgian Economic Trends* (www.geplac.org) is a quarterly with the best source of business news and information. It is published by the European Policy and Legal advice Center (Geplac) in English and Georgian.

Broadcasting

Georgian Public Broadcasting (GPB) (www.gpb.ge) provides national coverage.

Radio: The GPB (www.gpb.ge) has two radio stations, Public Radio offering a range of news, cultural and entertainment programmes and Radio Two offers Georgian music programmes, with part of the daytime schedule given over to educational, social and entertainment programmes. Private, commercial stations include, Radio Imedi (www.radio-imedi.ge) a national news and speech network and Fortuna FM (www.fortuna.ge) with local and international music of most genre.

Television: Most Georgians rely on TV to provide their news and information. The GPB (www.gpb.ge) has two TV stations, Public TV has a full range of programmes from news and current affairs to children's TV and sport and Channel Two has specialist programming but does not reach all regions of the country. There are a several commercial TV stations including Rustavi 2 (www.rustavi2.com.ge) is the most popular TV channel, Imedi TV (www.imedi.ge) and Mze TV (http://mze.ge), all providing locally produced and imported programmes.

A new Russian language TV news station, Kanal Pik (http://pik.tv/en), began broadcasting on 25 January 2011 from Tbilisi. It has a mandate to provide Georgian views on cross-border matters and to counter negative Russian reports concerning Georgia.

Other news agencies: Prime-News: http://eng.primenewsonline.com
Civil Georgia: www.civil.ge

Economy

The economy is dominated by the service sector, which constituted 66.4 per cent of GDP in 2014, with industry contributing 24.4 per cent, of which manufacturing accounted for 13 per cent and agriculture 9.2 per cent. Agriculture employs over 50 per cent of the total work force. Major export commodities include wine and nuts, as well as ores, finished metals and electricity. However, Georgia remains reliant on imported fuel, food and pharmaceuticals to meet domestic demands.

Georgia's economy has been hit by a combination of severe external shocks: the Russia-Ukraine crisis, the deepening recession in Russia and currency devaluations in trading partner countries. Because of these shocks, Georgia's exports are 30 per cent lower than in 2013–14, and remittances from Georgian workers abroad are down 25 per cent.

The economy is slowing as a result. While growth in 2015 is projected to reach 2 percent, it is subject to risks. The economies of many of Georgia's main trading partners are slowing by even more, and the depreciation of their exchange rates is hurting Georgia's competitiveness. GDP growth was 6.2 per cent in 2012. This figure fell to 3.3 in 2013 before rising again to 4.8 per cent in 2014.

The Baku-Tbilisi-Ceyhan oil pipeline, which commenced operations in 2005, crosses 248km of Georgia; there are plans to either run a parallel gas pipeline or ship liquefied natural gas (LNG) to Europe via Georgia. In all of these programmes Georgia benefits, not only financially from transit fees for the supply of hydrocarbons from its neighbours to allies in Europe, but also by having a secure supply of fuel, which also avoids relying on Russian supplies for its domestic consumption.

External trade

Georgia had traditional ties with Russia which were, following the break-up of the Soviet Union, formalised through the Commonwealth of Independent States (CIS), however relations first became strained when Georgia moved towards the West and Russia imposed restrictions on Georgian imports and transport access. There was a military confrontation in 2008. The destination of exports to Russia has steadily switched to Turkey, Europe and the US.

Georgia is an important transit country for goods and hydrocarbons through Central Asia.

Imports

Imports typically include fuels, machinery and parts, transport equipment, grain and other foods and pharmaceuticals.

Main sources: Turkey (20.1 per cent of total in 2014), China (8.5 per cent), Azerbaijan (7.4 per cent)

Exports

Merchandise exported includes vehicles, ferro-alloys, fertilisers, nuts, scrap metal, gold and copper ores.

Main destinations: Azerbaijan (19 per cent of total in 2014), Armenia (10.1 per cent), Russia (9.6 per cent), Turkey (8.4 per cent) and the US (7.3 per cent).

Re-exports

Fuel, citrus fruits and wine.

Agriculture

Farming

The agricultural sector typically contributes 10 per cent to GDP and employs about 50 per cent of the workforce.

Georgia is a major agricultural producer and the warm climate favours the growing of a range of sub-tropical crops in the coastal region. Crops include tea, grapes, tobacco and fruit.

Georgia is perennially the number one state in the nation in the production of peanuts, chickens, pecans and blueberries. We are also at or near the top when it comes to cotton, watermelon, peaches, eggs, rye, sweet corn, bell peppers, tomatoes, onions, cantaloupes and cabbage. Producers across the state raise cattle, horses, goats, sheep, hogs, poultry, turkeys and alligators.

A great deal of Georgia's produce is exported to other former Soviet republics in return for much-needed supplies of manufactured goods.

Forestry

Over two-fifths of the land is covered by forests and woodland, of which only a fifth is available for wood production and another fifth is classified as primeval forest untouched by man. Around 60 per cent of Georgia's trees are broadleaf, including beech, oak, hornbeam and chestnut, and the rest are coniferous, mainly spruce and pine. Forests are important to protecting soil and water. The state owns all forests by law.

Georgia produces and exports roundwood (typically 65 per cent of forestry exports) and sawnwood (27 per cent) from hardwood species.

Industry and manufacturing

Industry accounts for a quarter of GDP and employs about 20 per cent of the workforce. Light industrial activities include food-processing and drinks production, metallurgy, shipbuilding, car production, consumer durables, garment manufacturing and oil-processing. Other industries include mining, chemicals, heavy engineering and steel-making. Levels of self-sufficiency in the manufacturing sector are low and export manufacturing potential is limited. The sector is troubled by a periodic lack of finance, the slow pace of rehabilitation of enterprises and low levels of management.

Tourism

The prospects for tourism in Georgia have not been constrained by the political environment and Georgia's relations with its powerful neighbour, Russia. Some Western governments advise their citizens not to travel to the breakaway regions of South Ossetia and Abkhazia. The Georgian government boosted its investment after the conflict with Russia in 2008, promoting local resorts and tourist infrastructure and the EU allocated ?17 million (US$23.8 million) in developing the industry in 2009.

Over 5 million people visited Georgia in 2013, a large increase of 22 per cent from the previous year. Georgia offers historic buildings (particularly medieval) and landscapes dating back into antiquity; tourists will probably ignore the unappealing Soviet architecture in some towns and cities suburbs. There are three medieval sites included on UNESCO's World Heritage List. Many visit the popular Black Sea coastline which offers relaxation and water activities, while others may visit for a specific purpose, such as wine lovers going to Kakheti, the centre of

wine production, or those interested in early Christian history or those interested in the ancient route of the Silk Road, in the east of Georgia on the border with Azerbaijan.
The Tbilisi International Airport has undergone redevelopment, increasing its capacity to 2.5 million passengers per year and offering more services within the terminals. In February 2012, direct flights from Russia resumed, after a three and half-year hiatus; charter flights had previously been available.
The total contribution to GDP was 20 per cent in 2014. This meant that over 300,000 people were employed by the industry in the same year, or 16.9 per cent of total employment.

Mining

Georgia has major mineral deposits, notably manganese, copper and lead. Small quantities of iron ore are extracted.
There are reserves of about 200 million tonnes of manganese ore in Chiatura, of which 60 per cent is recoverable through underground mining and 40 per cent through open-pit mining. The Madneuli mining plant at Kazreti in southern Georgia is the country's only producer of copper concentrate. The Madneuli deposit contains the bulk of copper reserves, with reserves of around 460,000 tonnes of ore.

Hydrocarbons

Georgia has limited known oil reserves, estimated at 35 million barrels, but it is believed to have greater potential. Exploration is underway both offshore in the Black Sea as well as onshore. Georgia, which consumes 14,000 barrels per day (bpd), produces around 1,000bpd and relies on imports from Russia and Azerbaijan.
Georgia has always been an obvious transport route for the oil from the Caspian Sea to the Black Sea and the Mediterranean. The 1,768km Baku-Tibilisi-Ceyhan (BTC) oil pipeline, was inaugurated in 2005 and carries 1 million bpd, 1 per cent of the world's oil requirements.
Georgia had proven natural gas reserves of 0.3 trillion cubic feet. However, production is small and the country is dependent on imports of natural gas from Russia, although consumption has been falling since 2005, consumption rose 72 billion cubic feet in 2013 from 63 the previous year.
Coal reserves are estimated at 800 million tonnes, of which over a half can be located at Tkibuli-Shaorskoye.

Energy

Total installed generating capacity is 4.4GW, of which 81 per cent is produced by 53 hydroelectric power stations, the remainder by three thermal power plants. Fuel shortages and a deteriorating infrastructure means the electricity sector operates below capacity and there are frequent power cuts. In order to meet demand, Georgia imports electricity from Armenia, Azerbaijan and Russia and has run up considerable debt on these imports, resulting in disputes with the suppliers. Poor electricity supply and high rates have prompted widespread non-payment among Georgian electricity customers. The Russian state utility entity, Unified Energy Systems (UES), has bought 75 per cent of the electricity network and several generating facilities, effectively taking control of the energy market.

Financial markets

Stock exchange

Georgian Stock Exchange (GSE)

Banking and insurance

The banking sector has undergone reform since 1995 and the central bank, the National Bank of Georgia (NBG), has assumed a supervisory role. The NBG has concentrated on consolidating the banking sector to clamp down on poor management, corruption and non-performing loans. It has also progressively raised the minimum capital requirement, which has caused a dramatic fall in the number of banks operating in the country and forced many to seek foreign participation to survive.

Central bank

National Bank of Georgia (NBG)

Time

GMT plus three hours

Geography

Georgia is situated in west and central Transcaucasia on both sides of the Suram range. There are frontiers with Turkey and Armenia in the south, and with Azerbaijan in the south-east. The Black Sea coast is to the west. To the west of the Surams lies the more mountainous Kura basin. The Rion, which flows westwards into the Black Sea, and the Kura which flows eastwards through Azerbaijan into the Caspian Sea, are the country's two main rivers.

Hemisphere

Northern.

Climate

Hot and humid summers and mild winters. Georgia is protected against the cold air from the north by the Great Caucasus mountains. Temperatures range from 21 degrees Celsius (C) to 33C in July and from 0C to 10C in January. The west, including the Black Sea coast, lies in a sub-tropical zone with high humidity and heavy rainfall; temperatures average 5C in winter and 22C in summer. Eastern Georgia is more equable with lower humidity; temperatures average 2–4C in winter and 20–25C in summer. The mountain regions are dryer and cooler, while above 3,600m snow and ice prevail year-round.

Entry requirements

Passports

Required by all. Passports must be valid for six months after date of departure.

Visa

Required by all, except nationals of EU countries, CIS countries (other than Russia and Turkmenistan), Canada, Israel, Japan, Switzerland and US.
Business visas may in some cases require a letter of invitation from a local company or organisation and a letter of introduction from the employer.
Do not overstay the limit of the visa. The Georgian authorities can impose heavy penalties for non-compliance, including detention, fines and deportation, and all removals at the traveller's expense.

Currency advice/regulations

There are no restrictions on the import and export of local currency. The import of foreign currency is allowed, but export is limited to US$500.
Almost all payments are made in cash (US dollar notes are the most useful). Most foreign currency can be exchanged at special exchange shops in the streets of large towns.

Customs

Small amount of personal goods duty-free. On arrival declare all foreign currency and valuable items such as jewellery, cameras, computers and musical instruments.

Health (for visitors)

A reciprocal health agreement for urgent medical treatment exists with the United Kingdom. Some proof of UK residence will be required. Rabies is a health risk.

Mandatory precautions

A vaccination certificate is required for yellow fever if travelling from an infected area.

Advisable precautions

Water precautions are recommended (water purification tablets may be useful).
It is advisable to be in date for the following immunisations: tetanus (within 10 years), typhoid fever, hepatitis A (moderate risk only), hepatitis B, meningitis.
Any required medicines should be carried by the visitor, and it could be wise to have precautionary antibiotics if going outside major urban centres.
A travel kit including a disposable syringe is a reasonable precaution.

Credit cards

Only one or two outlets in Tbilisi can handle credit cards.

Public holidays (national)

Fixed dates

1 Jan (New Year's Day), 7 Jan (Orthodox Christmas Day), 19 Jan (Orthodox Epiphany), 3 Mar (Mothers' Day), 8 Mar (Women's Day), 9 Apr (Restoration Day), 9 May (Victory Day), 12 May (St Andrew's Day), 26 May (Independence Day), 28 Aug (Orthodox Assumption of the Virgin/Mariamoba), 14 Oct (Svetitskhovloba), 23 Nov (St George's Day/Giorgoba).

Variable dates

Orthodox Easter Monday

Working hours

Banking

Mon–Fri: 0930–1730.

Business

Mon–Fri: 0900–1800.

Shops

Mon–Sat: 0900–1700.

Electricity supply

220V AC 50Hz

Weights and measures

Metric system

Social customs/useful tips

Georgians are excellent hosts. Feasting is a central part of Georgian tradition. If you go to a dinner as the guest of honour, it is not unusual to be asked to sing a song or recite a romantic poem. When Georgians show friendship, it is sincere.

Security

There is a risk of terrorist activity, especially on the border with Chechnya.There has been an increase in the number of robberies, kidnappings and assaults involving foreigners, especially business people, in and around the capital, Tbilisi. Travellers should exercise caution in crowded places and markets, and when using public transportation. It is advisable not to walk alone at night and to avoid unofficial taxis.

Travellers should avoid unnecessary travel outside Tbilisi, especially at night. Train travel to Armenia, which is prone to incidents of theft and crime, should be avoided.

Getting there

Travellers intending to stay in Tbilisi for longer than three days must register with the Ministry of the Interior.

Air

National airline: Georgian Airways.

International airport/s: Tbilisi International Airport (TBS), 18km from city centre.

Airport tax: None

Surface

Road: Highways connect Georgia to the Russian Federation via the Caucasian Road Tunnel and the Georgian Military Highway to north Ossetia. The Verkhny Lars-Kazbegi border checkpoint between Georgia and Russia, which had been closed in July 2006, was reopened in March 2010.

Rail: Tbilisi has railway connections with Azerbaijan, Armenia and Iran. The conflict in Abkhazia has affected the rail link with the Russian Federation.

Water: International connections to main ports from the Black Sea ports of Odessa, Sochi, Trabzon and Istanbul. Connections are also available with the Mediterranean ports of Genoa and Piraeus.

Main port/s: The main ports are Batumi (deals mainly with oil exports), Poti and Sukhumi.

Getting about

National transport

Road: Difficult terrain and weather conditions restrict road links. Note that reliable road maps and signposts do not exist. Independent drivers should note that fuel can be difficult to obtain without specialist local knowledge. An international driving permit is required.

Buses: Buses operate between major towns and cities. There is a small underground system in Tbilisi.

Rail: There is approximately 1,583km of track with a double-track railway between Marelisi and Sagandzile. There are regular services between Tbilisi, Azerbaijan and Russia. Reservations are required for all trains.

City transport

There are many forms of cheap public transport in Tbilisi. A knowledge of the local language with its own script could be very helpful.

Taxis: Both official and unofficial taxis are plentiful.

Fares should always be agreed in advance as fares for foreigners can be set extremely high. It is advisable to use only official taxis and not share with strangers.

Car hire

Although the roads are severely pot-holed, hiring a car and driver through your guide or business associate is the quickest form of transport. It is not recommended to drive yourself.

BUSINESS DIRECTORY

The addresses listed below are a selection only. While World of Information makes every endeavour to check these addresses, we cannot guarantee that changes have not been made, especially to telephone numbers and area codes. We would welcome any corrections.

Telephone area codes

The international direct dialling code (IDD) for Georgia is +995, followed by area code and subscriber's number:

Kutaisi	331	Tbilisi	32

Useful telephone numbers

Police: 02
Fire: 01
Ambulance: 03

Chambers of Commerce

American Chamber of Commerce in Georgia, 1 Nustubidze Street, 0177 Tbilisi (tel: 312-110; fax: 312-105; e-mail: amcham@amcham.ge).

Georgian Chamber of Commerce and Industry, 11 Chavchavadze Avenue, 0179 Tbilisi (tel: 230-045; fax: 235-760; e-mail: info@gcci.ge).

Banking

Bank of Georgia, 3 Aleksander Pushkin Street, 0105 Tbilisi (tel: 444-1729; fax: 444-182; e-mail: welcome@bog.ge).

People's Bank of Georgia, 74 Chavchavadze Avenue, Tbilisi 0162 (tel: 555-500; e-mail: info@peobge.com).

ProCredit Bank, 154 Agmashenebeli Avenue, Tbilisi 0112 (tel/fax: 202-222; e-mail: central@procreditbank.ge).

TBC Bank, 7 Marjanishvili Street, Tbilisi 0102 (tel: 777-000; fax: 772-774; e-mail: marjanishvili@tbcbank.com.ge).

United Georgian Bank, 37 Uznadze Street, Tbilisi 0102 (tel: 505-505; fax: 999-139; e-mail: admin@ugb.com.ge).

Central bank

National Bank of Georgia, 3/5 Leonidze Street, 0105 Tbilisi (tel: 996-505; fax: 999-346; e-mail: info@nbg.gov.ge).

Stock exchange

Georgian Stock Exchange (GSE), www.gse.ge

Travel information

Georgian Airways, 12 Rustaveli Prospect, Tbilisi (tel: 485-560; fax: 999-660; e-mail: info@georgian-airways.com).

National tourist organisation offices

Georgian National Tourism Agency, 12 Kasbegi Avenue, 0061 Tbilisi (tel: 525-301; internet: www.gnta.ge)

Ministries

Ministry of Agriculture and Food, Kostava 41, Tbilisi (tel: 996-261; fax: 933-300).

Ministry of Communications and Post, 2.9 April St, Tbilisi (tel: 999-528; fax: 934-419).

Ministry of Culture, 37 Rustaveli Ave, Tbilisi (tel: 937-433; fax: 999-037).

Ministry of Defence, 2 University St, Tbilisi (tel: 303-163; fax: 983-929).

Ministry of the Economy, 12 Czhanturia St, Tbilisi (tel: 230-925; fax: 982-743).

Ministry of Education, 52 Chkheizze St, Tbilisi (tel: 958-886; fax: 770-073).

Ministry of Environmental Protection and Natural Resources, 68a Kostava St, Tbilisi (tel: 230-664; fax: 983-425).

Ministry of Finance, 170 Barnovi, Tbilisi (tel: 226-805; fax: 292-368).

Ministry of Foreign Affairs, 4 Chitadze St, Tbilisi (tel: 989-377; fax: 997-249).

Ministry of Health, 30 Gamsakhurdia Ave, Tbilisi (tel: 387-071; fax: 389-802).

Ministry of Industry, 28 Gamsakhurdia Ave, Tbilisi (tel: 931-045, 386-558).

Ministry of the Interior, 10 D/Kheivnis St, Tbilisi (tel: 996-296; fax: 986-532).

Ministry of Justice, 19 Griboedov St, Tbilisi (tel: 989-252; fax: 990-225).

Ministry of Refugees and Accommodation, 30 Dadiani St, Tbilisi (tel: 663-302).

Ministry of Social Security, Labour and Employment, 7/2 Leonidze St, Tbilisi (tel: 938-989; fax: 936-150).

Ministry of State Property Management, 64 Czhavczhavadze Ave, Tbilisi (tel: 294-875; fax: 225-209).

Ministry of State Security, 4.9 April St, Tbilisi (tel: 982-383; fax: 932-791).

Ministry of Trade and Foreign Economic Relations, 42 Kazbegi Ave, Tbilisi (tel: 389-667; fax: 398-882).

Ministry of Urbanisation and Construction, 16 V Pshavela Ave, Tbilisi (tel: 374-276; fax: 220-541).

Other useful addresses

British Embassy, GMT Plaza, 4 Freedom Square, 0105 Tbilisi (tel: 274-747; fax: 274-792; e-mail: British.Embassy.Tbilisi@fco.gov.uk).

Business Communication Centre (BCC), 47 Kostava Street, Tbilisi (tel: 988-371; fax: 987-601).

Business Support Centre (BSC) Kutaisi, 124 Rustaveli Avenue, Kutaisi (tel: 310-1001; fax: 331-1001; e-mail: BSC@iberiapac.ge).

Committee for Socio-Economic Information of Georgia, 4 K Gamsakhurdia Avenue, Tbilisi (tel: 361-450, 938-936; fax: 995-892, 995-622).

Georgian Embassy (USA), Suite 300, 1615 New Hampshire Avenue NW, Washington DC 20009 (tel: (1+202)-387-2390; fax: (1+202)-393-4537; e-mail: georgiaemb@hotmail.com).

Georgian Stock Exchange, 74a Chavchavadze Avenue, Tbilisi 0162 (tel: 220=718; fax: 251-876; e-mail: info@gse.ge).

Independent Agency for the Development of Municipal Services, 89/24 D Agmashenebeli Ave, Tbilisi (tel: 951-003; fax: 986-950).

Sakenergo (state hydroelectricity company), 1 Vekua Street, Tbilisi (tel: 989-814; fax: 940-676).

Saknavtobi (state oil company), 65 M Kostava Street, Tbilisi 0175 (tel: 942-887; fax: 332-509).

Saktransgasmretsvi (state gas company), 22 Delisi III Lane, Tbilisi (tel: 932-981; fax: 227-746).

Telecom Georgia, Tbilisi (tel: 999-197; fax: 442-929; e-mail: info@telecom.ge).

Prime-News: http://eng.primenewsonline.com

Civil Georgia: www.civil.ge

Internet sites

Information on government, elected officials and economic information: www.parliament.ge

Press office of the President of Georgia: www.presidpress.gov.ge

Georgian Investment Centre: web.sanet.ge/gic

Germany

KEY FACTS

Official name: Bundesrepublik Deutschland (Federal Republic of Germany)

Head of State: President Joachim Gauck (from 18 Mar 2012)

Head of government: Federal Chancellor Angela Merkel (CDU) (elected 2005; re-elected 27 Sep 2009, 22 Sep 2013)

Ruling party: Coalition lead by Christlich-Demokratische Union Deutschlands (Christian Democratic Union of Germany) (CDU)/Christlich-Soziale Union in Bayern (CSU) (Christian Social Union of Bavaria) with Sozialdemokratische Partei Deutschlands (SPD) (Social Democratic Party of Germany) (from 22 Sep 2013)

Area: 357,041 square km

Population: 81.10 million (2014)*

Capital: Berlin

Official language: German

Currency: Euro (€) = 100 cents (from 1 Jan 2002; previous currency Deutsche mark, locked at DM1.96 per euro)

Exchange rate: €0.89 per US$ (Sep 2015)

GDP per capita: US$47,590 (2014)*

GDP real growth: 1.61% (2014)

GDP: US$3,859.55 billion (2014)*

Labour force: 44.98 million (2014)*

Unemployment: 4.98% (2014)*

Inflation: 0.79% (2014)

Natural gas production: 7.70 billion cum (2014)

Balance of trade: US$304.15 billion (2014)

* estimated figure

November 2014 saw the twenty-fifth anniversary of the fall of the Berlin Wall, to be followed in October 2015 by the anniversary of German reunification in 1990. The country's reunification, masterminded by Chancellor Helmut Kohl, saw no less than 17 million East Germans become integrated into a greater Bundesrepublik. It was, in most respects, a resounding success. Twenty-five years later, in the early months of 2015, Angela Merkel was riding high in the popularity polls, internationally acknowledged as Europe's *de-facto* senior statesperson and leader in times of trouble – which in the first half of 2015 had meant dealing with the future of Greece and the euro-zone's currency, the euro.

Weaknesses

So what could go wrong? There were moments, however, when Mrs Merkel – 'Mutti' to her followers – must have wondered how long it was all going to last. The performance of her Christlich Demokratische Union Deutschlands (CDU) (Christian Democratic Union) in Hamburg's February regional elections was less than stellar, its support dropping from the 21.9 per cent gained in 2011 to 15.9 per cent. Mrs Merkel referred to the result, the party's worst ever in Hamburg, as 'bitter'; it had been given a beating on three fronts, reportedly losing votes in roughly equal proportions to the Freie Demokratische Partei (FDP) (Free Democrat Party), perceived to be more pro-business, to the newer Alternative für Deutschland (AfD) (Alternative for Germany Party) to be anti-European Union (EU) and – perhaps predictably – to the Sozialdemokratische Partei Deutschlands (SPD) (Social Democrats), the CDU's closest rival which was the clear front runner in the election with 45.7 per cent of the vote, enabling it to retain power. A report in the London *Economist* suggested that the fault lay with Mrs Merkel, who – attempting to poach voters from the SDP, had pushed the CDU to left of centre. According to the *Economist*, it appeared that this had in fact caused voters to return to the SPD; meanwhile, those looking for more centrist policies felt abandoned by the CDU and voted for the upstart AfD or the FDP.

Not that all was well within the right wing camp. Following open warfare in July between the AfD party's best-known politician, Bernd Lucke and the equally visible and loud, Frauke Petry, Mr Lucke packed his bags and left the ship. In the view of many of those who left with Mr Lucke, under the leadership of Ms Petry the AfD was bent on shifting rightwards with a populist agenda. In mid-2015 it remained to be seen whether a new party would be formed by Mr Lucke and his supporters.

In mid-2015 Mrs Merkel had been in power for a ten year period of influence, struggle and learning. The missing element has been charisma; Mrs Merkel is not given to revealing emotions, rarely even indicating that she holds them. This may be a product of growing up in the GDR (the former communist 'East' Germany). However, Mrs Merkel's stoicism proved an asset during the global financial crisis, enabling her rapidly to establish herself as Europe's stable leader, leading the European 'project', a reference to the use of the euro as a common currency throughout the borderless Schengen continent, despite the huge economic differences apparent in each country.

Everybody's Mutti

On becoming Chancellor, it soon became apparent that Mrs Merkel's strength was not in her country's foreign affairs. Her sheltered background growing up in East Germany had meant that opportunities to travel the world were, by Western standards, limited. She was only seven when the Berlin wall was built in 1960. Her understanding of English was better than her speaking ability. She does, however, have one trump card – her fluency in Russian. As the crisis with Russia developed, following the invasion of Crimea and Mr Putin's probing military adventures in eastern Ukraine continued, Mrs Merkel became the West's spokesperson, negotiator and even protector. Mr Putin knew that in Mrs Merkel he had more than met his match. At a G20 summit in Australia in late 2014 Mrs Merkel was reported to have lost her cool with Putin; the London *Economist* reported her as saying that the Russian leader 'tramples with his feet on international law'. She continued with her views on a range of Russian inspired problems, the Balkans, Moldova and what she described as a 'wider conflagration'. In so doing she was declaring herself to be more than just Europe's foreign minister. Germany had, it was clear, replaced the US as the frontline negotiating state when it came to Russian affairs. In the Russian context at least, Mrs Merkel had replaced President Obama as leader.

Foreign affairs

It was not difficult to see that Mrs Merkel's growing international standing and presence placed her as head girl with a diplomatic and ambassadorial team who were little more than sub-prefects. Changing this situation meant reform: reform from the top by giving ambassadors a more proactive role and from the bottom by making the German public aware of the initiatives that their country was taking overseas and the interventions it was making. Germany's low-profile foreign minister Frank-Walter Steimeier was detailed to organise a public consultation called Review 2014.

Crisis – Order – Europe was the title of the final report, published in February 2015. The Review's findings were expressed in predictably bland and vague terms: 'As Germany's clout increases, so too does interest in Germany's foreign policy debates.' The answer, it appeared, was to instigate a 'Change in the federal Foreign Office's corporate culture. Herein lies its greatest potential, as well as a challenge to each and every member of staff. Modern diplomacy must exhibit greater flexibility and agility and become more open and transparent. This is how the Federal Foreign Office wants to meet the challenges and expectations that the experts, the public and its own staff have detailed for German foreign policy. To ensure Germany's place as a leading European nation that is willing to shoulder responsibility world-wide for a peaceful and free international order – and which constantly sets out anew to seek and find innovative methods to do just that.' The *Economist* observed that German foreign policy suffered from a 'culture of atonement'. This was reflected by a perceived need to always act alongside partners and institutions. In 2015, for obvious historical reasons, Germany had still to come to

KEY INDICATORS Germany

	Unit	2011	2012	2013	2014	**2015
Population	m	81.78	*80.52	80.77	*81.10	*81.36
Gross domestic product (GDP)	US$bn	3,577.00	3,427.85	3,731.43	*3,859.55	*0.00
GDP per capita	US$	43,742	42,569	46,200	*47,590	*41,955
GDP real growth	%	3.1	0.9	0.2	*1.6	*1.6
Inflation	%	2.5	2.1	1.6	0.8	*0.2
Unemployment	%	7.1	5.5	5.2	*5.0	*4.9
Natural gas output	bn cum	10.0	9.0	8.2	7.7	–
Coal output	mtoe	44.6	45.7	43.0	43.8	–
Exports (fob) (goods)	US$m	1,493,740	1,460,120	1,506,330	4,192,160	–
Imports (fob) (goods)	US$m	1,273,470	1,221,960	1,248,550	1,188,010	–
Balance of trade	US$m	220,280	238,160	257,780	304,150	–
Current account	US$m	202,730	255,277	251,343	*287,549	*286,778
Total reserves minus gold	US$m	65,163.0	67,422.0	67,365.0	62,266.0	–
Foreign exchange	US$m	38,001.0	37,964.0	38,725.0		–
Exchange rate	per US$	0.75	0.77	0.73	0.82	–

* estimated figure ** forecast figure

terms with the blunt fact that diplomacy could often only work when backed up by a military presence or threat. Although Germany's standing army is bigger than those of the UK and France, its defence budget is smaller both in absolute terms or as a percentage of gross domestic product (GDP) where it fell well behind the North Atlantic Treaty Organisation's (Nato) requirement of 2 per cent.

A sidenote from Dirk Messner of the Deutsche Institut für Entwicklungspolitik (DIE) (German Development Insitute) commendably included in the Review's concluding pages stated very clearly that 'Rising external expectations on those responsible for foreign and global policy can easily lead to a kitchen sink approach: help shape things a bit everywhere, be a bit present everywhere, try not to disappoint anyone. Ad-hocism is, however, the opposite of strategic action.'

The perceived weakness of Germany's foreign office can probably be related to the poor performance of its universities. On the QS international university ranking, the highest ranked German university was Munich's Ludwig-Maximilians Universitat, which placed 75. The highest ranked continental European universities were the EPFL in Lausanne (14) and the Ecole Normale Supérieure in Paris (23). On the equally respected Shanghai rankings, the highest placed German university was Heidelberg, ranked 46. The highest placed European universities were the Swiss Federal Institute of Technology (20) and the University of Copenhagen (35). German students have long complained of inadequate university facilities and outdated teacher-pupil relations. Germany's foreign service has been criticised for being similarly behind the times.

The Importance of Being Schäuble

Leader she may be, but the influential Munich-based *SudDeutsche Zeitung* pointed out that when Angela Merkel was general secretary of the CDU and Wolfgang Schäuble was party chairman, the two party stalwarts had appeared together on a campaign poster over the slogan: 'Europe is like us – we don't always agree but we take the same path'. Mr Schäuble has been Mrs Merkel's finance minister since 2009. He is also perceived to be her confidant and advisor, despite the fact that relations between the two politicians have remained cool, occasionally frosty. The Bavarian newspaper had dubbed Mr Schäuble the *Nebenkanzler* or co-Chancellor, reflecting his importance in government. However, the tide seems to have flowed in Mr Schäuble's direction. Originally known for her gradualism, on many matters – notably the Greek rescue negotiations and the Russian problem – Mrs Merkel appears to have adopted the harder line advocated by Mr Schäuble.

Mr Schäuble had certainly been the visible target for most of the criticism aimed at Germany during the 2015 rescue discussions with Greece. Not all the criticism emanated from Greece or elsewhere in the euro-zone. Within Germany his so called *Sparpolitik* (translated by the *Economist* as 'savings policy', was considered by many left wing Germans as unnecessarily severe. At one stage in the rescue negotiations Mr Schäuble had advocated a temporary Greek exit from the euro within which to get its house in order. His own CDU party seemed divided over the idea and the SPD coalition partners suggested simply that every option be considered. As reported in the *Economist*, a July 2015 poll saw 85 per cent of Germans take the view that a Greek bankruptcy would damage the German economy seriously. Germans had taken exception to suggestions that Greece should receive the same 'haircut' treatment as that given to Germany immediately after the Second World War.

The refugees

The wave of refugees, for the most part Syrians heading for Germany, escalated dramatically in September 2015. Mrs Merkel certainly connected with a majority of Germans who felt that something needed to be done for them. Mrs Merkel went on record with a promise 'to succeed', which as the numbers swelled began to place Germany's infrastructure under severe pressure. Local government began to reproach the Chancellor for a lack of foresight and planning; within Mrs Merkel's own CDU party there were murmurings and misgivings. In mid-September, Manfred Schmidt, the man at the head of Germany's office for immigration and refugees resigned, citing health reasons. Mr Schmidt was not the only official to be criticised; his immediate boss, the interior minister and close ally of Mrs Merkel, Thomas de Maisiere, was also accused of negligence. The sharpest criticism came from the SDP and from the CDU's coalition partner, the Christlich-Soziale Union in Bayern (CSU) (Christian Social Union of Bavaria). Many politicians considered Mrs Merkel's decision to welcome the refugees as a serious mistake.

As winter approached, the question that had to be answered was just how adequate accommodation could be found across Germany for as many as 800,000 refugees. Refuting the steadily growing criticism, Mrs Merkel firmly stated: 'If we are going to have to beg forgiveness for having shown a friendly face in an emergency situation, this is no longer my country.'

The economy

In 2014 Germany was the fourth-largest economy in the world by GDP, after the United States, China and Japan. Much of German economic policy dates back to influences formed in Germany and Austria in the 1930s and contradicting the Keynsian theories that were being espoused in the US and the UK. Thus in the post-financial crash world, where the UK, the US and even Japan, resorted to quantitative easing, in Germany fiscal austerity was the order of the day. Monetary policy was all about price stability and little else. In the view of the Organisation for Economic Co-operation and Development (OECD), the favourable development of the German labour market since 2009 had continued during 2014. Employment rates had reached 74 per cent, a historical peak level and unemployment as well as youth unemployment had continued to fall.

The OECD noted that unemployment rates now stood at 4.7 per cent, the lowest level in 25 years and among the lowest levels in the OECD. Youth unemployment was the third-lowest in the OECD. However, the incidence of long-term unemployment remained stubbornly high: almost every second unemployed person in Germany had been without a job for at least one year, that is above the OECD average and twice as high as, for example, in the United States. In January 2015, Germany became the twenty-sixth OECD country to establish a statutory minimum wage. At around 50 per cent of median average earnings, the €8.50 (US$9.55) per hour minimum in Germany was close to the OECD average value.

This reform was a response to the increase in in-work poverty and the declining ability of the German collective bargaining system to create an effective wage floor. However, its effective anti-poverty impact was reduced by the relatively high taxes on labour in Germany. In the view of the OECD, attention would have to be paid to any negative effects of the new country-wide minimum wage on labour demand in economically depressed areas and for young adults. In eastern Germany, in 2014 – according to the OECD – one in five workers were paid less than the new minimum and even up to two-thirds in the hotels and restaurants sector. The new law therefore implies an increase in the total wage bill of over 10 per cent in some sectors/regions. In 2015 German unemployment was at its lowest for 20 years. That was the good news, as was the fact that budget surpluses seemed to be the order of the day (see below). However, public investment had been wheeled, or rather not been wheeled in, to shore things up. In 1970 in what was then West Germany, public investment was a healthy six per cent of GDP. By 2015 the figure had fallen to 2 per cent. German hesitancy about investment in general could be attributed to nervousness on a number of fronts – Russia, China, Greece were at the top of the list. But the major hesitancy emanated from the Chancellor's office; much of public investment has been sacrificed on the altar of finance minister Schäuble's obsession with balancing the federal books, an objective he had secured ahead of his own schedule, in 2014.

In a June 2015 survey of aspects of the German economy, the International Monetary Fund (IMF) noted that Germany's current large and sustained surpluses began in 2004 and continued into 2015. Although it was difficult to predict the future evolution of Germany's current account, the latest projections suggested that both its duration and size would exceed previous performance. In fact, according to the IMF, compared to the continuing surplus instances in Europe, Germany's surplus did not stand out in terms of its size or duration. Sweden, the Netherlands and Denmark had all experienced large and sustained surpluses since 1995, 2001 and 2008 respectively, with average current account surpluses of 5.7, 6.6 and 5.3 per cent of GDP, respectively. Germany's surplus, with an average size of 6 per cent, was close to the average of these countries. Germany had achieved a previous large and sustained surplus episode during 1985–91.

Germany's record on macro-economic management was without question, pretty exceptional. There were, however, signs in the early months of 2015 that something was not quite right. In 2014, the national airline, Lufthansa, was forced to cancel thousands of flights because of a pay dispute with its pilots. In a large country such as Germany, air travel is seen as a business (and leisure) necessity. In May 2015 it was another form of transport – trains – that ground to a halt. The railway dispute was not a lightning, one day affair; it was the ninth walkout in an 11 month period, which had included a five day strike earlier in 2015, the longest labour dispute in the national rail system – Deutsche Bahn's – 21-year history. Two thirds of long-distance trains and hundreds of commuter services had to be cancelled. This time the leader of the Gewerkschaft Deutscher Lokomotivführer (GDL) (Railway Drivers Union) Klaus Weselsky gave no end date for the strike, but said it would 'last a little longer' than the previous five-day strike.

The GDL had sought a 5 per cent pay rise for its 20,000 drivers and a shorter working week. Deutsche Bahn, which employs 200,000 people, had offered the drivers a 4.7 per cent pay rise plus a one-off €1,000 (US$1,120) payment, but had refused to allow GDL to negotiate on behalf of other workers. An estimated 5.5 million people travell by train each day in Germany and according to the London BBC, economists had estimated that an earlier strike had cost the German economy some €750 million (US$843 million) in lost activity.

Germany's low unemployment rate, estimated by the IMF to be 6.5 per cent in April 2015, has emboldened the country's labour force to the extent that average wages had risen by 2.7 per cent in 2014. Wage growth was expected to accelerate over the second half of 2015 and into 2016 by most observers. In July 2015, the IMF in its annual assessment of the German economy, concluded that the German economy's continued upturn was benefiting from the euro depreciation and lower energy prices and was underpinned by a healthy fiscal position and sound corporate and household balance sheets.

Employment growth has been robust, supported by strong immigration and the unemployment rate hit another post-reunification low at 4.7 per cent. The oil price drop brought inflation temporarily close to zero, which had contributed to lift wage growth to a twenty-year high. The current account surplus reached a new high in 2014, as the oil and gas trade deficit narrowed. Fiscal policy had been mildly contractionary in 2014 and it was expected to turn moderately expansionary in 2015.

While credit conditions remained very favourable, credit growth has been lukewarm, reflecting low demand despite the more dynamic housing market. The ECB Comprehensive Assessment revealed only minor shortcomings in large banks' loan classification or provisioning. The persistent low interest rate environment was putting pressure on banks' profitability and life insurers' solvency.

The IMF expected the current moderate growth momentum to continue as robust real wages boosted private consumption and the euro depreciation strengthened exports, opening up the possibility of a recovery in machinery and equipment investment. All in all, GDP was expected to grow by 1.6 per cent in 2015 and by 1.7 per cent in 2016. Together with a better anchoring of expectations because of the ECB quantitative easing programme, this should gradually push up core and headline inflation. Growth in the medium term, however, was expected to remain constrained by the still weak international environment and fast approaching adverse demographic developments. The anticipation of the ECB's quantitative easing (QE) programme had significantly lowered interest rates and term spreads, weakened the euro and, together with the drop in energy prices, helped overcome the unexpected slowdown of mid-2014. By the end of 2014 and into the first quarter of 2015, investment picked up again while consumption was supported by above-trend disposable income growth. The latter benefited from robust wage growth, a strong labour market and the positive demand effects of the pension reform implemented in 2014 (higher pensions for some mothers and earlier statutory retirement for some categories of workers). The regained domestic demand momentum boosted imports, while the weaker euro during the second half of the year helped strengthen export performance in spite of a slowdown in emerging markets.

With inflation temporarily close to zero (thanks to the oil price drop), core inflation was low and stable at around one per cent, while real compensation per employee increased by 1.7 per cent in 2014. Employment kept growing strongly – although the trend in total hours worked was less dynamic – and the unemployment rate hit another post-reunification low at 4.7 per cent, while Germany became the second largest migration destination in the world after the US in 2014. Recent collective agreements and continuing wage negotiations suggested continued significant real wage growth in 2015. The new minimum wage, introduced in January 2015 and implemented over two years, had had no visible impact on total employment.

Germany's current account surplus continued to grow in 2014, reaching 7.6 per cent of GDP. The narrowing of the oil and gas trade deficit was the main contributor to the expansion in the surplus, which was the largest in the world in US dollar terms. The surplus vis-à-vis euro-zone economies with high borrowing spreads during the 2010–11 sovereign debt crisis (Greece, Ireland, Italy, Portugal and Spain) was stable after declining substantially during the crisis.

The CPI-based real effective exchange rate was roughly stable in 2014, but has since depreciated by six per cent from its 2014 average primarily because of nominal depreciation vis-à-vis the dollar and the Chinese renminbi. Germany's net international investment position (NIIP) continued to grow in 2014, reflecting stronger direct and portfolio investment positions. Yet, monetary and financial institutions cut back their net foreign lending positions, continuing a trend observed since 2009.

Germany's fiscal policy was mildly contractionary in 2014, while it was conversely expected to turn a degree expansionary in 2015. The government presented a balanced federal budget for 2015, one year ahead of schedule. The general government surplus rose to 0.6 per cent of GDP in 2014 – a structural improvement of 0.3 per cent relative to 2013 – owing to lower-than-expected interest payments and one-off revenue items. A negative interest rate–growth rate differential pushed the debt ratio further down, to 74.7 per cent of GDP. The structural fiscal position for 2015 was expected to remain comfortably within the boundaries set by the constitutional debt brake rule at the federal level and the European Medium-Term Objective (MTO) at the general government level (maximum structural deficits of 0.35 per cent and 0.5 per cent of GDP, respectively).

Credit growth remained lukewarm despite record-low interest rates. The yield on 10-year bonds, after reaching a trough of 0.1 per cent in mid-April, recently rebounded sharply as market volatility suddenly jumped – possibly reflecting lower market liquidity – but remained very low from a historical perspective. Already historically low bank lending rates have fallen further with the anticipation of QE, while stock prices have accelerated sharply. So far, however, credit growth has remained subdued, especially in the corporate sector, where companies could finance a large share of their investment needs from retained earnings and cash reserves, resulting in low credit demand. A more dynamic housing market over the previous few years has been accompanied by tepid aggregate mortgage lending growth, although there are signs of acceleration in recent months

The more favourable external environment should support the growth momentum. The robust private consumption dynamics of the previous three quarters is projected to persist with the help of lower energy prices and strong real wage growth. The euro depreciation and lower real interest rate (as QE pushes up inflation expectations) is expected to strengthen exports as well as the long-awaited recovery in machinery and equipment investment. Although corporate credit demand is expected to remain muted in a context of cash-rich corporate balance sheets and increasing profit margins for exporters, QE-induced lower real interest rates are expected to translate into somewhat firmer credit growth.

The fiscal stance is expected to remain slightly expansionary in 2016. Employment growth is likely to slow down as the adverse effect of the lower statutory retirement age for some categories of workers on labour force participation kicks in fully and the already low unemployment rate becomes harder to reduce further. All in all, GDP is expected to grow by 1.6 per cent in 2015 and by 1.7 per cent in 2016. Although German inflation is likely to exceed that in the rest of the euro-zone throughout the forecast horizon, it is not projected to rise above the ECB price stability objective.

Fiscal balances are set to remain comfortably within the boundaries of the fiscal rules. For the remainder of the legislature (2015–17) and beyond, budget plans are centred on a zero balance at the federal level with small surpluses for the general government, backed by buoyant revenue forecasts. The IMF expected larger surpluses than the German authorities, mostly on account of lower projected interest payments, enough to bring public debt below 60 per cent of GDP by 2020.

The almost iconic current account surplus is projected to grow further in 2015 and decline only moderately in the medium term. The oil and gas trade balance is expected to continue to improve as energy prices remain lower on average than in 2014 (see Energy below). In addition, the real exchange rate depreciation (of 6 per cent in effective terms relative to 2014) would also put upward pressure on the external balance. As a result, the surplus is expected to exceed 8 per cent of GDP, a record high, and decline gradually to 6.7 per cent in 2020, as the terms of trade windfall is gradually spent, private investment recover modestly and stronger wage growth relative to euro-zone trading partners contributes to realign competitiveness. The IMF concluded its report by noting that the risks confronting the German economy are more balanced than a year earlier, but that uncertainties remained. There could be benefits arising should the expected stimulus from monetary policy and oil prices that are already in the pipeline proved more effective than expected. On the downside, as noted above, a number of external risks could affect Germany adversely, with their possible impact ranging from low to moderate.

Energy

Germany may not be an oil or gas producer, but it nevertheless plays an important role in the international hydrocarbons business. According to the United States government Energy Information Administration, Germany had more than 2.1 million barrels per day of crude refining capacity at the end of 2014, making it one of the largest refiners in the world and the second largest in Europe and Eurasia after Russia. Germany imports oil for consumption or in transit through several crude oil pipelines and sea ports. The two largest pipelines are the Druzhba pipeline from Russia via Belarus and Poland and the Trans Alpine pipeline from Trieste, on the Adriatic Sea. Wilhelmshaven, Germany's sole deep-water port, handles most of Germany's international oil trade.

According to the BP Statistical Review of World Energy, Germany was the largest energy consumer in Europe and the seventh-largest energy consumer in the world in 2014. Its size and location give it a considerable influence over the European Union's energy sector. However, Germany relies on imports to meet the majority of its energy demand.

Petroleum and other liquids continue to be Germany's main source of energy. In 2014, Germany consumed 2.4 million barrels per day, making up 36 per cent of the country's total primary energy consumption in 2014, according to BP.

The transport sector accounts for the largest share of petroleum product demand. The German government has a goal of putting one million electric vehicles on the road by 2020 and six million by 2030. At the end of 2014, there were some 24,000 electric vehicles registered in Germany.

Risk assessment

Economy	Good
Politics	Good
Regional stability	Good

Muslims in Germany

% of population	3.7
Sunni (% of Muslims)	87.5
Shi'a (% of Muslims)	12.5

COUNTRY PROFILE

1871 Germany was unified under the Prussian royal house of the Hohenzollerns. Wilhelm I was appointed Germany's first Kaiser. After defeating France in the Franco-Prussian War, Alsace-Lorraine was annexed by Germany.
1880–1900 After Germany became Europe's leading industrial power, it attempted to expand territorially and become a world power, establishing colonies in Africa and trying to influence politics in the Balkans.
1914–18 Germany invaded Belgium and then France. The UK intervened, but the war in France became one of attrition until 1917, when US troops joined British and French forces. The First World War ended in 1918 with Germany's defeat. Kaiser Wilhelm II went into exile in the Netherlands. The Weimar Republic, a federation of 19 states, was declared in November 1918.
1919 Friedrich Ebert was appointed Germany's first president. Germany was called on to make massive financial reparations and to cede Alsace-Lorraine to France and parts of the Saarland to Poland, as part of the Treaty of Versailles. The Rhineland was de-militarised and occupied by the Western European powers.
1920s Germany was gripped by an economic depression, suffering from hyperinflation and high unemployment. As it could not afford to pay war reparations, France and Belgium occupied the industrialised Rhur as a protest.
1931 The instability of the economy and of democratic government led to the fascist National-Sozialistische Deutsche Arbeiterpartei (NSDAP) (Nationalist Socialist German Workers' Party) or Nazis, led by Austrian Adolf Hitler, becoming the largest party in the German parliament.
1933 Adolf Hitler was appointed chancellor of Germany.
1934 The Nazis consolidated their power. Hitler established himself as the führer (leader) of the Third Reich. The economy was rebuilt, all other political parties were banned and Hitler's opponents – Jews and other minorities – were placed in concentration camps.
1936 German troops re-took the Rhineland and provided military aid to Spanish nationalists fighting the Spanish Civil War. Germany, Italy and Japan formed an alliance.
1938 Austria became part of the German Third Reich after its pro-Nazi chancellor, Arthur von Seyss Inquart, invited German troops into the country. Annexation of Sudetanland, Czechoslovakia.
1939 Germany signed a non-aggression pact with the Soviet Union. Britain and France declared war on Germany after German troops invaded Poland.
1940 Germany captured most of Western Europe while most of Eastern Europe had pro-German puppet governments installed.
1941 Germany invaded the Soviet Union. Following Japan's attack on Pearl Harbor, the US declared a state of war with Japan; three days later, Japan's allies, Germany and Italy, declared war on the US.
1944–45 The US, Britain and the Soviet Union liberated Nazi-occupied Europe. Adolf Hitler committed suicide in Berlin. Following the end of the Second World War, Germany was occupied by the Allied powers.
1949 The Federal Republic of Germany (FRG) was established in the western zone by unifying the British, French and American zones of control, and the Deutsche Demokratische Republik (DDR) (German Democratic Republic (GDR)) was established in the east, under the Sozialistische Einheitspartei Deutschlands (SED) (Socialist Unity Party), following failure of negotiations to establish a unified administration. Konrad Adenauer became federal chancellor. Waltar Ulbricht became general secretary of the GDR's ruling communist party until 1971 when Erich Honeker replaced him.
1951 The FRG and France merged their coal and steel industries through the European Coal and Steel Community (ECSC).
1953 Severe food shortages and the policy of 'sovietisation' in GDR led to uprisings and strikes, suppressed by Soviet troops, causing large numbers of refugees to begin fleeing to the West.
1954 The FRG was admitted to NATO.
1955 The GDR became a member of the Soviet Union's Warsaw Pact.
1957 The FRG declared Berlin its capital. Bonn became the seat of government until reunification.
1958 The FRG became a founding member of the forerunner of the EU, the European Economic Community (EEC).
1961 The GDR constructed the Berlin Wall between eastern and western sectors to stem the flow of refugees to West Berlin.
1963–66 Ludwig Erhard succeeded Adenauer as federal chancellor.
1966–69 Federal Chancellor Kurt Georg Kiesinger's coalition comprised the two largest parties, Christlich-Demokratische Union (CDU) (Christian Democratic Union)/Christlich-Soziale Union (CSU) (Christian Social Union) and the Sozialdemokratische Partei Deutschland (SPD) (Social Democratic Party of Germany). He chose the mayor of Berlin, Willi Brandt, as his foreign minister.
1969 Willi Brandt (SPD) became chancellor. He implemented a policy of *ostpolitik*, orienting FRG foreign policy towards Eastern Europe and détente with the GDR.
1971 Erich Honecker became leader of the GDR, which became one of the most hardline members of the Warsaw Pact. In the late 1980s, Honecker resisted calls for democratisation on the Russian *glasnost* pattern.
1973 The FRG and GDR joined the UN.
1974 Helmut Schmidt became federal chancellor after the fall of Brandt in a security scandal. Disputes over the deteriorating economic situation, nuclear power and defence policy led to coalition instability and the withdrawal of the Freie Demokratische Partei (FDP) (Free Democratic Party)
1982 The CDU leader, Helmut Kohl, became federal chancellor.
1989–90 The Soviet Union withdrew support for the Honecker regime, prompting his resignation. With growing pressure for reunification, the Berlin wall was breached on 9 November in a dramatic show of people-power as border guards declined to hold back protestors. After a further 11 months and a negotiated treaty the GDR acceded to the FDR and the two entities were officially reunified on 3 October 1990. Germany, France and the Benelux countries signed the Schengen Agreement abolishing passport controls between them. Helmut Kohl won the first free German election since 1931.
1994 Federal elections resulted in a narrow victory for Chancellor Kohl and his CDU-led coalition.
1998 The SPD gained the largest share of the vote in the elections. Gerhard Schröder became chancellor and formed a coalition government with Bündis 90 (Alliance 90) and Die Grünen (Greens).
1999 Germany became a founding member of the European Economic and Monetary Union (Emu). Johannes Rau was elected as federal president.
2000 Helmut Kohl resigned as chairman of the CDU following revelations about illicit funding to the party during his time as chancellor. He was replaced by Angela Merkel.
2002 The euro replaced the Deutschemark. Gerhard Schröder was re-elected as chancellor by one of the narrowest margins in German election history.
2003 The Constitutional Court rejected a government request to ban the neo-Nazi National Democratic Party, after accusations that state agents had infiltrated the party's ranks, acting as *agents provocateurs* to discredit it.

2004 Horst Köhler took office as federal president.
2005 Chancellor Schröder called early elections which were deemed inconclusive with the CDU/CSU winning 35.2 per cent of the vote and the SPD 34.2 per cent. Angela Merkel became chancellor, leading a coalition government of CDU/CSU and SPD. She also became Germany's first woman chancellor and the first chancellor from the former communist eastern part of Germany.
2006 Parliament approved proposals to amend the constitution to reform the working of the federal structure. The government decided that German armed forces should engage actively in an international security role.
2007 China's economic growth overtook Germany's to become the world's third leading trading nation after the US.
2008 Chancellor Merkel addressed the Israeli parliament, the first given by a German head of government, during Israel's celebrations marking 60 years since its founding. The government came up with US$68 billion to save one of Germany's largest banks, Hypo Real Estate, from collapse. The German economy officially fell into recession.
2009 The government introduced a US$63 billion stimulus package to help shore up the economy. Horst Köhler was re-elected as Federal President. The German economy officially grew out of recession. In parliamentary elections the CDU/CSU won 38.4 per cent of the vote (239 seats of 622). Chancellor Merkel headed a CDU/CSU coalition government with FDP, to form a conservative, pro-business, liberal government.
2010 Chancellor Merkel persuaded parliament to commit €22.4 billion (US$30.68 billion) of German money to an EU fund providing a loan to Greece; there was popular discontent at the move. President Köhler resigned, following a political row sparked by his statement that Germany must sometimes deploy its military to protect its international interests 'for example free trade routes'. President of the Bundesrat, Jens Böhrnsen, became acting president, until the Federal Convention elected Christian Wulff; he took office.
2011 In May, the government announced that all of Germany's nuclear reactors would be closed down by 2022. A virulent strain of E-coli killed 37 people and laid low over 3,228 people by 15 June; the outbreak was traced to a farm in Lower Saxony. German agricultural exports to Russia and Taiwan were suspended. In June, Germany led Europe's second Greek bailout of US$126.5 billion (€90 billion), when the risk of Greece defaulting rocked European money markets and investors.
2012 Horst Seehofer became acting president on 17 February after President Wulff resigned, amid the latest in a series of scandals involving alleged political favours and financial impropriety while Wulff was premier of Lower Saxony. A legal investigation into the allegations was underway and the public prosecutor's office considered there was initial suspicion of bribes given and received. On 18 March, Joachim Gauck, a former Lutheran pastor from East Germany, was elected by parliament as president; he won 991 votes out of 1,232. The opening of the newly revamped Berlin Brandenburg airport was postponed from June to March 2013, due to the delay in completing the fire safety system. The €2.5 billion (US$3.1 billion) upgraded airport project has been subject to a number of postponements, beginning in 2011. On 12 September, the Constitutional Court rejected a lawsuit to block funding of the European Stability Mechanism (ESM) by the federal government. The motion argued that that such funding constituted higher payment by Germany, which needed ratification by referendum and without this the funding violated the constitution. However the court did impose conditions, which included a cap on Germany's contribution to the ESM that could not be overruled by parliament. On 19 October, Chancellor Merkel proposed a European banking supervisor to heads of government at an EU summit. She explained that a mechanism to be used by the supervisor had to be in place before Eurozone banks are allowed to directly access EU rescue funds.
2013 A new political party, Alternative for Germany (founded by Bernd Lucke in March) held its first national conference in April. The party is opposed to the single European currency and wants the euro abolished, with states returning to their original currencies. Germany and the US called for the release of deposed president Morsi on 12 July. The 22 September elections were won convincingly by the Christlich-Demokratische Union Deutschlands (CDU) (Christian Democratic Union of Germany/Christian Social Union of Bavaria) coalition with 311 seats, just five seats short of an absolute majority. Her former partner in government, the FDP, won no seats. On 4 October Mrs Merkel began talks with the SPD. The talks were attended by seven members each from the CDU, the SPD and the CSU. Mrs Merkel also held talks with the Greens, but they failed on 15 October. On 21 October a group of SPD members backed a statement agreeing to the start of formal talks, including agreeing to a series of economic demands. Parliament re-convened on 22 October with Mrs Merkel presiding over a caretaker government until a governing coalition can be established. Revelations that the US may have been listening in to Mrs Merkel's mobile telephone lead to a cooling of relations in October. Together with France, Germany called for talks with the US about intelligence gathering activities. Mrs Merkel said at an EU summit in Brussels on 24 October that once the seeds of mistrust had been sown it made intelligence co-operation more difficult.
2015 The leader of the 'anti-Islamisation' movement Pegida, Lutz Bachmann, resigned on 21 January after he reportedly described refugees 'animals' and 'scumbags' in Facebook comments.

Political structure

Constitution

Federal republic; under the 1949 *Grundgesetz* (constitution), Germany has a high degree of devolution.

The federal structure is formed from 16 *Bundesländer* (regional states), including the city of Berlin. Each state has its own constitution, an elected legislature and a government with responsibilities including education and public order.

Form of state

Federal parliamentary democratic republic

The executive

Executive authority is held by the Bundesregierung (federal government). The chief executive and head of government is the Bundeskanzler (federal chancellor), chosen by the Bundestag (lower house of the federal assembly) and usually the leader of the ruling party, who then appoints his own ministers. The Bundespräsident (federal president) is elected for a five-year term by the members of the Bundesversammlung (federal assembly), but has largely ceremonial duties.

National legislature

The bicameral, Bundesversammlung (federal assembly), consists of the Bundestag (lower house) and Bundesrat (upper house). The Bundestag nominally has 598 members, of which 299 are elected in single seat constituencies and 299 allocated through party lists by proportional representation. Voters vote for both one candidate and one party per election. All members are elected for the term of the parliament, up to four-years.

The Bundesrat consists of 69 members chosen by the 16 state governors or landtags.

Legal system

The Federal Constitutional Court rules on constitutional issues, taking appeals from the lower courts. German law is largely code law that traces its roots to the Roman legal system. The court system below the Constitutional Court includes five branches: ordinary, labour, administrative, social and fiscal courts. Civil and criminal cases are normally in the jurisdiction of the ordinary court system, which is organised in local, regional and state tiers with a federal tribunal (Bundesgerichtshof), presiding over the system. Since the signing of the Single European Act in 1986, the European Court of Justice (ECJ) has been the highest court of appeal for rulings on matters affected by EU law.

Last elections

2 July 2010 (presidential, indirect); 22 September 2013 (parliamentary)

Results: Parliamentary (2013): Christlich-Demokratische Union Deutschlands (Christian Democratic Union of Germany) (CDU) won 40.5 per cent of the vote (255 seats out of 630), Christlich-Soziale Union in Bayern (CSU) (Christian Social Union of Bavaria) 8.9 per cent (56), Sozialdemokratische Partei Deutschlands (SPD) (Social Democratic Party of Germany) 30.5 per cent (192), Freie Demokratische Partei (FDP) (Free Democratic Party) 4.8 per cent (0), Die Linkspartei (The Left Party) 10.2 per cent (64), Die Grünen (The Greens) 10.0 per cent (63). Turnout was 71.5 per cent.

Federal President: Joachim Gauck won 80.4 per cent of the votes in the Federal Convention (991 out of 1228), Beat Klarsfeld won 10.2 per cent (126) and Olaf Rose won 0.2 per cent (3). Turnout was 99.4 per cent.

Next elections

June 2017 (presidential); no later than 22 October 2017 (parliamentary).

Political parties

Ruling party

Coalition lead by Christlich-Demokratische Union Deutschlands (Christian Democratic Union of Germany) (CDU)/Christlich-Soziale Union in Bayern (CSU) (Christian Social Union of Bavaria) with Sozialdemokratische Partei Deutschlands (SPD) (Social Democratic Party of Germany) (from 22 Sep 2013)

Main opposition party

Sozialdemokratische Partei Deutschlands (SPD) (Social Democratic Party of Germany)

Population

80.80 million (2013)*

Last census: March 2004: 82,491,000

Population density: 235 inhabitants per square km. Urban population 74 per cent (2010 Unicef).

Annual growth rate: 0.2 per cent, 1990–2010 (Unicef).

Ethnic make-up

The majority of the population is Germanic. There is a small ethnic Slavonic (Sorbian) enclave in the south-east state of Saxony (approximately 60,000) and a Danish minority in the northern state of Schleswig-Holstein (approximately 50,000). There are an estimated 70,000 Sinti and Roma German nationals, mainly in the state's cities and towns . Some neighbourhoods in industrial cities are dominated by guest workers, mostly from Turkey, the Balkans and southern Europe.

Religions

The two principal religions are Roman Catholicism and Protestantism. The German Evangelical (Lutheran) church dominates in the overwhelmingly Protestant eastern, northern and central parts of the country. Members of the Catholic church form a majority in the south and west.

Education

Participation levels in primary and secondary education are almost 100 per cent, while 45 per cent attend some form of tertiary education. Approximately 4.8 per cent of GNP is spent on public education.

The public school system is administered by the individual states. Primary education is free and grants are made available for secondary education in institutions where fees are charged.

A year of kindergarten is followed by four years of primary school (*Grundschule*). Pupils are then screened for later admission into either advanced study or specialised and vocational training. Those in the advanced track continue at a *Gymnasium* to the age of 19, and then take the *Arbitur* comprehensive academic examination for admission to university. The majority of pupils attend vocational college after the age of 16.

In June 2004, the German cabinet agreed to give 10 of the country's leading unversities and researsh centres an extra US$2.3 billion, over five years, from 2006.

Compulsory years: Six to 16

Pupils per teacher: 17 in primary schools

Health

There is no national health service, instead comprehensive healthcare is administered by the individual states. Health insurance provides 100 per cent of workers' salary for six weeks then drops to 80 per cent for 78 weeks. Health insurance also covers maternity and death benefits. Health insurance premiums, split by worker and employer in the case of those with high salaries, average 12.5 per cent of gross earnings.

HIV/Aids

HIV prevalence: 0.1 per cent aged 15–49 in 2003 (World Bank)

Life expectancy: 79 years, 2004 (WHO 2006)

Fertility rate/Maternal mortality rate: 1.4 births per woman, 2010 (Unicef)

Birth rate/Death rate: 8.6 births per 1,000 population; 10.3 deaths per 1,000 population (2003).

Child (under 5 years) mortality rate (per 1,000): 4 per 1,000 live births (WHO 2012)

Head of population per physician: 3.37 physicians per 1,000 people, 2003 (WHO 2006)

Welfare

Germany's health and social security systems are among the most generous in the world. Health, unemployment and retirement insurance are mandatory for most ordinary wage-earners under a wide-ranging social insurance system that has developed over more than a century. The system operates on a payroll withholding plan with contributions from workers, employers and government.

The welfare system provides assistance for all needy people who are unable to fend for themselves. There are funds for the support of widows, orphans and disabled people. The state makes available housing allowances for the poor in addition to its subsidies to low-income housing construction.

Changes introduced in 2005 affected the newly unemployed and those without work for more than a year, who received only a flat rate benefit and any additional sum was means tested, while measures to supervise and support those seeking work was stepped up. These measures were introduced to reduce the financial burden of the welfare system.

The Constitutional Court ruled that workers with children should pay a lower premium for the compulsory nursing insurance scheme than childless people.

Pensions

Of major concern is the rapidly changing demographic balance. As Germany's population continues to shrink, a smaller working population will have to bear the burden of an ever increasing number of pensioners. Pensions cost Germany the equivalent of 11–12 per cent of annual GDP and this is projected to rise to 18–19 per cent by 2040.

Contributions to the state pension scheme, which is mandatory except for workers with high salaries, range up to 18.7 per cent of gross income and are shared equally by worker and employer. The normal retirement age is 63 for men and 60 for women.

Main cities
Berlin (capital, estimated population 3.5 million (m) in 2012), Hamburg (1.8m), Munich (1.4m, Bavaria), Cologne (1.0m), Frankfurt am Main (687,107), Stuttgart (611,342), Düsseldorf (591,122), Dortmund (591,122), Essen (572,962), Bremen (546,952).

Languages spoken
English is widely spoken, especially in business circles; French is also spoken, particularly in the Saarland. In the north in Schleswig-Holstein, Danish is spoken by the Danish minority and taught in schools. Regional dialects often differ markedly from standard German. There is an ongoing debate on language reform in Germany. It is almost 100 years since language laws were last comprehensively reformed.
Sorbian, North and West Frisian, Romani, Turkish and Kurdish are also spoken.

Official language/s
German

Media
The constitution guaranteed freedom of the press. Germany has several international conglomerates that produce material for all media outlets, including Bertelsmann, ProSiebenSat.1 and Axel Springer.

Press
There are few national newspapers, most publications are regionally based and may be distributed nationally. Although newspaper circulations at over 21 million the figure has been falling since the 1990s. There are hundreds of newspaper titles, most of which are locally produced. Tabloid newspapers are referred to as 'boulevard press'. Most newspapers are subscribed to rather than purchased daily.
Dailies: Major national publications include, in German, *Bild* (www.bild.de) a tabloid with the highest circulation, *Süddeutsche Zeitung* (SZ) (www.sueddeutsche.de), *Frankfurter Allegemeine Zeitung* (FAZ) (www.faz.net), *Frankfurter Rundschau* (www.fr-online.de) and *Tageszeitung* (www.taz.de).
Foreign language newspapers are published in Berlin, in French and Spanish.
Weeklies: In German, an influential newspaper with more analysis and background information is *Die Zeit* (www.zeit.de); other news magazines include *Der Spiegel* (www.spiegel.de) with the largest circulation and has an English-language edition, *Stern* (www.stern.de), *Focus* (www.focus.de) and the illustrated magazine *Superillu* (www.superillu.de). A few of the national dailies produce Sunday papers
Business: In German, *Börsen Zeitung* (www.boersen-zeitung.com) published Tuesday–Saturday is a financial newspaper, *Handelsblatt* (www.handelsblatt.com) and *Aktiv* (www.aktiv-online.info) for general business news; most national daily newspapers have sections on business and finance, including. Weekly publications include *WirtschaftsWoche* (www.wiwo.de) a economic magazine covering many aspects of business and *Kapital*, which looks at economic issues from a political standpoint; they are both published by the GWP Media Group (www.gwp.de).
There are numerous trade and business publications. The German Institute of Business Management publishes a range of periodical of specific interest, on company law and governance.
Periodicals: There are over 800 general magazines and 1,000 specialist periodicals of offer.
In German, the monthly, *NinetoFive* is an imprint of *WirtschaftsWoche* (www.wiwo.de) with lifestyle contents for the office worker. *Lieraturen* (www.literaturen-online.de) is a literary monthly magazine and *Brigitte* (www.brigitte.de) is a women's magazine published fortnightly.
In English, *Exberliner* (www.exberliner.com) is published bi-monthly.

Broadcasting
Public broadcasting is funded by licence fees.
Radio: ARD (www.ard.de) is a consortium of national, public broadcasters providing a nationwide service with regional based programmes; some collaborate to produce shows of common interest. Most produce their own programmes of news and genre music. Most operate on the FM bandwidth and some are available digitally (DAB). Another public network is DeutschlandRadio (www.dradio.de) operates two national networks, with news and cultural programmes and a music channel. Deutsche Welle (www.dwelle.de) provides an international service in seven foreign languages, with news in 23 other languages, broadcasting via radio, internet and mobile/cell phones.
There are an abundance of private, commercial regional radio stations. Large media conglomerates operate radio stations and well as private interests catering for all genres.
Television: Germany has the largest and most competitive television market in Europe. Two of the largest television channel, ZDF (www.zdf.de) and ARD (www.ard.de), are national public services. ARD is a network of regional channels while ZDF is a nationwide channel that also broadcasts in Austria, Luxembourg and Switzerland. Both produce their own contents in a full range of programmes. There are private, commercial channels including Europe's largest TV, radio and production company, RTL Television (www.rtl.de), Sat.1 (www.sat1.de) and pay-to-view channels, specialising in genres such as films (Premiere (www.premiere.de)), sport (Arena (www.arena.tv)), documentaries and music. All public and private, major networks deliver German satellite TV programmes to international subscribers.
Germany plans to begin halting analogue TV transmission from 2008, as regional digital services are made available, completing the switch by 2010.
National news agency: DPA (Deutsche Presse-Agentur)
Other news agencies: Pressetext Deutschland (business news):www.pressetext.de

Economy
In 2014, the German economy was the fourth largest in the world; it is certainly the largest economy in Europe and is a leading member of the EU's European Monetary Union (EMU).
Typical for advanced economies, the service sector constitutes over 69 per cent of GDP, agriculture has fallen progressively to around 1 per cent and the remainder is industry and manufacturing. Germany has many world-class products with global brands, including vehicles, pharmaceuticals, biotechnology and medical and genetic engineering, aerospace and precision machinery, electronics, building materials, beverages and foodstuffs and textiles. Primary industries include iron and steel, coal and natural gas production.
In 2010 Germany pulled out of deep recession (GDP growth was -5.6 per cent in 2009) reaching an expansion of 4.1 per cent - the highest since the 1980s. However, after this peak, GDP growth started to fall steadily, dropping to as low as 0.1 per cent in 2013, before recovering slightly to the moderate growth rate of 1.6 per cent in 2014 when a weaker euro helped to make German exports more competitive. Boosted growth is expected in 2015 on account of extremely low inflation due to low global energy prices and a weak euro.
The banking sector was caught up in the crisis from the beginning, when in 2007, the Sachsen Landsbank, a regional bank, was sold, as it neared collapse, to another larger banking entity, and had to rely on €17 billion (US$23.15 billion) of public funding. Other financial institutions were also hit by so-called toxic debts due to the sub-prime mortgage failure in the US. In 2008, Germany's second largest bank, Commerzbank, was forced to write-off US$1.1 billion; the Deutsche Bank warned of credit losses of US$3.9 billion

and Hypo Real Estate was saved by a US$38.7 billion take-over deal with another private bank. Germany was the first advanced economy to fall into recession, but it was also one of first to climb out, due to government stimulus packages plus growing exports and increasing consumer spending.
Germany became the reluctant paymaster of the euro-zone as the economic crisis in Greece, from April–May 2010, threatened to destabilise the euro unless it received financial assistance from other members of the EMU. Despite unwillingness by the German public to underwrite a profligate economy, large amounts of Greek debt held in German banks were bought-up by the German government, as a US$146.2 billion (€110 billion) three-year loan was agreed, backed by the International Monetary Fund (IMF), plus another €130 billion (US$165 billion) from 2012-14. In an effort to stabilise the euro the government in May 2010 banned temporarily its ten most important financial institutions from selling naked credit default swaps and the short-selling of government bonds, which, it claimed, was exacerbating the European debt crisis resulting in the euro plummeting to a four-year low.
In order to address the fact the German economy is suffering from low levels of investment, the government has planned to invest €15 billion over 2016–18, primarily on investment.

External trade

As a member of the European Union, Germany operates within a community-wide free trade area, with tariffs set as a whole. Internationally, the EU has free trade agreements with a number of nations and trading blocs worldwide. It is Europe's leading export trader and the world's third largest vehicle exporter. Exports accounted for 45.6 per cent of GDP in 2014.

Imports

Include machinery, vehicles, chemicals, foodstuffs, textiles and metals raw materials.

Main sources: The Netherlands (12.9 per cent of total in 2014), France (7.8 per cent), China (6.6 per cent)

Exports

Principal exports include machinery, vehicles and aerospace, chemicals and pharmaceuticals, electrical and electronic equipment and plastics.

Main destinations: France (8.9 per cent of total in 2014), US (8.5 per cent), UK (7.0 per cent)

Agriculture

Farming

Germany has always provided incentives and subsidies for agriculture, which is generally regarded as a national resource.
Most of Germany's agriculture is now governed by the EU's fundamental reform to the Common Agricultural Policy (CAP), which was introduced in Germany in 2005. The subsidies paid on farm output, which tended to benefit large farms and encourage overproduction, were replaced by single farm payments not conditional on production.
Livestock production has long been the most important part of the sector, but it is steadily declining.
Agriculture now contributes 0.9 per cent to GDP and employs only 2 per cent of the workforce.

Fishing

West German sea fishing has experienced a sharp decline in recent decades. The government has made some subsidies available, but policy is largely an EU matter. The total seafood catch declined rapidly to just over 300,000 tonnes per annum during the mid-1990s. Since then catches have fallen to around 250,000 tonnes per year. Freshwater catches have also seen a drop in quantity of about one-fifth over the same period.
The homeports of the East German deep-sea fishing fleets are Rostock-Marienehe and Sassnitz. The fleets work the waters off Iceland, Greenland, Labrador and Newfoundland and off the coast of West Africa. Inland fisheries account for only 4 per cent of the annual catch.

Forestry

Forest accounts for nearly a third of the land area estimated at around 11 million hectares (ha). These are located mainly in the south, centre and east of the country, with relatively little on the northern plain. Most of the forest area is available for wood supply. The growing stock per hectare is high and has been increasing. About 50 per cent of forests are publicly owned.
Germany has a strong forest industry and is one of the leading producers of wood-based panels and paper in the global market. The large-scale engineered wood product industry is dependent partially on sawnwood imports. Paper production is also partly based on imported wood pulp. It is one of the largest exporters and consumers of recycled paper.

Industry and manufacturing

The industrial sector accounts for 30.2 per cent of GDP and employs approximately 30 per cent of the workforce.
Germany is a leading European producer of motor vehicles and accessories, industrial plant, machine tools, electrical goods, scientific instruments, chemicals, pharmaceuticals and consumer goods.
Traditional industries (steel, shipbuilding) have contracted because of foreign competition and weaker demand.
Some companies have moved into entirely new industries in order to take advantage of government deregulation and growth in service industries.
Strenuous efforts are being made to modernise industry in western Germany through the use of electronics and more flexible production techniques, and to restructure industry in eastern Germany which has shown a increase in competitiveness, in terms of price and quality.

Tourism

With a complex history and culture, mixed landscape and cities, Germany can offer a full range of tourist activities to visitors and its own population. There are over 30 archaeological, ancient and historic sites and three natural sites included on Unesco's World Heritage List. Germany's strong economic performance has resulted in a buoyant tourism industry. Germany is at the same time the top country for outbound tourism. Business travel is an important component of the sector, with conference centres located in all major cities and good transport links including the famed *autobahn*, a high speed rail network and ancillary airports.
Travel and tourism directly contributed 3.8 per cent of GDP (US$123.7 billion) in 2014 and in total, including indirect contribution, was 8.9 per cent. The industry directly and indirectly employed 11.7 per cent (5.0 million jobs) of the total work force.

Mining

Deposits of lignite are huge and located in eastern Germany, along with significant deposits of the more valuable anthracite, potassium salts and uranium ore. However, there are relatively few feasibly accessible natural resources other than large supplies of black and brown coal, so Germany is largely dependent on imports.
High extraction costs mean that exploitation of small deposits of iron ore, copper, lead, tin and zinc are limited.

Hydrocarbons

Total proven oil reserves stood at 232.6 million barrels in 2014, however with consumption at 2.4 million barrels per day (bpd) and crude oil production at around 100,000bpd Germany has to import a major proportion of its oil requirements. Germany is a major oil refining country with 14 sites and a total capacity of 2.1 million bpd. Germany is also the world's largest producer of bio-diesel, producing around 33,000bpd.

Proven natural gas reserves were 42.5 billion cubic metres (cum) at the end of 2014, located onshore in the north-western state of Niedersachsen. Offshore reserves, in the North Sea, are subjected to tight environmental regulations that curtail further exploration, development and production. Germany is one of the world's largest consumers of natural gas, with supplies imported from Russia, Norway and The Netherlands. The direct 1,200km, Nord Stream, natural gas pipeline underneath the Baltic Sea that transports Russian gas between the Russian town of Vyborg to the German town of Greifswald became operational in November 2011. It bypasses existing pipelines that traverse the Ukraine, thereby minimising disruption caused by third-party, foreign disputes. The project finally cost US$7.7 billion, with German companies controlling a 49 per cent stake in the pipeline and the remainder in Russian hands.
Coal is Germany's main hydrocarbon resource. In 2014, coal reserves stood at 40.5 billion tonnes and production totalled 43.8 million tonnes oil equivalent (toe), a decrease of 2.1 per cent on the 2013 figure. The majority of its coal is the less valuable sub-bituminous and lignite (brown coal), which is typically used in power stations, but is a heavy atmospheric pollutant.

Energy

There are over 2,800 power plants in Germany with an installed generating capacity of over 179 gigawatts (GW), producing over 625 billion-kilowatt hours (kWh) of electricity in 2014, over a quarter of which came from renewable resources. The energy mix is divided between domestically produced brown coal (24.9 per cent), nuclear energy (15.5 per cent) and imported hard coal (18.9 per cent); the remainder is produced from gas and renewable sources such as hydropower and wind. Germany has 17 nuclear reactors, which provided 22 million tonnes oil equivalent (mtoe) in 2014. In March 2011 four stations were closed following the earthquake and tsunami at the Fukushima plant in Japan. Then in May the government announced that the seven oldest reactors, which were already subject to a moratorium, and the Kruemmel nuclear power plant, would end production. Six other plants will be closed in 2021 and the last three in 2022.

Financial markets

There are eight German stock exchanges – located in Frankfurt, Dusseldorf, Munich, Berlin, Hamburg, Stuttgart, Hanover and Bremen. The Frankfurt Stock Exchange is the dominant trading floor with more than half the volume traded. Combined volume on the eight German exchanges exceeds that of all other European financial centres except London.

Stock exchange
Frankfurter Wertpapierbörse (FWB) Frankfurt Stock Exchange

Commodity exchange
Risk Management Exchange (RMX)

Banking and insurance

A sophisticated banking system underpins the country's economic strength.
There are three main categories: central bank; multi-purpose banks, including commercial, co-operative and (publicly owned) regional Landesbanks and savings banks; and specialist banks, including mortgage banks and instalment credit houses.
Many banks have important shareholdings in industrial companies and bankers sit on the supervisory boards of many companies.
In 2003, Josef Ackermann, the chief executive of Germany's main bank Deutsche Bundesbank, was put on trial for corruption. Although initially cleared, a retrial was ordered in December 2005 and Ackermann is facing increasing calls for his resignation.

Central bank
Deutsche Bundesbank; European Central Bank (ECB)

Time

GMT plus one hour (daylight saving, late March to late October, GMT plus two hours)

Geography

The Alps form the southern border with Switzerland and Austria. Germany's southern and eastern borders facing the Czech Republic are also demarcated by mountain ranges. The eastern border with Poland follows the Oder and Neisse rivers. The north is a low, wide coastal plain along the North and Baltic seas, which are separated by Denmark's Jutland peninsula. Germany's western borders join (in an anti-clockwise direction) the Netherlands, Belgium, Luxembourg, France and Switzerland.
Picturesque, forested highlands dominate the central and southern regions. The country is drained by the Danube, Rhine, Elbe, Weser and Oder river systems.
The highest mountain, with an elevation of 2,962 metres, is an alpine peak called Zugspitze, straddling the border with Austria. The main centres of population are concentrated in the west, along the middle and lower Rhine from Karlsruhe, near the French border, and from there northward through the highly industrialised Ruhr conurbation, to the Netherlands border. The German segment of the Rhine is 865km long, all of it navigable. On the south-east side of Europe's continental divide or watershed, the Danube flows eastward from its source in the Black Forest, through 647km of west Germany, to leave the country at the Austrian border at Passau on its way to the Black Sea. There is an important canal system allowing ships to sail from the Oder to the Elbe (to Prague).

Hemisphere
Northern

Climate

Moderate summers and rainy, bleak winters. Most of the country has a typical north-west coastal climate, heavily influenced by moist maritime air masses from the Atlantic. The eastern fringe of the country is sometimes influenced by the continental high pressure centre, making for somewhat colder winters and warmer summers. Prevailing winds are usually from the west.

Dress codes

It is customary to wear a suit and tie in banks, businesses and government offices.

Entry requirements

Passports
Required by all except citizens of Schengen agreement countries who may travel with national ID cards.

Visa
Required by all, except tourist and business visitors from EU, North America, Australasia and most of Europe for up to three months. For confirmation of exceptions and requirements see: www.auswaertiges-amt.de/ the website of the consular section of the German ministry of foreign affairs.
Germany is a member of the Schengen visa accord and all visitors that require a visa must apply to a Germany consulate; when a visa has been issued a visitor may travel to any other Schengen zone without further visas. A Schengen visa application (offered in several languages) can be downloaded from http://europa.eu/abc/travel/ see 'documents you will need'.

Currency advice/regulations
There are no restrictions on the import or export of local or foreign currency.

Customs
Personal items are duty-free. There are no duties levied on alcohol and tobacco between EU member states, providing amounts imported are for personal consumption.

Health (for visitors)

Nationals of the European Economic Area (EEA) countries and Switzerland can access reduced cost and sometimes free medical treatment using a European

Health Insurance Card (EHIC) while visiting the EEA. Exceptions include nationals of the 10 countries which joined the EU in 2004 whose EHIC is not valid in Switzerland. Applications for the EHIC should be made before travelling.

Mandatory precautions

Vaccination certificates are not usually required, unless arriving from infected area.

Hotels

No official rating system. 10–15 per cent service charge. Advisable to book in advance, especially when trade fairs are being held. All major credit cards accepted.

Public holidays (national)

Fixed dates

1 Jan (New Year's Day), *6 January (Epiphany), 1 May (Labour Day), *15 Aug (Assumption Day), 3 Oct (German Unity Day), *31 Oct (Day of Reformation), *1 Nov (All Saints' Day), 25 Dec (Christmas Day), 26 Dec (Boxing Day).

Although not official holidays, many shops and businesses are also closed on Christmas Eve and New Year's Eve.

Variable dates

Good Friday, Easter Monday, *Ascension Day, Whit Monday, *Corpus Christi (May/Jun)

* Holiday in certain areas only

Working hours

Banking

Mon–Fri: various hours between 0830–1300, 1400–1600; Thu: 0830–1300, 1400–1730. City centre branches do not close for lunch. Exchange bureaux: 0600–2200.

Business

Mon–Fri: usually 0800–1730.

Government

Mon–Fri: usually 0800–1700.

Shops

Mon–Fri: 0900–2000; Sat: 0900–2000. Sunday opening hours vary from state to state and can be limited.

Telecommunications

Mobile/cell phones

There are G3, 900 and 1800 services throughout the country.

Electricity supply

220V AC, 50 Hz. European-style round two-pin plugs are in use.

Social customs/useful tips

Handshaking is universal at the beginning and end of every social or business encounter. Germans acknowledge others, even strangers, with a standard greeting when entering or leaving a room, office, shop or railway compartment.

The focal point of German social life is frequently club membership. The thick web of traditional clubs, which are based on activities including pre-Lenten carnival and sports, card playing, animal husbandry and marksmanship, strongly contribute to social life. It is known as *Vereinsleben*, or club culture.

Germans are extremely aggressive drivers and politeness on the road is not rewarded. There is no speed limit on some parts of the *autobahn* (motorway network). Verbal public insults can result in lawsuits. There are also strict laws against racial slurs, especially anti-Semitism.

Do not try to pay bill if invited to a restaurant during business hours. If dining at a German's home, it is considered impolite to arrive late; a gift of flowers is a social 'must'; do not drink until the host has his or her glass. It is regarded as bad manners to keep your hands in your pockets when talking to someone.

Getting there

Air

National airline: Lufthansa

International airport/s: Berlin airports are small and do not receive intercontinental flights, arrivals are via continental or connecting flights. Frankfurt Airport (FRA), the principal German airport, is 13km south-west of the city, facilities include banks, post office, duty-free shops, restaurants and business suites. Extensive access to the city and other German connections are provided by trains (including international rail links), buses and taxis. Car hire and limousine services are available.

Other airport/s: Bremen (BRE) 4km south of city; Berlin-Tempelhof (THF), Berlin-Tegel (TXL) and Berlin-Schönefeld (SXF). Berlin-Schönefeld, in 2006, began redevelopment to replaced Berlin's three airports with the Berlin-Brandenburg International airport to be completed by 2011; Cologne/Bonn-Konrad Adenauer (CGN) 20km north of Bonn and 14km south-east of Cologne; Düsseldorf (DUS) 8km north of city; Hamburg (HAM) 13km north of city; Hanover (HAJ) 11km from city; Leipzig/Halle (LEJ); Munich (MUC) 11km north-east of city; Nuremberg (NUE) 8km north of city; Stuttgart Echterdingen (STR) 14km south of city.

Airport tax: None.

Surface

Road: There are good quality motorways and main roads linking all surrounding countries.

Water: Ships provide regular passenger services and cruises on the Danube between Regensburg, Vienna, Bratislava and Budapest and from Passau via Austria, Slovakia, Hungary, Serbia, Bulgaria to Romania and the Black Sea.

Main port/s: Bremen, Bremerhaven, Hamburg, Kiel, Rostock, Stralsund, Wilhelmshaven and Wismar.

Getting about

National transport

Air: Frequent services link Berlin, Hanover, Cologne/Bonn, Düsseldorf, Frankfurt, Hamburg, Bremen, Munich, Nuremberg and Stuttgart. Early morning flights provide direct links between many of these centres. Domestic flights are not cheap, but competition is bringing down prices.

Road: There are over 487,000km of roads with a modern network of motorways (*autobahnen*) linking all cities. Secondary roads in eastern Germany may not be of comparable standard with the west.

Buses: Good nationwide coach services are operated by Deutsche Bahn (DB) and other companies.

Rail: DB runs reliable Intercity Express and Sprinter services, with high-speed trains between major cities which include faster east–west links. First and second class travel is available and it is advisable to book in advance. For long-distance travel, trains can often be a quicker option than flying.

Water: Seaports on the Baltic and North Sea coasts are linked to inland waterways and railways. Navigable inland waterways are used extensively.

City transport

There are buses, trams, metro and electric railway services in many towns.

A Welcome Card entitles travellers to 48 hours of bus and rail travel. It can be bought at hotels or VBB (bus and train) offices. Otherwise, machines dispense tickets permitting three consecutive hours' travel on buses and trains.

Taxis: Good taxi services run in all main cities. In Berlin, the metered cabs are beige Mercedes with yellow taxi signs, available outside hotels or at well-signed ranks.

Car hire

Speed limits: built up areas 50kph, normal roads 100kph, *autobahns* 'recommended' top speed of 130kph.

Information is available from automobile clubs such as Allgemeiner Deutscher Automobil Club eV (ADAC), Automobil Club von Deutschland eV (AvD) and Deutscher Touring Automobil Club eV.

The wearing of seat belts is compulsory.

BUSINESS DIRECTORY

The addresses listed below are a selection only. While World of Information makes every endeavour to check these addresses, we cannot guarantee that changes have not been made, especially to telephone numbers and area codes. We would welcome any corrections.

Telephone area codes

The international direct dialling (IDD) code for Germany is +49 followed by the area code:

Berlin	30	Hamburg	40
Bonn	228	Hanover	511
Bremen	421	Leipzig	341
Cologne	221	Munich	89
Dortmund	231	Münster	251
Dresden	351	Nuremberg	911
Düsseldorf	211	Potsdam	331
Essen	201	Stuttgart	711
Frankfurt (Main)	69		

Useful telephone numbers

Police: 110
Fire: 112

Chambers of Commerce

American Chamber of Commerce in Germany, 12 Rossmarkt, 60311 Frankfurt am Main (tel: 929-1040; fax: 929-10411; e-mail: info@amcham.de).

Association of German Chambers of Industry and Commerce, 29 Breite Strasse, 10178 Berlin (tel: 203-080; fax: 203-081000; e-mail: dihk@berlin.dihk.de).

Berlin Chamber of Industry and Commerce, 85 Fasanenstrasse, 10623 Berlin (tel: 315-10666; fax: 315-10166; e-mail: service@berlin.ihk.de).

Bonn/Rhein-Sieg Chamber of Industry and Commerce, 17 Bonner Talweg, 53113 Bonn, (tel: 228-40; fax: 228-4170; e-mail: info@bonn.ihk.de).

British Chamber of Commerce in Germany, 60 Severinstrasse, 50678 Cologne (tel: 314-458; fax: 315-335; e-mail: info@bccg.de).

Cologne Chamber of Industry and Commerce, Unter Sachsenhausen 10-26, 50667 Cologne, (tel: 164-0551; fax:164-0129; e-mail: my@koeln.ihk.de).

Düsseldorf Chamber of Industry and Commerce, 1 Ernst-Schneider- Platz, 40212 Düsseldorf (tel: 355-70; fax: 355-7401; e-mail: ihkdus@duesseldorf.ihk.de).

Frankfurt am Main Chamber of Industry and Commerce, 4 Börsenplatz, 60313 Frankfurt am Main (tel: 219-70; fax: 219-71424; e-mail: info@frankfurt-main.ihk.de).

Hamburg Chamber of Industry and Commerce, 1 Adolphsplatz, 20457 Hamburg (tel: 361-38138; fax: 361-38401; e-mail: service@hk24.de).

Hanover Chamber of Industry and Commerce, 49 Schiffgraben, 30175 Hanover (tel: 31-070; fax: 310-7333; e-mail: schrage@hannover.ihk.de).

Munich Chamber of Industry and Commerce, 2 Max Joseph Strasse, 80333 Munich (tel: 511-6368; fax: 511-6290; e-mail: alberts@muenchen.ihk.de).

Münster Chamber of Industry and Commerce, 61 Sentmaringer Weg, 48151 Münster (tel: 707-0; fax: 707-325; e-mail: international@muenster.ihk.de).

Nuremberg Chamber of Industry and Commerce, 25–27 Am Hauptmarkt, 90403 Nuremberg (tel: 133-50; fax: 133-5200; e-mail: info@ihk-nuernberg.de).

Stuttgart Chamber of Industry and Commerce, 30 Jägerstrasse, 70174 Stuttgart (tel: 200-50; fax: 200-5354; e-mail: info@stuttgart.ihk.de).

Banking

Bayerische Landesbank, 18 Briennerstrasse, 80333 Munich (tel: 217-101; fax: 217-123579; e-mail: info@bayernlb.de).

Bremer Landesbank, 26 Domshof, 28195 Bremen (tel: 332-0; fax: 332-2322; e-mail: kontakt@bremerlandesbank.de).

Commerzbank, Kaiserplatz, 60261 Frankfurt am Main (tel: 136-20; fax: 285-389; e-mail: info@commerxbank.com).

Deutsche Bank, 12 Taunuslage, 60262 Frankfurt am Main (tel: 910-00; fax: 910-34225; e-mail: deutsche.bank@db.com).

Dresdner Bank, 1 Jürgen Ponto Platz, 60301 Frankfurt am Main (tel: 263-0; fax: 263-4831; e-mail: dresdner-bank@dresdner-bank.com).

DZ Bank, Platz der Republik, 60265 Frankfurt am Main (tel: 744-701; fax: 744-71685; e-mail: mail@dzbank.de).

Hamburgische Landesbank, 50 Gerhart Hauptmann Platz, 20095 Hamburg (tel: 333-30; fax: 333-32707; e-mail: info@hamburglb,de).

Hypovereinsbank, 16 Am Tucherpark, 80538 Munich (tel: 378-0; e-mail: info@hypovereinsbank.de).

Landesbank Baden-Württemberg, 2 Am Hauptbahnhof, 70173 Stuttgart (tel: 127-0; fax: 127-3278; e-mail: kontakt@lbbw.de).

Landesbank Berlin, 171 Bundesallee, 10889 Berlin (tel: 869-801; fax: 869-83074; e-mail: information@lbb.de).

Landesbank Hessen-Thuringen, 52-58 Neue Mainzer Strasse, 60311 Frankfurt am Main (tel: 913-201; fax: 291-517; e-mail: presse@helaba.de).

Landesbank Rheinland-Pfalz, 54-56 Grosse Bleiche, 55116 Mainz (tel: 113-01; fax: 113-2724; e-mail: lrp@lrp.de).

Landesbank Saar, 2 Ursulinenstrasse, 66111 Saarbrücken (tel: 383-01; fax: 383-1200; e-mail: service@saarlb.de).

Landesbank Schleswig-Holstein, 6 Martinsdamm, 24103 Kiel (tel: 900-01; fax: 900-2446; e-mail: info@lb-kiel.de).

Norddeutsche Landesbank, 10 Friedrichwall, 30159 Hannover (tel: 361-0; fax: 361-2502; e-mail: info@nordlb.de).

Westdeutsche Landesbank, 15 Herzogstrasse, 40217 Düsseldorf (tel: 826-2449; fax: 826-9683; e-mail: presse@westlb.de).

Central bank

Deutsche Bundesbank, Wilhelm Epstein Strasse 14, 60431 Frankfurt am Main (tel: 9566-3511; fax: 9566-4679; email: presse-information@bundesbank.de).

European Central Bank (ECB), Kaiserstrasse 29, 60311 Frankfurt am Main (tel: 13-440; fax: 1344-6000; email: info@ecb.int).

Stock exchange

Frankfurter Wertpapierbörse (FWB) Frankfurt Stock Exchange, http://deutsche-boerse.com

Börse Stuttgart (Stuttgart Stock Exchange), www.boerse-stuttgart.de

Börse Düsseldorf (Düsseldorf Stock Exchange), www.boerse-duesseldorf.de

Hamburger Börse (Hamburg Stock Exchange), www.hamburger-boerse.de

Berliner Börse (Berlin Stock Exchange), www.equiduct-trading.com

Börse München (Munich Stock Exchange), www.boerse-muenchen.de

Commodity exchange

Risk Management Exchange (RMX), www.rmx.eu/cnt

Travel information

Allgemeiner Deutscher Automobil Club (ADAC), 8 Am Westpark, 81373 Munich (tel: 767-60; fax: 767-62500; e-mail: adac@adac.de).

Automobil Club von Deutschland (AvD), 16 Lyoner Strasse 60528 Frankfurt am Main (tel: 660-60; fax: 660-6789; e-mail: avd@avd.de).

Deutsche Bahn (railway operator), 2 Potsdamer Platz, 10785 Berlin (tel: 297-0; fax: 297-1961; e-mail: info@bahn.de; internet site: http://www.bahn.de/index_e.html).

Lufthansa, 2-6 Von Gablenz Strasse, 50679 Cologne (tel: 696-0; fax: 696-3002; internet site: http://www.lufthansa.co.uk).

National tourist organisation offices

Deutsche Zentrale für Tourismus, Beethovenstrasse 69, 60325 Frankfurt am Main (tel: 757-20; fax: 751-903; e-mail: info@d-z-t.com).

Ministries

Office of the Federal Chancellor, 1 Schlossplatz, 10178 Berlin (tel: 400-0;

fax: 400-01818; e-mail: internetpost@bundeskanzler.de).

Ministry of Consumer Protection, Food and Agriculture, Rochusstrasse 1, 53123 Bonn (tel: 529-05291; fax: 529-4262; e-mail: internet@bmvel.bund.de).

Ministry of Defence, 18 Stauffenbergstrasse, 10785 Berlin (tel: 200-400; fax: 200-48333; e-mail: poststelle@bmvg.bund.400.de).

Ministry of Economic Co-operation and Development, 40 Friedrich Ebert Allee, 53113 Bonn (tel: 535-0; fax: 535-3500; e-mail: poststelle@bmz.bund.de).

Ministry of Economy and Labour, 36 Scharnhorststrasse, 10115 Berlin (tel: 615-0; fax: 615-7010; e-mail: info@bmwa.bund.de).

Ministry of Education and Research, 2 Heinemannstrasse, 53175 Bonn-Bad Godesberg (tel: 57-0; fax: 573-601; e-mail:bmbf@bmbf.bund.de).

Ministry of the Environment, Nature Conservation and Nuclear Safety, 6 Alexanderplatz, 10178 Berlin (tel: 305-0; fax: 305-4375; e-mail: service@bmu.de).

Ministry of Families, Senior Citizens, Women and Youth, 42 Taubenstrasse, 10117 Berlin (tel: 206-550; fax: 206-551145; e-mail: poststelle@bmfsfj.bund.de).

Ministry of Finance, 97 Wilhelmstrasse, 10117 Berlin (tel: 682-0; fax: 682-4420; e-mail: poststelle@bmf.bund.de).

Ministry of Foreign Affairs, 1 Werderscher Markt, 10117 Berlin (tel: 500-000; fax: 500-3402; e-mail: poststelle@auswaertiges-amt.de).

Ministry of Health, 78a Am Propsthof, 53121 Bonn (tel: 941-0; fax: 941-4900; e-mail: info@bmg.bund.de).

Ministry of the Interior, 101 Alt-Moabit, 10559 Berlin (tel: 681-0; fax: 681-2926; e-mail: poststelle@bmi.bund.de).

Ministry of Justice, 37 Mohrenstrasse, 10117 Berlin (tel: 202-570; fax: 259-525; e-mail: poststelle@bmj.bund.de).

Ministry of Transport, Construction and Housing, 44 Invalidenstrasse, 10115 Berlin (tel: 200-80; fax: 200-81920; e-mail: buergerinfo@bmvbw.bund.de).

Deutsche Bundestag, Platz der Republik 1, 11011 Berlin (tel.: 227-0; fax: 2273-6878 or 2273-6979; internet: www.bundestag.de).

Other useful addresses

American Embassy, 4-5 Neustädtische Kirchstrasse , 10117 Berlin (tel: 830-50; fax: 238-6290).

Aussenhandelsvereinigung des Deutschen Einzelhandels (Ave) (foreign trade association of the German retail trade), 1 Mauritiussteinweg, 50676 Cologne 1 (tel: 921-8340; fax: 921-8346; e-mail: info@ave-koeln.de).

Ausstellungs-und Messe-Ausschuss der Deutschen Wirtschaft (Auma) (trade fair industry association), 9 Littenstrasse, 10179 Berlin (tel: 240-000; fax: 240-00263; e-mail: info@auma.de).

British Embassy, 70-71 Wilhelmstrasse, 10117 Berlin (tel: 201-840; fax: 201-84123; e-mail: info@britischebotschaft.de).

Bundesagentur für Aussenwirtschaft (bfai) (German Office for Foreign Trade), 87-93 Agrippastrasse, 50676 Cologne (tel: 205-70; fax: 205-7212; e-mail: info@bfai.de).

Bundesanstalt für Arbeit (federal labour office), 106 Regensburger Strasse, 90478 Nuremberg (tel: 179-0; fax: 179-3600; e-mail: zentralamt@arbeitsamt.de).

Bundesverband der Deutschen Industrie (Bdi) (industry federation), Haus der Deutschen Wirtschaft, 29 Breite Strasse, 10178 Berlin (tel: 202-80; fax: 202-82450; e-mail: info@bdi-online.de).

Bundesverband des Deutschen Gross-und Aussenhandels (wholesale and foreign trade federation), Haus des Handels, 1A Am Weidendamm, 10117 Berlin (tel: 590-09950; fax: 590-099519; e-mail: info@bga.de).

Bundesvereinigung der Deutschen Arbeitgeberverbände (BDA) (employers' associations federation), Haus der Deutschen Wirtschaft, 29 Breite Strasse, 10178 Berlin (tel: 203-30; fax: 203-31055; e-mail: info@bda-online.de).

Büro des Beauftragten für Auslandsinvestitionen in Deutschland (foreign investment in Germany), 34 Markgrafenstrasse, 10117 Berlin (tel: 206-570; fax: 206-57111; e-mail: office@fdin.de).

Deutscher Gewerkschaftsbund (DGB) (trades unions federation), 2 Henrietta Herz Platz , 10178 Berlin (tel: 240-600; fax: 240-60324; e-mail: info@bundesvorstand.dgb.de).

Deutsches Institut für Wirtschaftsforschung (DIW) (economic research institute), 5 Königin Luise Strasse, 14195 Berlin (tel: 879-890; fax: 897-89200; e-mail: postmaster@diw.de).

Deutsche Presse-Agentur (dpa) (news agency), 38 Mittelweg, 20148 Hamburg (tel: 411-30; fax: 411-32219; e-mail: info@hbg.dpa.de).

German Convention Bureau, 48 Münchener Strasse, 60329 Frankfurt am Main (tel: 242-9300; fax: 242-93026; e-mail: info@gcb.de).

German Embassy (US), 4645 Reservoir Road, NW, Washington DC 20007 (tel: (+1-202) 298-4000; fax: (+1-202) 298-4249; e-mail: ge-embus@ix.netcom.com).

Industrial Investment Council (IIC), 57 Charlottenstrasse, 10117 Berlin (tel: 209-45660; fax: 209-45666; e-mail: info@iic.de).

Presse- und Informationsamt der Bundesregierung (government press office), 84 Dorotheenstrasse, 10117 Berlin (tel: 272-0; fax: 272-1365; e-mail: InternetPost@bundesregierung).

Statisches Bundesamt (federal statistical office), 11 Gustav Stresemann Ring, 65189 Wiesbaden (tel: 752-405; fax: 724-000; e-mail: pressestelle@stba.bund400.de; internet site: www.statistik-bund.de/e_home.htm).

Wirtschaftsförderung Berlin (Berlin Business Development Corpration), Ludwig Erhard Haus, 85 Fasanenstrasse, 10623 Berlin (tel: 399-800; fax: 399-80239; e-mail: info@wf-berlin.de).

Zentralverband der Deutschen Werbewirtschaft (ZAW) (advertising industry federation), 17 Villichgasse, 53177 Bonn (tel: 820-920; fax: 357-583; e-mail: zaw@zaw.de).

National news agency: DPA (Deutsche Presse-Agentur), PO Box 13 02 82, 20102; Mittelweg 38 20148, Hamburg (tel: 404-113; email: info@dpa.com).

Pressetext Deutschland (business news):www.pressetext.de

Internet sites

Gateway site to web directory (in German with translation facilities): www.dino-online.de

German-British Chamber of Commerce: www.germanbritishchamber.co.uk

German Government Website: www.bundesregierung.de

Germany Business Finder: www.infospace.com/uk.telegr/intldb/bizfindint.htm?QO=DE

Germany Technical Corporation: www.gtz.de/home/english/index.html

Rentenbank: www.rentenbank.de

State Bank of Baden-Württemberg: www.l-bank.de

Tourist Board: www.germany-tourism.de

Yellow pages: http://english.branchenbuch.com

Ghana

KEY FACTS

Official name: Republic of Ghana

Head of State: President John Dramani Mahama (NDC) (from 24 Jul 2012, on death of John Atta Mills; elected 7 Dec 2012, sworn-in 7 Jan 2013)

Head of government: President John Dramani Mahama (NDC)

Ruling party: National Democratic Congress (NDC) (from 7 Jan 2008, re-elected 7 Dec 2012)

Area: 239,460 square km

Population: 26.22 million (2014)*

Capital: Accra

Official language: English

Currency: Cedi (GH¢) = 100 pesewas

Exchange rate: GH¢3.85 per US$ (Sep 2015)

GDP per capita: US$1,474 (2014)*

GDP real growth: 4.16% (2014)*

GDP: US$38.65 billion (2014)*

Inflation: 15.49% (2014)*

Balance of trade: -US$3.85 billion (2014)

* estimated figure

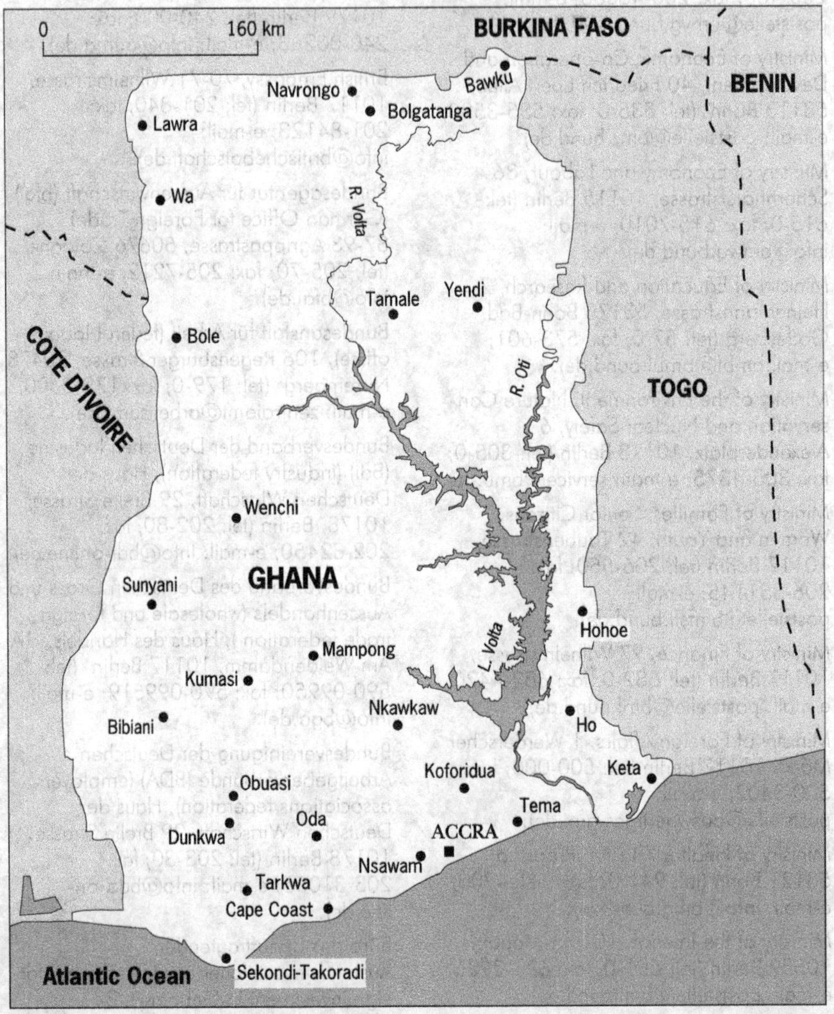

Ghana was formed from a merger between the British colony of the Gold Coast and the Togoland trust territory, and in 1957, it became the first sub-Saharan country in colonial Africa to gain its independence. Ghana endured a long series of coups prior to Flt Lt Jerry Rawlings who came to power after a second *coup* in 1981 and banned political parties and ruled through the Provisional National Defence Council (PNDC). After approving a new constitution and restoring multiparty politics in 1992, Rawlings won presidential elections in 1992 and 1996 but was constitutionally prevented from running a third time in 2000. The current president of Ghana is John Mahama who won the December 2012 election. Mahama faces an enormous challenge for the upcoming 2016 presidential elections as public dissatisfaction is very high in the midst of economic austerity.

In the first decade of the twenty-first century Ghanaians had become accustomed to seeing their country held up as an economic and political model for other African states to emulate. By 2014, however, much of the gloss had been rubbed off, as Ghanaians watched the value of their currency, the cedi, slump by some 30 per cent in the first nine months of 2014 and interest rates soar. Inflation has also increased substantially from 13.5 per cent in 2013 to 17 per cent in

2014 with some traders demanding payment in US dollars. High growth rates over recent years have been accompanied by the build-up of macroeconomic imbalances. In 2014, current accounts and fiscal deficits widened to 9.2 per cent and 10.4 per cent of GDP respectively. The continued growth in the budget deficit resulted in public debt increasing from 55.8 per cent of GDP in December 2013 to 67.1 per cent by the end of December 2014.

Ghana has a market-based economy with relatively few policy barriers to trade and investment in comparison with other countries in the region. Ghana is rich in natural resources with a large number of gold and cocoa exports. Despite the opportunity for Ghana to grow its industrial and services sector (in terms of employment), agriculture still employs more than half of the workforce, although it accounts for only 20 per cent of GDP. Coupled with exports, remittances also represent a fairly significant source of foreign exchange. Remittances amounted to US$119 million (0.3 per cent of GDP) in 2013. Although the economy is growing (4.2 per cent in 2014), it is slowing at an unprecedented rate, economic growth has almost halved from 8 per cent in 2012 and 7.3 per cent in 2013. Ghana's economy is expected to slow down for the fourth consecutive year to an estimate 3.9 per cent growth rate in 2015. In order to address its growing economic crisis, Ghana signed a US$920 million extended credit facility with the International Monetary Fund (IMF) in April 2015. The IMF fiscal targets will require Ghana to reduce its deficit by cutting government subsidies, decreasing the bloated public sector wage bill, strengthening revenue administration, and increasing revenues.

Expansion of Ghana's nascent oil industry has boosted economic growth, but the recent oil price crash has reduced by half Ghana's anticipated oil revenue. Ghana's largest offshore oil field, Jubilee, currently has a production rate of 110,000 barrels per day (bpd) having begun operations in mid-December 2010. Proven reserves of oil were 660 million barrels in 2015 with all production being located at the Jubilee field. Ghana exports approximately 84,000bpd and imports 24,000bpd. The country's first gas processing plant at Atubao is also producing the natural gas from the Jubilee field, providing power to several of Ghana's thermal power plants. Ghana's proven natural gas reserves stood at 22.7 billion cubic metres (cum) in 2014 with no production in 2014 although there has been production in 2015. Ghana imports all of its natural gas and this constitutes around 430 million cum.

Ghana is expected to produce 14 million cum of natural gas annually by 2019 that will be enough to power about 3,000MW of electricity generation in the country. The minister of petroleum, Emmanuel Armah-Kofi Buah, said that the ministry was undertaking a US$18 million project to produce 4.8 million cum in Ghana. The main objective of this is to promote the use of LPG in the three northern regions where there is a large dependence on firewood and charcoal for domestic fuel.

Although the energy sector is expanding, access to consistent electricity is still a major problem for Ghanaians, it is holding back the economy and preventing the country from reaching its potential. The Mahama administration has been taking steps to improve the situation but it will take until 2016 before any major changes are made. Ghana needs to expand its installed electricity capacity and distribution system if it is to provide electricity to the almost 30 per cent of its population that does not have access to electricity, according to World Bank data. Many Ghanaians, particularly in rural areas, rely on traditional biomass and waste, particularly firewood, for household cooking and heating. Firewood accounts for slightly more than 40 per cent of Ghana's total primary energy consumption, according to Ghana's national energy statistics.

God willing, the barge will arrive in Ghana

Such is Ghana's shortage of power that the Electricity Company of Ghana (ECG) signed an agreement in 2014 with Karpowership Company Limited of Turkey for the construction and supply of two Karpower barges which will supply a total of 450MW of power. The barges are each said to be the size of a shopping mall. The first barge, the *Black Marlin* finally set sail for the port of Tema on 6 November 2015. As of 2 November however, the government was still looking for a partnership for the provision of fuel, on which the power barge would run upon arrival in the harbour's man-made semi-submerged maritime structure that will prevent the barge from drifting to shallow ground.

Over the medium term, the economy is projected to recover, bolstered mainly by higher oil and gas production, combined with increased private sector and public infrastructure investments, as well as an improved macroeconomic framework and political stability. Although Ghana's current economic situation is dire, its growth over the past decade has helped the country to achieve the Millennium Development Goal of halving poverty, never the less, there is evidence of growing disparities in income inequality across regions, especially in the three northern regions. Progress in the achievement of other MDGs remains mixed, with the 2015 targets likely to be missed. The total population in multi-dimensional poverty was 30.5 per cent in 2014 with 28.6 per cent of the population living below US$1.25 a day. Economic growth is expected to recover in 2016, registering a rate of around 6 per cent.

According to the IMF, the main priority is to restore macro-economic stability by addressing the 'short-term vulnerabilities'

KEY INDICATORS — Ghana

	Unit	2011	2012	2013	2014	**2015
Population	m	24.30	*24.93	*25.56	*26.22	*26.89
Gross domestic product (GDP)	US$bn	37.20	40.44	48.59	*38.65	*39.22
GDP per capita	US$	1,529	1,622	1,901	*1,474	*1,459
GDP real growth	%	13.6	7.9	7.3	*4.2	*3.5
Inflation	%	8.7	9.2	11.7	*15.5	*12.2
Exports (fob) (goods)	US$m	12,785.4	13,543.4	13,751.9	–	–
Imports (fob) (goods)	US$m	15,842.7	17,763.2	17,600.3	–	–
Balance of trade	US$m	-3,057.3	-4,219.8	-3,848.4	–	–
Current account	US$m	-3,050.5	-4,924.0	-5,704.0	*-3,562.0	*-2,759.0
Total reserves minus gold	US$m	–	5,367.5	5,249.3	–	–
Foreign exchange	US$m	–	4,969.0	4,882.6	–	–
Exchange rate	per US$	1.49	1.88	2.34	3.22	–

* estimated figure ** forecast figure

that put Ghana's transformation agenda at risk. Ghana had experienced strong and broadly inclusive growth over the past two decades, regularly outperforming regional peers in reducing poverty and improving social indicators. A 'robust' political background and a highly rated business climate had helped attract significant foreign direct investment (FDI), supporting strong growth and a national graduation to lower middle-income status. FDI was US$3.4 billion in 2014, a slight increase from the US$3.2 billion in 2013. Ghana's numerous economic challenges may have put off foreign investors as FDI declined in the third quarter of 2015 as compared to 2014. Foreign projects in Ghana accounted for 43 out of 56 total projects as recorded in the third quarter of 2014 and this reduced to 37 out of 52 projects during the same period in 2015. FDI also dropped to US$802 million in the third quarter of 2015, a decrease of US$500 million from the third quarter in 2014. The major investment for the third quarter in 2015 has been power generation by Aska Energy Ltd investing US$301 million. Other projects were conducted by an agricultural trading company, Jubaili Agrotec Ltd and Safi Sana Ghana Ltd, providers of communal water electricity and organic fertilizers.

In 2013, some of the economic changes the Ghanaian government adopted to deal with the perceived problems affecting the economy had been to impose levies on a number of import items and on the profits of specific sectors. It also eliminated fuel subsidies, raised electricity and water tariffs as well as containing other expenditure.

The 2014 budget had focussed both on gathering additional revenues, as well as containing primary expenditure. The value-added tax (VAT) rate was raised and the coverage was broadened to include previously exempted items and activities. There was also an increased effort to control the wage bill. In April 2014 the government had issued a policy document outlining a strategy targeting public sector reform, which included the rationalisation of the public service, hiving off subsidised (public service) agencies from the payroll, restructuring statutory funds to reduce budget rigidities and revenue administration reform to increase tax compliance. The Bank of Ghana (central bank) had further tightened its monetary policy in early 2014, increasing both interest rates and reserve requirements.

The ministry of food and agriculture has said that efforts put in place by public and private institutions would help raise output of cashew nuts from the current 50,000 tonnes to 150,000 tonnes by 2025. In order to achieve this goal, the government has said it will increase supplies of cashew seedlings to farmers with the introduction of improved and high-yielding varieties. Sixty districts in the country are conducive for cashew production whereas only districts in the Brong Afhafo region have been properly utilised, with 90 per cent of national output coming from that area alone. Advocates for the local cashew industry have said that the government also needs to support cashew farmers with mass spraying exercises, supply of fertilisers and soft loans. By revitalising the cashew industry, Ghana would be able to compete with Côte d'Ivoire which is the second largest cashew producer in Africa behind Nigeria.

Risk assessment

Politics	Good
Economy	Fair/good
Regional stability	Good

Muslims in Ghana

% of population	15.9
Sunni (% of Muslims)	83
Shi'a (% of Muslims)	1

COUNTRY PROFILE

1482 A trading settlement was set up by the Portuguese at Elmina.
1821 The British Gold Coast was formed. The area under British influence grew with the addition of the Danish Gold Coast in 1850 and the Dutch Gold Coast in 1871. Four wars were fought with the Ashanti people between 1863 and 1896.
1874 The British proclaimed the coastal area a crown colony.
1914 The German Protectorate of Togoland (1884–1914) surrendered to British and French troops in August.
1916 Togoland was separated into French Togoland and British Togoland following the ratification of the Treaty of Versailles on 20 July 1922 when Togoland became a League of Nations Class B Mandate.
1925 First legislative council elections took place.
1945–1957 An independence movement grew under British rule.
1956 In a May plebiscite 58 per cent of residents of British Togoland voted to join Ghana on independence.
1957 Ghana (formerly The Gold Coast) was granted independence from Britain with Dr Kwame Nkrumah as prime minister.
1960 The country voted to become a republic. Dr Kwame Nkrumah of the People's Convention Party became president.
1964 Nkrumah declared the country a single political party state.
1966 The military overthrew Nkrumah and installed the National Liberation Council, a transitional government.
1969 Dr Kofi Busia secured victory in the parliamentary elections and became prime minister.
1972 After another military coup, Col Ignatius Acheampong took control of the country.
1978 Acheampong was deposed by the military and Lt-Gen F Akuffo, previously chief of the defence staff, became president.
1979 Akuffo's government was destabilised in an unsuccessful coup launched by Flt-Lt Jerry J Rawlings. Dr Hilla Limann of the People's National Party (PNP) was later elected as president. A new constitution was promulgated.
1981 Jerry J Rawlings took power through a second military coup, dissolved parliament and ruled through the Provisional National Defence Council (PNDC).
1983–89 Discontent with the regime and its economic ineffectiveness led to a series of attempted coups, student unrest and alleged anti-government conspiracies. The government attempted to impose fiscal and monetary discipline and bring the economy into alignment with market trends and influences. The cedi was devalued by 6,300 per cent in 1987. Over 1.1 million Ghanaians were expelled from Nigeria and returned home, placing great strain on limited resources.
1990 A national referendum on the restoration of multi-party politics was demanded.
1992 A referendum endorsed a new constitution to allow a multi-party system. Jerry Rawlings was elected president and his National Democratic Congress (NDC) secured an overall majority in legislative elections.
1993 The constitution came into force and the Fourth Republic was inaugurated.
1996 Jerry Rawlings won the presidential election and his party, the NDC, won the legislative elections.
1997 Ghanaian diplomat, Kofi Annan was appointed General Secretary of the United Nations.
2000 John Kufuor and the New Patriotic Party (NPP) took power. Kufuor became the first elected president in Ghana's history to succeed another elected president.
2002 Ethnic battles in the north led to the murder of Ghana's second most important tribal king, Ya Naa Yakubu Andani of the Dagbon people. His death led to the resignation of two senior government ministers.

2004 The former president, Jerry Rawlings, testified before the National Reconciliation Commission investigating human rights offences during the early years of his rule. Incumbent John Kufuor (NPP) and the ruling NPP retained power.
2005 The first fall in HIV/Aids infection rates in five years was reported.
2007 The cedi was re-valued when four zeros were removed. The new banknote was referred to as the Ghana Cedi. 'Substantial oil deposits' were found in Ghanaian territorial waters.
2008 Tribal violence between the Kusasi and Mamprusi people led to the deaths of 13 people in Bawku. A heavy military presence and a curfew were needed to bring peace, while the president called for talks over a contested chieftaincy to be resolved. In parliamentary elections the opposition NDC won 114 seats (out of 230), the ruling NPP 107; after two rounds of presidential elections opposition leader John Evans Atta Mills (NDC) won 50.23 per cent and his rival, Nana Addo Dankwa Akufo-Addo (NPP) won 49.77 per cent.
2009 President Atta Mills took office. US President Obama visited and addressed parliament, citing four key areas that were critical to Africa's success: democracy, opportunity, health and the peaceful resolution of conflict. The IMF agreed to a three-year loan of US$600 million, to help Ghana grappled with the global economic crisis.
2010 The World Bank agreed to fund the US$258 million refurbishment of the 998.8km West African coastal corridor road, running through Ghana from Abidjan (Côte d'Ivoire) to Lagos (Nigeria). Equatorial Guinea began export of two million barrels of crude oil a year to Ghana. Dividends from the operators of the Prestea-Bogoso and Wassa mines in the west of the country amounted to US$6.6 million by the second half of the year. Production of the first oil from the offshore Jubilee Field began.
2011 In July, the African Development Bank approved a US$70 million loan and US$41.3 grant to finance the poverty reduction and business environment support programme (PRBESP), with the intention of improving the private sector business environment and public financial management. Approval followed GDP growth figures for 2010 of 7.7 per cent.
2012 On 24 July, President John Atta Mills died of throat cancer in hospital in Accra. Vice president John Dramani Mahama assumed the office and was sworn in as president on the same day. On 6 August Kwesi Bekoe Amissah-Arthur was sworn into office as vice president. On 18 October, eight candidates were endorsed to contest the 7 December presidential election; the wife of former president Jerry Rawlings, Nana Konadu Rawlings, was barred despite having been chosen by the National Democratic Party (NDP) to represent it. The presidential and parliamentary elections held on 7 December were, according to Ecowas, held in a 'free and fair' manner. They were the first biometric elections to be held in Ghana. The presidential election was won by John Dramani Mahama (50.7 per cent) with Nana Akufo-Addo a close second (47.74 per cent). The NDC returned to power in the parliamentary elections with 147 seats (out of 275) to the NPP's 123 seats, four independents and one seat to the People's National Convention (PNC). Mr Mahama will be inaugurated on 7 January 2013. Turnout was some 80 per cent. The NPP challenged the result.
2013 President John Mahama, the National Democratic Congress (NDC), was inaugurated on 7 January. Poet Kofi Awoonor was one of the victims of the al Shabab attack on the Westgate shopping centre in Nairobi on 21 September. Deputy communications minister, Victoria Hammah, was sacked on 8 November after allegedly saying she would stay in politics until she had made US$1 million.
2014 On 21 October Addo Dankwa Akufo-Addo was nominated as the candidate for the NPP in the 2016 presidential election.
2015 The International Tribunal for the Law of the Sea ruled in April that Ghana should not start drilling for oil in waters that are in dispute with Côte d'Ivoire, although Ghana could continue developing current oilfields, including the so called-Ten fields, part owned by UK firm Tullow Oil. The tribunal ruled that suspending all drilling, as demanded by Côte d'Ivoire, would risk 'considerable financial loss' to Ghana. Rather it ruled that Ghana should 'take all necessary steps to ensure that no new drilling either by Ghana or under its control takes place in the disputed area' and to 'refrain from granting any new permit for oil exploration and exploitation in the disputed area'.

Political structure

Constitution
The constitution came into force on 7 January 1993. It is based on the US model. It allows for a multi-party system.
Ghana has 10 administrative regions which are subdivided into districts. Between 2000–04, 30 new constituencies were created.

Form of state
Unitary republic

The executive
Executive power is vested in the president, vice president and Council of Ministers; both the vice president and the Council of Ministers are appointed by the president. The president is elected by universal suffrage for a maximum of two four-year terms.
If no candidate receives more than 50 per cent of votes in the presidential election, a new election between the two candidates with the highest number of votes is to take place within 21 days.

National legislature
The unicameral Parliament of Ghana has 275 members directly elected in single-seat constituencies to serve four-year terms.

Legal system
The legal system is based on English common law and local customary law.

Last elections
7 December 2012 (parliamentary and presidential)

Results: Parliamentary: National Democratic Congress (NDC) won 147 seats (out of 275), New Patriotic Party (NPP) 123, Independents four and People's National Convention (PNC) one.
Presidential (first round): John Dramani Mahama (NDC) 50.7 per cent; Nana Addo Dankwa Akufo-Addo 47.74 per cent; turnout was 80 per cent.

Next elections
7 December 2016 (parliamentary and presidential)

Political parties

Ruling party
National Democratic Congress (NDC) (from 7 Jan 2008, re-elected 7 Dec 2012)

Main opposition party
New Patriotic Party (NPP)

Population

24.93 million (2012)* About 44 per cent of the population is under 15 years.
The highest population densities are in the urban areas. The cocoa processing and mining areas in the south have relatively large populations.

Last census: 26 March 2010: 24,658,823

Population density: 79 inhabitants per square km. Urban population 51 per cent (2010 Unicef).

Annual growth rate: 2.5 per cent, 1990–2010 (Unicef).

Ethnic make-up
Akan (including Ashanti) (44 per cent), Dagomba (16 per cent), Ewe (13 per cent), Ga-Adangbe (8.3 per cent), Guan (3.7 per cent), Gurma (3.5 per cent).

Religions
Christian (43 per cent), traditional religions (38 per cent), Muslim (12 per cent). There is complete freedom of worship in Ghana.

Education
Since the government removed school fees for primary education in 2005, record numbers of children have been enrolled. Over 600,000 more children of ages 5–13 were enrolled, with girls being the greater proportion of new students. The World Bank is due to give a grant of US$11 million in 2006, to provide more teachers, build new classrooms and purchase textbooks, in recognition for the government's efforts in achieving an objective of the UN Millennium Development Goals in education.
Government expenditure on education is about a quarter of total government spending.
Ghana boasts the oldest university in sub-Saharan Africa – at Legon in Accra.
Literacy rate: 74 per cent adult rate; 92 per cent youth rate (15–24) (Unesco 2005).
Enrolment rate: 69 per cent primary enrollment (2005–06 academic year, up from 59 per cent in 2004–05) (2006).
Pupils per teacher: 33 in primary schools.

Health
In 2012, Ghana became the first African country to begin using a double vaccination for Rotavirus and pneumococcal disease to protect children. These diseases kill up to 20 per cent of all Ghanaian children under the age of five years. This combined vaccine, coupled with those used for polio, measles and tuberculosis is expected to cut childhood mortality by over 60 per cent by 2015.

HIV/Aids
The fragile infection rate trend was down from 3.6 per cent in 2003 to 3.1 in 2004. Officials will not laud the result as a victory until the trend shows a three-year steady decline. In the meantime infection rates of other sexually transmitter deseases (STD) are showing a rise among young people indicating unprotected sex. Authorities are planning to switch emphasis A survey in 2003 indicated there were over 350,000 people living with HIV (UNAIDS).
HIV prevalence: 3.1 per cent aged 15–49 in 2004. Prevalence in the north is lower averaging 1.8 per cent, while in the south it is 6.5 per cent (government figures).
Life expectancy: 57 years, 2004 (WHO 2006)
Fertility rate/Maternal mortality rate: 4.2 births per woman, 2010 (Unicef)
Child (under 5 years) mortality rate (per 1,000): 72 per 1,000 live births (WHO 2012); 25 per cent of children aged under five are malnourished (World Bank).
Head of population per physician: 0.15 physicians per 1,000 people, 2004 (WHO 2006)

Welfare
The government's policies of structural adjustment have hit urban Ghanaians hard as the contraction of industry and the removal of state subsidies have led to increased unemployment, crime and poverty. In a bid to dampen the impact of reform, the government adopted a US$100 million Programme of Action to Mitigate the Social Costs of Adjustment (Pamscad) in the late 1990s to help cushion the shock of redundancies or redeployment as a result of the ERP. It involves 23 projects under five main categories: community initiatives, employment (including food-for-work schemes), redeployment (compensation for those made redundant), basic needs (self-help schemes) and education. Medium-term strategies are centred on the provision of primary health care.

Main cities
Accra (capital, estimated population 2.3 million (m) in 2012), Kumasi (2.0m), Tamale (537,986), Tamale (537,986), Ashiaman (284,518), Takoradi (260,635), Cape Coast (217,032), Obuasi (175,043), Teshi (160,939).

Languages spoken
There are over 25 major languages with numerous dialects. The principal languages spoken are Twi and Fante (spoken by the Akans), Ga, Hausa, Dagbani, Ewe and Nzema.
There is an official policy to encourage Ghanaians to be multilingual so English is also taught in most schools.

Official language/s
English

Media
Press freedom is respected and Ghana has a reputation as 'one of the most unfettered' in Africa. A government appointed commission regulates all media.

Press
Dailies: There are many newspapers on offer, all chasing a constricted advertising market hampered by government advertising being limited to state-owned publications and other advertisers tending to do business with only the larger publications. In English, the *Daily Graphic* (www.graphicghana.com) and *Ghanaian Times* (www.newtimesonline.com) are state-owned; the *Daily Guide* (http://dailyguideghana.com) is a tabloid, the conservative publication *The Statesman* (www.thestatesmanonline.com) is one of the oldest (although with a broken record) newspapers with a full range of articles, and the *Accra Daily Mail* (http://news.accra-mail.com).
Weeklies: In English, independent publications include the *The Ghanaian Chronicle* (www.ghanaian-chronicle.com), *Ghana Palaver* (www.ghana-palaver.com), with news and current affairs, *Public Agenda* (www.ghanaweb.com/public_agenda) is published twice weekly with social stories and *The Spectator* (http://spectator.newtimesonline.com) is a weekend edition of entertainment news. *The Mirror* is state-owned.
Business: In English, the *Business and Financial Times* (http://bftghanaonline.com), provides comprehensive information. Major newspapers have sections on business and finance.
Periodicals: In English, *The Heritage* (www.theheritagenews.com) is a month political review and the *Christian Messenger* is a conservative Presbyterian monthly. The *Ghana Review International* (http://ghanareview.com) is a foreign publication of national news.

Broadcasting
The state-run Ghana Broadcasting Corporation (GBC) is the national public operator.
Radio: GBC Radio (www.gbcghana.com) has a network of three stations with radio service in English, Hausa and other African languages and an external radio service in English, French and Hausa.
Private, commercial stations include Vibe FM (www.vibefm.com.gh) Citi FM (www.citifmonline.com), Solid FM (www.mysolidonline.com) and Space FM (www.spacefmradio.com).
Television: GBC operates Ghana TV (GTV) (www.gbcghana.com), which produces 80 per cent of locally made programmes. There are several private TV stations including TV3 (www.tv3.com.gh), Crystal TV and Media TV.
National news agency: Ghana News Agency

Economy
The Ghanaian economy is sustained primarily by agriculture, Ghana is the world's second-largest producer of cocoa after Côte d'Ivoire and exports palm oil, timber, coffee and coconuts, as well as other, non-traditional produce including pineapples, cashews and peppers. Domestic crops include cassava, yams, rice and plantains. Agriculture constitutes over 30 per cent of GDP and industry around 20 per cent. Ghana's natural resources in gold, oil, diamonds, bauxite and timber have resulted in an advanced extraction industry with the service industries that support them. The service sector constitutes 50 per cent of GDP, led by government services and finance and energy production. The manufacturing sector, which is relatively small (just over 6 per

cent of GDP), processes agricultural produce, as well as producing garments, steel (using scrap metal), timber products, simple consumer goods and vehicles assembly.
GDP growth reached 4.2 per cent in 2014, which, whilst high, indicated a deceleration compared to the growth of 7.3 per cent in the previous year. Economic growth in 2015 is expected to remain around 3.5 per cent, with low cocoa and gold production balanced by increased hydrocarbon production. Increased address to the electricity shortages that dampen economic development and activity has been achieved through new privately financed power plants.
In 2009 the IMF agreed to a three-year general loan of US$600 million and a further US$450 through a special facility set up to help poorer countries. The money was intended to reduce the budget deficit and support the currency. Ghanaian exports of cocoa and gold left the economy 'relatively resilient' during the global economic crisis and oil production, beginning in 2010, has played a positive role in Ghana's economic success since. The IMF will provide Ghana with loans worth about $940m in instalments, beginning in April 2015. This bailout is considered necessary for the restoration of investor confidence in a struggling economy beset by crippling electricity blackouts. Harsh austerity measures are likely to follow to the dismay of the people of Ghana.

In 2014, the UN Human Development Index (HDI) ranked Ghana 138 (out of 187) for national development in health, education and income. Since 2000, Ghana's progress has grown steadily and has outstripped other sub-Saharan African countries. In 2013, 20 per cent of the population were deemed to be below the national poverty line.
Remittances from migrant workers amounted to US$119 million in 2014.
With its modern port, Ghana's importance as a trading hub has grown for foreign investors. However, it needs to improve roads and port efficiency before it can take full advantage of all that this facility can provide for the country.

External trade

Ghana is a member of the Economic Community of West African States (Ecowas), which was set up to promote economic integration among members. It is a member of the Anglophone, West African Monetary Zone (WAMZ), which is due to introduce a common currency. WAMZ will eventually be merged with the Francophone-members' currency to produce a single currency (the eco) for the region.

Imports

Principal imports are refined petroleum, capital equipment and foodstuffs.
Main sources: China (25.5 per cent total of total in 2014), Nigeria (13.1 per cent), Netherlands (8.2 per cent), Cote d'Ivoire (7.2 per cent) and the United States (6.9 per cent).

Exports

Principal exports are oil, gold, timber, tuna, bauxite, aluminium, manganese ore, diamonds and horticultural products.
Main destinations: China (10.7 per cent of total in 2014), France (9 per cent), Netherlands (7.3 per cent), India (7.3 per cent), South Africa (6.6 per cent) and Italy (6.5 per cent).

Agriculture

Farming

Agricultural land – around 14,600 hectares (ha) – accounts for almost 65 per cent of the total land area. There is over 6330ha of arable and permanently cultivated land and around 8350ha of pastureland.
Ghana is one of the leading cocoa producers in the world, providing 19 per cent of the total. Cocoa is still a major component of the economy providing around 60 per cent of export earnings. Government monopoly on cocoa sales was removed in 1993; private trading companies purchase directly from farms.
Other cash crops for export include bananas, kola nuts, limes, coffee, copra and palm kernels.
Crops grown for the local agribusiness include rubber, sugar, cotton, and oil palms.
Subsistence farming of food crops (cassava, plantains, rice, maize, sorghum, millet, yams) has been affected by prolonged drought and shortages of fertilisers, but there has been a recovery, particularly in maize and rice production.

Fishing

The annual domestic fish catch averages 300,000 tonnes, satisfying over 75 per cent of domestic demand. Fish farms have been set up in the north in an effort to achieve total fish self-sufficiency.
Tuna is one of Ghana's non-traditional exports, but the maximum sustainable yield from the 28,000 square km territorial waters is far from being realised.

Forestry

Forests cover around 23 per cent of the landmass of Ghana. There are over 200 species of tropical hardwood. The forestry sector contributes about 6 per cent to Ghana's GDP, employing around 120,000 people directly. At the deforestation rate of 65,000ha–130,000ha per annum, the remaining forests in Ghana are concentrated in the south of the country.
Most commercial forestry is concentrated in the south. The extent of productive forest reserves is put at 1.2 million hectares, containing 190 million cubic metres of potential wood volume in trees over 30cm in diameter. Timber is Ghana's third-largest export commodity. The current export level of commercially viable species and sizes (trees with diameters of 70cm or more) can only be maintained if reliance on popular hardwoods is lessened and exploitation of lesser known species is increased. Domestic demand for wood for fuel is far greater than the permissible cut of one million cubic metres.
The National Forests Protection Strategy resulted in decreasing deforestation during the 1990s. The strategy plans to make the private sector responsible for the costs of forest depletion. The Environmental Protection Agency (EPA) monitors developments and policy affecting wildlife, forests and mining activities.
A local non-government body is developing a bamboo and rattan industry instead of available timber.
In 2009 the European Union (EU) and Ghana signed an agreement that ensures only legally harvested timber is exported to Ghana's most valuable markets in the EU. Around 43 per cent of total exports and 33 per cent of total volume of Ghanaian timber is sold to the EU and the agreement is expected to further the country's reforms of its forestry sector, promoting investment, sustainability and poverty alleviation.

Industry and manufacturing

The industrial sector accounts for approximately 27.2 per cent of annual GDP and accounted for 23.4 per cent of the country's growth achieved in 2004. Services are the second largest sector in the country and accounted for 32.4 per cent of the economy and was responsible for 25.9 per cent of overall growth in 2004. Manufacturing only contributes 9.0 per cent to GDP, electricity, gas and water 2.6 per cent and construction 8.5 per cent.
The privatisation and commercialisation of Ghana's public sector since the mid-1990s led to a severe contraction in manufacturing as jobs were shed, firms liquidated and the economy flooded by cheap imports. Officials believe foreign investment offers the key to the development of the sector.
Ghana's medium-sized manufacturing industries include aluminium smelting, paper and cement manufacturing and petroleum refining. The aluminium smelter at Tema, the Volta Aluminium Company (Valco), is the country's most capital-intensive enterprise. Potential production

capacity is 200,000 tonnes, but only a fraction of this has been produced in recent years.

The government is seeking to expand important agri-based industries and textile manufacturing. It is also encouraging the establishment of more industries geared to processing local raw materials to replace imported inputs.

Tourism

Ghana is a ranked third as West Africa's most popular destination for tourists (after Senegal and Nigeria). Not only does Ghana offer traditional African cultural activities, historic sites (of which two are included on Unesco's World Heritage List) and modern resorts, healthcare has also become an important component of tourism. New, internationally operated luxury hotels have opened, mostly in and around Accra.

Travel and tourism contributed an estimated 6.7 per cent of GDP in 2011 and employed 5.9 per cent (319,000 jobs) of total employed. Visitor revenue was 12.3 per cent of total foreign exchange and attracted 4 per cent of total capital investment in 2011.

Mining

Mining typically accounts for 18 per cent of GDP and employs 3 per cent of the workforce. Minerals resources include gold, manganese, diamonds, bauxite, iron ore, limestone, silica, columbite, tantalite and several rich clays.

Gold is the principal mineral export and Ghana is Africa's second-largest gold producer, after South Africa. Ashanti Goldfields Corporation (AGC) accounts for 85 per cent of total output. The other major producer is the State Gold Mines Corporation. Recoverable gold reserves are estimated at 57,000 tonnes. AGC has invested US$200 million in two new mines, while Newmont (the largest mining company globally) was given the go-ahead to begin the Ahafo South Project, a greenfields site, in 2005.

The US-based, World Food Association Organisation (WFAO) began purchasing the mineral rights to 300 acres of alluvial gold mines in 2009 as it expanded its farming operations in Ghana. The mines, some pre-existing that are being refurbished, are in Kibi (in the southeast of the country) and each are expected to produce 10–20kg of gold dust per month. With the proceeds from the mines, WFAO intends to set up large farming entities with local people as co-operators.

Diamonds and manganese each account for 1–2 per cent of export earnings. Diamonds (mostly industrial) are mined by Ghana Consolidated Diamonds Ltd in the Birim Basin. Ghana is the eighth-largest diamond producer in the world.

Manganese ore is mined at Nsuta by the National Manganese Corporation. Manganese production averages 280,000 tonnes per annum.

Ghana has vast bauxite reserves near Kibi, but heavy transport/extraction costs have limited commercial development of local bauxite for use by the Valco aluminium smelter.

Ghana granted mining licences in its protected forest reserves to attract new foreign investment.

The reductions in gold prices and increased regulation in recent years has led to many miners experiencing financial insecurity.

Hydrocarbons

Proven oil reserves have rapidly grown since 2000 when joint government and commercial oil companies began exploring Ghanaian territory. In 2007 commercial quantities of oil were found offshore in the Tano Basin by a consortium of Kosmos Energy, Anadarko Petroleum and Tullow Ghana in partnership with Ghana National Petroleum Corporation (GNPC), estimated at 2 billion barrels, although analysts believe undiscovered reserves are even greater. The US oil and gas company, ExxonMobil acquired a US$4 billion stake in the Jubilee Field, Africa's biggest deep-water offshore oil field, in October 2009. Production began in December 2010, beginning at 55,000 barrels per day (bpd) rising to 120,000bpd by mid-2011 and a maximum 250,000bpd at full production. The US-Kosmos Energy Company announced confirmation of oil in its Odum drilling site, discovered offshore in Ghana's territorial waters, in December 2009.

The International Tribunal for the Law of the Sea ruled in April 2015 that Ghana should not start drilling for oil in waters that are in dispute with Côte d'Ivoire, although Ghana could continue developing current oilfields, including the so called-Ten fields, part owned by the UK firm, Tullow Oil. The tribunal ruled that suspending all drilling, as demanded by Côte d'Ivoire, would risk 'considerable financial loss' to Ghana. Rather it ruled that Ghana should 'take all necessary steps to ensure than no new drilling either by Ghana or under its control takes place in the disputed area' and to 'refrain from granting any new permit for oil exploration and exploitation in the disputed area'.

Until domestic supplies are available, a substantial proportion of Ghana's 46,000bpd oil requirement is imported from Nigeria. Petroleum products account for about a quarter of the country's energy requirements.

The Tema Oil Refinery has a capacity of 45,000bpd. A residual catalytic cracking (RCC) unit has been installed to boost productivity and produce petroleum and liquefied petroleum gas (LPG) for export.

Natural gas reserves totalled 23.8 billion cubic metres, primarily located in the Tano fields. Natural gas is not used in domestic consumption, but rather is used to produce electricity for use domestically and commercially. The West African Gas Pipeline Project (WAGP) which links Nigeria, Ghana, Togo and Benin, supplying gas from Nigeria's gas fields, began delivering natural gas to Ghana in December 2008.

Ghana does not produce coal but imports minimal amounts of around 3,000 tonnes annually.

Energy

Ghana's installed electricity generating capacity is 2.8 million (kW) in 2015, producing 8.8 billion kilowatt hours (kWh) per annum, the majority of which is produced by hydropower, to a total of 1.2GW. The Volta River Authority (VRA) has responsibility for the development, generation and national distribution of electricity. The 912MW Akosombo hydropower plant and the 160MW Kpong plant are run at full capacity. The Chinese-funded Black Volta River, 400MW hydroelectric dam at Bui, was agreed in 2007, and was inaugurated by 2013. Construction of the US$600m dam continues despite concerns about the environmental and social effects of the dam. 54 per cent of total installed capacity in 2015 was generated via hydroelectric power.

The thermal power station near Takoradi produces 300MW and is linked to the (WAGP) natural gas pipeline from Nigeria. Ghana is a net exporter of electricity to the power grids in Benin and Togo, from the Akosombo Plant on the Volta River.

Around 60 per cent of the population has access to electricity. In September 2008 a US$350 million credit facility was granted by the US to fund the implementation of the latest rural electrification programme, which has been underway since the 1980s.

Financial markets

Stock exchange

Ghana Stock Exchange (GSE)

Banking and insurance

Stability in money markets and low inflationary expectations following petroleum deregulation, led to a reduction in the prime interest rate of 16.5 per cent on 30 May 2005, down from 18.5 per cent which had remained unchanged since May 2004.

It was announced in March 2005 that the introduction of the shared currency, the Eco, in Ghana, Guinea, Nigeria, Sierra Leone and The Gambia, which was due in July 2005, would be postponed. The currency was proposed to facilitate trade and growth with an ultimate plan to merge it with the CFA franc.

Central bank
Bank of Ghana

Main financial centre
Accra

Time
GMT

Geography
Ghana's southern border is the Gulf of Guinea. To the north, east and west lie the states of Burkina Faso, Togo and Côte d'Ivoire. From north to south the country extends a distance of about 680 km.
The River Volta, which flows from the north to the south-east, is the most conspicuous landmark. There is a coastal area of thicket and mangrove which gives way in the east and north-east to more open plains and semi-deciduous forest. To the west and north-west of the coastal strip is high forest, which still covers the greater part of Ashanti and part of the Northern Region. The forest gives way in the north to Guinea savannah woodland; the extreme north-eastern corner of Ghana forms part of the drier Sudan savannah woodland.

Hemisphere
Northern

Climate
Ghana lies entirely within the tropics. In the northern savannah the climate is hot and dry, with intermittent rainfall during March–September. In the hot and humid forest regions there are two rainy seasons, during March–June and September–November. At the coast, which is only 4.5 degrees from the Equator, the heat is intense.
The capital city, Accra, is only 65 metres above sea level. The capital's hottest month is March, with temperatures of 24–32 degrees Celsius (C); August is the coldest month, with temperatures of 21–27 C. The annual rainfall in the capital averages 865mm. The driest month is December when rainfall averages 18mm, and the wettest month is June when rainfall averages 235mm.

Dress codes
Western-style clothes are usually worn for business purposes, including shorts for outdoor occupations. On social or ceremonial occasions, traditional costume or Western-style clothes are equally acceptable.
Local dress includes the expensive, hand-woven Kente cloth for which Ghana is famous: this is worn by men like a toga. Wearing any military clothing, such as camouflage jackets or trousers, or any clothing or items that may appear military in nature, is strictly prohibited.

Entry requirements
Passports
Required by all, except by members of the Economic Community of West African States (Ecowas) with a valid travel certificate.

Visa
Required by all, except nationals of Ecowas countries, Kenya, Zimbabwe, Egypt, Mauritius, Singapore and Hong Kong.
Visas are valid for three-month periods. An application for a business visa must contain a letter of confirmation from the representative's employer and itinerary, plus an invitation from a local host. All visitors must have return/onward passage.

Currency advice/regulations
It is advisable to check the latest currency regulations prior to visit.
It is easy to exchange US dollar bills for cedis. Visa cards can be used to withdraw cedis from Barclays Bank automatic teller machines (ATMs).
Unlimited import of foreign currency, but it must be declared. Unused foreign currency, travellers cheques, etc, declared on arrival, can be exported. Foreign currency must be exchanged with authorised dealers only. Keep the foreign exchange form. Import of local currency is prohibited and export is limited to C5,000, which must be recorded in passport.
Unused cedis can be re-exchanged into foreign currency by local banks or the Bank of Ghana, but the declaration form T.5 must show that the monies were obtained while in Ghana from an authorised dealer in foreign exchange.

Health (for visitors)
Mandatory precautions
A yellow fever vaccination certificate must be presented on arrival. A cholera vaccination may be required, depending on local circumstances.

Advisable precautions
Cholera is seasonal. Typhoid, polio, tetanus, hepatitis A and meningitis vaccinations are recommended. A hepatitis B vaccination is recommended if staying in Ghana over six months. A vaccination for rabies is recommended if travelling to rural areas. Malaria prophylaxis should be taken as risk exists throughout the country. Water precautions are essential. There is a bilharzia risk and swimming in rivers is not advisable. HIV/Aids is present in Ghana. Guinea worm is rife and increasing in northern regions.
Emergency facilities are extremely limited. Insurance is vital and emergency evacuation should be included.

Hotels
Available in Accra, Kumasi, Takoradi and other regional capitals. Prices are high. A 10 per cent government tax is added. Tipping is permitted in hotels, restaurants, etc. It is rarely added to the bill.

Credit cards
The most widely accepted credit cards are American Express, Diners' and Visa. They may be used for payment at nearly all airlines, leading hotels and major supermarkets.
Many restaurants and airlines prefer to be paid in cash.

Public holidays (national)
Fixed dates
1 Jan (New Year's Day), 6 Mar (Independence Day), 1 May (Labour Day), 25 May (Africa Day), 4 Jun (1979 Coup Anniversary), 1 Jul (Republic Day), 25 Dec (Christmas Day), 26 Dec (Boxing Day), 31 Dec (Revolution Day).

Variable dates
Good Friday, Easter Monday, National Farmers' Day, Eid al Adha, Eid al Fitr.

Islamic year 1437 (15 Oct 2015–2 Oct 2016):: The Islamic year contains 354 or 355 days, with the result that Muslim feasts advance by 10–12 days against the Gregorian calendar. Dates of feasts vary according to the sighting of the new moon, so cannot be forecast exactly.

Working hours
Banking
Mon–Thu: 0830–1400; Fri: 0830–1500.

Business
Mon–Fri: 0800–1200, 1400–1700. Sat: 0830–1200.

Government
Mon–Fri: 0800–1230, 1330–1700.

Shops
Mon–Tue and Thu–Fri: 0800–1200, 1400–1730. Wed and Sat: 0800–1300. Closed on Sundays.

Electricity supply
220V AC, 50 cycles

Social customs/useful tips
It is traditional to arrive with a gift when accepting private hospitality, particularly in rural areas. It is customary to use the right hand when presenting an object to another person, particularly in the case of food or a gift.
In northern Ghana, where the population tends to be Muslim, Islamic customs should be respected: it is considered unclean to eat or drink with the left hand; it is insulting to point the sole of your shoe at a Muslim. Older people are treated with special respect in Ghana.

It is inadvisable for foreigners to refer to tribalism or ethnic affiliations when discussing current affairs.

Body language differences include the custom of a greater degree of physical contact – touching and holding hands – between men and between women.

Business people need patience when dealing with bureaucracy. There are regular power cuts in Accra.

There are no unusual or particularly strict laws, but foreign visitors should observe all rules and regulations as Ghana does not take ignorance of the law as an excuse for non-observance. It is prudent to carry proof of identity.

Security

Violent crime has risen, particularly in and around Accra. Visitors are advised to exercise a high level of vigilance in public areas and when travelling in vehicles. If possible, avoid travelling alone in taxis after dark. Be wary when withdrawing cash from the few cash points in central Accra. Thefts of both luggage and travel documents occur at Kotoka International Airport. Ensure your documents are kept secured (particularly when leaving the airport) and never leave your baggage unattended.

Be wary of all offers of unsolicited assistance at the airport unless from uniformed porters or officials who, as with all other permanent staff, wear a current ID card bearing their name and photograph. ID cards without photographs are not valid.

Taking photographs near sensitive installations, including military sites and government buildings, is prohibited. Permission should be obtained before taking photographs of anyone in uniform.

Getting there

Air

National airline: Ghana International Airlines

International airport/s: Accra-Kotoka International (ACC), 5km from city; duty-free shop, bar, buffet, restaurant, bank, post office, taxis.

Airport tax: International departures C22,000; domestic departures C500.

Surface

Road: The coastal road runs from Lagos (Nigeria) through Cotonou (Benin) and Lomé (Togo) to Accra. The condition of this road is variable. A generally good road links Abidjan (Côte d'Ivoire) with Kumasi.

Main port/s: The main ports are Tema and Takoradi. Ships connect Tema, 25km east of Accra, with ports in Nigeria, Côte d'Ivoire, Cameroon and South Africa.

Getting about

National transport

Transport in northern Ghana can be more difficult than in southern Ghana.

Air: Several airlines fly domestic routes from Kotoka to Kumasi and Tamale.

Road: There are over 30,000km of classified roads — 15,000km of these are trunk roads, the remainder being feeder roads. There are also around 6,000km of unclassified tracks. Of the total road network, approximately 6,000km are paved. There are reasonable roads between Accra and the main towns.

The main routes are Accra-Tema, Accra-Takoradi, Accra-Kumasi, Accra-Koforidua, Accra-Ho. Roads are often potholed and badly marked.

Buses: State-run bus services connect major centres. They are subject to delays and cancellation and are not recommended for business users.

Rail: The total network is about 1,000km, connecting Tema-Accra through Nsawam-Koforidua-Nkawkaw (Eastern Region) to Kumasi (Ashanti Region) through to Dunkwa and Prestea, Tarkwa and Sekondi-Takoradi (Western Region). Another line runs from Huni Valley (Western Region) to Kade (Eastern Region).

Two classes; air-conditioning and restaurant cars not available; sleeping accommodation available on some services.

Water: A weekly ferry, the *Yapei Queen*, plies Lake Volta between Yeji in the north and Akosombo, more than 200km to the south, a two-day journey. Ferries connect Yeji with Makongo and Buipe.

City transport

Taxis: There are cheap and reliable taxis in Accra.

Tipping is not usual; taxis are unmetered – fare is by negotiation; rates are often posted in hotels.

Buses, trams & metro: The bus services in Accra are run by the city authority and private operators.

Car hire

Car hire is expensive. An international driving licence is recommended; this must be endorsed by Police Licensing Office if stay exceeds 90 days. Traffic drives on the right.

Driving at night is not advised.

BUSINESS DIRECTORY

The addresses listed below are a selection only. While World of Information makes every endeavour to check these addresses, we cannot guarantee that changes have not been made, especially to telephone numbers and area codes. We would welcome any corrections.

Telephone area codes

The international direct dialling code (IDD) for Ghana is +233, followed by area code and subscriber's number:

Accra	21	Takoradi	31
Koforidua	81	Tamale	71
Kumasi	51	Tema	22

Useful telephone numbers

Police, fire and ambulance: 999.

Chambers of Commerce

Accra District Chamber of Commerce, Trade Fair Centre, PO Box 2325, Accra (tel: 662-427).

British-Ghana Chamber of Commerce and Industry, PO Box GP 21101, Accra (tel: 674-762; fax: 296-836; e-mail: info@ghanabritishchamber.com).

Ghana National Chamber of Commerce, 65 Kojo Thompson Road, PO Box 2325, Accra (tel: 662-427; fax: 662-210; e-mail: gncc@ncs.com.gh).

Banking

Agricultural Development Bank, PO Box 4191, Cedi House, Liberia Road, Accra (tel: 662-758, 662-762; fax: 662-912, 662-846).

Amalgamated Bank Limited, PO Box C1541, C131/3 Farrar Avenue, Accra (tel: 249-690; fax: 249-697; e-mail: amalbank@ighmail.com).

Barclays Bank of Ghana Ltd, PO Box 2949, Barclays House, High Street, Accra (tel: 664-901/4, 665-382; fax: 667-420).

CAL Merchant Bank Ltd, PO Box 14596, 45 Independence Avenue, Accra (tel: 221-056, 231-098, 222-345, 221-091, 231-912-7; fax: 231-104, 231-913).

Ecobank Ghana Ltd, 19 Seventh Avenue, Ridge West, Private Mail Bag, GPO, Accra (tel: 229-532, 228-812, 221-103, 667-109; fax: 667-127, 232-086).

First Atlantic Merchant Bank Ltd, PO Box C1620, Atlantic Place, No. 1 Seventh Avenue, Ridge West, Cantonments, Accra (tel: 231-433-5, 245-647, 245-660, 232-566; fax: 231-399).

Ghana Commercial Bank Ltd, PO Box 134, Accra (tel: 664-914 (5 lines), 664-911, 664-918; fax: 662-168).

International Commercial Bank Ltd, PO Box 20057, Accra (tel: 666-190, 665-779; fax: 668-221).

Merchant Bank (Ghana) Ltd, PO Box 401, Merban House, 44 Kwame Nkrumah Ave, Accra (tel: 666-331/2, 666-336; fax: 663-398).

Metropolitan and Allied Bank (GH) Ltd, PO Box C 1778, Valco Trust House, Castle Road Branch, Cantonments, Accra (tel: 232-770, 232-776; fax: 232-728).

National Investment Bank Ltd, PO Box 3726, 37 Kwame Nkrumah Avenue, Accra (tel: 240-001, 240-024; fax: 240-030/34).

Prudential Bank Ltd, PO Box 9820, Airport, Accra (tel: 226-322, 226-803; fax: 226-803).

SSB Bank Ltd, 1 Cola Avenue, Kokomlemle, Accra (tel: 222-564/223-375/222-136; fax: 222-136).

Stanbic Bank Ghana Limited, PO Box CT 2344, Valco Trust House, Castle Road, Ridge, Accra (tel: 234-683-4, 234-679, 250-066-7, 250-070-5; fax: 234-685).

Standard Chartered Bank Ghana Ltd, PO Box 768, 3rd Floor, Accra High Street Building, Accra (tel: 664-591-8, 672-210; fax: 667-751, 663-560).

The Trust Bank Ltd, PO Box 1862, Re-insurance House, 68 Kwame Nkrumah Avenue, Accra (tel: 240-049–052; fax: 240-056, 240-059).

Central bank

Bank of Ghana, PO Box 2674, Thorpe Road, Accra (tel: 666-174; fax: 662-996; e-mail: secretary@bog.gov.gh).

Stock exchange

Ghana Stock Exchange (GSE), www.gse.com.gh

Travel information

Accra Kotoka International Airport, PO Box 87, Accra (tel: 776-171).

Ghana International Airlines, Silver Star Tower, PO Box 78, Kotoka International Airport, Accra (tel: 213-555; fax: 767-744).

Ghana Tourist Development Co Ltd, PO Box 8710, Accra (tel: 772-084; fax: 772-093).

Ministry of tourism

Ministry of Tourism, PO Box 4386, Accra (tel: 666-314, 666-426; fax: 666-826).

National tourist organisation offices

Ghana Tourist Board, PO Box 3106, Accra (tel: 238-330; fax: 231-779; e-mail: gtb@africa-on-line.com.gh).

Ministries

Ministry of Communications: PO Box M.41, Accra (tel: 229-870; fax: 229-786).

Ministry of Defence, Burma Camp, Accra (tel: 774-727; fax: 773-951).

Ministry of Education, PO Box M45, Accra (tel: 662-772; fax: 664-067).

Ministry of Employment and Social Welfare, PO Box M84, Accra (tel: 665-421; fax: 667-251).

Ministry of Environment, Science and Technology, PO Box M39, Accra (tel: 662-626; fax: 666-828).

Ministry of Finance and Economic Planning, PO Box M40, Accra (tel: 665-441, 665-587, 666-512; fax: 667-069; internet: www.finance.gov.gh).

Ministry of Food and Agriculture, PO Box M37, Accra (tel: 663-036, 665-421; fax: 663-250).

Ministry of Foreign Affairs, PO Box M53, Accra (tel: 664-008; fax: 665-363; internet: www.mfa.gov.gh/).

Ministry of Health, PO Box M44, Accra (tel: 665-323; fax: 663-810).

Ministry of Information, PO Box M41, Accra (tel: 228-0211).

Ministry of Interior, PO Box M42, Accra (tel: 665-421; fax: 662-688).

Ministry of Justice & Attorney General, PO Box M60, Accra (tel: 665-051).

Ministry of Land and Forestry, PO Box M212, Accra (tel: 665-949; fax: 666-801, 666-896).

Ministry of Local Government, Rural Development and Co-op, PO Box M50, Accra (tel: 664-763; fax: 667-911).

Ministry of Mines and Energy, PO Box 40, Stadium Post Office, Accra (tel: 667-090; fax: 668-262).

Ministry of Mobilisation (tel: 665-349; fax: 667-251).

Ministry of Roads and Transport, PO Box M43, Accra (tel: 666-465; fax: 667-911).

Ministry of Tourism, PO Box 4386, Accra (tel: 666-314; fax: 666-182; e-mail: MOT@ghana.com; internet site: http://www.estghana.gov.gh; www.africaonline.com.gh/Tourism).

Ministry of Trade and Industry, PO Box M47, Accra (tel: 663-327; fax: 665-114).

Ministry of Works and Housing, PO Box M43, Accra (tel: 662-242; fax: 663-268).

Ministry of Youth and Sports, PO Box M 252, Accra (tel: 664-71; fax: 663-927).

Other useful addresses

Accra International Conference Centre, PO Box C1054, Accra (tel: 669-600; fax: 669-825).

Ashanti Goldfields Co Ltd, Gold House, Patrice Lumumba Road, Roman Ridge, PO Box 2665, Accra (tel: 772-190, 776-224, 778-155; fax: 775-947).

Association of Ghanaian Industry, PO Box 8624, Accra (tel: 777-283; fax: 773-143).

Black Star Line, PO Box 2760, Accra (tel: 776-161; fax: 775-140).

British Diplomatic Mission, Accra (tel: 221-665).

Civil Aviation Authority, Kotoka International Airport, PO Box 87, Accra (tel: 773-283).

Coffee, Sheanuts Exporters' Association, c/o Mr J W Biney, Agrotrade Ltd., PO Box 226, Accra (tel: 224-820; fax: 224-564).

Customs, Excise and Preventive Service, PO Box 68, Accra (tel: 666-841; fax: 660-019).

Department of Co-operatives, PO Box M150, Accra (tel: 666-212).

Department of Urban Roads, Ministry of Roads and Transport, PO Box 38, Accra (tel: 230-381, 223-908; fax: 234-522).

Divestiture Implementation Committee, F35/5 Ring Road East, North Labone, PO Box CT102, Cantonments, Accra (tel: 772-049, 773-119, 760-281; fax: 773-126; e-mail: dicgh@ncs.com.gh).

Export Finance Company, Bank of Ghana, PO Box 2674, Accra (tel: 666-902; fax: 662-996).

Federation of Association of Ghanaian Exporters (FAGE), c/o Kiku Ltd., PO Box M378, Accra (tel: 223-215; fax: 776-755).

Finsap Implementation Secretariat, Private Mail Bag (PMB), Ministries Post Office, Accra (tel: 666-254, 664-976; fax: 667-448; e-mail: finsap@gh.com).

Ghana Assorted Foodstuffs Exporters Assocation, PO Box 16073, Airport - Accra (tel: 220-746; fax: 223-663).

Ghana Chamber of Mines, PO Box 991, Accra (tel: 665-355; fax: 662-926).

Ghana Civil Aviation Authority, Private Mail Bag, Kotoka International Airport, Accra (tel: 776-171; fax: 773-293; e-mail: centre-GCAA@ighmail.com; internet site: http://www.gcaa.com.gh).

Ghana Cocoa Board, PO Box 933, Accra (tel: 221-212; fax: 667-104, 665-076; e-mail: cocobod@africaonline.com.gh).

Ghana Export Promotion Council, Republic House, Tudu, PO Box M 146, Accra (tel: 228-813/830/623; fax: 668-263, 233-715; e-mail: gepc@ighmail.com).

Ghana Free-Zones Board, PO Box M626, Accra (tel: 670-532/5; fax: 670-536; e-mail: freezone@africaonline.com.gh; internet site: http://www.ghanaclassified.com.ghzb).

Ghana Furniture Producers/Exporters Association, PO Box 32, Trade Fair Centre, Accra (tel: 775-311).

Ghana Highway Authority, PO Box 1641, Accra (tel: 666-591; fax: 665-571).

Ghana Investment Promotion Centre (GIPC), PO Box M193, Accra (tel: 665-125/9; fax: 663-801; e-mail: gipc@ghana.com; internet site: http://www.gipc.org.gh).

Ghana Liaison Office, Cotecna Inspection S A, 10 Drake Avenue, Airport Residential

Area, PO Box C2212, Cantonments, Accra (tel: 775-698; fax: 553-522).

Ghana National Petroleum Corporation (GNPC), Private Mail Bag, Tema (tel: 232-056; fax: 774-143).

Ghana National Procurement Agency, Ministries Post Office, Private Mail Bag, Accra (tel: 220-851; fax: 221-049).

Ghana Shippers Council, Private Mail Bag, Ministries Post Office, Accra (tel: 666-915; fax: 668-768).

Ghana Stock Exchange, Marketing Department, 5th Floor, Cedi House, Liberia Road, Accra (tel: 669-914; fax: 669-913; e-mail: stockex@ncs.com.gh; internet site; http://www.gse.com.gh).

Ghana Trade and Investment Gateway Project (GHATIG), PO Box M47, Accra (tel: 663-439, 664-074; fax: 665-423; e-mail: gateway1@ghana.com).

Ghana Yam Producers and Exporters' Association, PO Box 5233, Accra (tel: 775-311; fax: 668-263).

Ghanaian Embassy (USA), 3512 International Drive, NW, Washington DC 20008 (tel: (+1-202)-686-4520; fax: (+1-202)-686-4527; e-mail: hagan@cais.com).

Horticulturists' Association of Ghana, PO Box 9303, Accra (tel: 772-139; fax: 772-350).

Institute of Economic Affairs (tel: 776-641; fax: 776-724).

Internal Revenue Services, PO Box 2202, Accra (tel: 664-961; fax: 664-938).

Organisation for Export Development for Seafood, c/o Signotrade Ltd., PO Box 16851, Accra (tel: 712-762; fax: 668-263).

Precious Metals Marketing Corporation, PO Box M108, Accra (tel: 664-931; fax: 772-350).

Private Enterprises Foundation (PEF), PO Box C1671, Cantoments, Accra (tel: 222-313; fax: 231-487).

Registar-General's Department, PO Box 118, Accra (tel: 666-469).

US Diplomatic Mission, Accra (tel: 228-440).

Vegetables Exporters' Association, c/o Ghana Export Promotion Council, PO Box M146, Accra (tel: 221-212; fax: 668-263).

Volta River Authority, PO Box MB77, Accra (tel: 664-941, 221-124; fax: 662-610; e-mail: orgsrv@accra.vra.com).

National news agency: Ghana News Agency, PO Box 2118, Accra (tel: 662-381, 665-135/6/7; fax: 669-841; email: ghnews@ghana.com; internet: www.ghananewsagency.org).

Internet sites

Africa Business Network: http://www.ifc.org/abn

Ghana Forestry Commision: http://ghanatimber.org/

AllAfrica.com: http://allafrica.com

African Development Bank: http://www.afdb.org

Mbendi AfroPaedia (information on companies, countries, industries and stock exchanges in Africa): http://mbendi.co.za

Yellow Pages: http://www.ghanaforum.com/directory.htm

Gibraltar

The Gibraltar government's 2015 budget paper announced that the growth in gross domestic product (GDP) for the previous financial year 2014/15 was estimated by the Statistics Office at G£1.64 billion (US$2.53 billion), which represents a GDP growth of 10.3 per cent in money terms for that year. This increased level of growth in the economy during the previous three years, at an average growth rate of over 10 per cent per annum, meant that Gibraltar continued to rank among the fastest growing economies in the world.

Gibraltar's 2015 estimated GDP per capita is G£50,941 (US$78,400) using the latest published figure of population of 32,194 people, published in the mid-2015 Census. Gibraltar maintained its third place on the International Monetary Fund (IMF) *World Economic Outlook Database* of GDP per capita rankings, ahead of Kuwait, the United Arab Emirates, Singapore, Brunei and Norway and only behind Qatar and Luxembourg. The main drivers for this positive growth are primarily the continuing increases in employment and turnover in the predominant online gaming and financial services industries and the increased levels of construction in the economy with the private sector now taking more of the lead in that respect.

According to the government, the number of jobs in Gibraltar was at a record high of 24,422 in mid-2015. This represented a 16.4 per cent increase since 2010. The number of unemployed in Gibraltar was just under 200. This year's out-turn reflected a surplus of revenue over expenditure of G£51.3 million (US$78.9 million). Out of this record surplus for the year, a sum of G£30 million US$46.1 million) had been earmarked by the government as a contribution to the Gibraltar Community Care Trust, bringing the government's total contributions to the Trust during the previous three financial years to G£134 million (US$206 million). Government revenue during the previous financial year had exceeded the original budget by around G£24 million (US$40 million). As a reflection of the continuing growth in the economy, income tax receipts were up by around G£8 million (US$12.3 million), over the budgeted figure and company tax receipts were up by around G£9 million (US$13.8 million). In 2015 Gibraltar continued to be largely about making money. The level of turnover beyond which audited accounts are required had been raised from £1,000,000 to £1,250,000 (US$1,538,400–1,915,400), an indicator of the encouragement given by the Gibraltar government to start-up companies.

Airport troubles

At an informal meeting in Riga June 2015, the Spanish minister for foreign affairs and co-operation, José Manuel García-Margallo, expressed the wish to his fellow ministers that Spain and the United Kingdom could reach some form of agreement on the use of Gibraltar's airport that would apply the European Union's Open Skies policy. Mr García-Margallo said that 'The solution I have proposed, which has been well received by our colleagues, is that all aviation regulations, including the agreement with Ukraine, be applied to all European airports except to that of Gibraltar, until some agreement is reached between England and Spain.'

The Spanish minister confirmed that he had had a conversation with the British minister, Philip Hammond, about the possibility of applying European traffic regulations to Gibraltar's airport, where a Spanish veto had prevented the liberalisation of air traffic with Ukraine. 'The United Kingdom has expressed its opinion, as I have mine,' said the Spanish minister,' who insisted that the airport in question 'is built on the isthmus, which is not a territory ceded (to the UK) by the treaty of Utrecht.' Which was why Spain 'Could not accept any gesture that presupposed any recognition of sovereignty' in the zone. For the Spanish minister reaching an agreement was 'very feasible' since there existed 'known European formulae' such as those governing the use of the French-Swiss Basel airport. 'Spain is perfectly well disposed to finding a solution to the problem along these lines' said Mr García-Margallo, referring to the possible shared use of Gibraltar's airport by Britain and Spain. The European Commission has maintained a neutral stance on the issue,

KEY FACTS

Official name: Gibraltar

Head of State: Queen Elizabeth II, represented by Governor Sir James Dutton (from 6 Dec 2013)

Head of government: Chief Minister Fabian Picardo (GSL) (from 9 Dec 2011)

Ruling party: Gibraltar Socialist Labour Party-Liberal Party (GSL-LP) alliance (from 9 Dec 2011)

Area: 7 square km

Population: 32,194 (census, mid-2015)

Capital: Gibraltar

Official language: English

Currency: Pound sterling (£) = 100 pence (the euro also circulates and is accepted informally)

Exchange rate: £0.65 per US$ (Sep 2015)

in the hope that parties will eventually reach some sort of bilateral agreement.

Anachronism?

For both the British and Spanish governments, Gibraltar is an anachronism that will not go away. For twenty-first century Britain it is more of a liability than an asset, for Spanish governments, it is an annoying irritation used by each of the major parties to highlight the shortcomings of the other. The 32,200 population crammed into 2.5 square miles (6.5 square km) on Spain's southernmost point is a mixture of Italian (mostly of Genoese ancestry), Moorish (from nearby Morocco), Jewish (who had been expelled from Spain), Maltese, Portuguese and Hindi cultures – everything, in fact, except Spanish. There are relatively small numbers of British residents, although an increasing number of Britons work in the colony. Many of the Gibraltarian work force, although Gibraltarian taxpayers, actually live in Spain. Defending the border restrictions Mr Rajoy also announced that the tax status of those living in Spain would be closely investigated for what was described as 'Fiscal Fraud'. More than one per cent of Gibraltar's residents are millionaires from abroad, attracted by Gibraltar's Category Two tax status awarded to people with net assets of US$3.5 million. Under this scheme qualifying residents must buy or rent a property; they then pay a maximum of US$40,000 in annual income tax.

Financial centre

For decades now 'The Rock' has held a significant share of the global offshore sector. Developing Gibraltar as an offshore centre has been a key part of the government's strategy, even in the face of reservations and obstruction from Madrid. In September 2006 the banking sector in Gibraltar held assets in the vicinity of some US$15 billion and made up a third of the economy. The advantages of offshore banking in Gibraltar include its favourable tax status (bank interest is not taxed in Gibraltar, even when paid to residents), the lack of exchange controls, communications, stable government and EU membership. The EU's Savings Tax Directive, which came into force on 1 July 2005, means that for all citizens of EU member states there is an exchange of information between the Gibraltar authorities and the individuals' home tax authorities in regard to payments of interest and other returns on savings. Importantly, the directive does not apply to payments to corporate bodies. Gibraltar is beginning to develop corporate big business, which it is hoped will reduce the colony's reliance on providing more standard – and less remunerative – business for private clients.

Much of the banking activity in Gibraltar is directed to asset management for high-net-worth individuals, not least because Gibraltar has tried hard to attract such people with special tax regimes. In its financial services regulations, Gibraltar aims to match UK standards. An example of this is the local money laundering legislation which implemented the EU Directive and was extended as in the UK to encompass all crimes. Accordingly, all banking supervision regulations are the same as those in the UK and procedures for opening an account are much the same. Under EU legislation, a Gibraltar-licensed bank may set up branches elsewhere in Europe. Most of the twenty banks established in Gibraltar are branches of major UK, European or US banks.

Risk assessment

Economy	Good
Politics	Fair
Regional stability	Fair

COUNTRY PROFILE

1704 Gibraltar, commonly referred to as the Rock, was captured by the UK from Spain.

1713 Gibraltar was ceded to Britain in the Treaty of Utrecht. The Treaty stipulated that the Rock would become a part of Spain if Britain gave up sovereignty.

1830 Gibraltar became a crown colony.

1869 The opening of the Suez Canal increased Gibraltar's importance in guarding the route to India and the Far East.

1939–45 Gibraltar was a busy naval base in the Second World War. After the war, Spain continued to press for the return of Gibraltar, but rejected the UK's offer to refer the matter to the International Court of Justice.

1967 More than 12,000 Gibraltarians voted to remain British; only 44 opted for Spanish rule. The dispute continued to disrupt friendly relations between Spain and UK; for a while, Spain closed the frontier. Both countries sought a peaceful settlement, and the Gibraltarian people maintained their wish to remain British.

1969 Gibraltar adopted a new constitution that devolved a measure of power from the UK to local ministers. Spain closed the border in protest.

1975 The death of Spain's dictator, General Franco, led to more friendly relations with Spain, but there was still no resolution of the sovereignty issue.

1982 Spain allowed pedestrians to pass through the border.

1984 The Brussels Agreement was signed between Spain and the UK, establishing a negotiating process over the issue of Gibraltar's sovereignty.

1985 Spain lifted its border blockade.

1996 The Gibraltar Social Democrats (GSD) were elected; Peter Caruana became chief minister.

1998 Spanish proposals for joint sovereignty were rejected by the UK.

2000 The UK and Spain reached an agreement over Gibraltar's administrative status, which allowed Spanish recognition of documents and passports issued in Gibraltar.

2001 The Royal Navy dockyard was sold to Cammell Laird (Gibraltar) Limited.

2002 Spain and UK held talks to consider grounds for sharing sovereignty of Gibraltar.

2004 The 300th anniversary of the British occupation of Gibraltar was commemorated amid continued tensions with Spain. A trilateral forum, of the UK, Spain and Gibraltar, began talks on the territory's future.

2005 Gibraltarians took part in their first European Union (EU) elections.

2006 An agreement easing border controls allowed flights from Spain to land in Gibraltar.

2007 A constitution amendment required that a majority of 60 per cent of votes was requisite for changes to the constitution. The GSD were re-elected.

2008 Cammell Laird invested US$34.9 million in its shipyards to develop its market in super-yacht building and refitting.

2009 The foreign ministers of Spain and UK and Chief Minister Caruana held talks in Gibraltar over greater cross-border co-operation in maritime, financial and judicial matters. Sovereignty of the territory was not discussed. A move by Spain to denote the seas around Gibraltar as Spanish in an environmental directive submitted to the European Commission almost scuttled the visit before it began. This was the first visit by a Spanish minister since 1704. Sir Adrian Johns became the new governor.

2010 A new passenger ferry service to Algeciras (Cadiz) was launched. The neighbouring Spanish town of La Línea de la Concepción (La Línea), Cadiz Province, announced plans to impose a road toll tax for all vehicles entering from Gibraltar. Residents of La Línea will be granted waivers to commute into Gibraltar but no reciprocating waiver for Gibraltarian commuters was proposed.

2011 The corporate tax system for non-resident operated companies was phased out in January and replaced with a flat-rate corporate tax of 10 per cent.

Online gaming operators are expected to be disadvantaged by this new regime, introduced as a requirement of the UK tax authority. In July, the owners of the Algeciras ferry announced that it would expand the service to carry freight; this will allow Gibraltarian exports to Spain to avoid the restrictive land-border crossing at La Línea. In parliamentary elections held in December the opposition alliance of the Gibraltar Socialist Labour Party-Liberal Party (GSL-LP) won 48.9 per cent of the vote (10 seats of 17) and ousted the ruling GSD. Fabian Picardo (GSL) was sworn in as chief minister.

2012 On 15 October, the UK government condemned the action of Spanish border police which delayed traffic into Gibraltar by up to six hours on 13–14 October, and called the holdups 'unacceptable'. The Spanish authorities said an anti-smuggling operation had caused the problems, however no warning was given that any such action was due. The UK continues to demand that as both Spain and the UK (which includes its Gibraltarian territory) are members of the EU the right of passage between member-states is maintained.

2013 There were long delays at the Spanish-Gibraltar border due to increased vehicle searches by the Spanish authorities from 6 August. The Spanish were objecting to the creation of an artificial reef in the waters off Gibraltar and said they had been '… fulfilling [Spain's] duties under European law to monitor its borders and to abide by rules set up to avoid the illegal traffic of illicit goods and prevent smuggling.' Traffic began to flow again after the foreign ministers of the UK and Spain held discussions. The delays had affected tourists and thousands of people who go in and out of the territory every day to work. However, by 12 August the UK government was considering legal action against Spain after additional border checks were again imposed over the weekend. A government spokesman said Spain might take the dispute to the UN Security Council where it could seek the support of Argentina, which has a dispute with the UK over the Falkland Islands. He said that there were similarities between the two disputes. On 23 August Governor Sir Adrian Johns of Gibraltar criticised Spain for sending police divers to explore the artificial reef in waters which Spain claims and which Spanish fishermen say is damaging their industry. Six EU inspectors visited Gibraltar to investigate the row on 25 September.

2014 A poll carried out by *The Telegraph*, a London daily newspaper, in January asked whether Gibraltar is British of Spanish. Voting results appeared to show a majority voting for Spain. However, analysis of the voters showed that over 5,000 of the votes in favour of Spain appeared to come from computers of the Spanish ministry of defence. In addition a social media campaign run in Spain at the time of the poll was considered to have skewed the voting.

2015 At an informal meeting in Riga in June, Spain's foreign minister, José Manuel García- Margallo, expressed the wish to his fellow ministers that Spain and the UK could reach some form of agreement on the use of Gibraltar's airport.

Political structure

Constitution

A new constitution was promulgated on 2 January 2007, which modernises the UK-Gibraltar relationship. Some responsibilities undertaken by the governor are limited, particularly those areas of external affairs, defence, internal security and the public service. The house of Assembly became the Gibraltar Parliament, which determines its own size and new commissions were create to undertake the appointments to the judiciary and public service and a new police authority was created, which will undertake greater local input.

Form of state

British Overseas Territory (BOT)

The executive

The governor does not take an active role in governmental affairs.

The Chief Minister is the head of the Gibraltar government and holds much of the power.

National legislature

The unicameral Gibraltar Parliament is governed by the 2006 constitution. It has at least 17 elected members serving four-year terms plus a speaker, appointed by parliament, who does not have a casting vote. The governor appoints as chief minister the member of parliament (MP) most likely to command the largest political block.

There are no constituencies and all votes are cast for individual candidates that may make up block votes. Every voter has a maximum 10 votes, to cast among all candidates standing. Universal suffrage is at aged 18.

Legal system

It is based on English common law coupled to statutes. The civil courts in Gibraltar are the Court of First Instance, the Supreme Court, the Court of Appeal and ultimately, the Privy Council in the UK.

Last elections

8 December 2011 (parliamentary)

Results: Parliamentary: the Gibraltar Socialist Labour Party-Liberal Party (GSL-LP) alliance won 48.9 per cent of the vote (10 seats of 17), the Gibraltar Social Democrats (GSD) 46.8 per cent (7), and the Progressive Democratic Party (PDP) 4.4 per cent (0); turnout was 82.5 per cent.

Next elections

2015 (parliamentary)

Political parties

Ruling party

Gibraltar Socialist Labour Party-Liberal Party (GSL-LP) alliance (from 9 Dec 2011)

Main opposition party

Gibraltar Social Democrats (GSD)

Political situation

Success of the new constitution, which gives the territory, not only increased status, but also practical power in 2007 encourages Gibraltar to apply for membership of the United Nations. This of course is yet another thorny issue for Spain that sees the territory as a wayward entity that should be firmly under its jurisdiction. But Gibraltar has an historic tie to the UK, which has consistently said it won't give away Gibraltar's future of self-determination without a referendum in agreement. In the meantime, Gibraltar is taking progressively more decisions for itself and may never want to give up its, admittedly circumscribed, freedom.

Population

32,194 (2015)

Last census: 32,194 (mid-2015)

Annual growth rate: 0.2 per cent (2003)

Ethnic make-up

English, Italian, Maltese, Portuguese, Spanish.

Religions

Roman Catholic (77 per cent), Church of England (7 per cent), Muslim (7 per cent), Jewish (2 per cent).

Education

Gibraltar has a comprehensive system of education, based on the UK model. Bayside (merged with three separate schools), is the only secondary school for boys between the ages of 12 and 18. Westside School, the Gibraltar Girls' Comprehensive School caters for 900 students between the ages of 12 to 18. Many children are likely to receive third level education in the UK through several grant facilities, resulting in the high incidence of returning professional graduates.

Health

Health conditions are generally good and broadly comparable to most of Western Europe. Heart diseases and cancers account for most mortality. Gibraltar's health services are closely modelled on the UK's National Health Service, with which it maintains professional and service links. There is provision for a full range of primary care and secondary care services, available through the Primary Care Centre. Medical cases requiring

tertiary care are usually referred to the UK or Spain. The St Bernard's Hospital is the only general hospital, with 170 beds providing outpatient services, emergency facilities and investigative facilities.
Government expenditure towards healthcare amounted is around £30 million (US$45.2 million) per annum
Life expectancy: 79 years (estimate 2003)
Fertility rate/Maternal mortality rate: 1.7 births per woman (2003)
Birth rate/Death rate: 11 births per 1,000 population; nine deaths per 1,000 population (2003).
Child (under 5 years) mortality rate (per 1,000): Five per 1,000 live births (2003)

Welfare
A social insurance funds all state pensions and benefits, with contributions and other earnings on investments meeting the cost of the scheme. The government's investment in capital projects towards social and economic development is funded by the Improvement and Development Fund, 12 per cent of which is allocated for housing.

Main cities
Gibraltar (estimated population 26,936 in 2012).

Languages spoken
Spanish, Italian, Portuguese and Malti; English is used in schools and for official purposes.

Official language/s
English

Media

Press
Dailies: Gibraltar's oldest daily newspaper is the *Gibraltar Chronicle* (www.chronicle.gi).
Weeklies: There are several magazines including *Panorama* (www.panorama.gi), *Vox* (www.vox.gi), which also publishes a Spanish section, *The New People* (www.thenewpeople.net) with political reports and the satirical *Gibraltar Inquirer* (www.gibinquirer.net).
Business: The *Gibraltar International* (www.gibraltarfinance.com) is a quarterly magazine covering finance and business matters.
Periodicals: Magazines include the monthly *Insight* (www.insight-gibraltar.com) with lifestyle news and *The Gibraltar Magazine* (www.thegibraltarmagazine.com) with business and leisure articles.

Broadcasting
Public radio and television services are provided by the Gibraltar Broadcaster Corporation (GBC) (www.gbc.gi), funded partly by revenue from TV licence fees and also through advertising fees and the UK military broadcaster, BFBS (www.ssvc.com/bfbs).
Radio: Two station networks broadcast within the territory Radio Gibraltar (www.gbc.gi) and the BFBS Radio and Radio 2 (www.ssvc.com/bfbs). There are a number of external services from Spain that can be received.
Television: GBC (www.gbc.gi) operates one channel and BFBS offers access to pay-to-view TV and satellite services.

Economy
Gibraltar has few natural resources, with almost no part of its land area capable of sustaining agriculture. It has a significant absence of heavy manufacturing activity, apart from ship repair. The economy is dependent on imports of food, consumer goods, building materials, construction equipment and fuel. As such, the economy is service-based, in particular dependent on the financial and tourist sectors (over 5 million tourists annually – including day-visitors from Spain); shipping services fees, and duties on consumer goods. The first three sectors contribute 25–30 per cent of GDP. Telecommunications accounts for another 10 per cent.
The gambling sector has been a growth industry since the first gambling business began operating in 1989. An agreement reached with Spain in 2006 finally broke a 30-year ban on flights between Gibraltar and Spain. Spain also agreed to recognise Gibraltar's Internet suffix '.gi' and mobile (cell) phone signals across the border.
In 2013 visitors to Gibraltar spent £207 million (US$318 million) – 71 per cent of which came from visitors from the Campo -- whilst residents of Gibraltar spent £46 million (US$71 million) elsewhere in the region.
Gibraltar has a small population, boosted by a large pool of foreign workers recruited for the financial sector. The economy is dependent on offshore financial services. It is in competition with a number of tax havens within the EU and outside, and is subject to international limits on money transactions, while maintaining a reputation for probity and turning a profit in order to continue to flourish.

External trade
Gibraltar is a member of the European Community as an overseas territory of the UK, however it does not participate in the customs union, common commercial policy (free movement of goods do not apply), and the levy of VAT. Nevertheless community rulings are implemented through UK local legislation.
Its regular trade deficit is largely offset by invisible earnings in financial services, ship-repairs, internet gambling and telecommunications.

Imports
Main imports are petroleum, manufactured goods, vehicles, machinery and foodstuffs.
Main sources: Spain (typically 24 per cent of total), Russia (12 per cent), Italy (12 per cent).

Exports
Manufactured goods dominate exports.
Main destinations: UK (typically 30 per cent of total), Spain (23 per cent), Germany (14 per cent).

Re-exports
Petroleum (over 50 per cent of total), tobacco, manufactured goods and wine.

Industry and manufacturing
The shipbuilding company, Cammell Laird (Gibralter) Ltd ownes and operates the shipyard and dry dock. The port provides an important source of income. The Gibraltar government has encouraged the setting up of light industries there, by making available a package of incentives and other benefits to successful companies. Gibraltar also has a wine bottling plant and a satellite control system.
The New Harbours, a free-port zone where there are no duties or taxes on imported materials and low rates of tax on profits, comprises warehousing, industrial workshops and office space, available to rent or purchase for exporting companies.

Tourism
This tiny ex-British colony on the tip of the Iberian peninsular is staunchly independent of its Spanish neighbour. Travel and tourism is an important component of the economy for Gibraltar, constituting around 60 per cent of GDP. Visitors can arrive by air, sea or land. Gibraltar is a destination for the yachting enthusiast as it is within range of both the Atlantic Ocean and Mediterranean Sea. Cruise liner visitors, day-trip tax-free shoppers and military history enthusiasts are among the estimated annual seven million visitors.
In 2013 visitors to Gibraltar spent £207 million (US$318 million) – 71 per cent of which came from visitors from the Campo -- whilst residents of Gibraltar spent £46 million (US$71 million) elsewhere in the region.
Spain has a constricting influence on Gibraltar's tourism industry as road visitors can experience delays at the border with Spain.

Hydrocarbons
Gibraltar does not produce oil, gas or coal. It imports petroleum products to meet its energy needs, which were around 20,220 barrels per day in 2013; however it does not import either gas or coal.

Energy
The Gibraltar Electricity Authority is responsible for generation, transmission and supply of electricity. It had a total installed generating capacity of 43MW in 2013. It also takes electricity from a privately owned company. Total consumption was 160 million kilowatt hours (kWh) in 2013.

Banking and insurance
Gibraltar has a well-developed financial services sector, which has grown due to its independent jurisdiction under the EU's Treaty of Rome and its sound fiscal regime.
Gibraltar is a signatory of the EU tax agreement whereby it passes on, to the tax department of an EU citizen's country, information concerning the amount of money in savings accounts, to allow tax to be levied from the account holder's home country.
There are over 20 licenced banks and some 18 insurance companies operating.

Offshore facilities
There is a well established offshore banking sector in Gibraltar, although by 2008 the number of banks in operation dropped from 26 in 1996 to 17. Gibraltar complies with the European Union (EU) agreement on withholding tax for saving accounts held by EU citizens.

Time
GMT plus one hour (daylight saving, late-March to late-September, GMT plus two hours).

Geography
Gibraltar is situated at the southernmost tip of the Iberian Peninsula in southern Europe. The territory consists of a narrow peninsula running southwards from the south-west coast of Spain, to which it is connected by a sandy isthmus. About 8km (five miles) across the bay, to the west, lies Algeciras, the Spanish port, and 32km (20 miles) to the south, across the Strait of Gibraltar, is Morocco. The Mediterranean Sea is to the east.

Hemisphere
Northern

Climate
At the junction between the Mediterranean and Atlantic Ocean the climate in Gibraltar is heavily influenced by these and its local topography. Two local winds the *levanter* and *poniente* determine conditions. The easterly *levanter* produces warm, humid weather with sea fogs. The westerly *poniente* produces hot and mostly dry weather. Temperatures in summer average 25 degrees Celsius (C), although it can rise to over 30 degrees C; in winter it averages 14 degrees C.

Entry requirements
Passports
Required by all, except EU nationals travelling with valid national ID cards.

Visa
As an overseas territory of the UK, visa requirements are the same. Visas are required by all, except nationals of North America, Australasia, Japan and other EU members. For further exceptions and advice visit www.ukvisas.gov.uk/ (includes application forms). All visas must be applied for before travelling.
Gibraltar is outside the Schengen Agreement area. Visitors should ensure they have the right to return to Spain on their Schengen visa before entering Gibraltar from Spain.

Currency advice/regulations
There are no restrictions on the import or export of local or foreign currencies. Local bank notes are not accepted in the UK and should be exchanged before leaving Gibralter.
Travellers cheques are widely accepted and should be in pound sterling to avoid extra exchange fees.

Hotels
There is an official rating system in either stars or diamonds. Reservations should be made in advance, especially during summer (April–October).

Public holidays (national)
Fixed dates
1 Jan (New Year's Day), 8 Mar (Commonwealth Day), 1 May (May Day), 10 Sep (Gibraltar National Day), 25–26 Dec (Christmas).
Holidays that fall on the weekend are taken on the next Monday.

Variable dates
Good Friday, Easter Monday (Mar/Apr), Spring Bank Holiday (last Monday in May), Queen's Official Birthday (Jun), August Bank Holiday (last Monday in Aug).

Working hours
Banking
Mon–Thur: 0900–1530; Fri: 0900–1700.

Business
Mon–Fri: 0900–1700 (0800–1400, summer). Sat: 0900–1300.

Government
Mon—Fri: (winter) 0800—1615; (summer) 0730—1330.

Shops
Mon–Fri: Most shops open from 0900–1930 and some open from 0900–1300 and 1500–1900, Sat: 1000–1300.

Telecommunications
Mobile/cell phones
GSM 900 is available throughout the territory.

Electricity supply
240V AC, with UK style flat, thee-pin plugs.

Security
Violence and street crime is rare.

Getting there
Air
British Airways and Monarch Airlines operate daily direct flights from the UK.
National airline: GB Airways
International airport/s: Gibraltar (GIB) North Front airport, 1km from town centre. Facilities include duty-free shops, restaurants, bank and car hire. Taxis and hotel coaches are available. The airport is a ten minute walk from the centre of town.
Airport tax: None

Surface
Access is from Málaga, through the Spanish frontier at La Línea, which only opens 0900–1700 (Mon–Fri) and at weekends for longer hours.
Rail: There are no railways in Gibraltar but there are links to the Spanish national railway across the border, accessible within a few minutes.
Water: There are regular ferry services from Tangier in Morocco.

Getting about
National transport
Bus and taxi services are available. Taxi drivers are obliged by law to produce, on demand, a copy of the taxi fares. Gibraltar has a total of about 45km of roads. There is no railway network.

City transport
Taxis: Taxis are available from the airport to the town centre.
Buses, trams & metro: There is a bus service which operates from the airport to the town centre, journey time 15 minutes.

Car hire
Local car hire is available. A valid EU or international driving licence and evidence of insurance are required (third party). An age limit may be imposed usually 23–70 years. Traffic drives on the right. The speed limit is 50kph (31mph), except where indicated. Dipped headlights are compulsory at night time and seat belts are compulsory.
Additional conditions apply for travel into Spain.

BUSINESS DIRECTORY
The addresses listed below are a selection only. While World of Information makes every endeavour to check these addresses, we cannot guarantee that changes have not been made, especially to telephone numbers and area codes. We would welcome any corrections.

Telephone area codes
The international direct dialling code (IDD) for Gibraltar is +350 followed by

subscriber's number. (The IDD for Gibraltar is not recognised by Spain).

Chambers of Commerce

Gibraltar Chamber of Commerce, Don House, 38 Main Street, PO Box 29, Gibraltar (tel: 78-376; fax: 78-403; e-mail: gichacom@gibnet.gi).

Banking

Abbey National (Gibraltar) Ltd, 237 Main Street (tel: 76-090; fax: 72-028).

ABN Amro Bank (Gibraltar) Ltd, PO Box 100, 2-6 Main Street (tel: 79-220/79-370; fax: 78-512).

Baltica Bank (Gibraltar) Ltd, 215a Neptune House, Marina Bay (tel: 42-670; fax: 42-676).

Banco Atlántico (Gibraltar) Ltd, Eurolife Building, 1 Corral Road (tel: 40-117; fax: 40-110).

Banco Bilbao Vizcaya International (Gibraltar) Ltd, 3rd Floor, Hadfield House, Library Street (tel: 79-420; fax: 73-870).

Banco Bilbao Vizcaya (Gibraltar) Ltd, 260/262 Main Street (tel: 77-797, 77-871, 77-896).

Banco Central Sa, 198/200 Main Street (tel: 73-625, 73-650, 73-675; fax: 73-707).

Banco Español de Crédito, 114 Main Street (tel: 76-518; fax: 73-947).

Banque Indosuez, 206/210 Main Street (tel: 75-090; fax: 79-618).

Barclays Bank plc, 84/90 Main Street (tel: 78-565; fax: 79-509).

Crédit Suisse (Gibraltar) Ltd, Neptune House, Marina Bay (tel: 76-606; fax: 76-027).

Gibraltar Private Bank Ltd, PO Box 407, 10th Floor, ICC, Casemates (tel: 73-350; fax: 73-475).

Hambros Bank Ltd, PO Box 375, 32 Line Wall Road (tel: 74-850; fax: 79-037).

Hispano Commerzbank (Gibraltar) Ltd, Suite 14, 30/38 Main Street (tel: 74-199; fax: 74-174).

Lloyds Bank plc, 323 Main Street (tel: 77-373; fax: 70-023).

Midland Bank Trust Corporation (Gibraltar) Ltd, PO Box 19, Hadfield House, Library Street (tel: 79-500; fax: 72-090).

National Westminster Bank, 57 Line Wall Road (tel: 77-737; fax: 74-557).

Republic National Bank of New York (Gibraltar) Ltd, Neptune House, Marina Bay, PO Box 5578 (tel: 79-374; fax: 75-684).

Royal Bank of Scotland (Gibraltar) Ltd, 1 Corral Road (tel: 73-200; fax: 70-152).

Varde Bank International (Gibraltar) Ltd, PO Box 476, Suite E, Regal House, 3 Queensway (tel: 42-455; fax: 42-456).

Travel information

GB Airways, Iain Stewart Centre, Beehive Ring Road, Gatwick Airport, West Sussex RG6 0PB, UK (tel: (1293)664-239; fax: (1293)664-218).

London Passport Office, Globe House, 89 Ecclestone Square, London SW1V 1PN, UK (tel: (0870) 521-0410 (24-hour UK national advice line); (+44-20) 7901-2150 (international visa enquiries for British Overseas Territories. Opening hours: Mon-Fri 0730-1900; Sat 0900-1600); internet: www.passport.gov.uk; www.ukpa.gov.uk).

National tourist organisation offices

Gibraltar Tourist Board, Duke of Kent House, Cathedral Square (tel: 74-950; fax: 74-943; e-mail: tourism@gibnet.gi; internet site: www.gibraltar.gi).

Ministries

Government of Gibraltar, UK Office, 179 Strand, London WC2R 1EL, UK (tel: (+44-20) 7836-0777; fax: (+44-20) 7240-6612; e-mail: info@gibraltar.gov.uk; internet site: www.gibraltar.gov.uk).

Government Secretariat, 6 Convent Place (tel: 70-071; fax: 74-524).

Governor's Office, The Convent, Main Street (tel: 45-440; e-mail: convent@gibnet.gi).

Ministry of Tourism and Transport, Duke of Kent House, Cathedral Square (tel: 74-950; fax: 74-943).

Ministry of Trade, Industry and Telecommunications, Suite 771, Europort (tel: 52-052; fax: 71-406; e-mail: dticomm@gibnet.gi; internet site: www.gibraltar.gov.gi).

Other useful addresses

Economic Planning and Statistics Office, 6 Convent Place (tel: 75-515, 70-071).

Gibraltar Finance Centre, Suite 771, Europort (tel: 50-011; fax: 47-677; e-mail: fsc@gibnet.gi).

Gibraltar Information Bureau, Arundel Great Court, 179 Strand, London WC2R 1EH (tel: (+44-20) 7836-0777; fax: (+44-20) 7240-6612).

Gibraltar Telecommunications International Ltd, Mount Pleasant, 25 South Barrack Road (tel: 59-609; fax: 59-644).

Gibtelecom, Suite 942, Europort (tel: 52-200; fax: 71-673; internet site: www.gibtele.com).

Internet sites

Audio site – Talking about Gibraltar: www.gibnynex.gi/info/gibtalk

Business in Gibraltar: www.Gibraltarian.com/Gibraltar_business.asp

Government of Gibraltar: www.gibraltar.gov.gi

Gibraltar Broadcasting Corporation (GBC): www.gbc.gi

Offshore facilities: www.Gibraltaroffshore.com/

Greece

KEY FACTS

Official name: I Elliniki Dimokratia (The Hellenic Republic)

Head of State: President Prokopis Pavlopoulos (elected 18 Feb 2015)

Head of government: Prime Minister Alexis Tsipras (Synaspismos tis Rizospastikis Aristeras (Syriza)) (from 26 Jan 2015)

Ruling party: Coalition led by Synaspismos tis Rizospastikis Aristeras (Syriza) and Anexartitoi Ellines (ANEL) (Independent Greeks) (from 26 Jan 2015)

Area: 131,957 square km

Population: 10.99 million (2014)*

Capital: Athens

Official language: Greek

Currency: Euro (€) = 100 cents (from 1 Jan 2002; previous currency drachma, locked at Dr340.75 per euro)

Exchange rate: €0.89 per US$ (Sep 2015)

GDP per capita: US$21,653 (2014)

GDP real growth: 0.77% (2014)

GDP: US$238.02 billion (2014)

Labour force: 4.77 million (2014)*

Unemployment: 26.49% (2014)

Inflation: -1.43% (2014)*

Balance of trade: -US$23.73 billion (2014)

* estimated figure

Entering yet another 'last chance saloon' in early June and, having already withheld a payment of €500 million (US$562 million) to its nervous creditors (in this case the International Monetary Fund (IMF)), Greece presented so-called *troika* – the European Commission (EC), IMF and European Central Bank (ECB) – with yet another new set of proposals aimed at releasing funds that might permit the country to avoid default.

Compromise, compromise as the clock ticks

The proposals represented yet another attempt by Prime Minister Alexis Tsipras to gain some time by suggesting a more accommodating attitude towards lenders as the clock ticked on towards bankruptcy. This apparently more conciliatory mood boiled down to accepting Greece's creditors insistence on raising value added tax (VAT) rates and introducing higher budget surplus targets to bridge the gap with lenders.

Time was of the essence, as Greece's bailout programme ended on 30 June 2015, a moment when Athens would have to find substantial sums to repay its creditors while retaining the support of a population that had suffered badly during five years of economic crisis. But Greece showed no sign of yielding to the creditors' demands that Athens cut pensions.

Never never land

The dictionary definition of 'never never land' is: 'an imaginary place where everything is pleasant or perfect in a way that is impossible to achieve in real life.' Sadly, Greece is not an imaginary place, but in every other respect, the description fits. Both Greece and its creditors seemed to be in a state of denial. Simple arithmetic demonstrated that in all probability Greece would never be able to repay its existing debts, never mind the new loans that the Syriza government of Alexis Tsipras had agreed. Any enthusiasm its creditors had for further bail-outs had little to do with addressing the problems of the Greek people – the unemployment, unpaid pensions, under-resourced hospitals were at the top of a long list.

An article by Roger Cohen in the *New York Times* summed up the situation: 'Forcing Greece and Germany to co-exist in a currency union will always be an exercise in smoke and mirrors. Their economies are mismatched, their temperaments even more so.' Addressing the possibility of a formal Greek bankruptcy, Mr Cohen accepted that it 'sounds terrible, but I'm not sure. It would represent reality rather than the repetitive evasion of it.' Making the point that Greece was fortunate to be a unique tourist destination: 'A Greek meltdown is not the same as a Slovakian meltdown.' Mr Cohen also noted that 'So many mistakes have been made. They began with the sentimental illusion that the cradle of civilisation was also an economy competitive enough to join the euro. It was not.'

The Age of Uncertainty

Uncertainty had prevailed in Greece at the end of 2014. The failure of Greek parliamentarians to agree on the appointment of a new President meant that a general election would be called. In most European countries, this would not necessarily be a dramatic development. In Greece, however, the electoral outcome threatened to be significant; leading in the opinion polls was the coalition headed by the Syriza left wing, populist party. Central to Syrisa's electoral platform was the requirement that half of Greece's international debt be written off. Easily said, but the consequences of such a step looked to add up to an exit from the euro – despite Syrisa's assurances to the contrary. The political crisis neatly coincided with the visit of European Union (EU) economics commissioner Pierre Moscovi (a former French finance minister) traipsing from photo-call to photo call on construction sites and factory floors, bravely avoiding answering questions on the country's economic future.

As the January 2015 election approached, Syriza representatives appeared to be expressing their position in more 'rational' terms. While sticking to their core position that Greece's debt levels were so disproportionate that the economy's obvious difficulties were in addition to the social costs of people starving and sleeping on Athens' streets. The blunt truth that in the view of Syriza was ignored by Brussels, Berlin and Frankfurt, was that a country with a debt level around 170 per cent of GDP and rising could never achieve economic – or social – stability. None the less, in the offices of the IMF, the European Central Bank (ECB) and the Bundesrat the stated position was quite simply that the existing agreements signed by Greece had to be adhered to. Syriza won the election, in large measure because it claimed that the EU imposed austerity programme had brought the country and its people to their knees.

In a brief comment on the elections, the credit ratings agency Moodys summed up the situation, noting that Greece had endured tough budget cuts in return for its 2010 bailout, worth €240 billion (US$269 billion) and negotiated with the so-called troika – the European Commission (EC), IMF and ECB. The economy had shrunk drastically since the 2008 global financial crisis and increasing unemployment had thrown many Greeks into abject poverty.

For most of the 40 years since the end of Greece's military junta, political power had been the domain of a limited number of families. Notable among these élite social groupings had been the socialist Papandreu and the conservative Karamanlis, tidily alternating in power. Under their guidance, corruption prevailed, characterised by an idle and mercenary public service balanced by widespread tax evasion. In Greece it had become quite normal to pay a heart surgeon in cash for carrying out a routine operation. On the Transparency International *Corruption Perceptions Index* for 2014 Greece ranked 69 out of the 175 countries surveyed, a drop of 29 places from 2013, placing Greece behind Rwanda and Lesotho and only just above Sao Tomé and Principe and Benin. The only European countries to rank lower were Albania, Belarus, Bosnia and Kosovo – and of course Russia (if it could be considered properly European), which ranked 136.

Central bank caution

In its annual appraisal of the Greek economy the Bank of Greece (BG) (central bank) adopted a surprisingly upbeat tone. Its published summary opened ironically with the word 'Exit', a term that had been on the minds of virtually every observer of and participant in the Greek economy for months, if not years. But the BG wasn't talking about an exit from the euro – the Grexit as it had become known – but of what it described as Greece's 'Exit from the crisis'. If only.

None the less, the BG continued, claiming that after six years of severe recession, the downturn came to an end in 2014, as economic activity resumed positive growth rates. In the view of the BG, this development, combined with the elimination of the fiscal and current high account deficits and the implementation of significant structural reforms, arguably suggested that conditions were ripe for a

KEY INDICATORS — Greece

	Unit	2011	2012	2013	2014	**2015
Population	m	10.79	11.12	11.06	10.99	*10.98
Gross domestic product (GDP)	US$bn	303.10	248.56	242.31	238.02	*207.15
GDP per capita	US$	27,073	22,347	21,903	21,653	*18,863
GDP real growth	%	-6.9	-7.0	-3.9	0.8	*2.5
Inflation	%	3.1	1.5	-1.0	*-1.4	*-0.3
Unemployment	%	17.5	24.2	27.5	26.5	*24.8
Coal output	mtoe	7.4	7.9	6.9	6.3	–
Exports (fob) (goods)	US$m	27,954.0	27,954.0	29,678.0	31,168.0	–
Imports (fob) (goods)	US$m	65,838.0	53,369.0	52,582.0	54,896.0	–
Balance of trade	US$m	-37,884.0	-25,281.0	-22,904.0	-23,729.0	–
Current account	US$m	-29,353.0	-5,933.0	1,409.0	2,202.0	*2,807.0
Total reserves minus gold	US$m	1,388.4	1,269.6	1,419.6	1,876.6	–
Foreign exchange	US$m	65.5	48.8	371.0	–	–
Exchange rate	per US$	0.75	0.77	0.73	0.82	–

* estimated figure ** forecast figure

'definitive exit from the crisis and for accelerated growth in the immediate future.'

However, the Bank also noted that its optimistic outlook was clouded by the uncertainty surrounding the continued re-negotiation of the loan agreements with the EC, the ECB and the IMF. In the Bank's view, the outcome of these negotiations could ultimately determine Greece's future for the years ahead. The Bank advocated a co-ordinated national effort with the European and international institutions 'to ensure that the sacrifices made by Greek citizens have not been in vain' (a statement worthy of former finance minister Yanis Varoufakis) and to facilitate the economic re-structuring needed for sustainable growth.

The central bank also noted that 2014 had seen the return of economic activity to positive growth rates after no less than six years of recession, during which Greece's gross domestic product (GDP) had contracted by more than 25 per cent. According to the central bank, year-on-year growth in 2014 had returned to positive rates (0.8 per cent) for the first time since 2007, driven by higher exports of goods and services and increased private consumption. In the period from January to September 2014 exports rose by 8.4 per cent, largely as a result of improved competitiveness and strong showings by tourism and shipping exports. Private consumption rose by 1.5 per cent, supported by more stable disposable incomes, declining prices and lower uncertainty.

In 2014 the number of unemployed decreased for the first time since 2008, by 3.3 per cent. This still left the level of unemployment unacceptably high, the highest in the EU. Other positive labour data in 2014 included lower unit labour costs as well as the increased competitiveness already referred to above. According to the World Economic Forum's global competitiveness index, Greece moved up the ranking to 81, ten places higher than its 2012 ranking. On the World Bank's *Ease of Doing Business Index* Greece moved up to 61, from 65 and 89 respectively in the previous two years.

IMF approval?

In a February 2015 letter to the Dutch finance minister Jeroen Dijsselbloem in his capacity of President of the Eurogroup finance ministers, the managing director of the IMF, Christine Lagarde advised that the IMF had reviewed the list of measures that the Greek authorities had prepared in the expectation of receiving further assistance. Ms Lagarde advised that the IMF considered it covered the broad topics that should be on the new government's agenda. She confirmed that the IMF would certainly be able to support the conclusion that the list 'was sufficiently comprehensive to be a valid starting point for a successful conclusion of the review', as called for by the Eurogroup at its last meeting. But a determination in this regard should of course rest primarily on an assessment by Member States themselves and by the relevant European institutions.

Ms Lagarde went on to observe that while the (Greek) authorities' list was 'comprehensive', it was generally not very specific, 'perhaps to be expected considering that the government is new in office.' In some areas, like combating tax evasion and corruption, the IMF's managing director was encouraged with what appeared to be a stronger resolve on the part of the new authorities in Athens. The IMF looked forward to learning more about their plans. In quite a few areas, however, including perhaps the most important ones, the (Greek) letter was not felt to be conveying clear assurances that the government intended to undertake the reforms envisaged in the Memorandum on Economic and Financial Policies. 'We note in particular' said Ms Lagarde, 'that there are neither clear commitments to design and implement the envisaged comprehensive pension and VAT policy reforms, nor unequivocal undertakings to continue already-agreed policies for opening up closed sectors, for administrative reforms, for privatisation and for labour market reforms.' According to Ms Lagarde, the IMF considered such commitments and undertakings to be critical for Greece's ability to meet the basic objectives of its IMF-supported programme, which was why these were the areas subject to most of the structural benchmarks agreed with the IMF. Ms Lagarde concluded her letter by underlining that 'It was important' for her to emphasise 'that for the discussions on a completion of the review to be successful they could not be confined within the policy perimeters outlined in the government's list.'

Last chance saloon?

In simple terms, the nub of all the discussions between the Greek government and its international creditors was Greece's initial demand that its debt should be cut in half. Understandably enough, the countries which had lent money to Greece – of which there were a lot – were at best reluctant to see their money flushed away to help out a country – if not a government – that in their view had been profligate. Some confusion surrounded the discussion, which didn't help. Mr Varoufakis was quoted as saying that the Greek government wouldn't negotiate with the Troika of creditors. This turned out to be a 'misunderstanding in translation'. Writing in the London *Daily Telegraph* Ben Wright quoted the then Finnish prime minister, Cai-Göra Alexander Stubb, as saying that: 'The starting principle is that we will not extend any debt forgiveness.' Mr Stubb promptly contradicted himself by adding that 'But we are ready to discuss programme extensions and loan period extensions.'

By June 2015 Greece's financial position seemed more precarious than ever, to the extent that Jack Lew, the US treasury secretary was reported to have remarked that the never-ending delays in reaching any sort of agreement had reached the point that, as reported by the London *Financial Times*, the threat of an 'accident' could 'force Greece out of the euro-zone. However, Greece's major creditors, the IMF, the EC and the ECB continued to insist that the Greek government needed to present a comprehensive reform programme if a further tranche – this time of no less than €7.2 billion (US$8.1 billion) – was to be handed over.

Brass tacks?

At the beginning of June 2015 the Greek push had come face to face with the European shove in the negotiations with the EU, which had become the *de facto* negotiator with Greece. The show-boating days of finance minister Yanis Varoufakis (see below), who was perceived by many of those involved to be as much a liability as an asset, had ended with his side-lining by Syriza leader and Prime Minister Alexis Tsipras. The thorny negotiations appeared to have reached a climax – or a spectacular anti-climax – with a midnight meeting between Mr Tsipras and the President of the EC, Jean-Claude Juncker. However, later in the week it was reported that Mr Juncker was no longer taking Mr Tsipras' telephone calls.

Curiously, although once entrusted with the final negotiations, Mr Juncker's EC was not itself a Greek creditor, which is probably why, after a brief opening chat, Mr Juncker – against Mr Tsipras' wishes – had Mr Dijsselbloem of the Eurogroup join the meeting. The sticking points in the way of reaching an agreement were not insubstantial. Greece was insisting on being granted more room for manoeuvre in implementing its social (for which, read 'anti-austerity') programme which would involve adjusting its budget surplus (it was no mean feat that the Greek government had managed to generate a budget surplus) to one per cent of gross domestic product in 2015 and to two per cent in 2016. The original figures had been three per cent and four per cent respectively. Off the record, Greece had claimed that both France and Germany supported this measure.

Next on the troika's list came labour reforms. Brussels was first demanding an end to early retirements (which in Greece were accompanied by some of the euro-zone's highest levels of pensions) and second requiring the immediate introduction of lower pension levels. The Syriza government had countered with proposals for a gradual lowering of pensions over the period up to 2020. The authorities also planned to re-introduce collective wage bargaining for Greek companies.

Third and possibly the thorniest of all, came the question of value added tax (VAT) reforms (or rationalisations). Mr Tsipras wished to maintain the three-level system currently in place. Government projections posited an increase of €1,000 million (US$1,124 million) in collections. The troika's figures were based on a simplification of the VAT rates to two, which they considered should produce an additional €2,000 million (US$2,247 milliom).

Both the EC and other official sources played down their expectations. Coolest of all in his interpretation of the progress made – or not made – was the German finance minister, Wolfgang Schäuble, who simply announced that he had not 'received any information indicating that there had been a substantive change.' France's President Hollande, however, was almost over-optimistic: 'We are within a few days or even hours of an agreement.' The Spanish finance minister, Luis de Guindos, said that 'I am completely sure that we will reach an agreement with Greece. Completely sure. In the euro-zone club, you join, but you never leave.' This approximated to the definition of purgatory once adopted by the Spanish Inquisition.

The Syriza government was well aware that whatever agreement it reached with the Troika would be deeply unpopular with a large segment of its party. Syriza's parliamentary spokesman, Nikos Filis, prematurely announced that Greece would not pay the IMF the money due in early June (€300 million (US$337 million) out of the €1,600 million (US$1,798 million) due by the end of the month) if there was no sign of an agreement. The Syriza party's internal divisions (it held a total of 149 seats) very much hinged on what was in any agreement. The party planned to hold a meeting to debate the conditions on the due day. Playing to the more extreme wing of Syriza, Mr Filis baldly announced that if there was no prospect of an agreement, that Greece simply 'would not pay.' The Syriza veteran and Euro-MP struck a more pragmatic tone, saying that: 'If the creditors show the same realism as that shown by the Greek government, then we should be able to reach an agreement by the end of the week.' When the 'end of the week' arrived, however, no agreement had been reached. The Greek government announced that it would not be paying the €305 million (US$343 million) payment to the IMF in a show of defiance as a deal between Athens and its creditors remains out of reach. Greece was formally within its rights to delay the payment, invoking a rule created by the IMF in the 1970s that allowed it to bundle all of its €1.6 billion (US$1.8 billion) payments due in June 2015 into one. Gerry Rice, the IMF's chief spokesman announced that 'The Greek authorities have informed the Fund today that they plan to bundle the country's four June payments into one, which is now due on June 30. IMF Member states are allowed to bundle together principal payments (but not interest payments) falling due in a calendar month.' The clause had not been invoked since Zambia in the mid-1980s. Greece had to decide whether to delay three further payments of €312 million (US$350 million) due on 12 June 12, €573 million (US$644 million) on June 16 and €343 million (US$385 million) on 19 June. If the sums due to the IMF were mounting up, at the end of June the Greek government also had to find some €1.5 billion (US$1 7 billion) in public sector pensions and wages at the end of June 2015.

The payment deferral appeared to have surprised the IMF. The Greek finance ministry, which was at the time led by Yanis Varoufakis (see below) said that: 'After four months of negotiations, creditor institutions submitted proposals which can't solve the riddle of the economic crisis caused by the policies implemented in the last five years.'

Varoufakis sidelined

Sporting an open-neck shirt fashionably hanging outside his jeans and a long black overcoat, Mr Varoufakis had become something resembling the Greek government's court jester. Forlornly arguing the case for a debt write-off, he had looked out of place in meetings with the great and the good of European finance. And it was not only his appearance. A self declared 'Libertarian Marxist' Varoufakis rapidly gained fame for his one-liners, none the less often striking a chord with European voters. On austerity and Greece's €240 billion (US$270 billion) bailout he noted that 'Europe, in its infinite wisdom, decided to deal with this bankruptcy by loading the largest loan in human history on the weakest of shoulders... What we've been having ever since is a kind of fiscal waterboarding that has turned this nation into a debt colony.' He had anticipated Mr de Guindos' remarks that 'In the euro-zone club, you join, but you never leave' by quoting the eagles' song, Hotel California: ' You can check out any time you like, but you can never leave.' Varoufakis' relations with the Troika were hardly improved by his description of its members as 'A committee built on rotten foundations.'

At one point Mr Varoufakis admitted that he wanted a deal with hedge funds, bankers and the financial establishment. But: 'Forging alliances with reactionary forces, as I think we should do to stabilise Europe today, brings us up against the risk of becoming co-opted, of shedding our radicalism through the warm glow of having 'arrived' in the corridors of power.' 'We are going to destroy', he told London's Channel 4 News 'the basis upon which they have built for decade after decade a system, a network that viciously sucks the energy and the economic power from everybody else in society.'

Not altogether surprisingly, the unpredictable Varoufakis was given the microphone less and less as the debt negotiations proceeded. It was reported that Mr Tsipras had reined him in, to minimise the risk of an accident being triggered by one of the finance minister's spontaneous comments.

Mr Varoufakis was succeeded by Euclid Tsakalotos as finance minister on 23 September 2015.

From Russia, with... not much

In April 2015 Mr Tsipras, a humble tie-less prime minister sat down in the Kremlin with Russia's President Putin, who of course was wearing a neatly knotted tie. Quite what the agenda consisted of was unclear, but the principal backdrops were Greece's near bankruptcy and

Russia's irritation at having sanctions placed upon it by the EU, of which Greece is a member. Trade between the two countries risked disappearing altogether if nothing was done to stimulate it – in 2014 it fell by some 40 per cent.

After the visit Mr Tsipras denied that Greece had asked for funding. He put forward the view that the EU sanctions against Russia were a dead end street. The sanctions on Russia were due to be renewed in July 2015, a move which would require the unanimous support of all 28 EU members. The fear in Brussels was that Greece might threaten to use its veto, although Mr Tsipras had not referred to such a response. In the event the sanctions were renewed, on June 22, for a further six months

If Greece had hoped to secure some 'soft' energy deals from Russia, this did not happen. Almost 60 per cent of Greek gas consumption is supplied by Russia's Gazprom. Russia had endeavoured to interest Greece in joining the Turkish Stream gas pipeline. Whatever the economics, the pipeline's name made it less than straightforward for any Greek prime minister to sign on the dotted line. Mr Putin did offer some putative investment in Greece by Russian companies, notably in Greece's railway system and in the port of Thessalonika. But Russia did not overlook Greece's position in the EU; thus, no concessions were granted on the import of Greek agricultural produce. Mr Putin claimed that 'no exceptions could be made.'

Mr Tsipras was aware, however, that the eyes of most European leaders were upon him during his visit to Moscow, especially those of Angela Merkel. He also knew that with one false remark his chances of a debt-restructuring might simply vanish. He also knew that Greece needed the EU support desperately. And he certainly knew that an impoverished Russia was no replacement.

Scraping the barrel

Most members of Greece's Syriza party government considered, however, that Greece had gone as far as it could in accommodating its creditors. The budgetary barrel had been scraped dry, to the extent that at the end of April 2015 the Greek treasury had resorted to robbing Peter to pay Paul. Funds allocated as an IMF reserve were used to pay… the IMF. This fiscal legerdemain did little to encourage lenders that there was any prospect of further reforms. The *Financial Times* reported that domestic deposit withdrawals in the first quarter of 2015 from Greece's four major banks – Alpha Bank, Eurobank, the National Bank of Greece and Piraeus Bank – had added up to over €25 billion (US$18 billion). To retain liquidity, the banks had resorted to central bank funding of €113 billion (US$127 billion) in the first four months of 2015, €74 billion (US$83 billion) of which was emergency liquidity. This state of affairs exposed Greece to the possibility of the ECB ruling that the loans had been supplied without adequate collateral. The danger of a banking liquidity crisis becoming a banking solvency crisis was ever present.

Risk assessment

Politics	Poor
Economy	Poor
Regional stability	Good

COUNTRY PROFILE

1454 After the fall of Constantinople to Suleiman the Magnificent, Greece and most of the eastern Mediterranean were occupied by the Ottoman Empire.
1829 Following a war against the Ottomans lasting eight years, Greece declared its independence as a monarchy.
1913 The London Conference reduced the amount of ethnic Albanian-dominated territory of the former Ottoman Empire and Cameria (Chamouria) was granted to Greece.
1917 Greece entered the First World War on the side of the Allies and made territorial gains.
1923 Greece signed the Lausanne Peace Treaty with Turkey. The Treaty outlined the territory of each country and provided Greece with a number of islands in the Aegean Sea.
1939 Greece rejected Italy's ultimatum seeking free passage for its troops in the Second World War and repelled its attack, but was occupied by Germany. The government and the King went into exile. Mass armed resistance grew out of various political groupings.
1944 Liberation from the Nazis. The returned National Unity government under George Papandreou fought a civil war against the Communists.
1949 Constitutional monarchy was re-established. There were territorial gains from the war, the last of which was the Dodecanese islands in the south-eastern Aegean Sea.
1967–72 A military coup led by right-wing army officers deposed King Konstantinos II. An attempted counter-coup by the King failed, and he went into exile. Colonel Georgios Papadopoulos appointed himself prime minister. The regime was brutal and repressive with all political activity banned.
1973 Greece was declared a republic with Papadopoulos as president. General Demetrios Ioannides led a bloodless coup; Papadopoulos was overthrown. Partial civilian rule was allowed. General Phaidon Gizikis was appointed president.
1974 Civil war in Cyprus and the Turkish invasion of the island brought Greece close to war with Turkey and caused the downfall of the military junta. Elections resulted in a decisive victory for Nea Dimokratia (ND) (New Democracy). A referendum rejected proposals for a return to constitutional monarchy.
1975 A republican constitution providing for a parliamentary democracy was promulgated and Konstantinos Tsatsos was elected president.
1977 The ND was re-elected with a reduced majority.
1980 In May, Constantine Karamanlis was elected president. Greece joined the EU.
1981 The Panellino Socialistiko Kinima (Pasok) (Pan-Hellenic Socialist Movement) gained an absolute majority in parliament in the elections. The Pasok government, led by Andreas Papandreou, was the first socialist government in Greek history.
1985 President Karamanlis resigned and Christos Sartzetakis became president. Pasok was returned to power and implemented proposed constitutional changes. The government's programme of economic austerity became very unpopular and resulted in widespread industrial unrest.
1986 Constitutional amendments limited the powers of the president.
1989 ND won the largest proportion of votes in the elections.
1993 The ND government was forced to resign after losing its one seat parliamentary majority. Pasok regained power.
1995 Costis Stephanopoulos was elected president.
1996 Prime Minister Papandreou resigned due to ill health and Costas Simitis became prime minister. Andreas Papandreou died, ending an era of authoritarian control over Pasok, which won the parliamentary elections.
2000 Incumbent president, Stephanopoulos, was re-elected. Pasok was re-elected, becoming the first party to win three successive elections. Greece's application to join the Economic and Monetary Union (Emu) was accepted.
2001 Greece officially joined the Emu.
2002 The euro currency replaced the drachma.
2004 The ND, led by Costas Karamanlis, won the parliamentary elections.

2005 Karolos Papoulias was elected president. Newly introduced labour laws ended 'jobs for life'.
2007 A series of forest fires swept through areas in southern Greece and killed over 60 people and destroyed over 4,500 homes. The prime minister called an early election and the ruling ND won but with a reduced majority. Karamanlis remained prime minister.
2008 Greece blocked the Former Yugoslav Republic of Macedonia's (FYROM) membership of NATO, due to the unresolved issue of FYROM using Macedonia in its name. Eight days of rioting in Athens resulted in the death of a youth during protests about the growing unemployment rate.
2009 GDP growth fell to 1 per cent; unemployment reached 9.4 per cent. Tourism, which typically employed 20 per cent of the working population, suffered due in most part to a strong euro and a drop in the number of visitors by 15–20 per cent. The former state-owned Olympic Airlines was privatised following an agreement with the EU to write-off US$3.87 billion (€2.6 billion) in accumulated debt; it was re-launched as Olympic Air. In snap parliamentary elections the ruling ND lost to Pasok and Georgios Papandreou became prime minister. The credit rating agency Fitch reduced Greece's sovereign debt rating to BBB+.
2010 Parliament re-elected Karolos Papoulias as president. The government made further cuts in public spending. The domestic economic crisis grew into a eurozone problem when the government informed the European Central Bank (ECB) that its deficit was unsustainable and it was in danger of defaulting on its public debts. Several international rating agencies downgraded Greece's sovereign ratings to 'junk bond' status. The euro came under international pressure. Greece only just avoided insolvency when a US$147 billion three-year loan was arranged with the ECB and IMF, under a newly created European Financial Stability Facility (EFSF). The government implemented stringent austerity measures, including cuts in pensions and salaries of government workers, which resulted in widespread strikes and street protests. Greek truckers went on strike, protesting against the government's move to liberalise road transport. The strike ended after a week when the government threatened to revoke their licences; armed forces were ordered to deliver fuel to petrol stations.
2011 Rioting broke out in Athens in June as the prime minister announced the next phase in an economic austerity plan, required before further aid would be available. Over two days, parliament voted to approve the five-year austerity plan, which would qualify Greece for €110 billion (US$80.3 billion) in external financial aid from the ECB and IMF, or risk defaulting on its debts. A 48-hour general strike was held at the same time to protest at measures that included raised taxes and salary cuts for public employees at a time when unemployment was over 16 per cent. The ECB restructuring plan was implemented but by July money markets and investors were still concerned about Greece's ability to fund the debt. Germany appeared unsympathetic to Greece's continued financial needs. In August the planned merger of Greece's second and third largest banks, Eurobank EFG and Alpha Bank, was announced. The merger created the biggest bank in south-east Europe, with assets of US$212 billion and around 1,300 branches. Prime Minister Papandreou caused consternation in November when he declared that any agreement for further fiscal austerity measures, concluded with European Monetary Union (EMU) leaders to allow the next instalment of the bailout (US$11 billion), would be put to a referendum. In parliament both his supporters and the opposition attacked his handling of the crisis and in November he only narrowly won a vote of confidence (153 to 145). Parliament agreed to pass austerity legislation on the proviso that Papandreou stepped-down as prime minister after the formation of a government of unity. The proposed referendum was abandoned. Parliament selected Lucas Papademos as prime minister following days of wrangling between the ruling the Pasok and opposition ND to find an acceptable candidate to replace Georgios Papandreou; he took office on 11 November. Mr Papademos was a technocrat and a vice president of the European Central Bank (ECB). He secured bail-out-funds and implemented budget cuts to avert economic collapse.
2012 After months of volatility and a series of austerity budgets parliamentary elections were held on 6 May, which brought to prominence the conservative ND with 18.9 per cent of the vote (108 seats out of 300). Pasok lost 119 seats when it polled just 13.2 per cent (41) and was beaten into third place by Synaspismós Rizospastikís Aristerás (Syriza) (Coalition of the Radical Left) with 16.8 per cent (52). Antonio Samaras (ND) was given three days to form a coalition government, but failed. He was followed by Alexis Tsipras (Syriza) who likewise could not gather enough support for his far-left bloc. EU partners warned all political parties attempting to form a government that Greece must keep to the tough terms of the international financial bailout. On 10 May, Pasok's leader attempted to form a coalition government. On 17 May, a new caretaker government of technocrats, led by Panagiotis Pikramenos, was sworn into office, after the top three political parties in the last election failed to form a coalition; general elections were set for 17 June. A second general election was held on 17 June, following the political impasse when no government could be formed after the 6 May elections. The outcome of this election was considered to hold the key to Greece's membership of the EMU and not only Greece but the remainder of the euro-zone if Greece were forced to leave. ND won extra seats in this election, 129 seats out of 300 (with 29.7 per cent of the vote) and began coalition talks immediately. On 20 June a new government was sworn into office with Antonis Samaras as the new prime minister. He reiterated his undertaking to uphold the austerity commitments that Greece had previously accepted. On 31 October, the government submitted its budget for 2013, which proposed public spending cuts of up to €13.5 billion (US$17.4 billion). A two-day general strike by public and private workers began on 6 November. Parliament agreed to the latest austerity package to save €13.5 billion (US$17 billion) by 2016.
2013 An anti-austerity strike was staged by trade unions on 1 May. On 11 June the government shut Ellinikí Radiophonía Tileórassi (ERT) (Hellenic Radio and Television), the state-owned, public broadcaster. The move, part of government austerity measures, included the external service, Voice of Greece. All 2,700 workers were made redundent, although they were told they could apply for work when the corporation relaunches as a smaller, independent public broadcaster. On 13 June a 24-hour strike took place, called by trade unions and all media unions. On 17 June the Council of State (Greece's top administrative court) ordered that the signal be restored so that ERT could start broadcasting again. However, the court also upheld Prime Minister Samaras's plan to replace ERT with a new broadcaster later in the year. On 17 July parliament narrowly (by 153-140) approved a public sector reform bill that will mean thousands of people losing their jobs. The bill is tied to a further €6.8 billion (US$5.2 billon) of bailout loans, needed to keep the country afloat. Thousands of protesters rallied outside the parliament during the debate. In its fourth review of Greece published at the end of July the IMF backed the latest traunch of €1.7 billion (US$2.3 billion). It also reported that Greece needs to deliver 'rapidly on structural reforms to unlock growth and create jobs'. Greece's economy showed a slight improvement in the three months to the

end of June with GDP growth at -4.6 per cent, compared to -5.6 per in the first quarter. On 25 August the Greek finance minister was reported as saying that the country may need another €10 billion (US$13.4 billion); he also said that the Greece could not accept any further austerity measures. Anti-racist musician, Pavlos Fyssas, was stabbed to death by a man claiming to be a member of the far right Popular Association – Golden Dawn party on 18 September. On 28 September Nikolaos Michaloliakos, leader of Golden Dawn, was charged with belonging to a criminal organisation. Nineteen other party members, including four members of parliament, were also charged. Parliament voted on 22 October to suspend state funds to the Golden Dawn party. Police moved in on the ERT headquarters on 7 November and cleared it of all former employees and protestors.

2014 Greece held local elections on 18 and 25 May (first and second rounds). Néa Dimokratía (ND) (New Democracy) achieved an overall win of 26.3 per cent nationwide, followed by Synaspismós Rizospastikís Aristerás (Syriza) with 17.7 per cent and Pasok (Panhellenic Socialist Movement) with 16.2 per cent. Syriza also did well in the European parliament elections, winning six seats, up from one seat at the last election. The ND won five seats (down from eight) and the Golden Dawn party won their first three seats. On 8 December Prime Minister Samaras called for early presidential elections to be held on 17 December (first round), 23 December and 29 December (second and third rounds, if necessary). Stavros Dimas (ND) was the only candidate but he failed to win the necessary 180 votes in parliament. As a result and according to the constitution, on 31 December, incumbent President Karolos Papoulias dissolved the parliament by decree and set the date for the snap election to be held on 25 January and the new parliament to reconvene on 5 February 2015.

2015 The anti-austerity Syriza party won a surprisingly clear victory in the 25 January general election with 36.34 per cent of votes cast to 27.81 per cent for the outgoing ND and 6.28 per cent for Golden Dawn. In terms of seats Syriza was allocated 99 seats (out of 250) by proportional representation, which with the 50 seats allocated to the party winning the most seats, gave Syriza 149 seats in the 300 seat parliament, just 2 short of an absolute majority. The ND won 73 seats, Golden Dawn and Potami (The River) 17 seats each, Kommounistikó Kómma Elládas (KKE) (Communist Party of Greece) 15, ANEL and PASOK-DP 13 each. No other party achieved the 3 per cent threshold for entry into parliament. Syriza leader, Alexis Tsipras, became prime minister. After parliament was reconvened with a Syriza-ANEL coalition government, the presidential election resumed, and on 18 February, veteran ND politician Prokopis Pavlopoulos, backed by the coalition government, was elected with 233 votes. Syriza sought to renegotiate the terms of the country's €240 billion (US$260 billion) bailout from the IMF and EU. But by April negotiators had still not succeeded in satisfying Greece's international creditors that the scope of the proposed economic reforms required before the EU hands over the latest €7.2 billion (US$8 billion) tranche of the bailout, which the government needed to pay its bills, were strong enough. Finance minister Yanis Varoufakis was left isolated at an EU finance ministers' meeting in Latvia on 24 April. He skipped a state dinner and later tweeted a line from late US President Franklin Roosevelt: 'They are unanimous in their hate for me; and I welcome their hatred.' Nevertheless, Prime Minister Alexis Tsipras expressed support for Mr Varoufakis, saying Greece was in the final, critical stretch of talks with its international creditors and that he believed an interim deal would be in place by 9 May. Prime Minister Tsipras announced his resignation on 20 August.

Political structure

Constitution

The constitution of 1975 has been revised on several occasions in line with contemporary circumstances. It sets out the rights and responsibilities of the parliament, judiciary, people and church. The constitution is enshrined in law.

In March 1986, parliament ratified changes to the 1975 constitution, limiting the president's power in relation to parliament.

Independence date

1921, declared independence

Form of state

Parliamentary democratic republic

The executive

The president of the republic is Head of State, and is elected by parliament for a five-year term, for a maximum of two terms. The president must be elected by a two-thirds majority, or on the third ballot by a three-fifths majority.

Since 1985 when presidential power was reduced, *de facto* executive power is wielded by the prime minister and cabinet. The cabinet is named by the prime minister.

National legislature

Legislative power rests with the 300-member unicameral Vouli ton Ellinon (parliament), elected for four years by universal and compulsory adult suffrage.

Legal system

Greek law is based on codified Roman law with the judiciary divided into civil, criminal, and administrative courts. Judicial independence is guaranteed under the constitution.

Last elections

18 February 2015 (presidential); 25 January 2015 (parliamentary)

Results: Presidential (2015): Prokopis Pavlopoulos was elected president (by parliament, receiving 233 votes out of 300).

Parliamentary (2015): Synaspismós Rizospastikís Aristerás (Syriza) (Coalition of the Radical Left) 36.34 per cent of the vote (99 + 50 = 149 seats total, out of 300), Néa Dimokratía (ND) (New Democracy) won 27.81 per cent (73), Chrysi Avgi (CA) (Golden Dawn) 6.28 per cent (17), Potami (The River) 6.05 per cent (17), Kommounistikó Kómma Elládas (KKE) (Communist Party of Greece) 5.47 per cent (15), ANEL 4.75 per cent (13), PASOK-DP alliance 4.68 per cent (13). No other party achieved the 3 per cent threshold for entry into parliament.

Next elections

2016 (parliamentary); 2015 (presidential)

Political parties

Ruling party

Coalition led by Synaspismos tis Rizospastikis Aristeras (Syriza) and Anexartitoi Ellines (ANEL) (Independent Greeks) (from 26 Jan 2015)

Main opposition party

Synaspismós Rizospastikís Aristerás (Syriza) (Coalition of the Radical Left)

Population

11.06 million (2013)*

Last census: 24 May 2011: 10,787,690

Population density: 81 inhabitants per square km. Urban population 61 per cent (2010 Unicef).

Annual growth rate: 0.6 per cent, 1990–2010 (Unicef).

Ethnic make-up

Greece is a very homogenous state and the vast majority of its citizens regard themselves as ethnic Greek. However, there are also small numbers of Turks, Pomaks, Gypsies, Vlaks and an increasing numbers of illegal Albanian economic refugees (some 300,000 are believed to live in Athens).

Religions

Over 95 per cent of the population are baptised in the Greek Orthodox Church. There are small Muslim, Catholic and Jewish communities.

Education

Primary education lasts for six years. Secondary education generally lasts for six years and is divided into two equal periods. Approximately 47 per cent of the relevant age group participate in some form of tertiary education. Overcrowded classes at public high schools and a lack of facilities mean that students take private tuition or attend night school to improve their chances of going to university, for which entrance is fiercely competitive. Women comprise almost 60 per cent of Greek graduates.

Public education expenditure is equivalent to just over 3 per cent of GDP.

Literacy rate: 98 per cent, male; 96 per cent, female; adult rates (World Bank).

Enrolment rate: 93 per cent at primary level and 95 per cent at secondary level (of the relevant age groups).

Pupils per teacher: 14 in primary schools

Health

Although basic healthcare is provided free of charge, many Greeks find standards unsatisfactory and prefer to go to private doctors and clinics, or even to pay the high cost of treatment abroad.

HIV/Aids

HIV prevalence: 0.2 per aged 15–49 in 2003 (World Bank)

Life expectancy: 79 years, 2004 (WHO 2006)

Fertility rate/Maternal mortality rate: 1.5 births per woman, 2010 (Unicef)

Child (under 5 years) mortality rate (per 1,000): 5 per 1,000 live births (WHO 2012)

Head of population per physician: 4.38 physicians per 1,000 people, 2001 (WHO 2006)

Welfare

Social security is handled by more than 350 state-run or state-supervised social insurance funds, which together cover almost all the Greek population. The largest of these funds is the general social security scheme, run by the Idryma Koinonikis Asfalisis (IKA) (Social Security Institute). The scheme covers 1.8 million wage earners, pays pensions and operates a network of hospitals and out patient clinics.

Parliament approved the restructuring of the debt-burdened and complex state pension system in June. Greece has a growing aged population, which will become problematic.

At 9 per cent of the total labour force, the proportion of Greek employees living in conditions of poverty is one of the highest in the EU.

Main cities

Athens (capital, estimated population 762,698 in 2012), Thessaloniki (363,987), Piraeus (179,479), Patras (168,906), Peristerion (suburb of Athens) (147,598), Iráklion (capital of Crete, 139,890), Lárisa (138,264), Kallithéa (111,714).

Languages spoken

Macedonian, Albanian, Turkish, Aroumanian, Bulgarian and Pomak are spoken by their resident populations. Most people in the business community also speak English, French or German.

Official language/s

Greek

Media

Press

Although the media has considerable freedom, a public prosecutor may stop circulation of an edition of a newspaper on the grounds that it is blasphemous, offends public decency, reveals military or state secrets or offends the Greek president.

Dailies: There are 34 national daily newspapers and most publish Sunday editions. Most newspapers have political party affiliations.

In Greek, high circulation newspapers include *Ethnos* (*Nation*) (www.ethnos.gr), *Kathimerini* (*Daily*) (www.kathimerini.gr), *To Vima*, (*The Tribune*) (www.tovima.gr), *Eleftheros Typos* (*Free Press*) (www.e-tipos.com) and two evening publications include *Eleftherotypia* (*Press Freedom*) (www.enet.gr) and *Ta Nea*, (*The News*) (www.tanea.gr). Some offer online articles in English.

Weeklies: Many daily newspapers publish weekend editions. In Greek, *To Proto Thema* (www.protothema.gr) is a tabloid newspaper and *Stochos* (www.stoxos.gr) is a nationalist publication. In English *Athens News* (www.athensnews.gr); Big News Network is an internet site (www.bignewsnetwork.com).

Business: In Greek, there are several business newspapers, *Naftemboriki* (www.naftemporiki.gr) is a financial daily, *Kerdos* (www.kerdos.gr), *Reporter* (www.reporter.gr) reports on financial markets, others include *Express* (www.express.gr), *Imerissia* (www.imerisia.gr), *Isotimia* (www.isotimia.gr) and *Oikonomikos Tachydromos* (http://oikonomikos.dolnet.gr), a magazine for economic and policy analysis. Regional publications include *Thrakiki Agora* (www.thrakikiagora.gr) and *Thrakiki Gi* (www.thrakikigi.gr) from Komotini in the north-east. Industry publications include *Naftika Chronika* (www.naftikachronika.gr) concerning Greek shipping. Some offer online articles in English.

Periodicals: In Greek, for women, monthly magazines include *Gynaika*, the oldest women's publication and *Praktiki* for articles on the home.

Broadcasting

Ellinikí Radiophonía Tileórassi (ERT) (Hellenic Radio and Television) (www.ert.gr) is the state-owned, public broadcaster. As part of its austerity measures, on 11 June 2013 the government shut ERT, calling it 'a haven of waste'. All 2,700 workers were made redundent, although they were told they could apply for work when the corporation relaunches as a smaller, independent public broadcaster. On 17 June the Council of State (Greece's top administrative court) ordered that the signal be restored so that ERT could start broadcasting again. However, the court also upheld Prime Minister Samaras's plan to replace ERT with a new broadcaster later in the year.

Radio: ERT (http://tvradio.ert.gr) operates five radio channels, ERA 1–5, with nationwide coverage. ERA5 is an overseas network called 'Voice of Greece', while Filia (Friendship) broadcasts to immigrants in 12 languages, mainly European but includes Arabic, providing news, information and entertainment. There are over 400 commercial radio stations, many unregulated by government, providing programmes of music, sport and news and talk.

Television: ERT (www.ert.gr) operates three TV channels; two, ET1 and NET are broadcast from Athens and ET3 broadcasts from Thessaloniki with regional programmes for Northern Greece. New technologies include ERT Digital and ERT World (via satellite) with programmes broadcast around the world.

There are dozen commercial, private, digital and satellite channels based regionally, including Mega Channel (www.megatv.com), Skai TV (www.skai.gr), ANT1 Gold (www.gold.antenna.gr), Nova Cinema (www.novacinema.gr) and Nova Sport (www.novasport.gr).

In 2008 there were no cable TV services, although two services are available via high-speed internet connections.

Other news agencies: ANA-MPA: www.ana-mpa.gr

Economy

Greece's mixed economy is heavily dependent on tourism, agriculture and shipping. The service sector contributes around 80 per cent of GDP, industry around 16 per cent and agriculture less than 4 per cent. The tourist industry is based on Greece's ancient historic sites inland and its Mediterranean coastal resorts and islands. According to the World Travel and Tourism Council (WTTC) data, some 18 per cent of all employment in Greece is related to the tourist accommodation sector and provides around 16 per cent to GDP. In 2014, Greece's commercial shipping fleet was the largest (ahead of Japan) in the world, with around 4,900 registered vessels, over 16 per cent of the world's carrying capacity. The sector contributes some 5–6 per cent to GDP and employs around 160,000 people or 4 per cent of the total working population. After tourism it is the largest contributor to GDP.

As the global economic crisis struck, Greece fell into a 6-year recession beginning in 2008 and ending in 2014. By the end of this extended contraction, the Greek economy had shrunk by a quarter of its original size, with a trough in GDP growth of -8.9 per cent in 2011. The crisis resulted in a credit restriction, weakening world trade and a fall in domestic consumption and ultimately an uncompetitive economy. As a member of the euro-zone, the Greek economy is supposed to remain within a 3 per cent deficit margin as set by the European Central Bank (ECB), but as the crisis depressed the economy, government debt grew to 13.6 per cent of GDP and public debt burgeoned to 115.1 per cent of GDP. In 2011, in order to combat the growing debt (165 per cent of GDP at this point), the government initiated a three-year reform programme, under pressure from the EU, that included spending cuts, higher taxes, reducing the size of the public sector while freezing wages and introducing fiscal measures such as tackling tax evasion, reducing welfare payments in health, and pensions. However, by the end of 2014 the debt ratio to GDP was still growing at 177.1 per cent. Unemployment also reached an all-time high in 2014 of 28 per cent.

In 2012 as the EU dithered and could not find a financial mechanism to extricate Greece from its depression, there were calls for Greece to quit the EMU club. While some EU members, led by France, considered Greece's membership to be vital, many outsiders pondered the very survival of the euro if this crisis could not be resolved.

The outlook for recovery in 2014 improved greatly, enough to give the government confidence to cut some austerity taxes and predict a return to growth. This prediction came to fruition, as their GDP growth reached 0.8 per cent in 2014. In 2015, a new anti-austerity left-wing party, Syrzia, was brought into power with promises of renegotiating the EU-IMF bailouts. In February 2015 a four-month extension to Greece's bailout was negotiated by the government, however, it was on the condition that some anti-austerity measures were dropped and the undertaking of a Eurozone-approved reform programme. In June of that year the European Central Bank ended its emergency funding. Capital controls were put in place and banks were closed – people living in Greece were limited to withdrawing €60 (US$68) a day. In a July referendum EU bailout terms were overwhelmingly outvoted. In August a third bailout was agreed between Greece and its international creditors, one that imposed further spending cuts in order to avoid exit from the Eurozone and bankruptcy.

Despite being the first to downgrade Greece's credit rating to junk status in 2010, credit rating agency Standard and Poor's lifted the rating by two levels in 2015. The increase from triple-C minus to triple-C plus was credited to the three-year loan programme and €7.16 billion (US$7.84 billion) three-month bridge financing that had been secured.

External trade

As a member of the European Union, Greece operates within a community-wide free trade area, with tariffs set as a whole. Internationally, the EU has free trade agreements with a number of nations and trading blocs worldwide. It is Europe's largest producer of tobacco and the fifth largest exporter of cotton worldwide. Exports accounted for 33.0 per cent of Greece's GDP in 2014.

Imports

Principal imports include raw materials, fuels and lubricants, chemicals, machinery and transport equipment, foodstuffs, basic manufactures and consumer goods.

Main sources: Russia (10.3 per cent of total in 2014), Germany (9.9 per cent), Iraq (8.3 per cent)

Exports

Principal exports include tobacco, electrical and manufactured goods, petroleum products, chemicals, textiles and agricultural products, fruit and vegetables and live animals.

Main destinations: Turkey (12.2 per cent of total in 2014), Italy (9.2 per cent), Germany (6.6 per cent)

Agriculture

Farming

Agriculture is an important but diminishing sector of the economy. In 2014 agriculture contributed 3.8 per cent to GDP and employed around 13 per cent of the labour force.

The government's agricultural policy is, to a large extent, shaped by the EU's fundamental reform to the Common Agricultural Policy (CAP), which was introduced in Greece in 2005. The subsidies paid on farm output, which tended to benefit large farms and encourage overproduction, were replaced by single farm payments not conditional on production.

Main crops include wheat, barley, maize, fruit (especially olives), vegetables, oil seeds, tobacco, cotton and sugar beet.

Traditionally, farm co-operatives have played a large role in agriculture as a source of purchasing seeds, renting machinery and selling products. Larger co-operatives also handle basic processing and marketing. Attempts to restructure the co-operatives have largely failed, with weak management and widespread corruption preventing their modernisation and development.

The sector is also handicapped by weak infrastructure, low levels of technology and generally poor soil. However, with the exception of meat, dairy products and animal feed, Greece is self-sufficient in foodstuffs.

Fishing

Fish production is important for domestic consumption and export. The annual freshwater fish catch is around 25,000 tonnes, with a marine catch of approximately 270,000 tonnes. Coastal fish farms produce sea bass and gilthead bream.

Although Greece has an expanding aquaculture sector, its processing and marketing sector remains underdeveloped. Following the EU's common fisheries policy, the country benefits from the EU structural fund that covers the whole sector and also includes the development of the processing and marketing of products.

Forestry

Forest and other wooded land accounts for over 30 per cent of the land area, with forest cover estimated at 3.7 million hectares (ha). Most of the forest is in the northern and western part of the mainland and about 90 per cent is available for wood supply. Significant quantities of roundwood production are used for fuel consumption.

More than three-quarters of the forest and other wooded land is under public ownership, and only about 20 per cent is privately owned. The forest sector is rather small and all types of forest products are imported, mainly comprising sawnwood and paper products.

Industry and manufacturing

Industry typically accounts for 16 per cent of GDP and employs 17 per cent of the labour force. Within the industrial sector, manufacturing accounts for 57 per cent of output and construction 32 per cent. The remaining 11 per cent of industrial output is accounted for by the minerals and utilities sectors.

Manufacturing, which contributes around 10 per cent to overall GDP, is dominated by small family-owned companies, most of which are situated around Athens or in export-oriented zones around the port of Thessaloniki.

The number of mergers and acquisitions of Greek firms by foreign investors has increased in recent years, with greater numbers of companies making initial public offerings (IPOs) on the Athens Stock Exchange. However, production has been sluggish and relatively few industries are competitive on a European level.

Tourism

Greece attracts not only sea and sun-worshipers to its many islands, it also has many other attractions including classical ruins, Byzantine monuments, many of which are on the UN World Heritage list. Greece is one of Europe's top-ten destinations for foreign travellers.

Tourism is an important component of GDP, which in 2014 had a total contribution of 17.3 per cent. Tourism directly employs 9.4 per cent of the labour force in Greece (340,500 jobs) and indirectly employs a total of 19.4 per cent of the labour force (700,000 jobs).

In 2009, the former state-owned Olympic Airlines was privatised following an agreement with the EU to write-off US$3.87 billion in accumulated debt; it was re-launched as Olympic Air. It began operations as a competitive, full-service airline for southern Europe and the east Mediterranean.

Mining

There is some wealth of natural resources including large deposits of bauxite (aluminium ore), marble, lignite, magnesite, ferro-chrome, ferro-nickel, lead, zinc, uranium and manganese. Mining activity is small-scale and the sector typically contributes only 3 per cent to GDP and employs only 1 per cent of the workforce.

New gold resources have been found at Skouries (an ancient copper mine), estimated to contain five–seven million ounces of gold.

Hydrocarbons

Greece, situated as it is at the southern end of Europe, has more potential as an oil and gas transit country from the Caucasus and Caspian region than as a producer itself. It has oil reserves of around 10 million barrels (2014), produces around 500,000 barrels per day (bpd) of refined petroleum products and consumes 289,000bpd annually. Most oil production comes from the Prinos fields, which are exploited by North Aegean Petroleum Company (NAPC) consortium.

Total natural gas reserves stood at 991 million cubic metres (cum) in 2014. The Greek natural gas sector is controlled by the Greek Public Gas Company (DEPA).

A pipeline from Russia via Bulgaria delivers some 2.5 billion cum per year of natural gas, while a US$366 million natural gas pipeline from Turkey was completed in 2007 and was extended to Italy. In July 2015 Greece finally admitted it had plans for a €2 billion pipeline with Russia.

Greece's oil industry is dominated by Hellenic Petroleum (HP). The state owns approximately 60 per cent of HP.

Greece had coal reserves of 3 billion tonnes in 2014. Reserves are comprised wholly of low quality lignite, with high extraction costs. Coal production was 6.3 million tonnes oil equivalent (toe) in 2014, down 8.7 per cent from the 2013 figure.

Energy

Greece generates approximately 55 billion KW of electricity annually; around 75 per cent is thermal, 21 per cent hydro and 4 per cent solar. The majority of thermal power stations are fuelled by domestically produced lignite coal, with the remainder supplied by imported oil. Growth in electricity has increased by 50 per cent since 1995 and the energy authorities estimate that Greece will need an extra 6,000MW of additional capacity by the end of 2015.

Greece is the EU's second-largest solar collector (after Germany), with 20 per cent of households using solar powered water heaters.

The national Public Power Corporation (PPC) is the country's largest energy company and sole power supplier, operating 34 electricity-generating stations in an interconnected power grid as well as 60 autonomous power plants on Greek islands. The government has sold its assets in PPC but retained statutory control of its operations. The national electricity grid is connected to the networks of Albania, Bulgaria, Macedonia and Kosovo.

Financial markets

Stock exchange

Athens Stock Exchange (ASE)

Commodity exchange

ADEX (Athens Derivatives Exchange)

Banking and insurance

Liberalisation of the banking system was initiated in 1987. Interest rates are fully freed and commercial banks permitted to handle forward dealing in foreign exchange. Companies can borrow in foreign exchange without restriction.

On 29 August 2011 the planned merger of Greece's second and third largest banks, Eurobank EFG and Alpha Bank, was announced. The merger created the biggest bank in south-east Europe, with assets of US$212 billion and around 1,300 branches.

Central bank

Bank of Greece; European Central Bank (ECB).

Time

GMT plus two hours (daylight saving, late-March to late-September, GMT plus three hours)

Geography

Greece lies in south-eastern Europe. The country consists mainly of a mountainous peninsula between the Mediterranean Sea and the Aegean Sea. It is bounded by Albania, Macedonia (FYROM) and Bulgaria to the north, Turkey to the north-east, the Aegean Sea to the east, the Sea of Crete to the south and the Ionian Sea to the west. To the south, east and west of the mainland are many Greek islands, the largest being Crete.

Hemisphere

Northern

Climate

Coastal regions and the islands have typical Mediterranean conditions, with mild, rainy winters and hot, dry, sunny summers. Rainfall comes almost entirely in the winter months, although amounts vary widely according to position and relief.

Continental conditions affect the northern mountainous areas, with severe winters, deep snow cover and heavy precipitation, but summers are hot.

Athens: 9 degrees Celsius (C) (January); 28 degrees C (July); annual rainfall 414mm.

Dress codes

A suit and tie or formal clothing are necessary for business meetings, even during the hot summer months.

Women tend to dress smartly in the evening and men wear either suits or smart, casual clothes.

Entry requirements

Passports

Required by all, except nationals of EU/EEA countries, Switzerland and Monaco holding valid national identity cards. Passports must be valid for at least three months beyond length of stay.

Visa

Required by all, except nationals of Schengen agreement signatory countries and citizens of most of the Americas, Europe and many Asian countries. For confirmation of exceptions, contact the consular section of the nearest embassy. For those applying for a business visa, contact the consulate before travelling to determine requirements. A Schengen visa application (offered in several languages) can be downloaded from http://europa.eu/abc/travel/ see 'documents you will need'.

Currency advice/regulations

There are no restrictions on the import and export of local or foreign currency. Foreign currency over US$1,000 or equivalent must be declared on arrival.

Customs
Personal items are duty-free. There are no duties levied on alcohol and tobacco between EU member states, providing amounts imported are for personal consumption.
Strict regulations apply concerning the export of antiquities, including rocks from archaeological sites. Penalties range from large fines to prison terms.

Health (for visitors)
Nationals of the European Economic Area (EEA) countries and Switzerland can access reduced cost and sometimes free medical treatment using a European Health Insurance Card (EHIC) while visiting the EEA. Exceptions include nationals of the 10 countries which joined the EU in 2004 whose EHICs are not valid in Switzerland. Application for the EHIC should be made before travelling.

Mandatory precautions
Yellow fever vaccination certificate is required if travelling from infected area.

Advisable precautions
Long-term visitors should consider hepatitis A immunisation. Drinking water is not always purified .
Comprehensive travel insurance is advisable, in case of medical or other emergencies.

Hotels
Numerous hotels in all main towns, classified as de luxe, A,B,C,D and E. There is a 15 per cent service charge. A small tip will be expected. It is advisable to make reservations well in advance, especially between May and September.

Credit cards
All major credit cards are accepted.

Public holidays (national)
Fixed dates
1 Jan (New Year's Day), 6 Jan (Epiphany), 25 Mar (Independence Day), 1 May (Labour Day), 15 Aug (Assumption Day), 28 Oct (Ochi Day/National Day), 25 Dec (Christmas Day), 26 Dec (St Stephen's Day).

Variable dates
Greek Orthodox Shrove Monday, Greek Orthodox Good Friday, Greek Orthodox Easter Monday, Greek Orthodox Whit Monday, Greek Orthodox Pentecost.

Working hours
Banking
Mon–Fri: 0800–1400.

Business
Mon–Fri: generally 0800–1400 and 1700–2000; tend to close earlier during summer and on Mon and Wed afternoons.

Government
Mon–Fri: usually 0800–1500.

Shops
Mon, Wed and Sat: 0800–1400; Tue, Thu and Fri: 0800–1400 and 1800–2100.

Telecommunications
Mobile/cell phones
There are GSM roaming facilities available in 900/1800 band widths, with coverage throughout the country, including the island territories.

Electricity supply
220V AC

Social customs/useful tips
Personal contact is an important way of conducting business in Greece.
Greek bureaucracy can be slow. Identification documents and various authorisation letters or seals are necessary.
It is forbidden to photograph military installations and aircraft. Penalties for breaking the law can be severe.

Security
Visitors should be alert to the presence of pickpockets and purse-snatchers in tourist sites, particularly in Athens. As with the rest of Europe, there is a threat from terrorist activity, but Greece has its own anarchists, who occasionally engage in violence.

Getting there
Air
Greece has a strong tourist industry that relies on 80 per cent of international visitors arriving by air. Airports are located on the mainland as well as the islands.
National airline: Olympic Air
International airport/s: Eleftherios Venizelos Airport (ATH), sited in Sparta, 27km north-west of Athens. Facilities include: business centre, shops, duty-free shops, restaurants and car hire. Further information can be obtained at www.aia.gr. Express bus routes carry passengers into Athens or the port of Pireaus. The international airport on Crete is the Heraklion-Nikos Kazantzakis International Airport.
Other airport/s: Alexandroupolis (AXD), 7km from city; Corfu (CFU), 1.6km from city; Heraklion (HER), 5km from city; Ioannina (IOA), 5km from city; Kos (KGS), 27km from city; Mykonos (JMK); Paros (PAS); Rhodes (RHO), 16km south-west of Rhodes; Thessaloniki Makedonia (SKG), 16km from city; Skiathos (JSI); Thira (JTR).
Airport tax: International €12.5; domestic €8.51

Surface
Road: The Greek road network is accessible via Italy, Bulgaria and Macedonia (FYROM) (border crossing at Medzitlija, near Bitola).
Rail: The Greek rail network is connected to most European routes via Italy, Bulgaria and Macedonia (FYROM). There is a daily service between Athens and Istanbul.
Water: Frequent passenger ferry services operate from Italy to Piraeus. A car ferry service runs between Ancona and Brindisi (Italy) and Igoumenitsa and Patras.
There is a ferry from Marmaris, Turkey, to the island of Rhodes.
Main port/s: Heraklion, Igoumenitsa, Patras, Piraeus, Rafina, Salonika and Volos.

Getting about
National transport
Air: As well as the international airports, there are a further 25 other airports all connected by regular services operated by Olympic Airways.
Road: There are 117,000km of roads in Greece, of which about 9,000km are unpaved. There are 470km of motorways, including a route from Athens to Thessaloniki.
Rail: Over 2,500km of track is operated by Hellenic Railways Organisation Ltd, with services to most towns.
Water: About 80km of navigable inland waterways are used, as well as several regular ferry services along the coast and connecting the various islands.

City transport
Taxis: Taxis are plentiful in Athens, but avoid rush hours. There is an extra charge for each piece of luggage, waiting time, journeys outside Athens/Piraeus and journeys after midnight. Yellow taxis run from the airport to downtown Athens.
Buses, trams & metro: There is a good, but often busy, bus network in Athens with a standard flat rate within city limits. Tickets are available at blue booths situated near the bus stops, or at many kiosks throughout the city. These tickets must be inserted into a machine inside the bus to be valid. Double-decker buses run between the airport and downtown Athens, operating every 20 minutes from 0600 until midnight.
The Attico Metro runs from 0530 to midnight daily, approximately every four minutes during rush hour and every 10 minutes at other times. Tickets must be purchased before entering the metro and must be cancelled upon entry.
An extension to the subway system was inaugurated in 2000 as part of the subway grid built for the 2004 Olympic Games.

Car hire
All major car hire companies have offices in Athens and some other main towns. Rates vary depending on size of car, length of hire and season. International driving licences are recognised, but UK, Belgian, Austrian and German full licences are also accepted. International

insurance Green Card is valid, provided Greece is mentioned. The wearing of seatbelts is compulsory. Traffic drives on the right.
Extreme care is necessary if riding a motorbike.

BUSINESS DIRECTORY

The addresses listed below are a selection only. While World of Information makes every endeavour to check these addresses, we cannot guarantee that changes have not been made, especially to telephone numbers and area codes. We would welcome any corrections.

Telephone area codes

The international direct dialling code (IDD) for Greece is +30, followed by area code and subscriber's number:

Athens	210	Samos	273
Heraklion	81	Thessaloniki	31

Useful telephone numbers

Police: 100
Fire: 199
Hospitals: 106
Emergency services (24-hours; information in English, French and Greek, to request ambulances, fire department, police and coastguard): 112

Chambers of Commerce

American-Hellenic Chamber of Commerce, 109 Messoghion Avenue, 11526 Athens (tel: 699-3559; fax: 698-5686; e-mail: info@amcham.gr).

Athens Chamber of Commerce and Industry, 7 Akademias Street, 10671 Athens (tel: 360-4815; fax: 361-6408; e-mail: info@acci.gr).

British-Hellenic Chamber of Commerce, 25 Vassilissis Sophia Avenue, 10674 Athens (tel: 721-0361; fax: 722-2119; e-mail: info@bhcc.gr).

Heraklion Chamber of Commerce and Industry, 9 Koronaiou Street, 71202 Heraclion, Crete (tel: 022-9013; fax: 022-2914; e-mail: info@ebeh.gr).

Samos Chamber of Commerce and Industry, 19 Koundourioti Street, 83100 Samos (tel: 087-970; fax: 022-784; e-mail: samcci@otonet.gr).

Thessaloniki Chamber of Commerce and Industry, 29 Tsimiski Street, 54624 Thessaloniki (tel: 037-0100; fax: 037-0166; e-mail: root@ebeth.gr).

Union of Hellenic Chambers of Commerce and Industry, 7 Akademias Street, 10671 Athens (tel: 363-2702; fax: 362-2320; e-mail: hellas@uhcci.gr).

Banking

Agricultural Bank of Greece SA, Panepistimiou 23, 105-64 Athens (tel: 939-9911; fax: 323-9611).

Alpha Bank, 40 Stadiou Street, 102-52 Athens (tel: 326-0000; fax: 326-5438).

Commerical Bank of Greece, 11 Sophocleous Street, 102-35 Athens (tel: 328-4000; fax: 325-3746).

Egnatia Bank, Omirou 22, 106-72 Athens (tel: 360-6914; fax: 362-7945).

General Bank, Panepistimiou 9, 105-64 Athens (tel: 324-1289; fax: 322-2271).

National Bank of Greece, Aeolou 86, 150-51 Athens (tel: 334-1000; fax: 321-3119; internet site: http://www.nbg.gr).

Post-Office Savings Bank, Pesmazoglou 2-6, 105-59 Athens (tel: 323-0621; fax: 323-1055).

Central bank

Bank of Greece, 21 E Venizelos Avenue, GR 102-50 Athens (tel: 320-1111; fax: 323-2239; e-mail: secretariat@bankofgreece.gr).

European Central Bank (ECB), Kaiserstrasse 29, D-60311 Frankfurt am Main, Germany (tel: (+49-69) 13-440; fax: (+49-69) 1344-6000; e-mail: info@ecb.int).

Stock exchange

Athens Stock Exchange (ASE), www.ase.gr

Commodity exchange

ADEX (Athens Derivatives Exchange), www.adex.ase.gr

Travel information

Athens Airport (East), Helliniko, 167-00 Athens (tel: 969-9111; fax: 966-6162).

Athens Airport (West), Helliniko, 167-00 Athens (tel: 936-9111; fax: 936-3328).

Athens International Airport (Eleftherios Venizelos), 5th km Spata, Loutsa Ave, 190 04 Spata (tel: 369-8300; fax: 369-8883; internet site: http://www.aia.gr).

Hellenic Chamber of Hotels, 24 Stadiou Street, 10564 Athens (tel: 331-0022/33; fax: 323-6962, 322-5449).

Olympic Airways, Syngrou Ave 96-100, 117-41 Athens (tel: 926-9111; fax: 926-7154).

Ministry of tourism

Ministry of Tourism, Amerikis 2B, 105-64 Athens (tel: 322-3111; fax: 322-4148).

National tourist organisation offices

Ellinikos Organismos Tourismou (GNTO) (Greek National Tourist Organisation), Odos Amerikis 2, Athens 10564 (tel: 322-3111/9).

Ministries

Ministry of Aegean, Syngrou Ave 49, 117-43 Athens (tel: 923-7970; fax: 923-8200).

Ministry of Agriculture, Acharnon 2, 101-76 Athens (tel: 529-1111; fax: 524-0475).

Ministry of Commerce, Caningos Square, 106-77 Athens (tel: 381-6242; fax: 384-2642).

Ministry of Culture, Bouboulinas 20, 106-82 Athens (tel: 820-1100; fax: 820-1337).

Ministry of Education and Religious Affairs, Mitropoleos 15, 101-85 Athens (tel: 325-4221; fax: 324-8264).

Ministry of Environment, Town Planning and Public Works, Amaliados 17, 115-23 Athens (tel: 643-1461; fax: 644-7608).

Ministry of Finance, Karageorgi Servias 10, 101-84 Athens (tel: 331-3400; fax: 323-8657).

Ministry of Foreign Affairs, Academias 1, 106-71 Athens (tel: 361-0584; fax: 645-0028).

Ministry of Health, Welfare and Social Security, Aristotelous 17, 101-87 Athens (tel: 524-9010; fax: 522-3246).

Ministry of Industry, Energy and Technology, Michalakopoulou 80, 101-92 Athens (tel: 748-2770; fax: 770-8003).

General Secretariat for Energy and Technology, Mesogeion Ave 14-18, 115-10 Athens (tel: 775-2221; fax: 771-4153).

Ministry of Interior, Dragatsaniou 2, 105-59 Athens (tel: 322-3521; fax: 324-1180).

Ministry of Justice, Mesogeion 96, 115-27 Athens (tel: 775-7619; fax: 779-6055).

Ministry of Labour, Pireos 40, 101-82 Athens (tel: 523-3110; fax: 524-9805).

Ministry of National Defence, Papagou Camp, Mesogeion 227-229, 154-51 Athens (tel: 646-5201; fax: 646-5584).

Ministry of National Economy: Division for Foreign Capital and Attracting Investments, Syntagma Square, 101-80 Athens (tel: 333-2000; fax: 333-2130; internet site: http://www.dos.gr/welcome_en.htm).

Division for Private Investment Policy, Syntagma Square, 101-80 Athens (tel: 333-2252/3; fax: 333-2326).

Regional Development Divisions of Attica, Thiras 60, 112-52 Athens (tel: 862-9810; fax: 862-9742).

Ministry of Press and Mass Media, Zalokosta 10, 101-63 Athens (tel: 363-0911; fax: 360-6969).

Ministry of Prime Minister's Office, Vas Sofias, 106-74 Athens (tel: 339-3000; fax: 339-3020).

Ministry of Public Order, Pan Kanellopoulou 4, 101-77 Athens (tel: 692-8510; fax: 692-1675).

Ministry of Transport and Communications, Xenofontos 13, 105-57 Athens (tel: 325-1211; fax: 324-7400).

Prime Minister's Office, Maximos Mansion, Herod Atticus 19, 106-74 Athens (tel: 671-7071; fax: 671-5799).

Other useful addresses

Athenagence (ANA) (news agency), Odos Pindarou 5, Athens 10671 (tel: 363-9816).

Athens and Piraeus Electric Railways (ISAP), Athinas 67, 105-52 Athens (tel: 324-8311; fax: 322-3935).

Athens and Piraeus Trolleys (ILPAP), Admitou 17, 104-46 Athens (tel: 821-6305; fax: 883-7445).

Athens and Piraeus Water Company (EYDAP), Oropou 156, 111-46 Athens (tel: 253-3402; fax: 253-3124).

Athens Municipal Gas Corporation (DEFA), Orfeos 2, 118-54 Athens (tel: 346-1194; fax: 346-1400).

Athens Stock Exchange, Sofokleous 10, 105-59 Athens (tel: 321-1301; fax: 321-3938; internet site: http://www.ase.gr/).

British Embassy, I Ploutarchou Street, 106-75 Athens (tel: 727-2600).

Centre for Planning and Economic Research (KEPE), Hippokratous St 22, 106-80 Athens (tel: 362-7321; fax: 361-1136; e-mail: kepe@kepe.gr).

Cotton Organisation (OBA), Syngrou Ave 150, 176-71 Athens (tel: 923-4314; fax: 924-3676).

'Democritus' Nuclear Research Centre, Ag Paraskevi, 153-10 Athens (tel: 651-8911; fax: 651-9180).

Department of Press and Information, Ministry to The Prime Minister's Office, Odos Zalokosta 10, Athens (tel: 363-0911).

Economic and Industrial Research Institute (IOBE), Tsami Karatasi 11, 117-42 Athens (tel: 924-1378; fax: 923-3977).

Export Promotion Organisation (OPE), Mar Antippa 86-88, 163-46 Athens (tel: 996-1900; fax: 991-5392).

Federation of Greek Industry (SEB), Xenofontos 5, 105-57 Athens (tel: 323-7325; fax: 322-2929).

Geological and Mineral Research Institute (IGME), Mesogion Ave 70, 115-27 Athens (tel: 779-8412; fax: 775-2211).

Greek Atomic Energy Commission, Ag Paraskevi, 153-10 Athens (tel: 651-8911; fax: 651-9180).

Greek Embassy (USA), 2221 Massachusetts Avenue, NW, Washington DC 20008 (tel: (+1-202)-939-5800; fax: (+1-202)-939-5824; e-mail: greece@greekembassy.org).

Greek Post Offices (ELTA), Apellou 1, 101-88 Athens (tel: 324-3311; fax: 324-1228).

Greek Radio and Television (ET 1), Mesogion Ave 432, 153-42 Athens (tel: 639-0772; fax: 639-0652).

Greek Radio and Television (ET 2), Mesogion Ave 136, 115-62 Athens (tel: 770-1911; fax: 777-6239).

Greek Railways Organisation (OSE), Sina 6, 106-72 Athens (tel: 362-4402; fax: 362-8933).

Hellenic Aerospace Industry (EAB), Mesogion Ave 2-4, 115-27 Athens (tel: 779-9679; fax: 779-7670).

Hellenic Centre for Investment (HCI), 3 Mitropoleos Str, GR-105 57 Athens (tel: 324-2070; fax: 324-2079).

Hellenic Organisation for Small- and Medium-Size Enterprises and Handicraft Undertakings (EOMMEX), Xenias 16, 115-28 Athens (tel: 771-5002; fax: 771-5025).

Hellenic Organisation for the Promotion of Exports (HOPE), 1 Mitropoleos Street, 10557 Athens (tel: 324-7011/16).

Hellenic Standardisation Organisation (ELOT), Acharnon 313, 111-45 Athens (tel: 201-5025; fax: 202-0776).

Hellenic Telecommunications Organisation (OTE), Kifissias 99, 151-24 Athens (tel: 611-7466; fax: 681-0899).

Hellenic Tobacco Organisation (EOK), Kapodistriou 36, 104-32 Athens (tel: 524-7311; fax: 524-7318).

National Statistical Service , Lykourgou 14-16, 101-66 Athens (tel: 324-85118; fax: 324-1098; internet site: http://www.statistics.gr/).

Panhellenic Confederation of Farmers' Co-operatives (PASEGES), Kifissias 16, 115-26 Athens (tel: 770-4737; fax: 777-9313).

Panhellenic Exporters' Association, Kratinou 11, 105-52 Athens (tel: 522-8925; fax: 522-9403).

Public Materials Administration Organisation (ODDY), Stadiou 60, 105-64 Athens (tel: 324-4231; fax: 324;2970).

Public Petroleum Corporation (DEP), Mesogion Ave 357-359, 152-31 Athens (tel: 650-1340; fax: 650-1383).

Public Power Corporation (PPC), Halkokondyli 30, 104-32 Athens (tel: 523-4301; fax: 523-5307).

Union of Commercial Agents, Voulis 15, Athens (tel: 322-3148).

Urban Transport Organisation (OAS), Metsovou 15, 106-82 Athens (tel: 883-6077; fax: 821-2219).

ANA-MPA: www.ana-mpa.gr

Internet sites

Bridge to Greece and Cyprus: http://greekvillage.com/bridge/bridge.htm

EFG Eurobank Ergasias: http://www.eurobank.gr

Greek telephone directory: http://www.hellasyellow.gr/

Greenland

KEY FACTS

Official name: Greenland (Kalaallit Nunaat)

Head of State: Queen Margrethe II of Denmark, represented by High Commissioner Mikaela Engell (since 1 Feb 2011)

Head of government: Prime Minister Kim Kielsen (Siumut) (from 10 Dec 2014)

Ruling party: Coalition lead by Siumut (Forward) with Atassut (Solidarity) and Demokraatit (Democrats) (from 28 November 2014)

Area: 2,166,086 square km, of which 410,449 square km is not covered by permanent ice

Population: 56,744 (2011)*
(56,452; census figure 2010)

Capital: Nuuk (Godthåb)

Official language: Greenlandic Inuit and Danish

Currency: Danish krone (Kr) = 100 ore

Exchange rate: Kr6.67 per US$ (Sep 2015)

GDP per capita: US$37,517 (2011)

GDP real growth: -5.40% (2009)

GDP: US$1.27 billion (2009)

Labour force: 28,240 (2009)

Inflation: -19.00% (2009)

* estimated figure

Greenland, the world's largest island, is about 81 per cent ice-capped. Vikings reached the island in the tenth century from Iceland before Danish colonisation began in the eighteenth century. Greenland became an integral part of the Danish realm in 1953 and joined the European Community (now the EU) with Denmark in 1973, however, it withdrew in 1985 over a dispute centred on stringent fishing quotas. Greenland was granted self-governance by the Danish parliament in 1979 and it has voted in favour of increased self-rule in November 2008 and acquired greater responsibility when the Act on Greenland Self-Government was signed into law in June 2009. Despite the increased devolution and move towards independence, Denmark continues to exercise control over several areas on behalf of Greenland, including foreign affairs, security, and financial policy in consultation with Greenland's Self-Rule Government.

On 2 October 2014, Prime Minister Aleqa Hammond resigned, after being accused of spending US$17,000 on personal expenses including hotels and air tickets for family members, according to *Sermitsiaq* newspaper. Two ministers from Ms Hammond's Siumut Partii party, including the mining and natural resources minister Jens-Erik Kierkegaard, and two ministers from the Atassut party also resigned. The parliamentary coalition collapsed, as many members of Atassut crossed to the opposition party, Inuit Ataqatigiit (IA). Kierkegaard cancelled a visit to China to meet with investors. Siumut party member Kim Kielsen, minister for nature and the environment, took over as acting prime minister.

As a result a general election was held on 28 November. Siumut (Forward) and Inuit Ataqatigiit (IA) (Community of the People) emerged as the largest parties both winning 11 of the 31 seats. A three party coalition government was formed consisting of the incumbent Siumut and Atassut (Solidarity) parties alongside the Demokraatit (Democrats). Kim Kielsen, leader of the Siumut Partii, became prime minister of Greenland on 10 December.

The economy

Greenland's economy remains highly dependent on exports of shrimp and fish, income from resource exploration and extraction, and on a substantial subsidy from the Danish government. The latest figures from 2012 suggest that the subsidy was budgeted to be about US$651 million, 56 per cent of government revenues that year. The Greenlandic economy has benefited from increasing catches and exports of shrimp, Greenland halibut, and more recently, crabs. Due to the country's continued dependence on exports of fish – which accounted for 89 per cent of exports in 2010 – the economy is highly sensitive to external demand. Greenland weathered the global economic crisis with relative ease due to increased hydrocarbon and mineral and extraction activities, a high level of construction activity in the Nuuk area and the increasing price of shrimp and fish. International studies indicate the potential for oil and gas fields in northern and north-eastern Greenland, however, no extraction of hydrocarbons has commenced as of November 2015. A US aluminium producer concluded a memorandum of understanding with Greenland's government in 2007 to build a uranium smelter and a power generation facility, which would take advantage of Greenland's abundant hydropower potential; however, the plans were scrapped. Tourism also offers another avenue of economic growth for Greenland, with increasing numbers of cruise liners now operating in Greenland's western and southern waters during the peak summer tourism season.

All major political parties in Greenland support the development of a mining industry, however, the two main parties have been divided on the issue of uranium mining. The Inuit Ataqatigiit party has opposed it on environmental grounds while the Siumut Party along with its coalition supports uranium mining. London Mining's Greenland operations were purchased in December 2014 by a Chinese investment and trading group in Hong Kong. China is unlikely to pursue Greenland's plans to develop mining projects. Investment in rare earth projects outside of China has largely been driven by expectations of limited supply in China, where production capacity has been restricted by quotas on both production and export. The removal of the export quotas is likely to reduce China's interest in international rare earth projects, including the two in Greenland. London Mining originally planned to build uranium mines in Greenland, however, its bankruptcy in 2014 due to incurring heavy losses at its Sierra Leone mine due to the Ebola crisis prevented any further action.

As of September 2015, only one mine in Greenland is currently being constructed. Reaching it requires a four-hour boat ride from Nuuk along a barren coast and glaciers, to the Aappaluttoq deposit, where miners drill for pink sapphires and rubies. The ministry of mineral resources has reviewed hundreds of mining licence requests since 2013 and it is now moving forward with five of them, aiming to have up to 10 mines operating by 2018 and seeking new deposits. In the south of Greenland, Greenland Minerals and Energy and Tanbreez, two Australian-owned companies, have put forward the largest proposals of the 24 submitted for active exploration. The Greenland Minerals and Energy project is more contentious because it plans to extract uranium along with rare-earth elements and to create a chemical processing plant on site. This mine would represent the only open-pit uranium mine in the Arctic and its location on top of a mountain would make it more risky, as dust and water used in the mining could trickle down the slopes and disseminate.

Risk assessment

Politics	Fair
Economy	Fair
Regional stability	Good

COUNTRY PROFILE

1940 During the German occupation of Denmark in the Second World War, Greenland came under US protection. Denmark re-assumed control of Greenland but with continued military use of bases by the US and later NATO.
1953 Greenland ceased to be a colony and became an autonomous province of the Danish Kingdom under the Home Rule Constitution. Native Inuit were expelled, by Danish officials, from their ancestral lands in the north to make way for expansion of the US airbase at Thule.
1973 Greenland joined the EEC (later EU) as part of Denmark.
1979 Full home rule was granted to Greenland; Denmark retained control of constitutional matters, foreign relations and defence.
1985 Greenland left the EEC following two referenda.
1987 A disagreement with Denmark over the presence of a US military radar system in Thule led to the fall of the coalition government.
1991 Parliamentary elections resulted in a coalition government composed of the Siumit (Forward) party and the Inuit Ataqatigiit (IA) (Inuit Brotherhood).
1995 The IA formed a coalition with Attasut. Lars Emil Johansen became prime minister.
1999 The Danish High Court concluded the Inuit were illegally removed from their land around Thule in 1953, but their right to return was denied.
2000 NASA scientists found that the ice sheet which covers 85 per cent of Greenland's territory was melting by one metre per year.
2002 A coalition government was formed comprising the Siumut and IA parties; Hans Enoksen, became prime minister.
2003 The short-lived coalition collapsed amid allegations of corruption and the use of a native shaman. A new coalition of Siumut and the Atassut party was formed, but it failed within months during a row over the budget. Siumut resumed its coalition with the IA. Inuits lost their appeal to the Danish Supreme Court for return of their land.
2004 Denmark signed an agreement with the US to refurbish the US airbase at Thule.
2005 Prime Minister Enoksen was returned to power in early elections, called in response to allegations of misuse of public funds by ministers and failure of budgetary discussions.
2006 Official studies declared the Greenland ice sheets were melting at an increased rate.
2007 Plans by Greenland Inuits to increase their quota for whale hunting deadlocked the International Whaling Commission negotiations. Critics accused Greenland of expanding for commercial reasons rather than for cultural and nutritional values of native whaling.
2008 The five countries surrounding the Arctic met in Greenland to discuss territorial claims. The talks were aimed at reducing the detrimental effect of unrestrained exploration for oil and gas and forming an agreement concerning access to the north-west passage between the Atlantic and Pacific oceans. A referendum on more autonomy from Denmark was agreed by 75 per cent. Under the new arrangement Greenlanders are recognised as a separate people under international law and the local government was given more control of resources, including a bigger share of oil revenues, and control of internal security.
2009 Early general elections were called so that a new administration would be in place to implement the new self-governing reforms. The left-wing opposition IA won 43.7 per cent of the vote, the ruling Siumut 26.5 per cent. Jakob Edvard Kuupik Kleist (IA) became prime minister.
2010 The Scotland-based exploration company Cairn Energy began drilling for oil offshore between Greenland and Baffin Island. Following the hottest six months of global recorded temperatures, the biggest ice island to break from the Arctic ice sheet since 1962, broke away from northern Greenland. Estimated at around 250 square kilometres and 180m deep the island slowly drifted into the Atlantic Ocean and melted down. Cairn Energy announced that it had found natural gas and oil-bearing sands (containing crude oil) off the coast of Greenland.
2011 Mikaela Engell became High Commissioner in February. The leader of the environmental activist group Greenpeace, Kumi Naidoo, was arrested in June, having breached a court-imposed exclusion zone and scaled the Cairn Energy's Greenland exploration oil rig.
2012 In June an international conference that included scientists, business people and politicians, was held in Svalbard (Norway), close to the North Pole, to discuss the implication of industrial development, global warming, ecosystems and livelihoods during rapid change. Oil exploration is already underway offshore in Greenland's Arctic waters. On 25 July, satellite images of Greenland, produced by the US's Nasa, showed the unprecedented rapid melting of a huge ice sheet.
2013 Elections were held on 12 March. The result was a win for the Siumut party with 42.8 per cent of the vote (14 out of 31 seats) with the previous ruling party Inuit Ataqatigiit second with 34.4 per cent (11). Turnout was 74.2 per cent. Aleqa Hammond became prime minister, forming a coalition with the Atassut (Solidarity/Community Spirit) and the new Partii Inuit (Inuit Party), which each won 2 seats. On 24 October London Mining was awarded a licence to build and run an iron ore mine. The controversial project, known as Isua, is some 150km from Nuuk and will have an associated deep water port to export the expected 15 million tonnes annual production of high-grade iron ore. London Mining has said it expects to use Chinese construction companies, which will entail bringing in some 3,000 Chinese workers. Environmentalists have said they want reassurances that the exploitation of the deposits will not come at the cost of extensive environmental damage.

2014 Aleqa Hammond stepped down as prime minister on 30 September after being accused of misuse of public funds. Kim Kielsen became acting prime minister pending an election called for 28 November. elections were held on 14 November.
2015 Throughout 2015 Greenlanders continued to be divided over whether or not to develop their mining potential, or whether the risk to the environment would be too high.

Political structure

Constitution

The Home Rule constitution, enacted on 2 June 1953, altered the status of Greenland from a colony to an autonomous province of Denmark. In 1979 full powers were granted with executive, judicial and legislative branches. Denmark retained control of constitutional matters, foreign relations and defence. Following a 26 November 2008 referendum, Greenlanders became recognised as a separate people under international law and the local government gained more control of resources, including a bigger share of oil revenues, and control of internal security. Self-government came into effect on 21 June 2009.
Greenland elects two members to the Danish parliament.

Form of state

Parliamentary democratic dependency

The executive

The Danish monarch is head of state and is represented by a High Commissioner appointed by the monarch.
Executive power is exercised by a prime minister who heads the government, which is composed by the majority political party or parties in parliament.
There are seven Landsstyremaend (ministers) headed by the Landsstyreformanden (prime minister).

National legislature

The unicameral Landstingets (parliament) has 31 members, elected by proportional representation for four-year terms.

Last elections

28 November 2014
Results: Parliamentary: Siumut (Forward) won 34.6 per cent of the vote (11 out of 31 seats), Inuit Ataqatigiit (IA) (Community of the People) 33.5 per cent (11), Demokraatit (Democrats) 11.9 per cent (4), Partii Naleraq 11.7 per cent (3) and Atassut (Solidarity) 6.6 per cent (2). The Inuit Party and independents failed to win any seats. Turnout was 72.9 per cent.

Next elections

2018 (parliamentary)

Political parties

Ruling party

Coalition lead by Siumut (Forward) with Atassut (Solidarity) and Demokraatit (Democrats) (from 28 November 2014)

Main opposition party

Inuit Ataqatigiit (Community of the People)

Population

56,744 (2011)* (56,452; census figure 2010)
Last census: 1 January 2008: 56,462
Population density: Seven inhabitants per square km (2001) (icecap excluded).
Annual growth rate: 0.2 per cent (2003)

Ethnic make-up

Eighty-eight per cent of the population are Inuit and Greenland-born whites and the remainder are primarily Danes.

Religions

Ninety-six per cent belong to the Evangelical Lutheran Church of Denmark.

Education

US$102 million was spent on education in 2002.
Pupils per teacher: 10 in primary schools.

Health

Life expectancy: 68.9 years (estimate 2003)
Fertility rate/Maternal mortality rate: 2.4 births per woman (World Bank)
Birth rate/Death rate: 16 births per 1,000 population; eight deaths per 1,000 population (2003).
Child (under 5 years) mortality rate (per 1,000): 17 per 1,000 live births (2003)

Main cities

Nuuk (Godthåb) (capital, estimated population 16,225 in 2012), Sisimiut (Holsteinsborg) (5,532), Ilulissat (Jakobshavn) (4,658), Aasiaat (Ededesminde) (3,220), Qaqortoq (Julianehåb) (3,161).

Languages spoken

Danish and Greenlandic Inuit, which is an eastern branch of the East-Eskimo language categorised by linguists as Inupik, which is spoken on the northern coasts of Canada and Alaska and the eastern-most tip of Siberia. Greenlanders connected with tourism often speak English.

Official language/s

Greenlandic Inuit and Danish

Media

Press

In Greenlandic (although with Danish and sometimes English online editions), there are only two newspapers, Atuagagdliutit Gronlandsposten (www.ag.gl) is published twice weekly and Sermitsiak is published weekly; *Niviarsiaq* is published monthly.
Dailies: There are no daily newspapers.
Weeklies: *Grønlandsposten/Atuagagdliutit* and *Sermitsiak*.
Periodicals: *Grønland* is a general interest periodical, published 10 times a year.

Broadcasting

The national public broadcaster is Kalaallit Nunaata Radioa (KNR) (Greenland Broadcasting Company). It is financed through government funding, advertising and sponsorship and broadcasts a range of cultural, news, music and entertainment programmes.
Radio: Greenland Radio (KNR) broadcasts in Greenlandic and Danish with both local productions and Danish programmes.
Television: KNR TV broadcasts in Greenlandic and Danish with domestic productions of cultural and youth programmes and imported (mostly Danish) shows.

Economy

There are over 400 licensed fishing vessels operating in Greenland, where 89 per cent of all exports are derived from fish products, and therefore, fishing is the primary industry. Although Greenland draws on subsidies from Denmark, in the form of block grants, the government maintains a tight fiscal policy to create public budget surpluses and low inflation. The total financial package received from Denmark is around US$650 million annually, providing 60 per cent of government revenues.
The service sector is an important component of the economy, constituting around 67 per cent of GDP, of which public service is a leading factor. Although not a mass-market destination, Greenland is a destination for particular travellers and has a growing tourism sector.
Greenland's aboriginal population is involved in subsistence whaling. Catch limits on whaling are set by the International Whaling Commission (IWC), in order to maintain the sustainability of whaling and to ensure the continued growth of stocks is not impeded. However, no quotas have been set for the period 2013–18, leaving Greenland in an awkward situation.
Greenland has abundant thermal and hydropower, and investigation to utilise them as export elements is being undertaken. The US aluminium producer, Alcoa, is building a smelter, using a thermal power facility. The smelter is expected to come into production by the end of 2015 and together with the related power station will employ some 600 workers.
Natural gas and oil deposits were discovered offshore in Greenland territorial waters in mid-2010. The prospecting company, Cairn Energy, described the find as 'North Sea-scale' and likely to be significant, with an estimated 20 billion barrels of oil. However, drilling in 2014 has since proved unsuccessful.

External trade
Greenland is not a member of the European Union, despite being an overseas territory of Denmark. However, it has a fishing agreement with the EU, which allows it to sell its fish products as non-dutiable goods in the EU. It also has leased fishing rights to the EU.
While Canada provides Greenland with fresh fruit and vegetables Greenland does not produce anything that Canada does not already have, so trade is generally one-way.

Imports
Imports include machinery and transport equipment, food, manufactured goods and petroleum products.
Main sources: Denmark (60.4 per cent of total in 2014), Sweden (16.9 per cent) and Iceland (10.6 per cent).

Exports
Principal exports are crustaceans, metals (10 per cent), non-fillet frozen fish, fish fillets and other processed crustaceans and fish products (89 per cent).
Main destinations: Denmark (60.7 per cent of total in 2014), Japan (10.4 per cent) and China (8.4 per cent).

Agriculture

Farming
The agricultural sector, comprising around 60 farms, is largely confined to sheep farming in the south and small-scale reindeer farming. Livestock production is around 360 tonnes of mutton and lamb. The production of lamb and reindeer meat is mainly for domestic consumption. Arable areas mainly produce hay for fodder.

Fishing
Fishing is the mainstay of the economy, accounting for 89 per cent of exports and giving employment to a quarter of the population. Principal products include shrimp, halibut, cod and seal. Typical annual catches include over 142,000 tonnes (t) shrimps and 197,000t fish. Halibut is increasingly important, while cod has declined in importance. Traditional sea mammal catches include 115,000 seals annually.
The fishing industry employs over 6,000 people. The principal export markets are Denmark, Japan and China.
Catch limits on whaling are set by the International Whaling Commission (IWC), in order to maintain the sustainability of whaling and to ensure the continued growth of stocks is not impeded. The quotas for the period 2008–12 were an annual strike limit of 190 minke whales, 2 bowhead whales, 10 fin whales, and 9 humpback whales. In July 2012, the IWC had its 64th meeting to come to an agreement on the quotas for the period 2013–18. However, a decision on the update of catch limits for aboriginal subsistence was not reached, leaving Greenland in an awkward situation. In 2014, subsistence whaling continues on a temporary basis following scientific advice from the IWC.

Industry and manufacturing
Industry is centred on fish processing and packaging. Most of the sector is controlled by the government-owned Royal Greenland Company, which manages factories and smaller plants in both Greenland and Denmark. Some tanning and leatherworking takes place in the south. The industrial sector accounts for around 30 per cent of GDP.
Infrastructure improvements have provided a boost to construction activity, in particular the development of new airstrips.

Tourism
There are two tourist seasons, the principal one is during the warm spring-summer months when visitors make the journey to see the spectacular landscapes of the Arctic and semi-Arctic of glaciers, icebergs, Arctic wildlife and activities that include dog-sledding, whale watching, plus experiencing a little of the indigenous Inuit culture. While hardier visitors may visit during the frozen depths of winter for the chance to see the *aurora borealis* (northern lights), although this phenomena may be seen at other times of the year and in less strenuous circumstances.

Mining
There are known reserves of zinc, lead, copper, cobalt, uranium, iron ore, gold and diamonds. Mineral exploration is actively encouraged and the administration has reformed its mining regulations. Large quantities of two of the world's most rare metals, niobium and tantalum, exist in Greenland. Exploitation of the minerals becomes more likely as the ice-sheet retreats due to global warming.
In 2014 London Mining was awarded a licence to build and run an iron ore mine. The controversial project, known as Isua, is some 150km from Nuuk and will have an associated deep-water port to export the expected 15 million tonnes annual production of high-grade iron ore. London Mining has said it expects to use Chinese construction companies, which will entail bringing in some 3,000 Chinese workers. Environmentalists have said they want reassurances that the exploitation of the deposits will not come at the cost of extensive environmental damage. However, global events continued to conspire against Greenland's efforts to develop a mining industry. London Mining went bankrupt and was placed into receivership after incurring heavy losses at its Sierra Leone mine due to the Ebola crisis.
Since gaining political autonomy from the Kingdom of Denmark in 2009, successive governments in Greenland have been aggressively promoting the development of a mining industry as a solution to its deep and worsening economic issues. Greenland is likely to develop large-scale mining and energy projects eventually, but the pace of development will be much slower than the government of Greenland has anticipated due to steep declines in iron ore prices and unrealistic expectations of demand for rare earth elements.
China's decision at the start of 2015 to drop export quotas is likely to prove detrimental to Greenland's plans to develop mining projects.

Hydrocarbons
Greenland still hopes that oil and gas might become one of the mainstays of its economy. In 2013 it relied on imports of 3,980 barrels per day. Oil exploration began in the 1970s and the government is encouraging further exploration offshore of West Greenland. Arctic climatic conditions and deep waters make the task difficult. Greenland does not produce or import gas and coal.
Natural gas and oil deposits were discovered offshore in Greenland territorial waters in mid-2010. The prospecting company, Cairn Energy, described the find as 'North Sea-scale' and likely to be significant, with an estimated 20 billion barrels of oil. However, drilling in 2014 has since proved unsuccessful.

Energy
Total installed generating capacity is some 137MW; electricity production was over 320 million kilowatt hours in 2013, the majority of which was produced by thermal power plants. There is a hydroelectric station in Buksefjorden, which supplies Nuuk; there are others at Tasiilaq, Qorlortorsuaq and Sisimiut whilst there are other hydroelectric plants are under construction or being planned.

Banking and insurance
NUNA Bank A/S is an independent bank that was formerly a subsidiary of the Danish bank Sparekasse Bikuben AS. The two banks share a strong business relationship. The other major bank in Greenland is Grønlandsbanken, which is owned by Danish banks.

Central bank
Monetary policy and administration is handled by the Danish central bank (Danmarks Nationalbank).

Time
Greenland has four time zones:

East Greenland and Scoresbysund – GMT minus one hour (daylight saving, end March to end September, GMT)
Central Greenland, Godthåb – GMT minus three hours (daylight saving, GMT minus two hours)
Western Greenland, Thule – GMT minus four hours (no daylight saving)
Danmarkshavn – GMT (no daylight saving)

Geography

Greenland is the world's largest island, although much of the surrounding seas are permently frozen forming the arctic shelf. Greenland lies in the North Atlantic Ocean, to the east of Canada and to the west of Iceland. Around 85 per cent of the landmass is permanently covered by ice up to 3,375 metres (m) thick. A snow peaked central range of mountains run north/south, with the highest peak reaching 3,200m above sea-level. There are 410,449 square km of coastland that is habitable.

Hemisphere

Northern

Climate

Arctic; temperatures at Nuuk/Godthåb vary between about minus 12 degrees Celsius (C) and 11 degrees C.

Entry requirements

Entry requirements are the same as for Denmark.

Passports

Required by all, except EU visitors travelling on national ID cards.

Visa

Even though a Danish territory, visas are not valid for Greenland unless specified in the permit. For a business visa, an original letter of invitation from a local company or organisation, giving details about purpose of visit and duration of stay must accompany an application, along with evidence of hotel reservations.
Approval must be obtained from the Greenland Home Rule administration, PO Box 1015, 3900 Nuuk, Greenland, for entry into the military defence areas including the gateways of Sondre Stromfjord and Thule (unless in direct transit to points outside the airport of Sondre Stromfjord) and entry for the purpose of mountain/glacier climbing or geological/archaeological research.

Health (for visitors)

Mandatory precautions

Vaccination certificates are not usually required.

Public holidays (national)

Fixed dates

1 Jan (New Year's Day), 6 Jan (Epiphany), 21 Jun (National Day), 24–26 Dec (Christmas).

Variable dates

Maundy Thursday, Good Friday, Easter Monday, Great Prayer Day (Apr/May), Ascension Day, Whit Monday.

Working hours

Banking

Mon–Fri: 0930–1600 (Thu 1800).

Business

Mon–Fri: 0800–1600 or 0830–1630.

Government

Mon–Fri: generally 0900–1700.

Shops

Mon–Fri: 0800–1700 or 0900–1730, Sat: close at 1300 or 1400.

Telecommunications

Mobile/cell phones

There is a 900 GSM service in populated areas only.

Electricity supply

220V AC, 50Hz.

Getting there

Air

National airline: Air Greenland
International airport/s: Kangerlussuaq (Sondre Stromfjord) (SFJ) international airport, is on the west coast close to Sisimiut and the capital, Nuuk. Facilities include: bureau de change, restaurant, duty-free shops, post office and car rental.
Other airport/s: Narsarsuaq (UAK) is an airport for stopover flights between Europe and North America and internal flights, with few facilities.
Kulusuk (KUS), on the east coast receives some internal flights but most come from Iceland.
Airport tax: None

Surface

Water: Comfortable cruise ships sail during the summer season.

Main port/s: Nuuk/Godthåb

Getting about

National transport

Air: Air Greenland flies routes along the western coast from Pituffik and Qaanaaq in the north to Paamiut in the south and across to Kulusuk and Tasiilaq in the east. The regularity of services is dependent on the weather. Helicopter services link other, more remote, settlements.
Road: There are virtually no roads connecting towns in Greenland. Only 60km of paved roads exist, realistically the best means of transport is the traditional sea and air travel where available.
Dog-sledges and snow mobiles can be hired for variable periods.
Water: Greenland Trade operates two passenger liners on the west coast. Villages are served by local boats, some of which are for private hire.

BUSINESS DIRECTORY

The addresses listed below are a selection only. While World of Information makes every endeavour to check these addresses, we cannot guarantee that changes have not been made, especially to telephone numbers and area codes. We would welcome any corrections.

Telephone area codes

The international direct dialling (IDD) code for Greenland is +299, followed by the subscriber's number.

Banking

Grønlandsbanken (Bank of Greenland) 29 Skibshavnsvej, PO Box 1033, DK-3900 Nuuk (tel: 347-700; fax 347-706).

Central bank

Danmarks Nationalbank, Havnegade 5, DK-1093 Copenhagen (tel: (+45) 3363-6363; fax: (+45) 3363-7103; e-mail: info@nationalbanken.dk).

Travel information

Greenland Tourism Main Office, 29 Hans Egedesvej, PO Box 1615, Nuuk DK-3900 (tel: 342-820; fax: 322-877; e-mail: info@greenland.com).

National tourist organisation offices

Greenland Tourism a/s, Main Office, PO Box 1552, 3900 Nuuk (tel: 322-888; fax: 322-877; e-mail: info@visitgreenland.com).

Ministries

Grønlands Hjemmestyre (Greenland Home Rule administration), PO Box 1015, 3900 Nuuk (tel: 345-000; e-mail: info@gh.gl; internet site: www.gh.gl).

Greenland Home Rule Government Denmark Office, Sjaeleboderne 2, 1122 Copenhagen K, Denmark (tel: (+45) 3313-4224; fax: (+45) 3332-2024).

Prime Minister's Office, Greenland Department, 3 Hausergade, DK-1128 Copenhagen K, Denmark (tel: (+45) 3393-2200).

Other useful addresses

Ministry of Foreign Affairs, Asiatisk Plads 2, DK-1448 Copenhagen, Denmark (tel: (+45) 3392-0000; internet: www.um.dk/en).

Greenland Trade Shipping Department, Grønlandshavnen, DK-9220 Aalborg Ost (tel: (+45) 9815-7677).

Kalaallit Nunaata Radioa (Grønlands Radio) (KNR) (Radio Greenland), H J Rinksvej 35, PO Box 1007, 3900 Nuuk (tel: 321-172; fax: 324-703).

Internet sites

Bureau of minerals and petroleum: http://bmp.gl/
Greenland Tourism: http://www.greenland-guide.gl

Grenada

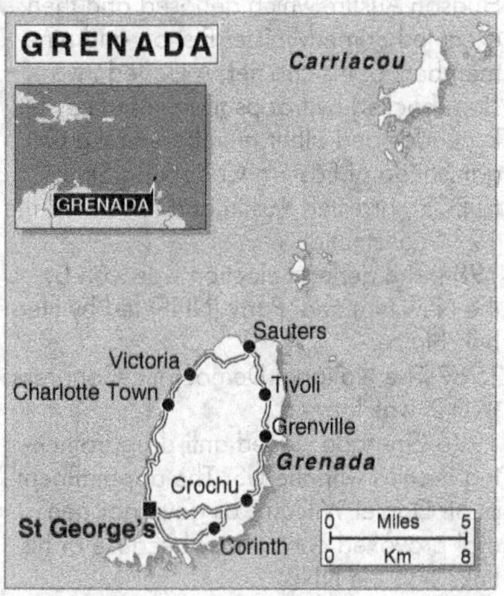

In 2015 Reuters reported that Grenada had found what was described as an 'innovative' way to resolve a sovereign debt problem. Whatever the validity of the innovation, it did at least have the advantage of getting Grenada into the headlines of the region, if not of the world.

The 1983 invasion

In 1983 Grenada had certainly hit the headlines when President Ronald Reagan gave the go-ahead for a military invasion of Grenada apparently unaware that it's head of state was Queen Elizabeth and that it was a member of the Commonwealth. Reagan later apologised to the then British prime minister, Margaret Thatcher, for not having consulted her, saying that he was 'sorry for any embarrassment that we caused you.' He had continued by lamely explaining 'that it was just our fear of our own weakness over here with regard to secrecy.' The US government had decided that the small island's nominally Marxist government posed a threat to the 1,000 Americans on the island (most of whom were students at St George's University medical school). Grenada had been a fly in the US ointment since its Constitution was suspended following a 1979 *coup* by the New Jewel Movement and its closer alignment with Cuba.

In 1983 no less than 1,900 US troops had landed at Grenada's Pearls airport, followed some hours later by 300 soldiers from six other Caribbean countries. To the irritation of the US, the United Kingdom had decided not to participate in the invasion. Confused reports arose from the invasion – one that three US soldiers had been killed in an action against Cuban workers at Point Salinas Airport. Other reports announced that 30 Soviet advisers and 600 Cubans had been arrested. The Caribbean Broadcasting Corp owned by the Barbados government reported that four Cubans had been killed in the invasion. Justifying the action, President Reagan said that the US had taken military action after an appeal by the Organisation of East Caribbean States (OECS), Jamaica and Barbados, who were worried about the security of the region.

Debt restructuring…

Grenada's uncomfortably high levels of debt – 111 per cent of gross domestic product (GDP) in 2014 – have obliged it to enter discussions with its creditors to accept what has become known in debt trading circles as a 'haircut', aka a loss on their debt repayment. The amount in question – US$193 million – was as nothing compared to the sums owed by larger countries. Creditors were being invited to take a 'hit' of 25 per cent immediately, followed by a further loss of 25 per cent once Grenada reached agreement with the International Monetary Fund (IMF) on future funding.

Additionally according to the Reuters report, creditors might be offered warrants linked to the government's revenue from its 'citizenship programme'. This was a scheme that allowed foreigners to purchase property on Grenada in return for citizenship. The warrants would stipulate that once the government reached a specific target, creditors would receive a payment.

… IMF approval

As part of its June 2015 assessment of the Grenadian economy, the IMF completed the second review of Grenada's economic performance under a three-year programme supported by an arrangement under the Extended Credit Facility (ECF). The completion of the review enabled the

KEY FACTS

Official name: Grenada

Head of State: Queen Elizabeth II, represented by Governor General Dr Cecile La Grenade (since 7 May 2013)

Head of government: Prime Minister Dr Keith Mitchell (took office 20 Feb 2013)

Ruling party: New National Party (NNP) (from 20 Feb 2013)

Area: 345 square km

Population: 106,000 (2014)*

Capital: St George's

Official language: English

Currency: East Caribbean dollar (EC$) = 100 cents

Exchange rate: EC$2.70 per US$ (fixed); (Jul 2014)

GDP per capita: US$8,125 (2014)*

GDP real growth: 1.52% (2014)*

GDP: US$862.00 million (2014)*

Inflation: -0.90% (2014)*

Balance of trade: -US$277.70 million (2013)

Annual FDI: US$41.44 million (2011)

* estimated figure

disbursement of SDR2 million (about US$2.8 million), bringing total disbursements under the arrangement to SDR6.04 million (about US$8.5 million).

This ECF arrangement, which corresponded to some US$21.7 million, or 120 per cent of Grenada's quota at the IMF, was approved by the IMF in June 2014. The IMF noted that the Grenadian authorities had achieved important results in the context of their Fund-supported economic programme. Fiscal targets had been exceeded, important reforms of the fiscal policy framework had been put in place and significant progress had been made in restructuring public debt. Stronger economic activity had supported the programme implementation, although Grenada's unemployment remained high. Maintaining social cohesion and support from all stakeholders remained critical to completing the reforms and putting Grenada on 'a higher, sustainable and more inclusive growth path.'

According to the IMF, Grenada was well advanced in its ambitious fiscal adjustment and in restoring its debt sustainability (See above). Safeguarding the fiscal performance already achieved, and carefully monitoring budget execution, would help achieve the 2015 fiscal objectives. A final round of adjustment would be needed, as planned, to achieve the programme's fiscal targets for 2016. An agreement on debt relief with the remaining stakeholders would also be necessary to return public debt to a sustainable level.

In the view of the IMF, recent reforms to the fiscal policy framework had been a major step forward to promote durable fiscal discipline and support debt sustainability over the medium-term. These comprehensive reforms included the introduction of fiscal responsibility and public debt management legislation and the reforms both of the tax incentive regime and of the framework governing state-owned enterprises and other parastatal entities.

In the context of the exchange rate peg, the IMF considered that continued structural reforms were needed to strengthen competitiveness and boost potential growth. These reforms needed to focus on lowering production costs, including in the energy sector, and improving the investment environment. Strengthening social protection programmes should also aim at promoting inclusive growth.

Concluding its summary report, the IMF reported that good progress has been achieved in advancing the regional strategy to strengthen the banking system, co-ordinated by the Eastern Caribbean Central Bank. Full implementation of the strategy was considered essential to preserving financial stability.

Risk assessment

Economy	Fair
Politics	Fair
Regional stability	Good

COUNTRY PROFILE

1762 Grenada was initially colonised by the French until captured by the British.
1783 British control of the islands was recognised.
1958 Grenada joined the Federation of the West Indies.
1967 Internal self-government was granted.
1974 Eric Gairy became prime minister of a newly independent Grenada.
1979 A coup deposed Gairy; Maurice Bishop, leading the socialist New Jewel Movement, took power.
1983 Civil disturbances, anti-government protests, media restrictions and a power struggle within the left-wing government resulted in a *coup d'etat*, led by General Hudson Austin, which deposed and then executed Prime Minister Bishop and nine members of his cabinet. A US-led invasion, backed by troops from Jamaica, Barbados and other members of the Organisation of Eastern Caribbean States (OECS), arrested Austin and reinstated the 1974 constitution.
1984 The general election was won by the New National Party (NNP) led by Herbert Blaize.
1987 The National Democratic Congress (NDC) was formed.
1996 Grenada signed anti-drug trafficking treaties with the US. The appointment of Sir Daniel Williams as governor general provoked controversy because of his links with the NNP.
1999 The NNP won the general election, winning every seat in the House of Representatives.
2001 Grenada was blacklisted by the Organisation for Economic Co-operation and Development (OECD)'s Financial Action Task Force (FATF) for not doing enough to combat money laundering. A review of offshore banking was begun.
2002 The government revoked the licences of 36 offshore banks in an attempt to secure Grenada's removal from the FATF blacklist. Grenada was hit by tropical storm Lili, causing damage estimated at around 2 per cent of GDP.
2003 Grenada was removed from the FATF's blacklist. The NNP was re-elected.
2004 Prime Minister Mitchell was accused of taking a US$500,000 bribe from a German citizen. Hurricane Ivan struck Grenada damaging 85 per cent of the island's housing.
2005 Grenada-born, army Private Johnson Beharry received Britain's highest military bravery awarded, the Victoria Cross, for his service in Iraq. Hurricane Emily struck the island, causing extensive damage.
2006 The EU granted around US$11 million for the rehabilitation of schools devastated by Hurricanes Ivan and Emily.
2008 Sir Eric Gairy was named as Grenada's first National Hero. He founded the Grenada United Labour Party in 1950 and steered the island to independence in 1974, becoming Grenada's first prime minister. The opposition NDC won the elections, ousting the former ruling party, the NNP. Tillman Thomas became prime minister. Sir Daniel Williams retired as

KEY INDICATORS — Grenada

	Unit	2011	2012	2013	2014	**2015
Population	m	*0.10	*0.11	*0.11	*0.11	0.11
Gross domestic product (GDP)	US$bn	1.45	0.80	0.84	*0.86	*0.88
GDP per capita	US$	7,878	7,605	*7,904	*8,125	*8,294
GDP real growth	%	1.1	-1.8	2.4	*1.5	*1.5
Inflation	%	3.0	2.4	–	*-0.9	*-1.5
Exports (fob) (goods)	US$m	36.4	42.8	46.5	–	–
Imports (fob) (goods)	US$m	296.3	300.3	324.2	–	–
Balance of trade	US$m	-260.0	-257.5	-277.7	–	–
Current account	US$m	-182.0	-154.0	-226.0	*-204.0	*-154.0
Total reserves minus gold	US$m	109.4	119.5	150.6	169.9	–
Foreign exchange	US$m	92.4	104.0	135.4	–	–
Exchange rate	per US$	2.70	2.70	2.70	2.70	–

* estimated figure ** forecast figure

governor general and was replaced by Carlyle Glean.

2009 The Point Salines international airport was renamed after former prime minister, Maurice Bishop, who had been executed in 1983 as a result of a coup *d'etat*, led by General Hudson Austin. A number of the perpetrators of the *coup d'etat* were released from jail after serving their 25 year sentences.

2010 The Organisation of Petroleum Exporting Countries (Opec) Fund for International Development approved a US$8.5 million loan for the second phase of an infrastructure programme of 25 agricultural feeder roads. The location of Grenada's new parliament and judiciary was announced, to be at Mount Wheldale, St George; work to be funded by the Australian government. The 4,645 square metre building will house both chambers of parliament, separated since hurricane Ivan in 2004 damaged the previous parliament; work is scheduled to be completed by 2013.

2011 In May, Grenada signed the Rome Statute of the International Criminal Court (ICC), the articles necessary to become a member. In June the World Band agreed to a zero interest loan of US$5.6 million to fund an improved electricity distribution system and diversity of energy production (including renewable energy sources). In July Grenada became a full member of the International Renewable Energy Agency (Irena). In August citizens of the Organisation of Eastern Caribbean States (OECS) – Antigua and Barbuda, Dominica, Grenada, St Kitts and Nevis, St Lucia and St Vincent and the Grenadines – were granted freedom of movement, allowing them to reside, work, establish businesses and provide services throughout the organisation. During the Commonwealth Heads of Government summit, in October, the 16 countries in which the British monarch is Head of State unanimously agreed to change the royal line of succession from that of first born son to the first born child (regardless of its gender). The change will be enacted after the succession of Prince William (currently second in line to the throne, after his father Prince Charles).

2012 During the NDC's annual convention, held on 30 September, seven senior members (including several parliamentary members) and its general secretary, were expelled from the party. The political turmoil in the party follows a failed coup by former minister Peter David to unseat Prime Minister Tillman Thomas.

2013 The general elections held on 19 February were won by the New National Party with all 15 seats (58.82 per cent), the first time this has happened since 1999. The National Democratic Congress was runner-up with 40.69 per cent. In September the Grenada Board of Tourism became the Tourism Authority of Grenada. Tourism Minister Alexandra Otway-Noel said the transition would lead to 'Increased marketing opportunities, greater potential for earning and better partnership with airlines and cruise ships' among other benefits.

2014 The opposition National Democratic Congress (NDC) elected former finance minister, Nazim Burke, as their leader on 2 February. In March Grenada reached staff level agreement with the IMF. The programme would be supported by a three year credit facility of some US$21.9 million. In July an initial report on changes to the constitution was submitted to the cabinet by the Constitution Reform Advisory Committee; a referendum on gthe changes was set for 10 February 2015. In September the minister responsible for civil aviation announced that, after months of negotiations, American Airlines had agreed to start daily flights from the US from December.

2015 In January the government confirmed an agreement with the Export-Import (ExIm) Bank of Taiwan whereby its US$36.6 million debt would be restructered. The amount of the debt itself would be halved and the balance repaid, at an interest rate of 7 per cent, over 15 years, including a grace period of three and a half years. The agreement also allows for a delay in payments in the event of a natural disaster such as a hurricane. A short-stay visa waiver agreement signed between the EU and a number of ACP countries on 28 May will allow citizens of Grenada to travel visa free to the Schengen area. The government's long term development plan, the 2030 National Plan, is expected to be tabled in parliament in mid-2015, and presented to cabinet by June 2016.

Political structure

Constitution

A referendum on changes to the constitution was supposed to be held on 10 February 2015 but has been delayed due to lack of support and financial difficulties. The report proposed 25 areas for change, of which 12 were recommended for Cabinet approval in July 2014. These included recognizing the Caribbean Court of Justice (CCJ) as Grenada's final court of appeal, and a change of the official country name from the 'State of Grenada' to 'Grenada, Carriacou and Petite Martinique'. As of September 2015, no exact date has been set for the proposed referendum.

Form of state

Parliamentary democracy under constitutional monarchy; it is a member of the Commonwealth.

The executive

The British monarch is the head of state, represented by the governor general appointed by the monarch. Executive power is vested in the cabinet, led by the prime minister. The cabinet is appointed by the governor general on the advice of the prime minister and is responsible to parliament. Following legislative elections, the leader of the majority party or the leader of the majority coalition is usually appointed prime minister by the governor general.

National legislature

The bicameral parliament consists of a 15-member House of Representatives (members are elected by popular vote to serve five-year terms) and an upper, 13-member, Senate (10 senators appointed by the government and three by the leader of the opposition)

Legal system

The legal system is based on English common law. Grenada is responsible for its own magistrate's courts. The regional Eastern Caribbean Supreme Court is responsible for the high court and the court of appeals. The final court of appeal is to the Privy Council in the UK.

Last elections

19 February 2013

Results: Parliamentary: The New National Party (NNP) won all 15 seats (58.82 per cent). The National Democratic Congress was runner-up with 40.69 per cent.

Next elections

2018 (parliamentary)

Political parties

Ruling party

New National Party (NNP) (from 20 Feb 2013)

Main opposition party

National Democratic Party (NDP) (leader from 2 Feb 2014 Nazim Burke)

Political situation

Prime Minister Keith Mitchell has an apparent penchant for persistent misfortune. Firstly, in 2004 he was accused of accepting US$500,000 from a German citizen in return for the post of general ambassador to Grenada and a diplomatic passport. An accusation he denied and was never proven. The second accusation is not only more convoluted but also has a wider implication if proved true.

In 2007, in a US criminal trial Prime Minister Mitchell was sited as a recipient of US$1 million from a US swindler. In the documents submitted to court it was asserted that Mitchell was or had been a US citizen. The news of this resulted in a question mark over Mitchell's Grenadian citizenship and his legitimacy as a Grenadian politician (only Grenadian citizens may be politicians). As of March 2008 the prime minister had not revealed the circumstances regarding his citizenship and whether he had revoked US citizenship at the time of his first election to the parliament of Grenada.

Population

105,000 (2012)* Approximately 35 per cent of the population is under 15 years.
Last census: May 2001: 102,632
Population density: 285 inhabitants per square km. Urban population 39 per cent (2010 Unicef).
Annual growth rate: 0.4 per cent, 1990–2010 (Unicef).

Ethnic make-up

Black (82 per cent), mixed black and European (13 per cent), European and East Indian (5 per cent) and a small number of Arawak/Carib.

Religions

Roman Catholic (53 per cent), Anglican (13.8 per cent), other Protestants (33.2 per cent).

Education

Education in Grenada is based on the English GCSE and A level system. There are several excellent local schools and an international primary school.
In total, there are 79 schools, 59 primary, 19 secondary and one tertiary institution. TA Marryshow Community College has a school of agriculture and a teacher's training college.
The St George's University School of Medicine is run by a US firm and offers medical training as well as non-medical courses.
Compulsory years: Five to 16.
Enrolment rate: 95 per cent gross primary enrolment of relevant age groups (including repeaters) (World Bank 2003).

Health

Grenada is divided into seven health districts, six of which have a health centre responsible for primary care. In addition, there are several medical stations throughout the country.
Medical care is limited, but everyone has access to some form of healthcare, regardless of ability to pay.
Life expectancy: 68 years, 2004 (WHO 2006)
Fertility rate/Maternal mortality rate: 2.2 births per woman, 2010 (Unicef)
Birth rate/Death rate: 23 births per 1,000 population; 7.5 deaths per 1,000 population (2003).
Child (under 5 years) mortality rate (per 1,000): 14 per 1,000 live births (WHO 2012)

Welfare

The social welfare department of the ministry of labour administers social work programmes to families and gives financial aid to three private children's homes. There is also a women's shelter in the northern part of the island. There are a number of government social service agencies that monitor the welfare of children, women and those with disabilities.

Main cities

St George's (capital, estimated population 5,731 in 2012), Gouyave (2,995), Grenville (2,403), Victoria (2,317).

Languages spoken

English and French patois

Official language/s

English

Media

Freedom of the press is guaranteed by law.

Press

The monthly *The Barnacle* publishes business news. There are no daily newspapers. *The Grenada Guardian* is sponsored by the Grenada United Labour political Party.
Weeklies: Weeklies include *The Grenadain Voice* (www.granadianvoce.com), *The Grenada Informer* (www.belgrafix.com) and *Grenada Today*.
Periodicals: *The Barnacle* (www.barnaclegrenada.com) is published monthly.

Broadcasting

The Grenada Broadcasting Network (GBN) (www.klassicgrenada.com) provides the national, public service, and is partly owned by the government and partly by the Caribbean Communications Network (CCN) (www.onecaribbeanmedia.net).
Radio: GBC operates two radio stations, Klassic Radio and Hott FM (www.klassicgrenada.com). Klassic Radio has 43 per cent of the audience listening figures and can be received by surrounding islands. Hott FM has a younger audience than its associate station.
Commercial radio includes City Sound FM (www.citysoundfm.com) and Voice of Grenada (www.spiceislander.com/vog), religious stations include Harbour Light Radio (www.harbourlightradio.org) and the Catholic Radio Upgrade.
Television: GBC Television (www.klassicgrenada.com) operates one channel and Gayelle TV is a the private cable service from Trinidad and Tobago.
Other news agencies: Caribbean Net News: www.caribbeannetnews.com

Economy

The economy is dominated by the service sector, in particular tourism, which attracts most foreign direct investment (FDI), particularly in construction of holiday facilities. The service sector constituted 83.2 per cent of GDP in 2014, with industry contributing 10.9 per cent, of which manufacturing was around 5 per cent and agriculture 5.9 per cent. St George's University, in Grenada, is prized as the combined Caribbean islands' centralised university, offers medical, veterinarian and other science courses as well as business and arts courses to 11,000 students from 140 countries.
In 2009 the economy fell into a deep recession with GDP growth at -5.7 per cent as the global economic crisis cut tourism numbers. The economy remained in recession in 2010, at -1.3 per cent, despite a pickup in global trade and an increase in tourist numbers visiting the Caribbean. The economy climbed out of recession in 2011, with growth of 1.1 per cent. However, in 2012 the country dropped back into negative growth recording a contraction of -1.2 per cent, before increasing to 2.4 per cent in 2013 and posting slow growth of 1.5 per cent in 2014. Unemployment in 2013 was 33.5 per cent nationally and 55.6 per cent among workers aged 16–25.
The government's long-term development plan, the 2030 National Plan, was launched in June 2015. The plan will build on other existing plans such as the Poverty Reduction and Growth Strategy in order to focus on the extensive development of the island over the proceeding 15 years.
The government has introduced fiscal measures to balance the economy, including replacing, in 2008, a general consumption tax, with a valued added tax (VAT). The International Monetary Fund (IMF) agreed around US$21.9 million in a three-year extended credit facility in 2014, in an 'ambitious programme' to help Grenada recover from the economic crisis, boost growth, reduce poverty and strengthen the private sector and business climate, while reducing weaknesses in the financial sector.
The government has invested heavily in the agricultural sector, bringing on the self-labelled title 'Isle of Spice', with attention paid to neglected farms and access roads and assistance given for land clearance. These undertakings paid off as production of Grenada's principal agricultural exports – cocoa, nutmeg and mace – have increased. And despite an overall decline in global trade these products sold well. Cocoa production is normally around 500,000 tonnes annually. In 2011, the Cocoa Farming Future Initiative (CFFI) was created to help the cocoa industry make a comeback after

production was stunted by the heavy hurricane seasons in 2004 and 2005.
Livestock farming and the fishing industry both enjoyed increased output, but domestic food crops were adversely affected by bad weather and consumer's low purchasing power.
In January 2015 the government confirmed an agreement with the Export-Import (ExIm) Bank of Taiwan whereby its US$36.6 million debt would be restructured. The amount of the debt itself would be halved and the balance repaid, at an interest rate of 7 per cent, over 15 years, including a grace period of three and a half years. The agreement also allows for a delay in payments in the event of a natural disaster such as a hurricane.

External trade

As a member of the Caribbean Community (Caricom), Grenada operates within the single market (Caribbean Single Market and Economy (CSME)), which it joined in 2006 and has a common currency as a member of the Eastern Caribbean Central Bank (ECCB). Caricom has a common external tariff and offers duty-free trade among its members. Grenada is a member of the Organisation of East Caribbean States (OECS); set up to promote regional development and economic integration. It is also a member of the World Trade Organisation (WTO).

Imports

Main imports are food, manufactured consumer goods, machinery, chemicals, petroleum and construction materials.
Main sources: Trinidad and Tobago (48.6 per cent of total in 2014), US (15.8 per cent), Barbados (3.4 per cent)

Exports

Main agricultural exports include cocoa, nutmeg and mace, bananas, tropical fruit, vegetables, fish and meat products, manufactured goods include clothing, light industrial products and foodstuffs.
Main destinations: Nigeria (45.0 per cent of total in 2014), St. Lucia (11.2 per cent), Antigua and Barbuda (7.6 per cent)

Agriculture

Farming

The agricultural sector contributed 5.9 per cent to GDP in 2014 and accounted for around 68 per cent of exports.
Activity centres on the traditional farming of nutmeg/mace (one of the world's largest producers), cocoa and bananas. Nutmeg and cocoa exports have benefited from a decline in world supply due to political problems in global suppliers (Indonesia and Côte d'Ivoire), as opposed to improvements in output.
Agricultural development policy is geared towards the rehabilitation of the cocoa and nutmeg industries, the promotion of new export crops, greater provision of fertilisers and other inputs and privatisation of state farms.

Fishing

There is a small fishing industry.
The typical total annual fish catch is around 2,500 tonnes (t). Shellfish, molluscs and cephalopods account for another 40t per annum.

Industry and manufacturing

The industrial sector accounted for around 15.8 per cent of GDP in 2013, of which manufacturing constitutes around 5 per cent.
Manufacturing activities include the production of garments, beverages, flour, wheat-bran, animal feed, furniture, paints and varnishes, sugar, rum, coconut oil, lime juice and honey. Furniture, handicrafts and garments are also manufactured for export to the Caricom market.
The government is committed to achieving growth in the manufacturing sector and to this end is endeavouring to attract foreign firms to use Grenada as a base for exports to extra-regional markets. Joint ventures are encouraged between local private sector and foreign investors in order to assist local manufacturers to access capital, technology and marketing channels.

Tourism

Grenada offers relaxing beach holidays, ocean activities, eco-friendly exploration of its landscapes and exciting local colour and culture. In 2013 there were 120,000 visitors to the island, and in the first half of 2014 there was a 12 per cent increase on the number of arrivals by cruise ship compared to the same period in 2013.
Travel and tourism is an important component of GDP, of which it constituted 24.2 per cent in total in 2013. The sector even contributed a similar amount during the global economic crisis. This may be in part due to the range of holidays it offers for all wallets and partly to the decrease in other sectors of GDP. Visitor exports in 2014 were US$109 million, which was 47.8 per cent of total exports. Employment in the industry was at 22.1 per cent in 2014, the equivalent of 10,500 jobs.
In September 2013 the Grenada Board of Tourism became the Tourism Authority of Grenada. Tourism Minister Alexandra Otway-Noel said the transition would lead to 'Increased marketing opportunities, greater potential for earning and better partnership with airlines and cruise ships' among other benefits.
The US visitor outnumbers all other visitors by a factor of five, with the UK the next largest contingent.
Capital investment in travel and tourism rose from a low of 4.2 per cent of total investment in 2002 to a high of 7.6 per cent in 2009, reflecting that other sectors may be losing out to an industry that still offers viable returns for investors. By 2014, this figure had reached 13.7 per cent of total investment.
In September 2014 the minister responsible for civil aviation announced that, after months of negotiations, American Airlines had agreed to start daily flights from the US from December. Both cruise arrivals and expenditure in Grenada increased by 29 per cent in 2014, compared to 2013. Preliminary data show that 162 cruise calls and 254,248 cruise passengers visited ports in Grenada and Carriacou, contributing EC$28 million (US$10.4 million) to the economy.

Hydrocarbons

There are no known hydrocarbon reserves. Consumption of oil was 2,590 barrels per day (bpd) in 2013, all of which was imported. In 2005, Grenada, plus a number of other Caribbean states, signed an agreement with Venezuela to establish PetroCaribe, a multi-national oil company, owned by the participating states. PetroCaribe buys low-priced Venezuelan crude oil under long-term payment plans. However, due to the falling oil prices, in late 2014 the Venezuelan authorities cut the subsidies for PetroCaribe members.
Any use of natural gas or coal is commercially insignificant. Trinidad and Tobago has had a plan to build a US$500 million, 965km natural gas pipeline linking the eastern Caribbean islands, which would open possibilities of importing natural gas into Grenada.

Energy

Thermal power plants produce a total installed electricity generating capacity of 49.7MW. The infrastructure damage caused during hurricane seasons has hampered the country's attempts at finding alternative sources of energy. The potential of solar and wind power are recognised but investment is constrained by their fragile characteristics. Providing energy through individual installations offers an option that could avoid wholesale public generating capacity devastation. Cuba already has a system of distributed generation (DG), whereby small-scale plants are located around the country and closer to their end users. This has allowed Cuba to recover from Caribbean hurricanes much more rapidly than other countries, which adopted more centralised power generation plants.
Plans for the commercial development of a geothermal-fuelled power plant, developed by the Eastern Caribbean Geothermal Development Project (ECGDP) (or Geo-Caraïbes), which is estimated will provide 60–120MW overall, will be operated by the West Indies Power Limited

(WIPL), which is owned by ECGDP countries. On 20 June 2011, the World Bank agreed to a zero interest loan of US$5.6 million to fund an improved electricity distribution system and diversity of energy production (including renewable energy sources).
Grenada became a full member of the International Renewable Energy Agency (Irena) in July 2011.
In September 2014, a Memorandum of Understanding (MOU) was signed between the United States and Grenada to support Grenada's efforts to transition to renewable energies, and away from reliance on imported petroleum.

Financial markets

Stock exchange
Eastern Caribbean Securities Exchange (ECSE)

Banking and insurance

The seven members of the Organisation of Eastern Caribbean States (OECS), Antigua and Barbuda, Dominica, Grenada, Montserrat, St Kitts and Nevis, St Lucia and St Vincent and the Grenadines, share a common currency (the East Caribbean dollar (EC$) and central bank. The British Virgin Islands and Anguilla are associate members.

Central bank
Eastern Caribbean Central Bank, St Kitts and Nevis.

Offshore facilities
The strengthening of the regulatory framework by the Grenada International Financial Services Authority (GIFSA) led to significant improvement and in 2003 Grenada was removed from the blacklist drawn up by the Organisation for Economic Co-operation and Development (OECD).

Time

GMT minus four hours

Geography

Grenada is a mountainous, heavily forested island. It is the most southerly of the Windward Islands in the West Indies. The country also includes some of the small islands known as the Grenadines, which lie to the north-east of Grenada, the largest of these being the low-lying island of Carriacou.

Hemisphere
Northern

Climate

Tropical marine with an annual mean temperature of 28 degrees Celsius. Rain occurs mainly from June–December. Driest from February–May.

Entry requirements

Passports
Required by all and must be valid for six months from the date of departure. Proof of return/onward passage is necessary.

Visa
Not required by nationals of most of the Americas, Europe, Australasia and Japan, for both tourist and business trips, valid for three months. Business visitors should supply extra information: letter of introduction from foreign company and letter of invitation from a local host. For further details and exceptions contact the consular section of the nearest High Commission or Embassy.

Currency advice/regulations
The import and export of foreign currencies is unrestricted, however large amounts should be declared.
Travellers cheques are widely accepted. To avoid extra exchange fees US dollar denominations are advised.

Health (for visitors)

Mandatory precautions
Yellow fever certificate required if arriving from an infected area.

Advisable precautions
Immunisation against hepatitis A, B and diphtheria may be recommended.
Medical attention can cost several thousand dollars and doctors often expect immediate cash payments; insurance is advisable.

Hotels

There are a wide variety of hotels from luxurious to one star. Except for town hotels, most are located near beaches, all hotels should be booked well in advance. An 8 per cent sales tax on food and beverages and 10 per cent service charge are added to the bill.

Public holidays (national)

Fixed dates
1 Jan (New Year's Day), 7 Feb (Independence Day), 1 May (Labour Day), 25 Oct (Thanksgiving Day), 25–26 Dec (Christmas).

Variable dates
Good Friday, Easter Monday (Mar/Apr), Whit Monday, Corpus Christi (May/Jun), Emancipation Day (first Mon in Aug), Carnival (two days, Aug).

Working hours

Banking
Mon–Thu: 0800–1400; Fri: 0800–1300, 1430–1700.

Business
Mon–Thu: 0800–1145, 1300–1600; Fri: 0800–1145, 1300–1700.

Government
Mon–Thu: 0800–1145, 1300–1600; Fri: 0800–1145, 1300–1700.

Shops
Mon–Fri: 0800–1145, 1300–1600; Sat: 0800–1145.

Telecommunications

Mobile/cell phones
GSM 850 900/1800/1900 services cover all of St George.

Electricity supply

220/240V AC, 50 cycles

Getting there

Air

International airport/s: Maurice Bishop International Airport (previously Point Salines, renamed in 2009) (GND), 8km from St George's; bureau de change, duty-free shops, restaurant, shops and car rental.
Taxis are available.

Airport tax: Departure tax EC$50, payable in local currency only.

Surface

Water: Many cruise lines call at Grenada. Regular boat services from St Vincent, Martinique and Trinidad. There is a ferry service to Carriacou Island.

Main port/s: St George's.

Getting about

National transport

Road: There are approximately 1,050km of roads, of which 650km are paved, although most main roads are narrow and winding.

Buses: Public transport is provided by small private operators, with a system covering the entire country. Cheap but often slow and few run during the late afternoons, evenings and Sundays.

City transport

Taxis: Widely available. Fares are regulated.

Car hire
International licence required or local permit obtained (valid national licence must be presented to local Traffic Department), a minimum age of 25 applies. Traffic drives on the left.

BUSINESS DIRECTORY

The addresses listed below are a selection only. While World of Information makes every endeavour to check these addresses, we cannot guarantee that changes have not been made, especially to telephone numbers and area codes. We would welcome any corrections.

Telephone area codes

The international direct dialling code (IDD) for Grenada is +1 473, followed by subscriber's number.

Chambers of Commerce

Grenada Chamber of Industry and Commerce, PO Box 129, St George's (tel: 440-2937; fax: 440-6621; e-mail: gcic@caribsurf.com).

Banking

Bank of Nova Scotia, PO Box 194, Grand Anse, St George's (tel: 440-3274).

Barclays Bank, PO Box 37, Grand Anse, St George's (tel: 440-3232; fax: 440-3232).

Grenada Bank of Commerce, PO Box 4, Grand Anse, St George's (tel: 440-3521; fax: 440-4153).

Grenada Co-operative Bank, Church Street, St George's (tel: 440-2111, 440-3549; fax: 440-6600).

Grenada Development Bank, Halifax Street, St George's (tel: 440-2382/1620).

National Commercial Bank of Grenada, Halifax Street, St George's (tel: 440-3566/8).

Scotiabank, Halifax Street, St George's (tel: 440-3274).

Central bank

Eastern Caribbean Central Bank, Agency Office, Monckton Street, St George's (tel: 440-3016; fax: 40-6721).

Stock exchange

Eastern Caribbean Securities Exchange (ECSE), www.ecseonline.com

Travel information

Grenada Hotel Association, Ross Point Inn, Lagoon Road, St George's (tel: 444-1353; fax: 444-4847).

Ministry of tourism

Ministry of Tourism, Civil Aviation, Social Security, Culture, Gender and Family, Ministerial Complex, 4th Floor, St. George's, (tel: 440-0366; fax: 440-0443).

National tourist organisation offices

Grenada Tourism Authority, P.O. Box 293, St George, Grenada (tel: 440-2279/2001; fax: 440-6637; email: info@grenadagrenadines.com; internet: www.grenadagrenadines.com).

Grenada Tourism Authority, Main Street, Hillsborough, Carriacou (tel: 443-7948; fax: 443-6127).

Ministries

Ministry of Agriculture, Ministerial Complex, 2nd and 3rd Floors, St George's (tel: 440-27008 fax: 440-4191).

Ministry of Carriacou and Petit Martinique Affairs, Beausejour, Carriacou (tel: 443-6026; fax: 443-6040).

Ministry of Communication & Works, Ministerial Complex, 4th Floor, St George's (tel: 440-2181; fax: 440-4122).

Ministry of Education, Botanical Gardens, St George's (tel: 440-2166; fax: 440-6650).

Ministry of Finance, Trade, Industry and Planning, Financial Complex, St George's (tel: 440-2731; fax: 440-4115).

Ministry of Foreign Affairs and International Trade, Ministerial Complex, 4th Floor, St George's (tel: 440-2640; fax: 440-4184).

Ministry of Health and Environment, Ministerial Complex, 1st and 2nd Floords, St George's (tel: 440-2649; fax: 440-4127).

Ministry of Housing, Social Services and Co-operatives, Ministerial Complex, 1st and 2nd Floors, St George's (tel: 440-6917; fax: 440-7990).

Ministry of Implementation, Ministerial Complex, 6th Floor, St George's (tel: 440-2255; fax: 440-4116).

Ministry of Labour and Local Government, Ministerial Complex, 3rd Floor, St George's (tel: 440-2532).

Ministry of Legal Affairs, Attorney General's Office, Church Street, St. George's (tel: 440-2050; fax: 440-6630).

Ministry of Youth, Sports and Community Development, Ministerial Complex, 2nd Floor, St George's (tel: 440-6917; fax: 440-6924).

Office of the Prime Minister, Ministerial Complex, 6th Floor, St George's (tel: 440-2225; fax: 440-4116).

Other useful addresses

Export Development Unit, Ministry of Trade, Lagoon Road, St George's (tel: 440-2101; fax: 440-4115).

Grenada Cocoa Board, Scott St, St George's (tel: 440-2234).

Grenada Co-operative Banana Society, Scott St, St George's (tel: 440-2117).

Grenada Co-operative Nutmeg Association, PO Box 160, St George's (tel: 440-2097).

Grenada Industrial Development Corporation, Frequente Industrial Park, True Blue, St. George's (tel: 444-1035; fax: 444-4828; e-mail: gidc@caribsurf.com; internet site: www.grenadaworld.com).

Grenada International Financial Services Authority (GIFSA), PO Box 39713, Carenage (tel: 440-8717; fax: 440-4780; e-mail: grenoffshore@caribsurf.com).

Grenada Manufacturers' Council, PO Box 129, St George's (tel: 444-4485/2937; fax: 440-6627).

Grenadan Embassy (US), 1701 New Hampshire Avenue, NW, Washington DC 20009 (tel: 202-265-2561).

Caribbean Net News: www.caribbeannetnews.com

Internet sites

Blue Horizons Cottage Hotel: www.cpscaribnet.com/ads/blue/blue.html

Calabash Hotel: www.cpscaribnet.com/ads/calabash/calabash.html

Coyaba Beach Resort: www.cpscaribnet.com/ads/coyaba/coyaba.html

Guadeloupe

KEY FACTS

Official name: Guadeloupe

Head of State: President of France François Hollande (PS) (from 15 May 2012) represented by *préfet* Amaury de Saint-Quentin (from 11 Sep 2011)

Head of government: President of Conseil Général Jacques Gillot (since 23 Mar 2001); President of Conseil Régional Josette Borel-Lincertin (since 2 April 2015)

Ruling party: Objectif Guadeloupe

Area: 1,780 square km

Population: 503,274 (2011)*

Capital: Basse Terre

Official language: French

Currency: Euro (€) = 100 cents (from 1 Jan 2002; previous currency French franc, locked at Ff6.56 per euro)

Exchange rate: €0.89 per US$ (Sep 2015)

* estimated figure

The French territory of Guadeloupe, once known as *Karukera*, or 'Island of Beautiful Waters', is a centre of Caribbean Creole culture. There are a mixture of French, African and Caribbean influences which show in its music, dance, food and the widely-spoken *patois*.

Guadeloupe's economy is kept afloat by public salaries and credits from Paris. Unemployment has been a long-running malaise, although its effects are tempered by France's generous social security system.

Agriculture used to revolve around sugar cane and bananas. However, since the phasing out of preferential European quotas both bananas and sugar cane have suffered from regional competition as larger and more efficient growers have taken their markets. In 2014 Cirad research station in Guadeloupe became part of the Caribbean's preparation against Panama Disease (Fusarium Wilt).

Tourism is important. Visitors, most of them from France, are drawn to Guadeloupe's resorts, beaches, waterfalls and forests and the territory is a port of call for cruise ships.

COUNTRY PROFILE

Guadeloupe is situated within the Lesser Antilles. The first inhabitants were the Arawak Indians and Carib Indians. The Carib name for the island was Karukera (island of beautiful water).

1493–1600 Columbus was the first European visitor. Spain made two attempts to colonise the islands of Guadeloupe but was unsuccessful, due to strong indigenous resistance.

1635 France conquered the islands and established its first settlement.

1654 The French welcomed a small number of Dutch who settled in Guadeloupe. They proved vital to the turnaround of Guadeloupe's economy by developing its sugar industry. Black African slaves were brought to the island to work on plantations.

1674 Guadeloupe became part of the French Crown Colonies.

1700s Guadeloupe was the scene of many battles between the French and British, who repeatedly fought for possession.

1808–1814 Guadeloupe was occupied by the British.

1816 The islands were handed back to France by the Treaty of Vienna.

1854–1885 Following the abolition of slavery in 1847, workers were brought to Guadeloupe from India. During this period, blacks were allowed to participate in Guadeloupe's politics and Guadeloupe was allowed representation in the French parliament.

1946 Guadeloupe became a French Département d'Outre-Mer (DOM) (Overseas Department).

1974 Guadeloupe was further incorporated into the French political system and granted the status of region of France.

1983 Guadeloupe was granted devolution. A Regional Council was established under the French decentralisation policy.

1998 Hurricane Georges wreaked havoc on the islands

1999 The Basse Terre declaration by Guadeloupe, Martinique and French Guiana called for greater local control. The country was hit by hurricane Lenny.

2002 Guadeloupe adopted the euro as its official currency. In the French presidential elections, Guadeloupe's support for Jacques Chirac was overwhelming (91 per cent of the vote).

2003 A referendum in Guadeloupe and Martinique rejected a French government-backed reform plan to streamline the system of local government and give the islands a new status. Guadeloupe's dependencies, St Barthélémy and St Maarten, voted to become overseas collectives.

2004 Victorin Lurel took office as president of the regional council and Jacques Gillot as president of the general council. Paul Girot de Langlade took office as *préfet*.

2006 Jean-Jacque Brot became *préfet*.

2007 Emmanuel Berthier became *préfet*. A new desalination unit, capable of producing 4,000 cubic metres of drinkable water from seawater, was installed on St Barthélémy. Hurricane Dean destroyed 80 per cent of all banana plantations. St Barthélémy and St Maarten became French overseas collectives.

2008 Guadeloupe and Dominica agreed to develop and deliver geothermal energy from Dominica, via undersea electricity cables.

2009 A general strike in protest against low pay and rising prices caused civil

unrest. Riot police from mainland France were deployed, including four French military police units of 260 officers. The France-based minister of overseas territories arrived to negotiate a solution. After 44 days the general strike ended with the promise of higher wages for workers. The protests affected tourism as a reported 10,000 tourists cancelled holidays.
2011 Amaury de Saint-Quentin took office as *préfet* in September. The new, year-round, Jeans Ferry Service operated by L' Express Des Il, between Dominica, St Lucia, Martinique and Guadeloupe, began operations.
2012 The French presidential elections held in April and May (in the Americas), were won by François Hollande (Parti Socialiste (PS) (Socialist Party)) with 51.63 per cent; incumbent Nicolas Sarkozy (UMP) won 48.37 per cent of the vote; turnout was 80.35 per cent. On 15 May François Hollande took office as president and head of state.
2013 A report released in St Lucia in April proposed that Guadeloupe and Martinique should become members of the Organisation of Eastern Caribbean States. At the summit of heads of state of the Association of Caribbean States (ACS) in Haiti an application for associate membership was presented by Martinique and Guadeloupe. France had approved the application for membership by the two French Overseas Territories in December 2012.
2014 Guadeloupe officially became an associate member of the Association of Caribbean States (ACS) in its own right on 14 April.
2015 In January the three French Caribbean countries (French Guiana, Guadeloupe and Martinique) began discussions on becoming associate members of Caricom.

Political structure

Constitution

28 September 1958 (French Fifth Republic).
Under the 1946 constitution of the French Fourth Republic, Guadeloupe became a Département d'Outre-Mer (DOM) (Overseas Department) of France. In 1974, it was granted additional status as a region of France.
Guadeloupe is represented in the French National Assembly by four deputies and in the Senate by two senators.
Since 1983, following the French government's policy of decentralisation, regional councils have been elected with powers similar to those of the regions.
Administration is by a *préfet* appointed by the government in Paris.
The local government comprises a Conseil Régional (Regional Council) of 39 members and a 42-member Conseil Général (General Council), both directly elected for six-year terms.
Dependencies: Marie Galante, Les Saintes, Désirade, St Barthélémy and St Martin, Grand Bourg (on Marie Galante).
In a 2003 referendum, voters on Guadeloupe's dependencies, St Barthélémy and St Martin, approved a referendum which streamlined the islands' local government and gave them a new status as French overseas collectives in 2007.

Form of state

Département d'Outre-Mer (DOM) (Overseas Department) of France, with additional status as a *région* (region) of France.

National legislature

The Conseil Régional (regional council) has 41 members elected for four-years by proportional representation. All members of the Conseil Général (general council) are elected for six-year terms in single seat constituencies. The two councils have diverging powers over local and departmental legislation.

Legal system

French legal system

Last elections

21–22 March 2010 (Conseil Général and Conseil Régional)
Results: General council: Parti Socialiste (PS) (Socialist Party) won 56.51 per cent (31 seats out of 41), Divers Gauche (DVG) (Miscellaneous Left) 14.01 per cent (four), Collectif Des Inkoruptibles (DdI) (The Incorruptible Party) 6.96 per cent (two); five other political parties each won less than 3 per cent of votes and gained no seats.

Next elections

2016 (Conseil Général and Conseil Régional)

Political parties

Ruling party

Objectif Guadeloupe

Political situation

In a region dominated by either the English or Spanish language, official measures to support the Francophone West Indies now includes not only a French language training programme offered by the Université des Antilles et de la Guyane to students from the Organisation of Eastern Caribbean States (OECS) region but also a French-speaking mobile (cell) phone network set up in 2007–08, by the Digicel Group, for the French West Indies and French Guiana.
503,274 (2011)*

Population

About 25 per cent of the total population is under 14 years.
Last census: 1 January 2006: 400,736
Population density: 250 inhabitants per square km.
Annual growth rate: 1 per cent (2003)

Ethnic make-up

Black or mixed race (90 per cent), white (5 per cent), East Indian and others (5 per cent).

Religions

Roman Catholic (95 per cent), other: Hindu, African animist, Protestant (5 per cent).

Education

Many students pursue higher education in the islands or in France. The islands have a teacher's training college, a school of law, and a school of science.
Literacy rate: Over 90 per cent
Compulsory years: 6 to 17.

Health

In addition to several hospitals, Guadeloupe has a Pasteur Institute for the study of tropical diseases. The consumption of crack cocaine has increased steadily with a large number of drug addicts being treated regularly by the health and social services.
Life expectancy: 77.5 years (estimate 2003)
Fertility rate/Maternal mortality rate: Two births per woman (2003)
Birth rate/Death rate: 16 births per 1,000 population; six deaths per 1,000 population (2003).
Child (under 5 years) mortality rate (per 1,000): Nine per 1,000 live births (2003)

Welfare

The existence of a state homecare policy and a traditional lifestyle enable most people aged 60 and over to live at home. The people are highly dependent on French social welfare programmes and development funds. About one-third of children under the age of 17 are brought up in single-parent families. Financial assistance is often available to needy families for their children's basic needs and to enable children to attend school at an early age.

Main cities

Basse-Terre (capital, on Basse Terre, estimated population 9,678 in 2012); Les Abymes (58,439), Le Gosier (30,816) and Sainte-Anne (24,248), Capesterre (18,636) (on Grande Terre),
Pointe-à-Pitre (commercial centre, straddles islands of Grande Terre and Basse Terre, 14,342), Baie-Mahault (38,578).
Dependencies include Marie Galante, Les Saintes, Désirade, St Barthélémy and St Martin, Grand Bourg (on Marie Galante).

Languages spoken
French (99 per cent); Creole patois is also spoken.
Official language/s
French

Media
Press
The only daily newspaper is the regional publication *France Antilles*. Local newspapers include *Le Journal de St Barth* (www.st-barths.com/jsb/headlinesfr.html), with a weekly edition.
Broadcasting
The French overseas broadcaster RFO (www.rfo.fr) provides locally produced radio and television news (http://guadeloupe.rfo.fr) and imported French programmes, as well as internet TV services.
Radio: Private radio stations include Radio Caraibes International (www.rci.gp), NRJ Antilles (www.nrjantilles.com) and Radyo Tanbou (www.radyotanbou.com).

Economy
Guadeloupe is heavily dependent on aid from France, which has prevented any significant macroeconomic adjustment to local conditions. The services sector dominates the economy, providing almost 70 per cent of GDP and over 60 per cent of employment. Tourism is the prominent sector with 493,000 visitors in 2013 (latest figures), most originating from the US; cruise ships are providing an increasing number of tourists. In 2014, tourism and travel contributed a total of 16.0 per cent to GDP and a total contribution to employment, including jobs indirectly supported by the industry, of 21,500 jobs (16.5 per cent of total employment).
Agriculture is important; sugarcane has lost its dominance and has being replaced by bananas, aubergines (eggplants) and flowers. Industry includes light manufacturing and foodstuffs using mostly local ingredients. Unemployment, particularly among the young, has been a long-running malaise and is high at over 25 per cent. The country is periodically inflicted with hurricanes, causing adverse affects to the agricultural sector.

External trade
As a département d'outre-mer (DOM) of France, Guadeloupe has the status within the European Union as one of its members; it has free trade within the EU and observes other trade agreements through the EU.
The rising trade deficit is only partially offset by earnings from tourism and aid flows from France aimed particularly at lowering the unemployment rate.
Imports
Principal imports are machinery and transport equipment, foodstuffs and live animals, basic manufactures, miscellaneous manufactures, road vehicles and parts, chemicals and related products.
Main sources: France (typically over 60 per cent of total), US (5 per cent), Germany (3 per cent).
Exports
Principal exports are bananas, aubergines (eggplants) and flowers, rum, basic manufactures and sugar.
Main destinations: France (typically over 60 per cent of total), Martinique (18 per cent), US (4 per cent).

Agriculture
Farming
Agriculture contributes around 15 per cent to GDP and employs around 15 per cent of the population. Guadeloupe is not self-sufficient, relying heavily on food imports from France.
An estimated 36 per cent of the total area is cultivated arable land, 10 per cent is pasture and 15 per cent woodland/forest (including national park land of around 3,000 hectares).
The export of bananas has been a prime activity accounting for around 50 per cent of foreign earnings. However, it has relied on preferential access to the EU, and in 2012 the World Trade Organisation (WTO) ruled that this access was illegal. Sugar, flowers and melons are also cultivated.
Fishing
Offshore fishing is a traditional source of food. The main fish catch includes lobsters, crab and octopus. The sector is underdeveloped, although demand is growing.
The typical total annual fish catch is over 10,000 tonnes (t). Shellfish, molluscs and cephalopods account for another 700t per annum.

Industry and manufacturing
The industrial sector contributes around 17 per cent to GDP and employs around 20 per cent of the workforce.
Manufacturing industries are small and centre on the processing of raw materials. Main activities include sugar refining, rum distilling, food processing, cement and brick manufacture, mineral water bottling and ship repair. The construction industry employs 12 per cent of the workforce and is the third-largest sector of activity.
There is an industrial free port at Jarry.

Tourism
The French department of Guadeloupe offers European culture in a Caribbean setting. The island offers a variety of holidays using different attractions on the five islands, to a variety of visitors and their budgets.
Travel and tourism is very important to the economy constituting 16.0 per cent of GDP in 2014, relatively constant since 2007 when the global economic crisis had an adverse effect on tourism worldwide. The industry provided employment to 16.5 per cent (21,500 jobs) of the workforce in 2014. Capital investment in tourism has fallen since 2008, from 9 per cent (US$252 million) of total investment to 7.3 per cent (US$196.3 million) in 2014, which may reflect the economic condition of France more than any local inaction.
A new passenger ferry was launched at the beginning of the 2011–12 tourist season, with links to other French departments as well as Dominica and St Lucia. Room night occupancy increased by 26 per cent in 2013.

Environment
In 2010, the French-based, Agence des Aires Marines Protégées (Marine Areas Protection Agency) announced the creation of a marine mammals' sanctuary (known as Agoa) in the territorial waters and the economic exclusion zone of the French West Indies (Guadeloupe, Martinique, St Martin, and St Barthélémy). The 138,000 square km marine habitat will require any proposed development to include consideration of their impact on marine mammals, such as whales.

Mining
Guadeloupe has no mineral resources.

Hydrocarbons
Guadeloupe relies entirely on imported petroleum products, which amounted to 16,380 barrels per day in 2013. It does not import coal or natural gas.
A proposed pipeline from Trinidad and Tobago to Guadeloupe and Martinique opens possibilities for the future import of natural gas; but the project still remained a scheme in 2014.

Energy
Total installed generating capacity is over 400MW, produced by thermal power stations.

Banking and insurance
Central bank
Caisse Centrale de Co-opération Economique; European Central Bank (ECB)

Time
GMT minus four hours

Geography
Guadeloupe is the most northerly of the Windward Islands group in the West Indies. Dominica lies to the south, and Antigua and Montserrat to the north-west. Guadeloupe is formed by two large islands, Grande Terre (mountainous) and Basse Terre, separated by a narrow sea channel, with two smaller islands, Marie

Galante, to the south-east, and La Désirade, to the east. St Barthélémy and the northern half of St Maarten (the remainder being part of the Netherlands Antilles) Maarten became French overseas collectives in 2007 (they were previously French dependences).

Hemisphere

Northern

Climate

Sub-tropical with annual mean temperature of 27 degrees Celsius. Levels of humidity and rainfall highest around Basse-Terre. Refreshing trade winds all year round. Humid season – *hivernage* – is between September and November.

Entry requirements

Passports

Required by all.

Visa

As an overseas region of France entry requirements are the same as those for France.

Visas required by all, except citizens of EU, North America, Australasia and Japan, for stays up to one month; this includes business trips by representatives of foreign entities with an invitation from a local company or organisation. Proof of adequate funds for stay, an itinerary, a guarantee of repatriation if necessary and return/onward ticket are also required. For further exceptions, full details and a copy of the application form visit www.diplomatie.gouv.fr/en/ and follow the path (going to France) on the legend.

Currency advice/regulations

There are no restrictions on the import and export of foreign currency but the amount imported must be declared. The amount of foreign currency, other than euros, that may be taken out must not exceed that imported.

ATMs are readily available. Travellers cheques in euros are accepted everywhere, however cheques in other currencies if accepted, may attract extra exchange fees.

Prohibited imports

Illegal drugs.

Health (for visitors)

Mandatory precautions

A yellow fever vaccination certificate is required if travelling from an infected area.

Advisable precautions

Hepatitis, typhoid, tetanus and polio vaccinations. Water precautions should be taken.

Hotels

There is a good range of quality hotels in Guadeloupe, as well as more basic accommodation. If a service charge is not added, a 15 per cent tip is usual.

Credit cards

Credit and charge cards are accepted in may places.

Public holidays (national)

Fixed dates

1 Jan (New Year's Day), 1 May (Labour Day), 8 May (Victory Day), 27 May (Abolition Day), 14 Jul (Bastille Day), 21 Jul (Schoelcher Day), 15 Aug (Assumption Day), ^1 Nov (All Saints' Day), 2 Nov (All Souls' Day), 11 Nov (Armistice Day), 25 Dec (Christmas).

Variable dates

Carnival (Feb, two days), ^Ash Wednesday (Feb/Mar), Good Friday (Mar/Apr), ^Easter Monday, ^Ascension Day, Whit Monday.

^ Religious holiday.

Working hours

Banking

Mon–Fri: 0800–1200, 1400–1600.

Some banks open Sat: 0800–1200, but these close 1200 Wed.

Banks close at noon on the day preceding a bank holiday.

Business

Mon–Fri: 0800–1200, 1400–1800.

Business visits are best between January–March and June–September.

Government

Mon–Fri: 0800–1300, 1500–1800.

Shops

Mon–Sat: 0800–1200, 1430–1700.

Telecommunications

Mobile/cell phones

GSM 900 and 1800 services are available on Basse Terre.

Electricity supply

220/380V AC, 50 and 60 cycles

Getting there

Air

National airline: Air Caraibes.

International airport/s: Pointe-à-Pitre Le Raizet International Airport (PTP), 3km from Pointe-à-Pitre; duty-free shop, restaurant, buffet, bank, post office, shops, hotel reservations, car hire.

Airport tax: None

Surface

Water: A new, year-round, 137-passenger, Jeans Ferry Service operated by L' Express Des Il, between Dominica, St Lucia, Martinique and Guadeloupe will begin on 20 October 2011.

Getting about

National transport

Air: Air Guadeloupe, Air St Barthélémy and Liat operate frequent services to all the dependent islands from Pointe-à-Pitre.

Road: The total network is around 3,000km – including about 500km of national highway; secondary roads can be tortuous.

Buses: There are several private bus lines that connect Pointe-à-Pitre or Basse Terre with all villages. There are no timetables; a hand gesture is needed to stop buses.

City transport

Taxis: Plentiful but generally regarded as expensive, particularly in rural areas.

Car hire

Reservations for car rental are advisable, especially between December and April. An international licence is required and one year's experience driving.

BUSINESS DIRECTORY

The addresses listed below are a selection only. While World of Information makes every endeavour to check these addresses, we cannot guarantee that changes have not been made, especially to telephone numbers and area codes. We would welcome any corrections.

Telephone area codes

The international direct dialling code (IDD) for Guadeloupe is +590, followed by another 590 and subscriber's number.

Chambers of Commerce

Basse Terre Chamber of Commerce and Industry, 6 Rue Victor Hugues, 97100 Basse Terre (tel: 994-444; fax: 812-117; e-mail: ccibt:ais.gp).

Pointe-à-Pitre Chamber of Commerce and Industry, Hôtel Consulaire, Rue Félix Eboué, 97159 Pointe-à-Pitre (tel: 937-600; fax: 902-187; e-mail: contacts@cci-pap.org).

Banking

Caisse Régionale de Crédit Agricole Mutuel de la Guadeloupe, BP 134, Zone Artisanale de Petit Perou, 97154 Pointe-à-Pitre (tel: 906-565).

Central bank

European Central Bank (ECB), Kaiserstrasse 29, D-60311 Frankfurt am Main, Germany (tel: (+49-69) 13-440; fax: (+49-69) 1344-6000).

Travel information

Air Caraibes, Morne Vergain, 97139 Abymes (tel: 824-747; fax: 824-749; e-mail: direction@aircaraibes.com).

Ministry of tourism

Bureau Industrie et Tourisme, Préfecture de la Guadeloupe, Rue de Lardenoy, 97109 Basse Terre (tel: 817-681).

Direction de la Promotion Touristique, Préfecture de la Guadeloupe, Rue Lardenoy, 97100 Basse Terre (tel: 811-560).

National tourist organisation offices

Office Départemental du Tourisme (Guadeloupe Tourism Board), 5 Square de la Banque, PO Box 1099, 97181 Pointe-á-Pitre (tel: 894-689, 820-930; fax: 838-922).

Other useful addresses

Agence pour la Promotion Industrielle de la Guadeloupe (APRIGA), BP 1229, 97184 Pointe-à-Pitre (tel: 834-897; fax: 902-187).

Chambre d'Agriculture de la Guadeloupe, 27 rue Sadi-Carnot, 97110 Pointe-à-Pitre (tel: 821-130; fax: 918-873).

Port Autonome de la Guadeloupe, Boulevard Pointe Jarry, Zone de Commerce International, Basse Terre (tel: 213-971; fax: 213-979).

Port Autonome de Pointe-á-Pitre, Gare maritime, 97165 Pointe-á-Pitre Cedex (tel: 213-900; fax: 213-969; internet site: http://www.port-guadeloupe.com).

Syndicat des Producteurs-Exportateurs de Sucre et de Rhum de la Guadeloupe et Dépendances, Zone Industrielle de la Pointe Jarry, 97122 Baie Mahault, BP 2015, 97191 Pointe-à-Pitre (tel: 266-212).

Internet sites

L' Express Des Iles ferry service: express-des-iles.com

Local government: http://guadeloupe.pref.gouv.fr

Guam

COUNTRY PROFILE

Guam is the largest of the Marianas islands, which were occupied by the Chamorro Indians, a Malayo-Polynesian people, around 1500 BC.
1521 The Spanish seized control of Guam, which became a port of call for its galleons travelling between Mexico and the Philippines.
1898 Spain ceded Guam to the US after it lost the Spanish-American war. Guam was transformed into a strategic naval base.
1941 The US were forced out by the Japanese during the Second World War.
1944 US rule was reinstated after three years of fighting. Guam has remained an important military base since then.
1950 The Organic Act of Guam granted the island internal self-government and the islanders US citizenship, but not voting rights in US elections.
1962 The US passed the Naval Clearing Act which opened Guam's ports to foreign visitors.
1975 More than 100,000 evacuees from the fall of Vietnam were repatriated via Guam.
1996 Around 7,000 Kurdish refugees, fearing retaliation from Iraqi leader Saddam Hussein were housed on Guam.
1997 The strongest ever recorded typhoon ripped through Guam, leaving thousands homeless.
2002 Felix Camacho (Republican) was elected governor. Super-typhoon Pongsona struck in December.
2004 A state of emergency was declared after typhoon Tingting hit the island, leaving it almost completely flooded; weeks later super-typhoon Chaba struck. The Republicans won control of the legislature.
2006 Governor Camacho won re-election with 50 per cent of the vote.
2008 The Democratic Party won a majority in the legislature.
2009 The US launched marine protected areas (MPA), totalling 500,000 square km of sea and sea floor, around its Pacific islands. Mining and commercial fishing out to 50 nautical miles (54.26km) from shore was banned. A lost Chamorro-English dictionary was found on Guam and re-published to help preserve Guam's indigenous language. The dictionary had been compiled by Chamorro elders in the late 1970s, in longhand, then stored away and lost. The US Environmental Protection Agency (EPA) ordered the oil company Shell to clean up its site in the west of Guam, which had contaminated groundwater with hazardous waste.
2010 Governor Camacho proposed that Guam's name should be changed to Guahan, a spelling, which he said, was a more indigenous spelling and pronunciation of the island. Official correspondence with the governor already uses the alternative spelling and other government departments are being encouraged to adopt the practice. The resident population took part in the United States census, which, after personal details, included questions on race, housing and internet and mobile phone access. The US decided to increase its military forces on Guam with the addition of an expanded dock for a nuclear-powered aircraft carrier and missile defence system. It was seen as a response to China's increased spending on its military. In gubernatorial elections held in November, Eddie Calvo (Republican) won 50.6 per cent of the vote, Carl Gutierrez (Democrat) 49.4 per cent.
2011 Governor Eddie Calvo took office in January. Following a proposal by the state authorities in Guam to include visitors from China and Russia in the visa-waiver programme, federal officials began evaluating the impact on US national security in July. Results of the census were released in August, showing a population of 159,358.
2012 On 2 October, the legislature passed a health insurance bill for government employees. Tourism statistics released in November show 1.38 million visitors had arrived from South Korea, the strongest market, and was the best ever year on record.
2013 Bank of Guam's chief economist, Joseph Bradley, said in April that despite the estimated US$85.4 billion in US federal budget cuts, which will mean a fall in civilian allocations for Guam, because of the perceived increase in threat from North Korea, military spending is likely to increase. The Guam Visitors Bureau announced at the end of May that tourist arrivals during the month had increased by 7.1 per cent over May 2012 to more than 64,000. The top five markets were Japan (which actually fell by 2.9 per cent), Korea

KEY FACTS

Official name: Territory of Guam (Guahan)

Head of State: President of the United States of America Barack Obama (from 20 Jan 2009)

Head of government: Governor Eddie Calvo (Republican) (from 3 Jan 2011; re-elected)

Ruling party: Democratic Party (elected 4 Nov 2008)

Area: 549 square km

Population: 160,378 (July 2013)*; (159,358; 2010, census figure)

Capital: Agaña

Official language: Chamorro and English

Currency: US dollar (US$) = 100 cents

Exchange rate: US$1.00 per US$ (Sep 2015)

* estimated figure

(up by 72 per cent), Taiwan (down 4 per cent), the People's Republic of China (up almost 60 per cent) and the United States mainland (down 14 per cent).

2014 Discussions with the US on when, or even whether, the troops from the US base on Okinawa would move to Guam continued in 2014. The associated construction projects would boost the Guam economy.

2015 2015 In August the US said it would be deploying three B-2 nuclear-capable bombers to Guam amid heightened tensions on the Korean Peninsula. The move is part of a general build up of service members to Andersen Air Force Base, including 8,000 Marines and 9,000 of their dependents from Okinawa, Japan.

Political structure

Constitution

Guam is represented by an elected non-voting delegate to the US House of Representatives; elections are every two years. Its inhabitants are US citizens but are not allowed to vote in US elections. In June 2004, a new process for the island's primary elections was approved, which prevents voters from crossing over between political parties on the ballot; voters can, however, keep their political affiliations confidential.

Form of state

Although it is administered by the department of the interior, Guam is virtually a self-governing unincorporated territory of the US.

The executive

Local executive power rests with a governor, elected by popular vote to a four-year term, who heads a cabinet made up of departmental directors.

National legislature

The unicameral, Liheslaturan Guåhan (in Chamorro) (Legislature of Guam) has 15 members, elected to a two-year term by popular vote, within one constituency that covers the whole island. It deals with legislation on local matters.

Last elections

4 November 2014 (parliamentary and gubernational)

Results: Parliamentary: Democratic Party (Dem) won 9 seats (out of 15), Republican Party (Rep) 6.

Gubernatorial: Eddie Calvo (Rep) won 63.69 per cent, Carl Gutierrez 35.97 per cent.

US House of Representatives: Madeleine ZBordallo (Dem) won 57.84 per cent of the vote, Magaret Metcalfe (Rep) 41.84 per cent.

Next elections

November 2016 (parliamentary and gubernatorial)

Political parties

Ruling party

Democratic Party (elected 4 Nov 2008)

Main opposition party

Republican Party

Political situation

The US House of Representatives passed an economic stimulus plan, whereby tax rebate cheques began to be sent to all tax payers in mid-2008, to stimulate the local economy and encourage consumer spending. Most households in Guam were looking forward to sums between US$300–600 for singles and US$1,200 for couples but 247 were disappointed when the Guam administration garnished their cheques for outstanding local tax duties.

The recovered US$100,788 was much needed, to cover costs for the Memorial Hospital, Guam Housing, an Urban Renew plan and child support.

In March 2011, the Republican controlled US-Congress voted to rescind the voting rites of representations of Guam effectively disenfranchising their electorate in policies that directly affect them.

160,378 (July 2013)*; (159,358; 2010, census figure)

Population

Last census: 1 April 2010: 159,358

Population density: 276 inhabitants per square km.

Annual growth rate: 1.5 per cent (2003)

Ethnic make-up

Native Chamorros comprise 37 per cent of the population, Filipinos (26 per cent), white (10 per cent), Chinese, Japanese, Korean and others (27 per cent). There is tension between the Chamorros and guest workers from the Philippines and other Asian countries.

Religions

Roman Catholic (85 per cent)

Education

The education system is similar to that of the US but is poorly managed, with drop-out rates at around 50 per cent. Schools lack basic equipment and essential books.

Education is a high priority for parents and is considered the key to success in Chamorro life. Despite ongoing criticisms of the flaws in the system, the government has implemented no major reforms.

An agreement between the education departments of Guam and the Marshall Islands, signed in October 2010, will allow an exchange of students to study at the University of Guam and the College of the Marshall Islands.

Compulsory years: Five to 16

Health

With a young and growing population the government is faced with the challenge of developing a health care system that will meet their needs. Health services are funded by the US government and the World Health Organisation (WHO).

Health services are good but there is a shortage of adequately trained medical staff. Training of medical personnel was a government priority throughout 2002–05. There are high incidents of mental retardation and thyroid cancers, blamed on nuclear contamination when naval ships were sent for decontamination to Guam.

Life expectancy: 77.9 years (World Bank)

Fertility rate/Maternal mortality rate: 3.7 births per woman (World Bank)

Birth rate/Death rate: 23 births and four deaths per 1,000 population (2003)

Child (under 5 years) mortality rate (per 1,000): 6.5 per 1,000 live births (2003)

Welfare

Welfare is unevenly distributed among the population. The Chamorros are the main beneficiaries of welfare while Filipinos receive less than 10 per cent of government money, however in a 2005 a survey over 50 per cent found to be homeless were Chamorros.

Main cities

Agaña (capital, estimated population 1,001 in 2012), Yigo (12,190), Tamuning (11,990), Mangilao (10,819), Astumbo (6,970), Ordot (5,571), Barrigada (5,049).

Languages spoken

English, Chamorro, Chinese, Japanese and Korean.

Official language/s

Chamorro and English

Media

Press

The *Guam Business News* is a monthly publication.

Dailies: In English the *Pacific Daily News* (www.guampdn.com) is the only national newspaper. The US Navy has its own publication *Navigator* with news and stories relevant to its readership.

Weeklies: There are several weeklies available. In English, *Micro Call*, *Guam Shopper's Guide*, *Pacific Crossroads*, *Pacific Voice* (published on Sundays for the Catholic community), *Pacific Sunday News* and *Tropic Topics*. In Japanese, *Guam Shinbun* and *Guam Kyodo News Service*, which provides a facsimile news service twice daily for the Japanese community and tourists. In Korean, the *Korean Community News* and *Korean News*.

Business: *Guam Business News* is a monthly publication.

Periodicals: In English, *Latte Magazine* is a quarterly, featuring contemporary life and multiculturalism; *Micronesica* is a bi-annual and *Manila, Manila* is a glossy news and lifestyle magazine catering to the Filipino community.

Broadcasting

The US Federal Communications Commission is responsible for broadcasting regulations.

Radio: There are several radio stations, the largest are K57 (KGUM) (www.k57.com) and KAUM (www.kuam.com), with news and talk shows, and these are parts of larger broadcasting media enterprises. KTKB Mega Mixx (www.ktkb.com) and Loud Radio 88 (http://loudradio88.homestead.com) are private stations. Several Christian radio stations provide music and entertainment, Light 91, Joy 92 and Adventist World Radio.

Television: Commercial TV stations include K57 (www.k57.com) and KAUM (www.kuam.com), with locally produced news and imported entertainment programmes. A cable service is provided by MSNBC KUAM (www.msnbc.msn.com)

Other news agencies: ABC Pacific Beat: www.radioaustralia.net.au/pacbeat
Pacific Magazine:
www.pacificmagazine.net
Pacific Islands New Association (Pina):
www.pina.com.fj

Economy

Guam remains one of the most prosperous islands in the Pacific and has the second highest GDP per capita of the region, Hawaii having the highest. About 60 per cent of Guam's income comes from US federal spending, which has, since 2006, grown with the decision to open a new military base. The Marines' base was scheduled to open in 2012, to be home to around 8,000 military personnel. However in February 2012 the plan was stalled due to on-going negotiations with Japan concerning the Marines' redeployment from the US military base on Okinawa, Japan. US$1 billion per annum for 6–10 years (2006–16) was allocated for the construction of the military base but in 2014 the US congress approved funding to complete the transfer of troops from Okinawa to Guam. An additional US$400 million was allocated to Guam for civil purposes and general infrastructure. The US military owns roughly one third of the land in Guam.

Tourism is the single largest component of the service sector with Guam increasingly being seen as a reasonable destination for Japanese visitors on a limited budget. Tourism accounts for around 30 per cent of total employment and 13.3 per cent to GDP (US$651 million).

Aside from tourism, the only other significant source of income is the fishing industry, although the cement and construction industries have continued to prosper due to the damage to buildings and infrastructure by natural disasters, as well as construction of the US military base.

External trade

Guam exports products free of duty to a number of countries, including Australia, Japan and the US.

Imports

Main imports are petroleum and petroleum products, food and manufactured goods.

Main sources: Singapore (typically 50 per cent of total), South Korea (21 per cent), Japan (14 per cent).

Exports

Main exports are construction materials, fish, food and beverage products.

Main destinations: Japan (typically 67 per cent of total), Singapore (7 per cent), UK (5 per cent).

Re-exports

Food re-exports for distribution throughout the Pacific provide the mainstay of export income along with refined petroleum products.

Agriculture

Farming

The agriculture sector typically accounts for around 5 per cent of GDP. Most agricultural activity is part-time market gardening on smallholdings.

Fishing

Fishing is an important source of protein. Future areas for growth include salmon and trout farming. Typical annual catches include over 200 tonnes (t) freshwater fish, over 300t marine fish, and 30t of all other seafood.

Industry and manufacturing

Industry typically accounts for 15 per cent of GDP and employs about 3 per cent of the labour force. Most industrial goods are imported.

Main industries include US military, tourism, construction, transshipment services, concrete products, printing and publishing, food processing and textiles.

Government policy is attempting to focus on attracting foreign investment, particularly from Asian manufacturers, in order to develop the industrial base.

Tourism

Among Guam's natural attractions are its unspoilt coral reefs, white sand beaches, lagoons and waterfalls. The brown tree snake, accidentally introduced in the 1940's has, however, decimated its bird-life and eradication programmes are carried out regularly. Guam is ideal for water sports including surfing, canoeing, jet skiing, and deep-sea fishing, in waters that are clear and warm. On the land, there are seven golf courses and good hiking tracks. It is one of the best diving destinations in the world with shipwrecks and coral reefs. On Cocos Island, two miles off the Southern tip of Guam, there is a Spanish galleon wreck with billions of dollars worth of treasure that has still to be recovered.

Most visitors to Guam come from Japan and South Korea, with new arrivals from China boosting visitor numbers since 2010 when Continental Micronesia began more flights and routes within the Pacific region. These flights are in competition with new low-cost carriers, Fly Guam, Jinair (a subsidiary of Korean Air) and PacificFlier, that have also begun operations. In 2013 there were 1,283,000 visitors to Guam.

Tourism constitutes an important component of GDP and after several years of negative growth by 2010 expansion in the sector reached double digits. The Guam Visitor's Bureau began to apply a uniform approach towards visitors so that they gain a more comprehensive experience of the Micronesian culture. In 2014 Tourism contributed 13.3 per cent to GDP (US$651 million) and some 30 per cent of total employment.

Environment

In May 2005 a US research study confirmed that Guam had received measurable radioactive fallout during nuclear testing from 1946–62. The government confirmed that residents would be eligible under the Radiation Exposure Compensation Act. Radioactive polution was also acknowledged in Apra Habour, caused when military ships were decontaminated by washing down after testing.

Military expansion of the Andersen Air Force Base will cause the loss of some pristine native forest at a time when several endangered bird species are being reintroduced into the area.

Mining

Mining contributes less than 5 per cent to GDP. Rock and cement production supplies the construction industry.

Hydrocarbons

Guam does not produce or refine oil; it relies entirely on imports, which amounted to around 12,000 barrels per day in 2013 (latest figures).

Any use of imported natural gas or coal is commercially insignificant.

Energy

Total installed electricity generating capacity was over 552MW in 2013 (latest figures), produced in thermal power stations; consumption is around 1.6 billion kilowatt hours.

Banking and insurance

Central bank

Federal Reserve Bank of San Francisco

Time

GMT plus ten hours

Geography

Guam is the southernmost and largest of the Marianas, situated about 2,170km (1,350 miles) south of Tokyo, Japan, and 5,300km (3,300 miles) west of Honolulu, Hawaii.

The island consists of two ancient volcanoes of which the southern peak is 407 metres at its tallest. In the north and between the summits are limestone plateaux with deep gorges that drop to the narrow coastal shelf.

The world's deepest chasm in the deepest ocean, the Marianas Trench, lies around 400km south-west of Guam.

Hemisphere

Northern

Climate

Guam is warm and humid with temperatures averaging between 24–30 degrees Celsius. Dec–May is generally cooler and drier. Rainfall, up to 300mm per month, averages 2,000mm per annum. The heaviest rainfall is usually between Jul–Sep. There are occasional tropical storms. The tropical humidity is tempered somewhat by the prevailing north-westerly trade winds.

Dress codes

Informal, lightweight clothing is acceptable.

Entry requirements

Passports

Required by all.

Visa

US entry requirements apply. Visas required by all, except US citizens and foreign nationals of countries that have visa free entry to the US and are in possession of machine readable passports with biometric data, under the Visa Waiver Program (VWP) introduced in 2005. All other visitors and passport holders must apply for a visa. Visas, for both tourism and business, are valid for up to 90 days. A return/onward ticket is also required. Further information can be found at http://travel.state.gov/ including information on temporary business visas. More detailed information can be found at http://uscis.gov/graphics/services/visa_info.htm.

Currency advice/regulations

There are no restrictions on import or export of foreign or local currency. However amounts over US$10,000 or equivalent must be declared.

Customs

Personal items are duty-free.

Prohibited imports

Plant material, meat products, illegal drugs and any material that breaches US copyright laws.

Health (for visitors)

Mandatory precautions

Vaccination certificates required for yellow fever if travelling from infected area.

Advisable precautions

Dengue fever is endemic; it is advisable to cover up at dawn and dusk and prophylaxis should be used. Vaccinations for diphtheria, tuberculosis, hepatitis A and B, tetanus, typhoid fever should be considered. No cases of polio have been reported since the 1990s. There is a rabies risk in rural areas.

Ciguatera poisoning is possible if eating tropical reef-fish – toxins are not removed through cooking – avoiding barracuda, grouper, snapper and amberjack will reduce the risk.

Medical insurance is necessary as all healthcare costs are high. All continuous medication should be carried along with its packaging and prescription.

Public holidays (national)

Fixed dates

1 Jan (New Year's Day), 4 Jul (US Independence Day), 21 Jul (Liberation Day), 2 Nov (All Souls' Day), 11 Nov (Veterans' Day), 8 Dec (Lady of Camarin Day), 25 Dec (Christmas).

Variable dates

Martin Luther King Day (third Mon in Jan), President's Day (second Mon in Feb), Guam Discovery Day (first Mon in Mar), Good Friday, Memorial Day (last Mon in May), Labour Day (first Mon in Sep), Columbus Day (first Mon in Oct), Thanksgiving Day (fourth Thu in Nov).

Working hours

Banking

Mon–Thu: 1000–1500; Fri: 1000–1800; Sat 0900–1200. ATMs are available.

Business

Mon–Fri: 0730/0830–1730/1800; Sat: 0830–1200.

Government

Mon–Fri: 0730/0830–1730/1800; Sat: 0830–1200.

Shops

Mon–Fri: 0800–1700; Sat: 0800–1300.

Telecommunications

Mobile/cell phones

GSM 1900 and 850 services cover most of the island.

Electricity supply

110V AC, 60Hz

Weights and measures

US system

Getting there

Air

Korean Air, Continental Micronesia, All Nippon Airlines and Japan Airlines all serve Guam.

International airport/s: The Antonio B Won Pat International Airport (GUM), 11km from Agaña; duty-free shop, first-class lounge, restaurant, currency exchange, hotel reservations and car hire.

Airport tax: None

Surface

Main port/s: Apra Harbour.

Getting about

National transport

Road: The roads and highways are third-rate and bumpy, with some 600km surfaced.

Buses: A reasonable service connects almost all villiages, however services do not run on Sundays or public holidays.

Taxis: Are readily available and fares are metered.

Car hire

Available through most major companies. In general, charges are based on time, mileage and insurance. An international driving licence is required.

BUSINESS DIRECTORY

The addresses listed below are a selection only. While World of Information makes every endeavour to check these addresses, we cannot guarantee that changes have not been made, especially to telephone numbers and area codes. We would welcome any corrections.

Telephone area codes

The international direct dialling code (IDD) for Guam is +1 671, followed by subscriber's number.

Chambers of Commerce

Guam Chamber of Commerce, 173 Aspinall Avenue, Ada Plaza Center, PO Box 283, Agana 96932 (tel: 472-6311; fax: 472-6202; e-mail: gchamber@guamchamber.com.gu).

Banking

Bank of Hawaii, PO Box BH, Agaña 96910 (tel: 4779-781; fax: 4777-533).

First Commercial Bank, 1st Floor, 330 Hernan Cortes Ave, Agaña 96910 (tel: 4726-864/5; fax: 4778-921).

Union Bank of California NA, 194 Hernan Cortes Ave, Agaña 96910 (tel: 4778-811; fax: 4723-284).

Central bank

Federal Reserve System, 20th Street and Constitution Avenue, NW, Washington DC 20551 (tel: (202) 452-3000; fax: (202) 452-3819).

Travel information

Dive Rota, PO Box 941, Rota MP 96951 (email: mark@diverota.com; internet: www.diverota.com).

Freedom Air, PO Box 1578, Hagatna, 96932 (tel: 647-8360/1; fax; 472-8080; email: freedom@ite.net).

National tourist organisation offices

Guam Visitors Bureau, PO Box 3520; 401 Pale San Vitores Road, Tamuning 96913 (tel: 646-5278/9; fax: 646-8861: internet: www.visitguam.org).

Other useful addresses

Guam Economic Development Authority, Suite 911, ITC Building, 590 South Marine Drive, Tamuning, Guam 96911 (tel: 649-4141; fax: 649-4146).

ABC Pacific Beat: www.radioaustralia.net.au/pacbeat

Pacific Magazine: www.pacificmagazine.net

Pacific Islands New Association (Pina): www.pina.com.fj

Internet sites

The Pacific Daily News: www.guampdn.com

KUAM Broadcasting News: www.kuam.com

US Office of Insular affairs: www.doi.gov/oia

Guatemala

KEY FACTS

Official name: República de Guatemala (Republic of Guatemala)

Head of State: Acting President Alejandro Maldonado Aguirre (since 3 Sep 2015) following resignation of President Otto Pérez Molina on 3 Sep 2015. President elect Jimmy Morales (FCN-Nación) (elected 25 Oct 2015)

Head of government: Acting President Alejandro Maldonado Aguirre (since 3 Sep 2015) following resignation of President Otto Pérez Molina on 3 Sep 2015. President elect Jimmy Morales (FCN-Nación) (elected 25 Oct 2015)

Ruling party: Libertad Democrática Renovada (LIDER) (Renewed Democratic Liberty) (won most seats (44, out of 158) in 6 Sep 2015 election)

Area: 108,890 square km

Population: 15.87 million (2014)*

Capital: Guatemala City

Official language: Spanish

Currency: Quetzal (Q) = 100 centavos

Exchange rate: Q7.73 per US$ (Sep 2015)

GDP per capita: US$3,807 (2014)*

GDP real growth: 4.00% (2014)*

GDP: US$60.42 billion (2014)*

Inflation: 3.42% (2014)*

Balance of trade: -US$6.06 billion (2014)

* estimated figure

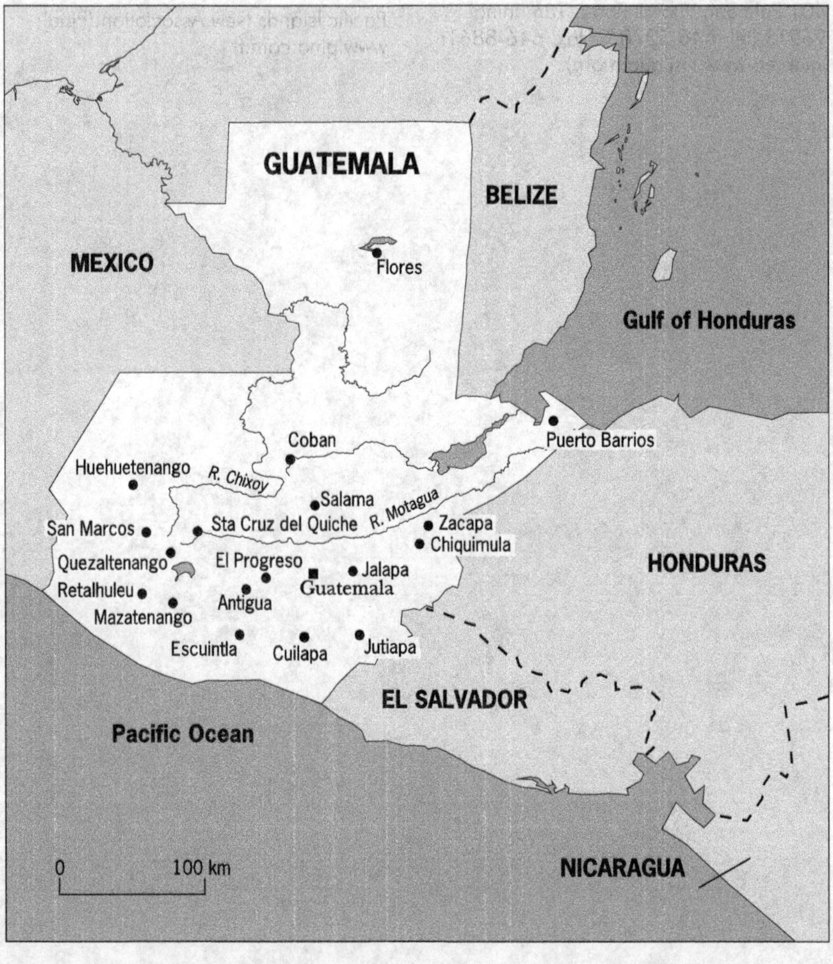

Early September 2015 saw the destitution of the Guatemalan President. This time it was President Otto Pérez Molina who, as Guatemalans put it, 'went to bed in a palace and woke up in a police cell.' Events moved quickly following the President's removal on charges of corruption. Mr Pérez Molina was removed from office on a Thursday and on the following Sunday Vice President Alejandro Maldonado was appointed caretaker President.

The Primavera del Descontento (Springtime of Anger)

The growing wave of anger in Guatemala burst its banks in April 2015 with a demonstration in front of the old government palace in Guatemala City to demand that President Otto Pérez Molina clean up his government. A fraud and bribery conspiracy in Guatemala's tax agency, allegedly organised by a corrupt gang of officials, had been revealed. Protests soon sprang up in other Guatemalan cities, eventually costing Vice President Roxana Baldetti her job in May when her name began to appear in the investigation. Ms Baldetti was suspected of involvement in a kick-back scheme organised by a senior aide. Resigning in May, in August 2015 she was charged with corruption offences, which included illicit association, fraud and graft, defrauding the Guatemalan state of millions of dollars. State investigators estimated that that in one week's operation, bribes paid to Guatemalan customs officials could have totalled over US$250,000. At the heart of the scandal was a group of criminals collectively known as *La Línea*, allegedly led by (former) Vice President's aide, Juan Carlos Monzón Rojas, who had disappeared. Mr Monzón was allegedly the architect of the scheme.

As if losing a vice president wasn't bad enough, the prosecutors were also seeking to have President Pérez Molina's immunity of office withdrawn, as the Attorney General, Thelma Adana bravely went on record to announce that it was 'highly probable that the President of the Republic may have participated in the same scheme.' President Pérez Molina promptly denied any involvement and the initial efforts to lift his immunity predictably failed. Presidential elections had already been scheduled for September. Guatemalan presidents are limited to a single four-year term, so Sr Pérez Molina was ineligible to run for re-election. His term of office was due to end in January 2016, when he would normally have handed over to his successor.

A Facebook revolution?

When businesswoman Lucía Mendizábal heard of the ministerial involvement in the fraud, she decided that she had had enough. She posted a Facebook message: 'This time we should do something.' She had a number of replies, one of which asked: 'Where and when?' She decided, with the help of half a dozen friends, to organise a demonstration. The small group described themselves as 'Indignant Citizens', with no political affiliation simply a determination to rid their country of corruption. No small task: Guatemala ranked 115 out of the 175 countries surveyed on the 2014 Transparency International *Corruption Perceptions Index*.

Ms Mendizábal and her friends had certainly touched a nerve. Within a few days the Indignant Citizens had over 35,000 Facebook followers. When they all met up on 25 April there were tens of thousands of demonstrators, many banging saucepans and blowing whistles in the park where they met. For a country where 60 per cent of the population live in poverty and where the murder rate is 50 times higher than in Europe, this was no small achievement. The Vice President's resignation was attributed to the demonstration; their next objective was the resignation of the President. From its inception, the Indignant Citizens movement had the close support of the United Nations International Commission against Impunity in Guatemala (CICIG). On 21 August the CICIG accused President Pérez Molina of being the real leader of the customs corruption scandal. This was the turning point – the following day crowds gathered to demand the President's resignation. Over 40 per cent of businesses in Guatemala City were estimated to have closed, including – a new icon for Guatemalan protests – the McDonald's chain. It was manifestly clear where the support and sympathy of the Guatemalan people lay – and it was not with the President. His immunity was taken from him in a parliamentary vote of 131 for, one against. The decision to strip the President of his immunity was welcomed by street celebrations and messages of support from business organisations, the Catholic Church, student organisations and trades unions. The following day a judge ordered the President's arrest. The Facebook message had deposed the President. On few occasions in Latin American history had political events moved so quickly. The catalyst was certainly the backroom presence, if not the obvious intervention, of the CICIG.

In addition to these ministerial scalps, CICIG could also take most of the credit for the May arrest of Guatemala's central bank chief, Julio Suárez, who was arrested along with the entire board of Guatemala's social security institute on which he also sat. The scandal, surrounding a US$15 million contract for the Guatemalan social security system had already resulted in the resignation of the bank's vice president, as well as the energy and mines minister. To simplify matters, the entire board of the social security institute had been arrested. The CICIG had certainly stiffened the sinews of the Guatemalan judiciary. In the run up to the ministerial arrests, the UN organisation had taped over 65,000 telephone conversations and intercepted over 6,000 e-mails. Added to this was the political climate created by Mrs Mendizábal and her legion of followers. This now vocal grouping had placed Guatemala's infamous political class firmly on the back foot.

In reality, the social conflict was not between Guatemalans and their ministers, it was between Guatemalans and the mafia like gangs that had suborned their representatives, including ministers. The statistics surrounding the shift in power away from a corrupt military towards an even more corrupt organised crime system are almost beyond belief. Writing in *El País* (Madrid) Joaquín Villalobos (a former guerrilla insurgent in El Salvador) summed up the situation. Guatemala, according to Mr Villalobos, had hundreds of private aerodromes and the second largest fleet of private aircraft in Latin America.

Added to this, within a period of 50 years, 59 political parties have simply disappeared in Guatemala. Even so, there were, in 2015, 28 political parties, for the most part temporary coalitions built around a single *Caudillo* or leader. In a period of 30 years, not one political party had been in power more than once.

During his election campaign, President Pérez Molina had made much of plans to legalise the production, sales and distribution and consumption of marijuana. Once in power, these plans were speedily

KEY INDICATORS Guatemala

	Unit	2011	2012	2013	2014	**2015
Population	m	*14.74	*15.11	*15.48	*15.87	*16.27
Gross domestic product (GDP)	US$bn	46.90	50.24	53.85	*60.42	*66.04
GDP per capita	US$	3,182	3,326	3,478	*3,807	*4,060
GDP real growth	%	3.8	3.0	3.7	*4.0	*4.0
Inflation	%	6.2	3.8	4.3	*3.4	*3.0
Exports (fob) (goods)	US$m	10,517.3	10,102.7	10,190.3	10,993.6	–
Imports (fob) (goods)	US$m	15,481.9	15,837.7	16,355.6	17,052.0	–
Balance of trade	US$m	-4,964.5	-5,735.0	-6,165.2	-6,058.4	–
Current account	US$m	-1,528.9	-1,310.0	-1,351.0	*-1,394.0	*-1,026.0
Total reserves minus gold	US$m	5,968.2	–	7,002.3	7,063.6	–
Foreign exchange	US$m	5,690.6	–	6,731.8	–	–
Exchange rate	per US$	7.76	7.84	7.86	7.60	–

* estimated figure ** forecast figure

dropped, not – according to Mr Villalobos – because of any intellectual rethink. Pérez Molina was no José Mujica. His thinking was determined by the strength of the Guatemalan criminal organisations and the money they were making.

New elections for old

Only days after the President's arrest and deposition, in early September 2015 came the scheduled first round of the Presidential election. Jimmy Morales, a comic actor with no political background, won a surprise victory in the first crowded round of voting. However, Sr Morales didn't secure enough votes to avoid an October run-off. With virtually all votes counted Mr Morales had won 24 per cent of the vote. Second came the left of centre Sandra Torres with 19 per cent, marginally ahead of the right-wing businessman Manuel Baldizón. The second, final round, was due to be held in late October 2015.

Same old story?

In 2013 Guatemalans had been taken aback by the events surrounding the conviction, arrest and subsequent discharge of former President Efraín Ríos Montt on charges of genocide which had succeeded in pushing Guatemalan politics back into the dark days of the 1980s. Mr Ríos Montt's subsequent release also revealed quite how close knit is the politico-legal coterie that still lurks behind the façade of a new, but fragile, democracy. This revelation was strengthened by the decision, in August 2015, that although Ríos Montt can stand trial on charges of genocide and crimes against humanity, he cannot be sentenced because he suffers from dementia.

The History Boys

Although Mr Ríos Montt served as his country's president from 1982 to 1983, he was never actually elected. In true Guatemalan style he entered office through a *golpe de estado* (*coup d'état*) in March 1982, only to be booted out of office by another *golpe de estado*, this time by his defence minister, Oscar Humberto Mejía Victores, 15 months later. Mr Ríos Montt continued to seek some sort of political respectability by running – unsuccessfully – in the 2003 presidential elections as the candidate of the Frente Republicano Guatemalteco (FRG) (Guatemalan Republican Front) (since renamed Partido Republicano Institucional (PRI) (Institutional Republican Party). Possibly as a move to obtain immunity from prosecution, in 2007 Mr Ríos Montt returned to public office as a member of Congress. However, his immunity ended in January 2012, at the end of his term in office.

Mr Ríos Montt's release on 'procedural grounds' which were never satisfactorily explained came as a massive disappointment for those Guatemalans who had hoped their country was turning a new page. Mr Ríos Montt's indictment was a first. Never before, anywhere in the world, had a former president been convicted of war crimes. Widespread protests broke out across the country, especially in those areas where the peasantry were already protesting over land grabbing and the random development of massive hydro-electric plants with minimum local consultation. There were further protests in 2015 when a medical examiner's report declared Mr Montt to be mentally incompetent and unfit for trial.

Guatemala's elite, had endeavoured since the mid-1990s to enter the political process with the simple objective of making sure that Guatemala's democracy produces conservatism and economic libertarianism. This phenomenon, according to Martin Rodríguez Pellecer has produced some weirdly radical opinions; Mr Rodríguez quotes the more radical elements as saying that 'the answer to the security crisis is more violence.' Writing on the *OpenDemocracy* website, Mr Rodríguez quotes a member of Guatemala's 'ruling' élite as saying: 'We'd better get involved in politics before the people rise up against us.' Whatever the motivation, the depressing outcome seemed to be that the strategy was meeting with some success as Guatemala's 'own brand' democracy, organised crime and the return of violence combined to make Guatemala one of the world's bloodiest countries again.

The almost iconic figure and appropriately named Claudia Paz y Paz was the judge who had had the temerity to send the former president to the cells. The behind the scenes machinations of the élite succeeded in having Judge Paz removed from office. Additionally, the commission appointed to choose a new attorney general had managed to remove her from the candidates, despite the fact that she was recognised as at least the second most qualified candidate for the post. Quoted by Anita Isaacs writing in the *New York Times* the appointment commission's President when asked if 'politics had intervened in the process' answered 'It is possible.' Politics certainly seemed to have had its say in the eventual appointment. Mrs Thelma Aldana, the successful candidate was known to have close links with the ruling élite.

The economy

Guatemala is the country with the lowest amount of tax collected in Latin America, as well as a business community which has fiercely resisted any tax reforms. This has inevitably resulted in a weak civil service, obeying the instructions of ministers and senior civil servants who are in turn beholden to their mafia overlords. The Guatemalan economy can only benefit from the end of the crippling levels of corruption and inequitably distorted taxation system.

According to the United Nations Economic Commission for Latin America and the Caribbean (ECLAC) Guatemala's gross domestic product (GDP) grew by an estimated 4.0 per cent in real terms in 2014, up from 3.7 per cent in 2013. The Banco de Guatemala (central bank) forecast average annual inflation of 3.5 per cent (compared with 4.3 per cent in 2013), within the target range of 3 per cent to 5 per cent. The fiscal deficit was expected to stand at 2.0 per cent of GDP (slightly down on the 2013 level), with the balance-of-payments current account deficit narrowing from 2.7 per cent of GDP in 2013 to 2.5 per cent in 2014. ECLAC estimated that the economy would grow by 4.0 per cent in 2015, given expectations of continued growth in exports and domestic demand, the latter primarily attributable to private consumption.

According to ECLAC, total central government income grew by 6.2 per cent in real terms to September 2014, while total expenditure rose by 6.8 per cent, driven by a surge in capital expenditure (17.5 per cent) and rising current spending (4.3 per cent). As a result of difficulties in the customs service and in tax collection over the year, the ministry of finance had forecast a tax burden of around 10.7 per cent of GDP by the end of 2014, compared with 11.0 per cent in 2013. External public debt as of September totalled US$6.985 billion, an increase of 5.8 per cent on the September 2013 figure. Domestic public debt was up by 8.7 per cent on the same period of 2013. The Banco de Guatemala forecast that total debt would reach 25.4 per cent of GDP by the end of 2014, up from 24.8 per cent in 2013.

In late November 2014, the Guatemalan Congress approved the general State budget for the 2015 fiscal year, which amounted to Q70.6 billion (US$9.1

billion). The agreement reached in Congress provided for reforms to the royalty percentages in the Mining Act, a higher rate of tax on fixed and mobile telephone lines, amendments to the Criminal Code and changes to the Specific Cement Distribution Tax Act, with a view to increasing ordinary tax revenue to fund spending in 2015. Budgetary appropriations for communications, foreign affairs, agriculture, culture, social development and presidential secretariats were cut. The issuance, negotiation and placement of Q2.8 billion (US$0.36 billion) in treasury bonds were authorised for fiscal year 2014 to cover obligations and transfers to public bodies. The main annual interest rate was held steady at 5.0 per cent until March 2014, when the Monetary Policy Committee (MCP) cut it to 4.75 per cent. Given that inflationary pressures and international oil, maize and wheat prices were trending downward and the pace of global recovery remained moderate, the MCP again reduced the base rate, to 4.5 per cent at its June session and then to 4.0 per cent at its November session. Bank interest rates remained stable over 2014.

ECLAC also noted that in nominal terms, the deposit rate stood at 5.49 per cent in October 2014 (versus 5.47 per cent in October 2013) and the lending rate at 13.73 per cent (compared with 13.66 per cent in the same month of 2013). Bank lending to the private sector was up 8.0 per cent year-on-year in nominal terms (4.2 per cent in real terms) in October – compared to 15.7 per cent in October 2013 (or 11.1 per cent in real terms) – owing primarily to consumer credit growth.

The exchange rate was 7.58 quetzales to the dollar at the end of October 2014, compared to 7.90 quetzales in October 2013), a nominal appreciation of 4.0 per cent over the same period in 2013. Net international reserves stood at US$7.098 billion at the end of October 2014 (up 6.6 per cent year-on-year on 2013), sufficient to cover 4.6 months of imports. Bank interest rates remained stable over 2014. In nominal terms, the deposit rate stood at 5.49 per cent in October (versus 5.47 per cent in October 2013) and the lending rate at 13.73 per cent (compared with 13.66 per cent in the same month of 2013). Bank lending to the private sector was up 8.0 per cent year-on-year in nominal terms (4.2 per cent in real terms) in October – compared to 15.7 per cent in October 2013 (or 11.1 per cent in real terms) – owing primarily to consumer credit growth.

Exports expanded 7.0 per cent by value to September 2014 (as against growth of just 0.2 per cent in the same period in 2013) owing to strong volume growth (19.5 per cent), since average prices fell by 10.4 per cent as a result of movements in those of core items such as sugar, precious and semi-precious stones and metals. Exports of traditional products fell by 3.0 per cent over the period to September, while those of non-traditional products grew by 11.2 per cent. Imports grew 3.8 per cent by value to September (compared to 4.0 per cent in 2013), mainly as a result of a rise in volume (8.4 per cent). The average price of imports also fell, by 4.4 per cent, to the same month. The goods and services trade balance for the entire year was therefore expected to be in deficit by the equivalent of 11.2 per cent of GDP (compared with 11.5 per cent in 2013), with a balance-of payments current account deficit equivalent to 2.5 per cent of GDP, down from 2.7 per cent in 2013. Family remittances rose 8.6 per cent in the period between January and October 2014 over the same period of 2013 to reach US$4.65 billion, maintaining steady, moderate growth as the United States labour market picked up. Foreign direct investment (FDI) amounted to US$713.4 million in the first half of 2014, mainly originating from Canada (especially investment in agriculture, mining and quarrying), the United States and the United Kingdom (chiefly in commerce) and Colombia (mainly in the financial sector). FDI was expected to have grown 8.0 per cent by the end of 2014 (up from 5.2 per cent growth in 2013).

ECLAC estimated GDP growth of 4.0 per cent for 2014, driven by buoyant activity in mining and quarrying (up 27.1 per cent), finance, insurance and business services (9.9 per cent), construction (4.8 per cent), private services (3.6 per cent), commerce (3.2 per cent), agriculture (3.1 per cent) and manufacturing (3.1 per cent). On the demand side, the highest rates of growth are expected in exports, private consumption and public and private investment. GDP expanded by 3.5 per cent in the first quarter of 2014 (compared with 3.0 per cent in the same period in 2013) then by 4.3 per cent in the second quarter (down from 4.7 per cent in the same period of 2013). In September, the trend-cycle series of the monthly index of economic activity (IMAE) was up 4.7 per cent year on year. Growth in the consumer price index to October was 3.64 per cent, compared with 4.15 per cent in October 2013, driven by food price inflation of 8.9 per cent. Average annual inflation by the end of the year was estimated at 3.5 per cent. In January 2014, the minimum wage was increased by 5 per cent in nominal terms (or by 1.3 per cent in real terms) to 74.97 quetzales (US$9.70) per day in the agricultural and non-agricultural sectors and 68.91 quetzales (US$8.91) in the *máquila* sector. Growth in the country's economy pushed the open unemployment rate down slightly to around 2.9 per cent in April and May 2014 (versus 3.2 per cent in the same period of 2013), while the urban unemployment rate increased slightly.

Risk assessment

Economy	Fair
Politics	Poor
Regional stability	Good

People to watch

Jimmy Morales, a comic actor with no political background who won a surprise victory in the first round of voting in the September 2015 presidential elections.

COUNTRY PROFILE

1523–24 Pedro de Alvarado defeated the indigenous Mayan peoples and created Guatemala as a Spanish colony.

1821 The Central American provinces (Costa Rica, Guatemala, Honduras, Nicaragua and El Salvador) declared independence from Spain.

1822 Central American provinces annexed to the Mexican Empire, under General Agustín de Iturbde, later Emperor Agustín I.

1823 Agustín I was overthrown and Mexico became a republic. The Central American states formed the United Provinces of Central America.

1825 Costa Rica, Guatemala, Honduras, Nicaragua and El Salvador formed the Central American Federation (CAF).

1838 The CAF was dissolved and Guatemala became a fully independent republic.

1844–65 Guatemala was ruled by conservative dictator Rafael Carrera.

1873–85 Liberal, Rufino Barrios, became president, he attempted to modernise the country by developing an army and introducing coffee plantations.

1930 General Jorge Ubico began his repressive dictatorship.

1941 Guatemala declared war on the Axis Powers.

1944 Ubico was overthrown in a popular revolution. Juan José Arevalo headed a new government that introduced social reforms, including a social security system and land redistribution.

1951 Jacobo Arbenz Guzmán became president and stepped up the reforms.

1954 A US-backed *coup d'état*, led by Colonel Carlos Castillo Armas and prompted by the US United Fruit Company when disused land it owned was nationalised, overthrew the democratically elected government. A military dictatorship was installed.
1957 Castillo Armas was assassinated.
1958 Miguel Ramon Ydígoras Fentes took control and his autocratic rule led to a failed military revolt by junior officers in 1960. Most leaders of armed insurrection for the next 36 years of civil war were part of this group.
1963 Enrique Peralta became president following a coup and civilian administration was completely assumed by the military whose power and influence increased. Widespread repression of opposition groups increased as leaders were targeted for assassination or 'disappearance'. Insurgents countered with sabotage and violent guerrilla tactics.
1966 Civilian rule was restored when César Méndez of the Revolucionario Partido (PR) (Revolutionary Party) was elected president. Nevertheless, the military launched a major counterinsurgency campaign, which crippled the guerrilla movement in the countryside.
1970 Carlos Arena, backed by the military and the US, was elected president.
1976 An earthquake struck just south-west of Guatemala City killing around 27,000 people and leaving one million citizens homeless.
1978–1984 Over 90 per cent of all atrocities occurred during this time as government forces and insurgents battled. The most frequent victims were the ethnic Mayan population who were attacked by both sides and accused of being collaborators or sympathisers of the opposition.
1980 Thirty seven people died in the Spanish Embassy siege in Guatemala City, when Mayan peasant farmers were protesting about military repression.
1981 Left-wing insurgent groups unified to become Unidad Revolucionaria Nacional Guatemalteca (URNG) (National Guatemalan Revolutionary Unit).
1982 General Efraín Ríos Montt seized power in a military coup. His dictatorship was in power during the bloodiest period of the civil war.
1983 Montt was ousted by General Mejía Victores, who declared an amnesty on guerrillas.
1985 Marco Vinicio Cerezo was elected president and Democracia Cristiana Guatemalteco (DCG) (Guatemalan Christian Democracy) won legislative elections.
1989 An attempt to overthrow Cerezo failed.
1991 Jorge Serrano Elias was elected president.
1993 Serrano's attempt to impose an authoritarian regime led to mass demonstrations and he was forced to resign. Ramiro de Leon Carpio was elected president by the legislature.
1994 Peace talks began between the government and the URNG.
1995 The URNG declared a cease-fire. The UN and the US criticised the government for widespread human rights violations and the deaths of more than 200,000 civilians during the civil war.
1996 After a civil war lasting 36 years, a peace treaty was signed. Alvaro Arzú and his Partido de Avanzada Nacional (PAN) (National Advancement Party) won the subsequent presidential and National Congress elections. Arzú began a purge on senior military officers implicated in human rights violations.
1999 A UN-sponsored investigation found that the security forces were responsible for 93 per cent of all human rights atrocities committed during the civil war and that the military had overseen 626 massacres in Mayan villages. Alfonso Portillo of the Frente Republicano Guatemalteco (FRG) (Guatemalan Republican Front) was elected president.
2000 Portillo was sworn in as president.
2001 A foreign exchange law allowed the free circulation of US dollars; citizens and companies were allowed to hold US dollar bank deposits without prior authorisation. The government paid US$1.8 million in compensation to the families of 226 victims killed by soldiers and death squads in the village of Las Dos Erres in 1982.
2003 The ruling FRG was defeated by the Gran Alianza Nacional (GANA) (Grand National Alliance) in the parliamentary elections. Óscar Berger Perdomo (GANA) became president.
2004 Former dictator, Ríos Montt, was put under house arrest on charges of inciting a riot, and genocide relating to atrocities carried out when he was in power. The State accepted responsibility for more human rights violations during the civil war; US$3.5 million was paid out to victims.
2005 The government signed the Central American Free Trade Agreement (Cafta) with the US and five other Central American and Caribbean states, amid anti-US demonstrations. Hurricane Stan hit the region causing 699 deaths; over 35,000 homes were destroyed and there were numerous landslides and extensive flooding. In the US, Guatemala's top anti-drugs investigator was arrested on drug trafficking charges.
2006 Manslaughter charges against Ríos Montt were dropped.
2007 In parliamentary elections the opposition Unidad Nacional de la Esperanza (UNE) (National Union of Hope) won 48 seats out of 158. Álvaro Colom (UNE) won the presidential election.
2008 Former president Alfonso Portillo Cabrera was extradited from Mexico to face fraud charges over the loss of US$15 million of government money. Premium Guatemalan coffee reached a record US$80.20 per pound, the highest price offered in the world.
2009 The IMF approved a US$935 million credit line to Guatemala as a stand-by arrangement providing a liquidity cushion during the global economic crisis.
2010 Tropical storm Agatha, killed more than 90 people and around 4,000 people were forced to evacuate their homes, while a 30m-diametre, 60m deep sinkhole swallowed a three-storey building in Guatemala City. Many bridges were swept away and mudslides closed the traffic along 100km stretch of the Pan-American Highway. Further heavy rains caused by Hurricane Frank, resulted in mudslides in the highlands that killed dozens and the Pan-American Highway was again cut, in over 30 places. Work carried out after the May storm was mostly undone. At the end of a year of natural disasters that caused an estimated US$1.55 billion in damages and a loss of 4.1 per cent of GDP, the World Bank approved a US$100 million loan to provide emergency assistance and preserve health and education services in Guatemala.
2011 In March US Secretary General Ban Ki-moon voiced anxiety at the deterioration in personal security in Guatemala, with one of the World's highest rates of gun-crime and deaths, as well as reported human rights abuses. In March, President Colom's wife, Sandra Torres de Colom, confirmed that she would be divorcing her husband so she could stand for election to succeed him. The constitution bans close relatives of the president from standing. In April a court put the divorce on hold after complaints it was aimed at bypassing the constitution; nevertheless a family court granted the divorce. In June the Organisation of American States (OAS) called on member-states to co-operate to improve citizen security and endorse measures to stop drugs, arms and people trafficking. In August, the Constitutional Court ruled that Sandra Torres was ineligible to run as president, despite her divorce from Álvaro Colom, which they regarded as a political ploy. Ten candidates took part in the first round of presidential elections held on 11 September in which Otto Pérez Molina (PP) won 31.1 per cent of the vote, Manuel Baldizón (Lider) 22.68 per cent and Eduardo Suger (CREO) 16.62 per cent; as none won more than 50 per cent of the vote a runoff

was held on 6 November in which Molina won 53.74 per cent and Baldizón 46.26 per cent.
2012 President Otto Pérez Molina (PP) took office 14 January. On 27 January former dictator Efraín Ríos Montt was charged with genocide and crimes against humanity for the deaths of over 1,700 indigenous people in 1982–83. On 23 October, parliament approved a US$8.5 billion, 2013 budget that included a 23 per cent increase in defence spending. The government plans to open five new military bases, to train 2,500 more soldiers (before 2016) to deal with drug cartels and street gangs.
2013 General Rios Montt was convicted on 10 May of ordering the deaths of 1,771 people of the Ixil Maya ethnic group during his time in office in 1982–83. However the conviction was overturned by Guatemala's top court on 21 May. On 5 November the trial of General Montt, who is 87, was rescheduled for January 2015, after it was said all judges were busy in 2014.
2014 An earthquake of magnitude 6.5 at a depth of 95km struck off the west coast of Guatemala on 6 September.
2015 On 1 September Congress voted to strip Mr Molina of his immunity from prosecution. Two days later he resigned the presidency and was arrested, appearing in court where a judge ordered his continued detention while allegations that he was the mastermind of a customs corruption scheme called *La Linea* (The Line) were investigated. Mr Molina denies the charges. Alejandro Maldonado Aguirre became Acting President on 3 September. A general election was hels on 6 September. The Libertad Democrática Renovada (LIDER) (Renewed Democratic Liberty) (won 44 seats (out of 158), followed by Unidad Nacional de la Esperanza (UNE) (National Unity of Hope) 36, Todos 18, Partido Patriota (PP) (Patriotic Party) 17, Frente de Convergencia Nacional (FCN-Nación) (National Convergence Front 11; another eight parties won under 10 seats each. Turnout was 71.13 per cent. The first found of the presidential election was also held on 6 September. The result had comedian Jimmy Morales in the lead with 23.85 per cent of the vote, followed by Sandra Torres (19.76 per cent) and Manuel Antonio Baldizón Méndez (19.64 per cent). No other candidate won more than 10 per cent and since no candidate won the necessary 50 per cent a second round was held on 25 September when Jimmy Morales won with 67.44 to Ms Torres' 32.56.

Political structure

In addition to their unicameral national parliaments, El Salvador, Guatemala, Honduras, Nicaragua, Panama and Dominican Republic also return directly-elected deputies to the supranational Central American Parliament.

Constitution

The constitution, which came into effect in 1986 (replacing the 1966 constitution suspended in 1982), created a representative system of government in which power is exercised equally by the legislative, executive and judicial arms.
Guatemala is divided into 22 provinces, subdivided into municipalities.

Form of state

Presidential democratic republic

The executive

Executive power is held by the president, directly elected by absolute majority popular vote in two rounds if required for four years, assisted by a vice president and an appointed cabinet.

National legislature

The unicameral Congreso de la República (Congress of the Republic), has 158 directly elected deputies, of which 31 are elected from a nationwide list by proportional representation vote and the remainder are directly elected in multi-seat constituencies within each of the country's 22 departments by simple majority vote. All deputies serve for four-year terms. No political party can win outright power and must form a coalition.
Congress is responsible for all legislative matters, including approving the budget and decreeing taxes by means of an absolute majority. All laws involving constitutional change or any international treaty or agreement affecting the sovereignty of the state must secure a two-thirds majority.

Legal system

Guatemala has a civil law system with judicial review of legislative acts. The Supreme Court serves as the highest appeal court in the country; there is also a separate Court of Constitutionality and a Supreme Electoral Tribunal. The country does not accept the compulsory jurisdiction of the International Court of Justice.

Last elections

6 Sept 2015: general election for parliament and first round presidential. 25 Oct 2015: second round presidential eletion.
Results: Presidential (2015) (first round): Jimmy Morales (FCN-Nación) won 23.9 per cent of the vote, Sandra Torres (UNE) 19.8 per cent, Manuel Baldizón (LIDER) 19.7 per cent, Alejandro Giammattei (Fuerza) 6.5 per cent, Zury Ríos (Vision with Values) 5.9 per cent, Lizardo Sosa (Todos) 5.3 per cent; the remaining eight presidential candidates failed to win any more than five per cent of the vote. Turnout was 71.2 per cent. (second round) Jimmy Morales (FCN-Nación) 67.4 per cent, Sandra Torres (UNE) 32.56 per cent.
Parliamentary (2015): Libertad Democrática Renovada (LIDER) (Renewed Democratic Liberty) won 19.1 per cent of the vote (44 seats, out of 158), Unidad Nacional de la Esperanza (UNE) (National Unity of Hope) 14.8 per cent (36), Todos 9.8 per cent (18), Partido Patriota (PP) (Patriotic Party) 9.4 per cent (17), Frente de Convergencia Nacional (FCN-Nación) (National Convergence Front) 8.8 per cent (11); the remaining twelve parties won less than seven per cent of the vote and failed to gain more than seven seats. Turnout was 71.1 per cent.

Next elections

2020 (presidential and parliamentary)

Political parties

Ruling party

Libertad Democrática Renovada (LIDER) (Renewed Democratic Liberty) (won most seats (44, out of 158) in 6 Sep 2015 election)

Main opposition party

Not applicable presently.

Population

15.87 million (2014)*
Last census: November 2002: 11,237,196
Population density: 101.8 inhabitants per square km. Urban population 49 per cent (2010 Unicef).
Annual growth rate: 2.4 per cent, 1990–2010 (Unicef).

Internally Displaced Persons (IDP)

250,000 (UNHCR 2004)

Ethnic make-up

A high proportion of the population belongs to 22 Mayan ethno-linguistic groups, conserving the cultural heritage of their ancestors. Their numbers are disputed but they constitute at least 45 per cent of the population and possibly as much as 60 per cent. Many of the inhabitants of the Caribbean coast are of Afro-Caribbean origin.

Religions

The constitution guarantees freedom of worship. Catholicism is the most widespread religion, although large numbers of conversions have been made in recent years by Protestant churches, including mainstream non-conformists and US-based fundamentalist sects. Protestant leaders claim to have converted some 30 per cent of the population and are playing an increasingly active role in the country's politics. Some indigenous communities hold services combining Catholicism with pre-Columbian rites.

Education

Elementary education is free and lasts for six years and secondary education, which begins at age 13, for a further six years, divided into two three-year courses. There are five universities, three of which are private, located in Guatemala City and Quetzaltenango, the country's second-largest city.

Literacy rate: 70 per cent adult rate; 80 per cent youth rate (15–24) (Unesco 2005).

Compulsory years: Seven to 14 in urban areas only.

Enrolment rate: 90 per cent total primary enrolment of the relevant age group; 26 per cent total enrolment in secondary schools, of the relevant age group; enrolment in tertiary education is less than 10 per cent.

Pupils per teacher: 35 in primary schools.

Health

Healthcare remains inadequate with 80 per cent of spending and hospitals confined in the two major cities.

HIV/Aids

HIV prevalence: 1.1 per cent aged 15–49 in 2003 (World Bank)

Life expectancy: 68 years, 2004 (WHO 2006)

Fertility rate/Maternal mortality rate: 4.0 births per woman, 2010 (Unicef); maternal mortality 2.9 per 1,000 live births (World Bank).

Child (under 5 years) mortality rate (per 1,000): 32 per 1,000 live births (WHO 2012); 44 per cent of children aged under five are malnourished (World Bank).

Welfare

Social security, which is compulsory, covers health and hospital care as well as industrial accidents, disability and widowhood for registered workers. All employers with five or more workers are required by law to register with the State Institute of Social Security.

Main cities

Guatemala City (capital, estimated population 1.1million in 2012), Villa Nueva (846,473), Mixco (769,040), Chinautla (178,428), Quezaltenango (167,200), Escuintla (166,830), Chimaltenango (159,839).

Languages spoken

Approximately 22 Indian languages are widely spoken throughout the highlands, including Quiché, Cakchiquel, Mam and Kekchi. About 40 per cent of all Guatemalan children enter school with no knowledge of Spanish.

English is spoken in almost all tourist areas.

Official language/s

Spanish

Media

The constitution guarantees freedom of the press. Private, independently owned media outlets dominate the market.

Press

Most of Guatemala's media is privately owned. Journalists have reported incidents of intimidation particularly following articles exposing corruption.

Dailies: In Spanish, national newspapers include *Prensa Libre* (www.prensalibre.com), *La Hora* (www.lahora.com.gt) and *El Periodico* and are broadsheets with articles on business and finance, while *Siglo Veintiuno* (www.sigloxxi.com) is a tabloid style newspaper.

Regional newspapers, in Spanish, include *El Metropolitano* (www.elmetropolitano.net) with local editions in five cities. Other local publications such as *Diario de Centroamérica* (www.dca.gob.gt), *Nuestro Diario* (www.nuestrodiario.com) and *El Qeutzalteco* (www.elquetzalteco.com.gt) are tabloid style newspapers.

In English, the Guatemala Times (www.guatemala-times.com) is an online publication.

Broadcasting

The state-owned Radiodifusión y Televisión Nacional operates public broadcasting.

Radio: The state-owned Radio TGW (www.radiotgw.gob.gt) operates a network of five radio stations, providing news, educational and cultural programmes, however it has low audience numbers. It competes with dozens of commercial stations, located regionally and locally and many of them broadcasting at least part of the time in indigenous languages. In Spanish, news and information stations include Emiroras Unidas (http://radio.emisorasunidas.com), a national network, Radio Sonora (www.sonora.com.gt) and Radio Punto (www.radiopunto.com).

Christian churches operate several radio stations which broadcast from rural areas, including Radio Cultural TGN (www.radiocultural.com), broadcasting in several languages.

Television: There is no public TV. The majority of commercial TV is owned by a few elites. TV channels broadcasting on terrestrial and satellite include Canal 3 (www.canal3.com.gt), Televisiete (www.canal7.com.gt), Vea Canal (www.veacanal.com), Guatevision (www.guatevision.com), TeleOnce, Trecevision and Latitud.

The Comtech cable TV channel operates Claro TV (www.comtech.net.gt) in Guatemala City.

Other news agencies: Inforpress (in Spanish and English): www.inforpressca.com

Prensa Latina (from Cuba, in six languages): www.prensa-latina.com.ar

Economy

The 1996 peace accords which ended 36 years of civil war removed a major obstacle to foreign investment, and since then Guatemala has pursued important reforms and macroeconomic stabilisation. Despite joining the Dominican Republic-Central America Free Trade Agreement and adopting progressive reforms, concerns over security, the lack of skilled workers, and poor infrastructure continue to hamper foreign direct investment (FDI). FDI was US$1.4 billion in 2014, a slight increase from US$1.3 billion in 2013.

The distribution of income remains highly unequal with the richest 20 per cent of the population accounting for more than 51 per cent of Guatemala's overall consumption. More than half of the population is below the poverty line, and 13 per cent of the population lives in extreme poverty. 73 per cent of the indigenous population (which accounts for 40 per cent overall) lives in poverty and 22 per cent live in extreme poverty. Guatemala is the top remittance recipient in Central America as a result of Guatemala's large expatriate community in the United States. Remittances amounted to US$5.4 billion in 2014 (9 per cent of GDP), an 8.6 per cent increase on the US$5.1 billion received in 2013. In November 2014, along with his counterparts from El Salvador and Honduras, President Perez Molina announced the Plan of the Alliance for Prosperity in the Northern Triangle. The Plan seeks to address the challenges facing the three Northern Triangle countries (El Salvador, Guatemala and Honduras), including steps the government will take to stimulate economic growth, increase transparency and fiscal responsibility, reduce violence, modernise the justice system, improve infrastructure, and promote educational opportunities over the next several years.

The economy is driven by the service sector, which made up 63 per cent of GDP in 2014; agriculture contributed 13.3 per cent and industry 24 per cent. Cash crops for export include coffee, bananas and sugar which are typically produced on commercial farms. However, the majority of farming is subsistence as multinational agri-businesses occupy much of the prime agricultural land. The remaining agricultural products are corn, beans, cardamom; cattle, sheep, pigs and chickens.

Industry is dominated by light manufacturing establishments, many of which are located in free-trade-zones, including textiles, general assembly of machinery and equipment, electronic equipment and electrical appliances, sugar, chemicals, clothing, furniture, petroleum, metals, rubber and tourism.

GDP growth was 3.3 per cent in 2008, falling to a low of 0.5 per cent in 2009. The economy did not fall into recession, despite the drop in international trade during the global economic crisis. The economy grew by 2.8 per cent in 2010 and higher still to an estimated 3.8 per cent in 2011. GDP growth fell to a moderate 3 per cent in 2012 before rebounding to 3.7 per cent in 2013 and 4 per cent in 2014.

Inequality and social outcomes in Guatemala are particularly stark. In 2014, the UN Human Development Index (HDI) ranked Guatemala 125 (out of 187), a fall of six places from 2011, for national development in health, education and income. According to the Central American Centre for Economic and Social Rights, 50 per cent of children under the age of five suffer from chronic malnutrition and one in three do not complete primary education. Since 2000, Guatemala's HDI progress has strengthened but has not matched the improvement of other countries in Latin American and Caribbean countries.

External trade

Guatemala is a member of the Central America Free Trade Agreement (DR-Cafta), which includes the Dominican Republic, Costa Rica, El Salvador and Honduras and the US. It is also a member of the Central American Common Market (CACM), along with Costa Rica, El Salvador, Honduras and Nicaragua.

Imports

Principal imports are fuels, machinery and transport equipment, construction materials, grain, fertilizers, electricity, mineral products, chemical products, plastic materials and products.

Main sources: US (40.3 per cent of total in 2014), Mexico (10.7 per cent), China (9.8 per cent) and El Salvador (4.6 per cent).

Exports

Principal exports are sugar, coffee, petroleum, apparel, bananas, fruits and vegetables, cardamom, manufacturing products, precious stones, metals and electricity.

Main destinations: US (36.1 per cent of total in 2014), El Salvador (11.8 per cent), Honduras (8.3 per cent), Nicaragua (4.8 per cent) and Mexico (4.1 per cent).

Agriculture

Farming

One of Guatemala's most important economic sectors is agriculture. The sector accounts for approximately 13 per cent of total GDP and employs 38 per cent of the country's total workforce. Despite the agricultural sector's high employment level, the number of jobs in the sector is falling due to increased mechanisation. Approximately 17 per cent of Guatemala's total land mass is cultivated arable land, 10 per cent pasture and 35 per cent forest.

Throughout the 1990s, Guatemala was relatively successful in establishing agricultural diversification, in an effort to buttress export earnings against commodity price fluctuations. It also sought to encourage the development of processing and packaging plants so as to upgrade the value of farm exports. Most of this took place in the highland areas where there is a good supply of land and labour. The production of fresh and frozen vegetables and ornamental plants and flowers has been particularly successful.

Production is mainly export-oriented, the major cash crops being coffee (the largest single earner of foreign exchange), sugar cane, bananas, cotton, cardamom (Guatemala accounts for over 90 per cent of world trade in cardamom) and tobacco. Vegetables such as mangetout, broccoli and asparagus, as well as a wide variety of fruits, are exported to the US and Europe.

Coffee has suffered from poor global commodity prices, although rising output has helped offset some of the losses.

Maize is the main food crop, although rice and wheat are also grown. Agricultural produce also includes cocoa, beans and flowers.

Foreign investment has so far been limited as a result of the absence of a domestic land market. Land is regarded as an indication of wealth and most owners leave it fallow if they choose not to plant. Land distribution is uneven, with just under 80 per cent of all farms under 3.5 hectares (ha) and 1 per cent over 2,500ha. Most foreign participation is concentrated on the non-traditional agricultural crops now emerging as major export earners.

Fishing

Guatemala's typical catch is approximately 14,300 tonnes (t), 9,800t freshwater fish inclusive.

Forestry

Approximately 35 per cent of Guatemala's total land mass is covered by forests. Some 20 per cent of Guatemala's land area is protected against industrial exploitation.

Softwood conifers account for 22 per cent with broad-leaved species, including valuable hardwoods such as mahogany, cedar and rosewood, accounting for the rest. Other forest products include rubber and chicle, an important chewing gum base, which is extracted in the forested Petén region.

The majority of timber production is consumed as domestic fuel, while a modest amount of sawnwood is exported. Much of the domestic demand for paper is met by imports.

Industry and manufacturing

Guatemala has a well developed industrial sector and the sector as a whole contributes approximately one fifth to GDP in a typical year. Industry contributes around 20 per cent to GDP (manufacturing contributes around 14 per cent) and employs 15 per cent of the workforce. Industry is primarily involved in activities related to agricultural inputs for major firms involved in food and drink processing, rubber, textiles, pottery, paper and pharmaceuticals. Other important industries are the assembly of electronic products, manufacture of furniture, canned goods, oil refining, cement, metals (especially steel), electrical goods assembly, plastics, chemicals, fertilisers and cigarettes.

Social and industrial unrest, high energy costs, shortages of imported materials and a slump in private and public investment have severely hampered industrial production. However, major government house building and infrastructural repair plans since the end of the civil war seem to have given a signficant boost to the construction industry, although construction as a proportion of GDP has shrunk in recent years.

Tourism

Guatemala has many archaeological sites, natural reserves and mountains, a stretch of the Pacific Ocean coast, as well as a much smaller stretch that opens to the Caribbean Sea to attract visitors. It is bordered by four countries that allow visitors overland access, as well as welcoming cruise ships and international flights. There are three sites in Guatemala included on Unesco's World Heritage List, including a historic town centre, ruins of the Mayan civilisation and Tikal National Park, home to jungle flora and fauna.

Travel and tourism accounted for around 8.8 per cent of GDP (US$5.2 billion) in 2014, and employed 8 per cent of the total workforce (489,000 jobs). In 2014 visitor revenue was US$1.7 billion, while domestic travel spending was US$2.2 billion.

Mining

The Alta Verapaz copper mine represents the main mining operation in Guatemala. In addition to copper, tungsten and antimony there are also exploitable reserves of marble and sulphur. Deposits of lead, zinc, gold and silver are also known to exist.

Lead is mined at Ballena and Penasco by Cía Minas de Oriente SA (Minersa).

Reserves are estimated at 2.2 million tonnes and contain 86 grammes per tonne of silver. Minas de Guatemala operates the Annabella and Los Lirios antimony and tungsten mines, producing about 1,800 tonnes per month of ore (6 per cent antimony, 0.5 per cent lead). The Oxec copper mine, worked by Transmetales in Alta Verapaz, has a capacity of 150,000 tonnes per year. The country's major mineral resource is laterite, with the El Estor deposits estimated at 50 million tonnes.

Hydrocarbons

Guatemala is one of only two oil-producing countries in Central America. Proven oil reserves were 83 million barrels in 2014, though actual reserves are thought to be as much as 1 billion barrels. Oil production was 14,100 barrels per day (bpd) in 2014. Most production occurs in the northern jungle areas, near to the border with Mexico. Guatemala exports approximately 5,000bpd of refined petroleum but it imports 71,000bpd, and therefore, it is a net importer of oil.

Guatemala does not produce or consume natural gas although it has estimated reserves of 3 billion cubic metres.

Energy

Guatemala has a total electricity generation capacity of approximately 2.7GW. The San José power station is Central America's largest coal-fired power plant. Net installed capacity of 739kW is supplied by hydropower.

Electricity consumption was 557kWh per capita in 2014, while electricity exports amounted to approximately 346 million kWh.

Financial markets

Stock exchange

BVN (Bolsa de Valores Naciónal) (Guatemala Stock Exchange)

Banking and insurance

The Guatemalan banking and financial services sector is organised under a central banking system, above which is the higher authority of the Monetary Board. There are 35 private commercial banks in Guatemala, but the banking market is dominated by a handful of large institutions. Some 40 per cent of total assets are in the hands of the five largest banks.

Guatemala is no longer on the OECD Financial Action Task Force (FATF) list of non-co-operative countries regarding money laundering.

Central bank

Banco de Guatemala

Time

GMT minus six hours

Geography

Guatemala has five distinct geographical zones. The first is the lowland Pacific strip running the length of the coastline, where the climate is tropical and summer rains are heavy. Most of the country's large sugar, banana and cotton farms are based here. Some 50km in from the coast the land rises to form the first of two mountain ranges running north-west to south-east. This range includes a string of volcanoes. A plateau formed by a series of volcanic basins at an average height of 1,500 metres above sea level forms the third zone; the capital, Guatemala City, and most of the country's population are to be found here.

Another mountain range with peaks of over 4,000 metres forms the basis of the north-west highlands, tapering down to the border with Honduras and El Salvador at its south-east extremity, where most of the country's more than four million indigenous people live. Beyond the mountains the land falls rapidly into a flat expanse of tropical forest. This area, which accounts for the northern part of the departments of Izabal, El Quiche, and Alta Verapaz and all the 36,400 square km of El Petén department, remains one of the region's last wildernesses.

Hemisphere

Northern

Climate

The climate varies with altitude but is essentially sub-tropical with little variation between the seasons. The hottest month is May when the average daily minimum and maximum temperatures are 16 degrees Celsius (C) and 29 degrees C. The coldest month is January when the temperature varies between 12 degrees C and 23 degrees C. The driest month is February and the wettest June, when there is an average of 274mm of rainfall.

Dress codes

Guatemalans are generally conservative in dress. Tropical lightweight suits are the accepted dress in business circles in the capital. Extremes of fashion should be avoided.

Entry requirements

Passports

Required by all.

Visa

Visas are not required by most nationals of the Americas, EU, Australasia, and a few Asian countries, for between 1–3 months.

A business visa, requiring additional information to the visitor's visa, must be applied for before arrival. The application should include a company letter as proof of business intentions.

Currency advice/regulations

No restrictions on import/export of foreign currency. There is free circulation of US dollars.

Health (for visitors)

Mandatory precautions

Cholera and yellow fever vaccination certificates are required from citizens of infected countries.

Advisable precautions

Malaria is prevalent in the low-lying areas outside the city, prophylaxes are recommended. Dengue fever is endemic, although there is no preventive medication, mosquito repellent and clothing covering as much skin as possible at dawn and dusk should help. Inoculations are recommended against typhoid, hepatitis A and B and typhoid.

Guatemalan hospitals are reluctant to give medical treatment unless a patient has medical insurance, so evidence of insurance cover should be carried at all times. State-funded hospitals are regarded as understaffed, ill-equipped and often unhygienic. Private clinics should be used where possible.

Bottled water should be used. Milk is often unpasteurised and should be boiled; avoid dairy products which are likely to have been made from unboiled milk. Only eat hot well-cooked meat and fish. Pork, salad and mayonnaise carry increased risk. Vegetables should be cooked and fruit peeled. There is a rabies risk.

Hotels

In the main cities there are a range of good hotels, the range can be limited in provincial towns. Most charge 20 per cent room tax; 10 per cent is added where service charges are not levied.

Public holidays (national)

Fixed dates

1 Jan (New Year), 1 May (Labour Day), 30 Jun (Army Day), 15 Aug (Assumption Day), 15 Sep (Independence Day), 20 Oct (Revolution Day), 1 Nov (All Saints' Day), 24 Dec (half-day), 25 Dec, 31 Dec (half-day).

Variable dates

Easter (Wed–Fri; Mar/Apr)

Working hours

Banking

Generally Mon–Fri: 0900–1500.

Business

Mon–Fri: 0800–1600. Private companies Mon–Fri: 0800–1200, 1400–1800.

Government

Mon–Fri: 0800–1600.

Shops

Shopping centres (Mon–Sun) 0900–2000.

Telecommunications

Mobile/cell phones

GSM 850/1900 services are available.

Electricity supply

110V AC, 60 cycles

Social customs/useful tips

Customs and social mores tend to mirror those of Catholic Europe or the more conservative southern states of the United States. Punctuality is not one of most Guatemalans' strongest points, although Western propensity for good time keeping is recognised in their phrase 'English time'.

Security

Security in the capital has become much more of a problem in recent years as street crime and house break-ins have risen. Armed mugging and gratuitous violence is common and most companies have armed guards and watchmen.

Getting there

Air

National airline: TACA – an amalgamation of the flag airlines of Guatemala (Aviateca), Costa Rica (Lacsa) and Nicaragua (Nica).

International airport/s: Guatemala City-Aurora (GUA), 6km from the city; duty-free shop, bank, bar, restaurant, bank, hotel reservations, post office, shops, car hire.

Airport tax: Departures tax US$30; not applicable to 24 hour transit passengers.

Surface

Road: The Pan-American Highway runs through the country from Mexico to El Salvador, stretching 511km. There are other roads from El Salvador, Honduras and Mexico and there is a route via Melchor de Mencos from Belize. Plans for any journey should be made in the light of prevailing road conditions.

Rail: It is possible to use scheduled train services but some of these are often subject to suspension.

Main port/s: Champerico, Puerto Barrios, San José, Santo Tomás de Castilla and the Quetzal Port.

Getting about

National transport

Air: TACA operates a domestic service to major centres.

Road: Total network is 13,238km, only 26 per cent of which is paved; using unpaved roads can be difficult. Paved roads are of fair quality.

Buses: Bus services connect major towns.

City transport

Taxis: There is a good taxi service in Guatemala City. Fares are generally negotiated but there are set rates for journeys from the airport to certain destinations. Tipping (5–10 per cent) is discretionary.

Buses, trams & metro: Numerous services within Guatemala City – said to be (outside usual rush hours) less crowded than some cities.

Car hire

Any valid licence is usually acceptable. Many of the international rental agencies have offices both at La Aurora airport and in Guatemala City centre.

BUSINESS DIRECTORY

The addresses listed below are a selection only. While World of Information makes every endeavour to check these addresses, we cannot guarantee that changes have not been made, especially to telephone numbers and area codes. We would welcome any corrections.

Telephone area codes

The international direct dialling code (IDD) for Guatemala is +502, followed by subscriber's number. Telephones and faxes have been eight digits since Septermber 2004.

Chambers of Commerce

American Chamber of Commerce in Guatemala, Avenida las Americas 18-81, Zona 14, 01014 Guatemala City (tel: 2363-1774; fax: 2367-3414; e-mail: director@amchamguate.com).

Guatemala Chamber of Commerce, 10a Calle 3-80, Zona 1, 01001 Guatemala City (tel: 2253-5353; fax: 2220-9393; e-mail: info@camaradecomercio.org.gt).

Banking

Banco Nacional de Desarrollo Agrícola (BANDESA), 9 Calle 9-47, Zona 1, 01001.

Banco Nacional de la Vivienda (BANVI), 6 Ave 1-22, Zona 4, 01004.

Credito Hipotecario Nacional, 7 Ave 22-77, Zona 1, 01001.

Banco de Occidente, 7 Ave 11-15, Zona 1, 01001.

Banco del Agro, 9 Calle 5-39, Zona 1, 01001 (tel: 2251-4026; fax: 2230-0322).

Banco del Café SA, Ave La Reforma 9-00, Zona 9, 01009.

Banco del Quetzal SA, Plaza El Robel, 7 Ave 6-26, Zona 9, 01009.

Banco Granai & Townson SA, 7 Ave 1-86, Zona 4, 1004.

Banco Industrial SA, 7 Ave 5-10, Zona 4, 01004.

Citibank, Ave La Reforma 15-45, Zona 10, 01010.

Lloyds Bank International, 6 Ave 9-51, Zona 9, 01009.

Central bank

Banco de Guatemala, 7 Avenida 22-01, Zona 1, PO Box 365, 01001 Guatemala City (tel: 2230-6222; fax: 2253-4035; email: webmaster@banguat.gob.gt).

Stock exchange

BVN (Bolsa de Valores Naciónal) (Guatemala Stock Exchange), www.bvnsa.com.gt

Travel information

Asociación Guatemalteca de Agentes de Viajes (AGAV) (Guatemalan Association of Travel Agents), 6a Avenida 8-41, Zona 9, Apdo 2735, Guatemala City.

TACA, Avenida Hincapié 12-22, Aeropuerto La Aurora, Zona 13, Guatemala City (internet (including email) www.taca.com).

National tourist organisation offices

Instituto Guatemalteco de Turismo (INGUAT) (Guatemalan Tourism Institute), 7 Avenida 1-17, Zona 4, Centro Cívico 01004, Guatemala City (tel: 2331-1333; fax: 2331-8893; e-mail: inguat@guate.net; internet: www.visitguatemala.com).

Ministries

Ministry of Agriculture, Livestock and Food, Avenida Reforma 4-47, Zona 10, Guatemala City.

Ministry of Communications, Transport and Public Works, Avenida Reforma 4-47, Zona 10, Guatemala City (tel: 2362-6051; fax: 2362-6059).

Ministry of Culture and Sport, 5 Calle 4-33, Zona 1, Plaza Rabi, Guatemala City.

Ministry of Defence, Avenida Reforma 4-47, Zona 10, Guatemala City (tel: 2360-9907; fax: 2360-9909).

Ministry of Economy, 8 Avenida 10-43, Zona 1, Guatemala City (tel: 2238-3331/2/3; fax: 2251-5055).

Ministry of Education, Avenida Reforma 4-47, Zona 10, Guatemala City.

Ministry of Employment and Social Security, 14 Calle 5-49, Zona 1, Edificio Nasa, Guatemala City (tel: 2230-5592/4; fax: 2251-3559).

Ministry of Energy and Mines, Diagonal 17, 29-78, Zona 11, Guatemala City (tel: 2477-0382, 2476-0680).

Ministry of Finance, Entre 8 Avenida y 21 calle, Zona 1, Centro Cívico, Guatemala City (tel: 2230-5180, 2230-5202; fax: 2251-6514).

Ministry of Foreign Affairs, Avenida Reforma 4-47, Zona 10, Guatemala City.

Ministry of Health and Social Assistance, Avenida Reforma 4-47, Zona 10, Guatemala City (tel: 2232-4509).

Ministry of the Interior, Avenida Reforma 4-47, Zona 10, Guatemala City.

Other useful addresses

Agroindustrias de Exportación, 14 Calle 7-46, Zona 10, Guatemala City

Asociación de Gerentes de Guatemala, 10a Calle 3-17, Zona 10, Edificio Aseguradora General, Nivel 70, Apartado Postal 2373, Guatemala City, 01010.

Bolsa Agrícola Nacional, 4a Calle 6-55, Zona 9, Guatemala City.

Bolsa de Valores Global, Av La Reforma 9-76, Zona 9, Edificio SCI Centre, Nivel 70, Guatemala City, 01009.

Bolsa de Valores Nacional, SA, 7a Av 5-10, Zona 4, Centro Financiero, Torre II, Nivel 20, Guatemala City, 01004.

British Embassy, Edificio Torre Internacional, Nivel 11, 16 Calle 0-55, Zona 10, Guatemala City (tel: 2367-5425–9; fax: 2367-5430; email: embassy@intelnett.com).

Centro de Investigaciones Económicas Nacionales (CIEN), 5 Av 15-45, Zona 10, Centro Empresarial, Torre 1, Of 302, Apartado Postal 260-C, Guatemala City.

Centro Nacional de Promoción de las Exportaciones, 6A Avenida Torre Profesional, Zona 14, Apdo 1237, Guatemala City.

Comité Co-ordinador de Asociaciones Agrícolas, Comerciales, Industriales y Financieras (CACIF), Ruta 6 9-21, Zona 4, Nivel 90, Guatemala City.

Coperex (international marketing fair), 8 Calle 2-33, Zona 9, Parque de la Industria, Guatemala City.

Dirección General de Radiodifusión y Televisión Nacional, 5a Avenida Zona 1, Guatemala City.

Empresa Eléctrica de Guatemala (EEGSA), 8a Calle y 6a Avenida Esquina, Zona 1, Guatemala City.

Empresa Municipal de Agua (Empagua), 7a Avenida 1-20, Zona 4, Edificio Torre Café, Nivel 16, Guatemala City.

Fundación para el Desarrollo de Guatemala (FUNDESA), Parque Gerencial Las Margaritas, Diagonal 6, 10-65, Zona 10, Of 402, Guatemala City.

Guatemala–US Trade Association (GUSTA), 299 Alhambra Circle, Suite 207, Coral Gables, Florida 33134, USA (tel: (+1-305) 443-0343; fax: (+1-305) 433-0699).

Guatemalan Embassy (USA), 2220 R Street, NW, Washington DC 20008 (tel: (+1-202) 745-4952; fax: (+1-202) 745-1908; e-mail: info@guatemala-embassy.org).

Inforpress Centroamericana, 9a Calle A 3-56, Guatemala City 01001.

Instituto Centroamericano de Investigación y Tecnología Industrial (ICAITI), Avenida La Reforma 4-47, Zona 10, Guatemala City.

Instituto Nacional de Electrificación (INDE), 7a Avenida 2-29, Zona 9, Guatemala City.

International Investment Securities Corporation, Edificio Galerías Reforma 8-60, Zona 9, Torre 1, Nivel 90, Guatemala City.

Telgua (Empresa de Telecomunicaciones de Guatemala), 5 Calle Avenida Reforma, Zona 9, Guatemala City (tel: 2331-8999/6599, 2230-1050).

United States Department of Commerce, Guatemala Desk, Department of Commerce H3025, Washington DC 20230, USA (tel: (+1-202) 377-2627; fax: (+1-202) 377-3718).

US Embassy, Avenida La Reforma 7-01, Zona 10, Guatemala City.

Inforpress (in Spanish and English): www.inforpressca.com

Prensa Latina (from Cuba, in six languages): www.prensa-latina.com.ar

Internet sites

Guatemalan portals: http://mi-guatemala.tripod.com

www.elcafecito.com/Zonas_geograficas/Paises/Guatemala

Business information: www.tradepoint.org.gt

Tourist office for Central American: http://centralamerica-tourism.com/

Guinea

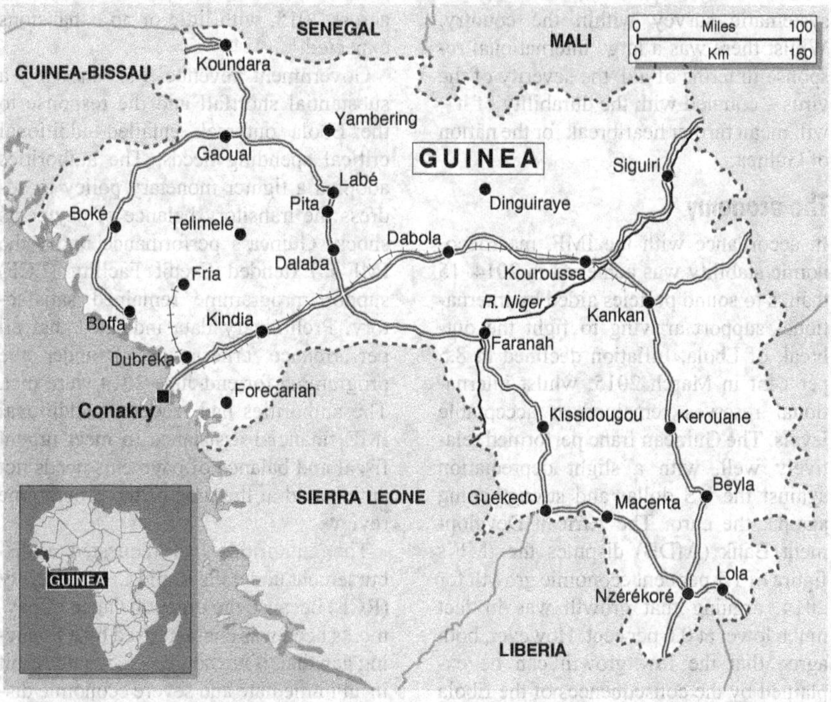

Guinea has an abundance of mineral wealth, making it potentially one of Africa's richest nations. Despite this, the residents of the country rank among the poorest, with poverty and malnutrition rates at alarming levels. This is especially true for rural residents, as vast socio-economic issues have caused a variety of issues for the people as well as a rank of 179 out of 187 countries in the United Nations Development programme (UNDP) Human Development Index.

Adding to this, Guinea has often been left affected by socio-political instabilities in neighbouring countries. Conflicts in Liberia, Sierra Leone and Cote d'Ivoire saw the arrival of around 700,000 refugees in the 1990s. Natural resources, relations and wealth have suffered as a result. This is despite most of the refugees returning to their countries of origin. The country is vulnerable to inter-ethnic violence, with clashes peaking in Nzérékoré, inJuly 2013. At least 58 people were killed in 3 days of violence between the ethnic Kpelle, who are predominantly Christian or animist, and ethnic Koninke, who are generally Muslim. The violence eventually ended after the Guinea military imposed a curfew and President Alpha Condé made a televised appeal for calm.

Condé became Guinea's first democratically elected President in 2010 after a lifetime battle against despotic and military regimes, which saw him sent into exile and prison. His political career began in the 1950s when he campaigned, to populist opinion, for independence from France. Independence was eventually achieved in 1958.

Condé took over from a military Junta, which followed the death of former President Lasansa Conte in 2008. However, the vote kindled a new form of ethnic tensions. Condé's origins lie in the Malinke ethic group, which comprise around 35 per cent of the population. His defeated opposition, Cellou Dalein Diallo, is a member of the Peul ethnic group, to which 40 per cent of Guineans belong. Diallo accused Condé of sidelining his constituents; the tensions eventually climaxed with an unsuccessful attack on the President's residence in 2011.

KEY FACTS

Official name: République de Guinée (Republic of Guinea)

Head of State: President Alpha Condé (RPG) (from 21 Dec 2010)

Head of government: Prime Minister Mohamed Said Fofana (from 24 Dec 2010)

Ruling party: A transitional council has served as a parliament since 2010, pending postponed elections. In the meantime, the President's party, the Rassemblement du Peuple Guinéen (RPG) (People's Party of Guinea) is the main party.

Area: 245,857 square km

Population: 11.40 million (2014)*

Capital: Conakry

Official language: French

Currency: Guinean franc (Gf)

Exchange rate: Gf7,699.00 per US$ (Sep 2015)

GDP per capita: US$573 (2014)*

GDP real growth: 0.40% (2014)*

GDP: US$6.53 billion (2014)*

Inflation: 9.72% (2014)

Balance of trade: -US$250.30 million (2013)

Annual FDI: US$896.45 million (2011)

* estimated figure

Ebola outbreak

In 2014, Guinea was devastated by an outbreak of Ebola, which claimed many lives and inflicted a large socio-economic toll. The International Monetary Fund (IMF) reported in its 2015 assessment that economic growth had slowed to 1.1 per cent for 2014, despite strong performances in the agricultural sector. As of 14 July 2015, 2,444 people had lost their lives to the Ebola virus. Guinea has the unfortunate claim of being the first West African country to represent an outbreak of the virus.

Following the recognition and emergence of Ebola, President Condé declared a national health emergency. Efforts to control the spread included forbidding Ebola patients from leaving their homes, border controls, travel restrictions and hospitalisations. He also banned the transporting of dead between towns. This particular outbreak was so striking due to the fact that it occurred in such a densely populated and mobile area within the Nzérékoré region. Border closures and flight bans were relatively ineffective, as Sierra Leone, Liberia and other countries reported incidences of Ebola.

The World Health Organization (WHO) reported in 2015 that the severity of the disease, compounded by fear within and beyond the affected countries, caused schools, markets, businesses, airline and shipping routes, and borders to close. Tourism shut down and a health crisis quickly snowballed into a humanitarian, social, economic and security crisis. Under the weight of the disease, Guinea's health system shut down. People stopped seeking help for deadlier diseases, such as malaria. A major paper from infectious disease experts reported in 2015 that as many as 74,000 fewer people were diagnosed and offered treatment than would have been expected. In the areas of Guinea hit worst by the Ebola outbreak, the numbers of people seeking treatment at outpatient clinics dropped by up to 42 per cent. Even more substantial, the numbers seeking care for suspected malaria were down by 69 per cent, according to a systematic survey within the country. Whilst there was a large international response in terms of aid, the severity of the virus – coupled with the durability of it – will mean further heartbreak for the nation of Guinea.

The economy

In accordance with the IMF, macroeconomic stability was achieved in 2014–15 thanks to sound policies aided by international support arriving to fight the outbreak of Ebola. Inflation declined to 8.5 per cent in March 2015, whilst international reserves remained at acceptable levels. The Guinean franc performed relatively well, with a slight depreciation against the US dollar and strengthening against the euro. The African Development Bank (AfDB) disputes the IMF's figure of 1.1 per cent economic growth for 2014, arguing that growth was in fact much lower at 0.6 per cent. However, both agree that the low growth can be explained by the consequences of the Ebola epidemic, delays in the implementation of structural reforms and electricity shortages. The AfDB also reports that growth should reach 0.9 per cent in 2015 and 4.3 per cent in 2016 thanks to public investments, increased mining and a better supply of electricity.

Executing the reforms designated by the IMF Extended Credit Facility (ECF) has proceeded successfully. The IMF reported that Guinea should be supported by a seventh disbursement of SDR18.36 million (US$26 million). However, it also reported that 2015 will prove to be another difficult year for the Guinean economy. The outbreak of Ebola is still not under control, and low commodity prices and political uncertainty only fuel further detriments. Growth is expected to be zero across 2015, with little or no expansions expected.

Government revenue was showing a substantial shortfall and the response to the Ebola outbreak entailed additional critical spending needs. The authorities adopted a tighter monetary policy to address the transitory balance of payments shock. Guinea's performance under the IMF's Extended Credit Facility (ECF) support programme remained satisfactory. Preliminary data indicated that all performance criteria (PCs) under the programme for end-June 2014 were met. The authorities had requested additional IMF financial assistance to meet urgent fiscal and balance of payments needs not anticipated at the time of the programme review.

The authorities had requested a disbursement under the Rapid Credit Facility (RCF) because the urgent balance of payments need was characterised by a financing gap that, if not addressed, would result in an immediate and severe economic disruption. Moreover, Guinea's balance of payments difficulties were caused not by a withdrawal of financial support by donors, but primarily by a sudden exogenous shock. Successful macroeconomic stabilisation and the start of reforms to boost the productive sector and the business climate have not been enough to register clear economic and social gains. Poverty still affects 55.2 per cent of the population more than half a century after independence (1958), and governance is still inadequate. Guinea ranks 164 out of 182 countries in Transparency International's *Corruption Perceptions Index*.

The government had adopted its third poverty reduction strategy paper (PRSP 3) in 2013 aimed at speeding up reforms in natural resource management and the productive sector (agriculture, energy and water supply, mining, investment and business) to remove economic transformation obstacles such as low farm labour productivity. The primary sector employs three-quarters of the workforce but only provides a fifth of GDP. A weak industrial sector, unsuitable infrastructure and poor energy supply limits the country's inclusion in global value chains (GVC). Low

KEY INDICATORS — Guinea

	Unit	2011	2012	2013	2014	**2015
Population	m	*10.59	*10.85	*11.13	*11.40	*11.69
Gross domestic product (GDP)	US$bn	5.20	5.63	*6.23	*6.53	*7.16
GDP per capita	US$	492	519	*560	*573	*612
GDP real growth	%	3.6	3.8	*2.3	*0.4	*-0.3
Inflation	%	21.5	15.2	12.0	9.7	*9.1
Exports (fob) (goods)	US$m	1,428.4	1,927.6	1,886.3	–	–
Imports (fob) (goods)	US$m	2,097.1	2,244.0	2,136.5	–	–
Balance of trade	US$m	-668.8	-316.4	-250.3	–	–
Current account	US$m	-1,049.0	-1,856.0	-1,336.0	*0.0	*-1,198.0
Exchange rate	per US$	6,940.00	7,237.50	7,030.00	7,025.00	–

* estimated figure ** forecast figure

capital productivity and a large, inefficient and unmotivated bureaucracy are other blocks. The end of the political transition and a new quest for social cohesion seem promising for the success of the PRSP 3.

Risk assessment

Politics	Poor
Economy	Fair
Regional stability	Fair

Muslims in Guinea

% of population	85
Sunni (% of Muslims)	88
Shi'a (% of Muslims)	1

COUNTRY PROFILE

From the thirteenth to fifteenth centuries Guinea was part of the Mali Empire which covered a large part of West Africa.

1450s The coastal region began to be settled by European traders.

1849 The French declared the area around Boké a protectorate. France's influence grew as it took over most of the rest of the country calling it Rivières du Sud (rivers of the south).

1891 French Guinea was formally constituted a colony, separate from Senegal.

1956 In a referendum Guinea voted to opt out of the French Community.

1958 Guinea became independent under the leadership of Sekou Touré. France severed all financial and technical ties.

1960s Despite having the backing of the Soviet Union, Guinea expelled the Soviet ambassador for interference in internal matters. Guinea began to improve its relations with the West although it remained a non-aligned, Marxist, one-party state.

1977 Private trade had been banned until demonstrations by traders in the market women's revolt led to a change in government policy.

1984 Touré died. In a bloodless coup, Colonel Lansana Conté became president and introduced IMF-backed austerity measures as well as a new currency, the Guinean franc, which replaced the syli. The Second Republic came into being on 3 April.

1990 A new constitution was approved and the Third Republic established.

1991 Union des Forces Démocratiques de Guinée (UFDG) (Union of Democratic Forces of Guinea) was formed.

1993 Conté won the presidency in multi-party elections, which were marred by killings and alleged fraud.

1995 The Parti de l'Unité et du Progrès (PUP) (Party of Unity and Progress), led by President Conté, won the multi-party legislative elections.

1996 As much as a quarter of the army mutinied due largely to low pay.

1998 President Lansana Conté was re-elected.

1999 Lamine Sidime (PUP) was appointed prime minister.

2001 The government accused neighbouring Liberia and rebels from Sierra Leone of aiding its army mutineers and attempting to destabilise the country. The number of displaced peoples, locally and from abroad, grew. There were rebel attacks along the borders between Guinea and Liberia, and Sierra Leone. A constitutional referendum permitted Conté to retain the presidency and run for a third and extended term (from five to seven years).

2002 The ruling PUP won parliamentary elections, delayed by two years allegedly due to the fighting between Guinea and Sierra Leone, and Liberia.

2003 Incumbent Lansana Conté won the presidential elections. The National Assembly voted unanimously for an amnesty for those convicted of political crimes, allowing them to stand for positions in national politics.

2004 Cellou Dalein Diallo was named prime minister.

2006 A general strike lasted five days. A power struggle among Conté's inner circle resulted in Prime Minister Diallo's sacking and the post of prime minister being dropped with its responsibilities given to other, expanded ministries. Fode Bangoura became minister of presidential affairs, with control of the military and the economy.

2007 An 18-day general strike disrupted the vital bauxite industry causing President Conté to dismiss his long-term supporter, Fode Bangoura, in an effort to placate the unions. Eugène Camara (a hard-line supporter of the president) was appointed to the vacant post of prime minister. Camara's appointment sparked riots. Martial law was imposed as another national general strike began and opposition and union leaders called on the president to resign. Lansana Kouyaté, a candidate acceptable to the opposition, was appointed prime minister, ending the general strike.

2008 President Conté sacked Prime Minister Kouyaté; Ahmed Tidiane Souaré became prime minister. Parliamentary elections were postponed by the electoral commission as voter registration was incomplete. President Conté died, of natural causes. The army launched a *coup d'état* and suspended the constitution. Coup leader Captain Moussa Dadis Camara seized the presidency, taking control through Le Conseil National de Défense et de Développement (CNDD) (the National Council for Defence and Development); he appointed Kabiné Komara as prime minister. Although the coup led to the African Union (AU) suspending Guinea from its organisation, the Economic Community of West African States (Ecowas) took a more positive attitude, trusting the transfer of power would allow 'democratic growth'.

2009 All mining operations, including Guinea's huge bauxite reserves and gold, diamond and ferrous metals, were suspended until 'renegotiations' of existing contracts had been agreed. Ousmane Conté, the son of the late president Lansana Conté, confessed to drug trafficking on state television. Hundreds of opposition protesters were wounded and dozens were shot dead or trampled to death attempting to flee from a sport stadium in the capital, Conakry, after security forces had opened fire and used teargas. Thousands were attending a rally in the stadium demanding a return to civilian rule and objecting to Captain Camara standing in forthcoming presidential elections. President Camara received medical attention in Morocco following an assassination attempt by an *aide-de-camp*.

2010 The Joint Ouagadougou Declaration confirmed Sékouba Konaté as interim president and the ruling military council appointed Jean-Marie Doré was as prime minister. Parliamentary elections, originally scheduled to take place in 2009 were, by agreement, postponed until after presidential elections took place. Presidential elections, postponed twice, were finally held; 24 candidates took part including four former prime ministers. Cellou Dalein Diallo (UFDG) won 39.72 per cent and his closest rival, Alpha Condé (Rassemblement du Peuple Guinéen (RPG) (People's Party of Guinea) (a party mainly based among the Mandinka population) 20.67 per cent. As no candidate won 50 per cent of the vote, a second round was scheduled, but was postponed as Condé challenged the results, claiming the election was 'flawed'. The Supreme Court confirmed the results of the first round. The runoff was postponed twice but when it was due to be held, a week of street violence between rival political supporters forced the elections to be postponed two more times. In the run-off, held on 7 November opposition leader Condé won 52.52 per cent of the vote and Diallo 47.48 per cent; turnout was 68.87 per cent. Diallo conceded defeat, after the Supreme Court rejected his complaint of election fraud.

2011 In February, President Condé declared the previous ruling military junta (2008–10) had bankrupted the country, so that the economy was in tatters, with no agricultural production and unpaid customs officials. President Conde's private residence was attacked in July. Up to 37 soldiers, some of who had been close to the members of the military junta who

had handed over power in 2010, were arrested the following day. The president was not injured.
2012 On 28 April, President Condé postponed indefinitely parliamentary elections due on 8 July. He cited 'technical problems' for the decision. The European Union warned that without democratic elections it would not release aid funds to Guinea. On 25 October 2012, the Paris Club of creditor nations agreed to cancel nearly all of Guinea's debt with it of up to US$356.3 million and also provide additional relief aid. This move followed the securing of US$2.1 billion in debt relief from the World Bank and IMF in September. On 29 October President Condé appointed a 25-person electoral body to organise preparations for parliamentary elections. The opposition cried foul, because their 10 nominees for inclusion in the body had been rejected by the president, contrary to the compromise deal agreed after the previous commission was deemed biased towards the RPG.
2013 Clashes in July between the Guerze and Konianke tribes in the south-east resulted in the deaths of some 54 persons. The government deployed troops to quell the disorder. The elections initially due in 2009 finally took place on 28 September. Initial results showed President Alpha Condé's ruling party, the RPG, had won 53 seats (out of 114) and the UFDG 37. The result was finally confirmed by the Supreme Court on 15 November.
2014 Guinea announced the first cases of Ebola virus in Conakry on 27 March; some 62 deaths had already been confirmed in rural areas. The sale and consumption of fruit bats, believed to be carriers of the virus, was banned by the government on 25 March. By July the total number of deaths across the region, including Sierra Leone, Liberia and Guinea, had reached over 670. Deaths from the Ebola virus in Guinea up to 29 October were said, by WHO, to be 1,018 (out of a total for West Africa of 4,951).
2015 Deaths in Guinea since the ebola outbreak started in 2014 were reported by the WHO to be 3,391 (out of a total of 11,079 'probable, confirmed or suspected deaths') by 9 May. Opposition leader, Cellou Dalein Diallo, called for an election re-run after the 11 October presidential election. There were claims of ballot box stuffing and that as many as 400 polling stations did not open.

Political structure

Constitution

The constitution was promulgated in 1990. In 2001 a constitutional amendment revised the length of the presidential term from five years to seven, with no legal limit to the number of terms a president may sit.

Form of state

Republic

The executive

Prior to the constitutional amendments, made in 2001, the president was elected for a five-year term, renewable only once. Following the changes, the mandate increased to a seven-year term with no legal limit as to the number of times that it could be renewed.
The prime minister and the Council of Ministers are appointed by the president.

National legislature

The unicameral Assemblée Nationale Populaire (People's National Assembly) was dissolved in December 2008; it will be re-convened following new elections, originally scheduled for 2009, but not held until 28 September 2013. Membership is 114, of which 76 are directly elected by proportional representation from party lists and 38 are elected in single seat constituencies by simple majority. All members serve five-year terms.

Legal system

The legal system is based on French civil law, customary law and decree.

Last elections

27 June and 7 November 2010 (presidential, first and second round); 28 September 2013 (parliamentary)
Results: Presidential: (first round) Cellou Dalein Diallo (UFDG) won 39.72 per cent, Alpha Condé (Rassemblement du Peuple Guinéen (RPG) (People's Party of Guinea)) 20.67 per cent, Sidya Touré (L'Union des Forces Républicaines (UFR) (Union of Republican Forces)) 15.6 per cent, Lansana Kouyaté (Parti de l'Espoir pour le Développement National (PEDN) (Hope Party for National Development)) 7.75 per cent, 20 other candidates each won less than 5 per cent. Second round: Alpha Condé won 52.52 per cent, Cellou Dalein Diallo 47.48 per cent. Turnout was 67.87 per cent.
Parliamentary: Rassemblement du Peuple Guinéen (RPG) (Rally of the Guinean People) won 53 seats (out of 114), Union des Forces Démocratiques de Guinée (UFDG) (Union of Democratic Forces of Guinea) 37, Union des Forces Républicaines (UFR) (Union of Republic Forces) 10, Partí de l'Espoir pur le National Développment National (PEDN) Party of Hope for National Development 2, Union pour le Progrès de la Guinée (UPG) (Union for the Progress of Guinea) 2. 10 other parties won one seat each, while a further 16 failed to gain any. Turnout was 64 per cent.

Next elections

11 October 2015 (presidential); 2018 (parliamentary)

Political parties

Political parties were legalised from 1992.

Ruling party

A transitional council has served as a parliament since 2010, pending postponed elections. In the meantime, the President's party, the Rassemblement du Peuple Guinéen (RPG) (People's Party of Guinea) is the main party.

Main opposition party

Union des Forces Démocratiques de Guinée (UFDG) (Union of Democratic Forces of Guinea)
About 47 per cent of the total population is under 15 years.

Population

10.85 million (2012)*
Last census: December 1996: 7,156,406 (provisional)
Population density: 28 inhabitants per square km. Urban population 35 per cent (2010 Unicef).
Annual growth rate: 2.7 per cent, 1990–2010 (Unicef).

Internally Displaced Persons (IDP)

100,000 (UNHCR 2004)

Ethnic make-up

Fulani (35 per cent), Malinke (30 per cent), Soussou (20 per cent).

Religions

Islam (85 per cent), a small number of Roman Catholics (8 per cent) and traditional beliefs (7 per cent).

Education

Guinea shows an upward trend in gross enrolment rate with increasing demand for teachers, school facilities, and other resources. The government has initiated the third phase of the project Basic Education for All (2001—2012) focussing on increased access, improved quality and efficiency through decentralisation processes.
Despite significant urban/rural and gender disparities in enrolment ratios, there is overall improvement. The crisis in teacher supply persists despite the World Bank and the government's intensive teacher-training programme (FIMG), which had planned recruitment of approximately 6,000 teachers for the entire 1998-2001 period.
Government expenditure on education is about 25–26 per cent of the total national budget.
Enrolment rate: 45.2 per cent net enrolment in primary; 11.9 per cent net enrolment in secondary schooling (World Bank).
In rural areas the enrolment rate for girls remains at only 26 per cent.
Pupils per teacher: 49 in primary schools.

Health

Improved water sources and sanitation facilities are available to 48 per cent and 58 per cent of the population, respectively.

HIV/Aids

HIV/Aids infection is currently concentrated in urban areas. Overall 2.8 per cent of pregnant women, 42 per cent of sex workers and 2.5 per cent of young adults (aged 15–24) are HIV positive. With governmental initiatives and local education, it is hoped to avert a potential pandemic if the rates in rural areas follow the urban trend.

HIV prevalence: 3.2 per cent aged 15–49 in 2003 (World Bank)

Life expectancy: 53 years, 2004 (WHO 2006)

Fertility rate/Maternal mortality rate: 5.2 births per woman, 2010 (Unicef); maternal mortality 620 per 100,000 live births (World Bank).

Child (under 5 years) mortality rate (per 1,000): 101 per 1,000 live births (WHO 2012); 23 per cent of children under aged five are malnourished (World Bank).

Head of population per physician: 0.11 physicians per 1,000 people, 2004 (WHO 2006)

Welfare

Guinea's social insurance system provides coverage for unemployed people, pensions, old-age benefits and survivor benefits (payable to widows, orphans and dependant relatives). Old age pensions are applicable to all those aged 55 and over. The system also provides sickness and maternity benefits as well as allowance for those families with children under the age of 17.

Main cities

Conakry (capital, estimated population 2.2 million in 2012), Guékédou (346,908), Nzérékoré (280,256), Kankan (240,635), Kindia (218,160), Boké (159,152).

Languages spoken

African languages are in daily use. English is seldom used.

Official language/s

French

Media

The government maintains a tight control of the media, with censorship of newspapers and controls to close private radio stations and interrupt international relays, while the military has a secure hold of the national broadcaster.

Press

The high cost of printing hampers and restricts independent publishing and disrupts regular print runs.

In French, the only business publication is the *Sud Economic* (http://sud-economie.press-guinee.com), other general news publications include *Le Diplomate* (www.nouvelle-tribune.com), *L'Enqueteur* (http://enqueteur.boubah.com), *La Nouvelle Tribune* (www.nouvelle-tribune.com), *L'Observateur* (www.observateur-guinee.com) and *Le Populaire* (http://lepopulaire.press-guinee.com). The *Sanakou* (http://sanakou.press-guinee.com) is published in Labé. The *Le Lynx* (www.mirinet.net.gn/lynx) is an independent satirical weekly.

Broadcasting

Radio: The state-owned, commercial Radiodiffusion-Télévision Guinéenne (RTG) operates Radio Guinenne in several languages including French, English, Arabic, Portuguese and a series of Radio Rurale in local languages. Private stations include Familia FM, Liberte FM, Radio Nostralie Guinea and Soleil FM. Radio France Internationale and BBC World Service can both be received.

Television: The state-owned, commercial Radiodiffusion-Télévision Guinéenne (RTG) has one channel.

National news agency: Agence Guineenne de Presse

Other news agencies: APA: www.apanews.net
Panapress: www.panapress.com

Economy

Guinea has the potential to become a wealthy country; an abundance of mineral wealth and fertile land gives the country a strong advantage and model for growth. Despite this, it remains one of the World's poorest and underdeveloped nations. A rank of 179 out of 187 countries in the United Nations Development programme (UNDP) Human Development Index is a very low score which is not reflective of the resources available within Guinea. The country possesses around 50 per cent of the world's bauxite reserves, also diamonds, iron ore, salt and uranium. The agriculture sector includes rice, coffee, bananas, palm oil, cattle, sheep and goats, fish and timber. There is a lot of room for improvements for hydroelectricity in Guinea, which was recorded at 32.2 per cent of total installed capacity in 2011. The mining of bauxite and iron ore along with other minerals accounts for around 80 per cent of foreign earnings.

In 2014, the emergence of Ebola inflicted losses to both the population and economy of Guinea. The International Monetary Fund (IMF) reported in 2015 that economic growth slowed to 1.1 per cent for the previous year. Unfortunately for the nation, Guinea was the first West African country to experience the outbreak of the virus, which has, as of July 2015, claimed 2,444 lives. Macroeconomic stability was achieved in 2014—15 despite the presence and emergence of Ebola.

Despite the potential for large-scale investment projects in agriculture, mining and hydroelectricity Guinea's political instability, corruption and poor resource management has limited foreign direct investment (FDI). FDI fell from US$386 million in 2007 to US$50 million in 2009, before growing, in 2010, to US$101 million, due largely to the state of the global economy. FDI was reported to be at US$148 million at the end of 2014.

In 2013, the UN Human Development Index (HDI) ranked Guinea 179 (out of 187) for national development in health, education and income. Since 2005, Guinea has progressed, but has not matched the improvement of other sub-Saharan countries. Headcount poverty is very high, with statistics from 2012 showing that 55.2 per cent of the population lived on less than the equivalent of US$1.25 per day.

Remittances from migrant workers amounted to US$60 million (1.3 per cent of GDP) in 2010 and was estimated to have reached US$61 million in 2011.

External trade

Guinea is a member of the Economic Community of West African States (Ecowas), which was setup to promote economic integration among members. It is a member of the Anglophone, West African Monetary Zone (WAMZ), which is due to introduce a common currency (although in January 2011 it had only just undertaken a feasibility study). WAMZ will eventually be merged with the Francophone-members' (Communauté financière d'Afrique (CFA) (Financial Community of Africa)) currency to produce a single currency (the eco) for the region. Achievement of this is now set for 2020.

Guinea has around 50 per cent of the world's reserves of bauxite and is the second largest supplier. Although diamond exports are rising, the balance of payments situation is precarious, especially since large volumes of concessionary assistance from the World Bank, IMF and foreign aid donors were suspended in 2009. Guinea's recent balance of payments difficulties were caused not by a withdrawal of financial support by donors, but primarily by a sudden exogenous shock mainly in the form of the Ebola virus.

Imports

Principal imports are petroleum products, metals, machinery, vehicles and parts, textiles, foodstuffs and grain.

Main sources: China (18.4 per cent of total in 2014), The Netherlands (6.6 per cent), India (4.3 per cent).

Exports

Exports are dominated by: bauxite and aluminium ore, gold, diamonds, coffee, fish, fresh fruit, vegetables and timber.

Main destinations: South Korea (27 per cent), India (20.9 per cent), Spain (6.6 per cent), Ireland (5.1 per cent) and Germany (4.4 per cent).

Agriculture

Farming

Traditional farming generates around 20.4 per cent of GDP and around 70 per cent of the population is engaged in subsistence farming.

Only 7 per cent of land is cultivated, although there is considerable potential for development.

Main cash crops are sugar cane, groundnuts, oil palm, cotton, citrus fruits and coffee. Main subsistence crops are rice (60 per cent of cultivated land), cassava, maize and vegetables.

Output has stagnated due to transport problems, low levels of mechanisation, poor marketing and a lack of vital inputs. Although infrastructural projects have rectified some problems, the country is in need of further investment to improve roads linking agricultural areas to domestic and foreign markets.

The fishing, forestry and livestock sectors are small. There is potential for lucrative fishing but the fishing fleet has suffered from lack of funds.

Industry and manufacturing

The industrial sector contributes around 46.5 per cent to GDP and employs 25 per cent of the workforce. Industrial production growth rates, as of 2013, were estimated at 4.6 per cent for Guinea.

The industrial sector contributes around 46.5 per cent to GDP and employs 25 per cent of the workforce. Industrial production growth rates, as of 2013, were estimated at 4.6 per cent for Guinea. The main industrial products are bauxite, gold, diamonds and iron, whilst aluminium refining, light manufacturing and agricultural production are small scare operations designed to meet local requirements. Political uncertainly and corruption claims are limits to the potential of growth within the sector.

The other main industries, textiles, food processing and plywood, are handicapped by supply bottlenecks and shortages of skilled labour.

The investment code and economic liberalisation are expected to attract more foreign capital.

Tourism

As an African destination, Guinea has many traditional, historic and cultural sites to interest visitors. It has an Atlantic Ocean coastline and the Mount Nimba Strict Nature Reserve (included on Unesco's World Heritage List) and a preserved section of the African Timbo slave route, with many landmarks along its way. The direct contribution of Travel & Tourism to GDP was GNF979.5bn (1.9% of total GDP) in 2014, and is forecast to rise by 1.6 per cent in 2015, and to rise by 6.5 per cent per annum, from 2015-2025, to GNF1, 870.8bn (1.9 per cent of total GDP) in 2025. In 2014 travel and tourism directly supported 38,500 jobs (1.5 per cent of total employment). The sector has a lot of potential, however the impact of Ebola has damaged the industry with hotel cancellation rates reaching 60 per cent in the winter season of 2014.

The African Cup of Nations took place in Guinea in 2015, which is likely to contribute to greater tourism in the country. Most visitors arrive by air as land access is considered unsafe.

Mining

Being the 24th largest oil exporter in the world (right behind Indonesia) and sending out 319,100 barrels per day, the country's economy is heavily reliant on crude oil and is therefore exposed to market volatility. Simandou, a mountainous area in the south, has a vast supply of iron ore. It is the world's largest known untapped deposit, with enough ore to sustain annual production of 200m tonnes – or 7 per cent of global iron-ore output. The potential projected cost for the mine and railway (and port) is upwards of US$20 billion, making it Africa's largest ever proposed mining venture. Over the years 2009–2014, Guinea has received investments of around US$2.5 billion, which is relatively low compared to its other mineral-rich neighbors. Numerous international firms, such as BSG Resources (BSGR), have adopted a delayed approach due to uncertain and political instability. Mining contributed 21.6 per cent to GDP in 2012, and 90 per cent towards total exports.

Exploration licenses were awarded for blocks at Simandou to Rio Tinto in 1997. Controversy surrounds the northern two blocks, which were assigned to BSGR with no upfront payment requirements. After the death of President Conté, BSGR sold 51 per cent of its interest to Vale for US$2.5 billion. Reviews led by the new government in 2010 found that BSGR got its blocks through bribery, and as a result, the firm was stripped of its concession in 2014. A new deal was struck with Rio and its Chinese partner, Chinalco, to develop the southern blocks. No solution has yet been found, as many lawsuits are now taking place. Rio has a racketeering suit against BSGR and Vale (Brazilian mining company and investor), whilst BSGR has an arbitration suit against Guinea; Vale also has one against BSGR. Simandou would prop up Guinea's economy via productions of iron-ore that would produce tens of thousands of jobs and, thanks to a railway, make agri-business competitive. It is key for Guinea to provide investment security however.

BSGR's Guinea director, Asher Avidan, has been banned from entering Guinea and two more local managers have been detained in a prison. Nevertheless, BSGR and managing director Beny Steinmetz both vigorously deny paying bribes and any wrongdoing. In 2013 Steinmetz's spokesman, Frederic Cilins, was arrested after meeting Conté's widow in Florida and, unbeknownst to the wire she was wearing, offered a large bribe to destroy substantial evidence. Steinmetz argues that the allegations against him are rooted in envy of his great success, which is valued at US$4 billion with some claiming it is actually twice this amount.

Guinea is rich in uranium, titanium, copper, manganese, iron ore, gold and diamonds. Diamond reserves are estimated at 40 million carats (93 per cent gem quality). The Aredor diamond mine, near Banankore, is 50 per cent owned by the government and 50 per cent by a consortium led by Bridge Oil of Australia and produces around 25,000 carats per year. Diamond mining capacity in Guinea is far lower than recorded exports. It is thought that many gems exported from Guinea have been smuggled from neighbouring countries into Guinea. Key sites of precious stones include Siguiri, Mandiana, Dinguiraye, Kissidougou and Kérouané, and along the rivers of Baoulé, Milo and Diani.

Hydrocarbons

There are no known hydrocarbon reserves and all petroleum needs must be imported, which amounted to 9,000 barrels per day in 2007, primarily for use in vehicles.

Any use of imported natural gas or coal is commercially insignificant.

Energy

There is considerable potential for hydroelectric power from several large rivers. Chinese and Guinean workers are building the country's largest dam on the Konkouré River in order to improve the supply of water to the capital Conakry and the surrounding area. Over one kilometer long, the dam will have a capacity of 240 MW. The hydropower project, named the Kaleta dam, will provide economic benefits constituting the first step towards greater energy independence. 32.2 per cent of total installed capacity in Guinea (2011) was generated by hydroelectric power, with the remaining 67.8 per cent of total installed capacity generated by fossil fuels.

Banking and insurance

It was announced in March 2005 that the introduction of the shared currency, the Eco, in Guinea, Ghana, Nigeria, Sierra Leone and The Gambia, which was due in July 2005, would be postponed. The currency was proposed to facilitate trade and growth with an ultimate plan to merge it with the CFA franc. Successful macroeconomic stabilisation and the start of reforms to boost the productive sector and the business climate have not been enough to register clear economic and social gains. Guinea needs to provide a stable climate in order to ensure the private sector can grow.

Central bank

Banque Centrale de la République de Guinée

Main financial centre

Conakry

Time

GMT

Geography

Guinea lies on the west coast of Africa, with Sierra Leone and Liberia to the south, Senegal to the north, and Mali and Côte d'Ivoire inland to the east.

The country is curved in shape, with Sierra Leone occupying a large chunk of the central region. It can be divided into four geographic zones: the furthest from the coast is bio-diverse rain forest, which turns into savannah in the centre. There is a northern hill region and a coastal zone with an Atlantic coast of 320km. The highest mountain is Mont Nimba (1,752 metres), which is at the centre of an internationally recognised nature reserve, on the border with Côte d'Ivoire and Liberia. There are 22 rivers that begin life in Guinea, including the Senegal, Gambia and Niger rivers.

Hemisphere

Northern

Climate

The climate is tropical and humid. In the south the rainy season falls in June–October; rainfall is particularly heavy in Conakry, average temperatures range from 22–30 degrees Celsius (C). The dry season is from November–April, likely temperature range 24–35 degrees C. The north is generally cooler and drier.

Entry requirements

Passports

Required by all and must have six months validity from the date of departure.

Visa

Required by all except nationals of some African countries. Applications for visas must be made to a Guinea Consulate before travelling. Business visas should included proof of sufficient funds, a business letter with a full itenerary, and an invitation from a local company or organisation. Contact the nearest embassy for further details.

Currency advice/regulations

There are no restrictions on the import of foreign currency but the amount must be declared; export may not exceed the amount imported. It is a requirement to exchange an amount of foreign currency into Gf, depending on the length of stay. Local currency up to Gf1,000 may be imported provided a valid declaration for its previous export can be provided.

Traveller's cheques have limited outlets in banks and large hotels. To avoid extra exchange fees US dollars and Euros are recommended.

Health (for visitors)

Mandatory precautions

Yellow fever vaccination certificate.

Advisable precautions

Malaria prophylaxes are essential as risk exists throughout the country. Immunisations or booster shots are necessary for diphtheria, tetanus, polio, hepatitis A, typhoid and yellow fever. Vaccinations may be needed for hepatitis B, TB, meningitis and cholera. Rabies is a risk in rural areas.

Use only bottled or boiled water for drinks, washing teeth and making ice. Eat only well cooked meals, preferably served hot; vegetables should be cooked and fruit peeled. Avoid pork, salad and food from street vendors. A full first-aid kit would be useful.

Hotels

Limited first-class accommodation is available in Conakry and Kankan; good hotels are expensive. Hotel bills may be paid in foreign currency or by credit card. A service charge is usually included in the bill. Tipping is optional.

Public holidays (national)

Fixed dates

1 Jan (New Year's Day), 1 May (Labour Day), *15 Aug (Assumption Day), 27 Aug (Anniversary of Women's Revolt), 28 Sep (Referendum Day), 2 Oct (Republic Day), 1 Nov (All Saints' Day), 25 Dec (Christmas).

Variable dates

*Easter Monday, Eid al Adha, Birth of the Prophet, *Ascension Day, Day after the Night's Vigil (Nov), Eid al Fitr (three days).

* Christian holiday only

Islamic year 1437 (15 Oct 2015–2 Oct 2016):: The Islamic year contains 354 or 355 days, with the result that Muslim feasts advance by 10–12 days against the Gregorian calendar. Dates of feasts vary according to the sighting of the new moon, so cannot be forecast exactly.

Working hours

Banking

Mon–Fri: 0800–1230, 1430–1700.

Business

Mon–Thu: 0830–1730; Fri: 0800–1300.

Government

Mon–Thu: 0800–1500; Fri: 0800–1300; Sat: 0800–1500.

Telecommunications

Mobile/cell phones

GSM 900 services are available.

Electricity supply

220V AC, 50 cycles

Social customs/useful tips

Showing respect for people will enhance your regard. Always greet people and never go straight into conversation without pleasantries beforehand. It is considered polite to use people's titles.

Security

Visitors are advised not travel to border areas where security is weak and there is a risk of kidnapping.

Always carry an identity card or passport, if stopped you are obliged to show ID.

Pickpocketing, muggings and armed break-ins occur in the city; avoid carrying valuables in public and remain vigilant.

There are numerous confidence tricksters typically attempting to dupe foreigners into buying precious gems (which, even if authentic, need export licences), gold and counterfeit goods.

Getting there

Air

National airline: Air Guinée (government owned) flies domestic routes only. International flights are regional or European.

International airport/s: Conakry (CKY), 13km from city, bank, and car hire. Taxis are to city.

Airport tax: None

Surface

Road: Best route is the coastal road from Sierra Leone (Freetown) to Conakry. Roads from Ganta (Liberia) to N'zérékoré and from Mali (to Kankan and Siguiri) can be difficult.

Getting about

National transport

Air: Air Guinée operates regular domestic service between Conakry, Boké, Kankan, Kissidougou, Labé, Macenta, N'zérékoré, Siguiri.

Road: A few main roads are surfaced, eg from Conakry north to Kindia and Kissidougou, and parts of the road east to Freetown in Sierra Leone. Most roads are laterite and become impassable during the rainy season (Jun–Oct).

Buses: Coach services include Conakry-Kindia-Gaoual and Dabola-N'zérékoré.

Rail: Narrow-gauge railway from Conakry to Kindia and Kankan, which is in poor condition.

City transport

Taxis: Available in Conakry, limited availability elsewhere; can be hired from hotels by the hour or day. Standard fares apply within towns, but for longer journeys fares should be agreed in advance. Tipping is optional.

Car hire

International and national driving licence required. Driving outside city limits with chauffeur and special authorisation only.

BUSINESS DIRECTORY

The addresses listed below are a selection only. While World of Information makes every endeavour to check these addresses, we cannot guarantee that changes have not been made, especially to telephone numbers and area codes. We would welcome any corrections.

Telephone area codes

The international dialling code (IDD) for Guinea is + 224, followed by subscriber's number.
All telephone/fax numbers became eight digits from 2005.

Chambers of Commerce

Guinea Chamber of Commerce, Industry and Handicrafts, PO Box 545, Conakry (email: cciag@sotelgui.net.gn).

Banking

Banque Internationale pour le Commerce et l'Industrie de la Guinée SA; PO Box 1484, Avenue de la République, Conakry (tel: 3041-2908/3643).

Banque Islamique de Guinee; PO Box 1247, 6è Avenue de la Republique, Conakry (tel: 3041-4581, 3046-2075).

Banque Populaire Maroco-Guineenne; PO Box 4400, Avenue de la Republique, Conakry-360 (tel: 3041-1599/2360/2552).

Ecobank-Guinee; PO Box 5687, Avenue de la Republique, Conakry (tel: 3045-5876).

International Commercial Bank; PO Box 3547, Cité Chemin de Fer, Conakry (tel: 3041-2590.

Société Générale de Banques en Guinée; PO Box 1514, Kaloum Coronthie Immeuble Boffa, Cité Chemin de Fer, Conakry (tel: 3041-1746).

Union Internationale de Banque en Guinée UIBG; PO Box 324, Angle 5è Boulevard, 6è Avenue de la République, Conakry (tel: 3041-2096/4309).

Central bank

Banque Centrale de la République de Guinée; PO Box 622, 3 Boulevard du Commerce, Conakry (tel: 3041-2651; fax: 3041-4898).

Travel information

Air France, BP 590, Ave de la Republique, Conakry (tel: 3046-4535)

Air Guinée, Route du Niger, BP 12, 12 Côte Commissariat Central, Conakry (tel: 3045-3662).

Other useful addresses

Bureau Veritas, BP 1451, Conakry (tel: 3044-1841, 3044-2202; fax: 3041-2112).

Chambre Economique de Guinée, BP 609, Conakry.

Comité d'Etat pour la Co-opération avec l'Europe Occidentale, Conakry.

Direction Nationale des Marchés Publics et du Portefeuille de l'Etat (privatisation office), La Division du Portefeuille du Ministère des Finances, avenue de la République, Face á l'Hôpital Ignace DEEN, BP 2006, Conakry (tel: 3041-3957; fax: 3041-4220).

ENTRAT (state forwarding firm), BP 315, Conakry.

Entreprise Nationale Import–Export (Importex), BP 152, Conakry (tel: 3044-2813, 3044-2809).

French Commercial Department, Ambassade de France, BP 373, Conakry (tel: 3041-1605, 3041-1655; fax: 3041-2708).

Guinea Embassy (US), 2112 Leroy Place, NW, Washington DC 20008 (tel: (+1-202) 483-9420; fax: (+1-202) 483-8688; e-mail: emgui@sysnet.net).

Office National des Hydrocarbures (Onah), Conakry.

L'Office de Promotion des Investissement Privés – Guichet Unique (OPIP) (assistance for foreign investors), BP 2024, Conakry (tel: 3045-1830, 3041-4985; fax: 3041-3990; e-mail: dg@opip.org.gn).

Port Autonome, BP 805, Conakry (tel: 3044-2728, 3044-2737; fax: 3041-4564).

Radio-Télévision Guinéenne (RTG), BP 391, Conakry.

Statistical Office, Bureau du Premier Ministre, Conakry (tel: 3044-2148).

National news agency: Agence Guineenne de Presse

Address: BP 1535; Anciens locaux d'Enelgui, 2ème boulevard, 5ème avenue, Conakry (tel: 144-434; 430-549; email: info@agpguinee.net)

APA: www.apanews.net

Panapress: www.panapress.com

Internet sites

Africa Business Network: www.ifc.org/abn

AllAfrica.com: http://allafrica.com

African Development Bank: www.afdb.org

Africa Online: www.africaonline.com

Mbendi AfroPaedia (information on companies, countries, industries and stock exchanges in Africa): http://mbendi.co.za

Online news www.guineenews.org/

Guinea-Bissau

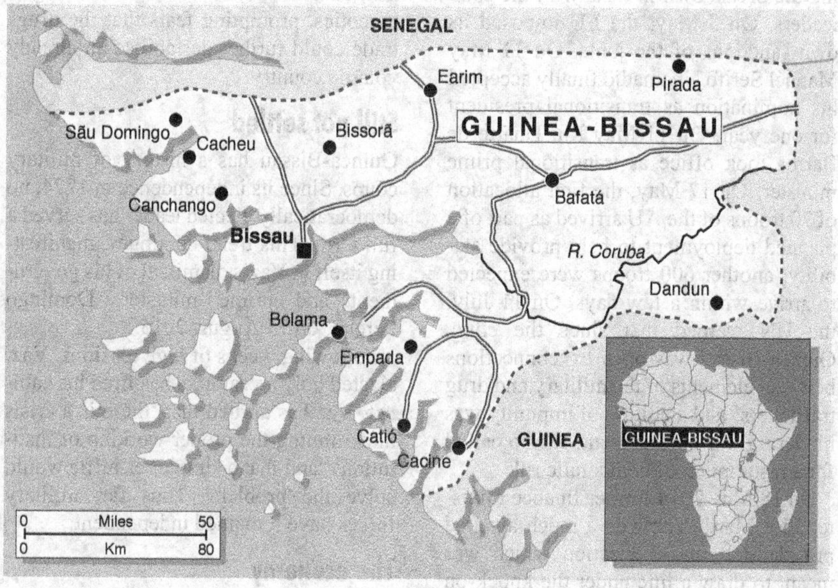

The recent history of Guinea-Bissau has been characterised by uncertainty, insecurity and *coups d'état.* Plagued by a massive foreign debt and reliance on foreign aid, Guinea-Bissau, which was once hailed as a model for development, has deteriorated and become one of the poorest nations in Africa. Since independence from Portugal in 1974, Guinea-Bissau has experienced vast political and military upheavals. For the next six years post-independence leader Luis Cabral officiated over a command economy. A military *coup* in 1980 ended Cabral's time in office, establishing the authoritarian dictator João Bernardo 'Nino' Vieira as President. Vieira led the country towards a market economy and multi-party system, but was accused of autocracy and corruption. His regime has been cited by the characterisation of suppression concerning both his political opponents and rivals.

Several *coup* attempts followed in the next two decades, failing in causing any unrest. In 1994, Vieira was elected president in the first free elections in the country. However, just five years later he was ousted after dismissing his army chief in the previous year, thereby plunging the nation into a crippling civil war. Foreign mediation led to a truce and free elections in January 2000. A transitional government turned over power to the opposition leader Kumba Ialá , after he was elected in a transparent polling. In 2003, after three years, Ialá was overthrown in another military *coup* – in this case a bloodless one.

Vieira was re-elected president in 2005; he was assassinated in 2009. An emergency election took place, with Malam Sanha becoming president. President Malam Bacai Sanhá died in Paris on 9 January 2012, where he had been receiving treatment. Under the constitution, the leader of the National People's Assembly (in this case Raimundo Pereira) becomes interim president when the president is incapacitated. However, the opposition coalition rejected Pereira's interim presidency; despite this, Pereira remained in office. Prime Minister Júnior resigned on 10 February, to become a presidential candidate; Adiato Djaló Nandigna became acting prime minister.

The first round of the presidential election was held on 18 March 2014, with nine candidates in contention. Former prime minister Carlos Gomes Júnior (Partido Africano da Independência de Guiné e

KEY FACTS

Official name: República da Guiné-Bissau (Republic of Guinea-Bissau)

Head of State: President José Mário Vaz (from 23 Jun 2014)

Head of government: Prime Minister Carlos Correia (sworn in 17 Sep 2015)

Ruling party: Partido Africano da Independência de Guiné e Cabo Verde (PAIGC) (African Independence Party of Guinea and Cape Verde) (from 13 April 2014)

Area: 36,125 square km

Population: 1.74 million (2014)*

Capital: Bissau

Official language: Portuguese

Currency: CFA franc (CFAf) = 100 centimes (Communauté Financière Africaine (African Financial Community) franc).

Exchange rate: CFAf586.44 per US$ (Sep 2015)

GDP per capita: US$589 (2014)*

GDP real growth: 2.54% (2014)*

GDP: US$1.02 billion (2014)*

Inflation: -1.03% (2014)*

Balance of trade: -US$50.40 million (2010)

* estimated figure

Cabo Verde (PAIGC) (African Independence Party of Guinea and Cape Verde)) won 48.97 per cent, Kumba Ialá (PRS) 23.36 per cent and Manuel Serifo Nhamadjo 15.74 per cent. A runoff was scheduled for 22 April. On 23 March, former president, Kumba Ialá announced that he would boycott the presidential runoff, due to what he claimed was the unfairness of the first round and that a new voter registration list must be produced before he would participate. Foreign electoral observers had declared that voting in the first round had been largely free and fair.

On 12 April, a *coup d'état*, led by General Mamadu Ture Kuruma, deposed interim President Pereira. On 16 April the military junta proposed all institutions be dissolved in favour of a National Transitional Council (NTC), until democratic power could be re-established (later determined to be in 2014) and the scheduled presidential run-off was cancelled. While most political parties were invited to participate in the NTC, PAIGC was specifically excluded. Of the 35 political parties that form the opposition, leaders of 22 of them agreed to join the NTC. The junta leaders claimed they had presidential candidates Carlos Gomes and Kumba Ialá in custody. On 17 April, the African Union suspended Guinea-Bissau's membership. On 19 April Manuel Serifo Nhamadjo (who was defeated when he came third in the presidential elections) was named transitional president. On 20 April several organisations, including Ecowas, the World Bank and the African Development Bank, condemned the appointment of Nhamadjo as 'illegal'. They also suspended financial aid, worth millions of US dollars.

On 20 April, Mr Nhamadjo rejected his appointment as transitional president, saying he had not been consulted before the announcement by *coup* leaders. Ecowas imposed sanctions on 30 April that specifically targeted the military junta, following the breakdown in talks with the *coup* leaders. On 3 May, the EU imposed its own sanctions of the junta. On 11 May Manuel Serifo Nhamadjo finally accepted his nomination as transitional president for one year. On 11 May Rui Duarte de Barros took office as transitional prime minister. On 17 May, the first allocation of 70 troops of the AU arrived as part of a planned deployment to help provide stability; another 600 troops were expected to arrive within a few days. On 11 July, the UN warned that since the *coup*, Guinea-Bissau was open to 'connections between elements of the military and drug traffickers' and a culture of impunity was hindering law enforcement. It also called for a resumption of democratic rule.

On 18 May 2014 former finance minister José Mário Vaz won a much awaited presidential run-off election which was meant to draw a line under the knock-on effects of the last – 2012 – *coup*. Although Mr Vaz was deemed to have won the election by the national elections commission, the losing candidate, Nuno Gomes Nabiam, initially rejected the result, finally conceding on 22 May. The dispute over the outcome of the vote had threatened to stir further unrest in the chronically unstable country as it set about repairing its fraught relations with both regional and international partners. Mr Vaz, the candidate of the PAIGC, took 61.9 per cent of votes.

The political insecurity of the nation has made the former Portuguese colony a safe haven for smugglers of Latin American cocaine destined for Europe. This has done little for the country's image or reputation. Several senior military figures are alleged to be involved in the trafficking of narcotics, prompting fears that the drugs trade could further destabilise an already volatile country.

Still not settled

Guinea-Bissau has a history of military coups. Since its independence in 1974, no democratically elected leader has served a full term. This trend continues, manifesting itself in Vaz's dismissal of his government and prime minister, Domingo Pereira, on 13 August 2015.

Following weeks of high tensions, Vaz, elected only a year ago, has fired his cabinet. Vaz has argued that 'there is a crisis undermining the proper working of institutions' and that a simple reshuffle would solve the problem. Thus far, military forces have remained independent.

The economy

The return to constitutional order has benefited Guinea-Bissau. According to a 2015 African Development Bank (AfDB) report, growth estimates averaged at 2.6 per cent for the year 2014. This is a large increase from the previous year's 0.9 per cent. The economic upturn is projected to continue to 3.9 per cent for 2015.

Political normalisation and export-driven growth in cashew nuts were major contributors to economic progression for Guinea-Bissau in 2014. These factors, as well as improvements in fiscal governance, can be considered the most important elements for the coming years.

Low tax burdens and high income-to-payroll ratios mean that the state's ability to meet and manage its fiscal resources and payroll are crucial. Food security is also a potential issue; threats arising from the unpredictable nature of the harvest coupled with lower rice production increased reliance on imports. The upturn in growth remains relatively fragile because of many structural problems, deficiencies in infrastructure and governance. The spread of Ebola from neighbouring countries also threatened development within the country.

An International Monetary Fund (IMF) mission in 2014 stressed the importance of improving the business environment and enhancing the opportunities for

KEY INDICATORS — Guinea-Bissau

	Unit	2011	2012	2013	2014	**2015
Population	m	*1.68	*1.58	*1.70	*1.74	*1.78
Gross domestic product (GDP)	US$bn	0.97	0.82	*0.95	*1.02	*0.98
GDP per capita	US$	629	521	*557	*589	*553
GDP real growth	%	5.3	-1.5	*0.3	*2.5	*4.5
Inflation	%	5.4	2.1	*0.8	*-1.0	*1.3
Exports (fob) (goods)	US$m	–	131.4	–	–	–
Imports (fob) (goods)	US$m	–	181.8	–	–	–
Balance of trade	US$m	–	-50.4	–	–	–
Current account	US$m	-61.5	-54.0	*-133.0	*-102.0	*-111.0
Total reserves minus gold	US$m	183.0	164.6	186.3	286.9	–
Foreign exchange	US$m	163.1	145.5	166.7	–	–
Exchange rate	per US$	466.82	505.65	480.26	542.07	–

* estimated figure ** forecast figure

inclusive growth. In this regard, the mission noted that high export taxes on cashew exports had increased rural poverty and smuggling through neighbouring countries and reiterated a call for eliminating the contributions toward the cashew industrialisation programme (FUNPI) (part of a five year Private Sector Rehabilitation and Agribusiness Development Project).

The legal economy is based on farming and fishing, but illegal logging and narcotic trafficking are also important economic activities. Some 66 per cent of Guinea-Bissau's population live below the absolute poverty line. Although there is a great potential for the development of mineral resources, structural challenges still remain. Cashew nuts generate more than 80 per cent of exports and are the main source of income for rural farmers.

Guinea-Bisseau has one of the lowest GDP per capita rates, reported by the United Nations to be US$510.4 as of 2010. Guinea-Bissau's 2012 Human Development Index (HDI) of 0.364 is below the average of 0.466 for countries in the low human development group and below the average of 0.475 for countries in Sub-Saharan Africa. Guinea-Bissau was ranked 177 out of 187 countries in 2014.

Risk assessment

Politics	Poor/fair
Economy	Poor/fair
Regional stability	Fair

Muslims in Guinea-Bissau

% of population	50
Sunni (% of Muslims)	90
Shi'a (% of Muslims)	1

COUNTRY PROFILE

1400s Until Portuguese traders first came to Guinea-Bissau, the country was part of the Mali Empire. It was administered as part of the Portuguese Cape Verde Islands, the Guinea area was important in the slave-trade.
1879 Guinea became a separate colony.
1951 Guinea declared a province of Portugal.
1915 The Portuguese had colonised only the coastal regions until the nineteenth century but finally gained control of the interior. Unlike its other colonies, Portugal made little attempt to develop the then Portuguese Guinea.
1956 The liberation movement, Partido Africano da Independência de Guiné e Cabo Verde (PAIGC) (African Independence Party of Guinea and Cape Verde), was founded by Amilcar Cabral.
1973 Amilcar Cabral was assassinated. PAIGC, which controlled much of the interior of the country, announced a unilateral declaration of independence. PAIGC dropped the name Portuguese from the country's name in favour of Guinea-Bissau.
1974 Portugal had long refused to relinquish power, extending Africa's longest war of independence, but it was finally granted after a *coup d'état* deposed the Portuguese prime minister, Marcello Caetano, in Lisbon, Portugal. Luis Cabral, (brother of the PAIGC founder, Amilcar Cabral), became president.
1980 PAIGC was committed to the unification of Guinea-Bissau and Cape Verde, but this aim was dropped when President Cabral was removed and replaced by his prime minister, João Bernardo Vieira (Nino).
1990 Parliament revoked the PAIGC sole legitimate party status.
1994 Vieira was elected president in the first free elections and PAIGC won the parliamentary elections.
1997 Formal entry to the Communauté Financière Africaine when the CFA franc replaced the peso as national currency.
1998 A civil war began. General Ansumane Mane attempted a coup against Vieira following an army uprising, when Vieira had tried to sack the general for smuggling arms into the neighbouring Senegalese province of Casamance. Senegalese and Guinea troops supported the government and after a month of fighting a cease-fire was agreed.
1999 Ecowas forces arrived to keep the peace, but fighting broke out again and President Vieira was ousted. Malam Bacai Sanhá became interim president. The Partido para a Renovaçao Social (PRS) (Party for Social Renewal) won the parliamentary elections.
2000 Kumba Ialá (Yala), leader of the PRS, was elected president.
2003 President Kumba Ialá was deposed in a bloodless coup.
2004 The opposition PAIGC won the parliamentary elections and Carlos Domingos Gomes Júnior (Carlos Gomes) was sworn in as prime minister.
2005 Former military leader and deposed president, João Bernardo 'Nino' Vieira, won presidential elections and almost immediately sacked Prime Minister Carlos Gomes; Aristides Gomes (no relation) was named as prime minister.
2006 The World Bank suspended a US$15 million funding for infrastructure, due to a lack of transparency in contracts.
2007 Prime Minister Aristides Gomes resigned, following a no-confidence vote in the legislature. Martinho Ndafa Kabi took office as prime minister. A law was enacted that guaranteed amnesty to the perpetrators of violence committed between 1980–2004 during the period of political unrest.
2008 The UN Office on Drugs and Crime (UNODC) declared Guinea-Bissau as the new hub for drugs from South America for onward distribution into Europe. The president appointed Carlos Correia as prime minister. The ruling PAIGC won 49.8 per cent of the votes (67 seats out of 100) in elections. President Vieira survived an attack by mutinous soldiers on his family compound. He appointed Carlos Gomes as prime minister.
2009 President João Bernardo Vieira was shot dead by soldiers loyal to the Army Chief of Staff, General Tagme Na Waie, who had been killed hours earlier in a bomb blast. Raimundo Pereira was sworn-in as acting president. Former president Luis Cabral died in Portugal; he had been the first post-independence president in 1974. Malam Bacai Sanhá won the runoff presidential election with 63.31 per cent of the vote. EU observers declared the polling as 'calm and orderly'.
2010 The prime minister was detained briefly by soldiers during a failed coup. The EU decided to end its security mission, which had been set up in 2008 to fund defence and security and sector reform (SSR) of the defence and police forces as well as the judiciary. Political instability and the deteriorating standards of law and order were cited as the reasons to end the mission following the appointment of one of the failed coup leaders, General Antonio Indjai, as head of the army. Head of the air force, Ibraima Papa Camara and former naval chief, Jose Americo Bubo Na Tchuto, were named by the US as 'drug kingpins'; their assets in the US were frozen and they were put on a US list of people with whom US citizens may not do business.
2011 In May the Paris Club of international creditors cancelled US$256 million in debt, as a result of government efforts in tackling poverty and boosting growth. A further US$27 million of bilateral debt was also waived. Following agreements with donor countries to provide the funds, military pensions will be paid from September. The income is considered important in deterring military coups and uprisings. When President Malam Bacai Sanhá became unwell Raimundo Pereira became interim president in September.
2012 President Malam Bacai Sanhá died in Paris on 9 January, where he had been receiving treatment. Under the constitution, the leader of the National People's Assembly becomes interim president when the president is incapacitated. However, the opposition coalition rejected Pereira's interim presidency; despite this, Pereira remained in office. Prime Minister Júnior

resigned on 10 February, to become a presidential candidate; Adiato Djaló Nandigna became acting prime minister. The first round of the presidential election was held on 18 March, with nine candidates in contention. Former prime minister Carlos Gomes Júnior (PAIGC) won 48.97 per cent, Kumba Ialá (PRS) 23.36 per cent and Manuel Serifo Nhamadjo 15.74 per cent. A runoff was scheduled for 22 April. On 23 March, former president, Kumba Ialá announced that he would boycott the presidential runoff, due to what he claimed was the unfairness of the first round and that a new voter registration list must be produced before he would participate. Foreign electoral observers had declared that voting in the first round had been largely free and fair. On 12 April, a *coup d'état*, led by General Mamadu Ture Kuruma, deposed interim president Pereira. On 17 April, the African Union suspended Guinea-Bissau's membership. On 16 April the military junta proposed all institutions be dissolved in favour of a National Transitional Council (NTC), until democratic power could be re-established (later determined to be in 2014) and the scheduled presidential run-off was cancelled. While most political parties were invited to participate in the NTC, PAIGC was specifically excluded. Of the 35 political parties that form the opposition, leaders of 22 of them agreed to join the NTC. The junta leaders claimed they had presidential candidates Carlos Gomes and Kumba Yala in custody. On 19 April Manuel Serifo Nhamadjo (who was defeated when he came third in the presidential elections) was named transitional president. On 20 April several organisations, including Ecowas, the World Bank and the African Development Bank, condemned the appointment of Nhamadjo as 'illegal'. They also suspended financial aid, worth millions of US dollars. On 20 April, Manuel Serifo Nhamadjo rejected his appointment as transitional president, saying he had not been consulted before the announcement by coup leaders. Ecowas imposed sanctions on 30 April that specifically targeted the military junta, following the breakdown in talks with the coup leaders. On 3 May, the EU imposed its own sanctions of the junta. On 11 May Manuel Serifo Nhamadjo finally accepted his nomination as transitional president for one year. On 11 May Rui Duarte de Barros took office as transitional prime minister. On 17 May, the first allocation of 70 troops of the AU arrived as part of a planned deployment to help provide stability; another 600 troops were expected to arrive within a few days. On 11 July, the UN warned that since the coup, Guinea-Bissau was open to 'connections between elements of the military and drug traffickers' and a culture of impunity was hindering law enforcement. It also called for a resumption of democratic rule.

2013 A slump in cashew nut prices for the 2012 harvest left nearly half of the population severly short of cash and having to resort to selling livestock in order to survive until the next harvest in September.

2014 Elections to the National Assembly and the first round of presidential elections were held on 13 April, with the runoff of the presidential election on 18 May. José Mário Vaz won 40.89 per cent in the first round of the presidential election, followed by two independents – Nuno Gomes Nabiam with 24.79 per cent and Paulo Gomes 10.40 per cent. No other candidate won more than 10 per cent. Mr Vaz won the runoff with 61.92 per cent to Mr Nabiam's 38.08 per cent. The PAIGC won the general election with 47.98 per cent (57 seats, out of 102), ahead of the PRS with 30.76 per cent (41), Partido da Nova Democracia (PND) (New Democracy Party) 4.87 (1), Partido da Convergência Democrática (PCD) (Democratic Convergence Party) 3.37 per cent (2) and União para a Mudança (UM) (Union for Change) 1.84 per cent (1). Domingos Simões Pereira became prime minister on 3 July.

2015 President José Mário Vaz dismissed Prime Minister Domingos Simoes Pereira on 12 August. He was replaced by Baciro Dja, who lasted just three weeks before the Supreme Court declared his appointment unconstitutional. Carlos Correia was sworn in as prime minister on 17 September.

Political structure

Constitution

The 1984 constitution has been revised five times. The 1999 amendment reserves the highest posts in the country for 'native Bissau-Guineans'.

Independence date

24 September 1973 (proclaimed unilaterally); 10 September 1974 (de jure from Portugal).

Form of state

Unitary republic

The executive

Executive power rests with the president, who is the head of state and serves a five-year term. The president appoints the prime minister, who presides over the Council of Ministers.

National legislature

The unicameral Assembleia Nacional Popular (National People's Assembly) has 102 members of which 100 are elected by proportional representation by party lists; two seats are reserved for expatriate citizens. All members serve for five-year terms.

Legal system

The legal system is based on the 1984 constitution, revised in 1993.

Last elections

13 April and 18 May 2014 (presidential, first round and runoff); 13 April 2014 (parliamentary

Results: Presidential (first round): José Mário Vaz (PAIGC) 40.89 per cent, Nuno Gomes Nabiam (Independent) 24.79 per cent, Paulo Gomes (Independent) 10.40 per cent. No other candidate won more than 10 per cent. Turnout was 89.29 per cent. Mr Vaz won the runoff with 61.92 per cent to Mr Nabiam's 38.08 per cent. Turnout was 78.21.

Parliamentary: Partido Africano da Independência de Guiné e Cabo Verde (PAIGC) (African Party for the Independence of Guinea and Cape Verde) won 47.98 per cent of the votes (57 seats out of 102), the Partido para a Renovaçao Social (PRS) (Party for Social Renewal) 30.76 per cent (41), Partido da Nova Democracia (PND) (New Democracy Party) 4.87 (1), Partido da Convergência Democrática (PCD) (Democratic Convergence Party) 3.37 per cent (2) and União para a Mudança (UM) (Union for Change) 1.84 per cent (1); no other party won parliamentary seats. Turnout was 88.57 per cent.

Next elections

2019 (presidential) and 2018 (parliament), although these are likely to change given the military's history of interfering in elections

Political parties

Ruling party

Partido Africano da Independência de Guiné e Cabo Verde (PAIGC) (African Independence Party of Guinea and Cape Verde) (from 13 April 2013

Main opposition party

Partido Unido Social Democrático (PUSD) (United Social Democratic Party)

Approximately 44 per cent of the total population is under 15 years.

Population

1.61 million (2013)*

Last census: December 1991: 983,367

Population density: 31 inhabitants per square km. Urban population 30 per cent (2010 Unicef).

Annual growth rate: 2.0 per cent, 1990–2010 (Unicef).

Ethnic make-up

Balanta (30 per cent), Fula (20 per cent), Manjaca (14 per cent), Mandinga 13 per cent, Papel 7 per cent.

Religions

Some 65 per cent of the population are animist, 30 per cent Muslim and 5 per cent Christian.

Education
Education in Guinea-Bissau has been seriously disrupted by chronic political turmoil since indepence in 1974. UNICEF reported that in 2010 only 22 per cent of children complete secondary education. In 2013 the then minister of education admitted that the interim government had '... embarked on free education without regard to the financial implications.'
Literacy rate: 59 per cent, total; 26.2 per cent female adult rates (World Bank).

Health
Improved water sources are available to 49 per cent of the population.
HIV/Aids
HIV prevalence: 2.8 per cent (UNAIDS estimate 2004)
Life expectancy: 47 years, 2004 (WHO 2006)
Fertility rate/Maternal mortality rate: 5.1 births per woman, 2010 (Unicef); maternal mortality 910 deaths per 100,000 live births (World Bank).
Child (under 5 years) mortality rate (per 1,000): 129 per 1,000 live births (WHO 2012)
Head of population per physician: 0.12 physicians per 1,000 people, 2004 (WHO 2006)

Main cities
Bissau (capital, estimated population 419,004 in 2012), Gabú (38,998), Bafatá (36,086), Canchungo (17,167), Farim (10,502).

Languages spoken
Crioulo (a hybrid of medieval Portuguese and local words) is the common language. Balanta, Bijago and Fulani are also spoken. French is more widely spoken than English. All correspondence and documentation should be in Portuguese and French.
Official language/s
Portuguese

Media
Despite the constitution guaranteeing freedom of the press, the government has not always respected this and journalists are known to practice self-censorship. Journalists that have reported on drug trafficking have been subject to harassment.
The small and weak media scene is hampered by the country's financial constraints.
Press
Newspaper and magazines include *No Pintcha*, *Correio de Bissau Fraskera* and *Banobero*.
Broadcasting
The state-owned Radio Televisao de Guinea-Bissau (RTGB) is the public broadcaster.
Radio: RTGB operates the only Radiodifusão Nacional public radio station. International radio is provided by RTP in Portuguese and RFI in French. Private radio stations include Radio Pidjiquiti, Bombolom FM both very popular and Voice of Quelele.
Television: The state-owned RTGB broadcasts locally. RTP Africa (ww1.rtp.pt) is funded by Portugal, with donated equipment, but managed locally by Bissau-Guineans.
National news agency: ABMP (Agência Bissau Media e Publiçacões)
Other news agencies: Bissau Digital: www.bissaudigital.com
Guine-Bissau: www.guine-bissau.com

Economy
Guinea-Bissau, once seen as a potential model for development in Africa, is one of the poorest countries in the world with an economy heavily dependent on foreign aid. The main economic activity is farming – crops include cashew nuts, peanuts, rice and palm kernels. Although fishing is another component of the economy, very little is undertaken by domestic fishermen, but rather fishing rights are licensed to foreign trawlers.
GDP growth was 2.6 per cent in 2014, which is a large increase from the 0.9 per cent recorded in the previous year. Improvements in fiscal governance coupled with export driven growth of cashew nuts, which rose by 40 per cent over 2013–14 to 70,000 tonnes, has contributed vastly towards this economic upturn.
Guinea-Bissau has one of the lowest GDP per capita rates, reported by the United Nations to be US$510.4 as of 2010. Guinea-Bissau's 2013 Human Development Index (HDI) of 0.396 is below the average of 0.466 for countries in the low human development group. An International Monetary Fund (IMF) mission in 2014 stressed the importance of improving the business environment and enhancing the opportunities for inclusive growth, mainly through tax reductions on cashew nuts.
In 2013, the UN Human Development Index (HDI) ranked Guinea-Bissau 177 (out of 187) for national development in health, education and income. Since 2000, Guinea-Bissau has hardly progressed and has not matched the improvement of other sub-Saharan countries. Remittances from migrant workers amounted to US$46 million (5 per cent of GDP) in 2011 and were estimated to have dropped to US$42 million in 2012. The informal economy has been estimated as larger than the formal market, with remittances providing families with vital, focused income that may represent their only tangible means of livelihood.
The military conflict of 1998–99, which damaged the infrastructure, still impacts on production, but has been eased through internationally backed projects of repair and expansion. Investment in energy has also aided growth.

External trade
Guinea-Bissau is a member of the Economic Community of West African States (Ecowas), and is also a member of the West African Economic and Monetary Union (WAEMU) using the common currency, the CFA franc.
Guinea-Bissau has a large trade deficit and heavy dependence on foreign aid and credits.
Imports
Principal imports are foodstuffs, machinery and transport equipment and petroleum products.
Main sources: Portugal (20.6 per cent of total in 2014), Senegal (17.5 per cent) and the United Kingdom (16.1 per cent).
Exports
Principal exports are fish, shrimp, cashews, peanuts, palm kernels and raw and sawn lumber. Fish is harvested by foreign trawlers, who pay for fishing rights.
Main destinations: India (52.3 per cent of total in 2014), Nigeria (20.7 per cent), China (16.3 per cent) and Togo (5.5 per cent).

Agriculture
Farming
Only 8.2 per cent of total area is arable; inland areas are largely savannah and coastal areas are forest and mangrove swamps. Nevertheless, the agricultural sector (including fishing) is the principal economic activity, accounting for 44.8 per cent of GDP and over 90 per cent of total exports and employing around 82 per cent of the workforce.
There are chronic food shortages, despite the emphasis on food self-sufficiency and co-operative farming.
The main food crop is paddy rice (19 per cent of cultivated land); other food crops include millet, sorghum, plantains, root crops, some maize and groundnuts.
Guinea-Bissau is one of the world's largest producers of cashew nuts. Other cash crops include palm kernels, coconuts, tobacco, and sugar.
In mid-2013, aid groups were reporting that a slump in cashew nut prices in 2012 had left nearly half of the population having to sell livestock in order to survive until the 2013 harvest in September.
In May 2014, the World Bank Board of Executive Directors approved an US$8.2 million credit from the International Development Association (IDA) to Guinea Bissau to help create jobs and combat

food insecurity. The funds are destined for the country's cashew industry, increasing the supply of rice production and entrepreneurship in other sectors of the economy.
The Guinea-Bissau government expects to export a total of 250,000 tons of cashew nuts in 2015. To achieve this, the government has fixed the purchase price from farmers at 300 CFA Francs, against the 250 CFA Francs from previous years. This, they hope, will curb the amount of smuggled nuts entering neighbouring Senegal.

Fishing

The fishing sector is important. Exports of fish and shellfish are expected to increase as the country's large marine resources are exploited. The European Development Fund gave a total of US$130 million over the period 2008–13 in aid to develop the fishing industry, including an ice-making plant. Fish worth between US$300–600 million are caught in the waters each year, but value added production on-shore is minimal.
The European Union and Guinea Bissau agreed to revive the ratification process for a fisheries partnership agreement (FPA) between the two parties in 2014. The parties had negotiated a three-year protocol in 2012, but it was never ratified due to political turmoil in Guinea Bissau. More investment is needed to refurbish the main port, damaged during the civil war, to enable fish processing for export to Europe or to neighbouring countries for processing and re-export.

Industry and manufacturing

The industrial sector contributed 7.5 per cent to GDP in 2014 and employs 18 per cent of the workforce. Production is mostly agri-related: processing groundnuts, fish processing, rice dehusking and sugar refining. There is also a large brewery plant, a small Citroën assembly plant, brick making and textile industries. Since the end of the civil war, there has been a drive to modernise transport facilities. Former Prime Minister, Domingos Simoes Pereira argued that a 2015 review to mine timber was aimed at diversifying investment in services such as maritime transport and telecoms, dominated by former colonial power Portugal.

Tourism

The country has two distinct tourist destinations to offer visitors – the archipelago islands of the capital Bissau offering coastal and marine holidays, and the remainder of the country, on mainland Africa, with its typical offerings of wildlife and traditional cultural sites to visit.
The government has recognised tourism as a growth industry and has called for capital investment in a dozen proposed enterprises. Among others they include 15 tourist zones throughout the country, national parks and reserves, sport and fishing tourism, conference facilities and hotels, a cruise ship port on Bubaque (one of the Bijagós islands) and a resort project in Saltinho.
To gain fully from the improvement tourism can provide, the level of infrastructure must also improve, with development of local roads, an upgrade of the international airport and development of internet facilities.
The government may have to show its determination to deal with the growing problem of South American drug cartels moving into the region or see legitimate tourism replaced by illegal drug trafficking as the main source of national income.

Mining

There are some 200 million tonnes of bauxite reserves in the region of Boé, but exploration costs are too high to justify extraction. There are also known deposits of phosphate near Farim, as well as gold and possibly diamonds. The main barrier to investment in the mining sector is the country's poor infrastructure.
Test drilling at the Farim phosphate deposit indicated it was commercially viable with high phosphate recovery rates (84.1 per cent).

Hydrocarbons

There are no known commercially viable oil reserves although exploration is ongoing. Consumption of oil was 3,020 barrels per day in 2013, all of which was imported.
The state-owned PetroGuin (formerly called Petrominas) is the national oil company, which controls downstream facilities.
Neither natural gas nor coal are produced, any imports are commercially negligible.

Energy

Total installed generating capacity was 26MW in 2013, producing 60 million kilowatt hours. Only a very small proportion of the population has access to electricity. Energy particularly in rural areas is mainly derived from charcoal and wood.
The World Bank and the West African Development Bank is supporting the Electricidade e Aguas da Guine-Bissau (EAGB) in restructuring and developing the sector with loans of US$20 million and US$5 million respectively. Integration with the West African Power Pool (WAPP), operated by the Economic Community of West African States (Ecowas), and the Gambia River Development Organisation project is expected to enhance EAGB's longer term prospects.

Financial markets

Stock exchange

Afribourse (Bourse Régionale des Valeurs Moblières) (BRVM)

Banking and insurance

Central bank

Banque Centrale des Etats de l'Afrique de l'Ouest

Main financial centre

Bissau

Time

GMT

Geography

Guinea-Bissau lies on the west coast of Africa, with Senegal to the north and Guinea to the east and south. The terrain is mainly low coastal plain with thick forest and mangrove swamps, rising to hills in the east, where savannah prevails; the highest elevation is approximately 300 metres. Guinea-Bissau also includes Bolama island and the Bijagós archipelago of 15 main islands, lying over 40km out in the Atlantic Ocean.

Hemisphere

Northern.

Climate

Tropical with rainy season from mid-May to November and dry season from December–April. Average temperatures range from 20–38 degrees Celsius (C) in April–May, and from 15–33 degrees C in December–January. High humidity from July–September.

Entry requirements

Passports

Required by all, valid for six months.

Visa

Required by all, except nationals of Ecowas countries for stay of one month. Applications for business visas should include a letter from the visitor's company accepting responsibility for any expenses incurred, and a full itinerary. For further details, contact the nearest embassy.

Currency advice/regulations

Import and export of local currency is prohibited. There is no restriction on the import of foreign currency, but amounts should be declared; export of foreign currency is allowed up to the declared amount.

Health (for visitors)

Medical facilities are limited.

Mandatory precautions

Yellow fever vaccination certificate.

Advisable precautions

Malaria prophylaxes are essential as risk exists throughout the country. Immunisations or booster shots are necessary for diphtheria, tetanus, polio, hepatitis A, typhoid and yellow fever. Vaccinations may be needed for hepatitis B, TB, meningitis and cholera. Rabies is a risk in rural areas.

Use only bottled or boiled water for drinks, washing teeth and making ice. Eat only well cooked meals, preferably served hot; vegetables should be cooked and fruit peeled. Avoid pork, salad and food from street vendors. A full first-aid kit would be useful.

Hotels

Accommodation is very limited and difficult to obtain at short notice. Reservations should be made well in advance, preferably through business contacts. Hotel tariffs are liable to change at short notice, therefore confirmation of booking is recommended.

Credit cards

Credit cards cannot be used.

Public holidays (national)

Fixed dates

1 Jan (New Year's Day), 20 Jan (Death of Amilcar Cabral), 8 Mar (Women's Day), 1 May (Labour Day), 3 Aug (Colonisation Martyrs' Day), 24 Sep (National Day), 14 Nov (Readjustment Movement Day), 25 Dec (Christmas Day).

Variable dates

Eid al Adha, Eid al Fitr

Islamic year 1437 (15 Oct 2015–2 Oct 2016):: The Islamic year contains 354 or 355 days, with the result that Muslim feasts advance by 10–12 days against the Gregorian calendar. Dates of feasts vary according to the sighting of the new moon, so cannot be forecast exactly.

Working hours

Banking

Mon–Fri: 0830–1430.

Business

Mon–Fri: 0830–1430.

Government

Mon–Fri: 0830–1430.

Shops

Mon–Fri: 0730–1230, 1430–1830.

Telecommunications

Telephone/fax

Communications are poor.

Mobile/cell phones

GSM 900 roaming facilities are available.

Getting there

Air

International airport/s: Bissau-Osvaldo Vieira Airport (OXB), 8km from city. Taxis and minibuses are available to take visitors to the city.

Airport tax: None.

Surface

Road: The road from Guinea is mostly paved; however, that which is not, from the border to Labé, gets boggy in the rainy season. Petrol is readily available only in the cities.

A 720-metre bridge over the Mansoa river has improved the traffic flow on the trans-African coastal road between Dakar, Senegal and Bissau.

Water: There are sea links between Cape Verde and Guinea-Bissau.

Main port/s: Bissau

Getting about

National transport

Air: There are no mainland internal flights. Flights go between Bissau and Bubaque Island and a small plane flies to Orango Island from Bissau.

Road: Total road network is over 3,250km, of which about a third is all-weather.

Buses: Minibuses operate on the main roads.

Taxis: Long-distance taxis leave from the market square in Bissau.

Water: Boats serve most towns on the coast and up-river. Tickets available from the Guinémar Office.

City transport

Taxis: Taxis are available in Bissau and serve all main towns.

BUSINESS DIRECTORY

The addresses listed below are a selection only. While World of Information makes every endeavour to check these addresses, we cannot guarantee that changes have not been made, especially to telephone numbers and area codes. We would welcome any corrections.

Telephone area codes

The international dialling code (IDD) for Guinea-Bissau is + 245 followed by subscriber's number.

Chambers of Commerce

Guini-Bissau Associação Comercial, Industrial e Agricola, PO Box 88, Bissau (tel: 222-276).

Guini-Bissau Camara do Comercio, Industria e Agricultura, PO Box 361, Bissau (tel: 212-844; fax: 201-602).

Banking

Central bank

Banque Centrale des Etats de l'Afrique de l'Ouest, Direction Nationale, Avenue Amilcar Cabral 124, PO Box 38, Bissau (tel: 215-548; fax: 201-305).

Stock exchange

Afribourse (Bourse Régionale des Valeurs Moblières) (BRVM), www.brvm.org

Ministries

Ministry of Economy and Finance, Rua Justino Lopes 74A, Bissau (tel: 203-495; fax: 203-496).

Ministry of Finance, Avenue Domingos Ramos, Caixa Postal 67, Bissau (tel/fax: 201-037).

Ministry of Mines and Energy, Caixa Postal 387, Bissau.

Other useful addresses

Empresa Nacional de Comércio Geral, CP 5, Bissau (tel: 212-925).

Empresa Nacional de Pesquisas e Exploração Petroliferas e Mineiras (Petrominas), 58 Rua Eduardo Mondlane, Bissau (tel: 212-279).

Guinea-Bissau Embassy (USA), 15929 Yukon Lane, Rockville MD 20855 (tel: (+1-202) 947-3958).

Guinémar Office, 21A Rua Guerra Mendes, Bissau.

Petroguin, Caixa Postal 387 Bissau (tel: 221-155, 222-625; fax: 221-155, 222-625).

Radiodifusão Nacional da República da Guiné-Bissau, CP 191, Bissau.

National news agency: ABMP (Agência Bissau Media e Publiçacões), CP1069; Rua Euardo Mondlane 52, Bissau (tel: 206-147; email: agenciabissau@agenciabissau.com; internet: www.agenciabissau.com).

Bissau Digital: www.bissaudigital.com

Guine-Bissau: www.guine-bissau.com

Internet sites

Africa Business Network: www.ifc.org/abn

AllAfrica.com: http://allafrica.com

African Development Bank: www.afdb.org

Africa Online: www.africaonline.com

Mbendi AfroPaedia (information on companies, countries, industries and stock exchanges in Africa): http://mbendi.co.za

Guyana

KEY FACTS

Official name: Co-operative Republic of Guyana

Head of State: President David A Granger (APNU) (sworn in 16 May 2015)

Head of government: Prime Minister Moses Veerasammy Nagamootoo (APNU) (sworn in 20 May 2015)

Ruling party: A Partnership for National Unity–Alliance for Change (APNU–AFC) (elected 11 May 2015)

Area: 214,970 square km

Population: 800,000 (2014)*

Capital: Georgetown

Official language: English

Currency: Guyana dollar (G$) = 100 cents

Exchange rate: G$206.12 per US$ (Sep 2015)

GDP per capita: US$3,748 (2014)*

GDP real growth: 3.83% (2014)*

GDP: US$3.00 billion (2014)*

Inflation: 1.02% (2014)*

Balance of trade: -US$471.40 million (2013)

* estimated figure

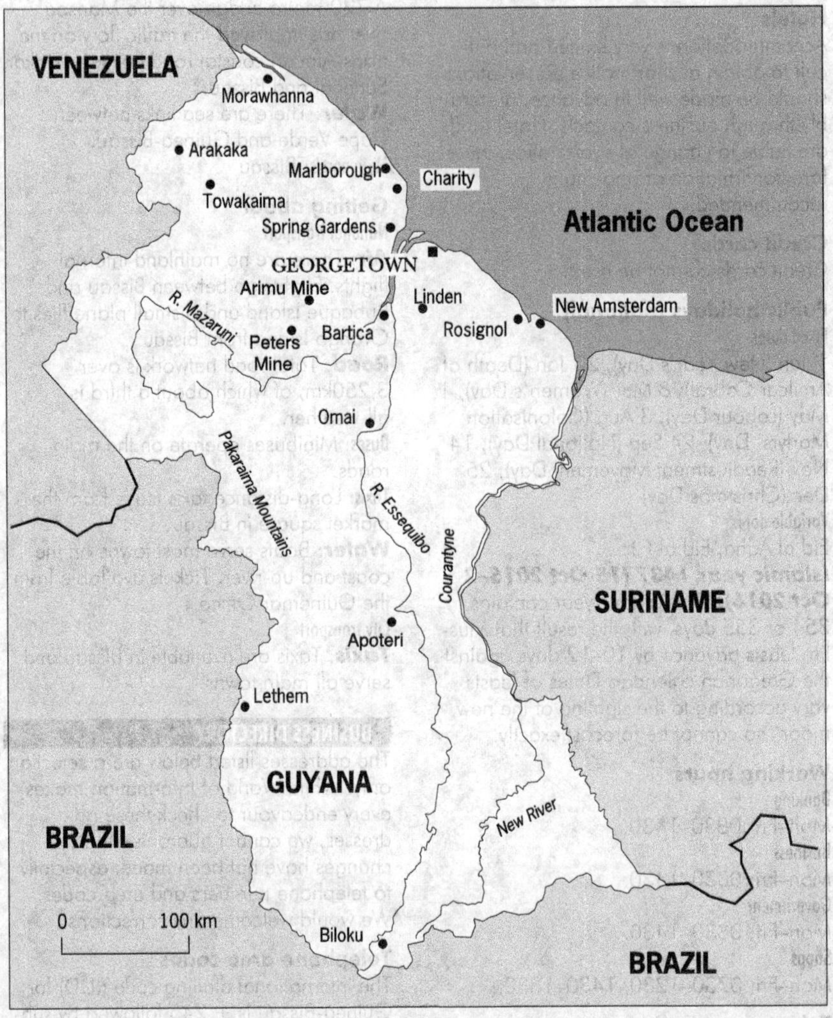

In the twenty-first century, around half Guyana's population live in urban centres, with more than a quarter in the capital city, Georgetown. The East Indian community are for the most part resident in agricultural areas, with the Afro-Guyanese mostly resident in towns. The balance of the population are of European or Chinese heritage, or Amerindians, most of whom live in the west and south or on reserves. Although the east Indians and the Afro-Guyanese are the dominant groups, Guyana is often referred to as the 'land of six peoples', reflecting the multi-ethnic composition of its population. The East Indians account for about 51 per cent of the population and are for the most part descendants of indentured labourers from India. The Afro-Guyanese, or simply 'Africans' make up about 38 per cent. The other ethnic groups are the Chinese, the Europeans (mostly Portuguese) and the Amerindians. The Portuguese came to Guyana as indentured labourers from Madeira, the Azores and Cape Verde. During the colonial era, they were regarded as a separate group from the other Europeans (mainly British), no doubt because of their origins as indentured labourers. There is inevitably a large racially mixed group.

These six groups have co-habited in Guyana for over 150 years. There is an obvious geographical separation, the Indians staying mainly in the rural areas, the Africans going to the cities. There was also functional separation, the Indians remaining on the plantation as sugar workers and dominating the rice industry, the Africans going into the civil service and the professions and becoming workers in Guyana's urban industries and bauxite; the Portuguese and the Chinese in general commerce, the Amerindian staying mainly in the interior. But in the latter years of the twentieth century, a gradual process of integration had appeared to be under way. Large numbers of Indians had settled in the cities, entered the civil service and the professions or taken clerical jobs. However, this increasing integration may paradoxically have created new stresses as there is more direct competition (for jobs, housing and social services) and the races mix more intimately and freely.

May elections

President Donald Ramotar announced general and local elections would be held early after he had defied spending cuts imposed by the National Assembly and the legislature had called for a motion of no confidence. On 24 February 2015 Mr Ramotar announced he had signed the proclamation to dissolve parliament on February 28. Local elections have not been held since 1994. Commonwealth Secretary General Kamalesh Sharma agreed an observer group would be in the country to observe the election from 3–19 May. The Commonwealth group would act impartially and make an independent assessment of the electoral process. The general election held on 11 May was narrowly won by A Partnership for National Unity–Alliance for Change (APNU–AFC) with 50.29 per cent (33 seats, out of 65), dislodging the People's Progressive Party/Civic (PPP/Civic) party which had held power since 1997 and which won 49.20 per cent (32 seats). David A Granger, leader of the APNU, was sworn in as President on 16 May and Moses Veerasammy Nagamootoo (APNU) was sworn in as prime minister four days later.

Corruption

Guyana ranks a lowly 136 out of the 175 countries surveyed in Transparency International's 2014 *Corruption Perceptions Index*, the lowest ranked South American country with the single exception of almost basket-case Venezuela, ranked 160. An article in the kaieteurnewsonline.com referred to the collapse of plans to complete the construction of a new Marriot hotel following allegations of fraud and cronyism. Local Guyanese contractors appeared to have been the losers in a major scam. This involved awarding the contract to an individual or firm with connections to the ruling party with no consideration to their competence in getting the contracted works done. What normally seemed to happen was that after a period of 'activity', alarm bells were sounded about performance failures and missed deadlines terminating in a decision to withdraw the contract and either re-tender or, worse still, award it to another favourite. These charades were described as 'only the tip of the graft and kickbacks iceberg.' Neither civil society, nor the political opposition has proved able to pursue these matters, probably because they lack the technical competence to do so.

This generally leaves the incumbent head of state to pick up the pieces that are left from the plans and plots of his predecessor. So it was that former president Donald Ramotar, in office December 2011–May 2015, had been left to sort out the myriad deals struck during the Bharrat Jagdeo administration, mostly shrouded in secrecy and for the most part involving the National Investment Company Limited (NICIL).

Corruption also seemed to be widespread at the lower levels of the bureaucracy, emulating the example set on high. Eyebrows had often been raised when public servants were known to be buying a home worth tens of millions of Guyana dollars (G$) while earning a salary of less than one tenth of a million dollars; or public servants apparently able to build homes for their children. In Guyana, Public perceptions of corruption often accurately mirror the reality therof, even if they sometimes underestimate it and therefore it behoves any incumbent or aspirant to public office to behave in a manner consistent with due regard for universally accepted professional norms and values.

Border disputes

The border dispute between Venezuela and Guyana (formerly 'British' Guyana) has over the past century often come close to provoking war – not only between Guyana and Venezuela, but at one stage between the US and Britain. The underlying interest relates, unsurprisingly, to the possibility of oil deposits. In mid-2015 tensions rose and there were hastily organised military exercises conducted by both countries. This sabre-rattling came ahead of an expected meeting between the presidents of the two countries the UN General Assembly in New York.

Venezuela had long laid claim to a vast chunk of Guyana's territory, 4 the Essequibo, which makes up no less than almost 40 per cent of Guyana's territory. The UN talks were expected to calm things down rather than resolve the issue. It had been suggested at one stage that the two countries follow the example of Kuwait and Saudi Arabia, who share oil revenues from a jointly administered territory in the Arabian Gulf.

The notional border between Venezuela and Guyana is improbably known as the Schomburgk Line, named after a German explorer called Robert Schomburgk, who

KEY INDICATORS — Guyana

	Unit	2011	2012	2013	2014	**2015
Population	m	*0.78	*0.80	*0.80	*0.80	*0.80
Gross domestic product (GDP)	US$bn	2.48	2.85	2.98	*3.00	*3.15
GDP per capita	US$	3,202	3,581	3,730	*3,748	*3,924
GDP real growth	%	4.2	4.8	5.2	*3.8	*3.8
Inflation	%	5.7	2.4	2.2	*1.0	*1.2
Exports (fob) (goods)	US$m	1,129.1	1,395.7	1,357.9	–	–
Imports (fob) (goods)	US$m	1,770.5	1,977.7	1,847.3	–	–
Balance of trade	US$m	-641.4	-581.9	-471.4	–	–
Current account	US$m	-344.0	-378.0	-395.0	*-477.0	*-517.0
Total reserves minus gold	US$m	784.1	864.0	783.6	667.9	–
Foreign exchange	US$m	778.8	862.2	776.9	–	–
Exchange rate	per US$	203.96	204.50	202.95	202.00	–

* estimated figure ** forecast figure

was commissioned by the United Kingdom as long ago as 1835 to conduct a geological survey of the territory. The Schomburk line was not accepted by Venezuela, which was backed by the fledgling United States. Eventually, the two parties agreed to have the dispute settled by international arbitration.

The outcome of the 1899 tribunal had at first appeared to settle the dispute between Venezuela and Guyana; a commission of officials from each country worked out the details of the boundary in 1905. However, after four dormant decades, the dispute flared up again in 1949 with the publication of a memorandum written by a US lawyer acting for Venezuela. The memorandum claimed that the tribunal result had favoured Britain's claims, alleging corruption and collusion between London and the Russian chairman of the tribunal.

The economy

According to the United Nations Economic Commission for Latin America and the Caribbean (CEPAL/ECLAC) in 2014 the Guyanese economy continued to improve and was on track for its ninth consecutive year of growth in 2014, having expanded by 5.2 per cent in 2013 and by 3.2 per cent in the first six months of 2014. GDP was expected to grow by 4.5 per cent in total for 2014 due to increased government spending and a strong performance in agriculture, manufacturing and construction. The government was projected to run a fiscal deficit of 4.9 per cent of GDP in 2014. External public debt at end-June 2014 was down 1.7 per cent compared to end-June 2013 and stood at 41.2 per cent of GDP. Steps had been taken to diversify the economy and to add value to products produced in Guyana.

The government ran a fiscal deficit of 0.3 per cent of GDP during the first half of 2014. Expenditure was up 27.8 per cent on the same period in 2013, primarily due to increases in purchases of goods and services (chiefly materials, equipment and supplies, electricity charges and other miscellaneous expenses), transfer payments (due to an increase in contributions to local and international organisations and pensions) and employee costs (due to increases in both public-sector employment, especially in core public services and wages). Revenue rose by 3.6 per cent over the same period due to increases in both direct and indirect tax receipts. However, this deficit was expected to widen to 4.9 per cent of projected GDP by the end of 2014, compared with the 4.4 per cent deficit posted in 2013.

The money supply as measured by M1 grew by 9.8 per cent from September 2013 to September 2014, in large part due to a net redemption of treasury bills in the first half of 2014. The banking reserve rate was set at 12 per cent, as it had been since 2002. A stable exchange rate was a priority goal of monetary policy in Guyana. The Guyanese dollar had depreciated by 0.12 per cent against the United States dollar to G$206.6 to US$1.00. Foreign exchange reserves held by the public sector had decreased in 2014, as they have every quarter since 2009, having been drawn down to US$671 million, or 3.9 months of import cover to finance the balance of payments deficit. However, foreign exchange held by private sector banks has increased due to a surplus of this in the market.

The current account deficit shrank by 23.7 per cent in the first half of 2014 compared to January–June 2013 due to improvements in the merchandise and services trade balances and to transfer payments. The capital and financial account surplus decreased by 27.5 per cent because of lower net capital transfers and short term capital inflows and despite increases in private capital inflows. Overall, the balance of payments deficit shrank by 36.1 per cent, to 3.1 per cent of GDP. The remaining deficit was largely financed by sales of foreign reserves.

Growth prospects for 2014 in most of the key agricultural sectors were good, in part due to favourable international commodity prices and weather conditions. The sugar sector was expected to rebound to 2012 levels in 2014 after a very poor performance in 2013. Record rice yields were expected, in part due to increased activity by small and medium-sized enterprises and investments in drainage and irrigation networks. The primary challenge for rice growers was to find markets for their exports, though a significant amount of rice is sold to Venezuela as part of the PetroCaribe arrangement. Forestry output was dramatically up on 2013, due to increased international demand and favourable prices. Fisheries output declined, while livestock output increased marginally. Growth in 2014 looked likely to be held back somewhat by a lacklustre performance in the extractive industries, as gold output dropped moderately from record highs in 2013 due to a price decline, which had resulted in lower net gold receipts. Diamond output also decreased due to lower investment in the sector and bauxite output was down due to lower prices.

Tourism arrivals fell in the first half of 2014. Guyana continued to focus on nature tourism and ecotourism; the biggest obstacle to developing the tourist industry is a lack of airline flights to Guyana from Europe and North America. This situation should improve following an expansion of the country's primary airport, which was scheduled to be completed in August 2015. Another boost to tourism was expected from the opening of a Marriott hotel in late 2014. The manufacturing and construction sectors were expected to post strong growth of 8.1 per cent and 12.0 per cent, respectively, in 2014.

Inflation in the first half of 2014 was very low at -0.4 per cent, owing largely to flat housing prices and slight declines in the prices of food, transport and communication and furniture. Inflation expectations are also low because inflation was restrained in 2013, at 0.9 per cent. Inflation for the whole of 2014 was projected to be 1 per cent. Though no official data on unemployment were available, it was likely to decrease in 2014 due to rising economic activity in key sectors, including increased government spending.

Risk assessment

Economy	Good
Politics	Fair
Regional stability	Fair

COUNTRY PROFILE

The area before European settlement was inhabited by semi-nomadic, hunter-gatherer Amerindian tribes, notably Arawaks and Caribs.

1498 Christopher Columbus first sighted Guyana.

1616 The Dutch built the first fort.

1640 The first African slaves arrived to work on sugar plantations. Settlements grew up in Essequibo, Demerara and Berbice and were sustained by trade through the Dutch West India Company.

1763 The Berbice slave rebellion began on one plantation and spread to others along the Berbice River.

1781–1803 The Three colonies of Essequibo, Demerara and Berbice passed into the hands of the English, briefly to the French, back to the Dutch, then the English, then the Dutch and lastly back to the English.

1814 After the Napoleonic Wars the colonies of were ceded to Britain.

1831 The British administration merged the three colonies into British Guiana, but retained the Dutch administrative, legislative and legal system.

1834 Britain abolished slavery in all its territories. Many Indian and smaller numbers of Chinese and Japanese indentured labourers were brought to work on the estates.
1920 Indentured labour ended.
1953 The General election was won by the People's Progressive Party (PPP), led by Cheddi Jagan and Forbes Burnham. The British government deemed the government as pro-Communist and suspended the constitution. The PPP spilt and Burnham founded the People's National Congress/Reform (PNC) party.
1957 and 1961 The PPP won both general elections. Support began to grow for independence.
1964 Guyana's political system was generally viewed as fraudulent with Guyana a *de facto* one-party state and an 'administrative dictatorship'.
1965 The PPP won most seats in the general election; however a coalition of PNC and another minor, conservative, party formed a government. Burnham became prime minister and stayed in post in an increasingly authoritarian manner, until 1980
1966 Guyana gained independence.
1971 A UN tribunal convened to try and resolve the long-standing border dispute with neighbouring Venezuela concerning the oil-rich Essequibo region.
1980 A new constitution introduced the post of executive president, and Forbes Burnham became the first.
1985 President Burnham died. Desmond Hoyte became president. The one-party state and radical socialism was gradually replaced by a market economy. Austerity measures introduced in the late 1980s resulted in great civil unrest.
1992 The National Assembly and Regional Council were elected in the first free and fair general elections. Hoyte lost the presidency to former Marxist, Dr Cheddi Jagan (PPP).
1997 A PPP/Civic (PPC/C) coalition won the election, but PNC refused to accept the election results. Cheddi Jagan died in March. Samuel Hinds became president until December when Jagan's widow Janet was elected president.
1998 After boycotting parliament since the 1997 election, the PNC returned to the National Assembly, following intervention by the Caribbean Community (Caricom), which carried out an independent audit of the election results and brokered an accord with the PNC, which also catered for a new constitution and fresh elections.
1999 Janet Jagan resigned the presidency due to ill-health; she was succeeded by Bharrat Jagdeo.
2000 Guyana had an agreement with the Canadian oil company CGX Energy to drill within waters also claimed by neighbouring Suriname. Suriname gunboats raided the exploration oil-rig sparking international tension; diplomatic proposals for joint exploration and exploitation failed.
2001 The general election was won by President Jagdeo's ruling PPC/C.
2002 A high-profile television presenter, Mark Benschop, was charged with treason after he was accused of inciting demonstrators to storm the presidential offices compound. The demonstrators were complaining of discrimination against Afro-Guyanese.
2003 A UN tribunal convened and tried, without success, to resolve the maritime border dispute with Suriname.
2004 CGX Energy announced it had begun exploration of inshore waters along the Cortenyne Coast, with drilling in the disputed Berbice area about to begin. A key witness in the trial of home affairs minister Ronald Gajraj was shot dead before he could testify about allegations of extra-judicial killings. The minister had stepped down after several months of procrastination and opposition inquiry. Guyana joined 12 South American countries in the launch of an economic and political bloc called the South American Community of Nations.
2005 Severe flooding affected half the country's population. The economic effect was shown to be a 2.2 per cent reduction in the year's economic growth, costing the nation about US$65 million. Ronald Gajraj was reinstated as home affairs minister, following a ruling by a presidential commission acquitting him of any wrongdoing; however the decision to reinstall the minister provoked international criticism. Gajraj resigned his position.
2006 The agriculture minister, Satyadeow Sawh, was murdered. President Jagdeo was re-elected with 54.6 per cent of the vote while his PPP/C party won a majority in parliament.
2007 The UN ruled that both Suriname and Guyana should share the disputed, possibly oil-rich, offshore territory.
2008 Guyana signed a trade agreement with the EU.
2009 Local elections were postponed until 2010 due to revisions necessary in the voter list, new identification cards and the demarcation and delineation of electoral boundaries. The new Takutu River Bridge, across the border with Brazil, was opened.
2010 A new, flood-resistant rice, developed for the Guyana Rice Development Board (GRDB) in the Guyana-based Burma Rice Research Station, began testing in local conditions. It was designed to survive being completely submerged for up to 17 days. The government and the China Development Bank signed a loan agreement (for an undisclosed amount) to begin the Amaila Falls Hydro-Electric Project (AFHEP), for which the Inter-American Development Bank (IDB) also approved US$1.2 million for project preparation.
2011 In July, at the close of President Jagdeo's second and final term in office, he addressed the conference of heads of government attending the Caricom meeting urging them to focus on outcomes rather than processes, 'people judge us by results' he said, and exhorted other leaders to 'always ascertain the value added to the process before plunging into new initiatives'. Presidential and parliamentary elections were held on 28 November, in which the PPP/Civic won 49 per cent of the vote (32 seats out of 65), the coalition of four parties called A Partnership for National Unity (APNU) won 41 per cent (26) and the AFC seven seats. PPP/Civic was given a mandate to appoint its presidential candidate, Donald Ramotar as president.
2012 On 12 September, a joint agreement was signed by the finance minister, private equity fund, Sithe Global and the engineering company, China Railway First Group, for the construction of the AFHEP, with an approximately 165MW capacity. The US$506 million project is the largest infrastructure contract ever undertaken by Guyana. On 6 October the minister of natural resources reported that gold production for the year had increased year-on-year by 23 per cent, to 314,000 ounces (up from 207,000 ounces in 2011).
2013 Guyana accused the Venezuelan navy of violating its sovereignty when it entered Guyanese territorial waters in October and detained the *Teknik Perdana*, a vessel contracted out to Texas-based company Anadarko. Anadarko has a contract to look for oil in the area. The government said that the Venezuelan actions in the disputed Essequibo region constituted 'a serious threat to peace in the region', while Venezuela said the ship was operating illegally in its waters. The vessel was released on 15 October.
2014 On 18 August Guyana banned all persons travelling from the West Africa countries where the ebola virus is present – Guinea, Liberia, Sierra Leone, Senegal and Nigeria – until further notice. The president prorogued parliament on 11 November. In his annual address to the nation on 31 December, President Ramotar assured the populace that the government '... will deliver the Amaila Falls Hydropower project to the Guyanese people, along with all its attendant benefits. Within months, we expect to achieve financial close and commence construction, and this project will come into operation during our new term in office.'

2015 On 20 January Ramatar announced general and local elections would be held on 11 May; he did not confirm whether or not he would stand himself. Local elections have not been held since 1994. On 24 February President Ramotar announced he had signed the proclamation to dissolve parliament on February 28. The departure from Louisiana in February of Exxon/Mobil's Deepwater Champion oil exploration rig heading for the Liza field, part of the Stabroek Block, lead to objections from Venezuela. The dispute dates back to the century-old quarrel over Essequibo, a potentially oil rich area claimed by Venezuela but administered by Guyana. The government warned Venezuela to refrain from taking any actions that might hinder the 'development of Guyana and its people and that would be in contravention of international law.' Commonwealth Secretary General Kamalesh Sharma agreed an observer group would be in the country to observe the election from 3–19 May. The Commonwealth group will act impartially and make an independent assessment of the electoral process. The general election held on 11 May was narrowly won by the APNU–Alliance for Change with 50.29 per cent (33 seats, out of 65), dislodging the PPP/Civic party which had held power since 1997 and which won 49.20 per cent (32 seats). David A Granger, leader of the APNU, was sworn in as President on 16 May. In July Kamla Persad-Bissessar, prime minister of Trinidad and Tobago, declared her country's full support of Guyana in its dispute Venezuela.

Political structure

Constitution

The Constitution was enacted in 1980, a decade after Guyana became a co-operative republic and 14 years after joining the Commonwealth.

Guyana is divided into 10 regions, each headed by a chairman who presides over a regional democratic council. Local communities are administered by village or city councils.

Independence date

26 May 1966

Form of state

Co-operative republic

The executive

Executive power rests with the president, who appoints and supervises the prime minister and other ministers. The president is the presidential candidate indirectly elected by the National Assembly from party lists to serve five-year terms without limits. Most cabinet ministers are also members of the National Assembly; the Constitution limits non-member technocrat ministers to five years. Technocrat ministers serve as non-elected members, allowing them to debate, but not to vote.

National legislature

The unicameral National Assembly is comprised of 65 members directly elected in multi-seat constituencies and a single nationwide constituency by proportional representation vote. The president may dissolve the Assembly and call new elections at any time, but no later than five years from its first sitting. All laws passed by the assembly must be endorsed by the president. From 2012 The executive is obliged to discuss and agree new laws with the National Assembly. Members serve five-year terms.

Legal system

Guyana's legal system is based on Roman Dutch law modified by English common law. The country has a series of magistrates' courts and further appellate courts, a Court of Appeal, headed by a chancellor of the judiciary, and a High Court, presided over by a chief justice. The chancellor and the chief justice are appointed by the president.

An ombudsman investigates complaints against government departments or other authorities.

Last elections

11 May 2015 (presidential and parliamentary)

Results: Presidential: candidates win depending on party list votes for parliamentary constituencies, in order of parliamentary voting, therefore the winner was David Granger (APNU) with Donald Ramotar (PPP/Civic) as runner-up.

Parliamentary (2015): A Partnership for National Unity–Alliance for Change (APNU–AFC) 50.29 per cent (33 seats, out of 65), People's Progressive Party/Civic (PPP) 49.20 per cent (32 seats), the United Force 0.26 per cent (none). The remaining three parties won less than 0.2 per cent of the vote and failed to win any seats. Turnout was 71 per cent

Next elections

2020 (presidential and parliamentary)

Political parties

Ruling party

A Partnership for National Unity–Alliance for Change (APNU–AFC) (elected 11 May 2015)

Main opposition party

People's Progressive Party

Population

796,000 (2013)*

Last census: September 2002: 751,223

Population density: Four inhabitants per square km. Urban population 29 per cent (2010 Unicef).

Overall population density is low although population distribution is very uneven with a high concentration of people along the coastal strip and many inland areas virtually uninhabited. More than one-quarter of the total population live in the capital, Georgetown.

Annual growth rate: 0.2 per cent, 1990–2010 (Unicef).

Ethnic make-up

East Indian (51 per cent) (resident mostly in agricultural areas) and Afro-Guyanese (30 per cent) (resident mostly in towns) make up the majority. The remainder are of Chinese and European heritage, or Amerindians, most of whom live in the west and south or on reserves.

The main groups of Amerindians are Arawak, Carib, Wapisiana and Warao. The Caribs include Akawaio, Macushi, Patamona and Waiwai.

Religions

Christian (approximately 50 per cent), Hindu (35 per cent) and Muslim (10 per cent).

Education

Education includes primary school, four to six years of secondary school and between three to four years of higher academic or practical education. Students are usually expected to remain in the school system until the age of 16. There are around 900 schools in Guyana.

Increased access to secondary education is supported by two bilateral funded education projects – the Guyana Education Access Programme (GEAP) and the Guyana Building Equity Project (GBET).

The Minister of Labour announced on 29 June 2011 that the schedule to distribute one laptop computer per family by October 2011 was on target. Computer trainers were also being recruited to go into communities and target groups that were required to undertake coaching in the new technology.

Literacy rate: 98.7 per cent, total; 98.3 per cent, female: adult rates in 2002 (World Bank).

Compulsory years: Five to 14

Enrolment rate: 97.4 per cent net primary enrolment (World Bank).

Health

The government has stepped up provisions for drugs and medical supplies in all hospitals and health centres including facilities in the Georgetown Public Hospital Corporation (GPHC).

In June 2011, the Inter-American Development Bank approved a US$12 million loan to improve the water supply to Guyana's second city Linden. Overall, the plans include water pressure to be improved, quality sustained and a reduction in water loss achieved. Over five years (2011–16) the annual cost of water supply to Linden (100km inland from the coast) is estimated to fall from US$232,000 to US$140,000.

HIV/Aids
By 2001 46 per cent of sex workers were living with HIV/Aids and the probability of the virus passing into the wider population is considered by UNAID/WHO as high.
HIV prevalence: 3.2 per cent aged 15–49 in 2003 (World Bank)
Life expectancy: 63 years, 2004 (WHO 2006)
Fertility rate/Maternal mortality rate: 2.3 births per woman, 2010 (Unicef)
Birth rate/Death rate: 9 deaths and 18 births, per 1,000 population (World Bank).
Child (under 5 years) mortality rate (per 1,000): 35 deaths per 1,000 live births (WHO 2012); 12 per cent of children aged under five are malnourished (World Bank).

Welfare
The government has been developing new housing schemes, including distributing over 20,000 housing lots for a Low Income Settlement Project. The private sector has also been encouraged to assist in the development of the housing sector.

Main cities
Georgetown (capital, estimated population 142,484 in 2012), Linden (30,875), New Amsterdam (15,283), Anna Regina (14,088), Golden Grove (11,042), Corriverton (10,313).

Languages spoken
Guyana is the only English-speaking country in South America. Urdu, Hindi, Amerindian languages and Creole are also spoken. Along the Brazilian border, many Guyanese also speak Portuguese.
Official language/s
English

Media
Press
Dailies: In English, the *Guyana Chronicle* (www.guyanachronicle.com) is state-owned, private newspapers include *Stabroek News* (www.stabroeknews.com) and *Kaieteur News* (www.kaieteurnews.com).
Weeklies: All daily newspapers publish a weekend edition. In English, other newspapers include The *Catholic Standard* and the *Mirror* (www.mirrornewsonline.com) published twice weekly.
Broadcasting
The state-owned National Communications Network (NCN) (www.ncnguyana.com) operates radio and television services.
Radio: The (NCN) (www.ncnguyana.com) operates two radio stations, Hot FM (http://98hotfm.co.gy) broadcasting modern music. The Voice of Guyana (http://voiceofguyana.com) broadcasts internationally (http://vog560am.co.gy).
Television: The (NCN) (www.ncnguyana.com) operates a public TV station (http://ncn.co.gy). A number of TV channels are received from neighbouring countries. There are international satellite TV channels available.
National news agency: GINA (Government Information Agency)
Other news agencies: Caribbean Net News: www.caribbeannetnews.com
Guyana Journal: www.guyanajournal.com

Economy
Although the service sector is the major component of the economy, constituting 44.6 per cent of GDP in 2014, agriculture is still an important factor accounting for 21.5 per cent of GDP. The industry sector contributed 33.9 per cent, of which manufacturing was around 5 per cent.
Agriculture provides employment for around 30 per cent of the workforce with traditional production of sugar and rice remaining major exports. There is on-going development and investment in new enterprises, including sea and freshwater fishing and shrimp and crawfish, raw timber and finished lumber. Mining of bauxite and gold constitutes most of industrial activity, with open cast mines operating for both minerals.
GDP growth was a record high of 7.0 per cent in 2007, falling to 2.0 per cent in 2008 as the global economic crisis cut world trade, particularly in commodities. However, Guyana avoided the worst of the downturn and in 2009 GDP growth picked up to 3.3 per cent, and further still to 4.4 per cent in 2010; increasing steadily to an estimated growth in 2013 of 5.2 per cent before dropping to 3.8 per cent in 2014.
Guyana has since the early 1990s been working to transform itself from a state-dominated economy to a largely free-market enterprise driven economy. In 2010, the government announced an Agricultural Export Diversification Programme (ADP), funded by US$21.9 million from a loan from the Inter-American Development Bank (IADB), with US$1.1 million of public funds, to develop non-traditional agricultural exports, including fruit and vegetables, livestock and farm and sea-caught fish. Despite the government priority of promoting foreign investment and membership of the Caribbean Community (Caricom), inward investment has been slow. Social and political unrest between ethnic divisions of the country has proved a deterrent to foreign investors.
In 2014, the UN Human Development Index (HDI) ranked Guyana 121 (out of 187) for national development in health, education and income. Since 2000, Guyana's progress has grown but has not matched the improvement of other countries in Latin America (it was 117 in 2011). In 2014, roughly 8 per cent of the population lived in multidimensional poverty.
Migrant workers provided US$469 million in remittances in 2012 (15.5 per cent of GDP). Remittances not only stimulate the economy in general but also directly support family budgets. They were estimated to have dropped to US$328 million in 2013 before rising to US$415 million in 2014.

External trade
Along with 11 other members of the Caribbean Community (Caricom), Guyana operates within the single market (Caribbean Single Market and Economy (CSME)), which became operational in 2006. CSME includes the free movement of goods and services, a common trade policy and external tariff.
Imports
Principal imports include fuels and lubricants, machinery and transport equipment, consumer goods, food and chemicals.
Main sources: US (25.4 per cent of total in 2014), Trinidad and Tobago (19.8 per cent), Venezuela (10.1 per cent)
Exports
Principal exports include gold, sugar, bauxite and alumina, shrimps, rice, rum, timber and diamonds.
Main destinations: US (26.9 per cent total of total in 2014), Venezuela (12.1 per cent), UK (9.6 per cent)

Agriculture
Farming
Agriculture is a very important economic activity in Guyana. The sector employs approximately 30 per cent of the workforce and contributes 21.5 per cent to the country's total GDP.
The sugar industry is an important export earner, responsible for around 8 per cent of total exports. Rice accounts for 12 per cent of Guyana's export earnings and 19 per cent of its agricultural contribution to GDP.
About 2 per cent of the total land area is under cultivation. Cultivation of cash crops is confined to the alluvial coastal plain. The main cash crops are sugar, rice and shrimps.
Guyana is self-sufficient in sugar, rice, vegetables, fish, meat and fruit and increased government investment in the sector has improved production of many other products. Cassava is the principal crop grown in the interior. Emphasis is also being placed on the cultivation of oil palms, soya beans and corn, and on the development of dairy farming.

There is a national herd of livestock of between 200,000–250,000 head, which are ranched on the Rupununi savannah in the southeast.

A flood-resistant rice, developed for the Guyana Rice Development Board (GRDB) in the Guyana-based Burma Rice Research Station, began testing in local conditions in 2010. It was designed to survive being completely submerged for up to 17 days. In 2011, yields from this rice had risen by 10 per cent. In 2013, rice production reached its highest rate in history, producing over 400,000 tonnes.

Fishing

The fishing industry represents a valuable source of income to the economy of Guyana. Produce is sold on both domestic and international markets and the industry employs approximately 5 per cent of the country's total workforce.

Guyana is the region's largest exporter of shrimp, making up some 14 per cent of total exports. Government initiatives in the fishing sector include the improvement of fisheries management and the encouragement of investment in unexploited marine stocks.

Forestry

Guyana is one of the most densely forested countries in the world. Approximately 95 per cent of the country's total land mass is covered by forest and woodland.

All the forests are state-owned. Sawnwood and plywood are the principal forest products; pulp and paper, however, are imported.

Industry and manufacturing

The expansion of the industrial sector has traditionally been hampered by a lack of domestic energy supplies together with a dearth of technical and managerial personnel. At present the sector contributes roughly 38.5 per cent of total GDP and employs approximately 20 per cent of the total work force.

Previously, a serious shortage of foreign exchange had also caused the closure of many firms relying on imported inputs. However, the government is trying to expand the country's industrial base with a policy of diversification and greater encouragement of foreign investors to work with the predominant state sector.

Guyana's manufacturing industry is dominated by the processing of raw materials. Activity related to the mining sector (predominantly bauxite, gold and diamonds) and the processing of agricultural products such as sugar, rice, coconuts and timber, together account for about three-quarters of manufacturing activity. The remainder is accounted for by small-scale import substitution production for the local market. A shortfall in investment is a recurring problem.

Tourism

As South America's only English-speaking country Guyana has a natural advantage of familiarity to visitors from North America and elsewhere. Tourist facilities are almost exclusively located along the Atlantic Coast and around the capital, Georgetown, where the main dock welcomes a growing number of cruise liner visitors. The Tourism Ministry and the Guyana Tourism Authority recorded 2014 as the most successful year in terms of arrivals to Guyana, with numbers in November alone increasing by 13 per cent year-on-year. The interior of the country offers sites of pristine rainforest to explore but is sparsely populated and suitable only for the experienced outdoor visitor.

In February 2012 Guyana joined the Amazon Co-operation Treaty Organisation (Acto), which develops strategies to integrate tourism in the Amazon region, focussing on Brazil, Guyana and Suriname. The emphasis is due to change from wholly local packaged holiday destinations to one that incorporates greater use of the wider Amazon tourist opportunities.

Guyana has experienced a downturn in its tourist industry since 2006 when travel and tourism represented 13.6 per cent of GDP (a figure that had itself grown from 13.7 per cent in 2000). Since then a five-year decline reduced its contribution to 9.1 per cent by 2010. By 2014, travel and tourism's contribution had fallen to 8.0 per cent of GDP. Tourism has been an important long-term employer, but it too matched the decline, with an overall employment rate of 12.2 per cent (32,600 jobs) in 2006 down to 8 per cent (24,800 jobs) in 2010; this figure was maintained in 2014 (20,000 jobs).

Mining

Both mining and quarrying are of great importance to Guyana's economy. Both activities combined, amount to 25 per cent of total GDP and account for approximately 12 per cent of the country's total work force.

Annual gold production averages 440,000 ounces, 70 per cent of which comes from Omai Gold Mines, a US$300 million venture. Cambior and Golden Star Resources – Canadian companies – own 65 per cent and 30 per cent of Omai, respectively, and the Guyana government owns 5 per cent. In mid-2003, residents of western Guyana began legal action against Omai for allegedly allowing a dam to collapse on the Essequibo river in 1995, pouring 2.9 million cubic metres of cyanide-tainted slurry into the river. Around 23,000 residents supporting the writ want Omai to pay US$2 billion in damages and are demanding an end to the dumping of toxic waste into the river. A similar writ was issued in 2000, but was thrown out by the courts on technical grounds. In 2006 the High Court of the Supreme Court of Judicature of Guyana ordered the dismissal of the action, and ordered the plaintiffs to pay the defendants legal costs.

Royalties paid to Guyana's Gold Board are linked to world gold prices. An estimated one-fifth of gold production is smuggled across the borders to Venezuela, Brazil and Suriname by local miners. There is also inefficient alluvial mining by some 10,000 miners using dredgers and suctions.

Bauxite is the country's most important mineral, typically accounting for around a quarter of total export earnings. Production slumped in the early 1980s, prompting the government to seek outside help for the management of the industry.

There are known deposits of kaolin, molybdenum, uranium, copper, semi-precious stones, talc, soapstone and high-silica sand, which the government would like to develop.

On 6 October 2012, the minister of natural resources reported that gold production for the year had increased year-on-year by 23 per cent, to 314,000 ounces (up from 207,000 ounces in 2011).

Guyana Goldfields Inc. in 2015 was developing the Aurora Gold Project, a mine plan that is expected to produce 3.29 million ounces of gold, averaging 194,000 ounces per year over. The first gold pour is expected to come before the end of 2015.

Hydrocarbons

There are no proven hydrocarbon reserves. Consumption of oil was around 10,000 barrels per day (bpd) in 2014, all of which was imported.

In 2005, Guyana, plus a number of other Caribbean states, signed an agreement with Venezuela to establish PetroCaribe, a multi-national oil company, owned by the participating states. PetroCaribe buys low-priced Venezuelan crude oil under long-term payment plans. However, due to the weakened state of its economy, the Venezuelan government stated in 2014 that the subsidies to the PetroCaribe members might have to be reduced, which would cause adverse affects to the Guyanese trade balance.

In 2015, oil exploration was on-going, and despite no viable finds being made, oil companies remain hopeful about prospects in Guyana.

Although exploration initiatives for natural gas have also been undertaken by, among others, Total of France and Mobil

of the United States, the projects have yet to yield any significant production.
In June 2015, the Venezuelan president Nicolas Maduro demanded that Guyana stopped its oil exploration in the disputed offshore territory west of the Essequibo River.
Any use of natural gas or coal is commercially insignificant.

Energy

Total installed generating capacity was 362.5MW in 2013, the majority of which was produced by thermal power plants. Consumption is typically around 520 million kilowatt hours. A large proportion of the population don't have access to an electricity supply and self-reliance on individual power sources is widespread. The country has two centres of generation, the Berbice and Demerara Systems; the government has plans to integrate them.
Guyana continues to be heavily dependent on imported oil from both Venezuela and Trinidad and Tobago in order to meet its energy needs. Guyana Electricity Corporation (GEC) is government-subsidised. The Inter-American Development Bank (IDB) has provided loans to rehabilitate a number of GEC's existing thermal stations, as well as expanding the power grid.
Renewable energy includes a wind farm on the east coast supplying 4MW. The country has considerable potential for hydroelectric power generation, but significant investment remains dubious due to the lack of existing, extensive infrastructure.
In 2010, the government and the China Development Bank signed a loan agreement (for an undisclosed amount) to begin the Amaila Falls Hydro-Electric Project (AFHEP), for which the Inter-American Development Bank (IDB) also approved US$1.2 million for project preparation.
On 12 September 2012, a joint agreement was signed by the finance minister, private equity fund, Sithe Global and the engineering company, China Railway First Group, for the construction of the AFHEP, with an approximately 165MW capacity. The US$506 million project would have been the largest infrastructure contract ever undertaken by Guyana. However, in August 2013 the opposition A Partnership for National Unity (APNU) vetoed the project in parliament. However, in his annual address to the nation on 31 December 2014, President Ramotar assured the populace that the government '... will deliver the Amaila Falls Hydropower project to the Guyanese people, along with all its attendant benefits. Within months, we expect to achieve financial close and commence construction, and this project will come into operation during our new term in office.'
The project involves the construction of a hydropower plant in the area of west-central Guyana, where the Amaila and Kuribrong rivers meet. Electricity produced at the plant will be delivered to Georgetown and Linden by an electric transmission line. Once operational, approximately GY$9 billion (US$44 million) will be saved annually in fuel imports.

Financial markets

Stock exchange

Gasci (Guyana Association of Securities Companies and Intermediaries Incorporated)

Banking and insurance

Guyana's banking and financial services industry is concentrated in the capital Georgetown. The Central Bank of Guyana regulates the industry.

Central bank

Bank of Guyana

Main financial centre

Georgetown

Time

GMT minus four hours.

Geography

A plain about 15km wide runs along the 320km northern (Atlantic) coast and extends west into Venezuela and east into Suriname. This strip, which lies some 1.5 metres below sea level and is protected by a system of dykes, is intensively farmed and contains 90 per cent of the population. To the south of this area the land is mountainous, heavily forested and covered with a network of fast-flowing rivers with numerous rapids and falls, including the Kaietur Falls on the Potaro River which is seven times higher than Niagara. There are substantial reserves of bauxite, gold and diamonds in this area. To the south-west along the border with Venezuela is a region of upland savannah, the Rupununi, where the rest of the population, predominantly Amerindian, engages in limited agriculture and cattle-raising.

Hemisphere

Northern.

Climate

The climate is tropical, with a mean monthly temperature of 26–28 degrees Celsius (C) throughout the year on the coast (28 degrees C in the interior). Temperatures of above 32 degrees C or below 24 degrees C at any time of day or any season are rare. Rainfall is between 200–280mm per year on the coast, mainly in two sharply defined wet seasons, May to August and November to January. In the south there is a single rainy season from April to September, but rainfall is lower – averaging 150mm per year.

Dress codes

Among local businessmen the *shirtjac suit* – based upon a civilian version of the bush jacket – is widely worn in preference to the traditional business suit. It is perfectly acceptable to wear an open-necked shirt without a jacket on all but the most formal of occasions, but shorts are frowned upon.

Entry requirements

Passports

Required by all and valid for at least six months beyond intended stay.

Visa

Visas are required by all, except nationals of North America, Western Europe, Australasia, some Asian and all Caricom countries. For full details see: www.guyana.org/govt/visa_requirements.html.

Currency advice/regulations

The import and export of local currency is limited to G$200. The import of foreign currency is unlimited, subject to declaration on arrival; export is limited to amount declared.

Health (for visitors)

On 18 August Guyana banned all person travelling from the West Africa countries where the ebola virus is present – Guinea, Liberia, Sierra Leone, Senegal and Nigeria until further notice.

Mandatory precautions

A yellow fever vaccination certificate is required if arriving from an infected area.

Advisable precautions

Vaccination against yellow fever is encouraged for travellers to rural areas. There is a risk of malaria in some areas of the interior, and adequate precautions should be taken. Water in urban areas is chlorinated, but typhoid is a risk in rural areas so drinking water should be boiled; bottled water is widely available. Dairy products are likely to be made from unpasteurised milk.
Various hepatitis strains are common. B and D stains are endemic in the Amazon basin and precautions are necessary. Tropical parasites, TB, and dengue fever all occur in certain areas. Professional advice concerning precautions should be sort before travelling to Guyana.
Hospital conditions may not match those in developed countries; health insurance, including repatriation is recommended. Travellers should carry enough prescription and medical supplies for the duration of their stay.

Hotels

Hotels are available in Georgetown, Linden and New Amsterdam. Rooms are generally in short supply. A 10 per cent tip is usual.

Public holidays (national)

Fixed dates

1 Jan (New Year's Day), 23 Feb (Republic Day), 1 May (Labour Day), 5 May (Arrival Day), 26 May (Independence Day), 25–26 Dec (Christmas).

When a public holiday falls on a Sunday, the following Monday is taken as the holiday.

Variable dates

Holi (Hindu, Mar), Good Friday, Easter Monday, Caricom Day (first Mon in Jul), Liberty Day (first Mon in Aug), Diwali (Hindu, Oct/Nov), Eid al Adha, Birth of the Prophet.

Hindu and Muslim festivals are timed according to local sightings of various phases of the moon.

Working hours

Banking

Mon–Thu: 0800–1230; Fri: 0800–1230, 1500–1700.

Business

Mon–Thu: 0800–1600; Fri: 0800–1200.

Government

Mon–Thu: 0800–1200, 1300–1630; Fri: 0800–1200, 1300–1530.

Shops

Mon–Fri: 0800–1130, 1300–1600; Sat: 0800–1130.

Electricity supply

Electricity supply is not standardised; Georgetown generally 110V AC 60Hz, but some supplies are 220V AC, 50Hz. Elsewhere supply is 110V AC at either 50 or 60 cycles.

Weights and measures

The metric system is official, but imperial measures are often preferred.

Social customs/useful tips

Business is often conducted in a relaxed atmosphere and an emphasis is placed upon personal contact. At the same time, careful observance of polite formalities such as handshaking and formal use of titles (such as Mr, etc) is appreciated. All officials should be treated with careful respect. Attention to detail in the making and keeping of appointments is also appreciated, although punctuality may not be reciprocated.

Invitations to the homes of business contacts are regularly offered since Guyanese pride themselves upon their hospitality. It is customary for visitors to return the invitation in a hotel or to a restaurant.

Hotel and restaurant staff and taxi drivers customarily receive a 10 per cent tip; airport porters are tipped by the bag.

Security

The streets of Georgetown can be unsafe after dark due to street robbery, and the use of taxis is recommended. Ostentatious display of wealth such as expensive wristwatches or jewellery and the carrying of large amounts of cash should be avoided. As in all cities, it is unwise to leave articles unattended in parked cars or hotel rooms.

Getting there

Air

International airport/s: Cheddi Jagan International Airport (GEO), 40km from Georgetown; bank, duty free, restaurants and car hire.

Airport tax: G$4,000 for international departures; not applicable to transit passengers.

Surface

Road: A coastal road runs from the Suriname border to Georgetown, via a ferry across the Berbice River at New Amsterdam.

Entry from Brazil is possible at Lethem where international border controls are in place. A bridge being constructed across the Takutu river will eventually connect Bonfim in Roraima State (Brazil) to Lethem. There are unsealed roads in current use. There are no road connections to Venezuela.

Water: There is a ferry service between Guyana-Suriname.

Main port/s: Georgetown, New Amsterdam and Springlands.

Getting about

National transport

Air: Air travel is the only efficient method of reaching the interior of the country. Trans Guyana Airways operates both regional and interior flights, but occasionally permits are needed from the ministry of the interior for non-nationals. Early booking is essential.

Charter facilities are available at Georgetown. Larger towns and mining companies have airports or landing strips.

Road: There are all-weather, asphalt roads along the coast and some brick roads inland. A coastal road links Georgetown, Rossignol, New Amsterdam and the Suriname border. Another coast road runs west from Georgetown, via the Demerara River, to Parika. A sealed highway to the Brazilian border via Lethem is in the initial stage of construction; only unsealed roads exist currently.

Buses: Buses are operated privately and run regularly and are generally reliable (although crowded). Services run along the coast. Private *tapir* minibuses, mine buses and bush buses (into the interior) are also available.

Rail: There is no passenger rail service, although some mining companies have private goods lines.

Water: Passenger and cargo vessels travel up the Demerara, Essequibo and Berbice rivers, and also along the coast between the rivers. Ferries link Parika-Bartica on the Essequibo River; Rosignol-New Amsterdam on the Berbice River; Corriverton-Suriname on the Corentyne River. These services include New Amsterdam-Ituni, Georgetown-Bartica, Rosignol-New Amsterdam. River taxis (small wooden boats) service the same areas as the ferries. The taxis are faster and more expensive, they may also be chartered.

City transport

Taxis: Taxis are widely available in major towns and can be found on ranks. They have standard fares for inner city journeys; fares for longer trips should be negotiated in advance. A 10 per cent tip is usual.

For early morning flights from Timehri, make taxi arrangements the previous day.

Buses, trams & metro: Minibuses are a cheap mode of transport. They connect Timehri airport with Georgetown and are safe in the day. At night it is wiser to use a taxi.

Car hire

Car hire facilities are limited. They are available in Georgetown but must be booked well in advance. An international driving licence is required. Traffic drives on the left.

BUSINESS DIRECTORY

The addresses listed below are a selection only. While World of Information makes every endeavour to check these addresses, we cannot guarantee that changes have not been made, especially to telephone numbers and area codes. We would welcome any corrections.

Telephone area codes

The international dialling code (IDD) for Guyana is +592, followed by subscriber's number:

Chambers of Commerce

Berbice Chamber of Commerce, 12 Chapel Street, New Amsterdam, Berbice (tel: 227-6340; fax: 226-4535).

Georgetown Chamber of Commerce and Industry, PO Box 10110, 156 Waterloo Street, North Cummingsburg, Georgetown (tel: 225-5864; fax: 226-3519; e-mail: info@georgetownchamberofcommerce.org).

Banking

Bank of Baroda, Avenue of the Republic & Regent Street, Georgetown (tel: 226-4005).

Bank of Nova Scotia, Regent & Hinck Streets, Georgetown (tel: 640-312; fax: 225-7985).

Citizens Bank Guyana Ltd, 201 Camp & Charlotte Sts, Georgetown (tel: 226-1705/6; fax: 226-1719).

Demerara Bank Ltd, 230 Camp St & South Rd, Georgetown (tel: 225-0610/9; fax 225-0601).

Guyana Bank for Trade & Industry, 47-48 Water Street, Georgetown (tel: 226-8430/9; fax: 227-1612).

Guyana Co-operative Agricultural & Industrial Development Bank, 126 Barrack & Parade Streets, Kingston, Georgetown (tel: 225-8806/9; fax: 226-8260).

Guyana National Co-operative Bank, Lombard & Cornhill Streets, Georgetown (tel: 225-7810/9).

National Bank of Industry & Commerce, 38-40 Water Street, Georgetown (tel: 226-4091/5; fax: 227-2921).

Central bank

Bank of Guyana, 1 Church Street & Avenue of the Republic, PO Box 1003, Georgetown (tel: 226-3250; fax: 227-2965; e-mail: comminications@bankofguyana.org.gy).

Stock exchange

Gasci (Guyana Association of Securities Companies and Intermediaries Incorporated), www.gasci.com

Travel information

Air Services Ltd, Wights Lane, Kingston, Georgetown (tel: 226-1767, 226-5759).

Guyana Overland Tours, PO Box 10173, 6 Avenue of the Republic, Robbstown, Georgetown (tel: 226-9876).

Roraima Airways, 101 Cummings Street, Georgetown (tel: 225-9647; fax: 225-9646).

Tourism Association of Guyana, 228 South Road, Lacytown, Georgetown (tel: 225-0807; fax: 225-0817).

Ministry of tourism

Ministry of Tourism, Industry and Commerce, 229 South Road, Lacytown, Georgetown (tel: 226-8629; fax: 225-9898; e-mail: ministry@mintic.gov.gy).

National tourist organisation offices

Guyana Tourism Office, Sophia Exhibition Complex, Georgetown (tel: 223-6351 fax: 231-6351).

Ministries

Ministry of Agriculture, Regent Road, Bourda, Georgetown (tel: 223-7844; fax: 225-0599; e-mail: moa@sdnp.org.gov.gy).

Ministry of Amerindian Affairs, 236 Thomas and Quamina Streets, Georgetown (tel: 227-5067; fax: 223-1616; e-mail: moaa@networksgy.com).

Ministry of Culture, Youth and Sports, 71 Main Street, Georgetown (tel: 227-7866; fax: 226-8549; e-mail: psmincys@guyana.net.gy).

Ministry of Education, 26 Brickdam, Stabroek, Georgetown (tel: 223-7900; fax: 225-8511; e-mail: moegyweb@yahoo.com).

Ministry of Finance, Main Street, Kingston, Georgetown (tel: 225-6088; fax: 226-1284; e-mail: guyanadmd@solutions2000.net).

Ministry of Fisheries, Crops & Livestock, Regent Road, Bourda, Georgetown (tel: 226-1565; fax: 227-2978; e-mail: minfci@sdnp.org.gy).

Ministry of Foreign Affairs, 254 South Road & New Garden Street, Georgetown (tel: 226-9080; fax: 223-5241; e-mail: minfor@sdnp.org.gy).

Ministry of Foreign Trade, 254 South Road & New Garden Street, Georgetown (tel: 226-1607; fax: 223-0900; e-mail: moftic@moftic.gov.gy).

Ministry of Health and Labour, Brickdam, Stabroek, Georgetown (tel: 226-1560; fax: 225-4505; e-mail: moh@sdnp.org.gy).

Ministry of Home Affairs, Brickdam, Stabroek, Georgetown (tel: 225-7270; fax: 227-4806).

Ministry of Housing and Water, 41 Brickdam, Stabroek, Georgetown (tel: 225-7192; fax: 227-3455; e-mail: housing@guyana.net.gy).

Ministry of Information, Area B Homestretch Avenue, Georgetown (tel: 226-8996; fax: 226-4003; e-mail: gis@sdnp.org.gy).

Ministry of Labour, Human Services and Social Security, 1 Water and Cornhill Streets, Stabroek, Georgetown (tel: 225-0655; fax: 227-1308; e-mail: nrdocgd@sdnp.org.gy).

Ministry of Legal Affairs, 95 Carmichael Street, Georgetown (tel: 223-7355; fax: 227-5419).

Ministry of Local Government and Regional Development, Fort Street, Kingston, Georgetown (tel: 225-8621; fax: 226-5070).

Ministry of Parliamentary Affairs, Office of the President, New Garden Street, Georgetown (tel: 226-6453).

Ministry of Public Service Management, 164 Waterloo Street, Georgetown (tel 227-1193; fax: 227-2700; e-mail: psm@sdnp.org.gy).

Ministry of Transport and Hydraulics, Wights Lane, Kingston, Georgetown (tel: 226-1875; fax: 225-8395; e-mail: minoth@networksgy.com).

Office of the President, New Garden Street, Bourda, Georgetown (tel: 225-1573; 227-3050; e-mail: op-iu@sdnp.org.gy).

Office of the Prime Minister, Wights Lane, Kingston, Georgetown (tel: 226-6695; fax: 226-7573; pmoffice@sdnp.org.gov.gy).

Other useful addresses

Association of Non-Traditional Exporters of Guyana (ANTEG), (tel: 226-0779; fax: 226-1063).

Bauxite Industry Development Co, 71 Main Street, Georgetown (tel: 225-7780; fax: 226-7413).

British High Commission, 44 Main Street, PO Box 10849, Georgetown (tel: 226-5881; fax: 225-0671; e-mail: bhcguyana@networksgy.com).

Caribbean Community Secretariat, PO Box 10827, Turkeyen, Georgetown (tel: 222-0001; fax: 222-0171; e-mail: info@caricom.org).

Consultative Association of Guyanese Industry, East Street, PO Box 10730, Georgetown.

Forest Products Association of Guyana (tel: 226-9848).

Forestry Commission, 1 Water Street, Georgetown (tel: 226-7271; fax: 226-8956; e-mail: forstry@sdnp.org.gy).

Geology and Mines Commission, PO Box 1028, Brickdam, Georgetown (tel: 225-3047; fax: 225-2274; e-mail: ggmc@sdnp.org.gy).

Guyana Broadcasting Corporation, PO Box 10760, Georgetown (tel: 226-9231).

Guyana Embassy (USA), 2490 Tracy Place, NW, Washington DC 20008 (tel: (+1-202) 265-6900; fax: (+1-202) 232-1297; e-mail: guyanaemb@aol.com).

Guyana Export Promotion Council, Sophia National Exhibition Park, Sophia, Georgetown (tel: 225-9443, 227-3394, 226-8526; fax: 226-3400).

Guyana Manufacturers' Association (GMA), 62 Main Street, Georgetown (tel: 227-4295; fax: 227-0670).

Guyana Mining Enterprise Ltd, Linden, Georgetown.

Guyana Office for Investment, Go-Invest, 190 Camp & Church Streets, Georgetown (tel: 225-0658, 227-0653; fax: 225-0655).

Guyana Rice Producers' Association (tel: 226-4411, 227-6957).

Guyana Rice Board, 1-2 Water Street, Georgetown (tel: 226-6822).

Guyana State Corporation, 45-47 Water Street, Georgetown (tel: 226-0530).

Guyana Sugar Corporation, 201 Camp Street, Cummingsburg, PO Box 10547, Georgetown (tel: 226-0571; fax: 225-7274).

Institute of Private Enterprise Development, (IPED), Georgetown (tel: 225-8949, 225-3067, 226-4765).

New Guyana Marketing Corporation, Robb Street, Georgetown.

Omai Gold Mines Limited, 176-D Middle Street, Cummingsburg, Georgetown (tel: 226-8129, 226-5898; fax: 226-6468).

Private Sector Commission (PSC), Georgetown (tel: 225-7170, 64-603; fax: 227-0725).

Public Corporations Secretariat, PO Box 1020, 45-7 Water Street, Georgetown (tel: 226-0536/9).

Shipping Association of Georgetown, 28 Main and Holmes Streets, Georgetown (tel: 226-2632).

United States Embassy, 31 Main Street, Georgetown (tel: 225-4900; fax: 225-8497).

National news agency: GINA (Government Information Agency)

Address: Area B Homestretch Ave, D' Urban Backlands, Georgetown (tel: 226-6715; fax: 226-4003; internet: www.gina.gov.gy).

Caribbean Net News: www.caribbeannetnews.com

Guyana Journal: www.guyanajournal.com

Internet sites

Berbice online newspaper: http://www.berbicenews.com

Guyana News and Information: http://www.guyana.org/

Economic Commission for Latin America and the Caribbean: http://www.eclac.cl/index1.html

Inter-American Development Bank: http://www.iadb.org

Organisation of American States: http://www.oas.org

Latin World: http://www.latinworld.com

Latin Trade Online://www.latintrade.com

Local web directory: http://sdnp.org.gy/guylink.html

Haiti

First-round presidential and second-round legislative elections will be held in Haiti on 25 October 2015, after the first round of legislative elections held on 9 August turned out pretty inconclusively. The votes scheduled for 25 October include the first round of the presidential election, a second round of legislative elections for 119 seats in Haiti's lower house (the chamber of deputies) and 20 in its upper house (the senate) and municipal elections. Of the 5.8 million people registered to vote a mere 1.05 million valid votes had been cast in August (less than 18 per cent turn-out). The expectation was that the presidential election would require a runoff second-round vote. Were that to be so, it would take place at the end of December 2015.

Not that the run-up to the elections has been entirely smooth. Pre-election violence has led to the deaths of at least 15 people, including two pregnant women. The violence appeared to be politically motivated, according to government officials; local activists said that politicians were distributing money to gangs in an effort to influence voting. During the first round of legislative elections, violence had forced several polling stations in Port-au-Prince to close.

KEY FACTS

Official name: République d'Haiti (Republic of Haiti)

Head of State: President Michel Martelly (from 14 May 2011)

Head of government: Prime Minister Evans Paul, nominated by President Martelly (since 16 January 2015)

Ruling party: Acting coalition led by Fwon Lespwa (Front for Hope) (formed 7 June 2006)

Area: 27,750 square km

Population: 10.32 million (2014)*

Capital: Port-au-Prince

Official language: French and Creole

Currency: Gourde (G) = 100 centimes

Exchange rate: G51.68 per US$ (Sep 2015)

GDP per capita: US$833 (2014)*

GDP real growth: 2.75% (2014)*

GDP: US$8.71 billion (2014)*

Inflation: 3.94% (2014)*

Balance of trade: -US$2.30 billion (2013)*

* estimated figure

Polling before the election showed vastly different results concerning who would be the frontrunner. In order to avoid a second round, a presidential candidate would need to achieve a margin of victory of more than 25 percentage points over his or her closest rival. It was thought to be unlikely that any candidate would achieve this. However, the close field will raise the risk of fraud accusations and another two months of campaigning will not alleviate a tense and fractious political climate.

In late 2014 protesters in Haiti had taken to the streets as they renewed calls for President Michel Martelly to resign and hold long overdue elections. Parliamentary polls should have been called three years earlier, but had been repeatedly delayed amid political deadlock in the country. President Michel Martelly was obliged to reach a deal with the senate and the chamber of deputies to avert an even greater political crisis over the delayed elections. It was reported that the President had signed an agreement with the presidents of the two chambers to extend their mandate.

Under the agreement, Haiti's deputies would be extended in their posts until 24 April and senators until 9 September. The deal came just two weeks after Prime Minister Laurent Lamothe had resigned following the protests at the delayed mid-term senate elections. These had originally been scheduled for May 2012. Haiti's municipal elections were also three years behind schedule and were postponed yet again in October 2014, on the very day they were due to be held, ostensibly because of a continuing dispute between the government and a group of opposition senators over an electoral law. The President's critics accused him of delaying the elections to enable him to rule by decree. Mr Martelly had appointed Evans Paul, a former radio journalist, to replace Mr Lamothe. However, before he could begin to form a government Mr Paul's appointment also had to be confirmed by parliament.

The earthquake

Haiti was thoroughly unprepared when the 7.0 magnitude earthquake had hit in January 2010. The earthquake devastated the island, leaving millions homeless. Five years on Haiti was still picking up the pieces.

In August 2014 Sam Hillesta of the Borgen Project in the US prepared a comprehensive list of the damage and effects of the earthquake that were still being dealt with five years on. Mr Hillesta noted that even before the earthquake, Haiti was one of the poorest countries in the world, ranking 145 out of the 169 countries surveyed in the UN Human Development Index, with over 70 per cent of Haiti's population living under the poverty line. The death toll estimates varied from 220,000 to 316,000. According to Mr Hillesta, over one million people were initially displaced and about 500,000 remained homeless in mid-2014.

Despite being built upon a major fault line, Haiti had no building codes and therefore had no way to ensure that its buildings were safe from earthquakes. As a result, much of Haiti's infrastructure was demolished and nearly 300,000 homes were badly damaged or destroyed. The earthquake struck near Port-au-Prince, destroying many of the most important government buildings, hospitals and roads. Over 4,000 schools, about one quarter of the total, were damaged or destroyed.

To make matters worse, a cholera outbreak occurred in October 2010. By June 2013, over 8,000 people had died from cholera out of the 664,282 cases registered. Ninety-six UN peacekeepers died in the earthquake, along with 122 US citizens. The international community responded well to the crisis. From 2010 to 2012, international donors raised US$6.43 billion for Haitian reconstruction. USAID contributed US$450 million in aid to Haiti. By mid-2014, aid organisations had rebuilt about 21,000 houses and made 100,000 temporary shelters. Fifty per cent of the rubble had been removed and 650 schools had been repaired. The American Red Cross had provided 369,000 people with clean water, 2.4 million with health and hygiene education and three million with cholera treatment and prevention.

Sadly, issues with transparency and supervision had made it difficult to track where all the reconstruction funds had gone. Seventy-five per cent of all foreign aid went to non-governmental organisations (NGOs) that spent the money inefficiently and with limited results. Experts have said that it will be another 10 years before 'serious results' can finally be seen. Only half of the money that international governments had promised was ever paid.

The economy

Haiti's economic growth slowed to 2.7 per cent in 2014 from 4.2 per cent the previous year. More than 6 million out of Haiti's 10.4 million people live below the poverty line of US$2.42 a day and one-quarter of Haitians live on less than US$1.23 per day, according to the World Bank. A key issue for Haiti was the sustainable development of its economy. In the wake of the 2010 earthquake, international donor funds had come flooding in, but much of the money was frittered away or simply 'disappeared'. Since 2012 support has subsided substantially as Haiti came to terms with the need to make use of its own resources to generate economic and social development.

In 2014 Transparency International ranked Haiti 161 out of the 175 countries surveyed on is *Corruption perceptions Index*, making it the most corrupt country in the Caribbean region. In 2015 Haiti lacked a robust judicial system and suffered from very limited transparency and

KEY INDICATORS — Haiti

	Unit	2011	2012	2013	2014	**2015
Population	m	*10.01	*10.17	*10.32	*10.46	*10.60
Gross domestic product (GDP)	US$bn	7.40	7.89	8.45	*8.71	*9.15
GDP per capita	US$	738	775	819	*833	*863
GDP real growth	%	5.6	2.9	4.2	*2.8	*3.3
Inflation	%	7.4	6.8	6.8	*3.9	*6.4
Exports (fob) (goods)	US$m	768.1	785.0	778.8	–	–
Imports (fob) (goods)	US$m	3,014.0	2,679.3	3,079.3	–	–
Balance of trade	US$m	-2,245.9	-1,894.4	-2,300.5	–	–
Current account	US$m	-339.0	-426.0	-569.0	*-502.0	*-275.0
Total reserves minus gold	US$m	1,388.0	1,284.5	1,735.6	1,916.4	–
Foreign exchange	US$m	1,277.7	1,178.6	1,629.5	–	–
Exchange rate	per US$	40.28	42.47	43.88	46.76	–

* estimated figure ** forecast figure

accountability in governance. Financial corruption was systemic in both the private and public sectors. Aggravated by the late adoption (in May 2015) of the 2014 budget, the main macro-economic variables of the Haitian economy have performed relatively well, albeit less impressively than the authorities had initially expected. Gross domestic product (GDP) grew by 3.5 per cent (versus 4.3 per cent in 2013), driven by expansions in manufacturing (7.3 per cent), construction (9.2 per cent) and commerce (12.8 per cent), as well as the expected good performance of the agricultural sector. The fiscal deficit rose to 4.6 per cent of GDP (on a cash basis), but remains below expected levels set out in the Extended Credit Facility arrangement with the International Monetary Fund (IMF), whose eighth and final review was completed in November. Average annual inflation between October 2013 and September 2014 (3.7 per cent) was half of that in the corresponding period between 2012 and 2013, attributable to a significant drop in the prices of certain imported products (rice, wheat and cooking oils) and a supply-side improvement in domestic agricultural production.

According to the United Nations Economic Commission for Latin America and the Caribbean (CEPAL/ECLAC), a slowdown in exports and imports (which grew by 5.3 per cent and 1.1 per cent, respectively) in 2014 and buoyant remittances (up by 11 per cent) led to a slight narrowing (-4 per cent) in the balance-of-payments current account deficit to 6.2 per cent of GDP.

Tax receipts grew by 5.3 per cent in nominal terms – despite the reduction (of 5.8 per cent) in tariff revenues – on the back of a rise (of 19.7 per cent) in direct collection. Current expenditure was up by 15 per cent, driven by increased out-goings in wages (13 per cent) and operating expenses (17 per cent). In stark contrast to the forecast acceleration in public investment, spending on public works from Treasury resources was slashed (by 45 per cent) as the public investment programme was frozen pending the adoption of the new budget. This was, however, partially offset by payments (to the tune of US$175 million) made under the Petrocaribe energy co-operation agreement and untied aid contributions (US$98 million) in the last quarter of the year.

ECLAC noted that the average increases in domestic oil and gas prices (7.7 per cent in October 2014), after three and a half years of freezes, would reduce the amount of subsidies and transfers paid out of the public purse, although the effects will not be felt until the 2014/15 fiscal year. The state-owned utility, Électricité d'Haïti (EDH) received subsidies and transfers to the tune of US$98 million in 2014.

The Bank of the Republic of Haiti (BRH) continued to implement a contractionary monetary policy, limiting growth in the monetary base to just 0.1 per cent by tightening legal reserve requirements, although the M1 monetary aggregate, at 9.8 per cent, was almost double that of 2013. Private lending expanded by 5.5 per cent in real terms, a slowdown on growth of 11.4 per cent seen in 2013 and the dollarisation rate grew (from 40 per cent to 43 per cent of the total offered amount). The BRH provided substantial monetary financing to the central authorities (1.3 per cent of GDP, up from 0.7 per cent of GDP in 2013). The gourde fell by 3.5 per cent between fiscal year 2013 and fiscal year 2014 (after depreciation of 3.7 per cent in 2013), leading the BRH to take action (by selling foreign exchange). Net international reserves (US$1 billion at the end of the fiscal year) were down by 18 per cent (or US$222 million) in respect of fiscal year 2013.

The balance-of-payments current account deficit (6.2 per cent of GDP) was practically unchanged on 2013, as a result of a reduction of the trade deficit and, more importantly, a surge in remittances, which at US$1,977 billion represented three times the amount received in donations. Haiti's terms of trade improved by 5.7 per cent according to ECLAC, recovering from the fall (of 6.2 per cent) seen in 2013. This was attributable to reductions or modest increases in the prices of Haiti's main import goods (hydrocarbons, rice, wheat and cooking oils) and price rises in goods in its export basket, namely *máquila* textile products (4.1 per cent), essential oils (26 per cent), mangoes (6.5 per cent), cocoa (27 per cent) and coffee (21 per cent).

The balance-of-payments financial account (standing at US$495 million) included US$99 million in foreign direct investment (FDI) – compared to US$160 million in 2013 – and was most affected by net outflows (of US$377 million) to service debt taken out under the Petrocaribe credit agreement with Venezuela. Overall public external debt stood at US$1.829 billion and had spiralled since 2011 (when it was US$657 million). The downward trend in international oil prices in 2014/15 (a cumulative fall of 11 per cent since July 2014) could lead to a restructuring of outstanding payments under the Petrocaribe agreement (50 per cent in cash and soft loan financing the remaining 50 per cent); if international prices reach a level between 50 and 80 dollars per barrel, Haiti would be required to pay 60 per cent of its oil bill in cash.

Estimates for GDP growth in 2014 (3.5 per cent) were chiefly reliant on the good performance of agriculture (which looked set, however, to be less buoyant than in 2013) and improved (or largely unchanged) trends in three other key sectors – manufacturing, construction and trade – between the end of the third quarter (in June) and the close of the fiscal year in September 2014.

Forecasts made for the agricultural sector in recent reports of the National Food Security Co-ordination Body (CNSA) are no more than moderately optimistic, since the spring harvest (June to August) of a considerable number of staple crops such as cereals (maize, sorghum and rice), legumes and tubers was markedly less abundant than in 2013. This was due both to climate-related factors (a water shortage in the principally rain-fed system of agriculture) and the greater scarcity of financial resources and inputs (fertilisers and seeds) which should have been provided by the public authorities (namely the ministry of agriculture). In 2014, growth in the industrial sector (7.3 per cent) was slightly stronger than in 2013 (6.7 per cent), but under-performed the government's initial forecasts. A major contributing factor was the under-whelming performance of *máquila* textile exports, both in terms of value (which increased by 3.3 per cent, down on 14 per cent in 2013) and volume (contracting by 0.9 per cent after growing by 20.7 per cent in 2013).

The construction sector expanded significantly (9.2 per cent) – albeit at a slower rate than in 2013 (11 per cent) – despite the delays in carrying out the public investment programme and disbursements of Petrocaribe funds, which were chiefly made in the last quarter of the fiscal year (between June and September). Commercial activity – both formal and, to a large extent, informal – accounted for 28 per cent of GDP. Important drivers of growth (of 12.8 per cent in real terms) in commercial activity were buoyant consumption, partially attributable to household remittances (which grew by 11 per cent in nominal terms) and an increase in wages (8.5 per cent) in the formal sectors of the economy in the wake of a rise of

12.5 per cent in minimum wages in May 2014 (to 225 gourdes, the equivalent of US$5 per working day). Another contributing factor was the rally in job creation in the *maquila* industry (36,340 jobs created) and in temporary jobs under various contractual arrangements (such as cash for work) in urban and rural areas and the funding provided as part of public social assistance programmes and by NGOs.

The fall in inflation (annual average rate of 3.7 per cent, compared to 7 per cent in 2013) might be a result of reductions in the international price of some core products in the local market, as shown by comparisons between year-on-year inflation (at the end of the fiscal year in September) in domestically produced (5.3 per cent) and imported (2.5 per cent) foodstuffs.

Immigration

In the first half of 2015 over 200,000 Haitians and Dominicans of Haitian descent had decided to flee the Dominican Republic when faced with a risk of deportation. This situation had been easy enough to anticipate following a 2013 ruling by the Dominican Constitutional Court that effectively meant that those with Haitian nationality or ancestry had been stripped of their Dominican citizenship. The ruling meant that those who could not comply with the new 'guidelines', became 'illegal'; Dominican citizenship was given to anyone born in the country. Although the new law affected many different migrant groups in the country, most immediately saw it as a clumsy move to deport black Dominicans of Haitian descent.

Surprisingly, given the already extensive population shifts in the region, the new law had created the largest stateless population in the Western Hemisphere. The favourite destination for those leaving was the area of Haiti close to the Dominican border. However, the sudden arrival of so many refugee families had not proved popular with their new Haitian neighbours, or with the Haitian government.

One casualty of the migrant situation was the United States diplomatic service; US ambassadors in both Haiti and the Dominican Republic, having visited the area, declared that there was 'no evidence' of any humanitarian calamity. Reporting in the US periodical, *Foreign Affairs* Lauran Carasik drew attention to this apparent failure: the US Ambassador James Brewster, had posed for photos with the heads of the Dominican army, border patrol and migration directorate, praising the Dominican security forces and denying that the Dominican Republic was violating human rights. This assessment curiously corresponded neatly with that of Brewster's counterpart in Haiti, where US Ambassador Pamela Ann White also claimed that there was no evidence of a humanitarian crisis.

Concerned at US inaction, according to Ms Carasik's report, over 550 former Peace Corps volunteers and three former Peace Corps country directors for the Dominican Republic signed a letter to Secretary of State John Kerry in August 2015, suggesting that the United States stopped its security aid to the Dominican Republic, which added up to US$17.5 million since 2013, until the Dominican government improved its record.

Risk assessment

Economy	Fair/good
Politics	Fair
Regional stability	Good/fair

COUNTRY PROFILE

1492 Christopher Columbus landed and named the island Hispaniola, or 'little Spain'.

1496 The Spanish established the first European settlement in the Western hemisphere at Santo Domingo, now the capital of the Dominican Republic.

1697 The island of Hispaniola was divided between France and Spain. The western half became Haiti (Land of Mountains).

1801 A former black slave, Toussaint Louverture, led a guerrilla rebellion, conquering Haiti, abolishing slavery and proclaiming himself governor general of all Hispaniola. He was captured by the French and died in their custody.

1804 Independence was declared by former slave Jean-Jacques Dessalines, who declared himself emperor. There were various monarchical periods until 1859.

1806 Dessalines was assassinated and Haiti became divided into the black-controlled north and the mulatto-controlled south.

1818–43 Pierre Boyer unified Haiti, but excluded blacks from power.

1915 The US invaded Haiti claiming it was protecting its property and investments threatened by clashes between blacks and mulattos.

1934 The US withdrew its troops.

1956 François 'Papa Doc' Duvalier, a voodoo physician, seized power in a military coup and became president in the following year.

1964 Duvalier declared himself president-for-life and established a dictatorship with the help of the violent Tontons Macoute militias.

1971 Duvalier died and was succeeded by his son, the 19-year-old Jean-Claude 'Baby Doc' Duvalier, who declared himself president-for-life.

1986 Baby Doc fled Haiti amid riots and a multitude of coup attempts. Lieutenant General Henri Namphy assumed power as the head of a governing junta.

1988 Leslie Manigat became president but was overthrown in a coup led by Brigadier General Prosper Avril, who installed a civilian government under military control.

1990 Jean-Bertrand Aristide was elected president.

1991 Aristide was expelled from the country following a military coup headed by Brigadier-General Raoul Cedras. The new junta promised elections at a future date. The US, France and Canada suspended aid to Haiti and refused to recognise the new government.

1992 Marc Louis Bazin served as interim prime minister in 1992–93.

1993 The UN imposed sanctions on Haiti after the military regime rejected an accord designed to facilitate Aristide's return to power.

1994 After US forces removed the military government of General Raoul Cedras, Aristide returned from exile and was reinstalled as president. He was not permitted by law to stand for re-election in 1995.

1995 René Préval was elected to replace Aristide.

1997 US troops left Haiti. Prime Minister Rosny Smarth resigned.

Former prime minister, Marc Louis Bazin, who was known as 'Mr Clean' for his attempts to improve the lot of ordinary Haitians during his term as interim prime minister in 1992–93, died in August.

1999 President Préval dissolved the legislature and a Provisional Electoral Council (CEP) was created to organise elections; Jacques Eduard Aléxis was appointed prime minister and a government was sworn in.

2000 The Fanmi Lavalas (FL) (Lavalas Family) party won control of the Senate and President Jean-Bertrand Aristide won the controversial presidential election.

2001 President Aristide appointed Jean-Marie Chérestal as prime minister. Aristide agreed to hold new parliamentary elections in return for the Organisation of American States (OAS) helping Haiti to receive the US$500 million of suspended aid. There was an unsuccessful coup attempt.

2002 Prime Minister Chérestal resigned amid allegations of corruption and incompetence. Aristide appointed Yvon Neptune as prime minister. Government and opposition factions clashed violently, with attacks by government loyalists on civic groups and armed anti-government gangs.

2004 Opposition rebels, led by Guy Philippe, won control of several towns. President Aristide resigned and left the country; Chief Justice Boniface Alexandre became caretaker president. The UN approved a multi-national security force to restore law and order. Gérard Latortue became prime minister. Hurricane Mitch devastated large areas and left a death toll of around 2,000. UN forces assumed Haiti peacekeeping duties. The US made available US$9 million to Haiti to assist in election preparations for 2005. Hurricane Jeanne swept through Haiti, killing as many as 1,500 Haitians.

2006 Presidential and legislative elections, postponed since 2005, finally took place and former president René Préval won. Fwon Lespwa (Lespwa) (Front de l'Espoir) won the largest share of votes in parliamentary elections in both the Senate and the Chamber of Deputies.

Jacques-Edouard Alexis became prime minister and formed a six-party coalition cabinet under Lespwa leadership.

2008 Prime Minister Alexis lost support in the Senate following widespread rioting over soaring food prices and the perceived lack of government action to increase national food production. Both houses of parliament accepted President Préval's third nomine, Michèle Pierre-Louis, as prime minister. A series of two tropical storms, Hanna and Fay, and two hurricanes, Gustav and Ike, collectively killed over 800 Haitians and left more than one million homeless. The hurricanes were estimated to have caused almost US$1 billion in damage.

2009 Swiss banks agreed to return the frozen assets of former dictator Jean-Claude Duvalier (US$6 million, sequestered since 1986). An aid package of US$324 million was agreed by international donors to help Haiti recover from the damage and food shortages caused by the 2008 storm damage. Prime Minister Pierre-Louis lost a vote of no-confidence in parliament and was dismissed; parliament unanimously voted for Jean-Max Bellerive as her replacement.

2010 A massive 7.0 point magnitude earthquake struck on 13 January, centred close to the capital, Port au Prince, causing extensive damage and loss of life. Around three million people were in need of initial aid. There were over 230,000 confirmed deaths and 1.5 million homeless. The government estimated that US$11.5 billion would be needed to rebuild the country. Following a donor meeting, US$9.9 billon was pledged in immediate and long-term aid for reconstruction in Haiti. The money was to be provided in three stages with the first focussing on rebuilding infrastructure, government buildings, hospitals and schools. Long-term plans included environmental reconstruction and agricultural recovery and services and help for the maimed. The IMF agreed to cancel Haiti's US$268 million debt and to lend a further US$60 million. Election campaigning for parliament and the presidency got underway, despite concern by democracy advocates that the country was too disrupted to undertake free and fair elections.

A cholera outbreak in a refugee camp spread to others in Port au Prince. The number of deaths and infection grew steadily, killing over 2,000 people and infecting a further 90,000 within eight weeks. A cholera awareness campaign was initiated. Local people attacked UN and relief workers accusing them of bringing cholera to Haiti. Aid flights and water purification projects around the country were suspended until order was restored. In the first round of presidential elections held in November no candidate won more than 23 per cent; 12 of the 18 candidates denounced the election results as fraudulent. In the parliamentary elections held at the same time, political parties formed and merged to back individual presidential candidates. The new Inité (Unity) won 33 seats (out of 99), Alternative pour le Progrés (Altnativ) (Alternative for Progress and Democracy) 14, Ansanm Nou Fò nine, L'Ayiti an Aksyon (AAA) (Haiti in Action) eight and Lavni Organisation (Lavni) seven. There were reports of voters unable to cast a vote as their names were missing from voter-lists, general mismanagement, with vote stuffing by some officials, and violence in voting stations. However, observers from the OAS declared the elections valid, despite 'serious irregularities' which were not reason enough to cancel the election.

A French epidemiologist concluded that Nepalese troops were the source of the cholera outbreak; the UN continued to deny a link between the arrival of these troops and Haiti's first ever outbreak of cholera. Jude Celestin and Mirlande Manigat were approved to contest the runoff presidential election. The announcement caused violent protests in the capital by supporters of Michel Martelly (known as 'Sweet Micky' in his musical career) who had narrowly missed the runoff.

2011 In January, Jean-Claude 'Baby Doc' Duvalier returned to Haiti from exile in France, 25 years after being overthrown by a popular revolt. The state prosecutors charged him with corruption and embezzlement. A former UN spokeswoman, Michele Montas, and three other Haitians brought a suit of torture against him. Duvalier denied all accusations. In February Jude Celestin (Inité (Unity)) withdrew from the second round of the presidential election allowing Michel Martelly to contest the runoff. Officials said that former president Jean-Bertrand Aristide would be given a diplomatic passport, allowing him to return to Haiti. A Swiss bank froze the assets of Jean-Claude Duvalier; he claimed the US$6 million involved was not his, but belonged to a foundation set up by his family and should be released and used to rebuild Haiti. Aristide returned from exile in South Africa in March.

Parliament approved an extension of President Préval's mandate in office until May, to cover the time necessary to complete the presidential election and the official handover in administration. Mirlande Manigat and Michel Martelly were officially named as the candidates to contest the runoff, which was eventually held on 28 May, after two postponements. Michel Martelly won 67.6 per cent of the vote, Manigat 31.74 per cent. None of the new political parties, Inité, Altnativ, AAA or Lavni that had won seats in the new parliament had backed either of the two run-off candidates. President Michel Martelly was sworn into office in May and proposed Daniel-Gerard Rouzier as prime minister. A USAID report was leaked to the media in May, which stated that there had been significantly fewer deaths (46,000–85,000) during the 2010 earthquake and not 361,000 as previously estimated. However, it also stated that the majority of survivors were still living in tent cities 18 months later. The report used a door-to-door survey carried out over most of January. In June parliament rejected Rouzier's nomination as prime minister. In July, Rouzier was again proposed, and rejected, as prime minister. In September, President Martelly nominated Garry Conille as his third choice for prime minister. In September hundreds of demonstrators were dispersed by security forces while protesting in Port-au-Prince against the UN peace-keeping force, demanding that it be removed. In October and after months of procrastination parliament finally approved Garry Conille as prime minister together with his new cabinet.

2012 Prime Minister Garry Conille resigned on 24 February, following a power struggle and division within the government. A source of conflict was the number of parliamentarians, some in senior positions, who have dual nationality contrary to the constitution. The UN noted that Conille's resignation could hamper Haiti's efforts to achieve foreign investment for redevelopment and a stronger civic society. The president appointed Laurent Lamothe as prime minister-designate on 1 March. On 10 April parliament endorsed

Lamothe's appointment. On 20 July, the US Congress called on the UN to take responsibility for the cholera epidemic in Haiti since the arrival of Nepalese UN peacekeepers in 2010 and which was estimated to have killed 7,500 victims. Congress called on the UN to raise money to build a water and sewage system to combat the disease. On 18 September, the Inter-American Development Bank (IDB) granted an initial US$50 million to the second phase of the Caracol Industrial Park (CIP), a major job-creation project. By 2018 the IDB expects to invest up to US$180 million in the CIP, providing employment for up to 40,000 workers. On 11 October, the IDB gave a grant of US$53 million to upgrade RN1, between Gonaïves and Ennery, part of the principal highway between the capital and Cap Haitien. Although the death toll from Hurricane Sandy, which hit on 27 October, was 54, the damage to already makeshift homes and agricultural production was extensive. Over 70 per cent of the total crop output (of maize, plantains and bananas) was destroyed in the south of Haiti and caused an immediate rise in food prices. On 5 November, the government again called for international emergency aid to help it deal with the aftermath of Hurricane Sandy. On 12 December, the UN launched a US$2 billion fund to fight the cholera epidemic, which is currently the world's worst outbreak and in a country with no innate immunity.

2013 On 10 October a lawsuit against the UN was filed in New York on behalf of victims of the cholera epidemic. The UN had rejected claims for compensation and said that it is immune from prosecution. In December Simon Dieuseul Desras, president of the Senate, was accused of treason by writing to the president of the Chilean National Assembly, Jorge Pizarro Soto, on 6 November asking him to use his influence to ensure Chilean UN troops would take the side of demonstrators seeking to overthrow the government. Desras, an opponent of the government, reportedly wrote that 'The Haitian Parliament is convinced that the troops from your country would choose, should it be necessary, to defend the Haitian people, thirsty for democracy, against the excesses of an arbitrary and totalitarian regime.'

2014 Haiti's new National Defence Force became active in early 2014 with the Corps of Military Engineering (CME) involved in road building and other development and civil protection projects. President Martelly had promised to reinstate the army, which had been disbanded in 1995 by then-president Jean-Bertrand Aristide and while Haiti does not currently have the means of forming a full defence force, the CME is considered a useful starting platform. In April José Miguel Insulza, secretary general of the Organization of American States (OAS), called for Haiti to held elections before the end of the year. On 12 August the Provisional Electoral Council (CEP) announced the 26 October election would not take place. On 13 August an arrest warrant was issued against former president Jean Bertrand Aristide; he is being investigated for corruption, misappropriation of public funds and laundering of drug money. In September Prime Minister Lamothe, who gave up the lavish motorcade he inherited from his predecessor, reminded his cabinet members against buying luxurious cars, arguing that all cabinet members should fully comply with the government's philosophy, which is to prioritise the needs of the most vulnerable and to work toward establishing a reign of social justice, in a country where the social and economic rights of the poor majority have always been denied. Former president Jean-Bertrand Aristide was placed under house arrest on 9 September. He is facing charges of corruption, drug smuggling and money laundering. Jean-Claude 'Baby Doc' Duvalier died on 4 October. Prime Minister Lamothe resigned on 14 December, following weeks of violent anti-government protests. Further protests took place on 25 December with demonstrators calling for the resignation of President Martelly for his failure to call elections. On 23 December the President appointed Florence Guillaume interim Prime Minister.

2015 On 8 January a report from Amnesty International (AI) said that five years since the earthquake tens of thousands of people still remained homeless. AI put this down to failed government policies, forced evictions and unsuccessful short-term solutions. The report, *15 minutes to leave*, said that according to the latest available data, 123 camps for internally displaced people (IDPs) remain open, housing 85,432 people. It concludes that although the number of those in camps has reduced significantly since 2010, more than 22,000 households are still without adequate housing. On 10 January police in Port-au-Prince fired tear gas and sprayed water on hundreds of protesters calling for the resignation of President Martelly over long-delayed elections. On 11 January Mr Martelly said he had come to an agreement with opposition parties on the holding of an election. However, key left-wing opposition party Fanmi Lavala was not part of the deal and it foundered. On 14 January parliament was dissolved after the President failed to resolve the issue of a new electoral law which would have postponed elections again. He will now rule the country by decree until his term of office runs out in 2016. However, on 16 January Martelly said he had reached a deal with the opposition to form a consensus government within the next 48 hours. The consensus government of 20 ministers and 12 secretaries of state was signed in on 20 January with Evans Paul as prime minister. A two day general strike organised by the opposition ended on 10 February, the same day the electoral council announced that the first round of legislative elections would take place in July with the second round on 25 October, the same day as the first round of the presidential election. The run-off, if needed, would be in January 2016. A copy of the decree issued by President Martelly and his cabinet was handed to the Provisional Electoral Council (CEP) by Prime Minister Paul on 5 March. The decree sets out the legal framework for the holding of elections to renew elected members in Parliament and local government entities. On 15 March a new electoral decree stated that the new Chamber of Deputies will comprise of 118 members, and the Senate will retain the 30 members. Observers from the OAS and EU described the first round of the general election held on 9 August as valid despite the violence (at least 10 persons were killed), technical problems and irregularities. The second round of legislative elections and the first round of the presidential election are scheduled for 25 October.

Political structure

Constitution

Under the 1987 Constitution, executive power is held by an elected president, serving a five-year term, and a cabinet of ministers.

On 13 March 2015 the electoral law changed so that the number of seats in the Haitian Chamber of Deputies increased from 99 to 119.

Independence date

1 January 1804

Form of state

Republic

The executive

The president is elected for a five-year term by universal suffrage. A president may be elected for a maximum of two, non-continuous terms by absolute majority popular vote in two rounds if needed. The prime minister is appointed by the president from among members of the majority party in the National Assembly whose decision is ratified by the senate.

National legislature

The bicameral Assemblée Nationale (National Assembly) consists of the Chambre des Députés (House of Representatives) (lower house) with 99 members directly elected every four years in single-seat constituencies by absolute majority vote in two rounds if needed. The 30-members that make up the Sénat (Senate) (upper house), are elected in multi-seat constituencies by absolute majority vote in two rounds if needed for six years (one-third renewed every two years, although in 2015 two-thirds were up for election since the 2012 election had been cancelled).

Legal system

Haiti's judicial system is based on the French Napoleonic Code. Judges are appointed by the president. The supreme court is the Court de Cassation, which may make rulings on constitutional matters. There is a court of appeal and civil courts in the major administrative centres.

Last elections

9 August 2015 (Parliamentary), two-thirds of the Senate and all members of the Chamber of Deputies were up for election. 28 November 2010 (Presidential).

Results: Parliamentary (2015): the result of the first, inconclusive, round of election held on 9 August, were announced on 28 September by the Electoral Committee. One senator from Ayiti an Aksyon (AAA) (Haiti in Action) and one from Ligue Dessalines (LIDE) were elected. Eight deputies were elected: 4 candidates from Parti Haitien Tet Kale (PHTK), 2 from AAA, one from VERITE (Truth) and one from Inite Patriyotik (Patriotic Unity) were elected. Elections were cancelled in 22 constituencies, and therefore there were no results for those districts. The electoral Committee found that there were 1.05 million valid votes for an electorate of 5.85 million which represented an 18 per cent turnout. The second round of the legislative election will take place on 25 October, along with the first round of the presidential election and the first round of the legislative election on the constituencies where the August election were cancelled.

Presidential (2010): Second round: Martelly won 67.57 per cent of the vote, Manigat 31.74 per cent.

Next elections

25 October 2015 (presidential and second round legislative elections)

Political parties

Ruling party

Acting coalition led by Fwon Lespwa (Front for Hope) (formed 7 June 2006)

An estimated 40 per cent of the total population is under 15 years. Life expectancy is 52 years.

Haiti is the poorest country in the western hemisphere. In 2002, it was estimated that 23 per cent of children under the age of five suffered from chronic malnutrition with a 30 per cent increase in cases of severe malnutrition in some areas.

Population

10.32 million (2014)*

Last census: January 2003: 8,373,750

Population density: 283 inhabitants per square km. Urban population 52 per cent (2010 Unicef).

Annual growth rate: 1.7 per cent, 1990–2010 (Unicef).

Ethnic make-up

Approximately 95 per cent are Afro-Caribbean; the remainder are white or of mixed race.

Religions

Roman Catholic (80 per cent), Protestant (16 per cent). Around half the population also practices voodoo, an African-derived belief.

Education

Only 20 per cent of the population complete primary schooling which is theoretically compulsory; the pass rate for secondary school exams is 7–8 per cent. Secondary education is provided by the state and *lycées* (private secondary schools). There are also vocational training and domestic science establishments. There is a state-run university and an administration and management institute (which offers courses in medical subjects, agricultural and veterinary sciences, law, economics and ethnology) and an Institute of Administration and Management.

The government launched a literacy campaign in 2014 to reach 225,000 annually over the following two years. The secretary of state for literacy reported at the same time that over 282,000 illiterate had been taught to read and write since President Martelly took office in 2011.

Literacy rate: 52 per cent adult rate; 66 per cent youth rate (15–24) (Unesco 2005).

Compulsory years: 6 to 15.

Enrolment rate: 64 per cent total primary school enrolment of the relevant age group (including repetition rates) (World Bank).

Pupils per teacher: 35 in primary schools.

Health

According to the UN's food aid agency, in 2006, over 50 per cent of women suffer from anaemia, most of which is often caused by insufficient iron in their generally poor diet, plus worm infestation and malaria. The percentage of pregnant women suffering from anaemia is even higher at two out of three and is the leading cause of spontaneous miscarriage and infant mortality during delivery.

An outbreak of cholera in refugee camps had, by December 2010, killed over 2,000 people and infected a further 90,000. A cholera awareness campaign was initiated, urging everyone to boil food and water, avoid raw vegetables and wash their hands regularly with soap. By January 2012, around 7,000 people were reported to have died of the disease.

HIV/Aids

HIV/Aids has become a leading cause of death, and urban infection rates are over twice the number of rural population infection rates.

For the first time, in June 2004, a joint mission was undertaken by the UN and UNAids, who have sent teams into the field with peacekeepers, in an attempt to limit HIV in a conflict zone. This initiative is designed to pre-empt the spread of the desease before the main contingent of peacekeepers arrive. There are fears that as 1 in 20 Haitians are HIV positive and with the arrival of a peacekeeping force with an almost inevitable sex-industry that will develop, Haiti could become a flashpoint of transmission. UNAids provides condoms, education and testing services to the peacekeepers.

HIV prevalence: 5.6 per cent aged 15–49 in 2003 (World Bank).

Life expectancy: 55 years, 2004 (WHO 2006)

Fertility rate/Maternal mortality rate: 3.3 births per woman, 2010 (Unicef)

Birth rate/Death rate: 34 births per 1,000 population; 13.4 deaths per 1,000 population (2003).

Child (under 5 years) mortality rate (per 1,000): 76 per 1,000 live births (WHO 2012)

Welfare

Since 80 per cent of Haiti's population live below the poverty line and its social and economic indicators remain far lower than the average for Latin America and the Caribbean, the country is not eligible for the IMF's Heavily Indebted Poor Countries (HIPC) debt relief initiative.

In the public sector, still only 20 per cent of resources go to rural areas, where approximately two-thirds of the people live. Poor welfare provision is one factor which causes migration both from the countryside to the capital and out of the country. As many as 330,000 Haitians are thought to be living in the US.

Incidences of crime and violence are very high in Haiti. The strengthening of the Haitian police force with improvements in the penal system is likely to improve the situation. The government will need to spread the cost of maintaining social welfare services including those on education, health, water, sanitation and family planning with private sectors.

Main cities

Port-au-Prince (capital, estimated population 807,301 in 2012), Carrefour (541,511), Delmas (425,509), Gonaïves

(154,140), Pétionville (142,999), Cap Haïtien (132,772).

Languages spoken

Official language/s

French and Creole

Media

Freedom of the press was a casualty of political instability, nevertheless, as the situation improved self-censorship has remained as journalists avoided reporting on politicians and commercial sponsors.

Press

Dailies: In French, private newspapers include *Le Nouvelliste* (www.lenouvelliste.com) and *Le Matin* (www.lematinhaiti.com).

Weeklies: In French, *Haiti Progrès* (www.haiti-progres.com) has online editions in English and Creole. In English Haitian Times (www.haitiantimes.com).

Business: In French, *Haiti en Marche* (www.haitienmarche.com) is a weekly newspaper.

Broadcasting

The Conseil National des Télécommunications (www.conatel.gouv.ht) is responsible for broadcasting regulations. The national, public broadcaster is Radio Télévision Nationale d'Haiti (RTNH).

Radio: With a low literacy rate radio is the principal medium for news and information. There are over 250 radio stations in operation in both private and public service. The government-owned Radio Nationale d'Haiti (www.radionationalehaiti.net) broadcasts in French. Private, independent radio stations include Radyo Atlantik (www.atlantikhaiti.com), Radio Metropole Haiti (www.metropolehaiti.com) and Signal FM (www.signalfmhaiti.com).

Television: Télévision Nationale D'Haiti (www.tnh.ht) has a tie-in with the pay-to-view Jump-TV, the international TV cable and satellite service. Private, commercial TV stations include Télé-Haiti (www.telehaitionline.com), which is a cable station relaying captured satellite signals on four channels, Tele Quisqueya Saint-Marc (TQ) (www.haitipal.com/tq) and PVS Antenne.

National news agency: Agence Haitienne de Presse

Other news agencies: Caribbean Net News: www.caribbeannetnews.com
Haiti Press Network (in French): www.haitipressnetwork.com

Economy

Before the devastating earthquake that struck close to the capital, Port au Prince, in 2010, Haiti was deemed the poorest country in the western hemisphere. After the massive 7.0 magnitude earthquake struck, when the country lost vital infrastructure including parliament and government buildings, roads, bridges, the presidential palace and homes for around 1.5 million people, its prospects fell further. In the aftermath of the destruction that killed around 230,000 people (some 2.5 per cent of the population) and injured a further 311,000, international aid amounting to US$9.9 billon was pledged in short and long-term aid for reconstruction of Haiti. The money was to be provided in three stages, with the first focussing on rebuilding infrastructure, government buildings, hospitals and schools. Long-term plans included environmental reconstruction and agricultural recovery and services and help for the maimed.

The United Nations Economic Commission for Latin America and the Caribbean (Eclac), estimated that 15 per cent of the population were made homeless and the total damage caused by the earthquake was around US$7.8 billion, equivalent to over 120 per cent of 2009 GDP.

In July 2010 the IMF announced it had agreed to cancel Haiti's US$268 million debt and would lend a further US$60 million.

GDP growth, which had been 2.9 per cent in 2009, dropped to -5.4 per cent in 2010 as supply and production were disrupted. However, as reconstruction got underway GDP growth reached an estimated 5.6 per cent in 2011. By 2013, this figure had reduced to 4.3 per cent.

High unemployment has been a long-term problem, with a typical rate of 40 per cent. With the destruction of so many businesses, unemployment has inevitably grown.

Haiti's public sector was in disarray and the country's infrastructure network badly fragmented and in need of significant investment even before the earthquake, so that the work to be undertaken provided the opportunity to provide a better environment for the population and economic growth. The Inter-American Development Bank and the Water and Sanitation Spanish Co-operation Fund provided an initial US$35 million to repair reservoirs and pumping stations and refurbish and expand Port au Prince's drinking water and sanitation system, as well as construct water projects in rural communities.

In 2014, the UN Human Development Index (HDI) ranked Haiti 168 (out of 187) for national development in health, education and income. Since 2005, Haiti's progress has grown but has not matched the improvement of other countries in Latin America and the Caribbean. In 2014, 50.2 per cent of the population lived in multidimensional poverty. Migrant workers provided US$1.9 billion in remittances in 2012, which was estimated to have reached US$1.8 billion in 2013.

External trade

Although Haiti is member of the Caribbean Community (Caricom), it did not adopt the single market and economy (CSME), which was ratified by 12 other member states in 2006.

The main Haitian port and secondary port facilities along the coast from Port-au-Prince were damaged in the January 2010 earthquake. Two piers in the capital's port collapsed and containers fell into the harbour. Imports and exports by sea have been hampered until work to clear up and re-construct the damaged facilities was completed. Likewise, roads and bridges were damaged along with business premises and electrical installations, all of which need repair or replacement before Haiti returns to pre-earthquake productivity.

Imports

Main imports are foodstuffs, manufactured goods, machinery and transport equipment, fuels and raw materials.

Post-earthquake imports include construction materials, communications equipment and primary products, such as food and fuels.

Main sources: Dominican Republic (33.4 per cent of total in 2014), US (27.3 per cent), Netherlands Antilles (8.9 per cent)

Exports

Main exports are clothing, mangoes, manufactured goods, leather and raw hides, seafood and cocoa.

Main destinations: US (83.0 per cent of total in 2014), Canada (3.4 per cent), Mexico (2.2 per cent)

Agriculture

Farming

Before the 2010 earthquake, agriculture accounted for around 27 per cent of GDP and employed two-thirds of the working population. The main cash crops are coffee, sisal and sugar.

An estimated 47 per cent of the total land area is cultivated and 20 per cent is pasture. Subsistence farming and animal husbandry predominate. Only 10 per cent of cultivation is carried out on large plantations. Maize, rice, sorghum, millet, beans, fruit and vegetables are grown. Production is largely outside the cash economy. Recurrent drought, insufficient irrigation, low producer prices and a weak infrastructure have kept production levels down and necessitated the import of foodstuffs, particularly cereals.

By 2014, agriculture's contribution to GDP had returned to approximately 25 per cent.

Fishing
The total annual fish catch is typically around 5,000 tonnes, three-quarters of which is through marine fishing. Around 10 per cent is exported.

Forestry
Forests cover around 88,000 hectares (ha) or 1 per cent of the total land area. This compares to around 40 per cent of land area in 1940. Deforestation is causing serious soil erosion and desertification. The rapid decline of the forests is partly due to the demand for fuel wood. There are no large-scale forest industries. The local demand for industrial wood and paper products is mainly met by imports.

Industry and manufacturing
The industrial sector contributes around a fifth of GDP and employs 10 per cent of the workforce. It is concentrated in Port-au-Prince.
Besides the traditional food processing, construction and textile industries, there is an important artisan manufacturing sector producing handicrafts. Haiti is the world's leading producer of baseballs and one of the Caribbean's largest suppliers of garments and electronic components to the US market. There is very little production for local consumption and workers are typically paid less than US$3 per day in the industrial sector.
Many US-owned light manufacturing and assembly plants operate as offshore 'cheap labour' industries (mainly assembling sports goods, toys, electrical components) and in the past significantly contributed to foreign exchange earnings. Manufacturing output in Haiti continues to suffer from the uncertain political and business climate and the resulting international pressures for massive internal structural reforms.
The manufacturing industry consists largely of an assembly sector. Assembly operations are concentrated in electronic and electrical equipment, sporting goods, toys and garments. There is also a domestic manufacturing sector which is mainly devoted to import substitution and the processing of agricultural products such as sugar and fruit, although there is an important artisan manufacturing sector producing handicrafts such as baskets, leather goods, brushes, and rugs.

Tourism
With a reputation as the Caribbean and Latin America's poorest nation, plus endemic street violence and political instability, Haiti was not a destination many tourists chose. Following the devastating earthquake in 2010 tourism along with the rest of economy had not fully recovered by the mid-2015, with infrastructure damaged and a large number of Haitians still living in tents and other temporary structures, leaving little available for visitors. Many Western governments advise their citizens not to visit the most badly affected areas of Port-au-Prince and other larger towns.
In 2014, the travel and tourism industry contributed around US$760 million to GDP (9.5 per cent), which has exceeded the US$600 million in 2009 before the earthquake. The industry directly supplied employment to 142,000 workers in the same year, or 2.7 per cent of the total workforce.

Mining
The mining and export of bauxite ceased in 1983 with the closure of Reynolds mine at Miragoane. There are known, but not commercially viable, deposits of copper, silver, gold, marble, lignite and natural asphalt.

Hydrocarbons
Haiti relies on imported petroleum products to meet domestic demand, which was around 14,000 barrels per day in 2014. Most of this is supplied by Mexico and Venezuela, which sell oil to 11 Caribbean and Central American countries on favourable terms under the San José Pact of 1980.
Any use of imported natural gas or coal is commercially insignificant.

Energy
Total installed generating capacity was over 130MW in 2013 (latest available figures), of which over two-thirds is produced by thermal power stations and the remainder is produced by hydropower, although dry seasons can limit production. The electricity supply is restricted to main towns as the country lacks a national power grid. Power cuts are experienced on a regular basis, as the purchase of imported petroleum is restricted by foreign-exchange shortages. Local wood provides three-quarters of total domestic energy and is a major cause of deforestation and soil erosion. Around 40 per cent of the population had access to electricity, a number that grows by around 5 per cent a year.

Financial markets
Stock exchange
Haitian Stock Exchange

Banking and insurance
The banking sector is underdeveloped and in disarray. The crowding out of private sector credit has undermined the banks' ability to function as an important part of the economy. Few people have bank accounts and the large informal sector and black market tends to keep the savings ratio and therefore banks' capital at low levels.

Central bank
Banque Nationale de la République d'Haiti

Main financial centre
Port-au-Prince

Time
GMT minus five hours.

Geography
Haiti occupies the western part of the Caribbean island of Hispaniola (the Dominican Republic occupies the remaining two-thirds), and some smaller offshore islands. Cuba is to the west and is less than 80km away.
Much of Haiti's land area is covered by mountains, which rise up to about 3,000 metres. Environmental damage caused primarily by population pressure has reduced the area of forests to about 6–8 per cent of land area. A number of rivers flow vigorously during the rainy season only, and there are large lakes in the centre of the country close to the border with the Dominican Republic.

Hemisphere
Northern

Climate
Year-round temperatures in Port-au-Prince varies only slightly from 24–27 degrees Celsius (C). The rainy season is from May–November. The climate is tropical, with the rainy seasons in October–November and May–June. May is the wettest month (231mm average rainfall) and December to February the driest and coldest. Temperatures vary from around 22 degrees C on the coast in January to 34 degrees C in July.

Dress codes
Jackets (tropical weight) and ties are normally worn for business. Swimwear is only worn at beaches and pools. Dresses of at least knee-length are recommended for women.

Entry requirements
Passports
Passports are required by all and must have at least six months validity beyond the date of departure. Proof of return/onward passage is required.

Visa
Required by all. Business and tourist visas are not required by citizens of North America or Argentina.
Business visitors from other destinations should supply a letter of introduction from their company and proof of sufficient funds for length of stay. For further information contact the nearest embassy.

Currency advice/regulations
There are no restrictions on the import or export of foreign or local currency. Nevertheless, amounts over G200,000 should be declared.

Travellers cheques are widely accepted, however it is difficult in banks, hotels and shops to exchange foreign currency other than US dollars.

Health (for visitors)

The rate of HIV/Aids is high and precautions should always be taken.

Mandatory precautions

Yellow fever vaccination is required if arriving from an infected area.

Anti-malaria precautions are essential.

Tap water is not safe to drink, and therefore ice, salads, raw vegetables and unpeeled fruits are suspect.

Advisable precautions

Inoculations against typhoid, polio and tetanus are recommended. Malaria prophylaxis and a mosquito net may be necessary. There is a very high prevalence of HIV/Aids. Use only bottled or boiled water for drinks, washing teeth and be wary of ice in restaurants. Eat only well cooked meals, preferably served hot; vegetables should be cooked and fruit peeled.

Medical facilities are very limited and offer a poor standard of care. Adequate supplies of essential medicines should be carried by visitors, with their prescription details. Local emergency services are inadequate, so full travel insurance, which includes emergency medical evacuation, should be obtained.

Hotels

There is not a good range of accommodation, the best hotels are in the capital and in tourist resorts. Hotels are fully booked during Carnival. There is a government tax of 10 per cent and hotels add a 5 per cent service charge to bills.

Credit cards

Major credit cards are accepted.

Public holidays (national)

Fixed dates

1 Jan (Independence Day), 2 Jan (Ancestors' Day), 14 Apr (Pan American Day), 1 May (Labour Day), 18 May (Flag and University Day), 15 Aug (Assumption Day), 17 Oct (Dessalines Day), 24 Oct (United Nations Day), 1 Nov (All Saints' Day), 2 Nov (All Souls' Day), 18 Nov (Vertières Battle Day), 25 Dec (Christmas Day).

Variable dates

Carnival (two days, Feb), Ash Wednesday, Good Friday (Mar/Apr), Ascension Day, Corpus Christi (May/Jun).

Working hours

Banking

Mon–Fri: 0900–1300, 1500–1700; Sat: 0900–1300.

Business

Mon–Fri: 0800–1600. (Visits are best arranged between November–March).

Government

Mon–Fri: 0800–1400.

Telecommunications

Mobile/cell phones

There is a 850 GSM service in operation.

Electricity supply

110-220V AC

Weights and measures

Officially the metric system is in force but many US measures are also used.

Social customs/useful tips

Careful observance of polite formalities such as handshaking, direct eye contact, formal use of titles such as Monsieur, etc, is essential, and offence may be taken if they are not observed. All officials should be treated with careful respect.

Security

Crime is widespread and often violent. The kidnapping of foreign nationals for ransom money is increasingly common. Random shootings, during robbery, has become more common, and pickpockets are numerous. Do not leave property in vehicles and always travel with doors locked and windows up. Armed hold-ups of vehicles take place, even in daylight, in busy parts of Port-au-Prince.

Some areas of Port-au-Prince should be avoided at all times. Whenever possible avoid going out after dark.

Whenever possible leave documents in a safety deposit box.

Getting there

Air

National airline: Haiti Trans Air offers limited flights to the US.

International airport/s: Port-au-Prince International Airport (PAP), 10km from city; duty-free shop, bar, bank, car hire. Cap-Haitien (CAP), 10km from the city.

Airport tax: Departure tax US$30 and security charge G10, excluding transit passengers.

Surface

Road: Access is possible from Dominican Republic, although sometimes, bureaucratic delays can occur.

Main port/s: Port-au-Prince, Cap Haitien, Gonaives.

Getting about

National transport

Air: Caribintair flies to Cap Haitien. Other towns can be reached from Port-au-Prince by charter flights.

Road: The total road network is around 4,000km, although not all passable/practicable in wet weather. There are surfaced roads from Port-au-Prince to Cap Haitien, Jacmel and Les Cayes.

Camionettes (large, out-of-town taxis) are available.

Buses: Unscheduled services operate from Port-au-Prince to Les Cayes, Jacmel, Jérémie, Hinche, Port de Paix and Cap Haitien.

City transport

Taxis: *Publiques* (shared taxis) can be identified by red ribbon in the window and registration number beginning 'P'. Tipping is not usual.

Car hire

Cars can be hired in Port-au-Prince and Petionville, at the airport and from hotels. International licence is required. Petrol is hard to find outside cities. Hire cars have registration numbers beginning with 'L'.

BUSINESS DIRECTORY

The addresses listed below are a selection only. While World of Information makes every endeavour to check these addresses, we cannot guarantee that changes have not been made, especially to telephone numbers and area codes. We would welcome any corrections.

Telephone area codes

The international direct dialling code (IDD) for Haiti is +509, followed by subscriber's number.

Chambers of Commerce

Haiti Chamber of Commerce and Industry, Boulevard Harry Truman, PO Box 982, Port-au-Prince (tel: 222-8661; fax: 222-0281; e-mail: ccih@acn2.net).

Banking

Banque Commerciale d'Haiti, Champ de Mars, Port-au-Prince.

Central bank

Banque de la République d'Haiti, Rues des Miracles et du Magasin de l'Etat et , PO Box 1570, Port-au-Prince (tel: 299-1200; fax: 299-1045; e-mail: webmaster@brh.net).

Stock exchange

Haitian Stock Exchange, www.haitianstockexchange.com

Travel information

Air Haiti, 35 ave Marie-Jeanne, Port-au-Prince.

Association Hotelière et Touristique d'Haiti, Hotel Montana, rue F. Cardozo, route de Pétionville, BP 2562, Port-au-Prince.

National tourist organisation offices

Office National du Tourisme d'Haiti, Avenue Marie Jeanne, Port-au-Prince (tel: 223-5631).

Ministries

Ministry of Economy and Finance, Palais des Ministères, Port-au-Prince.

Ministry of Information and Co-ordination, 300 Route de Delmas, Port-au-Prince.

Other useful addresses

Association des Industries d'Haiti (ADIH), Delmas 31 et 33, Etase Galeria 128, BP 2568, Port-au-Prince.

Association des Producteurs Agricoles (APA), c/o Chambre de Commerce et d'Industrie d'Haiti, blvd Harry S. Truman, Cite de l'Exposition, Port-au-Prince.

Centre de Promotion des Investissements et des Exportations Haitiennes (Prominex), Angle rue Lamarre et ave John Brown, Port-au-Prince.

Haitian Embassy (USA), 2311 Massachusetts Avenue, NW, Washington DC 20008 (tel: (+1-202) 332-4090; fax: (+1-202) 745-7215; e-mail: embassy@haiti.org).

Haitian International Business Center, 444 Brickell Avenue, Brickell Suite 650, Miami, Florida 33131, USA (tel: (+1-305) 374-8300).

National news agency: Agence Haitienne de Presse

Address: 6 Rue Fernand, Port-au-Prince (tel: 245-7222; fax: 245-5836; internet: www.ahphaiti.org).

Caribbean Net News: www.caribbeannetnews.com

Haiti Press Network (in French): www.haitipressnetwork.com

Internet sites

Embassy of Haiti: www.haiti.org

Haiti Business Directory: www.ascnet.net/haiti/directory.htm

Haiti website (in French): www.haitiwebs.com/

Latin America Network Information Center: www.lanic.utexas.edu

Honduras

KEY FACTS

Official name: República de Honduras (Republic of Honduras)

Head of State: President Juan Orlando Hernández (Partido Nacional de Honduras (PNH) (National Party of Honduras)) (elected 24 Nov 2013, inaugurated 27 Jan 2014)

Head of government: President Juan Orlando Hernández (inaugurated 27 Jan 2014)

Ruling party: Partido Nacional de Honduras (PNH) (National Party of Honduras) (from Jan 2010, re-elected 24 Nov 2013)

Area: 112,088 square km

Population: 8.26 million (2014)*

Capital: Tegucigalpa

Official language: Spanish

Currency: Lempira (L) = 100 centavos

Exchange rate: L21.94 per US$ (Sep 2015)

GDP per capita: US$2,361 (2014)*

GDP real growth: 3.08% (2014)*

GDP: US$19.51 billion (2014)*

Unemployment: 4.50% (2014)*

Inflation: 6.08% (2014)*

Balance of trade: -US$4.48 billion (2013)

Annual FDI: US$1.04 billion (2011)

* estimated figure

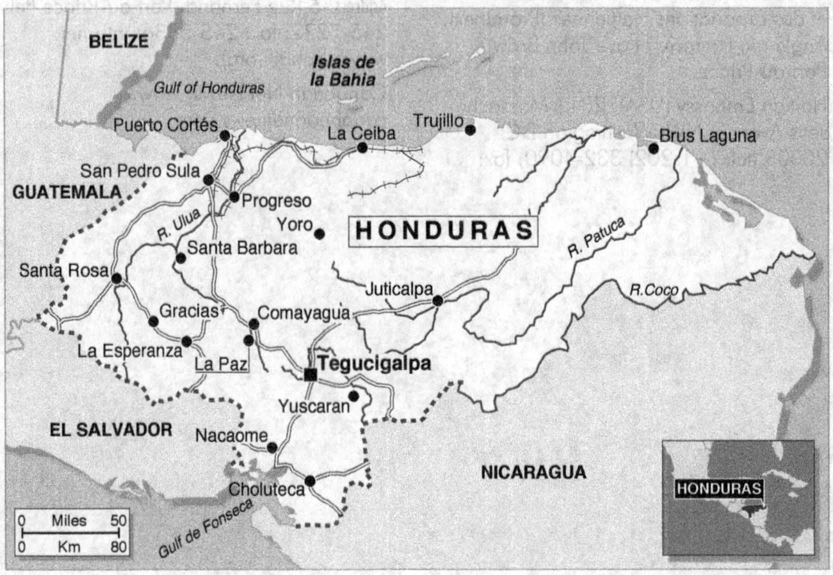

In regional terms, Honduras has always been a bit of a backwater, no precious metals were to be found, so the country was left to its landowners and farmers. Revolutions and uprisings constituted the country's earlier years – one calculation puts the number of governments claiming to rule the country at over one hundred. In the early 1900s, traders from Boston in the US began to develop the cultivation of the banana. Before long, the United Fruit Company was created (later to become United Brands) and there developed an uncomfortably close relationship between the US and Honduras. Honduras' 20 cent coin, worth 10 US cents and exactly the same size as a US dime, became commonly known as the *diemeh*. Thus was coined the expression 'banana republic' as sales of the Chiquita brand banana prospered and production on the 250,000 hectares or so owned by the company boomed. In 1911 a US grower Samuel Zemurray was alleged to have financed the overthrow of the Honduran President in order to gain more land. Over 60 years later, in 1975, United Brands were accused of paying a Honduran official over a million US dollars for a tax reduction. From 1963 until 1981 what democracy there was in Honduras took a back seat during a period of almost continuous military rule.

Carry on president

In April 2015, the Honduran Supreme Court ruled that Article 239 of the national constitution was no longer applicable. The article in question prohibited the re-election of presidents, who were constitutionally limited to a single four-year term and also noted that any president 'directly or indirectly' supporting a modification of the article would be immediately removed from his post and banned from public office for 10 years. In a number of Latin American (and African) republics there have, in recent years, been similar moves – occasionally successful – to extend presidential terms. There was a certain irony in the case of Honduras, as when President Zelaya was overthrown in 2009, it was article 239 that provided the constitutional framework for his arrest. At the time it was alleged that Zelaya was seeking to extend his presidency in contravention of clause 239.

Failed state?

It is therefore unsurprising that Honduras, the region's poorest country, in 2013 reportedly had the world's highest per-capita murder rate (79 per 100,000 inhabitants according to the Observatorio de la Violencia of the Universidad Nacional Autónoma de Honduras). Four years after the event, the strange saga of the 2009 *coup d'état* (*golpe de estado*) that deposed the left wing President Zelaya still had repercussions. Nowhere were these more obvious than in the November 2013 presidential election. The Libertad y Refundación (Libre) (Liberty and Refoundation) coalition's candidate was Mrs Castro de Zelaya, wife of the former – and deposed – President Zelaya. In mid-2013 Mrs Castro had seemed to hold a small lead in the opinion polls. However, the polls were less than reliable, as this was the first Honduran election with so many parties – eight in all – presenting candidates. The opinion polls clearly suggested that there were two major contenders, Mrs Castro for the Libre grouping and Juan Orlando Hernández for the Partido Nacional de Honduras (PNH) (National Party of Honduras). 'Evita' theories abounded as speculation grew over the extent to which the former president was the power behind Mrs Castro's candidacy. At political gatherings Libre party supporters often cheered more for the former president than they did for his wife. Mrs Castro, meanwhile, had pledged to 'rebuild' Honduras, attributing the parlous state of Honduras' politics and its economy to a century of rule by the two traditional parties. In the event Mrs Castro had lost by 28.78 per cent to the 36.89 per cent of Mr Hernández. After the April Supreme Court ruling Mr Hernández was said to be considering whether or not to stand again in the 2017 presidential election.

The economy

According to the United Nations Economic Commission for Latin America and the Caribbean (ECLAC/CEPAL) the Honduran economy was expected to show growth of 3.0 per cent in 2014 (compared with 2.6 per cent in 2013). A number of factors influenced this estimate, most particularly the recovery of coffee production in the country and an improvement in external conditions. Conversely, a sharp fiscal adjustment over the course of the year held growth in check.

The central government deficit for 2014 was forecast to be 5.2 per cent of gross domestic product (GDP) at year-end, a sizeable improvement on the deficit of 7.9 per cent of GDP posted in 2013. Inflation picked up slightly, but was projected to remain within the target range set by the Banco Central de Honduras (Central Bank of Honduras) (5.5 per cent to 7.5 per cent).

A major economic landmark under the administration of President Juan Orlando Hernández was the negotiations on a new agreement with the International Monetary Fund (IMF), culminating in December 2014 with the Fund's approval of a three-year stand-by arrangement worth a total of US$188.6 million. By signing the agreement, Honduras also became eligible for budget support loans from the Inter American Development Bank (IDB), the World Bank and the European Union (EU) worth US$220 million in 2014.

For 2015, ECLAC anticipated a growth rate similar to that of 2014, at around 3.0 per cent. The deep fiscal adjustment from a deficit of 7.9 per cent of GDP in 2013 to a projected deficit of 5.2 per cent of GDP at year-end 2014 was chiefly achieved by implementing the fiscal reform approved in late 2013 (the Act to Strengthen Public Finances, Control Tax Exemptions and Combat Evasion), which was designed to achieve higher tax revenues and greater control over public expenditure. On the income side, measures included a rise in the sales tax rate from 12 per cent to 15 per cent. These changes led to a 19.4 per cent year-on-year increase in total central government revenue in the period between January and August, with indirect tax revenues up 24.7 per cent during that period. It was estimated that the tax burden would rise from 15.1 per cent of GDP in 2013 to 16.8 per cent in 2014. On the spending side, total expenditure to August decreased by a modest 0.7 per cent from the figure to August 2013, with a 7.0 per cent year-on-year drop in capital expenditure being a major factor. Current expenditure edged up 0.6 per cent, with higher debt interest payments (up 20.6 per cent) making a significant contribution, partially offset by a 16.1 per cent fall in spending on goods and services. There was a rise in transfers, most of which were disbursed to balance the financial accounts of state-owned enterprises, notably the Empresa Nacional de Energía Eléctrica (ENEE) (National Electric Power Company), whose losses (estimated at 32 per cent of total sales in 2013) accounted for a large proportion of the overall public-sector deficit. Despite the adjustment over the year, the central government deficit remained high and was worrisome insofar as it quickened the growth of public debt and drove up debt servicing costs as a proportion of central government expenditure. In the third quarter of 2014, Honduras's total public debt stood at US$7.892 billion, equivalent to 41 per cent of GDP (of which 26 percentage points were external debt and 15 percentage points domestic debt). In the third quarter of 2014, total expenditure on public debt servicing accounted for almost 30 per cent of total central government revenue.

The central bank has kept the monetary policy rate unchanged at 7 per cent since May 2012. During this period, open market operations (mainly bond issues) had been the main monetary policy instrument used by the central bank to absorb the excess liquidity arising in the system. As regards interest rates, in the third quarter of 2014 the nominal deposit rate and real lending and deposit rates dropped below the levels observed in the fourth quarter of

KEY INDICATORS — Honduras

	Unit	2011	2012	2013	2014	**2015
Population	m	*8.21	*7.94	*8.10	*8.26	*8.43
Gross domestic product (GDP)	US$bn	17.40	18.50	18.50	*19.51	*19.98
GDP per capita	US$	2,116	2,331	2,284	*2,361	*2,369
GDP real growth	%	3.6	3.9	2.8	*3.1	*3.3
Inflation	%	6.8	5.2	5.2	*6.1	*4.1
Unemployment	%	4.4	4.4	4.4	*4.5	*4.5
Exports (fob) (goods)	US$m	3,913.6	4,438.6	3,950.3	–	–
Imports (fob) (goods)	US$m	8,297.2	8,808.2	8,429.7	–	–
Balance of trade	US$m	-4,383.6	-4,369.6	-4,479.4	–	–
Current account	US$m	-1,503.2	-1,587.0	-1,763.0	*-1,444.0	*-1,304.0
Total reserves minus gold	US$m	2,924.7	2,495.2	2,981.9	3,431.8	–
Foreign exchange	US$m	2,747.0	2,333.9	2,826.5	–	–
Exchange rate	per US$	18.90	19.85	20.23	21.02	–

* estimated figure ** forecast figure

2013, while the nominal lending rate rose slightly. Total credit to the private sector was up 10.7 per cent year on year in September in nominal terms, a slightly slower rate of increase than in 2013.

The central bank continued to use the exchange-rate band, which has a margin of plus or minus 7 per cent relative to a base price, and carried on allocating foreign currency by auction. In October 2014, the lempira showed a 3.4 per cent nominal depreciation against the dollar compared with the rate at year-end 2013. Where trade policy is concerned, the free trade agreement signed between Honduras and Canada in late 2013 entered into force in September 2014, with the consequence that Honduran products now receive preferential access to all North American markets.

Both exports and imports of goods (fob) made modest gains (1.7 per cent and 1.0 per cent, respectively) in the first half of 2014 compared with the same period the year before. Among traditional exports, coffee lost 2.8 per cent in value terms and this small decline came despite a 1.4 per cent price rise, owing to a 4.1 per cent drop in volume caused by coffee-leaf rust, which adversely affected production in 2013 and continued to weigh on exports in the early months of 2014. The central bank forecast that the balance-of-payments current account deficit would narrow from 9.6 per cent of GDP in 2013 to 7.5 per cent of GDP in 2014. On its financial account, Honduras received US$542 million in foreign direct investment (FDI) in the first half of 2014, a rise of 0.9 per cent on the same period in 2013. International reserves amounted to US$3.055 billion as of 13 November; this was almost the same as the figure at the end of 2013 and represented over three months of import cover. Family remittances showed year-on-year growth of 8.3 per cent in September, down slightly on the 9.2 per cent posted in the same period in 2013. Stronger remittance inflows largely reflected the improving labour market situation in the United States, the main destination for Honduran migrants.

According to quarterly GDP data, the economy expanded by 3.1 per cent in the first half of 2014, compared with 2.3 per cent in the first half of 2013. Construction and mining activity fell particularly heavily (by 9.7 per cent and 9.5 per cent respectively), although the strong performance of the agriculture, communications and financial intermediation sectors was enough to offset these contractions. On the demand side, total consumption rose by a modest 1.0 per cent during the first half of the year, as private consumption expanded by 2.1 per cent and public consumption dropped by 4.4 per cent.

Gross fixed investment rose by 3.9 per cent. In 2015, ECLAC projects a growth rate similar to that of 2014, in the region of 3.0 per cent. In October 2014, year-on-year inflation stood at 6.3 per cent, having quickened since October 2013 (4.6 per cent). Price rises were largely a temporary effect arising from the increase in the value added tax (VAT) rate from 12 per cent to 15 per cent as part of the fiscal reform approved in 2013. The category that most affected inflation was food and non-alcoholic beverages, whose contribution to the inflation rate in October stood at 2.4 percentage points. The inflation rate was 6.5 per cent in December 2014.

Risk assessment

Economy	Good
Politics	Fair
Regional stability	Good

COUNTRY PROFILE

1821 The Central American provinces (Costa Rica, Guatemala, Honduras, Nicaragua and El Salvador) declared independence from Spain.
1822 The five provinces annexed themselves to the Mexican Empire, under General Agustín de Iturbde, later Emperor Agustín I.
1823 Agustín I was overthrown and Mexico became a republic. The Central American states formed the United Provinces of Central America.
1825 Costa Rica, Guatemala, Honduras, Nicaragua and El Salvador formed the Central American Federation (CAF).
1838 The CAF was dissolved and Honduras became a fully independent republic.
1840–1957 Honduras was ruled by a military and civilian élite.
1957 The first democratic presidential election was won by Ramon Villeda Morales, a popular moderate reformist.
1963 Morales was ousted by Colonel Osvaldo Lopez Arellano in a military coup. Military rule continued until 1980.
1969 Honduras and El Salvador fought what became known as the 'soccer war', which was prompted by land disputes and El Salvador's win in the World Cup play-offs between the two countries. Over 3,000 people died.
1981 Presidential elections were won by Roberto Suazo Cordova of the Partido Liberal de Honduras (PLH) (Liberal Party of Honduras), although real power remained in the hands of the army under General Gustavo Alvarez.
1985 José Azcona Hoyo (PLH) won the presidential election, following a change in the constitution which limited the presidency to a maximum of one term.
1989 Rafael Leonardo Callejas Romero of the Partido Nacional de Honduras (PNH) (National Party of Honduras) the right-wing opposition party, was elected president.
1993 Carlos Roberto Reina Idiáquez (PLH) won the presidential election.
1997 Carlos Roberto Flores Facussé (PLH) was elected president.
1998 Hurricane Mitch killed around 11,000 people and left 1.3 million homeless.
1999 The constitution was amended to make the president the commander-in-chief of the armed forces.
2001 Ricardo Maduro Joest (PN) was elected president.
2002 Honduras renewed diplomatic ties with Cuba, with whom it had cut relations in 1961. Persistent drought and the decline in world coffee prices left around 300,000 Hondurans suffering from hunger.
2004 More than 100 prisoners, many of them gang members, were killed in a fire at San Pedro Sula prison. Honduras withdrew its troops from the coalition forces in Iraq.
2005 The PLH won the presidential and legislative elections.
2006 President Manuel Zelaya Rosales (PLH) was inaugurated. The Central American Free Trade Agreement (Cafta) came into effect.
2007 After eight years of conflict, the International Court of Justice ruled on a new maritime boundary between Honduras and Nicaragua. The result gave both countries equal access to the rich fishing grounds and oil and gas exploration waters in the area.
2008 Honduras signed a free trade agreement with Taiwan.
2009 Just hours before a referendum to change the constitution and allow an incumbent president to stand for a second term in office, the military deposed President Zelaya and flew him into exile in Costa Rica. Honduras was suspended from the Organisation of American States (OAS). Zelaya successfully returned, in secret, and took refuge in the Brazilian embassy in Tegucigalpa, which became a focal point for his supporters. A state of emergency was declared and lifted amid signs of reconciliation and negotiation. Porfirio Lobo Sosa (known as Pepe Lobo) (PNH) won the scheduled presidential election; Zelaya was constitutionally barred from standing under Article 239 of the constitution, which restricts a president to one four year term in office.

2010 President Lobo was sworn into office as ex-president Zelaya went into exile in the Dominican Republic. The PNH became the ruling party. The Central Bank of Economic Integration (BCIE) approved funds of US$288 million for social and welfare programmes, providing for education, health and nutrition, including school meals. The military was deployed in cities around the country to counter violent criminal gang activity (linked to Mexican drug cartels), following the murder of 18 people in a shoe factory in San Pedro Sula.
2011 All charges of fraud and falsifying documents laid against former president Zelaya were dismissed in May. Zelaya returned from exile in May. The OAS lifted its suspension of Honduras in June. In August, clashes between farmers and farm workers over land rights in the Aguan region in the north-east, resulted in the deaths of 11 people (in addition to the 35 farm workers and farm guards who had already died). Security forces were deployed to impose calm. In August Secundino Ruiz, a leader of the farm workers was shot dead.
2012 A fire that broke out in the prison of Comayagua on 14 February killed over 350 inmates; many locked in their cells and burned beyond recognition. On 18 April thousands of rural workers occupied large farms throughout the country in a co-ordinated invasion. The farm workers claimed they had occupied public lands where poor farmers had the right to grow food, under Honduran law. However the government said the invasion and occupations were illegal.
2013 In May the two largest and most dangerous street gangs in Honduras declared a truce, offering the government peace in exchange for rehabilitation and jobs. A Mara Salvatrucha spokesman said both his gang and the 18th Street gang would commit to zero violence and zero crime in the streets as a show of good faith. Presidential and parliamentary elections were held on 24 November. The presidentail election was won by Juan Orlando Hernández (PNH) with 36.89 per cent, followed by Xiomara Castro (wife of former president Manuel Zelaya) (Libre) with 28.78 per cent.
2014 An IMF mission visited Honduras during 2–12 September to discuss a three-year Fund-supported programme.
2015 On 23 April the Constitutional Chamber of the Supreme Court of Honduras ruled that Articles 239 and 240 should no longer apply. Article 239 had prevented a president from standing for another term in office and 240 said that any person attempting to recind Article 239 would be barred from public office for 10 years. The move to change the constitution had been initiated by a petition filed by former president (1990–94), Rafael Leonardo Callejas. Mr Callejas said he would be revitalising the National Callejista Movement (Monarca) which had brought him to power in 1990 and preparing to run in the internal elections of the great Partido Nacional de Honduras (PNH) (National Party of Honduras)'.

Political structure

In addition to their unicameral national parliaments, El Salvador, Guatemala, Honduras, Nicaragua, Panama and Dominican Republic also return directly-elected deputies to the supranational Central American Parliament.

Constitution

The Constitution was promulgated in 1982 and amended in 1999, making the president the commander-in-chief of the armed forces.
Voting is by secret ballot and is compulsory for all citizens aged 18 or over. Members of the security forces are barred from voting. Municipal elections and elections of representatives in the 18 departments are held every two years.

Form of state

Presidential democratic republic

The executive

Power is divided between a strong executive, a unicameral national assembly and an independent judiciary. The president, three vice presidents and members of the national assembly serve parallel four-year terms. The president is directly elected by simple majority popular vote for a single four-year term.

National legislature

The unicameral Congreso Nacional (National Congress) has 128 deputies directly elected in multi-seat constituencies by proportional representation vote. Members serve four-year terms.

Legal system

The legal system is based on Roman and Spanish civil law. Honduran laws are set out in the 'Cordigoes' or codes. The civil code covers dealings between people. The business code covers all matters relating to business while the penal code covers crime and punishment. The legal system is in desperate need of reform.

Last elections

24 November 2013 (parliamentary and presidential)
Results: Parliamentary: Partido Nacional de Honduras (PNH) (National Party of Honduras) won 48 seats (out of 128) (33.64 per cent), Libertad y Refundación (Libre) (Liberty and Refoundation) 37 seats (27.51 per cent), Partido Liberal de Honduras (PLH) (Liberal Party of Honduras) 27 seats (16.97 per cent); Partido Anticorrupción (PAC) (Anti-Corruption Party) 13 seats (15.15 per cent); three other political parties won the remaining 3 seats. Turnout was 59.14 per cent.
Presidential: Juan Orlando Hernández (Partido Nacional de Honduras (PNH) (National Party of Honduras)) 36.89 per cent, Xiomara Castro (Libertad y Refundación (Libre)) (Liberty and Refoundation) 28.78 per cent, Mauricio Villeda (Partido Liberal de Honduras (PLH) (Liberal Party of Honduras)) 20.30 per cent, Salvador Nasralla (Anti-Corruption Party) 13.43 per cent, the remaining four candidates won less than 1.0 between them. Turnout was 61.2 per cent.

Next elections

2017 (presidential), 2017 (parliamentary).

Political parties

Ruling party

Partido Nacional de Honduras (PNH) (National Party of Honduras) (from Jan 2010, re-elected 24 Nov 2013)

Main opposition party

Libertad y Refundación (LIBRE) (Liberty and Refoundation).
Approximately 53 per cent of the total population is aged between 15 and 64 years; 44 per cent under 14 years.
There were 633,401 Hondurans registered as residents in the 2010 US census.

Population

8.26 million (2014)*
Last census: July 2001: 6,071,200 (provisional)
Population density: 56 inhabitants per square km. Urban population 52 per cent (2010 Unicef).
Annual growth rate: 2.2 per cent, 1990–2010 (Unicef).

Ethnic make-up

Around 90 per cent are *mestizos*, with minorities of Indians, blacks, whites and others. The largest indigenous group is the Garifuna, descendants of African slaves and Arawak Indian women from San Vicente, who live along the north coast. The Miskitos live in the Mosquitia – wetland, rainforest country – and the Lencas live around Copan.

Religions

More than 90 per cent of the population are Roman Catholics. There is freedom of worship.

Education

Primary education is compulsory and free of charge. Secondary education, from 13 years to 17 years, is not compulsory.
Literacy rate: 80 per cent adult rate; 89 per cent youth rate (15–24) (Unesco 2005).
Compulsory years: Seven to 12
Enrolment rate: 110 per cent gross primary enrolment, of the relevant age group (including repetition rate); 32 per

cent gross secondary enrolment; 9 per cent gross tertiary enrolment (World Bank).

Pupils per teacher: 35 in primary schools

Health

In Honduras the quality of, and access to, healthcare is directly tied to income levels. Adequate health care is available to those able to pay the high cost. Health care for the urban and rural poor is limited.

The ministry of health manages 28 hospitals with 4,093 beds. There are also 31 hospitals managed by the private sector. The private sector generally concentrates on individual care and does not participate in general public sector health activities. A national policy was formulated to make sure people have access to safe, quality drugs. This policy however, has not been implemented.

The relatively young population places an extra burden on health facilities. Nearly two-thirds of the population have no access to essential drugs.

Infectious and parasitic diseases are the leading causes of death. Gastroenteritis and tuberculosis are serious problems. Approximately one-third of the population has no access to safe water or sanitation facilities.

HIV/Aids

The disease is spread predominantly through heterosexual intercourse. A study showed that the HIV prevalence in female sex workers was over 10 per cent (USCF – Centre for HIV Information, 2005).

HIV prevalence: 1.8 per cent aged 15–49 in 2003 (World Bank)

Life expectancy: 67 years, 2004 (WHO 2006)

Fertility rate/Maternal mortality rate: 3.1 births per woman, 2010 (Unicef); maternal mortality 110 per 100,000 live births (World Bank).

Child (under 5 years) mortality rate (per 1,000): 23 per 1,000 live births (WHO 2012); 25 per cent of children aged under five are malnourished (World Bank).

Welfare

Honduras is classified as a low-income country by the World Bank – 50 per cent of its inhabitants live below the poverty line. Social security benefits, mainly for pensions and health care, cover around 12 per cent of the Honduran population and account for around 1 per cent of GDP. Social security is mainly limited to urban centres. About 80 per cent of those covered live either in the capital, Tegucigalpa, or in the northern city of San Pedro Sula.

Organised social security started operations in 1962. Contributors are covered for general illness, maternity, accidents at work, professional illnesses, invalidity, old age and funeral expenses. There is no unemployment benefit.

Dependants, who account for 60 per cent of those covered, get some access to health care and pensions. Children under five years get free health treatment and wives of contributors receive maternity care in hospitals run by the social security institute. The widows of contributors receive pensions and there are more restricted pensions for widowers. Orphans, usually up to the age of 14 years, receive some support.

Main cities

Tegucigalpa (capital, estimated population 1.1 million in 2012), San Pedro Sula (687,018), Choloma (260,439), La Ceiba (189,078), El Progreso (141,077).

Languages spoken

English is common in some parts of the north coast and the Caribbean Islas de la Bahía.

Official language/s

Spanish

Media

While the constitution guarantees freedom of speech and the press, there are punitive defamation laws that tend to restrict journalism and journalists are known to practice self-censorship. Journalists reporting on corruption, drug trafficking and human rights abuses have been targeted not only for harassment but also by laws that require them to divulge their sources. Media outlets have been the object of political attacks with death threats issued to journalists and managers. Corruption of the media has also included bribes to journalists, selective government advertising and access and denial of public officials.

In 2005, the Supreme Court declared that defamation laws that protected public officials were unconstitutional.

Press

Ownership of newspapers in held by a few conglomerates with political and economic ties to the elite.

Dailies: The most popular newspapers are, in Spanish, *El Heraldo* (www.heraldohn.com) and *El Tiempo* (www.tiempo.hn), others include *La Tribuna* (www.latribuna.hn) and *La Prensa* (www.laprensahn.com). Articles include financial and business news.

Weeklies: In Spanish, government announcements are published in *La Gaceta*. In English, *Honduras This Week* (www.marrder.com/htw) covers news from Central America.

Broadcasting

Radio and television play a key role in Honduras, where literacy is around 60 per cent. Television is all privately owned and operated; there is one state-owned radio station.

Radio: There are five stations broadcasting nationally and over 280 local radio stations.

The biggest stations include Radio HRN (www.radiohrn.hn), Radio América (www.radioamerica.hn) and Power FM (www.powerfm.hn). The public radio network broadcasts under the collective name of Radio Corporación.

Television: There are six nationwide TV stations and some with more than one channel. The ones with the biggest market share are Televicentro (www.televicentrotv.net) with several channels and digital services and CBC Canal 6 (www.noti6.com), Vica TV (www.vicatv.hn) and Soptel Canal 11 (www.canal11.hn).

Economy

The service sector constituted 59.3 per cent of GDP in 2014, with industrial activity at 27.3 per cent (of which manufacturing is around 18 per cent of total GDP) and agriculture at 13.4 per cent. The importance of the *maquila* sector has grown since being introduced in the late 1980s, so that by 2014 it accounted for over 50 per cent of merchandise exports, of which 90 per cent were textile products. Around 80 per cent of *maquila* exports were destined for the US. Of the remaining exports, two-thirds are agricultural products; including coffee, bananas and crustaceans, and the remaining one-third are general manufactured goods, such as machinery and vehicle parts.

GDP growth was 6.2 per cent in 2007, falling to 4.1 per cent in 2008 as the global economic crisis cut world trade and exports fell. Honduras entered recession in 2009 with growth of -2.1 per cent, but regained strength in 2010 with a rate of 2.8 per cent and an estimated 3.6 per cent in 2011. In 2012 the economy went into recession, shrinking by -3.0 per cent. However, by 2014 growth was positive again reaching 3.5 per cent. Remittances in 2013 totalled US$3.1 billion (17 per cent of GDP), and at the end of 2014 the Central Bank of Honduras reported a rise to US$3.4 billion (18 per cent of GDP).

Inflation has been a long-term problem for Honduras, reaching a peak of 11.5 per cent in 2008, before falling to 8.7 per cent in 2009 and further to 4.7 per cent in 2010. In 2011 inflation climbed to 6.8 per cent, and following two years at 5.2 per cent rose to 6.1 per cent in 2014.

In 2014, the UN Human Development Index (HDI) ranked Honduras 129 (out of 187) for national development in health, education and income. Since 2000, Honduras's progress has grown but has not matched the improvement of other countries in Latin America. In 2014, 20.7 per cent of the population lived in multidimensional poverty.

External trade

Honduras is a member of the Central America Free Trade Agreement (DR-Cafta), which includes Dominican Republic, Costa Rica, El Salvador, Guatemala and the US; it is working to remove all tariffs and barriers between members by 2024. It is also a member of the World Trade Organisation (WTO). Honduras has free-trade agreements with Chile, Colombia, US, Mexico, Panama, the Dominican Republic and Taiwan.

A *maquila* industry, which began in the late 1980s, produces clothing for export, mainly to the US. Other non-traditional exports include cultivated cash crops, farmed shrimps and melons.

Imports

Principal imports are petroleum, machinery and vehicles, pharmaceuticals, industrial raw materials and foodstuffs.

Main sources: US (43.4 per cent of total in 2014), Guatemala (9.0 per cent), El Salvador (5.7 per cent)

Exports

Principal exports include clothing, coffee, bananas and crustaceans, palm oil, fruit and vegetable, timber and gold and machinery and vehicle parts.

Main destinations: US (36.1 per cent of total in 2014), El Salvador (8.5 per cent), Germany (7.0 per cent)

Agriculture

Farming

Agriculture is one of the most important economic activities in Honduras. The sector accounts for around 80 per cent of total exports, constitutes 14 per cent of total GDP and employs around 35 per cent of the country's workforce.

Sugar cane, bananas (grown on the northern lowland) and coffee are the main agricultural exports. The government is encouraging the growth of new banana varieties but it is likely to be a number of years before new crops become profitable exports.

The main food crops are maize, rice, sorghum and beans. Production of these staples has steadily risen, though food imports are still necessary to meet domestic demand.

Emphasis has been on land reform and the cultivation of new crops such as cocoa, allspice, cardamom, melons and citrus fruits.

Fishing

Honduras' annual fish catch is typically over 18,000 tonnes (t), of which approximately 12,000t is shellfish. The country's main fish exports are crustaceans such as shrimp and lobster, harvested by divers who spend up to seven hours a day on the sea bed. The lobsters are mainly exported to the US. Legislation requires all divers to undergo specific instruction and boat owners to hold licences to carry trained divers only. The government is expected to promote the potential of Honduras' fishing industry in order to attract investment and curtail growing unemployment along the country's coasts, which has forced fishermen to dive for lobsters. Improved regulation would benefit the lobster colonies, which are in danger of being depleted.

Forestry

Honduras does not have a great deal of energy resources and consequently wood is widely used as an inexpensive form of fuel. This has led to a widespread problem of deforestation in Honduras.

During 1990–95, the average rate of deforestation was 2.3 per cent, the third highest rate in the Western hemisphere after Haiti and Paraguay. Although it is estimated that 7.4 million hectares of land were covered by forest in 1987, annual deforestation in the 1980s was thought to be in the region of 70,000 hectares. Over the period 2000–2005, the annual deforestation had risen to 3.1 per cent. Since then the government has been keen to redress the rate of deforestation through education and development programmes.

According to the UN Food and Agriculture Organisation, in between 1990 and 2010, Honduras lost 36.4 per cent of its forest cover, averaging a deforestation rate of almost 2 per cent per year.

The government has promoted the protection of Honduras' forests by agreeing with foreign companies such as Stone Container Corporation (US), to establish a comprehensive forestry management plan enabling Honduras to increase the size of its forest coverage.

In a typical year, exports of forest materials amount to US$43.1 million, while imports amount to US$100 million.

Industry and manufacturing

The industrial sector, which is the smallest in Central America, typically contributes 27.3 per cent to GDP and employs 15 per cent of the workforce.

Government responsibility for the industrial sector has traditionally been divided between the Ministry of Economy's General Directorate of Industry, the Central Bank and various other official institutions. In the late 1980s government introduced policies aimed at stimulating Honduran labour-intensive industries, especially agro-industry, while boosting investment and exports to combat high unemployment. The authorities since then have continued to try and release Honduras from dependency on certain commodities such as bananas and coffee.

Virtually no production equipment is manufactured; capital goods need to be imported from foreign suppliers. The demand for capital goods cannot be funded without the government's help and the need to expand is being frustrated by financial constraints.

Manufacturing remains heavily dependent on imports of capital goods, raw materials and foreign technology; the biggest growth in the sector has been the *maquilla* (in-bond assembly and manufacturing) industries. The four main areas of manufacturing in Honduras are concentrated around food processing, agro-export, *maquilla* and chemicals. However, capacity utilisation is still low on account of Honduras' narrow domestic market and lack of international competitiveness. The key to helping the growth of the Honduran industrial sector has been the government-funded Free Trade Zones (FTZ) and privately funded Export Processing Zones (EPZs). Ninety per cent of all merchandise currently manufactured in the zones is clothing. Cloth is manufactured in the US and exported to Honduras from where it is then re-exported as garments, often duty free, to the US.

Tourism

The Mayan site of Copan and the Río Plátano Biospere Reserve are both included on Unesco's World Heritage List and are at the centre of Honduras' tourism industry. With coastlines on both the Caribbean Sea and, to a smaller extent, the Pacific Ocean, holidays are typically based on resorts with marine activities, with access to historic and natural sites, which include conservation sites of jaguars and a marine sanctuary for sharks. Many beach resorts are located offshore on the island of Roatán (often called the Big Island), which is also an important cruise liner destination and scuba diving site.

The sector has continued to grow in importance to the economy and by 2014 it represented 15.9 per cent of GDP and in total contributed 14.0 per cent of employment (447,500 jobs). Travel and tourism attracted 9.1 per cent of total capital investment in 2014.

Honduras has a reputation for street crime, which has led to visitors being segregated and protected in enclosed holiday resorts.

Mining

At present the mining sector employs approximately 2 per cent of Honduras' total workforce. The country has large reserves of tin, iron, copper and coal. There are small reserves of gold, silver, lead and zinc that are extracted for export.

Hydrocarbons
Honduras does not produce oil at significant level, despite extensive offshore exploration aimed at locating deposits.
Consumption was around 60,000 barrels per day in 2014, all of which was imported.
There are no refineries in Honduras.
There are no natural gas reserves and Honduras does not import natural gas.
Honduras imports around 125,000 tonnes of coal per year.

Energy
Total installed generating capacity was 1,815MW in 2013 (latest available figures), of which 38 per cent is publicly owned and the remainder privately. Of those in public ownership, 30 per cent are hydroelectric. Just over 85 per cent of the population has access to mains electricity, of which 94 per cent are in urban areas and 45 per cent in rural areas. Generating capacity is less than installed capacity due to ageing and under-performing power plants. There are several expansion projects of various energy mixes including hydro, coal, diesel, wind, geothermal, biomass and natural gas, to be installed by the end of 2015.
Honduras does not possess an integrated electricity supply system as local and regional electricity companies vie for business. However it has a limited connection with El Salvador, Guatemala and Nicaragua from where it imports electricity.

Financial markets
Stock exchange
Bolsa Honduras de Valores (BHV) (Honduran Stock Exchange)

Banking and insurance
The regulators of the banking and financial services sector of Honduras retain tight restrictions on bank ownership of fixed assets and limits on buying corporate shares. Foreign banks wishing to set up in Honduras must obtain approval from the president. Domestic and foreign-owned banks operate under identical rules, and historically there has been little difference in the type of business they conduct.
Central bank
Banco Central de Honduras
Main financial centre
Tegucigalpa

Time
GMT minus six hours

Geography
Honduras is in the middle of the Central American isthmus. It has a long northern coastline on the Caribbean Sea and a narrow southern outlet to the Pacific Ocean. Guatemala is to the west, El Salvador to the south-west and Nicaragua to the south-east. Covering 112,088 square km, Honduras is the second largest country in Central America after neighbouring Nicaragua. Much of the country is covered by thick forests and mountains, while around a quarter of the land is suitable for farming. Apart from a low coastal plain in the north-east, the country is crossed by numerous ranges of mountains and hills. The highest peak is the Cerro de las Minas at 2,866 metres in the western Sierra de Celaque.
Hemisphere
Northern.

Climate
Honduras has a tropical climate on the coast and a temperate climate in the mountainous interior. Temperatures in the capital Tegucigalpa, at 960 metres, are usually between 15 degrees Celsius (C) and 30 degrees C. Rain falls throughout the year on the north coast, while the rest of the country has heaviest rains between May and November. The average rainfall is 3,037mm per year. During the rainy season, May–November, the climate is temperate; in March and April the warm days are punctuated by cool nights; and in December–February it is cool and dry during the day, but chilly at night. The best time to visit is April–May.

Entry requirements
Passports
Required by all, valid for three months on arrival.
Visa
Visas are not required by nationals of most of the Americas and Europe (excluding Schengen agreement states), Australasia, Japan and some other Asian countries. Business visas should be accompanied by a company letter as proof of business intentions, and a full itinerary. For confirmation and requirements, contact the local embassy.
Currency advice/regulations
There are no restrictions on the import and export of local and foreign currency. US dollars should be declared on arrival; re-export is allowed up to the declared amount.

Health (for visitors)
Mandatory precautions
A yellow fever vaccination certificate is required if arriving from an infected area.
Advisable precautions
Typhoid, tetanus and polio vaccinations are advisable. There is a risk of malaria, especially in rural areas – prophylaxis is recommended. Water precautions are essential throughout the country.

Hotels
Hotel standards are reasonable in Tegucigalpa and San Pedro Sula. Hotel bills are subject to 16 per cent sales tax.

Public holidays (national)
Fixed dates
1 Jan (New Year's Day), 14 Apr (Americas Day), 1 May (Labour Day), 15 Sep (Independence Day), 3 Oct (Morozán Day), 12 Oct (Columbus Day), 21 Oct (Armed Forces Day), 25 Dec (Christmas Day).
Variable dates
Maundy Thursday, Good Friday.

Working hours
Banking
Mon–Fri: 0900–1500.
Business
Mon–Fri: 0800–1200, 1330/1400–1700; Sat: 0800–1100.
Government
Mon–Fri: 0800–1200, 1330/1400–1700; Sat: 0800–1100.

Electricity supply
110 or 220V AC, 60 cycles.

Social customs/useful tips
Handshaking is the main form of greeting. Embracing is frowned upon by both men and women.
Mothers are regarded as the leading family figures. It is a grave offence to insult someone's mother. Women rather than men are often the principal family breadwinners. Grandparents and elders are highly respected. The extended family plays an important social role by providing a sense of unity.
It is customary to send flowers to the hostess if invited to dinner or as a guest to someone's home.
Professional persons should be addressed by their title. Graduates are known as *Licenciados*.

Security
There is widespread petty and violent crime, including armed robbery, car hijacking, burglary and sexual assaults. Visitors are advised to exercise vigilance and caution in all areas, not to carry large amounts of money, take only what is necessary, keep the rest deposited at the hotel and not to resist robbery attempts.

Getting there
Air
National airline: Sol Air.
International airport/s: Tegucigalpa-Toncontín (TGU), 5km from city; duty-free shop, bar, restaurant, bank, post office, vaccination centre, shops, car hire.
Airport tax: US$32.
Surface
Road: It is possible to reach Tegucigalpa via the Pan-American Highway from Goascorán (on the border with El Salvador) and from El Espino and Guasaule (on the border with Nicaragua). Bus services run from most Central American

countries. Entry from Guatemala is possible via the Western Highway.

Main port/s: Ampala, La Ceiba, Cortés, Roatan, Castilla, Tela, Lorenzo.

Getting about

National transport

Air: Isleñas Airlines, Sosa Airlines and Rollins Air are the three local airlines, operating numerous flights between Tegucigalpa, San Pedro Sula, Roatan, La Ceiba, Trujillo and Tela. To reach more remote areas using other services, local enquiries should be made.

Road: Network of 10,468km, concentrated along coast (roughly San Pedro Sula to Trujillo) and the area between San Pedro Sula and Tegucigalpa and the Guatemalan border. The main highways are paved, although roads are of varying quality. Travel on unpaved roads is not recommended.

Buses: Frequent services San Pedro Sula to Tegucigalpa; also linking with Juticalpa, Danlí, Choluteca.

Rail: There are passenger train services in the north, running between San Pedro Sula, Puerto Cortés and Tela, although they are somewhat ramshackle and the service is slow.

Water: Water transport is commonly used to travel between Honduras, the Caribbean islands and the bay islands. In Mosquitia almost all transport is along the waterways due to poor road infrastructure.

City transport

Taxis: Can be hailed, ordered by telephone or found at ranks; also possible to hail and share a taxi; fares by negotiation (sometimes a flat rate). Tipping is not usual.

Buses, trams & metro: Buses stop outside the entrance to the Toncontín international airport. All buses in and around the capital operate between 0500 and 2100.

Car hire

A national or international licence is required. Rental cars are available in Tegucigalpa, San Pedro Sula, La Ceiba and on the island of Roatán.

BUSINESS DIRECTORY

The addresses listed below are a selection only. While World of Information makes every endeavour to check these addresses, we cannot guarantee that changes have not been made, especially to telephone numbers and area codes. We would welcome any corrections.

Telephone area codes

The international direct dialling code (IDD) for Honduras is +504 followed by the customer number.

Chambers of Commerce

American-Honduran Chamber of Commerce, Hotel Honduras Maya, PO Box 1838, Tegucigalpa (tel: 232-7043; fax: 232-2031; e-mail: amcham@t.hn2.com).

Cortes Camará de Comercio e Industrias, 17 Avenida Circunvalación, PO Box 14, San Pedro Sula (tel: 553-0761; fax: 533-3777; e-mail: ccic@ccichonduras.org).

Honduras Federación de Camarás de Comercio e Industrias, Edificio Castañito, Bulevar Morazan, Tegucigalpa, PO Box 3393 (tel: 232-6083; fax: 232-1870; e-mail: fedecamara@sigmant.hn).

Tegucigalpa Camará de Comercio e Industrias, Bulevar Centramérica, PO Box 3444, Tegucigalpa (tel: 232-4200; fax: 232-0159; e-mail: infoccit@ccit.hn).

Banking

Banco Atlántida SA, PO Box 3164, Plaza Bancatlan, Tegucigalpa (tel: 321-742; fax: 321-273).

Banco CentroAmericano de Integración Económico, Edificio Midence Soto, Nivel 10, PO Box 772, Tegucigalpa, M D C Honduras (tel: 372-230; fax: 311-906).

Banco Continental SA, PO Box 390, San Pedro Sula, Cortes (tel: 531-310; fax: 522-750).

Banco del Comercio SA (Bancomer), PO Box 160, San Pedro Sula, Cortes (tel: 533-600; fax: 533-128).

Banco de El Ahorro Hondureño SA, PO Box 3185, Tegucigalpa (tel: 375-161; fax: 374-638).

Banco de Honduras SA, PO Box 3434, Tegucigalpa (tel: 326-122; fax: 326-164).

Banco de la Exportación SA (Banexpo), PO Box 3988, Tegucigalpa (tel: 394-256; fax: 394-265).

Banco de las Fuerzas Armadas SA (Banffaa), PO Box 877, Tegucigalpa (tel: 312-051; fax: 313-832).

Banco de Los Trabajadores SA, PO Box 3246, Tegucigalpa (tel: 379-501; fax: 378-422).

Banco de Occidente SA, PO Box 3284, Tegucigalpa (tel: 370-310; fax: 370-486).

Banco del País SA, PO Box 314, San Pedro Sula, Cortes (tel: 525-202; fax: 525-229).

Banco Hondureño del Café (Banhcafe), PO Box 583, Tegucigalpa (tel: 328-370; fax: 328-332).

Banco Financiera Centroamericana SA (Ficensa), PO Box 1432, Tegucigalpa (tel: 381-661; fax: 381-630).

Banco La Capitalizadora Hondureña SA (Bancahsa), PO Box 344, Tegucigalpa (tel: 371-171; fax: 372-775).

Banco Mercantil SA (Bamer), PO Box 116, Tegucigalpa (tel: 320-006; fax: 323-137).

Banco Sogerín SA, PO Box 440, San Pedro Sula, Cortes (tel: 533-888; fax: 572-001).

Lloyds Bank, PO Box 3136, Tegucigalpa (tel: 366-864; fax: 366-417).

Central bank

Banco Central de Honduras, PO Box 3165, Tegucigalpa MDC (tel: 237-2270; fax: 237-1876; e-mail: webmaster@mail.bch.hn).

Stock exchange

Bolsa Honduras de Valores (BHV) (Honduran Stock Exchange)

Stock exchange 2

Bolsa Centroamericana de Valores (BCV) (Central American Stock Exchange Securities), www.bcv.hn

Travel information

National tourist organisation offices

Instituto Hondureño de Turismo, Col San Carlos, Edificio Europa, PO Box 3261, Tegucigalpa (tel: 222-2124 ext 502; fax: 222-2124 ext 501; e-mail: tourisminfo@iht.hn).

Ministries

Ministry of Agriculture, Boulevard Miraflores, Tegucigalpa, MDC (tel: 32-8394; fax: 325-375).

Ministry of Culture, Arts and Sport, Ave La Paz, Tegucigalpa, MDC (tel: 369-738; fax: 369-738).

Ministry of Defence, 4c, 5a Tegucigalpa, MDC (tel: 380-065; fax: 380-238).

Ministry of Education, 1C 2-3A Comaguela (tel: 228-517; fax: 374-312).

Ministry of External Relations, Antigua Casa Presidencial, Centro Civico Gubernamental, Tegucigalpa, MDC (tel: 343-297; fax: 341-484).

Ministry of Health, 3C 4A Tegucigalpa, MDC (tel: 228-518; fax: 384-141).

Ministry of Industry, Trade and Tourism, 5A, 4C Edif Salame, Tegucigalpa, MDC (tel: 382-025; fax: 372-836).

Ministry of Labour and Social Security, 7C 2-3 Ave Comayaguela (tel: 379-778; fax: 223-220).

Ministry of Natural Resources and Environment, Barrio la Fuente, Tegucigalpa, MDC (tel: 375-664; fax: 375-726).

Ministry of Public Works, Transport and Housing, Barrio la Bolsa, Comayaguela (tel: 33-7690; fax: 252-227).

Presidential Office, Palacio José Cecilio del Valle, Bd Juan Pablo II, Tegucigapa, MDC (tel: 326-282; fax: 31-0097).

Other useful addresses

Asociación Nacional de Industriales, Boulevard los Proceres, 4a Avenida, Colonia Lara, Tegucigalpa.

Asociación Hondureña de Productores de Café (Coffee Producers' Association), 10a Avenida, 6a Calle, Apdo 959, Tegucigalpa.

British Embassy, Edif Palmira, 3rd Floor, Colonia Palmira, Tegucigalpa (tel: 320-612, 320-618; fax: 325-480).

Consejo Hondureño de la Empresa Privada, Barrio la Plozuela, 5th Floor, Edificio San Miguel, Tegucigalpa.

Corporación Nacional de Inversiones (CONADI), Apdo 842, Tegucigalpa (tx: 1192).

División Estudios Económicos, Banco Atlántida, Apdo 57-C, Boulevard Centroamérica, Tegucigalpa.

Home Office, Palacio Nacional, 2o Piso, Tegucigalpa, MDC (tel: 228-604; fax: 37-1121).

Honduran Embassy (US), 3007 Tilden Street, NW, Washington DC 20008 (tel: (+1-202) 966-7702; fax: (+1-202) 966-9751; e-mail: embassy@hondurasemb.org).

Honduras Stock Exchange, PO Box 161, San Pedro Sula (tel: 534-410; fax: 534-480).

Secretary of the Treasury, 3C, 5A Tegucigalpa, MDC (tel: 220-111; fax: 382-309).

Secretaria de Planificación y Presupuesto (SECPLAN), 2 Avenida 9 y 10 Calle Comayaguela, Tegucigalpa.

US Embassy, Avenida La Paz, Apdo 26-C, Tegucigalpa (tel: 323-120; fax: 320-027).

Internet sites

Cámara de Comercio e Industrias de Cortes (Cortes Chamber of Commerce and Industry) (local, national and international business issues in Spanish only): http://www.123.hn/

Honduras yellow pages: http://www.only-honduras.com

Latin America Network Information Center: http://www.lanic.utexas.edu/

Hong Kong (China)

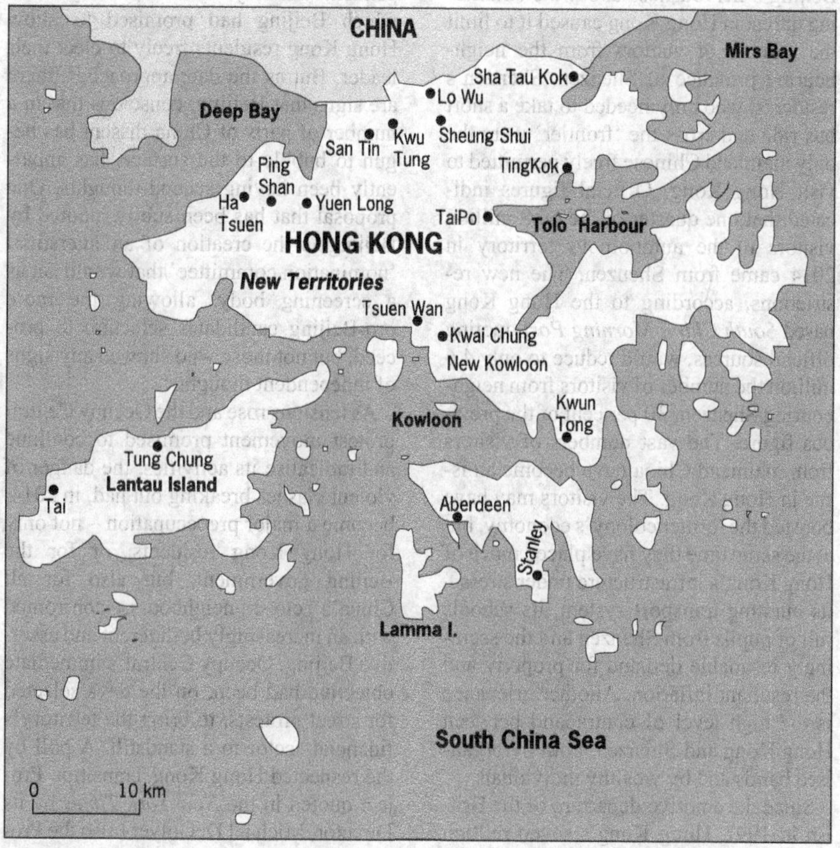

Uniquely within China, Hong Kong has its own legal system and rights including the freedom of assembly and free speech which are both protected. The territory's 'mini-constitution', known as the Basic Law, says that 'the ultimate aim' is to elect the chief executive 'by universal suffrage upon nomination by a broadly representative nominating committee in accordance with democratic procedures'. In April 2015 the Chinese government had opted to maintain its hard line in the early run up to the 2017 election for the new Chief Executive. A decision had been taken not to make any concessions to the pro-democracy movement that had blocked the territory's streets for two months in late 2014. The street protests had demanded free elections and there was a resurgence of the demonstrations in 2015.

The Umbrella Revolution

Six months after the so called Umbrella Revolution broke out, Carrie Lam, the deputy leader of the Hong Kong government was charged with presenting to Hong Kong's Legislative Council the electoral reforms proposed by Beijing. Ms Lam set out an electoral procedure that would conform to the 'strictest respect' for the regulations adopted by China's Peoples' Assembly in August 2014, which while it incorporated the 'one voice, one vote' principle, did so only for a limited number of candidates. It would be the first occasion in the ex-colony's history, that its inhabitants – or at least some of them – could vote for their 'leader'.

In fact the elections will be far from any principles resembling universal suffrage. Ms Lam underlined that only the two or

KEY FACTS

Official name: Xianggang Tebie Xingzhengqu (Hong Kong Special Administrative Region (SAR) of China)

Head of State: State President of China XI Jinping (in Beijing) (from 14 March 2013)

Head of government: Chief Executive-elect (CY) Leung Chun-ying (from 1 Jul 2012)

Ruling party: Coalition government (approved by the Zhongguo Gongchandang (Chinese Communist Party))

Area: 1,070 square km (including 235 islands)

Population: 7.26 million (2014)*

Capital: The Legislative Council building is situated in the central district, on Hong Kong Island

Official language: Chinese (Mandarin, Beijing dialect *de jure*; Cantonese *de facto*) and English

Currency: Hong Kong dollar (HK$) = 100 cents

Exchange rate: HK$7.75 per US$ (Sep 2015)

GDP per capita: US$39,871 (2014)

GDP real growth: 2.32% (2014)

GDP: US$289.63 billion (2014)

Labour force: 3.68 million (2010)

Unemployment: 3.23% (2014)

Inflation: 4.42% (2014)

Balance of trade: -US$30.14 billion (2014)*

* estimated figure

three candidates selected by an electoral committee of 1,200 members supposedly representing Hong Kong's different social sectors would stand for election as Chief Executive. The new electoral structure was remarkably similar to that endorsed by the pro-Beijing committee that had previously chosen the colony's leader. Ms Lam's announcement caused little surprise among Hong Kong's pro-democracy parliamentarians, who registered their disapproval by departing the Legislative Council in protest, a gesture that predicted lively debates on the proposed reforms.

Alan Leong, the leader of Hong Kong's Civic Party announced that 'We will initiate a campaign opposing these proposals and we will ask Hong Kong's population to continue demanding genuine universal suffrage.' These sentiments were echoed by Hong Kong's student leader, Joshua Wong, who did not rule out new street mobilisation when the reforms were to be debated in the Legislative Council. Anticipating this response, Ms Lam advised that the Hong Kong government was prepared for 'new and aggressive' protests, reiterating that there was no possibility that Beijing would withdraw its electoral reform plan.

The pro-democracy parliamentarians held thirty seats of the total 70 and had announced that they would not vote on the reforms. This meant that they would block the reforms, which required a two thirds majority to pass legislation. This would create a climate of uncertainty, which it was thought would favour the protestors' demands for free elections. In the face of this looming scenario, Leung Chun Ying the head of Hong Kong's executive described as 'uncertain' the territory's future if the reforms were not approved, a process he described as an 'important milestone for the city's future democratic development.'

Shutting the shop

Beijing's nervousness about the simmering unrest in Hong Kong caused it to limit the number of visitors from the neighbouring province of Shenzen. Shenzen's residents, who only needed to take a short bus ride and cross the 'frontier' were the only mainland Chinese freely permitted to visit Hong Kong. Official figures indicated that one quarter of the 60.8 million visitors to the autonomous territory in 2014 came from Shenzen. The new restrictions, according to the Hong Kong based *South China Morning Post* quoting official sources, would reduce to only 4.6 million the number of visitors from neighbouring Shenzen, 30 per cent of the previous figure. The vast numbers of visitors from mainland China have become an issue in Hong Kong. The visitors may have boosted the former colony's economy, but at the same time they have placed much of Hong Kong's infrastructure under stress – its bursting transport system, its schools full of pupils from Shenzen and the seemingly insatiable demand for property and the resultant inflation. Another grievance is the high level of contraband between Hong Kong and Shenzen, both by organised bands and by wealthy individuals.

Since the emotive departure of the British in 1997, Hong Kong's seven million residents have enjoyed a remarkably relaxed political environment, with surprisingly little direct interference from Beijing. But all good things come to an end and by 2013 a colder Beijing hand appeared to be tightening its grip on the island's affairs. The key date, the date which promises to be the litmus test of Hong Kong's theoretical status as an independent territory is 2017, the year in which Beijing had promised to allow Hong Kong residents freely to elect their leader. But as the date approaches, there are signs that Beijing, conscious that in a number of parts of China dissent has begun to bubble to the surface, has apparently been having second-thoughts. One proposal that has been subtly mooted by Beijing is the creation of an interstitial 'nomination committee' that would act as a screening body, allowing the more pro-Beijing candidates selection to proceed, but not those who showed any signs of independent thought.

As tensions rose and the Occupy Central protest movement promised to continue and radicalise its activities, the danger of violent clashes breaking out had, in 2014, become a major preoccupation – not only for Hong Kong residents, or for the Beijing government, but also for all China's close neighbours, confronted with an increasingly belligerent and assertive Beijing. Occupy Central's immediate objective had been, on the days selected for street protests, to bring the territory's financial sector to a standstill. A poll by the respected Hong Kong Transition Project quoted in the *New York Times* by its Director, Michael DeGolyer (also the Professor of government and International Studies at the Hong Kong Baptist University) had suggested that 40 per cent of Hong Kong residents planned to support the protest movement. The poll also pointed out that most of these people were under the age of 30. The gut feeling of most Hong Kong residents was that sooner or later Beijing would have to come to terms with Hong Kong's insatiable desire for free elections. The local government's popular campaign goes under the rather weak and wordy slogan: 'Let's talk and Achieve Universal Suffrage'.

Referendum rules

The Hong Kong authorities were both wrong-footed and disquieted by an unofficial referendum on Hong Kong's future democratic arrangements held in late June 2015, in which almost 800,000 votes were cast. The referendum was part of the civil campaign that had been declared illegal

KEY INDICATORS — Hong Kong (China)

	Unit	2011	2012	2013	2014	**2015
Population	m	*7.15	*7.18	7.22	*7.26	*7.31
Gross domestic product (GDP)	US$bn	243.30	262.64	274.86	289.63	*310.07
GDP per capita	US$	34,049	36,590	38,060	39,871	*42,437
GDP real growth	%	5.0	1.6	2.9	2.3	*2.8
Inflation	%	5.3	4.1	4.3	4.4	*3.2
Unemployment	%	3.4	3.3	3.4	3.2	*3.2
Exports (fob) (goods)	US$m	102,183.0	464,641.0	508,679.0	519,325.0	–
Imports (fob) (goods)	US$m	114,229.0	487,372.0	534,887.0	549,460.0	–
Balance of trade	US$m	-12,047.0	-22,731.0	-26,207.0	-30,136.0	–
Current account	US$m	12,908.0	7,333.0	4,149.0	*4,544.0	*6,325.0
Total reserves minus gold	US$m	277,105.0	317,251.0	311,129.0	328,436.0	–
Foreign exchange	US$m	277,086.0	317,189.0	311,061.0	–	–
Exchange rate	per US$	7.78	7.75	7.75	7.75	–

* estimated figure ** forecast figure

by both the local and the Beijing authorities. Hong Kong's democracy activists wanted the nomination process to be open to everyone. Beijing's continuing fear was the protestors threat to close down the Central area (the territory's business heartland) if Beijing refused to accept their demands for more genuinely democratic procedures for electing the next Chief Executive. The unofficial vote, organised by pro-democracy activists, was impressively well managed. Voting was mainly online and voters were asked for their identification number to prevent cheating.

Some pro-Beijing supporters appeared to denounce the vote; a pro-Beijing group, calling itself 'Caring Hong Kong Power', marched through Causeway Bay carrying bright orange balloons and urging people not to vote. The group handed in a petition against the anti-Beijing movement, allegedly signed by 30,000 people. The referendum voters had three choices, all of which involved allowing citizens to nominate candidates, who would then be presented to the Beijing government. Simple enough? The winning proposal, which mustered 42 per cent of the votes, was put forward by a grouping calling itself the Alliance for True Democracy, allowed candidates to be nominated by 35,000 registered voters, or by any political party which had secured a minimum of at least 5 per cent of the vote in the previous election for Hong Kong's legislative committee.

The referendum closed two days ahead of the annual 1 July 'anniversary' demonstration, (the anniversary of Hong Kong's return to Chinese rule), an occasion for citizens to protest generally, but specifically and principally against what is seen as government hedging on the question of democratic representation. Hong Kong's lawyers had marched through the city wearing black in protest against the wording of a Beijing white paper in which it was mooted that being patriotic and 'loving the country' were essential requirements for the city's administrators – and lawyers.

The economy

According to the Asian Development bank (ADB), Hong Kong's economy grew by 2.3 per cent in 2014, down from 2.9 per cent in 2013. Sluggish economic performance in Europe and moderating growth in the People's Republic of China (PRC) had dampened growth in the first half of the year, but a US economy performing better than expected and higher demand in Asia for exports lifted growth in the second half. Domestic demand was nevertheless the main engine of growth in 2014.

The ADB noted that private consumption had contributed 1.8 percentage points to growth, supported by rising real incomes, moderating underlying inflation and unemployment at a 17-year low of 3.2 per cent. These factors outweighed the drag on retail sales from a shift from more expensive items to cheaper consumer goods in the spending of PRC tourists, who make up 78 per cent of all arrivals. According to the ADB, the contribution of government consumption remained unchanged at 0.3 percentage points despite cutbacks to one-off relief measures from the previous year. Investment grew by 2.8 per cent, mainly for inventory accumulation and contributed 0.7 percentage points to growth. A business tendency survey had found cautious business sentiment holding down machinery and equipment acquisition.

Building and construction rebounded to 6.5 per cent, however, on large public infrastructure works and private housing projects. Net exports declined for the sixth consecutive year, subtracting 0.4 percentage points from gross domestic product (GDP) growth. Export growth moderated because of weak external demand. Another factor could have been 4.0 per cent nominal effective appreciation of the local dollar. Import growth also slowed in tandem with moderating GDP growth but outpaced that of exports.

Consumer price inflation was up marginally at 4.4 per cent. Subdued global inflation and softer rental growth kept inflation at bay, although residential property prices rose by 13.5 per cent, reflecting the continuing low interest rate environment and a tight demand – supply balance. Excluding the one-off relief measures implemented in 2014, including payment of 1 month's rent for public housing tenants and rates concession for two quarters, the adjusted overall inflation rate was 3.5 per cent. The current account surplus was estimated to have narrowed to 0.2 per cent of GDP owing to weak external demand, the appreciation of the local dollar and slowing growth in net services receipts. Growth in transport services and offshore trade was offset by lower tourism receipts and a slowdown in financial and other business service receipts in a sluggish trading environment. The overall balance of payments was expected to record a surplus largely on sustained net portfolio inflows. Gross official reserves rose to nearly US$329 billion, or cover for 7.2 months of imports.

On the policy front, according to the ADB, the budget was estimated at a surplus equivalent to 2.8 per cent of GDP in FY2014 (ending 31 March 2015), with fiscal reserves reaching HK$819.6 billion (US$105.8 billion). Revenue was estimated at 9.4 per cent higher than the original estimate for FY2014, mainly because of larger receipts from stamp duties and profits taxes. Expenditure was estimated to be lower at 17.7 per cent of GDP and within the planned target of 20.0 per cent of GDP. As the Hong Kong dollar is pegged to the US dollar, accommodative monetary policy in the US kept local interest rates low. Domestic credit rose by 12.1 per cent as loans for manufacturing, utilities and retail and wholesale trade rose. Growth in the broad money supply (M2) decelerated to 9.5 per cent from 12.4 per cent in 2013. The Hong Kong Monetary Authority introduced a requirement in 2014 that banks hold sufficient stable funds to support their lending business. Several rounds of macro-prudential and tax measures introduced since October 2009 have successfully dampened mortgage loan growth and speculation in the property market, curtailing short-term resale.

In the view of the ADB, shifting market sentiment caused the Hang Seng Index, the main index of the stock exchange, to swing from a low in March 2014 to a 6-year high in early September and close the year higher by 1.3 per cent. Hong Kong remained a top-ranked fund-raising hub, second only to New York, with more than HK$232 billion (US$30 billion) raised in initial public offerings in 2014, a 38 per cent rise on 2013. A US$1 billion Islamic government bond was successfully issued in September.

The city's role as the premier centre for offshore renminbi trading was bolstered as the monetary authority lifted the daily conversion limit on renminbi for residents and as a link with the Shanghai Stock Exchange commenced operation, facilitating trade on the two exchanges by investors located in either city. The local monetary authority and the central bank of the PRC renewed the currency swap agreement for a further 3 years.

GDP growth was forecast to improve slightly to 2.8 per cent in 2015 and to 2.9 per cent in 2016, still below its 5-year average of 3.7 per cent. Forecasts were premised on a strengthening US economy, sustained resilience in Asian economies and slowing but healthy growth in the

PRC. Domestic demand was set to be the engine of growth, spurred by strengthening private consumption underpinned by stable real income and full employment. Investment growth would find support in improving business sentiment and several ongoing big-ticket infrastructure projects, including the expansion of the mass transit railway, public housing and a bridge across the vast Pearl River estuary. Growth in tourism was expected to compensate for any weakness in trade.

Inflation was forecast to decelerate to 3.3 per cent in 2015 and then rebound slightly to 3.4 per cent in 2016. Lower prices for imported food and oil and the knock-on effects of the expected drop in housing prices looked likely to outweigh inflationary pressure from the rise in the statutory minimum wage in January 2015. A further drop in housing prices, lower rents and only a slight rise in world oil and commodity prices would keep the inflation rate stable in 2016.

Risk assessment

Economy	Good
Politics	Fair
Regional stability	Fair

COUNTRY PROFILE

1839 China impounded opium stocks and blocked further shipments. Major traders, Jardine Matheson, called on the British government to exert its right to trade. The British navy blockaded Chinese ports, sparking the first Opium War.
1842 China ceded Hong Kong to Great Britain under provision of the *Treaty of Nanking*, following defeat in the first Opium War, which it fought to wipe out the illicit smuggling of opium into the country. Hong Kong was already a sizeable local fishing community with 3,000 inhabitants and 2,000 fishermen. Hong Kong became an important British naval base and attracted merchants from mainland China; the colony became an important regional *entrepôt*.
1856–60 The second Opium War was fought in which the British and French defeated China.
1860 The Kowloon Peninsula was acquired under the *Convention of Peking*.
1898 The New Territories were leased from China for a period of 99 years.
1900s Immigration from the mainland increased as social turmoil due to the Boxer rebellion and general insecurity in China grew. The prospects of employment in Hong Kong's light industries increased.
1937 Outbreak of the Sino-Japanese War. As the Japanese army advanced further into China, more Chinese fled to Hong Kong. It is estimated that over 500,000 Chinese entered the territory at this time.
1941 Hong Kong fell to the Japanese.
1945 After Japan's defeat in the Second World War, Britain resumed control of the territory.
1984 The UK conceded that from July 1997, on the expiry of the lease on the New Territories, China would regain sovereignty over the whole of Hong Kong. The Sino-British Joint Declaration contained detailed assurances on the future of Hong Kong.
1997 On 1 July Hong Kong became a Special Administrative Region (SAR) of the People's Republic of China in an arrangement to last for 50 years. The Hong Kong stock market crashed; a fear that currency speculators would trade the Hong Kong dollar down in value prompted authorities to raise interest rates.
1998 Only 23 per cent of eligible voters turned out to choose an 800-member election committee with powers to nominate the chief executive and 10 legislators. The election process was criticised as complicated and undemocratic. Hong Kong International Airport on Lantau Island opened.
1999 Beijing redefined the constitution, ruling who had the right to live in Hong Kong. This constitutional change sparked protests.
2000 There was a low turnout in the LegCo elections; the Democratic Party (DP) lost a seat to the pro-Beijing Democratic Alliance for the Betterment of Hong Kong (DAB).
2001 Chief Secretary Anson Chan, holder of the SAR's second most powerful office, resigned, amid concerns that pressure from Beijing had made her position untenable. Donald Tsang replaced Chan as chief secretary.
2002 Chief Executive Tung Chee-hwa was appointed for a second five-year term.
2003 Around 500,000 people protested over a proposed anti-subversion law, which many believe threatened basic rights; another demonstration of 50,000 people called for universal suffrage and the dismissal of Chief Executive Tung Chee-hwa.
2004 Chinese legislators ruled out direct elections for a Hong Kong leader in 2007.
2005 Chief Executive Tung Chee-hwa resigned due to ill health; he was replaced by Chief Secretary Donald Tsang.
2007 Donald Tsang won a second term as chief executive. The former Chief Secretary, Ms Anson Chan, won a seat in the legislature with 55 per cent of the vote against China-backed Regina Ip (43 per cent) and six other candidates. Ms Chan campaigned for universal suffrage and full democracy. Donald Tsang submitted his report on democratic reform in Hong Kong to Beijing.
2008 In Legislative Council (LegCo) elections, pro-democrats won 58.99 per cent of the vote (23 seats out of 60), pro-Beijing parties 41.01 per cent (35) and independents 2.72 per cent (2). Hong Kong's economy officially fell into recession.
2009 The economy pulled out of recession in the second quarter. Construction began on a new, six-lane bridge, linking Hong Kong and Macao to China's mainland province of Guangdong; when completed (2016) it will be the longest sea-crossing bridge in the world (almost 50kms).
2010 Air pollution levels reached a record high, caused by severe sandstorms in Northern China, and prompting authorities to warn Hong Kong citizens to avoid going out. To dampen a possible property bubble, stamp duty on properties of over US$2.6 million was increased by 0.50 per cent (up to 4.25 per cent). A by-election was held following the resignation of five pro-democracy party legislative councillors. They had complained about the slow pace of democratisation, in particular the failure to introduce universal suffrage. All five members were re-elected; Beijing branded the elections 'illegal'. Protests in both Hong Kong and Guangdong took place over concerns that central government plans to insist that the regional dialect of Cantonese should be replaced by the national dialect of Mandarin in mainstream, primetime broadcasting. The worry for the protestors was that Cantonese will become marginalised.
2011 A minimum wage of HK$28 (US$3.60) per hour was introduced in Hong Kong in May. Around 270,000 low-paid workers (10 per cent of the working population) were expected to benefit from the change. A voluntary minimum wage scheme had been introduced in 2006, but never achieved widespread success. The five-yearly national census began in June, with completion in July. On 13 December, the Swiss-based, World Economic Forum voted Hong Kong as the world's leading financial centre in its annual survey of global financial development. This is the first time an Asian city had outstripped the traditional leading centres of Wall Street (New York) and the City of London (UK).
2012 On 1 February the membership of the electoral college was increased from 800 to 1,200, of which 1,044 members are elected from 35 subsectors, 60 members are nominated by religious bodies and 96 are *ex officio* members of the National People's Congress (in Beijing) (36) and the Hong Kong LegCo (60). Results

of the census were published on 21 February, showing a resident population of 6,635,558 people. Elections for the post of chief executive were held on 25 March. Businessman, (CY) Leung Chun-ying won with 689 votes (out of 1,200); Henry Tang won 285, the third candidate Albert Ho won 76 votes. On 1 July CY Leung was sworn in as the new chief executive. An additional five seats were added to the geographic constituencies (GCs) (making a total of 35), while the functional constituencies (FCs) remained the same (total of 35). The changes were implemented ahead of the elections for the LegCo held on 9 September. The pan-Democrats won 27 seats out of 70 (56.24 per cent of the vote) and the pro-Beijing bloc 43 seats (42.66 per cent). The result allowed pro-democracy parties to retain their power of veto over new laws in the LegCo.

2013 Chief Executive Leung Chun-ying paid a visit to the US in June. On 26 August the *South China Morning Post* reported criticism by James Tien, Liberal Party leader, that highlighted the split in the pro-establishment camp over the chief executive's dismal job performance ratings. Mr Tien was commenting on Mr Leung's rating of 45.7 points out of 100 in a July poll.

2014 Organisers said that a pro-democracy rally held on 1 July drew some 510,000 protesters. However, the police said the number was more like 98,600 at the peak of the march. A referendum held a week earlier drew almost 800,000 reponses. Some 42 per cent of the voters were in favour of the public, a nominating committee, and political parties naming candidates for the leader. China has said that the public can directly choose its chief executive in the 2017 election, but only from a list of candidates pre-selected by the nominating committee, which the public will not have elected. A pro-government rally was held on 17 August. The National People's Congress (Chinese parliament) confirmed on 31 August that the process of choosing Hong Kong's leader would not change. On 28 September the pro-democracy group Occupy Central joined forces with student protestors to take over Central Hong Kong. On 12 October hundreds of police moved in with chainsaws and bolt-cutters to dismantle barricades put up by the pro-democracy activists near the government offices. Chief Executive CY Leung said there was no chance that the mainland government would change its mind, and that he himself would not resign. On 11 December bailiffs backed by police finally moved in to clear the main camp near government buildings in Admiralty.

2015 Pro-democracy demonstrators returned to the streets on 1 February, although not in the high numbers of previous demonstrations. On 22 April Chief Secretary Carrie Lam announced the proposed reforms for the 2017 election in which for the first time the chief executive will be elected by the general population. However, these do not concede to pro-democracy demands for a fully free vote, rather they comply with guidelines from China's legislature that candidates will be screened. The legislature will vote on the proposals, but opposition democrats have vowed to veto it.

Political structure

Constitution

The Basic Law, promulgated by the People's Republic of China (PRC) in 1990, effectively became Hong Kong's Constitution after sovereignty of the former British colony was handed over to mainland China in July 1997. The Basic Law pledges to maintain Hong Kong's economic, social and political distinctiveness for a period of 50 years after the handover to the PRC, under the principle of 'one country, two systems'. Foreign affairs and defence are the responsibility of the central government in Beijing.

Form of state

Special Administrative Region (SAR) of the People's Republic of China

The executive

Hong Kong is administered by a Beijing-appointed chief executive, who represents the Chinese Politburo. The 13-member Executive Council (ExCo) serves in an advisory role for the Chief Executive.

On 1 February 2012 the membership of the electoral college that votes for candidates for the post of chief executive was increased from 800 to 1,200, of which 1,044 members are elected from 35 subsectors (representative bodies such as trades unions, professional bodies and health and educational faculties), 60 members are nominated by religious governing bodies and 96 are *ex officio* members of the National People's Congress (in Beijing) (36) and the Hong Kong LegCo (60).

On 22 April 2015 Chief Secretary Carrie Lam announced the proposed reforms for the 2017 election in which for the first time the chief executive will be elected by the general population. However, these do not concede to pro-democracy demands for a fully free vote, rather they comply with guidelines from China's legislature that candidates will be screened. According to Ms Lam, the 'proposals are in strict compliance with the Basic Law and the relevant decisions of [China's] standing committee of the National People's Congress. There will be two stages:

- A primary vote among the 1,200 members of the largely pro-Beijing nominating committee will produce a shortlist of 5–10 candidates with at least 120 votes, up to a maximum of 240 votes.
- These candidates will face a second round of voting by the nominating committee and the two or three candidates who win the most votes, a minimum of 601 votes, will then be eligible to run in the public election.

National legislature

The 60-seat unicameral Legislative Council (LegCo) has 60 members, of which 30 are elected by proportional representation in geographical constituencies and 30 by majority voting in functional constituencies (trade unions, professional and business associations). All members serve four-year terms.

Legal system

Under the Basic Law, Hong Kong's legal system is guaranteed independence from the Chinese judiciary. A Hong Kong Court of Final Appeal replaced the Privy Council in the United Kingdom as the highest court. The autonomy of this institution was seriously undermined in 1999 after a bitter dispute between the executive and the court over the migration of dependants from mainland China, in which China's legislature, the National People's Congress (NPC), overruled the Court of Final Appeal. However, the government in Beijing declared that recourse to the NPC would be kept a rare and exceptional act, and has not been invoked since.

Last elections

9 September 2012 (Legislative Council (LegCo)); 25 March 2012 (chief executive)

Results: LegCo: pan-Democrats (10 parties and three independents) won 56.24 per cent of the vote (27 seats out of 70), the pro-Beijing bloc (10 parties and 11 independents) won 42.66 per cent (43); turnout was 50.85 per cent.

Chief executive: (CY) Leung Chun-ying won with 689 votes (out of 1,200), Henry Tang 285, Albert Ho 76. Turnout was 94.9 per cent.

Next elections

September 2016 (LegCo), 2017 (Chief Executive).

Political parties

Ruling party

Coalition government (approved by the Zhongguo Gongchandang (Chinese Communist Party))

Main opposition party

Pro-democracy bloc.

Approximately 71 per cent of the population is aged between 15 and 64 years.

Some 20 per cent of the population resides on Hong Kong Island, a third in Kowloon and the remainder in the New Territories.

Population
7.26 million (2014)*

Last census: 14 March 2006: 6,864,958

Population density: 6,400 inhabitants per square km (2010), one of the highest densities in the world.

Annual growth rate: Projected growth 1 per cent per annum (2000–15).

Ethnic make-up
Approximately 98 per cent of the population is of Chinese descent. There are Caucasian, Indian and Filipino minorities, perhaps totalling more than 200,000, but many of these are seasonal migrant workers.

Religions
Buddhism and Taoism (74 per cent); Confucianism, Islam and Hinduism (17 per cent); Christianity (9 per cent). There are places of worship for most other religious groups. Falun Gong, the sect banned in mainland China, is legal in Hong Kong.

Education
Primary education is provided free in all government schools and in most government-assisted schools from the ages of six to 11 years. Secondary schools are divided into junior and senior levels, for 12–14-year-olds and 15–16-year-olds, respectively. The secondary school system consists of Anglo-Chinese grammar schools, Chinese middle schools, secondary technical schools and pre-vocational schools. There are a number of universities, several of which used to be technical colleges. After the British handover in 1997, 24 of Hong Kong's 124 secondary schools which taught in English were ordered to change to Cantonese.
Government expenditure on education amounts to over 20 per cent of the SAR government budget. The largest proportion of the budget is spent on basic education, accounting for 68.8 per cent of total spending on education.

Literacy rate: 93.8 per cent total, 90.1 per cent female; adult rates (World Bank).

Health
Government efforts have been mainly geared to the continuous development of the primary health care services.
Eighteen health centres and 18 visiting health teams provide services to the elderly and their carers. There are three types of hospital in Hong Kong: public, government-assisted and private. Provision of hospital service at nominal cost is made universally accessible to all people. Hong Kong's health care service faces a huge financial strain due to its ageing population and escalating medical costs.

Life expectancy: 80.1 years (estimate 2003)

Fertility rate/Maternal mortality rate: 1.0 birth per woman; maternal mortality 5.6 per 100,000 total births (World Bank).

Birth rate/Death rate: 7.9 births and 5 deaths and per 1,000 people (World Bank)

Child (under 5 years) mortality rate (per 1,000): 2.7 per 1,000 live births (World Bank)

Welfare
The social security schemes available in Hong Kong cover a broad range of developmental, support and remedial services, and financial assistance to those in need. The Comprehensive Social Security Assistance Scheme is means-tested and non-contributory. The Scheme provides cash assistance to individuals and families to meet their basic and essential needs. The recipients are also helped through various initiatives to establish self-reliance. The Social Security Allowance Scheme aims to meet the special needs of the elderly and people with disabilities. The Accident Compensation Schemes provide short-term assistance to families or individuals in cases of reduced or lost earnings.

Main cities
Xianggang (Victoria, Hong Kong Island) (estimated population 1.3 million (m) in 2012); Juilong (Kowloon) (1.8m), Tuen Mun (526,384), Sha Tin (682,368), Fanling (610,654).

Languages spoken
Cantonese is the Chinese language spoken at home by more than 90 per cent of the population. Mandarin Chinese (Putonghua), the official language of the People's Republic of China, is widely understood.
English is universally understood in business and commerce.

Official language/s
Chinese (Mandarin, Beijing dialect *de jure*; Cantonese *de facto*) and English

Media
The freedom on the press is guaranteed in basic law.

Press
Hong Kong has retained its press freedom since being reunited with China and is a major centre for print journalism with one of the world's largest press industries. It does not impose prior censorship on its newspapers or television and radio news reports.

Dailies: There are over 50 daily newspapers, most of which are published in Chinese.
In English, the *South China Morning Post* (www.scmp.com) has the largest circulation, *China Daily* (www.chinadaily.com.cn) is published by the Chinese communist party.
In Chinese, broadsheets include *Ming Pao* (www.mingpaonews.com) and *Sing Tao* (www.singtao.com). Newspapers considered pro-Beijing include *Ta Kung Pao* (www.takungpao.com.hk), *Sing Pao* (www.singpao.com) and *Wen Wek Po* (www.wenweipo.com). The newspapers with the highest circulations are tabloid and informal, including *The Sun* (http://the-sun.on.cc), the *Oriental Daily* and *Apple Daily* (http://home.atnext.com).

Weeklies: In Chinese and with the highest circulation *Next Magazine* (http://next.atnext.com) is tabloid in style that not only covers entertainment but also current affairs, economic and business issues. Others include *Easy Finder* (http://face.atnext.com), *East Touch*, *East Week* and *Him Magazine* (www.him.com.hk). The only Chinese newsweekly, *Yazhou Zhoukan (Asia Weekly)* (www.yzzk.com) has broad contents of economic and international news.

Business: In English, the free-issue *The Standard* (www.thestandard.com.hk) covers financial markets and news and the *Far Eastern Economic Review* (Feer) (www.feer.com), is an influential monthly covering all aspects of the news throughout Asia. In Chinese newspapers include *Hong Kong Commercial Daily* (www.hkcd.com.hk) with the largest circulation in Mainland China, *Hong Kong Economic Journal* (www.hkej.com) and *Hong Kong Economic Times* cover financial news.

Periodicals: There are over 500 periodicals in circulation. In English, the monthly *Prestige Hong Kong* (www.prestigehk.com), is a glossy lifestyle and society magazine and *Muse* (www.musemag.hk) covers art and culture.

Broadcasting
The Hong Kong Broadcasting Authority (BA) is responsible for regulating and licensing all broadcasting outlets, while standards are maintained by the Television and Entertainment Licensing Authority (TELA).
The government-funded, but independent, Radio Television Hong Kong (RTHK) (www.rthk.org.hk) provides public broadcasting.

Radio: RTHK (www.rthk.org.hk) provides seven radio channels (RTHK Radio 1–6 and Radio Putonghua), with a full range of locally produced programmes in Cantonese, English and Mandarin. RTHK Radio 6 relays the BBC World Service. There are two private, commercial radio stations. Commercial Radio Hong Kong

(CRHK) (www.crhk.com.hk) has three channels and a full range of programmes to rival RTHK. The other station is Metro (www.metroradio.com.hk) with three channels, Metro- Finance, Showbiz and Plus.

Television: RTHK (www.rthk.org.hk) produces locally made educational, entertainment and news and current affairs programmes that are shown on other TV stations.

The two private, free-to-air TV stations are Asia Television (ATV) and Television Broadcasts (TVB), each with one channel in English and one in Chinese. There are several subscription networks which between them offer over 200 channels, showing locally produced and international programmes, the largest of which is Cable TV Hong Kong (www.cabletv.com.hk), which produces more programmes than any other broadcaster.

National news agency: Xinhua News Agency, Hong Kong Branch

Other news agencies: Hong Kong China News Agency (HKCNA): www.chinanews.com.hk

Economy

Hong Kong is one of the most densely populated islands in the world; it is also one of the most economically dynamic. The economy is founded on financial services, light engineering and assembly-line manufacturing, property and trading; Hong Kong has the world's third largest harbour and the world's largest container port (processing 21 million containers annually), which accords Hong Kong its status as a major transportation hub.

Although the global economic crisis affected all sectors, Hong Kong's economy only registered recession in the third quarter of 2008, as annual GDP growth fell from 6.4 per cent in 2007 to 2.3 per cent in 2008. It fell further to -2.6 per cent in 2009 as global investment weakened. GDP growth jumped to 7 per cent in 2010 as global trade recovered but by 2012 had fallen to 1.7 per cent as Western economies failed to expand as forecast. Growth made a small recover in 2013 at 3.5 per cent before dropping down to 2.7 per cent in 2014.

Hong Kong's relationship with China is mixed. On the one hand, it benefits from China's booming economy that sees inward investment by some of China's newly created wealthy tycoons buying property and investing in businesses in the region. In 2010 property prices were rising rapidly, 47 per cent (January 2009–August 2010), as mortgages rate fell to their lowest since the early 1990s – a result of the Hong Kong dollar's peg to a weakening US dollar. An estimated 20 per cent of buyers of new residential property were from mainland China. The risk of an overheated property market prompted the government to increase the equity-ratio at the beginning of the transaction in October 2010. On the other hand, China's vast manufacturing sector can out-perform anything Hong Kong has to offer the world if it chooses. Although Hong Kong could be subsumed into China's leviathan business machine, the authorities in Beijing see Hong Kong as its banking and commercial arm that allows it to operate an energetic world-class stock exchange that processes not only currency and business transactions for China but also for many overseas entities. In 2010, the Hong Kong Stock Exchange (KHEx) had a combined market capitalisation of US$2.3 trillion, ranking it second behind Tokyo (Japan) in Asian stock exchanges; KHEx was ranked sixth in world stock exchanges. In 2014, KHEx was still the world's sixth largest stock exchange (and Asia's third largest) with market capitalisation of US$3.33 trillion.

In the 2014–15 Global Competitiveness Index, the Swiss-based World Economic Forum voted Hong Kong as the world's seventh most competitive financial centre in its annual survey of global financial development. This was a fall from being the leading financial centre in 2011- the first time an Asian city had outstripped the traditional leading centres of Wall Street (New York) and the City of London (UK).

External trade

Hong Kong, as an independent customs territory separate from the rest of China, can enter into international commercial and economic agreements on it own behalf. As an economic entity it participates in full membership of a number of international organisations including the Asia Pacific Economic Co-operation forum (APEC).

Under the Closer Economic Partnership Arrangement (CEPA), Hong Kong has a trade alliance with China's nine southernmost provinces and Macao through the pan-Pearl River Delta (PRD) trade bloc, which has been described as 'the largest and most export-oriented of China's regions' with a regional GDP of over US$270 billion. It has a free trade agreement with China, which allows the trade of goods of Hong Kong origin entry at zero tariff, as well as preferential treatment in 27 service sectors.

Hong Kong's manufacturing base has relocated to mainland China where raw materials are readily available and labour is cheaper. Its service industry has grown, in part to compete against China's own growing financial centres.

Imports

Main imports are petroleum, raw materials and semi-manufactures, capital goods and foodstuffs.

Main sources: China (43.8 per cent of total in 2014), Taiwan (7.8 per cent), Japan (6.6 per cent)

Exports

Exports include electrical machinery and appliances – telecommunications, sound recording and electronic components – textiles, clothing, footwear, watches and clocks, toys, plastics, precious stones and printed material.

Main destinations: China (57.3 per cent of total in 2014), US (8.4 per cent), Japan (3.3 per cent)

Re-exports

These include consumer goods, clothing, electrical machinery and appliances.

Agriculture

Farming

Agriculture accounts for around 0.1 per cent of GDP. The land area is mountainous, with fertile soils when they are watered. Agricultural land, including 600 hectares of orchards, accounts for 7 per cent of the total land area.

Main crops include sweet potatoes, yams, taro, sugar cane, white cabbage, flowering cabbage, lettuce, Chinese kale, radishes and watercress.

Fishing

Hong Kong has a fishing fleet of about 4,900 vessels, most of which are mechanised. The fishing sector employs about 24,000 fishermen, who are provided with training organised by the Agriculture and Fisheries Conservation Department (AFCD) in order to enhance the competitiveness of the sector. Pond and marine fish farming in the New Territories accounts for 3 per cent of total production. Seafood production can reach up to 200,000 tonnes per annum. Freshwater fish production is more limited, typically 4,000 tonnes or less per annum. In addition, Hong Kong imports in the region of 60,000 tonnes of freshwater fish per annum and some 500,000 tonnes of seafood, of which 300,000 tonnes are typically re-exported.

Industry and manufacturing

Industry accounts for around 11 per cent of GDP and employs 18 per cent of the workforce. The relocation of manufacturing operations from Hong Kong to mainland China is causing a long-term decline in the sector. The re-export sector, in contrast, has grown due to growing consumer demand and industrial production on the mainland.

Tourism

The influence of the British on the island is overlaid with Chinese culture, so that although the tiny island of Hong Kong is a vibrant Asian city that has all the bustle that shopping, restaurants and late night shopping can offer, many of its buildings and layout appear European. The combined islands and new territories offer activities that fuse Western with Eastern cultures from horse racing and cricket, to dragon boat racing and tai chi in the park. Hong Kong Disneyland is a resort beside Penny's Bay on Lantau Island. Hong Kong is topped by The Peak from which most surrounding territories can be viewed. At night the neon and halogen lighted cityscape offers a stunning vista best seen from tall skyscrapers.

Travel and tourism is an important component of the economy. Tourism grew by 11.7 per cent in 2013, as 54.3 million visitors arrived, of which around 20 millions stayed overnight. The majority of visitor came from mainland-China. In 2014 tourism accounted for 22.0 per cent of GDP, and was expected to increase by 1.3 per cent in 2015. The industry employs directly and indirectly around 19.8 per cent of the workforce (745,500 jobs). The tourist board is responsible for worldwide promotion through its website www.discoverhongkong.com with information offered in over a dozen languages. It supports the volunteer programme 'Hong Kong Pals', in which local citizens are encouraged to provide personal tips and recommendations to visitors on the delights of the city.

Environment

Hong Kong is suffering air pollution as a result of pollution from southern China; visibility has declined over the past 30 years and continues to worsen. Although Hong Kong has sharply reduced its own emissions, it lies at the southern end of a vast industrial conurbation that includes Guangzhou and Shenzhen.

Mining

Mining accounts for less than 0.05 per cent of GDP, producing mainly kaolin (around 44,500 tonnes) and feldspar (around 5,500 tonnes).

Hydrocarbons

Hong Kong relies entirely on imports of hydrocarbons. Consumption of petroleum products was 354,000 barrels per day in 2013. Natural gas is imported via a pipeline from the South China Sea offshore gas field and is used for power generation. Consumption was 2.6 billion cubic metres in 2013. Annual coal imports of around 13 million tonnes meet 20 per cent of energy consumption.

Energy

Total installed generating capacity is around 10.7GW, with consumption at 44.2 billion kilowatt hours (kWh) in 2013. Two commercial companies own and operate the power stations located within Hong Kong. CLP Power uses diesel, natural gas and nuclear energy, while HK Electric uses natural gas, coal and operates the only wind turbine, which became operational in 2006. HK Electric is a public company, responsible for generation, distribution and sale of electricity; there are other, private companies also supplying electricity. The upgrade completed in 2007 had introduced gas-fired turbines, and the wind-turbine.

Financial markets

Stock exchange

HKEx (Hong Kong Exchanges and Clearing) operates Hong Kong Stock Exchange and Hong Kong Futures Exchange.

Banking and insurance

Domestic banks in Hong Kong have tended to rely on the property sector for their earnings. Mortgages and other property-related lending still account for 40 to 50 per cent of total loans. Banking practice codes were revised in 2001 to make banking more transparent and consumer friendly. In 2002, some of the criteria for entry to the banking sector were relaxed. The aim was to attract a wider range of domestic and international banks to become involved in the SAR.

Hong Kong is an excellent location for insurers and has the largest number of insurance companies in Asia. Mainland Chinese insurers are linking up with foreign insurers in Hong Kong to cater for China's insurance market. By 2003, there were around 7,000 insurance establishments in the SAR with a total premium income of US$7 billion. French AXA group, the world's biggest insurance company, has its regional headquarters in Hong Kong.

Central bank

Hong Kong has no finance ministry or official central bank. The Hong Kong Monetary Authority (HKMA) oversees the monetary and banking system.

Main financial centre

Central District

Time

GMT plus eight hours

Geography

Hong Kong comprises some 235 islands and islets and a portion of the Chinese mainland, adjoining China's southern province of Guangdong. It consists of three areas: Hong Kong Island, the Kowloon Peninsula and the New Territories, which account for 92 per cent of the territory. About 75 per cent of Hong Kong's land is unsuitable for food production, consisting of hills that rise from sea level to 900 metres.

Hemisphere

Northern

Climate

Hong Kong is subtropical and monsoonal. Summer (May to mid-September) is hot and humid with a risk of typhoons. July and August can be very hot. Autumn (September to December) is generally sunny, but drier, and the most pleasant time of year. Winter (December to February) is dry, but can get uncomfortably cold, with an average temperature of 15 degrees Celsius (C). Spring (March and April) is moderately warm and damp. The average annual temperature is about 23 degrees C, while rainfall averages 2,224mm per year, and humidity is often above 83 per cent.

Dress codes

Business dress is formal as appearance is taken seriously. Very smart dress is also *de rigueur* for ladies; skirts are advisable, rather than trousers.

Entry requirements

Passports

A valid passport is required by all. Passports must be valid for six months after arrival.

Visa

Visas required by all, with some exceptions see www.immd.gov.hk/ehtml/hkvisas.htm for further details.

Business and tourist visas are considered the same, up to the minimum time allowed to visit. For further clarification email: enquiry@immd.gov.hk; or contact the local Chinese embassy.

Regulations regarding entry into Hong Kong are extensive owing to the high level of illegal immigration. Travellers are advised to obtain up-to-date information before any journey.

Currency advice/regulations

There are no currency restrictions. Travellers cheques are readily accepted.

Customs

Personal effects are duty-free. Visitors wishing to purchase ivory products in Hong Kong will need an export licence from the Hong Kong authorities, and will also need to show an import licence for their final destination.

Prohibited imports

Illegal drugs, fireworks, firearms, counterfeit items, textiles, ivory products, animals and plants, game, meat and poultry. Live animals are strictly controlled. Antibiotics may not be imported without an accompanying doctor's letter.

Visitors entering from China should expect searches for fireworks.

Health (for visitors)

Mandatory precautions

Yellow fever and cholera inoculation if travelling from infected areas.

Advisable precautions

Vaccinations are recommended for diphtheria, tuberculosis, hepatitis A and B, polio, tetanus and typhoid. Dengue fever is increasing, however the risk of malaria has been reduced. Tap water is safe to drink.

A HK$580 fee is imposed on any visitor who has to use accident and emergency hospital services. Medical insurance is recommended.

Hotels

A wide range of hotels are available; advance bookings are recommended between May–November. A 10 per cent service charge and 5 per cent tax are added to hotel bills.

Credit cards

Major international credit cards are widely accepted, although cash prices may be lower.

Public holidays (national)

Fixed dates

1 Jan (New Year's Day), 5 Apr (Ching Ming/Tomb Sweeping Day), ^1 May (Labour Day), 1 Jul (HKSAR Establishment Day), 1 Oct (National Day), 25–26 Dec (Christmas).

^ Holidays falling on Sunday are taken on Monday.

Variable dates

Chinese New Year (Jan/Feb, three days), Good Friday and Easter Monday (Mar/Apr), Birth of Buddha (May), Tuen Ng (Dragon Boat festival, May/Jun), Chinese Mid-Autumn Festival (Sep/Oct), Chung Yeung Festival (Oct).

Working hours

Banking

Mon–Fri: 0900–1630; Sat: 0900–1230.

Business

Mon–Fri: 0900–1300, 1400–1700; Sat: 0900–1300.

Government

Mon–Fri: 0900–1300, 1400–1700; Sat: 0900–1230.

Shops

Central District 1000–1900; Causeway Bay and Wanchai 1000–2130; Tsimshatsui East 1000–1930; Tsimshatsui, Yaumatei and Mong Kok 1000–2100. Most department stores and shops open Sundays. Some Japanese stores close one day per week, and street markets operate all day and into the night.

Telecommunications

Mobile/cell phones

GSM 900/1800 services are available throughout the islands and territories.

Electricity supply

200V AC, 50Hz. No uniformity in plug design.

Weights and measures

Metric system (Imperial system and local units also in use).

Social customs/useful tips

Western influence in Hong Kong has produced ways of doing business that are similar to other major business capitals. However, behind the facade of modern office blocks and neon-lit shopping malls, ancient Chinese customs still survive and have become part of the life of the foreign community.

Business cards are handed out liberally as a method of developing a network of professional contacts. A Chinese translation on the reverse side is a worthwhile addition. Use both hands when offering a business card, as passing it with one hand is seen as impolite.

Appearances of wealth are considered important in a territory that is dedicated to making money. Business contacts are ostentatiously wined and dined. Most entertaining is done in restaurants. It is considered bad manners to divide the bill after a meal. If you go to a dinner as the guest of honour, you should rise and thank the host briefly for his hospitality.

Personal friendships and family ties oil the wheels of business. The wealthy keep a high social profile, donating large sums of money to charity.

Punctuality is helpful as most people have packed days, although some allowances are made for the heavy traffic.

Policemen who speak English have a red shoulder badge.

Security

The level of crime against visitors is relatively low. Theft, mainly by pickpockets, is a problem on the streets.

Getting there

Air

National airline: Cathay Pacific Airways

International airport/s: Hong Kong International (HKG), 34km from the centre. Post office, bank, bureau de change, restaurants/cafeterias, duty free shop, taxis.

Airport tax: HK$120, excluding transit passengers.

Surface

The business district and commercial centre of Hong Kong is located on Hong Kong island. Kowloon and the new territories across the harbour are part of the Asia mainland, with road links providing connections.

Road: Bus services link Guangzhou to the Hong Kong border.

Rail: The Kowloon-Canton Railway Corporation (KCR) is the main carrier of passengers to and from China, with express trains serving Kowloon-Guangzhou and Kowloon-Lowu.

Water: Hovercraft services operate four times a day to and from Guangzhou and several times daily to and from Zhuhai. There are frequent daily services to and from Macao by hovercraft (75 minutes), jetcats (75 minutes), high speed ferry (90 minutes) and jetfoil (60 minutes).

Main port/s: Victoria Harbour (Hong Kong Island) and Tolo Harbour (New Territories).

Getting about

National transport

Air: Dragonair flies to 23 mainland Chinese destinations, as well as other regional capitals in Asia.

Hong Kong maintains separate immigration and customs policies from the mainland and flights between them are treated as international and not domestic flights.

Road: Hong Kong's road network is extensive and of high quality but often congested in central areas.

Buses: Bus services are inexpensive and convenient.There are three main private bus companies, China Motor Bus (CMB), Citybus and Kowloon Motor Bus (KMB, Kowloon only), and private minibus services.

Rail: There are three rail systems which operate outside urban areas. The KCR runs a passenger service between Kowloon and Guangzhou (China) and a suburban service to the new towns of the north-eastern New Territories; KCR also operates the Light Rail Transit network in the north-western New Territories; a cable-hauled funicular railway operates on Hong Kong Island between Garden Road in the Central District to Victoria Gap on the Peak.

The Airport Express is a dedicated high-speed train link, with a journey time of 24 minutes from central Hong Kong to the airport. Operating hours: 0550–0115 daily.

Water: There are extensive ferry, hovercraft, hydrofoil and coastal services between the islands of Hong Kong.

City transport

Taxis: Metered taxis (that calculate time and distance) are readily available in most areas of the territory. They carry four to five passengers. Cabs are painted green and silver in the New Territories, and red and silver in town. Hong Kong taxis are reasonably priced. It is advisable to have the destination written in Chinese. Tips are discretionary. Taxi drivers retain odd cents of change as a matter of course. A ride to or from the airport–

Central District will include an extra toll charge of HK$30 plus any tunnel tolls.

Buses, trams & metro: There are regular shuttle buses to and from the airport to both Central District (Hong Kong Island) and Tsimshatsui (Kowloon). They are cheaper than taxis and serve five routes every 12–15 minutes. Airport bus routes A11 and A12 operate 0600–2359 hours to Central District, journey time 70 minutes.

Trams: A flat fare system operates on Hong Kong Island's double-decker five-line tram system. The trams are crowded at rush hour, but afford good views of Hong Kong at other times.

Ferry: There are regular ferry services across the narrow strip of water from Star Ferry terminal at the north of Hong Kong Island to Kowloon.

Car hire

A valid driving licence issued in the country of origin may be used for up to 12 months. Parking difficulties and traffic congestion should be taken into account when planning to drive in Hong Kong. Chauffeur-driven and self-drive car hire is available.

BUSINESS DIRECTORY

The addresses listed below are a selection only. While World of Information makes every endeavour to check these addresses, we cannot guarantee that changes have not been made, especially to telephone numbers and area codes. We would welcome any corrections.

Telephone area codes

The international direct dialling code (IDD) for Hong Kong is +852, followed by subscriber's number.

Useful telephone numbers

Emergencies	999
Directory enquiries	108
Problems	109
International calls	010
Calls to China	012
Collect (reversed charge) calls	011
Tourist information	2801-7177
International direct dialling code enquiries	013

Chambers of Commerce

American Chamber of Commerce in Hong Kong, 1904 Bank of America Tower, 12 Harcourt Road, Central (tel: 2526-0165; fax: 2810-1289; e-mail: amcham@amcham.org.hk).

British Chamber of Commerce in Hong Kong, Emperor Group Centre, 288 Hennessy Road, Wan Chai (tel: 2824-2211; fax: 2824-1333; e-mail: info@britcham.com).

Banking

Bank of East Asia Ltd, GPO Box 31, 10 Des Voeux Road, Central (tel: 2842-3200; fax: 2845-9333).

Bank of China (Hong Kong) Ltd; Bank of China Tower, 1 Garden Road, Hong Kong (tel: 2826-6350; fax: 2530-3875).

DBS Bank (Hong Kong) Ltd, 99 Queen's Road Central, Central (tel: 2218-2706).

Hang Seng Bank Ltd, Hang Seng Bank Headquarters, 83 Des Voeux Road, Central (tel: 2825-5111; fax: 2845-9301).

HSBC, 1 Queen's Road, Central (tel: 2822-1111; fax: 2868-1646; internet: www.hsbcnet.com).

Nanyang Commercial Bank Ltd, 151 Des Voeux Road, Central (tel: 2852-0888; fax: 2815-3333).

Shanghai Commercial Bank Ltd, 12 Queen's Road, Central (tel: 2841-5415).

Wing Lung Bank Ltd, 45 Des Voeux Road, Central (tel: 2826-8333; fax: 2810-0592).

Central bank

Hong Kong Monetary Authority, 3 Garden Road, Central (tel: 2878-8196; fax: 2878-8197; e-mail: hkma@hkma.gov.hk).

Stock exchange

HKEx (Hong Kong Exchanges and Clearing) operates Hong Kong Stock Exchange and Hong Kong Futures Exchange. www.hkex.com.hk

Travel information

Cathay Pacific Airways, Swire House, 9 Connaught Road, Central (tel: 2747-5000; fax: 2810-6563).

Hong Kong Automobile Association, March Road, Wanchai (tel: 2574-3394).

Star Ferry Concourse, Kowloon; Shop 8, Basement Jardine House, Central (tel: 2801-7177 (visitor hotline); fax: 2810-4877).

National tourist organisation offices

Hong Kong Tourist Board (HKTB), 9-11th Floor, Citicorp Centre, 18 Whitfield Road, North Point (tel: 2807-6543, 2807-6177 (tourist information); fax: 2807-6582; internet: www.discoverhongkong.com).

Other useful addresses

Agriculture and Fisheries Department, 13/F Canton Road Government Offices, 393 Canton Road, Kowloon (tel: 2733-2174; fax: 2311-3731).

Banking, Securities, Insurance & Companies Division, 24th Floor Admiralty Centre, Tower II, Central (tel: 2527-8337; fax: 2865-6146).

Buildings Department, 3-12/F Murray Building Garden Road, Central (tel: 2848-2327; fax: 2840-0451).

Business and Industrial Trade Fairs Ltd, 51 Gloucester Road, Wanchai (tel: 2865-2633; fax: 2866-1770, 2865-5513).

Census and Statistics Department, Wanchai Tower 1, 12 Harbour Road, Wanchai (tel: 2823-4807).

Chinese Manufacturers' Association of Hong Kong, 3rd and 4th Floor CMA Bldg, 64 Connaught Road, Central (tel: 2545-6166).

Civil Aviation department, 46/F Queensway Government Offices, 66 Queensway (tel: 2867-4332; fax: 2869-0093).

Consumer Council, 22/F, K Wah Centre, 191 Java Road, North Point (tel: 2856-3113; fax: 2856-3611).

Department of Health, 17 & 21/F Wu Chung House, 213 Queen's Road East, Wan Chai (tel: 2961-8989; fax: 2836-0071).

Environmental Protection Department, 24-28/F Southorn Centre, 130 Hennessy Road, Wan Chai (tel: 2835-1018; fax: 2838-2155).

Exchange Fund Division, 24th Floor Admiralty Centre, Tower II, Central (tel: 2529-0024; fax: 2865-6146).

Federation of Hong Kong Industries, 4/F Hankow Centre, 5-15 Hankow Road, Kowloon (tel: 2723-0818).

Finance Branch, Government Secretariat, Central Government Offices, Lower Albert Road, Central (tel: 2810-2540; fax: 2810-1530).

Hong Kong Convention & Incentive Travel Bureau (trade fairs), 35th Floor Jardine House, Central (tel: 2801-7111; fax: 2810-4877).

Hong Kong Exporters' Association, Room 825 Star House, 3 Salisbury Road, Tsim Sha Tsui, Kowloon (tel: 2730-9851).

Hong Kong Government Industry Department, 'One-Stop' Unit, 14th Floor, Ocean Centre, 5 Canton Road, Kowloon (tel: 2737-2434; fax: 2730-4633).

Hong Kong Economic and Trade Office, 6 Grafton Street, London W1S 4EQ (tel: (+044-20) 7499-9821; fax: (+044-20) 7495-5033; email: general@hketolondon.gov.hk).

Hong Kong Industrial Estates Corporation, 107 Estate Centre Building, 19 Dai Cheong Street, Tai Po Industrial Estate, Tai Po, New Territories (tel: 2664-1183).

Hong Kong Productivity Council, 78 Tat Chee Avenue, HKCP Bldg, Kowloon (tel: 2788-5678).

Hong Kong Standards and Testing Centre, 10 Dai Wang Street, Tai Po Industrial

Estate, Tai Po, New Territories (tel: 2667-0021).

Hong Kong Telecom Association, GPO Box 13461 (tel: 2881-2333; fax: 2881-2332).

Hong Kong Trade Development Council, Research Department, 36-39/F Office Tower, Convention Plaza, 1 Harbour Road, Wan Chai (tel: 2584-4333; fax: 2824-0249; internet site: http://www.tdc.org.hk/).

Industry Department, 14/F Ocean Centre, 5 Canton Road, Tsim Sha Tsui (tel: 2737-2216; fax: 2377-0730).

Labour Department, 16/F Harbour Building, 38 Pier Road, Central (tel: 2852-3511).

Securities & Futures Commission, 38/F Two Exchange Square, 8 Connaught Place (tel: 2840-9202; fax: 2845-9553).

Stock Exchange of Hong Kong Ltd, 1/F, 1 and 2 Exchange Square, 8 Connaught Place, PO Box 8888 (tel: 2522-1122; fax: 2868-1308).

Telecommunications Authority, 29th Floor, Wu Chung House, 213 Queens Road East, Wan Chai (tel: 2961-6333; fax: 2803-5110).

Trade Department, Ocean Centre, 5 Canton Road, Kowloon (tel: 2722-2333).

US General Consulate, 26 Garden Road (tel: 2523-9011; fax: 2845-1598).

Visa Office, Ministry of Foreign Affairs, 5th Floor, Lower Block, 26 Harbour Road, Wanchai (tel: 2835-3794).

National news agency: Xinhua News Agency, Hong Kong Branch

Address: 381 Queen's Road East, Hong Kong

Hong Kong China News Agency (HKCNA): www.chinanews.com.hk

Internet sites

Economic Services Bureau: www.info.gov.hk/esb/content.htm

Hong Kong Airport: www.hongkongairport.com

Hong Kong Shipping directory: www.info.gov.hk/mardep/sdfiles/shipdir.ht

Hong Kong Statistics: www.info.gov.hk/censtatd/eindex.htm

Hungary

KEY FACTS

Official name: Magyar Köztársaság (Republic of Hungary)

Head of State: President János Áder (from 2 May 2012)

Head of government: Prime Minister Victor Orbán (Fidesz) (from 29 May 2010, re-elected 6 Apr 2014)

Ruling party: Coalition of Fidesz–Magyar Polgári Szövetség (Fidesz) (Fidesz–Hungarian Civic Union) and Kereszténydemokrata Néppárt (KDNP) (Christian Democratic People's Party) (Fidesz-KDNP) (from 6 Apr 2014)

Area: 93,033 square km

Population: 9.88 million (2014)*

Capital: Budapest

Official language: Hungarian (Magyar)

Currency: Forint (Ft)

Exchange rate: Ft280.34 per US$ (Sep 2015)

GDP per capita: US$13,881 (2014)*

GDP real growth: 3.64% (2014)*

GDP: US$137.10 billion (2014)*

Labour force: 4.46 million (2014)*

Unemployment: 7.76% (2014)*

Inflation: -0.30% (2014)*

Balance of trade: US$3.59 billion (2014)

* estimated figure

In their thousands, the refugees kept on entering Hungary in 2015. Many were from Syria, desperate to obtain security and prosperity in virtually any European Union (EU) country. In an effort to control their numbers, at the end of July 2015 the Hungarian government had begun building a 175km fence along the border with Serbia. Government estimates put at 100,000 the number of refugees, for the most part from Syria, who had entered the country since the beginning of the year. In June 2015, Hungary's Prime Minister Viktor Orban, not known for his liberal values, had to mobilise the army in order to complete the barrier by the end of August.

For all the wrong reasons, the barrier had become one of the most closely watched construction projects in central Europe. Combined with a law that would make illegal crossing a criminal offence, the border barrier represented the most visible aspect of the controversial plan by Hungary's populist government to halt the tide of thousands of migrants entering Hungary.

After weeks of delays, conflicting rumours and statements, Mr Orban had announced that 'the period of tolerance is over', saying that troops would be deployed along Hungary's southern border to enforce new measures, which included prison sentences of up to three years for illegal border crossings after mid-September. Mr Orban also sacked his defence minister Hende Csaba for taking too long to finish the fence.

Good fences make… problems?

The announcement of the barrier's construction was in itself enough to increase the numbers crossing daily, to an estimated 1,500. According to Hungary's immigration office, in 2014 43,000 refugees had entered the country; in 2012 the figure had been 2,000. Hungary's 'foreign' population is minimally small, estimated to be 1.5 per cent of the population. The majority of refugees entering the country do not intend to stay; they are fleeing the civil wars in Syria and Libya, tribal tensions in Afghanistan and religious divisions in Iraq in an effort to reach Germany, Europe's overwhelming population magnet.

Serbia had formally protested to Hungary about the barrier's construction, claiming – with some justification – that its completion would leave Serbia with a 'bubble' of refugees arriving via Greece and the Balkans who, if denied access to the EU would not wish to return whence they came. It was also clear that the Hungarian barrier could only be a short term solution. Refugees who had escaped civil wars, crossed hostile countries and risked their lives in small craft crossing the Mediterranean were unlikely to be thwarted by a man-made fence. Nevertheless, the Serbian social affairs minister, Aleksandar Vulin, told Reuters that the barrier's construction would be a humanitarian catastrophe if thousands of people seeking to leave Serbia were unable to do so.'

Mr Orban's barrier project was also viewed with opprobrium by the EU; for many it harked back to the days of the Iron Curtain that had divided Europe until 1998. But of greater concern was the nationalist posture adopted by the Orban government and its flagrantly hostile attitude not only to economic migrants (seeking jobs and security) and registered refugees who in the first instance simply sought peace and security. In late July Mr Orban made a speech in which he stated that if it depended on him, he would wish to 'keep Europe for the Europeans', and would always strive to defend 'Hungary for the Hungarians'. Budapest was at pains to claim that the barrier's construction did not infringe any international law and that both Bulgaria and Greece had taken similar steps to control Turkish immigration. The Hungarian foreign minister, Peter Szijjarto, also noted that 'Spanish cities in the North of Africa (a reference to Ceuta and Melilla) defended themselves in the same way against migratory pressure.

The immigration crisis inadvertently pitted Hungary against the EU's 'old guard', Mr Orban's office declaring that the manner in which the European Commission (EC) had distributed funds to cope with the crisis was 'humiliating' for Hungary: 'the older member states have appropriated money due to the newer sates' said the head of the Prime Minister's cabinet office, János Lázár. Budapest had requested an additional €8 million (US$9 million), over and above the €61 million (US$68.5 million) already awarded. Brussels had sent immigration and refugee officials from its Frontex and Europol agencies to process the flow of immigrants coming in to Catania (Sicily) and Piraeus (Greece), but Hungary was not considered an immigration 'front line' state. Despite Mr Orban's claims, an EU spokesperson added that Brussels had not received a request for the creation of an immigration processing point in Hungary. The EU did confirm that it was looking into two alleged cases of failure to implement EU immigration directives in Hungary. New and planned anti-immigration legislation allowed the police to arrest summarily and to inspect private properties without a search warrant.

Fidesz

In 2015 the ruling party Magyar Polgári Szövetség ((Fidesz) (Hungarian Civic Alliance) was sitting on its second (the first ran from 2010–14) 'super majority' which gave the party, in coalition with the Kereszténydemokrata Néppárt (KDNP) (Christian Democratic People's Party) (Fidesz-KDNP), an absolute majority the size of which had never been seen in Hungarian politics. Its two-thirds majority had enabled Fidesz to mount a fiercely xenophobic publicity campaign, with taxpayers money, playing to Hungarians' baser preoccupations. The advertisements claimed to be protecting their interests in television and billboards, with 'welcoming' slogans such as 'If you come to Hungary, you mustn't steal Hungarians' jobs' and 'If you come to Hungary you must respect our laws'. The fact that all the posters were in Hungarian rather gave the political game away, however.

The irony was that in the previous five or six years, over half a million Hungarians had emigrated in search of jobs; some were young professionals, others older. More Hungarians had emigrated in the twenty-first century than did so during and after the 1956 popular rising which brought Russian tanks to the streets of Budapest, resulting in as many as 30,000 deaths.

The anarchic opposition grouping (it could hardly be called a party), the Magyar Kétfarkú Kutya Párt (MKKP) (Two Tailed Dog Party), founded by Gergely Kovács in 2006, countered the government's poster campaign with one of its own, for which it sought public donations of three million forint (US$10.700) to cover costs. Within days it had received donations totalling over 34 million forint (US$121,500). In the absence of much competition, it seemed that the MKKP had little competition as the opposition's leading voice. The first poster in the anti-immigration protests asked visitors to 'Please excuse our prime minister'.

The economy – the IMF approves...

In its March 2015 annual assessment of the Hungarian economy, the International Monetary Fund (IMF) noted that the Hungarian economy was growing at a strong pace helped by accommodative macro-economic policies and improved market sentiment. Driven by strong domestic demand, output grew by 3.6 per cent in 2014. Unemployment declined sharply, reflecting the expansion of the public works programmes and job creation in the private sector. Headline and core inflation decelerated sharply and inflation expectations fell below the Magyar Nemzeti Bank (MNB) (National Bank of Hungary)'s inflation target. Improving

KEY INDICATORS — **Hungary**

	Unit	2011	2012	2013	2014	**2015
Population	m	*10.00	*9.93	9.91	9.88	*9.86
Gross domestic product (GDP)	US$bn	140.30	124.59	133.42	*137.10	*126.69
GDP per capita	US$	14,050	12,544	13,465	*13,881	*12,853
GDP real growth	%	1.7	-1.7	1.5	*3.6	*2.7
Inflation	%	3.9	5.7	1.7	*-0.3	*0.0
Unemployment	%	11.3	10.9	10.2	7.8	*7.6
Coal output	mtoe	2.0	1.9	2.0	2.0	–
Exports (fob) (goods)	US$m	98,955.9	88,373.2	95,192.4	100,014.6	–
Imports (fob) (goods)	US$m	95,203.9	86,549.1	91,386.4	96,424.2	–
Balance of trade	US$m	3,752.0	1,824.0	3,806.0	3,590.3	–
Current account	US$m	1,320.4	1,306.0	5,527.0	*5,824.0	*6,036.0
Total reserves minus gold	US$m	51,383.0	44,506.0	46,389.0	41,901.0	–
Foreign exchange	US$m	50,224.0	44,028.0	46,254.0	–	–
Exchange rate	per US$	191.46	218.50	218.21	261.28	–

* estimated figure ** forecast figure

terms of trade and strong export volume growth also helped maintain a sizeable current account surplus. Private sector credit continued to contract and the banking sector remains under pressure reflecting the heavy tax burden and high non-performing loans.

According to the IMF, Hungary's economic vulnerabilities continued to decline thanks to large and persistent current account surpluses and recent policy measures, including the conversion of foreign exchange mortgages into local currency loans. However, debt levels remained high and the associated financing requirements, together with a heavy reliance on non-resident financing, the large concentration of the investor base and the economy's large open foreign exchange position continued to pose risks. At the same time, the state had been increasing its role in the economy, notably through the acquisition of stakes in the banking and energy sectors, thereby contributing to a build-up of contingent liabilities.

Hungary's 2014 fiscal deficit came in below target, as revenues were propelled by accelerating economic activity and tax administration improvements and were only partially offset by higher expenditures. However, the fiscal stance eased significantly and public debt declined only moderately to just below 77 per cent of gross domestic product (GDP). For 2015, the deficit was projected at 2.7 per cent of GDP, implying a broadly neutral fiscal stance despite the relatively favourable cyclical conditions; the debt ratio was expected to decline only modestly.

Comforted by decelerating inflation, low risk premiums and a negative output gap, the MNB had kept its policy interest rate at 2.10 per cent since July 2014 and cut it to 1.95 per cent in March 2015. It also doubled the allocation for the second phase of the Funding for Growth Scheme (FGS) and extended the programme to the end of 2015.

The IMF expected output growth to decelerate to 2.75 per cent in 2015, on account of a smaller domestic-demand impetus due to less supportive fiscal stance and lower investment growth. Private consumption was expected to continue to grow, reflecting lower household indebtedness, accommodative monetary conditions and higher employment levels. Headline inflation was projected to remain very low on account of a still negative output gap and lower import prices. Over the medium-term, in the view of the IMF, growth prospects remained subdued, as private consumption was still constrained by the continued deleveraging; while the difficult business environment also continued to weigh on private investment. Labour participation, while increasing somewhat, remained low, particularly among women and older workers. These challenges were further compounded by competitiveness pressures and the lack of attractiveness for foreign direct investment (FDI).

.... and so does the EBRD

In its 2014 *Transition Report* the European Bank for Reconstruction and Development (EBRD) noted that following the second post-crisis recession that extended throughout 2012, Hungary had shown a strong recovery. GDP grew by 1.5 per cent in 2013 and by a further 3.8 per cent in annual terms in the first half of 2014. However, GDP still remained about 4 per cent below its pre-crisis peak of mid-2008. A number of temporary factors had, in the view of the EBRD, supported growth, notably cuts in utility tariffs, which had boosted household disposable income and increased public spending as funds under the previous EU financial programmes were being fully disbursed.

Hungary's export sector continued to strengthen the economy as export volumes grew strongly up to mid-2014, along with industrial production, as important capacity came on stream in a number of car plants. Since then the downturn in key export markets, such as Germany, has translated into much weaker industrial activity. Prices have been stagnant since early 2014, largely due to the three successive rounds of utility price cuts. Core inflation still remained at 2.6 per cent in annual terms in July 2014. Given the still high levels of household debt, protracted deflation could be a concern for aggregate demand and financial stability. Against this background the MNB persevered with its interest rate easing policy in July 2014, with a cut taking the key policy rate to 2.1 per cent and again in March 2015 to 1.95 per cent, well down from 7 per cent seen three years earlier.

Labour market developments had, in the view of the EBRD, been positive. Unemployment fell to 7.8 per cent in July 2014 and the employment rate rose to 66.5 per cent in the second quarter of 2014. The expansion of the government's public works programme had played a major role in these trends. At the end of 2013 slightly over 400,000 individuals, or about 10 per cent of the workforce, were enrolled in this programme. However, while the programme had had some success in raising employment in the more remote regions in the east of the country, the EBRD doubted that sustainable employment in the regular labour market had been created. Hungary continued to suffer from considerable skill mis-matches that explained the country's relatively high rate of long-term unemployment.

Credit conditions remained difficult despite the continued disbursement of the central bank's subsidised facility for lending to small- and medium-sized enterprises (SMEs). Hungary's net corporate credit also showed a further decline in the first half of 2014. Surveys continued to point towards risk aversion and restrictive conditions in terms of collateral requirements. As Hungary's banks continued to be held back by high taxes and recurring initiatives in household debt restructuring and with credit demand remaining low, liquidity continued to flow out of the country. In the first quarter of 2014, foreign banks withdrew €2.9 billion (US$3.3 billion) in liquidity, equivalent to 2.9 per cent of Hungary's GDP. Even though the pace of withdrawal has slowed, as in other central European economies, Hungary continues to see the second worst rate of outflows in the region. Similarly, FDI inflows remained much below pre-crisis levels, with inflows accounting for only about 2.4 per cent of GDP in 2013 and the value of green field investment projects having shrunk drastically.

The EBRD projects that over the medium term the momentum of growth is likely to diminish, as structural fundamentals such as the distortionary tax system, a still-impaired banking sector and growing state involvement under the Fidesz government reassert themselves. Downside risks could also materialise from the euro-zone export markets.

Hungary's share of high-tech exports remains very high (at over 17.3 per cent of total exports). However, Organisation for Economic Co-operation and Development (OECD) indicators suggest that only about 13 per cent of local SMEs invest in innovation and research and development. Productivity growth remains constrained by this still low investment rate, which declined steadily between 2007 and 2012 and only picked up again in 2013. These indicators underline the competitive nature of Hungary's FDI sector, as well as the considerable potential to improve innovation in domestic SMEs.

The EBRD considers that the Hungarian government remains committed to its plan to convert utility services into non-profit companies. Only any small profit generated would be used to cover innovation and upgrades to the distribution network. In March 2014 the prime minister had announced the establishment of a state utility provider, to distribute electricity, gas and district heating. To this end, the authorities decreed cuts on municipal utility tariffs. In April 2014 the government announced a third round of utility price cuts, thereby reducing the household price of gas, electricity and district heating by a further 6.5 per cent, 5.7 per cent and 3.3 per cent, respectively. According to the government the previous round of cuts resulted in household savings of Ft250 billion (US$0.89 billion), about 0.8 per cent of GDP, while the third cut was estimated to save just under 0.5 per cent of GDP. The government also implemented a stricter policy on consumer protection, which included transparency requirements on pricing.

The government has also advanced its agenda to reduce vulnerabilities in household foreign exchange debt. In June 2014 the Hungarian Supreme Court ruled on the long-running dispute over bank charges on foreign currency loan contracts. Based on this ruling, unilateral changes by banks to the terms of a contract, such as interest rate rises, could be considered unfair and hence void unless conditions for such changes had been comprehensively set out upon signing the contract. Meanwhile, the bid/ask spread that was typically applied by banks in disbursements of and repayment on, such loans was deemed illegal. Consequently, the government prepared new legislation within weeks, which obliged banks to refund borrowers who had suffered from interest rate rises and the bid/ask spreads that had been charged on foreign exchange loans. The deputy governor of the MNB estimated that this might cost the banks up to Ft900 billion (US$3.2 billion) (about 3 per cent of GDP). The central bank also extended its subsidised lending programme in September 2013.This extension was more focused on new lending, as opposed to refinancing and loosening eligibility criteria. While these funds were almost fully allocated to commercial banks, disbursements to SMEs was very slow. A fixed margin in the lending rate and a slow and cumbersome process in guaranteeing loans remained key impediments. In addition, other state banks were expanding into the SME market, principally targeting high-quality clients.

Risk assessment

Economy	Fair/good
Politics	Fair
Regional stability	Fair

COUNTRY PROFILE

The Hungarian (Magyar) peoples settled on the Hungarian plains in the seventh century AD, arriving from the Black Sea coast and southern Russia. The Hungarian language belongs to the Finno-Ugric family and is one of the few languages of the European Union that are not of Indo-European origin.

From the mid-eighteenth century, Hungary, together with Austria and a large area of central and Eastern Europe, was part of the dual monarchy ruled by the Habsburgs.

1914–18 After the assassination of Archduke Ferdinand, the heir to the Austro-Hungarian throne, Austro-Hungary declared war on Serbia in June 1914, with the support of Germany. In November 1918, after the Austro-Hungarian Empire was defeated in the First World War, Hungary declared its independence, King Karl IV stood down as head of state of Hungary and the Entente powers carved-up Hungary as a punishment for its role in the First World War, taking two-thirds of its territory and nearly 60 per cent of its pre-war population.

1919 Communists seized power and declared the Hungarian Soviet Republic but were defeated by Admiral Miklos Horthy, who governed as Regent from 1920 until 1944.

1920 Hungary signed the *Treaty of Trianon*, confirming its territorial losses to Romania, Yugoslavia, Czechoslovakia and Austria.

1939–45 During the Second World War Hungary initially allied with Germany and acquired territory through the partitioning of Czechoslovakia and the Axis invasion of Yugoslavia. Having sought to break the alliance, Hungary was occupied by Germany in 1944 before being invaded by the Soviets later in the same year. Following the end of the Second World War, Hungary's territory was reduced to pre-war boundaries and severe reparations exacted.

1947 Communists were the largest single party in the general election.

1949 The Communist, People's Republic of Hungary was established. With Matyas Rakosi as prime minister, purges and political trials on the Stalinist model followed. Agriculture was collectivised along the Soviet pattern and industry was nationalised.

1953 The more liberal Imre Nagy became prime minister, but fell out of favour with the Soviet politburo and was ousted in favour of András Hegedüs in 1955.

1956 During a period of anti-Soviet agitation, Imre Nagy returned, by popular demand, as prime minister. He moved to introduce multi-party politics and then announced Hungary's withdrawal from the Warsaw Pact. He appealed to the West for Hungary to be recognised as a neutral state. Soviet tanks rolled into Budapest and crushed the Hungarian Revolution. Nagy and others took sanctuary in the Yugoslav embassy but he was subsequently arrested by Russian forces and taken to Romania. The communist Magyar Szocialista Mukaspart Partja (MSzMP) (Hungarian Socialist Workers' Party), returned to power with János Kádár as prime minister.

1958 Nagy was executed in Romania. Árpád Szákasits, as chairman of the Presidential Council, became the Head of State.

1960s Kádár introduced a number of minor liberal reforms such as dismantling collective farms, raising wages and introducing some intellectual freedom.

1988 Dissatisfaction among party members with the remoteness of the leadership led to the resignation of Kádár and moves towards 'Socialist Pluralism'.

1989 In May the border with Austria was opened and thousands of East Germans fled to the West, breaching the 'Iron Curtain'. The Communist state of Hungary was dismantled and a transition to a multi-party democracy begun. The MSzMP was re-named the Magyar Szocialista Párt (MSzP) (Hungarian Socialist Party). Mátyás Szürös became Hungary's interim president.

1990 First free multi-party parliamentary elections for 43 years resulted in the formation of a coalition government led by József Antall of the Magyar Demokrata Fórum (MDF) (Hungarian Democratic Forum). Mátyás Szürös was replaced as president by Árpád Göncz

1994 The general election resulted in a coalition government led by Gyula Horn of the MSzP.

1998 The centre-right Fiatal Demokraták Szövetsége-Magyar Polgári Párt (Fidesz-MPP) (Federation of Young Democrats-Hungarian Civic Party), led by Viktor Orbán, unexpectedly won the general election.

1999 Hungary became one of the first former Soviet satellite states to join NATO.

2000 Ferenc Mádl was elected president by parliament, replacing Árpád Göncz.

2001 The government introduced the Status Law, giving the four million ethnic Hungarians in neighbouring countries the right to work and study in Hungary.

2002 Péter Médgyessy (MSzP) became prime minister of a coalition government, comprising MSzP and Szabad Demokratak Szovetsege (SzDSz) (Alliance of Free Democrats).

2003 In a referendum with a 46 per cent turnout, 84 per cent voted in favour of EU membership.

2004 Hungary joined the EU. After the ruling MSzP withdrew support for him, Prime Minister Péter Medgyessy resigned. Ferenc Gyurcsány became prime minister.
2005 László Sólyom became president.
2006 Prime Minister Gyurcsány was re-elected. Rioting followed his admission that he had lied about the economy during the election, but he defied demands for his resignation. He later won a vote of confidence in parliament.
2007 Hungary became a member of the European Union Schengen area whereby all travellers may cross borders without a passport or visa.
2008 An agreement for visa-free visits of citizens to the US was signed. The IMF led a consortium to lend Hungary US$25.1 billion to aid the economy.
2009 Prime Minister Ferenc Gyurcsány resigned. His government's popularity had plummeted and he declared that he was an obstacle to the changes necessary to rectify the economy and bring about social reforms. Gordon György Bajnai (an independent), became prime minster. A new political party, Lehet Más a Politika (LMP) (Politics Can Be Different), was founded, espousing environmental protection and sustainable development.
2010 In parliamentary elections, the opposition coalition of Fidesz won an overwhelming majority of 262 seats out of 386. This was enough to enact major changes without relying on the support of other political parties. The outgoing MSzP won 59 seats in total, and the far-right nationalist Jobbik Magyarországért Mozgalom (Jobbik) (Movement for a better Hungary) won 47 seats. Prime Minister Victor Orbán (Fidesz) took office and parliament voted for Pál Schmitt (Fidesz) as president, by 263 votes (out of 386).
2011 In April, parliament voted to change the constitution and bring to an end the transitional government implemented after the fall of Communist rule in 1989. Two opposition political parties boycotted the vote, claiming the ruling Fidesz were imposing divisive right-wing ideology on the country. Other critics characterised the constitution as 'socially and fiscally conservative', while human rights campaigners opposed articles that limited freedoms, banned same-sex marriages (although partnerships may be legally registered) and awarded legal protection for foetuses from conception. Economic analysts, however, were supportive of the articles that provided for the national deficit to be kept below 50 per cent of GDP and an opening of government operations to private enterprise.
2012 The national airline Malév was declared bankrupt and ceased operations on 3 February, after it was unable to pay running costs and planes were held in foreign airports *in lieu* of debts, it was also unable to repay a number of state aided packages (2007–10) of €130 million (US$171 million), as demanded by the European Commission. Around 7,500 passengers were stranded aboard. On 2 April, President Pál Schmitt resigned after losing his doctorate, which had been shown to have been largely plagiarised. László Kövér became acting president on 2 April. On 2 May János Áder was elected president by parliament (262 votes out of 386). He was sworn in immediately but took office on 10 May. On 6 September, Prime Minister Orbán rejected the conditions set out for a new US$19 billion IMF loan in 2012. He said that they included pension cuts and a withdrawal of taxes on banks and that he would present alternative proposals for the loan repayment.
2013 In a move hoped to both improve the health of Hungarians, and raise revenue, the government imposed taxes on salt, sugar and the ingredients in energy drinks. The IMF closed its office in August, on the suggestion of central bank governor, György Matolcsy.
2014 General elections held on 6 April were won by the coalition of Fidesz-Magyar Polgári Szövetség (Fidesz) (Fidesz-Hungarian Civic Union) and Kereszténydemokrata Néppárt (KDNP) (Christian Democratic People's Party) (Fidesz-KDNP) with 37 (out of 93) party list seats and 96 (out of 106) constituency seats. Local elections held on 13 October were convincingly won by Fidesz although the far-right Jobbik party made some gains, winning control of 14 towns and villages.
2015 On 17 June the government ordered the closure of its border with Serbia, and the construction of a fence along the frontier to keep out migrants. According to the government some 54,000 people have already crossed from Serbia this year. Hungary closed its border with Croatia on 16 October.

Political structure

Constitution

In 1989 the 1949 constitution was amended so that Hungary was formally re-titled the Hungarian Republic, concluding 40 years as a People's Republic.
Under the amended constitution, Hungary has a multi-party system.
Supreme power is vested in parliament.
The Constitutional Court has the power to overturn decisions or decrees that are considered unconstitutional.
On 18 April 2011, parliament voted to change the constitution and bring to an end the transitional government implemented after the fall of Communist rule (1989). Among the articles adopted were a limit on the powers of the Constitutional Court and the head of the central bank, any changes to tax and pension laws to require a two-thirds majority in parliament, government operations to be opened up to private enterprise, the national deficit to be kept below 50 per cent of GDP, legal protection for foetuses from the time of conception, a ban on same-sex marriages (although partnerships may be legally registered), discrimination to be outlawed (but excluded age and sexual orientation). The new constitution came into force on 1 January 2012.
The new electoral law went into force at the same time. Future elections will have a single round, with voters electing 199 MPs instead of previous 386 lawmakers.

Form of state

Parliamentary democratic republic

The executive

The prime minister is chosen by the National Assembly and heads the executive Council of Ministers or cabinet. The prime minister's control of the cabinet has been enhanced by the creation of a minister for the prime minister's office.
The president is also elected by the National Assembly for a five-year term. The president has no executive power, and is not able to dissolve parliament.

National legislature

The unicameral Országgyüles (National Assembly) has 199 members (under the electoral law that came into force on 1 January 2012) in total – 93 elected from party lists (with a 5 per cent minimum threashold) and 106 constituency seats elected in the first-passed-the-post method. (Prior to this there were 386 members, of which 176 are elected in single seat constituencies; 152 by proportional representation in multi-seat constituencies and 58 for what are called compensation seats. Voting for the national assembly was in two rounds.)

Legal system

The legal system is based on the amended 1949 constitution.
Civil and criminal cases are brought before district and county courts and the Supreme Court in Budapest. District courts are courts of first instance whereas county courts may act either as courts of first instance or as appeal courts. The Supreme Court is usually an appeal court, but can also take cases submitted to it by the Public Prosecutor and act as a court of first instance. All courts of first instance have one professional judge and two lay assessors. Appeal courts have three professional judges. The district and county judges are elected by district or county councils. All members of the Supreme Court are elected by parliament.

Last elections
6 April 2014, 29 June 2010 (presidential – indirect)
Results: Presidential: Pál Schmitt won 263 votes, András Bologh 58.
Parliamentary: Coalition of Fidesz – Magyar Polgári Szövetség (Fidesz) (Fidesz – Hungarian Civic Union) and Kereszténydemokrata Néppárt (KDNP) (Christian Democratic People's Party) (Fidesz-KDNP) 55.54 per cent of the party list vote (37 (of 93) seats) plus 96 (out of 106) constituency seats giving a total of 133 seats (66.83 per cent of total vote), Összefogás (Unity) Coalition 25.99 per cent (28 seats) plus 10 giving a total of 38 seats (19.10 per cent), Jobbik Magyarországért Mozgalom (Jobbik) (Movement for a better Hungary) 20.54 per cent (23 seats) no constituency seats, total 23 seats (11.56 per cent), Lehet Más a Politika (LMP) (Politics Can Be Different) 5.26 per cent (5 seats), no constituency seats, total 5 seats (2.51 per cent). No other parties achieved the minimum 5 per cent of the vote. Turnout was 61.73 per cent.
Next elections
2015 (presidential); 2014 (parliamentary).

Political parties
Ruling party
Coalition of Fidesz–Magyar Polgári Szövetség (Fidesz) (Fidesz–Hungarian Civic Union) and Kereszténydemokrata Néppárt (KDNP) (Christian Democratic People's Party) (Fidesz-KDNP) (from 6 Apr 2014)
Main opposition party
Magyar Szocialista Párt (MSzP) (Hungarian Socialist Party)

Population
9.88 million (2013)*
Last census: February 2001: 10,198,315
Population density: 110 inhabitants per square km. Urban population 68 per cent (2010 Unicef).
Annual growth rate: -0.2 per cent, 1990–2010 (Unicef).
Ethnic make-up
The population is almost entirely made up of ethnic Hungarians. Small groups of Germans, Slovaks, Romanians, Serbs and Gypsies (Roma) make up about 4 per cent of the population. Roma are not recognised as an official ethnic group, although they are estimated to number between 360,000 and 600,000.
Religions
There is no official national religion. Roman Catholic (67.5 per cent), Calvinist (20 per cent) and Lutheran (5 per cent). There are approximately six million Roman Catholics, two million Calvinists, 430,000 Lutherans, and 80,000 Jews in Hungary.

Education
Compulsory education starts at six years of age and most children complete secondary education. There are four types of secondary school, offering either academic or vocational education. Apprentice training schools are attached to factories and agricultural co-operatives. There are 57 higher education institutes, including 10 universities and nine technical universities. Some privatisation of education is taking place as church and other private schools are created. Public expenditure on education is equivalent to around 5 per cent of annual gross national income (GNI), and includes subsidies to private education at the primary, secondary and tertiary levels.
Literacy rate: 99.4 per cent total, 99.2 per cent female, adult rates in 2002 (World Bank).
Compulsory years: Six to 18
Enrolment rate: 89.7 per cent net primary enrolment, 84.9 per cent net secondary enrolment (World Bank 2003).
Pupils per teacher: 12 in primary schools.

Health
The health system is run by the State Health Fund, an entity with substantial operational autonomy and no effective accountability. It is financed by payroll taxes of 15 per cent from employers and 4 per cent from employees, although transfers from the budget have been necessary due to a large funding gap.
Service delivery remains poor. Although healthcare is free in Hungary, patients regularly hand over cash bribes to poorly-paid medical staff in order to gain proper access. There are reports of doctors recommending dangerous treatments in exchange for bribes. A major area of concern is the heavy subsidisation of medicine, which patients often obtain freely and then sell on.
HIV/Aids
HIV prevalence: 0.1 per cent aged 15–49 in 2003 (World Bank)
Life expectancy: 73 years, 2004 (WHO 2006)
Fertility rate/Maternal mortality rate: 1.4 births per woman, 2010 (Unicef); maternal mortality 15 per 100,000 live births (World Bank).
Child (under 5 years) mortality rate (per 1,000): 6 per 1,000 live births (WHO 2012)
Head of population per physician: 3.33 physicians per 1,000 people, 2003 (WHO 2006)

Welfare
Economic reforms have included a pioneering reorganisation of the pension system, with a new 'multi-pillar' system launched in 1996, supported by a World Bank US$150 million loan. Employees make mandatory contributions to the existing pay-as-you-go (PAYG) system and to a fully funded second pillar, based on a system of personal savings accounts held in privately managed pension funds. Those joining the work force after June 1998 were obliged to participate in the new system. In 2001, the government made both systems voluntary. The new scheme has proved highly popular. The largest private pension fund is managed by Nationale-Nederlanden (NN), with 257,000 members and Ft4 billion (US$16.4 million) in managed assets. Social security contributions on salaries are paid by the employer (39 per cent) and by the employee (10 per cent). Employer contributions must also be made to the unemployment solidarity fund (4.5 per cent) and by the employee (1.5 per cent).

Main cities
Budapest (capital, estimated population 1.6 million in 2012), Debrecen (204,383), Miskolc (171,843), Szeged (160,766), Pécs (153,696), Györ (130,724), Nyíregyháza (114,508), Kecskemét (104,816), Székesfehérvár (104,599).

Languages spoken
Slovak, Croatian, Serbian, Slovene, Romani are also spoken.
The main foreign language is German, followed by English, Russian and French.
Official language/s
Hungarian (Magyar)

Media
Press
Foreign ownership dominates the print media and all newspapers are privately owned. While the market in tabloid news is growing, quality newspapers are in decline.
Dailies: There are over 30 dailies of which 10 are national newspapers. Local newspapers have a strong market lead and national broadsheets are considered partisan.
In Hungarian, the most popular national newspaper is the free issue *Metro* (www.metro.hu); the most popular quality newspapers are the *Népszabadság* (www.nol.hu) and *Magyar Nemzet* (www.mno.hu), with *Magyar Hirlap* (ww.magyarhirlap.hu), *Népszava* (www.nepszava.hu) and *Reggel* (www.reggel.hu), which include articles on business and finance.
Weeklies: In Hungarian, magazines for news and current affairs include *168 Óra*

(www.168ora.hu), *Hírek* (www.miep.hu), *Magyar Demokrata* (www.demokrata.hu) and *HVG* (http://hvg.hu); for women, *Hölgyvilág* (www.holgyvilag.hu), *Nok Lapja* (www.nlcafe.hu); *Hócipo* (www.hocipo.hu) is a satirical magazine.

Business: In Hungarian, the leading business and financial newspapers are the *Napi Gazdaság* (www.napi.hu), *Magyar Tokepiac* (www.magyartokepiac.hu) and *Világgazdaság* (www.vilaggazdasag.hu). Magazines include *Adó* (www.ado.hu) and *Bank & Tözsde* (www.bankestozsde.hu).

In English, the weekly *Budapest Business Journal* (www.bbj.hu), has a round up of news and comprehensive industry and company information.

Periodicals: In Hungarian the monthly *Közéleti Krónika* (www.kronika.matav.hu) covers general interest.

Broadcasting

The state-owned media has lost its monopoly and, since 1996, most of its market. Its reputation has been damaged with accusation of political interference by government.

Radio: The state-run Magyar Rádió (www.radio.hu) operates three national public stations, Bartok (www.mr3-bartok.hu), Kossuth (www.mr1-kossuth.hu) and Petofi (www.mr2.hu), which include specialist interest broadcasts of parliamentary proceedings and religion. The two private, national commercial stations Danubius (www.danubius.hu) and Sláger (www.slager.hu) are also those with the highest listener figures. There are many local radio stations, either private, public and community, with intense competition for listeners.

Television: Television is the most popular medium for news, information and entertainment.

Magyar Televízió (MTV) (www.mtv.hu) has two channels M1 and M2. Funding for these services is provided by government grants and advertising revenue. MTV is chronically under-funded and the quality and quantity of programming is weak. Private commercial TV is led by RTLKlub (www.rtlklub.hu) and TV2 (http://tv2.hu), which offer a wide range of locally produced programmes and well as imported TV shows. Hir TV (www.hirtv.net) is a 24-hour news channel. There are dozens of pay-to-view TV channels offering programmes in most genres.

National news agency: Magyar Távirati Iroda (MTI) (Hungarian News Agency): http://english.mti.hu

Other news agencies: Havaria Press (in Hungarian): www.havariapress.hu

Economy

Hungary has an open market economy, built up since the mid-1990s, and can boast one of the most successful growth rates in Central Europe. It has a large industrial base including automobile manufacturing, mining and metallurgy, energy production and food processing. The Great Hungarian Plain and Little Hungarian Plain together make up 75 per cent of the land available for cultivation, and with their rich farming soils enable the production of, among other crops, grapes, fruit, grain, as well as providing pastures for livestock. However, over 65.4 per cent of Hungary's economy is based in the tertiary service sector, with tourism comprising a major component. The private sector accounts for around 80 per cent of GDP, with a high level of foreign ownership and foreign investment.

Exports, the backbone of the economy, fell sharply in 2008 and continued in a slump until 2010 when world trade picked up, and the total value of exports by 2014 had reached over US$100 billion. However in 2007, as world fuel and food costs soared, GDP growth fell to 0.1 per cent (down from 3.9 per cent in 2006), with a slight improvement to 0.9 per cent in 2008. Low domestic consumption and government austerity measures meant the economy fell into recession in the first quarter of 2009 with annual GDP growth of -6.8 per cent for the year. Growth picked up to 1.3 per cent in 2010 along with global expansion and was estimated to have remained positive at 1.7 per cent growth in 2011. The economy dropped into recession in 2012 following a loss of momentum, before returning to positive growth with the improvement of the global markets, reaching 3.6 per cent by 2014.

The currency had weakened – over 2008–11 the florin fell by 40 per cent against the Swiss franc. On 23 January 2012, both lenders agreed in principal to a new funding deal of EUR17–20 billion (US$21.9–25.8 billion) by March–April. The IMF and the EU used the loan to apply pressure on the government to change newly introduced laws on the courts, the central bank and the media, which were said to undermine their independence and breach EU rules.

On 1 January 2012, the rate of value added tax (VAT) was raised from 25 per cent to 27 per cent (reduced rates on certain goods and services remained at the same rate).

On 13 March 2012, the EU decided to suspend EUR495 million (US$655 million) from its funding due to Hungary's budget deficit. The EU gave Hungary three months to initiate further budget cuts before a review of the decision. The EU's excessive deficit procedure (EDP) requires member states to keep budget deficits below 3 per cent of national output and government debts below, or significantly declining towards, 60 per cent of GDP. Prime Minister Orban accused the EU of 'colonial' interference and said that Hungarians 'will not live as foreigners dictate it, (they) will not give up their independence or their freedom'.

The prime minister rejected the conditions set out for a new US$19 billion IMF loan, in September 2012. He said that they included pension cuts and a withdrawal of taxes on banks and that he would present alternative proposals for the loan repayment.

External trade

As a member of the European Union, Hungary operates within a community-wide free trade area, with tariffs set as a whole. Internationally, the EU has free trade agreements with a number of nations and trading blocs worldwide.

The economy is dependent on export trade, of which 75 per cent goes to the EU, mainly Germany. Major sectors include vehicle assembly and electronics, which account for a third of exports. Hungarian wine and fruit are consumed throughout the EU.

Imports

Principal imports are capital goods, machinery and equipment, fuels and electricity, food products, raw materials, energy (natural gas and electricity).

Main sources: Germany (25.2 per cent of total in 2014), Austria (7.3 per cent), Russia (7.1 per cent).

Exports

Principal exports are machinery and equipment, manufactured goods, foodstuffs and agricultural produce, raw materials, energy (refined oil and electricity).

Main destinations: Germany (27.4 per cent of total in 2014), Austria (5.5 per cent), Romania (5.4 per cent).

Agriculture

Farming

The agricultural sector contributes 3.5 per cent to GDP and employs around 10 per cent of the workforce. Agriculture and animal husbandry dominate in the Great Plain in central and eastern Hungary. The western region of Transdanubia – which includes Lake Balaton, the largest lake in Central Europe – is dominated by intensive agriculture and animal husbandry. Farming is largely socialised; co-operatives are the dominant form of production. The agriculture and food industry produces on average 50 per cent more food than is consumed domestically. Principal crops include wheat, maize, barley, sugar beet and potatoes. The livestock sector is also important. Crop cultivation, especially wheat, maize, potatoes, fruit and

vegetables, accounts for around half of Hungary's agricultural output. Processed and unprocessed meat, dairy products and wine are the other main products. The agriculture and food industry produces, on average, 50 per cent more than is needed for domestic consumption. After EU accession in 2004, Hungary is eligible for EU agricultural subsidies and rural development through the Common Agricultural Policy (CAP). However, it only received the full amount by the end of a 10-year transition period finishing in 2013.
During its transitional entry stage Hungary has decided to implement the reform of the CAP in January 2009. The reform was introduced throughout most of the EU in 2005, when subsidies on farm output, which tended to benefit large farms and encourage overproduction, were replaced by single farm payments, not conditional on production. The change is expected to reward farms that provide and maintain a healthy environment, food safety and animal welfare standards. The changes are also intended to encourage market conscious production and cut the cost of CAP to the EU taxpayer.

Fishing

Hungary is a landlocked country and although there is some fishing from lakes and rivers, most of the country's consumption needs are met through imports. Fish production in Hungary is mostly concentrated in the available 140,000 hectares (ha) of natural water and 20,000ha of man-made fishponds. The fish production sector primarily involves common carp and African catfish and remains a small and special sub-sector of agriculture. The sector traditionally supports less than 0.5 per cent of the total labour force and contributes below 2 per cent of the total for agricultural production. Annual consumption per capita is typically less than 3kg.

Forestry

Forests account for a fifth of Hungary's land area but the industry amounts to only 0.3 per cent of GDP. Forestry agriculture largely concentrates on production using hardwood species of trees, mostly being used for energy purposes. Oak and black locust are most prevalent. The state owns about 60 per cent of forests and and employs 20,000 workers on this land. Hungary is a net importer of all primary forest products as a result of not undertaking softwood and pulp production.

Industry and manufacturing

Mechanical engineering, chemicals, pulp and paper industries, as well as the iron and steel industry and metal processing are particularly successful sectors. Other industries include building materials, food processing and textiles. One of the fastest growing sectors in Hungary, as the country moves away from heavy industry, is motor vehicle components and assembly. The economy is upgrading to high-tech production. In 2014, industrial production rose by over 7 per cent and was predicted to repeat this achievement in 2015.
Foreign direct investment (FDI) has contributed greatly to industrial output in Hungary, concentrating in areas such as machinery, vehicles, computers, telecommunications equipment, electrical and electronic goods. These successes have been concentrated in a relatively small number of capital-intensive companies. Multinational companies are relocating some support services such as human resources and customer relations to Hungary. Analysts warn that the country could be in danger of developing a two-tier economy, with a prosperous, predominantly foreign-owned sector of larger enterprises and a struggling, locally-owned sector of small- and medium-sized enterprises (SMEs). However, high levels of FDI have not been sustained. Investors are now turning to Slovakia and the Czech Republic where corporate taxes are lower. Other problems with business conditions in Hungary include a lack of financial transparency between government and populace, excessive bureaucracy and a workforce neither sufficiently skilled nor mobile.
In the past, government policy focussed on the development of heavy industry and agriculture. In the late-1990s, this shifted towards the development of SMEs. These accounted for 53.9 per cent of GDP in 2014 and represent around 70 per cent of employment. The main problem facing smaller enterprises is the growing black market. This is due to a constantly changing and, thus far, largely unfavourable tax system in which evasion is widespread. Law-abiding SMEs are finding it difficult to compete with black market labour.
In recent years the government has addressed the problems of declining foreign investment and adverse business conditions for SMEs. It has launched The Hungarian National Development Program (NDP), the Smart Hungary Programme and the Europe Plan. The NDP has coffers of EUR5.4 billion, which it will invest in the development of Hungarian SMEs. 1,500 businesses have applied for such assistance, in the hope of sharpening their competitive edge. At its outset the Smart Hungary Programme had a budget of 1.2 billion forint and the aim of providing incentives to foreign investors. This money was directed towards creating subsidies, tax cuts for up to five years and a simplification of investment bureaucracy. It also promoted the implementation of environmentally friendly systems. The Europe Plan meanwhile seeks to prepare SMEs for the single currency.

Tourism

Hungary has a long cultural history. Its capital Budapest was Central Europe's most important city during the Austro-Hungarian Empire. It has many thermal springs that were first built during the Roman Empire, which developed spa baths, and through the ages visitors have enjoyed their hot mineral waters. There are seven cultural sites and one natural site on Unesco's World Heritage List, from historic buildings to the Caves of Aggtelek Karst.
Travel and tourism constituted 10.3 per cent of GDP in 2014. Around 9.8 per cent of the workforce is engaged in the tourism industry (415,500 jobs in 2014). Since 2009, the National Tourist Office has established a policy of decentralisation for tourism related issues and of fostering initiatives to encourage greater local participation in decisions in tourism development. The ultimate plan is to have individual, identifiable regional strategies so that marketing can be targeted at specific tourists and groups.

Mining

The mining sector accounts for around 5 per cent of GDP and employs 3 per cent of the workforce.
Hungary is a major European producer of bauxite, and also a small-scale producer of lignite and manganese ore. In the Northern Hills, iron ore and copper are mined.

Hydrocarbons

Hungary is a small-scale producer of coal, oil and natural gas. In the Great Plain in central and eastern Hungary, there are natural gas and oil deposits while brown coal is mined in the Northern Hills region.
Proven reserves were 27.3 million barrels of oil in 2014, producing around 23,000 barrels per day (bpd), with consumption at 132 billion bpd the balance is provided by imports. There is one oil refinery with a capacity of 161,000bpd; US$59 million has been invested to create a new hydro-desulphurisation unit in line with EU standards for low sulphur petrol and diesel.
Proven reserves of natural gas was 7.84 billion cubic metres (cum) in 2014. Consumption was 12 billion cum and production some 8.4 billion cum per annum. Imports of natural gas come primarily from Russia. Gas storage capacity is well developed and can hold 120 days of peak winter imports.
In February 2012, the multinational, South Stream Transport group,

announced the expected construction of the South Stream pipeline, to transport Russian natural gas to Western and Central Europe (and bypassing Ukraine) would begin in December 2012; however, the project was abandoned in December 2014.

Coal reserves totalled 1.66 billion tonnes in 2014; coal production was 2 million tonnes oil equivalent. Hungarian coal is the less valuable sub-bituminous and lignite composition that is typically used in power stations, but is a large atmospheric pollutant.

Energy

Total electricity generating capacity was over 9,900MW in 2013. Electricity generation has moved away from large, central production sites to small to medium locally placed cogeneration plants, of less than 50MW, producing electricity and heat, which in 2008 provided 25 per cent of the country's total generating capacity. Power stations are predominately fuelled by natural gas, 3,000 million tonnes oil equivalent (mtoe) per annum, as lignite coal has fallen (from over 25,000mtoe in 2003 to less than 17,000mtoe in 2005). Hungary has one nuclear power plant, near Paks, producing 3.3mtoe. The plant provides 40 per cent of domestic energy needs and is dependent on enrichment and processing facilities from the Russian Federation. Renewable wind energy has been growing in use. However, in 2011 (latest figures), renewable energy only contribute 9.5 per cent of total installed capacity.

Financial markets

Stock exchange

Budapesti Értéktözsde (Budapest Stock Exchange) (BSE)

Banking and insurance

Hungary has the most developed financial sector in Eastern Europe, with the Magyar Nemzeti Bank (MNB) (National Bank of Hungary) (central bank) playing an important role in economic and financial management of the economy. The country privatised banking services from 1994–97 in order to attract foreign investment.

About 30 of the 38 banks in Hungary are foreign-owned and are led by the OTP Bank (formely known as the National Savings Bank). Foreign-owned banks control 90 per cent of the country's total banking assets. OTP Bank, with an extensive branch network, offers banking for the general public, and also foreigners needing foreign exchange accounts.

Foreign trade and currency transactions are conducted by the Magyar Külkereskedelmi Bank (MKB) (formerly the Hungarian Foreign Trade Bank) and by some other banks.

The Central-European International Bank is an internationally active offshore bank owned by the central bank and six foreign banks.

Hungary adopted a German model for the banking system in 1999, allowing banks to engage in both commercial and investment banking.

Central bank

Magyar Nemzeti Bank (MNB) (National Bank of Hungary)

Main financial centre

Budapest

Time

GMT plus one hour (daylight saving, late March to late October, GMT plus two hours)

Geography

Hungary is a landlocked country in central Europe surrounded by the Alps, the Carpathians and the Dinaric Mountains. The Danube and Tisza rivers run through the country, which is bounded by Slovakia to the north, Ukraine to the north-east, Romania to the east, Serbia, Croatia and Slovenia to the south and Austria to the west.

The River Danube forms Hungary's north-western border with Slovakia and then flows south through Budapest, bisecting the country. More than half of the land surface consists of plains less than 200 metres above sea level. The highest point is Kekes at 1,015 metres in the Matra hills to the north, while the lowest point is on the southern edge of Szeged along the River Tisza (the longest tributary of the Danube) at 77 metres.

The major regions of the country are: the Pannonian or Great Hungarian Plain (central and eastern Hungary), east of the River Danube and also drained by the Tisza; Transdanubia (western Hungary, including Lake Balaton, the largest lake in central Europe); the Little Hungarian Plains in the north-west between the mountains and the Danube; and along Hungary's northern border are the Matras, foothills of the Carpathian Mountains.

Hemisphere

Northern

Climate

The temperate continental climate of Hungary is under the varying influence of three climatic zones: continental, Atlantic and Mediterranean. The annual median temperature in Budapest is 11 degrees Celsius (C). The warmest month is July, with an average of 22 degrees C, the coldest January, with minus 1 degrees C. Averaging 1,988 hours of sunshine a year, Hungary experiences more sun than most of the countries in Western Europe. Average annual rainfall is 630mm, but distribution is unpredictable. Most rain usually falls in May and June, but the south-west regions may have more in October. May is the wettest month, and September the driest. The central parts of the Great Plains are the driest with 200–500mm, the hilly western area of Koeszeg and Sopron the wettest with 900–1,000mm.

Dress codes

Hungarians used to dress more formally than West Europeans, but blazers, sports coats and flannels are as acceptable as lounge suits for visiting businessmen. Do not be offended if Hungarians ask where you bought your clothes or how much they cost.

Advisable clothing: medium to heavyweight and heavy topcoat for winter; lightweight clothing for summer. A raincoat will be needed in spring and autumn.

Entry requirements

Passports

Passport required by all; must be valid for six months beyond date of departure.

Visa

Required by all, except nationals of EU and Schengen area signatory countries, North America, Australasia and Japan. For further exceptions contact the nearest embassy. A Schengen visa application (offered in several languages) can be downloaded from http://europa.eu/abc/travel/ see 'documents you will need'. Business trips may be made visa-free, or on short-term visas. For terms and conditions see: www.mfa.gov.hu/kum/en/bal/ and follow links to consular services.

Transit passengers must have onward/return passage.

Currency advice/regulations

The import and export of local currency is limited to Ft200,000, provided the amount is declared. The import of foreign currency is unlimited, although amounts over Ft1 million must be declared. The export of foreign currency cannot exceed the amount imported and must be exported no later than three months after import. There is no compulsory money exchange on departure, however only 50 per cent of a visitor's forints can be re-exchanged (up to a limit of US$450, and with exchange receipts) at any authorised *bureaux de change*, or branch of the National Savings Bank.

Customs

Personal items are duty-free. There are no duties levied on alcohol and tobacco between EU member states, providing amounts imported are for personal consumption.

Health (for visitors)

Nationals of the European Economic Area (EEA) countries and Switzerland can access reduced cost and sometimes free medical treatment using a European Health Insurance Card (EHIC) while visiting the EEA. Exceptions include nationals of the 10 countries, which joined the EU in 2004, whose EHIC is not valid in Switzerland. Applications for the EHIC should be made before travelling.

Mandatory precautions

There are no special requirements.

Advisable precautions

There are no specific precautions necessary although a hepatitis A immunisation might be useful.

Hotels

There is a full range of hotels in Budapest. Reservations can be made in advance directly or through IBUSZ.

All hotels charge a 1–2 per cent tourism tax for guests staying more than one night. Tipping usually 10–15 per cent. Good hotels are concentrated in Pest, the business half of Budapest.

Credit cards

Credit cards are accepted and can be used for cash advances.

Public holidays (national)

Fixed dates

1 Jan (New Year's Day), 15 Mar (National Day), 1 May (Labour Day), 20 Aug (National Constitution/St Stephen's Day), 23 Oct (Remembrance Day), 1 Nov (All Saints' Day), 25–26 Dec (Christmas).

Variable dates

Easter Monday, Whit Monday.

Working hours

Banking

Mon–Thu: 0800–1500; Fri: 0800–1300.

Business

Mon–Thu: 0800–1600.

Government

Mon–Fri: 0800–1630.

Shops

Mon, Tue, Wed & Fri: 1000–1800, Thu: 1000–2000, Sat: 1000–1300.

Shops may have varied opening hours. Food shops open at 0600–0700 and may not close until 2000.

Telecommunications

Mobile/cell phones

There is a GSM dual band of 900 and 1800 with coverage throughout the country.

Electricity supply

220V AC, 50 cycles

Social customs/useful tips

Business people are expected to dress smartly. Local business people are generally friendly and hospitable and it is usual for visitors to be invited to lunch or dinner in a restaurant. Business cards are widely distributed and visitors are advised to have a supply available in Hungarian.

Best months for business visits are September to May and appointments should always be made. Interpreter and translation services may be booked through travel agents. In business Hungarians expect people to speak their mind. Giving and receiving gifts is very common; take promotional gifts with you.

Punctuality is appreciated.

If you are invited to a Hungarian home, take flowers for the hostess and wine or liquor for the host.

Hungarian law requires visitors to carry passports or other ID at all times.

Security

There has been an increase in street crime in Budapest, although levels are still below those in many Western capitals. Bag-snatching and pickpocketing are common in Budapest. Criminals at times pose as police officers, and credentials should be requested for inspection.

Getting there

Air

National airline: Malév (Hungarian Airlines) (defunct February 2012)

International airport/s: Budapest-Ferihegy (BUD, 16km from city; duty-free shop, restaurants and bar, bank/bureaux de change, tourist information centre, post office and car hire. Scheduled bus services run to the city centre; minibuses run to and from any address in the city. The 93 bus runs an express service between the underground terminus at Kobánya-Kispest and the Ferihegy terminals; a pre-purchased or season ticket is required. Taxis are available at all times.

Airport tax: None

Surface

Hungary is included in the Pan-European Corridor 5 scheme. The project has some 3,270km of railways, linking Kiev in the Ukraine with western Europe via Italy, and 2,850 of new and upgraded roads.

Water: A hydrofoil service is available on the Danube between Vienna and Budapest in the summer. Ships provide regular passenger service and cruises starting at Passau and Regensburg (Germany) to Budapest, passing through Austria and Slovakia. There are also links with the rivers Rhine and Main and the Black Sea.

Getting about

National transport

Road: Generally the road system is good. Tolls are payable on some roads and all motorways for which season tickets can be purchased. There are eight arterial roads: all but the M8 start from central Budapest. From Budapest the two main highways are the M1 to Györ (then to Austria) and the M7 along Lake Balaton. The M3 connects Budapest with eastern Hungary.

Buses: Budapest is linked to all major towns. Tickets are available from Volán offices throughout the country.

Rail: Services are operated by MÁV. All cities are linked by efficient services, but facilities are often inadequate. Supplements are payable on intercity (IC) and express trains and reservations are compulsory on IC trains and recommended for express trains, particularly in summer. Tickets and seat reservations can be bought 60 days in advance at domestic railway stations.

Water: Ferries run several times daily between Budapest and Visegrád over the summer; one service extends to Esztergom.

City transport

Most government offices, business centres and main hotels are located in Pest, on the eastern side of the Danube. The public transport system is good and it is rarely necessary to take a taxi, especially as the city centre is quite compact.

Buda, the hilly, western part of the city, is more difficult to get around without a car.

Taxis: Taxis are available from ranks, by telephone or can be hailed in the street. Taxis are metered. Avoid all unmarked cabs as they not only demand payment for mileage covered, but also for the return journey to their starting point.

A taxi from the airport to the centre of Budapest takes between 40 minutes and one hour; always agree your fare in advance. Non-airport taxis are plentiful and inexpensive although rates vary widely (watch out for meters being on the 'night' rate during the day). Tipping of 15–20 per cent is expected.

Buses, trams & metro: There is good public transport in all the main towns, including tramways in some.

Budapest has bus, trolleybus, tramway, suburban railway (HEV), a three-line metro and boat services. The metro has ticket barriers at all stations. The bus-trolleybus-tramway system has pre-purchase flat fares with ticket puncher on board. Day passes and season tickets are available for all the transport modes in the city. Trams and buses generally run from 0430–2300. Some night services also operate. The metro runs from 0430–2310; stations are identified by a large 'M'.

Trains: Main railway stations: Déli Pu (Southern RW Terminal), Krisztina krt 37/a, Budapest I.

Keleti Pu (Eastern RW Terminal), Baross Tér (tel: 142-9150).

Nyugati Pu (Western RW Terminal), Teréz krt 111 (tel: 122-7860).

Ferry: The Danube provides a ready highway for ferries and sightseeing cruises.

Car hire

Hire cars are available from the airport, hotels and IBUSZ travel company. The speed limit is 50kph in built up areas, 90kph on main roads, 110kph on highways and 130kph on motorways. There is an absolute ban on drinking and driving, headlights must be kept dipped, mobile phones can only be used with headsets and seat belts are compulsory. An international driving licence is recommended. For travel on the M1 and M3 motorways, drivers require a motorway *vignette*, obtainable from the Hungarian Auto Klub, petrol stations, post offices, and some motorway access points; without one, drivers may be fined.

BUSINESS DIRECTORY

The addresses listed below are a selection only. While World of Information makes every endeavour to check these addresses, we cannot guarantee that changes have not been made, especially to telephone numbers and area codes. We would welcome any corrections.

Telephone area codes

The international direct dialling code (IDD) for Hungary is +36, followed by area code and subscriber's number:

Budapest	1	Pecs	72
Debrecen	52	Salgotarjan	32
Gyor	96	Szeged	62
Miskolc	46	Szekesfehervar	22
Nyiregyhaza	42	Szombathely	94

Useful telephone numbers

Ambulance, Police, Fire: 112

24-hour emergency service (English-speaking): 118-8212

24-hour multi-lingual crime reporting service: 0800—2000: 438-8080; after hours: 06-80-660-044

Fotaxi (tel: 222-2222)

City Taxi (tel: 211-1111)

Volantaxi (tel: 166-6666)

Chambers of Commerce

American Chamber of Commerce in Hungary, 10 Deak Ferencu utca, 1052 Budapest (tel: 266-9880; fax: 266-9888; e-mail: info@amcham.hu).

Borsod-Abauj-Zemplen County Chamber of Commerce and Industry, 1 Szentpali u, 3530 Miskolc (tel: 328-539; fax: 328-722; e-mail: bokik@mail.bokik,hu).

British Chamber of Commerce in Hungary, 6 Bank utca, 1054 Budapest (tel: 302-5200; fax: 302-3069; e-mail: bcch@bcch.com).

Budapest Chamber of Commerce and Industry, Krisztina krt 99, 1016 Budapest (tel: 488-2000; fax: 488-2119; e-mail: bkik@bkik.hu).

Czongrád Chamber of Commerce and Industry, 2-4 Tisza Lajos krt, 6701 Csongrád (tel: 426-343; fax: 426-149; info@csmkik.hu).

Fejér County Chamber of Commerce, 4-6 Hosszusetater, 8000 Székesfehérvár (tel: 510-310; fax: 510-312; e-mail: fmkik@mail.fmkik.hu).

Gyor-Moson-Sopron County Chamber of Commerce and Industry, 10/A Szent Istvan ut, 9021 Gyor (tel: 520-202; fax: 520-291; e-mail: kamara@gymskik.hu).

Hajdu-Bihar County Chamber of Commerce and Industry, 10 Petofi ter, 4025 Debrecen (tel: 500-721; fax: 500-720; e-mail: info@hbkik.hu).

Hungarian Chamber of Commerce and Industry, 6-8 Kossuth Lajos ter, 1055 Budapest (tel: 474-5101; fax: 474-5105; e-mail: mkik@mkik.hu).

Pecs-Baranya Chamber of Commerce and Industry, 36 Majorossy I ut, 7625 Pécs (tel: 507-149; fax: 507-152; e-mail: pbkik@pbkik.hu).

Pest County Chamber of Commerce and Inustry, 40 Vaci utca, 1051 Budapest (tel: 317-7666; fax: 317-7755; e-mail: titkarsag@pmkik.hu).

Sopron Chamber of Commerce and Industry, 14 Deak ter, 9400 Sopron (tel: 523-570; fax: 523-581; e-mail: k-kamara@sopron.hu).

Vas County Chamber of Commerce and Industry, 2 Honved ter, 9700 Szombathely (tel: 312-356; fax: 316-936; e-mail: vmkik@vmkik.hu).

Veszprem Chamber of Commerce, 3 Budapesti u, 8200 Veszprém (tel: 429-008; fax: 412-150; e-mail: vkik@iveszpremikamara.hu).

Zala County Chamber of Commerce and Industry, 24 Petofi Sandor ut, 8900 Zalaegerszeg (tel: 550-514; fax: 550-525; e-mail: zmkik@zmkik.hu).

Banking

General Banking and Trust Co Ltd, Markó ut 9, H-1055 Budapest (tel: 269-1450; fax: 260-1440).

Magyar Külkereskedelmi Bank (commercial bank), St István ter 11, H-1821 Budapest (tel: 269-0922; fax: 269-0959).

OTP Bank, Nádor ut 16, H-1876 Budapest (tel: 153-1444; fax: 112-6858).

Raiffeisen Bank, PO Box 173, H-1054 Budapest (tel: 484-4400; fax: 484-4444).

Central bank

Magyar Nemzeti Bank (National Bank of Hungary), 1054 Szabadság tér 8-9, 1850 Budapest (tel:428-2752; fax: 302-3000).

Stock exchange

Budapesti Értéktözsde (Budapest Stock Exchange) (BSE), www.bse.hu

Travel information

Ferihegy International Airport flight enquiries (tel: 157-7155); passenger service (tel: 157-8555; fax: 157-8993).

Hungarian Automobile Club, Francis ut 38, Budapest XIV (tel: 691-8310).

IBUSZ – Hungarian Travel Agency (main Budapest office), Tanács krt 3/c, Budapest VII (tel: 142-3140).

Lufthansa Airport Office (tel: 157-0290, 157-6506; fax: 157-6192); town office, V ci utca 19-21, Budapest (tel: 266-4511; fax: 266-8669).

Malév Hungarian Airlines, (headquarters), 1097 Könyves Kálmán Krt 12-14 (tel: 235-3535); (customer service) Váci út 26, Budapest 11532 (tel: 235-3222; fax: 235-3244; email: centrum@malev.hu).

Police Tourinfo Office (service in English and German), Vigado Utca 6, 1051 Budapest.

Secretariat of the Hungarian Tourist Council, 6th floor, Margit krt 85, H-1024 Budapest (tel: 1175-1682; fax: 1175-38190).

National tourist organisation offices

Tourinform (Hungarian Tourist Board), Suto ut 2, H-1052 Budapest (tel: 117-9800; fax: 117-9578; e-mail: tourinform@mail.hungarytourism.hu; internet site: http://www.hungarytourism.hu).

Ministries

Ministry of Agriculture and Regional Development, Kossuth Lajos tér 11, H-1055 Budapest (tel: 302-0000; fax: 302-0402).

Ministry of Defence, Balaton ut 7-11, H-1055 Budapest (tel: 332-2500; fax: 311-0182).

Ministry of Economic Affairs, Honved U 13-14, H-1055 Budapest (tel: 302-2355; fax: 302-2394; internet site: http://www.gm.hu/english).

Ministry of Education, Szalay U 10-14, H-1055 Budapest (tel: 302-0600; fax: 302-2002).

Ministry of Environmental Protection, Fo ut 44-50, H-1011 Budapest (tel: 457-3300).

Ministry of Finance, József Nádor tér 2-4, H-1051 Budapest (tel: 118-2066, 138-2633; fax: 118-2570).

Ministry of Foreign Affairs, Bem rkp 47, H-1027 Budapest (tel: 458-1000; fax: 155-9693).

Ministry of Health, Arany János u 6-8, H-1051 Budapest (tel: 332-3100; fax: 302-0925).

Ministry of Home Affairs, József Attila u 2-4, H-1051 Budapest (tel: 331-3700, 332-5790; fax: 118-2870).

Ministry of Justice, Kossuth Lajos ter 4, H-1055 Budapest (tel: 268-3003).

Ministry of Transport, Telecommunications & Water Management, Dob ut 74-81, H-1077 Budapest (tel: 322-0220, 341-4300; fax: 322-8695).

Office of the President, Kossuth Lajos Ter 3-5, Budapest (tel: 268-4000).

Pressinform (information bureau for foreign journalists), Budakeszi ut 41, H-1021 Budapest (tel: 175-1890; fax: 175-1178).

Prime Minister's Office, Kossuth Lajos tér 1-3, H-1055 Budapest (tel: 268-3000; fax: 268-3050).

Other useful addresses

Allami Biztosító (state insurance company), Ullöi ut 1, H-1813 Budapest (tel: 117-8566).

Amex, Deak Ferenc ut 10, 1050 Budapest (tel: 117-8008).

British Embassy, 6 Harmincad utca, Budapest 1051 (tel: 266-2888; fax: 429-6360).

Budapest Stock Exchange, Deak Ferenc ut 5, H-1052 Budapest (tel: 117-5226; fax: 118-1737; internet site: www.fornax.hu/fmon/index.html).

Central Statistical Office, International Relations Department, Keleti Károly utca 5–7, , PO Box 51, H-1525 Budapest (tel: 212-6136; fax: 212-6378; internet site: www.ksh.hu/eng/index.htm).

Federation of Scientific and Technical Societies (MTESZ), Kossuth Lajos tér 6–8, Budapest V (tel: 153-3333).

Hungarian Aluminium Industrial Co Ltd (Hungalu), Privatisation Directorate, Room 419, 85 Margit krt, Budapest 1024 (tel: 175-6528; fax: 175-5802).

Hungária Biztosító (Hungária Insurance Company), Bánk ut 17–6, H-1115 Budapest (tel: 182-0750).

Hungarian Embassy (USA), 3910 Shoemaker Street, NW, Washington DC 20008 (tel: (+1-202) 362-6730; fax: (+1-202) 686-6412; e-mail: office@huembwas.org).

Hungarian Foundation for Enterprise Promotion, Etele ut 68, Budapest H-1115 (tel: 203-0348/60; fax: 203-0377).

Hungarian Investment and Trade Development Agency (ITD), Euro Information Correspondence Centre, Dorottya ut 4, 1051 Budapest (tel: 118-1712/6064; fax: 118-6198; e-mail: itdheicc@mail.datanet.hu; internet site: www.itd.hu/index.htm).

Hungarian Privatisation and Foreign Investment, APV, Pozsonyi ut 56, H-1133 Budapest (tel: 269-8600; fax: 267-0079).

Hungary EU Energy Centre (Thermie), Konyves Kalman Krt 76, 1087 Budapest VIII (tel: 269-9067, 133-1304; fax: 269-9065).

Hungexpo International Fair Centre, Dobi Istvan ut 10, Budapest X.

Magyar Tavirati Iroda (Hungarian news agency) (MTI), Fem utca 507, 1016 Budapest (tel: 155-6722).

Mineralimpex Hungarian Oil and Gas Co, Benczur u 13, 1068 Budapest (tel: 131-6720; fax: 153-1779, 142-3584).

US Embassy, Szabadsag ter 12, 1054 Budapest (tel: 267-4400; fax: 269-9326 or 269-9337 (Consular Section).

National news agency: Magyar Távirati Iroda (MTI) (Hungarian News Agency): http://english.mti.hu
Havaria Press (in Hungarian): www.havariapress.hu

Internet sites

Budapest Network: www.budapestnetwork.com

Budapest Sun: www.budapestsun.com

Hungary Network: www.hungary.com

Online financial journal: www.portfolio.hu/en

Virtual Hungary: virtualhungary.com

Iceland

KEY FACTS

Official name: Lyoveldio Island (Republic of Iceland)

Head of State: President Ólafur Ragnar Grímsson (Independent) (from 1996; re-elected 30 Jun 2012)

Head of government: Prime Minister Sigmundur Davíð Gunnlaugsson (FSF) (elected 27 Apr 2013)

Ruling party: Coalition of Sjálfstæðisflokkurinn (SSF) (Independence Party) and Framsóknarflokkurinn (FSF) (Progressive Party) (elected 27 Apr 2013)

Area: 103,100 square km

Population: 326,000 (2014)*

Capital: Reykjavík

Official language: Icelandic

Currency: Icelandic krona (Ikr) = 100 aurar

Exchange rate: Ikr128.67 per US$ (Sep 2015)

GDP per capita: US$51,262 (2014)*

GDP real growth: 1.75% (2014)*

GDP: US$16.69 billion (2014)*

Labour force: 186,000 (2014)*

Unemployment: 4.96% (2014)*

Inflation: 2.04% (2014)*

Balance of trade: -US$105.30 million (2014)

* estimated figure

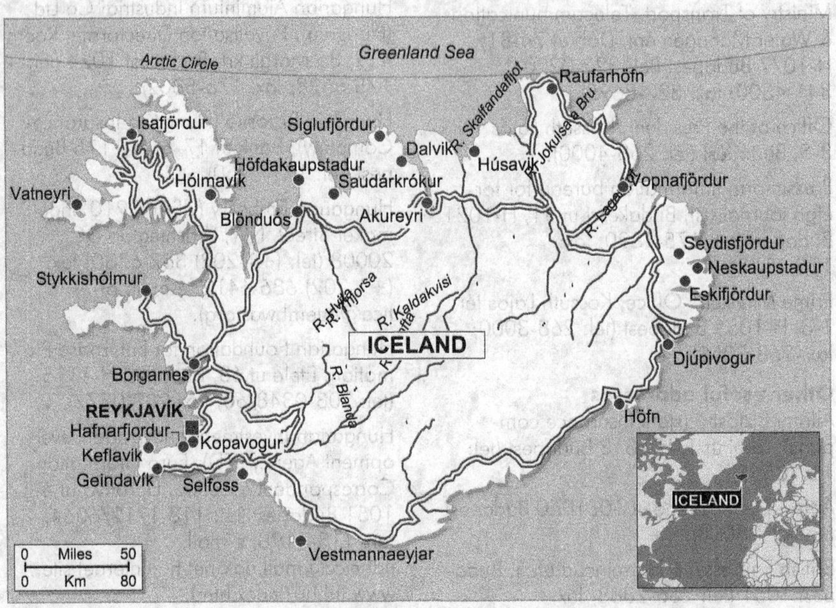

The twenty-first century has turned out to be something of a roller coaster for Iceland's 320,000 population. In a short space of time Iceland went from being one of the world's most expensive countries, to one of its most spectacularly bankrupt. Having once claimed high profile assets worth over 10 times Iceland's gross domestic product (GDP), the household names of Landsbanki, Kaupthing and Glitnir all rapidly imploded. Hubris abounded as the crisis dragged Iceland into bankruptcy in October 2008.

The aftermath

The ruling Samfylkingin (SF) (Social Democratic Alliance) managed to 'stabilise' the economy, although no-one was altogether sure what that implied. In a sense, Iceland was re-writing the economics textbooks. Unemployment reached record levels and Iceland's currency – the krona – was only saved by capital controls that tied in reluctant foreign investors for longer than they would have wished. Iceland's bailout package was described as exemplary by the International Monetary Fund (IMF) – hardly a surprise since the IMF had largely been the architect of the rescue plan – but policy mistakes, unwelcome tax rises and overt leniency toward foreign creditors made the Social Democrats unpopular. Despite this, in the 2009 elections the Social Democrats had still managed to gather enough votes to stay in power until 2013.

However, in the 2013 general election things turned out differently; when counting had been completed (not a massive task in a country where the electorate turnout –.at an impressive 81.44 per cent – is still less than 240,000) the Sjálfstæðisflokkurinn (SSF) (Independence Party) with 26.7 per cent had obtained the most votes, just ahead of the Framsóknarflokkurinn (FSF) (Progressive Party) with 24.43 per cent, pushing the Social Democrats into third place with only 12.85 per cent. This was the biggest defeat to any ruling party since independence from Denmark in 1944. Iceland's parliament, the Althing, claims to be the world's oldest parliamentary institution.

It looked as though a coalition of centre-right parties would form the new government, promising to end years of austerity and provide debt relief to households. and only arguing about which one of them should lead the government. In Iceland coalitions are usually formed in just days and commentators expressed the view that the new government would be no exception. It fell to Olafur Ragnar Grimsson Iceland's re-elected President to decide who he would ask to form the government. It was perhaps ironic that support for the Independence Party had grown despite the fact that many people blamed it for backing economic liberalisation and creating the cronyism that were seen by many as having led to the crisis. Sigmundur Davíð Gunnlaugsson became prime minister on 23 May 2013 after his centre-right Progressive Party and the conservative Independence Party of Bjarni Benediktsson had both won 19 seats in the 63-seat Althing. The two parties formed a coalition after the election, taking over power from the Social Democrats.

An Oxford-educated former journalist, Mr Gunnlaugsson belonged to a new breed of politicians who had emerged after the 2008 financial crisis and his elevation to the premiership marked a generational shift in the Icelandic government. His predecessor, Johanna Sigurdardottir, was 70 at the time of the election, while Mr Gunnlaugsson, aged 38 when he took office, became one of the youngest serving heads of government in the world.

Bye-bye Brussels

Iceland had first applied for EU membership in 2009 when the left of centre government was still recovering from the economic crisis that had seen the krona halve in value. Iceland's small economy was thought by many to need bolstering, specifically by membership of an apparently stable euro-zone. Iceland's final membership would eventually need to be ratified by parliament.

However, by 2015 the ruling coalition was made up of the conservative Independence Party and the agrarian Progressive Party and opinion polls were beginning to show a steady majority opposed to EU membership. So much so that in March the government announced that it was dropping Iceland's application for membership of the EU. The announcement lead to protests, not because of the withdrawal, but the fact that the coalition government had taken such a major decision without any public consultation. That membership was to be called off was in line with the manifesto promises made in 2013 by the new government; as was a promise to seek popular approval of whatever decision was reached. Some observers considered it premature to write off membership until the electorate had been able to see what had – or had not – been agreed and what were the sticking points. However, the government's decision to cease negotiations meant that it was unlikely that all would be revealed. The government's bald assertion that 'Iceland's interests are better served outside the European Union', certainly left a lot of questions unanswered. And of concern was the likelihood that on learning of the coalition's move, Brussels would remove Iceland's name from the list of aspirant countries, requiring it to recommence the whole lengthy process in the event of a change of policy.

Iceland's current membership of the European Economic Area (EEA) was in many respects considered a *de facto* EU membership, covering some 85 per cent of EU legislation. This allowed Iceland to export seafood to the EU tariff-free; it also boosted tourism, which was also a key foreign exchange earner. But what it did not do was to allow Iceland to take part in the discussions and negotiations on matters that might affect Iceland's interests. However, in EU membership terms, the tricky issue of fishing interests was the deal-breaker. The fishing industry's prosperity is essential to that of Iceland as a whole and it strangely seemed not to have been on the agenda in the EU discussions.

The decision, in April 2015, not to proceed with its membership of the European Union may have been popular with most of Iceland's electorate. But the manner in which the country's government decided to call a halt to its negotiations with Brussels certainly wasn't. The popular disaffection was considered by many to have been the cause for the rapid rise of the so called 'Pirate' Party, which – according to the opinion polls – had risen from obscurity to be Iceland's principal political movement. Its general voter support had risen from around 5 per cent in 2013 to almost 25 per cent according to newspaper reports.

The economy

By 2015 Iceland had managed to return from the chaos surrounding the demise of its overblown financial sector in 2008. Government figures showed that 2014 gross domestic product (GDP) growth reached a record 1.9 per cent, beating a GDP growth record dating back to pre-crisis levels according to Statistics Iceland. None the less, GDP per capita remained lower than in 2008, the year in which Iceland became the first Western European nation in 25 years to appeal to the IMF for help.

In its June 2015 Economic forecast summary the Paris-based Organisation for Economic Co-operation and Development (OECD) noted that Iceland's economy had entered its seventh year of economic growth, with a pick-up in private consumption and fixed investment and a boom in tourism. Large investments in energy-intensive projects and fiscal support for households were expected to sustain growth in 2015 and 2016. Inflationary pressures would, in the view of the OECD, mount as the labour market tightened. Fiscal policy had made significant progress in reducing government debt. The pace of fiscal consolidation was likely, in the view of the OECD, to slow in 2015, but debt would still fall further

KEY INDICATORS — Iceland

	Unit	2011	2012	2013	2014	**2015
Population	m	*0.33	0.32	0.32	*0.33	*0.33
Gross domestic product (GDP)	US$bn	14.00	13.58	15.33	*16.69	*17.81
GDP per capita	US$	43,088	42,482	47,630	*51,262	*54,331
GDP real growth	%	3.1	1.4	3.5	*1.8	*3.5
Inflation	%	4.0	5.2	3.9	*2.0	0.8
Unemployment	%	8.6	5.8	5.4	*5.0	*4.0
Exports (fob) (goods)	US$m	5,343.6	5,048.8	4,996.1	4,848.3	–
Imports (fob) (goods)	US$m	4,505.9	4,443.4	4,432.6	4,953.6	–
Balance of trade	US$m	837.7	605.4	563.5	-105.3	–
Current account	US$m	-972.8	-678.0	849.0	*789.0	*1,080.0
Total reserves minus gold	US$m	7,304.7	4,085.3	4,160.8	4,100.1	–
Foreign exchange	US$m	6,954.0	4,042.8	4,123.6	–	–
Exchange rate	per US$	115.19	125.83	115.62	127.49	–

* estimated figure ** forecast figure

under current plans. Containing public spending pressures will be important in maintaining an appropriate budgetary stance. With spare capacity disappearing, interest rates would need to rise as sizeable wage settlements unleashed inflationary pressures. Structural reforms were needed to enhance the investment environment.

The hair-cut...

Many observers had long felt that any realistic progress in lifting of capital controls would send a positive signal to investors. Thus, the government's plan to roll back the capital controls installed in 2008 was broadly welcomed. The controls objective had been to prevent capital leaving Iceland and further worsen the crisis. They had originally been introduced for only six months. The decision facing the Icelandic government had not been simple: the combined assets of Iceland's failed banks added up to some US$16.7 billion, 60 per cent or so held outside Iceland and almost 40 per cent held in Iceland itself. Under the deal proposed by the government, creditors were asked to relinquish, or give up (or take a 'hair cut') of an estimated US$6.8 billion in claims against the estates of the failed banks and of Icelandic residents. Having taken this 'hit', those creditors would be at liberty to move however much they liked from Iceland.

... and the IMF

In its June 2015 assessment of the Icelandic economy, the IMF took the view that Iceland's economy was 'facing two major challenges'. The first was the implementation of the new capital account liberalisation strategy (see Hair Cut above), aiming for full reintegration with global financial markets. The second challenge was the avoidance of significant wage increases that looked likely to disrupt Iceland's otherwise strong and stable economic position. The updated capital account liberalisation strategy, in the view of the IMF, took a staged approach, starting with steps to address the balance of payments (BOP) overhang of the old bank estates – prioritising a co-operative approach with incentives – in a manner consistent with maintaining stability. The next two stages were to address the remaining offshore liquid krona (OLK) holders, using an auction format. The final stage was dealing with Icelandic residents. If successfully implemented, the updated strategy would help speed up the pace of liberalisation.

The IMF noted that growth was accelerating in 2015 and was expected to reach 4.1 per cent, backed by significant investment, wage- and debt relief-fuelled consumption and booming tourism. Inflation in mid-2015 was low at 1.6 per cent – contained by imported deflation – but inflation expectations had picked up. Large wage rises were projected to push inflation well above the Central Bank of Iceland's (CBI) 2.5 per cent inflation target. The CBI's Monetary Policy Committee (MPC) raised its base interest rate by 50 basis points at its June 2015 meeting and signalled further possible raises in response to significant wage increases. Growth was expected to slow significantly in 2016–17 as efforts to dampen excess domestic demand and inflation pressures took hold. The CBI had stepped up its foreign exchange purchases in 2015.

Risks to growth were, in the view of the IMF, tilted to the downside, given the uncertainty of the impact of wage increases on the economy. Nonetheless, Iceland appeared ready to advance capital account liberalisation. The external current account balance – currently supported by favourable terms of trade – was projected to weaken but remain positive over the medium-term.

Several important financial sector reforms were under way, including draft legislation to further strengthen financial safety nets and the macro-prudential policy framework. Efforts to strengthen financial supervision capacity were continuing. Final agreement on the fate of the loss-making government-owned Housing Financing Fund was also pending.

Risk assessment

Economy	Fair
Politics	Fair
Regional stability	Good

COUNTRY PROFILE

Settled by Norwegians and Celtic (Scottish and Irish) immigrants during the late ninth and tenth centuries, Iceland boasts the world's oldest parliament, the Althingi. Iceland was under Norwegian, then Danish, rule from the thirteenth century. The severity of Iceland's terrain was frequently compounded by natural disasters leading, in the nineteenth century, to large-scale emigration to the USA and Canada. The island was granted its own constitution in the 1840s.

1903 Iceland was granted Home rule from Denmark.

1918 Iceland became a sovereign state in union with Denmark.

1940 Germany invaded Denmark. British troops were stationed in Iceland.

1944 Iceland terminated the convention linking it with Denmark and declared itself a republic.

1948 Iceland joined the International Whaling Commission (IWC).

1949 Iceland joined NATO and the Council of Europe. A large US airbase was established at Keflavík.

1953 Iceland became a founding member of the Nordic Council.

1959–71 The Coalition of Independence and Social Democratic Parties remained in power.

1960s–70s Iceland's unilateral extensions of its territorial waters to protect its fishing grounds led to the 'Cod Wars' with the UK, and in 1976, caused a temporary break in diplomatic relations, the first such break between NATO members.

1980 Vigdís Finnbogadóttir was elected president, the world's first popularly elected female head of state.

1985 Iceland was declared a nuclear-free zone, barring entry to all nuclear weapons.

1987 Thorsteinn Pálsson was appointed prime minister.

1991 Iceland quit the IWC after the organisation refused to consider Icelandic proposals for moderate catch quotas.

1996 Ólafur Ragnar Grímsson was elected president.

1999 The elections again returned a centre-right coalition of Sjálfstaeðisflokkurinn (SSF) (Independence Party) and Framsóknarflokkurinn (FSF) (Progressive Party).

2000 Ólafur Ragnar Grímsson was re-elected president unopposed.

2002 Iceland's bid to rejoin the IWC, without signing up to the moratorium on commercial whaling, was rejected.

2003 Prime Minister Oddsson's SSF won the parliamentary elections.

2004 Incumbent Ólafur Ragnar Grímsson was re-elected in the presidential elections. Halldór Ásgrímsson (FSF) became prime minister.

2005 The government granted Icelandic citizenship to Bobby Fischer, the chess grandmaster and US fugitive of 10 years, he died later in 2008.

2006 Halldór Ásgrímsson resigned as prime minister and Geir Haarde (SSF) replaced him. The US closed its naval base at Keflavík.

2007 In general elections, the SSF retained power.

2008 President Grímsson was re-elected unopposed. Following the collapse of Iceland's largest bank, Landsbanki, the UK government made available a loan of £100 million (US$174 million) to help repay the bank's UK creditors. The Sedlabanki (central bank) rate was raised to 18 per cent from 12 per cent in a move to stave off the collapse of Iceland's banking system. Iceland came under IMF administration.

2009 The central bank rate was raised to a record high of 21 per cent. Prime Minister Haarde resigned, following the collapse of the coalition government. The president called on the Samfylkingin (Social Democratic Alliance) (SDA) and VG to form a minority coalition, interim government. Jóhanna Sigurðardóttir (SDA) became prime minister and was endorsed into office following early parliamentary elections. Iceland formally applied for European Union membership. Moody's Investors Service cut Iceland's credit rating to the lowest investment grade. In one year, a record 5,027 babies were born in Iceland.

2010 The Eyjafjallajökull volcano erupted; volcanic ash thrown up into the atmosphere as high as 20,000 feet caused the shutdown of air traffic in 11 western and northern European countries, leading to severe disruption of passengers and cargo. Former directors of the bankrupt bank Glitnir, including Jón Ásgeir Jóhannesson, a retail magnate, were sued for US$2 billion in a US lawsuit, accused of a 'sweeping conspiracy' and draining cash from its assets. The lawsuit followed a year of forensic accountancy of the bank's books that supported the allegation of robbery 'from the inside'. The central bank interest rate was cut to 7 per cent, as inflation fell and the currency strengthened.

2011 In February the President announced that a referendum would be held on the latest plan to repay the Dutch and UK governments the US$4 billion lost in 2009 when the Icesave Bank collapsed. Parliament voted to accept the plan, but narrowly voted against a referendum. President Grimmson was against the repayment plan and refused to sign the deal, thereby triggering the April referendum. The government lost the referendum by a vote of 59.77 to 40.22; turnout was 75.34. The Dutch and UK governments said they would go to court to recover the lost US$4 billion.

2012 On 5 March, the trial of former prime minister Geir Haarde began. He was charged with failing to prevent the 2008 banking crisis and of failing his ministerial duties of managing the repercussions of the collapse of the Icelandic economy while he was in charge of the country. On 23 April, Haarde was found not guilty on three major charges of negligence. He was found guilty of a lesser crime, which does not carry a prison sentence, of not holding a dedicated cabinet meeting before the collapse. All legal expenses incurred by Haarde were paid for by the state. A presidential election was held on 30 June, in which six candidates took part. Ólafur Ragnar Grímsson was re-elected for a fifth consecutive term, with 52.78 per cent of the vote and Thóra Arnórsdóttir 33.16 per cent; turnout was 69.2 per cent. On 20 October, a constitutional referendum was held, with six proposals, including provisions for drafting a new constitution; declaring all non-privately owned natural resources to be national property; and allowing a referendum to be held providing a certain proportion of the electorate demands it. All six propositions were agreed.

2013 Elections were held on 27 April in which the ruling party lost to Sjálfstæðisflokkurinn (SSF) (Independence Party) with 26.7 per cent of the vote (19 seats out of 63) and Framsóknarflokkurinn (FSF) (Progressive Party) 24.43 per cent (also 19). Other successful parties were Samfylkingin (SF) (Social Democratic Alliance) 12.85 per cent (9); Vinstrihreyfingin – grænt framboð (VG) (Left-Green Movement) 10.87 per cent (7); Björt framtíð (Bright Future) 8.25 per cent (6); Píratar Pirate Party) 5.10 per cent (3). Nine other parties failed to win enough votes to secure any seats. Turnout was 81.44 per cent. A coalition government was formed between the SSF and the FSF. Sigmundur Davíð Gunnlaugsson (FSF) became prime minister. In October the Sedlabanki Íslands (Central Bank of Iceland) said the country was in danger of running out of foreign exchange to pay its debts.

2014 A free trade agreement (FTA) between Iceland and China came into force on 1 July. Icelandic companies believe the FTA will lower consumer prices in Iceland and boost the trade between the countries.

2015 In March the government announced that it was withdrawing Iceland's application for membership gto the EU.

Political structure

Constitution

The constitution was adopted 17 June 1944.

The parliament and office of president jointly exercise legislative power, with due adherence to the constitution. The judiciary is guaranteed independence.

Elections are by proportional representation with universal direct suffrage over the age of 18.

The constitution recognises the Evangelical Lutheran Church as the state church.

Independence date

17 June 1944

Form of state

Parliamentary democratic republic

The executive

Executive power is vested jointly in the offices of the president as Head of State, directly elected for a four-year term, and the prime minister as head of government (appointed by the president); the prime minister appoints a cabinet, which is approved by parliament).

Any citizen aged over 35 may become president, by popular vote (if more than one candidate stands for the post; without a challenge a candidate is duly elected without a vote).

National legislature

The unicameral Althingi (parliament) has 63 members elected for a four-year term, by a two-tier proportional representation system. Six constituencies each elect nine members (54), based on party lists with rankings that may be changed or candidates rejected; the remaining nine members are allocated as weighting seats (one for each constituency) equalising all votes for a party, which ensure total national votes reflect the number of seats gained by a political party.

Legislative power is held jointly by the president and the Althingi.

Legal system

The legal system is based on the 1944 constitution; the civil law system is based on Danish law.

Last elections

30 June 2012 (presidential); 2013 (parliamentary).

Results: 27 April 2013 (parliamentary): Sjálfstæðisflokkurinn (SSF) (Independence Party) 26.7 per cent of the vote (19 seats out of 63); Framsóknarflokkurinn (FSF) (Progressive Party) 24.43 per cent (19); Samfylkingin (SF) (Social Democratic Alliance) 12.85 per cent (9); Vinstrihreyfingin – grænt framboð (VG) (Left-Green Movement) 10.87 per cent (7); Björt framtíð (Bright Future) 8.25 per cent (6); Píratar Pirate Party) 5.10 per cent (3). Nine other parties failed to win enough votes to secure any seats. Turnout was 81.44 per cent.

Presidential: Ólafur Ragnar Grímsson won 52.78 per cent of the vote, Thóra Arnórsdóttir 33.16 per cent, Ari Trausti Guðmundsson 8.64 per cent; three other candidates each won less than 3 per cent. Turnout was 69.2 per cent.

Next elections

2016 (presidential); 2017 (parliamentary)

Political parties

Ruling party

Coalition of Sjálfstæðisflokkurinn (SSF) (Independence Party) and Framsóknarflokkurinn (FSF) (Progressive Party) (elected 27 Apr 2013)

Main opposition party

Framsóknarflokkurinn (FSF) (Progressive Party)

Population
327,000 (2012)*
Last census: July 2000: 281,154
Population density: 2.7 inhabitants per square km. Urban population 93 per cent (2010 Unicef).
Annual growth rate: 1.1 per cent, 1990–2010 (Unicef).

Ethnic make-up
Almost the entire population are descendants of Norwegians and Celts.

Religions
Lutherans (96 per cent), Protestants and Catholics (3 per cent).

Education
Pre-schooling is offered to children aged between one and six years when compulsory primary education begins. This leads into lower secondary school until aged 16 when students choose upper secondary education – either academic grammar or comprehensive schooling or vocational industrial or specialised training. Upper secondary education covers four years and is open to anyone who has completed compulsory school. Grammar and comprehensive attainment leads to higher education facilities at age 20.
Icelandic municipalities are responsible for delivering education in different regions.
There are eight higher education institutions in Iceland, most of which are run by the state and require no tuition fees. Private parties with state support run three institutions that charge tuition fees. About 16 per cent of Icelandic students in higher education study abroad.
The total public expenditure in education is typically 5—6 per cent of GDP.
Compulsory years: Six to 16.
Enrolment rate: 99 per cent net primary enrolment; 85.3 per cent net secondary enrolment (World Bank 2003).

Health
The country is divided into health care regions, each with their own primary health care centres, some of which are run jointly with the local community hospital; hospitalisation is free of charge. The number of Icelandic physicians has increased steadily during the last decade.

HIV/Aids
HIV prevalence: 0.2 per cent aged 15–49 in 2003 (World Bank)
Life expectancy: 81 years, 2004 (WHO 2006)
Fertility rate/Maternal mortality rate: 2.1 births per woman, 2010 (Unicef)
Child (under 5 years) mortality rate (per 1,000): 2 per 1,000 live births (WHO 2012)
Head of population per physician: 3.62 physicians per 1,000 people, 2004 (WHO 2006)

Welfare
Iceland follows the Nordic social security system, which aims to provide universal social welfare and health services.
The social security system covers pension, occupational injury, health and maternity insurance. Most pensions are covered by private pension funds. There is generous coverage for maternity leave for both men and women.
Special attention has been given to women's employment and special grants have been provided to women for running businesses.

Main cities
Reykjavík (capital, estimated population 119,474 in 2012), Kópavogur (33,045), Hafnarfjörður (28,085), Akureyri (17,770), Garðabær (11,420).

Languages spoken
The Icelandic language belongs to the North Germanic branch of the Indo-European family.

Official language/s
Icelandic

Media
The constitution guarantees freedom of the press.

Press
Dailies: In Icelandic popular newspapers include *Morgunbladid* (www.mbl.is), *Frettabladid* (www.visir.is), *DV* (www.dv.is) is an evening newspaper.
Weeklies: In Icelandic, regional newspapers include *FréttirWO (www.sudurlandid.is/Eyjafrettir) from Sudland, Vikurfrettir* (www.vf.is), from Sudurnes, *Tidis* (www.patreksfjordur.is), from Vestfirdir and *Skessuhorn* (www.skessuhorn.is) from Vesturland. *Sed og Heyrt* is a tabloid magazine.
Business: In Icelandic, *Viðskiptablaðið* (www.vb.is), is a daily, *Markadurinn* (http://vefmidlar.visir.is), is published weekly. Marine industry publications include *Aegir* and *Fiskifrettir*.
Periodicals: In Icelandic, the monthly *Mannlíf* (www.mannlif.is) covers news and current affairs and for women, *Birtíngur* (www.birtingur.is) is published 10 times a year.

Broadcasting
The Ríkisútvarpið (RÚV) (Icelandic National Broadcasting Service) is the public network providing services from a number of regional centres.
Radio: RÚV (www.ruv.is) operates two radio stations Rás 1 and Rás 2. The largest private commercial radio network is Bylgjan (http://lettbylgjan.is).
Television: Sjónvarpið/RÚV (www.ruv.is) operates the national television service and locally producing Icelandic language shows as well as transmitting imported TV shows. It transmits for around eight hours per day during the week and 16 hours per day during the weekend. Private commercial TV stations includes Stöð 2 (www.stod2.visir.is) with five channels and Skjárinn (http://skjarinn.is) with three channels.

Economy
The banking sector was privatised in 2003, from which time the banks increased their assets from just over 100 per cent of GDP to more than 1,000 per cent of GDP in 2008, with banks taking ever higher risks, outstripping the government's ability to act as lender of last resort. As the global crisis struck in 2008, investors quickly withdrew their funds and three banks failed, causing a crash of the Icelandic krona, which fell in value by over 70 per cent. The stock market lost 80 per cent of its value. Effectively the country was left bankrupt. GDP growth fell from a healthy 6 per cent in 2007, slowing to 1.3 per cent in 2008 before plunging into a recession of -6.8 per cent in 2009. Although the situation remained serious in 2010, the recession slowed to -4.0 per cent. In 2011, GDP growth rose to 3.1 per cent before steadily falling to 2.9 per cent in 2013 and further to 1.9 per cent in 2014. Iceland crashed from an economy with one of the highest GDP per capita rates in Europe of US$64,833 in 2007, to US$55,462 in 2008 and further still to US$37,853 in 2009; there has been a rise following this and per capita income reached US$52,111 in 2014 as the situation improved.
Unemployment had begun rising shortly after the economy floundered in 2008, so that in 2009 around 1 per cent of the workforce (2,000 people), were unemployed; by 2010, 8 per cent (16,000 people) were unemployed. However, the situation has improved and by mid-2015 unemployment was at 4.3 per cent.
The International Monetary Fund (IMF) approved an initial emergency financing loan of US$2.1 billion in 2008; the two-year Stand-By Arrangement was used to stabilise the krona as successive governments set about making swingeing cuts to public spending. The government, which had come to power in early 2009, quickly recapitalised two of the three largest failed domestic banks and introduced tighter banking regulations. Moody's Investors Service cut Iceland's credit rating to the lowest investment grade in November 2009. The interest rate was cut to 7 per cent on 18 August 2010, as inflation fell and the currency strengthened. The interest rate was dropped further in 2011 to just over 4 per cent before being raised to 6 per cent in 2013 and further to 6.2 in August 2015.

Iceland's non-financial economy is an open market economy based largely on fishing (although cod stocks are falling), tourism (expanding fast) and aluminium smelting (based on abundant geothermal power and water). The fishing industry typically makes up around 31 per cent of exports and contributes 10 per cent of GDP. However, with the level of cod catches falling there has been a knock-on effect for the processing industry. The large fish processing company, Samherji, now has its operations in Grimsby (UK), rather than Dalvík. When the move was made in 2006 it took advantage of lower UK wages (30–40 per cent less), and also lower transport costs; however, by 2009 unemployment had become higher and wages lower in Iceland than in the UK which was still the case in 2014.

The Alcoa Fjardaál aluminium smelting plant started operations in 2007. At full production it smelts up to 320,000 tonnes per year (tpy). In May 2012, plans were announced to enlarge the facility to increase production to 370,000tpy expected to be operational by 2018, with investment of US$95 million. In 2014 raw aluminium exports represented 32 per cent of total exports.

External trade

Iceland is a member of the European Economic Area (EEA), which maintains an internal market with, although not actually joining, the EU. The EU consults EEA members before making its decisions on community legislation. The EEA agreement allows freedom of movement of goods (excluding, to a significant degree, agriculture and fisheries), persons, services and capital.

In an attempt to move away from primary industries, which are subject to world prices and dwindling stocks, Iceland has developed interests in software production and biotechnology.

Imports

Principal imports include capital goods, vehicles, consumer goods, petroleum, foodstuffs and clothing.

Main sources: Norway (14.6 per cent of total in 2014), US (10.1 per cent), Germany (7.6 per cent)

Exports

Principal imports include raw aluminium and other minerals – ferrosilicon and diatomite, fish and marine products, manufactured goods.

Main destinations: The Netherlands (29.3 per cent of total in 2014), UK (11.3 per cent), Spain (7.6 per cent)

Agriculture

Farming

Some 20 per cent of Iceland's land area is suitable for the raising of livestock and for fodder production. Only 6 per cent of the area is used for the cultivation of, principally, hay and potatoes.

Arable land is scarce, but good grazing allows for self-sufficiency in meat (mostly lamb), milk, poultry, eggs, cheese and butter.

The sector is small-scale, heavily subsidised and organised into co-operatives. High import tariffs protect domestic production from foreign competition.

Fishing

Fishing replaced farming early in this century as the dominant sector of the economy. The fishing industry (including processing) is the second most important export earner, accounting for 31 per cent of Iceland's exports. The large modernised trawler fleet supplies over 110 freezing plants, which produce white fish fillets, frozen shrimps, capelin, scampi, scallops, fish oil and fish meal.

The Icelandic Freezing Plants Corporation and Iceland Seafood Ltd are the leading fish exporters.

There is rapid growth of inland and offshore fish farming.

Industry and manufacturing

The industrial sector contributes 22.9 per cent to GDP and employs 18 per cent of the workforce.

It is centred on fish and food processing. A salmon fish processing plant on Iceland's east coast is the first to use state-of-the-art technology to process salmon for export to the EU and US.

Other major industrial activity focuses on aluminium smelting, ferro-silicon alloys, diatomite production and light manufacturing. The demands of the fishing industry have lead to developments in the country's computer, software and electronics industries and have also encouraged developments in biotechnology and pharmaceuticals.

With abundant hydroelectric and geothermal power, Iceland has led to power-intensive industries, the largest of which is aluminium smelting. In June 2007 the US-owned Alcoa smelter opened in eastern Iceland, with a capacity of 320,000 tonnes per year (tpy) when fully operational. In May 2012, plans were announced to enlarge the facility to increase production to 550,000tpy, with investment of US$95 million.

Tourism

The 'land of ice and fire' has become Iceland's apt description. To any visitor, it offers spectacular natural sites of hot springs and volcanoes, plus the Blue Lagoon geothermal spa resort that offers outside hot baths even in the depths of winter. The chance to see the *aurora borealis* (northern lights) is now included in advertising campaigns, as are Arctic pursuits and winter sports such as dog-sledging and cross-country skiing.

Iceland suffered a catastrophic economic collapse in 2008 and since then travel and tourism has become a more important component of GDP. The tourism sector represented 23.3 per cent of GDP in 2014, rising from 14.3 per cent in 2007; the revenue from tourism in 2007 was US$2.9 billion, whereas in 2014 revenue was US$3.5 billion. Employment in tourism in 2007 was 14.5 per cent of total (25,700 jobs), which rose to 23.7 per cent (42,000 jobs) in 2014. The share of capital investment in the tourist industry was 19.7 per cent in 2014.

With the expansion of airline destinations into Iceland and the depreciation of the krona, Iceland has become an attractive location to visit for tourists. Many come from the United States.

Hydrocarbons

Iceland does not produce any hydrocarbons. Exploration of offshore sites proved unsuccessful. Imports of petroleum products are around 20,000 barrels per day every year.

No natural gas is imported.

Around 150,000 tonnes of coal is imported for electricity generation.

The government is committed to replacing as much as possible of the country's imported fossil fuels with renewable energy sources, so the consumption of oil and coal is likely to decrease as this industry grows.

Energy

Total installed generating capacity is around 2.6 gigawatts (GW) with production around 17.2 billion kilowatt hours. The energy is produced in 11 hydroelectric stations, 63 geothermal stations and two oil fired-powered stations. Hydro-power produces around 90 per cent of all electricity whilst geothermal power produces 6 per cent. Imported hydrocarbons are still used for spare power generation in emergencies.

Iceland is not only self-sufficient in energy requirements but has the potential to be a major exporter of electricity. It is estimated that only 12 per cent of Iceland's energy potential has been harnessed. Iceland aims to become the first fossil-fuel free economy by 2020 and plans to develop a fully hydrogen-powered transport system by 2035; new technology in hydrogen-fuelled buses began trials in 2000. Around 85 per cent of homes have geothermal heating. Despite so little dependence on fossil fuels, the fishing fleet still requires imported oil.

Landsvirkjun is the national electricity company, responsible for production, transmission and sale of electricity to commercial and domestic customers.

Financial markets

Stock exchange

ICEX (Kauphöll Íslands) (Iceland Stock Exchange)

Banking and insurance

In addition to the central bank, there are four commercial banks operating: the Búnadarbanki Íslands (Agricultural Bank), Icebank Ltd, Islandsbanki Ltd and Landsbanki Íslands (National Bank of Iceland) are privately owned.

Kaupthing, an investment bank, and the Búnadarbanki merged in May 2003 to form the Kaupthing Búnadarbanki.

Central bank

Sedlabanki Íslands (Central Bank of Iceland)

Time

GMT

Geography

Iceland comprises one large island, with an area of 103,000 square km, and numerous smaller ones, situated near the Arctic Circle in the North Atlantic Ocean. The main island lies about 300km (190 miles) south-east of Greenland, about 1,000km (620 miles) west of Norway and about 800km (500 miles) north of Scotland. The Gulf Stream keeps Iceland warmer than might be expected.

A geologically young island, Iceland is volcanically and geothermally active. The largest volcanoes are Hekla and Snaefellsness. The terrain has a rugged aspect. As much as half of it is mountainous lava desert and wasteland. The central highlands are barren and interspersed with mountains and glaciers. 11 per cent of Iceland is covered by glaciers. The most extensive glacier, located in the south-east of the island, is Vatnajökull, which covers an area of 8,500 square km. The highest point in Iceland, Hvannadalshnúkur, which rises to 2,119m, is in this region. There are numerous lakes and fast-flowing, unnavigable rivers, some of which rise in the glaciers, while others are spring-fed.

The coastline is irregular, with bays and fjords, affording good natural harbours, though some parts are sandy with lagoons. The populated areas are are restricted to less than a fifth of the land, around the coasts and in the valleys, especially in the Reykjavik area.

The largest islands are the Westmann Isles to the south, Hrísey to the north and Grímsey in the Arctic Circle.

Hemisphere

Northern.

Climate

Temperate, with mild but stormy winters and cool summers. Rainy in the south. Average temperatures vary between about minus 1 and 12 degrees Celsius.

Dress codes

Medium-weight throughout year, plus a topcoat and raincoat for winter.

Entry requirements

Passports

Required by all, except nationals of Nordic and Schengen Accord countries. Passports must be valid three months after date of departure.

Visa

Required by all, except nationals of EU/EEA and other European countries, North America, Australasia and some Latin American and Asian countries. For a full list of exceptions visit: www.utl.is/english. A Schengen visa application (offered in several languages) can be downloaded from http://europa.eu/abc/travel/ see 'documents you will need'.

Currency advice/regulations

There are no restrictions on the import and export of local and foreign currency.

Customs

Visitors may bring in personal effects and limited quantities of tobacco products and alcohol free of duty. Fishing and riding equipment must be accompanied by a certificate of disinfection issued by an authorised veterinary authority.

Health (for visitors)

Nationals of the European Economic Area (EEA) countries and Switzerland can access reduced cost and sometimes free medical treatment using a European Health Insurance Card (EHIC) while visiting the EEA. Exceptions include nationals of the 10 countries which joined the EU in 2005 whose EHIC is not valid in Switzerland. Applications for the EHIC should be made before travelling.

Mandatory precautions

There are no compulsory vaccinations.

Advisable precautions

Travellers should have up-to-date tetanus and polio immunisations.

Hotels

Most towns have hotels and guest houses. Between June and September university hostels and boarding schools are also used as hotels. Some hostels and many farms provide bed and breakfast service. The rating system is one-star (basic) to five -star (luxury). Tipping is not customary.

Credit cards

All major credit cards, such as American Express, Diners', Eurocard, Visa and Master Card, are accepted.

Public holidays (national)

Fixed dates

1 Jan (New Year's Day), 1 May (Labour Day), 17 Jun (National Day), 24 Dec (Christmas Eve, from mid-day), 25 Dec (Christmas Day), 26 Dec (Boxing Day), New Year's Eve (from mid-day).

Variable dates

Maundy Thursday, Good Friday, Easter Monday, First Day of Summer, Ascension Day, Whit Monday, Commerce Day (first Mon in Aug).

Working hours

Banking

Mon–Fri: 0915–1600 (winter), 0800–1600 (summer), plus 1700–1800 on Thu (Co-operative Bank, National Bank, Agricultural Bank (Kringlam).

Business

Mon–Fri: usually 0900–1700.

Government

Mon–Fri: usually 0900–1700.

Shops

Mon–Fri: 1000–1800. Most also open Sat 1000–1400/1600 (winter only, Oct to end May). Kiosks remain open until 2330 or even later.

Telecommunications

Mobile/cell phones

GSM 900/1800 services are available in populated areas.

Electricity supply

220V AC

Social customs/useful tips

Icelanders are generally self-confident, self-reliant and reserved. However, once the initial contact has been made people are more than likely to be friendly. Handshaking is customary on arrival and departure.

Getting there

Air

National airline: Icelandair

International airport/s: Keflavík International Airport (KEF), 51km south-west of Reykjavík; bank, restaraunts, shops, car hire.

Airport tax: A security fee of Ikr620 (Ikr285 for children two to 12 years of age) is charged on departure.

Surface

Water: There are ferry services to Iceland from Denmark, Norway and the Shetland Isles.

Getting about

National transport

Air: Air Iceland and Landsflug operate domestic services throughout the island to destinations which link with regional carriers in the west, north and east of the country. Light aircraft readily available for charter and sightseeing.

Road: There are approximately 1,350km of roads. Main highways (approximately one quarter of total) follow the coastline and are hard-surfaced; the rest are gravel-surfaced. Regular coach services link even the remote inland areas.

Water: Regular cargo coastal services link all major ports. Passenger and car ferries sail several times a day between

Reykjavík and Akranes and between Thorlakshöta and Vestmannaeyian.

City transport

Taxis: These are used extensively and usually summoned by telephone, although they can be hailed in the street. The journey time from the airport to the city centre is about 40 minutes.

Buses, trams & metro: There are excellent regular services covering the centre and suburbs of Reykjavík. There is a standard fare for any length of journey, even if it involves more than one bus route. Journey time from the airport to the city centre is about 45 minutes.

Car hire

Car hire is available in Reykjavík and several other towns. Rates vary depending on the type of car. Minimum age 20 years, and an international driving licence is usually required. Advance reservations are necessary between June and August. Self-drive cars not recommended as a method of national transport as road surfaces tend to be poor.

BUSINESS DIRECTORY

The addresses listed below are a selection only. While World of Information makes every endeavour to check these addresses, we cannot guarantee that changes have not been made, especially to telephone numbers and area codes. We would welcome any corrections.

Telephone area codes

The international direct dialling code (IDD) for Iceland is +354, followed by subscriber's number.

Chambers of Commerce

Iceland Chamber of Commerce, House of Commerce, Kringlan 7, 103 Reykjavík (tel: 510-7100; fax: 568-6564; e-mail: info@chamber.is).

Banking

Kaupthing Búnadarbanki, Austurstraeti 3, 101 Reykjavík (tel: 525-6000; fax: 525-6209).

Íslandsbanki (Bank of Iceland), Kringlunni, 155 Reykjavík (tel: 560-8000; fax: 560-8150).

Landsbanki Íslands (National Bank of Iceland), Laugavegur 77, 155 Reykjavík (tel: 560-6400; fax: 552-9882; internet site: http://www.landsbanki.is).

Central bank

Sedlabanki Íslands, Kalkofnsvegi 1, 150 Reykjavík (tel: 569-9600; fax: 569-9605; e-mail: sedlabanki@sedlabanki.is).

Stock exchange

ICEX (Kauphöll Íslands) (Iceland Stock Exchange), www.omxnordicexchange.com

Travel information

Airport Authority, Leifur Eiriksson Passenger Terminal, Keflavík Airport, 235 Keflavík.

BSI Travel (buses), Umferdarmidstödin v/Hringbraut, 101 Reykjavík.

Icelandair (Flugleidir), Reykjavík Airport, Reykjavík IS-101 (tel: 505-0200; fax: 505-0300; internet site: http://www.icelandair.com).

National tourist organisation offices

Icelandic Tourist Board, Laekjargotu 3, 101 Reykjavík (tel: 535-5500; fax: 535-5501; e-mail:info@icetourist.is).

Ministries

Ministry of Agriculture, 4th Floor, Sölvhólsgötu 7, 150 Reykjavík (tel: 560-9750; fax: 552-1160).

Ministry of Commerce and Industry, Arnarhváli, 150 Reykjavík (tel: 560-9070, 560-9420; fax: 562-1289).

Ministry of Communication, Hafnarhúsinu vio Tryggvagötu, 150 Reykjavík (tel: 560-9630; fax: 562-1702).

Ministry of Culture and Education, Sölvhólsgötu 4, 150 Reykjavík (tel: 560-9504; fax: 562-3068).

Ministry of the Environment, Vonarstraeti 4, 150 Reykjavík (tel: 560-9600; fax: 562-4566).

Ministry of Finance, Arnarhválli, 150 Reykjavík (tel: 560-9200; fax: 562-8280).

Ministry of Fisheries, Skúlagötu 4, 150 Reykjavík (tel: 560-9670; fax: 562-1853).

Ministry for Foreign Affairs, Rauoarásti\01g 25, 150 Reykjavík (tel: 560-9900; fax: 562-2373, 562-2386).

Ministry for Foreign Affairs, Trade Department, Hverfisgata 115, 105 Reykjavík (tel: 560-9930; fax: 562-4878).

Ministry of Health and Social Security, Laugavegi 116, 150 Reykjavík (tel: 560-9700; fax: 551-9165).

Ministry of Industry, Arnarhváli, 150 Reykjavík (tel: 560-9420; fax: 562-6859).

Ministry of Justice, Arnarhváli, 150 Reykjavík (tel: 560-9010; fax: 552-7340).

Ministry of Social Affairs, Hafnarhúsinu vio Tryggvagötu, 150 Reykjavík (tel: 560-9100; fax: 552-4804).

Office of the Prime Minister (Stjórnarráoshúsinu vio Laekjargötu), 150 Reykjavík (tel: 560-9400, 560-9403; fax: 562-4014, 562-8626).

Other useful addresses

Association of Icelandic Importers, Exporters & Wholesale Merchants, (Félag Íslands Storkaupmanna), Húsi verslunarinnar, 103 Reykjavík (tel: 567-8910; fax: 468-8441).

British Embassy, Laufásvegur 31, PO Box 460, 101 Reykjavík (tel: 550-5100; fax: 550-5105; e-mail: britemb@centrum.is).

Customs Department, Tolhusid, Tryggvagata 19, 150 Reykjavík (tel: 560-0300; fax: 562-5826).

Embassy of the United States of America, Laufásvegur 21, Reykjavík (tel: 629-100; fax: 29-139).

Export Council of Iceland, Lagmuli 5, Box 8796, 129 Reykjavík (tel: 568-8777; fax: 568-9197).

Federation of Icelandic Co-operative Societies (Samband of Iceland), Import Division, v/Holtavegur, 104 Reykjavík (tel: 568-1266; fax: 568-0290).

Icelandic Embassy (USA), Suite 1200, 1156 15th Street, NW, Washington DC 20005 (tel: (+1-202)-265-6653; fax: (+1-202)-265-6656; e-mail: icemb.wash@utn.stjr.is).

Icelandic Energy Marketing Agency, Haaleitisbraut 68, 103 Reykjavík (tel: 515-9000; fax: 515-9003; e-mail: landsvirkjun@lv.is).

Iceland Management Association, Ananaust 15, 121 Reykjavík (tel: 562-1066).

Invest in Iceland Bureau (privatisation and foreign investment), Hallveigarstigur 1, PO Box 1000, IS-121 Reykjavík (tel: 511-4000; fax: 511-4040; internet site: http://www.invest.is/us/index.htm; e-mail: Invest@icetrade.is).

National Economic Institute (for information on economic development corporations), Thjodhagsstofnun, Kalkofnsvegi 1, Reykjavík (tel: 569-9500; fax: 562-6540).

Retailers' Association of Iceland, Hus Verslunarinnar, Kringlan 7, 103 Reykjavík (tel: 568-7811; fax: 568-5569).

Samband islenskra auglysingastofa (Association of Icelandic Advertising Companies), Borgartún 35, 105 Reykjavík (tel: 562-9588; internet: www.sia.is/SIA/English).

Statistical Bureau in Iceland, Hagstofa Íslands, Skuggasund 3, 150 Reykjavík (tel: 560-9800; fax: 562-8865; internet site: http://www.statice.is/).

Internet sites

Iceland Reporter: www.centrum.is/icerev

Iceland websites: www.iceland.vefur.is

The Trade Council of Iceland: www.icetrade.is

India

KEY FACTS

Official name: Republic of India (Bharat Ganarajya from Sanskrit)

Head of State: President Pranab Kumar Mukherjee (Congress) (from 25 Jul 2012)

Head of government: Prime Minister Narendra Modi (BJP) (from 16 May 2014)

Ruling party: Bharatiya Janata Party (BJP) (from 16 May 2014)

Area: 3,287,590 square km

Population: 1.26 billion (2014)*

Capital: New Delhi

Official language: Hindi and English; 15 other languages are recognised for official use in regional areas.

Currency: Rupee (Rs) = 100 paisa

Exchange rate: Rs66.55 per US$ (Sep 2015)

GDP per capita: US$1,627 (2014)*

GDP real growth: 7.17% (2014)

GDP: US$2,049.50 billion (2014)

Inflation: 5.99% (2014)

Oil production: 895,000 bpd (2014)

Natural gas production: 31.70 billion cum (2014)

Balance of trade: -US$75.49 billion (2014)

Annual FDI: US$32.19 billion (2011)

* estimated figure

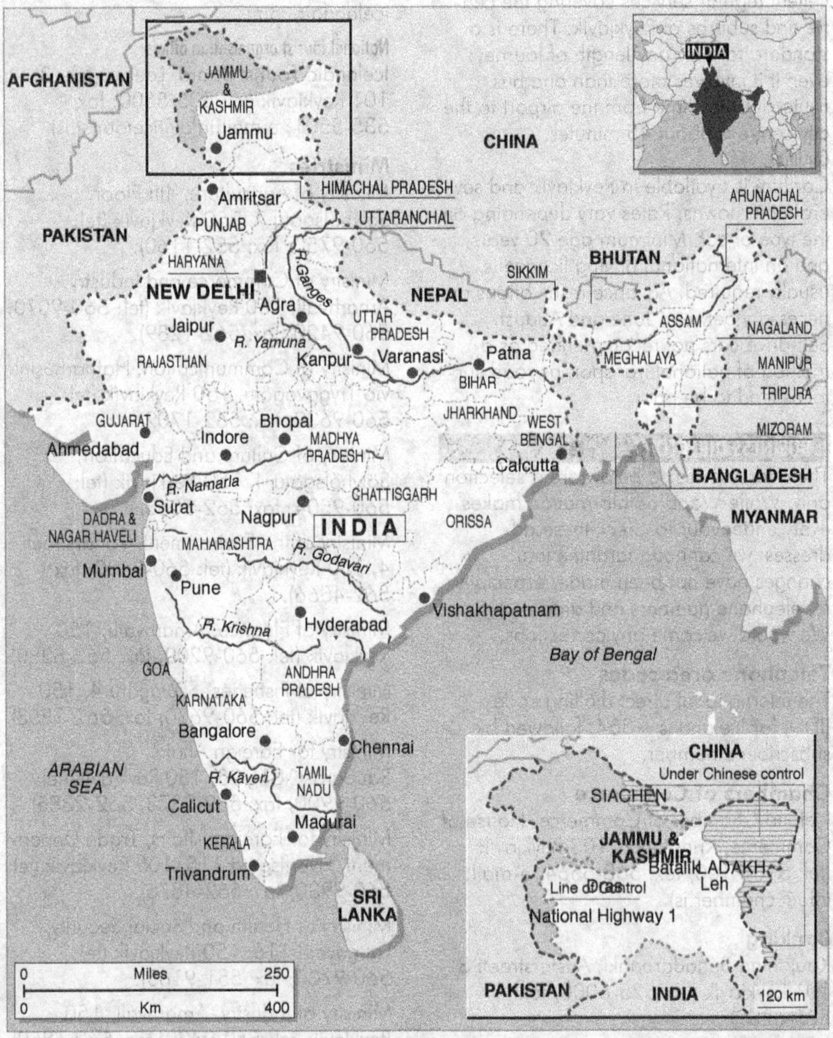

India had expressed two major preoccupations when voting for Prime Minister Narenda Modi in 2014, they were the revitalisation of the economy and a tightening up of India's regional role and its relationships with its neighbours. It was not long before the obvious comparisons with Japan's prime minister, Shinzo Abe were made. Both men confronted similar problems, particularly in their countries' relationships with China. Mr Modi also represented a new generation of political power in India. Like his Japanese counterpart, he was the first prime minister to have been born after India's independence in 1947. Contemporaries they may be, but Mr Modi's background could hardly have been more different from that of Mr Abe, whose grandfather and great-grandfather had both been prime minister, and his father minister of foreign affairs.

Possibly spotting an opportunity as relations between India and the US cooled (see below) Japan leant over backwards to encourage trade between the two countries. As prime minister in Gujarat Mr Modi paid two visits to Japan, in 2007 and 2012, happily inviting Japanese companies to set up shop in Gujarat. A by-product of these visits was the warm relationship that had grown up between Messrs Modi and Abe.

India awakening

A year after his election victory, there was cause for concern. On being elected, Mr Modi (not one for modesty or humility) had boldly stated that 'Ten years is all that is needed' to sort out India's many problems. After a year some Indians were wondering if Mr Modi himself might turn out to be the problem rather than the solution. Mr Modi had never been a Delhi 'insider'. His approach to running a country with a population approaching 1.3 billion was inevitably based on and formed by, his years of running Gujarat (population 62.7 million). Mr Modi was not a natural delegator, preferring to accumulate power around the office of prime minster. Nowhere was this more apparent than in the vital sphere of the economy. Modi's appointment as finance minister, Arun Jaitley, may be a perfectly competent minister, but the February 2015 budget was reportedly drawn up in some detail by the prime minister himself.

Mr Modi had also taken it upon himself to impart a new direction to India's foreign relations at a time when China, Asia's other population giant, was asserting itself to the extent of replacing India in its own backyard. Nepal, Sri Lanka and the Maldives had all been seduced by Chinese loans, grants and investments. Bhutan remained India's only true ally in South Asia. But China and Pakistan, the unpredictable next door neighbour, both possessed nuclear weapons. In China it was the Communist Party and its 'Princelings' that determined foreign policy; in Pakistan it was the mysteriously dark Inter-Services Intelligence (ISI) agency that called the shots, often using 'franchised' terrorist groups to achieve its objectives. The Indian government could not forget that the origins and the planning of the 2008 terrorist attack on Bombay were traced back to Pakistani terror groups with close links to ISI.

India and Pakistan have gone to war three times since their independence from Britain and division into two states. Initially, Pakistan appeared to have responded positively to Mr Modi's election victory. Mr Modi even invited his Pakistani counterpart, Nawaz Sharif to attend the ceremony, a first in the tetchy history of the two countries. Mr Sharif, elected for the third time in 2011, was invited along with eight other leaders of the South Asia Association for Regional Co-operation (SAARC). India's relations with Pakistan had seemed to be improving in 2014 but, almost inevitably, they deteriorated sharply as artillery fire was exchanged along their shared, but disputed, border.

Under the previous administration, India's relations with the US had hardly bloomed, often bogged down by commercial differences and avoidable diplomatic tensions. But Mr Modi's overtly pro-business stance looked likely to restore normality and, it was hoped, open up new opportunities for Indian business. There was only one fly in the ointment – in 2005 Washington had accused Mr Modi (apparently without any firm evidence) of being involved in the 2002 clashes between the Hindu and Muslim communities. The Indian Supreme Court had not found any proof of the allegations against the prime minister, but none the less the US authorities revoked his visa.

The Party's over

Mr Modi's 2014 election had been a resounding triumph for his Bharatiya Janata Party (BJP). The BJP won an impressive 282 seats out of 543, giving it an absolute majority and relegating the Congress Party to second best. It was the first time that any party other than congress had an overall majority. In the interregnum between general elections, the BJP would only have the controlling input in eight larger states. Congress were left with more states – nine – most of which had relatively small populations. The net of it was that with the support of its allies in a further six states, the BJP could command the support of a very respectable 41 per cent of the population. In terms of seats, the election had been an embarrassment for Congress, only mustering 44 seats. Blame was heaped on the party's leader, Rahul Gandhi, who had simply looked inadequate, causing voters to ask if the election represented the dying days of the Gandhi dynasty. The only remaining member of the Gandhi family that might offer some prospect of an improvement might have been Rahul's sister, Priyanka. However, her husband's involvement in corruption allegations had seemingly dished her chances.

Waiting in the wings, however, was a new face. No corruption allegations were likely to be made against moustachioed Arvind Kejriwal, the leader of the Aam Aadmi Party (AAP). (Common Man). Mr Kejriwal's fortunes seemed to blow hot and cold, at one stage in early 2014 taking control of the Delhi assembly, only to resign less than two months later after a disorganised period in power. In the 2014 general election, the AAP fared badly, only managing to win four seats. Most observers thought that was the end of the AAP and possibly of Mr Kejriwal's political prospects. Not so: in the February 2015 Delhi Assembly elections, the AAP almost had a clean sweep, winning 67 of the 70 seats, the highest majority since independence. For the time being, at least, both the BJP and Congress were swept off the capital's political map.

KEY INDICATORS — India

	Unit	2011	2012	2013	2014	**2015
Population	m	1,210.19	1,227.19	1,243.34	*1,259.70	*1,276.27
Gross domestic product (GDP)	US$bn	1,676.10	1,858.75	1,875.16	2,049.50	*2,308.02
GDP per capita	US$	1,389	1,515	1,508	*1,627	*1,808
GDP real growth	%	7.1	4.7	6.9	7.2	*7.5
Inflation	%	8.6	10.2	10.0	6.0	*6.1
Oil output	'000 bpd	858.0	894.0	894.0	895.0	–
Natural gas output	bn cum	46.1	40.2	33.7	31.7	–
Coal output	mtoe	222.4	228.8	228.8	243.5	–
Exports (fob) (goods)	US$m	299,387.0	298,320.6	319,109.8	329,633.3	–
Imports (fob) (goods)	US$m	415,799.8	450,249.4	433,760.3	405,122.2	–
Balance of trade	US$m	-116,412.8	-151,928.8	-114,650.6	-75,488.8	–
Current account	US$m	-60,038.0	-88,163.0	-32,397.0	*-29,473.0	*-29,408.0
Total reserves minus gold	US$m	285,009.1	270,587.0	276,493.0	303,455.0	–
Foreign exchange	US$m	276,873.8	261,656.0	267,703.0	–	–
Exchange rate	per US$	44.91	54.19	62.21	63.19	–

* estimated figure ** forecast figure

Mr Kejriwal is diametrically opposed to Mr Modi in every possible way – he represents modesty rather than arrogance, he is pro-poor rather than pro-business. Where Mr Modi sports expensive suits, Mr Kejriwal wears a simple scarf, earning him the nickname 'Mufflerman'. Politically, the two men were made for each other, providing ample fodder for jibes and criticism on an intensely public stage.

Sales tax

For decades Indian businesses had pressed for a national sales tax, seeking to replace the chaotic structure that inflates costs and halts lorries at state borders while state duty payments are made. However, as the goods and services tax (GST) bill came before parliament, doubts emerged. In something of a volte-face, Indian businesses began to call for a slowdown in the process. Finance minister, Arun Jaitley had been left by Prime Minister Modi to push through parliament what he described as India's biggest tax reform since independence. Business had called for improvements to be made to the bill, but Mr Jaitley would brook no delays and had marked April 2016 as the deadline for launching the reform, which he had claimed would boost annual economic growth by 2 percentage points.

The proposed goods and services tax would subsume at least 14 federal and state levies, according to the government. Caving in to the opposition to the GST bill, the Modi government had agreed to a one per cent additional levy by states on the cross-border transport of goods, even on a company shipping products from one plant to another. This was seen as a backward step, as the present system requires no such tax payments between plants.

The Modi government risked ending up with a watered down reform, but was committed to introducing the GST legislation, which had passed through the lower house of parliament and had been referred to an upper house committee. The upper house was expected to approve the legislation. Indian businesses feared that with no compensatory offsets under the proposed tax regime, they could face double-taxation on construction materials that often accounted for nearly 40 per cent of the cost of a new factory. The Modi government discreetly recognised the shortcomings of the legislation. Arvind Subramanian, Jaitley's chief economic adviser, warned that the proposed interstate charge could derail Mr Modi's ambitious plans for a manufacturing boom.

The Economy – the OECD

In its November 2014 Overview of the Indian economy, the Paris-based Organisation for Economic Co-operation and Development (OECD) noted that India had experienced strong inclusive growth between 2003 and 2011, with average growth in gross domestic product (GDP) above 8 per cent and the incidence of poverty spectacularly cut in half. This progress reflected gains from past structural reforms, strong capital inflows up to 2007 and expansionary fiscal and monetary policies since 2009. These growth engines faltered in 2012. However, according to the OECD, stubbornly high inflation as well as large current and fiscal deficits left little room for monetary and fiscal stimulus to revive growth. The prospect of 'tapering' (ie the winding down of) monetary stimulus in OECD countries and the reversal in capital inflows, as well as the difficulty to pass reforms to remove growth bottlenecks in the run-up to the 2014 general, elections had further affected India's economic performance.

In 2014, the economy had shown some signs of a turnaround and imbalances had lessened. Fiscal consolidation at the central government level had been accompanied by a decline in both inflation and the current account deficit. Confidence had been boosted by continuing reforms to the monetary policy framework, with more weight given to inflation. The large depreciation in the rupee also helped revive exports.

The exchange rate of the Indian rupee is determined by two baskets of currencies constantly monitored by the Reserve Bank of India (RBI) (central bank). One is a basket of six currencies – the US dollar, euro, Japanese yen, pound sterling, Swiss franc and the Australian dollar. The other basket contains no less than 36 currencies; these are countries with which India has major external trade. The RBI keeps an eye on inflation in these countries compared to India. For India's export trade to remain competitive, the currency of the country in which inflation is high needs, theoretically, to depreciate against the currency of the country where the inflation is lower.

However, since April 2014, the rupee has depreciated against the US dollar by only 4.5 per cent, due to the huge inflows of funds through investments both in equities and in debt. By comparison, the US dollar appreciated against other major currencies by much larger margins. Against the euro by 24 per cent, against sterling by 14 per cent and the yen by about 15–16 per cent.

Industrial production rebounded and business sentiment surged, triggered by less political uncertainty. Further reducing macro-economic imbalances was, in the view of the OECD, the key to sustaining consumer and investor confidence and to containing external vulnerabilities – this would require adherence to the fiscal roadmap and the implementation of the proposed changes to the monetary policy framework.

The OECD also considered that structural reforms would raise India's economic growth rate. In their absence, however, in the immediate future, growth was expected to remain below the 8 per cent mark seen in the previous decade. Both growth and job creation were, according to the OECD, being impeded by infrastructure bottlenecks, the cumbersome business environment, complex and distorting taxes, inadequate education and training and outdated labour laws. A May 2015 report in the London *Economist* listed the objectives that Mr Modi had set himself. Around half of the projects on this daunting list were scheduled for completion by 2019, the time of the next general election. Another half seemed alarmingly prone to bureaucratic delays. The construction of 30km of new roads every day and the commitment of state banks to open millions of new accounts were singled out by the *Economist* as vulnerable.

Female economic participation remained, according to the OECD, exceptionally low, holding down incomes and resulting in severe gender inequalities. Although India's absolute poverty has declined, it remains high and income inequality has in fact risen since the early 1990s. Inefficient subsidy programmes for food, energy and fertilisers have increased steadily while public spending on health care and education has remained low. Spending on public health was actually cut by the Modi government in the 2015 budget; this despite the obvious fact that health expenditure is inadequate and as a whole, the system is desperately underfunded. In contrast, a significant investment commitment is that to provide vocational training for no less than 500 million students by 2022.

Although the economic slowdown since mid-2011 has been more marked in India than in many other emerging economies, in 2013 India's GDP growth was at its weakest since 2003 – 4.7 per cent compared to the average of 8 per cent over the period 2003–11. The vital manufacturing sector had contracted in volume terms for the first time since 1991. In contrast, the OECD noted that financial and business services continued to grow at rates of 10 per cent or more. On the demand side, investment and private consumption has, in the view of the OECD, been weak, while exports rebounded in the second half of 2013 following the rupee depreciation.

Weaker exports of goods during the first months of 2014, however, suggested that competitiveness remained an issue. Structural bottlenecks had taken a toll on economic growth and on the manufacturing sector in particular. As an illustration, in 2012 due to unreliable power supply, around half of India's manufacturing companies experienced power cuts for more than 5 hours each week. Lengthy authorisation processes and uncertainty surrounding land acquisition held back infrastructure investment, while corporate investment suffered from rising input prices which squeezed corporate margins.

Job creation has also been sluggish and most jobs remain informal despite some pick-up in formal employment, mostly in services. One estimate, quoted by the *Economist* put at 10 million, the number of new jobs that needed to be created every year. In India urban drift has become more of a tidal wave, as labour desert agriculture for the more rewarding, if less agreeable, prospects of urban employment.

Consumer price inflation has remained much higher than in the OECD area and in other BRICS (Brazil, Russia, India, China and South Africa.). A series of one-off factors has contributed to inflation, including: adverse weather conditions, adjustment in administrative prices for core food items, oil products, electricity and railways; the extension of the National Rural Employment Guarantee Scheme (NREGS) which established a wage floor in rural areas; the rupee depreciation in the summer of 2013. Supply-side constraints in the food sector – including the lack of cold storage and refrigerated transport facilities – have also contributed to food price volatility. The decline in inflation in the first half of 2014 had been encouraging but inflation expectations have remained stubbornly high.

Figures, statistics and… confusion

According to official sources, India's economy grew at an annual rate of 7.5 per cent in the first quarter of 2015. However, there were those who doubted that the figures were sound, claiming that they seemed not to chime with other more empirical indicators. The government attributed the impressive figure to a strengthening of the economy in the final months of the financial year. But at the same time, the growth figure for the period October–December 2014 was revised downwards, from 7.5 per cent to 6.6 per cent.

According to the London *Financial Times* (FT), the figures and the doubt surrounding India's economic statistics dated back to the 2013–14 financial year when the official growth figure was declared to be 6.9 per cent for the year, well up on the initial official figure of 4.7 per cent. The FT wen on to note that even India's top economics advisor, Arvind Subramaian had described the figures as 'mystifying'. However, officials adhered to the official version, saying that the growth was largely due to an 8.4 per cent increase in manufacturing and a 14 per cent increase in the services sector. The FT quoted an analyst at Moody's credit rating agency as observing that 'rather than painting a healthy picture of the economy, we believe the new GDP figure merely shifts the goalposts.'

ADB Optimism

Striking a generally more positive note, the Asian Development Bank (ADB) in its annual assessment of the Indian economy noted that economic expansion picked up in 2014, inflation markedly declined and the external position was comfortable, helped by positive policies and lower global oil prices. The outlook was for economic strengthening through higher infrastructure spending, increased fiscal devolution to states and continued reform to financial and monetary policy. As mentioned above, the government emphasised its intention to move steadily to tackle politically difficult structural issues that have stalled investment and limited economic performance in recent years.

According to the ADB, a more robust economic performance than was earlier indicated emerged from revised data based on an updated base year, wider coverage of goods and services and the inclusion of tax data to estimate economic activity. Growth was previously estimated as a change in volume, but the new series estimated value added at each stage. The government's initial estimates for the 2014 fiscal year (ending 31 March 2015) showed that economic growth actually accelerated to 7.4 per cent. Agricultural growth fell to 1.1 per cent in 2014 largely because the monsoon was erratic, particularly affecting the summer crop. The production of food grains contracted by 3.2 per cent in relation to 2013.

In contrast, after reaching 4.5 per cent in FY2013, industrial growth accelerated to 5.9 per cent in 2014, helped by a 6.8 per cent expansion in manufacturing. However, these estimates may be optimistic, as they assumed manufacturing growth to have exceeded 10 per cent in the final quarter of 2014. Monthly industrial production estimates indicated a more modest upturn. The production of capital goods expanded after 3 years in the red. However, consumer durables continued to decline. Improved coal production helped double the growth of electricity generation over the previous year's rate.

According to the ADB, growth in the services sector rose to 10.6 per cent in 2014. The financial sector received a boost from the government's new financial inclusion scheme, under which new depositors had reportedly opened 125 million accounts. An increase in industrial activity enhanced the growth of trade and transport services.

Private consumption growth increased to 7.1 per cent. Declining oil prices, weakening food inflation, improved job prospects and a stable currency helped lift consumer confidence, though moderation in rural wage growth might have dampened rural consumption. Despite the policy momentum toward resolving issues that had constrained investment, growth in capital formation inched up only to 4.1 per cent in 2014. While the pace slowed as the year progressed, the initial estimates pointed to a recovery in the last quarter of FY2014. Consumer price inflation fell sharply over the course of the year, according to the ADB, to average below 7 per cent in 2014. Food inflation moderated considerably, helped by a limited increase in minimum support prices for food grains, muted rural wage growth and the government's offloading of food stocks. A sharp drop in global oil prices helped moderate fuel inflation, though rises in excise duty limited the pass-through of global oil prices to domestic retail prices. The central bank's strong anti-inflationary stance and the declining trend in the fiscal deficit boded well for core inflation, which dropped to below 5 per cent.

After maintaining an anti-inflationary stance during most of 2014, despite retail inflation declining by almost 400 basis points from April to December 2014, the central bank reduced key interest rates by 50 basis points in the fourth quarter of

FY2014. The move came after inflation had fallen significantly below the 8 per cent target for January 2015 and because inflation was likely to continue to average less than 6 per cent to January 2016. The central bank eased requirements on the portion of deposits that banks must invest in government bonds by 50 basis points to 21.5 per cent, to encourage banks to lend for productive uses.

February 2015 saw a monetary policy framework formalised under which the primary objective was to maintain price stability while remaining mindful of growth. The RBI was expected to bring consumer price inflation down to 6 per cent by January 2016, with the target for inflation being plus or minus 4 per cent with a two per cent margin from 2016.

The central government's budget deficit was estimated at 4.1 per cent in 2014, below the 4.4 per cent recorded in 2013. The reduction in the deficit came largely from curtailed expenditure, as revenue growth remained sluggish. While most major tax revenue segments under-performed their original targets, growth in corporate and service taxes was especially subdued. The sharp drop in global oil prices provided an opportunity to garner additional revenue by raising excise duty on various petroleum products. Receipts from asset sales increased in the last quarter of 2014 but still fell well below target. Expenditure grew by 7.8 per cent in 2014, less than the targeted 12.9 per cent. However, as in previous years, much of the burden of expenditure compression fell on capital expenditure, which grew by 2.5 per cent, only a fraction of the 20.8 per cent growth target. In contrast, current expenditure grew by 8.5 per cent. The drop in global oil prices, deregulation of diesel prices and limited increase in minimum support prices helped contain the subsidy bill, which was 2.1 per cent of GDP.

A commission set up by the government every 5 years to advise on revenue distribution between the centre and the states, as well as among the states, had recommended increasing the share of tax devolved from the centre to the states from the current 32 per cent to 42 per cent. It advised local bodies and states to explore municipal bonds for funding infrastructure. With a view to facilitating the introduction of the uniform goods and services tax, the commission recommended a tapering compensation package for the states for five years to reimburse their lost revenues.

After moderating to 1.7 per cent of GDP in 2013 from record highs in the previous 2 years, the current account deficit was estimated to have narrowed further to 1.5 per cent of GDP in FY2014. The improvement largely reflected a reduced trade deficit in 2014 as imports grew by only 2.0 per cent. Oil imports, which accounted for nearly one-third of all imports, declined by about 15 per cent as global prices fell sharply. The relaxation of restrictions on gold imports imposed in FY2013 spurred gold import growth over the previous year, which was more than offset by the decline in oil imports.

Export growth moderated to 2.3 per cent in FY2014. The double-digit growth witnessed in the first quarter slowed considerably in subsequent months, reflecting the slowdowns in the People's Republic of China and the European Union (EU) that cramped external demand and declining oil prices because they affected exports of refined petroleum products. Higher services exports and a slight increase in remittances helped to narrow the current account deficit.

According to the ADB, the decisive election result, improved fiscal and current account deficits and some movement toward resolving structural bottlenecks had buoyed investor sentiment and foreign capital inflows. Net portfolio investment inflow recovered strongly to over US$35 billion in 2014, after being unusually low in 2013. Foreign direct investment (FDI) revived on improved growth prospects, while low interest rates in advanced economies aided external commercial borrowings. The improved current account deficit and boisterous capital flows helped reserves increase by US$33 billion in FY2014 to over US$337 billion. Despite the rise in reserves, import cover continued to be well short of historical norms.

The demand for energy

The BJP government faces numerous challenges to meet India's massive energy demand both in securing affordable energy supplies and in attracting investment for infrastructure development. The check-list of reforms pending is long, including regulated fuel prices, expensive fuel subsidies and inconsistent attempts at energy sector reform. According to the United States government Energy Information Administration (EIA) some parts of the energy sector, chiefly coal production, remain virtually closed to private and foreign investment. Others such as electric power, petroleum and other liquids and natural gas have regulated price structures that discourage private investment.

Despite its large coal reserves and healthy growth in natural gas production, India is increasingly dependent on imported fossil fuels. In 2013, the then petroleum and natural gas minister, Veerappa Moily, announced an action plan to make India energy independent by 2030 through increased fossil fuel production, development of resources such as coalbed methane and shale gas, foreign acquisitions by domestic Indian companies of upstream hydrocarbon reserves, reduced subsidies on motor fuels and oil and natural gas pricing reforms. The current petroleum and natural gas minister, Dharmendra Pradhan, who took office in late May 2014, reiterated the goal of making India self-sufficient in energy resources.

The size of the task is vast; primary energy consumption more than doubled between 1990 and 2012. India's per capita energy consumption is one-third of the global average, according to the International Energy Agency (IEA), indicating potentially higher energy demand in the long term. The EIA predicts that India and China would account for about half of global energy demand growth in the period up to 2040, as India's energy demand grows at a forecast rate of 2.8 per cent per year. India's National Sample Survey Organisation estimated that about 25 per cent of the population (over 300 million people) lack basic access to electricity, while those areas with access suffered from regular electricity blackouts. The government seeks to balance the country's growing need for electricity with environmental concerns from the use of coal and other energy sources to produce that electricity.

India was the fourth-largest consumer of oil and petroleum products after the United States, China and Japan in 2013 and the fourth-largest net importer of crude oil and petroleum products. The gap between India's oil demand and supply has been widening, as demand reached nearly 3.7 million barrels per day (bpd) in 2013 compared to less than 1 million bpd of total liquids production. The EIA has projected that India's demand would more than double to 8.2 million bpd by 2040, while domestic production will remain relatively flat, hovering around 1 million bpd. The high degree of dependence on imported crude oil has led Indian energy companies to diversify their supply sources. The majority of India's imports continue to come from the Middle East.

The Indian government embarked on its New Economic Policy in 1991, that pushing for open market competition across a variety of energy sectors. The government introduced the New Exploration Licensing Policy (NELP) in 1999 that allowed investors to bid on development blocks with up to 100 per cent foreign control. International investment remains relatively low and most analysts agree that the NELP has had only limited success in reducing India's oil dependence.

According to the Oil & Gas Journal (OGJ), India held nearly 5.7 billion barrels of proved oil reserves at the beginning of 2015. About 44 per cent of reserves are onshore resources, while 56 per cent are offshore. Most reserves are found in the western part of India, particularly the Western offshore area near Gujarat and Rajasthan. The Assam-Arakan basin in the north-eastern part of the country is also an important oil-producing region and contains more than 23 per cent of the country's reserves and 12 per cent of the production.

Natural gas mainly serves as a substitute for coal for electricity generation and as an alternative for LPG and other petroleum products in the fertiliser and other sectors. India was self-sufficient in natural gas until 2004, when it began to import liquefied natural gas (LNG) from Qatar. Because it has not been able to create sufficient natural gas infrastructure on a national level or produce adequate domestic natural gas to meet domestic demand, India increasingly relies on imported LNG. It was the world's fourth-largest LNG importer in 2013, following Japan, South Korea and China and consumed almost 6 per cent of the global market, according to data from IHS Energy. Indian companies hold both long-term supply contracts and more expensive spot LNG contracts.

Natural gas consumption grew at an annual rate of 8 per cent from 2000 and 2012, although supply disruptions starting in 2011 resulted in declining consumption. Natural gas consumption in India was tied closely to domestic production until imports became available in 2004. In 2012, India consumed 2.1 trillion cubic feet (tcf) of natural gas. LNG imports accounted for about 29 per cent of 2012 demand and LNG is expected to account for an increasing portion of demand in the next several years. The majority of natural gas demand in 2012 came from the power sector (33 per cent), the fertiliser industry (28 per cent) and the replacement of LPG for cooking oil and other uses in the residential sector (15 per cent), according to India's Ministry of petroleum and natural Gas (MOPNG).

Risk assessment

Economy	Good/fair
Politics	Good/fair
Regional stability	Fair

Muslims in India

% of population	13.4
Sunni (% of Muslims)	85
Shi'a (% of Muslims)	15

Extras

Fair skin ideals

As of 2010 India's skin-whitening market was worth US$432 million and growing 18 per cent annually. Consuming over 250 tonnes of the product per year, Indian demand for skin-whitening products has outstripped that of Coca Cola. Nina Davuluri, a dark-skinned Indian-American, won the Miss America pageant in 2014. Yet even with her obvious natural beauty some sections of the Indian press questioned the result and insinuations were made that, had the contest been in India, she would not have won.

Famous Bollywood actress, Nandita Das, has fronted the Dark is Beautiful Campaign – aimed at reducing darker skin insecurities. 'Indians are very racist. It's deeply ingrained.' Argues Das, '[Film directors] always say to me 'don't worry we will lighten you. We're really good at it.'' Das links the skin-whitening fad to class culture, '[There is] a stereotype that only fair-skinned women can be educated and successful.' However, the Dark is Beautiful campaign has seen limited success hitherto and cosmetic brands continue to invest heavily in the lucrative Indian skin-whitening market.

COUNTRY PROFILE

1200 The start of five-and-a-half centuries of Muslim rule over the region, beginning with the Sultanate era.

1757 The region gradually came under the influence of British rule after the battle of Plassey.

1858 India came under the direct rule of the British crown after a failed mutiny.

1885 The Indian National Congress was founded by Indian nationalists.

1911 Delhi replaced Kolkata (Calcutta) as capital of India.

1920s Nationalist leader, Mohandas Karamachand Gandhi, launched a campaign of civil disobedience against British rule.

1927 Delhi was renamed New Delhi.

1931 New Delhi was inaugurated on 13 February.

1942 Congress launched its 'Quit India' campaign.

1947 The Union of India was granted independence by Britain. The partition of the sub-continent into mainly Hindu India and the Muslim-majority state of Pakistan led to the death of hundreds of thousands as communal violence followed independence. Jawaharlal Nehru of the Congress became India's first prime minister. The Hindu ruler of Muslim-majority Jammu and Kashmir joined secular India rather than Islamic Pakistan when the sub-continent was partitioned at the end of British rule.

1948 Gandhi was assassinated by a Hindu fundamentalist. India and Pakistan went to war in Kashmir for the first time.

1950 India became a republic. It remained a member of the Commonwealth. The constitution of India was adopted. France transferred sovereignty of Chandernagore to India.

1951–52 Congress Party won first general elections under leadership of Jawaharlal Nehru.

1954 France ceded its four remaining Indian settlements (Pondicherry, Yanam, Mahe and Karaikal).

1961 Indian forces overran the Portuguese territories of Goa, Daman and Diu and they were annexed by India.

1962 India lost a border war with China.

1964 Nehru died and was succeeded by Lal Bahadur Shastri.

1965 India and Pakistan fought a second war over Kashmir.

1966 Shastri died and Nehru's daughter, Indira Gandhi, became prime minister.

1971 India-Pakistan war over East Pakistan (later Bangladesh). A Treaty of Friendship was signed with the Soviet Union.

1972 The Simla peace agreement set a new Line of Control (LoC) in Kashmir, separating India- and Pakistan-controlled areas.

1974 India exploded its first nuclear device in underground tests.

1975 Indira Gandhi was found guilty of instigating electoral malpractice and was barred from office.

1977 Congress lost elections for the first time.

1980 Indira Gandhi was reinstated as prime minister heading a Congress splinter group, Congress (Indira). There followed years of widespread political and religious disturbances in several states.

1984 Indira Gandhi was assassinated by her Sikh bodyguard after troops stormed the Golden Temple, the Sikhs' most holy shrine, to arrest Sikh separatists. Her son, Rajiv Gandhi, was sworn in as prime minister. Widespread violence continued. The world's worst industrial accident, a gas leak, killed thousands of people living around the US-owned and operated, Union Carbide pesticide plant in Bhopal.

1987 India deployed peace-keeping troops in Sri Lanka.

1989 After an election in which over 100 people died, VP Singh was sworn in as

prime minister. His government was the first minority government in Indian history.
1990 The Indian army opened fire in Srinagar during a protest against a crack-down on separatism, killing 38 and giving impetus to rebel campaigns. Singh resigned and Chandra Shekhar was sworn in as prime minister. Indian troops withdrew from Sri Lanka. Muslim separatists, trained and armed by Pakistan, began a campaign of violence in Kashmir.
1991 Shekhar resigned, and the reformist government of PV Narashima Rao came to power. Former prime minister, Rajiv Gandhi, was assassinated by a supporter of the Sri Lankan Tamil separatists.
1996 Congress was defeated in elections and the largest single party in parliament became the Hindu fundamentalist Bharatiya Janata Party (BJP) (Indian Nationalist Party), which attempted and failed to form a government, after which the United Front (UF), a 13-party coalition, succeeded.
1997 Kocheril Raman Narayanan was elected president. He was the first Dalit (untouchable) to become president. The UF government was toppled after Congress withdrew its support in the lower house.
1998 BJP formed a coalition government and Atal Behari Vajpayee was appointed prime minister. Sonia Gandhi became leader of the opposition in the Lok Sabha on 19 March. India and Pakistan each conducted underground nuclear tests, leading to widespread international condemnation and US sanctions. Sonia Gandhi became president of the Indian National Congress Party.
1999 Prime Minister Vajpayee made a historic bus ride to Pakistan for a peace summit with Prime Minister Nawaz Sharif. Vajpayee lost a confidence vote, but was reaffirmed following general elections. Pakistan and India fought a brief war in Kargil in Indian-controlled Kashmir.
2000 India celebrated the birth of its one-billionth citizen. New states – Chattisgarh (part of Madhya Pradesh), Uttaranchal (in the north) and Jharkand (part of the eastern state of Bihar) – were created.
2001 The US lifted sanctions on Pakistan and India as a reward for supporting its attacks on Afghanistan.
2002 An attack on an Indian army camp in Kashmir killed more than 30 people. India threatened retaliation and moved troops to the border with Pakistan. The tension eased when India lifted its five-month ban on direct flights to Pakistan and ordered its naval battleships back to port. A P J Abdul Kalam was sworn in as president.
2003 India and China reached a *de facto* agreement over the status of Tibet and Sikkim in a cross-border trade agreement. The Indian and Pakistani armies began a cease-fire across the LoC dividing the disputed state of Kashmir and the Himalayan glacier of Siachen.
2004 Prime Minister Vajpayee visited Pakistan. Kashmiri separatist leaders agreed that all violence in the Himalayan region should stop. The Congress Party won parliamentary elections and Manmohan Singh was named prime minister. An earthquake off the island of Sumatra caused a *tsunami* that devastated coastal areas in the region. The final toll for India was estimated to be 12,407 dead or missing, 647,599 displaced.
2005 The first bus-link for 57 years between cities in divided Kashmir began. India, along with Bangladesh, Bhutan, Maldives, Nepal, Pakistan and Sri Lanka, signed the South Asia Free Trade Agreement (Safta).
2006 The third bus link between India and Pakistan was launched, providing the first direct link across the divided Punjab since partition in 1947. Agreement was reached with the US giving India access to American civilian nuclear technology.
2007 Pratibha Patil became India's first female president and Head of State. She was elected by state and federal parliaments. Severe monsoon flooding in Bihar caused death and destruction and left around 11 million Indian villagers affected. India celebrated 60 years of independence from Britain.
2008 The first passenger train since 1965 began operations between Dhaka (Bangladesh) and Kolkata. A number of Indian cities were targeted by Islamist bombers, killing dozens and injuring many more. India launched an unmanned spacecraft to the moon. Pakistani Islamist terrorist teams attacked a series of famous and important targets in Mumbai, lasting 60 hours and killing around 52 people and injuring hundreds more.
2009 Parliamentary elections held for the Lok Sabha (lower house), were won by the United Progressive Alliance (UPA) with 262 seats (out of 543). The UPA's leading party, Congress, won 206 seats, an increase of 61 seats on the 2004 election. The National Democratic Alliance won 159 seats, losing 17 seats overall; its leading party the Bharatiya Janata Party (BJP) won 116 seats, a loss of 22 seats from 2004. On 11 December a new state of Telengana, with a population of 35 million people, was created from 10 districts of Andhra Pradesh, with Hyderabad as the new capital. L K Advani stepped down as leader of the BJP.
2010 The biggest military operation began in what is called the 'red corridor' of 164 contiguous districts of eastern states under the control of the Naxalite-Maoists. A force of 75,000 paramilitaries and thousands of police moved against the communist insurgency as violence by the Naxalite-Maoists increased. Since the insurgency began in 1989 a total of 10,529 deaths have been caused by violence on both sides of the conflict. The first phase of the population and house-listing census began. The only surviving terrorist of the 2008 Mumbai attacks was convicted of possessing explosives, murder and 'waging war on India'. (An appeal was rejected and he was hanged in 2012). Although he had pleaded guilty at his trial in 2009, he later appealed his sentence. In a move to defuse tension India began removing some of the 200 paramilitary bunkers in Kashmir's main city. The world's largest diamond exchange, the Bharat Diamond Bourse, opened in Mumbai. The US-based Global Financial Integrity group reported that India had lost an estimated US$462 billion in 'illegal capital flows' (corruption) since independence in 1947. The report also estimated the underground economy at around 50 per cent of GDP (US$640 billion in 2008).
2011 In March, Prime Minister Manmohan Singh and Pakistan Prime Minister Yousuf Raza Gilani together watched the Indian cricket team beat Pakistan in a World Cup semi-final played in the Indian city of Mohali. In discussions the two premiers pledged to 'normalise relations'. The second phase of the census was undertaken in February, including, for the first time, collection of biometric information. The provisional population figure published on 31 March was 1,210,193,422, a 10-year growth rate of 17.64 per cent. Bangladesh and India held a joint census in July, in an attempt to determine just how many Indians there are in the 51 enclaves in Bangladesh and how many Bangladeshis in the 100 or so Indian enclaves. There are possibly as many as tens of thousands of people on the wrong side of each border in enclaves which are historical anomalies of the partition of the subcontinent in 1947. A change to the rules governing export earnings was announced in September, although the date the change would become effective was not given. The new rules will require companies to repatriate foreign currency earnings from exports, and to hold the earnings in domestic bank accounts. It is estimated that the amount concerned could be as high as US$33 billion. India successfully launched a new satellite, called Megha-Tropiques, in October, to study the patterns of the annual monsoon. Information from Megha-Tropiques will be shared with meteorological organisations in the US and Europe. The first section of the new metro service,

Namma (Our), was launched in Bangalore in October, with an initial six stations in the business district, from MG Road in the west, to Baiyappanahalli Terminal in the east of the city.
2012 The leaders of the Bric countries met in Delhi on 29 March to discuss their position regarding the control the US and Europe has on the World Bank and the IMF. Prime Minister Manmohan Singh reported that 'The Brics countries have agreed to examine in greater detail a proposal to set up a South-South development bank, funded and managed by the Brics and other developing countries.' On 26 April India launched its first all-weather radar imaging satellite. The RISAT-1, was developed wholly by India and launched using its own rocket from Sriharikota (Andhra Pradesh). On 19 July parliament elected Pranab Mukherjee (Congress) as president with 713,763 votes. His only rival, Purno Agitok Sangma (National Democratic Alliance (NDA)), won 315,987 votes. President-elect Mukherjee took office on 25 July. On 18 September, the All India Trinamool Congress withdrew from the government coalition, in protest at the proposed Foreign Direct Investment reforms (allowing the FDI limit in retail enterprises to rise to 51 per cent), as well as fuel price rises.
2013 The government approved the formation of India's 29th state on 30 July. Telangana will be formed from 10 districts in southern Andhra Pradesh, including the current capital, Hyderabad. There were a number of resignations from the state legislature as a result, and protests throughout the state. A submarine, the INS Sindhurakshak, sank in a Mumbai dockyard on 14 August. It was feared that at least 18 submariners died. The Lok Sabha passed the Food Security Bill on 26 August. The controversial bill aims to relieve hunger among India's 800 million poor by supplying 5 kilos of grain each month at a cost per kilo of rice at three rupees, wheat at two rupees and millet at one rupee. Congress Party leader, Sonia Gandhi, was taken to hospital after making a speech in favour of the bill; she was later released. The bill was approved by the upper house on 2 September. The cost of the scheme is expected to be some US$19.7 billion per year. As concerns for the economy grew, the rupee fell to 68.7 to the US dollar by late August. Raghuram Rajan took over as head of the Reserve Bank of India (the central bank) on 4 September. On 13 September the BJP named Narendra Modi as its prime ministerial candidate for the 2014 elections. Sachin Tendulka, the 'Little Master', announced he was retiring from cricket after playing his 200th test match in November. Over 500,000 people were evacuated as Cyclone Phailin, rated 'very severe', headed for India's east coast on 12 October. As a result, deaths were less than 50 although structural damage was severe. In Orissa state heavy rainfall following the cyclone killed a number of people and destroyed livestock and crops. The Kudankulam nuclear plant in Tamil Nadu state begun producing electricity on 22 October. Prime Minister Manmohan said he would not be attending the Commonwealth Heads of Government meeting in Sri Lanka in November in protest over alleged human rights abuses.
2014 Voting started in the parliamentary election on 7 April continuing until 12 May with counting starting on 16 May. There are more than 800 million registered voters. The two main parties battling for supremacy were the Congress Party (led by Rahul Gandhi after Prime Minister Manmahon said he was stepping down) and the BJP (led by Narendra Modi). The new Aam Aadmi Party (AAP) (Common Man's Party) was also expected to make a strong showing. The results announced on 16 May showed a landslide victory for the BJP with 282 seats (out of 543), the United Progressive Alliance won 59 seats (of which the Indian Congress Party won 44 seats), the All India Anna Dravida Munnetra Kazhagam (AIADMK) came in third with 28 seats. The AAP, which had been expected to do well, won 4 seats. The results gave the BJP a majority with 51.9 per cent in the Lok Sabha (the first time since 1984 that a single party has won a majority); Congress 8.1 per cent and the AIADMK 6.8 per cent. Hindustan Motors halted production of the iconic Ambassador salon car on 25 May. Once the symbol of success throughout India it retained its distinctive curved design of the Oxford Morris of the 1950s. Narendra Modi was sworn in as prime minister on 26 May. Mr Modi invited the leaders of all India's South Asian neighbours to attend the ceremony, including Prime Minister Nawaz Sharif of Pakistan. The two leaders met for private talks the following day. On 2 June the new state (India's 29th) of Telangana officially came into being when Andhra Pradesh was split into two. K Chandrasekhar Rao, of the Telangana Rashtra Samithi party (TRS), was sworn in as chief minister in Hyderabad, which will remain as joint capital for the next 10 years. Finance Minister Arun Jaitley presented the new government's first budget to parliament in 10 July. He said it would be a 'budget for growth' and spoke about plans to introduce a goods and services tax (GST). A bomb blast, on the Pakistan side of the one road border crossing with Pakistan, killed as many as 50 and injured over 100 on 2 November. Elections to elect 87 members to the Jammu and Kashmir Legislative Assembly were held in five phases between 25 November and 20 December. Turnout was higher than previous elections despite calls for a boycott by separatist leaders. Members sit for six-year terms.
2015 On 3 March President Mukherjee approved a bill banning the slaughter of cows and the sale and consumption of beef in the state of Maharashtra. In state elections held in Bihar in November the Rashtriya Janata Dal won 80 seats, ahead of the Janata Dal (United) with 71.

Political structure

Constitution

The Constitution of India was inaugurated on 26 January 1950. The Preamble declares that the people of India solemnly resolve to constitute a 'sovereign socialist secular democratic republic' and to secure to all its citizens, justice, liberty, equality and fraternity. India has 29 self-governing states and seven union territories with a federal form of government. India's constitution is the longest and most detailed in the world. As such, since 1950, there have been over 120 amendments to the constitution. On average, the text is adjusted twice a year in minor matters that most other states have decided not to include in their constitution.

Any citizen aged 18 years and over is eligible to vote. India is the world's largest democracy

Independence date

15 August 1947

Form of state

Secular, democratic republic

The executive

Executive power lies with the prime minister, who is appointed by the president, who has a largely ceremonial role and serves a five-year term. The prime minister nominates a 20-member Council of Ministers (cabinet).

National legislature

The bicameral parliament consists of the Lok Sabha (House of the People) (lower chamber) with a maximum 552 members (including up to 20 representatives of India's Union Territories and two representatives of the Anglo-Indian community appointed at the discretion of the president); all serve for five-year terms, and the Rajya Sabha (Council of States) (upper chamber), with a maximum 250 members, of which 238 are elected by state and territorial legislatures and 12 nominated members chosen by the president to provide cultural and scientific expertise. An alternate one third of the membership is elected every two years. In March 2010 parliament voted to guarantee one-third of all seats of the Lok Sabha be reserved for women.

Although the constitution allows for 552 members in the Lok Sabha, current laws have restricted the number to 545. By the same token, Rajya Sabha, at the moment, has only 245 members.

The legislative field is divided between the Union (central government) and the states. The Union possesses exclusive powers to make laws with respect to matters grouped under 97 headings in the constitution, including foreign affairs, defence, citizenship and trade with other countries. The Union territories are administered by the federal government based in New Delhi. Major legislation requires passage through both houses of parliament.

Each state has its own governor and elected state assembly, with a chief minister and council of ministers. Policy in areas such as agriculture, education and law and order are determined at the state level.

Legal system

The legal system is based on English common law. There is limited judicial review of legislative acts.

The judiciary is independent and known for delivering verdicts which may not necessarily please the government in power. The Chief Justice presides over the Supreme Court, which is the highest court in the land. Each state has its own high court.

Last elections

7 April–12 May 2014 (parliamentary); 19 July 2012 (presidential (indirect))

Results: Parliamentary (2014): Bharatiya Janata Party (BJP) 282 seats (31 per cent), Indian National Congress (INC) 44 seats (19.3 per cent), All India Anna Dravida Munnetra Kazhagam (AIADMK) 37 seats (3.3 per cent), All India Trinamool Congress (AITC) 34 seats (3.8 per cent), Biju Janata Dal (BJD) 20 seats (1.7 per cent), Shiv Sena (SS) 18 seats (1.9 per cent), TDP 16 seats (2.5 per cent), Telangana Rashtra Samithi (TRS) 11 seats (1.2 per cent), Communist Party of India (Marxist) (CPM) nine seats (3.2 per cent), YSR Congress Party (YSRCP) nine seats (2.5 per cent). No other party won more than six seats. Turnout was 66.4 per cent.

Presidential (2012): Pranab Mukherjee (Congress) 713,763 votes, Purno Agitok Sangma (National Democratic Alliance (NDA)) 315,987.

Next elections

2019 (parliamentary); 2017 (presidential)

Political parties

Ruling party

Bharatiya Janata Party (BJP) (from 16 May 2014)

Main opposition party

Indian National Congress (INC)

Population

1.22 billion (2012)*. Some 60 per cent of the population is designated as low-caste, of which a significant minority are *dalits* or scheduled castes, formerly known as 'untouchables'. The *brahmin* priestly caste makes up about 10–15 per cent of the Hindu population. According to the UN India's population will overtake China's in 2028, when both countries will reach 1.45 billion and India will continue to grow and China's to decrease.

Last census: 1 March 2011: 1,210,193,422

The 2011 census began in 2010 with the fingerprinting and photographing of every individual over the age of 15 in order to build up a national biometric database. The information was used to issue identity cards with a 16-digit identity number, beginning in November 2010. The ID process was expected to take one year, classifying gender, religion, occupation and education.

Population density: 360 inhabitants per square km (2010). Urban population 30 per cent (2010 Unicef).

Annual growth rate: 1.7 per cent, 1990–2010 (Unicef).

Internally Displaced Persons (IDP)

650,000 (UNHCR 2004)

Ethnic make-up

Indo-Aryan (72 per cent), Dravidian (25 per cent), Mongoloid and others (3 per cent).

Religions

Hindu (84 per cent), Muslim (13 per cent), Christian, Sikh, Buddhist, Jain.

Education

A Constitutional Amendment act passed in 2001 made education for all children aged six to 14 a fundamental right. The government earmarked 8 per cent of GNP for education, of which at least 50 per cent would be allocated to primary education. The government is also aiming for universal elementary education by 2010. Accordingly, the department of elementary education and literacy was allocated Rs4,900 crore (US$1,067 million) for 2002/03.

Primary education up to the age of 14 is compulsory in most states and lasts for eight years. Lower primary education between aged six and 11 is free in all states, but upper primary education from 11 to 14 years is free in only 12 states.

Secondary and higher education spending is forecast at Rs49.5 billion (US$1 billion) in 2003/04, of which, Rs17.7 billion (US$388 million) is allocated to higher education spending.

Gender differences, ethnic minorities, caste discrimination and regional disparities have contributed largely to wide inequalities in the development of basic education between Indian states. Independent surveys at the grassroots level show that despite the rhetoric of policy makers, expenditure in the education sector has been falling and typically 6,600,000 working children are still denied the right to primary education. Micro-level strategies for basic education in rural areas are developed through concerted co-operation between local communities, NGOs, government, and international donors.

In April 2010 the federal government introduced laws that gave all children aged six to 14 years the right to free education and announced that enough funds would be made available to ensure that the estimated eight million school-aged children can attend schools. A US$2 billion education fund was established by computer software tycoon Azim Premji in December 2010. The money will be used to found a university in Bangalore to produce 2,000 teaching and education graduates per year.

In September 2011 the Tamil Nadu State began a five-year programme of issuing free laptop computers to an estimated 6.8 million schoolchildren who attend government-funded schools and colleges. This was India's first such programme and is based in a state with a high use of information technology in general.

Literacy rate: 61 per cent adult rate (Unesco 2005)

Compulsory years: Six to 14. Compulsory education is enforced in eight States/Union Territories (UT) when it covers entirely primary schooling; in four States/UT compulsory education is only enforced between ages six to 11; while in March 2003, the ministry of education confirmed that as many as 20 States/UT had not introduced any measure of compulsion.

Enrolment rate: 92 per cent gross primary enrolment; 58 per cent for upper primary enrolment.

Pupils per teacher: 62 in primary schools.

Health

The size and complexity of the Indian population renders universal healthcare difficult to achieve.

India, with its large migrant workforce, is one of only two countries that exports polio (the other is Nigeria), according to the World Health Organisation – Global Polio Eradication Initiative (WHO – Polio Eradication). In particular the state of Uttar Pradesh, where the disease is endemic, saw an outbreak infecting over 400 people in 2006, which was spreading into neighbouring states. India represented 28 per cent of worldwide polio cases in 2006 an increase of 3 per cent from 2005.

In 2004 a new drug treatment for tuberculosis, the first in 40-years, which kills one million sufferers in India and 10 million worldwide, was announced. The medication was developed, and will be manufactured, in India as part of its positioning as a major location for cost-effective, bio-medical research.

In October 2007 the government launched a plan for insurance covering disability, health and life for India's 400m working poor. The plan is part of the government's 'New Deal' for rural India.

HIV/Aids

The World Bank warned India that without greater measures to prevent the spread of HIV through the use of condoms, infections rates and subsequent deaths from Aids could surpass all other pathogens. Indian authorities say infection rates are falling, though critics claim that the factors that lead to high rates in sub-Saharan Africa are all present in India: large pools of migrant labour, large numbers of prostitutes and stigma about sex and the Aids disease. Condom use has levelled out at 50 per cent and without an increased use new infections could grow by 3 million before 2013. Nationwide policies to tackle the disease are not apparent, with each state tackling the threat locally and some seemingly unable to change old habits.

A UNAids report, published in May 2006, claimed that there were 5.7 million people HIV positive in India, overtaking the 5.5 million infected in South Africa.

In April 2005 the head of the UN backed Global Fund to Fight Aids, Tuberculosis and Malaria, Richard Feacham, said official Indian statistics on the disease were wrong. Stating that Indian had more infections than registered, due to underreporting and that India's infection rates had surpassed that of South Africa. He rejected India's estimate of 5.1 million HIV sufferers, saying that the etimate was a 'conservative figure based on limited data', and he did not believe that India had adequate surveillance measures. The Global Fund has contributed US$265 million for Aids control (2004–09). The government increased the Naco spending to US$95.8 million, however it is estimated that per capita spending on Aids control in India is only US0.29, half the rate spent in Thailand.

While India's infection rate is only 1 per cent, in some of its most populous states the infection rates are up to 20 per cent. The UK endorsed the Naco assertion that more foreign aid would be spent on HIV/Aids sufferers. Of the £123 million (US$219), donated by the UK to fight the disease, £95 million (US$169 million) is still scheduled to be spent by March 2007.

HIV prevalence: 0.9 per cent aged 15–49 in 2003 (World Bank)

Life expectancy: 62 years, 2004 (WHO 2006)

Fertility rate/Maternal mortality rate: 2.6 births per woman, 2010 (Unicef); maternal mortality 410 per 100,000 live births (World Bank).

Birth rate/Death rate: 9 deaths to 27 births per 1,000 head of population.

Child (under 5 years) mortality rate (per 1,000): 56 per 1,000 live births (WHO 2012); 45 per cent of children aged under five are malnourished (World Bank).

Head of population per physician: 0.6 physicians per 1,000 people, 2005 (WHO 2006)

Welfare

The between 60–115 million children toiling as bonded workers in India. Most are agricultural labourers while others work in factories or as domestics. The majority of these children are *Dalit* caste (the untouchables) and may be bound to their employer for years to pay back loans incurred by their parents. While these children are working they do not attend school which perpetuates their deprivation in later life.

The are estimates of between 60–115 million children toiling as bonded workers in India. Most are agricultural labourers while others work in factories or as domestics. The majority of these children are *Dalit* caste (the untouchables) and may be bound to their employer for years to pay back loans incurred by their parents. While these children are working they do not attend school, which perpetuates their deprivation in later life.

Homeless children, widows, the elderly, and the disabled (who often occupy the strata of the most destitute people in India) do not have any explicit protection in the constitution, and consequently not enough demand for any government - (whether local, state or national) to extend care to them. The National Nutrition Mission, distributes food grains at subsidised prices to poor families.

World Bank estimates that India has 40 per cent of the World's poor. The government estimates that 85 per cent of the population is in need of some form of welfare support; 25 per cent of the population belongs to either scheduled castes (SC) or scheduled tribes (ST) and these people have been ascribed special welfare measures. The National SC and ST Finance and Development Corporation provides funds for developing entrepreneurial and other skills.

The central government's expenditure on social services accounts for 1.66 per cent of GDP. India's population suffers periodic problems of floods, droughts and other natural disasters.

Pensions

The 2003/04 budget planned a massive overhaul of the pension system. From 1 January 2004, new employees in the public and private sector stopped paying into state pensions and were made to pay into privately managed funds.

The public sector finance organisation, Life Insurance Corporation of India (LIC), also ran a new pension scheme, the The state-subsidised scheme will be available to workers above the age of 55, guaranteeing an annual return of 9 per cent and a maximum pension of Rs2,000 (US$43) per month.

An assurance scheme called *Janaraksha* has been designed by the LIC to provide life insurance for farmers and workers with irregular incomes.

Main cities

New Delhi (capital, estimated population 11.3 million (m) in 2012); state capitals: Mumbai, (Maharashtra) (14.3m), Bangalore (Karnataka) (6.4m), Chennai (was Madras, Tamil Nadu) (4.7m) Kolkata (West Bengal) (4.5m), Hyderabad (Andhra Pradesh) (3.9m), Pune (Maharashtra) (3.7m), Jaipur (Rajasthan) (3.4m), Kanpur (Uttar Pradesh) (3.2m), Patna (Bihar) (2.0m). Other populous cities: Ahmadabad (Gujarat) (4.1m), Surat (Gujarat) (3.9m), Kanpur (Uttar Pradesh) (3.4m).

Languages spoken

Hindi is spoken by almost a third of the population. English is widely spoken and is often the main language of business, with over 350 million Indians using it as the *lingua franca*. Most central government documents are in both Hindi and English. Government policy is to encourage wider use of Hindi.

There are 15 local official languages in the various states, of which the most widely spoken are Punjabi, Telugu, Bengali, Marathi, Tamil, Urdu and Gujarati. There are 1,652 languages spoken throughout the country.

In August a ruling by the mayor of Mumbai, Shubha Raul, made Marathi the official language of local government in Mumbai. Concern was expressed by a number of elected officials with a limited grasp of Marathi, who felt they would be put at a disadvantage. There was also concern that the move would hamper Mumbai's aspirations of becoming an international financial centre, and that it would encourage a resurgence of regional politics. All documents for the

Municipal Corporation of Greater Mumbai (BMC) have to be written in Marathi.

Official language/s

Hindi and English; 15 other languages are recognised for official use in regional areas.

Media

The government guarantees the freedom of the press. The market is huge and has been expanding as the economy has grown.

Press

India has a large middle class and newspaper circulation has expanded with new titles being added.

Dailies: Newspaper titles may be published in English and a local language, editions in English have national readerships, whereas local language newspapers are often regionally limited.

Circulation figures for top newspapers are in the millions.

In English, *The Times of India* (http://timesofindia.indiatimes.com) is the leading broadsheet, followed by *Hindustan Times* (http://timesofindia.indiatimes.com), *The Hindu* (www.thehindu.com), *New Delhi Times* (www.newdelhitimes.org) and *Early Times* (www.earlytimes.in).

Regional newspapers include *The Indian Express* (www.indianexpress.com) and *The Asian Age* (www.asianage.com) from New Delhi, *The Statesman* (www.thestatesman.net) and *The Telegraph* (www.telegraphindia.com) from Kolkata, *Kashmir Observer* (www.kashmirobserver.com) from Srinagar and *Deccan Herald* (www.deccanherald.com) from Bangalore.

Weeklies: There are no major national weeklies, but a huge number of all genre published at local level.

Business: There are several financial and business newspapers, including, in English, *Mint* (www.livemint.com), is a national newspaper, regional newspapers include *The Economic Times* (http://economictimes.indiatimes.com) and *The Financial Express* (www.financialexpress.com) are based in Mumbai and *Business Line* (www.blonnet.com) is based in Chennai. *Business Today* (http://businesstoday.digitaltoday.in) is a national magazine.

Periodicals: In English, the monthly *Diplomatist* (www.diplomatist.com) covers international relations and trade, *Frontline* covers news and current affairs, published fortnightly, the monthly *Verve* (www.verveonline.com) is the oldest publication for women.

Broadcasting

Radio: India has the largest radio network, worldwide. It has hundreds of FM radio stations, broadcasting, most music programmes, in local languages Only All India Radio (http://allindiaradio.org) the public network, with over 200 local stations may broadcast the news. Major commercial networks include Radio Mirchi (www.enil.co.in) with a network of 32 stations and Radio City (www.radiocity.in) with 18 stations. Meow FM is a talk radio station in Delhi and Mumbai for women.

Television: The national, public broadcaster is Noordarshan (www.ddindia.gov.in) with eight regional centres. There are large media groups that operate TV channels, including Zee TV (www.zeetelevision.com), Star TV (http://starnews.indya.com) and Sun Network (www.sunnetwork.org), which broadcast via satellite and cable, with schedules including locally produced and imported TV shows. India has the largest cable TV market in the world, with over 60 million subscribers.

Other news agencies: There are over 40 domestic news agencies.

Press Trust of India: www.ptinews.com

United News of India: www.uniindia.com

Economy

India weathered the global economic crisis of 2008-10 relatively well, compared to its neighbours in the Asian market, due mostly to speedy intervention by the government and Reserve Bank of India (RBI). Policy changes included measures to increase liquidity in the rupee and foreign currencies, increasing the availability of credit and encouraging capital inflows supported by national fiscal measures. India is one of the BRIC (Brazil, Russia, India and China) emerging economies, which have 40 per cent of the world's population, account for 25 per cent of global GDP and which do not rely on exports as there are sizeable domestic markets to maintain production. Merchandise trade accounts for one-third of India's GDP and trade between BRIC countries has grown, so that China is India's primary trading partner. The advantage of this is that while so many of India's other trading partners experienced either a severe downturn in GDP growth or even a recession; India's economy growth fell from a record high of 10 per cent in 2007, to a manageable 6–7 per cent in 2008–09, before rebounding to 10.8 per cent in 2010. By 2014 GDP growth had slowed but was still strong at 7.4 per cent.

Services provide 57.0 per cent of GDP and agriculture 18.2 per cent, whereas industry supplies 24.8 per cent, of which manufacturing is around 13 per cent. Manufacturing companies have emerged as efficient, low cost producers through a large increase in the number of small- to medium-sized Indian companies that are competing on the world market, with Indian entrepreneurs buying internationally recognised companies. India now competes with the West for 'intellectual capital' by investing in value-added, technology intensive industries at home and abroad, which utilise the graduates of its new universities and the successful Indian diaspora. Although per capita income is well over US$1,000, the country still has a large underclass of unemployed and underemployed workers. Agriculture employs almost 50 per cent of the workforce; the government is attempting to increase growth, necessary to achieve food security, by providing farmers with cheap credit and an expansion of the rural jobs guarantee scheme.

In 2010, the RBI raised its key interest rate by 0.25 per cent to 5.25 per cent in a measure to curb inflation, which had peaked to 10.9 per cent in 2009. However, inflation rose to 12 per cent in 2010 but had fallen to 6.4 per cent by 2014.

In 2014, the UN Human Development Index (HDI) ranked India 135 (out of 187) for national development in health, education and income. Since 2000, India's progress has grown steadily and matches the improvement of other countries in South Asia. However 32.7 per cent of the population still live below the poverty line and India has round 30 per cent of the world's poorest people.

Remittances from migrant workers amounted to US$70 billion in 2013, the highest of any country in the world.

In an effort to reduce inflation, the new governor of the Reserve Bank of India, Raghuram Rajan, raised key interest rates by a quarter of a percentage point, from 7.25 per cent to 7.50 per cent in 2013.

Finance Minister Arun Jaitley presented the new government's first budget to parliament in 10 July 2014. He said it would be a 'budget for growth' and spoke about plans to introduce a goods and services tax (GST).

External trade

India is a member of South Asia Association for Regional Co-operation (SAARC), which operates the SAARC agreement on preferential trading arrangements (Sapta) that covers over 6,000 products. The South Asia Free Trade Area was agreed to on by the seven member states (India, Pakistan, Bhutan, Nepal, Bangladesh, Sri Lanka and Maldives), it will be implemented in 2016.

Traditional products such as jewellery and gems (around 80 per cent of cut diamonds worldwide are produced in India), textiles, clothes and footwear, foodstuffs, metal manufacture and leather products remain leading exports but the rapidly growing software sector, including IT services in outsourced call centres, have assumed a large proportion of export trade.

On 16 February 2011, Japan and India signed a free trade agreement (FTA), which will cut tariffs on 94 per cent of goods by 2020. Among the goods to benefit are textiles, pharmaceuticals and vehicles, as well as services, are prominent.

In August 2012, restrictions on foreign direct investment (FDI) by Pakistani citizens in the Indian economy (excluding defence, space and atomic energy sectors) were lifted.

Imports

Main imports include crude oil, machinery, precious stones, fertiliser and chemicals.

Main sources: China (12.6 per cent total in 2014), Saudi Arabia (7.1 per cent), UAE (5.9 per cent)

Exports

Principal exports include textiles, gem stones and jewellery, engineering goods, organic chemicals and leather manufactures.

Main destinations: US (13.3 per cent total in 2014), UAE (10.4 per cent), Hong Kong (SAR of China) (4.3 per cent)

Agriculture

Farming

Agriculture accounted for 18.2 per cent of GDP in 2014. Main crops are wheat, rice, pulses, tea, sugar cane, cotton, jute, coffee, oilseeds, tobacco, rubber and potatoes. The southern state of Kerala accounts for 93 per cent of the natural rubber production. Dairy farming has made India self-sufficient in milk powder and butter (*ghee*).

Despite being the world's second largest producer of fruit and vegetables after China, in 2015 it was estimated by the UN Food and Agricultural Organisation (FAO) that 40 per cent of India's agricultural produce (US$8 billion) goes to waste every year.

Domestic demand and consumption patterns within the country have shifted from cereals to non-cereals including oilseeds, pulses, fruits, vegetables and dairy products. This shift calls for diversification of agricultural production and rural development to sustain future growth. While emphasis on minimum price support for rice and wheat has been beneficial, crop diversification and removal of restrictions on stock limits allowing greater flexibility in marketing are some of the key issues requiring more attention.

Of the 181 million hectares (ha) of agricultural land available, 162 million ha is arable and 11 million ha is permanent pasture. Land legislation has ensured that agriculture remains a fragmented sector, with the typical holding about one hectare. The land ceiling does not extend to farmland used for the cultivation of plantation crops, such as tea, coffee and rubber. Other problems for the sector include a lack of technological modernisation and infrastructural bottlenecks related to irrigation and rural electrification.

Use of improved seed varieties, irrigation and fertilisers has made India self-sufficient in most grains. Land for extending cultivation is limited, but there is scope for productivity improvements in other crops. The sector is dependent on annual monsoon levels and if rains are poor during the July sowing season production can suffer.

In a move to improve the income of the poorest farmers the government had, in its 2008 budget, cancelled the debt of small farmers, in a scheme of loan cancellations costing US$15 billion.

India accounts for almost half of the world spice market in terms of volume and 30 per cent of the value of the world spice market.

Fishing

India's share in the world seafood market largely depends on its shrimp exports. The crustacea catch is typically around 600,000 tonnes, and the fish catch is typically around six million tonnes, the export value of which is approximately US$65 million and US$80 million respectively. India is the world's third-largest fish producer.

The government has given increased attention to the development of other fishery resources including squid, cuttlefish and finfish. Export of frozen items has enabled India to penetrate into markets of Western Europe, North America and South-east Asia.

About a third of exports comprise low-value finfish varieties and another third are frozen shrimp. Japan remains the largest importer of Indian seafood, although the emergence of the South-East Asian market due to import liberalisation has boosted the industry. The US is also a major buyer of frozen seafood, accounting for around 15 per cent of the value of marine products exported.

The sector is likely to witness steady growth as the organised corporate sector has become increasingly involved in the preservation, processing and export of coastal fish. The introduction of several resource specific vessels will enlarge the scope of marine fish landings.

Forestry

India has vast and diverse forest resources, comprising around 23 per cent of the total land area and ranging from tropical moist and dry deciduous types to evergreen, alpine, thorn and mangrove forests. Forest cover is estimated at 64 million hectares (ha). India has more than 12 million ha of forest plantations, used mainly for fuel consumption. There are about 80 national parks and around 450 wildlife sanctuaries.

Wood is an important source of fuel: India is the world's largest consumer of wood for fuel. India has a very low level of industrial wood consumption in per capita terms. The forestry industry consists of small production units with low operating efficiency. There is an acute shortage of raw material, particularly for the manufacture of pulp and paper.

Industry and manufacturing

The steady removal of protection by the state since the early 1990s has meant large state-controlled enterprises have lost some ground to smaller enterprises. Main heavy industries include steel, chemicals, cement and heavy engineering. Further developments in petrochemicals and fertilisers are expected. Textiles account for 30 per cent of India's exports.

Small companies are moving into high-technology products including computers, as well as traditional light engineering and textiles; import controls have been relaxed on raw materials and services necessary for increased export trade. The entire system of industrial licensing has been revised to promote freer competition and many companies are now turning to private capital markets for expansion funding.

In mid-2015 there was speculation as to whether India was to replace China as the 'factory of the world'. China's official media cited this to its economic downturn, forcing companies to turn to India for manufacturing. Phone making companies Xiaomi (Chinese) and Foxconn's (Taiwanese) plans to invest in India suggested a movement of Chinese firms wanting to take advantage of the growing Indian market.

Tourism

India is a continental sized country with an ancient history and a huge population so that its tourist industry is complex, wide-ranging and diverse. Not only can India offer destinations for a single purpose such as beach holidays, it can also cater for niche interests such as cultural and historical, nature and wildlife, architectural and culinary tours. It is also an important destination of the Indian diaspora.

India has 23 cultural, ancient and historic sites, plus five national parks and sanctuaries throughout the country included on UNESCO's World Heritage List.

In 2014, some 7.7 million inbound visitors arrived, a rise of 10 per cent from 2013. Around 90 per cent of visitors arrived by air. On top of this India has a large domestic tourism market, as India's middle class is rapidly expanding.

The travel and tourism sector accounted for 2.2 per cent of GDP directly in 2014, and including indirect contributions the total was 6.7 per cent of GDP. Tourism is an important source of employment, providing 23 million jobs (5.5 per cent of total employment) directly in the industry and a further 37.4 million jobs (8.7 per cent of total employment) if secondary employment is included. Investment in the tourist industry in 2014 was INR2, 107.2 billion (USD32.2 billion), 6.2 per cent of total investment.

In August 2015 India released the world's first solar powered airport in the southern state of Kerala. The government has also directed other airports to begin incorporating solar energy into their daily operations.

Environment

Since 2002 the number of Indian tigers has fallen drastically from 3,642 to 1,411, due to poaching and urbanisation. India is home to 40 per cent of the World's tigers and has 23 tiger reserves in 17 states. The government sponsored a protection unit in 2007, but wildlife experts have said that urgent efforts should be made to save more tigers with inviolate areas and well armed forest guards. The poaching is for body parts for Chinese medicine, with tiger pelts valued up to US$12,500 in China.

The 160,000 square km mountain range, which includes non-equatorial tropical evergreen forests, of Western Ghats (running along the western coast of India) was added to Unesco's World Heritage List on 2 July 2012. The mountains are ranked eighth in the world for their biological diversity and the forest's influence on the annual monsoon.

Mining

India is well endowed with mineral resources, mainly iron ore, manganese, uranium, good-quality bauxite (an estimated 2.65 billion tonnes of reserves, the world's fourth largest) and chromite, but they are not fully exploited. Other minerals present include lead, zinc, tin, silver, mercury and cobalt.

Most of India's raw materials are for domestic consumption. The only exports of any significance are iron ore, mica and manganese ore. India's major markets for iron ore are Japan, South Korea and China. India's reserves of copper, zinc and lead are of relatively low quality.

The world's largest diamond exchange, the Bharat Diamond Bourse, opened in Mumbai in 2010. India already cuts, polishes and processes around 11 out of 12 diamonds in the world and it is hoped that the new Bourse will enable India to compete with Israel and Belgium diamond trading.

Hydrocarbons

India had 5.7 billion barrels of oil reserves in 2014, and produced 895,000 barrels per day (bpd) and consumed 3.8 million bpd, which was an increase of 1.2 per cent on the 2012 figure. Oil consumption has risen dramatically from 1.7 million bpd in 1997 in line with the country's economic growth. However, oil production has remained relatively stable while imported petroleum products have mainly fuelled growth.

A 360 mile-long (580km) heated pipeline from the Thar deserts of Rajasthan to the Gujarat coast was completed, by Cairn India, in 2010. The pipeline allows oil to be pumped directly to refineries with increased production from the Mangala field resulting.

In an effort to reduce dependence on imports, India is encouraging further exploration and production. In August 2013 India's biggest oil explorer, Oil and Natural Gas Corporation (ONGC), agreed a deal to buy 10 per cent of an offshore gas field in Mozambique from US Anadarko Petroleum. The state-controlled ONGC paid US$2.6 billion.

India had a refinery capacity of 4.3 million bpd in 2013, which is expected to rise to 6.2 million bpd by 2017. Most of the oil reserves are located in the Mumbai High, Upper Assam, Cambay, Krisha-Godavari and Cauvery basins.

India had proven natural gas reserves of 1.4 trillion cubic metres (cum) in 2014 and produced 31.7 billion cubic metres. Consumption rose from 20 billion cum in 1997 to 50.6 billion cum in 2014. Much of this increase is attributed to greater use of gas in electricity power generation. Consumption could be higher, but problems in financing liquefied natural gas (LNG) import projects have led to downward revisions of forecasts.

Over two-thirds of India's gas reserves are located in the Mumbai High basin and Gujarat.

Total proven coal reserves were 60.6 billion tonnes in 2014 with production of 243.5 million tonnes oil equivalent (toe). India is the world's fifth-largest coal producer. The main coalfields are in Bihar, West Bengal and Madhya Pradesh.

Around 90 per cent of coal is produced by Coal India Ltd (CIL). Power generation accounts for around 70 per cent of coal consumption; the second-largest consumer is heavy industry.

Energy

India has installed generating capacity of 208,100GW, of which 54.5 per cent comes from coal sources, 39.5 per cent from crude oil, 7.7 per cent from natural gas and the rest is from various other sources.

Although around 80 per cent of the population has access to electricity, the supply is unreliable and interruptions are frequent. More efficient stoves, solar cookers and biogas plants are being developed to address the problem of energy shortages. Other renewable sources are being explored, including wind and solar generators.

The government announced in 2009 that it was preparing to build the world's largest photovoltaic (solar) panels power complex in Gujarat State. The 3,000MW project, estimated at US$10 billion, will be endorsed by the US-based Clinton Foundation, which will provide support in raising the funds necessary to complete the development. The Charanka site, the largest site within the project, has over 600MW commissioned generating capacity.

The demand for electricity is expected to grow five-fold by 2030 and India aims to install an additional 20,000MW of solar power by 2020.

India experienced its worst energy crisis for over 50 years in July 2012, when the electricity supply was cut to 620 million people across 20 (out of 28) states. Three regional grids collapsed as summer demand outstripped supply.

On 22 October 2013 the controversial Kudankulam nuclear plant in Tamil Nadu state began producing electricity and was connected to the grid. The plant is one of many that India hopes to build as part of its aim of generating 63,000MW of nuclear power by 2032.

Financial markets

Stock exchange

National Stock Exchange of India (NSE)

Commodity exchange

Multi-Commodity Exchange (MCX)

Banking and insurance

Indian banking has traditionally been strongly directed from the centre; even private sector banks (excluding foreign banks) are required to lend to national priority projects. In February 2005 the remaining 27 banks in government hands were given freedom to manage themselves, including the ability to acquire foreign assets and close down unprofitable accounts. The government had nationalised the country's 14 major domestic

banks in 1969. Since the mid-1980s there has been a relaxation and improved profitability due to the deregulation of interest rates and the removal of credit allocation obligation, except for quotas for priority sectors. Reforms made since the mid-1990s have led to a growth in private sector banking activity.
Financial reforms implemented in 2001 focussed on tightening regulations on capital adequacy, income recognition, non-performing assets (NPAs), disclosure and transparency in accounting and risk management. The 2002 budget allowed foreign banks to establish subsidiaries in India for the first time, and sector caps on portfolio investments made by foreign institutional investors were eased.

Central bank
The Reserve Bank of India (RBI) controls India's financial system on a day-to-day basis.

Main financial centre
Mumbai is the main financial centre; New Delhi, Kolkata and Chennai are also important.

Time
GMT plus 5.5 hours

Geography
India is a bounded by Pakistan in the north-west, China in the north, the Himalayan Kingdoms of Nepal (administered by China) and Bhutan in the north and north-east. Bangladesh is surrounded on three sides by a bulge of Indian states that border China in the north-east and Myanmar in the east to south, with the Bay of Bengal separating it from the mainland. In the Indian Ocean India's neighbours are Sri Lanka and the Maldives.
India is a large landmass with four distinct regions. The northern Himalayan regions rise to a peak of 7,757 metres before falling away towards the east. The great rivers, Ganges and Brahmaputra begin life in these mountains before draining through a flat alluvial plain into the Bay of Bengal. On the other side of the country, the Great Indian or Thar Desert separates India and Pakistan. In the south the Deccan tableland is bordered by ranges of hills, the Western and Eastern Ghats and Nilgiri Hills in the south, and their coastal belts.

Hemisphere
Northern

Climate
India's winter is January–February, with hot weather increasing from March–May, south-western monsoons from June–September, and post monsoons or north-east monsoons in the southern peninsula from October–December. Temperatures vary from sub-zero in the far north during winter to constant tropical heat in southern regions. Average summer temperatures on the plains are approximately 27 degrees Celsius.

Dress codes
Dress is mostly informal in India except in winter months in New Delhi, where suits and coats are more usually worn. Women are expected to dress with modesty even in very hot weather. Businessmen can expect to wear suits and ties to meetings all year as most buildings have air conditioning.

Entry requirements
Passports
Required by all.

Visa
Required by all, and must be obtained before travelling as visas cannot be issued on arrival. Foreign nationals arriving on long-term, multiple visas are required to register with the nearest Foreigners Regional Registration Officer within 14 days of arrival. Those overstaying their visa entitlement will be fined and may be prosecuted.
For business visas a letter, issued by the local host company or organisation, giving details of itinerary, and traveller's company, a summary of purpose of trip, and the acceptance of full responsibility for any expenses incurred during the term of stay, should be submitted with the application. Business visas, valid for 10 years with multiple entries, are available to foreign businessmen who have set up or intend setting up joint ventures in India.
Long-term visa requirements were changed in December 2009; as a result all visitors on long-term visas (over 180 days) must leave the country and reapply for a visa from abroad.
For further details of various visas and restrictions see www.indianembassy.org or www.hcilondon.net. Nationals of Pakistan and Bangladesh are advised to seek further advice before travelling to, or via, India.

Currency advice/regulations
Import and export of local currency is prohibited; the exception is rupees that visitors may take to Nepal – notes must be less than Rs100, and Bangladesh and Sri Lanka – up to Rs20 per person.
Import of foreign currency is unlimited; amounts below US$1,000 (or equivalent) need not be declared, however, amounts over US$5,000 must be declared and registered on a *encashment certificate* on arrival. Export of foreign currency is limited to the amount declared, therefore all currency transaction receipts should be retained.
Travellers cheques are widely accepted. Currency may only be exchanged at banks or authorised money changers.

Customs
The export of products over 100 years old need a permit. Animal products from endangered species are illegal.

Health (for visitors)
Mandatory precautions
Vaccination certificates for yellow fever if travelling from an infected area.

Advisable precautions
Vaccinations for cholera, dysentery, Japanese B encephalitis and typhoid are recommended. Other vaccinations that may be recommended are diphtheria, tuberculosis, hepatitis A and B, meningitis and tetanus. Malaria, hepatitis B, dengue and chikungunya fever are caused by mosquitoes, precautions including mosquito repellents, nets and clothing covering the body, should be used, especially at night. There is a risk of rabies in rural areas. Polio is endemic in certain states and precautions, including booster shots, should be taken.
Use only bottled or boiled water for drinks, washing teeth and making ice. Eat only well cooked meals, preferably served hot; vegetables should be cooked and fruit peeled. Avoid pork and salad and food from street vendors. A full first-aid kit would be useful.
Locally manufactured Western proprietary medicines are easily obtainable, but visitors on regular medication should bring their own supplies – amounts for the length of the visit only.

Hotels
International-standard accommodation is widely available. Hotel bills must be paid in foreign exchange or in rupees proved to have been purchased in India with foreign exchange. Hotels in main cities are usually heavily booked, and it is advisable to book well in advance.
Extra charges may be applied to hotel bills, including variable service charges plus 10 per cent expenditure tax and 15 per cent luxury tax.

Credit cards
Major credit cards are accepted by larger hotels, travel agencies and airline offices, as well as some larger stores. The Central Card is issued by the Reserve Bank of India and is widely accepted.

Public holidays (national)
Fixed dates
1 Jan (New Year's Day), *26 Jan (Republic Day), *15 Aug (Independence Day), *2 Oct (Mahatma Gandhi's Birthday), 26 Nov (Guru Nanak's Birthday), 25 Dec (Christmas Day).

Variable dates
Good Friday (Mar/Apr), Mahavira's Birthday (Feb/Mar), Holi (Hindu, Mar), Sri Rama's Birthday (Apr), Buddha Purnima (May), Vijaya Dasami/Dussera (Sep/Oct),

Diwali (Hindu, Oct/Nov), Eid al Adha, Eid al Fitr, Islamic New Year, Birth of the Prophet Mohammed.
* Recognised official national holiday. All other holidays are either state, religious or informal holidays and may be observed at locally determined times dependent on sightings of various phases of the moon, or by adherents only.

Working hours

Banking
Mon–Fri: 1000–1400; Sat: 1000–1200, in New Delhi, Kolkata and Chennai. Mon–Fri: 1100–1500; Sat: 1100–1300 in Mumbai.

Business
Mon–Fri: 1000–1700, in New Delhi and Chennai; 0930–1700 in Kolkata; 1000–1730 in Mumbai.

Government
Mon–Fri: 1000–1730, in New Delhi, Kolkata and Chennai; 0930–1630 in Mumbai.

Shops
Mon–Fri: 0930–1930 in New Delhi; 1000–1830 in Kolkata; 1000–1830 in Mumbai; 0900–1930 in Chennai.

Telecommunications

Telegrams were finally discontinued on 15 July 2013 because of 'falling business'.

Mobile/cell phones
There are 900 and 1800 GSM services available, most are regionally based within cities and towns. A temporary ban imposed on imports of Chinese equipment was lifted in August 2010 when the government allowed Tata Teleservices and Reliance Communications to bring in equipment from Huawei and ZTA. In return the Chinese companies agreed to give Indian security agences access to their network source codes.

Electricity supply

Usually 220V AC, 50Hz; some areas have a DC supply for domestic use. Plugs used are of the round two- and three-pin type.

Weights and measures

Metric system

Social customs/useful tips

Namaste is the usual greeting (palms together as in prayer). Visiting cards are exchanged – use the right hand when giving or receiving items. It is not customary for business associates to be entertained at home. Hotels, which provide virtually the only bars in India, require non-resident foreigners to pay their bills in foreign currency.
Business and official contacts are addressed by their last name – *Sri* (Mr), *Srimati* (Mrs or Ms).
Cows are sacred to Hindus, and many Hindus are vegetarian. Sikhs and Parsees do not smoke tobacco. Muslims do not eat pig's flesh in any form, and orthodox Muslims do not drink alcoholic beverages. Officially the government follows a strictly secular policy, with religion considered a private affair.
Smoking is banned in public places, including all offices and restaurants (since October 2008).

Security

Generally, travel in India is quite safe, but travel to Jammu and Kashmir regions is not recommended. Mumbai is the safest city in India. Its police force is known to be the most efficient in the country. It is reasonably safe to travel by taxi until midnight anywhere in the city except slums and red-light districts.

Getting there

Air
National airline: Air India (Air India and Indian Airlines, which flies domestic routes, are to merge in mid-2007).
International airport/s: There are five international airports: Indira Gandhi International (DEL), 20km south of Delhi; Sahar International (BOM), 36km north of Mumbai; Netaji Subhas Chandra Bose International (CCU), 27km north-east of Kolkata; Meenambakkam (MAA), 14km south-east of Chennai; Patna (PAT), 8km from Patna. Dabolim (GOA) airport receives international chartered flights.
All international airports have duty-free shopping, bars, restaurants, currency exchanges, post offices and business centres that include telecommunications and rest facilities.
The Airport Metro rail link between Delhi's Indira Gandhi International airport and the city centre was opened in March 2011. Trains run every 20 minutes from 06.00 to 22.00 and take 20 minutes, compared to over an hour by car.
Airport tax: International flights, Foreign Travel Tax (FTT) Rs500; neighbouring countries only, FFT Rs150; excluding transit passengers.

Surface
Road: Overland access is possible through Nepal and Bangladesh, there is only one access point from Pakistan at Wagah – it may be dangerous crossing the border at any other place. The status of border crossing points and opening hours should be checked before travelling.
Rail: Rail connections exist between India and Bangladesh, although the journey is difficult.
The train service between Pakistan and India was restored in 2004 – one train a week between Lahore in Pakistan and Attari in India.
Water: Ferry services between Colombo and Tuticorin in Tamil Nadu state of India were resumed on 14 June after almost 30 years of having been suspended due to the security situation. There will be two round trips per week initially.
Main port/s: India has 12 major ports: five on the east coast, Kolkata-Haldia, Paradip, Visakhapatnam, Chennai and Tuticorin and seven on the west coast, Kandla, Mumbai, Jawaharlal Nehru, Mormugao, New Mangalore and Cochin.

Getting about

National transport
Air: The only time-efficient way to get between the large cities and even some smaller ones is by plane. The cost of air travel is reasonable and there are several domestic carriers. Airline tickets may now be bought at the airport, at least one hour before a flight.
Smoking and drinking are banned on board all internal flights.
Road: There are two million kilometres of road, including 833,000km of surfaced roads and 35,000km of national highways connecting main cities. Chauffeur driven cars can be hired in the big cities.
Buses: A number of long-distance express bus services operate, and air conditioning is becoming increasingly available. Poor roads make travel uncomfortable.
Rail: The Indian rail network covers over 64,000km and is the main form of domestic transport. Rail connections are available between all major towns and cities, with air-conditioned coaches and sleeper accommodation available on some routes. Some train journeys take 24 hours or more.
Water: There are coastal shipping and ferry services.

City transport
Taxis: Local taxis of varying standards are usually available. In main cities, metered taxis may not always show current rates, and fares should be negotiated in advance. Tipping is officially discouraged, but is practiced.
Other transport includes motorised trishaws.
Buses, trams & metro: There are over 40 stations in the New Delhi metro network, which will eventually cover 60km and is due to be completed by 2010. The first section of elevated track was opened in 2002 and in 2005 another 11km stretch of underground lines, from the government areas of the capital, via the commercial area, to the old city, was opened. A completed 32km section was opened in December 2005. When completed it is expected to cut a journey across the city from one hour at rush-hour, to 15 minutes.
There are surburban metro systems in Mumbai, Kolkata and Chennai (a monorail rapid transit system). The first section

of the new metro service, Namma (Our), was launched in Bangalore in October 2011, with an initial six stations in the business district, from MG Road in the west, to Baiyappanahalli Terminal in the east of the city.

Car hire

Self-drive hire cars are available in Mumbai and chauffeur-driven car hire is available in main cities.

BUSINESS DIRECTORY

The addresses listed below are a selection only. While World of Information makes every endeavour to check these addresses, we cannot guarantee that changes have not been made, especially to telephone numbers and area codes. We would welcome any corrections.

Telephone area codes

The international direct dialling (IDD) code for India is +91, followed by area code and subscriber's number:

Ahmedabad	79	Jammu	191
Amritsar	183	Kolkata	33
Bangalore	80	Lucknow	522
Bhopal	755	Madurai	452
Chandigarh	172	Mumbai	22
Chennai	44	Nagpur	712
Cochin	484	New Delhi	11
Goa	832	Patna	612
Hyderabad	40	Pune	212
Jaipur	141	Rajkot	281
Jallunder	181	Varanasi	542
Kanpur	512	Vishakhapatnam	891

Useful telephone numbers

Police: 100
Ambulance: 102
Fire: 101
Operator: 199
Directory enquiries: 197
International enquiries: 187

Chambers of Commerce

American Chamber of Commerce in India, Maurya Sheraton Hotel, Sardar Patel Marg, New Delhi 110021 (tel: 2302-3102; fax: 2302-3109; e-mail: usamcham@bol.net.in).

Associated Chambers of Commerce and Industry of India, 147B Gautam Nagar, Gulmohar Enclave, New Delhi 110049 (tel: 2651-2477; fax: 2651-2154; e-mail: assocham@sansad.nic.in).

Bengal National Chamber of Commerce and Industry, 23 RN Mukherjee Road, Kolkata 700001 (tel: 248-2951; fax: 248-7058; e-mail: bncci@bncci.com).

Bombay Chamber of Commerce and Industry, Mackinnon Mackenzie Building, Shoorji Vallabhdas Road, Mumbai 400001 (tel: 2261-4681; fax: 2262-1213; e-mail: bcci@bombaychamber.com).

Cochin Chamber of Commerce and Industry, Bristow Road, PO Box 503, Cochin 682003 (tel: 266-8650; fax: 266-8651; e-mail: chamber@md2.vsnl.net.in).

Federation of Indian Chambers of Commerce and Industry, Federation House, Tansen Marg, New Delhi 110001 (tel 2373-8760; fax@ 2332-0714; e-mail: ficci@ficci.com).

Goa Chamber of Commerce and Industry, Goa Chamber Building, Rua de Ormuz, Panaji-Goa 403001 (tel: 222-4223; fax: 242-9010; e-mail: gcci@sancharnet.in).

Gujarat Chamber of Commerce and Industry, Ashram Road, PO Box 4045, Ahmedabad 380009 (tel: 658-2301; fax: 658-7992; e-mail: gcci@gujaratchamber.org).

Indian Chamber of Commerce and Industry, Indian Chamber Road, Mattancherry, PO Box 236, Cochin 682002 (tel: 222-4335; fax: 222-4203; e-mail: mail@iccicochin.com).

Madras Chamber of Commerce and Industry, Karumuttu, 634 Anna Salai, Chennai 600035 (tel: 2434-9452; fax: 2434-9164; e-mail: mascham@md3.vsnl.net.in).

Mahratta Chamber of Commerce, Industries and Agriculture, 14 Tilak Road, Pune 411002 (tel: 444-0371; fax: 444-7902; e-mail: mccipune@vsnl.com).

PHD Chamber of Commerce and Industry, PHD House, opposite Asian Games Village, New Delhi 110016 (tel: 685-2416; fax: 686-3135; e-mail: phdcci@del2.vsnl.net.in).

Rajasthan Chamber of Commerce and Industry, Chamber Bhawan, MI Road, Jaipur 302003 (tel: 256-163; fax: 256-1419; e-mail: info@rajchamber.com).

Banking

Allahabad Bank, 2 Netaji Subhas Road, Kolkata 700 001 (tel: 220-0283; fax: 221-4598; email: homktg@allahabadbank.co.in).

Bank of Baroda, Suraj Plaza-1, Sayaji Ganj, Baroda 390 005 (tel: 361-852; 362-395).

Bank of India, Express Towers, Nariman Point, Mumbai 400 021(tel: 2202-3020; fax: 2202-3167; email: cmdboi@bom5.vsnl.net.in).

Canara Bank, Canara Bank Buildings, 112 Jayachamarajendra Road, PO Box 6648, Bangalore 560 002 (tel: 222-1581; fax: 222-2704; email: canbank@blr.vsnl.net.in).

Central Bank of India, Chandermukhi, Nariman Point, Mumbai 400 021 (tel: 2202-6428).

Corporation Bank, Mangalore 575 001 (tel: 426-416; fax: 441-208; email: corpho@corpbank.com).

ICIC, 163 Backbay Reclamation, Mumbai 400 020 (tel: 2202-5115; fax: 2204-6582).

Oriental Bank of Commerce, Harsha Bhawan, E-Block, Connaught Place, New Delhi 110 001 (tel: 2332-3444; fax: 2371-3244; email: obc@obcindia.com).

Punjab National Bank, 5 Sansad Marg, New Delhi 110 066 (tel: 2371-6032; fax: 2332-1305; email: pnbibd@ndf.vsnl.net.in).

State Bank of India, Madame Cama Road, PO Box 10121, Mumbai 400 021 (tel: 2202-2059; fax: 2204-0073).

Union Bank of India, Union Bank Bhavan, 239 Vidhan Bhavan Marg, Nariman Ponit, Mumbai 400 021 (tel: 2202-4647, 2202-6049; email: ibdhelpdesk@unionbankofindia.co).

Central bank

Reserve Bank of India, Central Office Building, Shahid Bhagat Singh Road, Mumbai 400 001 (tel: 286-1602; fax: 266-2105; e-mail: helpprd@rbi.org.in).

Stock exchange

National Stock Exchange of India (NSE), www.nse-india.com

Bombay Stock Exchange (BSE), www.bseindia.com

Ahmedadad Stock Exchange (ASE)
Madras Stock Exchange (MSE)

Delhi Stock Exchange (DSE), www.dseindia.org.in

Commodity exchange

Multi-Commodity Exchange (MCX), www.mcxindia.com

National Multi-Commodity Exchange of India Limited (NMCE), www.nmce.com

National Commodity & Derivatives Exchange Limited (NCDEX), www.ncdex.com

Travel information

Indian Airlines, Airlines House, 113 Gurdwara Rakabganj Road, New Delhi 110 001 (tel: 2335-7307; fax: 2371-9484).

Ministry of tourism

Department of Tourism of the Government of India, Ministry of Tourism, Transport Bhawan, 1 Parliament Street, New Delhi 110001 (tel: 371-0379; fax: 371-0518; internet: www.tourismindia.com).

National tourist organisation offices

India Tourism Development Corporation Ltd, SCOPE Complex, Core VIII, 6th

Floor, 7 Lodi Road, New Delhi 110003 (tel: 436-0303; fax: 436-0233).

Ministries

Ministry of Agriculture, Krishi Bhavan, Dr Rajendra Prasad Road, New Delhi 110 001 (tel: 2378-2691; fax: 2338-8006).

Ministry of Chemicals and Fertilisers, Shastri Bhavan, Dr Rajendra Prasad Road, New Delhi 110 001 (tel: 2338-6519; fax: 2338-6364).

Ministry of Civil Aviation, Rajiv Ghandi Bhavan, Safdarjung Airport Complex, New Delhi 110 003 (tel: 2463-2991; fax: 2461-0354; e-mail: secy@civilav.delhi.nic.in).

Ministry of Commerce and Industry, Udyog Bhavan, Rafi Marg, New Delhi 110 001 (tel: 2301-0261; fax: 2301-4418; e-mail: commerce@ hub.nic.in).

Ministry of Communications, Dak Bhavan, Parliament Street, New Delhi 110 001 (tel: 2371-0350; fax: 2371-2333).

Ministry of Consumer Affairs, Food and Public Distribution, Krishi Bhavan, Dr Rajendra Prasad Road, New Delhi 110 001 (tel: 2338-5723; fax: 2378-2213).

Ministry of Defence, South Block, New Delhi 110 011 (tel: 2301-6220; fax: 2301-5403).

Ministry of the Environment and Forests, Paryavaran Bhavan, CGO Complex, Lodhi Road, New Delhi 110 003 (tel: 2436-1896; fax: 2436-2222; e-mail: secy@menf.delhi.nic.in).

Ministry of External Affairs, South Block, New Delhi 110 011 (tel: 2301-6660; fax: 2301-0700).

Ministry of Finance, North Block, New Delhi 110 001 (tel: 2301-2810; fax: 2301-3289; internet site: http://wwwmnic.in/finmin/).

Ministry of Health and Family Welfare, Nirman Bhavan, Maulana Azad Road, New Delhi 110 011 (tel: 2301-4751; fax: 2301-6648).

Ministry of Heavy Industries and Public Enterprises, Udyog Bhavan, Rafi Marg, New Delhi 110 001 (tel: 2301-4598; fax: 2301-3086; e-mail: nic-dpe@hub.nic.in).

Ministry of Home Affairs, North Block, New Delhi 110 001 (tel: 2301-1011; fax: 2301-5750).

Ministry of Human Resource Development, Shastri Bhavan, Dr Rajendra Prasad Road, New Delhi 110 001 (tel: 2378-2698; fax: 2338-1355; e-mail:ksm@sb.nic.in).

Ministry of Information and Broadcasting, Shastri Bhavan, Dr Rajendra Prasad Road, New Delhi 110 001 (tel: 2338-4782; fax: 2378-3513).

Ministry of Labour, Shram Shakti Bhavan, Rafi Marg, New Delhi 110 001 (tel: 2371-7515; fax: 2371-1708; e-mail: labour@lisd.delhi.nic.in).

Ministry of Law, Justice and Company Affairs, Shastri Bhavan, Dr Rajendra Prasad Road, New Delhi 110 001 (tel: 2338-7557; fax: 2338-4241; e-mail: lawmin@caselaw.delhi.nic.in).

Ministry of Mines, Shastri Bhavan, Dr Rajendra Prasad Road, New Delhi 110 001 (tel: 2338-3082; fax: 2338-6402; e-mail: dom@sb.nic.in).

Ministry of Ocean Development, Mahasagar Bhavan, CGO Complex, Lodhi Road, New Delhi 110 003 (tel: 2436-0874; fax: 2436-0779).

Ministry of Parliamentary Affairs, Parliament House, New Delhi 110 001 (tel: 2301-7798; fax: 2301-7726; e-mail: parlmin@sansad.nic.in).

Ministry of Petroleum and Natural Gas, Shastri Bhavan, Dr Rajendra Prasad Road, New Delhi 110 001 (tel: 2338-3100; fax: 2338-6550).

Ministry of Power, Shastri Bhavan, Dr Rajendra Prasad Road, New Delhi 110 001 (tel: 2371-4168; fax: 2371-7519).

Ministry of Railways, Rail Bhawan, Parliament Street, New Delhi 110 001 (tel: 2338-2323; fax: 2330-3871).

Ministry of Science and Technology, Technology Bhavan, New Mehrauli Street, New Delhi 110 016 (tel: 2301-4999; fax: 2686-3847).

Ministry of Space, Lok Nayak Bhavan, New Delhi 110 003 (tel: 2469-7130; fax: 2461-7377).

Ministry of Surface Transport, Transport Bhavan, Parliament Street, New Delhi 110 001(tel: 2371-4095; fax: 2373-1270).

Ministry of Textiles, Udyog Bhavan, Rafi Marg, New Delhi 110 001 (tel: 2301-3779; fax: 2301-3711).

Ministry of Tourism, Transport Bhawan, Parliament Street, New Delhi 110 001 (tel: 2338-4173; fax: 2338-5115).

Ministry of Urban Development and Poverty Alleviation, Nirman Bhavan, Maulana Azad Road, New Delhi 110 011 (tel: 2301-8495; fax: 2301-4459; e-mail: muae@urban.delhi.nic.in).

Ministry of Water Resources, Shram Shakti Bhawan, Rafi Marg, New Delhi 110 001 (tel: 2371-4200; fax: 2371-0253; e-mail: webmaster@mowr.delhi.nic.in).

Ministry of Youth Affairs and Sport, Shastri Bhavan, Dr Rajendra Prasad Road, New Delhi 110 001 (tel: 2338-4183; e-mail: web.yas.@sb.nic.in).

Prime Minister's Office, South block, New Delhi 110 011 (tel: 2301-2312; fax: 2301-6857).

Other useful addresses

Asian Development Bank, India Resident Mission, 37 Golf Links, New Delhi 110 003 (tel: 2469-2578; fax: 2463-6175; e-mail:adbinrm@mail.asiandevbank.org).

British Deputy High Commission, Maker Chambers IV, 222 Jamnalal Bajaj Road, PO Box 11714, Nariman Point, Mumbai 400021 (tel: 2283-0517, 2283-2330, 2283-3602; fax: 2202-7940).

British High Commission, Shanti Path, Chanakyapuri, New Delhi 110 021 (tel: 2687-2161; fax: 2687-2882).

British Deputy High Commission, 1 Ho Chi Minh Sarani, Kolkata 700016 (tel: 242-5171; fax: 242-3435).

British Deputy High Commission, 24 Anderson Road, Chennai 600006 (tel: 827-3136/7; fax: 826-9004).

British Trade Office, 37/7 Cunningham Road, Bangalore 560052 (tel: 2220-4844; fax: 2220-4855).

Delhi Stock Exchange Association Ltd, 3 and 4/4B Asaf Ali Rd, New Delhi 110 002 (tel: 2327-9000/1302; fax: 2332-6182).

Delhi Tourism and Transport Development Corporation Ltd, 18A DDA, SCO Complex, Defence Colony, New Delhi 24 (tel: 2461-4354; fax: 2469-7352).

Department of Atomic Energy, South Block, New Delhi 110 011 (tel: 2301-1773; fax: 2301-3843).

Department of Electronics, Electronics Niketan, 6 CGO Complex, New Delhi 110 003 (tel: 2436-3101; fax: 2436-3083).

Federation of Indian Exports Organisation (FIEO), 56 Asiad Village, New Delhi 110 016 (tel: 2649-3220).

Foreign Investment Promotion Board, Prime Minister's Office, South Block, New Delhi 110 011 (tel: 2301-7839; fax: 2301-6857).

India Investment Centre, Jeewan vihar Building, Sansad Marg, New Delhi 110 001 (tel: 2373-3673; fax: 2373-245).

Indian Airlines, Stores and Purchases Department, Safdarjung Airport, New Delhi 110 003 (tel: 2461-1293; fax: 2462-1776; e-mail: sinha.ial@gems.vsnl.net.in).

Indian Embassy (USA), 2107 Massachusetts Avenue, NW, Washington DC 20008 (tel: (+1-202) 939-7000; fax: (+1-202) 265-4351; e-mail: indembwash@indiagov.org).

Infrastructure Leasing and Financial Services, East Court, Zone VI, 4th Floor,

India Habitat Centre, Lodhi Road, New Delhi 110 003 (tel: 2463-6637/41/42).

Power Grid Corporation of India Ltd, 10th Floor, Hemkunt Chambers 89, Nehru Place, New Delhi 110 019 (tel: 2622-2995, 2646-6806; fax: 2647-3332, 2642-8357).

Silk and Rayon Export Promotion Council, Resham Bhavan 78, Veer Nariman Rd, Mumbai 400020 (tel: 2294-792).

State Trading Corporation of India, Jawahar Vyapar Bhavan, Tolstoy Marg, New Delhi 110 001 (tel: 2331-3177; fax: 2332-6741).

The Stock Exchange (BSE), Phiroze Jeejeebhoy Towers, Dalal Street, Mumbai 400001 (tel: 2272-1233/4; fax: 2272-1552; e-mail: info@bseindia.com; internet site: http://www.bseindia.com).

Trade Development Authority, PO Box 767, Bank of Baroda Building, Parliament St, New Delhi 110 001 (tel: 2332-0214).

US Embassy, Shanti Path, Chanakyapuri, New Delhi 110 021(tel: 2687-6500; fax: 2687-6579, 2687-0031 (Consular Section)).

There are over 40 domestic news agencies.

Press Trust of India: www.ptinews.com

United News of India: www.uniindia.com

Internet sites

Explore India: http://www.exploreindia.com

General Information: http://www.hcidhaka.org

India Department of Commerce: http://www.nic.in/eximpol/

India On-line: http://indiaonline.com/index.html

Indian business: http://www.indiamart.com/allindia/

Indian company information: http://www.tradeaccess.com/general.htm

Indian Economy and Business links: http://www.ib-net.com/links/economy.htm

India Opportunity: http://www.DocuWeb.ca/India

Indian Press Information Bureau: http://www.nic.in/India-Image/PIB/

Indian weather service: http://weather.nic.in

Indonesia

KEY FACTS

Official name: Republik Indonesia (Republic of Indonesia)

Head of State: President Joko 'Jokowi' Widodo (PDI-P) (elected 22 Jul, took office 20 Oct 2014)

Head of government: President Joko 'Jokowi' Widodo (PDI-P) (elected 22 Jul, took office 20 Oct 2014)

Ruling party: Minority Coalition led by Partai Demokrasi Indonesia-Perjuangan, (PDI-P) (Indonesian Democratic Party-Struggle) (from Nov 2014)

Area: 1,919,443 square km (17,508 islands)

Population: 251.49 million (2014)*

Capital: Jakarta, on Java

Official language: Bahasa Indonesia

Currency: Rupiah (Rp) = 100 sen

Exchange rate: Rp14,280.00 per US$ (Sep 2015)

GDP per capita: US$3,534 (2014)*

GDP real growth: 5.03% (2014)

GDP: US$888.65 billion (2014)

Unemployment: 6.10% (2014)*

Inflation: 6.39% (2014)

Oil production: 852,000 bpd (2014)*

Natural gas production: 73.40 billion cum (2014)

Balance of trade: US$6.98 billion (2014)*

* estimated figure

Joko 'Jokowi' Widodo, who took office as president in late October 2014, represented a breath of fresh air in Indonesia's often claustrophobic politics. His political career only dated back nine years; before that he was in the furniture business – his father was a carpenter. Despite his relative inexperience, once elected mayor of the nondescript town of Solo in central Java, in no time at all – in 2012 – he became governor of Indonesia's capital, Jakarta. His new broom image had stood him in good stead, he was set to become Indonesia's first leader not to have emerged from the political or military elite. In his early political career he did have the key support of former President Megawati Sukarnoputri.

Reuters reported that Jokowi's rise through the ranks of local government could be attributed to 'his refusal to be intimidated by entrenched interests.' His famous impromptu visits around Jakarta had endeared him to a broad swathe of Indonesians, in particular the poor and minority groups. Reuters also quoted Paul Rowland, a Jakarta base political analyst: 'Jokowi's the first genuinely post-Suharto figure (while) everybody else comes from that era, including Prabowo. He is a different generation of politician and there's a market for politicians like him who are lower-key but who get things done.'

While president-elect he had told Reuters that he would continue to shake things up as president. He promised to 'beef up' Indonesia's inadequate infrastructure, simplify Indonesia's often impenetrable regulations and sack ministers if they aren't up to the job. 'If (ministers don't succeed) there are more than a thousand other good people in Indonesia to replace them. I can cut and then replace them. It's very simple for me,' he announced.

Mosaics

As the Middle East imploded over the Sunni-Shi'a divide, Indonesia's position as the country with the world's largest Muslim population bore particular scrutiny. It is also the world's fourth most populated country and third biggest democracy. The relatively smooth electoral process challenged the idea that Islam and democracy are incompatible. But also in the context of Indonesia's weight in the Islamic world, it is warmly welcomed that Indonesia's outgoing President, Susilo Bambang Yudhoyono, had condemned the Islamic State (IS) , which was challenging the *status quo* of the Middle East. The former president had called the IS an 'embarrassment to Islam' and had committed Indonesia to fighting extremism. It remained to be seen whether the criticism, which for many was a welcome contrast with the silence of the leaders of most other Muslim countries and organisations, such as the Organisation of Islamic States and the Arab League, would gain traction. But it clearly determined Indonesia's position.

Certainly, Jokowi looked unlikely to shift his country's external position one way or the other. He is seen to be a devout Muslim – in the immediate run up to the election when campaigning was not allowed, he had made a quick trip to Mecca. According to a report in the London *Economist*, Jokowi 'far outpolled Mr Prabowo among Indonesia's religious minorities.'

Jokowi's not joking

Joko Widodo began 2015 knowing that he will now have trillions of fresh rupiah to spend that his predecessors had lacked. Having trimmed petrol subsidies in November 2014, Mr Jokowi, scrapped them entirely from the beginning of January 2015. Small subsidies (1,000 rupiah, or eight US cents, per litre) were to remain in place for diesel fuel, used extensively for public transport and by Indonesia's millions of fishermen. But for the first time in decades, the price of petrol (gasoline) would reflect global market prices.

The move was not, however, without political risk. Furious protests had broken out when Jokowi's predecessor, Susilo Bambang Yudhoyono, attempted to raise fuel prices. Smaller protests had greeted Jokowi's November 2014 move. But in January, there were no protests at all. Falling global oil prices had cushioned the effect: the price of an unsubsidised litre of petrol in March cost Rp7,600 (US$0.53), well down on the subsidised price of

Rp8,500 (US$0.60) in December 2014. Even so, after the removal of the fuel subsidies, President Jokowi's popularity ratings had fallen – from 75 per cent to 46 per cent by October 2015.

Removing the fuel subsidies gave the government more fiscal room for manoeuvre. Amazingly, energy subsidies had often accounted for as much as one fifth of total government spending, more than its spending on infrastructure and social-welfare programmes combined. And the benefits typically flowed not to the poor, which was their supposed justification, but to Indonesia's car-owning middle classes.

Finance minister Bambang Brodjonegoro had claimed that the savings would be of the order of Rp200 trillion, almost US$16 billion. Roughly half of the windfall was already accounted for, destined to items such as the delayed payments of the previous year's subsidies, cash transfers to the poor to compensate for the subsidy cuts and funds owed to Indonesia's villages under a law enacted by the previous administration.

Some of these disbursements were 'one off' payments, which would not recur. But even after these had been made, there was enough left in the government's kitty to achieve quite a lot. The details were to be revealed in the 2016 budget. But the broad lines were already known; the priorities were increased spending on health, education and infrastructure and the reduction of the budget deficit to below two per cent of gross domestic product (GDP).

The 2015 abolition of fuel subsidies followed three programmes that were already under way: the Indonesia Health Card, the Indonesia Smart Card and the Family Welfare Fund. Between them, these three gave free health insurance to Indonesia's poor, guaranteed 12 years of free schooling as well as tertiary education to students accepted to university and provided cash transfers to poor Indonesians to help with the phasing-out of fuel subsidies. Indonesia had made some efforts to promote foreign direct investment (FDI) to fund a number of infrastructure projects. However, some of Indonesia's infrastructure needs, such as port and rail construction in remote areas would not be of commercial interest. .

President Jokowi had also voiced the need to restore Indonesia to a healthier growth rate of 7 per cent a year. Many analysts considered this to be an unrealistic target; growth levels like that had not been seen for some twenty years. In 2015 commodity prices had slumped and Chinese growth had slowed. The World Bank had forecast Indonesian growth at 5.2 per cent in 2015.

In its March 2015 assessment of the Indonesian economy, the International Monetary Fund (IMF) noted that since mid-2013, Indonesia had taken significant steps to strengthen policy and reserve buffers, in the face of strong headwinds confronting major commodity exporters and the periods of heightened market volatility in emerging market economies (EMEs). Aided by enhanced policy credibility and global push factors, external inflows to Indonesia had been supportive during the previous 18 months. Equity prices had rebounded, government bond yields had stabilised, with the fixed-income market buoyed by strong foreign inflows, which had led to an increase in reserves and helped keep the rupiah relatively stable against the US dollar.

However, in the view of the IMF the Indonesian economy continued to be affected by changing terms of trade against commodity exporters, with 'significant macro-financial implications'. The commodity down-cycle had weakened the current account, restricted new investment and resulted in a growth slowdown.

As a consequence, the IMF noted, corporate cash flows had been constrained, which had caused bank deposit growth to slow sharply and had contributed to funding pressures. More recently, credit growth had decelerated, in part due to monetary and macro-prudential policy measures, which have led to a moderate tightening in financial conditions. Household demand for credit had also slowed, according to the IMF, affecting private consumption and property prices. At the same time, private external borrowing had risen, with companies taking advantage of lower borrowing costs abroad.

The Jokowi administration, according to the IMF, appeared keen to ease the longstanding supply bottlenecks through a reform strategy that aimed to raise potential growth. As a first step, as detailed above, it had taken action to remove most fuel subsidies with a view to freeing up space in the government budget for what the IMF described as more growth-critical spending. In keeping with this, the authorities had tried to maintain macro-economic and financial stability, as Indonesia moved away from commodity-supported to competition-driven growth in a challenging global environment. Growth in Indonesia moderated to 5.1 per cent in 2014 from 5.7 per cent in 2013 – in line with the IMF's expectations and to its slowest pace in five years. While the growth in domestic demand was broadly unchanged, the contribution from net exports was significantly weaker in 2014 owing to slowing EME growth, notably in China and the raw mineral ore export ban. However, the current account deficit appeared to have narrowed moderately in 2014, owing to the effects of the exchange rate (REER) depreciation (about 7 per cent since mid-2013) and of lower oil prices on imports. Headline inflation had moved back above the Bank of Indonesia's target band towards end 2014 following the ending of fuel subsidies.

The IMF considered that the near-term outlook would continue to be complicated by cross currents in the global economy affecting financial conditions and commodity prices. While growth was expected to be weighed down by commodity-related activities, prospects were expected to improve as the domestic reform momentum gathered pace. The impact of the fall in oil prices was also expected to dampen inflation pressures and strengthen the current account through lower oil imports.

GDP growth was projected to rise to 5.2 per cent in 2015. Net exports were likely to remain constrained by weak external demand, notwithstanding one-off factors that were expected to boost oil and mineral exports. Private consumption growth was expected to slow due mainly to reduced commodity incomes. While total investment growth should rise moderately, the impetus was expected to come mainly from higher public infrastructure spending. Private investment growth would probably remain subdued because of funding constraints. Without some improvement in public investment, GDP growth might even be lower in 2015.

Funding pressures might also intensify if capital inflows were lower than envisaged and/or budgetary pressures affected liquidity, limiting space for new lending. Headline inflation was expected to decline in 2015, with reductions in retail gasoline and diesel prices under the new fuel price regime along with the passing through of the earlier price increase expected to bring inflation back within the BI's target band (4.0±1 per cent) by the end of 2015, if supported by the maintenance of a relatively tight monetary stance.

The current account deficit was projected to narrow slightly in 2015, mainly due to a reduction in net oil imports, but adjustment was expected to be partially offset by lower non-fuel commodity prices and weak external demand. The balance of payments recorded a sizeable surplus in 2014 following strong capital inflows, but a smaller surplus was expected in 2015 on shifts in global financial conditions. Indonesia' reserves at the end of 2014 were US$111.9 billion, equivalent to 7 months of prospective imports of goods and services or 160 per cent of the IMF's reserve metric for a floating currency, which should be sufficient to deal with most shocks.

Growth was projected by the IMF to rise to 6 per cent by 2018, factoring in positive reform momentum, which was also expected to raise growth potential through increases in factor productivity and capital stock. The current account deficit would narrow to 2.5 per cent of GDP in the medium term, factoring in increased investment-related imports as well as a subdued outlook for commodity prices. Gross FDI would continue to grow while portfolio inflows would remain supportive, with reserves expected to remain above six months of imports. Risks to this outlook were moderately on the downside, given the possibility of less supportive global financial conditions, more muted growth in major trading partners and slower and narrower reforms than envisaged in the current baseline.

The Indonesia authorities generally agreed with the IMF on macro-economic prospects for 2014, but were more optimistic on the growth outlook in 2015 on expectations of a faster rise in public investment. The IMF and Indonesian authorities' views were broadly aligned on the inflation forecast and the external outlook. The authorities also agreed with the IMF on its assessment of the major risks facing the economy and the appropriate policy responses, noting that since mid-2013 the Indonesia economy had weathered several mini-episodes of EME turbulence comparatively well.

Politicians

If his country's economy seemed to be moving slowly, at least it was doing so relatively smoothly. However, the same could not be said of his cabinet. No sooner had the business-like Joko Widodo called on his ministers to set aside their egos, than his new cabinet was beset by renewed squabbles, threatening to undo Presidential attempts to revive an economy that was growing at its slowest pace for some six years.

Risal Ramli, the new co-ordinating minister for maritime affairs, had been admonished by President Widodo after publicly criticising Vice President Jusuf Kalla and state-owned enterprises minister, Rini Soemarno. The president told Mr Ramli to voice his concerns privately at cabinet meetings in future, according to the presidential spokesman. President Widodo's critics claimed that the economy had actually gone into reverse, largely because of the bickering and sniping between ministers and bureaucrats.

In the second quarter of 2015, Indonesia's growth had slipped to an annual 4.67

KEY INDICATORS — Indonesia

	Unit	2011	2012	2013	2014	**2015
Population	m	241.03	*244.47	*247.95	*251.49	*255.08
Gross domestic product (GDP)	US$bn	845.70	877.80	912.50	888.65	*895.68
GDP per capita	US$	3,509	3,591	3,680	*3,534	0
GDP real growth	%	6.5	6.3	5.6	5.0	*5.2
GNP per capita	US$	0	0	0	0	*3,511
Inflation	%	5.4	4.0	6.4	6.4	*6.8
Unemployment	%	6.6	6.1	6.3	*6.1	*5.8
Oil output	'000 bpd	942.0	918.0	882.0	852.0	–
Natural gas output	bn cum	75.6	71.1	70.4	73.4	–
Coal output	mtoe	199.8	237.4	258.9	281.7	–
Exports (fob) (goods)	US$m	191,713.1	187,346.5	–	175,292.7	–
Imports (fob) (goods)	US$m	156,869.3	178,670.3	–	168,310.2	–
Balance of trade	US$m	34,843.8	8,676.2	–	6,982.5	–
Current account	US$m	2,070.0	-24,419.0	-29,115.0	*-26,233.0	*-27,058.0
Total reserves minus gold	US$m	105,000.3	108,837.0	96,364.0	108,836.0	–
Foreign exchange	US$m	101,966.8	105,907.0	93,427.0	–	–
Exchange rate	per US$	9,740.66	9,628.40	12,160.00	12,421.80	–

per cent, its slowest pace in six years and by mid-2015 the rupiah had dropped by 10 per cent against the US dollar to a 17-year low, making it South-east Asia's worst performing currency after Malaysia's ringgit.

Mr Ramli, one of six new ministers brought into office in a cabinet reshuffle had meant to assuage investors' concerns about policy muddles, by challenging Mr Kalla to debate the vice president's 'unrealistic' plans to build power plants capable of generating 35,000 megawatts over a five year period. Twice a minister under former President Abdurrahman Wahid, Mr Ramli was known for his forthright views on the economy. Thought to be close to Megawati Sukarnoputri, the titular head of the Partai Demokrasi Indonesia-Perjuangan (PDI-P) (Indonesian Democratic Party-Struggle) President Widodo's political party, Mr Ramli was responsible for a number of ministries, including energy, transport and tourism. He had also criticised plans by Indonesia's national airline, Garuda, to buy 30 Airbus passenger aircraft with US$44.5 billion in loans. The political consultant Kevin O'Rourke noted that: 'The major deficiency of the cabinet reshuffle is the return of Ramli to national office… Ramli is likely to continue provoking discord between ministers.'

Energy

Formerly a net oil exporter and a member of the Organisation of the Petroleum Exporting Countries (OPEC) for several decades, by the twenty-first century, Indonesia was finding it difficult to attract sufficient investment to meet growing domestic energy consumption. According to the United States Energy Information Administration, this was largely due to inadequate infrastructure and a complex regulatory environment. After suspending its OPEC membership in 2008, Indonesia looked set to rejoin the cartel by 2016 as it attempted to secure more crude oil supplies for its swiftly rising demand and greater investment from OPEC's Middle Eastern members in its downstream infrastructure projects. Despite Indonesia's energy struggles, the EIA reported that it was the world's largest exporter of coal by weight and the fifth-largest exporter of liquid natural gas (LNG) in 2014. As Indonesia seeks to meet its energy export obligations and earn revenues through international market sales, the country is also trying to meet energy demand at home.

Indonesia's total primary energy consumption grew by 43 per cent between 2003 and 2013, according to the Indonesian government. Petroleum continued to account for the highest portion of Indonesia's energy mix at 38 per cent in 2013. In the previous decade, coal consumption had more than doubled, surpassing natural gas consumption and becoming the second most consumed fossil fuel as Indonesia turned to less expensive sources of indigenous fuels. Indonesia intended to reduce its reliance on petroleum in its energy consumption portfolio to a 25 per cent maximum share while raising the coal and natural gas portions to at least 30 per cent and 22 per cent, respectively, by 2025.

The EIA noted that Indonesia's energy sector continued to influence the economy to a large degree, although the decline in oil and natural gas production during the previous few years had lowered its impact. Oil and natural gas alone constituted 15 per cent of merchandise exports in 2014, a decline from 23 per cent in 2000. In addition, revenues from the oil and gas sector, which historically accounted for about 20 per cent of total state revenues, fell below 20 per cent after 2008 and were less than 12 per cent in 2014, despite high oil prices during most of the year. The significant drop in global crude oil prices, which started in June 2014, was expected to reduce Indonesia's oil and gas revenues by at least one-third in 2015. A combination of healthy growth, some market reforms, higher hydrocarbon prices and a stable government encouraged rapid investment, particularly in the commodity sector until around 2010. Factors that have greatly hindered foreign investment in the past few years include more technically challenging oil and natural gas extraction, rising domestic energy demand and accompanying limitations on exports, higher taxes on exploration and production and lengthier processes to procure and renew contracts.

Despite the government's emphasis on more private sector involvement in infrastructure expansion, many infrastructure projects continue to be delayed, because regulatory challenges and uncertainties have reduced predictability for foreign investors. Indonesia's recently elected government under President Joko Widodo is attempting several energy sector reforms to address the country's regulatory burdens and lack of legal transparency and to attract much-needed foreign investment for its more capital-intensive and technically challenging energy projects.

President Widodo's new reforms attempt to address corruption and informal markets, streamline the regulatory process for investors, make domestic prices more competitive with international markets and reduce upstream oil and natural gas costs for investors. However, Indonesia's energy security policy of retaining more of its hydrocarbon production for domestic use and maintaining local content requirements will continue to hamper investment from international companies.

Exececutions

Andrew Chan and Myuran Sukumaran attempted to smuggle narcotics into Australia from Indonesia in 2005. Both Australians were promptly arrested and imprisoned by Indonesian authorities. On 28 April 2015, Chan and Sukumaran, along with six others (including five more foreigners), were executed by firing squad. One of the other victims was a 50-year-old Nigerian man who was caught carrying just 50g of heroin.

Repeated attempts by the Australian government to suspend their death sentences were met with deaf ears. Allegations have also been made that Indonesian judges requested bribes, and that the decision had been made for them by governmental people higher up.

International outrage followed the executions, especially as Chan and Sukumaran were widely believed to be reformed men, an assessment backed up by their Indonesian prison guards. Chan had married his girlfriend the day before his death, while Sukumaran had almost completed a fine arts degree.

The verdict and subsequent execution has increased calls for foreign aid to be more dependent on a country's human rights record.

People to watch

Risal Ramli, the co-ordinating minister for maritime affairs

Risk assessment

Economy	Good/fair
Politics	Good/fair
Regional stability	Good

Muslims in Indonesia

% of population	86.1
Sunni (% of Muslims)	99
Shi'a (% of Muslims)	1

COUNTRY PROFILE

It is thought that Negroid peoples came to Irian Jaya from East Africa around 30,000 years ago. Melanesians arrived later; the resultant population migrated throughout the islands of what is now Indonesia. Later settlers arrived from India, Burma and China. Islam spread to Indonesia as a result of strong trading links with the Arabian Peninsula.

1511 The Portuguese arrived in Indonesia, looking for spices. The Spaniards followed, bringing Christianity to the region.

1799 The Dutch spread control of the territory through the United East India Company. They gradually extended their control throughout the entire region. The Portuguese maintained East Timor.

1924 The Partai Kommunis Indonesia (PKI) (Indonesian Communist Party) was established. It was first active among trade unionists and rural villagers. The rural areas came to be the PKI's main power base.

1942–45 The islands of the Dutch East Indies were occupied by the Japanese. After the Second World War the Dutch regained control. Nationalist leader Ahmed Sukarno returned from internal exile and organised the fight for independence from Dutch colonial rule.

1945 In a speech in July Sukarno urged the adoption of the *Panca Sila* (Five Principles) as the ideological basis of the new state. The five principles were nationalism, internationalism (or humanitarianism), democracy, social justice, and belief in God.

1949 After four years of insurgency The Netherlands recognised the independence of Indonesia. A federal constitution was introduced, giving limited self-government to the 16 constituent regions. Ahmed Sukarno as leader of the Partai Nasional Indonesia (PNI) (Indonesian Nationalist Party), assumed the presidency. The Dutch retained control of West Papua; the Portuguese retained control of East Timor.

1950 The constitution was dissolved and the country adopted a unitary political structure. Sukarno was elected president.

1955 Sukarno won Indonesia's first general election. Political instability prompted Sukarno to dissolve parliament and a period of autocratic rule ensued.

1962 Dutch authority for West Papua was passed to UN administration.

1963 Authority for West Papua was transferred to Indonesia.

1964 Indonesia laid claim to areas of Borneo which had been granted to Malaysia on its independence, leading to a three-year guerrilla conflict on the Malaysian border, which severely damaged the Indonesian economy.

1965 A failed *coup d'état* by the PKI resulted in the deaths of hundreds of thousands of left-wing activists.

1967 Sukarno transferred full emergency power to General Suharto, commander of the Indonesian armed forces.

1968 General Suharto became president.

1975 Portugal granted independence to its colony of East Timor.

1976 East Timor was invaded by Indonesia and became a province. This annexation was never officially recognised by the UN.

1985 Australia recognised Indonesia's incorporation of East Timor.

1997 The South-East Asian economic crisis caused the rupiah to plummet in value.

1998 Suharto, re-elected in March, was forced to resign on 21 May after accusations of corruption and widespread public disturbances as the country's economy reached near collapse. He was succeeded by Bacharuddin Jusuf Habibie.

1999 A UN sponsored referendum on independence was supported by the population of East Timor. Anti-independence militia rampaged through East Timor until UN administration is imposed and the Indonesian government agreed to grant it independence. Abdurrahman Wahid was elected president of Indonesia by the People's Consultative Assembly.

2000 Ex-president Suharto's trial, on corruption charges, collapsed. Ethnic, religious and separatist violence in several provinces grew.

2001 The IMF halted further loans citing the government's inability to tackle corruption. Wahid was voted out of office for his alleged involvement in two financial scandals. Vice President Megawati Sukarnoputri (daughter of Indonesia's first president, Ahmed Sukarno) was sworn in as president.

2002 Indonesia, Malaysia and the Philippines signed a pact to counter terrorism. The government and separatist rebels in Aceh province signed a peace agreement giving greater autonomy and free elections to Aceh in exchange for disarmament by rebels. Constitutional changes included the posts of president and vice president to be by popular vote. A bomb planted by Islamic fundamentalists on the island of Bali, and targeted at Western tourists, killed 202 people. The International Court of Justice awarded the disputed islands of Sipadan and Ligitan to Malaysia.

2003 The Aceh peace accord failed; martial law was imposed. Three Bali bomb suspects were found guilty and sentenced to death.

2004 Susilo Bambang Yudhoyono won the presidential elections. An earthquake off the island of Sumatra caused a devastating *tsunami* that struck coastal areas throughout the region, particularly the peninsula of Aceh on Sumatra island. The final estimate for Indonesia was 167,000 dead or missing and 572,126 displaced.

2005 An agreement was signed between the leaders of Indonesia and Timor-Leste, recognising the location of their shared land border. The government withdrew the last troops from Aceh province, following the disbanding of the military wing of the Gerakan Aceh Merdeka (GAM) (Free Aceh Movement) a few days earlier.

2006 Legislation was introduced extending partial home rule to Aceh. Local elections were held in Aceh for a governor and other officials. The Partai Hati Nurani Rakyat (Partai Hanura) (People's Conscience Party) was founded by retired General Wiranto, formerly of the Golkar party.

2008 Former president (1967–98) Suharto died. The government was forced to raise fuel prices by around 30 per cent, in line with global prices; this lead to civil unrest. Global oil prices fell at the end of the year allowing subsidies to be re-introduced.

2009 In parliamentary elections, 38 political parties and 11,219 candidates (of which 30 per cent were required to be women candidates), took part. Incumbent, President Susilo Bambang Yudhoyono (commonly known as SBY) (DP coalition) was re-elected with 60.8 per cent of the vote. A 10-party coalition was formed from all political parties that won seats in the elections. An earthquake of 7.9 magnitude struck centred off the island of Sumatra, killing over 500 people, as buildings collapsed in the city of Padang.

2010 Darmin Nasution was approved as governor of Bank Indonesia (the central bank). There had been no permanent governor for 14 months. Religious violence increased in secular Indonesia, as the hard-line Front Pembela Islam (FPI) (Islamic Defenders Front) targeted Christians and other minority religious minorities and popular night-time entertainment venues. All illegally harvested wood and wood products were banned from export; official certificates, proving timber was legally sourced became mandatory. A *tsunami* struck the islands of Mentawai, off the west coast of Sumatra, killing over 400 people. The volcano Merapi erupted on the central island of Java, killing dozens of people.

2011 In June, following the execution of an Indonesian domestic worker by Saudi Arabia, a ban was placed on all Indonesian citizens working as domestic servants in Saudi Arabia from August. In June, President Yudhoyono announced that neither he, nor his wife or sons would run in presidential elections in 2014.

2012 The government announced on 12 March that the Indonesian rupiah would be redenominated in 2013, removing three zeros from the currency. On 8 June, Australia banned live cattle exports to Indonesia until animal welfare safeguards in Indonesian abattoirs can be assured. On 21 June Umar Patek was sentenced to 20 years imprisonment for the 2002 Bali bombings that killed 202 people. On 30 October, ethnic violence caused the evacuation of two villages in Lampung Province as hundreds of homes were destroyed and at least 10 people killed. Local Lampung people have been in conflict with migrant communities of Balinese descent on the island of Sumatra. On 6 November, the Supreme Court granted an injunction that stopped a 20 per cent export tax on mineral commodities (excluding coal), being applied by the government. The tax was intended to encourage value added processes to the minerals before export.

2013 On 17 June parliament finally passed a revised budget which cut fuel subsidies by an average 44 per cent. At the same time a handout of US$15 per month to the poor was agreed to help for four months after the rise.

2014 Parliamentary elections were held on 9 April. The main results were Partai Demokrasi Indonesia Perjuangan (PDI–P) (Indonesian Democratic Party-Struggle) 109 seats (out of 560) (19.46 per cent of seats), Partai Golongan Karya (Golkar Party) (Party of the Functioning Groups) 91 seats (16.25 per cent), Partai Demokrat (PD) (Democratic Party) 61 seats (10.89 per cent). Both candidates in the presidential election held on 8 July claimed victory the following day even though votes were still being counted. Turnout was 75.11 per cent. The result was announced on 22 July and was a win for Joko 'Jokowi' Widodo (PDI-P) with 53.15 per cent of the vote, followed by Prabowo Subianto (Gerindra) with 46.85 per cent. Turnout was 69.58 per cent. Mr Widodo took office on 20 October.

2015 In January President Widodo confirmed in an interview with CNN that he would not compromise on the death penalties handed down by the courts for drug smuggling. There were six executions in January. Despite appeals from the governments of Australia, Brazil, Nigeria and Ghana eight further executions of drug smugglers were carried out on 27 April. Australia withdrew their ambassador after the execution of two Australian nationals.

Political structure

Constitution

The system of government is based on the 1945 constitution which underlines the unity of Indonesia as a republic, supplemented by the General Elections Law of 1969.

The constitution provides for five branches of government: the president, the Dewan Perwakilan Rakyat (DPR) (House of People's Representatives), the Supreme Audit Board, the Supreme Court and the Supreme Advisory Council. Despite geographic diversity and the limited reach of the political centre, Indonesia has not implemented a federal system, an option tarnished by association with the colonial era under Dutch rule. Instead, each of the 27 provinces is headed by a governor who is responsible to the president through the minister of home affairs, and represents the central government in his province. The north Sumatran province of Aceh, the territory of Jogjakarta in central Java, and the capital, Jakarta, have a special status.

Since 1985, by law, all major organisations, including political parties, religious groups and trade unions, must include acknowledgement of *Pancasila* (the Five Principles) as their sole guiding ideology in their constitutions. It emphasises tolerance among different religious groups and a political system based on consensus.

All Indonesian citizens over the age of 17 are eligible to vote, as well as those citizens under the age of 17 who are married. To stand for election, a citizen must be at least 21 years old.

In August 2002, 14 amendments were made to the constitution, to take effect with the next elections. The revisions included the abolition of the reservation of 38 parliamentary seats for military personnel.

In July 2003, parliament passed legislation setting the parameters for the first direct presidential election.

Independence date

17 August 1945

Form of state

Democratic republic

The executive

Supreme power is vested in the President of Indonesia, who is both head of state and head of government, directly elected for a term of five years with re-election allowed once. The president may appoint and dismiss ministers (which may be partisan or largely composed of technocrats without an independent power base) and create laws, in agreement with the legislature. The president is head of the military and has the power to declare war, peace and sign treaties.

National legislature

The bicameral Majelis Permusyawaratan Rakyat (MPR) (People's Consultative Assembly) consists of Dewan Perwakilan Rakyat (DPR) (house of representatives) and Dewan Perwakilan Daerah (DPD) (consultative assembly). Since 2009, the DPR has 560 members, directly elected by proportional representation in multi-seat constituencies, to serve for a five-year term. The DPD has 136 members, each of the 34 provinces directly electing four candidates to serve for a four-year term. All statutes and the state budget must be approved by the DPR, which has the right to initiate legislation. All legislation relating to provincial matters is referred to the DPD for consideration and counsel.

Legal system

The judicial powers of the state are exercised by the Supreme Court.

Last elections

22 July 2014 (presidential); 9 April 2014 (parliamentary)

Results: Presidential: Joko 'Jokowi' Widodo (PDI-P) won 53.15 per cent of the vote, Prabowo Subianto (Gerindra) 46.85 per cent. Turnout was 69.58 per cent.

Parliamentary: Partai Demokrasi Indonesia Perjuangan (PDI–P) (Indonesian Democratic Party-Struggle) 109 seats (out of 560) (19.46 per cent of seats), Partai Golongan Karya (Golkar Party) (Party of the Functioning Groups) 91 seats (16.25 per cent), Partai Demokrat (PD) (Democratic Party) 61 seats (10.89 per cent), Partai Amanat Nasional (PAN) (National Mandate Party) 49 seats (8.75 per cent), Partai Kebangkitan Bangsa (PKB) (National Awakening Party) 47 seats (8.39 per cent), Partai Keadilan Sejahtera (PKS) (Prosperous Justice Party) 40 seats (7.14 per cent), Partai Persatuan Pembangunan (PPP) (United Development Party) 39 seats (6.96 per cent), Partai Nasdem (Nasdem) (Nasdem Party) 36 seats (6.25 per cent), Partai Hati Nurani Rakyat (Hanura) (People's Conscience Party) 16 seats (2.86 per cent). Turnout was 75.11 per cent.

Next elections

2019 (parliamentary and presidential)

Political parties

Ruling party

Minority Coalition led by Partai Demokrasi Indonesia-Perjuangan, (PDI-P) (Indonesian Democratic Party-Struggle) (from Nov 2014)

Main opposition party

The government is composed of all political parties that won seats in the general election. There is no official opposition

Population

247.95 million (2013)*

Last census: 1 May 2010: 237,641,326

Population density: 123 inhabitants per square km (2010). Urban population 44 per cent (2010 Unicef).

Annual growth rate: 1.3 per cent, 1990–2010 (Unicef).

Internally Displaced Persons (IDP)

535,000 (UNHCR 2004)

Ethnic make-up

Although 95 per cent of the population are of Malay origin, there are some 300 minorities, including Melanesian, Proto-Austranesian, Polynesian and Micronesian; there are approximately four million ethnic Chinese. Indonesia encompasses the Islamic people of Aceh on the northern tip of Sumatra, the densely populated main island of Java, the tourist resorts of Bali, the island of Flores and the primitive tribes of Irian Jaya in the east.

Religions

Only six faiths are officially recognised in Indonesia - Islam (87 per cent), Catholic and Protestant Christianity (10 per cent), Hinduism (2 per cent, mainly in Bali), Buddhism (1 per cent), and Confucianism.

Indonesia has the world's largest Muslim population, although Hindu-derived and indigenous religious variations are common. Religious violence has spread in line with political uncertainty. Animist beliefs are held in remote areas.

Education

Free universal primary education has been a long-term aim of the government. Almost 100 per cent of eligible children attend such schools, compared to only 40 per cent when President Suharto came to power in 1968. The overall literacy rate has increased by 31 per cent, up from 54 per cent in 1970.

Secondary education consists of two three-year cycles; over 50 per cent of eligible students are in secondary education. Tertiary education has also expanded, with 11 per cent of eligible students in school, up from 1 per cent in the late 1960s. The vast majority of tertiary institutions are privately owned, although there is a network of state institutions around the country. The quality of these universities and colleges varies enormously and large numbers of Indonesian students go overseas for their tertiary education. Despite improvements, the Indonesian education system is not supplying enough technicians and scientists for the country's ambitious plans.

Public expenditure on education typically amounts to 1.4 per cent of annual GDP. In April 2003, the Islamic Development Bank approved a US$31 million loan to Indonesia to finance university expansion.

Literacy rate: 88 per cent adult rate; 98 per cent youth rate (15–24) (Unesco 2005).

Compulsory years: 7 to 16

Enrolment rate: 113 per cent gross primary enrolment of the relevant age group (including repeaters); 56 per cent gross secondary enrolment (World Bank).

Pupils per teacher: 22 in primary schools.

Health

While basic healthcare has improved immeasurably over the past 30 years, it remains an urban rather than rural phenomenon. Inadequate numbers of trained staff remain the rule. Expatriates and wealthier Indonesians usually go to Singapore or Australia for operations.

State healthcare is rudimentary. According to government figures, there are about 1,350 hospitals in Indonesia with 110,200 beds. There are approximately 0.7 hospital beds per 1,000 people, which is low even by regional standards (India has 0.8 beds per 1,000).

Improved water sources are available to 74 per cent of the population.

There were cases of polio reported to the World Health Organisation – Global Polio Eradication Initiative in 2006; the country had previously been free of the disease and its re-emergence was due to infected travellers.

HIV/Aids

Government health figures in December 2009 showed that at least 290,000 people in Indonesia are HIV positive.

HIV prevalence: 0.1 per cent aged 15–49 in 2003 (World Bank)

Life expectancy: 67 years, 2004 (WHO 2006)

Fertility rate/Maternal mortality rate: 2.1 births per woman, 2010 (Unicef); maternal mortality 230 per 100,000 live births (World Bank).

Child (under 5 years) mortality rate (per 1,000): 31 per 1,000 live births (WHO 2012); 27.3 per cent of children aged under five are malnourished (World Bank).

Head of population per physician: 0.13 physicians per 1,000 people, 2003 (WHO 2006)

Welfare

Although poverty has been greatly reduced, the decline in living standards during the economic contraction of 1998 has yet to be reversed. The government has no plans to provide comprehensive welfare for the country's population of over 200 million. Instead, the government attempts to subsidise the cost of living of the poor through price controls, although these are being phased out in line with IMF commitments on goods such as kerosene. The state-run Workers' Accident Insurance and Provident Fund (*Jamsostek*) is the only form of social security in Indonesia. The insurance covers accident, sickness, pensions, unemployment, health and housing benefits. Outside *Jamsostek* there are other welfare programmes provided by private insurance companies, but they are not compulsory.

Main cities

Jakarta (capital, on island of Java, estimated population 9.8 million (m) in 2012); Surabaya (2.8m), Bekasi (2.6m), Bandung (2.5m), Medan (on Sumatra) (2.2m), Depok (1.9m), Tangerang (1.9m), Semarang (on Java) (1.6m), Palembang (on Sumatra) (1.5m), Ujung Pandang (Makassar) (on Sulawesi) (1.4m).

Languages spoken

Bahasa Indonesia has existed as an official language for the past 70 years, and is still in the process of developing, with new words constantly being added. For simplicity's sake, the use of English words is common, particularly in the banking, insurance and technology sectors. However, the government wishes to promote Indonesian language development and reduce the use of foreign words.

English is widely spoken in government and business circles and by the younger generation. Many older Indonesians speak Dutch as a second language.

Each ethnic group has its own language. Altogether, more than 580 languages and dialects are spoken, including Javanese, Sundanese, Arabic and Chinese.

Official language/s

Bahasa Indonesia

Media

The constitution provides for freedom of the press and speech, however, the government has occasionally restricted these rights. The Constitution Court struck down several laws in 2006–07 that criminalised defamation of the government, president and vice president, which had been used to curtail reporting. The government restricts the movement of journalist around the country and special permits must be obtained to visit, for example, West Papua.

Press

Dailies: In Indonesian, the largest newspapers include *Kompas* (http://kompas.com), *Media Indonesia* (www.mediaindonesia.com), *Koran Tempo* (www.korantempo.com), *Republik* (www.republika.co.id), *Pos Kota* (www.poskota.co.id) and *Rakyat Merdeka* (www.rakyatmerdeka.co.id) a tabloid. In English *The Jakarta Post* (www.thejakartapost.com), which includes business and financial news.

There are many more regional and local newspapers available.

Weeklies: In Indonesian, magazines include *Tempo* (www.tempointeractive.com) with English online edition, *Gatra* (www.gatra.com) for news and current affairs, *Tabloid Nova* (www.tabloidnova.com) and *Hanyawanita* (www.hanyawanita.com), is for women.

Business: In Indonesian, newspapers and magazines include *Bisnis Indonesia* (http://web.bisnis.com), *Bisnis Bali* (www.bisnisbali.com) and *SWA* (www.swa.co.id); the *JIEF Economic Monthly* (www.jief.biz) is also in Japanese and *Warta Ekonomi* (www.wartaekonomi.com). In English, publications include the *Standard Trade and Industry Directory of Indonesia Indonesian Commercial Newsletter*.

Periodicals: In Indonesian, the monthly *Femina* (www.femina-online.com) is for women. *Intisari* is a science monthly. In English, the quarterly *Inside Indonesia* (http://insideindonesia.org) has in-depth articles on politics and social issues and the monthly *Latitudes Magazine* has features on culture, travel and the arts.

Broadcasting

The government bans live news coverage and relayed international live news programmes on radio and television. However, digital news via the internet is a growing market.

Radio: There are many radio stations operating in FM and AM frequencies. A few digital audio broadcasting (DAB) stations have begun operations in Jakarta and Surabaya, since 2006.

The national public broadcaster is Radio Republik Indonesia (RRI) (www.rri-online.com), with six networks including the international channel, Voice of Indonesia. Private, commercial stations include Kiss FM (www.kissfm.co.id), Oz Radio Bali (www.ozradio.net) and Radio Otomotion (www.otomotionfm.com) for news.

Television: There are around a dozen national TV networks competing with the publicly owned Televisi Republik Indonesia (TVRI), (www.tvri.co.id), which broadcast free-to-air, cable and satellite TV. Major private TV channels include RCTI (www.rcti.tv) with a variety of locally produced shows including news, entertainment and religion. With similar content, SCTV (www.sctv.co.id) is known for its entertaining serials and Indosiar (www.indosiar.com) known for its cultural programmes and foreign language dramas.

National news agency: Antara National News Agency

Other news agencies: Indoexchange (for stock market news): www.indoexchange.com

Economy

The economy has prospered relatively well since 2006, when Indonesia repaid US$3.2 billion of the US$11.1 billion loan it had incurred during the 1997 Asian financial crisis. This was four years ahead of schedule and just in time to confront the next, and greater, global financial crisis. Indonesia is ranked 16 in the world by GDP, at over US$896 billion, a figure that grew 5.0 per cent on 2013's. It has a market economy in which the government plays an important role through state-owned entities and direct influence through regulation of prices of basic foodstuffs, utilities and fuel.

Within the structure of the economy, the service sector at 39.9 per cent of GDP lies just behind industry at 45.7 per cent. Exports are dominated by oil, natural gas and mineral products at around 40 per cent, with manufactured goods at around 15 per cent. Agriculture provides around 14.4 per cent of GDP, a figure that has been steadily falling since 1985.

GDP growth was 6 per cent in 2008 as domestic consumption and fiscal stimuli counteracted the weak external conditions. In 2009, growth fell to 4.6 per cent reflecting the lack of domestic demand; growth rebounded in 2010 to 6.2 per cent as global trade resumed and remained steady at 5.6 per cent in 2013 before dropping to 5.0 per cent in 2014.

The fiscal stimulus package introduced in 2008, as part of the globally co-ordinated response to the financial crisis, was US$6 billion. Total external debt in 2014 was US$293 billion (32.7 per cent of GDP). Foreign direct investment grew from US$18.2 billion in 2011 to US$23.3 billion in 2013.

External trade

Indonesia is a member of the Asian and Pacific Economic Co-operation (Apec) and belongs to the Asian Free Trade Area (Afta) operated by the Association of Southeast Asian Nations (Asean), which was set up to attract foreign direct investment (FDI) and the elimination of tariffs within the membership.

The US-owned Freeport-McMoran mine Grasberg, located in Papua province, contains the largest single reserve of copper and gold in the world.

Plans to establish Indonesia as a world hub for halal-labelled food products was announced by the minister of economy in March 2012. An estimated 1.4 billion Muslims and non-Muslims purchase halal products worldwide each year and delivering a standard of quality of halal food products from Indonesia would provide a significant boost to the economy. Indonesia has the world's largest population of Muslims.

Imports

Main imports include machinery and equipment, petroleum and chemicals, foodstuffs.

Main sources: China (17.2 per cent total in 2014), Singapore (14.1 per cent), Japan (9.5 per cent)

Exports

One of the most successful export sectors has been consumer electronics and home appliances. Indonesia is the world's leading exporter of coal for power stations, as well as palm oil. Major exports also include oil and gas, plywood, textiles and rubber, copper, gold and other minerals.

A change to the rules governing export earnings became effective on 2 January 2012. The rules require companies to repatriate foreign currency earnings from exports, and to hold the earnings in domestic bank accounts. It is estimated that the amount concerned will be as high as US$33 billion.

Main destinations: Japan (13.1 per cent total in 2014), China (10.0 per cent), Singapore (9.5 per cent)

Agriculture

Farming

Agriculture accounts for around 14.4 per cent of GDP and employs around 35 per cent of the labour force. Agricultural products make up 25 per cent of non-oil export earnings.

After planting more high-yield varieties, investing in irrigation systems, doubling the use of fertilisers and trebling the use of pesticides, Indonesia has achieved self-sufficiency in rice. Poor harvests can still result in rice and other cereals having to be imported to rebuild stocks.

Cassava, maize, sugar, sweet potatoes, bananas and many other fruits and vegetables are grown for local consumption. Self-sufficiency in sugar is a government goal.

It is estimated that there are 1.2 million clove farmers. Indonesia consumes 95 per cent of worldwide clove production, used in the manufacture of *kretek* (clove/tobacco mix) cigarettes. The clove cigarette industry is one of the country's major employers and the government has tariffs in place to restrict the import of cloves, mainly from Madagascar and Zanzibar, in an attempt to maintain its sustainability when over 80 per cent of the cloves consumed is home grown.

Large estates that have undergone rehabilitation produce coffee, tea, rubber, coconuts and palm oil nuts, mostly for export.

Indonesia is the world's largest producer of coconuts and the second-largest of palm oil, copra and natural rubber. It is the third-largest in rice, coffee and cocoa.

Fishing

Foreign aid organisations have assisted the government in rehabilitating the fishing sector. Foreign fishing trawlers are not permitted to operate in Indonesian waters, as these would obstruct traditional coastal fishermen.

Indonesia's fishing industry is plagued by corruption and illegal fishing methods, such as the use of bottle bombs to increase the size of the catch. Ineffective monitoring of fishing techniques means that these practices are likely to continue.

Shrimp and tuna fish are important exports. Other species include scad, Indian mackerel and sea catfish. Indonesia is the fifth largest producer of tuna in the world and has become one of the world's biggest exporters of shrimps and prawns.

Following the annual meeting of the Commission for the Conservation of

Southern Bluefin Tuna (CCSBT), held on Cheju Island, South Korea, all members agreed to a 20 per cut in the roughly 17,000 tonnes in 2009 bluefin tuna catches from 2010. Scientists had warned that without a cut, fish stocks could crash as numbers had become dangerously low.

In 2014, Indonesia's Ministry of Marine Affairs and Fisheries (MMAF) successfully gained membership to the Western and Central Pacific Fisheries Commission. This membership gives Indonesia a stronger bargaining position in relation to tuna management and habitat utilisation.

Forestry

Forest products are the third most important export earner. Indonesia has some of the world's largest remaining reserves of tropical hardwoods. Legislation aims to reduce the rate of felling and to ban the export of logs, and has increased the proportion used locally in timber processing. Illegal logging remains a problem and has doubled the deforestation rate. It is estimated that Indonesia is losing up to two million hectares (ha) of forest annually. It has been estimated that 300,000 cubic metres (cum) of hardwood is illegally felled each year in the state of New Guinea and shipped to China for processing. Indonesia's decentralisation programme could worsen the situation since local governments do not have the ability to manage their resources effectively. The military have also been implicated in the illegal logging trade with corruption and entrenched interests underpinning the activity. Indonesia is under pressure from international organisations to reform its forestry policy and to control the unprecedented rate at which its forests are depleted. Indonesia has 10 per cent of the world's plants but as of 2014 Indonesia surpassed Brazil to become the country with the highest amount of deforestation. In the last 12 years Indonesia has lost 60,000 square metres of virgin forest, an area about the size of Ireland.

Industry and manufacturing

The industrial sector typically contributes 39.9 per cent to Indonesia's GDP and is export-oriented. Important industries include cement production, motor and motorcycle assembly, textiles and garments, high technology industries, industrial chemicals, machinery and appliances. Other industries include food processing, fertilisers, basic metals, wood processing (mainly plywood) and paper products.

Indonesia is an important oil producer and the world's largest exporter of liquefied natural gas (LNG). Indonesia also exports large quantities of copper ore, nickel matte, coal and aluminium. There is a growing aircraft industry that produces small, fixed-wing aircraft and helicopters. These are sold to buyers world-wide.

Most manufacturing is concentrated in Java and Jakarta. These areas have good infrastructure and affluent markets so remain an attractive location for manufacturers. These factors have thwarted government attempts to develop manufacturing outside these areas. Foreign Direct Investment (FDI) has been weak following the Asian Financial Crisis and the government has done little to promote it. This is mainly due to continuing social unrest in the region.

Tourism

With hundreds of islands offering diverse scenery and a historical and cultural heritage, Indonesia can be a land of contrasts. The island of Bali is the most important centre for overseas visitors and has adapted to catering for a relaxed clientele. However, Indonesia is also an important Muslim country and cultures can clash. Tourism is a significant component in the economy and the government is reluctant to enforce a strict Islamic code that could deter visitors. One strategy to overcome the conundrum of culture verses tourism has been the emphasis Indonesia has placed on attracting visitors from the Arab Gulf states. However, with over seven million visitors each year the immediate response by authorities has been to emphasise cultural diversity and respect.

In July 2012, the Bali Province cultural landscape, including the *Subak* system of traditional agriculture and water temples, was added to Unesco's World Heritage List.

Travel and tourism accounted for 9.3 per cent of GDP in 2014 (US$67.8 billion). Employment in the sector was 8.4 per cent (9.8 million jobs) of total workforce, of which 2.9 per cent (3.3 million jobs) were directly employed in the industry.

Environment

Indonesia is ranked first in the world for its range and variety of corals, and together with the Philippines, Australia, Papua New Guinea and Solomon Islands for coral reef fish species.

In 2007 Indonesia was warned by Greenpeace that the drainage of peat wetlands in favour of plantations producing palm oil (used in foods and bio-fuel) was causing greater release of carbon dioxide (a greenhouse gas) than forest clearances by burning alone. Indonesia is planning to become the world's leading producer of palm oil, with a huge project planned for Borneo. In the face of international critisism of deforestation, and Indonesia's ranking as the world's third largest greenhouse emitter, around 80 million trees were planted nationwide in November.

In February 2011 the government admitted that rampant, illegal logging was beyond its control.

Mining

In a move to encourage domestic investment in mining projects the energy and mineral resources ministry announced in February 2012 that foreign investment in mines would in future be limited to 49 per cent. Current foreign mining licence holders will have to cut their stake down from 80 per cent within 10 years. Some alarm was expressed that this will threaten Indonesia's mining investment climate.

The archipelago of Indonesia produces tin, copper and chromium ore. Indonesia is the world's second-largest producer of tin (after China), producing typically 46,000 tonnes of tin concentrate. In addition to other precious metals, it is also a major producer of copper, bauxite and nickel. Mining and quarrying typically accounts for around 13 per cent of GDP. Mining's share of GDP has fallen continuously in recent years as production has dropped in response to depressed world prices. Increasing world demand for copper and rising prices have encouraged mines to be restarted and new mines opened.

The government is eager to increase investment in gold, copper and nickel exploitation, although complex issues are involved in mineral exploitation throughout the archipelago. Indonesia is by far the largest gold producing nation in Asia and one of the top 10 producers in the world. Gold is mined at Lebong Tandai in Sumatra and is produced as a by-product from the Freeport copper mine in the highlands of Irian Jaya. Most of Indonesia's gold mines have a short life span. Instability, particularly in separatist areas such as Aceh and Papua, has halted exploration projects in the past. The majority of gold comes from PT Freeport's mining facility in Irian Jaya.

Nickel is mined from new, large deposits in central Sulawesi and Irian Jaya; much of it becomes ferro-nickel and nickel matte, primarily for export. Bauxite production is carried out at Asahan in north Sumatra, for export to Japan.

Tin mining is carried out by state-owned PT Tambang Timah and joint-venture company PT Koba Tin (25 per cent owned by PT Tambang Timah and 75 per cent owned by Iluka Mining Corporation). PT Tambang Timah is the world's largest tin producer, producing tin from Bangka Island, including dredging operations at Karimun and Kundur islands in the Riau Province. The company has tin reserves estimated at around 382,000 tonnes, of which 60 per cent is located

Hydrocarbons
The role of oil and gas peaked in the early 1980s when it contributed to over four-fifths of total exports. Although oil and gas earnings are still significant, their contribution to GDP is declining. Nevertheless, the oil sector remains very important and Indonesia is the major oil producer in south-east Asia. Nevertheless, the country became a net importer of petroleum products in 2004.

Proven oil reserves were 3.7 billion barrels at the end of 2014, with production of 852,000 barrels per day (bpd) and consumption at 1.64 million bpd. The state-owned oil company, Pertamina, dominates the sector, although foreign involvement has steadily increased. In the downstream sector, Indonesia has nine refineries with a combined capacity of 1.06 million bpd in 2014. The refinery in Balikpapan, East Kalimantan, is to be upgraded in an estimated US$1.7 billion investment plan.

Proven natural gas reserves were 2.9 trillion cubic metres (cum) in 2014 and produced 73.4 billion cum, consumption stood at 38.4 billion cum. Natural gas is supplied from two very large fields at Arun in North Sumatra and Badak in East Kalimantan, although large offshore discoveries have been made around the Natuna Islands in the South China Sea.

Exports of liquefied natural gas (LNG) in 2013 were 23.2 billion cum, making Indonesia the world's fourth-largest LNG exporter in the world, after Qatar, Malaysia and Australia. However, Indonesia's share of world LNG exports has declined heavily since being 20 per cent in 1993 to around 7 per cent in 2014.

In 2014 Indonesia was the world's second largest coal exporter, after Australia, with an 18.7 per cent share of world total. Indonesia exports around 75 per cent of its 258.9 million tonnes oil equivalent (toe) production. Reserves stood at 28 billion tonnes in 2014 and consumption was 60.8 million toe.

Energy
Despite one of the largest populations in Asia, Indonesia has an installed electricity-generating capacity of only 39.9GW, and power shortage outside Jakarta (on Java) has grown due to underinvestment. Access to electricity was over 96 per cent of the population in 2014. Generation is mainly by oil-fired power plants and some hydro-power. Projects are planned to develop coal, gas-fired and hydro-electric power generation in order to preserve oil for export.

Financial markets
Stock exchange

Bursa Efek Indonesia (Indonesia Stock Exchange) (IDX)

Banking and insurance
In July 2006 the central bank announced plans to restructure the banking system by limiting the number of banks investors may control to one. The Indonesia Bank Restructuring Agency (IBRA) was given the task of enhancing public confidence in the banking industry, which had reached a low in 2002, before the sale of Bank Central Asia (BCA), Indonesia's largest bank. Following the sale the IMF commended the government's restructuring policies, which restored solvency to the banking system with net earnings becoming positive for the first time since the 1998 Asia economic crisis. It also advised the government to strengthening standards of corporate governance within the sector.

Indonesia released its first Islamic bond, for individual or retail investors, in February 2009. The government will invest the projected US$6 billion raised to stimulate the economy.

Central bank

Bank Indonesia

Main financial centre

Jakarta

Time
Indonesia has three time zones.

Java, Sumatra, west and central Kalimantan and Madura: GMT plus seven hours – West Zone

Bali, south and east Kalimantan, Sulawesi: GMT plus eight hours – Central Zone

Aru, Kai, Moluccas, Tanimbar, Irian Jaya: GMT plus nine hours – East Zone

Geography
The Indonesian archipelago has 17,508 islands and is the largest in the world, extending about 5,150km (3,200 miles) from Sumatra in the west to Irian Jaya, the western half of New Guinea, in the east. The main islands are Sumatra, Java, Bali, Sulawesi (the Celebes) and Timor. Kalimantan, the Indonesian part of Borneo island shared with Malaysia and Brunei, forms a major part of Indonesian territory. Now independent, the former Portuguese colony of East Timor became the youngest province in 1976. Indonesia's neighbours are Malaysia, Singapore, Papua New Guinea, the Philippines and Australia.

Part of the so-called volcanic 'ring of fire' on the Pacific rim, Indonesia has hundreds of volcanoes, 70 of them still active, and hardly a year passes without a major eruption. Earthquakes are also frequent, but rarely cause significant damage.

The country has the world's second largest area of primary rainforest after Brazil, with species of plant and animal life as diverse as anywhere on the planet. On Borneo alone, there are 3,000 different tree species. It also has an extraordinary diversity of animal life, with an estimated 500 species of mammals, including tigers, elephants, hairy rhinoceros, warthogs, small leopards, civets, mouse deer, orangutans, baboons and monkeys. Birds of Paradise, hornbills, peacocks and cockatoos are among the 1,500 species of known birds. The Komodo dragon is three metres long and weighs up to 150kg. It is the world's largest lizard and it is found only on the east Indonesian island of Komodo.

Hemisphere

Straddles the equator

Climate
All of the islands in the archipelago lie within the tropical zone, with average temperatures of 26 degrees Celsius (C). The dry season usually lasts from May to September, the wet season from October to April. In the hill regions west of Jakarta, average temperatures drop to a pleasant 21 degrees C. Indonesia straddles the equator and days are all the same length and rain is frequent. Yearly rainfall in Jakarta is about 300mm and humidity is more than 80 per cent. The islands east of Bali have a much drier climate, and tropical vegetation and jungles give way to rocky savannahs.

Dress codes
Foreigners are expected to dress for business as they would at home, despite the heat, although men can get away without ties and jackets during the day. Formal attire includes suits, or traditional *batik* shirts. Women are advised to dress conservatively as do their Indonesian counterparts. Although Indonesia is Muslim, there is little of the radicalism found elsewhere. At least in Jakarta, the only women wearing veils will be strict Islamic schoolgirls. The dress traditionally worn by men and women, is the *sarong*. This length of fabric wraps around the waist and is topped by elaborate blouses or shirts. Halter tops and shorts are frowned upon in most places except around sports facilities or on the beach. Proper decorum should especially be observed when visiting places of worship.

Entry requirements
Passports

Required by all and must have at least six months validity from date of entry, with proof of return/onward passage and sufficient funds for length of stay.

Visa

Required by all.

Nationals of Apec countries may obtain business visas for up to six months depending on the country of origin. Travellers should contact an Indonesian Consulate for details.

Business visitors arriving from countries with reciprical visa-free facilities on short-term visits need to supply an itinery, letter of business intent from their employer and a letter from a local sponsor. All other visitors should contact an Indonesian Consulate for visa details.

Currency advice/regulations

The import of local currency is limited to Rp50,000 and must be declared, amounts over Rp10 million must be authorised; export is limited to the amount declared on import. Import and export of foreign currency is unlimited.

Major currencies or travellers cheques may be exchanged at most banks, except in the provinces. It is advisable to carry rupiahs in sufficient amount before travelling to outer provinces or minor towns.

Customs

Personal effects are allowed entry; cameras must be declared. Video cameras, tape recorders, binoculars, portable radios, typewriters and sports equipment may be imported on condition that they are exported on departure.

Prohibited imports

These include illegal drugs and narcotics, firearms, ammunition, TV sets, pornography, publications in Chinese characters and Chinese medicine.

Health (for visitors)

Mandatory precautions

Vaccination certificates for yellow fever if travelling from infected area.

Advisable precautions

Vaccinations that are necessary include: cholera, diphtheria, tetanus, hepatitis A, polio and typhoid. Vaccinations that may be advised include: hepatitis B, tuberculosis, Japanese B encephalitis and rabies.

Anti-malarial precautions should be taken; the use of mosquito nets and repellents and covering up the body after dark can help avoid malaria, hepatitis B and dengue fever. Only well-maintained and chlorinated swimming pools are safe in which to swim.

Use only bottled or boiled water for drinks, washing teeth and making ice. Eat only well cooked meals, preferably served hot; vegetables should be cooked and fruit peeled. Avoid dairy products, salad and food from street vendors. A full, first-aid kit would be useful.

Tap water must be treated as unsafe unless boiled and filtered (bottled water is available in the main cities). Eat only well cooked meals, preferably served hot; vegetables should be cooked and fruit peeled. Dairy products are unpasteurised and should be avoided

Medical insurance is essential, including emergency evacuation, and an adequate supply of personal medicines is necessary.

Hotels

International-standard hotels have air-conditioning and often business centres, where translation and secretarial services are normally available. A 10 per cent service charge is normally added to the bill, so tipping with small change is usual. Where no service charge has been added, a tip of 5–10 per cent would be appropriate.

Credit cards

Credit and charge cards are widely accepted and ATMs are available in city centres.

Public holidays (national)

Fixed dates

*1 Jan (New Year), *17 Aug (Independence Day), *25 Dec (Christmas Day).

Variable dates

*Chinese New Year (Jan/Feb), Nyepi (Hindu New Year, Mar/Apr), Waisak Day (Birth of the Lord Buddha, May), Good Friday (Mar/Apr), Ascension Day, Eid al Adha, Islamic New Year, Birth of the Prophet Mohammed, Ascent of Prophet Mohammed, *Eid al Fitr (two days).

*Official national holidays, holidays that fall on Friday are taken the next day. The remainder, Muslim, Hindu and Christian, are informal holidays taken by adherents.

Islamic year 1437 (15 Oct 2015–2 Oct 2016):: The Islamic year contains 354 or 355 days, with the result that Muslim feasts advance by 10–12 days against the Gregorian calendar. Dates of feasts vary according to the sighting of the new moon, so cannot be forecast exactly.

Working hours

Banking

Mon–Fri: 0830–1530/1730; Sat: 0930–1230. Hotel banks may remain open longer.

Business

Mon–Fri: 0800–1600; Sat: 0830–1230. Fri: it is difficult to make an appointment after 1100 although businessmen sometimes meet people in the late afternoon and early evening.

Government

Mon–Thu: 0800–1500; Fri: 0800–1130; Sat: 0800–1400.

Shops

0800/1000–2100/2200 (some close at 1730).

Telecommunications

Mobile/cell phones

There are limited 900/1800 GSM services around Jakata. A G3 system in planned.

Electricity supply

Generally 220V 50Hz, with two-pronged plug. However, some hotels in the provinces may still be using 110V AC, 50Hz. It is better to check before using an appliance.

Weights and measures

Metric system

Social customs/useful tips

Indonesia is predominantly Muslim and alcohol is not considered essential to social intercourse. Care should be taken to respect Muslim, Hindu and other religious conventions. Footwear should be removed before entering places of worship and temples and sometimes also private homes.

Handshaking with the right hand is customary both for men and women. It is conventional to shake hands and give a slight bow with the head on meeting and taking leave. Punctuality is appreciated on social occasions.

Pork is forbidden for the Muslim population and beef for the Balinese Hindus. Do not start to consume food or drink until invited by the host to do so.

Pribumi is used to describe anything indigenous or native to Indonesia, and occurs in commercial or business contexts with reference to local participation, local capital investment or local loans.

In Indonesia, Western-style beckoning is considered rude; instead, turn your hand palm down, and waggle your fingers – like an upside-down wave. Putting your hands on your hips is considered an overt sign of aggression or contempt.

The word 'no' is regarded as impolite; often people use the word *belum*, which means 'not yet'.

Security

Since 2000, Indonesia has been experiencing unrest and violence. There has been sectarian and ethnic strife in Aceh, Irian Jaya, Central and West Kalimantan, Maluku, North Maluku, Central and South Sulawesi and tension in West Timor.

Since October 2002, terrorist attacks have deliberately targetted Western tourists.

Getting there

Air

National airline: Garuda Indonesia (GA) and Merpati Nusantara Airlines (MZ). *In July 2007 the European Union banned all Indonesian airlines from EU air space, due to safety concerns and warned its citizens not to use these airlines elsewhere in the world.*

International airport/s:

Soekarno-Hatta International (CGK), 28km north-west of Jakarta, banks/bureaux de change, a post office, duty-free shops, gift shops, 24-hour restaurants, snack bars, car hire and 24-hour medical/vaccination facilities; Denpasar Bali Ngurah Rai International (DPS), 13km south-west of the city, is the main airport on Bali; Bandung Husein (BDO); Cirebon Penggung (CBN); Ketapang (KTG); Pontianak Supadio (PNK); Semarang Uani (SRG); Surabaya Juanda (SUB).

Airport tax: International departures: Rp100,000.

Surface

Water: High-speed ferries run between Sumatra and Malaysia. Routes are either Medan–Penang or Dumai–Melaka. There are also services between Mandalo (Sulawesi) and the Philippines. Maritime piracy is a problem in some Indonesian waters.

Main port/s: Tanjung Priok, Jakarta; Tanjung Perak, Surabaya; Belawan, on Sumatra.

Getting about

National transport

Air: Garuda Indonesia operates extensive domestic services, including daily services between Jakarta, Surabaya and Medan. Other routes are also served by Sempati Air and Merpati Nusantara Airlines.

Road: Extensive road network includes over 370,000km of road, 25 per cent of which is surfaced. A 525km highway links key areas in Jambi and South Sumatra. Motorways and toll roads are good, but roads are narrower and poorly maintained in rural areas and remote regions. Secondary roads are frequently impassable in the rainy season. Driving outside major cities at night can be hazardous.

Buses: Express coach services link the main cities. Local bus services are inexpensive, but their use is complicated, they are often crowded, and service may be interrupted in the rainy season.

Rail: The rail network, limited to Java, Sumatra and Madura, comprises 8,600km of track. Java and parts of Sumatra have air-conditioned express rail services with sleeping and dining cars only between major cities. Fares are comparatively cheap but higher on air-conditioned trains. There are several trains daily from Jakarta to Bandung and Surabaya. Ordinary services can be slow, with many stops.

Water: There are extensive scheduled and non-scheduled inter-island sailings.

City transport

Roads in major cities are good.

Taxis: Taxis are plentiful but in various states of disrepair. Wherever possible, opt for Blue Bird or Silver Bird taxis and check the driver switches on the meter before starting the journey.

Taxis can be obtained at hotels, airports and railway stations. From Sukarno-Hatta airport to Jakarta, taxis add a surcharge and toll.

There are metered taxis only in Jakarta, Surabaya, Bandung, Solo, Semarang and Jogjakarta, but it may be necessary to insist on the use of the meter. Fares are very reasonable. Taxis may also be hired by the hour, which is less expensive for longer journeys.

In Jakarta it can be difficult to hail taxis, so engage one at the hotel and retain it until returning. A 10 per cent tip is usual. There are also minicabs for two passengers, the *bemo* (small bus) which plies regular routes, and the *becak*, all of which need advance bargaining to come to a mutually accepted fare.

From city centre to Jakarta

Soekarno-Hatta airport taxi journey times are about 45 minutes.

Buses, trams & metro: Journey time on the bus from city centre to Jakarta Soekarno-Hatta International Airport is about 60 minutes.

Trains: Women-only carriages (recognisable by their brightly covered pink seats) were introduced on busy commuter routes in Jakarta in 2010.

Car hire

Car hire, mostly chauffeur-driven, is available in major towns and cities. Except for international car hire operators which accept credit cards, full payment for car hire is made up-front. Traffic drives on the left. Driving at night can be dangerous outside major urban areas as it is common to encounter drivers who do not use their lights.

BUSINESS DIRECTORY

The addresses listed below are a selection only. While World of Information makes every endeavour to check these addresses, we cannot guarantee that changes have not been made, especially to telephone numbers and area codes. We would welcome any corrections.

Telephone area codes

The international direct dialling (IDD) code for Indonesia is +62, followed by the area code and subscriber's number:

Balik Papan	542	Manado	431
Bandung	22	Medan	61
Banjarmasin	511	Padang	751
Denpasar	361	Palembang	711
Jakarta	21		

Useful telephone numbers

Police: 110
Ambulance:118
Fire113
Directory (local):108
Directory (other Indonesian):106
International information102
International operator:101
Domestic connections:100

Chambers of Commerce

American Chamber of Commerce in Indonesia, World Trade Centre, Jalan Jend Sudirman Kav 29-31, Jakarta 12920 (tel: 526-2860; fax: 526-2861; e-mail: info@amcham.or.id).

Bali Chamber of Commerce and Industry, Gedung Merdeka, Jalan Surapati 7, Denpasar 80232 (tel: 233-053; fax: 227-020; e-mail: kadin_bali@balinetwork.com).

British Chamber of Commerce in Indonesia, World Trade Centre, Jalan Jend Sudirman Kav 31, Jakarta 12920 (tel: 522-9453; fax: 527-9135; e-mail: bisnis@britcham.or.id).

Indonesian Chamber of Commerce and Industry, Menara Kadin Indonesia, Jalan HR Rasuna Said X-5 Kav 2-3, Jakarta 12950 (tel: 916-5535; fax: 527-4485; e-mail: info@kadin.net.id).

Jakarta Chamber of Commerce and Industry, Majapahit Permai B21-23, Jalan Majapahit 18-22, PO Box 3077, Jakarta 10160 (tel: 380-8091; fax: 384-4549; e-mail: kadin_jkt@indosat.net.id).

Banking

Bank Dagang Nasional Indonesia (BDNI), Jl Hayam Wuruk No 8, Jakarta (tel: 231-1221/0530/0886; fax: 380-5725).

Bank Danamon, Jl Kebon Sirih No 15, Jakarta 10340 (tel: 231-1331, 230-1901/2; fax: 230-1883/5).

BankExim, Jl Lapangan Setasiun No 1, Jakarta 11110 (tel: 692-3122, 690-0991; fax: 692-3047, 690-5328).

Bank Internasional Indonesia (BII), Jl MH Thamrin Kav 22 No 51, Jakarta Pusat (tel: 230-0888/0666; fax: 230-1426).

Bank Mandiri, Jakarta (e-mail: corp.communications@bankmandiri.co.id; internet site: http://www.bankmandiri.co.id).

Bank Negara Indonesia (BNI), Jl Jend Sudirman Kav 1, Jakarta 10220 (tel: 251-1946; fax: 251-1214).

Bank Umum Nasional, 135 Jl Senen Raya, Jakarta 10410 (tel: 231-2828; fax: 231-2929).

Indonesian Bank Restructuring Agency, Komplek Bank Indonesia, Jl Budi Kemuliaan, Building D, 10th Floor, Jakarta (fax: 231-1478).

PT Bank Pembangunan Indonesia, JL RP Soeroso No 2-4, Jakarta 10011 (tel: 230-1908; fax: 230-1242/3, 230-0154).

PT Bank Bali Tbk, 17th Floor, Gedung Bank Bali, Jalan Jenderal Sudirman Kav 27, Jakarta 12920 (tel: 523-7899; fax: 250-0811).

PT Bank Buana Indonesia, Jalan Asemka 32-36, Jakarta 11110 (tel: 260-1051, 260-1055; fax: 260-1014).

Central bank

Bank Indonesia, 2 Jalan MH Thamrin, Jakarta 10110 (tel: 381-7187; fax: 350-1867; e-mail: humasbi@bi.go.id).

Stock exchange

Bursa Efek Indonesia (Indonesia Stock Exchange) (IDX), www.idx.co.id

Travel information

Bouraq Indonesia Airlines, PO Box 2965, Jalan Angkasa 1-3, Kernayoran, Jakarta 10720 (tel: 629-5289; fax: 629-5364).

Garuda Indonesia, Jl. Merdeka Selatan 13, Jakarta 10110 (tel: 380-1901; fax: 380-6652; internet site: http://www.garuda-indonesia.com).

Ikatan Motor Indonesia (IMI), Gedung KONI, Pusat Senayan, Kotakpos 609, Jakarta (tel: 591-102).

Merpati Nusantara Airlines, PO Box 323, Jalan Angkasa 2, Jakarta 10013 (tel: 413-608; fax: 420-7311).

Sempati Air Transport, Jalan Medan Merdeka Timur No 7, PO Box 2068, Jakarta 13610 (tel: 348-760; fax: 809-4420).

National tourist organisation offices

Direktorat Jenderal Pariwisata Indonesia (Directorate-General of Tourism), 16/19 Jalan Medan Merdeka-Barat, Jakarta 10110 (tel: 386-0934; fax: 386-0828; internet site: http://www.tourismindonesia.com).

Ministries

Ministry of Agriculture, Jalal Harsono RM 3, Ragunan, Pasar Minggu, Jakarta 12550 (tel: 781-5380; fax: 781-6385).

Ministry of Defence, Jalal Medan Merdeka Barat 13-14, Jakarta 10110 (tel: 384-0889; fax: 384-5178).

Ministry of Economy, Jalal Lapangan Banteng Timur 2-4, Jakarta 10310 (tel: 319-01152; fax: 319-01151).

Ministry of Education, Jalal Jend Sudirman, Senayan, Jakarta (tel: 573-1618; fax: 573-6870).

Ministry of Energy and Mineral Resources, Jalal Medan Merdeka Selatan 16, Jakarta 10110 (tel: 380-4242; fax: 384-7461).

Ministry of Finance, Jalall Lapangan Banteng Timur 2, Jakarta 10170 (tel: 344-9230; fax: 381-4324).

Minstry of Fisheries and Maritime Affairs, Jalal Veteran, 3rd Floor, Jakarta (tel: 385-7009; fax: 344-6733).

Ministry of Foreign Affairs, Jalal Taman Pejambon 6, Jakarta 10111 (tel: 344-1508; fax: 385-1193).

Ministry of Forestry and Estate Crops, Jalal Jend Gatot Subroto, Senayan, Jakarta (tel: 573-1820; fax: 570-0226).

Ministry of Health, Jalal HR Rasuna Said Blok X-5 Kav 4-9, Jakarta 12950 (tel: 520-1590; fax: 520-1591).

Ministry of Home Affairs, Jalal Medan Merdeka Utara 7, Jakarta 10110 (tel: 384-2222; fax: 385-1193).

Ministry of Justice and Human Rights, Jalal Jend HR Rasuna Said Kav 4-5, Kuningan, Jakarta (tel: 525-3006; fax: 525-3090).

Ministry of Manpower and Transmigration, Jalal Taman Makam Pahlawan 17, Jakarta (tel: 798-9912; fax: 799-2629).

Ministry of Political, Social and Security Affairs, Jalal Medan Merdeka Utara 7, Jakarta 10110 (tel: 384-9453; fax: 345-0918).

Ministry of Religious Affairs, Jalal Lapangan Banteng Barat 3-4, Jakarta 10710 (tel: 381-1679; fax: 381-1436).

Ministry of Resettlement and Regional Infrastructure, Jalal Pattimura 20, Kebayoran Baru, Jakarta 12110 (tel: 720-3962; fax: 726-0769).

Ministry of Social Affairs, Jalal Rasuna Said blok X-5 Kav 4-9, Jakarta 12950 (tel: 310-3781; fax: 310-3783).

Ministry of Trade and Industry, Jalal Jend Gatot Subroto Kav 52-53, Jakarta 12950 (tel: 525-6548; fax: 522-9592).

Ministry of Welfare, Jalal Salemba Raya 28, Jakarta 10430 (tel: 310-3781; fax: 310-3783).

Other useful addresses

Asean Investment Promotion Agency, The Investment Co-ordinating Board (BKPM), Jalan Gatot Subroto No 44, PO Box 3186, Jakarta (tel: 512-008, 515-041, 517-022, 510-023; fax: 514-945).

Asean Secretariat, 70 A Jalan Sisingamangaraja, Jakarta 12110 (tel: 726-2991, 724-3372; fax: 724-3504, 739-8234; e-mail: asean.or.id).

Asian Development Bank, Indonesia Resident Mission, Gedung BRI II, 7th Floor, Jl. Jend Sudirman Kav. 44-46, Jakarta 10210 (tel: 251-2721; fax: 251-2749; e-mail: adbirm@mail.asiandevbank.org).

Badan Ko-ordinasi Penanaman Modal (BKPM) (Co-ordinating Board for Capital Investment), Jalan Jend Gatot Subroto 44, Jakarta Selatan (tel: 525-4981, 525-4619; fax: 525-4945).

Badan Pelaksana Bursa Komoditi (ICEB) (Indonesian Commodity Exchange Board), Bursa Building, 2nd and 4th floors, Jalan Medan Merdeka Selatan 14, Jakarta 10110 (tel: 371-921; fax: 380-4426).

Badan Pelaksana Pasar Modal (BAPEPAM) (Capital Market Operation Board), Jalan Medan Merdeka Selatan 14, Jakarta 10110 (tel: 365-509).

British Consular enquiries: British Embassy, Deutsche Bank Building, 19th Floor, 80 Jalan Imam Bonjol, Jakarta 10310, Indonesia (tel: (62 21) 390-7484; fax: (62 21) 316-0850; internet site: www.britain.in.indonesia.or.id).

Business Advisory Services, Kuningan Plaza Building, Jalan Rasuna Said Kav C-11-14, Jakarta (tel: 517-7295).

Central Bureau of Statistics, Jl Dr Sutomo 18, Jakarta (tel: 372-808; internet site: http://www.bps.go.id).

Commander-in-Chief of the Armed Forces, ABRI Headquarters, Mabes ABRI Cilangkap, Jakarta Timur (tel: 384-2679, 840-1243; fax: 380-6711).

Indonesia-British Business Association, C/O Ernst & Young International, Jakarta Stock Exchange Building 23rd Floor, J1 Jenderal Sudirman, Kav 52-53, Jakarta 12190 (tel: 515-1984; fax: 515-1985).

Indonesia Science Institute, Jl Jend. Gatot Subroto No. 10, Jakarta 12710 (tel: 525-1831).

Indonesian Bank Restructuring Agency, Komplek Bank Indonesia, JL Budi Kemuliaan, building D, 10th Floor, Jakarta (fax: 231-1478).

Indonesian Embassy (USA), 2020 Massachusetts Avenue, NW, Wasahington DC 20036 (tel: (+1-202) 775-5200; fax: (+1-202) 775-5365; e-mail: indonesia@dgs.dgsys.com).

Jakarta Stock Exchange (JSE), Jalan Mendeka Selatan 14, Jakarta Pusat (internet site: http://www.jsx.co.id).

Office of the National Land Agency (BPN), Jl Sisingamangaraja 2, Jakarta Selatan (tel: 722-2420, 739-3939).

Subroto, Kav 52-53, Jakarta (tel: 520-1613; fax: 520-1606).

US Embassy, Medan Merdeka Selatan 5, Jakarta (tel: 344-2211; fax: 386-2259; e-mail: jakconsul@state.gov; internet site: http://www.usembassyjakarta.org).

National news agency: Antara National News Agency, Wisma Antara Building, Floor 3, 19, 20, Ji. Medan Merdeika Selatan 17, Jakarta (tel: 384-3051; fax 386-5577; internet: www.antara.co.id/en).

Indoexchange (for stock market news): www.indoexchange.com

Iran

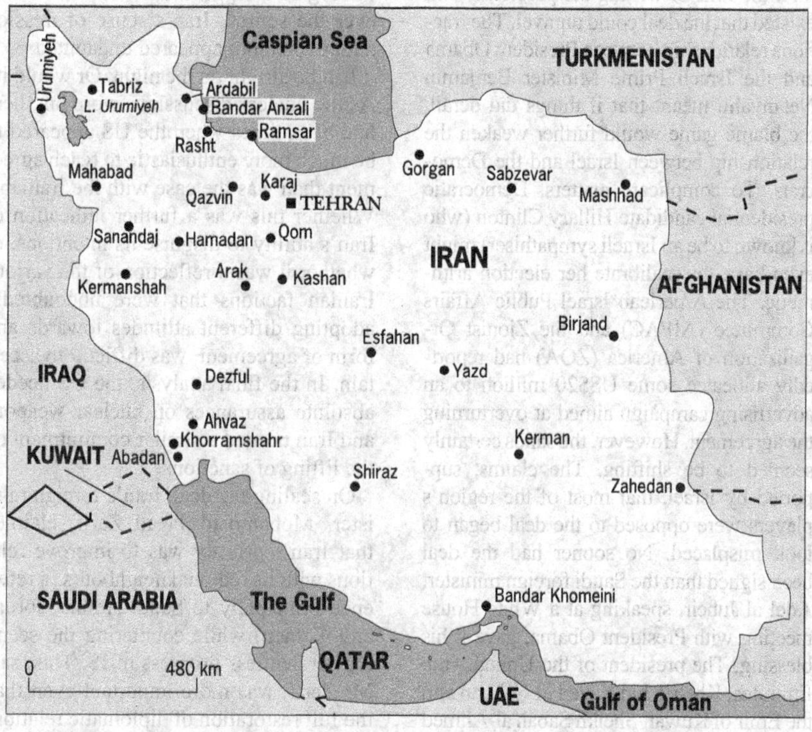

Iran is, in many respects a country in disguise; its leaders' disguise enables them to portray themselves as an almost medieval theocracy while enjoying the material creature comforts of the twenty-first century. It also enables the middle classes – for the most part – to act in public as a happy band of Islamic believers while wearing Prada or Tommy Hilfinger or enjoying an occasional illicit whisky when relaxing at home.

The real deal

In July 2015, however, there was little disguise about the relief felt by most Iranians on hearing that after months of negotiations, the non-nuclear agreement between Iran and the P5+1 group of countries (the five permanent members of the United Nations Security Council plus Germany) six-nation negotiating team was finally signed. Under the deal, once ratified, Iran would end the enrichment of uranium over the figure of 3.67 per cent for a period of 15 years and would destroy advanced production equipment. Iran's uranium enrichment programme was to be reduced to one facility, that at Nantaz. This would reduce the number of functioning centrifuges by two thirds. The nuclear enrichment site at Fordow was to become a research centre. Inspectors from the International Atomic Energy Agency (IAEA) would in future be able to demand access to any Iranian nuclear site. Any refusal on the part of Iran would be immediately passed to an independent arbitration panel.

In return, the restrictions on Iranian banks would end and some US$150 billion of overseas Iranian assets would be released. The oil embargoes, trade restrictions and financial sanctions in place would all be waived. However, in the case of a breach of its undertakings by Iran, the sanctions would be instantly reinstated. After a period of five years during which Iran had fulfilled its obligations, the United Nations arms embargo would be ended and the parallel limitations on missile technology development would also be ended. After a period of ten years, the

KEY FACTS

Official name: Jomhoori e Islami e Iran (Islamic Republic of Iran)

Head of State: Supreme Leader, Grand Ayatollah Seyyed Ali Khamenei (from 4 June 1989)

Head of government: President Hassan Rouhani (from 3 August 2013)

Ruling party: Conservatives (coalition of five political parties led by United Front of Conservatives (UFC)) (from 2004; re-elected 2 Mar 2012)

Area: 1,648,195 square km

Population: 77.97 million (2014)*

Capital: Tehran

Official language: Farsi (Persian)

Currency: Rial (IR) 10 rials = 1 toman

Exchange rate: IR29,900.00 per US$ (Sep 2015)

GDP per capita: US$5,183 (2014)*

GDP real growth: 2.97% (2014)*

GDP: US$404.13 billion (2014)*

Unemployment: 11.21% (2014)*

Inflation: 15.55% (2014)

Oil production: 3.61 million bpd (2014)

Natural gas production: 172.60 billion cum (2014)

Balance of trade: US$55.65 billion (2011)

* estimated figure

restrictions on nuclear activities would come to an end.

The possibility still existed that the US Congress might vote against the deal – it had a period of 60 days in which to do so. This would almost certainly trigger a presidential veto. That in turn might cause the Republican majority in Congress to seek to override the veto, which in turn would require a two thirds majority of senators. This is a scenario that supporters of the deal could barely contemplate. It would not simply represent the biggest foreign policy failure of the Obama presidency. It would also be a humiliation for the United States and mark the beginning of a Middle East arms race, lead by Iran and Saudi Arabia. Israel, firmly and vociferously opposed to the deal, was known to be well ahead in terms of nuclear weapons, although the exact number is unknown.

Crude oil prices had fallen as the reality of an agreement became more likely. Those involved in the negotiations were at pains to stress that sanctions relief was contingent upon Iranian co-operation. President Obama said that 'sanctions can be snapped back into place' if Iran cheated on the terms of the deal. While the agreement makes clear that Iran will be welcomed back into the international oil market and financial system if it complies with the agreed-upon nuclear restrictions, it remained unclear how long that process of rehabilitation might take. Once the designated changes to Iran's nuclear programme had been verified by international inspectors, the European Union would lift all financial sanctions. The European sanctions, which were put in place in 2012, blocked Iranian banks from using SWIFT, the messaging system banks use for cross-border transactions. The United States would also lift the secondary sanctions that blacklisted any foreign bank that did business with Iran. The US and European restrictions limited Iran's oil exports to about one million barrels per day, less than half the amount previously exported by Iran.

At the time of writing the possibility still existed that the deal could unravel. The fractious relationship between President Obama and the Israeli Prime Minister Benjamin Netanyahu meant that if things did derail, the blame game would further weaken the relationship between Israel and the Democrats. To complicate matters, Democratic presidential candidate Hillary Clinton (who is known to be an Israeli sympathiser) might even have to recalibrate her election arithmetic. The American Israel Public Affairs Committee (AIPAC) and the Zionist Organisation of America (ZOA) had reportedly allocated some US$20 million to an advertising campaign aimed at overturning the agreement. However, the sands certainly seemed to be shifting. The claims, supported by Israel, that most of the region's players were opposed to the deal began to look misplaced. No sooner had the deal been signed than the Saudi foreign minister, Adel al Jubeir, speaking at a White House meeting with President Obama, gave it his blessing. The president of the United Arab Emirates, Khalifa bin Zayed al Nahyan and the Emir of Kuwait Sheikh Sabah al-Ahmed al-Jabir al-Sabah sent notes of congratulation to Iran.

Foreign affairs (1)

Undoubtedly, since the end of the Iran-Iraq war in 1988, the Iranian influence in the Middle East had become significant. In Lebanon, the Shi'ite militia Hezbollah (which was founded and largely funded by Iran) had gained not just military, but also political, influence. Inevitably, this had resulted in the characterisation of Iran as an aggressive, terrorism sponsoring, state. But whatever the degree of opposition to Iran and whatever the source, Iran's sense of mission and momentum appeared undaunted.

It'll be alright on the night. Or would it? As the nuclear discussions wore on, there had been times when the US appeared to be much more enthusiastic to reach agreement than was the case with the Iranians. Whether this was a further indication of Iran's ability to disguise its intentions, or whether it was a reflection of the various Iranian factions that were undoubtedly adopting different attitudes towards any form of agreement, was difficult to ascertain. In the final analysis, the US needed absolute assurances on nuclear weapons and Iran needed a similar commitment on the lifting of sanctions.

On sealing the deal, Iran's foreign minister, Mohammad Javad Zarif, claimed that Iran's priority was to improve relations with its regional neighbours (a reference principally to Saudi Arabia, Jordan and Yemen) while countering the seemingly relentless progress of IS. This, said Mr Zarif, was more important even than the full restoration of diplomatic relations with the US. 'I believe it can be done.' Said Mr Zarif optimistically.

The economy – History, Boys

Quite simply, the extent to which anything could 'be done' in Iran depended not only on the will to do it, but critically on the cash being available to do it. And that availability depended fundamentally on the funds flowing into – and out of – the government's coffers. When the nuclear negotiations had started, the Iranian government was certainly conscious of the strengths and weaknesses of the national economy. By 2015, however, it was the weaknesses that were the priority. It had been rumoured that the Iranian exchequer was down to five months' cover of government expenses. Government projections for 2015–16 had been based on an oil price of US$72.00 per barrel. By the end of June the oil price was firmly rooted around the US$60.00 mark, a shortfall of almost 20 per cent. Iran might not be so dependent on oil as some of its neighbours – but oil revenues still made up over 40 per cent of government revenues.

KEY INDICATORS — Iran

	Unit	2011	2012	2013	2014	**2015
Population	m	*75.86	76.12	*76.98	*77.97	*78.97
Gross domestic product (GDP)	US$bn	482.40	398.03	380.35	*404.13	*0.00
GDP per capita	US$	6,360	5,229	*4,941	*5,183	*4,983
GDP real growth	%	2.0	-5.6	-1.9	*3.0	*0.6
Inflation	%	21.3	30.5	34.7	15.5	*16.5
Unemployment	%	12.3	12.2	10.4	*11.2	*12.3
Oil output	'000 bpd	4,321.0	3,680.0	3,558.0	3,614.0	–
Natural gas output	bn cum	151.8	106.5	166.6	172.6	–
Exports (fob) (goods)	US$m	131,795.0	–	–	–	–
Imports (fob) (goods)	US$m	76,148.0	–	–	–	–
Balance of trade	US$m	55,647.0	–	–	–	–
Current account	US$m	59,382.0	26,272.0	27,963.0	*15,407.0	*3,063.0
Exchange rate	per US$	10,512.57	12,260.00	12,386.50	27,136.78	–

* estimated figure ** forecast figure

There was no lack of whistling in the wind on the part of President Rouhani, who made the case for foreign investment. But with budget cuts of over 10 per cent the projects available for investment were few. On top of this investment scarcity, was the entrenched opposition of many senior clerics, to whom any kind of foreign investment was anathema.

According to the World Bank, Iran's business environment also remained a challenge; Iran ranked 130 out of the 189 countries surveyed in the Bank's 2015 *Doing Business Report*. One major obstacle was that the mindset of many of the senior clerics had been formed sixty years earlier in the short-lived rule of Prime Minister Mossadeq. Iranians had elected Mossadeq prime minister in 1951 and he had quickly moved to re-nationalise the country's oil production, which had been under British control through the Anglo-Persian Oil Company – which later became British Petroleum or BP. The re-nationalisation was a major source of concern to the US and the UK, both of which saw Iranian oil as key to its post-war economic rebuilding.

The Cold War was also a factor in the two countries' calculations. In Washington and Whitehall, there existed the fear that Iran might align itself to Moscow. The two countries set about removing Mossadeq, readying the exiled Shah Mohammad Reza Pahlavi to take over. The Shah had fled Iran after losing his power struggle with Mossadeq. Following the *coup* that deposed Mossadeq, he returned as head of state, becoming a close ally of the UK and the US. Thus the Shah returned to rule until he was deposed in 1979 by the forces of the Islamic Revolution.

In Iran's theocratic circles, Prime Minister Mossadeq's ousting was a deep wound. The *éminences grises* behind the 1953 *coup* were, without question, the UK and the US, who in Iranian political circles were perceived to be interested in oil and little else. Although in Islamic Revolutionary circles the idea of inviting investment from either country had long been anathema, without it the eventual lifting of sanctions might end up being less than half the story. Despite the internal divisions that beset the idea of attracting investment, Iran's business community and President Hassan Rouhani himself, seemed keen to encourage Western investment. The reforms passed in the previous twenty years would, it was thought, offer an attractive environment. Following the signature in July 2015 of the nuclear agreement, it appeared that the President and his Ministers had a single economic objective – investment.

The IMF

In its April 2014 survey of the Iranian economy, the first for over two years, the International Monetary Fund (IMF) noted that Iran had made progress toward stabilising its economy, but needed to introduce comprehensive reforms in order to lay the basis for a return to growth and create needed jobs. In dealing with the IMF, the Iranian government had little scope for disguise; in their health check of the Iranian economy, the IMF's economists had no need to pull their punches, bluntly asserting that Iran's near-term economic outlook remained uncertain. Facing continued constrained prospects for oil revenues and international transactions, Iran was expected to see its gross domestic product (GDP) growth begin to stabilise in the 2014 fiscal year after two consecutive years of sharp contraction. The still-weak recovery was expected by the IMF to benefit from potential improvements in the external environment and some early signs of modest revival in growth in domestic demand.

According to he IMF, the Iranian administration that took office in August 2013 had made some headway in improving the external environment and confidence in the outlook. At the beginning of 2014, the Iranian authorities had reached an interim agreement with the P5+1 group. This agreement (which took effect in January 2014 and provided for a limited, temporary easing of sanctions) allowing Iran to stabilise its oil exports, granted limited access to Iran's funds held abroad and temporarily waived sanctions on petrochemical automobile exports. In the view of the IMF, Iran now needed to focus on the domestic reform agenda to fully benefit from the country's economic potential.

A combination of large shocks and weak macro-economic management had, in the view of the IMF, had a significant impact on economic stability and growth in the previous few years, despite Iran's considerable progress in raising per capita income and living standards in the preceding decades. A combination of shocks, associated with the implementation of the first phase of energy subsidy reform, plus ambitious and inadequately funded social programmes and a marked deterioration in the external environment stemming from the intensification of trade and financial sanctions – had significantly weakened the economy.

The Iranian authorities, suggested the IMF, now needed to focus on how to address some of the longstanding challenges in the structure of the economy to achieve growth. The IMF noted that the government had begun taking important steps in this direction.

To reduce and stabilise inflation, the Bank Markazi Jomhouri Islami Iran (central bank) had kept tighter control over base money in the previous seven months. This effort had been supported by the agreement to remove the financing of the Mehr Housing Project – an ambitious affordable housing project launched in 2007 – from the central bank's balance sheet. These measures to control inflation, along with favourable global food prices and the appreciation of the currency, had allowed Iran to lower the 12-month inflation rate to about 23 per cent in early 2014, sharply down from the 45 per cent of June 2013.

However, more reforms were needed to get Iran's economy back on a sustainable growth track. The authorities needed to avoid postponing reforms and 'muddling through' in the hope of an improved external environment, according to the IMF.

A three-pronged strategy to fight the twin problems of low growth and high inflation should be centred on tightening monetary policy, balanced fiscal consolidation and structural reforms.

The 2014 budget boded well for this strategy by providing a good balance between disinflation and supporting the economy. Measures to begin broadening the revenue base away from oil – such as the authorities' decision to bring forward and increase the scheduled value-added tax (VAT) rate, as well as reforms to strengthen tax administration and reduce exemptions – would help lay the ground for a sustainable fiscal policy. The IMF report also observed that reforms to the fiscal policy framework should strengthen its counter-cyclical role, limit fiscal risks and enhance macro-economic co-ordination.

Reforms to the monetary policy framework were also essential to establish solid economic stability, as was the intended move to unify the foreign exchange market by mid-2015. Progress in simplifying and refocussing the central bank's mandate toward price stability and steps to restructure institutional decision making would be key in the success of these reforms.

At the same time, reforms to boost productivity were, in the view of the IMF, needed to unleash Iran's entrepreneurial and human capital potential to create much-needed new jobs. High unemployment of about 24 per cent among youth required reforms to the labour market. There was large scope to improve the business environment, the IMF noted and this could provide a significant boost to productivity and growth.

The implementation of Iran's subsidy reforms also remained a priority, the IMF report noted. The design of the reforms – replacing price subsidies with universal cash transfers to households – had been exemplary, even though the first phase had faced significant difficulties. It would be vital to ensure that the second phase of the reform proceeded with the right supporting framework and macro-economic policies.

A February 2015 report on the Iranian economy saw the IMF registering a marked improvement in macro-economic conditions when compared to the previous year, with a rebound in economic activity and a decline in inflation. However, the sharp drop in global oil prices and an uncertain external environment looked likely to bring significant challenges to the outlook.

The IMF also noted that the Iranian authorities recognised these challenges and remained determined to sustain the improvements in macro-economic conditions. The discussions focussed on the policies needed for preserving disinflation gains and for supporting the economy in its adjustment to lower oil prices. In this respect, the IMF considered that Iran's fiscal policy should aim at limiting the budget deficit in the next fiscal year (2016) to around 2.5 per cent of GDP. Monetary policy should continue to aim at keeping inflation expectations anchored, by pre-emptively targeting liquidity growth at prudent levels. This policy mix would help absorb shocks and provide more room for credit to flow to the economy. Maintaining exchange rate flexibility would also help smooth the transition to an environment reflecting lower oil prices. The IMF stressed the need for pressing ahead with reforms and with the Iranian authorities' plans in the banking sector to address non-performing loans and strengthen the efficiency of financial intermediation.

Inequalities – the rich get rich and the poor…

However indifferently the economy was performing, one aspect of Iran's economic development that the theocratic government could barely disguise was the increasing incidence of inequality. 'The rich get rich, the poor get poorer' runs the song and so does Iranian society. An Instagram page 'The Rich Kids of Tehran' which had gone viral, showed Iran's *jeunesse dorée* partying, showing off their Ferraris and Lamborghinis and their expensive swimwear. Reportedly, Iran's Supreme Leader Ayatollah Ali Khameini had criticised this phenomenon, saying that 'I hear that young people from the generation of wealth, a generation intoxicated by their money, are driving luxury cars and parading in the streets, making the streets insecure. This is an example of psychological insecurity.' The Supreme Leader was well aware that the 'rich kids' were a political liability, an aspect of Iranian society that urgently needed to be covered up and disguised. But for the bazaar, Tehran's recognised centre of rumour and intrigue, the Rich Kids' wealth and behaviour was already common knowledge.

The régime's disguise had once again slipped when the driver of an expensive Maserati killed in a crash turned out to be the grandson of Ayatollah Rabbani Shirazi, a political associate of the 1979 revolution's leader, Ayatollah Khomaini. One commentator noted that the Supreme Leader's criticism did not appear to be directed at the massive accumulation of wealth by the clerics running Iran's theocracy, so much as at its flamboyant display. This contrasted sharply with the miserably low wages, lack of job security, scarcity of medication and even food experienced by Iranians on a daily basis. The Rich Kids behaviour simply added insult to injury, as reported by the *New York Times* journalist Sharzad Elghanyan who observed that 'It was not just the wealth that struck me, but how freely Iran's 'one per centers' flaunted the symbols of Western decadence without fear of government retribution.' Ms Elghayan's report continued: 'Thirty-five years after a revolution that promised an egalitarian utopia and vowed to root out *gharbzadegi* (which translates as 'Westoxification', 'West-struck-ness' or 'Westitis') – the modern Westernised lifestyles of Iran's cosmopolitans – how have some people become so rich?'

Ayatolla Rohan is, by Iranian standards, internationally aware. That awareness has enabled him to follow the rise and the fall, of the Arab Spring movement. He could hardly have failed to note that there were some important lessons to be learned. The most important of these was that it was economic deprivation, chronic unemployment and deep rooted inequalities that had fuelled the uprisings in Tunisia, Libya, Yemen and Syria, where the super-rich were often identified as pro-Western, decadent and anti-Islamic. Rouhani is on record as advocating a greater involvement by the private sector in the economy. Rouhani, in contrast to his predecessor Ahmadinejad, is no lefty trades unionist, saying that 'The private sector understands the economy much better and it knows where to invest.'

Foreign affairs (2)

The fondness of Middle East political observers for conspiracy theories is nowhere more apparent than in assessments of Iran, which is held responsible, *inter alia*, for the rise of the Houthi movement in Yemen, the militias of Iraq, Hezbollah in Lebanon and even the Syrian Arab Army of President al Assad. The so-called 'Shi'ite Crescent' represented for the region's Sunni regimes a perceptibly serious threat. This overlooks the more demonstrably real threat of ISIL, which massacres not only Shi'a, but also members of any other religion that get in its way. In neither Iraq nor Syria has Iran invaded or even sent infantry, rather supplying some special operations forces in aid of local Iraqi and Syrian initiatives, at government request. In both countries, Iran has Sunni clients as well as Shi'ite ones. In both countries, local forces reached out to Iran for patronage in the face of local challenges, not the other way around.

Energy

Since 2012, Iranian oil exports have been reduced by sanctions, a financial restriction that has eaten into revenue and brought Iran to the negotiating table. Iranian officials have claimed that once the sanctions are lifted they could quickly increase crude production from 2.7 million barrels a day (bpd) to 4 million barrels a day and thus channel more exports to customers in Asia. China and India have apparently expressed interest in buying discounted Iranian crude. Iran also had an estimated 30 million barrels of oil stored on tankers waiting to be sold. However, the likelihood of substantial amounts of Iranian oil entering an already oversupplied market look unlikely. Most analysts consider that it would take months to fully unwind the oil sanctions, recommence production in antiquated Iranian oil fields, not to mention secure new contracts with buyers in Asia.

All this at a time when the global oil market was still oversupplied and prices had fallen by around 50 per cent. Organisation of the Petroleum Exporting Countries (Opec) oil production was at its highest level since mid-2014; Saudi Arabia's output was close to its all-time record of 10 million barrels a day and oil producers were vying for market share at a time when demand had shown no signs of recovering. Delivering additional oil would a challenge for an industry that has been deprived of Western investment and technology for some years. One analyst forecast that simply meeting the terms of the agreement and then securing verification by the International Atomic Energy Agency (IAEA) would delay a full return until at least 2016.

According to the US government Energy Information Administration (EIA) Iran holds the world's fourth-largest proved crude oil reserves and the world's second-largest natural gas reserves. Despite these abundant reserves, Iran's crude oil production has substantially declined and natural gas production growth has been slower than expected over the past few years. The international sanctions had seriously affected Iran's energy sector as a whole and had prompted a number of cancellations or delays of upstream oil and gas projects. The state-owned National Iranian Oil Company (NIOC) is responsible for all upstream oil and natural gas projects. The Iranian constitution prohibits foreign or private ownership of natural resources. However, international oil companies (IOCs) can participate in the exploration and development phases through buy-back contracts. Iran had been planning to change its oil contract model to allow IOCs to participate in all phases of an upstream project, including production. However, as previously mentioned, international sanctions had affected foreign investment in Iran's energy sector, limiting the technology and expertise needed to expand capacity at oil and natural gas fields.

Iran holds almost 10 per cent of the world's crude oil reserves and 13 per cent of Opec reserves. About 70 per cent of Iran's crude oil reserves are located onshore, with the remainder mostly located offshore in the Persian Gulf. Iran also holds proved reserves in the Caspian Sea, although exploration has been at a standstill.

Iran produced 3.4 million bpd of petroleum and other liquids in 2014, of which 2.8 million bpd was crude oil and the remainder was condensate and natural gas plant liquids. Iran's crude oil production fell dramatically from nearly 3.7 million bpd in 2011 to 2.7 million bpd in 2013 because of sanctions.

Human Rights

During the initial to-and-fro between Mr Obama and President Hassan Rouhani many Iranians had expressed hopes that the nuclear agreement might bring with it an improvement in Iran's human rights behaviour. Their optimism looked to be misplaced despite the fact that in 2010, the US had been instrumental in the appointment of a UN special *rapporteur* on human rights in Iran. When Mr Rouhani won the presidency in 2013, in Washington there was some increased optimism as during his campaign Mr Rouhani had promised to enforce the rights spelt out in the Iranian Constitution. Disappointingly, according to the special *rapporteur*, Ahmed Shaheed, in a 2015 report, President Rouhani's rights record has been less than positive. In 2014, Iran executed an estimated 753 people, according to Mr Shaheed. A large proportion were drug offenders. The figure for 2015 promises to be even worse. Alongside Mr Shaheed's observations, a February 2015 report by UN Secretary General Ban Ki-moon listed the dismal state of women's rights in Iran, noting that no less than two-thirds of women had been subjected to domestic violence and more than 50,000 a year were married off before they were 15. A major concern is that Iran might achieve a degree of international acceptance that enables it to continue with these and similar human rights abuses unchallenged.

The political outlook

Iran's internal debates over human rights reflected a wider debate over the country's political future. Tehran's conservatives are thought to fear that the moderates of the Reformist party, who constituted the backbone of the 2009 Green Movement, are endeavouring to take control of the next Majles (parliament) and the Assembly of Experts, a body tasked – *inter alia* – with electing the supreme leader should the incumbent die. The elections for the Majles and the Assembly of Experts are due to take place in March 2016.

A December 2014 article entitled *Seditionists dreaming to come back to power* published on *Basirat*, the Revolutionary Guards' website, took the view that the June 2013 elections and the advent of the Rouhani administration were the thin end of a moderate wedge. Detailing the activities of the moderates and Reformists, in a blinding glimpse of the obvious, the article claimed that these activities were aimed at winning the tenth parliament and the fifth Assembly of Experts. In the period leading up to the disputed 2009 election, the majority of political parties subscribed to the moderate and Reformist movement. This movement was now represented politically by the Council for Co-ordinating the Reformist Front, a coalition of some 20 parties.

Risk assessment

Economy	Poor
Politics	Poor
Regional stability	Poor

Muslims in Iran

% of population	98
Sunni (% of Muslims)	7.5
Shi'a (% of Muslims)	92.5

People to watch

Mohammad Reza Aref: the Reformist presidential candidate who withdrew in favour of President Rouhani in 2013

Akbar Hashemi Rafsanjani: Former moderate President, now leader and founder of the Servants of Construction Party.

Mohammad Khatami: former leader of the Reformist Party, now leader of the Association of Combatant Clerics

Sadegh Kharazi: Former diplomat and adviser to Mohammad Khatami, leader of the newly formed Voice of Iranians party

COUNTRY PROFILE

1907 A constitution was introduced, limiting the royal absolutism of the ruler. An Anglo-Russian agreement (annulled after the First World War) divided Iran into spheres of influence, one Soviet and the other British.

1909–13 Following the discovery of a large oil field in Masjet Soleiman, the Anglo-Persian Oil Company (APOC) was founded in 1909. A licence to search for, refine, produce and export oil was granted to APOC in 1913.

1921–26 A Cossack officer, Reza Khan, carried out a military coup, becoming prime minister in 1923. Parliament subsequently proclaimed him the Shah, to be called Reza Shah Pahlavi, ushering in the Pahlavi era. His eldest son, Mohammed Reza was proclaimed crown prince.

1935 Persia was renamed Iran. APOC changed its name to the Anglo-Iranian Oil Company (AIOC); it was a British enterprise, owned jointly by the private sector and the British government. Later, the company was renamed British Petroleum (BP).

1941 In the Second World War, after Reza Shah demonstrated allegiance to Germany, the British and Soviets entered Iran and removed him from power. They permitted his son, Mohammad Reza Shah Pahlavi, to succeed to the throne.
1949 The power of the Shah was increased following an attempted assassination by the Tudeh communist party, which was then banned.
1950 Mohammed Mosaddeq, a leading advocate of oil nationalisation, was installed as prime minister, following the assassination of his predecessor.
1951 Iran's Assembly approved the nationalisation of the oil industry, which was formerly controlled by Britain. As a result, Britain boycotted the purchase of Iranian oil. A contest for control of the government began between the young Shah and the nationalistic Mosaddeq.
1953–54 Mainly due to oil interests, the British persuaded the US to help the Shah remove Mosaddeq. Large sectors of Iranian public opinion condemned the US and Britain for this coup and Mosaddeq became a folk hero of Iranian nationalism. Drilling concessions were granted to eight foreign oil companies.
1963 The Shah assumed complete control of the government and launched a programme of land reform and social and economic modernisation. He used Savak (the secret police) to control opposition to his reforms.
1978 Following several years of growing opposition to the Shah's rule, martial law was imposed.
1979 The Shah was overthrown by forces loyal to the exiled religious leader, Ayatollah Khomeini, who became *Valy e Faqih* (supreme spiritual leader) of Iran. The Shah and his family were forced into exile. The Islamic Republic of Iran was proclaimed following a referendum. Fifty-two staff members at the US Embassy in Tehran were taken hostage by Islamic militants, who demanded the extradition of the Shah from the US, where he was having medical treatment.
1980 Abolhassan Beni Sadr was elected president. The former shah died of cancer.
1980–88 The Iran-Iraq War broke out after Iraq invaded Iran over disputed border areas.
1981 The US Embassy hostages in Tehran were released.
1989 After Ayatollah Khomeini's death, Grand Ayatollah Seyyed Ali Khamenei was sworn in as Supreme Leader (Head of State). Ali Akbar Hashemi Rafsanjani was elected president on 3 August.
1990 A peace agreement with Iraq was signed.
1993 Ali Akbar Hashemi Rafsanjani was elected to a second term as president.
1995 Oil and trade sanctions were imposed by the US, which alleged that Iran had sponsored terrorist groups throughout the region, had sought to acquire nuclear arms and destabilised the Middle East peace process.
1996 The Combatant Clergy Society (CCS) remained the largest single political group in parliament.
1997 Moderate cleric Mohammad Khatami, was elected president.
2000 Elections to an expanded Majlis returned a majority for reformist candidates. Ayatollah Ali Khamenei halted a bill that would have revived Iran's banned reformist newspapers. The Oil Stabilisation Fund (OSF) was established, to use money accumulated when oil prices rise above a set level, to level out fluctuations in prices and to promote the private sector.
2001 President Khatami was re-elected for a second term. Saudi Arabia and Iran signed a security accord to combat terrorism, drug trafficking and organised crime.
2002 Iran released nearly 700 Iraqi prisoners held since the 1980–88 war. President Bush included Iran in an 'axis of evil' due to its supposed development of weapons of mass destruction (WMD). Iran began construction of its first nuclear reactor.
2003 Parliament passed a bill guaranteeing free parliamentary elections. Iran came under pressure from the International Atomic Energy Agency (IAEA) over its nuclear energy programme. Subsequent IAEA inspections concluded there was no evidence of a weapons programme. A major earthquake hit the city of Bam in the southeast, killing 40,000 people and leaving the city in ruins.
2004 Over a third of parliament resigned after the Council of Guardians upheld the disqualification of more than 2,000 prospective reformist candidates hoping to stand in parliamentary elections, which were won by conservative candidates.
2005 Three villages were destroyed and 40 badly damaged when an earthquake struck central Iran. Mahmoud Ahmadinejad was elected president. He caused international concern when he suggested that Israel should be 'wiped off the map'.
2006 The UN Security Council (UNSC) voted to impose sanctions over Iran's refusal to stop uranium enrichment.
2007 The state-owned Bank Sepah was blacklisted by the US, accused of being the 'financial lynchpin' in Iran's efforts to procure material for its missile programme.
2008 President Ahmadinejad visited Iraq, the first visit by a president since the Iran/Iraq war in the 1980s. In parliamentary elections, candidates with a conservative affiliation won most seats. Iran test-fired nine missiles, including Shahab 3, which, with a range of over 2,000 kilometres, could reach Israel. The French oil company Total announced it would not be investing in Iran because the political situation was too risky. The company had been considering an investment in developing gas fields in the south of the country. Traders in Tehran's bazaar shut down for a month in protest at a new value added tax; traders in Isfahan, Mashad and Tabriz also shut down.
2009 Iran's first domestically produced telecommunications satellite was launched. Mahmoud Ahmadinejad won the presidential elections. There were immediate claims of vote rigging by opposition candidates but Iran's Supreme Leader Ayatollah Ali Khamenei endorsed the result and urged the defeated rivals against 'provocations'. Days of violence on the streets of Tehran followed, the Supreme Leader eventually ordered an inquiry into claims of vote rigging. However the Guardian Council, the top judicial body in Iran, confirmed Ahmadinejad as president. The government announced that there had been another successful test-fire of the Shahab-3 missile, at the same time as international condemnation was growing of Iran's nuclear programme, including the (suspected) enrichment of low-grade uranium into weapons-grade uranium. Iran joined negotiations with the six major nuclear powers (US, Russia, China, UK, France and Germany) concerning its nuclear programme. IAEA inspectors were allowed to view Iran's nuclear sites including the known site, near the holy city of Qom.
2010 The highest denomination bank note was raised to IR100,000 (US$10). The UNSC voted to impose further sanctions against Iran, for its lack of compliance with earlier UN resolutions to ensure the peaceful nature of Iran's nuclear programme. Foreign minister Manouchehr Mottaki was sacked by President Ahmadinejad in December while on an official visit to Senegal. Top nuclear official, Ali Akbar Salehi, was appointed as a temporary replacement. The government cut food and fuel subsidies – the cost of these subsidies was put at around US$100 billion.
2011 Ali Reza Pahlavi, the younger son of the last Shah of Iran, committed suicide in January. His sister Leila had also committed suicide, in 2001. Akbar Hashemi Rafsanjani was replaced as head of the Assembly of Experts by Ayatollah Mohammad Reza Mahdavi Kani. In April intelligence minister Heydar Moslehi resigned unexpectedly. Although his resignation was accepted by President Ahmadinejed, he was rapidly reinstated by

Ayatollah Ali Khamenei, (the highest authority in state affairs). In May Ahmadinejad declared himself 'acting' oil minister but said he would not attend the June Opec meeting in Vienna, even though Iran held the rotating chairmanship. Ahmadinejad supporter, Mohammad Sharif Malekzadeh, quit as deputy foreign minister three days after he took office. He was arrested a few days later, accused of corruption. The Iranian oil bourse, the Kish International Commodity Exchange, was officially launched in July, with 600,000 barrels of heavy crude oil for sale. The opening ended the government's complete control of the country's oil trade. In November the IAEA published its quarterly report which stated Iran appeared to be on a 'structured programme' which included computer models exclusively used to develop a trigger for a nuclear bomb. Iran rejected the report as 'unbalanced, unprofessional with political motivation...' The UK suspended all banking transactions with Iran in November as part of a series of international sanctions; France announced that it would no longer buy Iranian oil on a 'national basis', which had amounted to some 49,000 barrels per year. The British embassy in Tehran and a British diplomatic compound in northern Tehran were stormed by hundreds of protestors, angry at British sanctions against Iran. All UK diplomatic staff and their families were evacuated on 30 November; all Iranian embassy staff in London were told to quit the UK within 48 hours. The foreign minister called the UK action 'hasty' and that appropriate action would be taken against the protestors. In December, the US disrupted a principal conduit for processing Iranian oil sales when it pressured the Noor Islamic Bank, based in Dubai (United Arab Emirates) to close the oil receipts facility provided to Iran. The loss was estimated to be up to 60 per cent of Iran's foreign oil sales and within a week of the end of transactions the rial fell by 12 per cent in value against a basket of foreign currencies.

2012 On 6 January international tensions rose when Iran announced that after the completion of 10 days of naval war-games in the Strait of Hormuz, which had included test flights of its missiles, it would hold further exercises from 21 January–19 February. It also threatened to block the Strait if the EU put an embargo on Iranian oil imports. In a tit-for-tat move that a Western official described as being simply to 'illustrate international resolve' to maintain free movement of shipping, six warships (four American, one British and one French) sailed through the Strait on 23 January.

On 24 January the IAEA said that the Iranian authorities had failed to clear up questions on the possible military aspects of its nuclear programme. On the same day the EU imposed sanctions on Iran's central bank and a ban on Iranian oil imports (scheduled for introduction on 1 July). The move was in response to Iran's stance on the enrichment of uranium. Insurance for oil tankers was increased by major UK companies in February. Inspectors from the IAEA arrived in Iran on 20 February for discussions with the government concerning Iran's nuclear programme and to clarify any 'possible military dimensions'. On 22 February the IAEA inspectors left Iran, having been denied access to inspect the Parchin site south of Tehran. In February, Iran proposed fresh talks on its nuclear programme.

Parliamentary (lower house) elections were held on 2 March, in which 3,400 candidates competed for 290 seats, representing 31 provinces. As few reforming candidates ran for election, the contest became largely one between those who supported President Ahmadinejad and those supporting Supreme Leader, Grand Ayatollah Ali Khamenei, both within the Conservative coalition. International observers considered that the power struggle had been won by Ayatollah Khamenei. A rerun of 65 constituencies where no candidate won a minimum of 25 per cent of the vote was scheduled for April.

Israel's Prime Minister Netanyahu met US President Obama on 6 March to discuss the repercussions of Iran becoming an armed nuclear power in the Middle East. While Obama said the US would take military action to protect its interests in the region, Netanyahu said little to counter concerns that Israel might use first-strike action against Iran before the end of 2012.

On 5 June the conservative critic of Ahmadinejad, Ali Larijani, was re-elected as Speaker of parliament (by 177 votes to 89 in parliament). Two earthquakes, minutes apart, struck in the north-west near Tabriz and Ahar, with most casualties in villages surrounding the towns. The initial casualties list was 180 dead and 1,300 injured, plus 50 per cent damage to 60 villages.

On 1 October the rial fell further – by around 18 per cent – and reached its lowest level against the US dollar; at one point the exchange rate was IR35,000 per US$1. The rial has lost 80 per cent of its value since the end of 2011. On 2 October, President Ahmadinejad accused 'enemies' and Western sanctions on Iran for the sharp fall. He called the sanctions economic war.

2013 Hassan Rouhani won the presidential election held on 14 June. He secured just over 50 per cent of the vote thereby avoiding the need for a run-off; second placed was Mohammad Bagher Ghalibaf with 16 per cent with one-time favourite Saeed Jalili third with 11 per cent; reformist Mohammad Reza Aref withdrew before the election. Turn out was 72.2 per cent. He was congratulated by Supreme Leader Ayatollah Ali Khamenei and the result was greeted with enthusiasm by the people of Tehran who surged into the streets in celebration. Mr Rouhani himself, who has said that he will work for greater engagement with Western powers, said: 'This victory is a victory for wisdom, moderation and maturity... over extremism.' Hassan Rouhani was sworn in as President on 3 August and inaugurated on 4 August. At a press conference on 6 August President Rouhani called for 'serious and substantive' negotiations with the international community about its nuclear programme. In a move that may presage a less hardline attitude towards the West, President Rouhani announced in September that the foreign ministry would in future take charge of nuclear negotiations with the West, previously handled by the Supreme National Security Council. The European Court of Justice (ECJ) ruled on 6 September that the EU should lift the sanctions on the assets of a number of banks and businesses. The court said there was insufficient evidence they were involved in nuclear proliferation. President Rouhani told the US broadcaster NBC that Iran would never build nuclear weapons, and that he had full authority to negotiate with the West over Tehran's controversial uranium enrichment programme. He also ordered the release of 11 political prisoners. In an historic speech to the UNSC President Rouhani said that although he considered the sanctions against Iran were 'violent', he was still prepared to enter into 'time-bound and results-oriented' talks on its nuclear programme. A hand shake with President Obama did not materialise, but a 15-minute telephone call was said to be cordial. President Rouhani's visit to the UN was widely hailed internationally as a success. On his return to Tehran President Rouhani was met by hardline protestors chanting 'Death to America' and throwing shoes and eggs, as well as supporters, including senior adviser to Supreme Leader Ayatollah Ali Khamenei, Ali Akbar Velayati. Supreme Leader Khamenei endorsed on his website diplomatic overtures to the US made last month by President Rouhani during his visit to New York. However, he also said that some of what had occurred 'was not appropriate'. British foreign secretary, William Hague, announced on 8

October that a *charge d'affaires* will be appointed to work with Iran, the first diplomatic appoint since the embassies were closed in November 2011. Iran will in turn appoint a *charge d'affaires* to work with the UK. Two days of talks (October 15 and 16) between Iran and world powers held in Geneva were discribed by the EU's top foreign policy official, Catherine Ashton, as 'the most detailed talks ever' on Iran's nuclear programme. Foreign minister, Mohammad Javad Zarif, called the talks 'substantive and forward-looking'. Further talks between Iran and the five UN Security Council members, plus Germany, were held in Geneva in early November. The talks ended without an agreement on 9 November. A further meeting was set for 20 November.

2014 The US refused to grant a visa to Iran's new ambassador to the UN, Hamid Aboutalebi on 8 April. The US accused Mr Aboutalebi of being involved with the students who siezed the US embassy in Tehran in 1979. Mr Aboutalebi said he only acted as an interpreter; the Iranian government said the Americans were acting illegally and they would 'pursue the matter via legal mechanisms' with the UN.

2015 On 14 July, in Vienna, Iran and the P5+1 finally signed the Joint Comprehensive Plan of Action, which will lead to the lifting of international sanctions on Iran.

Political structure

Constitution

Iran became an Islamic Republic in April 1979, having previously been a monarchy under the Shah. The constitution of the Islamic Republic was formally adopted in December 1979. The constitution also provides for representation in the Majlis Shura-e-Islami (Islamic Consultative Assembly) of non-Islamic minorities, Zoroastrians, Jews and Christians. However, power is wielded mainly by the Shi'a clergy.

It has been amended only once, in 1989. Approved by 97.57 per cent of the population the referendum elimated the need for the supreme leader to be directly elected, got rid of the post of Prime Minister and created a Supreme National Security Council.

Form of state

Islamic republic

The executive

The Wali Faqih (Supreme Leader of the Islamic Revolution) retains overall control of all branches of government, including the judiciary and the revolutionary guard. He declares war and peace and can veto presidential nominations. His role combines spiritual leader, theological protector and supreme authority. The structure of the constitution is effectively split between the president, who is elected every four years, and the Supreme Leader, who has overall control. The Supreme Leader, in his role as theological protector, appoints the Council for the Protection of the Constitution. All legislation adopted by the Majlis Shura-e-Islami is scrutinised by the council to ensure that it is in keeping with Islamic principles and laws. The council consists of six religious lawyers.

The Council of Guardians, composed of 12 jurists and clerics, has supervisory powers over elections and a right of veto over all legislation if it does not conform with Islamic law and the constitution. It is independent of the Supreme Leader.

In 1986, the Expediency Council was established to mediate between the Majlis and the Council of Guardians. It is designed to resolve political decisions which cannot be solved through the main channels, but it is controlled by the spiritual leader.

A further adjunct to the Supreme Leader's power is the Assembly of Experts which consists of 83 clerics who elect the next Supreme Leader, interpret the constitution and approve Majlis decisions. The cumulative effect of this plethora of legislative institutions is that despite the enhancement of the president's power, following reform in 1989, he remains tightly constrained by these institutional checks and balances.

National legislature

The unicameral Majlis Shura e Islami (Islamic Consultative Assembly) has 290 members, elected for four-year terms. Although members of parliament are technically independent, the Majlis is now very loosely divided along party political lines between the conservative clergy groupings and reformists. The Majlis is elected by universal suffrage, with a voting age of 15.

The Majles e Khobregan (Assembly of Experts) is a body of 86 Islamic scholars who deliberate the election and dismissal of the Supreme Leader of Iran and supervise his activities. Members are popularly and directly elected from a government approved list, for eight-year terms in office.

Legal system

The judiciary is organised independently of the other branches of government. There are two types of courts: public and special. The Penal Courts, Special Civil Court and Islamic Revolution Courts adjudicate on the basis of Islamic laws, fixed since 1979 for a wide range of crimes.

Last elections

14 June 2013 (presidential); 2 March and 4 May 2012 (parliamentary and re-runs)

Results: Presidential: Hassan Rouhani (Combatant Clergy Association) (50.88 per cent), Mohammad Bagher Ghalibaf (Islamic Society of Engineers) (16.46 per cent), Saeed Jalili (Front of Islamic Revolutionary Stability) (11.31 per cent), Mohsen Rezaee (Moderation and Development Party) (10.55 per cent), Ali Akbar Velayati (6.16 per cent). Turn out was 72.7 per cent.

Parliamentary: Conservatives (coalition of five political parties led by United Front of Conservatives (UFC)) won a combined total of 59.7 per cent of the vote (143 seats out of 290), Reformists (coalition of three parties led by Democratic Coalition of Reformists (DCR)) total 35.5 per cent (59), Religious minorities (coalition of four parties) 2.1 per cent (14), independents 2.5 per cent (nine); turnout was 64.2 per cent. Reruns (in 65 constituencies where no candidate won a minimum of 25 per cent of the vote): UFC won an additional 39 seats, Reformists 16, independents 19.

Next elections

2017 (presidential); 2016 (parliamentary)

Political parties

Mohammad Khatami: former leader of the Reformist Party, now (2015) leader of the Association of Combatant Clerics

Sadegh Kharazi: Former diplomat and adviser to Mohammad Khatami, leader of the newly (2015) formed Voice of Iranians party.

Ruling party

Conservatives (coalition of five political parties led by United Front of Conservatives (UFC)) (from 2004; re-elected 2 Mar 2012)

Main opposition party

Reformists (coalition of three parties led by Democratic Coalition of Reformists (DCR))

Population

76.12 million (2012)*

Last census: 28 October 2006: 70,495,782

Population density: 65 inhabitants per cent (1995–2001). Urban population 71 per cent (2010 Unicef).

Annual growth rate: 1.5 per cent, 1990–2010 (Unicef).

Ethnic make-up

The population is predominantly Persian (55 per cent), with the second largest group being Azeris, concentrated in the north-west. There are also Afghans (approximately two million Afghan refugees were repatriated by the UN refugee organisation in 2002), Kurds, Baluchis, Lurs, Turkmen, Arabs and nomads.

Religions

Islam of the Twelver Shi'a sect is dominant. A Sunni Muslim minority is concentrated in fringe areas of Iran. There are also small Baha'i, Christian, Jewish and Zoroastran communities.

Education
Government expenditure on education was 37.2 per cent of the annual budget in 1999/2000, with 7.4 per cent for higher education and 4.0 per cent for research. Education is compulsory for eight years from the ages of six. This is not fully effective in rural areas. Primary education is free and lasts for five years. Secondary education begins at 11 years and lasts for up to seven years, with a first course of three years and a second course of four years.
Secondary education is split between intermediate (or 'guidance') schools and secondary schools. There are also technical, business and other specialised vocational schools.
Iran has 116 higher education institutes, 23 of which are full universities. Enrolment in the universities accounts for 68 per cent of Iran's 123,000 students, with the remainder enrolled in other institutes of higher education. Secondary education (Reform system) covers three years and a one-year pre-university programme.
Higher education is provided by comprehensive universities, specialised universities, universities of technology, medical universities, teacher training centres and private institutions. The Islamic Open University was established in 1981. It has around 100,000 students in 70 Iranian cities and towns. In addition, there are 131 teacher-training colleges, 107 teacher colleges for rural areas, 10 colleges for technical and vocational teachers, and 19 institutes of technology.
Education became a state monopoly following the 1979 Revolution, but a law passed in 1987 provided for the creation of private schools under certain conditions. To keep pace with population growth, 10,000 new university educated teachers are required each year.
Literacy rate: 78.1 per cent total; 71.4 per cent female, adult rates in 2002 (World Bank).
Compulsory years: 6 to 14.
Enrolment rate: 98 per cent total primary enrolment of relevant age group; 77 per cent total secondary enrolment (World Bank).
Pupils per teacher: 30 in primary schools.

Health
The combined ministry of hygiene, medical care and education is the authority responsible for health and medical care, controlling all related offices and organisations in the private sector as well as those directly funded by the state. The Social Security Organisation (SSO) offers health insurance and runs 60 hospitals, 260 clinics and 30 medical record registration offices in the country.
Iran has adequate healthcare facilities in the cities, although it is generally insufficient in rural areas. The government has, however, created a large number of health clinics in small towns, as well as in villages, to serve the population of the surrounding area. The ministry has undertaken a national hygiene campaign by setting up 'hygiene houses' in many villages and towns.
Drug abuse is a serious problem in Iran, due to imports of cheap heroin and opium from Afghanistan, and there are an estimated two million drug addicts.

HIV/Aids
Intravenous drug users in Iranian prisons accounted for 65 per cent of HIV infections in the country. A programme has been implemented, by non-governmental agencies, working to reduce the harm of HIV/Aids among this group.
Rates of HIV/Aids infection among tuberculosis patients also rose and reached 4.2 per cent by mid-2001 (UNAID/WHO).
HIV prevalence: 0.1 per cent aged 15–49 in 2003 (World Bank)
Life expectancy: 70 years, 2004 (WHO 2006)
Fertility rate/Maternal mortality rate: 1.7 births per woman, 2010 (Unicef); maternal mortality 30 deaths per 100,000 live births (2008) (World Bank).
Child (under 5 years) mortality rate (per 1,000): 18 per 1,000 live births (WHO 2012); 11 per cent of children aged under five are malnourished (World Bank).
Head of population per physician: 0.45 physicians per 1,000 people, 2004 (WHO 2006)

Welfare
A large number of organisations, usually autonomous, are responsible for social welfare. Various foundations manage sequestered property worth billions of US dollars. They are responsible for the care of families of men killed in the war with Iraq, for war refugees and for rural development. At the local level in the cities and towns, mosque committees (*komitehs*) have funds, which are made available for poorer families. The country's rationing system, that includes giving coupons for limited quantities of staple foods and other items at heavily subsidised prices, is also run through mosques.
Iran's Social Security Organisation (SSO) provides a list of services, including survivor's pension, subsidies to large families, retirement, unemployment and disability benefits.
The social security scheme covers some 260,000 factories, workshops and offices. The Foundation for the Refugees of the Imposed War operates under the authority of Iran's ministry of labour and social affairs. It is responsible for the welfare of over two million of the country's internal refugees, or displaced persons, from the Iran-Iraq war.

Main cities
Tehran (capital, estimated population 8.8 million (m) in 2012), Mashhad (2.6m), Esfahan (1.8m), Karaj (2.7m), Tabriz (1.5m), Shiraz (1.3m), Qom (1.1m), Ahvaz (1.1m).

Languages spoken
Azeri Turkish is the second most popular language. English and Arabic are widely taught in high schools. In the cities, French and German are also spoken.

Official language/s
Farsi (Persian)

Media
The government maintains strict control of the media and imposes censorship, particularly of material with Western influence and any divergence from religious regulations. In 2007 the US-based human right's watchdog, Freedom House, rated Iran as 'not free', with one of the lowest scores worldwide, as all publications must be licensed and can be subject to closure, with criminal penalties for journalists for reporting 'propaganda against the state' and the intimidation of publishers, editors and journalist has included detaining, fines and in some cases torture.

Press
There are a large number of daily and weekly newspapers, which had a wide range of political stances; however since 2006 the government began a crack down on reformist publications. Newspapers are challenged by a falling readership, the small advertising market and the shortage of imported and locally produced paper.
Dailies: In Farsi, the main conservative newspapers include *Kayhan* (www.kayhannews.ir) the oldest and run by the office of the supreme leader, *Resalat* (www.resalat-news.com), favours a market economy, and *Jomhouri Eslami* (www.jomhourieslami.com), is linked to Ayatollah Ali Khamene'i with radical views on foreign policies. *Jaam e Jam* (www.jamejamonline.ir), has the largest circulation and is published by IRIB. Reformist newspapers include *Etemaad* (www.etemaad.com) and *Aftab e Yazd* (www.aftab-yazd.com). In English, *Iran News* (www.irannewsdaily.com), the *Tehran Times* (www.tehrantimes.com), is government-run, *Iran Daily* (www.iran-daily.com), is published by IRNA.
Weeklies: Magazines tend to be special interest publications. In Farsi, the *Chelcheragh* (www.40cheragh.org) is a social magazine and *Gozaresh*

(www.gozaresh.com), covers computers and technology.
Periodicals: The quarterly *Azari Majedi* (www.azarmajedi.com) in Farsi, English and French, for articles on culture, the monthly *Donya e Bazi* (www.dbazi.com) covers computer games.

Broadcasting

The national public broadcaster is the Islamic Republic of Iran Broadcaster (IRIB) (www.irib.ir).
Radio: The state-run IRIB (www.irib.ir) has eight national networks with provincial services and an external service that broadcasts in 27 languages.
Television: Around 80 per cent of the population watch TV, with the youth TV having the largest audience. The state-run IRIB (www.irib.ir) has four national networks with provincial services, plus an international channel and three satellite channels. IRIB also has a motion picture production company, Sima Film. In 2007, an alternative, state-run TV network, Press TV (www.presstv.com), based in Tehran, with 24-hour news was introduced.
National news agency: IRNA (Islamic Republic News Agency): www2.irna.ir
Other news agencies: IRIB: www.irib.ir
Iranian Students News Agency (ISNA): http://isna.ir
Press TV: www.presstv.com

Economy

Hydrocarbon exports are the mainstay of Iran's economy, accounting for around 25 per cent of GDP and 20 per cent of government revenue. The country has the world's fourth-largest proven oil reserve at 157.8 billion barrels at the end of 2014, with production at over 3.61 million barrels per day (bpd). Iran's oil sector is, however, severely hampered by its inability to increase production due to insufficient investment as a result of sanctions imposed by the UN. GDP growth of 6.4 per cent in 2007 fell sharply in 2008 to 0.6 per cent before recovering in 2009 to register 4 per cent. As global trade picked up in 2010, growth increased to 5.9 per cent, before falling into negative figures in 2013 at -1.9 per cent because of economic sanctions and Government mismanagement. Growth accelerated out of recession in 2014, reaching 1.5 per cent.
On-going international sanctions against a number of Iranian institutions have resulted in difficulties in trading, consequently the profitability of some financial entities has been hindered. International sanctions have also discouraged foreign investment. Despite the fall-backs, foreign direct investment (FDI) rose from US$1.6 billion in 2008 to US$3.5 billion in 2013, before falling to US$2.1 billion in 2014. However, in July 2015, the UN Security Council passed a resolution which set out to suspend and eventually lift the sanctions, its success is dependent on Iranian cooperation. Simultaneously, foreign direct investment in the country has increased in the first financial quarter of 2015 year-on-year, reaching US$3 billion.
The ability of the Bank Markazi Jomhouri Islami Iran (the Central Bank of Iran) (CBI) to influence monetary policy decisions was curtailed in 2008 as the policy board, which oversaw monetary and credit supply, was integrated into the government's supreme council for economic management and planning. The government had planned to introduce a value added tax (VAT) in 2008, beginning at 3 per cent. However, after days of political protests the president announced he would delay the VAT introduction until 2009/10. Months of opposition to VAT forced a further delay, but it was finally introduced in March 2011, at 4 per cent, but raised to 7 per cent by 2014 and expected to be raised to 10 per cent by the end of 2015 in order to combat crashing oil prices.
The economy is protected by high external tariffs, price controls and subsidies. The International Monetary Fund (IMF) advised, in 2008, that large state-owned banks and private smaller banks would have to be recapitalised and banking procedures would have to be aligned to World Trade Organisation (WTO) standards if Iran was to be integrated in the global banking sector. Anti-money laundering regulations were introduced in 2008, but the IMF still regards the law as deficient in some aspects. Although Iran submitted an application to form the WTO in 1996, and a working party was set up by the WTO in 2005, in 2015 Iran is still not a member.
Political and religious charities, *bonyads*, established at the founding of the Iranian Islamic state, which had appropriated assets of the former Shah and that were to be used to provide welfare payments to disadvantaged groups in society, have evolved into huge private monopolies, which have no governmental oversight of their operations but contribute to the ideological and cultural needs of the Islamic state. They dominate the economy, particularly the non-oil sector. They are allocated around two-thirds of the budget each year and own or control all the country's transport, oil, petrochemical and mining companies.
The service sector accounts for 45.3 per cent of GDP, with industry 44.5 per cent and agriculture 10.2 per cent. Iran has had to find employment for around 750,000 new workers each year; unemployment consistently averages over 10 per cent, reaching 11.5 per cent in the first quarter of 2015.
Among the noteworthy export products outside the petrochemical industry are motor vehicles and highly prized carpets. Pistachio nuts account for around 8 per cent of non-oil GDP with exports of over 200 tonnes per year.
The highest denomination bank note was raised to IR100,000 (US$10) in 2010, due to inflation of 12.4 per cent (falling from a high of 25.4 per cent in 2008), with around 150 million bank notes being printed for distribution. In 2013 inflation had risen to a staggering 39.3 per cent before more than halving in 2014 to 17.2 per cent.
On 17 September 2012, Iranian rial plunged by almost 8 per cent against the US dollar; the news was suppressed by the media. The street exchange rate had been Rh24,000 per US$1 on 16 September, but within 24 hours the informal rate had fallen to Rh26,400 per US$1. An officially maintained fixed rate of Rh12,260 per US$1 is reserved for government business and a few privileged businesses; everyone else relies on the informal rate and imports have risen in cost accordingly. On 1 October the rial weakened further to Rh34,700 per dollar. By then the currency had lost 80 per cent of its value since the end of 2011. By August 2015 the exchange rate had risen to Rh29,860 per US$1, although this was still higher than what would be preferred by the Iranian government.

External trade

Iran was a founding member, in 1985, of the Economic Co-operation Organisation (ECO), with Turkey and Pakistan. Seven other countries (Afghanistan, Azerbaijan, Kazakhstan, Kyrgyzstan, Tajikistan, Turkmenistan and Uzbekistan) Joined in 1992. The ECO has plans to create a free trade zone. Iran also has bilateral trade agreements with, among others, Venezuela, Cuba, Iraq and South Africa.
Oil dominates the Iranian economy and is the biggest source of revenue in terms of exports. Shortages of foreign currency have produced a boom in counter (barter) trade, which obscures the extent of foreign trade.

Imports

Main imports include industrial supplies, intermediate goods, electrical and electronic equipment, foodstuffs and other consumer goods, technical services and military supplies.
Main sources: UAE (30.6 per cent of total in 2014), China (25.5 per cent), Algeria (8.3 per cent), India (4.6 per cent), South Korea (4.4 per cent) and Turkey (4.1 per cent).

Exports

Petroleum and chemical and petrochemical products; non-oil items include iron and steel, carpets, pistachio nuts, dates, cement, ore and caviar.

Iran and Pakistan signed a deal to build a US$7.5 billion gas pipeline in 2008 and in May 2009 signed a trade agreement for an initial 30 million cubic metres per day of Iranian natural gas (increasing to 60 million cum) to be transferred to Pakistan. The project had a deadline of December 2014 to be completed, however more realistic predictions state that 2017 is more likely.

Main destinations: China (29.0 per cent total in 2014), India (11.9 per cent), Turkey (10.4 per cent), Japan (6.5 per cent) and South Korea (4.8 per cent).

Agriculture

Farming

Since the 1979 revolution, land ownership has been in dispute. Meanwhile, people have moved from the countryside to the city. This has left a shortage of agricultural labour, despite high unemployment in the economy as a whole. On many farms, particularly those in the private sector near Tehran, immigrant Afghan workers have replaced Iranians. In 2014 agriculture contributed 10.2 per cent to GDP and employed around a quarter of the workforce. Iran's main agricultural goods are wheat, rice, other grains and sugar beet.

Since it was set up in the 1980s, the Bonyad-e Mostazafin (Foundation for the Oppressed and Deprived) has brought new facilities, especially water, electricity and roads, to thousands of rural villages. Government efforts to stimulate sluggish private investment in agriculture have made little headway. As half of Iran's farmers belong to 3,000 rural co-operatives, grouped into 180 unions and benefiting from cheap credit made available by the state, they are reluctant to embrace private sector competition.

The government wants to reduce the import bill for food and agricultural inputs. Iran imports large quantities of meat, rice, vegetables, oil, sugar and tea, as well as cattle fodder, fertilisers, machinery and tractors. It is encouraging the expansion of cotton and sugar cane plantations, livestock production and downstream processing industries for these products.

Fishing

There are few river systems in Iran, and most freshwater fishing is for subsistence purposes. There is commercial fishing on the Persian Gulf and the Caspian Sea. Iran produces around 444,000 tonnes of seafood per year. Main species are sturgeon, tuna, mackerel, shrimps, lobster and crayfish. Iran is the world's largest producer and exporter of caviar, producing some 300 tonnes annually.

Forestry

There is some forestation in the north of the country, near the Caspian Sea, but limited commercial exploitation is generally for domestic purposes only. Forests cover 6.8 per cent of Iran's land area, a figure that has remained constant for a number of decades.

Industry and manufacturing

The government's goal in the past has been to build up basic industries as a means of import substitution and to develop a broad industrial base to reduce reliance on oil. The government has also given priority to the development of downstream industries in the oil and gas sectors and to the development of mining and metals processing.

State companies dominate industry. During the Iran-Iraq war, their role was strengthened as the government requisitioned factories, such as vehicle plants, for the war effort. Since the war, politically run state conglomerates called bonyad have dominated the economy. They are allocated two-thirds of the budget each year, have preferential access to scarce foreign exchange, and own or control all the country's transport, oil, petrochemical and mining companies.

Despite this, the private sector remains surprisingly resilient. Many new private-sector companies have been formed since the revolution. The government hopes that Iranian expatriates will form the spearhead of 'foreign' private-sector investment in the development of manufacturing capacity. The government also hopes to increase Iran's industrial competitiveness and exports by encouraging privatisation. In 2014, the Rouhani government privatised 27 huge companies, 76 large companies, 31 medium companies, and 31 companies of other sizes.

Tehran and Isfahan are the main industrial centres. The largest industrial conglomerate is the National Iranian Industries Organisation (NIIO), a state-owned group which is directly responsible for 380 companies in manufacturing, services and trading. The NIIO companies are in nine industrial groups: textiles, chemicals, pharmaceuticals, food, footwear and leather, electrical goods, construction, cement and celluloid. They produce about 23 per cent of total industrial output.

Tourism

Iran has a history reaching back into antiquity, from the ruins of Persepolis, founded by Darius the Great, including cuneiform inscriptions (the first form of writing in the world), to religious sites pre-dating Islam to the cultural and architectural artefacts from the height of the Persian Empire, most of which are included on Unesco's World Heritage List. Iran was also an important staging post along the Silk Road.

Due to the political situation in Iran and its on-going differences with Western powers, many countries have advised their citizens not to travel to Iran, while travel companies are prohibited from dealing with Iran as part of UN economic sanctions. Most tourists are domestic visitors who use the large network of public transport to visit other parts of Iran.

Travel and tourism contributed a steady 6.3 per cent to GDP in 2014. The industry employs a consistent 5.3 per cent of total employment (1.2 million jobs in 2014) with around 2 per cent of direct employment (413,000 jobs in 2014).

Environment

Tehran is susceptable to severe air polution as the population has greatly increased and there is a growing number of cars on the roads – many of them old. The city is wedged between mountains, meaning dirty air can get trapped when there is no wind or rain.

Mining

Iran is one of the world's 15 major mineral-rich countries and the mining sector employs directly over 107,000 workers. Production has a market value of over US$4 billion. The government is trying to encourage private investment in mineral exploration and production.

The majority of the large-scale mines and major industries, including steelworks, copper, lead and zinc, are partially or totally state-owned. The government has sought to develop the country's abundant mineral resources as an alternative to oil- and gas-based industrial development. However, as in other sectors, expansion of mineral production has suffered from shortages of foreign currency for machinery and spare parts, power cuts, and the lack of mining experts. Consequently, Iran is still obliged to import many raw materials, which it could produce from its own resources, given appropriate investment and manpower skills.

The Iranian government has strongly encouraged foreign investment on 'buy-back' terms that enables foreign investors to recoup capital through receipt of the project's output. Substantial improvement is targeted for the non-ferrous metals sector including aluminium, copper and zinc. Iran has 60 lead and zinc mines, 30 coal mines, 20 copper mines and 40 deposits of chromite, fluorine and sulphur. It also has an important industrial mineral sector, and is the third largest producer of gypsum in the world.

In March 2015 two large iron ore and coal reserves were found in the Sangan mine in the eastern province of Khorasan

Razavi. There is an expected 200 million tons of iron ore and 120 million tons of coal.

Hydrocarbons

Proven oil reserves were 157.8 billion barrels in 2014, which constitutes 9.3 per cent of the world's total petroleum reserves. Production in 2014 was 3.61 million barrels per day (bpd), an annual increase of 2 per cent from 2013. Although a new oil and gas field was discovered in 2009, in the Khorramabad block, in western Iran, with estimated proven natural gas reserves of 26.8 trillion cum (second only to Russia's gas reserves) the industry is still faced with maturing oil fields, limited investment and international sanctions imposed on the country. In 2015 production had still not started on these fields.

Oil consumption is around 2 million bpd but mainly in light fuels, petrol and diesel. Iran increased its refining capacity to 2 million bpd in 2013, sufficient to satisfy its domestic requirements.

Iran was a founding member of the Organisation of the Petroleum Exporting Countries (Opec) and is its second largest exporter (after Saudi Arabia). The Ministry of Petroleum has responsibility for oil and natural gas exploration and production through the state-owned National Iranian Oil Company (NIOC). International oil companies are involved in developing Iran's oil fields on a buyback basis, which entails the contractor funding all investment in return for an allocated production share from NIOC. The operation of the oil field is transferred to the NIOC once the contract is completed.

In the downstream sector, the government's strategy is to develop petrochemicals as part of a plan to add value to hydrocarbon exports; it is encouraging foreign investment into the industry but in 2015 was still hampered by sanctions.

The US Energy Information Administration (EIA) considers the Strait of Hormuz as 'the world's most important oil chokepoint' and any threat to the free movement of oil tankers would be considered a provocation. In 2013, 35 per cent of all seaborne traded oil (and 20 per cent of all traded oil) flowed through the strait.

Proven gas reserves were 34.0 trillion cubic metres in 2014, the world's largest natural gas reserve. Production was 172.6 billion cubic metres (cum), an increase of 5.2 per cent on the 2013 figure. Around 60 per cent of all reserves are undeveloped. Consumption was 170.2 billion cum in 2013, showing a steady growth from 47 billion in 1997. The government is keen to expand export markets, particularly in Asia. The massive South Pars gas field, which is shared with Qatar, is being developed in 25 stages over 25 years.

In November 2012, Iran announced that it had begun to build a new 225km, US$3 billion, natural gas pipeline to its border with Iraq. Iran, Iraq and Syria had signed a US$10 billion agreement in 2011 to build an extended, 1,500km gas pipeline through Iraq (close to Baghdad) to Damascus in Syria, with the ultimate sale of 110 million cum per day. However due to the civil war in Syria construction has experienced many problems and there is no completion date.

Production of coal is less than one million tonnes per year (tpy) but with consumption at approximately 2 million tpy imports complete the supply. In 2009, Iran's first mechanised underground coal mine at Tabas was begun. At full production, it is expected to produce around 1.5 million tonnes of coking coal for steel production each year, however production hadn't started in 2015.

In March 2015, a coal field with 120 million tons of reserves was discovered in the Sangan mine in the eastern province of Khorasan Razavi.

Energy

Total installed generating capacity is 62.1GW in 2013 with production of typically around 239 billion KWh; 98 per cent is produced by thermal power stations of which natural gas accounts for two thirds and oil the remaining; hydroelectricity makes up 5 per cent of the energy mix and coal 1 per cent. Iran's demand is growing rapidly at 7–9 per cent per annum and this will require a doubling of electricity generating capacity in the next few years.

Financial markets

Stock exchange

Tehran Stock Exchange (TSE)

Commodity exchange

Kish International Commodity Exchange

Banking and insurance

Before the revolution, Iran's banking system was handicapped by the small number of banks, by heavy indebtedness (both to the central bank and to foreign creditors) and by the high levels of non-performing assets, a legacy of the virtual absence of regulatory controls under the Shah's regime. After the reorganisation in 1979, the sector's weakness was further aggravated by economic recession, the freezing of Iranian assets held abroad and the long war with Iraq.

The government recognises that the state-owned banking system is unable to provide sufficient credit for economic growth. Non-banking credit institutions (NBCIs) will legally do what *bazaaris* have been doing for two decades. Foreign banks, a number of which have a representative office in Tehran, became more active as oil exports revived and financing became available for the reconstruction programme. Reconstruction requires imported goods and services. French banks are keen to regain the dominance they enjoyed in foreign trade financing in Iran before 1983, when France's supply of weapons to Iraq caused a breakdown in relations between France and Iran. Several French banks are on the approved list of the National Iranian Oil Company (NIOC). The most active are Banque Paribas, Société Générale and Banque Nationale de Paris.

As part of the 2000—04 economic development programme, the banking sector is being opened up to foreign participation and in 2002, Bank Markazi (the central bank) agreed to license the first fully foreign-owned banks since the 1979 revolution.

Bank Sepah was blacklisted by the US. The state-owned bank was accused of being the 'financial lynchpin' in Iran's efforts to procure material for its missile programme.

The Iran-Europe Commercial Bank (ICB) opened for business on the 27 May 2008, with the Iranian Bank of Industry and Mines (San'at va Ma'dan) as a major shareholder, and registered in Germany as a lender. The ICB was the first of six foreign banks allowed to operate in Iran (and not just on the island of Kish Free Trade Zone).

Central bank

Bank Markazi Jomhouri Islami Iran

Main financial centre

Tehran

Time

GMT plus 3.5 hours

Geography

Iran is a large and varied country. Much of it is desert wilderness, with mountainous regions along the western borders with Iraq and in the north with Turkey. Around 11 per cent of Iran is forested, notably in the northern regions of the Caspian Sea and Zagros mountains.

By the early part of the twentieth century, the majority of the population were villagers living in fertile fringes of Iran's great central plateau, which is made up of vast sand and salt deserts. However, rapid urbanisation, especially the growth of the capital Tehran, has changed the distribution of the population and the activities in which it is engaged.

Water is scarce in most of Iran and its availability dictates the density of the population in settled areas. There are very few towns of any size in central and eastern Iran, although there are lush oases scattered across the sand and salt deserts. There is a traditional system of subterranean water channels, cut from the water tables in mountains for irrigation.

Hemisphere

Northern

Climate

The climate for most of the country is dry and hot in summer before abruptly changing to a bitterly cold winter. The best season for visiting is around the Persian New Year (Nowruz). Temperatures range from 51 degrees Celsius (C) in summer at the head of the Gulf to minus 14 degrees C in winter in the interior. The mean temperatures are 3 degrees C in January and 29 degrees C in July. The Gulf area becomes very hot and humid in summer.

Dress codes

Since the 1979 Islamic Revolution, ties are shunned by Iranians but suits are acceptable. Informal dress is acceptable for men (not shorts). Women should always dress discreetly in public and avoid make-up.

Iranian women are required to cover all their hair and to disguise the shape of their bodies by wearing long, loose fitting clothes. Men can be stopped for having inappropriate hairstyles. Punishment can take the form of imprisonment, lashes or fines.

Entry requirements

Passports

Required by all, valid for six months beyond period of visit.

Visa

Visas are required by all, except nationals of Turkey and some other countries subject to change, and are valid for 30 days. Business visas must have an invitation letter from a local, sponsoring company, to be submitted to the foreign ministry in Tehran for approval. When authorised, the host company can obtain a reference number which is forwarded to the applicant. After one week, the visitor should contact the consulate quoting the reference number, and confirm the approval. Once confirmed, the application and documents can be submitted to the consular section for further action.

Prohibited entry

Israeli citizens or anyone with Israeli stamps in their passport will be rejected.

Currency advice/regulations

Import and export of local currency is limited to IR200,000. No restrictions on the import of foreign currency, but over US$1,000 must be declared on arrival; export is limited up to amount declared. Currency should be exchanged by authorised banks and exchange dealers and the receipts presented on departure.

Customs

The export of all antiques (over 50 years old) is prohibited, including gems, coins, handwritten manuscripts and other artifacts.

Prohibited imports

The import of all alcohol, firearms and ammunitions, video tapes and obscene publications.

Health (for visitors)

Mandatory precautions

A yellow fever certificate is required if travelling from an infected area. An AIDS certificate is required if staying more than three months.

Advisable precautions

Cholera is a high risk and precautions are required. Typhoid, dysentery and typhoid fever are common.

Hotels

The situation and status of hotels should be carefully checked. The use of the name of an international management chain does not imply a current connection with the chain, but may indicate only a previous link or the usual name by which the hotel is known. Most hotels are utilitarian. Evening entertainment is very rare.

Credit cards

Mastercard and visa are accepted in major locations.

Public holidays (national)

Solar Hijri year 1393: 21 March 2014–20 March 2015;

Fixed dates

11 Feb (Victory of Islamic Revolution, 1979), 20 Mar (Oil Nationalisation Day), 1 Apr (Islamic Republic Day), 2 Apr (Public Outing Day), 4 Jun (Death of Imam Khomeini), 5 Jun (Anniversary of Uprising against the Shah).

Variable dates

Nowruz (Persian New Year), Martyrdom of Imam Hassan Mojtaba, Martyrdom of Imam Reza, Martyrdom of Hazrat Fatemeh, Birthday of Imam Ali, Prophet Mohammad received his calling, Birthday of Imam Mahdi (12th Imam), Martyrdom of Imam Ali, Eid al Fitr, Martyrdom of Imam Sadegh, Eid e Ghorban (Eid al Ahda), Eid e Ghadir Khom, Tassoua, Ashura, Arbeen, Demise of Prophet Mohammad, Martyrdom of Imam Reza.

Iran uses the solar Persian calendar, which differs from the Gregorian calendar: there are 31 days in each of the first six months of the Persian calendar, 30 days in each of the next five months and 29 days in the last month, except in leap year when it has 30 days. The year always begins on the spring equinox (around 21 March).

The Persian calendar dates from the Arab/Muslim invasion and the introduction of Islam into the country. The calendar (known as the *Hejrieh Shamsi*) is very precise; it was devised by the renowned Persian mathematician, Omar Khayyam. The months are: Farvardin, Ordibehesht, Khordad, Tir, Mordad, Shahrivar, Mehr, Aban, Azar, Day, Bahman, Esfand. The Iranian calendar year was briefly changed in commemoration of the 2,500th anniversary of the Persian Empire in 1971. The year was changed from 1350 Hejrieh Shamsi to 2530 Melli (national). This calendar was unpopular and the nation reverted to the old calendar soon afterwards.

Persian year 1393: 21 March 2014 to 20 March 2015).

Working hours

Friday is the Muslim day of religious observance (weekly holiday).

Banking

Sat–Wed: 0800–1700; Thu: 0800–1200; closed on Friday.

Business

Sat–Wed: 0700/0800–1300, 1600–1900. Closed on Thursday and Friday.

Government

Sat–Wed: 0700/0800–1300, 1600–1900. Closed on Thursday and Friday.

Shops

Sat–Wed: 0800–2000; Thu: 0800–1200; most bakeries and some food shops stay open on Fridays while the rest close.

Electricity supply

230V AC, 50 cycles

Weights and measures

Metric system

Social customs/useful tips

Visitors for business engagements are expected to arrive on time for appointments. However, it is by no means uncommon to be kept waiting, or even for appointments to be cancelled without notice. Tehran is susceptable to severe air polution as the population has greatly increased and there is a growing number of cars on the roads – many of them old. The city is wedged between mountains, meaning dirty air can get trapped when there is no wind or rain. The government can declare a public holiday when the polution is particularly bad.

The Gulf is never called Arabian, but is usually identified as Persian.

Normal Muslim customs prevail within most areas of the country. Alcohol is forbidden, although tolerance is shown to non-Muslims who may drink it at home. Women must sit at the back of buses. Men and women who are not married must not touch, therefore a business deal with a woman may not be sealed with a handshake.

Business negotiations can take a long time. A good lawyer and a detailed contract are essential.

Prostitution, casual sex and especially homosexual sex, are punishable with death or long prison sentences. Foreign visitors are not exempt from these laws.

Security

There is little violent street crime in Tehran, but visitors should take great care of their wallets and bags. Keep passports separate from other valuables.

Getting there

Air

National airline: IranAir

International airport/s: Mehrabad (THR), 5km west of Tehran, with duty-free shop, restaurant, bank, post office, shops; Shiraz (SYZ), 15km from city, with currency exchange, post office, shops.

Airport tax: Departure tax: IR70,000.

Surface

Road: There are roads from Iraq, Turkey, Armenia, Afghanistan and Pakistan, although these routes are not always passable.

Rail: There is a link with Turkey and Syria. A rail route runs nearly 300km from Mashhad into Turkmenistan, crossing the border at Sarakhs to join the Soviet-era Turksib railway at Tedzhen.

Water: Ferries run between Iran and United Arab Emirates, Manama (Bahrain) and Kuwait City.

Main port/s: The large ports on the Gulf include the country's main oil terminal at Kharg Island, the largest port Khorramshahr, Bandar Shahid Rajai, Bushehr, Bandar Khomeini and Chah Bahar. The main ports on the Caspian Sea are Bandar Anzali and Bandar Nowshahr.

Getting about

National transport

Air: IranAir and Aseman Airlines run frequent services between most cities and Tehran.

Road: Surfaced roads serve main centres; condition of secondary roads may vary.

Buses: There is an extensive, comfortable and cheap bus network that runs throughout the country. Scheduled long-distance coach services vary in their routes, but usually travel between all the main towns.

Rail: Rail services on the 5,500km network may vary, but there are usually various classes of service, with sleeping accommodation, air-conditioning and restaurant services available.

City transport

Taxis: Taxis are not metered and frequently shared. Those hired by telephone or by hotels are more expensive. Tipping is not expected.

Car hire

An international driving licence (along with two photographs) is required.

BUSINESS DIRECTORY

The addresses listed below are a selection only. While World of Information makes every endeavour to check these addresses, we cannot guarantee that changes have not been made, especially to telephone numbers and area codes. We would welcome any corrections.

Telephone area codes

The international direct dialling (IDD) code for Iran is +98, followed by area code and subscriber's number:

Abadan	631	Isfahan	311
Ahvaz	611	Kerman	342
Arak	262	Mashad	511
Babol	111	Shiraz	711
Bakhtaran	431	Tabriz	411
Hamadán	811	Tehran	21

Useful telephone numbers

Ambulance: 123

Fire: 125

General emergencies: 123

Police: 110

Traffic accidents: 197

Chambers of Commerce

Iran Chamber of Commerce, Industries & Mines, 254 Taleghani Avenue, Tehran 15814 (tel:8884-6031; fax: 8882-5111; e-mail: info@iccm.org).

Irano-British Chamber of Commerce, Industries and Mines, 254 Taleghani Avenue, Tehran 15814 (tel 8881-0525; fax: 8881-0526; e-mail: info@ibchamber.org).

Shiraz Chamber of Commerce, Industries and Mines, Zand Street, Shiraz 71356-53564 (tel: 2230-4415; fax: 2233-1220; e-mail: info@sccim.com).

Tehran Chamber of Commerce, Industries and Mines, 254 Taleghani Avenue, Tehran 15814 (tel: 8884-6031; fax: 882-5111; e-mail: info@tccim.com).

Banking

Bank Maskan, Ferdowsi Avenue, PO Box 11365-3499, Tehran (tel: 6670-9658; fax: 6670-9684; e-mail: info@bank-maskan.ir).

Bank Mellat, Head Office Bldg, 327 Taleghani Ave, 15817 Tehran (tel: 8296-2700).

Bank Melli Iran, Ferdowsi Avenue, PO Box 11365-171, Tehran (tel: 3231; fax: 3391-2813).

Bank Refah Kargaran, 40 Northern Shirazi Street, Mollasadra Avenue, Tehran (tel: 8804-2926; fax: 8804-2926).

Bank Saderat Iran, Sepehr Tower, 43 Somayeh Avenue, PO Box 15745-631, Tehran (tel: 8829-9469; fax: 8883-9534).

Bank Sepah, Imam Khomeini Square, PO Box 11364-9569, Tehran (tel: 6674-3761; fax: 6674-3282; e-mail: info@banksepah.ir). (Bank Sepah was blacklisted by the US. The state-owned bank was accused of being the 'financial lynchpin' in Iran's efforts to procure material for its missile programme.)

Bank Tejarat, PO Box 11365-5416, 130 Taleghani Avenue, Nejatoullahie, 15994 Tehran (tel: 8882-6690; fax: 8889-3641).

Central bank

Bank Markazi Jomhouri Islami Iran, PO Box 11365-8551, Tehran (tel: 29-951; fax: 673-5674;e-mail: g.secdept@cbi.ir).

Stock exchange

Tehran Stock Exchange (TSE), www.iranbourse.com

Commodity exchange

Kish International Commodity Exchange

Travel information

Irpedia, 6 Kachouee Avenue, Chamran Highway, Tehran (tel: 200-8189; e-mail: info@irpedia.com).

Pars Tourist Agency, Zand Sreet 71358, Shiraz (tel: 222-3163; fax: 224-0645; e-mail: info@key2persia.com).

Ministry of tourism

Ministry of Culture and Islamic Guidance, Baharestan Square, Kamal-al-Molk Avenue, Avenue Kamalolmolk, Tehran (tel: 3851-2583; fax: 3311-7535).

National tourist organisation offices

Iran Tourist Co, 257 Motahari Avenue, Tehran 15868 (tel: 8873-6762/5; fax: 8873-6158; e-mail: info@ irantouristco.com; internet site: http://www.irantouristco.com).

Ministries

Ministry of Commerce, 492 Valieasr Avenue, Tehran (tel: 8889-3553; fax: 8890-3943).

Ministry of Foreign Affairs, Imam Khomeini Square, Tehran (tel: 6673-9191; fax: 6674-3149; e-mail: matbuat@mfa.gov.ir).

Ministry of Information and Communication Technology (MICT), Sharlati St, PO Box 15875-4415, 16314 Tehran (tel: 8846 9000; fax: 8846 8131).

Ministry of Petroleum, Hafez Crossing, Taleghani Street, Tehran (tel: 6615-2606; fax: 6615-4977; e-mail: public-relations@mop.ir).

Ministry of Science, Research and Technology, Unit 2, Ostad Nejatollahi Street, Teheran (tel: 8890-2024; fax: 8890-2027; e-mail: msrt@mche.or.ir).

Other useful addresses

Export Promotion Centre of Iran, PO Box 11-48, Tajrish, Tehran (tel: 2205-1437; fax: 2205-1438; e-mail: epc-iran@epc-iran.com).

Iranian Interests Section (USA), 2209 Wisconsin Avenue, NW, Washington DC 20007 (tel:(+1-202)-965-4990; fax: (+1-202)-965-1073; e-mail: requests@daftar.org).

National Iranian Oil Company (NIOC), Taleghani Avenue, PO Box 1853, Tehran (tel: 6615-2275; fax: 6641-0916; e-mail: public-relation@nioc.com).

Statistical Centre of Iran, Dr Fatemi Ave, PO Box 14155-6133 Tehran (tel: 8896-5061; fax: 8896-5070; e-mail: sci@sci/org.ir).

Tehran Stock Exchange, 228 Hafez Avenue, Tehran (tel: 6670-4130; fax:6670-2524; e-mail: info@tse.ir).

National news agency: IRNA (Islamic Republic News Agency): www2.irna.ir

IRIB: www.irib.ir

Iranian Students News Agency (ISNA): http://isna.ir

Press TV: www.presstv.com

Internet sites

Customs Administration: http://www.irica.gov.ir

General information: http://www.salamiran.org

General political information: http://www.netiran.com

Islamic Republic News Agency: http://www.irna.ir

Iraq

KEY FACTS

Official name: Al Jumhouriya al Iraqia (The Republic of Iraq)

Head of State: President Fuad Masum (PUK) (from 24 Jul 2014)

Head of government: Prime Minister Haider al Abadi (Dawa) (from 8 Sep 2014)

Ruling party: National Alliance coalition, led by Al Iraqiya (Iraqi National Movement), with I'tilaf Dawlat al Qanon (State of Law Coalition) and Al Ittilaf al Watani al Iraqi (National Iraqi Alliance) (known as Watani List) (from 14 Jun 2010)

Area: 434,924 square km

Population: 35.87 million (2014)*

Capital: Baghdad

Official language: Arabic and Kurdish

Currency: New Iraqi dinar (ID) 1,000 fils

Exchange rate: ID1,188.00 per US$ (Sep 2015)

GDP per capita: US$6,165 (2014)*

GDP real growth: -2.40% (2014)

GDP: US$221.13 billion (2014)

Labour force: 7.54 million (2011)

Unemployment: 27.50% (Average figure, does not include underemployment)

Inflation: 2.24% (2014)

Oil production: 3.29 million bpd (2014)

Natural gas production: 1.30 billion cum (2014)

Balance of trade: US$4.41 billion (2012)

Annual FDI: US$1.40 billion (2011)

* estimated figure

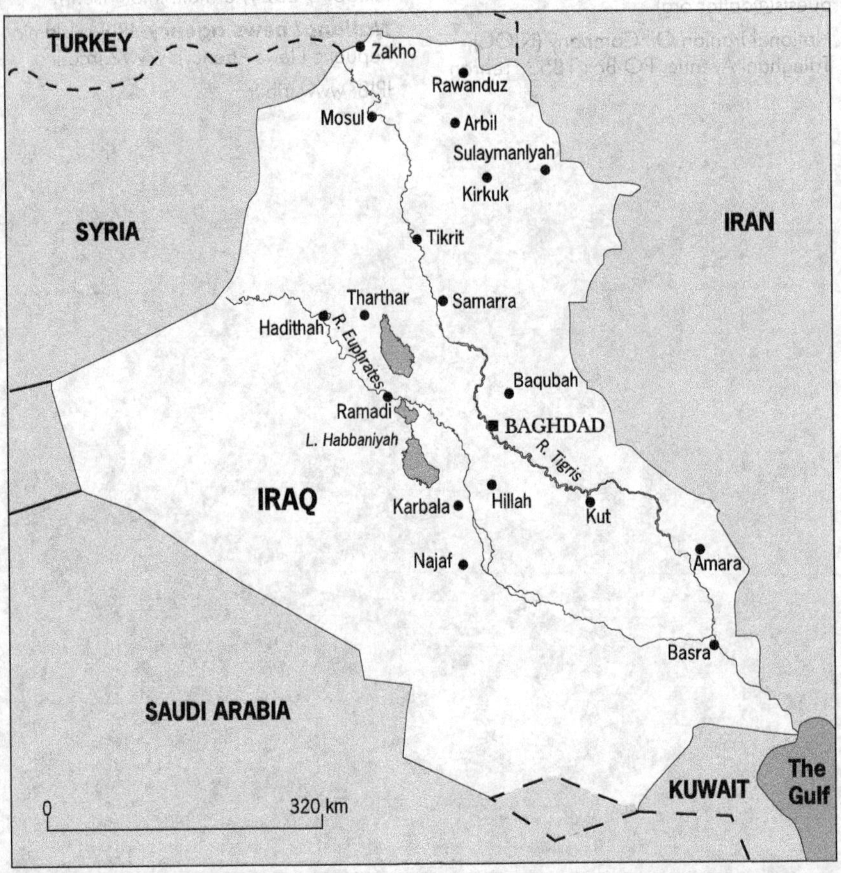

Four years after the withdrawal of US troops from Iraq, President Obama found himself – in the light of constant gains by the so called Islamic State (IS) (or Islamic State of Iraq and the Levant (ISIL), Islamic State of Iraq and Syria (ISIS) and DAESH (which is the Arabic acronym for ISIL)) – obliged to reinforce the 3,500 US military advisors already in Iraq with a further 450 troops.

The US strategy had been elaborated by the discredited Paul Wolfowitz, a one-time ultra conservative advisor of George Bush. The policy was described by the Algerian political commentator Sami Naïr as 'based on the trivialisation of Iraq' as some sort of antidote to a perceived 'secular, potentially anti-imperialist, nationalism and authoritarianism.' According to Mr Naïr this interpretation of events resulted in an attempt to impose a 'Western' approach on Arab geopolitics. The objective was to install a democracy of sorts, but one that permitted the fragmentation of the Iraqi body politic into a complex mosaic of ethnic and religious divisions. What Mr Naïr described as 'the Iraqi tragedy' demonstrated the failure of this strategy.

An army implodes

The dramatic implosion of the Iraqi army in the first half of 2015 lead to countless theories and explanations being put forward as to why the Iraqi army simply gave in to IS insurgents, allowing them to capture no less than four cities and all that came with them – cash, arms and hostages. The biggest losses were undoubtedly those endured by local populations, where non-Muslims were simply lined up and shot and where women were abducted as deemed necessary. This was human tragedy at its worst. Following the defeat in Mosul, Iraq's military headquarters in Baghdad had to admit that not only had Mosul's main military base and headquarters been stripped bare, but hundreds of prisoners – in jail for a variety of reasons – had been released and an estimated US$480 million in banknotes had gone missing from Mosul's banks. Mosul, Iraq's second city, was not a small town; its population of 660,000 (around a million with its suburbs) was large by Middle Eastern standards. Isis killed many of its Shi'a or Yazidi opponents, driving Christians out of Mosul and surrounding towns. It claimed to offer 'forgiveness' to Sunni Muslims who publicly showed repentance for having worked for the Iraqi army or local government.

According to the London *Guardian* newspaper, in the province of Anbar, when faced with an IS attack by no more than 800 insurgents, two divisions of Iraqi soldiers, around 30,000 troops, ran for their lives. The *Guardian* also reported that officials in Baghdad had accused the army command of betrayal. Quite apart from the loss of matériel and cash, the rout demonstrated just how out of touch the US advisors were when it came to assessing the competence of the Iraqi army. US claims to have established a unified and competent military began to look dangerously off the mark. This state of affairs also called into question the effectiveness of the trillion or so dollars that had been spent invading and shoring up Iraq. US public opinion – the Iraq war and its incompetent 'stabilisation' had cost the lives of more than 4,500 of its soldiers – was firmly against any further military involvement. However unacceptable that figure was, it did not compare with the estimated loss of over 100,000 Iraqi lives since the invasion in 2003.

Rumours and whispers abounded in Iraq, making it impossible to predict what was likely to happen in other cities such as Tikrit. US intelligence services seemed to be either non-existent or incompetent; worse, the US military had at no stage shown, or even had access to, any real awareness of Arab-Muslim cultures and concerns. Since the Iraqi invasion of Kuwait in 1990 – an event involving 100,000 troops and over 700 tanks – which took the US and other Western countries by surprise, it might have been expected that the US would invest some resources and time in gaining a better understanding of what made Iraq and its people tick – or not, as the case may be. But this did not happen. Thus the growth of – and support for – IS seemed to take both Washington and North Atlantic Treaty Organisation (NATO) by surprise. The chaotic consequences were, however (as pointed out by Mr Naïr), well suited to the continuation of the almost medieval systems of government found in Saudi Arabia and the Gulf states. In none of these countries had the leadership wished to see a modern democratic government imposed upon them. The example of Iraq said it all; the majority Shi'a government had established a corrupt, militarily ineffective, largely totalitarian system of power (rather than of government) – sustained by two allies (the US and Iran) with virtually nothing in common – quite the contrary. The two were opposed in almost every respect. In 2015 the US wanted to maintain a tribal structure in Iraq, having abandoned its ambitious plans for democracies that did not work. Iran wished to strengthen Iraqi Shi'as against the Sunnis in general and against the IS *sunami* in particular.

However, the Iraqi body politic now seemed incapable of confronting any serious threat. The return of the US to the Iraqi battlefields, if it were to succeed, would almost certainly have to be expanded. But the IS rise could be attributed to what Mr Naïr described as a 'double decomposition' – that of Iraq as a body politic or 'state' and that of its Sunni community which had never been homogenous, in contrast to the Shi'a community. The deposed Saddam Hussain had been well aware of this eventuality, claimed Mr Naïr, opting for a rigid dictatorship that controlled each and every community, albeit by means of separation. In a blunt conclusion, Mr Naïr noted that a 'democratic' solution for Iraq would be unlikely. Iraq was simply not capable of being transformed into a 'Western' democracy. The collapse of the Arab Spring – with the possible exception of Tunisia – demonstrated the relative soundness of this theory.

The case of the Yazidis attracted extensive press and media coverage. The IS was not, it emerged, in the business of taking prisoners from among its enemies. The IS gains had resulted in waves of refugees fleeing to what they hoped was safety. An estimated three million, as many as there were in the months after the US-led invasion when sectarian warfare had created the first waves of 'internal' refugees. Many of those refugees had headed for Syria, then seen as a safe haven. However, the civil war in Syria now meant that that option no longer existed; the situation was further complicated by the (Shi'a) authorities' decision to limit the areas of Iraq that would accept internal refugees. Many observers felt that this limitation was a mistake, as it risked the marginalisation of large numbers of Sunnis, widening the sectarian breach that lay at the heart of so many of Iraq's problems. Petty authoritarian restrictions also created tensions – refugees from Anbar province, where in June 2015 the Iraqi army had simply melted away when the province's capital Ramadi had come under attack, were not allowed to make their way to Baghdad. Anbar refugees not only had to show that they had a close relative in the capital, they had to be escorted into the capital by that relative. In

KEY INDICATORS — Iraq

	Unit	2011	2012	2013	2014	**2015
Population	m	*32.85	33.70	34.78	*35.87	*36.98
Gross domestic product (GDP)	US$bn	482.40	216.04	232.50	221.13	*173.82
GDP per capita	US$	3,513	6,410	6,686	*6,165	*4,701
GDP real growth	%	9.9	10.3	6.6	-2.4	*1.3
Inflation	%	6.0	6.1	1.9	2.2	*3.0
Oil output	'000 bpd	2,798.0	3,115.0	3,141.0	3,285.0	–
Natural gas output	bn cum	1.9	0.8	0.6	1.3	–
Exports (fob) (goods)	US$m	79,683.6	94,207.0	–	–	–
Imports (fob) (goods)	US$m	40,632.5	50,155.0	–	–	–
Balance of trade	US$m	39,051.1	4,405.2	–	–	–
Current account	US$m	26,202.7	14,494.0	*3,052.0	*-7,748.0	*-16,636.0
Total reserves minus gold	US$m	53,915.8	68,733.4	76,112.2	62,885.9	–
Foreign exchange	US$m	51,812.1	66,746.1	74,296.3	–	–
Exchange rate	per US$	1,170.00	1,166.00	1,163.20	1,144.20	–

* estimated figure ** forecast figure

Baghdad, 32 mosques had been designated refugee shelters. The city's largest Sunni mosque, the Umm al Qura (Mother of All Cities) in the Sunni-populated al Adel area was hosting 900 refugees. Many refugees had complained that the Iraqi government was doing very little to help them.

The economy

In its July 2015 assessment of the Iraqi economy, the International Monetary Fund (IMF) concluded that Iraq was facing a double shock arising from the IS insurgency and the plunge in global oil prices. In 2014, gross domestic product (GDP) had contracted by 2.1 per cent mainly due to the impact of the conflict, while oil production and exports had increased slightly compared to 2013. In 2015, overall economic activity was expected to see a modest recovery of 0.5 per cent thanks to oil sector expansion, while non-oil activity was expected to contract further.

The decline in oil prices had driven the decline of Iraq's international reserves (including the Development Fund for Iraq) from US$84 billion at end-2013 to US$67 billion at the end of 2014. Fiscal pressures were intensifying, with the government deficit expected to expand from 5.3 per cent of GDP in 2014 to 18.4 per cent of GDP in 2015 due to continuing weak oil prices and rising humanitarian and security spending.

The authorities had therefore maintained Iraq's exchange rate peg. Liberalisation steps taken by the Central Bank of Iraq had lead to a decline in the parallel market spread to less than two per cent by the end of 2014. The imposition of new restrictions triggered significant market volatility and a sharply wider spread in the first months of 2015, but their later removal had helped narrow the spread back to 4 per cent by July 2015.

Medium term growth prospects remained positive in the view of the IMF, although less favourable than before the crisis. Growth would be driven by the projected increase in oil production and the rebound in non-oil growth supported by the expected improvement in security and the implementation of structural reforms. Risks remained very high, however, arising primarily from an escalation of the conflict, political tensions and poor policy implementation. According to data collected by the World Bank's *Doing Business* index, starting a business in Iraq required 10 separate procedures, takes 29 days, costs 38.2 per cent of income per capita and required paid-up capital of 12.8 per cent of income per capita. Globally, Iraq ranked 142 out of 189 countries on the ease of starting a business.

Quite apart from the disastrous security situation, in Iraq corruption constitutes a major obstacle for companies wishing to do business of any kind. On Transparency International's 2014 *Corruption perceptions Index* Iraq ranked 170 out of the 175 countries surveyed.

Energy – and cash

The closing months of 2014 saw Baghdad and the Kurdish Regional government (KRG), with its capital in Erbil, reach some sort of an agreement over the vexed question of Kurdish exports of crude oil. Baghdad had considered these to be at best unconstitutional, at worst illegal and had gone so far as to blacklist the purchasers. Since January 2013 the Baghdad government had suspended payment of the funds constitutionally due to Kurdistan. Things changed with the election of Haider al Abadi as Iraqi prime minister in September 2014. Apparently more competent and effective, the al Abadi's appointment saw a negotiated solution to the stand-off, enabling the salaries of Kurdish civil servants to be paid. At the end of the year, the contentious question of who held title to the Kurdish oil remained unsettled.

According to the Kurdish authorities, Baghdad had agreed to transfer US$500 million to the KRG as a payment on account in respect of unpaid budgetary payments. In return, the KRG agreed to make half its crude production – some 150,000 barrels per day (bpd) – available to Baghdad. It was also announced that the KRG's prime minister, Nercheveran Barzani would be going to Baghdad to negotiate a 'constitutional settlement'.

The US$500 million was a small part (around 17 per cent) of the US$12,000 million that Kurdistan was allocated annually by Iraq's constitution. Given that the KRG was not being paid in full, it was not altogether clear why it was handing over half the oil. One KRG spokesman described it as a 'goodwill gesture'. Ruba Husari, Director of the Iraqi Oil Forum considered it 'not to be the answer to an historic problem.' At the heart of the matter was still the question of title. The KRG's interpretation of the Constitution allowed the exploitation and export of the oil; in Baghdad things were seen differently – the oil was an Iraqi resource and as such could only be sold through the national Oil Marketing Company (SOMO). The KRG had refused to work with SOMO.

Strapped for cash, in mid-2015, the Kurds had decided to paddle their own canoe, selling some 40 million barrels of oil to international brokers operating in the Turkish port of Ceyhan. This left Baghdad, already faced with a disintegrating country and body politic, with a dilemma. While it badly needed the oil revenues (all shipped via pipeline, providing the KRG with funds in the conflict with IS) it also needed the KRG's military support through its renowned Pesh Merga military brigades. A report in the London *Financial Times* (FT) indicated that crude oil sales from Iraqi Kurdistan and northern Iraq had averaged 450,000bpd since May 2015.

According to the FT, quoting KRG sources, crude oil exports through the pipeline to Ceyhan had become the KRG's principal means of survival. Kurdistan's revenues from oil sales fell below its 17 per cent share of the federal budget, but were greater than several hundred million dollars a month that Baghdad had been transferring at the start of 2015. The KRG was reported to have acknowledged that it had received more than US$1.5 billion in payments from oil dealers in the previous two months.

According to the US government's Energy Information Administration (EIA), Iraq was the second-largest crude oil producer in the Organisation of the Petroleum Exporting Countries (OPEC) in 2014. It also held the world's fifth largest proved crude oil reserves, behind Venezuela, Saudi Arabia, Canada and Iran. The EIA noted that most of Iraq's major known fields were producing or in development, although much of its known hydrocarbon resources had not yet been fully exploited. All Iraq's known oil fields were located onshore and for the most part had relatively low extraction costs.

Iraq's crude oil production grew by 950,000 barrels per day (bpd) in the period 2009–14, increasing from around 2.4 million bpd in 2010 to almost 3.4 million bpd in 2014. These estimated figures included oil produced in the Iraqi Kurdistan Region. Despite this growth, Iraq's production has grown at a slower rate than originally expected, due to infrastructure bottlenecks in the south, supply disruptions in the north and delays in awarding contracts.

The Iraqi government had set ambitious (probably optimistic) oil production targets. The government had been re-negotiating field production targets set in

Iraqi Kurdistan

The Iraqi Kurds have experienced a long a bloody road to establishing a self-autonomous region in the north of Iraq. The initial step towards a self governed region for the Kurds began in 1970 when the Kurdish Democratic Party (KDP) signed an agreement with the Iraqi government after almost a decade of heavy clashes between the two parties during the First Iraqi-Kurdish War, which resulted in some 100,000 casualties. The initial euphoria of success for the Kurds did not, however, last very long as the agreement was never implemented or enforced and by 1974 Northern Iraq again descended into heavy fighting between the Kurdish forces and the Arab-led government in the south. This marked the beginning of the Second Iraqi-Kurdish War which lasted for a year and saw up to 20,000 casualties and resulted in the exiling of the KDP from Iraq.

After the Second Iraqi-Kurdish War the Kurdish population had suffered serious blows and was insecure in their own country. To add to this hardship, the Iran-Iraq war of 1980–88 saw some of the greatest atrocities on the Kurdish population that had ever been carried out. In 1986 Saddam Hussein launched the Al-Anfal Campaign, otherwise known as the Kurdish Genocide, in Northern Iraq during the last stages of the Iran-Iraq conflict. Hussein used poison gas, concentration and extermination camps, and the Arabisation of the Kurdish region to displace and exterminate the Kurdish population of Iraq. By the end of the campaign 4,500 villages had been destroyed and 50,000–100,000 people killed as Hussein left the Kurdish population harrowed and broken.

Hussein's attempted annexation of Kuwait in 1990 caused the largest military coalition since World War Two to be formed in order to tackle Hussein's expansionary foreign policies. The Peshmerga, the Kurdish military, success's during and after the First Gulf War laid the foundations for the autonomous region that the Kurds enjoy today as they established No-Fly zones and fought back the weakened Iraqi Army from Northern Iraq during the 1991 uprisings in Iraq in retaliation to Hussein's social injustices. The chasing out of the Iraqi army allowed the Kurds to set up a *de facto autonomous region and in 1992 the KDP and the Patriotic Union of Kurdistan (PUK) established the semi-autonomous Kurdish Regional Government (KRG).*

The Western invasion of Iraq in 2003 led to the drafting and ratification of the new Iraqi Constitution in 2005 which defines Iraqi Kurdistan as a federal entity of Iraq. Nechirvan Idris Barzani, KDP, has been the prime minister of the region since january 2012 and is serving his third term.

Though the Kurds have made huge progress towards establishing a state for themselves, their successes have again been impeded in recent years due to renewed instability and violence in the region. The rise of the Islamic State of Iraq and the Levant (ISIL, now more commonly refered to as IS) (Al-Dawla Al-Islamiya fi al-Iraq wa al-Sham in Arabic (DAESH)) in the region in 2014 has meant that reluctant Kurdish forces have again had to take up arms in order to defend their region and have lost territory to the organisation. By August 2014 IS, by now known for their relentless brutality, stood only 30km away form the Kurdish capital of Erbil after they captured the city of Mosul, which now acts as one of the the organisation's strongholds, and small parts of the Kurdish autonomous region around the city of Dohuk in the north. The rise of IS to a significantly influential and dangerous organisation has prompted fear of their intentions in the Western world, and as a result the Kurdish forces have received much military aid in the form of arms and training. The potential effects of the IS conflict are as yet difficult to predict. The organisation now has significant territorial control in both Iraq and Syria, as well as affiliate groups in 9 other countries, in total controlling an area inhabited by over 10 million people.

The Kurdish Autonomous Region in Northern Iraq is one of four Kurdish regions in the Middle East. Iraqi Kurds inhabit Southern Kurdistan, the Kurds in northern Syria inhabit Western Kurdistan, in south-eastern Turkey Kurds occupy Northern Kurdistan, and in western Iran the Kurds live in Eastern Kurdistan; all together they amount to a population of some 28 million. Kurdish nationalism and a fight for an independent, or at least autonomous, state has not been as successful in Turkey as it has been in Iraq. Tensions between the Turks and Kurds still run high within the country, although the Kurds have made some significant steps in gaining an increase in influence and power. Traditionally many Kurdish groups have been viewed as threats to the peace of the nation by the Turkish governments but in the 2015 general election the Kurdish minority, 20 per cent of the population, managed to achieve the 10 per cent threshold to get into parliament as Halklarin Demokratik Partisi (HDP) (Peoples Democratic Party), who represent Kurdish interests, won 80 seats in the election, up form 51. This signifies a significant opportunity for the Kurds as the Turkish President Recep, Erdogan, and his Adalet ve Kalkinma Partisi (AKP) (Justice and Development Party), who represent Turkish nationalism, suffered their biggest political set back in thirteen years. This success, however, was short-lived and in the second election on 1 November 2015 the HDP lost 21 of their 80 seats, reducing the number of seats to 59.

Economy

The economy of Iraqi Kurdistan is dominated by oil, agriculture and tourism. The Iraqi Kurdistani economy is more highly developed than that of the rest of the Iraq as it has a more liberal, modern, and stable government, making it more in line with the economies of neighbouring Turkey than of Iraq.

Oil is the leading source of revenue as it is cheap to drill. However, in the current climate it is not the drilling that is a potential problem. The rise of IS has meant that oil wells and pipelines are under constant threat of being captured and taken over. The Kurdistani region of Iraq was estimated to have reserves of 45 billion barrels of oil at the end of 2014 and despite the security threat the regional government reports that oil production rose 60 per cent in the same year. However, the Kurdistani region and the Iraqi government have fallen out over an agreement the Kurds have with the Turks to channel much of the oil out through Turkish pipelines as opposed to using the Iraqi ones that had been used before.

Technical Service Contracts (TSCs) previously signed with international oil companies (IOCs). Based on some of the target revisions that had already been announced, the Energy Intelligence Group estimated that Iraq was aiming for a crude oil output figure of 9.0 million bpd by 2020. However, the Iraqi government faces a number of challenges to achieve this target: these include expanding the southern export infrastructure and storage capacity, building a large common water supply and re-injection system also in the south and passing a new hydrocarbon law. Iraq's slow administrative process cries out for reform, as do the unattractive contract terms that have often failed to attract IOCs to invest in new projects. Above all, Iraq's political instability, sectarian violence and the threat of the Islamic State's activities spreading to other areas of Iraq pose significant uncertainty for Iraq's future energy revenues.

According to the *Oil & Gas Journal* (OGJ), Iraq held 144 billion barrels of proved crude oil reserves in January 2015, representing 18 per cent of proved reserves in the Middle East and almost 9 per cent of global reserves. However, Iraq's resources are not evenly divided across sectarian-demographic lines. Most known oil and natural gas resources are concentrated in the Shi'ite areas of the south and the ethnically Kurdish region in the north, with few known resources in the control of the Sunni minority in central/western Iraq.

Iraq has five super-giant fields (defined as holding more than 5 billion barrels of oil reserves) in the south that account for about 60 per cent of the country's total proved oil reserves. An estimated 17 per cent of oil reserves are in the north of Iraq, near Kirkuk, Mosul and Khanaqin. The International Energy Agency (IEA) estimates that the Iraqi Kurdistan Region contained four billion barrels of proved reserves. According to the EIA, the KRG's estimate was much higher because it was a resource estimate that includes unproved resources. In 2015 the KRG increased its oil resource estimate from 45 billion barrels to 60 billion barrels, although this has not been independently verified. The ministry of oil in Baghdad oversees oil and natural gas development and production in all but the Kurdish territory through its operating entities, the North Oil Company (NOC) and the Midland Oil Company (MDOC) in the north and central regions and the South Oil Company (SOC) and the Missan Oil Company (MOC) in southern regions. In the Iraqi Kurdistan Region, the KRG, through its ministry of natural resources, oversees oil and gas development and production. IOCs are very active in Iraq, including the Iraqi Kurdistan Region.

Iraq's crude oil production increased by more than 300,000bpd in 2014, compared with the previous year, averaging almost 3.4 million bpd in 2014. Supply disruptions in the north escalated in 2014 after the Iraq-Turkey (IT) pipeline flows were completely halted in March 2015. The IS offensive caused more northern production to shut down in June 2015. However, increased output at fields in southern Iraq and in the Iraqi Kurdistan Region more than offset disrupted volumes. Iraq also produces about 30,000bpd of non-crude liquids. The production growth in 2014 was a significant improvement from 2013 when year-over-year production grew by only 70,000bpd. Poor oil production growth in 2013was attributed to infrastructure bottlenecks in the south and an increase in supply disruptions to northern fields because of frequent attacks on the IT pipeline. Production in the northern region controlled by the KRG in the past has tended to fluctuate because of disputes with the central Iraqi government, but recently it has steadily increased. The EIA estimated that the KRG's crude oil production averaged 350,000bpd during the second half of 2014.

Overcoming IS

Iraq's oil and its oil revenues make an obvious and attractive target for the insurgent IS. The IS attack in June 2014 that had captured Mosul, Iraq's second city and subsequently other nearby towns, affected northern Iraqi (not including the Iraqi Kurdistan Region) production and refinery operations, but it did not affect southern production and exports, which accounted for about 95 per cent of Iraq's total crude oil exports in 2014. According to the EIA, the IS initially took over some smaller northern Iraqi oil fields, including Ajeel, Hamrin, Qayara, Balad, Ain Zalah, Batma and Najma, but later lost control of a number of fields following the US-led air strikes that had begun in August 2014. The Ajeel field, with a capacity of 28,000bpd, was one of IS's main sources of Iraqi production, but it was bombed in August 2014, causing significant damage to the field's control room. After the bombing, according to the EIA, an Iraqi official reported that the IS production in Iraq was less than 15,000bpd. The IS continued to sell oil on the black market, most of which ended up in small refineries in northern Iraq and Turkey. Both the KRG and Turkey have taken steps to restrict oil smuggling.

During the second half of June 2015, the IS attacked Baiji, Iraq's largest oil refinery, halting operations. The Iraqi government later regained control of Baiji, although the refinery was not operational. The closure of the Baiji refinery caused a near halt to commercial production in northern Iraq (not including the Iraqi Kurdistan Region). The Iraq portion of the Kirkuk to Ceyhan pipeline (IT pipeline) had already been severely damaged after being sabotaged by militants and it had not operated since March 2014. With the closure of both the Baiji refinery and the Iraq portion of the IT pipeline, northern Iraqi oil production (the Kirkuk and Bai Hassan fields) lacked a significant commercial outlet for several months.

In 2014, Iraq consumed 760,000bpd of petroleum and other liquids. Iraq's oil consumption, which has increased by two-thirds since 2003, slightly declined in 2014 mostly because of the attacks in Iraq by ISIL that led to the shutdown of Iraq's largest refinery and fuel shortages in northern Iraq. Most of Iraq's petroleum consumption derives from its domestic oil refineries, which are fuelled by domestically produced oil. Iraq also imported roughly 100,000bpd of petroleum products in 2013 and 2014. Iraq burns crude oil for power generation, averaging about 70,000bpd in 2013 and 2014.

Total Iraqi crude oil exports averaged 2.6 million bpd in 2014, 0.2 million bpd higher than the previous year, based on Lloyd's List Intelligence (APEX tanker data). Asia (China, India and South Korea) was the main destination for Iraq's crude oil, importing 58 per cent of the total in 2014. The United States is the third-largest importer of Iraq's crude, although the volume has fallen over the past decade. The United States imported an average of 355,000bpd of crude from Iraq in 2014, 30 per cent lower than the volume received 10 years before in 2005. In 2014, about 95 per cent of Iraq's exports came from its southern export terminals in the Gulf. The KRG started to export crude via its independent pipeline for the first time in May 2014.

Natural gas

According to the EIA, Iraqi gross natural gas production was 724 billion cubic feet (bcf) in 2012, of which 423bcf (58 per cent) was vented and flared. In 2011, Iraq was ranked as the fourth-largest natural gas-flaring country in the world. Natural gas is flared because of a lack of sufficient pipelines and other infrastructure to transport it for consumption and export. Natural gas that is not flared is mostly used for reinjection into oil wells to increase oil recovery rates. To reduce flaring, Iraq's state-owned South Gas Company signed an agreement with Royal Dutch Shell and Mitsubishi to create a new joint venture, Basrah Gas Company, to capture flared gas at three large southern oil fields at Rumaila, West Qurna 1 and Zubair. The 25-year venture, which was estimated at a cost of US$17 billion, entailed upgrading current facilities and building new facilities and processing plants to increase gas processing capacity to 2 bcf per day. The joint venture was considering the construction of a liquefied natural gas (LNG) exporting facility, the Basra Gas LNG Project. Under the agreement, processed gas would go first to the South Gas Company for power generation. Any gas not bought for use by Iraqi power plants could be exported via the LNG plant. The implementation of this agreement was also necessary for the new oil development projects, which would use some of the natural gas for reinjection. The Akkas field, in the volatile western part of the country, has had its operations disrupted by attacks. In June 2014, the IS offensive in northern Iraq disrupted operations at both the Akkas and al Mansuriyah fields. Plans to export natural gas remain controversial because natural gas is needed as fuel for Iraq's electric power plants. The shortage of adequate gas has resulted in idle and sub-optimal electricity generation in Iraq.

Before the 1990–91 Gulf War, Iraq exported natural gas to Kuwait. The gas came from the Rumaila field through a 105-mile, 400 million cubic feet per day pipeline to Kuwait's central processing centre at Ahmadi. The ministry of oil has discussed reviving the mothballed pipeline, but no firm plans have been made to do this. The Iraqi government has also considered proposals to build a transcontinental pipeline to export natural gas to Europe via nearby countries, but there were no firm plans for this either.

Risk assessment

Economy	Fair/poor
Politics	Poor
Regional stability	Poor

Muslims in Iraq

% of population	97
Sunni (% of Muslims)	32.5
Shi'a (% of Muslims)	67.5

COUNTRY PROFILE

For 400 years, until the end of the First World War, the region was part of the Ottoman Empire.

1920 Iraq was placed under British mandate. The Great Iraqi Revolution began in May as a revolt against British rule. It united Sunnis, Shi'as and tribal groupings but by the end of the year had failed.

1921 Amir Faisal ibn Hussain (a member of the Arab Hashemite dynasty) was proclaimed Iraq's first King.

1932 Iraq became an independent state.

1933 King Faisal died and was succeeded by his son, Ghazi.

1939 King Ghazi was killed in a car crash and was succeeded by the infant Faisal II, whose uncle, Prince Abd al Ilah, acted as regent.

1953 King Faisal II assumed full powers.

1958 A military coup overthrew the monarchy and a republic was proclaimed.

1963 Pan-Arab elements in the armed forces staged a coup and formed a government under Colonel (later Field Marshal) Abd as Salem Muhammad Aref.

1966 Aref was killed in an airplane crash and was succeeded by his brother, Major General Abd ar Rahman Muhammad Aref.

1968 Major General Aref was removed from office in a coup organised by the Hizb al Ba'ath al Arabiyah al Ishtiraki (Ba'ath) (Socialist Arab Rebirth Party). The Ba'ath government was headed by Major General Ahmad Hassan al Bakr (a former prime minister) and supreme authority was vested in the Revolutionary Command Council (RCC).

1970 The RCC and the leader of the Kurdistan Democratic Party (KDP) signed a peace agreement.

1972 Iraq nationalised the Iraq Petroleum Company (IPC).

1979 The vice president of the RCC, Saddam Hussein (already the real power in Iraq), replaced Al Bakr as president.

1980–88 The Iran-Iraq War broke out after Iraq invaded Iran over a disputed border area.

1988 A chemical attack ordered by Saddam Hussein on the northern Kurdish town of Halabja, killed 5,000 people.

1990 Iraq invaded Kuwait on 2 August. The invasion was condemned by the international community. Iraqi troops destroyed over 400 oil wells, causing environmental and economic havoc. Following the invasion, the United Nations Security Council (UNSC) imposed an arms embargo and economic sanctions on Iraq (Resolution 661) and passed Resolution 678, which authorised member states to use force if Iraq had not withdrawn from Kuwait by 15 January 1991.

1991 The Gulf War started in the early hours of 17 January when coalition forces launched an aerial bombing campaign against Iraq and Iraqi forces in Kuwait. US-led ground forces (from around 30 countries, including Syria, Egypt and Morocco) moved into Kuwait on 24 February and drove the Iraqi forces there back into Iraq. The UN maintained the arms embargo and economic sanctions on Iraq after the end of the War in an attempt to force it to disarm of weapons of mass destruction (WMD). After a Kurdish and Shi'a Muslim-led uprising was brutally quashed by Saddam Hussein's regime, the US, UK and France imposed 'no-fly zones' on Iraq to protect the Kurds in the north and the Shi'as in the south. The UN administered the three northern provinces of Dahuk, Arbil and As Sulaymaniyah, which allowed the Kurds to develop their own semi-autonomous Kurdish enclave, with its own parliament.

1993 The US launched 24 cruise missiles at targets in Baghdad after an alleged Iraqi plot to assassinate former US president George Bush was uncovered.

1994 Saddam Hussein appointed himself prime minister as well as president.

1995 The population voted in a referendum on Saddam Hussein's presidency and, inevitably, supported him. The Iraq oil-for-food programme, administered by the UN, began.

1996 Saddam Hussein's son-in-law, his brother and their families, were granted asylum in Jordan; the two men were subsequently promised a pardon by Saddam Hussein, but were killed on their return to Baghdad. Saddam Hussein's eldest son, Uday, survived an assassination attempt.

1998 Various disputes arose between Iraq and the UN over UN inspections to verify the termination of Iraq's WMD programme; Saddam Hussein excluded the weapons inspectors from Iraq. As a result, the US and the UK launched their largest military attack against Iraq since the Gulf War, bombing installations throughout Iraq.

1999 The spiritual leader of the Shi'a community, Ayatollah Mohammed Sadiq al Sadr, was assassinated in Najaf.

2000 In his capacity as head of the Organisation of the Petroleum Exporting Countries (Opec), President Hugo Chávez Frías of Venezuela travelled overland to Baghdad – the first democratically elected head of state to enter Iraq since the Gulf War.

2001 Five UN officials working for the UN oil-for-food programme were expelled by Iraqi authorities on charges of spying.

2002 A presidential referendum extended Saddam Hussein's rule for a further seven years. US President Bush demanded that Hussein must prove to the UN weapons inspectors that all WMD had been destroyed, as stipulated in the UN resolution after the First Gulf War – if not the US would launch a war against Iraq. UN weapons inspectors returned to Iraq for the first time in four years, however the information they were shown was not sufficient to convince the US that there were no WMD. President Bush included Iraq, North Korea with Iran in a list of countries that supported terrorism as an 'axis of evil'.

2003 After diplomatic efforts to force Iraq to disarm failed and the expiry of an US ultimatum giving Hussein and his sons 48 hours to leave the country, US-led coalition forces invaded Iraq. Within 20 days central Baghdad was under US control and the Hussein government had collapsed. The Ba'ath party was abolished, together with institutions of the former regime. The UN Security Council lifted economic sanctions and a 25-member Iraq Governing Council (IGC) was appointed, with a rotating nine-member presidency. Hussein's sons, Uday and Qusay, were killed in a skirmish with US troops attempting to arrest them. The leader of the Shi'as, Ayatollah Mohammed Baqr al Hakim, was killed in Najaf. An amended US resolution on Iraq, legitimising the US-led administration, was approved by the UN, which stressed early transfer of power to the Iraqis. The security situation deteriorated as guerrilla warfare intensified. At the end of the year, Saddam Hussein was captured in Tikrit.

2004 After the president of the IGC was killed in a car bomb attack, Iyad Allawi (a Shi'a) was designated prime minister and Ghazi al Yawar (a Sunni tribal leader) was chosen as president. An interim 36-member cabinet was appointment to Transitional Government, until elections for a fully independent government could be held; it had power-sharing responsibilities with the US-led multinational forces in matters of security. The US handed over sovereignty to the Iraqi interim government. Hussein was transferred into Iraqi legal custody. There was heavy fighting for more than a week in an uprising against coalition troops by Shi'a militia loyal to radical cleric, Moqtada al Sadr, in the holy city of Najaf.

2005 The Transitional Government of Iraq recognised the Kurdish Autonomous Region, along with the sovereignty of its government. An estimated eight million people voted in the elections for a Transitional National Assembly. Many Sunni Moslems boycotted the elections, and the Shi'a United Iraqi Alliance won most seats. Iraq's first freely elected parliament in half a century began its opening session after a series of explosions targeted the gathering. Kurdish leader Jalal Talabani was named president. Former president, and Sunni leader, Ghazi al Yawar, and Shi'ite leader, Adel Abdul Mahdi, were named as deputies. The Shi'ite leader, Ibrahim Jaafari, was named prime minister. The Kurdish parliament unanimously elected Massoud Barzani as president of the autonomous region of Kurdistan. In his trial, former president, Saddam Hussein, was accused, along with seven others, of murdering 148 people in 1982 in the Shi'a town of Dujail. Parliamentary elections were held.

2006 With little progress made in forming a new government, the interim prime minister, Ibrahim Jaafari, relinquished the office and was replaced by Nouri al Maliki (Islamic Dawa Party) (a leading party within the Shi'ite grouping, United Iraqi Alliance). The chief judge in Saddam Hussein's trial, Abdullah al Amiri, was removed as being 'no longer neutral', after he made court statements that Saddam had not been a dictator; he was replaced by Muhammad al Uraiybi. Saddam Hussein was executed by hanging on 30 December, after being found guilty of crimes against humanity. An unauthorised recording was broadcast on the Internet of the event, showing him being taunted by his captors.

2007 US President Bush dispatched a further 21,500 soldiers, specifically to police Baghdad. Civilian deaths in the four weeks before their arrival were 1,440, which dropped to 265 in the following four weeks. Iraqi-US forces targeted the followers of the Shi'a cleric, Moqtada al Sadr, known as the Mahdi army, as its leadership fled to Iran. Former vice president, Taha Yassin Ramadan, was executed for crimes against humanity. Seventeen Sunni government members either quit or suspended their involvement in the Unity Government, leaving it weak and vulnerable. The Kurdish government, in northern Iraq, signed four exploration and two refinery contracts, worth about US$800 million, with several international energy companies. The deals were signed ahead of Iraqi national oil and gas laws and increased tension between the central government and the Kurdish territory.

2008 Final approval by the Presidency Council allowed former Ba'ath party members to return to public life. Russia announced that it was writing off US$12 billion of debt which had built up under Saddam Hussein. President Ahmadinejad made the first official visit by an Iranian president since the Iran-Iraq war in the 1980s. The Christian Archbishop of Mosul, Paulos Faraj Rahho, was kidnapped and killed. The leader of al Qaeda in Iraq, Ahmed Ali Ahmed (known as Abu Omar) was sentenced to death for the murder of Archbishop Rahho. Parliament approved a draft law for provincial elections to be held, despite a boycott by the Kurdish bloc and a few Shi'a MPs. Anbar Province was officially handed over to Iraqi control by the US. The province had been one of the most militant and dangerous for US troops until the Sunni population took control of their own security by helping to fight al Qaeda insurgents. The Kuwaiti ambassador took up residence in Iraq, after an 18-year gap since the Iraqi invasion of Kuwait; diplomatic relations had been restored in 2003.

2009 The US embassy, its largest in the world, was officially opened in Baghdad. Responsibility for security for the central Baghdad Green Zone was handed over to Iraqi forces. Provincial elections were held and won by those candidates that supported the ruling administration of Prime Minister al Maliki. US military personnel withdrew from Iraqi cities, prior to a full re-deployment to the US. In elections for Iraqi Kurdistan, Massoud Barzini won the presidency and the Kurdistani List alliance won the leadership of the Kurdish National Assembly (KNA). The government released the first official estimate of violent deaths during 2004–08, of 85,694, based on death certificates issued by the ministry of health, including some 15,000 unidentified bodies. Barham Salih became prime minister of the Kurdistan autonomous region.

2010 Ali Hassan al-Majid (Chemical Ali), Saddam Hussein's notorious cousin, was hanged for crimes against humanity. In parliamentary elections the Al Iraqiya (Iraqi National Movement) won 25.87 per cent of the vote (91 seats out of 325) and the ruling I'tilaf Dawlat al Qanon (State of Law Coalition) 25.76 per cent (89). The Iraq High Electoral Commission (IHEC) banned 52 members of the Watani Alliance from serving in parliament due to their links to the outlawed Ba'ath Party. Their votes were recalculated and allocated to other candidates of the Watani Alliance. Iraqi Airways was declared bankrupt. The Supreme Court endorsed the election results and Al Iraqiya were given the right to begin negotiations to form a government. The new coalition, the National Alliance, included the two major Shi'a political parties (Al Iraqiya and I'tilaf Dawlat al Qanon) as well as a number of other Shi'a parties including the Watani List. A new parliament was convened and the 325 members were sworn in, even though there was as yet no government. Iraq's General Chief of Staff, Lieutenant General Babakir voiced his concern that Iraqi troops were not ready to take over security following the planned US troop withdrawal, which he considered premature. The last US combat troops left Iraq on 19 August, although 50,000 advisory troops were to remain until 2011. By 13 September a coalition government had still to be formed. Tariq Aziz, the most senior Christian to serve Saddam Hussein (deputy prime minister and foreign minister) was found guilty of the persecution of religious parties and sentenced to death. A power-sharing agreement was forged between former prime ministers Iyad Allawi and Nouri al Maliki, so that Maliki was re-appointed prime minister, while Allawi was appointed head of the National Council for Strategic Policies; four Sunni politicians were reinstated, having been banned as former Ba'ath party members. President Talabani said he would refuse to sign the execution order on Tariq Aziz. The new government finally began parliament's first session on 21 November, after an eight month delay. The UN lifted the last sanctions against Iraq, which had first been imposed in 1991.

2011 In January, radical cleric Moqtada al Sadr, returned from four years of self-imposed exile in Iran. Sheikh Nasser al Mohammed al Sabah became the first prime minister of Kuwait to visit Iraq since the 1990 invasion. Prime ministerial discussions covered border issues, finance and security as well as the payment of war reparations said to amount to amount to billions of US dollars. The UK military operations in Iraq ended completely in May, when 81 naval trainers of the Royal Navy left the country, having completed their training of Iraqi sailors, ready to defend Iraqi territorial waters and its shipping. In July, in a ceremony held in Washington, some Babylonian antiquities that had been looted from the Iraqi Museum in 2003 and found in the US, were formally returned. The central bank announced on August that the Iraqi dinar was to have three zeros removed. The authorities said 30 trillion (US$26 billion) banknotes were being printed to replace existing notes. In September, the CBI declared its intention of implementing the change in 2013. The US military operations were formally ended on 18 December, as the last 4,000 soldiers left Iraq (200 soldiers remain as advisors). However, 15,000 US personnel will remain the US embassy in Bagdad.

2012 In January a wave of bombings killed almost 200 people, mostly Shia Muslims. On 2 February, the government imposed a ban on smoking in public buildings, including schools, hospitals, offices, theatres and markets. The law will come into effect after April. A dispute between Kurdistan and the central government over control over the right to export oil came to a head on 28 March when Kurdistan threatened to halt all oil exports from its region if the central government continued to withhold payment for the oil from Kurdistan. The threat was repeated in August and for the same reason. On 22 October, Kurdistan began selling its oil into international markets as an independent producer. The first sale of this oil was transported by road-tankers to Turkey; the loads of around 12,000 tonnes were worth around US$10 million. Central government condemned the sale and characterised it as smuggling.

2013 Hundreds of prisoners escaped from Taji and Abu Ghraib jails on 22 July; many of them were serving death sentences for violence. On 29 July a wave of car bombs killed at least 51 people in mostly Shi'a areas of Baghdad and other cities around the country. Figures published in early August by the United Nations mission in Baghdad suggest 1,057 Iraqis were killed in July, making it the deadliest month in years. A further wave of bombings on 25 August killed as many as 46 people. Another wave of bombings hit most Shi'a areas of Baghdad on 28 August. More than 50 people died. Parliamentary elections held on 21 September in Kurdistan Region were won by the Kurdistan Democratic Party (KDP) of regional President Massoud Barzani with 38 seats, followed by The Change Movement with 24 seats. The Patriotic Union of Kurdistan (PUK) (the party of President Jalal Talabani) came third with 18 seats. It was not immediately clear whether KDP and PUK would be able to continue their power sharing arrangement. At least 50 Shi'a died in another suicide bomb attach in the Adhamiyah district of Baghdad on 5 October.

2014 The Abu Ghraib prison was closed on 15 April. Parliamentary elections were held on 30 April. The results were a win for Mr Malaki's I'tilaf Dawlat al Qanon (Dawlat) (State of Law Coalition) with 92 seats (out of 328). Shi'as won a total of 174 seats, Sunnis 36 seats, Kurds 69, Secular 29, Turkmen 2, Reserved 18. Militant fighters from the Islamic State of Iraq and the Levant (ISIL, but more commonly known as ISIS) over ran the city of Mosul on 10 June, causing alarm throughout the Middle East. As many as 500,000 residents fled, largely to Irbil and other cities in Kurdistan. ISIS fighters moved rapidly towards Baghdad, meeting little resistance from the Iraqi army. By July, when ISIS had renamed itself Islamic State (IS) and captured Mosul Dam, Iraq's largest, just an hour's drive from Irbil (capital of semi-autonomous Iraqi Kurdistan), the West was becoming more concerned. On 24 July Kurdish politician Fuad Masum was elected by parliament (211 votes to 17) as president. In August there were reports of IS massacres of Yazidis (a little known group with a faith including many elements of Christianity and Islam) as they fled up Mt Sinjar. The IS were said to be forcing Christians to either become Muslims, pay a religious tax or be killed. There were reports of atrocities in towns and villages across Nineveh province. In August the West took steps to halt the IS advance and rescue the refugees stranded up Mt Sinjar. The US began strikes against IS targets using drones. Both US President Obama and British Prime Minister Cameron have said they want to avoid 'boots on the ground.' Iraqi and Peshmerga troops recaptured the Mosul dam on 18 August. On 15 August Mr Maliki finally agreed to step down in favour of Haider al Abadi, a deputy speaker of parliament. President Fuad Masum asked Mr Abadi to form a new government within 30 days. He became prime minister on 8 September.

2015 The night-time curfew in place for the last several years was lifted on 7 February. On 10 March officials reported that Iraqi forces had retaken some areas of the city of Tikrit, initially taken by IS militants in June 2014. Prime Minister Abadi announced a number of major reforms on 9 August, aimed at reducing government costs and fighting corruption. The reforms included abolishing the posts of vice president (presently two Shi'a and one Sunni) and deputy prime minister and ensuring that government positions be political independents appointed on merit rather than party or sectarian affiliation. The reforms were approved by the cabinet before the announcement, but stilled needed parliamentary approval. Ayaollah Sistani has also impressed on the prime minster the need to 'stike with an iron fist' against corruption.

Political structure

Constitution

A public referendum approved a new permanent constitution on 15 October 2005. It came into effect when the elections for the Council of Representatives took place on 15 December 2005.

The constitution declares that the Republic of Iraq is an independent, sovereign nation, and its system of governance is democratic, federal, and representative (parliamentary). Islam is the official religion of the state and is a basic source of legislation. Iraq is part of the Arab nation and the Islamic world.

Universal suffrage begins at aged 18.

The country is divided into 18 provinces (*muhafazat, singular muhafazahW0): al Anbar, al Basrah, al Muthanna, al Qadisiyah, An Najaf, Arbil, As Sulaymaniyah, At Ta'mim, Babil, Baghdad, Dahuk, Dhi Qar, Diyala, Karbala', Maysan, Ninawa, Salah ad Din and Wasit.*

Independence date

3 October 1932, independent Kingdom; 14 July 1958, Republic.

Form of state
Republic, federal
The executive
Executive authority consists of the Presidency Council, the Council of Ministers, presided over by the prime minister. The Presidency Council consists of the president and two deputies; they are elected by the national assembly.
National legislature
The unicameral Majlis al Watani (National Assembly), with 275 members (the constitution defines the number ratio as one representative per 100,000 Iraqi citizens), elected by proportional representation from party lists. All members serve for four-year terms.
Kurdish Autonomous Region (known as Iraqi Kurdistan): the unicameral Civata Nîstimanî Kurdistan (Perleman) (Al Majlis al Watani Li Kurdistan) (Kurdistan National Assembly) (KNA) has 111 members, elected by proportional representation from party lists, with each political party allocated seats in proportion to their share of the vote. By law, 25 per cent of membership must be female and 11 seats are reserved for minority people's candidates. Elections take place every four years. The KNA shares federal power with the Iraqi National Assembly but has a dominant role and responsibility for indigenous matters, including the economy and investment of the region.
Legal system
Under the constitution the Judiciary is independent and represented by courts of different kinds and levels, issuing their rulings according to law. No authority can interfere in the judiciary or in the affairs of justice.
The Federal Judiciary includes the Supreme Judiciary Council, and the Supreme Federal Court.The Iraqi court system is divided into the Civil Courts, Courts of Personal Status, and Criminal Courts.
Last elections
21 January 2010 (presidential) postponed until 24 July 2014; 30 April 2014 (parliamentary)
Results: Presidential: On 24 July 2014 Kurdish politician Fuad Masum was elected by parliament (211 votes to 17).
National Assembly: I'tilaf Dawlat al Qanon (State of Law Coalition) 92 seats (out of 328); the Muqtada al-Sadr (Sadrist Movements) including Kotlat Al-Ahrar (Al-Ahrar Bloc) 28, al-Kawadir wal-Nukhab al-Wataniyya (Nukhab) 3 and Sharaka (National Partnership Gathering) 3; Al-Muwatin Coalition (Islamic Supreme Council of Iraq) 29; I'tilaf Muttaidun lil-Islah (Muttaidun) (Uniters for Reform Coalition) 23; Al-Wataniya (National Coalition) 21; Kurdistan Democratic Party (KDP) 25; Patriotic Union of Kurdistan (PUK) 21; Al-Arabiya Coalition (Arabic Coalition) 10; Bizûtinewey Gorran (Gorran) (Movement for Change) 9; Hizb al-Fadhila al-Islami (Islamic Virtue Party) 6; Tayyar al Islah (National Reform Trend) 6; Diyala Huwia (Diyala is Our Identity) 5; Etelaf Al-Iraq (Iraq Alliance) 5; Kurdistan Islamic Union (KIU) 4; Kurdistan Islamic Group (KIG) 3; Nineveh National Alliance (allied with Ammar al-Hakim) 3; Civil Democratic Alliance 3; Loyalty to Al-Anbar 3; Iraqi Turkmen Front, Al Wafaa al Iraqi (Iraqi Loyalty Alliance), Kafaat wa Jamahir (Competences and People Gathering) and Wahdat Abnaa al-Iraq (Unity of the Iraqis) each won 2 seats and a further 10 groups won 1 seat each; 5 seats are reserved for Christians and 1each for the Mandaeans, Yezidis and Shabaks.

Al Iraqiya (Iraqi National Movement) won 25.87 per cent of the vote (91 seats out of 325); ; Al Ittilaf al Watani al Iraqi (National Iraqi Alliance) (known as Watani List) 19.43 per cent (70); Lîstî Kurdistan (Kurdistan List) 15.27 per cent (43); Gorran (Movement for Change) 4.36 per cent (8); Al Tawafuq (Iraqi Accord Front) 2.72 per cent (six); three other political parties won less than five seats each and eight independents failed to win any seats. Turnout was 62.4 per cent.
On 26 April 2010 the Iraq High Electoral Commission (IHEC) banned 52 members of the Watani Alliance from serving in parliament due to their links to the outlawed Ba'ath Party. The votes within constituencies were recalculated and allocated to other candidates of the Watani alliance.
KNA: Kurdistani List alliance 57.34 per cent (59 seats out of 111), Change List 23.75 per cent (25), Service and Reform List 12.8 per cent (13), IMK List 1.45 per cent (2), Turkmen Democratic Movement 0.99 per cent (3), Social Justice and Freedom List 0.82 per cent (1), Chaldean Syriac Assryrian Popular Council 0.58 per cent (3), Reform Turkmen List 0.38 per cent (1), National Rafidain List 0.3 per cent (2), Aram Shahine Dawood (independent Armenian) 0.22 per cent (1) and Erbil Turkmen (independent Turk) 0.21 per cent; 13 other political parties failed to win any seats.
Iraqi Kurdistan presidential: Massoud Barzani won 69.6 per cent, Kamal Mirawdily 25.3 per cent, Halow Ibrahim Ahmed 3.5 per cent, Ahmed Mohammed Rasul 1.4 per cent, Hussein Garmiyani 0.6 per cent.
Next elections
21 January 2010 (presidential) postponed; 2014 (parliamentary)

Political parties
Ruling party
National Alliance coalition, led by Al Iraqiya (Iraqi National Movement), with I'tilaf Dawlat al Qanon (State of Law Coalition) and Al Ittilaf al Watani al Iraqi (National Iraqi Alliance) (known as Watani List) (from 14 Jun 2010)
Main opposition party
Hizb al Fadhila al Islamiyah (Islamic Virtue Party)
About 42 per cent of the population is aged under 14 years; 55 per cent aged 15–64; 3 per cent aged over 65.
In 2009, the government released the first official estimate of violent deaths during 2004–08, of 85,694, based on death certificates issued by the ministry of health, including some 15,000 unidentified bodies. The figure includes violent deaths of security forces and civilians, but not insurgents or foreigners in general; it also does not include deaths during the first months of the 2003 US-led invasion when there was no functioning Iraqi government to record such details. The number of people injured was estimated at 148,000.
In August 2012, a Kurdish spokesman called on the national government to hold a census. The census had originally been scheduled for October 2010, but was postponed, initially until the end of 2011. The reason for the delay was said to be the ongoing dispute between the minority Kurds and majority Arabs over land and oil in the northern provinces of Anbar, Kirkuk and Nineveh.

Population
33.70 million (2012)* (Figure includes the UN estimated 4.6 million living in exile)
Last census: October 1997: 19,184,543 (excluding data for autonomous northern regions)
Population density: 49 inhabitants per square km. Urban population 66 per cent (2010 Unicef).
Annual growth rate: 3.0 per cent, 1990–2010 (Unicef).
Internally Displaced Persons (IDP)
900,000 (UNHCR 2004)
Ethnic make-up
Arabs comprise 75 per cent of the population, with Kurds representing a further 20 per cent (mostly located in northern Iraq) and Turkmen, Assyrian and other minorities making up the remaining 5 per cent.
Religions
Shi'a (also known as Shi'ite, Shiite, Shi'is) Muslims are the largest religious group, comprising 54 per cent of the population. Sunni Muslims were politically dominant in the Saddam Hussein period, although accounting for only 42 per cent of the

total. There is a significant number of Christians and a small number of Yazidis and others.

Education

After the 2003 Iraq War, attempts began to re-build Iraq's education system, as the US Agency for International Development (USAID) granted US$2 million to provide immediate educational needs.

Free education is provided for children between the ages of six and 18.

Literacy rate: 40.1 per cent total, 24.1 per cent female, adult rates in 2002 (World Bank).

Compulsory years: Six and 12

Enrolment rate: 46 per cent in primary education. Only 37 per cent of girls attend school. (Unicef, 2008)

Pupils per teacher: 20 in primary schools.

Health

The Health Ministry announced in January 2012 that 18 new hospitals, costing a total of US$2 billion, were to be built. The majority will be at least 100-beds each and constructed to world standards. Some will be specialist medical centres, for heart disease, maternity, burns units and psychiatric treatment.

HIV/Aids

HIV prevalence: 0.1 per cent aged 15–49 in 2003 (World Bank)

Life expectancy: 55 years, 2004 (WHO 2006)

Fertility rate/Maternal mortality rate: 4.7 births per woman, 2010 (Unicef)

Child (under 5 years) mortality rate (per 1,000): 34 per 1,000 live births (WHO 2012)

Head of population per physician: 0.66 physicians per 1,000 people, 2004 (WHO 2006)

Welfare

Iraq is struggling to repair its social infrastructure, welfare and pensions are being administered in an *ad hoc* manner until the newly elected government can get to grips with the economy and implement nationwide policies.

All political parties, during the January 2005 election campaign, advocated the introduction of comprehensive state subsidies and welfare measures and to aleviate the widespread poverty the government may have to invest heavily in its welfare programmes.

In 2008 there were an estimated 1.9 million internally displaced persons.

Main cities

Baghdad (capital, estimated population 5.5 million (m) in 2012), Mosul (3.0m), Basra (2.0m), Arbil (1.5m), Sulaymaniyah (901,028), Kirkuk (890,034).

Languages spoken

French and English are spoken in business.

Official language/s

Arabic and Kurdish

Media

The media has been liberated from official sanctions and there has been a rapid growth in all mediums. Private media outlets are typically linked to political, religious and ethnic groupings.

Press

Dailies: In Arabic, newspapers with the highest circulations include *Al Mada* (www.almadapaper.com), *Al Sabah* (www.alsabaah.com), *Al Mashriq* (www.al-mashriq.net), *Al Ahali* (www.ahali-iraq.net). In Kurdish, *Al Ittihad* (www.alitthad.com) and *Khabat* (www.xebat.net), published by the Kurdistan Democratic Party. Iraqi newspapers with English online editions include *Al Sabah* and *Azzaman* (www.azzaman.com).

Broadcasting

The Iraqi Media Net (www.iraqimedianet.net) is the national public radio and television broadcaster.

Radio: The Republic of Iraq Radio (www.iraqimedianet.net), known as Iraqi Radio has two networks RI 1 and H Quraan. There are many local radio stations in operation, including Radio Annas (www.radioannas.com), Al Huda Radio (www.al-hodaonline.com), Radio Sawa (www.radiosawa.com) and Radio Nawa Kurdish (www.radionawa.com). There are international services provided by France, UK and the US available via local relays.

Television: Around 70 per cent of the TV audience watch satellite TV with pan-Arab stations taking the majority share of ratings. Iraqi Media Net (www.iraqimedianet.net) operates three channels of Al Iraqiya TV, TV2 and Sports TV. Private stations include *Al Sharqiya* (www.alsharqiya.com) and Al Sumaria (www.alsumaria.tv). In the semi-autonomous Kurdistan there are three satellite stations, Kurdistan Satellite Channel (www.kurdistan.tv), KurdSat (www.kurdsat.tv) and Zagros (www.zagrostv.com).

Other news agencies: Nina (National Iraqi News Agency): www.ninanews.com Voices of Iraq: www.aswataliraq.info

Economy

With huge proven oil reserves, 150 billion barrels of oil and 3.6 trillion cubic metres of natural gas at the end of 2014, Iraq has the potential to have a modern well-funded economy. However, the problems created under the old regime and the disruption to the economy since 2003 left a huge legacy of poverty, unemployment and underinvestment. The government is still struggling to address the country's problems and has begun to initiate change, rebuilding its infrastructure and providing commodities for its people.

In early 2008 global oil prices were at a record high and in Iraq rebuilding was underway so GDP growth was 9.5 per cent as Iraq expanded oil production (by an extra 285,000 barrels per day). However as the global economic crisis cut production worldwide, in 2009 GDP growth fell to 4.2 per cent, which decreased to 0.8 per cent in 2010, but by 2013 had picked up again to 4.2 per cent. In 2014, due to the on going security crisis in Iraq, economic growth shrunk to -2.4 per cent. Oil typically provides over 99 per cent of all exports and in 2014 export of oil was estimated at US$41.3 billion (up from US$38.4 in 2009), however, the figure shrank to US$40.4 billion in 2014.

As the economy has gradually been brought under control, inflation, which had peaked at a record 30.8 per cent in 2007, was quickly brought down to single digits predominately by maintaining a stable exchange rate. By 2013 Iraq's inflation rate had stabilised at 1.9 per cent and was mostly contained in 2014 at 2.2 per cent.

The government operates under a system whereby oil revenue is shared among the regions dominated by the three principal ethnic/religious groups (Shi'a, Sunni and Kurdish). It had been hoped this measure would ensure unity and a cessation in sectarian bloodshed, as current oil fields are located in the predominately Shi'a region in the south while the best prospects for oil in the future are in the Kurdish region of the north.

External trade

In 2005 the Greater Arab Free Trade Area (Gafta) was ratified by 17 members, including Iraq, creating an Arab economic bloc. A customs union was established whereby tariffs within Gafta were to be reduced by a percentage each year, until none remain. By mid-2015 Iraq was still in negotiation with the WTO for membership.

Iraq has an open trade investment regime whereby a duty of 5 per cent is levied on all import goods, except primary commodities such as food, medicines, clothing and humanitarian items.

Construction work on a new railway began in April 2012. The service is specifically designed for freight, referred to as a 'dry canal' from Basra to Turkey. The US$1.4 billion project, backed by a loan from the World Bank, will be part of an integrated transport system linking the

Mediterranean with the Gulf and East Asia and was completed in 2014.

Imports

Commodities include food, medicines and manufactured goods.

Main sources: Turkey (25.4 per cent of total in 2014), Syria (18.0 per cent), China (14.6 per cent)

Exports

Main exports include crude oil (over 95 per cent), non-oil items include raw materials, food and live animals.

Main destinations: India (21.7 per cent of total in 2014), China (19.8 per cent), US (14.7 per cent)

Agriculture

Farming

The area of cultivatable land in Iraq is estimated to be around 12 million hectares (ha). About four million ha of this arable land consists of rain-fed agriculture and the remaining eight million depends on irrigation. Less than 50 per cent of this land is actually cultivated. However, irrigation systems are badly in need of repair and salinity is increasingly affecting large areas of arable land.

The most important crops are barley and wheat (yields of each exceed one million tonnes in a good year) and rice; and after cereals, which account for most of the arable land, cotton, dates, vegetables and fruit.

Historically, dates were the most valuable exports after oil (with an annual value of around US$75 million). Production plummeted during the war with Iran (1980–88) while pollution has negatively affected millions of trees in the south, following the 1991 Gulf War. Agriculture contributes around 3 per cent to GDP and employs around a fifth of the work force.

Fishing

There is a small fishing industry, mostly based on the Tigris and Euphrates rivers. Without import and export activities it will remain insignificant.

Forestry

Forests cover around 800,000ha, or 1.9 per cent of the land area and are mainly confined to the northern part of the country. There is no significant commercial exploitation.

Industry and manufacturing

Iraq's pre-Gulf War major industries centred on the petroleum, chemical, textile, construction and food processing sectors. Much of Iraq's industrial base has been affected by war and the sanctions imposed by Western states during them. Before 1991, Iraq was second only to Saudi Arabia in terms of oil production and reserves. Iraq's oil industry has been boosted and re-invested into by the UN oil-for-food programme, although it still remains far from pre-1991 levels.

State-owned chemical plants were hampered in their production of nerve agents for warfare by UN weapons inspection teams in mid-1990s. Many chemical plants were also bombed during the Gulf War. In the run-up to the 2003 Iraq War, the US claimed that Iraq's chemical production facilities had been re-built sufficiently for the country to undertake production of chemical weapons. Following the collapse of the Saddam Hussein regime, further investigation of the facilities found no evidence of chemical production for military use.

Tourism

Iraq has much to offer visitors who enjoy historic sites and museums. It has two of the world's major rivers (Tigris and Euphrates) flowing through it, ending in the Mesopotamian Marshes that were restored after 2003, and containing the unique culture of the Marsh Arabs.

However, Iraq is still considered too dangerous for most travellers and Western governments continue to issue warnings to their citizens not to undertake visits unless absolutely necessary. As such the tourist industry is constrained by Iraq's recent history and continued unrest. Nevertheless, the government is engaged in attracting foreign investment in capital works and infrastructure to provide for tourists. One plan, proposed in 2010, is to convert some of Saddam Hussein's former palaces into tourist resorts.

To improve the quality of care, educational courses in tourism studies and conference organisation have been instigated.

In 2014 tourism contributed 6.9 per cent to GDP in total, 2.6 per cent directly, and employed 5.6 per cent of total employment (446,500 jobs)

Iraq is the home of important Shi'a holy sites, which attract around 12 million Muslims visitors annually.

Mining

The mining sector contributes about 8 per cent to GDP and employs 4 per cent of the working population.

Iraq has huge resources of phosphate and its sulphur reserves are among the world's largest; there is significant potential for sulphur exports.

Other minerals include glass sand, raw materials for the construction industry, and modest quantities of iron ore, lead, copper and gypsum.

Hydrocarbons

Proven oil reserves were 150 billion barrels of oil at the end of 2014, with production of 3.3 million barrels per day (bpd). It is considered, by experts in the field, that Iraq has known and unknown reserves of oil yet to be exploited, which may contain anything from 45–100 billion bpd of recoverable oil. War damage to the northern oil fields around Kirkuk caused a significant drop in production from the pre-war level of 680,000bpd to 206,000bpd in 2007 and by 2014 had only reached 400,000bpd. In March 2012, the deputy prime minister announced that Iraq was now producing 3 million bpd and that it was increasing production to 3.4 million bpd, with exports expected at 2.6 million bpd. Oil output in July 2012 was three million bpd, ranking Iraq second in the world for oil output and outperforming Iran for the first time since the 1980s, however by 2013 Iran was once again out performing Iraq. Iraq's medium-term target is to produce 12 million bpd by 2017.

The Russian energy company, Lukoil, began production drilling and constructing a central processing facility at the West Qurna-2 oil field on 25 April 2012. The site has a production of 150,000bpd and is expected to produce over 1.8 million barrels over a 13-year period. West Qurna-2 is the world's second largest undeveloped oil field with recoverable reserves of 14 billion barrels of oil.

In 2009 the UK-based oil company Heritage announced it had discovered an oil field of 2.3–4.2 billion barrels in Kurdish Iraq. It was announced in January 2011 that a significant find of natural gas, estimated at 348 billion cubic metres (cum), in the Kurdistan region of northern Iraq. In June, following the completion of an oil pipeline exporting oil from the region, China's Sinopec out-bid South Korea's National Oil Company, with an offer of US$7.8 billion to purchase Addax Petroleum Corporation, which has large oil assets in Kurdish Iraq. In 2009, the minister of oil announced that oil capacity was predicted to reach 12 million bpd by 2017 following the signing of a number of contracts: the Russian Lukoil and Norwegian Statoil firms won a joint contract to exploit the supergiant West Quran field (with around 13 billion barrels of oil), the Anglo-Dutch Shell oil will develop the Majnoon field (with around 12.6 billion barrels of oil), and the Chinese state oil company CNPC now has the rights to the Halfaya field (with 4.1 billion barrels of oil). The Al Ahdab oil field in central Iraq began production in 2011 with 60,000bpd, according to its operator the CNPC. When fully operational, by December 2011, production rose to 120,000bpd.

Refining capacity had grown to 1.1 million bpd in 2013, an increase of 8.3 per cent on the 2012 figures.

In 2014 the Islamic extremist group Islamic State of Iraq and the Levant (ISIL) had a detrimental effect on the northern

Iraq oil sector. In early June 2014, an attack was launched on Mosul by ISIL resulting with the city and its neighbouring towns being taken over, and impacting the refinery and production of oil in that region. However 95 per cent of Iraq's crude oil exports derive from the southern regions of Iraq, which were not impacted by ISIL's attacks.
Proven natural gas reserves were 3.6 trillion cum at the end of 2014. However, probable reserves are considerably higher, they could be as much as 8.4 trillion cum. Approximately 70 per cent of Iraq's natural gas supplies are by-products of oil production. Natural gas production was 1.3 billion cum in 2014, having shown a steady decline since the 3.2 billion cum in 2000. The largest gas fields are in the north at Kirkuk, and in Rumaila and Zubair in the south. Iraq signed a multi-million dollar purchase agreement for Iranian natural gas (25 million cum per day) on 7 June 2011, to be delivered to two Iraqi power plants in the north-east via a new gas pipeline, the project was completed in 2012.
In November 2012, Iran announced that it had begun to build a new 225km, US$3 billion, natural gas pipeline to its border with Iraq to be completed in June 2013. Iran, Iraq and Syria had signed a US$10 billion agreement in 2011 to build an extended, 1,500km gas pipeline through Iraq (close to Bagdad) and then to Syria, with the ultimate sale of 110 million cum per day. However the recent unrest in Syria has meant that the project has experienced many disruptions and it is unlikely that it will be completed any time in the near future.
Iraq has some small low-grade coal deposits, with some limited exploitation before 1990 supplying the domestic chemicals industry. These mines are thought to have fallen into disuse following the destruction of industrial capacity and imposition of UN sanctions in the 1990s.

Energy
Total installed generating capacity was 10.1GW in 2013. Consumption was 53.41 billion KWh. The electricity infrastructure is undergoing refurbishment and expansion; however an estimate US$20–25 billion will have to be spent to bring the system into full operation with electricity supplied to all.
A parliamentary committee submitted a report to the council of ministers in August 2012, concerning the money spent on the electricity sector. The report stated that US$27 billion had been spent since 2003 'but electricity has only increased by 1,000MW. The Kurdistan Region has spent US$1 billion and gained 2,000MWs more.' The report further stated that 'there is huge corruption in the electricity sector in Iraq.'

Financial markets
Stock exchange
Iraq Stock Exchange (ISX)

Banking and insurance
The banking systems, according to the IMF in 2005, is weak and barely functioning. It comprises the Central Bank of Iraq and 26 chartered banks. Two state-owned banks, the Rafidain and Rashid Banks, account for over 90 per cent of the commercial banking assets and 75 per cent of the local branch network. These institutions are heavily over-staffed with too many staff under-skilled and the government may invite foreign involvement in restructuring them. It may also amalgamate four of the smaller, and specialised banks into two regional development banks and well establishing new Islamic banks.
In 2003, the Trade Bank of Iraq (TBI) was established to provide financial and related services to facilitate imports and exports. It is independent of the Central Bank of Iraq.
The authorities will be implementing international accounting and auditing standards, and improving disclosure requirements, to adhere to recognised practices in good governance.
The Iraqi Central Bank (IBC) paid off a total of US$2.7 billion to 3,500 commercial creditors in February 2011, to ensure protection for the Iraqi dinar on foreign currency markets.
On 2 February 2011, the ICB confirmed that six private and publicly owned banks were using electronic banking systems and that it had allocated US$10 million to state banks to activate the system. By 2010, 85 per cent of government financial transactions were processed through state banks.
Parliament's Economic Commission announced on 20 March 2011 that it will introduce legislation to organise the work of private and publicly owned banks, to enhance financial and economic development and avoid the growth of irregular business practices.
Central bank
Central Bank of Iraq

Time
GMT plus three hours (daylight saving, April–September, GMT plus four hours)

Geography
Iraq is bounded by Turkey to the north, Iran to the east, Kuwait to the south-east, and Saudi Arabia, Jordan and Syria to the west. There is also a neutral zone between Iraq and Saudi Arabia administered jointly by the two countries with Iraq's portion covering 3,522 square km. The country's most fertile area and heartland is the flood plain of the Tigris and Euphrates rivers, which flow in parallel for most of their length from the Turkish and Syrian borders respectively, to the Gulf. The north-east of Iraq is mountainous while the large western desert area is sparsely populated and undeveloped.
Hemisphere
Northern

Climate
There is an excessively hot sub-tropical period with no rainfall from May–September (38–49 degrees Celsius (C)). Dry and pleasantly warm from October–April (20–25 degrees C), with occasional heavy rain. Continental conditions affect the northern mountainous areas which experience severe winters, but the southern plains have warm winters with some rain and very hot, dry summers. The temperature in Baghdad ranges from between 4 degrees C and 16 degrees C in January, to between 24 degrees C and 33 degrees C in July and August. Average annual rainfall is 300mm.

Dress codes
Conservative and modest dress should be worn in public in conformity with local Islamic traditions. Safari suits or short-sleeved suits are acceptable for men at work or at informal meetings; lounge suits in light materials are worn for formal meetings and in the evening.

Entry requirements
All requirements are subject to change and should be thoroughly checked before departure.
Passports
Passports are required by all.
Visa
There are only a few countries designated to issue visas and only to certain authorised visitors. See *Entry Visa Regulations* in the consular section at www.iraqembassy.org for a list.
Prohibited entry
Nationals of Israel and holders of passports with evidence of travel in Israel are denied entry.
Currency advice/regulations
A currency declaration form must be completed on arrival and departure. The import and export of local currency is restricted to small coins only. The import of foreign currency is unlimited but amounts must be declared. Export cannot exceed the amount declared on entry. Travellers cheques are little used.
Customs
Beyond the allotted duty-free allowance, the total value of imports must not exceed ID100. Electrial goods (not for personal use), commercial artifacts and fruits and plant material are subject to import duty.

The export of antiques and artefacts is prohibited.

Health (for visitors)

Travellers should be aware of the poor capacity of Iraqi hospitals to extend medical care and that communications and essential services, including power and water cannot be relied on. Comprehensive medical insurance covering repatriation is essential. There are severe shortages of essential drugs. Detailed health advice should be sought before visiting Iraq.

Mandatory precautions

A certificate of vaccination against yellow fever, if travelling from an infected area.

Advisable precautions

Precautions should include vaccinations, or booster shots, for typhoid, diphtheria, tetanus, polio and hepatitis A; some vaccines may be advised including hepatitis B, TB, cholera and rabies. Anti-malarial precautions should be taken; the use of mosquito nets and repellents and covering up the body after dark can help avoid malaria and hepatitis B.

All water should be regarded as being potentially contaminated. Water used for drinking, brushing teeth or making ice should be boiled or otherwise sterilised. Dairy products are likely to be unpasteurised and should be avoided. Eat only well-cooked meat and fish, preferably served hot. Vegetables should be cooked and fruit peeled. Pork, salad and mayonnaise may carry increased risk.

Hotels

There are few and should be booked in advance. Payment in hard currency is required and a 10 per cent service charge is added.

Credit cards

Not in use.

Public holidays (national)

Fixed dates

1 Jan (New Year's Day), 17 Apr (FAO Day), 1 May (Labour Day), 14 Jul (Republic Day).

Variable dates

Eid al Adha (four days), Islamic New Year, Birth of the Prophet, Eid al Fitr (two days).

Islamic year 1437 (15 Oct 2015–2 Oct 2016):: The Islamic year contains 354 or 355 days, with the result that Muslim feasts advance by 10–12 days against the Gregorian calendar. Dates of feasts vary according to the sighting of the new moon, so cannot be forecast exactly.

Working hours

The weekly closing day is Friday.

Banking

Sat–Wed: 0800–1230; Thur: 0800–1100. During Ramadan: 0800–1000.

Business

Sat–Wed: 0800–1400; Thursday: 0800–1300.

Government

Summer hours: Sat–Wed: 0800–1230; Thu: 0800–1100. Winter hours: Sat–Wed: 0830–1430 Thu: 0830–1330.

Shops

Small shops tend to open very early, close during the middle of the day and then reopen from around 1600–1900 or later. Food markets open around 0900 and close at mid-day or when supplies are exhausted.

Telecommunications

The first subsea cable, providing digital connectivity, landed in mid-January 2012. It was Iraq's first cable and is a milestone in providing a high-capacity system with speed and reliability.

Mobile/cell phones

GSM 900 services are available. Numbers begin 7801/2/3/4, plus 6 digits.

Electricity supply

220V AC, 50 cycles

Weights and measures

Metric system.

Social customs/useful tips

Traditional Islamic culture predominates, with Quranic law playing an active role in the day-to-day life of the country. Visitors should be careful to respect this and act accordingly. They should always address their hosts by full name and title. Traditional Arab hospitality is generally offered. In business meetings formal courtesies are expected. Visiting cards are regularly exchanged and these should be printed in Arabic as well as English. Meetings may not always be on a one-to-one basis and it is often difficult to confine conversation to the business in hand, as many topics may be discussed in order to assess the character of potential business partners. Patience and good humour are required. Always refer to the stretch of water south of Iraq as the Arabian Gulf or the Gulf – never the Persian Gulf.

It is unwise to discuss religion or politics, and desirable to have an informed view on contemporary issues (such as Israel) in case such subjects arise.

During the Ramadan fasting month, both smoking and drinking in public are forbidden.

Security

Visitors should keep in touch with developments in the Middle East as any increase in regional tension might affect travel advice. The security situation in Iraq remains dangerous with insurgent forces targetting coalition interests and personnel as well as international agencies, such as the UN and the Red Cross. There are daily bombings in central and southern Iraq.

Getting there

Air

National airline: Iraqi Airways

International airport/s: Baghdad International Airport (BGW), 18km west of Baghdad; Basra International Airport.

Other airport/s: Smaller airfields exist at Hadithah, Kirkuk and Mosul.

Airport tax: Departure tax: ID2,000.

Surface

Road: The only two borders open are the highway from Amman, Jordan, to Baghdad (2,331km across the desert) and from Turkey via the road through Zakho and Mosul; this crosses Iraqi Kurdistan territory and the Kurds sometimes impose taxes on goods carried.

Travel by road remains hazardous and is not recommended.

Rail: The line between Mosul and Aleppo, Syria was reopened, although the service was suspended.

Water: All ports remain closed to civilian traffic.

Main port/s: Umm Qasr and Khor al Zubair are the major commercial ports.

Getting about

National transport

Air: Services are subject to US military restrictions. Prior to 2003 Iraqi Airways flew from Baghdad to Basra. There are domestic airports at Mosul and Kirkuk.

Road: Despite the Iraq War, the country's 40,800km road system is in relatively good condition with 84 per cent paved.

Rail: Prior to 2003, the rail network included three-class services with sleeping accommodation, restaurant cars and air-conditioning. Rail links between most major centres include Baghdad-Mosul, Baghdad-Arbil and Baghdad-Basra.

In June 2011 a preliminary deal was signed by French engineering company Alstom to build a high-speed rail line linking Basra and Baghdad. The line would also connect with Karbala and Najaf in a total network of 650km.

City transport

Taxis: Prior to 2003, taxis were available in major cities and at hotels. There were shared and regular taxis. There was a standard fare system and taxis were meters. A surcharge was made after 2200 hours. Fares should be clearly agreed in advance. Tipping is not expected.

BUSINESS DIRECTORY

The addresses listed below are a selection only. While World of Information makes every endeavour to check these addresses, we cannot guarantee that changes have not been made, especially to telephone numbers and area codes. We would welcome any corrections.

Readers should be aware that the details following may not be current. Telephone numbers probably won't work.

Telephone area codes

The international direct dialling code (IDD) for Iraq is +964, followed by area code and subscriber's number:

Baghdad	1	Mosul	60
Basra	40	Najaf	33
Erbil	66	Nasiriya	42
Kirkuk	50	Sulayimaniya	53
Kut	23	Tikrit	21

Useful telephone numbers

Police: 104
Fire: 115
Ambulance: 122
Emergency hospital: 719-5191
Operator: 537-2191
Directory enquiries: 102
International operator: 105

Chambers of Commerce

Federation of Iraqi Chambers of Commerce, Sadoon Street, PO Box 3388 Al-Alwia, Baghdad (tel: 718-7348; fax: 718-1115; e-mail: union@uruklink.net).

Baghdad Chamber of Commerce, Mustansir Street, PO Box 24168 Almsarif, Baghdad (tel: 887-6111; fax: 887-9563).

Basrah Chamber of Commerce, Al-Azizyah Street, Alashad, Basrah (tel: 211-343; fax: 212-478).

Mosul Chamber of Commerce, Khalid Ibn Al-Waleed, PO Box 35, Mosul (tel: 774-771; fax: 771-359).

Banking

Bank of Baghdad, PO 3192, Alawiyah (tel: 822-7083).

Credit Bank of Iraq, PO Box 3420, Baghdad (tel: 360-0494).

Dar Es Salaam Investment Bank, PO Box 3067, Alawiyah (tel: 360-4646).

Industrial Bank of Iraq, al Khullani Square, PO Box 5825, Baghdad (tel: 887-2181).

Iraq Middle East Investment Bank, PO Box 10379, Baghdad (tel: 360-4242).

Rafidain Bank, New Banks' Street, Massarif, PO Box 11360, Baghdad (tel: 887-0522: fax: 415-8616).

Rashid Bank, PO Box 7177, Tourism Building, Haifa Street, Baghdad (tel: 884-5287, 885-3433; fax: 882-6201).

Central bank

Central Bank of Iraq, PO Box 64, Rashid Street, Baghdad, Iraq (tel: 886-5171; fax: 886-6802).

Stock exchange

Iraq Stock Exchange (ISX), www.isx-iq.net

Travel information

Baghdad International Airport, Baghdad (tel: 887-2500, 886-3999; fax: 887-5808).

Ministries

Ministry of Foreign Affairs (email: press@iraqmofamail.net; internet: wwww.iraqmofa.net).

Directorate of Foreign Economic Relations, Ministry of Trade, Khulafa Street, al Khullani Square, Baghdad (tel: 887-2682).

Ministry of Industry and Military Industrialisation, Nidhal Street, near Sa'adoun Petrol Station, Baghdad (tel: 887-2006).

Ministry of Oil, al Mansour, PO Box 6178, Baghdad (tel: 541-0031).

Other useful addresses

Iraqi Embassy (in the UK), 169 Knightsbridge, London SW7 1DW (tel: (+44-20) 7602-8456 and 7581 2264; fax: (+44-20) 7589-3356).

Iraqi Embassy (in the USA), 1801 P Street, NW, Washington, DC 20036 (tel: (+1-202) 483 7500; internet: www.iraqiembassy.org).

Iraq National Oil Company, al Khullani Square, PO Box 476, Baghdad (tel: 887-1115).

Iraqi Federation of Industries, Iraqi Federation of Industries Building, al Khullani Square, Baghdad.

Nina (National Iraqi News Agency): www.ninanews.com

Voices of Iraq: www.aswataliraq.info

Internet sites

Guide to Iraqi businesses: www.iraqdirectory.com

Iraq Stock Exchange: www.isx-iq.net

Iraq portal: www.portaliraq.com

Ireland

KEY FACTS

Official name: Éire (Ireland)

Head of State: President Michael D Higgins (from 11 Nov 2011)

Head of government: Prime Minister (*Taoiseach*) Enda Kelly (FG) (from 9 Mar 2011)

Ruling party: Coalition led by Fine Gael (FG) (United Ireland Party) with Labour Party (LP) (from 9 Mar 2011)

Area: 70,283 square km

Population: 4.61 million (2014)

Capital: Dublin

Official language: Irish (Gaelic) and English

Currency: Euro (€) = 100 cents (from 1 Jan 2002; previous currency, punt, locked at IR£0.79 per euro)

Exchange rate: €0.89 per US$ (Sep 2015)

GDP per capita: US$53,462 (2014)

GDP real growth: 4.78% (2014)

GDP: US$246.44 billion (2014)

Labour force: 2.13 million (2014)*

Unemployment: 11.26% (2014)

Inflation: 0.31% (2014)

Balance of trade: US$5.00 billion (2013)

* estimated figure

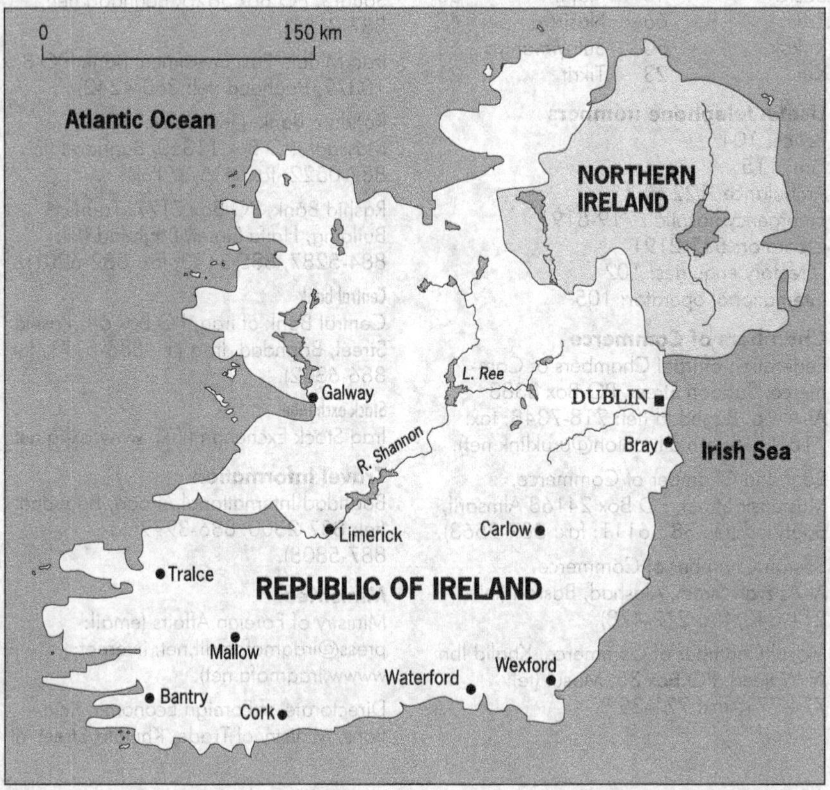

As those Irish who could afford it returned from their summer holidays in August 2015, it looked as though the incumbent Taoiseach (prime minister) Enda Kenny, would emerge as winner from the elections that were due to take place between November 2015 and April 2016. The unanswered issue was the exact formation of his next coalition government.

Not beyond Our Ken?

Mr Kenny is a seasoned political operator. The leader of the Fine Gael party, he has been the Taoiseach since March 2011 and has lead his party since 2002. He has worked his way up the ranks, serving as minister for tourism and trade from 1994 to 1997 and as vice president of the European People's Party. No other member of parliament (Teachta Dála (TD)) can pull rank on him, he has been the representative for Mayo since 1975, making him the longest serving TD, which also makes him the incumbent 'Father of the Dail'.

If Mr Kenny can relax about his eventual election prospects, he can not rest easily when facing the political programme that awaits him. His saving grace is the incipient recovery of the economy, which at least gives him extra money to spend – reportedly in the region of €1.2–1.5 billion (US$1.3–1.7 billion). The general expectation is that the extra expenditure would be divided between tax cuts and increased spending. A large part of the available funds have been earmarked for pay rises for civil servants in an attempt to restore – even if only partially – their salaries to the pre-2008 levels. Mr Kenny's fellow ministers were already queuing up with requests for higher allocations in early 2015. Ireland's health services were known to be seeking an additional €1.9 billion (US$2.1 billion) and other ministries such as defence and agriculture – both headed up by the same minister,

Simon Coveney – were also looking for more.

Gay at last

When it came to it, Ireland's May 2015 vote in favour of homosexual marriage was conclusive, as just over 62 per cent of the electorate returned a 'yes' vote. The referendum had divided Ireland between young and old, the religious and the agnostic or atheist, the urban and the rural populations. Those over 40 and the country-dwellers – particularly those from Donegal, Cork, Galway, Mayo and Sligo – for the most part voted 'no', reluctant to give their approval to a totally new concept of matrimony. It was also a victory for the Irish diaspora, although only those who had lived abroad for less than eighteen months were entitled to vote (on condition that they did so in person). The turnout was high, reaching around the 60 per cent mark in most major cities.

Although civil partnerships between homosexual couples had been legal for some years, by voting in favour of gay marriage Ireland had turned a significant page. The major loser in the debate was the Catholic Church, long accustomed to calling the political as well as the ecclesiastical shots in Ireland. In many respects the Catholic Church could only blame itself. In the twenty-first century it was picking up the tab for years of turning a blind eye to paedophilia in its seminaries, schools and other institutions, for condemning many children and teenagers to a life of virtual imprisonment in outdated institutions, often run by priests who themselves were far from scandal-free.

There was also an actuarial aspect: Ireland is one of the world's 'youngest' societies and there was little doubt about how its youth wished to vote. The Catholic Church mounted a strong campaign for a 'no' vote, but it found itself outmanoeuvred by the country's body politic, as all the major political parties – Fine Gael, Labour, Fianna Fail and Sinn Fein – advocated voting 'yes'. The approval of gay marriage meant that there only remained one hurdle for the more 'progressive' elements of Irish society to clear – that of abortion. This was the Church's last stand and until things changed, Irish women would have to continue travelling to Great Britain, Holland or other countries that offered the possibility of abortion. Prime minister Enda Kenny tweeted his pride in announcing that he and his wife had voted 'yes', as did health minister, Leo Varadkar, who in January 2015 had declared himself gay.

The economy – Apple

Ireland's business community has often found itself hamstrung by regulations and government intervention. In October 2014 the European Union (EU) expressed the view that Ireland had entered into an illegal arrangement with the computer giant Apple. Apple's headquarters for Europe, Africa and the Middle East is located in Cork. The US company had secured a change in its fiscal status that enabled it to lower its tax bill in return for investment and the maintenance of its payroll –1,000 jobs in late 2014 – in Ireland. Documents published by the EU confirmed that on two occasions, in 1990 and again in 2007, legislation was changed to suit Apple's requirements. The EU noted that 'through these changes, Ireland granted advantages to Apple'. Following an investigation into Apple's status in Ireland Brussels wrote to the Irish government to advise that EU treaties allowed for special treatment 'in exceptional cases' but expressed 'doubts' about Apple's eligibility. Companies that considered themselves to have been prejudiced by the changes in the legislation were able to seek legal redress. In theory, Brussels could force the Irish government to recover 100 per cent of the unpaid tax.

The economy – Cattle...

Dairy and beef cattle production dominates agriculture in Ireland. The cattle herd is approximately seven million and has remained fairly stable over the years. This can be partly attributed to the support mechanisms of the EU – milk quota, suckler cow and steer/bull premia – which have capped milk production and encouraged the maintenance of the beef cattle herd. The cattle herd is spread fairly evenly throughout the country

Irish beef exports in 2014 added up to €2.3 billion (US$2.6 billion), constituting around 20 per cent of the country's food and drink exports. Often overlooked, Ireland is Europe's largest beef exporter; however, until 2014 the world's largest market (the US) was closed to Ireland in the aftermath of the mad cow disease (BSE) in the late 1990's. Hopes were irrationally high that the end of the ban would represent something of an El Dorado for Irish beef farmers. In the US beef prices were reportedly higher – by as much as €1.00 (US$1.12) per kilo. US consumers get through around 11 billion kilos of beef a year, so even a small percentage could represent a quantum leap for Ireland's farmers .

... and Sheep

Ireland is the fifth largest sheep producer in the EU and is the region's largest net exporter. However, after rapid growth in breeding ewes from fewer than two million in 1980 to a peak of almost five million in 1992, there has been a steady decline and the breeding ewe flock stood at three million in 2007. This decline had accelerated as EU payments were de-coupled from production and profitability declined. In 2006 there were 35,277 sheep flocks with an average flock size of 102. Sheep production in Ireland can be classified into hill or lowland. The lowland

KEY INDICATORS — Ireland

	Unit	2011	2012	2013	2014	**2015
Population	m	4.59	4.59	4.59	4.61	*4.65
Gross domestic product (GDP)	US$bn	217.70	210.75	232.15	246.44	*220.01
GDP per capita	US$	47,513	45,962	50,543	53,462	*47,329
GDP real growth	%	0.7	0.2	0.2	4.8	*3.9
Inflation	%	1.1	1.9	0.5	0.3	*0.2
Unemployment	%	14.7	14.7	13.0	11.3	*9.8
Exports (fob) (goods)	US$m	126,704.0	*119,203.0	116,091.0	–	–
Imports (fob) (goods)	US$m	67,111.0	*64,138.0	66,101.0	–	–
Balance of trade	US$m	59,593.0	*55,065.0	4,999.0	–	–
Current account	US$m	2,514.0	9,320.0	10,138.0	15,241.0	*10,719.0
Total reserves minus gold	US$m	1,857.0	*1,386.0	1,403.0	1,517.0	–
Foreign exchange	US$m	439.0	*3.0	4.0	–	–
Exchange rate	per US$	0.75	*0.77	0.73	0.82	–

* estimated figure ** forecast figure

sector accounts for 75 per cent of the ewes and 85 per cent of the output. Lowland sheep production is predominantly grass based, with most ewes lambing in the spring and most lambs sold for slaughter before the end of the grazing season. In most hill sheep systems, lambs are sold at weaning for finishing in the lowland sector. Often, ewe lambs from the hill sheep are used for breeding in the lowland sector. All sheep are meat breeds, with none bred specifically for wool production; very few sheep are milked in Ireland.

The economy – Irish Tiger?

The Irish government, meanwhile, issued a delayed report on its economic performance in the first quarter of 2015. It showed a 1.4 per cent month-on-month growth auguring a stunning 6.5 per cent annual rate, a pace more associated with an emerging market economy. In its June 2015 assessment of the Irish economy, the International Monetary Fund (IMF) considered that Ireland's strong economic recovery was continuing in 2015, following the robust growth of 4.8 per cent in 2014. In the view of the IMF, a range of high frequency indicators pointed to an extension of the solid recovery momentum into 2015, with growth increasingly driven by domestic demand as well as by exports. Job creation continued with employment growth of 2.2 per cent year-on-year in the first quarter of 2015, bringing the unemployment rate down to 9.8 per cent in May 2015. According to the IMF, tax revenues rose by 11 per cent year-on-year during the first five months of 2015, while expenditure remained within budget profiles, so the fiscal deficit for 2015 was expected to be 2.3 per cent of GDP, out-performing the budget targets.

Owing to the European Central Bank (ECB)'s quantitative easing measures, financial conditions remained highly supportive despite some bond market volatility. House price increases had moderated following the announcement of new macro-prudential regulations, but commercial real estate prices were still rising rapidly on the back of strong demand from non-bank investors. Although the health of Ireland's banks had improved, reported the ECB, operating profitability remained weak and, despite progress in the resolution of mortgages in arrears, 17.1 per cent of mortgages had been in arrears for over 90 days and of these, almost 60 per cent had been in arrears for over 2 years.

In mid-2015 the ECB expressed its concerns over the political pressure that Ireland's still weakened banks were under to lower the mortgage interest rates that were considered to be too high by the government. In May 2015, the chief executives of Ireland's banks found themselves summoned to meetings with finance minister, Michael Noonan, to be told that the authorities might well take charge of setting mortgage rates or even impose financial penalties if no action was taken. Following the meeting, Ireland's two largest lenders – Bank of Ireland and Allied Irish Banks which had returned to profit in 2014 for the first time since the 2008 financial crisis – had announced rate cuts.

However, the banking system was, according to most reports, still 'quite fragile' and lenders were exposed to very large non-performing loans. The head of financial regulation at Ireland's Central Bank, Cyril Roux, was quoted by Reuters as saying to a parliamentary enquiry about the banking crisis: 'They have weak profitability and I have to say that political pressure is built on them to reduce yet further their profitability and that's something that worries the ECB. If they're not profitable, then they will veer away from their restructuring plans and that will spell a lot of trouble for these banks. We monitor them very closely and, at some point, we can say 'You're no longer viable'.'

In its *Economic Policy Reforms 2015: Going for Growth* report, the Paris-based Organisation for Economic Co-operation and Development (OECD) noted that GDP per capita had remained steady in recent years at close to the average of the upper half of the OECD member countries. Ireland's fall in labour utilisation had been offset by a rise in labour productivity. In the view of the OECD Ireland's bankruptcy framework had been improved with the introduction of a new personal insolvency procedure.

The OECD considered that enhancing job-search assistance and retraining opportunities would help raise employment. The removal of barriers to entrepreneurship and competition and fostering innovation would encourage a more dynamic and cost-competitive home grown business sector. The OECD also recommended continued efforts to improve labour market activation.

Risk assessment

Economy	Good
Politics	Good
Regional stability	Good

COUNTRY PROFILE

In the twelfth century, the Norman invasion began a long period of foreign domination. Over the centuries, Irish Catholic hostility increased along with English control, following the seizure of land, the Protestant Reformation and the loss of religious and political freedoms.

1801 Ireland was united with Great Britain through the Act of Union.

1840s The potato crop suffered from blight over several years, leading to severe famine. Combined with emigration, this reduced the population by one-third. The decade also saw the beginnings of a republican movement.

1916 The British army suppressed the republican Easter Rising, provoking the formation of Sinn Féin (Ourselves Alone).

1919–21 The Anglo-Irish War was fought against British troops and police by the military arm of Sinn Féin, the Irish Republican Army (IRA).

1921 The Irish Free State was formed, under the British crown, by partition of 26 southern counties from six north-eastern counties that remained part of the UK.

1922 The Dáil Eireann (Irish parliament) ratified the treaty establishing the Free State, sparking a civil war with nationalists, led by Eamonn De Valera, who advocated full independence.

1927 De Valera entered parliament as the head of the newly-created Fianna Fáil (Soldiers of Destiny).

1932 Fianna Fáil won the elections. De Valera began to work towards full independence from Britain.

1937 The constitution was promulgated, abolishing the Free State and declaring Ireland as an independent state.

1938 Douglas Hyde became the country's first president, with De Valera as prime minister.

1939–45 Ireland remained neutral during the Second World War, although many Irish citizens fought in the British Army.

1948 Fianna Fáil lost the election and De Valera was replaced by John Costello as prime minister.

1949 A republic was proclaimed and Ireland left the Commonwealth. Partition remained contentious and the IRA mounted a terrorist campaign for reunification with the six northern counties.

1955 Ireland joined the UN.

1957 De Valera was voted back into office as prime minister; he said that the union of Northern Ireland with the Republic could not be achieved through violence.

1959 De Valera became president.

1971 Around 8,000 Catholics fled to Ireland from Northern Ireland, due to violence by sectarian paramilitaries following the introduction of internment of IRA suspects in the North.

1973 Ireland joined the forerunner of the EU, the European Economic Community (EEC). Fianna Fáil, the traditional party of government, lost power in the general election and Jack Lynch resigned. Liam Cosgrave formed a coalition between his party, Fine Gael, and the Labour Party. The IRA became active again after a long period of decline, as inter-communal fighting intensified in the north, under the Unionist-run regime and later, direct rule from London.
1977 Fianna Fáil won the general election and Jack Lynch again became prime minister.
1980s None of a succession of elections produced a single-party majority government.
1985 The Ango-Irish Agreement established regular participation by the Irish government in political, legal, security and cross-border matters in Northern Ireland.
1990 Mary Robinson was the first woman and the first left-winger to be elected president.
1992 In a referendum, Irish voters agreed to relax the abortion laws, enabling women to travel abroad to have an abortion.
1993 The Downing Street Declaration by the Irish and British governments offered talks to all parties in Northern Ireland if they renounced political violence.
1995 A referendum to change the 1937 constitution narrowly approved the lifting of the ban on divorce.
1997 Mary McAleese, (born in Northern Ireland), was elected president of the Irish Republic.
1998 In a referendum, nearly 95 per cent of voters approved the Good Friday Agreement, which entailed Ireland giving up its constitutional claim to Northern Ireland.
2002 The euro replaced the punt. After parliamentary elections, Bertie Ahern was confirmed as prime minister and formed a coalition government led by Fianna Fáil. At the second attempt, Ireland voted in favour of the EU's *Treaty of Nice*.
2003 The population of Ireland reached four million.
2004 President Mary McAleese was returned unopposed for a second term as president.
2005 Irish was adopted as an official working language of the EU.
2006 An official tribunal found that former prime minister, Charles Haughey, had 'accepted bribes and followed unethical business practices' and accepted 'cash from wealthy businessmen over a 17-year period, including eight years as *taoiseach*'.
2007 Fianna Fáil led a coalition government.
2008 Brian Cowen (FF) replaced Bertie Ahern following his resignation as prime minister. Voters rejected the Lisbon Treaty in a referendum held on reform of the EU. The Progressive Democrats disbanded, due to its low national support base. Ireland was the first of the eurozone economies to succumb to recession during the global economic crisis. GDP growth fell to -3.0 per cent as both government deficit and unemployment grew. An early budget introduced austerity measures.
2009 The credit rating agency, Standard and Poor's (S&P) cut the Ireland debt rating from AAA to AA+. The government introduced an aggressive emergency budget; it cut government spending by €3.3 billion (US$4.3 billion) and raised taxes, which combined amounted to 5 per cent of GDP. After two referenda within 16 months, the Irish electorate sanctioned the EU *Lisbon Treaty*. A catalogue of sexual and physical assaults, mostly on children, perpetrated by Roman Catholic priests and church officials between 1975–2004 was published, causing widespread condemnation of those in authority for their failure to protect vulnerable youngsters while covering up abuse and suppressing investigations. A new, National Asset Management Agency (Nama) was set up to rehabilitate the banking sector by removing toxic debt from bank ledgers. Annual GDP growth was -7.1 per cent. There was a 24 per cent year-on-year increase in the suicide rate.
2010 The credit ratings agency S&P downgraded Ireland's economy to AA-, following the US$63 million recapitalisation of the banking system and the strain it put on the economy; it warned that another downgrade was possible. On 1 October the government announced that the total cost of bailing out the country's loss-making banks had to be revised upward to just under €50 billion (US$65.5 billion) and was likely to cost over 30 per cent of GDP. Nama paid banks €30.2 billion (US$42.4 billion) for 11,500 non-performing loans, belonging to 850 debtors, each with an average of 13 loans.
2011 Revelations that Prime Minister Cowan had had personal contact with Sean Fitzpatrick, former head of Anglo Irish Bank, during the period of maximum financial loss caused widespread controversy. Although Cowan won a vote of confidence from his political party (FF) in January, several cabinet members resigned, resulting in Cowan calling an early general election; he announced that he would not stand for re-election. However, he was determined to see the passing of the finance bill, necessary for the December 2010 IMF loan to be paid, before stepping down. The Greens withdrew from the government coalition on 24 January, leaving Prime Minister Cowan in charge of a minority administration. The general election was held in February, the opposition FG won 36.1 per cent (76 seats out of 166) and immediately began coalition talks, which were successfully concluded with the Labour Party in March. The Greens lost all their seats from the previous election. In March, the governor of the Bank of Ireland (BOI) announced that following 'stress tests' of the banking system a further €24 billion (US$33.65 billion) would have to be injected into the top four banks to ensure stability as a whole. This brought the total amount of recapitalisation by the Irish economy to €70 billion (US$98.13 billion). Loans to fund their bailout came from the EU and IMF and the BOI, which will be forced to sell off €30 billion (US42.1 billion) in assets by 2013. The UK's Queen Elizabeth made a state-visit to the Irish Republic in May, the first by a British monarch since 1911. In September Sinn Féin nominated former IRA commander Martin McGuiness as their candidate for the presidential elections, which were held in October; five candidates took part. Following the ballot and elimination of the lesser candidates who transferred their votes to the two strongest candidates Michael D Higgins (LP) won a total of 56.8 per cent and Sean Gallagher (independent) 35.5 per cent; President Higgins took office in November.
2012 In a referendum held on 1 June 60 per cent of voters backed the new EU fiscal treaty, which imposes strict budget rules with deficit limits and includes penalties that can be applied if the treaty is broken. Bankrupt, former billionaire, Sean Quinn, was jailed on 2 November for failing to disclose assets hidden abroad and preventing the Irish Banking Resolution Corporation (formerly known as the Anglo Irish Bank) from seizing foreign property assets worth an estimated €500 million (US$649 million). A constitutional referendum was held on 10 November, concerning the rights of children. The proposal that set out provisions for duty of care was agreed by 58.01 per cent (41.99 per cent against), with a turnout of 33.5 per cent.
2013 A Fine Gael Labour coalition government proposal ro abolish the Seanad Éireann (upper house of parliament) was narrowly defeated in a referendum held on 4 October by 51.7 per cent to 48.3 per cent, even though the proposal was supported by Sinn Féin. The defeat, on a turnout of 40 per cent was unexpected. Court of Appeal and other changes to the courts system were approved. Ireland is due to make a clean break from its three-year €85 billion (US$113 billion) bailout programme in December.

2015 In a referendum held on 23 May Ireland became the first EI country to vote on whether to legalise same-sex marriage. The result was over 62 per cent in favour.

Political structure

Constitution

The Constitution was drawn up in 1937. The Uchtarán na Eireann (president), directly elected every seven years, is guardian of the Constitution, and may submit a bill to the people in a referendum or to the Supreme Court if it is felt that legislation might contravene the constitution.
The constitution was amended three times by referendum in the 1990s, to loosen anti-abortion laws, legalise divorce and give up Ireland's territorial claim to Northern Ireland in favour of the principle of unity by consent.

Form of state

Parliamentary democratic republic

The executive

Executive power is exercised by the cabinet, led by the *Taoiseach* (prime minister) who is appointed by the president on the recommendation of the Dáil Eireann (House of Representatives). The president is directly elected by a majority popular vote for a 7-year term.

National legislature

The bicameral Oireachtas (National Parliament), consists of the Seanad (Senate, upper house) and the Dáil.
The Dáil (House of Representatives) (lower chamber) has 166 members (known as Teachta Dála (TD)), elected in multi-seat constituencies by proportional representation vote, using single transferable votes (STV) in multi-seat constituencies. Members serve for up to five years. The Dáil has responsibility for electing the cabinet, consisting of between 7–15 members, proposing a budget, ratifying treaties and declaring war or permitting participation in a war.
The Seanad, with 60 members, is elected by a system of electoral colleges, its periods corresponding with that of the Dáil. The *taoiseach* (prime minister) nominates 11 members, 43 are elected by panels representing vocational and cultural interests and six are elected by Ireland's universities. Six are elected by graduates of the University of Dublin and the National University of Ireland. Members serve 5-year terms.
A Fine Gael Labour coalition government proposal to abolish the Seanad was narrowly defeated in a referendum held on 4 October 2013 by 51.7 per cent to 48.3 per cent, even though the proposal was supported by Sinn Féin. Turnout was 40 per cent.

Legal system

The Irish constitution declares that every person living in Ireland has certain fundamental personal rights, listed in articles. Every constitutional right has the same status and value, however when a conflict arises between constitutional rights the courts have the prerogative to adjudicate which constitutional right is more important in which particular case.
Much civil and criminal law is derived from English common law and remains in force if it is consistent with the Constitution.
The courts are made up of District, Circuit and the High Court. District Courts deal with summary offences and minor civil cases. Circuit Courts deal with civil cases of a more serious nature and criminal cases are presented before a judge with a jury of 12 citizens.
The High Court has full jurisdiction in civil and criminal cases and can act as an appeal court from the Circuit Court. When exercising criminal jurisdiction, it is called the Central Criminal Court. Under the Offences Against the State Act 1939, Special Criminal Courts were set up; these sit without a jury.
The Supreme Court, the court of final appeal, consists of a Chief Justice and five other judges who can hear appeals on all High Court decisions. It is also the final arbiter on the interpretation of the constitution.
A referendum held on 4 October 2013 agreed to the establishment of a Court of Appeal. The vote in favour was 65 per cent on a turnout of 40 per cent.

Last elections

27 October 2011 (presidential); 25 February 2011 (parliamentary).
Results: Presidential: Michael D Higgins (LP) won 39.6 per cent of the vote, Sean Gallagher (independent) 28.5 per cent, Martine McGuinness (Sinn Féin) 13.7 per cent, Gay Mitchell (Fine Gael) 6.4 per cent, David Norris (independent) 6.2 per cent; turnout was 56.1 per cent. After elimination, lesser candidates transferred their votes: Higgins won a total of 56.8 per cent and Gallagher 35.5 per cent.
Parliamentary: Fine Gael (FG) (United Ireland Party) won 36.1 per cent (76 seats out of 166), Labour Party 19.4 per cent (37), Fianna Fáil 19.4 per cent (20), Sinn Féin 9.9 per cent (14), United Left Alliance (ULA) per cent (five), Independents 5.7 per cent (14). Turnout was 70 per cent.

Next elections

2018 (presidential); 2016 (parliamentary).

Political parties

Ruling party

Coalition led by Fine Gael (FG) (United Ireland Party) with Labour Party (LP) (from 9 Mar 2011)

Main opposition party

Fine Gael (FG) (United Ireland Party)

Population

4.59 million (2012)* (4,588,252; 2011; census figure)
Last census: 10 April 2011: 4,588,252
Population density: 54 inhabitants per square km. Urban population 69 per cent (2010 Unicef).
Annual growth rate: 1.2 per cent, 1990–2010 (Unicef).

Ethnic make-up

Ireland is predominantly white. Only recently has it seen non-white immigration.

Religions

Roman Catholic (95 per cent); Church of Ireland (2.8 per cent); Presbyterian (0.4 per cent) Jewish (0.1 per cent); others (0.3 per cent); no religion (1.2 per cent).

Education

Education is divided into three levels: primary, secondary and tertiary. Primary schooling (including, although not compulsory, infant pre-schooling from age four), lasts for eight years. Secondary schooling starts age 12 for either five or six years, and includes a junior and a senior cycle with examinations at the end of each. About 81 per cent of Irish students complete the senior cycle and almost 50 per cent go on to tertiary education, which can be either academic or vocational.
Ireland has a higher proportion of graduates with scientific skills in the 25–34 age group than any other OECD member, except Japan.
Compulsory years: Six to 15.
Enrolment rate: 105 per cent gross primary enrolment of relevant age group; 118 per cent gross secondary enrolment (including repeaters) (World Bank).
Pupils per teacher: 22 in primary schools.

Health

Eight regional health boards administer Ireland's health system, which is funded by the central government, through the department of health, which in turn is under the control of the minister of health. Various community welfare services operate for the chronically sick, the elderly and the disabled. Almost 38 per cent of the population – those on lower incomes – receive medical services free of charge. The remainder receive public hospital services for a minimum charge. Charges are also made to the better-off for visits to the family doctor and to hospital consultants.

HIV/Aids

HIV prevalence: 0.1 per cent aged 15–49 in 2003 (World Bank)
Life expectancy: 78 years, 2004 (WHO 2006)

Fertility rate/Maternal mortality rate: 2.1 births per woman, 2010 (Unicef); maternal mortality, 5 per 100,000 live births (World Bank).

Child (under 5 years) mortality rate (per 1,000): 4 per 1,000 live births (WHO 2012)

Head of population per physician: 2.79 physicians per 1,000 people, 2004 (WHO 2006)

Welfare

Social insurance is compulsory for employees and the self-employed. The principal benefits are unemployment, disability and maternity payments plus pay-related benefits to supplement those on low incomes, invalidity pension (for those on disability benefit), widows' payments (contributory and non-contributory), orphans' payments, deserted wives' payments, old age pensions (contributory and non-contributory), medical treatment benefits, including dental and optical, an occupational injuries scheme and certain free schemes for the elderly. Employees in the private sector contribute at the highest rate.

Main cities

Dublin (capital, estimated population 1.1 million in 2012), Cork (194,184), Galway (80,695), Waterford (49,710), Swords (44,241), Limerick (40,169).

Languages spoken

Official documents are printed in both English and Irish.

Five per cent of the population speak Irish as their first language.

Official language/s

Irish (Gaelic) and English

Media

Press

In 2007 less than 50 per cent of the population read a daily newspaper, however, access of newspaper websites rose by 27 per cent.

There are over 50 newspapers and over 100 magazines. The circulation figures for morning newspapers have remained stable but figures for evening newspapers have been falling.

Dailies: The newspapers with the highest circulations are the *Irish Independent* (www.independent.ie), *The Irish Times* (www.irishtimes.com) and the *Irish Examiner* (www.irishexaminer.com). The free issue *Metro* (www.metroireland.ie) has taken a lead in circulation figures in Dublin.

Weeklies: In Gaelic *Foinse* (www.foinse.ie) is published in Galway. In English, *Woman's Way* (www.harmonia.ie) is the leading woman's magazine, *An Phoblacht Republican* (www.anphoblacht.com) takes with an Irish Republican perspective on national and international affairs. A number of local or regional newspapers, owned by few conglomerates including North West of Ireland Printing and Publishing (www.nwipp-newspapers.com) published weeklies such as *Donegal News* and *GaelicLife* and Independent News and Media. (www.independent.ie). Other smaller newspapers include *Waterford Today* (www.waterford-today.ie), *Limerick Post* (www2.limerickpost.ie) and *Anglo Celt* (www.anglocelt.ie) from Cavan. There are also many specialist, genre magazines available.

Business: Dublin has a small number of business publications. The weekly newspaper *Sunday Business Post* (www.sbpost.ie) provides Ireland's financial, political, The monthly *Marine Times* (www.marinetimes.ie) covers the fishing industry and aquaculture industries and communities and *ShelfLife* (www.mediateam.ie) for retail news. A magazine aimed at directors *Decision* (www.decisionireland.com) is published six times a year.

Periodicals: The monthly *Image* (www.image.ie) is a glossy women's magazine. *U* (www.harmonia.ie) is a tabloid, published fortnightly. Of general interest, the scholarly *History Ireland* (www.historyireland.com) and *Irish Roots Magazine* (www.irishrootsmedia.com) on genealogy and ZenthOptimedia (www.zenithoptimedia.com.sg) publishes entertainment guides *GV Magazine* and *Newsline*.

Broadcasting

The Broadcasting Authority is responsible for regulating public and private broadcasting. Broadcasting laws lay down rules regarding the balance of news and current affairs and culture in broadcasting, in addition to the prohibition of matters which the minister for telecommunications considers likely to promote or incite crime. Radio Telefís Éireann (RTE) (www.rte.ie) is the national public broadcaster, funded by a license fee and advertising revenue.

Radio: There are around 60 radio stations located around the country. Almost three million adults listen to the radio every day and of the top 20 shows, 18 are broadcast by RTE (www.rte.ie), which has four networks including popular music, classical and cultural, talk and an Irish-language station. Private, commercial radio includes Today FM (www.rte.ie), NewsTalk (http://newstalk.ie) and 98FM (www.dublins98.ie) from Dublin, Red FM (www.redfm.ie) from Cork and Galway Bay FM (www.galwaybayfm.ie).

Television: The RTE (www.rte.ie) has two television channels (RTE 1 and Network 2) and provides locally produced shows as well as imported programmes. It has a 57 per cent share of the advertising market and its main local competitor TV3 (www.tv3.ie) has 20 per cent, followed by TG4 (www.tg4.ie) the Irish language station. Overall, RTE's principal competition is from UK digital TV providers.

Digital TV is received by 58 per cent of households, but free-to-air digital services is expected to begin in 2009. One-third of homes are cabled, however satellite TV is becoming popular, carrying further UK channels.

Economy

Ireland has an open economy with principle exports in goods and services producing 70.8 per cent of GDP. Tourism, as the major service industry, typically contributes over 9.0 per cent of GDP. Alongside the successful high-tech industries is an agricultural sector that accounts for around 10 per cent of GDP and around 7 per cent of exports. Ireland has a highly skilled labour pool. A national development plan is focussed on IT, life sciences, medical technologies, engineering, financial and international services, Internet based activity and digital businesses. Of the 1,100 foreign-owned companies operating in Ireland around half are American, while the combined numbers of UK and German companies make up around 25 per cent. Those industries that have shown most growth in exports are computers and electrical machinery and chemical and pharmaceutical production. However, Ireland's economy was one of the hardest hit by the 2008 global financial crisis and was the first EU country to enter recession. The crisis exposed an ultimately unsustainable economy, fuelled as it was by expansionary bank credit, which promoted a boom in construction that led to rising property prices and excessive domestic spending.

The annualised GDP growth from 1990–2007 was 10.37 per cent, according to UN statistics, but in 2008 it plunged to -3 per cent, as the current account lurched abruptly from surplus to deficit. GDP growth fell further to -7.0 per cent in 2009, at which point the government introduced an aggressive emergency budget, which in April 2009 cut government spending by EUR3.3 billion (US$4.3 billion) and raised taxes which, combined, amounted to 5 per cent of GDP. Salaries of private sector workers began falling, while public worker's salaries fell by 7 per cent. This produced the official end of the recession in the first quarter of 2010 with GDP growth of 2.7 per cent for the period; however, the annual rate was -0.4 per cent in 2010 and at 2.8 per cent in 2011. Since then the economy has struggled to settle into a state of steady growth, shrinking by 0.3 per cent in 2012, growing slowly by 0.2 per cent in 2013 and

jumping to a growth of 4.8 per cent in 2014.
According to the Organisation for Economic Co-operation and Development (OECD), annual unemployment increased from 6.3 per cent in 2007 to 11.9 per cent in 2009 (particularly in the construction industry (the housing market slumped by 24 per cent in 2008, which at its most productive, in 2006, contributed 15 per cent to GDP); the highest ever number of registered unemployed, 326,100, was recorded in January 2009. Unemployment climbed to 13.7 per cent in 2010. The rate in 2011 was 14.3 per cent, peaking in March–May. There was an inevitable impact on government revenue with reduced tax returns, both corporate and personal. The rising unemployment rates prompted a rise in migration (particularly to the US and Australia), although immigration from other European nations maintained the level of the workforce until 2009–10. Following on from 2011, the unemployment has been falling and in July 2015 reached a 6-year low of 9.5 per cent.
The government established the National Asset Management Agency (Nama) in late 2009. The chief aims of the agency were to rehabilitate the banking sector by removing toxic debt from bank ledgers, channel credit to productive sectors of the economy, underpinning activity, and strengthen employment prospects. In November 2009, US$80 billion was made available for Nama to set up a bank to buy up the loans of defaulting borrowers held by other commercial banks. In March 2010 the Anglo Irish Bank reported the loss of US$17.2 billion in assets, making it the largest corporate loss in Irish commercial history.
The government agreed to inject EUR8.3 billion (US$11.2 billion) to recapitalise the bank as 'the least bad option'. Nama took EUR10 billion (US$13.5 billion) in bad debts, while the European Union regulators began an investigation into the help offered by the government for the Anglo Irish Bank.
On 1 October 2010, the government announced that the total cost of bailing out the country's loss-making banks had to be revised upward to just under EUR50 billion (US$65.5 billion) and was likely to cost over 30 per cent of GDP. On 21 November 2010, the government formally applied for a US$140 billion EU/IMF loan to guarantee its credit worthiness. On 24 November, a new austerity budget was introduced, slashing US$20 billion in public spending over four years, including among other things, welfare cuts, public job losses, a drop in the minimum wage, an increased VAT rate to 23 per cent and a new property tax on homeowners.
On 31 March 2011, the governor of the Bank of Ireland (BoI) announced that following 'stress tests' of the banking system a further EUR24 billion (US$33.65 billion) would have to be injected into the top four banks to ensure stability as a whole. This brought the total amount of recapitalisation by the Irish economy to more than EUR70 billion (US$98.13 billion). Loans to fund their bailout came from the EU and IMF. The BoI will be forced to sell off EUR30 billion (US42.1 billion) in assets by 2013. Restructuring of the banking system began in April 2011; the number of domestic banks was reduced from four to two core banks based around the Allied Irish Bank (AIB) and BoI. A rate cut was given to Ireland by the EU and IMF on the US$572 million emergency loan in May 2011.
From 5–6 December 2011, an interim, austerity budget was introduced which further reduced public spending by over EUR1 billion (US$1.34) and raised income through tax increases of EUR1.6 billion (US$2.14 billion). VAT was raised from 21 per cent to 23 per cent in January 2012.
An eighth austerity budget was introduced in 2013, which consisted of more moderate policies than the previous ones as a result of the economic fatigue experienced by the Irish. This proved successful as the positive growth of 4.8 per cent achieved in 2014 was one of the highest posted in Europe.

External trade

As a member of the European Union (EU), Ireland operates within a community-wide free trade area, with tariffs set across the whole community. Internationally, the EU has free trade agreements with a number of nations and trading blocs worldwide.
Ireland is an exporter of electronic and IT equipment and pharmaceutical and biotechnology products produced by multinational and start-up hi-tech companies utilising a highly educated workforce.
Ireland is the fourth largest producer of salmon in Europe and exports 60 per cent of its meat production.

Imports

Imports consist of data processing equipment, other machinery and equipment, chemicals, petroleum and petroleum products, textiles and clothing.
Main sources: UK (38.5 per cent of total in 2014), US (10.3 per cent), Germany (8.4 per cent)

Exports

Exports consist mainly of machinery and equipment, computers, chemicals, pharmaceuticals, live animals and animal products and natural gas (to Northern Ireland).
Main destinations: US (22.3 per cent of total in 2014), UK (15.1 per cent), Belgium (13.3 per cent)

Agriculture

Farming

Agricultural earnings equate to only 1.6 per cent of annual GDP and around 5 per cent of export earnings. The sector employs 7.5 per cent of the labour force.
With its temperate climate and relatively high levels of rainfall, Ireland is suited to stock raising, with the result that there is a predominance of livestock production in Irish agriculture. Approximately 70 per cent of all land is devoted to pasture while 10 per cent is tilled. Irish farms tend to be owner-occupied, with an average size of just over 25 hectares.
The EU's Fundamental reform to the Common Agricultural Policy (CAP) was introduced in Ireland in 2005. The subsidies paid on farm output, which tended to benefit large farms and encourage overproduction, were replaced by single farm payments not conditional on production.
Ireland is a net exporter of agricultural goods. Main exports include meat, vegetables, milk, butter and alcoholic beverages. Main agricultural imports include rice and maize.

Fishing

The sea fishing industry makes an important contribution to the agricultural economy. Mackerel accounts for about 35 per cent of total catch, and is the most important species landed. Ireland is also one of Europe's leading salmon producers.

Forestry

With forest cover estimated at 659,000 hectares (ha), it occupies less than a tenth of the total land area. Though Ireland is traditionally one of Europe's least forested countries, massive afforestation programmes have contributed to an annual average increase of 3.03 per cent, the equivalent of 17,000ha of forest cover. Private ownership in new planting areas has been rising with around two-thirds of the forest remaining under state ownership. Employment in the forest and wood products industry is about 13,000.
Most of the forest is available for wood supply. Roundwood production has considerably increased with the expansion of forest cover. Much of the production consists of softwood logs for the domestic sawn wood and panel industry. Ireland imports most of its paper and sawn wood.

Industry and manufacturing

The industrial sector accounts for 27.6 per cent of GDP, around 80 per cent of the value of annual exports and approximately a quarter of employment.
Ireland's indigenous manufacturing base is relatively small. Traditional industries,

such as food and beverages, textiles, paper, non-metallic minerals and machinery, dominate, although there has been rapid growth in new export-oriented chemicals as well as electronic engineering industries. Most of the new capital and skill-intensive industries are subsidiaries of large US and European multinationals and are heavily reliant on imported primary and intermediate inputs.

Tourism

Ireland is a popular destination for its diaspora and other visitors wishing to enjoy the culture, history and landscape of the island. Dublin is the main tourist destination, followed by Cork and the west counties. All parts of the Republic benefit from the expansion of tourism, which has become an important factor in regional development, bringing employment and business to otherwise economically-deprived areas.
Travel and tourism constituted 9.0 per cent of GDP in 2014, which despite the serious downturn in tourist numbers since 2007 has remained constant. Income from the sector was EUR16.5 billion (US$20.6 billion) in 2014, which is the same value of the contribution in 2007, showing that the industry has recovered. Direct employment in the industry has also remained steady at 2.1 per cent (40,500 jobs) and 9.0 per cent of total employment (171,500 jobs) in 2014.
The National Tourism Development Authority has been concerned about the cost and quality of the tourism product and has been seeking to sharpen the sector's competitiveness. The industry attracted a growing share of capital investment into 2010, reaching a record 27.5 per cent of total investment, however the figure has been falling since and in 2014 it was 17.2 per cent of total.

Mining

Mining accounts for about 1 per cent of GDP and 1 per cent of the workforce. Europe's largest zinc and lead deposits are located at Navan, County Meath, and are operated by Tara Mines. Production has continued since the mid-1970s.
Ireland is Europe's leading producer of zinc. There are also reserves of gypsum, barytes, dolomite, silica sand, limestone, coal, marble and small amounts of silver. Gypsum is extracted from an open-pit at Knocknacran, Co Monaghan. Gold and base metals have been discovered at Clontibret, County Monaghan.

Hydrocarbons

Dependence on imported petroleum has been reduced due to the exploitation of domestic gas and peat reserves. Imports of oil in 2012 were 61,000 barrels per day (bpd), down from 202,000 (bpd) in 2007. In 2009, UK Serica Energy announced an oil find off the west coast; the size of the well was undetermined.
On 27 February 2012, the Irish oil exploration company, Providence, announced the discovery of oil offshore of the south-east coast. Providence said the discovery was of high-quality light crude oil and that test drilling would begin immediately. On 15 March 2012 it was confirmed that the well had produced the first commercial oil flows for Ireland. On 10 October 2012, Providence estimated the field should yield around 280 million barrels.
Ireland's total proven gas reserves amount to around 9.9 billion cubic metres (cum). However, Ireland still continues to import natural gas primarily from Britain, at over 4 billion cum. Natural gas represents around 23 per cent of primary energy consumption. Indigenous reserves of natural gas are located in the Kinsale Head gas field and the smaller Ballycotton field off the Cork coast. Other sites for exploration were opened up in 2009.
There are two sub-sea interconnector pipelines (Moffat and Twynholm), owned and operated by Bord Gáis Éireann (Irish Gas Board), which links Ireland's transmission system to that of the UK.

Energy

Ireland has, in effect, a stand-alone electricity grid, although a connection with Northern Ireland was re-commissioned in 1995 to manage peak demand supply. As electricity demand has grown the industry was challenged to increase generation resources accordingly. The electricity market has been opened up to competition in line with EU regulations.
The Single Electricity Market (SEM) operates between the Irish Republic and Northern Ireland, uniting the wholesale electricity market, with all generated power pooled and suppliers buying from it. Total installed generating capacity is over 8.3 gigawatts (GW); installed generating capacity in Northern Ireland is over 3.2GW. The largest power station is gas-fired and located in Country Antrim (Northern Ireland), producing 50 per cent of the North's energy and 17 per cent of both Irish and Northern Irish capacity.
Two natural gas pipeline projects link the country to the UK and provide security of supply to meet industry and power generation demands.

Financial markets

Stock exchange

Stocmhalartán na hÉireann (Irish Stock Exchange) (ISE)

Banking and insurance

The governor of the Bank of Ireland (BOI) announced on 31 March 2011 that banks were to be restructured to 'put the banking system on a firm footing for the future…' This followed five attempts to recapitalise the system that cost the economy a total of €70 billion (US$98.13 billion). The number of domestic banks was reduced from four to two core banks based around the AIB (Allied Irish Bank) and BOI. The AIB was merged with the EBS Building Society to form a second banking group.
The governor also said that 'significant contributions' would be sought from the bank's subordinate bondholders to aid recapitalisation and banking officials may re-examine the legitimacy of imposing losses on major bondholders at AIB, if the bank required additional capital.
The Irish Life and Permanent insurance company will be restructured and broken up as it sells its profitable pensions division, Irish Life.
In April 2011, the international credit ratings agency Moody's downgraded AIB and Irish Life and Permanents' long-term deposit ratings to Ba2; the Bank of Ireland was downgraded to Ba1

Central bank

Central Bank of Ireland; European Central Bank (ECB).

Time

GMT (daylight saving, end March to end October, GMT plus one hour)

Geography

Ireland is situated in the north-west of Europe, bordered in the east by the Irish Sea, in the west by the Atlantic Ocean and in the south by the Celtic Sea. The landmass is bounded by mountains and has a low-lying central plain.
The island of Ireland consists of 32 counties, of which six, in the north east, belong to Northern Ireland, part of the United Kingdom.

Hemisphere

Northern

Climate

Ireland is in the temperate zone, with moderate south-westerly winds, influenced by the warm waters of the Gulf Stream, which produce a mild climate with rain throughout the year and annual rainfall varying between 800–1,200mm. The driest months are May and June.
The coldest months are January and February, when temperatures average between 4 and 7 degrees Celsius (C); the warmest months are July and August, when temperatures average between 14 and 17 degrees C.

Dress codes

While dress tends to be informal, business people normally wear suits, and evening social events can be quite formal. A medium-weight raincoat is advised throughout the year.

Entry requirements

Passports

Required by all, except UK-born nationals, who require official photographic identification, and other EU visitors with a valid national ID card.

Visa

Visas are not required by nationals of the EU, the Americas, Australasia and many Asian countries. For confirmation see www.irlgov.ie/iveagh and see Service. Other business travellers should contact the consulate of the nearest Irish Embassy for further information.

Currency advice/regulations

The import of local and foreign currency is unrestricted.

Travellers cheques are widely accepted.

Customs

Personal items are duty-free. There are no duties levied on alcohol and tobacco between EU member states, providing amounts imported are for personal consumption.

Prohibited imports

A wide range of items, including firearms, offensive weapons, ammunition and explosives, pornography, meat and meat products, live or dead animals (including birds and poultry), hay and straw (including used in packing) and endangered species.

UK residents only may be accompanied by a domestic dog, which has its necessary passport of health.

Health (for visitors)

Nationals of the European Economic Area (EEA) countries and Switzerland can access reduced cost and sometimes free medical treatment using a European Health Insurance Card (EHIC) while visiting the EEA. Exceptions include nationals of the 10 countries, which joined the EU in 2004, whose EHIC is not valid in Switzerland. Applications for the EHIC should be made before travelling.

Mandatory precautions

There are no requirements.

Advisable precautions

Travel insurance for those not entitled to free emergency cover.

Hotels

Classified into three categories: Star A, B and C. Reservations should be made in advance. Tipping: 10 per cent is customary.

Credit cards

All international credit and debit cards are widely accepted. ATMs are available in most town.

Public holidays (national)

Fixed dates

1 Jan (New Year's Day), 17 Mar (St Patrick's Day), 25–26 Dec (Christmas).

Variable dates

Good Friday, Easter Monday, May Bank Holiday (first Mon in May); June Bank Holiday (first Mon in Jun), Summer Bank Holiday (first Mon in Aug), Halloween Bank Holiday (last Mon in Oct).

Working hours

Banking

Mon–Fri: 0900–1600 (banks open later one evening a week, in Dublin on Thursdays until 1700, may vary in other cities).

Business

Mon–Fri: 0900–1700.

Government

Mon–Fri: 0915–1300, 1415–1715.

Shops

Mon–Fri: 0900–1730; late night shopping in city centres usually occurs once a week when shops are open to 2100. Supermarkets Mon–Wed: 0830–1900; Thu–Sat: 0830–2100/2000/1900; Sun: 1200–1800.

Telecommunications

Mobile/cell phones

GSM 900/1800 operate throughout the country.

Electricity supply

220V AC, with UK style, flat, three-pin plugs.

Social customs/useful tips

The hold of the Catholic Church over Ireland has diminished in recent years and the country now has an air of moderate social liberalism, although there are more conservative attitudes in rural areas. Smoking is banned in pubs and restaurants.

Getting there

Air

National airline: Aer Lingus

International airport/s: Dublin (DUB), 10km north of city. Airport express coaches and taxis are available to the city centre.

Shannon (SNN), 26 km from Limerick. Bus services are available every hour to and from both Limerick and Clare, (60 minutes duration). A daily express coach travels between both Shannon and Limerick, or Galway. A taxi service is also available to Limerick.

Airport facilities at both airports include duty-free shopping, bank, *bureau de change*, bar, restaurant and tourist information centre.

Other airport/s: Cork (ORK), 5 km from city; Horan (NOC) at Knock, Co Mayo, Connaught Province.

Airport tax: None

Surface

Road: Bus Éireann and National Express operate services from London, and many other UK centres, to Dublin and other destinations.

Rail: Most rail-ferry services to Ireland depart from London. There are a number of services across the Northern Ireland border including the regular, direct intercity Belfast-Dublin service (duration 2.15 hours).

Water: In addition to conventional ferry crossings, there are high-speed catamaran sailings. Routes include links with Scotland, England and Wales to alternative destinations in Ireland. Continental connections include routes to north-western France.

Rail links provide connections from the major seaports.

Main port/s: The main ports are Dun Laoghaire, Dublin, Rosslare and Cork.

Getting about

National transport

Air: Daily services between Dublin and Shannon, and Dublin and Cork operated by Aer Lingus. Also one flight daily between Dublin and Horan Airport, Knock. Charter services are available. Domestic airports include Waterford (WAT), Galway (GWY), Sligo (SXL), Carrickfinn (CFN) and Kerry (KIR). In addition, there are also various small airstrips which receive passenger services.

Road: The Irish road network carries the overwhelming part of Irish imports and exports. A good highway system links all cities.

Buses: Bus Éireann is the national bus line, with services all over the south and north. Winter bus schedule is often drastically reduced and many routes simply disappear after September.

Rail: Ireland's rail network is not extensive. Irishrail is the main operator, with routes which fan out from Dublin.

Water: There are ferry services to outlying islands off the west coast and across rivers.

City transport

Taxis: Taxis in Ireland tend to be expensive. There are metered taxis in Cork, Dublin, Galway and Limerick, but in other places fares must be agreed beforehand. If a taxi is booked by telephone there may be a small pick-up charge.

Buses, trams & metro: There are comprehensive bus services in all towns and cities, combined in Dublin with a fast, surburban rail service, the Dart.

Two tram services – the Luas – were inaugurated in 2004. The red line runs from Connelly Street in Dublin's city centre, west then south-west, to Tallaght. The green line runs from St Steven's Green, in the administrative district of Dublin, south to Cherrywood.

Car hire

Available in all main towns, but heavy demand during tourist season. All international hire companies are represented in Ireland. Drivers must be aged between 21 and 75. A national or international driving licence is required and the driver is generally required to have had at least two years experience. Speed limits 30mph (48kph) in built-up areas and 60mph (96kph) on main roads. Driving is on the left.

BUSINESS DIRECTORY

The addresses listed below are a selection only. While World of Information makes every endeavour to check these addresses, we cannot guarantee that changes have not been made, especially to telephone numbers and area codes. We would welcome any corrections.

Telephone area codes

The international direct dialling (IDD) code for Ireland is +353 followed by area code and subscriber's number:

Cork	21	Mullingar	44
Donegal	73	Shannon	61
Dublin	1	Sligo	71
Galway	91	Tipperary	62
Kilkenny	56	Waterford	51
Killarney	64	Wexford	53
Limerick	61	Wicklow	404

Chambers of Commerce

American Chamber of Commerce Ireland, 6 Wilton Place, Dublin 2 (tel: 661-6201; fax: 661-6217; e-mail: ifo@amcham.ie).

Chambers of Commerce of Ireland, 17 Merrion Square, Dublin 2 (tel: 661-2888; fax: 661-2811; e-mail: info@chambersireland.ie).

Cork Chamber of Commerce, Fitzgerald House, Summerhill North, Cork (tel: 450-9044; fax: 450-8568; e-mail: info@corkchamber.ie).

Dublin Chamber of Commerce, 7 Clare Street, Dublin 2 (tel: 644-7200; fax: 676-6043; info@dublinchamber.ie).

Dun Laoghaire Rathdown Chamber of Commerce, Kilcullen House, 1 Haigh Terrace, Dun Laoghaire (tel: 284-5066; 284-5034; e-mail: info@dirchamber.ie).

Dundalk Chamber of Commerce, Hagan House, Ramparts Road, Dundalk (tel: 933-6343; fax: 933-2085; info@dundalk.ie).

Limerick Chamber of Commerce, 96 O'Connell Street, Limerick (tel: 415-180; fax: 415-785; e-mail: info@limchamber.ie).

Mullingar Chamber of Commerce, ACC House, Dominick Street, Mullingar (tel: 44-044; fax: 44-045; e-mail: info@mullingar-chamber.ie).

Sligo Chamber of Commerce and Industry, 16 Quay Street, Sligo (tel: 916-1274; fax: 916-0912; e-mail: sligochamber@eircom.net).

Waterford Chamber of Commerce, Georges Street, Waterford (tel: 311-136; fax: 876-002; e-mail: info@waterfordchamber.ie).

Wexford Chamber of Industry and Commerce, The Ballast Office, Crescent Quay, Wexford (tel: 22-226; fax:241-70; e-mail: info@wexchamber.iol.ie).

Banking

Allied Irish Bank Ltd, Bankcentre, PO Box 452, Ballsbridge, Dublin 4 (tel: 660-0311; fax: 668-2508).

Allied Irish Investment Bank plc, Bankcentre, Ballsbridge, Dublin 4 (tel: 660-4733).

Bank of Ireland, Lower Baggot Street, Dublin 2 (tel: 661-5933; fax: 661-5671).

The Institute of Bankers in Ireland (banking association), Nassau House, Nassau Street, Dublin 2 (tel: 679-3311).

Investment Bank of Ireland Ltd, 26 Fitzwilliam Place, Dublin 2 (tel: 661-6433; fax: 661-6433).

National Irish Bank, 7/8 Wilton Terrace, Dublin 2 (tel: 678-5066; fax: 661-3324).

Ulster Bank, 33 College Green, Dublin 2 (tel: 677-7623).

Ulster Investment Bank Ltd, 2 Hume Street, Dublin 2 (tel: 661-3444; fax: 676-3021).

Central bank

Central Bank and Financial Services Authority of Ireland, PO Box 559, Dame Street, Dublin 2 (tel: 434-4000; fax: 671-6561; e-mail: enquiries@centralbank.ie).

European Central Bank (ECB), Kaiserstrasse 29, D-60311 Frankfurt am Main, Germany (tel: (+49-69) 13-440; fax: (+49-69) 1344-6000; e-mail: info@ecb.int).

Stock exchange

Stocmhalartán na hÉireann (Irish Stock Exchange) (ISE), www.ise.ie

Travel information

Aer Lingus, Head Office Block, Dublin Airport (tel: 705-2222; fax: 705-3832; internet site: www.aerlingus.ie).

Cork Airport (tel: 431-3131; internet: www.corkairport.com)

Dublin Airport (tel: 814-1111; internet: www.iol.ie).

Irishrail (internet: www.iarnrodeireann.ie and www.irishrail.ie)

Ryanair, Corporate Head Office Building, Dublin Airport (tel: 844-4489, 844-4400; fax: 844-4402; internet: www.ryanair.com).

Shannon Airport (tel:712-000; internet: www.shannonairport.com).

Ministry of tourism

Department of Arts, Sport and Tourism, 23 Kildare Street, Dublin 2 (tel: 631-3800; fax: 661-1201; internet: www.arts-sport-tourism.gov.ie).

National tourist organisation offices

Irish Tourist Board, Baggot Street Bridge, Dublin 2 (tel: 676-5871, 661-6500; fax: 676-4764, 676-4765; internet site: www.irland.ie).

Ministries

Department of Agriculture and Food, Agriculture House, Kildare Street, Dublin 2 (tel: 607-2000; internet: www.agriculture.gov.ie).

Department of Defence, Colaiste Caoimhin, Mobhi Road, Glasnevin, Dublin 9 (tel: 804-210; fax: 804-5000; email: info@defence.irlgov.ie).

Department of Education and Science, Marlborough Street, Dublin 1 (tel: 889-6400; email: info@education.gov.ie).

Department of Enterprise, Trade and Employment, 23 Kildare Street, Dublin 2 (tel: 631-2121; fax: 631-2827; email: info@entemp.ie).

Department of Environment, Heritage and Local Government, Custom House, Dublin 1 (tel: 888-2000; internet: www.environ.ie).

Department of Finance, Government Bldgs, Upper Merrion Street, Dublin 2 (tel: 676-7571; fax: 678-9936; email: webmaster@finance.irlgov.ie).

Department of Foreign Affairs, 80 St Stephen's Green, Dublin 2 (tel: 478-0822; fax: 478-1484; internet: http://foreignaffairs.gov.ie).

Department of Transport, Transport House, 44 Kildare Street, Dublin 2 (tel: 670-7444; email: info@transport.ie).

Department of Taoiseach, Government Buildings, Upper Merrion Street, Dublin 2 (tel: 662-4888; fax: 678-9791; email: webmaster@taoiseach.gov.ie).

Department of Arts, Sport and Tourism, 23 Kildare Street, Dublin 2 (tel: 631-3800; fax: 661-1201; internet: www.arts-sport-tourism.gov.ie).

Other useful addresses

Central Statistics Office, Skehard Road, Cork (tel: 359-000; fax: 359-090; internet site: www.cso.ie).

Confederation of Irish Industry, Confederation House, Kildare Street, Dublin 2 (tel: 660-1011).

Enterprise Ireland, Glasnevin, Dublin 9 (tel: 808-2000; fax: 808-2020; internet site: www.enterprise-ireland.com).

IDA Ireland (Industrial Development Agency), Wilton Park House, Wilton Place, Dublin 2 (tel: 668-6633; fax: 660-3703).

Irish Business and Employers' Confederation, 84 Lower Baggot Street, Dublin 2 (tel: 660-1011; fax: 660-1717).

Irish Embassy (USA), 2234 Massachusetts Avenue, NW, Washington DC 20008 (tel: (+1-202) 462-3939; fax: (+1-202) 232-5993; e-mail: embirlus@aol.com).

Provincial Newspapers' Association of Ireland, 33 Parkgate Street, Dublin 8 (tel: 679-3679).

RTÉ (Irish broadcasting), Donnybrook, Dublin 4 (tel: 208-3111; fax: 208-3080; internet: rte.ie)

The Stock Exchange, 24-28 Anglesea Street, Dublin 2 (tel: 677-8808; fax: 677-6045).

Internet sites

Access Ireland: www.visunet.ie

Business information: www.factfinder.ie

Doras web directory: www.doras.ie

Ireland On-Line: www.home.iol.ie

Irish Government website: irlgov.ie

Irish Times: www.irish-times.com

Irish trade web (information on Irelands' top 1000 companies): www.itw.ie

Israel

Times change: sands shift. Since its creation as an independent state in 1948 Israel's foreign policy has largely been determined by two major influences. First, its understandably sensitive relationship with the neighbouring Palestinian community and by extension the region's other Arab states. The second major influence has, for decades, been the United States (US). Since Israel's early days, the US has looked upon Israel as a haven of democracy in a largely dictatorial region. Add to that the sympathy and regret felt by all the Western democracies for the Holocaust victims and the presence in the US of a hugely influential Jewish diaspora. Since 2008, however, three factors in the equation changed. One was the arrival of President Obama in the White House, which – without actually diminishing practical and emotional support for Israel – tilted US foreign policy a degree or two towards the situation of the Palestinians. The second was the return of Benjamin Netanyahu to office as prime minister in 2009. The chemistry between Obama and Netanyahu simply did not work, creating a rift at the top for the first time in US-Israeli relations. Third, was the perceived emergence of Iran as a major threat to Israeli security. As the international community's nuclear negotiations wore on, it seemed to many Israelis that the US was warming to Iran, possibly at the expense of its relations with Saudi Arabia but more probably at the expense of its once cordial relationship with Israel.

Times change: for some. In June 2015 the new Saudi Arabian King Salman, addressing the Doha Forum, directed part of his speech to Israel. The newly crowned King's message was that he reiterated 'the Saudi peace proposals, claiming that it was time that Israel accepted them.' This was no more than the confirmation of proposals that had already been submitted to the Israeli delegation to the Forum by Saudi Arabian General Anuar Eshki, director of the Saudi Centre for Strategic Studies. The Saudi proposal was unlikely to be accepted by Israel, since it involved Israel's withdrawal to its 1967 borders, in return for the restoration of diplomatic relations with all 22 Arab states and the world's 20 Muslim countries. That there should be any sort of dialogue between Israel and its Arab neighbours might not necessarily be described as promising, but it at least established some tentative relationships.

Only the Lonely

In the first half of 2015, when the final touches to the ground-breaking agreement with Tehran were being made, Israel found itself desperately isolated. It had

KEY FACTS

Official name: Medinat Israel (State of Israel)

Head of State: President Reuven Rivlin (Likud) (sworn in 24 July 2014)

Head of government: Prime Minister Benjamin Netanyahu (from 1 Apr 2009, re-elected 22 Jan 2013 and 17 Mar 2015)

Ruling party: Coalition led by Likud Yisrael Beiteinu and including Hatnuah (The Movement) and others.

Area: 20,700 square km (excluding occupied territories)

Population: 8.21 million (2014)

Capital: Jerusalem (Israel regards the entire city as its capital although it is not recognised by the UN); Tel Aviv, administrative and diplomatic centre

Official language: Hebrew

Currency: New shekel (NIS) = 100 agorot

Exchange rate: NIS3.91 per US$ (Sep 2015)

GDP per capita: US$36,991 (2014)

GDP real growth: 2.75% (2014)

GDP: US$303.77 billion (2014)

Labour force: 3.80 million (2014)*

Unemployment: 5.95% (2014)

Inflation: 0.48% (2014)

Balance of trade: -US$7.86 billion (2014)

* estimated figure

succeeded in distancing itself, not only from the European Union (EU) but more catastrophically, from the United States. Traditionally, the warmth in relationships between Israeli premiers and American presidents had been based on shared values, understanding and respect. Mr Netanyahu's relationship with President Obama had reached breaking point when Mr Netanyahu accepted a Republican party inspired invitation to address a joint session of Congress on 3 March 2015 (two weeks before Israel's 17 March general election) without first advising or consulting the White House. If Mr Netanyahu had friends in the US, it had become clear that, increasingly, they came from the Republican benches. His long-standing friendship with the leader of the Senate, Mitch McConnell, was one obvious example. His critics claimed that that his pre-election speech in Congress on 3 March had turned Israel from the recipient of bipartisan US support, to a pawn in a political game between the two US parties. Israel's Channel 2 broadcast an interview with President Obama in which he observed that Mr Netanyahu's declarations on the Palestine Peace Process 'contained so many reservations and qualifications that it would be unrealistic to expect progress in the near future.' The President went on to note that 'The current danger is that Israel, as a whole, ends up losing credibility.'

Quoted in the *Atlantic* magazine, Mr Netanyahu had reportedly 'written off' the Obama administration. The feeling was mutual; White House officials expressed their 'red-hot anger' at the Netanyahu administration for pursuing its expansive settlement policies on the West Bank and its intrusive building policies in Jerusalem. US officials believed that this disregard for the views of its closest ally, as well as for those of the wider international community, had torpedoed Secretary of State John Kerry's peace process.

The author of the article in the journal *Atlantic*, Jeffery Goldberg, reported that Obama administration officials had described Mr Netanyahu as 'recalcitrant, myopic, reactionary, obtuse, blustering, pompous and Aspergery'. (Many Aspergers affected people find it difficult to understand what other people think and how they feel.) Mr Goldberg noted how, from time to time, administration officials had described Mr Netanyahu as a national leader who acted as though he was the Mayor of Jerusalem, which was to say 'a no-vision small-timer who worries mainly about pleasing the hardest core of his political constituency.' Mr Goldberg reported that President Obama in interviews had alluded to Mr Netanyahu's 'lack of political courage'. A White House official was quoted as saying that 'The bad thing about him is that he won't do anything to reach an accommodation with the Palestinians or with the Sunni Arab states. The only thing he's interested in is protecting himself from political defeat. He's not [Yitzhak] Rabin, he's not [Ariel] Sharon, he's certainly no [Menachem] Begin.'

The Prime Minister's insensitivity also had its critics within Israel: quoted in the *New York Times*, Efraim Halevy, the former head of the Mossad national intelligence agency, publically asserted that those Israeli politicians who had been critical of President Obama should 'Change their tone'. Later, speaking on Israel's Army Radio, Mr Halevy added that Israel had had three months in which to lobby to improve the international agreement with Iran: 'In order to influence, you have to act with a certain kind of respect for your partner.' Quite apart from the behaviour of its Prime Minister, which had failed to produce any results as far as the agreement with Iran was concerned, Israel's position was further weakened by its own failure to sign up to the Nuclear Non Proliferation Treaty. Israel is a member of the International Atomic Energy Agency (IAEA) although it has never acknowledged the possession of nuclear arms, preferring to maintain an official policy of 'nuclear ambiguity'. Israel's objections to the nuclear agreement were lengthy. They focussed on the negotiators' failure to link any ending of sanctions to a shift in Iran's attitude towards Israel, the international negotiators' apparent willingness to lift sanctions rapidly and the failure to deal with Iran's intercontinental ballistic missile programme, which allegedly also threatened the US.

Coalition? When?

Until the day of the 17 March election, Mr Netanyahu had been widely expected to lose and had already become a lame duck in the eyes of many in his party as well as among the opposition. Returning to government as the winner, following his narrow election victory, Mr Netanyahu had been obliged to embark on lengthily complex coalition discussions. At one point it emerged that the negotiations were failing following a fall-out with his originally designated finance minister, Moshe Kahlon, chairman of the Kulanu Party. At issue was the scope of Mr Kahlon's authority in a coalition government.

However, Mr Netanyahu's approach to the coalition discussions seemed to be one of 'when the going gets tough, revert to the nuclear agreement.' One commentator described the Iranian nuclear issue as Mr Netanyahu's 'comfort zone' to which he could repair, in statesman-like fashion, to avoid unwelcome coalition disagreements. Public statements were invariably related to the negotiations with Iran, not to the difficulties in his negotiations with Kahlon or to Israel's housing and cost-of-living problems. But for most Israeli politicians and its electorate, an agreement with Iran was not their first electoral priority. The Iranian nuclear issue had, however, helped Mr Netanyahu

KEY INDICATORS — Israel

	Unit	2011	2012	2013	2014	**2015
Population	m	*7.59	7.70	8.06	8.21	*8.37
Gross domestic product (GDP)	US$bn	242.90	257.62	290.55	303.77	*306.87
GDP per capita	US$	31,986	33,451	36,066	36,991	*36,659
GDP real growth	%	4.7	3.4	3.2	2.8	*3.5
Inflation	%	3.5	1.7	1.5	0.5	*-0.2
Unemployment	%	7.0	6.8	6.3	6.0	*5.5
Exports (fob) (goods)	US$m	62,854.9	62,320.6	61,956.7	63,334.9	–
Imports (fob) (goods)	US$m	71,931.8	71,665.5	71,296.5	71,196.8	–
Balance of trade	US$m	-9,076.9	-9,344.9	-9,339.8	-7,861.9	–
Current account	US$m	3,384.0	849.0	6,893.0	9,026.0	*13,779.0
Total reserves minus gold	US$m	77,941.8	75,907.6	81,785.5	86,101.3	–
Foreign exchange	US$m	76,100.0	74,040.0	79,591.0	–	–
Exchange rate	per US$	3.51	3.84	3.49	3.91	–

* estimated figure ** forecast figure

win in the final stages of the election despite the polls demoting it as an electoral priority. Elected for the fourth time as prime minister, Mr Netanyahu was also fortunate that the Israeli electorate failed to believe that the Zionist Party leader Isaac Herzog was enough of a statesman.

Not that Mr Netanyahu had completely ignored the electorate's main preoccupations. In the closing days of his campaign he had linked up with Moshe Kahlon in an effort to recover the votes of Likud Yisrael Beiteinu (Likud) members who had defected to Kulanu. The prospect of Mr Kahlon becoming a coalition minister, mixed with less precise undertakings to sort out the housing crisis gained him victory, just.

Whatever the positive gloss that Mr Netanyahu and his Likud party placed on the March 2015 electoral victory, many commentators saw the result as an opportunity for the electorate to advance its demands for an improved socio-economic performance from the government. Mr Kahlon's minority Kulanu party won 10 seats, one less than the 11 won by the former television presenter Yair Lapid and his Yesh Atid party. These were votes driven by the social protest movement that began in the summer of 2011. In the 2013 elections, the telegenic Mr Lapid had managed 19 seats by virtue of the fact that he was widely viewed as the saviour of the Israeli middle class. His subsequent performance as finance minister had been disappointing. In the previous two election campaigns Mr Netanyahu had been forced to deal with a tide of dissatisfaction that he had not dealt with Israel's perceived real-estate bubble and the high cost of living. The Israeli electorate's disappointment with Netanyahu's continued failure to deliver on domestic matters had none the less fallen far short of dislodging him from the premiership.

With only two days to go before the deadline for forming a government, the Likud leader – whose party had only mustered 30 seats in the 17 March election – had only managed to reach agreement with two possible coalition partners. Had it failed to form a coherent grouping of at least 61 seats in the Knesset, Israel's President Reuven Rivlin would have had to ask the leader of the Labour Party, runner up Isaac Herzog, to form a government. Mr Netanyahu, striving to obtain the fourth mandate that would make him Israel's longest serving prime minister, simply could not face defeat. To put a coalition group together meant swallowing his pride and coming to terms with the ultra-Orthodox Ashkenazis from the Union for the Torah and Judaism (Yahadut Hatorah) with six seats, to whom Netanyahu had promised the health portfolio. In exchange for their support the ultra-Orthodox parties would see increased state funding for the rabbinical schools or Yeshiva. There would also be a VAT exemption for basic necessities and an undertaking that no orthodox Jew would be punished for failing to turn up for military service, which is still compulsory in Israel. At one stage Mr Kahlon had boycotted the coalition negotiations in protest over Netanyahu's appointment of a Yahadut HaTorah politician to the chairmanship of the Finance Committee.

As the deadline for completing the coalition approached, Mr Netanyahu was still in negotiation with three other minority parties. The left of centre newspaper *Haaretz* reported a Likud official as despairing that their 'requirements are mind-boggling, the territory of extorsionists'. Another ultra-orthodox party, the Shas (Shomrei Sfarad meaning Sephardi Guards) which had seven seats and spoke for the Sephardic Jews and the nationalists of Jewish Home (HaBayit HaYehudi) lead by Naftali Bennet looked close to signing up. With all of these disparate parties on board, Mr Netanyahu could just manage the 61 seats needed to form an absolute majority. One potential sticking point had been over the possible inclusion of former foreign minister, Avigdor Lieberman. However, having failed to get what he wanted, the maverick Mr Lieberman had stormed off. Following Mr Liberman's sudden announcement, the Likud party held its final coalition talks with Shas and HaBayit HaYehudi to complete the process of building the government by the 8 pm deadline.

The Joint List

The March 2015 election had one remarkable result. The Joint List party emerged as the third-largest political party in the Knesset. The Joint List was not a new party but a grouping of the four parties representing Palestinians, who are around 20 per cent of Israel's population, a percentage which is increasing. The decision to join forces was in response to the Knesset's decision to increase the electoral threshold (to be allocated seats) to 3.25 per cent of the vote (from its earlier 2 per cent). The transparent objective of the new legislation had been to prevent minority parties from gaining representation.

With little choice, the Palestinian parties got together, forming the Joint List under the leadership of Ayman Odeh, from the left-wing Hadash party. As a result the Joint List secured 14 seats in the March election. It was reported that the Palestinian electoral turnout increased to 64 per cent. If nothing else, the List's success was a rebuke to Mr Lieberman's anti-Arab ranting. It also showed up Mr Netanyahu – particularly internationally – when the Likud party released a rather racist video that baldly declared that 'Right-wing rule is in danger. Arab voters are streaming in huge quantities to the polling stations.' On the day before his re-election, Mr Netanyahu, in full electoral swing, had announced that there would never be a Palestinian state while he was prime minister. One neutral commentator suggested that the key to understanding Mr Netanyahu's personality was to appreciate that he cared 'about only two things: staying in power and maintaining Israeli control over the Golan and the occupied Palestinian territories.'

Washington responded that Israel would face consequences in the diplomatic arena for having repudiated the two-state solution. *Haaretz* had also reported on a leaked EU document that specified the sanctions to be imposed on Israel should it officially reject negotiating a withdrawal from the West Bank and the establishment of a Palestinian state. Just when it looked as though Mr Netanyahu had stepped over a White House red line and with the elections two days behind him Mr Netanyahu announced on a US television channel that he had not repudiated the idea of two states. Rather, he claimed, the reality had changed. Palestinian President Mahmoud Abbas had refused to acknowledge Israel as the Jewish state and furthermore he had made a pact with Hamas to destroy Israel. Sadly, neither comment was true.

The economy

In its 2015 summary *Economic Survey of Israel* the Paris-based Organisation for Economic Co-operation and Development (OECD) noted that Israel's economic growth had slowed in 2014, but picked up again strongly at the end of the year and looked likely to strengthen to a growth rate of around 3.5 per cent of gross domestic product (GDP) in 2015 and 2016, helping to keep unemployment low. Lower oil prices, further cuts in interest rates and a significant revaluation of the minimum wage were expected to shore up domestic demand, while the gradual improvement of the global economy should increase exports. The OECD suggested that an accommodative monetary policy was still appropriate to support current growth and prevent any undesirable appreciation of the shekel. But the probable temporary nature of the price falls seen in early 2015 argued against any further monetary relaxation involving unconventional measures. Israel's public debt reduction policy was still needed to increase the room for fiscal manoeuvre, but it needed recourse to greater revenue increases; the OECD recommended that the current rule constraining expenditure needed to be reviewed. Structural reforms were also essential to enhance competition on product markets and formal education and skills, especially among the Ultra-Orthodox and Arab populations, to stimulate productivity and to make growth more inclusive. Increased investment in infrastructure – especially in public transport and in the natural gas distribution network, but also in education – was needed to lift some of the barriers to private investment and boost potential growth. In the view of the OECD, the government should also pursue efforts to improve the co-ordination of public intervention in the property sector to better respond to housing demand by increasing supply and thus reducing prices.

According to the International Monetary Fund (IMF) in its annual assessment of the Israeli economy, Israel's exports account for one third of GDP, with the United States, Europe and emerging Asia its major trade partners. Israel has strong comparative advantages in the high-tech industry, which accounts for more than 40 per cent of total manufacturing exports, but economy-wide labour productivity is low and the poverty rate is among the highest in the OECD. Israel was less affected by the 2009 global financial crisis than many other countries, in part due to the absence of pre-crisis asset and lending booms. It is the only advanced economy where growth has exceeded pre-crisis *World Economic Outlook* (WEO) projections. According to the IMF, unemployment had continued to decline, to 5.3 per cent in the first quarter of 2015 a 'multi-decade' low. Thus continued what the IMF described as the Israeli employment miracle: in the previous 25 years, employment had grown by 3.5 per cent annually. Growth had slowed in recent years to around 3 per cent. Both potential and actual growth have slowed – the latter held back by sluggish partner country growth, the strong shekel and – in 2014 – the conflict in Gaza. In per capita terms, annual growth was about one per cent.

In the view of the IMF, Israeli policy makers were confronted with several problems: first, that despite relatively high growth post-crisis, Israel had one of the highest structural fiscal deficits in the OECD. Repeated upward revisions to fiscal targets had delayed progress in deficit reduction. Second, Israeli inflation was negative, but house prices kept soaring. Over the previous three years, the Bank of Israel (BOI) (central bank) had cut the monetary interest rate from 3.25 to 0.10 per cent. Low energy prices and an appreciating shekel had dampened inflation, although recent data showed an upturn in inflation and inflation expectations. Low interest rates had also contributed to the housing price boom, with prices nearly doubling since the beginning of 2007. Finally, the IMF noted that labour productivity was low and the gap relative to the United States was widening. Productivity looked likely to come under further pressure from the rapidly rising share in the population of the Haredi and Israeli Arabs – both groups with generally lower-than-average education levels. Israel's income inequality was high. This reflected both the high inequality of labour and income, with a high share of both high-paying and low-paying jobs relative to other countries; as well as less redistribution through the tax/transfer system than was the case in other countries. Poverty was also concentrated among the Israeli-Arab and Haredi populations, which have lower labour force participation rates, less education and larger families; even among the non-Haredi Jews, income inequality was higher than in almost all advanced economies. The IMF expected growth of 3 per cent in 2015, as rapid employment growth, falling import prices and near-zero interest rates boosted private consumption. Weak partner country growth and strong demand for imports continued to weigh on net exports in the near term. The output gap was near zero and inflation was projected to recover to around 0.7 per cent at the end of the year. Beyond 2015, medium-term growth was projected at around 3–3.25 per cent a year – in line with potential GDP growth.

The IMF also considered that the risks to the economic outlook were balanced. External negative risks included disappointing growth in Israel's trading partners, geopolitical tensions in the Middle East and a renewed appreciation of the shekel resulting from a longer episode of loose monetary policy in large advanced economies. In this context, prospective US monetary tightening could actually help Israel, as it would probably diminish re-emerging appreciation pressures on the shekel, especially if it reflected stronger growth prospects in the United States. Contagion from Greece was likely to be limited in Israel, as there were few financial and trade links. Domestic risks included a housing price crash, which could affect growth and financial system stability. Upside 'risks' included a faster- and stronger-than-expected recovery in the global economy and a further increase in natural gas investment. (See: 'Energy' below)

The economic outlook

Overall, in the view of the IMF, Israel's economy had been doing well and short-term growth prospects were favourable. The central government had met the original deficit target of 2.8 per cent of GDP in 2014. However, the government had raised the deficit targets for 2015 and 2016 to 2.9 per cent of GDP for both years (almost 4 per cent of GDP based on international accounting standards), compared with 2.5 and 2.0 per cent of GDP previously. Debt had declined to 67 per cent of GDP from a peak of 94 per cent of GDP in 2003 but was expected to increase for the first time since 2009, following upward revisions to the deficit targets.

The BOI had kept interest rates on hold in August 2015, as inflation was expected to return to the target band in 2016. Housing prices had continued to increase by around 4 per cent year-on-year, owing largely to supply constraints. In response, the government had announced a variety of initiatives to boost housing supply. Macro-prudential measures had been successful in containing the increase in household leverage and the ratio of household credit to GDP had remained low (at around 40 per cent of GDP) compared to other advanced economies. However, labour productivity growth and levels were low, affecting growth prospects, and income inequality was among the highest in advanced countries. Acknowledging the challenges to medium-term growth and poverty, the new government has prioritised boosting competition in several sectors and better integrating the rapidly growing Israeli-Arab and Ultra-Orthodox Jewish (Haredi) populations into the labour force.

Energy

In 2015, Israel, once dependent on imports to supply its energy, had a growing natural gas industry. Discoveries of offshore natural gas fields had, according to the US government Energy Information Administration (EIA), the potential to provide adequate amounts of energy to meet domestic demand, while allowing the country to export excess volumes. In 2014, Israel's primary energy consumption came mainly from petroleum and other liquids (42 per cent), coal (29 per cent) and natural gas (28 per cent), according to the *BP Statistical Review of World Energy*.

In the ten years from 2004 to 2014, Israel's energy consumption from coal had decreased by 14 per cent. At the same time, energy consumption from natural gas had grown more than fivefold. While coal had long been the country's primary source of electricity, it was likely that its use would decline as Israel's natural gas sector continues its rapid growth and natural gas-fired generating capacity supplants coal-fired generating capacity. In January 2015, Israel had estimated proved reserves of oil at 14 million barrels. However, Israel had, according to the EIA, virtually no crude oil and condensate production. In February 2015, exploratory drilling for oil began in the southern part of the Golan Heights. In 2014, Israel consumed 235 thousand barrels per day (bpd), all met by imports. The majority of Israel's oil imports are from crude oil and the country exports small quantities of refined products. Israel plans to reduce its dependence on oil imports through an expansion of its rapidly-growing natural gas sector.

Natural gas

At the end of 2014, Israel had proven natural gas reserves of 6.7 trillion cubic feet (tcf). Energy exploration over the previous few years had uncovered significant natural gas resources in Israel, primarily in the country's offshore areas.

The Mari-B field – discovered in 2000 – provided the first significant volumes of domestically-produced natural gas to Israel's markets. However, in 2012 production plummeted as the field rapidly entered the final stages of depletion. In prior years, the Mari-B field met up to 40 per cent of Israel's natural gas demand. The Tamar field was discovered offshore near Haifa in 2009. Israel began commercial production from this field in late March 2013. The natural gas produced from the Tamar field travels through existing onshore facilities at Ashdod via a pipeline that links to existing infrastructure at the Mari-B development site.

In 2013, the Tamar South-west field was discovered 8 miles south-west of the Tamar field. This was a smaller, separate field that was approved for development in 2013 and was estimated to contain 700 bcf of natural gas. However, the most significant find in offshore Israel is the Leviathan field, located approximately 80 miles off the coast and situated in water that is more than 5,000 feet deep. Assessments of the Leviathan field indicate that it holds around 22tcf of recoverable natural gas. Exports from the Leviathan are expected to begin by 2019. More recently, the Royee field was discovered nearly 100 miles off the coast. Best estimates place Royee's reserves at 3.2tcf, but range from 1.9tcf and 5tcf. The drilling of an exploration well looked likely to start in December 2015.

Historically, Israel has been an importer of energy, with a substantial portion of its natural gas needs supplied through the Arish-Ashkelon pipeline from Egypt and a small amount from LNG imports from a floating regasification terminal installed in 2013. The recent discoveries of natural gas fields are expected to provide enough fuel to meet the rising needs of Israel's domestic needs and extra gas resources would probably be exported. In 2014, Israel consumed 267bcf of natural gas, nearly all met by domestic production.

There are competing proposals to develop pipelines and LNG infrastructure to support natural gas exports, but according to the EIA, deliberations about how Israel would get its natural gas to market were continuing. In January 2014, the Israeli government approved plans to supply the Palestinian Authority with natural gas from the Leviathan field once production commenced. Noble Energy of the US had signed a natural gas sales agreement with two Jordanian companies to provide supplies from the Tamar field in early 2014. The initial term of the agreement with Jordan was for 15 years, for a total gross quantity of 66bcf, with exports due to begin in 2016. In June 2013, the Israeli Cabinet approved exports of 40 per cent of the country's natural gas reserves. With the 40 per cent cap in place, Israel's reserves are estimated to be able to supply the country for 25 years.

Risk assessment

The Economy	Good
Politics	Good/fair
Regional stability	Poor

Muslims in Israel

% of population	16.8
Sunni (% of Muslims)	97
Shi'a (% of Muslims)	0

People to watch

Moshe Kahlon, chairman of the Kulanu party

Naftali Bennet, leader of the HaBayit HaYehudi (Jewish Home) party

COUNTRY PROFILE

The struggle between the Israelis and the Palestinians over historic claims to land is one of the most enduring of all the world's conflicts.

1917 The Balfour Declaration suggested the establishment in Palestine of a national home for the Jewish people.

1922 The Council of the League of Nations assigned to Britain a mandate for the Ottoman Arab territory of Palestine, a region that covered present-day Israel and Jordan, plus the Golan Heights region (claimed by Syria). The British divided the mandate into two parts, designating all lands west of the Jordan River as Palestine and those easts of the river as Transjordan. The League of Nations mandate also addressed the goal of restoring a Jewish homeland in Palestine.

1929 Riots in Jerusalem between Arab Palestinians and Jews were sparked by a dispute over the use of the western wall of the Al Aqsa Mosque (the site is sacred to Muslims, and Jews claim it as part of their temple).

1936–39 The Arab Higher Committee opposed Jewish immigration to Palestine and the Peel Commission concluded that the mandate in Palestine was unworkable. Legislation limiting the number of Jewish immigrants into Palestine was introduced by the British government.

1945–46 Many Jews who had survived the Nazi German Holocaust arrived in Palestine and Jewish extremists began to oppose Britain's immigration legislation. Transjordan became independent and was later re-named Jordan.

1947 The UN adopted Resolution 181, establishing Jewish and Arab states within Palestine. A partition plan was based solely on population, with Jerusalem as an international zone under UN jurisdiction. The Jews agreed to the partition; the Arabs refused. Britain withdrew from Palestine.

1948 Conflict ensued between Arabs and Jews. Jewish leaders announced the formation of the State of Israel, open to the immigration of Jews from all countries. Egypt, Iraq, Lebanon, Syria and Jordan joined Palestinian and other Arab guerrillas and invaded Israel. The armistice agreements extended the territory under Israel's control beyond the UN partition boundaries. Many Arabs fled Israel to become refugees in the surrounding Arab countries, ending the Arab majority in the new Jewish state.

1956 Egypt nationalised the Suez Canal and blockaded the Red Sea port of Eilat. Israeli forces attacked and occupied the Sinai Peninsula, later being joined by Britain and France, seeking to regain control of the Canal Zone. In the face of strong international opposition, particularly from the US, all three withdrew their forces.
1967 Egypt blockaded Eilat again. Israel launched and won the Six Day War taking control of the Sinai peninsular and the Gaza Strip, which had been Egyptian territory, together with the Golan Heights, formerly claimed by Syria, and the West Bank, including East Jerusalem, which had been united with Jordan since 1950. Around 300,000 Palestinian Arabs fled to Jordan. Israel's settlement policy began with occupation of all territory seized including East Jerusalem, re-unifying the city; such areas became known as the occupied territories.
1968–70 The War of Attrition was a limited war fought between Egypt and Israel, initiated by Egypt as a way to recapture the Sinai from Israel. The war ended without changes to the borders.
1969 Golda Meir became prime minister.
1973 Lebanon was used by the Palestinians as a base for activities against Israel. In retaliation, Israeli commandos raided Beirut, killing three associates of Palestine Liberation Organisation (PLO) chairman, Yasser Arafat. In the 6 October War (also known as the Yom Kippur War), Egypt and Syria invaded Israel to reclaim some of the land lost in the Six Day War, but despite some early strategic gains by Egypt and Syria, Israel counter-attacked and repelled the invasion, re-conquering the Golan Heights from Syria.
1974 Golda Meir resigned and was succeeded as prime minister by Yitzhak Rabin. Jordan and other Arab countries recognised the PLO as the sole legitimate representative of the Palestinian people.
1977 President Sadat of Egypt visited Jerusalem.
1978 Prime Minister Menachim Begin and Egyptian Prime Minister Anwar Sadat signed peace accords at Camp David in the US. Israel agreed to withdraw from the Sinai.
1981 Israel annexed East Jerusalem and the Golan Heights.
1982–85 The Sinai peninsular was returned to Egypt in 1982. Israel launched a full-scale invasion of Lebanon. Despite subsequently withdrawing from most of the territory, Israel maintained some troops in Lebanon in order to help secure its own northern border.
1987 The Palestinians launched an *intifida* (uprising) against the Israelis.
1988 The Harakat al Muqawama al Islamia (Hamas) (Islamic Resistance Movement) was formed and began armed resistance to Israeli rule in the occupied territories of the West Bank and Gaza Strip.
1989 Mass immigration of Jews from the Soviet Union began; many settled in the occupied territories.
1991–93 Israel and the PLO conducted secret negotiations in Oslo (Norway), agreeing an interim peace accord, which was signed in the US. The Oslo Peace Accords laid the basis for transfer of authority from the Israeli military administration to the PLO in the Gaza Strip and an undefined area around the town of Jericho in the West Bank. President Ezer Weizman took office.
1995–96 A follow-up treaty, Oslo II, (known collectively, with the first, as the Accord), envisaged Palestinian autonomy, with Israeli troop units withdrawn from the West Bank. Yasser Arafat was elected president of the Palestinian Legislative Council (PLC), the assembly of the Palestinian National Authority (PNA).
2000 President Ezer Weizman resigned and Moshe Katsav, (Likud), was elected president. Israel withdrew from southern Lebanon without reaching an agreement with Syria on the future of the Golan Heights, still under Israeli control. The Camp David summit aimed at pushing forward the Accord failed when no agreement could be reached; the Palestinians claimed sovereignty over all of east Jerusalem, including Judaism's holiest place of Temple Mount. The right-wing opposition leader, Ariel Sharon, made a provocative visit to Palestinian controlled Temple Mount (called al Haram as Sharif by Arabs) and the second *intifada* was launched. A total blockade was imposed by Israel on the West Bank and Gaza.
2001 Ariel Sharon was elected prime minister. He declared the PNA a terrorist-supporting organisation and launched Operation 'Defensive Shield', invading the PNA-controlled West Bank and Gaza Strip, attacking its institutions and besieging Yasser Arafat's headquarters.
2002 Saudi Arabia proposed a peace initiative, whereby Israel could have normal relations, peace and security with the Arab world if Israel withdrew from captured territories and agreed to recognise a Palestinian state. Israel began building a 640km security barrier, claiming it was the only way to control the infiltration of militant terrorists.
2003 US President Bush unveiled the Middle East Road Map to Peace, to run between 2003–05, with a cease-fire, an end to Jewish settlements in the occupied territories and the creation of an independent Palestinian state. However neither side kept to its timetable and it, *de facto*, failed.
2004 The International Court of Justice ruled that the West Bank security barrier was illegal. Palestinian President Yasser Arafat died.
2005 Sharon and the newly elected Palestinian president, Mahmoud Abbas, signed a truce that planned to bring to an end four years of violence between the two states. Egypt and Jordan agreed to return their ambassadors to Israel. The cabinet approved the removal of Jewish illegal settlers from the Gaza Strip and part of the West Bank. Hamas bombed targets in Israel claiming it was not party to the truce. Abbas ordered a crackdown and sacked senior security chiefs. Israeli troops began clearing Jewish settlements from Gaza. Most commercial buildings were left standing but some homes and synagogues were destroyed. Sharon left Likud, a party he had helped found, to form a centrist party, Kadima, a right-of-centre party. Binyamin Netanyahu was elected leader of Likud.
2006 Sharon suffered a massive stroke and was hospitalised; Ehud Olmert became acting prime minister. Kadima won parliamentary elections. Olmert became prime minister after Sharon was declared 'permanently incapacitated' in a coma. Israel became a member of the International Red Cross, adopting a diamond-shaped red crystal as its symbol. Hezbollah paramilitary forces based in southern Lebanon crossed the border and captured two Israeli soldiers. Israel retaliated by invading Lebanon in an attempt to retrieve its soldiers; it inflicted massive damage, especially in the south, to infrastructure, with thousands of homes destroyed and hundreds of civilian casualties. The conflict lasted for 34 days. The Israeli soldiers were not recovered and the whole exercise was considered a failure on behalf of the Israeli Defence Force (IDF).
2007 Raleb Majadele (Labour) was the first Arab Muslim to hold office in Israel. The head of Israel's armed forces General Halutz resigned following an enquiry that criticised poor planning, strategy and execution of the 2006 invasion of Lebanon. A criminal inquiry into Ehud Olmert's role in the privatisation of Bank Leumi began. President Moshe Katsav resigned; Shimon Peres became president. Binjamin Netanyahu was re-elected leader of Likud.
2008 Ehud Olmert resigned as prime minister, due to a damaging corruption case. Tzipi Livni (Kadima) became acting prime minister but was unable to form a coalition government within a constitutionally set period. Israel launched an offensive into the Gaza Strip on 27 December, to deter on-going Hamas rocket attacks on its territories. Despite Israel's claims of targeting Hamas weapons

dumps, tunnels running between Gaza and Egypt and Hamas officials, casualties were highest among civilians. In August the government halted the immigration scheme which had allowed Ethiopians of Jewish descent to settle in Israel.
2009 An Israeli invasion of the Gaza Strip left over 1,000 Gaza Palestinians dead and 4,700 wounded, as well as 13 Israelis including two civilians killed by rocket attacks. UN and EU representatives called for a halt to the military action and humanitarian aid to be supplied to Gaza. Israel agreed to a daily aid convoy during a three-hour cease-fire. Israel declared a cease-fire and Hamas announcement it would stop launching missiles into Israel. Early general elections were held. Although Kadima won the most seats in the Knesset it could not form a coalition and became the official opposition. President Peres asked Benjamin Netanyahu (Likud) to form a coalition government, which finally included nationalist and ultra-orthodox Jewish political parties. The UN investigated alleged violations of international law during Israel's conflict in the Gaza Strip and concluded Israeli military action had 'involved varying degrees of negligence or recklessness' and accused the military of war crimes and possible crimes against humanity. Israel rejected the report as showing bias and claiming that Hamas had hidden fighters among civilians in the vicinity of UN properties. The government confirmed that construction of Jewish settlements in the West Bank would resume, even if peace talks with the Palestinians were renewed.
2010 The Organisation for Economic Co-operation and Development (OECD) voted unanimously to admit Israel as a member, despite strong opposition from the Palestinian government. Nine activists were killed by Israeli security forces when they stormed a ship in international waters, attempting to break the blockade of Gaza, resulting in US condemnation. Israel announced that it would ease the Gaza Strip blockade and allow more civilian items into the territory. Israel and Palestine agreed to resume peace talks after a two year gap. Talks began between Prime Minister Netanyahu and Palestinian President Mohmoud Abbas in Washington, hosted by President Obama and chaired by Secretary of State, Hillary Clinton. President Obama criticised plans to build a further 1,300 homes in East Jerusalem. The government approved a scheme that would allow a further 8,000 Ethiopians of the Falash Mura community and of Jewish descent to settle in Israel by 2013. Construction began of a barrier along the border with Egypt. The government estimated that up to 700 illegal immigrants cross into Israel from Egypt each week.
2011 In March, despite international disapproval and condemnation by Palestinian authorities, the government approved the construction of hundreds of Jewish settlers' homes in the occupied West Bank. The so-called 'Nakba' ('catastrophe') bill, which refuses funding to organisations that deny Israel's existence as a Jewish state, was passed in parliament by a majority of 37–25. The construction of a further 942 homes in the Jewish settlement of Gilo on the outskirts of Jerusalem was approved in April, just days before President Peres was due to meet President Obama in Washington. A group of 21 prominent Israelis signed an open letter in May calling on the international community to recognise a Palestinian state in Jerusalem, the West Bank and Gaza. In a speech in May, US President Obama said that any future settlement with Palestine must be based on 1967 borders, although 'with mutually agreed swaps, so that secure and recognised borders are established for both states.' Prime Minister Netanyahu rejected the proposal in a speech to the US Congress, saying that 'Israel will be generous on the size of a Palestinian state but will be very firm on where we put the border'. His office had earlier said that President Obama should refrain from demanding Israel withdraw to 'indefensible' 1967 borders. In July parliament passed, by 47 votes to 36, a law banning the boycotting of West Bank settlements. A legal challenge to the ban was announced by civil-rights groups that called it 'deeply undemocratic'. A prisoner swap deal between the government and Hamas involving the young Israeli soldier, Gilad Shalit, and 'hundreds' of Palestinian prisoners was agreed in the Knesset by 26–3 votes on 11 October. Sargeant Shalit had been held for five years.
2012 Benyamin Netanyahu was re-elected leader of the Likud party on 31 January. Prime Minster Netanyahu condemned the Palestinian deal announced on 7 February under which Hamas-Fatah formed a unity government, saying 'If President Abbas (Fatah) moves to implement what was signed today in Doha, he will abandon the path of peace and join forces with the enemies of peace. You can't have it both ways. It is either a pact with Hamas, or peace with Israel.' A Turkish court began the trial, *in absentia*, of four senior Israeli military commanders for the deaths of nine Turkish activists in 2010. Israel refused to co-operate with the prosecution, but if the military commanders are found guilty of the charges an international warrant of arrest could be issued. On 13 June, the State Comptroller criticised Prime Minister Netanyahu regarding the navy's interception of the Free-Gaza Flotilla, with supplies and aid, saying the decision taken by Netanyahu had 'serious shortcomings'. On 15 October parliament voted to hold early general elections on 22 January 2013; parliament was dissolved. Israel launched air and artillery weapons on Gaza on 13 November in retaliation of Hamas missiles launched at Israel since 4 November. On 17 November, the government mobilised up to 75,000 army reservists. Prime Minister Netanyahu said he was ready to expand the military operation. A ceasefire was agreed on 21 November.
2013 The UN Disengagement Observer Force (Undof), which monitors the only open border crossing between the Israeli-controlled Golan Heights and Syria, lost a number of international peacekeepers as the violence in Syria spread. Austria began withdrawing its 377 UN soldiers from the mission on 12 June, following the withdrawal of troops by Canada, Croatia and Japan. Troops from the Philippines and India remain. On 22 July Mr Netanyahu said he would put any future peace deal with the Palestinians to a referendum. After months of shuttle diplomacy by US secretary of state John Kerry, Israeli and Palestinian negotiators resumed stalled (since 2010) peace talks about talks in Washington. As part of the deal the Israeli cabinet approved (by 13 votes to seven) the release of some 104 long-term Palestinian prisoners. The prisoners will be released in four stages over a number of months and will be linked to progress in the talks. On 12 August the government announced the names of 26 Palestinians due to be released. In a speech to the UN General Assembly on 1 October Mr Netanyahu warned against treating with the Iranian government, describing President Rouhani of Iran as a 'wolf in sheep's clothing' and reiterating that Israel would not allow Iran to develop nuclear weapons. The second of four groups of Palestinians, 26 who had served 19-28 years in prison, was freed on 30 October. On the same day Israel announced approval for the construction of 1,500 housing units at Ramat Shlomo. On 30 October Israeli aircraft attacked a site near Latakia in Syria, destroying missiles intended for the Lebanese militant group Hezbollah. On 12 November plans for the construction of a further 20,000 houses on the West Bank were put on hold by Prime Minister Netanyahu just hours after they had been announced by the housing minister. Mr Netanyahu said they would create unnecessary friction with the international community at a time when peace talks with the Palestinians were at a delicate stage.

2014 On 10 June the Knesset elected Reuven Rivlin president by 63 votes to 53 in a runoff against Meir Sheetrit. Mr Rivlin was sworn in as President on 24 July. Israel sealed off the Al-Aqsa Mosque (Temple Mount) on 30 October, after an attack on a Jewish activist the previous day. Mahmoud Abbas said the closure was tantamount to a declaration of war.
2015 In the election held on 17 March Benjamin Netanyahu won a fourth term in office. Violence escalated in Jerusalem throughout the year with both Israelis and Paketinians being killed.

Political structure

Constitution

Israel passed the Law and Administration Ordinance on attaining independence, in 1948. In the Declaration of the Establishment of the State of Israel that embodied the principals of law, it was recognised that these principals would evolve in time and circumstances.
Basic laws set out the powers of the executive, legislative and judicial branches. The country functions without a written Constitution as Israel's founders wanted to avoid creating problems between religious and secular Jews and between Jews and the non-Jewish minority.

Independence date

14 May 1948

Form of state

Parliamentary democracy

The executive

Executive power rests with the government (a cabinet of ministers), headed by a prime minister as Head of government. The government may determine its own agenda and executive procedures.
The prime minister is directly elected for four years and cannot be deposed from office without fresh elections.
The prime minister chooses members of the cabinet from either inside or outside the Knesset (parliament). The cabinet is responsible to the Knesset.
The president is Head of State and has a largely ceremonial role; indirectly elected by the Knesset every seven years for a maximum of one term.

National legislature

The 120-seat unicameral Knesset is elected in a single nationwide constituency by proportional representation for a maximum of four years. The country is divided into six *mezoh* (administrative districts).

Legal system

The law is based on English common law, components of Jewish religious law and some features of other systems, as appropriate.
The judiciary has constitutionally guaranteed independence. The court system has three levels: the Supreme Court, district courts and magistrates' courts. The court system does not employ juries in Israel. There is also a separate system of limited and specific tribunals that deal with military, labour law and religious, civil matters.

Last elections

17 March 2015 (parliament); 10 June 2014 (presidential).

Results: Parliament (2015): Likud Yisrael Beiteinu won 23.4 per cent of the vote (30 seats out of 120), HaMahane HaZioni (Zionist Union) 18.7 per cent (24), HaReshima HaMeshutefet (Joint List) 10.6 per cent (13), Yesh Atid (There is a Future) 8.8 per cent (11), Kulanu (All of Us) 7.5 per cent (10), HaBayit HaYehudi (The Jewish Home) 6.7 per cent (eight), Shas 5.7 per cent (seven), Yisrael Beiteinu (Israel is our Home) 5.1 per cent (six), Yahadut HaTorah HaMeukhedet (United Torah Judaism) (UTJ) 5 per cent (six), Meretz 3.9 per cent (five); the remaining fifteen parties won less than three percent of the vote and failed to win any seats. Turnout was 72.3 per cent.
Presidential: (first round) Reuven Rivlin won 44 votes (out of 119), Meir Sheetrit 31, Dalia Itzik 28, Dalia Dorner 13 and Dan Shechtman 1. Second round: Rivlin won 63 votes and Meir Sheetrit 53.

Next elections

2021 (presidential); 2017 (Knesset)

Political parties

Ruling party

Coalition led by Likud Yisrael Beiteinu and including Hatnuah (The Movement) and others.

Main opposition party

Kadima (Forward)

Population

7.87 million (2013)*

Last census: November 1995: 5,548,523 (including residents of East Jerusalem and Israelis in Palestinian territories).

Population density: 302 inhabitants per square km. Urban population 92 per cent (2010 Unicef).

Annual growth rate: 2.5 per cent, 1990–2010 (Unicef).

Internally Displaced Persons (IDP)

150,000–300,000 (UNHCR 2004)

Ethnic make-up

European, Middle Eastern and North African Jews, Arabs and Druze.

Religions

The Jewish, Muslim, Catholic, Greek Orthodox, Druze, Protestant and Baha'i faiths are all represented. Non-Jews make up 18 per cent of the population. They include 635,000 Muslims, 105,000 Christians (almost all Arabs) and 78,000 Druze. The ultra-orthodox Jewish, or charedi, population has nearly doubled since 1990 to about 600,000, or 10 per cent of Israel's population.

Education

Education is provided free of charge and is organised by the state. Primary schooling lasts until aged 11.
Secondary schools are divided into four groups: state schools, which are attended by the majority, state religious schools, Arab and Druze schools and Torah schools for ultra-orthodox Jews. Youth Aliya schools specialise in educating new immigrants.
Demand for tertiary education consistently outstrips domestic supply, so that more Israelis study at universities abroad than at home, giving the country a ratio of graduates that is one of the highest in the world.
Public expenditure on education typically amounts to around 8 per cent of GDP.

Literacy rate: 95 per cent adult rate; 100 per cent youth rate (15–24) (Unesco 2005).

Compulsory years: Five to 16

Enrolment rate: 98 per cent total primary enrolment, of relevant age group (including repeaters); 88 per cent total secondary enrolment (World Bank).

Pupils per teacher: 14 in primary schools

Health

The ministry of health, the large municipalities, private, non-profit institutions and health insurance funds cater to different medical facilities. Companies are required to contribute to insurance for their employees to cover hospital treatment.
The Histadrut (General Federation of Labour) whose members include 90 per cent of Jewish workers, provide sickness benefits and medical care. About 95 per cent of the population are covered by a health insurance plan.
Smoking is prevalent among 45 per cent of men and 30 per cent of women causing health hazards. It is estimated that 99 per cent of the population have access to safe water and sanitation facilities are universal.

HIV/Aids

HIV prevalence: 0.1 per cent aged 15–49 in 2003 (World Bank)

Life expectancy: 80 years, 2004 (WHO 2006)

Fertility rate/Maternal mortality rate: 2.9 births per woman, 2010 (Unicef); maternal mortality 5 per 100,000 live births (World Bank).

Birth rate/Death rate: 6 death and 21 births per 1,000 people (World Bank)

Child (under 5 years) mortality rate (per 1,000): 4 per 1,000 live births (WHO 2012)

Head of population per physician: 3.82 physicians per 1,000 people, 2003 (WHO 2006)

Welfare

There is a state-sponsored social welfare system, the National Insurance Institute, which covers the entire population. It is largely financed by compulsory monthly fees collected under the National Insurance Law, with the government providing the remaining funds. The system provides pensions, general disability payments, work injury compensation, child support and other allowances. The Institute also reimburses employers for salaries paid to employees during annual military reserve duty. Citizens disabled during military service are entitled to additional benefits from the defence ministry.

Main cities

Jerusalem (*de facto* capital, estimated population 783,791 in 2012). *Although Israel regards the city as its capital, Palestinians regard a large part of it as their territory; the international community does not recognised it as Israel's capital.*
Tel Aviv (the diplomatic centre), estimated population 390,750 in 2012). Other cities include Haifa (269,502), Ashdod (255,708), Rishon LeZiyyon (250,296), Bersheva (203,787), Netanya (188,601).

Languages spoken

English and European languages are widely spoken. Arabic is the most common language among non-Jews.

Official language/s

Hebrew

Media

Press

The press has more freedom than in any of its neighbours and the government respects its media.
The mix of newspapers reflects the diversity of the population with Hebrew national dailies vying with Arabic, English and the Russian language newspapers for their readership, although non are exclusive and crossover readership is common.
Dailies: In Hebrew *Yediot Aharonot* (www.ynet.co.il), a tabloid has the largest circulation, *Haaretz* (www.haaretz.co.il), has a reputation for quality reporting, *Maariv* (www.nrg.co.il) is a popular tabloid. In English *The Jerusalem Post* (www.jpost.com), is a broadsheet and *Vesti* is a popular Russian language newspaper.
Weeklies: In Arabic *Kul al Arab* (www.kul-alarab.com) is a popular publication of news and current affairs.
Business: In Hebrew, *Globes* (www.globes.co.il), with an English online edition, is a weekly publication along with *The Marker* (www.themarker.com). An online site *Bull* (www.bull.co.il) covers news from the stock market.
Periodicals: In English and German, *Challenge* (www.challenge-mag.com), is a magazine concerning the Israeli-Palestinian conflict, published six times a year.

Broadcasting

The Israel Broadcasting Authority (IBA) (www.iba.org.il) is the national, public broadcaster, which is funded by licence fees, sponsorship and radio adverts.
Al Jazeera broadcasts were restricted in Israel in February 2009 following Qatar's decision to cut ties with Israel. Visas for al Jazeera correspondents were not renewed and access to news briefings were curtailed.
Radio: The IBA (www.iba.org.il) operates a network referred to as Kol Yisrael (Voice of Israel), of eight different stations, the four popular, domestic services include in Hebrew (Network A, B and C) broadcasting news, talk radio, music and (Network D) is an Arabic service. There is also a station for recent immigrants to Israel broadcasting in 13 languages, predominantly Russian. The other three are devoted to classical music, education and Jazz.
Independent radio stations include Arutz 7 (www.inn.co.il) a national network, all other stations are locally based including 90FM (www.90fm.co.il) in Jerusalem, Galgalatz (http://glz.msn.co.il) in Beersheva and Radio Haifa (http://1075.fm).
Television: The IBA (www.iba.org.il) has two channels, one broadcasting in Hebrew and the other in Arabic. There are other, pubic commercial stations including Channel 2, with weekly schedules operated by Keshet TV (www.keshet-tv.com) and Reshet TV (www.rashet.tv), Channel 10 (www.nana10.co.il) and Israel Plus (www.israel-plus.com) which broadcasts in Russian. There are several cable services and one local satellite service, Yes (www.yes.co.il). Other, international satellite services are available.
Other news agencies: Israel National News: www.israelnationalnews.com
Israel News Agency (INA): www.israelnewsagency.com
Israeli News Now: www.israelinewsnow.com
PR Newswire: www.prnewswire.co.il

Economy

Israel has a thriving modern economy, based on high technology and communication industries, which is orientated towards exports. The markets for its products lie outside the Middle East, mainly in North America, Western Europe and East Asia. The US is the principal market. As well as high technology equipment, the predominant exports are cut diamonds, agricultural produce and pharmaceuticals. Israel is reliant on imports for raw materials and oil. Grains also have to be imported, although Israel is otherwise self-sufficient in agricultural produce.
The IMF judged Israel's banking sector to have come through the global economic crisis relatively unscathed, due to its conservative establishment practices and supervisory regulations that saw much of the selling of asset-backed securities (ABS) in early 2008 before the critical peak of the crisis stuck later that year.
Despite falling into a brief recession as a result of the global economic crisis, between 2004 and 2013 Israel's average growth in GDP was 5 per cent a year. However, by 2014 growth had slowed down to 2.8 per cent.
Israel is a leading trader in raw diamonds with approximately half of all polished diamonds worldwide being processed in Israel. The industry accounted for US$4.07 billion in exports of polished diamonds in 2014, through the export of 5.2 billion carats; rough diamond exports amounted to US$3.9 billion (14.7 billion carats). However, the industries' contribution to GDP has reduced in recent years, from over 10 per cent in 2012 to 7.5 per cent in 2014.
Israel benefits from strong overseas investment, and pioneered the harnessing of investment by its diaspora through the issuing of 'Israel Bonds'. Net inflows of foreign direct investment in 2014 were US$6.7 billion.

External trade

Israel has bilateral free trade agreements with, among others, the EU, Turkey, the US, Canada and Mexico.
Exports provide over 36 per cent of GDP, of which 40 per cent are hi-tech industry output and pharmaceutical companies producing generic medicines whilst cut and dressed precious and semi-precious gems and pearls provide over 35 per cent. Israel has a free trade agreement with the US and is also a signatory of the Euro-Mediterranean Partnership agreement, which provides for the introduction of free trade between the EU and 10 Mediterranean countries.

Imports

Principal imports include raw materials, military equipment, investment goods, rough diamonds, fuels, grain and consumer goods.
Main sources: US (11.8 per cent of total in 2014), China (8.3 per cent), Switzerland (7.2 per cent)

Exports

Principal exports are machinery and equipment, software, cut and polished diamonds, agricultural products, chemicals, textiles and clothes.
Main destinations: US (26.9 per cent of total in 2014), Hong Kong (8.9 per cent), UK (5.8 per cent)

Agriculture

Farming

The agricultural sector contributes around 2 per cent to GDP and employs 2 per cent of the working population.

Israel is largely self-sufficient in food, importing some cereals, sugar beet and animal feeds. Food, beverages and tobacco are exported.

Farms are relatively small but mostly part of *kibbutzim* (larger co-operatives) or *moshavim* (co-operative smallholder villages), sharing machinery etc. The *kibbutz* and *moshav* movement formed the backbone of early Jewish settlement in Palestine before the State's creation in 1948.

The *Keren Kayemeth Le Yisrael* (Jewish National Fund) was created in 1901 to buy land for the settlers. Since 1948 it has become involved in land development, especially land reclamation and forestry.

Israel's agricultural miracle of the 1950s and early 1960s, with annual growth levels of around 12 per cent, was based on intensive irrigated farming, the rise in domestic demand from new immigrants and the expansion of export markets. From the late 1960s, growth slowed to stagnation by the 1980s. Many blamed the bureaucratic marketing organisations for stifling incentives and others blamed an over emphasis on heavily irrigated cash crops, such as cotton, which have become increasingly costly to produce and are vulnerable to international competition.

The major crops are fruits (30 per cent of total production), vegetables (14 per cent) and livestock (42 per cent).

About 40 per cent of farm produce is sold locally, 26 per cent to industry for processing and another 26 per cent is exported directly.

Of the total cultivated land area (4,400 square km), over half is under irrigation.

The general trend in agriculture is towards greater mechanisation and many agricultural workers have transferred to industry.

Fishing

There is some fish farming; approximately 85 per cent of the total catch of fish is consumed locally.

Forestry

Between 60,000–70,000 tonnes of timber are harvested annually.

Industry and manufacturing

Israeli governments have historically worked with trade unions and employers to plan economic policy. Key policy elements have been to build up basic industry with state or trade union funds and high-tech industries that are either state-owned (a spin-off from the important arms industry) or privately-owned, but which benefit from government incentives aimed specifically at attracting foreign technology. Industry has long been supported with protective tariffs and subsidies, but Israel is progressively exposing its domestic market to competition from abroad as a result of growing trade with the European Union (EU) and the US. Exports are vitally important to Israeli industry on account of the small size of the domestic market.

The strength of Israeli manufacturing industry is increasingly in high technology. Traditional industries such as food processing, textiles, metals, rubber and plastics and chemicals are well developed but the future manufacturing base is likely to be in heavy and hi-tech industries, particularly the defence industry. Government policy is to shift from low value labour intensive industries to high value high tech industries. These have become increasingly important as labour intensive industries such as the textile industry relocate to more competitive economies such as Jordan, Egypt and Turkey where labour costs are lower.

Tourism

Israel offers its visitors a range of religious centres of pilgrimage, as well as ancient, historic and cultural sites and coastal beach resorts. There are six sites on Unesco's World Heritage List, including prehistoric, Phoenician, Roman and modern sites.

Travel and tourism contributed a total of 7.3 per cent to GDP in 2014, which has remained fairly constant since 2001. Employment in the industry in 2014 was 7.8 per cent of the total workforce (275,000 jobs) and investment in the industry was 4.5 per cent of total capital investment.

The ability of the tourism industry to expand and grow will depend on the security and political situation in not only Israel but also the Middle East as a whole.

Mining

The mining sector typically contributes 1 per cent to GDP and employs 1 per cent of the workforce.

There are vast reserves of potash, bromine and periclase in the area of the Dead Sea, the world's most saline lake, and deposits of 600 million tonnes of phosphate rock in the Negev Desert. These evaporites are produced for fertilisers and industrial minerals. Phosphates are mined at Oron (around 1.2 million tonnes per annum); potash is extracted from the Dead Sea at Sodom (approximately 3.5 million tonnes per annum). Israel is the world's second-largest producer of bromine and produces 20 per cent of world output.

Hydrocarbons

Israel has no oil production of its own and for political and security reasons is reluctant to obtain its hydrocarbons from one single source, particularly one from the Middle East. Currently, Israel obtains most of its oil from Russia and central Asia – Turkmenistan and Kazakhstan. Other sources include Mexico, Egypt, Angola and the UK. It imports around 270,000 barrels per day (bpd) and it had 11.5 million barrels of oil reserves, located underneath gas reserves. There has been significant oil exploration onshore and in the Mediterranean (with the drilling of over 350 wells).

Israel has two oil refineries, at Haifa and Ashdod, with a joint capacity of 286,000bpd, which is sufficient for all of the countries' refined oil needs. If the Israeli-Palestinian conflict is resolved then Israel could provide an alternative route for Middle Eastern oil exports from the Gulf to the West. At present, oil exports travel by tanker through the Suez Canal or around South Africa.

Israel has an estimated 600 million tonnes of recoverable oil shale, producing around 9,000bpd. This reserve is located mainly in the Rotem basin region.

Proven natural gas reserves were 200 billion cubic metres (cum) in 2014, found in deposits off the Israeli coast and Gaza Strip coast. An agreement for the start of 1.7 billion cum of natural gas imports (over 20 years) from Egypt via the el Arish-Ashkelon pipeline began in 2008. In April 2012, Egyptian officials said they had scrapped an agreement with Israel to supply natural gas; the gas had amounted to around 40 per cent of Israel's electricity generating needs. The Israeli company Ampal that bought the natural gas called the termination of the contract 'unlawful and in bad faith'.

Imports of coal were 7.3 million tonnes oil equivalent (toe) in 2013, providing approximately 32 per cent of Israel's energy requirements. All coal imports come primarily from South Africa, Columbia, Australia and Indonesia.

Energy

Total installed generating capacity was 16.3 billion GW in 2014, with production at 64.4 billion kilowatt hours (kWh) and consumption at 59.8 billion kWh. Around 70 per cent of electricity comes from coal-fired power stations, 25 per cent from oil-fired stations and the remainder by gas-oil and independent power producers (IPPs). Approximately 97 per cent of fuel requirements are met from imports.

Israel's energy security is severely compromised by the lack of peace between Israel and its Arab population and neighbours. The energy infrastructure, including offshore exploration, onshore installations and proposed pipelines connecting Central Asia with Europe are vulnerable to continued attacks.

The Israel Electric Corporation (IEC) is responsible for generating and supplying energy. The government hopes to increase the participation of the private sector, with the aim of 10 per cent of electricity to be generated by IPPs. A programme of converting oil and coal-fired power stations to natural gas has begun. The delivery of Egyptian gas is subject to production problems and political opposition. Renewable energy supplies include primarily solar which is widely used for domestic hot water heating, although not in commercial generation of electricity.

Financial markets

Stock exchange

Tel Aviv Stock Exchange (TASE)

Banking and insurance

The government introduce structural reforms to the banking system in 2005 with the legislation to break the dominance of the largest banks over capital markets. It is intended to open up the banking sector to foreign competition. The top two banks, Hapoalim and Leumi, will be required to sell their mutual funds before 2009 and provident funds by 2008. Smaller institutions have longer to do the same.

Central bank

The Bank of Israel (BOI), Jerusalem. It has the sole right to issue currency, create and implement monetary policy, regulate and supervise commercial and other banks, control foreign exchange, maintain foreign currency reserves and publish the only representative exchange rate for the shekel versus foreign currencies.

Main financial centre

Tel Aviv

Time

GMT plus two hours (daylight saving GMT plus three hours)

Geography

Israel is at the eastern end of the Mediterranean Sea, with a coastline of about 270km from the Lebanese border in the north to the north-eastern tip of the Sinai Desert in the south. Israel has borders with Lebanon in the north, Syria in the north-east, Jordan in the east and south-east and Egypt is in the south west. There is a short coastline on the Gulf of Aqaba in the south

Within these internationally recognised borders there are disputed borders between Israel and State of Palestine. Gaza is a strip (around 40km wide) of coastline in the south-west and the West Bank is an area west of the Jordan River, containing Jerusalem and areas west and north of the city, the borders of which have been in dispute since the Six Day War in 1967.

The country can be divided into four regions, the coastal plain, the central highlands, the Jordan Rift Valley (which includes Lake Tiberias (also known as the Sea of Galilee in the bible and Lake Kinneret by Israelis) and the Negev Desert (an area including the Dead Sea, the lowest land point on the planet at 399 metres below sea level). The desert comprises over half the country's landmass and is an extension of the greater Sinai Desert.

Hemisphere

Northern

Climate

Two climates exist, Mediterranean in the north and an arid sub-tropical in the south. Jerusalem, situated in the central highlands, has summer temperatures in July–August of 19–29 degrees Celsius (C) and 6–14 degrees C in winter (December–January). Tel Aviv on the coast has a more humid climate with summer temperatures of 24–35 degrees C and 19–30 degrees C in winter. Eilat, on the Gulf of Aqaba, records the hottest average summer temperatures of 40 degrees C.

Dress codes

Business dress is fairly relaxed, except on formal occasions. In Jerusalem even in the height of summer a sweater is often necessary at night. Tel Aviv, along the coast, is far more humid and evenings are warmer.

It is recommended that business women should wear respectable clothing; bare arms, trousers and short skirts may cause offence to some community members.

Entry requirements

Passports

All travellers require passports with at least six months validity from the date of entry; proof of return/onward passage and sufficient funds for stay are also required.

The Israeli Ministry of the Interior insists that Israeli citizens holding dual nationality must enter and leave Israel on their Israeli passport.

NB When crossing into Israel from any border other than the West Bank, it is important to note that an Israeli stamp, or exit stamp from any of the neighbouring countries, will mean entry is barred to almost any other Arab country. It is possible to request that the passport should not be stamped and a separate form is stamped instead and attached to the passport; the form can be removed when exiting the country.

Visa

Israel has agreements with 65 countries for visa-free travel, including most citizens from Europe, the Americas, Australasia and some Asian countries. Transit passengers with onward passage within 24 hours do not require visas. Contact the nearest Israeli consulate for further information.

Prohibited entry

Persons carrying a Palestinian identity number will not be permitted to enter Israel through Ben Gurion International Airport if their last departure was through the Allenby Bridge or Rafah border crossings.

Currency advice/regulations

There are no restrictions on the import of local and foreign currencies but amounts to be exported should not exceed the amount imported.

Money should only be changed at authorised exchanged outlets.

Travellers cheques are widely accepted.

Customs

Video cameras and other electronic items must be declared on entry.

Prohibited imports

Fresh meat and fruit and vegetables from Africa.

Health (for visitors)

Mandatory precautions

There are no vaccinations required.

Advisable precautions

Inoculations and boosters should be current for tetanus and hepatitis A. There may be a need for vaccinations for typhoid, tuberculosis, diphtheria and hepatitis B. Rabies is a risk.

Mains water is normally safe to drink but readily available bottled water is advised for the first few weeks of a visit.

A supply of any regular medicines required should be carried, with their prescription details; medical insurance, which includes emergency evacuation, is recommended.

Hotels

There are plenty of hotels in business and tourist centres. Service charge of 15 per cent usually added to bill. Settlement of bills in foreign currency will avoid payment of local taxes. Many hotels quote prices in US dollars.

Credit cards

All major credit and charge cards are widely accepted. ATMs are widely available.

Public holidays (national)

Variable dates

Purim (Mar), First day of Passover (Apr), Last day of Passover (Apr), Independence Day (May), Shavuot (Pentecost) (Jun), Tisha B'Av (Aug), Rosh Hashanah (Jewish New Year) (Sep/Oct), Yom Kippur (Day of Atonement) (Oct), First day of Succoth (Feast of Tabernacles) (Oct), Last day of Sukkot (Oct), Shemini Atzeret (Celebration of Renewal and Thanksgiving) (Oct).

The Jewish calendar is based on the lunar and solar cycle. Each month begins with a new moon and runs for either 29 or 30 days; this results in years that are either

12 or 13 months long. The Jewish new year begins in March or April.
The Jewish religious day is Saturday – the *Sabbath* – which begins at nightfall on Friday until nightfall on Saturday. Most public services and shops close early on Friday.
Muslim and Christian holidays are also observed by their respective populations. Thus, depending on the district, the day of rest falls on Friday, Saturday or Sunday.
Jewish year – 5767 (23 Sep 2006–12 Sep 2007): the Jewish calendar is lunar and loses approximately 12 days per year against the Gregorian calendar, therefore every three years a leap or intercalary month is inserted to re-align the calenders.

Working hours

Banking
Sun–Fri: 0830–1200; Sun/Tue/Thu: 1600–1800.

Business
Sun—Thu: 0800–1730. On Fridays, some businesses stay open until 1230, but most close all day.

Government
Sun–Thu: 0730–1430 (Jun—Oct); 0730–1300, 1345–1600 (Nov–May). All government offices close on Friday afternoon and all day on Saturday.

Shops
Sun—Fri: 0800—1900; some shops close 1300—1600. Jewish shops observe closing time near sunset Friday evenings; Arabic stores are closed on Friday; Christian shops are closed on Sunday. Shops in hotels are often open until midnight.

Telecommunications

Mobile/cell phones
There are GSM 900/1800 roaming facilities available, with coverage throughout Israel and the West Bank.

Electricity supply

220V AC, 50 cycles. Most sockets are round and three-pronged so a European adaptor is necessary.

Weights and measures

Metric system, but area is usually measured in dunam (1,000 sq metres).

Social customs/useful tips

People are hospitable and informal and culturally diverse. Jewish traditions and customs are generally adhered to.
Israel is largely secular in character and Mediterranean in style. The Jewish *Sabbath*, from Friday dusk until Saturday dusk is, however, widely observed. Shops close on Friday and do not open again until Sunday morning. Most cinemas and restaurants are closed on Friday night. In most cities over the *Sabbath* there is no public transport (except for taxis), postal service, or banking service. Some religious sections in Jerusalem and the Tel Aviv suburb of Bnei Brak, as well as Tel Aviv's main street, Rehov Dizengoff, are closed to traffic. The same is true on six Jewish religious holidays.
Punctuality is not a strong point and business visitors should not be surprised to be kept waiting. Business meetings are less formal in character than in northern Europe but the normal courtesies are observed.
It is considered by many a violation of the *Sabbath* to smoke in public places such as restaurants and hotels.

Security

Security is tight owing to the threat of terrorist activity, and delays in the ongoing peace process have increased tensions. Business travellers often encounter delays because of security alerts. Prolonged questioning and detailed searches may take place at the time of entry and/or departure. Do not leave bags unattended.
In Jerusalem, tourists should exercise caution at religious sites on holy days. Visitors are advised to avoid demonstrations and areas where large crowds are gathering.
The theft of passports, credit cards and valuables from public beaches is commonplace. Visitors should carry passports at all times as a form of identity. Money and valuables should be kept out of sight.

Getting there

Air
National airline: El Al
El Al has an intensive security check and passengers are advised to arrive for flights in plenty of time.
International airport/s: Ben Gurion International (TLV), 20km south-east of Tel Aviv (50k west of Jerusalem); duty-free shop, ATMs, currency exchange, bar, restaurant, hotel reservations, post office, shops, car hire. A rail service to Tel Aviv operates between 0300–0000, journey time 15 minutes. Taxis and buses are available to Jerusalem and Tel Aviv.
Other airport/s: Eilat Central Airport (ETH)
Airport tax: None

Surface
Road: Tourists from Jordan can cross into Israel after obtaining a 'bridge pass' from the Jordanian Interior Ministry in Amman. It is also possible to cross the border at Eilat on the Red Sea coast. The road and bus route, via Cairo and Rafa (Gaza Strip), has been closed.
There is an exit tax of US$16 at all land border crossings.
Water: There are ferry services from Piraeus (Greece) and Larnaca (Cyprus) to Haifa.
Main port/s: Haifa, Ashdod and Eilat.

Getting about

National transport
Air: Arkia operate daily services from Tel Aviv to Jerusalem, Haifa, Eilat, and other major cities.
Road: Main roads are good. Maximum speed 90km per hour.
Buses: Buses connect all centres of population; they are frequent and cheap but can be crowded. Buses do not operate from sunset on Friday to sunset on Saturday.
Rail: Services between Tel Aviv and Haifa (hourly). Seats can be reserved. No service Friday evenings or Saturday.

City transport
Taxis: Taxis are metered but flat rates often apply so it is advisable to check before any long trips.
From Ben Gurion airport to Tel Aviv centre takes about 30 minutes.
Many offices close on Fridays and consequently traffic flows are better.
For inter-city travel (including Saturdays), *sherut* (share taxis) run between central points in main cities and are not expensive. Some *sherut* companies, including Arieh and Aviv, will accept advance bookings.

Car hire
International companies have offices in main cities and at Ben Gurion airport. Drivers must be over 21 years and have an international credit card and national or international licence. Seat belts are compulsory for drivers and front-seat passengers. Most road signs on major roads are in English.

BUSINESS DIRECTORY

The addresses listed below are a selection only. While World of Information makes every endeavour to check these addresses, we cannot guarantee that changes have not been made, especially to telephone numbers and area codes. We would welcome any corrections.

Telephone area codes

The international direct dialling (IDD) code for Israel is +972, followed by area code and subscriber's number:

Afula	4	Kfar Saba	9
Ashdod	8	Natanya	9
Ashkelon	8	Nazareth	4
Beersheva	8	Raanana	9
Briei Brak	3	Ramat Gan	3
Eilat	8	Rehovot	8
Haifa	4	Safed	4
Holon	3	Tel Aviv	3
Jerusalem	2		

Useful telephone numbers

International operator: 188
Directory enquiries: 144
Collect calls: 142
Overseas operator: 188
Ambulance: 101
Fire: 102

Police: 100
Correct time: 155

Chambers of Commerce

America-Israel Chamber of Commerce and Industry, 35 Shaul Hamelech Boulevard, PO Box 33174, Tel Aviv 61333 (tel: 695-2341; fax: 695-1272; email: amcham@amcham.co.il).

British-Israel Chamber of Commerce, 29 Hamered Street, PO Box 50321, Tel Aviv 61502 (tel: 510-9424; fax: 510-9540; email: isrbrit@bezeqint.net).

Federation of Israeli Chambers of Commerce, 84 Ha'ashmonaim Street, PO Box 20027, Tel Aviv 61200 (tel: 563-1020; fax: 561-9027; chamber@chamber.org.il).

Haifa and the North Chamber of Commerce and Industry, 53 Ha'atzmaut Road, PO Box 33176, Haifa 31331 (tel: 862-6364; fax: 864-5424; email: main@haifachamber.org.il).

Banking

Bank Hapoalim BM, 50 Rothschild Blvd, Tel Aviv 66883 (tel: 567-5777; fax: 567-6015; internet site: www.bankhapoalim.co.il).

Bank Leumi Le-Israel BM, 24-32 Yehuda Halevi St, Tel Aviv 65546 (tel: 514-8111; fax: 566-1872).

The First International Bank of Israel Ltd, Shalom Tower, 9 Ahad Haam St, Tel Aviv 65251 (tel: 519-6111; fax: 510-0316).

Investec Bank (Israel) Ltd; PO Box 677, 38 Rothschild Boulevard, Tel Aviv 61006 (tel: 564-5645; fax: 564-5210).

Israel Discount Bank Ltd, 27-31 Yehuda Halevi Street, Tel Aviv 65136 (tel: 514-5555; fax: 514-5346; internet site: www.discountbank.net).

Union Bank of Israel Ltd, 6-8 Ahuzat Bayit Street, Tel Aviv 65143 (tel: 519-1111; fax: 519-1421).

Central bank

Bank of Israel, PO Box 780, Kiryat Ben-Gurion, Jerusalem 91007 (tel: 655-2211; fax: 652-8805; e-mail: webmaster@bankisrael.gov.il).

Stock exchange

Tel Aviv Stock Exchange (TASE), www.tase.co.il

Travel information

Arkia Israeli Airlines Ltd, (Charter Airline), Sde Dov, PO Box 39301, Tel Aviv, 61392 (tel: 690-2222; fax: 699-1512).

Automobile and Touring Club of Israel (MEMSI), 20 Harakevet Street, PO Box 65144, Tel Aviv 65117 (tel: 564-1122; fax: 566-0493).

Bus Station, Levinsky and Levanda intersection, Nava Sha'anan, Tel Aviv.

Dan Co-operative Society for Public Transport Ltd. (City buses), 39 Shaul Hamelech Blvd., Tel Aviv, 64928 (tel: 693-3333; fax: 693-3511).

Egged Israel Transport Co-operative Ltd (Intercity buses), 142 Petach Tikvah Road, Tel Aviv, 64921 (tel: 692-2211; fax: 696-5354).

El Al Israel Airlines Ltd, Ben Gurion Airport, Lod, 71285 (tel: 971-6111; fax: 972-1442; internet site: www.elal.co.il).

Israel Airports Authority, Ben Gurion Airport, PO Box 137 70100 (tel: 975-5555; fax: 973-1650; www.iaa.gov.il).

Israel Ports and Railway Authority, 74 Derech Petach Tikva, POB 20121, Tel Aviv, 61201 (tel: 565-7000; fax: 512-1048).

Israel Railways, PO Box 18085, Tel Aviv, 61180 (tel: 542-1515; fax: 695-8176).

Ministry of tourism

Ministry of Tourism, 24 King George Street, PO Box 1018, Jerusalem 94262 (tel: 675-4811; fax: 625-3407; e-mail: doar@tourism.gov.il; internet site: www.travelnet.co.il).

Ministries

Prime Minister's Office, 3 Kaplan Street, PO Box 187, Kiryat Ben-Gurion, Jerusalem 91919 (tel: 670-5555; fax: 651-2631; email: markal@pmo.gov.il).

Ministry of Agriculture, Agricultural Centre, PO Box 50200, Bet-Dagan (tel: 948-5555; email: pniot@moag.gov.il).

Ministry of Communications, 23 Jaffa Street, Jerusalem 91999 (tel: 670-6320; fax: 670-6372; email: intmocil@moc.gov.il).

Ministry of Construction and Housing, Kiryat Hamemshala, PO Box 18110, Jerusalem 91180 (tel: 584-7211; fax: 581-1904).

Ministry of Defence, Kaplan Street, Hakirya, Tel-Aviv 61909 (tel: 569-2010; fax: 691-6940).

Ministry of Education, 34 Shivtei Israel Street, PO Box 292, Jerusalem 91911 (tel: 560-2222; fax: 560-2223; email: info@education.gov.il).

Ministry of the Environment, 5 Kanfei Nesharim Street, Givat Shaul, PO Box 34033, Jerusalem 95464 (tel: 655-3777; fax: 653-5934).

Ministry of Finance, 1 Kaplan Street, Kyriat Ben-Gurion, PO Box 13195, Jerusalem 91008 (tel: 531-7111; fax: 563-7891; email: webmaster@mof.gov.il).

Ministry of Foreign Affairs, Hakirya, Romema, Jerusalem 91950 (tel: 530-3111; fax: 530-33367; email: markal@mofa.gov.il; internet site: (Information) www.israel.org).

Ministry of Health, 2 Ben-Tabai Street, PO Box 1176, Jerusalem 91010 (tel: 670-5705; fax: 623-3026).

Ministry of Industry and Trade, 30 Agron Street, PO Box 299, Jerusalem 91002 (tel: 622-0220; fax: 624-5110).

Ministry of the Interior, 2 Kaplan Street, PO Box 6158, Kiryat Ben-Gurion, Jerusalem 91061 (tel: 670-1411; fax: 670-1628).

Ministry of Justice, 29 Salah A-din Street, Jerusalem 91010 (tel: 670-8511; fax: 628-8618; email: feedback@justice.gov.il).

Ministry of Labour and Social Welfare, 2 Kaplan Street, PO Box 915, Kiryat Ben-Gurion, Jerusalem 91008 (tel: 675-2311; fax: 675-2803).

Ministry of National Infrastructure, 216 Jaffa Street, Jerusalem 91130 (tel: 500-6777; fax: 500-6888).

Ministry of Public Security, Kiryat Hamemshala, PO Box 18182, Jerusalem 91181 (tel: 530-9999; fax: 584-7872).

Ministry of Religious Affairs, 236 Jaffa Street, PO Box 13059, Jerusalem 91130 (tel: 531-1171; fax: 531-1183; email: tsibor@religinfoserv.gov.il).

Ministry of Science, Culture and Sport, Kiryat Hamemshala Hamizrahit, POB 49100, Jerusalem 91181 (tel: 541-1111).

Ministry of Transport, 97 Jaffa Street, Jerusalem 91000 (tel: 622-8211; fax: 622-8693).

Office of the President, 3 Hanassi Street, Jerusalem 92188 (tel: 670-7211; fax: 561-0037).

The Knesset, Kiryat Ben-Gurion, Jerusalem 91950 (tel: 675-3333; fax: 652-1599).

Other useful addresses

Administration of Rabbinical Courts, 9 Koresh Street, Jerusalem 91012 (tel: 624-8603; fax: 624-5019).

British Embassy, 192 Hayarkon Street, Tel Aviv 63405 (tel: 524-9171; fax: 524-3313).

Central Bureau of Statistics, 3 Kaplan Street, PO Box 187, Kiryat Ben-Gurion, Jerusalem 91919 (tel: 655-3553; fax: 655-3325).

Israeli Academy of Sciences and Humanities, Albert Einstein Square, Talbieh, PO Box 4040, Jerusalem 91040 (tel: 563-6211).

Israel Airports Authority, Ben Gurion Airport (tel: 971-2804; fax: 971-2436). For information on taxes and tariffs (tel: 971-5596).

Israel Convention Bureau (ISCOB), Israel Tourism Administration, PO Box 1018, Jerusalem.

Israeli Broadcasting Authority, Klal Building, 97 Jaffa Street, PO Box 6387, Jerusalem 91063 (tel: 529-1888).

Israel Chemicals Ltd, 123 Hahashmonaim Street, Tel Aviv, 67133 (tel: 563-0232; fax: 561-5391).

Israel Electric Corporation Ltd, 2 Hahagana Boulevard, Haifa, 35254 (tel: 854-8548; fax: 853-8149).

Israel Fuel Corporation Ltd (Delek), Prof. Y. Kaufman Street, PO Box 50250, Tel Aviv, 61500 (tel: 591-5555; fax: 510-2072).

Israel Land Administration (part of the National Infrastructure Ministry), 6 Shamai Street, POB 2600, Jerusalem 94631 (tel: 520-8422; fax: 523-4960).

Israel Shipyards Ltd, Po Box 10630, Haifa Bay, 26118 (tel: 846-0245; fax: 841-0572).

Israel Telecommunication Corporation, PO Box 1088, Jerusalem, 91010 (tel: 539-5333; fax: 625-2506).

Israel Trade Fairs Centre/Israel Convention Centre, PO Box 21075, 61210 Tel Aviv (tel: 422-422).

Israeli Embassy (US), 3514 International Drive, NW, Washington DC 20008 (tel: (+1-202) 364-5500; fax: (+1-202) 364-5560; email: ask@israelemb.org).

Manufacturers' Association of Israel, Industry House, PO Box 50022, 29 Hamered Street, Tel Aviv (tel: 650-121).

National Coal Supply Corporation Ltd, 155 Bialik Street, Ramat Gan, 52523 (tel: 751-2261; fax: 751-0119).

National Insurance Institute, 13 Weizmann Blvd, Jerusalem 91909 (tel: 670-9211; fax: 670-9792).

National Water Company (Mekorot), 9 Lincoln Street, Tel Aviv, 67134 (tel: 623-0555; fax: 623-0833).

Oil Refineries Ltd, PO Box 4, Industrial Zone, Haifa, 31000 (tel: 878-8111; fax: 872-8319).

Ormat Industries Ltd, Po Box 68, Szydlowksi Road, New Industrial Area, Yavne, 70650 (tel: 433-777; fax: 439-901).

Pama Development for Energy and Sources, PO Box 20118, 14 Kalman Magen Street, Tel Aviv, 61200 (tel: 695-8129; fax: 695-8131).

Paz Oil Company Ltd, PO Box 434, 4 Hagefen Street, Haifa, 31003 (tel: 856-7111; fax: 852-2390).

Postal Authority, 237 Jaffa Street, Jerusalem 91999 (tel: 629-0800; fax: 629-0921).

State Comptroller, POB 1081, Jerusalem 91010 (tel: 531-5111).

Tahal Consulting Engineers Ltd (Water), PO Box 11170, 54 Ibn Gvirol Street, Tel Aviv, 61111 (tel: 692-4434; fax: 696-9969).

The Tel Aviv Stock Exchange (TASE), 54 Ahad Ha'am Street, Tel Aviv 65202; PO Box 29060, Tel Aviv 61290 (tel: 567-7411; fax: 510-5379; internet site: www.tase.co.il).

Zim Israel Navigation Co. Ltd, 7-9 Pal Yam Avenue, Haifa, 31000 (tel: 865-2111; fax: 865-2956).

Israel National News: www.israelnationalnews.com

Israel News Agency (INA): www.israelnewsagency.com

Israeli News Now: www.israelinewsnow.com

PR Newswire: www.prnewswire.co.il

Internet sites

Mercantile Discount Bank: www.mercantile.co.il

Yellow and White Pages: www.yellowpages.co.il

Italy

To become prime minister of Italy in the knowledge that your government is the sixty-third in the sixty-nine years of Italy's post Second World War history cannot inspire confidence.

Italian Prime Minister Matteo Renzi's already daunting problems were compounded in August 2015 when official Italian data suggested that the long-awaited economic recovery was already losing steam. The news agency Reuters summed up the situation by noting that 'not much had been going right for Renzi in 2015.' His approval ratings had fallen dramatically, his governing Partito Democratico (PD) (Democratic Party) was deeply divided, his parliamentary majority was fragile and his economic reforms were struggling to make an impact. Italy's sovereign debt had reached a staggering €2.16 trillion (US$2.43 trillion).

Whistlers in the wind?

Mr Renzi and the Italian economy minister, Pier Carlo Padoan, had been at pains to advise that they expected 'positive surprises' as the recovery got under way after

KEY FACTS

Official name: Repubblica Italiana (Italian Republic)

Head of State: President Sergio Mattarella (since 3 February 2015 following Giorgio Napolitano's resignation on 14 January 2015)

Head of government: Prime Minister Matteo Renzi (Partito Democratico (PD) (Democratic Party) (from 22 Feb 2014)

Ruling party: Coalition led by the Italia. Bene Comune (IBC) (Italy. Common Good) alliance (including the Partito Democratico (PD) (Democratic Party)), the Coalizione del Centrodestra (Centre-right Coalition) (including the Il Popolo della Libertà (the People of Freedom)) and Con Monti per l'Italia (CMI) (With Monti for Italy) (including Scelta Civica (Civic Choice)) (from Feb 2013).

Area: 301,277 square km

Population: 59.69 million (2014)

Capital: Rome

Official language: Italian

Currency: Euro (€) = 100 cents (from 1 Jan 2002; previous currency lira, locked at L1,936.27 per euro) (Campione d'Italia, an Italian enclave near Lake Lugano in Switzerland, uses the Swiss franc, although the euro also circulates)

Exchange rate: €0.89 per US$ (Sep 2015)

GDP per capita: US$35,823 (2014)

GDP real growth: -0.42% (2014)

GDP: US$2,147.95 billion (2014)

Labour force: 25.77 million (2014)*

Unemployment: 12.80% (2014)

Inflation: 0.22% (2014)

Oil production: 121,000 bpd (2014)

Natural gas production: 6.60 billion cum (2014)

Balance of trade: US$65.31 billion (2014)*

* estimated figure

three years of dreary recession. However, the latest data provides little by way of comfort. Growth was just 0.2 per cent between April and June 2015, according to the national statistics bureau ISTAT, well below analysts' expectations and down on the 0.3 per cent seen in the first quarter. Forlornly, Italy had posted virtually no growth since adopting the euro-zone as a founder member. This made Italy the most sluggish performer in the bloc, surprisingly even worse than Greece. Whistling in the wind, Italy's economy ministry said the data left Italy on track to reach the government's 0.7 per cent growth target for 2015. But even this, according to Reuters, would still be less than half the projected euro-zone average.

The perception worsened when the euro's weakness was taken into account. In theory, the currency's fall against the US dollar and other currencies should have boosted Italian exports. Low oil prices and rock-bottom interest rates should have had a similar effect. But Italy's feeble 'recovery', if it could be so described, would still not be enough to improve noticeably living standards or lower the country's unacceptably high levels of unemployment. Reuters also reported that Giorgio Squinzi, the president of the employers' lobby Confindustria, had dampened Italian spirits by commenting that the new data 'unfortunately confirmed that there is no real recovery.'

Things appeared to have worsened for Mr Renzi since the PD won a record 41 per cent at European elections in May 2014. The cornerstone reform agenda had run out of steam when faced with the Machiavellian intrigues of Italian politics. Mr Renzi's 'one reform every month' slogan rang hollow by mid-2015. Mr Renzi countered this perception by claiming that 'no one has ever done so many reforms in such a short period in the history of Italy.' The opinion polls certainly suggested that Mr Renzi's ambitious plans no longer convinced quite so many Italians. His approval ratings had fallen by around 35 percentage points over the previous 12 months.

The reform programme certainly seemed to be bogged down. There were few signs that in the labour market or in the education system things were improving. The changes in the ability of companies to hire and fire didn't seem to have gained much traction, despite the so called 'Jobs Act' – which granted some degree of financial protection to young workers while enabling employers the right to sack workers when times became hard. Unsurprisingly, there did not seem to be any significant change for the better in the unemployment statistics. On the contrary, mid-2015 data indicated a jobless rate of 12.7 per cent in June, up from 12.3 per cent at the start of the year when the reforms were introduced. The unemployment rate among job-seekers aged 25 or less reached a high of 44 per cent, which boded ill for the future.

Disaffected DP rebels claimed that Mr Renzi and his Palazzo Chigi (the prime minister's official residence) chums had moved the DP too far to the right; there were rumblings that the party's rebels would endeavour to thwart Renzi's plans to abolish the Senate as an elected chamber when parliament resumed in September 2015. The situation was complicated by the arithmetic – which suggested that without the full support of the DP, Renzi might no longer enjoy a majority in the Senate, where an estimated 176 of the 315 members had said they favoured maintaining a system of direct election. In mid-2015 the DP was still Italy's largest party, although its lead over the eccentrically charismatic Beppe Grillo's Movimento Cinque Stelle (M5S) (Five Star Movement) had shrunk to only 6 points.

By announcing sweeping changes and then failing to achieve them, Mr Renzi's ability to occupy the commanding heights of Italian politics looked a little uncertain. As already noted, by mid-2015 a nagging doubt continued to persist that perhaps Mr Renzi was another Prince Charming, clad in Emperor's clothes but lacking the strength and the substance needed to sort out his country's problems. Mr Renzi had never been a Rome 'insider'. In this respect he suffered from what US politicians once called the Carter conundrum – and latterly known as the Obama problem. Neither of these US Presidents was a Washington insider. Obama had cut his political teeth in the South Side of Chicago, Carter was more at home in rural Georgia. Mr Renzo's background was in Florence, 280km from Rome where, in a short period of time, he had risen to be mayor. Arriving in Rome, where he soon became Italy's youngest prime minister, he was not only confronted by substantial economic challenges, but also the reluctant inertia of a government machine that simply did not work, or even want to work. And Mr Renzi, by not bringing his family to Rome, appeared to distance himself from the capital and its politics.

An excellent article in the *New Yorker* by Jane Kramer entitled 'The Demolition Man' traced the influences and experience that had allowed Matteo Renzi to become prime minister. The title, 'Demolition Man' referred to the term 'Il Rottamatore' used by Renzi's political enemies. Ms Kramer quoted Mr Renzi as describing himself as 'the scrapper. I'm cleaning up the swamp.' And what a swamp.

Political reforms

In May 2015 the Italian parliament approved one of Mr Renzi's reforms that it had been hoped would turn out to be the most important of all. The objective had

KEY INDICATORS — Italy

	Unit	2011	2012	2013	2014	**2015
Population	m	*60.63	59.39	59.69	59.96	*60.24
Gross domestic product (GDP)	US$bn	2,198.70	2,014.38	2,137.62	2,147.95	*1,842.84
GDP per capita	US$	36,267	33,915	35,815	35,823	*30,594
GDP real growth	%	0.4	-2.4	-1.7	-0.4	*0.5
Inflation	%	2.9	3.3	1.3	0.2	*0.0
Unemployment	%	8.4	10.7	12.2	12.8	*12.6
Oil output	'000 bpd	110.0	112.0	116.0	121.0	–
Natural gas output	bn cum	7.7	7.8	7.1	6.6	–
Exports (fob) (goods)	US$m	502,978.0	478,932.0	501,687.0	513,716.0	–
Imports (fob) (goods)	US$m	523,076.0	453,531.0	453,594.0	448,402.0	–
Balance of trade	US$m	-20,098.0	25,402.0	48,092.0	65,314.0	–
Current account	US$m	-67,366.0	-7,717.0	20,545.0	*38,940.0	*48,409.0
Total reserves minus gold	US$m	48,968.0	50,499.0	50,775.0	47,689.0	–
Foreign exchange	US$m	34,334.0	34,816.0	35,516.0	–	–
Exchange rate	per US$	0.75	0.77	0.73	0.82	–

* estimated figure ** forecast figure

been for the Italian system to have greater political stability and the ability to act more decisively. Under a new set of rules, any political party that secures a minimum of 40 per cent of the vote will be granted 'bonus' seats enabling it to obtain a majority of 340 seats in the 630 seat parliament. In the event that no single party reaches the 40 per cent mark, then there would be a run-off between the two parties with the most votes to decide which had the greater level of support. This fundamental electoral change was due to take effect from July 2016, when the party that controlled the lower house (the effective legislative house) would assume control of the country. There was substantial resistance to the move – including opposition from within the DP. While giving Italians a more transparent system, the changes would provide less opportunity for the political machinations of coalition government. The resistance was for the most part cloaked in an objection to a perceived 'one party state'. Neutral observers attributed much of the resistance to Mr Renzi's largely common sense reforms either to a fear of the unknown or a realisation that accountability was to become the order of the day.

While endeavouring to steer his country towards a more transparent, accountable system of government – no mean challenge in a country where the terms 'government' and 'accountability' rarely featured on the same page. Mr Renzi also had to cope with often surreal cases of corruption and graft. In some cases these emanated from within his own PD. In one case relating to the apparent bankruptcy of a nursing home company, theatre seemed to overtake reality with the arrest of two nuns on money laundering charges. Much of the wave of corruption cases related to the capital city, Rome, where the Mafia appeared to have established an unshakable hold. This, despite the presence of a new mayor, Ignazio Marino, untainted by the mafia, but administratively ineffectual in dealing with strikes by garbage workers and other municipal workers. Dirty and disorganised, Rome was once more in decline. The city's administration was reportedly 'paralysed' by allegations of Mafia infiltration. Basic services, notably waste collection and treatment, were failing. Rome's main airport – Leonardo da Vinci Airport (at Fiumicino) – was partially closed, following a fire in early May. Two months later, 40 per cent of all flights were still being cancelled every day because of a dispute over the danger posed by contaminants unleashed by the flames. Magistrates had ordered the site sealed for weeks to measure the air quality.

Doubts

As already noted, doubts were circulating about the prime minister's ability to convert intentions into achievements. In her *New Yorker* article Ms Kramer wrote that 'Italians who admired Mr Renzi called him 'our best hope.' More sceptical Italians say, 'Well maybe our only hope.' He is not only confronted by substantial economic challenges – but also the reluctant inertia of a government machine that simply does not work, or even want to work. Just as his neighbour, Pope Francis, was taking on the Curia, so Matteo Renzi needed to start a root and branches reform of his civil service.

According to the London '*Economist*' a report prepared by the PD's president, one Matteo Orfini, advised that in 27 of the party's 110 branches, the principal concern was 'power for the sake of power.' The damning report on the party's activities in Rome raised questions about the party's activities elsewhere in Italy. In the end-May 2015 regional elections, Mr Renzi's PD won five out of seven regions; however, the party's share of the vote was estimated to have fallen by almost ten per cent. The regional elections may have showed the PD to be the front runner, but not far behind came Grillo's Five Star Movement.

The economy

To mis-quote Winston Churchill (who in this case was actually talking about Russia), Italy's economy is 'a riddle, wrapped in a mystery, inside an enigma'. Corruption in Italy is rife: in its 2014 *Corruption Perceptions Index*, the Berlin-based Transparency International ranked Italy 69 out of the 175 countries surveyed. This placed Italy embarrassingly alongside the European Union's two most corrupt countries, Bulgaria and Romania. Faced with what was a hugely daunting scenario, Prime Minister Renzi had come up with an ambitious series of proposed reforms, while conducting a tricky balancing act aimed at keeping the budget deficit below the three per cent mark. In its February 2015 Economic Survey, the Paris-based Organisation for Economic Co-operation and Development (OECD) reported that after a long period of stagnation that had left the economy vulnerable when the financial crisis hit, Italy was undertaking broad-based and ambitious reforms to boost growth, taking advantage of what the OECD described as 'synergies across policies' (a rather meaningless phrase which it failed to clarify or explain). Worryingly for Mr Renzi, The OECD noted that in the past, many good reform projects were not fully implemented, depriving the economy of their full benefits. In a statement of the obvious, the OECD considered that the Italian government was 'focusing on changes in the political and institutional frameworks and judicial system to remove previous impediments to full implementation of reforms.'

The OECD went on to say that the key challenges were to make the economy more productive, more competitive and more adaptable, thereby raising the living standards and well-being of all Italians. The immediate priority was to reform the labour market, where too much rigidity prevented job creation and the efficient matching of skills; according to the OECD, the Italian government intended to complete this task by mid-2015. The OECD noted that the government under Matteo Renzi intended to transfer the responsibility for active labour market policy from local governments to the central government, so as to increase effectiveness. There were also structural weaknesses in other areas, notably competition and regulation, which the Renzi government intends to tackle with broad-based reforms over the two years to 2017. These steps are needed to reverse previous declines in productivity and put the economy back on a path of steady growth. In the (possibly optimistic) view of the OECD, if fully implemented, they might well increase the level of gross domestic production (GDP) by 6 per cent within 10 years. A small fiscal surplus, combined with renewed growth, would bring down public debt. Meanwhile, sustained public expenditure restraint and tax increases have gone a long way to strengthen the fiscal position. Together with renewed growth and low interest rates, this would help to bring down the public debt burden.

In its July 2015 assessment of the Italian economy, the International Monetary Fund (IMF) expressed the view that Italy was emerging gradually from a prolonged recession. Financial market sentiment and confidence indicators had, at least in the view of the IMF, improved substantially since the end of 2014. Despite bouts of volatility, sovereign bond yields had fallen to pre-crisis levels, buoyed by the European Central Bank's quantitative easing (QE). Bank and corporate funding costs had also declined. Rising business and consumer confidence had stemmed the decline in domestic demand. Against this backdrop, the economy was expected to recover moderately, with GDP projected to expand by 0.7 per cent in 2015, supported by domestic demand and net exports. With the favourable tailwinds from QE continuing and investment gaining further momentum, growth was projected by the IMF to pick up to 1.2 per cent in 2016.

According to the IMF, the policies implemented at the European level, such as QE and greater flexibility in the Stability and Growth Pact, had been instrumental in supporting demand. At the national level, Prime Minister Matteo Renzi's government had set out an ambitious agenda to overhaul Italy's political and economic system. The Jobs Act (see above), an overhaul of Italy's labour market, was approved by parliament in December 2014 and, said the IMF, had been 'largely implemented'. A new law to convert Italy's largest co-operative banks into joint stock companies had spurred expectations of consolidation in the sector. Reforms of the product and services markets, public administration, education, judicial and tax system were also progressing.

In the view of the IMF, there was now a window of opportunity to push ahead with deeper reforms to re-ignite growth. This, said the IMF, required 'continued actions and strong implementation efforts on multiple fronts, which were mutually reinforcing.' A wide-ranging reform to raise the efficiency of public services was envisaged and would help tackle the long standing productivity problem. Product market reforms in sectors that remained highly regulated, such as transport, would also improve productivity.

However, in a subsequent report by different authors, the IMF noted that Italy's productivity had been stagnant since the late 1990s. Labour productivity, defined as GDP per hour worked, increased by a meagre 3.5 per cent, while Trade Facilitation Programmes (TFPs) had fallen by a cumulative 7.5 per cent since Italy adopted the euro in 1998. As a result, a wide gap had emerged between Italy's productivity and that of most major OECD economies. Addressing this productivity problem was essential to boost growth in Italy. A recovery in investment and employment creation would expand output in the near term as the economy emerged from its deep recession. However, productivity gains were necessary to lay the foundations for sustainable growth in the long run.

The IMF report's authors considered that identifying the key source of Italy's low productivity was difficult. Many hypotheses had been put forth in trying to explain Italy's lack of productivity growth – structural deficiencies related to the sectoral specialisation of Italian manufacturing and a business model which relied predominantly on micro and small firms and institutional factors, such as labour regulations, judicial inefficiency and the availability of key factors of production, such as human and entrepreneurship capital and managerial know-how. Other analysts had examined systematically the various possible explanations of Italy's productivity slowdown. Using industry level data across 23 sectors in 15 countries, they had concluded that the main cause of Italy's 'disease' was the inability of small firms to adjust to the global change of the 2000s, namely the rise of China and the information and communications technology (ICT) revolution, due to a lack of managerial talent. This weakness was in turn the outcome of a deeply-rooted system of 'familism' and cronyism.

The report questioned whether public sector inefficiency might be holding back firm productivity. Italy lagged behind other advanced economies on various measures of public sector efficiency. Among OECD economies, Italy achieved some of the lowest scores on direct efficiency measures as experienced by firms on the ground, such as the number of days and cost to get a construction permit, enforce a contract, obtain electricity supplies or pay taxes, according to the World Bank's *Doing Business* indicators. Perception based measures of efficiency, as compiled by the World Economic Forum's *Global Competitiveness Survey*, painted a similar picture, with Italy ranking amongst the worst on measures of government efficiency, wastefulness of government spending, diversion of public funds, etc. As government services were inputs into firms' production processes, their inefficient provision might lower the marginal productivity of labour and capital employed by the firm.

The report provided new evidence on the role of Italy's inefficient public sector in explaining its low levels of productivity. Exploiting the significant variation that existed in the efficiency of the government service provision across Italian provinces, the inter-industry differences in government dependence and detailed enterprise level data, the questions that needed to be addressed included whether public sector inefficiency resulted in lower private sector productivity. A further question was which types of firms were more affected by government inefficiency and what types of services mattered the most. Finally, what would be the macro-economic gains from raising the efficiency of the public sector?

Risk assessment

Economy	Poor
Politics	Poor
Regional stability	Fair/good

COUNTRY PROFILE

1796–1806 The French, under Emperor Napoléon Bonaparte, occupied Italy. The country was carved up and ruled by Napoléon, his relatives and Pope Pius VII.
1814–15 Following Napoléon's defeat by the Austrians, British, Prussians and Russians, Italy returned to its feudal status under the terms of the Congress of Vienna. Regions of northern Italy were also handed to Austria.
1848 A rise in nationalism and rebellion against Austrian rule began, known locally as the Risorgimento (Revival). A key figure in this process was Giuseppe Garibaldi.
1859–61 A partially unified Italy (Sardina, Piedmont, Genoa and Savoy) was created under the King of Sardina, Vittorio Emmanuelle II.
1870. Italian nationalists liberated Rome from French rule and proclaimed it the capital of a unified Italy under Vittorio Emmanuelle II.
1889–90 Italy established colonies in Africa (Somalia and Eritrea) through military conquests.
1901 Italy secured a territorial concession in the Chinese city of Tientsin.
1911–12 Italy gained Tripolitania and Cyrenaica (later Libya) and the Dodekanesa (Dodecanese) Islands from the Ottoman Empire.
1916–18 Italy eventually fought alongside the Allies in the First World War. Ensuing disorder and economic weakness fostered the rise of Benito Mussolini and the Partito Nazionale Fascista (PNF) (National Fascist Party).
1919 Italy gained Trentino-Südtirol (South Tyrol), the Istrian peninsula and Trieste, which had been parts of the Austro-Hungarian Empire, under the terms of the Treaty of Versailles. Italian nationalists later seized control of the former Austro-Hungarian city of Fiume (now Rijeka), in the face of Yugoslav claims.
1922 After Italian fascists marched on Rome, Mussolini and the PNF were invited to form a government by King Vittorio Emmanuele III.

1924–26 Mussolini increased his prime ministerial powers, effectively making his rule a dictatorship.
1929 Three Lateran Treaties granted Roman Catholicism special status in Italy. The Vatican City state, under the rule of the Pope, was created within Rome.
1935–36 Italy invaded Abyssinia (now Ethiopia).
1936 Italy supported General Franco's nationalists in the Spanish Civil War, until they won in 1939.
1940–42 Italy was part of the Axis powers, assisting Nazi Germany's military campaigns in Europe and Africa. It also invaded British Somaliland in East Africa in 1940.
1943 Allied forces invaded southern Italy and its African colonies. Mussolini was removed from government, imprisoned, and Pietro Badoglio was appointed prime minister. After escaping from prison, Mussolini declared the creation of the Repubblica Sociale Italiana (Social Republic of Italy) in German-controlled northern Italy.
1945 The fascist regime collapsed as the allies liberated the whole of Italy. Mussolini was executed by Italian partisans.
1946 In May, Vittorio Emmanuele III abdicated from the Italian throne and was temporarily replaced by Umberto II. After a referendum the Italian monarchy was abolished and a republic was declared. Enrico De Nicola was appointed as temporary head of state.

1948 De Nicola was elected the Republic's first president. The constitution, which established a parliament, was promulgated.
1949–82 A succession of short-lived coalitions followed, involving the Democrazia Cristiana (DC) (Christian Democrats) and up to four other major parties, frequently producing several regroupings and new cabinets in a year.
1978 Former prime minister and then president of the DC, Aldo Moro, was assassinated by the Red Brigades.
1983–87 Bettino Craxi, of the Partito Socialista Italiano (PSI) (Italian Socialist Party), headed what was then the longest-running post-war Italian government.
1989 The DC returned to government and Giulio Andreotti became prime minister for the third time.
1992–93 Italy had two prime ministers in two years, Giuliano Amato and Carlo Azeglio Ciampi. Both were forced to resign after political and corruption scandals.
1994 Silvio Berlusconi, of the Forza Italia (FI) (Go Italy!) – a party he largely created and funded, was elected prime minister for nine months. A transitional government was formed led by Lamberto Dina (independent).
1996 The centre-left Ulivo (Olive Tree) coalition won the parliamentary elections and Romano Prodi, was appointed prime minister.
1997 A constitutional reform commission, drawn from both houses of parliament, altered the Italian political system by introducing direct elections for the office of president.
1998 The Democratici di Sinistra's (DS) (Democrats of the Left) Massimo d'Alema succeeded Romano Prodi.
1999 The government fell and d'Alema resigned. He was reinstated by the newly-elected president, Carlo Ciampi.
2000 D'Alema resigned and was replaced by Giuliano Amato, heading a new centre-left 12-party coalition government.
2001 The Casa delle Libertà (House of Freedom) coalition won elections and Silvio Berlusconi became prime minister for a second time. Voters approved a referendum on constitutional changes to give more power to the regions.
2002 The euro currency replaced the lira. A controversial bill, allowing Berlusconi to retain control of his media empire, was passed in parliament.
2003 The Parmalat dairy food-manufacturing giant – one of Italy's blue-chip companies – was declared insolvent when a US$11 billion-plus accountancy fraud was discovered.
2004 The Constitutional Court threw out the immunity from prosecution law granting Mr Berlusconi and other top state post holders immunity from prosecution and Berlusconi's trial on corruption charges resumed; he was found not guilty.
2005 Romano Prodi became leader of the renamed centre-Left bloc, L'Unione (The Union), formerly Ulivo. Reform of the electoral system was passed: in future all parliamentary seats will determined by proportional representation and only parties winning a minimum of 2 per cent of the vote will be allocated seats
2006 Romano Prodi and the coalition L'Unione won national elections. Giorgio Napolitano was elected president by the Electoral College; he was the first former Communist to be elected president of Italy.
2007 Prodi resigned as prime minister, following a defeat in the senate on his foreign policy of enhancing NATO's deployment in Afghanistan. Prodi won a vote of confidence and was reinstated
2008 FI merged with Alleanza Nazionale (AN) (National Alliance) to form Il Popolo della Libertà (PdL) (The People of Freedom) and formed a three-party coalition with Partito Democratico (PD) (Democratic Party) and Lega Nord (LN) (Northern League) and won the national elections with a combined 46.81 per cent of the votes (340 seats out of 630). Silvio Berlusconi became prime minister for a second time. Italy apologised for damage inflicted during its occupation of Libya and agreed to invest US$5 billion as compensation. The state-owned Alitalia airline filed for bankruptcy.
2009 Prime Minister Berlusconi was stripped of his immunity from prosecution by the Constitutional Court, which rejected legislation that gave immunity to top government officials while they are in office, on the grounds that all Italians must be equal before the law and that the legislation had not been subject to greater scrutiny before being enacted.
2010 Futuro e Libertà (FLI) (Future and Freedom), a new political party, was formed by followers of its founder Gianfranco Fini, who broke away from Berlusconi's PdL-led coalition government.
2011 From January, thousands of migrants and refugees from Africa made the Mediterranean Sea crossing to reach the EU and landed on the Italian island of Lampedusa, overwhelming local resources and immigration procedures. Italy called on the EU for increased funds to deal with the influx. On 19 March, Italy joined in a five-country coalition (with Canada, France, the UK and the US) to impose a no-fly zone over Libya. On 4 April Italy became the third country (after France and Qatar) to recognise the Transitional National Council (TNC) as the legitimate government of Libya. Investors in the Italian economy were losing confidence in its viability as, on 15 July, the government's austerity budget, designed to cut the deficit by €47 billion (US$65.98 billion) by 2014, was adopted by parliament. However on 28 July, unforgiving bond markets forced the Italian treasury to pay more for sovereign bonds than previous rates. On 20 September, Standard & Poor's downgraded Italy's sovereign debt rating from A+ to A, and added an economic outlook for the country of 'negative', saying it feared for the government's ability to cut state spending and reduce the deficit. The government responded by saying the downgrade was 'politically motivated'. Moody's cut Italy's credit rating from Aa2 to A2, with a negative outlook. Italy's sovereign debt crisis came to a head on 10 November following weeks when the government failed to implement agreed austerity measures (on 15 July and 14 September) aimed at saving €124 billion (US$174.7 billion) in government spending. Italian government bonds were sold at an interest rate of 6.087 per cent (for one year) meaning the government will have to pay an extra €28 billion

(US$38.5 billion) to service the new debt. Prime Minister Berlusconi narrowly won a vote of confidence on 5 November but his support and position were critically undermined. Silvio Berlusconi resigned on 13 November and on 14 November the president appointed Mario Monti, a technocrat, as prime minister. Parliament approved public spending cuts amounting to €33 billion (US$43 billion) in December, as well as tax rises and measures to counter tax evasion.

2012 Employment reforms were introduced in January to promote a more meritocratic system and reduce youth unemployment. On 14 May, the ratings agency Moody's cut the credit ratings of two of Italy's largest lending banks, Unicredit and Intesa Sanpaolo, from A3 to A2. The ratings of 24 other Italian banks were also cut by up to four points. All the banks were put on negative credit watch, with further downgrading possible. An earthquake of magnitude six struck on 20 May, its epicentre was in the flat plains of the River Po, north of Bologna. The earthquake, and its aftershocks, killed seven people and injured 50 others and destroyed or badly damaged many historic buildings in the small towns around the area. On 26 October, former prime minister Berlusconi was found guilty of tax fraud and sentenced to four years in prison (later reduced to one year due to an amnesty law).

2013 the 24–25 February elections were won by The Italia. Bene Comune (IBC) (Italy. Common Good) alliance lead by the Partito Democratico (PD) (Democratic Party) 25.42 per cent (292 out of 630 seats) and including Sinistra Ecologia Libertà (Left Ecology Freedom) 3.2 per cent (37), Centro Democratico (Democratic Centre) 0.49 per cent (6) and Partito Popolare Sudtirolese (South Tyrolean People's Party) 0.43 per cent (5) won a total of 340 seats; followed by former president Berlusconi's Coalizione del Centrodestra (Centre-right Coalition) consisting of Il Popolo della Libertà (the People of Freedom) 21.56 per cent (97 seats), the Lega Nord (North League) 4.08 per cent (18), the Fratelli d'Italia (Brothers of Italy) 1.95 per cent (9) with a total of 124 seats; third was Giuseppe Piero 'Beppe' Grillo's Movimento Cinque Stelle (Five Star Movement) with 25.55 per cent (108). The only other coalition to win seats was the Con Monti per l'Italia (CMI) (With Monti for Italy) lead by Scelta Civica (Civic Choice) 8.3 per cent (37) and Unione di Centro (Union of the Centre) 1.78 per vent (8) with a total of 45 seats. Eventually a ruling coalition of the centre-left (Italia. Bene Comune), centre (Con Monti per l'Italia) and centre-right (Centre-right Coalition) was formed. Although asked to form a coalition with the IBC, Beppe Grillo had refused. Senate results were IBC 31.63 per cent (113 seats out of 315) (lead by PD 29.32 per cent (105 seats)), CC 30.71 per cent (116) (lead by IPL 22.3 per cent (98), M5S 23.79 per cent (54), CMI 9.13 per cent (18). Presidential elections on 18–20 April were won by Giorgio Napolitano (738 out of 1007) after he was persuaded to run again. On 1 August Berlusconi lost his appeal to the highest court; in an angry broadcast he said he was the innocent victim of 'an incredible series of accusations and trials that had nothing to do with reality'. The 76-year old is likely to serve some form of house arrest and community service. A move by supporters of Mr Berlusconi to block his disqualification from parliament (after his conviction for fraud) failed on 19 September. Mr Berlusconi withdrew his five ministers on 28 September and the government collapsed. President Napolitano was said to be trying to form another coalition rather than call elections. However, on 29 September Prime Minister Letta called a confidence vote for 2 October, which he won after Mr Berlusconi was forced to back down when several of his ministers said they would support the government. the vote was 235 to 70 in favour of the government. On 3 October a boat laden with migrants from Africa sank off the coast of Lampadusa. Over 300 people are thought to have drowned. On 4 October a cross-party panel of the Senate recommended the expulsion of Mr Berlusconi from the chamber over his conviction for tax fraud. The Italian airline Alitalia was rescued from bankruptcy after the airline's board agreed to a US$678 million rescue package. The Four of the planned 78 mobile flood barriers designed to protect Venice from flooding were successfully tested on 12 October. Construction of the barriers started 10 years ago and have so far cost some US$7 billion. Completion is scheduled for 2016, although this will depend on financing arrangements. On 14 October defence minister Mario Mauro said Italy would triple its presence in the southern Mediterranean. The refugees would be rescued rather than told 'to stay where they are' said Emma Bonino, Italy's foreign minister. On 19 September A court in Milan banned Berlusconi from holding public office for two years, following his conviction for tax fraud; the ban must be approved by parliament before taking effect. On 26 October at a leaders' meeting of the PdL, Mr Berlusconi relaunched Forza Italia after a vote to suspend the PdL. There were a number of notable absentees, including Deputy Prime Minister Angelino Alfano, suggesting party divisions.

2014 Matteo Renzi (Partito Democratico (PD) (Democratic Party) became prime minister on 22 February.

2015 Parliament elected constitutional court judge Sergio Mattarella as president on 13 January, after Giorgio Napolitano, stood down early (his term would not have ended until 2020) on 30 January citing 'signs of fatigue'. On 10 March the Court of Cassation rejected prosecutors' appeals to overturn the acquittal of Silvio Berlusconi in 2014 on charges of abuse of office and paying for sex with an underage prostitute (the so-called 'bunga-bunga' trial) and hold a fresh trial; Mr Berlusconi had been found guilty in 2013.

Political structure

Constitution

Under the terms of the 1948 Constitution, Italy's legislative power is held by a bicameral parliament.

Italy is divided into 20 regions which enjoy a large degree of autonomy. Each region has a regional council elected every five years by universal suffrage.

In 2001, the Constitution was amended by the federalist reform bill which increased the decision-making power of the regions.

In 2005 proportional representation was introduced to elect both houses of parliament.

On May 4 2015, the Italian parliament approved a constitutional reform which will lead to a two-party or even a one-party political system. The new rules will give a party that wins 40 per cent of the vote bonus seats to create a majority of 340 in the 630-seat Chamber of Deputies. If no group can reach the threshold, a run-off will be held between the two biggest parties to decide which gets the absolute majority. The electoral change will take effect in July 2016, it is one of a series of reforms planned by Prime Minister Renzi to weaken the power of the Senate.

Form of state

Parliamentary democratic republic

The executive

Executive power is held by the prime minister, who is usually the leader of the largest party in the lower house of the parliament, and by a cabinet of ministers chosen by him.

The president, who must be more than 50 years old, holds a seven-year term of office and is elected by an electoral college consisting of both chambers of parliament and regional representatives. From the presidential term due to start in 2006, presidents will be directly elected. The president nominates a number of Supreme Court judges and has the power to dissolve parliament but has no other executive powers.

National legislature
Parliament consists of the *Camera dei Deputati* (Chamber of Deputies) and the Senato della Repubblica (Senate of the Republic). The chamber of deputies is comprised of 630 members, of which 629 are directly elected in single- and multi-seat constituencies by proportional representation vote. One member from Valle d'Aosta is elected by simple majority vote. The senate has 322 seats of which 315 members are directly elected in single- and multi-seat constituencies by proportional representation vote. Seven ex-officio members are appointed by the president of the Republic to serve for life. Members of both houses are elected for five-year terms.

Legal system
The legal system is based on the constitution of 1948.
The Constitutional Court, set up in 1955, is the final arbiter of the constitutionality of laws and decrees. It defines the powers of the state and regions and passes judgements in disputes between them. It can also try the president and government ministers. The court consists of 15 judges. Five are appointed by the president, five by parliament and the remainder by the highest law and administrative courts.
The highest court of cassation is divided into 23 appeal court districts, with three other sections. These are then further divided into 159 tribunal districts which, together, are divided into 899 magistracies. There are 90 first degree assize courts and 26 assize courts of appeal.

Last elections
24-25 February 2013 (parliamentary); 29-31 January 2015 (presidential).
Results: Presidential: Sergio Mattarella, elected president by the Electoral College, with 665 votes (out of 1009), Ferdinando Imposimato won 127 votes, Vittorio Feltri won 46 votes and Stefano Rodota won 17; the remaining candidates each won two or less votes.
Parliamentary (Chamber of Deputies): The Italia. Bene Comune (IBC) (Italy. Common Good) alliance lead by the Partito Democratico (PD) (Democratic Party) 25.42 per cent (292 out of 630 seats) and including Sinistra Ecologia Libertà (Left Ecology Freedom) 3.2 per cent (37), Centro Democratico (Democratic Centre) 0.49 per cent (6) and Partito Popolare Sudtirolese (South Tyrolean People's Party) 0.43 per cent (5) won a total of 340 seats; followed by former president Berlusconi's Coalizione del Centrodestra (CC) (Centre-right Coalition) consisting of Il Popolo della Libertà (IPL) (the People of Freedom) 21.56 per cent (97 seats), the Lega Nord (North League) 4.08 per cent (18), the Fratelli d'Italia (Brothers of Italy) 1.95 per cent (9) with a total of 124 seats; third was Giuseppe Piero 'Beppe' Grillo's MoVimento 5 Stelle M5S) (Five Star Movement) with 25.55 per cent (108). The only other coalition to win seats was the Con Monti per l'Italia (CMI) (With Monti for Italy) lead by Scelta Civica (Civic Choice) 8.3 per cent (37) and Unione di Centro (Union of the Centre) 1.78 per vent (8) with a total of 45 seats. Eventually a ruling coalition of the centre-left (Italia. Bene Comune), centre (Con Monti per l'Italia) and centre-right (Centre-right Coalition) was formed. Turnout was 75.19 per cent.
Senate: IBC 31.63 per cent (113 seats out of 315) (lead by PD 29.32 per cent (105 seats)); CC 30.71 per cent (116) (lead by IPL 22.3 per cent (98)); M5S 23.79 per cent (54); CMI 9.13 per cent (18). Turnout was 75.11 per cent.

Next elections
No later than 23 May 2018 (parliamentary); 2020 (presidential).

Political parties

Ruling party
Coalition led by the Italia. Bene Comune (IBC) (Italy. Common Good) alliance (including the Partito Democratico (PD) (Democratic Party)), the Coalizione del Centrodestra (Centre-right Coalition) (including the Il Popolo della Libertà (the People of Freedom)) and Con Monti per l'Italia (CMI) (With Monti for Italy) (including Scelta Civica (Civic Choice)) (from Feb 2013).

Main opposition party
Opposition in the chamber of deputies and the senate – coalition led by Partito Democratico (PD) (Democratic Party) with Italia dei Valori (IdV) (Italy of Values)
Between 2002–2015, the sections of the population aged between 0–14 and 15–64 are expected to contract by an annual 0.9 and 0.4 per cent respectively. Meanwhile, the population aged over 65 is projected to grow by an annual 1 per cent. At current demographic trends the population aged 65 and above will constitute 21.1 per cent of the total population by 2015.
Approximately 44.4 per cent of the population are resident in northern Italy, 19.2 per cent in central Italy and 36.4 per cent in southern Italy.

Population

59.69 million (2014)
Last census: October 2001: 57,110,144
Population density: 196 inhabitants per square km. Urban population 68 per cent (2010 Unicef).
Annual growth rate: 0.3 per cent, 1990–2010 (Unicef).

Ethnic make-up
Centuries of colonisation have meant that Italy has many ethnic heritages and groups, including Arberesh (Albanian) (around 100,000, mainly in southern Italy), French (around 100,000, mainly in Valle d'Aosta), German (around 290,000, mainly in Trentino-Alto Adige), Friulian (around 600,000, mainly in Friuli-Venezia Giulia), and Greek (around 4,000, mainly in Calabria). The country has been a destination for immigrants from all over the world. There are an estimated one million foreigners residing in Italy.

Religions
97.5 per cent Roman Catholic.

Education

Schooling is free of charge and compulsory from age six. Primary schooling lasts until age 11 years, and lower secondary schools from age 11 to 14 years. Only the first year of upper secondary schooling is compulsory.
Higher secondary schools, from age 14, provide five-year courses in the arts, sciences and teacher training. Specialised secondary schools run four-year courses, and vocational and professional training programmes lasting for three and five years, respectively.
Graduation from higher secondary school automatically gives a student a place at university. Besides universities, a wide range of professional training establishments also provide higher education.
Most of the existing universities were directly established by the state, although some private institutions are recognised. There are 51 state universities and three technical universities.
Public expenditure on education typically amounts to 4.9 per cent of annual gross national income.
Literacy rate: 98.5 per cent total; 98.2 per cent female, adult rates (World Bank).
Compulsory years: Six to 15
Enrolment rate: 101 gross primary enrolment of relevant age group (including repeaters); 95 per cent gross secondary enrolment (World Bank).
Pupils per teacher: 11 in primary schools

Health

The healthcare system is regionally based, providing universal coverage free of charge at the point of service. There are deep regional inequalities in healthcare expenditure and in supply and utilisation of healthcare services.
Healthcare is financed through general taxation collected centrally, various other regional taxes and users' payments, which replaced the previous system of social health insurance contributions. The National Solidarity Fund was developed to transfer funds to the regions unable to raise sufficient resources. The Fund was authorised to spend 10 per cent of the overall regional funding.

HIV/Aids

HIV prevalence: 0.5 per cent aged 15–49 in 2003 (World Bank)

Life expectancy: 81 years, 2004 (WHO 2006)

Fertility rate/Maternal mortality rate: 1.4 births per woman, 2010 (Unicef); maternal mortality 11 per 100,000 live births (World Bank).

Birth rate/Death rate: 10 deaths to nine births per 1,000 people (World Bank)

Child (under 5 years) mortality rate (per 1,000): 4 per 1,000 live births (WHO 2012)

Head of population per physician: 4.2 physicians per 1,000 people, 2004 (WHO 2006)

Welfare

Italy has a fully comprehensive social security system with benefits covering unemployment, retirement pensions, disability, family allowances and health services.

The social security system is financed by contributions made by the state, employers and employees, and forms part of the government's overall budget.

The pension system is contribution-based calculated on the basis of the social security contributions paid over the course of working life. The system assures equal benefits for both public and private sector employees. There is increasing government expenditure on old-age pensions and survivorship annuities due to its ageing population.

There have been promising developments in the regulation of family allowances and income maintenance programmes. The Family Allowance fund, replaced by the Family Unit Allowance, differentiates the allowance in relation to the number of members of the family and the make-up of the family unit's income.

Pensions

The long-awaited pension reform bill was passed in July 2004. Italy was spending 14 per cent of GDP on pensions and the bill is expected to save 0.7 per cent of GDP annually from 2013–30.

The requirements for employees will be that they must pay 40 years of contributions into the fund before receiving benefits at aged 57, or retire later at aged 60 with a minimum 35 years contributions. This reform will be implemented by 2008.

Main cities

Rome (capital, estimated population 2.4 million in 2012), Milan (1.3 million), Naples (937,501), Turin (854,299), Palermo (633,182), Genoa (575,087), Florence (380,802), Bologna (371,088), Bari (301,521), Venice (261,532).

Languages spoken

German is spoken in South Tyrol on the Austrian border. Slovene is spoken by a minority in Trieste. French is spoken in the Val d'Aosta, bordering France and Switzerland. Albanian is spoken in some areas of Basilicata, Calabria and Sicily. An increasing number of business people also speak English, replacing French as the second commercial language.

Official language/s

Italian

Media

Press

There are approximately 125 newspapers, which reach 42.5 per cent of the adult population, and an estimated 10,000 magazines.

Italy's press is highly regionalised and controlled directly or indirectly by either major media groups, political parties or corporate entities. The Agnelli family (which owns Fiat) controls the Turin-based *La Stampa*, Milan's *Corriere della Sera* and the sports daily *Gazzetta dello Sport*; the multinational, Ferruzzi group owns *Il Messagero in Rome* and *Italia Oggi*; Fininvest controls the Milan-based *Il Giornale*; Carlo de Benedetti, chairman of Gruppo Editoriale L'Espresso, owns *La Repubblica* and over 12 regional newspapers.

Dailies: There are around 150 dailies newspapers, of which 20 are distributed nationally. In Italian, those with the highest circulations include, *Il Corriere della Sera* (*Evening Courier*) (www.corriere.it), *La Repubblica* (www.repubblica.it), *La Stampa* (*The Press*) (www.lastampa.it) and *Il Messaggero* (www.ilmessaggero.it). All regions produce their own dailies including *Barisera* (www.barisera.it) in Puglia, *L'Arena* (www.larena.it) in Verona, *Gazzetta del Sud* (www.gazzettadelsud.it) in Sicily and *In Umbria* (www.inumbria.it) in Perugia. Free issue newspapers have become popular and many centres have their own editions within a national format (www.epolis.sm). Italy does not have tabloid newspapers but the sports newspaper *La Gazzetta dello Sport* (www.gazzetta.it) has one of the largest circulations.

Weeklies: There are over 50 weekly magazines, with an average of 15 million copies produced. In Italian, general interest weeklies and special interest magazines include *Gente* (*People*), *Panorama*, *Famiglia Cristiana* (www.sanpaolo.org/fc), for Roman Catholic views and *Oggi* (*Today*), *Panorama* (http://www.panorama.it) and *L'Espresso* (http://espresso.repubblica.it) for news and current affairs.

Business: In Italian, there are several newspapers from Milan, including the respected *Milano Finanza* (www.milanofinanza.it), *Il Sole 24 Ore* (www.ilsole24ore.com), *24 Minuti* (www.24minuti.ilsole24ore.com) and *Affari Italiani* (www.affaritaliani.it), which also offers tabloid news and from Naples *Il Denaro* (www.denaro.it) and in German *Sudtiroler Wirtschaftszeitung* (www.swz.it) from South Tyrol. In Italian, weekly magazines include *Il Mondo* (www.ilmondo.rcs.it) concerned with the economy, business and politics and a supplement of *La Repubblica* (www.repubblica.it), *Affari & Finanza*.

Periodicals: There are around 100 monthly magazines published catering for all genres. In recent years 'gossip' magazines such as, in Italian, *Gossip News* (www.gossipnews.it) and *Kiss Me* (www.kissme.it), have grown in popularity. Mondodori Media (www.mondadori.it) publishes a range of general periodicals on life-style, consumer, cuisine, entertainment and commercial interests including *Grazia*, and *Cucina*, other publications include *Donna Moderna* (www.donnamoderna.com).

Broadcasting

The national public broadcaster is Rai (Radiotelevisione Italiana) (www.rai.it).

Radio: There are numerous radio stations, of which over a dozen form national networks. Rai (www.rai.it) has three stations which offer entertainment, culture and news from parliament. National commercial stations include 105 Classic (www.105classics.net), CNR (www.radiocnr.it), a news network, Radio Cuore (www.radiocuore.it) and Radio Italia (www.radioitalia.it) is a community radio station.

Television: Rai (www.rai.it) has three channels (Rai Uno, Due, Tre) and has a market share of around 50 per cent, with funding derived from public funding (through TV licences, general taxes and donations) and advertising, providing locally produced and imported programmes. The main competitors are Mediaset (www.mediaset.it), owned by Silvio Belusconi, the biggest national, commercial network with three channels and La7 (www.la7.it).

Analogue transmissions are due to end in 2010, in favour of digital terrestrial transmission. There are many cable TV and Satellite, pay-to-view broadcasting is almost entirely provided by US-based Sky; , ing locally produced and imported programmes.

National news agency: ANSA (Agenzia Nazionale Stampa Associata)

Other news agencies: AGI (Agenzia Giornalistica Italia) (in Italian): www.agenziaitalia.it

Economy

According to the International Monetary Fund (IMF) and the World Bank, Italy, with a gross domestic product (GDP) of over US$2.1 trillion in 2014, was ranked eighth in the world and fourth in Europe (but down from seventh in 2008). Italy is a leading industrialised country with an economy that is driven by the manufacture of high-quality goods. Export of these goods is crucial to the health of the economy, accounting for approximately 29.4 per cent of GDP in 2014, so that Italy's fortunes have been hard hit by the worldwide recession that cut exports as demand fell in all sectors. From 2009, exports have been particularly hard hit, with the loss of billions of euros to the economy. In 2014, the services sector constituted an estimated 73.9 per cent of GDP, with industry accounting for 23.9 per cent and agriculture 2.2 per cent. Italy's largest companies include businesses in energy, banking and insurance, utilities, telecommunications, aerospace and defence and manufactured consumer durables.

The Italian government was the first of the G8 countries to instigate a stimulus package, of US$102 billion when it went into recession in 2008, which included public works, mortgage relief and tax cuts for poorer families, which in turn left it with the world's third-largest debt burden – 106.1 per cent of GDP in 2008 and reaching an estimated 132.1 per cent in 2014. Italy's recession deepened to -5.5 per cent in 2009 as the global economic crisis worsened. As world trade picked up, GDP growth returned to a positive 1.7 per cent in 2010. However, since 2011 growth has been negative, shrinking by 2.8 per cent in 2012 and 0.4 per cent in 2014. Inflation did not spiral out of control as a result of the recession, and following a peak of 3.0 per cent in 2012, inflation had dropped to 0.2 per cent in 2014.

Mezzogiorno, in the south, has much lower per capita income levels and higher unemployment rates than the more industrialised north, despite many years of heavy government subsidies; this severe regional imbalance in Italy's labour market causes on-going problems for the economy. Unemployment has been rising since 2009, peaking at 13.2 per cent towards the end of 2014 before dropping to 12.4 per cent by the second quarter of 2015. Remittances in 2013 were US$2.7 billion and were estimated to have dropped to US$2.5 billion in 2014.

The services sector, particularly tourism, is important to overall economic performance; in 2008 tourist numbers fell by 25 per cent as the economic situation in home countries limited discretionary spending, plus the euro remained relatively strong against other currencies, so making holidays costlier. In 2010 the industry began to revive as tourists returned reaching 43.6 million arrivals, and by 2014 this had grown to 47.7 million.

An austerity budget was passed on in 2011, including cuts to public spending of US$67 billion. The measure was planned to reduce the national deficit, which had grown to 115 per cent of GDP in 2010. In September 2011, Standard & Poor's downgraded Italy's sovereign debt rating from A+ to A, and added an economic outlook for the country of 'negative', saying it feared for the government's ability to cut state spending and reduce the deficit. The government responded by saying the downgrade was 'politically motivated'. Italy's sovereign debt crisis came to a head in the following weeks when the government failed to implement agreed austerity measures (due on 15 July and 14 September) aimed at saving EUR124 billion (US$174.7 billion) in government spending. Italian government bonds were sold at an interest rate of 6.087 per cent (for one year). Financial markets were worried at Italy's public debt, of EUR1.9 trillion (US$2.6 trillion), for which EUR173.3 billion (US$238 billion) in short- and long-term debt was coming to maturity in 2011. By 2014, Standard & Poor's rating of Italy had decreased even further to BBB, and in December of that year it was downgraded again to BBB- – one level above junk, or non-investment grade, status. However, Italy's outlook was stated as 'stable' as Standard and Poor's expected the country to exit recession and begin a period of slow growth. On 14 May 2012, the ratings agency Moody's cut the credit ratings of two of Italy's largest lending banks, Unicredit and Intesa Sanpaolo, from A3 to A2. The ratings of 24 other Italian banks were also cut by up to four points. All the banks were put on negative credit watch, with further downgrading possible.

External trade

As a member of the European Union (EU), Italy operates within a community-wide free trade area, with tariffs set across the whole community. Internationally, the EU has free trade agreements with a number of nations and trading blocs worldwide. Exports provided 29.4 per cent of GDP in 2014, with manufactured goods representing around 97 per cent, despite lacking most raw materials and energy needed to sustain the trade; nevertheless it is renowned for its luxury goods and quality manufactures. Italy is the world's second largest exporter of wine after France and Europe's premier exporter of rice, fruit and vegetables.

Imports

Main imports are capital goods, consumer products, chemicals, transport equipment, energy products, minerals and non-ferrous metals, textiles and clothing, food, wine, tobacco and raw materials.

Main sources: Germany (15.4 per cent total in 2014), France (8.6 per cent), China (7.0 per cent).

Exports

Main exports are refined petroleum, machinery, vehicles and vehicle parts, metal products, gold, textiles and foodstuffs.

Main destinations: Germany (12.5 per cent total in 2014), France (10.5 per cent), US (7.5 per cent).

Re-exports

Re-fined oil and petroleum products

Agriculture

Farming

Italian farming is characterised by substantial regional differences. Farms in the north are closer to their counterparts in north European countries – in terms of technology, culture and economy – than Italian farmers in the south. Italy's programme for developing agriculture in the south of the country includes drainage and irrigation schemes, and building up co-operatives and integrated agribusiness ventures to improve trading opportunities.

The EU's Fundamental reform to the Common Agricultural Policy (CAP) was introduced in Italy in 2005. The subsidies that paid on farm output, which tended to benefit large farms and encourage overproduction, were replaced by single farm payments not conditional on production.

Only 20 per cent of Italy is fertile arable land and farms are mostly small-scale. Regions with the most labour intensive farms are Sicily and Apulia. Capital intensive farms are most common in the northern province of Emilia Romagna, but the overall proportion of agricultural employment is the same in the north and south.

In mountainous areas, which stretch throughout the peninsula and on the islands, agricultural activity concentrates on forestry and livestock. The climate is ideal for vineyards and Italy vies with France as one the world's biggest wine producers. The plains of the north and of Apulia, the heel of Italy, are also important areas for wheat, olives and fruit. Half of total agricultural income is generated in the Po valley and the plains in the north. The area produces the entire rice crop, cereals such as wheat and corn, fodder and livestock. In central Italy, wine-making and wheat-growing are the main activities. Most citrus fruit and olives are grown in the south, where vegetables and cereals are also grown.

Fishing

The fishing industry has a turnover of around US$4 billion, but it remains a neglected sector of the economy. Sicily and the Adriatic coast produce around three quarters of the country's fish. The most important fish commercially are sardines and anchovies.

Forestry

Forest and wooded land account for less than 40 per cent of land area. Sixty per cent of the forest is available for wood supply. Broadleaved species account for 66 per cent of the growing stock, the main species being beech, deciduous and evergreen oaks, poplars and chestnut. Common coniferous species include pine, Norway spruce and European larch.

Italy is one of the major consumers, producers and traders of forest products in the EU. It accounts for nearly ten per cent of the EU's total paper and wood-based panel production.

Industry and manufacturing

The industrial sector contributed 23.9 per cent to GDP in 2014 and employed around a third of the labour force. Subdivided by sector, manufacturing contributes approximately 16 per cent to annual GDP, with construction accounting for a further 6 per cent. The sector is dominated by the automobile manufacturer Fiat, Eni and the food conglomerate Ferruzzi Finanziaria.

Problems in the sector include growing competition in traditional products from developing countries, and the small share of the export market taken up by value added high technology products. Efforts to attract industrial investment to the depressed southern region, the *Mezzogiorno*, has been met with only partial success, despite large subsidies.

Tourism

Italy has one of the world's largest collections included on Unesco's World Heritage List, containing a wealth of ancient, classical, medieval and Renaissance art, artefacts and architecture. It is a destination for pilgrims as the centre of Catholicism and home to the origins of many institutions of the Catholic Church.

The global economic crisis, which began in 2008, impacted on the tourist sector as growth fell from 0.9 per cent in 2007 to -7.7 per cent in 2008, and -8.2 per cent in 2009. It rebounded with a modest 0.5 per cent growth rate in 2010, as tourism improved throughout Europe. Whilst still not providing as much to GDP as it did before the crisis struck, the tourist industry's contribution to GDP is currently increasing; in 2014 it contributed 10.1 per cent, expected to rise by 1.7 per cent in 2015. Tourism is a major source of income; in 2014 tourism receipts were at a high of US$51.5 billion, forecast to have risen by 2.5 per cent in 2015. Around 4.8 per cent of employment is directly related to tourism and 11.4 per cent of the workforce is indirectly employed by tourism.

The regions of Venice and Emilia-Romagna are typically the top destinations for visitors staying overnight. These destinations include the established holiday regions on the Adriatic Sea of Rimini and Pesaro, favoured by Italians and foreign visitors alike. Most visitors are from other European countries, followed by North America. In 2014 there were 47.7 million arrivals.

Mining

The mining sector accounts for less than 1 per cent of GDP and employs a similar percentage of the workforce. Italy has relatively poor mineral resources, although large quantities of iron ore and pyrites, mercury, lead, zinc, bauxite, aluminium, sulphur, gravel, alabaster and marble exist.

Sardinia (Cagliari, Sassari and Iglesias) is the main mining area and holds the only large sulphur deposit in Europe, but mining it is not economically viable. Bauxite is mined mainly in Abruzzi, Campania and Apulia, though output has dropped due to falling demand from the aluminium industry. Output of lead, zinc and particularly copper has all increased. Quarrying activity is strong, with marble and gravel much in demand for the construction and road building industries.

In 2013, the mining and quarrying industry produced a turnover of approximately EUR70.7 billion (US$94.7 billion).

Hydrocarbons

Italy relies heavily on energy imports although there is a plan under way to develop indigenous hydrocarbon resources, which are scattered along its peninsula, offshore, and on Sicily.

Proven oil reserves stood at 600 million barrels in 2014, producing 121,000 barrels per day (bpd), well below consumption of 1.2 million bpd. Italy is therefore one of the largest oil importers in Europe with 90 per cent of its consumption dependent on imports.

Italy has a refining capacity of around 2.3 million bpd. The most important oil reserves are in Val d'Agri (Potenza) southern Italy and Villafortuna-Trecate (Novara) northern Italy. The Italian multinational energy company ENI let a contract in 2009 to purchase two of the world's largest refinery reactors for its refinery in Sannazzaro (Sicily), which will increase production of middle distillates.

Italy produced 6.6 billion cubic metres (cum) of natural gas in 2014, a fall of 7.6 per cent on the amount produced in 2013. Production has been falling consistently for a decade – 11.9 billion cum in 2004 – along with reserves. In 2004 Italy had 100 billion cum in reserves, most of which were in and off Sicily, however, by the end of 2014 these had dwindled to less than 50 billion cum. Despite resources falling, natural gas still accounts for 46.1 per cent of all electricity generation.

A call for tenders for the Italian section of the Trans-Adriatic Pipeline (TAP) was issued in May 2011, which is expected to start production in 2020. Existing international pipelines deliver gas from Norway, The Netherlands, Algeria and Russia. In February 2012, the multinational, South Stream Transport group, announced the expected construction of the South Stream pipeline, to transport Russian natural gas to Western and Central Europe (and bypassing Ukraine) that should have begun in December 2012, however it got delayed until 2014 because of the numerous obstacles and sanctions imposed by the EU and Bulgaria. Russia has since abandoned the project.

Most domestic coal production is used in electricity generation; coal accounts for less than 10 per cent of total domestic energy consumption.

Energy

Total installed electricity generating capacity was 122.3GW in 2013, producing around 299.3 billion kilowatt hours (kWh). Natural gas accounts for 46.1 per cent of electricity generation and the government plans for renewable sources to account for 26 per cent by 2020.

Enel, the former state-owned energy monopoly, is the largest power company in Italy, producing over 50 per cent of domestic electricity needs. It produces and sells electricity throughout Italy and operates an international power grid trading energy from Italy-France and Italy-Slovenia. Enel began a programme of converting its huge oil-fired power plant in Civitavecchia to coal, which has increased the coal contribution to electricity generation from 14 per cent in 2014 to 16 per cent by 2013.

Italy had four nuclear power stations but they are not currently in operation – the last two were shutdown in 1990 -- nor expected to be reopened.

Financial markets

Stock exchange

Borsa Italiana (Italian Stock Exchange)

Banking and insurance

Scandal hit the Central Bank in July 2005 when the governor, Antonio Fazio, refused to allow a cross-border banking takeover and was subsequently placed under investigation in two criminal inquiries. He refused to resign for several months, receiving strong support from one of Italy's governing parties, the Lega Nord, and the Catholic Church, but was eventually replaced by Mario Draghi in December. Unlike Mr Fazio, who held an open-ended mandate, Mr Draghi will serve a six-year term, renewable once.

Central bank
Banca d'Italia; European Central Bank (ECB).

Time
GMT plus one hour (daylight saving, late March to late October, GMT plus two hours)

Geography
Italy consists of a peninsula stretching from southern Europe into the Mediterranean and includes a number of adjacent islands, including Sicily in the south-west and Sardinia in the west. The country stretches 1,200km from north to south and has 7,456km of coastline.
The distinctive boot-shaped peninsula is dominated by two extensive mountain ranges, accounting for about 75 per cent of the land area. The Alps form a natural barrier separating Italy from Slovenia in the north-east, Austria and Switzerland in the north and France in the north-west. The Apennines form the backbone of the peninsula.
Italy experiences frequent minor earthquakes, especially in the south, and its active volcanoes include Vesuvius in the Naples district, Etna in Sicily and Stromboli in the Aeolian Islands.
Two autonomous countries lie within Italy's frontiers, the Vatican City in Rome, home of the Holy See, and the tiny republic of San Marino in the north-east.

Hemisphere
Northern

Climate
While Italy lies in a temperate zone, the climates of the north and south vary. Summers are uniformly hot, although summers in the south can be extremely hot and dry. In the winter, the south is generally mild, while the north can be extremely cold – particularly near the Alps and Po Valley. Temperatures range from about 4–30 degrees Celsius.

Dress codes
Particular attention is paid to dress, although dress codes are not rigid. Most businessmen wear suits and ties during business hours.

Entry requirements
Passports
Required by most; passports must be valid for three months from arrival. Nationals of countries which are signatories of the Schengen Accords, which includes most EU/EEA member states, San Marino and Croatia, may visit on national IDs.

Visa
No visa requirements for citizens of most of Europe, the Americas, Australasia and some Asian countries, visiting for up to 90 days. For a full list, and further information for those citizens not included on the list of visa-free travel, visit www.ambwashingtondc.esteri.it and see consular services. A Schengen visa application (offered in several languages) can be downloaded from http://europa.eu/abc/travel/ see 'documents you will need'.
Business travel is also allowed for those enjoying visa-free travel. Those who do not have visa-free arrangements must provide a letter from their employer guaranteeing travel expenses, including full itinery and purpose of the trip. Letters of invitation from all Italian companies to be visited, and a current (not over 90 days) *Visura Camerale* issued by the Italian Chamber of Commerce should be attached; a return/onward ticket must be produced before collection of the passport and visa from the issuing consulate; which may request any additional documents at its discretion.
Within eight days of arrival in Italy the visa traveller must appear before local police authorities to receive a Residency Permit and will also need to show proof of health insurance.

Currency advice/regulations
Import and export of local and foreign currency up to eur12,000 (or foreign equivalent) is permitted. Imports and export of amounts greater than this must be declared within 48 hours of arrival or departure.
Travellers cheques are widely accepted.

Customs
Personal items are duty-free. There are no duties levied on alcohol and tobacco between EU member states, providing amounts imported are for personal consumption.

Health (for visitors)
Nationals of the European Economic Area (EEA) countries and Switzerland can access reduced cost and sometimes free medical treatment using a European Health Insurance Card (EHIC) while visiting the EEA. Exceptions include nationals of the 10 countries, which joined the EU in 2004 whose EHIC is not valid in Switzerland. Applications for the EHIC should be made before travelling.

Mandatory precautions
None.

Advisable precautions
No special immunisations are needed.
Pharmacists are usually open from 0830 to 1300 and 1600 to 2000.

Hotels
Classified into five star categories. Rates are fixed by the Provincial Tourist Board, and vary according to class, season, services available and locality. A service charge of 15–18 per cent is added to bills, but additional tips are also expected for individual services. Restaurants expect 15 per cent on top of the bill.

Credit cards
International credit cards are widely accepted.

Public holidays (national)
Fixed dates
1 Jan (New Year's Day), 6 Jan (Epiphany), 25 April (Liberation Day), 1 May (Labour Day), 2 Jun (National Day), 15 Aug (Assumption Day), 1 Nov (All Saints' Day), 8 Dec (Immaculate Conception), 25–26 Dec (Christmas).

Variable dates
Easter Monday

Working hours
Business travellers would do best to avoid August when Italians desert the stifling heat of the big cities for the beaches and mountains. The mass exodus usually begins in mid-July and lasts at least until after the *Ferragosto* festival (August 15).
Most factories, government offices, shops and restaurants close for all of August or are run by minimal staff.
The afternoon siesta is still very much part of the Italian way of life in Rome and the south. In northern Italy, there is a trend towards standard European business hours of 0900 to 1700, at least in offices.

Banking
Mon–Fri: 0830–1300; 1500–1600.
Banks in tourist areas may not close for lunch.

Business
Northern Italy: 0930–1300 and 1400–1800.
Central and southern Italy: 0830–1245 and 1630–2000.

Government
Post offices: Mon–Fri: 0830–1345 and Sat: 0830–1200; central city post offices stay open until 2100.
Government offices: Mon–Sat: 0830–1345.

Shops
Mon–Sat: 0830–1230, 1500–1800; Sat: 0900–1230.

Telecommunications
Mobile/cell phones
There are 3G, 900/1800 GSM services throughout the country.

Electricity supply
220V AC, 50Hz

Social customs/useful tips
Italians always shake hands on meeting and leaving. Exchanging business cards is also normal practice as it helps to reinforce the informal network of personal contacts which permeates Italian business. Businessmen prefer that written communication, either by e-mail, facsimile or letter, be sent before a telephone discussion. Personal titles are considered important,

although often more prestigious than professionally accurate. Small luxury goods are frequently exchanged as gifts in business. Smoking is still fashionable, with fewer restrictions than in many other Western countries.

Italians are required to carry identification on them at all times and foreigners are recommended to do likewise.

Security

Handbag snatching and pickpocketing are widespread, particularly in popular tourist spots in Rome and Naples. It is advisable not to wear conspicuous jewellery or carry personal valuables. In general the level of violent crime is low, but drug-related crime is on the increase in Milan, Rome and Naples. With this in mind, visitors to Rome are advised to avoid the streets around the central railway station at night.

Getting there

Air

National airline: Alitalia

International airport/s: Leonardo da Vinci (Fiumicino) Rome (FCO) 26km south-west of Rome. There is a direct rail link to the central railway station (duration 35 minutes), and express buses into Rome. Licensed, metered taxis are also available to the city.

Milan Malpensa (MXP) 45km north-west of Milan. Both airport facilities include duty-free shops, bar, restaurant, car hire, bank, *bureau de change* and business centre.

Other airport/s: Pisa (PSA), 2km from city, (an hour by train from Florence); Turin International (TRN), 16km north-west of city; Venice Marco Polo (VCE), 13km north-west of city; Bologna G Marconi (BLQ); Milan Linate (LIN); Naples Capodichino (NAP); Genoa Cristoforo Colombo (GOA); Palermo (PMO).

Airport tax: None

Surface

Italy is included in the Pan-European Corridor 5 scheme. The project has some 3,270km of railways, linking Kiev in the Ukraine with western Europe via Italy, and 2,850 of new and upgraded roads.

Road: Italy can be entered by road from France, Switzerland, Austria and Slovenia. However, several passes are closed during winter. In addition to the Riviera coastal motorway, access from France and Switzerland is maintained via the St Bernard, Mont Blanc and Fréjus tunnels.

Rail: There are daily services, run by Ferrovie dello Stato (FS) (Italian State Railways) that run from France, Switzerland and Austria, which are linked to the European rail network.

The high-speed Lyon-Turin Ferroviaire rail link, consisting of two linked tunnel sections, which are due to join the north-south, east-west transport network hub in Lyon, is expected to be completed by 2012.

Water: There are regular ferry service connections to Greece, Albania, North Africa, Croatia and France.

Main port/s: Genoa, Trieste, Augusta, Taranto, Leghorn, Savona, Ancona, Bari, Brindisi, Civitavecchia, Venice, La Spezia, Naples, Palermo (Sicily), and Cagliari and Porto Torres (Sardinia).

Getting about

National transport

Air: Alitalia and Aero Transporti Italiani (ATI) operate services connecting Rome to most major towns. Alisarda operates services connecting Rome, Milan and Turin with Sardinia.

Road: There is a road network of over 300,000km, of which 6,000km are motorways (*autostrade*) with tolls, connecting most cities.

Buses: Extensive bus services, operated by several companies, link all major towns.

Rail: Trenitalia operates an extensive network in all regions. Express trains, which provide buffet carriages, have seats to be booked in advance. Larger railway stations provide left luggage, banks, ATMs and refreshment facilities.

Water: Ferryboat and hydrofoil services linking the mainland with Sicily, Sardinia and the smaller islands are operated by several lines including the State Railways.

City transport

Taxis: Available in all towns and tourist resorts, usually in ranks at railway stations, or can be called by phone. Fares vary considerably, and unmetered cabs should be avoided. Drivers round up their fares; gratuities are not necessary.

Buses, trams & metro: All major cities have bus services with one standard fare. Day and monthly tickets are available. Bus tickets can also be bought in packs of five and then fed into a machine upon boarding.

There are metros in Rome and Milan with standard single fares as for buses. In Milan tickets last for 70 minutes and can be used on both metro lines and all bus routes. A daily or monthly ticket usable for all Rome services is available. The metro journey from Malpensa international airport, Milan, to the city centre takes around 30 minutes.

Tram services are available in Milan, Naples and Turin.

Car hire

Self-drive cars are available; the daily rate depends on the engine size, plus an additional charge per kilometre. Special weekly tariffs are available. VAT is charged. Official translation of driving licence required. Driving is on the right. Maximum speed is 50kph in towns, 90/110kph on country roads and 130kph on motorways. There are legal obligations for wearing seat belts while driving and warning waistcoats (fluorescent jackets) when leaving a vehicle during a breakdown or emergency.

Road signs are international.

BUSINESS DIRECTORY

The addresses listed below are a selection only. While World of Information makes every endeavour to check these addresses, we cannot guarantee that changes have not been made, especially to telephone numbers and area codes. We would welcome any corrections.

Telephone area codes

The international direct dialling code (IDD) for Italy is +39, followed by area code, including the first zero:

Bologna	051	Pisa	050
Capri	081	Rome	06
Florence	055	Trieste	040
Genoa	010	Turin	011
Milan	02	Venice	041
Naples	081	Verona	045

Useful telephone numbers

Police, fire and ambulance: 113

Chambers of Commerce

American Chamber of Commerce in Italy, 1 Via Cantù, 20123 Milan (tel: 869-0661; fax: 805-7737; email: amcham@amcham.it).

Bergamo Camera di Commercio, 16 Largo Belotti, 24121 Bergamo (tel: 422-5111; fax: 226-023; email: info@bg.camcom.it).

Bologna Camera di Commercio, Palazzo Mercanzia, 4 Piazza Mercanzia, 40125 Bologna (tel: 609-3111; fax: 609-3451; email: segreteria.generale@bo.camcom.it).

Brescia Camera di Commercio, 3 Via Orzinuovi, 25125 Brescia (tel: 351-41; fax: 351-4222; email: brescia@bs.camcom.it).

British Chamber of Commerce for Italy, 12 Via Dante, 20121 Milan (tel: 877-798; fax: 8646-1885; email: bcci@britchamitaly.com).

Ferrara Camera di Commercio, 11 Via Borgoleoni, 44100 Ferrara (tel: 783-711; fax: 240-204; email: cciaa.ferrara@fe.camcom.it).

Florence Camera di Commercio, 3 Piazza dei Giudici, 50122 Florence (tel: 2795-1; fax: 2795-259; email: info@fi.camcom.it).

Genoa Camera di Commercio, 4 Via Garibaldi, 16124 Genoa (tel: 270-41; fax: 270-4300; email: camera.genova@ge.camcom.it).

Mantua Camera di Commercio, 28 Via Pietro Fortunato Calvi, 46100 Mantua (tel: 234-1; fax: 234-234; email: mantova@mn.camcom.it).

Milan Camera di Commercio, 9b Via Meravigli, 20123 Milan (tel: 8515-1; fax: 8515-4232; email: infohighway@mi.camcom.it).

Naples Camera di Commercio, 2 Via S Aspreno, 80133 Naples (tel: 760-7111; fax: 552-6940; email: segretaria.generale@na.camcom.it)

Padua Camera di Commercio, 34 Via E Filiberto, 35122 Padua (tel: 820-8111; fax: 820-8290; email: info@pd.camcom.it).

Parma Camera di Commercio, 2 Via Verde, 43100 Parma (tel: 210-11; fax: 282-168; email: segretaria.generale@pr.camcom.it).

Pavia Camera di Commercio, 27 Via Mentana, 27199 Pavia (tel: 393-1; fax: 304-559; email: pavia@pv.camcom.it).

Rome Camera di Commercio, 147 Via De' Burrò, 00186 Rome (tel: 520-2630; fax: 520-82617; email: info@rm.camcom.it).

Siena Camera di Commercio, 30 Piazza Matteotti, 53100 Siena (tel: 202-511; fax: 270-981; email: cciaa@si.camcom.it).

Treieste Camera di Commercio, 14 Piazza della Borsa, 34121 Trieste (tel: 670-1111; fax: 670-1321; email: info@ts.camcom.it).

Turin Camera di Commercio, 24 Via San Francesco da Paola, 10123 Turin (tel: 571-6405; fax: 571-6404; email: urp@to.camcom.it).

Unione Italiana delle Camere di Commercio, Industria, Artigianato e Agricoltura, 21 Piazza Sallustio, 00187 Rome (tel: 470-41; fax: 470-4240; email: segretaria.generale@unioncamere.it).

Venice Camera di Commercio, 2032 Via XXII Marzo, San Marco, 30124 Venice (tel: 786-111; fax: 786-330; email: segretaria.generale@ve.camcom.it).

Verona Camera di Commercio, 96 Corso Porta Nuova, 37122 Verona (tel: 808-5011; fax: 594-648; email: cciaavr@vr.camcom.it).

Banking

Banca Commerciale Italiana, Via del Corso, 226 C.A.P. 00186 Rome (tel: 67-121; fax: 6712-4925).

Banca di Napoli, Via Toledo 177–188, 80132 Naples (tel: 791-1111).

Banca Nazionale del Lavoro, Via Vittoro Veneto 119, 00187 Rome (tel: 47-021; fax: 4702-6263).

Banca Nazionale dell'Agricoltura SPA, Via Salaria 231, 00199 Rome (tel: 85-881; fax: 8588-3396).

Banca Popolare Commercio E Industria Scarl, Via Casifina 1790, 00132 Rome (tel: 207-1712; fax: 207-2676).

Banca di Roma, Via del Corso 320, 00186 Rome (tel: 67-071; fax: 6707-3783).

Cassa di Risparmio delle Provincie Lombarde, Piazza Barberini 21, 00167 Rome (tel: 46-781; fax 486-884).

Cassa di Risparmio di Roma, 320 Via del Corso, 00186 Rome (tel: 67-071; fax: 6707-3783).

Cassa di Risparmio di Torino, 31 Via XX Settembre, 10121 Torino (tel: 57-661; fax: 638-203).

Credito Italiano, 00144 Piazzale dell'Industria 46 (tel: 54-631; fax: 5423-7006).

European Investment Bank, via Saroagna 36, 100187 Rome (tel: 47-191; fax: 487-3438).

Istituto Centrale Delle Banche Di Credito Cooperativo, Via Torino 146, 00184 Rome (tel: 47-161; fax: 4716-5583).

Istituto Di Credito Delle Casse Di Rigparmio Italiane, Via San Basilo 15, 00187 Rome (tel: 47-151).

Mediocredito Centrale, Via Piemonte 51, 00187 Rome (tel: 47-911; fax: 479-1626).

Monte dei Paschi di Siena, Piazza Salimbeni, Siena (tel: 294-111).

Nuovo Banco Ambrosiano, Piazza Paolo Ferrari 10, 20121 Milan (tel: 85-941).

UBAE Arab Italian Bak SpA, Piazza Venezia 11, 00187 Rome (tel: 67-5921; fax: 678-4606).

Central bank

Banca d'Italia, Via Nazionale 91, 00184 Rome (tel: 47-921; fax: 479-22983; internet: www.bancaditalia.it).

European Central Bank (ECB), Kaiserstrasse 29, D-60311 Frankfurt am Main, Germany (tel: (+49-69) 13-440; fax: (+49-69) 1344-6000; email: info@ecb.int).

Stock exchange

Borsa Italiana (Italian Stock Exchange), www.borsaitaliana.it

Travel information

Alitalia (Linee Aeree Italiane), Centro Direzionale, Viale Alissandro Marchetti, 111, Rome 100148 (tel: 709-2780; fax: 709-3065).
Leonardo da Vinci (Fiumicino) Airport, Via dell'Aeroporto di Fiumicino 320, PO Box 68, 00050, Fiumicino (tel: 5951; fax: 595-5707; email: info@adr.it; internet: www.adr.it).
Milan Malpensa Airport, 21010 Varese (tel: 7485-2200; fax: 7485-4010: email: communication@sea-aeroportimilano.it; internet: www.sea-aeroportimilano.it/eng).
Trenitalia, 1 Piazza della Croce Rossa, Rome (tel: 892-021; internet: www.trenitalia.com).

Ministry of tourism

Ministry of Industry and Tourism, Via Molise 2, 00187 Rome (tel: 47-051; fax: 4705-2215).

National tourist organisation offices

Ente Nazionale Italiano per il Turismo (ENIT), 2/6Via Marghera, 00185 Rome (tel: 49-711; fax: 446-3379; email: sedecentrale@cert.ent.it; internet: www.enit.it).

Ministries

Ministry of Agriculture and Forests, Via XX Settembre 20, 00187 Rome (tel: 46-651; fax: 592-314).

Ministry of Defence, Via XX Settembre 8, 00187 Rome (tel: 488-2126; fax: 474-7775).

Ministry of Education, Viale Trastevere 76/A, 00153 Rome (tel: 58-491; fax: 580-3381).

Ministry of Employment and Social Welfare, Via Flavia 6, 00187 Rome (tel: 46-831; fax: 4788-7174).

Ministry of the Environment, Piazza Venezia 11, 00187 Rome (tel: 70-361; fax: 678-3844).

Ministry of Equal Opportunities, c/o Presidenza del Consiglio dei Ministry, Palazzo Chigi, 00187 Rome (tel: 67-791; fax: 678-3998).

Ministry of Finance, Viale Europa 242, 00144 Rome (tel: 59-971; fax: 501-5714).

Ministry of Foreign Affairs, Piazzale della Farnesina, 00194 Rome (tel: 36-911; fax: 323-6258).

Ministry of Foreign Trade, Viale America 341, 00144 Rome (tel: 59-931; fax: 5964-7504).

Ministry of Health, Viale dell'Industria 20, 00144 Rome (tel: 59-941; fax: 5964-7649).

Ministry of Industry and Tourism, Via Molise 2, 00187 Rome (tel: 47-051; fax: 4705-2215).

Ministry of the Interior, Piazzale del Viminale, 00184 Rome (tel: 6451; fax: 482-5792).

Ministry of Justice, Via Arenula 71, 00186 Rome (tel: 68-851; fax: 5227-8550).

Ministry of Posts and Telecommunications, Viale America 201, 00144 Rome (tel: 59-581; fax: 594-274).

Ministry of Public Administration, Palazzo Vidoni, Corso Vittorio Emanuele 116, 00186 Rome (tel: 680-031).

Ministry of Public Works, Piazza Porta Pia 1, 00198 Rome (tel: 44-121; fax: 4426-7275).

Ministry of Transport, Piazza della Croce Rossa 1, 00161 Rome (tel: 84-901; fax: 4424-1539).

Ministry of the Treasury and Budget, Via XX Settembre 97, 00187 Rome (tel: 47-611; fax: 488-2146).

Ministry for University, Scientific and Technological Research, Piazzale Kennedy 20, 00144 Rome (tel: 59-911; fax: 591-5493).

Office of the President, Palazzo del Quirinale, 00187 Rome (tel: 4699).

Prime Minister's Office, Palazzo Chigi, Piazza Colonna 370, 00187 Rome (tel: 67-791; fax: 678-3998).

Other useful addresses

Agenzia Nazionale Stampa Associata (news agency), Via della Dataria 94, 00187 Rome (tel: 678-6161).

Borsa Valori di Milano, Piazza Degli Affari, 20100 Milan (tel: 8534).

British Embassy, Via XX Settembre 80/A, 00187 Rome (tel: 482-5551, 482-5441; fax: 487-3324).

Commissione Nazionale per le Società e la Borsa (Commission for Companies and the Stock Exchange), Milan (tel: 877-841).

Confederazione Generale dell'Industria Italiana (General Confederation of Italian Industry), Viale dell'Astronomia 30, 00144 Rome (tel: 59-031).

Confederazione Generale Italiana del Commercio (General Confederation of Italian Commerce), Piazza G.C. Belli 2, Rome (tel: 588-783, 580-192).

Ente Nazionale Idrocarburi (ENI), Piazzalo E. Mattei, 00144 Rome (tel: 59-001).

Ente Partecipazioni e Finanziamento Industria Manifatturiera (EFIM), Via XXIV Maggio 43–45, 00187 Rome (tel: 47-101).

Istituto Nazionale di Statistica (ISTAT) (national statistics office), Via Cesare Balbo 16, 00100 Rome (tel: 46-731; fax: 4673-4177).

Istituto per la Ricostruzione Industriale (IRI) Via Vittorio Veneto 85, 00187 Rome (tel: 47-271).

Istituto Nazionale per il Commercio Estero (Italian government agency for promotion of foreign trade), 21 Via Liszt, 00100 Rome (tel: 59-921).

Italian Embassy (US), 3000 Whitehaven Street, NW, Washington DC 20008 (tel: (+1-202) 612-4400; fax: (+1-202) 518-2154; email: stampa@itwash.org).

US Embassy, Via Vittorio Veneto 119A, 00187 Rome (tel: 46-741; fax: 4674-2356).

National news agency: ANSA (Agenzia Nazionale Stampa Associata)

Address: Via della Dataria 94, 00187 Rome (tel: 677-41; fax: 677-4638; internet: www.ansa.it).

AGI (Agenzia Giornalistica Italia) (in Italian): www.agenziaitalia.it

Internet sites

City of Venice Gateway: www.venetia.it

City of Florence information: www.aboutflorence.com

Gateway site of servers listed by city (launches into Italian language sites): www.cilea.it/WWW-map

Italian Central Bank: www.bancaditalia.it

Italian Statistics: www.istat.it

Italian Embassy in the US (includes economic and trade data) www.italyemb.org

Ministry of Foreign Affairs: www.esteri.it/eng/index/htm

The Uffizi Museum: www.uffizi.firenze.it

Yellow pages Online: www.paginegialle.it

Jamaica

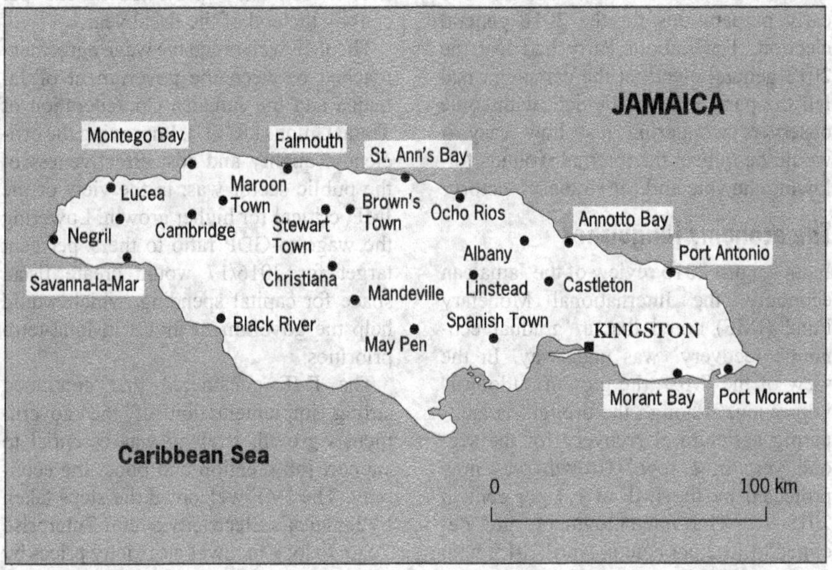

Political commentaries on Jamaica in 2015 inevitably focussed on the country's obstinate crime rate and its chronic unemployment. But the single issue that preoccupied most Jamaicans was the date of the next general election. In a monthly press conference, the chairman of the government's Economic Programme Oversight Committee (EPOC), Richard Byles, expressed the views of the majority when he said that 'If the government intends to call a general election, then it should do so and take the country out of its current state of limbo. The last thing Jamaica needs at this point is a stop-and-start process, first yes and then no, prolonging the period of political uncertainty.'

No elections – no election fever?

Public speculation about whether the ruling People's National Party (PNP) would call an election before the end of 2015 had intensified, particularly in the run up to the party's 77th annual conference in September 2015. However, despite intimations that she would reveal the date, Prime Minister Portia Simpson Miller ('PSM' for short), the PNP president failed to do so. Under the Jamaican Constitution, only the prime minister is able to decide upon the date of an election. Despite all the speculation, the prime minister still had another eighteen months before she had to call the election, which was constitutionally due between 29 December 2016 and 16 April 2017.

In the meantime, in the 'phony election' period, both sides of the political divide – both the ruling PNP and the opposition Labour Party – had been making preparations as Jamaica found itself aware of the inevitability of elections, but unaware of when they might take place. The ruling PNP had reportedly completed the selection of its 63 candidates. In similar pre-election vein, Jamaica's Director of Elections had confirmed that by the end of September 2015 the Electoral Office of Jamaica (EOJ) would be in a position to run an election. The most up to date voters' list was scheduled for publication at the end of November 2015. At the end of May 2015, there had been 1,793,039 Jamaicans registered to vote..

Prime Minister Portia Simpson Miller's term in office (she had taken over from the outgoing labour prime minister, Andrew Holness, in January 2012) was remarkably uneventful. However, PSM was considered by many observers to be a less than impressive prime minister. By March 2013 one Jamaican blogger was already

KEY FACTS

Official name: Jamaica

Head of State: Queen Elizabeth II (since 1952); represented by Governor General Patrick Allen (from 26 Feb 2009)

Head of government: Prime Minister Portia Simpson Miller (from 5 Jan 2012)

Ruling party: People's National Party (PNP) (from 5 Jan 2012)

Area: 10,989 square km

Population: 2.80 million (2014)*

Capital: Kingston

Official language: English

Currency: Jamaican dollar (J$) = 100 cents

Exchange rate: J$117.74 per US$ (Sep 2015)

GDP per capita: US$4,926 (2014)*

GDP real growth: 0.52% (2014)*

GDP: US$13.79 billion (2014)*

Labour force: 1.25 million (2010)

Unemployment: 15.28% (2014)*

Inflation: 7.09% (2014)

Balance of trade: -US$3.72 billion (2014)

* estimated figure

asking 'how on earth did she become prime minister of Jamaica?' Under the Jamaican political system, by virtue of being party leader PSM had automatically become the prime minister as the party she 'leads' won the general election.

According to the blogger Jay Warren (*commonsenseja.wordpress.com*), Ms Simpson Miller – one of the Caribbean's richest women – 'constantly hides from the media, will not take questions in parliament unless given two weeks notice, refuses to speak to the Jamaican public on national issues and is insistent on hiding behind her large whatnot.' According to Mr Warren, the prime minister had held five 'Whatnot' (a peculiarly Jamaican use of the term to mean 'general' or 'unspecific') retreats in 15 months and not once has she emerged 'with a cohesive economic plan and or direction.'

When asked why she was not speaking to the people of Jamaica the prime minister responded that 'When you don't hear from me, I am working, working, working.' The perceived problem was that it was hard for the Jamaican electorate to see or judge the efforts of her work. PSM answered criticism of her work by saying that she didn't '... listen to negative criticism. I only listen to the positives ones. My husband filters the news for me and tells me what news cast I need to listen to and what to avoid. Furthermore those persons who are critics are nothing but failures themselves.' According to the opposition spokesman on finance, Audley Shaw, the price of basic food items like sardines and corn-beef had increased by more than 30 per cent since the PNP came to power.

Labour party reforms

The principal political activity in 2014 concerned the challenge to Jamaica's opposition leader (and former prime minister) Andrew Holness, from Labour Party's Audley Shaw, one of his deputies and the party's chief economic spokesman. The unrest in the Labour Party was related to early preparations for the 2016 general election. The Labour Party had lost the 2012 general election; the campaign had left the party bitterly divided, with some observers wondering just how easy it would be to heal the internal wounds following the vote and Mr Holness' victory.

The economy languishes

In its August 2015 review of the Jamaican economy, the International Monetary Fund (IMF) noted that a 'gradual economic recovery' was underway. In the view of the IMF, 'the growth outlook is improving, although the drought is hampering agricultural recovery for the second year in a row.' Growth was now projected by the IMF at 1.4 per cent in 2015–16. The unemployment rate declined to 13.2 per cent in April 2015, with strong employment growth in tourism and in the business process outsourcing (BPO) sector. Inflation remained at a historic low of 4 per cent in July, in spite of higher food prices on account of the drought. International reserves had continued to increase, standing at US$2.4 billion at the end of July 2015.

The IMF also noted that 'The recent PetroCaribe liability management operation was an important step in reducing Jamaica's public debt.' The buyback had immediately reduced the debt-to-GDP ratio by about 10 per cent of GDP and the Net Present Value (NPV) gain of the transaction was estimated at about US$300 million. This pro-active operation would help keep public debt on a clear downward trajectory, with debt-to-GDP now projected at 125 per cent by the end of the fiscal year.

The IMF welcomed the wage agreement reached between the government of Jamaica and the Jamaica Confederation of Trade Unions (JCTU). Improving the efficiency, quality and cost effectiveness of the public sector was, in the view of the IMF, critical for higher growth. Lowering the wage-to-GDP ratio to the 9 per cent target for 2016/17 would create fiscal space for capital spending, which would help the government invest in long-term priorities.

The IMF considered that continued strong implementation of the government's growth strategy was essential to support job creation and boost the economy. The IMF welcomed the steps taken by Jamaica's Electricity Sector Enterprise Team to lock in lower electricity prices by diversifying sources of energy used for electricity generation beyond oil. There was also scope for further improvements in the business climate. Enhancing access to credit for small- and medium-sized enterprises would improve financial inclusion and support private investment.

According to the IMF, Jamaica's financial sector stability was being strengthened through the implementation of the Banking Services Act and continued reforms in the securities dealers sector. Additionally the transition of retail repos to a trust was nearing completion and should make this investment more secure and transparent.

In its annual overview of what the Fitch rating agency described as Jamaica's 'small and weak economy' the United Nations Economic Commission for Latin America and the Caribbean (ECLAC) noted that the Jamaican economy posted growth rates of 1.6 per cent in the first quarter of 2014 and 1.2 per cent in the April to June quarter. It was anticipated that this growth would continue to build gradually, with the IMF Extended Fund Facility (EFF) in place and with growing confidence in the domestic private sector. Overall growth was expected to be 1.2 per cent in 2014 and 1.6 per cent in 2015. Meanwhile, inflation in 2014 was likely to be 9 per cent, provided there were no adverse exchange-rate movements. The

KEY INDICATORS — Jamaica

	Unit	2011	2012	2013	2014	**2015
Population	m	*2.74	2.77	2.78	*2.80	*2.81
Gross domestic product (GDP)	US$bn	14.80	14.75	14.20	*13.79	*13.85
GDP per capita	US$	5,402	5,328	5,100	*4,926	*4,922
GDP real growth	%	1.5	-0.5	0.2	*0.5	*1.7
Inflation	%	7.5	6.9	9.4	7.1	*5.8
Unemployment	%	12.9	13.9	15.3	*15.3	*15.3
Exports (fob) (goods)	US$m	1,666.1	1,746.7	1,597.3	1,482.2	–
Imports (fob) (goods)	US$m	5,881.4	5,904.7	5,573.4	5,199.9	–
Balance of trade	US$m	-4,215.3	-4,158.0	-3,976.2	-3,717.7	–
Current account	US$m	-2,063.2	-1,920.0	-1,265.0	*-879.0	*-697.0
Total reserves minus gold	US$m	2,883.0	1,980.8	1,818.4	2,473.0	–
Foreign exchange	US$m	2,547.1	1,674.3	1,522.3	–	–
Exchange rate	per US$	85.65	91.23	106.05	114.33	–

* estimated figure ** forecast figure

exchange rate was likely to depreciate more slowly, as the economy had met a number of quantitative targets and completed a number of reforms under the EFF programme.

A recent World Bank report suggested a significant rise in the *Doing Business Index* which, together with a number of structural reforms, should increase the confidence of both domestic and international investors in the Jamaican economy. ECLAC considered the continuing fiscal challenges to be the most significant as Jamaica sought to control its public finances. In June 2014, the IMF had concluded its fourth review of the EFF programme and confirmed that Jamaica had successfully met a number of quarterly quantitative targets and structural benchmarks.

Central to this programme was expenditure restraint. Over the period from April to September 2014, expenditure and revenues were down by 6.1 per cent and 3.7 per cent, respectively, relative to the budget estimates. At the same time, the fiscal deficit, at J$18.9 billion (US$0.161 billion), was some 24.9 per cent below the budgeted amount over this period. ECLAC stressed the importance of the fact that income and profit taxes as a whole and taxes on companies other than those in the bauxite industry, were below the government's targets by 3.7 per cent and 30.0 per cent, respectively, suggesting that growth was still lacklustre despite some improvement in business confidence relative to that seen two years earlier. It was important to note also that capital expenditure was 43.7 per cent below target, suggesting considerable compression of such spending. Due to the efforts to contain public expenditure, the central government's overall deficit was projected to narrow in 2014 and further improvements are expected in 2015. For these reasons, Standard & Poor's had revised Jamaica's B rating from stable to positive.

The total debt stock in the fiscal year 2013/14 was 131.9 per cent of GDP and a figure of 129.3 per cent was projected for the following fiscal year. Given its high share of foreign-currency denominated debt, devaluations of the Jamaican dollar could further increase the external debt burden. The debt-to-GDP ratio would remain high for some time and, despite efforts to increase primary surpluses, the lack of robust growth had meant that it could not be brought down swiftly. It was projected at a still considerable 122.7 per cent of GDP in the fiscal year 2015/16.

By the end of June 2014, the rate of depreciation had slowed to 10.61 per cent from the 10.81 per cent registered in the previous quarter. The weighted average selling rate of the Jamaican dollar against the United States dollar was US$1.00 = J$ 112.20. The decline was due to slower imports and a reduced demand for financing of balance-of-payments transactions. In addition, inflows from current transfers in the second quarter had increased by 4.4 per cent relative to the corresponding quarter of the previous year.

As regards monetary policy, the Bank of Jamaica (central bank) held its base bank rate, which was the 30-day certificate of deposit, at 5.25 per cent, compared with a rate of 6.26 per cent in 2012. The base rate had been kept unchanged since March 2013 as a way of countering weak domestic demand by helping to stimulate investment. Positive growth in lending to the private sector was only observed in distribution and in agriculture and fisheries. In response to concerns about liquidity constraints in the June quarter, the Bank of Jamaica had also been entering the foreign exchange market, injecting J$31.8 billion (US$0.270 billion) and J$12.4 billion (US$0.) into the system in the first and second quarters, respectively. This had also created a downward impact on selected market interest rates. Meanwhile, the weighted average lending rate declined from 16.72 per cent in June 2013 to 14.76 per cent in June 2014, while the average deposit rate fell from 1.50 per cent to 1.40 per cent over a similar period. Growth in lending to the private sector was lower in the June quarter than the quarter before, despite increased liquidity in the banking system. It was also observed that the ratio of non-performing loans to total private-sector loans fell by 11 per cent on an annual basis.

Net international reserves stood at US$1.0 billion at the end of the first quarter and had risen to US$1.4 billion by the end of the second quarter, or slightly less than 12 weeks of import cover. Reserves were up to US$2.0 billion by the end of November 2014, buoyed by a US$800 million Eurobond issue on the international capital market. Some US$68 million were also received for budgetary support under the EFF after the country passed the IMF test in September 2014. The balance of payments was estimated to have remained broadly unchanged in 2013 and 2014, with the current account balance holding steady at about 10 per cent of GDP. Growing confidence in the private sector and greater international demand were likely to lead to a better performance in 2015.

Growth rates in the first two quarters of 2014 were 1.6 per cent and 1.2 per cent, respectively. When the data were disaggregated to reveal the contribution of the goods (25 per cent) and service (75 per cent) sectors to real GDP, it was observed that the goods sector grew by 5.6 per cent and 3.6 per cent, respectively, in the two quarters, while for services the growth rates were 0.3 per cent and 0.5 per cent, respectively. In the first quarter, only manufacturing declined in the goods sector, while agriculture grew by 18 per cent. For services, the only decline was in government, a drop that was unsurprising given the fiscal consolidation programme put in place by the IMF. In the second quarter, mining and manufacturing declined and agriculture grew by 12 per cent, while in services electricity and water showed some decline alongside government. The World Bank had reported a significant improvement in the *Doing Business Index* for Jamaica and this was likely to translate into better growth outcomes in the medium term, especially given the strong commitment of policymakers to the IMF programme. The ECLAC projections were for 1.2 per cent growth in 2014 and 1.6 per cent in 2015, based on the expectation that international and domestic demand will improve slightly in 2015.

The inflation rate was 9.5 per cent in 2013 and the Bank of Jamaica's projection was that inflation in 2014 would be between 7 per cent and 9 per cent. Factors that could cause inflation to rise above this range were higher oil prices and utility rates and exchange-rate depreciation. On the other hand, weaker than expected commodity demand, a fall-off in commodity import prices and expansion in local agriculture were, in ECLAC's view, factors that could reduce inflation. Exchange-rate pressure was perhaps the factor most likely to push inflation outside the target range.

Risk assessment

Politics	Fair
Economy	Fair
Regional stability	Good

COUNTRY PROFILE

1494 Jamaica was sighted by members of an expedition led by Christopher Columbus.

1509 Jamaica was occupied by Spaniards. Most of the indigenous Arawak community died from exposure to European diseases. African slaves were

brought in to work on the sugar plantations.
1655 The British captured the island. Jamaica became a slave-based economy producing sugar and some coffee for export.
1692 Jamaican capital, Port Royal, sunk into the sea after an earthquake and Spanish Town became the new capital.
1834 Slavery was abolished.
1865 A major revolt against Jamaican landowners among freed slaves living in hardship was brutally put down by the British. The local legislature surrendered its powers and Jamaica became a crown colony.
1870 Plantations began to replace sugar cane with banana production, due to increased sugar beet production in Europe.
1884 A new constitution marked the revival of Jamaican autonomy.
1930s The worldwide economic depression and greater international competition further undermined the Jamaican sugar industry.
1938 Popular uprisings caused by unemployment and resentment of racial British policies led to the establishment of the People's National Party (PNP) by Norman Manley.
1943 The Jamaica Labour Party (JLP) was founded.
1944 Universal adult suffrage was introduced and a new constitution allowed for the election of the House of Representatives.
1958 Jamaica became part of the attempted West Indies Federation.
1962 At the insistence of Prime Minister Alexander Bustamante, Jamaica left the West Indies Federation and gained separate independence. It became a member of the Commonwealth. Kingston became the capital city.
1968–69 Protests against poor housing conditions turned into serious riots in Kingston.
1972 Michael Manley became prime minister and pursued a policy of economic self-reliance.
1976 The PNP won another term following elections marked by violence and proceeded to nationalise businesses and build closer ties with Cuba.
1980 The JLP won the elections and Edward Seaga became prime minister reversing the nationalisation policies of the previous government. The US granted the Seaga government substantial aid after it distanced itself from Cuba.
1988 Hurricane Gilbert caused an estimated US$3 billion damage to much of the island.
1989 The PNP ousted the JLP in elections, returning Michael Manley as prime minister. Manley, however, chose to continue Seaga's policies.
1992 Manley retired on health grounds and was succeeded by Percival Patterson.
1993 The PNP was returned to office with an increased majority.
1997 The PNP won a third term in office.
1999 Protests against a new fuel tax spilled over into rioting in several areas. The Jamaican Defence Force (JDF) was ordered onto the streets to tackle the high rate of crime.
2001 Violence broke out in Kingston. There were gun battles between the police and gangs with political links. The army was called out after 25 people had been killed.
2002 The ruling PNP won parliamentary elections.
2004 Extra police were drafted into St James, the island's tourism capital, to tackle an escalating crime wave. Ivan, the worst hurricane since 1988, struck Jamaica, damaging thousands of homes and killing 15 people.
2005 Jamaica and Venezuela signed a US$200 million agreement to modernise and expand the Petrojam oil refinery in Kingston.
2007 In parliamentary elections, the opposition JLP won 50.1 per cent, 33 seats (out of 60); the ruling PNP won 49.8 per cent (27). Bruce Golding became prime minister.
2008 Parliament voted to continue the death penalty; Jamaica has one of the world's highest murder rates.
2009 Dr Patrick Allen, pastor and president of the Adventist Church's West Indies Union became Governor General.
2010 A state of emergency was declared in parts of the capital after several police stations were attacked. Security forces stormed the Kingston suburb of Tivoli Gardens, to arrest Christopher 'Dudus' Coke, an alleged drugs baron. The resulting gun-battle killed 73 people. The US had issued an international arrest warrant for Coke for drugs smuggling and gang-related offences. He was extradited, without opposition, to the US. The state of emergency was ended in mid-July after the government failed to get enough votes in Parliament to extend it. All suspects arrested during the disturbances had to be released. In July, Jamaica announced it was establishing an embassy in Kuwait.
2011 In May Prime Minister Golding announced that Jamaica was officially out of recession, following modest GDP growth in the first quarter. In June parliament approved the increase of fees charged to airline passengers visiting Jamaica from US$10 to US$20. Prime Minister Golding announced his resignation in September and in October, the JLP voted for Andrew Holness as his replacement as both leader of the party and therefore the country. During the Commonwealth Heads of Government summit, in October, the 16 countries in which the British monarch is Head of State unanimously agreed to change the royal line of succession from that of first born son to the first born child (regardless of its gender). The change will be enacted after the succession of Prince William (currently second in line to the throne, after his father Charles Prince of Wales). An early, snap, general election was held on 29 December in which the opposition PNP won 53.32 per cent of the vote (41 seats out of 63); the ruling JLP won 46.56 per cent (22 seats).
2012 Portia Simpson-Miller took office as prime minister on 5 January. During her inaugural speech she advocated replacing the monarch in favour of a presidency for Jamaica. On 24 October, Hurricane Sandy struck with heavy rains and winds of up to 125kph. On 1 November damage by Hurricane Sandy was estimated at over US$55 million. Agriculture was the hardest hit sector (over US$10 million), with significant losses of livestock as well as banana, plantain, cocoa, coffee and other cash crop production.
2013 In April the IMF agreed a US$1 billion, 48-month arrangement under an Extended Fund Facility (EFF). In December the Labour Party held its leadership election, won by Andrew Holness by 2,704 votes to 2,012 for Audley Shaw.
2014 In March the IMF completed its third review of Jamaica's economic performance under its EFF arrangement. This allowed for the disbursement of a further US$71.4 million, bringing the total disbursed under the EFF to US$345.8 million (out of a total of US$958 million). In May the IMF reported that the success of Jamaica's economic reform programme (ERP) had put the country on course to pass its fourth quarterly review (January to March 2014) to secure a further, fifth, drawdown of US$71 million, under the four-year EFF agreement. Standard and Poor's improved its outlook on Jamaica from stable to positive in September. In October Alcoa and Noble Group Ltd signed an agreement that will result in Alcoa World Alumina and Chemicals (AWAC) selling 100 per cent of its ownership stake in the Jamalco bauxite mining and alumina refining joint venture to Noble for US$140 million. AWAC will continue as the managing operator for three years and the government will retain its 45 per cent through Clarendon Alumina Production Ltd.
2015 The government took the first step towards legalising marijuana when the Dangerous Drugs (Amendment) Act, 2015, was tabled on 23 January, including a provision to establish a Cannabis Licensing Authority to regulate the proposed hemp and medical marijuana industry.

While on a visit to Jamaica in September the UK prime minister, David Cameroon, ruled out majing reparations for the slave trade.

Political structure

Constitution

Jamaica is a parliamentary democracy and independent state within the Commonwealth. The British monarch is the titular head of state and is represented by a governor general appointed on the advice of the prime minister. The governor general's role is mainly ceremonial and is guided in most cases by the prime minister, who as head of government effectively exercises executive power. Duties include appointing the leader of the opposition from among members of parliament who do not support the government. The governor general must have no affiliation with any political party while holding office.

Local governments in the 14 parishes are due for election every three years. The minimum voting age is 18. Voting is by secret ballot and the candidate who wins the most votes in each constituency is elected in a first-past-the-post electoral system.

Form of state

Constitutional monarchy

The executive

The head of state is the British monarch who is represented by the Governor General of Jamaica. The prime minister is selected by the governor general from the House of Representatives as the member best able to command the support of the House. Executive power rests with the cabinet – made up of the prime minister and at least 11 ministers. Cabinet ministers are chosen by the prime minister.

National legislature

The legislature is a bicameral parliament. It consists of a 63-member House of Representatives, elected every five years, and a 21-member Senate, appointed to a parallel term. The prime minister, who is also leader of the majority in the House of Representatives, appoints 13 senators, while the remaining eight are named by the leader of the opposition. The Senate mainly reviews legislation passed by the House of Representatives, although it can also initiate legislation, except on financial matters.

Voting must be held within three months of the dissolution of parliament. There have been eight parliaments since 1962, when Jamaica became the first English-speaking West Indian island to gain independence from the UK.

Legal system

The judiciary is headed by a Supreme Court and a Court of Appeal. The governor general, acting under the guidance of a six-member Privy Council based in London, UK, can grant pardons to convicted criminals. The final appeal is to the Judicial Committee of the Privy Council in the UK.

Last elections

29 December 2011 (parliamentary)

Results: Parliamentary: People's National Party (PNP) won 53.32 per cent of the vote (41 seats out of 63), the Jamaica Labour Party (JLP) won 46.56 per cent (22); four other political parties each won less than 1 per cent and failed to win any seats.

Next elections

On a date in between 29 December 2016 and 16 April 2017 (parliamentary)

Political parties

Ruling party

People's National Party (PNP) (from 5 Jan 2012)

Main opposition party

Jamaica Labour Party (JLP)

Approximately 30 per cent of the total population is under 14 years of age.

Population

2.75 million (2012)*

Last census: September 2001: 2,607632

Population density: 209 inhabitants per square km. Urban population 52 per cent (2010 Unicef).

Annual growth rate: 0.7 per cent, 1990–2010 (Unicef).

Ethnic make-up

Afro-Caribbean (90.9 per cent), East Indian (1.3 per cent), European (0.2 per cent), Chinese (0.2 per cent), mixed (7.3 per cent) and other (0.1 per cent).

Religions

Jamaica is home to a number of Christian denominations, mostly Protestant (over 61 per cent of the population). These include the Church of God (21 per cent), Baptist (9 per cent), Anglican (6 per cent) and Seventh-Day Adventist (9 per cent) churches. Roman Catholics (4 per cent) and spiritual cults (35 per cent) make up the other principal religious groups.

Education

The quality of schooling has slowly deteriorated over the last 20 years as debt reduction and other fiscal issues take higher priority. Jamaica's education system is based on the British system. Schooling consists of a two year pre-primary from aged 4, then a compulsory primary cycle of six years. Secondary schooling is divided into three phases, at the end of each, students either leave or move up to the next grade. They enter a 'first cycle' secondary school for three years, then a sixth form education of two-years and finally a 'second cycle' secondary school of two years; GSE 'O' and 'A' level examinations conclude the latter two. The education system accommodates a variety of public and private schools.

The main beneficiary of the government's spending on education is the primary school system, which enjoys a higher per capita expenditure than secondary and tertiary education.

Free places are offered in secondary schools through an annual common entrance examination, but a shortage of places has meant that not all children who qualify can be accommodated.

Post-secondary education is available at three universities and a number of community and teacher-training colleges. Opportunities for tertiary education remain limited, with only 8 per cent of high school graduates going to university or other higher institutions.

The primary and secondary education system was affected by the structural adjustment programme agreed with the IMF during the 1990s, which resulted in general cutbacks in social services expenditure. However, education has also benefitted from direct support from multilateral institutions. In 1996, the World Bank initiated a US$28 million student loan project, and has sponsored reform of secondary education. In 2000, the Inter-American Development Bank (IDB) approved a US$31 million loan to support the development of the primary school system.

Literacy rate: 88 per cent adult rate; 95 per cent youth rate (15–24) (Unesco 2005).

Compulsory years: Six to 12

Enrolment rate: 101 per cent gross primary enrolment, of relevant age group (including repeaters) (World Bank)

Pupils per teacher: 31 in primary schools.

Health

Jamaica's health care is affordable and improving dramatically; increasing life expectancy and lowering infant mortality rates to some of the best figures in the Caribbean. Unfortunately, money has been taken out of the funding for the public education system.

Improved water sources and sanitation facilities are available to 71 per cent and 84 per cent of the population, respectively.

HIV/Aids

HIV prevalence: 1.2 per cent aged 15–49 in 2003 (World Bank)

Life expectancy: 72 years, 2004 (WHO 2006)

Fertility rate/Maternal mortality rate: 1.4 births per woman, 2010 (Unicef)

Birth rate/Death rate: 17.4 births per 1,000 population; 5.4 deaths per 1,000 population (2003).

Child (under 5 years) mortality rate (per 1,000): 17 per 1,000 live births (WHO 2012)
Head of population per physician: 0.85 physicians per 1,000 people, 2003 (WHO 2006)

Welfare

Welfare is provided under the National Insurance Scheme (NIS) and the Social Assistance Programme. The NIS is contributory and provides protection against loss of income for men aged 18 to 70 years and women aged 18 to 65 years. There has also been multilateral involvement in welfare provision, including a US$20 million Jamaica Social Investment Fund (JSIF) initiated by the World Bank in 1996. JSIF is part of a national programme aimed at eliminating poverty and generating social funds. The Bank has initiated a social assessment programme for the inner cities, to allow the JSIF to target poverty more effectively. The Jamaican government has mobilised support from several non-governmental organisations and other charities towards the administration of social security and welfare measures. It is open to collaboration and partnership with stakeholders, both locally and abroad to improve the quality of services delivered to the poor. Such organisations include, Food for the Poor, which was involved in a massive programme to build 2,000 homes for poor families across Jamaica.

Main cities

Kingston (capital, estimated population 575,946 in 2012), Spanish Town (170,325), Portmore (132,777), Montego Bay (78,998), May Pen (49,471), Mandeville (48,849).

Languages spoken

English and a local patois, influenced by Elizabethan English.

Official language/s

English

Media

The media is free from censorship, athough the government has wide involvement in television, it has little control over radio and none in the print media.

Press

Dailies: There of the three dailies, two are published in the morning, *The Jamaica Gleaner* (www.jamaica-gleaner.com) and *The Jamaica Observer* (www.jamaicaobserver.com), *The Jamaica Star* (an afternoon tabloid) (www.jamaica-star.com).
Weeklies: There are several publications for local communities as well as one national newspaper, *Sunday Herald* (www.sunheraldja.com), *North Star Times* and *Mandeville Weekly*. The *Xtra-News* (www.xnewsjamaica.com) is an entertainment magazine.
Business: The monthly *Investor's Choice* magazine serving a diverse audience. Daily and weekly newspapers have local business news articles.
Periodicals: A monthly magazine, *The Commentator* (www.thecommentatorjm.com) publishes submitted articles on a variety of historical and current topics.

Broadcasting

Radio: All radio stations are independently owned and commercially operated. RJR Communications Group (www.rjrgroup.com) operates Radio Jamaica with a network of three stations including RJR (www.rjr94fm.com) for news and talk radio, Fame FM (www.famefm.fm) for innovative music and Hitz 92. Other stations include NewsTalk (www.newstalk.com.jm), Kool 97 FM (http://kool97fm.com) and Irie FM (www.iriefm.net).
Television: There are three TV stations in operation, of which TVJ (www.televisionjamaica.com) and CVM TV (www.cvmtv.com) are the other major broadcasters providing locally produced and imported TV programmes, Love TV (www.love101.org) is a religious broadcaster. Cable and satellite TV is available for subscribers, including CETV, Hype TV and RJR (http://rjrgroup.com).
National news agency: Jamaica Information Service
Other news agencies: Caribbean Net News: www.caribbeannetnews.com Jamaica New Bulletin: (www.jamaicanewsbulletin.com)

Economy

The economy is primarily based on services (72.0 cent of GDP in 2014), centred on tourism, with a record number of visitors in 2014 – 2.1 million – a 3.6 per cent increase on 2013. Agricultural production constituted 6.9 per cent of the economy with exports that include bananas, coffee, sugar, rum and spices. The industrial sector constituted 21.1 per cent of GDP, of which manufacturing contributed around 10 per cent in 2014. Alumina and bauxite exports provide valuable foreign earnings, combined they represented just under 50 per cent of total exports in 2014.
Jamaica's economy has a history of slow growth and recession, which has been worse since the global economic crisis struck in 2007. On top of this, the country is hampered by high crime and corruption, high unemployment and a debt equivalent to 130 per cent of its GDP. Over the 2008–10 period GDP growth averaged -1.8 per cent before briefly jumping out of recession in 2011 with growth of 1.7 per cent. Jamaica fell back into recession in 2012 with a contraction of -0.5 per cent, however, in 2013 growth became positive but stagnant at 0.2 per cent and 0.5 per cent in 2014. Inflation remains high, averaging 8.0 per cent over 2011–14.
Damage from hurricanes and tropical storms create continued economic shocks and have an adverse effect on the Jamaican economy. Tropical storm Gustav, which struck in 2008, destroyed many plantations and halted all exports. However, by 2010 exports of commodities had recovered and resulted in a US$667.2 million surplus.
Remittances in 2013 were US$2.16 billion (15.0 per cent of GDP), rising to US$2.26 billion in 2014 (16.4 per cent of GDP).
On 26 February 2014 Fitch Ratings Agency upgraded Jamaica's long term foreign currency and local currency issuer default ratings to B- from CCC.
In March 2014 the IMF completed its third review of Jamaica's economic performance under its Extended Fund Facility (EFF) arrangement. This allowed for the disbursement of a further US$71.4 million, bringing the total disbursed under the EFF to US$345.8 million. Standard and Poor's improved its rating for Jamaica from B- to B in June 2015.

External trade

Along with 11 other members in the Caribbean Community (Caricom), Jamaica operates within the single market (Caribbean Single Market and Economy (CSME)), which became operational in 2006. CSME includes the free movement of goods and services, a common trade policy and external tariff.
There is a heavy reliance on commodity exports while Jamaica's dependency on energy imports continues to cause severe balance of payments difficulties, although the PetroCaribe Energy Co-operation Agreement with Venezuela helps to ease these difficulties. However, due to falling oil prices, in 2014 the Venezuelan government cut the subsidies to the PetroCaribe.

Imports

Principal imports are foodstuffs, petroleum, capital goods and industrial supplies, vehicles, machinery and transport equipment, construction materials and consumer goods.
Main sources: US (39.3 per cent of total in 2014), Venezuela (11.5 per cent), Trinidad and Tobago (10.2 per cent)

Exports

Principal exports are aluminium, bauxite and chemicals, rum, coffee, sugar, bananas and yams, manufactured clothes.

Main destinations: US (39.5 per cent of total in 2014), Canada (15.3 per cent), Netherlands (5.7 per cent)

Re-exports

Re-exports including chemicals, machinery, transport equipment and miscellaneous manufactures represent 3.5 per cent of total value.

Agriculture

Farming

The agricultural sector, including forestry and fishing, contributed 6.9 per cent to GDP in 2014 and employs approximately 18 per cent of the workforce. Agricultural production is often affected by adverse weather conditions.

Blue Mountain coffee, one of the most expensive in the world, is grown in Jamaica. The 2012 annual crop of the famous coffee was severely damaged by the African Coffee Berry Borer beetle (*Hypothenemus hampei*). The Coffee Industry Board (CIB) revised its projection for coffee output from 234,000 boxes to 150,000–180,000 as a result of the infestation. The estimate to coffee growers is reduced production of 30–50 per cent and an industry loss of J$432.5 million (US$5 million).

Fishing

The produce of the fish industry is mostly consumed domestically. Estimates show that annual output could increase to 6.6 million pounds of freshwater fish, enabling Jamaica to compete on the world market.

The typical annual marine fish catch is around 5,000 tonnes (t) and around 600t shellfish.

Industry and manufacturing

The industrial sector contributed 21.1 per cent to GDP in 2014, of which manufacturing contributed an estimated 12 per cent. In addition to bauxite refining, agro-industries dominate, particularly food processing and sugar refining. The re-export manufacturing sector concentrates on textiles and garments, which are destined for markets in North America. However, this sector has suffered due to competition with Central American and Mexican producers, which enjoy freer trade links with the US. Other important manufacturing industries include chemicals, machinery and tools, glass, cement and metal products. Most companies in these industries are foreign-owned and heavily dependent on imported materials and components.

The Patterson government has been trying to direct industrial output to take advantage of preferential access for a range of products shipped to the US, Canada and the EU, in order to increase foreign earnings and employment. Further moves towards a free market economy are expected; the privatisation programme includes over 60 state-owned enterprises. Among public concerns already privatised are Caribbean Cement Company, Southern Processors and several hotels.

The industrial sector has not benefited significantly from the structural adjustment programme implemented since 1981, in agreement with the IMF. The programme has emphasised agro-industrial expansion to raise industrial exports while cutting the volume of imported raw materials. However, the sector has suffered from a prohibitive interest rate policy, high costs for factory construction and rental, out-dated technology and machinery and unfair competition from illicit imports and from dumping.

Tourism

Jamaica has been a leading Caribbean holiday destination for decades and has an established tourism infrastructure. It offers a wide range of accommodation and cultural and sports activities such as carnivals, yachting regattas and sports fishing. Jamaica was the home of the creator of James Bond, Ian Fleming, and Noel Coward, whose home Firefly Estate is a national heritage site.

Jamaica's tourism sector is an important component of the economy and constituted 27.2 per cent of GDP in 2014. In 2014 the number of visitors increased by 3.6 per cent on 2013, reaching 2.1 million. Over 60 per cent of visitors come from the US and over 15 per cent from Canada. Europe accounts for 15 per cent of all visitors, of which the UK represents 10 per cent. Employment in the travel and tourism sector was 24.7 per cent in 2014. Visitor exports were US$2.06 billion in 2014 and were projected to rise by 5.2 per cent in 2015.

Legislation was passed in October 2011 for gaming regulation and the opening of two casinos.

Mining

The mining sector generates around half of export earnings and contributes approximately 9 per cent to GDP. Mining and quarrying employs approximately 1 per cent of the workforce.

Activity is centred on the extraction of bauxite and alumina refining. Known reserves of bauxite are around two billion tonnes, although most is of relatively low quality. Other minerals exploited include gypsum, marble, silica and clays. In 2014, just under 50 per cent of all exports were accounted for by alumina and bauxite.

Hydrocarbons

There are no known oil or natural gas reserves. Consumption of oil was 69,310 barrels per day (bpd) in 2013, almost all of which was imported. In 2005, Jamaica, plus a number of other Caribbean states, signed an agreement with Venezuela to establish PetroCaribe, a multi-national oil company, owned by the participating states. PetroCaribe buys low-priced Venezuelan crude oil under long-term payment plans. However, due to falling oil prices, in 2014 the Venezuelan government cut the subsidies to the PetroCaribe.

The state-owned Petroleum Corporation of Jamaica (PCJ) is responsible for the management, exploration and importation of oil. Petrojam operates the only oil refinery on the island in Kingston, with a capacity of up to 50,000 barrels per day (bpd). The refinery was bought from Exxon in 1982 for US$42 million, including stocks, after the government refused to allow Esso a guaranteed profit margin under a new operating contract.

The government is planning to import liquefied natural gas (LNG) and has had talks with Trinidad and Tobago to ensure stable supplies remain at competitive prices. LNG is seen as a less expensive and less polluting energy source that could reduce the country's dependence on oil. Imports were expected to begin in early 2016.

Coal imports were 123,000 tonnes in 2012, used in power generation.

Energy

Total installed generating capacity was 1,175MW in 2013, generating over 4.75 billion kilowatt hours (kWh). The commercial company, Jamaica Public Service Company (JPS) is the sole distributor of electricity and owns four power stations and an additional eight-hydropower stations producing only 23.8MW of electricity, but which has a further installed potential of 100MW. There are five alternative, private independent power producers.

Almost all the country's energy needs are imported, with an estimated 70 per cent of foreign exchange earnings spent on oil. Oil is supplied at concessionary rates by Mexico and Venezuela. The major consumer is the alumina industry, where energy accounts for around 48 per cent of production costs. There is a strategy to move from oil to liquefied natural gas as the country's main source of energy for electricity generation; however this is dependent on the construction of either an undersea gas pipeline from Trinidad and Tobago, or a liquefied national gas processing plant for supplies from elsewhere. Other renewable sources of power are being considered.

Financial markets

Stock exchange

Jamaica Stock Exchange (JSE)

Banking and insurance

The banking sector has undergone extensive restructuring since 1997, when the government intervened to prevent a complete collapse of the country's financial institutions. The sector's problems arose from a lack of proper risk management which created inherent weaknesses. These were exposed when the monetary authorities raised interest rates to stem the tide of inflation causing asset values to plummet. The restructuring of the financial sector was completed by the Financial Sector Adjustment Company (Finsac) in 2002 at an estimated cost of around 30 per cent of GDP. In the restructuring process, Finsac merged banks and sold them to the Royal Bank of Trinidad and Tobago. Consequently, foreign banks have a high presence in Jamaica, controlling around 80 per cent of total bank deposits.

Central bank

The Bank of Jamaica

Time

GMT minus five hours

Geography

Jamaica, with an area of 10,989 square km, is the third largest island in the Caribbean. Covered with dense tropical vegetation, it is 234km long and 82km across at the widest point. The island lies about 145km south of Cuba and 160km west of Hispaniola. Mountain ranges snake across the island from south-east to north-west, with many long spurs to north and south. The highest summits are at the eastern end of the island, with the Blue Mountain Peak the tallest at 2,256 metres. The longest river, the Rio Minho, flows south from its source in the centre of the country, and is 92km long.

Hemisphere

Northern

Climate

Jamaica is around 5 degrees south of the Tropic of Cancer and has a maritime tropical climate characterised by warm trade winds. Average coastal and lowland temperatures are around 27 degrees Celsius, with little seasonal variation. Mean annual rainfall is about 200mm, with the main rainy season in October and a second one in May. Jamaica may be subject to the tropical storms and hurricanes typical of the Caribbean basin weather system.

Dress codes

Dress codes are mainly informal. Officials wear a jacket and tie or loose-fitting lightweight clothes when the climate is hot and humid. A sweater is rarely needed, even on cooler evenings. Light rainwear is useful. On social occasions, dress as for business meetings unless otherwise indicated.

Entry requirements

Passports

Required by all, valid for six months from date of departure, except nationals of the US and Canada, who require only proof of identity and nationality, (all US and Canadian nationals require a passport for re-entry to their country from January 2007).

Visa

No visa requirements for nationals of EU/EEA countries, North America, Australasia, and some Latin American and Asian countries. For details, see www.jhcuk.com/newguide-fr.html. Business visas require a letter from the employer, an itinerary and evidence of sufficient funds.

Currency advice/regulations

The import and export of local currency is prohibited. The import and export of foreign currency is allowed, subject to declaration.

Prohibited imports

Obscene images and publications. The following items are restricted and require permits: meat, ground provisions, fruit and vegetables, pharmaceuticals, firearms, used tyres, two-way radios, coconut derivatives, motor vehicles, explosives, bulk alcohol, sugar, human remains, pesticides and live animals.

Health (for visitors)

Mandatory precautions

A yellow fever vaccination certificate is required if arriving from an infected area.

Advisable precautions

Hepatitis A and B, tetanus, TB, typhoid and polio vaccinations are recommended. Drinking water from the public supply is safe.

Foreigners visiting the island can use public health services, but are advised to seek private medical attention. Insurance to cover the latter which can be expensive is highly recommended.

Hotels

Hotels and guest houses are graded and mostly geared towards holidaymakers. There are also numerous resort villas and apartments.

Public holidays (national)

Fixed dates

1 Jan (New Year's Day), 23 May (Labour Day), 1 Aug (Emancipation Day), 6 Aug (Independence Day), 25–26 Dec (Christmas).

Variable dates

Ash Wednesday, Good Friday, Easter Monday, National Heroes' Day (third Mon in Oct).

Working hours

Banking

Mon–Thu: 0900–1400; Fri 0900–1500. Branches of some banks open on Sat.

Business

Mon–Fri: 0830–1630/1700. Some offices open Sat.

Government

Mon–Fri: 0830–1630/1700. Some offices open Sat.

Shops

Mon–Sat: 0830–1630/1700.

Telecommunications

Mobile/cell phones

There are several GSM 850, 900, 1800 and 1900 services available throughout the country.

Electricity supply

110/220V AC, 50 cycles

Social customs/useful tips

Appointments should be made in advance. Punctuality is appreciated. An additional 10 per cent tip is usual, even where a 10–15 per cent service charge is billed automatically. Penalties for drug offences are severe, with possession of even small quantities possibly leading to imprisonment. Luggage should be packed without the help of others and only your own should be carried through customs.

Security

It is advisable not to walk around after dark due to street crime. Some parts of Kingston are considered dangerous even during the daytime, avoid exploring nightlife away from main hotels and restaurants, unless accompanied by Jamaican friends. Only taxis, authorised by the Jamaica Union of Travellers Association (Juta) should be used and preferably ordered through hotels.

Getting there

Air

National airline: Air Jamaica.

International airport/s: Kingston-Norman Manley International (KIN), 17km south-east of city, duty-free shop, bars, restaurants, bank, post office, car hire.

Other airport/s: Montego Bay-Sangster International (MBJ), 3km north of Montego Bay.

Airport tax: J$1,000.

Surface

Water: The island has several ports catering for international shipping and local ferries.

Main port/s: Kingston, Montego Bay, Ocho Rios and Port Antonio.

Getting about

National transport

Air: Air Jamaica serves several destinations. TimAir Ltd and International Air Link provide charter services.

Road: There is an extensive network of surfaced, all-weather roads, accounting for 70 per cent of the total of around 18,000km.

Buses: Minibuses in towns are generally cheap but crowded; in the country they are often considered slow, crowded and sometimes dangerous. There are regular, scheduled services over longer distances (eg Kingston-Montego Bay; journey time varies, to some extent dependent on route).
Rail: Jamaica has 272km of track. Passenger services have been suspended since 1992. A privately-owned portion of the network is used for transport of bauxite.

City transport

Taxis: All taxis have red PPV plates. It is advisable to negotiate fares (J$) in advance. Taxis in Kingston no longer use meters. A 10 per cent tip is usual.

Car hire

Widely available. International or national licence accepted; traffic drives on the left.

BUSINESS DIRECTORY

The addresses listed below are a selection only. While World of Information makes every endeavour to check these addresses, we cannot guarantee that changes have not been made, especially to telephone numbers and area codes. We would welcome any corrections.

Telephone area codes

International direct dialling code (IDD) for Jamaica is +1 876, followed by subscriber's number.

Chambers of Commerce

American Chamber of Commerce of Jamaica, Le Méridien Jamaica Pegasus Hotel, 81 Knutsford Boulevard, Kingston (tel: 929-7866; fax: 929-8597; e-mail: info@amchamjamaica.org).

Jamaica Chamber of Commerce, 85a Duke Street, Kingston (tel: 922-0150; fax: 924-9056; e-mail: jamcham@cwjamaica.com).

Montego Bay Chamber of Commerce and Industry, 4-7 Overton Plaza, PO Box 213, Montego Bay (tel: 952-6045; fax: 952-2784).

Banking

National Investment Bank of Jamaica, 32 Trafalgar Road, Kingston 10 (tel. 929-9050).

Bank of Nova Scotia Jamaica, Scotia Centre, Port Royal Street, Kingston (tel: 922-1000).

CIBC Jamaica, 23-27 Knutsford Boulevard, Kingston 5 (tel: 929-9310).

Citibank N.A., 63-67 Knutsford Boulevard, Kingston 5 (tel: 926-3270/3285; fax: 929-3745).

National Commercial Bank of Jamaica, The Atrium, 32 Trafalgar Road, Kingston 10 (tel: 929-9050).

RBTT Bank Jamaica, 17 Dominica Drive, Kingston 5 (tel: 960-2340; e-mail: rbtt@cwjamaica.com).

The Financial Sector Adjustment Company, PO Box 54, 76 Knutsford Boulevard, Kingston 5: (tel: 906-1809; fax: 906-1822; info@FINSAC.com).

Trafalgar Commercial Bank, 60 Knutsford Boulevard, Kingston 5 (tel: 929-3383, 929-3511, 929-3521; fax: 929-3654).

Central bank

Bank of Jamaica, Nethersole Place, PO Box 621, Kingston (tel: 922-0750; fax: 922-0854; e-mail: info@boj.org.jm).

Stock exchange

Jamaica Stock Exchange (JSE), www.jamstockex.com

Travel information

Air Jamaica Ltd, 72–76 Harbour St, Kingston (tel: 922-3460; fax: 967-3125; pr@airjamaica.com).

Jamaica Hotel and Tourist Association, 2 Ardenne Road, Kingston 10 (tel: 926-3635; fax: 929-1054; e-mail: info@jhta.org).

National tourist organisation offices

Jamaica Tourist Board, Knutsford Boulevard, Kingston 5 (tel: 929-9200; fax: 929-9375; e-mail: info@visitjamaica.com).

Ministries

Office of The Prime Minister, Jamaica House, 1 Devon Road, Kingston 6 (tel: 927-9941/3; fax: 929-0005).

Ministry of Agriculture, Hope Gardens, Kingston 6 (tel: 927-1731/45; fax: 927-1904).

Ministry of Education and Culture, 2 National Heroes Circle, Kingston 4 (tel: 922-1400/19; fax: 967-1837).

Ministry of Finance and Planning, 30 National Heroes Circle, Kingston 4 (tel: 922-8600/15; fax: 922-7097).

Ministry of Foreign Affairs and Foreign Trade, 21 Dominica Drive, Kingston 5 (tel: 926-4220/8; fax: 929-5112; e-mail: mfaftjam@cwjamaica.com).

Ministry of Health, Oceana Hotel Complex, 2 King Street, Kingston (tel: 967-1092; fax: 967-7293).

Ministry of Industry, Commerce and Technology, 36 Trafalgar Road, Kingston 10 (tel: 929-8990/9; fax: 960-1623; e-mail: gojmii@infochan.com).

Ministry of Labour and Social Security, 1f North Street, Kingston (tel: 922-9500, 967-1900; fax: 922-6902).

Ministry of Land and Environment, 2 Hagley Park Road, Kingston 10 (tel: 926-1590, 926-7008; fax: 926-2591; e-mail: mehsys@hotmail.com).

Ministry of Local Government, Youth & Community Development, 85 Hagley Park, Kingston 10 (tel: 754-0994; fax: 960-0725).

Ministry of Mining and Energy, 36 Trafalgar Road, Kingston 10 (tel: 926-9170/7; fax: 968-2082; e-mail: hmme@cwjamaica.com).

Ministry of National Security and Justice, Mutual Life Building, North Tower, 2 Oxford Road, Kingston 5 (tel: 906-4908/33; fax: 906-1724; e-mail: inform@infochan.com).

Ministry of Tourism and Sports, 64 Knutsford Boulevard, Kingston 5 (tel: 920-4956; fax: 920-4944; e-mail: opmt@cwjamaica.com).

Ministry of Transportation and Works, 1c-1f Pawsey Place, New Kingston (tel: 754-1900; fax: 927-8763).

Ministry of Water and Housing, 7th Floor, Island Life Building, 6 St Lucia Avenue, Kingston 5 (tel: 754-0973; fax: 754-0975; e-mail: prumow@cwjamaica.com).

Attorney General's Department, Mutual Life Building, North Tower, 2 Oxford Road, Kingston 5 (tel: 906-2416/7) and 79-83 Barry Street, Kingston (tel: 922-6140; fax: 922-5109).

Other useful addresses

All-Island Jamaica Cane Farmers' Association, 4 North Ave, Kingston 4 (tel: 922-3010; fax: 922-077).

Banana Export Co (BECO), 10 South Ave, Kingston 4 (tel: 922-5490).

British High Commission, Trafalgar Road, PO Box 575, Kingston 10 (tel: 926-9050; fax: 929-7869).

Cabinet Office, 1 Devon Road, Kingston 10 (tel: 927-9941/3; fax: 929-8459).

Cocoa Industry Board, Marcus Garvey Drive, PO Box 68, Kingston 15 (tel: 923-6411).

Coffee Industry Board, Marcus Garvey Drive, Kingston 15 (tel: 923-7211).

Jamaica Bauxite Institute, Hope Gdns, PO Box 355, Kingston 6 (tel: 927-2073; fax: 927-159).

Jamaica Exporters' Association (JEA), 13 Dominica Drive, PO Box 9, Kingston 5 (tel: 929-1292; fax: 929-831).

Jamaica Information Service, Kingston (tel: 926-3740, 926-3590; fax: 926-715).

Jamaica Manufacturers' Association, 85a Duke Street, Kingston (tel: 922-8880/2).

Jamaica Promotion Corporation (Jampro Limited), 35 Trafalgar Road, Kingston 10 (tel: 929-9450, 929-9452/6; fax: 924-9650; e-mail: jamprouk@investjamaica.com).

Jamaica Stock Exchange, 40 Harbour Street, Kingston (tel: 922-0806; fax: 922-6966; e-mail: info-jse@jamstockex.com).

Jamaican Embassy (USA), 1520 New Hampshire Avenue, NW, Washington DC 20006 (tel: (+1-202)-452-0660; fax: (+1-202)-452-0081; e-mail: emjam@sysnet.net).

Kingston Free Zone, Lot 27, Shannon Drive, Kingston 15 (tel: 923-5274).

The Planning Institute of Jamaica, 39 Barbados Ave, Kingston 5 (tel: 926-1480; fax: 926-4670).

US Embassy, Mutual Life Centre, 2 Oxford Road, Kingston 5 (tel: 929-4850).

National news agency: Jamaica Information Service, 58a Half Way Tree Road, Kingston 10 (tel: 926-3740; fax: 926-6715; email: jis@jis.gov.jm; internet: www.jis.gov.jm).

Caribbean Net News: www.caribbeannetnews.com

Jamaica New Bulletin: (www.jamaicanewsbulletin.com)

Internet sites

Export Jamaica: http://www.exportjamaica.org

Jamaica Stock Exchange: http://www.jamstockex.com

CVM Television: http://www.cvmtv.com/top_news1.htm

Jamaica and Jamaican Top 5 Sites: http://www.top5jamaica.com

Jamaicamarket (business gateway): http://www.jamaicamarket.com

Jamaica Promotions Corporation (Jampro) (export and investment promotion agency): http://www.investjamaica.com

Japan

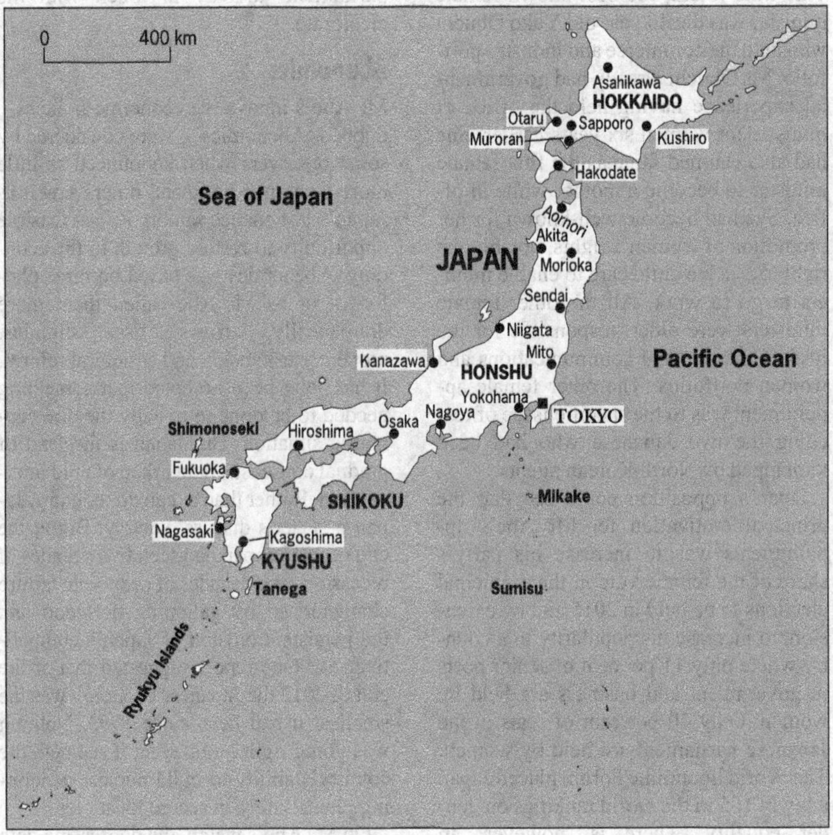

KEY FACTS

Official name: Nippon or Nihon (Japan)

Head of State: Emperor Tsegu no Miya Akihito (since 1989)

Head of government: Prime Minister Shinzo Abe (LDP) (from 16 Dec 2012)

Ruling party: Liberal Democratic Party-New Komeito Party (LDP-NKP coalition) from 16 Dec 2012)

Area: 377,728 square km (3,900 small islands)

Population: 127.06 million (2014)

Capital: Tokyo

Official language: Japanese

Currency: Yen (¥)

Exchange rate: ¥119.75 per US$ (Sep 2015)

GDP per capita: US$36,332 (2014)

GDP real growth: -0.06% (2014)

GDP: US$4,616.34 billion (2014)

Labour force: 65.93 million (2014)*

Unemployment: 3.58% (2014)

Inflation: 2.74% (2014)

Balance of trade: -US$99.20 billion (2014)

* estimated figure

Although China has pushed it into third place, Japan still has a mighty economy and is one of the world's richest countries.

Poverty? Here?

However, by 2015, life-time employment, or 'employment for life' had virtually disappeared in Japan, replaced by the insecurity of contractual employment and often short term contracts at that. Clearly there are plenty of pockets of wealth and prosperity in Japan, but none the less an estimated one in six Japanese children now live in poverty – one of the worst rates in the industrialised world. A piece for the Australian Broadcasting Corporation (ABC) by North Asia correspondent Matthew Carney reported that in 2015 Japan more than half a million single mothers live below the poverty line, earning less than US$12,000 a year.

As the case with many social problems in Japan, poverty is often hidden. To acknowledge poverty is a matter of great shame, a major loss of face. The poverty issue cuts across age-groups and across gender. But unquestionably, by 2015 it was no longer just a social problem, it had spilled over into Japan's ability to shake off deflation and create an economic revival.

The London *Economist* also reported that in 2014 the Japanese government recorded relative poverty rates of 16 per cent – defined as the share of the population living on less than half the national median income. That was the highest on record. According to the *Economist*, this was not a totally new phenomenon: poverty levels had been growing at a rate of 1.3 per cent a year since the mid-1980s. A poverty study by the Organisation for Economic Co-operation and

Development (OECD) in 2011 ranked Japan sixth from the bottom among its 34 members.

At first sight, at least in the macro-economic picture, things might have appeared to be improving in 2015 Japan. Unemployment was respectably low, below 4 per cent and new jobs were being generated against a background of quantitative easing. But as noted above, the second rate quality of new jobs – or at least the contracts that govern them – was not helping much. Since Prime Minister Shinzo Abe took office in 2012, the number of irregular workers – some earning less than half the pay of their full-time counterparts with permanent employment contracts – had jumped by over 1.5 million. Casual and part-time employees now accounted for approaching 40 per cent of the Japanese workforce.

Gender bender

The government appointed by Prime Minister Shinzo Abe in September 2014 represented an attempt at change from its predecessors. The fact that there were five female ministers in the cabinet, over one quarter, was seen as more than a simple gesture towards Japan's female population. Outside observers had long been aware of the dichotomy between the level of competence of Japan's women and their level of representation both in government and in business.

Mr Abe had gone on record that the government's target for female senior representation in both areas of activity should be a minimum 30 per cent, saying that 'Creating a society in which women can shine is a great challenge which the government is taking on.' However, Japan's progress has been slow. In 2001 the then prime minister, Jumichiro Koizumi, had made an attempt, appointing the same number of women to his cabinet; but tradition prevailed in subsequent cabinets. This time round, the best known female minister was the 40 year old Yuko Obuchi who held the commerce and industry portfolio. Ms Obuchi already had governmental experience having held the office of minister for women six years earlier. She had also claimed fame as the first female minister to become a mother while in office. She had become well-known for her promotion of women's rights, notably the right to receive child care to enable mothers to go to work. All the other female ministers were older, responsible for the justice, interior and communications and women portfolios. The other female appointment was to the specific issue of rescuing the two Japanese who had been kidnapped by North Korean agents.

Japan's opposition could see that the principal motivation for Mr Abe's appointments was to increase his party's share of the female vote in the municipal elections to be held in 2015 and by extension, to increase his popularity in a country where only 11 per cent of senior posts in government and business are held by women. Only 10 per cent of seats in the Japanese parliament are held by women. The World Economic Forum placed Japan a lowly 105 in the world rankings on gender equality. There is, however, an important underlying factor: Japan is facing a rapid ageing of its population which in turn places heavier demands on the social security system. Furthermore, the birth rate is low meaning that the pool of potential politicians is also smaller; promoting more women would (theoretically) enable the political parties and the parliament, to stay in touch with the electorate.

Abenomics

Mr Abe's innovative economic policies – dubbed 'Abenomics' – were considered by some observers when announced as little more than an experiment, others saw it as Japan's last chance saloon, its last feasible opportunity to restore growth to the economy. Abenomics was based on three platforms, or as Mr Abe called them more dramatically, 'arrows': fiscal stimulus, monetary expansion and structural reform. It had long been accepted that something needed to be done to remedy the dire economic situation. But Japan is the land of gradual consensus rather than of bold intervention. Rather than a 'can do' country, Japan is a 'let's discuss' society. But at the end of 2013 Japan had seen two decades of recession, two decades of economic failure characterised by galloping deflation and the persistent erosion of Japan's competitiveness. One report suggested that at the end of 2012 the Japanese economy was the smallest it had been since 1993. Nothing was going right – not even, it seemed, the country's ability to build nuclear generating plants safely in secure locations.

On Mr Abe's watch, the depressing data that used to be regularly churned out had, it was hoped, become history. Since December 2012, when Mr Abe became prime minister, things had changed in a way that few expected. Japan's economic growth rate had averaged an annual 4 per cent, the consumer price index had risen by 2 per cent and salaries were expected to increase by one per cent in 2014. In the month of June 2014 the Nikkei Index rose by an impressive 4.5 per cent. Mid-2014 was the moment designated under Abenomics when Japan embarked on the third phase of the 'experiment'. This was the most ambitious and far reaching: the implementation of structural reforms. The two earlier phases were engineering the depreciation of the yen and unprecedented injections of capital into the economy – quantitative easing.

It was in anticipation of Abenomics' third 'arrow' that the Japanese stock exchange had picked up after a period of stagnation in the first months of 2014. The

KEY INDICATORS — Japan

	Unit	2011	2012	2013	2014	**2015
Population	m	*127.82	127.61	127.34	127.06	*126.73
Gross domestic product (GDP)	US$bn	5,869.50	5,937.77	4,919.56	4,616.34	*4,210.36
GDP per capita	US$	45,920	46,530	38,633	36,332	*33,223
GDP real growth	%	-0.7	1.4	1.6	-0.1	*1.0
Inflation	%	-0.3	*0.0	0.4	2.7	*1.0
Unemployment	%	4.5	4.3	4.0	3.6	*3.7
Coal output	mtoe	0.7	0.7	0.7	0.7	–
Exports (fob) (goods)	US$m	789,950	776,640	694,940	699,450	–
Imports (fob) (goods)	US$m	794,420	830,120	784,590	798,650	–
Balance of trade	US$m	-4,470	-53,480	-89,650	-99,200	–
Current account	US$m	119,060	60,446	33,634	24,280	81,568
Total reserves minus gold	US$m	1,110,795	1,227,147	1,237,218	1,231,010	–
Foreign exchange	US$m	1,071,993	1,193,578	1,202,924	–	–
Exchange rate	per US$	81.63	81.11	105.03	119.86	–

* estimated figure ** forecast figure

proposed structural reforms included a revision of the public pension system, encouraging private investment in Japan's equity markets, a progressive reduction of as much as six per cent in corporate taxation and measures to improve corporate governance and transparency. Overall, corporate and governmental transparency in Japan was relatively good. On the 2013 Transparency International (TI) *Corruption Perceptions Index* Japan ranked fifteenth out of the 175 countries surveyed, ahead of France, Hong Kong and the US. However, a new and unpopular secrecy law appeared to run counter to both popular and media sentiment. The planned legislation would apply to all senior Japanese civil servants, including diplomats. and embrace defence, counter-terrorism and counter-espionage. The net effect, according to most Japanese newspapers, would be that the Japanese public would have less access to information than before.

The financial community certainly endorsed Mr Abe's moves, some going so far as to predict a rise of 2–3,000 points in the Nikkei Index, from the 15,000 level pertaining in mid-2014 to well over 17,000 by mid-2015. As it turned out, despite the turmoil in the Chinese stock markets, the Nikkei outperformed Mr Abe's target, reaching over 18,000 by early September 2015. It appeared that many of Japan's mid-level equity investors had emerged from the woodwork and, reassured by Mr Abe's policies, begun to play a more active investment role. It was assumed that the Bank of Japan would continue its quantitative easing activity (the scale of which was proportionately bigger than that seen in the UK or the US). A major incentive to invest in Japanese equities was provided by the seemingly unanimous view of the market that Japanese equities remained undervalued.

The economy – OECD concerns

In its 2015 *Economic Survey of Japan*, the Paris based Organisation for Economic Co-operation and Development (OECD) noted that two decades of sluggish growth and persistent deflation had reduced Japanese living standards below the OECD average. Gross government debt had risen to 226 per cent of gross domestic product (GDP), the highest in the OECD, driven by rising social spending and inadequate revenues. Rapid population ageing was putting continued pressure on public spending, while pushing down Japan's potential growth rate to around 0.75 per cent. Abenomics, flexible fiscal policy and growth strategy, all aimed at revitalising the economy and ending deflation – had had an immediately positive effect in 2013. Growth was interrupted in the wake of the tax increase in April 2014, but resumed later in the year.

In the view of the OECD, fundamental structural reforms urgently needed to be stepped up to raise output growth, which was essential for fiscal consolidation and improved living standards. The role of women was limited by a range of factors, including their concentration in non-regular jobs and disincentives in the tax system. Japan remains internationally isolated with the lowest share of inward foreign direct investment (FDI – as a per cent of GDP) in the OECD area. Low rates of business creation and exit reflected a lack of economic dynamism in the business sector. Venture capital investment was at an early stage of development and the small and medium-sized enterprise sector was lagging.

With a primary deficit of nearly 7 per cent of GDP in 2014, Japan's public debt remained on an upward path. The impact of the high debt was mitigated by low long-term interest rates, although weakening confidence might cause interest rates to rise substantially. A rise in interest rates would increase debt rapidly and destabilise the financial sector and the real economy. Large-scale revenue increases were, in the opinion of the OECD, indispensable, although they would tend to temporarily hold back GDP growth. Constraining spending was difficult but crucial, given the upward pressure on social outlays, notably for health and long-term care and the need to promote social cohesion.

The IMF: economic health check

In its July 2015 survey of the Japanese economy, the International Monetary Fund (IMF) noted that Japan's prospects had improved, but also considered that the introduction of stronger structural reforms was critical to meet long-term challenges. The IMF also felt that there was a need for balanced, credible, fiscal consolidation while at the same time supporting growth. In the view of the IMF, Abenomics 'had lifted Japan out of the doldrums.' But there was still the need to 'end the lingering deflationary mindset, raise growth, restore fiscal sustainability and maintain financial stability without undue reliance on yen depreciation.'

The IMF reported that Abenomics' three-pronged strategy of aggressive monetary easing, flexible fiscal policy and structural reforms had been a clear break from previous incremental efforts. But that 'despite initial positive results', the pace of GDP growth had remained at about one per cent – similar to the post-bubble period – and deflation risks remained

The negative impact of the consumption tax rate increase in 2014 had lasted longer than expected in the view of the IMF, but structural impediments had also played a role. These included sluggish wage growth, production being moved to other countries through FDI and the problems posed by Japan's ageing and declining population.

The IMF expected the economy to grow by 0.8 and 1.2 per cent in 2015 and 2016, provided higher real wages supported consumption and that business investment rose reflecting lower production costs from falling oil prices, higher corporate profits, continuing corporate governance reforms and the abundant availability of credit.

Japan also faced short-term risks from lower-than-expected growth in China and the United States and the possible yen appreciation in the event of global financial turbulence given its status as a safe-haven currency.

Structural reforms had progressed in a number of areas, notably in female labour force participation (see above). Although this had been rising gradually since the mid-2000s, it had received a further high-profile boost from Abenomics. The IMF considered that the government could also address labour shortages by facilitating more foreign labour and relaxing immigration restrictions, as well as providing incentives for older workers to remain in the workforce.

Rather stating the obvious, the IMF suggested that 'The financial sector should become a catalyst for growth.' This alluded to corporate governance reforms to unwind cross-shareholdings, foster consolidation in the enterprise sector and 'promote the exit of unviable enterprises.'

The IMF report's author acknowledged that in Japan 'Raising inflation has proven to be a marathon rather than a sprint.' According to the report, market-based measures of inflation expectations had declined since mid-2014 and stabilised at around one per cent, suggesting the hoped for 'regime change' had not fully materialised. However, the report suggested that several factors would put upward pressure on prices in the near term, including a recovery in oil and commodity prices, the eventual effect of the recent episode of yen weakening and the closing of the output gap – or the difference between the potential output of an economy and its actual output. The IMF expected inflation to rise gradually to 1.5 per cent over the medium term.

Stock market confidence?

In the second week of September 2015 the main index of the Japanese Stock Exchange, the Nikkei, registered its greatest one day rise for seven years. There was something counter- intuitive about the rise, which seemed to be largely fuelled by the general optimism of stock markets around the world. As governments, notably those in emerging markets, announced that they would be resorting to stimulus measures to assist their languishing economies, investors appeared to be piling in, despite the aftermath of the turmoil in Japan's largest neighbour, China. This had left stock prices at their lowest levels for seven months. In one September day alone, the Nikkei jumped up by 7.71 per cent, closing at 18,770.51 points.

One important factor in Japanese market confidence was the 9 September 2015 announcement by Mr Abe that corporation taxes would be lowered by at least 3.3 per cent over the following two financial years. Japanese optimism was buttressed both by the possibility that the US Federal Reserve would decide to delay raising interest rates and the intention of the Chinese authorities to increase public expenditure to counter the economy's apparent deceleration. Almost 99 per cent of the companies listed on the Tokyo Stock Exchange had registered increases, lead by the pharmaceutical companies, banking, finance, automobiles and informatics. A day earlier, the Nikkei had registered a fall of 2.43 per cent following the downwards revision of GDP in the second quarter of 2015 which, although smaller than expected, none the less raised doubts about the actual strength of the economy. A number of analysts noted that the share price leap was also due to the buying opportunities that had arisen after the continued fall in share prices. In August 2015, prompted by the dramatic falls of the Chinese Stock Exchange, the Nikkei had dropped by an unparalleled 15 per cent.

Second quarter uncertainty

In September 2015, Reuters reported that Japan's economy had shrunk less than expected in the second quarter, although capital expenditure fell more than originally forecast. This left Mr Abe's government under some pressure to do more to stimulate the fragile recovery. Most analysts expected that any rebound in the third quarter would be weak. Japan's factory output had unexpectedly fallen in July and the marked slowdown in China held out little hope for an export recovery.

The Japanese economy had shrunk by an annualised 1.2 per cent in April–June 2015, slightly lower than the initial estimate of a 1.6 per cent contraction. In fact most analysts had finally forecast a 1.8 per cent contraction. A negative note was that capital expenditure had fallen 0.9 per cent from the previous quarter, more than the preliminary 0.1 per cent drop forecast. However, the weakness in capital spending was offset by gains in inventories, which were expected to contribute 0.3 per cent to economic growth.

The hope was that companies would use the record profits they had earned from the weakened yen and from lower energy costs to boost wages and investment, triggering a positive cycle of rising income and higher spending. However, data existed to cast doubt on any optimism, including the Bank of Japan's assertion that a recovery would help accelerate inflation to its 2 per cent target by September 2016.

Energy

Japan's energy profile is rather one-sided. It is the world's largest liquefied natural gas importer, second-largest coal importer and third-largest net importer of crude oil and oil products. It is also the third-largest petroleum consumer in the world, relying almost entirely on imports to meet its oil consumption needs; its own oil resources are extremely limited. The US government's Energy Information Administration (EIA) noted that Japan's energy strategy plan encouraged Japanese companies to increase energy exploration and development projects around the world to secure a stable supply of oil and natural gas.

Japan remains highly dependent on a volatile Middle East for most of its energy supplies. Efforts are being made to diversify its supply sources in Russia, south-east Asia and west Africa. Japan relies on LNG imports for virtually all of its natural gas supply.

The nuclear question

According to the EIA, before the Fukushima accident (in March 2011), Japan ranked as the third-largest nuclear power generator in the world behind the United States and France. However, since the Fukushima disaster, Japan has lost all of its nuclear generation capacity as its facilities have been removed from service either because of earthquake damage or for regular maintenance. Japan currently has 48 operable nuclear reactors at 16 power plants with a total installed generating capacity of more than 42GW, down from 54 reactors with about 47GW of capacity in 2010. More than 10GW of nuclear capacity at the Fukushima, Onagawa and Tokai facilities ceased operations immediately following the earthquake and *tsunami* and some of the reactors were permanently damaged from emergency seawater pumping efforts and were no longer scheduled to return to service. The government officially decommissioned the 6 reactors at the Fukushima Daiichi nuclear plant where the accident occurred, which had a combined capacity of 4.6GW.

General maintenance standards in Japan require facilities to come offline every 13 months for inspections. According to the EIA, following the Fukushima disaster, the Japanese government required facilities to pass stress tests as well as obtain local government approval. As reactors were removed from operation, they remained offline. By May 2012, Japan had no nuclear generation at all for the first time in more than 40 years. The government returned two reactors, Kansai Electric's Ohi 3 and Ohi 4, to service in July 2012, leaving Japan with only 2.4GW of capacity for slightly more than a year. These two reactors were again removed from service in September 2013, leaving Japan with no operational nuclear capacity for a second time. Ministry of economy, trade and industry (METI) and the Federation of Electric Power Companies (FEPC) estimate that Japan produced less than 10 TWh of nuclear-generated electricity in fiscal year 2013 (April 2012–March 2013), down from about 288TWh in FY 2010.

The EIA noted that Japan's 2010 Energy Plan had called for at least a dozen new nuclear reactors to be constructed by 2020 and for the share of nuclear-fired electric generation to increase to 50 per cent by 2030 as Japan attempted to reduce greenhouse gas emissions. However, the Fukushima catastrophe created greater public concerns and revealed potential dangers of an aggressive nuclear policy. The previous government led by former prime minister Noda had, in 2012, pledged a no-nuclear policy that encountered opposition from the business sector. The Abe administration supported the idea of nuclear power providing at least 15 per cent of power generation. Prime Minister Abe and industrial interests in Japan favour re-commissioning nuclear power to lower energy costs. However, they need to consider increased safety concerns as well as the resistance from anti-nuclear government factions and the wider public. In August 2015 Kyushu Electric Power restarted the Sendai nuclear plant in southern Japan, the first to begin operation since the 2011 Fukushima meltdowns, and despite anti-nuclear protests

Islands in the cold

The haggling between Moscow and Tokyo over four disputed Pacific islands has strained relations since the end of the Second World War. In theory the two countries are still at war, because no peace treaty was ever signed between them to mark the end of hostlities. The cause of this is the island chain generally known as the Kurils which stretches north across the Pacific Ocean from the Japanese island of Hokkaido to the southern tip of Russia's Kamchatka Peninsula. Four islands, called the Southern Kurils by Russia, the 'Northern Territories' by Japan, lie at the heart of the dispute. They are known in Japan as Kunashiri, Etorofu, Shikotan and the Habomai islets.

According to the *Diplomat* magazine, quoting sources at Japan's defence ministry, in the year up to March 2015 Japan's fighter jet scrambles 'had reached Cold War-levels' partly due to the increased number of operations against Russian aircraft in the Kuril Islands airspace. Although more recent figures showed a fall in the number of air manoeuvres directed against Russian planes, Japanese officials stressed that this should not be seen as reflecting a slowdown in Russian military activities in the region. Tokyo had noted what was described as 'a dramatic change' in Russian behaviour. Russian ships had been detected close to Japanese waters with increasing frequency; Japanese jets had been scrambled against Russian aircraft amid 'a notable rise in flights, exercises and training near Japan.'

In June 2015, shortly after Mr Abe became the first Japanese prime minister to visit Ukraine, Russia announced that it would speed up the construction of military facilities in the islands. Earlier in 2015, Japan had objected to the Russian Prime Minister Dmitry Medvedev's visit to one of the islands, postponing a planned visit by the Japanese foreign minister Fumio Kishida.

The Kuril dispute was not Japan's only international headache. The stand-off with China over the Senkaku/Diaoyu Islands in the East China Sea was of as much, if not more, concern. This time, the disagreement centred on eight uninhabited islands and rocks in the East China Sea. With a total area of no more than 7 square kilometres, the islands lie north-east of Taiwan, east of the Chinese mainland and south-west of Japan's southern-most prefecture, Okinawa. The islands are controlled by Japan, but China has called that control into question and physically challenged it with landings. The islands are important for a number of reasons. First, because they lie close to major shipping lanes; second because they hold plentiful fishing grounds and third, because they are near potential oil and gas reserves. The elephant in the room – the importance that does not get mentioned but is very much both countries minds is the islands' strategic importance at a time when the rivalry between the US and China for military hegemony in the region is increasing. The islands came under US trusteeship at the end of the Second World War and were returned to Japan in 1971 under what was known as the Okinawa reversion deal. Japan claims that China raised no objections to this agreement. The Japanese believe that it has only been since the question of oil resources in the area emerged that the Chinese, and to a lesser degree, the Taiwanese, authorities have begun to press their claims.

Risk assessment

Economy	Fair
Politics	Good
Regional stability	Fair

People to watch

Junichiro Koizumi (Lionheart) Japanese prime minster 2001–06. In 2006 Mr Koizumi appointed Mr Abe as his successor, but by 2014 he was challenging Mr Abe's leadership.

COUNTRY PROFILE

1600 The unification of Japan began in the Tokugawa period (1600–1868), during which a national administrative hierarchy was formed.

1868 The restoration of the imperial family from political obscurity ended the Tokugawa Shogunate and began the Meiji era. Key reforms were initiated to orient Japan to the West and end centuries of isolation.

1894 Japan defeated imperial China in a brief war.

1895 China ceded Taiwan to Japan and allowed Japan to trade in China.

1904–05 Japan went to war with Russia and won.

1910 After three years of fighting, Japan annexed Korea.

1914–19 Japan had limited participation in the First World War on the side of Britain and the allies. The Treaty of Versailles gave Japan some territory in the Pacific.

1920–32 Since the late 1920s, extreme nationalism had increased. In 1931, Japan invaded Manchuria (northern China), renaming it and installing a puppet regime. The Japanese prime minister was assassinated in 1932 by ultra-nationalists. The military held increasing influence in the country.

1938–41 Japanese forces occupied large parts of China and south-east Asia, forcing the British out of Singapore, Malaysia and Hong Kong.

1945 Following its defeat in the Second World War, the subsequent armistice ceded control over many of Japan's outer islands, and the country was placed under US military occupation.

1947 Under direction and influence of the US occupying administration a new democratic constitution was enacted, with many aspects based on the US constitution. Foremost of which had Japan renouncing all military activity outside Japan and the Emperor being stripped of all political power; women were enfranchised and civil liberties were enshrined in law.

1951 Following the signing of the peace treaty, Japan regained its sovereignty. Sovereignty over the Tokara Archipelago and the Amami islands were also restored.

1955 The Liberal Democratic Party (LDP, also known as Jiminto) was formed by a coalition of centre-right groups; it remained in power until its first defeat in 1993.

1956 Japan joined the UN.

1964 Prime Minister Hayato Ikeda was succeeded by Eisaku Sato, who was to become the longest-serving prime minister in Japanese history, remaining in office until 1972.

1972 The Bonin Islands and the remainder of the Ryukyu Islands (including Okinawa), which had been under US administration since 1945, were finally returned to Japan. Kakuei Tanaka became prime minister; he resigned in 1974.

1976 Kakuei Tanaka was arrested on charges of accepting bribes. The scandal damaged the LDP, which, in the elections, lost its overall majority for the first time.

1983 Following seven years of judicial proceedings, Tanaka was found guilty of accepting bribes. He began appeal proceedings and refused to resign his legislative seat, forcing a premature general election.

1986 The LDP recovered its absolute majority in the Diet

1987 The high court upheld the 1983 decision, finding Tanaka guilty of accepting bribes.
1989 The Showa era ended with the death of Emperor Hirohito, who had reigned since 1926. He was succeeded by his son, Akihito, beginning the Heisei era.
1993 The LDP lost its majority in the lower house in the national elections and a coalition government was formed.
1994 Tomiichi Murayama, leader of the Social Democratic Party of Japan (SDPJ), became Japan's fourth prime minister in a year.
1997 Ryutaro Hashimoto of the LDP were elected for a second term. The economy entered a severe recession.
1998 Keizo Obuchi succeeded Hashimoto.
2000 Obuchi died and was replaced by Yoshiro Mori. The LDP lost its parliamentary majority, forcing Mori to rely on coalition partners.
2001 Mori, rocked by scandals and an unpopular image, resigned as prime minister and party leader. Junichiro Koizumi became prime minister and leader of the LDP. He helped turn around the fortunes of the LDP.
2002 Koizumi's opinion poll ratings plummeted as his 'reform' agenda prove unpopular.
2003 The LDP was re-elected in the parliamentary elections.
2004 The opposition won the upper house partial elections; however, the LDP-led coalition retained its majority in both houses. Japanese non-combat troops were sent to Iraq. Huge earthquakes killed 30 people in the north.
2005 Early elections were called after the prime minister's proposal to privatise Japan Post was defeated in the upper house. The LDP won an increased majority in the Diet (parliament). Relations with China were strained as a result of controversial Japanese textbooks, Koizumi's visits to a war shrine commemorating war criminals and China's exploration of disputed areas of the East China Sea.
2006 Shinzo Abe won the LDP's party presidency. Koizumi resigned from the premiership and was replaced by Abe. The Japan Defence Agency became the Ministry of Defence.
2007 Satsuki Eda (Democratic Party of Japan) (DPJ) became the first opposition politician to be president of the upper house. Shinzo Abe resigned as prime minister and Yasuo Fukuda (LDP), was appointed as his successor.
2008 Indigenous people of the northern island of Hokkaido, the Ainu, were granted full recognition. A four-year bilateral dispute was settled when Japan and China agreed to the joint development of a gas field in the East China Sea. Fukuda resigned as prime minister and was replaced by Taro Aso.
2009 Following a decisive defeat for LDP in local elections, Prime Minister Aso called early general elections for 30 August, in which the opposition DPJ won a solid victory with 42.4 per cent of the vote (308 seats of 480). Yukio Hatoyama (DPJ) was elected prime minister.
2010 Japan Airlines (JAL) filed for bankruptcy; it was the largest corporate failure in Japan's business history. However, the government decided to revitalise JAL with US$3.3 billion in reorganisation, US$8 billion in debt waivers and a line of credit of over US$6.5 billion. Prime Minister Yukio Hatoyama resigned, following his inability to close the unpopular US military base in Okinawa, which had been an election campaign pledge, and a funding scandal involving government aides. Parliament elected Naoto Kan (DPJ) as prime minister. The state-funded deposit insurance agency announced that only the first US$120 million of depositor's money in the insolvent Incubator Bank of Japan (IBJ) was guaranteed to be refunded, while around US$130 million of 3,423 depositor's money was uninsured. The IBJ was a private lender to small businesses and the first bank failure since 2003.
2011 A massive earthquake, of magnitude 8.9 (the biggest since 1871) struck offshore of the north-eastern coast of Honshu in March. A *tsunami* that followed caused extensive damage onshore, not only killing thousands of people and leaving hundreds of thousands homeless, but also causing explosions in the Fukushima nuclear power station. Another earthquake of 7.1-magnitude hit in April, causing localised damage. The severity rating of the nuclear crisis for the Fukushima nuclear plant was raised to the highest level for such accidents (seven) in April. However officials said radiation leakage were a tenth of that from the 1986 Chernobyl disaster. The government made it illegal to enter a 20km evacuation zone around the stricken Fukushima nuclear reactor. An emergency budget of ¥4 trillion (US$48.9 billion) was proposed in April. Monies intended for pension funds, child allowances and reducing highway tolls were diverted to the emergency budget. Analysts estimated that the final cost to the economy of the disaster could be US$309 billion. By the beginning of May, 14,704 people were confirmed dead and 10,969 people were still missing and tens of thousands of people were in need of re-housing. The disaster was estimated to have cost the equivalent of 6 per cent of its 2010 economic output and forced the economy to fall back into recession in the first quarter of 2011. In July, children that were living in Fukushima City (60km from the damaged Fukushima nuclear power plant) tested positive for trace amounts of radioactive substances. The sluggish economy and slow clean-up and recovery undermined the authority of Prime Minister Kan, who resigned in August; he was replaced by Yoshihiko Noda (DPJ). Japan confirmed in early October that it would be sending its whaling fleet fishing back to the Antarctic. The move was condemned by the New Zealand government while the anti-whaling campaigning group, Sea Shepherd, said they would continue to hassle the boats.
2012 Emperor Akihito underwent successful heart by-pass surgery in a Tokyo hospital on 18 February. Japan's trade surplus rose to a record ¥32.9 trillion ($394 billion) in February, following on a deficit of ¥1.5 trillion (US$17.9 billion) in January. In April the governments of the US and Japan reached an agreement whereby around 9,000 US marines will be relocated outside Japan, leaving a force of 10,000 on the island of Okinawa. The final date of closure of the USAF Futenma airbase (Okinawa) remains to be decided. On 1 July, the Fukushima nuclear reactor was reactivated, despite local protests. On 11 July, a new political party called Kokumin no Seikatsu ga Daiichi (KSD) (Putting People's Lives First) was founded by 48 members defecting from the DPJ. They opposed the doubling of the consumption tax (to 10 per cent), as imposed by the DPJ. On 15 July devastating floods, which followed torrential rains, caused the evacuation of 250,000 persons and the deaths of 26 from the southern island of Kyushu. On 23 September, China cancelled diplomatic events celebrating 40 years of normalised relations with Japan, due to a dispute over ownership of the Senkaku (known in China as Diaoyu) Islands. On 25 October, Shintaro Islihara, governor of Tokyo, resigned to form a new political party to contest the 2013 elections. He stated his motivation was that Japan's pacifist post-war constitution needed reforming. Parliament was dissolved on 16 November and early general elections were held on 16 December in which the opposition coalition of two parties led by LDP won a total of 67.7 per cent (325 seats, out of 480) and the ruling coalition of eight parties lead by the DPJ (plus other representatives) won 31.3 per cent (150 seats). Shinzo Abe, leader of the LDP, became prime minister designate.
2013 In August officials reported that some 300 tonnes of radioactive water may be leaking daily from the damaged Fukushima nuclear plant. The prime minister pledged action on a rapid clean-up. Cabinet ministers visited the Yasukuni

shrine on 15 August, the anniversary of Japan's surrender in World War II. Although Prime Minister Abe did not join them, the Chinese government summoned the Japanese ambassador to register a complaint. Although the government has said it would like talks with China on the future of the disputed East China Sea islands, deputy foreign minister Li Baodong has said that China is not in favour of a meeting at the G20 meeting in early September. The governement announced on 2 September that it was allocating US$473 million to fix the leaking tanks at the Fukushima nuclear plant. Tokyo was announced as the venue for the 2020 Olympic Games on 7 September. Japan's last nuclear reactor, Reactor 4 at Ohi in western Japan, was shut down on 16 September.

2014 The cabinet agreed on 1 July to reinterpret the Article 9 peace clause of Japan's constitution to recognise the exercise of collective self-defence under limited circumstances. Presidents Abe and Xi of China met at the Asia-Pacific Economic Co-operation (Apec) summit held in Beijing in November. They held formal talks after more than two years of severe tension over a territorial dispute. On 18 November President Abe called a snap general election to be held on 14 December. The LDP won a total (Local Constituency Vote plus PR Block vote) of 61.26 per cent of the vote (291 out of 475 seats), which together with the NKP's 7.37 per cent (35) gave the coalition, 68.63 per cent (326 seats).

2015 On 20 January Prime Minister Abe condemned an apparent threat by the Islamic State (IS) group to kill two Japanese hostages unless a ransom is paid. Kyushu Electric Power restarted the number one reactor at its Sendai plant on 11 August, after passing new safety tests. The government is encouraging the restarting of nuclear reactors to alleviate the high cost of imported fossil fuels and growing CO2 emissions, although there is still public concern about their safety. On 18 September parliament voted to allow Japan's military to act overseas under certain conditions. Despite considerable opposition the bill passed in the upper house by 148 votes in favour to 40 against. The government of Prime Minister Abe has said that the changes in defence policy are vital to meet new military challenges such as those posed from a rising China.

Political structure

Constitution

The Japanese constitution came into force in 1947. It may be amended only if the proposed alteration is passed with a two-thirds majority by the Diet (parliament) and then submitted to the people for ratification, either in a referendum or by election. Religion and state are constitutionally separate.

The imperial succession crisis caused by the lack of any male heir being born for over 40 years was eased following the birth of Prince Hisahito in 2006 (son of the Emperor's cousin and third in line to the throne, Prince Akishino). Since 2005 there has been much discussion about amending the constitution to allow equal primogeniture so that the Emperor's daughter Princess Aiko can ascend to the imperial throne.

Form of state

Constitutional monarchy

The executive

Executive power is vested in the cabinet, which consists of the prime minister and not more than 20 ministers of state (including ministers without portfolio and the chief cabinet secretary) and is collectively responsible to the Diet.

By convention, the chosen president of the majority party becomes prime minister; the Emperor appoints the prime minister, who must already have been approved by the Diet. The prime minister appoints the cabinet, the majority of whom must be members of the Diet; the cabinet remains collectively responsible to the Diet.

The Emperor is the head of state under the constitution, but is primarily a national figurehead

National legislature

The bicameral Kokkai (National Diet) (parliament) is the highest organ of state power and the sole lawmaking authority, comprising two chambers, both directly elected by independent and separate voting systems. The Sangi-in (House of Representatives) (lower house), has 475 members in 2014 (five less than the 480 members in the previous election), of which 295 members are directly elected in single-seat constituencies and 180 are elected by proportional representation within 11 multi-member constituencies; all members serve for four-year terms.

The Shugi-in (House of Councillors) (upper house) has 242 members, of which 96 are elected by proportional representation in a single nationwide electoral district. The remaining 146 are elected in 47 constituencies each returning 2–10 members. All candidates must be aged at least 30 years and voters must by aged at least 20 years, although discussions have been going on for a several years to lower the age to 18. All members serve for a fixed six-year term, with an alternate half the number elected every three years. This chamber cannot be dissolved by the prime minister.

Both houses must be in agreement for legislation to be enacted, although when the Diet is in deadlock the lower house takes precedence.

Legal system

The judiciary is independent, but the role of bureaucratic interpretation and the reluctance of the Japanese to get involved in litigation mean that judges are less influential than in Western democracies. All judicial power is vested in the Supreme Court and four types of inferior court – High, District, Family and Summary Courts.

The judges of the Supreme Court, except the chief judge, who is appointed by the Emperor, are appointed by the cabinet. The judges of inferior courts are also appointed by the cabinet, but only from a list of persons nominated by the Supreme Court.

Last elections

14 December 2014 (parliamentary, lower house); 21 July 2013 (parliament: upper house)

Results: Parliamentary 2014 (lower house): Prospective coalition (Liberal Democratic Party-New Komeito Party) (LDP-NKP coalition) won 68.63 per cent of total vote (326 seats, out of 475); the Democratic Party of Japan (DPJ) won 15.37 per cent (73). No other party won over 10 per cent.

Parliamentary (upper house – 50 per cent of membership): the coalition of LDP, NKP and New Renaissance Party (NRP) won 105 seats overall (out of 242 in house); LDP won 51 seats (to achieve an overall 84); the NKP nine (19 overall), NRP 1 (2 overall), the coalition of DJP, PNP and New Party Nippon won 44, out of 110 overall (out of total 242 in house) DPJ 44 overall, PNP nil (three overall), NPN nil (one overall); Your Party (YP) 10 (11 overall), JCP three (six overall), SDP two (four overall), Sunrise Party of Japan (SPJ) one (three overall), Happiness Realisation Party one (one overall), independents two (two overall). Turnout was between 48–73 per cent.

Next elections

2018 (parliamentary, the lower house of the National Diet); 2016 50 per cent of members (parliamentary, the upper house of the National Diet)

Political parties

Ruling party

Liberal Democratic Party-New Komeito Party (LDP-NKP coalition) from 16 Dec 2012)

Main opposition party

Liberal-Democratic Party (L-DP)

Approximately 80 per cent of the population live on the northern island of Honshu, and the density in the major cities (Tokyo, Osaka, Nagoya) is high. Approximately five million Japanese live outside Japan.

Population
127.61 million (2012) (128,056,000; 2010, census)
Last census: 1 October 2010: 128,056,000
Population density: 337 inhabitants per square km. Urban population 67 per cent (2010 Unicef).
Annual growth rate: 0.2 per cent, 1990–2010 (Unicef).

Ethnic make-up
Japan is generally recognised to be racially homogenous, however there are small numbers of Ainu (indigenous people) and almost one million Koreans.
The 1980s saw an influx of illegal immigrants into Japan, notably from the Philippines. Immigration levels have remained low relative to other industrialised countries, with non-Japanese making up only 2 per cent of the population.

Religions
Shintoism and Buddhism (majority), Christianity (minority). Many people profess both Shintoism and Buddhism, observing Shinto rites for birth and marriage and Buddhism for funerals. Both religions continue to play a significant role in cultural, philosophical and even business and political spheres. There are approximately 1.7 million Christians.

Education
Japan follows the American educational cycle of 6-3-3-4 years, where the six, elementary (primary) years and three junior high school years are free of charge and mandatory.
Even though competition is fierce, 97 per cent of students enrol for non-compulsory high school at aged 15. Valued places in prestigious high schools virtually guarantee a direct path into universities and other institutes of higher education. High school lasts for three years. There are a number of private international schools.
At 62.6 per cent, Japan has the highest rate, of any industrialised country, for students going into higher education. There are three types of institutes of higher education: university, junior college and technical college.
There are also kindergartens for pre-school children, and miscellaneous schools for vocational and practical training, and special education schools for the physically and mentally handicapped.
Admission is highly competitive at every stage of schooling and there have been many critics who question whether the intensive school curriculum enables students to confront a dynamic, modern world.
Changes have been introduced to encourage a greater flexibility in both teaching and learning. The academic year has been amended to five days a week and 210 days a year.
Public expenditure on education typically amounts to 3.6 per cent of annual gross national income.
Compulsory years: Six to 15
Enrolment rate: 101 per cent gross primary enrolment, 103 gross secondary enrolment; of the relevant age groups (including repeater) (World Bank).
Pupils per teacher: 19 in primary schools

Health
Medical facilities in Japan are excellent, with around 97 per cent of all medical services covered by plans such as National Health Insurance, which is also available to foreigners with residence or work visas.
Japan has a low fertility rate reflecting trends in all developed countries as its population ages rapidly. In a 2005 study the recorded number of Japanese men fell by 0.01 per cent, as the population rose by 0.05 per cent, these figures are the smallest seen (apart from the war years when statistics of military deaths were withheld) since records began in 1920. The fall in the number of men could be explained by many working abroad, however what is sure is the number of Japanese aged over 65, in 2004, reached a record high of 19.5 per cent, as those aged under 14 fell to an all-time low of 13.9 per cent. The concerns in the changing demographics has prompted reform of the state pension where amendments implemented in 2004 steadily reduce benefits, as premiums increase.

HIV/Aids
There are signs that the sexual behaviour of youth in Japan could be changing significantly and putting this group at greater risk of HIV infection.
HIV prevalence: 0.1 per cent aged 15–49 in 2003 (World Bank)
Life expectancy: 82 years, 2004 (WHO 2006)
Fertility rate/Maternal mortality rate: 1.4 births per woman, 2010 (Unicef); maternal mortality eight per 100,000 live births (World Bank)
Birth rate/Death rate: 1.26. In 2007 forecasters said the population could fall by 20 per cent by 2050.
Child (under 5 years) mortality rate (per 1,000): 3 per 1,000 live births (WHO 2012)
Head of population per physician: 1.98 physicians per 1,000 people, 2002 (WHO 2006)

Welfare
Japan's social security system is divided into five parts: public assistance, welfare services, social insurance (medical care, pensions, child allowances, unemployment insurance and workers' accident compensation), public health, public service pensions and assistance for war victims.
There are some 26,000 social welfare institutions (excluding day nursery facilities), of which around 16,600 are public and 9,400 private.

Pensions
The falling birth rate and ageing population has increased the pressure on the pension scheme, which relies on contributions paid by those working, too many of whom have opted out.
The welfare ministry estimates that social security costs will increase fourfold by 2025, from ¥65 trillion (US$608 billion) in 1995 to ¥274 trillion (US$2.6 trillion) in 2025. To compound the problem, the stagnating economy in the 1990s resulted in a huge pension liabilities gap – underfunded pension liabilities are thought to total ¥419 trillion (US$3.9 trillion). To fill the gap, the government has raised corporate taxes and scaled back the benefits.
The pension reform bill was opposed by those who claimed that the underlying assumptions on which it was based were flawed. About 40 per cent of self-employed workers are said to have failed to pay contributions, many believe they would be unlikely to see any retirement benefits. Without a unified pension, which covers all workers, the funding remains problematic, although a sales tax has been proposed to add to the funding.

Family support
A social security reform bill was passed in June 2004, in which corporate tax will be increased gradually from 13.58 per cent in 2004 to 18.3 per cent in 2017, while benefits will be reduced, with payments at only 50 per cent of the average take-home pay. Opposition say increased tax will encourage employers to hire part-time workers who are covered by another scheme.

Main cities
Tokyo, (capital, estimated population 8.9 million (m) in 2012); Yokohama, (3.8m), Osaka (2.7m), Nagoya, (2.3m), Sapporo (1.9m), Kobe (1.6m), Fukuoka (1.5m), Kyoto (1.5m), Kawasaka (1.4m), Hiroshima (1.2m).

Languages spoken
It is hard to operate in Japan without some knowledge of Japanese or the services of an interpreter.
Pupils are taught English in school for seven years but this involves a formal grammatical knowledge rather than spoken English.

Official language/s
Japanese

Media

Press

Around 80 per cent of the population read a daily newspaper, of which there are over 120 to choose from, with a combined publish run of around 70 million. In the largest markets, such as Tokyo, there can be three editions published per day. Nevertheless, the number of subscribers is declining and this trend is expected to continue.

Dailies: In Japanese (with English online editions) the major nationals include *Yomiuri Shimbun* (www.yomiuri.co.jp/dy), the leading newspaper with a circulation of around 10 million and is affiliated to Nippon TV, *Asahi Shimbun* (www.asahi.com/english) is affiliated to Asahi TV and *Mainichi Shimbun* (http://mdn.mainichi.jp) is affiliated to TBS. Other major newspapers are regionally based including *Hokkaido Shimbun* (www.hokkaido-np.co.jp), *The Kyoto Shimbun* (www.kyoto-np.co.jp) and *Sankei Shimbun* (www.sankei-kansai.com) from Osaka.

The *Japan Times* (www.japantimes.co.jp) is the only exclusively English language newspaper published, while Japan Today (www.japantoday.com) is a comprehensive online publication.

Weeklies: Some Japanese newspapers publish an English weekly edition. The *Tokyo Journal* (www.tokyo.to), *Tokyo Weekender* (www.weekender.co.jp) and *Metropolis* (www.metropolis.co.jp), are published for foreigners living in Japan, and in particular the capital.

There are weekend or Sunday editions of daily newspapers, including. *Aera* (www3.asahi.com) and *Sekai* (www.iwanami.co.jp).

Business: In Japanese, the *Nikkan Kogyo Shimbun* (www.nikkan.co.jp) and *Nihon Keizai Shimbun* (www.nikkei.co.jp) are leading financial newspapers from Tokyo of which *The Nikkei Weekly* (www.nikkei4946.com) is the English-language weekly edition of the latter. All quality newspapers cover business and economic news.

A trade-press of 7–8,000 publications covers most aspects of business and the economy.

The Japan Economic Institute of America (www.jei.org) publishes articles and analysis of the business environment from a US perspective.

Periodicals: Japanese Anime and Manga magazines featuring illustrative, cartoon stories are very popular and cater for all ages.

Broadcasting

NHK (Nippon Hoso Kyokai) (www.nhk.or.jp) is only one of five national terrestrial broadcasters all of which compete strenuously for audiences. TBS (www.tbs.co.jp) provides national radio and television services.

Radio: NHK (www.nhk.or.jp) has a network of three stations, Radio 1 for news a talk radio, Radio 2 for cultural and educational programmes and FM Radio for classical music. It also operates an external network, Radio Japan; the First Services broadcasts in Japanese and English to Asia and the Second Service which broadcasts in 20 other languages throughout Asia. There are numerous commercial radio stations located regionally including Tokyo FM (www.tfm.co.jp) TBS Radio (www.tbs.co.jp/radio), FM Cocolo (www.cocolo.co.jp) from Osaka, Zip FM (http://zip-fm.co.jp) from Nagoya and FMii (www.fmii.co.jp) from Morioka. The American Forces Network (AFN) operates from US military bases, offering English-language programmes from Yokata Air Base (www.yokota.af.mil/afn). Digital radio services are available, provided by all major broadcasters.

Television: NHK (www.nhk.or.jp) is the only public TV service, funded largely by a licence fee. It is at the forefront in providing new technological transmissions and analogue signals will be completely replaced by digitals signals by 2011. Japan was the first country to introduce high definition (HD) TV services and NHK has a channel exclusively for these transmissions. Of the other major national TV networks all are commercial, including Nippon Television Network (NTV) (www.ntv.co.jp), the Tokyo Broadcasting System (TBS) (www.tbs.co.jp), Fuji Television (www.fujitv.co.jp) and TV Asahi (www.tv-asahi.co.jp).

Locally produced TV programmes dominate the schedules and foreign shows may have an influence on production although they do not get screened.

Millions of viewers subscribe to cable and satellite TV.

Other news agencies: Jiji Press (in Japanese): www.jiji.com

Kyodo News: http://home.kyodo.co.jp

Nikkei Net (business and stock market news): www.nni.nikkei.co.jp

Economy

Japan's economy is the third largest in the world (after the US and China). It is an advanced industry-led economy, dependent on exports to remain expansionary. Between 2002, when it came out of a decade-long recession, and late 2007 the economy grew steadily. However the shock of the global financial crisis of 2008–09 left it in a precarious state, with a return to negative GDP growth of -1.0 per cent in 2008; in 2009 growth contracted further falling to -5.5 per cent, before pulling out of recession in 2010, with a growth rate of 4.4 per cent, as global trade picked up. In 2011, after the tsunami disaster, GDP growth fell to -0.5 per cent and after a period of slow growth in 2012–13 fell back into a recession of -0.1 per cent in 2014.

An earthquake, the biggest since 1871, with a magnitude of 8.9, struck offshore of the north-eastern coast of Honshu Island on 11 March 2011, followed by a massive *tsunami*. The tsunami caused extensive damage onshore, killing as many as 16,000 people and leaving tens of thousands of people in need of re-housing, and leading to explosions in the Fukushima nuclear power station. The Fukushima Daiichi nuclear disaster represents the largest nuclear meltdown since the Chernobyl disaster (1986). The nuclear meltdown is also the second disaster (after Chernobyl) to be given Level 7 Event classification.

In response, the government announced an emergency budget of 4 trillion yen (US$48.9 billion) on 22 April 2011. Monies intended for pension funds, child allowances and reducing highway tolls were diverted to the emergency budget. On 21 March, the World Bank estimated that Japan may need up to five years to recover from the earthquake and *tsunami* that damaged industrial output, wrecking ports, steel works and vehicle parts and electronic manufacturing.

The disaster was estimated to have cost Japan the equivalent of 6 per cent of its 2010 economic output and forced the economy to fall back into recession estimated at -0.7 per cent in 2011. On 24 October 2011, the government approved a ¥12.1 trillion (US$157 billion) budget for the reconstruction of the area devastated by the March earthquake and *tsunami* and to decontaminate the damaged Fukushima nuclear power station. This was the third supplementary budget (and the second largest ever to be presented to parliament). The economy rebounded in the third quarter of 2011, recording GDP growth of 1.5 per cent after the previous three-quarters of contraction. By July 2011, 73 per cent of the farms and 36 per cent of the fisheries that had been affected by the tsunami reopened for business. Despite managing to save some businesses, by March 2012, 644 of them had been forced into bankruptcy. A total of 11,500 jobs were lost and in 2014, the effects were still having their toll with 270,000 people still homeless as a result of the disaster.

As reconstruction of the earthquake and *tsunami* damage began to take effect, the economy responded positively with a solid recovery due in 2012, despite a dampening of demand caused by the European debt crisis. However by the second quarter of 2012, industrial output had dropped by

1.2 per cent and manufacturing output was at its lowest since the earthquake of 2011, plus Japan's annual inflationary target of 1 per cent was virtually unattainable.
Inflation matched the growth trend, falling from 1.4 per cent in 2008 to -1.1 per cent in 2009. The government, in concert with other G8 countries, committed US$100 billion in a fiscal stimulus plan to fight deflation. The package was followed by three months of the fastest ever contraction in the economy, with the trade deficit in January (US$9.9 billion) the worst since records began in 1980. Exports of automobiles fell by 69 per cent (Toyota, the world's largest vehicle manufacturer, made its worst annual loss in 2008/09, losing a net US$4.4 billion, compared to record profits in 2007/08; as a result production was cut across a number of its manufacturing sites both in Japan and overseas). Exports in general dropped by 45.7 per cent. Industrial production fell by 10 per cent in January 2009, the fourth consecutive monthly drop in factory output. By August 2009 the economy had begun to pick up and GDP growth rose to 0.9 per cent in the second quarter. Deflation continued in 2010, at -0.7 per cent and, before the earthquake in March 2011, the economy was expected to continue this trend. The Bank of Japan reacted to the global economic crisis by implementing measures to reduce interest rates, ensure stability in financial markets and engender corporate financing, as well as buying up stocks held by banks and providing subordinate loans to banks. In 2013 inflation was low at 0.4 per cent before it rose to 2.7 per cent in 2014.
On 26 January 2011, the international rating agency, Standard & Poor's, downgraded Japan from AA to AA-. In 2012 the government's debt was 196 per cent of Japans GDP. Japans debt has got considerably worse since, reaching 246 per cent of GDP in mid-2015 and is expected to be in excess of 400 per cent by 2030 unless policymakers implement vital reforms.
The trend in unemployment continued to rise during 2008–09 with the annual average rate of 4.0 per cent in 2008 rising to 5.1 per cent in 2009 and remaining constant in 2010. However, as global trade has picked up the rate fell to 5 per cent by 2011 and went down further to 3.4 per cent by mid-2015. There has been a corresponding change in work patterns, from long-term, full-time employment, to part-time, casual or contract employment.
In March 2012, Japan and China agreed to swap the equivalent of US$339 billion in each of their currencies in a measure intended to safeguard them in the face of another global economic crisis and strengthen trade ties. Both central banks will be able to exchange each other's currency (up to the US$339 billion) without consideration of fluctuation in the money markets. Despite this apparent burst of co-operation, tension rose between the two countries in September over disputed islands (known as Senkaku in Japan and Diaoyu in China) in the East China Sea. There were a number of anti-Japan demonstrations throughout China and a number of Japanese factories, including Toyota, closed temporarily.

External trade

Japan is a member of the Asia-Pacific Economic Co-operation (Apec) which is a forum for discussing regional economic, investment and trade matters. It does not belong to any free trade zone but does have bilateral trade agreements with several countries and regional blocs worldwide.
The open market economy is predicated on external trade, which provides around 25 per cent of GDP, allowing for the purchase of the raw materials that Japan does not produce; the majority of exports are finished goods. Japan is highly dependent on imported energy and minerals.
Japan has the world's largest fishing fleet which accounts for around 15 per cent of the global catch; the Japanese consume more seafood than any other nation. Japan is the second largest producer of paper (after the US).
In 2011, Japan and India signed a free trade agreement (FTA), which will cut tariffs on 94 per cent of goods by 2020. Among the goods to benefit are textiles, pharmaceuticals and vehicles, as well as services.
In the first quarter of 2015, Japanese exports rose by 7.6 per cent on the previous year however, imports only fell by 3.6 per cent, which was less than expected. The resulting US$2.2 billion deficit has exacerbated the country's already sizeable debt.

Imports

Principal imports are fuels, industrial raw materials, machinery and equipment, textiles, foodstuffs – rice, other grains, fish products, meat products, chemicals and non-ferrous ores and ash.
Main sources: China (22.3 per cent total in 2014), US (8.8 per cent), Australia (5.9 per cent)

Exports

Principal exports are vehicles and transport equipment, semiconductors, electronic and electrical machinery, optical and measuring equipment.
Main destinations: US (18.6 per cent total in 2014), China (18.3 per cent), South Korea (7.5 per cent)

Agriculture

Farming

The agricultural sector accounted for approximately 1.2 per cent of GDP in 2014 and employed less than 4 per cent of the workforce (down from 50 per cent at the end of the Second World War). Most people in farm employment supplement their income with non-farm employment.
Only about 12.5 per cent of the land area is available for agriculture and stock-rearing and this is constantly in demand for residential use. Agricultural labour is highly intensive, making considerable use of technology and capital investment.
Wet cultivation of rice is the main activity (virtually self-sufficient), with a trend toward production of beef, citrus fruits and tobacco. Wheat, barley, soya beans, potatoes, sweet potatoes, vegetables, fruit, tea and silkworms are also produced.
The price of rice has declined and it is difficult for the paddy farmers to make a profit. In addition, consumers' tastes have changed and they are eating more potatoes, bread, pasta and noodles instead of rice.
Japanese farming is heavily protected by government subsidies and high import tariffs, despite the fact that Japan is dependent on food imports. The political influence of farmers has frequently stalled free trade negotiations with other countries which are deemed as competitors to the Japanese farming sector.

Fishing

Japan is one of the world's great fishing nations and there are some 3,000 fishing ports dotted around its coasts. Its methods of driftnet fishing, which drags up sea fauna indiscriminately from the ocean, have been criticised throughout the world. The establishment of 200-mile economic zones at sea by a number of countries has meant that Japan has had to go further afield for fishing grounds: half the catch now comes from outside Japanese waters and Japanese boats have increasingly been accused of predatory practices.
Fishing contributes substantially to domestic food supply and export earnings. Japanese fishermen catch pollock, pilchards, cod, salmon, mackerel and other fish throughout the north and central Pacific, and are second only to the former USSR in whaling. The total annual marine catch can be up to seven million tonnes per year, with a further 5 per cent of demand imported. Aquaculture is well developed and there are inshore fisheries for squid, clams, crustaceans, shallow-water fish and dolphins.

Japan remains a whaling nation and has been criticised for using overseas aid to manipulate countries into voting in favour of maintaining whaling in international waters. The typical import value of aquatic mammals amounts to over US$176 million yearly, while total fish imports average over US$2 billion.

In 2007, the Japanese whaling fleet had a quota to kill up to 1,000 whales. There was considerable international condemnation, especially from the US, Australia and New Zealand that the quota included the slaughtering of humpback and fin whales. By April 2008 the fleet had failed to catch its quota due to interference by anti-whaling activists. There had been a moratorium on commercial whaling since 1986, and on the killing of humpback whales since 1963. The Japanese maintain that they are whaling in the name of scientific research. In March 2014, the International Court of Justice ruled that Japan must cease all fishing in the Arctic, saying that whaling for scientific research is not compatible with international law.

Following the annual meeting of the Commission for the Conservation of Southern Bluefin Tuna (CCSBT), held on Cheju Island, South Korea, all members agreed to a 20 per cut in the roughly 17,000 tonnes of 2009 Bluefin tuna catches caught in 2010. Scientists had warned that without a cut fish stocks could crash as numbers had become dangerously low.

Forestry

Japan is heavily forested, with forests covering around 69 per cent of the total land area. The variation in climate across Japan means that the country enjoys a diverse range of forests. Plantations account for around 44 per cent of total forested area. About 42 per cent of forests are in public ownership.

Japan is a major consumer of wood and paper products. Despite being heavily forested, Japan is one of the world's largest importers of forest products and by far the largest importer of tropical logs and wood products. The production costs involved in the extraction of Japanese wood are high, so the country is forced to rely on imports.

Industry and manufacturing

Manufacturing contributes approximately 20 per cent of GDP and employs nearly 24 per cent of the workforce. This compares to 16 per cent of the labour force in the US and an average of 18 per cent in OECD countries. In the past, industry has benefited from innovative technology and, in some less competitive sectors such as chemicals, aircraft and software, from considerable financial backing from the government. Japan has also traditionally led the world in automated production processes, which has helped to reduce the industrial workforce and re-deploy workers into the tertiary sector. Toyota is one of the world's most successful car manufacturers while Nippon Steel is also a world-leader. However, one of the main long-term problems in Japanese industry is its inefficiency. The Nikkei-300 non-financial companies have typically had a return on equity of just 4 per cent, compared to 20 per cent in the US. Sony and Sanyo have been forced to restructure as a response to bad sales. The IT and telecommunications sector suffered after strong sales in 2004, particularly in mobile phones and digital cameras.

Part of the root cause of inefficiency is the prevailing culture. The Japanese are admired for their discipline and patience, but these qualities have not resulted in increased productivity; and whereas Japanese product innovation and development is excellent, sales and marketing have lagged behind. Instead of aggressive and inspirational advertising, the Japanese tend to release a lot of new products and invest in those which prove most successful. However, this is labour-intensive. A 'convoy' system has tended to operate in under-competing, protected sectors, where firms have paced their development to keep step with the slowest.

Another concern is the rapid ascent of China and other East Asian rivals. Korea and China have mimicked the successes of Japanese manufacturing and are now producing more quickly and more cheaply. As well as East Asian improvements in quality and efficiency, the strong yen was another factor prompting investors to abandon Japan. Traditionally the Japanese have not embraced foreign trade with the same openness as its rivals: off-putting tariffs are applied to imports. Although the government, as well as companies themselves, are coming round to seeing the benefit of alliances with foreign firms in order to compete on the international stage, the process is slow. Moreover, communication issues surrounding Japan's complex corporate culture can act as something of a barrier to merger and acquisition activities between Japanese and foreign firms.

Nevertheless, as the cross-holding structure typical of Japan's famous *keiretsu* (business networks in which firms own stakes in one another) unravels, Japanese firms in general are coming under pressure to prioritise profits over their traditional relationships. Firms kept alive by their banks after they have lost all hope of financial viability – often termed the 'walking dead' by Asian business journalists – are gradually reducing.

Tourism

Boarding the Shinkansen (bullet train) that takes visitors from one city to another through a landscape that may not have changed in millennia typifies Japan's appeal. Japan has a reputation for its respect of the environment and historic monuments as well as an ancient culture that coexists with modernity. Visitors are drawn as much to the well preserved temples, castles and historic villages as they are to the neon-bright cities with all the latest technology on show. Japan has 16 sites included on Unesco's World Heritage List, some dating back into pre-history but also including the Hiroshima Peace Memorial (Genbaku Dome) at the site of the first atomic bomb dropped on an inhabited city. Japan also has a world renowned cuisine and love of most foods from the sea.

Travel and tourism is an important component of the economy and constituted 7.5 per cent of GDP in 2014. It also provided 7.0 per cent of total employment (4.4 million jobs) in 2014, a figure which has remained fairly constant since 2006.

In April 2015 there was a record number of monthly visitors to Japan, reaching 1.7 million arrivals, a 43.3 per cent increase on the same period of the previous year. This was the third record breaking month in a row, as Japan is experiencing a boom in tourism.

The Japanese National Tourism Organisation (JNTO) offers international travellers a website to inform, schedule and book trips to and throughout Japan.

Mining

Mining accounts for 0.5 per cent of GDP and 1 per cent of total employment. There are few exploitable mineral resources. Molybdenum, manganese, zinc, copper and iron are mined on a small scale. Japan is self-sufficient in sulphur and limestone.

Hydrocarbons

Japan has virtually no domestic hydrocarbon reserves and must rely on imports for its needs; it was the world's third highest oil consumer in 2014 (after the US and China) at 4.3 million barrels per day. Most of Japan's oil is sourced from the Middle East, however as this area is politically volatile and supplies may be subject to outside interference, Japan has been looking elsewhere for supplies. It entered into negotiations with Russia to buy Russian oil, via the East Siberian-Pacific Ocean (ESPO) pipeline. An agreement for buying this oil would have included investment in completing the pipeline, but during the 2008–09 financial crisis, when Japan's economy contracted, China intercepted and signed a deal on 18 February 2009, whereby the pipeline will be routed from its Russian terminal in Yakutia and south into China. It was completed in 2010.

In June 2012, Qatargas agreed to a long-term contract to supply one million tonnes of liquefied natural gas (LNG) per year to Tepco, beginning in 2012.

In 2008, Japan and China agreed to jointly develop and share the profits of gas fields in the East China Sea, with estimated reserves of some 56 million cubic metres (cum). Japan imported almost 116 billion cubic metres of LNG from 13 different countries in 2014, the bulk of which was bought from other Asian countries.

All of Japan's coalmines are closed; there are reserves of 347 million tonnes of black coal. Coal imports account for 25 per cent of the country's electricity generation and most of it is imported from Australia.

Energy

Japan has a total generating capacity of around 287GW, producing over 1 trillion kilowatt hours (kWh). Around 70 per cent of total generation is produced by conventional thermal plants, 11 per cent by hydroelectric dams and the rest from geothermal, solar and wind power.

Following the earthquake of 11 March 2011 and subsequent damage to the Fukushima nuclear power plant, its owners, Tokyo Electric Power (Tepco), announced on 30 March that it would decommission reactors 1–4, due to harmful levels of radioactivity detected in the power plant's location.

On 7 May 2012, Japan's last working nuclear reactor (the third reactor at the Tomari plant) was shut for routine maintenance. The shutdown removed a major source of electricity from Japan's energy mix – until the 2011 *tsunami* Japan received 30 per cent of its energy from its nuclear power stations. Although the shutdown was said to be for 'routine maintenance', marchers in Tokyo, waved banners to celebrate what they hoped would be the end of nuclear power in Japan. By 2013 only around 1 per cent of energy came from nuclear sources.

Liquefied natural gas (LNG) is likely to become an important source of energy for electricity generation in the long-term.

Japan's electricity prices are among the highest in the world, but prices are falling due to cuts in capital investment. The country is served by 10 vertically integrated utility companies which have monopolies over different regions; Japan has no national grid. The regional organisation of grids has a limited number of inter-connections. The utilities market has been de-regularised and made more efficient, leading to significant price cuts.

The Japanese government signed the Kyoto Protocol on reducing greenhouse gases and is committed to energy efficiency.

Financial markets

Stock exchange

Tokyo Shoken Torihikisho (Tokyo Stock Exchange) (TSE)

Commodity exchange

The Tokyo Grain Exchange

Banking and insurance

In the 1990s the bubble burst in the Japanese economy and banks were the major casualties. They became burdened with huge amounts of non-performing loans (NPL) and bad debt.

In efforts to bounce back and also to prevent future risk, a series of mergers and takeovers took place in the banking sector. The fifteen banks that had existed during the financial crash were reduced to four. The biggest bank, Mizuho Bank, was created when Dai-Ichi Kangyo Bank, Fuji Bank and the Industrial Bank of Japan merged. The other three are: Mitsubishi Tokyo Financial Group, Sumitomo Mitsui Banking and the United Financial of Japan Group (UFG). However, the biggest 'bank' in the world is the Japanese post office, which is in the process of privatisation.

The Bank of Japan (BoJ) was granted independence from the government in 1998. However, in 2005 the government applied acute pressure to the BoJ to ensure that it did not raise interest rates above zero before economic growth was proven to be steady. The finance ministry reacted to the BoJ's reluctance by threatening to rescind its independence. The government's distrust of the Bank's monetary policy stems from 2000 when the Bank prematurely raised interest rates against the will of domestic finance officials and the IMF.

Central bank

Nippon Ginko (Bank of Japan).

Main financial centre

Tokyo, Osaka and Nagoya.

Time

GMT plus nine hours

Geography

Japan lies off the north-east coast of Asia and consists of four main islands – Hokkaido, Honshu, Shikoku and Kyushu – and thousands of smaller islands running in an arc from north (latitude 45 33'N) to south (latitude 24 25'N). Japan is mainly mountainous with only 29 per cent of the national land area consisting of plains and basins. It has about 10 per cent of the world's active volcanoes and its highest mountain, Mount Fuji (3,776 metres), is a dormant volcano. Japan occupies less than 0.3 per cent of the earth's total land area: it is only 4 per cent of the size of the United States and one and a half times bigger than the United Kingdom.

Hemisphere

Northern

Climate

The general climate is temperate, except for part of Hokkaido in the north and some of the southernmost islands. Spring is March–May, with average temperatures of 6 degrees Celsius (C) (minimum) and 21 degrees C (maximum). The rainy season is mid-June–mid-July. Summer is June–August, with temperatures between 20 degrees C and 28 degrees C. Autumn is September–November, with temperatures ranging from 10 degrees C to 24 degrees C. Rainfall is heaviest June and August–September. Winter is December–February, with temperatures from minus 5.1 degrees C to 16 degrees C. Annual rainfall is 1,000–2,500mm. South and central Japan can be subject to typhoons in late summer and early autumn.

Dress codes

In modern Japan, dark business suits and Western dress are the normal rule.

Traditional Japanese dress consisted of kimonos for both men and women. On for formal occasions women often wear kimonos, while men usually wear morning dress, but occasionally also wear kimonos for weddings etc.

Entry requirements

Passports

Required by all. Passports must be valid for the duration of stay.

Visa

No visa requirements for citizens of most of Europe, the Americas, Australasia and some Asian countries, visiting for up to 90 days. For a full list, and application form, plus further information for those citizens not included on the list of visa-free travel, see www.mofa.go.jp/j_info/visit/visa/index.html.

Business travel is allowed for those enjoying visa-free travel for the minimum period. Those who do not must provide business letters, itinerary and invitations from Japanese hosts.

Foreigners arriving in Japan (both visitors and residents) are fingerprinted and photographed. The move was introduced in November 2007 as an anti-terrorist measure.

Currency advice/regulations

There are no restrictions on currency import or export. However, amounts in excess of ¥1 million (or equivalent) must be declared. All money exchanged must be through authorised banks and money changers. The money exchange counter at Narita airport is open from 0900–2300.

Travellers cheques are accepted in larger bank branches, hotels and duty-free shops. To avoid extra exchange fee, US dollars and Japanese yen are best.

Customs

Personal effects duty-free. Visitors may purchase souvenir items (pearls, cameras, transistor radios) free of sales tax at designated shops, but they must be taken out of the country within six months.

Prohibited imports

Firearms, ammunition, illegal drugs, pornography including films. Counterfeit or altered currencies. Animal, plant/soil and food products.

Health (for visitors)

There are no mandatory precautions. Japan has extensive health facilities with high standards, although medical services are expensive and insurance is essential. The International Association of Medical Assistance to Travellers provide English speaking doctors.

Advisable precautions

Inoculations may be useful for the occasional occurrence of typhoid hepatitis A and C and TB.

Hotels

Hotels should be booked well in advance. Service charges and taxes are added to the bill, and tipping is not customary. In addition to Western-style hotels, there are traditional Japanese-style inns (*ryokan*) in Tokyo and Osaka.

Credit cards

International credit and charge cards are widely accepted. ATMs, may not accept foreign cards, although Citbank ATMs do and are open 24 hours.

Public holidays (national)

Fixed dates

31 Dec–3 Jan (New Year holidays), 11 Feb (Foundation Day), 29 Apr (Greenery Day), 3–5 May (Constitution Day/Citizens' Day of Rest/Children's Day), 20 Jul (Marine Day), 15 Sep (Respect for the Aged Day), 23 Sep (Autumnal Equinox), 3 Nov (Culture Day), 23 Nov (Labour Thanksgiving Day), 23 Dec (Emperor's Birthday).

With the exception of New Year's Day, if a holiday falls on a Sunday, the following day is treated as a holiday instead. When there is a single day between two national holidays, it is also taken as a holiday.

Avoid visits during Golden Week (Apr–May) and the Obon festive season (late Jul–third week in Aug), when everywhere is very crowded.

Variable dates

Coming of Age Day (Seijin-no-hi) (Jan), Vernal Equinox (Shunbun-no-hi) (Mar), Physical Fitness Day (Oct).

Working hours

Banking

Mon–Fri: 0900–1500.

Business

Mon–Fri: 0900–1700; Sat: 0900–1200 (most companies close on Saturdays).

Government

Mon–Fri: 1000–1700; Sat: 1000–1200.

Shops

1000–1900 (many closed on Wed or Thu).

Telecommunications

Mobile/cell phones

3G services are available in most cities.

Electricity supply

100V AC, 60 cycles in west Japan (Osaka) and 100V AC, 50 cycles in east Japan (Tokyo), with flat two-pin plug fittings.

Weights and measures

Metric system

Social customs/useful tips

The Japanese are a polite and reserved people. They do not expect overseas visitors to understand or adopt their customs – but they do value courtesy and friendliness and efforts to follow their customs are appreciated. The suffix san is added to the surname (ie Suzuki-san instead of Mr Suzuki) in polite conversation.

In most Japanese homes, in Japanese-style inns and frequently in traditional restaurants, it is taboo to wear outdoor shoes; instead slippers are provided. It is considered bad etiquette to step on the door sill or the borders of the *tatami* mats.

Japan has become thoroughly Westernised on the surface but the people still celebrate numerous traditional festivals. These range from the informal – cherry blossom viewing in the spring and kite flying – to formal festivals such as celebrating a person's coming of age.

The Japanese insist on punctuality and punctiliousness in business behaviour. It is essential to carry *meishi* or name cards (preferably with your name in Japanese on the reverse). When receiving name cards at formal meetings, the correct procedure is to study them carefully and then place them in front of you on the table.

Seating arrangements are particularly important in Japan. The place of honour is generally that furthest from the door.

Gift giving is a pleasant Japanese custom and for Japanese businessmen the exchange of gifts at New Year is very important. Ideally, gifts should consist of something personal, and be given, unopened, at the start of meetings. Whisky is now so widely sold and discounted in Japan that it is not a particularly attractive gift. When receiving gifts the Japanese practice is to treat them as objects of great reverence, but never to open them in front of the donor.

Late night business entertainment is common, but being invited to a Japanese home is rare. Restaurants are the usual venue for private social entertaining.

Drinking has its own rituals: it is bad manners for a visitor to pour a drink for himself. It is impolite to blow your nose in public. Kissing in public, standing too close to someone while talking and eating while walking down the street are also considered impolite. Do not point with your index finger – use the whole hand, palm turned upwards, in a flowing movement.

Security

Japanese cities are safe despite recent increases in crime. Burglaries are uncommon. Late night travel is usually perfectly safe, even for unaccompanied women, though drunks are to be avoided.

Getting there

Air

National airline: Japan Airlines (JAL); Japan Air System (JAS); All Nippon Airways (ANA)

International airport/s: Tokyo International, Narita (NRT), 60km east of Tokyo, with duty-free shops, bank/bureau de change (0900–2300), car hire, restaurants and tourist information centres with multilingual staff. There is a free shuttle bus connecting the two terminals.

Osaka Kansai International (KIX), 50km south-west of city; duty-free shops, car hire, banks/bureaux de change, tourist information (0900–2100) and bar/restaurant. Travel time by Nankai Express to Nama station in central Osaka 29 minutes. Tickets for trains, which connect with the Shinkansen Bullet train network, must be pre-booked.

Fukuoka, Itazuke (FUK), 10km from city; Nagoya, Komaki (NGO), 18km from city; Kagoshima (KOJ), 6km from city; Kumamoto (KMJ), 8km from city; Okinawa (OKA) 3km from Naha; Osaka International (OSA); Kobe; Kyoto.

Limousine bus services link Kansai International Airport with Osaka city centre and various other points including Kobe, Hikone and Nara.

Other airport/s: Haneda (HND), the former international airport, serves largely as a domestic airport, 19km south of Tokyo. China Airlines flights from Taipei, Taiwan, arrive here.

Airport tax: Tokyo Narita International Airport levies a tax of ¥2,040, which is usually included in the ticket price.

Getting about

National transport

Air: Most domestic flights from Tokyo to Osaka and other Japanese cities are from

Haneda, 19km from Tokyo. Extensive air services provided by a number of local airlines link all main cities and provincial towns. Tickets can be purchased by automatic machines at Tokyo and Osaka International Airports' domestic departure counters.

Road: Road transport is the main form of domestic access. The network consists of 1.2 million km of road. There are good motorways linking Tokyo, Osaka, Kobe, Hiroshima, Yamaguchi, Shimonoseki, Moji, Fukuoka, Kumamoto and Morioka. Tolls are payable on certain roads. Long-distance travel by road is not recommended (travel time from Tokyo to Nagasaki by car is 18 hours, by train 9 hours and by plane less than 2 hours), road signs are in Japanese and roads are frequently very crowded outside main cities.

Buses: An extensive network of frequent coach services link main centres via express motorways, but visitors are advised against coach travel in view of language difficulties and the complexity and number of routes available.

Rail: Japan Railways run national routes from the terminal located beneath the airport.

It is easy to travel by rail to all regions. Express and limited express trains are best for intercity travel with very frequent services run on the main routes. *Shinkansen*, the *Bullet Trains*, are the fastest, with compartments for wheelchair passengers, diners and buffet facilities. Supplements are payable on the three classes of express train and in green (first-class) cars of principal trains, for which reservations must be made well in advance; two pieces of ordinary luggage may be carried free, but there are restrictions on size and weight. Other types of train include *Tokkyu* (Limited Express), *Kyuko* (Express), *Kaisoku* (Rapid Train) and *Futsu* (Local Train). For short-distance trains, tickets can only be bought at vending machines outside train stations.

Long-distance one-way tickets generally do not permit stopovers and ticket refunds are not made after the time of the planned journey. Foreign visitors can make considerable savings by buying a Japan Rail exchange voucher, which is sold only outside Japan.

All Japan Railways (JR) stations display station names in both Japanese and Roman letters. The station's name is at the top centre of the signboard, in large letters; the names of the previous station and the next station are at the bottom of the signboard, in smaller letters.

Water: Jetfoil services to Kobe. There is also a jetfoil from Kansai International Airport to Osaka Port, with a journey time of around 40 minutes.

City transport

Taxis: Metered taxis can be easily hired in large cities at hotel entrances or by flagging them down in the street, but do not try to open or close the driver-controlled passenger door. Tipping is not required. Journey times: from Narita International Airport to Tokyo city centre around 90 minutes; from Kansai International Airport to Osaka city centre about 60 minutes. There is a surcharge after 2200 and an additional time charge is levied for traffic jams. Taxis are five times more expensive than trains.

Few taxi drivers understand foreign languages or read Roman lettering, so it is advisable to have your destination, including the name of a nearby landmark, written down in Japanese, along with the telephone number if possible. Hotels can often help with this. A map showing the location of the destination is also helpful.

Buses, trams & metro: Limousine buses depart several times an hour from Narita airport to city-centre hotels; journey time is about two hours. There is also a bus to the Tokyo City Air Terminal (TCAT). Tickets for all services can be bought in the terminals.

Buses can be confusing and are best used with someone who knows the system. Efficient underground railway services operate in Tokyo, Yokohama, Osaka, Kyoto, Kobe, Nagoya, Sapporo and Fukuoka, with station names displayed in Roman as well as Japanese lettering.

Trains: JR and Keisei railway lines provide frequent services from Narita airport to the city centre, journey time 60–90 minutes.

Car hire

An international driving licence is required. Driving is on the left. Chauffeur-driven cars are often recommended for visitors without command of Japanese and knowledge of the area, as traffic and navigation can be difficult. Symbolic road signs have the expected international meanings, but few signs are written in the Roman alphabet. A red triangle with white script means 'stop', while a white triangle with a red border and blue script means 'proceed slowly'.

BUSINESS DIRECTORY

The addresses listed below are a selection only. While World of Information makes every endeavour to check these addresses, we cannot guarantee that changes have not been made, especially to telephone numbers and area codes. We would welcome any corrections.

Telephone area codes

The international direct dialling (IDD) code for Japan is +81, followed by area code and subscriber's number:

Fukuoka	92	Nagoya	52
Hiroshima	82	Okayama	862
Kawasaki	44	Osaka	66
Kobe	78	Sapparo	11
Kyoto	75	Tokyo	3
Nagasaki	958	Yokohama	45

Useful telephone numbers

Emergency
Police: 110.
Ambulance/Fire: 119
Overseas calls
Tokyo to south-east Asia: 3211-4211.
Tokyo operator: 0051.
Tokyo telegraph office: 3211-5588.
Nagoya telegraph office: 203-3311.
Osaka telegraph office: 228-2151.

Chambers of Commerce

American Chamber of Commerce in Japan, Masonic 39 MT Building, 2-4-5 Azabudai, Minato-ku, Tokyo 106-0041 (tel: 3433-5381; fax: 3433-8454; e-mail: info@accj.or.jp).

British Chamber of Commerce in Japan, Kenkyusha Eigo Centre Building, 1-2, Kagurazaka, Shinjuku-ku, Tokyo 162-0825 (tel: 3267-1901; fax: 3267-1903; e-mail: info@bccjapan.com).

Fukuoka Chamber of Commerce and Industry, 2-9-28 Hakata-ekimae, Hakata-ku, Fukuoka 812-8505 (tel: 441-1110; fax: 474-3200; e-mail: fksomu@fukunet.or.jp).

Kobe Chamber of Commerce and Industry, 6-1 Minato-jima Naka-machi, Chuo-ku, Kobe 650-8543 (tel: 303-5801; fax: 303-2312; e-mail: info@kcci-iic.ne.jp).

Nagoya Chamber of Commerce and Industry, 2-10-19 Sakae, Naka-ku, Nagoya (tel: 223-5611; fax: 231-6768; e-mail: info@nagoya-cci.or.jp).

Yokohama Chamber of Commerce and Industry, 2 Yamashita-cho, Naka-ku, Yokohama 231-8524 (tel: 671-7400; fax: 671-7410; e-mail: info@yokohama-cci.or.jp).

Banking

Mitsubishi Tokyo Financial Group, 1-3-2 Nihonbashi-Hongkucho, Chuo-ku, Tokyo (tel: 3245-1111; fax: 3246-1708); 7-1 Marunouchi 2-chome, Chiyoda-ku, Tokyo 100 (tel: 3240-1111; fax: 3211-6645).

Mizuho Bank, 1-1-5 Uchisaiwaicho, Chiyoda-ku, Tokyo 100 (tel: 3596-111).

Sumitomo Mitsui Banking Corporation, 1-2 Yurakucho, 1-chome, Chiyoda-ku, Tokyo 100-0006 (tel: 2501-1111).

Central bank

Bank of Japan (Nippon Ginko), 2-1-1 Nihonbashi-Hongokucho, Chuo-ku, Tokyo 103 (tel: 3279-1111; fax: 3277-1473).

Stock exchange

Tokyo Shoken Torihikisho (Tokyo Stock Exchange) (TSE), www.tse.or.jp

Kabushiki-gaisha Osaka Shoken Torihikijo (Osaka Securities Exchange) (OSE), www.ose.or.jp

Nagoya Shoken Torihikijo (Nagoya Securities Exchange) (NSE), www.nse.or.jp

JASDAQ (Jasudakku Shoken Torihikisho), www.jasdaq.co.jp

Commodity exchange

The Tokyo Grain Exchange, www.tge.or.jp

Tokyo Commodity Exchange (Tocom), www.tocom.or.jp

Central Japan Commodity Exchange (C-Com), www.c-com.or.jp

Kansai Commodities Exchange (Kanex), http://kanex.or.jp

Travel information

Japan Airlines (JAL), Tokyo Building, Marunouchi 2-7-3, Chiyoda-ku, Tokyo 100 (tel: 3284-2610; fax: 3284-2659; internet site: http://www.spin.ad.jp/jal/home-e.html).

Japan Automobile Federation, Shiba-Koen, 3-5-8 Minato-ku, Tokyo 105 (tel: 3436-2811).

Tourist Information Centre, 1-6-6 Yurakucho 1-chome, Chiyoda-Ku, Tokyo 100 (tel: 3502-1461); Kyoto Tower Building, Higashi-Shiokojicho, Shimogyo-ku, Kyoto 600 (tel: 371-5649).

Japan Travel Phone is a nationwide telephone service for English-language assistance and travel information. Available from 0900–1700 daily, the service is toll-free from outside Tokyo or Kyoto: information on eastern Japan: 0088-222-800 (or 0120-222-800); information on western Japan: 0088-22-4800 (or 0120-444-800). Tokyo: 3503-4400. Kyoto: 371-5649. Tokyo; French-language assistance: 3503-2926.

Tokyo: Japan Railways (JR) English-language information service, (Mon–Fri, except holidays) 1000–1800; reservations cannot be accepted by telephone service: 3423-0111. (Narita Express has a free phone connection to this service).

National tourist organisation offices

Japan National Tourist Organisation, 2-10-1 Yuraku-cho, Chiyodaku, Tokyo (tel: 3201-3331; fax: 3201-3347; internet: www.jnto.go.jp).

Ministries

Ministry of Agriculture, Forestry and Fisheries, 1-2-1 Kasumigaseki, Chiyoda-ku, Tokyo 100-8950 (tel: 3502-8111; fax: 3592-7697; e-mail: white56@maff.go.jp).

Ministry of Education, Culture, Sports, Science and Technology, 3-2-2 Kasumigaseki, Chiyoda-ku, Tokyo 100-8959 (tel: 3581-4211; fax: 3595-2017).

Ministry of the Environment, 1-2-2 Kasumigaseki, Chiyoda-ku, Tokyo 100-8975 (tel: 3581-3351; e-mail: MOE@eanet.go.jp).

Ministry of Foreign Affairs, 2-2-1, Kasumigaseki, Chiyoda-ku, Tokyo 100-8919 (tel: 3580-3311; fax: 3581-2667; e-mail: webmaster@mofa.go.jp).

Ministry of Health, Labour and Welfare, 1-2-2 Kasumigaseki, Chiyoda-ku, Tokyo 100-8916 (tel: 5253-1111; fax: 3501-2532).

Ministry of Justice, 1-1-1 Kasumigaseki, Chiyoda-ku, Tokyo 100-8977 (tel: 3580-4111; fax: 3592-7011; e-mail: webmaster@moj.go.jp).

Ministry of Land, Infrastructure and Transport, 2-1-3 Kasumigaseki, Chiyoda-ku, Tokyo 100-8918 (tel: 5253-8111; fax: 3580-7982; e-mail: webmaster@mlit.go.jp).

Ministry of Public Management, Home Affairs, Posts and Telecommunications, 2-1-2 Kasumigaseki, Chiyoda-ku, Tokyo 100-8926 (tel: 5253-5111; fax: 3504-0265; e-mail: feedback@mpt.go.jp).

Defence Agency, 5-1 Ichigaya, Honmura-cho, Shinjuku-ku, Tokyo 162-8801 (tel: 3268-3111; e-mail: info@jda.go.jp).

National Public Safety Commission, 2-1-2 Kasumigaseki, Chiyoda-ku, Tokyo 100-8974 (tel: 3581-0141).

Prime Minister's Office, 1-6-1, Nagata-cho, Chiyoda-ku, Tokyo 100-8914 (tel: 3581-2361; fax: 3593-1784).

Other useful addresses

Asian Development Bank, Japanese Representative Office, Second Floor, Yamato Seimei Building, 1-7 Uchisaiwaicho 1-Chome, Chiyoda-ku, Tokyo 100 (tel: 3504-3160; fax: 3504-3165; E-mail: adbjro@mail.asiandevbank.org).

Association for the Promotion of International Trade, Nihon Building, 6-2 Otemachi 2-chome, Chiyoda-ku, Tokyo (tel: 3245-1561).

British Embassy, No 1 Ichiban-cho, Chiyoda-ku, Tokyo 102 (tel: 3265-6340; fax: 5275-0346).

Council of All-Japan Exporters' Association, Kikai Shinko Kaikan Building, 5-8 Shibakaen 3-chome, Minato-ku, Tokyo.

Defence Agency, 9-7-45 Akasaka, Minato-ku, Tokyo 107-0052 (tel: 3408-5211; fax: 3408-6480).

Economic Planning Agency, 3-1-1 Kasumigaseki, Chiyoda-ku, Tokyo 100-0013 (tel: 3581-0261; fax: 3581-0838).

Environment Agency, 1-2-2 Kasumigaseki, Chiyoda-ku, Tokyo 100-0013 (tel: 3581-3351; fax: 3502-0308).

Fair Trade Commission, 2-2-1 Kasumigaseki, Chiyoda-ku, Tokyo 100-0013 (tel: 3581-5471; fax: 3581-1963).

Federation of Economic Organisations (Keidanren), 9-4 Othe-machi 1-chome, Chiyoda-ku 100, Tokyo (tel: 3279-1411; fax: 5255-6250).

Hokkaido Development Agency, 3-1-1 Kasumigaseki, Chiyoda-ku, Tokyo 100-8922 (tel: 3581-9111; fax: 3581-1208; e-mail: info1@had.go.jp).

House of Councillors, 1-7-1 Nagata-cho, Chiyoda-ku, Tokyo 100-0014 (tel: 3581-3111; fax: 3581-2900).

House of Representitives, 1-7-1 Nagata-cho, Chiyoda-ku, Tokyo 100-0014 (tel: 3581-5111; fax: 3581-2900).

Imperial Household Agency, 1-1 Chiyoda, Chiyoda-ku, Tokyo 100-0001 (tel: 3213-1111; fax: 3282-1407).

Japan Commercial Arbitration Association, Tosho Building, 2-2 Marunouchi 3-chome, Chiyoda-ku, Tokyo (tel: 3214-0641).

Japan Committee for Economic Development, Kogo Club Building 4-6 Marunouchi 1-chome, Chiyoda-ku, Tokyo (tel: 3211-1271).

Japan External Trade Organisation (JETRO), 2-5 Toranomon 2-chome, Minato-ku 105, Tokyo (tel: 3582-5511).

Japan Federation of Economic Organisations (Keidanren), 9-4 Otemachi 1-chome, Chiyoda-ku, Tokyo (tel: 3279-1411).

Japan Federation of Importers' Organisation, Nihombashi Daiwa Building, 1-6-1 Nihombashi Hon-Cho, Chuo-ku, Tokyo (tel: 3270-2020).

Japan Federation of Smaller Enterprise Organisation, 8-4 Nihonbashi Kayaba-cho 2-chome, Chuo-ku 103, Tokyo (tel: 3669-6862; fax: 3668-2957).

Japan Foreign Trade Council, World Trade Centre Building, 4-1 Hamamatsu-cho 2-chome, Minato-ku 105, Tokyo (tel: 3435-5952; fax: 3435-5979).

Japan Guide Association (interpreter and translation services), Shin Kokusai Building, 4-1 Marunouchi 3-chome, Chiyoda-ku, Tokyo (tel: 213-2706).

Japan International Co-operation System, 5th Floor, Shinjuku Sanshin Bldg, 4-9 Yoyogi 2-chome, Shibuya-ku, Tokyo 151 (tel: 5981-5988; fax: 5981-5994).

Japan Productivity Centre, 1-1 Shibuya 3-chome, Shibuya-ku 150, Tokyo (tel: 3409-1111; fax: 3409-4128).

Japan Securities Dealers Association, 5-8 Nihombashi Kayabacho 1-chome, Chuo-ku, Tokyo (tel: 3667-8459; fax: 3666-8009).

Japanese Embassy (USA), 2520 Massachusetts Avenue, NW, Washington DC 20008 (tel: (+1-202) 238-6700; fax: (+1-202) 328-2187).

Kansai Economic Federation, Nakanoshima Centre Bldg, 2-27 Nakanoshima 6-chome, Kita-ku, Osaka 530 (tel: 253-2351; 253-1678).

Management and Co-ordination Agency, 3-1-1 Kasumigaseki Chiyoda-ku, Tokyo 100-0013 (tel: 3581-6361; fax: 3593-1620).

Okinawa Development Agency, 1-6-1 Nagata-cho, Chiyoda-ku, Tokyo 100-0014 (tel: 3581-2361; fax: 3581-4783).

Science and Technology Agency, 2-2-1 Kasumigaseki, Chiyoda-ku, Tokyo 100-8966 (tel: 3581-5271; fax: 3593-1371; e-mail: www@sta.go.jp).

Statistics Bureau & Statistics Centre Management & Coordination Agency, 19-1 Wakamatsu-cho, Shinjuku-ku, Tokyo 162 (tel: 3202-1111; fax: 5273-1180).

Supreme Court, 4-2 Hayabusa-cho, Chiyoda-ku, Tokyo 102-0092 (tel: 3264-8111; fax: 3221-8975).

Tokyo International Trade Fair Commission, 7-24 Harumi 4-chome, Chuo-ku, Tokyo 103 (tel: 3666-0141, 3531-3371; fax: 3663-0625).

Tokyo Stock Exchange, 2-1 Nihombashi Kabutocho 1-chome, Chuo-ku, Tokyo (tel: 3666-0141; fax: 3663-0625, 3666-0141; internet site: http://www.tse.or.jp).

West Japan Railway Company, 4-24 Shibata 2-chome, Kita-ku, Osaka 530-8341 (tel: 375-8981; fax: 375-8919).

World Trade Centre of Japan, 4-1 2-chome Hamamatsu-cho, Minato-ku, Tokyo (tel: 3435-5651).

Jiji Press (in Japanese): www.jiji.com

Kyodo News: http://home.kyodo.co.jp

Nikkei Net (business and stock market news): www.nni.nikkei.co.jp

Internet sites

Asahi Shimbun: www.adv.asahi.com/english

Japan access: www.keidanren.or.jp/A2J/index.html

Japan Company Record: www.japancompanyrecord.com/

Japan Hotel Association: www.j-hotel.or.jp

Japan Information Network: http://jin.jcic.or.jp

Japan Statistics:www.stat.go.jp/1.htm

JETRO Homepage (Japanese Trade Promotion): www.jetro.go.jp

Sanwa Bank: www.sanwabank.co.jp

Jordan

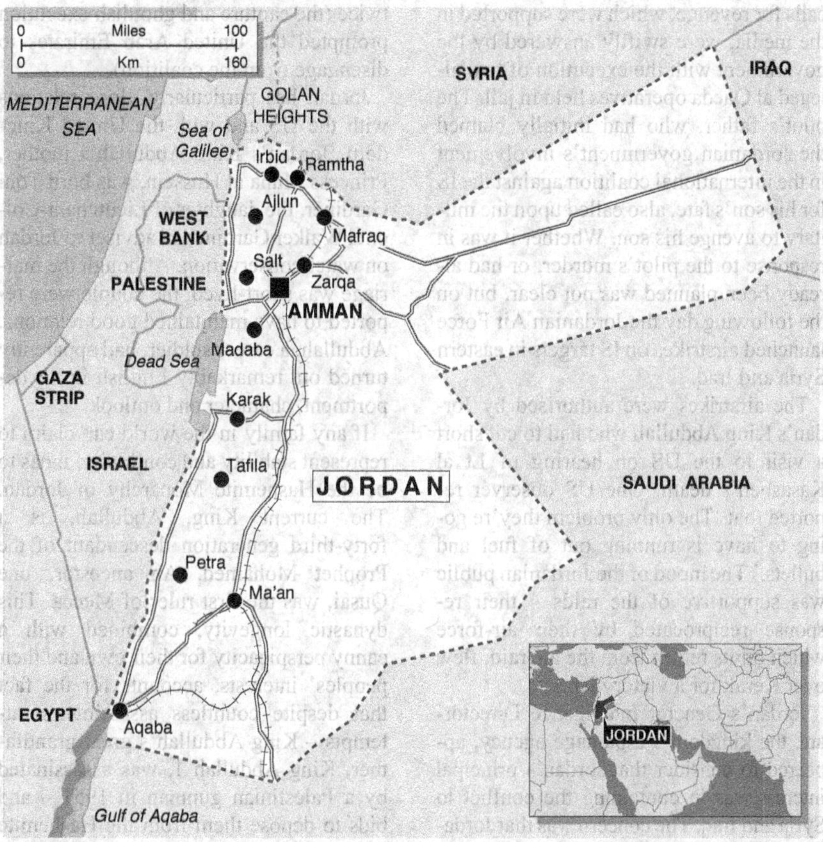

According to the United Nations High Commission for refugees (UNHCR) in September 2015 there were 625,000 Syrian refugees in Jordan – some 10 per cent of Jordan's population – for the most part housed in tents, with inadequate sanitation and offering little winter shelter. Adding to the refugees' misery, the World Food Programme (WFP) which had been providing much of the refugees' food requirements had almost run out of money, facing a funding gap of some US$340 million. The refugees' plight and perspectives, were beginning to change, or even come full circle, according to a WFP spokesperson. Refugees arriving in Jordan in 2011 or 2012 still hoped to return to Syria after a few weeks or months. The weeks and months had then become years as the uprising in Syria became a full-blown civil war. In 2015 such was the desperation of many refugees that they were beginning to drift back to Syria, despite the fact that the whole country could be classed as an active war-zone. Their resources limited, living on as little as US$0.50 cents per day (a WFP figure quoted in the London *Guardian* newspaper) had been the proverbial last straw. Reportedly many refugees were taking their children out of school and putting them on Amman's streets to beg. Working to earn a living was prohibited for refugees in Jordan. One report suggested that the number of refugees leaving Jordan to try and return home had doubled to 120 persons a day.

Refugee plight, or respite?

According to the International Labour Organisation (ILO) the largest numbers of Syrian refugees were located in Jordan's northern governorates. The Amman, Irbid and Mafraq governorates were hosting

KEY FACTS

Official name: Al Mamlaka al Urduniya al Hashemiya (The Hashemite Kingdom of Jordan)

Head of State: King Abdullah II (crowned 1999), Crown Prince Hussein (born 28 June 1994), eldest son of King Abdullah II

Head of government: Prime Minister Abdullah Ensour (from 10 Oct 2012, reappointed Jan 2013)

Ruling party: National Constitutional Party (NCP) (pro-monarchy coalition formed from a union of independent members of parliament and nine centrist parties)

Area: 91,860 square km

Population: 6.67 million (2014)*

Capital: Amman

Official language: Arabic

Currency: Jordanian dinar (JD) = 1,000 fils

Exchange rate: JD0.71 per US$ (Sep 2015)

GDP per capita: US$5,358 (2014)*

GDP real growth: 3.10% (2014)*

GDP: US$35.77 billion (2014)*

Unemployment: 11.90% (2014)*

Inflation: 2.90% (2014)

Balance of trade: -US$11.47 billion (2013)

* estimated figure

over 75 per cent of the total Syrian refugee population. Syrian refugees constituted 52 per cent of the total population of Mafraq, 12 per cent of the total population of Irbid and seven per cent of the total population of the Amman governorate. Press reports suggested that Syrian refugees were having significant impacts on the Jordanian labour market, raising concerns about the effects on available job opportunities, wage levels, working conditions, access to work and other aspects of the labour market.

These concerns were not altogether new; the Jordanian labour market already had a number of challenges before the Syrian crisis started. In 2010, the national unemployment rate was 12.7 per cent. To make matters worse, Jordan had one of the lowest labour force participation rates in the world and one of the lowest female participation rates, with only 14 per cent of women participating in the labour force, compared to 65 per cent of men. Jordan's youth unemployment rate was estimated by the ILO to be over 40 per cent. What jobs there were tended to be at the bottom end of the scale, attracting low-skilled foreign workers. At the beginning of the Syrian crisis, according to the ILO, 335,000 foreign workers were officially employed in Jordan, of whom almost 90 per cent were illiterate. Seventy per cent of the foreign workers in Jordan in 2009 were Egyptians. Over 95 per cent of foreign workers received wages of less than JD199 in 2009.

For Jordan, the year 2015 started badly, with the burning to death of the Jordanian Air Force officer Lieutenant Moaz al Kasasbeh by the members of the Islamic State (IS) grouping in early January. Jordanians responded to the young pilot's death by calling for revenge. Demonstrations broke out across Jordan, focussed on the seat of government, Amman, and in Lieutenant al Kasasbeh's hometown of Kerak. The rallies, which supported the government were well attended and their calls for revenge, which were supported in the media, were swiftly answered by the government with the execution of two alleged al Qaeda operatives held in jail. The pilot's father, who had initially blamed the Jordanian government's involvement in the international coalition against the IS for his son's fate, also called upon the military to avenge his son. Whether it was in response to the pilot's murder, or had already been planned was not clear, but on the following day the Jordanian Air Force launched airstrikes on IS targets in eastern Syria and Iraq.

The airstrikes were authorised by Jordan's King Abdullah who had to cut short a visit to the US on hearing of Lt al Kasasbeh's death. One US observer reported that 'The only problem they're going to have is running out of fuel and bullets.' The mood of the Jordanian public was supportive of the raids – their response reciprocated by their air-force which on its return from the air-raid, flew over Kerak for a victory lap.

Jordan's General Intelligence Directorate, the kingdom's espionage agency, appeared to consider that Jordan's principal interest was in containing the conflict to Syria and Iraq. The concern was that Jordanian public opinion could quickly change.

KEY INDICATORS — Jordan

	Unit	2011	2012	2013	2014	**2015
Population	m	*6.25	*6.40	6.53	*6.67	*6.82
Gross domestic product (GDP)	US$bn	29.20	30.98	33.64	*35.77	*3.81
GDP per capita	US$	4,675	4,843	5,152	*5,358	*5,590
GDP real growth	%	2.5	2.7	2.8	*3.1	*3.8
Inflation	%	4.4	4.6	5.8	*2.9	*1.1
Unemployment	%	12.9	12.2	12.6	*11.9	–
Exports (fob) (goods)	US$m	2,001.6	7,886.6	7,910.8	–	–
Imports (fob) (goods)	US$m	4,206.5	18,430.9	19,380.7	–	–
Balance of trade	US$m	-2,204.9	-10,544.3	-11,469.8	–	–
Current account	US$m	3,475.0	-5,612.0	-3,453.0	*-2,512.0	*-2,907.0
Total reserves minus gold	US$m	12,206.4	8,089.5	13,223.8	15,299.5	–
Foreign exchange	US$m	11,972.8	7,868.7	13,009.7	–	–
Exchange rate	per US$	0.71	0.71	0.71	0.71	–

* estimated figure ** forecast figure

Lt al Kasasbeh's death had, for a period at least, caused outrage and grief. The young pilot's barbaric death had served to remind the Jordanian public of how costly its government's anti-IS policies might prove to be. As Arab nations go, Jordan is not thought of as faint-hearted. Lt al Kasasbeh's death might have caused other members of the US-led coalition to think twice (the capture and ghoulish execution prompted the United Arab Emirates to disengage from the coalition).

Jordan has particularly close relations with the US and with the United Kingdom. Jordan's King Abdullah's mother, Princess Muna al Hussein, was born Toni Gardiner, the daughter of Lieutenant-Colonel Walker Gardiner an adviser to Jordan on water conservation. Although the marriage was short-lived, the couple were reported to have maintained good relations. Abdullah, a career soldier, had apparently turned out remarkably English in his deportment, character and outlook.

If any family in the world can claim to represent stability and continuity, it has to be the Hashemite Monarchy of Jordan. The current King, Abdullah, is a forty-third generation descendant of the Prophet Mohamed. An ancestor, one Qusai, was the first ruler of Mecca. This dynastic longevity, combined with a canny perspicacity for their own and their peoples' interests, accounts for the fact that despite countless assassination attempts – King Abdullah's great grandfather, King Abdullah 1, was assassinated by a Palestinian gunman in 1951 – and bids to depose them from the Hashemite throne, the family continue to call the shots.

Robust, but exposed

Although Jordan's monarchy is considered one of the region's more robust regimes, it is also one of the most exposed. The Palestinian presence in the country is hugely significant. An estimated 4.5 million Palestinians live in Jordan, of whom 3.5 million have acquired Jordanian citizenship. The influx of Palestinians into Jordan has meant that the traditional Bedouin community of 3 million finds itself to be a minority in its own country. The balance of power is currently maintained by an electoral system that denies Palestinians full voting rights. Underlying the Palestinian presence in Jordan is the 'right of return' that is a *sine qua non* of all Israeli-Palestinian negotiations. Until the 2014 peace negotiations came to a stop, many Jordanians – both Bedu and Palestinians – feared that under US pressure their representatives in the negotiations might forego their insistence on the right to return for the sake of a wider peace agreement. This would inevitably mean that the Jordanian Palestinians, many of whom had been resident in the country for as many as three or four generations, would settle permanently in Jordan – thereby changing the whole political dynamic of the country.

The economy

Jordan has been hit by a series of severe shocks over the past few years. The conflicts in neighbouring Syria and Iraq have created considerable economic and social pressures; the Jordanian authorities have published estimates that Jordan was hosting as many as 1.4 million Syrians, which was over one fifth of Jordan's non-refugee population. However, international organisations put the Syrian refugee number at 625,000.

In its annual review of the Jordanian economy, the International Monetary Fund (IMF) noted that Jordan's annual gross domestic product (GDP) growth dropped to 2 per cent in the first quarter of 2015, very much reflecting the flared up regional tensions linked to IS early in the year adversely affecting Jordan's exports and tourism. The country was also affected by a weather-related contraction in construction, delays in government spending and a slowdown in mining (after a rebound in 2014). Despite a drop in labour force participation, unemployment increased, pointing to a decline in employment in the first quarter. The deteriorating regional environment and uncertainty were certainly damaging both output and jobs.

Jordan's inflation remains low, headline CPI inflation rebounding to an annual 0.3 per cent in June 2015, from -1.7 per cent in February, reflecting primarily a partial recovery in transport costs from higher oil prices and an acceleration in food prices. Core inflation continued its gradual descent, to an annual 3.4 per cent. There was a slight upturn in private sector credit growth. Excluding Jordan's refinery – which repaid loans after NEPCO cleared its arrears – credit growth had been gradually increasing since early this year, reaching an annual 4.8 per cent in April 2015. Corporate credit growth picked up in the first quarter and some firms were said to have sought credit from abroad to benefit from low interest rates. Mortgages slowed down in tandem with real estate prices; the exposure of banks to real estate credit risk remained limited.

Energy imports fell by one third in the first quarter of 2015 and remittance inflows increased. (See 'Energy' below). According to the IMF, this more than offset the decline in merchandise exports and tourism receipts, probably reflecting a stronger-than-expected impact of the Iraq crisis (which had started to have a more pronounced impact on Jordan in the second half of 2014). Largely mirroring a stronger US dollar, the exchange rate had been appreciating since mid-2014.

Growth for 2015 was revised down by the IMF, from 3.8 per cent to about 3 per cent following the drop in the first quarter. Risks were to the downside as the IMF projection assumed that investor sentiment and tourism would recover quickly, while low oil prices would continue to support private consumption. The IMF assumed a gradual easing of the Syria and Iraq conflicts starting in 2017, one year later than had been originally assumed. As a result, growth, supported by public and private investment and a rebound in exports and tourism, was only expected to reach its potential in 2017. At the same time, imports and consumption were expected to slow down as refugees started returning and related economic pressures ease.

In summary, the IMF expected inflation to move into positive territory by the end of 2015, peaking at an annual 2.5 per cent in 2016. Thereafter, it was projected to gradually decelerate to an annual two per cent as consumption slowed down. The decline in the current account deficit was expected to be about 11 per cent of GDP in 2015, smaller than previously envisaged as lower imports would only partially offset a drop in travel receipts and exports throughout the year. The deficit was expected to steadily decline to about 9 per cent of GDP by 2020 because of continued public sector consolidation, further savings from the energy import bill and increases in both tourism and exports.

Energy

Jordan is almost an exception among Middle East states in not having substantial energy resources. In January 2014, the *Oil & Gas Journal* (OGJ) estimated Jordan's proved oil reserves at just one million barrels and its proved natural gas reserves at slightly more than 200 billion cubic feet (bcf). According to the United States government Energy Information Administration (EIA) oil shale resources had the potential to increase Jordan's reserves significantly; it was planned to build the first oil shale-fired electricity generation facility in the Middle East after 2017.

As a result of its lack of significant energy resources, Jordan inevitably relies heavily on imports of crude oil, petroleum products and natural gas to meet domestic energy demand. Government sources have indicated that energy imports meet more than 90 per cent of Jordan's energy demand and that the energy imports account for more than 40 per cent of the country's budget.

Government statistics also indicate that in 2012 the use of crude oil and oil products accounted for approximately 88 per cent of Jordan's total primary energy demand, but that domestic sources of oil and natural gas met less than 2 per cent of that demand.

Jordan was pursuing several pipeline deals, notably with Iraq, to help bolster its energy security. One proposal would send Iraqi oil from the area around Basra to the Jordanian port of Aqaba on the Red Sea. If constructed, the pipeline would initially carry up to 1 million barrels per day (bpd) of oil, including more than 100,000bpd available for use inside Jordan. The plan also called for a natural gas pipeline to run along the same route as the oil pipeline, with up to 100 million cubic feet per day (MMcf/d) being allocated to help meet Jordanian demand.

The Arab Gas Pipeline (AGP) – which runs through Jordan from Egypt – had been the principal source of Jordanian natural gas imports, until volumes fell dramatically from 89 billion cubic feet (bcf) in 2010 to 17bcf in 2012 as a result of unrest in the Sinai Peninsula and in Syria. Jordan's economy was hit hard by the end of these low-cost gas imports from Egypt, creating the need for more expensive fuel imports, which in turn led to large losses by the electricity company NEPCO.

Risk assessment

Economy	Fair
Politics	Fair
Regional stability	Poor

Muslims in Jordan

% of population	92
Sunni (% of Muslims)	95
Shi'a (% of Muslims)	0

COUNTRY PROFILE

1928 Transjordan obtained qualified independence in a treaty with Britain.

1946 Transjordan achieved full independence as the Hashemite Kingdom of Jordan under the Emir, who took the title of King Abdullah.

1948 Jewish leaders announced the formation of the State of Israel in British-mandate Palestine and thousands of Palestinian Arabs fled to Jordan and the West Bank.
1950 A post-war agreement united Jordan with the part of Palestine remaining in Arab hands (the West Bank, including East Jerusalem, but excluding the Gaza Strip).
1951 King Abdullah was assassinated and was succeeded by his son, Talal bin Abdullah.
1952 Hussein bin Talal formally took power as King Hussein after his father, Talal bin Abdullah, stepped down due to mental illness.
1956 King Hussein banned political parties.
1957 British troops completed their withdrawal from Jordan.
1967 Six Day War with Israel. Israel occupied the West Bank and Gaza Strip and re-unified Jerusalem; around 300,000 Palestinian Arab refugees entered Jordan.
1970 Civil war (Black September) between the Jordanian army and Palestinians followed airplane hijackings by the Palestine Liberation Organisation (PLO) resistance group. The PLO was forcefully expelled from its bases in Jordan and moved to Lebanon
1972 An attempted military coup was thwarted.
1974 Jordan and other Arab countries recognised the PLO as the sole legitimate representative of the Palestinian people.
1978–84 The House of Representatives (parliament) was temporarily replaced during these years by a National Consultative Council appointed by the King.
1986 King Hussein severed political links with the PLO and ordered its main offices to shut.
1988 The House of Representatives was dissolved, prior to King Hussein's announcement of the severance of all administrative and legal ties with the West Bank. The King publicly backed the Palestinian *intifada* against Israeli rule.
1989 The first general elections since 1967 were contested only by independent candidates.
1992 Parliament authorised political parties for the first time since they were banned by King Hussein 36 years previously.
1993 Multi-party elections were held.
1994 The Jordan-Israel Peace Treaty was signed at Wadi Araba, Jordan, following the opening of the first border crossing between Aqaba (Jordan) and Eilat (Israel).
1997 Parliamentary elections were boycotted by nine opposition parties, led by the Islamic Action Front (IAF). The Islamists said the electoral law favoured the rural constituencies, where support for the King was strong, over the towns, where nearly half of Jordan's population lived. The elections were won by the National Constitutional Party (NCP), a pro-monarchy coalition formed from the union of nine centrist parties.
1999 King Hussein appointed his eldest son, Abdullah bin Hussein, as crown prince and heir, replacing Prince Hassan, the King's brother, who had been appointed crown prince in 1965. King Hussein, who had been treated for cancer for many years, died, and Abdullah bin Hussein was sworn in as King.
2000 King Abdullah II made a historic visit to the state of Israel. Jordan joined the World Trade Organisation (WTO).
2002 Senior US diplomat, Laurence Foley, was shot dead outside his home in Amman. Many political activists were arrested.
2003 King Abdullah II ratified an amended law adding six women members to the women's share in parliament. Independent candidates, allies of the King, won two-thirds of the seats in the parliamentary elections. The King appointed Faisal al Fayez as prime minister and three female ministers.
2005 Jordan returned its ambassador to Israel after a truce was signed by Israel and Palestine.
2006 The joint Jordanian-Syrian Wahdah Dam project was completed.
2007 New entry regulations stemmed the flow of refugees from Iraq; over one million Iraqis had taken up residence since 2003.
2008 George Habash, the (founder of militant Popular Front for the Liberation of Palestine) (PFLP) died in Amman. King Abdullah became the first Gulf-Arab leader to visit Iraq.
2009 Hussein bin Al Abdullah, eldest son of King Abdullah II, was declared Crown Prince by royal decree; when he ascends to the throne, he will become King Hussein II. Pope Benedict XVI visited, holding an open air mass for some 25,000 celebrants. King Abdullah dissolved parliament and called for early elections. Prime Minister Dahabi resigned and Samir al Rifai was appointed as his replacement.
2010 The King set up the National Dialogue Committee, chaired by the Senate president, Taher Masri, to consider a range of reforms proposed by King Abdullah II. Recommendations were submitted to Prime Minister Marouf Al Bakhit that included a proposal for an increase in the number of seats in parliament from 120 to 130; and the establishment of an independent panel of retired judges (appointed by royal decree) to oversee elections, instead of the interior ministry; a draft law was proposed making it easier to form political parties and to encourage participation by women. Talks with a French-Japanese consortium regarding Jordan's nuclear power programme entered its second stage, concerning commissioning the plant and logistics. The main opposition IAF boycotted parliamentary elections, held one-year earlier than planned, calling them unfair, due to election laws that gave undue weight to votes from rural, sparsely populated areas. Of the 763 candidates standing for election, three-quarters were previous members of the legislature; all stood as independents. Only 17 candidates elected (out of 120 seats) were members of political parties; 78 elected candidates were new to parliament. Samir al Rifai became prime minister.
2011 In February, when demonstrations in the Middle East had toppled the regimes in Tunisia and Egypt during the Arab Spring, anti-government unrest caused King Abdullah to dismiss the government and appointed Marouf al Bakhit as prime minister. In June King Abdullah announced that he would relinquish his right to appoint prime ministers, and future government cabinet posts, which instead will be formed by an elected parliamentary majority. On 25 July, Prince Rashid Bin El Hassan (son of the former Crown Prince El Hassan bin Talaal) married Zeina Shaban. In October, Prime Minister Maarouf al Bakhit resigned and King Abdullah appointed a former judge of the International Court of Justice (ICJ), Awn al Khasawneh as prime minister.
2012 Awn Khasawneh resigned as prime minister on 26 April; the King appointed Fayez Tarawneh as the new prime minister. A fight broke out on 17 June between members in parliament during a debate on draft election laws, when an amendment was proposed, by the opposition, to increase the number of seats allocated to candidates who run on party lists. In July the Muslim Brotherhoo affiliated Islamic Action Front announced that the party would boycott the elections, stating that the changes to the electoral law increasing the number of seats for political parties did not go far enough and that the constituency system favoured tribal candidates. On 4 October King Abdullah dissolved parliament a day ahead of a demonstration led by the IAF, calling on the King for political reforms. On 11 October a new government, led by Abdullah Ensour as prime minister was sworn into office. The date for early general elections on 13 January 2013 was announced on 16 October.
2013 A general election was held on 23 January. Out of the 150 seats, 123 were won by independents. Of the parties

standing, the Hizb Al-Wasat Al-Islamiy (Muslim Centre Party) won 3 seats, the Stronger Jordan party, The Homeland party and the National Union Party each won 2 seats and and further 18 parties won one seat each. Interim Prime Minister Abdullah Ensour was appointed to the post on a permanent basis. For the first time King Abdullah consulted Parliament on membership of the cabinet. With 19 members, the new cabinet was the smallest in four decades. In October the number of members in the upper house of parliament was increased from 40 to 75.
2014 By June it was estimated that there were over 600,000 Syrian refugees in the country. Former minister of information, Abdallah Abu Romman, said that the refugee crisis 'is turning into a security situation,' as the government worried that armed fighters, regime intelligence agents and smugglers would hide among the refugees. The government was also concerned at the strain the refugees were putting on water supplies especially.
2015 Video of Jordanian pilot Moaz al Kasasbeh, captured by Islamic State (IS) when his fighter jet crashed in Syria on 24 December 2014, being burned to death in a cage was released by IS on 3 February. The Jordanian government had earlier offered to release Sajida al Rishawi, an Iraqi militant sentenced to death in Jordan after a failed suicide bombing, in exchange for Lt Kasasbeh. However, it appears that he had probably already been murdered. Ms Rishawi was hung the following day, and the government announced that it had carried out its first air strikes on IS on 5 February.

Political structure

Constitution

Under a revised constitution of January 1952, the throne passes by male descent to heirs above the age of 18. A Regent or Council of Regency exercises power on behalf of the heir if he is below the age of 18 on succeeding to the throne.
Jordan is divided into eight governorates, each headed by a governor and consisting of districts, sub-districts and counties. At local government level there are 152 municipalities, including Greater Amman, and 340 village councils. Local affairs are managed by city or village councils. Councils are under the supervision of the ministry of municipal and rural affairs.
A national charter, published by King Hussein in 1991, enshrined the principle of political freedom. It also underscored the ultimate power of the monarchy.
In 2003, King Abdullah II ratified an amended law adding six women members to the parliament. This number was increased to 12 in the 2010 electoral law. The new law also increased the total number of parliamentary seats to 120, including adding four seats each to Amman, Irbid, and Zarqa. Nine seats are reserved for Christians and three more for Jordan's Circassian or Cherkess minority. In 2012 the number of seats in the House of Representative was increased to 150. In 2013 the number of members of the upper house, all appointed by the King, was increased to 75.

Independence date

25 May 1946

Form of state

Monarchy with limited parliamentary democracy.

The executive

The King is Head of State and commander-in-chief of the armed forces. The King has the power to declare war or conclude peace treaties, order elections, inaugurate, adjourn and prorogue the lower house of parliament as well as to appoint the prime minister, cabinet and speaker of the upper house of parliament. The cabinet is appointed by the prime minister in consultation with the monarch.

National legislature

The bicameral Majlis al Umma (National Assembly) consists of the Majlis al-Nuwab (House of Representatives) (lower house) with 150 seats and the Majlis al A'ayan (Assembly of Senators) (upper house) with 75 members. Of the 150 seats, 108 members are directly elected in single- and multi-seat constituencies by simple majority vote, 27 members are directly elected in a single national constituency by proportional representation vote, and 15 seats are reserved for women. The electoral law enacted in July 2012 allocated an additional ten seats – 6 for women, 2 for Amman, and one seat each for the cities of Zarqa and Irbid; unchanged are nine seats reserved for Christian candidates, nine for Bedouin candidates, and three for Jordanians of Chechen or Circassian descent. Members serve four-year terms.
The 75 members of the upper house are appointed by the King. The number was increased to 75 in October 2013 and cannot exceed 50 per cent of the members of the lower house. Members also serve four-year terms.

Legal system

Judges are appointed by royal decree and are independent of the legislature and the executive. The King has the right of clemency and must confirm death sentences.

Last elections

23 January 2013

Results: Parliamentary: 123 seats were won by independents, the Hizb Al-Wasat Al-Islamiy (Muslim Centre Party) won 3 seats, the Stronger Jordan party, The Homeland party and the National Union Party each won 2 seats and and further 18 parties won one seat each. Abdullah Ensour (independent) won the election with the majority number of seats. Turnout was 56.6 per cent.

Next elections

2017 (parliamentary)

Political parties

Ruling party

National Constitutional Party (NCP) (pro-monarchy coalition formed from a union of independent members of parliament and nine centrist parties)

Main opposition party

Islamic Action Front (IAF) (the political wing of the Muslim Brotherhood)

Population

6.67 million (2014)*
Last census: October 2004: 5,100,981
Population density: 53 inhabitants per square km. Urban population 79 per cent (2010 Unicef).
Annual growth rate: 3.0 per cent, 1990–2010 (Unicef).

Ethnic make-up

The population is predominantly Arab, with small minorities of Circassians, Armenians and Kurds. No official figures are kept but it is generally accepted that Palestinians constitute 60 to 70 per cent of Jordan's population.

Religions

Over 80 per cent of the population are Sunni Muslims. There is a Christian minority, mainly Roman Catholic, Coptic and Greek Orthodox, and smaller numbers of other Muslims.

Education

The government has instituted a programme to revise and upgrade the state school system, involving teacher retraining, new curricula and substantial school construction. University students tend to concentrate on science, mathematics and computer programming. Consequently, Jordan has a steady supply of young people with the necessary skills in computer programming, as well as those with training in basic technical education.
Literacy rate: 91 per cent adult rate; 99 per cent youth rate (15–24) (Unesco 2005).
Compulsory years: 6 to 14; elementary aged 6–11 and preparatory 12–14.
Enrolment rate: 70 per cent for boys and 72 per cent for girls total primary school enrolment, (including repetition rates) of the relevant age group (World Bank estimates 1994–2000).
Pupils per teacher: 21 in primary schools.

Health

Improved water sources and sanitation facilities are available to 99 per cent and 96 per cent of the population, respectively.

HIV/Aids

HIV prevalence: 0.1 per cent aged 15–49 in 2003 (World Bank)

Life expectancy: 71 years, 2004 (WHO 2006)

Fertility rate/Maternal mortality rate: 3.1 births per woman, 2010 (Unicef); maternal mortality 41 per 100,000 live births (World Bank).

Birth rate/Death rate: 4 deaths and 30 births per 1,000 population.

Child (under 5 years) mortality rate (per 1,000): 19 per 1,000 live births (WHO 2012)

Head of population per physician: 2.03 physicians per 1,000 people, 2004 (WHO 2006)

Welfare

Social security in Jordan has few beneficiaries relative to contributing workers and it only first started paying benefits in 1995.

All workers in non-government establishments that employ more than five persons are obliged to contribute to the state social security fund. Those in smaller establishments may contribute voluntarily.

Lump-sum payments and hospital expenses are made in the case of work-related injury, death and retirement pensions. The Social Security Corporation (SCC) provides two types of insurance — old age disability and work-related injuries insurance. It collects revenues directly from wages and is not reliant on the government budget. It covers both the private sector and any public employees hired after 1995.

Main cities

Amman (capital, estimated population 1.2 million in 2012), Zarqa (486,042), Russeifa (369,165), Irbid (325,996), Al Quwaysimah (248,017), Wadi Essier (175,133), Khraibet Essooq (174,719), Aqaba (108,561).

Languages spoken

English is the second language and is widely spoken; most people in business can both speak and correspond in English. French is spoken to a lesser extent.

Official language/s

Arabic

Media

Press

A press and publications law was passed in late 1992. The law banned a wide range of items including those which harm the King or his family or reveal information about the armed forces. The ban on hurting national unity, insulting Arab or Muslim heads of state or transgressing so-called 'public ethics' caused the most controversy.

The law also forced all Jordanian journalists to become members of the Jordan Press Association and denies them the right to protect their sources. The law came as media activity surged with a dozen newspapers licensed or applying for licences and the legalisation of domestic satellite dishes opening Jordanians to uncensored world television.

The Jordan News Agency (Petra) provides news to local and foreign media. The Ministry of Information, which Petra had been a part of, ceased to exist in early 2002. A new media policy is being drawn-up by the Jordanian Media Higher Council, which was established in December 2001.

Dailies: Jordan has both Arabic and English dailies, all published nationally. The Arabic newspapers are *Sawt al Shaab*, *al Ra'i Daily* (both government-owned), *al Dustour*, *al Aswaq* and *al Arab Alyawm*. The English newspapers are *Arab Daily*, *Assabeel Jordan Times* and *Jordan Times*.

Weeklies: There are several weeklies in Arabic, including *Akhbar al Usbu*, *Amman al Masa*, *Assabeel Weekly* and *al Hawadith*. English language weeklies include *The Star* and there is also a French weekly supplement to *The Jordan Times*.

Broadcasting

Broadcasting is run by state bodies and the press is licensed by the government. Restrictions on the press eased considerably in the early 1990s and many areas have been opened to active discussion. A certain amount of self-censorship remains and some subjects – including information on military and security establishments and criticism of the royal family – are strictly taboo.

Radio: The state radio service broadcasts domestic and external programmes in Arabic and English.

Television: The state television service runs one Arabic channel and one foreign channel which broadcasts programmes in English, French and Hebrew.

Economy

Jordan is not rich in resources: unlike its neighbours it has no oil, water is scarce and agricultural land is limited. Its geographic location at the centre of the Middle Eastern region means that its fortunes are strongly influenced by regional circumstances. Unlike many Arab states, Jordan has strong trade links with its neighbours. Intra-Arab trade and remittances from overseas workers, especially those in the Gulf States, make a significant contribution to the economy. Jordan has long served as a transit route for goods destined for Iraq, from which it formerly received subsidised oil.

In 2008 the government removed subsidies on oil and foodstuffs, which reduced its overall fiscal deficit and allowed for an increase in spending in 2009. GDP growth averaged 6 per cent from 2000–07 and despite the global economic recession growth was still 5.5 per cent in 2009. However, since 2009 growth has been slower in line with the weaker global outlook – in 2012 GDP grew by 2.7 per cent, increasing slightly to 2.8 per cent in 2013 and further to 3.1 per cent in 2014. Inflation peaked at 13.9 per cent in 2008, before plummeting to -0.7 per cent in 2009 as domestic spending weakened, however it picked-up in 2010 to 5 per cent as commodity prices began to increase and remained largely at this rate until 2014 when it dropped to 2.8 per cent.

Substantial remittances from expatriate workers amounted to US$3.64 billion (10.8 per cent of GDP) in 2013, a 4.4 per cent rise on the 2012 figure. Tourism is a major earner of foreign exchange. Number of tourist arrivals reached 5.4 million in 2013, of which around four million arrived by land (mostly from other Arab Gulf States). In 2014 numbers fell slightly by 1.2 per cent, however, the tourist industry still contributed 23.0 per cent of GDP in total. Jordan exports potash and phosphate, which are its only available natural resources, as well as fertilisers, pharmaceuticals, clothing and fruit. It is however, dependent on imports, especially for basic foodstuffs and oil and runs a large trade deficit.

The Islamic Development Bank (IDB) and the World Bank announced in 2010, that they were setting up a regional initiative of up to US$1 billion to help close the infrastructure gap in the Middle East and North African region (Mena) and help boost economic growth. The World Bank considers that the Mena region requires US$75–100 billion per year to sustain the growth of recent years and boost economic competitiveness. Private sector investment is limited and the new initiative should address the shortfall in investment, through Sharia-compliant and conventional investment. The initiative should benefit Egypt, Morocco, Jordan and Tunisia in particular. In 2014 the World Bank lent Jordan US$467 million in commitments in order to for the country to take further steps in enhancing the investment climate and ease of doing business.

Saudi Arabia has also agreed to give grants to Jordan in order to decrease its budget deficit. The grants were paid in two tranches of US$400,000 in June 2011 and US$1 billion in July, with more help provided through the supply of crude oil at a discounted price. The Ministry of Planning and International Cooperation claimed the overall amount of foreign assistance received by Jordan from international donors was US$1.74 billion by the end of 2014.

External trade

Jordan has signed the Agadir Agreement which proposed to set up a free trade zone (FTZ) between Egypt, Jordan, Tunisia and Morocco. In 2005 the Greater Arab Free Trade Area (Gafta) was ratified by 17 members, including Jordan, creating an Arab economic bloc. A customs union was established whereby tariffs within Gafta will be reduced by a percentage each year, until none remain. A new free-trade zone, including visa-free travel for their nationals, was agreed in June 2010, between Turkey, Lebanon, Jordan and Syria. A co-operation council will be established to 'develop a long-term strategic partnership' to encourage free movement of goods and persons.

It is also a signatory of the Euro-Mediterranean Partnership agreement, which provides for the introduction of free trade between the EU and 10 Mediterranean countries, including Jordan.

Exports contributed 43.3 per cent of GDP in 2014.

Imports

Main imports are crude oil, textiles, machinery, vehicles, capital goods and manufactured goods.

Main sources: Saudi Arabia (19.6 per cent of total in 2014), China (10.5 per cent), US (5.8 per cent)

Exports

Main exports are manufactured clothing, phosphates, fertilisers and potash, vegetables, manufactured goods and pharmaceuticals.

Main destinations: US (15.8 per cent of total in 2014), Iraq (15.3 per cent), Saudi Arabia (12.4 per cent)

Agriculture

Farming

Jordan became a net importer of foodstuffs when it no longer had access to its principal growing areas on the West Bank of the River Jordan. More than 91 per cent of the total land area is classified as desert and only 6 per cent is cultivable. The sector is vulnerable to drought. Extreme variations in seasonal rainfall in the highland areas led to severe fluctuations in yields from year to year. Highland farmers are one of the poorest groups of people in the country. Irrigated farming in the Jordan Valley has been a success in production terms, but marketing has suffered from periods of overproduction and fluctuation in exports.

Jordan has two distinct agricultural zones: the irrigated Jordan Valley and the rain-fed highlands. Government policy has been to encourage intensive fruit and vegetable growing in the Jordan Valley, both for local consumption and as a major export earner, and to boost cereal and fodder production in the highlands in an effort to reduce a high food import bill. Farming is a private sector activity, but the state-owned Agricultural Marketing and Processing Company (AMPC) plays a regulatory role in fresh produce imports. The government buys cereal and fodder crops at fixed prices, with prices of other crops set according to supply and demand.

Since 1986, state land in southern Jordan has been leased to private farmers for sophisticated irrigation projects conceived at a time when the Arab world was placing heavy emphasis on food self-sufficiency. The projects rely on ground water reserves and there is increasing concern that the benefits of increased production are outweighed by the depletion of scarce water supplies.

Fishing

Jordan's only seaboard is in the south at Aqaba, on the Red Sea. The number of fishermen and vessels is negligible and the catches are consumed locally for the most part. A number of fish farming projects have been started, but with little success. The level of the Jordan River is frequently very low, contributing to the difficulties of fish farming. The majority of Jordan's fish for consumption is imported.

Forestry

Active afforestation programmes are under way in some areas in an effort to control soil erosion and desertification. There is little commercial exploitation of forests.

Industry and manufacturing

Industry contributed around 29.3 per cent to GDP in 2014. Industries include phosphate fertilisers and minerals, food processing, building materials, petroleum products, pharmaceuticals, plastics and furniture. Apart from several major minerals producers, most industries are small-to-medium scale. Commercial and industrial development has been adversely influenced by its geographical location. The 1991 Gulf War, the Israel-Palestinian conflict and the 2003 Iraq War have all adversely affected Jordan's business. It is understandable that the government believes that industrial expansion depends on developing new overseas markets beyond the region. The minerals sector has successfully developed secure markets in the Indian sub-continent and in Southeast Asia. Most other Jordanian industry relies on highly volatile Arab markets. State industries have become a particular burden.

Tourism

Jordan offers a range of historical sites to visitors, ranging in age from the classical, Byzantine and early Muslim eras. It also has several natural reserves with species adapted to arid conditions. Jordan has four sites on Unesco's World Heritage List, including the pink rock city of Petra, the most popular of its tourist destinations.

Travel and tourism is a major component of the economy and accounted for an average of 22.6 per cent of GDP (2006–10). However in 2011, as tourists were put off from visiting due to the disturbances in the region during the Arab Spring, there was a downturn in tourism numbers and the industry only accounted for 18.8 per cent of GDP. By 2014, the contribution had returned to pre-2011 figures at 23.0 per cent in total. The industry provided an average 20 per cent of total employment (average 314,740 jobs) (2006–10), but in 2011 it recorded lower employment figures of 16.8 per cent of the workforce (282,100 jobs). This figure also restored to pre-2011 figures by 2014 reaching 20.0 per cent of total employment (310,000 jobs).

The government has invested in promoting Jordan, and niche marketing has included eco-tourism specifically geared to animal and bird watching, adventure tours, trekking and marine sports in Jordan's Red Sea coast.

Jordan is a member of the Euromed Heritage Programme, a computerisation project, sponsored by the EU, which focuses on cultural tourists of archaeology, arts and history, promoting sites through the internet. It encourages local communities in promoting their culture and history.

Environment

Water is the single greatest challenge to Jordan's long-term well-being. The available figures on supply and demand present a disturbing picture. Agriculture remains the largest consumer of water resources, accounting for over 70 per cent of total water use. The acute water shortage means that Jordan is heavily reliant on ground water, of which 45 per cent is irreplaceable. In the long-term, water consumption at the present rates cannot be sustained. With an increasing population rate in Jordan, the government has estimated that per capita water supply will fall from the current 200 cubic metres per person to only 91 cubic metres by 2025. A programme of dam building has improved supply but it is clear that a solution to the problem will have to come from better regional arrangements for water sharing. Jordan receives 215 million cubic metres annually from Israel through dams and pipelines. The Israeli-Palestinian conflict has not disrupted these water supplies and the government has done its utmost not to offend Israel over the conflict in order to prevent a repeat of Israel's decision in 1999 to cut water supplies to Jordan . The building of the Wahdeh (formerly known as Maqarin) dam on the Jordanian-Syrian border cannot proceed

without the agreement of Israel, which stands to lose water as a result of the project.
The water and irrigation ministry has invested some US$5billion to boost supply, which will be invested in a number of projects until 2010.

Mining
The Jordanian government earmarked the mining and minerals industry as a priority sector for investment and development.
The Natural Resources Authority (NRA) is the main policy-making body in the mineral sector, which promotes investment and undertakes operations. The agency has benefited from the UN Conference on Trade and Development's (Unctad) technical assistance and is able to attract foreign investment into the sector. The NRA has identified a range of metallic and non-metallic minerals, of which Jordan has substantial reserves. The EU is funding a project to identify the economic potential of non-oil mineral resources, including copper, a granitoid complex and ornamental stone.
The phosphate and potash industries in Jordan are key contributors to the economy. The Eshidiya deposit owned by Jordan Phosphate Mining Corporation (JPMC) has a proved phosphate reserve of 1,200 million tonnes. The Arab Potash Company (APC), which accounts for 4.4 per cent of the world's total potash production, produces 1.8 million tonnes of potash annually in Jordan. Almost 1.4 million tonnes is exported to 28 countries (mostly Asian).
The Jordan Safi Salt Company (Jossco) produces 1.2 million tonnes per year of industrial salt. Jordan is also an important exporter of calcium carbonate to other Middle Eastern states. Mineral production is largely of industrial minerals derived from the overlying sediments and volcanics. The most important mineral resources, which merit development and provide investment opportunities, are silica sand, tripoli, gypsum, ornamental stone (Ajlun limestone) and zeolite.

Hydrocarbons
Jordan, unlike its neighbours Iraq and Saudi Arabia, is not blessed with huge gas or oil reserves and has to import the 96 per cent of its fuel requirements to meet domestic demand. Imports were 127,000 barrels per day (bpd) of oil in 2013.
Proven oil reserves are small at 1 million barrels in 2014 and there is no oil production. The rise in global oil prices encouraged the consideration of production from oil shale, located in west central Jordan and amenable to open cast mining.
Jordan had 6.03 billion cubic meters (cum) of natural gas reserves in 2014; production in 2013 was 225,000 cum of natural gas from the Risheh field, for both domestic consumption as well as to a thermal power station. Jordan received natural gas from Egypt, through the Arab Gas Pipeline (AGP), until July 2014 when it was halted due to repeated attacks on the pipeline.
Jordan does not produce or import coal.

Energy
Total installed generating capacity was 3.14 gigawatts (GW) in 2013. Consumption has grown steadily from 8.5 billion kilowatt hours (kWh) in 2007 to 17.3 billion kWh in 2013. This is despite government policy, which has been to restrain energy consumption while increasing efforts to develop domestic energy sources and lessen dependence on costly oil imports. However, in 2013 99.6 per cent of energy was generated using fossil fuels.
The state-owned National Electric Power Company (Nepco) is split into three independent operating companies, responsible for generation, distribution and sales. The majority of electricity generated is supplied by three power plants, the Hussein Thermal Power Station outside Amman, the Aqaba Thermal Power Station in the south and at Rihab in the west. Around 80 per cent of all electricity generated was fuelled by Egyptian natural gas received via the Arab Gas Pipeline (AGP) until July 2014 when it was brought to a halt due to repeated attacks on the pipeline. The power grids of Jordan, Syria and Egypt are linked.
Other options for producing electricity are being considered, including solid waste, wind and biomass.
In March 2015 Jordan signed a US$10 billion deal with Russia to build the kingdom's first nuclear power plant with two 1,000MW reactors. Construction of the plant, in Amra, is expected to be finished in 2022, with hopes that it will be fuelled with uranium mined in Jordan.

Financial markets
Stock exchange
Amman Stock Exchange (ASE)

Banking and insurance
Central bank
Central Bank of Jordan (CBJ)
Main financial centre
Amman

Time
GMT plus two hours (daylight saving GMT plus three hours)

Geography
Jordan is bounded by Syria to the north, Iraq to the east, Saudi Arabia to the south and Israel, the West Bank and Gaza Strip to the west. The only access to the sea is at Aqaba at the northern tip of the Gulf of Aqaba and about 400km south of the capital Amman.
There are three major geographical regions – the Jordan Rift Valley, the Eastern Uplands and the desert. Settlement is concentrated in northern and central sections of the uplands which run in a narrow strip from the Syrian border in the north to the Shubak/Petra area in the south.
Hemisphere
Northern

Climate
The climate is Mediterranean with dry, warm to hot summers and wet, mild to cool winters. There are noticeable variations due to altitude with temperatures in the Jordan Valley and Aqaba region around 10 degrees Celsius (C) higher on average than the highlands area throughout the year. Daytime temperatures in the highlands range from 25 to 32 degrees C in summer and from 7 to 15 degrees C in winter. Rainfall ranges from 40cm annually in the northern highlands to 10cm in the south and 20cm in the Jordan Valley.

Dress codes
Lightweight clothing is needed during the hottest months and warm clothing in winter when snow is not uncommon. Both men and women should dress discreetly in public.

Entry requirements
Passports
Required by all and must have at least six months validity.
Visa
Required by all, except most citizens of the Middle East. Many nationals may obtain a visa at the port of entry (for stays up to 14 days) and all others must apply in advance. Visit www.mfa.gov.jo and follow path from Ministry to Consular Affairs Department, for a full list of each category.
Business visas should be applied for in advance and require a business letter outlining purpose of visit and an itinerary.
Visas are not issued at the King Hussein Bridge across the Jordan River from Israel.
Currency advice/regulations
There are no restrictions on the import or export of foreign or local currency.
Travellers cheques are accepted in banks.
Prohibited imports
Illegal drugs. Firearms require export permission for country of origin and prior approval for import into Jordan. Permitted weapons must be transported as baggage.

Health (for visitors)
Mandatory precautions
There are no automatic health checks at entry points, but travellers arriving from areas with infectious diseases such as cholera are expected to have had appropriate vaccinations. Travellers coming

from an infected area require a yellow fever vaccination certificate.

Advisable precautions

Vaccination against typhoid, polio and hepatitis is advisable. Tap water is generally of a good standard, but short-stay visitors may prefer bottled water.

Hotels

There is a good selection of hotels in Amman. A number of new hotels are being built in Amman, around the Dead Sea and in Aqaba. The main tourist centres are Aqaba and the ancient city of Petra. A service charge of 10–12 per cent is usually added to the bill plus a government tax of 10 per cent on all services at three-, four- and five-star hotels and restaurants.

Extra tips are discretionary. Porters' and drivers' tips are about 8 per cent.

Credit cards

Major credit cards are accepted at hotels and restaurants.

Public holidays (national)

Fixed dates

1 Jan (New Year's Day), 30 Jan (King Abdullah II's Birthday), 1 May (Labour Day), 25 May (Independence Day), 14 Nov (King Hussein's Birthday), 25 Dec (Christmas Day).

Variable dates

Eid al Adha (four days), Islamic New Year, Birth of the Prophet, Ascent of the Prophet, Eid al Fitr (three days).

Islamic year 1437 (15 Oct 2015–2 Oct 2016):: The Islamic year contains 354 or 355 days, with the result that Muslim feasts advance by 10–12 days against the Gregorian calendar. Dates of feasts vary according to the sighting of the new moon, so cannot be forecast exactly.

Working hours

Friday is the official day of rest.

Banking

0830–1230 (Sat–Thu); some banks open for two hours in the afternoon, generally from 1500–1700.

Business

Summer: 0800–1300, 1500–1900 (Sat–Thu); winter: 0800–1330 (Sat–Thu). During Ramadan, most firms operate only from 0900–1600. Christian businesses may close on Sunday afternoon.

Government

0800–1400 (Sat–Thu).

Shops

0800–2000/2100 or 0930–1330, 1530–1800 daily. Some shops close Fridays and public holidays.

Telecommunications

Mobile/cell phones

GSM 900 and 1800 services cover almost all of the country.

Internet/e-mail

Internet access is available in Amman, Aqaba and other major business districts.

Electricity supply

Domestic 220V, 50 cycles AC. Industrial 220–380V 50 cycles AC.

Lamp sockets are screw-type, and there is a wide range of wall sockets. Bring a universal adapter.

Weights and measures

Metric system. Land is measured in dunums (1,000sq metres).

Social customs/useful tips

Jordanian society operates a mixture of traditional and modern attitudes and habits, and a foreigner needs to be aware which apply in any given situation. Business appointments are usually respected, though most people keep an open door and interruptions must be expected. All meetings are prefaced by an extended exchange of pleasantries allowing both sides the chance to assess each other.

Tea and coffee are offered in all offices, and should be accepted; however, on the third or fourth appointment during a morning it is acceptable to excuse oneself and accept just a glass of water. It is still not customary to refer directly to a man's wife unless you have actually met her; it is safer to enquire after the welfare of 'the family'. It is forbidden to eat, drink or smoke in public in daylight hours during Ramadan.

Handshaking is the customary form of greeting. Jordanians are proud of their Arab culture and are hospitable and courteous. A small gift is quite acceptable in return for hospitality.

Islam plays an important role in society. Be discreet when drinking alcohol and do not drink in public places. Women are expected to dress modestly, and for both women and men beachwear must only be worn on the beach or by the poolside.

Security

Visitors should keep in touch with developments in the Middle East as any increase in regional tension might affect travel advice.

Street crime is rare in Jordan, with mugging virtually unheard of. However, housebreaking and car theft is on the increase and reasonable precautions must be observed. There are occasional small-scale bomb attacks against cinemas and nightclubs in Amman. Women do not usually walk alone in Amman after about 2200, but driving alone is safe. A woman alone wanting a taxi late at night is advised to telephone a taxi office with which she is familiar.

Getting there

Air

National airline: Royal Jordanian Airlines

International airport/s: Amman-Queen Alia International (AMM), 32km east of Amman (35 minutes from city centre).

Airport tax: Departure tax: JD4

Surface

Road: King Hussein Bridge is the only way to cross the Jordan river from Israel, and only the official minibus services are allowed to cross it. There are also buses and taxis from Syria, where the only border crossing point is at Ramtha/Der'a. There are a number of routes into Jordan from Jeddah and Riyadh in Saudi Arabia.

Rail: There is an elderly and decrepit rail link between Damascus (Syria) and Mecca (Saudi Arabia), via Amman but the journey time can be two–three times the length of time taken to drive the same route.

Water: There are ferry services, including car ferries, between Aqaba and Nuweiba in Egypt.

Main port/s: Aqaba is the country's only port.

Getting about

National transport

Air: The only internal air route is between Amman and Aqaba. Royal Jordanian Airlines operate regular flights. Arab Wings offer a charter service.

Road: The road network is good, with well-surfaced main roads connecting all the major towns and cities.

Buses: The Jordanian Express Tourist Transport Company (Jett) runs extensive services.

Rail: The rail network is no longer viable for the traveller.

Water: There are no passenger services along the Jordan river.

City transport

Taxis: Metered taxis are readily available in Amman and other cities (do not let your driver forget to switch on his meter). Can be hired for the journey or the day for an agreed sum. Do not use a taxi without a meter before agreeing the fare with the driver. There are also many service taxis offering a standard charge for any journey. Since there are few street names outside Amman, destinations are generally described in relation to landmarks.

Tipping is approximately 10 per cent.

Car hire

National or international driving licence required. Driver must be at least 25 years old and not over 60. Speed limit is 100kph. Insurance is compulsory.

BUSINESS DIRECTORY

The addresses listed below are a selection only. While World of Information makes every endeavour to check these

addresses, we cannot guarantee that changes have not been made, especially to telephone numbers and area codes. We would welcome any corrections.

Telephone area codes

The international direct dialling (IDD) code for Jordan is +962 followed by the area code:

Amman	6	Madaba	8
Aqaba	3	Mafraq	4
Balga (Salt)	5	Petra	3
Irbid	2	Ramtha	2
Karak	3	Zarqa	5

Mobile pones – Fastnet 79

Mobile phones – Mobilecom 77

Useful telephone numbers

Ambulance: 193

Fire: 193

Police: 192

Chambers of Commerce

American Chamber of Commerce in Jordan, 23 Salem Al-Hindawi Street, Shmeisani, PO Box 840817, Amman 11184 (tel: 565-1860; fax: 565-1862; e-mail: mail@jaba.org.jo).

Amman Chamber of Commerce, Al-Sharif Shaker Bin Zaid Street, PO Box 287, Amman 11118 (tel: 566-6151; fax: 566-6155; e-mail: info@ammanchamber.org.jo).

Amman Chamber of Industry, 2nd Circle Amman, PO Box 1800, Amman 11118 (tel: 464-3001; fax: 464-7852; e-mail: aci@aci.org.jo).

Aqaba Chamber of Commerce, PO Box 12, Aqaba 77110 (tel: 201-2235; fax 201-3070; e-mail: ask@index.com.jo).

Federation of Jordanian Chambers of Commerce, Al-Sharif Shaker Bin Zaid Street, PO Box 7029, Amman 11118 (tel: 566-5492; fax: 568-5997; e-mail: fjcc@nets.com.jo).

Irbid Chamber of Commerce, PO Box 13, Irbid (tel: 724-2077; fax: 724-2072; e-mail:icc@go.com.jo).

Jerash Chamber of Commerce, PO Box 195, Jerash (tel/fax: 635-1278).

Madaba Chamber of Commerce, PO Box 120, Madaba (tel: 544-120; fax: 545-878).

Mafraq Chamber of Commerce, PO Box 21, Mafraq (tel: 623-4197; fax: 623-1135).

Zarqa Chamber of Commerce, PO Box 77, Zarqa (tel: 385-3307; fax: 385-4617).

Banking

Arab Bank Plc, PO Box 950545, 11195 Amman (tel: 560-7231; fax: 560-6793; e-mail: international@arabbank.com.jo).

Arab Banking Corporation (Jordan), PO Box 926691, 11190 Amman (tel: 5 66-4183; fax: 568-6291; e-mail: info@arabbanking.com.jo).

Arab Jordan Investment Bank, PO Box 8797, 11121 Amman (tel: 560-7126; fax: 568-1482; e-mail: info@ajib.com).

Bank of Jordan, PO Box 2140, 11181 Amman (tel: 569-6277; fax: 569-6291; boj@go.com.jo).

Cairo Amman Bank, PO Box 950661, 11195 Amman (tel: 461-6910; fax: 464-2890; e-mail: cainfo@ca_bank.com.jo).

Export and Finance Bank, PO Box 941283, 11194 Amman (tel: 569-4250; fax: 569-2062; e-mail: info@efbank.com.jo).

Housing Bank for Trade and Finance, PO Box 7693, 11118 Amman (tel: 560-7315; fax: 567-8121; e-mail: quality@hbtf.com.jo).

Jordan Gulf Bank, PO Box 9989, 11191 Amman (tel: 5 60-3931; fax: 566-4110; e-mail: jgb@jkbank.com.jo).

Jordan Investment and Finance Bank, PO Box 950601, 11195 Amman (tel: 566-5145; fax: 568-1410; e-mail: jifbank@jifbank.com.jo).

Jordan Kuwait Bank, PO Box 9776, 11191Amman (tel: 568-8814; fax: 569-5604; e-mail: webmaster@jkbank.com.jo).

Jordan National Bank, PO Box 3103, 11181 Amman (tel: 562-2282; fax: 562-2281; ingo@inb.com.jo).

Union Bank for Saving and Investment, PO Box 35104, 11180 Amman (tel: 560-7011; fax: 566-6149; e-mail: info@unionbankjo.com).

Central bank

Central Bank of Jordan , PO Box 37, 11118 Amman (tel: 463-0301–10; fax: 463-8889; e-mail: banksuper@cbj.gov.jo).

Stock exchange

Amman Stock Exchange (ASE), www.ase.com.jo

Travel information

Royal Jordanian Airlines, PO Box 302, Amman (tel: 672-872).

Ministry of tourism

Ministry of Tourism & Antiquities, PO Box 224, Amman (tel: 464-2311/4; fax: 464-8465; e-mail: tourism@mota.gov.jo).

National tourist organisation offices

Jordan Tourism Board, PO Box 830688, Amman 11183 (tel: 567-8294; fax: 567-8295; e-mail: jtb@nets.com.jo; internet: www.see-jordan.com).

Ministries

Ministry of Agriculture, University of Jordan Street, PO Box 2099, Amman (tel: 568-6431, 568-6151; fax: 568-6310).

Ministry of Awqaf and Islamic Affairs, POB 659, Amman (tel: 566-141; fax: 560-2254).

Ministry of Communications and Postal Affairs, PO Box 35214 (tel: 560-7111; fax: 560-6233).

Ministry of Culture, PO Box 6140, Amman (tel: 463-6392/3569-6588; fax: 569-6598).

Ministry of Defence, PO Box 80, Amman (tel: 464-1211, 462-2131; fax: 464-2520).

Ministry of Development Affairs, PO Box 1577, Amman (tel: 464-361; fax: 464-8825).

Ministry of Education, PO Box 1646, Amman (tel: 847-671; fax: 566-6019).

Ministry of Energy and Mineral Resources, PO Box 2310 (tel: 586-3326/9; fax: 586-5714, 581-5615).

Ministry of Finance, PO Box 85, Amman (tel: 463-6321, 463-6502, 463-7781/2; fax: 464-3132, 464-3121).

Ministry of Foreign Affairs, 3rd Circle, PO Box 35217, Amman (tel: 464-4361, 464-4311; fax: 464-8825; internet www.mfa.gov.jo/).

Ministry of Health, PO Box 86, Amman (tel: 566-5131; fax: 568-8373).

Ministry of Industry and Trade, PO Box 2019, Amman (tel: 560-7191; fax: 560-3721).

Ministry of Information, PO Box 1794, Amman (tel: 464-1467; fax: 464-8895).

Ministry of the Interior, PO Box 100, Amman (tel: 463-8849, 566-3111, 569-1141; fax: 560-6908).

Ministry of Justice, PO Box 6040, Amman (tel: 566-3101; fax: 568-0238).

Ministry of Labour, PO Box 9052, Amman (tel: 560-7481; fax: 566-7193).

Ministry of Municipal, Rural and Environmental Affairs, 3rd Circle, PO Box 1799, Amman (tel: 464-1393/7; fax: 467-2135).

Ministry of Parliamentary Affairs, Jabal, Amman (tel: 464-1211; fax: 464-2520).

Ministry of Planning, PO Box 555, Amman (tel: 464-4466/7; fax: 464-9341).

Ministry of Public Works and Housing, PO Box 1220, Amman (tel: 585-0470, 585-0479; fax: 585-7590).

Ministry of Social Development, PO Box 6720, Amman (tel: 593-1391; fax: 567-3198).

Ministry of Supply, PO Box 830, Amman (tel: 560-2121, 560-2135; fax: 560-4691).

Ministry of Tourism & Antiquities, PO Box 224, Amman (tel: 464-2311/4; fax: 464-8465; e-mail: tourism@mota.gov.jo).

Ministry of Trade and Industry, PO Box 2019, Amman (tel: 663-191; fax: 603-721).

Ministry of Transport, PO Box 35214, Amman (tel: 551-8111; fax: 552-7233).

Ministry of Water and Irrigation, PO Box 2412, Amman (tel: 568-0100, 568-0117; fax: 567-9143).

Ministry of Youth, PO Box 1794 (tel: 604-701; fax: 604-717).

Prime Minister's Office, PO Box 80, Amman (tel: 641-211; fax: 642-520).

Other useful addresses

Amman Financial Market (AFM), PO Box 8802, Amman (tel: 660-170; fax: 686-830).

Amman World Trade Centre, PO Box 962140, Amman (tel: 560-5791/2; fax: 560-5793).

Arab Potash Company (APC), PO Box 1470, Amman (tel: 566-6165; fax: 567-4416).

British Embassy, PO Box 87, Abdoun, Amman (tel: 592-3100; fax: 592-3759; e-mail: british@nets.com.jo).

British Embassy, Commercial Section, PO Box 6062, Amman (tel: 592-3100; fax: 592-3759; e-mail: becommercial@nets.com.jo).

Chief of the Royal Court, PO Box 80, Amman (tel: 464-1211, 462-7421; fax: 464-2520).

Civil Aviation Authority, PO Box 7547, Amman (tel: 92-282; fax: 891-653).

Customs Department, PO Box 90, Amman (tel: 463-8358; fax: 464-7791; internet site: www.customs.gov.jo).

Indo-Jordan Chemicals Company, PO Box 926787, Amman (tel: 568-5732; fax: 568-5730).

Institution for Standards and Metrology, PO Box 941287, Amman 11194 (tel: 568-0139; fax: 568-1099).

Investment Promotion Council, PO Box 893, Amman 11821 (tel: 553-1081/2/3; fax: 552-1084; e-mail: ipc@amra.nic.gov.jo).

Jordan Dead Sea Industries Company (JODICO), PO Box 941260, Amman (tel: 569-941; fax: 569-5939).

Jordan Europe Business Association, PO Box 910751, Amman (tel: 568-5433; fax: 566-6550).

Jordan Export Development and Commercial Centres Corporation (JEDCO), PO Box 7704, Amman (tel: 560-3507; fax: 568-4568; internet site: www.jedco.gov.jo).

Jordan Fertilisers Industrial Company, PO Box 409, Aqaba (tel: 201-4156; fax: 201-7008).

Jordan Magnesia Company (JORMAG), PO Box 941260, Amman (tel: 569-5941; fax: 569-5939).

Jordan Phosphate Mines Company (JPMC), PO Box 30, Amman (tel: 560-7141; fax: 568-2290).

Jordanian Business Association, PO Box 926182, Amman (tel: 568-0855; fax: 566-0663).

Jordanian Embassy (USA), 3504 International Drive, NW, Washington DC 20008 (tel: (+1-202) 966-2664; fax: (+1-202) 966-3110; e-mail: hkjembassydc@aol,com).

National Electric Power Company (NEPCO), PO Box 2310, Amman 1181 (tel: 558-615; fax: 518-336).

Nippon Jordan Fertilisers Company Ltd., Po Box 926861, Amman (tel: 569-1708; fax: 568-4127).

US Embassy, PO Box 354, Jabal, Amman 11118 (tel: 592-0101; fax: 592-0163).

Internet sites

Arabia On-line: www.arabia.com

ArabNet: www.arab.net/

Global Chamber of Commerce: www.gcc.net

Jordan information site: www.kinghussein.gov.jo

Kazakhstan

KEY FACTS

Official name: Kazakstan Respublikasy (Republic of Kazakhstan)

Head of State: President Nursultan Äbishuly Nazarbayev (Nur Otan) (from 1990; re-elected Apr 2015)

Head of government: Prime Minister Karim Massimov (appointed 2 April 2014)

Ruling party: Nur Otan (National Democratic Party) (NDC) (since 1999; re-elected 15 Jan 2012)

Area: 2,717,300 square km

Population: 17.42 million (2014)*

Capital: Astana (seat of government) (renamed 1998; formerly called Akmola; inaugurated as the new capital 1997); Almaty (formerly Alma Ata, commercial capital)

Official language: Kazakh

Currency: Tenge (T) = 100 tein (introduced Nov 1993)

Exchange rate: T245.05 per US$ (Sep 2015)

GDP per capita: US$12,184 (2014)*

GDP real growth: 4.30% (2014)*

GDP: US$212.26 billion (2014)*

Labour force: 8.12 million (2010)

Unemployment: 5.22% (2014)*

Inflation: 6.72% (2014)*

Oil production: 1.70 million bpd (2014)

Natural gas production: 19.30 billion cum (2014)

Balance of trade: US$33.69 billion (2013)

* estimated figure

Politics in Kazakhstan is a dangerous business. Mixing politics with business or banking seemed to be doubly dangerous. Becoming an opposition politician almost tantamount to suicide. Marrying into this cocktail could also well prove fatal if the case of Rakhat Aliev was anything to go by. In February 2015 Mr Aliev, a former son-in-law of President Nursultan Nazarbaev, who had served as ambassador in Vienna and was once the deputy head of his country's secret service organisation (National Security Committee or KNB), was found dead in his prison cell in Vienna.

Risky business

Mr Aliev, who had made the mistake of becoming an opponent of the long-ruling Kazakh president, was at first declared by Austrian officials to have committed suicide. However, his lawyers cast doubt on the assumption and demanded a fuller investigation.

Aliev had fled to Austria, where he had once served as ambassador, amid an investigation into the abduction and killing of the two Kazakh bankers (Kazakh Nurbank) in 2007. Six years before handing himself in to the police in June 2014; in 2008 a Kazakh court had sentenced him in absentia to 40 years in prison after convicting him of plotting to overthrow the government and organising a criminal abduction group. The Austrian authorities had repeatedly refused to extradite Mr Aliev, citing concerns that he might not face a fair trial in Kazakhstan. They had opened their own investigation in 2011 and charged him with the murders in December 2014. Mr Aliev had dismissed the charges against him as politically motivated. He had been married to Nazarbaev's eldest daughter, Darigha.

Ring, ring

In 2015, if car ownership in Almaty and the surrounding region was anything to judge by, the Kazakh economy was booming. The ownership figure had risen from 617,000 in 2007 to 936,000 in 2011. The irritating side affect was that Almaty descended into gridlock in the morning and evening rush hours. The preferred solution was to build a ring-road round the city, popularly known as the *Bakad*, which had been on the drawing board for some years. The US$680 million project represented something more than the answer to Almaty's traffic problems, it was to be Kazakhstan's first internationally-tendered public-private partnership (PPP). The government hoped that the PPP solution might become a wider source of funding for Kazakhstan's infrastructure projects. (Particular reference was made to a light rail system in Almaty and an operating and maintenance contract for the western China-to-Russia highway.) The European Bank for

Reconstruction and Development (EBRD) enthusiastically described the road scheme's finance as 'absolutely ground-breaking.' In an advertising supplement published in the *International New York Times* in May 2015 the EBRD's Director for Kazakhstan, Janet Heckman heaped praise on 'the commitment of Kazakhstan's leadership to real structural reform.' Ms Heckman continued her statement by adding that 'The reforms that Kazakhstan has embarked on in the past 18 months are bringing real and significant change. This is evident in the new foreign investment legislation, progress on the reduction of non-performing loans (NPL) and agreements signed with the European Union (EU) and the Organisation for Economic Co-operation and Development (OECD).'

The economy

According to the Asian Development Bank (ADB) Kazakhstan's growth moderated in 2014 to 4.3 per cent from the 6.0 per cent seen in 2013, mainly because slow global growth cut demand for Kazakhstan's main export commodities: oil, coal, metals, chemicals and grain. Economic conditions worsened with the sharp decline in oil prices and the knock-on effects from the sanctions imposed by the EU and the US on the Russian Federation, Kazakhstan's major trading partner. On the supply side, industry grew by only 0.3 per cent, versus 3.0 per cent in 2013, as mining and manufacturing performed poorly. Construction, driven by government programmes, expanded by 4.1 per cent, up from 3.5 per cent a year earlier. The expansion in agriculture slowed sharply to 0.8 per cent from 11.2 per cent in 2013 as poor weather limited grain production. Services grew by 6.0 per cent, versus 6.8 per cent in 2013, reflecting slowdowns in transport, trade and communication.

On the demand side, 9 months of data showed that lower real income and constricted access to credit cut consumption growth to 2.5 per cent from 12.8 per cent in the same period of 2013. Private consumption grew only marginally by 0.4 per cent, but higher government spending, including a pay increase after currency devaluation, boosted public consumption by 11.2 per cent. Investment growth slowed to 3.9 per cent from 6.2 per cent in 2013 as public investment expanded by 24.9 per cent but private investment declined by 0.3 per cent. Meanwhile, a 15.6 per cent drop in imports against a fall in exports half as steep – at 8.6 per cent, reflecting weaker external demand for oil, coal and metals – meant net exports improved by 7.5 per cent, reversing the 12.7 per cent drop in 2013.

Although price administration limited the impact of the devaluation of the Kazakh tenge in February 2014, inflation accelerated to 6.7 per cent from 5.8 per cent in 2013, reflecting price rises for food and other goods. Inflation in services slowed because of restrictions on utility tariffs. The 12-month inflation rate, December to December, was 7.4 per cent, up from 4.8 per cent in 2013. The fiscal deficit in the budget expanded to 2.8 per cent of GDP from 2.0 per cent in 2013. Revenue reached 15.5 per cent of GDP, up from 14.7 per cent in 2013, reflecting larger transfers from the National Fund of the Republic of Kazakhstan (NFRK), equivalent to 4.8 per cent of GDP and a 13.3 per cent rise in corporate income tax revenue expenditure to 18.4 per cent of GDP from 16.7 per cent a year earlier. However, the post devaluation pay rise and higher pensions and social transfers boosted expenditure to 18.4 per cent of GDP from 16.7 per cent a year earlier. In October, Kazakhstan sold US$2.5 billion in eurobonds, pushing public and publicly guaranteed debt to an estimated 15.0 per cent of GDP from 13.0 per cent in 2013. State enterprise debt declined to equal 13.4 per cent of GDP at the end of September from 14.3 per cent at the end of 2013. Kazakh monetary policy aimed to combat inflation and rehabilitate the country's banking system while preventing a post-devaluation downturn; the policy interest rate was maintained. Broad money grew by 10.5 per cent, versus 10.2 per cent in 2013, despite credit growth slowing to 7.2 per cent from 13.4 per cent in 2013. Lending to large firms declined by 6.1 per cent, while loans to small and medium-sized enterprises rose by 38.7 per cent and to households by 12.5 per cent. Deposits expanded by 15.9 per cent but a shift into foreign currency accounts limited the supply of long-term loans denominated in tenge. Interest rates on tenge deposits rose in most banks. To boost tenge liquidity, the National Bank of Kazakhstan (NBK) (the central bank), opened in July a US$10 billion window for tenge/US dollar swaps with commercial banks at an implied interest rate of 3 per cent. Following the devaluation in February, the tenge/US dollar exchange rate remained stable within a band of T182–188 per US dollar. In September, the central bank widened the band to T170–188. The rapid depreciation of the rouble against the major currencies in the second half of 2014 caused it to depreciate sharply against the tenge as well. The resulting downward pressure on the tenge against the US dollar induced many firms and households to convert tenge deposits into foreign currency, raising foreign currency deposits by more than 70 per cent to account for 55.6 per cent of all deposits.

KEY INDICATORS — Kazakhstan

	Unit	2011	2012	2013	2014	**2015
Population	m	16.67	16.91	17.16	*17.42	*17.68
Gross domestic product (GDP)	US$bn	178.30	203.52	231.88	*212.26	*203.14
GDP per capita	US$	10,694	12,034	13,509	*12,184	*11,488
GDP real growth	%	7.5	5.0	6.0	*4.3	*2.0
Inflation	%	8.3	5.1	5.8	*6.7	*5.2
Unemployment	%	5.5	5.3	5.2	*5.2	*5.2
Oil output	'000 bpd	1,841.0	1,728.0	1,785.0	1,701.0	–
Natural gas output	bn cum	19.3	19.7	18.5	19.3	–
Coal output	mtoe	58.0	58.8	58.4	55.3	–
Exports (fob) (goods)	US$m	22,116.7	92,065.9	83,406.9	–	–
Imports (fob) (goods)	US$m	10,290.8	47,359.3	49,715.4	–	–
Balance of trade	US$m	11,825.9	44,706.6	33,691.5	–	–
Current account	US$m	13,600.0	641.0	1,122.0	*3,392.0	*-8,269.0
Total reserves minus gold	US$m	33,490.5	22,131.5	19,126.6	21,524.5	–
Foreign exchange	US$m	32,939.5	21,600.3	18,590.2	–	–
Exchange rate	per US$	145.99	150.44	154.35	182.51	–

* estimated figure ** forecast figure

To prevent speculation and excessive reserve losses, the central bank halted swap operations with banks.

Lending slowed in the second half of the year and some banks stopped lending in tenge. Despite banks' efforts to cut NPLs, devaluation helped push the NPL ratio to 33.7 per cent in April from 26.3 per cent in November 2013. In response, the central bank asked commercial banks with significant NPLs to develop and implement action plans under its supervision. The discontinuation of tax disincentives for writing off bad loans helped rein in NPLs to 23.6 per cent by the end of 2014. In addition, T250 billion (US$1.02 billion) was allocated from the National Fund of the Republic of Kazakhstan (NFRK) to capitalise the central bank's fund for purchasing NPLs from banks.

The current account surplus was estimated to have widened to 1.8 per cent of GDP from 0.5 per cent in 2013. Devaluation initially boosted exports, but declining commodity prices offset the gains and caused export revenue to fall by 8.6 per cent, versus a 1.5 per cent decline in 2013. Imports also fell, by 18.9 per cent, following a 4.1 per cent increase in 2013, as imports of food, chemicals, metal products and machinery all declined.

Gross reserves rose to US$28.9 billion from US$24.7 billion at the end of 2013 and NFRK assets reached US$73.6 billion, though heavier use of NFRK funds for budgetary support and infrastructure spending cut growth in NFRK assets to 3.9 per cent from 22.1 per cent in 2013. External debt including inter-company loans reached an estimated 74.3 per cent of GDP from 64.8 per cent in 2013, while public and publicly guaranteed external debt rose to 3.9 per cent of GDP from 2.7 per cent a year earlier.

Economic prospects

The ADB noted that despite the launch of the Eurasian Economic Union with Armenia, Belarus and the Russian Federation, growth looked likely to slow to 1.9 per cent in 2015. This reflected the slumping oil prices, economic weakness in the Russian Federation and tenge appreciation against the rouble, which had hurt the competitiveness of Kazakh exports and boosted imports from the Russian Federation. Growth was projected to recover to 3.8 per cent in 2016 as the economy adjusts to low oil prices and as stimulus measures take hold. On the supply side, mining was forecast to contract by 10.0 per cent in 2015 and remain unchanged in 2016, dragging down industry by 5.3 per cent in the first year and allowing marginal growth of 0.4 per cent in the second. The slowdown will limit growth in services to 5.0 per cent in both years.

Investments in housing and infrastructure under a state programme for regional development were projected by the ADB to boost construction by 4.0 per cent annually and earlier investment under the Agriculture 2020 development programme was projected to expand agriculture by 2.7 per cent in 2015 and 4.0 per cent in 2016. On the demand side, government interventions were expected by the ADB to propel consumption growth by 4.2 per cent in 2015 and 5.0 per cent in 2016. Counter-cyclical policy will likely see investment supported by NFRK resources rise by 4.0 per cent in 2015 and 4.8 per cent in 2016, as Expo 2017 nears. Net exports were forecast to fall by 15.5 per cent in 2015 on low oil prices and a weak grain crop, which would shrink agricultural exports and export revenue and by 8.0 per cent in 2016, as imports rose by 5 per cent and exports remained unchanged.

Hydrocarbons

In August 2014, Kazakhstan's long serving president, Nursultan Nazarbayev, announced an extensive government reorganisation with the intention of creating a more compact and effective government. The number of ministries in the government was reduced from 17 to 12 and a ministry of energy was created, subsuming the various ministries and government agencies that had previously been responsible for the country's energy resources and their exploration, exploitation and development.

In its report on the Kazakhstan hydrocarbons sector, the US government's Energy Information Authority (EIA) noted that Kazakhstan is a major oil producer. Estimated total petroleum and other liquids production was 1.70 million barrels per day (bpd) in 2014. The key to its continued growth in liquids production from this level would be the development of its giant Tengiz, Karachaganak and Kashagan fields. The development of additional export capacity would also be necessary for production growth.

Although Kazakhstan became an oil producer in 1911, according to the EIA, production did not increase to a meaningful level until the 1960s and 1970s, when it stuck at nearly 500,000bpd, a pre-Soviet independence record production level. Since the mid-1990s and with the help of major international oil companies, Kazakhstan's production first exceeded 1 million bpd in 2003. Rising natural gas production over the past decade has also boosted oil recovery (as a significant volume of natural gas is reinjected into oil reservoirs) and decreased Kazakhstan's reliance on natural gas imports.

The Kashagan field, the largest known oil field outside the Middle East and the fifth largest in the world in terms of reserves, is located off the northern shore of the Caspian Sea near the city of Atyrau, Kazakhstan. Kashagan's recoverable reserves had been estimated at 7 to 13 billion barrels of crude oil. On 11 September 2013, production from the super-giant field commenced, eight years after the original scheduled start-up date. In October 2013, just a few weeks after production began, production had to be halted because of leaks in the pipeline that transported natural gas from the field to shore. Production was not expected to resume until the second half of 2016.

The EIA noted that Kazakhstan is landlocked and is distant from international oil markets. The lack of access to the open ocean makes it largely dependent on pipelines to transport its hydrocarbons to world markets. Kazakhstan is also a transit country for natural gas pipeline exports from Turkmenistan and Uzbekistan. According to the *Oil & Gas Journal* (OGJ), Kazakhstan had proved crude oil reserves of 30 billion barrels in January 2014 – the second largest endowment in Eurasia after Russia and the twelfth largest in the world, just behind the United States. Kazakhstan's current oil production is dominated by two giant onshore fields in the north-west of the country: Tengiz and Karachaganak, which produce about half of Kazakhstan's total petroleum liquids output. The offshore Kashagan field, in Kazakhstan's part of the Caspian Sea, was also expected to play a major role in Kazakhstan's future liquids production. .

In 2013, Kazakhstan exported nearly 1.4 million bpd of crude oil and condensate, according to the Global Trade Information Service. More than three-quarters of Kazakhstan's crude exports travel around or across the Caspian Sea headed to European markets. An additional 16 per cent of Kazakhstan's crude exports head east via a pipeline to China. Kazakhstan's exports looked likely to increase, as production began at Kashagan and expanded at Tengiz and Karachaganak. However, the rapid growth of oil production and exports would require an expansion of export capacity.

Natural gas

The OGJ estimated Kazakhstan's proven natural gas reserves at 85 trillion cubic feet (tcf) in January 2014. The majority of Kazakhstan's gas reserves are in crude or condensate-rich fields. The two largest petroleum liquids fields, Karachaganak and Tengiz, are also the two largest natural gas fields. Over the previous decade, annual gross natural gas production almost tripled, from 0.6tcf in 2003 to 1.6tcf in 2012. Reinjected natural gas had accounted for most of the increase in gross production, while dry natural gas production had remained relatively stable. In 2012, reinjected natural gas production was more than double dry natural gas production.

In 2013, the Karachaganak and Tengiz fields combined accounted for more than 90 per cent of Kazakhstan's raw marketed natural gas production. The Tengiz project included a gas processing plant, which according to Chevron produced 251 billion cubic feet (bcf) of dry marketed natural gas in 2013 that was sold to local consumers. The Karachaganak project has insufficient gas processing capacity. Most of the raw marketed production from the Karachaganak field had to be exported to Russia to be processed at a gas processing plant in Orenberg. In 2013, about 30 per cent of this processed gas was sold in Russia, with the remainder of the dry gas returned to Kazakhstan to help meet local demand. The next phase of development at Karachaganak originally included plans for facilities to process its own gas and boost dry natural gas supplies to consumers within Kazakhstan. However, the project developers have since changed their plans and gas produced under Karachaganak's next expansion will largely be reinjected into the field to boost liquids recovery. When it comes online, the first phase of the Kashagan project is expected to marginally boost supplies of dry gas to consumers in Kazakhstan. However, like the Karachaganak and Tengiz projects, much of the gas produced from Kashagan would either be reinjected into the well to boost liquids recovery, or used at the project site to produce electricity.

Risk assessment

Economy	Fair
Politics	Poor/dangerous
Regional stability	Good/fair

Muslims in Kazakhstan

% of population	47
Sunni (% of Muslims)	97
Shi'a (% of Muslims)	2

COUNTRY PROFILE

1854 The Russian garrison town of Verny, now Almaty, was established. Russian and Ukrainian peasants were brought in to settle the Kazakh lands and the first industrial enterprises were set up.

1916 A major anti-Russian rebellion was suppressed, with about 150,000 people killed and more than 300,000 fleeing abroad.

1917 After the October Revolution in Russia, the Russian ruler, Lenin, gave the peoples of Central Asia the right of self-determination.

1920s–30s Kazakhstan was granted autonomous status as part of the USSR in 1920. Soviet nationalities policy under the direction of Joseph Stalin saw Soviet rule enforced from Moscow by Red Army troops who put down Muslim revolts throughout Central Asia after the Russian civil war. Industrialisation and collectivisation of agriculture began. One million mainly nomadic Kazakhs died of starvation in the central government's campaign to enforce permanent settlements and build collective farms.

1930s–40s Kazakhstan was granted full Soviet Socialist Republic status in 1936. The country was transformed into a major producer of non-ferrous metals, coal and oil, as well as a region of developed agriculture.

1940s–50s Koreans, Crimean Tatars, Germans and others were forcibly moved to Kazakhstan. The first nuclear test explosion was carried out in 1949 at Semipalatinsk in eastern Kazakhstan.

1950s–60s Russian President Nikita Khruschev's 'Virgin Lands' scheme began. It brought agriculture to much of the Kazakh steppe and made the Kazakhs a minority in their own republic, as Russian and Ukrainian settlers were sent to run the collective farms. In 1961, the first manned spacecraft took off from Baykonur cosmodrome in central Kazakhstan.

1986 Riots in Almaty over the replacement of Dinmukhamed Kunayev (an ethnic Kazakh) with Gennady Kolbin (an ethnic Russian) as head of the Kommunisticheskaya Partiya Kazakhstana (KPK) (Communist Party of Kazakhstan) were the first signs of ethnic and nationalist unrest in Central Asia.

1989 Nursultan Nazarbayev, an ethnic Kazakh, was appointed leader of the KPK. Kazakh was declared an official language and Russian a language of inter-ethnic communication.

1990 Kazakhstan's Supreme Soviet appointed Nazarbayev as the country's first president and declared state sovereignty.

1991 Nazarbayev won uncontested presidential elections. President Nazarbayev had supported Gorbachev's efforts to keep the Soviet Union intact and Kazakhstan was the last Soviet Republic to declare full independence. Kazakhstan joined the Commonwealth of Independent States (CIS), an association which grew out of the remnants of the Soviet Union. The President signed a decree closing the Semipalatinsk nuclear testing ground.

1992 Kazakhstan became a member of the UN.

1993 A programme of national privatisation began.

1994 The first multi-party parliamentary elections were held for a full-time professional legislature, the Kenges (parliament). Results returned a predominantly pro-Nazarbayev assembly. Kazakhstan signed an economic, military and social co-operation treaty with Uzbekistan and Kyrgyzstan.

1995 President Nazarbayev dissolved parliament following a ruling by the Constitutional Court that the 1994 parliamentary elections were invalid. The president's term of office was extended to 2000 and a referendum endorsed the introduction of a new constitution.

1996 Uzbekistan, Kazakhstan and Kyrgyzstan agreed to create a single economic market.

1997 Oil agreements were signed with China. Kazakhstan's capital was moved from Almaty to Akmola, formerly known as Tselinograd.

1998 The new capital was renamed Astana. The constitution was amended to extend the presidential term from five to seven years and to remove the upper age limit for a president.

1999 In early presidential elections Nazarbayev was re-elected after his main rival was barred from standing. International observers claimed there were serious irregularities in the parliamentary elections. An attempt by ethnic Russians in north-east Kazakhstan to form a separate state failed.

2000 A law was passed granting Nazarbayev life-long powers and privileges. Belarus, Kazakhstan, Kyrgyzstan, Russia and Tajikistan (formerly the Customs Five) established the Eurasian Economic Community (EEC). Internal security and border controls were increased following incursions by Islamic militants from Kyrgyzstan and Uzbekistan.

2001 The country's first major pipeline running from the large Tengiz oil field to the Black Sea was opened. Nazarbayev purged the government of officials accused of joining the newly formed Qazaqstannyn Demokratiyalyk Tandau (QDT) (Democratic Choice (of Kazakhstan)) reform movement. Pope John Paul II paid his first visit to Kazakhstan. Tajikistan, China, Russia, Kazakhstan, Kyrgyzstan and Uzbekistan formed the Shanghai Co-operation Organisation (SCO) and agreed to fight ethnic and religious militancy, while promoting investment and trade.

2003 A bill allowing private ownership of land was passed. Russia, Ukraine, Kazakhstan and Belarus signed an economic union treaty.
2004 A deal was signed with China on the construction of an oil pipeline to the Chinese border. Nazarbayev's Otan (Fatherland) party was re-elected in the Majlis elections; international observers considered them flawed.
2005 Nursultan Nazarbayev was re-elected president. Democratic Choice was ordered by the supreme court to be dissolved because it had encouraged protests against the parliamentary election results.
2006 Galymzhan Zhakiyanov, one of the founders of Democratic Choice, was released from prison. Asar (All Together), the small political party of President Nazarbayev's daughter, merged with the president's ruling party, Otan; two other small parties merged with Otan, which was re-named Nur-Otan (Fatherland's Ray of Light).
2007 Karim Masimov replaced Daniyal Akhmetov as prime minister. The constitution was amended so that a president may serve an unlimited number of terms. The ruling Nur-Otan won early parliamentary elections and ratified the constitution.
2008 Newly elected Russian president, Dmitry Medvedev, made his first state visit to Kazakhstan and obtained agreement that Kazakhstan-produced oil should be routed through Russia to the energy hungry markets in Europe.
2009 President Nazarbayev offered to site a nuclear fuel bank on Kazakh territory.
2010 At the beginning of the year, the Organisation for Security and Co-operation in Europe (OSCE) elected Kazakhstan, its first ex-Soviet republic, to take the chair as president. Talks between the IAEA and Kazak authorities on siting a low enriched uranium fuel bank began in January. A lawsuit was filed in the UK, by a subsidiary of the Russian company, Polyus, which had bought a 50.1 per cent share of KazakhGold for US$254 million, claiming that the previous owners, a prominent Kazakh family, the Assaubayevs, had inflated the assets of the goldfield. The claim demanded US$450 million in compensation. While the court case was on-going, the UK-assets of the Assaubayevs were frozen. Export of wild caviar began again, but under a strict quota agreement.
2011 In January, the lower house of parliament voted to hold a referendum to extend the term in office of President Nazarbayev until 2020. The constitutional court dismissed the grounds for the referendum. President Nazarbayev, who had not supported the referendum, called early presidential elections in April, in which four candidates took part. The incumbent Nursultan Nazarbayev (Nur Otan) won 95.55 per cent of the vote and the three other candidates won less than 2 per cent each. Observers from the OSCE declared that there had been a lack of transparency and competition in the vote. In July the upper house of parliament agreed to hold a referendum on extending President Nazarbayev's term in office. In November, the presidents of Russia, Belarus and Kazakhstan signed an agreement to set targets for setting up an internal market, the Eurasian Union, by 2015.
2012 On 1 January a Eurasian Commission begin an oversight role for integration of the internal market. Parliamentary elections were held on 15 January, with seven political parties competing. Nur Otan, led by President Nazarbayev, won a majority of the seats (83 out of 108); the opposition Ak Zhol won eight seats and the communist party seven. Turnout was 75.4 per cent. International monitors considered the elections failed to meet basic democratic principles. In September, Kazakhstan, Russia and Kyrgyzstan signed an agreement to build the Kambarata-1 hydroelectric power plant. The power station will be built in Upper Naryn (in Kyrgyzstan) and is due to be completed in 2020. On 24 September, Prime Minister Masimov resigned and Serik Akhmetov was appointed as his replacement. On 8 October, the most prominent opposition political figure and leader of the unregistered political party (Alga!), Vladimir Kozlov was sentenced to seven and a half years in jail on charges of orchestrating unrest among oil workers. Kozlov claimed the accusations were politically motivated.
2014 The National Bank of Kazakhstan devalued the tenge by 18.9 per cent on 11 February.
2015 Presidential elections were held on 26 April, a year ahead of schedule. Incumbent President Nazaebayev campaigned on a promise of economic and social stability; his two opponents were seen as pro-government.

Political structure

Constitution

On 21 May 2007 amendments to the constitution were approved by parliament. Some presidential power was transferred to parliament, whereby it now influences the formation of government, the constitutional court and the central election committee. The number of Majilis (lower house) members was increased to 154: 98 deputies by proportional representation (with 10 per cent reserved for women), nine seats exclusively reserved for ethnic representatives. Elections for the Majilis are to be five-year terms. The president can now become involved with political parties during his time in office. Parliament voted to allow President Nazarbayev an exception from the two-term restriction and allow him to stand for a third term, while presidential terms will be reduced from seven years to five, from 2012. The majority parliamentary party will determine the government. State funding of political parties was introduced for parties that received over 7 per cent of the popular vote in previous elections. Political candidates may only use specifically allocated election funds but media coverage will be granted to all candidates. The role of the Senate (upper house) will assume full powers when the Majilis is in recess. The president shall appoint 15 senators (instead of seven). The power and independence of the judiciary was increased.

Independence date

16 December 1991

Form of state

Secular democratic republic

The executive

The power of the executive was redistributed in 2007. The president is elected for seven years (to be reduced to five-year terms from 2012). The prime minister and the Council of Ministers are appointed by the president and approved by parliament.

National legislature

The bicameral parliament consists of the Majilis (lower house) with 77 members, of which 67 are popularly elected in single seat constituencies and 10 are elected from party lists, members serve four-year terms; the Senate (upper house) has 39 members, as each regional legislature elects two members as their representative senators (32 in total) and the remaining seven senators are appointed by the president; members serve six-year terms. All former presidents and *ex officio* members are senators for life.

Legal system

The legal system is based on the civil law system. The country has a Supreme Court (44 members), and a Constitutional Council (seven members).

Last elections

26 April 2015 (presidential); 15 January 2012 (parliamentary).

Results: Presidential: Nursultan Äbishuly Nazarbayev (Nur Otan) won 97.75 per cent of the vote, Turgun Syzdykov (Communist Party of Kazakhstan) 1.61 per cent, Abelgazi Kusainov (Independent) 1.36 per cent; turnout was 95.21 per cent.
Parliamentary (lower house): Nur Otan (National Democratic Party) (NDC) won 80.99 per cent of the vote (83 seats out of 108), Ak Zhol (Democratic Party) (DP) 7.47 per cent (eight), Communist People's Party (CPP) 7.19 per cent (seven);

four other political parties each won less than 2 per cent and failed to win any seats. Turnout was 75.4 per cent.
The Organization for Security and Co-operation in Europe (OSCE) has argued that the elections failed to meet 'fundamental principles of democratic elections'.

Next elections

2020 (presidential); 2017 (parliamentary)

Political parties

President Nazarbayev's ruling party, Otan (Fatherland), merged with the small Asar (All Together), Civic and Agrarian parties in 2006, and was re-named Nur-Otan (Fatherland's Ray of Light). The defunct Civic Party and Agrarian Party had jointly contested the 2004 election as the Agrarian and Industrial Union of Workers Bloc.

Ruling party

Nur Otan (National Democratic Party) (NDC) (since 1999; re-elected 15 Jan 2012)

Main opposition party

Ak Zhol (Democratic Party) (DP)
About 29 per cent of the population is under 14 years; 64 per cent 15–64; 7 per cent over 65.

Population

17.16 million (2013)*
Last census: February 1999: 14,953,126
Population density: Six inhabitants per square km (one of the most sparsely populated countries in the world) (2010). Urban population 59 per cent (2010 Unicef).
Annual growth rate: -0.2 per cent, 1990–2010 (Unicef).

Ethnic make-up

Kazakh (Qazaq) (45 per cent, principally in the south), Russian (36 per cent, principally in the north), Ukrainian (5 per cent), German (4 per cent), Uzbek (2 per cent), Tartars (2 per cent), Uighur (1 per cent), Korean (0.6 per cent).

Religions

Muslim (47 per cent), Russian Orthodox (44 per cent), Protestant (2 per cent) and other (7 per cent). Kazakhstan is officially a secular state along Turkish lines. Kazakhs are predominantly Islamic (Sunni), while Russians belong to the Orthodox Church. Islam, not of a fundamentalist nature, is strongest in the countryside. North American and European evangelical organisations are very active throughout the country.

Education

Although the 99 per cent literacy rate claimed by the Soviet authorities for Central Asia was exaggerated, particularly in rural areas, education in Central Asia surpasses that of neighbouring countries to the south.
Primary education starts from the age of six and lasts for four years followed by basic secondary education for five years and general secondary, which is not compulsory, lasting for another two years. Secondary professional education is offered in special professional or technical schools, lyceums or colleges and vocational schools. The Academy of Sciences in Almaty is the republic's principal college of higher education. Several private institutions offering higher education have been licensed. The Academy of Sciences is the republic's principal college of higher education.
All classes are now officially conducted in Kazakh, but many schools have been allowed to continue teaching in Russian after strong Russian protests. The argument is somewhat academic, however, as most educated Kazakhs converse in Russian and all ethnic groups are eager to learn English. Plans to introduce the Latin script, bringing the republic closer to Turkey, are unlikely to be realised for some years.
Literacy rate: 99 per cent adult rate; 100 per cent youth rate (15–24) (Unesco 2005).
Compulsory years: Six to 15
Enrolment rate: 89 per cent, total primary school enrolment of the relevant age group, including repetition rates (World Bank estimates 1994–2000).
Pupils per teacher: 18 in primary schools.

Health

Kazakhstan's healthcare system is highly decentralised with a separate development model for every region. Public funds available for reforming the system are limited and do not cover the basic needs of the population, including access to primary healthcare services.
The healthcare services sector consists of public and private providers, including hospitals, offices and clinics of medical doctors, other specialised healthcare facilities and health insurance providers. The number of public hospitals has fallen leaving 63.8 beds available per 10,000 people. This reduction corresponded to a growth of small out-patient facilities (so-called family healthcare units); with the network numbering 1,752 facilities. The number of private hospitals has increased by over 30 per cent since 2000. More than half of private clinics and hospitals concluded contracts with regional healthcare departments to provide certain medical services to be paid from regional state budgets.
In the Semipalatinsk area in northern Kazakhstan, a former nuclear testing area, cases of cancer and birth defects are widespread. During the Soviet era, the military tested the local population before and after nuclear tests to assess the consequences of exposure to radiation. The high levels of plutonium in the soil stem from the numerous tests and cause, among other things, immune-deficiency which is passed from generation to generation.
Respiratory diseases are the most common illnesses because of the republic's myriad environmental problems.
Improved water sources are available to 91 per cent of the population. Funds to provide improved water supplies to over 500,000 people, in four regions of Kazakhstan, was jointly provided by the Asian Development Bank (ADB), the Islamic Development Bank and the government – US$34.6 million, US$9.5 million, US$20.9 million respectively. The average per capita investment for water services is US$125 for surface facilities such as construction of pumping stations and treatment facilities and US$90 for groundwater services, including repairing pipes, sewage and wastewater drainage. In 2009, hygiene and sanitation education programmes were run along with the infrastructure programme and works.

HIV/Aids

HIV prevalence: 0.2 per cent aged 15–49 in 2003 (World Bank)
Life expectancy: 61 years, 2004 (WHO 2006)
Fertility rate/Maternal mortality rate: 2.6 births per woman, 2010 (Unicef); maternal mortality 70 per 100,000 live births (World Bank).
Child (under 5 years) mortality rate (per 1,000): 19 per 1,000 live births (WHO 2012); 4.2 per cent of children aged under five are malnourished (World Bank).
Head of population per physician: 3.54 physicians per 1,000 people, 2003 (WHO 2006)

Welfare

The former Soviet Union developed an extensive welfare system, but price liberalisation has rendered pensions, unemployment benefit and money paid out to single parent families virtually worthless. Most Kazakhstanis hold down two or three jobs and rely heavily on privately grown food. The government has said it intends to cushion low-income groups from the heaviest blows of economic reform, but is under pressure not to stretch the budget for fear of hyperinflation.
Kazakhstan has emerged as a role model in pension reform in the Commonwealth of Independent States (CIS). In January 1998, a pay-as-you-go (PAYG) system was replaced with a privately managed and fully-funded system (similar to that introduced by Chile in the 1980s). Under the new system, employees pay a

compulsory 10 per cent of their wages into a personal retirement account. This is in addition to existing pension liabilities funded through a 15 per cent payroll tax which will be cut to 5 per cent by 2009. The reform initially increased the pension fund deficit, as the state had to make up for the contributions that were diverted to the private funds. In 1998, the World Bank approved a US$300 million loan to support the government's efforts to finance the transition to a fully-funded pension system by financing part of the estimated 1.7 per cent of GDP fiscal deficit. Nevertheless, the programme is regarded as highly successful, with participation levels and the yields on investments remaining high.

By the end of 2001, the assets accumulated in Kazakhstan's pension funds reached T182.5 billion (US$1.2 billion). At the same time, the share of state pension funds fell from 39 per cent to 32 per cent over 2001. On the other hand, the minimum capital required to invest in private pension funds doubled in 2000 to T180 million (US$1.2 billion), leading to the merger of private funds with stronger institutions, and the share of private funds grew to 68 per cent in 2001.

Main cities

Astana (capital, estimated population 425,806 in 2012); Almaty (commercial capital, 1.4 million), Shymkent (476,066), Taraz (427,469), Karaganda (421,250), Pavlodar (360,050), Öskemen (349,713), Semey (311,687).

Languages spoken

Kazakh (Turkic) is only spoken by around 40 per cent of the population. Russian is the language of inter-ethnic communication, spoken by two-thirds of the population and used in everyday business.

Official language/s

Kazakh

Media

Although the constitution guarantees freedom of the press, private owned and opposition media outlets are subject to harassment and censorship. Presidential prerogative includes his private life, health and financial dealings being designated state secrets and criminal charges can be incurred for 'insulting' the president and public officials. The government has control of most printing presses and transmission facilities for radio and television.

Press

According to government statistics, there are 990 privately owned newspapers and 418 privately owned magazines. Most are supportive of the government with members of President Nazarbayeva's family owning some of the largest circulating newspapers.

Dailies: There are several daily and weekly newspapers in both Russian and Kazakh including: *Kazakhstanskaya Pravda* (www.kazpravda.kz), *Karavan* (www.caravan.kz), *Ekspress-K* (www.express-k.kz), *Vremya* (www.time.kz), *Liter* (www.liter.kz) and *Zhas Alash* (www.zhasalash.kz).

Business: In Cyrillic, *Delovaya Nedelya* (www.dn.kz), *Panarama* (www.panorama.vkkz.com) are Russian-language publications. The US-based news agency EIN News (www.einnews.com) also provides business and economic news, in English.

Broadcasting

A law was introduced in 2002 requiring that at least 50 per cent of all television and radio broadcasts must be in the Kazakh language other languages include Russian and Chinese. The Turkish Radio and Television Corporation (TRT) also broadcasts programmes for Kazakhstan.

Radio: Kazakh Radio is state-run, private stations including Europa Plus (www.europaplus.kz) with a nationwide network, Khabar Hit FM and Russkoye Radio-Aziya are owned by President Nazarbayeva's daughter. Other, private stations include Radio 31 (www.31.kz/radio31), Radio Tekc (www.radiotex.net) and Auto Radio (www.avtoradio.kz).

International radio networks including the BBC (www.bbc.co.uk/worldservice) and Radio Free Europe (www.rferl.org) are available.

Television: Of there are five television channels available all are either government owned by family members of President Nazarbayeva. The state-run Kazakh TV has two channels. The Khabar news agency owns Khabar TV (www.khabar.kz), Yel Arna (for cultural programmes) and Caspionet (www.caspionet.kz) a satellite station. KTK (www.ktk.kz) is a commercial channel. Other private stations include Channel 31 TV (www.31.kz), Alma TV, the first cable TV station in Almaty and Perviy Kanal Evraziya a local channel.

Imported US TV programmes are popular.

National news agency: Kazinform

Other news agencies:

Interfax-Kazakhstan: www.interfax.kz

Economy

Kazakhstan's economy is characterised as being resource-rich, with a large oil fund (US$76.8 billion in October 2014, 36 per cent of GDP). Proven oil reserves were 30 billion barrels at the end of 2014, with production of 1.7 million barrels per day. Proven natural gas reserves were 1.5 trillion cubic metres (cum), with production of 19.3 billion cum in 2014, of which typically over half is shipped via pipelines to Russia (for onward sale to the European energy market). It also has large deposits of coal, 33.6 trillion tonnes in 2014, with production of 55.3 million tonnes oil equivalent. Kazakhstan remains an attractive destination for foreign direct investment, which was around US$10 trillion in 2013 (and never fell below US$10 trillion during the global economic crisis). The principal challenge for Kazakhstan in the latter stages of the global recession was the impact of the fall in world commodity prices, particularly oil, on its economy. Kazakhstan managed to keep GDP growth positive throughout the global economic crisis, reaching a low of 1.2 per cent in 2009. As global production and trade picked up growth rebounded to 7.3 per cent in 2010, a high growth rate that was maintained in 2011 at 7.5 per cent. Despite remaining strong after 2011, growth has been falling due to weak global performance reducing the demand for Kazakhstan's main export commodities (oil, gas, coal, metals, chemicals and grains) so that by 2014 the economy grew by 4.3 per cent.

There is a largely domestically owned banking system with external debt at almost 75 per cent of GDP, of which around 40 per cent is internal company debt within the mining and hydrocarbon sectors.

Agricultural products include dairy goods, leather, meat, wool and grain. Kazakhstan is usually one of the largest producers of wheat in the world, typically producing 15–16 million tonnes per annum. However in 2012, adverse weather conditions caused a fall in wheat harvests estimated by up to 52 per cent. In 2013 wheat production rebounded by around 42 per cent before falling by 7 per cent in 2014.

In 2010, Russia launched a customs union with Belarus and Kazakhstan, looking to further integrate with the former Soviet bloc. The customs union plans a single currency in the next ten years.

External trade

Following two decades of negotiations, in July 2015 Kazakhstan became the 162nd member of the World Trade Organisation (WTO). It belongs to the Eurasian Economic Community (EurAsec or EAEC), which was set up in 2000 to promote a customs union between its six member states (Belarus, Kazakhstan, Kyrgyzstan, Russia, Tajikistan and Uzbekistan) and, among other objectives, to introduce a standardised currency exchange and rules for trade in goods and service. The EAEC evolved out of the Commonwealth of Independent States (CIS) Customs Union and has begun the process of merging with the Central Asian Co-operation Organisation (CACO). On 19 October

2011, a free trade agreement (FTA) was signed by Russia with seven of its former Soviet republics: Armenia, Belarus, Kazakhstan, Kyrgyzstan, Moldova and Tajikistan.

In May 2014 the Eurasian Economic Union (EEU) was signed between Kazakhstan, Belarus and Russia and came into action in January 2015. Armenia and Kyrgyzstan's accession to the EEU was signed in October 2014. The EEU has an integrated single market of 176 million people and a GDP of over US$4 trillion.

Kazakhstan has plentiful natural resources, including oil and gas, coal, copper, silver, uranium and zinc, all of which are export commodities. Over 50 per cent of all exports is oil, which provides around 30 per cent of GDP. As the manufacturing sector is underdeveloped imports are dominated by capital and consumer goods.

Imports

Principal imports include machinery and equipment (over 40 per cent), typically for the extractive industries; vehicles, machinery, iron and steel, appliances and electronic products and fuel.

Main sources: Russia (33.3 per cent total in 2014), China (17.9 per cent), Germany (5.6 per cent)

Exports

Principal exports are dominated by primary products including oil and oil products (over 50 per cent), ferrous metals (around 25 per cent), chemicals, machinery, grain, wool, meat and coal.

Main destinations: Italy (20.5 per cent total in 2014), China (12.5 per cent), The Netherlands (11.2 per cent).

Agriculture

Farming

Agriculture contributed approximately 4.9 per cent to GDP in 2014 and employed around a quarter of the working population.

Kazakhstan's farming area constituted 16 per cent of the former Soviet Union's farm land. The cultivation of the 'Virgin Lands' in the north during the Soviet period introduced a high level of mechanisation and Kazakhstan used to provide around 14 per cent of Soviet grain.

There are still many problems in the agricultural sector, including weaknesses in input supply (such as fertilisers), poor incentives for farm production and failure to restructure farm enterprises. Privatisation is proceeding slowly. Small-scale private farming has been introduced in the south, while production in the north remains more centralised. While agricultural land may be leased long-term, attempts to introduce private land ownership is unpopular.

Irrigated land in the south and east produces fruit, vegetables, sugar beet, rice, tobacco, mustard and natural rubber. Wheat, cotton and oilseeds are the main crops produced. Dairy farming, horse breeding and sheep breeding are also undertaken.

Fishing

In the north-eastern part of Kazakhstan cold water fish are found in the River Ob catchment area, including the Altai Mountains drainage of the Irtysh River, Mountain Rivers of the Tien Shan range and in Lake Balkhash, which has a mix of cold water and temperate water fish stocks.

The fishing of streams and rivers is largely unmanaged, but considerable effort has been put into maintaining reasonably high fish catches in some lakes and reservoirs. Kazakhstan has concentrated largely on the exploitation of indigenous fish stocks. The typical annual fish catch is over 31,000mt.

Forestry

Forest and other wooded land account for a small part of the total land area, around 1.2 per cent in 2012. Forests cover around 12.1 million hectares, which has increased by an average of 2.22 per cent per annum.

The increasing demand for forest products is met by imports, mainly from the Russian Federation.

Industry and manufacturing

Kazakhstan's industrial capacity is largely inherited from the Soviet era and the firms are battling to replace redundant machinery and attract foreign direct investment (FDI). As a result of Soviet planning, Kazakhstan specialises in the production of phosphate fertiliser, rolled metal, military equipment, radio cables, tractors and bulldozers. Military-related industries produced and processed beryllium, uranium, machine guns, anti-ship missiles, torpedoes, chemical and biological weapons, equipment for launching missiles and armoured vehicles. Since independence, the defence industry has been in decline with many plants closing or producing non-military electronic equipment and machines. The industrial sector shrank dramatically throughout the 1990s due to a decrease in demand from Russia, the country's main customer. More than three-quarters of Kazakhstan's industrial exports are destined for Russia. From 2011–15, industrial output rose on average by around 1.5 per cent per year.

Kazakhstan has earned a prominent place in astronautics and space flight. The Baykonur Space Centre (formerly the Baikonur Cosmodrome) was the principle launch site for Soviet rockets and satellites. Following an agreement in March 1994, Russia paid Kazakhstan US$115 million per year for the rental of the centre for a 20-year period. The long-term future of Baykonur is uncertain. The number of Russian rocket launches steadily fell in the 1990s due to lack of finance and military satellites are now launched from Russia's Plesetsk Cosmodrome, which is also increasingly being used as a launch site for civilian-use satellites. Baykonur's location is also a major problem as due-east launches are forbidden because spent booster rockets would drop on Chinese territory. In those launch corridors which are used, tens of thousands of tonnes of spent boosters, many with toxic residual propellants still on board, now litter the countryside. Any attempt to tackle the environmental impact of rocket launches would mean severely restricting launches from Baykonur.

Tourism

Kazakhstan is a huge country with varied terrain that includes the Altay Mountains, glaciers, the Taiga coniferous forests, deserts, lakes and the world's largest dry steppe region. It can offer visitors adventure holidays, including mountaineering, trekking and fishing. However, tourist facilities in general are underdeveloped and require visitors to organise their own tours. Attractions include the Silk Road and the former capital of Almaty as popular destinations for visitors.

Travel and tourism has the potential for greater contribution to GDP then the 5.6 per cent it provided in 2014. Employment in the sector accounted for only 5.3 per cent (453,500 jobs) of total employment in 2014. In July 2014 the authorities of Astana announced they were planning to invest up to US$10 billion (including US$6 billion from private investors) on developing the tourism sector by 2020. Total investment in the tourism and travel industry in 2014 was US$2.25 billion, or 4.9 per cent of total investment.

Environment

The Aral Sea was subject to a loss of up to 50 per cent of its water, dropping by up to 19 metres, due to the overuse of water from the two main rivers which fed into it. A UN study published in 2004 reported that there was no possibility of restoring the water and the need must be on preserving what is left. A World Bank funded project to build, reconstruct and rehabilitate waterworks along the river Syr Darya has reversed the damaged in the northern section of the sea. A sluice will be installed to supply water to the parched southern section.

Plans are underway to improve irrigation in the farmland around the sea.

Potentially, revenue may be earned from the sale of hydroelectic power.

A meeting was held in April 2009 to determine water sharing between Tajikistan, Kyrgyzstan, Uzbekistan, Turkmenistan and Kazakhstan failed, as negotiators were unable to find a trade in water for energy and hydrocarbons. Tajikistan and Kyrgyzstan hold around 80 per cent of the water in the Aral Sea but suffer from lack of electricity during freezing winters, while the remaining three states downstream are semi-arid and need water for their cotton industries and agriculture.

Mining

Mining contributes around 15 per cent to GDP and employs around 8 per cent of the workforce.

Rich in mineral resources, Kazakhstan produces some 40 per cent of the world's chrome ore, second only to South Africa. There are also important deposits of iron ore, nickel, cobalt, vanadium, titanium, copper, lead, wolfram, zinc, gold, silver, tin, tungsten, molybdenum, uranium (Kazakhstan overtook Canada and Australia as the world's biggest uranium miner in 2009), cadmium, bismuth, pyrophyllite, barite, phosphorites, magnesium, phosphorous, asbestos, rare earths and sizeable manganese deposits in eastern and northern Kazakhstan. There are significant bauxite reserves in southern Kazakhstan.

In 2014, Kazakhstan fine-tuned legislation concerning the mining industry in order to attract foreign attention to its natural resources. In 2015 the country began awarding 50–100 licences to foreign companies. Investment in the mining sector is expected to reach US$30 billion by 2017.

Hydrocarbons

Kazakhstan is believed to have the world's largest untapped oil and gas reserves.

Since the 1990s the government has concentrated its efforts on attracting foreign investment to the hydrocarbons sector.

Upstream production is funded by foreign oil companies in association with the government. However, in 2007 an amendment was passed into law whereby the government could unilaterally break contracts with oil companies, either by forcing a renegotiation of contracts or the outright termination of contracts. The new law was seen as a move to stimulate greater urgency for production and a greater return on royalties.

There were 30 billion barrels of proven oil reserves in 2014, with production at 1.7 million barrels per day (bpd). Production in the country's main oil field, Tengiz, is expected to double and an additional 1 million bpd is anticipated from the Kashagan field (the largest outside the Middle East), as long as construction in vital infrastructure is maintained. Around 75 per cent of production is exported and accounts for around a quarter of GDP.

There are three major refineries, at Pavlador, Atyrau and Shymkent, all largely owned by the state and lacking in any significant foreign direct investment, so that by 2010 their joint capacity had fallen below commercially recorded levels.

Oil from the Tengiz oilfield was first pumped down the Caspian Pipeline Consortium (CPC) pipeline in 2001. The oil was sent to a Russian marine terminal on the Black Sea near Novorossiysk. This effectively stopped Kazak hydrocarbons from becoming a direct competitor to Russian oil and gas. In 2010 CPC shareholders agreed a further investment of US$4.5 billion to increase capacity to 1.5 million bpd. The US and Europe had originally been negotiating to build a pipeline beneath the Caspian Sea to avoid Russia altogether. There is another pipeline supplying oil to China, jointly owned by the China Nation Petroleum Corporation (CNPC) and KazMunaiGas (KMG).

Kazakhstan had proven natural gas reserves of 1.5 trillion cubic metres in 2014 and produced 19.3 billion cubic metres, an increase of 3.4 per cent on the figure for 2013. The largest gas field is Karachaganak in the north. The gas reserves in the Tengiz and Kashagan fields are almost entirely 'associated gas' produced by drilling for oil and as the country has insufficient pipeline infrastructure excess production that is not exported or used locally is being re-injected into crude oil bore holes to maintain pressure for oil extraction. Eventually, this gas can be recovered, when commercial exploitation is viable. In the meantime Kazakhstan is the world fifth-largest flarer of excess gas.

The government targeted the sector for expansion – the country became a net exporter of natural gas as late as 2008, which was still the case in 2012. Distribution of gas is divided, with natural gas from the northern Karachaganak fields being exported to Russia, via the Karachaganak-Atyrau pipeline, while gas from the other fields is used domestically or exported via the Baku-Tibilisi-Ceyhan pipeline to Europe.

Kazakhstan has Central Asia's largest reserves of recoverable coal, of 33.6 trillion tonnes in 2014, the majority of which is the higher quality anthracite. Production in 2014 was 55.3 million tonnes of oil equivalent (toe), a fall of 4.9 per cent on the 2013 production level. Russia is a major importer of Kazak coal.

Coal is the largest domestic source of energy (75 per cent in 2013); production is hampered by the lack of investment in new and existing mines. Many of the high-cost underground coalmines have been closed, and the more competitive open (surface) mines are owned and operated by international energy companies.

Energy

Total electricity generating capacity was 18.73GW in 2013. Around three quarters of electricity in the country was produced using coal in 2013, gas accounted for 10 per cent, hydropower accounted for 10 per cent and oil accounted for the remaining 5 per cent. The sector is faced with large amounts of inefficient or redundant equipment and needs considerable investment if it is to reverse the decline in output and halt the frequent power stoppages experienced since the 1990s.

Kazakhstan closed down its only nuclear station in 1999 and government plans for constructing a new 1,500MW nuclear power plant in the south-east near Lake Balkash remains long-term and as of 2015, Kazakhstan produced no nuclear energy.

Financial markets

Stock exchange

Kazakhstan Stock Exchange (KASE)

Banking and insurance

The National Bank of Kazakhstan was given powers, from late 2007, to undertake measures to strengthen regulations and improve corporate governance over banks as they were restructured and recapitalised. Nevertheless the banking system was still caught up in the crisis and the International Monetary Fund (IMF) said in 2009 that, since 2007, total losses to the banking system had been US$40 billion (in foreign debt). In October 2009 the state news agency Interfax reported that the total net loss to the banking system between January–September 2009 was T2.8 trillion (about US$19 billion). In October 2009 the government secured a deal with creditors of the Alliance Bank for US$4 billion of gross debt in exchange for equity in the Alliance Bank's reconstruction.

Central bank

National Bank of Kazakhstan

Time

Western Kazakhstan: GMT plus four hours

Central Kazakhstan, Astana: GMT plus five hours

Eastern Kazakhstan, Almaty: GMT plus six hours

Geography

Kazakhstan, in Central Asia, is a landlocked country but with a coastline on the Caspian Sea, (the largest lake in the world). It is the second-largest country in the region, extending some 1,900km (1,200 miles) from the Volga river in Europe, in the west, to the Altai mountains, in the east, and about 1,300km (800 miles) from the Siberian plain in the north

to the Central Asian deserts in the south. Kazakhstan's 2.7 million square km are equivalent to the size of Western Europe and comprise rolling steppes to the north, desert to the south and part of the western edge of the Tien Shan mountains to the south-east.
Kazakhstan is bordered by the Russian Federation to the north, China to the east, Kyrgyzstan, Uzbekistan and Turkmenistan to the south. In the south-west there is almost a 1,000km coastline on the Caspian Sea. Half of the Aral Sea lies within Kazakhstan, the other half in Uzbekistan.

Hemisphere
Northern

Climate
The temperature varies greatly from temperate steppe in the north to desert in the south. Temperatures in southern Kazakhstan average minus 3 degrees Celsius (C) in January and 29 degrees C in June. Average temperatures in Almaty range from minus 5 degrees C to 35 degrees C. Rainfall averages 200–300mm per annum in the north of the country and 400–500mm in the south.

Dress codes
Not overly formal during business hours, although women must dress modestly. Formal wear may be expected when visiting the theatre or attending a dinner party. Shorts should not be worn except in a sporting environment.

Entry requirements
Passports
Required by all visitors, valid for six months beyond intended length of stay.

Visa
Required by all, except nationals of CIS countries and Turkey. Business visas are issued after an invitation from a local company has been registered with the consular department of the Ministry of Foreign Affairs in Kazakhstan. When authorised, the host company obtains a reference number which is forwarded to the applicant who submits the application form along with a business letter of intent, a full itinerary and an undertaking of financial responsibility for expenses incurred by the representative. Details can be obtained from the consular section of the nearest embassy.
Tourist visits over five days require registration by the local authorities on arrival.

Currency advice/regulations
There are no restrictions on the import and export of local currency. Import of foreign currency is allowed subject to declaration on arrival; export is limited to amount declared.

Customs
A customs declaration form must be completed on arrival and retained until departure. Items for declaration are articles intended for personal use (currency, jewellery, cameras, computers, etc), which must be exported when leaving. It is advisable to keep receipts for goods purchased locally.

Prohibited imports
Military weapons and ammunition, illegal drugs, pornography, live animals, photographs or printed material detrimental to the image of Kazakhstan, loose pearls or anything carried for a third party.

Health (for visitors)
Mandatory precautions
Vaccination certificates are required for yellow fever if travelling from an infected area. For stays over one month and applications for visas for stays over three months, an AIDS certificate is required.

Advisable precautions
It is advisable to be in date for the following immunisations: polio (within 10 years), tetanus (within 10 years), typhoid fever, TB, hepatitis A, tick-borne encephalitis. Anti-malarial precautions advisable. Any medicines required by the traveller should be taken by the visitor, and it could be wise to have precautionary antibiotics if going outside major urban centres. A travel kit including a disposable syringe is a reasonable precaution. Water precautions recommended: water purification tablets may be useful or drink bottled water. Rabies is a health risk.

Hotels
Advisable to book at least a month in advance through Intourist or other specialist travel agents. There are many luxury Western-style hotels in Almaty. Gratuities are becoming more customary, particularly in international hotels.

Credit cards
More widely accepted than anywhere else in Central Asia; as well as being welcomed in shops and hotels, they can be used for cash advances.

Public holidays (national)
Fixed dates
1–2 Jan (New Year), 8 Mar (Women's Day), 22 Mar (Nauryz Meyrami/Traditional Spring Holiday/Persian New Year), 1 May (Unity Day), 9 May (Victory Day), 30 Aug (Constitution Day), 25 Oct (Republic Day), 16 Dec (Independence Day).

Variable dates
Eid al Adha

Working hours
Banking
Mon–Fri: 0930–1730.

Business
Mon–Fri: 0900–1800.

Government
Mon–Fri: 0900–1730.

Shops
Mon–Sat: 0900–1700.

Electricity supply
220V AC.

Social customs/useful tips
Kazakhistanis are very hospitable and courteous. It is best to book appointments for meetings in the morning. Cancellation, even at the last minute, is fairly common. Russian is the everyday business language. Business and politics are intertwined, with negotiations and deals often 'arranged'.

Security
It is unwise to venture out on the streets alone at night. Dress inconspicuously as wealthy-looking foreigners can be a target for muggers.
It may be preferable to travel by intercity bus rather than train, as robberies are making rail travel increasingly hazardous.

Getting there
Air
Almaty is the principal gateway to the country and well-served, with the most developed air routes through Turkey and Russia.
National airline: Air Astana.
International airport/s: Almaty International (ALA), 10km north-east of the city; hotel, car hire, duty-free shops, cafeterias. Atyrau International (GUW), 8km west of the city; bank, post office, restaurant, car hire. Astana (TSE), 17 km south of the city; facilities include duty-free shop and restaurant. Buses and taxis connect to the city centre.
Other airport/s: There are fifteen other airports.
Airport tax: None

Surface
Road: There are generally good international road connections to the surrounding countries. The north-east area is well served by roads to the Urals and the North Caucasus.
The Regional Road Corridor Improvement Project, estimated at US$18 billion, to improve Central Asian roads, airports, railway lines and seaports and provide a vital transit route between Europe and Asia was agreed, on 3 November 2007. Six new transit corridors, between Afghanistan, Azerbaijan, China, Kazakhstan, Kyrgyzstan, Mongolia, Tajikistan and Uzbekistan, of mainly roads and rail links, will be constructed, or existing resources upgraded, by 2013. Half the costs with be provided by the Asian Development Bank and other multilateral organisations and the other half by participating countries.
Rail: A railway line was completed in 1991 between Almaty and Urumchi in China. There are also rail connections to Russia, Kyrgystan and Turkmenistan. A

new railway line is being built to connect Iran and Turkey with Kazakhstan. Foreign visitors should use caution when travelling by train, other than the Almaty-Moscow line, as violent crime against westerners is on the increase.

Main port/s: Aktau (formerly Shevchenko) on the Caspian Sea is the main oil port and trans-shipment centre.

Getting about

National transport

Air: There are fifteen domestic/local airports located around the regions that are served by scheduled internal flights. It should be noted that maintenance procedures for aircraft on internal flights may not conform to internationally accepted standards.

Planes and helicopters can be chartered for nominal prices provided you have a good local contact.

Road: Primary and secondary roads are of poor quality, particularly in desert and semi-desert regions. However, the Oral region is well served by road links to the Urals, European Russia and the North Caucasus. Road transport is subject to cancellation and delay. Passengers are advised to travel in groups. Petrol supplies are adequate. Kazakhstan has 189,000km of paved and gravelled roads, 108,100km of unpaved roads and 80,900km of earth roads.

Buses: There are regular bus services between all the main cities.

Rail: Rail links are extensive but slow. There are 14,460km of railway, excluding industrial lines, in Kazakhstan. The Turksib railway connects Almaty with the Trans-Siberian line to the north at Novisibirsk, while the principal rail connection with Moscow runs through Chimkent and Uralsk.

City transport

Taxis: Unless Russian or Kazakh is spoken, ensure any taxi taken is booked through the hotel reception desk and that the price is agreed beforehand.

Buses, trams & metro: Swift and cheap trolley-bus and bus network in Almaty.

Car hire

A national driver's licence with an authorised translation or an international driving permit is required.

BUSINESS DIRECTORY

The addresses listed below are a selection only. While World of Information makes every endeavour to check these addresses, we cannot guarantee that changes have not been made, especially to telephone numbers and area codes. We would welcome any corrections.

Telephone area codes

The international direct dialling code (IDD) for Kazakhstan is +7, followed by area code and subscriber's number:

Almaty	327	Shimkent	325
Aktau	329	Taldykorgan	328
Astana	317	Uralsk	311
Karaganda	321	Ust-Kamenogorsk	323
Leninsk	336	Zhambyl	326
Petropavlovsk	315	Zhezkazgan	310

Useful telephone numbers

Police: 02

Fire: 01

Ambulance: 03

Chambers of Commerce

Almaty Chamber of Commerce and Industry, 45 Tole bi Street, Almaty 480091 (tel: 620-301; fax: 611-404; e-mail: alcci@nursat.kz).

American Chamber of Commerce in Kazakhstan, 531 Seifullina Prospect, Almaty 480091 (tel: 587-938; fax: 587-939; e-mail: information@amcham.kz).

East Kazakhstan Chamber of Commerce and Industry, PO Box 177, 3 Novatorov Street, Ust-Kamenogorsk 492000 (tel: 265-310; fax:267-247; e-mail@cci@ustk.kz).

Kazakhstan Union of Chambers of Commerce and Industry, 26 Masanchi Street, Almaty 480091 (tel: 920-052; fax: 507-029; e-mail: tpprkaz@online.ru).

North Kazakhstan Chamber of Commerce and Industry, 112 Mira Street, Petropavlovsk 642015 (tel: 460-568; fax: 465-443; e-mail: tpp@petropavl.kz).

Semipalatinsk Chamber of Commerce and Industry, 92/22 Abai Street, Semipalatinsk 490050 (tel/fax: 627-887; e-mail: tpp@relcom.kz).

South Kazakhstan Chamber of Commerce and Industry, 31 Tauke khan Street, Shimkent 486050 (tel: 211-405; fax: 211-403).

West Kazakhstan Chamber of Commerce and Industry, 67 Kuibyshev Street, Uralsk 417000 (tel: 504-440; fax: 513-537; e-mail: zktpp@kaznet.kz).

Banking

ATF Bank, 100 Furmanov Str, 480091 Almaty (tel: 503-765; fax: 501-995).

Bank Centercredit, 100 Shevchenko Street, 480072 Almaty (tel: 634-605, 680-140; fax: 507-813).

Central Asian Bank for Co-operation and Development, 115-a Abay Ave, Almaty (tel: 422-737; fax: 428-627).

Demir Kazakhstan Bank, 61A Kurmangazy Street, 480091 Almaty (tel: 508-550, 508-527; fax: 508-525).

Export-Import Bank of Kazakhstan, 118 Pushkin Street, 480021 Almaty (tel: 622-815, 633-767, 634-300; fax: 631-985).

Halyk Savings Bank of Kazakhstan; 97 Rozybakieva St, 480046 Almaty (tel: 509-991; fax: 679-738).

Kazkommertsbank, 135 Gagarin Avenue, 480060 Almaty (tel: 585-101; fax: 585-281; internet site: http://www.kkb.kz).

Temirbank, 68/74 Abay Ave, 480008 Almaty (tel: 587-888; fax: 590-529; e-mail: board@temirbank.kz; internet site: http://www.temirbank.kz).

Central bank

National Bank of Kazakhstan, 21 Koktem-3, 480090 Almaty (tel: 504-631; fax: 506-090; e-mail: info@nationalbank.kz).

Stock exchange

Kazakhstan Stock Exchange (KASE), www.kase.kz

Travel information

Aeroflot, 111 Zhibek Zhola Street, Almaty (tel: 390-594).

Air Kazakhstan, 59 Mira Street, 480003 Almaty (tel: 335-518; fax: 335-506).

Flight information (24 hours) (tel: 541-555).

Intourist, Hotel Ostrar, Gogolya 65, Almaty (tel: 330-045, 330-076).

Almaty Airport, Mailin Street 2B, 480040 Almaty (tel: 571-300; fax: 571-281).

Astana International Airport, PO Box 1968, 473026 Astana (tel: 333-709; fax: 333-741).

Kazakhstan Tourist Agency, 22 Kosmonautov Street, 480083 Almaty (tel: 390-318; fax: 390-257).

Travel Bureau, Hotel Irtysh, Ulitsa Abai 97, Semipalatinsk, Almaty (tel: 447-529, 447-531).

National tourist organisation offices

Department of Tourism, 4 Republic Square, Almaty 4860065 (tel/fax: 620-030; e-mail: dep_tour@nursat.kz; internet: www.kaztour.kz).

Ministries

Ministry of Agriculture, 49 Abai Street, 473000 Astana (tel: 323-763; fax: 324-541).

Ministry of Culture, Information and Public Accord, 22 Beibitshilik Street, 473000 Astana (tel: 322-495; fax: 326-203).

Ministry of Defence, 49 Auezova Street, 473000 Astana (tel: 337-845;fax: 337-892).

Ministry of Economy and Trade, 2 Beibitshilik Street, 473000 Astana (tel/fax: 333-003).

Ministry of Education and Science, 83 Kenesary Street, 473000 Astana (tel: 322-540; fax: 326-482).

Ministry of Employment and Social Security, 2 Manasa Street, 473000 Astana (tel: 153-602; fax: 341-270).

Ministry of Energy and Mineral Resources, 37 Beibitshilik Street, 473000 Astana (tel: 337-133; fax: 337-164).

Ministry of Finance, 60 Republic Avenue, 473000 Astana (tel: 334-186;fax: 280-321).

Ministry of Foreign Affairs, 10 Beibitshilik Street, 473000 Astana (tel: 327-669; fax: 327-667).

Ministry of Internal Affairs, 4 Manasa Street, 473000 Astana (tel: 343-601; fax: 341-738).

Ministry of Justice, 45 Pobeda Street, 473000 Astana (tel: 391-213; fax: 321-554).

Ministry of Natural Resources and Environmental Protection, 81 Karl Marx Street, 475000 Kokshetau (tel: 54-265; fax: 50-620).

Ministry of State Revenues, 48 Abai Avenue (tel: 326-951;fax: 326-963).

Ministry of Transport and Communications, 49 Abai Street, 473000 Astana (tel: 326-277; fax: 321-058).

Prime Minister's Office, 11 Beibitshilik Street, 473000 Astana (tel: 320-985;fax: 152-028).

Other useful addresses

Atomic Energy Agency, 13 Republic Square, 480013 Almaty (tel: 637-626; fax: 633-356).

Board for Investment Projects, Department of Transport, Room 124, Gogol Str 86, 480091 Almaty (tel: 323-661, 324-769; fax: 322-679, 324-449).

Business Communication Centre, 89 Michurina Street, Almaty 480059 (tel: 476-803, 347-549; fax: 347-798).

Centre for Economic Reforms, 4 Republic Square, Almaty (tel: 621-836).

Committee for the use of Foreign Capital, 152 Bogenbai Batyr, 3rd Floord, Ablay Khan Street 97, 480091 Almaty (tel: 627-326; fax: 696-152).

Kazakh Centre of Business Co-operation 'Atakent', 42 Timiryazeve Street, Almaty 480058 (tel: 473-113; fax: 509-238).

Kazakh Embassy (USA), 1401 16th Street, NW, Washington DC 20036 (tel: (+1-202)-232-5488; fax: (+1-202)-232-5845; e-mail: kazakh@intr.net).

Kazakhgas, 521 Seifullin Street, Almaty (tel: 324-288; fax: 325-442).

Kazakhstan Caspishelf, 211 Mukhanov Street, Almaty (tel: 416-034; fax: 416-430).

Kazakhstan Commerce (import-export), Zhibek Zholy 64, 480002 Almaty (tel: 333-871; fax: 331-483).

Kazakhstan Foreign Trade Organisation, v/o Kazakhintorg, Gogolya 111, Almaty (tel: 328-381).

Kazakhstanmunaigas (oil and gas refining), 458 Seifullin Street, Almaty (tel: 695-800; fax: 626-630).

Kazakh Academy of Sciences Engineering Institute, 80 Bogenbay Batyr Street, Almaty 480100 (tel: 541-281; fax: 695-769).

Kazakhstan Stock Exchange, Ulitsa Timipiazeva 42, Almaty (tel: 441-043; fax: 447-809).

Kazakh State TV and Radio, Ulitsa Mira 175, Almaty (tel: 633-716).

Kazchrome Transnational Corporation, 56 Kunaev Street, Almaty, 480002.

KazMunayGaz, 142 Bogenbai Batyr Street, 470091 Almaty (tel: 626-080; fax: 695-405).

Kazpisprom (a joint-stock company representing food producers), 92 Internatsionalnaya Street, Almaty (tel: 629-482; fax: 628-652).

Kaztag (state news agency), 77 Ablai Han Street, Almaty (tel: 625-037).

Kazvetmet (represents metal producers), 111 Gogol Street, 480003 Almaty (tel: 622-318; fax: 328-488).

Market Economy Group (privatisation committee), President's Office, Government House, Almaty (tel: 621-022).

State Property and Privatisation Committee, Ministry of Finance, 36 Auezov Street, 473024 Astana (tel: 334-397; fax: 320-937).

Union of Manufacturers and Businessmen, 4/450 Republic Square, Almaty (tel: 622-307; fax: 665-490).

National news agency: Kazinform

Address: 10 Beibitshilik Street, 010000 Astana (tel: 717-232-7567; email: subs@inform.kz).

Interfax-Kazakhstan: www.interfax.kz

Internet sites

Kazakhstan local navigator: http://reenic.utexas.edu/reenic/countries/kazakhstan/kazakhstan/html

Kazakhstan government website: http://www.president.kz/

KEY FACTS

Official name: Jamhuri ya Kenya (Republic of Kenya)

Head of State: President Uhuru Kenyatta (elected 4 Mar 2013)

Head of government: President Uhuru Kenyatta (elected 4 Mar 2013)

Ruling party: Jubilee Alliance, a coalition led by The National Alliance (TNA) and including the United Republican Party (URP) and National Alliance of Rainbow Coalition (NARC) (elected 4 Mar 2013)

Area: 582,646 square km

Population: 429,270 (2014)*

Capital: Nairobi

Official language: KiSwahili and English

Currency: Kenyan shilling (Ksh) = 100 cents (convertible with currencies of Tanzania and Uganda)

Exchange rate: Ksh105.45 per US$ (Sep 2015)

GDP per capita: US$1,416 (2014)*

GDP real growth: 5.28% (2014)

GDP: US$60.77 billion (2014)

Inflation: 6.88% (2014)

Balance of trade: -US$11.44 billion (2014)

* estimated figure

Kenya

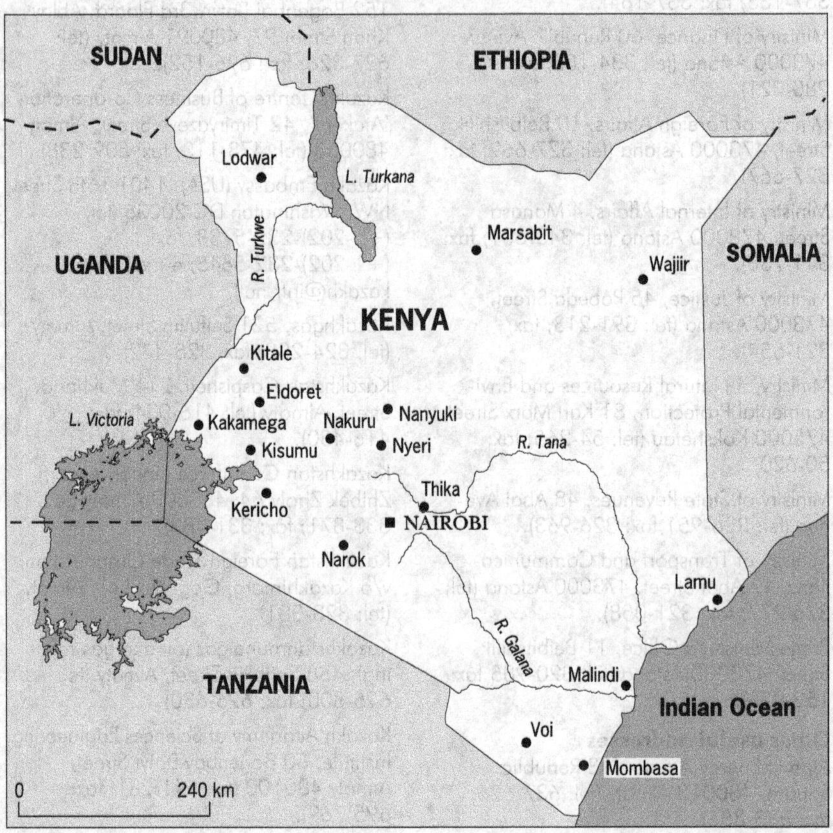

On his first presidential visit to Kenya, his father's homeland, in July 2015 the US President Barack Obama told Kenyans that there was 'no limit to what you can achieve.' Not many Kenyans could aspire to the presidency of their own country, never mind that of the US, but the US President's exhortation was aimed at improving the lot of the average Kenyan, by greater genuine democracy, reducing 'the cancer of corruption' and ending any social and political exclusion that was based on class, gender or ethnicity.

After a morning of talks with President Uhuru Kenyatta the US President was introduced to an audience of over 4,000 Kenyans by his sister, Auma Obama. The President told them that he was in Kenya 'As President of a country that sees Kenya as an important partner. I'm here as a friend who wants Kenya to succeed.'

Corruption

If Kenya was to succeed in any sense at all, then the most obvious area for improvement had to be that of corruption. According to an audit of the government finances, corruption in Kenya was simply sliding out of control – from an already low starting point. On the Transparency International 2014 *Corruption Perceptions Index* Kenya ranked an unsatisfactory 145 out of the 175 countries surveyed, down from 136 it had held in 2013. The slippage certainly endorsed the comments made in an interview with Agence France Presse by Kenya's high profile anti-corruption activist, John Githongo.

The interview was prompted by the publication of an official audit which found that only one per cent of Kenya government expenditure and one quarter of the entire US$16 billion budget was actually accounted for. Mr Githongo had made the claim that since President Kenyatta came to power in 2013, 'Corruption in Kenya had deepened and widened.' Alongside the depressing findings of the Auditor-General's report, there had been extensive press coverage of a number of other scandals related to government procurement and land grabbing.

Although the Kenyatta government had insisted that it was fighting corruption and had even suspended some ministers and officials on corruption charges. Mr Githongo dismissed the government's actions as simply paying 'lip service' to fighting corruption. President Obama had not stopped at his reference to describing corruption as a 'cancer'. In the same speech he had noted that 'Corruption is tolerated because that's how things have always been done.' President Obama said that money spent on bribes would be better paid to someone 'doing an honest day's work.'

Mr Githongo agreed, accepting that paying bribes to police and bureaucrats remained routine for ordinary Kenyans, but alleging that the current level of corruption was at a higher level than ever: ' It's clear we have reached a scale of looting that surpasses anything we've had in Kenyan history.'

Ironically, in 2002 Mr Githongo had been appointed 'anti-corruption czar' by the then Kenyan President Mwai Kibaki. Three years after his appointment, he had left the country after uncovering a US$770 million fraud. The earlier government of Daniel arap Moi, who had ruled for 24 years until 2002, was tainted by the US$1 billion gold subsidy fiddle known as Goldenberg. More recently, parliament had seen fit to query the tendering behind the new US$13.5 billion Mombasa-Nairobi railway line, a huge infrastructure project seen as essential to Kenya's economic growth. There had been suspicions that the railway was 'from the very beginning... engineered as a corrupt project.'

In response to the criticism, finance minister Henry Rotich had simply dismissed the auditor's report in a three-page statement that stated that his ministry 'had since established that there were no resources lost.'

Al Shabab

President Obama spoke of Kenya's challenge in dealing with attacks by the Somali Islamist militant group al Shabab and promised the United States would stand by Kenya as a 'partner'. In a speech on 25 July, he offered extra counter-terrorism training and funds.

Kenya's tourist industry has been hammered by attacks by al Shabab, which had raided a Nairobi shopping mall in 2013. The worst attack to date by al Shabab was that at the north-eastern Garissa University campus in April 2015. At least 147 people, mostly students, were killed by the Islamic extremists who after killing two security guards opened fire indiscriminately on students. Four of the gunman were eventually surrounded in a dormitory and died when their suicide vests detonated. This was the deadliest attack anywhere by the Somalia based al Shabab. Reportedly, the militants singled out Christians and shot them. Over 500 students managed to escape, 79 of whom were injured.

According to the London based British Broadcasting Corporation (BBC) al Shabab had attacked the university claiming to be at war with Kenya. Kenyan troops had entered Somalia in October 2011 attempting to stop the Islamists from crossing the border between the two countries and kidnapping Kenyans. However, this had achieved the opposite, prompting al Shabab to intensify its activity in Kenya. The group had been behind the 2013 Westgate shopping mall attack, when 67 people were killed.

In June 2014 Shabab militia had attacked Kenya's coastal population centres, this time killing over 60 people. The attacks apparently targeted non-Muslim Kikuyus, the tribe of President Uhuru Kenyatta. One high profile result of the attacks – which were close to the popular coastal resort of Lamu – was a sharp drop in tourism, which normally accounted for about 15 per cent of Kenya's gross domestic product (GDP). Inexplicably, President Kenyatta – after two days of silence – blamed the attacks on local political interests. This was interpreted as a political ploy to deflect blame on to the opposition at a time of unpopularity for the ruling Jubilee coalition.

Political activity in 2014 centred mostly on the call by both the opposition party, Coalition for Reforms and Democracy (CORD) and county governments – the latter mainly seeking amendments of the constitution – to raise national government financial transfers to county governments from 15 per cent to 45 per cent, as well as on the trials at the International Criminal Court (ICC) of the President of the Republic of Kenya, his deputy and a journalist. In December 2014, the trial of the president was dismissed because of insufficient evidence. The trial of his deputy and the journalist were continuing in 2015.

Spatial inclusion had been a challenge in Kenya since independence because of major differences in access to economic, political and social services, leading to political and ethnic conflicts with serious cases of fighting and displacement of persons in 1992, 1997 and 2007–08. The 2010 constitution attempted to address these differences by introducing 47 county governments and putting political, economic and social structures in place aimed at introducing equity in resource distribution. The national government was due to allocate at least 15 per cent of the latest audited accounts to the annual budgets of the county governments. The constitution also addressed marginalisation through affirmative

KEY INDICATORS — Kenya

	Unit	2011	2012	2013	2014	**2015
Population	m	*40.91	43.18	*41.80	*0.43	*44.08
Gross domestic product (GDP)	US$bn	34.80	40.70	55.24	60.77	*65.90
GDP per capita	US$	851	943	1,322	*1,416	*1,495
GDP real growth	%	5.0	4.6	5.7	5.3	*6.9
Inflation	%	14.0	9.4	5.7	6.9	*5.1
Exports (fob) (goods)	US$m	5,791.8	6,164.7	5,803.0	6,173.8	–
Imports (fob) (goods)	US$m	14,162.1	15,472.4	16,024.0	17,609.6	–
Balance of trade	US$m	-8,370.3	-9,307.8	-10,221.0	-11,435.8	–
Current account	US$m	-3,333.2	-4,253.0	-4,788.0	*-5,604.0	*-5,047.0
Total reserves minus gold	US$m	4,181.2	5,711.0	6,598.2	7,910.5	–
Foreign exchange	US$m	41,380.0	5,681.9	6,547.3	–	–
Exchange rate	per US$	84.99	85.58	86.85	90.56	–

* estimated figure ** forecast figure

action programmes and policies designed to redress any historical disadvantages.

The economy

In its 2015 *Africa Economic Outlook*, the African Development Bank (AfDB) noted that Kenya's GDP growth remained robust in 2013 at 5.7 per cent based on rebased statistics and stood at 4.4 per cent, 5.8 per cent and 5.5 per cent in the first three quarters of 2014 compared with 6.4 per cent, 7.2 per cent and 6.2 per cent in comparable quarters of 2013. According to the Central Bank of Kenya's (CBK) economic monthly review of November 2014, growth was mainly supported by expansion in construction, manufacturing, finance and insurance, information, communications and technology and wholesale and retail trade. The economy slowed in the third quarter of 2014, partly due to a sharp drop in tourism following the terrorist attacks in the country. Overall GDP growth was expected to amount to 6.5 per cent and 6.3 per cent in 2015 and 2016, respectively. Consumer price index (CPI) inflation was expected to remain in single digits, at around 5 per cent, during the same period.

The short- to medium-term positive growth projections were based on assumptions of increased rainfall for enhanced agricultural production, a stable macro-economic environment, continued low international oil prices, stability of the Kenya shilling, improvement in the security situation for a positive influence on the tourism sector; and reforms in the areas of governance and justice.

In its September 2015 overview of the Kenyan economy, the International Monetary Fund (IMF) considered Kenya's economic performance to have remained satisfactory despite headwinds from rising volatility in global markets and domestic security challenges. GDP growth has been robust and, notwithstanding the recent shilling depreciation, inflation had remained within the authorities' target range. External buffers to date had remained adequate.

In the view of the IMF, the Kenyan authorities' fiscal programme for 2015/16 sought to address persistent security challenges and infrastructure bottlenecks while preserving macro-economic stability. The authorities' commitments to contain current spending and mobilise additional revenue were welcomed by the IMF and were expected to contribute to mitigating excess demand pressures. Over the medium term, continued efforts were needed to boost fiscal space to accommodate development priorities and an orderly process for devolving fiscal responsibility to lower tiers of government while maintaining public debt sustainability.

Public financial management reforms – in particular the strengthening of capacity at the National Treasury's Debt Management Office and the introduction of the Treasury Single Account – should be decisively implemented. The authorities had taken a number of steps to strengthen expenditure control and improve the efficiency of public spending. However, the regional counties' access to the CBK's overdraft facility might complicate monetary policy implementation.

In conclusion, the IMF viewed recent decisive steps by the central bank to tighten monetary policy as appropriate. These steps would help contain the impact of the shilling depreciation on domestic prices and anchor inflationary expectations. The central bank remained committed to refraining from intervening in the foreign exchange market except for smoothing excessive exchange rate volatility.

Risk assessment

Economy	Fair
Politics	Fair
Regional stability	Fair

Muslims in Kenya

% of population	10
Sunni (% of Muslims)	93
Shi'a (% of Muslims)	5

COUNTRY PROFILE

1944 The Kenyan African Union (KAU) was formed to voice local demands for the return of native lands.
1947 KAU was led by Jomo Kenyatta, a prominent member of the Kikuyu tribe.
1952 A state of emergency was announced in response to guerrilla activity by the Kikuyu-led secret society, the Mau Mau. More than 13,500 Africans were killed during the uprising, compared to less than 100 Europeans.
1953 The KAU was suspended. Kenyatta was detained.
1957 Africans were elected to the Legislative Council and offered ministerial posts.
1960 A new constitution gave Africans a majority in the Legislative Council. The KAU split; the Kenya African National Union (Kanu) (which had a strong Kikuyu and Luo membership) and the Kenya African Democratic Union (Kadu) were established.
1961 Kenyatta was freed and became president of Kanu and leader of an all-party African government.
1963 The Republic of Kenya was proclaimed and Kenyatta became president.
1964 Kadu was dissolved.
1978 Jomo Kenyatta died and was succeeded as president by Daniel arap Moi.
1979, 1983 and 1988 Only Daniel arap Moi stood in presidential elections and was elected unopposed.
1992 After a lengthy period as, effectively, a one-party state, multi-party elections were held and President Moi was re-elected.
1997 President Moi and Kanu won the presidential and parliamentary elections.
1998 Terrorists blew up the US embassy in Nairobi; 244 people were killed and over 4,000 people were injured.
2001 President Daniel arap Moi appointed the opposition National Development Party (NDP) leader, Raila Odinga, to his 26-member cabinet, forming Kenya's first coalition government. International aid was withheld by the IMF when the government failed to implement anti-corruption measures.
2002 The NDP and Kanu announced a merger in the run-up to the general election. Uhuru Kenyatta became Kanu's presidential candidate, leading to a wave of defections, including Raila Odinga. Emilio Mwai Kibaki of the opposition, National Rainbow Coalition (Narc), won the presidential elections with 62.3 per cent of the vote.
2003 A draft constitution was presented to parliament, proposing a number of reforms.
2004 The deadline for the enactment of the long-awaited new constitution, which proposed restricting presidential powers and creating a post of prime minister, was missed. In a corruption survey Kenya was rated 129, out of 146, by the watchdog Transparency International, which said the problem remained 'rampant'.
2005 Justice and constitutional affairs minister, Martha Karua, was asked to prepare a bill for a new constitution. The Orange Democratic Movement (ODM) was formed, led by Raila Odinga and Kalonzo Musyoka.
2006 Finance minister, David Mwiraria, resigned in a corruption scandal. The police raided and closed down the premises of the Standard Media Group (publishers of the daily *The Standard* newspaper), drawing widespread international condemnation. The Chinese president, on a visit to Kenya, signed an offshore oil exploration agreement with Kenya. Uhuru Kenyatta was replaced as Kanu chairman by Nicholas Biwott; the High Court blocked the elections, pending a hearing of a challenge by Kenyatta.
2007 A new political party was formed, the Party of National Unity (PNU) out of the ruling Kanu coalition and other

pro-Kibaki political parties. In presidential elections the incumbent Mwai Kibaki (PNU coalition) won 46.6 per cent of the vote and his closest rival Raila Odinga (ODM) won 44.3 per cent. Widespread rioting broke out following the results and while international observers reported that polling had been 'relatively orderly and generally positive', the chief EU monitor said the Electoral Commission of Kenya had 'not succeeded in establishing the credibility of the tallying process'.

2008 An estimated 1,500 people died and 600,000 people were displaced in the violence following the presidential election, as distrust increased between the main tribal groups. President Kibaki opened parliament and called for members to become 'ambassadors of peace' in their constituencies and urged them to pass the four bills (the National Accord and Reconciliation Bill, the Constitutional Amendment Bill, the Truth Justice and Reconciliation Bill and the Ethnic Commission Bill) which formed part of the Kofi Annan-brokered agreement, whereby the ODM shared power with the PNU. President Kibaki announced a new cabinet, naming Raila Odinga (ODM) as prime minister. The formation of a tribunal to consider the violence during the last general elections was announced and parliament was given a deadline of 45 days to enact the tribunal or a sealed list of accused ringleaders would be given to the International Criminal Court (ICC). Some prominent politicians were thought to be on the list, making parliament wary of instigating further inquiries.

2009 A national emergency was declared as drought in the east threatened almost 10 million people with food shortages. Martha Karua, the first coalition minister, resigned as minister of justice. She had been a close ally of President Kibaki and resigned after he had appointed a number of judges without consulting her. After two years of low annual rainfall the Masinga dam hydroelectric power station was shut down for only the second time in the plant's 28-year history. The government decided to use local courts rather than a special tribunal to deal with post-election violence. However, the ICC confirmed it would proceed with prosecution of the leaders of post-election violence, saying Kenya had failed, for the third time, to set a deadline to establish the agreed tribunal. The ICC accused the police force, judiciary and Attorney General of failure to prosecute suspects locally. The US and EU imposed restrictions on senior officials travelling to the US and Europe.

2010 The US suspended US$7 million of funding for free primary schools. Prime Minister Odinga suspended William Ruto and Sam Ongeri, the ministers of agriculture and education for alleged corruption, only for President Kibaki to reinstate them a few hours later. A new constitution was agreed by 68.55 per cent of voters. The Second Republic was inaugurated. Although both political parties within the coalition government supported the new constitution, voting was generally along tribal lines with Kenya's largest tribe, the Kikuyu, voting 'yes', supported by the Luo, Luhya and coastal Muslims and Somalis. The Kalenjin voted against. In future a presidential candidate will require 50 per cent of the national vote and over 25 per cent of the vote in more than half of the electoral constituencies to succeed to the presidency. This was designed to achieve greater acceptance and appeal from a more diverse electorate for any presidential winner. The new constitution also includes significant reform to the judiciary. The ICC named six people they suspected of being behind the violence after the 2007 elections. The six included deputy prime minister and finance minister, Uhuru Kenyatta.

2011 One of the ministers named by the ICC, Henry Kosgey, resigned in January; he said he was stepping down to allow the accusations to be 'fully investigated'. Another of the accused, William Ruto, had already resigned. In March the ICC issued summonses for six persons accused of being behind the violence after the 2007 elections; they were ordered to attend the court in The Hague in April. In March, Kenya announced that it would challenge the ICC's right to prosecute six of its nationals, summoned to appear before it. In March, the General Service Union of the Kenyan police force crossed into Somalia at the border town of Liboi, to confront the militant forces of the al Shabab. It was the first time that Kenyan forces had directly fought al Shabab, which was accused of raids into Kenya. Four Kenyans who allege they were tortured during the suppression of the Mau Mau uprising of 1952–61 began legal proceedings against the UK government in April. Deputy Prime Minister Uhuru Kenyatta appeared at the ICC in April, along with two other supporters of the president. The three supporters of Raila Odinga had already appeared. Three refugee camps at Dadaab on Kenya's northern border were inundated by Somalis and Ethiopians seeking help as a two-year drought (the worst since late-1940s) caused widespread failure in crop and animal production. The camps, designed to house 90,000 people, had by July grown to 350,000. The UN estimated that 10 million people in the Horn of Africa were affected by drought and food insecurity. The first African woman to win the Nobel Peace Prize, Wangari Maathai, died in Nairobi in September. A conservationist, she founded the Green Belt Movement which has planted 20–30 million trees across the continent.

2012 The Kenyan army attacked al Shabab forces in Somalia in early January, following a warning from Western governments to their citizens of a credible risk of terrorist attack in Nairobi. This was the latest report of military activity by Kenya, which had been operating in southern Somalia since October 2011, in its efforts to deter insurgency and criminal activity threatening Kenya's tourist industry. On 21 January, the ICC ruled that six prominent Kenyans accused (in 2010) of orchestrating post-election violence in 2007 must stand trial. On 25 April, four senior judges were declared unfit for office by a newly formed committee that investigated the impartiality of the judiciary. The committee was constituted as part of the 2008 post-election agreement on political and judicial reform. In July, half a tonne of Kenyan ivory, worth an estimated US$700,000 was seized by Thai customs officials, being smuggled through Bangkok's airport. On 18 September, two mass graves of over 100 people were found in the village of Kilelengwani, the centre of a long-running dispute over water and grazing rights, between the mostly farming Pokomo people and the semi-nomadic cattle herders of the Orma in the coastal Tana Delta region. A number of politicians were accused of inciting violence ahead of parliamentary elections in March 2013. On 5 October, a UK High Court ruled that the three elderly Kenyans (who had started proceedings in 2011) had the right to sue the UK government for damages after they had been detained and tortured during the 1950s Mau Mau rebellion. Cattle rustlers in northern Samburu ambushed police officers, killing at least 42 and injuring others on 12 November. The authorities were attempting to retrieve stolen cattle when sophisticated weapons (including, rocket propelled grenades, anti-personnel mines and machine guns) were used to resist the recovery. On 13 November 2012, a new commuter train began operations, running from the centre of Nairobi to the suburb of Syokimau, where a new station was opened.

2013 On 9 March Uhuru Kenyatta was confirmed as the winner of the 4 March presidential election with 50.07 per cent. The result was unsuccessfully challenged by his main rival, Raila Odinga. President Kenyatta was sworn in on 9 April; William Ruto was signed in as Deputy President at the same time. The general election was won by President Kenyatta's Jubilee 3-party coalition (TNA, URP, and NARC) with a total of 167 seats (of 349 seats), followed by the CORD coalition with 141 seats. The Amani coalition came third with 24 seats. The Salaries and Remuneration Commission (SRC) announced on 12 June that an agreement had been reached to cut MP's salaries by US$45,000 to US$75,000 after a public outcry; protesters had denounced MPs as 'MPigs'. Kenyan MPs are among the highest paid in the world. A fire at Jomo Kenyatta International Airport in Nairobi on 7 August gutted the arrivals hall. Flights were diverted to Mombasa and Eldoret; there were concerns about fresh flower exports – Kenyan flowers account for 35 per cent of flowers imported into the EU. Restricted international flights resumed some 24 hours later. On 5 September an emergency debate to remove Kenya from the ICC was approved; the opposition Cord boycotted the debate. A bill is expected to be put to Parliament. Deputy President William Ruto left Nairobi for the Hague on 9 September. His trial started on 10 September. Two large aquifers have been found in the Turkana Basin and Lotikipi Basin in the northern Turkana region. The discovery was announced by Judi Wakhungu, the environment minister, at a meeting of Unesco in early September. She said the source could supply the country with water for the next 70 years. An attack by al Shabab militants on the Westgate shopping centre in Nairobi on 21 September resulted in the death of at least 67 people. The ICC agreed Mr Ruto could return to Nairobi for a week. Three days of mourning began on 25 September. On 28 September local media reported that the government had been warned of possible attacks in Nairobi and Mombasa. On 2 October the ICC ordered the arrest of a Kenyan journalist, Walter Osapiri Barasa, on charges that he had attempted to bribe witnesses in the trial of Deputy President Ruto. ICC chief prosecutor Fatou Bensouda called on Kenya to immediately arrest and transfer Mr Barasa to The Hague. Ojn 10 October lawyers of the President called for his trial to be abandoned after defence witnesses claimed they had been intimidated. On 18 September the ICC ruled that President Kenyatta is only required to be present at certain key parts of the case. Prosecutors successfully appealed against a decision by the ICC which would have allowed Deputy President Ruto to remain in Kenya. The ruling on 26 October said he could be excused only on a 'case by case' basis. Despite continued denials by the army that there had been any 'widespread looting' by its forces during the Westgate seige, two soldiers were reported sacked and jailed for looting, the army chief said on 29 October. At the end of October the ICC announced that President Kenyatta's trial would be postponed until 5 February 2014. A resolution to suspend for one year the trials of the president and vice-president at the ICC was rejected by the Security Council on 15 November.

2014 A single cross-border tourist visa for Burundi, Kenya and Uganda was launched on 20 February. The visa costs US$100 and is valid for 90 days. Tanzania and Rwanda are expected to join in the future. Uhuru Kenyatta appeared at the ICC on 8 October. He was present in a personal capacity having handed the presidency to Vice President Ruto while he was out of the country. This was the first time a serving president had appeared before the Court. Mr Kenyatta faces five charges relating to the ethnic massacres after the 2007 election. He is specifically accused of organising the Mungiki sect, an ethnic Kikuyu gang, to attack rival groups supporting Raila Odinga. Kenyan academic and pan-Africanist Ali Mazrui died on 13 October. A series of attacks by al Shabab, including 28 non-Muslem bus passengers on 22 November and 36 sleeping quarry workers near the town of Mandera in the north-east in the early hours of 2 December, lead to the resignation of police chief David Kimaiyo, and the dismissal of interior minister Joseph Ole Lenko on 3 December by the President. President Kenyatta had made an uncompromsing speech the day before, saying his country was fighting a 'war on terrorism'. On 5 December the ICC announced it was withdrawing charges of crimes against humanity against President Kenyatta. Lack of co-operation by the Kenyan government was cited as the main reason.

2015 US President Barack Obama arrived for a visit on 24 July.

Political structure

Constitution

The constitution was promulgated in 1963. In 1997, a number of constitutional changes took place; these allowed the formation of a coalition government, the review of the constitution by an independent commission and increased the number of directly elected seats in the Kenyan National Assembly from 188 to 210. A further 12 seats are nominated by the government.

A constitutional amendment affirming the National Assembly's supremacy and curbing the powers of the presidency was approved in 1999. This removed the president's right to appoint the clerk of the house, enabling the legislature to appoint and dismiss the clerk, who is no longer answerable to the president's office. The clerk manages everything from the National Assembly's agenda to its budget.

The country is divided into seven provinces run by provincial commissioners appointed by the president. The provinces are divided into districts run by district commissioners. Towns and districts have municipal and country councils, which are partly elected and partly nominated, but the commissioner has wider powers than the councils. The Nairobi area has a separate government-appointed city commission.

A referendum on constitutional amendments, held on 4 August 2013, passed by a majority of around two to one. It was signed into law by President Kenyatta on 27 August. In future a presidential candidate will require 50 per cent of the national vote and over 25 per cent of the vote in more than half of the electoral constituencies to succeed to the presidency. This is expected to achieve greater acceptance and appeal from a more diverse electorate for any presidential winner. The new constitution also includes significant reform to the judiciary. Other changes included a Deputy President, abolishing the prime minister and restoring the Senate as the upper house of parliament.

Form of state

Republic

The executive

Executive power in Kenya is in the hands of the president, assisted by the deputy president and cabinet, both named by the president. The president and deputy president are directly elected on the same ballot by qualified majority popular vote for a five-year term (eligible for a second term). As well as being required to win an absolute majority, a presidential candidate must also win 25 percent of the votes cast in each of more than half of the 47 counties to avoid a runoff.

National legislature

The bicameral Parliament includes the National Assembly (lower house) with 349 seats consisting of 290 members who are directly elected in single-seat constituencies by simple majority vote. 47 seats are reserved for women who are directly elected in single-seat constituencies by simple majority vote. The twelve remaining members are nominated by the National Assembly of which six represent youth and six represent the disabled. Members serve five-year terms.

The Senate (upper house, re-established under the 2010 constitution) consists of 67 seats of which 47 members are directly elected in single-seat constituencies by simple majority vote. 20 are directly elected by proportional representation vote made up of sixteen women, two representing youth and two representing the disabled. Members serve five-year terms.

Legal system

Kenya's legal system is based on English common law, Islamic law and tribal law, with a High Court and Court of Appeal. The Chief Justice of the Court of Appeal is appointed by the president.

Last elections

4 March 2013 (presidential and parliamentary).

Results: Presidential: Uhuru Kenyatta won 50.51 per cent of the vote, Raila Odinga won 43.70 per cent, all other candidates won less than 10 per cent.

Parliamentary (National Assembly): Orange Democratic Movement (ODM) total of 96 seats, including directly elected, women and nominated, (out of 349), The National Alliance (TNA) 89, United Republican Party (URP) of Kenya 75, Wiper Democratic Movement–Kenya (WDM-K) 26, United Democratic Forum Party (UDFP) 12, Forum for the Restoration of Democracy–Kenya (FORD–K) 10, Kenya African National Union (KANU) 6, New Ford Kenya (NFK) 6, Alliance Party of Kenya (APK) 5, Forum for the Restoration of Democracy–People (FORD–P) 4, Federal Party of Kenya (FPK) 3, National Alliance of Rainbow Coalition (NARC) 3. A coalition government (the Jubilee Coalition) was formed of the TNA, URP and NARC.

Parliamentary (Senate): Jubilee Coalition 30 seats out of 67 (21 elected + 9 nominated), CORD 27 seats (19 + 8), Amani 6 (4 + 2), APK 3 (2 + 1)

Next elections

2018 (presidential and parliamentary).

Political parties

Ruling party

Jubilee Alliance, a coalition led by The National Alliance (TNA) and including the United Republican Party (URP) and National Alliance of Rainbow Coalition (NARC) (elected 4 Mar 2013)

Main opposition party

Kenya African National Union (Kanu)

The high population density exerts pressure on land resources. It is estimated that 75 per cent of the population is confined to 10 per cent of the land area as most of the country is classified semi-arid or arid. Northern Kenya is arid and sparsely populated and most of its people lead a nomadic life.

Population

44.53 million (2013)

Last census: August 1999: 28,686,607

Population density: 52 inhabitants per square km. Urban population 22 per cent (2010 Unicef).

Annual growth rate: 2.7 per cent, 1990–2010 (Unicef).

Internally Displaced Persons (IDP)

350,000 (UNHCR 2004)

Ethnic make-up

Kenya is a multi-cultural society. Most of Kenya's people belong to 13 ethnic groups although there are a further 27 smaller groups. The majority of Kenyans belong to Bantu tribes such as the Kikuyu (22 per cent), Luhya (14 per cent) and Kamba (11 per cent). The Luo (13 per cent) are of Nilotic origin, as are the smaller Kalenjin (12 per cent), Maasai, Turkana and others.

The Kikuyu live in the central highlands and have traditionally been dominant in commerce and politics, although this is changing. A small European settler population remains in the highlands, involved in farming and commerce. In the north live the Somalis and the nomadic Hamitic peoples (Turkana, Rendille and Samburu); Kamba and Maasai peoples are concentrated in the south and eastern lowlands, and the Luo live around Lake Victoria.

Religions

Protestant (38 per cent), Roman Catholic (28 per cent), animist (26 per cent), Muslim (6 per cent), others (including small Hindu, Sikh and Jain minorities) (2 per cent).

Education

Education has expanded rapidly since independence in 1963. The number of primary schools has more than doubled, while that of secondary schools has increased eighteen-fold. Enrolment at primary schools has declined by 20 per cent since 1980, when the gross enrolment rate was 115 per cent (including repeaters).

Primary education begins at the age of six and is provided free of charge at state schools, however the lack of state funds compels schools to charge fees for books, electricity, water and upkeep, forcing children of poor families to either abandon learning early on or develop an erratic attendance record.

It has been estimated by Oxfam that 75 per cent of children aged six to 11 will enrol for school by 2015.

Secondary school enrolment has grown since 1980, when it was 20 per cent, but still covers only a small proportion of the relevant age group.

The present government, elected in December 2002, has pledged to introduce universal, free and compulsory primary education, an aim which will require higher levels of expenditure then currently spent.

Literacy rate: 84 per cent adult rate; 96 per cent youth rate (15–24) (Unesco 2005).

Enrolment rate: Unicef says the primary school population jumped from 5.9 million in 2002 to 7.6 million in 2005.

Pupils per teacher: 31 in primary schools.

Health

Improved water sources are available to 48 per cent of the population.

There were cases of polio reported to the World Health Organisation – Global Polio Eradication Initiative (WHO – Polio Eradication) in 2006; the country had previously been free of the disease and its re-emergence was due to infected travellers. In a synchronised campaign with Ethiopia and Somalia, inoculation began for under fives by WHO – Polio Eradication and the country's health authorities in 2006.

In 2007, it was estimated that around 10 per cent of the population were suffering from diabetes, but only 3.5 per cent were diagnosed. Around 85 per cent of the cases were type II diabetes, linked to an unhealthy diet of too much starchy food, high in sugars, salts and fats, and lack of exercise.

HIV/Aids

The number of HIV positive cases have fallen from a high of 4.5 million in 2000 to 2.1 million in 2004. HIV testing also improved with a 10-fold increase between 2002–04. Kenyan businesses were rated as best in the region for having HIV prevention programmes and providing their workers with condoms. In June 2006 the fee for anti-retroviral (ARV) drugs was removed in hospital and public clinics; this is expected to boost the number of Aids sufferers who undertake the course of treatment.

The national level of HIV/Aids infections is mixed, in urban areas rates have declined, however, infection figures for rural areas have yet to peak. Added to which, food shortages due to East Africa's worst drought in a decade, hampers Aids patients with their ARV treatment.

The annual loss in terms of GDP per capita growth are projected to be 1.3 per cent per annum between 2000–10.

Households, in which one family member dies of Aids, are estimated to lose between 49–78 per cent of their annual income.

Kenya's Population Council has reported that many women surveyed, knowing they were HIV positive had not disclosed their condition to their partners for fear of violence or abandonment.

The Kenyan government's annual expenditure on HIV/Aids amounts to 6.5 per cent of the annual healthcare budget.

HIV prevalence: 4 per cent (2006), down from 14 per cent in 1997 (UNAids 2006).

Life expectancy: 51 years, 2004 (WHO 2006)
Fertility rate/Maternal mortality rate: 4.7 births per woman, 2010 (Unicef); maternal mortality 590 per 100,000 live births (World Bank).
Child (under 5 years) mortality rate (per 1,000): 73 per 1,000 live births (WHO 2012)
Head of population per physician: 0.14 physician per 1,000 people, 2004 (WHO 2006)

Welfare

Approximately 47 per cent of the total population is under 15 years. Around 50 per cent of the population is thought to live on less than US$1 a day. Around 80 per cent of the population is at risk from drought, famine and HIV/Aids.
A social security system, administered separately from the government budget, covers only government employees and workers in the small modern sector of the economy. The welfare system is financed by the National Social Security Fund (NSSF), set up in 1965. The NSSF has approximately 2.7 million members. In theory, social security contributions are compulsory and are deducted from wages at source. Deductions range from one-thirtieth to one-tenth of earnings. The employer pays half of each employee's contribution. In practice, few families or small businesses enrol their servants or workers. In November 2001, President Moi announced the establishment of a mandatory National Social Health Insurance (NSHI) scheme that would cover all Kenyans.
Social security benefits are limited to survivor's benefit (paid on the death of contributor), invalidity benefit, withdrawal benefit (a fixed sum paid on retirement) and an emigration grant. There is no unemployment benefit. Every Kenyan is entitled to supplementary health benefit under the National Hospital Insurance scheme, founded in 1966.

Main cities

Nairobi (capital, estimated population 3.5 million in 2012, some 1,650 metres above sea-level), Mombasa (966,413), Nakuru (284,840), Eldoret (269,574), Kisumu (236,394), Ruiru (182,598), Thika (110,336).

Languages spoken

KiSwahili is the lingua franca. In addition, most tribes have their own language. English is universally used in business and spoken by most people in the tourist industry. Other languages are Gikuyu, Kiluhya, Dholuo, Kikamba, Maasai and Somali.

Official language/s

KiSwahili and English

Media

The press is lively and mostly free but can be subjected to extra-legal intimidation if it incurs the wrath of the authorities.
In August 2007 President Kibaki refused to sign a bill which could have forced reporters to reveal their sources. The bill was returned to parliament. Kenya has a lively media which has exposed corruption in government in the past.
On 31 October 2013 parliament passed a bill to set up a communications tribunal with the power to impose fines for breaching a code of conduct. It has still to be approved by the President before coming into law.

Press

Dailies: The Nation Media Group publishes the independent *Daily Nation* (www.nation.co.ke) in English and in KiSwahili *Taifa Leo*, other private publications include, in English, *The Standard* (www.eastandard.net) which is the oldest newspapers; the *Kenya Times* (www.timesnews.co.ke) and *The People Daily* are owned by political entities.
Weeklies: Some daily newspapers publish weekend editions, others include *Coastweek* (www.coastweek.com) from Mombassa and the *Weekly Advertiser*.
Business: The Nation Media Group publishes the *Business Daily* (www.bdafrica.com) and the weekly *The East African* (www.theeastafrican.co.ke). The *Business Mirror* is a fortnightly, promotional trade publication. The Centre for Business Information in Kenya (CBIK) (www.epckenya.org) publishes a number of specific marketing, sales, exports and business information pamphlets.
Periodicals: There are a number of general and specialised periodicals.

Broadcasting

The Kenya Broadcasting Corporation (KBC) (www.kbc.co.ke) is the state-run radio and television provider.
Radio: With high levels of poverty radio is the principal medium for news and information and with the significant expansion of FM radio, particularly ethnic stations which have increased public participation through call-in programmes radio provides an important medium for public debate. KBC (www.kbc.co.ke) operates extensive national services in English, Hindi, KiSwahili and 14 other local languages. Private radio stations include Capital FM (www.capitalfm.co.ke), Kiss FM (www.kissfm.co.ke) and a Christian station Family FM (www.familykenya.com). Coro FM and Radio Citizen in Kikuyu and East FM in Hindi.
Television: KBC (www.kbc.co.ke) operates one channel with programmes in KiSwahili and English it also runs Metro TV with a younger target audience. The satellite channel, Kenya Television Network (KTN) (www.ktnkenya.tv) broadcasts imported and locally produced programmes. Other, private TV stations include the Christian Family TV (www.familykenya.com), Stella TV and NTV (http://politics.nationmedia.com) run by Nation Media Group.
The Africa-wide Business Africa (www.business-africa.net) broadcasts news and business items over the internet in French and English.
National news agency: Office of Public Communications

Economy

Kenya is East Africa's largest economy, despite it being a predominantly rural (48.2 per cent of all land used for agriculture), low-income economy. Although heavily indebted to international lenders, Kenya managed to reschedule its Paris Club debts, to be paid within 20 years with 10-years grace, from 2004. Agriculture in 2014 provided over 29.3 per cent of GDP, rising from almost 25 per cent of GDP in 2007. With 75 per cent of the land area arid or semi-arid there is a high urban population, notably in the large shantytowns that skirt the major cities such as Nairobi.
As global trade picked up in 2010, Kenya recorded a peak growth in GDP of 8.4 per cent. The economy's expansion has slowed down since, but it has still been maintained at a high level. In 2012 growth had fallen to 4.6 per cent before increasing to 5.7 per cent in 2013. In 2014 growth was still robust at 5.3 per cent. According to the central bank growth was mainly supported by expansion in construction, manufacturing, finance and insurance, information, communications and technology, and wholesale and retail trade. Deceleration in the economy struck in the third quarter of 2014 as terrorist attacks led to a sharp drop in tourism.
In 2014, the UN Human Development Index (HDI) ranked Kenya 147 (out of 187) for national development in health, education and income. Since 2000, Kenya's progress has improved more than other sub-Saharan African countries. In 2014, 48 per cent of the population lived in multidimensional poverty, while 43 per cent lived on less than the equivalent of US$1.25 per day; the headcount poverty rate was 47.8 per cent of the population (2000–10). Unemployment remains high at around 40 per cent.
Remittances from migrant workers amounted to US$1.30 billion (5.4 per cent of GDP) in 2013, rising to US$1.44 billion in 2014 (2.4 per cent of GDP). Industrial activity provided 17.7 per cent of GDP in 2014, including

manufacturing's 10 per cent contribution to total GDP. The industrial sector is more diversified than in neighbouring countries and includes more private sector involvement. Industries include food processing, tobacco, beverages and transport. There are over 40 export-processing zones that provide facilities for manufacturers with over 70 per cent of all output exported to the US, under its African Growth and Opportunity Act.

There is a strong service sector, which accounts for over 53 per cent of GDP in mainly tourism and financial services and is a major source of employment and foreign exchange. Kenya's tourism industry was once again rocked in 2014 as Somali Islamic insurgents and pirates targeted Kenya's coastal resorts.

A serious obstacle to Kenya's development is the level of corruption and nepotism, in both government and business. Kenya is ranked 145, out of 175, in the Transparency International's Corruption Perceptions Index.

External trade

Kenya is a member of the East African Community (EAC) (with Burundi, Rwanda, Tanzania and Uganda). The East African Community Common Market Protocol (EACMP) was launched on 1 July 2010, which will lead to the free movement of labour, capital, goods and services between member states as well as employment opportunities and easier flow of investment capital. The signed protocol now requires that legislation in all states must be harmonised to conform to its jurisdiction.

Kenya is also a member of the Common Market for Eastern and Southern Africa (Comesa), which operates a free trade zone with 13 of the 19 member states and belongs to the InterGovernmental Authority on Development (IGAD), which offers regional help to members during times of drought and natural disasters as well as economic co-operation and integration.

Around 65 per cent of all exports are fresh flowers, fruit and vegetables, which are flown to European markets within hours of harvesting. This heavy reliance on airfreight leaves Kenya open to air traffic disruption – the Icelandic volcano eruption in 2010 cost Kenya millions of dollars of lost exports.

Exports accounted for 16.4 per cent of GDP in 2014, down from 17.9 per cent in 2013.

Imports

Principal imports are machinery and vehicles, petroleum, iron and steel, resins and plastics.

Main sources: India (18.3 per cent of total in 2013), China (12.9 per cent), UAE (8.3 per cent)

Exports

Principal exports are tea (typically over 25 per cent of total), horticultural products and coffee. Other exports include petroleum products, fruit and vegetables, cement and sisal.

Main destinations: Uganda (11.9 per cent of total in 2013), UK (7.9 per cent), Tanzania (7.7 per cent)

Agriculture

Farming

The agriculture sector generates some 60 per cent of export earnings and gives employment to 62 per cent of the workforce. Less than 20 per cent of Kenya's land surface is arable. There is an acute shortage of arable land and uneven distribution has resulted in most farmers working plots of two hectares or less. Population growth and rapid urbanisation has placed increasing pressure on food production and distribution to meet demand at affordable prices. In addition, there is an ecological risk to some of the most fertile areas of western and central Kenya, which are already severely overpopulated. Given the pressure on land, increased food production depends on the development of new high-yielding crops.

The principal cash crops are tea, coffee (mainly arabica grown by smallholders), sugar, cotton, sisal, tobacco, pineapples and wattle. Kenya produces high quality coffee, an average of one million bags per annum. Horticultural production has increased in importance and it is the second-largest export earner after tea with flowers making up the largest share (close to 40,000 tonnes).

Kenya's 200,000 or so farmers, who used to grow the natural pesticide, pyrethrum, have been badly let down over the years. The once globally dominant industry (as much as 70 per cent of world production) has dwindled as mismanagement of the Pyrethrum Board of Kenya (PBK) has forced farmers, many of whom haven't been paid for three years, to uproot their crops. In 2011 there was a move towards liberalisation of the industry, which would provide an alternative to the PBK, which had a monopoly on buying, processing and marketing the plant.

Kenya's growers of fresh flowers and vegetables are vulnerable to disruption of airfreight. For instance, the shutdown of air travel in Europe in April 2010, caused by the Icelandic volcanic ash cloud, resulted in the horticultural sector losing around US$3–4 million per day over the six-day period of closure. Millions of flowers and hundreds of tonnes of vegetables had to be discarded. From one refrigeration plant alone, in a two-day period, almost 65 tonnes of vegetables and 400,000 roses were dumped.

Despite the insecurity and harassing from bandits, a booming trade in livestock has thrived for more than two decades along the borders between Somalia, Ethiopia and Kenya. However, in 2011, this trade was badly affected by the drought, which covered the Horn of Africa region and the resultant high numbers of refugees who fled south from Somalia and Ethiopia into Kenya.

Fishing

Kenya has a coastline of 680km, as well as territorial waters in Lake Victoria and Lake Takana. Some 20,000 small fishermen along the coast have complained that large foreign boats are depriving them of their living. Although 60 boats, mostly from Europe and the Far East, have been licensed to fish, local fisherman estimate that some 200 boats are fishing in a single season. Most of the ships target prawns, yellow fin tuna and sharks. A report by the World Wide Fund for Nature (WWF) in 2014 shows that Kenya loses about US$118 million through illegal fishing by foreign boats each year. To tackle this the Kenyan government plans to invest in larger boats for Kenyan fisherman who would then be able to tackle larger catches and larger fish. It is hoped that this could drive out the illegal competition.

Forestry

Kenya has only 6.1 per cent of forest cover. Deforestation is a major problem along with desertification in northern regions.

Fuel wood and charcoal meet more than 75 per cent of the domestic energy requirement. The government is attempting to protect timber resources, which are being depleted by excessive demands. The government estimates that only 70 per cent of Kenya's wood fuel demands are met by regenerative growth. Meanwhile, the need for land for other purposes is placing increasing pressure on Kenya's forestry reserves.

Industry and manufacturing

Foreign investment, particularly from the UK, Japan and the US, plays a significant role. Emphasis is on developing joint venture, export-oriented industries and encouraging greater utilisation of local raw materials and other inputs. Large sections of industry continue to operate well below full capacity as a result of import controls, rising costs and marketing difficulties. Principal industries include food and tobacco processing, beverages, chemicals, machinery and transport equipment, textiles, glass, vehicle assembly and construction materials.

In 2014 the industrial sector contributed 17.7 per cent to GDP, around 10 per cent of which was derived from manufacturing. Industrial production grew by 4.7 per cent in 2014.

Tourism

The tourist industry is well established and Kenya offers a wide range of holiday destinations and for various pockets. Kenya's tourist assets are its wildlife, mostly accessible through a system of parks and reserves, extensive white sand beaches protected by coral reefs, and dramatic scenery from deserts to tropical rain forest. There are six sites on Unesco's World Heritage List.

Tourism is continually hampered by the insecurity derived from terrorist attacks. Visitor numbers in the first three quarters of 2015 fell by 4.3 per cent on the same period in 2014. In 2011, the country attracted 1.75 million international arrivals, down to 1.43 million by 2013.

Travel and tourism in total contributed 10.5 per cent of GDP in 2014, whilst employment directly and indirectly in tourism provided 543,500 jobs (9.2 per cent of the workforce).

In a move calculated to encourage tourists, Kenya, Rwanda and Uganda announced in November 2013 a joint visa scheme. The single cross-border tourist visa for Rwanda, Kenya and Uganda was launched on 20 February 2014. The visa costs US$100 and is valid for 90 days (see http://www.visiteastafrica.org/visa/ for details). Tanzania and Burundi are expected to join in the future.

Environment

Almost five tonnes of confiscated elephant ivory tusks, worth US$16 million, were destroyed on 20 July 2011. President Kibaki set the torch that burned the tusks, which were seized in Singapore, in a public display of combating the illegal poaching trade.

In July 2012 Thai customs officials seized almost 500,000 tonnes of Kenyan ivory, worth an estimated US$700,000, being smuggled through Bangkok's airport. The raw elephant tusks, poached in Kenya, were expected to be turned into jewellery or decorative carvings or used in traditional medicines.

Mining

Mining accounts for just 1 per cent of GDP. The sector is dominated by the production of industrial minerals such as soda ash, flourspar, kaolin and some gemstones. Gold is also produced in small quantities by artisanal gold miners. The government's policy is to encourage private sector participation in further exploration, prospecting and development of the mineral resources sector.

The most promising mining prospects are within the licences held by the Canadian mining company Tiomin Resources for deposits spanning four areas – Mambrui, Sokoke, Vipingo and Kwale – which hold 12 per cent of the world's rutile and ilmenite resources.

In August 2013 commissioner of mines, Moses Masibo, was suspended after the government revoked all prospecting and mining licences granted during the first five months of the year after complaints about the issuing process. Najib Balala, the mining minister, was reported as saying the licences in question had been issued in a hurry and without transparency.

Although Kenya is not considered a mineral rich country, recent discoveries of the rare mineral Niobium have encouraged a rush by local and international speculators. Mr Balala said that new legislation in the sector would include an increase in royalties on gold to 5 per cent of gross sales value from the current level of 2.5-3 per cent. Including rare earths, niobium and titanium ores, this would see royalties rise from 3 per cent of gross sales value to 10 per cent.

Hydrocarbons

Kenyan oil requirements are met by imports, which were 81,000 barrels per day (bpd) in 2013.

There has been limited exploration, but without tangible results. Interest has been ignited by discoveries in Sudan, which shares Kenya's geology, and by the increase in world oil prices. Companies from a number of countries, including China, are becoming increasingly involved in the possibility of locating reserves of oil and gas. The search is also being extended offshore to the Lamu basin.

A memorandum of understanding (MOU) was signed between South Sudan and Kenya on 24 January 2012, to build a new oil pipeline, taking South Sudanese oil to a Kenyan port for export. The pipeline will be built and owned by South Sudan and the two countries will negotiate transit fees for the oil through Kenya. On 2 March construction began on the US$23 billion port and oil refinery project in Lamu District. The presidents of Kenya, South Sudan and Ethiopia were at the launching ceremony, amid tight security in an area close to the border with war-torn Somalia. The project, known as the Lamu Port South Sudan Ethiopia Transit Corridor (Lapsset), is due to be completed by 2016, with initial investment from all three countries, with plans to attract international investment. Lapsset will be one of Africa's largest civil engineering projects. Lamu old town is included on Unesco's World Heritage List, leading to warnings from critics that the project could damage one of East Africa's most unspoiled environments.

Kenya does not currently produce or import natural gas.

Several Chinese firms have won deals to explore for coal in the Kitui basin. The Kitui basin is split into four blocks – A, B, C and D. In 2010 an estimated 400 million tonnes of coal reserves were confirmed in block C.

Energy

Installed generating capacity in 2013 was 1.7GW. Total electricity production in 2013 was 7.8 billion kWh, of which 67.3 per cent comes from renewable sources and the remainder from oil sources.

There are hydroelectric plants in the Tana River basin, a geothermal station at Olkaria, and at Kipevu, on the coast and a 75MW oil-fired plant, which was opened in 1999. In June 2008, the president announced that a plan to install around 1,700MW of geothermal energy by 2018 would begin and increase capacity by 150 per cent. The project is underway and centred just north of Nairobi.

The government has invested US$1.2 billion jointly with private companies to build solar power plants across the country. The plans include nine sites that in 2014 were claimed to provide half the country's electricity by 2016.

Financial markets

The NSE is small and somewhat speculative. It was established in 1954 and is sub-Saharan Africa's fourth-largest bourse. It originally operated as an association of stockbrokers with no trading floor until October 1991. The introduction of the trading floor has led to a substantial increase in trading volumes and dramatic upward movement in the various indexes. In 1995, foreign investors were allowed back into the NSE for the first time in 30 years. The NSE has been instrumental in enabling the public and private sectors in Kenya to raise large amounts of capital for expansion projects and for the financing of new businesses.

The public sale of shares in the mobile/cell phone company Safaricom, which was set at Ks5, when they went on sale on 9 June 2008, rose by 60 per cent in one day to Ks8. It was Kenya's record biggest stock market flotation and earned the government around US$833 from its 25 per cent stake in the company. The sale was over-subscribed by more than 500 per cent, with those successful receiving around 20 shares.

Stock exchange

Nairobi Stock Exchange (NSE). The Nairobi Stock Exchange was formed in 1954. It became fully automated in December 2007. The NSE 20 share index is expected to be joined by an all-share index in 2008.

Banking and insurance
Kenya contains a thriving community of foreign banks, which were attracted during the 1970s and 1980s by its reputation for political and commercial stability, good telecommunications infrastructure and the large number of multinationals based in the country. However, the sector is plagued by high levels of non-performing loans which threaten to undermine banking liquidity, affecting the wider economy.

Central bank

Central Bank of Kenya

Main financial centre

Nairobi

Time
GMT plus three hours

Geography
Kenya lies on the east coast of Africa. It is bounded by Ethiopia and Sudan to the north, Uganda and Lake Victoria to the west, Tanzania to the south and Somalia and the Indian Ocean to the east.

From the Indian Ocean, the land rises gradually through dry bush to the arable land of the highlands. The highest peak is Mount Kenya at 5,200 metres. The west of the country is dissected by the Great Rift Valley, partly filled by a chain of lakes.

Hemisphere

Straddles the equator

Climate
The climate is tropical in low-lying districts, especially along the coast, but is more temperate on the plateau and in the highlands. Kenya has two rainy seasons when temperatures can fall sharply: the long rains from April to June and the short rains in October and November. The hottest month is February, with temperatures of 20–30 degrees Celsius (C), while the coolest month is July, with temperatures of 11–22 degrees C. Nairobi, at an altitude of 1,661 metres, has a mean annual temperature of 17 degrees C and annual rainfall averaging 864mm.

Dress codes
A lightweight suit, collar and tie or other formal clothing should be worn for business meetings. Despite a hot tropical climate, nights can be cool and it is advisable to have a sweater to cover day wear, which should be light cotton casual at the coast. Warmer clothing is needed especially in June and July. Evening dress should normally be smart casual. Nairobi is considerably cooler than Mombasa.

Entry requirements
Passports

Required by all, valid for three months from date of entry.

Visa

Required by all, with the exception of nationals of some Commonwealth and other countries. Visas may be obtained from Kenyan missions or at the port of entry, although nationals of certain specified countries nationals must apply well in advance for referral to Nairobi. For a full list of each category and further details, visit www.kenyaembassy.co.uk.

In a move calculated to encourage tourists, a single cross-border tourist visa for Rwanda, Kenya and Uganda was launched on 20 February 2014. The visa costs US$100 and is valid for 90 days (see http://www.visiteastafrica.org/visa/ for details).

Currency advice/regulations

There are no restrictions on the import and export of local and foreign currencies, subject to declaration of amounts in excess of Ksh100,000.

US dollar or other hard currency travellers cheques are recommended.

Health (for visitors)
Mandatory precautions

Yellow fever vaccination certificate if arriving from an infected area.

Advisable precautions

Yellow fever, typhoid, tetanus, hepatitis A, meningitis and polio vaccinations. Malaria prophylaxis necessary for coastal and other lower altitude regions. Water precautions should be taken – bilharzia is present. Rabies is a risk in rural areas and vaccinations must be administered following a bites from any mammal.

Hotels
There is a wide range available in main centres. It is advisable to book well in advance during peak season (November–April).

Credit cards
Major cards are widely accepted.

Public holidays (national)
Fixed dates

1 Jan (New Year's Day), 1 May (Labour Day), 1 Jun (Madaraka Day), 10 Oct (Moi Day), 20 Oct (Mashujaa (Heroes) Day), 12 Dec (Independence/Jamhuri Day), 25–26 Dec (Christmas).

Holidays falling on a Sunday are observed the following Monday.

Variable dates

Good Friday, Easter Monday, Eid al Fitr.

Working hours
Banking

Mon–Fri: 0900–1400. Open first and last Sat in each month 0900–1100.

Barclays Bank, Kenyatta Avenue, Nairobi, open daily for foreign exchange until 1600.

Airport banks are open until midnight every day.

Business

Mon–Fri: 0800–1300, 1400–1700; Sat: 0830–1200/1230. Mombasa offices normally open and close half-an-hour earlier.

Government

Mon–Fri: 0800–1300, 1400–1700; Sat: 0830–1200/1230. Mombasa offices normally open and close half-an-hour earlier.

Shops

Mon-Fri: 0800–1700; Sat: 0830–1300. Many shops open outside these hours.

Telecommunications
Mobile/cell phones

GSM 900/1800 services are available, particularly in the south of the country.

Electricity supply
230/240V AC, 50 cycles. Subject to power surges outside main centres. Sockets are usually three-pin square (British type).

Social customs/useful tips
Personal contact is an important way of doing business in Kenya.

Bureaucracy can be frustratingly slow, although persistence pays. Going in person to the relevant office is often the best way of getting things done. Government and commercial offices are within easy walking distance of the main hotels.

Outside the major towns local customs vary from place to place. In the game parks and bush, some tribes do not like being photographed, although in areas where tourism is more developed, some tribe members will allow photographs for a fee. Visitors to game parks should not leave their vehicles without permission from the guide. There is a large Arab influence on the coast and most hotels display government signs saying nudity is banned. Topless bathing for women is, however, tolerated in areas where there are large concentrations of hotels.

Kenyans are friendly and open, and the greeting, *jambo*, will be returned with a smile.

It is prohibited to photograph the president or his residence, military, police or related installations.

Security
Security is not a problem in the major towns during the day but flashy displays of jewellery are not recommended. Do not carry large amounts of cash.

Nairobi is practically deserted after 2200. Walking around the African quarters of town without a guide or in the shanty towns around the capital is not advised.

Visitors are advised to avoid political meetings and demonstrations.

Incidents of armed car-hijacking are prevalent in Nairobi and Mombasa.

Do not attempt to escape from hijackers or resist their demands.

Getting there

A fire at Jomo Kenyatta International Airport in Nairobi on 7 August 2013 gutted the arrivals hall. Flights were diverted to Mombasa and Eldoret; there were concerns over fresh flower exports – Kenyan flowers account for 35 per cent of flowers imported into the EU. Restricted international flights resumed some 24 hours later.

Air

National airline: Kenya Airways

International airport/s: Nairobi – Jomo Kenyatta International (NBO), 17km from city, duty-free shop, bar, restaurant, buffet, bank, post office, shops, car hire. Mombasa – Moi International Airport (MBA), duty-free shop, bar, restaurant, buffet, bank, post office, shops, car hire. Eldoret International Airport (EDL), 16km from city, open 03.30-17.30 only (2013), mainly cargo.

Other airport/s: Mombasa – Moi International (MBA), 13km south-east of city, duty-free shop, bar, restaurant, bank, post office, shops, car hire. Medium-sized airports have also been developed at Eldoret, Kisumu and Malindi.

Airport tax: US$20, usually included in ticket price.

Surface

Road: Entry by road from Uganda, Ethiopia, Sudan and Tanzania can be difficult. Regulations and conditions should be checked with Kenyan authorities before travelling.

An all-weather road links Nairobi to Addis Ababa (Ethiopia) and there is a 590km road link between Kitale and Juba (Sudan).

In rural areas, some of the unsurfaced roads can be difficult in wet weather.

Rail: A 1,085km main line runs from the port of Mombasa through Nairobi, Nakuru and Eldoret to Uganda. There is also a link to Moshi (Tanzania).

Main port/s: Mombasa

Getting about

National transport

Air: Kenya Airways operates regular services linking Mombasa, Malindi, Kisumu and other major centres with Nairobi. Local light aircraft companies fly regular services to smaller airfields, such as Lamu, a tourist attraction on the coast.

Charter flights are also available to game reserves, such as Maasai Mara, and main centres.

Road: The growth in road transportation has led to overloading of some highways, and both the maintenance and improvement of these routes have been neglected. This also applies to roads which come under the jurisdiction of town authorities.

Nearly all main towns are connected by good surfaced roads. In rural areas some of the unsurfaced roads can be difficult in wet weather.

Long-distance (Peugeot) taxi service operates between towns. Cars can be shared, although it is not generally recommended.

Buses: Coach services operate on all major routes between towns and cities and into Tanzania, Ethiopia and Uganda.

Rail: The Kenya Railways system comprises approximately 1,920km of one metre gauge single track.

There are departures daily, with first- and second-class service, from Nairobi to Mombasa; the overnight service is popular. Journey time is approximately 14 hours. Trains often run late, but are fairly comfortable. It is advisable to book sleeping compartments in advance.

Two Uganda-Kenya railway agreements were signed in April 2006. In Uganda a concession agreement covers the freight services of Uganda Railways Corporation (URC), while an Interface agreement covers matters common to the Kenya freight and passenger concession and the Uganda freight concession. The Rift Valley Railways Consortium (RVRC) will invest US$15 million over the first five years and a further US$75 million over the remainder of the agreement in Uganda and US$45 and US$300 million respectively in Kenya.

City transport

Taxis: Available in most major towns. Some licensed taxis are metered and often shared, with fares according to time and distance. Fares for long trips should be agreed in advance.

Buses, trams & metro: Good and fairly cheap services operate regularly in Nairobi and Mombasa and between towns and cities, as well as across the borders to Tanzania, Ethiopia and Uganda. Minibuses and vans (*matatu*) are unregulated and can be overcrowded; they are not recommended for visitors.

Trains: A fast communter train between the eastern suburb of Syokimau and Nairobi's city centre was inaugurated by President Kibaki in November 2012. The journey takes 15 minutes compared to a two hour road trip in rush-hour.

Car hire

Can be hired from travel operators and hotels in Nairobi, Mombasa and Malindi. A national or international driving licence which has been held for at least two years without endorsements, including the period of visit to Kenya, is required .

BUSINESS DIRECTORY

The addresses listed below are a selection only. While World of Information makes every endeavour to check these addresses, we cannot guarantee that changes have not been made, especially to telephone numbers and area codes. We would welcome any corrections.

Telephone area codes

The international direct dialling (IDD) code for Kenya is +254, followed by area code and subscriber's number:

Eldoret	53	Malindi	42
Garissa	46	Mombasa	41
Kajiado	45	Nairobi	20
Kericho	52	Naivasha	50
Kisumu	57	Nakuru	51
Kwale	40	Voi	43

Mobile phones – Celtel: 733

Mobile phones – Safaricom 722

Chambers of Commerce

Kenya National Chamber of Commerce & Industry, Ufanisi House, Haile Selassie Avenue, PO Box 47024, Nairobi (tel: 220-867; fax: 334-2934; e-mail: kncci@swiftkenya.com).

Banking

African Banking Corporation Ltd, PO Box 46452, Mezzanine Floor, ABC-Bank, Koingange Street, Nairobi (tel: 223-922, 251-540/1, 226-712, 248-978; fax: 222-437).

Barclays Bank of Kenya Ltd, PO Box 30120, Barclays Plaza, Loita St, Nairobi (tel: 214-270, 313-405; fax: 213-915, 215-418).

The Co-operative Bank of Kenya Ltd, PO Box 48231, Union Towers, Kenya-Re Plaza - Taifa Rd, Moi Ave, Nairobi (tel: 225-579, 228-453/7, 251290/9; fax: 229-38, 246-635, 227-747).

Commercial Bank of Africa Ltd, Commercial Bank Building, Standard/Wabera Streets, Nairobi (tel: 228-881; fax: 335-827, 340-157).

Development Bank of Kenya Ltd, PO Box 30483, Finance House, Loita Street, Nairobi (tel: 340-401, 340-402, 340-403; fax: 338-426).

Imperial Bank Ltd, PO Box 44905, 8th Floor, IPS Bldg, Kimathi St, Nairobi (tel: 252-175/6/7/8, 252-184/5, 225-060; fax: 230-994, 250-137).

Investments & Mortgages Bank Ltd, PO Box 30238, I & M Bank House, 2nd Ngong Avenue, Nairobi (tel: 711-994-8, 310-105-7; fax: 713-757, 716-372).

Kenya Commercial Bank Ltd, PO Box 48400, Moi Avenue, Nairobi (tel: 339-441; fax: 215-565).

National Bank of Kenya Ltd, PO Box 72866, National Bank Building, Harambee Avenue, Nairobi.

Standard Chartered Bank Kenya Ltd, PO Box 30003, Stanbank House, Moi Avenue, Nairobi (tel: 330-200, 331-210; fax: 214-086).

Central bank
Central Bank of Kenya, Haile Selassie Avenue, PO Box 60000-0200 Nairobi (tel: 286-1000; fax: 340-192; e-mail: info@centralbank.go.ke).

Stock exchange
Nairobi Stock Exchange, Kimathi Street, IPS Building, 2nd Floor, PO Box 43833, Nairobi (tel: 230-692; fax: 224-200). www.nse.co.ke

Travel information

Automobile Association of Kenya, AA House, Embakasi, PO Box 40087, Nairobi (tel: 825-060; fax: 825-068; e-mail: aakenya@africaonline.co.ke).

Air Kenya, Wilson Airport, PO Box 30357, Nairobi (tel: 605-745; fax: 602-951; e-mail: resvns@airkenya.com).

Kenya Airways, Airport North Road, Embakasi, PO Box 19142, Nairobi (tel: 642-2000; fax: 823-488).

Kenya Railways, PO Box 30121, Nairobi (tel: 221-211; fax: 340-049).

Ministry of tourism
Ministry of Tourism and Wildlife, Utalii House, Uhuru Highway, PO Box 30027, Nairobi (tel: 333-555; fax: 318-045; e-mail:info@tourism.go.ke).

National tourist organisation offices
Kenya Tourist Board, Kenya-Re Towers, Ragati Road, PO Box 30630, Nairobi (tel: 711-262; fax: 719-925; e-mail: info@kenyatourism.org).

Ministries

Ministry of Agriculture, Livestock Development and Marketing, Kilimo House, Cathedral Road, PO Box 30028, Nairobi (tel: 718-870; fax: 725-774).

Ministry of Commerce and Industry, Co-operative House, Haile Selassie Avenue, PO Box 30430, Nairobi (tel: 340-010, 340-224; fax: 218-845).

Ministry of Energy, Nyayo House, Kenyatta Avenue, PO Box 30582, Nairobi (tel: 333-551).

Ministry of the Environment and Natural Resources, Kencom House, Moi Avenue, PO Box 30126, Nairobi (tel: 229-261).

Ministry of Finance, Treasury House, Harambee Avenue, PO Box 30007, Nairobi (tel: 338-111; fax: 330-426).

Ministry of Information and Broadcasting, Jogoo House 'A', Taifa Road, PO Box 30025, Nairobi (tel: 334-688; fax: 340-659).

Ministry of Planning and National Development, PO Box 3007, Nairobi (tel: 338-111; fax: 330-426).

Ministry of Transport and Communications, Transcom House, Ngong Road, PO Box 52692, Nairobi (tel: 729-200; fax: 726-362).

Office of the President, Harambee House, Harambee Avenue, PO Box 30510, Nairobi (tel: 227-411; fax: 723-666).

Other useful addresses

Agricultural Development Corporation, PO Box 30367, Nairobi (tel: 338-530).

Attorney-General's Office, State Law Office, Harambee Avenue, PO Box 40112, Nairobi (tel: 227-461; fax: 211-082).

British High Commission, Bruce House, Standard Street, PO Box 30465, Nairobi (tel: 335-944; fax: 333-196); Commercial Section, Upper Hill Road, PO Box 30133, Nairobi (tel: 714-699; fax: 719-082; e-mail: bhctrade@users.africaonline.co.ke).

Capital Markets Authority (CMA), Re-Insurance Plaza, Taifa Rd, PO Box 74800, Nairobi (tel: 221-910/869; fax: 216-681).

Central Police Station, University Way, Nairobi (tel: 222-222).

Central Reference Library, Ministry of Information, Department of Information, PO Box 8053 or 30025, Nairobi (tel: 223-201).

Communications Commission of Kenya (CCK), 5th Floor, Longonot Place, Kijabe Street, PO Box 14448, Nairobi 00800 (tel: 240-165, 250-173, 310-083/4; fax: 252-547; internet site: http://www.cck.go.ke).

Customs and Excise, PO Box 40160, Nairobi.

Development Finance Company of Kenya, Finance House, Loita Street, PO Box 30483, Nairobi (tel: 340-401; fax: 338-246).

East African Report on Trade and Industry, PO Box 30339, Nairobi.

Economic Development for Equatorial and Southern Africa, PO Box 56038, Nairobi (tel: 822-920/4; fax: 822-925/907).

Executive Secretariat and Technical Unit (ESTU), Anniversary Towers, University Way, 7th Floor, PO Box 34542, Nairobi (tel: 222-127/57/68; fax: 216-945).

Export Processing Zones Authority (EPZA), British American Centre, Mara Rd, PO Box 50563, Nairobi (tel: 712-800/6; fax: 713-704).

Export Promotion Council (EPC), Anniversary Towers, 1st Floor, University Way, PO Box 40247, Nairobi (tel: 228-534/5; fax: 218-013).

Federation of Kenya Employers (FKE), Argwings Kodhek Road, PO Box 48311, Nairobi (tel: 721-929; fax: 721-948).

Horticultural Crops Development Authority (HCDA), Uniafric House, Koinange St, PO Box 42601, Nairobi (tel: 337-381/3).

Industrial and Commercial Development Corporation, Uchumi House, Nkrumah Avenue, PO Box 45519, Nairobi (tel: 229-213; fax: 333-880).

International Finance Corporation, View Park Towers, PO Box 30577, Nairobi (tel: 224-726; fax: 219-980).

Kenya Association of Manufacturers (KAM), Mpaka Rd, Westland, PO Box 30225, Nairobi (tel: 746-005/7; fax: 746-028).

Kenya Association of Tour Operators (for information on conference facilities throughout Kenya), PO Box 48461, Nairobi (tel: 227-005).

Kenya External Trade Authority, PO Box 43137, Nairobi (tel: 226-016).

Kenya Investment Authority, National Bank of Kenya Building, Harambee Avenue, PO Box 55704, Nairobi (tel: 221-401; fax: 243-862; e-mail: info@investmentkenya.com).

Kenya Power Company Limited, Stima Plaza, Kolobot Road, PO Box 47936, Nairobi (tel: 741-181/9; fax: 337-351).

Kenya Revenue Authority, Tax Programmes and New Business Initiatives, Nairobi (tel: 715-428; fax: 715-432).

Kenya Tea Development Authority, Commonwealth House, Moi Avenue, Nairobi (tel: 221-441).

Kenyan Embassy (USA), 2249 R Street, NW, Washington DC 20008 (tel: (+1-202)-387-6101; fax: (+1-202)-462-3829; e-mail: info@kenyaembassy.com).

Kenyatta International Conference Centre, PO Box 30746, Nairobi (tel: 332-383).

US Embassy, Corner Moi and Haile Selassie Avenues, PO Box 30137, Nairobi (tel: 334-141; fax: 340-838).

National news agency: Office of Public Communications, PO Box 45617; KICC Building, 3 Floor, 8 Harambee Ave, 00100 Nairobi (tel: 202 224-0488; fax: 202 240-600; email: comms@comms.go.ke).

Internet sites

Africa Business Network: http://www.ifc.org/abn

AllAfrica.com: http://allafrica.com

African Development Bank: http://www.afdb.org

Africa Online: http://www.africaonline.com

KenyaWeb: http://www.kenyaweb.com/

Kiribati

KEY FACTS

Official name: Ripaberikan Kiribati (Republic of Kiribati) (pronounced Kiribas)

Head of State: President (Beretitenti) Anote Tong (BTK) (since 2003: re-elected 13 Jan 2012)

Head of government: President (Beretitenti) Anote Tong

Ruling party: Boutokan te Koaua (BTK) (Pillars of Truth) (since 2003; re-elected 28 Oct 2011)

Area: 810 square km (33 islands and atolls)

Population: 110,000 (2014)*

Capital: Bairiki (on Tarawa)

Official language: I-Kiribati, English

Currency: Australian dollar (A$) = 100 cents)

Exchange rate: A$1.43 per US$ (Sep 2015)

GDP per capita: US$1,647 (2014)*

GDP real growth: 3.80% (2014)*

GDP: US$181.00 million (2014)*

Inflation: 2.09% (2014)*

Balance of trade: -US$88.96 million (2012)

Foreign debt: US$34.00 million (2012)*

* estimated figure

Gross domestic product (GDP) growth in 2014 was 3.0 per cent, slightly upfrom 2 per cent in 2013, largely due to a 34 per cent increase in fishing licence revenues and continued construction projects largely financed by aid.

Revenues from fishing licence fees continued their strong performance for a third consecutive year, with 2014 revenues again exceeding budget projections. As parties to the Nauru Agreement, Kiribati benefits from rising rates under a vessel day scheme, wherein foreign fishing vessels are charged by the number of days they spend in Kiribati waters. Never the less, Kiribati recorded a large current account deficit, equivalent to 30.2 per cent of GDP, from substantial imbalances in the merchandise and services accounts.

A weaker Australian dollar, particularly in the middle of 2013, brought inflation back to Kiribati, but it remained low at 2.0 per. Inflation is generally expected to be similar to that experienced in Australia, which targets inflation within a band of 2–3 per cent. Over 2014 and 2015, inflation is projected to remain at 2.5 per cent.

Infrastructure upgrades are expected to drive growth over the next 2 years so that the economy is projected to grow by 3.0 per cent in 2014 and 2.0 per cent in 2015 as construction picks up on projects funded by development partners, including upgrades of the airports at Tarawa and Kiritimati and of the South Tarawa Road, and the extension of Betio Port.

The government plans higher recurrent expenditures, to be financed in part by the continuing strength of fishing licence revenues and budget support grants, and higher capital spending associated with ongoing infrastructure projects.

COUNTRY PROFILE

1892 Kiribati became part of the British colony of the Gilbert and Ellice Islands and was administered by the West Pacific High Commission in Fiji.

1942 The islands were occupied by the Japanese during World War II.

1957 Christmas Island (now renamed Kiritimati) became a site for British nuclear testing. The tests went on for six years.

1963 Transition to independence began, with the formation of legislative and executive councils under the supervision of a British governor general.

1975 Ellice Islands seceded and formed the separate entity of Tuvalu.

1979 Became the fully independent Republic of Kiribati.

1982–91 Iremia Tabai won the first three post-independence presidential elections in 1982, 1983 and 1987. Constitutional restrictions prevented Tabai contesting the 1991 elections that were won by Teatao Teannaki.

1994 Teburoro Tito of the Mwaneaaban te Mauri Party (MMP) was elected president.

1995 The government unilaterally moved the International Date Line eastwards to ensure the country's collection of islands were all designated as being within the same day.

1997 China built a satellite-tracking base on Kiribati's main atoll on a 15-year lease.

1998 President Tito was elected to his second term.

2000 Caroline Island was the first inhabited place to greet the new century, the name of the island was changed in celebration of the event to New Millennium.

2001 The Pacific Islands Forum, of which Kiribati is a member completed its negotiations to bring 14 Pacific island countries into a free trade agreement, known as the Pacific Islands Countries Trade Agreement (PICTA). The government of President Tito suffered heavy losses in the second round of parliamentary elections.

2002 Parliament passed newspaper registration laws, giving powers to ban the publication of newspapers that face complaints.

2003 Teburoro Tito (MMP) won presidential elections. President Tito lost a motion of no confidence and parliament was dissolved. In the resulting general elections the ruling MMP won 16 seats, the Boutokaan te Koaua (BTK) (Pillars of Truth) won 17. Anote Tong (BTK) was elected president. Kiribati established diplomatic relations with Taiwan, but also offered to honour the lease of the satellite tracking station with China; however, China rejected the offer, dismantled the station and severed diplomatic relations.

2005 Kiribati joined the International Whaling Commission.
2006 Kiribati designated an area of 184,700 square km in the Phoenix Islands as the world's third largest marine reserve. Kiribati appealed to the United Nations for action on global warming amid concerns about rising sea levels.
2007 The BTK won parliamentary elections with 18 seats. MTM won seven and independents 19 seats. In presidential elections, incumbent Anote Tong won about 65 per cent of the vote, his next closest rival, Nabuti Mwemwenikarawa, won about 33 per cent.
2008 The Phoenix Islands Protected Area was increased to 410,500 square kilometres to become the world's largest marine reserve.
2010 Air Pacific resumed its services (cancelled in 2008) following the upgrade of the airstrip on the island of Kiritimati. The UK's *The Sunday Times* alleged that Kiribati (among other countries) was bribed by Japan to vote in favour of Japan's killing of whales for scientific reasons at the International Whaling Commission. The denial by Kiribati of the allegation was based on the government's stance that 'everything has to be harvested in a sustainable manner' and all travel expenses were paid for from a fund provided by donor countries.
2011 The World Bank provided US$2 million in emergency funding for importing food for 60,000 people (60 per cent of the population) due to food shortages that resulted from a government funding shortfall for shipping costs. Since 2008, Kiribati experienced both extreme weather and adverse financial conditions that drained public coffers so that rising shipping costs reduced the quantity of affordable foods. The grant paid for shipping costs, specifically to outer islands. In parliamentary elections held in October, the BTK won 15 seats, United Coalition Party (UCP) 10, Maurin Kirbati Pati three; all remaining seats were won by independents.
2012 In the presidential election held on 13 January, incumbent Anote Tong (BTK) won 42.18 per cent of the vote, Tetaua Taitai 35 per cent and Rimeta Beniamina 22.8 per cent; turnout was around 68 per cent. On 9 March the government approved the purchase 6,000 acres of land in Fiji to accommodate the entire population of Kiribati. According to President Tong, this measure is a last resort to be used when rising sea levels inundate Kiribati. On 12 April the Kiribati Development Plan 2012–15 (KDP) was approved by the cabinet. On 24 July, the plane wreckage of US aviator Amelia Earhart was located on a reef off a remote Kiribati island.
2013 In early October President Tong said that he was concerned by the new government in Australia's scrapping of its Climate Commission. He pointed out that Australia, unlike many of the low-lying Pacific islands, was not so vunerable to the effects of climate change.
2014 King tides caused damage to five islands in Kiribati on 3 March. Most of the damage was to Marakei Atoll (population 2,872), with approximately 44 homes damaged and evacuees sheltering in community halls. There is also damage to sea walls and causeways on the main island, Tarawa. Access to clean drinking water is a key concern as groundwater sources have been contaminated.
2015 Cyclone Pam passed over Kiribati on 11 March, causing some damage and flooding, destroying causeways between the islets.

Political structure

Constitution
The 1979 constitution created an independent republic with a president as head of state, executive government, judicature and public service. A provision for citizenship of Kiribati also includes special status of Banaba and Banabans, as well as fundamental rights of freedom for individuals.

Form of state
Independent democratic republic; it is a member of the Commonwealth.

The executive
Executive power is exercised by a popularly elected *beretitenti* (president), for a four-year term, limited to three terms. The president is elected by the people from among three candidates nominated by the Maneaba (house of assembly) from its ranks. The president is head of state and head of government and appoints a cabinet composed of a president, vice president, 10 ministers from the house of assembly and an *ex officio* attorney general.

National legislature
The unicameral Maneaba Ni Maungatabu (House of Assembly) consists of 46 members elected for four-year terms in multi-seat constituencies, with 44 directly elected. One appointed member represents the Banaban community (most of whose inhabitants were evacuated from the Banaba Island during phosphate mining and now live on Rabi Island in Fiji). The speaker is an appointed post from outside the membership of the house of assembly and the attorney general is an *ex officio* post.
Universal suffrage begins at aged 18.

Last elections
21/28 October 2011 (parliamentary); 13 January 2012 (presidential)
Results: Parliamentary: Boutakaan Te Koaua (BTK) (Pillars of Truth) won 15 seats (out of 44), United Coalition Party (UCP) 10, Maurin Kirbati Pati (MKP) three, Independents won the remaining 16 seats.
Presidential: Anote Tong (BTK) won 42.18 per cent of the vote, Tetaua Taitai 35.02 per cent and Rimeta Beniamina 22.80 per cent; turnout was around 68 per cent.

Next elections
October 2015 (parliamentary); 2017 (presidential)

Political parties

Ruling party
Boutokan te Koaua (BTK) (Pillars of Truth) (since 2003; re-elected 28 Oct 2011)

Main opposition party
United Coalition Party (UCP)
Overpopulation is a problem, particularly on Tarawa, which has some 30,000 inhabitants. Nearly 3,000 i-Kiribati have resettled on Kiritimati (formerly Christmas Island), the country's easternmost island, the largest coral atoll in the world. Tabuaeran (formerly Washington) and Teraina (formerly Fanning) are also being resettled.

KEY INDICATORS — Kiribati

	Unit	2011	2012	2013	2014	**2015
Population	m	*0.11	*0.11	0.11	*0.11	*0.11
Gross domestic product (GDP)	US$bn	0.17	0.17	0.18	*0.18	*0.17
GDP per capita	US$	1,593	1,633	1,676	*1,647	*1,511
GDP real growth	%	1.8	2.8	2.4	*3.8	*2.9
Inflation	%	2.8	-3.4	-1.5	2.1	*1.4
Exports (fob) (goods)	US$m	11.5	10.2	–	–	–
Imports (fob) (goods)	US$m	86.3	99.2	–	–	–
Balance of trade	US$m	-74.8	-89.0	–	–	–
Current account	US$m	-38.0	-51.0	*-39.0	*7.0	*-41.0
Exchange rate	per US$	0.96	0.95	1.12	1.43	–

* estimated figure ** forecast figure

Population

105,000 (2012)*
Last census: 7 December 2005: 92,533
Population density: 124 inhabitants per square km (2010). Urban population 44 per cent (2010 Unicef).
Annual growth rate: 1.6 per cent, 1990–2010 (Unicef).

Ethnic make-up

Predominantly Micronesian, with some Polynesian.

Religions

Roman Catholic (52 per cent), Protestant (Congregational) (40 per cent), Seventh-Day Adventist, Islam, Baha'i Faith, Latter-day Saints and Church of God.

Education

The Junior Secondary School (JSS) programme aims to provide universal access to basic secondary education. Almost all the outer islands (except Teraina and Tabuaeran) and South Tarawa have junior secondary schools.
Higher education, including both university level programmes and post-secondary vocational/technical training, is provided by the government and the regional institution, University of the South Pacific (USP). The government also operates two tertiary institutions on South Tarawa: Tarawa Technical Institute and Kiribati Teachers College.
Literacy rate: 92.2 per cent, adult rate.
Compulsory years: six to 15
Enrolment rate: 67.8 per cent gross school enrolment.

Health

The government has collaborated with the World Health Organisation (WHO) to strengthen its primary healthcare services. WHO's technical support has brought down the infant mortality rate and increased life expectancy.
Improved water sources are available to 47 per cent of the population.
There is one general hospital in Tarawa and a number of health centres in the more populated islands. There are few doctors. Medical facilities are of the most basic kind and there are no pharmacies.
Excessive alcohol consumption has become a very severe problem both socially and medically. Diabetes linked to a western diet is widespread.

HIV/Aids

There has been a significant increase in infections on Tarawa.
Life expectancy: 65 years, 2004 (WHO 2006)
Fertility rate/Maternal mortality rate: 4.1 births per woman, 2004 (WHO 2006)
Birth rate/Death rate: 31 births per 1,000 population; 8.6 deaths per 1,000 population (2003).
Child (under 5 years) mortality rate (per 1,000): 60 per 1,000 live births (WHO 2012)

Welfare

The government has instituted a bonding system requiring all trained personnel to serve the country for at least the same number of years that it has funded their training. The retirement age, which was previously 50 years for all government employees, has been increased to 60 years for doctors and 55 for other categories.

Main cities

Bairiki, (capital, on Tarawa, estimated population 50,171 in 2012), Taburao (4,409), Bonriki (4,191), Temaraia (3,076), Butaritari (2,607), Tabukiniberu (2,117).

Languages spoken

English is used for official communications and is widely understood in the capital, Tarawa. It is used less on the outer islands where i-Kiribati is the norm. In the i-Kiribati language the letters 'ti' are pronounced 's' (Kiribati is pronounced Kiribas).

Official language/s

I-Kiribati, English

Media

Despite the lack of independent news outlets the government-owned radio and newspaper provide an appropriate level of press freedom.

Press

Tthe Newspaper Registration Amendment Bill allows publications to be deregister and stopped when faced with complaints. The *Kiribati Independent* was closed down on 22 June 2012, due to a breach in its newspaper registration requirements. Observers claim the closure was politically motivated following several articles exposing government corruption and mismanagement.
Weeklies: The government-owned *Te Uekera* is published in I-Kiribati and English; the *Kiribati New Star* is an independent newspaper.
Periodicals: There are no newsagents and only limited copies of overseas papers and magazines are sold in shops. Religious organisations publish newsletters and periodicals in I-Kiribati with local news and stories relevant to their readership. *Te Itoi ni Kiribati* and *Kaotan te Ota* for Catholic and Protestant communities respectively.

Broadcasting

Kiribati is a member of the Commonwealth Broadcasting Association (www.cba.org.uk), which promotes best practices in broadcasting.
Radio: The only radio stating in operation is Radio Kiribati broadcasting in AM and FM, which provides a national, public network. External services from the BBC and VOA may be received on short-wave radios.
Other news agencies: ABC Pacific Beat: www.radioaustralia.net.au/pacbeat
Pacific News: www.pacificmagazine.net
Pacific Islands New Association (Pina): www.pina.com.fj

Economy

Kiribati lacks both human and natural resources; the infrastructure is weak, the islands remote and the soil poor, with frequent droughts. This, together with a traditional land tenure structure, makes the islands unattractive to large-scale agricultural activity. The principal source of foreign exchange comes from the Revenue Equalisation Reserve Fund (RERF), which was set up to invest funds from the now depleted phosphate mining operation on Banaba Island. Income from the RERF enables the government to cover fiscal deficits and to buffer year-to-year movements on the current account. The RERF seeks to accumulate funds my holding investments in over 20 foreign currencies and in 2013 (latest figures) the RERF balance stood at US$668 million, 381 per cent of GDP.
Like many small islands states, Kiribati is vulnerable to external shocks that directly affects its economy and as a result it spiralled into recession after the global economic crash and suffered negative growth from 2008-10. Since then, however, the economy has improved as the global economic climate improved and over the last four years Kiribati has enjoyed positive economic growth that is typically around 3 per cent, where it remained in 2014.
According to the International Monetary Fund (IMF) external risks have increased for Kiribati. The main sources of income – investments, fishing licence fees, remittances, (which accounts to some 6 per cent of GDP) and tourism, which together accounts for over half of GDP – can easily be adversely affected by the global economy. In 2012 (latest figures) the service sector accounted for 64.5 per cent of GDP while industry and agriculture, including fishing, accounted for 9.2 per cent and 26.3 per cent respectively.
The agricultural sector is mostly subsistence farming. Almost all manufactured goods are imported, while commodity exports include copra (coconut flesh), seaweed and fish.
Kiribati's large (around 3.5 million square kilometres – some six times the area of France) Exclusive Economic Zone (EEZ) is a major source of fishing licence revenue. Tourism could be a major source of foreign earnings but its isolation in the Pacific Ocean and the lack of infrastructure

has limited its development. Game fishing and bird watching are an attraction for visitors to the island.

Kiritimati (Christmas) Island has been used for landings of unmanned space shuttles operated by the Japan Aerospace Exploration Agency (Jaxa). Japan is leasing land on Kiritimati to build a spaceport, and according to the agreement will spend US$12.9 million, however, by 2015 construction had not yet started and the future of the project looked to be in danger. Japan is also funding the building of storage and handling areas at the island's fishing port.

External trade

Kiribati is a member of the South Pacific Regional Trade and Economic Co-operation Agreement (Sparteca) along with 12 other regional nations, which allows products duty free access by Pacific Island Forum members to Australian and New Zealand markets (subject to the country of origin restrictions).

Much of Kiribati's foreign revenue is provided through leased fishing rights, remittances and international aid and operates with a trade deficit that is not balanced by export trade.

Imports

Principal imports are food, machinery and equipment, miscellaneous manufactured goods and fuel.

Main sources: Australia (26.8 per cent of total in 2013 (latest figures)), Singapore (21.1 per cent), Fiji (14.9 per cent) and New Zealand (13.2 per cent).

Exports

Principal exports are copra (over 60 per cent), aquarium fish, dried shark fins and seaweed. Tuna is exported from Kiribati waters by foreign fleets under licence.

Main destinations: Morocco (24.2 per cent of total in 2013 (latest figures)), Marshall Islands (12.8 per cent), Philippines (12.5 per cent) and Australia (9.4 per cent).

Agriculture

Farming

The agricultural sector, including fishing, accounts for about 26.3 per cent of GDP and around 60 per cent of exports.

Agricultural development is limited by poor soil quality. There are commercial and government-owned copra plantations on Teraina (Washington) and Tabuaeran (Fanning) islands, but peasant smallholdings are more usual. Most copra is exported to Europe by the Copra Co-operative Society (CCS).

Flour, sugar and rice are replacing the traditional breadfruit and taro in the national diet, increasing reliance on imports.

Fishing

There are programmes to upgrade subsistence fisheries to small commercial enterprises. Foreign fleets under licence in the immense Kiribati Exclusive Economic Zone (EEZ) carry out deep-sea fishing.

In September 2006, a second Kiribati and EU contract under which Spanish, French and Portuguese purse seine and long-line fishing boats are to be allowed to catch tuna in the EEZ. The latest deal emphasises the promotion of sustainable and responsible fishing.

Typically, the annual catch for home consumption is over 32,000t including both fish and other seafood.

In April 2010 the Parties to the Nauru Agreement (PNA) (eight island states including Kiribati) collectively agreed to permit *purse seine* fishing in 4.55 million square kilometres of high seas, from 1 January 2011, to vessels with the necessary license. The area involved stretches from Palau and Papua New Guinea in the west to Kiribati in the east, from the Marshall Islands in the north to Tuvalu in the south; it holds an estimated 25 per cent of the world's tuna supply.

On 12 April 2011, a summit of the Parties to the Nauru Agreement (PNA) concluded its strategy for a policy of sustainable fishing in the Pacific. The PNA treaty, which was established in 1989 and expired in 2012, is in need of an overhaul. As a collective region (FSM, Kiribati, Marshall Islands, Nauru, Palau, PNG, Solomon Islands and Tuvalu) it controls around 25–30 per cent of world stocks of tuna. Only 5 per cent of sales revenue is returned to the PNA and ministers have called for specific changes, including receiving an increased share of profits for PNA crews on-board *purse seine* vessels (minimum 10 per cent). Other suggested changes included conservation and management measures including a limit to fish trapping (fish aggregating devices (FADs), net mesh rules and the establishment of an observer agency and fisheries information management system.

Industry and manufacturing

Small-scale manufacturing industries include clothing, furniture and handicrafts.

Tourism

The Phoenix Island Protected Area is included on UNESCO's World Heritage List as the largest designated marine protection site. It conserves one of the largest intact oceanic coral archipelago ecosystems in the world. The Millennium Islands are located just over the International Date Line and are the first islands in the world to celebrate the New Year.

Tourism has become a much needed lifeline for the economy, with direct contribution to GDP rising year-on-year, standing at AUD18.5 million in 2014 (US$17.5 million) or 10 per cent of GDP. Total contribution to GDP, including industries indirectly affected by the travel and tourism industry, stood at AUD44.o million (US$41.5 million), or 23.7 per cent of GDP. Visitor exports also amounted to 23.4 per cent of total exports in 2014 at AUD7.4 million (US$7.0 million).

Direct employment in the tourism industry stood at 2,000 jobs in 2014 (8.2 per cent of total employment) and total contribution, including jobs indirectly linked to the industry, stood at 5,500 jobs (20.3 per cent of total employment).

Although Kiribati has all of the assets that a tropic paradise could offer visitors, palm fringed lagoons with white sandy beaches it is also at risk from global warming and rising seas, Kiribati experienced flooding due to Cyclone Pam in early 2015.

Its infrastructure is underdeveloped and there are water restrictions in place, so that a significant increase in tourist numbers could damage or overwhelm the picturesque but fragile tropical idyll.

Nevertheless, upgrades of the international airports on Tarawa and Kirimati began in 2011 as work also began on upgrading two major roads on Tarawa.

Environment

The South Pacific Regional Environment Programme (SPREP) reported in 1999 that, due to global warming, two uninhabited islands in the Kiribati group, Tebua Tarawa and Abanuea, had disappeared beneath the waves, others have almost gone, and the main islands suffer severe floods from high tides.

The Phoenix Islands Protected Area, the world's largest marine reserve of 410,500 square kilometres was created by Kiribati in 2008. It includes the planet's biggest intact coral archipelagos with an estimated 120 species of coral, 520 species of fish, some of which have only recently been discovered, large sea turtle populations and important seabird nesting sites.

Kiribati is one of the low lying islands with most to loose through global warming and the government was unhappy at the lack of commitment by countries worldwide to limit their emission of greenhouse gases, outlined by the Kyoto agreement and the UN-backed conference in Copenhagen (Denmark) in December 2009.

Two uninhabited islands in the Kiribati group, Tebua Tarawa and Abanuea, disappeared beneath the waves in 1999 and others have almost gone, the main islands suffer severe floods at high and king tides.

Hydrocarbons

There are no known hydrocarbon reserves and Kiribati does not import natural gas or coal. It relies entirely on imported oil products, of distillate, jet fuel and gasoline, to meet its fuel requirements at around 230 barrels per day.

Energy
There are publicly owned generators on Tarawa and Christmas Island and private generators on Banaba and others, producing annually around 6.5 million kilowatt hours.

Banking and insurance
There is no central bank in Kiribati and the sole commercial bank is the Bank of Kiribati. The government does not buy and sell foreign exchange.

Time
GMT plus twelve hours

Geography
Kiribati comprises 33 atolls in three principal groups, within an area of about 3.6 million square km (two million square miles) in the mid-Pacific Ocean. The country extends about 3,870km (2,400 miles) from east to west and about 2,050km (1,275 miles) from north to south. Nauru lies to the west and Tuvalu and Tokelau to the south.
Most islands are low-lying coral outcrops covered in poor soil, except for Banaba, which rises to 80m with good planting. Kiribati has no hills or freshwater streams on any of its islands and relies on wells and stored rainwater.
Hemisphere
Straddles the equator, with most islands in the southern hemisphere.

Climate
Temperatures range from 25–33 Celsius. The wet season extends from Dec–May and rainfall variation is high in most of the islands. A gentle breeze from the easterly quarter is predominant. The westerly gale (Oct–Mar) can be unpleasant.

Entry requirements
Passports
Required by all and must have six months validity from date of arrival.
Proof of return/onward passage and sufficient funds are also required.
Visa
Required by all, except citizens of UK and most Commonwealth countries and Pacific Islanders, for up to either 20 or 30 days, dependent on business, tourist and nationality criteria. Contact the nearest consulate for further information (some details are given at www.embassy-avenue.jp/kiri/visa/index.html). Citizens of Australia, Japan and US require visas.
Currency advice/regulations
There are no restriction on the import or export of foreign or local currencies
Travellers cheques in Australian dollars avoid extra exchange fees; they are accepted in main banks and some shops.
Customs
Personal effects are allowed duty-free.
Strict quarantine laws govern the import of plants, or parts of plants, vegetable matter or soil, clay or earth, animals and/or animal products.
Visitors are not allowed to take out of the country human remains, artefacts over 30 years old, traditional fighting swords, traditional tools, dancing ornaments or suits of armour.
Prohibited imports
Firearms, ammunition, explosives and indecent publications.

Health (for visitors)
Mandatory precautions
Vaccination certificate for yellow fever is required if travelling from an infected zone.
Advisable precautions
Vaccination for diphtheria, tuberculosis, hepatitis A and B, polio, tetanus, typhoid are recommended. There is also a rabies risk. It is advisable to boil water before drinking. Dengue fever is occasionally reported.

Hotels
In addition to the islands' four hotels, there are rudimentary rest houses. All hotels provide laundry services. Travellers cheques are seldom accepted.
A 10 per cent service charge is added to all hotel bills. Tipping is not customary.

Public holidays (national)
Fixed dates
1 Jan (New Year's Day), 8 Mar (Women's Day), 18 Apr (Health Day), 12 Jul (Independence Day – three days), 7 Aug (Youth Day), 7 Oct (Education Day), 25–26 Dec (Christmas).
Variable dates
Good Friday and Easter Monday (Mar/Apr) Gospel Day (Jul), Human Rights Day (Dec).

Working hours
Banking
Mon–Fri: 0930–1500 for all branches of Bank of Kiribati except Bikenibeu which opens from 0900–1400 and Kiritimati Island branch which opens between 1230 and 1330.
Business
Mon–Fri: 0800–1230, 1330–1615.
Government
Mon–Fri: 0800–1230, 1330–1615.
Shops
Shopping on Tarawa is very limited.
Mon–Sat: 0700–1900 (some shops open until 2030).

Telecommunications
Telephone/fax
A telephone service is available throughout urban Tarawa. Radio telephone links available to most outer islands.
Mobile/cell phones
There is a limited GSM 900 service available.

Electricity supply
240V AC, 50 cycles. Appliances with the standard Australian type three-pin plug will operate within South Tarawa.

Weights and measures
Metric system (Imperial units also used).

Social customs/useful tips
In official correspondence i-Kiribati adopt the western convention of signing their names with initials and surname, but it is customary (and more polite) to address people by their first name.
Women should not go out in shorts or short dresses especially on the outer islands. Bikinis should not be worn.

Getting there
Air
National airline: Air Kiribati
International airport/s: Bonriki International (TRW) on Tarawa.
Other airport/s: An upgrade to the airstrip on the island of Kiritimati in 2010 resulted in the resumption of an air service by Air Pacific, which had been cancelled since 2008.
Airport tax: Departure tax A$20; except transit passengers.
Surface
Government ships operate between Fiji and Kiribati. The remoteness of the islands restricts the number of large vessels which call. The international ports are Betio (on Tarawa), Banaba and Kirimati.

Getting about
National transport
Air: Air Kiribati provides inter-island plane connections several times a week to most of the islands. Charter flights can be arranged.
Road: There are 30km of asphalt road on Tarawa and Christmas Island.
Buses: A large fleet of privately owned buses operates an efficient and inexpensive mode of public transport from the airport to the main centres on South Tarawa. They may be flagged down anywhere on the main road; users may get off anywhere they wish. Buses operate daily from Betio to Buota 0600–2100.
Water: Passenger ferries operate between the islands.
City transport
Taxis: Taxis are available on Tarawa but cannot be booked, nor do they have meters. Charges are high.
Car hire
An international driving licence is required. Driving is on the left side of the road. In general, car hire is available on urban Tarawa and Kiritimati only.

BUSINESS DIRECTORY
The addresses listed below are a selection only. While World of Information makes every endeavour to check these

addresses, we cannot guarantee that changes have not been made, especially to telephone numbers and area codes. We would welcome any corrections.

Telephone area codes

The international direct dialling (IDD) code for Kiribati is +686, followed by area code (below) then subscriber's number.

Abaiang: 33
Abaokoro, Tarawa: 31, 32
Abemama: 41
Aranuka: 40
Arorae: 49
Bairiki, Tarawa: 21, 22, 23, 24
Betio, Tarawa: 25, 26
Bekenibeu, Tarawa: 28, 29
Fanning, Tabuaeran: 83
Kirimati: 81, 82
Onotoa: 45
Tabiteuea, North: 43
Tabiteuea, South 44

Useful telephone numbers

Fire, police, ambulance: 999
Tungaru Central Hospital, Nawerewere, South Tarawa: 28-100.

Chambers of Commerce

Kiribati Chamber of Commerce, PO Box 550, Betio, Tarawa (tel: 26-351; fax: 26-332; e-mail: kcc@tski.net.ki).

Banking

Bank of Kiribati Ltd, PO Box 66, Bairiki, Tarawa (tel: 21-095; fax: 21-200; e-mail: bankofkiribati@tksl.net.ki).

Development Bank of Kiribati, PO Box 33, Bairiki, Tarawa (tel: 81-224; fax: 81-444; e-mail: bokxmas@tksl.net.ki).

Travel information

Air Kiribati, PO Box 274, Bikenibeu, Tarawa (tel: 28-088/093; fax: 26-204).

Air Marshall, PO Box 104, Bairike, Tarawa (tel: 21-578; fax: 21-579).

Air Nauru, Tobaraoi Travel, Tarawa (tel: 26-567; fax: 26-000).

Air Tungaru Corporation, PO Box 274, Bikenibeu, Tarawa (tel: general 28-088; reservations 21-214).

Authentic Atoll Tours, PO Box 296, Banganteburе, Bikenibeu, Tarawa (tel and fax: 28-454).

Tarawa Agency, PO Box 274, Bikenibeu, Tarawa (tel: 28-088, 28-165; fax: 28-216).

National tourist organisation offices

Kiribati Visitors Bureau, PO Box 261, Bikenibeu, Tarawa (tel: 28-287/288; fax: 26-193).

Ministries

Ministry of Commerce, Industry and Tourism, PO Box 510, Betio, Tarawa (tel: 26-157, 26-158; fax: 26-233).

Ministry of Education, Bikenibeu, Tarawa (tel: 28-091; fax: 28-222).

Ministry of Environment, Bairiki, Tarawa (tel: 21-099; fax: 21-120).

Ministry of Finance and Economic Planning, PO Box 67, Bairiki, Tarawa (tel: 21-082; fax: 21-307).

Ministry of Foreign Affairs, PO Box 68, Bairiki, Tarawa (tel: 21-342; fax: 21-466; email: mfa@tskl.net.ki).

Ministry of Health and Family Planning, Bikenibeu, Tarawa (tel: 28-081; fax: 28-152).

Ministry of Line and Phoenix Group, Bairiki, Tarawa (tel: 21-449).

Ministry of Trade, Industry and Labour, Bairiki, Tarawa (tel: 21-097; fax: 21-167).

Ministry of Transport and Communications, Betio, Tarawa (tel: 26-435; fax: 26-193).

Ministry of Works and Energy, Betio, Tarawa (tel: 26-192; fax: 26-343).

Other useful addresses

Abamakoro Trading Ltd, PO Box 492, Betio, Tarawa (tel: 26-568; fax: 26-415).

Asian Development Bank (ADB), South Pacific Regional Mission, La Casa di Andrea, Fr. Dr. W. H. Lini Highway; PO Box 127, Port Vila (tel: (+678-2) 23-300; fax: (+678-2) 23-183; email: adbsprm@adb.org; internet: http://www.adb.org/SPRM).

British High Commission, PO Box 61, Bairiki, Tarawa (tel: 21-327; fax: 21-488).

Broadcasting and Publications Authority, PO Box 78, Bairiki, Tarawa.

General Post Office, Bairiki (tel: 21-080).

Kiribati Co-operative Wholesale Society (tel: 26-092; fax: 26-224).

Kiribati National Library and Archives, PO Box 6, Bairiki, Tarawa (tel: 21-245; fax: 28-222).

Kiribati Shipping Corporation, PO Box 495, Betio, Tarawa (tel: 26-195; fax: 26-204).

Office of the Attorney General, Bairiki, Tarawa (tel: 21-242).

Philatelic Bureau, Ministry of Transport and Communications, PO Box 494, Betio, Tarawa (tel: 26-515; fax: 26-193).

Telecom Kiribati Ltd, PO Box 72, Bairiki, Tarawa (tel: 21-287; fax: 21-010).

Tungaru Central Hospital, Bikenibeu, Tarawa (tel: 28-081).

ABC Pacific Beat: www.radioaustralia.net.au/pacbeat

Pacific News: www.pacificmagazine.net

Pacific Islands New Association (Pina): www.pina.com.fj

Internet sites

South Pacific Tourism Organisation: http://www.tcsp.com/kiribati/index.html

Kiribati homepage: http://www.trussel.com/f_kir.htm

Government site: http://www.tskl.net.ki/kiribati/

North Korea

KEY FACTS

Official name: Chosun Minchu-chui Inmin Konghwa-guk (Democratic People's Republic of Korea) (DPRK)

Head of State: General Secretary of KWP Kim Jong-un (from 19 Dec 2011). In 1998, his grandfather, Kim Il-sung, who died in 1994, was named President of North Korea for Life.

Head of government: Premier Pak Pong-ju (from 2 April 2013)

Ruling party: Chosun Rodongdang (Korean Workers' Party) (KWP)

Area: 122,400 square km

Population: 24.45 million (2011)*

Capital: Pyongyang

Official language: Korean

Currency: Won (W) = 100 chon

Exchange rate: W900.00 per US$ (Nov 2015)

GDP per capita: US$508 (2010)

GDP real growth: 2.50% (2011)*

GDP: US$12.30 billion (2010)

Annual FDI: US$55.00 million (2011)

* estimated figure

The two Koreas, pitted against each other for decades, have with time become the international community's mismatched 'Odd Couple'. North Korea assuming the role of the uptight, overly neat and tidy Felix Ungar, memorably played by Jack Lemmon, South Korea the more easy going Oscar Madison, as portrayed by Walter Matthau. As in the film, the two rub along next to each other, for the most part more irritated than angry. When anger between the two takes over, it is often expressed in the strangest of ways.

Your mines, our loudspeakers

In August 2015, justifiable anger flared up on the part of South Korea when three North Korean anti-personnel landmines maimed two South Korean soldiers patrolling a neutral section of the demilitarised zone (DMZ) between the two countries. The soldiers' legs were reportedly blown off. After almost a week's interval following the incident the authorities in Seoul launched their response: loudspeakers along the border began to broadcast propaganda, news and the inevitable 'Gangnam Style' pop music sung by the South Korean pop star, Psy. Such is the power of the loudspeakers that the broadcasts could be heard for miles. Whether or not the response was 'proportionate' was almost immaterial. The South Korean authorities had long been aware that the immature Kim Jong-un's régime would be hyper-sensitive to the broadcasts, which informed North Koreans within earshot that there was little international respect, or even time, for their leader and his sycophantic clique of advisers. News that famines were almost a thing of the past throughout most of the world came as a shock to North Koreans, many of whose compatriots lived in a state bordering on permanent famine. The loudspeaker system had been carefully maintained, but not used, during the 11 years since tensions had flared up in 2004. The last occasion on which the pot had boiled over was in 2010, when North Korea sank the *Cheonan*, a South Korean warship, in March and then shelled Yeonpyeong island in November.

When the North Korean response did come, it was hardly one of calm submission. It was anger rather than sorrow – and with a vengeance, as the sound of artillery fire obliterated the South's broadcasts. The Southern response to the explosive outbreak was in kind. It was difficult to ascertain whether artillery attacks were the North just huffing and puffing, or whether this was simply a negotiating ploy. The answer came when the North declared what it described as a state of 'quasi war' between the two Koreas. This looked like something more than show. The declaration added that there would be a full military response, to begin on 22 August unless the South undertook to silence and dismantle the loudspeakers. It issued a deadline of 5 pm 'local' time, which meant, the new time zone, (half an hour behind that of South Korea), which had only been announced a month earlier.

Conversations were held over the hot-line between 'the couple' and reason appeared to have prevailed. The two countries agreed to meet in Panmunjon at 6 pm with a view to lowering tensions. The meeting was taking place only 30 minutes after the North Korean deadline. The seriousness of the meeting, however, could be judged by the fact that on both sides of the table those participating were certainly not junior officers. South Korea was represented by Kim Kwanjin, head of the National Security Agency (NSA) and the unification minister, Hong Yong-pyo. Pyongyang was to be represented by Vice Marshal Hwan Pyong-so, considered to be Kim Jong-un's right hand man, and Kim Yang Gon, its head of relations with Seoul. According to Kim Kyo-hyun, the deputy head of the NSA, North Korea had suggested the meeting a day earlier. The South Korean government had made counter-proposals to ensure the participation of Mr Hwan.

Both sides were well aware that tensions had been running high for five years or so. According to the version of the South Korean ministry of defence, the North had launched four rounds of artillery missiles in response to the loudspeaker broadcasts. Seoul had responded with 29 rounds. There were no casualties or material damage, suggesting that neither side wished to raise tensions any higher. Pyongyang had sent an 'ultimatum' to Seoul to cease the broadcasts; Kim Jong-un had placed his forces on alert. South Korea had insisted it would continue broadcasting until it received an apology from the North. South Korea's President Park Cheung-hye cancelled her appointments, donned a military uniform and, just for good measure, arranged to visit a military base.

Propaganda broadcasts had been a part of daily life on both sides of the border since the end of the war in Korea in 1953. The war did not, however, end with a peace treaty but just with an armistice, leaving the two sides technically at war. The broadcasts were discontinued by mutual agreement as recently as 2004, at the beginning of a rapprochement between the sides which came to an end in 2010 when 46 South Korean sailors died when their warship was sunk, allegedly by North Korea. Since then, relations have gone from bad to worse; however, although the rhetoric had reached new levels of aggression, both sides have retained a sense of prudence, or at least enough reserve to prevent events becoming too bellicose.

South Korea sought an admission of responsibility and apology, for the anti-personnel landmines. Their use (although South Korea was reported to be equally guilty of using them) was a violation of the terms of the armistice; a United Nations (UN) investigation confirmed that the landmines used were of the North Korean 'wooden-box' type. Not that South Korea could adopt a 'holier than thou' attitude. Both sides had reportedly littered the DMZ with a million or more mines. South Korea resolutely claimed that North Korea had sent troops into the DMZ to plant them. Rumours abounded, claiming that North Korea sought to derail the annual military manoeuvres between South Korea and the US which were already under way. Or even to prejudice a state visit by Ms Park scheduled for early September 2015.

After 43 hours of discussion, agreement was reached between the two sides. In theory, at any rate, both sides got what they wanted. The joint communiqué signed by both Koreas stated that on the following mid-day Seoul would cease its broadcasting and Pyongyang would publicly express its 'lament' at the maiming of the two soldiers. The apology had been the possible deal breaker for South Korea The agreement put an end to the prevailing state of 'semi-war' between the Koreas, in which North Korea had mobilised some 50 submarines and had doubled the deployment of troops on the demarcation border.

South Korea's willingness to discuss any of its actions was not altogether clear. Ms Park was on record that she wanted to improve relations with the North, a not unpopular notion. But not much had actually happened in this respect. The London *Economist* reported that the joint ventures between the two countries operating in North Korea continued to function.

Regional tension

In May 2015 North Korea had notched up another military first by successfully launching a submarine ballistic missile. The bulletin announcing the achievement predictably featured a photograph of the 32 year old Kim Jong-un knowledgeably pointing at the missile as it surfaced. Bordering on paranoia, the bulletin added that 'The army now disposed of a strategic weapon of an international standard that would enable it to attack and annihilate any hostile forces that threatened the sovereignty and the dignity of North Korea.' Almost as an afterthought, the bulletin added that 'It would also enable submarine operations.'

An article in the *Wall Street Journal* (WSJ) by Richard Haass, the President of the US Council on Foreign Relations, summed up North Korea as a 'cyber-vandal', an unauthorised nuclear power and the possessor of a large conventional army. Oh, and a former sponsor of international terrorism. Significantly, at the beginning of 2015 – four years after his inauguration, President Kim had yet to be invited to China (or indeed anywhere else). This was in sharp contrast to his Southern counterpart, Ms Park Geun-hye, who has a close relationship with China's Xi Jinping.

The economy: Capitalism 1–Ideology 0

Reliable economic information on North Korea is hard to come by. In 2015 in some ways, North Korea's economy did appear to be improving slightly. Unobtrusively, Kim Jong-un began to change the country's economy, more or less following the Chinese model of the late 1970s. As a result, in 2013, North Korea had the best harvest in 25 years. South Korea's central bank reported the North's economy grew at just over 1 per cent in 2012 and 2013. It estimated North Korea's GDP at about US$30 billion. In the absence of any official figures from the North, the estimates compiled by various South Korean agencies are generally regarded as the only answer. However, figures emanating from South Korea are predictably dismissed out of hand by Pyongyang and not always considered reliable by international commentators. The income gap between North and South Korea is thought to be the largest income gap in the world between two countries which share a land border. If you believe the optimists, it's 1 to 15. If you believe the pessimists, it's 1 to 40. The income gap between the former East and West Germanys was between 1 to 2 and 1 to 3.

North Korea watchers reported in 2015 that there were signs that what could be described as 'capitalist features' were slowly starting to show themselves in the economy. The principal source for the reports was the veteran North Korea watcher Andrei Lankov, the author of *The Real North Korea: Life and Politics in the Failed Stalinist Utopia*. (Oxford University Press. 2013) According to Mr Lankov, in the 1990s the North Korean economy had to seek new answers. Mr Lankov notes that the implosion of North Korea's principal backer, the USSR (Soviet Union) coincided with the devastating famine that killed hundreds of thousands of North Koreans. In desperation many North Koreans turned to the black market. Similarly, the state was forced to consider different policies in respect of the market. According to Lankov, President Kim Jong-un is happy to cohabit with them. Mr Lankov's theory is that Kim Jong-un's government has been seeking to adopt the economic reforms followed by China in the 1970s and 1980s. However, the economic reforms also constituted a potential threat to the regime's hold on power in Mr Lankov's view. So, paradoxically, the North Korean government would at the same time need to tighten its grip on North Korea's long suffering inhabitants.

Two publications, reviewed by the *Financial Times*'s Seoul correspondent, Simon Munday, threw some light on the way in which the country was moving. While some of its developments – not least the faintly ridiculous appearance of its leader, were cause for mirth, the laughter faded quickly at the realisation, highlighted by Mr Lankov, that when Kim Jong-un's father died in December 2011, seven senior *apparatchiks* accompanied the funeral cortege. Within two years all of them had either been executed or 'purged' (relieved of their responsibilities). It was even rumoured that the former minister for the armed forces was executed with an anti-aircraft gun, apparently because he had fallen asleep while Kim Jong-un was speaking. One South Korean source, quoted in the new *York Times* alleged that as many as 70 senior North Korean officials had met their maker.

Commenting on the first book, *A Kim Jong-Il Production* by Paul Fischer, which broadly endorsed Mr Lankov's views, Mr Munday notes that 'The daily charade of life in North Korea has taken on a new character since the 1990s when the state, in effect, gave up feeding most of its people, as sharp cuts to aid compounded the effects of decades of economic mismanagement.' Mr Munday links this observation to others made in the second book, *North Korea Confidential* in which the authors relate how their interviews with defectors confirm the view that capitalism, often in its most primitive forms, had become a part of Korean daily life.

According to Mr Munday, the book's authors – Messrs Tudor and Pearson – considered that Kim Jong-un's regime was happy to '... harness the shifts in the economy for its own ends, with public-private capitalism allowing the leadership to build patronage and loyalty in an era where ideology no longer matters.' Their conclusion on future trends in North Korean society is hardly optimistic. Tudor and Pearson write that 'The new rising capitalist class generally seeks to join the exiting élite, rather than undermine it.'r

Risk assessment

Economy	Poor/catastrophic
Politics	Poor/catastrophic
Regional stability	Poor

COUNTRY PROFILE

1910 Japan formalised its annexation of Korea after gaining responsibility for its security following victory in the Russo-Japanese war of 1905.
1919 Japan suppressed the mass March First movement for self-determination.
1930s–1940s Japan imposed measures designed to assimilate the Korean population, including the outlawing of the Korean language and family names. Korea suffered under military occupation but gained the benefits of forced industrialisation.
1945 Liberation at the hands of Allied forces was a prelude to partition of the peninsula as the victorious powers encouraged friendly governments north and south of the 38th parallel. The US occupied the south while the north was taken over by the Soviet Union. As the two powers did not wish to give independence to Korea, feeling that the Korean people needed political and social re-education, a line of demarcation was established.
1947 The Chosun Rodongdang (Korean Workers' Party) (KWP) was established by Kim il-Sung (known as the 'Great Leader').
1948 The Democratic People's Republic of Korea (DPRK) was established as an independent communist state.
1950 North Korea, backed by Soviet and Chinese Communist forces, invaded South Korea after it had declared independence. War ensued.
1953 A cease-fire was signed on 27 July; a peace treaty was never signed.
1972 A constitution was laid down.
1990s Ten years of famine began after the fall of the Soviet Union, which had been supporting the DPRK regime. It lasted for most of the decade and due to lack of verifiable statistics it killed anywhere between 800,000 and 3.5 million people from starvation and hunger-related illness; deaths peak in 1997. At the height of the famine, the UN estimated one-third of the population received food aid and half the population were malnourished.
1994 Kim il-Sung, who spent his last two decades in power, died. He was succeeded by his son Kim Jong-il (he did not take the title of president but became known as the 'Dear Leader').
1995–96 Floods destroyed 16 per cent of arable land.
1997 Kim Jong-il formally assumed power. He was elected general secretary of the KWP.
1998 Kim il-Sung, who died in 1994, was named president of North Korea for life.
2000 Australia, the Philippines and Italy restored diplomatic ties with DPRK. South Korea President Kim Dae-Jung visited Pyongyang and met Kim Jong-il in an unprecedented and much fêted meeting of the two Korean leaders. The then US secretary of state, Madeleine Albright, visited Kim Jong-il. North Korea and the UK established diplomatic relations.
2001 An EU delegation held talks with Kim Jong-il. Talks started by the US administration in 2000 were suspended. Talks on opening the first land route between the Republic of Korea and Korea DPR broke down. After the worst winter in 50 years and a summer drought harvests were devastated, the UN WFP called for over US$300 million in food aid.
2002 DPRK was included on the list of countries that were an 'axis of evil' due to their development of weapons of mass destruction (WMD). Inter-Korean relations progressed, as the two sides agreed to

resume the engagement process after the South Korean envoy, Lim Dong-won visited DPRK. The accord included plans for economic co-operation, continuing family reunions and a revival of a cross-border railway project linking the two countries.
2003 China began talks in an effort to persuade North Korea to end its nuclear arms programme. All 687 KWP candidates, standing unopposed, won 100 per cent of the votes in elections to the National Assembly. Pak Pong Ju became premier. The Kaesong Industrial Complex (KIC) was launched in a free zone between the two countries. Largely financed by the South to increase co-operation North Koreans would be employed in manufacturing industries, with goods exported to the South
2004 A train carrying volatile materials exploded killing at least 161 people and injuring over 1,000. South and North Korea temporarily opened their borders. The Gyeongui railway line was under refurbishment and a new line, Donghae Bukbu (Tonghae Pukpu), began construction.
2005 A short-range missile was test-fired in the general direction of Japan. International talks led to an agreement whereby the nuclear weapons programme would be terminated in return for aid and security guarantees. Further negotiations were vetoed due to international sanctions that had frozen DPRK assets in a Macau bank, which the US alleged was responsible for laundering millions of US dollars' worth of counterfeit and illegally earned money and which effectively denied DPRK access to the international banking system.
2006 The DPRK government listed its central bank on the London Stock exchange in an attempt to circumvent financial sanctions and sold an estimated US$28 million in gold bullion on international markets. A limited nuclear explosion of less than one kiloton was detonated in DPRK, resulting in international financial sanctions.
2007 The UN suspended all aid until an audit was completed, following US accusation that the aid was 'perverted for the benefit of the Kim Jong Il regime' instead of being spent on the people of DPRK. An agreement was reached whereby two contentious nuclear reactors would be closed down, to be verified by international inspectors, in return for the supply of 50,000 tonnes of heavy fuel oil, plus food and other aid. It would also allow DPRK access to the international banking system and a formal end to the 1950–53 Korean War. North and South Korea resumed ministerial meetings. Pak Pong Ju was replaced as prime minister by Kim Yong Il. UN inspectors confirmed that the Yongbyon nuclear reactor had been shut down. Floods killed over 100 people and left 300,000 people temporarily homeless. A summit of leaders of North and South Korea took place in Pyongyang. The South Korea delegation included industrialists, bureaucrats, poets and clerics. US technicians began the process of disabling the Yongbyon nuclear complex. The end-of-year deadline to disclose its nuclear programme was missed.
2008 International negotiations on the nuclear weapons programme ground to a halt, as verification of work cessation could not be agreed.
2009 All political and military agreements with South Korea were scraped, due to what the DPRK saw as 'hostile intent' by South Korea. Legislative elections were announced, with the supreme leader picking one candidate for each constituency, to be voted on by the electorate. In the parliamentary elections, 687 candidates were elected unopposed; turnout was said to be 99.98 per cent. The US called the launch of a DPRK satellite rocket 'provocative', even though the US and South Korea said the launch had been unsuccessful. Contrary to all agreements a large nuclear test took place, estimated at 20 kilotons; the UN Security Council condemned the test. DPRK declared that it was 'no longer bound by the 'armistice' of 1953, following South Korea's participation in the Proliferation Security Initiative (PSI) that included measures to search ships suspected of carrying nuclear materials. North Korea considered such searches 'hostile' acts against its 'peaceful vessels' and an infringement of its sovereignty. New, UN sanctions were imposed on named DPRK citizens and businesses, as well as some foreign firms doing business with DPRK. A decree was issued ordering all bank notes be exchanged for new, lower re-valued bank notes. The re-valuation was reasoned to be a move by the government to counter black-market money traders.
2010 The finance official overseeing the re-valuation of the won in 2009, Pak Nam-ki, was sacked due to the chaotic process that wiped out many people's savings and caused food shortages; he was later executed. The report by an international investigation team, led by South Korea, concluded that DPRK had torpedoed a South Korean warship, with the loss of all 46 sailors aboard. DPRK denied the accusation, as condemnation by UN members followed. China, North Korea's principal ally, and Japan agreed to impose financial sanctions on DPRK. Choe Yong-Rim became premier (head of government), replacing Kim Yong-il, who stepped down following the bungled currency reforms. South Korea staged five days of military drills off the penisular's west coast. The move infuriated the North Koreans, who in retaliation fired off over 100 rounds of artillery close to the disputed sea border between the two countries. Kim Jong-il and his son, Kim Jong-un, travelled to China again. There was speculation that Kim Jong-il was looking for approval of Kim Jong-un as his successor. Four people, including two civilians, were killed after DPRK fired artillery shells at the island of Yeonpyeong in South Korea.
2011 An outbreak of foot and mouth struck livestock and weakened an already fragile food supply. In February, the government appealed for foreign aid to feed its people. The 'Elders' a group of four international statesmen, (former presidents Jimmy Carter (US), Martti Ahtisaari (Finland) and Mary Robinson (Ireland), with prime minister Gro Brundtland (Norway)) paid a three day visit in April, in an effort to revive the six-party talks on North Korea's nuclear programme, and to ease tensions with South Korea. In June the government closed all universities and sent students to factories, farms and construction sites in an attempt to rebuild the economy, but also to limit any opposition moves caused by uprisings elsewhere in the world. In August DPRK called for a resumption of the six-party nuclear negotiations 'without preconditions'. President Jong-il travelled by train to the Russian border town of Khasan in August. He held talks with the Russian president, Dmitry Medvedev and visited a dam north of Vladivostock. In September Kim Jong-un made a rare public appearance when he stood with his father at the national celebrations of DPRK's 63rd anniversary of its founding. The General Secretary of KWP (known as Dear Leader) Kim Jong-il, chairman of the National Defence Commission (*de facto* leader), died on 17 December.
2012 On 12 April, state media announced that Kim Jong-un had been named as chairman of the National Defence Commission (NDC), a standing member of the politburo of the KWP and Supreme Leader. A long-range missile, launched on 13 April, exploded over the Yellow Sea shortly after take-off. The US condemned the launch as provocative and suspended the shipment of 240,000 tonnes of food aid to DPRK. Other members of the UN Security Council condemned the launch as violating three UN resolutions banning the testing of ballistic missile technology. On 3 August, the UN announced that DPRK had requested immediate food aid to provide for the tens of thousands of people, around the city of Anju and Songchon County, made homeless by severe flooding in July. A rare second sitting of parliament (within one year) was held in private on 25 September. The

session endorsed an extension to compulsory education by one year. No announcements on other reforms, including to the economy, were made. On 9 October, DPRK announced that it had a missile that could reach the US mainland, two days after South Korea announced that it had upgraded its missile capabilities, with the agreement of the US. On 12 December, North Korea successfully launched a long-range rocket defying international warnings against continued development of intercontinental ballistic missile technology.

2013 On 11 June high level talks that had been agreed the day before to be held in Seoul were suspended by North Korea over the choice of delegates. Seoul attempted to call the North on the restored Red Cross hotline at 09.00 on 12 June but there was no answer. The two Koreas had spoken twice a day at 0900 and 1600 until the hotline had been cut by the North on 10 March. In mid-April the North effectively closed the KIC, which since its inception in 2003 had grown to include some 120 factories employing over 53,000 North Korean workers. On 6 July officials from North and South Korea began talks on reopening the KIC. By 10 July the two sides had agreed in principle to restart operations. However, within days the talks fell through. On 7 August North Korea again offered talks, for 14 August, saying its workers would return to the joint complex and the safety of South Korean staff would be guaranteed. The offer came shortly after the South Korean government announced insurance payments to companies affected by the stoppage – a move seen as paving the way for a formal closure of the site. It was also a day after Seoul said it was providing US$6 million in aid to North Korea. On 18 August the government announced they had agreed that reunions between families separated since the 1950–53 war will take place in a North Korean tourist resort on 19 September. Officials in Seoul announced on 23 August that reunions would take place on 25–30 September at the North's Mount Kumgang resort. Steam was seen rising from the Yongbyon nuclear facility on 11 September, suggesting that the government was preparing to re-start production of plutonium, which can be used in the production of nuclear weapons. On 21 September North Korea announced it was indefinitely postponing the scheduled family reunions. On 24 September China announced that it was banning the export of technologies that could be used in the development of nuclear weapons.

2014 Pyongyang threatened to cancel the family reunions agreed for February because of the annual military exercises between South Korea and the US, also planned for February. The first high-level talks between North and South Korea since 2007 were held on 12 February and were expected to discuss family visits. Two medium-range ballistic missiles (Nodongs) were test-fired on 26 March. The US, South Korea and Japan happened to be meeting in the Netherlands at the same time. After speculation on his health and whereabouts, on 13 October Kim Jong-un was seen in public for the first time since 3 September visiting the Wisong Scientists Residential District. He was walking with a stick but otherwise appeared in good spirits, despite being reported as having suffered some 'discomfort'. South Korea's Yonhap news agency reported on 15 October that talks had taken place between senior military officials of the two Koreas in the truce village of Panmunjom in the Demilitarised Zone. The last two Americans held in North Korea, one arrested in November 2012 and the second in April this year, were released on 8 November.

2015 Tensions between the Norh and South increased during the year. The 70th anniversary of the founding of the Chosun Rodongdang (Korean Workers' Party was celegrated with a grand parade in Pyongyang on 10 October.

Political structure

Constitution

Under the terms of the 1972 constitution, nominal political authority is held by a unicameral Supreme People's Assembly (SPA).

Local government is vested in nine provincial and three municipal elected people's assemblies.

Government at all levels is dominated by the Chosun Rodongdang (Korean Workers' Party) (KWP).

A 1998 amendment appointed Kim Il-sung eternal president.

In 2009, the Korean word for 'communism' was dropped from the Economy and Culture sections of the constitution

Amendments in 2012 and 2013 labelled North Korea a 'nuclear-armed state'.

The executive

The head of state holds executive power and governs in conjunction with a Central People's Committee and an appointed Administrative Council (cabinet).

The head of state is no longer president since the title was given to Kim il-Sung, after he had died, for life.

Kim Jong-il was given administrative powers in 1994 and formally assumed power as head of state after being elected general secretary of the ruling KWP in 1997.

National legislature

A unicameral, Supreme People's Assembly (SPA) exercises nominal legislative power. Its 687 members are elected every four years from a single list of candidates, sanctioned by the General Secretary of the KWP.

The SPA, which elects a standing committee to represent it when not in session, also elects the head of government.

Legal system

The legal system is based on the German civil law system with Japanese influences and Communist legal theory.

Last elections

9 March 2014 (parliamentary)

Results: Although there are technically four parties in North Korea all belong to the Democratic Front for the Reunification of Korea alliance, with each candidate requiring approval from the alliance in order to run.

Chosun Rodongdang (Korean Workers' Party) (KWP) gained 607 seats (out of 687), Choson Sahoe Minjudang (Korean Social Democratic Party) (KSDP) 50 seats, Chondoist Chongu Party (Korean Chondoist Chongu Party) 22 seats, Independents (sanctioned by the KWP) got the remaining 8. Turnout was 99.97 per cent.

Next elections

March 2019 (parliamentary)

Political parties

No political parties, other than the KWP, are permitted to operate.

Ruling party

Chosun Rodongdang (Korean Workers' Party) (KWP)

Approximately 68 per cent of the population is aged between 15 and 64 years. Unicef estimates that around 16 per cent of the population suffer from acute malnutrition, with hardship concentrated in urban areas. The government encourages the urban population to leave the cities. In South Korea, there is a growing number of refugees who have escaped from the harsh conditions of North Korea.

Population

24.45 million (2011)*

Last census: 1 October 2008: 24,051,403 (provisional)

Population density: 186 inhabitants per square km. Urban population 60 per cent (2010 Unicef).

Annual growth rate: 0.9 per cent, 1990–2010 (Unicef).

Ethnic make-up

The Korean DPR (DPRK) has a highly homogeneous population descended from migratory groups who entered the Korean Peninsula from Siberia, Manchuria and inner Asia. There is a small Chinese community and a few ethnic Japanese.

Religions

The constitution provides for 'freedom of religious belief' but, in practice, organised religious activity is discouraged, except for certain government-sponsored religious groups. Traditional religions are Buddhism, Confucianism, Daoism, Shamanism and Chondogyo.

Education

The is a national Education for All Forum (EFA) that organises consultations with organisations such as the Youth League, the Women's Union and the Academy of Educational Science.

Education in Korea consists of six years of elementary education, three years of junior high school, three years of senior high school, and four years of college education. The government has established a free educational system and plans to extend this to the remote areas of the country. However, school attendance in some areas has reportedly dropped to between 60—80 per cent, due to extreme economic hardship not only, in families through lack of food, but also in school facilities with inadequately trained teachers, poor heating and scarce learning materials.

Competition for college entry is fierce. There are three universities. These are the Kim Il-Sung, Kim Chaek Polytechnic and Korryo-Songgyungwan. There are also around 280 colleges.

It is common for students to opt for military service after graduation. This is not compulsory, but can positively affect an individual's future career.

Literacy rate: 95–99 per cent, adult rate.

Health

There is an extensive, free medical care system, but the quality of care has declined.

Water and sanitation sector, one of the key priority areas, remains poorly funded at only 18 per cent of the requirement.

A nutrition survey conducted by Unicef, in 2002, indicated that 40 per cent of children under five were chronically malnourished or stunted (a fall from the previous high of 45 per cent in 2000) and in 2003 nationwide, 5 million people, especially children, the elderly and pregnant females were dependent on foreign food aid. The mortality rate for those aged under 5 was 55 per 1,000 children; maternal mortality continues to increase as estimates show that the nutritional status of some 480,000 pregnant and nursing women is poor.

Life expectancy: 66 years, 2004 (WHO 2006)

Fertility rate/Maternal mortality rate: 2.0 births per woman, 2010 (Unicef)

Birth rate/Death rate: 17.6 births per 1,000 population; seven deaths per 1,000 population (World Bank 2003).

Child (under 5 years) mortality rate (per 1,000): 29 per 1,000 live births (WHO 2012)

Welfare

A large segment of the civilian population rely on the government-run public distribution system. In 2003 the meagre food ration was further reduced to 250–380 grammes per person daily – half the minimum daily energy requirement. People are required to rely on independently procured supplements; families in urban, industrial areas have fared worst.

Main cities

Pyongyang (capital, estimated population 3.4 million (m) in 2012), Hamhung (597,037), Namp'o (478,999m), Hungnam (369,594), Kaesong (361,338m), Wonsan (348,092), Ch'ongjin (331,552), Sunch'on (283,552).

Languages spoken

English, amoung other international languages, is used in business.

Official language/s

Korean

Media

Despite a constitution that guarantees freedom of the press, media is a severely restricted as the government prohibits and controls information and the means of distribution. In 2008 the Paris-based Reporters Without Borders condemned North Korea as isolating its population from the world and subjecting it to 'propaganda worthy of a bygone age'. Criticism of the state leader and government is not tolerated as news is heavily censored; typically all media reinforces the personality cult of the leader, Kim Jong-il.

Press

All publications are state-owned or controlled, including *Rodong Shinmun* (*Labour Daily*), *Minju Choson* (*Democratic Korea*), *Joson Inmingun* (*Korean People's Army Daily*) and *Rodongja Sinmum* (*Worker's Newspaper*). In English, *People's Korea* (www.korea-np.co.jp/pk) is a government online publication.

Dailies: These include *Rodong Shinmun*, *Minju Choson*, *Rodong Chongnyon* and *Pyongyang Times*. The Korean News Service in Tokyo also provides an internet service *Korean News* at www.kcna.co.jp/index-e.htm.

Business: The Foreign Trade Publishing House publishes a monthly journal, *Foreign Trade of the DPRK*, which includes listings of specialised corporations, giving telegraphic and telex addresses.

Periodicals: A semimonthly, Tokyo-based unofficial mouthpiece of the Korea DPR government, *The People's Korea*, reports on Korean affairs.

Broadcasting

All radios and television sets are pre-tuned to state-run stations and there are heavy penalties for anyone caught listening to a foreign broadcast.

There are two radio stations, the Korean Central Broadcasting Station and the external service Voice of Korea, both are state-run. The Korean Workers' Party operates Korean Central TV; Mansudae TV is a cultural service.

Radio: National and locally-produced programmes are widely disseminated (factory, outdoor loudspeakers); there are external services in several languages.

Television: There are two stations, plus a third channel at weekends. Viewing foreign channels is illegal for Korean DPR nationals.

National news agency: Korean Central News Agency (KCNA): www.kcna.co.jp

Economy

North Korea has probably the world's most highly centralised planned economy; the regime is highly secretive and does not publish national accounts, which might reflect poorly on its dogmatic political philosophy. The concentration of economic policy on the development of heavy industry reflects the continued implementation of out-dated Soviet-style priorities, wholly unsuited to present conditions which are characterised as under-invested and outmoded and which have led to a moribund industrial sector that is considered beyond rescue. Energy output is, likewise, declining. Industry accounts for 47.2 per cent of GDP, services over 29.4 per cent and agricultural and fisheries 23.4 per cent (2014).

GDP growth in 2007 was -1.2 per cent due to severe flooding that devastated harvests and forced North Korea to petition for food aid. Following a *rapprochement* with South Korea in 2008 the economy grew by an estimated 3.1 per cent largely due to the inter-Korean economic co-operation, whereby South Korea provided investment and collaboration in setting up the Kaesong Industrial Complex (KIC), to the north of the border with South Korea. By 2009 there were 117 South Korean companies manufacturing goods in North Korea and employing over 42,000 local workers. However, when KPRK's leader, Kim Jong-Il, became unwell all political and military agreements were scrapped, also ending business ties by the end of 2009. This caused the economy to return to recessionary growth of -0.9 per cent. Growth in 2010 was still negative at -0.5 per cent, however, it became positive in 2011 and was maintained at an average of 1.1 per cent up in to 2014.

Foreign investment in industry, construction, technology and tourism is officially encouraged, but there have been few firms willing to invest in North Korea.

Without investment in infrastructure, North Korea, with its low-cost, relatively educated workforce, cannot become the centre for competitively-priced exports to Russia and China that its geographic location could provide.

After the death of Kim Jong-Il in December 2011, and the subsequent succession of his son, Kim Jong-un, reports stated that North Korea was moving towards a less centralised and more liberalised economy. However, more recent reports from 2014, conflict with previous reports and show that the economy remains very much centralised.

In 2014 there were more than 120 factories in the Kaesong Industrial Complex (KIC), employing some 53,000 North Koreans, earning over US$80 million a year in wages from South Korean companies. The KIC makes up for 99 per cent of all inter-Korean trade. Goods are mostly exported to the South. In the second quarter of 2015, inter-Korean trade volumes had fallen by 10 per cent due to a wage dispute between the two countries. However, in mid-August 2015 the dispute came to an end, and a South Korean industry representative announced a 5 per cent increase in North Korean worker's wages.

External trade

North Korea's foreign trade accounts for less than 10 per cent of GDP. There is a special economic zone (SEZ), Rajin-Sonbong, near Rason on the north-eastern border with China and Russia, allowing free trade access in return for investment. Although in 2014, after the December execution of Kim Jong-un's uncle, Jang Song-Thaek, on charges of plotting to overthrow the communist regime, and the subsequent purge of his family, there was a clamp down on foreign investors by the authorities.

The imposition of extra taxes on Chinese investors in the SEZ has been unsettling since China is now North Korea's biggest trading partner; in 2013 North Korean exports to China amounted to US$3 billion, a 17 per cent rise from the 2012 figure.

The trade in illicit drugs is thought to be an important source of foreign currency within the grey economy.

Imports

Vital supplies of food aid are still required. Main imports are petroleum and coking coal, crude rubber, textiles, machinery and equipment, alloying elements, sulphur, halite, grain, cotton, sugar and palm oil.

Main sources: China (79.3 per cent of total in 2014), South Korea (11 per cent), Republic of Congo (4.5 per cent)

Exports

Exports are clothing (many fur products), medicinal products, iron and steel, armaments, machinery and equipment, textiles, non-ferrous metals, manufactured goods, fireproof bricks, anthracite, magnetite cakes, cement, magnesia clinker and machine tools.

Main destinations: China (54.9 per cent of total in 2014), Algeria (30 per cent), South Korea (16 per cent)

Agriculture

Farming

The agriculture sector accounts for an estimated 23.4 per cent of GDP and is thought to employ around 35 per cent of the workforce (2014). Only 20 per cent of North Korean land is arable.

Agriculture is mostly practised on large-scale collective and state farms, which have been fatally mismanaged. Main crops are rice, maize and potatoes. Other crops include wheat, barley, rape, sugar, millet, sorghum, pulses, sweet potatoes, vegetables, tobacco and silkworms. Extra grain supplies are necessary.

Since the mid-1990s, North Korea has been affected by adverse climatic conditions, with a series of floods and droughts destroying crops. Other problems affecting the sector include severe deforestation, which has caused silting of rivers, a lack of fertilisers and pesticides and low levels of mechanisation. This has led to a serious food deficit at a time when North Korea's increasing political isolation has affected aid flows.

Industry and manufacturing

The industrial sector accounts for an estimated 42.9 per cent of GDP and is thought to employ around 20 per cent of the workforce (2012).

Major manufacturing activities have been diversified to include production of steel, iron, non-ferrous metals, machinery and equipment, fertilisers, plastics and cement. Light industrial products include silk, cotton and rayon textiles, chemicals, processed food, machine tools, hardware and machinery.

Development projects in western and eastern industrial zones have included a vinalon factory in Sunchon with productive capacity of 100,000 tonnes per annum, a potash fertiliser complex in Sariwon, a coal mining complex in Anju, steel complexes in Nampo and Chongjin and synthetic rubber plants in Hamhung and Namhung.

Tourism

North Korea is a closed, insular country that only allows limited access to a limited number of non-Korean visitors, who are tightly chaperoned during specified tours, either in groups or singly. The historic Koguryo Tombs, in the Pyongyang region, are included on Unesco's World Heritage List.

Around 3,000 people, excluding Chinese nationals, are allowed to visit each year, for up to nine days per trip. Tours often begin in Beijing and include either a train journey or connecting flight into North Korea. There are three- and four-star tourist hotels in major cities. Since December 2013 North Korea has been open to tourists in the winter with the opening of the Masikryong ski resort.

In 2010 it was announced that an increased number of US visitors would be allowed to visit throughout the year, instead of only at the time of the Arirang mass games (when thousands of performers create slogans and mosaics with colourful cards).

In July 2015, plans were formed for a North Korean surfing expedition available to tourists. A professional Italian surfer and tourism agency based in New Jersey created a training camp for September 2015.

Mining

The mining sector is thought to account for some 10 per cent of GDP and to employ 5 per cent of the workforce. North Korea is well-endowed with mineral resources, including refractory clays, phosphates, sulphur and graphite and ores of iron, magnesium, tungsten, copper, lead, zinc, silver, gold, magnesite and nickel. Non-ferrous metals are an important foreign exchange earner, with 70 per cent of zinc, lead and copper production in the Hamhung district.

Hydrocarbons

There are no known oil or natural gas reserves. North Korea relies entirely on imports of oil (70,000 barrels per day (bpd) in 2013) for its requirements, which were 14,920 bpd in 2013; it does not import natural gas.

Coal reserves are conservatively estimated at around 600 million tonnes at the end of 2014, with annual production at over 100 million tonnes, and small amounts imported. Coal provides around a third of domestic electricity.

Energy

Total installed generating capacity was 9.5GW in 2014, two-thirds of which is provided by hydropower and the rest by coal-fired plants. Capacity is under-utilised and consumption has declined over the years. Infrastructures, including power plants and the transmission grid, have deteriorated due to lack of investment causing frequent outages and falls in transmissions (brownouts).

North Korea's first nuclear power plant, producing a maximum 5MW at peak periods, but which produced fissile material in 2006, has been a cause of intense negotiations in bringing North Korea under the regulation of the International Atomic Energy Agency. There was international condemnation when North Korea disregarded agreements made for its closure. In 2014 North Korea had still not committed to denuclearisation.

Banking and insurance

There are no private banks in North Korea. The euro replaced the US dollar as the official foreign exchange currency in 2002; the Japanese yen is an unofficial exchange currency.

Central bank

Central Bank of the Peoples' Repubic of Korea

Main financial centre

Pyongyang

Time

GMT plus 8.5 hours (from 15 August 2015)

Geography

North Korea occupies the northern part of the Korean peninsula, bordered to the north by the People's Republic of China and to the south by South Korea. It has a series of mountain ranges, covering up to 80 per cent of the land, across the Korean peninsula and includes all the tallest peaks of over 2,000 metres. A ridge of mountains, the Nangnim Range, runs north-south and makes communication between the east and west coast difficult.
Most of the habitable areas are either in the lowlands or the coastal plains, which are, in turn, limited; the two largest plains – P'yongyang and Chaeryng – are only 500 square kilometres each. Most rivers run in a westerly direction due to the lie of the mountains. The Yalu River is the longest at 790km and flows west into Korea Bay in the Yellow Sea.

Hemisphere

Northern

Climate

Winters are cold, with temperatures ranging from minus 3 degrees Celsius (C) to minus 8 degrees C in January and falling as low as minus 20 degrees C at night. Summers are warm and humid, with an average temperature in August of 25 degrees C. Most rainfall is from June–September.

Entry requirements

Passports

Required by all.

Visa

Required by all. Applications for visas should be made well in advance. It is impossible to visit Korea DPR except by official invitation or by joining group tours from certain countries. Contact the nearest embassy for further details.

Currency advice/regulations

Import and export of local currency is prohibited. Import and export of foreign currency is unlimited, but must be declared. The euro has replaced the US dollar as the official foreign exchange currency; all other currencies will be exchanged at unfavourable rates.

Customs

Single shot cameras, laptop computers (without internet connections) and personal electronic music players are allowed but must be declared.

Prohibited imports

Illegal drugs, firearms and explosives, animals, plants, video cameras, camera lens over 150mm and pornography. Any mass printed documents, literature, audio and videotapes, compact discs and letters deemed political or intended for religious proselytising are also prohibited.
Mobile telephones and global positioning satellite systems and radios are not permitted and must be deposited on entry and collected on departure at the Customs checkpoint.

Health (for visitors)

Mandatory precautions

No compulsory vaccinations.

Advisable precautions

Malaria and cholera are a risk and precautions are essential. Vaccinations against diphtheria, hepatitis A and B, Japanese B encephalitis, polio, tuberculosis, tetanus and typhoid are recommended. Rabies is a risk.
There is a foreigners' hospital in Pyongyang, with higher standards then elsewhere in North Korea where hospitals often lack heat, medicine and supplies and suffer from frequent power loss and outbreaks of infection. In these hospitals one should avoid any invasive surgery. It is strongly recommend that visitors obtain comprehensive health insurance before travelling to DPRK, including emergency medical evacuation as necessary.
All medication necessary should be taken (in their original packaging) in sufficient quantities, as it is not possible to purchase supplies locally.
Drink only bottled or sterilised water, avoid dairy products, which are probably unpasturised. Eat only hot, cooked meat, fish and vegetables, or peeled fruit, and avoid pork, salads and mayonnaise.

Hotels

Pyongyang has *deluxe* hotels that are equivalent to Western 3 stars hotels. Hotels outside Pyongyang are not as well developed but include the traditional Korean hotel *Minsok*.

Credit cards

The main hotels in Pyongyang will take credit and debit cards (Visa and Mastercard but not American Express). Travellers' cheques are not accepted. Hotels generally insist on full payment in advance when checking-in.
Tipping is officially frowned upon, but is increasingly expected by some hotel staff.

Public holidays (national)

Fixed dates

1 Jan (New Year's Day), 16–17 Feb (Kim Jong-il's Birthday), 15 Apr (Kim il-Sung's Birthday), 25 Apr (Army Day), 1 May (Labour Day), 27 Jul (Victory Day), 15 Aug (Liberation Day), 9 Sep (Independence Day), 10 Oct (Foundation of the Korean Workers' Party), 27 Dec (Constitution Day).

Working hours

Banking

0900–1700. The Trade Bank of the DPRK situated near Kim Il-Sung Square in Sungni Street, Pyongyang, is open in the morning every day except Sunday.

Business

0800–1200, 1300–1700.

Government

0800–1200, 1300–1700.

Shops

1000–1800.

Telecommunications

Mobile/cell phones

A basic network has been in operation since 2002, but only available to senior party members. In 2004, the use of mobile phones was banned. A new G3 (third generation) mobile/cell phone network was launched by Egyptian telecom firm, Orascom in December. Despite plans to build a network of 22 million customers, handsets are expected to remain withheld from the general public by being overpriced.

Electricity supply

The electric current on the national grid is 220V AC and 60Hz. 220V and 110V power points are available in hotels.

Weights and measures

Metric system

Social customs/useful tips

Koreans give a short bow or nod as a sign of respect when greeting or departing, although foreigners are usually greeted with a handshake.
When anything is handed over to or received from another person, including business cards, it is polite to use both hands. The card should be read and not immediately put away.
The surname precedes the given name in Korean, but may be transposed for the benefit of foreigners.

Chopsticks should never be placed upright in rice: this is only done at funerals.
In homes and traditional restaurants, shoes are removed and slippers worn.
The Korean word for 'four' is similar to that for death and considered unlucky. Many public buildings and all hospitals omit the fourth floor.
Names should never be written in red ink, a traditional symbol of death.

Security
Government agencies closely supervise visitors to North Korea. Hotel rooms, telephones and fax machines may be monitored, and personal possessions in hotel rooms may be searched. Photographing roads, bridges, airports, railway stations, or anything other than designated public tourist sites may be perceived as espionage and could result in confiscation of cameras and film or even detention.

Getting there
Air
It is essential to reconfirm ticket bookings for a journey some days in advance, as an issued air ticket does not guarantee a seat, unless it has been confirmed and endorsed prior to travel. For most travellers this will be done by their travel agents or inviting organisation in the DPRK.
National airline: Air Koryo
International airport/s: Sunan (FNJ), 24 km from Pyongyang.
Airport tax: None.
Surface
Rail: Rail services operate to/from Beijing and Moscow. Cargo trains started running between North and South Korea on 11 December 2007.
Main port/s: Chongjin, Haeju, Hungnam, Najin, Nampo, Wonsan. The two Koreas are discussing expansion of shipping routes. Nampo and Wonsan may become special import-export zones.

Getting about
National transport
It can be difficult to reach many areas of the interior, although the system is developing.
Air: Air Koryo operates domestic services.
Road: The road network (75,112km) includes motorways between Pyongyang and Wonsan and Pyongyang and Nampo.
Rail: The rail network is estimated at 8,533km, 89 per cent of which is electrified, with two classes of accommodation. Rail travel is slow.
Water: Rivers, canals and sea transport provide important internal links.
City transport
Taxis: Taxis are available and should be booked through the hotel.
Buses, trams & metro: There is a four-line underground system in Pyongyang with a hub at Jonu Station.

BUSINESS DIRECTORY
The addresses listed below are a selection only. While World of Information makes every endeavour to check these addresses, we cannot guarantee that changes have not been made, especially to telephone numbers and area codes. We would welcome any corrections.

Telephone area codes
The international direct dialling (IDD) code for PDR Korea is +850, followed by area code and subscriber's number.

Pyongyang	2	Hamchon	9

Banking
Changgwang Credit Bank Chukzen 1-dong, Mangyongdae District, Pyongyang (fax: 381-4793).

Credit Bank of Korea, Chongryu 1-Dong, Munsu Street, Otan-dong, Central District, Pyongyang (tel: 381-8285; fax: 381-7806).

Foreign Trade Bank of the Democratic People's Republic of Korea, FTB Building, Jungsong dong, Central District, Pyongyang (tel: 381-5270; fax: 381-4467).

The International Industrial Development Bank, Mansu-dong, Central District, Pyongyang (tel: 381-8610).

Korea Daesong Bank, Segori-dong, Gyongheung Street, Pyongyang.

Korea Joint Bank, Ryugyong 1 dong, Pothonggang District, Pyongyang (tel: 381-8151; fax: 381-4410).

Koryo Bank, Pong-Hwa Dong, Potonggang District, Pyongyang (tel: 381-8168; fax: 381-4033).

Central bank
Central Bank of the Democratic People's Republic of Korea, Mansu-dong, 58-1 Sungri Street, Central District, Pyongyang, (fax: 381-4624).

Travel information
Air Koryo, Sunan Airport, Sunan District, Pyongyang (fax: 381-4410 ext 4625).

Kumgangsan International Tourist Company, Central District, Pyongyang (fax: 381-2100).

Tourist Advertisement and Information Agency, Songuja-dong, Mangyongdae District, Pyongyang

National tourist organisation offices
State General Bureau of Tourism of the DPRK, Central District, Pyongyang.

Other useful addresses
Committee for the Promotion of International Trade of the Democratic People's Republic of Korea, Central District, Pyongyang.

Foreign Languages Publishing House, Sosong District, Pyongyang.

Foreign Trade Publishing House, Pyongyang District, Pyongyang.

Korea-Europe Technology & Economy Services, 15 Sojae-chon, Konguk-dong, Potonggang District, Pyongyang (e-mail: ketes@ketes.org).

Korean Central News Agency (KCNA), Potonggang District, Pyongyang.

Korean Committee for Solidarity with World People, 8-120 Yonggwang Street, Central District, Pyongyang.

Korean General Company for Economic Co-operation, Central District, Pyongyang.

Korean General Merchandise Export and Import Corporation, Central District, Pyongyang.

Korean Publications Exchange Association, PO Box 222, Pyongyang 20691.

Korean Publications Export and Import Corporation, Central District, Pyongyang.

Permanent Representative of the DPRK to the United Nations, 515 East 72nd Street, 38-F, New York, NY 10021 (tel: (+1-212) 972-3106; fax: (+1-212) 972-3154; email: prkun@undp.org).

National news agency: Korean Central News Agency (KCNA): www.kcna.co.jp

Internet sites
Korean Friendship Association (for business trips): www.korea-dpr.com

Koryo Group, British company in Beijing, China, arranging tourism to North Korea: www.koryogroup.com

South Korea

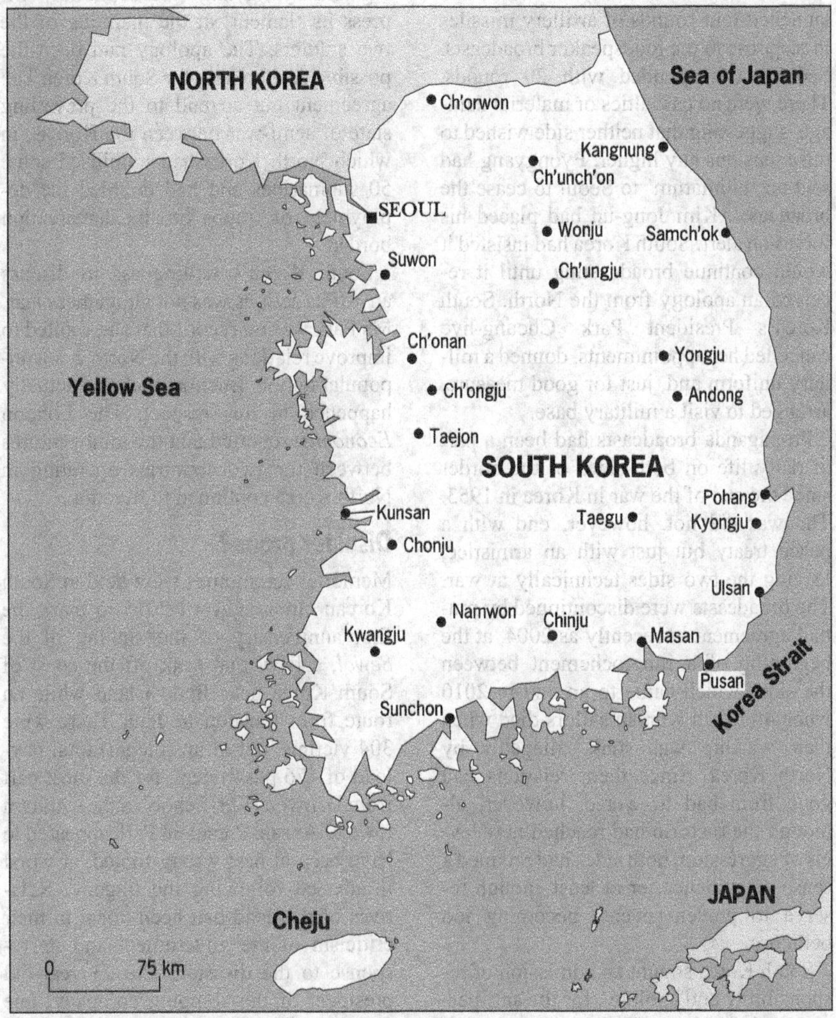

The two Koreas, pitted against each other for decades, have with time become the international community's mismatched 'Odd Couple'. North Korea assuming the role of the uptight, overly neat and tidy Felix Ungar, memorably played by Jack Lemmon, South Korea the more easy going Oscar Madison, as portrayed by Walter Matthau. As in the film, the two rub along next to each other, for the most part more irritated than angry. When anger between the two takes over, it is often expressed in the strangest of ways.

In August 2015, justifiable anger flared up on the part of South Korea when three North Korean anti-personnel landmines maimed two South Korean soldiers patrolling a neutral section of the demilitarised zone (DMZ) between the two countries. The soldiers' legs were reportedly blown off.

Your mines, our loudspeakers

After almost a week's interval following the incident the authorities in Seoul launched their response: loudspeakers along the border began to broadcast propaganda, news and the inevitable 'Gangnam Style' pop music sung by the South Korean pop star, Psy. Such is the power of the loudspeakers that the broadcasts could be heard for miles. Whether or

KEY FACTS

Official name: Daehan Min-kuk (Republic of Korea) (ROK) (known as South Korea)

Head of State: President Park Geun-hye (NF) (from 19 Dec 2012; took office 25 Feb 2013)

Head of government: Prime Minister Lee Wan-koo (Saenuri) (from 21 Apr 2015)

Ruling party: Coalition led by Saenuri (New Frontier) (NF) (formerly known as Hannara Dang (Grand National Party) (GNP) with Seonijin Tongil-dang (Advancement Unification Party) (AUP) (formerly known as Jayu Seonjin-dang (Liberty Forward Party) (LFP) (from 2008; re-elected 19 Dec 2012)

Area: 99,091 square km

Population: 50.42 million (2014)

Capital: Seoul

Official language: Korean

Currency: Won (W) = 100 chon

Exchange rate: W1,148.99 per US$ (Nov 2015)

GDP per capita: US$28,101 (2014)

GDP real growth: 3.32% (2014)

GDP: US$1,416.95 billion (2014)

Labour force: 26.62 million (2014)*

Unemployment: 3.54% (2014)

Inflation: 1.27% (2014)

Balance of trade: US$92.69 billion (2014)*

Annual FDI: US$4.66 billion (2011)

* estimated figure

not the response was a 'proportionate' was almost immaterial. The South Korean authorities had long been aware that the immature Kim Jong-un's régime would be hyper-sensitive to the broadcasts, which informed North Koreans within earshot that there was little international respect, or even time, for their leader and his sycophantic clique of advisers. News that famines were almost a thing of the past throughout most of the world came as a shock to North Koreans, many of whom lived in a state bordering on permanent famine. The loudspeaker system had been carefully maintained, but not used, during the ten years since tensions had flared up in 2004. The last occasion on which the pot had boiled over was in 2010, when North Korea sank the *Cheonan*, a South Korean warship, in March and then shelled Yeonpyeong Island in November.

When the North Korean response did come, it was hardly one of calm submission. It was anger rather than sorrow – and with a vengeance, as the sound of artillery fire obliterated the South's broadcasts. The Southern response to the explosive outbreak was in kind. It was difficult to ascertain whether artillery attacks were the North just huffing and puffing, or whether this was simply a negotiating ploy. The answer came when the North declared what it described as a state of 'quasi war' between the two Koreas. This looked like something more than show. The declaration added that there would be a full military response, to begin on 22 August unless the South undertook to silence and dismantle the loudspeakers. It issued a deadline of 5 pm 'local' time, which meant 'Pyongyang', time, the new time zone (half an hour behind that of South Korea) which had only been announced a month earlier.

Conversations were held over the hot-line between 'the couple' and reason appeared to have prevailed. The two countries agreed to meet in Panmunjon at 6 pm with a view to lowering tensions. The meeting was taking place only 30 minutes after the North Korean deadline. The seriousness of the meeting, however, could be judged by the fact that on both sides of the table those participating were certainly not junior officers. South Korea was represented by Kim Kwanjin, head of the National Security Agency and the unification minister, Hong Yong-pyo. Pyongyang was to be represented by Vice Marshal Hwan Pyong-so, considered to be Kim Jong-un's right hand man and Kim Yang Gon, its head of relations with Seoul. According to Kim Kyo-hyun, the deputy head of the National Security Agency North Korea had suggested the meeting a day earlier. The South Korean government had made counter-proposals to ensure the participation of Mr Hwan.

Both sides were well aware that tensions had been running high for five years or so. According to the version of the South Korean ministry of defence, the North had launched four rounds of artillery missiles in response to the loudspeaker broadcasts. Seoul had responded with 29 rounds. There were no casualties or material damage, suggesting that neither side wished to raise tensions any higher. Pyongyang had sent an 'ultimatum' to Seoul to cease the broadcasts; Kim Jong-un had placed his forces on alert. South Korea had insisted it would continue broadcasting until it received an apology from the North. South Korea's President Park Cheung-hye cancelled her appointments, donned a military uniform and, just for good measure, arranged to visit a military base.

Propaganda broadcasts had been a part of daily life on both sides of the border since the end of the war in Korea in 1953. The war did not, however, end with a peace treaty but just with an armistice, leaving the two sides technically at war. The broadcasts were discontinued by mutual agreement as recently as 2004, at the beginning of a rapprochement between the sides which came to an end in 2010 when 46 South Korean sailors died when their warship was sunk, allegedly by North Korea. Since then, relations had gone from bad to worse; however, although the rhetoric had reached new levels of aggression, both sides had retained a sense of prudence, or at least enough reserve to prevent events becoming too bellicose.

South Korea sought an admission of responsibility and apology, for the anti-personnel landmines. Their use (although South Korea was reported to be equally guilty of using them) was deemed to be a violation of the terms of the armistice; a United Nations (UN) investigation confirmed that the landmines used were of the North Korean 'wooden-box' type. Not that South Korea could adopt a 'holier than thou' attitude. Both sides had reportedly littered the DMZ with a million or more mines. South Korea resolutely claimed that North Korea had sent troops into the DMZ to plant them. Rumours abounded, claiming that North Korea sought to derail the annual military manoeuvres between South Korea and the US which were already under way. Or even to prejudice a state visit to China by Ms Park scheduled for early September 2015.

After 43 hours of discussion, agreement was reached between the two sides. In theory, at any rate, both sides got what they wanted. The joint communiqué signed by both Koreas stated that on the following midday Seoul would cease its broadcasting and Pyongyang would publicly express its 'lament' at the maiming of the two soldiers. The apology had been the possible deal breaker for South Korea The agreement put an end to the prevailing state of semi-war between the Koreas, in which North Korea had mobilised some 50 submarines and had doubled the deployment of troops on the demarcation border.

South Korea's willingness to discuss any of its actions was not altogether clear. Ms Park was on record that she wanted to improve relations with the North, a not unpopular notion. But not much had actually happened in this respect. The London *Economist* reported that the joint ventures between the two countries operating in North Korea continued to function.

Disaster prone?

Memorial ceremonies were held in South Korean cities in April 2015 to mark the first anniversary of the sinking of the *Sewol*, a ferry that sank off the coast of South Korea near Jindo island while en route from Incheon to Jeju. There were 304 victims, out of an (illegal) total payload of 476 passengers, for the most part from Danwon High School in the southern town of Ansan. President Park appeared to have been at best wrong-footed, at worst ill-advised following the tragedy. Relatives of the dead had been vocal in their criticism of the government and its response to the disaster. The 23 year-old president of the shipping company, one Yoo Byung-un disappeared and was later found dead, presumably by his own hand. The *Sewol*'s captain, Lee Joon-seok was tried in court and sentenced to life imprisonment.

Misjudging public sentiment, the government had originally declined to have the ship raised, claiming that the US$110 million cost was excessive. This despite the fact that there were nine bodies still trapped on board. In a damage control exercise, speaking at a memorial service in the port of Jindo, President Park Guen-hye announced that the ship would be raised after all. On the April anniversary of the disaster the government faced public anger, with relatives cancelling at least one memorial service in protest. Many bereaved families had left Jindo port before the President arrived, a painful gesture of disapproval. One grudge focussed on the apparent political interference with the official investigation. One protestor welcomed the President by shouting out that 'the Republic of Korea is rotten.' Embarrassingly, Korea's Prime Minister Lee Wan-koo was prevented from entering the memorial area by relatives of those who had died. A memorial service in the city of Ansan was cancelled because the President was not present.

In 2015 another disaster not of its making threatened to damage public confidence in the government. In May 2015 a medical condition known as the Middle East Respiratory Syndrome (MERS) was detected following the return of a 68 year old man to Korea from the Middle East. At first his condition defied Korea's doctors, until the fourth hospital he was sent to was able to confirm his condition. By then, in late May eleven people had died from MERS, with 120 confirmed cases and some 3,600 people in quarantine. By the end of May there had been 14 deaths, for the most part among elderly people who had an existing medical condition that the MERS virus aggravated. Any optimism expressed by the Korean authorities was quashed by the World Health Organisation (WHO), which announced that it expected the number of cases to rise. Probably responding to a media fuelled exaggeration, in some parts of South Korea schools were closed and even whole villages were isolated. In responding to the epidemic, Ms Park's government were between hell and a hard place, the public's perception of its government's disaster handling competence still conditioned by the hopeless bungling of the *Sewol* sinking. But in the MERS case there was cause for criticism: following the first diagnosis, the administration made no official statement for over two weeks. Then as more cases emerged, no further information was made available, no bulletins issued. Matters were made worse by the fact that when, finally, a further announcement was made, it was full of errors as to where cases had been confirmed. The discovery that virus detection equipment had been installed at Seoul's Blue House, the President's official residence was interpreted as self protection at the expense of Korean citizens.

As Ms Park's popularity ratings slumped to around 30 per cent, for the President the two disasters had the effect of heightening awareness that all was not well with Korean politics and business. In its 2014 *Corruption Perceptions Index* the Berlin based NGO Transparency International ranked South Korea 45, one place behind the African state of Cape Verde. Little cause for celebration there. Not too much cause, either, in South Korea's relations with the respected NGO, Human Rights Watch, which – in May 2015 – wrote to the government expressing concern that its social policies discriminated against lesbian and gay youth, violating the right to education, information and health. HRW considered that new legislation violated South Korea's international human rights commitments. This, claimed HRW, ran contrary to South Korea's 'commendable' leadership role at the United Nations (UN), where it had voted for both the 2011 and 2014 Human Rights Council resolutions to address violence and discrimination on the basis of sexual orientation and gender identity. In July 2015, noted HRW, South Korea had also reaffirmed the government's 'international commitment to upholding the rights to education, information and health for all' by supporting a UN resolution on violence against women – the first-ever UN resolution to mention comprehensive sexuality education. This was seen as commendable, but the sharp contrast between these positions taken at the UN versus official policy and practice within South Korea was disappointing.

The economy

In May 2015 the International Monetary Fund (IMF) published its annual review of the South Korean economy, noting that performance had been on a declining trend after decades of robust and sustained growth. Potential output had decreased from around seven per cent during 1990–97 to 4.75 per cent during 2000–07 and had been running at about 3.5–4 per cent since then. While this rate still exceeded that of many of Korea's peers, prosperity was concentrated within the highly competitive export-oriented conglomerates employing a small share of the population, whereas household income growth and service sector productivity have been sluggish. In the view of the IMF, population ageing risked becoming a major brake on potential growth: on current trends the working age population was projected to peak in 2016 and Korea's population was expected to become one of the oldest among the OECD countries by 2050. The IMF noted that even reaching its projection for potential growth of 3.75 per cent would require increased productivity playing a more significant role than at present.

In the view of the IMF exports were at the centre of these trends, accounting for both the period of rapid growth and the slowdown. Korea's gross exports had risen steadily since the early 2000s and by 2015 they exceeded 50 per cent of gross domestic product (GDP), significantly higher than the OECD average. This growth was driven in large part by the emergence of Korea's flagship companies to world-class status and accompanied by a sizeable gain in global market share. It was unlikely, however, that Korea could continue to rely on this growth model going forward – indeed, according to the IMF, Korea's market share has been at a standstill since 2011 with continued gains in electronics offset by stable or falling shares for other leading export products. Korea's future prosperity will therefore depend on success in fostering more broad-based productivity growth. The IMF considered that the resilience of the Korean financial system had increased since 2008 and what it described as 'near-term vulnerabilities' were limited. Korea's banks remained well capitalised with the capital adequacy ratio at around 15 per cent in June 2014 and their funding and liquidity conditions were stable. The banking sector's profitability had improved somewhat in 2014 driven by lower provisions and impairment losses, although the return on assets was still below the historical average. The aggregate bank non-performing loan (NPL) ratio had increased in 2013, albeit from a low level, driven by a rise in NPLs to large companies in the shipbuilding and construction sectors, but since then the banks' asset quality had improved somewhat with the decline in new bad loans and the write-offs and sales of old loans. Growth in the non-bank financial institutions had slowed considerably and their profitability continued to weaken, in part from low interest rates and the strengthening of regulations. Overall, the banks' short-term external debt increased in 2014 although it remained well below the pre-crisis levels and the sizes of the banks' foreign currency and maturity mismatches continued to decline. However, Korean banks still relied heavily on offshore funding and any tightening of global financial conditions could lead to funding pressures.

For its part, the Asian Development Bank (ADB) in its annual overview of the South Korean economy noted that economic expansion accelerated slightly from 3.0 per cent in 2013 to an estimated

3.3 per cent in 2014. Unexpected weakness in the world economy slowed down the anticipated export-led rebound. The contribution of net exports to GDP growth fell by two-thirds, from 1.5 percentage points in 2013 to 0.5. According to the ADB, domestic demand accounted for the bulk of GDP growth in 2014. Investment, mainly in plant and equipment, contributed 1.5 percentage points, a marked turnaround from 2013, when its contribution was nil. Private consumption added another 0.9 percentage points and the government's consumption contribution held steady at 0.4 percentage points. Quarter on quarter, growth momentum failed to gain traction during 2014, as the pace of expansion slackened from 0.9 per cent in the first quarter to 0.4 per cent in the fourth, mainly reflecting subdued domestic demand following the *Sewol* ferry disaster. Mirroring the continued general weakness of domestic demand and abetted by falling global oil prices, consumer price inflation remained low at 1.3 per cent in 2014, below the central bank target band of 2.5 per cent ±1.0 percentage point. Core inflation, which strips out food and energy, was at 2.0 per cent.

Plant and equipment investment grew by 5.9 per cent after shrinking slightly in 2013. Construction investment decelerated sharply to 1.1 per cent in 2014 from 6.7 per cent in 2013, with both residential construction and civic works in the doldrums. Private consumption growth slowed further to 1.7 per cent in 2014, owing to the Sewol ferry disaster, a reduction in a mobile phone subsidy that hurt sales and sluggish wage growth despite the strong rise in employment.

Merchandise exports in real local currency terms rose by a mere 2.2 per cent in 2014 (0.5 per cent in nominal US dollars), halving from 4.5 per cent in 2013 as export growth slowed and turned negative in the second half of the year. The gathering recovery in the US, the sole bright spot in a generally bleak export environment, could not offset the sluggishness of other main export markets, including the PRC and the European Union (EU). In line with stuttering domestic demand and lower oil prices, merchandise imports grew by even less than merchandise exports, helping to push the current account surplus to a record equal to 6.3 per cent of GDP – this despite the services account recording a deficit, partly because intellectual property rights payments increased. The won appreciated during the first half of the year but closed the year lower in nominal terms at W1,099 per US dollar. In real effective terms, it had appreciated by 1.8 per cent during the year.

With slow growth a bigger concern than inflation, the Bank of Korea (central bank) cut its benchmark base interest rate from 2.50 per cent to 2.25 per cent in August, 2.00 per cent in October and a 4-year low of 1.75 per cent in March 2015. Fiscal policy was also expansionary in 2014. The fiscal deficit rose to 1.8 per cent of GDP from 1.5 per cent in 2013 and the ratio of public debt to GDP nudged up to 35.1 per cent. A US$40 billion stimulus was unveiled in July and the government signalled its intention to actively support growth through fiscal measures. Reflecting the low budget deficit and public debt in the Republic of Korea, rating agency Moody's upgraded its sovereign credit rating in 2014, as did Standard and Poor's.

In the view of the ADB, both external and internal factors pointed to only modest recovery in 2015 that was unlikely to dispel concerns about the economy's loss of momentum since the global financial crisis. GDP growth was expected by the ADB to rise slightly to 3.5 per cent in 2015 as global output and trade began to stir. Domestic demand was likely to rebound, buoyed by the improved terms of trade, much lower global oil prices (as the Republic of Korea imports virtually all of its energy – see 'Energy' below) and a modest recovery in the housing market. GDP growth was expected to rise further to 3.7 per cent in 2016, supported by a strengthening global economy. Subdued inflation and a strong fiscal position would allow both monetary and fiscal policy to support growth.

Energy

Rather like Japan, South Korea is not endowed with energy resources, relying on imports to meet about 97 per cent of its total primary energy consumption as a result of insufficient domestic resources. South Korea is, according to the US government's Energy Information Administration (EIA) one of the world's leading energy importers. It has a large oil refining sector, but relies almost entirely on crude oil imports to fuel its refineries. South Korea is the second-largest importer of liquefied natural gas in the world behind Japan. Rising coal consumption and negligible domestic production have resulted in South Korea having to rely heavily on coal imports in recent years. In 2014, South Korea was the fourth-largest global coal importer. Fossil fuel sources account for nearly two-thirds of South Korea's electricity generation, while nuclear accounts for 30 per cent.

Risk assessment

Politics	Fair
Economy	Good
Regional stability	Fair

COUNTRY PROFILE

1910 Japan formalised its annexation of Korea after gaining responsibility for its security following victory in the Russo-Japanese war of 1905.

1919 Japan suppressed the mass March First movement for self-determination.

1930s–1940s Japan imposed measures designed to assimilate the Korean population, including the outlawing of the Korean language and family names. Korea suffered under military occupation but gained the benefits of forced industrialisation.

1945 Liberation at the hands of allied forces was a prelude to partition of the peninsula as the victorious powers encouraged friendly governments north and south of the 38th parallel. The US occupied the south while the north was taken over by the Soviet Union. As the two powers did not wish to give independence to Korea, feeling that the Korean people needed political and social re-education, a line of demarcation was established.

1948 Political divisions in the peninsula deepened. In the south, the Republic of Korea became independent after UN-supervised elections were held. Dr Syngman Rhee, leader of the Liberal Party, became the country's first president. The declaration of the Democratic People's Republic of Korea (DPRK) in the north followed, with Kim il-Sung as premier and Head of State.

1950 North Korea invaded the South with backing from China and the Soviet Union, prompting US-led intervention under a UN mandate.

1953 A cease-fire was agreed, but a peace-treaty was not signed.

1960 President Rhee was forced to resign.

1961 The government was deposed by a military coup led by General Park Chung-Hee.

1963 After the military dictatorship, a new constitution was enacted. General Park Chung-Hee became president.

1980 Demonstrations by students led to martial law being imposed throughout the country. The National Assembly was closed and all political activity banned.

1981 Martial law was lifted and political parties were formed.

1985 The election results transformed the political scene with the emergence for the first time of a relatively powerful parliamentary opposition.

1986 The opposition launched a campaign demanding constitutional reform.
1987 Roh Tae-Woo was elected president.
1988 The Constitution of the Sixth Republic was adopted, following sustained popular unrest during 1987.
1993 President Roh was succeeded by Kim Young-Sam.
1994 President of DPRK, Kim il-Sung died
1997 The Asian financial crisis precipitated the near collapse in South Korea's economy, as its credit rating plunged from A1 to BAA2; the won was devalued and the IMF and G-7 countries provided a US$57 billion loan. The resultant political upheaval led to the defeat of the Hannara Dang, (Grand National Party) (GNP) as opposition leader Kim Dae-Jung was elected president.
2000 President Kim Dae-Jung visited Pyongyang, DPRK (North Korea) and met President Kim Jong-il, in an unprecedented meeting of the two Korean leaders. President Kim Dae-Jung won the Nobel peace prize. Family reunions were allowed between the north and south for the first time since the Korean War.
2001 The government resigned after a vote of no-confidence threatened Lim Dong-Won, the unification minister and chief architect of the 'Sunshine' policy promoting engagement with North Korea. The president subsequently returned Lim to government as a presidential advisor and appointed five new ministers and retained Lee Han-Dong as prime minister.
2002 Key inter-Korean relations developed after the South Korean envoy Lim Dong-Won visited North Korea. Kim Suk Soo became prime minister. Roh Moo-Hyun won the presidential elections.
2003 Goh Kun became prime minister. President Roh resigned from the ruling Saecheonnyeonminju Dang (SMD) (Millennium Democratic Party) for the Uri Dang (UD) (Our Party). Hundreds of South Koreans crossed the demilitarised zone into North Korea in a declaration of unity.
2004 The National Assembly impeached President Roh; Prime Minister Goh Kun became acting president. The left-leaning liberal UD won National Assembly elections. The Constitutional Court overturned President Roh's impeachment. Prime Minister Goh Kun resigned and Lee Hai Chan became prime minister. South and North Korea agreed to open cross-border roads and to make test runs on two railways. The supreme court rejected the proposal that Yeongi-Kongju region, in the central south province of Chungchong, would be the site of the new capital city. The government compromised and decided to move just 36 ministries and agencies instead.
2005 Street protests in Seoul followed Japan's confirmation of its claim to a small group of uninhabited islands called Dokdo, which South Korea also claimed. Chairman of Daewoo, Kim Woo-chong was convicted on fraud charges and ordered to pay back US$22 billion, for his part in the company's US$70 billion collapse.
2006 Han Myung-sook of the Daetongham Minjusin-dang (DM) (United New Democratic Party) became the first female prime minister. Ban Ki-moon was appointed secretary general of the United Nations. Five spies for the DPRK were convicted, the biggest case of espionage since the North and South Korean reconciliation in 2000.
2007 North and South Korea resumed ministerial meetings following the DPRK's nuclear closure deal. The chairman of Hyundai was convicted of embezzlement. South Korea agreed to assume operational control of its military forces, in the event of a war, after 2012. A US-South Korea FTA was signed. The first passenger trains since 1953 crossed the north-south border. A summit of leaders of North and South Korea took place, the first in 15 years. They agreed to formally end the Korean War. The South Korean delegation included industrialists, bureaucrats, poets and clerics. Lee Myung-bak (GNP) won the presidential election with 48.7 per cent. The UD collapsed and broke into splinter groups.
2008 One of the country's great cultural treasures, the Namdaemun Gate, was destroyed by fire. The Minju-dang (Democratic Party) (DEP) political party was formed from a merger between the DM and the UD. Relations between DPRK and South Korea deteriorated after DPRK expelled managers of joint industrial enterprises and test fired short-range missiles. In parliamentary elections the GNP won a slim majority of 153 seats (out of 299).
2009 All political and military agreements with South Korea were scrapped by DPRK, due to what DPRK saw as 'hostile intent' by South Korea. Former president Roh Moo-Hyun committed suicide while under investigation for alleged corruption. President Lee appointed Chung Un Chan as prime minister, to carry forward his planned programme of reforms.
2010 The Constitutional Court, South Korea's highest court, ruled that the death penalty does not violate the constitution and should continue. A report by an international investigation team, led by South Korea, concluded that North Korea torpedoed a South Korean warship in March, with the loss of all 46 sailors aboard. North Korea angrily denied the accusation, as condemnation by UN members followed swiftly. In a major cabinet re-shuffle, President Lee replaced seven ministers and nominated Kim Tae-ho as prime minister after Prime Minister Chung Un-Change resigned, citing parliament's failure to endorse his policy to found a science-business park in a central region. South Korea staged five days of military drills off its west coast. The move infuriated the North Koreans, who, in retaliation, fired off over 100 rounds of artillery close to the disputed sea border between the two countries. A South Korean fishing vessel, which may have strayed across the border, was seized by North Korea; the government in South Korea demanded the vessel's immediate and safe return. On Liberation Day, President Lee called for a fund to be started towards the cost of unification with the north. Kim Hwang-sik became prime minister. Four people, including two civilians, were killed after North Korea fired artillery shells at the island of Yeonpyeong in South Korea. Damage to homes and businesses was widespread and hundreds of people fled the island. Korean observers consider the aggression by North Korea could be seen as endorsing the succession of Kim Jong-un and a measure of the significance the North places on fishing rights in the rich seas around the island. The attack on the island came just days after news that North Korea had built a modern plant to enrich uranium, for possible use in nuclear weapons.
2011 North and South Korean military talks collapsed in February within hours of commencing, following South Korea insistence that North Korea must apologise for shelling Yeonpyeong Island in 2010. DPRK had agreed to talks under pressure from China and by its need to secure food and fuel aid. In July Pyeongchang was awarded the 2018 Winter Olympics. The EU signed a free trade agreement with South Korea, its biggest with any Asian country, as South Korea agreed to end the 20 per cent import duty on alcohol and its complicated rules on labelling and storage. In August DPRK called for a resumption of the six-party nuclear negotiations 'without preconditions'. A trade agreement with the US was agreed by both houses of the US congress in October. In December, the Democratic Labor Party and a faction of the New Progressive Party called the People's Participation Party, merged to form the Tonghapjinbodang (United Progressive Party) (UPP). The DM merged with the smaller, Citizens Unity Party sic) to form Minju Tonghabdang (Democratic United Party) (DUP).
2012 On 2 February, the ruling GNP was renamed the Saenuri (New Frontier) (NF) party. The change was deemed necessary to counter voter-apathy, while its interim

leader Park Geun-hye said it would allow the party to be 'reborn as a completely new party' and heralded deep-seated reforms. In parliamentary elections held on 11 April the ruling NF won 42.8 per cent of the vote (152 seats, out of 300) and the newly formed DUP 36.5 per cent (127); turnout was 54.3 per cent. On 3 July, the new, Special Autonomous City of Sejong was officially opened by the prime minister. By 2014, 36 government agencies and nine ministries should have moved into offices in the city, beginning with the prime minister's office. On 7 October, South Korea announced an agreement with the US to increase the range of its ballistic missile system, to counter the threat from the DPRK. On 9 October, DPRK announced that it had successfully launched a missile that could reach the US mainland. National elections were held on 19 December. Six candidates took part in the presidential election; Park Geun-hye (NF) won 51.6 per cent and her closest rival Moon Jae-in (DUP) 48.0 per cent, with a turnout of 75.8 per cent. In parliamentary elections the conservative coalition of three political parties, led by NF, won a total of 157 seats (out of 300), the liberal coalition of two parties won 127 seats, the progressive coalition won 13 seats and others the remaining three. Turnout was 54.3 per cent.

2013 President Park Geun-hye took office 25 Feb 2013. On 11 June high level talks that had been agreed the day before to be held in Seoul were suspended by North Korea over the choice of delegates. Seoul attempted to call the North on the restored Red Cross hotline at 09.00 on 12 June but there was no answer. The two Koreas had spoken twice a day at 0900 and 1600 until the hotline had been cut by the North on 10 March. On 6 July officials from North and South Korea began talks on reopening the KIC. By 10 July the two sides had agreed in principle to restart operations. However, within days the talks fell through. On 7 August North Korea again offered talks, for 14 August, saying its workers would return to the joint complex and the safety of South Korean staff would be guaranteed. The offer came shortly after the South Korean government announced insurance payments to companies affected by the stoppage – a move seen as paving the way for a formal closure of the site. It was also a day after Seoul said it was providing US$6 million in aid to North Korea. On 14 August the two governments agreed to re-open the Kaesong complex, although no date was set. On 15 August President Park called for the resumption of the reuniting of families divided by the partitioning of the Korean peninsula. Joint exercises with the US began on 19 August. North Korea was notified well in advance and it was not thought that the drills would affect the re-opening of the Kaesong Industrial Complex. Officials in Seoul announced on 23 August that reunions between families separated since the 1950–53 war would take place on 25–30 September at the North's Mount Kumgang resort. On 21 September North Korea announced it was indefinitely postponing the scheduled family reunions. In an interview with the BBC on 3 November President Park Geun-hye highlighted the deep rift with Japan over 'wrongdoings' committed by the Japanese during the war and for which there has been no apology.

2014 Pyongyang threatened to cancel the family reunions agreed for February because of the annual military exercises between South Korea and the US, also planned for February. The first high-level talks between North and South Korea since 2007 were held on 12 February and were expected to discuss family visits. A ferry sank on 16 April, killing at least 300 people, mostly children on a school outing. Prime Minister Chung Hong-won resigned on 27 April saying he felt responsible for the government's poor response to the sinking of the ferry. However, President Park Geun-hye was unable to replace him immediately and he remained in post as acting prime minister. North Korea threatened a 'merciless' retaliatory strike against South Korea as the 12-day Ulchi Freedom Guardian annual drills with the US military began on 18 August. Pope Francis, on a visit at the same time, called for reconciliation on the Korean peninsular. He had earlier beatified 124 South Korean Catholic martyrs during a large open-air mass in Seoul on 16 August. In November the captain of the ferry that had sunk in April was sentanced to 36 years in prison after being found guilty of gross negligence.

2015 On 23 January the president appointed Lee Wan-koo as prime minister. On 20 April Prime Minister Lee Wan-koo offered to resign after being accused of accepting US$27,700 in illegal campaign funds. On 28 April an appeals court increased the sentence of the ferry captain to life in prison on a murder charge, strengthening the November 2014 sentence. Fourteen crew membershad their sentences reduced. A number of three day 'family visits' to North Korea took place in October.

Political structure

Constitution

A new constitution, allowing direct presidential elections and thus providing a framework for civilian rule, took effect in 1988 after receiving overwhelming approval in a referendum. The constitution removed the president's sweeping emergency powers that included the right to dissolve parliament. It also enhanced the authority of the legislature and judiciary. It provided for more civil liberties, including restoration of *habeas corpus*, while the National Assembly was empowered to supervise and investigate state affairs. Free presidential elections replaced the electoral college system, which had favoured the ruling party candidate. In addition, the constitution requires that the armed forces must maintain political neutrality.

The constitution provides for greater checks and balances among the executive, legislative and judiciary powers. A Board of Audit and Inspection was set up to monitor all government expenditure, revenue and agencies. The chairperson is appointed by the president but only with the National Assembly's approval.

A constitutional court has judgement on the constitutionality of any legislation.

Form of state

Democratic republic

The executive

Executive power is held by the president, who is popularly elected for a single term of five years and governs with the assistance of the State Council, normally composed of 15–30 ministers and headed by the prime minister. The State Council is appointed by the president on the advice of the prime minister. It does not have to be composed entirely of members of the National Assembly. No active member of the armed forces may serve on the State Council.

The president has veto power over legislation, but the National Assembly can override this by a two-thirds vote.

Other presidential powers include the appointment of officials such as judges, ministers, the mayors of five cities (Seoul, Pusan, Taegu, Inchon and Kwangu) and the governors of nine provinces.

National legislature

The unicameral Kuk Hoe (National Assembly) has 299 members, of which 245 are directly elected in single-seat constituencies and 54 are elected by proportional representation; all serve for four-year terms.

Legal system

There is a three-tier legal system, headed by a Supreme Court. This Court is composed of a chief justice (for a six-year term) and 13 justices (on recommendation by the chief justice), all appointed by the president, with the consent of the National Assembly. Below the Supreme Court are High Courts (intermediate appelate courts) and, below these, District Courts. High Courts and District Courts are divided into geographic districts. Korea also has a number of specialised courts, such as a Family Court and an Administrative Court.

Last elections

19 December 2012 (parliamentary and presidential)

Results: Parliamentary: the conservative coalition of three political parties won 157 seats (out of 300), of which its senior party, Saenuri (New Frontier) (NF) had won 152 seats, the liberal coalition of two parties won 127 seats, of which Minju Tonghabdang (Democratic United Party) (DUP) won 127 seats, the progressive coalition of two parties won 13 seats, of which Tonghapjinbodang (United Progressive Party) (UPP) won 13, others won three. Turnout was 54.3 per cent.

Presidential: Park Geun-hye (NF) won 51.55 per cent, Moon Jae-in (DUP) 48.0 per cent; four other candidates each won less than 1 per cent. Turnout of 75.8 per cent.

Next elections

13 April 2016 (parliamentary); 2017 (presidential)

Political parties

Ruling party

Coalition led by Saenuri (New Frontier) (NF) (formerly known as Hannara Dang (Grand National Party) (GNP) with Seonijin Tongil-dang (Advancement Unification Party) (AUP) (formerly known as Jayu Seonjin-dang (Liberty Forward Party) (LFP) (from 2008; re-elected 19 Dec 2012)

Main opposition party

United Democratic Party (UDP)

Nearly 60 per cent of the population is under 25 years of age. The US plans to withdraw 12,500 of its 37,000 troops stationed in South Korea by 2006.

Population

50.22 million (2013)*

Last census: 1 November 2010: 48,219,172

Population density: 490 inhabitants per square km. Urban population 83 per cent (2010 Unicef).

Annual growth rate: 0.6 per cent, 1990–2010 (Unicef).

Ethnic make-up

Koreans, although apparently homogeneous, have complex ethnic origins, with much genetic input from the nomadic tribes of Mongolia and Central Asia. There are over 25,000 Chinese, the only major foreign ethnic community besides the 37,000 US troops stationed in South Korea. In addition, there are some 230,000 migrant labourers from a variety of countries such as Kazakhstan, Morocco and China. There is also a growing number of refugees who have escaped from the harsh conditions of North Korea.

Religions

There is no state religion and the country is tolerant of various religious faiths. Although census and churchgoing data conflict, the most recent information available indicates that up to 49 per cent of the population professes to be Christian, 47 per cent Mahayana Buddhist, 3 per cent Confucianist.

Education

Public expenditure on education amounts to 3.6 per cent of GDP. Universal primary education and gender parity, at this level and in secondary schools, have been achieved.

Primary schooling lasts until a child is 12, middle secondary schooling lasts for three years, these constitute compulsory education. Upper secondary high schools offer either, an academic, special purpose (combined academic and vocational courses), or a wholly vocational programme, lasting for three years.

There are five types of public and private teriary institutions including junior colleges and universities.

Literacy rate: 98 per cent, male; 96.8 per cent, female; adult rates (World Bank).

Compulsory years: 6 to 15

Enrolment rate: 110 per cent, gross primary enrolment, of relevant age group (including repeaters); 102 per cent, gross secondary enrolment (World Bank).

Pupils per teacher: 31, in primary schools

Health

There are around 19,500 private clinics complementing the country's hospitals, of which a significant number are university-affiliated. Improved water sources and sanitation facilities are available to 92 per cent and 63 per cent of the population resectively.

Life expectancy: 77 years, 2004 (WHO 2006)

Fertility rate/Maternal mortality rate: 1.3 births per woman, 2010 (Unicef); maternal mortality 20 deaths per 100,000 live births (World Bank).

Birth rate/Death rate: 6 deaths and 14 births per 1,000 population (World Bank estimates).

Child (under 5 years) mortality rate (per 1,000): 4 per 1,000 live births (WHO 2012)

Welfare

The National Basic Livelihood Protection Law makes social assistance a legal right for the unemployed, based on a concept of 'productive welfare' which combines means-testing with self-support plans to facilitate re-entry to the workforce.

Public pensions provision, introduced in 1988, is set to increase as the system confronts an ageing population with a 12-fold increase in the expected number of beneficiaries by 2010. Contributions will have to double to 18 per cent of salary to maintain an actuarial balance, according to the Organisation for Economic Co-Operation and Development (OECD). The South Korean government may consider alternative options, such as privately-managed pensions funds, paid into by the allowances firms are obliged to award departing employees.

Main cities

Seoul (capital, estimated population 9.8 million (m) in 2012), Pusan (3.7m), Inchon (2.7m), Taegu (2.4m), Taejon (1.5m), Kwangju (1.5m), Changwon (1.1m), Suwon, Ulsan (1.1m), Yongin (1.0m).

In 2012, many government ministries were relocated to the city of Chungcheongnam.

Languages spoken

The Korean language is a member of the Altaic family with origins in Mongolia. Approximately 60 per cent of the vocabulary is borrowed from Chinese. The written language employs its own phonetic character system, Hangul.

English is spoken to a limited extent in government and business circles. The older generation often speak Japanese.

Official language/s

Korean

Media

The Korean media, reputedly notorious for their appetite for influence, are thought, by civic campaigners, to be a constituency in need of urgent reform. Efforts made in the past to curtail publishers and their various backers have not succeeded. The sector has a long tradition of collaborating with South Korea's authoritarian regimes and is sensitive about criticism of bias.

Press

Much of the Korean press is controlled by industrial conglomerates. Readership is high and there are over 100 national and local dailies to choose from.

Dailies: The 'Big Three' nationals published in Seoul are *Chosun Ilbo* (http://english.chosun.com) is considered a conservative publication, *JoongAng Ilbo* (http://joongangdaily.joins.com) and *Donga Ilbo* (http://english.donga.com), take an independent line. In Korean, other regional publication include from Pusan *Pusan Ilbo* (www.busanilbo.com), *Kookje Shinmun* (www.kookje.co.kr); from Inch'on *Inchon Ilbo* (http://news.itimes.co.kr); from Taegu *Kyongbuk Ilbo* (www.kyongbuk.co.kr), *Maeil Shinmun* (www.imaeil.com) and *Morning News* (www.morningnews.co.kr).

In English, *The Seoul Times* (www.theseoultimes.com).

Weeklies: Many foreign magazines have Korean sections, local news magazines include *Korea Newsreview*, which publishes articles from the government-owned *Korea Herald* (www.koreaherald.co.kr), in English.

Business: In Korean, *Hankyung* (www.hankyung.com), *Financial News Daily* (www.fnnews.com), *Seoul Economic Daily* (www.hankooki.com) and *Maeil Business Newspaper* (http://news.mk.co.kr, with online English edition. Most national newspapers also provide business news some with online English editions.

Periodicals: *Dong-A Herald* is a bi-monthly student newspaper. *The Granite Tower* is a monthly English language tabloid.

Broadcasting

Radio: The public service is the Korea Broadcasting System (http://english.kbs.co.kr), which operates six networks including Radio Korea International (http://world.kbs.co.kr) offering programmes in 11 languages.

There are over 200 local radio stations some of which are relayed nationwide. Around 30 per cent of all stations are privately owned and commercial. There are national networks that are educational and religious. The American Forces Network (AFN) Korea (http://afnkorea.net) is operated by the US military.

Television: There are over 30 television stations run by the country's networks, of which the most important are Korea Broadcasting System (KBS) and Munwha Broadcasting Corporation (MBC). The longest-running stations are KBS 1, 2, 3 (an educational station), MBC and AFKN-TV (operated by the US military for its personnel and their dependants). Other networks operating in South Korea include Asia-Pacific broadcaster Arirang TV, which provides English-language programming, the youth-oriented Mnet, Korea Music Television, Seoul Broadcasting System (SBS) and the News Channel of Korea. Around 90 per cent of the population subscribe to cable TV.

Yonhap News Agency, 85-1, Susong-dong, Jongro-gu, Seoul (fax: 398-3463/3567; internet: http://english.yonhapnews.co.kr).

Economy

South Korea, which is one of Asia's largest economies, is open and mixed and heavily geared to exporting manufactured goods, particularly vehicles and shipbuilding, textiles, steel, electronics and computers, bioengineering, fine chemistry and aerospace items. However with its lack of hydrocarbons and an economy dependent on exports South Korea is vulnerable to external shocks, as it requires the import of oil and natural gas, while being subject to the vagaries and volatile market needs of international trading.

The global economic crisis brought on the worst decrease in exports since 2001, falling in January 2008 by 35 per cent year-on-year from the same period in 2007. Investment and domestic consumption fell as a result and the economy suffered one of the sharpest contractions of any country. However, South Korea had learned from the two previous recessions of 1997 and 2001, both of which had been characterised by massive capital outflows and a slump in exports. As a result the government swiftly adopted measures to curtail serious damage to the economy by initially setting aside US$55 billion in foreign exchange reserves to provide loans to banks and trade-related businesses. It also administered major monetary and fiscal stimuli (to stop any slide in confidence). To shield the banking sector it established a bank to buy up toxic assets and recapitalise bank funds. By 2009 GDP growth was down to 0.3 per cent. Nevertheless South Korea avoided falling into recession and in 2010 the economy rebounded with growth of 6.3 per cent as exports increased and oil imports were less expensive than previously anticipated. The Central Bank of South Korea lifted its key interest rate to 2.25 per cent in 2010, the first increase since August 2008 when it was dropped to a record low of 2 per cent. Growth continued at a steady rate following this, averaging 3.1 per cent from 2011–14.

External trade

South Korea is a member of the Asia-Pacific Economic Co-operation (Apec) forum, which is a group of 21 countries that border the Pacific. The objective of Apec is to facilitate trade, economic growth and investment in the region.

A revised, Korea-US Free Trade Agreement (Korus FTA) was announced in 2010; the original having been signed in 2006. US exports to South Korea were expected to rise to US$11 billion annually. The agreement allows the import of vehicle-parts that had been, until the revision, blocked but denied import of beef aged over 30-months. The Korus FTA, under negotiation for 16 years, was finally ratified by the US Congress on 13 October 2011 and by the South Korean parliament on 15 March 2012. Under the FTA, 80 per cent of traded goods had their tariffs removed and a further 15 per cent will so by 2017.

Main export sectors include semiconductors, telecommunications, computers, steel making, shipbuilding, vehicle assembly, organic chemicals and textile manufacturing. In 2014, electronics accounted for 24.1 per cent of all exports, with road vehicles accounting for 12.8 per cent and machinery 11.0 per cent.

Imports

Principal imports are petroleum and natural gas, machinery, electronics and electrical equipment, petroleum, steel, plastics, transport equipment, iron and steel.

Main sources: China (17.1 per cent of total in 2014), Japan (10.2 per cent), US (8.6 per cent)

Exports

Principal exports are semiconductors, telecommunications equipment, vehicles, computers, steel, ships and petrochemicals.

Main destinations: China (25.4 per cent of total in 2014), US (12.3 per cent), Japan (5.6 per cent)

Agriculture

Farming

The agricultural sector accounts for 2.3 per cent of GDP and employs around 15 per cent of the workforce. Farming remains essentially subsistence-based and is inherently uncompetitive. While, by comparison, farmers are richer than their counterparts elsewhere in Asia, the average farm holding is big enough to support only a small family and the disparity in incomes between the urban and rural populations is growing.

Price-support policies for farmers are being reduced in line with South Korea's international commitments. Increasing the average size of farms and decoupling production decisions from government aid are likely to be vital in promoting efficiency in farming.

The main crops grown are rice, sweet potatoes, barley, soya beans and a wide range of fruit and vegetables. Despite considerable efforts, the country depends on imports for animal feed grains. Ginseng, tobacco, pears and processed noodles are among other South Korean exports.

Fishing

The fishing industry is an important source of export earnings but international restriction of fishing zones has limited potential growth. South Korean fishing vessels are mostly active in the South Pacific. The annual catch, of which some 60 per cent is marine fish, totals up to 2.6 million tonnes.

Following the annual meeting of the Commission for the Conservation of Southern Bluefin Tuna (CCSBT), held on Cheju Island, South Korea, all members agreed to a 20 per cut in the roughly 17,000 tonnes in 2009 bluefin tuna

catches from 2010. Scientists had warned that without a cut fish stocks could crash as numbers had become dangerously low.
In July 2012, the government announced that it was lifting the prohibition on fishing for whales off the Korean coast. The decision drew condemnation from the International Whaling Commission (IWC).
In 2014, tune exports rose 42.1 per cent year-on-year, up from 141,000 tonnes in 2013 to 200,000 tonnes in 2014.

Forestry

Forests, around half of which are conifer, cover some 65 per cent of the total land area. Much of the forest owes its existence to large-scale replanting programmes implemented after the Second World War and since the end of the Korean War in 1953. The latter conflict, together with logging under the Japanese occupation, and demand for fuelwood, badly degraded the native forest.
South Korea and Indonesia have an agreement for forestry co-operation. This involves projects such as tree planting, fighting forest fires, skills development and eco-tourism investment.

Industry and manufacturing

Korea's industrialisation programme made it the world's eleventh richest economy during the 1990s, when it became the world's largest shipbuilder and producer of DRAM memory chips, the fourth biggest car exporter and the sixth largest steelmaker. The industrial sector accounts for around 40 per cent of GDP and employs around a fifth of the workforce.
The manufacture of iron and steel products, the automobile industry, shipbuilding, petrochemicals and electronics continue to be central to export-led growth. Other main products include fertilisers and other industrial chemicals, rubber, synthetic and natural textiles, garments, footwear and processed foods.
The industrial structure continues to be haunted by the legacy of rapid state-guided industrialisation protected from overseas competition. The government has struggled to limit the economic power of the 30 largest leading companies (*chaebol*), which still dominate national industry.
In the first quarter of 2012, Samsung became the world's largest seller of mobile phones with sales of 93 million units, overtaking the Finnish company Nokia which had sales in 83 million units. Samsung also had its highest profits at US$4.5 billion (net), which was an increase of 81 per cent on 2011.

Tourism

South Korea has an ancient culture that resides alongside a modern, developed country, so that historic temples, shrines and traditional buildings are juxtaposed with contemporary cities. South Koreans celebrate many festivals, centred on the natural environment which include Korean cuisine. There are ten sites listed on Unesco's World Heritage List. In 2008 the Namdaemun (Great South Gate), the oldest timber structure in Seoul (constructed in 1398) was burned down in an arson attack. By February 2012 restoration work on the Namdaemun, on what has been designated as South Korea's first national treasure, was almost complete, at a cost of US$20 million.
Domestic tourism is a healthy component of the sector with outbound South Koreans being one of the top travelling nationalities, although their tendency is to stay in Asia and the Pacific region.
Travel and tourism in total contributed 5.8 per cent of GDP in 2014. In 2014, there were a record 11.9 million arrivals. In 2014, the Chinese constituted 43.1 per cent of the total arrivals, followed by the Japanese with 13.6 per cent. Employment in the industry was 6.3 per cent (around 1.6 million jobs) in 2014.
The travel and tourism industry typically attracts over US$6 billion in capital investment. The country has also attracted international amusement park chains.

Mining

There are no significant mineral resources. South Korea relies mainly on imports to meet its increasing domestic demand. The major mineral imports are iron ore, copper and zinc ore concentrates. Cement is a major export commodity to the US, as there is surplus in the domestic market.
LG-Nikko Copper Incorporated, a joint venture established by LG and Japan Korea Joint Smelting Company, a Japanese consortium, is the only copper smelting and refining operation in South Korea. Each company was obliged to invest US$20 million in the joint venture that took control of LG's Changhang and Onsan copper smelting and refining operations, which had an estimated value of US$830 million.
Domestic iron ore supplies only make up about one per cent of South Korea's needs. The Pohang Iron and Steel Company (Posco), the largest crude steel producer in South Korea and the only integrated iron and steel producer, formed a strategic alliance with Nippon Steel Corp, to expand research and development, and also encouraged other Asian companies to join the alliance. Posco employs more than 5,000 employees at production plants in Pohang and Kwangyang, producing more than 23.4 million tonnes of steel products annually for customers in over 60 countries. Its products range from electrical steel sheets to stainless steel products.
The only lead and zinc mine, at Kumba, supplies about 10 per cent of the demand for lead and zinc concentrates. Korea Zinc, which is one of the largest primary zinc producers in the world, completed the expansion of its zinc plant complex at Onsan, and is able to produce over 350,000 tonnes per year. Young Poong Corporation, its parent company, increased zinc metal output at the Sukpo zinc refinery, in the North Kyongsang Province, by over 198,300 tonnes per year.
The non-metal mineral sector accounts for around half of the total mining industry. Other industrial mineral production includes limestone, silica stone, kaolin, serpentine, feldspar and zeolite. Major imports consist of potash, asbestos and manganese ores and concentrates.

Hydrocarbons

There are no domestic oil reserves. Oil consumption was 2.46 million barrels per day (bpd) in 2014, making it the world's eleventh largest consumer and fifth largest importer of oil, of which 20 per cent is exported as refined. The country has a strategic petroleum reserve of over 110 million barrels of oil, which covers 90 days of imports, in order to offset any disruption to supply; in 2009 the reserve is expected to total over 146 million barrels. The state-owned Korea National Oil Corporation (KNOC) has, in an effort to secure the country's oil supply, bought up stakes in oil companies throughout the world and is involved in 32 foreign exploration and production projects, of which six are producing oil. South Korea has an oil refining capacity of 2.6 million bpd, from six facilities, with plans for another 480,000bpd plant in Sosan.
Domestic gas production has ceased and in 2009 South Korea was the world's second largest importer of liquefied natural gas (LNG) importing 88.8 billion cubic metres in 2007 mostly provided by Qatar, Oman, Malaysia and Indonesia.
Proven coal reserves were 146 million tonnes in 2014, all of which is the less valuable brown coal typically used in power plants. Domestic production has declined from 10 million tonnes in the mid-1980s to less than 800,000 tonnes in 2014. Metallurgical coal for steelmaking comes mainly from China and Australia, where the Korean Electric Power Corporation (Kepco) has invested in a number of mines.

Energy

Total installed electricity generation was 84.7 gigawatts (GW) in 2013, of which around two-thirds was produced by conventional thermal power stations, with

nuclear reactors producing around 12 per cent of all energy. There are four operational nuclear power stations in South Korea.
The privatisation of the state-owned electricity utility, Korean Electric Power Corporation (Kepco), has moved at a slow pace but Kepco has been broken into six generating companies with the government retaining control of the Korea Hydro and Nuclear Power Company (KHNPC). Auctioning off of the other five companies has been repeatedly postponed. Foreign ownership is limited to 30 per cent of any single power company.

Financial markets

Stock exchange

Koria Exchange (KRX)

Banking and insurance

The 1997/98 financial crisis revealed underlying structural problems in South Korea's banking system. The crisis led to the creation of the Financial Restructuring Committee (FRC), which reported a large ratio of non-performing loans (NPLs) to total loans and poor accounting standards. The government was forced to nationalise the country's five largest banks so that by 2002/03 at 7.5 per cent, South Korea had the second-lowest NPL ratio in East Asia after Hong Kong. The estimated recovery rate on South Korean NPLs is 35 per cent, compared to Singapore and Hong Kong at 75 per cent and 50 per cent respectively.
Although the financial system is in better health, controversies linger over bank privatisation. Arguments also surround banking regulation, with President Roh reluctant to allow the *chaebol* to regain their influence over the sector. Roh favours increasing the powers of independent directors and shareholders as well as encouraging greater foreign ownership, although there is little foreign interest in South Korea's banking sector which is seen as risky.
Another pressing concern for the government is consolidating the banking sector into three or four large banks.

Central bank

Bank of Korea

Main financial centre

Seoul

Time

GMT plus nine hours

Geography

South Korea forms the southern part of the Korean peninsula, in north-east Asia, with the Democratic People's Republic of Korea to the north. To the west is the Yellow Sea, the East China Sea is to the south and the Sea of Japan is to the east. The Korea Strait separates the peninsula from Japan in the south-east. The country's portion of the peninsula is dominated by rugged terrain and mountains, culminating in the T'aebaek-sanmaek mountain range which runs from north to south along the eastern coast. Two major rivers originate in this range, the Naktong flowing to the Korea Strait and the Han river to the Yellow Sea. Plains are few and far between, mostly concentrated in the west, with the coastal strips in the east and south typically narrow. There are a number of islands off the southern and western coasts. Of these the largest is Cheju, over 1,800 square km in size and home to South Korea's highest peak, Mount Hallasan (1,950 metres).

Hemisphere

Northern

Climate

Winters are dry and very cold, with temperatures well below 0 degrees Celsius (C) between December–February. Korean summers are typically hot and humid, with monsoon rains, tropical storms and occasional typhoons from June–September. The average July temperature range is 22–29 degrees C. The narrow southernmost coastal plain has the mildest climate and is home to vegetation such as bamboo and evergreen oak.

Entry requirements

Passports

Required by all and must be valid for six months from the date of departure.

Visa

Not required by tourists from North America, Japan, Australia and many citizens of EU for up to 60 days. See http://english.tour2korea.com and the link to *Entry Info* for a full list and entitlements. For business travellers and those not eligible for visa-free travel, visit www.mofat.go.kr/me/index.jsp and see *visa control*. Applications must be submitted to the nearest Korean consulate.

Currency advice/regulations

The import of local and foreign currency greater than US$10,000 must be declared; permission for the export of local and foreign currency larger than US$10,000 (or equivalent, including travellers cheques) must be obtained from customs or the Bank of Korea; export is limited to the amount declared on arrival. Exchange receipts should be retained for verification.
Travellers cheques are accepted in banks, hotels and larger shops in major towns.

Customs

Personal effects are duty free, including high-value items (cameras, watches etc) which should be recorded on a baggage declaration form on arrival.
A certificate from the Cultural Properties Preservation Bureau is necessary for exporting antiques. Permission for trade imports or exports must be obtained from the trade and industry ministry or from authorised foreign exchange banks, and certain items may be restricted or prohibited (such as ginseng and cuttlefish).

Prohibited imports

Illegal drugs and pornography. Firearms and ammunition, fruit, vegetables soil and seeds all require licences, obtained before arrival.

Health (for visitors)

Health facilities in South Korea are generally good. The high level of pollution may be a serious problem for those suffering from respiratory conditions.

Mandatory precautions

An HIV/Aids-free certificate is required for stays of over three months.

Advisable precautions

Vaccinations are recommended for diphtheria, tuberculosis, hepatitis A and B, Japanese B encephalitis, polio, tetanus and typhoid. There is rabies risk and travellers should avoid stray animals.

Hotels

Luxury hotels include a 10 per cent service charge in the bill. Tipping is not usual, although it is on the increase in Western-style hotels.

Credit cards

Major hotels accept credit cards, but check when booking which ones are accepted for settlement of hotel bills. Also accepted in major department stores, supermarkets etc.
The Korea Travel Card, a pre-paid debit card allows visitors to pay for goods and services throughout the country at favourable rates. The card is obtained through tourist outlets.

Public holidays (national)

Fixed dates

1 Jan (New Year's Day), 1 Mar (Independence Movement Day), *1 May (Labour Day), 5 May (Children's Day), 6 Jun (Memorial Day), 17 Jul (Constitution Day), 15 Aug (Liberation Day), 3 Oct (National Foundation Day), 25 Dec (Christmas Day).
* Bank and business organisations holiday.
The summer vacation is the last week in July and the first week in August.

Variable dates

Soellal (Lunar New Year, Jan/Feb, three days), Birth of Buddha (May), Chu'seok (Harvest Moon Festival, Sep/Oct, three days).

Working hours

Banking

Mon–Fri: 0900–1700.

Business

Mon–Fri: 0900–1800.

Government
Mon–Fri: 0900–1800.
Shops
Sun–Sat: 1030–2000 (department stores, closed one day per month, typically Mon, different stores choose different days). Small shops open from early morning till late evening every day of the week.

Telecommunications
Mobile/cell phones
There are 3G GSM services available.

Electricity supply
220V AC, 60 cycles, with round two-pin plugs.

Weights and measures
Metric system used in commerce; local system also in use, especially relating to land and buildings.

Social customs/useful tips
Korean surnames precede given names, and given names are never used alone, except by intimates. The family names, 'Kim', 'Lee' and 'Park', cover more than half the population and may have variant spellings. Business associates are normally addressed by title (eg Director Kim or Manager Lee).
Business entertaining usually takes place in restaurants and wives do not participate. Business visitors should carry a good supply of business cards, which are exchanged on introduction. Hotels can provide bilingual business cards overnight.
Note the official romanisation of Korean words has been altered to more accurately reflect pronunciation (eg Gimpo international airport rather than Kimpo, Busan instead of Pusan and Gimchi instead of Kimchi, Korea's signature spiced cabbage dish). However, the former romanisations are still widely used, with some major newspapers declaring a complete boycott of the new system.
Business etiquette is very formal. Punctuality and a smart appearance are important. Jackets and ties are required, even in summer. However, the ritual of getting drunk with a potential business partner may be expected. You should appear respectful at all times and keep smiling even if negotiations are slow. Business associates like to spend time getting to know you. Confirm agreements in writing.
It is impolite to refuse food or drink. Use the right hand when giving or receiving. Outdoor shoes should never be worn inside a house.
There are certain areas, particularly near the demilitarised zone, where entry and photography are forbidden.

Getting there
Air
National airline: Korean Air and Asiana Airlines
International airport/s: Seoul-Inchon International Airport (ICN), 40km west of Inchon and 52km from Seoul. Facilities include, duty-free shopping, restaurant, bar, banks, business centre, medical services and car hire. It is connected to the city by rail, taxi (30–60 mins) buses and ferry. Pusan (PUS) 27km from city, with flights arriving mainly from Japan. Cheju (CJU) on the island of Cheju.
Airport tax: Departure tax: W10,000, not applicable to transit passengers.
Surface
Road: There are no land borders with any other country except North Korea; all border crossing are closed.
Rail: Cargo trains started running between North and South Korea on 11 December 2007.
Water: There is a daily ferry service between Pusan and Shiminoseki, Japan.
Main port/s: Pusan, Inchon, Masan, Ulsan, Mokpo, Kunsan, Yosu.

Getting about
National transport
Air: Gimpo Airport, located close to Gimpo, west of Seoul, is used for all domestic flights. Korean Air operates daily services between Seoul and Pusan (50 minutes), Taegu, Cheju, Ulsan and Kwangju, with less frequent services to other centres. Other services are provided by Asiana Airlines. Expect to be searched for firearms when embarking on internal flights.
Road: The road network contains more than 60,000km of highways and lesser roads. More than half of roads are paved. Major cities are linked by motorways, but minor roads may be poorly maintained. Pusan is over five hours distant from Seoul by road, compared to four hours by rail.
Buses: Air-conditioned express *Chwasok* buses operate between major cities, in competition with trains. Villages are often connected by a network of local buses.
Rail: Korean National Railroads offers normal and super-express trains between major cities. The super-express train (*Saemaul-ho*) runs between Seoul and Pusan, Chongju, Yosu and Inchon. Timetables and station signs are often in English. Many trains have sleeping and dining cars.
Water: Various services are available. Mokpo and Pusan are linked by a steamer service twice weekly. The *Angel Line*, a hydrofoil service, runs between Pusan and Yosu five times daily, via Chongmy. The island of Cheju is linked to the mainland by daily ferries, including car ferries, three times per week.
City transport
Public transport in Seoul is well-developed, but becomes crowded at rush-hour.
Taxis: Registered taxis carry meters and are clearly marked on the roof. Taxis are plentiful, and available at ranks, by telephone or hailed in the steet. A 20 per cent surcharge applies between 0000–0400. Taxi drivers suspend use of meters for journeys outside town, so negotiate the fare for such trips in advance. It is advisable to carry written instructions in Korean if possible.
Buses, trams & metro: The Korean Air limousine shuttle bus calls at 20 Seoul locations, including major hotels.
City buses, though cheap and convenient, are crowded. Purple and white buses have few seats. Green and beige 'seat buses' make fewer stops and are more comfortable and air-conditioned. Tokens are available at most stops. There are English-language signs on city-centre buses only.
Seoul has an extensive metro system with eight lines accessing most parts of the city and provides a rapid means of travelling between places. First and last trains are around 0500–2400 depending on individual lines. Comprehensive information is given at www.seoulmetro.co.kr/eng/ with maps and related links. Signs are in English and Korean.
Pusan, Daegu and Incheon have metro systems and Gwangju and Daejeon have systems under construction.
Car hire
International driving licences are acceptable, but chauffeur-driven car hire is recommended in the main cities.

BUSINESS DIRECTORY
The addresses listed below are a selection only. While World of Information makes every endeavour to check these addresses, we cannot guarantee that changes have not been made, especially to telephone numbers and area codes. We would welcome any corrections.

Telephone area codes
The international direct dialling (IDD) code for the Republic of Korea, is +82, followed by area code and subscriber's number:

Inchon	32	Seoul	2
Pusan	51	Taegu	53

Useful telephone numbers
Police: 112
Fire: 119
Medical emergency 1339
Directory inquiries: 114
International calls: 1035/1037
Tourist helpline: 1330

Chambers of Commerce
American Chamber of Commerce in Korea, 4501 Trade Tower, 159-1 Samsung-dong, Kangnam-gu, Seoul

135-729 (tel: 564-2040; fax: 564-2050; e-mail: info@amchamkorea.org).

British Chamber of Commerce in Korea, 21/F Seoul Finance Centre, 84 Taepyoung-ro 1-ga, Chung-gu, Seoul 100-101 (tel: 720-9406; fax: 720-9411; e-mail: bcck@bcck.or.kr).

European Union Chamber of Commerce in Korea, Kyobo Building, 1 Chongro 1-ga, Chongro-gu, Seoul, 110-714 (tel: 725-9880; fax: 725-9886; e-mail: eucck@eucck.org).

Inchon Chamber of Commerce and Industry, 447 Nonhyon-dong, Namdong-gu, Inchon 405-300 (tel: 810-2800; fax: 810-2807; e-mail: ebiz@incci.co.kr).

Korea Chamber of Commerce and Industry, 45 Namdaemunro 4-ga, Chung-gu, Seoul 100-743 (tel: 316-3114; fax: 771-3267; e-mail: info@korcham.net).

Pusan Chamber of Commerce and Industry, 853-1 Pomchon-dong, Pusanjin-gu, Pusan 614-021 (tel: 645-7771; fax: 645-3003; e-mail: julyjang@pcci.or.kr).

Taegu Chamber of Commerce and Industry, 107 Sinchon 3-dong, Tong-gu, Taegu 701-023 (tel: 755-0041; fax: 795-5774; e-mail: mrlee@dcci.or.kr).

Banking

Bank of Seoul, 10-1, 2-ka, Namdaemun-ro, Chung-gu, Seoul (fax: 756-6389).

Cho Hung Bank Ltd., 14, 1-ka, Namdaemun-ro, Chung-gu, Seoul (tel: 733-2000; fax: 732-0835).

Citizens National Bank, 9-1, 2-ka, Namdaemun-ro, Chung-gu, Seoul (fax: 757-3679).

Commercial Bank of Korea, 111-1, 2-ka, Namdaemun-ro, Chung-gu, Seoul (tel: 754-3920; fax: 754-9203).

Export-Import Bank of Korea, 16-1, Yoido-dong, Youngdungpo-gu, Seoul 150-010 (tel: 779-6114; fax: 784-1030).

Hanil Bank, 130, 2-ka, Namdaemun-ro, Chung-gu, Seoul (tel: 754-0479).

Hana Bank, 101-1, 1-ga Ulchiro, Chung-gu, Seoul 100-191 (tel: 754-2121; fax: 756-6358).

Korea Development Bank, 10-2, Kwanchul-dong, Chongro-gu, Seoul (tel: 398-6369; fax: 720-0015).

Korea Exchange Bank, 181, 2-ka, Ulji-ro, Chung-gu, Seoul.

Korea First Bank, 100 Kongpyong-dong, Chongro-gu, Seoul (tel: 733-0070; fax: 736-8092).

Shinhan Bank, 120, 2-ga, Taepyung-ro, Chung-gu, Seoul (tel: 756-0505; fax: 774-7013).

Central bank

Bank of Korea, 110, 3-KA Namdaemun-ro, Chung-ku, Seoul 100-794 (tel: 759-4114; fax: 759-4060; e-mail:bokdplp@bok.or.kr).

Stock exchange

Koria Exchange (KRX), www.krx.co.kr

Travel information

Korea Automobile Association, 1, PO Box 2008, Seoul (tel: 785-5051).

Korean Air, 41-3 Seosomun-Dong, Chung-gu, Seoul (tel: 755-2221; fax: 751-7799; internet: www.koreanair.com).

Ministry of tourism

Ministry of Culture and Tourism, 82-1 Sejongno, Chongno-gu, Seoul (tel: 736-7946; fax: 736-8513).

National tourist organisation offices

Korean National Tourism Organisation (KNTO), 40 Cheongyecheonmo, Chung-gu, Seoul 100-180 (tel: 729 9497; fax: 319 0086; e-mail: webmaster@mail.knto.or.kr; internet site: www.tour2korea.com).

Ministries

Ministry of Agriculture and Forestry, 1 Jungang-dong, Kwachon, Kyongki-do 427-760 (tel: 500-1587; fax: 503-7249; e-mail: webmaster@maf.go.kr).

Ministry of Construction and Transportation, 1 Jungang-dong, Kwachon, Kyongki-do 427-712 (tel: 504-9031; fax: 504-6825; e-mail: webmaster@moct.go.kr).

Ministry of Culture and Tourism, 82-1 Sejongno, Jongno-gu, Seoul 110-703 (tel: 3704-9114; fax: 3704-9119; e-mail: webmaster@mct.go.kr).

Ministry of Defence, 1 Yongsan-dong, Yongsan-gu, Seoul 140-701 (tel: 795-0071; fax: 703-3109; e-mail: cyber@mnd.go.kr).

Ministry of Education and Human Resources Development, 77-6 Sejong-no, Jongno-gu, Seoul 110-760 (tel: 3703-2114; fax: 2100-6133; e-mail: webmaster@moe.go.kr).

Ministry of Environment, 1 Jungang-dong, Kwachon, Kyongki-do 427-729 (tel: 2110-6546; fax: 504-9206; e-mail: shinae@me.go.kr).

Ministry of Finance and Economy, 1 Chungang-dong, Kwachon City, Kyonggi-Do, Seoul (tel: 503-7171; fax: 502-0193; internet site: www.mofe.go.kr/mofe/eng).

Ministry of Finance, Jungang-dong, Kwachon, Kyongki-do 427-725 (tel: 503-9032; fax: 503-9033; e-mail: fppr@mofe.go.kr).

Ministry of Foreign Affairs and Trade, Doryeom-dong Jongno-gu Seoul 110-787 (tel: 100-2114; fax 100-7999:email: web@mofat.go.kr; internet: www.mofat.go.kr/me/index.jsp).

Ministry of Gender Equality, 77-6 Sejong-no, Jongno-gu, Seoul 110-760 (tel: 3703-2500; fax: 2106-5145; e-mail: webadmin@moge.go.kr).

Ministry of Government Administration and Home Affairs, 77-6 Sejong-no, Jongno-gu, Seoul 110-760 (tel: 3703-2114; fax: 3703-5502; e-mail: webmaster@mogaha.go.kr).

Ministry of Government Legislation, 77-6 Sejong-no, Jongno-gu, Seoul 110-760 (tel: 3703-2114; fax: 738-2649; e-mail: lawinfo@moleg.go.kr).

Ministry of Health and Welfare, 1 Jungang-dong, Kwachon, Kyongki-do 427-760 (tel: 503-7524; fax: 504-6418; e-mail: m_mohw@mohw.go.kr).

Ministry of Information and Communication, 100 Sejong-no, Jongno-gu, Seoul 110-777 (tel 750-2114; fax: 750-2915; e-mail: webmaster@mic.go.kr).

Ministry of Justice, 1 Jungang-dong, Kwachon, Kyongki-do 427-760 (tel: 503-7023; fax: 2110-3079; webmaster@moj.go.kr).

Ministry of Labour, 1 Jungang-dong, Kwachon, Kyongki-do 427-716 (tel: 2110-2114; fax: 503-9772; e-mail: webmaster@molab.go.kr).

Ministry of Maritime Affairs and Fisheries, 50 Chungjeongno, Saedaemun-gu, Seoul 120-715 (tel: 3148-6114; fax: 3148-6044; e-mail: webmaster@momaf.go.kr).

Ministry of Planning and Budget, 520-3 Banpo-dong, Seocho-gu. Seoul 137-756 (tel: 3480-7990; fax: 3480-7600; e-mail: nara@mpb.go.kr).

Ministry of Science and Technology, 2 Jungang-dong, Kwachon, Kyongki-do 427-715 (tel: 503-7600; fax: 503-7673; e-mail: webadmin@most.go.kr).

Ministry of Trade, Industry and Energy, 1 Jungang-dong, Kwachon, Kyongki-do 427-760 (tel: 2110-5061; fax: 503-9496; e-mail: webmocie@mocie.go.kr).

Ministry of Unification, 77-6 Sejong-no, Jongno-gu, Seoul 110-760 (tel: 3703-2433; fax: 739-5047; e-mail: webmaster@unikorea.go.kr).

Other useful addresses

Association of Foreign Trading Agents in Korea, 218 Hangangro 2-ka,

Youngsan-gu, Seoul (tel: 792-1581; fax: 749-1830).

Board of Audit and Inspection, 25-23 Samchong-dong, Jongno-gu, soul (tel: 721-9114; fax: 721-9299).

British Embassy, 4 Chung-dong-Chung-gu, Seoul (tel: 735-7341/3; fax: 736-6241).

Customs Administration, 71 Nonhyun-dong, Kangnam-gu, Seoul (tel: 512-0011; fax: 512-2322).

Economic Planning Board, 1 Chungang-dong, Kwach'on City, Kyonggi, Seoul (tel: 503-7171).

Emergency Planning Committee, 1 Chungang-dong, Kwachon-City, Kyonggi-Do (tel: 503-7723; fax: 503-7727).

Fair Trade Commission, 1 Chungang-dong, Kwachon-City, Kyonggi-Do (tel: 503-7171; fax: 504-5144).

Foreign Investment Policy Division, Rm 203, Complex No 3, 1 Chungang-dong, Kwacheon City, Kyongki-do (tel: 503-9276/7; fax: 503-9324).

Institute of Foreign Affairs and National Security, 1376-2 Seocho-dong, Seocho-gu, Seoul (tel: 571-1020; fax: 571-1019).

Invest Korea, Kotra Bldg 300-9 Yomgok-dong, Seocho-gu, Seoul 137-70 (tel: 3460-7545; fax: 3460–7946; internet: www.investkorea.org).

Korean Exhibition Centre, 65 Samsung-dong, Gangnam-gu, Seoul (tel: 553-7907/8; fax: 557-5784).

Korean Foreign Trade Association, TCPO Box 100, Seoul (tel: 551-5114; fax: 551-5100/5200).

Korean Information Service, 82-1 Sejongno, Jongno-gu, Seoul 110-703 (internet site: www.korea.net).

Korean Republic Embassy (US), 2450 Massachusetts Avenue, NW, Washington DC 20008, USA (tel: (+1-202) 939-5600; fax: (+1-202) 797-0595; e-mail: information_usa@mofat.go.kr).

Korea Stock Exchange, 33, Yoido-dong, Youngdeungpo-gu, KR-Seoul 150-010 (tel: 780-2271; fax: 786-0263; internet site: www.kse.or.kr/e_index.html).

Korean Trade Promotion Corporation, CPO Box 1621 10-1, 2-ka Hoehyun-dong, Chung-gu, Seoul (tel: 753-4180/9; internet site: www.kotra.or.kr/eng/index.php3).

Meteorological Administration, 1 Songwall-dong, Jongno-gu, Seoul (tel: 738-0345; fax: 723-8731).

National Statistical Office, Hanta Building, 645-15 Yoksam-dong, Kangnam-gu, Seoul (tel: 222-1901; fax: 538-3874; internet site: www.nso.go.kr/eindex.htm).

National Tax Administration, 108-4 Susong-dong, Jongno-gu, Seoul (tel: 397-1200; fax: 720-0278).

Overseas Aircargo Service Inc, 1–6 Fl. Daishin Bldg, 93–62 Bukchang-dong, PO Box 2757, Chung-gu, Seoul (tel: 753-8374/6; fax: 756-9400).

Rural Development Administratin, 250 Socun-dong, Suwon-City, Kyonggi-Do (tel: 292-4370; fax: 292-4163).

Securities Exchange Commission, 28-1 Yoido-dong, Yongdongpo-gu, Seoul (tel: 785-7593; fax: 785-3475).

Small and Medium Business Administration, 2 Chungang-dong, Kwachon-City, Kyonggi-Do (tel: 509-7114; fax: 503-7941).

Internet sites

Asiana Airlines: http://us.flyasiana.com

EC21 (Internet trade site): www.ec21.net

Korea Air: www.koreanair.com

Korea Asset Management Corporation: www.kamco.or.kr/eng/index.htm

Korea Infogate: www.koreainfogate.co.kr

Korean Travel (internet: http://english.tour2korea.com/).

Inchon International Airport, www.airport.or.kr/eng/airport/

Samsung Economic Research Institute: www.koreaeconomy.org

Kosovo

KEY FACTS

Official name: Republic of Kosovo

Head of State: President Atifete Jahjaga (from 7 Apr 2011)

Head of government: Prime Minister Isa Mustafa (from 9 December 2014)

Ruling party: Coalition led by Partia Demokratike e Kosovës (PDK) (Democratic Party of Kosovo), Lidhja Demokratike e Kosovës (LDK) (Democratic League of Kosovo) and Aleanca Kosova e Re (AKR) (New Kosovo Alliance)

Area: 10,887 square km

Population: 1.73 million (2011; census figure)

Capital: Pristina

Official language: Albanian, Serbian (English was the official language of the UN Interim Administration Mission in Kosovo (UNMIK))

Currency: Euro (€) = 100 cents

Exchange rate: €0.89 per US$ (Sep 2015)

GDP per capita: US$3,693 (2011)*

GDP real growth: 2.74% (2014)*

GDP: US$7.32 billion (2014)*

Unemployment: 40.00% (2010)*

Inflation: 0.43% (2014)*

Balance of trade: -US$2.73 billion (2014)*

* estimated figure

In late October 2015 the European Union (EU) was thought to be about to sign an agreement with Kosovo which would pave the way for the accession of Kosovo to the pan-European grouping, a move which was also perceived to be helpful in bringing prospective member country Serbia closer to the EU.

Concerns

However, many observers expected the move towards Kosovar membership to cause concern in a number of EU member states that were struggling with internal separatist movements. Notable among these were Spain (where the Catalan independence movement had become a thorn in the government's side, Cyprus (still divided into two ethnic groups), Romania (where the Trans Dniester territory remained an issue). Greece and Slovakia had still not recognised Kosovo since its secession from Serbia in 2008, almost a decade after its majority ethnic Albanians had launched a guerrilla campaign against Belgrade.

None of these problems and issues had, however, prevented the EU giving the all-clear to opening negotiations with Kosovo, which, it was hoped, would pacify the Balkans' often simmering nationalist tensions. Kosovo had concluded talks with the EU in July 2014 for a Stabilisation and Association Agreement, a key step on the path to eventual EU membership. The Kosovo government hoped that signature would further calm the ethnic tensions that dogged the Balkans. The signing ceremony on 27 October 2015 was attended by the EU's head of foreign affairs, Italy's Federica Mogherini and the EU Enlargement Commissioner Johannes Hahn of Austria. Kosovo's membership seemed to be happening despite itself and regardless of a number of negatives, notably Kosovo's lack of progress in a number of key policy sectors. 'The rule of law in Kosovo, including judicial independence and limited results in the fight against organised crime and corruption, remains a major concern,' the European Commission had clearly stated in its last report on Kosovo in October 2014. If concessions appeared to be being made in the case of Kosovo, the same was not the case with Serbian membership. This was because Serbia still formally regarded Kosovo as part of its territory.

For Kosovo to join the EU, 35 chapters on topics ranging from fundamental rights to economic issues need to be opened and successfully closed with the unanimous support of member states. A tall order.

The politics

When, in June 2014 Kosovo went to the polls to elect a new government a much larger proportion of the Serbian community seemed to have participated than had been the case in the previous elections. Furthermore, the elections were seen to be encouragingly free and above board by both local and visiting observers. This contrasted with the November 2013 regional elections, when around 20 polling stations were found to have illegalities – particularly ballot paper stuffing – so hopes for a corruption free 2014 election had not been riding high.

The incumbent Prime Minister, Hashim Thaci, was seeking a third term, but he was by no means a shoe-in, facing a closer contest from the opposition. Mr Thaci had sought to woo voters with a programme labelled the 'New Mission', which rather optimistically promised €1.5 billion (US$1.7 billion) in investment and 200,000 new jobs for the small country with 35 per cent unemployment and widespread poverty. Mr Thaci had become a seasoned Kosovo politician, an architect of Kosovo's fractious declaration of independence from Serbia in 2008. The challenge, according to Mr Thaci's election campaign, was what he referred to as the 'third battle: economic development, creation of new jobs and enhancing social well-being.' Kosovo's electoral law made it virtually impossible for a single party to rule on its own – a coalition government was almost inevitably always required.

Unsurprisingly, both Kosovo's political opposition and its few independent analysts described Mr Thaci's election promises as outrageous. Quoted by the Agence France Press (AFP) press agency, analyst Lumir Abdixhiku estimated that 'Kosovo would need to have at least 20 per cent annual growth, seven times more than it registered during Mr Thaci's previous mandates.' To make matters worse, several members of Mr Thaci's Partia Demokratike e Kosovës (PDK) (Democratic Party of Kosovo) had been accused of having links to organised crime and to lining their pockets. Mr Thaci, who had lead the political wing of the pro-Albanian, anti-Serb Kosovo Liberation Army (KLA) guerrilla movement was no angel – currently facing gruesome EU allegations of the trafficking of body parts from Serbian prisoners of war from the 1998–99 conflict.

Less gruesome was a report in the London *Independent* describing how the candidates standing for mayor of Kosovo's capital city, Pristina, in the November regional elections appeared on television. Asked why they wanted to become mayor, the principal candidates claimed that their motivation was the public good or similar generalisations. That is with the exception of Kosovo's answer to Beppe Grillo, Visar Arifaj, leader of the so called 'Party of the Strong' who announced that he wanted to be mayor 'so he could gain power and get rich.' This certainly struck a chord with the audience who were reported to have 'laughed uproariously.' None the less, despite public cynicism, Kosovans voted in favour of the mixture as before. The preliminary 2014 election results confirmed that Mr Thaci's PDK had won the elections with more than 30 per cent of the votes. The Lidhja Demokratike e Kosovës (LDK) (Democratic League of Kosovo) received 26 per cent and the radical Vetevendosje (Self Determination) movement, came third with 13.5 per cent.

Not quite the mixture as before as Mr Thaci became foreign minister in the new coalition government of Prime Minister Isa Mustafa who took office on 9 December 2014. Mr Mustafa has a PhD in economics and has said that his government will be focused on the economic development of the country. He is a member of the LDK, which had come second in the election. He ran into trouble in September 2015 when addressing the Kosovo Assembly on an autonomy agreement for the ethnic Serb minority – he was pelted with eggs by opposition members and had to continue his address while being shielded with an umbrella by his bodyguard

The economy

In May 2015 the International Monetary Fund (IMF) had concluded its key Article IV Consultation with the Kosovar authorities. The IMF noted that 'Growth in Kosovo has proven relatively resilient and stronger than in its Western Balkan neighbours, averaging slightly more than three per cent over the last five years.' Much of this economic success was the consequence of the remittances made from the Diaspora living in Western Europe, which continued to be a key driver of growth, supporting both private consumption and investment. Nonetheless, according to the IMF, Kosovo's medium-term growth prospects of some 3.5 per cent per year, while reasonable, were not strong enough to steadily lift incomes towards regional standards, or even to create enough jobs in a country with very high unemployment.

However, the IMF reported that Kosovo continued to enjoy a low public debt and the 2014 budget deficit had complied with the fiscal rule's limit. However, promises made in the run up to the general elections risked pushing the 2015 deficit above the limit. Moreover, the composition of the budget had worsened considerably, with unproductive current spending crowding out spending on infrastructure, education and health.

Kosovo's banks remained liquid, well capitalised and profitable. Non performing loan (NPL) ratios were on the high side, at 8.4 per cent, but were stable and fully provisioned. The Banka Qendrore e Repubukës së Kosovës (BQK) (Central Bank of Kosovo) had, in the view of the IMF, made commendable progress in strengthening bank supervision as well as in developing the framework for emergency liquidity assistance. However, there were obstacles to the provision of credit, despite high levels of liquidity in the banks. In particular, inefficient court proceedings on bank cases contributed to high interest margins and high collateral requirements. High levels of informality also deterred credit provision via the concomitant lack of reliable financial statements.

Kosovo's productive and export capacity was, in the view of the IMF, currently low owing to the country's significant wage and non-wage competitiveness gap. The former was related to unsustainable wage pressures in the public sector, which made it difficult for the private sector to attract talent. The latter involved a looming energy deficit, limited access to and quality of, education and vocational training and remaining issues in the business environment, including perceptions of corruption. On the Transparency International 2014 *Corruption Perceptions Index* Kosovo ranked 110 out of the 175 countries surveyed, level with Albania, but behind both Serbia (78) and Montenegro (76).

According to the European Bank for Economic Reconstruction and Development (EBRD) in its annual *Transition Report*, Kosovo's economy had been relatively shielded from adverse external developments during the global economic crisis. As a result, while most countries in the region performed poorly, the economy of Kosovo grew at about 4 per cent on average for the period between 2009 and 2011. However, GDP growth later moderated to an average of 3.1 per cent, which was attributable to both domestic and external demand dropping slightly. At the same time, according to the EBRD, inflation had slowed significantly, remaining below 0.5 per cent year-on-year since December 2013.

KEY INDICATORS — Kosovo

	Unit	2011	2012	2013	2014	**2015
Population	m	1.73	–	–	–	–
Gross domestic product (GDP)	US$bn	6.40	6.32	7.08	*7.32	*6.47
GDP per capita	US$	3,690	0	0	0	0
GDP real growth	%	5.0	2.5	3.4	*2.7	*3.3
Inflation	%	7.3	2.5	1.8	*0.4	*0.3
Exports (fob) (goods)	US$m	441.2	362.1	386.9	–	–
Imports (fob) (goods)	US$m	3,289.1	2,990.3	3,038.5	–	–
Balance of trade	US$m	-2,847.9	-2,628.2	-2,651.6	–	–
Current account	US$m	-1,028.2	-489.0	-450.0	*-522.0	*-473.0
Total reserves minus gold	US$m	965.8	1,108.1	1,102.9	–	–
Foreign exchange	US$m	855.7	1,002.8	999.0	–	–
Exchange rate	per US$	0.75	0.77	0.73	0.83	–

* estimated figure ** forecast figure

In terms of fiscal policy, Kosovo had been less prudent in 2014. In the light of Kosovo's unilateral adoption of the euro, the EBRD considered that a sound fiscal policy had been important for maintaining macro-economic stability. The IMF had supported the establishment of Kosovo's fiscal programme and framework. In April 2012, the IMF had approved a 20-month €106.6 million (US$119.7 million) Stand-By Arrangement (SBA) for Kosovo. To lock in the adjustments achieved under the IMF programmes, from 2014 fiscal policy was anchored by a fiscal rule that set a ceiling of two per cent of GDP on the general government deficit (with very limited exceptions allowed) and a cap of 40 per cent of GDP on the public debt. However, although the rule was likely to be observed in 2015, large pre-election increases in public sector wages, pensions and other benefits had come at the cost of a major reduction in capital expenditure.

The EBRD expected Kosovo's growth to remain moderate in 2014. Output was forecast to be about 3.5 per cent in 2014 supported by strong remittance inflows and a rise in external demand. Kosovo was the poorest country in south-eastern Europe (SEE) and it therefore had more catch-up potential than other countries in the region. However, negative risks were substantial due to a range of internal problems and the continuing economic difficulties experienced by the euro-zone. Negative contagion effects had been limited, but Kosovo's dependence on remittances from its diaspora still made it vulnerable to external factors. Furthermore, major infrastructure projects were highly dependent on official foreign funding sources as domestic capital markets were still underdeveloped.

Less good news was that the privatisation of the PTK, Kosovo's principal telecommunications company, had failed. In December 2013 parliament had failed to approve the sale of a majority stake in PTK. The winning bid of €227 million (US$255 million) for a 75 per cent stake had been submitted by a US-German consortium in April 2013, after an open tender. However, amid significant political opposition to the deal, the government's attempt to privatise the company failed for the second time within four years. This was a serious setback to Kosovo's efforts to privatise state-owned assets and attract much-needed foreign direct investment (FDI). In general, progress on privatisation has been weak. Many key state-owned companies have still not been privatised. At the end of 2013 the Privatisation Agency of Kosovo (PAK) still had 585 'socially-owned' companies in it 'for sale'. During 2013 PAK had held three privatisation waves but progress on this front has been limited, not least because of political instability and the economic slow-down, which has further dampened investor interest, but also due to the failure to fill positions on PAK's board. In addition, the challenging business environment is a major deterrent to investment in Kosovo; although Kosovo had made notable progress over the previous year in improving business conditions, it still lagged behind most other countries in the region. Kosovo's ranking on the World Bank *Doing Business 2015* report showed an improvement over recent years, up to 75 (out of 189 countries). The change in ranking was particularly significant when it came to starting a business, where its ranking climbed from 100 to 42 in the latest report. Nonetheless, Kosovo still lagged behind its regional peers on most competitiveness indicators. Financial management and corporate governance were, however, improving for some of the larger companies, with a higher number of acceptable corporate financial reports produced throughout 2013. Demonstrating social responsibility and good governance (management boards) had also been recognised by some companies as a marketing tool and as a way to gain access to finance. However, rule of law implementation remained weak in many areas and the level of corruption was perceived to be high. These factors, alongside widespread informality in the economy, constrained private investment and sustainable economic development.

Keeping the lights on

The EBRD considered that Kosovo had considerable potential to improve energy efficiency and to increase the proportion of renewables in power generation. In mid-2015 nearly all the electricity produced came from two old, inefficient and highly polluting lignite-fired thermal power plants (TPP). The Kosovo A TPP was considered one of the worst polluters in the region and was scheduled to be shut down in 2017. The 40-year-old thermal power plant experienced a major explosion in June 2014 that killed two people, threatening the stability of the power system and costing an estimated €60 million (US$67 million) in damages. The construction of a new thermal power station close to the capital, Pristina, has been announced. Improvements are also needed in transmission infrastructure, particularly in increasing interconnection capacity, which is one of the key factors constraining imports. In addition, although the present electricity tariffs are partly subsidised by the state (and hence are not reflective of costs), network losses, which have been mainly non-technical in character, accounted for almost 40 per cent of the electricity produced.

In the view of the EBRD, there remained major transition gaps in 2015 in providing critical infrastructure services to both businesses and households. Kosovo has made some progress in addressing part of the investment needs in the wastewater sector, with support from the KfW Development Bank and the German and Swiss governments. However, a discussion with the EU within the Stabilisation and Association Process framework in May 2014 highlighted the overall slow progress in the transport, environment, energy, climate and regional development sectors. To date, little investment and local capacity building has occurred in these areas and private participation has been limited.

The banking sector remained commendably stable reported the EBRD. The banks' capital adequacy ratio stood at 17.4 per cent at the end of March 2014. Although this was the lowest in the region, non performing loans had continued to edge up, reaching 8.6 per cent of total loans. They were, however, well provisioned. Kosovo's banking sector is largely foreign owned, with the parent banks coming from the Euro-zone and Turkey. For the most part, lending is funded from deposits, so the risks of contagious cross border financing are limited.

Risk assessment

Politics	Fair
Economy	Fair
Regional stability	Poor

Muslims in Kosovo

% of population	95
Sunni (% of Muslims)	99
Shi'a (% of Muslims)	1

COUNTRY PROFILE

1389 The battle of Kosovo was lost by the Serbian people and the Turkish Ottoman Empire began a 500-year rule. During this time the population changed from Christian Serbs to Muslim Albanians.

1912 During the Balkan Wars Serbia regained control of Kosovo.

1918 Kosovo became part of the Kingdom of Serbs, Croats and Slovenes.

1941 During World War II the Italian army controlled the entire region.
1945 The Federal People's Republic of Yugoslavia was formed into a communist republic by Josip Broz Tito, and included the province of Kosovo with its own constitutional rights.
1974 Yugoslavia increased the autonomy of constituent republics, allowing Kosovo *de facto* self-government.
1980 Tito died.
1987 Serbian nationalist politician, Slobodan Milosevic, incited Serbian Kosovans to protest at alleged harassment by the majority ethnic Albanians.
1989 Yugoslav president Milosevic stripped Kosovo of its constitutional rights.
1990 Ethnic Albanians declared Kosovo independent. The Yugoslav government dissolved the Kosovo government and sacked 100,000 workers, which led to a general strike.
1991 Two major Yugoslav republics (Slovenia and Croatia) declared their independence. Slovenia became independent with little dispute. Croatia with its 12 per cent Serbian population fought the remaining Yugoslav army and evicted its Serbs to gain its independence. The Yugoslav government in Belgrade began a process of disenfranchising Albanian Kosovans by closing down schools and marginalising the Albanian language.
1992 Macedonia and Bosnia and Hercegovina (BiH) declared their independence. Nationalist and ethnic tensions in BiH, the most ethnically diverse Yugoslav republic, strained until the territory erupted into war. Thousands died in 'ethnic cleansing' as one faction tried to clear a region of civilians of another faction; a million people were displaced. Ibrahim Rugova was elected president of the self-proclaimed Republic of Kosovo.
1996 The Ushtria Çlirimtare e Kosovës (UÇK) (Kosovo Liberation Army) began attacking Serbian police.
1998 Confrontation between Serbian forces and the UÇK increased, culminating in a brutal crackdown by Serbian police and paramilitary units which resulted in massacres and thousands of civilians being driven from their homes. NATO gave the Milosevic government an ultimatum to halt the crackdown or risk air attacks.
1999 An international peace deal failed and NATO began air attacks on Serbia, which finally agreed to withdraw troops and the UN Kosovo Peace Implementation Force (Kfor) began peace-keeping operations. The UN Interim Administration Mission in Kosovo (UNMIK) came into operation, charged with determining the future of Kosovo. The UÇK agreed to disarm, while Serb civilians fled the province in the face of revenge attacks.
2000 Local elections were won by the Lidhja Demokratike e Kosovës (LDK) (Democratic League of Kosovo), led by Ibrahim Rugova.
2002 The parliament elected Ibrahim Rugova as president and Bajram Rexhepi of the Partia Demokratike e Kosovës (PDK) (Democratic Party of Kosovo) was elected prime minister of a power-sharing 10-member cabinet.
2003 Official negotiations between Kosovo and Serbia began. Conditions for the talks to determine Kosovo's final status were announced by the UN in December.
2004 The LDK won parliamentary elections and incumbent President Ibrahim Rugova was re-elected. Ramush Haradinaj became prime minister. Serbian Kosovans boycotted the elections. The worst inter-ethnic violence since 1999 erupted in Mitrovica, with up to 22 people killed and hundreds injured.
2005 Prime minister Haradinaj resigned and Adem Salihaj replaced him.
2006 President Ibrahim Rugova died; as a moderate Kosovan leader his death just as negotiations on Kosovo's future were about to start, was a setback. He was succeeded by Fatmir Sejdiu. Agim Çeku became prime minister. Joachim Rucker took office as the head of UNMIK.
2007 The UN Special Envoy Martti Ahtisaari submitted a *Comprehensive Proposal for the Kosovo Status Settlement* (the Ahtisaari Plan) for the independence of Kosovo which also focused on protecting the rights, identity and culture of Kosovo's non-Albanian communities, including establishing a framework for their active participation in public life. Ahtisaari also proposed that Kosovo become independent, subject to a period of international supervision. Agim Çeku said that no unilateral declaration of independence would be made (by ethnic Albanian leaders) without the support of the EU and US. No agreement was reached during the first round of talks concerning the future of Kosovo: Serbian authorities offered broad autonomy while the province's ethnic Albanians demanded full independence. Parliamentary elections were won by the PDK with 34.3 per cent of the vote (37 seats out of 120), led by Hashim Thaçi, former leader of the UÇK.
2008 President Sejdiu resigned and took part in fresh elections, held on the same day, under Kosovo's new constitutional framework. After three rounds he won a simple majority of 61 votes to become president for a second time. The Kosovo Assembly issued a unilateral declaration of independence (UDI), in line with the Ahtisaari Plan. The new constitution came into force and the Kosovo government took over most of the powers previously held by the UN. Although Russia initially rejected the deployment of the EU Law and Order Mission (Eulex), a 2,200 policing force, it was eventually used after UN agreement. Ethnic Serbs insisted that the new constitution did not apply to them and as a last act of the outgoing government in Serbia, the Serbian minister for Kosovo set up a new parliament in the divided city of Mitrovica for minority Serbs. The new Kosovan Serb Assembly may challenge the legitimacy of the Kosovan Assembly and entrench *de facto* partition of Kosovo. The issuing of Kosovan passports began. Kosovo's UDI was referred to the International Court of Justice (ICJ) by the UN General Assembly to give its opinion.
2009 A new 2,500-strong Kosovo Security Force (KSV), trained by the UN, became operational. Members of the KSV were drawn from all members of the community to undertake civil protection and crisis response. Serbian President Boris Tadic attended a religious service at the Serb Orthodox monastery of Visoki Decani. Kosovo was offered membership of the International Monetary Fund (IMF). The number of NATO (Kfor) troops was reduced from around 14,000 to 10,000.
2010 Former prime minister Haradinaj was ordered to stand trial for a second time, as his earlier acquittal on murder and torture charges was ruled to have been a miscarriage of justice, due to the intimidation of prosecution witnesses. The ICJ ruled that Kosovo's UDI from Serbia did not violate international law. The ruling should allow more countries to recognise Kosovo as a sovereign state. Serbia rejected the ruling and called for fresh talks at the UN over Kosovo's status. The number of Kfor troops was reduced from around 10,000 to 6,300. The constitutional court ruled that the leader of a political party may not serve as president. This caused Fatmir Sejdiu (LDK) to step down as president and for him to withdraw the LDK from the coalition government. Prime Minister Hashim Thaçi lost a vote of no-confidence by 66–1, which resulted in a snap general election, in which the PDK again won the largest share of the vote (32.1 per cent; 34 seats out of 120) and began coalition negotiations with the next largest party LDK.
2011 PDK and LDK agreed a coalition with Aleanca Kosova e Re (AKR) (New Kosovo Alliance) in February. Parliament re-elected Hashim Thaçi (PDK) as prime minister, after three rounds of voting. Behgjet Pacolli was elected as president, despite most opposition members boycotting the vote. He replaced Jakup Krasniqi who had been acting-president since former president Sejdiu had been forced to step down. In March the Constitutional Court ruled that the election of President

Pacolli was unconstitutional as there was not a quorum in parliament when the vote to elect him was taken. On 7 April, parliament elected Atifete Jahjaga president by 80 votes (with 10 for Suzanna Novoberdaliu); she was sworn in the same day. The first state census was completed on 15 April and preliminary results published in July showed a total population of 1,733,872 with 295,070 households. The Kosovo police attempted to replace Kosovan-Serbs manning the border crossing between Kosovo and Serbia in July, but were repelled by the Kosovan-Serbs. NATO-led peacekeepers were required to restore order. The EU and US criticised Kosovo for this unannounced move to assert its authority in Northern Kosovo. Ramush Haradinaj re-appeared before the ICJ in August, along with two other defendants, on charges of joint criminal enterprise during the civil war; all three were acquitted of the charges in November 2012. Forces, led by NATO-peacekeepers, dispersed Kosovan-Serb protestors and dismantled their barricades in October. In December, an EU-mediated the integrated border management (IBM) agreement was reached between Serbia and Kosovo to jointly manage and to 'gradually set up joint, integrated, single and secure posts at all their common crossing points.'

2012 On 24 February, Serbia and Kosovo reached an agreement whereby Kosovo can be represented at any regional forum without provoking a Serbian boycott. The complex formula has Kosovo registered under its name but with an addendum saying that giving the name and status does not prejudge UN Resolution 1244 and the ICJ opinion on Kosovo's UDI. This agreement concludes a technical protocol on the implementation of the IBM deal, reached in December 2011. On 7 June, the Constitutional Court ruled that changes to the constitution, which scrapped 21 amendments and ended Kosovo's international supervised independence by the end of 2012, was legitimate. The Court also ruled these changes did not undermine any fundamental right or freedoms that the constitution guaranteed. On 2 August, the government announced that the mandate for Eulex will cease, following a transitional period managed in three stages. The first begins in September and runs through to March 2013, with the second stage following-on until September 2013 and the final one running up to 15 June 2014, at which time all personnel will have been withdrawn. On 19 September, Prime Minister Hashim Thaci met Prime Minister Dacic of Serbia. This was the first meeting of the two leaders since Kosovo's UDI in 2008.

2013 On 10 April agreement was finally reached with Serbia on future relations. Under the 15-point deal signed by parliament on 21 April Serbs in Mitrovica will have their own police commander and appeal court. Kosovo began the long road to EU membership in October when negotiations for a Stabilisation and Association Agreement were opened. Municipal elections were held on 3 November. The government in Serbia , which is applying for membership of the EU, encouraged ethnic Serbs to vote, in line with an agreement between Kosovo and Serbia to normalise relations. However, turnout was low and ballot boxes were destroyed in violent episodes, including in Mitrovica in the north. On 6 November the electoral commission annulled results from three polling stations in the Serb-dominated town of Mitrovica, after ballot boxes were damaged. A re-run of the election was held on 17 November and although it went off relatively peacefully, very few Serbs voted.

2014 On 7 May President Atifete Jahjaga disolved parliament and called elections for 8 June. The results were a win for an alliance headed by the PDK and including the PD–LB–PSHDK–PK with 37 seats (out of 120), closely followed by the Lidhja Demokratike e Kosovës (LDK) (Democratic League of Kosovo) with 30 seats and Vetëvendosje! (Self-determination) with 9 seats. A coalition led by Partia Demokratike e Kosovës (PDK) (Democratic Party of Kosovo) with Lidhja Demokratike e Kosovës (LDK) (Democratic League of Kosovo) and Aleanca Kosova e Re (AKR) (New Kosovo Alliance) took power and Isa Mustafa (LDK) was sworn in as prime minister on 9 December.

2015 On 22 September Prime Minister Mustafa was pelted with eggs by opposition members and had to continue his address on an autonomy agreement for the ethnic Serb minority while being shielded with an umbrella by his bodyguard.

Political structure

Constitution

An interim Constitutional framework was ratified in 2001 providing legitamacy for the provisional institutions of self-government, with deferral to the UN Special Representative based on the UN Security Council Resolution 1244.

A draft Constitution was being prepared in 2008.

On 7 June 2012 the Constitutional Court ruled that changes to the constitution, which scrapped 21 amendments and ended Kosovo's international supervised independence by the end of 2012, was legitimate. The Court also ruled these changes did not undermine any fundamental right or freedoms that the constitution guaranteed. However of one amendment (referring to Article 156), dealing with refugees and internally displaced persons (IDPs), this was judged could not be deleted.

Independence date

17 February 2008

Form of state

Parliamentary democracy

The executive

The president is indirectly elected by two-thirds majority vote of the Assembly for a five year term (eligible for a second term). The president represents the country in foreign affairs and in domestic matters acts on the advice of the prime minister and cabinet.

The executive branch of government is headed by the prime minister, deputy prime ministers and all other ministers. The Prime Minister is indirectly elected by the Assembly.

National legislature

The unicameral Assembly of Kosovo (Kuvendi i Kosovës) has 120 seats; 100 membersdirectly elected by the proportional representation vote with twenty seats reserved for ethnic minorities: ten seats are reserved for Serbs and ten seats for other ethnic groups. Legislative power is vested in the assembly and government. Members serve four-year terms.

Last elections

9 June 2014 (parliamentary); 7 April 2011 (presidential).

Results: Parliamentary: the Partia Demokratike e Kosovës (PDK) (Democratic Party of Kosovo) won 30.38 per cent of the vote (37 seats out of 120), Lidhja Demokratike e Kosovës (LDK) (Democratic League of Kosovo) 25.24 per cent (30), Vetëvendosje! (Self-Determination) 13.59 per cent (16), Aleanca për Ardhmërinë e Kosovës (AAK) (Alliance for the Future of Kosovo) 9.54 per cent (11), Serbian List 5.22 per cent (9), Nisma për Kosovën (Nisma) (Initiative for Kosovo) 5.15 per cent (6), the Turkish Democratic Party of Kosovo and the Vakat Coalition won two seats each, seven other parties won one seat each. Turnout was 42.63 per cent.

Presidential (2011): Behgjet Pacolli was elected as president on the third round, despite most opposition members boycotting the vote. However, the Constitutional Court ruled that the election unconstitutional as there was not a quorum in parliament when the vote was taken. On 7 April, parliament elected Atifete Jahjaga president by 80 votes (with 10 for Suzanna Novoberdaliu).

Next elections

June 2018 (parliamentary); 2016 (presidential)

Political parties

Ruling party

Coalition led by Partia Demokratike e Kosovës (PDK) (Democratic Party of Kosovo), Lidhja Demokratike e Kosovës (LDK) (Democratic League of Kosovo) and Aleanca Kosova e Re (AKR) (New Kosovo Alliance)

Main opposition party

Lidhja Demokratike e Kosovës (LDK) (Democratic League of Kosovo)

The first national census was undertaken on 15 April 2011 with the final results published in 2012.

Population

1.73 million (2011; census figure)

Last census: 1991: 1,956,000 (during political troubles)

2001: 2,400,000 (estimate: Office for Security and Co-operation in Europe)

Population density: 202 per square km

Internally Displaced Persons (IDP)

Internal Displacement Monitoring Centre

Ethnic make-up

Estimated demographics: Albanian (92 per cent) Serbian (5.3 per cent) and others (Croats, Roma, Turks) (2.7 per cent).

Religions

Muslim 90 per cent, the majority of which are Sunni, Christian Orthodox 5 per cent.

Education

Before 1991 educational institutions were administered independently of Serbian influence by Kosovan authorities, which were at liberty to construct a national curriculum and system of education. All levels of education were provided in the Albanian and Serbian languages and schools were charged with maintaining levels of instruction for all minority communities. Enrolment rates where typically almost 100 per cent and this resulted in literacy levels that matched the average of surrounding territories. From 1991, the independence of Kosovo's education service was abolished by Serbian authorities, which closed down schools and dismissed over 14,000 primary and 4,000 secondary school teachers plus over 860 university lecturers of Albanian ethnicity and required all teaching to be in the Serbian language. A parallel schooling system developed whereby Serbian schools were enhanced at the expense of Albanian schools which began to lag behind in books and equipment. Albanian students were denied access to Serbian libraries and so took up informal learning provided by sacked teachers. However, at this time Serbian investment was cut due to the economic crisis following the conflict in Croatia and even the Serbian schools became poorly stocked and maintained.

The University of Pristina was badly damaged by vandalism and looting during the NATO attacks on Serbia in 1999, but was finally reopened to all students by 2000. Around 45 per cent of all schools were severely damaged or destroyed and many were within minefields which prevented their use until cleared. When the 2000/01 school-year began only around 50 per cent of school students attended remedial classes; the percentage began to rise as facilities improved. Apart from war damage, the previous nine years of under-investment also added to the problems of rehabilitation for the UN Administration authorities (UNMIK).

UNMIK began the reconstruction of the educational system with a three-way split into priority areas of consideration, which included the physical (buildings, books and equipment), legal aspects (new teaching structures that provided for or moderated opposing orthodoxy) and academic reform (curricula development and educational management). Teacher training was implemented under UN-sponsored programmes from 2004/05.

Finding an ongoing consensus was hampered in 2006 following the Serbian constitutional referendum (that excluded Kosovans), which voted to enshrine the Cyrillic alphabet as the official script for all territories; Albanians use the Latin script.

In 2007 Unesco stated that less than 10 per cent of 3–6 year olds had access to early childhood education, with the majority of facilities located in larger urban areas.

The conflict with Serbia led to a massive population shift from the country to towns and resulted in the overcrowding of many primary schools, which have had to operate at least a two shift system.

Literacy rate: 89.8 per cent female rate; 97.7 per cent male. Around 14 per cent of rural females are illiterate (Unesco 2007).

Compulsory years: Six to 14

Enrolment rate: 97.5 per cent (Albanian), 99 per cent (Serbian), 77 per cent (all others, of which only 69 per cent female) (Unesco 2007).

Pupils per teacher: The average was 19 per class (in primary schools) before 1999; the average has increased to 35 students per class.

Health

Kosovo, as one of the poorest territories in Europe has, as a UN report in 2007 reported, 37 per cent of the population living in poverty and 15.2 per cent in absolute poverty. The healthcare system is chronically under funded with a lack of medical equipment and drugs. Poorly educated mothers and lack of access to facilities has resulted in Kosovo having the highest fertility rate in Europe, and also the highest maternal mortality rate, despite 95 per cent of all births taking place in medical facilities. Measures to reach UN Millennium Development Goals (MDG) have been included in necessary restoration policies since 1999. Childhood immunisation reached levels of 90 per cent by 2007, although parents in some minority ethnic communities delayed vaccinations.

In 2005 a total of 72.4 per cent of the population had access to clean water, of which 96 per cent were urban dwellers, around 70 per cent of total households were connected to the sewage system, of which 95 per cent were urban dwellers.

HIV/Aids

The young have not been or are poorly informed about HIV/Aids, sex education and the risks of drugs. Less than 41 per cent of sexually active young people used a condom, according to a 2007 Unesco report.

Life expectancy: 68.8 years (67.8 male; 69.9 female) (2006 Kosovo Government)

Fertility rate/Maternal mortality rate: Separate figures from Serbia for Kosovo are unavailable.

Child (under 5 years) mortality rate (per 1,000): 69 per 1,000 (estimated, Unicef 2006)

Head of population per physician: 1 doctor per 840 head of population (2004, Kosovo Statistics Office)

Welfare

At a time when Europe's populations are ageing Kosovo's average age is 22–23 years, with around 33 per cent less than 15 years old. This group will be an ongoing burden of responsibility for the government to educate, find work and house at a time of economic hardship. There is no social welfare although international donors provide funds for programmes to aid the vulnerable. There are high levels of unemployment and poor prospects for improvement.

Main cities

Priština (capital, estimated population 172,033 in 2012), Prizren (102,117), Urosevac (81,988), Pec (75,411), Mitrovica (71,162), Dakovica (65,282), Gnjilane (57,432).

Languages spoken

Albanian, Serbian, Bosniak and Turkish. Since the arrival of the UN English has increased in popularity.

Official language/s

Albanian, Serbian (English was the official language of the UN Interim Administration Mission in Kosovo (UNMIK))

Media

Press

Periodicals: UNMIK started the publication of a quarterly *Focus* (www.euinkosovo.org) with a variety of background articles on people and events in Kosovo.

Broadcasting

The national, public broadcaster is RTK (www.rtklive.com).

Radio: RTK operates two stations, Radio Kosova and Radio Blue Sky. Other, private radio stations in operation include Radio Dukagjini (www.radio-dukagjini.com), Radio Kim (www.kimradio.net) and Radio Tema (www.radiotema.net).

National news agency: Kosova Press

Other news agencies: Kosovalive: www.kosovalive.com

Kosova Information Center: www.kosova.com

Economy

Since declaring unilateral independence in 2007, the fledgling economy has had to contend with the severe downturn in the global economy. Kosovo has the lowest per capita income in Europe, as low as US$4,000 in 2014. It has begun to set up the infrastructure to provide financial services necessary. The Central Bank of Kosovo (CBK) began work in 1999 and by 2009 there were eight commercial banks, 19 micro-financial institutions, 11 insurance companies and two pension funds in operation. Kosovo became a member of the International Monetary Fund (IMF) in June 2009, with an initial capital subscription of US$91.5 million, which amounted to 0.027 per cent of the total fund membership quota.

Kosovo's economy has achieved a rate of steady growth since the global economic crisis, averaging 3.5 per cent between 2011 and 2014. There is high unemployment at around 30 per cent, which encourages emigration; remittances from migrant workers account for about 15 per cent of GDP. International donor assistance accounts for a further 10 per cent of GDP.

Investment is a priority for Kosovo. Political relations with Serbia and the tensions between the majority ethnic Albanian and minority Serbian populations have dampened the prospects of much needed foreign direct investment and risks leading to a stagnating economy. Kosovo needs a higher inflow of FDI in order to balance its current account deficit. FDI was approximately US$175 million in 2014, a significant decrease from the US$274 million in 2013.

With the world's fifth largest stock of lignite coal, Kosovo is planning to privatise two existing coal plants, to realise around US$4.8 billion, and construct another. Sales of other assets are also under consideration, such as the mobile/cell operator Vala.

Around 60 per cent of the population live in rural areas with agriculture contributing 25 per cent of GDP; it is also an important sector for employment. Industrial production is centred on mining, agribusiness, including wood processing, and manufacturing of textiles and automotive components. Tourism is still nascent, but has the potential for strong growth when the infrastructure is brought up to international standards. The official unemployment rate for 2013 was 31 per cent.

External trade

Kosovo has a customs-free access to the European Union market, based on an EU Autonomous Trade Preference (ATP) regime. It also has free trade agreements (FTA) with Albania, Croatia, Bosnia and Hercegovina and Macedonia (FYROM). Around 20 per cent of all exports are agricultural, including wheat, meat and wine.

Major trading partners include the European Union, Balkans region, Turkey and the US.

Imports

Main imports include foodstuffs, livestock, wood, petroleum, chemicals, machinery, minerals, textiles, stone, ceramic and glass products and electrical equipment.

Main sources: Germany (11.9 per cent of total in 2014), Macedonia (11.5 per cent), Serbia (11.1 per cent)

Exports

Principal exports are base metals (including scrap) (50 per cent), leather goods (18 per cent), food stuffs (15 per cent), plastics and rubber (10 per cent).

Main destinations: Italy (25.8 per cent of total in 2014), Albania (14.6 per cent), Macedonia (9.6 per cent)

Agriculture

Farming

Of the 1.1 million hectares (ha) of Kosova land, 53 per cent (577,000ha) is arable. Over 85 per cent is privately owned, however the average size of land per rural household is 3ha. Of the arable land 51 per cent is grain, 45 per cent pastures and meadows, 2 per cent orchards and less than 1 per cent vineyards. Principal crops are wheat, corn, potatoes, watermelons and lucerne (animal fodder).

The government regards small farms as less than 5ha and large farms over 5ha, around 96 per cent of farming households work small farms. Many farms were abandoned in 1999 and rural infrastructure is in disrepair. There is an urgent need to modernise traditional practices that provide little more than subsistence production. Around 65 per cent of the working population is employed in agriculture, providing 30 per cent of GDP. Kosovo has fallen from being a net exporter of agriculture products to foodstuffs accounting for around 30 per cent of all imports, the largest single import segment.

Since the early 1990s the number of livestock has fallen and the trend has continued. Small farms have now mostly invested in beef cattle, donkeys and beehives; larger farms have invested in breeding pigs and donkeys, all other farm animals have fallen in number. Government statistics acknowledge that all but the largest of farms fail to keep records and the number of animals reported may be incorrect.

Forestry

Forests represent an important resource but historic mismanagement has resulted in heavy degradation; the high demand for timber following the conflict with Serbia has increased the pressure on forestry's long-term sustainability.

Timbered areas make up 47 per cent of all land, of which forests are 460,800ha. Around 62 per cent of forests are publicly owned. Forest products, before the break-up of Yugoslavia, were a significant export sector.

Industry and manufacturing

Industrial development was historically dictated by the economic interests of firstly Yugoslavia and later Serbia, with widespread exploitation of natural resources. Mining and forestry products formed the majority of intra-exports.

Due to war damage and the lack of investment in what were state-owned industries and manufacturing, food processing, tobacco, wood processing and textiles were all disrupted and non-productive by 2006. Privatisation was begun but the problems may be long term as poor transport infrastructure, with 25 per cent of the road network in serious need of remedial work, a serious impediment to redevelopment.

Kosovo has limited water resources, as most rivers run out of the country, any process that requires water to facilitate production will be severely hampered.

Tourism

Kosovo has had positive growth in tourism since 2007, albeit from a low base. Leisure tourism has grown to replace business trips for most reasons to visit, as the political situation has settled down.

Kosovo has spectacular natural landscapes and historic architecture of both Ottoman and Christian Orthodox religious sites. Three sites of Byzantine-Romanesque medieval monuments are included on Unesco's World Heritage List. In January 2012, the Illyria Hotel in Pristina was reopened following a US$51.6 million refurbishment and renamed the Swiss Diamond Pristina. The luxury hotel has spa facilities, bars, a restaurant and an executive club. Plans for a new ski resort close to Brezovica were proposed by Ecosign Europa in February 2012, and presented to the European Commission, which recognised the location as having the greatest potential for development in the Balkans. The resort could provide up to 3,000 new jobs and generate hundreds of millions of euros from the planned new mountain resort with a ski village, five major lifts and over 25km of pistes.

Environment

The US committed an initial US$15.5 million to repairing war damage, which included water contamination, minefields and unexploded ordinance (UXO). In 2007, the ongoing clearance programme concentrated on unmarked minefields and UXO in forested areas.

Archaic communist industrial practices degraded land, water and air quality and until production plants are either upgraded or closed the pollution is likely to continue. A government environmental plan was proposed in 2006 to introduce legislation to develop policies and guidelines for international funding and donor communities to deal with the problems and plan for the future. It was also recognised that a full inventory of fauna and flora for Kosovo was needed.

Kosovo, in 2006, had one national park and 11 natural reserves, 37 natural monuments and two protected landscapes totalling 46,000ha (4.27 per cent of the country). The richest area for wildlife is the Sharr Mountains and the Bjeshkët e Nemuna area.

Rivers around industrial regions are heavily polluted and denuded of aquatic life.

Energy production is the major polluter in Kosovo, producing acid rain and contaminated water with high concentrates of phenols.

Mining

The large industrial complex of Trepca, near the town of Mitrovica, is a conglomerate of 40 mines, foundries, refineries and subsidiary plants. It has one of Europe's richest deposits of lignite, lead, zinc and non-ferrous ores, as well as gold, silver and over 1.6 billion tonnes of coal, valued at an estimated EUR13 billion (US$18.9 billion). However, the only railway capable of transporting coal is through Serbia and an alternative route through Albania or Macedonia is not expected for many years. Trepca had previously been the source of much of former Yugoslavia's mining wealth and after the 1999 conflict was realised as Kosovo's principal economic asset, despite the need for investment to revitalise its infrastructure.

There are large stocks of decorative stone, including onyx, white, grey and black marble, grey granite and other stone such as gneiss, magnesite, quartzite and porphyry which could become important export commodities, however, they are yet to be fully exploited.

Mining production, which was once the backbone of the economy, has decline due to lack of investment and ageing equipment.

Hydrocarbons

Kosovo has no hydrocarbon resources or refineries. All petroleum products must be imported from neighbouring countries, where refining capacity allows.

There are large deposits, estimated at around 18 billion tonnes, of lignite coal typically used in power stations.

Energy

Total installed generating capacity in 2014 was 5.3 billion kWh. The Kosovo Energy Corporation (KEK), operates two large coal-fired power plants. These power stations are close to the open cast lignite mines of Bardhi and Mirash and burn 7 million tonnes per annum. Energy production is the major polluter in Kosovo, producing acid rain and contaminated water with high concentrates of phenols. A 1,000MW coal-fired power plant was put out to tender in 2010. The plant is expected to take around five years to complete and is scheduled to be operational by 2015/16.

Long-term energy development and electricity supply is also being provided for as Kosovo's national power grid is brought up to international standards.

Banking and insurance

The World Bank is providing grants and technical assistance to the Central Banking Authority to oversee the financial system and provide stability and development, including supervision of banks and non-bank financial institutions (insurance and pension funds).

Central bank

Banka Qendrore e Repubukës së Kosovës (BQK) (Central Bank of Kosovo)

Main financial centre

Pristina

Time

GMT plus one hour (daylight saving, late March to late October, GMT plus two hours)

Geography

This land-locked country, roughly square in shape standing on a corner is surrounded by Serbia from the north to the south-east, Macedonia (FYROM) in the south, Albania to the west and Montenegro in the north-west. The average altitude is 800 metres above sea level, however, there are several mountain ranges encircling the country, with the highest ranges in the south-west, north-west and north. The highest mountain, Gjeravica, in Peja in the south-west, is 2,656 metres high, with deep, wide valleys and the largest river, the White Drin at 122 km, flowing down into the central plain, on which most of the urban areas are located. The largest lake, Gazivoda, in Mitrovica, is 9.1 square km.

Hemisphere

Northern

Climate

With a continental climate summers in Kosovo are warm and winters are cold. Temperature ranges average from +30 degrees Celsius (summer July–August) to -10 degrees C (winter December–January). Snowfalls are typical between November and March even on the lowland flat plains. The large mountain ranges also produce local variations and rainfall distributions.

Entry requirements

Passports

Required by all and must be valid for up to 90 days from date of entry.

Serbian authorities will not allow entry to Serbia from Kosovo, unless as a through journey from Albania or Macedonia, or as part of a return journey.

Visa

As of February 2008, for visits of less than 90 days, visitors with US passports do not require visas. EU citizens from countries that recognised Kosovo's independence also do not require visas. All other visitors and those staying over 90 days must provide documentary evidence for purpose of visit, such as employment or education. A 90-day entry stamp will be issued at the border.

For further information see www.unmikonline.org/regulations/ADMDIRECT/2005/ADE2005_08.pdf or visitors should contact the consular section of their own ministry of foreign affairs for advice.

Currency advice/regulations

The banking system is embryonic and a cash economy exists so visitors should expect to travel with enough cash for their stay. There are a few ATMs in Pristina; credit cards are not widely accepted.

The Serbian dinar is in use in Serbian-populated regions.

Customs

UNMIK has been responsible for customs, before trained Kosovan officials are deployed.

Consumer items are limited and should be declared, including jewellery, only two cameras (including a video camera allowed), binoculars, one bicycle and camping equipment, electronic equipment such as laptops and musical players. Sporting equipment may have added restrictions and further information should be obtained.

Prohibited imports

Regulations may be altered with little notice, check details before travelling.

Weapons and ammunitions. Animals may be imported with a vet certificate and proof of healthy condition.

Health (for visitors)

Mandatory precautions

None

Advisable precautions

It is advisable to be in date for the following immunisations: diphtheria, polio and tetanus (within 10 years), typhoid fever, hepatitis A (moderate risk only), hepatitis B and tuberculosis; rabies is a risk. Crimean Congo Haemorrhagic Fever (CCHF) is endemic, particularly in the central Kosovo region and visitors suffering from flu-like systems with a red rash or bleeding in the mouth should seek medical advice.

The health system is severely under funded and care may not reach visitors expectations, so comprehensive travel insurance, including medical evacuation, should be purchased before travelling.

There is a shortage of medicines and visitors should travel with all necessary medications for the duration of their stay.

Hotels

There are no four- or fire-star hotels, Pristina has the largest stock of hotels, but elsewhere there is little choice beyond mid-range and budget accommodation.

Credit cards

Are not widely accepted.

Public holidays (national)

Public holidays that fall at the weekend are taken on the following Monday.

Fixed dates

1–2 January (News Year), 7 January (Orthodox Christmas), 17 February (Independence Day), 1–2 May (Labour Day), 28 November (Flag Day), 25 December (Christmas Day)

Variable dates

Orthodox Christmas, Easter Monday, (first Monday in May), Start of Ramadan, Eid al Fitr, Eid al Adha.

Working hours

Banking

Mon–Fri 0800–1900; Sat 0800–1500; a few open on Sun.

Business

Mon–Fri: 0700/0800–1500/1600.

Government

Mon–Fri: 0700/0800–1500/1600.

Shops

Mon–Fri: 0800–1200, 1500–2000; Sat: 0800–1500. Supermarkets and food shops open for longer.

Telecommunications

Mobile/cell phones

There is an uneven coverage of GSM 900/1800 services.

Electricity supply

230 volts AC, 50Hz. Type C electrical outlets (two-pin plugs).

Social customs/useful tips

A 10 per cent tip is expected.

Avoid taking photographs of military installations and obvious war damage.

Security

In 2008, landmines and unexploded ordinance (UXO) still posed a threat, particularly in border areas with Albania, the Dulje Pass area (in central Kosovo) and in the west and south of the country. All roads and tracks have been cleared.

Political demonstrations have been known to spill over into violence and should be avoided. Criminal activity is largely centred on pickpockets and theft of vehicles, particularly four-wheel drive and luxury cars.

Getting there

Air

National airline: Kosova Airlines (HHI)

International airport/s: Pristina International Airport (PRN), 18km south-west of the capital, with a business lounge, duty free, restaurants, car hire and banking. Taxis from the airport are available between 0500–2230 for a 20 minute journey; airport buses start running two hours before the first flights at 0500 up to 2300. It handled 1.2 million passengers in 2008, and 14,000 aircraft operations. In 2009 the government announced it was looking to agree a design-build-finance-operate-transfer (DBFOT) contract with a private operator to expand the infrastructure, including a new landmark terminal, and thereafter manage and maintain the airport.

Airport tax: A eur15 departure tax is typically included in the price of a ticket.

Surface

Road: There are several frontier posts between Serbia, a few between Albania and Macedonia of which delays are common due to the poor road conditions.

Rail: The railway system operates an irregular service and should not be considered reliable.

Getting about

National transport

Road: There is a 1,925km network of two-lane main and secondary roads of which 1,576km is paved, but even the standard of this is fair to poor and conditions deteriorate in rural areas and after bad weather.

Rail: The railway system operates an irregular service and should not be considered reliable. A 300km single-track railway runs north-south and from the north to the east-west. These are part of the railway that ran from Serbia to either Macedonia or Albania through Kosovo. Domestic services are poor and slow in winter and prone to delays.

City transport

Taxis: As most people's first choice for any distance most taxis are marked and have metres. The destination should be written in Albanian, as English is not spoken by all and the condition of taxis and standard of driving varies.

Buses, trams & metro: Public transport is limited.

Car hire

International car hire firms offer modern vehicles from Pristina and its airport. The European Green Card vehicle insurance is not valid in Kosovo and vehicle insurance, preferably comprehensive, is necessary and should be purchased before driving. It is unlikely that credit cards or travellers cheques will be accepted everywhere so sufficient euro should be carried to pay for insurance and petrol.

Traffic and local drivers may pose a hazard to unwary foreign drivers and travelling at night can be risky. Fuel, although widely available, varies in quality.

In summer during dry hot weather there is a danger of forest fires and care must be taken when driving through wooded areas and lighted cigarette ends should not be thrown away.

Note that Serbian car hire firms do not permit their rented vehicles to enter Kosovo.

BUSINESS DIRECTORY

Telephone area codes

The international direct dialling code (IDD) for Kosovo is +381, followed by area code and the subscriber's number. In August 2015 Kosovo was allocated +383 as its IDD, although the northern, Serbian, areas will be able to continue to use the +381 Serbian IDD code.

Ferizaj	29	Peja	39
Gjakova	390	Pristina	38
Gjilan	280	Prizren	29
Mitrovica	28		

Useful telephone numbers

Emergency number	112
Police	92
Fire service	93
First aid	94

Chambers of Commerce

Kosovo Chamber of Commerce, Mother Theresa No 20, Pristina 10000 (tel:

+381 224-741; fax: +381 224-299; email: info@oek-kcc.org; internet: www.oek-kcc.org).

Banking

Bank for Business, UÇK Street No 41, 10000 Pristina (tel: 244-666).

Economic Bank, Migjeni Street No 1, 10000 Pristina (tel: 244-396).

KASA Bank, Rexhep Luci Street No 5, 10000 Pristina (tel: 246-180).

New Bank of Kosova, Nëna Terezë Street No 49a, Pristina 10000 Pristina (tel: 223-976).

ProCredit Bank, Skenderbeu Street, 10000 Pristina (tel: 240-248).

Raiffeisen Bank Kosovo UÇK Street No 51, 10000 Pristina (tel: 226-400/1

Central bank

Central Bank of Kosovo, 33 Garibaldi Street, Pristina (tel: 222-055; fax: 243-763; email: publicrelations@ bpk-kos.org; internet: www.cbak-kos.org).

Travel information

Kosova Airline, Vellusha e Poshtme 17, Te Kino Rinia (tel: 249-184/5; fax: 249-186; email: info@kosovaairlines.com; internet: www.flyksa.com).

Kosovo Railways, Sheshi i Lirisë pn, Fushë Kosovë (tel: 536-355; fax: 536-307; email: info@kosovorailway.com; internet: www.kosovorailway.com).

Ministries

Ministry of Trade and Industry, Perandori Justinian Street, Pejton Square, 3–5 Pristina (tel: 38 20 036-015; internet: www.mit-ks.org)

Other useful addresses

Auditor General, Gazmend Zajmi No 59, 10000 Pristina (internet: www.ks-gov.net/oag).

Community Development Fund Rruga Perandori Justinian No 4, Pristina (tel: 249-677/8; fax: 249-679; internet: www.kcdf.org).

Constitutional Secretariat, New Bld, 8th Floor, Office 803, Skenderbeg Square, 10000 Pristina (tel: email: info@kushtetutakosoves.info; internet: www.kushtetutakosoves.info).

Economic Initiative for Kosovo (ECIKS), Nussdorfer Strasse 20–23, A-1090 Vienna, Austria (+43 1-890-5026; internet: www.eciks.org).

British Consulate, Ismail Qemajli 6, Arbëri Dragodan, Pristina (tel: 254-700; fax: 249-799; email: britishoffice.pristina@fco.gov.uk).

Independent Media Commission, Gazmend Zajmi Street, No 1 Pristina (tel: 245-031; fax: 245-034; email: info@imc-ko.org; internet: www.imc-ko.org).

Investment Promotion Agency of Kosovo, Perandori Justinian No 3-5, Qyteza Pejton, Pristina (tel/fax: 38 200-360; email: infor@invest-ks.org; internet: www.invest-ks.org).

National Assembly (Media Office), Mother Theresa No 20, Pristina 10000 (tel: 211-186/189; fax: 211-188; internet: www.assembly-kosova.org).

Statistics Office of Kosovo, Zenel Salihu Street No 4, Pristina (tel: 235-111; fax: 235-545; email: esk@ks-gov.net; internet: www.ks-gov.net/esk).

United Nations Development Programme (UNDP), (internet: www.ks.undp.org).

National news agency: Kosova Press, No 20, Mother Teresa Square, 10000 Pristina (tel/fax: 38 248-721; internet: www.kosovapress.com).

Kosovalive: www.kosovalive.com

Kosova Information Center: www.kosova.com

Internet sites

Department of Tourism, Visit Kosovo, (internet: www.visitkosova.org).

Hotel Pristina: www.hotelprishtina.com

Grand Hotel Pristina: www.grandhotel-pr.com

Kosovo Force (KFOR): www.nato.int/KFOR

Kosovo map: http://kosova.org/maps/atlas/index.asp

Kosovo postal codes: http://kosova.org/docs/pdf/Kodet_Postare.pdf

Kosova Tourism Association: www.kotas-ks.org

Ministry of Trade and Industry, (internet: www.mti-ks.org).

OSCE: http://www.osce.org/kosovo

Republic of Kosovo Assembly: www.assembly-kosova.org

UNMIK: www.unmikonline.org

Kuwait

KEY FACTS

Official name: State of Kuwait

Head of State: Sheikh Sabah al-Ahmed al-Jabir al-Sabah (since 29 January 2006)

Head of government: Prime Minister Jabir Al-Mubarak al-Hamad al-Sabah (from 30 November 2011, re-appointed 5 Dec 2013)

Ruling party: 15-member Council of Ministers

Area: 17,818 square km (including neutral zone)

Population: 4.00 million (2014)*

Capital: Kuwait City

Official language: Arabic

Currency: Kuwaiti dinar (KD) = 1,000 fils

Exchange rate: KD0.30 per US$ (Sep 2015)

GDP per capita: US$43,103 (2014)*

GDP real growth: 1.30% (2014)*

GDP: US$172.35 billion (2014)*

Unemployment: 2.07% (2014)*

Inflation: 2.94% (2014)*

Oil production: 3.12 million bpd (2014)

Natural gas production: 16.40 billion cum (2014)

Balance of trade: US$77.41 billion (2014)

* estimated figure

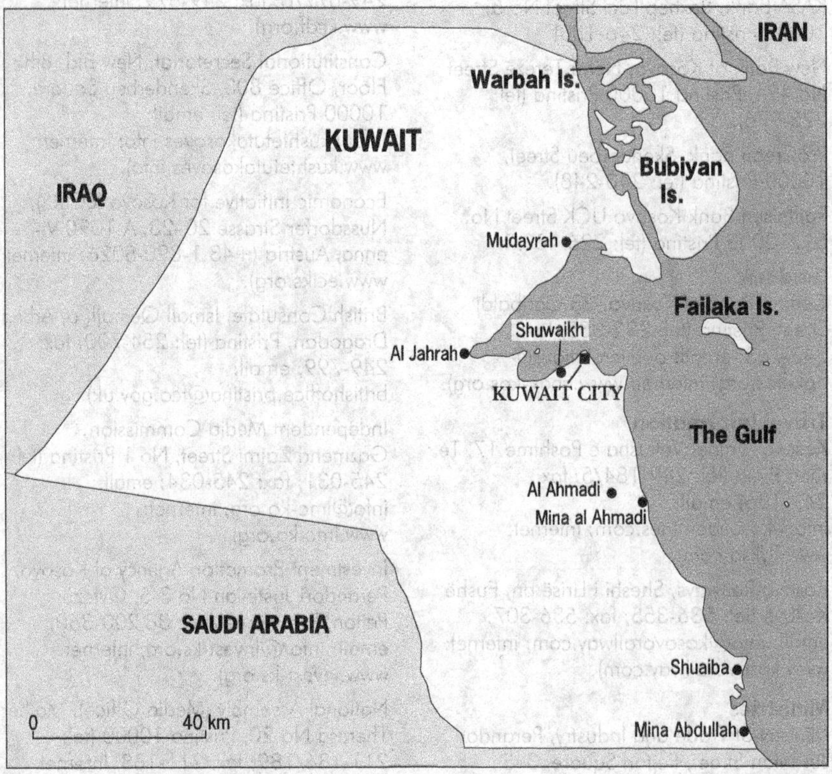

Since the invasion by Iraq in August 1990, Kuwait's international profile had been kept deliberately low. The invasion had come as a shock both for the Kuwaiti population and its government, triggering the Gulf War, which lasted until February 1991. So it was in 2015 that when, on 26 June the worst terrorist attack in Kuwaiti history took place, the immediate response was one of shock and confusion. A suicide bomber killed 27 Shi'a worshippers at the Imam al Sadeq Mosque. The attack was attributed to supporters of the so-called Islamic State (IS). If the attackers' motivation was to drive a wedge between Kuwait's Sunni and Shi'a communities, then it seemed to have failed. In a television broadcast, the Emir, Sheikh Sabah al Ahmad al Sabah, reassured Kuwaitis a few days later that they had 'Foiled a desperate attempt to stir sectarian tensions.' After the trauma of the 1990 invasion, Kuwaitis seemed better able to cope with the unexpected. Kuwait's 'paper democracy' still functioned, despite the introduction of legislation designed to stifle, rather than encourage, political dissent.

Democracy?

Following the attack, Kuwait's social media reportedly erupted with denunciations of sectarian rifts and Sunni and Shi'a held prayers side by side. The suicide bombers seemed unlikely to achieve what the attackers, claiming allegiance to Najd Province IS group in Saudi Arabia, intended. Yet behind the calming talk, officials mentioned their concerns that tensions were in fact on the rise. Hoping to stem the trend, Kuwait's security forces had cracked down. 'We are in a state of war,' Muhammad al Khaled al Sabah, the interior minister, told parliament after the attacks. The increased vigilance may well be warranted, but a series of new laws and a string of arrests threatened to crush dissent in Kuwait – long the Gulf region's most open, 'almost' democratic state.

It was perhaps understandable that shortly after the attack, the Kuwaiti parliament passed its new counter-terrorism legislation. This appeared to have already been in preparation, requiring not only citizens, but also residents and visitors to Kuwait to provide a DNA sample for the national database. The government also proposed extending the period during which the police might detain suspects without charge. Not long before the terrorist attack the parliament had given its approval to a new cyber-security law that critics claimed would make it easier for the government to silence critical media.

Old Gulf hands had always seen Kuwait as one of, if not the, most mature of the Arabian Gulf states. Your correspondent remembers welcoming Kuwaiti pupils, gold watches and all, to a North London grammar school in the 1950s. Despite its wealth, British expatriates would fondly describe Kuwait as 'Stevenage in the Sun', a jocular reference to the ring-roads and roundabouts (similar to those of Stevenage) that surrounded Kuwait City. Following complete independence from Britain in 1961, British protection as set out in the Anglo-Kuwait agreement of 1899 was formally withdrawn; the treaty was abrogated in an exchange of letters between the ruler of Kuwait and the British Political Resident. Until the independence of India in 1947, the Kuwait Political Resident had been answerable to New Delhi rather than to London. Prior to 1961, for some time Kuwait had already been responsible for its own international relations. In this respect, Kuwait was refreshingly independent: the flags of China and North Korea happily fluttered over their Kuwait embassies, alongside those of the UK and the US, the DDR and the Bundesrepublik.

The economy

The news was almost without precedent. Before 2017 Kuwait would probably post a budget deficit, due to falling oil prices, the country's finance minister Anas al Saleh had advised the Kuwaiti parliament. So it was that Kuwait's parliament approved a state budget for the 2015/16 fiscal year that envisaged a budget deficit of KD8.18 billion (US$27.0 billion) – nearly half the country's total spending – largely because of the low oil prices.

Reuters reported that the budget for the year that began in April 2015 featured spending of KD19.17 billion (US$63.26 billion) and revenues of only KD12.2 billion (US$40.26 billion), assuming an average oil price of US$45 a barrel during the course of the year. The deficit of KD8.18 billion would be reached after the transfer of 10 per cent of state revenues to the Future Generations Fund, part of Kuwait's sovereign wealth fund.

Reuters reported that the actual deficit might not turn out to be nearly as large – in mid-2015 Brent crude oil was trading above US$60 per barrel. The deficit would be about KD4.5 billion (US$14.85 billion) if oil stayed in the mid-US$60s, according to Anas al Saleh. In previous years Kuwait had often underspent its budget because of bureaucratic red tape and the tensions between the cabinet and parliament that had slowed down economic projects. Nevertheless, the budget plan revealed the dramatic change in Kuwait's finances due to the fall in oil prices, which had severely reduced its export earnings. The government had posted an estimated deficit of KD2.31 billion (US$7.62 billion) in the previous (2014/15) fiscal year, after contributions to the Future Generations Fund – its first deficit since the 1999/2000 fiscal year. No decision had been taken on how to fund the year's deficit according to the minister.

Kuwait is well known to be highly dependent on its oil as a means of income, with no less than 95 per cent of its public revenues being derived from it. Lower oil prices have been affecting the government's ability to indulge in welfare spending as freely as before, when a barrel of oil hovered around the US$100 per barrel mark. The minister added that in the previous fiscal year, Kuwait spent up to KD5 billion (US$16.5 billion) in subsidies, up 25 per cent from KD864 million (US$2.85 billion) spent in the fiscal year of 2004.

In order to reduce the strain on its coffers, Kuwait slashed the subsidies on diesel, kerosene and aviation fuel from January 2015. The government was also considering a phase-out of subsidies on petrol and other utilities, although no concrete steps had been taken at the time of writing. The reduction in subsidies had led to production costs soaring among businesses, triggering a wave of price rises. As a result, the parliament had urged the government to halt the removal of any more subsidies or grants over fears of further price rises in the economy. Parliamentary deputies also called on the government to conduct a comprehensive study to ensure that the subsidy removal would not affect citizens' living standards. Despite such steps towards austerity, Kuwait was not expected to go into a spending freeze. The Kuwaiti authorities had announced that it had set apart KD45.5 billion (US$150.15 billion) in the national five year developmental plan to spend on various projects and on human resource development. The amount was expected to finance 523 projects between the years 2015 to 2020. Out of the total amount, KD29.5 billion (US$97.35 billion) would be spent on

KEY INDICATORS — Kuwait

	Unit	2011	2012	2013	2014	**2015
Population	m	*3.68	3.79	3.89	*4.00	*4.11
Gross domestic product (GDP)	US$bn	176.70	184.54	175.79	*172.35	*134.48
GDP per capita	US$	47,982	48,761	45,189	*43,103	*32,720
GDP real growth	%	8.2	6.2	1.5	*1.3	*1.7
Inflation	%	4.7	3.2	2.7	2.9	*3.3
Unemployment	%	2.0	2.1	3.9	*2.1	*2.1
Oil output	'000 bpd	2,865.0	3,127.0	3,126.0	3,123.0	–
Natural gas output	bn cum	13.0	14.5	15.6	16.4	–
Exports (fob) (goods)	US$m	102,854.7	119,275.2	115,854.1	–	–
Imports (fob) (goods)	US$m	22,597.2	22,464.3	25,861.9	–	–
Balance of trade	US$m	80,257.5	96,810.9	89,992.1	–	–
Current account	US$m	70,800.0	79,768.0	69,612.0	*60,922.0	*21,114.0
Total reserves minus gold	US$m	25,800.5	28,885.7	32,184.4	–	–
Foreign exchange	US$m	22,859.0	25,964.1	29,179.9	–	–
Exchange rate	per US$	0.28	0.28	0.28	0.29	–

* estimated figure ** forecast figure

economic development and KD15.5 billion (US$51.15 billion) on human resource development. The remaining amount of KD500 million (US$1.65 billion) would be spent on administrative development.

Energy

In mid-2015 the Kuwait National Petroleum Co (KNPC) awarded 3.48 billion dinars (US$11.5 billion) worth of contracts to build the al Zour oil refinery, which would be one of the largest in the Middle East according to the national news agency KUNA. This was seen by most analysts as a critically optimistic initiative by the Kuwaiti government. Construction of the 615,000 barrels per day (bpd) refinery was expected to be a major boost to Kuwait's economy, which had slowed in recent years reflecting political tensions; on top of political bickering, the country now had to cope with the blow to state finances represented by low oil prices.

The al Zour project was originally planned more than a decade earlier, ago but had been delayed repeatedly by bureaucratic and political problems, including conflict between Kuwait's parliament and the cabinet. The state-owned KNPC had commissioned a consortium including Spain's Técnicas Reunidas, China's Sinopec and South Korea's Hanwha Engineering and Construction to build the main process units of the refinery, with a contract worth a total of KD1.28 billion (US$4.22 billion).

Another consortium, including Daewoo Engineering and Construction, Hyundai Heavy Industries (both from South Korea) and Fluor Corp of the United States would build support units and infrastructure services. A third consortium made up of Hyundai Engineering and Construction (South Korea), SK Engineering and Construction (UK) and Italy's Saipem was awarded the contract to build a marine export terminal. All the ancillary contracts for the project were to be awarded by early October 2015.

Kuwait's Supreme Petroleum Council had agreed to increase al Zour's total budget to KD4.87 billion (US$16 billion) from about KD4 billion (US$13.2 billion) . The refinery was due to start up by late 2018 or early 2019, providing low-sulphur fuel to power stations, but it is not clear if that timeframe can still be met.

According to the *BP Statistical Review of World Energy* of June 2015 (BP15) Kuwait was the world's seventh largest petroleum producer in 2014. Despite being the second smallest in land area among the Organisation of the Petroleum Exporting Countries (Opec) member countries, Kuwait exports the fifth-largest volume of crude oil and condensates after Saudi Arabia, the United Arab Emirates (UAE), Iraq and Nigeria. The national economy is heavily dependent on petroleum export revenues, which account for nearly 60 per cent its gross domestic product (GDP) and for about 94 per cent of export revenues, according to Opec and International Monetary Fund (IMF) data. The US government's Energy Information Administration (EIA) estimated these revenues to have been US$92 billion in 2013. Kuwait seeks to remain one of the world's top oil producers as the country targets crude oil and condensate production of 4 million barrels per day (bpd) by 2020. However, Kuwait has struggled to boost oil and natural gas production for more than a decade because of upstream project delays and insufficient foreign investment.

To diversify its oil-heavy economy, Kuwait has increased efforts to explore and develop its non-associated natural gas fields, which make up a small portion of its natural gas production. Greater natural gas production would increase Kuwait's feedstock for its struggling electricity sector, which frequently cannot meet demand in peak times. Kuwait has increased the share of natural gas in its primary energy consumption from 34 per cent in 2009 to 42 per cent in 2012 (see below), while the remaining share, consisting solely of petroleum and other liquids, has declined.

Despite Kuwait's constitutional ban on foreign ownership of its resources and revenues, the government has taken measures to increase foreign participation in the oil and natural gas sectors through what are known as technical and service contracts. Kuwait's frequent delays of major energy projects have been the result of political disagreements between the Emir and parliament over contract management, especially those contracts involving foreign companies and project logistics. The ministry of petroleum supervises all aspects of policy implementation in the upstream and downstream portions of the oil and natural gas sectors.

According to the BP15 Review, in January 2015, Kuwait had an estimated 101.5 billion barrels of proved oil reserves, roughly 6 per cent of the world total and seventh among all countries. Additional reserves were held in the Partitioned Neutral Zone (PNZ), which Kuwait shares on a 50–50 basis with Saudi Arabia (see below). The PNZ holds 5 billion barrels of proved reserves, bringing Kuwait's total oil reserves to 104.5 billion barrels. Kuwait's oil reserves include approximately 13 billion barrels of heavy oil, located primarily in northern Kuwait, with other reserves concentrated in the PNZ.

The Kuwait Petroleum Corporation (KPC) manages domestic and foreign oil investments. The Kuwait Oil Company (KOC), the upstream subsidiary of KPC, was taken over by the Kuwaiti government in 1975 and manages all upstream development in the oil and natural gas sectors. The Kuwait National Petroleum Company (KNPC) controls the downstream sector, while the Petrochemical Industries Company (PIC) is in charge of the petrochemical sector. Export operations are overseen by both KNPC and the Kuwait Oil Tanker Company (KOTC). Foreign interests of KPC are handled by the Kuwait Foreign Petroleum Exploration Company (Kufpec) and international upstream development and downstream operations are controlled by Kuwait Petroleum International (KPI). Kuwait Energy Company (KEC) is a privately-held company that has developed a number of foreign interests over the past decade, including interests in Yemen, Egypt, Russia, Pakistan and Oman. The PNZ has its own managing companies, separated by onshore and offshore activities.

In 2014, Kuwait's petroleum production was approximately 3,123 million barrels per day (bpd), including its share of approximately 250,000bpd of oil production from the PNZ. Of the country's 2013 production, approximately 2.6 million bpd was crude oil and nearly 200,000bpd was non-crude liquids. About half of Kuwaiti crude oil production in 2014 came from the south-east region of the country, largely from the Burgan field, which has a production capacity of 1.7 million bpd. Current crude oil production capacity from the northern fields has increased to approximately 700,000bpd according to the Middle East Economic Survey (MEES). In early 2011, as one of the few Opec members with spare capacity, Kuwait increased its oil production to compensate for the loss of Libyan supplies. Because of the constitutional ban on foreign ownership of Kuwait's natural resources, development of domestic fields had stalled.

Many hopes had at one stage been pinned on the government's 'Project Kuwait' scheme, which aimed to be the focal point of Kuwait's aspirations to attain a production capacity of 4 million bpd. Proposed in 1998, Project Kuwait was seen as a concerted effort to create proper incentives to attract foreign participation, particularly for the country's northern fields. The contract structure that resulted was challenged as unconstitutional and the National Assembly impeded any progress on Project Kuwait for a number of years. Kuwait's constitution barred foreign ownership of the country's natural resources, which precluded the product-sharing agreements (PSAs) that provide the desired incentive for IOC investment. To allow IOC involvement, an incentivised buy-back contract (IBBC) arrangement was created, which did not involve production sharing or concessions. In principle, the structure of the IBBC agreements allowed the Kuwaiti government to retain full ownership of oil reserves, control over oil production levels and strategic management of the ventures.

The PNZ had been established in 1922 to settle a territorial dispute between Kuwait and Saudi Arabia. It encompasses a 6,200 square-mile area that contains 1 trillion cubic feet (tcf) of natural gas in addition to the estimated 5 billion barrels of oil, according to *Oil & Gas Journal* (OGJ). Oil production capacity in the PNZ was 520,000bpd in 2013, all of which was divided equally between Saudi Arabia and Kuwait. Onshore production in the PNZ centres on the Wafra oil field, which began producing oil in 1954. Wafra is the largest of the PNZ's onshore fields with approximately 3.4 billion barrels in proved and probable reserves. Wafra has related production facilities and gathering centres with South Umm Gudair and South Fuwaris. Onshore production in the PNZ had a capacity of 300,000bpd, but is in decline. The production capacity of offshore fields in the PNZ was less than 300,000bpd and Khafji Joint Operations, the joint venture developing the offshore capacity of the PNZ, plans to increase production to 400,000bpd by 2019, according to the *Wall Street Journal*.

In 2013, Kuwaiti exports of crude oil were estimated at 1.9 million bpd, making Kuwait the sixth-largest exporter of crude oil among Opec producers behind Saudi Arabia, the United Arab Emirates, Iraq, Nigeria and Venezuela, according to tanker data from Lloyd's List Intelligence (LLI). Most Kuwaiti crude oil is sold on term contracts. Exports to the United States totaled 334,000bpd and Europe received around 83,000bpd, according to LLI. The largest importers were South Korea and India.

Natural gas

According to the OGJ, in January 2014, Kuwait had an estimated 63 trillion cubic feet (tcf) of proved natural gas reserves. Natural gas reserves have remained at the same level since 2006. Kuwait's intent to diversify its economy has spurred an extensive focus on natural gas exploration. Vast discoveries of non-associated gas in the northern region of the country has attracted interest from IOCs. However, contract structures and political uncertainty remain the principal impediments to any rapid expansion of either reserves or production. Additionally, new natural gas discoveries are geologically more complex, mainly tight and sour natural gas deposits that require more sophisticated development and have higher capital costs.

As in the oil sector, all of the natural gas resources are owned by the KPC. The Kuwaiti constitution prohibits any use of production-sharing agreements (PSAs) that allows for an equity stake by an IOC in development projects; therefore, Kuwait uses technical service agreements (TSAs) to bring in IOCs to develop the more difficult projects. In 2014, Kuwait produced 16.4 billion cubic metres per day (bcm/d) of natural gas, the highest on record and up about some 42 per cent from production in 2010. Domestic natural gas supplies started rising after 2009 with the introduction of non-associated production and higher oil output in tandem with associated gas production. Given the predominance of associated natural gas in Kuwaiti production, domestic natural gas supplies had relied on Opec crude oil production quotas. Kuwait required increasing supplies of natural gas for the generation of electricity, water desalination and petrochemicals, as well as for the increased use for enhanced oil recovery (EOR) techniques to boost oil production.

Risk assessment

Economy	Good
Politics	Fair
Regional stability	Fair

Muslims in Kuwait

% of population	85
Sunni (% of Muslims)	75
Shi'a (% of Muslims)	25

COUNTRY PROFILE

1600s The north-east Arabian Peninsula, including what is now Kuwait, was part of the Ottoman Empire.
1756 The Al-Sabah family took control of Kuwait and there was a degree of semi-autonomy from Ottoman Turkey.
1899 Sheikh Mubarak 'the Great' accepted British protection in order to counter the spread of Turkish influence. Kuwait became a British protectorate but control of external relations remained with Britain.
1918 The end of the First World War saw the end of what was already only nominal Turkish control over Kuwait.
1938 Oil was first discovered by the US-British Kuwait Oil Company. Further exploration was interrupted by the Second World War.
1940s–50s Drilling resumed after the War and Kuwait soon developed into a thriving commercial centre. The government began using oil revenues to develop the country's infrastructure and a modern and comprehensive welfare system.
1961 Kuwait's status as a British protectorate ended and it became an independent country. The ruling Sheikh became the Emir and assumed full executive power. Iraq claimed Kuwait as part of its territory, but backed down after British military intervention.
1963 The constitution was promulgated and National Assembly elections were held.
1976 The Emir suspended the National Assembly; he said it was not acting in the country's best interests.
1977 Sheikh Jaber al Ahmad al Sabah succeeded his cousin, Sheikh Sabah al Salem al Sabah as Emir.
1980 In the Iran-Iraq War, Kuwait supported Iraq.
1981 The political and economic union, Co-operation Council for the Arab States of the Gulf (CCASG) (known as Gulf Co-operation Council (GCC)) was formed by Bahrain, Kuwait, Oman, Qatar, Saudi Arabia and the United Arab Emirates (UAE). The National Assembly was recalled, but was again dissolved in 1986.
1985 The Emir survived an assassination attempt.
1990 Iraq invaded Kuwait and the Emir and cabinet fled to Saudi Arabia. The invasion was condemned by the international community which, led by the US, deployed armed forces to Saudi Arabia. UN Resolution 678 authorised member states to use force if Iraq did not withdraw by 15 January 1991.
1991 When Iraq did not withdraw, in the early hours of 17 January coalition forces launched an aerial bombing campaign against Iraq and Iraqi forces in Kuwait. US-led ground forces (from around 30 countries, including Syria, Egypt and Morocco) moved into Kuwait on 24 February and drove the Iraqi forces there back into Iraq. Iraq agreed to accept all UN resolutions concerning Kuwait.
1992 The Emir was pressurised into allowing National Assembly elections, in which the opposition fared well.
1999 Islamists and liberals swept to victory in parliamentary elections. A draft law granting women full political rights,

including the right to vote, was narrowly rejected by parliament. The National Assembly was suspended by the Emir, following a dispute over a misprinted state edition of the Quran.
2001 The Constitutional Court refused to grant women the vote.
2002 The Emir suffered a brain haemorrhage; he received treatment in London.
2003 US troops and allies massed in the border area of Kuwait before invading Iraq. Islamist and pro-government candidates were successful in parliamentary elections; liberal candidates suffered heavy losses. Emir Sheikh Jaber appointed his brother, Sheikh Sabah al Ahmad al Jaber al Sabah, as prime minister, separating the post from the role of heir to the throne for the first time since independence.
2005 A constitutional amendment gave women the right to vote and stand for parliament from 2007. For the first time, two women were named as members of the national assembly.
2006 Sheikh Sabah al Ahmed al Jaber al Sabah became Emir instead of ailing Crown Prince Sheikh Sa'ad al Abdullah al Sabah, who had been heir apparent since 1978. Sheikh Nasser al Mohammad al Ahmad (nephew of the Emir) was appointed prime minister. Women voted for the first time, in a council by-election. The Emir dissolved parliament and scheduled new elections; members opposed to the government's stance on electoral reform won 33 elected seats out of 50. A new reform bill reduced the number of parliamentary constituencies from 25 to five.
2007 The cabinet of Prime Minister Nasser al Sabah's resigned and was re-appointed to form another cabinet. As a counter-inflationary measure, the central bank ended the dinar's peg to the US dollar (adopted in 2003) in favour of a basket of currencies.
2008 A GCC common market was created by the six wealthiest Gulf States. Citizens of these countries are allowed to travel between, and live in any of the six states, where they may find employment, buy properties and businesses and use the educational and health facilities freely. Early elections were called as Prime Minister Nasser al Sabah's cabinet resigned. In parliamentary elections, Sunni Islamists won 21 seats, Shi'ite Islamists five, the National Action Bloc (liberals) seven, and independents 17. Incumbent Prime Minister Sheikh Nasser al Sabah formed a new government, with no change from the previous cabinet in the key portfolios. After an 18-year gap the Kuwaiti ambassador took up residence in Iraq; diplomatic relations had been restored in 2003. The prime minister and other cabinet members resigned rather than answer questions concerning a visiting Iranian cleric accused of insulting Sunni Muslims.
2009 Having been reappointed, the prime minister and cabinet resigned again, allegedly to avoid questions about the misuse of public funds. In early parliamentary elections independents won 21 seats (out of 50), Sunni Islamists 13, Liberals 7, Shi'a Islamists 6, and the Popular Bloc 3; turnout was 50 per cent. Two of the successful candidates were women, the first females to win entry to parliament. The Emir reappointed Nasser al Sabah as prime minister.
2010 Around 93,000 people (including about 31,000 Kuwaiti nationals) were banned from travel by the authorities due to outstanding debts to the state; the total owed was some KD784 million (US$2.7 billion). The first chairman of the Capital Market Authority, the first independent regulatory body to oversee the stock exchange, was appointed.
2011 In January, Sheikh Nasser al Mohammed al Sabah arrived in Bagdad and became the first prime minister of Kuwait to visit Iraq since the 1990 invasion. Discussions with his counterpart covered border issues, finance and security as well as the payment of war reparations said to amount to billions of US dollars. The entire government resigned in March, in a row with parliament that wanted to question three senior cabinet ministers and Al Sabah family members concerning allegations of corruption and failure to perform their duties. Sheikh Nasser Mohammad al Sabah was reappointed prime minister in April. In June parliament voted to spend around US$70 billion on subsidies for Kuwaiti citizens, of which 90 per cent was set aside to pay for fuel. Observers considered this a measure to forestall any opposition to the Al Sabah family rule during the Arab Spring protests elsewhere in the Middle East. In November, a group of campaigners stormed the parliamentary chamber in protest at the prime minister's leadership and corruption in general; hundreds more protested outside. Prime Minister Nasser Mohammad al Sabah resigned and Jabir Mubarak al Hamad al Sabah was appointed as prime minister; he took office on 4 December. The Emir dissolved parliament, citing 'deteriorating conditions' and on 18 December, called early general elections. As the campaign progressed opposition candidates called for sweeping reforms, including a new constitution that would turn the oil-rich, autocracy into a full democracy. Demands were made for a constitutional monarch with a multi-party parliament and a change in the current practice of important positions in the so called sovereign positions – ministries of defence, interior and foreign affairs – being reserved for members of the ruling al Sabah family.
2012 In early general elections held on 2 February, 34 seats out of 50 were won by opposition Islamists. Although a quota had been set for female candidates, only 24 women stood for election and not only did no new contenders win but four female parliamentarians lost their seats. The victory by Islamists was seen as public frustration with corruption and the rise in tribal power. Tribes, which constitute 55 per cent of the population (total 1.2 million), had been seen as traditional supporters of the al Sabah family but many had switched allegiance to become an important component of the opposition. Sheikh Jabir Mubarak Al Hamad Al Sabah resigned as prime minister on 5 February, but was reappointed by the Emir on the following day. On 18 May, the Emir vetoed a proposed amendment to the constitution that would have required all legislation to be *sharia* compliant. On 20 June the constitutional court ruled that the dissolution in 2011 of the previous parliament by Emir Sabah al Ahmed al Jaber al Sabah was unconstitutional and the results of the 2 February elections were therefore void. The government resigned (the ninth time since mid-2006) and the former parliament was reinstated. The Emir dissolved parliament on 7 October ahead of a new and early general election, due by 7 December. A new visa system (similar to the European Schengen agreement) allowing multiply entry for foreigners to the six Gulf Co-operation Council (GCC) countries was introduced in November. Sheikh Jaber al Mubarak al Sabah was reappointed as prime minister on 5 December, two days after resigning, following parliamentary elections held on 1 December which had been boycotted by the opposition. Rejecting the elections, opponents protested at electoral law amendments that had been introduced by the Emir in October. The turnout at 40.3 per cent was the lowest in Kuwait's history (the opposition claimed turnout was even lower at 26.7 per cent).
2013 The Constitutional Court dissolved parliament on 16 June. On 20 June the government called an election for 25 July, delayed until 27 July. In the election government supporting Independents won 30 seats, Shi'a candidates won just eight seats, down from 17, the Liberal bloc increased their seats by six to nine, the Sunnis won three. Turnout was 52.5 per cent.
2014 Government announced on 18 May that parliamentary by-elections would be held on 26 June to replace the five lawmakers who quit over a row about questioning Prime minister Jaber in parliament.

2015 A sucide attack on the Imam al Sadeq Mosque on 26 June killed 27 Shi'a worshippers and injured over 200. The perpetrator was later identified as a young Saudi Arabian who had arrived earlier in the day.

Political structure

Constitution

The Constitution was enacted on 29 January 1963. It authorises the ruling al Sabah family to choose an Emir, who holds executive power and can proclaim legislation by decree.

The Constitution ascribes the political system as democratic, with sovereignty residing in the people. Impartial personal liberty and equality of rights and duties before the law are guaranteed.

The Emir or one-third of the national assembly may propose amending the Constitution by deleting or adding new ones, except for the Emiri System and the principles of liberty and equality unless to increase provisions. Approval by a two-thirds majority is required for such a bill to succeed.

Males aged over 21 may vote; women aged over 21 were able to vote from 2007.

Independence date

19 June 1961

Form of state

Constitutional monarchy (Emirate)

The executive

Executive power resides with the Emir, who is Head of State and appoints a prime minister, acceptable to the national assembly. In consultation with the prime minister the Emir appoints the Council of Ministers, who may not be members of parliament, although they assume ex *officio* membership during their term of office.

The Emir rules by decrees agreed by the Council of Ministers and, approved by parliament. He is also supreme commander of the armed forces.

Since 2003, the office of prime minister has been separated from the office of the Crown Prince, allowing greater independence of the legislature.

National legislature

The unicameral Majlis al Umma (National Assembly) has 65 seats of which 50 members are directly elected in multi-seat constituencies by simple majority vote. The remaining fifteen members are ex-officio cabinet ministers appointed by the prime minister. All members serve four-year terms. Legislation must be confirmed by two-thirds of the National Assembly membership before being endorsed by the Emir.

There is a cabinet with a total of 15 members which may be elected from the National Assembly membership or appointed *ex officio*.

The February 2012 elections were declared invalid and an early general election was called for 1 December. In October 2012, six weeks ahead of the election the electoral system was changed, with voters restricted to voting for one candidate, having previously been allowed to vote for four candidates.

Legal system

The Judiciary is based on Egyptian laws, derived from French law. The legal system is a mix of *Sharia* (Islamic law) and Napoleonic law.

In 1960, a unified judicial system was adopted, establishing different levels of courts. There are three separate divisions including the Courts of First Instance subdivided into criminal, commercial and civil boards, the Constitutional Court and the Court of State Security. The judiciary is administered by a council of seven senior judges and minister.

Last elections

25 July 2013 (parliamentary)

Results: Parliamentary: all candidates stand as independents since political parties are banned. Pro-government candidates won 30 seats out of 50. The Liberals won nine seats, a big increase from their previous one seat, Shiites won eight seats and Sunni Islamists won three seats. Turnout was 51.9 per cent.

Next elections

July 2017 (parliamentary)

Political parties

No political parties are allowed, although informal groupings exist. Candidates standing for election to the National Assembly do so as individuals, although they maybe a member of a political group.

The largest such groupings are the Islamic Patriotic Coalition (a Shi'a fundamentalist group), two Sunni fundamentalist groups, the Islamic Constitutional Movement and the Islamic Popular Grouping (also known as the Salafi). The Kuwait Democratic Forum is the largest secular political group and has liberal and Arab nationalist opinions.

Ruling party

15-member Council of Ministers

According to government statistics foreign workers had outnumber Kuwaitis citizens by over 2:1 by 2008; 3,441,813 (total); 1,087,000 (citizens); 2,354,261 (expatriates) (Statistics Department at the Public Authority for Civil Information (Paci), December 2008) .

Population

4.00 million (2014)*

Last census: April 2005: 2,213,403 (880,774 Kuwaitis; 1,332,629 expatriates)

Population density: 102 inhabitants per square km. Urban population 98 per cent (2010 Unicef).

Annual growth rate: 1.4 per cent, 1990–2010 (Unicef).

Internally Displaced Persons (IDP)

21,000 (2006, Internal Displacement Monitoring Centre)

Ethnic make-up

Kuwaiti (37 per cent), other Arab (35 per cent), south Asian (9 per cent) and Iranian (4 per cent).

Religions

Sunni Muslim (45 per cent), Shi'ite Muslim (30 per cent), other Muslims (10 per cent); others, including Christian, Hindu and Parsi (15 per cent).

Education

There is state and private education at all levels; state schools are single-sex and only private schools may be co-educational. Tuition in the state sector is in Arabic.

Compulsory schooling begins at aged six and lasts until students have completed two four-year cycles in, first, elemental then intermediate schools. The last four-year cycle is not compulsory; as with the previous two stages, it is free of charge.

Pre-primary schools (also funded by the state) cater for four- to six-year-olds.

Public expenditure on education is typically equivalent to around 5 per cent of annual GNP and included subsidies to private education at primary, secondary and tertiary levels. Average public expenditure was estimated at 39.6 per cent of GDP per capita for primary level students, 5.5 per cent for secondary level and a higher expenditure of 87.9 per cent for tertiary level students.

Literacy rate: 83 per cent adult rate; 93 per cent youth rate (15–24) (Unesco 2005).

Compulsory years: Six to 14

Enrolment rate: 77 per cent gross primary enrolment of relevant age group (including repeaters); 65 per cent gross seconday enrolment (World Bank).

Pupils per teacher: 14 in primary schools

Health

Kuwait offers free, high quality health services through its clinics and hospitals, but charges for certain medical services for some residents and expatriates. The Ministry of Public Health (MPH) manages the health system and provides care on a referral basis through a network of local clinics, general and specialised services.

Life expectancy: 77 years, 2004 (WHO 2006)

Fertility rate/Maternal mortality rate: 2.3 births per woman, 2010 (Unicef);

maternal mortality 5 per 100,000 live births (World Bank).
Birth rate/Death rate: 3 deaths and 20 births per 1,000 people (World Bank)
Child (under 5 years) mortality rate (per 1,000): 11 per 1,000 live births (WHO 2012); 2 per cent of children aged under five years are malnourished (World Bank).
Head of population per physician: 1.53 physicians per 1,000 people, 2001 (WHO 2006)

Welfare

The social insurance system was set up as a basic scheme to include all employees with an addition supplementary scheme covering only those employees with an average monthly income above KD1,250. Disability benefits are provided up to 60-years of age. The survivor pension amounts to 33.3–100 per cent of the deceased person's earnings according to number of widows and family dependants. A widow or widower receives a minimum monthly benefit.

Pensions

The old age pension is calculated on the number of years of contribution, the age at retirement and average earnings. It is set at a minimum of 65 per cent, and by a maximum benefit of 95 per cent, of the last monthly earnings.

Main cities

Kuwait City (capital, estimated population in 2012), Farwaniya (86,236), Qalib ash Shuyukh (a town largely populated by foreign workers) (206,157), Subbah al Salem (176,754), Al Qurayn (163,556), As Salimiyah (145,068), Farwaniya (107,136), Hawali (91,618).

Languages spoken

English is widely spoken, especially in business circles.

Official language/s

Arabic

Media

In 2008 Kuwait was ranked first for press freedom among all Arab states, by the Amman Centre of Human Rights Studies. A press law prohibits references to God and the prophet Mohammed. Criticism of the Emir, the constitution, the judiciary and the 'tenets and mores of the society' can be prosecuted and imprisoned thus self-censorship is practised.

Press

The Ministry of Information issues licences to newspaper publishers.
Dailies: In Arabic, *Al Qabas* (www.alqabas.com.kw), *Al Rai al Amm* (www.alraialaam.com), *Al Watan* (www.alwatan.com.kw), *Annarar* (www.annaharkw.com), *Al Anba* (www.alanba.com.kw), *Al Seyassah* and *Al Taleea*. In English *Al Watan Daily* (www2.alwatan.com.kw), *Kuwait Times* (www.kuwaittimes.net) and *Arab Times* (www.arabtimesonline.com).
Weeklies: In Arabic, *Al Nahda* (www.al-nahda.com) and *Al Mujtammaa* (www.almujtamaa-mag.com) cover for current affairs.
Business: There are three regional business magazines which provide local and regional news on financial and business news, the Lebanon-based *Al Iktissad Wal Aamal* (www.iktissad.com), the UAE based *Zawya* (http://www.zawya.com) and the monthly *Investors* (http://mosgcc.com/english) published by the Gulf Co-operation Council. Local daily newspapers also publish business news.
Periodicals: In Arabic, the cultural review magazines *Dar al Yaqza* (www.alyaqza.com), *Al Arabi* (www.alarabimag.com) and *Anhar* (www.anhaar.com) are published monthly. The Quarterly *Thouq* (www.thouq.com) is a glossy magazine on fashion and lifestyles.

Broadcasting

State-run radio and television is operated by the Ministry of Information.
Radio: Radio Kuwait is the national public radio station providing several services of news, sports, religion, traditional and pop music and programmes in English. The only other local radio station is the private Marina FM (www.marinafm.com). Foreign radio stations available include the UK's BBC and BFBS, the US AFN and the French Monte Carlo Doualiya. There are numerous satellite radio stations available.
Television: The state-run Kuwait Televion has four channels, KTV1–4. Other, private broadcasters include the Al Watan (www.watan.tv), Al Resalah (www.alresalah.net), a religious channel and the first satellite TV service Al Rai, funded by the Al Rai Media Group (www.alraimedia.com) which has nationwide interests in TV, radio, publishing and advertising. Minority satellite TV interests include Bahry TV (www.bahry.com) with marine programmes and CNBC Arabiya (www.cnbcarabia.com) for business programmes. There are other smaller, local TV services available.
National news agency: Kuwait News Agency (Kuna): www.kuna.net.kw

Economy

Once described as 'an oil well masquerading as a country', the economy of Kuwait is centred on the oil and natural gas extraction industries. Kuwait has vast oil reserves (101.5 billion barrels of oil at the end of 2014, the seventh largest reserves in the world) with production of 3.1 million barrels per day. Proven natural gas reserves were 1.8 trillion cubic metres (cum) and production 16.4 billion cum at the end of 2014, all of which is consumed domestically.
The recovery of world oil prices in 2011 helped to alleviate Kuwait out of its 2009–10 recession, recording a strong GDP growth of 9.6 per cent. However, since this peak, growth has been decelerating, falling to 6.6 per cent in 2012 and further to 1.5 per cent in 2013. Growth in 2014 was largely maintained, posting a slow expansion in GDP of 1.3 per cent.
The Kuwaiti dinar (KD) was uncoupled from the US dollar in 2006 and pegged against a basket of currencies in 2007. Following the beginning of the global economic slowdown the dinar appreciated in value by 7 per cent in real terms.
The windfall income which came from oil at its high price led to substantial fiscal and current account surpluses. The government sets aside 10 per cent of all oil revenue annually, to be paid into the Reserve Fund for Future Generations (RFFG). The reserves are managed by the state-owned asset management company, Kuwait Investment Authority (KIC), which invests in projects aimed at diversifying Kuwait's economy. However, despite the government's plans to invest US$104 billion over four years in diversification, its uncertain political situation lead to a large proportion of the projects not materialising.
Arab finance ministers launched a US$2 billion Arab Development Fund (ADF) in 2010, administered by the Arab Fund for Economic and Social Development (AFESD) in Kuwait. The Fund finances small and medium investments in the 11 donor countries (including Kuwait) and is aimed at improving the circumstances of the some 140 million Arabs living below the poverty line.

External trade

Kuwait is a member of the Gulf Co-operation Council (along with Bahrain, Oman, Qatar, Saudi Arabia and the UAE), and the Greater Arab Free Trade Area (Gafta), which operates a customs union whereby tariffs within Gafta were reduced by a percentage each year, until none remained in 2005.
Around 90 per cent of all exports are oil and gas, while 90 per cent of all imports are consumer commodities and goods.

Imports

Food, construction materials, vehicles and parts, consumer goods and clothing.
Main sources: United States (12.7 per cent of total in 2014), China (11.9 per cent), Saudi Arabia (7.1 per cent), South Korea (6.9 per cent) and Japan (6.6 per cent).

Exports

Petroleum, refined oil-related and by-products, predominately plastics and fertilizers and electrical and electronic equipment.

Main destinations: South Korea (16.7 per cent of total in 2014), India (14.9 per cent), Japan (12.3 per cent), United States (11.3 per cent) and China (9.9 per cent).

Agriculture

Farming

Kuwait remains dependent on food imports. The sector as a whole accounts for only 0.4 per cent of GDP.

Fishing

Fish stocks have recovered after war-related pollution reduced stocks in the early 1990s. Fish forms a relatively major part of the national diet, and domestic production can satisfy only 40 per cent of domestic requirements.

Industry and manufacturing

Industrial areas are located in Shuaiba, Mina Abdullah (both in south Kuwait) and Shuwaikh. Efforts to foster growth of non-oil industries have been hindered by the small size of the domestic market and a lack of natural resources other than hydrocarbons. Industry has been growing very slowly as a proportion of GDP, to between 11 and 13 per cent of total output.

Tourism

Tourism is a sector that provides an alternative source of economic activity to hydrocarbon extraction. As a new industry the facilities for tourism are limited, based on existing amenities provided for the domestic market. Currently most visitors are either from neighbouring countries or expatriates or those on business trips. Kuwait City has a growing number of international luxury hotels and its transport system is improving.

Traditional and modern architecture, museums and grand mosques are among the sites to visit as well as the gold souks in the centre of Kuwait City. Temperatures in the height of summer can reach 46 degrees centigrade and many Western visitors are compelled to stay within the numerous air-conditioned shops and hotels by day before venturing out at night when temperatures fall to around 27 degrees centigrade.

Travel and tourism contributed a record 7.1 per cent of GDP in 2009, when 297,000 visitors arrived; this was an improvement on the 4.4 per cent when 259,000 visitors arrived in 2008. By 2014 the contribution had fallen to 3.5 per cent. Employment mirrors the level of arrivals – the number of jobs in tourism in 2009 was 163,300 (7.9 per cent of total), which fell to 90,000 (3.7 per cent) by 2014.

Hydrocarbons

In 2014, proven oil reserves were 101.5 billion barrels, with production at 3.1 billion barrels per day (bpd). Kuwait is the fourth largest oil producer in the Middle East.

Kuwait has three refineries with capacity of 936,000bpd in 2014; Amec won a five-year, US$8 billion contract to modernise them, to increase total domestic processing capacity and to allow for environmentally cleaner products.

Proven natural gas reserves were 1.8 trillion cubic metres (cum) in 2014; production totalled 16.4 billion cum. Currently all domestic natural gas production is consumed locally and to meet demand, Kuwait imports around 3 billion cum annually. Kuwait has plans to convert as much domestic consumption of energy as possible from oil to natural gas. This will free up more oil for foreign export earnings.

Kuwait used to import natural gas from Iraq and had also signed a memorandum of agreement with Qatar and Iran to import natural gas, following the completion of the necessary gas pipelines. However by early 2009 these plans were stalled and were subject to international boundary considerations, and by 2015 the situation had not changed. Kuwait relies on imported liquefied natural gas (LNG) from a variety of sources.

Any coal imported or used is commercially insignificant.

Energy

Total installed generating capacity is 12.7 gigawatts (GW), produced in five power stations. Kuwait has one of the world's largest per capita electricity consumption rates at 14,000 kilowatt hours (kWh) and is growing by 7–9 per cent annually. Not only is there heavy demand due to air conditioning and water desalination but electricity prices are subsidised. Total generating capacity will be increased by a further 1,000MW following the completion of the new Al Zour South power plant. Another 3,000MW will be added when the Al Zour North power plant is constructed, plus a further nine independent power stations to be built for 2017.

A Gulf Co-operation Council (GCC) project to link the six member states (Saudi Arabia, Qatar, Bahrain, Kuwait, Oman and the United Arab Emirates) to an integrated power-grid began in 2005. The first phase of the GCC power grid was completed in 2009 at a cost of US$1,095 million, linking Saudi Arabia, Bahrain, Kuwait and Qatar through 800km of transmission lines. Kuwait and Saudi Arabia will each receive an extra 1,200MW of power capacity and later, the UAE will receive 900MW, Qatar 750MW, Bahrain 600MW and Oman 400MW. In the first phase, a 400kV overhead line links Kuwait's Al Zour power station with Doha, and a 400kV submarine line to Saudi Arabia with Bahrain. The third and final phase of the project – completed in 2011 – linked the UAE and Oman with the rest of the GCC members.

The new, US$2.65 billion, Sabiyya electric power plant, capable of producing 1,200MW with six generating turbines, came on stream in July 2011. After becoming fully operational in 2012, the plant now produces 2,400MW and ensures that Kuwait's peak electricity demand in summer is met.

Financial markets

On 8 September 2010, the first chairman of the Capital Market Authority, the first independent regulatory body to oversee the stock exchange, was appointed.

Stock exchange

Kuwait Stock Exchange (KSE)

Banking and insurance

The IMF, Financial System Stability Assessment (FSSA), reported that the banking system was well capitalised with no immediate threat of instability. The capital adequacy ratio (CAR) was positive and quality assets were improving profits and returns on equity, which were increasing significantly. The financial institutional framework has been strengthened.

An agreement was reached between Saudi Arabia, Kuwait, Bahrain and Qatar to establish the Gulf Co-operation Council (GCC) Monetary Council to be established (originally in 2009), marking plans to set up a regional central bank, to be based in Riyadh (Saudi Arabia). The GCC Monetary Council will oversee the introduction of a monetary union, due to be in operation by 2013.

By June 2010, the Kuwaiti-owned Burgan Bank had completed the purchase of Tunis International Bank from the United Gulf Bank as part of its regional expansion strategy. The US$725 million purchase will allow the Burgan Bank access to other North African markets, to offer specifically investment banking and asset management.

Central bank

Central Bank of Kuwait

Main financial centre

Kuwait City

Time

GMT plus three hours

Geography

Kuwait lies at the north-west corner of the Gulf. To the south and south-west it shares a border with Saudi Arabia, and to the north and west with Iraq.

Kuwait is mainly flat desert with a scattering of oases. From east to west, the country is about 208km and from north to south, 185km. The al Mutla ridge is the only significant geographic feature. The desert is generally gravelly.

Hemisphere

Northern

Climate

Kuwait is less humid than other Gulf countries. However, the coast is more humid than inland, although the temperatures are lower.

Kuwait has four seasons. Mid-February to mid-April is spring; April to September (summer) is very hot (up to 49 degrees Celsius (C) in the shade); autumn is around mid-September to mid-November. The winter months are usually pleasant, with daytime temperatures around 18 degrees C and cold nights. Sandstorms occur, particularly in spring. Kuwait has an annual rainfall ranging from 10mm to 370mm which falls almost entirely between the months of November and April.

Dress codes

Lightweight or tropical clothes are worn in the summer, although in winter months a medium-weight jacket and a jumper are advisable. Women should dress modestly. A long-sleeved shirt and tie should be worn at business meetings but a jacket may be carried. On social occasions dress as for business meetings, unless otherwise indicated.

Entry requirements

Passports

Passports are required by all, and must be valid for six months from date of entry.

Visa

Required by all, except citizens of Gulf Co-operation Council countries. All other visitors should contact the nearest Kuwaiti Consulate for current exceptions and requirements.

Business visas, obtained before travelling, require an invitation from a sponsor in a local company or organisation. When completed it should be submitted to the issuing embassy, along with a business letter from the employer giving an account of the visitor's position and role within the foreign company, and full itinerary with purpose of visit and length of stay.

Tourist visas can be obtained at ports of entry, by nationals of the US, Western Europe, South East Asia and Australasia.

A new visa system (similar to the European Schengen agreement) allowing multiply entry for foreigners to the six Gulf Co-operation Council (GCC) countries was introduced in November 2012.

Currency advice/regulations

There are no restrictions on local and foreign currency imports or exports.

Customs

Personal effects and a limited supply of tobacco are duty-free.

Prohibited imports

Alcohol, illegal drugs, pornographic and/or politically subversive materials; pork products in any form; all non-tinned food and fresh fruit, vegetables and shellfish. Products that originate from Israel.

Health (for visitors)

Health facilities are excellent.

Mandatory precautions

There are no compulsory vaccinations.

Advisable precautions

Recommended immunisations are hepatitis A, polio and tetanus. There is a risk of rabies.

Hotels

Most visitors are business travellers. Five-star hotels have swimming pools and exercise/gymnasium facilities. Small tip for porters is customary. There is usually a 15 per cent service charge.

Credit cards

Major credit cards (American Express, Diners Club, Visa and Mastercard or Access) accepted at all hotels and many restaurants and shops.

Public holidays (national)

Fixed dates

1 Jan (New Year's Day), 25 Feb (National Day), 26 Feb (Liberation Day), 1 Jul (Bank Holiday).

Variable dates

Eid al Adha (four days), Islamic New Year, Birth of the Prophet, Ascent of the Prophet, Eid al Fitr (three days).

Islamic year 1437 (15 Oct 2015–2 Oct 2016):: The Islamic year has 354 or 355 days, with the result that Muslim feast advance by 10–12 days against the Gregorian calendar each year. Dates of the Muslim feast vary according to sightings of the new moon, so cannot be forecast exactly.

Working hours

Friday is the Muslim day of religious observance (weekly holiday).

Banking

Sun–Wed: 0800–1200; Sun–Wed, Ramadan: 0900–1230.

Business

Sat–Wed: 0830–1400; some businesses work 1700–2000.

Government

Sat–Wed, winter: 0700–1430; Sat–Wed (summer): 0700–1400; Ramadan: 0900–1300.

Shops

Sat–Thu: 0800–1230, 1630–2100.

Telecommunications

Mobile/cell phones

There are GSM roaming facilities available, with coverage throughout the country. The ministries of communications and commerce announced their intention to auction a 26 per cent share in the Third Mobile Telecommunications Company on 10 July 2007.

Electricity supply

240V AC; plug fittings normally three-pin flat type (British).

Weights and measures

Metric system (local units are also in use).

Social customs/useful tips

Appointments should be made in advance. Punctuality is appreciated. Personal introductions are advantageous. If the visiting executive is a woman, this must be clearly stated in initial correspondence. On the street, women should not respond to approaches by men and should avoid eye contact.

Men shake hands on meeting and taking leave. Conference visits are an accepted way of doing business and other visitors may be present. The host may hold several conversations at the same time. It is not customary to start talking business immediately. Business cards should have an Arabic translation on the reverse side. Islamic conventions apply. At meetings it is polite to drink coffee or tea when offered. It is the convention to use the right and not the left hand when shaking hands, eating, and passing or receiving anything. Almost everything may stop five times a day for prayers. Some people prefer not to shake hands with those of the opposite sex. When sitting cross-legged on sofas or cushions, soles of the feet must not be shown. A man should not enquire about another man's wife, only about the children. Pork and alcohol are forbidden.

Gratuities are around 10 per cent. Bargaining is not as common as in other countries. There are many restrictions on photography.

Security

Visitors should keep in touch with developments in the Middle East as any increase in regional tension might affect travel advice.

Kuwait is relatively safe but take normal travel precautions. Like the rest of the Middle East, there is a threat to westerners from possible terrorist attacks. Mines remain a problem outside Kuwait City.

Getting there

Air

National airline: Kuwait Airways.

International airport/s: Kuwait International (KWI), 16km south of city; duty-free shop, restaurant, banks, hotel reservations, post office, car hire. Taxis and hotel courtesy buses are available.

Airport tax: Departure tax: KD2, except transit passengers remaining in the airport.

Surface

Road: There are excellent roads from the Saudi Arabian and Iraqi borders.

Main port/s: Several commercial shipping lines call in at Kuwait City.

Getting about

National transport

Road: A network of 3,800km of good paved roads and expressways link towns.

Buses: Nationwide service operated by Kuwait Transport Company, generally rated good and inexpensive.

Rail: In February 2008 a plan to build a US$11 billion rail network was announced. The plan includes a metro system for Kuwait city.

City transport

Taxis: Taxis are not metered. Both private and shared taxis, which are orange and operate on set routes, are available. Taxis are more expensive from hotel ranks. There is a standard taxi fare in Kuwait City and drivers do not expect a tip. If hiring a taxi for a day or half-day agree the fare in advance. Call taxis are reliable and widely used.

Car hire

Locally approved/inspected international driving licence (valid for duration of entry permit) and insurance with Gulf Insurance Company or Kuwait Insurance Company are essential. Driving is on the right.

BUSINESS DIRECTORY

The addresses listed below are a selection only. While World of Information makes every endeavour to check these addresses, we cannot guarantee that changes have not been made, especially to telephone numbers and area codes. We would welcome any corrections.

Telephone area codes

The international direct dialling code (IDD) for Kuwait is +965, followed by subscriber's number.

Useful telephone numbers

Ambulance: 777
Telephone enquiries: 101
Directory enquiries: 023 or 244-4777

Chambers of Commerce

American Business Council of Kuwait, PO Box 29992, Safat 13159 (tel: 564-3149; fax: 563-8012; e-mail: abckuwait@hotmail.com).

Banking

Al-Ahli Bank of Kuwait KSC, PO Box 1387 Safat-13014, Mubarak Al-Kabir St, Kuwait City (tel: 241-1101/2; fax: 242-4557).

Commercial Bank of Kuwait SAK, PO Box 2861 Safat-13029, Mubarak Al-Kabir St, Kuwait City (tel: 241-1001; fax: 245-0150).

Gulf Bank KSC, PO Box 3200 Safat-13032, Raed Centre next to Awadi Tower, Kuwait City (tel: 244-9501; fax: 244-5212).

Industrial Bank of Kuwait KSC, PO Box 3146, Safat 13032, Kuwait City (tel: 245-7661; fax: 246-2057).

National Bank of Kuwait SAK, PO Box 95 Safat-13001, Ali Awadi Tower, Ahmed Al-Jaber St, Kuwait City (tel: 242-2011).

Central bank

Central Bank of Kuwait, PO Box 526, Abdulla Al-Salem Street, Safat 13006, Kuwait City (tel: 244-9200; fax: 244-0887; cbk@cbk.gov.kw).

Stock exchange

Kuwait Stock Exchange (KSE), www.kuwaitse.com

Travel information

Gulf Automobile Association, PO Box 827, Safat, Kuwait City (tel: 242-3864, 243-8640).

Kuwait Airways, PO Box 394, Safat, Kuwait International Airport, Safat 13004, Kuwait (tel: 434-5555; fax: 431-9204; internet site: www.kuwait-airways.com).

Kuwait International Airport (tel: 473-3625).

Ministry of tourism

Tourism Department, Ministry of Information, PO Box 193, Safat, Kuwait City (tel: 242-7141).

Ministries

Ministry of Awqaf and Islamic Affairs, PO Box 13, 13001 Safat, Kuwait City (tel: 248-0000; fax: 243-3750).

Ministry of Communications, PO Box 318, 13004 Safat, Kuwait City (tel: 481-9033; fax: 484-7058).

Ministry of Defence, PO Box 1170, 13012 Safat, Kuwait City (tel: 484-8300; fax: 483-7244).

Ministry of Education, PO Box 7, 13001 Safat, Kuwait City (tel: 483-6800; fax: 483-7829).

Ministry of Electricity and Water, PO Box 12, 13001 Safat, Kuwait City (tel: 537-1000; fax: 537-1420).

Ministry of Foreign Affairs, PO Box 3, 13001 Safat, Kuwait City (tel: 242-5141; fax: 241-2169; e-mail: info@mofa.org).

Ministry of Health, PO Box 5, 13001 Safat, Kuwait City (tel: 246-2900; fax: 243-2288).

Ministry of Higher Education, PO Box 27130, 13132 Safat, Kuwait City (tel: 240-1300; fax: 245-6319).

Ministry of Information, PO Box 193, 13002 Safat, Kuwait City (tel: 241-5300; fax: 241-9642; e-mail: info@moinfo.gov.kw).

Ministry of Interior, PO Box 12500, 71655 Safat, Kuwait City (tel: 243-3804; fax: 243-6570).

Ministry of Justice, PO Box 6, 13001 Safat, Kuwait City (tel: 248-0000; fax: 243-3750).

Ministry of Oil, PO Box 5077, 13051 Safat, Kuwait City (tel: 241-5201; fax: 241-7088).

Ministry of Planning, PO Box 15, 13001 Safat, Kuwait City (tel: 242-8200; fax: 240-7326).

Ministry of Public Works, PO Box 8, 13001 Safat, Kuwait City (tel: 538-5520; fax: 538-0829).

Ministry of Social Affairs & Labour, PO Box 563, 13006 Safat, Kuwait City (tel: 248-0000; fax: 241-9877).

Other useful addresses

Central Tenders Committee, PO Box 1070, 13011 Kuwait City (tel: 243-1719; fax: 241-6574).

Council of Ministers, PO Box 1397, 13014 Safat (tel: 245-5333; fax: 245-5002).

General Secretariat, PO Box 1397, Safat 13014 (tel: 245-5333; fax: 245-5002).

Kuwait Foreign Trading, Contracting & Investment Co, PO Box 5665, Kuwait 13057 (tel: 244-9031).

Kuwait National Industries Co, PO Box 417, Safat, Kuwait City (tel: 815-466, 812-455).

Kuwait National Petroleum Company, PO Box 70, 13001 Safat (tel: 326-2616; fax: 326-0280).

Kuwait Oil Company (KOC), PO Box 9758, 61008 Ahmadi (tel: 398-9111; fax: 398-3661).

Kuwait Parliament, The National Assembly (tel: 245-5422; fax: 243-9032).

Kuwait Petroleum Corp, PO Box 26565, Safat, Kuwait City (tel: 245-5455; fax: 246-7159).

Kuwaiti Embassy (USA), 2940 Tilden Street, NW, Washington DC 20008 (tel: (+1-202)-966-0702; fax: (+1-202)-364-2868).

Petrochemical Industries Board Co, PO Box 1084, Safat, Kuwait City (tel: 242-2141; fax: 246-0224).

Shuaiba Area Authority, PO Box 4690, Safat (tel: 960-903).

National news agency: Kuwait News Agency (Kuna): www.kuna.net.kw

Internet sites

Gulf Business Explorer: www.igulf.com
Kuwait Information: www.kuwait-info.org

Kyrgyzstan

KEY FACTS

Official name: Kyrgyz Respublikasy (Kyrgyz Republic)

Head of State: President Almazbek Sharshenovich Atembayev (SDPK) (took office 1 Dec 2011)

Head of government: Prime Minister Temir Sariyev (since 1 May 2015) has replaced Djoomart Otorbaev after the latter resigned on April 23 2015.

Ruling party: Coalition led by Sotsial-Demokraticheskaya Partiya Kyrgyzstana (SDPK) (Social Democratic Party of Kyrgyzstan), with Respublika (Republican Party) and Ata-Zhurt (Fatherland) (from 17 Dec 2010)

Area: 198,500 square km

Population: 5.70 million (2014)*

Capital: Bishkek (formerly Frunze)

Official language: Kyrgyz, Russian

Currency: Som (S) = 100 tyin

Exchange rate: S66.15 per US$ (Sep 2015)

GDP per capita: US$1,299 (2014)*

GDP real growth: 3.60% (2014)

GDP: US$7.40 billion (2014)

Labour force: 506,000 (2011)*

Unemployment: 7.55% (2014)*

Inflation: 7.53% (2014)

Balance of trade: -US$3.40 billion (2014)*

Annual FDI: US$391.00 million (2011)*

* estimated figure

Following the summary departure of President Kurmanbek Bakiyev in April 2010, a referendum was held under interim President Roza Otunbayeva of the Sotsial-Demokraticheskaya Partiya Kyrgyzstana (SDPK) (Social Democratic Party of Kyrgyzstan) in which Kyrgyzstan voted to become the first parliamentary democracy in Central Asia. The first parliamentary elections were held in 2010, after which various coalition governments came and went.

Elections again

In the October 2015 parliamentary elections the largely pro-Russia SPDK obtained 27.4 per cent of the vote, which gave it 38 seats in parliament. Five other parties passed the electoral threshold, gaining enough votes to give them seats in parliament. In second place, with 20.1 per cent of the votes, was the Respublika-Ata Jurt Party, with just over 20 per cent of the votes, giving it 28 seats. For the first time, biometric identity cards were used to identify voters – the cards were scanned using fingerprint recognition and although there were some technical problems (affecting between three and five per cent of those voting, the system appeared to work satisfactorily. Voting was overseen by the Organisation for Security and Co-operation in Europe (OCSE), which declared the election to have taken place fairly.

Since the ousting of President Bakiyev, Kyrgyzstan has certainly developed the most modern and effective political system in post-Soviet Central Asia. In 2014, the government leadership undertook to adhere to the electoral timetable in 2015 and 2017, which meant ending the decade-long pattern of early elections generally called to strengthen the position of the incumbent. No less than 14 political parties took part in the 2015 elections, some of which represented the interests of specific social groups, such as migrants and entrepreneurs, rather than those of political groupings.

However modern and liberal the system appeared to be, Kyrgyzstan remains a traditional society, with close links to Russia. It came as no surprise to seasoned observers that in 2014, the Bishtek parliament debated classifying those organisations and individuals receiving foreign grants as 'foreign agents', as well as forbidding the 'propaganda of non-traditional sexual relations.' Both the resultant bills were copycat legislation from Russia and entered the statute book. Despite some progress and modernisation, the respected US non-governmental organisation Freedom House noted that under the 2010 constitution: 'endemic institutional weaknesses of national and local government agencies, a lack of reform in the judicial sector and intermittent rule of law continue to hamper Kyrgyzstan's democratic gains.' Freedom House also reported that corruption and nepotism continued to plague government agencies.

Divisions

Sadly, Kyrgyzstan's geography does little to give it a national peace of mind. Claiming to be the home of the apple and the walnut (both grow wild in Kyrgyzstan's mountains) the former Soviet satellite borders international heavyweights such as China and high risk countries such as Afghanistan as well as its fellow ex-USSR sub-states Tajikistan, Uzbekistan and Kazakhstan. In the twenty years since 1991 and freedom from Soviet rule, Kyrgyzstan's domestic politics had hardly been stable or even benevolent. To make matters worse, Kyrgyzstan found itself pulled in different directions by its own minority ethnic groups, notably a number of Uzbek enclaves. Added to the mix had been Kyrgyzstan's almost unique international position of playing host to both US and Russian air bases. The Manat North Atlantic Treaty Organisation (NATO) air base was closed in mid-2014 with the departure of NATO forces from Afghanistan.

Not only is Kyrgyzstan divided geographically by its high mountain ranges. There are ethnic divisions as well, although to the outside world these had not appeared to be on the brink of violence. The larger part of Kyrgyzstan's estimated 800,000 Uzbeks live in the southern part of the country, to the west of Osh and centred on Andijan. In the fertile Fergana valley, Uzbeks are generally thought to be in a majority. One of the few advantages of Soviet rule was the tight grip maintained by the (essentially Russian) troop presence. Northern Kyrgyzstan was the most distinctly Russian part of the country. Despite its proximity, former President Atambayev had managed to resist Russian pressure to sign up to the Eurasian Economic Community (only members Russia, Kazakhstan and Belarus). Mr Atambayev had insisted on the union being a purely economic agreement, rather than the thinly veiled attempt to create a 'Greater Russia' that most observers considered it to be.

Kyrgyzstan's long and troubled, relationship with Russia once again came into he limelight in 2014, as the Kyrgyz people nervously watched what was happening in the Ukraine.

The economy

In a September 2015 assessment of the outlook and risks facing the Kyrgyz economy, the International monetary Fund (IMF) noted that in recent years the Kyrgyz Republic's economy had been resilient, but its growth momentum had waned due to a difficult international economic environment and the knock-on effects from regional conflicts. Non-gold gross domestic product (GDP) growth was expected to slow down in 2015 to about three per cent, as a result of the slowdown in major trading partners, turbulence in regional currency markets and uncertainty surrounding the economic impact of Kyrgyzstan's August 2015 accession to the Eurasian Economic Union (EEU). Inflation had dropped to 5.8 per cent in August 2015, but was expected to increase, driven by the som depreciation and the impact of higher EEU import tariffs. The overall fiscal deficit was expected by the IMF to rise to 2.6 per cent of GDP by the end of 2015, reflecting lower-than-projected revenue and higher-than-budgeted spending. With declining exports as well as falling remittance inflows, the external current account deficit was expected to rise to 18.4 per cent of GDP in 2015.

The IMF expected the economy to improve overall, but in its view there were critical downside risks. Economic growth was expected to average about 4 per cent over the medium term. However, several risks prevailed: the dependence on gold, remittances and foreign aid leaves the economy exposed to external shocks and unable to generate broader-based prosperity; any further regional economic slowdown could hurt economic activity; a loose fiscal policy combined with additional investment projects could undermine debt sustainability; and high credit growth, coupled with high dollarisation and som depreciation, could create risks for financial sector stability.

According to the Asian Development Bank (ADB) the 16 per cent decline in gold production at the main Kumtor gold mine cut GDP growth by two-thirds to 3.6 per cent in 2014 from 10.9 per cent in 2013. Apart from gold mining, GDP rose by 4.6 per cent, buoyed by expansion in services and industry. The ADB noted that on the supply side, growth in industry was 5.1 per cent, but this was a steep plunge from 30.5 per cent in 2013, in which gold output doubled. Lower gold production contributed to declines of 3.0 per cent in manufacturing and 0.5 per cent in mining, although industry growth remained positive because of expansion in food products by 8 per cent, construction by 24.9 per cent and minerals other than gold by 6.2 per cent. Services grew by 4.1 per cent as higher consumer demand and improved cross-border trade boosted retail and wholesale trade by 7.2 per cent, hotels and restaurants by 9.6 per cent and transportation by 4.3 per cent. Agriculture, by contrast, contracted by 0.6 per cent because of adverse weather. On the demand side, private consumption was estimated to have increased on rising retail trade. Investment expanded by 21.6 per cent, reflecting a jump in private housing construction.

Average annual inflation rose to 7.5 per cent from 6.6 per cent in 2013, as food prices rose by 13.9 per cent, led by wheat. Prices for most other items increased by

KEY INDICATORS — **Kyrgyzstan**

	Unit	2011	2012	2013	2014	**2015
Population	m	*5.51	*5.59	*5.64	*5.70	*5.76
Gross domestic product (GDP)	US$bn	5.92	6.60	7.33	7.40	*7.37
GDP per capita	US$	1,070	1,182	1,299	*1,299	*1,280
GDP real growth	%	5.7	-0.9	10.5	3.6	*1.7
Inflation	%	16.6	2.8	6.6	7.5	*10.7
Unemployment	%	7.9	7.7	7.6	*7.6	*7.5
Exports (fob) (goods)	US$m	2,271.2	1,920.6	2,048.4	1,891.6	–
Imports (fob) (goods)	US$m	3,935.9	4,966.5	5,613.6	5,290.2	–
Balance of trade	US$m	-1,664.7	-3,045.9	-3,565.2	-3,398.6	–
Current account	US$m	-371.0	-991.0	-1,101.0	-1,013.0	*-1,255.0
Total reserves minus gold	US$m	1,827.8	1,903.2	2,098.6	1,804.8	–
Foreign exchange	US$m	1,652.8	1,717.3	1,900.6	–	–
Exchange rate	per US$	46.55	47.25	39.19	58.89	–

* estimated figure ** forecast figure

6.8 per cent and utility charges by 5.9 per cent. Inflation accelerated mainly during the second half of the year, when the Kyrgyz som depreciated by 19.1 per cent against the US dollar; the 12-month inflation rate, December to December, jumped to 10.5 per cent from 4.0 per cent in 2013.

The ADB noted that the fiscal deficit increased to 4.3 per cent of GDP as growth slowed and revenue fell short. Higher grants and cuts in expenditure only partly offset the loss of non-tax revenue from the closing of the Transit Centre at Manas Airport in July 2014 as NATO ended operations in Afghanistan. Public external debt surged to an estimated 51.0 per cent of GDP at the end of 2014 from 43.7 per cent a year earlier, reflecting in part sharp currency depreciation. To limit inflation in the wake of currency depreciation, the National Bank of the Kyrgyz Republic, the central bank, sharply raised its base interest rate from 4.16 per cent at the beginning of the year to 10.50 per cent at year-end. However, the full impact of the rate hike was limited by extensive dollarisation, as more than half of all bank loans and deposits were in foreign currency and dollarisation increased as the currency weakened. The average deposit interest rate rose marginally, to 4.8 per cent from 4.3 per cent in 2013, but the average lending rate fell to 17.6 per cent from 18.4 per cent. Moreover, deposits expanded by 22.6 per cent and credit by 45.9 per cent. Non-performing loans declined to 4.5 per cent of all credit outstanding at the end of 2014 from 5.5 per cent a year earlier.

The Kyrgyz som depreciated in 2014 by 19.1 per cent, from S49.19 per US dollar to S58.59, despite more than 61 central bank interventions that cost US$516 million. By year-end, foreign exchange reserves had fallen to US$1.96 billion, equal to about 4 months of imports, from US$2.24 billion at the end of 2013.

The current account deficit was estimated to have risen to equal 15.0 per cent of GDP from 14.1 per cent in 2013. Data up to December 2014 showed a 6.3 per cent decline in exports, reflecting the drop in gold production and weaker sales of fruit, vegetables and textiles. Imports fell by 4.3 per cent as imports of petroleum products, coal and apparel declined. Remittances, equivalent to about a quarter of GDP, declined by an estimated 5 per cent to US$1.8 billion, largely during the last quarter. External debt rose to an estimated 53 per cent of GDP.

Looking at Kyrgyzstan's economic prospects the ADB took the view that growth was likely to slow further to 1.7 per cent in 2015, reflecting recession in the Russian Federation, sluggish performance in Kazakhstan and a further drop in gold production as the quality of extracted ore declines. Growth was expected to remain positive, however, with a recovery in agro-processing and textiles and more trade following membership of the EEU.

The government has been developing an action plan to support export-oriented industries such as textiles and agro-processing through fiscal incentives and tax waivers. Growth is projected at 2.0 per cent in 2016 on the assumption of some recovery in the Russian Federation and Kazakhstan and higher levels of remittances. The highly volatile external environment posed downside risks to growth. On the supply side, processing, light industry and construction should raise activity outside the gold sector. In addition, EEU accession might boost trade and transport, although the need to raise tariffs to EEU levels might discourage trade outside the EEU. On the demand side, entry into the EEU might also boost external demand, but lower remittances would reduce household incomes and, probably, domestic private consumption.

The economy also remains vulnerable to shocks from its largest enterprise, the Kumtor gold mine, which generated 7.4 per cent of GDP in 2014 and some 40 per cent of exports. A long-standing dispute over mine ownership poses risks to the current forecast and has damaged the investment climate.

Currency depreciation and tariff increases on imports to comply with the EEU were projected to keep average annual inflation at 10.5 per cent in 2015 and 10.0 per cent in 2016. Continued rouble depreciation could trigger further weakening of the som, which would likely worsen inflation and dollarisation. The fiscal deficit was projected by the ADB to reach at least 5.0 per cent of GDP in 2015 and 2016 as spending on teacher salaries and social protection rise, as announced, by half in 2015. With cautious revenue forecasts, the government has committed to limiting the deficit in the medium term by restraining expenditure on low-priority items. Revenue was projected at around 29 per cent of GDP in 2015 and 2016 on improved tax and customs administration. Expenditure is forecast at 34 per cent of GDP or higher, reflecting modest growth projections for 2015 and 2016 and higher current and capital spending partly related to the election year. Public debt was expected to rise further to 56 per cent of GDP in 2015.

Risk assessment

Politics	Good
Economy	Good/fair
Regional stability	Fair

Muslims in Kyrgyzstan

% of population	75
Sunni (% of Muslims)	86
Shi'a (% of Muslims)	4

COUNTRY PROFILE

1700s–1800s After being invaded by the Arabs, Mongols and the Chinese, Kyrgyzstan was ruled by the Khanate of Kokand (part of modern-day Uzbekistan).

1876 Tsarist troops conquered Kokand and incorporated Kyrgyzstan into the Russian Empire.

1916–17 Following the suppression of rebellion in Central Asia against Russian rule and the outbreak of civil war after the October Revolution in Russia, many Kyrgyz crossed the eastern border into China.

1918 Parts of Kyrgyzstan were absorbed into Russian-controlled Turkestan.

1920s–30s Soviet nationalities policy under the direction of Joseph Stalin saw Soviet rule enforced from Moscow by Red Army troops who put down Muslim revolts throughout Central Asia after the Russian civil war. All arable and grazing lands were consolidated into large state-owned farms, upsetting the traditional Kyrgyz way of life, based on nomadic livestock-herding. The Kyrgyz Communist Party was established as the sole legal party.

1924 Kyrgyzstan was designated the Kara-Kyrgyz Autonomous Region (renamed Kyrgyz Autonomous Region in 1925) and absorbed into the Russian Socialist Federated Soviet Republic (RSFSR).

1926 The Kyrgyz Autonomous Region was upgraded to an Autonomous Soviet Socialist Republic (ASSR).

1936 Kyrgyzstan became a constituent republic within the Union of Soviet Socialist Republics (USSR).

1940s–80s Kyrgyzstan was an important source of raw materials to the Soviet Union.

1990 Leaders of the Kyrgyz Communist Party opposed changes to the Soviet constitution as they would have allowed non-Communist parties to take part in political life. The Kyrgyz and Uzbek populations rioted in ethnically-divided Osh in southern Kyrgyzstan and a state of emergency was declared after several hundred people were killed. Askar Akayev, a liberal academic on the reform wing of the Kyrgyz Communist Party, was elected by

the legislature to the newly created post of president of the Kyrgyz Socialist Republic.
1991 Kyrgyzstan was the first Central Asian republic to declare independence from the USSR. Akayev stood alone in the country's presidential elections. Kyrgyzstan joined the Commonwealth of Independent States (CIS).
1992 An economic reform programme was launched. Kyrgyzstan joined the United Nations and the Conference on Security and Co-operation in Europe, the predecessor of the Organisation for Security and Co-operation in Europe (OSCE);
1993 Kyrgyzstan adopted its first post-Soviet constitution allowing for a parliamentary system of government. The som replaced the rouble as the unit of currency.
1994 Akayev won a resounding referendum victory, giving him the mandate to make the legislature a bicameral body. Uzbekistan signed an economic, military and social co-operation treaty with Kazakhstan and Kyrgyzstan.
1995 Akayev was re-elected for a second five-year term.
1996 A referendum gave the president the authority to appoint all top officials; parliamentary approval is only required for prime ministerial candidates. Uzbekistan, Kazakhstan and Kyrgyzstan agreed to create a single economic market.
1998 Constitutional changes were approved to change former communist farm collectives to private land ownership – the first time this was attempted by a Central Asian state. Kyrgyzstan became a member of the World Trade Organisation (WTO), the first of any former Soviet Union republics to join.
2000 President Akayev was elected for a third term, contrary to the constitution and amid allegations of electoral irregularities. The elections were followed by the harassment and imprisonment of opposition leaders and the closure of opposition newspapers. The presidents of Belarus, Kazakhstan, Kyrgyzstan, Russia and Tajikistan (formerly the Customs Five) established the Eurasian Economic Community (EEC).
2001 Tajikistan, China, Russia, Kazakhstan, Kyrgyzstan and Uzbekistan formed the Shanghai Co-operation Organisation (SCO) and agreed to fight ethnic and religious militancy, while promoting investment and trade.
2002 Prime Minister Kurmanbek Bakiyev resigned and Nikolai Tanayev was named as his replacement. Opposition protesters marched in the capital, demanding the President's resignation.
2003 President Akayev's constitutional reforms, which included extending the president's term of office were endorsed by 80 per cent of voters; the opposition said they restricted civil liberties and consolidated power in the hands of the president. Widespread voting irregularities were reported by international observers. Parliament granted President Akayev and two other Soviet era Communist leaders lifelong immunity from prosecution.
2005 Numerous independent and opposition candidates were barred from standing in parliamentary elections, sparking widespread demonstrations. Protests increased during the second round of voting as demonstrators occupied government buildings and calls were made for President Akayev to resign. When protesters occupied official buildings in the capital Akayev fled to Moscow. The supreme court cancelled the results of the elections, although later elected members took their seats. The acting president, Kurmanbek Bakiyev, won a landslide victory in presidential elections. Feliks Kulov became prime minister.
2006 President Bakiyev signed a new constitution after a week of mass protests for constitutional reforms and action to combat crime and corruption. Kyrgyzstan became a member of the World Trade Organisation (WTO). Bakiyev accepted the resignation of the entire cabinet in his long-running dispute with parliament. Parliament revised the latest constitution, reinstating some presidential powers concerning government appointments.
2007 Almazbek Atambayev became prime minister. A constitutional referendum agreed to a change in voting laws from first-past-the-post to party-list voting; it also endorsed constitutional changes, which had been invalidated by the Constitutional Court. Prime Minister Atambayev and his cabinet resigned; Iskenderbek Aidaraliyev became acting prime minister. In early parliamentary elections, the ruling Ak Zhol Eldik Partiyasy (Ak Zholor) (Bright Path Popular Party) won over 48 per cent of the vote. A presidential ruling required any political party to achieve a threshold 5 per cent of the national vote, of which 0.5 per cent of the vote had to be in every district in the country, to win seats. As no other party managed this, Ak Zholor would have had a clean sweep and taken all 90 seats. However, the Supreme Court revoked the 0.5 per cent aspect of the presidential ruling and Ata Menken Socialist Party (Fatherland Socialist Party) won several seats.
2009 Following an offer of US$1.4 billion in aid from Russia, the president asked parliament to terminate the US lease on its Manas air base, which the Americans used to transport material and personnel into Afghanistan. In presidential elections Kurmanbek Bakiyev won overwhelmingly with 77.8 per cent of the vote. Opposition candidate Almaz Atambaev withdrew from the election citing electoral fraud. The OSCE considered the elections to be flawed. Prime Minister Igor Chudinov resigned and Daniyar Üsönöv was appointed as his replacement.
2010 After a series of mass protests throughout the country, President Bakiyev was ousted and retreated to his home in the south of the country. He initially refused to step down as president but eventually fled to Kazakhstan and resigned from there. One of the interim government's first moves was to extend the US lease on the Manas air base. Communal violence in the city of Osh between ethnic Kyrgyz and Uzbeks resulted in the killing of 470 persons, mainly Uzbeks, and with hundreds injured. An estimated 400,000 fled into neighbouring Uzbekistan; the UN launched an aid appeal to raise US$71 million to help the refugees. In a constitutional referendum, 90 per cent voted in favour of proposals to remove a number of presidential powers and turn the country into a parliamentary republic, with a single six-year presidential term and parliamentary elections every five years. International observers declared the referendum as 'largely transparent and peaceful'. The amendments also included a new political system to prevent concentration of power in the executive, and set a limit of 50 on the number of parliamentary members from any one political party. Under the constitution the president is banned from deriving income from any source other than the presidential salary and the president and family lost their immunity from the law and their personal lives are not subsidised by the state. Roza Otunbayeva was sworn in as interim president under the terms of the new constitution. She had the responsibility of heading a cabinet until a new government was formed in elections scheduled for later in the year. The state of emergency, imposed in the southern region was lifted. In parliamentary elections, using the newly adopted system of proportional representation from political party lists, no party won overall power and talks on a coalition government began immediately. A military court sentenced Sanzhar Bakiyev, nephew of ousted president Kurmanbek Bakiyev, to 10 years in jail for plotting rebellion. Parliament approved the new government coalition led by Sotsial-Demokraticheskaya Partiya Kyrgyzstana (SDPK) (Social Democratic Party of Kyrgyzstan), with Respublika (Republican Party) and Ata-Zhurt (Fatherland) on 17 December; Almazbek Atambayev (SDPK) became the country's first prime minister as Kyrgyzstan became Central Asia's first parliamentary republic.
2011 The Kyrgyzstan Inquiry Commission (KIC) report into the ethnic violence in

Osh in 2010 was published in May. It concluded that political fanaticism mixed with ethno-nationalism had led to the violence and that the minority Uzbek community was the overwhelming victim of attack. The report also said that there was evidence of official complicity. It also determined that some acts could be considered as crimes against humanity, but not genocide. The official response was of acceptance of the KIC, but that the report was rushed and subjective. In early July, the Criminal Code was amended, removing libel as a criminal offence, a move expected to strengthen press freedom. In a move to allow him to run for president, Prime Minister Atambayev temporarily transferred his authority to First Deputy Prime Minister Omurbek Babanov in September. Presidential elections were held in October in which five candidates took part. Former prime minister and supporter of Russia, Almazbek Atambayev (SDPK) won an overwhelming majority with 62.9 per cent of the vote, his closest rivals Adahan Madomarov (Butun Kyrgyzstan (United Kyrgyzstan)) and Kamchybek Tashiev (Ata-Zhurt) won just over 14 per cent each. In November, Almazbek Atambayev resumed his duties as prime minister, prior to taking office as president in December when Roza Otunbayeva stepped down from the office. Omurbek Babanov was appointed as prime minister on the same day and parliament later confirmed the appointment.

2012 On 1 September Omurbek Babanov resigned as prime minister. On 5 September Zhantoro Satybaldiyev (an independent politician) took office as prime minister. In September, Kazakhstan, Russia and Kyrgyzstan signed an agreement to build the Kambarata-1 hydroelectric power plant. The power station will be built in Upper Naryn (in Kyrgyzstan) and is due to be completed in 2020. On 13 October, Maksim Bakiyev, the son of former president Kurmanbek Bakiyev, was arrested in London on a provisional warrant issued by the US, alleging his involvement in a conspiracy to defraud and pervert the course of justice.

2015 Parliamentary elections were held on 4 October. the result was a win for Sotsial-Demokraticheskaya Partiya Kyrgyzstana (SDPK) (Social Democratic Party of Kyrgyzstan) 27.56 per cent of the vote (38 seats, out of 120), followed by Respublika-Ata-Zhurt (Fatherland) with 20.26 per cent (28), and the Kyrgyzstan Party 13.07 per cent (18). Turnout was 57.56 per cent.

Political structure

Constitution

The Constitution was adopted in 1993 (amended in 1998, 2003, 2007 and 2010). It defines Kyrgyzstan as a sovereign, unitary, parliamentary democratic and secular republic. All land, airspace and natural resources are the property of the state unless assigned for private usage. Discrimination on the grounds of language is forbidden. There is universal direct adult suffrage by secret ballot.

There are six administrative *oblasts* (regions): Chu, Issyk-Kul, Osh, Talas, Jalal-Abad and Naryn. The capital, Bishkek, has special status and is not included in any oblast.

The 2003 consitutional amendment gave local authorities more power.

The 2007 consitutional amendment changed voting laws from first-past-the-post to party-list voting, as well as the constitutional changes, agreed in 2005, but which had been invalidated by the Constitutional Court.

The first 2010 consitutional amendment prevented authoritarianism and included a new political system that prevents concentration of power in the executive, a limit of 50 to the number of parliamentary members any one political party may have. The president must not derive income from any source except the presidential salary. The president and his family will lose their immunity from the law and his family's personal lives will not be subsidised by the state. The status of the country was changed to a parliamentary republic, with a single six-year presidential term of office and parliamentary elections to be held every five years.

Independence date

31 August 1991

Form of state

Parliamentary republic

The executive

The president is directly elected by absolute majority popular vote in two rounds if needed for a single six-year presidential term in office. The prime minister is nominated by the majority party or majority coalition in the Supreme Council, appointed by the president.

The constitution states that the president must be able to speak the Kyrgyz language. In 2010 executive power was ceded to parliament, under the leadership of the interim president.

National legislature

There are 120 seats in the unicameral, Jorgorku Kenesh (Supreme Council). All members are elected in a single nationwide constituency by proportional representation vote to serve five year terms. Seats are allocated to political parties obtaining over 5 per cent of the national vote and more than 0.5 per cent within each of the nine provinces and capped at 65 seats per party.

Legal system

The legal system is based on a civil law code. There are three ultimate legal authorities: the Constitutional Court, the Supreme Court and the Higher Arbitration Court. All are composed of judges with a 15-year term of office who must be approved by the national legislature and the executive. The Constitutional Court rules on the constitutionality of central and local government legislation and on the validity of elections. The Supreme Court is the highest court of appeal for civil, criminal and administrative cases previously heard in oblast, district, city and military courts. The Higher Arbitration Court oversees and rules on the operation of the regional and City of Bishkek arbitration courts.

Last elections

30 October 2011 (presidential); 4 October 2015 (parliamentary)

Results: Presidential: Almazbek Atambayev (SDPK) won 62.9 per cent of the vote, Adakhan Madomarov (Butun Kyrgyzstan (United Kyrgyzstan)) 14.9 per cent, Kamchybek Tashiev (Ata-Zhurt) 14.4 per cent; 14 other candidates each won less than 1 per cent. Turnout was 57 per cent.

Parliamentary: Sotsial-Demokraticheskaya Partiya Kyrgyzstana (SDPK) (Social Democratic Party of Kyrgyzstan) 27.56 per cent of the vote (38 seats, out of 120), Respublika-Ata-Zhurt (Fatherland) won 20.26 per cent (28), Kyrgyzstan Party 13.07 per cent (18), Onuguu–Progress 9.39 per cent (13), Bir Bol 8,59 per cent (12), Ata-Meken (Fatherland Socialist Party) 7.08 per cent (11). No other parties reached the electoral threshold of 7 per cent of votes cast. Turnout was 57.56 per cent.

Next elections

October 2020 (parliamentary); 2017 (presidential)

Political parties

Ruling party

Coalition led by Sotsial-Demokraticheskaya Partiya Kyrgyzstana (SDPK) (Social Democratic Party of Kyrgyzstan), with Respublika (Republican Party) and Ata-Zhurt (Fatherland) (from 17 Dec 2010)

Approximately 37 per cent of the population is under 14 years of age, 58 per cent 15–64 years and 5 per cent over 65. Over 400,000 people, mostly Slavs, emigrated from Kyrgyzstan between 1990 and 2000. It is estimated that 48 per cent of the population live in poverty with about three-quarters of the total poor living in the rural areas.

Population

5.70 million (2014)*

Last census: March 1999: 4,822,938

Population density: 27 inhabitants per square km (2010). Urban population 35 per cent (2010 Unicef).
Annual growth rate: 1.0 per cent, 1990–2010 (Unicef).

Ethnic make-up

Kyrgyz (54.0 per cent, originally a nomadic people of Turko-Mongolian origin who still dominate in rural areas), Russians (12.0 per cent), Ukrainians (2.5 per cent), Germans (2.0 per cent), Kazakh, Uighurs and others (29.5 per cent).

Religions

Predominantly Muslim (Sunni) (70 per cent of the population). There are also Russian Orthodox and Baptist churches.

Education

Primary education lasts for three years between the ages of seven and 10. Secondary education comprises of compulsory basic secondary (five years) and non-compulsory complete secondary (two years) which gives access to higher education. Vocational education is provided by professional schools which lasts for one-and-a-half years for those with complete secondary education.
There are 51 higher education institutions, of which 26 are run by the government. There are 13 non-governmental and 12 private higher education institutions.
Compulsory years: Seven to 15
Enrolment rate: 104 per cent gross primary enrolment of relevant age group (including repeaters); 79 per cent gross seceondary enrolment (World Bank).
Pupils per teacher: 20 in primary schools.

Health

The healthcare system in Kyrgyzstan continues to be based on practices developed in the Soviet era, which concentrate on primary care and are cost-inefficient. The primary health sector has been supported by international donors, including the International Development Association (IDA), Asian Development Bank (ADB) and the German and Swiss governments, to resist the tide of an overall decline. Primary healthcare has slowly been re-formed, by local people identifying their own needs and devising methods to improve health generally. Despite the best efforts of local committees, a scandal in the hospital system resulted in a known 78 babies and some of their nursing mothers being infected with the HIV virus during to poor hygiene and corrupt practises in 2006. It has been recognised that the millions of dollars spent in international aid in prevention programmes in Kyrgyzstan the health system was of more danger than the disease.
A mandatory medical health insurance fund provides for 70 per cent of the population, covering 65 hospitals and 350 groups of family doctors. In-patient treatment is provided through a system of referrals throughout several levels of the system. Patients are entitled to essential drugs free of charge. Medical equipment supplies only 20 per cent of the needs of medical institutions. Kyrgyzstani clinics and hospitals use outdated equipment, 75 per cent of which needs to be replaced or upgraded. There is a shortage of affordable drugs and vaccines and most of the drugs are imported by small traders who do not conform to strict safety rules.

HIV/Aids

HIV prevalence: 0.1 per cent aged 15–49 in 2003 (World Bank)
Life expectancy: 63 years, 2004 (WHO 2006)
Fertility rate/Maternal mortality rate: 2.7 births per woman, 2010 (Unicef); maternal mortality 65 per 100,000 live births (World Bank).
Child (under 5 years) mortality rate (per 1,000): 27 per 1,000 live births (WHO 2012); 7 per cent of children aged under five are malnourished (World Bank).
Head of population per physician: 2.51 physicians per 1,000 people, 2003 (WHO 2006)

Welfare

Like many other former Soviet countries, Kyrgyzstan has a large and complex social benefit system. Social spending, including expenditures of the social fund, makes up 28 per cent of the government budget and 7 per cent of GDP. Although the government budget subsidises the social fund, the payroll tax and the total costs of pensions are high. Pensions are often below subsistence level and the government believes that the current pension system is financially unsustainable. It is looking at cutting costs, preferably by reducing the number of beneficiaries, and aims to move to a system with a minimal state pension and a service pension based on payments into a pension insurance scheme.
Around 44.5 per cent of the population live below the poverty line. The aim of the Participatory Poverty Alleviation Programme (PPAP), set up by the UN Development Programme (UNDP), in co-operation with President Akayev's administration, is to reduce poverty in the country by 10 per cent by 2010.

Main cities

Bishkek (capital, estimated population 977,204 in 2012), Osh (246,881), Celalabad (81,280), Karakol (68,562), Tokmak (59,352), Karabalta (53,573).

Languages spoken

Kyrgyz is a Turkic language. Russian is widely spoken, even among ethnic Kyrgyz.

Official language/s

Kyrgyz, Russian

Media

A rise in pressure on the media in recent years from informal government censorship and large fines from legal action for slander has resulted in self-censorship in editorial content and a financial burden on media entities.

Press

Several daily and weekly newspapers include in Russian, *Slovo Kirgyzstana*, *Vecherni Bishkek* (www.vb.kg), *Komsomolskaya Pravda* (KP) (www.kp.kg), *Moya Stoltisa Novosti* (MSN) (www.msn.kg), *Obshchestvennyy Reyting* (www.pr.kg). In English *The Times of Central Asia* (www.timesca-europe.com) with regional news.

Broadcasting

Kyrgyz National TV and Radio Broadcasting Corporation is state-run. The government maintains control of broadcasting through licenses which can be revoked if political comment becomes provoking. Live broadcasts are restricted in what can be reported.
Radio: The state-run Kyrgyz Radio Broadcasting Corporation operates Radio 1 and 21 Vek. Most private stations operate from Bishkek, including AutoRadio, Europa Plus, Radio Max (www.max.kg) Ekho Bishkeka and Russkove Radio.
Television: There Kyrgyz National TV operates two channels. Other private stations include NTS (www.nts.kg), Piramida, Independent Bishkek TV and Broadcasts are in Kyrgyz and Russian. Osh TV is an independent TV company broadcasting in the southern regions of the country mostly in the Uzbek language.
National news agency: Kabar: http://en.kabar.kg
Other news agencies: AKIpress: www.akipress.com
24.Kg: http://eng.24.kg

Economy

Kyrgyzstan experienced a severe economic shock after the collapse of the former Soviet Union as trading links were severed and exports of its natural resources were markedly reduced. However, as trade began to grow again, with Russia and Kazakhstan and other new markets, the economy picked up and from 2000 onward Kyrgyzstan experienced relatively high GDP growth for a number of years. In 2012, the economy dropped into recession, recording a growth in GDP of -0.1 per cent. However, due to a substantial boost from a higher gold output, in 2013 Kyrgyzstan's GDP growth

accelerated to 10.5 per cent, before dropping to 3.6 per cent in 2014.
In 2009, the governor of the Bank of Kyrgyzstan (BoK) characterised the effect of the global crisis on the economy as having struck in three waves. Beginning in 2007, as global commodity prices rose, Kyrgyzstan was threatened with a severe shortage of foodstuffs, typically imported from other countries, which resulted in a sharp rise in inflation to over 20 per cent in late 2007. In 2008, a steep rise in fuel costs increased inflation to over 30 per cent before falling back to 14.4 per cent in 2009 as oil prices moderated.
Under President Atambaev, the government in coordination with international donors has created a plan for economic development. In 2014 expansion in capital investment fell from 13.5 per cent to 6.8 per cent, which was reflected by growth in construction halving from 20.0 per cent to 11.2 per cent. In August 2015, Kyrgyzstan became a fully-fledged member of the Eurasian Economic Union (EEU).
With its mountainous terrain and plentiful water resources, Kyrgyzstan has the potential to produce and export large quantities of electricity. However, it currently suffers from a shortfall in energy and water, which typically impacts on industrial output.

External trade

Kyrgyzstan is a member of the World Trade Organisation (WTO). It also belongs to the Eurasian Economic Community (EurAsec or EAEC), which was set up in 2000 to promote a customs union between its six member states (Belarus, Kazakhstan, Kyrgyzstan, Russia, Tajikistan and Uzbekistan) and among, other objectives, to introduce standardised currency exchange and rules for trade in goods and service.

Imports

Main imports are food, oil and gas, machinery and equipment, chemicals and foodstuffs.
Main sources: China (54.4 per cent of total in 2014), Russia (18.1 per cent), Kazakhstan (7.8 per cent), Turkey (4.4 per cent)

Exports

Principal exports are primary minerals, including mercury, antimony and rare-earth metals, chemicals, electricity and engineering goods, paper and timber products, agricultural products including woollens, vegetable oil, rice and meat.
Main destinations: Uzbekistan (29. 3 per cent of total in 2014), Kazakhstan (28.5 per cent), UAE (6.6 per cent), China (15 per cent), Russia (5.9 per cent)

Agriculture

Farming

Agriculture accounted for 19.3 per cent of GDP in 2014 and employs approximately 48 per cent of the labour force.
The total area of agricultural land is 10 million hectares (ha), but only 7 per cent is cultivated.
The main products are tobacco (55,000 tonnes per annum), wool, cotton, leather, silk, meat, grain (especially barley), fruit and vegetables.
Livestock production accounts for about 60 per cent of gross agricultural income. Kyrgyzstan is the third-largest wool producer in the former Soviet Union. Only 15 per cent is processed locally. Vegetable oil, milk products and baby foods are imported.
There are no price regulations and there is no duty on export products. Since the amendment of the constitution in 1998 to allow for the full private ownership of land, the government has worked on a plan to auction land under the Land Redistribution Fund (which administers about 25 per cent of all arable land) and to implement a scheme to eliminate the state monopoly on seed production.

Fishing

Fishing remains important for domestic consumption, but fish stocks have been drastically reduced by irrigation, pollution and a lack of investment. The typical annual catch is 200million tonnes.

Forestry

Forests cover four per cent of Kyrgyzstan's land area, or 7,000 square km. Conifers account for 40 per cent of forest composition. Almost half of the forests are mature and over-mature stands. All forests are state-owned. Despite commercial potential, there are no significant forest industries, although Kyrgyzstan has a co-operation agreement with Switzerland for forestry development.
The total forested area has remained stable for several decades and could probably absorb higher levels of exploitation. The government aims to increase production, both to meet domestic needs and to export to other Central Asian countries.

Industry and manufacturing

The industrial sector contributed 31.1 per cent to GDP in 2014, with manufacturing accounting for 19.8 per cent. In the first half of 2015, industrial output increased by 23.6 per cent due to strong mining and goods processing.
Prior to independence, Kyrgyzstan was a significant producer of agricultural machinery, military equipment and medical supplies. However, since fundamental manufacturing inputs came from other parts of the former Soviet Union, independence severely impacted upon the size of the industrial base.

Tourism

The geographical remoteness of Kyrgyzstan is an immediate obstacle to growth in the tourist sector. A rise in the number of visitors from other former Soviet states has encouraged a growth in accommodation for visitors. Inbound travellers make up the majority of tourists to Kyrgyzstan. The terrain is impressive and attracts those that love adventure and sightseeing holidays. The Sulaiman-Too Sacred Mountain is a backdrop to the city of Osh and dominates the Fergana Valley; it is also included on Unesco's World Heritage List. The Silk Road runs through Kyrgyzstan and visitors can follow its trail with the help of tour guides and in groups.
Travel and tourism provided 3.5 per cent of GDP in 2014. This figure was forecast to fall by 1.4 per cent in 2015. In 2014, 79,000 people were directly or indirectly employed by the industry, the equivalent of 3.3 per cent of the workforce.

Environment

The Aral Sea is drying up due to the overuse of water from the two main rivers which feed into it and has lost 40 per cent of its water, dropping by up to 19 metres. This has resulted in desertification of the surrounding land. A UN study published in 2004 reported that there was no possibility of restoring the water and the need must be on preserving what is left.
A meeting was held in April 2009 to determine water sharing between Tajikistan, Kyrgyzstan, Uzbekistan, Turkmenistan and Kazakhstan failed, as negotiators were unable to find a trade in water for energy and hydrocarbons. Tajikistan and Kyrgyzstan hold around 80 per cent of the water in the Aral Sea but suffer from lack of electricity during freezing winters, while the remaining three states downstream are semi-arid and need water for their cotton industries and agriculture.

Mining

Kyrgyzstan has deposits of gold, mercury, antimony, wolfram, tungsten, lead, zinc, uranium, rock salt and gypsum. Uranium oxide and molybdenum are produced at the Kara-Balta combine (Chu Valley). Metallic antimony (7,800 tonnes per year (tpy)) and antimony oxide (6,000 tpy) produced at the Kadamzhay combine (Osh Region), account for 13 per cent of world supply. Mercury is produced at the Khaidarkan combine (Osh Region), accounting for 21 per cent of world output. Kyrgyzstan has impressive reserves of tin and tungsten, which are concentrated in the Sary-Dzhaz river basin, in the east of the country, and have been prospected and prepared for commercial development.

Kyrgyzstan attracts foreign mining and metallurgical companies due to its lax environmental laws. Large mining and metallurgical plants have failed to take into account the hazards of mercury, cyanide, acids and other toxic substances used in the ore refining and enrichment process. This has caused environmental disasters and poses a threat to the health of workers and the local population.

Antimony manufactured at the Kadamzhay combine suffers from high production costs and is unable to compete with relatively cheap antimony available from Chinese producers. Three other undeveloped reserves include Nichkesu (with estimated reserves of 100,000 tonnes), Savoyardy (90,000 tonnes) and Aktyub (30,000 tonnes).

The Russian, Kyrgyzstani and Kazakhstani governments have co-operated to step up the extraction and processing of raw uranium. The state-owned Khaidarkan combine in the Osh region is the only mercury producer in Kyrgyzstan. It is responsible for the improvement of ore enrichment technology and the development of the Novoye deposit, which has a high concentration of mercury, antimony and fluoride.

Most of the gold reserves are concentrated in lode deposits. With substantial deposits in the Talas Mountains in the north and the Batken region in the south, together with relatively low production costs, gold is a key export for Kyrgyzstan.

Hydrocarbons

Proven oil reserves were at 40 million barrels in 2014, with production of around 1,000 barrels per day (bpd). The downstream industry consists of one crude oil refinery at Dzhalal-abad, south of Bishkek, which has a capacity of 10,000bpd, although supplies of crude are unreliable and the refinery operates below capacity.

Oil and Natural Gas exploitation has begun in the Naryn Basin in the centre of the country. By 2014 there had been a few discoveries, but any evaluation had yet to be determined.

Proven natural gas reserves were 5.7 billion cubic metres (cum) in 2014, with production at under 10 million cum.

Consumption was 428 million cum in 2012.

Coal reserves are estimated at 1.3 billion tonnes. There are sizeable coal deposits in Shurab, Kyzyl-Kiya, Naryn and Kok-Yangak. Further coal could be extracted from the Kara-Keche deposit in the north, but it would need foreign investment to cover the development costs.

Energy

Kyrgyzstan has an electricity generating capacity of 3.72GW. Hydropower accounts for over 80 per cent of electricity generated. If the country were to utilise its full hydropower potential it could produce 160 billion kilowatt hours (kWh) per year, whereas currently it uses only 10 per cent of this amount. There are 15 hydropower stations, of which five major plants are located on the Naryn River below the Tokogul dam, providing 97 per cent of hydroelectricity. There are two thermal power stations. Another two thermal power plants, with construction begun in 1980 but left incomplete in 1991, are being considered for addition to the production capacity.

The Electric Stations Open Joint Stock Company (OJSC) controls all major power stations and has a monopoly in electrical generation. The National Electric Network operates all power lines. Both companies are government-owned but in 2008 plans were initiated to privatise the hydro power plants.

A report in February 2009 by Eucam (EU Central Asia Monitoring) highlighted the energy emergency facing Kyrgyzstan. The country is reliant on hydropower but the 'outdated' and 'barely functioning' energy infrastructure is faced with collapse following the recent cycles of drought and harsh winters. The lack of energy threatens food security and could destabilise the country through social upheaval.

Kyrgyzstan has the second largest water resource in Central Asia and conflicts have arisen over the water taken for hydropower, which is also vital downstream in neighbouring countries.

Financial markets

Stock exchange

Kyrgyz Stock Exchange (KSE)

Banking and insurance

During the final years of the Soviet Union, the banking sector was one of the first economic activities to be liberalised.

Upon independence in 1991, Kyrgyzstan had a large number of small banks, many of which offered limited services and had poor ratios of reserves to deposits. Of the Central Asian countries, Kyrgyzstan has made the best progress towards tighter regulation and supervision of banks, although it continues to fall short of the progress made by the Baltic states and Eastern European countries.

Kyrgyzstan adopted the Basle capital requirements in 1995, since when the minimum capital requirement has been increased in stages. As regulation of the system has tightened, so the number of banks has fallen. Simultaneously, privatisation has progressed in Kyrgyzstan to the extent that less than 10 per cent of the banking market is controlled by state banks. Furthermore, 16–17 per cent of the market is controlled by the three foreign banks with a presence in the country. The largest investment bank is the Kairat Bank.

The Law on Banks and Banking Activity, enacted in 2003, strengthened the regulatory powers of the central bank to ensure good management and corporate governance in banks, improve financial disclosure, and control insider dealing.

Central bank

National Bank of the Kyrgyz Rebublic

Time

GMT plus five hours

Geography

Kyrgyzstan is a relatively small, landlocked country situated in eastern central Asia. There are border crossings with the People's Republic of China to the east and south-east, Kazakhstan to the north, Tajikistan to the south and south-west and Uzbekistan to the west.

The Tian Shan mountains, with glaciers, fast flowing rivers and deep lakes, account for most of the country's high alpine terrain, except for the eastern edge of the steppe bordering Kazakhstan and the fertile Osh Valley to the west. Lake Issyk-Kul in the north-east of the country is the second deepest crater lake in the world.

Hemisphere

Northern

Climate

Temperature varies from the temperate steppe to sub-zero temperatures in the mountains (Bishkek: minus 5–35 degrees Celsius). Depending on terrain, annual rainfall varies from 170mm and 265mm.

Dress codes

Dress in the business community is informal, European style.

Entry requirements

Passports

Passports are required by all and must be valid for a minimum of six months at the time of entry.

Visa

Required by all except some nationals of former communist states. For tourist purposes, it is advisable to obtain visas in advance even though some nationals can obtain a visa on arrival, without a letter of invitation.

For most visitors tourist and business visas require an invitation from a local sponsor or company or government organisation. Business visas require confirmation of the contacts to be met and their business addresses and telephone numbers. These should be submitted to the issuing embassy, along with a business letter from the employer giving an account of the visitor's position and role within the foreign company, and full itinerary with purpose of visit and length of stay. For individual business travellers, visa support is required from the Ministry of Foreign Affairs. More information should be gathered from the nearest consulate.

CIS transit visas are no longer valid to enter neighbouring countries; a visa for each state should be obtained in advance.

Currency advice/regulations

Only Kyrgyz residents may import and export local currency.

The import of foreign currency is unlimited but must be declared; export is limited to the amount declared.

Travellers cheques, in US dollars, have limited acceptance in banks in the capital.

Customs

A customs declaration form is issued on arrival and must be surrendered on departure; declare all foreign currency and valuable items such as jewellery, cameras, computers, etc.

Prohibited imports

Illegal drugs, precious metals and artefacts, fur, fruit and vegetables and printed material, including photographs, which are detrimental to Kyrgyzstan.

Firearms, ammunition, works of art and antiques and live animals are subject to special permits.

Health (for visitors)

A reciprocal health agreement for urgent medical treatment exists with the UK. Proof of UK residence will be required.

Mandatory precautions

Vaccination certificates are required for yellow fever if travelling from an infected area.

Advisable precautions

Water precautions are recommended: water purification tablets may be useful or drink bottled water. It is advisable to be in date for the following immunisations: polio (within 10 years), tetanus (within 10 years), typhoid fever, tuberculosis, hepatitis A (moderate risk only), hepatitis B, tick-borne encephalitis.

Any medicines required by the traveller should be stocked by the visitor, and it would be wise to have precautionary antibiotics if going outside major urban centres. A travel kit including a disposable syringe is a reasonable precaution. There is a risk of rabies.

Hotels

It is advisable to book in advance through specialist travel agents. Tips are becoming customary.

Credit cards

Credit cards are accepted in larger hotels and banks in Bishkek.

Public holidays (national)

Fixed dates

1 Jan (New Year's Day), 7 Jan (Orthodox Christmas Day), 8 Mar (Women's Day), 21 Mar (Noruz/Persian New Year), 24 Mar (National Day), 1 May (Labour Day), 5 May (Constitution Day), 9 May (Victory Day), 31 Aug (Independence Day), 7 Nov (Socialist Revolution Day).

Variable dates

Eid al Adha, Eid al Fitr.

Islamic year 1437 (15 Oct 2015–2 Oct 2016):: The Islamic year contains 354 or 355 days, with the result that Muslim feasts advance by 10–12 days against the Gregorian calendar. Dates of feast vary according to the sighting of the new moon, so cannot be forecast exactly.

Working hours

Banking

Mon–Fri: 0930–1730.

Business

Mon–Fri: 0900–1800.

Government

Mon–Fri: 0900–1800.

Shops

Mon–Fri: 0900–1700.

Telecommunications

Mobile/cell phones

GSM 900 and 1800 services are available in populated areas only.

Electricity supply

220V AC

Social customs/useful tips

There are many customs and traditions to be understood. Alcohol is available and smoking is widespread. Gratuities are becoming more customary, particularly in international hotels.

Security

Western nationals have been advised to be vigilant if staying in Kyrgyzstan. Close proximity to Afghanistan and the presence of Western troops in the country could make foreign travellers a target of Islamic rebels. Travellers have been particularly advised to stay away from the southern provincial capital of Osh and especially the surrounding area.

It is unwise to venture out on the streets alone at night. Keep expensive jewellery, watches, cameras, etc, out of sight. Avoid parks at night and use registered taxis only.

Getting there

Air

National airline: Kyrgyz Aba Zholdoru (Kyrgyzstan Airlines)

International airport/s: Bishkek-Manas airport (FRU), 30km north of city, *bureau de change*, duty-free shops, post office, restaurants.

Almaty International Airport (ALA), 10km north-east of the city. Facilities include VIP lounge, car hire, duty-free shops, restaurant and post office.

Airport tax: US$10

Surface

Road: There are roads and border crossings with China, Kazakhstan, Tajikistan and Uzbekistan. Roads can be hazardous in winter. The border crossings in the south-west of the country are considered insecure due to the activity by Islamic rebels.

The Regional Road Corridor Improvement Project, estimated at US$18 billion, to improve Central Asian roads, airports, railway lines and seaports and provide a vital transit route between Europe and Asia was agreed, on 3 November 2007. Six new transit corridors, between Afghanistan, Azerbaijan, China, Kazakhstan, Kyrgyzstan, Mongolia, Tajikistan and Uzbekistan, of mainly roads and rail links, will be constructed, or existing resources upgraded, by 2013. Half the costs with be provided by the Asian Development Bank and other multilateral organisations and the other half by participating countries.

Rail: Bishkek is linked by rail to Central Asia's transport hub, Tashkent, in Uzbekistan.

Getting about

National transport

Air: Kyrgyz Aba Zholdoru operates domestic services. There are regular flights from Bishkek to Osh.

Road: There are 21,000km of roads, only about 50 per cent of which are in reasonable condition. Travel by road is generally difficult because of the terrain and in spring, landslides are common in mountain areas, especially around Osh. Travel by horseback in the mountains. There are few garage facilities on the main roads to and from Bishkek. Care should be taken when travelling by road, especially if a breakdown is involved. Driving during the winter months in private vehicles can be hazardous and some routes could be closed at times. Taxis and private drivers are often willing to provide inter-city services at reasonable prices.

Buses: There are regular and convenient bus services between major towns and cities.

Rail: The only line in use for passenger services is the 340km line in the north of the country, which connects to the Kazakhstani border at both ends and passes through Bishkek. The service is unreliable and is not widely used.

City transport

Taxis: Few taxis have meters and a price should be agreed beforehand. It is sometimes possible to hire private cars, but visitors are recommended to travel only in official taxis.

Buses, trams & metro: Cheap trolley-buses. Service 153 from Bishkek-Manas airport to city centre, every 15 minutes.

Car hire
A national licence with authorised translation or an international driving permit is required. A rented car is often accompanied by a driver.

BUSINESS DIRECTORY

The addresses listed below are a selection only. While World of Information makes every endeavour to check these addresses, we cannot guarantee that changes have not been made, especially to telephone numbers and area codes. We would welcome any corrections.

Telephone area codes

The international direct dialling (IDD) code for Kyrgyzstan is +996, followed by area code and customer's number:

Bishkek	312	Osh	322

Useful telephone numbers

Fire: 101
Police: 102
Ambulance (free): 103
Ambulance (private): 151

Chambers of Commerce

Bishkek Chamber of Commerce, Industry and Hanicraft, 539 Jibek-Jolu, Bishkek (tel: 670-113; fax: 660-048; e-mail: bishkekchamber@netmail.kg).

Kyrgyzstan Chamber of Commerce and Industry, 107 Kievskaya Street, Bishkek 720001 (tel: 210-565; fax: 210-575; e-mail: cci-kr@imfiko.bishkek.su).

Banking

Bakai, 75 Isanov Street, Bishkek 720001 (tel: 660-610; 660-612; e-mail:bank@bakai.kg).

Demir Kyrgyz International, 245 Chui Boulevard, Bishkek 720040 (tel: 610-610; fax: 610-444; e-mail: dkib@demirbank.com.kg).

Eridan, 57 Kalyk-Akieva Street, Bishkek 720001 (tel: 650-610; fax: 650-654; e-mail: eridanbank@infotel.kg).

Kairat, 390 Frunze Street, Bishkek 720033 (tel: 218-932; fax: 218-955; e-mail: kairat@kairatbank.kg).

Kurulush, 28 Manas Street, Bishkek 720391 (tel: 219-736; fax: 219-743; e-mail: kurulush@bank.kg).

Kyrgyzstan, 54 Togolok Moldo Street, Bishkek 720001 (tel: 219-598; fax: 610-220; e-mail: akb@elcat.kg).

Central bank
National Bank of Kyrgyz Republic, 101 Umetalieva St, 720040 Bishkek (tel: 669-011; fax: 669-176; internet: www.nbkr.kg).

Stock exchange
Kyrgyz Stock Exchange (KSE), www.kse.kg

Travel information

Airport 'Manas', Bishkek 720062 (tel: 313-593; fax: 313-040; e-mail: manas@ch2m.bishkek.su).

AKC Kyrgyz Concept, 1000 Razzakova Street, Bishkek 720001 (tel 210-556; fax: 660-220; e-mail: akc@mail.elcat.kg).

Kyrgyzstan Aba Joldoru (national airline), Airport 'Manas', Bishkek 720062 (tel: 257-755; fax: 257-162; e-mail: mana@ch2m.bishkek.su).

Kyrgyzstan Airlines (domestic services), Airport 'Manas', Bishkek 720062 (tel: 696-600).

National tourist organisation offices
Kyrgyz State Agency for Tourism and Sport, 17 Togolok Moldo Street, Bishkek 720033 (tel: 220-657; fax: 212-845).

Ministries

Ministry of Agriculture and Water Resources, 96a Kievskaya Street, Bishkek 720040 (tel: 221-435; fax: 226-784).

Ministry of Environmental Protection, 131 Isanova Street, Bishkek 720033 (tel: 219-737; fax: 216-763).

Ministry of Finance, 58 Erkindik Boulevard, Bishkek 720002 (tel: 228-922; fax: 227-404, 620-955).

Ministry of Foreign Affairs, 59 Razzakopva Street, Bishkek 720040 (tel: 220-545; fax: 263-639).

Ministry of Foreign Trade and Industry, 106 Chui Boulevard, Bishkek 720002 (tel: 223-866; fax: 220-793, 252-747).

Ministry of Justice, 37 Orozbekova Street, Bishkek 720040 (tel: 228-489; fax: 261-115).

Ministry of Transport and Telecommunications, Isanova Street, Bishkek 720017 (tel: 216-672; fax: 213-667).

Other useful addresses

British Embassy, 173 Furmanova Street, Alma Ata, Kazakhstan (accredited to Kyrgyzstan) (tel: (7-3272) 506-191; fax: (7-3272) 506-260).

Free Economic Zone General Directorate, 303 Manas Street, Bishkek 720026 (tel: 670-511; fax: 670-512).

Goskominvest (State Committee on Foreign Investments and Economic Co-operation), 58A Erkindik Boulevard, Bishkek 720002 (tel: 223-292; fax: 620-017; e-mail:satc@imfiko.bishkek.su).

Kyrgyzstan Embassy (USA), 1732 Wisconsin Avenue, NW, Washington DC 20007 (tel: (+1-202) 338-5141; fax: (+1-202) 338-5139; e-mail: embassy@kyrgyzstan.org).

Kyrgyzvneshtorg (Foreign Trade Association), 276 Abdymomunova Street, Bishkek 720033 (tel: 215-701; fax: 620-836).

National Statistical Committee of the Kyrgyz Republic, 374 Frunze Street, Bishkek 720033 (tel: 226-363; fax: 220-759; e-mail: zkudabaev@nsc.bishkek.su).

State Property Fund, 57 Erkindik Boulevard, Bishkek 720002, (tel: 227-706; fax: 660-236; e-mail: spf@imfiko.bishkek.su).

Stock Exchange, 172 Moskvskaya Street, Bishkek 720010 (tel:665-059; fax: 661-595; e-mail: kse@kse.kg).

US Embassy, 171 Mira Boulevard, Bishkek 720016 (tel: 551-241; fax: 551-264; e-mail: mukambaevaibx@state.gov).

National news agency: Kabar: http://en.kabar.kg

AKIpress: www.akipress.com

24.Kg: http://eng.24.kg

Internet sites

The Times of Central Asia: http://www.times.kg

Government of Kyrgyzstan (list of departments in Cyrillic script, email addresses in Latin script): http://kenesh.bishkek.gov.kg/

Laos

KEY FACTS

Official name: Saathiaranarath Prachhathipatay Prachhachhon Lao (Lao People's Democratic Republic)

Head of State: President Lt. Gen. Choummaly Sayasone (since Jun 2006; re-elected 15 Jun 2011)

Head of government: Prime Minister Thongsing Thammavong (from 23 Dec 2010; re-elected 15 Jun 2011)

Ruling party: Phak Paxaxôn Pativat Lao (Lao People's Revolutionary Party) (LPRP) (since 1975; re-elected 30 April 2011)

Area: 236,800 square km

Population: 6.90 million (2014)*

Capital: Vientiane

Official language: Lao (English is the business language of the Lao government)

Currency: New kip (Nk) = 100 at

Exchange rate: Nk8,160.00 per US$ (Sep 2015)

GDP per capita: US$1,693 (2014)*

GDP real growth: 7.41% (2014)*

GDP: US$11.68 billion (2014)*

Inflation: 4.13% (2014)*

Balance of trade: -US$755.80 million (2013)

* estimated figure

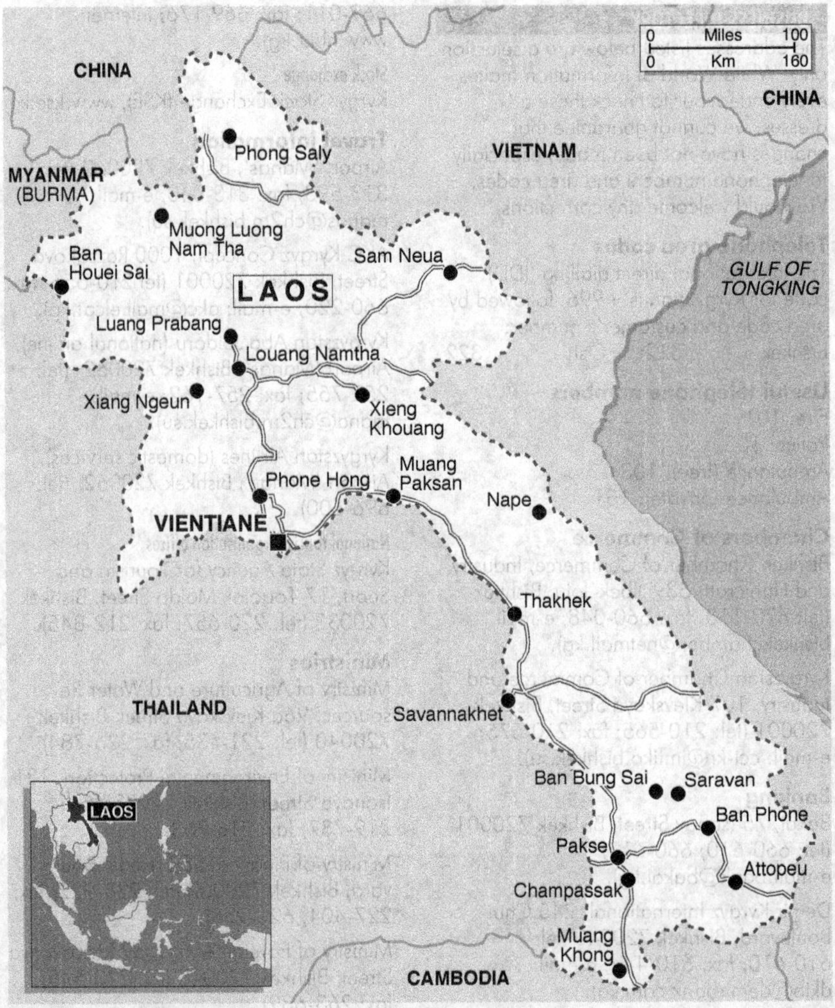

In September 2014 the Communist government of Laos issued a decree outlawing online criticism of policies of the ruling party or government. In this respect Laos was the latest in a line of south-east Asian countries to enact strict internet controls. The legislation, which had been approved by Prime Minister Thongsing Thammavong, meant that web users could face criminal action for spreading 'false' information aimed at discrediting the government. It also required subscribers to social media websites to use their real names when setting up accounts. The seemingly vague legislation stated that internet service providers could face legal action for providing 'available conditions' for any individual or group that had intentions of 'tarnishing the party and government's guidelines and policy.'

The decree came as Laos' mobile telephone and internet usage rose rapidly, keeping pace with economic growth, lower poverty rates and improved access to electricity. No doubt inspired by similar legislation in communist Vietnam, the legislation proscribed 'disseminating or circulating untrue information for negative purposes against the Lao Phak Paxaxôn Pativat Lao (Lao People's Revolutionary Party) (LPRP) and the Lao government, undermining peace, independence, sovereignty, unity and prosperity of the country.' As if that wasn't enough, it also banned uploading of pornography or 'inappropriate' photographs. The possible punishments under the legislation ranged from warnings to fines and unspecified legal redress.

Although the days of the Vietnam war, when Laos was regularly in the world's headlines, are long over, in the twenty-first century not a lot of information, be it political or economic, emerged from Laos. The relationship that no Laotian can ignore is, beyond question, that with neighbouring China. Given China's constant demand for natural resources, it would indeed be surprising to discover that Laos had emerged unaffected. Chinese enterprises, some of which are state-owned, have secured vast rubber concessions in Laos. In a 'normal' economic relationship, inward investment on this scale would be welcomed for its employment creation potential. Not so in Laos, where the Chinese plan is to create employment for thousands... of Chinese workers.

Last man standing?

It's not always easy being one of the last one-party Communist states on earth. To its credit, Laos has succeeded in purely economic terms, generating remarkable economic growth from strong commodity exports, huge infrastructure projects, large hydroelectric dams, as well as substantial investments from China, Thailand and Vietnam. Laos can also claim to have the world's smallest stock market and has regularly managed to notch up 8 per cent annual gross domestic product (GDP) growth over the past decade. Vientiane in 2015 has – in parts – a prosperous feel to it. The government embarked upon its economic decentralisation programme, fostering private enterprise, as long ago as 1986.

The Chinese presence in Laos cannot fail to be noticed. Chinese companies abound, as do its businessmen, shops and restaurants. But inequality is also evident, for the most part the boom businesses do not benefit average Laotians. Reuters reported that although poverty rates have fallen by as much as 33 per cent in 15 years, Laos is simply one of the world's poorest nations. The rural poor often lack access to safe drinking water, sanitation and hygiene services.

Rumours of corruption and bribery abound in Laos. Although the government has tried to address the issue, any country with such wide degrees of inequality would be prone to temptation. On the 2014 Transparency International *Corruption Perceptions Index* Laos ranked an embarrassing 145 out of the 175 countries surveyed.

The underlying tension that besets the government is the almost impossible balancing act of squaring the liberal, reformist economic policies of what is a remarkably flexible communist leadership with the LPRP's concern to maintain and extend political control. Ultimately, one of these will need to give way. As things stand, the greatest risks the economy faces are those of overheating and of fiscal imbalance as expenditure rises faster than income. Prime Minister Thongsing Thammavong has warned of the fiscal position and ordered his ministers to cut costs. But by 2015 all that had been done was a bit of trimming at the edges: the wages of state workers have been frozen, payments to contractors have been delayed. But the government's debt level remains high.

The economy

According to the Asian Development Bank (ADB), growth was maintained at above seven per cent for a ninth consecutive year in 2014, although fiscal tightening and weaker global demand for minerals moderated the pace by 0.5 percentage points to 7.4 per cent. Two decades of significant economic growth had helped to halve the national poverty rate from 46 per cent in 1992 to 23 per cent in 2013. The services sector expanded by 9.0 per cent in 2014. Wholesale and retail trading, public services and transport and communications recorded solid growth. A decline in tourism in neighbouring Thailand, owing to political unrest and street protests there saw fewer tourists taking side trips to Laos, causing the growth in total tourist arrivals to slow to 10.8 per cent in 2014.

Industry grew by 8.5 per cent in 2014, supported by foreign direct investment (FDI) to construct hydropower projects, residential and commercial developments and factories in special economic zones. Output of electricity, most of it sold to Thailand, rose by 7.7 per cent to 15.4 billion kilowatt-hours. Softer global demand and prices for minerals dampened growth in mining. Copper production from the two main mines in Laos rose by 3.1 per cent to 159,680 tons and silver output increased, but gold production fell by 23.2 per cent to 168,755 ounces, reflecting the end of gold production from the Sepon mine in December 2013. Better weather for agriculture, which employs nearly 70 per cent of the workforce but accounts for only 25 per cent of GDP, lifted this sector's production by 2.9 per cent.

The government tightened fiscal policy in reaction to a sharp widening of its fiscal deficit in FY2013 (ended 30 September 2013), when it had boosted wages and allowances for the civil service and then fell into arrears. In 2014 the government cancelled a cost-of-living allowance for the civil service, curbed off-budget spending and postponed some infrastructure projects. A second sharp rise in civil services wages went ahead, but the government cancelled a third wage rise that was to take effect in 2015. These measures narrowed the fiscal deficit, including

KEY INDICATORS **Laos**

	Unit	2011	2012	2013	2014	**2015
Population	m	*6.56	*6.65	*6.77	*6.90	*7.03
Gross domestic product (GDP)	US$bn	7.90	9.17	10.79	*11.68	*12.76
GDP per capita	US$	1,204	1,380	1,594	*1,693	*1,816
GDP real growth	%	8.3	7.9	8.0	*7.4	*7.3
Inflation	%	8.7	4.3	6.4	*4.1	*4.0
Exports (fob) (goods)	US$m	1,854.0	2,270.7	2,263.9	–	–
Imports (fob) (goods)	US$m	2,422.9	3,055.1	3,019.7	–	–
Balance of trade	US$m	-568.9	-784.4	-755.8	–	–
Current account	US$m	-1,773.0	-2,606.0	-3,123.0	*-2,907.0	*-2,570.0
Total reserves minus gold	US$m	–	–	721.6	875.1	–
Foreign exchange	US$m	–	–	643.0	–	–
Exchange rate	per US$	8,058.40	7,949.00	8,000.00	8,095.95	–

* estimated figure ** forecast figure

grants but excluding off-budget spending, to an estimated 4.2 per cent of GDP in 2014, down from 5.6 per cent in 2013.

The monetary authorities, concerned about rapid growth in credit and declining international reserves, restricted sales of foreign currency to the public and directed commercial banks to limit lending in foreign currency. The central bank also curbed its direct lending for infrastructure. Credit growth decelerated to 14.1 per cent at the end of 2014 from 35.7 per cent in 2013. Some businesses dealing with the public sector faced delays receiving payments that hurt their earnings and their capacity to service loans, which added to banks' non-performing loans. Inflationary pressures eased steadily in 2014 owing to better food supplies, lower fuel prices and the fiscal tightening. Inflation had abated to 2.4 per cent year on year by December 2014, bringing the average rate in 2014 down to 4.2 per cent, the lowest in 5 years.

Moderating domestic demand restrained growth in merchandise imports to 4.4 per cent in 2014, while merchandise exports grew by 6.1 per cent. The current account deficit narrowed to an estimated US$3.2 billion, or 25.0 per cent of GDP. FDI inflows contributed to a slight rebuilding of gross international reserves to an estimated US$815 million, cover for only 1.3 months of imports of goods and services. The Lao kip depreciated by 2.7 per cent against the US dollar during 2014, though it appreciated by 2.9 per cent against the Thai baht. In real effective terms, the kip had appreciated over recent years, hurting export competitiveness.

Growth was expected to moderate further in 2015 as lacklustre demand for minerals had its effect on mining and as fiscal constraints curbed public investment. Nevertheless, GDP growth was still forecast at 7.0 per cent in 2015, picking up to 7.2 per cent in 2016. Investment in power projects was expected to generate much of the growth over the forecast period. More than 20 power projects were under construction at the beginning of 2015, including the US$3.5 billion Xayaburi hydropower plant, scheduled for commissioning in 2019 with capacity to generate 1.3 gigawatts. Power generation was also set to get a boost when the large Hongsa lignite power plant, able to generate 1.9 gigawatts, came on stream later in 2015 and became fully operational in 2016. Total electricity production was projected to rise by 6 per cent in 2015, accelerating significantly in 2016 when six new plants were due to come online.

A recovery in Thailand and in particular in its tourism industry, would obviously benefit Laos. As would lower oil prices, as Laos imports all its oil, which comprises 15 per cent of merchandise imports. Services were expected to continue to expand at a strong pace, but agriculture was expected to record only slight growth in 2015. Weaker revenue from mining suggested that the fiscal deficit could widen to about 5 per cent of GDP. Public debt was projected to increase from 60 per cent of GDP to 65 per cent over the medium term. The International Monetary Fund (IMF) had reported that the risk of external debt distress worsened in 2014 but was still moderate.

Inflation eased further to 1.4 per cent in February 2015. Lower oil prices and slowing economic growth were forecast to trim year-average inflation to 3.5 per cent for the year. In 2016, inflation was forecast to quicken to 4.0 per cent as domestic demand picks up and the prices of imported oil and food begin to rise. Oil price declines were also expected to benefit the current account. While electricity exports are set to rise, the prices of metals and some other export commodities would probably stay soft. The deficit in the current account was expected to remain substantial but to narrow through the ADB's forecast period to the end of 2015.

Risk assessment

Economy	Good
Politics	Fair
Regional stability	Good/fair

COUNTRY PROFILE

Between the fourth and eighth centuries, communities along the Mekong River began to form into townships, called muang.

1353 This development culminated in the formation of the Lane Xang (the million elephants) Kingdom by King FaNgum and established Xieng Thong, now known as Luang Prabang as capital of Lane Xang Kingdom.

1548–71 During the reign of King Setthathirat, the capital was moved to Vientiane. During this period the That Luang Stupa, a venerated religious shrine and a temple to house the Phra Keo, the Emerald Buddha, were constructed.

1641 A Dutch merchant of the East India Company, Geritt Van Wuysthoff established the first European contact with the Kingdom. Later, Italian missionaries visited.

1893 Laos was put under French administration.

1945 Laos was briefly occupied by the Japanese towards the end of the Second World War.

1950 Laos was granted semi-autonomy as an associated state within the French union.

1954 Laos gained independence and became a constitutional monarchy. Civil war began between monarchists and communists of the Pathet Lao.

1960s Laos was subjected to intensive bombing by the US in its war against the North Vietnamese in one of the worst aerial bombardments in world history.

1973 The Vientiane cease-fire agreement led to renewed divisions between royalists and communists.

1975 The Pathet Lao (the Lao Communist movement) won the civil war. The Lao People's Democratic Republic (LDPR) was proclaimed by a National Congress of People's Representatives. Pathet Lao was renamed the Lao People's Revolutionary Party (LPRP), which became the sole legal political party. Kaysone Phomvihane was appointed prime minister and began a policy of socialist transformation of the economy.

1979 The government modified its approach following widespread food shortages and an exodus of Laotian refugees to Thailand.

1986 Laos introduced market reforms, encouraged by Soviet leader Mikhail Gorbachev.

1989 The first elections since 1975 were held, although all candidates had to be vetted by the LPRP. The LPRP retained power.

1991 A security and co-operation pact was signed with Thailand. A new constitution was promulgated. Kaysone Phomvihane became president and General Khamtai Siphandon became prime minister.

1992 President Phomvihane died. Siphandon became head of the LPRP.

1995 A 20-year aid embargo was lifted by the US.

1997 Laos became a member of the Association of Southeast Asian Nations (Asean). The Asian financial crisis undermined the value of the kip.

1998 Khamtai Siphandon became president.

2000 Anti-government demonstrations erupted and a series of terrorists bomb blasts killed over a dozen people. Laos celebrated 25 years of communist rule in December.

2001 Boungnang Vorachith was appointed prime minister and Khamtai was re-elected president. The death penalty was introduced for the possession of more than 500 grams of heroin. The UN's World Food Programme (WFP) launched

a three-year programme to feed 70,000 malnourished children in Laos.
2002 The LPRP was re-elected; Khamtai Siphandon was re-elected president.
2003 As part of reforms pledged to foreign donors in 2000, Laos' one-party parliament began a process of amending its constitution, to decentralise power.
2005 The World Bank approved funds for the construction of the US$1.2 billion Nam Theun Two hydroelectric dam. According to a UN report, the poppy crop in Laos has been reduced by 73 per cent since 1998 and the number of opium addicts has fallen by 42,000 to 21,000.
2006 President of the ruling LPRP Khamtay Siphandone resigned and was succeeded by Choummaly Sayasone; Bouasone Bouphavanh was appointed prime minister. A new bridge was opened across the Mekong River in the central region of Savannakhet.
2007 Former General Vang Pao, a leader among the ethnic Hmong people was arrested in the US, accused of planning a coup to overthrow the Lao government. The Hmong people backed the US in the Vietnam War during the 1960s and aid agencies in the region have reported that they have been subjected to human right's abuses since then.
2008 The government confirmed plans to increase the area of forest to 18.7 million hectares. Deforestation has reduced natural forests from 41 per cent of the country in 2002 to 35 per cent in 2008, due to changes in agriculture, hydroelectric projects, mining and illegal logging.
2009 A rail link was established between Thailand and Laos with a freight and passenger service officially opened.
2010 A ministerial conference of 13 countries in the south-east Asian region, including Laos, discussed conservation and co-ordinated measures, with targets set to boost the numbers needed to protect the indigenous wild tiger from extinction. Laos held the first official international convention on cluster munitions in Vientiane. Delegates from governments, the UN and non-governmental agencies as well as survivors of such bombs discussed a treaty on clearance and limited use. Prime Minister Bouasone Bouphavanh resigned and parliament elected Thongsing Thammavong as his replacement. The new Lao Securities Exchange Market building was opened.
2011 In parliamentary elections held in April the LPRP won 131 seats (out of 132), five independent candidates were allowed to stand and one won the remaining seat. The number of members of parliament (MPs) had increased by 17, due to the rise in population. A decision, by the four-country Mekong River Commission, to implement plans to build the controversial Mekong Xayaburi dam in Laos was due to be taken in April, but following ecologically and socially adverse reports the decision was postponed. The Mekong River is a food source for millions of people along its length; the dam would reduce food production in favour of electricity production. In June, President Choummaly Sayasone and Prime Minister Thammavong were re-elected by parliament.
2012 In April the Thai building company CH Karnchang signed a US$2.4 billion contract with the Lao government to begin construction of the dam for the Xayaburi hydroelectric power plant on the Mekong River. Over 90 per cent of the electricity generated would be exported to Thailand. On 20 April the Cambodian government responded to the news by threatening to take the Lao government to the international court of arbitration over its unilateral decision to begin work on the dam without regional consensus. On 11 July, for the first time since 1955 a US Secretary of State visited Laos and discussed environmental problems in the region. On 5 September, preparation work began on the construction of the Xayaburi hydroelectric dam, despite opposition from local and international activists. Approval was given and construction began of the Xayaburi dam on 7 November.
2013 Laos became a member of the World Trade Organsation on 1 February.
2014 Laos signed seven co-operative agreements with China on 28 July. The agreements included loans from China to fund power grids, hydropower projects and the prevention of cybercrime in Laos.

Political structure

Constitution

The first Constitution was endorsed in August 1991, enshrining the single-party rule of the Lao People's Revolutionary Party (LPRP).

The country is divided into provinces, municipalities, districts and villages. Each of these has a local administrative structure that is subject to the laws and policies of the national government.

Laos' one-party parliament is in the process of amending its Constitution in a move towards decentralisation.

Independence date

12 October 1954

The executive

The president and vice president are indirectly elected by the National Assembly every five years, there are no limits to how many terms they can remain in power. The president is the Head of State.

The Head of government is the prime minister, who is nominated by the president and elected by the National Assembly for a five year term. The Council of Ministers is also appointed by the president.

National legislature

The unicameral Sapha Heng Xat (National Assembly) has 132 seats of which members are directly elected in multi-seat constituencies by simple majority vote from candidate lists provided by the Lao People's Revolutionary Party. Members serve for a five-year term.

Last elections

30 April 2011 (parliamentary); June 2011 (presidential, indirect)

Results: Parliamentary: Phak Paxaxôn Pativat Lao (Lao People's Revolutionary Party) (LPRP) (the only legal party allowed) won 128 seats (out of 132), independent candidates were allowed to stand and they won the four remaining seats.

Presidential: parliament re-elected Choummaly Sayasone, unopposed.

Next elections

2016 (parliamentary and presidential)

Political parties

Effective political power is exercised by the leadership of the sole legal political organisation, the Lao People's Revolutionary Party (LPRP).

Ruling party

Phak Paxaxôn Pativat Lao (Lao People's Revolutionary Party) (LPRP) (since 1975; re-elected 30 April 2011)

Laos is one of the poorest countries in Asia. Around 70 per cent of the population are farmers.

Population

6.90 million (2014)*

Last census: 1 March 2005: 5,621,982

Population density: 26 inhabitants per square km (2010). Urban population 33 per cent (2010 Unicef).

Annual growth rate: 2.0 per cent, 1990–2010 (Unicef).

Ethnic make-up

There are three main ethnic groups: the Lao Loum (lowlanders), the Lao Theung (semi-nomadic people who live mainly on the mountain slopes) and the Lao Soung (hill tribes and minority elements).

Religions

The Lao Theung and the Lao Soung are animist, but the great majority of Lao are Theravada Buddhists; there are some Christians.

Education

Nearly 60 per cent of teachers in primary and secondary schools are underqualified.

Secondary education starts at the age of 11 and is divided into three-year lower secondary school and three-year upper secondary school. Higher education is provided by the National University of Laos, which has merged with 10 higher education institutions located in Vientiane.

There are also higher technical institutes and teacher training colleges.

Public expenditure on education typically amounts to 2.1 per cent of annual gross national income. In 2001, the Asian Development Bank approved a US$20 million loan to support a project partly that will enable over 550,000 children, especially girls and ethnic minorities to receive better primary education. The government is expected to fund the balance with the help of other international donors and complete the project by end-2007./10/04

Literacy rate: 66 per cent adult rate; 79 per cent youth rate (15–24) (Unesco 2005).

Compulsory years: Primary education is compulsory between the ages of six and 11.

Enrolment rate: 112 per cent gross primary enrolment of the relevant age group (including repeaters); 29 per cent gross secondary enrolment (World Bank).

Pupils per teacher: 30 in primary schools.

Health

Laos had one of the highest rates of maternal deaths in 2010, at 1 death per 33 births, due largely to a lack of skilled healthcare workers and emergency obstetric services. In a measure to reduce the rate the authorities, with the backing of the UN Population Fund, re-introduced midwifery training courses that were stopped in 1987. It also agreed that affordable and reliable antenatal services were needed and would be introduced in due course.

Improved water sources and sanitation facilities are available to 90 per cent and 46 per cent of the population, respectively.

HIV/Aids

HIV/Aids infection is one of the major public health challenges in the country, affecting almost all provinces and populations and is expected to triple in the next 20 years, unless preventive measures are undertaken.

HIV prevalence: 0.1 per cent aged 15–49 in 2003 (World Bank)

Life expectancy: 59 years, 2004 (WHO 2006)

Fertility rate/Maternal mortality rate: 2.7 births per woman, 2010 (Unicef); maternal mortality 650 per 100,000 live births (World Bank).

Child (under 5 years) mortality rate (per 1,000): 72 per 1,000 live births (WHO 2012); 40 per cent of children under aged five are malnourished (World Bank).

Welfare

About 40 per cent of the population live in poverty. The country is covered under the Asian Development Bank (ADB's) poverty reduction strategy that focusses on rural development, regional integration, human resource development, sustainable environmental management and private sector development. To achieve this, the ADB has lent Lao PDR about US$45—55 million annually on concessional terms for the period 2002–04, in addition to other technical assistance grants. Another US$1 million grant is provided by the Japan Fund for Poverty Reduction to help the landless poor increase their participation in farm-based production.

Main cities

Viangchan (Vientiane) (capital, estimated population 248,692 in 2012), Pakxe (108,079), Savannakhet (79,908), Louang Phrabang (53,792), Xam Nua (40,931), Thakek (Khammouan) (31,129).

Languages spoken

The adopted business language of the Lao government is English. Widely spoken languages other than Lao are: Thai, English, Vietnamese, Chinese, Russian, German, and to a much lesser extent, French; plus tribal languages.

Official language/s

Lao (English is the business language of the Lao government)

Media

The government owns and maintains strict control the print and broadcast media. Criticism of the government or communist party is restricts and criminal law can be applied for slandering the state, distorting communist party policies and spread false rumours.

Press

Dailies: In Lao, the *Vientiane Mai* (www.vientianemai.net) is state-run; *Pasason* (www.pasaxon.org.la) is owned by the Laos Communist Party. In English *Vientiane Times* (www.vientianetimes.org.la) is published biweekly and in French *Le Renovateur* (www.lerenovateur.org.la) are both state-owned.

Broadcasting

Lao National Radio (www.lnr.org.la) operates two nationwide stations FM1–2, relayed by satellite on FM and AM frequencies. Foreign radio can also be received. Although all domestic Lao National TV (TVNL) is owned by the state viewers have unrestricted access to foreign TV via satellite and internet channels.

National news agency: KPL (Khaosan Pathet Lao)

Economy

Laos' previously centrally planned communist economy was dropped in 1986 in favour of a free market economy. Monetary reforms were adopted along with fiscal expansion to improve their economy, however, the pace of change has been slow so that Laos still remains heavily dependent on international aid and is one of the poorest countries in the world. A third of the population exists outside the money economy and 80 per cent depend on subsistence agriculture, which contributed some 24 per cent of GDP in 2014. Rice is the main crop with tea and maize as important cash crops.

The service sector constituted 44.1 per cent of GDP and industry 32.2 per cent, of which manufacturing accounted for 9 per cent in 2014. The export of electricity to neighbouring countries is another major foreign exchange earner, along with mined ores, which have benefited from rising global prices.

Remittances from migrant workers were US$42 million (20.8 per cent of GDP) in 2010 and were estimated to have reached US$45 million in 2011. This figure has risen to US$59 million in 2013.

Despite the economic reforms, the economy is still burdened by low productivity, poor infrastructure and a dominant public sector. Tourism is beginning to have an impact as its share of GDP increases and the sector becomes an important source of foreign exchange. Without full integration in world markets, Laos was largely unaffected by the global economic crisis, so that GDP growth averaged 7.8 per cent over 2007–10, with an estimated growth of 8.3 per cent in 2011 and 7.5 per cent in 2014. Growth is forecasted to have grown by 7 per cent in 2015.

In 2014, the UN Human Development Index (HDI) ranked Laos 139 (out of 187) for national development in health, education and income. Since 1990, Laos's progress has improved but has not matched the growth of other countries in East Asia and the Pacific. In 2010, 56.5 per cent of the population experienced at least one indicator of poverty, while 33.9 per cent lived on less than the equivalent of US$1.25 per day; the headcount poverty rate was 47.2 per cent of the population (2000–10).

Laos became a member of the World Trade Organisation on 1 February 2013

Laos has made significant progress in poverty alleviation over the past 2 decades with poverty rates declining from 46 per cent in 1992 to 27.6 per cent in 2008. The country is on course to achieve the Millennium Development Goal target of halving poverty by 2015, however the challenge now is to ensure that all Lao people benefit from the country's development.

External trade

Laos belongs to the Association of Southeast Asian Nations (Asean) and the Asian Free Trade Area (Afta), which maintains a list of goods with preferential import duties between members and a programme of tariff reductions due to be introduced in the next few years. In 2013, Laos became a member of the World Trade Organisation.

There are transit agreements with Vietnam, Cambodia and Thailand allowing cargo, by bonded customs carriers, to travel by cross-border highways from the coast to landlocked Laos.

Imports

Principal imports are vehicles, machinery and equipment, capital goods, food, consumer goods and fuel.

Main sources: Thailand (55.2 per cent of total in 2014), China (25.6 per cent), Vietnam (6.6 per cent)

Exports

Principal exports are electricity (typically 40 per cent of total), garment and small-scale manufacturing, timber products, cassava, coffee and mined ore including gold, silver, tin, copper, nickel and zinc.

Main destinations: China (34.2 per cent of total in 2014), Thailand (27.4 per cent), Vietnam (15.7 per cent)

Agriculture

Farming

Agriculture contributes around 23.7 per cent of GDP and employs around 75 per cent of the workforce.

Rice, the main crop, is cultivated in irrigated lowland paddies and on drier hill farms.

Other crops include maize, sweet potatoes, cassava, pulses, groundnuts, fruit, vegetables, sugar cane, coffee, tobacco and cotton. Livestock raised includes cattle, buffaloes, pigs, goats and poultry.

Fishing

Forestry

Plans to increase the area of forest to 18.7 million hectares were confirmed by the government in 2008. Deforestation has reduced natural forests from 41 per cent of the country in 2002 to a current 35 per cent, due to changes in agriculture, hydroelectric projects, mining and illegal logging.

Industry and manufacturing

The industrial sector accounts for around 27 per cent of GDP and employs over 10 per cent of the workforce.

There is no heavy industry. The production of tin concentrates is the main industrial activity. Other major industries include textiles, bricks, cement, minerals and hydroelectricity.

Small-scale manufacturing industries produce beer, cigarettes, detergents, rubber footwear, plywood, matches, salt, animal feed, veterinary products, handicrafts, alcoholic beverages and soft drinks.

The growth sectors are garments, wood products, handicrafts and light industry, including vehicle assembly.

In June 2009 the US removed Laos from its economic black list and opened up opportunities for bilateral trade.

Tourism

Tourism has grown in importance as a source of income for many, at a time when interest by foreigners has grown in the South-east Asian region. Tourist numbers have grown in a decade from 259,000 to 1.23 million (1999–2009).

Nevertheless, most tourists are young and adventurous and ready to rough it as necessary, while the tourist infrastructure for the older, more discerning traveller is still being developed.

There are two sites on Unesco's World Heritage List, one a cultural landscape of a traditional temple complex and the other a fusion of European-Lao urban architecture in Luang Prabang. Trips and accommodation along the river and its environment are offered with agreement and participation from local communities.

As part of its promotion of ecotourism, the government has established the Laos Northern Heritage Route that provides tours looping around all of the major cultural and natural sites, including the caves used by Communist fighters (of independence) in Vieng Xai.

Travel and tourism contributed to 14.7 per cent of total GDP in 2014. Employment has progressed from 10.8 per cent in 2006 to 12.8 per cent in 2014. Capital investment in the industry has matched this trend – tourism attracted 9.3 per cent (US$320 million) of total investment in 2014, up from 6.2 per cent (US$60 million) in 2006.

Mining

Mining together with hydrocarbons contributes around 5 per cent to GDP. The sector employs 1 per cent of the workforce.

As with other economic sectors in Laos, resources have not been optimised because of bureaucracy, lack of infrastructure and inefficiency.

Principal minerals include tin, high-grade iron ore, gold, copper, potash, limestone, manganese, lead, zinc, gypsum and bauxite.

There is great potential for the extraction of gold. Pan Australian and CRA Exploration of Australia (a subsidiary of Rio Tinto Zinc) have conducted explorations in joint ventures with the Laos government. Commercial interest in gold mining has surged following the success of the Sepon project – 80 per cent Oxiana Resources and 20 per cent Rio Tinto – which started gold and copper production in 2003.

The Lao government expects to accept new mining investment proposals in 2015 after suspending the new investment projects a few years ago to review the approved mining projects and policy. After carrying out inspections, the Ministry of Energy and Mines estimated that 22.8 per cent of the mining projects are of a high grade, 45.6 per cent are medium and 26.3 per cent are low grade. Investments for low grade productions were encouraged in 2015.

Hydrocarbons

Laos does not produce any hydrocarbons. It relies on imports of petroleum products to meet domestic consumption levels.

Laos does not import either coal or natural gas. Imports of oil are typically 3,000 barrels per day.

Exploration for oil in 2008 was carried out by two companies from Vietnam and the UK. Large deposits of oil and natural gas are expected, but if found commercially viable production would take years to begin.

Energy

Laos has an installed generating capacity of 700MW, supplied mainly by hydropower, producing 1.64 billion kilowatt hours in 2006. Electricity supplies are restricted mainly to the capital and other large urban areas.

The potential for expansion of hydropower is enormous due to plentiful water and a mountainous terrain. An estimated 30,000MW could be developed, given the investment in plants and infrastructure. In 2015 the Lao government allowed local and overseas companies to invest in 357 hydropower development projects with a capacity generation expected to be around 26,000 megawatts. This will eventually comprise the major source of electricity exports within the country.

The construction of Nam Khanh 2 hydropower dam is nearing completion. The cost is worth more than US$350 million and is designed to generate 130 megawatts.

Financial markets

On 11 January the new Lao Securities Exchange Market opened, with two companies listed. It is expected that the stock exchange will raise US$8 billion in equity and bond sales to help fund investment in the country. Trading details are available through the website of Banque pour le Commerce Laos (www.bcel.com.la) and Laos' first brokerage firm, Lane Xang Securities Public Company.

Stock exchange

Laos Securities Exchange

Banking and insurance

Since the early 1990s, the number of banks in Laos has more than doubled, with a corresponding rise in business. There are eight state-run commercial banks, two joint venture banks, seven foreign banks and 32 private non-bank foreign exchange bureaux operating in Laos. Banks have adopted commercial lending practices. Restructuring from September 2002 included the phased recapitalisation of the state commercial banks, the merger of two smaller banks and a rationalisation of banking operations.

Central bank

Banque de la RDP Lao (Bank of Lao PDR)

Time

GMT plus seven hours

Geography

Laos is a landlocked country in south-east Asia, bordered by the People's Republic of China to the north, Vietnam to the east, Cambodia to the south, Thailand to the west and Myanmar (Burma) to the north-west.

It is largely a mountainous country with the Annam Range running like a spine down the length of the country producing a natural barrier, with only three mountain passes into Vietnam. The highest mountain is Pou Bia at 2,817m in the northern central region. In the south and west, along the Mekong River, large alluvial plains provide much of the country's agricultural produce. The Mekong runs for 1,805km through Laos and provides much of its border with Thailand.

Hemisphere

Northern

Climate

Most of the year is hot and humid. The climate is monsoonal and has three distinct seasons. The hot dry season begins in February, with temperatures up to 40 degrees Celsius (C), only broken by the odd shower of rain. A build-up of storm activity in April–May with increasing humidity heralds the wet season during June–October, typified by a more consistent pattern of rain and cloudy days through June, July and August. There can be as much as 250mm rainfall per month. Temperatures average 29 degrees C. During this time, the Mekong River rises and flooding of the surrounding area is not uncommon. The cool, dry season arrives in November with lower temperatures and reduced humidity. Average temperature may drop to 14–15 degrees C. The cool weather can continue until February. Always cooler in the mountains, especially at night.

Entry requirements

Passports

Required by all, valid for six months beyond departure date.

Visa

Tourist visas are only obtained abroad through a Laotian consulate or accredited tour operator and must be used within two months. However they can be issued for immediate use at most ports of entry for periods of up to 15 days. Business visas are only issued from Laos and require a completed application form with a letter of invitation from a local company or entity. Further information should be sought through the nearest embassy.

Currency advice/regulations

Import and export of local currency is prohibited; there are no restrictions on foreign currency but amounts over US$2,000 must be declared.

Travellers cheques are not widely accepted, the Thai baht and US dollar are easiest to exchange.

Customs

It is forbidden to take any antiques or Buddha images over 50-years-old out of the country. Such items brought into Laos from other countries have to be declared at Customs.

Health (for visitors)

Laos has few hospitals and medical facilities.

Mandatory precautions

Vaccination certificates for yellow fever if travelling from an infected area.

Advisable precautions

Anti-malaria precautions; malaria is endemic in many areas of Laos but is not found in Vientiane. Mosquito repellent is recommended as dengue fever can be caught in Vientiane all year round. Immunisations against diphtheria, hepatitis A and B, Japanese B encephalitis, TB, tetanus, polio and typhoid. Rabies is a health risk.

Comprehensive health insurance, including provision for air evacuation, is strongly advised.

Hotels

The hotel sector is at an early stage of development and is at present restricted mainly to Vientiane, Luang Prabang and Vang Vieng, where there are a number of tourist-standard and luxury hotels. Visitor accommodation around the country is in short supply, the main resource being village hostels and guesthouses, where available.

Credit cards

Major credit cards are accepted by main hotels and some restaurants. The handling fee of 1.5–3.0 per cent is generally passed on to the customer.

Public holidays (national)

Fixed dates

1–2 Jan (New Year's Day/National Day), 6 Jan (Pathet Lao Day), 20 Jan (Army Day), 8 Mar (Women's Day), 22 Mar (People's Party Day), 13–15 Apr (Lao New Year), 1 May (Labour Day), 1 Jun (Children's Day), 13 Aug (Day of the Free Laos), 12 Oct (Day of Liberation), 2 Dec (Republic Day).

Variable dates

Chinese New Year (Feb), Birth of Buddha (May), Buddhist Fast begins (Jun/Jul), Buddhist Fast ends (Oct).

Working hours

Banking

Mon–Fri: 0800–1200, 1330–1730.

Business

Mon–Sat: 0800–1200, 1300–1600.

Government

Mon–Sat: 0800–1200, 1400–1700.

Some ministries close at 1130 for lunch; others work a half-day Saturday.

Shops

(Mon–Sun) 0900–1700.

Telecommunications

Mobile/cell phones

There are GSM 900/1800 services available in major cities only.

Electricity supply

220V 50Hz. Power outlets are two-prong round or flat sockets.

Weights and measures

Metric system (local units also in use).

Social customs/useful tips

The generally accepted form of greeting among Lao people is the *nop*, performed by placing one's palms together in a position of praying at chest level, but not touching the body. The higher the hands, the greater the sign of respect. Nonetheless, the hands should not be held above the level of the nose. The *nop* is accompanied by a slight bow to show respect to persons of higher status and age. It is also used as an expression of thanks, regret or saying goodbye. But with Western people, it is acceptable to shake hands.

Since the head is considered the most sacred part of the body and the soles of the feet the least, one should not touch a person's head nor use one's foot to point at a person or any object. It is forbidden for a woman to touch a Buddhist monk.

Men and women rarely show affection in public.

Getting there

Air

National airline: Lao Airlines

International airport/s: Vientiane-Wattay International Airpirt (VTE), 4km from city centre.

Airport tax: Departure tax US$10

Surface

Road: The Mitraphap (Friendship) Bridge over the Mekong River at Nong Khai, situated 14km east of Vientiane, provides the first modern road link with Thailand. It also gave Laos road access to a port for the first time.

There are road crossings from all surrounding countries, although the roads via Cambodia and Myanmar are not recommended due to poor security. Road No 1 runs from Thailand, through Laos, to China; road No 9 runs from Thailand, through Laos, to Vietnam.

Major infrastructure and construction of the Chiang Rai-Kunming Road Improvement Project is underway. When complete, it will involve over 1,220km of road along the north axis of the subregion, and will provide road links from Yunnan Province, Laos, to Bangkok in Thailand.

Rail: A railway line runs up to the border of Laos near Vientiane, although it does not run in Laos.

Water: From Kunming or Xishuangbanna, China, it is possible to travel by boat along the Mekong river south into Bokeo Province.

Getting about

National transport

It is relatively easy to travel in northern Laos but in the south, public transport is extremely erratic.

Air: Travel by air is the most convenient means of transportation within Laos. Lao Aviation flies daily from Vientiane to Luang Prabang, Savannakhet, Xieng Khouang, Pakse and Oudomsay. There are several flights a week to Luang Namtha, Sayaboury, Houeixay, Sam Neua, Saravane, Lak Xao, Muangkhong and Attapeu.

Road: Laos has 18,153km of national roads, 2,500km of which are paved. The most important road is route No 13 which runs north-south from China to Cambodia. It links Pak Mong in the north with Khong in the south, passing through major urban areas of Luang Prabang, Vientiane, Savannakhet and Champassack.

Buses: There are services between main centres.

Rail: A line from Vientiane to Nong Khai is operating, including air-conditioned coaches.

Water: River transport is important, especially on the Mekong River, which flows through 1,865km of Laos.

City transport

The easiest way to travel around town is with a car and driver, usually arranged through your hotel.

Taxis: Three-wheeled *tuk-tuk* (motorcycle taxis) are easily found.

Taxis are available in Vientiane, but often operate along certain routes in the manner of buses. Individual hire may require negotiation. Tipping is discouraged.

Car hire

Arrangements are generally made through hotels.

BUSINESS DIRECTORY

The addresses listed below are a selection only. While World of Information makes every endeavour to check these addresses, we cannot guarantee that changes have not been made, especially to telephone numbers and area codes. We would welcome any corrections.

Telephone area codes

The international dialling code (IDD) for Laos is +856 followed by area code (Vientiane only) and subscriber's number:

Vientiane 21

Useful telephone numbers

Police: 191

Police (Immigration Office) emergency number: 212-520

Fire: 190

Ambulance: 195

International Medical Clinic: 214-018, 214-022, 214-025

Chambers of Commerce

Lao National Chamber of Commerce, Phonphanao village Saysettha, PO Box 4596, Vientiane (tel: 452-579, 453-311; fax: 452-580; e-mail: laocci@laotel.com).

Banking

Acleda Bank Lao Ltd, P O Box 1555, #372, Corner of Dongpalane and Dongpina Road, Unit 21, Phonesavanh Neua Village, Sisattanak District, Vientiane (tel: 264-994; fax: 264-995).

Banque de la République Democratique Populaire Lao, PO Box 19, Rue Yonnet, Vientiane (tel: 213-109, 213-110; fax: 213-108).

Banque Pour Le Commerce Exterieur La; PO Box 2925, N 1 Pang Kham Rd, Vientiane (tel: 213-200; fax: 213-202).

Joint Development Bank Ltd; 75/15 Lane Xang Ave, Vientiane (tel: 213-536; fax: 213-530).

Lane Xang Bank Ltd; 6-80 Setthathiilath, Vientiane (tel: 213-400, 212-186, 212-108, 212-105; fax: 213-404).

Vientiane Commercial Bank Ltd; 33 Lane Xang Ave, Hatsady, Chanthaboury, Vientiane (tel: 222-700; fax: 213-513).

Central bank

Banque de la République Democratique Populaire Lao, PO Box 19, Rue Yonnet, Vientiane (tel: 213-109; fax: 213-108; e-mail: bol@pan-laos.net.la).

Stock exchange

Laos Securities Exchange

Travel information

Lao Aviation, 2 Pangkham Road, PO Box 4169, Vientiane (tel: 212-055; fax: 212-056).

Ministry of tourism

Ministry of Trade and Tourism, Vientiane (tel: 412-003, 412-436; fax: 412-434).

National tourist organisation offices

National Tourism Authority of Lao PDR, PO Box 3556, PO Box 3556, Lane Xang Avenue, Vientiane (tel: 212-248, 212-251; fax: 212-769).

Ministries

Department of Foreign Trade, Ministry of Industry and Commerce, Vientiane.

Ministry of Agriculture and Forestry, Vientiane (tel: 412-358).

Ministry of Commerce and Tourism, Vientiane (tel: 107-484).

Ministry of Communications, Transport, Post and Construction, Vientiane (tel: 412-281); Foreign Relations Department (tel: 412-267).

Ministry of Defence, Vientiane (tel: 412-803); Foreign Relations Departments (tel: 412-805, 412-810).

Ministry of Education, Vientiane (tel: 216-000); Foreign Relations Department (tel: 216-005).

Ministry of External Economic Relations, Foreign Investment Adviser, Vientiane (tel: 169-804).

Ministry of Finance, Vientiane (tel: 412-142, 412-404, 412-417).

Ministry of Foreign Affairs, Vientiane (tel: 414-002, 414-003).

Ministry of Industry and Handicrafts, Vientiane (tel: 413-000, 413-004, 413-006); (Electricity Division) (tel: 413-010; fax: 413-013); (Industry Division) (tel: 414-332); (Geology and Mines Division) (tel: 212-080, 212-082; fax: 222-539).

Ministry of Information and Culture, Vientiane (tel: 212-898, 212-402); (Foreign Relations Director) (tel: 212-409).

Ministry of the Interior, Vientiane (tel: 212-503, 212-501); (Foreign Relations Division) (tel: 212-554).

Ministry of Justice, Vientiane (tel: 414-101).

Ministry of Labour and Social Welfare, Vientiane (tel: 213-001, 213-002).

Ministry of Public Health, Vientiane (tel: 412-985, 214-046).

Other useful addresses

ASEAN Investment Promotion Agency, Foreign Investment Management Committee in charge of Promotion Administration and Investment Services, Luang Prabang Road, Vientiane (tel: 216-663; fax: 215-491).

ASEAN Secretariat, 70 A J1 Sisingamangaraja, Jakarta 12110, Indonesia (tel: (+62-21) 726-2991,

724-3372; fax: (+62-21) 724-3504, 739-8234; e-mail: asean.or.id).

British Embassy, Commercial Section, 1031 Wireless Road, Bangkok 10330, Thailand (tel: (+66-2) 253-0191; fax: (+66-2) 255-8619).

British Trade Office, Vientiane, Pandit J Nehru Road, PO Box 6626, Vientiane (tel: 413-606; fax: 413-607).

Foreign Investment Management Committee, Luang Prabang Road, Vientiane (tel: 216-662, 216-663, 217-009, 217-018); fax: 215-491, 217-007, 217-013).

Lao Embassy (USA), 2222 S Street, NW, Washington DC 20008 (tel: (+1-202) 332-6416; fax: (+1-202) 332-4923).

Lao Import-Export Company, 43-47 Lanexang Road, Vientiane.

Lao National Radio, Vientiane (tel: 212-428, 212-429, 212-431, 212-430).

Lao National Television Channel 9, Vientiane (tel: 412-182).

Lao Water Authority, Commercial Division, Vientiane (tel: 412-885; fax: 414-378).

United Nations Development Programme (UNDP), Phon Kheng Road, PO Box 345, Vientiane (tel: 4101, 5605; fax: 5001).

US Embassy, Thatdam Bartholonie Road, Bane Thatdam, Vientiane (tel: 213-966, 212-581, 212-582, 212-585).

National news agency: KPL (Khaosan Pathet Lao), 80 Setthathirath Rd, Vientiane (tel: 215-402; fax: 212-446; internet: www.kpl.net.la).

Internet sites

Asian Development Bank: http://www.adb.org/lrm

Laos Business Centre: http://www.asiadragons.com/

Laos website: http://laos.asiaco.com/

Web directory: http://www.angelfire.com/ca/laoscom/

Web directory: http://www.laoworld.com/

Worldwide Gazeteer — Laos: http://www.c-allen.dircon.co.uk/Countries/Laos.htm

Latvia

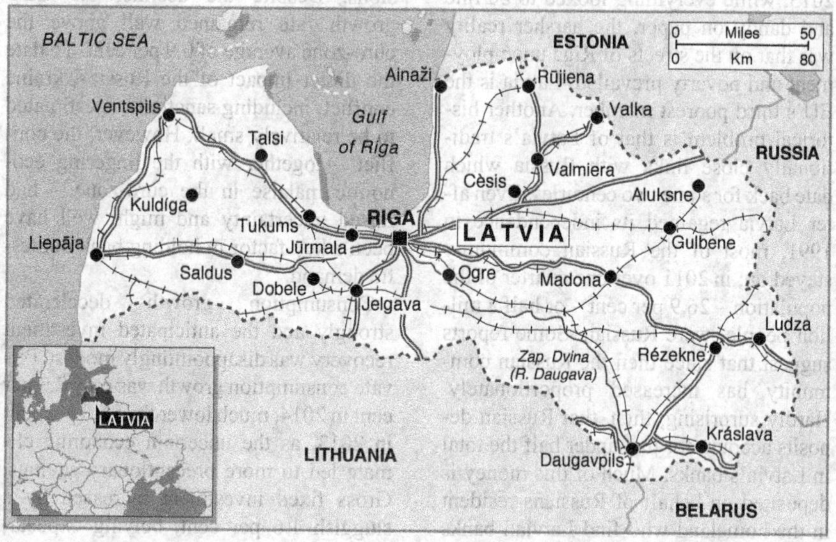

In its May 2015 assessment of the Latvian economy, the International Monetary Fund (IMF) was singing Latvia's praises. According to the IMF, Latvia had made remarkable economic progress since the financial crisis. The output gap had almost closed; unemployment, although still high, was now mainly structural in nature; and the real effective exchange rate was, in the view of the IMF, broadly in line with fundamentals. The current account – which was more than 20 per cent of GDP in deficit just before the output collapse – was close to balance. Fiscal policy was prudent and public debt was among the lowest in Europe. Latvia had experienced a smooth entry into the euro-zone. Policy continuity was likely, as the incumbent centre-right coalition remained in power following the parliamentary elections held in October 2014.

Nerves

Latvia was a nervous country in 2014, principally because Russian-speakers make up 40 per cent of the population. Latvia has the largest Russian-speaking population in the EU. But as the unrest created by the Russian President, Vladimir Putin, increased, Latvia's Russians emerged as – for the most part – a curiously pro-European grouping. Although Russian is still their first language and in many cases they supported Mr Putin's annexation of Crimea, they differed from Ukrainian Russian speakers in one cardinal respect: they did not want to join Russia. A report from the Riga correspondent of the London based British Broadcasting Corporation (BBC) noted that an organisation called the Movement of Russian Europeans had been established in Latvia to counter the vociferous support of Mr Putin's menaces that, it seemed, did not represent the views of the majority of Latvia's Russians.

However pro-European Latvia's Russian speakers may seem to be, many consider that they have suffered discrimination since the break-up of the Soviet Union in 1991. Many Russians – for various reasons – were not automatically granted Latvian citizenship even though they had supported Latvian independence. Instead they were obliged to take a Latvian language and culture citizenship test. In 2013 an estimated 300,000 Russian speakers – 15 per cent of Latvia's population – were humiliatingly classed as 'non-citizens'. Their situation is, of course, heaven sent for Mr Putin, who clearly sees it as an opportunity to drive a wedge between Latvians and their country's Russian population.

KEY FACTS

Official name: Latvijas Republika (Republic of Latvia)

Head of State: President Raimonds Vejonis (since 8 July 2015)

Head of government: Prime Minister Laimdota Straujuma (since 22 January 2014)

Ruling party: Coalition led by Vienotiba (Unity) with Zalo un Zemnieku savieniba (ZZS) (Union of Greens and Farmers) and Nacionala Apvieniba (NA) (National Alliance)

Area: 64,589 square km

Population: 2.03 million (2014)* (2,070,371; 2011; census figure)

Capital: Riga

Official language: Lettish

Currency: Euro (€) = 100 cents

Exchange rate: €0.89 per US$ (Sep 2015)

GDP per capita: US$15,729 (2014)*

GDP real growth: 2.36% (2014)*

GDP: US$31.97 billion (2014)*

Labour force: 983,000 (2014)*

Unemployment: 10.84% (2014)*

Inflation: 0.69% (2014)*

Balance of trade: -US$3.24 billion (2014)*

* estimated figure

Lats gone

At the beginning of January 2014 Latvia said goodbye to its currency, the lats and adopted the euro as its currency. This, at a moment when the grouping of currencies that had adopted the euro, the so-called euro-zone continued to languish economically. Having survived the threats to the very existence of the currency, the group now faced widespread deflation and stagnation. Latvia's leaders saw other benefits – in particular responding to strategy that the Russian invasion of eastern Ukraine had made clearer. For Latvia, with a border of almost 300km with Russia, the attraction was not really about prosperity or economic growth. Alongside their country's membership of North Atlantic Treaty Organisation (NATO) and the EU, adopting the euro was just as much about security. In similar vein, discussions were under way about membership of the Organisation for Economic Co-operation and Development.

Euro here

Many commentators had considered it strange that Valdis Dombrovskis, Latvia's prime minister at the time, should have been so set on taking his country into the euro-zone and adopting the euro as its currency. Latvia had fulfilled all the necessary Maastricht criteria for membership; its currency, the lats, had been pegged to the euro for some ten years and most of its international debt was euro designated. Of that, Mr Dombrovskis could be proud. There was less cause for pride, however, in Latvia's not so recent economic history. At the end of 2008 it had gone cap in hand to Brussels and to the International Monetary Fund (IMF) to seek a €75 billion (US$84 billion) bail-out. In 2009 the economy shrank by 17.7 per cent Tens of thousands of Latvians simply emigrated, something much easier to do as an EU member state, but leaving their country facing a brain drain it could ill afford. In 2013, while everything looked to be fine and dandy on paper, the harsher reality was that on the streets of Riga unemployment and poverty prevailed. Latvia is the EU's third poorest member. Another historical problem is that of Latvia's traditionally close links with Russia which date back for some two centuries. Even after Latvia regained its independence in 1991, most of the Russian community stayed on; in 2011 over one quarter of the population – 26.9 per cent – or half a million people, were Russian. Some reports suggest that since then the Russian community has increased proportionately. Hardly surprising, then, that Russian deposits account for just under half the total in Latvia's banks. Much of this money is deposited on behalf of Russians resident in the homeland who find Latvian banks to be more correct and business-like. This Russian preponderance inevitably drew comparisons between Latvia and Cyprus, where the banking sector also had close links with Russia. Many Latvians had been wary of changing currency again after little more than twenty years with the lats. Above all they feared inflation.

The economy

According to the IMF, Latvia's economic recovery slowed considerably in 2014 amid a deteriorating external environment. Gross domestic product (GDP) growth fell from 4.2 per cent in 2013 to an estimated 2.4 per cent, reflecting the prolonged closure of a large steel manufacturer Liepajas Metalurgs (LM) and weak economic performance in the euro-zone and Russia amid rising geopolitical tensions. Despite the decline, the GDP growth rate remained well above the euro-zone average of 0.9 per cent. To date the direct impact of the Russia-Ukraine conflict, including sanctions, is estimated to be relatively small. However, the conflict – together with the lingering economic malaise in the euro-zone – had raised uncertainty and might well have been a key factor in holding back domestic demand.

Consumption growth decelerated strongly and the anticipated investment recovery was disappointingly modest. Private consumption growth was only 2.3 per cent in 2014, much lower than 6.3 per cent in 2013, as the uncertain economic climate led to more precautionary savings. Gross fixed investment increased by a sluggish 1.6 per cent, belying expectations of a strong rebound from the 5.2 per cent contraction of 2013. Apart from weak external conditions, controversy over proposed amendments to the insolvency law probably contributed to an uncertain domestic environment. Exports remained subdued, due to luke-warm growth among trading partners and the full-year impact of the closure of LM in mid-2013, while the depreciation of the Russian rouble against the euro had a negative impact on export receipts, especially in the last quarter. The current account deficit widened slightly to about 3 per cent of GDP.

The unemployment rate had declined further to about 10.5 per cent by December 2014, down from 11.3 per cent a year earlier, while the participation rate stayed constant. Inflation recovered slightly on the back of robust core inflation. Headline inflation averaged only 0.7 per cent, following zero price growth in 2014. Despite a significant increase in core inflation to 1.5 per cent (from 0.2 per cent in 2013), reflecting strong wage growth, the continued decline in food and energy prices held back headline inflation. In comparison, core inflation in the euro-zone was 0.7 per cent in 2014.

According to the IMF, Latvia's banks continued to repair their balance sheets. Bank profitability improved further, while the overall non-performing loan (NPL) ratio declined to 6.8 per cent in December 2014 from 8.3 per cent a year earlier.

KEY INDICATORS — Latvia

	Unit	2011	2012	2013	2014	**2015
Population	m	2.07	2.04	2.04	*2.03	*2.03
Gross domestic product (GDP)	US$bn	28.30	28.38	30.84	*31.97	*28.36
GDP per capita	US$	12,671	15,048	15,126	*15,729	*13,996
GDP real growth	%	5.5	5.2	4.2	*2.4	*2.3
Inflation	%	4.2	2.0	–	*0.7	*0.5
Unemployment	%	16.2	15.0	11.9	*10.8	*10.4
Exports (fob) (goods)	US$m	2,874.7	12,232.6	13,058.6	13,410.1	–
Imports (fob) (goods)	US$m	3,685.0	15,151.3	15,979.8	16,652.4	–
Balance of trade	US$m	-810.3	-2,918.7	-2,921.2	-3,242.4	
Current account	US$m	-862.2	-705.0	-721.0	*-996.0	*-626.0
Total reserves minus gold	US$m	7,367.6	7,110.9	7,595.7	2,971.2	–
Foreign exchange	US$m	7,195.1	6,954.1	7,409.6	–	–
Exchange rate	per US$	0.50	0.54	0.73	0.82	–

* estimated figure ** forecast figure

However, deleveraging continued, with the stock of bank credit to the private sector declining by about 7.6 per cent (year-on-year) in December 2014. Moreover, the IMF noted that the issuance of new loans actually decreased in 2014. The shrinking stock of domestic credit – extended primarily by large Nordic subsidiary banks – was matched by the repatriation of funds to parent banks. Asset prices continued their gradual recovery, although both stock prices and property prices remained well under the levels reached immediately before the 2008/09 financial crisis.

According to the IMF, there was little evidence that geopolitical tensions had disrupted the flow of non-resident deposits (NRDs) into Latvia. NRD growth was stable in 2014 and accelerated slightly towards the end of the year. Excluding exchange rate effects, which were substantial due to the depreciation of the euro against the US dollar, the stock of NRDs increased by 14 per cent year-on-year in December 2014, broadly in line with the average rate of growth over the previous three years. The general government deficit widened by about 0.5 percentage points to around 1.4 per cent of GDP in 2014. While this exceeded the nominal budget target of 0.9 per cent of GDP, the breach was largely accounted for by a one-off payment related to the sale of Citadele Bank.

The IMF expected Latvia's lacklustre economic growth to continue into 2015. This reflected the adverse impact of the anaemic external environment, particularly Russia's sharp slowdown, on exports and investment. This would be mitigated but not fully offset by higher disposable income due to lower oil prices and robust real wages, which would tend to support private consumption. By mid-2015 LM had reopened and was gradually increasing production, but was not expected to reach full capacity until the fourth quarter of 2015. Given abundant liquidity in the banking system, the accommodative monetary stance of the European Central Bank (ECB) was unlikely to exercise much impact except through a weaker euro and expectations of a more robust recovery in the euro-zone. While inflation was expected to fall in 2015, reflecting the sharply lower oil price forecast, the liberalisation of electricity tariffs would support prices to some extent.

Over time, growth was expected to accelerate as the external climate improves and investment picks up, but this expectation is based on strong reform efforts. Annual medium-term growth of around 4 per cent – higher than in core economies – should be achievable as the economy converges towards euro-zone average income levels. This is conditional on measures to enhance competitiveness and continued prudent macro-economic management. Adverse demographics, including continuing emigration, would tend to reduce the labour force, so reforms aimed at reducing high structural unemployment would be needed simply to keep employment constant.

Robust growth would depend on capital accumulation – underpinned by a resumption of credit supply – and total factor productivity (TFP) growth. International evidence shows that while several countries at a similar level of development have been able to increase labour productivity rapidly and converge towards frontier income levels, others had failed to do so.

The IMF stressed that the outlook for Latvia was subject to significant downside risks. A prolonged slowdown in Russia and the euro-zone would further dampen confidence and prevent a pick-up in economic activity, while a further escalation of sanctions and counter-sanctions could disrupt trade settlements. A sharp supply-driven rise in oil prices would remove an important factor supporting projected growth, especially in the near-term. Resurgent sovereign stress arising from events in Greece could spill over to higher bond yields in Latvia.

Risk assessment

Politics	Good
Economy	Fair
Regional stability	Fair

COUNTRY PROFILE

Before being occupied by the Germans in the thirteenth century, Latvia had been part of an important Baltic-trading route and was a largely feudal and tribal society.

1561 Latvia came under Polish rule after the Livonian Order appealed to Poland-Lithuania for protection from Russia's Ivan the Terrible.

1620s Following the Polish-Swedish war, most of Latvia came under Swedish rule, except Courland in western Latvia where the dukes of Jelgava maintained allegiance to Poland until 1709.

1700–21 Russia's Peter the Great destroyed Swedish power in the Great Northern War. Latvia became part of the Russian empire.

1795 Apart from a brief period of French occupation in 1812, Courland was under Russian control until 1915 when the Germans occupied the province.

1914–18 During the First World War, Latvia alternated between Russian and German control five times. It was under Bolshevik Russian control in late 1918 by which time Latvian independence had been declared by nationalists.

1919 Joint British and German forces expelled Bolshevik Russian forces and democratic rule was introduced.

1922 Latvia's first constitution, including proportional representation, was adopted.

1934–39 Prime Minister Karlis Ulmanis declared a state of emergency, suspended parliament and banned all political parties. In 1936, he assumed the title of president, becoming an autocratic ruler.

1939 Through the German and Soviet Ribbentrop-Molotov pact, Latvia was forcibly incorporated back into the Soviet Union.

1940 Latvia was incorporated as a constituent republic of the USSR.

1941 The Germans invaded and occupied Latvia.

1944 The Soviet Union liberated Latvia from German rule.

1945–80s Mass deportation to Siberia of Latvian citizens by Stalin, following the war and resulting in an influx of Russian nationals as the Soviet Union introduced collective farming and developed heavy industries in Latvia.

1990 The Supreme Court declared *de jure* independence from the Soviet Union. The Latvijas Komunistiska Partija (LKP) (Latvian Communist Party) lost office.

1991 Elite Soviet troops were deployed in Riga, but were withdrawn following international pressure. Anatolijs Gorbunov of the Latvijas Tautas Fronte (LTF) (Latvian Popular Front) became head of state as chairman of the Latvian Supreme Council. Ivars Godmanis (LTF) became head of government as the chairman of the Council of Ministers, which declared Latvia's independence. Lativia joined the United Nations. Latvian citizenship was reinstated for all those who held it before 1940, including their dependents.

1993 A coalition led by Latvijas Cels (LC) (Latvia's Way) formed a government with the Latvijas Zemnieku Savienîa (LZS) (Latvian Farmers' Union). The 1922 Satversme (constitution) was fully reinstituted. Guntis Ulmanis (LZS) was elected the first post-Soviet Latvian president. Valdis Birkavs (LC) was appointed prime minister.

1995 Parliamentary elections led to political turmoil as the ruling LC lost its dominant position and no single party held a majority. A six-party coalition government was eventually formed, dominated by the two largest parties, the centrist LC and the left-wing Demokrâtiskâ Partija 'Saimnieks'

(DPS) (Master Democratic Party). After a lot of wrangling, Andris Skele (LC) became prime minister.
1996 President Ulmanis was re-elected by parliament for a second term in office.
1998 Latvians narrowly backed the liberalisation of the country's citizenship laws in a referendum held alongside general elections. A centre-right coalition was formed, with Vilis Kristopans (LC) as prime minister.
1999 Latvia became a member of the World Trade Organisation (WTO), the first of the Baltic states to join. Independent Vaira Vike-Freiberga was elected president. The minority centre-left coalition headed by Vilis Kristopans fell and a majority coalition government was formed under Prime Minister Andris Skele.
2000 Skele's coalition collapsed over plans to privatise the Latvian Shipping Company (Lasco).
2002 The president invited Einars Repše and his Jaunais Laiks (JL) (New Era) to form a coalition government following the general elections. It included Latvijas Pirmâ Partija (LPP) (Latvia's First Party), Zalo un Zemnieku Savieniba (ZZS) (Green and Farmers Union) (coalition of two parties) and the Apvienîba Tçvzemei un Brîvîbai'/Latvijas Nacionala Konservativa Partija (TB/LNNK) (Union for the Fatherland and Freedom/Latvian National Conservative Party).
2003 President Vaira Vike-Freiberga was re-elected. In a referendum 67 per cent voted to join the European Union (EU).
2004 The ruling coalition collapsed; Repše resigned. Indulis Emsis (ZZS) became prime minister and formed a minority coalition government. Latvia joined NATO and the EU. The government's draft budget was rejected and Emsis resigned. Aigars Kalvitis became prime minister.
2006 Citizenship laws were seen as more pressure on the minority Russian community. The ruling coalition won a majority in parliamentary elections.
2007 Latvia signed a treaty with Russia defining their mutual border. The parliament elected Valdis Zatlers as president with 59 votes, Aivars Endzins won 39 votes. Aleksijs Loskutovs, a leading anti-corruption investigator was sacked; large street demonstrations forced his reinstatement. Prime Minister Kalvitis resigned amid allegations of corruption and Ivars Godmanis was appointed prime minister. Latvia became a member of the EU Schengen area, whereby all travellers may cross borders without a passport or visa.
2008 An agreement for visa-free visits by citizens to the US was signed. The parliament approved the EU's Lisbon Treaty for community constitutional reforms.
2009 Prime Minister Ivars Godmanis and his government resigned, amid political turmoil caused by the global economic crisis. Parliament approved the appointment of Valdis Dombrovskis as prime minister. EU regulators began an investigation into the rescue of Latvia's second largest bank, JSC Parex Banka. The government had agreed to US$401 million in loan guarantees, which together with a loan from the European Bank for Reconstruction and Development (EBRD) may have given Parex Bank undue commercial advantage, contrary to EU trading regulations.
2010 The government coalition lost two constituent parties, following street riots, protesting at the country's severe economic state and the introduction of austerity measures that avoided devaluing the lat through a US$9.5 billion loan agreed by the International Monetary Fund (IMF) in 2009. EU investigators passed the government's rescue plan for JSC Parex Banka. Prime Minister Gadmanis resigned but the president rejected his resignation and Gadmanis invited other, smaller political parties to join his coalition. In parliamentary elections, the incumbent Vienotiba (Unity) coalition won 31.22 per cent of the vote (33 seats out of 100), which was not enough to hold power unaided. A coalition government was formed led by Par Labu Latviju! (For a Good Latvia) (a coalition which includes the prime minister's party Tautas Partija (People's Party), with ZZS and Tevzemei un Brivibai/LNNK (For Fatherland and Freedom/LNNK) of the Nacionala Apvieniba (NA) (National Alliance)).
2011 In May constitutional powers to dissolve parliament were used for the first time, by President Valdis Zatlers. The move followed a political crisis when the government failed to endorse a law to limit the immunity of one of its members accused of corruption. Parliament, in retaliation, replaced Zatlers with Andris Berzins (Zemnieku Savieniba (Farmers Union)) in an indirect presidential election in June; Berzinš won 50 votes (out of 100) and Zatlers 48. Later in June, in conjunction with a national referendum to endorse the dissolution of parliament, a second round of presidential elections took place. Berzinš was elected with 53 votes, while Zatlers won 41. In September parliamentary elections, the pro-Russian, centre-left Saskanas Centrs (Harmony Centre) won 28.36 per cent of the vote (31 seats out of 100), and the newly formed Zatlera Reformu Partija (ZRP) (Zatlers' Reform Party) 20.82 per cent (22). Unity, the previous ruling party, won 20 seats and lost 13, as it was seen to be the instigator of an austerity regime and a government with three, alleged, corrupt politicians at its centre. After weeks of unsuccessful coalition talks, undertaken by Nils Usakovs the leader of Harmony Centre, the president invited Prime Minister Dombrovskis (TP) to form a new government in October. President Berzinš also suggested that a coalition be formed to include politicians from all political parties that had won seats in the parliamentary elections. A coalition was formed between Unity with ZRP and NA, following Valdis Dombrovskis's re-appointment as prime minister; the government took office on 27 October
2012 A referendum held on 18 February on whether Russian should become Latvia's second official language was heavily defeated by 74.4 per cent agaisnt to 24.88 per cent in favour; turnout was 71.12 per cent. Russia criticised the result, saying it was biased since the referendum had excluded around 319,000 Russian-speaking 'non-citizens' from voting. It also expressed 'bewilderment' that Latvia had opposed a delegation of Russian observers monitoring the vote. On 20 February, the president and prime minister met to discuss changing the constitution to alter the procedure for initiating referenda. On 30 May, the European Central Bank (ECB) announced that none of the eight countries (including Latvia), which are scheduled to join the European single currency (euro) are ready.
2013 EU finance minsters set the seal on Latvia's application to become the 18th country to use the euro on 9 July; the application had already been approved by the European Commission and European Central Bank. Euro notes and coins will be issued in Latvia on 1 January 2014 at a rate of 0.702804 lats to one euro.
2014 The euro became the currency of Latvia on 1 January. Laimdota Straujuma became prime minister on 22 January. Parliamentary elections were held on 4 October. Socialdemokratiska Partija 'Saskana' won 23 per cent of the vote (24 seats out of 100), Vienotiba (Unity) 21.9 per cent (23), Zalo un Zemnieku savieniba (ZZS) (Green and Farmers Union) 19.5 per cent (21), Nacionala Apvieniba (NA) (National Alliance) 16.6 per cent (17), No sirds Latvijai (For Latvia from the Heart) 6.9 per cent (seven) and Latvijas Regionu Apvieniba (Latvian Association of Regions) 6.7 per cent (eight); seven other political parties each won less than two per cent and failed to win any seats. Turnout was 58.9 per cent.
2015 Latvia took on the presidency of the EU for six months from January, setting three priorities – a more competitive Europe, digital Europe and engaged Europe. However, as Prime Minister Laimdota Straujuma said at the end of the six months 'life brought in its corrections'

and terrorists attacks and the humanitarian crisis brought on by refugees and migrants on Europe's border, meant that priorities shifted.

Political structure

Constitution

In 1993, the Constitutional Law supplemented the 1922 Constitution. The constitution provides for basic rights and freedoms.

Latvian citizens 18 years and over and those residents that have lived in Latvia before 27 June 1940, are eligible to vote.

A constitutional referendum was held on 18 February 2012. The proposed amendment was to add Russian as the second official language as well as prescribe two working languages – Latvian and Russian for self-government institutions. 74.8 per cent voted no while 24.9 per cent voted yes. Turnout was 71.1 per cent.

Form of state

Parliamentary democratic republic

The executive

Executive powers are vested in the Cabinet of Ministers, nominated by the prime minister and appointed by and accountable to, parliament. The Cabinet of Ministers is led by the prime minister, who is appointed by the president but confirmed by Parliament.

The president is indirectly elected by parliament for a four-year term (eligible for a second term).

National legislature

The unicameral Saeima (parliament) has 100 members, they are directly elected in multi-seat constituencies for a four-year term by proportional representation in seats allocated to political parties which gain at least 5 per cent of the popular vote.

The president may dissolve parliament earlier than scheduled. General elections are held on the first Saturday of October.

Legal system

The legal system is based on a civil law system. The appointment of judges to the Supreme Court is confirmed by the Saiema.

Last elections

2 June 2011 (presidential, indirect); 23 July 2011 (referendum); 4 October 2014 (parliamentary)

Results: Presidential Fourth Round: Raimonds Vejonis (ZZS) won 46 votes (out of 100) and Egils Levits (NA) won 26 votes. Consequently, Levits was eliminated from the election and in the final round, Vejonis was elected with 55 votes for and 42 against. 99 lawmakers voted in total, but one vote was invalid.

Referendum: In the motion to dissolve parliament and hold another general election, 94.3 per cent voted yes; 5.48 per cent no.

Parliamentary: Socialdemokratiska Partija 'Saskana' won 23 per cent of the vote (24 seats out of 100), Vienotiba (Unity) 21.9 per cent (23), Zalo un Zemnieku savieniba (ZZS) (Green and Farmers Union) 19.5 per cent (21), Nacionala Apvieniba (NA) (National Alliance) 16.6 per cent (17), No sirds Latvijai (For Latvia from the Heart) 6.9 per cent (seven) and Latvijas Regionu Apvieniba (Latvian Association of Regions) 6.7 per cent (eight); seven other political parties each won less than two per cent and failed to win any seats. Turnout was 58.9 per cent.

Next elections

October 2018 (parliamentary), 2019 (presidential)

Political parties

Ruling party

Coalition led by Vienotiba (Unity) with Zalo un Zemnieku savieniba (ZZS) (Union of Greens and Farmers) and Nacionala Apvieniba (NA) (National Alliance)

Main opposition party

Socialdemokratiska Partija "Saskana" (SDPS) (Social Democratic Party "Harmony").

A population and housing census was held in March 2011, in which a population figure of 2,067,887 was recorded. It showed a decrease in the population of 309,000 (13 per cent) since the 2000 census.

Population

2.03 million (2014)* (2,070,371; 2011; census figure)

Last census: 1 March 2011: 2,070,371

Population density: 37.5 inhabitants per square km. Urban population 68 per cent (2010 Unicef).

Annual growth rate: -0.8 per cent, 1990–2010 (Unicef).

Ethnic make-up

The proportion of those that described themselves as ethnic Latvians increased from 57.7 (1,370,703) to 62.1 per cent (1,284,194) in the 2011 census. The number of resident Russians fell from 703,243 in 2000 (29.6 per cent of population) to 556,422 (26.9 per cent). Other resident nationalities recorded in 2011 were: Belarusians 68,174; Ukrainians 45,699; Polish 44,783; Lithuanians 24,426; all remaining nationalities combined 44,189.

Citizenship is granted to stateless children, even if their parents are not citizens, provided they have lived in Latvia for at least five years. Most ethnic Russians must still pass language examinations to become citizens.

Religions

Predominantly Protestant (Lutheran), with a Roman Catholic minority in the east of the country. Orthodox Christianity is the most common religious denomination among Russians in Latvia.

Education

Education has traditionally been important in Latvia and a high level of education enabled Latvia to become a centre of the Soviet communications and electronics industries.

For those who live in rural Latvia, educational opportunities are limited. About 25 per cent in the 18–24 age group receive only a basic education.

Basic education lasts for nine years. From this, students are channelled into either 1) a basic vocational school for a two-year course from age 16; or 2) a vocational school from age 15 for three years; or 3) a vocational secondary school at age 15 for four years. Each vocational school course has its relevant qualifications. Students undertaking academic study progress to a general secondary school from age 16 for four years. Students who graduate from either the general or vocational secondary school may undertake higher education.

There are four universities and a number of other higher education institutions in Latvia. All universities and 17 other higher education institutions are state-run. In addition, there are a number of private institutions of which 10 are state-recognised. Higher education institutions confer academic degrees and professional higher education qualifications.

Latvia has a higher proportion of undergraduates than many countries (including Japan, Poland and the Czech Republic). Engineering and science courses are well established, while commercial courses such as law, accountancy and business management, although in their infancy, are growing in popularity.

Annual total expenditure on education is around 7 per cent of GDP.

Literacy rate: 100 per cent adult rate; 100 per cent youth rate (15–24) (Unesco 2005).

Compulsory years: Seven to 18.

Enrolment rate: 96 per cent gross primary enrolment of the relevant age group (including repeaters); 84 per cent gross secondary enrolment (World Bank).

Pupils per teacher: 13 in primary schools.

Health

The Latvian healthcare system is set to become more expensive with the introduction of more payment-based services. However, the country has one of the highest ratios of doctors to population in the world.

Healthcare has largely deteriorated in Latvia. This has been due to a lack of primary healthcare provision, an over-stretched network of small hospitals, overstaffing and over-specialisation, the lack of modern management systems and the use of hospitals as dumping grounds for people with social rather than medical problems.

HIV/Aids

HIV prevalence: 0.6 per cent aged 15–49 in 2003 (World Bank)

Life expectancy: 71 years, 2004 (WHO 2006)

Fertility rate/Maternal mortality rate: 1.5 births per woman, 2010 (Unicef); maternal mortality 45 per 100,000 live births (World Bank).

Child (under 5 years) mortality rate (per 1,000): 9 per 1,000 live births (WHO 2012)

Head of population per physician: 3.01 physicians per 1,000 people, 2003 (WHO 2006)

Welfare

The social security system provides a state pension and a social insurance fund, for which there are mandatory contributions. The pension system has three tiers, composed of a modified pay-as-you-go (PAYG) system, stronger links with contributions, a mandatory state-funded system of privately managed savings accounts and voluntary privately managed pensions.

Legislation regulates private pension funds, which are supervised by the state insurance inspection department. Banks, life insurance companies, brokerages and investment companies are permitted to operate private pension funds, which allow saving in addition to the state pension scheme.

In March 2012 the government amended the age of retirement from 62 years to 65 years. The process begins in 2014 for people born from 1 January 1952, when an extra three months will be added to the retiree's age before eligibility for a state pension. In 2016 it will be raised to six months before eligibility and the process will be completed in 2020. The minimum term in employment for eligibility to receive a state pension will be raised from 10 years to 15 years, from 2014 and increased to 20 years from 2020.

Main cities

Riga (capital, estimated population 693,919 in 2012), Daugavpils (102,338), Liepaja (82,790), Jelgava (66,880), Jurmala (54,715), Ventspils (42,715), Rezekne (34,460).

Languages spoken

Russian, English and German are widely spoken (over 80 per cent of Latvians speak both Lettish and Russian); Lettish is required for citizenship. Belarusian, Ukrainian, Polish and Yiddish are also spoken. Some 150,000 Latvians speak Latgalian.

A law passed in February 2004 requires at least 60 per cent of teaching at minority schools to be in Latvian.

Official language/s

Lettish

Media

Press

After spectacular growth since 1995, consolidation became the typical development. The small press market is separated into two languages Latvian and Russian.

Dailies: In Latvian, *Diena* (www.diena.lv) is a prestigious, independent newspaper, which owns several local newspapers, as does *Neatkariga Rita Avize* (NRA) (www.nra.lv) which owns the evening tabloid *Vakara Zinas* among others, *Latvijas Avize* (www2.la.lv) is a daily tabloid. The free newspaper *5 Min* (published by *Diena*) has been steadily increasing its circulation since 2005.

In Russian *Vesti Segodnja (Today's News)* (http://rus.delfi.lv/news/press/vesti), is the largest circulating newspaper; *Chas* (www.chas-daily.com) from Rida and *Ventspils* (www.ventspils.lv) from Ventspilis.

Weeklies: In English, the independent weekly *The Baltic Times* (www.baltictimes.com) provides news from the region; *Tovary Optum* is published in Russia.

Business: In Latvian, the newspapers *Dienas Bizness* (www.db.lv), and in Russian *Biznez I Baltiya* (www.bb.lv), plus the magazine *Kapitals* (www.kapitals.lv) in Latvain provide comprehensive news and views on business and financial matters. Some daily newspapers include business articles.

Periodicals: There are around 190 magazine titles on offer of which *Lilit* (www.lilita.lv) is a leading women's monthly magazine.

Broadcasting

Radio: The national, public Latvian Radio (www.radio.org.lv) operates four stations, including Radio 1 and 2, plus Klasika and Latvia International. Private, commercial stations includes Gold FM (www2.goldfm.lv) and Radio Naba (www.naba.lv) from Riga, the public Saldus Radio (www.saldus.lv) and Alise Plus (www.aliseplus.lv) from Daugavpils in Russian.

Television: Private, commercial television dominates the market. TV3 Latvis (www.tv3.lv), launched in 1998, with programmes in Latvian, became the leading TV station in September 2007 overtaking the previous leader, Latvian Independent Television (LNT) (www.lnt.lv). The national, public Latvian Television (LTV) (www.ltv.lv) operates LVT 1 and 7, with 70 per cent funding provided by the government and the remainder by advertising and sales. Russian-based channels, although popular with large parts of the population, have increasingly faced opposition as the government – through its control of transmission rights – attempts to limit Russian influence on Latvia.

National news agency: LETA (Latvian News Agency)

Other news agencies: BNS: www.bns.lv Delfi (in Latvian and Russian):www.delfi.lv

Economy

Forests account for 54 per cent of Latvian productive land so that the country's principal export commodity is timber. Some 50 per cent or the forests are state-owned, with domestic production at around 5 per cent of GDP and 70 per cent of all production exported; typically, 10–11 million square metres of timber are harvested annually. The UK, Egypt and Germany are typically Latvian timber's principal markets. Industry in general is diverse and largely geared to serve local markets. Latvia's financial services are growing.

Latvia successfully transformed its economy from an integrated part of the former-Soviet Union's centrally planned economy to a free market economy. Despite a couple of setbacks in the 1990s, Latvia became the European Union's fastest growing economy after joining in 2004. However, it experienced a severe deterioration of its economy beginning in late 2007, in line with the global economic crisis. Despite recovering from the plummeting recession beginning in 2008 that saw GDP growth fall as low as -14.2 per cent in 2009, Latvia has still not returned to its pre-crisis performance levels. Growth in GDP averaged 4.7 per cent over the 2011–13 period, aided by strong growth especially in the export sector. In 2014, the economy decelerated and GDP growth was 2.4 per cent.

Latvia's unemployment rate in 2009 became one of the worst in the EU at almost 23 per cent and GDP per capita fell from US$14,833 to US$11,448 in 2009. It was estimated that from 2008–10 10 per cent of the workforce migrated to find work. Unemployment has improved but it is still high at 10.8 per cent in 2014, and GDP per capita has recovered, reaching US$23,700.

On 2 February 2012, the Japanese credit ratings agency, Rating and Investment Information Inc (R&I) increased Latvia's rating from BB+ to BBB-, which restored the country's rating to investment level. R&I stated that Latvia had 'increased the stability of its economic fundamentals through efforts to adjust its economic structures' since 2008. R&I also said that the government's fiscal consolidation was 'progressing better than scheduled' and that Latvia was less likely to be greatly shaken by any further deteriorations in the external environment.

Standard and Poor's upgraded Latvia's rating to A- in May 2014, citing its strong economy and improving public finances.

External trade

As a member of the European Union, Latvia operates within a community-wide free trade area, which sets import tariffs as a whole. The EU has free trade agreements with a number of nations and trading blocs worldwide.

Latvia has to import all of its energy and raw material; timber is Latvia's sole natural resource and is the single largest export, as either logs, finished panels or charcoal. External trade accounts for around 75 per cent of Latvia's GDP.

Imports

Principal imports are fuels and vehicles, iron ore, steel and capital goods.

Main sources: Lithuania (17.0 per cent of total in 2014), Germany (11.7 per cent), Poland (10.9 per cent)

Exports

Principal exports are timber (typically over 35 per cent of total), machinery, electrical and electronic and equipment, iron and steel, textiles and foodstuffs.

Main destinations: Lithuania (17.7 per cent of total in 2014), Russia (14.7 per cent), Estonia (11.2 per cent)

Agriculture

Farming

Latvia's agricultural sector still has remnants of the old Soviet central planning system and has suffered during the transition to a capitalist economic environment. With the majority of output going to the food-processing sector, demand has fallen considerably. With agriculture employing over 15 per cent of the workforce, its problems are becoming increasingly significant politically.

During its transitional entry stage Latvia has decided to implement the reform of CAP in January 2009. The reform was introduced throughout most of the EU in 2005, when subsidies on farm output, which tended to benefit large farms and encourage overproduction, were replaced by single farm payments, not conditional on production. The change is expected to reward farms that provide and maintain a healthy environment, food safety and animal welfare standards. The changes are also intended to encourage market conscious production and cut the cost of CAP to the EU taxpayer.

The sector is dominated by dairy farming, pig-breeding, grain production and potatoes. Latvia is self-sufficient in the production of cattle and dairy products, pork, sugar beet, flax and potatoes. Any surplus is exported to Russia, other republics of the CIS and the EU.

The reform of the agricultural sector has proceeded at a faster rate than in either Lithuania or Estonia and 95 per cent of agricultural production comes from the private sector. Crops cover about 28 per cent of the total land area and permanent pastures about 13 per cent.

Decreases in agricultural output have been caused by the structural reforms in the sector, a lack of modern technology and the money to buy it, problems in the distribution of produce – particularly from the small private farms – and an absence of bank credit combined with high interest rates.

Stock-breeding contributes over 50 per cent of gross agricultural production; however, this means that large amounts of fodder must be imported. Consequently the structure of the agricultural sector is changing with greater emphasis placed on grain production.

The reform of the agricultural sector has proceeded at a faster rate than in either Lithuania or Estonia and 95 per cent of agricultural production comes from the private sector. Crops cover about 28 per cent of the total land area and permanent pastures about 13 per cent.

Decreases in agricultural output have been caused by the structural reforms in the sector, a lack of modern technology and the money to buy it, problems in the distribution of produce – particularly from the small private farms – and an absence of bank credit combined with high interest rates.

Stock-breeding contributes over 50 per cent of gross agricultural production; however, this means that large amounts of fodder must be imported. Consequently the structure of the agricultural sector is changing with greater emphasis placed on grain production.

Fishing

Latvia's extensive coastline provides large fish catches. Principal catches include sprat, Baltic Sea pilchards, Riga Gulf pilchards, cod and salmon. Typical annual catches amount to some 145 million tonnes per year (tpy).

Thirty per cent of total fish production is used domestically while 70 per cent is exported. Latvia held discussions with Joe Borg, EU Commissioner for Fisheries, about conservation methods to protect overexploited and depleted cod stocks in the Baltic Sea.

Forestry

With forests covering approximately half of total land area, forestry has the potential to become one of the most important sectors of the economy. About 60 per cent of the forest is classified as soft wood (66 per cent pine forest and 34 per cent spruce) with the remaining hardwood mainly birch. Reforestation following cutting is compulsory.

Latvia's rich and extensive forests are mainly in areas of low population, making the felling, processing and export of timber relatively easy. There is potential to harvest 8.3 million cubic metres of timber a year, half of which would be available for pulp production. The timber and furniture industry accounts for about 8 per cent of GDP and employs around 51,000 people. Timber and furniture exports grew substantially in the 1990s and currently comprise around 35 per cent of total exports. In particular, growth in exports to the EU is the result of higher wood exports.

There are about 2,500 forest industry companies in Latvia, all but a few in private ownership; the majority concentrate on sawn wood milling, wood panel production and furniture. Progress in the timber industry has been made since independence, although there is still a lack of finance, management and design skills and many production techniques remain inefficient. Pulp and paper production does not meet domestic demand.

Even though Latvia is one of the top five countries in Europe in terms of forest resources per capita, it lacks a large processing plant for pulp and paper production, and consequently a large proportion of raw timber produce is exported to pulp mills in Sweden.

Industry and manufacturing

The industrial sector accounts for 24.8 per cent of GDP and employs around 24 per cent of the work force (2014).

Latvia is one of the most heavily industrialised areas of the former Soviet Union. A well-developed infrastructure and a broadly diversified industrial base includes both light and heavy industries including high-technology manufacturing and shipbuilding. Main industries are mechanical engineering, metal working, textiles and the food industry. Forestry, paper, chemicals, petrochemicals and communications are also important.

The manufacturing industry is concentrated on the production of railway carriages, buses, mopeds, washing machines and telephone systems. Mineral fertilisers are also produced. Industrial development is slow and only about half of the potential capacity is being utilised. Riga, Liepaja and Ventspils are the principal industrial centres.

Tourism

Latvia became a popular destination during the 2000s with tourist numbers rising from around 500,000 in the 1990s to a peak of 1.7 million in 2008, just before the global economic crisis depressed the market and visitor numbers began to fall (to 1.4 million in 2010). In 2012 the government launched a new, long term tourist strategy that identified and segmented the most important markets for inbound visitors. New marketing campaigns were tailored to their interests. The growth in both budget airlines and internet bookings allow visitors to organise their own tours and step outside the well-trod tourist paths. By 2014, there were 2 million visitors to Riga alone.

The short summer season could be considered a barrier to the industry's prospects. However, Riga is successfully marketed as a weekend destination for shopping, cultural activities and nightlife. This, coupled with the reduction in value added tax (VAT) on tourist services in 2010 and a strong programme of price reductions by hotels, has allowed Latvia to become a competitively priced destination. Visitors are mostly from Europe but there is an increasing number from North America.

Travel and tourism in total contributed 8.8 per cent to GDP in 2014, whilst 76,500 jobs were directly or indirectly involved in the industry (8.6 per cent of total employment). Visitor revenue jumped from US$874 million in 2007 to US$1.1 billion in 2008 which has remained the same up to 2014.

Mining

Mineral resources include limestone, clay for the cement industry, dolomite, gypsum, sand for glass, clay for pottery, sand for silicate products and gravel. The few minerals found in Latvia are used as building materials.

Mining and the quarrying of mineral resources account for approximately 0.5 per cent of annual GDP and have a negligible impact on the economy.

Hydrocarbons

Latvia no longer has any proven oil reserves; consumption was 34,000 barrels per day in 2013, mostly imported, largely from Belarus, Russia and Lithuania. As it has no refining capacity it imports all petroleum products necessary.

Latvia has no proven reserves of natural gas. Consumption was 1.5 billion cum in 2012. Latvia relies on Russian imports to meet domestic demand.

Latvia does not produce coal but does produce around 500,000 tonnes of peat per annum. Coal imports come mostly from Poland.

Energy

Total installed generating capacity was over 2.17GW in 2013, of which hydroelectric power provided 68 per cent. However, hydroelectric and thermal power plants do not provide the country with enough power to meet requirements and the country must rely on imports to meet its needs. While the energy market was opened up to competition in 2005 little progress has been made as the state-owned Latvenergo has a monopoly on the distribution of electricity and operates the generating hydro- and thermal-power plants, which provide 93 per cent of production.

The Estlink project, an underwater cable linking the Baltic States with the Scandinavian and Nordic power grids, was partly funded by the EU and became operational in 2007. The cable has helped to reduce Latvia's dependency on Russian supplies.

Latvia has the largest wind energy station in the Baltic, with a peak output of 2.5 million kilowatt hours of electricity per year (enough for over 1,500 households). The German energy company Preussen Elektra funded 70 per cent of the plant, which has a minimum operating life of 20 years. Over 500MW of wind energy is technically possible in the country, with only 20MW installed so far. National legislation facilitates investment in renewable energy.

Financial markets

Stock exchange

Rigas Fondsbørs (Riga Stock Exchange) (RSE)

Banking and insurance

The Bank of Latvia, the national central bank, is independent and manages the monetary supply and instigates governmental financial policy. The Financial Capital Markets Commission audits commercial banks. In the early 1990s most state banks were privatised and the sector proliferated. 1995 and 1998 saw major crises in the sector, involving mass insolvency and closures. Since then, regulation has been improved to stabilise Latvian banking and encourage investment by the West. Western owned banks control much of the country's finances. There are over 20 banks in operation.

Central bank

Latvijas Banka (Bank of Latvia)

Offshore facilities

Riga is popular with Russians seeking safe dollar accounts. Russian-linked banks have become influential in the sector.

Time

GMT plus two hours (daylight saving, late March to late September, GMT plus three hours)

Geography

Latvia is situated in north-eastern Europe on the east coast of the Baltic Sea. It is slightly larger than Switzerland at 64,589 sq km and is bordered by Estonia to the north, the Russian Federation to the east, Belarus to the south-east and Lithuania to the south and south-west. With rolling plains and gentle hills, half the country is less than 90 metres above sea level.

There are over 2,300 lakes and 12,000 rivers; the longest is the River Daugava. The largest lake is Lake Lubans which stretches over 81 square km. Latvia's highest point is in the south-east of the country where Latgale Upland reaches 289 metres.

Hemisphere

Northern

Climate

Temperate climate, but with considerable temperature variations. Mildest areas along the Baltic coast. Summer is warm with relatively mild weather in spring and autumn. Summer sunshine may be nine hours a day. Winter, which lasts from November to mid-March, can be very cold. Rainfall is distributed throughout the year with the heaviest rainfall in August. Snowfalls are common in winter months.

Dress codes

Warm clothing is essential in winter as are a raincoat and umbrella during spring and summer. Business dress is conservative but relatively informal, with a jacket and tie expected for meetings.

Entry requirements

Passports

Required by all and must be valid for at least six months. For identification purposes, a photocopy of the passport should be carried at all times.

Visa

Required by all, except nationals of EU and Schengen area signatory countries, North America, Australasia and Japan. For further exceptions contact the nearest consulate or see www.am.gov.lv/en/service/ for a full list. A Schengen visa application (offered in several languages) can be downloaded from http://europa.eu/abc/travel/ see 'documents you will need'. All visitors must have valid travel health insurance, including emergency repatriation cover.

Currency advice/regulations

There are no restrictions on import and export of local and foreign currency. Travellers cheques, in freely convertible currencies, preferably US dollars and euros, are accepted.

Customs

Personal items are duty-free. There are no duties levied on alcohol and tobacco between EU member states, providing amounts imported are for personal consumption.

It is advisable to declare valuable items such as jewellery, cameras, computers and musical instruments. Ensure that the

declaration is stamped by the customs officials.
A certificate must be obtained to export of art objects over 50 years old.

Prohibited imports
Illegal drugs; guns and ammunition (without a police import permit); fresh meat.

Health (for visitors)

Nationals of the European Economic Area (EEA) countries and Switzerland can access reduced cost and sometimes free medical treatment using a European Health Insurance Card (EHIC) while visiting the EEA. Exceptions include nationals of the 10 countries, which joined the EU in 2004, whose EHIC is not valid in Switzerland. Applications for the EHIC should be made before travelling.

Mandatory precautions
There are no special requirements.

Advisable precautions
It is advisable to be in date for the following immunisations: tuberculosis, hepatitis A and diphtheria.
Any medicines required by the traveller should be taken by the visitor, and it could be wise to have precautionary antibiotics if going outside major urban centres. Rabies is endemic.
A travel kit including a disposable syringe is a reasonable precaution. It is recommended to drink bottled water. The tap water is occasionally yellow.

Hotels

Riga has business-class hotels. Tips are included in restaurant bills.

Credit cards

Credit and charge cards are accepted in large hotels and restaurants and some shops. ATMs are widely found in towns and cities.

Public holidays (national)

Fixed dates
1 Jan (New Year), 1 May (Labour Day), 4 May (Restoration Day), 23 Jun (Ligo Day/Midsummer's Eve), 24 Jun (St John's Day/Summer Solstice), 18 Nov (National Day), 25–26 Dec (Christmas/Winter Solstice).

Variable dates
Good Friday, Easter Monday.

Working hours

Banking
Mon–Fri: 0900–1700. Some banks are open between 0900–1300 on Saturdays.

Business
Mon–Fri: 0830/0900–1730/1800.

Government
Mon–Fri: 0900–1700.

Shops
Mon–Fri: 1000–1900, Saturday: 1000–1600. Grocery and department stores are usually open from 0800 until 1900. There are quite a few food stores in Riga that provide 24-hour service.

Telecommunications

Mobile/cell phones
GSM 900/1800 services are available throughout most of the country.

Electricity supply

220V AC, 50 Hz. European-style two-pin plugs are in use.

Social customs/useful tips

Latvians can be reserved and formal, but hospitable. When meeting, shake hands and slightly nod your head. If invited to a private home, it is usual to bring flowers for the hostess. Business cards are widely used.
The informal custom of overcharging foreigners (particularly by taxi-drivers) has developed since 1991.
Taxi fares do not usually include a tip, whereas restaurant bills usually do. Tipping is generally expected. Carry small-denomination US dollar bills as well as local currency for tips, taxis etc.
Reference to Russia and Russians should be avoided, at least until you are sure of the ethnic background of your host. Many Latvians have strong feelings about Russia as many have relatives who were sent to Siberia during the Soviet period. It is also wise not to ask your host what they did before independence, as they may think you are asking whether they were in the Communist Party or even if they were sent to Siberia.

Security

As living standards have dropped, so the crime rate has risen since independence. Care should be taken not to display valuables when walking around the city.
When walking, travellers should be alert to the threat of pickpocketing and other forms of theft. Always avoid unlit streets and parks at night, and be extra vigilant if walking alone.
Wherever possible, guarded car-parks should be used and valuables kept out of sight.

Getting there

Air
National airline: Air Baltic (ABC)
International airport/s: Riga International (RIX) 8km west of Riga; facilities include currency exchange, car hire, post office, business lounge and duty-free. A courtesy shuttle bus and the number 22a bus (tickets available from the post office) run to city centre hotels; alternatively taxis are located in front of the terminal building, and the journey takes about 15 minutes.
Airport tax: None

Surface
Road: There are roads leading from all the surrounding countries, however not all have customs control and it is advisable to determine which border crossing has this facility before undertaking a fruitless journey. Visit http://www.transit.lv/ for details of the country's road network.
Rail: The Berlin to St Petersburg service passes through Daugavpils in south-eastern Latvia. Trains also link Riga with Moscow, St Petersburg and Minsk.
Water: There are direct ferries to Riga from Travemünde in Germany and Stockholm in Sweden.
Main port/s: Warm-water ports at Riga and Ventspils and Liepaja, (designated a Special Economic Zone (SEZ)).

Getting about

National transport
Air: Daily flights operate between Riga and Liepaja regional airport in the west.
Road: Latvia has a good road network, although secondary roads are in a variety of conditions.
Buses: The extensive bus network is a better form of transport than trains.
Rail: Riga is connected to all major towns and there are some cross country services. The railway terminal in Riga is Stacijas Laukums.

City transport
Taxis: Taxis can be flagged down or hired from taxis stands. All taxis have metres that should be used; there is a surcharge between 2200–0600. Some taxis accept credit cards and display a credit card sticker. Tipping is not usual.
Buses, trams & metro: There is an economic and extensive transport system, including buses, trams and trolley buses operating between 0530–2330 in Riga. In addition, some trolley bus and tram routes run an hourly night service. Tickets can be purchased from the driver or conductor. Routes are displayed on the Riga city map, available from most city kiosks.

Car hire
There are a number of international car hire firms in Riga. Either an international driving licence or an EU pink format licence is necessary and drivers have to be over 21 years old. Cars with drivers are also available. Traffic drives on the right, seat belts must be worn and car headlights must remain on at all times. Alcohol consumption and mobile phone use by drivers is strictly prohibited. Speed limits are 50kph in urban areas and 90kph on open roads.

BUSINESS DIRECTORY

The addresses listed below are a selection only. While World of Information makes every endeavour to check these addresses, we cannot guarantee that changes have not been made, especially to telephone numbers and area codes. We would welcome any corrections.

Telephone area codes

The international direct dialling (IDD) code for Latvia is +371, followed by area code

Daugavpils	54	Rezekne	46
Jelgava	30	Riga not required	
Liepaja	34	Ventspils	36

Useful telephone numbers

Fire brigade: 01
Police: 02
Ambulance: 03
National telephone operator: 116
International telephone operator: 115
Train information: 1181

Chambers of Commerce

American Chamber of Commerce in Latvia, 4 Torna iela, Riga 1050 (tel/fax: 721-2204; e-mail: amcham@amcham.lv).

British Chamber of Commerce in Latvia, Valdemara Centres, 21 Kr Valdemara iela, Riga 1010 (tel: 703-5202; fax: 703-5318; e-mail: info@bccl.lv).

Latvian Chamber of Commerce and Industry, 35 Kr Valdemara iela, Riga 1010 (tel: 722-5595; fax: 782-0092; e-mail: info@chamber.lv).

Banking

Hansabank, 26 Kalku Street, Riga LV-1050 (tel: 702-44444; fax: 702-4400; e-mail: info@hansabanka.lv).

Latvijas Krājbanka, 1 Palasta Street, Riga, LV-1954 (tel: 709-2020; fax: 721-2083).

Parex Banka, 3 Smilsu Street, Riga LV-1522 (tel: 701-0000; fax: 701-0001; e-mail: inquiry@parex.lv).

Saules Bank, 16 Smilsu Street, Riga (tel: 702-0500; fax: 702-0505; e-mail: office@saules.com).

Unibanka, 23 Pils Street, Riga (tel: 721-5555; fax: 721-5566; e-mail: atsauksmes@unibanka.lv).

Central bank

Latvijas Banka, K Valdemara iela 2a, LV-1050, Riga (tel: 702-2300; fax: 702-2420; e-mail: info@bank.lv).

Stock exchange

Rigas Fondsbørs (Riga Stock Exchange) (RSE), www.omxnordicexchange.com

Travel information

Air Baltic Corporation (ABC), Riga International Airport, Riga LV-1053 (tel: 207-777; fax: 207-505); Kalku iela 15, Riga LV-1050 (tel: 207-777; fax: 722-8284).

LDZ (Latvian Railways), 3 Gogola Street, Riga, LV-1547 (tel: 723-1181; fax: 782-0231; International booking: 721-664; internet: www.ldz.lv).

Latvian Tourism Development Agency, Pils laukums 4, Riga (tel: 722-9945; fax: 750-8468; e-mail: tda@latviatourism.lv).

Lidosta Airport flight enquiries (tel: 207-009; fax: 348-654).

Lufthansa Airport Office (tel: 207-183; fax: 207-026); city centre, Kr Barona iela 7-9, Riga LV-1442 (tel: 728-5614; fax: 782-8199).

Polish Airlines, Maza Pils iela 5, Riga LV 1863 (tel: 724-2870; fax: 724-2869).

Riga International Airport Information (tel: 720-7009; internet site: http://www.riga-airport.com).

Riair (Rigas Aeronavijas), 1 Melluzu Street, Riga LV-1067 (tel: 720-7325; fax: 786-0189).

Riga Bus Station (Autoosta) (tel: 721-3611, 721-3826).

Riga Tourist Information Centre, 22 Skarnu iela (tel: 722-1731; fax: 722-7680; internet: www.rigatourism.com).

SAS, Kalku iela 15, Riga LV 1050 (tel: 721-6139; fax: 722-4282).

Ministry of tourism

Ministry of Environmental Protection and Regional Development, Peldu iela 25, Riga (tel: 702-6492; fax: 782-0442; e-mail: tourism@varam.gov.lv).

National tourist organisation offices

Latvian Tourist Board, Riga 800 Office, Torna iela 4, 1B-103, Riga LV-1050 (tel: 732-0550; fax: 732-0609; e-mail: ltboard@latnet.lv; internet: www.latviatourism.lv).

Ministries

Department of Citizenship and Immigration, 6 Raina Blvd, Riga LV-1181 (tel: 721-9181; fax: 782-0156).

Latvian Customs Department Kr Valdemara iela 1a, Riga LV-1841 (tel: 732-0928; fax: 732-2440).

Ministry of Agriculture, Republikas Laukums 2, Riga LV-1981 (tel: 702-7107; fax: 702-7512).

Ministry of Culture, Kr Valdemara iela 11a, Riga LV-1364 (tel: 722-4772; fax: 722-7916).

Ministry of Defence, Kr Valdemara iela 10-12, Riga LV-1010 (tel: 721-0124; fax: 783-0236).

Ministry of Economics, Brivibas Boulevard 55, LV 1519 Riga (tel: 701-3109; fax: 728-0882); Department of Energy Development (tel: 728-7730, 722-0151; fax: 733-8026, 722-4794).

Ministry of Education, Vajnu iela 2, 1098 Riga (tel: 722-2415; fax: 721-3992; e-mail: vetpmu@com.latnet.lv).

Ministry of Environmental Protection and Regional Development, Peldu St 25, 1494 Riga (tel: 722-3612; fax: 782-0442; e-mail: Saule@varam.gov.lv).

Ministry of Finance, Smilsu iela 1, Riga LV-1919 (tel: 722-6672; fax: 721-1140); World Bank Technical Unit (tel: 722-0348; fax: 782-0168).

Ministry of Foreign Affairs, 36 Brivibas bulv, Riga LV-1395 (tel: 701-6210; fax: 728-2121; e-mail: info@info.gov.lv; internet site: http://www.mfa.gov.lv).

Ministry of the Interior, Raina bulv 6, Riga LV-1533 (tel: 728-7260; fax: 721-2255).

Ministry of Justice, Brivibas bulv 34, Riga LV-1536 (tel: 728-2607; fax: 728-5575).

Ministry of Transport, Gogola iela 3, 1743, Riga (tel: 702-8214; fax: 721-7180).

Ministry of Welfare, Skolas iela 28, Riga LV-1331 (tel: 729-2800; fax: 727-6445).

State Property Fund (privatisation), Ministry of Economics, 36 Brivibas Boulevard, LV 1519 Riga (tel: 213-501; fax: 280-882); external department (tel: 722-5426; fax: 828-223).

Other useful addresses

Association of Insurers, Valnu iela 1, Riga LV-1912 (tel: 722-4375, fax: 724-3286).

Baltic Data House Ltd (marketing research), Akas iela 5/7, Riga LV-1050 (tel: 227-6144; fax: 227-6246, 934-6442).

British Council, Blaumena iela 5a, LV-1050 Riga (tel: 232-0468; fax: 883-0031).

British Embassy, 5 Alunana iela, Riga LV-1010 (tel: 733-8126/31; fax: 733-8132).

Business Centre (to use fax, telex, xerox, e-mail, typing, international telephone) 55 Elizabetes, Hotel 'Latvia' (tel: 722-2211).

Central Statistical Bureau of Latvia, Lacplesa Str, 1 Riga (tel: 727-0126; fax: 782-0166; internet site: www.csb.lv/avidus.cfm).

Commercial Port of Riga, Eksporta iela 6, Riga LV-1242 (tel: 732-5350; fax: 783-0051).

Commercial Port of Ventspils, Dzintaru iela 22, Ventspils LV-3602 (tel: 22-821; 21-231).

Committee for Television & Radio Broadcasting, Doma Laukums 8, Riga LV-226935 (tel: 227-906; fax: 200-025).

Consular Department, Elizabetes iela 57, Riga (tel: 728-6815; 928-7398 (24 hours); fax: 782-8274).

Department of Customs, Kr Valdemara iela 1a, Riga LV-1181 (tel: 721-9639; fax: 733-1123; e-mail: pmlp@pmlp.gov.lv).

Enterprise Support Centre, Perses Str 2, 1011 Riga (tel: 722-7623, 728-9328; fax: 782-0442); External Adviser (tel: 701-3161; fax: 782-8251, 728-0882).

Fire Protection Agency, 5 Maskavas Street, Riga (tel: 220-1322).

Government Information Agency, 36 Brivibas bulv, Riga LV-1070 (tel: 728-2828; fax: 728-4450).

Interlatvija Foreign Trade Association, Komunaru Bulv 1, 226010 Riga (tel: 332-952, 333-597; fax 226-070).

International Advertising Association, Liela Pils iela 9, Riga LV-1755 (tel: 722-8361; fax: 722-9252).

Komunalprojekts AS, 148A Brivibas Blvd, Riga LV 1012 (tel/fax: 237-6920).

Latvian Association of Civil Construction Engineers, 22/24 Grecinieku Street, Riga LV 050 (tel: 721-2661; fax: 722-4832).

Latvian Association of Traders, Kr Barona 48/50, LV-1011 Riga (tel: 721-7372; fax: 782-1010).

Latvian Business Consultants' Association, Jauniela 24, Riga LV-1050 (tel: 722-0320, 782-0076; fax: 722-8926).

Latvian Business Union (commercial information), Bungada PO Box 475, 226001 Riga (tel: 320-888; fax: 217-633).

Latvian Development Agency, Business Information Institute, 2 Perses Street, Riga LV-1442 (tel: 728-3425; fax: 782-0458; e-mail: invest@lda.gov.lv; internet site: www.lda.gov.lv).

Latvian Embassy (USA), 4325 17th Street, NW, Washington DC 20011 (tel: (+1-202) 726-8213; fax: (+1-202) 726-6785; e-mail: embassy@latvia-usa.org).

Latvian Foreign Trade Centre, 2 Elizabetes Street, Riga (tel: 732-0619, 732-1818, 732-2816; fax: 783-0035, 732-3313).

Latvian Privatisation Agency, Kr Valdemara Street 31, Riga LV-1887 (tel: 732-2281, 733-2082; fax: 783-0363; e-mail: lpa@mail.bkc.lv).

Latvian Retailers' Association, Kr Barona iela 48/50, Riga LV-1011 (tel: 721-7372; fax: 782-1010).

Latvian State Radio, 8 Doma Laukums (tel: 720-6722; fax: 720-6709, 782-0216).

Liepaja Special Economic Zone Authority, 4 Feniksa iela, LV-3401 Liepaja (tel: 26-605; fax: 80-252).

Main Post Office, Brivibas Bulvaris 21, Riga (tel: 224-155; fax: 733-1920).

National Environmental Health Centre, 7 Klijanu Street, Riga (tel: 237-7473; fax: 237-5940).

Port of Liepaja, Feniksa iela 4, Liepaja LV-3400 (tel: 342-5887; fax: 789-3418).

Public Investment Unit, Brivibas Blv. 36, 1519 Riga (tel: 701-3122; fax: 782-0458).

Riga City Council, 3 kr Valdemara Street, Riga LV-1539 (tel: 232-0680; fax: 222-0785).

Riga Fairs, Conferences & Exhibitions (tel: 213-637).

Riga Commercial Port, 5a Katrinas Street, Riga LV-1227 (tel: 732-9224; fax: 783-0215; e-mail: rto@mail.bkc.lv).

Rigas Ostas Parvalde (Riga Port Authority), 6 Eksporta St, Riga LV-1010 (tel: 732-2644; fax: 783-0051).

Riga Stock Exchange, Doma Laukums 6, Riga LV-1885 (tel: 721-2431, 722-9449; fax: 722-4515).

Saeima (Parliament), 16 Jekaba (tel: 732-2938; fax: 721-1611).

US Embassy, Raina Bulvaris 7, LV-1050 Riga (tel: 721-0005, 722-0367, 722-9709; fax: 722-6530).

Ventspils Free Port Authority, 8 Uzavas Str, Ventspils LV3601 (tel: 362-2586; fax: 362-1297).

Ventspils Tirdznecibas Osta (Ventspils Commercial Port), 20a Dzintaru Street, Ventspils LV-3602 (tel: 366-8778; fax: 362-1231).

World Trade Centre, Elizabetes iela 2, Riga LV-1340 (tel: 322-242; fax: 7830-0385).

National news agency: LETA (Latvian News Agency), 2 Marijas Street, Riga (tel: 6722-2509; fax: 6722-3850; internet: www.leta.lv).
BNS: www.bns.lv

Delfi (in Latvian and Russian):www.delfi.lv

Internet sites
Baltic News Service: http://www.bns.ee

Business in the Baltic States:
http://www.binet.lv/english/database

Latvian information:
http://www.ciesin.ee/LATVIA/

Pirma banka: http://www.rkb.lv

Trasta Komercbanka: http://www.tkb.lv

Lebanon

KEY FACTS

Official name: Jumhouriya al Lubnaniya (Republic of Lebanon)

Head of State: There is no president currently. Michel Sulayman's term expired on 25 May 2014; the prime minister and his cabinet are temporarily assuming the duties of the president.

Head of government: Prime Minister Tamam Salam (from 14 Feb 2014))

Ruling party: On 15 February 2014, Salam announced a national unity government of 24 ministers including March 8 and March 14 alliances, and independents.

Area: 10,452 square km

Population: 4.51 million (2014)*

Capital: Beirut

Official language: Arabic

Currency: Lebanese pound (LL) = 100 piastres

Exchange rate: LL1,512.70 per US$ (Sep 2015)

GDP per capita: US$11,068 (2014)*

GDP real growth: 2.00% (2014)*

GDP: US$49.92 billion (2014)*

Inflation: 1.85% (2014)*

Balance of trade: -US$15.17 billion (2013)

* estimated figure

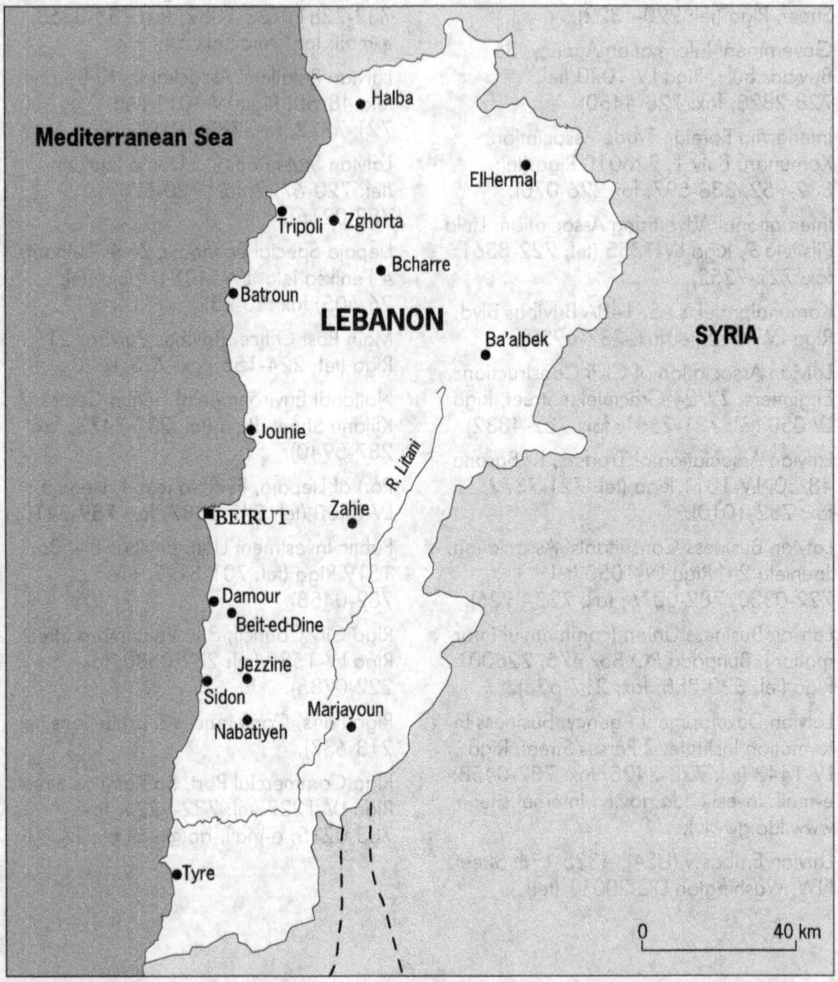

Some thirty odd years after the arrival of Syrian troops as 'peacekeepers' in a period of post civil war uncertainty, Lebanon found itself coping with a different kind of Syrian invasion. An estimated 1.5 million refugees had sought sanctuary in neighbouring – but much smaller – Lebanon. Anecdotal reports suggested that, initially at least, the refugees had been well received, despite the fact that Lebanon's resources, scant enough in the first place, had become seriously over stretched.

As if the problem of the refugees wasn't enough, Lebanon's proximity to what, by 2014 had become the Syrian civil war, hardly improved things. In 2014 Lebanon had to contend with cross border excursions from Syria by both the Islamic State (IS) and al Nusra forces, each content to kidnap and later execute, members of the harassed Lebanese army. By the end of 2014 just how long the initially tolerant reception shown to the Syrians would last was uncertain. When in mid-2014 the Assad regime held its phony elections, the Lebanese reaction to those Syrians who returned 'home' to vote (for Assad, it was assumed) was less than sympathetic.

The anachronism that works

Lebanon has always been seen as an anachronism – mostly by residents of the region that traditionally looked to it for financial probity and business acumen. In mid-2015 the Lebanese Presidency had been vacant since May 2014 and its parliament lacked sufficient consensus to convene to discuss key legislation. Without a president, cabinet can still enact legislation, but only if agreed unanimously by all 24 ministers – which had become very difficult given the current political fissures. The Lebanese constitution dictates that the President should be a Maronite Christian. By the end of May 2015 there had been 22 sessions of parliament since the end of Michel Suleiman's presidency a year earlier. This was not the first time the country had been without a president for any length of time – between 1988 and 1989 it had gone 408 days without. Mr Suleiman's presidency had followed an interval of 184 days without a head of state. Parliament's term has been extended (for a second time) to June 2017, adding to concerns as to its legitimacy. In this environment, a few targeted policy actions would send a strong signal about the country's will and determination to move forward despite the many challenges ahead.

And challenges there were in abundance. In 2015 Lebanon continued to suffer extensively, first from its domestic political stalemate. The parties involved were the March 14 grouping, lead by the Sunni politician Saad Hariri, the son of Rafic Hariri, who had served as prime minister from 2009 until 2011. Strongly influenced by Saudi Arabia, Mr Hariri's parliamentary allies were the Druze and some Christian factions. Opposing them were the March 8 group, headed up by the Christian General Michel Aun alongside Shi'a Hezbollah strongly influenced by Iran. The octogenarian General Aun held presidential aspirations.

And secondly, from the regional turmoil, particularly along its border with Syria. Although the influx of Syrian refugees had decelerated significantly following the government's decision to impose entry restrictions, the impact at street level was undeniable. A substantial black economy had proliferated within and around the refugee community. The United Nations High Commission for Refugees (UNHCR) had registered 1.1 million Syrian refugees by May 2015. Syrian refugees accounted for over 25 per cent of the population. It was not only entry requirements that had been tightened up. Spot checks and inspections by the security forces within Lebanon had resulted in the arrest and detention of an estimated 2,000 male Syrian refugees.

The economy

Lebanon's economic survival against all the odds can probably be attributed to one factor: its international diaspora is estimated to be some 10 million strong. The natural business acumen of the Lebanese has enabled them to prosper world-wide, not only in the Gulf states, but also in West Africa, Latin America, Asia and even Australia. The Lebanese nation has been described as one of 'rich refugees'.

If the international acumen and awareness of Lebanese banks is an important asset, so is their discretion. Beirut is the financial centre of first recourse for every Saudi Arabian merchant, self aggrandised Middle eastern politician, for the profits and revenues from Afghanistan's opium trade and from Somalia's tanker pirates. Most of the funds deposited in this way never show up in the annual macro-economic information. But it strengthens the balance sheets of Lebanon's banks and by extension, generates wealth and prosperity within the country.

According to the World Bank in the spring 2015 edition of its *Lebanon Economic Monitor*, economic activity picked up in the second half of 2014. The stronger economic performance and lower oil prices pushed gross domestic product (GDP) growth to an estimated 2.0 per cent in 2014, compared to 0.9 per cent in 2013, led by private demand. Renewed improvement in security conditions so far in 2015 and the launch of dialogue between opposing political parties were expected to generate consumer and investor confidence. In addition, the low oil prices were expected to have a positive net impact on the economy. As a result, real GDP growth in 2015 was projected to further accelerate to 2.5 per cent.

One-off cosmetic and unsustainable measures rather than policy actions also helped improve the fiscal balance in 2014. The World Bank estimated the overall fiscal deficit to have declined by 2.3 percentage points to reach 7.2 per cent of GDP and the primary balance to have reverted back to surplus after two years in deficit. An increase in domestic debt service, however, had driven public debt higher, albeit at a slower rate than a year earlier, to around 145.7 per cent of GDP by the end of 2014. In 2015, reduced transfers to Electricité du Liban (EdL) from falling oil prices are expected to be offset by higher debt servicing due to expected tightening of US interest rates to, leaving the fiscal position largely unchanged.

According to the World Bank, in 2014, a fall in merchandise imports induced a 4.4 per cent reduction in the current account deficit to a still-elevated 22.2 per cent of GDP. This trend was projected to continue in 2015 helped by falling oil prices and a depreciating euro, further narrowing the deficit by a projected 5.5 per cent. As a result, Lebanon's gross foreign reserves (excluding gold) at the Banque du Liban (BDL) (Bank of Lebanon) (central bank) reached US$32.4 billion (equivalent to 11.6 months of imported goods) by end-2014.

Headline inflation plummeted from 2.7 per cent in 2013 to 1.9 per cent in 2014 and was expected to remain tempered over the medium term. This, in addition to exchange rate stability and a sizable output gap, supported the government's

KEY INDICATORS — Lebanon

	Unit	2011	2012	2013	2014	**2015
Population	m	*3.96	*4.42	*4.47	*4.51	*4.55
Gross domestic product (GDP)	US$bn	39.00	42.52	47.60	*49.92	*54.67
GDP per capita	US$	9,862	9,609	10,655	*11,068	*12,006
GDP real growth	%	1.5	1.5	2.5	*2.0	*2.5
Inflation	%	5.0	5.9	4.8	*1.9	*1.1
Exports (fob) (goods)	US$m	5,385.5	5,615.3	4,498.8	–	–
Imports (fob) (goods)	US$m	19,304.4	20,326.9	19,672.3	–	–
Balance of trade	US$m	-13,918.9	-14,711.6	-15,173.5	–	–
Current account	US$m	-4,887.0	-6,696.0	-12,731.0	*-12,451.0	*-12,146.0
Total reserves minus gold	US$m	31,066.2	37,158.6	36,748.0	39,547.1	–
Foreign exchange	US$m	30,702.2	36,836.6	636,398.5	–	–
Exchange rate	per US$	1,507.50	1,507.50	1,503.00	1,512.00	–

* estimated figure ** forecast figure

continued expansionary monetary policy; the central bank injected US$800 million dollars in 2014, with an additional injection expected in 2015, in the form of subsidised loans primarily destined for the real estate sector.

However, the World Bank noted that Lebanon's economy continued to be exposed to external shocks. The border with Syria was increasingly menacing as co-ordinated attacks by IS and al Nusra are being launched more frequently from their bases in Syria. Moreover, with reasonable prospects of the US Federal Reserve tightening monetary policies in 2015, Lebanon would be bound to follow suit to maintain the margin on US$ deposits in Lebanon. This would have a negative impact on lending to the private sector and raise Lebanon's large debt service, as new debt would need to be contracted at higher interest rates given large gross financing needs.

Surprisingly, according to the World Bank, the evidence suggested that Lebanon's international trade had not been negatively impacted by the Syrian conflict. In the view of the Bank, the war seemed to have affected neither merchandise nor services exports. Where Lebanese exporters to Syria had suffered from a drop in demand in the Syrian market, other Lebanese exporters had started to export to Syria to fill the gap in Syrian production. Additionally, Syrian refugees in Lebanon provided an important impetus to Lebanese services exports.

Expensive electricity, water shortages

Inefficiencies in power generation imposed a sizable macro-economic cost on Lebanon. In the view of the World Bank, the Lebanese electricity sector had been under-performing for decades with considerable socio-economic costs. The macro-economic impact had been massive; accruing debt on investments in and transfers to EdL amounted to 40 per cent of Lebanon's gross public debt, while transfers have accounted for over half of the fiscal deficit. Going forward, transfers to EdL will be significantly lower on current oil prices. Some of the measures needed to improve EdL's financial situation are well known, such as increased investment, tariff reforms and corporatisation of EdL. Political and confessional obstacles, however, have so far hindered any progress. Since the beginning of the civil war in 1975 Lebanon has been without what would pass as a 'normal' supply of electricity. The destruction or collapse of basic infrastructure such as power stations has left the field open to privateers who can charge what they want to supply electricity when they can, or feel like doing so.

Water-supply shortages in what is the region's most water-rich country would seem to be an absurdity. However, despite the relative availability of water resources, Lebanon has long suffered from serious shortages of water supply. To make matters worse, the cost of inaction in the water sector has been estimated at about 1.8 per cent of GDP or 2.8 per cent of GDP if the cost of environmental degradation is included and in the opinion of the World Bank the Lebanese government needed to address the sector's priorities urgently.

In its annual assessment of the Lebanese economy, the International Monetary Fund (IMF) noted that growth had decelerated significantly. Following the fall from 8 per cent in 2010 to less than 1 per cent in 2011, growth had inched upward to around 2–3 per cent, but remained well short of its potential. Inflation had also declined sharply in 2014, owing to lower oil prices and a number of additional one-off developments, but was expected to return to a trend rate of about 3 per cent in 2015. In this regard, lower inflation had essentially offset the recent appreciation of the Lebanese pound (pegged to the US dollar), leaving Lebanon's effective exchange rate broadly unchanged.

The IMF considered that rising uncertainty was taking a toll on the economy, but incomes and consumption were receiving a temporary boost from lower oil prices. Lebanon's traditional growth sectors – tourism, real estate and construction – had all taken a significant blow and a strong rebound was unlikely in the immediate future. Indeed, early indications for 2015 pointed to a marked softening of the construction sector, particularly for high-end residential projects. However, the pass-through of global oil prices to local fuel prices is relatively high in Lebanon, so the recent drop in global prices would boost local incomes. Remittance inflows, a significant portion of which come from oil-exporting Gulf countries, had been stable in the face of volatile oil prices. Projections also suggested that activity in key oil exporting countries would remain steady, as financial buffers were expected to cushion any adverse impact on growth. Taking all these factors into account, the IMF estimated Lebanon's GDP growth at about 2 per cent in 2014 (slightly less than the previous year) and projected a similarly modest rate for 2015.

Domestic demand was expected to remain relatively subdued from 2016 onward and the economy's medium-term recovery would probably be driven mostly by the normalisation of broader global conditions. Thus, Lebanon's return to potential growth (4 per cent) was now unlikely before 2019. Exceptional factors had allowed for a welcome primary surplus in 2014, but without decisive action fiscal deterioration looked set to resume in 2015. At an unexpected 2.5 per cent of GDP, the 2014 primary surplus largely resulted from unusually high telecom transfers (part of which, estimated at about one per cent of GDP, would be transferred to Lebanon's municipalities in 2015), the non-implementation of a much-awaited salary increase for the public sector and, to some extent, withheld and delayed payments. Without a repetition of these one-off factors, the IMF projected that the country's primary balance would probably deteriorate to almost 1.25 per cent of GDP in 2015, with public debt remaining at 132 per cent of GDP, very high by international standards.

Hezbollah

Lebanon's Hezbollah is strongly aligned with Iran. It was formed around 1984 under the wing of the Iraqi Dawa Party in exile. Its main objective was ending the Israeli occupation of 10 per cent of Lebanon's territory, which began in 1982. Its rival, the Amal Party (now the Amal Movement), was more middle-class and less connected to Iran, even though it was also made up of Shi'ites. Exit polls suggest that roughly half of voters who vote for Hezbollah among Lebanese Shi'ites are non-religious; they are supporting it for nationalist reasons and seeking self-defence against Israeli incursions. Lebanon is a country of only 4 million and the Twelver Shi'ites are only about a third of the population, some 1.3 million, most of whom are children. The way in which Hezbollah has been built up in the Western imagination as a major force is a little bizarre, given that they have only a few thousand fighters. In 2015 Hezbollah maintained a strong alliance with Lebanese Christians and Druze because all three broadly support the government of Bashar al Assad in Syria. But Lebanese politics are kaleidoscopic and that political dominance could change abruptly. Lebanese Shi'ites are no more the pawns of Iran than are the Lebanese Christians, many of them now allied with the Shi'ites and Alawites as well.

Risk assessment

Economy	Fair
Politics	Poor
Regional stability	Poor

Muslims in Lebanon

% of population	59.7
Sunni (% of Muslims)	27
Shi'a (% of Muslims)	50

COUNTRY PROFILE

1926 The constitution was approved and the Lebanese Republic declared.
1940 Lebanon came under the control of the Vichy French government.
1941 After occupation by Free French and British troops, independence was declared.
1943 France agreed to the transfer of power to the Lebanese government with effect from 1944.
1948 A major influx of Arab refugees from Palestine built tensions between Christian Maronites and Muslim Shi'as.
1958 The first civil war erupted between Muslim and Christian groups
1964 Yasser Arafat established a Palestine Liberation Organisation (PLO) stronghold in Lebanon.
1970 Anti-Israeli terrorist attacks from Lebanese bases increased after the PLO was expelled from Jordan. Israeli retaliations further alienated leftist Muslims from conservative Maronites (the largest Christian sect) and undermined governmental legitimacy, with nine changes in three years.
1975 Full-scale civil war erupted between Muslims (with PLO aid) and Christians. Southern Lebanon and the western half of Beirut became bases for the PLO and other Muslim militias, while the Christians controlled East Beirut and the Christian section of Mt Lebanon.
1976 A 30,000-strong Arab Deterrent Force was established to restore peace.
1978 In reprisal for an attack by Palestinians based in Lebanon, Israel invaded and occupied the south of the country; the UN called on Israel to withdraw its troops; it handed over the territory to the mainly Christian Lebanese militia.
1982 Hezbollah (Party of God) was formed by Muslim clerics, backed by Iran and Syria, to respond to the Israeli invasion of Lebanon and to advocate the establishment of an Islamic government (it became a political movement in 1985 and entered parliament in 1992). Israel launched a full-scale invasion after an assassination attempt on Shlomo Argov, its ambassador to the UK. Syria, which maintained a large army in Lebanon, unsuccessfully fought Israel. Christian Phalangist militiamen, with Israeli compliance, massacred more than 1,000 Palestinian refugees in the Sabra and Shatila camps. A Western multinational force monitored the evacuation of the PLO to Tunis.
1983 Hostilities between Israel and Lebanon ended. Syrian forces remained in Lebanon.
1985 Despite withdrawing from most of the territory, Israel maintained some troops in support of the mainly Christian South Lebanon Army (SLA) (a militia set up and supported by Israel) in order to help secure its own northern border.
1986–90 Factional conflict worsened as various efforts at national reconciliation failed. Lebanon had two governments – one mainly Muslim in West Beirut, headed by Salim al Huss, the other, Christian, in East Beirut, led by the Maronite Commander-in-Chief of the Army, General Michel Aoun.
1989 Under the Ta'if Accord, a government of national reconciliation was formed with an equal number of Christian and Muslim members. Elias Hrawi was elected president.
1990 The civil war ended and General Aoun fled.
1992 President Hrawi appointed Rafik al Hariri as prime minister, heading a cabinet of technocrats. Al Hariri, a rich businessman, born in Sidon but with Saudi Arabian nationality, became the mastermind behind the reconstruction of Lebanon.
1993–97 The Oslo Peace Accords laid the basis for transfer of authority from the Israeli military administration to the PLO in the Gaza Strip and an undefined area around the town of Jericho in the West Bank. A follow-up treaty, Oslo II, envisaged Palestinian autonomy, with Israeli troop units withdrawing from the West Bank. Yasser Arafat was elected president of the Palestinian Legislative Council (PLC), the assembly of the Palestinian National Authority (PNA). Attacks and reprisals continued between Hezbollah and Palestinian guerrillas, and Israel.
1998 The National Assembly elected army chief of staff, General Émile Lahoud, as president, replacing Elias Hrawi. Following the resignation of Prime Minister al Hariri, Salim al Huss was appointed to the post.
2000 The Israeli army withdrew from southern Lebanon and the SLA disbanded. Sporadic clashes continued between Hezbollah and Israeli forces. Rafik al Hariri won convincingly at the elections and was re-appointed prime minister.
2003 Israeli warplanes and artillery attacked suspected Hezbollah positions in the disputed Shebaa Farms area in south Lebanon in retaliation for guerrilla attacks.
2004 Syria insisted that President Lahoud's term in office be extended until 2007, which was approved by parliament. UN Security Council resolution 1559 demanded that Syrian soldiers leave Lebanon and that Hezbollah disarm. Rafik al Hariri opposed the extension of Lahoud's term and stood down as prime minister; Omar Karami was nominated for the post.
2005 Former prime minister Rafik al Hariri was assassinated. Syria was accused of supporting the perpetrators. Thousands of protesters gathered in Beirut, demanding the withdrawal of Syrian troops; the pro-Syrian government resigned. Syria agreed to withdraw its troops to the Bekaa valley in eastern Lebanon. Najib Mikati became prime minister of a mixed pro- and anti-Syrian cabinet. Syrian troops pulled out of Lebanon. In parliamentary elections, Hariri-Jumblatt, the bloc led by Saad al Hariri (son of Rafik al Hariri), won 72 seats, the Shi'a Muslim bloc of Amal and Hezbollah won 35 seats and the anti-Syrian Michel Aoun and allies won 21 seats. Fouad Siniora became prime minister. He formed a cabinet which mostly included those opposed to Syrian involvement in Lebanon but also included – for the first time – ministers of the Hezbollah and Amal movements. Four pro-Syrian generals were charged with the assassination of Rafik al Hariri, following the findings of the UN's chief investigator.
2006 Israel bombed southern Lebanon after Hezbollah kidnapped two Israeli soldiers while raiding Israel. Israel invaded the south attempting to retrieve its soldiers but after 34 days of fighting without a conclusive victory and the death of approximately 1,000 Lebanese, the Israelis agreed to a truce. Israeli troops withdrew and the Lebanese army deployed along the border. Hezbollah claimed the war was 'a strategic and historical victory for Lebanon against the Israeli enemy'. Plans for a UN tribunal to prosecute the suspects in the Rafik al Hariri assassination led to the resignation of ministers of Hezbollah and the Amal.
2007 International donors pledged US$7.4 billion in aid towards reconstruction and the repayment of war debt at a conference held in Paris. The anti-Syrian politician, Antoine Ghanim, was assassinated. Syria denied responsibility. The death of Ghanim plus several more assassinations of anti-Syrian members of parliament reduced the government's majority and with the lack of a quorum forced the first presidential vote in parliament to be postponed. A compromise candidate for president, Michel Suleiman, won backing from all political parties. However, as a serving military officer, the constitution had to be amended to allow his candidacy. In order to gain enough support Suleiman had to agree a shortened

presidential term in office, to end in 2009 instead of 2013, and an appointed prime minister with neutral allegiances. Presidential elections were postponed several more times.

2008 The Lebanese National Dialogue Conference between religious blocs and political parties agreed to new electoral laws, whereby the128-seat Majlis al Nuwab (parliament) was allocated equally between Christians and Muslims with 64 seats each; while individual constituencies were elected by proportional representation among religious communities (confessionally distributed). Elections for president were again postponed until General Michel Suleiman was finally elected president; he received 118 votes out of 127 and was sworn in immediately. Prime Minister Siniora announced the formation of a national unity government with members from all political and religious blocs. An agreed common border was formally demarcated between Lebanon and Syria, in a move to improve diplomatic relations. Syria opened an embassy in Beirut.

2009 President Suleiman approved the appointment of Mr Ali Abdul Karim Ali as Syrian ambassador to Lebanon, thereby re-establishing full diplomatic relations for the first time since the 1940s. A former Syrian security officer suspected of assassinating Rafik al Hariri was detained in Dubai on an international arrest warrant. Before he could be extradited to Denmark to the Special Tribunal for Lebanon (STL) at the International Court of Justice (ICJ) he absconded. In parliamentary elections, within the 14 March Alliance (Christians), the Maronites won 34 seats, the Greek Orthodox 14; within the 8 March Alliance (Muslims) the Shi'a (Hezbollah) and Sunni each won 27 seats. Saad al Hariri was nominated as prime minister by President Suleiman; 86 members of parliament confirmed his appointment. Hezbollah agreed to join a unity government under Prime Minister Hariri, breaking a four month deadlock over the appointment of a government; 15 ministers were nominated from the 14 March Alliance and 10 from the 8 March Alliance; the president nominated five appointees for the remaining ministries.

2010 Prime Minister Hariri visited Syria to discuss bilateral relations and closer ties. Hariri said his accusation that Syria was responsible for the murder of his father was an error and that it was a 'political accusation'.

2011 In January, the Hezbollah group of 10 cabinet ministers resigned and therefore the whole cabinet was considered resigne; Saad Hariri remained care taker prime minister. In June, the chief prosecutor of the STL issued indictments for four senior members of Hezbollah – Assad Sabra, Hassan Issa, Salim Ayachhe and Moustaf Badredine accused of the assassination of former prime minister Rafiq Hariri in 2005. Hariri refused to reject the indictments and the president, with the agreement of 68 of 125 members of parliament, appointed Hezbollah-backed candidate, Najib Mikati, as the new prime minister. The authorities asked Hezbollah to hand over the suspects for trial; failing which they would be tried *in absentia*.

2012 On 2 February, the STL proceeded with the prosecution of the four Hezbollah suspects in the assassination of Rafik al Hariri *in absentia*. The STL said that Lebanese authorities had tried to apprehend the accused and give notice of the charges against them. The leaders of Hezbollah have refused to surrender the accused and deny any role in the killing of Hariri and 21 others. On 19 October, chief security officer Wissam al Hassan was assassinated in a car bomb in central Beirut. He was a leading critic of the Syrian regime and the suspicion was that Syria was responsible for his death.

2013 A car bomb wounded many people in a stronghold of Lebanon's Shi'a militant group Hezbollah in Beirut. Prime Minister Najib Mikati submitted his resignation on 22 March. On 7 April Tammam Salam was nominated as prime minister; he was backed by parties across the political spectrum, including Hezbollah. On 22 July the EU agreed to list the military wing of militant group Hezbollah as a terrorist organisation. A fifth person, Hassan Habib Merhi, was indicted in August on charges related to the murder of Rafik Hariri. On 22 August rockets were fired from the Shi'a (Hezbollah) area of southern Lebanon into Israel. In retaliation Israel said an air strike targeted a 'terror site' the following day. By mid-October, interim Prime Minister Tammam Salam had still to form a government.

2014 Tammam Salam was finally able to form a government and was sworn in as prime minister on 14 February. On 25 May President Michel Suleiman's term in office ended without a successor being named. Prime Minister Salam became Acting President the same day. On 5 November parliament extended its term until June 2017.

2015 In January the authorities moved to tighten entry requirements for Syrians entering the country. The United Nations High Commission for Refugees (UNHCR) reported it had registered 1.1 million Syrian refugees by May.

Political structure

Constitution

The Constitution was enacted in May 1926, and has since been amended on five occasions. A key amendment agreed under the Ta'if Agreement of 1989 reduced the authority of the president by transferring executive power to the cabinet. The prime minister must be a Sunni Muslim, with the cabinet made up of equal numbers of Muslims and Christians. An amendment to the Constitution was introduced in 2000, reducing the minimum age of a president from 40 to 34 years. Following the Lebanese National Dialogue Conference, in 2007, between religious blocs and political parties, an agreement was reached for new electoral laws, whereby the128-seat parliament is allocated equally between Christians and Muslims at 64 seats each; while individual constituencies are elected by proportional representation among religious communities (confessionally distributed).

Independence date

22 November 1943.

Form of state

Republic

The executive

As head of state, the president is indirectly elected for a single six-year term (eligible for non-consecutive terms) by the National Assembly. Under the constitution, the president chooses the prime minister upon recommendation from the parliament. The prime minister, who must be a Sunni Muslim, is responsible for choosing members of the 30-member Council of Ministers (cabinet). Ministers may be selected from inside or outside parliament.

National legislature

The Majlis al Nuwab (unicameral National Assembly) has 128 parliamentary members (MP), directly elected in multi-seat constituencies by majority vote for a four-year term. Seats are apportioned among the Christian and Muslim denominations.

Parliament tried to amend the voting age from 21 to 18 on 22 February 2010 but it failed to pass.

Legal system

The legal system is based on the 1926 constitution and the Commercial Code, the Civil Procedure Code, the Criminal Procedure Code and the Penal Code. French law has had a lasting impact on local legislation, while Ottoman law and Islamic law have also influenced Lebanon's legal system. Civil law is based on the Code of Obligations and Contracts and the Land Ownership Law. Various branches of the legal framework are being revised and updated. Lebanon has an independent judiciary.

Last elections

7 July 2009 (parliamentary); 23 April 2014 (presidential)

Results: Parliamentary: 14 March Alliance including Tayyar Al Mustaqbal (Future Movement) (Future) (Maronite), Hizb

al Taqadummi al Ishtiraki (Progressive Socialists Party) (PSP) (Druze), Al Quwat al Lubnaniyya (Lebanese Forces) (LF) (Maronite), Hizb al-Kataeb (Kataeb Party) and others won 71 seats (out of 128). The 8 March Alliance, including Hezbollah (Shi'a); Harakat Amal (Amal Movement) (Sunni); Al Hizb al Qawmi al souri al ijtima'I (Syrian Social Nationalist Party), Ba'arth (Arab Socialist Ba'arth Party) and others won 29 seats. Change and Reform alliance, including Tayyar Al Watani Al Horr (Free Patriotic Movement) (FPM) (Maronite), Marada Movement, Armenian Revolutionary Federation and Lebanese Democratic Party won 28 seats.
Presidential First Round: Samir Geagea (Quwwat al-Libnaniyah) (Lebanese Forces Party) won 48 votes (out of 128) (38 per cent), Henri Helou won 16 votes (13 per cent) and Amine Gemayel (Kataeb Party) won one vote (one per cent). No majority could be reached in this round or any subsequent round.
There is no president currently. Michel Sulayman's term expired on 25 May 2014; the prime minister and his cabinet are temporarily assuming the duties of the president. The next round of elections are to be held in 2020.

Next elections

2017 (parliamentary), 2020 (presidential).

Political parties

Ruling party

On 15 February 2014, Salam announced a national unity government of 24 ministers including March 8 and March 14 alliances, and independents.

Population

4.51 million (2014)*
Last census: 3 March 2007: 3,759,134 (excluding Palestinian refugees in camps)
Population density: Urban population 87 per cent (2010 Unicef).
Annual growth rate: 1.8 per cent, 1990–2010 (Unicef).

Internally Displaced Persons (IDP)

300,000 (UNHCR 2004)

Ethnic make-up

The Lebanese belong to a single ethnic grouping, Levanto Arab, which encompasses the people of the Levant coast from northern Syria to southern Palestine. Armenians and Kurds have settled in Lebanon and there are Syrian troops and many Syrian workers.

Religions

There are 17 recognised religious groupings in Lebanon. Five predominate: Shi'a Muslims, Sunni Muslims, Maronite (Catholic) Christians, Greek Orthodox Christians and Druze.

Education

Education is mainly run by private enterprises and the religious sector. State schools exist and are free of charge. Primary education lasts for nine years.
The civil war severely disrupted state education at all levels and by the end of the civil war in 1990, 1,270 schools throughout the country needed rehabilitation at an estimated cost of US$65 million. Public expenditure on education is equivalent to approximately 2.5 per cent of annual GNP.
There is a government-run Lebanese National University, but the major universities continue to be operated by the US, France and Egypt. There are over 10 universities in Beirut.
Literacy rate: 86.1 per cent total, 81.4 per cent female, adult rates (World Bank).
Compulsory years: None
Enrolment rate: 111 per cent total primary enrolment of the relevant age group (including repetition rates); 81 per cent total secondary enrolment (World Bank).

Health

A Social Security Fund covers the health expenses of workers.

HIV/Aids

HIV prevalence: 0.1 per cent aged 15–49 in 2003 (World Bank)
Life expectancy: 70 years, 2004 (WHO 2006)
Fertility rate/Maternal mortality rate: 1.8 births per woman, 2010 (Unicef); maternal mortality 100 per 100,000 live births (World Bank).
Child (under 5 years) mortality rate (per 1,000): 9 per 1,000 live births (WHO 2012); 3 per cent of children aged under five are malnourished (World Bank).
Head of population per physician: 3.25 physicians per 1,000 people, 2001 (WHO 2006)

Welfare

Since 1963, Lebanon has operated a social insurance system offering lump sum benefits only. Social insurance covers employees in industry, commerce and agriculture, but excludes temporary agricultural employees and those previously entitled to special benefits under the labour code.
In 1999, old age pensions were available to men aged over 60, but compulsory for those aged over 64. The benefit included a lump sum amount equivalent to the average monthly earnings during the last 12 months or the final month. The rate for disability benefit is a lump sum equal to the final month's earnings multiplied by the number of years in service. Widows receive 25 per cent of their former spouse's benefit. There are no sickness or maternity benefits. Workers receive medical benefits for up to 26 weeks or 52 weeks in special cases. Family allowances are employment-related and are available to employees with a non-working wife or with one to five children. The maximum monthly allowance is equivalent to 75 per cent of the minimum wage.

Main cities

Beirut (capital, estimated population 2.1 million in 2012), Tripoli (195,932), Jounieh 102,221), Sidon (59,948), Zahlé (55,081).

Languages spoken

French and English are widely spoken in business circles.

Official language/s

Arabic

Media

Freedom of the press is practiced but there are laws forbidding defaming the president and other heads of states and inciting sectarian strife.

Press

Dailies: In Arabic *An Nahar* (www.annahar.com), *Al Safir* (www.assafir.com), *Al Anwar* (www.alanwar.com), *Al Diyar* (www.journaladdiyar.com), *Al Mustaqbal* (http://almustaqbal.com) with affiliation to the Future Movement. In Armenian *Aztag Daily* (www.aztagdaily.com). In French *L'Orient-Le Jour* (www.lorient-lejour.com.lb) is the country's fifth-largest newspaper. In English *The Daily Star* (www.dailystar.com.lb).
Weeklies: In Arabic, *Al Shiraa Magazine* (www.alshiraa.com) and *Al Afkar* (www.alafkar.net) for politics; *Al Noujoum* (www.alnoujoum.com) for celebrity news and *Al Jaras* (www.aljaras.com) for entertainment news. In French, *L'Hebdo Magazine* (www.magazine.com.lb) for news and current affairs and *La Revue du Liban* (www.rdl.com.lb) is a news review In English *Monday Morning* (www.mmorning.com) for general news.
Business: In Arabic *Al Markazia* (www.immarwaiktissad.com) with articles on finance and current affairs and the monthly *Al Iktissad Wal Aamal* (www.iktissad.com) covers Arab business and economic news. In English, the UK-based monthly magazine *Executive* (http://executive-magazine.com) offers articles on Lebanese world of commerce in major sectors.
Periodicals: Monthly women's magazines include *Snob Magazine* (www.snobmagazine.com) in Arabic, is aimed at a young female audience and in French, *Femme* (www.femmemag.com.lb) is aimed at an older readership while *Noun* (www.noun.com.lb) is aimed at a sophisticated female market. In Arabic, *Al*

Mustiqbal Al Arabi (www.caus.org.lb) is an academic publication on Arab matters.

Broadcasting

The Lebanese Broadcasting Company (LBCI) is privately owned. In 1996, Lebanon banned broadcasts of political programmes and news by about 50 private television stations and 150 radio stations and ordered them to close. Political broadcasting is restricted to four TV stations and three radio outlets controlled by the pro-government establishment.

Radio: The government gives permission to operators to broadcast and limits which station may broadcasts the news.

Radio Liban (www.96-2.com) is state-run with nationwide reception. There are many private, commercial stations including Mix FM (www.mixfm.com.lb), NBN (www.nbn.com.lb) and NRG Beirut (www.nrjlebanon.com). International broadcasts are relayed through local stations.

Television: Viewing of satellite and cable television is widespread.

Tele-Liban is the state-run channel. Other, private, commercial channels include the Lebanese Broadcasting Corporation (LBC) (www.lbcgroup.tv) the market leader with regional and international coverage through satellite transmissions. Its political stance is towards the Christian community. Future Television (www.future.com.lb) is affiliated to a Sunni Muslim political movement (Tayyar Al Mustaqbal (Future Movement). Orange TV (www.otv.com.lb) is a publicly owned station which began broadcasting in 2007. Al Manar (www.almanar.com.lb) is a station affiliated to the Hezbollah. The Lebanon-based news station Al Jaheed (www.akjadeed.tv) broadcasts throughout the region.

Cable Vision (www.cablevision-leb.net) is the largest of the cable TV services.

National news agency: NNA (National News Agency): www.nna-leb.gov.lb

Other news agencies: Central News Agency: www.almarkazia.com

Economy

Lebanon has a strong tradition as an open market, trade-orientated economy. Coupled with strong banking laws and a high ratio of 50 per cent liquid assets to short-term loans its banking system has not been subject to the high level of toxic debts prevailing elsewhere. Thus, while the world experienced a global economic crisis and world trade fell, Lebanon experienced GDP growth of 0.6 per cent in 2006, rising to 7.5 per cent in 2007 as rebuilding after the Israeli invasion began. Lebanon's period of high growth continued from 2007–10, averaging 9.2 per cent, before dropping to 2.0 per cent in 2011, and remaining slow into 2014 at 2.0 per cent.

Lebanon is one of the world's largest recipients of remittances, which in 2013 was US$7.6 billion (17.4 per cent of GDP), increasing to US$8.9 billion in 2014 (19.5 per cent of GDP). Over 50 per cent of all remittances originate from Gulf Co-operation Council (GCC) states.

The service sector (mainly banking and tourism) is by far the dominant component of the economy at 72.6 per cent of GDP in 2014. Industry provides 21.1 per cent, of which manufacturing accounted for around 9 per cent of GDP, with the remainder provided by agriculture (6.3 per cent).

The main exports are manufactured goods, including jewellery, machinery, textiles and paper, plus chemicals and fruit and vegetables, such as citrus, grapes, tobacco and live animals. However, Lebanon has to import most of its commodities and typically maintains a negative current account balance (-US$12.5 billion in 2014).

A law allowing Palestinian refugees to work legally was passed by parliament in 2010; there are estimated to be some 400,000 Palestinians in Lebanon.

External trade

Lebanon belongs to the Greater Arab Free Trade Area (Gafta), which has 17 members, creating an Arab economic bloc. A customs union was established whereby tariffs within Gafta will be reduced by a percentage each year, until none remain. Lebanon is also a signatory of the Euro-Mediterranean Partnership agreement, which provides for the introduction of free trade between the EU and 10 Mediterranean countries. A new free-trade zone, including visa-free travel for their nationals, was agreed in June 2010, between Turkey, Lebanon, Jordan and Syria. A co-operation council will be established to 'develop a long-term strategic partnership' to encourage free movement of goods and persons.

In 2015 Lebanon was close to full membership of the WTO, having progressed to the outline phase for terms of membership.

Around 65 per cent of GDP is provided by foreign trade, with recent growth in the IT (information technology) sector, although financial services still provide the lion's share.

Imports

Major imports include petroleum products, vehicles, medicine, clothing, meat and live animals, consumer goods, paper, textiles and tobacco.

Main sources: China (11.8 per cent of total in 2014), Italy (7.7 per cent), France (6.2 per cent)

Exports

Commodity exports include gems and jewellery, electrical and electronic equipment, minerals such as salt and sulphur, iron and steel, consumer goods and construction materials.

Main destinations: Saudi Arabia (10.8 per cent of total in 2014), UAE (9.7 per cent) and Syria (8.7 per cent).

Agriculture

Farming

The agricultural sector contributes 6.3 per cent to GDP but the sector has still not recovered from the effects of the civil war. While agricultural exports have shown signs of recovery, they earn only around US$233 million compared with expenditure of US$1.5 billion on imports of agricultural produce. Main goods for export are surplus products such as apples, citrus fruit and potatoes.

Agricultural and farming activities are in private hands. The land tenure system and difficult terrain has resulted in the majority of farmland being divided into small relatively uneconomic units. This has acted as a disincentive to investment in irrigation and mechanisation. The government provides little aid to the sector, which has had to compete with heavily subsidised produce from other countries.

The relatively mild climate allows for diversified agricultural production. Main crops: wheat, barley, maize, vegetables, potatoes, fruit, olives and tobacco. Farmers have started the cultivation of advanced cash crops, such as avocados and flowers.

Goats, cattle and sheep are the main types of livestock raised in Lebanon.

One-third of Lebanon's land is cultivable with 400,000 hectares of arable land, of which 25 per cent is irrigated. The main agricultural areas are in the Beka'a valley, the Akkar plain, the coastal plain and the foothills of the central mountain range.

Most of these areas were badly affected by war. Agriculture in the south and in the Beka'a valley was particularly affected.

Agriculture remains an important source of income in rural areas, and although it is difficult to estimate the number of full-time farmers, most families conduct or participate in agriculture as a part-time activity.

Fishing

Despite Lebanon's extensive coastline, commercial fishing remains a minor activity, contributing less than one per cent to GDP annually.

Forestry

Forest cover amounts to less than 13.4 per cent of total land area.

Industry and manufacturing

Industry and manufacturing is small to medium scale. The sector accounts for

around 19.8 per cent of GDP and employs 21 per cent of the workforce. The main products are building materials, textiles and clothing, food processing and furniture.
Construction employs about 6 per cent of the workforce. Industry provides more than 40 per cent of Lebanon's merchandised export earnings.

Tourism
Beirut was once called the Paris of the Middle East for its liberal-minded, open, commercial and café society but, along with the rest of Lebanon, Beirut has suffered from the conflicts and violence in the region. Lebanon offers many historical sites reaching back into antiquity, of which several are included on Unesco's World Heritage List. It also offers modern activities for a large expatriate population and luxury accommodation for wealthy visitors from the region.
The travel and tourism sector has become less important to the economy, dropping from a contribution to GDP of 35.1 per cent in 2011 to 21.1 per cent in 2014. Likewise it provided employment to 448,300 in 2011, dropping to 313,000 jobs in 2014 (20.3 per cent of total employment). However the industry is beginning to rebound as number of arrivals increased by 6 per cent in 2014, reaching 1.35 million.
Lebanon is becoming a hub for health tourism, with services for dental, plastic surgery and other specialist medical and therapeutic treatments offered in dedicated spas and 'wellness' centres.

Mining
Lebanon has few natural resources. There are minor deposits of high-grade iron ore, asphalt, coal, lignite, phosphates and salt, all of which are exploited for internal consumption. There are also quarries for building-stone, and sand and lime suitable for use in construction.

Hydrocarbons
Lebanon relies on the import of refined oil to meet domestic demand. In 2013 it consumed 104,000 barrels per day (bpd) of oil. Explorations for oil remain unsuccessful and in 2013 Lebanon agreed with Cyprus to a seabed demarcation of their boundary to what are considered to be potentially rich oil and natural gas fields.
Lebanon does not produce natural gas. The 1,200km Arab Gas Pipeline (AGP) runs from Egypt to Jordan and Syria and to the border with Turkey; it has a spur to Lebanon, via Syria, which was completed in 2004, and is able to deliver over 1.5 million cubic metres (cum) of gas per day to the Beddawi power station in northern Lebanon. The pipeline returned to continuous operation in the spring of 2013 but due to gas shortages in Egypt the supply has been low.
Lebanon has no coal, but imports around 5.6 million tonnes per annum.

Energy
Total installed generating capacity is over 2.3GW. Electricity rationing is widespread and power cuts are common. The electricity supply is highly inefficient and expensive.
Electricité du Liban (EDL), the state-owned electricity provider, operates at an annual loss of some US$400 million a year. Electricity is produced using imported fuel oil, which accounts for around 70 per cent of EDL's total costs.

Financial markets
Stock exchange
Beirut Stock Exchange (BSE)

Banking and insurance
Before the civil war, Lebanon was the unrivalled financial centre in the Middle East. Lebanon's free exchange system, strict secrecy laws, and strong currency all served to attract regional and international institutions and customers. Favourable economic and financial conditions following the end of the civil war initially led to an improved monetary and banking situation. However, lack of dynamism in the sector has since discouraged most foreign investors.
Central bank
Banque du Liban (BDL) (Bank of Lebanon)
Main financial centre
Beirut

Time
GMT plus two hours (daylight saving GMT plus three hours)

Geography
Lebanon stretches approximately 140km along the eastern shore of the Mediterranean, bounded by Syria to the north and east and Israel to the south. Its terrain is mountainous, dominated by the parallel ranges of the Lebanon in the west and the Anti-Lebanon in the east, which run north-east to south-west. Between these ranges lies the Beka'a valley, broad in the north, narrowing in the south. The coastal plain is defined by the Lebanon range which in places plunges into the sea, dividing the coastal strip into segments. The major cities are: Tripoli in the north, Beirut on one of the wider segments halfway down the coast and Sidon and Tyre in the south.
Hemisphere
Northern

Climate
In the summer, temperatures range between 20–30 degrees Celsius (C); Beirut averages 27 degrees C. The coastal region is humid in the summer months. In the winter, temperatures in the coastal region range between 10–16 degrees C and it becomes colder inland. Snow is usual on mountains. Most rain falls between November and March. Lebanon enjoys an essentially Mediterranean climate with mild, rainy winters and long warm summers. It almost never rains between June and October, and there is an average of 300 sunny days every year. In summer it is possible to escape the heat and humidity of the coast and go to the mountains. Average annual rainfall is 893mm in Beirut, mostly occurring in winter.

Dress codes
Formal clothing is required for business meetings. Women should dress modestly.

Entry requirements
Passports
Required by all and must have six months validity from date of visit.
Visa
Required by all, with a few exceptions for regional nationals. Contact the nearest consulate for confirmation. Those who apply for a business visa must submit a business letter from the visitor's company with a letter or fax from a local business contact stating the purpose of the trip.
Prohibited entry
Entry is refused to holders of Israeli and Palestinian passports, holders of passports containing a visa for Israel, valid or expired, used or unused, and passports with entry stamps to Israel.
Currency advice/regulations
There are no restrictions on the import and export of local or foreign currencies.
Travellers cheques are not suitable for Lebanon as it takes two weeks for cheques to clear.
Customs
Duty-free allowances include amounts of alcohol, tobacco and perfume. Personal belonging may not exceed LL200,000.
Antiques require export permits.
Prohibited imports
Firearms, ammunition, illegal drugs and pornography.

Health (for visitors)
Mandatory precautions
Vaccination certificates for yellow fever are required if travelling from an infected area. There are no other mandatory vaccinations required to enter Lebanon.
Advisable precautions
It is recommended that visitors have preventative vaccinations for polio, typhoid, tetanus and hepatitis A.
Lebanon's medical services are generally modern, with most doctors speaking French or English. The private hospitals are the best, but more expensive, and it is

recommended that insurance is taken out by all visitors.

Hotels
The ministry of tourism assesses the quality of hotels and publishes an annual report. A full range of hotels were available before the Lebanese/Israeli conflict of 2006.

A 15 per cent service charge is usually added to the bill, with additional tipping optional.

Credit cards
International credit cards are accepted throughout the capital, and in the more developed areas across the country. ATMs are plentiful

Public holidays (national)
Fixed dates
1 Jan (New Year's Day), *9 Feb (Feast of St Maroun), 1 May (Labour Day), 6 May (Martyrs' Day), *15 Aug (Assumption Day), *1 Nov (All Saints' Day), 22 Nov (Independence Day), *25 Dec (Christmas Day).

* Observed by adherents only.

Holidays that fall at the weekend are taken on the Monday following.

Variable dates
Orthodox Christmas (Jan), Orthodox Easter (Mar/Apr, Fri–Mon), Eid al Adha (three days), Islamic New Year, Ashura (two days), Birth of the Prophet, Eid al Fitr (three days).

Islamic year 1437 (15 Oct 2015–2 Oct 2016):: The Islamic year contains 354 or 355 days, with the result that Muslim feasts advance by 10–12 days against the Gregorian calendar. Dates of feasts vary according to the sighting of the new moon, so cannot be forecast exactly.

Working hours
Banking
Mon–Fri: 0800–1230; Sat: 0800–1200.

Business
Mon–Fri: 0900–1600.

Government
Mon–Fri: 0800–1400; Sat: 0800–1300.

Shops
Mon–Sat: 0800–1900. Some shops open on Sundays.

Telecommunications
Mobile/cell phones
GSM 900 services cover the entire country.

Electricity supply
110V or 220V AC, 50 cycles. Supply is subject to fluctuations and blackouts. It is advisable to use a stabiliser when operating more advanced electronic equipment.

Weights and measures
Metric system

Social customs/useful tips
Punctuality is expected for business appointments but is less strictly observed for social engagements. The usual form of greeting is to shake hands. It is the custom to offer coffee or tea to visitors and it is considered rude to refuse. Muslim traditions are observed.

During Ramadan (the four weeks prior to the Eid al Fitr holiday) employees tend to work shorter hours. It is advisable to avoid business trips at this time.

Security
Visitors should keep in touch with developments in the Middle East as any increase in regional tension might affect travel advice.

Security in Lebanon is likely to remain hostage to the regional tensions over the Israeli-Palestinian and Iraqi conflicts. Visitors are advised to carry their passports.

Getting there
Air
National airline: Middle East Airlines (MEA).

International airport/s: The Rafik Hariri International Airport (renamed in June 2006) (BEY), is 16km from Beirut, with duty-free shops, VIP lounge, post office, restaurant *bureau de change*, hotel reservation and car hire.

Airport tax: Departure tax: LL100,000 first class, LL75,000 business class, LL50,000 economy class passengers

Surface
Road: Road access is possible through Turkey via Aleppo and Syria via the Bekaa valley. No access is possible via Israel.

Water: A ferry operates between Larnaca in Cyprus and Beirut.

Main port/s: Beirut, Tripoli, Saida (Sidon), Jounieh, Tyre and Byblos.

Getting about
National transport
Air: There are no domestic flights.

Road: Some 6,000km of roads and highways, excluding municipal roads. There are two international motorways with a total length of 570km. Some 40 per cent of the road network is in poor condition. New routes were under construction prior to the 2006 conflict with Israel.

Buses: Buses travel between Beirut and other major towns around the country. There are only limited daily departures.

Rail: There is no passenger railway network in Lebanon.

City transport
Taxis: There are taxis available throughout Beirut and most of the country. Service taxis usually follow established routes where one person will often share the taxi with up to four other passengers. Share taxis will stop on request. Ordinary taxis are not restricted to a set route and will take passengers anywhere in the country. The government has fixed charges for airport taxis.

Buses, trams & metro: A few buses are available to certain destinations. Not recommended for foreign visitors.

Car hire
There are several international car hire companies in Beirut, usually offering competitive rates. Rental companies can also provide drivers with their cars.

BUSINESS DIRECTORY
The addresses listed below are a selection only. While World of Information makes every endeavour to check these addresses, we cannot guarantee that changes have not been made, especially to telephone numbers and area codes. We would welcome any corrections.

Telephone area codes
The international direct dialling (IDD) code for Lebanon is +961, followed by area code:

Grand Beirut	1	Tripoli	6
Kerswan / Jbeil	9	Tyre	7
Sidon	7	Zahle	8

Chambers of Commerce
American Lebanese Chamber of Commerce,1153 Foch Street, PO Box 175093, Beirut (tel: 985-330; fax: 985-331; e-mail: amchamlb@cyberia.net.lb).

Beirut and Mount Lebanon Chamber of Commerce, Industry and Agriculture, Sanayeh, 1 Justinien Street, PO Box 11-1801, Beirut (tel: 353-390; fax: 353-395; e-mail: info@ccib.org.lb).

Federation of the Chambers of Commerce, Industry and Agriculture in Lebanon, Sanayeh, 1 Justinien Street, PO Box 11-1801, Beirut (tel: 745-288; fax: 341-328; e-mail: fccial@cci-fed.org.lb).

Sidon and South Lebanon Chamber of Commerce, Industry and Agriculture, Boulevard Maarouf Saad, PO Box 41, Sidon (tel: 720-123; fax: 722-986; e-mail: chamber@ccias.org.lb).

Tripoli and North Lebanon Chamber of Commerce, Industry and Agriculture, Bechara Khoury Street, PO Box 47, Tripoli (tel: 425-600; fax: 442-042; e-mail: comindeg@adm.net.lb).

Banking
ABN-AMRO Bank Lebanon, ABN AMRO Tower, Charles Malek Avenue, Achrafieh, Beirut (tel: 219-200; fax: 217-756/7).

Arab African International Bank, Riad El Solh, beirur (tel: 980-162/3, 980-264/5; fax: 633-912).

Bank of Beirut; PO Box 11-7354, Bank of Beirut sal Bldg, Foch Street, Beirut Central

District, Beirut (tel: 738767/68; fax: 602166).

Banque Audi, Banque Audi Plaza, Bab Idriss, 2021 8102 Beirut (tel: 200-250, 331-600; fax: 339-220).

British Arab Commercial Bank Ltd, ARESCO Centre, Banque du Liban Street, PO Box 113-5495, Hamra, Beirut (tel: 602-437; fax: 602-438).

HSBC Bank Middle East Ltd, PO Box 11-1380, St Georges Bay, Minet el Hosn, Beirut (tel: 377-477, 369-900; fax: 372-362).

Banque Libano-Française, PO Box 11808, Beirut Liberty Plaza Bldg, Roma Street, Ras Beirut, Beirut (tel: 791332; fax: 340355).

BLOM Bank, BLOM Banks's Bldg, Rashid Karami St, Verdun, Beirut, Lebanon (tel: 743-300, 738-938; fax: 738-946).

Banque de la Méditerranée; Méditerranée Group Building, Clemenceau Street, Kantari Beirut, 2022 9302 Beirut (tel: 373-937; fax: 362-706).

Central bank

Banque du Liban, PO Box 11-5544, Masraf Loubane Street, Beirut (tel: 750-000; fax: 478-2740; e-mail: bdlit@bdl.gov.lb).

Stock exchange

Beirut Stock Exchange (BSE), www.bse.com.lb

Travel information

Middle East Airlines, PO Box 206, Beirut International Airport.

Tourist Police (343-209).

Trans Mediterranean Airways, PO Box 11-3018, Beirut International Airport.

Ministry of tourism

Ministry of Tourism, Information Services, 550 Central Bank Street, PO Box 11-5344, Beirut (tel: 354-764; fax: 343-279; e-mail: mot@lebanon-tourismgov.lb; internet: www.destinationlebanon.gov.lb).

Ministries

Ministry of Agriculture, Georges Jaber Building, Badaro Street, Beirut (tel: 455-613; fax: 455-475; e-mail: ministry@agriculture.gov.lb).

Ministry of Defence, Yarzé, Beirut (tel: 452-963; fax: 457-920).

Ministry of the Displaced, Old Sidon Road, Damour (tel: 840-474; fax: 840-476; e-mail: mod@dm.net.lb).

Ministry of Economy and Trade, Assaf Building, Rue Artois, Beirut (tel: 340-504; fax: 354-640; e-mail: postmaster@economy.gov.lb).

Ministry of Education and Higher Education, Rue Georges Piko, Beirut (tel: 744-251; fax: 371-079).

Ministry of Electricity and Water Resources, Shiah, Beirut (tel: 565-040; fax: 449-639).

Ministry of the Environment, 550 Central Bank Street, Beirut (tel: 524-999; fax: 524-555).

Ministry of Finance, MOF Building, Riyad el Solh Square, Beirut (tel: 981-001; fax: 642-762; e-mail: infocenter@finance.gov.lb).

Ministry of Foreign Affairs, Rue Sursock, Beirut (tel: 334-400; fax: 584-098).

Ministry of Health, Museum Street, Beirut (tel: 615-701; fax: 645-099).

Ministry of Industry, Rue Sami Solh, Beirut (tel: 427-247; fax: 427-112).

Ministry of Information, Rue Hamra, Beirut (tel: 351-032; fax: 423-189).

Ministry of the Interior, Rue des Arts et Métiers, Sanayeh, Beirut (tel: 981-270; fax: 751-622).

Ministry of Justice, Rue Sami Solh, Beirut (tel: 425-670; fax: 422-957).

Ministry of Labour, Shiah, Beirut (tel: 556-831; fax: 556-832).

Ministry of Posts and Telecommunications, Rue Sami Shoh, Beirut (tel: 888-100; fax: 423-005; e-mail: webmaster@mpt.gov.lb).

Ministry of Public Works and Transport, Fiyadieh, Hazmieh, Beirut (tel: 458-975; fax: 459-434).

Ministry of Social Affairs, Rue Badaro, Beirut (tel: 395-561; fax: 396-148).

Ministry of Sports and Youth, Campus of Unesco, Beirut (tel: 790-529; fax: 840-440).

Ministry of Tourism, 550 Central Bank Street, Beirut (fax: 340-940; e-mail: mot@lebanon-tourism.gov.lb).

Office of the President, Presidential Palace, Beirut (tel: 220-0000; fax: 425-395).

Office of the Prime Minister, Riyad el Sol Square, Beirut (tel: 862-001; fax: 869-630).

Other useful addresses

Assocation of Lebanese Industrialists, PO Box 1520, Chamber of Commerce and Industry Building, Justinian Street, Beirut (tel: 350-280; fax: 351-167).

Board for Foreign Economic Relations, PO Box 11-5344, Beirut (tel: 483-391/5

British Embassy, Commercial Section, PO Box 60180, Coolrite Building, Autostrade, Jal El Dib, Beirut (tel: 406-330, 405-033, 402-035; fax: 402-033).

Council for Development and Reconstruction (CDR), Tallet El Serail, Beirut Central District (tel: 643-981; fax: 647-947, 864-494, 865-630).

Electricité du Liban, Nahr Street, Beirut (tel: 442-720; fax: 583-084).

Higher Council for Privatisation, Grand Serail, Beirut Central District, Beirut (tel: 987-500; fax: 983-061).

International Fairs and Promotions, SARL, PO Box 55576, Beirut.

Investment Development Authority of Lebanon, Presidency of the Council of Ministers, Liberty, Lyon Street, PO Box 113-7251, Sanayeh, Beirut (tel: 344-676, 344-403; fax: 344-463, 347-397).

Lebanese Embassy (USA), 2560 28th Street, NW, Washington DC 20008 (tel: (+1-202) 939-6300; fax: (+1-202) 939-6324; e-mail: info@lebanonembassy.org).

Solidére (development company for rebuilding Beirut), Industry and Labour Bank Building, Riyadh El-Solh Street, PO Box 11-9493, Beirut (tel: 346-891, 646-137/8/9; fax: 646-136).

National news agency: NNA (National News Agency): www.nna-leb.gov.lb

Central News Agency: www.almarkazia.com

Internet sites

Investment Development Authority of Lebanon (IDAL): www.idal.com.lb

Lebanon Online: www.lebanon.com

Ministry of Economy and Trade: www.economy.gov.lb

Ministry of Tourism: www.lebanon-tourism.gov.lb

Lesotho

KEY FACTS

Official name: Kingdom of Lesotho

Head of State: King Letsie III (since 7 Feb 1996)

Head of government: Prime Minister Pakalitha Mosisili (ABC) (sworn in 17 Mar 2015)

Ruling party: Coalition led by Democratic Congress (DC), with Lesotho Congress for Democracy (LCD), and a number of small parties (from March 2015)

Area: 30,355 square km

Population: 1.91 million (2014)*

Capital: Maseru

Official language: Sesotho and English

Currency: Loti (maloti, plural) (L) = 100 lisente; has parity with the South African rand, which is legal tender.

Exchange rate: L13.77 per US$ (Sep 2015)

GDP per capita: US$1,130 (2014)*

GDP real growth: 2.17% (2014)*

GDP: US$2.16 billion (2014)*

Inflation: 3.86% (2014)*

Balance of trade: -US$1.04 billion (2013)

* estimated figure

Since 2012, Lesotho had been led by a coalition government with a slim majority. In September 2014 Lesotho's disbanded parliament was due to reconvene, seen as the first step in a peace deal aimed at resolving what had become weeks of crisis triggered by an attempted military *coup*. The legislature had been suspended by Prime Minister Tom Thabane some four months earlier to circumnavigate a no-confidence vote that would have most likely seen him lose power.

One government spokesman claimed that the suspension was 'the first step in the right direction, in liberating our country from the danger that has surrounded us these past few months.' At the end of August 2014 the prime minister had fled the kingdom, which is entirely surrounded by South Africa, only hours before the military began to attack police installations, in what was seen as part of an orchestrated *putsch*. In the hours before fleeing, the prime minister had fired Lesotho's Defence Force commander, Lieutenant General Tlali Kamoli, who in September still refused to relinquish his command. Prime Minister Thabane returned on 3 September, accompanied by police, from a meeting of the 15-nation Southern African Development Community (SADC), which later mediated a peace deal between Lesotho's sparring factions.

Outlining the agreement, the SADC's chief mediator, South African Deputy President Cyril Ramaphosa declared Lesotho's parliament would begin preparing fresh elections for February 2015. As part of the agreement, the opposition agreed not to persist with the no-confidence vote against Mr Thabane. Instead, they allowed parliament to re-open (on 17 October) and to approve the budget, then officially dissolve in order for the country to prepare for early elections.

It was felt appropriate, in view of the continuing instability, to cancel the military parade that traditionally opens Parliament – formally overseen by King Letsie III. The decision to put the military parade on hold also avoided resolving the question as to who was in charge of Lesotho's armed forces.

The economy

According to the African Development Bank (AfDB) in its *Economic Outlook* for Lesotho, the prospects for Lesotho in 2014 and 2015 remained moderately positive with average growth of 4.4 per cent expected, although there were risks relating to the global demand for diamonds and the renewal of the United States' African Growth and Opportunity Act (AGOA), which is due to run out in 2015. The economy was estimated to have grown by 3.4 per cent in 2013, well below the strong 6.5 per cent recorded in 2012. Lesotho suffered from the economic uncertainty prevailing in Europe which constrained production activity in the mining sector. Growth is supported by booming construction activities, a strong recovery by textile and clothing, transport and communications and financial intermediation.

However, in the view of the AfDB, Lesotho's growth to date has not been inclusive enough and there is widespread unemployment, inequality and poverty, particularly in rural areas. The proportion of households living below the poverty line had increased from 56.6 per cent in 2003 to 57.1 per cent in 2013. The Gini inequality index coefficient remains high at 0.51. HIV/Aids continues to have a serious impact on the young. These factors have meant increasing numbers in need of social protection.

Lesotho's fiscal policy stance in 2013 remained tight because of the need to curb high spending. However, the fiscal consolidation, in the absence of strong private sector support, is likely to compromise the country's growth. Coupled with this is the government's weak capacity to implement a sound capital programme aligned to its development objectives. In the view of the AfDB, the government needs to undertake deep reforms to improve capacity, accountability and efficiency.

In its July 2014 assessment of the Lesotho economy, the International Monetary Fund (IMF) noted that the country has achieved strong economic growth in recent years, with only moderate inflation. International reserves have largely been rebuilt, thanks to a sustained period of fiscal restraint and recovery in revenues from the Southern African Customs Union (SACU). However, the IMF also considered unemployment to be high and poverty widespread, especially in rural areas. Growth is expected to be robust over the medium term – led by mining, construction and services – but there are risks, mainly arising from Lesotho's heavy dependence on volatile SACU revenues. A loosening of the fiscal stance in the budget for 2014/15 threatens to erode official international reserves. The budget also indicated that recurrent expenditures – most notably the government wage bill – would remain high over the medium term. The IMF recommended a more moderate easing in the fiscal stance than that prescribed in the budget and the reduction of recurrent expenditures to allow greater investment for a more inclusive growth. Preserving international reserves – to ensure a secure exchange rate peg – and debt sustainability were critical for macro-economic stability, stated the IMF. Over time a rules-based fiscal framework would strengthen stability. Overall, the financial sector indicators point to a sound banking system. Implementing the Financial Sector Development Strategy should improve access to financial services and support private sector development. An ambitious reform effort, particularly in the fiscal area, is needed to achieve a more efficient public sector and enable private sector-led growth.

Risk assessment

Politics	Poor
Economy	Fair
Regional stability	Good

COUNTRY PROFILE

1600s Modern-day Lesotho was settled by the Sotho people; the area was already home to the San people.

1800s European traders and missionaries arrived in the area, and were soon followed by the Boers on their Great Trek. The Boer trek coincided with the expansion of the Zulu state. King Moshoeshoe the Great ensured the survival of his people by taking them to a mountain stronghold in about 1820. The policy of assisting refugees on condition that they help in defence proved successful – by 1842 the King's people numbered around 40,000 and were protected by outlying refugee settlements.

1870 By the time King Moshoeshoe died, a Basuto nation of 150,000 had been established.

1910 After annexing Basutoland, the British established the Basutoland National Council comprising members nominated by chiefs.

1960 After a new constitution was introduced, elections were held, which were won by the Basutoland Congress Party (BCP) ahead of the Basutoland National Party (BNP) led by Chief Leabua Jonathan.

1965 The BCP lost the election to the BNP; Chief Jonathan became the first prime minister of the Kingdom of Lesotho. King Moshoeshoe II was stripped of most of his powers.

1966 Independence was granted.

1970 The constitution was suspended and opposition political parties banned.

1986 The government of Chief Leabua Jonathan was overthrown in a military coup by Major General J M Lekhanya. A military government chaired by Lekhanya ruled Lesotho in co-ordination with King Moshoeshoe II and a civilian cabinet appointed by the King. The new regime was more amenable to South Africa's wishes.

1990 A constituent assembly was set up to frame a new constitution; a timetable was announced for a return to civilian rule. King Moshoeshoe II was stripped of his executive and legislative powers and exiled by Lekhanya.

1991 Lekhanya was overthrown by a group of military officers led by Major General Elias Ramaema who took control. Because Moshoeshoe II initially refused to return under the new rules of the government, in which the King was given only ceremonial powers, Moshoeshoe's son was installed as King Letsie III.

1992 King Moshoeshoe returned from exile as a common citizen, in a deal with the military regime.

1993 A new constitution was adopted leaving the King as ceremonial head of the country. Elections signalled a return to democracy; the BCP won a convincing victory. King Letsie III became a purely constitutional monarch.

1994 After growing unrest, King Letsie III suspended the constitution. King Moshoeshoe, in collaboration with military supporters staged a coup but it was thwarted within a month. The settlement eventually negotiated allowed for both the re-establishment of parliamentary rule and King Letsie abdicated in favour of King Moshoeshoe.

1996 King Moshoeshoe II was killed in a road accident and was again succeeded by his son, who was sworn in as King Letsie III.

1997 King Letsie III was formally crowned.

1998 The Lesotho Congress for Democracy (LCD) won the elections. The result was rejected by opposition groups. After riots broke out in Maseru and reports circulated of an imminent military coup, 800 South African and Botswanan soldiers entered Lesotho with the aim of restoring order. Pakalitha Mosisili (LCD) became prime minister. The Interim Political Authority (IPA) was created to work alongside the government to prepare for elections.

KEY INDICATORS — Lesotho

	Unit	2011	2012	2013	2014	**2015
Population	m	*1.94	*1.90	*1.91	*1.91	*1.92
Gross domestic product (GDP)	US$bn	2.45	2.38	2.29	*2.16	*2.11
GDP per capita	US$	1,264	1,249	1,201	*1,130	*1,103
GDP real growth	%	4.2	6.0	3.5	*2.2	*4.0
Inflation	%	5.6	6.2	5.0	*3.9	*4.0
Exports (fob) (goods)	US$m	1,172.2	972.4	847.1	–	–
Imports (fob) (goods)	US$m	2,155.4	2,238.8	1,884.2	–	–
Balance of trade	US$m	-983.2	-1,266.4	-1,037.2	–	–
Current account	US$m	-520.1	-100.0	-97.0	*-143.0	*-114.0
Total reserves minus gold	US$m	–	–	1,055.2	1,070.8	–
Exchange rate	per US$	6.89	8.69	10.66	11.57	–

* estimated figure ** forecast figure

2000 King Letsie III married Karabo Motsoeneng.
2001 President Thabo Mbeki of South Africa visited Lesotho to mend diplomatic relations and develop economic links. Twenty-seven LCD members of parliament quit the party to form the Lesotho People's Congress (LPC).
2002 The first chamber of parliament was enlarged from 80 seats to 120.
2003 Families displaced by the Lesotho Highlands Water Project (LHWP), and resettled in the Maseru district, won a ruling that improvements to their schools should be made by the project's authority.
2004 Prime Minister Mosisili declared a state of emergency and appealed for food aid. The first phase of the LHWP was officially opened.
2006 Foreign Minister Monyane Moleleki was shot and wounded by a gunman. The Lesotho Promise, one of the world's largest diamonds, was sold uncut for US12.4 million. To celebrate 40 years of independence, Lesotho adopted a new flag to show it was 'at peace with itself and its neighbours' and replaced the one adopted in 1986 after a coup.
2007 The ruling LCD won parliamentary elections. The most severe drought since the 1970s caused widespread hunger, exacerbated by a drop in food production due to HIV/Aids. The annual cereal harvest was less than 25 per cent of the country's needs.
2008 The European Investment Bank (EIB) agreed a loan of US$22 million for 50 per cent of the cost of the expansion and rehabilitation of wastewater and sanitation facilities in the capital.
2009 The home of Prime Minister Mosisili was attacked and he was wounded by firearms.
2010 As South Africa closed its borders to Lesotho ahead of the Soccer World Cup, a petition was handed to the government and South African High Commission calling on South Africa to integrate Lesotho into its country. The reason for the petition was that signatories considered Lesotho to be a ruined state. HIV/Aids decimated the country, with up to 400,000 Aids orphans among the population of 2.5 million; life expectancy has fallen to 44.9 years and the population growth rate of 0.8 per cent is the lowest in Africa. The economy only survives through international aid and employment in South Africa. UNAids stated that the HIV infection rate for 15–24 year olds in Lesotho had fallen by over 30 per cent, due to prevention campaigns.
2011 In April, seven suspected mercenaries were remanded in custody, charged with attempting to assassinate Prime Minister Pakalitha Mosisili in 2009. In July, health workers were trained to use motorbikes to reach remote and rural areas that were unlikely to receive medical help otherwise.
2012 On 29 February, Prime Minister Mosisili resigned from the LCD, the political party he had led since 1998 (he remained in office as prime minister). He said he could no long contain the internal divisions and that the party was 'falling apart'. He joined and became deputy leader of the newly formed Democratic Congress (DC). The LCD became the main opposition. Parliamentary elections took place on 26 May, producing an inconclusive result, with the ruling DC winning 48 seats, ABC 30 and the LCD 26 seats (nine other parties won the remaining 16 seats); turnout was 50.04 per cent. Coalition talks began immediately. On 30 May the leader of ABC, Tom Thabane, said that he had reached an agreement with the LCD and several smaller parties to form a coalition. He was appointed prime minister and sworn into office on 8 June.
2013 A lack of winter snowfall in the highlands meant that rivers were running low and by August farmers were struggling to plough their parched land in preparation for spring planting.
2014 A coup by the army was reported to have taken place on 30 August. The army denied the report but Prime Minister Thomas Thabane fled to South Africa, saying that his life was in danger and he would not return until he knew he was 'not going to get killed'. He returned on 3 September, reportedly escorted by South African police. Parliament was scheduled to reopen on 19 September, but on 8 September Prime Minister Thabane said that the actions of an army general – who refused to step down and had seized army weapons – made parliament's reopening impossible. South Africa Deputy President Cyril Ramaphosa told reporters on 2 October that talks he led talks co-ordinated by the South African Development Community had made progress. King Letsie III eventually reopened parliament on 17 October. Parliament will consider the passing of the budget and how to facilitate a smooth election process. Parliament was disolved on 5 December and elections scheduled for 28 February 2015.
2015 Elections were held on 28 February. The result was close between the Democratic Congress (DC) with 218,573 votes (38.37 per cent) giving the party 37 (out of 80) first past the post constituency seats, + 10 (out of 40) proportional representation seats (total 47 seats (out of 120) and the All Basotho Convention (ABC) with 215,022 votes (37.75 per cent) 40 + 6 (total 46), Lesotho Congress for Democracy (LCD) 56,467 votes (9.91 per cent) 2 + 10 (total 12), Basotho National Party 31,508 votes (5.53 per cent) 1+ 6 (total 7). Six other parties won less that 1 per cent but sufficient for two seats (Popular Front for Democracy and the new Reformed Congress of Lesotho) and a single seat (National Independent Party, Marematlou Freedom Party, Basutoland Congress Party and Lesotho People's Congress). The DC formed a coalition government with the LCD and five small parties. Pakalitha Mosisili was sworn in as prime minister on 17 March.

Political structure

Constitution
A new constitution was adopted in 1993, which redefined the role of the monarchy and altered the legislative branch of the government.
The King, who is head of State, has no executive or legislative authority.

Form of state
Constitutional monarchy

The executive
Executive power is vested in the prime minister, leader of the majority parliamentary party, and the cabinet appointed by the prime minister.

National legislature
Legislative power is held by a bi-cameral National Assembly.
The first chamber, the Assembly has 120 seats, 80 of which are elected by a simple majority in single-member constituencies, while 40 seats are chosen by proportional representation through party lists.
The second chamber (Senate) is made up of 22 hereditary principal chiefs and 11 members are appointed by the King, on advice from the prime minister.
All members serve for a maximum 5-year term.

Legal system
The legal system is based on English common law and Roman-Dutch law.

Last elections
28 February 2015 (parliamentary)
Results: Parliamentary: Democratic Congress (DC) 218,573 votes (38.37 per cent) giving the party 37 (out of 80) first past the post constituency seats, + 10 (out of 40) proportional representation seats (total 47 seats (out of 120), All Basotho Convention (ABC) 215,022 votes (37.75 per cent) 40 + 6 (total 46), Lesotho Congress for Democracy (LCD) 56,467 votes (9.91 per cent) 2 + 10 (total 12), Basotho National Party 31,508 votes (5.53 per cent) 1+ 6 (total 7). Six other parties won less that 1 per cent but sufficient for two seats (Popular Front for Democracy and the new Reformed Congress of Lesotho) and a single seat (National Independent Party, Marematlou Freedom Party, Basutoland Congress Party and Lesotho People's Congress). Turnout was 47.75 per cent.

Next elections
2020 (parliamentary)

Political parties

Ruling party
Coalition led by Democratic Congress (DC), with Lesotho Congress for Democracy (LCD), and a number of small parties (from March 2015)

Main opposition party
All Basotho Convention (ABC)

Approximately 41 per cent of the population is below the age of 15 years.
Seventy per cent of the population live in the lowlands along the western strip.
Collectively the nationals are called Basotho, the singular of which is Mosotho.

Population

Last census: 1.91 million (2013)*
9 April 2006: 1,880,661 (provisional)
Population density: 66 inhabitants per square km. Urban population 27 per cent (2010 Unicef).
Annual growth rate: 1.4 per cent, 1990–2010 (Unicef).

Ethnic make-up
The Basotho nation is an amalgam of mainly Sesotho-speaking people. Some 45 per cent of the population is of Nguni origin. A number of smaller groups, including San Griqua, Indian and European, have also become naturalised Basotho.

Religions
Christianity (approximately 80 per cent, mainly Roman Catholic), various traditional beliefs and others (20 per cent).

Education

Primary education is free from the age of six.
Public expenditure on education typically amounts to around 8.5 per cent of gross national income (GNI). Lesotho has one university, located in the capital, Maseru.
Literacy rate: 81 per cent adult rate (Unesco 2005)
Compulsory years: Six to 13
Enrolment rate: 108 per cent gross primary enrolment, of the relevant age group (including repeaters); 31 per cent gross secondary enrolment (World Bank).
Pupils per teacher: 46 in primary schools.

Health

HIV/Aids
The HIV prevalence is one of the highest in the world. The government has undertaken a scheme to offer HIV counseling and testing for every household by 2007; seven thousand people will be trained in medical care and for the purpose of the campaign.
Lesotho has record success by exceeding epectations in its participation of the UN sponsored '3 by 5' campaign (worldwide, providing three million HIV sufferers with antiretroviral drugs by 2005).
HIV prevalence: 25 per cent in 2005
Life expectancy: 41 years, 2004 (WHO 2006)
Fertility rate/Maternal mortality rate: 3.2 births per woman, 2010 (Unicef); maternal mortality 530 per 100,000 live births (World Bank).
Child (under 5 years) mortality rate (per 1,000): 100 per 1,000 live births (WHO 2012); 16 per cent of children aged under five are malnourished (World Bank).
Head of population per physician: 0.05 physicians per 1,000 people, 2003 (WHO 2006)

Main cities

Maseru (capital, estimated population 267,559 in 2012), Hlotse (47,894), Mafeteng (43,200), Teyateyaneng (28,142), Molale's Hoek (23,481), Maputsoa (23,029).

Languages spoken

English becomes the medium of instruction from the fifth year of primary education.

Official language/s
Sesotho and English

Media

Press
Journalists and the print media are frequently subject to defamation lawsuits, which hampers their freedom to report. High publishing costs keep the number of publications limited and all on offer are weeklies.
In English, *Informative News* (www.informativenews.co.ls) is a business magazine published on Friday. For general news, *The Mirror* and *Public Eye* (www.publiceye.co.ls). In Sesotho *Makatolle*, *MoAfrica* and *Mohlanka*. *Mopheme* (*The Survivor*) is published in Sesotho and English.

Broadcasting
Radio: Radio provides the majority of the population with news, information and entertainment.
The national, state-run Radio Lesotho (www.radioles.co.ls) has programmes in Sesotho and English (in educational shows during the school year). There are several private radio stations including Lesotho NBS (www.radiolesotho.co.ls), PC FM (www.pcfm.co.ls), Joy Radio, Mo Afrika FM and Catholic Radio.
Television: The national, state-run Lesotho Television has a limited service. The South African Broadcasting Corporation (SABC) (www.sabc.co.za) is available.
National news agency: LENA (Lesotho News Agency)

Economy

Lesotho is a small, land-locked country, surrounded by South Africa, with few natural resources beyond its rivers. Its economy is fuelled by the sale of water and electricity to South Africa with the Lesotho Highlands Water Project (LHWP) being one of the largest and most ambitious multi-purpose water schemes anywhere in the world. Once completed it will provide South Africa with 79 cubic metres of water a second, by diverting the flow of the Senqu River and its tributaries northwards to South Africa. The first phase was completed when the Katse Dam began supplying the Muela hydroelectric power station in 1998, since then Lesotho has been self-sufficient in electricity. The Mohale Dam was completed in 2002, also supplying water to the Muela power station and the Katse Dam. The final phase, scheduled for completion in 2016, includes three more dams but in 2012 it was still in its feasibility study stage.
Other exports include manufactured goods, diamonds, mohair and wool and agricultural products including livestock.
The textile industry has dwindled in recent years from its peak in 2008, when exports of garment and textiles totalled US$340 million. An estimated one third of Lesotho's textile and clothing production will be lost if the African Growth and Opportunity Act (AGOA) is not ratified in late 2015. As around 80 per cent of exports are destined for the US, Lesotho finds itself dependent on the volatility of the US market. Before AGOA, the Lesotho textile and clothing industry employed around 20,000 people, with South Africa and Europe being the principle export-markets instead of the US which has monopolised Lesotho's export market since the introduction of the AGOA in 2000. Employment in the sector rose from 20,000 to around 55,000. This has fallen to 44,000, and the threat of a withdrawal from the AGOA could lead to a further loss of 15,000.
GDP growth remained relatively constant at 4 per cent for the second half of the 2000s, despite a fall in industrial production of -4.4 per cent. GDP growth was 4.4 per cent in 2014 and has positive prospects which expect it to rise to 4.9 per cent in the coming years. Inflation registered at 6.6 per cent for 2014.
A general election was held in Lesotho in February 2015, more than two years ahead of schedule due to a political crisis in 2014. King Letsie III dissolved the eighth parliament and called for a snap election, which was won under Pakalitha Mosisili who then formed a new coalition government.
Although the majority of the population live in rural areas, agriculture's share of

the economy has declined in recent decades to around 7.5 per cent of GDP. There has also been a loss of man-power and farming skills due to the spread of HIV/Aids. Almost one in five people suffer from HIV/Aids in Lesotho (largely as a result of migrant workers coming home from the mines in South Africa), which adversely affects both domestic and public economies. The industrial sector accounts for 35.7 per cent of GDP, of which manufacturing accounts for around 18 per cent, services account for 56.6 per cent. In 2014, the UN Human Development Index (HDI) ranked Lesotho 162 (out of 187) for national development in health, education and income. Since 2000, Lesotho's progress has improved to match the growth of other countries in sub-Saharan Africa. Nonetheless, the poverty rate remains very high at 57.1 per cent which is greater than many of its neighbours. The mainstay of the economy has proved to be remittances from migrant workers employed in South Africa. Total remittances amount to 30 to 40 per cent of GDP. South Africa has begun to reduce its reliance on imported labour, which may cause Lesotho's migrants to search elsewhere for work.

External trade

Lesotho's economy is heavily influenced by South Africa; all foreign trade is either with South Africa or has to pass through it to reach other markets. Lesotho is a member of the Southern African Customs Union (Sacu), with South Africa, Namibia, Swaziland and Botswana. Sacu sets customs duties for commodities passing between member states and members share the common pool of customs and excise revenue on all external trade.

Lesotho is also a member of the Southern African Development Community (SADC), the objectives of which include reduction in trade barriers, achieving regional development and economic growth and evolving common systems and institutions.

Lesotho produces more denim jeans (over 26 million pairs each year) than any other country in Africa. This is despite the fall in sales and the temporary loss of jobs following the end of the Multi-Fibre Agreement (MFA) in 2005, which saw world sales of Asian garments eliminate many markets for African manufacturers. Trade picked up later as the clothing industry was revitalised, mainly by new markets for ethical clothing.

Imports

Principal imports include petroleum, food, building materials, machinery and vehicles, pharmaceuticals and medical products.

Main sources: South Africa (88.9 per cent), Taiwan (4.7 per cent), China (2.8 per cent)

Exports

Principal exports are electricity and water (to South Africa), garment manufactures, vehicles parts, wool and mohair, food and live animals.

Main destinations: South Africa (47.3 per cent of total in 2009), US (43.9 per cent), Belgium (3.2 per cent)

Agriculture

Farming

The agricultural sector has traditionally been a major contributor to the economy. A series of programmes were implemented since 1996 to boost agricultural development through commercialisation and privatisation. Agriculture accounts for only 7.5 per cent of GDP (2014), through the primary products of corn, wheat, pulses, barley and livestock.

There are a number of factors constraining development such as the government's heavy involvement in production, marketing and processing of the sector. This involves controlling commodity prices as well as containing imports and exports. These policies have deterred private sector involvement and hampered growth. The country also faces a severe lack of land suitable for arable farming as well as poor soil fertility and unreliable rainfall. Poverty is widespread in rural areas, where households rely on miners' remittances to remain in operation. As more workers are being laid off in South African mines, the agricultural sector is finding it hard to maintain production levels high enough to feed the population.

Moreover, the construction of the Mohale dam as part of the Lesotho Highlands Water Project (LHWP) has meant flooding the most fertile land area, the only region producing a food surplus. The World Bank maintains that the US$55 million earned from water sales to South Africa will far exceed the US$2 million value of Mohale valley crops. Farmers from the Katse Dam area have been given food aid and skills training and communities have been resettled. Environmental organisations expressed concern over increased unemployment, food insecurity and water shortages downstream due to dams.

Industry and manufacturing

The industrial sector as a whole typically contributes around 35 per cent of GDP and employs around 14 per cent of the labour force.

Most firms are small and are in joint ventures with the Lesotho National Development Corporation (LNDC). Production is largely for export (clothing, footwear, textiles) or import substitution (food processing, bricks). Other enterprises include handicrafts, ceramics and furniture making. Pharmaceuticals and leather/hide processing are under development.

Industrial production growth was at 3.3 per cent for 2014.

Tourism

Lesotho is called the Kingdom of the Sky as the majority of its land is over 3,000 metres above sea-level. As such it offers visitors adventure activities in the highlands and for those less outdoor inclined there are casinos and relatively luxurious hotels in the capital, Maseru, located on the lowland plane, close to the border with South Africa.

In 2014 Travel & Tourism directly supported 23,500 jobs (4.7 per cent of total employment). This is expected to rise by 2.2 per cent in 2015. The direct contribution of Travel & Tourism to GDP was 5.5 per cent of total GDP.

Lesotho is a member of the Regional Tourism Organisation of Southern Africa (Retosa), organised as part of the SADC, which has proposed a tourist univisa (a single visa to visit all 15 member states) and which is expected to be in use by 2013.

Mining

The diamond industry is mainly based on the Letseng la Terae mine. Letseng Diamonds and the New Mining Corporation each have a 38 per cent share in the project while the government retains a 24 per cent share. The mine produces just three carats per 100 tonnes, compared to the global average of 50–100 carats per 100 tonnes. Production costs are at least 10 times greater than the world average. However, Letseng la Terae continues to be in operation due to the high number of large diamonds produced.

The diamond mining industry has been in existence in Lesotho since the late 1950s. The diamond mining industry has gone from contributing virtually zero towards economic growth in 2000 to around 4 per cent in 2010/2011. The diamond sector comprises five major mines, operating as foreign direct investment companies. The weighted diamond production index has shown growth from 13 089 carats in the first quarter of 2006 to 27 724 carats in the second quarter of 2012. This reflected the general increase in global commodity prices.

Hydrocarbons

Lesotho does not produce any hydrocarbons. Explorations for oil took place in 1970. These proved unsuccessful and no further attempts have been made. Currently it imports around 2,000 barrels per day of refined oil, primarily from South Africa.

Energy

The net energy consumption of Lesotho (2011) is 0.8 TW. Consumption of petroleum barrels is 1600 a day. 100 per cent of total installed capacity is derived from hydroelectric power. Electricity installed capacity was 80,000 kW (2011 est.)

Banking and insurance

Restructuring of the banking sector in the 1990s has strengthened the position of Lesotho's banking sector by improving asset management and the capital base of domestic banks. Along with the liberalisation of interest rates, restructuring has enabled domestic banks to respond to interest rate movements in South Africa and strengthened the Central Bank's ability to influence the money supply.

Central bank

Central Bank of Lesotho

Time

GMT plus two hours

Geography

Lesotho is a landlocked country, entirely surrounded by South African territory. It is a mountainous land situated at the highest part of the Drakensberg escarpment on the eastern rim of the South African plateau. To its west, the land falls through foothills to a lowland area where the majority of the population lives. Three large rivers, the Orange, the Caledon and the Tugela, rise in the mountains and flow through it.

Hemisphere

Southern

Climate

Temperate climate with well-marked seasons.

More than 85 per cent of the country's rainfall – averaging 700mm in mountain areas – falls from October to April. Spring comes in August. Summer from November–January with average temperature 27 degrees Centigrade (C), rising to 32 degrees C in lowland areas.

Autumn days are warm. Winter from May–July with temperatures as low as minus 7 degrees C in lowlands and minus 18 degrees C in highlands.

Snowfalls can occur on the highlands at any time of the year.

Dress codes

In summer, light, loose clothing is most comfortable, but include a raincoat.

Spring and autumn clothing should include a jersey for the cool evenings.

Heavy woollens, vests, windcheaters, socks and jackets are a must in winter.

Warm clothing is also essential for a journey into the Maloti where severe weather conditions can be encountered any time of the year.

Entry requirements

Passports

Required by all.

Visa

Required by all, except those (mostly Commonwealth) countries listed on the internet at www.lesotholondon.org.uk, in the consular section. Further information may be requested through the consulate, or application forms downloaded from consulate websites, within applicant's country.

A proposed tourist *univisa* (a single visa to visit all 15-member states of SADC: Angola, Botswana, DRC, Lesotho, Madagascar, Malawi, Mauritius, Mozambique, Namibia, South Africa, Seychelles, Swaziland, Tanzania, Zambia and Zimbabwe) is expected to be in use by 2013. Visitors should check with the appropriate consulates to confirm start of *univisas* and their scope before beginning a tour of southern Africa.

Currency advice/regulations

There are no restrictions on the import or export of local or foreign currency. The South African rand is interchangeable with the loti in Lesotho, but the loti cannot be used in South Africa.

Travellers cheques are widely accepted.

Customs

Personal items are exempt from duty.

Prohibited imports

Alcohol and firearms

Health (for visitors)

Mandatory precautions

Yellow fever vaccination for visitors from infected areas.

Advisable precautions

Immunisation and booster shots are advised for diphtheria, tetanus, typhoid and hepatitis A. Tuberculosis, polio and hepititis B may be advised. Malaria is not common. There is a rabies risk in rural areas. There is a very high prevalence of HIV/Aids.

Sun-burning is a problem for visitors at higher altitudes and sunscreens are recommended.

All medication necessary should be brought by a visitor.

Hotels

There are a number of comfortable, international-class hotels in Maseru. Throughout the rest of the country, accommodation ranges from medium-sized hotels to smaller tourist lodges.

Credit cards

Major credit and charge cards have acceptance.

Public holidays (national)

Fixed dates

1 Jan (New Year's Day), 11 Mar (Moshoeshoe's Day), 1 May (Workers' Day), 25 May (Heroes' Day), 17 Jul (King Letsie III's Birthday), 4 Oct (Independence Day), 24–25 Dec (Christmas).

Variable dates

Good Friday, Easter Monday, Ascension Day.

Working hours

Banking

Mon, Tue, Thu, Fri: 0830–1530; Wed: 0830–1300; Sat: 0830–1100.

Business

Mon–Fri: 0800–1245, 1400–1630; Sat: 0800–1300.

Government

Mon–Fri: 0800–1245, 1400–1630.

Shops

Mon–Fri: 0800–1700; Sat: 0800–1300.

Telecommunications

Mobile/cell phones

GSM 900 services are available in larger populated areas.

Getting there

Air

National airline: South African Airways provide regular scheduled flights via Johannesburg.

International airport/s:

Maseru-Moshoeshoe I (MSU), 18km south of Maseru. All international flights are via South Africa.

Airport tax: International departures M20; transit passengers are exempt.

Surface

Road: There are three good tarred roads from South Africa into the western region, via the Maseru Bridge, Ficksburg Bridge (both open 24 hours) and Caledonsport (open daytime only). With the implementation of the Highlands Water Project, the road network has being expanded.

There are several other border crossings but with limited opening hours.

A road tax of M5 exists for visitors leaving Lesotho by light vehicles.

Rail: Only freight traffic is carried on the rail system that links to the South African system via Maseru.

Getting about

National transport

Air: Charter flights are difficult to find. South African companies may provide a service.

Road: Over 3,500km of tarred, gravel and dirt roads. Approximately 500km are tarred.

Roads are being continuously upgraded, and tarred roads connect main towns in seven out of 10 districts.

Buses: A good service provided by mainly privately owned buses. Coach services operate Maseru-Welkom; Maseru-Qacha's Nek.

Car hire

Drivers must hold an international driving licence. Driving is on the left and seat belts are compulsory.

In winter, antifreeze is a wise precaution for all cars with watercooled engines. Chains are useful in mud and snow.

Petrol can be obtained in all District Headquarter towns but is not easily obtainable elsewhere.

For visitors using their own vehicles information should be obtained from Lesotho Tourist Board Information Office (www.lesotho.gov.ls).

BUSINESS DIRECTORY

The addresses listed below are a selection only. While World of Information makes every endeavour to check these addresses, we cannot guarantee that changes have not been made, especially to telephone numbers and area codes. We would welcome any corrections.

Telephone area codes

The international dialling code (IDD) for Lesotho is +266 followed by the subscriber's number.

Useful telephone numbers

Queen Elizabeth II Hospital:312-501
Police:123
Fire brigade:122
Ambulance:121

Chambers of Commerce

Lesotho Chamber of Commerce & Industry, PO Box 79, Fairways Centre, Kingsway Avenue, Maseru 100 (tel: 2232-3482; fax: 2231-0414; e-mail: lcci@lesoff.co.za).

Banking

Lesotho Bank Ltd; PO Box 1053, Kingsway, Maseru 100 (tel: 2231-4333; fax: 2231-0348).

Barclays Bank plc, PO Box 115, Kingsway, Maseru (tel: 2231-2423; fax: 2231-0068).

NedBank, 1st Floor, Standard Bank Bldg, Kingsway, PO Box 1001, Maseru 100 (tel: 2232-2696; fax: 2231-0025).

Central bank

Central Bank of Lesotho, PO Box 1184, Corner Airport and Moshoeshoe Roads, Maseru 100 (tel: 2231-4281; fax: 2231-0051; email: cbl@centralbank.org.ls/).

Travel information

Ministry of tourism

Ministry of Tourism, Environment and Culture, PO Box 52, Maseru 100 (tel: 2231-3034).

National tourist organisation offices

Lesotho Tourist Development Corporation, PO Box 1378, Maseru 100 (tel: 2231-2427; fax: 2232-3674; email: touristinfo@ltdc.org.ls; internet: www.ltdc.org.ls).

Ministries

Minister to the Prime Minister, PO Box 527, Maseru 100 (tel: 2231-1000; fax: 2231-0102).

Ministry of Agriculture, Co-ops, Marketing and Youth Affairs, PO Box 24, Maseru 100 (tel: 2232-3561; fax: 2231-0349).

Ministry of Defence and Public Service, PO Box 527, Maseru 100 (tel: 2231-1000; fax: 2231-0102).

Ministry of Education and Manpower Development, PO Box 47, Maseru 100 (tel: 2231-3045; fax: 2231-0206).

Ministry of Finance and Economic Planning, PO Box 395, Maseru 100 (tel: 22311-101; fax: 2231-0157).

Ministry of Foreign Affairs, PO Box 1378, Maseru 100 (tel: 2231-1150; fax: 2231-1150).

Ministry of Health and Social Welfare, PO Box 514, Maseru 100 (tel: 2232-4404; fax: 2231-0467).

Ministry of Home Affairs and Local Government, Rural and Urban Development, PO Box 174, Maseru 100 (tel: 2232-3771; fax: 2231-0319).

Ministry of Information and Broadcasting, PO Box 36, Maseru 100 (tel: 2232-3561; fax: 2231-0003).

Ministry of Justice, Human Rights, Law and Constitutional Affairs, PO Box 402, Maseru 100 (tel: 2232-2683).

Ministry of Labour and Employment, Private Bag A116, Maseru 100 (tel: 2232-2565).

Ministry of Natural Resources, PO Box 426, Maseru 100 (tel: 2231-3632).

Ministry of Tourism, Sports and Culture, PO Box 52, Maseru 100 (tel: 2231-3034).

Ministry of Trade and Industry, PO Box 747, Maseru 100 (tel: 2232-2138; fax: 2231-0326).

Ministry of Transport and Telecommunications, PO Box 413, Maseru 100 (tel: 2232-3691).

Ministry of Works, PO Box 20, Maseru 100 (tel: 2231-1362; fax: 2231-0125).

Other useful addresses

British High Commission, PO Box 521, Maseru 100 (tel: 22313-961; fax: 2231-0120).

Lesotho Embassy (USA), 2511 Massachusetts Avenue, NW, Washington DC 20008 (tel: (+1-202) 797-5533; fax: (+1-202) 234-6815).

Lesotho National Development Corporation, Private Mail Bag A96, Maseru 100 (tel: 2231-2012; fax: 22310-038; internet site: www.lndc.org.ls).

Lesotho National Insurance Corporation, Private Bag A96, Maseru 100 (tel: 2231-3031; fax: 2231-0007).

Livestock Marketing Corp, PO Box 800, Maseru (tel: 2232-2444) (sole marketing concern for all livestock and products, including mohair).

Multilateral Investment Guarantee Agency (MIGA), 1818 H Street NW, Washington DC 20433, USA (tel: (+1-202) 473-1079; fax: (+1-202) 334-0265).

Radio Lesotho, PO Box 552, Maseru (tel: 2232-3561).

Statistics Bureau, PO Box 455, Maseru (tel: 2232-3852).

Trade Promotion Unit, Ministry of Trade and Industry, PO Box 747, Maseru (tel: 2232-3414; fax: 2231-0121).

National news agency: LENA (Lesotho News Agency), PO Box 36; Lerotholi Street, Maseru 100 (tel: 2232-5317; fax: 2232-6408; internet: www.lena.gov.ls).

Internet sites

Africa Business Network: www.ifc.org/abn

AllAfrica.com: http://allafrica.com

African Development Bank: www.afdb.org

Africa Online: www.africaonline.com

Public Eye (on-line edition of daily newspaper): www.publiceye.co.ls

Lesotho news agency: www.lena.gov.ls/news.htm

Mopheme newspaper: www.lesoff.co.za/news/

Lesotho Council of Non-Governmental Organisations (LCN): www.lecongo.org.ls/

Lesotho Government online: www.lesotho.gov.ls

Liberia

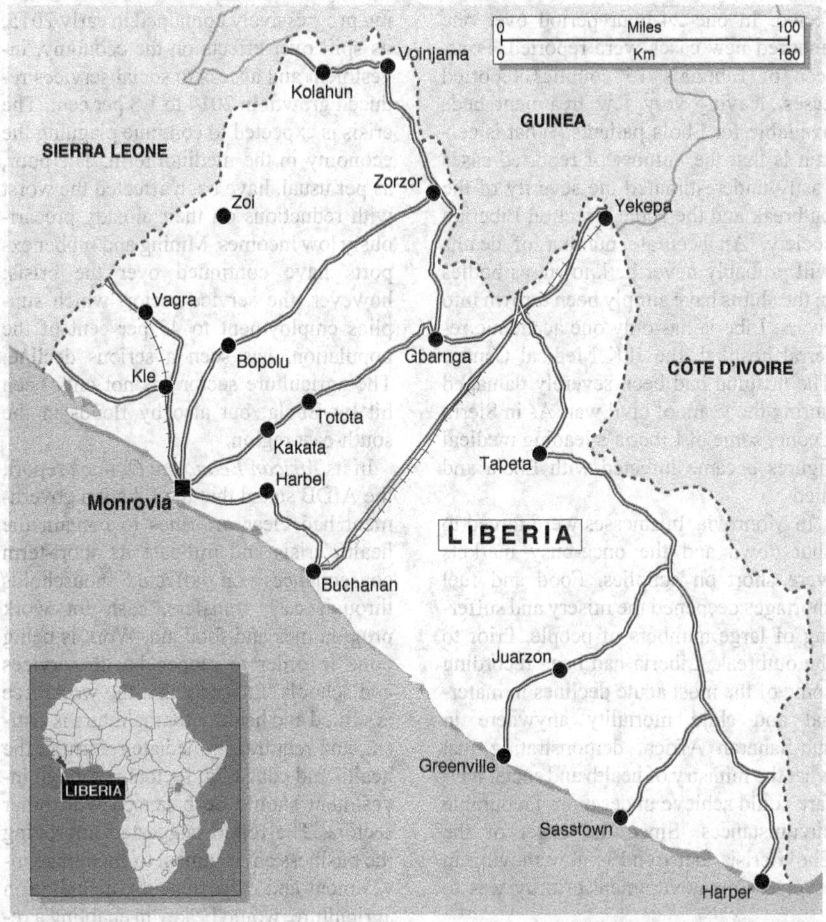

Many of Liberia's poverty-stricken inhabitants felt that their once popular leader, Ellen Johnson Sirleaf, and her government had not done enough to protect them from the deadly Ebola virus that in 2015 was still affecting countries in West Africa. And they were correct to be worried, as seven weeks after Liberia had been declared Ebola-free, a 17-year-old boy died from the disease on the 28 June 2015. Since December 2013 the death toll from the world's worst Ebola outbreak has reached over 4,000 in Liberia. The death of the young boy resulted in the quarantine of his village, Nedowein, which is only 48km from the capital.

Government response

This was not to say that the Liberian government's response to the Ebola outbreak was inadequate. The Elwa hospital in Monrovia was being run by Médecins Sans Frontiéres (MSF). A new 120-bed facility was opened in August 2014, and has since grown to accommodate more. The facility in the John F Kennedy (JFK) Medical Centre was functioning as a full Ebola treatment unit (ETU). The World Health Organisation (WHO) advised in September that an additional 40 beds had been opened in Monrovia. And as well as a holding unit at Redemption Hospital there was a 150-bed unit in the western suburb of Duala. An additional 120-bed ETU, run by the ministry of health (MoH) and WHO, opened in September at the Old Island Clinic on Bushrod Island, with an operational US Navy mobile laboratory. A 200-bed ETU was also opened before

KEY FACTS

Official name: Republic of Liberia

Head of State: President Ellen Johnson-Sirleaf (from 2005; re-elected 8 Nov 2011)

Head of government: President Ellen Johnson-Sirleaf

Ruling party: Coalition led by the Unity Party (UP) (re-elected 11 Oct 2011)

Area: 111,370 square km

Population: 4.19 million (2014)*

Capital: Monrovia

Official language: English

Currency: Liberian dollar (L$) = 100 cents

Exchange rate: L$87.00 per US$ (Sep 2015)

GDP per capita: US$484 (2014)*

GDP real growth: 0.50% (2014)*

GDP: US$2.03 billion (2014)*

Inflation: 9.86% (2014)*

Balance of trade: -US$395.20 million (2013)

Annual FDI: US$1.31 billion (2011)

* estimated figure

the end of 2014 at the ministry of defence in Oldest Congo Town.

However, despite the country getting to a position in which it was able to declare itself Ebola-free, the battle hadn't ended. Many patients are experiencing a host of 'post-Ebola' symptoms. In order to combat this, an Ebola Survivors Clinic was opened at the Redemption Hospital in Monrovia at which survivors could receive treatment and support, as well as health-care workers being able to gain experience working with the disease.

A Noble Peace Prize winner for her work on women's rights, Mrs Johnson Sirleaf had made gradual progress before the epidemic in rebuilding Liberia after the 1989–2003 civil war. Feted internationally since she became Africa's first female head of state in 2005, Johnson Sirleaf's reputation at home has been dogged by a slow improvement in living standards. Some critics say she is out of touch with poor Liberians, and the 75-year-old former World Bank official has faced mounting anger over her handling of the Ebola crisis. Her government has been criticised for causing food shortages by imposing quarantine on affected communities, while healthcare workers walked out on strike after several of their colleagues died. The President has also faced criticism for sending troops to quell protests in the ocean-front West Point slum of Monrovia. A 15-year-old boy was fatally shot after soldiers opened fire on a crowd trying to break out of a quarantine there.

Her political opponents called for Johnson Sirleaf to resign, but her government claimed to be doing everything possible, given the scant resources at its disposal.

In her defence, Mrs Johnson Sirleaf has taken a number of bold steps. Declaring a state of national emergency, she closed schools to prevent them becoming breeding grounds for infection and sent home all non-essential government staff.

The outbreak in Liberia, where case counts have increased exponentially, is by far the most worrisome of the countries affected. In one 24-hour period over one hundred new cases were reported. Fourteen of Liberia's 15 counties reported cases, leaving very few treatment beds available for Ebola patients. What is certain is that the number of reported cases vastly underestimated the severity of the outbreak and the acute effect on Liberian society. An accurate number of deaths will probably never be known, as bodies in the slums have simply been thrown into rivers. Liberia has only one academic referral hospital, the JFK Medical Centre. The hospital had been severely damaged during the years of civil war. As in Sierra Leone, some of Liberia's leading medical figures became infected with Ebola and died.

In Monrovia, businesses were forced to shut down and the once-busy markets were short on supplies. Food and fuel shortages deepened the misery and suffering of large numbers of people. Prior to the outbreak, Liberia had been recording some of the most acute declines in maternal and child mortality anywhere in sub-Saharan Africa, demonstrating just what the ministry of health and social welfare could achieve under more favourable circumstances. Since the onset of the Ebola crisis that trend is now moving in reverse. One government priority was to extend Ebola community care to more rural areas so that patients and the families who were caring for them, had support for safer and better treatment near their homes.

The economy

According to the African Development Bank (AfDB), despite the Ebola crisis being progressively contained in early 2015, its spill over effects on the economy, investment and access to social services reduced growth in 2014 to 1.8 per cent. The crisis is expected to continue plaguing the economy in the medium term. The poor, as per usual, have been affected the worst with reductions on their already precariously low incomes. Mining and rubber exports have continued over the crisis; however, the service sector, which supplies employment to 45 per cent of the population, has seen a serious decline. The agriculture sector has not only been hit by Ebola, but also by floods in the south-east region.

In its *African Economic Outlook* report, the AfDB stated that the Liberian government had clear priorities to contain the health crisis and mitigate its short-term consequences on affected households through cash transfers, cash for work programmes and food aid. Work is being done in order to reopen health services and schools. Ensuring that the workforce is skilled and healthy for the future is critical, and requires immediate reform in the health and education sectors, although investment should be balanced with other sectors. The report suggested improving the business environment to encourage investment and entrepreneurs, including in agriculture, would be key in enabling a return to stable growth beyond the immediate recovery. This especially needs attention since there is reduced demand for Liberia's exports and the additional stigma of the crisis decreasing potential investment. Resuming major road and energy infrastructure projects will help to overcome the constraints on growth.

The AfDB stated that improving services in rural areas would support long-term growth and stability. Despite Monrovia being the centre for economic activity, increasing the welfare of rural households will be key to the future of the country. The report stated that de-concentration of health services and education will be important factors in this. However, the weak infrastructure, low local capacity and the high financial costs will hinder this process and make the move to decentralisation take years.

KEY INDICATORS **Liberia**

	Unit	2011	2012	2013	2014	**2015
Population	m	*3.88	*3.98	*4.08	*4.19	*4.30
Gross domestic product (GDP)	US$bn	1.16	1.73	1.96	*2.03	*2.06
GDP per capita	US$	281	436	481	*484	*479
GDP real growth	%	8.5	8.3	8.7	*0.5	*-1.4
Inflation	%	9.9	6.8	7.6	*9.9	*7.9
Exports (fob) (goods)	US$m	645.7	–	624.3	–	–
Imports (fob) (goods)	US$m	2,068.4	–	1,019.6	–	–
Balance of trade	US$m	-1,422.8	–	-395.2	–	–
Current account	US$m	-525.0	-554.0	-554.0	*-646.0	*-826.0
Total reserves minus gold	US$m		497.2	493.1	–	–
Foreign exchange	US$m	–	255.2	226.3	–	–
Exchange rate	per US$	72.20	72.27	79.03	92.50	–

* estimated figure ** forecast figure

Risk assessment

Politics	Fair
Economy	Poor/fair
Regional stability	Good

Muslims in Liberia

% of population	20
Sunni (% of Muslims)	96
Shi'a (% of Muslims)	1

COUNTRY PROFILE

1822 Liberia was created by a number of US philanthropists with the idea that freed American and Caribbean slaves would be resettled in Africa. Many refused to go and those who did were met with hostility from the majority indigenous population.
1847 Liberia was established as an independent state with a constitution modelled on that of the United States.. The US did not formally recognise this status until 1862.
1944–71 Under President William Tubman of the True Whig party (which monopolised power from early in Liberia's existence), the country received massive foreign investment, but this only exacerbated tension between the descendants of the settlers and the indigenous people.
1963 The local people were enfranchised – around 97 per cent of the total population.
1971 Tubman was succeeded by William Tolbert.
1980 Following protests against the government the previous year, Tolbert's government was overthrown in a coup led by Master Sergeant Samuel Doe, who survived several coup attempts and won an 'election' held in 1985. His government proved widely unpopular.
1984 A new multi-party constitution was introduced.
1985 Samuel Doe was elected president.
1989 Charles Taylor led the National Patriotic Front of Liberia (NPFL) in an uprising.
1990 Opposition groups, led by Prince Johnson and Charles Taylor overran most of Liberia and captured Monrovia. With Johnson and Taylor both claiming the presidency, the West African peacekeeping force, the Economic Community of West African States Monitoring Group (Ecomog), installed Amos Sawyer as head of an Interim Government of National Unity (IGNU). The NPFL controlled around 90 per cent of Liberia; the remnants of Doe's supporters and Johnson's forces were both encamped within the capital. President Doe was executed by NPFL.
1993 After a period of heavy fighting, a UN-sponsored peace accord was signed, calling for the creation of a six-month transitional government representing the IGNU, the NPFL and Doe's supporters and the United Liberation Movement for Democracy (Ulimo).
1994–95 Several agreements were reached, none of which brought a final peace.
1996 An attempt to arrest one faction leader for breaking the truce led to two weeks of serious street fighting in Monrovia until Ecomog regained control. Following the renewed conflict, both the faction leaders and Ecowas agreed to hold elections in 1997.
1997 Charles Taylor and his NPFL won a landslide victory.
1999 The Ghanaian and Nigerian troops, who were part of Ecomog, withdrew from Liberia.
2000 President Charles Taylor announced that his government was forming a new army.
2001 There were rebel attacks on the border between Guinea and Liberia and Liberia closed its border with Sierra Leone.
2002 A state of emergency was declared after rebels (Liberians United for Reconciliation and Democracy (LURD)) attacked a town near the capital, Monrovia.
2003 The UN Security Council extended its arms embargo against Liberia for 12 months and added an export ban on raw timber. Foreign nationals were evacuated from Monrovia amid fighting by LURD rebels in their campaign against President Taylor, who initially refused to resign. President Taylor finally accepted Nigeria's asylum offer. West African peacekeepers entered Monrovia as President Taylor resigned and named Moses Blah as president. The government and two rebel groups selected Gyude Bryant, chairman of the Liberia Action Party (LAP), to head Liberia's interim post-war administration.
2004 International donors pledged more than US$500 million in reconstruction aid. The UN Security Council voted to freeze the assets of former president, Charles Taylor.
2005 The first elections since the end of the civil war were held; in the presidential run-off Ellen Johnson-Sirleaf (Unity Party) (UP) defeated George Weah (Liberal Party) (LP), becoming the first woman president in Africa. The UN Security Council extended its ban on arms sales to Liberia for a further 12 months and the sale of diamonds and timber for a further six months.
2006 Ellen Johnson-Sirleaf took office as president on 16 January. A Truth and Reconciliation Commission began work. Former president Charles Taylor was extradited from Nigeria into UN custody in Sierra Leone and indicted for war crimes before the UN-backed Special Court in The Hague (The Netherlands). The government concluded a mineral concession agreement with Indian-based, Mittal Steel.
2007 Personal banking arrived in the north-east border region of Ganta, with the opening of the first bank after 16 years of civil war, when most banks outside the capital region were looted and left defunct. Liberia inherited debts of US$3.7 billion – an unsustainable amount the World Bank said was 30 times the country's annual export earnings and eight times greater than its GDP. The US granted US$500 million in aid and agreed to cancel US$391 million in debt, then pledged US$200 million in further funds. The UN lifted a ban on the export of diamonds and the government lifted the moratorium on the mining, sale and export of diamonds. The vital Mano River Bridge, connecting Sierra Leone with Liberia, was officially re-opened.
2008 US President George W Bush became the first US president to visit in 30 years. The first census since 1984 was undertaken, which recorded a population of 3,489,072.
2009 A US court convicted Charles 'Chuckie' Taylor, son of former president Taylor, and sentenced him to 97 years in prison for torture and *ex officio* executions. Liberia reduced its foreign debt by a significant amount when it bought back US$1.2 billion in government debt at 97 per cent of its face value. The World Bank provided 50 per cent of the necessary payment and Germany, Norway, the UK and US provided the other 50 per cent between them. Former president, Charles Taylor, began his testimony in his trial, in The Hague, on charges of terrorism, murder, rape and torture. The Liberian Truth and Reconciliation Commission recommended that a 30-year ban should be placed on President Johnson-Sirleaf, and many other senior politicians, for backing Charles Taylor when he overthrew the previous administration in 1989. President Johnson-Sirleaf apologised for her support of Charles Taylor in 1989. In August, the members of parliament (MPs) said they would take one year to consult their constituents' views of President Johnson-Sirleaf, before making a decision about her future.
2010 President Johnson-Sirleaf received a number of plaudits by leading international publications, claiming she was one of the best leaders in the world and the best in Africa. Opposition parties and candidates claim her progress had been too little and too slow.
2011 In January the controversial 30-year ban from politics imposed on President Ellen Johnson-Sirleaf and a number of politicians and individuals by the now dissolved Truth and Reconciliation

Commission (TRC), for their alleged roles in the country's war, was declared unconstitutional by the Supreme Court. President Johnson-Sirleaf said that she would stand for re-election in the coming presidential elections. In February, one of Charles Taylor's lawyers, Courtenay Griffiths, walked out of Taylor's war trial, after Griffiths' final written brief, submitted 20 days late, was rejected by the judges. However in March the decision was reversed and the defence argument was completed. Two Liberians, found guilty of defrauding World Vision (funded by USAid) of food and construction materials for Liberia, valued at US$2 million, were jailed in the US for over 11 years. The first official rate of GDP since 1987 was published in August. President Johnson-Sirleaf and Liberian activist Leymah Gbowee were two of the three women (the third was Tawakkul Karman from the Yemen) to win the 2011 Nobel Peace Prize in October. The three women were honoured for 'their non-violent struggle for the safety of women and for women's rights to full participation in peace-building work'. Parliamentary elections were held in October, all seats in the lower house were in contention and half the seats in the Senate. The UP won most seats in the lower house, with a return of 24 candidates. The opposition CDC won 11 seats. Presidential elections were also held in October in which 16 candidates took part. Incumbent Ellen Johnson-Sirleaf (UP) won 43.9 per cent of the vote and her closest opponent, Winston Tubman (CDC) won 32.7 per cent. Winston Tubman withdrew from the runoff elections, alleging fraud; he called on his supporters to boycott the election. President Johnson-Sirleaf accused Tubman of violating the constitution by urging Liberians not to take part in the elections and advised all to participate. A runoff election took place in November between these two candidates and despite the appeal by the president for voters not to boycott the election, turnout was only 33 per cent; Johnson-Sirleaf won 90 per cent and Tubman around 9 per cent.

2012 On 31 March, former warlord George Boley was deported from the US to stand trial for human rights abuses during the civil war. On 26 April, the Special Court for Sierra Leone (SCSL) found former president Charles Taylor guilty of aiding and abetting war crimes perpetrated during the civil war in Sierra Leone. On 30 May the SCSL sentenced Charles Taylor to 50 years in jail, to be served in the UK. The senior judge said Taylor 'aided and abetted' RUF rebels in prolonging a conflict where 'the lives of many more innocent civilians in Sierra Leone were lost or destroyed as a direct result of his actions.' Nobel Laureate, Leymah Gbowee, resigned as head of the Peace and Reconciliation Commission in October. She wss replaced by George Weah, the popular ex-footballer and the opposition's Vice Presidential candidate in 2011, in December.

2013 Exam results showed that not one of the almost 25,000 students who sat exams for entrance to the University of Liberia passed. President Johnson-Sirleaf had already said that education in Liberia was 'in a mess'. After discussions with the university, the President said the university would nevertheless take on 1,800 students. Former president Taylor's appeal against his conviction for war crimes was rejected by the SCSL on 25 September. He is set to serve his term in a British prison, although on 14 October he requested he serve his term in Rwanda rather than the UK. He arrived in the UK on 15 October.

2014 Guinea announced an outbreak of the deadly Ebola virus in Conakry on 27 March; by July the total number of deaths across the region, including Sierra Leone, Liberia and Guinea, had reached over 670. The government confirmed the 16 August disappearance of 17 Ebola patients from a hospital in Monrovia. The WHO reported that the number of deaths had increased to over 1,100, with Sierra Leone suffering the most. President Sirleaf ordered an overnight curfew on 20 August in an attempt to halt the spread of the virus. Deaths from the Ebola virus in Liberia up to 29 October were said, by WHO, to be 2,413 (out of a total for West Africa of 4,951).

2015 The first large-scale trials of an experimental vaccine against Ebola began in Liberia in February. On 9 May the WHO declared Liberia free of the Ebola virus, confirming there had been no new cases for 42 days. Deaths in Liberia since the outbreak started in 2014 were reported by the WHO to be 4,769 (out of a total of 11,079 'probable, confirmed or suspected deaths'). A young Liberian died of Ebola on 30 June, and two new cases were thought to be confirmed a day later.

Political structure

Constitution

The multi-party 1984 constitution, approved by referendum, replaced the 1847 constitution which was suspended in April 1980.

The executive

Executive power rests with the president, elected by universal adult suffrage for a term of six years; the maximum number of terms is two. The president is head of state, head of government and commander-in-chief of the armed forces. The president must be a natural-born Liberian citizen of not less than 35 years of age, the owner of unencumbered property valued at not less than US$25,000 and resident in Liberia 10 years prior to the elections.

National legislature

The bicameral Legislature of Liberia consists of the House of Representatives (lower house) with 73 members directly elected by popular vote for six-year terms, and the Senate (upper house) with 30 members; each county (constituency) returns two candidates each (the winner is the senior senator and second placed is the junior senator). Senior senators serve for nine-year terms and junior senators for six-year terms.

Legal system

Liberia has a dual system of statutory law based on Anglo-American common law for the modern sector and customary law based on unwritten tribal practices for the indigenous sector.

Last elections

11 October and 8 November 2011 (House of Representatives, half of Senate and presidential and runoff); 20 December 2014 (second half of Senate)

Results: House of Representatives (lower house): Unity Party (UP) won 24 seats (out of 73), Congress of Democratic Change (CDC) 11, Liberty Party (LP) seven, National Union for Democratic Progress (NUDP) six, National Democratic Coalition (NDC) five, National Patriotic Party (NPP) three, Alliance for Peace and Democracy (APD) three, Movement for Progressive Change (MPC) two, independents nine; three other political parties each won one seat. Senate (50 per cent of membership): UP four (out of 15), NPP four, CDC two, four other parties and one independent each won one seat. Senate (upper house): Unity Party (UP) 10 seats (out of 30), National Patriotic Party (NPP) 6 seats, Congress of Democratic Change (CDC) 3 seats, National Union for Democratic Progress (NUDP) 2 seats, Alliance for Peace and Democracy (APD) 2 seats. Liberty Party (LP), National Democratic Coalition (NDC), Liberia Destiny Party (LDP), National Democratic Party (NDP) all won 1 seat each. Independents gained the remaining 3 seats. Presidential: Ellen Johnson Sirleaf (UP) won 43.9 per cent of the vote, Winston Tubman (CDC) 32.7 per cent, Prince Yormie Johnson (NUDP) 11.6 per cent, Charles Brumskine (LP) 5.5 per cent; 12 other candidates each won less that 1.5 per cent. Turnout was 71.64 per cent. Runoff: Sirleaf won 90 per cent, Tubman (boycotting runoff) around 9 per cent. Turnout was 33 per cent.

Next elections

2017 (presidential and House of Representatives); 2020 (senate)

Political parties

Ruling party

Coalition led by the Unity Party (UP) (re-elected 11 Oct 2011)

Main opposition party

Congress of Democratic Change (CDC)

Approximately 46 per cent of the total population are under 15 years.

Population

3.98 million (2012)*

Last census: 21 March 2008: 3,476,608

Population density: 32 inhabitants per square km. Urban population 48 per cent (2010 Unicef).

Annual growth rate: 3.2 per cent, 1990–2010 (Unicef).

Internally Displaced Persons (IDP)

500,000 (UNHCR 2004)

Ethnic make-up

Indigenous tribes (95 per cent), Americo-Liberians (5 per cent).

Religions

Christianity (68 per cent), traditional beliefs (18 per cent), Muslim (14 per cent).

Education

Primary education lasts for six years ending at age 12. Junior secondary school last for three years before successful students can progress onto senior secondary school for a further three years.

Higher education is provided principally by the Uninversity of Liberia in Monrovia, the African Methodist Episcopal University and Cuttington University College.

Not one of the almost 25,000 students who sat exams for entrance to the University of Liberia passed in 2013. President Johnson-Sirleaf had already said that education in Liberia was 'in a mess'. After discussions with the university, the President said the university would nevertheless take on 1,800 students.

Literacy rate: 56 per cent adult rate; 71 per cent youth rate (15–24) (Unesco 2005).

Compulsory years: Six to 16.

Health

In 2007, the health minister estimated that the country had only one-tenth of the doctors needed for its post-conflict society. Of the 120 doctors in post, 70 were foreign doctors serving with international medical organisations and charities.

Other healthcare professionals needed included nurses, midwives and laboratory technicians. Under-funding and lack of opportunity has led most trained healthcare workers to emigrate and many doctors resident in Liberia prefer to live in the coastal region leaving rural areas without medical cover. The government has offered a gratuity of US$1,000 (five times the current average salary) for any doctor who accepts assignments inland.

HIV/Aids

Altogether there were 96,000 adults, of which 54,000 women, and 8,000 children under the age of 15, living with HIV/Aids in 2003. Deaths from Aids totalled 7,200 and there were 36,000 orphans aged 0–17 created in 2003 (UCSF).

HIV prevalence: 5.9 per cent aged 15–49 in 2003 (World Bank)

Life expectancy: 42 years, 2004 (WHO 2006)

Fertility rate/Maternal mortality rate: 5.2 births per woman, 2010 (Unicef)

Child (under 5 years) mortality rate (per 1,000): 75 per 1,000 live births (WHO 2012)

Head of population per physician: 0.03 physicians per 1,000 people, 2004 (WHO 2006)

Main cities

Monrovia (capital, estimated population 1.1 million in 2012), Ganta (42,786), Buchanan (35,411), Kakata (34,749), Gbarnga (34,571), Voinjama (27,329).

Languages spoken

English is the business language. There are three main Liberian dialects – Golla, Bassa, Kpelle, Kru and Vai.

Official language/s

English

Media

The state of media in Liberia is still struggling to repair not only the damaged technology but also the proficiency and of the profession. Installations were either destroyed or looted during the civil war and the professionalism of journalists was corrupted as patronage was bestowed on only those that supported the former regime of Charles Taylor.

Press

Since the former president Taylor's departure, several independent newspapers have started publication.

Dailies: In English *The Inquirer* (www.theinquirer.com.lr), *The News* (www.thenews.com.lr), *The Analyst* (www.analystliberia.com), *Daily Observer* (www.liberianobserver.com) and *Poll Watch* are all published in Monrovia.

Weeklies: The private publication, *The Heritage*, is published in Monrovia.

Broadcasting

State-owned TV and radio suffered particularly from looting in the civil war and lost its TV and FM radio transmitters in 1991. The Liberia Broadcasting System (LBS) has one FM small transmitter that can reach only Monrovia, and no television.

The LCN controls a TV and radio network which uses the frequency 89FM, previously used by LBS, and which, by law, belongs to the state.

Radio: The public, Liberia Broadcasting System (ELBS) (www.liberiabroadcastingsystem.com) has a limited service but provides programmes in local languages, English and French. Others radio services include Star Radio (www.starradio.org.lr), Unmil Radio (http://unmil.org) operated by the United Nations mission, Sky FM and two Christian stations. Community radio services are operated, supported by international entities.

Television: There are three, private TV stations, Clar TV, Power TV and Real TV.

Other news agencies: APA: www.apanews.net

Panapress: www.panapress.com

Economy

Liberia has a number of marketable natural resources including iron ore, gold, diamonds, rubber, timber and recently discovered oil off its Atlantic coastline. It also has the world's second largest registered fleet (after Panama), licensing over 1,700 maritime vessels, including 35 per cent of the global tanker fleet. This has the potential to provide a reasonable standard of living for its people. Nevertheless, in 2014 the UN Human Development Index (HDI), ranked Liberia 175 out of 187 for national development in health, education and income. Liberia's economy has improved, but this progress has not matched the development of other countries in sub-Saharan Africa. In 2014, 82 per cent of the population lived in multidimensional poverty, while 83.8 per cent lived on less than the equivalent of US$1.25 per day.

Many years of mismanagement, before the end of the civil war in 2003, left Liberia with an unsustainable debt of around US$3.7 billion, or 800 per cent of GDP, or 3,000 per cent of total export earnings. Under the Paris Club's April 2008 agreement Liberia had been granted debt relief to clear US$1.5 billion. As it complies with economic reforms to attract investment it also aims at further debt relief through the Highly Indebted Poor Country (HIPC) initiative. In 2009 a British court ordered Liberia to pay US$20 million to two investment funds based in Caribbean tax-havens for debts dating back to 1978, an amount equivalent to 5 per cent of the government's 2009 budget. Liberia referred to these as 'vulture funds' (finance companies that buy up defaulted debts of poor countries and either harass the country or any entity trading with, or investing in, the country, demanding prompt repayment or risk seizure of monies through legal channels) and declared it had no money to pay the debt. In September 2010 the 19-nation Paris Club of creditors wrote-off a further US$1.2

billion in Liberian debt, a sum that had until then accounted for most of debt servicing within the national budget. In November the government came to an agreement with two 'vulture funds', to repay 3 per cent of US$43 million, to clear the debt. This follows rulings in the US and UK court rulings, both of which said Liberia must repay the debt. The finance minister said that since 2006 the government had 'not borrowed a dime from any country'.

As Liberia tried to rebuild, the cost of imports far outstripped exports, resulting in annual trade deficits of -US$379 million in 2009 and -US$459 million in 2010 of which the largest components were imported oil and rice. However, the situation is improving, as at the end of 2014 the trade deficit was –US$198 million.

Liberia is a large recipient of international aid, used to fund both public spending and social projects. GDP growth over the period 2011–13 was consistently high, averaging 8.3 per cent. However, due to the outbreak of the Ebola virus and its spill over effects, growth all but halted in 2014, dropping to 0.5 per cent.

Unemployment is estimated to be over 50 per cent. An IMF programme in 2011 included plans to improve broad-based employment, although Liberia suffers from a lack of educated and trained workers, many of whom left the country during the civil war. Remittances from migrant workers amounted to US$406 million (20 per cent of GDP) in 2014.

External trade

Liberia is a member of the Economic Community of Western African States (Ecowas), which was set up to promote economic integration among members. It has expressed an interest in joining four other Anglophone-members in setting up a single currency, which will eventually be merged with the Francophone-members' currency to produce a single currency (the eco) for the region.

The government has encouraged foreign direct investment (FDI) in mining with US$700 million in 2013. Natural rubber is the largest export product.

Imports

Principal imports include petroleum, rice and other foodstuffs, medicines and pharmaceuticals, machinery and transport equipment and manufactured goods.

Main sources: Singapore (33.9 per cent of total in 2014), South Korea (25.6 per cent), China (14.7 per cent)

Exports

Principal exports rubber, timber, iron, diamonds, cocoa and coffee.

Main destinations: China (31.9 per cent of total in 2014), Greece (8.8 per cent), US (8.6 per cent)

Agriculture

Farming

Hit by hostilities and migration from rural areas, production has been reduced from pre-war levels. Agriculture is still the most important sector of the economy, contributing approximately 40 per cent to GDP and employing around half of the workforce.

One of the country's principal cash crops is rubber, which provides a large proportion of exports. Although mostly grown in foreign-owned plantations, smallholders are responsible for over half the total acreage planted.

Coffee, cocoa and timber are also grown for export, but, as with rubber, earnings have been reduced due to falling world prices. The main food crops are rice, cassava and sweet potatoes, followed by eddoes and yams. The government has attempted to improve production to reduce the need for imports of rice, which have become necessary to meet domestic demand.

Fishing

Commercial ocean fishing is a growing activity, particularly fishing for shrimps.

Forestry

Despite international sanction prohibiting timber exports, imposed in 2001, revenue from the trade in timber played a vital role in providing funding to ex-president Charles Taylor, for illicit arms imports during the civil war. Following his defeat, all sanctions were lifted in 2006; at which time steps were undertaken to control the exploitation of forest recourses, including the cancellation of all previous logging concessions. The Forestry Development Authority began by introducing new, transparent contracts and a forestry reform programme. Forests cover 44 per cent of Liberia's land mass.

Industry and manufacturing

The small industrial sector contributes 4.9 per cent to GDP. The manufacturing sector is relatively underdeveloped, contributing 4 per cent to GDP. Activity is mainly confined to textiles, food and rubber processing, wood products, cement and chemicals.

The sector has been weakened by the country's upheavals, which damaged infrastructure and deterred investment. Growth in the sector is in any case constrained by the small size of the domestic market, the need to import practically all raw materials, shortage of skilled labour and financial problems.

Tourism

The tourist industry is slowly recovering from the country's civil war. The Robertsport-Madina road was refurbished by the end of 2009 and gives access to the beautiful scenery lying between the Atlantic Ocean and Lake Piso (a proposed wildlife sanctuary), an area that has the greatest potential for tourist development. There are ancient natural rock formations of interest, the Sapo National Park, containing up to 40 per cent of West Africa's rainforest, and African culture to experience.

International travellers to Liberia must be hardy and prepared as facilities, which could be expected in other more settled West African countries are missing in Liberia. Public transport and taxis from the Monrovia-Roberts International airport into Monrovia are absent and transfers must be arranged before arrival. The outbreak of the Ebola virus in 2014 led to sharp falls in tourism numbers.

Although Liberia requested that two Liberian sites, Sarpo National Park and Providence Island be added to Unesco's World Heritage List, by 2015 no decision had been made.

Environment

Liberia is involved in the Great Apes Survival Project (Grasp), in concert with Unesco, in the first concerted programme developed to counter a major extinction crisis of great apes. Liberia requested the UN Scientific and Cultural Organisation to add two Liberian sites, Sarpo National Park and Providence Island, to The World's Cultural Heritage.

Mining

Prior to the civil war, Liberia was one of the world's major producers of iron ore (mainly extracted from mines at Mount Nimba, Mano River and Bong), which accounted for around 30 per cent of GDP. Production ceased completely as a result of the war. Efforts are being made to revive the sector. In August 2005, an agreement was entered into with the Mittal Steel Company to develop reserves and associated infrastructure in western Liberia. In 2015 Endeavour Mining Company was granted three mineral reconnaissance licences.

Diamonds are mined, previously earning Liberia an estimated US$300 million annually. During the war, factions exploited production. Current production figures are hard to gauge due to the allegations of diamond smuggling with Sierra Leone, Guinea and Côte d'Ivoire. Liberia's diamond exports, along with timber, are subject to UN economic sanctions because of misuse of the revenues. Foreign investors, anticipating future stability, are showing interest in the sector.

A deal between the Israeli Diamond Institute (IDI) and the government was signed, whereby diamond experts from IDI will help in the search for local diamonds. The agreement was the first since a moratorium on mining, sales and export of

Liberian diamonds was lifted by the UN, imposed in 2001 in an effort to halt the trade in 'blood diamonds' used to fund the civil war.

Hydrocarbons

There are no known oil or gas reserves in Liberia although there is potential in the territorial waters in the Gulf of Guinea. Investigations are at an early stage – in 2014 Liberia concluded the bidding for four new blocks to add to the eight it had already sold exploration licenses to. There are a total of 30 blocks that have been mapped and could possibly be explored.
Oil consumption was 3,780 barrels per day (bpd) in 2013, but is likely to increase as development picks up since the end of the civil war.
Any uses of natural gas and coal imports are commercially insignificant.

Energy

The electricity generation and supply infrastructure was wrecked early in the civil war. Total installed generating capacity was 197MW in 2013.
A technical study was undertaken to determine sites for seven hydroelectricity plants, plus the development of a new 100MW facility at the existing Mount Coffee hydro location. Mini-hydro power plants are also being considered, throughout the country. When completed the country's generating capacity should be around 1.2GW.

Banking and insurance

The civil war has led to a virtual collapse of the banking system and lending services have declined dramatically. The country's five commercial banks have found it hard to attract capital savings, as the public and businesses have tended to hoard money rather than put it in banks due to a general crisis of confidence in the banking system. The subsequent lack of liquidity in the banking sector has led to a wide spread between the average deposit and lending rates. Lack of affordable bank credit has hampered growth across the economy, particularly the agricultural sector. Unless the government can ensure political stability and security and a policy is instituted to increase bank savings, Liberia's banking sector will remain in the doldrums.

Central bank

In October 1999 the National Legislature enacted a law creating the Central Bank of Liberia, which replaced the National Bank of Liberia. Monetary authority functions are undertaken by the central government.

Main financial centre

Monrovia

Time

GMT

Geography

Liberia lies on the west coast of Africa, with Sierra Leone and Guinea to the north and Côte d'Ivoire to the east.
Liberia's coastline extends for about 580km, over half of which comprises sandy beaches. The terrain is generally low-lying. Lagoons, creeks and mangrove swamps punctuate the low coastal plain, behind which the land rises to a gently rolling, grassy plateau. Further inland, in the north-east, is mountainous, where the highest point in the country at 1,380m is Mount Wuwve. The plateau and mountain regions are home to approximately 40 per cent of Africa's rainforest.

Hemisphere

Northern

Climate

Hot and tropical with high levels of humidity (85–90 per cent) and there is little temperature variation throughout the year. Average temperatures range between 20–22 degrees Celsius (C) at night and 28–32 degrees C during the day.
Wet season lasts from May–October with especially heavy rain June–July.

Entry requirements

Passports

Required by all, valid for six months from date of entry.

Visa

Required by all, except nationals of Ecowas countries, Israel, South Korea and Thailand.

Currency advice/regulations

There are no restrictions on import and export of local or foreign currencies. US dollars are legal tender.

Health (for visitors)

Mandatory precautions

Yellow fever vaccination certificate is required.

Advisable precautions

Typhoid, hepatitis A, tetanus and polio vaccinations are recommended. Malaria prophylaxis should be taken as risk exists throughout the country. There is a rabies risk. Drinking water should be boiled and filtered.

Hotels

The airport hotel and other major hotels in Monrovia should be booked in advance. Rates are expensive and tipping is optional.

Credit cards

There is limited acceptance of credit cards.

Public holidays (national)

Fixed dates

1 Jan (New Year's Day), 11 Feb (Armed Forces Day), 15 Mar (J J Roberts' Birthday), 12 Apr (National Redemption Day), 14 Apr (Fast and Prayer Day), 14 May (National Unification Day), 26 Jul (Independence Day), 24 Aug (Flag Day), 29 Nov (President Tubman's Birthday), 25 Dec (Christmas Day).

Variable dates

Decoration Day (Mar), Fast and Prayer Day (Apr), Thanksgiving Day (Nov)

Working hours

Banking

Mon–Thu: 0900–1200; Fri: 0800–1400.

Business

Mon–Fri: 0800–1200, 1400–1600.

Government

Mon–Fri: 0800–1200, 1300–1600.

Shops

Mon–Sat: 0800–1300, 1500–1800.

Telecommunications

Telephone/fax

The service is 100 per cent automatic but very limited outside Monrovia. In 2006, land line numbers (six digits, starting with a two) not yet restored.

Mobile/cell phones

Cell phone numbers (seven plus seven digits, six plus five digits) are working.

Weights and measures

Imperial system

Security

Crime is high in the capital, Monrovia, with theft and assault prevalent, particularly at night.

Getting there

Air

International airport/s: Monrovia-Roberts International (ROB), 60km from city; duty-free shop, bar, restaurant, buffet, post office, shops.
Airport tax: US$25

Surface

Road: The vital Mano River bridge connecting Sierre Leone with Liberia was officially reopened in June 2007.

Getting about

National transport

Air: Air taxi companies charter planes between Monrovia and airfields throughout the country.
Road: A network of 10,000km covers most areas, although many roads are untarred. Main highways are: Monrovia-Sanniquellie (with a branch Ganta-Harper) and Monrovia-Buchanan.
Rail: There are no passenger railways.
Water: Freight/passenger services between Monrovia and Buchanan.

City transport

There are buses and taxis available from the airport to the city centre.
Taxis: Zoning system in operation. Negotiate fares in advance for long-distance journeys. Tipping is not usual.

Car hire

Chauffeur-driven or self-drive cars are available in Monrovia. International

driving licence or national driving licence with permit (valid for up to 30 days) accepted. Traffic drives on the right.
Self-drive cars are not generally recommended.

BUSINESS DIRECTORY

The addresses listed below are a selection only. While World of Information makes every endeavour to check these addresses, we cannot guarantee that changes have not been made, especially to telephone numbers and area codes. We would welcome any corrections.

Telephone area codes

The international dialling code (IDD) for Liberia is +231, followed by subscriber's number.
In late-2006 land-line telephone numbers (6 digits beginning with a 2) were still not functioning. Cell phone numbers (7 + 7 digits and 6 + 5 digits) were working.

Chambers of Commerce

Liberia Chamber of Commerce, Capitol Hill, PO Box 92, Monrovia (tel: 223-738).

Banking

Liberian Bank for Development and Investment (LBDI), Corner of Randall and Ashmun Streets, PO Box 547, Monrovia (tel: 227-140; fax: 226-939).

International Bank (Liberia) Limited; 64 Broad Street, Monrovia (tel: 227-438; fax: 226-092/3).

Liberian Trading and Development Bank Ltd, PO Box 293, Tradevco Building, Ashmun Street, 1000 Monrovia 10 (tel: 226-072, 226-074; fax: 226-471).

Central bank

Central Bank of Liberia: PO Box 2048, Warren and Carey Streets, Monrovia (tel: 226-991; fax: 226-144).

Travel information

Ministry of tourism

Ministry of Information, Cultural Affairs and Tourism, United Nations Drive, Capitol Hill, PO Box 10-9021, 1000 Monrovia 10 (tel: 226-269; fax: 226-069; e-mail: webmaster@liberia.net).

Ministries

Ministry of Commerce, Industry, PO Box 10-9041, 1000 Monrovia 10 (tel: 226-283).

Ministry of Finance, Bureau of Customs and Excise, PO Box 10-9013, 1000 Monrovia 10.

Ministry of Foreign Affairs, PO Box 10-9002, 1000 Monrovia 10 (tel: 226-763, 221-029, 221-751).

Ministry of Information, Culture and Tourism, PO Box 10-9021, Capitol Hill, 1000 Monrovia 10 (tel: 226-045, 226-269, 227-349; fax: 226-045).

Ministry of Justice, Bureau of Immigration, PO Box 10-9006, Broad Street, 1000 Monrovia 10.

Ministry of Lands, Mines and Energy, PO Box 10-9024, 1000 Monrovia 10 (tel: 226-281, 221-580, 221-488, 221-460).

Ministry of Planning and Economic Affairs, PO Box 10-9016, 1000 Monrovia 10 (tel: 226-962, 227-987, 222-121, 222-331, 223-208, 221-971).

Ministry of Youth and Sports, PO Box 10-9040, 1000 Monrovia 10 (tel: 226-284).

Other useful addresses

ELTV (Liberian television system), PO Box 594, Monrovia.

Liberian Development Corporation, PO Box 9043, Monrovia.

Liberian Embassy (USA), 5201 16th Street, NW, Washington DC 20011 (tel: (+1-202)-723-0437; fax: (+1-202)-723-0436; e-mail: info@liberiaemb.org).

Liberian News Agency (LINA), Ministry of Information, PO Box 9021, Capitol Hill, Monrovia (tel: 222-229).

National Investment Commission, PO Box 10-9043, 1000 Monrovia 10 (tel: 226-685, 226-575).

National Ports Authority, PO Box 14, Monrovia.

Statistics Bureau, PO Box 9016, Monrovia (tel: 222-622).

APA: www.apanews.net

Panapress: www.panapress.com

Internet sites

Africa Business Network: www.ifc.org/abn
African Development Bank: www.afdb.org

Africa Online: www.africaonline.com

AllAfrica.com: http://allafrica.com

Mbendi AfroPaedia (information on companies, countries, industries and stock exchanges in Africa): http://mbendi.co.za

Libya

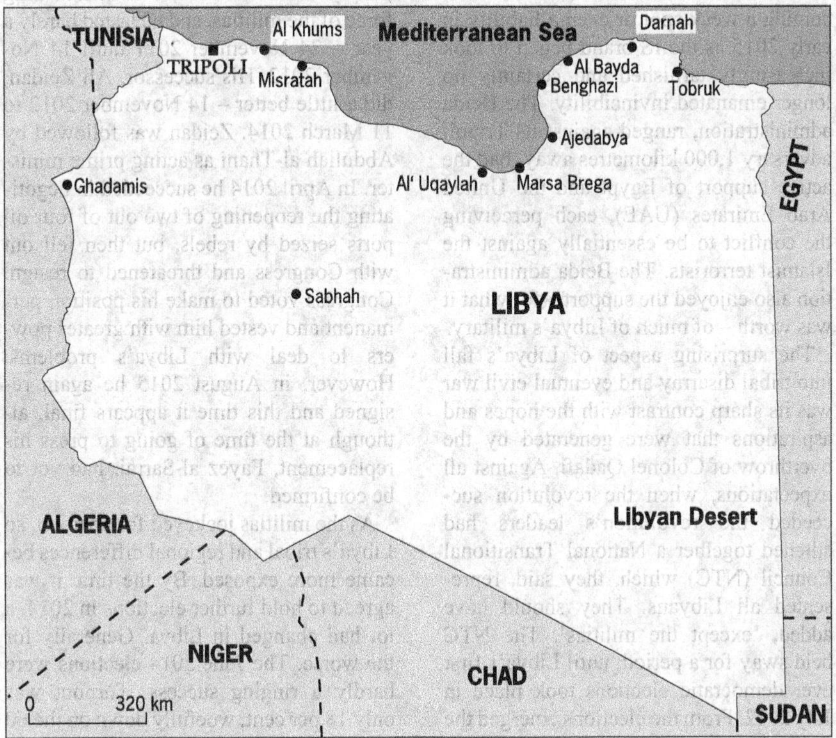

The importance of understanding a country's history has rarely been more evident than in Libya. Most countries represent a commonality of history and geography. Libya can best be described as a buffer zone between the Arab east (the Mashreq) and the Arab west (the Mahgreb). In the east, Cyrenaica was historically Greek or Hellenistic. In the west, Tripolitania, was Roman. However, there are obvious dangers in simplifying and generalising Libya's social make-up. It is also misleading to attribute political (rather than simply democratic) motivation to the warring factions. Col Qadafi's main support appeared to come from three major sources: the Warfalla, based 180km south-west of Tripoli, the largest tribe in the country with sizeable communities within Tripoli. The Warfalla also comprise the majority of well-educated Libyans. Qadafi's own tribe, centred in Sirte, 500km east of Tripoli, was another pillar of his support. The allegiance between Qadafi's tribe, the Gaddafa and the Warfalla has been described as a 'blood link'. Their ties predated Col Qadafi's rise to power and look like taking time to change in the post-Qadafi era. Prejudice against other tribes in Libya, particularly against the Misrata, make many Warfalla even more hardline than Col Qadafi was himself. Sizeable support for Col Qadafi also existed deep into Libya's south, notably around Sebh, the capital of the southern region.

This tribal mosaic still counts for a lot in Libya. Under the rule of King Idris, the east of the country with Benghazi as its capital was the country's political and commercial capital. With Qadafi, this changed: Tripoli became the capital. Libya has not had political parties for more than four decades; tribal loyalties are likely for some time to be the closest Libya comes to politics. Anything resembling civil society simply has not existed, nor for that matter, does the idea of loyalty to the state hold much of a grip. By mid-2015 Libya still lacked a

KEY FACTS

Official name: Libiya (Libya)

Head of State: Speaker of the House of Representatives Aqilah Salah Issa (since 5 August 2014)

Head of government: Prime Minister Abdullah al-Thinni (since 11 March 2014), however, on the 4 August 2015, Abdullah al-Thinni announced his intention to resign, although he has not yet officially resigned.

Ruling party: Party lists were forbidden under the electoral system.

Area: 1,775,500 square km

Population: 6.21 million (2014)

Capital: Tripoli

Official language: Arabic

Currency: Libyan dinar (LD) = 1,000 dirhams

Exchange rate: LD1.38 per US$ (Sep 2015)

GDP per capita: US$6,623 (2014)

GDP real growth: -2403.10% (2014)

GDP: US$41.15 billion (2014)

Inflation: 2.80% (2014)

Oil production: 498,000 bpd (2014)

Natural gas production: 12.20 billion cum (2014)

Balance of trade: US$11.97 billion (2013)

Annual FDI: US$1.80 billion (2010)

constitution, nor did there exist any nationally-accepted rule of law nor practical mechanism by which this vast country faced with a power vacuum might be guided. Nevertheless the Constitutional Drafting Assembly was working towards a constitution that has to be approved by a two-thirds majority in a referendum.

Barqa

By September 2013 things had taken such a chaotic turn that Libya's future as a body politic had to be questioned. Rebels from some hundred tribes had joined forces to impose a *de facto* sequestration of the vital oil industry. In August they had seized control of the principal oil terminals, swearing not to relinquish control until autonomy was granted to the Barqa region in Libya's east. The so-called Barqa Defence Force, headed up by Ibrahim al Jathran constituted the main rebel movement claimed to represent all the Eastern tribes and, significantly, was able to deploy naval units able to prevent oil tankers from berthing at Libyan oil terminals. Barqa's strikes at Libya's oil facilities risked starving Libya's government of essential cash flow.

Two Capitals, One Central Bank, One Oil Company

Were it not so tragic and so bloody, what had all the attributes of civil war in Libya also had aspects of tragicomedy about it. Two capitals – one recognised, the other not – a Central Bank that still managed to preserve some sort of neutrality by paying the salaries of government employees on both sides of the divide, a National Oil Company in the temporary administrative capital, Beida, that continued to collect oil revenues from Western oil companies, but was unable to pay its employees' salaries as the staff records were held in Tripoli.

The hopes that the Tripoli 'government' (aka 'Libya Dawn') had pinned on its alliance with the Islamic State (IS) risked becoming a weak spot or even a liability in early 2015 as the IS brand began to look increasingly tarnished and certainly no longer emanated invincibility. The Beida administration, ranged against its Tripoli adversary 1,000 kilometres away, had the active support of Egypt and the United Arab Emirates (UAE), each perceiving the conflict to be essentially against the Islamist terrorists. The Beida administration also enjoyed the support – for what it was worth – of much of Libya's military.

The surprising aspect of Libya's fall into tribal disarray and eventual civil war was its sharp contrast with the hopes and aspirations that were generated by the overthrow of Colonel Qadafi. Against all expectations, when the revolution succeeded the revolution's leaders had stitched together a National Transitional Council (NTC) which, they said, represented all Libyans. They should have added, 'except the militias'. The NTC held sway for a period, until Libya's first ever democratic elections took place in July 2012. From the elections emerged the General National Congress (GNC) charged with appointing the government. Meanwhile, militia membership had swelled dramatically in the period after Qadafi's overthrow, rising to around 200,000 by the time of the first election. Their strength on the ground allowed the militias to demand a number of senior ministerial posts, regardless of their apparent suitability or competence. Libya's first elected prime minister, the formerly exiled academic Abdurrahim al Keib, was simply no match for the swashbuckling force of the militias, and he lasted barely a year – 24 November 2011 until 14 November 2012. His successor, Ali Zeidan, did a little better – 14 November 2012 to 11 March 2014. Zeidan was followed by Abdullah al-Thani as acting prime minister. In April 2014 he succeeded in negotiating the reopening of two out of four oil ports seized by rebels, but then fell out with Congress and threatened to resign. Congress voted to make his position permanent and vested him with greater powers to deal with Libya's problems. However, in August 2015 he again resigned and this time it appears final, although at the time of going to press his replacement, Fayez al-Sarraj. had yet to be confirmed.

As the militias jockeyed for position, so Libya's tribal and regional differences became more exposed. By the time it was agreed to hold further elections in 2014, a lot had changed in Libya. Generally for the worse. The June 2014 elections were hardly a ringing success. Turnout was only 18 per cent, woefully down on the 60 per cent turnout seen in 2012. Even on the low turnout the Islamist parties did badly. The Libya Dawn grouping decided to take matters into its own military hands, laying siege to Tripoli for six weeks.

Hopes that a unity government might be formed blew hot and cold in 2015. Proposals had been drawn up to appoint a three man Presidential Council with an elected parliament and a constitutional assembly. However, in mid-2015 the Beida administration still clung to its tattered legitimacy, temporarily hunkered down in the city of Tobruq (better known in Europe and the US as Tobruk and made famous by the Second World War film *Taxi to Tobruk*). The IS had established African beachheads in Libya, first in Derna then in Sirte, the home town of former dictator Qadafi. Sirte was not only important to Libya's oil industry, but also worryingly close to Europe's southern border on the Mediterranean. The IS foothold was strategically threatening, possibly enabling IS to move southwards towards Nigeria in the West and Somalia in the East, both countries with an active, al Qadea inspired Islamist presence. In March 2015, as they began to

KEY INDICATORS — Libya

	Unit	2011	2012	2013	2014	**2015
Population	m	*6.48	*6.03	6.12	6.21	*6.30
Gross domestic product (GDP)	US$bn	36.90	81.92	65.52	41.15	*34.24
GDP per capita	US$	5,691	13,851	10,702	6,623	*5,430
GDP real growth	%	-61.0	104.5	-13.6	-24.0	*4.6
Inflation	%	14.1	6.1	2.6	2.8	*2.2
Oil output	'000 bpd	479.0	1,509.0	988.0	498.0	–
Natural gas output	bn cum	4.1	12.2	12.0	12.2	–
Exports (fob) (goods)	US$m	12,986.0	61,026.1	46,017.9	–	–
Imports (fob) (goods)	US$m	11,200.0	25,590.0	34,049.5	–	–
Balance of trade	US$m	1,786.0	35,436.1	11,968.4	–	–
Current account	US$m	3,173.0	28,973.0	8,895.0	-12,391.0	*-18,064.0
Total reserves minus gold	US$m	103,552.0	118,408.0	115,197.0	89,093.0	–
Foreign exchange	US$m	100,582.0	115,473.0	112,243.0	–	–
Exchange rate	per US$	1.21	1.26	1.24	1.32	–

* estimated figure ** forecast figure

probe inland, the IS had claimed attacks on both the Beida and the Tripoli administrations.

The Chaos Theory

What had become clear in Libya's first four post-Qadafi years was that the country's structures and leadership were not up to the job of democratic independence. After 42 years of brutal dictatorship with no model to follow and no resident leadership waiting in the wings, there was an awful lot to be done before even the simplest of governments could be appointed. Meanwhile, IS had taken advantage of the perceived security vacuum to take control of the oil port of Sirte. The United Nations special envoy to Libya, Mr Bernardino Leon, was reportedly preparing a fifth draft of a proposed peace agreement although the suspicion prevailed that the parties involved, be they militias, Islamists or war-lords, could hope for little in the way of influence when it came to negotiating.

Probably because many of those involved had adopted a seemingly nihilistic approach to their country's future, most observers in the first half of 2015 considered that Libya's fragmentation and chaotic disorder represented a more dangerous threat than did the IS. The talks in Skheirat, in Morocco to resolve the Libyan political crisis, did not look destined for success. It was almost certainly fanciful to imagine that any progress could emerge from the talks considering that General Haftar, who headed the Beida military forces had launched an air offensive against Tripoli, while the talks were still going on. The implication seemed to be that even if a political agreement for national unity was signed, the militias and factions on the ground would not recognise it. The militias would be unlikely to agree to disarmament. The need for Libya to achieve a political resolution made foreign intervention of any kind problematic. The West, Russia, Saudi Arabia and most of the Gulf States had recognised the Tobruk government as legitimate. However, the Supreme Court of Libya had dissented, calling it illegal. Meanwhile, Turkey and Qatar had recognised the government in Tripoli.

The gap that apparently lay between the ideals and the objectives and the harsher truth of life on the ground reflected the day to day reality into which Libya had sunk. The toxic, intractable mix of militias and sects, regional and international interests, seemed to make matters worse by the day. General Haftar's objectives had become entwined with those of Egyptian President al Sisi's campaign against the Muslim Brotherhood. There was no clear picture of what President al Sisi sought. In some Libyan quarters it was rumoured that he wished to keep Libya separated and ultimately secure the independence of the eastern province of Cyrenaica with its rich oil and gas resources. Cyrenaica could become a useful and highly profitable, adjunct to the activities of the Egyptian army. This would kill two birds with one stone, both feathering the military nest and protecting Egypt's western flank. It was thought that Saudi Arabia, a keen supporter of al Sisi, would lend its support to this strategy.

Il servitore di due padroni – Two Guv'nors, One Oil Company

The state of *de facto* civil war that pertained in early 2015 meant that the internationally recognised government based in the eastern town of Baida could at least claim to control what was left of the oil industry, even if Libya's National Oil Company (NOC) resided in the self declared – and unrecognised – capital city of Tripoli held by the so-called Libya Dawn. Any account or analysis of the state of Libya's oil industry in 2015 is inevitably speculative. Analysts could only focus on what was not happening and what used to happen. The current state of affairs is as vague as the future is likely to be. At the beginning of 2015, one preoccupation that Libya shared with many oil exporting countries was that the price of oil had sunk too far.

Despite the chaos surrounding the Libyan oil industry, at the beginning of October 2015 there was a small cause for optimism. Libya's export capacity had increased significantly with the re-opening of the eastern port of Zueitina. The port had begun to ship a cargo of 600,000 barrels of oil, its first shipments in six months, following protests that shut down the pipeline that supplied the terminal. The port has an export capacity of 70,000 barrels per day (bpd). The shut down was brought about by protesters seeking jobs at the state-run National Oil Company. This had shut down the pipeline that supplies Zueitina with crude. The protesters had agreed to reopen the export route after being promised jobs. Libya's largest port, Es Sider, remained inoperative. Despite the faltering progress of the peace discussions being held in Morocco, in 2015 any resumption of oil shipments to their 2012 levels looked unlikely.

With the largest amount of crude oil reserves in Africa and the fourth-largest amount of proved natural gas reserves on the continent, for decades Libya had been an important contributor to the global supply of light, sweet (low sulphur) crude oil, which Libya mostly exported to European markets. Whatever their potential, Libya's hydrocarbon production and exports had been substantially affected by civil unrest over the previous few years. In 2011, Libya's hydrocarbon exports suffered the almost total disruption of the Libyan civil war and the minimal and sporadic production that did take place was mostly consumed domestically. In response to the loss of Libya's oil supplies in the summer of 2011, the International Energy Agency (IEA) co-ordinated the release of 60 million barrels of oil from the emergency stocks of its member countries through the Libya Collective Action programme – the first such release since Hurricane Katrina in 2005.

According to the US government Energy Information Administration (EIA), Libya's oil production did recover to some extent in 2012, but it was still less than the levels seen before the civil war. In 2013 and 2014, Libya experienced major swings in its crude oil production, falling to its lowest level since the civil war of 0.2 million barrels per day (bpd) at the end of 2013. For almost a year, Libya's major eastern oil ports (Es Sidra, Ras Lanuf, Zueitina and Marsa al Hariga) were not able to export oil because of a blockade led by Ibrahim Jidran, a branch leader of the Petroleum Facilities Guard (PFG), which had been hired to protect the facilities. The port blockades began in late-July 2013 and ended after deals were made to reopen the ports in April 2014 (Zueitina and Marsa al Hariga) and June 2014 (Es Sidra and Ras Lanuf). In the western part of Libya, production at the 340,000bpd El Sharara field and, to a lesser extent, the 100,000bpd El Feel field had also been repeatedly shut down.

Libya's economy was in 2015 still heavily dependent on hydrocarbon production. According to the International Monetary Fund (IMF), oil and natural gas accounted for nearly 96 per cent of total government revenue and 98 per cent of export revenue in 2012. Roughly 79 per cent of Libya's export revenue traditionally came from crude oil exports, which brought in about US$4 billion per month of net revenues in 2012. The EIA fact sheet showed that Libya's net oil export revenues totalled US$4 billion during the first six months of 2014 following the drop in oil export volumes. During the 2011 civil war, the drop in oil and natural gas production led to an economic collapse and gross domestic product (GDP) declined by 62 per cent for the year. Libya's GDP growth rebounded in 2012, reflecting the relative stability of oil production, but it contracted again by almost 14 per cent in 2013. Projected oil production was expected to fall by another 20 per cent in 2014.

According to the *Oil & Gas Journal* (OGJ), Libya had proved crude oil reserves of 48.4 billion barrels in January 2015 – the largest endowment in Africa, accounting for 38 per cent for the continent's total and the ninth-largest amount globally. About 80 per cent of Libya's recoverable reserves are located in the Sirte basin, which also accounts for most of the country's oil output. Most of Libya remains unexplored and the civil unrest has prevented any large-scale exploration programmes.

Before the 2013 oil sector crisis, the Libyan government had made several announcements of plans to increase crude oil production capacity to 1.7 million bpd by the end of 2013 and to 2 million bpd over the following few years. In more peaceful times, the NOC had emphasised investing in enhanced oil recovery (EOR) methods to counter depletion of reserves and to expand production capacity at existing fields. The programme had aimed to boost total capacity by 775,000bpd from existing fields. However, plans to pursue any capital-intensive EOR projects in Libya have been postponed because of the unstable situation.

Libya's oil industry had, in principle, been run by the state-owned NOC, which was responsible for implementing Exploration and Production Sharing Agreements (EPSA) and related activities with international oil companies (IOCs). NOC subsidiaries included the Sirte Oil Company and the Arabian Gulf Oil Company (Agoco). Post Qadafi, the NOC continued to be the main body overseeing Libya's oil and natural gas industry. However, as noted above, the situation has become complicated by the existence of two rival parliaments. The precise role and responsibilities of the NOC has become unclear. In the view of the EIA, in the short term any involvement of international oil companies will first require the resolution of political issues, operational security and new regulatory legislation. Prior to the onset of hostilities in 2011, Libya had been producing an estimated 1.65 million bpd of mostly high-quality light, sweet crude oil. Libya's production had increased for most of the previous decade, from 1.4 million bpd in 2000 to 1.74 million bpd in 2008, but production remained well below peak levels of more than 3 million bpd achieved in the late 1960s. Oil production in Libya from the 1970s into the 2000s had been affected by the partial nationalisation of the industry and later by international sanctions.

The EIA estimated that Libya's current production capacity is slightly below 1.6 million bpd. Some of Libya's production was compromised from the prolonged closure of oil fields during the 2011 conflict, but a vast majority of production was restored and restarted quicker than most industry analysts expected. According to the EIA, from January 2014 to November 2014, Libya's crude oil production averaged 450,000bpd, nearly 500,000bpd lower than the 2013 average and 900,000bpd lower than the 2012 average. From mid-2013 to mid-2014, protests at major oil loading ports in the central and eastern regions of Libya forced the complete or partial shut-in of oil fields linked to the ports. Oil fields in the western part of the country were also closed intermittently during that time because of protests at the field level or along the pipeline that transports the crude to the export terminals. At the time of the EIA report Libya was still experiencing sporadic protests throughout the country that were affecting production. Libya also produced an estimated 50,000bpd to 100,000bpd of non-crude liquids, which include condensate and natural gas plants liquids.

In 2013, Libya exported an average of 875,000bpd of crude oil, including condensate, which is lower than the 2012 level of almost 1.3 million bpd but higher than the 2011 level of 400,000bpd during the deposition of Qadafi. In 2013, Libya's exports were curtailed because of disruptions to oil production that escalated in mid-2013 and continued into 2014. Typically, most (70 per cent to 80 per cent) of Libya's crude oil had been sold to European countries. In 2013, about 75 per cent of Libya's crude exports were sent to Europe; the leading single recipients were Italy, Germany and France. The United States restarted oil imports from Libya in 2004, after sanctions were lifted. The United States imported 43,000bpd of crude oil from Libya in 2013, representing only about 0.6 per cent of total imports during that year.

Natural gas

In January 2014 the OGJ estimated that Libya's proved natural gas reserves were almost 55 trillion cubic feet, making it the fifth-largest natural gas reserve holder in Africa. Before the events of 2011, new discoveries and investments in natural gas exploration had been expected to raise Libya's proved reserves in the near term. Many of the same entities involved in oversight and operations of the oil industry exercise similar functions for natural gas. Likewise, some of the same questions and uncertainties about the future are equally applicable to both sectors. Libya's natural gas sector is mostly state-run by the NOC and its Sirte Oil Company subsidiary. Italy's Eni is the only foreign oil company with a major stake in natural gas production. According to the EIA, Libya's dry natural gas production grew substantially from 194 billion cubic feet (bcf) in 2003 to 594 bcf in 2010. The Western Libya Gas Project (WLGP), which is operated by Eni and the NOC accounted for most of Libya's natural gas production growth after 2003. Most other natural gas output in Libya is produced by the NOC and its Sirte Oil Company subsidiary in the onshore Sirte Basin and is associated with oil production.

As with oil, Libya's natural gas production was almost entirely closed down for sustained periods in 2011. Dry natural gas production averaged 277bcf in 2011, more than a 50 per cent drop from the previous year. Natural gas production soon recovered to an average of 12.2 billion cubic metres (bcm) in 2012, fell to 11.0bcm in 2013 before rising to 12.2bcm again in 2014, according to the BP's *Statistical Review of World Energy* 2015. In 2013, Libya consumed about 223 billion cubic feet (bcf) of dry natural gas, or slightly more than half of what the country produced. Libya exported the surplus of its production (200 bcf in 2013) to Italy via the Greenstream pipeline. Natural gas production and exports had partially recovered since the 2011 war, but still remained lower than pre-war levels. In 2011, natural gas exports dropped to 85 bcf, about 75 per cent lower than the previous year. Before the 2011 events, Libya exported natural gas via pipeline to Italy and in the form of LNG to Spain. However, Libya's LNG plant was severely damaged during the 2011 civil war and Libya has not exported LNG since early 2011.

Risk assessment

Economy	Poor
Politics	Poor
Regional stability	Poor

Muslims in Libya

% of population	97
Sunni (% of Muslims)	98
Shi'a (% of Muslims)	1

COUNTRY PROFILE

1510 During the struggle between Hapsburg Spain and the Ottoman Turks for supremacy in the Mediterranean, Spanish forces captured and largely destroyed Tripoli.

1524 Tripoli was entrusted to the Knights of St John of Malta.

1551 The Knights were driven out of Tripolitania by the Turks who began consolidating their control over the Maghreb region. The three provinces of Tripolitania, Cyrenaica and Fezzan were combined into a single regency in Tripoli by the Ottomans.

1711–1835 Although nominally part of the Ottoman empire, the Turks in effect gave way to the local Karamanli dynasty until 1835, when the Turks strengthened their control again. The local rulers levied a toll on every Christian fleet using the Mediterranean.

1870–1911 The area was dominated by the Sanusi religious order, although the Turks and the Italians continued to invade periodically.

1911–42 By the time of the First World War in 1914, an Italian force had taken control of the coastal towns. After the War, Italy captured the Libyan nationalist hero, Omar Mukhtar, hanging him in 1931. Italy introduced an Italianisation programme. Italy's colonisation of Libya ended when the Italians and Germans lost the war in the Western Desert. The British took over Tripolitania and Cyrenaica and the French took over the Fezzan.

1951 Italy granted independence to Libya under King Idris (originally Mohammed Idris al Sanusi, a member of the Sanusi religious order).

1955 Oil exploration began.

1959 Oil was discovered.

1961 King Idris opened a 167km pipeline, which linked important oil fields in the interior to the Mediterranean Sea, making it possible for Libya to export oil.

1969 As pan-Arabism swept the Arab world, Colonel Muammar al Qadafi seized power as Leader of the Revolution. Most economic activities were nationalised, including the oil industry.

1970 The government closed the British airbase in Tobruk and the US Air Force base in Tripoli. Property belonging to Italian settlers was nationalised.

1971 The Federation of Arab Republics (FAR), comprising Libya, Egypt and Syria, was approved by national referendum, but was never realised.

1972 Libya and Egypt agreed to merge into a single state; but the plans were abandoned.

1973 Qadafi announced a cultural revolution in which people's committees were established throughout the country. Libyan forces invaded the Aozou Strip in northern Chad.

1974 A plan to unify Libya and Tunisia was agreed, but never implemented.

1977 Qadafi set up the General People's Congress (GPC) and the country was renamed the Great Socialist People's Libyan Arab Jamahiriya.

1981 The US shot down two Libyan aircraft that had challenged US warplanes over the Gulf of Sirte, claimed by Libya as its territorial waters.

1984 Police Constable Yvonne Fletcher was killed during demonstrations outside the Libyan embassy in London. The UK suspended diplomatic relations with Libya.

1986 An attempt to overthrow the Qadafi regime was unsuccessful. The US launched a major air strike on Tripoli, causing substantial damage. The US claimed its raids were in response to an alleged Libyan involvement in the bombing of a nightclub in Berlin, which was used by US military personnel. The US imposed economic sanctions on Libya.

1988 Libyan terrorists were blamed for the bomb that destroyed a Pan Am passenger aircraft over Lockerbie in Scotland.

1989 Algeria, Libya, Mauritania, Morocco and Tunisia formed the Arab Maghreb Union.

1992 UN sanctions were imposed on Libya for refusing to hand over two men suspected of the Lockerbie bombing.

1994 Libya returned the Aozou Strip to Chad.

1995 Qadafi ordered the expulsion of 30,000 Palestinians in protest at the Oslo accords signed by the Israeli government and the Palestine Liberation Organisation (PLO).

1999 UN and EU sanctions were suspended after Libya agreed to arrest and extradite Lockerbie bombing suspects. The UK re-established diplomatic links with Libya.

2000 Qadafi visited Arab states in North Africa and the Middle East, seeking to promote Arab co-operation. Libya was one of the key signatories for the creation of the African Union (AU) to replace the Organisation of African Unity (OAU).

2001 Abdelbaset Ali Mohmed al Megrahi, a Libyan intelligence agent, was found guilty of the Lockerbie bombing in a Scottish court based in The Netherlands, while his co-accused, al Amin Khalifa Fhimah, was acquitted. The US imposed a five-year extension to sanctions against Libya.

2002 Megrahi's appeal failed and he was sentenced to life imprisonment in a Scottish jail.

2003 Libya was chosen to chair the UN Human Rights Commission. The Libyan government and lawyers representing families of Lockerbie bombing victims signed a compensation agreement worth US$2.7 billion. Libya formally took responsibility for the bombing before the UN Security Council. The UN Security Council voted to lift the 11-year-old sanctions against Libya (already suspended). Libya announced that it would abandon its programmes to develop weapons of mass destruction (WMD).

2004 Libya agreed to compensate families of victims of the 1989 bombing of a French passenger aircraft and to pay US$35 million to victims of the bombing of a Berlin nightclub in 1986. The UK prime minister, Tony Blair, met Colonel Qadafi, the first visit of this kind since 1943. UN sanctions were finally lifted and the US and Libya restored diplomatic relations after a break of 24 years as US economic sanctions were lifted. President Chirac of France visited Libya, the first by a French president since 1951.

2005 Libya officially opened to tourist visitors. Leases on 26 oil fields were allocated to foreign companies.

2006 The US restored full diplomatic relations with Libya and rescinded Libya's designation as a state sponsor of terrorism.

2008 Muftah Mohammed Kaiba became secretary of the General People's Congress. Italian Prime Minister Silvio Berlusconi apologised for the damage caused to Libya during Italy's colonial reign and signed a US$5 billion investment plan to fund a coastal highway.

2009 Muammar al Qadafi was elected chairman of the African Union and later proposed a United States of Africa. Abdelbaset Ali Mohmed al Megrahi, imprisoned in Scotland since 2002 for the bombing of Pan Am Flight 103 over Lockerbie, was released, due to his failing health, to serve his prison term in Libya. Qadafi made an official visit to Italy.

2010 Muammar al Qadafi proposed that Nigeria should be split into two countries, one Muslim and the other Christian. The suggestion was vigorously rejected by Nigeria.

2011 Following the fall of authoritarian regimes in neighbouring Tunisia and Egypt in January, in February there was a call on the social network, Facebook, for peaceful demonstrations against the regime of Muammar al Qadafi. A number of demonstrations, triggered by the arrest of a lawyer acting for the families of prisoners believed to have been murdered in the Abu Salim prison in Tripoli, began in the east, centred on the second city of Benghazi. Police countered the demonstrations and there were a number of deaths reported.

On 18 February protesters gained control of Benghazi, while pro-government demonstrators held enthusiastic gatherings in

Tripoli. A report claimed 173 people had been killed by security forces and anti-government protests had spread to Tripoli. Qadafi's son, Saif al Islam, broadcast a warning to protesters that their actions could lead to a civil war. Abdel Fattah Younis, considered Qadafi's number two in his government, resigned and sided with the rebel movement.
The Transitional National Council (TNC) was established in Benghazi on 26 February, on the same day as the UN Security Council (UNSC) unanimously voted for an arms embargo, travel bans and asset freezes on Libyan regime leaders. The actions of Colonel Qadafi were referred to the International Criminal Court (ICC).
Foreign workers began to leave the country as the fighting grew more widespread. Libyan observers said that security forces had been supplemented by 'African mercenaries' who, it was said, had fired indiscriminately on protestors. Thousands of Egyptian workers fled home across the border as other nationals crossed into either Egypt or Tunisia for evacuation by the international community. The Indian government began evacuating its nationals. There were estimated to be 18,000 Indian nationals working in Libya, of which 3,000 were in Benghazi working for car companies and hospitals.
As the violence deepened, thousands of migrants and refugees from Somalia and Eritrea and other sub-Saharan countries caught up in the Libyan crisis, as well as Libyan citizens concerned by a possible regime change, crossed the Mediterranean Sea to reach the EU. They landed on the Italian island of Lampedusa, overwhelming local resources and immigration procedures. Malta also registered a steep rise in Libyans reaching its territory.
The battle for Misrata to the east of tripoli, the third city and most important business centre, began on 24 February. On 26 February, the EU imposed sanctions against the regime of Qadafi. NATO and its allies discussed a no-fly zone over Libya on 27 February. On 28 February, the US froze US$30 billion in assets belonging to the Libyan government. Qadafi launched a combined air and ground assault on Misrata on 1 March.
While other rebel leaders were debating whether to ask for Western military support, Abdul Fattah Younis said he would welcome foreign intervention by air strikes, but not a ground invasion. Four senior military commanders defected from Qadafi to the rebels. Qadafi sent food and medical supplies to Benghazi as a demonstration of national unity. On 2 March, the TNC formally requested that the UN impose a no-fly zone over Libya. On 3 March, the chief prosecutor of the ICC announced that he would investigate Qadafi, his sons and senior aids for crimes against humanity. Qadafi's forces attempted to retake the oil refineries of Zawiya on 4 March but were repelled with heavy losses on both sides. On 7 March, in the UNSC, France and the UK proposed a no-fly zone. Hundreds of Qadafi's forces, supported by tanks, entered Zawiya; following heavy fighting, they were beaten off. On 8 March the TNC told Qadafi that if he stopped his offensive, and he and his family left Libya, they would not face any future prosecution.
On 9 March the European Parliament called on all European countries to recognise the TNC as Libya's legitimate government. The EU agreed to extend sanctions against the Qadafi regime to include Libya's sovereign wealth fund and central bank. The measures would deny Qadafi funds from oil sales to buy armaments. The sanctions also included a weapons ban; any equipment that could be used for 'internal repression' had already been banned. On 10 March, Qadafi's forces began a concerted effort to retake cities along the coast west from Tripoli, starting with Zawiya.
On 12 March, Arab League foreign ministers meeting in Cairo endorsed calls for a UN no-fly-zone and formally recognised the TNC. Human rights observers accused Qadafi's security forces of arbitrary arrests, disappearances and torture following the fall of rebel towns. On 17 March the UNSC approved, by 10 votes (with five abstentions), UN Resolution 1973, which imposed a no-fly-zone over Libya, with 'all necessary measures' to protect civilians. An immediate ceasefire and an end to attacks on civilians were also demanded.
On 18 March Qadafi called a ceasefire and invited foreign observers to witness his actions. However, on 19 March his forces shelled the outer suburbs of Benghazi. At 1300 GMT, the first military flights by a five-country coalition (Canada, France, Italy, the UK and the US) attacked Libya's air defence systems and Libyan 'command and control' centres to impose the UN-sanctioned no-fly zone.
On 19 March the TNC designated the Central Bank of Benghazi (CBB) as its monetary authority and a governor was appointed. It also set up the Libyan Oil Company (LOC), headquartered in Benghazi, as the supervising authority for oil policy and production. From 23 March, LOC was able to sell all oil and natural gas within its control on the international market, depositing the proceeds in the CBB and denying any revenue to the Qadafi treasury. Qadafi forces continued their assault on Misrata and coalition fighters struck airfields and the road to Tobruk on 21 March.
Coalition air attacks followed for several days, while rebel forces took advantage of the safety being provided and began another campaign to capture towns between Benghazi and Tripoli. NATO took command of the no-fly zone and naval operations against Qadafi on 24 March.
On 3 April an envoy from Qadafi, deputy foreign minister Abdelati Obeidi, left for Athens on an apparent peace mission.
On 4 April Italy became the third country (after France and Qatar) to recognise the TNC. In a television broadcast on 29 April Qadafi vowed not to leave Libya. He also called for talks with NATO. The chief prosecutor for the ICC announced on 4 May that there were reasonable grounds for charges against Colonel Qadafi.
NATO damaged eight warships in three ports on 20 May; they were being used by Qadafi's forces to target civilians in Misrata and other towns.
On 30 May, South African President Jacob Zuma visited Colonel Qadafi in an attempt to mediate a cease-fire. Qadafi agreed to the cease-fire but would not relinquish power, as called for by the TNC. As a result the TNC rejected the agreement. The ICC issued an arrest warrant for Qadafi, accusing him of crimes against humanity. Warrants were also issued for Saif al Qadafi and intelligence chief Abdullah al Sanusi. On 29 June a supply of weapons (including assault rifles, machine guns and rocket launchers) was parachuted into rebel held territory of Libya by the French military. The AU condemned the move saying it put the whole region at risk. The French stated that this was a one-off decision to re-arm a town cut off from supplies from its allies.
On 3 July Turkey recognised the rebel TNC as the legitimate representatives of the Libyan people. US officials confirmed that they had held talks with representatives of Qadafi in mid-July, reiterating the US demand that Qadafi should step down. The TNC's military leader Abdel Fattah Younis was killed on 28 July. At first his death was blamed on Islamist-linked militia within TNC forces that did not trust him and thought he still had ties to Qadafi. On 1 August, France agreed to release US$259 million of frozen funds, banked by Qadafi, to the TNC for the express purchase of humanitarian materials (food and medicine). By 2 August, 63 people suspected of links to Qadafi had been arrested for murdering Younis. A draft constitution was published on 22 August 2011 that enshrined the form of state and its administration, plus rights of the family and judicial guarantees. Forces of the TNC took control of Tripoli on 23 August.

Mass graves began to be found around Tripoli. On 6 September, a large convoy of heavily armed and armoured vehicles, in the company of Tuareg fighters, crossed the Sahara and entered Niger. Mustafa Abdel Jalil, head of the TNC, arrived in Tripoli. He delivered his first public speech, in Martyrs' Square (the re-named Green Square where Qadafi used to harangue the nation), on 13 September. Although he said that *Sharia* (Islamic law) would be the main source of the law, he also said the TNC would not 'accept any extremist ideology, on the right or the left. We are a Muslim people, for a moderate Islam, and will stay on this road.' He also warned against reprisals by rebel forces against elements of the Qadafi regime.

UK Prime Minister David Cameron and French President Nicolas Sarkozy visited Libya on 15 September. Both leaders promised financial and practical support. A mass grave thought to contain the remains of over 1,200 prisoners from the Abu Salim prison murdered by the Qadafi regime in 1996 was found in Tripoli on 25 September. Libyan oil exports resumed in October. On 17 October, the pro-Qadafi TV station Arrai, confirmed that the youngest son of Colonel Qadafi, Khamis, had been killed by TNC fighters in August.

On 20 October, Muammar al Qadafi was caught and killed in his home town of Sirte, following weeks of intense fighting to capture it. Mustafa Abdul Jalil officially declared the national liberation of Libya in a ceremony held in Benghazi on 23 October. The TNC said that it would embark on building a democracy and would hold free elections in 2012.

On 23 October interim prime minister Jibril resigned, and the TNC voted for the consensus candidate, Abdurrahim al Keib (26 votes out of a total of 51), as interim prime minister on 1 November. Qadafi's body was taken away after dark on 25 October and buried at a secret location in the desert, to avoid his grave becoming a shrine for his supporters.

On 31 October, NATO officially ended its emergency mission to Libya – exactly seven months after its imposition of a naval blockade and no-fly zone. By 30 November, oil production had reached 750,000bpd.

2012 On 13 January, the governor of the central bank said the bank had begun to print a new Libyan currency and in the meantime was withdrawing the old currency, starting with 50 dinar notes (which many Libyans were refusing to use because of its image of Qadafi). Médicins Sans Frontières (MSF) suspended its work in prisons in Misrata on 26 January, due to the number of detainees being both tortured and presented for medical treatment before resumption of maltreatment and others denied urgent medical treatment following torture.

In February, the international human rights observer group, Amnesty International, warned that armed militias threatened the stability of Libya, as some former rebels were committing human rights violations, unchecked by the government.

On 6 March, during a conference attended by hundreds of people, the leaders of the eastern city of Benghazi declared their region to be a semi-autonomous state, to be known as Cyrenaica. According to the leaders, the oil-rich region had been neglected for decades with most development concentrated around Tripoli. He added that they were protecting their hard won independence. TNC leader, Mustafa Abdel Jalil, accused other Arab states of inciting those living in the east and of undermining the new regime by calling for federalism for Libya.

On 24 April the NTC enacted a law whereby no political party that was based on religious, tribal or ethnic principals would be allowed to form or contest elections.

On 1 July a mob ransacked the offices of the electoral authority in Benghazi, damaging ballot boxes and burning election papers, in advance of parliamentary elections. Pro-autonomy leaders from eastern Libya called for a boycott of the elections until a larger share in the new 200-member legislature that will draw up a new constitution was allocated to the east. The electoral law apportioned 60 seats to the eastern region, 102 seats for the western region and 38 seats for the remaining (Fezzan).

Elections for the General National Congress (GNC) took place on 7 July, having been postponed from 19 June. The newly elected GNC undertook to appoint a prime minister and cabinet within 30 days and provide governance while the (to be elected) Constitutional Assembly drafted Libya's new constitution, and new GNC elections could be held under the new rules. On 9 August the NTC handed power to the new GNC, which elected a moderate Islamist, Mohammed al Magarief, as its president on 10 August. His main task was to lead the GNC in appointing a prime minister and drafting a new constitution. US Ambassador J Christopher Stevens was killed by armed men within an angry mob that attacked the US Consulate in Benghazi on 11 September. Three other Americans and 10 Libyans were also killed as the building was shot at and fire-bombed. The mob was protesting at a film alleged to defame the Prophet Mohammed.

On 12 September, Mustafa Abushagur was elected prime minister by parliament (by 96 votes), narrowly defeating former interim prime minister Mahmoud Jibril (94 votes). Mr Abushagur will serve a fixed term in office, until March 2014.

On 16 September, over 50 people were arrested in connection with the unlawful death of US Ambassador Stevens.

On 22 September, police and protestors stormed the headquarters in Benghazi of the Islamist group Ansar al Sharia, held responsible for the death of the US ambassador, and drove them and other militia out of the city. On 23 September, the prime minister announced that all unauthorised camps and militia must be abandoned and disbanded. On 30 September, a range of over 600 different military hardware was handed over by hundreds of militia members following TV adverts promoting a collection.

On 4 October, parliament rejected Prime Minister Abushagur's proposed cabinet. On 8 October, Abushagur was dismissed as prime minister having twice failed to appoint a cabinet acceptable to parliament. On 14 October, parliament elected Ali Zidan prime minister, with a majority of 93 votes. He was given 14 days to propose a cabinet. On 14 November the cabinet of Prime Minister Zidan was sworn into office.

2013 Saif al Qadafi appeared in court on 2 May on criminal charges. On 25 June the national assembly elected Nouri Abusahmen as its president by 96 of 184 votes. Mr Abusahmen is the first Berber to be elected to the position. Over 1,000 prisoners were reported to have escaped from a jail in Benghazi on 27 July. On 13 August members of the Amazigh (Berbers) stormed parliament, demanding their language, culture and ethnicity be recognised in the constitution. Interior minister, Mohammed Khalifa al-Sheikh, resigned on 18 August, just three months after he was appointed. The ministry is under fire for not containing the violence that has flared up around the country. Mr Sheikh said he lacked support of the prime minister and complained of interference by members of the GNC. His resignation follows that of deputy prime minister, Awadh al-Barassi, on 4 August. Armed men shut down oil facilities in the western, Berber, region of Libya on 30 September. The Berber minority are concerned that they will be marginalised by the new constitution. In an interview with the BBC Newsnight programme on 8 October, Prime Minister Ali Zeidan asked for Western help to prevent the smuggling of weapons into Libya, which are then either used in the spread of militancy within Libya, or smuggled out of Libya into other north African countries. The day before the national congress had demanded the return of Anas al-Liby (also known as Nazih Abdul-Hamed al-Ruqai), captured in Tripoli by the US on 5 October. The Americans want Mr Liby to stand trial over the bombings of its embassies in Kenya and Tanzania in 1988. Prime Minister Ali Zeidan was kidnapped and briefly held by a group pf militia on 10 October. He was rescued by a different group. The incident illustrated the need for an effective police force or military to replace the militia groups supported by different ministries. Ali Zeidan himself called the kidnapping an 'attempted coup'. On 17 November, after clashes had left more than 40 people dead in Tripoli, militia groups from the city of Misrata were ordered to leave the capital.

2014 On February former Qadafi supporter but then commander of the anti-Qadafi supporters in the east, General Khalifa Haftar, called on television for Libyans to rise up against the GNC. There was no reaction and the general faded from view again. On 11 March Prime Minister Ali Zeidan lost a vote of confidence in parliament and Abdullah al Thani, formerly defence minister, was named as interim prime minister. He was sworn in the same day, for an initial two week period. The vote of confidence was called after the tanker *Morning Glory* managed to load some 234,000 barrels of oil from the eastern, rebel held, port of Sidra and then break through a naval blockade. Libyan officials had earlier reported that they had 'complete control' of the tanker. Zueitina and Hariga oil terminals in the east were reopened on 6 April after rebels agreed to partially lift their oil blockade in a deal reached with the government. Mr al Thani was confirmed as prime minister on 8 April. On 13 April Mr al Thani announced his resignation after he and his family were attacked. He said he and his caretaker ministers would continue working until a new prime minister could be named by parliament. However, Mr al Thani refused to cede power despite Ahmed Maiteeq being elected prime minister by the GMC in May. On 16 May supporters of General Haftar (Libyan National Army (LNA)) launched Operation Libyan Dignity, attacking bases in Benghazi of Ansar al-Sharia (AS), Rafallah al-Sahati and the February 17 Brigade. On 9 June the Supreme Court ruled that the election of Mr Maiteeq was 'unconstitutional' after the vote was described as 'chaotic'. Confused fighting continued throughout the country. At the end of July government Special Forces were over-run and forced from their base in Benghazi by militia fighters. Tripoli's head of police, Col Muhammad Suwaysi, was assassinated by unknown gunmen on 12 August. On 13 August parliament met in Tobruk in the east after violence in Tripoli and Benghazi. Members voted 111 to 13 to call for foreign intervention to protect civilians from clashes between rival militia groups. At the same time parliament voted to order the disbanding of all militia groups, although they do not have the means to enforce the ruling. Mr al Thani stepped down as prime minister on 29 August, in what he said was a ' move to end the power struggle in the country.' On 6 November the Supreme Court ruled that parliament was unconstitutional, 2015 Ansar al-Sharia, which calls for the implementation of Sharia law across Libya, announced the death of its leader, Mohammad al-Zahawi on 26 January. It is not known precisely when he died although it is thought that it was as a result of wounds received in October 2014.

Political structure

Constitution

A draft constitution was published on 22 August 2011 that enshrined the form of state and its administration, the rights of the family and judicial guarantees.

Independence date

17 February 2011 (as per draft constitution)

The executive

The prime minister and speaker of the house are elected by the House of Representatives. The current cabinet was approved by the House of Representatives in September 2014.

National legislature

The unicameral House of Representatives or Majlis Al Nuwab consists of 200 seats of which 32 are reserved for women. In the previous election, forty seats were elected by first-past-the-post in single-member constituencies, eighty were elected by single non-transferable vote in 29 multi-seat constituencies, and the remaining eighty were elected by proportional representation.

Legal system

The Libyan legal system is based on *Sharia* (Islamic law) and the Italian civil law system. There are separate religious courts and no constitutional provision for judicial review of legislative acts. The judicial system consists of the Supreme Court, courts of appeal, courts of first instance and summary courts. Libya has not accepted compulsory International Court of Justice (ICJ) jurisdiction.

Last elections

25 June 2014 (parliamentary – Council of Deputies), 20 February 2014 (parliamentary – Constitutional Assembly).

Results: Parliamentary – Council of Deputies: All 1,714 candidates were registered as independent candidates. Of the total 200 seats in the new parliament, 188 were set, while the remaining twelve seats were absent due to boycott or insecurity in some electoral districts. Secular factions had taken the most seats, while the Islamist lawmakers (Muslim Brotherhood), who had a bigger say in the old parliament only won around thirty seats this time. Abdullah al-Thinni won the election as an independent candidate. Turnout was 18 per cent, down from 60 per cent in the first post-Gaddafi election of July 2012.

Parliamentary – Constitutional Assembly: Political parties were not officially represented at the vote, only individuals were allowed to present themselves as candidates. Results suggest that liberal candidates did well in the capital Tripoli and the eastern city of Benghazi, where so much Islamist unrest had been present.

Next elections

To be announced.

Political parties

Ruling party

Party lists were forbidden under the electoral system.

Main opposition party

Not applicable.

Approximately 40 per cent of the population is under 14 years of age; 57 per cent 15–64 years; 3 per cent over 65.

Around 90 per cent of the population live in coastal regions, with half residing in Tripoli itself.

Population

6.21 million (2014)

Last census: August 1995: 4,404,986

Population density: Three inhabitants per square kilometre. Urban population 78 per cent (2010 Unicef).

Annual growth rate: 1.9 per cent, 1990–2010 (Unicef).

Ethnic make-up

Berber-Arab (97 per cent). There are small communities of Greeks, Maltese, Italians, Egyptians, Pakistanis, Turks, Indians and Tunisians.

Religions

Sunni Muslim (97 per cent). A third of Libya's Muslims are affilitated to the Sanusi religious sect, which had fought against European colonialism in the first half of the twentieth century.

Education

Libya has paid particular attention to its education system, with the aim of reducing illiteracy and improving the education available to women.

Education is free for all children during the compulsory years. Secondary schooling begins at aged 15 and the curriculum is divided into three- or four-year courses and comprises a number of secondary school types including both academic and specialised or vocational centres. English

and Arabic are the main languages for instruction.
Higher education is offered in 14 universities and 54 higher vocational institutes.
Literacy rate: 82 per cent adult rate; 97 per cent youth rate (15–24) (Unesco 2005).
Compulsory years: 6 to 15.

Health

The government provides free health services to all its citizens. UN sanctions had a detrimental impact on the quality and access to healthcare provision and many medical services and pharmaceutical products became unavailable. With the lifting of sanctions in 2004, these shortcomings were overcome to a certain extent. Many Libyans typically seek medical treatment in Tunisia, Egypt or in Western Europe. There are two large hospitals in Tripoli and Benghazi.

HIV/Aids

HIV prevalence: 0.3 per cent aged 15–49 in 2003 (World Bank)
Life expectancy: 72 years, 2004 (WHO 2006)
Fertility rate/Maternal mortality rate: 2.6 births per woman, 2010 (Unicef); maternal mortality 0.75 per 1,000 live births (World Bank).
Child (under 5 years) mortality rate (per 1,000): 15 per 1,000 live births (WHO 2012); 5 per cent of children aged under five are malnourished (World Bank).

Welfare

The government is theoretically committed to full provision of welfare services to all Libyan nationals. In reality, parts of the population are often not covered by welfare provisions. The most common welfare benefit is housing to those in need. The government provides a national social security system covering pensions and other social insurance, but the availability of such services regularly depends on annual oil receipts, which make up a large proportion of total government revenues.

Main cities

Tripoli (capital, estimated population 1.0 million in 2012), Benghazi (632,937), Misratah (Misurata) (285,759), Tobruk (138,535), Sabha (99,028), Bani Walid (90,769), Zawiyah (87,316), Sirte (78,215).

Languages spoken

Italian and English are spoken and there are also pockets of native Berber speakers.

Official language/s

Arabic

Media

The France-based media watchdog, Reporters Without Borders (RWB) assessed Libya's attitude to its news gathering, reporting and broadcasting services in 2006 and considered that the government 'maintains its monopoly of power, and the press continues to be just a propaganda tool'. In 2008 RWB noted that non-government media were allowed to operate but were firmly kept under its control, only foreign internet and satellite radio and television stations, particularly Al Jazeera, provide an independent viewpoint.
Change has begun, as the market is less tolerant of the political cant provided by the official media. Self-censorship by journalists is widespread.

Press

Private newspapers were only introduced in 2006, although censorship limits their news contents and no criticism of Colonel Qadafi is allowed.
In Arabic, newspapers controlled by the ministry of information include *Al Shames* (www.alshames.com), *Al Jamahiriya* (www.aljamahiria.com), *Al Fajr Al Jahideed* (www.alfajraljadeed.com) a bi-monthly and *Al Zahf Al Akhdar* (www.azzahfalakhder.com) which is controlled by the Revolutionary Committees Movement. Private newspapers produced by One Nine Media, owned by Saif al Islam Qadafi, include *Oea* (www.oealibya.com) and *Quryna* (www.quryna.com). In English, *The Tripoli Post* (www.tripolipost.com) is a weekly newspaper. The women's magazine *Kul Alfonoon* (www.kulalfonon.com) is a government publication.

Broadcasting

The state-owned, Libyan Jamahiriya Broadcasting Corporation (LJBC) (http://en.ljbc.net) is the national domestic broadcasting organisation.
Radio: The state-run Great Jamahiriya Radio operates four stations from major cities and includes a religious station. Its external service, Voice of Africa (www.voiceofafrica.com.ly), broadcasts in Arabic, French, Hausa and KiSwahili to countries in Africa with Muslim communities. The private, Allibya Radio broadcasting from Tripoli is operated by the organisation One Nine Media owned by Saif al Islam Qadafi.
Television: The state-run Great Jamahiriya Television operates several networks, with national coverage, providing different contents such as sport and entertainment. The only local, private TV station is Al Libiyah (www.allibiya.tv), provided via satellite and is operated by the organisation One Nine Media, owned by Saif al Islam Qadafi.
National news agency: Jamahiriya News Agency (Jana): www.jananews.ly

Economy

The economy is heavily dependent on its energy sector, which provides 96 per cent of government revenues (the remaining revenues are from primary mining products) and around 65 per cent of GDP. Following a global high in oil prices in 2007 Libya's current account balance was given a significant boost to US$35 billion in 2008, up from US$24 billion in 2007, even though oil production had been stable over the three years from 2006 at 1.8 million barrels per day (bpd) each year. Due to the fall in global oil prices more recently, Libya's current account has plummeted into negative, recording a figure of -US$2.7 billion in 2013, and -US$12.4 billion in 2014. Since 2011 Libya has experienced extremely unstable GDP growth due to civil unrest which has had a negative effect on growth, not only because international sanctions halted oil exports, but also because the rebel, Transitional National Council (TNC) (based in Benghazi) set up its own Libyan Oil Company (LOC) to export crude oil from wells within its region of influence. In 2011 GDP growth was as low as -62.1 per cent, before shooting up to 104.5 per cent in 2012. Since this peak plummeting oil prices have seen the economy enter a two-year recession, with GDP contractions of -13.6 per cent in 2013, and -24.0 per cent in 2014. According to the African Development Bank, GDP is expected to rise by 14.5 per cent in 2015, if an agreement is achieved relating to the opening of some of the major oil terminals, which would help to increase oil production.
Agriculture only contributes 2.0 per cent to GDP; Libya is still reliant on imported foodstuffs as it only produces around 25 per cent of its needs. Output is limited by poor soil and extreme climatic conditions that produce low rainfalls. To aid irrigation the Great Manmade River (GMR) project was created. The project is the largest underground network of pipes in the world and consists of more than 1,300 wells, most over 500 metres deep, and supplies 6.5 million cubic metres of fresh water per day to the capital and other major cities. The project supplies much needed water from underground aquifers beneath the Sahara to the Mediterranean coast and to some 135,000 hectares of cultivatable land. However, large resources are also spent on desalinisation research to meet growing demand.
The services sector accounted for 52.2 per cent of GDP in 2014, with significant foreign direct investment (FDI) in the tourism and real estate sectors. The industrial sector, including manufacturing

accounted for 45.8 per cent of GDP in 2014.
Some problems within the economy are yet to be addressed. It is still, largely, state controlled with minimal diversification highlighted by the fact that 75 per cent of all employment is in the public sector. Nevertheless Libya has liberalised its banking sector, given more independence to the Central Bank of Libya, with authority to allow foreign banks to operate, and enacted anti-money laundering laws. A privatisation programme has been broadened to include health, insurance, transport and downstream oil activities.

The non-oil sector, including construction accounts for over 20 per cent of GDP, with significant foreign direct investment (FDI) in the tourism and real estate sectors – over US$435 million for three projects in 2008.
Some problems within the economy have yet to be addressed. It is still, largely, state controlled with minimal diversification with around 75 per cent of all employment in the public sector. Nevertheless Libya has liberalised its banking sector, given more independence to the Central Bank of Libya, with authority to allow foreign banks to operate, and enacted anti-money laundering laws. A privatisation programme has been broadened to include health, insurance, transport and downstream oil activities.

External trade

Libya is a member of the Common Market of Eastern and Southern Africa (Comesa) with 18 other country members.
Comesa's objective is to formulate a large economic and trading union, which will be able to promote the interests of all members. Libya led the move towards a customs union, which became operational in 2009, in which all non-members are charged a common external tariff (CET).
Libya is also a member of the Arab Maghreb Union (AMU) and the Greater Arab Free Trade Area (Gafta) which operates a customs union whereby tariffs within Gafta will be reduced by a percentage each year, until none remain.
Libya applied for membership of the World Trade Organisation (WTO) in 2004 but in 2015 it is still undergoing economic and trade alignment required for full membership.

Imports

Goods imported include machinery, vehicles, semi-finished goods, food and consumer products.
Main sources: Italy (15.1 per cent of total in 2014), China (12.3 per cent), Turkey (11.8 per cent)

Exports

Principal commodities are crude oil, refined petroleum products, natural gas, gypsum, limestone and salt.
Main destinations: Italy (17.7 per cent of total in 2014), France (13.1 per cent), Germany (11.9 per cent)

Agriculture

Farming

Agriculture is estimated to employ around 3 per cent of the labour force.
Agricultural land (175.9 million hectares) is only 8.8 per cent of the total land area, of which 7.7 per cent is pasture, concentrated around oases and the northern coastal regions, especially near Benghazi and Tripoli.
Climatic conditions and irrigation problems limit output. Over 70 per cent of food requirements are imported. Libya is self-sufficient in fruit and vegetables, dairy products and poultry. The main crops are potatoes, wheat, barley, dates, tomatoes, almonds, oats, olives, citrus fruits and groundnuts.
To aid irrigation the Great Manmade River (GMR) project was created. The project is the largest underground network of pipes in the world and consists of more than 1,300 wells, most over 500 metres deep, and supplies 6.5 million cubic metres of fresh water per day to the capital and other major cities. The project supplies much needed water from underground aquifers beneath the Sahara to the Mediterranean coast and to some 135,000 hectares of cultivatable land. However, large resources are also spent on desalinisation research to meet growing demand.

Fishing

The total annual catch is typically 33,000 tonnes, of which up to 6,000 tonnes is exported with a total value of between US$15–30 million. Most of the catch is taken by artisanal boats with nets or hooks. There is negligible freshwater fishing, although the government has attempted to stock reservoirs with fish. Libya has a number of fish canning plants, which can tuna and sardines. Fishmeal is also produced.
Small quantities of fish are exported to Greece, Malta and Tunisia. There is a tuna cannery at Zanzur, and sardine canneries at Zuara and Khoms.

Forestry

Libya is very lightly forested, with less than 1 per cent of total land area covered by forest and woodland, from which small quantities of sawn timber and paper are produced. The majority of domestic demand for industrial wood products is met by imports. Experiments have been undertaken into tree planting, to halt the advance of the desert, but with mixed success; there has been some development of orchards.

Industry and manufacturing

The industrial sector contributed 45.8 per cent to GDP in 2014 and employs around 15 per cent of the workforce. Virtually all industry is state-owned.
Traditionally the industrial sector was limited to small-scale processing operations, mostly in food, wood and paper, textiles and soap. However, traditional small-scale agro-allied industries have given way to the growth of import substitution industries (such as building materials manufacture) and heavy industries (such as petrochemicals, iron and steel, concrete pipes and vehicle assembly). The National Petrochemicals Company has built up a substantial petrochemicals capacity since the late 1970s using local feedstock. Much industrial investment has gone into expanding capital-intensive chemicals capacity as a means of increasing the value added content of exports. Major metal smelting projects have been impeded by low incomes and depressed world prices in recent years. Other constraints to development are insufficiently trained Libyan manpower and the small domestic market.

Tourism

After the rapprochement with the West achieved in 2003 and the lifting of US sanctions in 2004, Libya officially opened to tourism in 2005.
Travel sanctions and political isolation has proved to represent a significant obstacle to the revival of Libya's tourism sector. Its tourist infrastructure had been neglected for many years and, while new resort and hotel projects have been initiated, more investment is needed to upgrade old resources. The Mediterranean beaches and ancient historical sites, together with its proximity to Europe and other developed North African tourist destinations, provide the country with good potential for expanding visitor numbers. Despite tourism being hampered by the on-going civil war, in 2014 5.5 per cent of GDP was derived from the travel and tourism industry, and it provided work to 4.4 per cent of the labour force.

Mining

Major mineral deposits include iron ore (which supplies the steel complex at Misrata), potassium, magnesium, sulphur, gypsum and phosphate. There are also potential uranium deposits. Commercial exploitation of minerals is restricted by high development costs.
Salt and construction materials are produced, but large reserves of iron ore at Wadi Shatti remain undeveloped, although this is being reconsidered.

Hydrocarbons

Proven oil reserves were 48.4 billion barrels at the end of 2014; Libya has one of the world's top ten highest oil reserves. Production was 498,000 barrels per day (bpd), which marked a decrease of 50 per cent from the 988,000 bpd produced in 2013. Hydrocarbon exports represent 95 per cent of total merchandised exports and 65 per cent of GDP.

Libya has Africa's largest proven oil reserves, but requires foreign investment of billions of US dollars in production and infrastructure to exploit its resources. The state-owned National Oil Company (NOC) is responsible for the oil industry, including exploration, production and distribution.

There are five domestic refineries, with a combined capacity of approximately 378,000bpd. They produce for the domestic market as well as the export of refined products. Libya also has oil refining operations overseas, mainly in Europe, operated by the state-owned Tamoil.

Proven natural gas reserves were 1.5 trillion cubic metres (cum) at the end of 2014, with production at 12.2 billion cum, an increase of 10.9 per cent on the 11.0 billion cum in 2013.

The government had been expanding gas production as it is attempting to replace oil with natural gas, so that more oil is made available for export. Plus, Libya, with its huge gas reserves is looking to Europe to build a market while using European energy companies to provide investment.

Any use of coal is commercially insignificant.

Energy

Electricity generating capacity was 6.7GW in 2013, and production is around 26 gigawatts hours (gWh) and supplies 100 per cent of the population; there is a totally interconnected system. While the vast majority of the 27 electricity-generating plants are gas-fired and steam-driven, some are still oil-fired but are located in rural, desert, areas. Crude oil is used in power plants located close to oil fields in remote desert areas.

The General Electricity Company of Libya (Gecol) has sole responsibility for generating and distributing electricity.

Power demand is growing rapidly at 9 per cent per annum, the government hopes to double generating capacity by 2020 as new, smaller power plants are opened in local areas. Gecol has allocated US$2.8 billion to upgrade the transmission system and construct sub-stations.

Financial markets

Stock exchange

The Libyan Exchange Stock Market

Banking and insurance

In April 2012 the Qatar National Bank announced that it had purchased a 49 per cent stake in a private in Libya, the Bank of Commerce and Development.

Central bank

Central Bank of Libya

Main financial centre

Tripoli

Time

GMT plus three hours

Geography

Libya is the fourth-largest country in Africa. It extends along the Mediterranean coast of North Africa with Tunisia and Algeria to the west, Niger and Chad to the south, Egypt to the east, and Sudan to the south-east. Most of the country is part of the Sahara Desert. Only the narrow coastal strip receives sufficient rainfall to be suitable for agriculture and it is here that 90 per cent of the population live.

In 1984, the Great Man-Made River Project was begun and when completed will transport daily 6.5 million cubic metres of fresh water, drawn from Sahara Desert aquifers in the south, to the coast in the north. The aquifer water is estimated to be over 40,000 years old. The irrigation will allow an increase in the land available for agriculture.

Hemisphere

Northern

Climate

The coastal areas enjoy a temperate Mediterranean climate. Summer (May–September) temperatures are up to 40 degrees Celsius (C), while winter (November–April) temperatures reach 25–32 degrees C during daytime but can fall to 4–5 degrees C at night. Otherwise, with 90 per cent of the country desert, very hot days (to 50 degrees C), cold nights and sandstorms are likely in May–June. There is low rainfall, mainly between October and March, in the highlands and semi-desert.

Dress codes

A lightweight suit or jacket and trousers are advised. A tie and a long-sleeved shirt should be worn at business meetings, but a jacket is not essential. Women should dress modestly, covering their arms and knees.

Entry requirements

Passports

Required by all. From 11 November 2007 all foreign passports require an Arabic translation. Visitors are advised to contact a Libyan consulate or tourist office for the latest official ruling before travelling.

Visa

Required by all and valid for three months. Exceptions granted for citizens of most Middle East countries, and a few other, African, states. For further information contact the nearest Libyan consulate.

All visitors must have an invitation from a Libyan contact – these can be obtained from a Libyan travel agent or Embassy – and essential information on the documentation must have Arab translations.

Business visitors should be sponsored by a Libyan company, which will organise the issue of a business visa.

Prohibited entry

Nationals of Israel and passport holders with Israeli visas may be refused entry, check status with a Libyan Consulate.

Currency advice/regulations

Import and export of local currency is prohibited. The import of foreign currency is unlimited but must be declared; export is limited to the amount declared.

Travellers cheques are not readily accepted. Carrying cash is the only realistic option, and the favoured currency is the US dollar. Penalties for the use of unauthorised currency dealers are severe.

Customs

There are strict customs regulations about the import or export of firearms, religious materials, antiquities and medications.

Prohibited imports

Alcohol and illegal drugs

Health (for visitors)

Mandatory precautions

Yellow fever vaccination certificate is required if travelling from an infected areas.

Advisable precautions

Vaccinations or booster shots are advised for typhoid, tetanus and hepatitis A. Other immunisation that may be advised are polio, TB, diphtheria, and hepatitis B. Malaria prophylaxis is recommended for visits to certain areas.

Avoid drinking tap water.

All necessary medication brought in by a visitor should be accompanied by a letter of explanation. A first-aid kit would be useful.

Hotels

Tripoli has a range of hotels.

Credit cards

Credit cards are not accepted.

Public holidays (national)

Fixed dates

9 Feb (Ashura), 3 Mar (Declaration of the People's Authority Day), 11 Jun (Evacuation Day), 1 Sep (Revolution Day), 7 Oct (Friendship Day), 26 Oct (Day of Mourning).

Variable dates

Eid al Adha (two days), Islamic New Year, Eid al Fitr (two days).

Islamic year 1437 (15 Oct 2015–2 Oct 2016):: The Islamic year contains 354 or 355 days, with the result that Muslim feasts advance by 10–12 days against the Gregorian calendar. Dates of feasts vary according to the sighting of the new moon, so cannot be forecast exactly.

Working hours

Friday is the Muslim holy day and all offices, businesses and banks are closed. The oil industry is also closed on Saturday.

Banking

Sat–Wed: 0800–1500 (winter); Sat–Wed: 0800–1200 and 1600–1700, Thu: 0800–1200 (summer).
Hours may be reduced during Ramadan.

Business

Sat–Thu: 0800–1600 (winter); Sat–Thu: 0700–1400 (summer).

Government

Sat–Thu: 0730–1430 (winter); Sat–Thu: 0700–1400 (summer).

Shops

Shops are mainly open 0800–1800, often closing for a few hours during the middle of the day.

Telecommunications

Mobile/cell phones

GSM 900 services are limited to populated areas.

Electricity supply

110 or 220V AC

Social customs/useful tips

Alcohol is banned throughout Libya and visitors arriving with alcohol will have it confiscated. Women often do not attend Arab social or business meetings, despite gender equality enshrined in the constitution.
Photography of public buildings and anything of military or security interest is not permitted. It is best to avoid criticism of the country, its leadership or Islam while in Libya since this could potentially result in a heavy-handed response from the authorities.
During Ramadan, eating, drinking and smoking in public is banned throughout the hours of daylight. Islamic and Arab customs prevail and must be respected by visitors. Pork is forbidden by Muslim law. Food is traditionally eaten with the right hand only.

Security

Crime is growing in Libya. The most common crimes are car theft and theft of items left in vehicles. Muggings have occurred on the beaches. Travel to remote areas is best undertaken in groups.

Getting there

Air

National airline: Libyan Arab Airlines.
International airport/s: Tripoli International airport (TIP), 35km from the city, facilities include duty-free shops, restaurants, post office and bank.
Benina International (BEN), 19km from Benghazi; Sebha (SEB), 11km from town.
Airport tax: Departure tax LD6, except for transit passenger. It may be included in the price of the ticket.

Surface

Road: There are entry points via Tunisia and Egypt by the main coast road, Algeria (via Sabhah and Ghat) and Niger and Chad (via Sabhah).
Water: There are ferry services from Malta to Tripoli. There are also occasional services from Casablanca (Morocco) and Alexandria (Egypt).
Main port/s: Benghazi, Misratah, Marsa Brega and Tripoli (free port).

Getting about

National transport

Air: Libyan Arab Airlines operates an hourly shuttle between Tripoli and Benghazi. Other scheduled routes include all major centres. Buraq Air also provides internal flights.
Road: There is a surfaced road system comprising an estimated 32,000km linking all main centres. The main roads include the 1,820km national coast road from the Tunisian border to the Egyptian border; Sabhah-Ghat; Tripoli-Sabhah; Agedabia-Kufra; Sabhah-Chad and Niger borders. Many rural roads have improved due to the infrastructure work carried out for the Great Man-Made River project.
Buses: There are services between main centres.
Rail: There has been no railway in operation since 1965 when the network was broken-up. There are plans to construct a new east-west railway line from the Tunisian border to Tripoli, extending it along the coast to Misratah and then on to Egypt via Tobruk. Another railway line is planned to run north-south from Misratah to Sabhah, and then on to Chad, however these projects are still little beyond their planning stages and may take several years before fruition. Meanwhile Libya has let contracts with private foreign companies to supply crossing and pointwork for the proposed east-west line.

City transport

Taxis: Yellow government taxis are generally cheaper than private taxis. It is advisable to negotiate the fare in advance. Taxis are often on a shared basis.
Buses, trams & metro: State-run bus services operate in Benghazi and Tripoli. They can be unreliable and overcrowded.

Car hire

There are car hire agencies in Tripoli and Benghazi, although rates can be quite high. Cars with drivers can be hired.

BUSINESS DIRECTORY

The addresses listed below are a selection only. While World of Information makes every endeavour to check these addresses, we cannot guarantee that changes have not been made, especially to telephone numbers and area codes. We would welcome any corrections.

Telephone area codes

The international direct dialling code (IDD) for Libya is +218, followed by area code and subscriber's number:

Benghazi	61	Tobruk	87
Misratah	51	Tripoli	21

Chambers of Commerce

Benghazi Chamber of Commerce, Trade, Industry and Agriculture, Issabri Street, PO Box 208, Benghazi (tel: 80-971; fax: 80-761; e-mail: benghaziccia@netscape.net).

Misurata Chamber of Commerce, Trade, Industry and Agriculture, Souweihli Street, PO Box 84, Misurata (tel: 616-497; fax: 620-340; e-mail: info@ccimisrata.org).

Tobruk Chamber of Commerce, Industry and Agriculture, Alfadel Abu Omar Street, PO Box 868, Tobruk (tel/fax: 24-835).

Tripoli Chamber of Commerce, Trade, Industry and Agriculture, 6 Najd Street, PO Box 2321, Tripoli (tel: 333-6855; fax: 333-2655).

Union of Chambers of Commerce, Trade, Industry and Agriculture, PO Box 12556, 26 Bandong Street, Tripoli (tel: 444-1613; fax: 444-1457; e-mail: unionchamber@hotmail.com).

Banking

Libyan Arab Foreign Bank, PO Box 2542, That al-Imad Administrative Complex, Tripoli (tel: 335-0155, 335-0160, 335-0086/7; fax: 335-0164/8).

Sahara Bank, PO Box 270, 10 First of September Street, Tripoli (tel: 333-9804; fax: 333-7922).

Wahda Bank, PO Box 452, Sharia Gamal Abd an-Naser, Benghazi (tel: 222-4122; fax: 222-4122, 222-4709).

Umma Bank Sal, PO Box 685, 1 Giaddat Omar El-Mokhtar Street, Tripoli (tel: 333-4031/35, 444-2541, 444-2544; fax: 333-2505, 444-2476).

Central bank

Central Bank of Libya, PO Box 1103, Tripoli (tel: 333-3591; fax: 444-1488; e-mail: info@cbl.gov.ly).

Stock exchange

The Libyan Exchange Stock Market

Travel information

Libyan Arab Airlines, PO Box 2555, Haiti Street, Tripoli (tel: 602-093, 608-860;

fax: 2-230-970; internet: www.libyanarabairline.com).

National tourist organisation offices
General People's Committee of Tourism, PO Box 82063, Tripoli (tel: 333-6452, 333-7576; fax: 334-2709; internet: www.libyan-tourism.org).

Other useful addresses
General National Organisation for Industrialisation, PO Box 4388, Tripoli (tel: 44-680, 34-995).

Kufrah & Serir Authority, Council of Agricultural Development, Benghazi.

National Oil Corporation, PO Box 2655, Tripoli (tel: 46-180).

National Trade Union Federation, PO Box 734, Tripoli.

National news agency: Jamahiriya News Agency (Jana): www.jananews.ly

Internet sites
Qadafi's official website: www.algathafi.org

Africa Business Network: www.ifc.org/abn

African Development Bank: www.afdb.org

Africa Online: www.africaonline.com

AllAfrica.com: http://allafrica.com

Buraq Air: www.buraqair.com

Libya on the Web: www.libyaweb.com/news.htm

Libyans Online: www.libyaonline.com

Libyan Mission at United Nations: www.un.int/libya/

Azar Libya Travel and Tour Company: www.angelfire.com/az/azartours/index.html

Juddaim Tourism Service: www.libya-juddaim.com/eng/index.html

Caravanserai Tours: www.caravanserai-tours.com

Liechtenstein

KEY FACTS

Official name: Fürstentum Liechtenstein (The Principality of Liechtenstein)

Head of State: Prince Hans-Adam II (titular), (since 1989; on 15 Aug 2004, Crown Prince Alois became acting Head of State)

Head of government: Prime Minister . Adrian Hasler (FBP) (from 27 Mar 2013)

Ruling party: Coalition led by Fortschrittliche Bürgerpartei (FBP) (Progressive Citizens' Party) with Vaterländische Union (VU) (Patriotic Union) (FBP since 2001; re-elected 2009 and 2013, VU since 2005; re-elected Feb 2009 and 2013)

Area: 160 square km

Population: 36,304 (2011)*

Capital: Vaduz

Official language: German

Currency: Swiss franc (Swf) = 100 centimes/rappen (the euro also circulates informally)

Exchange rate: Swf0.98 per US$ (Sep 2015)

GDP per capita: US$134,915 (2009)

GDP real growth: -1.20% (2009)

GDP: US$4.83 billion (2009)

Inflation: -0.50% (2009)

* estimated figure

On 25 June 2014 one of Liechtenstein's longest running legal cases was resolved when the government of the principality of Liechtenstein handed over to the Nigerian government €167 million (US$227 million), part of looted funds recovered from the Abacha family. The money had been stolen by former military dictator Sani Abacha and had been held by banks in Liechtenstein. The Nigerians had been frustrated by companies linked to the Abacha family which had filed a complaint before the European Court of Human Rights.

Sandwiched between Switzerland and Austria, tiny Liechtenstein (population just over 36,300, area 35 square kilometres) is Europe's only absolute monarchy. Crown Prince Alois, who became acting Head of State after his father Prince Hans-Adam stepped back in August 2004 has the power to hire and fire the government since the people of Liechtenstein voted in a constitutional referendum in March 2003 to give the head of state sweeping new powers.

Liechtenstein is known mostly for its financial services, and indeed they account for 33 per cent of gross domestic product (GDP). And since Liechtenstein was removed from the Organisation for Economic Co-operation and Development's (OECD) blacklist of non-co-operative tax havens in April 2009 it has been repositioning itself as a legitimate financial centre.

However, Liechtenstein's strongly export-oriented industry and manufacturing sector is the largest sector, contributing 36 per cent of GDP. Traditionally, Liechtenstein has focused on producing high-quality, specialist goods, including machine and tool engineering, precision instruments and the dental and food industries.

Liechtenstein is in a customs union with Switzerland and is a member of the four-nation European Free Trade Association (EFTA) which gives it trading preferences with the European Union.

Risk assessment

Economy	Fair
Politics	Fair
Regional stability	Good

COUNTRY PROFILE

Independence in 1719 was followed in the early nineteenth century by a period of French domination, then close connection with Austria until 1918.

1938–70 Fortschrittliche Bürgerpartei (FBP) (Progressive Citizens' Party) was the majority party in the coalition government.

1970–74 Vaterländische Union (VU) (Fatherland Union) was the majority party in coalition, followed by FBP in the 1974 elections.

1978 Liechtenstein was admitted to the Council of Europe. A VU-led coalition was formed.

1984 Prince Hans-Adam II took over executive power from his father. Women were granted the vote in national elections, but not in local elections.

1986 Women were given to right to vote in all elections.

1989 The VU gained a majority of one seat.

1993 FBP became the largest party

1997 The VU gained an outright majority in the elections, the first by any party for over 60 years, and Mario Frick became prime minister.

2001 FBP was elected and Otmar Hasler became prime minister.

2002 The Organisation for Economic Co-operation and Development's (OECD) included Liechtenstein on a list of seven states that were failing to meet international standards on financial transparency and information exchange. An agreement was signed with Monaco over the prevention of money laundering and terrorist financing.

2003 In a referendum, 64 per cent of voters agreed to give Prince Hans-Adam II more power, including the right to dismiss any government deemed incompetent. The vote followed a long-standing dispute between parliament and the monarch, who had threatened to leave the country if his constitutional reform proposals were not adopted.

2004 Liechtenstein adopted a new aubergine-coloured flag. Prince Hans-Adam II handed over day-to-day responsibility for running the country to his son, Prince Alois, while remaining head of state himself.

2005 Otmar Hasler of the ruling FBP was re-elected with 48.7 per cent of the vote

(12 seats out of 25). A coalition with the VU was formed.
2006 Liechtenstein celebrated the bi-centenary of its admission to the Confederation of the Rhine in 1806. After its borders were re-measured the size of the country was found to be greater than previously thought at 160 square km,
2007 The Swiss army, on night manoeuvres, accidentally trekked up to 2km into Liechtenstein before the error was noticed and the 171-man company returned to their own lands.
2008 An international arrest warrant was issued for the former employee of the LGT Bank, who allegedly sold client details to foreign governments. Germany, the UK and several other countries, have used these records to pursue tax evasion by their citizens. Liechtenstein announced it would modify its banking rules to allow 'comprehensive co-operation' with foreign finance ministries on tax issues. However, 'a culture of privacy' would still be maintained.
2009 In parliamentary elections, the VU won 47.6 per cent of the votes (13 seats out of 25). Otmar Hasler resigned as prime minister and was succeeded by Klaus Tschütscher. Liechtenstein was removed from the OECD's list of countries considered unco-operative tax havens.
2011 A rental scheme for the entire principality was launched in April for US$70,000 per night, with the offer of accommodation for 150 people, customised street signs and temporary currency. The marketing opportunities were identified following a refusal in 2010 by authorities in hiring the country as a backdrop to a music video for the Rap-star Snoop Dogg. In December, Liechtenstein became a member of the European Union Schengen area whereby all travellers may cross borders without a passport or visa.
2012 A constitutional referendum was held on 1 July to decide whether to remove the veto held by the Prince of Liechtenstein of any legislation. The motion was defeated by a vote of 76.1 per cent on a turnout of 82.9 per cent.
2013 The 3 February general election results were The Fortschrittliche Bürgerpartei (FBP) (Progressive Citizen's Party) won 40.0 per cent (10 seats out of 25), Vaterländische Union (VU) (Fatherland Union) 33.5 per cent (8), Die Unabhängigen (DU)(The Independents) 15.3 (4) and Freie Liste (FL) (Free List) 11.1 per cent (3). Turnout was 79.8 per cent. Attempts by Nigeria to repatriate US$250 million stolen by former military dictator Sani Abacha and being held by banks in Liechtenstein have been frustrated by companies linked to the Abacha family which have filed a complaint before the European Court of Human Rights.
2014 A Nigerian finance ministry statement confirmed that 'Nigeria will on 25 June 2014 receive the sum of euros 167 million (US$227 million) from the government of the principality of Liechtenstein, part of looted funds recovered from the Abacha family.' To secure the funds, Nigeria agreed to drop a legal case tied to Abacha's family.

Political structure

Constitution

The constitution dates from 1921.Voting rights for women on national issues were granted in 1984, and on local matters two years later.

In 2003, 64 per cent of voters were in favour of constitutional changes, which gave Prince Hans-Adam II power to veto the decisions of parliament and to sack the government, and powers over the appointment of judges, but it took away his right to rule by emergency decree for an unlimited period and to nominate government officials.

Form of state

Constitutional monarchy

The executive

The head of state is the monarch. The 2003 referendum conferred on the monarch the power to veto the decisions of parliament and to sack the government.

National legislature

The constitution provides for a unicameral Landtag (parliament) with 25 seats, elected by proportional representation in two multi-seat constituencies, for a four-year term. The Landtag elects a five-member government, which is thereafter officially approved by the head of state.

Legal system

The monarch appoints the country's judges.

Last elections

2013 (parliamentary)

Results: Parliament: The Fortschrittliche Bürgerpartei (FBP) (Progressive Citizen's Party) won 40.0 per cent (10 seats out of 25), Vaterländische Union (VU) (Fatherland Union) 33.5 per cent (8), Die Unabhängigen (DU) (The Independents) 15.3 (4) and Freie Liste (FL) (Free List) 11.1 per cent (3). Turnout was 79.8 per cent.

Next elections

2017 (parliamentary)

Political parties

Ruling party

Coalition led by Fortschrittliche Bürgerpartei (FBP) (Progressive Citizens' Party) with Vaterländische Union (VU) (Patriotic Union) (FBP since 2001; re-elected 2009 and 2013, VU since 2005; re-elected Feb 2009 and 2013)

Main opposition party

Fortschrittliche Bürgerpartei in Liechtenstein (FBP) (Progressive Citizens' Party in Liechtenstein)

Population

36,304 (2011)*

Last census: December 2000: 33,307

Population density: 200 inhabitants per square km. Urban population 14 per cent (2010 Unicef).

Annual growth rate: 1.1 per cent, 1990–2010 (Unicef).

Ethnic make-up

Alemannic (87.5 per cent), Italian, Turkish and other (12.5 per cent).

Religions

Roman Catholic (80 per cent), Protestant (7.4 per cent).

Education

Primary education lasts for five years. Secondary education, starting at aged 12, is provided through three school types: *Oberschule, Realschule* and *Gymnasium*. Each is geared to the attainment outcomes expected of their students.

On completing four years (compulsory) secondary education, a lower secondary school certificate is awarded. *Realschule* students either undertake a one year technical or vocational course leading to specialised schools of further education, or an academic course to attain the lower level Matura Certificate. Students of the *Gymnasium* complete a four year academic course, attaining the higher grade Matura Certificate which is recognised for university entrance either at home or in Switzerland, Austria and Germany.

Compulsory years: Seven to 16.

Health

Life expectancy: 79 years (estimate 2003)

Main cities

Vaduz (capital, estimated population 5,161 in 2012), Schaan (5,829), Triesen (4,738), Balzers (4,528), Eschen (4,347), Mauren (3,893).

Languages spoken

Allemannish – a dialect of German – is also spoken.

Official language/s

German

Media

Press

There two dailies newspapers are *Liechtensteiner Vaterland* (www.vaterland.li) and *Liechtensteiner Volksblatt* (www.volksblatt.li) and one weekly *Liewo Sonntagszeitung* which is published on Sunday.

Dailies: Two main dailies include the *Liechtensteiner Vaterland* (Vaduz) and *Liechtensteiner Volksblatt* (Schaan).

Weeklies: *Liechtenstein News* is the official weekly newspaper, providing tourist and hotel information in the principality.

Broadcasting

Radio Liechtenstein (www.radio.li) has a network of seven stations. Swiss radio signals are readily received in Liechtenstein including RTSI (www.rtsi.ch) and DSR, with seven stations. RTSI also broadcasts TV programmes.

Economy

Liechtenstein has a highly industrialised, export-based economy with a well developed banking sector. It ranks as one of the wealthiest countries by GDP per capita in the world. There is close economic inter-dependence with Switzerland through a customs and currency union (neither country is a member or the European Union).

Financial services contribute about 30 per cent of its GDP. It is home to some 17 banks, including Liechtenstein Global Trust (LGT), owned by the royal family.

The tourism sector is an important foreign exchange earner and together with the services sector enjoyed rapid expansion during the latter part of the 1990s to provide over 55 per cent of GDP.

Around 40 per cent of the workforce are employed in the service sector, with a large proportion of cross-border workers from Switzerland and Austria. Around 30,000 businesses are registered in Liechtenstein, which is not far short of one business per resident. There is an extremely high ratio of self-financing enjoyed by domestic businesses plus their ability, if necessary, to fall back on private wealth. A number of companies are research-focussed and are considered world leaders in their particular specialities.

Liechtenstein has repeatedly come under pressure due to its lack of transparency laws in relation to its banking system, especially from the US and Germany, and as a result Liechtenstein has had to sign multiple bilateral information-sharing agreements. This step to increasing co-operation and reaching European standards of banking has led to more openness from the small nation. Subsequently, they joined the open-border Schengen area in 2011.

External trade

Liechtenstein is one of the four members of the European Free Trade Association (EFTA) and European Economic Area (EEA) which allows access to the internal EU market. Approximately 70 per cent of Liechtenstein's exports goes to the internal EU market.

While the industrial sector produces goods of high value it is the financial services and tourism that make the most significant contributions to the balance of payments.

Imports

Main imports include agricultural products, raw materials, machinery, metal goods, textiles, foodstuffs and vehicles.

Main sources: EU, Switzerland

Exports

Principal commodities include small speciality machinery, audio and video parts, vehicle parts, dental and optical products, prepared foodstuffs, ceramics, hardware and electronic equipment.

Main destinations: EU (typically over 60 per cent in total – Germany (24 per cent) Austria (10 per cent), France (9 per cent), Italy (7 per cent), UK (5 per cent)), US (18.9 per cent), Switzerland (15.7 per cent)

Agriculture

Farming

Agriculture is small-scale, employing only about 1.7 per cent of the population (350 workers). Activity is concentrated on dairy farming and farming of fodder cereals although vegetable cultivation and wine production are also undertaken. Utilising methods such as technical rationalisation and intensive cultivation, yields have been steadily increasing. Production typically includes 150 tonnes (t) grapes and 12,000t milk.

Fishing

Forestry

Forested land accounts for 42 per cent of the principality and 0.3 per cent of the agricultural sector are employed in forestry. The forestry industry has grown since the late 1990s, doubling production to 22,167 cubic metres (cum) industrial roundwood and 18,000cum sawlogs and veneer logs and maintaining production of 4,000cum-fuel wood annually.

Industry and manufacturing

Industry and trade employs about 45 per cent of the workforce. Owing to lack of raw materials and a small domestic market, the sector is export-based and centred on specialised and high technology production. Manufacturing is focused on machine building, precision engineering and metal working industries. There are also traditional industries such as chemicals (mainly pharmaceuticals), textiles, ceramics and food processing. The production of materials for dental medicine, of micro-sections for optics and electronics, the manufacture of preserves and deep-frozen products, upholstery, and varnishes, have all attained growing importance. Liechtenstein is the world's largest exporter of false teeth.

Tourism

Liechtenstein receives over 50,000 tourist arrivals each year, mainly from Germany and Switzerland. In recent years the popularly of staying in the towns has risen, while those in the mountains have fallen. Most tourism activities on offer consist of outdoor pursuits geared to the seasons, such as winter sports and wildlife watching at other times of the year. Local and regional cuisine is promoted.

The State Art Collection (collected by the Princes of Liechtenstein) includes over a thousand art works and among them are paintings by Van Dyck and Rubens. Only a portion of the collection is on display to the visiting public at any one time.

Hydrocarbons

Liechtenstein does not produce any hydrocarbons. Over 90 per cent of energy imports are acquired from Switzerland and 46 per cent of Liechtenstein's primary energy consumption is met by oil imports. Gas contributes 27 per cent of energy consumption.

Energy

Liechtenstein is dependent on imported energy from Switzerland, which supplies over 90 per cent of the energy needed. The remainder is sourced from domestically generated hydropower (75 per cent) and wood (25 per cent). The country has ratified the Kyoto Protocol. The government has pledged to source 10 per cent of domestic energy requirements from renewable sources particularly biomass and solar.

Banking and insurance

Three main banks are in operation: Liechtensteinische Landesbank, LGT Bank in Liechtenstein and Verwaltungs und Privat-Bank (VP Bank) AG. These have a close association with the Swiss banking system. Secrecy laws are strict although new legislation has put an end to the old anonymous numbered accounts.

There are a total of 17 banking institutes in operation.

Liechtenstein is a signatory of an EU tax agreement introduced in 2005 in a number of non-EU countries. Liechtenstein will impose a withholding tax of up to 35 per cent, to be passed to the tax department of an EU citizen's country whilst retaining the anonymity of the saver. This means that the relevant EU country will not be informed about the amount of money in its citizens' bank accounts. In an effort to avoid joining the global list of non-co-operative tax havens, held by the Organisation of Economic Co-operation and Development (OECD), Liechtenstein eased its banking laws to allow the sharing of bank data that cracks down on offshore tax evasion.

Liechtenstein has also agreed to supply information on tax fraud, for criminal or civil trials, and notify EU member states about additional malpractice.

In 2005, a banking ombudsman was appointed in Liechtenstein, ending years of reliance on the Swiss banking ombudsman.

The insurance sector is a recent development. Eight companies make up the Liechtenstein Insurance Association, formed in 1998.

Central bank

Centrum Bank AG

Offshore facilities

Liechtenstein is a major international offshore financial centre, and the largest single supplier of fiduciary funds in Europe.

Time

GMT plus one hour (daylight saving, late March to late October, GMT plus two hours)

Geography

Liechtenstein is a tiny, land-locked country, surrounded by Switzerland (to the west and south) and Austria (to the east). The area of the principality is 160 square km. The river Rhine forms Liechtenstein's western frontier.

The western part of Liechtenstein is lowland, situated in the Rhine flood-plain. This has been drained, providing a wide range of soil types suitable for agriculture. The eastern half of the country is in the foothills of the Rhätikon mountains (Raetian Alps), which rise to snowy Alpine peaks. The highest point is the Grauspitz at 2,599m. Coniferous forests and alpine meadows cover the lower slopes. There are three main valleys in the mountains. The river Samina crosses the range south to north to join the Ill river in Austria.

Hemisphere

Northern

Climate

Varies with altitude, generally mild and often windy. Average summer temperature 17 degrees Celsius (C). Average winter temperature 1 degree C.

Dress codes

Medium-weight throughout the year, with a topcoat for winter.

Entry requirements

Passports

Swiss regulations apply. Passports are required by all, except nationals of EU countries. Passports must be valid for three months beyond intended stay.

Visa

Visas are required by all, except nationals of EU/EEA countries, Australasia, North America, Japan and some other countries. Contact the nearest embassy or consulate for details. A business visa for a citizen of a non-exempt country requires a letter of invitation from or evidence of correspondence with a Liechtenstein company.

Currency advice/regulations

There are no restrictions on the import and export of local and foreign currencies.

Customs

Restricted amounts of alcoholic beverages, tobacco and gifts (up to value of Swf300) may be imported duty free.

Health (for visitors)

Nationals of the European Economic Area (EEA) countries and Switzerland can access reduced cost and sometimes free necessary medical treatment using a European Health Insurance Card (EHIC) while visiting the EEA. Applications for the EHIC should be made before travelling.

The EHIC of nationals of the 10 countries which joined the EU in 2005 are not valid in Switzerland.

Mandatory precautions

None

Advisable precautions

Up-to-date tetanus and polio immunisations.

Hotels

Tips are included in hotel and restaurant bills.

Public holidays (national)

Fixed dates

1 Jan (New Year's Day), 2 Jan (St Berchtold's Day), 6 Jan (Epiphany), 2 Feb (Candlemas), 19 Mar (Feast of St Joseph), 1 May (Labour Day), 15 Aug (Assumption Day), 8 Sep (Nativity of Our Lady), 1 Nov (All Saints' Day), 8 Dec (Immaculate Conception), 24–26 Dec (Christmas), 31 Dec (New Year's Eve).

Variable dates

Shrove Tuesday, Good Friday, Easter Monday, Ascension Day, Whit Monday, Corpus Christi (May/Jun).

Working hours

Banking

Mon–Fri: 0800–1630.

Business

Mon–Fri: 0800–1200 and 1330–1730.

Government

Mon–Fri: 0800–1630.

Shops

Mon–Fri: 0800–1200, 1330–1830; Sat: 0800–1600.

Getting there

Air

International airport/s: There are no airports in Liechtenstein. The nearest international airport is Zürich-Unique (ZRH), Switzerland, approximately 130km from Vaduz. Travel to Liechtenstein can then be continued by road, rail or bus; an autoroute connects Zürich with Liechtenstein.

Surface

Road: Good road access from Switzerland and to a lesser extent Austria. Autoroute (N13) extends along Liechtenstein's Rhine border to Lake Constance, Austria and Germany in the north, continuing southwards towards St Moritz. In the west there are autoroutes to Zürich, Bern and Basel.

Motorway connections: Balzers, Vaduz, Schaan, Bendern, Ruggell.

Rail: The nearest rail stations to Vaduz are at Sargans and Buchs, in St Gallen, Switzerland. Another rail station is at Feldkirch in Austria.

Getting about

National transport

Buses: All villages can be reached by bus service.

Rail: Restricted rail network, with stations at Nendelny and halts at Schaan and Schaanwald.

Nearest main rail stations are at Buchs and Sargans in St Gallen, Switzerland, and Feldkirch in Austria.

City transport

There are regular and inexpensive bus services, and easily obtainable taxi services. Tipping is not customary.

Car hire

Service offered by Avis (Vaduz), Europcar (Eschen-Nendeln) and Nolo (Balzers). Driver must have held a valid driving licence for at least one year and be over 20 years of age. Speed limit 50kph in city, 80kph outside. Traffic drives on the right.

BUSINESS DIRECTORY

The addresses listed below are a selection only. While World of Information makes every endeavour to check these addresses, we cannot guarantee that changes have not been made, especially to telephone numbers and area codes. We would welcome any corrections.

Telephone area codes

The international direct dialling (IDD) code for Liechtenstein is +423, followed by subscriber's number.

Chambers of Commerce

Liechtenstein Chamber of Commerce and Industry, Altenbach 8, 9490 Vaduz (tel: 237-5511; fax: 237-5512; e-mail: info@lihk.li).

Banking

Centrum Bank AG, Heiligkreuz 8, FL-9490 Vaduz (tel: 235-8585; fax: 235-8686).

LGT Bank in Liechtenstein AG (prior to Jan 1996, known as BIL GT Group), Herrengasse 12, FL-9490 Vaduz (tel: 235-1122; fax: 235-1522).

Verwaltungs und Privat-Bank AG, Im Zentrum, Aeulestrasse 6, FL-9490 Vaduz (tel: 235-6655; fax: 235-6500).

Central bank

Liechtensteinische Landesbank, 44 Städtle, PO Box 384, FL-9490 Vaduz (tel: 236-8811; fax: 236-8822; e-mail: llb@llb.li).

Travel information

National tourist organisation offices

Liechtenstein Tourism, Städtle 38, PO Box 139, FL-9490 Vaduz (tel: 239-6300; fax: 239-6301; e-mail: info@tourismus.li).

Other useful addresses

Amt für Volkswirtschaft (national statistics office), Kirchastrasse 7, FL-9490 Vaduz (tel: 236-6871; fax: 236-6889).

Liechtenstein Embassy (USA), 633 Third Avenue, 27th Floor, New York, NY 10017 (tel: (+1-202)-599-0220; fax: (+1-202)-599-0064).

Postillion-Reisen AG, Landstrasse 9, FL-9494 Schaan (tel: 26-565; fax: 27-037).

Presse-und Informationsamt, Regierungsgebäude, FL-9490 Vaduz (tel: 236-6111; fax: 236-6460).

Internet sites

Liechtenstein News: http://www.news.li

Tourism information: http://www.tourismus.li/

Lithuania

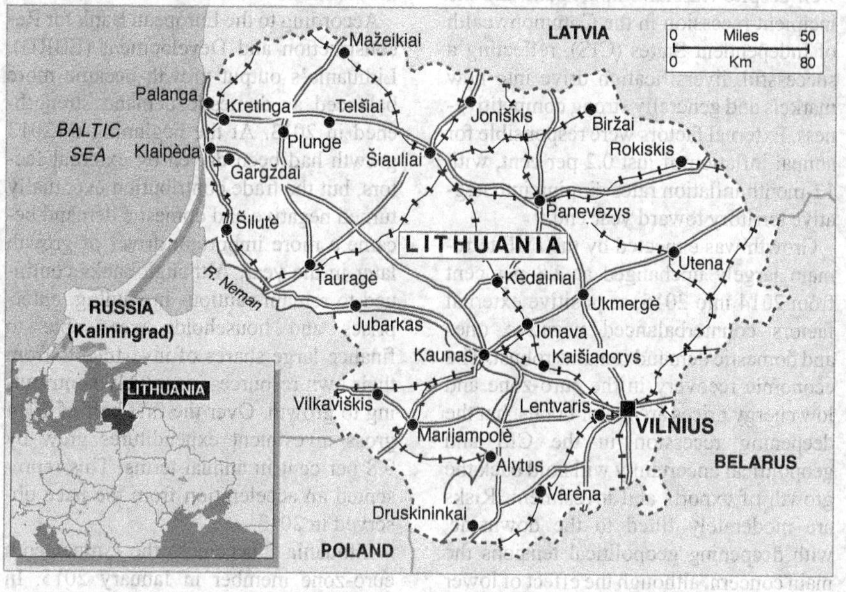

In Lithuania's May 2014 presidential elections the incumbent President Grybauskaitė obtained victory in the second round of voting. Ms Grybauskaitė was standing as an independent candidate. When the votes were counted, Dalia Grybauskaitė had won 58 per cent with her Social Democrat rival Zigmantas Balcytis 16 percentage points behind, on 42 per cent. It was the first time in Lithuania's history as an independent country that a president had been elected for two consecutive terms. The importance of the elections had been dramatically underlined by events in Ukraine and the annexation of Crimea by Russia. Ms Grybauskaitė had accused Russia of seeking 'confrontation, aggression and a review of post-war peace structures.' In late 2012, parliamentary elections had led to a change in government. This time round it was a coalition government lead by the Lietuvos Socialdemokratu Partija (LSDP) (Social Democratic Party of Lithuania), with Darbo Partija (DP) (Labour Party), Tvarka ir Teisingumas (TT) (Order and Justice) and Lietuvos Lenku Rinkimu Akcija (LLRA) (Electoral Action of Poles in Lithuania). Algirdas Butkevicius became prime minister. The four-party coalition had surprised many observers by its stability and decisiveness.

Any port in a storm

The arrival in a European port of a nondescript grey painted factory ship would not normally be a major occasion. But in late October 2014 the arrival of the 'floating storage with a regasification unit' (FSRU) vessel *Independence* in the Lithuanian port of Klaipeda was loaded with significance, both commercial, but also political and symbolic. The great and the good from half a dozen European countries – Lithuania, Latvia, Estonia, Norway – even the US – had turned up both to welcome the vessel, but also to show their support of the strategy that lay behind its arrival. The event marked the commissioning of the first Liquefied Natural Gas terminal in the Baltic and Nordic region. A report in the *New York Times* dubbed the ship the 'game changer'.

The new installation was, eventually, to enable Lithuania to survive without Russian gas, thereby: 'redrawing the energy map for the Baltic states', and ending the supply monopoly of Russia's Gazprom and Lithuania's effective isolation from the global gas markets. The terminal would enable Lithuania to meet all the gas needs of its three million citizens and also supply LNG to Baltic neighbours Latvia and Estonia. Initially, Lithuania planned

KEY FACTS

Official name: Lietuvos Respublika (Republic of Lithuania)

Head of State: President Dalia Grybauskaitė (from 12 Jul 2009, re-elected 25 May 2014)

Head of government: Prime Minister Algirdas Butkevicius (from 22 Nov 2012)

Ruling party: Coalition led by Lietuvos Socialdemokratu Partija (LSDP) (Social Democratic Party of Lithuania), with Darbo Partija (DP) (Labour Party), Tvarka ir Teisingumas (TT) (Order and Justice) and Lietuvos Lenku Rinkimu Akcija (LLRA) (Electoral Action of Poles in Lithuania) (from 22 Nov 2012)

Area: 65,200 square km

Population: 2.94 million (2014)*

Capital: Vilnius

Official language: Lithuanian

Currency: Litas (plural Litai) (Lt) = 100 cents

Exchange rate: Lt0.89 per US$ (Sep 2015)

GDP per capita: US$16,386 (2014)*

GDP real growth: 2.93% (2014)*

GDP: US$48.23 billion (2014)*

Labour force: 1.47 million (2014)*

Unemployment: 10.70% (2014)*

Inflation: 0.24% (2014)*

Balance of trade: -US$1.99 billion (2014)*

* estimated figure

to buy 0.54 billion cubic metres (bcm) of gas per year, enough to cover about a quarter of its gas needs, from Norway's Statoil. Legislation which stipulated that certain large Lithuanian domestic gas consumers would purchase 25 per cent of their supply from the terminal was challenged under European Union (EU) competition policies. As a result, the legislation had to be reversed, which risked diminishing the commercial viability of the project. Energy security had long been at or near the top of the Lithuanian political and economic agenda. Until the arrival of the *Independence* , 100 per cent of gas had been supplied to Lithuania by Gazprom. In the longer term, it was hoped that the LNG terminal would become the LNG hub for the Baltic Sea, open for third party access. The capacity of the terminal could expand to provide 75 per cent of the total natural gas demand in Lithuania, Latvia and Estonia.

As it happened, Lithuania's long-term gas supply contract with Gazprom was due to expire at the end of 2015. Lithuania had traditionally met about 60 per cent of its electricity needs via imports, the highest import dependency ratio in the EU and relied on Russia for its energy supplies. Lithuania's dependence on energy supplies from Russia will further diminish when it commissions the new 650MW sub-sea cable to Sweden, which is scheduled for the end of 2015.

The economy

In May 2015 the International Monetary Fund (IMF), in its annual assessment of the Lithuanian economy noted that growth had remained resilient, despite challenges in the external environment. Strong domestic demand growth on the back of improving labour market conditions had underpinned real gross domestic product (GDP) growth of 2.9 per cent in 2014. Exports had held up reasonably well despite Russian import bans and the incipient recession in the Commonwealth of Independent States (CIS), reflecting a successful diversification drive into new markets and generally strong competitiveness. External factors were responsible for annual inflation of just 0.2 per cent, with 12-month inflation rates dipping into negative territory toward year end.

Growth was expected by the IMF to remain largely unchanged at 2.8 per cent from 2014 into 2015, as positive external factors counterbalanced negative ones and domestic demand remains robust. The economic recovery in the euro-zone and low energy prices are major boons, but the deepening recession in the CIS and geopolitical uncertainty will hold back the growth of exports and investment. Risks are moderately tilted to the downside, with deepening geopolitical tensions the main concern, although the effect of lower energy prices could surprise on the upside. Inflation looked likely to turn positive again, but none the less average below zero for the year as a whole.

The main policy challenge will continue to be to secure reasonably rapid convergence with living standards in Western Europe. With macro-economic stability and strong policy frameworks in place, the onus is mainly on structural reforms: fiscal structural reforms to lift spending efficiency and shift the tax burden away from labour; investment and innovation promotion through use of EU funds and better focused policies; and making the most of demographically shrinking labour resources through education reform and a modernisation of the labour code.

According to the European Bank for Reconstruction and Development (EBRD), Lithuania's output growth became more balanced as domestic demand strengthened in 2013. At the beginning of 2013 growth had been driven by external factors, but the trade contribution eventually turned negative and domestic demand became a more important driver of growth later in the year. Although banks continued to remain cautious in lending, enterprises and households were able to finance large shares of investments from their own resources, positively contributing to growth. Over the first half of 2014 gross investment expenditures grew by 9.8 per cent in annual terms. This represented an acceleration from the pace observed in 2013.

Lithuania became the nineteenth euro-zone member in January 2015. In July 2014 the EU Council had given the final green light for Lithuania to join the single currency. Lithuania followed in the footsteps of its two Baltic neighbours, Estonia and Latvia, which had adopted the euro in 2011 and 2014, respectively. This step eliminated remaining currency risk premia in lending and credit risks resulting from independent currency regime exposures. Domestic banks gained access to the ECB's liquidity facilities and become subject to the Single Supervisory Mechanism. Surprisingly, public support for euro adoption had continued to increase, reaching 50 per cent of the population in June 2014, according to Eurobarometer. This trend was nevertheless in line with expectations, as euro-zone membership provided Lithuania with an additional safety net.

The EBRD noted that Lithuania's export performance had been volatile. In the first half of 2013 export volumes showed a double-digit growth of about 15 per cent in annual terms. However, volumes fell in the first half of 2014 as demand from Russia contracted and the loss-making Orlen Lietuva refinery, one of the largest exporting companies in the country, saw a reduction in sales.

Over the following next two years, growth was expected to remain well above the regional average at 3 and 3.4 per cent in

KEY INDICATORS — Lithuania

	Unit	2011	2012	2013	2014	**2015
Population	m	3.27	2.99	2.96	*2.94	*2.93
Gross domestic product (GDP)	US$bn	42.70	42.34	46.43	*48.23	*42.64
GDP per capita	US$	13,075	14,171	16,697	*16,386	0
GDP real growth	%	5.9	3.7	3.3	*2.9	*2.8
GNP per capita	US$	0	0	0	0	*14,560
Inflation	%	4.1	3.2	1.2	*0.2	*-0.3
Unemployment	%	17.2	13.4	11.8	*10.7	*10.6
Exports (fob) (goods)	US$m	27,029.0	28,764.6	31,816.8	31,548.8	–
Imports (fob) (goods)	US$m	29,523.5	30,438.8	33,436.6	33,543.3	–
Balance of trade	US$m	-2,494.5	-1,674.2	-1,619.8	-1,994.5	–
Current account	US$m	-619.1	-99.0	743.0	*-177.0	*91.0
Total reserves minus gold	US$m	–	8,218.2	7,847.3	8,503.9	–
Foreign exchange	US$m	–	8,007.1	7,635.8	–	–
Exchange rate	per US$	2.46	2.66	2.53	2.85	–

* estimated figure ** forecast figure

2014 and 2015 respectively. In the medium term, any prolonged economic slow-down in Russia combined with EU trade sanctions (against Russia) and Russian counter-sanctions could constitute a risk to growth, as Lithuania ships approximately 20 per cent of its total exports to Russia, although about 85 per cent of these consist of re-exports from other countries to Russia. The reform of state-owned enterprises has progressed. The main goals of the amendments to the 2012 State Owned Enterprise (SOE) law were to separate regulatory and ownership functions and commercial and non-commercial functions. Also, the legal constraints in hiring independent board members were to be loosened, thus leading to a higher degree of professionalism of boards that would positively impact on SOE performance. In December 2013 the government had approved a legal act compelling SOEs to deliver separate data for commercial and non-commercial operations in their annual reports. The separation of ownership and regulatory functions had been finalised, while plans to professionalise SOE boards had been expected to be completed by the end of 2014.

Lithuania's labour productivity is highest among the Baltic States, although the research and development (R&D) investment gap persists. Lithuania has a relatively large manufacturing sector, which generates about 20 per cent of the country's gross value added, the highest among its Baltic peers. It consists mainly of low and medium-technology sectors, which account for over 80 per cent of exports (for example, mineral fuels, transport and furniture). Exports of high-tech goods, by contrast, remain relatively low at only 5.6 per cent of total exports compared with the EU average of 15.4 per cent. Public and private R&D total expenditures remained at 0.9 per cent of GDP, significantly below the Europe 2020 target of 1.9 per cent. Labour productivity has been growing rapidly in the post crisis period and was the highest in the Baltic region, amounting to almost 75 per cent of the EU average. However, real unit costs had been rising at a pace well above productivity.

Risk assessment

Economy	Good/fair
Politics	Good
Regional stability	Fair

COUNTRY PROFILE

The Grand Duchy of Lithuania was in union with Poland from 1569; it was annexed by Russia between 1772 and 1795.

1795–1914 Lithuania became part of the Russian empire.

1914–18 The Russians were driven out of Lithuania by the Germans in the First World War.

1918 Lithuania declared independence.

1922 A constitution declared Lithuania a parliamentary republic with the Seimas as the parliamentary organ.

1926 In a military coup, Antanas Smetona came to power as the head of an authoritarian regime.

1940 Lithuania was invaded and occupied by the Soviet Union.

1941 Lithuania was occupied by the Germans, until it was re-annexed by the Soviets in 1944.

1988 A nationalist movement, the Lithuanian Reform Movement (Sàjudis), was set up by a group of writers and intellectuals; at a mass rally in Vilnius, the leaders declared that the USSR occupied Lithuania illegally.

1989 Parliament approved the declaration of Lithuanian sovereignty, stating that Lithuanian laws take precedence over Soviet laws.

1990 Sàjudis won the elections (the first free elections for 50 years). Vytautas Landsbergis was elected chairman of parliament, which declared Lithuania's independence. Fearing the impact that this would have on nationalist demands in the other Baltic republics, the Soviet Union immediately imposed an economic blockade; Lithuania agreed to suspend independence, pending talks.

1991 Talks with Moscow failed and the economy faced turmoil; Landsbergis ended the suspension of the declaration of independence. A referendum was held, resulting in an overwhelming vote for independence. Following a failed coup in Moscow, the USSR recognised Lithuania's independence. Lithuania, together with Latvia and Estonia, were admitted to the UN.

1992 A new constitution introducing a presidency was adopted by referendum. The Lietuvos Demokratine Darbo Partija (LDDP) (Democratic Labour Party of Lithuania) won more seats than Sàjudis in the elections – the LDDP was the first former communist party to return to power in central and eastern Europe.

1993 Algirdas Brazauskas, the former Lietuvos Komunistu Partija (LKP) (Lithuanian Communist Party) first secretary, won direct presidential elections and appointed Adolfas Slezevicius prime minister. Following the defeat of the Sàjudis organisation in the 1992 elections, the Homeland Union was established.

1996 Allegations of corruption led to the removal of Slezevicius and Mindaugas Stankevicius was appointed prime minister. After elections, the Tevynes Sajunga (TS) (Homeland Union) formed a centre-right coalition government with the Lietuvos Kricioniu Demokratu Partija (LKDP) (Lithuanian Christian Democratic Party) and the Lietuvos Centro Sajunga (LCS) (Centre Union of Lithuania). Gediminas Vagnorius was appointed prime minister.

1998 Valdas Adamkus was elected president.

1999 Vagnorius resigned, Rolandas Paksas substituted until a new government, under the leadership of Andrius Kubilius, came to power.

2000 Following the parliamentary elections, a minority coalition government was established, which included the Lietuvos Liberalu Sajunga (LLS) (Lithuanian Liberal Union), LCS and the Modernuju Kriscioni Demokratu Sajunga (MKDS) (Modern Christian-Democratic Union) with the support of other smaller parties. Rolandas Paksas, leader of the LLS, was again appointed prime minister.

2001 Prime Minister Rolandas Paksas' coalition government was brought down over differences about energy sector privatisations. A coalition government was formed, led by the Lietuvos Socialdemokratu Partija (LSDP) (Social-Democratic Party of Lithuania). The LSDP's Algirdas Brazauskas was appointed prime minister.

2002 The litas was re-pegged from the US dollar to the euro.

2003 Rolandas Paksas won the presidential election. Algirdas Brazauskas was re-appointed prime minister. In a referendum on membership of the European Union (EU), 90 per cent voted in favour; turnout was 60 per cent.

2004 Lithuania joined NATO and the EU. Parliament impeached President Paksas following an inquiry that concluded his alleged links with Russian organised crime was a threat to national security. Valdas Adamkus was re-elected president. In parliamentary elections, the Darbo Partija (DP) (Labour Party) formed a coalition government including the DP, LSDP, Naujoji Sajunga (NS) New Union and non-aligned members of parliament; Algirdas Brazauskas was re-appointed prime minister.

2005 The president declined an invitation to attend the ceremony in Moscow celebrating the end of the Second World War.

2006 Prime Minister Brazauskas's government resigned after the DP withdrew its support in protest against the president's statement that he did not trust two DP cabinet members. Gediminas Kirkilas became prime minister.

2007 Lithuania missed the start date for joining the European Monetary Union

(Emu), due to a higher than planned inflation rate. Lithuania became a member of the EU Schengen area whereby all travellers may cross borders without a passport or visa.
2008 An agreement for visa-free visits by citizens to the US was signed. Parliament passed a law making it an offence to display Soviet or Nazi images, including flags, emblems and badges with swastikas or the hammer and sickle. In general elections, Tevynes Sąjunga-Lietuvos Krikščionys Demokratai (Homeland Union-Lithuanian Christian Democrats) (TS-LKD) won the highest number of seats (45 out of 141), the ruling LSDP won 25. An alliance of TS, Tautos Prisikelimo Partija (TPP) (National Resurrection Party) and Lietuvos Respublikos Liberalu Sajudis (LRLS) (Liberals' Movement of Republic of Lithuania) formed a government led by Andrius Kubilius.
2009 Dalia Grybauskaité became Lithuania's first female head of state following presidential elections in which she won 68.18 per cent of the vote; her closest rival Algirdas Butkevicius won 11.8 per cent.
2010 Former president Algirdas Brazauskas died.
2011 In January, the European Court of Human Rights ruled against Lithuania for violating articles on free elections when former president Paksas had been prevented from standing for re-election. Lithuania will be required to prevent any future, similar violation. In August the government ratified a visa-free agreement for local residents of Lithuania and Belarus to cross the border with the minimum documentation. New, long-term travel permits replaced costly and time consuming to attain visas.
2012 Parliamentary elections took place on 14 and 28 October and after two rounds the LSDP had won 15 seats by proportional representation (PR) and 23 seats by constituency (C) (38 seats in total, out of 141) and the right to form a coalition government. However, allegations of tax fraud and vote buying by the DP forced President Grybauskaité on 29 October to veto the proposed coalition of LSDP, Tvarka ir Teisingumas (TT) (Order and Justice) and DP. In a referendum, held on 14 October, voters rejected the proposal to build a new nuclear power plant to replace the Ignalina Nuclear Power Plant (which had a similar design to the Chernobyl plant and which had been closed in 2009) by 64.77 per cent to 35.23 per cent in favour. The referendum was merely 'advisory' and the government may choose to carry on with the project. On 22 November, parliament endorsed the appointment of Algirdas Butkevicius as prime minister; he was supported by members of LSDP, DP, TT and Lietuvos Lenku Rinkimu Akcija (LLRA) (Electoral Action of Poles in Lithuania).
2013 The minimum wage was increased by 18 per cent in January.
2014 The first and second rounds of the presidential election were held on 11 and 25 May. Mrs Grybauskaité was re-elected in the second round, winning with 59.08 per cent to Zigmantas Balcytis's 40.92 per cent. In late October the 'floating storage with a regasification unit' (FSRU) vessel *Independence* arrived in the Lithuanian port of Klaipeda.
2015 On 29 January there was a bomb scare aimed at the *Independence*, disrupting the gas supply for several hours. No bomb was found.

Political structure

Constitution

The Constitution was adopted on 25 October 1992.

The written Constitution has precedence over all subsequent laws unless amended by referendum. The office of the president, parliamentary democracy and an independent judiciary are all guaranteed under the constitution, along with specific citizens' rights.

Independence date

16 February 1918, statehood; 11 March 1990 – from the USSR.

Form of state

Parliamentary democratic republic

The executive

The Head of State is the president, who is directly elected by absolute majority popular vote in 2 rounds if required and can serve for a maximum of two five-year terms. The president can dissolve parliament if it refuses to appoint a new government or, at the latter's request, if the parliament passes a vote of no confidence. The president cannot use this power during the last six months of the presidential term of office, or if an early election has taken place during the previous six months.

The prime minister is appointed or dismissed by the president, with the approval of the Seimas. Ministers are appointed and dismissed by the president on the recommendation of the prime minister.

National legislature

The unicameral Seimas (parliament) has 141 seats, of which 71 members are elected by in single-seat constituencies by absolute majority vote and 70 members are elected by proportional representation in a single nationwide constituency. All members serve for four-year terms.

The Seimas, on a two-to-three majority vote of its members, can decide to hold early elections.

Legal system

The Lithuanian legal code is based on civil law system with no judicial review of legislative acts. The court system consists of district and county courts, the Court of Appeal and the Supreme Court as well as the Administrative Court. The president participates in the process of appointment and dismissal of judges. Moreover, the president has the right to apply to the Constitutional Court concerning the conformity of the legal acts passed by the government. Judges are independent in administering justice.

Last elections

14 and 28 October 2012 (parliamentary); presidential first and second rounds: 11 and 25 May 2014.

Results: Presidential: first round: Dalia Grybauskaité (Independent) won 45.9 per cent of the vote, Zigmantas Balcytis 13.6 per cent, Arturas Paulauskas 12 per cent; Naglis Puteikis (Independent) 9.3 per cent, Valdemar Tomasevski 8.2 per cent, Arturas Zuokas 5.2 per cent, Bronis Rope 4.1 per cent. Turnout was 52.2 per cent. Second round: Dalia Grybauskaité 57.9 per cent, Zigmantas Balcytis 40 per cent. Turnout was 47.4 per cent.

Parliamentary: after two rounds, Lietuvos Socialdemokratu Partija (LSDP) (Social Democratic Party of Lithuania) 18.37 per cent of the vote (38 seats, out of 141), Tevynes Sajunga (TS) (Homeland Union) 15.08 per cent (33), Darbo Partija (DP) (Labour Party) 19.82 per cent, (17), Tvarka ir Teisingumas (TT) (Order and Justice) 7.31 per cent (11), Liberalu Sajudis (LS) (Liberal Movement) 8.57 per cent (10), Lietuvos Lenku Rinkimu Akcija (LLRA) (Electoral Action of Poles in Lithuania) 5.83 per cent (eight), Drasos Kelias (DK) (The Way of Courage) 7.99 per cent (seven), Lietuvos valsTleciu ir žaliuju Sajunga (LVŽS) (Lithuanian Peasant and Greens Union) 3.88 per cent (one), independents (three) and one seat unannounced; 10 other political parties failed to win any seats. Turnout was 52.93 per cent.

Next elections

May 2019 (presidential); October 2016 (parliamentary)

Political parties

Ruling party

Coalition led by Lietuvos socialdemokratu partija (LSDP) (Social Democratic Party of Lithuania), with Darbo Partija (DP) (Labour Party), Tvarka ir Teisingumas (TT) (Order and Justice) and Lietuvos Lenku Rinkimu Akcija (LLRA) (Electoral Action of Poles in Lithuania) (from 22 Nov 2012)

Main opposition party

Lietuvos Socialdemokratu Partija (LSDP) (Social-democratic Party of Lithuania)

Lithuania is the largest of the three Baltic states and has the highest population density.

Population
2.97 million (2013)*
Last census: April 2001: 3,483,972
Population density: 56.7 inhabitants per square km.Urban population 67 per cent (2010 Unicef).
Annual growth rate: -0.5 per cent, 1990–2010 (Unicef).

Ethnic make-up
Lithuanian (80.1 per cent), Russian (9.1 per cent), Polish (7 per cent), Belarussian (1.5 per cent) and others (2.3 per cent). There are long-standing cultural and political links with Poland, and many Poles live in the southern Vilnius region where they are in the majority, and have their own schools and newspapers.

Religions
Roman Catholic (primarily), Lutheran, Russian Orthodox, Protestant, Evangelical Christian Baptist, Muslim, Jewish.

Education
Primary school starts at age seven and is compulsory. There are three types of school, run by the state: primary (attended for four years), middle (five years) and secondary (three years). There are 17 higher education institutions in Lithuania. Vilnius University, founded in 1579, is the oldest university in Eastern Europe and also the largest in Lithuania.
Literacy rate: 100 per cent adult rate; 100 per cent youth rate (15–24) (Unesco 2005).
Compulsory years: Seven to 14
Enrolment rate: 98 per cent gross primary enrolment of relevant age group (including repeaters); 86 per cent secondary enrolment and 31 per cent at tertiary level (World Bank).
Pupils per teacher: 16 in primary schools.

Health
Lithuania is suffering from a lack of primary healthcare provision and an over-stretched network of small hospitals and large polyclinics. Over-specialisation of staff, low-quality equipment and a lack of investment have also put a strain on the health system.
The private sector accounts for only 2–3 per cent of total healthcare in Lithuania. Private clinics can charge 60 per cent more for any treatment than those funded by the state. The Lithuanian government sees these clinics as a threat to the state health care system.

HIV/Aids
HIV prevalence: 0.1 per cent aged 15–49 in 2003 (World Bank)
Life expectancy: 72 years, 2004 (WHO 2006)
Fertility rate/Maternal mortality rate: 1.5 births per woman, 2010 (Unicef); maternal mortality 18 per 100,000 live births (World Bank).
Child (under 5 years) mortality rate (per 1,000): 5 per 1,000 live births (WHO 2012)
Head of population per physician: 3.97 physicians per 1,000 people, 2003 (WHO 2006)

Welfare
The government is introduced a multi-pillar pension system, with voluntary public pension contributions for workers in 2004. A 2000 law enforces private voluntary pension funds.
The social security system provides pensions, sickness allowance, maternity and child care benefits and unemployment benefit. Small family grants are also provided that are not subject to means-testing. Contributions to the Lithuanian Social Insurance Fund are tax deductible. Employers contribute 30 per cent of the payroll of the company and employees pay 1 per cent of their wages.

Main cities
Vilnius (capital, estimated population 540,608 in 2012), Kaunas (340,316), Klaipeda (179,063), Siauliai (124,534), Panevezys (110,901), Alytus (67,151).

Languages spoken
By law, all transactions, contracts and company returns must be in Lithuanian. English is widely spoken by business people. Other languages spoken include Russian, Polish, Belarusian, Ukrainian, German and Yiddish.

Official language/s
Lithuanian

Media

Press
All newspapers are privately owned.
Dailies: There are over a dozen daily newspapers, of which the majority are published in Lithuanian; other languages include Russian, Polish and German.
In Lithuanian, major newspapers include *Lietuvos Rytas* (www.lrytas.lt), *Lietuvos Žinios* (www.lzinios.lt) and *Respublika*; tabloids include*Vakaro Zinios* (www.vakarozinios.lt) and *15 Min* (www.15min.lt) which was first published in 2005 and as a free issue newspaper quickly captured around 30 per cent of the readership to became the leading tabloid.
Weeklies: There are over 450 magazines published in various languages and covering all interests.
In Lithuanian, magazines with news and political analysis include *Ekstra* (www.lrytas.lt/ekstra), *Atgimimas* (www.atgimimas.lt) and *Veidas* (www.veidas.lt). Women's magazines include *Moteris* (www.moteris.lt) and *Panele* (www.panele.lt). In English, *The Baltic Times* (www.baltictimes.com), in Russian, *Litovskiy Kurier* (www.kurier.lt), in Polish, *Tygodnik Wilenszczyzny* (www.tygodnik.lt) and, in German, *Baltische Rundschau* (www.baltische-rundschau.eu) provide general local and international news.
Business: In Lithuanian, *Verslo Zinios* (http://vz.lt) is a comprehensive newspaper with local and international finance and business news. The agro-business magazine *Mano Ukis* (www.manoukis.lt) is published monthly; *Archiforma* is a quarterly architectural review. Verslo Savaite (www.verslosavaite.lt) is an online business publication with an English edition.

Broadcasting
The Radio and Television Commission of Lithuania (www.rtk.lt/en) has power to regulate and supervise all broadcasters, including satellite and internet providers. The national, public broadcaster is Lietuvos Radio ir Televizijos Centras (LRTC) (www.lrt.lt), which is funded by 57 per cent by government and the remainder by commercial sales.
Radio: LRTC (http://www.lrt.lt), operates three radio channels, LR, Klasika and Pus 3,— which includes Radijas. There are around 50 private, commercial radio stations, which include several national networks, Pukas (www.pukas.lt) with two channels broadcasting traditional and jazz music, Radio Centras (www.radiocentras.lt) and Ziniu Radijas (www.ziniur.lt).
Television: LRTC (http://www.lrt.lt), operates two TV stations (LTV1 and LTV2). Major, commercial channels includes LNK (www.lnk.lt), BTV (www.btv.lt) and TV3 (www.tv3.lt). Most programmes are locally produced by some foreign imports are included.
Other news agencies: ELTA (Lithuanian News Agency): www.elta.lt
Baltic News Service (BNS): www.bns.lt
Delfi: www.delfi.lt

Economy
The economy grew rapidly during the 1990s, moving from a centrally planned economy within the now defunct Soviet Union to an independent open market economy, characterised by increasing productivity, investment and innovation. Following Lithuania's accession to the European Union in 2004 there was a sharp rise in investment and capital inflow, which were channelled into the non-tradable sector (services) and real estate. Lithuania's trade with the EU and Commonwealth of Independent States (CIS) accounts for almost 90 per cent of its total trade.

The global economic crisis knocked Lithuania into a deep recession, recording a contraction in GDP of 14.8 per cent in 2009. However, since then the economy has rebounded and it has become one of the EU's fastest growing economies. In 2012 GDP expanded by 3.8 per cent, falling to 3.3 per cent in 2013 and slowed even further to 2.9 per cent in 2014 as poor economic performance in the EU and Russia impeded export growth.

In response to the crisis in 2009 the government implemented a US$2.3 billion stimulus plan along with severe budget cuts. The international credit ratings agency Standard and Poor's cut Lithuania's credit rating to BBB (the second lowest investment grade) in 2009 as the country's outlook deteriorated, with falling exports and a weakened banking system. At the same time Lithuania signed a US$1.45 billion loan with the European Investment Bank (EIB) to support EU-backed infrastructure, utilities, health and education sector projects. In April 2014, Standard and Poor's raised Lithuania's credit rating by two notches, increasing it to A- as a result of a stronger fiscal performance than expected. The improvement was also based on the prediction that the nation would qualify for adopting the euro in the proceeding year, which it did in January 2015.

Almost all of Lithuania's state-owned entities have been privatised, including the banks (of which 90 per cent are foreign controlled, mainly by Scandinavian interests); around 80 per cent of economic output is generated by the private sector. Around 12 per cent of GDP comes from fees for transit of oil from Russia to Western Europe.

External trade

As a member of the European Union, Lithuania operates within a communitywide free trade area, with tariffs set as a whole. Internationally, the EU has free trade agreements with a number of nations and trading blocs worldwide.

Despite the poor balance of trade, exports account for 60 per cent of GDP, of which around 10 per is provided by forest and timber products. Industrial production is in food processing, shipbuilding and manufacturing, with a growing sector in information technology.

Imports

Principal imports include fuels and oil, vehicles, machinery and equipment, chemicals, textiles and clothing and metals.

Main sources: Russia (21.7 per cent of total in 2014), Germany (11.0 per cent), Poland (9.5 per cent)

Exports

Principal exports are mineral products (over 20 per cent), textiles and clothing, machinery and electronic equipment, chemicals, timber products and foodstuffs.

Main destinations: Russia (20.9 per cent in total in 2014), Latvia (9.2 per cent), Estonia (8.3 per cent)

Re-exports

Oil (from Russia) around 150,000 barrels per day (bpd).

Agriculture

Farming

Agricultural land constitutes 53.4 per cent of total land area, estimated at 3.4 million hectares (ha). The industry employs about 8 per cent of the total labour force and contributed 3.7 per cent of GDP in 2014. Main products include grain, potatoes, sugar beet, dairy products, meat and silk.

Land restitution began soon after independence in 1990, with the creation of 104,000 private family farms. The break up of state-owned farms into small plots, the limited availability of capital and a lack of business skills have slowed the recovery and development of the agricultural sector.

Lithuania's European membership has significantly increased competitive pressures on its agriculture, with almost 70 per cent of exports heading to the EU. It has adopted the Swedish model of organic farming with policies that draw heavily on bilateral international projects. Environmental factors continue to affect agricultural reforms – 50 to 70 per cent of nitrogen and 10 to 20 per cent of phosphorus have been found in surface waters originating from farming activities.

Fishing

The opportunity to export fishery products to the EU market without any tariff barriers has attracted the interest of its seafood processing industry.

Redfish, mackerel, cod, red plaice, black halibut and shrimp are caught in the high seas. Baltic Sea catches include cod, sprat, Baltic sprat, plaice, turbot, salmon and smelt.

Forestry

Forest and other wooded land accounts for a third of the land area, with forest cover estimated at 1.9 million hectares (ha). Most of the forest is available for wood supply. About 80 per cent of the forest area is owned by the state, although private ownership has been rising since the early 1990s. Consumption of forest products per capita is below the European average level.

The sawmill industry, which exports half of its production, contributes largely to the national economy. Large volumes of roundwood, comprising mostly pulpwood, are exported mainly to Sweden and Germany. Although pulp and paper production is one of the oldest industries in Lithuania, most of the internal demand for high quality paper is met by imports. Chemical timber, furniture, wood-fibre and wood-chipboards are also produced, with chipboard materials in particular having strong export potential. Sawn hardwood is also used in the domestic furniture industry.

Industry and manufacturing

The industrial sector accounted for 28.2 per cent of GDP in 2014 and employs around 20 per cent of the workforce.

Manufacturing accounts for around 20 per cent of GDP. Main industries are shipbuilding, consumer electronics, metalworking, machine building, machine tools, scientific instruments, sulphuric acid, paper, meat, dairy products, food processing, textiles, clothing and furniture. One of Lithuania's priorities is the development of light industry, particularly furniture, using natural wood products.

The principal branches of existing light industry in Lithuania are textiles and knitwear, with the largest leather and footwear enterprises in Vilnius, Kaunas and Siauliai. Other areas offering potential for growth include electronics.

Tourism

Lithuania attracts tourists for its scenery and historic buildings, its traditional spa treatments and its value for money holiday experiences. It has four sites included on Unesco's World Heritage List, including the archaeological site of Kernave with its series of hill forts (called a Lithuanian Troy) and cultural landscape. Trakai was the medieval capital of Lithuania, in the country's lake district. The coastal resort of Palanga boasts sandy beaches as well as health and spa facilities, which are also found in Birstonas on the bank of the Nemunas River. Five national and nearly 30 regional parks are classified as protected areas.

In 2014 travel and tourism directly and indirectly contributed 4.8 per cent of GDP and was forecast to rise by 1.3 per cent in 2015. In the same period, the travel and tourism industry supplied employment to 61,000 people, or 4.6 per cent of total employment. There were 2.4 million visitors to Lithuania in 2014.

Mining

Lithuania is famous for its high quality deposits of amber, which supply the local jewellery industry. Amber deposits have been found in the coastal region of Curonian Bay and Juodkrante. The Juodkrante site covers 82 hectares; amber deposits are estimated at 112 tonnes.

Lithuania also has large reserves of high-quality iron ore in the south, but extraction is not economically viable.
Other raw materials found in small quantities include limestone, dolomite, gypsum, clay, sand and gravel.

Hydrocarbons

Lithuania reserves have been falling since the 1990s. Total, proven oil reserves were 12 million barrels of oil in 2014. Exploration has found only two new, small oilfields, in 2004 and 2005, close to existing oilfields; by 2008 exploration had ceased. The oil in production and the country's reserves so far are high quality, light crude, which is easy to convert into refined products.
The country imports most of its domestic consumption oil needs of approximately 70,000 barrels per day (bpd) from Russia, via the Druzhba pipeline, which terminates in Butinge, the site of the country's only oil refinery – Mazeikiu Nafta. It has a capacity of over 260,000bpd producing petrol, diesel and jet fuel.
Lithuania's natural gas situation is similar to that of oil: the country has scarce reserves and is heavily dependent on Russian imports to meet the country's domestic consumption demand of 3.3 billion cubic metres per annum.
Lithuania does not produce coal and has reduced its consumption, but still imports small quantities from Poland and Russia.

Energy

Total installed generating capacity was over 4.3GW in 2014, and the country produces around 12 terawatt hours annually.
The Lithuanian energy sector is dominated by Lietuvos Energija, the largest electric power company in the country. It is 96.2 per cent state-owned, with a minority stake held by Sweden's Vatenfall. The company is structured into separate companies, responsible for generation, distribution and transmission.
The Estlink project, an underwater cable linking the Baltic States with the Scandinavian and Nordic power grids, was partly funded by the EU and became operational in 2007. Lithuania has plans to interlink its power grid with those of Poland, Karliningrad (Russia) and eventually Western Europe.
On 17 May 2012 parliament overwhelmingly approved the building of the Visaginas nuclear power plant. The joint project (between Lithuania, Latvia and Estonia), sited at the eastern border of Lithuania, will be built by the Japanese engineering company Hitachi, with construction beginning in 2015 and energy production in 2020–21; the total project is expected to cost US$6.1 billion, of which Lithuania's share is US$2.1 billion.
The potential for geothermal energy production has been identified in west Lithuania, close to existing oil fields.

Financial markets

Stock exchange
Vilniaus Vertybiniu Popieriu Birza (Vilnius Stock Exchange) (VSE)

Banking and insurance

Lithuania has a two-tier banking system whereby the commercial and central bank functions of the state bank are separated. Foreign-owned banks may operate in the country. Commercial banking operations have been removed from the central bank, which has assumed the government's responsibility for setting interest policy. The Lietuvos Zemes Ukio Bankas (LZUB) (Lithuanian Agricultural Bank) was sold by the government in early-2002 — the end of state involvement in commercial banking.
Central bank
Lietuvos Banka (LB) (Bank of Lithuania)
Main financial centre
Vilnius

Time

GMT plus two hours (daylight saving, late March to late October, GMT plus three hours)

Geography

Lithuania is the largest of the three Baltic states, situated on the eastern coast of the Baltic Sea in north-eastern Europe. It is bordered by Latvia to the north, Belarus to the south-east, Poland to the south-west and the Russian Federation to the west. There is a dense network of waterways, the main river being the Nemunas, which flows south to north into the Baltic Sea. There are many lakes in the northern regions of the Baltic Highlands. The highest point is Juozapine Hill (294 metres) in the east of the country.
Hemisphere
Northern

Climate

Lithuania enjoys one of the mildest climates along the Baltic coast. Summer sunshine may last nine hours a day, but winters can be very cold. Annual rainfall averages 490mm and humidity 80 per cent.

Entry requirements

Passports
Required by all.
Visa
Required by all, except nationals of EU and Schengen area signatory countries, North America, Australasia and Japan. For further exceptions contact the nearest embassy. A Schengen visa application (offered in several languages) can be downloaded from http://europa.eu/abc/travel/ see 'documents you will need'.
Business visas for all other nationals must be applied for with an invitation from a local company or organisation and certified by the migration authorities in Lithuania (stamped and signed by a migration officer). A business letter, by the visitor's company, giving purpose of visit and full itinerary should also be included.
Currency advice/regulations
Import of local currency is unlimited but export is limited to Lt5,000. Import and export of foreign currency is unlimited although any amount over the equivalent of Lt40,000 must be declared.
Travellers cheques are not widely accepted.
Customs
Personal items are duty-free. There are no duties levied on alcohol and tobacco between EU member states, providing amounts imported are for personal consumption.
Prohibited imports
Military and hunting firearms, ammunition, fishing equipment require a permit. Meat and dairy products; illegal drugs are prohibited.

Health (for visitors)

Nationals of the European Economic Area (EEA) countries and Switzerland can access reduced cost and sometimes free medical treatment using a European Health Insurance Card (EHIC) while visiting the EEA. Exceptions include nationals of the 10 countries, which joined the EU in 2004, whose EHIC is not valid in Switzerland. Applications for the EHIC should be made before travelling.
Mandatory precautions
Vaccination certificates are required for cholera or yellow fever if travelling from an infected area.
Advisable precautions
It is advisable to be in date for the following immunisations: polio (within 10 years), tetanus (within 10 years), typhoid fever, hepatitis A (moderate risk only).
It is recommended that bottled water is used for drinking; tap water is occasionally brown.

Hotels

There are many hotels in Vilnius. Some have been restored or taken over. Most ask for payment in hard currency. Western-class hotels charge Western prices. Tipping is not widely practised.

Credit cards

Major credit cards are accepted in hotels, restaurants and shops. ATMs are found in many centres.

Public holidays (national)

Fixed dates
1 Jan (New Year), 16 Feb (Independence Day), 11 Mar (Restoration Day), 1 May (Labour Day), 8 May (Mother's Day), 26

May (Jonines), 6 Jul (Statehood Day), 15 Aug (Assumption Day), 1 Nov (All Saints' Day), 25–26 Dec (Christmas).

Variable dates

Easter (two days)

Working hours

Banking

Mon–Fri: 0900–1700. Some banks open on Sat: 0900–1300.

Business

Mon–Fri: 0900–1300 and 1400–1800; lunch break 1300–1400.

Shops

Mon–Fri: 1000–1400 and 1500–1900; Sat: 1000–1600.

Telecommunications

Mobile/cell phones

A GSM network covers the republic's eight largest cities.

Electricity supply

220V AC, 50Hz. European plugs are required.

Social customs/useful tips

Social behaviour is fairly informal. Lithuanians are open and hospitable. Straight professional questions receive straight answers. Business cards are used widely and shaking hands is the common form of greeting and farewell. Most Lithuanians are punctual – being late for a meeting can be a bad start.

Tipping has become more widespread, with waiters often expecting generous tips from westerners – avoid leaving hard currency.

Lithuanian-Russian relations are not as tense as those between Estonians and Latvians and Russians, although care should be taken when discussing Russia and its role in the region. Lithuanians also dislike being described as members of the Baltic states, rather than Lithuanian.

Security

Compared to other European capitals, the crime rate in Vilnius is relatively low, but street crime does occur. Make use of hotel safe deposit boxes and be careful not to show valuables when walking around the city. Car theft is common.

Getting there

Air

National airline: FlyLAL (Lithuanian Airlines)

International airport/s: Vilnius International (VNO), 5km from city; facilities include business and VIP lounges, duty-free shops, car hire, post office, *bureau de change*, restaurants, first aid. Taxis and buses are available.

Airport tax: Departure tax Lt60

Surface

Road: Lithuania has a good network of interconnecting roads, providing links to neighbouring countries.

Rail: There is a well developed rail network with Vilnius as the hub for rail connections in the region. There are train connections with Poland through Grodno in Belarus. There are regular trains to Russia (Moscow and St Petersburg). Rail travel between Lithuania, Latvia and Estonia can be slow.

Water: There are several regular ferry services from the main port of Klaipeda to UK, Russian Federation, Germany, Poland and Sweden. There are also many more irregular sea links to other foreign ports.

Getting about

National transport

Air: There are three domestic airports at Palanga, Kaunas and Siauliai but they have limited services.

Road: Paved roads are generally in good condition, however rural unpaved roads can be hazardous. There is a modern four-lane motorway connecting Vilnius with Kaunas, Laipeda and Panaeveys.

Buses: Buses are convenient and the cheapest way to travel as trains do not serve every town and village.

Rail: The rail system is being upgraded. Twice daily trains connect Vilnius with the Baltic coast.

Water: There is a coastal ferry linking Klaipeda and the Curonian Spit. There is also a dense network of rivers, the longest of which is the Nemunas River – total length 973km, 475km of which is in Lithuania – which is suitable for navigation in parts.

City transport

Taxis: Taxis display an illuminated *Taksi* sign and can be flagged down in the street or found at taxi-stands or booked by telephone. Meters should be in operation and visitors can insist that they be used. If not, fares must be negotiated and avoided being paid for in hard currency. Taxis are always more expensive from the airport, railway station, cathedral and the Vilnius Department Store.

Buses, trams & metro: There is a choice of buses and trolley buses within the city. Tickets can be purchased from kiosks (*spaudos kioskas*) and drivers; they must be inserted into a validating machine on board. Services operate from 0600 to 0030 or 0100.

The Vilnius railway station is a cosmopolitan marketplace and terminus, but it is not safe for visitors at night.

Car hire

Many of the major car rental companies operate in Lithuania. There are winter (Oct–Mar) and summer (Apr–Sep) speed limits on motorways: 110kph (winter), 130kph (summer); 90kph (all year) on open roads and 60kph on urban roads. National driving licences with photo IDs are required. Seat belts are compulsory and drink/driving is prohitited. Traffic drives on the right. It is advisable to make sure hire vehicles have an alarm and steering lock.

Drivers must pay a fee to use any road leading to Vilnius old town.

BUSINESS DIRECTORY

The addresses listed below are a selection only. While World of Information makes every endeavour to check these addresses, we cannot guarantee that changes have not been made, especially to telephone numbers and area codes. We would welcome any corrections.

Telephone area codes

The international direct dialling code (IDD) for Lithuania is +370, followed by area code and subscriber's number:

Kaunus	37	Panevezys	45
Klaipeda	46	Siauliai	41
Palanga	460	Vilnius	5

Useful telephone numbers

Directory enquiries: 09

International operator: 8-194

Fire: 01

Police: 02

Ambulance (greitoji pagalba): 03

Vilnius City Road Police, Giraites 3: 631-168

Chambers of Commerce

American Chamber of Commerce in Lithuania, 5 Lukiskiu Street, 2600 Vilnius (tel: 261-1181; fax: 212-6128; e-mail: acc@acc.lt).

Association of Lithuanian Chambers of Commerce, Industry and Crafts, 9 J Tumo-Vaizganto Street, 2001 Vilnius (tel: 261-2102; fax: 261-2112; e-mail: info@chambers.lt).

Kaunas Chamber of Commerce, Industry and Crafts, PO Box 2111, 8 K Donelaicis Street, 3000 Kaunas (tel: 229-212; fax: 208-330; e-mail: chamber@chamber.lt).

Klaipeda Chamber of Commerce, Industry and Crafts, 17 Danes Street, 5800 Klaipeda (tel: 390-861; fax: 410-626; e-mail: klaipeda@chambers.lt).

Panevezys Regional Chamber of Commerce, Industry and Crafts, 34 Respublikos Street, 5319 Panevezys (tel: 463-687; fax: 462-227; e-mail: panevezys@chambers.lt).

Siauliai Regional Chamber of Commerce, Industry and Crafts, 88 Vilniaus Street, 5400 Siauliai (tel: 525-504; fax: 523-903; siauliai@chambers.lt).

Vilnius Regional Chamber of Commerce, Industry and Crafts, 31 Algirdo Street, 2600 Vilnius (tel: 213-5550; fax: 213-5542; e-mail: vilnius@chambers.lt).

Banking

Bankas Snoras, 7A Vivulskio Street, 2600 Vilnius (tel: 216-2795).

Lietuvos Zemes Ukio Bankas (Lithuanian Agricultural Bank), Totoriu 4, 2600 Vilnius.

Lithuanian Commercial Banker's Association, Vilniaus 4/35, Vilnius 2001.

Lithuanian Development Bank, Stulginskio 4-7, 2600 Vilnius.

Lietuvos Taupomasis Bankas (Lithuanian Savings Bank), Savanoriu pr 19, 2015 Vilnius.

Lietuvos Valstybinis Komercinis Bankas (Lithuanian State Commercial Bank), Jogailos 14, 2001 Vilnius.

Vilniaus Bankas (commercial bank), Gedimino Avenue 12, 14, 2600 Vilnius.

Central bank

Lietuvos Bankas (Bank of Lithuania), 6 Gedimino Avenue, LT-01103 Vilnius (tel: 268-0029; fax: 262-8124; e-mail: info@lb.lt; internet: www.lb.lt).

Stock exchange

Vilniaus Vertybiniu Popieriu Birza (Vilnius Stock Exchange) (VSE), www.omxnordicexchange.com

Travel information

FlyLAL, 4 Gustaicio Avenue LT-02512 Vilnius (tel: 252-5555; email: info@flylal.com).

Krantas Travel Operator, 5 Teatro Street, LT-91247 Klaipeda (tel: 395-215)

Lithuanian Tourism Association, Pylimo 6, 2001 Vilnius.

Travel Bureau, Lietuva Hotel, Ukmerges 20, Vilnius.

Vilnius International Airport, Rodunios kelias 10A, LT- 02189, Vilnius (tel: 230-6666; fax: 232-9122; email: airport@vno.lt).

Vilnius Tourist Information Centre, (J-3) Didzioji 31, Town Hall, Vilnius (tel: 262-6470; email: turizm.info@vilnius.lt).

National tourist organisation offices

Lithuanian State Department of Tourism, A Juozapaviciaus 13, LT-09311 Vilnius (tel: 210-8796: fax:210-8753; email: vtd@tourism.lt; internet: www.tourism.lt).

Ministries

Ministry of Agriculture, Gedimino Avenue 19, LT-2025 Vilnius (email: zum@zum.lt).

Ministry of Culture, J Basanaviciaus Street 5, LT-5683 Vilnius (email: culture@muza.lt).

Ministry of Defence, Tortoriu 25/3, LT-2001 Vilnius (email: vis@kam.kam.lt).

Ministry of the Economy, Gedimino Avenue 38/2, LT-2600 Vilnius (email: pr@po.ekm.lt).

Ministry of Education and Science, A Volano Street 2/7, LT-2691 Vilnius (email: smmin@smm.lt).

Ministry of the Environment, A Jaksto Street 4/9, LT-2694 Vilnius (email: info@aplinkuma.lt).

Ministry of Finance, J Tumo-Vaizganto Street 8a/2, LT-2600 Vilnius (email: finmin@finmin.lt).

Ministry of Foreign Affairs, J Tumo-Vaizganto Street 2, LT-2600 Vilnius (email: urm@urm.lt).

Ministry of Health, Vilniaus Street 33, LT-2001 Vilnius (email: ministerija@sam.lt).

Ministry of the Interior, Sventaragio Street 5, LT-2600 Vilnius (email: infoskyrius@vrm/lt).

Ministry of Justice, Gediminio Avenue 30/1, LT-2600 Vilnius.

Ministry of Social Welfare and Labour, A Vivulskio Street 11, LT-2693 Vilnius (email: post@socmin.lt).

Ministry of Transport, Gediminio Avenue 17, LT-2679 Vilnius (email: transp@transp.lt).

Office of the President, S Daukanto Square 3, LT-2008 Vilnius (email: info@president.lt).

Office of the Prime Minister, Gedimino Avenue 11, LT-2039 Vilnius (email: kanceliarija@lrvk.lt).

Other useful addresses

Association of Light Industry Enterprises of Lithuania, Saltonishkiu 29/3, 2677 Vilnius.

Association of Lithuanian Entrepreneurs, A Jakshto 9, 2600 Vilnius.

BNS (English-language Baltic news service), Konarskio 49, Vilnius.

British Embassy, Antakalnio 2, Vilnius 2055 (tel: 222-070/1; fax: 727-579; e-mail: BE-VILNIUS@post.omnitel.net).

Central Post Office, Gedimino 7, Vilnius.

Commercial Court of the Republic of Lithuania, Gedimino pr 39/1, 2640 Vilnius.

Confederation of Lithuanian Industrialists, Saltonishkiu 19, 2600 Vilnius.

Construction Production Certification Centre, Linkmenu 28, 2600 Vilnius.

Department of Customs, A. Jaksto 1/25, 2600 Vilnius (internet: (foreign trade database) www.cust.lt/).

Department of Statistics, Gedimino pr 29, 2746 Vilnius.

Energy Agency, A Vienuolio 8/4, 2600 Vilnius.

Lithuanian Building Industry Association, Sevcenko 19, 2000 Vilnius.

Lithuanian Construction Association, Raugyklos 15, 2600 Vilnius.

Lithuanian Development Agency, Investment, Marketing and Public Relations Departments, Sv Jono Str 3 2600 Vilnius (email: lda@lda.lt; internet: www.lda.lt); Export Department, Algirdo 31, 2600 Vilnius (email: lda@lda.lt).

Lithuanian Economic and Foreign Investment Development Agency (FIDA), J Jasinskio 9, 4th floor, 2600 Vilnius.

Lithuanian Embassy (USA), 2622 16th Street, NW, Washington DC 20009 (tel: (+1-202) 234-5860; fax: (+1-202) 328-0466; email: info@ltembassyus.org).

Lithuanian Export Promotion Agency, J Tumo-Vaizganto 8a/2, 2739 Vilnius (email: lepa.epd@post.omnitel.net).

Lithuanian Free Market Institute, Birutes 56, 2600 Vilnius.

Lithuanian Information Institute, Kalvariju 3, 2659 Vilnius.

Lithuanian International Trade Agency, V Kudirkos st 18, 2600 Vilnius (email: LAITA@post.omnitel.net).

Lithuanian Investment Agency (LIA), Sv Jono 3, 2600 Vilnius.

Lithuanian Manufacturers' Confederation, Saltonishkiu 19, 2687 Vilnius.

Lithuanian Privatisation Agency, Gedimino 38/2, 2600 Vilnius.

Lithuanian Road Administration, State Property and Service Division, 36/2 Basanaviciaus Street, Vilnius LT-2009.

Lithuanian Standardisation Board, A Joksto g 1/25, 2600 Vilnius.

Lithuanian Television & Radio Broadcasting, Konarskio 49, 2674 Vilnius.

Securities Commission, Ukmerges g 41, 2600 Vilnius.

State Tax Inspection, Sermuksniu st 6, 2600 Vilnius.

Vilnius City Administration, Gedimino ave 9, 2600 Vilnius.

ELTA (Lithuanian News Agency): www.elta.lt

Baltic News Service (BNS): www.bns.lt

Delfi: www.delfi.lt

Internet sites

Lithuania on-line: www.aiva.lt/lol

Official travel guide: www.travel.lt

Port of Klaipeda: www.portofklaipeda.lt/en.php

Yellow pages: www.yellowpages.lt

Luxembourg

KEY FACTS

Official name: Groussherzogtom Lëtzebuerg, Grossherzogtum Luxemburg, Grand-Duché de Luxembourg (The Grand Duchy of Luxembourg)

Head of State: Grand Duke Henri of Luxembourg (acceeded Oct 2000)

Head of government: Prime Minister Xavier Bettel (DP) (named by Grand Duke Henri on 25 Oct 2013)

Ruling party: Coalition led by Demokratesch Partei (DP) (Democratic Party) and the Lëtzebuerger Sozialistesch Arbechterpartei (LSAP) (Luxembourg Socialist Workers' Party) with Die Grünen (the Greens) (elected 20 Oct 2013).

Area: 2,586 square km

Population: 559,000 (2014)*

Capital: Luxembourg-Ville

Official language: Lëtzebuergish (Luxembourgish); French and German are the administrative languages.

Currency: Euro (€) = 100 cents (from 1 Jan 2002; previous currency Luxembourg franc, locked at Lf40.34 per euro)

Exchange rate: €0.89 per US$ (Sep 2015)

GDP per capita: US$111,716 (2014)*

GDP real growth: 2.91% (2014)*

GDP: US$62.40 billion (2014)*

Labour force: 370,500 (2011)*

Unemployment: 7.12% (2014)*

Inflation: 0.70% (2014)

Balance of trade: -US$574.00 million (2014)

* estimated figure

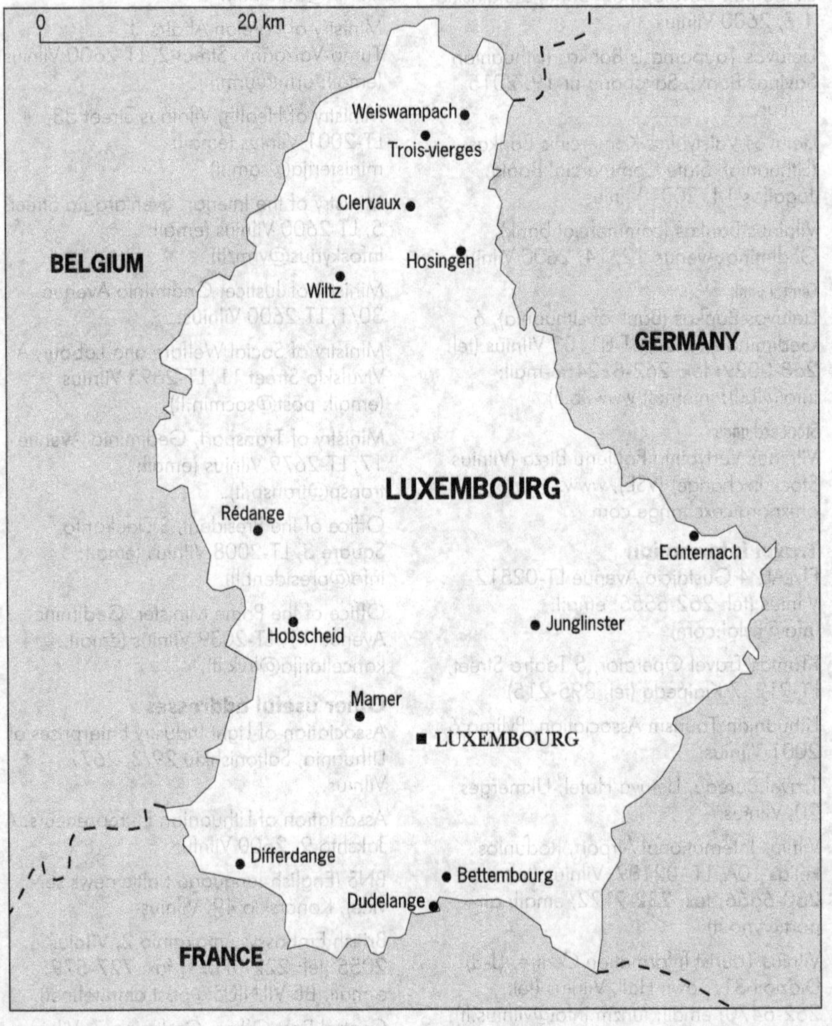

Founded in 963, Luxembourg became a grand duchy in 1815 and an independent state under the Netherlands. It lost more than half of its territory to Belgium in 1839 but gained a larger measure of autonomy. Full independence was attained in 1867, subsequently it was overrun by Germany in both world wars and it ended its neutrality in 1948 when it entered into the Benelux Customs Union and when it joined North Atlantic Treaty Organisation (NATO) the following year. In 1957, Luxembourg became one of the six founding countries of the European Economic Community (EEC), the successor to the European Coal and Steel Community (ECSC) – the original international organisation to be based on the principles of supra-nationalism (and which later became the European Union (EU)), and in 1999 it joined the euro currency area.

The small, stable, high-income economy has historically featured solid growth, low inflation, and low unemployment. The industrial sector has become increasingly diversified into chemicals, machinery and equipment and automotive components from steel production which used to be the dominant industry. The financial sector accounts for 36 per cent of gross domestic product (GDP) and constitutes the largest sector of the economy. Luxembourg depends on foreign and cross-border workers for approximately 39 per cent of its workforce. Since the global economic crisis has ended, growth has recovered at 2 per cent in 2013 and 2.9 per cent in 2014. Furthermore, unemployment has remained at a stable rate of 7.1 per cent in 2014 which remains below the EU average despite having increased from its historically low rate of 4 per cent in the 2000s. Luxembourg continues to enjoy an extremely high standard of living with GDP per capita at US$92,000 in 2014, the second largest in the world and not far behind Qatar. Luxembourg has one of the highest current account surpluses as a share of GDP in the euro-zone and it maintains a healthy budgetary position and the lowest public debt levels in the region. Luxembourg has lost a significant portion of its advantage as a favourable tax location because of Organisation for Economic Co-operation and Development (OECD) and EU pressure. In 2015, the government has had to comply with EU requirements to implement automatic exchange of tax information on savings accounts which has ended banking secrecy. As a result, bank activity has been depressed and GDP growth has slowed.

The political situation in Luxembourg politics has rarely been the stuff of excitement. With the exception of the five year period from 1974–79, the centre-right Chrëschtlech Sozial Vollekspartei (CSV) (Christian Social People's Party), the largest political party in Luxembourg, has been in government either in its own right or in coalition, since 1919. Until he resigned in December 2013, the prime minister was Mr Jean-Claude Juncker of the ruling CSV, who served in that role for a period of nearly 18 years, thereby making him the EU's longest-serving democratically-elected European leader in recent times. Mr Juncker went on to replace José Manuel Barroso as President of the European Commission.

The elections held in October 2013 brought to an end the domination of Luxembourg politics by the CSV. After the election a coalition government led by Demokratesch Partei (DP) (Democratic Party) and including the Lëtzebuerger Sozialistesch Arbechte (LSAP) (Luxembourg Socialist Workers' Party) and the Déi Gréng (Gréng) (The Greens) was sworn in in December. Mr Xavier Bettel became prime minister and Mr Etienne Schneider deputy prime minister. Mr Jean Asselborn retained the portfolio of minister for foreign affairs.

The IMF's executive summary for 2014 stated that Luxembourg's main challenge is to strengthen an economic model that has served it well. The model emphasises maintaining fiscal stability and openness, practising conservative prudential oversight, and responding to investor needs. Luxembourg has been viewed for a long time as an extremely attractive place for international financial businesses to invest. Assets under the management of Luxembourg's financial sector have doubled since 2008, to €3.5 trillion (US$3.9 trillion) in 2014. The IMF suggested Luxembourg should explore options to make the tax system more robust, and they should pursue further reforms to make the pension system more resilient to an ageing population. These policy initiatives should fortify Luxembourg's 'AAA' sovereign credit rating. In the short-term, growth will remain fairly high and consistent, helped by a firmer euro area recovery. In the medium-term, the success of the government's initiatives to diversify the economy will play out against a backdrop of lower potential growth. It is very important, therefore, that efforts are underway to better equip workers with relevant skills and to lift youth and women's participation in the labour force.

The Luxembourg government presented its 2016 budget on 14 October 2015 and it contains certain tax measures to be introduced over the next year. A progressive reduction of the corporate income tax rate (CIT) has also been announced for 2017 but no further details have been provided. Since the European Commission considers the Luxembourg minimum corporate income tax rules not to be in line with EU law, the government intends to abolish the CIT from 2016 and to replace it with a minimum net wealth tax (NWT) of the same amount. The objective here is to make Luxembourg's minimum tax rules EU-compliant and at the same time ensure that companies which have been subjected to the CIT rate to date will remain subject to the same amount of minimum tax in the future. The amounts of minimum NWT remain the same based on the minimum CIT rules, except that an increased amount of minimum NWT will apply, under certain conditions, to companies with a total balance sheet exceeding €30 million (US$33.7 million).

Refugees

On 4 November 2015, Greece sent 30 refugees in the first round of relocations under the EU's plan to redistribute migrants. The six families, from Syria and Iraq, are among the first to be moved under aims to share out nearly 160,000 migrants across the bloc. On arrival in Luxembourg the families will spend two days in a registration centre and then two or three months in temporary accommodation as the authorities help them to find a permanent home, schools and jobs. None of the refugees in Greece actually wanted to move to Luxembourg despite the fact that it is the EU's wealthiest country in per capita terms. Luxembourg chaired the EU's rotating president for the six months from July 2015 and Jean-Claude Juncker, its prime minister from 1995 to 2013, is head of the European Commission and one of the architects of the new quota system. Not all

KEY INDICATORS — Luxembourg

	Unit	2011	2012	2013	2014	**2015
Population	m	0.51	0.53	0.55	*0.56	*0.57
Gross domestic product (GDP)	US$bn	58.40	55.17	60.15	*62.40	*54.94
GDP per capita	US$	113,533	103,807	110,307	*111,716	*96,269
GDP real growth	%	1.0	-0.2	2.0	*2.9	*2.5
Inflation	%	3.4	2.9	1.7	0.7	*0.5
Unemployment	%	5.8	6.1	6.9	*7.1	*6.9
Exports (fob) (goods)	US$m	18,807.0	15,934.0	16,978.0	24,215.0	–
Imports (fob) (goods)	US$m	26,269.0	23,776.0	25,336.0	24,789.0	–
Balance of trade	US$m	-7,462.0	-7,842.0	-8,358.0	-574.0	–
Current account	US$m	4,199.0	3,642.0	2,918.0	*3,275.0	*2,582.0
Total reserves minus gold	US$m	957.8	871.0	876.4	776.8	–
Foreign exchange	US$m	272.4	151.1	184.8	–	–
Exchange rate	per US$	0.75	0.77	0.73	0.82	–

* estimated figure ** forecast figure

the countries in the EU support the 'resettlement' programme decided by the European Union with the Czech Republic, Hungary, Romania and Slovakia all objecting to it, urging the EU instead to reinforce the bloc's external borders. The European commissioner for immigration, Dimitris Avramopoulos, said that many of those selected to relocate to Luxembourg refused because they all wanted to go to Germany.

Risk assessment

Politics	Good
Economy	Good
Regional stability	Good

COUNTRY PROFILE

Modern-day Luxembourg was occupied by the Burgundians, Prussians, Spanish and French until the nineteenth century, when it came under German and Dutch control.

1867 Luxembourg was granted independence.

1914–18 Luxembourg was occupied by the Germans.

1921 The Belgian-Luxembourg Economic Union (BLEU) was formed.

1940–45 Nazi Germany occupied Luxembourg.

1948 The Benelux Economic Union (Benelux) was inaugurated between Belgium, Luxembourg and the Netherlands and became effective in 1960, establishing the three countries as a single customs area in 1970.

1949 Luxembourg became a founding member of NATO.

1957 Luxembourg became one of the founder members of the forerunner to the EU, the European Economic Community (EEC).

1964 Grand Duchess Charlotte abdicated after a reign of 45 years and was succeeded by her son, Prince Jean.

1974 After being in power since 1918, the Chrëschtlich Sozial Vollekspartei (CSV) (Christian Social People's Party) was defeated by the Demokratesch Partie (DP) (Democratic Party) in general elections.

1979 The CSV regained power.

1990 Luxembourg was an original signatory of the Schengen Agreement to remove all border controls.

1994 Jean-Claude Juncker became prime minister.

1999 A CSV/DP coalition government was formed after the CSV failed to win enough seats in the parliamentary elections to have an outright majority. Juncker remained as prime minister.

2000 Grand Duke Jean abdicated and was succeeded by his son, Prince Henri.

2002 Euro currency replaced the Luxembourg franc. Luxembourg was named by a French parliamentary committee as a haven for tax evasion and money laundering.

2003 After EU talks on new rules for the taxation of savings invested abroad, Luxembourg won the right to decide when they would drop the withholding tax and begin exchanging information.

2004 The CSV was re-elected.

2005 Voters approved the European Union constitution by 57 per cent to 43 per cent.

2006 Arcelor, Luxembourg's premier steel manufacture was sold to the Indian-owned Mittal Steel, for US$34 billion, which created one the world's largest steel manufacturers.

2008 President Chavez of Venezuela announced that the Luxembourg-based and Argentine-owned steel maker, Ternium, would be nationalised to bring a key industry under state ownership and drive its socialist economy. Executive power to veto legislation was removed from the Grand Duke Henri, due to his conscientious objection to a parliamentary bill to legalise euthanasia. The Grand Duke promulgates laws with his signature; his role became ceremonial with minimal executive powers.

2009 In parliamentary elections, the ruling CSV won 26 seats (out of 60), and formed a coalition with Lëtzebuerger Sozialistesch Arbechterpartei (LSAP) (Luxembourg Socialist Workers' Party). Prime Minister Juncker remained in office.

2012 Hereditary Grand Duke Guillaume (heir apparent) of Luxembourg and Countess Stéphanie de Lannoy were married on 19 October.

2013 Jean-Claude Juncker resigned as prime minister on 11 July. He was accused as allowing illegal security agency activity such as phone-taps and corruption. Grand Duke Henri called elections for 20 October. The results were CSV 23 seats (out of 60), LSAP and DP 13 seats each, Die Grünen (the Greens) 6, Alternativ Demokratesch Reformpartei (ADR) (Alternative Democratic Reform Party) (3), Déi Lénk (Lénk) (The Left) (1); turnout was 91.15 per cent. The DP, LSAP and the Greens formed a coalition. Xavier Bettel of the DP was named as prime minister by the Grand Duke Henri on 25 October, to take up his position in November.

Political structure

Constitution

The Constitution was adopted in 1868 and has been amended on four occasions (1919, 1994, 1996 and 1998). It can be amended when at least two thirds, of a minimum 75 per cent of parliamentary members, vote in agreement. A plebicite must ratify the amendment. The Constitution sets out the role of the hereditary crown as Head of State, and the rights of citzens before the law. Universal direct suffrage for all those registered and over the age of 18.

Independence date

1814

Form of state

Constitutional monarchy, unitary state.

The executive

The leader of the majority party or majority coalition is usually appointed prime minister by the monarch.

Executive power is vested in the prime minister and the council of ministers is recommended by the prime minister but appointed by the monarch. The prime minister and the deputy prime minister are responsible to the chamber of deputies. The Grand Duke promulgates laws with his signature; his role is ceremonial with minimal executive powers.

National legislature

Legislative power is exercised by a unicameral 60-member Châmber vun Députéirten / Chambre des Députés (Chamber of Deputies), which is elected for a five-year term by proportional representation in multi-seat constituencies.

A 21-member Council of State, chosen by the Grand Duke on the advice of the prime ministers, acts as an advisory body to the Chamber of Deputies and has some legislative functions.

Legal system

Loosely based on Napoleonic code, of inquisitorial justice. The highest court is th Superior Court of Justice. Justices of the peace, district court judges and members of the Superior Court are appointed for life by the Grand Duke. Special laws regulate military tribunals. Administrative courts have jurisdiction over tax and administrative matters. There is a Constitutional Court that decides on the conformity of laws within the constitution. The Grand Duke has the authority to revoke or reduce penalties awarded by judges.

Last elections

20 October 2013 (Parliamentary)

Results: Parliamentary: Chrëschtlech Sozial Vollekspartei (CSV) (Christian Social People's Party) (23 seats, out of 60), Lëtzebuergesch Sozialistesch Arbechterpartei (LSAP) (Luxembourg Socialist Workers' Party) (13), Demokratesch Partei (DP) (Democratic Party) (13), Déi Gréng (Gréng) (The Greens) (6), Alternativ Demokratesch Reformpartei (ADR) (Alternative Democratic Reform Party) (3), Déi Lénk (Lénk) (The Left) (1); turnout was 91.15 per cent.

Next elections

June 2018 (parliamentary).

Political parties
Ruling party
Coalition led by Demokratesch Partei (DP) (Democratic Party) and the Lëtzebuerger Sozialistesch Arbechterpartei (LSAP) (Luxembourg Socialist Workers' Party) with Die Grünen (the Greens) (elected 20 Oct 2013).
Main opposition party
Lëtzeburger Sozialistesch Arbechterpartei or Parti Ouvrier Socialiste Luxembourgeois (LSAP/POSL) (Luxembourg Socialist Workers' Party)
In 2011, the total number of immigrants was 220,522; over 130,000 workers commute to work daily from the neighbouring countries of France, Germany and Belgium.

Population
529,000 (2012)*
Last census: February 2001: 439,539
Population density: 202.9 inhabitants per square km. Urban population 85 per cent (2010 Unicef).
Annual growth rate: 1.4 per cent, 1990–2010 (Unicef).
Ethnic make-up
The inhabitants of Luxembourg are mostly of German and French origin, but have a distinct national consciousness. From just under 20 per cent in 1970, the percentage of foreign residents has risen to over 30 per cent. The Portuguese, who account for over 10 per cent of the total population, form the largest foreign community. The second largest immigrant community comes from Italy (5 per cent).
Religions
Approximately 97 per cent of the population is Roman Catholic.

Education
Primary education lasts for six years, until the age of 12. Instruction is initially given in German, and French is added in the second year. Secondary education can be obtained through either a lLycé, or *Lycé Technique*. The first offers general and technical schooling, for up to seven years with an initial period of three years then an advanced (and non-compulsory) programme of four years. The *Lycé Technique* offers complete seven-year courses. French replaces German in the classroom at secondary schooling.
Higher education in the Grand Duchy is limited in scope. Approximately 4,000 students attend foreign universities, predominantly in Belgium and France.
Compulsory years: Six to 15.
Enrolment rate: 85 per cent net primary enrolment (Unicef).

Health
HIV/Aids
HIV prevalence: 0.2 per cent aged 15–49 in 2003 (World Bank)
Life expectancy: 79 years, 2004 (WHO 2006)
Fertility rate/Maternal mortality rate: 1.6 births per woman, 2010 (Unicef)
Child (under 5 years) mortality rate (per 1,000): 2 per 1,000 live births (WHO 2012)
Head of population per physician: 2.66 physicians per 1,000 people, 2003 (WHO 2006)

Welfare
The social security system was built in several stages. It has been extended to include both the socio-professional categories and at risk groups. The minimum wage, which functions as a mechanism to guarantee resources, consists of a supplementary benefit paid up to a threshold determined according to the composition of the household. The benefit is awarded irrespective of the causes of the situation of need. Sickness benefits, in which patients pay only a small part of medical costs, as well as birth, family and unemployment payments, are included in the plans. Housing conditions are generally comparable to those found in other Western European countries. There has been some difficulty in assimilating the many thousands of foreign workers and their families.
Luxembourg conforms to the EU provisions dealing with social security based on the principle of free movement of workers within the EU that enables its workers to accept a job in another member state without suffering any inequality with regard to social security. The EU social security arrangements aim to co-ordinate the national social security schemes in all the member states of the EU and the European Economic Area (EEA).
The social security system covers benefits for sickness and maternity, pensions, insurance against accidents at work and occupational diseases, unemployment benefits and family allowances. The scheme is compulsory and covers all persons in paid employment as well as self-employed workers in the country. Half of the contribution due is payable by the worker and half by the employer. There is no contribution towards industrial accident insurance, family benefits or unemployment benefit. Contributions are payable for sickness and maternity insurance, disability insurance, old-age and survivor's pension, amounting to a certain percentage of his/her remuneration.

Main cities
Luxembourg-Ville (capital, estimated population 74,738 in 2012), Esch-sur-Alzette (29,616), Dudelange (18,898), Schifflange (8,556).

Languages spoken
Official language/s
Lëtzebuergish (Luxembourgish); French and German are the administrative languages.

Media
Press
The high level of newspapers per readership is based on subsidies provided by public money and political affiliates. The market is dominated by the Imprimerie Saint Paul (www.isp.lu) media group which controls around 90 per cent of the daily newspaper market.
Newspapers are published in the predominant language (either French or Germany) of the region in which they sold with an edition in the alternative language.
Dailies: The most popular newspaper the *Luxemburger Wort* (www.wort.lu) is owned by the Roman Catholic Church and has close ties to the Christian socialist political party. The newspaper with the second highest circulation is *Tageblatt* (http://news.tageblatt.lu), published by the trade unions and is closely linked the the socialist political party. Other publications include *Lëtzebuerger Journal* (www.journal.lu), *Zeitung vum Letzebuerger Vollek* (www.zlv.lu) and *La Voix du Luxembourg* (www.lavoix.lu). The French newspaper *Le Républicain-Lorrain* (www.republicain-lorrain.fr), which has an extensive Luxembourg section, is also widely read.
Weeklies: Those featuring general interest, news and current affairs include *Revue* (www.revue.lu), *d'Letzebuerger Land* (www.land.lu), and *Letzebuerger Gemengen* (www.gemengen.lu) and, in English, *352* (www.352.lu) provides general news for the expatriate community. *Den Neie Feierkrop* (www.feierkrop.lu) is a satirical magazine.
Business: In French with an online German edition *l'Echo de l'Industrie* (www.fedil.lu/Echo) is published by the Federation of Luxembourg Industrialists (Fedil) and *Le Jeudi* (http://hebdo.le-jeudi.lu) is a weekly publication of financial and business news.
Broadcasting
Luxembourg has a long tradition of broadcasting to huge audiences in Europe including France, Germany and the UK. The RTL Group (www.rtlgroup.com) is Europe's largest media organisation with over 40 television and 30 radio stations throughout Europe plus production companies in the US and elsewhere, producing gameshows and long-running domestic dramas. While RTL is a private entity it has a government agreement whereby RTL keeps certain operations located in Luxembourg plus provide

television and radio programmes for local audiences in exchange for freeing RTL from franchise fees and no third party being granted a licence by the government to broadcast if it competed with RTL international activities. The agreement runs until 2010.

Radio: There are a range of radio stations dedicated to the various official languages. Domestic radio is dominated by Radio Lëtzebuerg RTL (http://rtl.lu) with around 50 per cent of the audience share. Radio Ara (www.ara.lu) broadcasts alternative programming for marginal groups and foreign residents.

Television: Luxembourg was the first European country to switch completely from analogue signals to digital terrestrial television (DTT) signals, in 2006. Télé Lëtzebuerg RTL (http://rtl.lu) dominates with around 40 per cent of the audience in the local market and operates TV channels is each of the local languages. Other, commercial stations include Nordliicht TV (www.nordliicht.lu) and Satmode for interactive TV.

Economy

Luxembourg's financial sector is large by international standards and contributes substantially to GDP growth and trade. However, since the onset of the global economic recession GDP growth has contracted severely but in 2013 Luxembourg registered positive growth again and in 2014 growth stood at 2.7 per cent. Luxembourg also enjoys one of the highest GDP per capita's in the world, and the highest in the eurozone, at US$110,665. As a member of the European Union euro-zone Luxembourg undertook recapitalisation of its banks in 2008, while the European Central Bank (ECB) reduced interest rates and initiated 'supportive fiscal' policies that included unlimited term funding at fixed rates. The euro-zone moved out of recession by mid-2009. In January 2015 the government was pressured to undertake reforms to bring Luxembourg's banking regulations up to European standards in order to tackle money laundering by complying with EU requirement to have automatic exchange of tax information on savings accounts. This is expected to end Luxembourg's run as a tax and financial haven and is forecast to hamper economic growth as the financial sector, which contributes 36 per cent to GDP, becomes less attractive to foreign investors.

The other mainstay of Luxembourg's economy is steel production and as global trade fell, European crude steel production dropped by 39.9 per cent in 2009. However, following the merger of Luxembourg's largest steelmaker Acelor with India's Mittal Steel in 2006, becoming the world's largest steelmaker, production of steel in Luxembourg in 2009 rose 7.6 per cent. Sincethe global economic crisis steel production fell across Europe but has slowly been recovering. In 2013 (latest figures) Luxembourg produced 2.1 million tonnes of steel, the industry contributed 1.8 per cent to GDP and accounted for 29 per cent of all exports (excluding services).

The service sector (dominated by banking) contributed 87.7 per cent of GDP with industry providing around 12 per cent, of which manufacturing is about 5 per cent; agriculture provides less than 1 per cent.

Employment in Luxembourg is dynamic with cross-border workers living in neighbouring countries and returning each day, many employed in the financial sector. Luxembourg has generally always enjoyed unemployment below the EU average, at 7.1 per cent in 2014. Of all the labour force working in Luxembourg 39 per cent were foreign and commuted from Luxembourg's neighbouring countries.

External trade

As a member of the European Union, Luxembourg operates within a community-wide free trade union, with tariffs set as a whole. Internationally, the EU has free trade agreements with a number of nations and trading blocs worldwide.

The traditional steel industry provides around 29 per cent of exports (excluding services), despite depleted domestic iron ore reserves. Hi-tech industries have grown in importance; nevertheless, the financial services sector is a major provider of external revenue, which provides around 87.7 per cent of GDP.

Imports

Imports include petroleum, gas, vehicles, iron ore, minerals, metals, foodstuffs and quality consumer goods.

Main sources: Belgium (23.7 per cent of total in 2014), Germany (23.3 per cent), France (13.9 per cent).

Exports

Commodities include iron and steel, electrical and electronic equipment, machinery, glass, ceramics and plastics. Intermediate manufactured products account for around 80 per cent of total exports.

Main destinations: Germany (27.6 per cent of total in 2014), France (13.8 per cent), Belgium (13.2 per cent).

Agriculture

Farming

The country has gradually adapted and delegated much of its farm policy to the EU, through the Common Agricultural Policy (CAP). The EU's Fundamental reform to the CAP was introduced in Luxembourg in 2005. The subsidies paid on farm output, which tended to benefit large farms and encourage overproduction, were replaced by single farm payments not conditional on production.

Farming is concentrated on barley, oats and potatoes in the north, and fruit and grapes in the east.

Although agricultural output has tripled since the 1980s, its contribution to GDP has in the same period declined from 4 per cent in mid-1970s to around 1 per cent in late 1990s. The number of farms declined from 5,173 in 1980 to 2,950 in 1998 as high agricultural production costs and high employment in Luxembourg caused more people to leave the farming industry and farmland has subsequently been converted to other uses. This trend slowed in 2003–04 as the economy slowed and jobs were not so readily available. Three-quarters of the land is cultivated. Pasture accounts for 55 per cent of all cultivated farmland. In 2014 agriculture contributed a mere 0.3 per cent to GDP.

Food and wine account for about 1.9 per cent of exports.

Fishing

Luxembourg does not have any significant freshwater fishing industry.

Forestry

Largely driven back to the least productive soil and escarpments where viable development is precluded, woods cover some 89,000 hectares or around a third of the country. Extending over 4,500 hectares, the forest of Gruenwald is the largest continuous wooded area in the Grand Duchy. Forestry only plays a very modest role in the overall economy, the commercial explotation of private forests and those subject to the system of forest tenure only represent on average between 0.1 per cent and 0.2 per cent of GDP.

Industry and manufacturing

As with the agricultural sector, Luxembourg's industrial base has declined in proportion to the dominant services sector and accounts for only 30 per cent of GDP. The country's principal industries include steel, chemicals, rubber, plastics, processing, glass, aluminium, metalworking and vehicle spares manufacture.

Tourism

The Grand Duchy of Luxembourg is a small land-locked country that is a major crossroads between France, Germany and Belgium which surround it and from which it draws many of its influences. The old quarters and fortification of the capital of Luxembourg-ville are included on the UN list of World Heritage Sites.

Luxembourg is home to a large community of wealthy residents and has one of the world's highest per capita incomes. Although the travel and tourism sector is an important component of GDP, its contribution is only around 4.5 per cent of

the total, generating US$2.9 billion in 2014. Total employment in the industry was 6.0 per cent 2014 (14,500 jobs) and total investment in the sector accounted for 7.4 of total investment in the country (€590.7 million= US$809.2 million)
A new terminal was completed at Findel International Airport in 2008 to encourage more passengers to take direct flights to Luxembourg rather than to Frankfurt (Germany) or the other smaller, surrounding airports in Belgium and France.

Mining

Iron ore, discovered around 1850, made the fortune of modern Luxembourg's economy. The steel industry still serves as one of the most important sector of the economy, although its share of GDP fallen has since the early 2000s.

Hydrocarbons

Luxembourg does not have any oil, natural gas or coal reserves. The country imports all its hydrocarbons, totalling 60,000 barrels per day (bpd) of refined oil products, 1.3 billion cubic metres of natural gas and 153,000 tonnes of coal. These imports come primarily from within the EU.

Energy

Domestic production of electricity supplies 54.9 per cent of consumer needs; 45.1 per cent of supplies are imported from Germany, via a connection to its network. Installed generating capacity is over 1.16 gigawatts (GW); and consumption over 6.4 billion kilowatt hours (kWh)
The hydroelectric dam at Vianden is one of the largest hydro-power plants in Europe, producing 1.1GW. The biggest power company is Cegedel, supplying 69 per cent of all electricity consumed.

Financial markets

Stock exchange

Bourse de Luxembourg (Luxembourg Stock Exchange)

Banking and insurance

Luxembourg has a large banking sector. Activity is oriented towards wholesale banking services, with a large concentration of German and Scandinavian banks serving corporate customers in Europe. Private banking has rapidly increased. The financial sector accounts for around 36 per cent of GDP and banking employs 10 per cent of the workforce. Luxembourg's banking secrecy laws have been a source of complaint abroad; however rules allow authorities to investigate as necessary.
There were concerns that EU requirements for the deduction of a withholding tax from all foreign accounts would adversely affect the sector.
In an effort to avoid joining the global list of non-co-operative tax havens, held by the Organisation of Economic Co-operation and Development (OECD), Luxembourg eased its banking laws to allow the sharing of bank data that cracks down on offshore tax evasion.
In April 2013 Luxembourg announced that the secrecy surrounding its banks would be eased and rules on the automatic exchange of bank account information with its EU partners would be automatic from 2015. In January 2015 the government undertook these reforms to bring Luxembourg's banking regulations up to European standards in order to tackle money laundering by complying with EU requirement to have automatic exchange of tax information on savings accounts. This is expected to end Luxembourg's run as a tax and financial haven and is forecast to hamper economic growth as the financial sector, which contributes 36 per cent to GDP, becomes less attractive to foreign investors.

Central bank

The European Central Bank (ECB) acts as the central bank, issuing notes and coins and determining interest rates.

Time

GMT plus one hour (daylight saving, late March to late October, GMT plus two hours)

Geography

Luxembourg is a landlocked country in Western Europe, bounded by Belgium on the north and west, Germany to the east and France to the south. Luxembourg consists mainly of the upper basins of the Sauer (Sûre) and Alzette rivers. The highest point is Buurgplaatz (559 metres), in the Ardennes Plateau in the north. The southern two-thirds of the country is a rolling plateau, the Bon Pays.

Hemisphere

Northern

Climate

Luxembourg's climate is temperate, without extremes. Sea winds (south-west and north-west) shed a great part of their moisture before reaching the Luxembourg frontiers. May to mid-October is suitable for vacations; July and August are the warmest; May and June are the sunniest months; in September and October there is often an 'Indian summer'.

Dress codes

Medium-weight clothing is required throughout the year. A raincoat is useful.

Entry requirements

Passports

Passports are required by nationals of most countries. Exceptions include holders of national identity cards issued to nationals of some European countries.

Visa

Required by all, except nationals of Europe, North America, Australasia, or Japan. For a full list of visa-free citizens visit www.luxembourg-usa.org/consindex.html. Schengen visas cover all entry needs; for those requiring a business visa, a letter of business references and proof of sufficient funds to cover the cost of your intended stay should accompany the application. A Schengen visa application (offered in several languages) can be downloaded from http://europa.eu/abc/travel/ see 'documents you will need'.

Currency advice/regulations

There are no restrictions on the movement of local or foreign currencies.

Customs

Personal items are duty-free. There are no duties levied on alcohol and tobacco between EU member states, providing amounts imported are for personal consumption.
Passengers carrying weapons and transiting Luxembourg must hold an *Autorisation de Transit d'Armes* certificate issued by the Luxembourg Ministry of Justice.

Health (for visitors)

Nationals of the European Economic Area (EEA) countries and Switzerland can access reduced cost and sometimes free medical treatment using a European Health Insurance Card (EHIC) while visiting the EEA. Exceptions include nationals of the 10 countries, which joined the EU in 2004, whose EHIC is not valid in Switzerland. Applications for the EHIC should be made before travelling.

Mandatory precautions

None

Advisable precautions

It is recommended that travellers have up-to-date tetanus and polio immunisations.

Hotels

A one-to five-star rating system is partially in operation. Bills include the service charge. Tipping is optional.

Credit cards

All main credit cards are accepted.

Public holidays (national)

Fixed dates

1 Jan (New Year's Day), 1 May (May Day), 23 Jun (National Day), 15 Aug (Assumption Day), 1 Nov (All Saints' Day), 25-26 Dec (Christmas).
If a holiday falls on a Sunday, the Monday following is usually a holiday as well (maximum two per annum).

Variable dates

Carnival (Feb), Good Friday, Easter Monday, Ascension Day, Whit Monday, Luxembourg City Fair Day (Luxembourg City only, Sep).

Working hours

Banking
Mon–Fri: 0900–1630.

Business
Mon–Fri: 0800–1800, lunch 1200–1400.

Government
Mon–Fri: 0800–1800, lunch 1200–1400.

Shops
There are large variations in shop hours, but they are generally open 0900–2000, closed Mon morning.

Electricity supply
220V AC

Weights and measures
Metric system

Social customs/useful tips
Punctuality is appreciated. Business people are expected to wear suits. It is advisable to make prior appointments and business cards are widely used.

Security
Luxembourg has a low crime rate. However, during the tourist season pickpocketing and theft from vehicles do occur.

Getting there

Air
National airline: Luxair
International airport/s: Luxembourg-Findel (LUX), 5km east of city; restaraunts, post office shops, car hire.
Airport tax: None

Surface
Road: There are good road links with Brussels, Trier, Paris, Frankfurt and Saarbrücken. Luxembourg has open borders with all its immediate neighbours, namely Germany, France and Belgium.
Rail: There are rail connections with Brussels, Frankfurt, Amsterdam, Basle and Paris.

Getting about

National transport
Network tickets (*billets réseaux*), which allow unlimited travel for one day on all forms of transport throughout Luxembourg, are also available.
Road: Luxembourg has an extensive network of roads and motorways, all of which are paved.
Buses: Bus services link most towns and villages.
Rail: There are 280km of railway track. State-run railway services link the capital with most main towns.

City transport
Taxis: There is a metered taxi service with a minimum charge. Tipping is usually 10 per cent.
Buses, trams & metro: Regular flat-fare bus service operates in Luxembourg city. Tickets are valid for one hour or 10km and also allow connections with out-of-city connections.

Car hire
Car hire is available from the airport and hotels.

BUSINESS DIRECTORY

The addresses listed below are a selection only. While World of Information makes every endeavour to check these addresses, we cannot guarantee that changes have not been made, especially to telephone numbers and area codes. We would welcome any corrections.

Telephone area codes
The international direct dialling (IDD) code for Luxembourg is +352, followed by subscriber's number.

Chambers of Commerce
American Chamber of Commerce in Luxembourg, 6 Rue Antoine de Saint Exupéry, PO Box 542, L-1432 Luxembourg (tel/fax: 431-756; e-mail: info@amcham.lu).

British Chamber of Commerce for Luxembourg, 6 Rue Antoine de Saint Exupéry, L-1432 Luxembourg (tel: 465-466; fax: 220-384; e-mail: info@bcc.lu).

Luxembourg Chamber of Commerce, 7 Rue Alcide de Gaspari, L-2981 Luxembourg (tel: 423-939; fax: 438-326; e-mail: chamcom@cc.lu).

Banking
Association des Banques et Banquiers, 59 Boulevard Royal, PO Box 13, L-2010 Luxembourg (tel: 29-501, 463-6601; fax: 460-921).

Banque Continentale du Luxembourg SA, 2 Boulevard Emmanuel Servais, L-2535 Luxembourg (tel: 474-491; fax: 477-688-333).

Banque de Luxembourg SA, 80 Place de la Gare, BP 2221, L-1022 Luxembourg (tel: 499-241; fax: 494-820).

Banque et Caisse d'Epargne de l'Etat, 1 Place de Metz, PO Box 2105, L-2954 Luxembourg (tel: 4015-1; fax: 4015-2099; e-mail: info@bcee.lu).

Banque Générale du Luxembourg, Boulevard JF Kennedy, L-2951 Luxembourg (tel: 47-991, 42-421; fax: 4799-2579).

Banque Internationale à Luxembourg SA BIL), 2 Boulevard Royal, L-2953 Luxembourg (tel: 45-901; fax: 4791-2010).

Banque Nationale de Paris SA, 22-24 Boulevard Royal, L-2952 Luxembourg-Ville (tel: 47-641; fax: 26-480).

Caisse Centrale Raiffeisen SC, 28 Boulevard Royal, BP 111, L-2011 Luxembourg (tel: 462-151).

Fortuna, Société Co-opérative de Credit et d'Epargne, 128-132 Boulevard de la Pétrusse, BP 1203, L-1012 Luxembourg (tel: 488-888).

Kredietbank SA Luxembourgeoise, 43 Boulevard Royal, L-2953 Luxembourg (tel: 47-971; fax: 472-667).

Société Générale Bank and Trust, 11 Avenue Emile Reuter, PO Box 1271, L-2420 Luxembourg (tel: 479-3111; fax: 228-859; e-mail:sgbt.lu@socgen.com).

Société Nationale de Credit et d'Investissement, 7 Rue du St Esprit, BP 1207, L-1012 Luxembourg (tel: 461-9711).

Central bank
Banque Centrale du Luxembourg, 2 Boulevard Royal, L-2983 Luxembourg (tel: 4774-1; fax: 4774-4910; email: info@bcl.lu).

European Central Bank (ECB), Kaiserstrasse 29, D-60311 Frankfurt am Main, Germany (tel: (+49-69) 13-440; fax: (+49-69) 1344-6000; email: info@ecb.int).

Stock exchange
Bourse de Luxembourg (Luxembourg Stock Exchange), www.bourse.lu

Travel information
Luxair, Luxembourg Airport, 2987 Luxembourg (tel: 798-2311; fax: 443-2482e-mail: information@luxair.lu).

Luxembourg Airport, PO Box 635, L-2016 Luxembourg (tel: 2464-1; fax: 2464-2464; e-mail: mail@lux-airport.lu).

Luxembourg City Tourist Office, Place d'Armes, L-1136 Luxembourg (tel: 222-809; fax: 474-818; e-mail: touristinfo@luxembourg-city.lu).

Ministry of tourism
Department of Tourism, 6 Avenue Emile Reuter, L-2937 Luxembourg (tel: 478-4751; fax: 474-011; e-mail: info@mdt.public.lu).

National tourist organisation offices
Office National du Tourisme, Gare Centrale, Box 1001, L-1010 Luxembourg (tel: 4282-821; fax: 4282-8238; e-mail: info@visitluxembourg.lu).

Ministries
Ministère des Affaires Etrangères, du Commerce Extèrieur et de la Coopèration, 5 Rue Notre-Dame, L-2913 Luxembourg (tel: 4781; fax: 461-720).

Ministère de l'Agriculture, de la Viticulture et du Developpement Rural, 1 Rue de la Congrègation, L-2913 Luxembourg (tel: 4781; fax: 464-027).

Ministère de l'Amenagement du Territoire, 18 Montèe de la Pètrusse, L-2946 Luxembourg (tel: 4781; fax: 408-970).

Ministère de la Culture, 20 Montée de la Pétrusse, L-2912 Luxembourg (tel: 4781; fax: 402-427).

Ministère de l'Economie, 19-21 Boulevard Royal, L-2914 Luxembourg (tel: 478-4100; fax: 460-448).

Ministère de l'Education Nationale et de la Formation Professionnelle, 29 rue Aldringen, L-2926 Luxembourg (tel: 4781; fax: 478-5113).

Ministère de l'Education Physique et des Sports, 66 route de Treves, L-2916 Luxembourg (tel: 4781; fax: 434-599).

Ministère de l'Energie, 19 Boulevard Royal, L-2449 Luxembourg (tel: 4781).

Ministère de l'Environnement, 18 Montée de la Pètrusse, L-2918 Luxembourg (tel: 4781; fax: 400-410).

Ministère de la Famille, 14 Avenue de la Gare, L-2919 Luxembourg (tel: 4781; fax: 478-6570).

Ministère des Finances, 3 rue de la Congregation, L-2931 Luxembourg (tel: 4781; fax: 475-241).

Ministère de la Fonction Publique et de la Réforme Administrative, Plateau du St Esprit, L-2011 Luxembourg (tel: 4781; fax: 478-3122).

Ministère de la Force Publique, Plateau du St Esprit, Bâtiment Vauban, L-2915 Luxembourg (tel: 4781; fax: 462-682).

Ministère de l'Intèrieur, 19 Rue Beaumont, L-2933 Luxembourg (tel: 4781; fax: 418-46).

Ministère de la Jeunesse, 26 Rue Zithe, L-2943 Luxembourg (tel: 4781; fax: 467-454).

Ministère de la Justice, 16 Boulevard Royal, L-2934 Luxembourg (tel: 4781; fax: 227-661).

Ministère du Logement, 6 Avenue Emile Reuter, L-2942 Luxembourg (tel: 4781; fax: 478-4840).

Ministère de la Promotion Féminine, 33 Boulevard Prince Henri, L-2919 Luxembourg (tel: 4781; fax: 41-886).

Ministère de la Santé, 57 et 90 Boulevard de la Pétrusse, L-2320 Luxembourg (tel: 4781; fax: 484-903).

Ministère de la Sécurité Sociale, 26 Rue Zithe, L-2936 Luxembourg (tel: 4781; fax: 478-6328).

Ministère des Transports, 19-21 Boulevard Royal, L-2938 Luxembourg (tel: 4781; fax: 464-315).

Ministère des Travail et de l'Emploi, 26 rue Zithe, L-2939 Luxembourg (tel: 4781; fax: 478-6325).

Ministère des Travaux Publics, 4 Boulevard FD Roosevelt, L-2940 Luxembourg (tel: 4781; fax: 462-709).

Other useful addresses

Bourse de Luxembourg SA (stock exchange), 11 Avenue de la Porte-Neuve, L-2227 Luxembourg (tel: 477-9361; fax: 22-050; internet site: http://www.bourse.lu/).

Board of Economic Development, 19-21 Boulevard Royal, L-2914 Luxembourg (tel:478-4135/4141; fax: 460-448).

Confédération du Commerce Luxembourgeois, 23 Allée Scheffer, L-2520 Luxembourg (tel: 473-125).

Fédération des Industriels Luxembourgeois, 7 Rue Alcide de Gasperi, L-1615 Luxembourg (tel: 435-366; fax: 438-326).

Foires Internationales de Luxembourg, L-2088 Luxembourg (tel: 043-991; fax: 0439-9315).

Groupement des Industries Sidérurgiques Luxembourgeoises (Federation of Iron and Steel Industries in Luxembourg), 3 Rue Goethe, PO Box 1704, L-1637 Luxembourg (tel: 480-001).

Luxembourg Embassy (USA), 2200 Massechusetts Avenue, NW, Washington DC 20008 (tel: (+1-202)-265-4171; fax: (+1-202)-328-8270; e-mail: info@luxembourg-usa.org).

Offshore Company Registration Agents (Luxembourg) SA, PO Box 878, 19 Rue Aldringen, L-1118 Luxembourg (tel: 224-286; fax: 224-287).

Press and Information Service of the Government, 43 Boulevard Roosevelt, L-2450 Luxembourg (tel: 478-224, 478-321; fax: 470-285, 20-090).

Radio Télé-Luxembourg (RTL), Villa Louvigny, L-2850 Luxembourg (tel: 476-6242; fax: 4766-2737).

Service Central de la Statistique et des Etudes Economiques (STATEC), 6 Boulevard Royal, L-2013 Luxembourg (tel: 4781; fax: 464-289; internet site: http://statec.lu/).

Société Européenne des Satellites (SES), Château de Betzdorf, L-6815 Luxembourg (tel: 710-725/1; fax: 725-227; internet site: http://www.astra.lu).

Internet sites

Complete list of banks in Luxembourg: http://www.bank.lu

Government statistics: http://statec.gouvernement.lu

Luxembourg weekly publication (in English): http://www.352.lu

Luxembourg government: http://gouvernement.lu

The Station Network, online information (in English): http://www.station.lu

Web directory: http://Luxembourg.lu/

Macao (China)

KEY FACTS

Official name: Macao Special Administrative Region of China (Macao SAR)

Head of State: State President of China Xi Jinping (in Beijing) (since 14 March 2013)

Head of government: Chief Executive (Fernando) Chui Sai On (from 20 Dec 2009, re-elected 31 Aug 2014)

Ruling party: An executive committee of technocrats, policymakers and business representatives provide a government cabinet.

Area: 29 square km (Macao peninsula, Taipa and Coloane islands)

Population: 552,503 (2011)* (568,700 census 2012)

Capital: Macao City

Official language: Chinese (Mandarin, Beijing dialect *de jure*; Cantonese *de facto*) and Portuguese

Currency: Pataca (Pa) = 100 avos

Exchange rate: Pa7.98 per US$ (Sep 2015)

GDP per capita: US$60,667 (2011)*

GDP real growth: 20.70% (2011)*

GDP: US$36.40 billion (2011)*

Labour force: 406,000 (2014)*

Unemployment: 1.70% (2014)

Inflation: 5.31% (Aug 2013)*

Balance of trade: -US$10.18 billion (2014)

* estimated figure

Macau does not often hit the headlines. In the second quarter of 2015 it did so when it turned in what was probably the biggest economic contraction of any country or territory in the world. The one-dimensional game industry economy of this Chinese Special Administrative Region (SAR) shrank by a staggering 26.4 per cent. Unsurprisingly, the gaming industry sector's revenues also diminished by about the same amount. In the six months between January and June 2015, the city's gross domestic product (GDP) also contracted by 24.5 per cent.

Macau is considered to be the most densely populated territory on earth. A mere 600,000 inhabitants live in some 30 square kilometres. Until very recently the habitable area was only 16 square kilometres, but in 2015 Macau saw its land area virtually double as the neighbouring satellite islands of Coloane and Taipa were joined to the mainland. For readers wondering just what makes the economy tick, the answer is simple: gambling. Macau is the only place in China where gambling is legal. It has a market of millions on its doorstep. And gambling is to Chinese what vodka is to Russians – only more so. Despite the economy's dramatically sharp implosion in the first half of 2015, which had seen its GDP drop to 2011 levels, unemployment remained at around two per cent, one of the lowest levels in the world.

The fall in gaming revenues had accelerated during the course of 2015 reflecting China's economic slowdown. Virtually all the casino customers come from China, filling the former Portuguese colony's hotels and restaurants. But for fourteen consecutive months turnover had been falling. A poll of analysts conducted by the New York financial analysts and publishers Bloomberg put the industry's annual rate of decline at an astonishing 38 per cent. Were this figure to prove correct, it would mean that the chances of recovery to former levels were virtually zero.

Fortunately, the economy's collapse did not seem to have affected Macau's public finances to the same degree. At least the economy had avoided running a deficit. Nevertheless, the fiscal surplus had halved in the space of little more than a year as the gaming taxes diminished proportionately. The chief executive of the Macau SAR, Fernando Chui Sai On, announced that the Macau government would be taking steps to reduce public expenditure if there was no sign of an upturn in casino revenues.

According to the World Bank, at the end of 2013 Macau's annual per capita GDP was US$96,000 making it one of the richest territories in the world, after Qatar and Norway. This did not mean that every Macanese (or Macaense after the Portuguese nomenclature) was stinking rich – Macau's wealth is concentrated in a small number of individuals and companies. The bulk of the population may be happy to have a job which, by Chinese standards pays well, but the inequalities are remarkable. Also by Chinese standards, Macau is an extremely expensive place to live in. For the first half of the twenty-first century, under agreements signed by China and Portugal, Macau (like Hong Kong) is allowed to maintain its capitalist status and economy.

Even if their trade was suffering, in 2015 new projects abounded. As revenues plummeted in China's only legal gambling centre, global casino operators operating in Macau looked to Las Vegas for inspiration. The Las Vegas economy has steadily diversified into hotels, entertainment and retail outlets: this template has already been adopted by Hong Kong's Galaxy Entertainment Group. The company's two new resort projects, worth US$3.2 billion, included a Broadway-themed hotel, a street food market and a river adventure ride. Galaxy had originally applied for 400 gaming tables, but the Macau authorities had only approved 150.

In 2014 Las Vegas, non-gaming accounted for more than two-thirds of the territory's total revenue. In Macau, the motivation is different, the territory is not set on changing its image, but there is an urgency as gambling revenues are clearly waning. The decline is not totally due to the Chinese economy's travails; the Beijing government's anti-corruption campaign has resulted in less ostentation from would be high-rollers in Macau.

Macau operators have little option but to consider such moves, and by allocating gaming tables in new projects according to the proportion of on non-gaming amenities they hope to encourage more diversity. However, the industry consensus is that Macau is unlikely to match Las Vegas for non-gaming revenue growth. Macau has 29,000 hotel rooms, barely half the 60,000 or so in Las Vegas. The number of Michelin-starred restaurants in Macau has more than doubled since 2009. However, the one statistic that matters is the bottom line and Macau's position is strong; the turnover of its thirty casinos is greater than that of Las Vegas.

However exotic the territory's gambling attractions, there is another aspect of Macau that is even more rarely mentioned. Unesco has recognised the territory as a World heritage site. The colonial centre has twenty baroque churches, colonial mansions and entire streets that remain totally Portuguese. The Portuguese established themselves in Macau in 1557, after being granted permission by the Chinese authorities to land (initially they were only allowed to remain ashore during the day). Thus a *de facto* colony was set up, which remained Portuguese territory until 1997. Macau was the only Portuguese territory to remain loyal to the Portuguese crown during the 48 years of union with Spain.

Risk assessment

Economy	Fair
Politics	Poor
Regional stability	Good

COUNTRY PROFILE

1513 The first group of Portuguese arrived at the entrance to the Pearl River, the area that is now Macao.

1557 The colony of Macao was founded by the Portuguese with the apparent approval of the Chinese authorities.

1845 After years of Chinese rule, the Portuguese expelled the Chinese and announced Macao a free port. The territory enlarged to include the islands of Taipa and Coloane.

1860 The Portuguese introduced gambling licences to the territory.

1887 Macao's status was recognised by the Treaty of Amity and Commerce, signed between Portugal and China.

1939–45 Macao remained neutral during the Second World War and its economy prospered.

1976 The Portuguese government declared Macao a special territory and granted it a high degree of independence.

1987 The Sino-Portuguese Joint Declaration on the Question of Macao was signed.

1999 China resumed control over the territory. Edmund Ho Hau Wah became the first chief executive, as Macao became a Special Administrative Region (SAR) of China.

2001 The Associação de Novo Macau Democrático (ANMD) (New Democratic Macao Association), won two of the 10 directly elected seats in the legislature.

2002 As part of the move to liberalise the gambling sector, Macao issued three casino licences to private operators. This broke the monopoly of self-made billionaire and the world's most successful casino operator, Stanley Ho Hung San.

2004 Edmund Ho was re-elected chief executive. The American owned and operated Sands Macao Casino opened with more gaming tables than any other single casino in the world.

2005 The Banco Delta Asia had accounts of around US$7 million linked to North Korea frozen by the US, after the bank was branded a 'primary money-laundering concern' as having dealt in counterfeit and illicitly earned money. For almost a year before the suspension over US$49 million were transmitted through the bank on behalf of North Korean Daedong Credit Bank.

2009 A new security law prohibiting acts of treason, secession, sedition and subversion against China's central government was enacted. It also banned foreign political organisations from activities in Macao as well as Macao political organisations from establishing links with overseas bodies. Fernando Chui Sai On was the overwhelming winner of the vote for chief executive with 282 votes out of 296. There were no changes in the distribution of seats in legislative assembly elections (the pro-business block five seats (out of 29), pro-democracy block four, Traditionalists block three and others 17 seats. Construction of a new six-lane bridge linking Hong Kong and Macao to China's mainland province of Guangdong began, to be completed by 2016; when completed it will be the longest sea-crossing bridge in the world (almost 50kms).

2010 Macao denied the Internet site Google permission to gather and photograph street views, while the Macao Office of Personal Data Protection investigated the legitimacy of Google's image collecting activities.

2011 In March Google launched its street views of Macao. Statistics released on 28 July showed Macao's fiscal surplus as US$4.53 billion in the first half of the year, while its deficit reached US$560 million by June. Merchandise imports in June were US$77.9 million a year-on-year increase of 40 per cent. Exports in June fell year-on-year by 6.3 per cent to US$425 million, of which re-exports declined by 10.4 per cent. Total visitor arrivals for the first half of the year were 13,246,656, recording a year-on-year increase of 8.3 per cent.

2012 A census was undertaken on 30 June; the preliminary result was 568,700 people recorded. On 19 October the US-casino operator, MGM Macao completed a land deal to build a new casino on the territory's Cotai Strip. The land, acquired for US$56 million from the government, is the fastest growing gambling district of Macao. The Amendment to Electoral Law for the Legislative Assembly of the Macau (also known as the 2+2+100 law), increased the members of the Legislative Council from 29 to 33.

2013 Elections to the Legislative Assembly were held on 15 September. The results were a win for the pro-establishment bloc with 10 seats and 4 seats for the pro-democracy bloc.

2014 Macao's Chief Executive Fernando Chui won a second five-year term as the only candidate in an election held on 31 August. The newly expanded (to 400 members from 300) election committee voted 380 in favour, out of the 396 votes cast.

2015 In August it was announced that the 'Free Yacht Travel Scheme' between the Macau and Zhongshan in Guangdong will be delayed by two months to start its pilot run at the end of September.

Political structure

Constitution

The Basic Law, promulgated by the People's Republic of China (PRC) in 1993, effectively became Macao's Constitution after sovereignty of the former Portuguese Special Territory was handed over to PRC in December 1999. The Basic Law pledges to maintain Macao's economic, social and political distinctiveness for a period of 50 years after the handover to the PRC, under the principle of 'one country, two systems'.

Under the Basic Law, members of the executive and legislature must be permanent Macao residents. Private property, free speech and freedom of conscience are guaranteed.

The Legislative Assembly voted to expand the Election Committee to 400 from 300 seats in August 2012 for the 2014 election.

Form of state

Special Administrative Region (SAR) of the People's Republic of China.

The executive

Under the terms of the Basic Law of Macao SAR (MSAR), executive power is vested in the chief executive, except in foreign affairs and defence, which are the responsibility of the People's Republic of China (PRC) government.

The president is indirectly elected by National People's Congress for a five-year term (eligible for a second term).

The Chief Executive is chosen by a 400-member Election Committee for a five-year term (eligible for a second term).

National legislature

The Assembleia Legislativa da Região Administrativa Especial de Macau (Legislative Assembly to the Macao Special Administrative Region) is a unicameral legislative council which consists of 33 seats, of which 14 members are directly elected by proportional representation vote and 12 are indirectly elected by an electoral college of professional and commercial interest groups and seven are appointed by the chief executive. Members serve four-year term. Among other responsibilities, the assembly may enact, amend, suspend or repeal laws, review and approve the budget, decide on taxes and review the conduct of the chief executive.

The chief executive has the power to remove members and dissolve the Legislative Council under conditions of political deadlock.

Last elections

15 September 2013 (Legislative Assembly); 31 August 2014 (chief executive)

Results: Legislative assembly: the pan-establishment bloc, led by the United Citizens Association of Macau won 10 (out of 14) geographical seats and the pro-democracy bloc (lead by the Prosperous Democratic Macao Association) 4 seats.

Chief Executive: Chui Sai On won 380 votes (97 per cent) (out of 396 votes cast) from the 400-member election committee in the National People's Congress.

Next elections

September 2017 (Legislative Assembly). 2019 (chief executive)

Political parties

There are no formal political parties. However, pro-Chinese associations control a majority of the Assembly's elective seats. A number of civic associations exist. The Associacao de Novo Macao Democratio (ANMD) (New Democratic Macao Association) has a significant presence in the Assembly.

Ruling party

An executive committee of technocrats, policymakers and business representatives provide a government cabinet.

Main opposition party

Associação de Novo Macao Democrático (ANMD) (New Democrat Macao Association); Associação dos Cidadãos Unidos de Macao (ACUM) (United Citizens Association of Macao); União para o Desenvolvimento (UPD) (Union for Development); União Promotora para o Progresso (UNIPRO) (Union for Promoting Progress).

552,503 (2011)* (568,700 census 2012)

Population

Most of the population lives in Macao City; the remainder on the islands of Taipa and Coloane. The northern area of the peninsula is considered to have the highest population density in the world, with 120,000 people per square km.

Last census: 19 August 2006: 502,113

Population density: Over 20,000 inhabitants per square km. Urban population: 99 per cent.

Annual growth rate: 1 per cent (2003)

Ethnic make-up

Approximately 96 per cent of the territory's inhabitants are Chinese (mostly Cantonese from Guangdong province); the remainder are Mavanese (mixed Portuguese and Chinese).

Religions

Chinese Buddhism (45 per cent), Christianity (Roman Catholicism) (15 per cent).

Education

Primary education begins at age six and lasts until age 12. There are three stages of secondary schooling, beginning with junior, lasting for three years, then senior for two years and finally a pre-university one-year course. The first 10 years of education are free of charge.

Teaching may be given in Chinese, English or Portuguese.

Some 25 per cent of Macao's inhabitants attend any of 83 primary schools, 40 secondary schools, nine vocational technical colleges or nine institutes of higher education. The University of Macao has approximately 3,500 students in 80 undergraduate and post-graduate degree subjects.

Literacy rate: 94.3 per cent total, 91.7 per cent female, adult rates (World Bank).

Enrolment rate: 84.1 per cent net primary enrolment; 62.3 per cent net secondary enrolment (government statistics, 2005).

Pupils per teacher: 21.2 in primary/secondary schools; 9.3 in higher education.

Health

Macao's population is young, with around 60 per cent between the ages of 15 and 50. Approximately 9 per cent of the government budget is allocated to healthcare.

Life expectancy: 79.3 years (estimate 2003)

Fertility rate/Maternal mortality rate: 1.2 births per per woman (World Bank)

Child (under 5 years) mortality rate (per 1,000): Six per 1,000 live births (World Bank).

Welfare

Unemployment benefits, old age pensions and invalid benefits are administered by the Social Security Fund, which is financed through employer and employee contributions as well as government subsidies.

Public assistance centres are co-ordinated by the Macao Social Welfare Institute in conjunction with the Church and other civilian organisations.

Main cities

Macao City (capital, estimated population 433,337 in 2012).

Languages spoken

Only 1.8 per cent of the population speak Portuguese. English is widely spoken and used in business and tourist circles.

Official language/s

Chinese (Mandarin, Beijing dialect *de jure*; Cantonese *de facto*) and Portuguese

Media

Freedom of the press is guaranteed under the law and the government respects this. China's official Xinhua state news agency operates as the Liaison Offices of the Central People's Government for Macau and regulates broadcasting media.

Press

Dailies: In Portuguese, publications include *Hoje Macau* (www.hojemacau.com), *Jornal Tribuna de Macau* (www.jtm.com.mo) and *Ponto Final*. In Chinese, publications include *Macao Daily News* (www.macaodaily.com), with the highest circulation, the privately owned *Va Kio* (www.vakiodaily.com) and *Jornal Va Kio*, *Ou Mun*, *Si Man*, *Tai Chung Pou* and *Seng Pou*. The *Macau Post Daily* (www.macaupostdaily.com) is the oldest English language newspaper.

Weeklies: There are several magazines catering for all interests.

Business: In English, *Macau Business* (www.macaubusiness.com) is a monthly publication with sections dedicated to specific business interests such as banking, gaming and property. In Chinese *Business Intelligence* (www.bizintelligenceonline.com).

Periodicals: In Portuguese *Revista Macau* (www.revistamacau.com) is a quarterly magazine covering cultural matters. *Inside Asian Gaming*

(www.asgam.com) is a monthly publication concerned with industry development.

Broadcasting

Teledifusão de Macau (TDM) (www.tdm.com.mo) is the public broadcaster.

Radio: TDM (www.tdm.com.mo) operates Radio Macau in Cantonese and Portuguese. Radio Villa Verde (www.am738.com) is an independent station.

Overseas radio stations from China and Hong Kong are available.

Television: TDM (www.tdm.com.mo) operates two channels, broadcasting in Cantonese and Portuguese. There are several private TV stations broadcasting, via digital cables or satellite, which provide international programmes, including Macao Cable (www.macaucabletv.com) and Villa Verde Ltd.

Economy

Macao has an economy heavily dependent on tourism, principally based around gambling. Emphasis on the tourist sector remains at the heart of all future plans for development by the governments of SAR Macao and China. As part of the Pearl River Delta Region of southern China, which includes the cities of Guangzhou, Shenzhen and Zhuhai, and has a combined population of over 25 million, Macao is planning to diversify its economy. In 2014, Macau's gaming-related taxes accounted for more than 83 per cent of total government revenue.

Macau hosted nearly 31.5 million visitors in 2014. Around 65 per cent arrived from main land China. China's ongoing anti-corruption campaign has brought Macau's gambling boom to a halt, with spending in casinos contracting 2.6 per cent in 2014. As a result, Macau's GDP contracted 0.4 per cent from 2013, significantly down from double-digit expansion rates in 2010–13.

Macao's GDP in 2008 had fallen, from 14.4 per cent in 2007 to 3.4 per cent and fell further to 1.6 per cent in 2009. However in 2010 as global trade picked-up, GDP growth jumped to 27.1 per cent and remained high at an estimated 20.7 per cent in 2011. The inflation rate was 8.7 per cent in 2008, which fell to 1.1 per cent in 2009 as domestic consumption declined; it rose again in 2010, to 2.8 per cent, before climbing to an estimated 4.64 per cent in August 2015. Macao's GDP fell from 10.9 per cent in 2013 to -0.4 per cent of GDP in 2014.

A steep 24.5 per cent year-on-year drop in output in the first quarter of 2015 confirms the view that Macau will remain in recession in 2015. Nevertheless, new casino developments in the Cotai Strip are proceeding, providing some support to growth, and unemployment will remain very low. An economic recovery should be underway by 2016.

The Beijing government limits trips by Chinese citizens to Macao, the only Chinese territory with legal gambling.

There is a potential for greater scope in development into fields of not only existing enterprises, such as textile manufacturing (despite lower operating costs in Zhuhai), but particularly in labour-intensive processes. A number of enterprises, particularly textile manufacturers, have shifted to Zhuhai, but new hi-tech manufacturing such as telecommunications and more sophisticated, capital-intensive processes have tended to remain in Macao.

Shipping facilities were upgraded following the construction of the Ka Ho port with its container terminal and an oil terminal.

Macao has physically grown – by 2.9sq km of reclaimed land in 2006, joining with the island of Coloane to become one landmass, thereby increasing Macao's area by 18 per cent. The Cotai Strip is a large development of hotels and casinos, with some of the world's largest casino operators building state-of-the-art gambling facilities. The American owned and operated Sands Macao Casino is the largest casino in the world with more gaming tables than any other single casino. Casino operators must pay 35 per cent of gross revenue, as a special gaming tax, and a premium for their gaming concession. They also pay 1.6 per cent of their gross revenue to the Macao Foundation (a social fund to promote cultural activities). Over 70 per cent of the SAR government's total revenue is garnered from gaming taxes.

Macao offers tax and other incentives for investment in tourism and hotels, the electronics manufacturing industry, fishing industry and property development. It has certain competitive advantages over Hong Kong, for example, wage costs, factory rentals, office space and residential accommodation cost about half – in some cases a third – of Hong Kong equivalents.

External trade

Under the Closer Economic Partnership Arrangement (CEPA), Macau has a trade alliance with China's nine southernmost provinces and Hong Kong through the pan-Pearl River Delta (PRD) trade bloc.

Imports

Principle imports include raw materials and semi-manufactured goods, foodstuffs, tobacco, capital goods, mineral fuels and oils and alcohol.

Main sources: China (30.3 per cent of total in 2014), Hong Kong (10 per cent), Switzerland (9 per cent).

Exports

Principal exports include clothing, textiles, footwear, toys, electronics, machinery and parts and textile yarns.

Main destinations: Hong Kong (48.6 per cent of total in 2014), China (10.2 per cent), US (1 per cent)

Agriculture

Farming

The agriculture and fishing sectors typically account for 0.1 per cent of GDP and 0.2 per cent of the workforce.

Soils are generally meagre and there is little agricultural production. Macao imports its food and water requirements, mainly from China.

Fishing

Fish, prawns and other seafood are trawled for local consumption and export.

Industry and manufacturing

The textile and garment industries provide the bulk of Macao's exports, although they are subject to limitations such as EU quotas and some producers have been moving to Zhuhai. Other main products include toys, printing and packaging, leather products, electronics and opticals, food and beverages, furniture, woodware and ceramics.

Tourism

Macao has become a premier destination for all lovers of gaming and gambling in the new state of the art casinos that have been built since 2002. It is also home to the Macao Formula Three Grand Prix (held annually in November) and is the only street circuit racing event for both cars (including touring cars) and motorcycles. The historic centre of Macao, with a fusion of Chinese and Portuguese architecture, has been placed on the UN list of World Heritage Sites. The statue of the Buddhist Goddess, Kun Lam, is described as 'dainty but gigantic' it is a carving representing the mother goddess and is an attraction for many practicing Buddhists and other tourists.

Travel and tourism are vital components of GDP, constituting over 80 per cent since 2006, it also provides a similar share of total employment. In 2014, the total contribution to GDP was 87.6 per cent, whilst the total contribution to employment was 85.7 per cent.

Hydrocarbons

There are no known hydrocarbons reserves. Consumption of oil was 16,000 barrels per day in 2008, all of which was imported.

Any imports of coal are commercially insignificant.

Energy

Total installed generating capacity was 472MW in 2013, producing over 4.13

billion kilowatt hours. The private utility company Companhia de Electricidade de Macao (Cem) (Macao Electricity Company) remains the energy monopoly in Macao, responsible for generating, transmitting, distributing and selling electricity. It operates two thermal power stations on Coloane Island, which meet about 80 per cent of the total requirements; the remainder is imported from neighbouring Zhuhai City in China.

There are no proven reserves of natural gas. Imports totalled 371,000 cubic metres (cum) in 2013.

Banking and insurance

Since China took control of Macao in 1999, new banking laws intended to attract more foreign banks and allow a full range of offshore banking services have been enacted to ensure participation in financing the development of southern China. Macao enjoys some of the most liberal financial systems in the world.

Central bank

There is no central bank. The Monetary Authority of Macao (known as Autoridade Monetária e Cambial de Macao until 2000) is the monetary and foreign exchange authority of the territory.

Main financial centre

Macao City

Time

GMT plus eight hours

Geography

Macao comprises the peninsula of Macao and two nearby islands: Taipa, linked to the mainland by a bridge, and Coloane, which is connected to Taipa by a causeway. The territory lies opposite Hong Kong on the western side of the mouth of the Xijiang (Sikiang) river.

Hemisphere

Northern

Climate

Subtropical and monsoonal. Winter (November–April) is cool and dry, with an average temperature of 14–23 degrees Celsius (C). Summer (May–September) is hot, humid and rainy, with an average temperature of 27 degrees C. October and November are somewhat less humid. Average annual rainfall ranges from 1,000–2,000mm; monsoon rains from May–October.

Entry requirements

Passport and visa regulations are liable to change at short notice.

Passports

Valid passport required by all except holders of a Hong Kong Identity Card (HKIC) and nationals of China with a China Identity Card.

Visa

Required by all, except citizens of many European and Asian countries, North America and Australasia, arriving as tourists. Requirements for business visas should be obtained from the nearest Chinese consulate, well in advance of a business visit.

Currency advice/regulations

There are no restrictions on the import and export of local and foreign currencies.

Customs

Personal effects are allowed duty-free. Macao is a free port and there are no import duties, except on electrical appliances and equipment, which are subject to a 5 per cent *ad valorem* duty. Registration is required for all imports and an import licence for goods subject to consumption tax, such as beverages, coffee, rice, salt, sugar, wheat, matches, tobacco, bricks, cement and mineral oils, gases, vehicles. There are no export duties on articles purchased in Macao.

As inward and outward travel is generally through Hong Kong, export/import regulations of Hong Kong must be observed.

Health (for visitors)

Mandatory precautions

No compulsory vaccinations are required.

Advisable precautions

Vaccinations for diphtheria, tuberculosis, hepatitis A and B, Japanese B encephalitis, polio, tetanus and typhoid. Rabies is a risk.

Hotels

There are around 9,000 hotels rooms. A 10 per cent service charge and 5 per cent tax are added to the bill. It is customary to leave a small tip.

Credit cards

Most major credit cards are widely accepted.

Public holidays (national)

Fixed dates

1 Jan (New Year's Day), 5 Apr (Qing Ming Festival), 1 May (Labour Day), 1 Oct (National Day of China), 2 Nov (All Souls' Day), 8 Dec (Immaculate Conception), 20 Dec (Macao Special Administrative Region Establishment Day), 22 Dec (Winter Solstice), 24–25 Dec (Christmas).

Variable dates

Chinese New Year (Jan/Feb), Easter, Birth of Buddha (Apr/May), Dragon Boat Festival (May/Jun), Mid-Autumn Festival (Sep/Oct), Chung Yeung Festival (Oct).

Working hours

Banking

Mon–Fri: 0930–1600; Sat: 0930–1230.

Business

Mon–Fri: 0900–1300, 1500–1730; Sat: 0900–1230.

Government

Mon–Fri: 0930–1800.

Shops

Mon–Sat: 1000–1900.

Electricity supply

220V AC, 50Hz in new buildings and 110V AC for most domestic supply, with various types of plug fittings.

Weights and measures

Metric system

Social customs/useful tips

It is customary to shake hands on meeting and taking leave.

Getting there

Air

National airline: Air Macau

International airport/s: Macao International (MFM), on Taipa Island, seven km south of the city.

The airport is linked to Macao via a four-lane motorway and to mainland China via a dual-lane highway. Estimated travelling time into central Macao is 10 minutes and 20 minutes to the Chinese border.

Airport tax: Pa90, paid in local currency.

Surface

Road: Macao is connected to mainland China by a short causeway. Two bridges, the Friendship and Lotus, the latter carrying a six-lane highway, link the island of Taipa with the Zhuhai Special Economic Zone.

Water: Most visitors enter via Hong Kong. There are over 100 scheduled sailings both ways during the day, and jetfoils operate round the clock (journey time 55 minutes). It is advisable to book in advance.

Main port/s: Macao harbour.

Getting about

National transport

Buses: Bus services operate 0700–2400, with services between the ferry pier and the city centre and the islands.

Rail: The proposed light rail system will connect all major ports and tourist attractions along the coast of the Macao Peninsula and the new town, Cotai, terminating at Macao International Airport. The light rail system will also connect to the inter-city express railway transport system proposed by mainland China.

City transport

Central Macao is tiny and easily walkable. It is possible to hire two-passenger *triciclos* (pedal rickshaws), although they are unsuitable for climbing the hills. It is advisable to agree the fare before starting the journey.

Taxis: Taxis are inexpensive and readily available. Licensed, metered taxis are mostly painted black with cream-coloured tops. Radio taxis are painted yellow.

Buses, trams & metro: Good local bus services. Transmac AP1 service runs from airport to city centre every 30 minutes, journey time 30 minutes; STCM service 21 runs every 20 minutes, journey time 30 minutes.

Car hire

Car hire is available. Driving is on the left. An international driving permit is required. The minimum driving age is 21.

BUSINESS DIRECTORY

The addresses listed below are a selection only. While World of Information makes every endeavour to check these addresses, we cannot guarantee that changes have not been made, especially to telephone numbers and area codes. We would welcome any corrections.

Telephone area codes

The international direct dialling code (IDD) for Macao is +853, followed by subscriber's number.

Useful telephone numbers

Medical emergencies: 999
Police tourist hotline: 112
Fire: 999

Chambers of Commerce

Macao Chamber of Commerce, Edificio ACM, 175 Rua de Xangai, Macao (tel: 576-833; fax: 594-513; e-mail: acm@macauweb.com).

Banking

Banco Comercial de Macau SA, Rua da Praia Grande No 22, PO Box 545, Macao (tel: 569-622; fax: 580-967).

Banco Delta Asia SARL, 79 Avenida Conselheiro Ferreira de Almeida, Macao (tel: 559-898; fax: 570-068).

Banco Weng Hang SARL, 241 Avenida de Almeida Ribeiro, Macao (tel: 335-678; fax: 576-527).

Luso International Banking Ltd, 47 Avenida Dr Mário Soares, Macao (tel: 378-977; fax: 578-517).

Tai Fung Bank Ltd, Tai Fung Bank Headquarters Building, 418 Alameda Dr Carlos d'Assumpção, Macao (tel: 322-323; fax: 570-737).

Central bank

Monetary Authority of Macao, Calçada do Gaio 24-26, Macao City (tel: 568-288; fax: 325-432; e-mail: general@amcm.gov.mo).

Travel information

Administração de Aeropoertos (tel: 711-808; fax: 711-803).

Air Macao (tel: 396-5555; fax: 396-6866).

East Asia Airlines (tel: 790-7040).

Far East Jetfoils (tel: 790-7093).

Flight information (24 hours) (tel: 2886 1111).

Macao International Airport, R Dr Pedro Jose Lobo, 1—3, Edif Luso Internacional, 26 o andar, Macao (tel: 511-213; fax: 338-089; e-mail: aacm@aacm.gov.mo; www.macau-airport.com/en).

Sociedade de Turismo e Diversoes de Macao, 9 Largo do Senado, Macao (tel: 315-566; fax: 510-104).

National tourist organisation offices

Macau Government Tourist Office, PO Box 3006, 9 Edifício Largo do Leal Senado (tel: 375-156, 561-167, 555-424, fax: 510-104; internet: www.macoutourism.gov.mo).

Other useful addresses

Coastal International Exhibition Co Ltd, Room 3808, China Resources Building, 26 Harbour Road, Wanchai, Hong Kong (tel: (+852) 2827-6766; fax: + 852 2827-6870; e-mail: general@coastal.com.hk).

Macao Business Support Centre (tel: 728-212; fax: 727-123, 728-213; e-mail: mbsc@ipim.gov.mo).

Macao Commercial Association (Associacão Comercial de Macão), Edifício ACM, Rua da Xanghai, 5th Floor (tel: 576-833; fax: 594-513).

Macao Export Promotions Department, 1-3 Rua Pedro José Lobo, International Building (tel: 78-221).

Macao Importers and Exporters' Association, Av do Infante D Henrique No 60-62, 30 o andar, Centro Comercial Central, Macao (tel: 553-187, 375-859; fax: 512-174; e-mail: aeim@macau.ctm.net).

Macao Industrial Association, PO Box 70, Travessa da Praia Grande No. 56 (tel: 574-125; fax: 578-305).

Macao Statistics Department, PO Box 3022, Ground Floor, Rua Inácio Baptista, 4D-6, Seaview Garden (tel: 550-935; fax: 307-825; internet site: http://www.dsec.gov.mo).

Macao Trade and Investment Promotion Institute, 1—3 Rua Dr Pedro Jose Lobo (7th/8th Floor) (e-mail: ipim@ipim.gov.mo); Investment Promotion (tel: 340-090, 712-660; fax: 712-659; internet site: http://www.ipim.gov.mo); Trade Promotion: (tel: 378-221, 710-528; fax: 590-309).

Internet sites

Customs formalities: www.customs.gov.mo

Immigration formalities: www.fsm.gov.mo

Macao Environment Council: www.ambiente.gov.mo

Macao government: www.macau.gov.mo

Macao Tower Convention and Entertainment Centre: www.gaming-exhibition.com

Macedonia

KEY FACTS

Official name: Republika Makedonija (Former Yugoslav Republic of Macedonia) (FYROM)

Head of State: President Gjorgje Ivanov (VMRO–DPMNE) (from 12 May 2009) (re-elected on 27 April 2014)

Head of government: Prime Minister Nikola Gruevski (from 2006; re-elected 5 Jun 2011 and 27 Apr 2014)

Ruling party: Coalition (of 22 parties), led by Vnatrešno-Makedonska Revoluciona Organizacija-Demokratska Partija za Makedonsko Nacionalno Edintsvo (VMRO-DPMNE) (Internal Macedonian Revolutionary Organisation-Democratic Party for Macedonian National Unity) (from 2006; re-elected 5 Jun 2011 and 27 Apr 2014)

Area: 25,713 square km

Population: 2.07 million (2014)*

Capital: Skopje

Official language: Macedonian and Albanian.

Currency: Macedonian denar (Md) = 100 deni

Exchange rate: Md55.23 per US$ (Sep 2015)

GDP per capita: US$5,481 (2014)*

GDP real growth: 3.77% (2014)

GDP: US$11.34 billion (2014)

Labour force: 961,000 (2014)*

Unemployment: 28.45% (2014)

Inflation: -0.13% (2014)

Balance of trade: -US$2.47 billion (2014)*

* estimated figure

The Macedonian national flag features a curiously un-European motif of a rising – or possibly beaming – yellow sun on a red background. In a number of European countries the word Macedonia refers to a fruit salad rather than a country. In early 2015 things in Macedonia were looking decidedly pear-shaped. The promise once symbolised by the flag had, literally, flagged. Once hailed as a regional success story, Macedonia was showing signs of imploding under the democratic burden. Quite amazingly, in February 2015, rumours began to circulate that as many as 20,000 prominent Macedonians, ranging from the judiciary, through the diplomatic corps, to run of the mill politicians and journalists had been subjected to illegal surveillance. In some cases, according to the allegations, the spying had been carried on for some four years. The fingers of accusation, lead by the leader of the opposition, Zoran Zaev of the Socijaldemokratski sojuz na Makedonija (SDSM) (Social Democratic Union of Macedonia) all pointed at the incumbent Prime Minister Nikola Gruevski.

In an article in the *New York Times*, Macedonia's former ambassador to the US and the Netherlands, Nikola Dimitrov, went on to note that Mr Gruevski, perhaps predictably, had denied the allegations, claiming that they were the handiwork of an unidentified foreign intelligence service. It seemed to escape Mr Gruevski's radar that the notion of any foreign country mounting such an operation on such a tiny body politic as Macedonia was simply laughable. The prime minister's knee-jerk reaction was to accuse Mr Zaev of 'violence against representatives of the highest state authorities.' Mr Zaev was not the only Macedonian to face charges – five policeman and intelligence operatives were charged with espionage and one was sentenced to no less three years in prison.

In a number of respects – with the exception of their scale – there was nothing particularly surprising about the allegations. Macedonia ranks low on the Reporters Without Borders' *World Press Freedom Index*, 117 – the lowest European Union (EU) accession country and, for that matter, the lowest Balkan nation.

In 2006 Macedonia ranked 45. On the Transparency International *Corruption Perceptions Index* for 2014 it ranked 64 out of the 175 countries surveyed. Perhaps the biggest surprise was how the aspirations once generated and advocated by Mr Gruevski had evaporated in such a short space of time. In his excellent article, Mr Dimitrov notes how 'In 2006, when Mr Gruevski became Prime Minister, Macedonia was a functional, multi-ethnic democracy with a prospective future in both the European Union and NATO.' Mr Gruevski's electoral platform was based on improving the economy (he was a former finance minister) and fighting corruption.

Resignations

In May 2015 Prime Minister Gruevski 'accepted' the resignation of two ministers and his head of intelligence, apparently for their roles in the surveillance scandal. It was rumoured that the intelligence supremo, Saso Mijalkov (the prime minister's cousin) and the interior minister, Gordana Jankulovska, had led government attempts to control the press, judiciary and electoral officials through systematic phone tapping. The climate of uncertainty was aggravated by the clashes that also erupted between ethnic Albanians and police forces. Fourteen ethnic Albanians and eight police officers were killed in the fighting that followed a police raid on an ethnic Albanian neighbourhood in the northern town of Kumanovo. Mr Gruevski avoided giving a reason for the resignations.

Since its independence, Macedonia has had to fight the childish opposition of Greece to its use of the national name, insisting that it adhered to the wordy – and by 2015 quite meaningless and long-winded – Former Yugoslavia Republic of Macedonia – FYROM. Greece's northern province is also known as Macedonia. Macedonia's failure to make progress in its EU accession is in part due to Greek objections. At a time when Greece is on its knees economically, it seems strange that the EU authorities have not spelt out the absurdity of the Greek position over Macedonia. In the *New York Times*, Mr Dimitrov concluded his article by stating that 'Macedonia's path to EU membership must be freed from Greece's grip.'

Presidential elections

In April 2014, Macedonia had held the first round of its Presidential elections. The incumbent, Professor Gjorgje Ivanov, supported by the conservative Vnatrešno-Makedonska Revoluciona Organizacija-Demokratska Partija za Makedonsko Nacionalno Edintsvo (VMRO-DPMNE) (Internal Macedonian Revolutionary Organisation-Democratic Party for Macedonian National Unity), faced three challengers: Stevo Pendarovski supported by the former communist SDSM; Iljaz Halimi from the ethnic Albanian opposition party (Partia Demokratike Shqiptare (PDS) (Democratic Party of Albanians) and Zoran Popovski from the newly founded Grajanska Optsiya za Makedoniya) (GOM) (Citizen Option for Macedonia). The turnout was disappointing, 49 per cent, down from the 57 per cent registered in the first election in 2009. Macedonia's Electoral Code requires that 50 per cent+1 be gained for an outright victory. The incumbent Mr Ivanov won the first round by a long chalk, with 449,068 votes, ahead of Mr Pendarovski with 326,133. The lesser candidates Messrs Halimi and Popovski won 38,966 and 31,366 respectively. Thus the final presidential round was, unsurprisingly, to be a contest between the candidates of VMRO-DPMNE and SDSM. In the event, Macedonia's conservative ruling coalition party secured a third term in office, winning both the parliamentary and presidential elections. An idea of the complex structure and balance of Macedonian politics can be gained by a glance at the winning coalition's make-up: the VMRO-DPMNE coalition, lead by Nikola Gruevski, consisted – in a rather Ruritanian mold – of no less than 22 parties, which – for the record (and in English to demonstrate the 'fruit salad' nature of the politics) – were – VMRO-DPMNE, the Socialist party of Macedonia, the Democratic Union, the Democratic Renewal of Macedonia, the Democratic Party of Turks, the Democratic Party of Serbs in Macedonia, the Union of Roma in Macedonia, the United Party for Emancipation, the Party of Justice, the Party of the Democratic Action of Macedonia, the Party of the Vlachs from Macedonia, the Party for Integration of the Roma, the Bosniak Democratic Party, Democratic Forces of the Roma, Permanent Macedonian Radical Unification, the New Liberal Party, the People's Movement for Macedonia, VMRO–Democratic Party, VMRO-United, Fatherland's Macedonian Organisation for Radical Renewal–Vardar–Aegean–Pirin TMORO – VEP, Macedonian Alliance and VMRO–Macedonian. Prime Minister Gruevski had ruled the former Yugoslav republic of 2 million people since 2006, in coalition with ethnic Albanian party DUI.

The centre left SDSM coalition, lead by Zoran Zaev, could only gather 24 per cent of the vote. The SDSM members were rather fewer than the VMRO-DPMNE – it could only muster nine partners: the Social Democratic Union of Macedonia, the New Social Democratic Party, the Liberal Democratic Party, United for Macedonia, the Party for the Movement of the Turks in Macedonia, the Party for the full Emancipation of the Roma in Macedonia, the Serbian Party in Macedonia, the Democratic Alliance of the Vlachs in Macedonia and the Sandžak List

The economy – the IMF

KEY INDICATORS — Macedonia

	Unit	2011	2012	2013	2014	**2015
Population	m	*2.06	2.07	2.07	*2.07	*2.07
Gross domestic product (GDP)	US$bn	10.30	9.59	10.77	11.34	*10.15
GDP per capita	US$	5,016	4,638	5,215	*5,481	*4,896
GDP real growth	%	3.0	-0.4	2.7	3.8	*3.8
Inflation	%	3.9	3.3	2.8	-0.1	*0.1
Unemployment	%	31.2	31.3	29.0	28.5	*27.4
Exports (fob) (goods)	US$m	3,299.1	2,958.1	3,166.1	3,681.2	–
Imports (fob) (goods)	US$m	5,998.4	5,577.6	5,634.5	6,149.8	–
Balance of trade	US$m	-2,699.3	-2,619.5	-2,468.4	-2,468.6	–
Current account	US$m	-310.6	-290.0	-195.0	-151.0	*-203.0
Total reserves minus gold	US$m	2,539.8	2,528.2	2,484.6	2,700.5	–
Foreign exchange	US$m	2,538.1	2,526.6	2,480.0	–	–
Exchange rate	per US$	43.78	47.44	45.05	50.61	–

* estimated figure ** forecast figure

In its January 2015 assessment of the Macedonian economy, the International Monetary Fund (IMF) notes that the government's 'jobs and growth' agenda should remain a top policy priority, with efforts focused on relaxing key constraints for domestic firms. According to the IMF, the priorities should include properly implementing and monitoring recent initiatives to enforce payment discipline in both public and private sector contracts, as well as upgrading the professional status of inspection bodies, clarifying their mandate and streamlining their work. In the view of the IMF, the public-sector led growth strategy is likely to place pressure on other types of spending if consolidation is to proceed in the current low-tax environment.

Macedonia's investment spending should, in the view of the IMF, target gaps in transport and energy infrastructure to maximise the opportunities for medium-term growth. At the same time, with public debt rising steadily to over 50 per cent of gross domestic product (GDP) by 2017, fiscal policy should aim at reducing the deficit to below 2.6 per cent of GDP by 2016. In the absence of further tax policy changes to boost revenues, a comprehensive spending review that seeks to minimise the growth impact of current expenditure compression should therefore be undertaken. More comprehensive public debt management is needed to support external sustainability. To further reduce risks, particularly currency risk, the strategy should be expanded to cover the debt of state owned enterprises (SOEs) and contingent liabilities. Increased reliance on foreign currency borrowing also has important implications for central bank (Narodna banka na Republika Makedonija (NBRM) (National Bank of the Republic of Macedonia)) reserve developments and domestic liquidity that should be taken into account in evaluating government financing options. The monetary easing cycle has reached its end. The combination of relaxed financial conditions and tight prudential regulation has helped revive credit growth while preserving the health of the financial sector. While temporary supply-side developments have recently generated deflationary pressures, the focus of monetary policy henceforth should be on maintaining the attractiveness of holding denar-denominated assets in support of the exchange rate peg. Outstanding credit is scheduled to fall below 200 per cent of quota at end-year.

The economy – the EBRD

According to the European Bank for Reconstruction and Development (EBRD) Macedonia's economy recovered well after the 2012 recession. In sharp contrast to 2012, when GDP contracted by 0.4 per cent reflecting weaker export growth and lower private consumption, growth in 2013 was relatively strong. GDP rose by some three per cent, due in large measure to public investment; exports and private consumption which also grew.

However, the strength of the economy has not worked its way through to the labour market. Macedonia's unemployment remained high at around 30 per cent and the decline in inflation accelerated in the second half of 2013. In early 2014 the same trends appeared to be continuing, with mid-year growth almost hitting four per cent alongside low inflation which became negative in April. Macedonia's fiscal policy had relaxed significantly in the previous few years.

The EBRD noted that Macedonia's budget deficit rose from 2.5 per cent in 2011 to almost 4 per cent of GDP in 2012 and around 4.1 per cent in 2013. It was expected to remain high in the immediate future reflecting the government's continued high level of capital expenditure. Macedonia's public debt in August 2014 was considered moderate by regional standards at an estimated 46.8 per cent of GDP. None the less, this was twice the level seen in 2008, when the figure was 23 per cent. The government has started a process of imposing a constitutional ceiling on the budget deficit and on public debt at 3 per cent and 60 per cent of GDP respectively. The EBRD expected to see GDP growth of 3 per cent by the end of 2014. Macedonia continues to attract foreign direct investment (FDI) which contributes to Macedonia's growth prospects.

Any success in unblocking Macedonia's EU accession would further boost investor confidence. The dialogue continued, but the EBRD noted that the formal EU accession remained stalled. Despite Greek opposition, in October 2014 the European Commission – for the sixth year in succession – recommended the resumption of accession talks. Agreement for the privatisation of a tobacco company represented the most significant progress. In May 2014 the US tobacco giant Philip Morris took a 51 per cent holding in the Macedonian Tutunski Kombinat AD Prilep (YKP). In 2014 other privatisation deals appeared to be stalled.

Macedonia compares well with its regional neighbours on the World Bank's *Doing Business*, ranking 30 out of the 189 countries surveyed. Despite the slow progress in privatisation, FDI increased by a factor of three in 2013 and by 43 per cent year on year in the first four months of 2014. The investments came from the EU, Middle East, the US and Turkey. Hopes are also pinned on the car components where there have been a number of investments.

Two major road projects were approved in 2014; significantly these are to be financed by China Exim Bank and the works will be carried out by the Chinese company Sinohydro Corporation Ltd. The value of the two projects was put at €0.5 billion (US$0.56 billion). A positive aspect of the agreement is the condition that the project should have a minimum of 49 per cent local contractors and 51 per cent local labour. Macedonia's banking sector is dominated by foreign banks which, according to the EBRD, account for over 90 per cent of total banking assets. Banks have relied primarily of domestic deposits to fund lending.

Risk assessment

Politics	Fair
Economy	Fair
Regional stability	Fair

Muslims in Macedonia

% of population	34.9
Sunni (% of Muslims)	99
Shi'a (% of Muslims)	1

COUNTRY PROFILE

1371 The Ottoman Turks conquered the area and retained control until the nineteenth century.

1893 The Vnatrešno-Makedonska Revoluciona Organizacija (VMRO) (Internal Macedonian Revolutionary Organisation) was founded to gain independence from the Ottoman Empire.

1912–13 During the Balkan conflicts, the Turks were driven out and the area was divided between Serbia and Greece, with a small section being retained by Bulgaria.

1918 Macedonia became part of the new Kingdom of Serbs, Croats and Slovenes along with parts of Bosnia-Hercegovina, Croatia, parts of Dalmatia, Montenegro, Serbia, Slavonia and Slovenia.

1929 The Kingdom was renamed Yugoslavia.

1941–45 Macedonia was occupied by Bulgaria, under German direction. The Partisans, led by Josip Broz Tito – also leader of the Communist Party of

Yugoslavia (CPY) – eventually liberated the whole of Yugoslavia.
1945 Following the end of the Second World War, Macedonia became one of the constituent republics of a federated Yugoslavia. Tito assumed power and a Soviet-style constitution was adopted. The other republics were Bosnia-Hercegovina, Croatia, Slovenia, Montenegro, Serbia and the two autonomous regions of Vojvodina and Kosovo.
1953 Constitutions adopted in 1953, 1963 and 1974 increased the autonomy extended to the constituent republics.
1990 Following the collapse of communism in Yugoslavia, Macedonia held its first multi-party elections and the VMRO became the largest party in parliament.
1991 The first multi-party National Assembly was officially constituted. After a referendum in which the people voted overwhelmingly in favour of Macedonian sovereignty and independence, Macedonia declared its independence.
1992 Kiro Gligorov, the former communist leader, was elected president. A new currency, the denar, was adopted on 26 April.
1993 Greece showed consternation over Macedonia's choice of name and flag which the Greek government argued were a claim on its northern province of Macedonia. To accommodate Greek concerns, Macedonia eventually agreed to join the UN with the temporary prefix of 'Former Yugoslav Republic (of Macedonia (FYROM))' and an alternative national flag design was introduced.
1994 Kiro Gligorov was re-elected president. Greece imposed a partial trade embargo on Macedonia.
1995 An accord resulting in a normalisation of relations between Greece and Macedonia ensured that Macedonians had access to the northern Greek port of Thessaloniki, their nearest outlet to the sea.
1998 A coalition government under the leadership of Ljubco Georgievski was formed after elections.
1999 Amid accusations of electoral irregularities from the opposition, Boris Trajkovski of the Vnatrešno-Makedonska Revoluciona Organizacija-Demokratska Partija za Makedonsko Nacionalno Edintsvo (VMRO-DPMNE) (Internal Macedonian Revolutionary Organisation-Democratic Party for Macedonian National Unity) was elected president.
2000 A coalition government was formed, led by Prime Minister Georgievski.
2001 Ethnic Albanian guerrillas and police clashed in Tetovo and other parts of Macedonia. A cease-fire was brokered and a NATO force was sent to Macedonia to supervise the collection of arms handed in by ethnic Albanian rebels. The Ohrid Agreement was signed, paving the way for political reforms to enhance the status of the ethnic Albanian population within Macedonia. The government signed a Stabilisation and Association Agreement (SAA) with the EU, aimed at bringing Macedonia into line with EU political, economic and social norms.
2002 After parliamentary elections, the Socijaldemockratski Sojuz na Makedonija (SDSM) (Social Democratic Alliance of Macedonia) leader, Branko Crvenkovski, became prime minister, heading a multi-ethnic, 10-member coalition government.
2003 The EU took over NATO's military mission in Macedonia, overseeing the implementation of the Ohrid Agreement. Macedonia joined the World Trade Organisation (WTO).
2004 President Boris Trajkovski died in a plane crash; Ljupco Jordanovski became acting president. Macedonia formally submitted its application to join the EU. Branko Crvenkovski won the presidential elections. Hari Kostov became prime minister but later resigned following disputes within the ruling coalition; Vlado Buckovski became prime minister.
2005 Local elections were held, the first under redrawn electoral boundaries, as stipulated in the Ohrid Agreement. Despite fears of inter-communal tension, EU observers reported a high turnout and few irregularities. EU member states agreed to grant EU candidate status to Macedonia.
2008 The Skopje airport was renamed Skopje-Aleksandar Makedonski (Alexander of Macedonia, or Alexander the Great) Airport. Greece, unhappy with the exploitation of what it saw as its heritage and cultural iconography, criticised the decision and threatened to block Macedonia's membership of NATO unless it dropped the name. However, NATO believes membership for Macedonia will avert divisions within Macedonia, whereby the Slav majority in the east splits from the Albanian minority in the west. Following months of deadlock concerning the rights of the country's minority Albanian community, parliament was dissolved and early parliamentary elections held. For a Better Macedonia, a coalition (of 19 political parties), led by VMRO-DPMNE won 48.3 per cent of the vote (64 seats out of 120), the Sun–Coalition for Europe (coalition of eight parties), won 23.4 per cent (28 seats); turnout was 58 per cent. Nikola Gruevski (VMRO-DPMNE) remained as prime minister.
2009 Branko Crvenkovski decided not to stand in the presidential election. After two rounds George Ivanov (VMRO-DPNME) won the presidential elections with 63.41 per cent of the vote against Ljubomir Frckoski (SDSM) with 36.56 per cent. In the International Court of Justice (ICJ), Macedonia accused Greece of breaching the 1995 UN-brokered interim accord concerning the use of the name Macedonia, following Greece's blocking of Macedonia's membership of NATO.
2010 127 UN member countries recognised Macedonia by its constitutional name. However, Greece stubbornly required the UN to officially refer to Macedonia as FYROM until such time as Greece and Macedonia resolved their disagreement. Macedonia signed a protocol to jointly found a new company, called Cargo 10, with Serbia, Croatia and Slovenia to incorporate their railway companies.
2011 All opposition parties boycotted parliament in January, accusing the prime minister of authoritarian rule and curbing media freedom, and called for early elections. President Ivanov convened a meeting in February to resolve the political crisis. The opposition SDSM walked out of parliament, accusing the government of interference in the media. In March, Prime Minister Gruevski finally set a date for new elections. For the first time, three parliamentary seats were established for representatives of expatriate Macedonians (one each for those living in Europe, Americas and Asia), bringing the total number of parliamentary seats in contention to 123. In the elections, held in June, the VMRO-DPMNE ruling coalition won 39.0 per cent of the vote (56 seats out of 123), which less than the 64 seats was won in 2008, and not enough to rule outright. The SDSM won 32.78 per cent which at 42 was a higher number of seats than in 2008 (27), but still not enough for the right to form a coalition government. The national census was officially stopped by parliament in October, having already come to a stop (four days before its scheduled completion date), following the resignation of members of the State Census Commission (SCC). The 2002 census had been controversial, with the registration of over 20 per cent of the population as ethnic Albanians disputed; this would have allow them collective rights and privileges under the Ohrid Framework Agreement. A long-running political dispute grew, over whether the 2011 census would be a repeat of the previous one and without agreement the census was scrapped to be re-run in 2012.
2012 Two weeks of communal violence between ethnic Macedonian and Albanian youths in Skopje in March resulted in the arrest of 20 people and a dozen injured and a warning issued on 13 March from the EU that the fighting was likely to cause 'emotional consequences'. In April

the World Bank announced it would provide US$100 million to Macedonia to pursue economic reforms specific to health, education and welfare issues. On 3 November, the government adopted a budget of €2.7 billion (US$3.5 billion) for 2013.

2013 A trade row between Macedonia and Kosovo in September threatened to escalate into a political confrontation. Macedonia started it by imposing quantitative limitations on flour and wheat from Kosovo and other neighbours to protect local production. Kosovo responded by banning all food imports from Macedonia. Macedonia imposed a tax of €2 on Kosova citizens crossing into Macedonia, €5 per car and €10 per bus or truck. In the latest move, Kosova banned all border crossings.

2014 The first round of the presidential election was held on 13 April, followed by the second round and general elections on 27 April. The first round of the presidential election was won by the incumbant president, Gjorge Ivanov, with 51.69 per cent of the vote, but not more than 50 per cent of registered voters, necessitating a run-off vote two weeks later. Mr Ivanov successfully won the second round with 55.28 per cent. Turnout on both occasions was low at 48.86 per cent and 54.36 per cent respectively. The general election was won by Mr Ivanov's coalition of 22 parties with 42.98 per cent (61 seats, out of 123), followed by the SDSM coalition with 25.34 per cent (34) and the BDI with 13.71 per cent (19). Turnout was 62.98 per cent.

2015 The government declared a state of emergency on 20 August as migrants gathered on the border with Greece and attempted to enter Macedonia. Although most were wanting to travel north, as many as 3,500 people were entering each day.

Political structure

Constitution

Under the constitution, adopted on 17 November 1991, the Former Yugoslav Republic of Macedonia (FYROM) is a sovereign, independent, democratic and socially responsive state. There is universal suffrage from age 18. The constitution guarantees the free expression of national identity, the rule of law (including international law) and the legal protection of property. The principles of a free commercial market, urban and rural planning and environmental protection are also enshrined in the constitution.

Constitutional amendments to give the ethnic Albanian minority more rights were endorsed by parliament in November 2001.

Form of state

Parliamentary democratic republic

The executive

The executive is headed by the president, directly elected by absolute majority vote every five years in two rounds if needed (eligible for a second term). The prime minister is usually the leader of the majority party or majority coalition elected by the Assembly. The prime minister appoints a cabinet of 20 ministers, who must be approved by a majority of the country's national assembly.

National legislature

The unicameral Sobranje (National Assembly) has 120 members directly elected in multi-seat constituencies by proportional representation vote (six electoral districts returning 20 delegates each).

In 2011, for the first time, three parliamentary seats were established for representatives of expatriate Macedonians (one each for those living in Europe, Americas and Asia), bringing the total number of parliamentary seats in contention to 123. These members are directly elected in diaspora constituencies worldwide by simple majority vote. Members serve four-year terms.

Legal system

Judicial powers are vested in courts which are nominally independent of government under the terms of the 1991 constitution. In practice, the judiciary remains politicised, especially in cases involving ethnic Albanians and other minorities. All civil and criminal cases are dealt with by courts of general jurisdiction. The Supreme Court is the highest court. Elected by parliament, the Judicial Council appoints and dismisses all judges and other judicial officials. The judicial system is the administrative responsibility of the justice ministry. There is a public prosecutor. The Constitutional Court decides on the conformity of national legislation with the 1991 constitution.

Macedonia is aiming to harmonise its laws and judicial standards with those of the EU and the Council of Europe, but progress is slow.

Last elections

13 April / 27 April 2014 (presidential first round and runoff); 27 April 2014 (parliamentary).

Results: Presidential: (first round) Gjorgje Ivanov (VMRO–DPMNE) won 51.69 per cent, Stevo Pendarovski (Socijaldemokratski sojuz na Makedonija) (SDSM) (Social Democratic Union of Macedonia) 37.51 per cent, Ilijaz Halimi (Partia Demokratike Shqiptare (PDS) (Democratic Party of Albanians) 4.5 per cent, Zoran T Popovski (Grajanska Optsiya za Makedoniya) (GOM) (Citizen Option for Macedonia) 3.6 per cent. Turnout was 48.9 per cent. (Runoff): Ivanov won with 55.28 per cent of the vote; Pendarovski 41.14 per cent. Turnout was 54.4 per cent.

Parliamentary: Vnatrešno-Makedonska Revoluciona Organizacija-Demokratska Partija za Makedonsko Nacionalno Edintsvo (VMRO-DPMNE) (Internal Macedonian Revolutionary Organisation-Democratic Party for Macedonian National Unity) coalition (of 22 parties) won 42.98 per cent of the vote (61 seats out of 123), Socijaldemockratski Sojuz na Makedonija (SDSM) (Social Democratic Alliance of Macedonia) coalition 25.34 per cent (34), Bashkimi Demokratik për Integrim (BDI) (Democratic Union for Integration) 13.71 per cent (19), Partia Demokratike Shqiptare (PDS) (Democratic Party of Albania) 5.92 per cent (7); two other parties won a seat each. Turnout was 62.98 per cent.

Expatriate Macedonians living in Europe, the US and Australia each elected one candidate as their Member of Parliament (MP).

Next elections

2019 (presidential); 24 April 2016 (parliamentary)

Political parties

Ruling party

Coalition (of 22 parties), led by Vnatrešno-Makedonska Revoluciona Organizacija-Demokratska Partija za Makedonsko Nacionalno Edintsvo (VMRO-DPMNE) (Internal Macedonian Revolutionary Organisation-Democratic Party for Macedonian National Unity) (from 2006; re-elected 5 Jun 2011 and 27 Apr 2014)

Main opposition party

Socijaldemokratski sojuz na Makedonija (SDSM) (Social Democratic Union of Macedonia)

Nearly one-third of the total population of Macedonia lives in Skopje.

Population

2.07 million (2014)*

Last census: November 2002: 2,022,547

Population density: 79 inhabitants per square km. Urban population 59 per cent (2010 Unicef).

Annual growth rate: 0.4 per cent, 1990–2010 (Unicef).

Internally Displaced Persons (IDP)

3,000 (UNHCR 2004)

Ethnic make-up

Macedonian (63 per cent), Albanian (30 per cent), Turkish (4 per cent), Romanian (3 per cent). The Albanians are concentrated in Tetovo, Gostivar and other parts of the north-west.

Religions

The official religion is Macedonian Orthodox Christianity, which is practised by approximately two-thirds of the population.

Muslims (over a quarter of the population) and Roman Catholics practise openly.

Education

The educational system is entirely state-controlled. During the 1990s, independence from Yugoslavia meant an end to federal subsidies, resulting in declining educational provision in Macedonia. Politically, the issue of ethnic Albanian access to higher education in the Albanian language has been the cause of great controversy and even violence in Macedonia.

Primary schooling lasts for eight years and is followed by attendance at either a general secondary school for academic students or at a variety of technical, specialist or vocational schools. After four years, in whichever mode of school, students must undertake examination before advancement to the second, three-year stage. Courses may last until students are aged 19.

There are three universities in Macedonia: Skopje, Bitola and Tetovo. The Albanian-language University at Tetovo is legalised and classified by parliament as an accredited private institution.

Compulsory years: Seven to 15.

Enrolment rate: 99 per cent total primary enrolment of relevant age group (including repetition rates); 63 per cent total secondary enrolment (World Bank).

Health

The standard of state healthcare is low compared to the rest of the former Yugoslavia, the basic healthcare infrastructure has declined mainly due to the lack of funds to replace essential equipment and retain doctors in the state sector.

Healthcare provision has increasingly involved extra charges, notably for medication, leading to a large black market in healthcare services. Most healthcare professionals are either in semi-private or private practice and some parts of the healthcare system have been privatised.

Externally, Macedonia received considerable international aid for local healthcare during the 1990s.

Improved water sources and sanitation facilities are available to 99 per cent of the population.

HIV/Aids

HIV prevalence: 0.1 per cent aged 15–49 in 2003 (World Bank)

Life expectancy: 72 years, 2004 (WHO 2006)

Fertility rate/Maternal mortality rate: 1.4 births per woman, 2010 (Unicef); maternal mortality three per 100,000 live births (World Bank).

Child (under 5 years) mortality rate (per 1,000): 7 per 1,000 live births (WHO 2012); and 5.9 per cent of children aged under five are malnourished (World Bank).

Head of population per physician: 2.19 physicians per 1,000 people, 2001 (WHO 2006)

Welfare

Welfare provision was heavily subsidised by budgetary transfers from outside Macedonia during the Yugoslav period, when retirement pensions and other welfare benefits were relatively generous at around 80 per cent of average monthly income. Consequently, the state pension fund experienced major financial problems after independence. Welfare benefits declined sharply, aggravated by spells of high inflation. The IMF and other official creditors have made loans available in recent years for the state pension fund and unemployment benefit outlays. The foreign exchange remittances of emigrants plays a major role in the economic support of many Macedonians.

Main cities

Skopje (capital, estimated population 486,596 in 2012), Kumanovo (118,750), Bitola (84,867), Tetovo (76,895), Prilep (73,743), Veles (57,615), Ohrid (55,258), Gostivar (53,675).

Languages spoken

Macedonian (Slavic) is written using the Cyrillic alphabet.

The Albanian minority campaigned successfully to have its language officially recognised as the country's second language. Turkish, Serbian, Croatian and Romani are also spoken.

English, French and German are often understood.

Official language/s

Macedonian and Albanian.

Media

The constitution guarantees freedom of the press and access to information, there are laws that back up these rights although specific regulation concerning media can be loosely implemented, including the non-transparency of media ownership.

Press

The newspaper market is dominated by three major media groups; the German Westdeutsche Allgemeine Zeitung (WAZ), A1-Vreme and Vecer-Sitel-Cetis.

Dailies: In Macedonian, the most widely read newspapers are *Utrinski Vesnik* (www.utrinski.com.mk), *Dnevnik* (www.dnevnik.com.mk), *Vest* (www.vest.com.mk), other publications include *Vreme* (www.vreme.com.mk), *Nova Makedonija* (www.novamakedonija.com.mk), and the state-subsidised *Vecer* (www.vecer.com.mk) which is a tabloid.

Weeklies: In Macedonian, general interest publications include *Forum* (www.forum.com.mk) and *Makedonsko Sonce* (www.makedonskosonce.com), *Aktuel Start* and *Focus*.

Business: In Macedonian, *Kapital* (www.kapital.com.mk) is an economic weekly magazine.

Broadcasting

The national, public broadcaster is Makedonska Radiotelevizija (MRT) (www.mrt.com.mk).

Radio: MRT (www.mrt.com.mk) operates three stations providing programmes in Macedonian, eight foreign languages of the region and English. There are many licensed and unlicensed local radio stations in a market that is highly fragmented. Private, commercial stations include City FM (www.cityradio.com.mk), Radio Antenna 5 (www.antenna5.com.mk) and Radio Vati (www.vati.com.mk).

Television: MRT (www.mrt.com.mk) operates three stations providing national coverage. Although two channels provide programmes for the majority Macedonian population the last channel broadcasts in local, ethnic languages. Alsat-M (www.alsat-m.tv) provides programmes for the large minority Albanian population. Sitel (www.sitel.com.mk) is the leading commercial channel, followed by A1 (www.a1.com.mk) and Kanal 5 (www.kanal5.com.mk). English language programmes provided by cable and satellite broadcasters are becoming increasingly popular.

National news agency: MIA (Macedonian Information Agency

Other news agencies: Makfax: www.makfax.com.mk

Economy

Macedonia's economy is small with gross domestic production (GDP) of a little over US$10.2 billion in 2013, an increase of about 11 per cent on the US$9.2 billion per annum average from 2007–10. It had a GDP growth rate of 5 per cent in 2008, which fell to -0.9 per cent in 2009 as the global economic crisis struck and Macedonia was affected by falling exports and higher priced imports. In 2010, as global trade improved GDP growth rose to 1.8 per cent, with further growth of 3 per cent in 2011. Its economy dropped into recession again in 2012, before regaining pace and reaching 3.1 per cent growth in 2013 and 3.4 per cent in 2014.

In 2014 the services sector constituted 63.5 per cent of the economy, with the industrial sector providing 26.1 per cent of GDP and agriculture accounting for some 10.4 per cent. Although agriculture is the smallest component of the economy, it is characterised by small family farms that provide around 20 per cent of paid employment. Macedonia is a net exporter of processed vegetables, as well as fruits, cereals, tobacco and grapes for wine production.

Industrial production is largely centred on iron and steel, with manufacturing in clothing and footwear. Structural reforms to Macedonia's industrial sector have increased production and prosperity. Unemployment has represented a long-term problem with rates of over 30 per cent for the entire last half of the 2000s. However, despite remaining high, unemployment has improved and in the first quarter of 2015 27.3 per cent of the workforce were without work. However, many people work in the grey economy, which is estimated to constitute 20 per cent of GDP, with production consequently ignored with respect to affecting the legitimate economy. The lack of employment opportunities have also encouraged many skilled workers to seek work abroad. Remittances peaked in 2011 at US$434 million, and have slowly been decreasing, falling to US$366.5 million in 2014.

In April 2012, the World Bank announced it would provide US$100 million to Macedonia to pursue economic reforms specific to health, education and welfare issues. In April 2014, the World Bank guaranteed US$201.5 million in support of a commercial loan to Macedonia in order to improve the efficiency of public expenditures by strengthening public financial management practices.

External trade

Macedonia signed a Stabilisation and Association Agreement with the EU and has duty free access to EU markets. It was expected to become a full EU member by 2010, however in 2015 the relationship between Macedonia and the EU was still under High-Level Accession Dialogue that began in March 2012. It belongs to the World Trade Organisation and has free trade agreements with Turkey and Ukraine as well as membership in the Central European Free Trade Agreement (Cefta).

Macedonia is set to earn annual transit fees from the new 895km Balkan oil pipeline (AMBO), from Burgas, on the Black Sea (Bulgaria) to the port of Vlore, in southern Albania. The trilateral agreement contract was signed in 2007; the project is estimated to cost US$1.2 billion and has a supply target of 750,000 barrels per day. It will allow Caspian oil to by-pass Turkey's increasingly congested Bosporus and Dardanelles shipping lanes.

Imports

Principal imports are machinery and equipment, automobiles, chemicals, fuels and food products.

Main sources: United Kingdom (12.3 per cent of total in 2014), Germany (11.1 per cent), Greece (9.2 per cent), Serbia (8.2 per cent) and Italy (6.2 per cent).

Exports

Principal exports are foodstuffs, beverages, tobacco, textiles, miscellaneous manufactures, iron, steel and automotive parts.

Main destinations: Germany (41.4 per cent of total in 2014), Bulgaria (6.6 per cent), Italy (6.1 per cent), Serbia (5.2 per cent).

Agriculture

Farming

The agricultural sector accounts for 10.4 per cent of GDP and employs around 30 per cent of the workforce.

Agricultural land totals 1.3 million hectares (ha), of which approximately half is cultivable and half is pasture. Macedonia has propitious conditions for agriculture and is nearly self-sufficient in food production. The private sector accounts for over 75 per cent of agricultural production.

The government has allowed a systematic break-up of the old *agrokombinats*, or collectivised farms. As a result, privately owned farms now account for 90 per cent of annual output, although each farm is rarely more than 25ha. New private company formation in agriculture is also growing rapidly.

On the negative side, the state still directly controls 30 per cent of all arable land, or around 300,000ha. Markedly less productive than the private sector, state farms and co-operatives are scheduled to be privatised in due course, although this remains politically controversial. Local agriculture is one of the few sectors of interest to potential foreign investors due to the cultivation of higher value cash crops (particularly tobacco) with ready markets in the EU, and cheap labour costs. Economically, the government now regards agriculture as a major area for future growth and development, including increased foreign direct investment (FDI).

Fishing

Macedonia has a small fishing industry, which catches freshwater fish for domestic consumption.

Forestry

Forest and other wooded land account for about two-fifths of the land area, equivalent to approximately 906,000ha. More than four-fifths of the forest is available for wood supply. Forest resources supply an active forestry industry producing approximately 774,000 cubic metres (cum) of timber per annum.

Forest wood is mainly used for fuel, while hardwood processed in local sawmills is largely exported. Domestic demand for softwood and paper is met by imports.

Industry and manufacturing

Industry and manufacturing account for nearly 35 per cent of GDP. Macedonia retains a relatively industrialised economy inherited from the Yugoslav period. During the 1990s, the collapse of the Yugoslav market and subsequent regional conflict, the loss of former Soviet markets, the Greek economic blockade and resultant energy shortages all had devastating consequences for Macedonian industrial output.

Although privatisation of smaller industries has largely been completed, sell-offs of larger industries are still at an early stage. State industries suffer from overstaffing, slow growth, a slow rate of change in the structure of production and ailing technology.

Tourism

The attractions of Macedonia include Unesco's World Heritage listed natural and cultural Ohrid region, which includes Europe's oldest human settlement and the oldest Slav monastery located in the region with a wealth of Byzantine-style religious icons. The country has a landscape of lakes and rivers that have largely escaped industrialisation. Macedonia has the potential to draw in many visitors, although investment in the sector only attracts around 2 per cent of total capital investment, which is inadequate to develop the necessary tourist infrastructure to grow the industry. Cultural and heritage events such as folk, wedding and children's' festivals are held each year, primarily for Macedonians but to which everyone is invited.

Travel and tourism accounted for 5.2 per cent of GDP in 2014 with employment in the sector at around 4.7 per cent of total employment (33,000 jobs). Visitor exports were US$239 million but were expected to fall by 0.5 per cent 2015.

Environment

The Vardar, Macedonia's main river, collects the waste from several towns with no treatment facilities before flowing through Greece to the Aegean Sea. A system for monitoring the waterways and a project for communal water treatment for six towns have been initiated by the Macedonian government.

Macedonia and Albania participate in the Lake Ohrid Conservation Project (LOCP) which is a bilateral project supported by the World Bank.

Mining

Macedonia is an important producer of metals and mines significant quantities of copper and lead-zinc ores, ferroalloys and some silver. There is also some chromium production from reserves that overlap with those of nearby Albania. The aluminium and copper ore production is centred on Alumina AD in Skopje and 'Bucim' Radovis DM in Radovis respectively. There is also significant quarrying of decorative and architectural building stone.

The mining sector in Macedonia has had little room for growth due to regional instability and depressed market conditions. The various conflicts in the former Yugoslavia have created a regional dislocation of transportation of cargoes on the Danube River, shifting the route of exports through the port of Thessaloniki in Greece at a huge cost. This financial burden has diminished Macedonia's production of hot and cold rolled steel to about 30 per cent of capacity, and the export of finished products by Balkan Steel International (BSI).

However, it was not regional dislocation that affected some companies that have traditionally exported through Greece. Their production fell or ceased due to shortage of foreign investment and adverse market conditions. Foreign investment and participation has been restricted to the steel industry (Duferco and BSI), petroleum refining (Hellenic Petroleum) and cement manufacturing (Titan Cement and Holderbank Financiere Glaris).

Hydrocarbons

There are no commercial oil or gas reserves although exploration is ongoing. Consumption of oil in 2013 was 16,670 barrels per day (bpd) and consumption of natural gas was 158.6 million cubic metres (cum) all of which was imported. There is one oil refinery, located outside Skopje, with production of 50,000bpd. Although Macedonia signed a US$1.8 billion agreement with Bulgaria and Albania in 2004 to construct a trans-Balkan oil pipeline, it was not until 2007 that an agreement to begin construction in 2008 had been signed. Even so in 2015 planning work was still ongoing. The 984km pipeline will connect the Black Sea with the Adriatic, via the Bulgarian port of Burgas and the Albanian port of Vlores, and will transport Russian and Caspian oil that would otherwise have to be shipped through the Bosphorus. On 4 July 2012, Macedonia signed an agreement to participate in the Russian-led South Stream natural gas pipeline project. Natural gas will be piped via the Black Sea and through the Balkans and into the lucrative energy markets of Western Europe. Not only will countries involved in the transit of natural gas be able to access the gas but will also receive a transit fee.

Plans to use natural gas as a main source of energy include reconstruction of the existing Skopje-Oblic (Pristina) gas pipeline. Macedonia also has a gas pipeline of 100km from Deve Bair to Skopje with a connection to the international gas pipeline in Bulgaria. This pipeline transfers over 800 million cum per annum as part of a wider Russian gas export pipeline network in the Balkan region that supplies Greece with natural gas.

Macedonia has large reserves of coal, estimated at more than one billion tonnes, with an annual production rate of around 9 million tonnes. Most output is low-grade coal used extensively in domestic energy production. Higher quality anthracite coals and coke (approximately 130,000 tonnes per annum) are traded with Western European states.

Energy

Total installed generating capacity was 1,940MW in 2013 producing 5.68 billion kilowatt hours. Most of energy needs are met by domestic production, with hydropower supplying most at around 30 per cent, however, 30 per cent of annual electricity need is imported.

There are eight hydroelectric dams, with a total generating capacity of 634MW. Thermal power stations are typically old and due for upgrading or decommissioning.

A number of new hydroelectric power plants are being built and plans are being considered by the government to modernise some of Macedonia's older power plants.

Financial markets

Stock exchange

Makedonska Berza (Macedonia Stock Exchange) (MSE)

Banking and insurance

There are seven major public lending and savings banks in Macedonia, as well as several smaller private commercial credit banks. The sector is dominated by Stopanska Banka, which has approximately 65 per cent of domestic banking assets and 50 per cent of banking deposits.

The republic has a tiered banking structure. The Narodna banka na Republika Makedonija (NBRM) (National Bank of the Republic of Macedonia) is responsible for the money supply, the liquidity of financial institutions and foreign currency transactions and reserves. The banking system requires a major overhaul. Competition is being introduced with the emergence of private credit institutions such as Uniprokom. International institutions are providing loans.

Central bank

Narodna banka na Republika Makedonija (NBRM) (National Bank of the Republic of Macedonia)

Time

GMT plus one hour (daylight saving, late March to late September, GMT plus two hours)

Geography

Situated in south-eastern Europe on the Balkan peninsula, Macedonia, or Vardar Macedonia, is part of a wider historical and geographical region of the same name. Part of this ancient territory, known as Pirin Macedonia, is situated in modern-day Greece. Roughly rectangular in shape, Macedonia is bordered by Serbia to the north (Kosovo province to the north-west and Serbia to the north-east), Albania to the west, Bulgaria to the east and Greece to the south. Geographically, the republic is dominated by the Balkan Mountains and the Vardar River, which flows north-west to south-east.

Macedonia's strategic importance is out of all proportion to its small size, population and economic resources. On the negative side, its small size and lack of direct access to the sea makes Macedonia very vulnerable to its stronger neighbours in the southern Balkans.

Macedonia's major geographic characteristics are two large inland lakes, Ohrid and Prespa, which are shared with Albania and Greece. Lake Ohrid is a Unesco-designated World Heritage Site.

Hemisphere

Northern

Climate

The river valleys of Vardar and Strumica are temperate Mediterranean, as is the eastern region. Western and northern regions are temperate continental. However, temperatures may vary from 40 degrees Celsius (C) in the summer to minus 30 degrees C in the winter. Rainfall averages 742 millimetres annually, but around 450 millimetres in Skopje which has about 100 days of rain annually. Skopje can be very hot in the summer and shrouded in mist in the winter.

Dress codes

Informal dress is tolerated in Macedonia, but should be avoided in business contexts, notably in Skopje.

Entry requirements

Passports

Required by all, with three months validity beyond date of stay.

Visa

Required by all, except nationals of EU/EEA and most CIS countries, US, New Zealand, Japan, Malaysia, Israel, Botswana, Argentina, Cuba and Barbados. Visitors should contact the nearest consulate to confirm their visa status and requirements before travelling.

Business visas require a letter of invitation from a local company, submitted with the application.

Currency advice/regulations

There are no restrictions on the import and export of local or foreign currency.

Health (for visitors)

Medical care in private facilities or by private practitioners is not covered by insurance. Foreigners are entitled to medical care in state medical facilities and those staying for a year or more have a right to full medical coverage. Temporary visitors and those in transit are entitled to basic necessities and emergency first-aid treatment, but payment in cash is expected, regardless of insurance cover.

Mandatory precautions

None

Advisable precautions

Vaccinations are recommended for hepatitis A and, if expecting to eat or drink outside main hotels and restaurants, typhoid. Food and water precautions should be observed. Public health is poor in certain parts of Macedonia.

Hotels

There are around 90 hotels in Macedonia. There is one first-class hotel, in Skopje.

Public holidays (national)

Fixed dates

1–2 Jan (New Year), 6-7 Jan (Orthodox Christmas), 14 Jan (Orthodox New Year's Day), 8 Mar (Women's Day), 1 May (Labour Day), 24 May (SS Cyrilus and Methodius Day), 2 Aug (Ilinden Day), 8 Sep (Independence Day), 11 Oct (National Day).

Variable dates

Orthodox Easter Monday, Eid al Adha, Eid al Fitr.

Working hours

Banking

Mon–Fri: 0730–1930; Sat: 0800–1300.

Business

Mon–Fri: 0800–1600 or 0830–1630.

Government

Mon–Fri: 0700–1500 or 0730–1530.

Shops

Mon–Fri: 0800–1200 and 1700–2000/2100, but many shops open throughout day; Sat: 0800–1500.

Telecommunications

Mobile/cell phones

GSM 900 roaming facilities are available with coverage throughout the country. Services are provided by Cosmofon and MobiMak.

Electricity supply

220V AC 50Hz with two large round prongs.

Weights and measures

Metric system.

Social customs/useful tips

Macedonians are a friendly people, although less gregarious then their Serbian neighbours in the Balkans. Similar to the Bulgarians, they are also practically minded.

Political discussions of any sort are best avoided altogether by foreigners. There are strict laws against drinking and driving, speeding and other traffic offences. They are rigorously enforced.

Security

Car theft is very common. Local ownership of firearms is high. Visitors are advised to keep themselves informed of political developments.

Getting there

Air

National airline: Makedonski Aviotransport (MAT) (Macedonian Airlines)

International airport/s: Skopje (SKP), 25km from city, post office, restaurants, duty-free shop; Ohrid (OHD, 10km from city.

Air traffic control systems are not up to European standards and the airports are by-passed by many international carriers and used primarily by regional airlines.

Airport tax: None.

Surface

Road: Bus services operate along the main routes connecting Albania, Bulgaria, Greece and Serbia.

Rail: Several international railway lines pass through Skopje, including the Ljuljan-Athens and Budapest-Athens services. Intercity trains provide connections between Skopje and Belgrade (Serbia) and Thessaloniki (Greece).

Getting about

National transport

Air: There are no regular scheduled flights, although occasional flights between Ohrid and Skopje are available.

Road: There are 4,876km of modernised roads. The main road is between Ohrid and Tetovo.

Rail: There are 922km of railway lines, of which 231km are electrified. The main terminals are at Skopje, Bitola and Gevgelija on the Greek border, Kicevo in the west of the country and Kriva Palanka on the Bulgarian border.

City transport

Taxis: Good service operating in all main cities. Licensed taxis are metered, but the fare should be agreed before the journey. A 10 per cent tip is usual. Unmarked taxis should be avoided.

Buses, trams & metro: Most city centres are served by trams, and the suburbs by buses. The service is generally cheap and regular.

Car hire

Limited availability in Skopje, but very expensive. Special insurance is required for travel to certain parts of the country. An international driving licence is required. Hired cars generally have to be paid for in foreign exchange.

BUSINESS DIRECTORY

The addresses listed below are a selection only. While World of Information makes every endeavour to check these addresses, we cannot guarantee that changes have not been made, especially to telephone numbers and area codes. We would welcome any corrections.

Telephone area codes

The international direct diallng code (IDD) for Macedonia is +389 followed by the area code and subscriber's number:

Gostivar	42	Prilep	48
Kicevo	45	Skopje	2
Kochani	33	Tetovo	44
Kumanovo	31	Veles	43

Useful telephone numbers

Police: 92
Fire: 93
Ambulance: 94
Time: 95
Telegrams: 96
Telephone service: 977
Report emergencies: 985
Emergency road service: 987
Telephone information: 988

Chambers of Commerce

American Chamber of Commerce in Macedonia, 13 Juli Street 20, 1000 Skopje (tel: 3123-873; fax: 3123-872; e-mail: contact@amcham.com.mk).

Economic Chamber of Macedonia, Dimitrie Cupovski Street 13, PO Box 324, 1000 Skopje (tel: 3118-088; fax: 3116-210; e-mail: ic@ic.mchamber.org.mk).

Skopje Regional Chamber, Partizanski Odredi Boulevard 2, PO Box 509, 1000 Skopje (tel: 3112-511; fax: 3116-419; e-mail: regkomsk@regkom.org.mk).

Banking

Balkanska Banka, 6 Maksim Gorki, Skopje (tel: 3127-155; fax: 3132-186).

Eksport Import Banka, Dame Gruev 14, PO Box 836, Skopje (tel: 3133-411; fax: 3112-744; e-mail: info@eximpb.com.mk).

Invest Banka , Makedonija 9/11, Skopje (tel: 3114-166; fax: 3135-528).

Izvozna i Kreditna Banka, 11 Oktomvri 8, Skopje (tel: 3122-207; fax: 3122-393).

Komercijalna Banka, Kej Dimitar Vlahov 4, PO Box 563, Skopje (tel: 3112-077; fax: 3111-780; e-mail: international@kb.com.mk).

Kreditna Banka Skopje, Dame Gruev, Skopje (tel: 3116-433; fax: 3116-830).

Makedonska Banka, Bul. VMRO 3-12/2, Skopje (tel: 3117-111; fax: 3117-191; e-mail: info@makbanka.com.mk).

Radobank, Jurij Gagarin 17, Skopje (tel: 3393-300; fax: 3380-453; e-mail: radobank@radobank.com.mk).

Sileks Banka, Gradski Zid, Blok 9, Lokal 5, Skopje (tel: 3115-288; fax: 3114-891).

Stopanska Banka, 11 Oktomvri 7, Skopje (tel: 3191-191; fax: 3114-503; e-mail: sbank@stb.com.mk).

Teteks Bank, Naroden Front 19a, Skopje (tel: 3127-449; fax: 3131-419).

Tutunska Banka, 12 Udarna brigada bb, PO Box 702, Skopje (tel: 3105-600; fax: 3164-068; e-mail: tbanka@tb.com.mk).

Zemjodelska Banka, Vasil Glavinov 28/2, Skopje (tel: 3112-699; fax: 3224-844).

Central bank

National Bank of the Republic of Macedonia, PO Box 401, Kompleks banki bb, 1000 Skopje (tel: 3108-108; fax: 3108-357; e-mail: governorsoffice@nbrm.gov.mk).

Stock exchange

Makedonska Berza (Macedonia Stock Exchange) (MSE), www.mse.com.mk

Travel information

Macedonian Airlines (MAT), Vasil Glavinov 3, Skopje (tel: 3292-333; fax: 3229-576; e-mail: mathq@mat.com.mk).

Ohrid Airport, PO Box 134, Ohrid (tel: 252-820; fax: 252-840; e-mail: ohdap@airports.com.mk).

Skopje Airport, Skopje (tel: 148-300; fax: 148-360; e-mail: skpap@airports.com.mk).

Tourist Association of Skopje, Dame Gruev Gradski, Blok 3, PO Box 399, Skopje (tel: 3118-498; fax: 3230-803; e-mail: info@skopjetourism.org).

Ministries

Ministry of Agriculture, Forestry and Water, Leninova 2, Skopje (tel: 3134-477; fax: 3211-997).

Ministry of Culture, Bul. Ilinden bb, Skopje (tel: 3118-022; fax: 3127-112).

Ministry of Defence, Orce Nikolov bb, Skopje (tel: 3119-872; fax:3 221-808; e-mail: info@morm.gov.mk).

Ministry of Economy, Bote Bocevski bb, Skopje (tel: 3113-705; fax: 3111-541; e-mail: ms@mt.net.mk).

Ministry of Education and Science, Dimitrija Chupovski 9, Skopje (tel: 3117-277; fax: 3118-414; e-mail: contact@mofk.gov.mk).

Ministry of Environment and Urban Planning, Drezdenska 52, Skopje (tel: 3366-930; fax: 3366-931; e-mail: info@moe.gov.mk).

Ministry of Finance, Dame Gruev 14, Skopje (tel: 3117-288; fax: 3117-280).

Ministry of Foreign Affairs, Dame Gruev 6, Skopje (tel: 3110-330; fax: 3115-790; e-mail: mailmnr@mnr.gov.mk).

Ministry of Health, Vodnjanska bb, Skopje (tel: 3147-147; fax: 3113-014).

Ministry of Internal Affairs, Dimce Mircev bb, Skopje (tel: 3117-222; fax: 3112-468).

Ministry of Justice, Dimitrija Chupovski 9, Skopje (tel: 3117-277; fax: 3226-975).

Ministry of Labour and Social Policy, Dame Gruev 14, Skopje (tel: 3117-288; fax: 3118-242).

Ministry of Local Self-Government, Dimitrija Chupovski 9, Skopje (tel: 3117-288; fax: 3211-764)

Ministry of Transport and Communications, Crvena Skopska Opstina 4, Skopje (tel: 3128-200; fax: 3118-144).

Prime Minister's Office, Bul. Ilinden bb, Skopje (tel: 3115-389; fax: 3113-512).

Other useful addresses

Bank Rehabilitation Agency, Kompleks banki bb, Skopje (tel: 3126-323; fax: 3121-250).

British Embassy, Dimitrija Chupovski 26, 4th Floor, Skopje (tel: 3116-772; fax: 3117-005; e-mail: beskopje@mt.net.mk).

Customs Administration, Lazar Licenovski 13, Skopje (tel: 3224-467; fax: 3237-832).

Fund for National and Regional Roads, Dame Gruev 14, Skopje (tel: 3118-044; fax: 3220-535; e-mail: tanjam@.mpt.net.mk).

Macedonia Telecommunications, Orce Nikolov bb, Skopje (tel: 3141-000; fax: 3120-244).

Macedonian Embassy (USA), 3050 K Street, NW, Washington DC 20007 (tel: (+1-202)-337-3063; fax: (+1-202)-337-3093; e-mail: rmacedonia@aol.com).

Macedonian Stock Exchange, Mito Hadzivasilev 20, Skopje (tel: 3122-055; fax: 3122-069; e-mail: mse@unet.com.mk).

Privatisation Agency of the Republic of Macedonia, PO Box 410, Nikola Vapcarov 7, Skopje (tel: 3117-564; fax: 3126-022; e-mail: agency@mpa.org.mk).

Skopje Fair, Belasica bb, PO Box 356, Skopje (tel: 3118-288; fax: 3117-375; e-mail: skfair@mt.net.mk).

Skopje Free Economic Zone, Salvador Allende 73, Skopje (tel: 3176-170; fax: 3177-101; e-mail: sfez@mol.com.mk).

US Embassy, Bul. Ilinden bb, Skopje (tel: 3116-180; fax: 3117-103).

National news agency: MIA (Macedonian Information Agency

Address: PO Box 4; Bojmija K-2, 1000 Skopje (tel: 246-1600; fax: 246-4048; email: mia@mia.mk; internet: www.mia.mk).

Makfax: www.makfax.com.mk

Internet sites

Privatisation Agency of the Republic of Macedonia: http://www.mpa.org.mk

Economic Chamber of Macedonia: http://www.mchamber.org.mk

Government of FRY Macedonia: http://www.gov.mk/english

Agency of Information: http://www.sinf.gov.mk/defaulten.htm

National Bank of the Republic of Macedonia: http://www.nbrm.gov.mk

Macedonian Stock Exchange: http://www.mse.org.mk

Republic of Macedonia News Collection: http://b-info.com/places/Macedonia/republic/news/

Madagascar

KEY FACTS

Official name: Repoblikan'i Madagasikara (Republic of Madagascar)

Head of State: President Hery Rajaonarimampianina (Hery Vaovao ho an'i Madagasikara) (New Forces for Madagascar) (from 25 Jan 2014)

Head of government: Prime Minister Jean Ravelonarivo (since 17 January 2015) following the resignation of Roger Kolo and his cabinet on 13 January 2015.)

Ruling party: Together with President Andry Rajoelina

Area: 592,000 square km (the world's fourth-largest island)

Population: 23.57 million (2014)*

Capital: Antananarivo

Official language: Malagasy, French, English (from 2007)

Currency: Ariary (MGA) = 5 iraimbilanja

Exchange rate: MGA3,150.00 per US$ (Sep 2015)

GDP per capita: US$449 (2014)*

GDP real growth: 2.97% (2014)*

GDP: US$10.60 billion (2014)*

Inflation: 6.08% (2014)

Balance of trade: -US$851.30 million (2013)

* estimated figure

The Indian Ocean island nation of Madagascar with its 22 million people is famous for at least two things: its unique pristine biological diversity, and its recurrent political turmoil. But there's another striking feature about Madagascar that barely goes noticed even by its professional watchers: the relations between its political crises and its business cycles. Economic growth and politics apparently operate at cross-purposes. Growth spurts generate political crises in cyclical fashion. Economic prosperity in Madagascar displays a destructive impulse: elites fight over its spoils in a way that ends up sinking the whole country into periodic political turmoil and recessions.

The Madagascar cycle

As the country slowly recovered from one of its most damaging political crises, which started in 2009, Hery Rajaonarimampianina, the president as of January 2014, seemed to want do the right things. However, in May 2015 parliament voted to impeach the president, accusing him of violating the constitution and general misrule. The members of parliament said that the president had shown a lack of respect for the institution and the final straw was his refusal to expressly rule out dissolving parliament. Despite the risk of upsetting the country's recent relative political stability, the parliament went through with the impeachment and the request went to the High Constitutional Council. On 13 June the Court ruled the impeachment proceedings had 'no legal foundation' and that the president had not violated the constitution. Despite the result, the political unrest caused by the impeachment distracted the government from developing the country and lead to nervousness in potential investors and donors.

Sustained economic growth was the centrepiece of the Rajaonarimampianina agenda to reconstruct the country and build peace. But how growth interacts with the conflict systems remains a major threat. Remarkably, with the exception of the period 1978–80, the cyclical crises that have marked politics in the country (1972, 1991, 2002 and 2009) seem to immediately precede periods of relatively strong economic growth.

Economic growth, simply put, spurts with a curse. Periods of development boom have been short-lived. Higher levels of corruption and inequality coincide with times of prosperity, suggesting a destabilising role of élites in a business cycle – a conflict-vicious system. In good times, some people, interests and sectors are left out of 'the party'. Others fight back in a way that spoils the party for everyone. According to the Mo Ibrahim Governance Index, the rule of law score dropped substantially over the growth period of 2006–08 from 58.1 to 51.4. During the same business cycle, accountability – which includes corruption – declined from 56.0 to 53.3. In fact, accountability ratings in 2000 and 2008 barely changed: 50.3 and 50.2, respectively – all periods of peak economic performance. Over its two business cycles in the past decade, the country witnessed the most remarkable drop in its relative position against other countries on the Transparency International Corruption Index.

The footprints of élites were revealed at towards the end of the 2009 crisis. In contrast to previous crises, old grievances between the two major ethno-regional blocs, the Merinas and the Cotiers, did not hold water. The main protagonists, ex-presidents Ravalomanana and Rajoelina, were both élites from the highland Merina region. The crisis started when a military directorate took power from the former president, Marc Ravalomanana, and handed it over to the then Antananarivo mayor, Andry Rajoelina. The stand-off that followed was the worst since the coming of democracy to the country, marked by five-year-long sanctions by the international community. The previous crisis had lasted only 14 months.

While it is difficult to put an exact figure on the total cost of the recurrent crises, the World Bank estimates that the latest crisis (ending in 2014) cost the government almost US$6.3 billion over the period 2009–12 alone. This is more than half the gross domestic product (GDP) and 15 times what the government spends on healthcare a year. The per capita income dropped significantly over the past ten years too. In 1980, more than 85 per cent of the population lived below the official US$1.25 poverty line. And in 2010 – the date of the most up-to-date data – it was 75.3 per cent poverty (World Bank 2014). With more than 92 per cent of the population living under US$2 a day, Madagascar is now one of the poorest countries in the world. The cumulative impacts are dire. With only 1.9 per cent of the population classified as middle class against an African average of 33 per cent, the staying power of the recurrent conflicts is very high.

With poverty figures like this, Madagascar badly needs help. Unicef's country representative, Elke Wisch, said in 2016: 'We have a lot of other countries where for children the situation is not good but for some reason those countries get more attention than Madagascar. This is an island. There is no terrorism. There are no geopolitical interests. We are very much off the map. There is a need for an urgent priority list but Madagascar will probably never attract donor aid like Malawi or Tanzania or Uganda.'

Another curse in waiting

Despite conflicts, Madagascar's natural resource base remains rich and diverse with considerable room to bounce back and sustain long-term economic growth. The country is richly endowed with mineral deposits. According to the Economist Intelligence Unit (EIU) in 2014, mining is becoming an important foreign exchange earner – amplified by the recent discovery of nickel deposits whose processing and expected step-up in production in 2014 will make it one of the world's largest lateritic mines. In January 2014, the Ambatovy large-tonnage long-life nickel and cobalt mining enterprise reached commercial production. At US$7 billion, it is the largest-ever foreign investment in Madagascar and one of the biggest in sub-Saharan Africa. Development of the Malagasy oil industry is still in its early stages. The country has no proven offshore reserves of light crude at present. However, according to the EIU its location in the highly prospective East African region has prompted a new surge of interest, with Total and ExxonMobil among the 17 or so oil companies operating in the country. In April 2015, Madagascar Oil (MOIL) was given the go ahead for its Tsimiroro Development Plan following 11 years of exploration and the drilling of 138 wells. The exploring company is sitting on an estimated 1.7 billion barrels of oil and expects to be producing 10,000 barrels per day (bpd) by 2018.

How to translate the country's abundant resources into sustained generation of wealth in a way that significantly reduces massive poverty and deprivation? The consistently poor economic performance is at the root of structural violence. The economy is struggling to rebound from a negative trend that marked the crisis. The share of the national cake available to each citizen has been declining in absolute terms and, worst of all, is moving in the opposite direction of population growth – per capita GDP growth in 2013 was -0.17 per cent and continued to be negative in 2014.

A significant percentage of élites have made it a culture to grab the country's wealth illegally for themselves. According to the president, almost 40 per cent of the budget is lost to corruption. While the full extent of graft during the political crises remains unknown, the destabilising effect on the country's ecological stability and insecurity has raised alarm bells on a global scale. According to Global Witness, an international environmental NGO, the illegal trade of the country's timber alone is worth over US$460,000 a day, which averages over US$167 million a year, a very significant sum that disappears into private pockets. Shockingly, this is more than the budgets of the ministries of defence, education and health together. In fact, almost 100,000 of the 8.5 million hectares of pristine forest are lost yearly.

Too few encouraging steps

While the government has adopted a liberal approach with economic partners, it remains to be seen how this is going to play out in the polarised and corrupt context of economic and business rivalries. Business relations have reopened with the French and the Americans. China's business engagement, which stayed even during the period of sanctions, has grown significantly since 2000 when it was encouraged by Ravalomanana.

Whether the country's substantial mineral wealth and new discoveries will be

KEY INDICATORS — Madagascar

	Unit	2011	2012	2013	2014	**2015
Population	m	*21.85	*22.41	*22.93	*23.57	*24.23
Gross domestic product (GDP)	US$bn	10.00	9.88	10.61	*10.60	*10.75
GDP per capita	US$	459	441	463	*449	*444
GDP real growth	%	0.5	2.5	2.4	*3.0	*5.0
Inflation	%	10.6	5.8	5.8	6.1	*7.6
Exports (fob) (goods)	US$m	3,299.1	1,518.5	1,922.2	–	–
Imports (fob) (goods)	US$m	5,998.4	2,630.0	2,773.4	–	–
Balance of trade	US$m	-2,699.3	-1,111.6	-851.3	–	–
Current account	US$m	-310.6	-616.0	-593.0	-240.0	*-343.0
Total reserves minus gold	US$m	1,215.6	1,190.9	905.1	773.8	–
Foreign exchange	US$m	1,063.3	1,052.8	776.1	–	–
Exchange rate	per US$	1,994.34	2,236.80	2,242.45	2,596.73	–

* estimated figure ** forecast figure

subjected to full competitive bidding processes remains unclear. Even more so, whether the government will renege on the opaque contracts that were signed during the crisis is uncertain, too. For example, the licence for exploring the Soalala iron deposit was alleged to be under-priced to Wuhan Iron & Steel Co (WISCO), a Chinese company, in a deal in which it paid a US$100 million signing bonus. Meanwhile, unscrupulous Chinese businessmen, together with some Madagascar élites, have been held responsible for the illegal trade of the country's endangered wildlife, such as the tropical rosewood, which Global Witness has been decried internationally as an 'ecological massacre' of extinction scale.

Madagascar turns on its head the standard economic wisdom that a rising tide of economic growth would lift everyone. In fact, without clear rules or people-centred institutions to ensure that the whole boat of prosperity lifts all passengers, the haves will leverage their greed fighting over its spoils in a way that will only end up sinking the whole boat and harming everyone, in particular the have-nots. Plainly speaking, more of the same economic growth is bad for Madagascar's long-term stability and peace.

According to the African Development Bank's (AfDB) African Economic Outlook report for Madagascar, the main drivers of growth in 2013 and 2014 have been the extraction industries, agro-industry, banks, transport, livestock and fisheries. Inflation reached 6 per cent in 2014, increasing by 0.2 per cent from the previous year due to energy prices and imported goods. Both the budget deficit and the current account deficit decreased in 2014 thanks to healthy exports and steady imports. Growth is not expected to increase significantly in 2015, due to the political situation, energy shortages and floods damaging crops and infrastructure. Depending on the resolution of the governance constraints, growth in 2016 could reach 5.1 per cent in view of the AfDB.

Risk assessment

Politics	Fair
Economy	Fair
Regional stability	Fair

COUNTRY PROFILE

1500 The first Europeans landed in Madagascar.
1790s King Andrianampoinimerina unified the Merina tribe which soon became the island's dominant tribe, controlling nearly half of Madagascar.
1820 Britain signed a treaty recognising Madagascar as an independent state under Merina rule.
1890 An Anglo-French treaty gave control of the island to France.
1894 Queen Ranavalona III was forced to abdicate and Madagascar was declared a French colony.
1946 Madagascar became a Territoire d'Outre-Mer (TOM, overseas territory).
1947 After several decades of growing resentment and resistance to French rule, there was an armed rebellion. France crushed the revolt with the loss of several thousand lives.
1960 The Republic of Madagascar (known between 1960–72 as the Malagasy Republic) gained full independence on 26 June. Philibert Tsiranana became president.
1972 Tsiranana was forced from office; he dissolved parliament and was replaced by General Gabriel Ramanantsoa as head of a provisional government. He moved the country away from ties with France towards the Soviet Union.
1975 After a short tussle between pro- and anti-government forces a military coup replaced Ramantsoa with Didier Ratsiraka. The country was renamed the Democratic Republic of Madagascar; Ratsiraka was elected president for a seven-year term.
1976 Large parts of the economy were nationalised. The Andry sy Riana Enti-Manavotra an'i Madagasikara (Arema) (Association for the Rebirth of Madagascar) party was formed. Ratsiraka increased state control over the economy until 1986 when a market economy was encouraged.
1992 Following three years of protests and civil disturbances after Ratsiraka's third presidential election victory, a referendum endorsed a multi-party constitution which enshrined a unitary state and reduced the powers of the president.
1993 In the presidential election Ratsiraka was defeated by Albert Zafy.
1996 Zafy was impeached.
1997 Didier Ratsiraka beat Albert Zafy in the presidential election.
2000, Local elections were boycotted by 70 per cent of the electorate and Ratsiraka and his party retained considerable political power.
2001 The Senate reopened in May after 29 years, completing the government framework provided for in the 1992 constitution, which replaced the socialist revolutionary system.
2001 Both candidates, Ratsiraka and Marc Ravalomanana, declared themselves winners in the presidential election.
2002 Civil disturbance accompanied heated debate about the prospective winner of the presidential election. Ravalomanana was declared the winner by the Constitutional High Court, following a recount. Ravalomanana was recognised by the US as Head of State. Didier Ratsiraka fled to the Seychelles. President Marc Ravalomanana's Tiako i Madagasikara (TIM) (I Love and Care for Madagascar) won parliamentary elections.
2003 Prime Minister Jacques Sylla announced a new cabinet.
2004 The IMF agreed to write off debts of US$2 billion. Madagascar joined the Southern African Development Community (SADC).
2006 The president's plane was shot at as he returned home from France as General Andrianafidisoa (Fidy) attempted a military coup claiming the 2001 presidential election was illegitimate. President Ravalomanana won a second term in office.
2007 The president appointed General Charles Rabemananjara as prime minister. Constitutional amendments were agreed by referendum to increase presidential powers. Parliamentary elections were won by the ruling TIM. A US$3.3 billion nickel cobalt mine was opened in Tamatave.
2008 The UN launched an appeal to help the 332,391 people left homeless by Cyclone Ivan, one of the largest ever recorded. The first barrels of crude oil since the 1940s were produced. Madagascar issued 19 offshore exploration licences.
2009 Anti-government protests and political confrontation between the mayor of Antananarivo, Andry Rajoelina, and the president increased until the president sacked Rajoelina and appointed a city official as his replacement. Dissident soldiers joined Rajoelina and refused to take orders from the president and government. Police attempted to arrest Rajoelina, who took refuge in the French embassy. Troops stormed the presidential palace forcing Ravalomanana to resign and replacing him with Andry Rajoelina, who became president of the High Transitional Authority (HTA). The African Union (AU) suspended Madagascar, calling the regime change an 'unconstitutional coup'. The SADC said it would not recognise Rajoelina as the new president. An arrest warrant was issued by the HTA for former president Ravalomanana, who was living in exile in Swaziland. He was charged with misuse of government funds. Ravalomanana was sentenced, *in absentia*, to a four-year jail sentence and fined US$70 million for alleged abuse of office. UN-backed mediation talks began with HTA to reintroduce democratic principles and a unity government. President Rajoelina postponed parliamentary

elections and appointed Brigadier General Albert Camille Vital as prime minister.
2010 The US and AU imposed sanctions on President Rajoelina and 108 of his supporters in March, following Rajoelina's failure to meet a deadline to set up a unity government despite earlier agreements. Foreign assets were frozen and travel restrictions were imposed in the hope that further negotiations would take place. The European Union (EU) confirmed that its substantial aid programme would remain frozen until Madagascar returned to democratic rule. Following agreement at a mediated forum and despite the boycott by three major opposition parties, the date for a constitutional referendum was set for mid-2011, along with the presidential election. Although opposition political parties called for voters to boycott the referendum, 74.19 per cent voted yes. The referendum endorsed the presidency of Andry Rajoelina and lowered the age of a presidential candidate from 40 to 36 years (thus allowing Rajoelina to stand in new presidential elections). The Constitutional High Court rejected all opposition objections to the results and validated the referendum. The fourth Malagasy Republic was declared.
2011 President Rajoelina dismissed Prime Minister Albert Camille Vital in March, but he was re-appointed and asked to form a new cabinet. Presidential and parliamentary elections scheduled for May were postponed until September. In July the UN *rapporteur* called for international sanctions on Madagascar to be reconsidered, as they were threatening more of the population with food insecurity. An agreement was reached between politicians allowing elections to take place in 2012. The agreement kept President Rajoelina in post and also allow exiled former president Ravalomanana to return to Madagascar. Prime Minister Vital and his government resigned in October and President Rajoelina appointed Jean Omer Beriziky as prime minster. Beriziky took office in November. Former president, Didier Ratsiraka returned from exile (since 2002) in France in November. In 2003, a court had convicted Ratsiraka, *in absentia*, of corruption. He was sentenced to 10 year's hard labour. President Rajoelina consented to his return, without penalty. His return followed the formation of a unity government on 21 November and a possible end to the political deadlock.
2012 On 22 January, former president Marc Ravalomanana's aircraft had to return to South Africa when the airport in Antananariva was closed against him when he attempted to land. Cyclone Giovanna struck the island near Madagascar's principal sea port and the eastern city of Toamasina (200km north-east of the capital) on 14 February. The cyclone killed 35 people and caused damage to 60 per cent of the homes in the area as well as uprooting vegetation and damaging infrastructure. Another cyclone (Irena) hit on 6 March. It struck in the south eastern Ifanadiana district, killing over 65 people and making homeless 70,000. Over 300,000 people were made homeless from both cyclones. On 1 August, the National Election Commission of the Transition (NECT) announced that the first round of presidential elections would take place on 8 May 2013, with a runoff to be held on 3 July. The NECT also said that mayoral and urban and rural municipality elections would be held simultaneously, with municipal councillor elections to be held on 23 October 2013. In November the government declared a state of emergency across the country after locusts numhers increased to a crisis level. There were fears of a return to the locust infestations of 1997, which cost the government and international community US$60 million for the treatment of four million hectares over four years. Another such plague began in the 1950s and lasted 17 years because there was no coordinated action plan.
2013 On 3 May the Special Elections Court approved 41 candidates for the presidential election, including Andry Rajoelina; the wife of former president, Marc Ravalomanana, Lalao Ravalomanana; former president Didier Ratsiraka and two former prime ministers. On 4 May the Court announced the date for the election as 24 July 2013, which was later postponed until 25 October, with the second round, if no candidate wins 50 per cent of the vote, on 20 December, the same day as parliamentary elections. The first round of the presidential election, held on 25 October had no clear winner. The run-off was held on 20 December between Richard Jean-Louis Robinson of the Avana (Rainbow) party who had won 21.16 per cent of the first round vote, and Hery Martial Rokotoarimanana Rajaonarimampianina who had won 15.85 per cent. Mr Rajaonarimampianina had the support of Malagasy Tonga Saina (the Conscious Malagasies party) candidate Roland Ratsiraka – a nephew of former President Didier Ratsiraka – as well as the former minister of foreign affairs and presidential candidate, Pierrot Rajaonarivelo. Mr Robinson had the support of two more former presidential hopefuls – Saraha Georget Rabeharisoa of the Green Party of Madagascar, and former prime minister Camille Vital. Elections to the National Assembly were held at the same time. The results were: Party of Andry Rajoelina 49 seats (out of 151) (17.3 per cent), Ravalomanana Movement 20 seats (10.8 per cent), Vondrona Politika 13 seats (8.2 per cent), Parti Hiaraka Isika 5 seats (5 per cent), Madagascar Green Party 2 seats (3.5 per cent), Economic Liberalism 5 seats (2.8 per cent), independents 25 seats, no other party won more than 2 per cent but three parties won two seats and the rest one seat each. Turnout was 50.8 per cent.
2014 The result of the 20 December 2013 presidential election was announced on 3 January, and was a reversal of the first round with Mr Rajaonarimampianina winning with 53.5 per cent to Mr Robinson's 46.5 per cent. Mr Robinson alleged the election had been rigged and demanded a recount. A special court confirmed the result on 17 January. Mr Rajaonarimampianina was sworn in on 25 January. After consulting with parliament, Roger Laurent Christophe Kolo was named as prime minister in April; he took office on 16 April and named his 31-member cabinet, on 18 April. The cabinet included seven ministers who had served under former president, Andry Rajoelina, as well as two of the 32 unsuccessful presidential candidates – Mr Roland Ratsiraka and Mr Joseph Martin Randriamampionona. Former president Marc Ravalomanana returned to Madagascar on 13 October and was promptly arrested.
2015 Tropical Storm Chedza hit the west coast of Madagascar in January and quickly crossed the island, affecting over 80,000 lives. The formative stages of the cyclone caused heavy rainfall that exacerbated the conditions of already heavily flooded areas, leading to the death of 68 people and forcing 20,000 people to live in temporary shelters. Parliament voted to impeach President Rajaonarimampianina in May, but the High Constitutional Council ruled on 13 June that the impeachment proceedings had 'no legal foundation'.

Political structure

Constitution

The Fourth Malagasy Republic was declared in December 2010, following a Constitutional referendum on 17 November, which reduced the age restriction of presidential candidates.
Constitutional reforms in 1995 and 1998 gave the president the power to appoint or dismiss the prime minister and presidential terms in office were limited to three.

Independence date

26 June 1960

Form of state

Republic

The executive
The president is directly elected by absolute majority popular vote in 2 rounds if needed for a five-year term (eligible for a second term).
The prime minister is nominated by the National Assembly and appointed by the president.
National legislature
The bicameral parliament consists of the Antenimieram-Pirenena (Assemblée Nationale) (National Assembly) (lower chamber) with 151 members elected in single and multi-seat constituencies. The Antenimieran-Doholona (Sénat) has 33 members of which 22 are elected (one from each district) and 11 appointed by the President. Members serve five-year terms.
Legal system
The constitution guarantees judicial independence. The single judicial system is tiered, including in the first instance civil, criminal and military courts. Above these are the Court of Appeal, High Court of Justice, which tries high officials, and a High Constitutional Court. Finally overseeing all is the Supreme Court. *Dian* (traditional courts) handle some civil disputes, among rural peoples only, and decisions are not subject to formal procedural protection of the formal court system. Both parties must agree to abide by the *dian's* authority and ruling.
Last elections
25 October 2013 (presidential, first round) and 20 December 2013 (presidential, second round), 20 December 2013 (parliamentary)
Results: Parliamentary: Party of Andry Rajoelina won 49 seats (out of 151) (17.3 per cent), Ravalomanana Movement 20 seats (10.8 per cent), Vondrona Politika 13 seats (8.2 per cent), Parti Hiaraka Isika 5 seats (5 per cent), Madagascar Green Party 2 seats (3.5 per cent), Economic Liberalism 5 seats (2.8 per cent), independents 25 seats, no other party won more than 2 per cent but three parties won two seats and the rest one seat each. Turnout was 50.8 per cent.
Presidential (first round 25 Oct 2013): Since none of the 33 candidates achieved 50 per cent, the two leaders, Richard Jean-Louis Robinson (21.1 per cent) and Hery Martial Rakotoarimanana Rajaonarimampianina (15.9 per cent), stood in the second round on 20 December. Mr Rajaonarimampianina won with 53.49 per cent to Mr Robinson's 46.51 per cent. The result was challenged by Mr Robinson but his challenge was rejected by a special court on 17 January 2014. Mr Rajaonarimampianina was sworn in on 25 January. Turnout was 61.8 per cent.
Next elections
2017 (parliamentary), 2018 (presidential)

Political parties
Ruling party
Together with President Andry Rajoelina
Main opposition party
Ravalomanana Movement
Approximately 45 per cent of the total population are under 15 years.

Population
23.57 million (2014)*
Last census: August 1993: 12,238,914
Population density: 24 inhabitants per square km. Urban population 30 per cent (2010 Unicef).
Annual growth rate: 3.0 per cent, 1990–2010 (Unicef).
Ethnic make-up
The population comprises 18 separate ethnic groups, all deriving in varying degrees from Malayo-Indonesian origin, with African and Arab influences a particular feature in coastal areas. The Merinas (central highlands) represent about 26 per cent of the total, while the Betsimisaraka on the east coast account for 15 per cent and the Betsileo (southern highlands) 12 per cent. The other main groups are the Antankarana (north), Sakalava (west) and Mahafaly and Antandroy (far south). There is long-standing rivalry between the highland groups (particularly the Merina) and those of the coastal regions.
Religions
Traditional beliefs (45 per cent), Christianity (about 45 per cent), Islam (7 per cent).

Education
Primary education lasts for five years. Secondary schooling is divided into two, beginning with a four-year programme. When completed students may continue in either an acedemic or technical programme, for a further three years. Education may be given in either French or Madagasy.
The majority of those who do not attend school or who withdraw early come from the poorest sections of the population and those living in rural areas; illiteracy rates in women are a higher among the youngest; and nearly half of school age children are not enrolled in schools.
Public expenditure is around 3 per cent of GDP, of which around 40 per cent is spent on primary and 35 per cent on secondary education. Higher education expenses amount to only 0.5 per cent of GDP.
Literacy rate: 68.1 per cent total, 61.6 per cent female; adult rates (World Bank).
Compulsory years: Six to 11.
Enrolment rate: 120 per cent gross primary enrolment of relevant age group (including repeaters), World Bank.
Pupils per teacher: 47 in primary schools.

Health
About 60 per cent of the population live within 5km of, or about one hour's walk from, a public health centre.
Vaccination facilities remain poor with only 61 per cent of children immunised against measles, before aged one year.
More than three-quarters of the people have no ready access to drinking water.
HIV/Aids
The government has a national Aids policy that covers all economic sectors.
HIV prevalence: 1.7 per cent aged 15–49 in 2003 (World Bank)
Life expectancy: 57 years, 2004 (WHO 2006)
Fertility rate/Maternal mortality rate: 4.7 births per woman, 2010 (Unicef); maternal mortality 488 per 100,000 live births (World Bank).
Child (under 5 years) mortality rate (per 1,000): 58 per 1,000 live births (WHO 2012)
Head of population per physician: 0.29 physicians per 1,000 people, 2004 (WHO 2006)

Welfare
In 2004, three separate cyclones, including Cyclone Gafilo, estimated to have been the worst cyclone in 20 years, killed over 100 people and damaged more than 117,000 hectares of farmland as well as many schools and healthcare centres. Total damage from Cyclone Gafilo was estimated, by Government, at US$250 million.

Main cities
Antananarivo (capital, and principal business centre, estimated population 1.8 million in 2012), Toamasina (Tamatave), (236,748), Antsirabé (205,811), Fianarantsoa (194,287), Mahajanga (Majunga) (174,023), Toliara (formerly Tuléar) (128,629), Antsiranana (formerly Diégo-Suarez) (91,671).

Languages spoken
French is the usual business language and the medium for all documentation.
Very little English is spoken.
Official language/s
Malagasy, French, English (from 2007)

Media
National state radio and television is controlled by the office of the president. National broadcasting is a state monopoly.
Press
Most newspapers are privately owned and are published in French, with a minority number published in Malagasy.
Dailies: In French, *Midi-Madagasikara* (www.midi-madagasikara.mg), *Madagascar Tribune* (www.

madagascar-tribune.com), *Les Nouvelles* (www.les-nouvelles.com), *L'Express* (www.lexpressmada.com) and *La Gazette de la Grande Ile* (www.lagazette-dgi.com) and in Malagasy *Gazetiko*; all are published and circulated in Antananarivo.

Weeklies: In French, *Dans les Media Demain* www.dmd.mg) is a privately owned news digest, with a large circulation in the Madagascan Diaspora. In Malagasy, *Lakroa* (Cross) is a Roman Catholic publication reaching rural and remote areas, *Feon'ny Merina* (Voice of the Merina) promotes the interests of Merina people of Malay origin.

Periodicals: In French, the monthly *Jureco* has articles on legal and economic issues while *Madagascar Magazine* (www.madagascarmagazine.com) is a quarterly publication that covers politics and economic issues as well as tourist features. The news magazine *Revue de l'Ocean Indian* (www.madatours.com/roi) covering issues of Indian Ocean islands.

Broadcasting

Radio: Radio-Télévision Malagasy (RTM) operates the only national radio service. Private, local, commercial stations include Radio MBS (www.mbs.mg) owned by President Ravalomanana, Radio Don Bosco (www.radiodonbosco.mg) owned by the Catholic Church, Radio Feon'ny Merina, which promotes the interests of the Merina people and Radio Fahazavana.

Television: Radio-Télévision Malagasy (RTM) operates the only national TV station. Other, private local TV stations include Radio-Television Analamanga (RTA) (www.rta.mg), MBS TV (www.mbs.mg) and Madagascar TV (MATV).

Other news agencies: APA: www.apanews.net
Panapress: www.panapress.com
Reuters Africa: http://africa.reuters.com

Economy

Oil was discovered offshore in 2006, and with projected production of 60,000 barrels per day by 2010, energy analysts were predicting annual revenue of US$1 billion. However, as none was forthcoming, in March 2011, the minister for mines and hydrocarbons announced that all planned licensing for oil exploration had been suspended indefinitely for around 225 blocks across three basins. These sites had attracted major international exploration companies, some of which had discovered oil and were awaiting an improvement in the political situation before increasing their investment.

On 28 June it was announced that the French oil company Total had been given a one-year extension on its exploration licence. In June 2011, the UK-based production company (Madagascar Oil) resolved its dispute with the government concerning validity of the production sharing contract, with oil expected to begin extraction in 2012.

GDP growth was 6.2 per cent in 2007 and 7.1 per cent in 2008, which plummeted to -4.1 in 2009 as political turmoil undermined the economy at a time of global economic crisis. In 2010, as a fragile stability was re-established, GDP growth picked up and reached 0.5 per cent, which remained static at an estimated 0.5 per cent in 2011. Economic growth in Madagascar rebounded to an estimated 3 per cent in 2014. Inflation which had been in double digits for most of the 2000s, dipped to 9.2 per cent in 2008 and remained fairly constant until 2010. Since 2010, the inflation rate has decreased significantly and it was reported at 6.1 per cent in 2014.

Madagascar is a member of the Extractive Industries Transparency Initiative (EITI), a 'forum of oil producers and consumers seeking to promote accountability in oil revenue', which should supply the necessary support in Madagascan efforts to strengthen public financial management.

The service sector is the major generator of the economy at 54.9 per cent in 2009, with industry accounting for 16 per cent, of which manufacturing was 14.1 per cent; agriculture contributed 29.1 per cent. Madagascar overtook Nigeria as Africa's largest rice producer in 2009, but still needs to import a further 10 per cent to meet domestic demand. Other agricultural produce includes livestock, coffee, cotton, tobacco and sugar. It also produces around 1,800–2,000 tonnes of vanilla a year as an important cash crop, although overseas competition has arisen due to the discovery of new plantations and synthetic vanilla. Its industries consist of food processing, textiles and clothing, refined petroleum products, mining and manufactured goods.

Madagascar was ranked 151 (out of 187) in the UN Human Development Index (HDI) in 2011. Madagascar has 67.8 per cent of its population living on the equivalent of US$1.25 per day, and 53.3 per cent who experience multiple deprivations in the same household. Madagascar has reached the conditions for aid under the IMF Enhanced Heavily Indebted Poor Countries (HIPC) Initiative, which allows it to borrow funds backed by the Initiative's guarantee.

External trade

Madagascar was one of the founding members of the Common Market of Eastern and Southern Africa (Comesa) and since June 2009 operates a customs union whereby the goods and services of non-members attract a common external tariff (CET).

Madagascar is one of the World's largest exporter of vanilla (it lost its pre-eminence in 2000 when a cyclone destroyed much of its production). It has significant reserves of minerals and ores; investment in mineral extraction was bolstered in May 2007 when the African Development Bank agreed to a US$150 million loan to develop the Ambatovy nickel plant.

Imports

Principal imports are capital goods, petroleum, consumer goods and food.

Main sources: China (20.6 per cent of total in 2014), France (10.6 per cent), Algeria (6.3 per cent), India (5.4 per cent) and Bahrain (5 per cent).

Exports

Principal exports are coffee, vanilla, shellfish, sugar, cotton cloth, clothing, chromite and petroleum products.

Main destinations: France (17.7 per cent of total in 2014), United States (8.8 per cent), Belgium (6.8 per cent), Netherlands (6.4 per cent) and South Africa (5.7 per cent).

Agriculture

Farming

The agricultural sector dominates the economy.

Madagascar has a wide range of soil types and its main cash/export crops are prawns, coffee, cotton, cloves and vanilla, production of which has fluctuated due to recurrent droughts and cyclones. Vanilla used to be the country's main export crop but increased competition worldwide has reduced exports. Around 1,800–2,000 tonnes of vanilla a year is produced, but its cultivation has suffered a drop in value due to overseas competition from new plantations and synthetic vanilla.

Main food crops are rice, maize, bananas and sweet potatoes. Groundnuts, pineapples, coconuts and sugar are also grown, mostly for domestic use. The decline in coffee prices led to many growers switching production to rice, increasing production by 5 per cent, and making Madagascar self-sufficient in rice (the staple diet of the country) for the first time since the mid-1970s, with annual production at around 3.0 million tonnes per year.

Divestiture of vanilla, cotton and sugar parastatals was expected to encourage greater foreign investment. However, as vanilla prices fell from US$450—500 per kilo in 2003, to US$30 in 2007, financial co-operatives kept several thousand vanilla farmers afloat.

The livestock sector is dominant in the west and south of the country.

Fishing

In 2013 local conservation groups reported that since the mid-1990s overfishing has threatened the livelihoods of local fishermen. The groups blamed the government for a lack of regulation.

In a meeting of African ministers in Namibia, held in 2009, members discussed illegal and unregulated fishing, which is estimated to cost Africa US$1 billion per annum in lost revenue. It has also significantly increased threat to stocks and for the livelihoods of fishermen engaging in local artisan fishing.

Forestry

Only 15 per cent of Madagascar's ancient forest remains. Deforestation has left the hills exposed to the wind and rain which has stripped away the soil. Forest preservation and the creation of national parks are receiving large-scale international support.

Industry and manufacturing

The industrial sector contributes around 16 per cent of GDP and employs around 9 per cent of the workforce.

Industry is dominated by food processing and the manufacture of textiles for international markets. Other major sectors include rice milling, sugar refining, distilling, oil-seed crushing, meat, fruit and vegetable canning, processing of cashew nuts, fruit juices, milk products and jams, cigarettes, soap and rope manufacturing, cotton spinning and brewing. Major capital-intensive industries are oil refining, fertiliser and cement production.

There are 150 firms based in industrial free zones, representing mainly textile, food processing and information technology, and creating 6,000 jobs in the Antananarivo area alone. Many textile companies in Mauritius are relocating to Madagascar due to the cheaper labour rates.

Tourism

Political instability in Madagascar has dampened the tourist industry and visitors who would have considered visiting the largest island in Africa to see its exceptional flora and fauna have been deterred. Madagascar has three sites on Unesco's World Heritage List including the rainforests of the Atsinanana national parks with their unique biodiversity and the culturally vital Royal Hill of Ambohimanga.

Travel and tourism is an important component of the economy, contributing 11.8 per cent per annum of GDP (2008–10), and rising to 12.5 per cent in 2011. Employment in the industry remained at 11.8 per cent (522,500 jobs) from 2008–10, but rose to 12.5 per cent (577,000 jobs) in 2011. Foreign direct investment has grown since oil exploration began. Investment in hotels and other visitor infrastructure accounted for some of the increase in capital investment in travel and tourism, which increased from 8.8 per cent of total investment in 2009 to 15.8 per cent in 2010 (a figure sustained in 2011).

The political situation has improved, but while Madagascar is still suspended from a number of regional development bodies, its underdevelopment remains an inhibitor to tourism growth.

Environment

Madagascar has plants and wildlife found nowhere else on earth, and growth of both tourism and mining needs to be controlled to protect the fragile ecosystems.

Evidence from satellites, in March 2009, showed sediment flowing into the Mozambique Channel from the west coast of Madagascar. Deforestation for cultivation and pastureland since the 1960s has resulted in massive annual soil loss, estimated at 250 tonnes per hectare in some regions and the largest amount recorded anywhere in the world.

Mining

Excluding gold and gem production by artisanal miners, mining contributes less than 1 per cent of GDP and employs 1 per cent of the workforce. If the informal sector is included, the contribution to GDP is around 3 per cent.

Madagascar is rich in mineral resources, although it is still only a minor mineral producer by regional standards. There are sizeable deposits of a number of minerals, industrial ores and precious and semi-precious gemstones including chrome ore, mica, graphite, gold, bauxite, uranium, iron ore, ilmenite/titanium, quartz, nickel, copper, lead, platinum, labradorite, rock-crystal, rhodolite, marble, garnets, emeralds, rubies and sapphires. There are known deposits containing 100 million tonnes of bauxite and 400 million tonnes of iron ore, although these have not yet been developed due to the country's poor infrastructure.

Only chrome, mica and graphite have been exploited to any great extent, and export earnings from these are limited due to lack of demand. The world's largest known emerald cluster was discovered in Madagascar in 1996.

The region of Ilakaka in the southern interior has around 50 per cent of the world's sapphire reserves, while there are small quantities of semi-precious stones (garnets and amethysts) mined for export.

The state-owned Société Kraomita Malagasy (Kraoma) is Madagascar's main chromite producer. It extracts around 40,000 tonnes of concentrates and 80,000 tonnes of lumpy ore per year from the Andriamana complex and a further 20,000 tonnes from the Behandrinana mine.

There are some 100,000 individual gold miners and small syndicates. Although the government tolerates this form of mining, it is worried about its ecological effects which include a high level of mercury leaking into streams and rivers.

The country also produces graphite, 66 per cent of which comes from the Gallois mine. It exports up to 15,000tpy, mostly to the UK, US and Germany.

Hydrocarbons

No oil was being produced in 2010. However, oil exploration by international oil companies has been underway since the mid-2000s. Finds are expected to yield 9.8 billion barrels of recoverable reserves from the Bermolanga, and another 1.3 billion barrels from the Tsimiroro, oil fields.

On 4 March 2011, the minister for Office des Mines Nationales et des Industries Strategiques (Omnis) announced that all planned licensing for oil exploration had been suspended indefinitely for around 225 blocks across three basins. These sites had attracted major international exploration companies, some of which had discovered oil and were awaiting an improvement in the political situation before increasing their investment. On 29 March 2011, the US-based Madagascar Oil declared *force majeure* under its contractual agreements for four production-sharing blocks that it believes would be slated for expropriation by the government. Conditions deteriorated as Omnis failed to instruct the state regulatory authority to proceed with the 2011 Madagascar works programme. Discussions with the government had not improved the situation.

Consumption in 2008 was 20,000 barrels per day, all of which was imported.

Since the only oil refinery, in Toamasina, was privatised in 2000, it was upgraded and processes 540,000 tonnes of crude per year and provides 85 per cent of the country's refined oil needs.

Omnis is a government organisation responsible for policy, implementation and managing the country's hydrocarbons and mining assets.

Proven coal reserves were 137 million tonnes in 2008, but commercial production was limited as old facilities became uncompetitive. However renewed interest by foreign energy companies ready to invest in coal mining for power generation may invigorate the industry over the next decade.

Madagascar does not produce or import natural gas.

Energy

Total installed generating capacity was 227MW in 2007, producing 980 million kilowatt hours. Around 60 per cent of all energy is generated by hydropower, however only 15 per cent of the population have access to electricity; the majority rely on biomass, including fuel wood, for cooking and lighting. With demand increasing by 7 per cent per annum, government policy is to encourage growth in hydroelectric power, and it intends to increase hydropower to 70 per cent of the energy mix. Recent thermal power plants have been built by foreign companies using local coal, with all output used in the nickel mining industry.

There is no integrated power grid and each centre of population is served by its own power station, which either provides enough energy as needed or fails, resulting in outages. The state-owned national power and water utility Jiro sy Rano Malagasy (Jirama) is responsible for the provision of electricity and drinking water for the population of Madagascar. It is overseeing the installation of a mid-voltage transmission line between power plants. Solar-photovoltaic panels have been installed in rural communities to provide for localised energy needs.

Banking and insurance

Moves to strengthen banking supervision have been enhanced through the IMF backed Financial Sector Assessment Program.

Central bank

Banque Centrale de la République Malgache

Time

GMT plus three hours

Geography

Madagascar is situated in the western Indian Ocean, about 500km east of Mozambique in southern Africa. It comprises the island of Madagascar itself and several much smaller offshore islands. Madagascar is the fourth-largest island in the world. The terrain is dominated by a chain of mountains running the length of the island, with broad lowlands to the west and a narrow strip of lowlands to the east.

The highlands, which occupy around half of the total area, rise to 1,800m. A rift valley runs from north to south and includes lake Alaotra, which, at 40km in length, is the largest body of water in the country. The capital, Antananarivo, is located on the plateau.The highest elevations face east, forming an escarpment above the eastern lowlands. The east coast is narrow, averaging about 50km in width, and is heavily forested. The mountains slope gradually down towards the broad west coast, which is given over to savannah; unlike that of the east coast, the coastline is indented and provides harbourage.

The highest point of the island (2,880m) is in the Tsaratanana Massif at the northern end of the island. The coastline is contoured and is home to the natural harbour of Antsiranana. The southern end of the island is semi-desert with cactus-like plant species, which are unique to Madgascar.

Rivers flowing east from the highlands are short and fast with waterfalls. Those flowing down the gentler western terrain are longer and slower-moving.

Hemisphere

Southern

Climate

Tropical, cooler in highlands. The summer period spans the months of November to April. Numerous areas have their own micro-climates – the highlands are subject to mild freshness in the winter, while the eastern parts of the island experience high temperatures and humidity, with barren and arid conditions dominating the western sector.

In Antananarivo, the hottest month is December (15–28 Celsius (C)), coldest July (9–19 C). The wettest month is January. Winter in the capital lasts from April to October, when it is cold and dry.

Madagascar falls within the cyclone belt and cyclones tend to occur during the rainy season December–March, which is hotter than the rest of the year. It is rainy until June or July on the east coast and is very hot throughout the year. It is drier on the west coast.

Dress codes

In Antananarivo, in the winter months, normal weight clothing is suitable, with a woollen sweater/cardigan recommended. In the summer men should wear tropical suits and women, cotton dresses. On the coast, tropical clothing is recommended all year round.

Entry requirements

Passports

Required by all, valid for six months after date of entry.

Visa

Required by all, along with proof of return/onward passage. A proposed tourist *univisa* (a single visa to visit all 15-member states of SADC: Angola, Botswana, DRC, Lesotho, Madagascar, Malawi, Mauritius, Mozambique, Namibia, South Africa, Seychelles, Swaziland, Tanzania, Zambia and Zimbabwe) is expected to be in use by 2013. Visitors should check with the appropriate consulates to confirm start of *univisas* and their scope before beginning a tour of southern Africa.

A business visas requires a letter of recommendation from the employer, confirming the traveller's business activity and financial responsibility, to be submitted with the application.

Currency advice/regulations

Import of local currency is limited to MGA1,000; visitors are not allowed to export local currency. There is no limit on import of foreign currency, subject to declaration on arrival, and export is allowed up to the declared amount.

Health (for visitors)

Mandatory precautions

Yellow fever vaccination certificate required if arriving from an infected area.

Advisable precautions

Typhoid, polio, tetanus and hepatitis A vaccinations recommended. Malaria risk exists throughout the country and prophylaxis is necessary. There is a rabies risk. Water precautions should be taken.

Hotels

Good hotels are available in Antananarivo, Toamasina, Nosy Be, Ste Marie and Taolanaro. A service charge is added to bills at some hotels. Discretionary tipping is usual.

Credit cards

Credit cards are of limited use in Madagascar and few establishments accept them.

Public holidays (national)

Fixed dates

1 Jan (New Year's Day), 29 Mar (Commemoration Day – 1947), 1 May (Labour Day), 26 Jun (Independence Day), 15 Aug (Assumption Day), 1 Nov (All Saints' Day), 25 Dec (Christmas Day), 30 Dec (Republic Day).

Variable dates

Easter Monday, Ascension Day, Whit Monday.

Working hours

Banking

Mon–Fri: 0800–1100, 1400–1600.

Business

Mon–Fri: 0830–1200, 1400–1800.

Government

Mon–Fri: 0800–1200, 1400–1800.

Shops

Mon–Fri: 0800–1200, 1400–1800.

Telecommunications

Postal services

Air mail is advised. Surface mail can take between three and four months.

Electricity supply

110 or 220V AC, 50 cycles; also 380V AC, 50 cycles

Getting there

Air

National airline: Air Madagascar

International airport/s:

Antananarivo-Ivato (TNR), 14km from the city; restaurant, currency exchange.

Airport tax: None.

Surface

Water: There are few scheduled sea passages.

Main port/s: Toamasina (Tamatave), on the east coast, is the island's main port. It is used by numerous foreign shipping lines. Mahajanga (Majunga) is the west coast's main port. Antseranana (Diégo-Suarez) is in the extreme north of the island, and Toliara (Tuléar) is on the south-west coast.

Getting about

National transport

Air: Air Madagascar and TAM airlines fly more than 60 domestic routes. There are connections between all major towns, apart from Antsirabe. Air travel is the most used and generally recommended form of transport. There are over 100 airfields on the island, although many are just airstrips.

Road: Generally poor and in need of repair, and only passable in good weather (the dry season).
Fairly well-maintained main roads leave Antananarivo – the N4 to Mahajanga (Majunga), the RN2 to Toamasina (Tamatave), and the RN7 plateau route south to Fianarantsoa.

Rail: Two classes; light refreshments may be available; air-conditioning available on first-class trains.
Routes are: between Toamasina and Antsirabe, via Antananarivo, incorporating a connection between Moramanga and Lake Alaotra; and between Fianarantsoa and Manakara on the east coast. Daily services operate on most routes.

City transport

Taxis: Flat fare system for short journeys in most towns, otherwise by negotiation; tipping is not usual.

Car hire

Available in main centres. International driving licence required.

BUSINESS DIRECTORY

The addresses listed below are a selection only. While World of Information makes every endeavour to check these addresses, we cannot guarantee that changes have not been made, especially to telephone numbers and area codes. We would welcome any corrections.

Telephone area codes

The international dialling code (IDD) for Madagascar is +261 20 followed by operator and area codes and subscriber's number:

Antananarivo	22	Nosy-Be	86
Antsiranana	82	Toamasina	53
Fianarantsoa	75	Toliara	18
Mahajanga	62		

Useful telephone numbers

Police: 17
Fire: 18
Ambulance: 357-53

Chambers of Commerce

Antananarivo Chamber of Commerce, Industry and Agriculture, 20 Rue Paul Dussac, PO Box 166, 101 Antananarivo 101 (tel: 202-11; fax: 20213).

Antsiranana Chamber of Commerce, Industry and Agriculture, 3 Rue Colbert, PO Box 76, Antsiranana 201 (tel: 223-72; fax: 294-03).

Madagascar Federation of Chambers of Commerce, Industry and Agriculture, 20 Rue Paul Dussac, PO Box 166, Antananarivo 101 (tel: 20-211; fax: 20-213).

Mahajanga Chamber of Commerce, Industry and Agriculture, Boulevard Poincaré, PO Box 52, Mahajanga 401(tel: 226-21).

Nosy-Be Chamber of Commerce, Industry and Agriculture, Cours de Hell, PO Box 11, Nosy-Be 207 (tel: 610-26; fax: 610-56).

Toamasina Chamber of Commerce, Industry, Handicrafts and Agriculture, 4 Rue de Commerce, PO Box 108, Toamasina 501 (tel: 323-45; fax: 320-25).

Banking

BMOI, Place de l'Indépendence, BP 25 bis, Antananarivo 101 (tel: 346-09; fax: 346-10; e-mail:bmoi.sm@simicro.mg).

Bank of Africa-Madagascar, 2 Place de l'Independance, BP 183, Antananarivo 101 (tel: 391-00/; fax: 294-08).

Banque SBM Madagascar, 1 Rue Andrianary Ratianarivo Antsahavola, Antananarivo 101 (tel: 666-07; fax: 666-08).

BFV-Société Générale, 14 Lalana Jeneraly Rabehevitra, BP 196, Antananarivo 101 (tel: 206-91; fax: 345-54).

BNI-Crédit Lyonnais Madagascar, 74 Rue du 26 Juin 1960, BP 174, Antananarivo 101 (tel: 228-00; fax: 337-49).

Investco Southern Investment Bancorp, Immeuble NIAG, 8 Lalana Rainizanabololona, BP 8510, Antanimena, Antananarivo 101 (tel: 648-20; fax: 613-29).

Union Commercial Bank SA, 77 Rue Solombavambahoaka Frantsay, Antsahavola, BP 197, Antananarivo 101 (tel: 272-62; fax: 287-40).

Central bank

Banque Centrale de Madagascar, Avenue de la Révolution Socialiste, PO Box 550, Antananarivo (tel: 234-65; fax: 345-32; e-mail: b.c.m@simicro.mg).

Travel information

Air Madagascar, 31 Avenue de l'Indépendance, Analakely, Antananarivo 101 (tel: 222-22; fax: 337-60; e-mail: commercial@airmadagascar.com)

Association des Agences de Voyages de Madagascar, 5 Rue Ravveloary, Antananarivo (tel: 656-31; e-mail: aavm@wanadoo.mg).

Air Mauritius, 77 lalana Solombavabahoaka, Frantsay, Antsahavola, Antananarivo (tel: 359-00; fax: 357-73).

Réseau National des Chemins de Fer, BP 259, Soarano, Antananarivo (tel: 205-21).

Ministry of tourism

Ministry of Culture and Tourism, Rue Fernand Kasanga, BP 610, Tsimbazaza, Antananarivo (tel: 668-05; fax: 789-53; e-mail: mct@tourisme.gov.mg).

National tourist organisation offices

Maison du Tourisme de Madagascar (Madagascar Tourist Office), Place de l'Indépendance, Antaninarenina, PO Box 3224, Antananarivo (tel: 351-78; fax: 695-22; e-mail: mtm@simicro.gov.mg).

Ministries

Ministry of Private Sector Development and Privatisation, Comité de Privatisation, Zone III 1er étage, Ampefiloha, Antananarivo (tel: 666-67; fax: 601-38; e-mail: magpriv@dts.mg).

Other useful addresses

Agence Nationale d'Information 'Taratra' (ANTA), 3 rue du R P Callet, BP 386, Antananarivo (tel: 211-71).

Association of the Hotel Industry of Madagascar (SIHM), c/o Sofitrans – Soarano, Antananarivo (tel: 223-30).

Comité de Privatisation, Secrétariat Technique á la Privatisation Immeuble FIARO, Zone III 1er étage, Ampefiloha, 101 Antananarivo (fax: 2260-138).

Customs Services, Ivato Airport, Antananarivo (tel: 440-32).

Institut National de la Statistique et de la Recherche Economique (DGBDE), Direction Générale, BP 485, Antananarivo (tel: 216-52).

Madagascan Embassy (US), 2374 Massachusetts Avenue, NW, Wasghington DC 20008 (tel: (+1-202)-265-5525; fax: (+1-202)-265-3034; e-mail: malagasy@embassy.org).

Office Militaire National pour les Industries Stratégiques (monitors major industrial projects), 21 Lalana Razanakombana, Antananarivo.

Société d'Etude et de Réalisation pour le Développement Industriel, BP 3180, Antananarivo (tel: 213-35).

Syndicat de l'Industrie Hôteliére de Madagascar, BP 341, Antananarivo (tel: 202-02).

APA: www.apanews.net

Panapress: www.panapress.com

Reuters Africa: http://africa.reuters.com

Malawi

Malawi is currently on track to achieve four of the eight Millennium Development Goals (MDGs): reduce child mortality, combat HIV/Aids, malaria and numerous other diseases, ensure environmental sustainability, and develop a global partnership for development. However, the country still faces challenges in the form of fiscal disciplines, sustainable policies, a poor investment climate, a lack of diversification, a rising population and natural disasters. It also faces serious challenges in meeting the MDG targets relating to reducing gender inequality, maternal mortality and universal primary education.

Malawi experienced devastating floods at the start of 2015, with over a quarter of a million people affected. The United Nations reported that as many as 230,000 citizens were left unable to return to their homes. According to Unicef, around 64,000 hectares of land were left damaged, yet only half of one per cent of arable lands were affected by the floods. As most of Malawi's economy is heavily agro-based it is fortunate that the forecast dip in growth is set to be less severe than its might have been, with growth likely to slow to 5.5 per cent in 2015. This is from the previous year's 5.7 per cent increase in growth. This itself was a vast improvement from the 2.1 per cent growth in 2013; a strong recovery in tobacco output, Malawi's main export, improved agricultural sector growth.

The economy

Malawi's economy is beset by problems – the most significant of which is the blunt fact that the country depends on foreign donors for some 40 per cent of its budget. Before being able to free itself from this reliance on donor assistance, Malawi will need to address its complex labyrinth of state contracts, corruption, imports, backhanders, public sector procurement and vested interests.

Despite this, *African Economic Outlook 2015* (AEO), published by the African Development Bank (AfDB) determined that overall the 2014 calendar year was a success in terms of GDP growth. Malawi demonstrated overall recovery trends

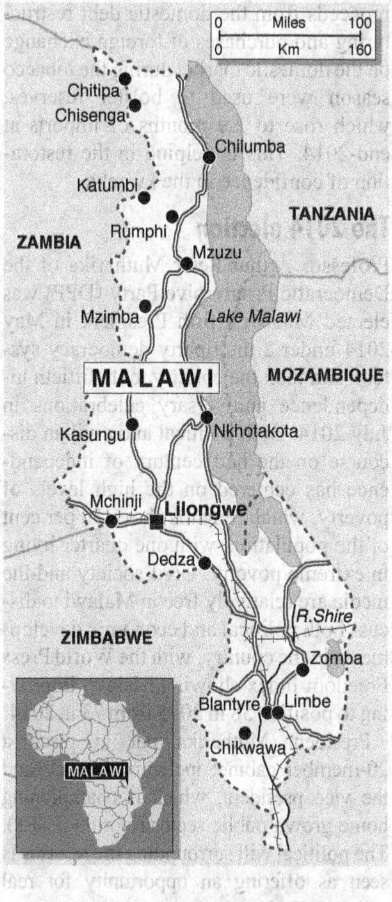

from the crisis of 2012. This is mainly due to the involvement of the International Monetary Fund (IMF), which has generated support to Malawi under an Extended Credit Facility (ECF) arrangement.

The discovery of a large theft of public funds in October 2013, locally known as 'Cashgate', exposed serious problems and deficiencies within the fiscal systems of Malawi. An estimated US$100 million had mysteriously disappeared from government funds. A large number of arrests were made and in the same month the then President, Mrs Banda, sacked her entire cabinet. It was rumoured, but never proved, that Mrs Banda herself had been involved in 'Cashgate'. Since the scandal, progress has occurred in the implementation of a short-term plan adopted in the aftermath of the scandal, aimed at securing co-ordinated prosecutions. However, the

KEY FACTS

Official name: Dziko la Malawi (Republic of Malawi)

Head of State: President Peter Mutharika (Democratic Progressive Party (DPP)) (from 31 May 2014)

Head of government: President Prof Peter Mutharika (DPP) (from 31 May 2014)

Ruling party: Democratic Progressive Party (DPP)

Area: 118,484 square km

Population: 17.60 million (2014)

Capital: Lilongwe

Official language: English

Currency: Kwacha (K) = 100 tambala

Exchange rate: K561.08 per US$ (Sep 2015)

GDP per capita: US$242 (2014)*

GDP real growth: 5.70% (2014)*

GDP: US$4.26 billion (2014)*

Inflation: 23.79% (2014)

Balance of trade: -US$1.02 billion (2012)

* estimated figure

scandal significantly damaged Malawi's economic outlook.

According to the IMF, the run up to the parliamentary and presidential elections in May 2014 left further governance concerns leaving macroeconomic policies adrift. This resulted in further suspension of donor budget support and, as a result, increased recourse to domestic financing, monetisation of the deficit and waning of confidence. The exchange rate of the domestic currency, the kwacha, depreciated further with inflation entrenched around 24 per cent for 2014. It is important for the government to sustain fiscal consolidation efforts to reduce the widening fiscal deficit (4.3 per cent in 2013–14 from 0.2 per cent in 2012–13) and interest rates. Tight monetary policy reflects the need to reduce the levels of inflation experienced by the kwacha.

Malawi's major exports consist predominantly of primary goods, such as tobacco, which form 80 per cent of the agricultural output of the nation. However, with globalisation, opportunities for exports of processed products have emerged. Nevertheless, the country has not yet re-positioned itself to exploit opportunities to integrate into global value chains (GVCs). Obstacles to integration into GVCs include poor infrastructure, low skills and a weak business climate. The government is implementing the national export strategy with a view to enhancing export competitiveness and promoting exports of processed agro-products to feed into regional and global value chains.

The current account deteriorated in 2014, mainly reflecting the large drop in official transfers. An improvement in the merchandise deficit by 2 percentage points to about 101 per cent of GDP owing to strong growth in traditional exports was more than offset by the sharp decline in net official transfers by 6 percentage points of GDP. As a result the current account deficit widened by 31 per cent to 5.1 percent of GDP and the exchange rate depreciated by 15 percent over 2014. The proceeds from the domestic debt restructuring and purchases of foreign exchange on the domestic market during the tobacco season were used to bolster reserves, which rose to 2.9 months of imports at end-2014. This is helping in the restoration of confidence in the kwacha.

The 2014 election

Professor Arthur Peter Mutharika of the Democratic Progressive Party (DPP) was elected Malawi's fifth President in May 2014 under a multiparty democracy system, and took the country to its fiftieth independence anniversary celebrations in July 2014. Both political and civilian discourse on the half century of independence has centered on the high levels of poverty, which remains above 50 per cent of the population, with one quarter living in extreme poverty. Civil society and the media are relatively free in Malawi to discuss both political and economic developments in the country, with the World Press Freedom Index showing Malawi improving to position 58 in 2015 from 73 in 2014.

President Mutharika put in place a 20-member cabinet including himself and the vice president, which is championing home grown public sector reforms (PSRs). The political will surrounding the reforms is seen as offering an opportunity for real change if well implemented. The PSRs were launched in February 2015 by the President, whilst the Vice President will continue as the overseer of the reform process.

The previous president, Joyce Banda, had, at the time, been only the second female head of state in Africa. In the elections, Mrs Banda was, by common consent, confronting humiliation and became the first female head of state to be voted out of power. Quite what had gone wrong for the internationally respected Mrs Banda was difficult to ascertain. There was no single trigger, rather a collection of self-made and inherited errors. Mrs Banda was never actually elected Malawi's president. As vice president, she assumed power on the death of President Bingu wa Mutharika, Peter Mutharika's brother.

Key issues

In April 2014 President Mutharika signed into law the raising of marriage age to 18, following a campaign against Malawi's high rate of child marriage. More than half of girls are married off as children, sometimes as at ages as early as nine. Gay rights activists were disappointed in that the law only recognises heterosexual marriage. Homosexual acts are illegal in Malawi, where most people hold deeply conservative religious and cultural beliefs.

According to the World Health Organisation (WHO) Malawi faces one of the highest HIV prevalence rates in the World. HIV is now the leading cause of death in the most productive age group, resulting in an estimated 86,000 deaths among adults and children annually. The epidemic has affected all sectors of society, especially social services.

Poverty is also widespread across most of Malawi, with the data from the World Bank reporting 50.7 per cent of the population as living within poverty (as of 2010).

Poor education and limited vocational training programmes mean there are few opportunities for Malawians to improve their situations. According to USAID 45 per cent of the country's children under the age of five are stunted due to the lack of adequate nutrition. Compounding the problem, many people live far from health care services and lack the transportation and money to access adequate care.

Risk assessment

Economy	Poor
Politics	Fair
Regional stability	Fair

KEY INDICATORS — Malawi

	Unit	2011	2012	2013	2014	**2015
Population	m	16.17	16.63	17.11	17.60	*18.11
Gross domestic product (GDP)	US$bn	5.70	4.17	*3.82	*4.26	*4.94
GDP per capita	US$	351	251	*223	*242	*273
GDP real growth	%	5.5	1.9	*5.2	*5.7	*5.5
Inflation	%	7.6	21.3	28.3	23.8	*17.3
Exports (fob) (goods)	US$m	1,530.9	1,284.6	–	–	–
Imports (fob) (goods)	US$m	2,629.6	2,302.4	–	–	–
Balance of trade	US$m	-1,098.7	-1,017.7	–	–	–
Current account	US$m	-764.7	-165.0	-68.0	*-216.0	*-168.0
Total reserves minus gold	US$m	–	223.2	413.1	602.4	–
Foreign exchange	US$m	–	218.5	400.6	–	–
Exchange rate	per US$	150.80	320.78	430.00	466.00	–

* estimated figure ** forecast figure

COUNTRY PROFILE

In the eighth century, the Bantu people of Nyasaland began trading with Portuguese merchants on the east African coast. The slave trade expanded rapidly over the period of 1790–1860.
1850 After David Livingstone, a Scottish missionary, visited the area he was followed by other missionaries and traders.
1891 The Nyasaland and District Protectorate was established by Britain. In the wake of David Livingstone's explorations an increasing number of Europeans went to Nyasaland, particularly missionaries. The settlers expropriated land and imposed taxes which led to ever growing numbers of Africans working on the coffee plantations or moving to the then Rhodesia or South Africa.
1893 Name was changed to the British Central African Protectorate.
1907 The Central African Protectorate became Nyasaland.
1944 Nationalists establish the Nyasaland African Congress (NAC).
1950s Opposition to colonial rule, which had begun in the southern highlands, became more widespread. The NAC opposed the planned Central African Federation (CAF) with Northern and Southern Rhodesia, and the heavy-handed interference by white settlers in traditional agricultural methods. The CAF came into being on 1 August 1953.
1954 The NAC grew rapidly upon the return from Britain of Dr Hastings Kamuzu Banda; within a year the colonial authorities had jailed him and other leaders.
1959 The NAC was banned after violence flared between supporters and government authorities. Banda and several other leaders were arrested and a state of emergency declared.
Malawi Congress Party (MCP) was founded as a successor to the NAC.
1961 Dr Banda was released and invited to London for a constitutional conference, at which Nyasaland was promised eventual independence regardless of constitutional developments in the rest of the CAF. Elections followed, which Dr Banda's MCP won.
1963 The CAF was officially dissolved, paving the way for independence in Nyasaland.
1964 Dr Banda became prime minister after independence was declared on 6 July.
1966 On 6 July Nyasaland became a republic and was renamed Malawi; Dr Banda became president. The constitution established a one-party state.
1971 Banda declared himself president for life.
1975 Zomba was replaced as the capital by Lilongwe
1978 Dr Banda and the MCP won the first election since independence. All candidates had to be members of the MCP and approved by Dr Banda.
1992 Catholic bishops condemned Banda and the one-party state and sparked mass demonstrations; humanitarian aid to the country was cut off.
1993 A referendum overwhelmingly backed a multi-party option and political parties began to develop.
1994 The United Democratic Front (UDF) beat the MCP in multi-party legislative elections and Bakili Muluzi became president. Dr Banda retired.
1995 Banda was acquitted of ordering the murder of three government ministers, he later apologised for any suffering he may have 'unknowingly caused'.
1997 Hastings Banda died in South Africa, where he was being treated for pneumonia.
1999 The UDF won the parliamentary elections and Muluzi retained the presidency for his last, five-year term.
2000 Corruption scandals began to threaten aid flow. Muluzi was forced to dismiss his government.
2002 Malawi's bishops condemned Muluzi's rule, warning that it was becoming a dictatorship. International aid was suspended due to a lack of reform and transparency. A drought caused widespread hunger; food aid was supplied by the UN.
2004 The government offered free anti-retroviral drugs to HIV/Aids sufferers. Bingu wa Mutharika (UDF), won presidential elections, while the MCP won most seats in the parliamentary elections. The elections were not considered free and fair by observers. A coalition government was formed, led by the UDF.
2005 President Mutharika founded the Democratic Progressive Party (DPP). Impeachment proceedings began against the president for corruption; he survived and many of the UDF-sponsors resigned from the party. The DPP won a number of by-elections in its support for the president.
2006 Vice President Cassim Chilumpha was arrested and charged with treason; it was alleged that he had hired a South African assassin to kill the president. Former president Bakili Muluzi was arrested for corruption, fraud and theft during his time in office.
2008 The government ended diplomatic relations with Taiwan, in favour of ties with China, stating it recognised Taiwan as 'an inalienable part of China's territory'. Aid worth several billion US dollars offered by China was thought to have persuaded Malawi to transfer its endorsement.
2009 In presidential elections, incumbent President Bingu wa Mutharika (DPP) won 2.7 million votes, against 1.3 million for John Zenus Ungapake Tembo (popularly known as JZU) (MCP). In parliamentary elections the DPP won 114 seats (out of 193) and remained in power.
2010 President Bingu wa Mutharika became chairman of the African Union (AU) for the year. Japan sponsored the distribution of photovoltaic (solar) panels for electricity generation in Kamuzu International Airport, in a programme to introduce 'green-energy' to Malawi. International condemnation was heaped on Malawi for the conviction of a homosexual couple who had declared their betrothal (in 2009). A presidential pardon was granted to the couple. Malawi's new flag was unveiled. The new flag consists of three broad bands of red, black and green, with a stylised white, fully risen sun with sun rays in the centre. The president said the change from red half-sun to white full-sun symbolised Malawi's progress from under-developed country to developed one.
2011 The trial of former president, Bakili Muluzi, began in March. He was accused of misappropriating some US$11 million of international donor funds. The UK's high commissioner was expelled in April after he was quoted in a leaked communication to London as saying President Mutharika was 'becoming ever more autocratic and intolerant of criticism'. In July the UK cut aid to Malawi; the IMF had also cut its aid. The recently passed austerity budget did not include any aid finance. In July riots broke out in a number of cities after a court ruled that protests against the high cost of living, and President Mutharika's government in general, were banned. The trial of Vice President Chilumpha, delayed since 2006, was scheduled to begin in July but Chilumpha sacked his second legal team, resulting in a further delay. In August, Vice President Joyce Banda founded a new political party, the People's Party (PP), following her expulsion from the UDF for refusing to endorse the presidential candidacy of Peter Mutharika (younger brother of President Mutharika) for the 2014 presidential election. The kwacha was devalued by 10 per cent in August. On 19 August, President Mutharika sacked his entire cabinet and took over the running of every ministry himself. In September, President Mutharika appointed new ministers for foreign, financial and domestic portfolios; the defence ministry was abolished.
2012 In a speech during a road-opening ceremony on 5 March, President Mutharika lashed out at foreign aid donors and non-governmental agencies (NGOs), accusing them of plotting with

his opponents to topple his government and that they could 'go to hell'. He said he was 'tired of being insulted' and urged his followers to prevent opposition protests adding 'I will not accept this nonsense any more'. President Mutharika died on 5 April, although this news was not announced until 7 April, when, under constitutional dictum, Vice President Joyce Banda took office as president. On 7 May the new government devalued the kwacha by 33 per cent. The Reserve Bank of Malawi (central bank) also announced that the peg to the US dollar would be scrapped. US$1 became worth K250 (up from K168). The devaluing had been advised by the IMF but the previous administration had rejected the proposal; international financial aid was restored. There was a rush by shoppers to buy basic goods and many shops ran out of staple foods. On 29 May, parliament voted to reinstate the rising sun flag (first hoisted at independence in 1964) that had been replaced by former president Mutharika (in 2010). In July a UN assessment report found 1.63 million people (11 per cent of the total population) were at serious risk of malnutrition. Prolonged drought in central and southern Malawi resulted in poor harvests, which by August had created widespread food shortages, particularly of the maize staple. The devalued currency also caused greater strain on family incomes to buy food. On 17 October, President Banda requested the African Union (AU) arbitrate in Malawi's dispute with Tanzania over sovereignty of Lake Malawi (also known as Lake Nyasa); Tanzania claims 50 per cent of the lake (the third largest in Africa) and its share of the potential for oil and gas discoveries.

2013 President Banda sacked the cabinet on 10 October after allegations of widespread corruption in government. According to the BBC several officials had been caught allegedly with money hidden under their beds and in their cars.

2014 Presidential and parliamentary elections were held on 20 May. The result was a win for Peter Mutharika (Democratic Progressive Party (DPP)) with 36.4 per cent of the vote, followed by Lazarus Chakwera (MCP) with 27.8 per cent and Joyce Banda with 20.2 per cent. Mr Mutharika is the younger brother of former president, Bingu wa Mutharika, who died in office in 2012. Peter Mutharika was later accused of an attempted coup when he asked the army to take over after the death of his brother. His treason trial is unlikely to be held since he now holds presidential immunity. Mr Mutharika was inaugurated on 2 June; former president, Joyce Banda, did not attend the ceremony, saying she had not been invited.

2015 Former army chief, Gen Henry Odillo, was arrested on 12 May over a multi-million dollar corruption allegation. He and his former deputy, Lt Col Clement Kafuwa, were accused of arranging a contract to supply military equipment which was never delivered. In October the opposition MCP called for the President to answer questions before Parliament.

Political structure

Constitution

The constitution dates from 1966. A multi-party political system was adopted in 1994.

Malawi is divided into 24 administrative divisions.

Form of state

Republic

The executive

The president is both the head of state and the head of government. The president names the 36-member Cabinet and is elected by popular vote for a five-year term.

National legislature

The unicameral 193-member National Assembly is elected by popular vote to serve a five-year term.

Legal system

The legal system is based on English common law.

Last elections

20 May 2014 (presidential and parliamentary)

Results: Presidential (2014): Prof Peter Mutharika (Democratic Progressive Party (DPP)) won with 36.4 per cent of the vote, followed by Lazarus Chakwera (MCP) with 27.8 per cent, Joyce Banda (PP) with 20.2 per cent and Atupele Muluzi (UDF) with 13.7 per cent. 8 other candidates failed to poll above 0.5 per cent. Turnout was 70.7 per cent.

Parliamentary (2014): the Democratic Progressive Party (DPP) won 21.98 per cent and 51 seats (out of 193), the Malawi Congress Party (MCP) 17.37 per cent and 48 seats, People's Party 18.15 per cent and 26 seats, United Democratic Front (UDF) 9.63 per cent and 14 seats, Alliance for Democracy 0.62 per cent and 1 seat, Chipani cha Pfuko 0.20 per cent and 1 seat and independents 29.68 per cent and 52 seats. Turnout was 70.25 per cent.

Next elections

2019 (presidential and parliamentary)

Political parties

Ruling party

Democratic Progressive Party (DPP)

Main opposition party

United Democratic Front (UDF) and the Malawi Congress Party (MCP)

Population

17.11 million (2013)

Last census: 5 June 2008: 13,066,320 (provisional)

Population density: 87 inhabitants per square km.Urban population 20 per cent (2010 Unicef).

Annual growth rate: 2.2 per cent, 1990–2010 (Unicef).

Ethnic make-up

Chewa (60 per cent), Lomwe (18 per cent), Yao (13 per cent), Ngoni (7 per cent).

Religions

Christianity (80 per cent), Islam (13 per cent), traditional beliefs (7 per cent).

Education

Primary education lasts for eight years. Junior secondary school follows, and if successful, students may progress to the senior secondary school, of which each stage lasts for two years. Instruction is given in English.

Educational attainment, defined as completion of standard eight (at the end of primary school), is only 11.2 per cent. While education is free, provision has not kept up with demand. In some rural areas children have to walk up to 13km to the nearest school. The government's decision to provide free primary education has brought a crisis in the system, placing severe restrictions on its education budget. Secondary schools have less than half the teachers they need and about two-thirds of these are not trained to teach at secondary level. The government proposes to convert Malawi Distance Education Centres (DECs) into Community Day Secondary Schools (CDSS) in order to alleviate the shortage of secondary school teachers.

The University of Malawi typically has approximately 3,000 students, with roughly 1,000 new enrolments every year.

Literacy rate: 62 per cent adult rate; 73 per cent youth rate (15–24) (Unesco 2005).

Compulsory years: 5 to 13.

Enrolment rate: 134 per cent gross primary enrolment, of relevant age group (including repeaters); 29 per cent gross secondary enrolment (World Bank).

Pupils per teacher: 59 in primary schools; in some classes the ratio has increased to 96:1 due to Aids related illness among teachers.

Health

Malaria is endemic; around four million new cases are reported each year. Malaria accounts for 18 per cent of all hospital deaths and 40 per cent of all outpatients visits. A programme to reduce the effect of the disease includes the provision of insecticide treated nets, more access to prompt treatment for children and increased availability of insulin potentiation therapy for pregnant women.

Malawi experienced a severe drought and locust plagues in 2004–05 that left in 2005, over 4.6 million people short of food. The UK has provided around US$18 million in food aid and in September 2005 announced it will provide an extra £5 million (US$9.1 million) to feed those affected by food shortages. The aid will provide 60,000 tonnes of maize from South Africa, and funds for Unicef to feed 3,500 severely malnourished children as well as subsidies for farmers to buy high-yield maize seed for next year's harvest.

Both the president and the UN World Food Programme have declared Malawi, to be in crisis. Funds required for food-aid are put at US$88 million but only US$28 million, has been pledged by international donors.

HIV/Aids

There were over one million children and adults infected, of which over 50 per cent are females (2005).

With the most productive section of the population at the highest risk from HIV infection in one of Africa's poorest countries, there is concern at the long-term effect on the country's political stability, social cohesion and economic growth.

Women, are the country's subsistence farmers, have been hard hit by the disease, which has had a catastrophic impact on agricultural output. It has been estimated that between a quarter and a half of civil servants may die from Aids by 2010, and the government's ability to implement health policies will be severely hampered in coming years.

Aids is the leading cause of death for those aged 20–49, with an estimated 50,000–70,000 adult and child deaths annually, and has left thousands of child-led households. Up to 70 per cent of hospital beds are occupied by patients who are HIV positive. The growing impact of Aids related deaths has driven up the state's health spending on the army and civil service by an estimated 50 per cent, diminishing the amount available to other section of the population.

In 2004 long-term funding was provided, by international donors, to provide more health workers, disease control, HIV testing, mother-to-child infection reduction and to dispense free antiretroviral drugs to HIV/Aids sufferers. Foreign donors had suspended aid funding in 2001 due to corruption and mismanagement and new funding is offered with the proviso of independent vetting.

HIV prevalence: 15 per cent of 15–49 year olds; 8.4 per cent national prevalence and 24 per cent females of reproductive age (The Global Fund).

Life expectancy: 41 years, 2004 (WHO 2006)

Fertility rate/Maternal mortality rate: 6.0 births per woman, 2010 (Unicef)

Child (under 5 years) mortality rate (per 1,000): 71 per 1,000 live births (WHO 2012)

Head of population per physician: 0.02 physicians per 1,000 people, 2004 (WHO 2006)

Welfare

Around 65 per cent of the population lives below the poverty line and deaths from Aids has killed many family breadwinners, fractured families and left communities vulnerable to social disintegration.

In 2002, the government launched a Poverty Reduction Strategy Paper (PRSP) to gain unqualified relief on its US$2.5 billion foreign debt under the controversial Highly Indebted Poor Countries (HIPC) initiative. Malawi launched its war on poverty at a time when the country was facing a severe food shortage. Two subsequent years of poor harvests and a drought in 2005 increased food shortages and threatens millions of people with starvation.

Main cities

Lilongwe (capital, estimated population 781,538 in 2012), Blantyre (728,285), Mzuzu (148,754), Zomba (96,460), Kasungu (51,082).

Languages spoken

English is the primary language in business. Chewa (or Chichewa, literally, language of the Chewa) is the major national language; Nyanja, Yao and Tumbuka are also spoken.

Official language/s

English

Media

Press

The government has a range of among others, libel laws, to curb journalists and newspapers from publishing hostile stories.

In English, there are two daily newspapers *The Nation* (www.nationmw.net) and *The Daily Times* (www.dailytimes.bppmw.com), which is owned by Blantyre Newspapers Limited, which also publishes the weekly *Sunday News* (ww.sundaytimes.bppmw.com) and *Malawi News* (www.malawinews.bppmw.com). In Chichewa, *Boma Lathu* is a monthly publication.

Broadcasting

The Malawi Broadcasting Corporation (MBC) operates the state-owned, public radio and television services.

Radio: Radio services are the main medium of mass communication and sources of news and information for most of the population.

MBC operates two national, radio stations, Radio One and Radio 2FM. Private, national networks include, Star FM (www.starradiomw.com), Power 101 and Capital Radio Malawi (www.capitalradiomalawi.com). Radio Maria Malawi (www.radiomaria.mw) is operated by the Catholic Church.

Television: MBC operates TV Malawi (www.tvmalawi.com), which is the only domestic TV channel. It transmits programmes over 24 hours and broadcasting via satellite signals.

National news agency: Mana (Malawi News Agency): www.malawi.gov.mw/information1/malawi_News_Agency.htm

Other news agencies: APA: www.apanews.net

Panapress: www.panapress.com

Reuters Africa: http://africa.reuters.com

Economy

The country's economy is heavily dependent on agriculture for around 30 per cent of gross domestic production (GDP) and 80 per cent of all exports. The sector also contributes around 64 per cent of total rural income as almost 90 per cent of the population are engaged in subsistence farming. This means, however, that Malawi is vulnerable to external shocks due to volatile global commodity prices as well as adverse weather conditions. Tobacco, tea and sugar are the principal cash crops and uranium is the main mineral exported.

Malawi's major exports consist predominantly of primary goods, such as tobacco, which constitutes 80 per cent of the agricultural output of the nation. However, with globalisation, opportunities for exports of processed products have emerged. Nevertheless, the country has not yet re-positioned itself to exploit opportunities to integrate into global value chains (GVCs). Obstacles to integration into GVCs include poor infrastructure, low skills and a weak business climate. The government is implementing the national export strategy with a view to enhancing export competitiveness and promoting exports of processed agro-products to feed into regional and global value chains.

GDP growth in 2014 was 5.7 per cent, which is predicted to fall to 5.5 per cent in 2015. Malawi experienced devastating floods at the start of 2015, with over a quarter of a million people affected. The United Nations reported that as much as 230,000 citizens have been left unable to return to their homes. According to Unicef, 64,000 hectares of land were left damaged, yet only half of one per cent of arable lands were affected by the floods.

As most of Malawi's economy is heavily agro-based it is fortunate that the forecasted dip in growth is set to be less severe than its potential, with growth likely to slow to 5.5 per cent in 2015. An assessment by the President in February 2015, showed that the damage caused by the flood disaster was estimated to have been 23.9 billion kwacha, excluding the cost of the relief program.

The discovery of a large theft of public funds in October 2013, colloquially known as 'Cashgate', damaged the reputation of the government and fiscal manoeuvrability. An estimated US$100 million had mysteriously disappeared from government funds. Since the scandal, progress has occurred in the implementation of a short-term plan adopted in the aftermath of the scandal, aimed at securing co-ordinated prosecutions. However, the scandal has significantly hindered Malawi's economic progress. The International Monetary Fund (IMF) has since helped via an extended arrangement, which has disbursed 52.06 million SDR to assist the economy.

High transport costs for this landlocked country can represent around 50 per cent of its import bill, impeding economic development and trade. There are few exploitable mineral resources (except for uranium, which is profitable but has a limited and controlled market). Industry accounts for over 20 per cent of GDP (of which manufacturing represents 15 per cent) and the service sector 45 per cent. Structural adjustments have not yet led to an increase in private domestic savings, which have diminished partly due to the HIV/Aids pandemic. Wealth is concentrated within a small elite.

Malawi was ranked 174 (out of 187) in the UN Human Development Index (HDI) in 2014. Of its population of just under 14 million, 52.8 per cent experience multiple deprivations in the same household.

Malawi met the Heavily Indebted Poor Countries (HIPC) completion point in 2006 and became eligible for further relief.

Malawi's creditors allowed debt relief of US$646 million under the enhanced HIPC initiative, an amount equivalent to US$3.1 billion in nominal terms of actual dollar value over a period of time. The IMF believes this initiative will save an average of US$50 million per year in debt service payments by 2020, an amount equivalent to around 2.5 per cent of annual GDP for 2001–09 and 1.2 per cent of annual GDP for the period 2010–20. The country's annual service payments on outstanding debt are estimated to average US$5 million (2005–25).

On 7 June 2012, the IMF announced that it would lend Malawi US$157 million, following reforms introduced by President Banda in May. This loan was offered days after the UK resumed its aid package with £33 million (US$51 million).

According to the IMF, the run up to the parliamentary and presidential elections of May 2014 left further governance concerns and left macroeconomic policies adrift. This resulted in further suspension of donor budget support and, as a result, increased recourse to domestic financing, monetization of the deficit and waning of confidence. The current account deteriorated in 2014, mainly reflecting the large drop in official transfers. As a result the current account deficit widened by 31 per cent to 5.1 percent of GDP and the exchange rate depreciated by 15 percent over 2014.

External trade

Malawi was one of the founding members of the Common Market of Eastern and Southern Africa (Comesa), which operates a free trade area (FTA) with eight out of the 20 Comesa members and a customs union (CU), which was launched in June 2009, with common external tariffs. Malawi is also a member of the Southern African Development Community (SADC), the objectives of which include reducing trade barriers, achieving regional development and economic growth and evolving common systems and institutions.

Malawi's major exports are tobacco (newly industrialising countries are increasingly important destinations for tobacco) and tea, which are susceptible to external shocks such as droughts and fluctuating world prices.

In April 2009 international donors pledged US$1 billion to upgrade transport links across eastern and southern Africa, in an initiative to speed up and reduce the cost of carrying goods to market. Not only will roads and rail links be improved, but also time-consuming official procedures will be streamlined for efficiency.

Imports

Principal imports are petroleum, food, products, semi-manufactures, consumer goods, transportation equipment and vehicles.

Main sources: South Africa (26.2 per cent of total in 2014), India (15.5 per cent), China (10 per cent), Zambia (9.8 per cent) and Tanzania (5.4 per cent).

Exports

Principal exports are tobacco (53 per cent), tea, sugar, cotton, coffee, peanuts, wood products and garments.

Main destinations: Belgium (12.4 per cent of total in 2014), Zimbabwe (10.4 per cent), South Africa (6.8 per cent), Germany (6.8 per cent), Russia (6.6 per cent), Canada (6.1 per cent) and the US (6 per cent).

Agriculture

Farming

The agricultural sector is an important sector of the economy, accounting for 30.1 per cent of GDP in 2014 and employing over 90 per cent of the workforce. The sector consists of two modes of production: smallholders, growing mainly food crops such as maize and groundnuts but also tobacco, and estate farmers, growing cash crops for export. Tobacco is important for the short-term growth of the economy as it accounts for over half of the country's exports. Other food crops include cassava, millet, sorghum and rice. Tobacco production generates 53 per cent of the country's exports.

Formerly a food exporter, Malawi has become a net importer due to the rising population, adverse weather conditions (especially drought), a decline in farming subsidies and smallholders switching to tobacco as their preferred crop.

In the long term, the country needs more investment in food production. Much of the investment in agriculture in the past has been directed at improving export-oriented production, while food production has been neglected.

Donors have been reluctant to give aid for investment due to the lack of transparency in previous years. The government and donor agencies will need to work together to ensure a more even pattern of investment in farming.

Fishing

Malawi has the western and southern shores of Lake Malawi, one of the world's largest lakes. The fishing industry is an important sector, providing much needed protein. Production can vary between 50–65,000 tonnes per year although catches have been falling since 1990 and as a consequence, fish imports have increased.

Catch from the lake is estimated to provide 20 per cent of the protein requirement for Malawi's population, with some 1.7 million Malawians relying 'exclusively', according to the Co-ordination Union for Rehabilitation of the Environment (CURE) NGO, on the lake. Tanzanians and Mozambicans also derive livelihoods from the lake.

A combination of overfishing and the use of illegal fishing gear has seen fish stocks in Lake Malawi dwindle to the point that local people's livelihoods and food security are now under threat. Fish stocks in Lake Malawi, the third largest lake in Africa, declined by up to 93 percent between 1990 and 2010 and, based on reports from locals, the situation appears to have deteriorated further since then. The reduction of fish stocks are threatening the livelihoods of about 60,000 Malawians directly employed as fishermen and a further 350,000 who are involved in fish processing, fish marketing, net making, boat building and engine repair, according to the Department of Fisheries. There are concerns that oil exploration activities by Tanzania in their section of the lake will damage the fishing industry before a comprehensive legislative regulatory framework can be installed.

Forestry

Around 35 per cent of Malawi's land area is forested and there are significant areas of plantation forests. There are nine national parks and game reserves and a large number of forest reserves, which provide varying levels of protection against deforestation. However, during 1990–2000, forest cover disappeared at a rate of 2.41 per cent per year, one of the highest rates of deforestation in the world. This is largely due to the use of wood as fuel for domestic and industrial uses. The increased emphasis upon the tobacco industry is to the detriment of increased deforestation within the area. About 15 per cent of Malawian tobacco is flue-cured, a process that burns a large amount of wood. Policies have been aimed towards afforestation, yet only 90 per cent of the seedlings have proved to survive.

Industry and manufacturing

The industrial sector contributes around 18.5 per cent to GDP and employs around 10 per cent of the workforce. The industrial sector is centred on agro-processing.

The major constraints on growth are the country's relatively limited resource base, small domestic market and difficulties in importing raw materials and intermediate goods.

The industrial production growth rate fell by 1.7 per cent in 2014.

Tourism

Malawi offers traditional African culture in a relatively unspoiled landscape, with wildlife and the scenery being the principal draw for visitors. There are two sites included on Unesco's World Heritage List, the ancient Chongoni rock-art area and Lake Malawi National Park. Tourism has grown in importance as part of the economy, particularly as a vital source of foreign exchange and employment.

Travel and tourism, in total, contributed an average 8.9 per cent to GDP in 2013 and was forecasted to rise by 3.7 per cent in 2014. The total contribution to employment, including jobs indirectly supported by the industry, was 7.6 per cent of total employment in 2013.

Mining

The mining sector is underdeveloped, but has potential in the extraction of heavy mineral sand, bauxite, phosphate, uranium and rare earth elements.

There are three heavy mineral sand deposits with considerable titanium resources: Tengani with over 100 million tonnes of heavy minerals, Mpyukyu/Kachulu with over four million tonnes of ilmenite, 300,000 tonnes of zircon and 10,000 tonnes of rutile and beach deposits along the shores of Lake Malawi.

The Australian owned Kayelekera uranium deposits has reserves of 11,000 tonnes of uranium ore at 0.16 per cent grade. The mines' total capital costs are estimated at up to US$65 million, while the revenue from the mine's 10-year lifespan is estimated to average between US$30–34 million per year.

Hydrocarbons

There are no known oil or natural gas reserves. Consumption was 13,040 barrels per day of oil in 2013, all of which was imported. Most of the country's fuel imports are supplied via Tanzanian and South African ports and delivered by tanker.

Mining contributes less than 1 per cent to Malawi's GDP as of 2015.

Any imported natural gas is used exclusively in the Blantyre power plant.

There are very small coal reserves; the main coal mine in Mchenga produces around 60,000 tonnes per annum of bituminous or brown coal, typically used in power stations.

Energy

Total installed generating capacity of electricity was 301,000 kW in 2011.

Over 90 per cent of all generation is provided by hydropower, of which the majority of plants are concentrated on the Shire River in the south of the country; a mini-hydro plant (4.5MW) exists on the Wovme River in the north. Thermal power plants are used as back-up for hydro plants. Less than 10 per cent of the population has access to electricity, the majority of which live in urban areas. The majority of the population relies on non-commercial biomass, mostly fuel wood, for cooking, lighting and power, which has led to deforestation. A planting programme was implemented to replace dwindling resources with shortages becoming acute in the southern region. As oil prices rise there is a corresponding increased pressure on wood resources.

The parastatal, Electricity Supply Corporation of Malawi (Escom), is responsible for generation, transmission, distribution and sale of electricity. Malawi is a member of the Southern African Development Community (SADC) and the Southern African Power Pool (Sapp), set up to provide reliable and economical energy supplies to all 12 members in the region. Imports of energy come from Tanzania and Mozambique.

Financial markets

Stock exchange

Malawi Stock Exchange (MSE)

Banking and insurance

The banking system is underdeveloped and the vast majority of lending is to the government and parastatals. There is little lending to private individuals. There are five commercial banks in operation in Malawi. Although the sector is open to foreign participation, few foreign banks have shown an interest in establishing operations in Malawi.

The commercial bank prime-lending rate of 29.5 per cent gives it a global rank of 4. The exchange rate between the Kwacha and the US dollar was 412.1 in 2014.

Central bank

Reserve Bank of Malawi

Main financial centre

Blantyre and Lilongwe

Time

GMT plus two hours

Geography

Malawi is a landlocked country in southern central Africa, with Zambia to the west, Mozambique to the south and east, and Tanzania to the north.

A fifth of the country is covered by lakes, including one of the largest in Africa, the 580km-long Lake Malawi (formerly Lake Nyasa), which borders on Tanzania and Mozambique. The lake is situated in the north-south Rift Valley and is drained by the Shire river, which flows south to meet the Zambezi in Mozambique. The terrain beyond the Rift Valley comprises plateaux and mountains, ranging from 1,000m to 3,000m high, with lower-lying land in the south. There are forests in the northern mountain areas. The Mulanje Massif, at 3,002m (Sapitwa Peak) the highest point in Malawi and central Africa, lies in the southern area, near Blantyre.

Hemisphere

Southern

Climate

On the shores of Lake Malawi and upper Shire River, the weather is pleasantly warm most of the year, hotter in the rainy season. It is more temperate in the highlands and on the plateaux, with cool nights all year. Around the lower Shire River and the south, it is more tropical and very hot during the rains.

The May–August period is cool and dry (the *Chiperoni* wind can be chilly during July and August). The hottest months are

September–November. The rainy season is November–April.

Dress codes

There are no restrictive dress codes and resort wear is informal. Travellers are advised to respect local sensibilities, especially when visiting remote areas. Formal attire is usual for business.

Entry requirements

Passports

Required by all, valid for six months beyond date of departure.

Visa

Required by all, except nationals of most EU and Commonwealth countries, Japan and US. For further details contact the nearest consulate. A proposed tourist *univisa* (a single visa to visit all 15-member states of SADC: Angola, Botswana, DRC, Lesotho, Madagascar, Malawi, Mauritius, Mozambique, Namibia, South Africa, Seychelles, Swaziland, Tanzania, Zambia and Zimbabwe) is expected to be in use by 2013. Visitors should check with the appropriate consulates to confirm start of *univisas* and their scope before beginning a tour of southern Africa.

All travellers must have return/onward passage.

Currency advice/regulations

There are no restrictions on the import of local currency, but export is limited to K200. There are no restrictions on the import of foreign currency, subject to declaration, and export is limited to the amount declared on arrival.

Travellers cheques and all major currencies are accepted by banks, authorised hotels and other institutions. Recommended travellers cheques are South African rand, UK sterling, euros and US dollars.

Health (for visitors)

Healthcare and facilities are basic and expatriate residents usually travel to South Africa when in need of anything but the most straightforward medical care. Medical insurance including emergency evacuation should be arranged prior to travel.

Mandatory precautions

Yellow fever vaccination certificate is required if arriving from an infected area.

Advisable precautions

Typhoid, polio, tetanus and hepatitis A vaccinations. HIV/Aids is endemic and precautions must be taken. Take malaria prophylactics and use mosquito nets at night when provided, as well as insect repellents, especially in lower-lying areas. Cholera and rabies are a risk in some areas; vaccinations are only recommended for those at particularly high risk. Bilharzia is an increasing problem, visitors should only swim in designated areas or in swimming pools.

Although tap water is safe to drink in Lilongwe, Blantyre, Limbe and Zomba, water should be boiled or purifying tablets used in rural areas.

It is advisable to carry a sterile first aid kit including syringes, as well as any prescribed medicines.

Hotels

Good hotels available in all main commercial centres. However, space can be limited so reservations should be made well in advance and a booking confirmation obtained. A 10 per cent service charge and government tax are added to bills, and a small tip is occasionally expected.

Credit cards

Credit cards are accepted in major hotels, restaurants and car hire companies in Blantyre and Lilongwe.

Public holidays (national)

Fixed dates

1 Jan (New Year's Day), 15 Jan (John Chilembwe Day), 3 Mar (Martyrs' Day), 1 May (Labour Day), 14 Jun (Freedom Day), 6 Jul (Republic Day), 25–26 Dec (Christmas).

If a public holiday falls on a Saturday, the preceding day will be a holiday; if on a Sunday, the next day will be a holiday.

Variable dates

Easter, Mothers' Day (second Mon in Oct), Arbor Day (second Mon in Dec).

Working hours

Banking

Mon–Fri: 0800–1400.

Business

Mon–Fri: 0730–1700, with one-hour lunch break 1200–1300.

Government

Mon–Fri: 0730–1700, with one-hour lunch break 1200–1300.

Shops

Mon–Fri: 0800–1700; Sat: 0800–1200.

Telecommunications

Telephone/fax

The telephone system is poor.

Mobile/cell phones

GSM 900 services are available throughout much of the country.

Electricity supply

230V/50Hz.

Security

Normal precautions should be taken. Travel after nightfall should be avoided.

Getting there

Air

National airline: Air Malawi.

International airport/s:

Lilongwe-Kamuzu International (LLW), 26km north of the city; bars, restaurants, bank, post office, shops, car hire.

Airport tax: US$30, paid in US dollars.

Surface

The lake-ship-road-rail Northern Corridor route to Dar es Salaam (Tanzania) carries half of Malawi's fuel imports. It has the potential capacity to carry up to two-thirds of foreign freight.

Road: Road border points with Zambia, Mozambique and Tanzania open 0600—1800. To bring a vehicle into Malawi, either a *carnet de passage* is required, or a temporary import permit (TIP) which can be obtained at border posts for a small fee. There are two main routes from Zambia: via Chipata on the Lilongwe to Lusaka road and, further north, via Chitipa on the Karonga to Nakonde road. Entry from Tanzania is via the Songwe river bridge, north of Kaporo. Roads also link with Mozambique.

Rail: Link with Nacala (Mozambique), but capacity is severely limited by poor track condition.

Getting about

National transport

Air: Air Malawi flies regular services linking Lilongwe, Blantyre, Mzuzu, Karonga, Nyika National Park and the southern lakeshore. There are also charter services to several locations.

Road: There are around 28,000km of roads with major highways linking main centres. The standard of the surfaces is variable and can be poor.

Buses: The bus network covers most of the country. Luxury coaches operate on the Blantyre-Zomba-Lilongwe route.

Rail: There is a limited rail network, largely used for freight. Passenger services are slow and crowded and not suitable for tourists.

Water: A passenger ferry boat operates on Lake Malawi travelling between Monkey Bay in the south and Chilumba in the north, stopping regularly in between. The round trip operates weekly.

City transport

Taxis: Taxis operate in the main towns, but are scarce. Fares should be agreed in advance of journey.

Buses, trams & metro: There are regular bus services in and between the main centres, including luxury services between Lilongwe and Blantyre and Lilongwe and Mzuzu.

Car hire

Car hire is available in main cities. Demand is high so cars should be booked in advance. Self-drive cars are hired at a daily rate, which includes the first 40km. A full international driver's licence is required and a minimum age of 25 with two years' driving experience. Seat belts must be worn in the front seats. Traffic drives on the left. General speed limit of 80kph, and 60kph in urban areas.

Chauffeurs charge a daily rate plus overtime after 1600 and at lunch-time.

BUSINESS DIRECTORY

The addresses listed below are a selection only. While World of Information makes every endeavour to check these addresses, we cannot guarantee that changes have not been made, especially to telephone numbers and area codes. We would welcome any corrections.

Telephone area codes

The international direct dialling code (IDD) for Malawi is +265, followed by the subscriber's number.

Useful telephone numbers

International operator: 102
Domestic operator: 0
Directory enquiries: 191
Emergencies (Blantyre, Lilongwe): 199

Chambers of Commerce

Central Region Chamber of Commerce, PO Box 31357, Lilongwe (tel: 1759-593; fax: 1758-982; e-mail: crcci@sdnp.org.mw).

Malawi Confederation of Chambers of Commerce and Industry, Masauko Chipembere Highway, Chichiri Trade Fair Grounds, PO Box 258, Blantyre (tel: 1671-988; fax:1671-147; e-mail: mcci@eomw.net).

Northern Region Chamber of Commerce, Private Bag 135, Mzuzu (tel: 3133-415; fax: 1334-619; e-mail: nrcci@sdnp.org.mw).

Southern Region Chamber of Commerce, PO Box 258, Blantyre (tel/fax: 1675-113; e-mail: srcci@sdnp.org.mw).

Banking

CBM Financial Services Limited, PO Box 2619, Victoria Avenue, Blantyre (tel: 1621-280; fax: 1624-525).

Stanbic Malawi, PO Box 1111, Capital City, Blantyre (tel: 6120-144; fax: 1620-117).

Finance Bank of Malawi, PO Box 421, Finance House, Victoria Avenue, Blantyre (tel: 1624-799; fax: 1622-957; email: makhan@malawi.net).

First Merchant Bank Limited, PO Box 122, First House, Glyn Jones Road, Blantyre (tel: 1622-787; fax: 1621-978).

Investment & Development Bank of Malawi, PO Box 358, Indebank House, Kaushong Road, Top Mandala, Blantyre (tel: 1620-055; fax: 1623-353).

Loita Investment Bank Ltd, Loita House, Victoria Avenue; Private Bag 389, Chichiri, Blantyre 3 (fax: 1622-683).

Malawi Savings Bank, PO Box 521, Umoyo House, Blantyre (tel: 1625-111 fax: 1621-929).

National Bank of Malawi, PO Box 945, Victoria Avenue, Blantyre (tel: 1620-622; fax: 1620-464).

Central bank

Reserve Bank of Malawi, Convention Drive, City Centre, PO Box 30063, Lilongwe 3 (tel: 1770-600; fax:1 772-752; e-mail: webmaster@rbm.mw).

Stock exchange

Malawi Stock Exchange (MSE), www.mse.co.mw

Travel information

Air Malawi, PO Box 84,4 Robins Road, Blantyre (tel: 1820-811; fax: 1820-042; e-mail: it@airmalawi.net).

Malawi Railways, PO Box 5492, Limbe (tel: 1640-844; fax: 1640-683).

Ministry of tourism

Ministry of Information and Tourism, Tourism House, Convention Drive, PO Box 326, Lilongwe (tel: 1775-499; fax: 1770-650; e-mail: psinfo@sdnp.org).

National tourist organisation offices

Malawi Tourism Association, Aquarius House, PO Box 1044, Lilongwe (tel: 1770-010; fax: 1770-131; e-mail: mta@malawi.net).

Ministries

Ministry of Economic Planning and Development, PO Box 30136, Capital City, Lilongwe 3 (tel: 1782-300; fax: 1782-224).

Ministry of Energy and Mining, Private Bag 309, Lilongwe 3 (tel: 1784-178; fax: 1784-236).

Ministry of Lands and Valuation, Tikwere House, Private Bag 311, Lilongwe 3 (tel: 1780-755; fax: 1780-727).

Ministry of Physical Planning and Surveys, PO Box 30385, Capital City, Lilongwe 3 (tel: 1784-655).

Ministry of Trade and Industry, PO Box 30366, Lilongwe 3 (tel: 1732-711; fax: 1732-551).

Other useful addresses

Agricultural Development & Marketing Corporation (ADMARC), PO Box 50512, Limbe (tel: 1640-500; fax: 1640-486).

Civil Service Commission, PO Box 30133, Capital City, Lilongwe 3 (tel: 1783-811).

Electricity Supply Commission of Malawi, PO Box 2047, Blantyre (tel: 1622-000; fax: 1622-008).

European Development Fund, Lingadzi House, PO Box 30102, Lilongwe 3 (tel: 1730-255).

Geological Survey Department, PO Box 27, Zomba (tel: 1522-166; fax: 1522-716).

Immigration Office, PO Box 331, Blantyre (tel: 1623-777; fax: 1623-065).

Malawi Broadcasting Corporation, PO Box 30133, Chichiri, Blantyre 3 (tel: 1671-222; fax: 1671-257).

Malawi Bureau of Standards, PO Box 946, Blantyre (tel: 1670-488; fax: 1670-756).

Malawi Development Corporation, Development House, PO Box 566, Blantyre (tel: 1620-100; fax: 1620-584).

Malawi Embassy (USA), 2408 Massachusetts Avenue, NW, Washington DC 20008 (tel: (+1-202)-797-1007; fax: (+1-202)-265-0976; e-mail: embassy@malawi.org).

Malawi Export Promotion Council, Delamere House, Victoria Avenue, PO Box 1299, Blantyre (tel: 1620-499).

Malawi Investment Promotion Agency, Private Bag 302, Lilongwe 3 (tel: 1780-800; fax: 1781-781).

Malawi Iron and Steel Corporation, PO Box 2165, Blantyre (tel: 671-455).

National Statistical Office, PO Box 333, Zomba (tel: 1522-377; fax: 1523-130).

Registrar General's Department (Companies etc), Private Bag 100, Blantyre (tel: 1635-077; fax: 1640-877).

United Nations Development Programme, Resident Representative, PO Box 30135, Capital City, Lilongwe 3 (tel: 1783-500; fax: 1783-637).

National news agency: Mana (Malawi News Agency): www.malawi.gov.mw/information1/malawi_News_Agency.htm

APA: www.apanews.net

Panapress: www.panapress.com

Reuters Africa: http://africa.reuters.com

Internet sites

Africa Business Network: http://www.ifc.org/abn

AllAfrica.com: http://allafrica.com

African Development Bank: http://www.afdb.org

Africa Online: http://www.africaonline.com

MalawiBiz.com: http://www.malawibiz.com/complist.html

Mbendi AfroPaedia (information on companies, countries, industries and stock exchanges in Africa): http://mbendi.co.za

Malaysia

KEY FACTS

Official name: Persekutuan Tanah Malaysia (Federation of Malaysia)

Head of State: Yang di Pertuan Agong (traditional ruler) Tuanku Abdul Halim Muadzam Shah ibni al Marhum Sultan Badlishah (from 13 Dec 2011)

Head of government: Datuk Sri Mohamed Najib bin Tun Haji Abdul Razak (UNMO) (appointed 3 Apr 2009)

Ruling party: Barisan Nasional (BN) (National Front) multi-racial coalition of 13 parties, led by Pertubuhan Kebangsaan Melayu Bersatu (United Malays National Organisation) (UMNO) (re-elected 5 May 2013)

Area: 330,434 square km

Population: 30.26 million (2014) (28,334,135; 2010, census figure)

Capital: Kuala Lumpur; Putrajaya (administrative capital)

Official language: Bahasa Malaysia

Currency: Ringgit (also known as Malaysian dollar) (M$) = 100 sen

Exchange rate: M$4.34 per US$ (Sep 2015)

GDP per capita: US$10,804 (2014)

GDP real growth: 6.02% (2014)

GDP: US$326.93 billion (2014)

Labour force: 12.90 million (2012)*

Unemployment: 2.90% (2014)

Inflation: 3.14% (2014)

Oil production: 666,000 bpd (2014)

Natural gas production: 66.40 billion cum (2014)

Balance of trade: US$32.49 billion (2013)

Annual FDI: US$10.80 billion (2011)

* estimated figure

For this well endowed nation of 30 million people 2014 and 2015 were not the best of times. The national airline, Malaysia Airlines, heavily subsidised to enable it boost the country's image and its tourism, lost not one, but two, large passenger jets in a period of four months. In March 2014 Malaysia Airlines flight MH370 from Kuala Lumpur to Beijing simply disappeared with 239 passengers and crew aboard. (In mid-2015 pieces of wreckage were found on the island of Réunion in the western Indian Ocean.) Four months later, in September 2014, flight MH17 flying from Amsterdam to Kuala Lumpur was shot down over eastern Ukraine, allegedly by a Russian fired missile. All 298 passengers and crew perished. The incidents put Malaysia on the map for all the wrong reasons – the government's handling of the disappearance of the first jet was inept. At least the same could not be said of the second loss.

Scandalous?

Since his appointment as prime minister in 2009, Dato' Sri Mohammad Najib bin Tun Haji Abdul Razak, (Mr Najib or Najib Razak, the son of Malaysia's second prime minister, Abdul Razak Hussein, and nephew of its third, Hussein Onn) had projected an image of modest self confidence. However, both the image and the persona were under severe pressure in August 2015 when a mass street protest under the name *Bersih* (Literally, 'clean') was being organised by an indignant population on the Prime Minster's admission that he had received the sum of US$700 million into his private bank account. Mr Razak was adamant that in receiving the money, which he claimed had been sent from a Middle Eastern donor, he had not broken the law. This account appeared not to be the whole truth; in failing to explain the purpose of the money, the Prime Minister had been perceived to be 'economic with the truth' – according to *The Wall Street Journal* and the *Sarawak Report* blog. Their reports alleged that the money might have been provided by Malaysian companies and banks to bail out the Prime Minister's pet project – 1Malaysia Development Berhad (1MDB), which was reported by the London *Financial Times* to be some US$11 billion in debt following a series of 'dud' investments in Malaysia and abroad.

In mid-2015 the jury was still out on Malaysia's 'damaged' prime minister. Outside the country, his polished manners and articulate English had enabled him to forge good relationships with a number of heads of state or of governments, notably the US's Barack Obama and UK's David Cameron. On the streets of Kuala Lumpur, however, his track record was judged to be 'dodgy', bordering on corrupt. Najib Razak, a member of parliament for almost 40 years, had become one of Malaysia's most astute and hardened, politicians. On becoming prime minister he managed to tighten his grip on power through a series of manoeuvres aimed at neutering dissent.

Reuters reported a government spokesman as claiming that: 'The attacks on 1MDB began out of political motivation and the ultimate aim is to remove Malaysia's democratically elected government.' The prime minister's fiercest critic was former prime minister, Mahathir Mohamad, who accused Najib Razak of seeking to 'subvert the institutions of government and make them instruments for sustaining himself.'

At the end of July 2015 Najib Razak had deftly outsmarted his critics by sacking Deputy Prime Minister Muhyiddin Yassin (around whom plotters interested in ousting Najib were reported to be gathering) and a number of other ministers, who had publicly questioned him. In a move perceived to simply gain time, Malaysia's attorney general responsible for investigating the affairs of 1MDB had been replaced. For good measure, two Malaysian newspapers had been closed down and internet access to the *Sarawak Report* blocked.

In March 2015, before the matter of the US$700 million had surfaced, the Malaysian authorities had formed a powerful task force led by the previous attorney-general supported by the Malaysian Anti-Corruption Commission (MACC) and the police force, to investigate 1MDB. In August, the MACC announced that the task force had been disbanded.

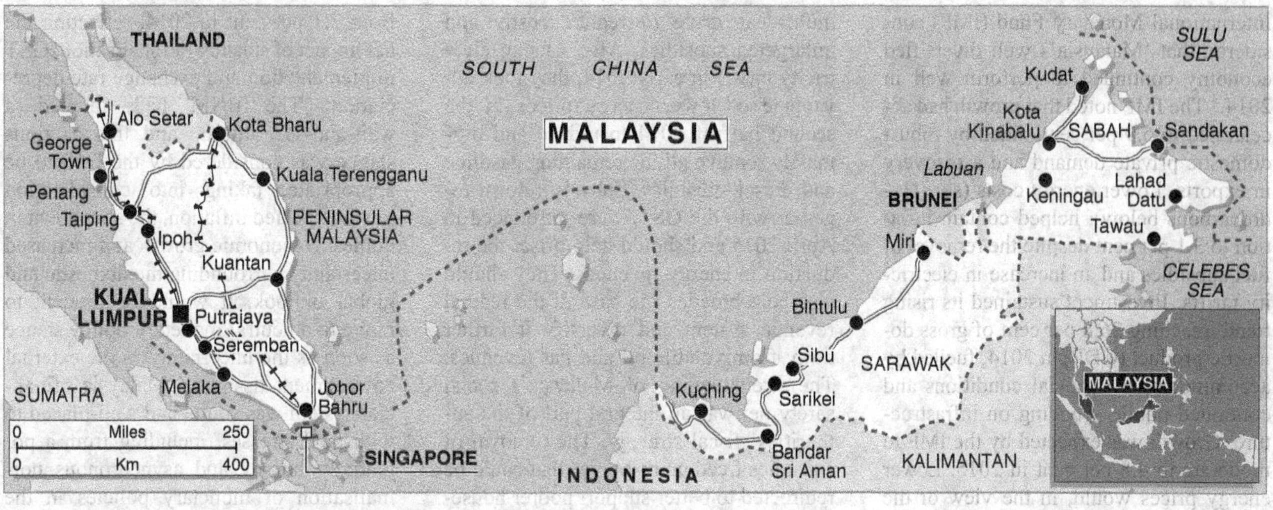

Najib retained significant support from the long-ruling Barisan Nasional (BN) (National Front) coalition and from within his party, United Malays National Organisation (UMNO).But his public support had fallen to 44 per cent in January 2015. It fell further in April 2015 when the proposed repeal of Malaysia's Internal Security Act turned out to be a curtain raiser for a replacement Prevention of Terror Act which gave the government wide ranging powers to arrest and detain without charge or trial. The political climate had been pulled away from the liberalisation once promised by Mr Najib towards something resembling a police state. In its 2014 *Corruption perceptions Index*, the Berlin-based NGO Transparency International ranked Malaysia a miserable 136 out of the 175 countries surveyed. Neighbouring Singapore came in seventh.

Anwar Ibrahim

The UMNO party, which had been in power since 1957, lost much of its popular vote for the first time in 2013 to the opposition alliance, Pakatan Rakyat, led by former deputy prime minister, Anwar Ibrahim. However, the alliance's success was short-lived as the coalition split in early 2015. Anwar Ibrahim, who represented the biggest (and the only) threat to the ruling coalition, was jailed for five years in February 2015 on sodomy charges, which he said were politically motivated. Later in 2015 Anwar Ibrahim's Parti Keadilan Rakyat (PKR) (People's Justice Party) and the Chinese-based Democratic Action Party (DAP) joined forces with the newly formed Parti Amanah Negara (PAN) (National Trust Party) to form a new coalition – Pakatan Harapan (Alliance of Hope).

Mr Anwar, had once belonged to the ruling BN coalition, but disputes within the party leadership resulted in him being summarily beaten, jailed and disgraced. Not one to give up, Mr Anwar emerged as the leader of the opposition Pakatan Rakyat alliance in the 2013 general election. The three-party coalition represented strongest-ever challenge to the ruling coalition. Although unable to defeat the ruling BN – it at least gave it a bloodied nose, scraping home with 133 of the 222 seats in parliament, its worst election performance. The opposition won 89 seats, seven more than in the previous election.

In March 2014, Mr Anwar's legal difficulties resurfaced, as the courts overturned his earlier acquittal for sodomy in response to a government appeal. Anwar launched a final appeal but the court upheld the original verdict and he was returned to jail.

Human rights activists alleged that the case formed part of a long-running campaign to destroy the former deputy premier. Malaysian law ruled that Anwar had lost his seat in parliament and would be disqualified from participating in the 2018 elections. Human Rights Watch (HRW) called it a 'travesty of justice', saying that 'Prime Minister Najib Razak's government has persisted in its politically motivated prosecution of opposition leader Anwar Ibrahim. Allowing this travesty of justice to stand will further undermine respect for rights and democracy in Malaysia.' Anwar Ibrahim's daughter, Nurul Izzah, a member of parliament was arrested 'on suspicion of sedition' for denouncing her father's arrest.

Rohingas

Called the 'most persecuted minority in the world' many of Myanmar's Rohinga Muslim community had risked travelling in flimsy craft the 1,500 kilometres to the Malaysian coast. The total Rohinga community in Malaysia was thought, in mid-2015, to number as many as 100,000. Quoted in the London *Economist*, the Rohinga's were described by the lobby group 'fortify Rights' as 'a community in hiding'. Malaysia granted them no legal status, unable to work and earn a living. Desperation leads to law-breaking as refugee Rohinga are exploited as domestic servants. Rohinga do not qualify for education or health care. In May 2015 Malaysia (and Indonesia), in response to international pressure, finally agreed to stop turning refugee boats away. An awareness of the demand for cheap labour in Malaysia exposed the Rohinga to people traffickers and employment sharks.

The economy

Although Malaysia has succeeded in reducing its dependence on oil and gas revenues (see: Hydrocarbons below), the black gold continued in 2014 to account for some 30 per cent of government revenues. The figure may have dropped, but the collapse in global oil prices still left something of a hole in Malaysia's finances. At the beginning of 2015 the government cut fuel subsidies and in January 2015 it promised to maintain the budget deficit at 3 per cent, even if that meant cutting expenditure here and there.

However, in mid-2015 Malaysia's economy was in a bad way. The ringitt was hovering at a 17 year low and Kuala Lumpur's stock exchange was on the slide. To cap it all, Malaysia Airlines's newly appointed chief executive had declared the airline 'technically bankrupt', embarking on a restructuring programme that would see the loss of around 6,000 jobs. In its annual report on the Malaysian economy, in February 2015, the

International Monetary Fund (IMF) considered that 'Malaysia's well diversified economy continued to perform well in 2014.' The IMF noted that growth had accelerated to 5.9 per cent, aided by robust domestic private demand and a recovery in exports. Lower energy costs (see: Hydrocarbons below), helped contain inflation to 3.1 per cent despite the removal of fuel subsidies and an increase in electricity tariffs. Investment sustained its rising trend, reaching 26.8 per cent of gross domestic product (GDP) in 2014, fuelled by accommodative financial conditions and continued public spending on infrastructure. Growth was expected by the IMF to moderate to 4.8 per cent in 2015. Lower energy prices would, in the view of the IMF, adversely affect oil and gas production, but should provide a boost to the large non-oil sector. Consumption growth was expected to moderate following the introduction of the goods and services tax (GST), although Malaysia's strong labour market and supportive – albeit gradually tightening – domestic financial conditions and lower energy costs should help consumers.

Malaysia's fiscal consolidation was, in the view of the IMF, well timed, appropriately paced and on track. The Malaysian authorities had revised the federal budget resulting in a slight change of the budget deficit ceiling, to 3.2 per cent from 3.0 per cent of GDP, in a timely and pragmatic response to the sharp decline in international crude oil prices. They took bold fiscal action in 2014, continuing a multi-year drive to reduce costly and untargeted subsidies. After raising electricity tariffs in early 2014, they took advantage of lower energy prices in the second half of 2014 to reduce and ultimately remove all the remaining gasoline and diesel subsidies. Subsidy reform together with the GST, were introduced in April 2015 and should help offset the reduction in energy revenues. They should also help broaden the base of the federal revenue system and diversify it further away from volatile oil and gas revenues. The strengthening of Malaysia's social safety net was an integral part of the authorities' fiscal strategy. The removal of subsidies freed up resources that could be redirected to better support poorer households through better targeted cash transfers. According to the IMF, Malaysia was also making progress in reforming its fiscal institutions. Top-down fiscal management and control were also being strengthened and the size of supplementary budgets had been substantially reduced. These reforms would help reinforce the sustainability of Malaysia's public finances and make the fiscal system more effective in promoting efficiency, equity and growth.

Bank Negara Malaysia (BNM) (central bank) took a step towards normalising monetary conditions in July 2015, but has since paused as the downside risks to growth increased and inflation remained low, while risks to financial stability abated. Headline inflation looked likely to increase slightly, to 3.2 per cent in 2015 from 3.1 per cent in 2014, reflecting the net impact of subsidy rationalisation, GST implementation and exchange rate depreciation. The BNM had adopted a wait-and-see attitude and this cautious stance was considered by the IMF to be appropriate, taking into consideration lower expected inflation, the slowdown in domestic economic growth and increased uncertainty surrounding the domestic and global outlook. It would be prudent to move to a neutral monetary policy stance as soon as the uncertainty in the external environment dissipated. Malaysia's financial system was sound and well-placed to withstand stresses, including from a potentially bumpy and asynchronous normalisation of monetary policies in the advanced economies. In the opinion of the IMF, the high level of household debt together with the large participation of foreign investors in Malaysia's financial markets warranted continued vigilance. The flexible exchange rate system and substantial financial buffers, as well as offsetting action by domestic institutional investors, provided multiple lines of defence against capital flow volatility.

In conclusion, the IMF suggested that Malaysia's favourable domestic economic conditions offered a window of opportunity to continue structural reforms to raise productivity growth by increasing innovation, raising the quality of education, addressing youth unemployment and increasing female labour force participation. Malaysia also stood to benefit from its outward economic orientation and the strengthening of regional economic and financial integration underway, including the creation of the Association of South-east Asian Nations (Asean) Economic Community in 2015 and other trade initiatives. Accelerating the pace of regional integration should help unleash both Malaysia's and Asean's, economic potential.

KEY INDICATORS — Malaysia

	Unit	2011	2012	2013	2014	**2015
Population	m	*28.73	29.34	29.95	30.26	*30.78
Gross domestic product (GDP)	US$bn	278.70	304.73	313.16	326.93	*327.89
GDP per capita	US$	9,700	10,387	10,466	10,804	*10,654
GDP real growth	%	5.1	5.6	4.7	6.0	*4.8
Inflation	%	3.2	1.7	2.1	3.1	*2.7
Unemployment	%	2.9	3.0	3.1	2.9	*3.0
Oil output	'000 bpd	573.0	657.0	657.0	666.0	–
Natural gas output	bn cum	61.8	65.2	69.1	66.4	–
Exports (fob) (goods)	US$m	227,646.1	227,663.9	219,199.0	–	–
Imports (fob) (goods)	US$m	179,241.1	186,944.2	186,705.0	–	–
Balance of trade	US$m	48,405.0	40,719.3	32,494.0	–	–
Current account	US$m	31,769.7	18,566.0	12,665.0	15,127.0	*6,908.0
Total reserves minus gold	US$m	133,674.0	137,784.0	133,444.0	114,572.0	–
Foreign exchange	US$m	130,817.0	134,940.0	130,492.0	–	–
Exchange rate	per US$	3.03	3.06	3.29	3.50	–

* estimated figure ** forecast figure

Hydrocarbons

According to the US government's Energy Information Administration (EIA), in 2014 Malaysia was the world's second-largest exporter of liquefied natural gas and the second-largest oil and natural gas producer in south-east Asia, as well as being strategically located amid important routes for seaborne energy trade. Malaysia's oil reserves are the fourth-highest in Asia-Pacific after China, India and Vietnam. Nearly all of Malaysia's oil comes from offshore fields.

Declines in production at Malaysia's major producing oil fields in the previous decade have led government efforts to encourage investment in enhanced oil recovery and development of smaller and marginal fields, as well as deep-water fields. As a result of rising regional and domestic demand for crude oil and oil products, Malaysia plans to become a regional oil trading and storage hub by increasing the country's refining and storage capacity. Malaysia produced negligible quantities of biofuels in 2013, although the country played a significant role in supplying palm oil, a key raw material used in biodiesel production. (See Biofuels below).

Malaysia's energy industry is a critical sector of growth for the entire economy, making up almost 20 per cent of the total GDP. New tax and investment incentives, starting in 2010, haf aimed to promote oil and natural gas exploration and development in the country's deep-water and marginal fields as well as promote energy efficiency measures and use of alternative energy sources. These fiscal incentives were part of the country's economic transformation programme to leverage its resources and geographic location to become one of Asia's top energy players by 2020. Another key pillar in Malaysia's energy strategy is to become a regional oil and natural gas storage, trading and development hub that would attract technical expertise and downstream services that could compete in Asia.

According to the *Oil & Gas Journal* (OGJ), Malaysia held proved oil reserves of 4 billion barrels in December 2014, the fourth-highest reserves in Asia-Pacific after China, India and Vietnam. Malaysia's national oil and gas company, Petroliam Nasional Berhad (Petronas), holds exclusive ownership rights to all oil and natural gas exploration and production projects in Malaysia and is responsible for managing all licencing procedures. The company is directed by the prime minister, who also controls appointments to the company board. Petronas holds stakes in the majority of oil and gas blocks in Malaysia and it is the single largest contributor to Malaysian government revenues, up to 45 per cent, by way of taxes and dividends. Since its incorporation in 1974, Petronas has grown to be a world-renowned integrated international oil and gas company with business interests in more than 30 countries. Under legislation enacted in 1985, Petronas is required to hold a 15 per cent minimum equity in production sharing contracts (PSC) with all foreign and private companies.

ExxonMobil, Shell and Murphy Oil are currently the largest foreign oil companies by production volume. New opportunities for investment in Malaysia's energy sector have attracted small- and medium-sized foreign oil independents such as Talisman Energy Canada), Lundin Petroleum (Sweden), Roc Oil Company (Australia) and Petrofac (UK). Malaysia is south-east Asia's second-largest oil producer behind Indonesia. Petroleum and other liquids production (including crude oil, lease condensates, natural gas liquids, biofuels and refinery processing gains) in 2013 was nearly 670,000 barrels per day (bpd), hovering around the same level since 2011, but down from the country's peak production of 844,000bpd in 2003.

Malaysia remained a net oil exporter of crude oil and petroleum products in 2014 despite the narrowing gap between production and consumption over the previous years. Malaysia exported about half of its crude oil production because the crude quality (light and sweet) is attractive to the Asian markets and fetched a higher premium compared to other crude oil blends. In return, Malaysia imported lower-cost heavy sour crude oil, about half from the Middle East and the rest from several other regions, for its refineries and domestic needs.

Biofuels

Although Malaysia produced no significant quantities of ethanol and only 6,000bpd of biodiesel in 2013, it played a significant role in the industry by supplying more than one-third of the world's total palm oil, a vegetable oil and key product used in biodiesel production. Collectively, Indonesia and Malaysia represent 85 per cent of global palm oil production. While a majority of this oil is used in food, both countries have also marketed their palm oil for biodiesel production.

Currently, only about 10 per cent of global palm oil supply goes towards biofuels production. However, palm oil is the second-largest feedstock (after soy oil) used to produce biodiesel. In contrast to Indonesia, Malaysia historically had not converted much of its raw palm oil to biodiesel locally. Instead, Malaysia exported the palm oil to be refined elsewhere, mostly in neighbouring Singapore or Europe. Singapore's large renewable diesel plant was a particularly good destination since its advanced hydro-treating capabilities resulted in a higher quality fuel product that could be used at high blend levels without operational issues.

Despite its low biodiesel fuel production, Malaysia has much higher production capacity. Some analysts estimate the country has up to 50,000bpd of capacity, which is 40 per cent of US capacity. However, since 2010, Malaysia's biodiesel capacity has been significantly under-utilised as many consuming nations have added land-use criteria for feedstocks used to comply with their biofuels mandates. Production has grown recently from an estimated 1,000bpd in 2011 to 6,000bpd in 2013 and is currently on target to increase production in the next few years.

Natural gas

According to the OGJ, Malaysia held 83 trillion cubic feet (tcf) of proved natural gas reserves in December 2014 and is the third-largest natural gas reserve holder in the Asia-Pacific region. More than half of the country's natural gas reserves atr located in its eastern areas, predominantly offshore Sarawak. Most of Malaysia's gas reserves atr associated with oil basins, although Sarawak and Sabah have an increasing amount of non-associated gas reserves that have offset some of the

Najib Razak and the question of US$682 million

July 2015 saw the revelation that US$682 million had allegedly ended up in the bank account of Malaysian leader, Najib Razak. A governmental anti-corruption committee found that the funds had come not from embezzled state funds, but rather a wealthy Middle Eastern donor.

Although this might sound like a let off, questions are now being raised of as to who exactly would want to 'donate' nearly three quarters of a billion dollars to the Malaysian prime minister. Najib has admitted to receiving the money but has thus far failed to adequately explain it. He has, however, fired both his deputy and attorney general.

At the moment, Najib seems content to let the scandal play itself out. With elections still three years away he knows, as head of UMNO (Malaysia's biggest and historically strongest party) that whatever revelations come to light in the next few months, he still has more than a fighting chance of retaining power come election time.

declines from mature oil and gas basins in offshore Peninsular Malaysia.

Although Malaysia's dry natural gas production had risen steadily over the previous two decades, reaching an estimated 2.3tcf in 2012, growth has slowed somewhat since 2007. Meanwhile domestic natural gas consumption has increased, reaching 1.1tcf in 2013, accounting for about 50 per cent of production. The power sector consumed about 51 per cent while the industrial sector accounted for 33 per cent of the Malaysia's natural gas market sales in 2013, according to FGE Energy Consultants. Demand for power, especially in Peninsular Malaysia, is expected to steadily increase and gas demand for industrial development likely to remain strong as the government pursues greater economic development. Rising domestic demand, particularly in Peninsular Malaysia and LNG export contract obligations have been placing pressure on the natural gas supply and driving Malaysia to seek investments for reservoir development.

Malaysia remains a key global LNG exporter as the second-largest exporter after Qatar in 2013. Malaysia has been developing sizeable reserves in its eastern region. However, growing natural gas supply shortages in demand centres in the western region prompted Petronas to construct the country's first LNG import terminal in the western region to augment the supply from pipelines.

Malaysia ships more than 1.2tcf/y of LNG and contributes some 11 per cent of LNG exports worldwide, according to IHS Energy. Key importers of Malaysia's LNG are Japan (60 per cent), South Korea (17 per cent), Taiwan (12 per cent) and China (11 per cent), all holding medium- or long-term supply contracts with Malaysia. Malaysia also has sold LNG cargoes to Petronas LNG Limited, a trading company based in Malaysia, which ships spot LNG cargoes to many locations around the world.

Risk assessment

Economy	Good
Politics	Fair
Regional stability	Good/fair

Muslims in Malaysia

% of population	61.4
Sunni (% of Muslims)	98
Shi'a (% of Muslims)	2

COUNTRY PROFILE

1511 The Portuguese took control of Malaysia's south-western state, Malacca, as part of their plans to monopolise the south-east Asian spice trade.

1641 Control of Malacca fell to the Dutch who came to control the entire spice trade.

1786 A port was established in Malacca as part of the British East India Company.

1795 The British took full control of Malacca.

1824 The Anglo-Dutch treaty peacefully divided rule of the peninsula between the Dutch and the British, with the British in control of Malacca.

1826 The states on Malacca, Penang and Singapore were combined to form the Straits Settlements.

1870's Britain brought the Malay states under direct rule. The Pangkor agreement signed with Malay leaders gave the British more control of the territory.

1895 Four Malay states combine to form the Federated Malay States.

1896 The Malay states were grouped together under a British general. During British control, public services, rubber and tin production were developed. The British brought Indian and Chinese labourers to the country to help with construction projects, altering the country's ethnic make-up.

1939–45 Malaysia was overrun by the Japanese. After their defeat, the British resumed control, but the Straits Settlements were abolished.

1948 The Federation of Malaya, comprising the 11 states of Peninsular Malaysia, was formed.

1951 Pressured by strong Malay nationalism, the British were forced to introduce elections.

1955 The first federal elections were held.

1957 Malaya was granted independence from the British. It remained part of the Commonwealth. Tunku Abdul Rahman became prime minister.

1963 The state changed its name to the Federation of Malaysia when Singapore, Sabah and Sarawak joined.

1965 Singapore withdrew from Malaysia. A communist insurgency began in Sarawak.

1969 Increasing frustration over the economic success of the ethnic Chinese lead to anti-Chinese riots by Malays.

1970 Abdul Rahman resigned and Tun Abdul Razak became prime minister. The Barisan Nasional (BN) (National Front) coalition was formed.

1977 Expulsion of the chief minister of Kelantan from the Parti Islam se Malaysia (PAS) (Islamic Party of Malaysia) resulted in violent demonstrations. Direct rule was imposed in Kelantan and PAS was expelled from the ruling BN coalition.

1981 Dr Mahathir Mohamad succeeded Hussein Onn as leader of the BN coalition and was formally elected as prime minister.

1986 Mahathir Mohamad was re-elected in the general election, despite internal party conflict caused by the resignation of the deputy prime minister, Musa Hitam.

1988 Constitutional amendments limiting the power of the judiciary to interpret laws were approved. The Security Law was introduced removing the right of persons detained under the Internal Security Act to have recourse to the courts.

1990 Mahathir Mohamad was re-elected.

1995 Mahathir Mohamad was elected for a third term.

1997–98 The ringgit plunged on worldwide money markets during the Asian financial crisis. The authorities imposed capital controls and a selective exchange rate regime, against the advice of the International Monetary Fund (IMF). Mahathir sacked his chosen successor; finance minister Anwar Ibrahim, after disagreements regarding economic management and political manoeuvring by some of Anwar's supporters. Anwar was arrested for corruption and sexual misconduct.

1999 Anwar was imprisoned. General elections returned the Pertubuhan Kebangsaan Melayu Bersatu (UMNO) (United Malay National Front)-controlled BN to power and brought Mahathir Mohamad's fourth election as prime minister, avowedly his last.

2001 The new federal territory of Putrajaya was created. Malaysian King, Sultan Salahuddin Abdul Aziz Shah of Selangor, one of nine hereditary rulers, died. The Conference of Rulers chose Syed Sirajuddin, the Raja of Perlis state, as the new King and head of state.

2002 King Syed Sirajuddin formally took office. Indonesia, Malaysia and the Philippines signed a pact to counter terrorism and to stop a network that is believed to be trying to turn all three into a single Islamic state.

2003 Mahathir Mohamad, who had been prime minister for 22 years, retired. The deputy prime minister, Abdullah Ahmad Badawi, was immediately appointed to be his successor.

2004 The ruling BN coalition was re-elected in parliamentary elections. An earthquake off the island of Sumatra caused a *tsunami*, which devastated coastal areas in the region. The final estimate for Malaysia was 75 dead or missing, 5,000 displaced.

2005 Malaysia's large population of illegal foreign workers was targeted for identification and removal, leaving the country short of labourers. A state of emergency was declared as the worst pollution since 1997, emanating from forest fires in Indonesia, spread over the country.

2006 Sultan Mizan Zainal Abidin ibni Almarhum Sultan Mahmud al Muktafi Billah Shah of Terengganu took office as the thirteenth *Yang di Pertuan Agong* (traditional ruler), and Head of State, a position he will hold until 2011 when the next Conference of Rulers choses another candidate.
2008 Early elections were called, a year before required. The ruling BN coalition (of 14 parties) was re-elected with 50.3 per cent of the vote (140 seats out of 222); the opposition Barisan Rakyat (People's Front) coalition (of three parties), led by Parti Keadilan Rakyat (PKR) (People's Justice Party, whose leader, Anwar Ibrahim, had been unable to contest the elections) won 46.75 per cent (82 seats). Abdullah Ahmad Badawi remained as prime minister. In what many claimed was a politically motivated police action, Anwar Ibrahim was arrested and charged with sodomy. Nevertheless, he won a landslide victory in the Penang by-election and maintained his innocence during months of investigations.
2009 Abdullah Badawi resigned as prime minister and leader of UNMO, Mohamed Najib Razak replaced him in both positions. Malaysia, was removed from the OECD's blacklist of secretive tax havens, and placed on a grey list of countries that have agreed to adhere to tax disclosure standards, although without legislation enacting it. The government instigated plans to build a new city at the southern tip of Malaysia in Johor State. The 20-year project is expected to cost over US$13 billion. The 2,217 square km area is planned to become the home and commercial centre for three million people. The high court refused to strike out the sodomy charge against Anwar Ibrahim.
2010 Tuanku Mahmud Iskandar ibni al Marhum Sultan Ismail, sultan of Johor died and his son Ibrahim Ismail Ibni Almarhum Sultan Mahmud Iskandar al Haj became the new Sultan. Anwar Ibrahim went on trial for a second time charged with sodomy; as the trial continued Anwar accused former prime minister Ahmad Badawi of political conspiracy.
2011 A bilateral agreement was signed in May between the governments of Australia and Malaysia for irregular maritime arrivals (IMAs) (asylum seekers and unauthorised migrants) attempting to land in Australia to be held in camps in Malaysia while their applications for settlement are processed. Around 900 IMAs are expected to be held in Malaysia annually. In July, the Vatican and Malaysia agreed to establish diplomatic ties. A rally by supporters of PKR demanding electoral reforms turned violent as police cordoned off the centre of Kuala Lumpur and used tear gas and water cannon. The trial of Anwar Ibrahim continued in August with earlier DNA evidence supporting his claim of innocence was dismissed by the trial judge. In September, Prime Minister Razak said that the *Internal Security Act*, a law that had been used to detain indefinitely opposition leaders, union activists and students since the colonial era, would be abolished to ensure a modern and functioning democracy. In October, the Sultan of Kedah, Tuanku Abdul Halim Muadzam Shah ibni al Marhum Sultan Badlishah, was named as the next paramount ruler (from 13 December), by the Conference of Rulers.
2012 On 9 January, Anwar Ibrahim was acquitted of the charge of sodomy, after the judge declared the evidence unreliable. On 12 July the government announced the repeal of the Sedition Act, often used to crackdown on free-speech of dissenters and the opposition. It will be replaced by a new National Harmony Act that will balance the right of freedom of expression and ensure all communities are protected. On 25 July Malaysia agreed to house 800 asylum seekers and 4,000 refugees on behalf of Australia, in exchange of a fee for each person held. On 26 October, the government said it would review its application of the mandatory death sentence for drug trafficking and consider prison terms instead.
2013 Elections were held on 5 May. The results were the ruling Barisan Nasional (BN) (National Front) coalition (of 13 parties) was re-elected with 47.38 per cent of the vote (133 seats out of 222); the opposition Pakatan Rakyat (PR) (People's Front) coalition (of three parties) won 50.87 per cent (89 seats). Turnout was 84.63 per cent. In a move to cut its budget deficit by as much as US$1 billion a year the government cut the subsidies on petrol and diesel by 20 sen a litre on 2 September. On 14 October a court overturned a 2009 ruling that non-Muslims could refer to their God as 'Allah'. A week later Prime Minister Najib Razak said that the ruling would not apply in Sabah and Sarawak states.
2014 On 8 March Malaysian Airlines flight MH370 disappeared on a flight from Kuala Lumpur to Beijing with 239 passengers and crew. Despite extensive efforts, the aircraft has never been found and the reason for the disappeance remains a mystery. Four months later a second Malaysian Airlines flight was lost. MH17, flying from Amsterday to Kuala Lumpur, carrying 298 passengers and crew, was shot down over eastern Ukraine on 17 July. The majority of the passengers were Dutch (196); other nationalities included Malaysians, Australians, New Zealanders, and Belgians. The Netherlands was asked to take on the investigation from the Ukraine and in September 2014 a preliminary report indicated MH17 was brought down by a great number of objects piercing the plane with high velocity; there was no evidence of human or technical failure. Accusations were made against both pro-Russian rebel troops and the Ukrainian military.
2015 Malaysia, Australia, the Netherlands, Belgium and Ukraine announced on 2 July that they intend to present a resolution in relation to the shooting down of flight MH17 to the UN. Malaysia has said that it wants a tribunal set up to find and prosecute those involved. Wreckage confirmed as being from an Airbus Protestors organised by Bersih (Clean) and dressed in yellow t-shirts took to the streets of Kuala Lumpur over the weekend of 29/30 August to protest against Prime Minister Najib Razak, accusing him of pocketing some US$700 million in funds from the 1Malaysia Development Berhad (1MDB) state investment fund, established when he became prime minister in 2009 to drive Malaysia towards a high income economy.

Political structure

Constitution

The Federal Constitution of Malaysia came into force in 1957. It guarantees basic human rights such as Freedom of Speech, equality and a right to life and liberty.
In 1992, the powers granted to the country's traditional rulers upon independence were modified to the advantage of the federal government.
In 1994, a Constitutional Amendment Bill reduced the power of the monarchy.
Each of the 13 states of the federation has its own constitution and legislative assembly. Malacca, Penang, Sabah and Sarawak are each headed by a governor appointed for a four-year term by the King. A Council of State or cabinet has executive authority in the state, and each state has a legislature which legislates on matters not reserved for the federal parliament.

Independence date

31 August 1957

Form of state

Federative republic; constitutional elective monarchy.

The executive

The supreme head of state, the Yang di-Pertuan Agong (King), is elected every five years by a Conference of Rulers (nine hereditary state rulers). The non-executive Conference of Rulers is made up of the Sultans of Kedah, Perak, Johor, Selangor, Pahang, Trengganu and Kelantan, the Besar of Negeri Sembilan and the Raja of Perlis.

Power is concentrated at the federal level of government in Kuala Lumpur, where a Federal Executive Council, or cabinet, is formed by the party or parties with a working majority in the Dewan Rakyat, the lower house of the federal parliament. The federal government and its premier deal with all federal matters.

National legislature
The bicameral parliment (the federal parliament) consists of the 222-member Dewan Rakyat (House of Representatives), elected every five years by universal suffrage, and the 69-member Dewan Negara (Senate) with two elected members from each state and 43 appointed by the King; senators serve a six-year term. Legislative power rests with the federal parliament, although the Dewan Negara can delay ordinary bills for up to a year. Supply bills, such as the budget, can be delayed for up to one month. The head of state can delay assent to legislation.

Legal system
The basis of the legal system is English common law.
The judiciary underwent major changes in the 1990s. By 1995, the jury system had been completely abolished. Constitutionally, judicial powers have been reduced to the advantage of the Executive. A code of conduct has been established for judges. Controversy has surrounded Malaysia's retention of the death penalty for certain offences.
Two states, Kelantan and Terengganu, have tried to implement a moderate form of Sharia (Islamic law). This move has been blocked by the federal government. The Federal Court is Malaysia's highest judicial authority, although the King may grant pardons.

Last elections
5 May 2013 (parliamentary)
Results: Parliamentary (Dewan Rakyat): the ruling Barisan Nasional (BN) (National Front) coalition (of 13 parties) was re-elected with 47.38 per cent of the vote (133 seats out of 222); the opposition Pakatan Rakyat (PR) (People's Front) coalition (of three parties) won 50.87 per cent (89 seats). Turnout was 84.63 per cent. State Assemblies (Dewan Undangan Negeri): BN 54 per cent (275 seats out of 505), BR 45 per cent (229).

Next elections
2018 (parliamentary)

Political parties

Ruling party
Barisan Nasional (BN) (National Front) multi-racial coalition of 13 parties, led by Pertubuhan Kebangsaan Melayu Bersatu (United Malays National Organisation) (UMNO) (re-elected 5 May 2013)

Main opposition party
Barisan Rakyat (People's Front) coalition led by Parti Tindakan Demokratik (PTD) (Democratic Action Party), with Parti Islam se Malaysia (PAS) (Pan Malaysian Islamic Party) and Parti Keadilan Rakyat (PKR) (People's Justice Party).
Malaysia's annual population increases are expected to be 1.6 per cent during 2000–2015. Nearly 70 per cent of the population is under 30 years of age. Population growth in Peninsular Malaysia, where 82 per cent of the population live, is slightly lower than in Sarawak and Sabah.

Population

29.46 million (2012) (28,334,135; 2010, census figure)
Last census: 6 July 2010: 28,334,135
Population density: 84 inhabitants per square km (2010). Urban population 72 per cent (2010 Unicef).
Annual growth rate: 2.2 per cent, 1990–2010 (Unicef).

Ethnic make-up
Malaysia is a multi-racial country, including Malay (50 per cent), Chinese (27 per cent) and Indian (9 per cent).
The political dominance of Malays, the 'bumiputeras' prominent in the civil service, military, and education, is accepted by the Chinese and Indian communities in exchange for relative freedom in the private sector. The Kadazans are the principal ethnic group in the state of Sabah, while the Ibans, Bidayuhs and Melanaus predominate in the state of Sarawak. Approximately one million Indonesians work in Malaysia.

Religions
The official religion is Islam (55 per cent), although Malaysia is constitutionally committed to being a secular state. Buddhism, Taoism, Confucianism, Ancestor Worship, Hinduism, Christianity and Sikhism are also practised. The constitution guarantees freedom of religion.
Malays are generally Muslim. Most of the Chinese are Buddhist or Taoist, a few are Christian. The majority of Indians are Hindu, but some are Muslim, Christian or Sikh. Eurasians are predominantly Christian.

Education

Compulsory education covers six years of primary education and three years of lower secondary education.
There is selective entry for upper secondary school that lasts two years for both academic schools and vocational training. Pre-university education lasts for a further year. Higher education is provided by universities, polytechnics and colleges. There are a few private universities with three foreign universities in the country including the Monash University, Curtin University and Nottingham University-Malaysian campus.
Public expenditure on education typically amounts to 4.9 per cent of annual gross national income.
Literacy rate: 89 per cent adult rate; 97 per cent youth rate (15–24) (Unesco 2005).
Compulsory years: 6 to 16.
Enrolment rate: 98.7 per cent net primary enrolment; 69.9 per cent net secondary enrolment (World Bank).
Pupils per teacher: 19 in primary schools.

Health

The Ministry of Health estimates that expenditure on health will reach 7 per cent of GDP by the year 2020. The World Health Organisation's (WHO) assistance to Malaysia for technical co-operation and improving national health strategies amounted to US$1.7 million.
Public hospitals treat about 24.3 million outpatients and 1.5 million inpatients yearly. 55 per cent of doctors are engaged in private practice although only 30 per cent of the population seek medical attention from them. There are 111 public hospitals with seven private medical institutions nationwide with a total of 33,338 beds. Public sector doctors are generally concentrated in urban areas. The government has also made a special allocation of M$1.74 billion (US$46 million) towards improving the rural health services. There is increasing pressure on consumers to draw up individual financing plans through health insurance schemes and managed care organisations.

HIV/Aids
HIV prevalence: 0.4 per cent aged 15–49 in 2003 (World Bank)
Life expectancy: 72 years, 2004 (WHO 2006)
Fertility rate/Maternal mortality rate: 2.6 births per woman, 2010 (Unicef)
Child (under 5 years) mortality rate (per 1,000): 9 per 1,000 live births (WHO 2012); 19 per cent of children aged under five were malnourished (World Bank)

Welfare

Malaysia's system of social welfare is not comparable to Western standards, but considerable legislation exists in health and safety, and protection for workers against arbitrary dismissal. The Employees Provident Fund (EPF) and Social Security Organisation (SSO) each have approximately 8.5 million contributors. There are also non-profit-making voluntary organisations and ethnic associations that do much community work among Malays, Chinese and Indians.

Main cities
Kuala Lumpur (capital, estimated population 1.6 million in 2012); Ipoh (capital of Perak, 441,628), Johor Bahru (capital of Johor, 441,239), Kuantan (356,153), Seremban (317,813), Kelang (254,919), Taiping (220,364), Kota Kinabalu (capital of Sabah, 208,779), Kuching (capital of Sarawak, 138,306).

Languages spoken
Bahasa Malaysia is the national language; it is almost identical to Bahasa Indonesia, the official language of Indonesia. English is common in commerce and industry. Chinese dialects (Cantonese, Mandarin and Hokkien) are widely used in Malaysia, and Tamil and Punjabi among Indians. Other languages include Itan Dusan and Bajau.

Official language/s
Bahasa Malaysia

Media
The state exercises a great deal of control over print and broadcast media through the workings of the internal security ministry. In the 2008 annual report, by Reporters without borders, it stated the ministry censored articles and arrested journalists under the internal security law, while pressure was applied to media outlets to under-report or ignore opposition events and their contrary stances.

Press
Censorship laws constrain journalistic freedom and each year newspapers must renew their publication licence.

Dailies: There are many newspapers published in major cities and regionally. In English, *New Straits Times* (www.nst.com.my), *The Star* (http://thestar.com.my) and from the eastern provinces, the *Daily Express* (www.dailyexpress.com.my) and *Borneo Post* (www.theborneopost.com). In Malay, *Utusan Malaysia* (www.utusan.com.my) and *Berita Harian* (www.bharian.com.my). In Chinese *China Press* (www.chinapress.com.my) and *International Times* (www.intimes.com.my). In Tamil *Tamil Nesan* (www.tamilnesan.com.my).

Weeklies: ACP Publishing has several international magazines titles adapted for Malaysia, including *The Malaysian Women's Weekly*.

Business: In English, daily newspapers include *Business Times* (www.btimes.com.my) and *The Edge Daily* (www.theedgedaily.com). The Institute of Bankers publishes *Banker's Journal Malaysia* (www.ibbm.org.my) (see knowledge resources) as a quarterly and SME (www.smemagazine.com.my) is a monthly magazine for small and medium enterprises. Other industry publications include *Malaysian Industry* and *The Planter*.

The Malaysia External Trade Development Corporation (Matrade) has a website for international trade: www.matrade.gov.my.

Periodicals: Berita Publishing (www.beritapublishing.com.my) has several magazines within its house, including *Anjung Seri* for interior design and women's magazines *Iremaia* and *Jelita*.

Broadcasting
The state-owned, national public broadcaster is Radio Television Malaysia (RTM) (www.rtm.net.my).

Radio: The multi-lingual population has stations broadcasting in community languages only including, Malay, Iban, Chinese, Tamil, Arabic and English with content also targeting interest groups such as the business community (BMF www.bfm.my), women (WFM) and the Iban community of east Malaysia (Cats FM www.cats.fm).

RTM (www.rtm.net.my) operates over 30 radio stations nationally, regionally and locally, plus the external service, Voice of Malaysia. There are a number of private and commercial stations operated by media groups providing national networks including Era (www.era.fm) Hitz (www.hitz.fm), Ai FM (www.aifm.net.my) and Minnal FM (www.minnalfm.com).

Television: Digital TV trials are expected to end in 2009 and a full launch of digital services should be completed by 2015 when the analogue signal is terminated. RTM (www.rtm.net.my) operates two TV channels, RTM1 and RTM2 broadcasting domestic and import TV shows. Other, free-to-air TV stations include TV3 (www.tv3.com.my), NTV7 (www.ntv7.com.my) 8TV (www.8tv.com.my) and TV9 (www.tv9.com.my). Pay-to-view TV is operated by Astro satellite TV (www.astro.com.my) with 19 channels. Political parties broadcast programmes over the internet.

National news agency: Bernama

Other news agencies: Bernama: www.bernama.com

Economy
Malaysia is abundantly endowed with natural resources including oil and gas, and has a climate conducive to growing export crops including rubber, palm oil, pepper and timber. It has a stable and fast-growing economy, with wealth creation formed by using its basic resources effectively. An example of this is how Malaysia has channelled tin into diversification of its economy through a rapidly expanding industrial sector. Malaysia already has a high level of technological development, including e-commerce and has a high level of manufacturing for export. Foreign direct investment (FDI) in 2014 reached a record high of US$17.9 billion, increasing from the previous record of US$11.6 billion in 2013. Production was hit hard when the global economic crisis struck, but Malaysia had built up sufficient foreign exchange reserves to allow it to commit US$20 billion in a series of stimulus packages between October 2008 and November 2009. These packages were intended to create jobs, provide tax incentives and giving businesses access to funds.

Nevertheless, GDP growth fell from 6.2 per cent in 2007 to 4.8 per cent in 2008, before falling into negative growth of -1.6 in 2009 as global trade weakened. As trade weakened due to the global economic crisis, Malaysia went from a period of strong economic performance to a recession in 2009 when GDP growth dropped by 1.6 per cent. In 2010 growth surged back to life at 7.2 per cent as the Asian economies quickly recovered from the crisis; growth continued at a stable level to 4.7 per cent in 2013 before jumping to 6.0 per cent in 2014. Inflation followed the economic trend, rising from 2 per cent in 2007 to 5.4 per cent in 2008, before dropping to 0.6 per cent in 2009 as domestic spending all but ceased; inflation rose again in 2010 to 1.7 per cent, remaining reasonably low at 3.1 per cent in 2013.

Malaysia relies heavily on oil and natural gas revenue. Proven oil reserves were 3.8 billion barrels at the end of 2014, with an annual production rate of 666,000 barrels per day. Proven natural gas reserves were 1.1 trillion cubic metres (cum) at the end of 2014, with an annual production rate of 66.4 billion cum, of which about half was exported as liquefied natural gas (LNG) to other Asian countries. The remainder was consumed domestically.

The government's priority is to improve its human capital in order to remain regionally competitive.

External trade
Malaysia belongs to the Association of Southeast Asian Nations (Asean) Free Trade Area (Afta) and maintains a list of goods that have preferential import duties between members and a programme of tariff reductions due to be introduced in the next few years.

It is a major exporter of manufactured goods, including semiconductor devices and electrical goods and appliances; the government is encouraging the expansion of hi-technology and software products to provide more skilled employment.

Rubber product exports reached 847,090 tonnes in 2013. Malaysia is the world's largest rubber glove manufacturer, constituting around 65 per cent of total worldwide rubber glove production. It became a key industry, matching palm oil for its importance along with tropical timber.

Imports

Main imports include electrical and electronic equipment, machinery, petroleum products and plastics, vehicles, iron and steel products and chemicals.

Main sources: China (16.9 per cent of total in 2014), Singapore (12.5 per cent), Japan (8.0 per cent).

Exports

Main exports include semiconductors and electronic equipment, palm oil, petroleum and liquefied natural gas, wood and wood products, palm oil, rubber, textiles, chemicals and solar panels.

Main destinations: Singapore (14.2 per cent of total in 2014), China (12.0 per cent), Japan (10.8 per cent).

Agriculture

Farming

Agriculture contributed around 9.3 per cent to GDP in 2014 and employed around 13 per cent of all those in employment. Labour shortages and migration from rural to urban areas are contributory factors in the decline of the sector in recent decades. 24 per cent of the total land area is cultivated. Malaysia is the world's largest producer of palm oil and natural rubber, the latter accounting for around 25 per cent of world production. Most rubber production (97 per cent) occurs in Peninsular Malaysia.

Smallholders account for 69 per cent of output. The government is looking to upgrade the sector from small-scale farming to high-scale farming involving the use of technology.

The government has encouraged diversification away from rubber, the colonial-era staple export, into palm oil production; Malaysia now accounts for over half of world output. World Bank aid has supported government initiatives to improve productivity, increase diversification and alleviate poverty in the agricultural sector.

In line with the government's emphasis on new sources of growth within the sector, the production of selected Malaysian tropical fruits and flowers has made a particular contribution. Production and export of cocoa and pepper has increased, as newly planted areas have improved yields.

Other main crops are coconuts, sugar cane, tobacco, vegetables, coffee, tea, maize and groundnuts. Sugar cane and tea are grown as plantation crops; for the rest, smallholders account for most cultivation.

The government is trying to encourage higher yields in rice, the main subsistence crop. The formerly state-owned Bernas group, a monopoly rice importer, has entered into joint ventures with Marditech, the commercial arm of the Malaysian Agricultural Research and Development Institute (Mardi), in a drive to produce high-class rice that could rival Thai varieties. The dominance of smallholdings in rice cultivation remains the biggest barrier to advanced rice cultivation.

The state-run Palm Oil Research Institute of Malaysia (Porim) is attempting to genetically modify the oil palm, in order to create more palm oil, used as refined cooking oil in India and China.

Fishing

Malaysia typically produces 1.5 million tonnes of fish and other aquatic life per year. It imports about 100,000 tonnes and exports over twice this amount, but the bulk of production is destined for domestic consumption. The main species of fish catch are freshwater fish, marine fish, squid, cuttlefish, octopus, shrimps and prawns. Malaysia is also experimenting with fish-farming.

Forestry

Around 62 per cent of Malaysia is covered by natural forest. Some 14 million hectares (ha), or 43 per cent of total land area is within designated Permanent Forest Estates, designed to ensure sustainable forestry. Of these some 10.5 million ha are productive forest, the remainder being protected. More than three million ha are designated as conversion forests, which will eventually be cleared and put into alternative use.

Malaysia is one of the world's largest exporters of tropical hardwood; Sarawak is the most important timber-producing area. New markets have been found in the Middle East. The sector is moving away from upstream operations into those with more value added, including furniture making, plywood, and sawn timber.

Malaysia is a member of the International Tropical Timber Organisation (ITTO) and is committed to sustainable forest management. Rattan, rubber and bamboo are alternatives to logging.

Industry and manufacturing

Manufacturing accounted for 24 per cent of GDP in 2014. It is the largest single contributor to the economy, and accounts for around 80 per cent of export earnings. Prime Minister Mahathir has encouraged the development of heavy industries based on the country's natural resources. There is also emphasis on the promotion of small and medium-sized firms, and measures are being undertaken to disperse industries to less developed states.

Conglomerate groups, often politically well-connected, used to control large parts of Malaysian industry. The ownership structure of many of Malaysia's largest companies were best described as tangled. Leading businessmen were believed to hold shares in proxy for government figures in a symbiotic relationship between business and government known as 'Malaysia Inc'. The bargain between private and public sectors saw businesses grant government extraordinary influence in investment and other decisions, in exchange for government contracts.

However, the recession tamed some of the excesses of this system. Several politically-connected conglomerates, such as Renong, which effectively acted as an investment vehicle for the ruling UMNO party, were creatures of the 1990s construction boom. Many have been restructured and old management replaced.

Meanwhile, many vanity projects, such as the construction of the world's longest building along the Kelang river (to complement two of the world's highest, the Petronas twin towers), and the construction of a new administrative capital for the federal government at Putrajaya, 25km south of Kuala Lumpur, have been cancelled.

Tourism

Malaysia is a popular destination for visitors from other south-east Asian countries, for its modern and traditional cities, tropical islands and beaches, historical buildings and national parks. There are three sites on Unesco's World Heritage List, as well as religious and secular festivals celebrated throughout the year. In July 2012, the Lenggong Valley, with four archaeological sites, was added to Unesco's World Heritage List.

In 2013 there were 25.7 million visitors, an increase of around 700,000 from the 2012 figure. In 2014, number of arrivals was expected to have risen by almost 10 per cent on the previous year, despite the number of Chinese tourists declining.

Travel and tourism contributed 14.9 per cent to GDP in 2014, a figure forecast to rise by 5.3 per cent in 2015. Employment has mirrored the trend in tourism; 13.0 per cent of the labour force were directly or indirectly provided jobs by the tourism sector in 2014. In the same year, investment in the tourist industry accounted for 6.8 per cent of total investment in Malaysia.

Mining

The leading minerals mining firm, the Malaysia Mining Corporation (MMC), is trying to diversify away from tin and is prospecting for base and precious metals on the east coast of peninsular Malaysia. Gold mining has been revived and the Penjom mine accounts for 70 per cent of annual gold production. Malaysia produces around 4,000kg of gold per year. Other resources mined include iron ore, bauxite and copper.

There are undisclosed reserves of gold and antimony in Bau in Sarawak. MMC has also found reserves of copper, silver, gold and bismuth in Pahang state and deposits of alluvial gold in Kelantan state. The mining sector output is declining, mainly as a result of falling tin, copper and petroleum output.

Hydrocarbons

Proven oil reserves were 3.8 billion barrels at the end of 2014, with production at 666,000 barrels per day (bpd). Consumption was 815,000bpd in 2014; the shortfall was made up by imports. There are over 50 oil fields in production, concentrated offshore around the Malaysian peninsula, with several others under development.

The state-owned Petronas has exclusive rights to all Malaysian petroleum reserves and is responsible for all oil and gas exploration and production undertaken through production sharing contracts (PSC) with international oil and gas companies. It is currently undertaking exploration outside Malaysia in over 25 countries, through a subsidiary company.

Oil reserves are in decline and analysts consider the alternative of constructing a new Sabah Oil and Gas Terminal (SOCT) near the first deep-water oil and natural gas field to handle around 300,000bpd of oil and 30 million cubic metres of natural gas destined for export worldwide.

Malaysia, along with China, Taiwan, Brunei, The Philippines and Vietnam, claims the potentially oil-rich Spratly Islands. In 2010, an agreement was reached between the governments of Brunei and Malaysia to share the revenue of two disputed oil blocks in territorial waters. The dispute had led to international oil companies declining to invest in exploration within the offshore waters while the countries haggled over its sovereign ownership.

There are six refineries in operation, with a total refining capacity of 854,000bpd, sufficient to meet domestic needs. In January 2015, Shell announced its plans to either sell or close down its refinery in Port Dickinson, on which it has spend large sums in modernisation in recent years.

Proven natural gas reserves were 1.1 trillion cum in 2014; production was 66.4 billion cum and consumption was 41 billion cum – all surplus was exported. Malaysia is the world's second largest liquefied natural gas (LNG) exporter (after Qatar), with the bulk of LNG exports going to Japan, South Korea, Taiwan and China.

Malaysia produced 2.9 million tonnes of coal in 2012 but consumed 24 million tonnes, therefore imports were required to make up the shortfall. The sector has been subject to underinvestment, and although the government has published plans for expanding domestic energy production through the use of coal, so that more oil and natural gas can be exported, the economic climate in 2009 forced deferral of the proposals.

Energy

In 2013, total installed generating capacity was 25.4GW, and total energy production was 130.1 billion kWh, of which 86 per cent is supplied by thermal plants and the rest by hydropower and renewable sources. Around 50 per cent of demand comes from the industrial sector, 25 per cent from transportation, 10 per cent from commercial sectors and 10 per cent from residential users.

Development of the coal reserves and hydropower potential is intended to diversify sources of energy and reduce the use of natural gas needed for export. Five independent power producers (IPPs) supply power alongside the established utilities in Sarawak, Sabah and Peninsular Malaysia.

Financial markets

Stock exchange

Bursa Malaysia (Malaysia Exchange)

Banking and insurance

Bank Negara Malaysia ordered a major consolidation programme in 2001. This involved creating 10 institutions from 31 commercial banks, 19 financial companies and 12 merchant banks. By end-2001, 51 financial institutions had successfully merged. As a result, Malaysia's banking system is well-capitalised to meet future demands for capital expenditure.

Central bank

Bank Negara Malaysia

Offshore facilities

Measures to enhance development of Labuan island, Malaysia's offshore banking centre, are planned. Approximately 1,000 financial institutions already have a presence in Labuan.

Time

GMT plus eight hours

Geography

Malaysia comprises 13 states in the Malay Peninsula situated south of Thailand, including Sabah and Sarawak states on the north coast of the island of Borneo, which is separated from the Peninsula by the South China Sea. Peninsular Malaysia extends 740km from Perlis state in the north to Johor state in the south. Sabah and Sarawak stretch some 1,120km from Tanjung Datu (Sarawak) in the west to Hog Point (Sabah) in the east.

Malaysia has a land frontier with Thailand to the north, is bordered by the Republic of Singapore to the south and by the Indonesian island of Sumatra across the Straits of Malacca to the west. Other important neighbours are the Philippines and Brunei which separates Sabah and Sarawak.

Hemisphere

Northern

Climate

The climate is tropical with high temperatures and high humidity throughout the year. Relative humidity averages about 80 per cent annually.

Average daily temperatures 21–32 degrees Celsius (C) in the lowlands; in the hill resorts they average 18–24 degrees C but can be as low as 16 degrees C.

November–February is the rainy season for the east coast of Peninsular Malaysia, the north-eastern part of Sabah and western part of Sarawak. In some years, rainfall is concentrated in short periods and some flooding can occur.

During the months of April, May and October, the west coast of the peninsula experiences occasional thunderstorms in the afternoons. Showers are heavy but they clear up as quickly as they come.

Rainfall averages around 2,300mm a year.

Dress codes

Lightweight clothing is worn all year. The dress code tends to be conservative and although jackets are not usually worn in offices, a tie and long-sleeved shirt are normal. For formal meetings, a full suit is required. Government officials often wear a safari-style short-sleeved suit. In deference to the Islamic culture, western business women should dress modestly at all times.

Entry requirements

Passports

Required by all, and must be valid six months from date of departure.

Visitors must have proof of return/onward passage and enough money to finance their stay.

Visa

Social visas are not required by nationals of most countries although the length of stay permitted varies by nationality. There are a number of exceptions, particularly African countries, and for a full list go to http://malaysia.embassyhomepage.com/malaysia_visa_malaysian_embassy_london_uk.htm

There are two categories: a visa with reference (VWR), issued in Malaysia and appropriate for business travellers, and a visa without reference (VWTR), issued in overseas countries. All visitors with a VWTR must enter Malaysia through an airport only.

A visitor's pass issued for entry into the Malaysia peninsular is not valid for entry into Sabah and Sarawak.

Prohibited entry

Holders of Israeli passports.

Currency advice/regulations

The import of local currency is limited to M$1,000, the import of foreign currency in amounts over M$1,000 or equivalent must be declared using a Travellers Declaration Form (TDF), which can be obtained from airports, tourist offices or Malaysian diplomatic missions. Export of local and foreign currency is limited to the amount declared on arrival.

Customs

Personal items and a limited amount of tobacco and alcohol may be imported duty-free.

Prohibited imports

Illegal drugs, firearms and ammunition, daggers and knives and pornographic materials. Malaysia enforces a very strict drug trafficking policy that includes capital punishment.

Health (for visitors)

Mandatory precautions

Valid certificate of vaccination against yellow fever if travelling from infected area.

Advisable precautions

Vaccinations are advisable for diphtheria, tuberculosis, typhoid, hepatitis A and B, Japanese A encephalitis, tetanus and polio. Tap water is boiled by many people before drinking, although it is generally regarded as safe.

There is a malaria risk in Sabah (northern Malaysia) and the eastern Malaysia province of Sarawak. There is a rabies risk.

Visitors with respiratory problems may be put at risk from the poor air quality caused by pollution.

Hotels

There are a range of good hotels in all main cities. A 5 per cent tax and 10 per cent service charge is added to hotel and restaurant meals. Tipping is not encouraged.

Credit cards

Extensive acceptance of all major cards, particularly in urban centres and hotels. Travellers cheques are also widely accepted.

Public holidays (national)

Fixed dates

1 Jan (New Year's Day), 1 May (Labour Day), 31 Aug (National Day), 25 Dec (Christmas Day).

Holidays falling on Sunday are celebrated the next day.

Malaysia's multi-ethnic and multi-religious population celebrates a variety of holidays – federal, Muslim, Christian, Buddhist, Hindu and others.

In addition to federal holidays, each state has 3–4 additional holidays, one of which is the birthday of its ruler.

1 Feb (City Day) is a holiday in the Federal Territory of Kuala Lumpur.

Variable dates

Chinese New Year (two days, Jan/Feb), Birth of Buddha (Apr), The King's Birthday (first Sat in Jun), Divali (Hindu, Oct/Nov), Eid al Adha, Islamic New Year, Birth of the Prophet Mohammed, Eid al Fitr (two days).

Islamic year 1437 (15 Oct 2015–2 Oct 2016):: The Islamic year contains 354 or 355 days, with the result that Muslim feasts advance by 10–12 days against the Gregorian calendar. Dates of feasts vary according to the sighting of the new moon, so cannot be forecast exactly.

Working hours

The Muslim weekly holiday is Thursday afternoon and Friday and is observed in the states of Johor, Kedah, Kelantan, Perlis and Terengganu. Other states have a Saturday–Sunday weekend.

Banking

Mon–Fri: 0930–1600, Sat: 0930–1130 (second and fourth Sat only).

Mon–Fri: 0800–1200, 1400–1600; Sat: 0800–1100 in Sabah only.

Business

Mon–Fri: 0900–170; Sat: 0900–1300, Malaysia Peninsular, times vary in East Malaysia.

Government

Mon–Fri: 0830–1630 in most provinces. Sat–Wed: 0830–1630; Thu 0830–1230 in Kedah, Kelantan and Terengganu.

Shops

Usually 1000–2200 (department stores and supermarkets), 0930–1900 (shops) in Peninsular Malaysia; Mon–Sat: 0800–1830 in Sabah; Mon–Fri: 0900–1800, Sat: 0900–1300 in Sarawak.

Telecommunications

Mobile/cell phones

There are 3G, 900 and 1800 GSM services available in most populated areas.

Electricity supply

220V AC, 50Hz. Three-pin square plug fittings and bayonet-type light fittings are generally used.

Weights and measures

Metric system

Social customs/useful tips

Appointments should be made in advance and punctuality is important. It is customary to shake hands on meeting and taking leave, although Muslim women avoid shaking hands with men and vice versa. Business cards are exchanged after introduction. By tradition, Malaysians are hospitable, open people and prefer to avoid arguments, which are seen as distasteful. Avoiding loss of face is an important consideration in business negotiations.

Malaysians place great importance on the correct use of titles. *Tunku* or *Tengku* indicates hereditary royalty; *Tun* denotes membership of a high order of chivalry. *Tan Sri an Datuk* (or *Datuk Seri* or *Dato*) indicate knighthood. *Tuan* or *Encik* is the equivalent of Mr, *Puan* of Mrs, *Cik* of Miss.

Visitors should be aware of the conventions of Muslims, Buddhists and Hindus, and other religious and ethnic groups. Muslims are not permitted to drink alcohol or eat pork. The fasting month of Ramadan is strictly observed. Use right hand only for receiving anything (food, drink, money etc) and for eating. Refusal of offered refreshment is considered discourteous. It is customary to bargain when shopping, except in department stores. Tipping is officially discouraged but is seen in the capital.

The authorities have a very strict attitude to drug abuse and there can be a mandatory death sentence for anyone, including foreigners, who is convicted of possession of even a very small amount of narcotics. Other punishments include whipping, in addition to any custodial sentence. Warning notices about *dadah* (drugs) are prominently displayed at the airport.

Security

Street crime is low compared with European cities, but is increasing. Bag snatching is becoming common generally, as is passport theft on aircraft and in airport buildings. Possessions should not be left unattended, even in vehicles with a locked boot. Credit card fraud is becoming more common, and care should be taken when paying by this method.

Visitors are advised to avoid street gatherings and demonstrations which could place them at risk, especially if gatherings lack police permission.

Getting there

Air

National airline: Malaysian Airlines (MAS).

International airport/s: Kuala Lumpur International Airport (KUL), 55km south of the city, near Putrajaya, duty-free shop, restaurant, ATMs, bank, business facilities, post office, shops, car hire. Taxis must be pre-paid in the airport arrivals area (travel time 40 minutes). There is also a 24-hour express bus service to and from the city centre (journey time 60 minutes). A high speed rail service, (the KLIA Ekspres), provides access to the city in 28 minutes. Tickets can be purchased onboard or at the KL air terminal office.

Kota Kinabalu (BKI), 7km from city, situated on the northern coast of Sabah state is the principal international airport of Sabah on the north-eastern part of Borneo Island of East Malaysia. Facilities include duty free, bank, restaurant and bars. Taxis have prices for zoned trips.

Other airport/s: Penang (Bayan Lepas) (PEN), 16km south of Georgetown, capital of small island off the north-west coast of the peninsula, duty-free shop, bar, restaurant, currency exchange, hotel reservations, shops, car hire; Kuantan (KUA), 16km from city; Kuching (KCH), 11km from the city, (situated in the west of Sarawak on the island of Borneo) and receives a limited number of international flights.

Airport tax: International departure tax: M$45

Surface

Road: There are two Asian highways that pass through Malaysia. The AH2 and AH18 combined, runs north-south along the eastern seaboard, from Thailand to Singapore.

The state of Johor is linked to Singapore by a causeway.

It is also possible to cross the land border between Malaysia and Indonesia between Pontianak in Kalimantan and Kuching in Sarawak.

Rail: A railway line runs from Singapore to Kuala Lumpur, Butterworth, and on into Thailand.

Water: The main ferry crossing from Singapore is between North Changi and Tanjung Belungkor. High-speed ferries run between Sumatra and Malaysia; routes are either Medan–Penang or Dumai–Melaka. A ferry from Port Kelang, Kuala Lumpur's port, goes to Belawan, on Sumatra. Yachts sail irregularly between Langkawi in Malaysia and Phuket in Thailand.

There are ferry connections between Brunei and Sabah.

Getting about

National transport

Air: There are over 20 domestic airports. MAS operates extensive network services to main centres and, particularly in Sabah and Sarawak, smaller towns.

Road: About 80—90 per cent of the 43,818km road network in Peninsular Malaysia is paved. All major cities and towns are linked by roads although in the monsoon season driving can be difficult.

Buses: Most long-distance bus services operate from Kuala Lumpur to all major cities and town. The buses are fast, economical and reasonably comfortable. Seats can be reserved. On many routes buses are air-conditioned, which cost a little more than the regular buses. In Sabah and Sarawak rural services are provided by four-wheel-drive vehicles.

Taxis: In almost every town there are long-distance taxi offices or *teksi* (taxi) ranks. They wait for the full complement of four passengers before leaving.

Rail: The capital city is the hub of the national railway system, which is modern, comfortable and economical. Day and night services link major cities in Peninsula Malaysia.

There is a line which branches off the Singapore-Kuala Lumpur-Butterworth-Thailand line at Gemas and runs through Kuala Lipis up to the north-east corner of Malaysia, near Kota Baharu. There are other branch lines which are not used very much.

There are express and ordinary trains. Express trains are air-conditioned and are generally first- and second-class only, and on night trains there is a choice of sleepers or seats.

Rail passes are only available to foreigners and can be purchased at a number of main railway stations.

Water: The Straits Steamship Company operates a passenger service between Port Kelang and Sabah and Sarawak every nine to 10 days. There are frequent ferry services between Penang and Butterworth. There are boats between the Peninsula and offshore islands, and along the rivers of Sabah and Sarawak.

City transport

Taxis: Travel vouchers for airport taxis are available at the airport counters at fixed rates.

Between midnight and 0600, an extra surcharge of 50 per cent applies. There is an extra charge for telephone bookings.

Taxi coupons at fixed prices to various destinations in the city and its vicinity are available at Platform Four of the Kuala Lumpur railway station.

There are bicycle rickshaws in many towns.

Buses, trams & metro: Kuala Lumpur has a 29km, fully automated, driverless, three line, light rail transit (LRT) system (known locally as the Putra, after its original operators): the Kelana Jaya Line, the Ampang Line and the Sri Petaling Line. There are other rail services within the city, including a monorail, a commuter service and two high-speed airport rail links.

Trains: The express rail link between central Kuala Lumpur and the international airport opened in April 2002.

Car hire

Car hire is available in all main cities. Driving is on the left-hand side of the road, and the use of seat belts in front seats is obligatory. International driving licences are required. Chauffeur-driven cars are available.

BUSINESS DIRECTORY

The addresses listed below are a selection only. While World of Information makes every endeavour to check these addresses, we cannot guarantee that changes have not been made, especially to telephone numbers and area codes. We would welcome any corrections.

Telephone area codes

The international direct dialling (IDD) code for Malaysia is +60, followed by area code and subscriber's number:

Ipoh5Melaka6
Johor Bahru7Penang4
Kota Kinabalu88Port Dickson6
Kuala Lumpur3Sandakan89
Kuantan9Sibu84
Kuching82Taiping5

Useful telephone numbers

Emergency: 999
Operator (trunk call enquiries): 102
Directory: 103
International service: 108
Tourist Police: 243-5522

Chambers of Commerce

American Malaysian Chamber of Commerce, Amoda Building, 22 Jalan Imbi, 55100 Kuala Lumpur (tel: 2148-2407; fax: 2148-8540; e-mail: info@amcham.com.my).

British Malaysian Chamber of Commerce, c/o British High Commission, 185 Jalan Ampang, 50450 Kuala Lumpur (tel: 2163-1784; fax: 2163-1781; e-mail: britcham@bmcc.org.my).

Kuala Lumpur Chamber of Commerce, 79 Kompleks Damai, Jalan Datuk Haji Eusoff, Kuala Lumpur (tel: 4042-4711; fax: 4042-1540; e-mail: dpmmbkl@tm.net.my).

Malay Chamber of Commerce Malaysia, Plaza Pekeliling,2 Jalan Tun Razak, 50400 Kuala Lumpur (tel: 4041-8522; fax: 4041-4502; e-mail: wmaster@dpmm.org.my).

Malaysian International Chamber of Commerce and Industry, Plaza Mont' Kiara, 2 Jalan Kiara, 50480 Kuala Lumpur (tel: 6201-7708; fax: 6210-7705; e-mail:micci@micci.com).

Banking

Affin Merchant Bank Berhad, PO Box 1124, 27th Floor, Menara Boustead, 69 Jalan Raja Chulan, 50200 Kuala Lumpur (tel: 2070-8080; fax: 2070-7592).

Bumiputra-Commerce Bank Berhad, 6 Jalan Tun Perak, 50050 Kuala Lumpur, (tel: 2693-1722; fax: 2698-6628).

Bank Kerjasama Rakyat Malaysia Bhd, Bangunan Bank Rakyat, Jalan Tangsi, 50480 Kuala Lumpur (tel: 2612-9600; fax: 2612-9576).

Bank Muamalat Malaysia Berhad, Menara Bumiputra, 21, Jalan Melaka,

PO Box 10407, 50913, Kuala Lumpur (tel: 2698-8787; fax: 2692-2000).

Bank Pembangunan & Infrastruktur Malaysia Berhad, PO Box 12352, Menara Bank Pembangunan, Jalan Sultan Ismail, 50774 Kuala Lumpur (tel: 2615-2020; fax: 2692-8520).

Bank Islam Malaysia Berhad, Level 11, Darul Takaful, Jalan Sultan Ismail, 50734 Kuala Lumpur (tel: 2616-8000; fax: 2698-0587).

Bank Simpanan Nasional, Wisma BSN, 117 Jalan Ampang, 50450 Kuala Lumpur (tel: 2162-3222; fax: 2710-7252).

Citibank Berhad, PO Box 10112, 165 Jalan Ampang, 50450 Kuala Lumpur (tel: 232-5334; fax: 232-8763).

Malayan Banking Berhad, PO Box 12010, 100 Jalan Tun Perak, 50050 Kuala Lumpur (tel: 2070-8833; fax: 2070-2611).

Bank Negara, Jalan Dato Onn, 50480 Kuala Lumpur (tel: 2698-8044; fax: 2691-2990).

Sabah Development Bank, PO Box 12172, 88824 Kota Kinabalu; SDB Tower, Wisma Tun Faud Stephens, Km 2.4, Jalan Tuaran, Sabah (tel: 232-177; fax: 261-852).

Southern Bank Bhd, Wisma Genting, Jalan Sultan Ismail, Peti Surat 12281, Kuala Lumpur (tel: 263-7000; fax: 232-5008).

Standard Chartered Bank, 2 Jalan Ampang, 50450 Kuala Lumpur (tel: 232-6555; fax: 238-3295).

Central bank

Bank Negara Malaysia, Jalan Dato' Onn, PO Box 10922, Kuala Lumpur 50929 (tel: 2698-8044; fax: 2691-2990; e-mail: info@bnm.gov.my).

Stock exchange

Bursa Malaysia (Malaysia Exchange), www.bursamalaysia.com

Travel information

Automobile Association of Malaysia, E-7-4, Megan Avenue 1, 189 Jalan Tun Razak, 50400 Kuala Lumpur (tel: 2162-5777; fax: 2162-5358; email: mru@aamhq.po.my; internet: www.aam.org.my).

KLIA Ekspres, Express Rail Link Sdn Bhd, L2, KL City Air Terminal, KL Sentral Station, 50470 Kuala Lumpur (tel: 2267-8088, customer enquiry: 2267-8000; fax: 2267-8910; email: air-rail@KLIAekspres.com; internet: www.kliaekspres.com).

Malaysia Airlines, Main Ticket Office, Bangunan MAS, Jalan Sultan Ismail, 50250, Kuala Lumpur (tel: 7846-3000; fax: 2162-9025; email customer@mas.com.my; internet: www.malaysiaairlines.com).

Rapid KL (Public Transport) 1 Jalan PJU 1A/46, Off Jalan Lapangan Terbang, Sultan Abdul Aziz Shah, 47301 Petaling Jaya, Selangor (tel: 7650-7788; fax: 7625-6667; email: suggest@rapidkl.com.my; internet: www.putralrt.com.my).

National tourist organisation offices

Malaysia Tourism Promotion Board, 17th Floor, Menara Dato' Onn, Putra World Trade Centre, 45, Jalan Tun Ismail, 50480 Kuala Lumpur (tel: 2615-8188; fax: 2693-5884; email: enquiries@tourism.gov.my; internet: www.tourism.gov.my).

Ministries

Ministry of Agriculture, Wisma Tani, Jl Sultan Salahuddin, 50624 Kuala Lumpur (tel: 2617 -5000; fax: 2691-3758; email: matdaud@agri.moa.my).

Ministry of Culture, Arts and Heritage, TH Perbadanan Tower, Maju Junction, 10110 Jl Sultan Ismail , 50694 Kuala Lumpur (tel: 2612-7600; fax: 2693-5114, 2697-6100; email: info@heritage.gov.my).

Ministry of Defence, Jl Padang Tembak, 50634 Kuala Lumpur (tel: 292-1333, 230-1033; fax: 298-4662, 298-5372).

Ministry of Domestic Trade and Consumer Affairs, Lot 2G3, Presint 2, Federal Goverment Administrative Centre, 62623 Putrajaya (tel: 8882-5500 ; fax: 8882-5763; email: nsuzana@kpdnhep.gov.my).

Ministry of Education, Level 5, Block E8 Parcel E, Federal Goverment Administrative Centre, 62604 Putrajaya (tel: 8884-6000; fax: 8889-5235; email: julina@bdpk.moe.gov.my).

Ministry of Energy, Water and Communications, Block E4/5, Government Complex, Parcel E , Federal Government Administrative Centre, 50668 Kuala Lumpur (tel: 8883-6000; fax: 8889-5235; email: norliza@ktak.gov.my).

Ministry of Entrepreneur Development and Co-operative Development, Lot 2G6, Precint 2, Federal Goverment Administrative Centre, 62100 Putrajaya (tel: 8880-5100; fax: 8880-5106; email: webmaster@mecd.gov.my).

Ministry of Federal Territories, Level 3, West block , Perdana Putra Building , Federal Government Administrative Centre, 62502 Putrajaya (tel: 8889-7844 ; fax: 8888-9140; email: admin@kwp.gov.my).

Ministry of Finance, Finance Ministry Complex, Precint 2, Federal Government Administrative Centre, 62592 Putrajaya (tel: 8882-3000; fax: 8882-3892/3894; email: webmaster@treasury.gov.my).

Ministry of Foreign Affairs, Wisma Putra , No 1, Jl Wisma Putra, Precint 2, 62602 Putrajaya (tel: 8887-4000/ 4570, 8889-2476; fax: 8889-1717/2816; email: webmaster@kln.gov.my; internet: www.kln.gov.my).

Ministry of Health, Block E1, E6, E7 and 10, Parcel E, Federal Government Administrative Centre, 62590 Putrajaya (tel: 8883-3888; fax: 2698-5964; email: iadam@moh.gov.my).

Ministry of Home Affairs, Block D2, Parcel D, Federal Government Administrative Centre, 62546 Putrajaya (tel: 8886-3000; fax: 8889-1613; email: pro@moha.gov.my).

Ministry of Human Resources, Level 6-9, Block D3, Parcel D, Federal Government Administrative Centre, 62502 Putrajaya (tel: 8886-5000; fax: 8889-2381; email: ksm@mohr.gov.my).

Ministry of Housing and Local Government, Level 3-7, Block K, Pusat Bandar Damansara, 50782 Kuala Lumpur (tel: 2094-7033; fax: 2094-9720; email: pro@kpkt.gov.my).

Ministry of Information, Angkasapuri, Bukit Putra, 50610 Kuala Lumpur (tel: 2282-5333; fax: 2282-1255; email: webmaster@kempen.gov.my).

Ministry of Internal Security, Level 3, Block D1 and D2, Parcel D, Federal Government Administrative Centre, 62546 Putrajaya (tel: 8886 8000; fax: 8889 1730; email: pro@mois.gov.my).

Ministry of Natural Resources and Environment, 13th Floor, Wisma Tanah,, Jl Semarak, 50574 Kuala Lumpur (tel: 2692-1566; fax: 2693-2166; email: webmaster@nre.gov.my).

Ministry of Plantation Industries and Commodities, Level 6–13, Lot 2G4, Precinct 2, Federal Government Administrative Centre, 62654 Putrajaya (tel: 8880-3300; fax: 8880-3482; email: info@kppk.gov.my).

Ministry of Rural and Regional Development, Level 5-9, Block D9, Parcel D, Federal Government Administrative Centre, 62606 Putrajaya (tel: 8886-3500/3700; fax: 8886-3801; email: webmaster@rurallink.gov.my).

Ministry of Science, Technology and Innovations, Level 1-7, Block C5, Federal Government Administrative Centre, 62662 Putrajaya (tel: 8885-8000; fax: 8888-9070; email: webmaster@mosti.gov.my).

Ministry of Transport, Level 5-7, Block D5, Parcel D, Federal Government Administrative Centre, 62502 Putrajaya (tel:

8886-6000/2597; fax: 8889-1569; email: saptuyah@mot.gov.my).

Ministry of Works, Level 4, Block B, Kompleks Kerja Raya, Jl Sultan Salahuddin, 50580 Kuala Lumpur (tel: 2711-1100/ 9309; fax: 2711-6612; email: pro@kkr.gov.my).

Ministry of Women, Family and Community Development, Level 1-6, Block E, Government Office Complex , Kompleks Pejabat Kerajaan Bukit Perdana, Jl Dato' Onn, 50515 Kuala Lumpur (tel: 2693-0095, 2693-0401; fax: 2693-4982; email: info@kpwkm.gov.my).

Ministry of Youth and Sports, Lot G4, Precinct 4, Federal Government Administrative Centre, 62570 Putrajaya (tel: 8871-3333; fax: 8888-8767; email: webmaster@kbs.gov.my).

Prime Minister's Department, Perdana Putra Building, Federal Government Administrative Centre, 62502 Putrajaya (tel: 8888-8000; fax: 8888-3444; email: ppmnun@pmo.gov.my).

Other useful addresses

Advertising Standards Authority of Malaysia, c/o Coopers and Lybrand, Hong Kong Bank Building, Leboh Pasar, Kuala Lumpur.

Asean Investment Promotion Agency, Malaysian Industrial Development Authority, 6th Floor, Wisma Damansara, Damansara Heights, PO Box 10618, 50720 Kuala Lumpur.

Asean Secretariat, 70 A Jl Sisingamangaraja, Jakarta 12110, Indonesia (tel: (+62-21) 726-2991, 724-3372; fax: (+62-21) 724-3504, 739-8234; internet: www.asean.or.id).

British Council, Jalan Bukit Aman, PO Box 10539, 50916 Kuala Lumpur.

British High Commission, PO Box 11030, 50732 KL; 185 Jalan Ampang, 50450 Kuala Lumpur (tel: 2170-2200; (Consular Section, tel: 2170-2345; email: consular2.kualalumpur@fco.gov.uk)).

British Malaysian Industry & Trade Association (BMITA), PO Box 12574, 50782 Kuala Lumpur.

Capital Issues Committee, Kementerian Kewangan, 11th Floor, Block 9, Khazanah Malaysia, Jl Duta, Kuala Lumpur.

Department of Immigration, Level 1-7 (Podium) Block 2G4, Precinct 2, Federal Government Administration Centre, 62550 Putrajaya, Federal Territory (tel: 8880-1000; fax: 8880-1200; internet: www.imi.gov.my).

Federal Land Development Authority, (FELDA), Wisma Felda, Jalan Perumahan Gurney, 54000 Kuala Lumpur (tel: 2693-5066; fax: 2692-0087; email: unitit.felda@felda.net.my).

Federation of Malaysian Manufacturers, Tingkat 7 Balai Felda, Jalan Gurney Satu (1), 54000 Kuala Lumpur (tel: 2698-7772; fax: 2693-0018; email: tohit.1@felda.net.my).

Foreign Investment Committee, Economic Planning Unit, Prime Minister's Dept, Jl Dato' Onn, Kuala Lumpur (tel: 230-0133).

Bursa Malaysia, (Kuala Lumpur Stock Exchange), Exchange Square, Bukit Kewangan, 50200 Kuala Lumpur (tel: 2034-7000; fax: 2732-0069; email: enquiries@bursamalaysia.com).

Malaysian Embassy (US), 2401 Massachusetts Avenue, NW, 20008 (tel: (+1-202) 328-2700; fax: (+1-202) 483-7661; email: mwwashdc@erols.com).

Malaysian Export Trade Centre, Ministry of Trade and Industry, Wisma PKNS, Jl Raja Laut, 50350.

Malaysian Industrial Development Authority (MIDA), Blk 4, Plaza Sentral, Jalan Stesen Sentral 5, Kuala Lumpur Sentral, 50470 Kuala Lumpur (tel: 2267-3633; fax: 2274-7970; email: promotion@mida.gov.my; internet: www.mida.gov.my).

Sarawak Economic Development Corporation, PO Box 400; 6-11th Floor, Menara SEDC, Jalan Tunku Abdul Rahman, 93902 Kuching, Sarawak, (tel: 416-777; fax: 424-330; email: ssedc@po.jaring.my; internet: www.sedc.com.my).

Securities Commission, 3 Persiaran Bukit Kiara, Bukit Kiara, 50490 Kuala Lumpur (tel: 6204-8510; fax: 6201-5078; internet: www.sc.com.my).

National news agency: Bernama Malaysian National News Agency, Wisma No 28, Jalan 1/65A, Off Jalan Tun Razak, 50400 Kuala Lumpur (tel: 03-2693-9933; fax: 03-2698-2332; internet: www.bernama.com).

Bernama: www.bernama.com

Internet sites

Malaysia Homepage: www.jaring.my

Malaysia portal: www.mycen.com.my

Malyasia yellow and white pages: www.tpsb.com.my/thome.htm

Maldives

KEY FACTS

Official name: Divehi Raajjeyge Jumhooriyyaa (Republic of Maldives)

Head of State: President Abdulla Yameen (elected 16 Nov 2013)

Head of government: President Abdulla Yameen

Ruling party: Progressive Party of Maldives (PPM) (from 22 March 2014)

Area: 298 square km (1,190 tiny atoll islands) – Malé: 1.5 square km

Population: 342,000 (2014)*

Capital: Malé, on Malé Island

Official language: Dhivehi (Maldivian)

Currency: Rufiyaa (MRf) = 100 laari

Exchange rate: MRf15.25 per US$ (Sep 2015)

GDP per capita: US$8,342 (2014)*

GDP real growth: 5.02% (2014)*

GDP: US$2.85 billion (2014)*

Inflation: 2.46% (2014)

Balance of trade: -US$1.66 billion (2014)

* estimated figure

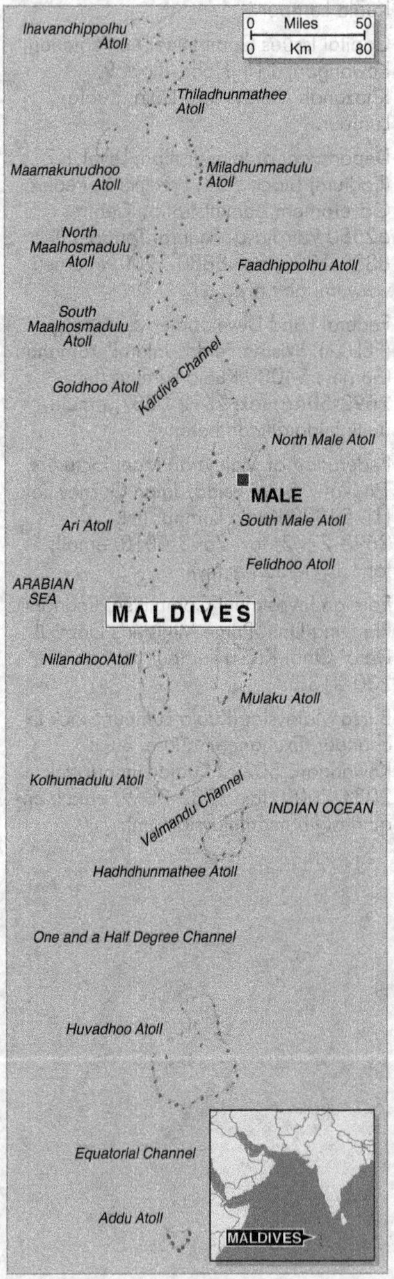

Probably few of the tourists visiting the Maldives in late 2015 were aware that the far flung island republic was in something of a state of turmoil. As they sped by boat from Ibrahim Nasir International Airport on Hulhule' Island to their expensive all-inclusive resort, there were few indications that the country was in a state of emergency, declared by President Abdulla Yameen – who is also head of government or prime minister and Commander in Chief of the Maldives' National Defence Force. Seven articles of the constitution had been suspended, including those guaranteeing citizens of the Indian Ocean island nation the rights of assembly, free expression, freedom from arbitrary detention and freedom of movement. The state of emergency was initially limited to 30 days. Critically, the decree gave the security forces sweeping powers to arrest suspects before a major anti-government rally that was planned within days. This was being organised by the main opposition Maldivian Democratic Party (MDP), whose leader Mohamed Nasheed was in jail following a conviction earlier in 2015 on terrorist charges. Nasheed had been deposed in 2012 amid protests, in what his supporters claimed was a *coup d'état*.

Paradise lost

The self-styled tourist paradise had been having a rough ride for some time, as its economy – posting what would have been satisfactory figures for most of the world's economies – under-performed. Although the Maldives remains a popular upmarket tourist destination (every year over a million tourists visit the Maldives), its image has been slightly dented due to the prolonged political unrest. However, although most of the tourists who did arrive were perfectly happy, the Maldives' citizens were anything but, with high unemployment rates (see 'Economy' below), overcrowding and reported drug problems. At the top of the political tree was a bitter struggle between the President and his deputy, Ahmed Adeeb. This had been going on for some time, since the president's election in 2013, with each party trying to raise support from different political actions and members of the army and police forces.

The infighting might have carried on had it not been for the apparent explosion that took place on the presidential launch carrying the President and his wife from the airport to Male on their return from a pilgrimage to Mecca. The President's wife and two of his party were reportedly injured. Initially the investigating authorities had announced that the explosion could have been the result of a mechanical failure, but they later claimed that it was an attempt to assassinate Gayoom and launched a criminal investigation.

One month later, in late October, Vice President Ahmed Adeeb was arrested, placed in detention and charged with high treason related to an alleged plot to assassinate the president. A criminal court later allowed police to detain Adeeb for 15 days for questioning. The offence of 'high treason' is not in fact specified in the Maldives penal code, but rather a generic term used applied to all offences against the state by government officials, politicians, judges and others.

Possibly in an attempt to show statesmanlike qualities, President Gayoom said that while he had dismissed Adeeb from heading some committees, he would not initiate an impeachment to strip him of the vice presidency until his case was decided by a court. Vice President Adeeb was not the only one arrested. Seven other people were held for questioning.

What could not be explained was the fact that the vice president had been known as a staunch supporter of President Gayoom. He was appointed vice president in July 2015 at the age of 33, promoted by the president to vice president after serving as tourism minister. In an address to the nation the President alleged that the vice president had provided the police with money and equipment outside of the state budget. He said that it was because of his influence over the police, it was considered that an impartial investigation could not be carried out with the vice president remaining in office.

The economy

According to the Asian Development Bank (ADB) official data showed economic growth to have accelerated to an estimated 6.8 per cent in 2014 from 4.7 per cent in the previous year. Tourism and related transport and communication remained key contributors to growth, while, in contrast with the previous two years, construction contributed substantially to expansion. Preliminary estimates showed that tourism expanded strongly by 6.8 per cent, still less than the 9.0 per cent growth recorded in 2013. Growth in tourist arrivals at 7.1 per cent in 2014 was much less robust than the 17.4 per cent seen in the previous year as European economies were sluggish and the People's Republic of China (PRC) experienced a slowdown. In 2014 Asian tourists made up 47 per cent of the market of 1.2 million visitors per year, most of them from the PRC. The share from Europe, which used to be the major market, had declined to 44 per cent. Transport grew robustly by 11.2 per cent and communication by 9.6 per cent, as reflected by the rapid increase in communication services such as mobile cellular and internet subscriptions. Government services likewise grew on increased social welfare spending and subsidies.

Construction rebounded substantially, by an estimated 20.6 per cent, after a 2.5 per cent contraction in 2013. The bulk of construction was in new resort projects and real estate development, notably on Hulhumalé to help relieve overcrowding in the nearby capital, Malé. Buoyant construction drove up imports of cement, wood and other construction materials by nearly 30.0 per cent. Bank lending to private construction firms rose accordingly. After growing at 5.1 per cent in 2013, agriculture slowed to 2.1 per cent as the fish catch declined. Fish exports, which accounted for essentially all domestic exports, fell by 2.8 per cent, compared with 22.1 per cent expansion in 2013. Average inflation moderated to 2.4 per cent in 2014 from 4.0 per cent in 2013, mainly on declining world commodity and fuel prices as well as weakening domestic fish prices. Monthly inflation throughout the year was low, ranging from 1.1 per cent to 3.5 per cent and trending downward in a see-saw pattern.

The ADB noted that the Maldives' fiscal policy was expansionary, with total expenditure increasing by 20.6 per cent from 3.5 per cent growth in 2013. Current expenditure, which made up over 80 per cent of total expenditure, rose by 17.1 per cent, largely on increased social welfare benefits, pension payments and subsidies for food, medicine, electricity. Capital expenditure increased by 40.4 per cent but still comprised only about 18 per cent of the fiscal budget. Revenue and grants grew rapidly by 25.3 per cent, owing mainly to increases in the business profits tax, the tourism goods and service tax and non-tax revenues. Based on reported fiscal data, the budget deficit was estimated to have narrowed to 3.2 per cent of GDP from 3.9 per cent in 2013. The International Monetary Fund (IMF) estimated, however, that the Maldives budget deficit widened to 11.6 per cent of GDP in 2014 from 7.8 per cent in 2013.

Government financing of the deficit was funded largely through Treasury bills bought primarily by domestic sources, mostly banks and other financial corporations. Total domestic claims on the central government increased from 40.7 per cent of GDP in 2013 to 44.3 per cent in 2014. Notably, all outstanding loans granted by the Maldives Monetary Authority (MMA) to the government were retired and replaced with Treasury bonds, which nearly doubled to Rf6.4 billion (US$0.42 billion).

External public debt increased by 5.6 per cent to US$789.5 million in 2014, amounting to 26.1 per cent of GDP. Total public debt was estimated at 70.4 per cent of GDP at the end of 2014, about 2 percentage points higher than a year earlier. The Maldives' monetary stance had been

KEY INDICATORS **Maldives**

	Unit	2011	2012	2013	2014	**2015
Population	m	0.33	*0.33	*0.34	*0.34	*0.35
Gross domestic product (GDP)	US$bn	1.94	2.11	2.70	*2.85	*3.03
GDP per capita	US$	5,973	6,378	8,023	*8,342	*8,717
GDP real growth	%	7.4	0.9	4.7	*5.0	*5.0
Inflation	%	12.1	10.9	4.0	2.5	*0.3
Exports (fob) (goods)	US$m	346.4	329.8	331.0	300.9	–
Imports (fob) (goods)	US$m	1,725.3	1,778.8	1,703.0	1,960.9	–
Balance of trade	US$m	-1,378.9	-1,449.1	-1,372.0	-1,660.0	–
Current account	US$m	-490.1	-484.0	-176.0	*-240.0	*-139.0
Total reserves minus gold	US$m	362.4	318.3	381.9	627.4	–
Foreign exchange	US$m	348.0	304.6	368.3	–	–
Exchange rate	per US$	14.05	15.36	15.41	15.40	–

* estimated figure ** forecast figure

accommodative because inflation was low and credit growth slowing. The MMA had moved to stimulate lending by reducing in February 2014 the minimum reserve requirements for banks from 25 per cent to 20 per cent, halving in September 2014 the overnight deposit facility interest rate to 1.5 per cent and cutting the overnight Lombard policy rate to 10 per cent from 12 per cent. Despite these efforts, bank lending rates for the private sector stayed elevated, though the rate eased somewhat for public corporations. The MMA reintroduced in April 2014 the fixed-rate tap system for issuing Treasury bills and the rates were subsequently set at 7.5 per cent for the 28-day bill and 8.0 per cent for the 91-day bill.

Credit to the private sector was depressed by net repayments for most of 2014 but began to pick up in the last quarter and, at year-end, was up slightly by 3.3 per cent as lending for construction and commerce increased while lending for tourism continued to fall. Growth in credit to the public sector slowed from 12.9 per cent in 2013 to 7.4 per cent in 2014. The large overall balance of payments surplus substantially increased the MMA's net foreign assets and with open market operations suspended from May 2014, banks' reserves with the MMA expanded by almost half and with them the banks' ability to lend. Growth in broad money eased to 14.7 per cent from 18.4 per cent in 2013.

The current account deficit was estimated to have widened to 9.6 per cent of GDP from 6.5 per cent in 2013 as higher imports outweighed increased tourism receipts. Merchandise imports rose by 16.8 per cent in 2014, much more than in the previous year, on robust imports of construction materials. This widened the trade deficit to 54.8 per cent of GDP as exports remained small. With capital and financial inflows double those of a year earlier, the overall balance of payments moved to a large surplus estimated at nearly US$250 million and gross international reserves climbed to US$614.7 million, sufficient to cover 3.7 months of merchandise imports. GDP growth was forecast by the ADB to average 6.3 per cent in 2015 and ease to 5.1 per cent in 2016. Tourism was projected to see growth rebound to 8.3 per cent in 2015 as the government forecast a 13.0 per cent growth in tourist arrivals. The launch of three new flights to the PRC in 2015 and a strengthened promotion campaign supported this projection. Tourism expansion was expected to moderate in 2016 in light of the low growth outlook in tourist source economies.

Growth in related transport and communication was expected to follow a similar trend. Construction was likely to continue to expand but at a moderate pace of 8.0 per cent in 2015 off the high base seen in 2014. Construction was expected to grow at a similar rate in 2016 as work gathers pace on government infrastructure and private investments connected with the new special economic zones.

Risk assessment

Economy	Good
Politics	Poor
Regional stability	Good

Muslims in Maldives

% of population	98.4
Sunni (% of Muslims)	99
Shi'a (% of Muslims)	1

COUNTRY PROFILE

1887 The islands were placed under British protection, with internal self-government.
1932 The first democratic constitution was proclaimed. The sultanate became an elected position.
1953 The Maldives became a republic and a member of the Commonwealth as the sultanate was abolished. However, the sultanate was restored within months.
1965 Gained full independence as a sultanate and left the Commonwealth.
1968 Following a referendum, the country reverted from a sultanate back to a republic. Ibrahim Nasir became president.
1975 The UK pulled out of its military base on Addu atoll. A proposal from the USSR to take over the base was rejected.
1978 Nasir retired and Maumoon Abdul Gayoom was elected president.
1980s The expansion in the tourist industry resulted in economic growth. An industrial zone was established on Gan.
1982 Rejoined the Commonwealth.
1988 An attempt by Sri Lankan Tamil mercenaries to depose the government was thwarted with the help of Indian army forces.
1994 Non-party elections to the Majlis (parliament) were held.
1997 A new constitution was passed.
1998 President Maumoon Abdul Gayoom was re-elected for a fifth consecutive term in office.
1999 Forty non-partisan members were elected to the Majlis. Over 120 candidates had stood in the November elections.
2002 The Maldivian and Indian governments began working together to implement a plan for poverty reduction in the Maldives.
2003 Amnesty International accused the government of political repression and torture. Riots broke out in Malé when prison inmates protested at alleged torture. President Gayoom won a sixth term with over 90 per cent of the vote.
2004 A special Majlis was formed to consider constitutional changes proposed by the President, including limiting his powers and allowing the formation of political parties. A referendum agreed to a presidential and parliamentary style of government. A state of emergency was declared after violence during a pro-democracy demonstration. An earthquake off the island of Sumatra caused a *tsunami* that devastated coastal areas in the region, including 20 inhabited islands of the Maldives. The final toll in the Maldives was estimated at 108 dead or missing and 29,577 displaced.
2005 In parliamentary elections, all candidates for the 42 seats ran officially as independents; parliament unanimously voted in favour of introducing multiparty politics. Five new political parties were registered: Dhivehi Rayyithunge Party (DRP) (Maldivian Peoples Party); Islamic Democratic Party (IDP); Adhaalath Party (AP) (Justice Party); Maldivian Democratic Party (MDP). Mohamed Nasheed (known as Anni) returned from exile to register the MDP; he was later arrested for terrorism and sedition.
2006 The South Asia Free Trade Agreement (Safta) between the Maldives, Bhutan, Bangladesh, India, Nepal, Sri Lanka and Pakistan came into effect.
2007 In a referendum, 60 per cent of the vote agreed to a presidential and parliamentary government system, while endorsing President Gayoom's continued administration.
2008 A new constitution that introduced key democratic changes, including multi-party presidential elections, the separation of power and a bill of rights, was ratified. In the first democratic presidential election since 1978, after two rounds Mohamed Nasheed won 54.2 per cent beating incumbent Maumoon Gayoom who won 45.8 per cent.
2009 In parliamentary elections, the DRP won 28 seats (out of 77), and President Nasheed's party, MDP 26, independents 13, the People's Alliance (PA), led by former president Gayoom's brother Abdullah Yameen, 7, the Republican Party 1 and the Dhivehi Qaumee Party 2.
2010 A 25-year lease agreement was signed by the government with the GMR-Malaysia Airport Holdings consortium to develop and manage the Male International Airport. A US$180 million agreement was signed with the US energy

company Merciel to provide electricity for all islands (three atolls) in the upper north province, using bio-fuelled generators.

2011 In April, by presidential decree, the rufiyaa exchange rate was floated against the US dollar (between MRf10.20–15.42). In May police used tear gas and batons to disperse several thousand people who had gathered to protest at the deteriorating economy and demand that President Mohamed Nasheed should quit. In June Bangladesh and the Maldives signed a memorandum of understanding to implement free trade between them. Import taxes on medicines from Bangladesh were removed. In August Sri Lanka gave a US$10 million import credit to the Maldives, to encourage the import of, particularly, fruit and vegetables for tourist hotels. India granted more credit than Sri Lanka, which felt they would lose out unless they increased their own credit. Sri Lanka also agreed to construct a road to help preparations for the South Asian Association for Regional Cooperation (SAARC) summit held in the Maldives in November.

2012 President Nasheed ordered the arrest of the Chief Justice of the criminal court (in January), accusing him of political bias and corruption. The arrest of the Chief Justice resulted in mass protests and the downfall of Nasheed who was forced to resign on 7 February during a televised press conference. This followed weeks of demonstrations and a mutiny by police who seized control of the state broadcaster in Male and broadcast support for former president, Maumoon Abdul Gayoom. Vice President Mohamed Waheed Hassan was sworn in as president within hours, while Nasheed was held under detention by security forces in the presidential palace. The vice president denied that Nasheed's replacement was a coup. An arrest warrant was issued for Nasheed on 10 February, as supporters surrounded his former house. The charges were unclear and President Hassan said that the warrant was not to be served unless it became necessary for Mr Nasheed's personal safety. The revised date for the next presidential election was set for July 2013. On 15 July former president Nasheed was charged with illegally arresting the Chief Justice. On 25 September, a travel ban was imposed on Nasheed, preventing him from leaving the capital to campaign ahead of presidential elections. On 1 October, the court case against Nasheed, for abuse of power while in office, began. Nasheed believed the charges against him were politically motivated, as any conviction would ban him from participating in any elections. Nasheed refused to appear before the special court, questioning its legitimacy and saying that he had appealed his case before the High Court and awaited its decision; an arrest warrant was issued by the special court on 8 October, which Nasheed defied. On 5 November, the High Court suspended the trial of the special court.

2013 The Puntland government signed piracy-transfer agreements with the governments of Seychelles, Mauritius and the Maldives, to bring convicted Somali pirates to complete their prison sentences in Puntland prisons. The United Nations Office on Drugs and Crime has overseen a prison construction project in Bosaso and Garowe for the purpose of housing convicted pirates. In the first round of the presidential election held on 7 September Mohamed Nasheed won 45 per cent and Abdulla Yameen 25 per cent. The second round was set for 28 September. However, electoral fraud was alleged by the third placed candidate, Qasim Ibrahim, who requested the Maldives Supreme Court to annul the results. The Court ordered the Elections Commission to postpone the second round while it considered a ruling. On 7 October the Court annulled the results of the first round and called for new elections by 20 October. On 12 October President Mohamed Waheed withdrew from the race, having received just 5 per cent of the vote, saying he was doing so for the 'greater interest' of the Maldives. The 20 October election failed to take place after police prevented ballot papers from being distributed. Mohamed Nasheed called for fresh elections under a caretaker leader. He called for President Waheed to resign to let the parliamentary speaker oversee the elections. On 21 October the electoral commission announced new dates as 9 November (first round) and 16 November (second round if necessary). Under the constitution a new president had to be elected by 11 November; it was not clear what the situation would be if a second round were needed. President Waheed confirmed that he would not be standing. Two members of parliament were ejected by the Supreme Court on 25 October. The main opposition party, the Maldivian Democratic Party (MDP), accused the government of harassment. On 6 November the three presidential candidates announced they had agreed to take part in elections on 9 November. Mr Nasheed polled nearly 47 per cent, just short of the 50 per cent needed to avoid a run-off on 10 November. However, the Supreme Court suspended the run-off for six days, after the runner-up, Abdulla Yameen, sought a delay, saying he needed time to campaign afresh. The second round, held on 16 November, was won by Abdulla Yameen with 51.3 per cent, Mohamed Nasheed 48.6 per cent.

2014 The Commonwealth Observer Group to observe the 22 March parliamentary elections was headed by Bruce Golding, former prime minister of Jamaica. The result was win for the Progressive Party of Maldives with 33 seats (out of 85) (27.72 per cent), followed by the Maldivian Democratic Party (MDP) 26 seats (40.78 per cent), Jumhooree Party 15 seats (13.55 per cent), Maldives Development Alliance 5 seats (4.04 per cent), Adhaalath Party 1 seat (2.65 per cent), independents 5 seats (10.93 per cent). The Dhivehi Rayyithunge Party (DRP) (Maldivian Peoples Party) lost all their seats. After the elections the Observer Group reported that 'Election day was orderly, peaceful and well administered. The competency of polling officials and the presence of observers and media enabled an efficient and transparent process. Voters appeared to be free to exercise their franchise.' However the Group was '... deeply concerned that, in the lead up to the elections, action was taken by the Supreme Court on 9 March to declare the Chair and the Vice Chair of the Elections Commission dismissed from their positions for contempt of court.' This 'inevitably had a negative effect on the overall electoral environment and created a level of uncertainty regarding the electoral process' reported the Group.

2015 Despite being cleared of the charges in February, on 13 March former president Mohamed Nasheed was found guilty of ordering the arrest of a judge (Abdulla Mohamed) while in office and sentenced to 13 years in prison. This will prevent him from standing for president again in 2018. On 9 September human rights lawyer, Amal Clooney, met with Mr Nasheed, prior to represting him in discussions with the government and the day before an appeal by the prosecutor general's office was to be heard by the high court. The prosecutor general's office said they had found some procedural irregularities. Around the same time he UN rights chief, Zeid Ra'ad Al-Hussein, called on the Yameen government to release Mr Nasheed, as well as calling for a review of criminal cases against several hundred of Nasheed's party supporters who have been arrested in protests since May in the Maldives. A bomb exploded on the President's boat as he was returning from Haj. His wife and a number of others on the boat were injured although the President himself was not. The police refered to the incident as 'an alleged plot to assassinate the president'. Vice President Ahmed Adeeb was arrested on 24 October, charged with treason over an alleged plot to assassinate the president.

Political structure

Constitution

The constitution dates from 1997, which provides power to the executive, the legislature and the judiciary, while these powers are vested from the people. The president also derives influence from the constitutional role as 'supreme authority to propagate the tenets of Islam'.

However critics argue that supreme power under the constitution is held by the president, who can appoint and dismiss the top posts in all branches of the administration. The constitution, it is argued, does not provide a guarantee that individuals' rights are not subject to subordinate laws and government practices.

In 2007 constitutional changes included the introduction of a US-style presidential form of government, where the president can only hold office for two terms and the introduction of a multiparty parliament.

In January 2008 the gender bar that allowed women to serve in the Majlis but not become a presidential candidate, was removed. A new constitution was ratified on 7 August which introduced key democratic changes, including multi-party presidential elections, the separation of power and a bill of rights.

Voting: universal suffrage over 21 years.

Local authority is vested in atoll chiefs and island headmen appointed by the president.

Independence date

26 July 1965

The executive

Executive power is held by the president, who is head of state and head of government, commander-in-chief of the armed forces, minister of defence and national security, and minister of finance and treasury.

Since 2008 the president has been elected for a renewable five-year term. The winner must achieve a vote of over 50 per cent, failing which a run-off must be held within three weeks.

National legislature

The unicameral Majlis (parliament) has 85 members, elected in single member constituencies by the first-past-the-post system. All members serve for five-year terms. The Majlis must ratify all legislation introduced by the government or parliamentary members (MP).

Legal system

The legal system is based on Islamic law with admixtures of English common law, primarily in commercial matters.

Last elections

9 and 16 November 2013 (presidential) first and second roundw; 22 March 2014 (parliamentary).

Results: Presidential (first round): Mohamed Nasheed 45.45 per cent (MDP), Abdulla Yameen (PPM) 25.35 per cent, Qasim Ibrahim (JP) 24.07 per cent, Mohammed Waheed Hassan (Independent) 5.13 per cent. Turnout was 88.44 per cent.

Presidential (second round): 16 November Abdulla Yameen 51.39 per cent, Mohamed Nasheed 48.61 per cent. Turnout was 91.41 per cent.

Parliamentary: Progressive Party of Maldives won 33 seats (27.72 per cent), Maldivian Democratic Party (MDP) 26 seats (40.78 per cent), Jumhooree Party 15 seats (13.55 per cent), Maldives Development Alliance 5 seats (4.04 per cent), Adhaalath Party 1 seat (2.65 per cent), independents 5 seats (10.93 per cent). The Dhivehi Rayyithunge Party (DRP) (Maldivian Peoples Party) lost all their seats.

Next elections

2019 (parliamentary), 2018 (presidential)

Political parties

Ruling party

Progressive Party of Maldives PPM) (from 22 March 2014)

Main opposition party

Maldivian Democratic Party (MDP)

Population

336,000 (2013)*

Last census: 21 March 2006: 298,968

Population density: 1,066 inhabitants per square km (2010). Urban population 40 per cent (2010 Unicef).

Annual growth rate: 1.8 per cent, 1990–2010 (Unicef).

Ethnic make-up

The majority of the population are Sinhalese or Dravidian, with significant Arab and smaller African minorities.

Religions

Islam (Sunni majority)

Education

Primary education is provided through either private or state schools; lessons are given in English, Arabic and Dhivehi.

The curriculum, for segregated (by gender) secondary education, is based on the British system and many schools prepare students to sit the General Certificate of Education at 'O' level and a few for 'A' level examinations. Students have to travel abroad for higher education.

President Gayoom has made improving education levels his top priority. There is an ongoing teacher training programme due to the shortage of qualified teachers.

Typically 2.4 per cent of the GNP is spent on primary education.

Literacy rate: 97.2 per cent total; adult rates (World Bank).

Enrolment rate: 98 per cent net primary enrolment (Unicef).

Pupils per teacher: 24 in primary schools.

Health

The Maldives has significantly improved health services and severe diseases such as malaria, childhood tuberculosis and leprosy have been eradicated.

There are two hospitals on the main island and six regional hospitals serving all the remaining islands. In addition, there are 45 health centres and 36 health posts serving the islands.

HIV/Aids

The first Maldivian with HIV was identified in 1991. There have been six deaths as a result of Aids. Although the HIV rate is very small, the Maldives is particularly vulnerable to the spread of the virus due to the high number of migrant workers that pass through the islands. Drug usage among young people is also on the rise.

Life expectancy: 67 years, 2004 (WHO 2006)

Fertility rate/Maternal mortality rate: 1.8 births per woman, 2010 (Unicef)

Child (under 5 years) mortality rate (per 1,000): 11 per 1,000 live births (WHO 2012); 45 per cent of children aged under five are malnourished (World Bank).

Head of population per physician: 0.92 physicians per 1,000 people, 2004 (WHO 2006)

Welfare

Due to the highly dispersed character of the country, it is difficult for the government to ensure that everyone receives benefits. The ministry of women's affairs and social welfare has responsibility for administering the welfare programme that covers women, children, the disabled and unemployed.

Main cities

Malé (capital, estimated population 134,232 in 2012); Hithadhoo (9,394), Fuvammulah (7,674), Kulhudhuffushi (7,434).

Languages spoken

The Maldivian language is Indo-Aryan.

Official language/s

Dhivehi (Maldivian)

Media

The government retains the power to close media outlets critical to its regime which has resulted in media self-regulation.

Press

There are several newspapers publishing in the Divehi language, and some with English online editions, including *Haveeru* (www.haveeru.com.mv) and *Miadhu* (www.miadhu.com.mv), *Aafathis Daily News* (www.aafathisnews.com.mv), is one of the oldest local newspapers and *Haama Daily* (www.haamadaily.com).

Broadcasting

Radio: There are only four radio stations broadcasting, two government owned, Voice of Maldives (www.vom.gov.mv) and Radio Eke and two private DhiFM (http://dhifm95.com) and Capital Radio (http://capital956.fm). An overseas radio operated by expatriates opposed to the government of President Gayoom broadcasts over the internet, Radio Minivan (www.minivannews.com).

Television: The only local television service, TVM Maldives, is government-run. Satellite TV is available.

Economy

The economy is based on tourism and commercial fishing. The service sector in 2014 constituted 77.4 per cent of GDP, of which, the tourist industry is typically the largest single component at around 50 per cent of GDP. Industry accounted for 13.2 per cent of GDP, of which manufacturing was 5 per cent and agriculture contributed 3.6 per cent of GDP.

The global economic crisis impacted the economy significantly as visitor numbers dropped. GDP growth was 12.2 per cent in 2008, but with a fall in foreign earnings from tourism. The Maldives plummeted into recession at -4.7 per cent in 2009. Positive GDP growth returned in 2010 at 5.7 per cent, as promotional programmes stimulated tourism, and the economies of the host countries recovered and tourists had more time and money to spend. Growth rose from 3.7 per cent in 2013 to 7.2 per cent in 2014 driven by stronger tourism activity. Higher tourism exports and low global fuel inflation have helped reduce the current account deficit to around 8.4 per cent of GDP in 2014.

There was a change of government in 2008, when long-term President Gayoom retired and a new political regime took over, changing the direction of the economy. The new government, under president Mohammed Nasheed, implemented reforms that included, in particular, a cut of around 9,000 public workers with a reduction in the public service wage bill, which had increased fourfold and grown to represent 28 per cent of GDP. These measures were welcomed by the International Monetary Fund (IMF), which extended to Maldives a loan of US$93.5 million in 2009, allowing the government to manage its large external debt and shore up its foreign reserves. However, by 2010, the IMF reported that tax reforms had been delayed and public wages had increased, which had resulted in 'significant fiscal slippages', which would need adjustments to the exchange rate and fiscal strategy to achieve a reduction in public debt. On 8 February 2012, President Nasheed was forced to step down in favour of Vice President Hassan, who in turn was succeeded by Abulla Yameen as president from 16 November 2013.

The largest project undertaken by the Maldives has been the Hulhumalé infrastructure project, which has reclaimed land close to the capital Malé, on Kafuul Atoll, for domestic, commercial and industrial expansion. By 2012, many housing units, mosques, roads and waste management for the development had been completed. Final completion of the project, which will include such facilities as a hospital, sports buildings and more housing is due by 2020.

External trade

The Maldives is a member of the South Asia Association for Regional Co-operation (SAARC), which operates a preferential trading arrangement that covers 6,000 products. It is also a member of the South Asia Free Trade Area (Safta) along with seven other member states (India, Pakistan, Bhutan, Nepal, Bangladesh and Sri Lanka), that in 2012 had a customs union.

Fishing is a major industrial sector, which provides foreign exchange, as well as revenue from licensing fishing rights to foreign fleets. Manufactured garments and boat building are important sectors. The agriculture sector is unable to feed the population and staple foods must be imported.

Imports

Main imports are petroleum, commodities and foodstuffs, intermediate and consumer goods, capital machinery and vehicles.

Main sources: UAE (23.7 per cent of total in 2014), Singapore (17.5 per cent), India (8.6 per cent)

Exports

Main exports include fish, garments and boats.

Main destinations: Thailand (32.2 per cent of total in 2014), France (14.5 per cent), United States (9 per cent)

Agriculture

Farming

Agriculture, including fishing, accounts for 3.6 per cent of GDP. Farming is at subsistence level on smallholdings, confined to field crops and fruit trees, with no livestock. Main crops are coconuts, bananas, watermelon, sweet potato, cucumber, cassava, pumpkin, cabbage and yam. Approximately 6 per cent of the total land area is under cultivation. The soil is shallow and highly alkaline, with poor water-retaining properties.

Fishing

The fishing sector is second to tourism in importance to the economy. Fish provide the main source of protein for the population with a 126,000 tonnes annual catch. Fishing employs over 20 per cent of the workforce.

Tourism

The tourist industry is the most important component of the economy, contributing 41.5 per cent to GDP directly and 78.1 per cent in total in 2014. Tourism provides 32.2 per cent of employment directly (48,000 jobs) and 62 per cent in total (92,000 jobs). The Maldives has promoted its tropical beauty to tourists from around the world with the islands receiving 1.2 million visitors in 2014. Over 70 per cent of all visitors come from Europe, with visitors from the UK, Italy and Germany pre-eminent.

The government is attempting to balance the interests and the long-term requirements of the people of the Maldives with the needs and expectations of visitors. However, sustainable tourism may not be possible as fragile environments and natural resources become overwhelmingly consumed by tourists.

Environment

It has been reported that the beaches of one-third of the Maldives' 200 inhabited islands could be swept away by rising sea levels, as global warming melts the fringes of polar ice caps. Another issue affecting the Maldives is the depletion of fresh water aquifiers which threatens water supply.

Hydrocarbons

There are no known hydrocarbon reserves and all domestic energy requirements are met by imports. Oil consumption was 7,310 barrels per day in 2013. Any natural gas or coal imports are commercially negligible.

Energy

Total installed generating capacity was 77MW in 2013, produced by imported oil, of which around half the capacity is concentrated in tourist resort areas. The State Electricity Company (Stelco) generates a third of the supply. Island Development Committees and private generators supply the rest.

In 2014, The World Bank approved a US$16 million IDA guarantee towards the Accelerating Sustainable Private Investment in Renewable Energy (ASPIRE) Project. The funding aims to develop new electricity generation capacity with renewable solar photovoltaic (PV) energy resources.

Financial markets

Stock exchange

Maldives Stock Exchange (MSE)

Banking and insurance

Central bank

Maldives Monetary Authority

Time
GMT plus five hours

Geography
The Republic of Maldives is one of the smallest countries in the world. Situated in the Indian Ocean, it lies about 675km (420 miles) south-west of Sri Lanka. The northern tip of the Maldives is about 600km south of India. Over 99 per cent of the territory is sea.
The Maldives consists of around 1,190 small islands grouped into 26 atolls, running north to south in a double chain 823km long and 129km wide. The total land area is around 298 square km. Most of the islands are coral outcrops perched on a submarine mountain range, although some are only sandbars. They are low-lying, reaching no higher than two metres above sea level. They are at risk of flooding from natural causes, most recently the *tsunami* of December 2004. The geography of the country can be affected in that islands can disappear as a result of flooding, as well as from erosion. The potential effects of global warming on sea levels puts the continued physical existence of the archipelago at risk.
Around 200 islands are inhabited. Many of these are covered by tropical vegetation, including coconut palms and breadfruit trees, while the uninhabitated islands are given over to scrub. Few islands in the archipelago are longer than 2km, the longest being Hithadhoo, which is 8km long. While most form atolls enclosing shallow lagoons, several are single islands with coral beaches.

Hemisphere
Northern

Climate
There is year-round sunshine, with temperatures ranging 26–30 degrees Celsius. Most rainfall occurs during the south-west monsoon season from April–October.

Entry requirements

Passports
Required by all, valid for six months.

Visa
Visas are issued free to all visitors on arrival at the airport in Malé for visits of up to 30 days (visas may be extended for a minimum of three months on payment of a fee). Proof of return/onward passage is necessary.

Currency advice/regulations
There are no restrictions on the import and export of local and foreign currencies.

Customs
Personal effects are allowed duty-free. Tortoise and articles produced using tortoise shells may not be exported.

Prohibited imports
Alcohol, pork, pharmaceuticals and goods at variance with Islamic culture are prohibited or subject to restrictions. Pornographic material may not be imported.

Health (for visitors)

Mandatory precautions
Vaccination certificate required for yellow fever if travelling from an infected area.

Advisable precautions
Anti-malarial precautions, outside Malé. Hepatitis A and B, tetanus and typhoid. There is a rabies risk.
Visitors are advised to use mosquito repellent, a mosquito net at night, and wear clothing covering as much skin as possible.

Hotels
The Maldives are a popular tourist destination. There are numerous first class hotels and island resorts.

Credit cards
All major credit cards, including American Express, Visa and MasterCard, are widely accepted on the islands.

Public holidays (national)

Fixed dates
1 Jan (New Year's Day), 26–27 Jul (Independence Days), 3 Nov (Victory Day), 11–12 Nov (Republic Day).

Variable dates
Hajj Day (Jan), Eid al Adha, Islamic New Year, National Day, Birth of the Prophet, Start of Ramadan, Eid al Fitr (End of Ramadan), Huravee Day (Jul), Martyrs' Day (Sep).

Islamic year 1437 (15 Oct 2015–2 Oct 2016):: The Islamic year contains 354 or 355 days, with the result that Muslim feasts advance by 10–12 days against the Gregorian calendar. Dates of feasts vary according to the sighting of the new moon, so cannot be forecast exactly.

Working hours

Banking
Sun–Thu: 0800–1330.

Business
Sun–Thu: 0730–1430. During the month of Ramadan 0900–1300.

Government
Sun–Thu: 0730–1430.

Shops
Sat–Thu: 0930–2300; Fri: 1400–2300.

Weights and measures
Metric system

Social customs/useful tips
Alcohol can only be consumed in holiday resorts.

Getting there

Air
National airline: Island Aviation Services
International airport/s: Malé International Airport (MLE), (renamed Ibrahim Nasir International Airport) on Hulule Island, 2km north-east of Malé; post office, bank, restarurants, duty-free shop.
Airport tax: US$12, usually included in price of ticket.

Surface
Main port/s: Gan, Uligamu and Malé.

Getting about

National transport
Air: Island Aviation Services operates regular domestic flights between Malé and island airports at Gan, Kaadedhdhoo, Kadhdhoo and Hanimaadhoo. Charter planes are also available.
Water: There is a public boat service from the airport to Malé city centre, with a journey time of 15 minutes. Resort islands have regular ferry services. Local boats can be hired; rates are negotiable. Charter vessels are available.

City transport
Due to the small size of the islands, there is little need for transportation. It is possible to walk to all places within the small area of Malé.
Taxis: Taxis are available in Malé.

BUSINESS DIRECTORY

The addresses listed below are a selection only. While World of Information makes every endeavour to check these addresses, we cannot guarantee that changes have not been made, especially to telephone numbers and area codes. We would welcome any corrections.

Telephone area codes
The international direct dialling code (IDD) for the Maldives is +960, followed by subscriber's number.

Useful telephone numbers
Police: 119
Fire: 118
Ambulance: 102

Chambers of Commerce
Maldives National Chamber of Commerce and Industry, G Viyafaari Hiya, Ameenee Magu, PO Box 92, Malé 2004 (tel: 332-6634; fax: 331-0233; e-mail: mncci@dhivehinet.net.mv).

Banking
Bank of Ceylon, 2 Boduthakurufaanu Magu, Malé (tel: 332-3045; fax: 332-0575; e-mail: bcmale@dhivehinet.net.mv).

Bank of Maldives, 11 Boduthakurufaanu Magu, Malé (tel: 333-0100; fax: 332-8233; e-mail: bmla@dhivehinet.net.mv).

Habib Bank Ltd, Ground Floor, Ship Plaza, 1/6 Orchid Magu , Malé (tel: 332-2051; fax: 332-6791; e-mail: hbmale@dhivehinet.net.mv).

State Bank of India, Boduthakurufaanu Magu, Malé (tel: 332-0860; fax: 332-3053; e-mail: sbimale@dhivehinet.net.mv).

Central bank

Maldives Monetary Authority, 3rd Floor, Umar Shopping Arcade, Chandhanee Magu, Malé 20156 (tel: 3312-343; fax: 3323-862; e-mail: mail@mma.gov.mv).

Stock exchange

Maldives Stock Exchange (MSE), www.maldivesstockexchange.com.mv

Travel information

Island Aviation Services, Malé (tel: 333-5566; fax: 331-4806; e-mail: sales@island.com.mv).

Maldives Tourism Promotion Board, 12 Boduthakurufaanu Magu, Malé (tel: 332-328; fax: 332-3229; e-mail: mtpb@visitmaldives.com).

Malé International Airport, Malé (tel: 332-5511; fax: 333-1515; e-mail: info@macinet.net).

Ministry of tourism

Ministry of Tourism, 2/F Ghazi Building, Orchid Magu, Henveiru, Malé (tel: 313-461).

Ministries

Ministry of Atolls Development, Faashanaa Bdg, Boduthakurufaanu Magu, Malé (tel: 332-3070; fax: 332-7750; e-mail: info@atolls.gov.mv).

Ministry of Communication, Science and Technology, 12 Boduthakurufaanu Magu, Malé (tel: 333-1695; fax: 333-1694; e-mail: secretariat@mcst.gov.mv).

Ministry of Economic Development and Trade, Ghazee Bdg, Ameeru Ahmed Magu, Malé (tel: 332-3668; fax: 332-3840; e-mail: contact@trademin.gov.mv).

Ministry of Fisheries, Agriculture and Marine Resources, Ghazee Bdg, Ameeru Ahmed Magu, Malé (tel: 332-2625; fax: 332-6558; e-mail: it@fishagri.gov.mv).

Ministry of Health, Ameenee Magu, Malé (tel: 332-5311; fax: 332-7793; e-mail: moh@dhivehinet.net.mv).

Ministry of Higher Education, Employment and Social Security, Haveeree Hingun, Malé (tel: 331-7172; fax: 333-1578; e-mail: admin@employment.gov.mv).

Ministry of Women's Affairs and Social Security, Umar Shopping Arcade, Chandhanee Magu, Malé (tel: 332-5956; fax: 331-6237; e-mail: info@urcmaldives.gov.mv).

Other useful addresses

Attorney General's Office, Huravee Bdg, Malé (tel: 332-3809; fax: 331-4109).

Maldives National Ship Management Ltd, 2/F, Ship Plaza, Male (tel: 332-3871; fax: 332-4323; e-mail@mnfl@dhivehinet.net.mv).

Maldives Association of Tourism Industry, Gadhamoo Bdg, Boduthakurufaanu Magu, Malé (tel: 332-6640; fax: 332-6641).

Maldives Traders' Association, G Viyafaari Hiyaa, Meenee Magu, Malé (tel: 332-6634; fax: 332-1889).

State Trading Organisation, Haveeree Higun, Malé (tel: 332-3279; fax: 332-5218; e-mail: sto@dhivehinet.net.mvo).

Internet sites

Maldives Consular Information: http://www.travel.state.gov/maldives.html

Maldives news online: http://maldivesculture.com

Maldives Yellow Pages: http://www.maldivesyellowpages.com

Mali

KEY FACTS

Official name: République du Mali (Republic of Mali)

Head of State: Interim President Ibrahim Boubacar Keita (from 11 Aug 2013)

Head of government: Prime Minister Modibo Keita (from 9 Jan 2015)

Ruling party: Rassemblement pour le Mali (RPM) (Rally for Mali)

Area: 1,241,238 square km

Population: 15.79 million (2014)*

Capital: Bamako

Official language: French

Currency: CFA franc (CFAf) = 100 centimes (Communauté Financière Africaine (African Financial Community) franc).

Exchange rate: CFAf586.44 per US$ (Sep 2015)

GDP per capita: US$755 (2014)*

GDP real growth: 6.83% (2014)*

GDP: US$11.91 billion (2014)*

Inflation: 0.89% (2014)*

Balance of trade: -US$248.60 million (2013)

* estimated figure

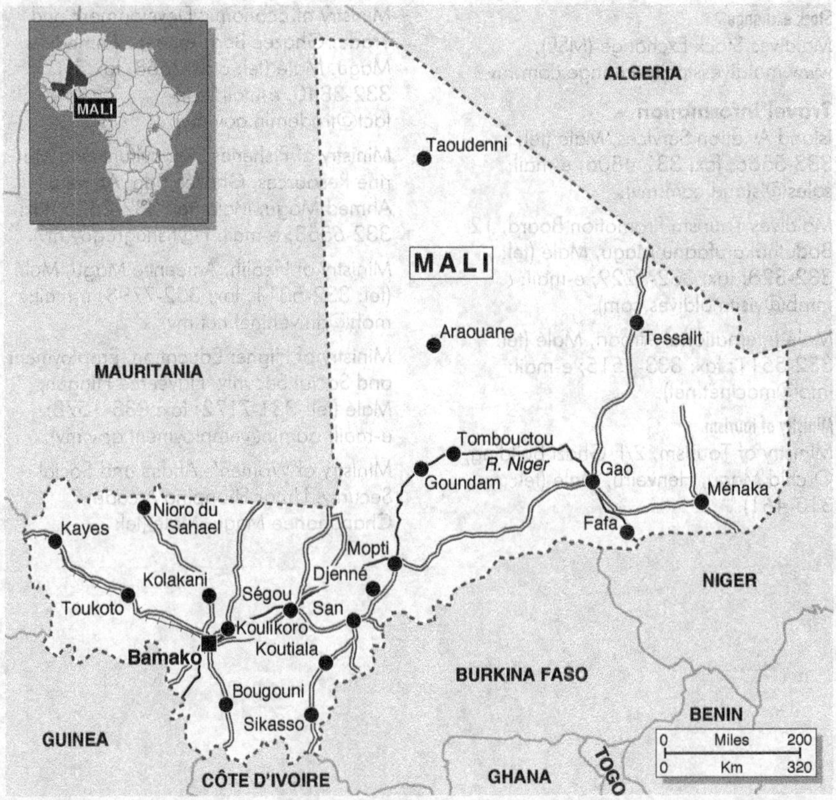

The long periods of military rule in Mali over the years have left the country largely devoid of mature politicians capable of running the country. The French had conquered Mali during the mid-nineteenth century. In 1958 it was proclaimed the Sudanese Republic and the following year it became the Mali Federation, after uniting with Senegal. However, Senegal seceded and Mali became independent in 1960. In 1985 Mali fought a brief border war with Burkina Faso and thirty years on, relations continue to be strained.

There had been an influx of arms in 2011 following the breakdown of law and order in Libya. The nomadic Tuareg to the north of the country began an insurgency concerning land and cultural rights, which has continued to this day. The Saharan branch of al Qaeda was quick to capitalise on this increasing lawlessness, seizing control of the Tuareg north after a March 2012 military coup. They then proceeded to impose a harsh form of Islamic law and advanced south. Alarmed at the capture of the town of Konna, the government in Bamako asked France to intervene. French troops overran the Islamist strongholds in the north. However, tensions still pervade much of the country and region, as both Tuareg separatists and Islamists remain sporadically active.

Following independence from France in 1960, democratic elections were finally held in 1992. Mali has suffered numerous times due to droughts, rebellions, and a dictatorship under Moussa Traoré that lasted for 23 years (1968–91). A military coup lead by Lieutenant Colonel Amadou Toumani Touré ended the dictatorship, ushering in a new era under democratically elected President Alpha Oumar Konaré in June 1992, which led to the arrival of rapid economic growth, a flourishing democracy and relative social stability. Amadou Toumani Touré came back on the scene when he won the 2002 presidential elections.

However, the gains made all hung in the balance by 2012, when the collapse of state control over the north of the country was followed by what the London BBC described as 'an inconclusive military coup'. A French military intervention against Islamist fighters that threatened to advance south also contributed to a feeling of unease and uncertainty within the region.

President Amadou Touré had been democratically elected to a second term in 2007. However, he was later overthrown owing to the frustrations of soldiers concerning the handling of the northern rebellion in 2012. Interim President Traore was appointed by a civilian administration. The post-coup chaos led to rebels expounding Malian militaries in three regions in the north, to be replaced by Islamist strongholds. An international effort to retake the regions the following year was, for the most part, successful. Ibrahim Boubacar Keïta was elected in the second round of the 2013 elections.

The economy

According to the African Development Bank (AfDB) in it's 2015 update, the economy of Mali remained firm in 2014. Gross domestic production (GDP) growth increased by an estimated 5.8 per cent after recovery began the previous year with an expansion of 1.7 per cent. This was mainly due to advances in the primary sector, which was up 9.4 per cent. Good harvests boosted agriculture by 13 per cent. The services sector also contributed, with a revival of activity in transport and telecommunications (up by 7.4 per cent), and commerce, (up 3 per cent).

The secondary sector performed poorly however. An increase of 1.8 per cent was low compared to the 5.5 per cent of 2013. The current account deficit worsened to 6.2 per cent of GDP in 2014, from 1.2 per cent the previous year. Lower oil prices might result in cheaper imports over 2015 and 2016, as terms of trade improve as well.

The political instability and occupation of the north in 2012 had quickly led to the deterioration of an already fragile social situation. The UN Development Programme's 2013 *Human Development Index* ranked Mali only 182 out of 187 countries. The slight drop in the poverty rate did not actually reduce the number of people affected, which grew from 5.7 million to 6.4 million between 2001 and 2010. The high fertility rate (6.7 children per woman) hampered poverty reduction and resulted in large dependency ratios, worsened maternal mortality and entrenched gender inequality in various sectors. It also placed great pressure on the government's ability to provide basic services for all, such as education, healthcare, social protection and security.

The International Monetary Fund's (IMF) publication in 2015 called for a steadfast implementation of reforms in order to further strengthen public financial management. The performance criteria for the end of 2014 relating to gross tax revenue and market financing of the government were not met owing to weaknesses at customs administrations. The IMF suggested that tax policy and administration reforms need to be accelerated to successfully raise the tax yield. Simplifying the tax and customs administrative procedures will help improve the overall business environment.

Mali had been on target to meet the 2015 Millennium Development Goals (MDGs) for universal primary education, controlling the spread of HIV/Aids and access to safe drinking water. But this progress made in recent years has been damaged by the occupation of the north and these MDGs may not now be achieved. The humanitarian situation in the north remains unstable, with more than 1,390,000 people needing urgent food aid, 496,000 children under five in danger of acute malnutrition and refugees and displaced people returning to their home regions in difficult conditions.

Risk assessment

Politics	Poor
Economy	Poor
Regional stability	Poor

Muslims in Mali

% of population	92.4
Sunni (% of Muslims)	98
Shi'a (% of Muslims)	1

COUNTRY PROFILE

900 Modern-day Mali was part of the empire of Ghana.

1250s Sundiata Keita, leader of the Mandinka people, established the Empire of Mali, which stretched from the Atlantic to the present-day borders of Nigeria and controlled most trans-Sahara trading routes by the fourteenth century.

1464 The Songhai Empire, centred around Gao, overwhelmed the Mali Empire and began to conquer the Sahel.

1591 After a Moroccan invasion, the Songhai Empire collapsed.

1890s Mali became a French colony.

1960 Mali gained independence from France as part of the Federation of Mali, which was dissolved a few weeks later when Senegal broke away. The Republic of Mali was established and Modibo Keita became the country's first president.

1968 Keita was overthrown by a military coup, led by Moussa Traoré, who became president.

1977 Protests erupted following Keita's death in prison.

1979 A new constitution provided for elections in which Traoré was elected as president.

1985 A border war erupted between Mali and Burkina Faso, but was ended after intervention by other African states.

1991 Following pro-democracy demonstrations, Traoré was deposed by a military coup. A 25-member military/civilian Transitional People's Salvation Committee

KEY INDICATORS — Mali

	Unit	2011	2012	2013	2014	**2015
Population	m	*15.85	*16.34	*15.30	*15.79	*16.30
Gross domestic product (GDP)	US$bn	10.60	10.44	11.07	*11.91	*10.97
GDP per capita	US$	669	639	723	*755	*673
GDP real growth	%	2.7	–	1.7	*6.8	*5.6
Inflation	%	3.1	5.3	-0.6	*0.9	*2.2
Unemployment	%	6.6	–	–	–	–
Exports (fob) (goods)	US$m	2,389.8	3,001.1	2,873.3	–	–
Imports (fob) (goods)	US$m	2,772.6	2,889.5	3,121.9	–	–
Balance of trade	US$m	-332.8	111.7	-248.6	–	–
Current account	US$m	-1,189.9	-340.0	-574.0	*-949.0	*-612.0
Total reserves minus gold	US$m	1,368.7	1,341.4	1,305.7	860.8	–
Foreign exchange	US$m	1,269.7	1,213.2	1,177.3	–	–
Exchange rate	per US$	466.82	505.65	480.26	542.07	–

came to power, led by Lieutenant Colonel Amadou Toumani Touré.
1992 Touré resigned and did not stand in the elections he organised. Alpha Oumar Konaré was democratically elected president.
1995 A peace agreement with Tuareg rebels led to the return of thousands of refugees from neighbouring African states.
1997 President Konaré was re-elected.
1999 Former president Traoré was sentenced to death for corruption, but his sentence was commuted to life imprisonment by Konaré, who also announced that he would not contest the next presidential election
2000 Mande Sidibe, a former International Monetary Fund (IMF) official, was appointed prime minister.
2001 Konaré announced the indefinite postponement of a constitutional referendum which proposed granting him immunity from prosecution.
2002 Amadou Toumani Touré (popularly known as ATT) won the presidential election and named Ahmed Mohamed Ag Hamani as prime minister. The Constitutional Court reversed the outcome of the parliamentary elections. The government resigned without explanation and a new government of national reconciliation took over.
2003 The IMF announced that Mali was to benefit from debt relief amounting to approximately US$675 million under the enhanced Heavily Indebted Poor Countries (HIPC) initiative.
2004 Ousmane Issoufi Maïga replaced Hamani as prime minister.
2006 Tuareg rebels, demanding greater autonomy, attacked government barracks in the north. The government signed a peace agreement, mediated by Algeria, with the rebels.
2007 President Amadou Toumani Touré was re-elected. The Congrès pour la Démocratie et le Progrès (CDP) (Alliance for Democracy and Progress) coalition (of 12 political parties) led by Alliance pour la Démocratie en Mali-Parti Pan-Africain pour la Solidarité et la Justice (ADEMA-PASJ) (Alliance for Democracy in Mali-African Party for Solidarity and Justice) won parliamentary elections The opposition Espoir 2002 (Hope 2002) was renamed Front pour la Démocratie et la République (FDR) (Front for a Democratic Republic) coalition (of two parties), won 11 seats. Prime Minister Ousmane Issoufi Maïga resigned and Modibo Sidibé was appointed as his replacement.
2009 In an official ceremony to mark a return to the peace process, around 700 Tuareg insurgents surrendered their arms, with an expectation of joining the regular army. The rebels had been fighting for greater political influence and economic development for their traditional Sahel homeland. The government agreed to more regional autonomy and investment. Ibrahim Ag Bahanga, the rebel leader, fled into exile; he could pose a future threat to peace.
2010 The IMF agreed to the disbursement of US$3.1 million under its Extended Credit Facility, after Mali successfully completed the IMF's second review of its economic performance. According to the International Organisation of Migration (IOM), Mali has lost 13 per cent of its population to emigration since 2000, an estimated 1.5 million people. The mining ministry announced that 80.47 per cent of export earnings in 2009 were from gold. However with relatively low taxation, the export earnings only account for 8 per cent of GDP. A prolonged drought in the north forced nomad herders to move further south and into neighbouring Niger and Burkina Faso. Construction began on another leg of the Sahel Highway, north of Timbuktu.
2011 The president appointed Cissé Mariam Kaïdama Sidibé as prime minister in April. In August the government announced that the threat of attacks by Al Qaeda on tourists had cost Mali around CFAf50 billion (US$108.8 million) in lost tourism receipts and 8,000 jobs since 2009. Many tourists have been drawn to spectacular desert-scapes and the ancient trading town of Timbuktu but the risk of kidnapping, sponsored by Al Qaeda, has grown.
2012 Thousands of people from northern Mali were forced to flee an uprising by ethnic Tuareg rebels in January. On 3 February the International Committee of the Red Cross reported that almost 10,000 Malian refugees had crossed into Niger, where living conditions were described as 'extremely difficult' with a lack of food and water.
Mutinous army soldiers (in the south) seized power in a *coup d'état* that overthrew President Touré on 22 March. A spokesman for the newly formed Comité National pour le Redressement de la Démocratie et la Restauration de l'Etat (CNRDR) (National Committee for the Return of Democracy and the Restoration of the State), Lieutenant Amadou Konare, claimed the *coup* was in response to the president's failure to quell the Tuareg separatist uprising in the north. The two Tuareg groups in rebellion, the Mouvement National pour la Libération de l'Azawad (MNLA) (National Movement for the Liberation of Azawad) and Ansar Dine, an Islamist group, which began to impose, in the towns they gained control of, *Sharia* (Islamic law). Captain Amadou Haya Sanogo was named as chairman of CNRDR. The UN Security Council straightaway called for an 'immediate restoration of constitutional rule and the democratically elected government'. On 30 March the regional economic body, Ecowas, announced an ultimatum of 72 hours for the CNRDR to relinquish power or face sanctions; land borders would be closed and Mali's assets held in the 15 Ecowas countries would be frozen. An Ecowas peacekeeping force was put on standby as CNRDR forces overran the international airport runway. Malian people were quickly seen to be withdrawing cash from their banks and stocking up on essential supplies.
On 2 April, rebel Tuareg, from the MNLA, overran the town of Timbuktu, the last stronghold of the national army in the north. A MNLA statement announced that they had 'control of the entire region' (the towns of Kidal and Gao had also been captured before Timbuktu) and had ended Mali's 'occupation' of Tuareg lands. The CNRDR said it intended to reinstate the constitution, but gave no clear indication of a timetable for transfer of power. Ecowas lifted sanctions on 8 April, as President Touré formally resigned from office, following a negotiated deal, mediated by Ecowas, with the CNRDR. Speaker of the national assembly, Dioncounda Traoré, was sworn in as interim president on the same day. According to the negotiated agreement, the coup leaders may step down without fear of prosecution and presidential elections will be held. On 11 April, Captain Sanogo (head of CNRDR) rejected a proposal that Ecowas troops should be used to help restore order in northern Mali. He cited the Ecowas agreement as sanctioning his continued involvement in the transitional power and would help decide how the country would be run following presidential elections set to be held by 21 May. On 17 April, Cheick Modibo Diarra was appointed as interim prime minister. Mr Diarra, a businessman, is a former US-Nasa astrophysicist and had been named as Microsoft Corporation's 'ambassador to Africa' in 2006. Ex-president Touré was released from detention on 19 April and along with his family fled to Senegal. On 26 April Ecowas decided to send 3,000 troops to Mali, to help secure the transitional government and defeat the Tuareg rebels.
In May, Islamist terrorists destroyed the tomb of a local Muslim saint (Sidi Mahmoud Ben Amar) in Timbuktu. The Islamist rebels that control Timbuktu announced that they would smash every mausoleum in the city, having judged them 'un-Islamic'. These centuries-old shrines to Islamic saints were included on Unesco's World Heritage List for their 'outstanding architectural wonders'. They

were placed on its list of endangered sites on 29 June.
On 21 August, a new government of unity was formed, led by Prime Minister Diarra and including five members allied to coup leader Captain Sanogo (CNRDR). On 29 August the UNHCR chief, Valerie Amos, stated that Mali had 500,000 internally displaced people (IDPs) and that it was in desperate need of humanitarian aid to deal with their needs.
On 12 October, the UN Security Council (UNSC) adopted a resolution that would allow military intervention to regain northern territory held by militants. To enable a formal endorsement of military action the UNSC required the submission of detailed operation plans by 26 November. On 24 October, the AU ended Mali's suspension in favour of working with the coup authorities to counter the rebel Islamist forces in the north.
On 13 November the AU endorsed a six-month plan to deploy its troops in northern Mali to oust Islamist and Tuareg forces. Government representatives took part in direct talks with Tuareg and Islamist rebels in December in efforts to find a platform for peace and national unity.
2013 The assistance of France in defending Mali's sovereignty was requested by the transitional authorities as the northern town of Konna was captured by extremist groups. As a result the French lead 'Operation Serval' began military operations alongside Malian forces on 11 January. The security situation rapidly improved. The French troops began withdrawing in April, leaving behind heavy patrol vehicles and tanks; a group of around 1,000 soldiers are expected to remain in a training role until the end of 2013. The government signed a peace deal with Tuareg rebels on 18 June. The deal called for an immediate ceasefire and government troops to return to the rebel-held northern town of Kidal. Officials reported the accord should also help pave the way for elections on 28 July. On 1 July the United Nations Multidimensional Integrated Stabilisation Mission in Mali (Minusma), established by Security Council resolution 2100 of 25 April 2013, took over authority from the African-led International Support Mission in Mali (Afisma). Under the terms of the resolution, the mission was to support the political process and carry out a number of security-related stabilisation tasks, with a focus on major population centres and lines of communication, protecting civilians, human rights monitoring, the creation of conditions for the provision of humanitarian assistance and the return of displaced persons, the extension of State authority and the preparation of free, inclusive and peaceful elections. The 12,600-strong peacekeeping force incorporated most of the 6,000 West African troops who had deployed to help the French operation. The state of emergency in place since January was lifted on 6 July. Presidential candidate Tiebele Drame withdrew from the election on 17 July. He had previously called for the elections to be delayed but said his party's application to the Constitutional Court had been met by a 'deafening silence'. His withdrawal left 27 other candidates. The presidential elections held on 28 July were hailed by France as a 'great success'. Since no candidate reached the 50 per cent needed for victory a run-off election between former prime minister Ibrahim Boubacar Keita (39.2 per cent in the first round) (Rassemblement pour le Mali (RPM) (Rally for Mali)) and ex-finance minister Soumaïla Cissé (19.4 per cent) (Union pour la République et la Démocratie (URD) (Union for the Republic and Democracy) was scheduled for 11 August. Despite heavy rain the run-off election went smoothly. Ibrahim Boubacar Keita was declared the winner (77.61 per cent) after Cissé (22.39 per cent) ceded defeat on 12 August, despite alleging serious irregularities in the voting, On 22 August the militant group headed by Algerian Mokhtar Belmokhtar, the Al Mulathameen (Masked Men Brigade), announced it had merged with the Mali-based Movement for Oneness and Jihad in West Africa (Mojwa) to form Al Murabitoun (the sentinels). A statement said that Al Murabitoun would take revenge against France for its actions in Mali. Oumar Tatam Ly was appointed as prime minister on 5 September. Government forces clashed with Tuareg rebels on 11 September, the first fighting since the June peace agreement. On 26 September the BBC reported that the National Movement for the Liberation of Azawad (MNLA) had accused the government of failing to honour its promises. MNLA want a separate Tuareg homeland. The Tuareg separatists were said to have withdrawn from the peace deal. Fighting broke out in the northern town of Kidal on 30 September. In mid-October the UN said that it still had only half of the 12,000 troops it had been mandated; it appealed for more men and equipmant after attacks in the north had again destabilised the country.
2014 Prime Minister Oumar Tatam Ly resigned on 5 April, along with his entire government. Moussa Mara was appointed as his successor the following day.
2015 A rocket attack on a UN base in northern Mali killed at least three people on 8 March, a day after an attack on a bar in Bamako killed at least five people, including a Belgian security official and a French national. On 26 September the International Criminal Court in The Hague (ICC) announced that the first case to be brought before it 'concerning the destruction of buildings dedicated to religion and historical monuments' would be that of Ahmad al Mahdi al Faq who is accused of the war crime of destroying religious monuments, specifically the destruction of nine mausoleums and a mosque in Timbuktu in 2012.

Political structure

Constitution

A referendum held in January 1992 approved a constitution establishing multi-party rule.
A two-round voting system for electing parliamentarians was established.
In 1997, a new electoral code introduced an Independent National Electoral Commission (CENI) comprising 34 members: 10 representatives of government services, 10 from civil society and 14 from the political parties (seven from the opposition and seven from the parliamentary majority).
Other changes included the authorisation of independent candidacies, the reduction in the number of voters per polling station to 700 and an increase in the number of deputies in the National Assembly from 116 to 147. The principle of sponsoring presidential candidates was ended, and correspondence or proxy voting and eligibility for other African nationals were annulled.
Administratively, Mali is divided into eight regions and the capital district of Bamako, each under the authority of an appointed governor.

Form of state

Republic

The executive

The directly-elected president serves a five-year term, with a limit of two terms. The president is head of state and commander-in-chief of the armed forces. The president appoints the prime minister and chairs the Council of Ministers.

National legislature

The unicameral National Assembly has 160-members in total, of which 147 are directly elected in single or multi-member constituencies through two rounds ending in a run-off election. Expatriate Malians are represented by 13 representatives. All members serve for five-year terms.

Legal system

Based on French civil law system and customary law. The legal system is constitutionally independent of the executive.

Last elections

24 November & 15 December 2013 (parliamentary); 28 July & 11 August 2013 (presidential)
Results: Parliamentary: Rassemblement pour le Mali (RPM) (Rally for Mali) won 66

seats (out of 147), Union pour le République et la Démocratie (URD) (Union for the Republic and Democracy) 17 seats, Alliance pour la Démocratie au Mali-Parti Pan-Africain pour la Liberté, la Solidarité et la Justice (ADEMA-PASJ) (Alliance for Demcoracy in Mali-Pan-African Party for Liberty, Solidarity and Justice) 16 seats, Forces Alternatives pour le Renouveau et l'Emergence (FARE) (Alternative Forces for Renewal and Emergence) 6 seats, Convergence pour le développement du Mali (CODEM) (Convergence for the Development of Mali) 5 seats, Solidarité Africaine pour la Démocratie et l'Indépendance (SADI) (African Solidarity for Democracy and Independence) 5 seats. 13 other parties shared 28 further seats and independents claimed the final 4. Turnout was 38.6 per cent.

Presidential: First round held on 28 July 2013 Ibrahim Boubacar Keita 39.23 per cent, Soumaïla Cissé 19.44 per cent; none of the other 26 candidates won more than 10 per cent. The second round, held on 11 August, saw Ibrahim Boubacar Keita win with 77.61 per cent, Soumaïla Cissé gained only 22.39 per cent.

Next elections

2018 (parliamentary and presidential)

Political parties

Ruling party

Rassemblement pour le Mali (RPM) (Rally for Mali)

Main opposition party

Union pour la République et la Démocratie (URD) (Union for the Republic and Democracy)

Approximately 47 per cent of the total population are under 15 years. Around 600,000 Tuareg Berbers live in Mali. There is a continuing population drift toward the Senegal and Niger Rivers.

The government's medium-term social objective is to achieve a broadly based improvement in living standards.

Population

16.85 million (2013)*

Last census: April 1998: 9,790,492

Population density: Eight inhabitants per square km. Urban population 36 per cent (2010 Unicef).

Annual growth rate: 2.9 per cent, 1990–2010 (Unicef).

Ethnic make-up

Mande (50 per cent), Peul (17 per cent), Voltaic (12 per cent).

Religions

Muslim (90 per cent), indigenous beliefs (9 per cent), Christian (1 per cent).

Education

Primary schooling is divided into two stages, with the first and compulsory stage lasting until aged 13, followed by three years of basic education. At age 16 students may follow either an academic path in a general secondary school, for three years, or specialisted education through a technical secondary school, for either two or three years. Four year vocational courses are also available.

Mali has one of the highest pupil-teacher ratio in the world, with an average of around 80 pupils per teacher.

Literacy rate: 19 per cent adult rate; 24 per cent youth rate (15–24) (Unesco 2005).

Compulsory years: Seven to 13

Enrolment rate: 29 per cent net primary enrolment (Unicef)

Pupils per teacher: 80 in primary schools.

Health

Improved water sources and sanitation facilities are available to 65 per cent and 30 per cent of the population respectively.

HIV/Aids

There are an estimated 100,000 people living with HIV/Aids in Mali – 5,000 are under the age of 15. Mali has so far escaped much of the African pandemic.

The African Development Fund (ADF) provided US$12.1 million for a programme to reduce the prevalence rate from 1.9 per cent in 2003 to 1 per cent by 2008. The money will be used to improved testing for the disease, antiretroviral drugs and training medical and research workers to monitor and manage the pandemic.

HIV prevalence: 1.9 per cent aged 15–49 in 2003 (World Bank)

Life expectancy: 46 years, 2004 (WHO 2006)

Fertility rate/Maternal mortality rate: 6.3 births per woman, 2010 (Unicef)

Child (under 5 years) mortality rate (per 1,000): 128 per 1,000 live births (WHO 2012); 25 per cent of children aged under five are malnourished (World Bank).

Head of population per physician: 0.08 physicians per 1,000 people, 2004 (WHO 2006)

Welfare

In the mid-1990s, it was estimated that 72.8 per cent of the population lived on less than US$1 per day and over 90 per cent lived on less than US$2 per day. The distribution of wealth in Mali is highly unequal and the highest 10 per cent of the population owns 56.2 per cent of the wealth.

In over 70 districts in Mali, one million people were affected by swarms of locust and suffered acute food shortages. Emergency food aid was provided from reserves while government officials estimated over 440,000 tonnes of the 2004 harvest to have been destroyed.

Main cities

Bamako (capital and main business centre, estimated population 1.9 million in 2012); Sikasso (213,977), Kayes (148,053), Mopti (105,646), Ségou (104,992), Nioro (100,239), Markala (90,516).

Languages spoken

Tamazight (the Berber language) is recognised as a national language. Tamazight belongs to the Afro-Asiatic family and is related to ancient Egyptian and Ethiopian. Arabic, Bambara, Fulani, Senoufo and Dogon are commonly spoken. Very little English is spoken.

Official language/s

French

Media

Although harsh penalties exist for slandering public officials they are rarely invoked so that Mali's media enjoys widespread freedom to report.

Press

Dailies: In French, *L'Essor* (www.essor.gov.ml) is state-owned, *Info-Matin* (www.info-matin.com), *Le Républicain* (www.lerepublicain.net.ml) *Le Ségovien* (www.lesegovien.com), *Les Echos* (www.jamana.org) and *L'Aurore*.

Weeklies: In French, *Courrier*. In Bambara, Fulani, Songhai and Arabic *Cauris* is a training pamphlet for farmers.

Broadcasting

The Office de Radiodiffusion Télévision Malienne (ORTM) (www.ortm.ml) is the national public broadcaster.

Radio: ORTM (www.ortm.ml) operates Radio Mali, which has a nationwide network of stations to provide national and local programming. There are many privately operated radio stations throughout the country, including Radio Canal 2000 and Radio Liberté from Bamako, Radio Kene from Sikasso and Radio Ania from Gao.

Television: ORTM (www.ortm.ml) operates one channel broadcasting locally produced programmes in 10 locally languages of news, culture and entertainment and well as imported TV shows (typically French). The private satellite channel, Africable is also available.

National news agency: Agence Malienne de Presse and de Publicité

Economy

The majority of the population is engaged in subsistence farming. Nevertheless the agricultural sector provides cash crops, primarily cotton and rice and livestock, for export and a range of foods for domestic consumption; the sector constituted over 38 per cent of GDP in 2013. The industrial sector constitutes around 24 per cent of GDP, of which gold mining in particular accounts for around 80 per cent of exports. Manufacturing comprises less than 10 per cent of GDP, with the processing of foodstuffs and other agricultural products such as tobacco, ground nuts and shea butter. Mali's climate is subject to drought, which has severely damaged the economy as herds and crops have failed. In 2010 a prolonged drought in the north forced nomad herders to move further south and into neighbouring Niger and Burkina Faso. According to the International Organisation of Migration (IOM), Mali has lost 13 per cent of its population to emigration since 2000, an estimated 1.5 million people.

In 2008 legislation was passed to privatise the Malian Textile Development Company, which was replaced by four new companies. In 2007–08 a drought affected the cotton crop and many farmers planned to switch to other crops in 2009. In 2010 world prices of cotton were at a record high as US and Chinese stocks had been depleted and farmers were able to claim higher prices at the farm gate. GDP growth was 5 per cent in 2008, which fell to 4.5 per cent in 2009 when world commodity prices fell. As global food prices had been at a record high in 2008, inflation peaked at 9.1 per cent before falling back to 2.2 per cent in 2009. However, by 2012 GDP growth had fallen to -1.2 per cent. The economy recovered from this recession in 2013, and by 2014 growth reached 7.2 per cent.

Mali is one of the world's poorest countries and is heavily dependent on foreign aid. Remittances from migrant workers amounted to US$454 million (5.1 per cent of GDP) in 2010 and reached US$473 million in 2011 (7.4 per cent of GDP).

In 2013, the UN Human Development Index (HDI) ranked Mali 176 (out of 187) for national development in health, education and income. Since 1995, Mali has achieved steady progress, albeit from a low base, but has not matched the improvement of other countries in sub-Saharan Africa. In 2013, 66.76 per cent of the population experienced at least one indicator of poverty, while 50.43 per cent lived on less than the equivalent of US$1.25 per day.

In 2009 the International Fund for Agricultural Development (Ifad) introduced a new US$25.04 million, microfinance fund, to expand the existing rural microfinance network of credit unions and to expand their reach.

The political turmoil in 2012 forced thousands of people from northern Mali to flee. By August, the UNHCR estimated that Mali had 500,000 internally displaced people (IDP).

External trade

Mali is a member of the Union Économique et Monétaire Ouest Africaine (UEMOA) (West African Economic and Monetary Union) (WAEMU). As a member of the Communauté financière d'Afrique (CFA) (Financial Community of Africa), it uses the CFA franc currency along with the seven other CFA members. It is also a member of the Economic Community of West African States (Ecowas).

Its primary exports, gold and cotton, are subject to world prices and along with livestock sales provide 80–90 per cent of export earnings. Remittances constitute an important portion of foreign revenue.

Imports

Principal imports are petroleum products, vehicles, machinery and equipment, pharmaceuticals, construction materials, foodstuffs and textiles.

Main sources: France (10.9 per cent of total in 2013), Senegal (9.9 per cent), Côte d'Ivoire (9.1 per cent).

Exports

The main exports are gold, cotton, livestock and foodstuffs.

Main destinations: China (30.1 per cent of total in 2013), India (15 per cent), Indonesia (8.5 per cent).

Agriculture

Farming

Agriculture is the mainstay of the economy, contributing 42.3 per cent of GDP, employing 73 per cent of the workforce (largely at subsistence levels). Only about 2 per cent of the total land area is cultivated, but approximately 20 per cent of the total land area along the Niger River is suitable for cultivation, with the most productive areas lying between Bamako and Mopti.

Principal food crops are millet, sorghum, paddy rice, maize and groundnuts. Supported by foreign aid, the government has co-ordinated a programme to expand production of rice as a staple food. There is a regular food deficit due to recurrent drought, crop smuggling and an inefficient marketing and distribution system.

The main export crops are cotton, groundnuts, cereals, fresh fruit and vegetables. Mali is Africa's second-largest cotton producer. Livestock exports have experienced growth in recent years following the abolition of export taxes on livestock. The livestock sector is a mainstay of the economy in the northern half of the country and contributes 20 per cent to GDP. Recent desertification caused by deforestation and global warming has shifted herding activity southwards.

Fishing

Fishing is an important livelihood along the Niger River. The annual fish catch is around 100,000 tonnes, of which 20 per cent is exported, mainly to Côte d'Ivoire. Production, through artisnal fishing, is vulnerable to drought, pollution and man-made obstructions across the river. Inland fisheries have been targeted for development as part of the national poverty reduction strategy. Fish processing and packaging centres and 10,000-hectare fishponds plus supporting developments are among the undertakings.

Industry and manufacturing

The industrial sector is growing, contributing around 22.7 per cent to GDP in 2013.

Manufacturing is concerned mainly with agricultural processing for domestic consumption and export. Other industries include soft drinks, textiles, soaps, plastics, cigarettes, cement, bricks and agricultural tools and equipment. Activity is concentrated in Bamako.

Around 90 per cent of production is accounted for by state enterprises, although rationalisation and privatisation plans are likely to continue.

Tourism

Mali has a mix of thriving, traditional cultures that include the Bambara (western Mali), the Songhai centred on the city of Timbuktu (Tombouctou), located on the southern edge of the Sahara Desert and the nomadic Tuareg, among others.

Tourism is an increasingly important sector of the economy, third only to gold and cotton. Its contribution to GDP averaged 9.8 per cent, jumping to 11.6 per cent in 2010 and to 12.1 per cent in 2012 as visitor numbers increased.

A military coup in March 2012 that toppled the president lead most Western governments to advise their citizens not to travel to Mali until the situation was resolved. This meant that tourism's contribution to GDP shrunk to 9.6 per cent in 2013. Employment in the tourist industry is 158,000 jobs (6.9 per cent of total employment).

Environment

In June 2010 the African Union backed a proposal to build the 'Great Green Wall' project, of a 15km wide, 7,775km long, continuous belt of trees from Senegal in the west to Djibouti in the east (traversing 11 countries) in an effort to halt the advance of the Sahara Desert. The trees to be used would be drought-adapted, preferably native to the area from a list of 37 possible species, and should help to slow soil erosion and filter rain water.

Mining

The mining sector typically contributes around 10 per cent to GDP and employs 0.5 per cent of the workforce. Gold is Mali's principal mineral resource and since the late 1990s has replaced cotton and livestock as the country's largest export earner.

Following the introduction of new mining laws in 1991, which helped expand gold production, Mali has become Africa's third largest gold producer after Ghana and South Africa. Total gold reserves are estimated at up to 700 tonnes and geologists claim there is potential for further discoveries. However, commercial exploitation is hampered by the lack of adequate physical infrastructure. Gold represents 80 per cent of the country's total mineral production.

The first privately owned gold mine was opened by BHP-Utah at Syama in 1990, but following operational difficulties it was sold to Randgold of South Africa in 1996. The mine underwent an investment programme and production peaked at 6.1 tonnes in 1999. However, in January 2001, Randgold decided to mothball Syama after extensive flooding led to financial losses.

Opened in 1997, the Sadiola Hill opencast mine, owned by AngloGold, IAMGold and the Mali government, has estimated reserves of around 130 tonnes. With average annual production estimated at around 10 tonnes per annum until 2010, it is the second largest gold mine in Africa and one of the biggest and lowest cost gold mines in the world.

The Yatela gold mine – owned jointly by AngloGold (40 per cent), IAMGold (40 per cent) and the Mali government (20 per cent) – lies 35km to the north of Sadiola, and was officially opened in September 2002. It has reserves of over 72 tonnes with estimated average annual production of 6 tonnes over a period of 12 years. In 2002, it produced 6.8 tonnes of gold.

The Morila gold mine, opened in early 2001, is forecast to produce an average of 10 tonnes per year over a period of 14 years and is jointly owned by Rangold (40 per cent), AngloGold (40 per cent) and the Mali government (20 per cent). In 2002, Morila produced 15.2 tonnes of gold. Feasibility studies are being conducted on the re-opening of the Kalana gold mine that could produce an estimated 430kg per annum. There are also large unexploited deposits at Kodieran (43 tonnes), Loulo (30.1 tonnes), Segala (15.4 tonnes) and Tabakto (1 tonne).

Artisanal gold mining has been practised in Mali for around 1,000 years and represents 0.6 per cent of GDP and employs around 150,000 seasonal workers. Much of this kind of mining is performed without permits and is generally dangerous.

Phosphate production is around 10,000 tonnes per annum. Small quantities of salt, limestone and uranium are also mined. There are known deposits of bauxite, manganese, iron and tin, and prospecting for lithium, diamonds and copper is under way. Lack of adequate infrastructure has deterred commercial exploitation.

Petroleum products (5,200 barrels per day in 2013) are imported from Côte d'Ivoire and Senegal. Mali has no oil refining capacity.

Hydrocarbons

Although there are no proven oil or gas reserves, in 2009 Algeria's Sonatrach and Canada's Selier Energy signed exploration deals for the Taoudeni basin. Oil and gas reserves were indicated from seismic and drilling tests undertaken in the 1970s, but civil unrest prevented earlier exploration.

Petroleum products (5,200 barrels per day in 2013) are imported from Côte d'Ivoire and Senegal. Mali has no oil refining capacity.

Energy

Total installed generating capacity was 300MW in 2011, producing 500 million-kilowatt hours. Senegal, Mali and Mauritania operate the Manantali Dam located on the Senegal River, it has five hydroelectric generators supplying around 200MW in a three-way split: Mali 52 per cent, Senegal 33 per cent and Mauritania 15 per cent. The energy from this facility meets the demand of the capital's population. There are small-scale, isolated diesel generators providing power for community facilities but the majority of the population relies on non-commercial biomass, mostly fuel wood for cooking, lighting and power. Mali has the capacity to use 200,000 tonnes of agricultural waste to produce biogas.

Financial markets

Stock exchange

Afribourse (Bourse Régionale des Valeurs Moblières) (BRVM)

Banking and insurance

Mali has an undeveloped banking sector with just nine banks and two financial institutions. Three of the banks are majority owned by the state while the state owns a minority share in three others. There are three privately owned banks. In recent years, the sector has undergone liberalisation.

Central bank

Banque Centrale du Mali

Main financial centre

Bamako

Time

GMT

Geography

Mali is a landlocked country in West Africa, with Algeria to the north, Mauritania and Senegal to the west, Guinea and Côte d'Ivoire to the south, and Burkina Faso and Niger to the east.

Mali is a landlocked country in West Africa, with Algeria to the north, Mauritania and Senegal to the west, Guinea and Côte d'Ivoire to the south, and Burkina Faso and Niger to the east.

There are three distinct topographic regions. The north is the arid Saharan zone, the semiarid Sahel (an Arab word to describe a border or margin) of savannah and scrubland in the centre, and in the south the fertile and cultivated Sudanese zone. The land rises from the south, typically flatland, through rolling plains to high plateaux in the north. Rugged hills no higher than 1,000 metres line the north-east boundary with Mauritania. The Niger River is 1,693 kilometres long and runs through most of the central and southern region and is considered by Malians as the country's lifeblood as it provides drinking water, aquaculture, irrigation and transport.

Hemisphere

Northern

Climate

There is considerable variation between southern, central and northern areas, rain being rare and sporadic in the far north, Sahara region. Bamako's rainy season runs from June to October with humidity reaching 80 per cent and temperatures ranging from 20 degrees Centigrade (C) to 36 degrees C. The warm, dry season runs from November to February followed by a hot, dry season between February and May with average temperatures of 35 degrees C.

Entry requirements

Passports

Required by all. Passport must be valid six months from date of entry.

Visa

Required by all; there are a few exceptions such as citizens of Ecowas countries. For further details and exceptions visit www.maliembassy-addis.org with its link to consular services. Business visas also require a covering company letter declaring the purpose of the trip and proof of return/onward passage.

Currency advice/regulations

The import and export of local currency is unlimited. Import and export of foreign currency is unlimited however amounts over the equivalent of CFAf25,000 must be declared.

Travellers cheques are accepted in banks.

Customs

Personal belongings and a small amount of tobacco and alcohol are permitted duty free. Cameras and films must be declared.
Sporting firearms and plants, excluding fruit and vegetables, need a certificate of import.

Health (for visitors)

Mandatory precautions

Yellow fever vaccination certificate is required by all.

Advisable precautions

Typhoid, tetanus, hepatitis A and polio vaccinations are recommended. Malaria prophylaxis should be taken as risk exists throughout the country. There is a rabies risk. Water precautions must be taken.

Hotels

There are only a few good hotels available and these can be expensive.

Credit cards

Major international credit and charge cards have limited acceptance in major hotels in the capital.

Public holidays (national)

Fixed dates

1 Jan (New Year's Day), 20 Jan (Armed Forces Day), 26 Mar (Day of Democracy), 1 May (Labour Day), 25 May (Africa Day), 22 Sep (Independence Day), 25 Dec (Christmas Day).

Variable dates

Easter Monday, Eid al Adha, Birth of the Prophet, Eid al Fitr.

Islamic year 1437 (15 Oct 2015–2 Oct 2016):: The Islamic year contains 354 or 355 days, with the result that Muslim feasts advance by 10–12 days against the Gregorian calendar. Dates of feasts vary according to the sighting of the new moon, so cannot be forecast exactly.

Working hours

Banking

Mon–Fri: 0730–1300; Mon–Thur 1400–1630; Fri 1500–1730.

Business

Mon–Thu: 0730–1230, 1300–1600. Fri: 0730–1230, 1430–1730.

Government

Mon–Thu, Sat: 0730–1430, Fri: 0730–1230.

Telecommunications

Telephone/fax

The internal service is unreliable.

Mobile/cell phones

GSM 900 services are available in the larger urban areas only.

Electricity supply

220V AC, 50 cycles.

Getting there

Air

National airline: Air Mali.

International airport/s: Bamako (BKO), 15km from city.

Airport tax: CFAf2,500 is payable on domestic flights; CFAf8,000 on international flights within Africa; and CFAf10,000 is payable for flights outside Africa. The airport tax may be collected at time of ticket sale and does not apply to transit passengers on the same flight and for children under two years.

Surface

Road: Good road from Niger (Niamey); condition of routes from Côte d'Ivoire and Burkina Faso varies; those from Senegal and Algeria are not generally recommended.

Rail: There is a regular twice weekly rail service from Senegal (Dakar) to Bamako (with sleeping and restaurant cars and facility for conveying vehicles). Journey takes up to 29 hours.

Main port/s: River ports of Bamako, Mopti, Tombouctou and Gao on the Niger.

Getting about

National transport

Air: There are no scheduled services between Bamako and other towns. Charter of light aircraft available from Société des Transports Aériens (STA). Tombouctou Air Service provides domestic flights.

Road: Main roads run from Sikasso and Bougouni in the south to Bamako, and from Bamako to Mopti and on to Gao via a tarred road. Conditions of roads are variable and secondary roads can be difficult.

Buses: Cheap but generally uncomfortable. Services run from Bamako to all main towns.

Rail: Main routes: Bamako-Koulikoro (59 km); Bamako-Kayes (494km). There are two classes: sleeping and restaurant facilities. Some air-conditioned cars are available.

Water: Three river steamers operate up and down the River Niger betwen August and late December, linking Koulikoro, Mopti, Tombouctou and Gao. Four classes are available, but first-class cabins must be booked in advance through SMERT, the tourist organisation.

City transport

Taxis: Cheap and widely available but not metered. Official standard fare system in Bamako. Tipping is not usual.

Car hire

International driving licence recommended. Hired cars are usually Renaults or Peugeots.

BUSINESS DIRECTORY

The addresses listed below are a selection only. While World of Information makes every endeavour to check these addresses, we cannot guarantee that changes have not been made, especially to telephone numbers and area codes. We would welcome any corrections.

Telephone area codes

The international dialling code (IDD) for Mali is +223, followed by subscriber's number.

Useful telephone numbers

Police: 17
Fire: 18
Ambulance: 225-002

Chambers of Commerce

Mali Chamber of Commerce and Industry, Place de la Liberté, BP 46, Bamako (tel: 222-9645; fax: 222-2120; e-mail: ccim@cefip.com).

Banking

Bank of Africa Mali, BP 2249, 418 Avenue de la Marne, Bamako (tel: 222-4672, 222-4088; fax: 222-4653).

Banque Commerciale du Sahel; BP 2372, 127 Rue, Bozola, Bamako (tel: 210-195/97, 225-536; fax: 222-5543, 222-0135).

Banque de Développement du Mali, BP 94, Ave Modibo Keita, Quartier du Fleuve, Bamako (tel: 222-2050, 222-4088; fax: 222-5085, 222-4250).

Banque de l'Habitat du Mali, BP 2614, Rue de Métal Soudan, Quartier du Fleuve, Bamako (tel: 222-9190, 222-9342; fax: 222-9350).

Banque Internationale du Mali; BP 15, Blvd de l'Indépendance, Bamako (tel: 222-5111, 222-5066; fax: 222-4566).

Banque Internationale pour le Commerce et l'Industrie du Mali; BP B72, Bd du Peuple, Immeuble Nimagala, Bamako (tel: 223-3370; fax: 223-3373).

Banque Malienne de Crédit et de Dépôts, BP 45, Avenue Modibo Keïta, Bamako (tel: 222-5336; fax: 222-7950).

Banque Nationale de Développement Agricole - Mali; BP 2424, Immeuble Dette Publique, Bamako (tel: 222-6464, 222-6611 fax: 222-2961).

Ecobank-Mali; BP 1272, Quartier du Fleuve, Place de la Nation, Bamako (tel: 223-3300; fax: 223-3305).

Central bank

Banque Centrale des Etats de l'Afrique de l'Ouest, Direction Nationale, PO Box 206, Avenue Moussa Travele, Bamako (tel: 222-3756; fax: 222-4786).

Stock exchange

Afribourse (Bourse Régionale des Valeurs Moblières) (BRVM), www.brvm.org

Travel information

Air Mali, Immeuble Scif, Square Lumumba, BP 27, Bamako (tel: 225-741/42; fax: 222-349).

Commissariat au Tourisme, BP 191, Bamako (tel: 225-673).

Delta Voyages SA, Immeuble Gamby (ex BNDA), BP 5005, Bamako (fax: 231-272).

Timbuctours, BP 222, Bamako (tel: 225-315).

Ministry of tourism

Ministry of Crafts Industry and Tourism, BP 2211, Bamako (tel: 223-6344, 223-6450; fax: 223-8201).

Ministries

Ministry of Agriculture, Breeding and Fishing, BP 61, Bamako (tel: 222-2979, 222-2785, 222-3006).

Ministry of Economy and Finances, BP 776, Bamako (tel: 222-9918, 222-8353; fax: 229-4440).

Ministry of Education, BP 71, Bamako, (tel: 222-2450; 222-2125; fax: 223-0545).

Ministry of Foreign Affairs, Bamako (fax: 230-327, 225-226).

Ministry of Industry and Trade, BP 1759, Bamako (tel: 221-6399, 222-8353; fax: 221-3114).

Ministry of Labour and Public Works, BP 80, Bamako, (tel: 222-4819; 222-1117; fax: 222-6548).

Ministry of Overseas Aid and International Co-operation, Bamako, (tel: 222-5092; 223-0056).

Other useful addresses

Direction Nationale du Plan et de la Statistique, Koulouba, Bamako (tel: 222-2753).

Government Press Office, Bamako, (tel: 222-0733).

Radiodiffusion-Télévision Malienne, BP 171, Bamako (tel: 222-2474).

Mali Embassy (USA), 2130 R Street, NW, Washington DC 20009 (tel: (+1-202) 332-2249; fax: (+1-202) 332-6603; e-mail: info@maliembassy-usa.org).

National news agency: Agence Malienne de Presse and de Publicité, BP 141 Bamako (tel: 222-2346; fax: 222-4774; internet: www.essor. gov.ml).

Internet sites

Africa Business Network: http://www.ifc.org/abn

African Development Bank: http://www.afdb.org

AllAfrica.com: http://www.allafrica.com

Africa Online: http://www.africaonline.com

Mbendi AfroPaedia (information on companies, countries, industries and stock exchanges in Africa): http://mbendi.co.za

Malta

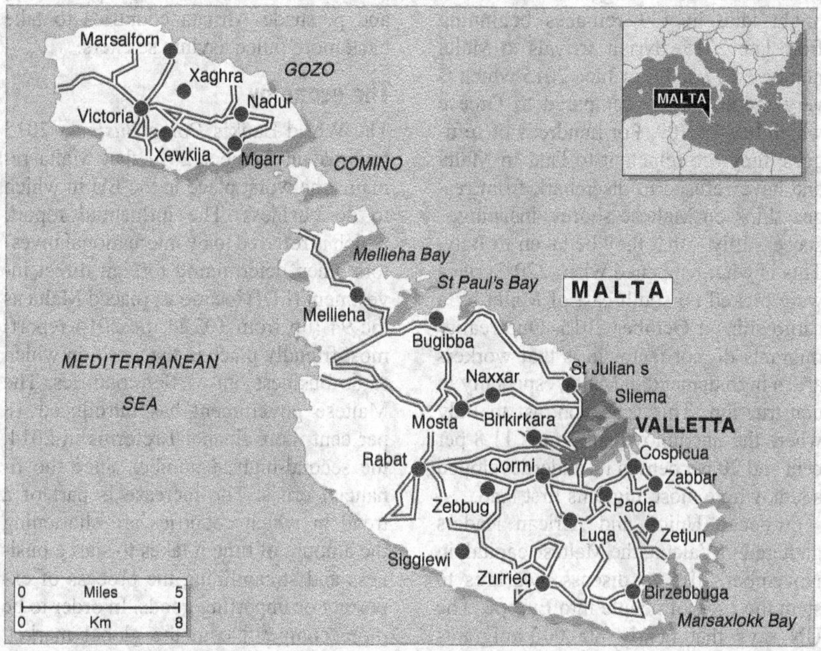

The United Kingdom (UK) formally acquired possession of Malta in 1814 and since then, the island has staunchly supported the UK through both world wars and remained in the Commonwealth when it became independent in 1964. In 1974, Malta declared itself to be a republic. Since the mid-1980s, Malta has transformed itself into a freight transshipment point, a financial centre, and a tourist destination. Meanwhile its key industries are moving towards more service-oriented activities. The island state became an European Union (EU) member in May 2004 and began using the euro as its currency in 2008.

Malta held its last general election in March 2013. The result had been a surprise to both parties. The Partit Laburista (PL) (Labour Party) came out victorious with a total of 167,533 first count votes, surpassing the Partit Nazzjonalista (PN) (Nationalist Party) by more than 35,000 votes – the largest gap since Maltese independence. The PL, led by Joseph Muscat – for whom this was the first election as party leader – won a total of 39 seats, comfortably ahead of the PN headed up by the former prime minister, Lawrence Gonzi, with 26 seats. Under Malta's system of proportional representation, which includes the so called casual election process – under which there is a re-count of votes where the difference in seats does not mirror the number of votes actually cast – Malta's Electoral Commission awarded an additional four seats to the PN making sure the number of seats is proportional to the number of first count votes gained. The two main political parties were in effect the only parties contesting the election. The only other party was the Democratic Alternative, a so-called 'Green' party, seeking to elect its first MP. A small number of independent candidates also ran for election.

Malta has the smallest economy in the euro-zone, it produces approximately 20 per cent of its food needs, has limited fresh water supplies, and has few domestic energy sources. Malta weathered the euro-zone crisis better than most EU member states due to a low debt-to-gross domestic product (GDP) ratio and a financially sound banking sector. Unemployment is low at just 5.9 per cent which is half the euro-zone average. GDP growth has recovered since the 2009 recession

KEY FACTS

Official name: Republic of Malta

Head of State: President Marie-Louise Coleiro Preca (from 4 April 2014)

Head of government: Prime Minister Joseph Muscat (from 9 Mar 2013)

Ruling party: Partit Laburista (PL) (Labour Party) (from 9 Mar 2013)

Area: 316 square km

Population: 425,000 (2014)*

Capital: Valletta

Official language: Malti (Maltese) and English

Currency: Euro (€) = 100 cents (from 1 Jan 2008; previous currency Maltese lira, locked at MI0.43 per euro)

Exchange rate: €0.89 per US$ (Sep 2015)

GDP per capita: US$24,876 (2014)*

GDP real growth: 3.55% (2014)*

GDP: US$10.58 billion (2014)*

Labour force: 191,000 (2014)*

Unemployment: 5.89% (2014)*

Inflation: 0.77% (2014)*

Balance of trade: -US$1.45 billion (2014)

Annual FDI: US$474.50 million (2011)

* estimated figure

and in 2014, Malta led the euro-zone in growth, expanding by 3.5 per cent. Also in 2014, the government began promoting public-private partnerships in the healthcare sector to establish Malta as a Mediterranean health hub for medical tourism, reduced residential and commercial energy tariffs by 25 per cent, and implemented a citizenship purchase programme to increase government revenue and attract foreign investors. The government has implemented new programmes including free child care, to encourage labour participation. The high cost of borrowing and the small labour market represents potential constraints to future economic growth. Furthermore, Malta's banking sector is seriously disproportionate to the size of its economy. The turnover of Malta's banking sector is eight times its GDP; were there to be a capital flight, the consequences would be frightening.

A major issue for Malta is the problem of water supplies. Both the main island of Malta, as well as the smaller Gozo, suffer water shortages. Half of Malta's water supplies come from its expensive desalination plants. Without these, Malta would only have an estimated four days' water supply.

Migration

Malta's geographic position between Europe and North Africa has made it a target for irregular migration, which has strained Malta's political and economic resources. Malta's fertility rate is below the EU average and, therefore, the population growth in recent years can be predominantly attributed to migration. Malta has Europe's second highest rate of granting asylum per capita and, the government's refugee commissioner, Mario Friggieri dismissed fears harboured by some migrants that they would languish for months in severe detention centres. A leaked quota plan prepared by the European Commission suggests that Malta might take in 133 refugees beginning from late 2015. Syrian arrivals to Malta numbered 77 so far in June 2015 which is very modest when compared to Greece which had 44,709. For hundreds of refugees, they are reluctant to land in Malta and have refused to disembark from rescue ships on Maltese shores, insisting – successfully – that they be taken to Italy. This is what happened when 220 Syrians were picked up south-east of Malta by a cargo ship in October 2015. One reality migrants do not factor in is that workers are in high demand in Malta, especially in construction. This is in contrast to Italy where the unemployment rate is 11.8 per cent and 20 per cent in its underdeveloped south, where most migrants first land.

European Union and African leaders gathered in Valetta, the Maltese capital, in November 2015 to discuss measures to stem the flow of people into Europe. The UN says that nearly 800,000 migrants have arrived in Europe by sea so far in 2015, while 3,440 have died or gone missing making the journey. Approximately 150,000 people from African countries such as Eritrea, Nigeria and Somalia have made the perilous journey across the Mediterranean from North Africa so far this year, arriving mainly in Italy and Malta. This number has been dwarfed by the arrival of 650,000 people – mostly Syrians – via Turkey and Greece. The European Commission is setting up a €1.8 billion (US$2.02 billion) trust fund for Africa and has urged member states to match that sum, however, it is unlikely that they will. The aim is to tackle the economic and security problems that cause people to flee, and persuade African countries to take back more failed asylum se ekers.

The economy

The World Bank's *Doing Business* 2015 reported in October 2014 that Malta remains the worst place in the EU in which to do business. The influential report, which is referred to by international investors when determining foreign direct investment (FDI) locations, placed Malta as the 94 (up from 103 in the 2014 report) most friendly place in the world in which to do business out of 189 countries. The Maltese government has introduced 18 per cent more financial reforms in 2014, the second-highest number since the financial crisis. The increase is part of a trend in which countries are shortening the amount of time it takes to start a business and streamlining the process of exporting or importing goods. In order to be more competitive in the global market, Malta has no choice but to drastically improve its 'ease of doing business rating' otherwise the economy will suffer. An example of Malta's previous lack of intent to make changes was that in 2013, they had undertaken just one reform that helped ease doing business.

The IMF has forecast a moderate acceleration in real GDP growth of 3.1 per cent for 2015, which means that Malta would continue to out-perform the euro-zone average. Private consumption was expected to increase as policy uncertainty diminished. The IMF expected the current account balance to remain slightly positive. Any protracted period of slower growth in Europe, or the re-emergence of euro-zone financial stress, would negatively affect the Maltese economy. Malta's close financial links with the euro-zone creates a potential spill-over risk. However, strong fundamentals in Malta, including a comfortable external position, low reliance on external financing by the government and a resilient financial system limit Malta's vulnerability. Furthermore, the IMF praised the free childcare service, the tapering of social benefits and measures taken in the employment sector. The IMF notes that Malta made impressive strides in improving its external balances

KEY INDICATORS **Malta**

	Unit	2011	2012	2013	2014	**2015
Population	m	0.42	0.42	0.42	*0.42	*0.43
Gross domestic product (GDP)	US$bn	8.90	8.85	10.06	*10.58	*9.51
GDP per capita	US$	21,028	21,227	23,865	*24,876	*22,319
GDP real growth	%	2.1	0.9	2.7	*3.5	*3.2
Inflation	%	2.4	3.2	1.0	*0.8	*1.1
Unemployment	%	6.6	6.4	6.4	*5.9	*6.1
Exports (fob) (goods)	US$m	3,549.6	4,231.5	37,771.6	3,467.0	–
Imports (fob) (goods)	US$m	4,967.1	5,450.8	5,255.8	4,920.4	–
Balance of trade	US$m	-1,417.6	-1,219.3	-1,484.3	-1,453.5	–
Current account	US$m	-46.0	186.0	321.0	*286.0	*291.0
Total reserves minus gold	US$m	542.2	688.3	584.9	615.6	–
Foreign exchange	US$m	328.3	474.8	367.6	–	–
Exchange rate	per US$	0.75	0.77	0.73	0.82	–

* estimated figure ** forecast figure

overturning its trade balance of 2.5 per cent in 2009 to a nine per cent surplus in 2014, the government deficit is also set to drop to 1.7 per cent in 2015, while debt would fall to less than 70 per cent this year and nearly 60 per cent by 2020. Inflation has also decreased from 1.4 per cent in 2013 to 0.3 per cent in 2014 as a result of lower water, electricity and fuel rates.

Recent events in Europe – particularly those relating to Cyprus – heightened perceptions about risks of hosting a large banking sector in a small country. In the case of Malta, these risks have been contained because the large international banking segment has limited balance sheet exposures to the Maltese economy. The authorities should, in the view of the IMF, continue monitoring banking developments, including the links between foreign parent banks and their Maltese entities. The Maltese authorities needed to be ready to take action if spill-overs from abroad became likely or Malta's internationally-oriented banks increased their exposure to the domestic economy. Any significant decline in house prices could have a sizeable impact on the domestic banking sector in the short-term.

Pension reform remains a priority to ease long-term fiscal pressures. In particular, reported the IMF, the retirement age needs to be aligned with life expectancy. Continued efforts are also needed to improve female labour participation and educational attainment. Continuing efforts to incentivise and support job search were also welcome. Education reforms should focus on promoting greater social inclusion and linking vocational training more closely with labour market needs.

The IMF concluded its assessment by observing that Malta's growth model had become increasingly dependent on financial and niche services; this meant that measures to broaden competitiveness would be needed to help diversify the economy. The government needed to ensure better alignment of wages and productivity, promote foreign direct investment (FDI), improve the judicial system and implement structural reforms. This was particularly important at a time when many of Malta's trading partners were undergoing internal devaluation, fiscal consolidation and structural reforms to restore their competitiveness. More generally, these reforms would make the economy less vulnerable to any sectoral setbacks and more resilient to any potential harmonisation of EU tax rates at the EU level.

Risk assessment

Economy	Good
Politics	Good
Regional stability	Fair

COUNTRY PROFILE

1814 Malta became a crown colony of the UK, with limited self-government.

1942 The islanders were awarded the George Cross for heroism during a three-year siege and severe bombing by Germans and Italians in the Second World War.

1947 Malta was granted full internal self-government.

1956 In a referendum, a majority voted in favour of integration with the UK as proposed by the Partit Laburista (Malta Labour Party) (MLP) under Dominic (Dom) Mintoff.

1959–62 Disturbances followed the rejection of Mintoff's integration proposals by the British, leading to his resignation. The British reinstated direct rule.

1964 Malta was granted full independence. It became a member of the Commonwealth, reinforced by defence and aid treaties with UK.

1971 A Labour government was elected under Dom Mintoff , who signed co-operative treaties with Eastern and Western countries and established close relations with Libya.

1974 Malta declared itself a republic.

1981 The MLP gained more seats but fewer votes than the Partit Nazzionalista (PN) (Nationalist Party), which mounted a campaign of civil disobedience and boycotted the House of Representatives for over a year.

1987 Following constitutional amendments, the PN, led by Eddie Fenech Adami, worked to maintain non-aligned status, while seeking closer ties with the West.

1990 Malta applied to join the EU.

1996 The EU application was frozen by Alfred Sant (MLP) when he took office as prime minister.

1998 Prime Minister Adami (PN) renewed the island's application to join the EU.

2003 The ruling PN won the parliamentary elections.

2004 Prime Minister Fenech Adami stepped down and Lawrence Gonzi was sworn in as prime minister. Eddie Fenech Adami took office as president. Malta joined the EU.

2005 The Maltese parliament ratified the European constitution in a unanimous vote.

2006 Increasing numbers of illegal immigrants from Africa forced Malta to seek stronger commitment from EU partners.

2007 The EU formally invited Malta to join the third stage of the European Monetary Union (EMU). Malta became a member of the European Union Schengen area whereby all travellers may cross borders without a passport or visa.

2008 Malta adopted the euro as its official currency. In parliamentary elections the PN won 49.3 per cent of the vote (35 seats out of 69), the MLP 48.8 per cent (34); turnout was 93 per cent.

2009 By unanimous approval, parliament elected George Abela as president.

2011 A referendum held in March was won by pro-divorce supporters. A bill was presented to parliament, and passed (by 52 votes to 11) on 25 July, making divorce legal so long as the couple have been separated for at least four years, that there was no chance of reconciliation, and adequate maintenance was agreed and the children were protected. It came into effect in October. Malta's call for a suspension of the 'Dublin regulation' and more help from the EU to cope with the unprecedented number of migrants and refugees arriving from North Africa since January, was given limited approval at the 23–24 June summit meeting. Malta argued that as the 'Dublin regulation' requires all EU members to return migrants and refugees to the first country of entry and as Malta was a frontline country of the EU it was likely to be disproportionately hit hard by the numbers to be processed. However, the summit did agree to a 'safeguard mechanism', which allowed the temporary re-introduction of border controls in exceptional circumstances in individual cases.

2012 On 13 January, the international credit ratings agency, Standard & Poor's, lowered its long term sovereign ratings for Malta from A to A- and its short term rating from A- to A-2, with a negative outlook, due to what it considered was the impact of deepening political and economic problems in the euro-zone. On 20 August, Dom Mintoff died, aged 96 years. He was one of Malta's prime movers for, and first prime minister after, independence. The international credit ratings agency, Fitch, confirmed Malta's rating of A+ on 25 September, with a stable outlook following a largely positive report by the International Monetary Fund in May. On 10 December parliament defeated the budget bill and the government fell.

2013 The elections held on 9 March were won by the opposition Partit Laburista (PL) (Labour Party) with 54.8 per cent of the vote (39 seats out of 65), followed by the former ruling Partit Nazzjonalista (PN) (Nationalist Party) with 43.3 per cent (26 seats). Joseph Muscat became Prime Minister. After over 300 people drowned when a boat sank off the coast of the Italian island of Lampadusa on 3 October, a boat believed to have been in Maltese

waters sank on 11 October, with the loss of at least 27 lives. Prime Minister Muscat said that European waters close to Africa were turning into a cemetery, and that Malta felt 'abandoned' by the rest of Europe and insisted that the EU take action to prevent such tragedies from happening.
2015 A meeting between some 60 African and EU countries was held in Valletta 11 and 12 November to discuss the number of refugees and migrants who were crossing the Mediterranian to get to Europe. The EU offered an African Trust Fund of €1.8 billion (US$2 billion) to encourage African governments to take migrants back and stop them from coming to Europe in the first place. Shortly after this meeting, the biennial Commonwealth Heads of Government Meeting (CHOGM) was held on 27–29 November.

Political structure

Constitution

The constitution was adopted in 1979. Under the Compact of Free Association (CFA), the Marshall Islands have control over all domestic and foreign affairs with the exception of defence which is the responsibility of the US.
Universal suffrage begins at aged 18.

Independence date

21 September 1964

Form of state

Self-governing territory in free association with the US.

The executive

Executive power rests with the president and the cabinet. The president is both head of state and head of government, elected by parliament for a four-year term. The president appoints the cabinet from members of the Nitijela (parliament).

National legislature

The bicameral system of government includes the Nitijela (lower house), with 33 senators of the Nitijela elected from 24 constituencies, for four-year terms. The Nitijela holds legislative power and elects the president.
The upper house, Council of Iroij (council of chiefs) is an advisory body, of 12 tribal chiefs, with consultative authority on matters relating to land and customs, who serves four-year terms.

Legal system

The judiciary is independent. Public law is based on English common law.

Last elections

21 November 2011 (parliamentary); 3 January 2012 (presidential, indirect)
Results: Parliamentary: United Democratic Party (UDP) won 15 seats, Aelon Kein Ad (AKA) (Our Islands) eight, United People's Party (UPP) seven and independents three.
Presidential (indirect): Christopher Loeak (independent) 21 votes, Jurelang Zedkaia (AKA) 11; one abstention.

Next elections

16 November 2015 (general and, in the weeks after, presidential)

Political parties

Ruling party

Partit Laburista (PL) (Labour Party) (from 9 Mar 2013)

Main opposition party

United Democratic Party (UDP)

Population

417,000 (2012)*
Last census: 27 November 2005: 404,962
Population density: 1,184 inhabitants per square km. Urban population 95 per cent (2010 Unicef).
Annual growth rate: 0.6 per cent, 1990–2010 (Unicef).

Ethnic make-up

Most Maltese are descendants of Phoenicians, with strong elements of Italian and other Mediterranean influences.

Religions

Roman Catholic (98 per cent).

Education

Primary education lasts for six years; secondary schooling lasts for five years, divided into a three-year orientation cycle and a two-year cycle of specialisation. There are two types of secondary education schools – junior Lyceums and area secondary schools; following either of these leads to a choice between academic or technical courses. Over 54 per cent of students continue with their education and training after the age of 16. Church schools are funded through the government and tuition is free.
Higher education is mainly provided by the University of Malta. The quality of education in Malta is high and attracts students from the Mediterranean and the Middle East.
Literacy rate: 92.6 per cent total; 93.4 per cent female, adult rates (World Bank).
Compulsory years: Five to 16.
Enrolment rate: 108 per cent (boys); 107 per cent (girls) gross primary enrolment of the relevant age group (including repetition rates) (World Bank).

Health

Public hospital services are adequate although there have been concerns over the long waiting times. Total bed capacity is around 2,000. An increasing number of doctors are resigning due to poor working conditions and wages. Due to the low numbers of doctors, some health centres have stopped operating on a 24-hour basis.
A programme of refurbishment and modernisation was undertaken in all government hospitals.

HIV/Aids

HIV prevalence: 0.2 per cent aged 15–49 in 2003 (World Bank)
Life expectancy: 79 years, 2004 (WHO 2006)
Fertility rate/Maternal mortality rate: 1.3 births per woman, 2010 (Unicef)
Child (under 5 years) mortality rate (per 1,000): 7 per 1,000 live births (WHO 2012)
Head of population per physician: 3.18 physicians per 1,000 people, 2003 (WHO 2006)

Welfare

The Maltese welfare system is poised for reform. There is a significant welfare gap in society.
The social security contribution rate paid by every Maltese employer is 10 per cent. The self-employed pay a rate of 15 per cent.
A Care Allowance was introduced for children living in institutions and was later extended to foster parents.

Main cities

Valletta (capital, estimated population 5,465 in 2012), Birkirkara (20,552), Mosta (19,644), San Pawl il Bahar (19,276), Qormi (15,300), Zabbar (14,546), Naxxar (13,405), Marsascala (13,328).

Languages spoken

Malti (Maltese), English and some Italian; most business correspondence is in English.

Official language/s

Malti (Maltese) and English

Media

Press

Dailies: Bilingualism has resulted in 50 per cent of the number of newspapers published in either Maltese or English. In Maltese, *L-orizzont* (www.l-orizzont.com) has the highest circulation, followed by *In-Nazzjon* (www.nazzjon.com.mt). While *The Times* (www.timesofmalta.com), *The Malta Independent* (www.independent.com.mt) and *Malta Today* (www.maltatoday.com.mt), are popular English newspapers.
Weeklies: In Maltese, *It Torca* (www.it-torca.com), published on Sunday, has the highest circulation followed by *Kull Hadd* (www.kullhadd.com) and *Lehen is-Sewwa* a Catholic publication. English dailies publish Sunday editions.
Business: Two publications include, in English, the daily *Business Today* (www.businesstoday.com.mt) and *The Malta Business Weekly* (www.maltabusinessweekly.com.mt).

Broadcasting

The Public Broadcasting Service (PBS) (www.pbs.com.mt) is funded by both a television license and advertising.

Radio: There are dozens of local stations broadcasting; however the market is dominated by those operated by either the government, political parties or the Catholic Church. PBS (www.pbs.com.mt) operates three stations including Radju Malta, Radju Parlament and Majic FM. Super One Radio (www.one.com.mt) is owned by the Maltese Labour Party, Radio 101 (www.radio101.com.mt) is operated by the Nationalist Party, RTK (www.rtk.org.mt) is owned by the Catholic Church and Campus FM (http://campusfm.um.edu.mt) is operated by the University of Malta.

Television: For revenue, television companies lease airtime to independently production houses which provided programmes of agreed topics. The TV market is diverse with broadcasts from Italian television received and over 80 per cent of homes subscribing to cable services.

PBS (www.pbs.com.mt) operates TVM, which mainly broadcasts externally produced programmes in both Maltese and English. Super One TV (www.super1.com) is owned by the Maltese Labour Party and Net TV (www.nettv.com.mt) is operated by the Nationalist Party.

Economy

The economy is largely structured on trade, tourism and financial services. The service sector contributed 65.4 per cent to GDP in 2013, while industry contributed 32.7 per cent and agriculture only 1.9 per cent.

GDP growth in 2008 was 4.1 per cent, falling into recession in 2009 with a rate of -2.7 per cent, before bouncing back in 2010, as tourism and global trade began to pick up, so that annual growth was 2.3 per cent. The rate remained constant at 2.4 per cent growth in 2013 before increasing to a healthy rate of 3.5 per cent in 2014. Inflation in 2008 was 4.7 per cent as imports of energy and food had risen; by 2009 it had dropped to 1.8 per cent as domestic demand fell; inflation in 2013 was recorded at 1 per cent before decreasing to 0.3 per cent in 2014.

The government introduced a financial stimulus package in 2009, which included support for the manufacturing and tourism sectors and increased public investment. Female participation in the workforce is the lowest in the European Union (EU) at just over 30 per cent (typically the highest enrolment rates are over 60 per cent), a personal income tax regime was modified to encourage their uptake of paid employment. Foreign direct investment (FDI) peaked in 2006 at US$1.84 billion (around 30 per cent of GDP), with much of the investment directed towards the innovation-driven sectors, specifically semiconductor manufacturing. FDI declined to US$832.6 million in 2008, before recording stronger investment in 2010 of US$998.9 million. In 2013 Malta had an FDI net inflow of -US$1.9 billion.

Transport-related services, such as trans-shipment and ship repair, are important to the economy. Malta is a flag of convenience state that has been under pressure from the EU to comply with its maritime standards.

External trade

As a member of the European Union, Malta operates within a communitywide free trade union, with tariffs set as a whole. Internationally, the EU has free trade agreements with a number of nations and trading blocs worldwide.

Manufactured commodities provide 50 per cent of total exports, while the tourist sector provides over 25 per cent of GDP. Malta has one of the world's largest registered merchant fleets and is actively encouraging growth in international banking and financial services and developing an offshore tax haven.

Imports

Principal imports are mineral fuels, oils and products; electrical machinery; aircraft/spacecraft and parts thereof; machinery and mechanical appliances; plastic and other semi-manufactured goods; vehicles and parts.

Main sources: Italy (22.8 per cent of total in 2014), US (8.6 per cent), UK (7.4 per cent), Germany (5.9 per cent) and Canada (5.6 per cent).

Exports

Major exports include machinery and mechanical appliances, mineral fuels, oils and petroleum products; pharmaceutical products; books and newspapers; aircraft/spacecraft and parts; toys, games, and sports equipment.

Main destinations: Germany (22.8 per cent of total in 2014), France (12.8 per cent), Italy (9.3 per cent), Libya (6.7 per cent) and the UK (6.6 per cent).

Agriculture

Farming

The agricultural sector accounts for around 1.9 per cent of GDP and employs some 1 per cent of the population.

Agricultural production supplies only about 20 per cent of Malta's food needs. There is a limited area of land available for agriculture and freshwater supplies are scarce. Potatoes and onions are the largest vegetable crops; potatoes are also the largest export crop. Grapes are the largest fruit crop and flower cultivation is flourishing.

Malta implemented the reform of the EU Common Agricultural Policy (CAP) on 1 January 2007. The reform was introduced throughout most of the EU in 2005, when there were subsidiaries on farm output, which tended to benefit large farms and encourage overproduction. They were replaced by single farm payments, not conditional on production. The change rewards farmers who provide and maintain a healthy environment, food safety and animal welfare standards. The changes are also intended to encourage market conscious production and cut the cost of CAP to the EU taxpayer.

Fishing

Around 1,000 tonnes of marine fish are landed annually, while aquaculture produces 2,000 tonnes. Around 370 people are registered as full-time fishermen, with 300 registered fishing vessels in operation. Another 1,500 boats are owned by part-time fishermen.

Forestry

Industry and manufacturing

The industrial sector contributes approximately 33 per cent to GDP and employs 22 per cent of the labour force.

Manufactures include textiles, clothing, synthetic fibres, footwear, wines and beer, furniture, electronic goods, automobile components, measuring/controlling equipment and tobacco products.

Tourism

Malta, strategically located in the middle of the Mediterranean, has been occupied or colonised down the ages by the Phoenicians, the Romans, Byzantines, Arabs, Normans, Crusaders, Napoleonic troops and the British. Each succeeding occupation left behind evidence of their passing. The Germans were the last to attack the islands, in the 1940s, subjecting the people to a blockade, the privations of which earned the island a Victory Cross (the highest award for bravery given by the UK). The capital Valetta is a UN World Heritage Site, which includes 320 monuments within an area of 55 hectares (one of the most concentrated historic areas in the world). Malta and Gozo's megalithic temples are also on the UN list.

With tourist numbers of over 1.5 million annually, for a population of some 415,000, the travel and tourism industry is a major component of the economy, which constituted 25.5 per cent of GDP in 2013 and employed 26.4 per cent of the total workforce (46,000 jobs).

Malta has been investing in its tourism industry and the total capital investment for travel and tourism has consistently attracted between 10–15 per cent per annum. Cruise ships dock at the Port of Valetta at newly refurbished buildings that once belonged to the Knights Hospitaller of Malta.

Mining

Malta has no exploitable natural resources.

Hydrocarbons

There are no known oil or gas reserves although oil and gas exploration is ongoing. All hydrocarbon needs are met by imports; consumption of oil was 39,280 barrels per day in 2013.

With the few reserves of coal that Malta may have, it has not been commercially recorded.

Energy

Total production in 2013 was 2.19 billion kilowatt hours. The Enemalta Corporation generates and distributes electricity nationwide. There are three traditional thermal power stations supplying electricity throughout Malta and by sub-marine cables to Gozo and Comino.

Many households buy bottled supplies of liquefied natural gas (LNG) for cooking and heating.

Financial markets

Stock exchange

Borza ta' Malta (Malta Stock Exchange) (MSE)

Banking and insurance

There are two major commercial banks — Bank of Valletta and the HSBC Bank Malta plc.

Central bank

Central Bank of Malta

Time

GMT plus one hour (daylight saving, late March to late October, GMT plus two hours)

Geography

The largest and only inhabited islands of the Maltese archipelago in the Mediterranean are Malta, Gozo and Comino. The main island, Malta, lies 93km (58 miles) south of the Italian island of Sicily and 290km (180 miles) north of the Libyan coast, with Tunisia to the west.

Malta is typically limestone rock with a series of low hills and slopes running toward the north-west and low-lying land to the south-east. The soil can be thin producing heathland, while terraced hills produce much of Malta's agricultural produce.

Hemisphere

Northern

Climate

Mediterranean, with hot summers and warm winters. Temperatures range from about 29 degrees Celsius (C) down to about 10 degrees C. January and February are the coldest months, July and August the hottest. August and September tend to be hot and humid, but usually with sea breezes in evening.

Dress codes

European clothing is suitable for winter, spring and autumn; tropical weight for summer.

Entry requirements

Passports

Required by all, excepted for citizens of EU and EEA with national ID cards. Passports must be valid for three month beyond the length of stay.

Visa

Required by all, except nationals of EU and Schengen area signatory countries, North America, Australasia and Japan. For further exceptions contact the nearest embassy or see www.foreign.gov.mt and follow the link to travel advice. A Schengen visa application (offered in several languages) can be downloaded from http://europa.eu/abc/travel/ see 'documents you will need'.

Currency advice/regulations

The import and export of local currency is limited to Lm5,000; the import of export of foreign currency is unlimited.

Travellers cheques are widely accepted.

Customs

Personal items are duty-free. There are no duties levied on alcohol and tobacco between EU member states, providing amounts imported are for personal consumption.

Health (for visitors)

Nationals of the European Economic Area (EEA) countries and Switzerland can access reduced cost and sometimes free medical treatment using a European Health Insurance Card (EHIC) while visiting the EEA. Exceptions include nationals of the 10 countries, which joined the EU in 2004, whose EHIC is not valid in Switzerland. Applications for the EHIC should be made before travelling.

Advisable precautions

There are no special requirements.

Hotels

Classified from five-star to one-star. All hotel staff speak English and many are multi-lingual.

Credit cards

All major credit and debit cards are accepted; ATMs are widely available.

Public holidays (national)

Fixed dates

1 Jan (New Year's Day), 10 Feb (St Paul's Shipwreck), 19 Mar (St Joseph's Day), 31 Mar (Freedom Day), 1 May (Labour Day), 7 Jun (Commemoration of the 1919 Uprising), 29 Jun (Feast of St Peter and St Paul), 15 Aug (Assumption Day), 8 Sep (Victory Day), 21 Sep (Independence Day), 8 Dec (Immaculate Conception), 13 Dec (Republic Day) and 25 Dec (Christmas Day).

Variable dates

Good Friday

Working hours

Banking

Mon–Fri: 0830–1230; Sat: 0830–1200.
Summer and winter opening hours may vary.

Business

Mon–Fri: 0830–1245 and 1430–1730.

Government

Mon–Fri: 0745–1230 and 1315–1715 (Jun to Sep Mon–Fri: 0730–1330).

Shops

Mon–Sat: 0900–1300 and 1600–1900.

Telecommunications

Mobile/cell phones

GSM 900 and 1800 services are available throughout the islands.

Electricity supply

240V AC

Weights and measures

The metric system is the main one in use. Sometimes the imperial system is also used and, on rare occasions, the old local measures.

Getting there

Air

National airline: Air Malta.

International airport/s: Malta (MLA) at Luqa, 5km from Valletta, facilities include *bureau de change*, duty-free shops, car hire and restaurant. Taxis and buses are available.

Airport tax: None

Surface

Water: There are regular car ferry services from Sicily and the Italian mainland.

Getting about

National transport

Air: Internal flights (by helicopter) operate between Malta and Gozo.

Buses: Regular bus services run from Valletta to most towns and villages on Malta and Gozo.

Water: Gozo Channel Company operates a regular round-the-clock daily ferry service between Malta and Gozo.

City transport

Metered taxis are available.

Car hire

Self-drive cars are available at daily, weekly and monthly rates with unlimited mileage and fully comprehensive insurance. A national or international driving licence is required, which must be endorsed at the Police Licensing Office, Floriana. Speed limits are 40kph in built-up areas and 64kph elsewhere. Driving is on the left.

BUSINESS DIRECTORY

The addresses listed below are a selection only. While World of Information makes every endeavour to check these addresses, we cannot guarantee that changes have not been made, especially to telephone numbers and area codes. We would welcome any corrections.

Telephone area codes

The international direct dialling (IDD) code for Malta is +356 followed by subscriber's number.

Useful telephone numbers

Police: 191
Ambulance: 196
Fire brigade: 199
Directory enquiries: 190
Overseas operator: 194
Time check: 195

Chambers of Commerce

Malta Chamber of Commerce and Enterprise, Exchange Buildings, Republic Street, Valletta VLT 05 (tel: 2123-3873; fax: 2124-5223; e-mail: admin@chamber.org.mt).

Maltese-American Chamber of Commerce, Exchange Buildings, Republic Street, Valletta VLT 05 (tel: 2124-7233; fax: 2124-5223; e-mail: president@malta-uschamber.com).

Banking

APS Bank ltd, 275 St Paul Street, Valletta VLT 07 (tel: 247-547; fax: 238-698).

Bank of Valletta Ltd, 58 Zachary Street, Valletta VLT 04 (tel: 243-261/7; fax: 230-894).

Bank of Valletta Group, BOV Centre, High Street, Sliema, SLM 16 (tel: 336-224; fax: 346-160; internet site: www.bov.com).

HSBC Bank Malta plc, 233 Republic Street, Valletta VLT 05 (tel: 485-713; fax: 489-425).

HSBC Bank Malta (Overseas) plc, 15 Republic Street, Valletta VLT 05 (tel: 249-801/4; fax: 249-805).

Investment Finance Bank Ltd, 168 Strait Street, Valletta VLT 07 (tel: 232-017, 233-349; fax: 242-014).

Lombard Bank (Malta) Ltd, Lombard House, 67 Republic Street, Valletta VLT 05 (tel: 248-411/8; fax: 246-600).

Valletta Investment Bank Ltd, 144 St Christopher Street, Valletta VLT 02 (tel: 2235-246; fax: 234-419).

Central bank

Central Bank of Malta, Pjazza Kastija, Valletta CMR 01 (tel: 2550-0000; fax: 2550-2500; e-mail: info@centralbankmalta.com).

Stock exchange

Borza ta' Malta (Malta Stock Exchange) (MSE), www.borzamalta.com.mt

Travel information

Air Malta, Head Office, Malta International Airport, Gudja (tel: 2299-9984, 2299-9885; fax: 2299-9368; internet site: www.airmalta.com).

Malta International Airport Ltd, Luqa LQA 05 (tel: 249-600; fax: 243-042; internet site: www.maltairport.com).

National tourist organisation offices

Malta Tourism Authority, 280 Republic Street, Valletta CMR 02 (tel: 224-444, 225-048/9; fax: 220-401; e-mail: info@visitmalta.com; internet site: http://www.visitmalta.com).

Ministries

Ministry of Investment, Industry and Information Technology, 168 Triq id-Dejqa, Valletta CMR 02 (tel: 2122-6808; fax: 2125-0700; email: miti@gov.mt).

Ministry of Foreign Affairs, Palazzo Parisio, Merchants Street, Valletta CMR 02 (tel: 2124-2853; fax: 2123-5032; email: info.mfa@gov.mt).

Ministry of Finance, Maison Demandols, South Street, Valletta CMR 02 (tel: 2124-9640/6; fax: 2122-4667; email info.mfin@gov.mt).

Ministry of Resources and Infrastructures, Block B, Floriana CMR 02 (tel: 2122-2378; fax: 2124-3306).

Other useful addresses

British High Commission, Whitehall Mansions, Ta'Xbiex Seafront, Ta'Xbiex, MSD 11, (tel: 2323-0000; fax: 622-001).

Department of Industry, St George's, Canon Road, St Venera (tel: 446-259).

Department of Information, Auberge de Castille, Valletta (tel: 225-241, 224-901; fax: 237-170).

Department of Trade, Lascaris, Valletta (tel: 224-411).

Embassy of the United States of America, PO Box 535, Valletta CMR O1 (tel: 2561-4000; fax: 2124-3229; email: usembmalta@state.gov).

Hotels and Restaurants Association, 7 Frederick Street, Valletta (tel: 336-843; fax: 237-253).

Malta Broadcasting Authority, National Rd, Blata 1-Bajda (tel: 221-281).

Maltacom (telecommunications), Spencer Hill, Marsa HMR12 (postal address: PO Box 40, Qormi, QRM01) (tel: 240-000; fax: 246-369; e-mail: mcintrel@maltacom.com; internet site: www.maltacom.com).

Malta Development Corporation, PO Box 141, Marsa GPO 01; head office: Triq l-Industrija, Qormi (tel: 441-888; fax: 441-887; e-mail: info@mdc.com.mt; internet site: www.investinmalta.com).

Malta Drydocks, The Docks (tel: 822-451, 822-491; fax: 800-021).

Malta Export Trade Corporation, Trade Centre, PO Box 8, San Gwann SGN 01 (tel: 446-186/7/8; fax: 496-687; internet site: www.metco.com.mt/main.htm).

Malta Federation of Industry, Development House, St Anne Street, Floriana VLT 01 (tel: 222-074, 234-428; fax: 240-702).

Malta Financial Services Centre (MFSC), Attard (tel: 441-155; fax: 441-188).

Malta Freeport Corporation Ltd, Freeport Centre, Port of Matrsaxlokk, Kalafrana BBG 07 (tel: 650-200; fax: 684-814).

Malta Investment Management Co Ltd (MIMCOL), Trade Centre, San Gwann Industrial Estate, Birkirkara SGN09 (tel: 497-970; fax: 499-568).

Malta Maritime Authority, Maritime House, Lascaris Wharf, Valletta VLT 01 (tel: 250-360/4; fax: 250-365).

Malta Shipbuilding Co Ltd, Marsa (tel: 220-051, 237-297; fax: 240-930).

Malta Stock Exchange, Pope Pius V Street, Valletta VLT 11 (tel: 244-051/5; fax: 244-071).

Malta Trade Fairs Corporation, The Fair Grounds, Naxxar NXR 02 (tel: 410-371/4; fax: 414-099).

Maltese Embassy (US), 2017 Connecticut Avenue, NW, Washington DC 20008 (tel: (+1-202) 462-3611; fax: (+1-202) 387-5470; e-mail: malta_embassy@compuserve.com).

Parliamentary Secretariat for Maritime and Offshore, House of Four Winds, Valletta (tel: 241-570).

Privatisation Unit, Ministry of Finance and Economic Affairs, Trade Centre, San Gwann Industrial Estate, San Gwann SGN 09 (internet site: www.maltacom.com).

Sea Malta Co Ltd, Sea Malta Building, Flagstone Wharf, Marsa HMR 12 (tel: 232-230/9; fax: 225-776).

Internet sites

Malta Government: http://www.magnet.mt/

Marshall Islands

KEY FACTS

Official name: Republic of the Marshall Islands

Head of State: President Christopher Loeak (from 10 Jan 2012)

Head of government: President Christopher Loeak

Ruling party: A loose coalition of the United People's Party (UPP) and Aelon Kein Ad (AKA) (Our Islands) (from 2008; re-elected Jan 2012)

Area: 183 square km consisting of 29 atolls and 1,225 islets

Population: 54,000 (2014)*

Capital: Majuro (on Majuro atoll)

Official language: Marshallese, English

Currency: US dollar (US$) = 100 cents)

GDP per capita: US$3,539 (2014)*

GDP real growth: 0.51% (2014)*

GDP: US$193.00 million (2014)*

Inflation: 1.10% (2014)*

Balance of trade: -US$41.08 million (2013)

Foreign debt: US$101.00 million (2012)

Annual FDI: US$7.37 million (2011)

* estimated figure

COUNTRY PROFILE

The Marshall Islands comprise over a thousand flat coral islands of white sand beaches and lagoons.

1788 The Marshall Islands were named after Captain John Marshall, who visited the islands on his way to China from Botany Bay.

1886 Germany established a protectorate over the Marshall Islands.

1914 The islands were captured from Germany by Japan.

1935 The Japanese transformed the islands into a military base.

1944 Allied troops occupied the islands.

1945 After the end of the Second World War, control of the Marshall Islands was granted to the US.

1946 The Marshall Islands were used as a nuclear testing ground by the US.

1947 Marshall Islands became one of six entities in the Trust Territory of the Pacific Islands (TTPI) established by the UN with the US as the Trustee.

1962 The US ended nuclear testing on the islands.

1965 The Congress of Micronesia was established, with representatives from all TTPI islands.

1978 The Marshall Islands' first constitution was adopted.

1979 The government of the Marshall Islands was officially established and the islands became self-governing. Amata Kabua was elected president.

1982 The official title of the islands became the Republic of the Marshall Islands (RMI).

1983 RMI voters approved the Compact of Free Association (CFA) with the US.

1986 The US Congress approved the CFA. The RMI was granted sovereignty, aid and US defence, in return for continued US military missile testing.

1990 The UN Security Council formally ended the trusteeship.

1991 The RMI joined the UN.

1995 President Kabua was re-elected for the fourth time.

1996 Amata Kabua died. He was succeeded by his cousin, Imata Kabua

1999 The United Democratic Party (UDP) won the general election.

2000 Kessai Note (UDP) was elected president.

2001 Former inhabitants of Bikini and the Enewetak atolls were awarded over US$1 billion in compensation for hardship suffered when they were evacuated and resettled in the 1940s to allow US nuclear tests on the islands.

2003 The RMI concluded negotiations with the US on the provisions of the CFA.

2004 Kessai Note was re-elected as president.

2006 Justin deBrum, a leading politician and presidential candidate died.

2007 The ruling UDP won the general elections. The OECD removed RMI from the blacklist of unco-operative tax havens.

2008 Parliament elected Litokwa Tomeing (representing coalition of United People's Party (UPP) and Aelon Kein Ad (AKA) (Our Islands)) as president by 18 to 15 votes. High tidal surges and a storm flooded low-lying areas resulting in the evacuation of over 300 people.

2009 Taiwan and Australia provided emergency funding and assistance for the flooding. The government-run retirement fund was declared to have a serious funding shortfall of US$231 million (a sum greater than the CMNI budget for 2009/10 of US$162 million). The superior court declared the government must fund the missing amount. President Litokwa Tomeing lost a vote of no-confidence in parliament and Jurelang Zedkaia became president.

2010 The first black pearls to be harvested since 2005 prompted renewed interest in the pearl fishing industry. A 1,300 unit haul, as part of a government-backed three-year project of growing oysters on a remote outer atoll, was valued at US$20,000. An expansion of the industry is planned to provide an annual 50,000 pearls.

2011 In February, the Director of the US Office of Insular Affairs conducted a joint US-Marshall Islands investigation into allegations of fraud involving US federal funds, resulting in the arrest of 10 people who were charged with misappropriation of over US$500,000. The national census, postponed since 2009, due to lack of funds to undertake the work, was concluded in April. Preliminary results recorded a population of just over 52,000. In October, an existing shark sanctuary was enlarged, to encompass an ocean area of almost two million square km around the Marshall Islands. At the same time, a new law was enacted, banning

commercial shark fishing and the trade in shark products. Parliamentary elections took place on 21 November, in which The United Democratic Party (UDP) won 15 seats, Aelon Kein Ad (AKA) (Our Islands) eight, United People's Party (UPP) seven and independents three.
2012 On 3 January, parliament elected Christopher Loeak (independent), as president, with 21 votes, against 11 votes for incumbent Jurelang Zedkaia. On 10 December Our Airline began weekly scheduled flights to Brisbane (Australia).
2013 The Luen Thai Fishing Venture, a multinational fishing company licensed to fish in Marshall Island waters was fined US$120,000 and stripped of its fishing licence for Marshall Islands waters after being found with shark fins on board their vessels. The annual meeting of the Pacific Forum was held in the first week of September. Representatives of the world's major climate change offenders attended and agreed that climate change is the greatest threat to the livelihoods, security and well being of the peoples of the region. The Majuro Declaration for Climate Leadership agreed at the end of the summit committed the Pacific nations to cut their own green house gas emissions and fight to combat climate change.
2014 In April the Marshall Islands announced it was suing the nine nuclear-armed nations (China, France, India, Israel, North Korea, Pakistan, Russia, UK and USA), demanding that they meet their obligations toward disarmament and accusing them of 'flagrant violations' of international law. The Islands had suffered the consequences of 12 years of US nuclear testing until they were ended in 1962. Announcing the lawsuits, foreign minister, Tony de Brum, said in a statement that 'Our people have suffered the catastrophic and irreparable damage of these weapons, and we vow to fight so that no one else on earth will ever again experience these atrocities.' The Islands are not seeking compensation, rather that the nine countries meet their obligations.
2015 In March a federal judge ruled that the law suit against the US to force it to dismantle its nuclear missiles should be dismissed since the Marshall Islands doesn't have standing to bring the case. On 2 April the government filed notice that it will appeal the judge's decision to dismiss the case.

Political structure

Constitution

The constitution was adopted in 1979. Under the Compact of Free Association (CFA), the Marshall Islands have control over all domestic and foreign affairs with the exception of defence which is the responsibility of the US.
Universal suffrage begins at aged 18.

Form of state

Self-governing territory in free association with the US.

The executive

Executive power rests with the president and the cabinet. The president is both head of state and head of government, elected by parliament for a four-year term. The president appoints the cabinet from members of the Nitijela (parliament).

National legislature

The bicameral system of government includes the Nitijela (lower house), with 33 senators of the Nitijela elected from 24 constituencies, for four-year terms. The Nitijela holds legislative power and elects the president.
The upper house, Council of Iroij (council of chiefs) is an advisory body, of 12 tribal chiefs, with consultative authority on matters relating to land and customs, who serves four-year terms.

Last elections

21 November 2011 (parliamentary); 3 January 2012 (presidential, indirect)
Results: Parliamentary: United Democratic Party (UDP) won 15 seats, Aelon Kein Ad (AKA) (Our Islands) eight, United People's Party (UPP) seven and independents three.
Presidential (indirect): Christopher Loeak (independent) 21 votes, Jurelang Zedkaia (AKA) 11; one abstention.

Next elections

16 November 2015 (general and, in the weeks after, presidential)

Political parties

Ruling party

A loose coalition of the United People's Party (UPP) and Aelon Kein Ad (AKA) (Our Islands) (from 2008; re-elected Jan 2012)

Main opposition party

United Democratic Party (UDP)

Political situation

The 2007 parliamentary elections resulted in two firsts. For the first time an unprecedented number of independent members were elected, leaving the government to be formed by a coalition, also for the first time. The result was determined to be a reaction by many landowners to the previous government's agreement with the US to lease, long-term, Kwajalein Atoll for missile testing. The landowners had consistently rejected the agreement for leasing the atoll until 2086 and said that unless there was an improvement in terms of conditions the agreement must end in 2016.
However by 2010 when a land use agreement (LUA) was thought to be ready for signing, in which landowners could be entitled to share the US$30 million from the leasing deal with the US military the LUA was found to be in abeyance since the landowners had included provision for funding a US$570 million infrastructure programme for the atoll. Neither the US military nor the RMI government were ready to sign the LUA, leaving all sides in need of further negotiations.
The island of Ebeye, part of Kwajalein atoll, is overcrowded, due to forced removals of people from atolls within the nuclear test zone. Between them, Ebeye and the urban area of Majuro make up around 10 per cent of the total land but are home to almost three-quarters of the population.
A national census, postponed since 2009, due to lack of funds to undertake the work, was concluded in April 2011. Preliminary results recorded a population of just over 52,000. Results of the census were published in May 2012, which showed that 30 per cent of all Marshallese reside in the US.

Population

55,000 (2012)*
Last census: June 1999: 50,848
Population density: 302 inhabitants per square km (2010). Urban population 72 per cent (2010 Unicef).
Annual growth rate: 0.7 per cent, 1990–2010 (Unicef).

KEY INDICATORS — Marshall Islands

	Unit	2011	2012	2013	2014	**2015
Population	m	*0.05	*0.05	–5	*0.05	*0.06
Gross domestic product (GDP)	US$bn	0.17	0.17	0.19	*0.19	*0.20
GDP per capita	US$	3,169	3,232	3,572	*3,539	*3,527
GDP real growth	%	5.0	3.2	3.0	*0.5	*1.7
Inflation	%	1.5	4.5	1.9	*1.1	*-0.6
Exports (fob) (goods)	US$m	60.5	98.6	92.9	–	–
Imports (fob) (goods)	US$m	117.5	121.6	134.0	–	–
Balance of trade	US$m	-57.0	-23.0	-41.1	–	–
Current account	US$m	-11.0	-14.0	-26.0	*-40.0	*3.0

* estimated figure ** forecast figure

Ethnic make-up
Micronesian
Religions
Christian (mostly Protestant).

Education
In 2009 the government announced that it would join the 'one laptop per child' programme (OLPC).
An agreement between the education departments of Guam and the Marshall Islands, signed in October 2010, will allow an exchange of students to study at the University of Guam and the College of the Marshall Islands.
Enrolment rate: 134 per cent (boys); 133 per cent (girls), gross primary enrolment of the relevant age group (including repetition rates) (Unicef).

Health
Type II diabetes (a disease associated with diet and lifestyle) became the leading cause of deaths among the Marshallese in 2011.
Over 80 per cent of children are immunised against measles. RMI has the highest per capita rate of leprosy in the world.
Life expectancy: 62 years, 2004 (WHO 2006)
Fertility rate/Maternal mortality rate: 4.4 births per woman, 2004 (WHO 2006)
Birth rate/Death rate: 34 births per 1,000 population; five deaths per 1,000 population (2003).
Child (under 5 years) mortality rate (per 1,000): 38 per 1,000 live births (WHO 2012)

Main cities
Majuro (capital, on Majuro atoll, Dalap-Uliga-Darrit Municipality, estimated population 20,301 in 2012), Ebeye (on Kwajalein) (9,627), Laura (3,046), Ajeltake (2,167).

Languages spoken
There are two main Marshallese dialects from the Malayo-Polynesian family. Marshallese is used by the government. English is taught in the schools and is widely spoken. Japanese is also spoken.
Official language/s
Marshallese, English

Media
Press
The *Marshall Islands Journal* (www.marshallislandsjournal.com) containing items in both Marshallese and English, is published every Friday and the government published *Marshall Islands Gazette* has official news.
Broadcasting
The government-owned radio station V7AB and MBC Television station are the only national broadcasters. Micronesia Heatwave is a commercial radio station and V7AA is a religious station.
Pay-to-view, cable TV is available in some areas.
Other news agencies: ABC Pacific Beat: www.radioaustralia.net.au/pacbeat
Pacific Magazine: www.pacificmagazine.net
Pacific Islands New Association (Pina): www.pina.com.fj

Economy
The Marshall Islands has a limited revenue base; most income is derived from payment by the US under the Compact of Free Association (CFA), the latest of which came into effect in 2004, and which commits the US to long-term financial support, international aid and a few commercial ventures. Following an initial US$29 million, the US will contribute US$7 million a year to the Intergenerational Investment Fund (IIF) until 2023. Together with government contributions the Fund should be able to provide investment for the islanders' future. However, in December 2009 the International Monetary Fund (IMF) warned that if the government persisted in deficit spending while at the same time denying substantial money to the fund, as seen over the past years, the country will end up with a major financial crisis by 2023.
The government employs over 45 per cent of the salaried workforce; unemployment is as high as 34 per cent. Agriculture, a small sector of GDP, is largely subsistence level production of food crops such as breadfruit, taro and pandanus; small quantities of commercial copra are processed but with limited means of trade. The Marshall Islands licenses ships as a flag of convenience and has around 1,200 ships registered through International Registries Inc, making it the fifth largest fleet in the world and earning about US$1 million annually.
The economy fell into recession in 2008, with GDP growth of -1.9 per cent. There was a slight improvement in 2009, to -1.3 per cent. The economy recovered with strong growth of 5.2 per cent in 2010, which moderated to 0.8 per cent in 2013 and 0.5 per cent in 2014.
The Chinese fishing company Shanghai Deep-Sea Fisheries invested US$8.5 million in a processing plant in Manuro in 2007. The plant is for skipjack tuna processing for the Asian market. In 2009 the Marshall Islands Service Corporation went ahead with plans to buy and operate modern fishing vessels for the island's tuna industry.

External trade
The Marshall Islands (RMI) is a member of the South Pacific Regional Trade and Economic Co-operation Agreement (Sparteca) along with 12 other regional nations, which allows products duty free access by Pacific Island Forum members to Australian and New Zealand markets (subject to the country of origin restrictions).
Semi-manufactured goods, assembled in the islands, enjoy preferential access to US markets under the Compact of Free Association. Light manufacturing includes soap, cooking oil, salad oil, margarine and cosmetics, using local processed coconut oil.
Imports
Principal imports, which far outstrip exports, are foodstuffs, petroleum, machinery and equipment, beverages and tobacco.
Main sources: US, Japan, Australia, New Zealand, Singapore, Fiji, China, Philippines.
Exports
Principal exports are copra cake, coconut oil, handicrafts and fish
Main destinations: US, Japan, Australia, China.

Agriculture
Farming
Subsistence farming of taro, breadfruit, bananas, yams, sweet potatoes and vegetables, along with pig and poultry raising, is the main occupation. Large areas of potentially arable land remain uncultivated.
Fishing
Fishing, particularly tuna, is important, supplying the principal source of protein as well as export revenues. A dozen-longline tuna boats built with Asian Development Bank money almost doubled the fleet in the mid-1990s. Tuna is supplied to the Pan Pacific Foods Plant in Majuro for processing.
A Hawaiian company, Black Pearl Inc, noted after extensive research the potential for breeding black pearl oysters. Some farms have opened but it will be several years before they can compete with world market leaders. Seaweed farming may offer an alternative. Typical pearl and shell harvest production is 100,000 units per annum.
On 12 April 2011, a summit of the Parties to the Nauru Agreement (PNA) concluded its strategy for a policy of sustainable fishing in the Pacific. The PNA treaty, which was established in 1989 and expired in 2012, is seen as in need of an overhaul. As a collective region, the PNA (FSM, Kiribati, Marshall Islands, Nauru, Palau, PNG, Solomon Islands and Tuvalu) control around 25–30 per cent of world stocks of tuna. Only 5 per cent of sales revenue is returned to the PNA and ministers called for specific changes, including an increased share of profits, PNA crews on-board purse seine vessels (minimum

10 per cent), conservation and management measures including a limit to fish trapping (fish aggregating devices (FADs)), net mesh rules and the establishment of an observer agency and fisheries information management system. The PNA met in May 2012 to discuss even stronger management measures to ensure even more sustainable tuna fisheries and minimise environmental damage. Many of the ideas put forward were implemented in January 2013, for example observation and monitoring of catches and environmental damage by 100 per cent independent bodies.

Forestry

Industry and manufacturing

Small-scale industries include handicrafts, fish processing, copra processing, bakeries and boat building and repairs. A tuna processing factory which opened in 1999 was a significant addition to industry.

Tourism

Tourism is relatively underdeveloped with the opportunity for growth dependent on air access. There were around 6,000 visitors in 2008; the industry typically employs around 10 per cent of the workforce.

A national holiday was declared for 1 March 2012, to mark the anniversary of the first hydrogen bomb testing on Bikini Atoll in 1954. The Atoll is included on UNESCO's World Heritage List as an important historic site at the start of the nuclear age.

Environment

In October 2011, an existing shark sanctuary was enlarged, to encompass an ocean area of almost two million square km around the Marshall Islands. At the same time, a new law was enacted, banning commercial shark fishing and the trade in shark products.

Mining

Small mineral deposits exist, but exploitation is hampered by a shortage of land to accommodate the displaced population and doubts about economic viability. Extraction of phosphate occurs at Ailinglaplap.

Hydrocarbons

There are no known hydrocarbon reserves; all petroleum products are imported to meet domestic needs.

Energy

The Marshall Energy Company is responsible for generation and supply of electricity on all but Ebeye where the Kwajalein Atoll Joint Utility Resource provides energy.

Solar-photovoltaic systems are funded through Japan's Pacific Environmental Community (PEC) fund, which supplies Majuro with renewable energy.

Banking and insurance

Growth in the Marshall Islands' banking sector is limited by the size of its population. Commercial bank lending in 2004 was some US$45 million while deposits were substantially greater at US$81 million.

Time

GMT plus twelve hours

Geography

The Marshall Islands are located in the area of the Pacific Ocean known as Micronesia (which includes Kiribati, Tuvalu and other territories). The islands lie about 3,200km (2,000 miles) south-west of Hawaii and about 2,100km (1,300 miles) south-east of Guam.

The Marshall Islands comprises around 1,200 coral islands and islets, of which five are single islands, the rest combining into 29 atolls. The territory extends over 750,000 square km of sea area in two parallel chains: Ratak (Sunrise) to the east and Ralik (Sunset) to the west. Total land mass of the system is around 183 square km. The mean height is two metres. The atolls are narrow and encircle large lagoons. Beaches are white sand.

Hemisphere

Northern

Climate

Tropical climate. Warm and humid, temperatures 23–30 degrees Celsius, humidity around 80 per cent. High temperatures are cooled by trade winds. Rainfall variable, minimum 250mm per year, can occur in downpours. Hurricanes are possible.

Entry requirements

Passports

Required by all, valid for six months beyond date of departure.

Visa

Required by all, except nationals of the US, Federated States of Micronesia and Palau. Tourist and business visas are issued on arrival for stays up to three months.

All visitors must have proof of adequate funds and return/onward passage. Special regulations may apply to some non-tourist destinations. Further information can be obtained through www.rmiembassyus.org.

Health (for visitors)

Advisable precautions

Vaccinations for hepatitis A and B and typhoid are recommended; those for tetanus and diphtheria should be updated as needed.

Hotels

There are a number of first class and other hotels, mainly on Majuro and Ebeye, and guesthouses, which are more widely distributed.

Credit cards

Visa, Mastercard and American Express are accepted by most major businesses.

Public holidays (national)

Fixed dates

1 Jan (New Year's Day), 1 Mar (Nuclear Survivors Day), 1 May (Constitution Day), 21 Oct (Compact Day), 17 Nov (President's Day), 25 Dec (Christmas Day).

Some dates vary from island to island.

Variable dates

Fishermen's Day (first Fri in Jul), Rijerbal/Labour Day (first Fri in Sep), Manit/Customs Day (last Fri in Sep), Gospel Day (first Fri in Dec).

Working hours

Banking

Mon–Fri: 1000–1500; Fri: 1000–1800.

Business

Mon–Fri: 0800–1700.

Government

Mon–Fri: 0800–1700.

Shops

Mon–Sat: 0800–2000; (Sun) 0800–1800.

Telecommunications

Telephone/fax

International satellite links provide fax and Internet facilities. Communication with the outer islands is by radio.

Postal services

There are US Postal Service offices on Majuro and Ebeye.

Mobile/cell phones

Cellular service is available on Maburo, Ebeye and Kwajalein.

Social customs/useful tips

In business an informal attitude prevails. Appointments should be made. Business cards are exchanged. Business is usually conducted in English. Permission should be sought before taking photographs of people. The minimum drinking age is 21 years. Swimsuits, shorts or short skirts should not be worn in urban areas. Tipping is optional.

Getting there

Air

National airline: Our Airline

International airport/s: Amata Kabua International International (MAJ), 25km from Majuro. There are buses, taxis and hotel transport from the airport to the city.

Airport tax: US$15.

Surface

Main port/s: Majuro and Kwajalein.

Getting about

National transport

Air: Air Marshall Islands flies services to most of the atolls.

Road: The main roads on the major islands are paved. Others are stone-, coral- or laterite-surfaced roads and tracks.

Water: The government operates several vessels, which link the islands on an irregular schedule. Inter-island cruises are available and boats can be hired privately.

City transport

Taxis: Taxis are plentiful and relatively cheap, but usually operate on a shared basis.

Car hire

There are many car hire operators. Driving is on the right.

BUSINESS DIRECTORY

The addresses listed below are a selection only. While World of Information makes every endeavour to check these addresses, we cannot guarantee that changes have not been made, especially to telephone numbers and area codes. We would welcome any corrections.

Telephone area codes

The international direct dialling (IDD) code for Marshall Islands is +692 followed by area code and subscriber's number:

Ebeye	329	Majuro	625

Chambers of Commerce

Majuro Chamber of Commerce, PO Box 1318, Majuro 96960 (tel: 625-3051; fax: 625-3343; e-mail: majurochamber@hotmail.com).

Banking

Bank of Marshall Islands, PO Box J, Majuro 96960 (tel: 625-3636; fax: 625-3661; e-mail: bankmar@ntamar.com).

Travel information

Air Marshall Islands, PO Box 1319, Majuro 96960 (tel: 625-3731; fax: 625-37; e-mail: amisales@ntamar.net).

Marshall Islands Visitors Authority, PO Box 5, Majuro 96960 (tel: 625-6482; fax: 625-6771; e-mail: tourism@ntamar.com).

Ministry of tourism

Ministry of Resources and Development, Tourism Office, PO Box 1727, Majuro 96960 (tel: 625-6482; fax: 625-3218).

Other useful addresses

Marshall Islands Embassy (USA), 2433 Massachusetts Avenue, NW, Washington DC 20008 (tel: (+1-202)-234-5414; fax: (+1-202)-232-3236: e-mail: info@rmiembassyus.org).

ABC Pacific Beat: www.radioaustralia.net.au/pacbeat

Pacific Magazine: www.pacificmagazine.net

Pacific Islands New Association (Pina): www.pina.com.fj

Internet sites

Our Airline: www.ourairline.com.au

Website of the Marshall Islands: www.rmiembassyus.org/

The Pacific business centre: http://cba.hawaii.edu/pbcp/

Martinique

COUNTRY PROFILE

1493 Columbus was the first European visitor.
1635 The island was settled by the French – in the face of indigenous Indian hostility.
1700s The island was seized by the British several times.
1763 Marie-Josephe Rose Tascher de la Pagerie – Napoleon's Empress Josephine – was born at Les Trois Ilets.
1814 The British gave up their attempts to control the island and it became a French possession under the Treaty of Paris.
1848 The Emancipation Proclamation abolished slavery in the West Indies.
1902 St Pierre was destroyed by an eruption of the volcano Mount Pelée.
1946 Martinique became a French Département d'Outre-Mer (DOM) (Overseas Department).
1974 Martinique was further incorporated into the French political system and granted the status of region of France.
1983 Martinique was granted devolution. A Regional Council was established under the French decentralisation policy.
1999–2001 The presidents of the regional assemblies of Martinique, Guadeloupe and French Guiana called for more autonomy from France.
2002 Martinique adopted the euro as its official currency.
2003 A referendum in Guadeloupe and Martinique rejected a French government-backed reform plan to streamline the system of local government and give the islands a new status.
2004 Martinique was the first port of call for Cunard's newest, and largest, cruise ship, *Queen Mary II*. Yves Dassonville took over as *Préfet*, replacing Michel Cadot.
2007 Ange Mancini was appointed *Préfet*.
2008 The poet, Aime Cesaire, a leading figure of not only the local but also the wider, international black empowerment and cultural community, died. President Sarkozy led the mourners in a state funeral in Fort-de-France.
2009 Civil unrest following a workers' strike in protest against low pay and rising prices resulted in the deployment of riot police from mainland France. As a result a reported 10,000 tourists cancelled their holidays. The France-based minister of overseas territories arrived to oversee negotiations.
2010 By 80–20 per cent (on a turnout of 55 per cent), voters rejected a referendum proposal to devolve more power to local government and grant more autonomy. Serge Letchimy was elected president of the Regional Council.
2011 In July, the EU agreed to allow Martinique to impose import duties from 1 July 2014, to protect local production of food and manufactured goods.
2012 Laurent Prévost was appointed as *Préfet* on 2 March. Ten candidates took part in the French presidential elections (held over two rounds on 21 April and 5 May); in the runoff, incumbent Nicolas Sarkozy (UMP) won 48.37 per cent of the vote and rival François Hollande (Parti Socialiste (PS) (Socialist Party)) 51.63 per cent. Turnout was 80.35 per cent. On 15 May François Hollande took office as president and head of state. On 10 November the town of Sainte Marie and the l'Office National des Forêt (ONF) (National Forestry Office) inaugurated the refurbished tourist development along the shoreline, including a new monument, an exhibition of the site's heritage and an artistic presentation.
2013 A report released in St Lucia in April proposed that Martinique and Guadeloupe should become members of the Organisation of Eastern Caribbean States. At the summit of heads of state of the Association of Caribbean States (ACS) in Haiti an application for associate membership was presented by Martinique and Guadeloupe. France had approved the application for membership by the two French Overseas Territories in December 2012.
2014 Martinique officially became an associate member of the Association of Caribbean States (ACS) in its own right on 11 April.
2015 In January the three French Caribbean countries (French Guiana, Guadeloupe and Martinique) began discussions on becoming associate members of Caricom. On 4 February Martinique became an associate member of the Organisation of Eastern Caribbean States (OECS), increasing the nine-member grouping to ten.

KEY FACTS

Official name: Martinique

Head of State: President of France François Hollande (PS) (from 15 May 2012), represented by *Préfet* Laurent Prévost (from 2 March 2012)

Head of government: President of Conseil Général Claude Lise (since 22 Mar 1992); President of Conseil Régional Serge Letchimy (from 26 Mar 2010)

Ruling party: Coalition led by Mouvement pour l'Indépendence de la Martinique (MIM), with Conseil National des Comités Populaires (CNCP) (since Mar 2004)

Area: 1,100 square km

Population: 406,000 (2010)

Capital: Fort-de-France

Official language: French

Currency: Euro (€) = 100 cents (from 1 Jan 2002; previous currency French franc, locked at Ff6.56 per euro)

Exchange rate: €0.89 per US$ (Sep 2015)

Political structure

Constitution

28 September 1958 (French Fifth Republic)

Under the 1946 constitution of the French Fourth Republic, Martinique became a Département d'Outre-Mer (DOM) (Overseas Department) of France. In 1974, it was granted additional status as a region of France.

Martinique is represented in the French National Assembly by four deputies and in the Senate by two senators.

Administration is by a préfet appointed by the government in Paris.

Since 1983, following the French government's policy of decentralisation, regional councils have been elected with powers similar to those of the regions.

Local administration is through a Conseil Régional (Regional Council) of 41 members and a 45-member Conseil Général (General Council), both directly elected for six-year terms.

Form of state

Département d'Outre-Mer (DOM) (Overseas Department) of France, with additional status as a région (region) of France.

The executive

The island is administered by a *préfet* (commissioner), appointed by the central government in Paris.

National legislature

The Conseil Régional (Regional Council) provides legislative administration for the island; it has 41 members elected by proportional representation for four-year terms.

Legal system

French law applies. The country has no supreme court but this role is filled by a nine-member Conseil Constitutionel (Constitutional Council). Its task is to ensure that law treaties and regulations are in keeping with the constitution and that elections are conducted in a regular manner. The highest court of appeal is the Cour de Cassation, which can overrule decisions in all lower courts, but not government legislation. Since the signing of the Single European Act in 1986, the European Court of Justice (ECJ) has been the highest authority in certain areas of French law.

Next elections

2016 (Regional council)

Political parties

Ruling party

Coalition led by Mouvement pour l'Indépendence de la Martinique (MIM), with Conseil National des Comités Populaires (CNCP) (since Mar 2004)

Main opposition party

Parti Progressiste Martiniquais (PPM) (Martinican Progressive Party)

Political situation

A referendum on a French government proposal held in Martinique in 2003 seemed straightforward. The proposal was twofold. First, it would streamline the local government apparatus and reduce the number of elected offices. The second effect would be a change in Martinique's relationship with France, which would effectively reduce its standing as a region of France. The proposal was made in response to a call made in 1999—2000 for more independence.

However, the proposal was rejected and the failure was thought to be due to voters' worry that any change in their status would ultimately result in a withdrawal of French central government funds needed, most particularly, for social security.

Population

406,000 (2010)

Last census: 1 January 2006: 397,732

Population density: 282 inhabitants per sq km.

Annual growth rate: 0.6 per cent (2003)

Ethnic make-up

African and mixed race (90 per cent), white (5 per cent), East Indian and others (5 per cent).

Religions

Roman Catholic (85 per cent), Protestant (10 per cent), Islam, Hindu, pagan African (5 per cent).

Education

There is 42 per cent enrolment in education for the 20- to 24-year age groups with a high rate of unemployment among them.

Literacy rate: 98 per cent, adult rate (2003)

Health

Water for consumption is subject to intensive controls and is of high quality.

There are three public hospitals including one teaching hospital, and three private clinics.

HIV/Aids

Martinique has a departmental Aids control scheme.

Life expectancy: 79 (estimate 2003)

Birth rate/Death rate: 15 births per 1,000 population; 6.4 deaths per 1,000 population (2003).

Child (under 5 years) mortality rate (per 1,000): 7.4 per 1,000 live births (2003)

Welfare

With unemployment ranging between 30 and 35 per cent among the youth, there has been a noticeable increase in the number of people calling for independence from France. The French social security system guarantees a high minimum wage, a 35-hour working week, five-week vacations, a 40 per cent incentive on salary and other social benefits.

Main cities

Fort-de-France (capital (prefecture), estimated population 84,440 in 2012), Le Lamentin (43,734), Le Robert (27,000), Schoelcher (22,076), Le Francois (20,860), Sainte Marie (20,515), Ducos (20,128).

Languages spoken

French and Creole patois (developed from French, English, Spanish and some African languages). English is widely understood.

Official language/s

French

Media

Press

In French, *France Antilles* is the only daily newspaper, which belongs to a French-based publishing house. Weekly publications include *Le Progressiste, Aujourd'hui Dimanche, Justice, Le Naif* and *Antilla*.

Broadcasting

The French overseas broadcaster RFO (www.rfo.fr) provides locally produced radio and television news (http://martinique.rfo.fr) and imported French programmes, as well as internet TV services.

Radio: Apart from the public RFO Martinique radio broadcasts, Radio Caraibes International (http://rci.fm) and NRJ Antilles (www.nrjantilles.com) are private radio stations.

Economy

Martinique has an open market economy, with the service sector providing over 80 per cent of employment and tourism providing 12.0 per cent of GDP in 2014. The tourist sector is a major employer and key source of foreign exchange; Martinique has not only increased its share of the cruise ship industry but has also become a leading provider of luxury holiday venues.

Agriculture accounts for almost 40 per cent of export earnings, of which bananas account for around half.

The local economy represents no more than 25 per cent of GDP, with French funding accounting for the remaining 75 per cent.

A French government 15-year economic development plan for the dependent territories, published in 2002, has led to greater improvements in infrastructure and has improved the island's investment climate.

Among the improvements was the construction of a land and sea transport terminal, next to Pointe Simon Cruise Terminal, which integrated water taxis and public transport at the Cap Est lagoon resort and spa.

External trade

As a département d'outre-mer (DOM) of France, Martinique is integrated as an outermost region of the European Union, which includes all EU trade agreements. The large trade deficit is only partly offset by invisible earnings from tourism, workers' remittances from abroad, and French aid aimed at developing the tourist trade and reducing unemployment.

Imports

Principal imports are petroleum products, crude oil, foodstuffs, construction materials, vehicles, clothing and other consumer goods.

Main sources: France (typically 60 per cent), Venezuela (6.0 per cent), Germany (4.0 per cent), Italy (4.0 per cent), US (3.0 per cent).

Exports

Principal exports are refined petroleum products, bananas, rum and pineapples.

Main destinations: France (typically 45 per cent), Guadeloupe (28 per cent).

Agriculture

Farming

Once the mainstay of the economy, the agricultural sector has declined in recent years. It employs 10 per cent of the workforce and contributes well under 10 per cent to GDP. Around 48 per cent of total land area is cultivated, 25 per cent is forest and 19 per cent savannah. The majority of farms are privately run by smallholders.

Activity is centred on the production of pineapples and bananas, mainly for industrial processing and export.

Crops such as sweet potatoes, yams, manioc, beans, cabbages and tomatoes are grown primarily for domestic consumption. Small quantities of aubergines and limes are exported. Virtually all the island's meat requirements are met by imports. Almost half of all agricultural exports are bananas.

Fishing

Fishing (lobster, crayfish, crab, and clams) is undertaken all year round. The typical total annual fish catch is over 6,250 tonnes (t). Shellfish, molluscs and cephalopods account for another 909t per annum.

Forestry

Industry and manufacturing

Major industries include an oil refinery (capacity 17,000 barrels per day (bpd) in 2013), a cement works, rum distilling, sugar refining, dairy produce, fruit canning, soft drinks manufacture, mineral water bottling and a polyethylene plant.

Industrial development has been poor and centres mainly on the manufacture of consumer goods for the local market. Five industrial zones have been set up and tax exemptions introduced to encourage light industrial development.

Tourism

Martinique offers a French culture in a Caribbean setting, which attracts around 500,000 visitors each year. However, over 60 per cent of all visitors arrive by cruise liners. The majority of visitors are from France (80 per cent), with citizens of other regional French departments (Guadeloupe, French Guiana) representing 9 per cent, but with no other nationality representing more than 2 per cent.

Travel and tourism represented over 12.0 per cent of GDP in 2014, with total employment at 12.3 per cent (16,000 jobs). Cruise passenger arrivals for January–December 2014 were up by 71.3 per cent over 2013, according to the Martinique Tourism Authority.

Martinique's Tourism Development Strategy took a big leap forward when three major airports in the northeast of the US (New York, Boston and Washington) announced in June 2015 they would be scheduling non-stop flights to the island.

Mining

Martinique has no mineral resources.

Hydrocarbons

There are no known hydrocarbons reserves. Oil imports were around 18,000 barrels per day (bpd) in 2014 all of which was refined on the island by Sara (Société Anonyme de Raffinerie des Antilles) in the only refinery. Consumption was around 19,000bpd.

Any imports of coal or natural gas are commercially insignificant. A proposed pipeline from Trinidad and Tobago to Martinique and Guadeloupe could open up possibilities for the future import of natural gas. The project was slated to begin in 2014 however by 2015 construction had not started.

Energy

Total installed generating capacity was 400MW in 2012, producing over 1.6 billion kilowatt hours, from two thermal power stations. The state-owned EDF (Electricité de France) is responsible for generation and distribution of electricity.

Banking and insurance

Central bank

Caisse Centrale de Co-opération Economique; European Central Bank (ECB)

Time

GMT minus four hours

Geography

Martinique is one of the Windward Islands in the West Indies, with Dominica to the north and St Lucia to the south. The island, which has an area of 1,100 square km, is bounded to the west by the calm Caribbean Sea and to the east by the choppier Atlantic Ocean.

The terrain rises from the south to the mountainous centre and the north. The highest point in the island, situated in the north, is an active volcano, Mount Pelée, which reaches 1,397m. The mountain areas are covered with rainforest. The Lamentin Plain, an area of hills and valleys, occupies the centre of the island. The northern beaches consist of volcanic ash and are grey, while those in the south, where the Salines Beach is located, are sandy and white. The southern Atlantic coastline is protected by coral reefs.

Hemisphere

Northern

Climate

Sub-tropical with an annual mean temperature of 26 degrees Celsius. Rain heaviest in the north. Rainy season from June–October. The island's temperature is moderated by trade winds.

Entry requirements

Passports

Required by all, valid for three months beyond the date of departure.

Visa

Required by all, except citizens of EU, North America, Australasia and Japan.

Business visas require an invitation from a local company or organisation. Proof of adequate funds for stay, an itinerary, a guarantee of repatriation if necessary and return/onward ticket are also required.

Currency advice/regulations

There are no restrictions on the import and export of local and foreign currencies, but amounts in excess of eur7,600 must be declared.

Health (for visitors)

Mandatory precautions

A yellow fever vaccination certificate is required if travelling from an infected area.

Advisable precautions

Hepatitis, typhoid, tetanus and polio vaccinations. Water precautions should be taken.

Hotels

There is a 5 per cent room tax. If service charge is not added, 15 per cent tip is usual.

Public holidays (national)

Fixed dates

1 Jan (New Year's Day), 1 May (Labour Day), 8 May (Victory Day), 22 May (Abolition of Slavery), 14 Jul (Bastille Day), 21 Jul (Schoelcher Day), 15 Aug (Assumption Day), 1 Nov (All Saints' Day), 11 Nov (Armistice Day), 25 Dec (Christmas Day).

Variable dates
Carnival (four days, Feb), Good Friday, Easter Monday, Ascension Day, Whit Monday.

Working hours

Banking
Mon–Fri: 0800–1200, 1400–1700. Banks close at noon on day preceding a bank holiday.

Business
Mon–Fri: 0800–1200, 1430–1700; Sat: 0800–1200.

Government
Mon–Fri: 0730–1300, 1500–1730.

Shops
Mon–Fri: 0900–1300, 1500–1800; Sat: 0900–1300.

Telecommunications

Telephone/fax
There is a 100 per cent automatic service.

Mobile/cell phones
There are several GSM 850, 900, 1800 and 1900 services available throughout the country.

Electricity supply

220V AC, 50 cycles

Getting there

Air

National airline: Air Caraibes.
International airport/s: Lamentin (FDF), 11km from Fort-de-France; restaurant, banks, shops, car hire.
Airport tax: None.

Surface

Main port/s: Fort-de-France is the only commercial port; other ports of entry include St Pierre, Anse Mitan and Le Marin.

Getting about

National transport

Road: Well-developed network of more than 2,000km of roads, three-quarters of which are paved and the rest gravel and earth.
Water: There are regular ferry services (*vedettes*) from Fort-de-France to Pointe de Bout and Anse Mitan.

Car hire
There are ample car rental facilities. A valid driving licence is required and also, for periods beyond 20 days, an international licence.

BUSINESS DIRECTORY

The addresses listed below are a selection only. While World of Information makes every endeavour to check these addresses, we cannot guarantee that changes have not been made, especially to telephone numbers and area codes. We would welcome any corrections.

Telephone area codes

The international direct dialling code (IDD) for Martinique is +596, followed by subscriber's number.

Useful telephone numbers

Ambulance: 15
Fire brigade: 18
Police: 17

Chambers of Commerce

Martinique Chamber of Commerce and Industry, 50 Rue Ernest Deproge, PO Box 478, Fort-de-France 97241 (tel: 552-800; fax: 606-668; e-mail: info@martinique.cci.fr).

Banking

Banque des Antilles Françaises, 34 rue Lamartine, BP 582, 97200 Fort-de-France (tel: 739-344; fax: 635-894).

Banque Française Commerciale, 6-10 rue Ernest Deproge, 97200 Fort-de-France (tel: 638-257).

Banque National de Paris, Avenue des Caraibes, 97200 Fort-de-France (tel: 737-111).

Chase Manhattan Bank, Place de Monseigheur Romero, 97200 Fort-de-France (tel: 602-424).

Crédit Martiniquais, rue de la Liberté, Fort-de-France (tel: 701-240).

Institut d'Emission des DOM (IEDOM), Boulevard General de Gaulle, BP 512, 97206 Fort-de-France (tel: 594-400; fax: 594-404).

Société Générale de Banque aux Antilles, rue de la Liberté, BP 408, 97200 Fort-de-France (tel: 716-983).

Central bank
European Central Bank (ECB), Kaiserstrasse 29, D-60311 Frankfurt am Main, Germany (tel: (+49-69)-13-440; fax: (+49-69)-1344-6000; e-mail: info@ecb.int).

Travel information

Agence Régionale pour le Développement du Tourisme de la Martinique (ARDTM), 4 Rue de l'école Hotellière, Anse Goureaud, 97233 Schoelcher (tel: 616-177; fax: 612-272).

Air Caraibes, Morne Vergain, 97139 Abymes (tel: (0590)-824-747; fax: (0490)-824-749; e-mail: direction@aircaraibes.com).

Délégation Régionale au Tourisme, 41 Rue Gabriel Péri, 97200 Fort-de-France (tel: 393-767; fax: 730-096).

Fort-de-France Office du Tourisme, 76 rue Lazare Carnot, 97206 Fort-de-France (tel: 602-773; fax: 602-795; e-mail: info@tourismefdf.com).

Lamentin Airport, 97200 Lamentin (tel: 421-600; fax: 421-877).

National tourist organisation offices
Comité Martiniquais du Tourisme, Immeuble Le Beaupré, Pointe de Jaham, 97233 Schoelcher (tel: 616-177; fax:612-272; e-mail: infos.cmt@martiniquetourisme.com).

Other useful addresses

Agence pour le Développement Economique de la Martinique, Immeuble Nayaradou, Plateau de Cluny, 97233 Schoelcher (tel: 734-581; fax: 724-138).
Bureau de l'Industrie de l'Artisanat, Préfecture, 97262 Fort-de France (tel: 713-627).
Chambre Départementale d'Agriculture, Place D'Armes, BP 312, 97286 Lamentin Cedex (tel: 517-575; fax: 519-342).
Chambre des Métiers, 2 Rue du Temple, Morne Tartenson, BP 1191, 97249 Fort-de-France (tel: 713-222; fax: 704-730).
Post Office, 132 boulevard Pasteur, Fort-de-France (tel: 599-600).
Préfecture, rue Victor Severe, BP 647-648, 97262 Fort-de-France (tel: 631-861; fax: 714-029; internet site: http://www.martinique.pref.gouv.fr/pages/somangl.html).

Internet sites

Regional Council of Martinique: http://www.cr-martinique.fr/anglais/accueil_anglais.html

Martinique Promotion Bureau: http://www.martinique.org

Martinique Shipping Services: http://www.marship.fr

Mauritania

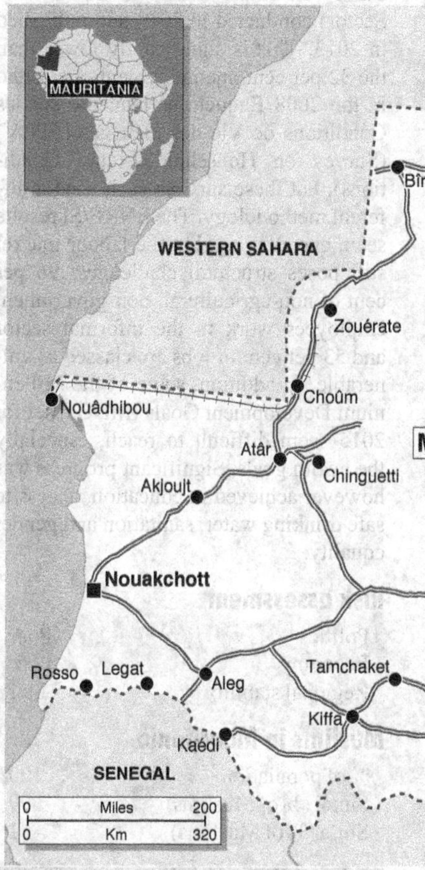

KEY FACTS

Official name: République Islamique Arabe et Africaine de Mauritanie (Islamic Republic of Mauritania)

Head of State: President Mohamed Ould Abdel Aziz (from 5 Aug 2009)

Head of government: Prime Minister Yahya Ould Hademine (appointed 20 Aug 2014)

Ruling party: Coalition of the majority led by Union pour la République (UPR) (Union for the Republic)

Area: 1,030,700 square km

Population: 3.62 million (2014)*

Capital: Nouakchott

Official language: Hassani Arabic and Wolof

Currency: Ouguiya (UM) = 5 khoums

Exchange rate: UM318.00 per US$ (Sep 2015)

GDP per capita: US$1,403 (2014)*

GDP real growth: 6.42% (2014)

GDP: US$5.08 billion (2014)

Inflation: 3.52% (2014)

Balance of trade: -US$392.90 million (2013)

* estimated figure

Mauritania is huge, its geography apparently purposeless. Three quarters of Mauritanians live along the northern banks of the Senegal River. The Sahel droughts have driven many thousands of peasants and nomads into the shanty-towns around Nouakchott. With a growth rate of 3 per cent per year and a per capita gross national income (GNI) of US$580 in 2005, Mauritania has an intricate dual culture, having traditional ties with the Maghreb countries in the North and with Senegal and Mali in the south and east. The socio-cultural landscape has recently undergone a rapid transformation. From a traditionally nomadic society at independence (1960) with only 5 per cent of the population in urban centres, the country is now urban-dominated, with over 60 per cent of the population (1.8 million) living in urban centres. This urbanisation was caused by migration from rural areas, particularly since the mid-1980s. Today, Nouakchott, the capital city, contains one-third of the total population. Live is hard in the slums of Nouakchott, with no amenities and scant chance of real employment.

Call it employment? Or slavery?

In 2014 Mauritania was one of the last and little known redoubts of slavery in the world. An excellent article by Alexis Okeowo in the *New Yorker* magazine drew readers' attention to the fact that it was only 1981 that Mauritania became the last country in the world to abolish slavery. That was a major step forward, but Mauritania had failed to take one other important step: no legal provision existed for punishing slave owners. It was some 26 years later, in 2007, that bowing to international pressure Mauritania passed a law that 'allowed' slaveholders to be punished. But seven years on, slavery still persists, benefiting from the country's low international profile. Quoted by Mr Okeowo, the Global Slavery Index's summary of the position states that: 'Mauritania, a West African nation with deeply entrenched hereditary slavery, is ranked number one in the Index. This reflects the high prevalence of slavery in Mauritania – it is estimated that there are between 140,000–160,000 people enslaved in Mauritania, a country with a population of just 3.8 million. This ranking also reflects high levels of child marriage and to a lesser extent, human trafficking.' These figures are, one imagines difficult to compile and probably subject to some inaccuracies. However, what is beyond doubt, as described by Mr Okeowo, is that 'many Mauritanians exist somewhere on a continuum between slavery and freedom. There is outright subjugation; there is indentured servitude and there is the freed slaves' struggle with what is politely referred to as the 'vestiges of slavery'.'

The origins of slavery in Mauritania are as old as its tribes. The Berbers and the Arabs who occupied the vast territory took African slaves as a matter of course. Over the centuries, blood-lines became confused and mingled, to the extent that Arab-Berbers became known as *Beydanes* and the slaves as *Haratin*, descriptive terms which are still used today. Unsurprisingly, the *Beydanes* occupy most of Mauritania's positions of wealth, power and influence. The darker *Haratin* are regarded as an underclass, no matter how well educated they are. This archaic social structure is a serious hindrance to Mauritania's economic development.

The economy

According to the African Development Bank (AfDB) in its 2014 *Economic Outlook*, the economic dynamism displayed by Mauritania in 2012 continued in 2013, fuelled by agriculture, mining and construction. Growth is estimated to have been at 6.8 per cent in 2013 and is projected at 6.9 per cent in 2014 and 7.3 per cent in 2015. This favourable outlook relies on a series of optimistic assumptions: new iron deposits available to the mining sector, good climate conditions and a positive impact of the country's new fishing agreement with the European Union (EU) signed in October 2013. Benefits are also expected from the Brussels talks held in 2010 to finance the government's economic and social programme under its Cadre Stratégique de Lutte contre la Pauvreté (CSLP III) (strategic framework to combat poverty). Strangely, the issue of slavery does not seem to have crossed the AfDB's radar. In the long run, however, the economy remains vulnerable to changes in the terms of trade.

The year 2013 was marked by a satisfactory implementation of the three-year programme supported by the International Monetary Fund (IMF)'s Extended Credit Facility (ECF). The programme was completed in June 2013 when national authorities had met almost all the quantitative performance criteria. Official reserves reached the equivalent of 7.3 months of imports at end-2013. In addition to good budgetary performance, macro-economic stability was supported by a prudent monetary policy aimed at absorbing the inflationary pressures resulting from excess bank liquidity.

Strong growth seems to have created jobs, bringing unemployment down to 10.1 per cent according to the Enquête nationale de référence sur l'emploi et le secteur informel (ENRE/SI) (National Survey on Employment and the Informal Sector) conducted in 2012 and published in 2013. This is significantly lower than the 32 per cent unemployment rate found in the 2008 Enquête permanente sur les Conditions de Vie des ménages (EPCV) (Survey on Household Living Conditions), but these surveys each used a different methodology. The ENRE/SI results seem encouraging, but the labour market still poses structural challenges: 96 per cent of non-agricultural, non-government employees work in the informal sector and 53 per cent of jobs are classed as vulnerable. In addition, some of the Millennium Development Goals (MDGs) set for 2015 seem difficult to reach, especially the health goals. Significant progress was however achieved in education, access to safe drinking water, sanitation and gender equality.

Risk assessment

Politics	Poor
Economy	Poor
Regional stability	Fair

Muslims in Mauritania

% of population	100
Sunni (% of Muslims)	99
Shi'a (% of Muslims)	1

KEY INDICATORS — Mauritania

	Unit	2011	2012	2013	2014	**2015
Population	m	*3.30	*3.63	*3.54	*3.62	*3.71
Gross domestic product (GDP)	US$bn	4.20	3.96	5.09	5.08	*4.99
GDP per capita	US$	1,247	1,092	*1,439	*1,403	*1,347
GDP real growth	%	3.6	7.0	5.7	6.4	*5.5
Inflation	%	5.7	4.9	4.1	3.5	*4.5
Exports (fob) (goods)	US$m	2,765.7	2,641.0	2,651.5	–	–
Imports (fob) (goods)	US$m	2,495.2	3,128.8	3,044.3	–	–
Balance of trade	US$m	270.5	-487.9	-392.9	–	–
Current account	US$m	-313.9	-1,286.0	-1,262.0	*-1,403.0	*-728.0
Total reserves minus gold	US$m	288.2	949.5	–	–	–
Foreign exchange	US$m	287.5	946.0	–	–	–
Exchange rate	per US$	278.30	300.44	292.50	290.97	–

* estimated figure ** forecast figure

COUNTRY PROFILE

1800s France took control first of southern Mauritania, ruling it from Senegal.
1904 Mauritania became a colonial territory of France.
1920 Mauritania became part of French West Africa.
1946 Mauritania became a Territoire d'Outre-Mer (TOM, overseas territory) of France.
1957 Limited self-government was granted under the Loi cadre. Nouakchott became the capital.
1960 Mauritania gained full independence from France on 28 November, under the regime of the Mauritanian People's Party. Mokhtar Ould Daddah became president.
1974 Mauritania withdrew from the CFAf currency zone and introduced the ouguiya.
1975 An agreement between Mauritania, Morocco and Spain led to the division of the Spanish Sahara (a Spanish colony and

the present-day Sahrawi Arab Republic (Western Sahara)) between Mauritania and Morocco.
1978 After fighting a largely unsuccessful war against the Frente para la Liberación de Saguia al Hamra y Río de Oro (Frente Polisario) (Popular Front for the Liberation of Saguia al Hamra and Río de Oro) rebels of the Western Sahara, President Daddah was overthrown.
1979 The government of President Haidallah agreed to renounce all territorial claims to Western Sahara.
1981 Slavery was banned in Mauritania.
1984 Haidallah was removed from office by Colonel Maaouya Ould Sid'Ahmed Taya.
1992 Multi-party elections were held in which President Taya was returned to office.
1996 The governing Parti Républicain Démocratique et Social (PRDS) (Social and Democratic Republican Party) won the elections.
1997 President Taya was re-elected.
1999 Full diplomatic relations were established with Israel. After criticism by Iraq, the foreign ministry announced that Mauritania had severed its relations with Iraq.
2001 The PRDS was re-elected.
2002 Famine increased due to three years of drought.
2003 The OPEC Fund for International Development donated US$300,000 to support an emergency operation by the World Food Programme (WFP). A coup attempt by rebels in Nouakchott was foiled by the President's troops. President Taya named Sghair Ould M'Bareck as the new prime minister. Incumbent Maaouya Ould Sid'Ahmed Taya was re-elected president. Prime Minister Sghair Ould M'Bareck was re-appointed.
2005 Mauritania lost its annual crop production after it was attacked by locust swarms. The UN called for food aid. While President Taya was out of the country, a military coup overthrew his regime. Colonel Ely Ould Mohamed Vall (leader of the military *Junta*) was declared president and head of the Military Council for Justice and Democracy.
2006 A referendum was held approving limitations on future presidential powers. Parliamentary and municipal elections took place.
2007 Sidi Mohamed Ould Cheikh Abdallahi won presidential elections and Zeine Ould Zeidane became prime minister.
2008 Prime Minister Zeine Ould Zeidane resigned and was replaced by Yahya Ould Ahmed El Waghef. A *coup d'etat* led by General Mohamed Ould Abdel Aziz removed President Abdallahi and Prime Minister El Waghef from power. Within a week, two-thirds of members of parliament had signed a document in support of the coup. A High Council of State was established, led by General Abdel Aziz. Moulaye Ould Mohamed Laghdaf was appointed prime minister. Former prime minister El Waghef was arrested, released and then rearrested a few days later and put on trial for malfeasance and later corruption.
2009 General Abdel Aziz resigned as president and chairman of the ruling High Council of State and Ba Mamadou dit M'Baré became interim president. The opposition agreed to participate in presidential elections on the condition that former prime minister El Waghef was released from gaol. Presidential elections were postponed but later Mohamed Ould Abdel Aziz (Union pour la Republique (UPR) (Union for the Republic)) won 52.58 per cent of the vote, his closest rival Messaoud Ould Boulkheir (APP) won 16.29 per cent. A unity government, headed by President Aziz, was formed to include opposition members.
2010 A *fatwa* (religious opinion), banning the practice of female genital mutilation was signed by 34 Islamic scholars. A UN-sponsored repatriation scheme for Mauritanian refugees in Senegal resumed.
2011 In June and July, there were a number of skirmishes between government troops and fighters of Al-Qaeda in the Islamic Maghreb (AQIM). The numbers wounded or killed varied according to sources. A national census was undertaken from 20 June, which sparked protests from the black African community in Mauritania and abroad. The census was branded as 'discriminatory' as it not only noted citizens within racial groupings (which, it was suspected, could be used to discriminate against various groupings in the future), but required a set of civil documents (including identity papers of parents and grandparents, which excluded anyone born outside Mauritania before 1945), before a person could be recorded (or 'enrolled').
2012 A Tuareg rebellion in northern Mali caused thousands of Malian refugees to flee into Mauritania. On 13 October, President Aziz was wounded when soldiers opened fire on his convoy. The president was flown to France for treatment. He returned home from France on 24 November.
2013 In May a deal to allow EU vessels to fish in Mauritanian waters in exchange for a €70 million (US$93 million) financial package was rejected by the Fisheries Committee as being a 'bad deal for taxpayers'. An alternative agreement is expected to be put forward later in the year. Heavy rainfall that began in August had by September flooded much of Nouakchott, and six of the surrounding regions. In the south-central region as many as 40 per cent of familes had been affected, while in the north herders in some regions had lost complete herds.
2015 Although Mauritania had officially abolished slavery in 1980–81, and in 2007 the practice was criminalised, it was not until 11 August 2015 that actual punishment for enslavement was legislated against, and slavery was defined as a crime against humanity. While the Mauritanian government continues to speak of 'vestiges' of slavery, local anti-slavery activists such as Boubacar Messaoud and Biram Dah Abeid continue to insist that slavery remains alive and well.

Political structure

Constitution

A new constitution was approved in 2006; a president is limited to two consecutive terms in office, which are cut from six to five years and there is a presidential age limit of 75 years. The oath of office includes a vow not to alter these changes.

Form of state

Islamic republic

The executive

The president is the head of state and is elected by universal suffrage for five-year terms. The president appoints the prime minister and presides over the Council of Ministers, who are recommended by the prime minister and appointed by the president. The president is the supreme chief of the armed forces.
The president, after consultation with the prime minister and the presidents of the assemblies, may pronounce the dissolution of the National Assembly.

National legislature

The bicameral Barlamane (parliament) is comprised of the Al Jamiya al Wataniyah (National Assembly), with 146 members, directly elected in single-seat constituencies for five-year terms and the Majlis al Shuyukh (Senate) with 56 members, of which 53 are elected by municipal councils for six-year terms. Three members are elected by expatriated Mauritanians. An alternate one-third of senators are re-elected every two years.
The prime minister, under the authority of the president, defines the policy of the government, divides the tasks among the ministers and directs and co-ordinates the action of the government.

Legal system

The legal system is based on the 1991 constitution and is strongly influenced by *Sharia* (Islamic law).

Last elections

21 June 2014 (presidential); 23 November/21 December 2013 (parliamentary)

Results: Presidential: Mohamed Ould Abdel Aziz (UPR) won 91.89 per cent of the vote, Biram Dah Abeid (IRA) 8.67 per cent, Boïdiel Ould Houmeit (El Wiam) 4.50 per cent, Ibrahima Moctar Sarr (AJD/MR) 4.44 per cent and Laila Maryam Mint Moulaye Idriss (Independent) 0.49 per cent. Turnout was 56.46 per cent.
Parliamentary: Union pour la République (UPR) (Union for the Republic) won 75 seats (out of 146), Tewassoul Party 16 seats, El Wiam 10 seats, Alliance populaire progessiste (APP) (People's Progressive Alliance) 7 seats, Union pour le Démocratie et le Progrès (UDP) (Union for Democracy and Progress) 6 seats, El Karam 6 seats. 12 other parties failed to gain five or more seats and shared the remaining 26 seats. 47 other parties didn't win a single seat. Turnout was 78.22 per cent

Next elections
2018 (parliamentary); 2019 (presidential)

Political parties

Political parties were legalised in July 1991 but were forbidden to be organised on racial or regional lines, or to be opposed to Islam.

Ruling party
All members of parliament are independents

Main opposition party
Tewassoul Party
3.63 million (2012)*

Population

Last census: November 2000: 2,548,157
Population density: Two inhabitants per square km. Urban population 41 per cent (2010 Unicef).
Annual growth rate: 2.8 per cent, 1990–2010 (Unicef).

Ethnic make-up
The population comprises a majority of Arabised Moors. The rest are ethnically linked with the peoples of Senegal and Mali. Moor-black (40 per cent), Moor (30 per cent), black (30 per cent).

Religions
Islam (99 per cent) is the state religion.

Education

Primary schooling lasts for six years. Progression to secondary education is through a competitive entrance examination. Secondary schooling lasts for six years, divided into two three-year cycles. Each stage requires further examination and students may graduate from either with academic or technical qualifications. Public expenditure on education typically amounts to around 5 per cent of gross national income (GNI).

Literacy rate: 41 per cent adult rate; 50 per cent youth rate (15–24) (Unesco 2005).
Compulsory years: Six to 16.
Enrolment rate: 87 per cent (boys); 82 per cent (girls) gross primary enrolment of the relevant age group (including repeaters), (Unicef).
Pupils per teacher: 50 in primary schools.

Health

Improved water sources and sanitation facilities are available to 37 per cent and 33 per cent of the population, respectively.

HIV/Aids
HIV prevalence: 0.6 per cent aged 15–49 in 2003 (World Bank)
Life expectancy: 58 years, 2004 (WHO 2006)
Fertility rate/Maternal mortality rate: 4.5 births per woman, 2010 (Unicef)
Child (under 5 years) mortality rate (per 1,000): 84 per 1,000 live births (WHO 2012); 32 per cent of children aged under five are malnourished (World Bank).
Head of population per physician: 0.11 physicians per 1,000 people, 2004 (WHO 2006)

Main cities

Nouakchott (administrative capital, estimated population 870,073 in 2012), Kifah (91,336), Nouadhibou (formerly Port-Etienne, 85,337), Rosso (80,936), Kayhaydi (59,942), Zuwarat (56,851).

Languages spoken

French is usually spoken in business circles; English is rarely spoken. Hassani Arabic, Pulaar, Soninke and Wolof are the major languages in everyday use.

Official language/s
Hassani Arabic and Wolof

Media

Since 2006 freedom of the press has been generally respected by two revolutionary regimes and has been described as 'partly free' by US-based human rights watchdog, Freedom House. Nevertheless, journalists are prohibited from publishing material that is anti-Islamic or threatens national security.

Press
There are three daily newspapers published by the state, two in Arabic *Chaab* (www.ami.mr/chaab) and *Akhbar Nouakchott* (www.ani.mr/anifr.php) and one in French, *Horizons* (www.ami.mr/horizons). Private dailies include, in French *Le Calame* (www.lecalame.info), *Le Quotidien de Nouakchott* (www.quotidien-nouakchott.com) and *Al Mourabit* (www.almourabit.mr); in Arabic *El Bedil Athalith*.

Broadcasting
The government operates the only national public broadcaster, operating Radio Mauritanie and Télévision de Mauritanie (TVM) (www.tvm.mr), which broadcast in Arabic and French.
National news agency: Mauritanian News Agency (in Arabic): www.ami.mr
Other news agencies: APA (African Press Agency): www.apanews.net

Economy

The service sector accounted for 36.9 per cent of GDP in 2014, industry constituted 46.1 per cent of which manufacturing amounted to 8 per cent and agriculture contributed 17 per cent of GDP. Mauritania has valuable deposits of iron ore, gold and copper, which combined, with hydrocarbons, account for 75 per cent of total export earnings. Iron ore contributes some 40 per cent of total exports, and iron ore constitutes around 15 per cent of GDP. The trade balance in 2014 was -US$1.4 billion, but is estimated to rise to -US$728. Foreign earnings also come from fish caught within Mauritania's territorial waters by licensed foreign vessels. Mauritania has been warned that its seas will become over-fished without strict monitoring.
Around 50 per cent of the population depend on agriculture (typically subsistence farming) for a livelihood; a series of droughts since the 1980s have forced nomads and subsistence farmers into urban areas.
GDP growth was 6.8 per cent in 2014, credited to foreign investment in the oil and mining industry. Mining now also accounts for some 29 per cent of government revenue.
Proven and probable oil reserves were estimated at 20 million barrels in 2013. Although Mauritania began producing oil in 2006 with an initial production of 75,000 barrels per day (bpd), this rapidly dropped to 6.6 bpd by 2012, largely due to technical difficulties offshore in the Chinguetti oil field and exhausting reserves.
Mauritania joined the Extractive Industries Transparency Initiative (EITI) – a forum of oil producers and consumers seeking to promote accountability in oil revenue – as part of the International Monetary Fund (IMF) sponsored growth programme in 2005 (full validation of EITI compliance will be in 2017). The IMF advised that oil funds should be used in accordance with Mauritania's own poverty reduction strategy plans, with a fund for investment in future generations.
In 2014, the UN Human Development Index (HDI) ranked Mauritania 161 (out of 187) for national development in health, education and income. Since 2000, Mauritania's progress has matched the

improvement of other countries in sub-Saharan Africa. In 2015, 23.4 per cent lived on less than the equivalent of US$1.25 per day; the headcount poverty rate was 66 per cent of the population (2000–15).

External trade

Mauritania is a member of the Arab Maghreb Union (AMU) (with Morocco, Tunisia, Algeria and Libya); however no economic integration or free trade agreement has been achieved between members.

Mauritania has valuable deposits of iron ore, gold and copper, which combined, with hydrocarbons, account for 75 per cent of total export earnings. An agreement was signed with the European Union (EU) to allow EU fishing fleets access to Mauritanian waters for €516 million (US$700 million) over 2006–12. However, talks to renew the agreement in 2014 broke down as an agreement was not met and the future of these negotiations is uncertain.

Imports

Principal imports are capital machinery and equipment, petroleum products, vehicles, foodstuffs and consumer goods.

Main sources: USA (23.8 per cent of total in 2014), UAE (18.5 per cent), France (10.0 per cent).

Exports

Principal exports are fish and fish products, crude oil, iron ore and gold.

Main destinations: China (32.7 per cent of total in 2014), Switzerland (17.1 per cent), Spain (6.6 per cent).

Agriculture

Farming

Agriculture accounts for some 17.0 per cent of GDP in 2014 and employs around 50 per cent of the population.

Production of food crops is restricted to irrigated land in the south along the north bank of the Senegal River. International aid and imported cereals have been vital in supplementing the main food crops – millet, sorghum, rice, maize, potatoes and dates.

Most of Mauritania consists of arid and semi-arid land and although it is unsuitable for crops, livestock rearing is an important sector. Nomadic herders comprise around 10 per cent of the population, although their numbers are dwindling. In 2005 Oxfam stated intermittent droughts since 2000 have affected nomadic herders and northern farming families, leading to food crises and a need of food and farming aid.

Fishing

Fishing contributes up to 10 per cent of GDP and provides an important source of food for Mauritanians. The coastal waters are among the richest in the world and joint venture fishing is one of the most important foreign exchange earners. The catch is mainly deep sea species and shellfish – particularly shrimp for the Japanese market.

Forestry

The majority of timber production is used as domestic firewood.

Industry and manufacturing

The industrial sector contributes around 46.1 per cent to GDP but employs only 2 per cent of the workforce.

The most important activities are related to the extraction industries. There are also various small import substitution industries (brewing, footwear, dairy processing etc), oil refining and a sugar refinery in Nouakchott.

Industrial production increased by 10 per cent in 2014.

Tourism

Mauritania has some ancient cities that have cultural and spiritual significance for both citizens and visitors to the country.

The city of Chinguetti was a famous centre of Koranic education that was renowned throughout the region and reached its height of fame during the 17th and 18th centuries. Today it is largely a city buried by the Sahara but some of the old city buildings remain. The trans-Saharan caravans were frequent visitor and towns that grew up along the trade routes can still be visited, including Ouadane, which is included on Unesco's World Heritage List, as part of the world inheritance to humanity.

Western governments have warned their citizens not to visit most of the country, including the historic towns and cities of central, eastern, northern and north-western Mauritania due to the high danger of kidnapping by lawless elements and terrorists. The south and south-west of the country are deemed merely unsafe.

Environment

In June 2010 the African Union backed a proposal to build the 'Great Green Wall' project, of a 15km wide, 7,775km long, continuous belt of trees from Senegal in the west to Djibouti in the east (traversing 11 countries) in an effort to halt the advance of the Sahara Desert. The trees to be used would be drought-adapted, preferably native to the area from a list of 37 possible species, and should help to slow soil erosion and filter rain water.

Mining

The mining sector contributes around 30 per cent to GDP in 2014, employs 5 per cent of the working population and generates, with hydrocarbons, 75 per cent of export earnings.

The annual output of iron ore is around 12 million tonnes, of which about 11 million tonnes is exported – 36 per cent to France, 26 per cent to Italy, 16 per cent to Belgium, 8 per cent to Germany, 4 per cent to Spain and 4 per cent to the UK.

The iron mines are located in the Tiris region in the north and are owned and operated by Société Nationale Industrielle et Minière (SNIM). Other mineral resources include copper (at Akjoujt); gold (also near Akjoujt); phosphates (deposits at Bofal), diamonds and uranium.

Hydrocarbons

Proven oil reserves were only 20 million barrels in 2013, with production at 6,750 barrels per day (bpd). Consumption was 17,870bpd with the shortfall covered by imports. Oil production began in 2006 from the small offshore Chinguetti oil field; the Tiof oil field, which is not under production, has reserves estimated at 350 million barrels. Exploration of offshore sites is ongoing.

The Société Mauritanienne des Hydrocarbures (SMH) is responsible for all matters dealing with exploration, production and marketing of oil and gas in Mauritania, with exclusive rights to negotiate on behalf of the state any exploitation of the country's hydrocarbon resources.

The Somir oil refinery in Nouadhibou, is the only refinery in operation. Owned by an Algerian company, it processes Algerian crude oil, with a capacity of 20,000bpd.

Proven natural gas reserves were 28.3 billion cubic metres (cum) in 2014, but production remains negligible. In January 2009 the government signed an agreement with Shell Gas and Power to evaluate the potential for developing the natural gas reserves but production has not yet begun.

Any imports of coal are insignificant and reserves are negligible.

Energy

Total installed generating capacity was 293MW in 2011, producing 930 million kilowatt hours (kWh). Hydropower accounts for around 50MW of primary energy; Mauritania receives around 30MW from the Manantali hydroelectric dam in Mali.

The Société Mauritanienne d'Electricité (Maurelec) is responsible for electricity generation, transmission and supply. The electricity network serves only a few people in urban areas. There is small-scale thermal electricity (generating capacity 110MW), most of which is provided by isolated diesel generators. The majority of the population relies on non-commercial biomass, mostly fuel wood for cooking, lighting and power.

Banking and insurance

In recent years, Mauritania's banking sector has undergone liberalisation with the

government selling its equity stake in commercial banks, making the sector more competitive. Reform of the banking sector has led to limits on bank lending and to new laws on debt recovery.
Domestic confidence in the banking sector remains low and 60 per cent of cash is still not placed in banks. However, this represents an enormous opportunity for the banking sector to increase savings and improve liquidity. An increase in the number of bank branches and the introduction of micro-banking schemes may transform the sector in coming years.

Central bank
Banque Centrale de Mauritanie

Main financial centre
Nouakchott

Time
GMT

Geography
Mauritania lies in north-west Africa, with the Atlantic Ocean to the west, Algeria and Western Sahara/Morocco to the north, Mali to the east and south, and Senegal to the south.
Mauritania extends over an area of 1,030,700 square km, around 75 per cent of which is covered with sand and scrub. South-west-facing scarps in the huge plains are home to oases. The general flatness is relieved by rocky plateaux, which rise to 500–600m. These are cut by ravines and punctuated by isolated peaks. The country's highest point is Kediet Ijill, which reaches 915m. The plateaux drop gradually north-eastwards to the Empty Quarter, heralding the onset of the Sahara. Westwards, between the plateaux and the Atlantic Ocean, the terrain alternates between areas of plains and dunes, which increase in size and movement to the north. The only area of permanent vegetation is in the south along the Senegal river, which forms the frontier with Senegal.

Hemisphere
Northern

Climate
The climate is hot and dry. The hottest month in Noukachott is September (24–34 degrees Celsius (C)); the coldest is December (12–29 degrees C); the wettest month is August.

Entry requirements

Passports
Required by all.

Visa
Required by all, except citizens of neighbouring states, contact the consular section of the nearest embassy for confirmation of exclusions. Business travellers may visit with a tourist visa, obtained in advance. An application should include a bank letter showing sufficient funds for the length of trip, an employer's letter of accreditation and an invitation from a local company or organisation. All travellers must have return/onward passage.

Currency advice/regulations
Unlimited foreign currency may be imported, but the amount must be declared on arrival. Unexchanged foreign currency may be exported. Declaration forms must be produced on departure. Import and export of local currency is strictly forbidden. Controls are constantly subject to modification.

Health (for visitors)

Mandatory precautions
Yellow fever vaccination certificate required if arriving from an infected area.

Advisable precautions
Yellow fever, hepatitis A, tetanus, typhoid and polio vaccinations. Malaria prophylaxis should be taken.
Water precautions are advisable. There is a rabies risk.

Hotels
Accommodation is limited and visitors should book well in advance. A service charge is normally included in the bill, otherwise a 15 per cent tip is usual.

Credit cards
Only accepted in main hotels.

Public holidays (national)

Fixed dates
1 Jan (New Year's Day), 1 May (Labour Day), 25 May (Africa Day), 10 Jul (Armed Forces Day), 28 Nov (Independence Day).

Variable dates
Eid al Adha, Islamic New Year, Birth of the Prophet, Eid al Fitr.
Islamic year 1437 (15 Oct 2015–2 Oct 2016):: The Islamic year contains 354 or 355 days, with the result that Muslim feasts advance by 10–12 days against the Gregorian calendar. Dates of feasts vary according to the sighting of the new moon, so cannot be forecast exactly.

Working hours
Although a Muslim country, Mauritania changed to a Western weekend from 1 October 2014. Most businesses close early on Friday.

Banking
Mon–Fri: 0800–1115; 1430–1630.

Business
Mon–Fri: 0800–1500. Some stop for a lunch-time break (usually 1200–1300).

Government
Mon–Thu: 0800–1500; Fri: 0800–1300.

Shops
Mon–Thu: 0800–1200; 1430–1800; Fri: 0800–1300.

Telecommunications

Telephone/fax
International telephone facilities are available in Nouakchott and Nouadhibou.

Electricity supply
127/220V AC, 50 cycles. Plugs and sockets mostly two-pin (round).

Getting there

Air
National airline: Air Mauritanie
International airport/s: Nouakchott (NKC), 4km from city; Nouadhibou (NDB), 4km from city.
Airport tax: UM270.

Surface
Road: Crossing the Mali and Western Sahara/Morocco borders may present difficulties and the Algerian frontier is closed. The best route is via Senegal. A surfaced road exists from Dakar (Senegal) to Nouakchott.
Main port/s: Nouadhibou and Nouakchott

Getting about

National transport
Air: Air Mauritanie provides mainly weekly services between most main centres.
Road: Most roads linking major centres are adequate, although four-wheel drive vehicles are recommended. Minor roads are usually impassable after the rainy season. There is a paved road between Rosso (on the Senegal River, where a ferry connects with the road to Dakar) and Akjoujt, via Nouakchott, and another, *La Route de l'Espoir*, running from Nouakchott to Mali.
Rail: A track runs inland from the coast (Nouakchott-Zouerate), mainly for freight, but there are some passenger services (single-class) scheduled; motor vehicles are sometimes carried.

City transport
Taxis: Taxis are numerous in the main towns. They are not metered, but the fares are standardised, although they should be checked before departure. A small tip is usual. Taxis can be rented by the hour.

Car hire
Cars can be rented in Nouakchott, Nouadhibou and Atar. An international or national driving licence is required. Out of town, a four-wheel drive vehicle with chauffeur, although expensive, is recommended.

BUSINESS DIRECTORY
The addresses listed below are a selection only. While World of Information makes every endeavour to check these addresses, we cannot guarantee that changes have not been made, especially to telephone numbers and area codes. We would welcome any corrections.

Telephone area codes
The international dialling (IDD) code for Mauritania is +222, followed by subscriber's number.

Chambers of Commerce
Mauritania Chamber of Commerce, Industry and Agriculture, Avenue de la République, PO Box 215, Nouakchott (tel: 525-2214; fax: 525-3895; e-mail: ccia@mauritel.mr).

Banking
Banque Mauritanienne pour le Commerce International, PO Box 622, Immeuble Afarco, Avenue Gamal Abdel Nasser, Nouakchott (tel: 525-4349; fax: 525-2045).

Banque Nationale de Mauritanie, PO Box 614, Avenue Gamal Abdel Nasser, Nouakchott (tel: 525-2602; fax: 525-3397).

Central bank
Banque Centrale de Mauritanie, PO Box 623, Avenue de l'Indépendence, Nouakchott (tel: 525-2206; fax: 525-2759; e-mail: info@bcm.mr).

Travel information
Air Mauritanie, Avenue Gamal Abdel Nasser, PO Box 41, Nouakchott (tel: 525-2721; e-mail: resa@airmauritanie.mr).

Ministry of tourism
Ministry of Trade, Handicrafts and Tourism, Directorate of Tourism, PO Box 246, Nouakchott (tel: 525-1367; fax: 525-1057).

National tourist organisation offices
Office National du Tourisme, PO Box 2884, Nouakchott (tel: 529-0344; fax: 529-0528; e-mail: ont@mauritel.mr).

Ministries
Ministry of Economic Affairs and Development, BP 238, Nouakchott (tel: 525-1612; fax: 525-5110; e-mail: infomaed@mauritania.mr).

Ministry of Education, PO Box 227, Nouakchott (tel: 525-8445; fax: 525-1222).

Ministry of Finance, PO Box 197, Nouakchott (tel: 525-4397; fax: 525-3114; e-mail: sidahd@mauritania.mr).

Ministry of Fishing and Maritime Economy, PO Box 137, Nouakchott (tel: 525-9970; fax: 525-3146).

Ministry of Foreign Affairs and Co-operation, PO Box 230, Nouakchott (tel: 525-2682).

Ministry of Health and Social Affairs, PO Box 169, Nouakchott (tel: 525-2052).

Ministry of Infrastructure and Transport, PO Box 237, Nouakchott (tel: 525-3337).

Ministry of the Interior, Post and Telecommunications, PO Box 195, Nouakchott (tel: 525-2020).

Ministry of Mines and Industry, PO Box 199, Nouakchott (tel: 525-3086; fax: 525-6937; e-mail: mmi@mauritania.mr).

Ministry of Trade, Artisans and Tourism, PO Box 182, Nouakchott (tel: 525-1057).

Ministry of Rural Development and Environment, PO Box 366, Nouakchott (tel: 525-1500; fax: 525-7574).

Prime Minister's Office, PO Box 237, Nouakchott (tel: 525-3337).

Other useful addresses
Centre d'Information Mauritanien pour le Developpement Economique et Technique, PO Box 2119, Nouakchott (tel: 525-8738; fax: 525-8648; e-mail: cimdet@pacdet.org).

Confédération Générale des Employeurs de Mauritanie (CGEM), PO Box 383, Nouakchott (tel: 525-2160; fax: 525-3301).

Fédération des Industries et Armement de Pêche (FIAP), PO Box 43, Nouadhibou (tel: 574-5089; fax: 574-5430).

Fédération des Industries et des Mines (FIM), PO Box 5501, Nouakchott (tel: 525-0304; fax: 525-6955).

Mauritanian Embassy (USA), 2129 Leroy Place, NW, Washington DC 20008 (tel: (+1-202)-232-5700; fax: (+1-202)-319-2623).

Mauritanienne d'Entreposage des Produits Pétroliers (MEPP), Nouakchott (tel: 525-2646; fax: 525-4608; e-mail: mepp@mauritel.mr).

National Statistics Office, BP 240, Nouakchott (tel: 525-5031; fax:525-5170; e-mail: webmaster@)ons.mr).

National news agency: Mauritanian News Agency (in Arabic): www.ami.mr

APA (African Press Agency): www.apanews.net

Internet sites
Africa Business Network: http://www.ifc.org/abn

AllAfrica.com: http://allafrica.com

African Development Bank: http://www.afdb.org

Africa Online: http://www.africaonline.com

Mbendi AfroPaedia (information on companies, countries, industries and stock exchanges in Africa): http://mbendi.co.za

Mauritius

KEY FACTS

Official name: Republic of Mauritius

Head of State: President Ameenah Gurib-Fakim (from 5 June 2015)

Head of government: Prime Minister Sir Anerood Jugnauth (from 17 December 2014)

Ruling party: Alliance Lepep (Alliance of the People) led by Mouvement Socialiste Militant (MSM) (Militant Socialist Movement), with Parti Mauricien Social Démocrate (PMSD) (Mauritian Social Democratic Party) and Muvman Liberater (ML)

Area: 1,865 square km

Population: 1.26 million (2014)* (1,286,051; 2011, initial census result)

Capital: Port Louis

Official language: English and French

Currency: Mauritian rupee (MR) = 100 cents

Exchange rate: MR35.17 per US$ (Sep 2015)

GDP per capita: US$10,517 (2014)*

GDP real growth: 3.24% (2014)*

GDP: US$13.24 billion (2014)*

Labour force: 581,000 (2010)

Unemployment: 7.80% (2014)*

Inflation: 2.96% (2014)*

Balance of trade: -US$2.25 billion (2014)

Visitor numbers: 980,000 (2010)

* estimated figure

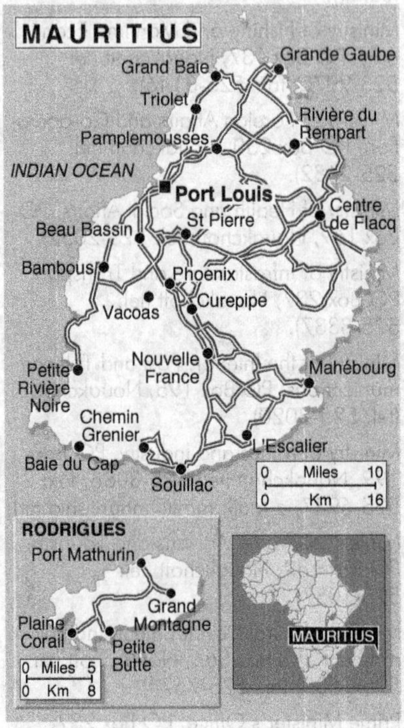

Mauritius remained the top ranking country in overall governance in Africa for the ninth consecutive year according to the Mo Ibrahim *Index of African Governance 2015*. Mauritius has scored the highest points with regards to global governance for the past 15 years.

The island was first explored by the Portuguese in the sixteenth century and subsequently settled by the Dutch who named it in honour of Prince Maurits van Nassau in the seventeenth century. It developed as an important naval base for the French who assumed control in 1715 and the British who captured the island in 1810, during the Napoleonic Wars. The island played an important role in World War II for anti-submarine and convoy operations, as well as the collection of signals' intelligence. In 1968, Mauritius gained independence from Britain and since then it has defied critics by maintaining a stable democracy with regular free elections and a positive human rights record. The country has attracted significant foreign direct investment (FDI) and it has one of Africa's highest per capita incomes.

Mauritius held its general election on 10 December 2014. The result was a victory for the Alliance Lepep (Alliance of the People) coalition, which secured 47 of the elected seats under the leadership of Sir Anerood Jugnauth, while the Parti Travailliste (PTR) (Labour Party)-Mauritian Militant Movement (Mouvement Militant Mauricien) coalition only won 13 seats. Alliance Lepep is a coalition led by the Mouvement Socialiste Militant (MSM) (Militant Socialist Movement) with other parties including the Parti Mauricien Social Démocrate (PMSD) (Mauritian Social Democratic Party) and Muvman Liberater (ML). The PTR (Labour Party) and MMM alliance led by Navin Ramgoolam was based on an agreement of power sharing and the implementation of a Second Republic with a more presidential system. The current system is largely based on the British style of government where the head of state (being the president) is a ceremonial figurehead with very few executive powers. The proposed changes would have given additional powers to the president which would include the prerogative to preside over the ministerial cabinet, the ability to dissolve the National Assembly and to offer recommendations in various institutions including the appointment of ministers. The President would also be elected for a 7-year term, as opposed to the five-year term served by the National Assembly. If the coalition were to win a three-quarters majority in parliament, a bill would be passed to implement the new republic, with Ramgoolam resigning to present himself as a presidential candidate while Paul Berenger would replace him as prime minister. For many people, the changes obviously favoured Navin Ramgoolam who had always favoured a presidential system of government. The Alliance Lepep coalition was formed as a response to the PTR-MMM alliance and to oppose the proposed constitutional changes. Surprisingly, the Alliance Lepep coalition won the election with Prime Minister Jugnauth saying that they will put the country back on track for another economic miracle.

The economy

Since independence in 1968, Mauritius has undergone a startling economic transformation from a low-income, agriculturally based economy to a diversified, upper middle-income economy with growing industrial, financial, and tourist sectors. The economy is dependent on sugar exports, tourism, financial services and textiles and apparel, and is expanding into fish processing, information and communication technology and hospitality and property development. Sugarcane is grown on 90 per cent of the cultivated land and accounts for 15 per cent of export earnings. Mauritius' textile sector has taken advantage of the US African Growth and Opportunity Act, with Mauritanian exports to the US growing by 400 per cent from 2001–12. The economy was not badly affected by the global economic crisis and it continues to expand its trade and investment outreach around the globe. Mauritius has also attracted more than 32,000 offshore entities, mostly aimed at commerce in India, South Africa, and China. Investment in the banking sector alone has reached over US$1 billion.

Fruit bat cull?

Mauritius has begun to cull the local bat population by 20 per cent (they started mid-October 2015) because the government believes that they have become a 'pest'. The hope is that by reducing the population of the endemic and vulnerable Mauritius fruit bat on the island, it will help reduce damage to fruits like mangoes and litchis in orchards and boost revenue for fruit farmers. Conservationists are calling this decision 'unacceptable' and 'disgraceful'. Implementation of the cull could be disastrous for the native bat species and it will threaten the native biodiversity of the country. It will damage the reputation of Mauritius as one of the world leaders in conservation. The government believes that there are 90,000 bats on the island and they aim to slaughter 18,000 of them, however, conservationists estimate that there are only around 50,000 bats. If this is the case then the cull will result in the killing of 36 per cent of the fruit bat population. The government's claim that bats are responsible for up to 70 per cent of the damage to mangoes and litchis is not backed up by scientific evidence. They are not taking into account birds, rats, monkeys, wind or fruit flies all of which feed on commercial fruits. In a study carried out by a conservationist from Bristol University, around 20 per cent of the fruits get damaged due to natural causes like wind or over-ripening, causing fruits to fall to the ground. Not only would killing these bats be unethical and inhumane, they also play an import role in the ecosystem – they pollinate plants and disperse seeds.

Not only has Mauritius proven to act unethically with bats but they are also one of the world's largest suppliers of primates for the international research industry, in particular the USA and Europe. The UK government's annual statistics for the number of animal experiments completed in 2014 revealed that 2,954 experiments involved long-tailed macaques. Over half (54 per cent) of the monkeys used (1,343) were imported from Mauritius. The UK Parliament has called for the existing ban on Great Apes to be extended to monkeys, and they also hope that members of the Mauritius parliament will take action to end the export of its country's primates. Thousands of monkeys, many of which have been captured from the wild, are held in farms across Mauritius, where they are used to breed offspring. The monkeys spend their lives behind bars on concrete and their offspring are exported overseas, in small wooden crates, as cargo on airlines.

While Mauritius is not a significant transhipment location of a global scale, the island state is increasingly seen as a regional hub for heroin distribution, often intended for onward movement into Europe and even the United States. Cannabis is the only illicit drug that is locally cultivated in large quantities, primarily by small groups or individuals for local consumption and is not exported. Heroin and subutex (a prescription drug used to treat heroin dependence) are brought into Mauritius for consumption with a small amount going for transhipment to other markets.

The future of Mauritius is positive, however, there are a number of macroeconomic challenges to overcome for it to improve further. First, there is a need to diversify and transform the economy, especially from its sugar and textile industries which are largely dependent on world demand for the commodities. Second, Mauritius must undertake structural reforms to increase labour market flexibility. Third, budget deficits need to be controlled and monitored so that solid medium-term fiscal sustainability and stability are to be preserved.

Risk assessment

Economy	Good
Politics	Good
Regional stability	Good

Muslims in Mauritius

% of population	16.6
Sunni (% of Muslims)	90
Shi'a (% of Muslims)	10

COUNTRY PROFILE

1598 A Dutch squadron landed at Grand Port and named the island Mauritius.
1638 Mauritius was settled by the Dutch. The island became an important port of call for Dutch, English and French trading ships. The Dutch introduced sugar cane and imported slaves to harvest it.
1710 The Dutch abandoned their settlement.

KEY INDICATORS — Mauritius

	Unit	2011	2012	2013	2014	**2015
Population	m	*1.29	1.30	*1.26	*1.26	*1.26
Gross domestic product (GDP)	US$bn	11.30	11.45	11.94	*13.24	*13.36
GDP per capita	US$	8,777	8,835	*9,484	*10,517	*10,609
GDP real growth	%	4.1	3.3	3.2	*3.2	*3.5
Inflation	%	6.5	3.9	3.5	*3.0	*1.7
Unemployment	%	8.3	8.0	8.0	*7.8	*7.8
Exports (fob) (goods)	US$m	2,646.5	2,672.8	2,971.9	3,107.3	–
Imports (fob) (goods)	US$m	4,925.4	5,104.2	5,141.2	5,353.4	–
Balance of trade	US$m	-2,278.9	-2,431.4	-2,269.3	-2,246.1	–
Current account	US$m	-1,421.8	-900.0	-1,188.0	*-956.0	*-838.0
Total reserves minus gold	US$m	2,713.8	2,836.7	3,340.2	3,614.7	–
Foreign exchange	US$m	2,508.5	2,631.4	3,128.1	–	–
Exchange rate	per US$	28.64	30.81	30.10	31.75	–

* estimated figure ** forecast figure

1721 France claimed the island; it also imported large numbers of slaves to harvest sugar cane, cotton and other crops.
1810 Britain defeated a French naval squadron and the island was ceded to Britain at the end of the Napoleonic Wars.
1835 Slavery was abolished. Most freed slaves left the plantations and settled in coastal towns; workers had to be imported from the Indian sub-continent to take their place, most of whom opted to remain on the island at the end of their contracts.
1936 The Labour Party (LP) was formed and organised strikes and protests between 1937–45.
1953 A group of Mauritians under Seewoosagur Ramgoolam rose to the leadership of the LP, which won the elections to the Legislative Council. Most Creoles joined the Parti Mauricien Social-Démocrate (PMSD) (Social Democratic Party of Mauritius).
1959 New political parties emerged including the Muslim Committee of Action (CAM). CAM formed an alliance with the LP.
1968 Mauritius gained independence from Britain.
1969 Ramgoolam's LP-CAM (Muslim) ruling alliance was strengthened when a coalition with the PMSD was formed. In response, the Mouvement Militante Mauricien (MMM) (Mauritian Militant Movement) was established.
1982 The LP lost power as the MMM, in alliance with the Parti Socialiste Mauricien (PSM), gained power under the premiership of Anerood Jugnauth.
1983 The MMM split and Jugnauth formed the Mouvement Socialiste Mauricien (MSM) (Mauritian Socialist Movement) which formed a government with the LP.
1990 The MMM and the MSM formed a political alliance.
1991 In December the Legislative Assembly approved the transition to a republic within the Commonwealth.
1992 Cassam Uteem was elected president.
1995 An alliance of the LP and the MMM, led by Navinchandra (Navin) Ramgoolam (son of the late Sir Seewoosagur Ramgoolam) and Paul Berenger, won the parliamentary elections. Ramgoolam became prime minister.
1997 The LP-MMM coalition broke up when the MMM left government and became the official opposition. Even so, the LP continued to hold an outright majority in the legislature and for the first time since independence, Mauritius was governed by a single party. Cassam Uteem was re-elected president.
2000 The opposition, MSM/MMM, won the parliamentary election. Sir Anerood Jugnauth, leader of the MMM, became prime minister for the second time. Mauritius revived a claim to sovereignty over Diego Garcia, the British Indian Ocean Territory.
2001 The WTO trade policy review encouraged Mauritius to further liberalise and diversify its economy. A constitutional amendment was introduced, allowing Rodrigues Island to have two representatives in the National Assembly and its own regional assembly.
2002 President Uteem resigned and Vice President Angidi Chettiar became interim president, but he also resigned; both men had refused to sign into law controversial anti-terrorism legislation. The National Assembly elected Karl Offman as president. On Rodrigues Island, the Rodrigues People's Organisation (RPO) won 10 seats out of 18 and the Mouvement Rodriguais (MR) (Rodrigues Movement) won eight seats in the first Rodrigues Regional Assembly election. The Rodrigues Regional Assembly opened with Jean Daniel Spéville as chief commissioner.
2003 Serge Clair became chief commissioner of Rodrigues Island. Sir Anerood Jugnauth resigned and Paul Bérenger replaced him as prime minister. Parliament elected Jugnauth as president.
2005 In parliamentary elections the opposition Alliance Sociale (AS) (Social Alliance) won 49 per cent of the vote (38 out of 62 constituencies) and the incumbent coalition MSM and MMM won 43 per cent (22). Turnout was 81.5 per cent. Navin Ramgoolam (Parti Travailliste (PT) (Labour Party)) became prime minister.
2006 Former residents of Diego Garcia in the Chagos Archipelago, evicted by the British for the island to be turned into a US military air base in the 1960s and living since in Mauritius, which also claims Diego Garcia, won the right to visit their island.
2007 The British High Court ruled that families of the expelled Diego Garcia islanders could return home.
2008 Le Morne Mountain was added to the list of Unesco World Heritage sites. The mountain was an important site of shelter and became a symbol of freedom for runaway slaves fleeing the eastern slave trade in the eighteenth and nineteenth centuries. Anerood Jugnauth was unanimously re-elected president by the national assembly. Chagos residents lost their rights to return to Diego Garcia in a legal battle with the UK government.
2009 The United States and Mauritius began negotiations towards a bilateral investment treaty. The intention was to strengthen investor protection in Mauritius and encourage market-oriented economic reforms.
2010 The world's largest marine reserve, around the Chagos Islands, was created by the British government. The 545,000 square kilometre reserve protects a rich marine ecosystem, including 220 coral species and over 1,000 species of reef fish. It excludes commercial fishing. There were objections from the Chagossian diaspora as the banning of commercial fishing makes it almost impossible for exiled Chagossians to return and earn a living from fishing. The Alliance de L'Avenir (Alliance of the Future) a coalition of three political parties led by the ruling PT won parliamentary elections. Prime Minister Ramgoolam remained in office.
2011 A national census took place between 20 June–31 July. In July Air Mauritius launched its first scheduled flight service to Shanghai (China).
2012 Anerood Jugnauth resigned from the ceremonial post of President of Mauritius on 31 March so that he could compete in party politics and challenge Prime Minister Navin Ramgoolam for control of the governing coalition. The coalition had accused Jugnauth of meddling in Mauritian politics. Monique Ohsan-Bellepeau Gosk became acting president from 31 March. On 21 July, parliament elected Rajkeswur (Kailash) Purryag as president (40 votes in favour). President Purryag took office on 21 July.
2013 The Puntland government has signed piracy-transfer agreements with the governments of Seychelles, Mauritius and Maldives, to bring convicted Somali pirates to complete their prison sentences in Puntland prisons, Puntland Counter-Piracy Director Abdirizak Mohamed Dirir has said. The United Nations Office on Drugs and Crime has overseen a prison construction project in Bosaso and Garowe for the purpose of housing convicted pirates. Prime Minister Ramgoolam said he would not be attending the Commonwealth Heads of Government meeting in Sri Lanka in November in protest over alleged human rights abuses.
2014 President Kailash Purryag dissolved parliament on 6 October in preparation for the 10 December parliamentary elections.

Political structure

Constitution

Mauritius is a republic with a president as head of state.
The president is elected by a simple majority of all the members of the National Assembly for a five-year term. The National Assembly is the supreme body that votes laws. The president's agreement

and signature is required to sign legislation into law.

Form of state

Republic

The executive

Executive power is vested in the prime minister, leader of the majority parliamentary party.

There is a Council of Ministers consisting of the prime minister and not more than 24 other ministers.

National legislature

The unicameral National Assembly has 69 members in total, of which 62 seats are elected in single seat constituencies for five years terms; eight members are appointed by the Supreme Court to represent minority ethnic and religious groups. The official language of the National Assembly is English but any member may address the Chair in French.

Last elections

10 December 2014 (general)

Results: Presidential: the National Assembly elected Ameenah Gurib-Fakim

Parliamentary: Alliance Lepep (MSM-PMSD-ML) (Alliance of the People) won 49.83 per cent of the vote and 51 seats (out of 69), PTR-MMM coalition 38.51 per cent and 16 seats, Organisation du Peuple Rodriguais (OPR) (Rodrigues People's Organization) 1.07 per cent and 2 seats. Other parties failed to win any seats.

Next elections

2019 (general)

Political parties

Ruling party

Coalition Alliance de L'Avenir (Alliance of the Future) led by Parti Travailliste (PT) (Labour Party), with Parti Mauricien Social-Démocrate (Mauritius Social Democratic Party) and Mouvement Socialiste Mauricien (Mauritian Socialist Movement)

Main opposition party

PTR-MMM coalition made up of Parti Travailliste (PTR) (Labour Party) and Mouvement Militant Mauricien (MMM) (Mauritian Militant Movement)

The population is expected to reach 1.4 million by 2025. Approximately 26 per cent of the total population is under 15 years.

Population

1.30 million (2012) (1,286,051; 2011, initial census result)

Last census: 2011: 1,286,051 initial census result

Population density: Population density: 588 per square km. The population densities of the island of Mauritius and the island of Rodrigues are 624 and 345, respectively. Urban population 42 per cent (2010 Unicef).

Annual growth rate: 1.0 per cent, 1990–2010 (Unicef).

Ethnic make-up

Indentured workers were brought from India to work on sugar estates and their descendants form a majority of the population, followed by Creoles (of mixed, predominantly African, origin), Muslim Indians, Chinese and Europeans. Hindu Indo-Mauritian (51 per cent), Creole (27 per cent), Muslim Indo-Mauritians (17 per cent), Chinese (2 per cent).

Religions

Hinduism (51 per cent), Christianity (Roman Catholic) (31.3 per cent), Muslim (16.6 per cent).

Education

Education is modelled on the English school system. Primary schooling lasts for six years until the age of 12; lower secondary schooling lasts for five years and upper secondary schooling for a further two years. Examinations are undertaken at each transition.

The expenditure allocated to education by central government was 16 per cent (Unicef estimates 1992–1999).

Literacy rate: 85.3 per cent total; 82.3 per cent female, adult rates (World Bank).

Compulsory years: Five to 12.

Enrolment rate: 93.6 per cent net primary enrolment, of the relevant age group; 62.9 per cent net secondary enrolment (World Bank).

Pupils per teacher: 24 in primary schools.

Health

Life expectancy: 72 years, 2004 (WHO 2006)

Fertility rate/Maternal mortality rate: 1.6 births per woman, 2010 (Unicef)

Child (under 5 years) mortality rate (per 1,000): 15 per 1,000 live births (WHO 2012); about 15 per cent of children aged under five are malnourished (World Bank).

Head of population per physician: 1.06 physicians per 1,000 people, 2004 (WHO 2006)

Main cities

Port Louis (capital, estimated population 158,965 in 2012), Beau Bassin/Rose Hill (112,215), Vascoas-Phoenix (108,103), Curepipe (85,259), Quatre Bornes (81,979).

Languages spoken

Creole and Bhojpuri are the predominant languages in everyday life.

Official language/s

English and French

Media

Freedom of the press is guaranteed by the constitution.

Press

Two media groups, Le Mauricien and La Sentinelle are dominant in the market. The French language predominates in newspapers but most either have online editions in English or have locally produced editions in other languages.

There are several dailies including *l'Express* (www.lexpress.mu), *Le Matinal* (www.lematinal.com), *L'Hebdo* (www.defimedia.info) and *Le Mauricien* (www.lemauricien.com), which also publishes a Sunday edition. Weekly newspapers include, in English *Mauritius Times* (www.mauritiustimes.com), *Sunday Vani* (http://sundayvani.intnet.mu) also in Creole and in French *Star* (www.mauriweb.com/star) and *Weekend* (www.lemauricien.com/weekend).

Broadcasting

The state-owned Mauritius Broadcasting Corporation (MBC) (mbc.intnet.mu), which is funded by both a license fee and advertising. Locally produced and imported programmes are broadcast in French, English, Hindi, Creole, Chinese and a number of indigenous Indian languages.

Radio: MBC (mbc.intnet.mu) operates seven stations including Radio Maurice (RM) 1 and 2, Taal FM and Kool FM. Other private, commercial radio stations include Radio One (www.r1.mu), Top FM (www.topfmradio.com) and Radio Plus.

Television: Digital TV services have become operational ahead of the total switch over from analogue to digital signals in 2011. MBC (mbc.intnet.mu) operates 12 TV channels, two of which are digital and free-to-air.

Other news agencies: APA: www.apanews.net

Panapress: www.panapress.com

Reuters Africa: http://africa.reuters.com

Economy

Mauritius' economy, one of the most vibrant in Africa, is founded on tourism, financial services, textiles and sugarcane. GDP growth was 5.5 per cent in 2008, falling to 3.0 per cent in 2009 as the global economic crisis cut visitor numbers, but recovering in 2010 with growth of 4.1 per cent, dropping slightly to 3.1 by 2013 and 3.2 per cent in 2014.

The government, in response to globalisation, initiated a reform strategy from 2006–09 which aimed to correct fiscal weaknesses and open up the economy to facilitate business and improve the investment climate. The strategy encouraged foreign direct investment (FDI) and expertise with FDI increasing from US$41.8 million in 2005 to US$106.8 million in 2006 and averaging US$352 million per annum from 2007–10. The information and communication technology

(ICT) and software development sector has expanded to over 350 ICT business entities, including French-speaking call centres. In 2013 the World Bank's *Ease of doing business* table ranked Mauritius as 20 (of 183) countries in the world.
Building on existing free port facilities of logistics and distribution, Mauritius is also promoting itself as a seafood hub for the region. With the end of textile quotas and preferential sugar sales these sectors have been restructured and modernised. The number of sugar plantations has been increased to 50–80 per cent of total land cultivated so that sugar can be processed into ethanol and other by-products to alleviate the islands' energy needs.
The service sector constitutes over 73 per cent of GDP, agriculture around 3.3 per cent and industry some 23 per cent, of which manufacturing is around 20 per cent. Tourism is an important sector and one the government regards as a growth industry. It has increased the number of airlines allowed to arrive in high-season, while encouraging conference and retail investment.

External trade

Mauritius was one of the founding members of the Common Market of Eastern and Southern Africa (Comesa), and operates a free trade area (FTA) with 13 other Comesa members. Internal duties were eliminated in 2000 and common external tariffs were introduced in June 2009 for some member states. Mauritius is also a member of the Southern African Development Community (SADC), the objectives of which include reducing trade barriers, achieving regional development and economic growth and evolving common systems and institutions.
The importance of sugar as an export commodity has been replaced by services, which generate more than 33 per cent of total foreign exchange earnings; tourism contributes the largest share and is growing. Nevertheless, production in 2012 was some 409,000 tonnes, most of which was exported.

Imports

Principal imports are manufactured goods, capital equipment, foodstuffs, petroleum products and chemicals.
Main sources: India (21.7 per cent of total in 2014), China (16.2 per cent), France (7.8 per cent) and South Africa (6.6 per cent).

Exports

Principal exports are clothing and textiles, sugar, cut flowers, molasses, fish and primates (for research).
Main destinations: France (14.6 per cent of total in 2014), UK (13.8 per cent), UAE (10.6 per cent), US (10.5 per cent), South Africa (7.1 per cent), Italy (6.6 per cent), Madagascar (6.5 per cent) and Spain (5.2 per cent).

Agriculture

Farming

The agricultural sector contributes around 3.3 per cent to GDP and employed 8 per cent of the workforce in 2013.
Sugar cane cultivation dominates the sector. Approximately 70 per cent of all cultivated land is devoted to the crop, and the sugar industry as a whole employs the majority of the workforce. Cultivation is undertaken both on large plantations and by smallholders.
The other major export crop is tea, grown by tenant farmers. Mauritius is the fourth-largest producer of tea per capita in the world. Around 75 per cent of tea production (green leaf) is controlled by the Tea Development Authority, of which commercial activities are privately run.
Tobacco is grown for the home market.
Main food crops include potatoes and other vegetables, output of which is sufficient to meet domestic demand.
Much of the island's meat requirement is imported. Around 75 per cent of food requirements are also imported.

Fishing

All fish-farming production and 90 per cent of marine fishing provides about 40 per cent of the nutritional requirement of the Mauritian population. Commercial aquaculture includes cultivation of giant freshwater prawns and oysters. Mauritius is a hub for longline tuna fishing fleets that dock to offload their cargo on freezer ships for transhipment which provides the local economy with foreign currency.
Total fish catches amount to over 10,000 tonnes per year with another 70 tonnes of other sea food. Over 70,000 cultivated oysters are produced each year.
Sports fishing has become a major influence, along with reef diving, which not only drives the local tourist industry but also employs boats and crews formerly used in fishing that were less capable of competing with modern replacement ships and mechanisation.

Forestry

Annual estimated production: 13,500 cubic metres (cum) roundwood, 3,000cum sawnwood, 5,000cum sawlogs and veneers, 6,000cum woodfuel, 100mt charcoal.

Industry and manufacturing

The industrial sector contributes 23.1 per cent to GDP and employed 28 per cent of the workforce in 2013.
The industrial sector is based on the Export Processing Zones (EPZ) which were opened in the 1970s to take advantage of the preferential treatment which Mauritius receives under the Cotonou Agreement.
Production of textiles, and in particular knitwear, was the most significant EPZ industry, and Mauritius was once the world's third-largest exporter of pure new wool products. However, as Mauritius lost it's preferential status and world markets looked elsewhere for cheaper manufacturers, Mauritius was forced to diversify, most successfully into ICT services.
Other industries include the manufacture of watches and clocks, jewellery, spectacle frames and leather goods.

Tourism

Mauritius is an island country that attracts wealthy tourists typically from Western Europe (over 65 per cent of total), particularly France, which has a historic connection.
Travel and tourism plays a vital role in the economy of Mauritius, providing 25.3 per cent of GDP in 2013. This was a fall from the record 35.7 per cent of GDP in 2007, before the global economic crisis. Employment in the industry has, likewise, been affected by the downturn. In 2007, 33.2 per cent of all jobs (174,200) were provided by tourism, whereas in 2013 the number had fallen to 137,000 jobs (23.9 per cent of total employment).

Hydrocarbons

There are no known oil or natural gas reserves. Consumption of oil was 25,000 barrels per day (bpd) in 2013, all of which was imported. The State Trading Corporation has a monopoly on importing strategic products, including petroleum.
Any use of natural gas is commercially insignificant.
Over 661,000 tonnes of coal is typically imported for use in power generation.

Energy

Total installed generating capacity was 900MW in 2011, producing over 2.54 billion kilowatt hours. Around 75 per cent of power is produced by conventional thermal stations using fossil fuels, the remainder is largely produced from bagasse (waste material from the sugar cane crop). Renewable sources, including hydro and wind generation, account for a very small percentage of production,
The state-owned Central Electricity Board is responsible for generation, transmission, distribution and sales of electricity.

Financial markets

Stock exchange

The Stock Exchange of Mauritius

Banking and insurance

In 1989 tax and duty incentives were introduced for foreign banks licensed to engage in offshore banking. Mauritius launched Africa's first offshore banking centre at the end of 1989 which continues to expand.

Central bank

Bank of Mauritius.

Main financial centre

Port Louis.

Time

GMT plus four hours

Geography

Mauritius lies in the Indian Ocean. The principal island, from which the country takes its name, lies about 800km (500 miles) east of Madagascar. The other main islands are Rodrigues, the Agalega Islands and the Cargados Carajos Shoals (St Brandon Islands).

The island of Mauritius is volcanic with a coastal plain sharply rising to a plateau of 275–580 metres (m). Piton de la Rivière Noire is the highest peak, at 828m and the Grand River South East is the longest river. Coral reefs surround the island from hundreds of metres to several kilometres off the coast.

Hemisphere

Southern

Climate

Maritime – tropical in summer (November–April), and sub-tropical for the rest of the year. High humidity especially in inland areas. Summer temperatures average 25–30 degrees Celsius (C) with maximum 35 degrees C in February. Highest rainfall occurs in summer (when cyclones are likely). From May–November, drier and warm with temperatures 19–27 degrees C. Lowest rainfall from September–November. Inland areas generally 5 degrees C cooler than coast and with higher rainfall.

Entry requirements

Passports

Passports must be valid for six months from date of entry.

Visa

Required by all except citizens of most Commonwealth countries, plus EU, US and others. For a full list and further information see www.gov.mu/portal/site/passportSite and follow link from *passport and visa requirements*. From 2009 EU citizens may make a short-stay visit, for up to three months, without a visa. Business travellers may visit with a tourist visa, obtained in advance. An application should include details of sufficient funds for the length of trip, an employer's letter of accreditation and an invitation from a local company or organisation.

A proposed tourist *univisa* (a single visa to visit all 15-member states of SADC: Angola, Botswana, DRC, Lesotho, Madagascar, Malawi, Mauritius, Mozambique, Namibia, South Africa, Seychelles, Swaziland, Tanzania, Zambia and Zimbabwe) is expected to be in use by 2013. Visitors should check with the appropriate consulates to confirm start of *univisas* and their scope before beginning a tour of southern Africa.

All travellers must have return/onward passage.

Currency advice/regulations

The import and export of local and foreign currency is unlimited.

Travellers cheques are accepted in banks, hotels and authorised dealers.

Prohibited imports

Sugar cane, invertebrates and soil micro-organisms and illegal drugs.

Firearms and ammunition require import permits and must be declared on arrival.

Health (for visitors)

Mandatory precautions

Yellow fever and cholera vaccination certificates are required if arriving from infected areas.

Advisable precautions

Typhoid, tetanus, hepatitis A and polio vaccinations. Water precautions should be taken.

Hotels

There is a wide choice available but relatively expensive. A value added tax of 15 per cent is added to hotel and restaurant bills. Tip is not compulsory.

Credit cards

International credit and charge cards are acceptable in many establishments. ATMs are available.

Public holidays (national)

Fixed dates

1–2 Jan (New Year), 1 Feb (Abolition of Slavery Day), 12 Mar (National Day), 1 May (Labour Day), 2 Nov (Arrival of Indentured Labourers), 25 Dec (Christmas Day).

Variable dates

Thaipoosam Cavadee (Jan/Feb), Chinese New Year (Jan/Feb), Maha Shivaratri (Feb/Mar), Ougadi (Mar/Apr), Ganesh Chaturthi (Aug/Sep), Diwali (Oct/Nov), Eid al Fitr.

There are a diversity of cultures, each with their own set of holidays. Muslim, Buddhist and Hindu festivals are timed according to local sightings of the moon and its phases.

Working hours

Banking

Mon–Thu: 0915–1515; Fri: 0915–1530; Sat: 0915–1115. Some banks open Mon–Fri: 0900–1700.

Business

Mon–Fri: 0830–1615, Sat: 0900–1200.

Government

Mon–Fri: 0900–1600; Sat 0900–1200 (minimal staff only).

Shops

Mon–Sat 0930–1930.

Telecommunications

Mobile/cell phones

GSM 900 and 3G services cover almost the entire area of Mauritius and Rodrigues.

Electricity supply

220V AC, 50 cycles.

Weights and measures

The metric system is in general use, but certain obsolete French measures are still used in connection with the measurement of land.

Getting there

Air

National airline: Air Mauritius.

International airport/s: Sir Seewoosagur Ramgoolam International (MRU) 3km from Mahébourg, 48km south-east of Port Louis; duty free, currency exchange, post office, shops, car hire, banks.

Airport tax: Departure tax: MR500

Surface

Main port/s: Port Louis is the island's only commercial port with five deep water quays. Its free port status underpins the island's offshore banking system.

Getting about

National transport

Air: Air Mauritius operates inter-island service between Mauritius and Rodrigues and Réunion. Two Air Mauritius Bell Jet helicopters are available for transfer from airport to hotel and tours.

Road: There is an extensive network throughout the island. About 93 per cent of the road network is paved. Occasional congestion. A dual highway links Port Louis and Phoenix, Port Louis and Mapou/Pamplemousses.

Buses: Good bus services cover the main island.

City transport

Taxis: Operate in all towns, villages and resorts. Generally unmetered so it is advisable to agree a fare before starting the journey. Tipping is not usual.

Car hire

Widely available. International or foreign licence accepted; traffic drives on the left.

BUSINESS DIRECTORY

The addresses listed below are a selection only. While World of Information makes every endeavour to check these addresses, we cannot guarantee that changes have not been made, especially to telephone numbers and area codes. We would welcome any corrections.

Telephone area codes
The international dialling code (IDD) for Mauritius is +230, followed by subscriber's number.

Useful telephone numbers
Emergency999
Fire995
Police208-7018

Chambers of Commerce
Mauritius Chamber of Commerce and Industry, 3 Royal Street, Port Louis (tel: 208-3301; fax: 208-0076; e-mail: mcci@intnet.mu).

Banking
African Asian Bank Limited, Office 5, 8th Floor, Max City Building, Corner Louis Pasteur & Remy Ollier Streets, Port Louis (tel: 240-7002, 240-7350; fax: 240-7009).

Bank of Baroda, African Asian Bank Limited, PO Box 553, Sir William Newton Street, Port Louis (tel: 208-1504; fax: 208-3892).

Banque Nationale de Paris Intercontinentale, 1 Sir William Newton Street, Port Louis (tel: 208-4147/8/9, 208-4151/2; fax: 208-8143).

Delphis Bank Limited, 16 Sir William Newton Street, Port Louis (tel: 208-5061; fax: 208-5388).

Development Bank of Mauritius Ltd, PO Box 157, Chaussée, Port Louis (tel: 208-0241; fax: 208-8498).

Indian Ocean International Bank Ltd, 34 Sir William Newton Street, Port Louis (tel: 208-0121; fax: 208-0127).

Mauritius Commercial Bank Ltd, 9-15 Sir William Newton St, Port Louis (tel: 202-5000; fax: 208-7054).

South East Asian Bank Ltd, 26 Bourbon Street, PO Box 13, Port Louis (tel: 208-8826/7/8, 212-2884/6/7; fax: 208-8825).

State Bank of Mauritius Ltd, PO Box 152, State Bank Tower, 1 Queen Elizabeth II Ave, Port Louis (tel: 202-1111; fax: 202-1234).

Central bank
Bank of Mauritius, Sir William Newton Street, Port Louis (tel: 208-4164 fax: 208-9204; e-mail: bomrd@bow.intnet.mu).

Stock exchange
The Stock Exchange of Mauritius www.stockexchangeofmauritius.com

Travel information
Air Mauritius, Rogers House, 5 President John F. Kennedy Street, PO Box 441, Port Louis (tel: 208-7700; fax: 208-8331).

Ministry of tourism
Ministry of Tourism, Emmanuel Anquetil Bldg, Sir Seewoosagur Ramgoolam St, Port Louis (tel: 201-2286).

National tourist organisation offices
Mauritius Tourism Promotion Authority, 11th Floor, Air Mauritius Centre, President John Kennedy Street, Port-Louis (tel: 210-1545; fax: 212-5142; e-mail: mtpa@intnet.mu; Internet: www.mauritius.net).

Ministries
Ministry of Agriculture and Natural Resources, NPF Bldg, 9th Floor, Port Louis (tel: 212-7946; fax: 212-4427).

Ministry of Arts, Culture, Leisure and Reform Institutions, Government Centre, Port Louis (tel: 201-2032).

Ministry of Civil Service Affairs and Employment, Government Centre, Port Louis (tel: 201-1035; fax: 212-9528).

Ministry of Co-operatives and Handicraft, Life Insurance Corporation of India Bldg, 3rd Floor, John Kennedy St, Port Louis (tel: 208-4812; fax: 208-9265).

Ministry of Economic Planning and Development, Emmanuel Anquetil Bldg, Sir Seewoosagur Ramgoolam St, Port Louis (tel: 201-1576; fax: 212-4124).

Ministry of Education and Science, Sun Trust Bldg, Edith Cavell St, Port Louis (tel: 212-8411; fax: 212-3783).

Ministry of Energy, Water Resources and Postal Services, Government Centre, Port Louis (tel: 201-1087; fax: 208-6497).

Ministry of the Environment and Quality of Life, Barracks St, Port Louis (tel: 212-8332; fax: 212-9407).

Ministry of External Affairs, Government Centre, Port Louis (tel: 201-1416; fax: 208-8087).

Ministry of Finance, Government Centre, Port Louis (tel: 201-1145; fax: 208-8622).

Ministry of Fisheries and Marine Resources, Port Louis.

Ministry of Health, Emmanuel Anquetil Bldg, Sir Seewoosagur Ramgoolam St, Port Louis (tel: 201-1910; fax: 208-0376).

Ministry of Housing, Lands and Town and Country Planning, Moorgate House, Port Louis (tel: 212-6022; fax: 212-7482).

Ministry of Industry and Industrial Technology, Government Centre, Port Louis (tel: 201-1221; fax: 212-8201).

Ministry of Information, Government Centre, Port Louis (tel: 201-1278; fax: 208-8243).

Ministry of Internal and External Communications, Emmanuel Anquetil Bldg, 10th Floor, Sir Seewoosagur Ramgoolam St, Port Louis (tel: 201-1089; fax: 212-1673).

Ministry of Justice, Jules Koenig St, Port Louis (tel: 208-5321).

Ministry of Labour and Industrial Relations, Ming Court, cnr Eugène Laurent and GMD Atchia Sts, Port Louis (tel: 212-3049; fax: 212-3070).

Ministry of Local Government, Government Centre, Port Louis (tel: 201-1215).

Ministry of Manpower Resources and Vocational and Technical Training, Jade House, Remy Ollier St, Port Louis (tel: 242-1462).

Ministry for Rodrigues Island, Fon Sing Bldg, Edith Cavell St, Port Louis (tel: 208-8472; fax: 212-6329).

Ministry of Social Security and National Solidarity, cnr Maillard and Jules Koenig Sts, Port Louis (tel: 212-3006).

Ministry of Trade and Shipping, Government Centre, Port Louis (tel: 201-1067; fax: 212-6386).

Ministry of Women's Rights, Child Development and Family Welfare, Rainbow House, cnr Edith Cavell and Brown Sequard Sts, Port Louis (tel: 208-2061; fax: 208-8250).

Ministry of Works, Treasury Bldg, Port Louis (tel: 208-0281; fax: 212-8373).

Ministry of Youth and Sports, Emmanuel Anquetil Bldg, Sir Seewoosagur Ramgoolam St, Port Louis (tel: 201-1242; fax: 212-6506).

Prime Minister's Office, Government Centre, Port Louis (tel: 201-1001; fax: 208-8619).

Other useful addresses
British High Commission, Commercial Section, 7th Floor, Les Cascades Building, Edith Cavell Street, Port Louis (tel: 208-9850/1; fax: 212-8470).

Export Processing Zone Development Authority, 5th Floor, Les Cascades, Edith Cavell St, Port Louis (tel: 212-9760; fax: 212-9767).

Mauritius Embassy (USA), Suite 441, 4301 Connecticut Avenue, NW, Washington DC 20008 (tel: (+1-202) 244-1491; fax: (+1-202) 966-0983; e-mail: mauritius.embassy@prodigy.net).

Mauritius Employers' Federation, Cerné House, Chausse, Port Louis (tel: 212-1599; fax: 212-6725).

Mauritius Export Processing Zone Association, 42 Sir William Newton St, Port Louis (tel: 208-5216; fax: 212-1853).

Mauritius Free Port Authority, 2nd Floor, Deramann Tower, Sir William Newton St,

Port Louis (tel: 212-9627; fax: 212-9629).

Mauritius Industrial Development Authority, Level 2, BAI Bldg, 25 Pope Hennessy St, Port Louis (tel: 208-7750; fax: 208-5965; e-mail: mida@media.intnet.mu).

Mauritius Offshore Business Activities Authority, 1st Floor, Deramann Tower, 30 Sir William Newton St, Port Louis (tel: 212-9650; fax: 212-9459).

Mauritius Standards Bureau, Ministry of Industry and Industrial Technology, Réduit (tel: 454-1933; fax: 464-7675).

APA: www.apanews.net

Panapress: www.panapress.com

Reuters Africa: http://africa.reuters.com

Internet sites

Africa Business Network: www.ifc.org/abn

AllAfrica.com: http://allafrica.com

African Development Bank: www.afdb.org

Business Directory: www.mauritius.co.uk/

Mbendi AfroPaedia (information on companies, countries, industries and stock exchanges in Africa): http://mbendi.co.za

Mexico

KEY FACTS

Official name: Estados Unidos Mexicanos (United Mexican States)

Head of State: President Enrique Peña Neito (PRI) (elected 1 July, inaugurated 1 Dec 2012)

Head of government: President Enrique Peña Neito (PRI) (from 1 Dec 2012)

Ruling party: Three party coalition led by Partido Revolucionario Institucional (PRI). Other parties are Partido Verde Ecologista de México (PVEM) and Partido Nueva Alianza (PNA) (from 7 June 2015)

Area: 1,958,201 square km

Population: 119.72 million (2014) (112,336,538; 2010, census figure)

Capital: Mexico City (DF)

Official language: Spanish

Currency: Mexican peso (Mex$) = 100 centavos

Exchange rate: Mex$16.82 per US$ (Sep 2015)

GDP per capita: US$10,715 (2014)

GDP real growth: 2.13% (2014)

GDP: US$1,282.73 billion (2014)

Labour force: 46.20 million (2009)

Unemployment: 4.75% (2014) (plus additional underemployment)

Inflation: 4.02% (2014)

Oil production: 2.78 million bpd (2014)

Natural gas production: 58.10 billion cum (2014)

Balance of trade: -US$2.57 billion (2014)

Annual FDI: US$20.36 billion (2011)

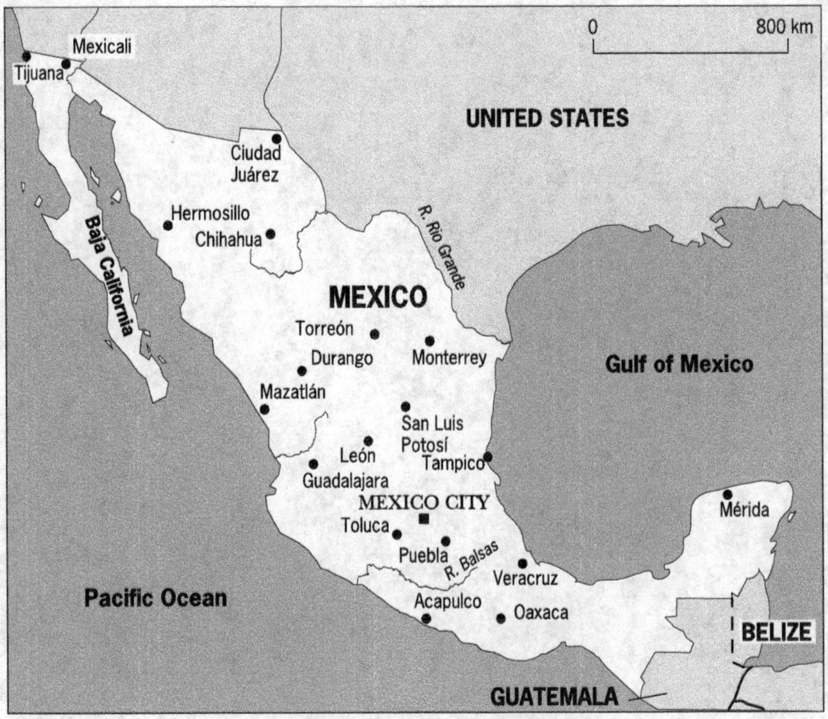

In June 2015 Mexico's President Peña Nieto could breathe a sigh of relief when the results of the June mid-term elections came in. He had not been handed a blank cheque, but he had at least managed to maintain the parliamentary majority of the Partido Revolucionario Institucional (PRI) (Institutional Revolutionary Party). However, the reduction of the majority was a shot across the PRI's bows, warning him that in his three remaining years as President he would need to devote more attention to Mexico's acute social problems, particularly its pervasive corruption and scant regard for human rights. One positive sign provided by the election results was that all three of the 'major' parties, the centrist PRI, with 30 per cent, the right wing Partido Acción Nacional (PAN) (National Action Party), 22 per cent and the left wing Partido de la Revolución Democrática (PRD) (Democratic Revolution Party), 11 per cent, saw their number of deputies fall, while the number of successful independent candidates had risen. Another interesting development was the arrival of the Morena Party, a breakaway group from the PRD, headed by Andrés Manuel López Obrador (twice a presidential candidate), which in its electoral debut had managed to secure 8 per cent of the votes. The election of Jaime Rodríguez was the only independent governor (of Nueva León).

Mr Peña Nieto had begun his presidency by promising to introduce widespread reforms. Many of the proposed reforms were perceived to be essential by most Mexicans; however, three years into his presidency a large number of the reforms were still on the drawing board. Worse, in some cases – notably education – the reform process appeared to have gone into reverse. The lesson that the president appeared not to have learnt was that Mexicans wanted more than economic reforms, they wanted to see an end to the corruption and violence that in many parts of Mexico made a functioning democracy impossible. Mexicans were tired of newspaper headlines that repetitively focussed on the murder of students, on new corruption scandals, the arrival of new drug *carteles*, bloody clashes between Mexican troops and organised crime. The statistics were frightening – some 100,000 killed or disappeared since 2008 in the so called '*guerra contra el narco*' (anti-drug war). There were also the high profile student deaths in Ayotzinapa and Apatzingán, deaths directly attributed to the police force. The United Nations, not known for precipitous interventions in the affairs of member countries had published a report that accused the Mexican state of practising torture. Another gloomy statistic was the sentencing rate – it appeared that only three per cent of the Mexicans arrested and accused were ever sentenced. In the 2015 election campaigning, eight candidates had been assassinated.

President Peña Nieto's much vaunted reform programme had one central irony. Many of the political reforms envisaged would undermine the very system that had enabled the PRI – and its president – to be elected. This included the *caciquismo* (cronyism), sinecure appointments, the corporate approach to government which saw election success as a passport to enrichment and which had survived the adoption of democracy in the 1990s. Jorge Zepeda the editor of the digital *Sin Embargo* (*None the Less*) wrote that what had initially been seen as a 'film, a new documentary,' had turned into a 'still life photo' of the moment in 2012 when the three main parties, the PRI, the PAN and the PRD signed the *Pacto para México*. President Peña Nieto had only three years in which to introduce his reforms. What was really required was the re-creation of Mexico as a functioning democracy. There was a long way to go – on the 2014 *Corruption Perceptions Index* published by Transparency International, Mexico ranked 103 of the 175 countries surveyed.

Democracy wins… just

The 2015 mid-term elections offered Mexicans a glimmer of optimism, the knowledge that however tarnished, their democracy was at least still alive. The elections were also seen as an opportunity to pass judgement on the PRI government. The turnout, at 47 per cent, was slightly up on the previous mid-term elections in 2009. There were more female candidates; the range of parties was wider. In five of the nine elections for state governors, the winner was not a mainstream party candidate. In the northern state of Nueva León where the turnout was 59 per cent, the winner was the maverick Jaime Rodríguez, (also known as 'El Bronco', a title which defies translation) as governor, with 49 per cent of the vote. El Bronco's victory was widely anticipated – Nueva León has often been in the vanguard of social change in Mexico. In 2015 the city had already formed an alternative police service, financed by the business community, to counter the gang culture. In Mr Rodríguez's home town of García the police had been 'purged' and a new rapid response group formed. El Bronco had, before being elected governor, been on the sharp end of two attempts on his life. Students of Latin American history could be forgiven for seeing in El Bronco signs of the populist Caudillismo that had long prevailed throughout Latin America. His electoral appeal had more to do with his personality than his policies, about which little had been revealed. But such was his appeal that following his victory rumours spread that he might be standing as an independent candidate for the presidency in 2018. In the Distrito Federal (Mexico's capital district) a majority of the administrations went to non-PRI candidates. To maintain its parliamentary majority, the PRI had to seek the support of two minority parties.

In his September 2014 address to the nation, President Peña Nieto had listed the successes of his first 21 months in office, giving particular attention to the war on crime and on hunger; he also covered his administration's successes in education and foreign policy, as well as launching in to a rugged defence of his energy policy. But pride of place was reserved for the infrastructural programme. The administration was open enough about the policy's objective: to shake the Mexican economy from its lethargy – growth forecasts for 2014 had been scaled back in successive steps to an unsatisfactory 2.7 per cent (see below), some way off the President's cherished target of 5 per cent. Peña Nieto said that: 'The economy is moving in the right direction, but we haven't yet reached what is needed. The target of accelerated, sustained and sustainable growth can only be achieved if we make fundamental changes. And reforming implies taking decisions.'

In contrast to the almost immediate results likely to be generated by the major increase in infrastructure expenditure, the historic legislative packet approved in August 2014 – after 18 months' deliberation – would probably need years before it produced any tangible results. The plan was also kicking in at a moment when the administration was under-performing in the opinion polls, allowing it to regain the initiative on topics close to voters' hearts, such as transport and infrastructure. But the topic closest to most Mexicans' hearts was that of security. Their president had made references enough to 'crime', but less emphasis had been placed on 'corruption'.

El Chapo – Part 2, El Mencho Part 1

For the Mexican prison system to allow a drugs cartel leader to escape from prison

KEY INDICATORS — Mexico

	Unit	2011	2012	2013	2014	**2015
Population	m	*113.74	117.06	118.40	119.72	*121.08
Gross domestic product (GDP)	US$bn	1,154.80	1,183.51	1,262.25	1,282.73	*1,231.98
GDP per capita	US$	10,153	10,111	10,661	10,715	*10,174
GDP real growth	%	3.9	3.9	1.4	2.1	*3.0
Inflation	%	3.4	4.1	3.8	4.0	*3.2
Unemployment	%	5.2	5.0	4.9	4.8	*4.3
Oil output	'000 bpd	2,938.0	2,911.0	2,875.0	2,784.0	–
Natural gas output	bn cum	52.5	58.5	56.6	58.1	–
Coal output	mtoe	7.6	6.6	8.3	6.9	–
Exports (fob) (goods)	US$m	349,946.0	371,378.0	380,903.0	397,866.0	–
Imports (fob) (goods)	US$m	351,116.0	371,028.0	381,638.0	400,440.0	–
Balance of trade	US$m	-1,171.0	350.0	-736.0	-2,573.0	–
Current account	US$m	-9,671.0	-14,767.0	-29,682.0	-26,545.0	*-26,595.0
Total reserves minus gold	US$m	132,962.0	160,413.0	175,432.0	190,923.0	–
Foreign exchange	US$m	126,659.0	153,473.0	168,613.0	–	–
Exchange rate	per US$	11.87	12.94	13.09	14.75	–

* estimated figure ** forecast figure

once could perhaps be put down to carelessness or incompetence. However, quoting Oscar Wilde on carelessness was simply not enough. There were no words adequate when the same drug cartel leader, El Chapo, escaped for a second time, this time from Mexico's only high security prison. But El Chapo Guzmán was no ordinary drug dealer, nor was he any ordinary prison escapee. His second escape, this time from the Altiplano prison, was via a tunnel big enough to allow a rudimentary vehicle to pass through, expertly dug, cemented and ventilated. Such was the sophistication involved – described by President Peña Nieto as 'incredible and unpardonable' that it reflected more on Mexico's unacceptably high levels of corruption than it did on the incompetence of its prison officials. It implied that corruption had taken an almost unshakeable grip on the affairs of state. Mexico's government had surely been aware that having escaped once, El Chapo was likely to do so again. In the first place, it seemed beyond belief that this prisoner had not been given a chip to enable him to be constantly located. Secondly, when it emerged that the security cameras had been doctored to permit the tunnel to be built, it also emerged that no checks were ever made to ensure that the cameras were working. That the incompetence check list was so long suggested not so much the incompetence of the state, it symbolised its total disappearance from much of Mexico's everyday life.

Mexico's drug problem was not simply one of trying to eliminate existing drug gangs. The cartel cancer ran deep and as with the disease, new operations would continuously spring up. In May 2015 a new threat emerged, this time from the Jalisco Nueva Generación (CJNG) cartel that had simply taken control of a run-down *barrío* in the city of Guadalajara, Mexico's second largest conurbation. 'Taking control' in this case was more sinister than it sounded. The CJNG, led by one Nemesio Oseguera aka '*El Mencho*', would round up any small time drug dealers not on their approved payroll and simply 'eliminate' them. In an exchange of fire with the police force, the CJNG managed to bring down a police helicopter with a rocket launcher, as well as killing 17 police and soldiers. El Mencho had himself once been a policeman in the Pacific district of Cabo Corrientes. He appeared to have departed the police force to join the Milenio drug cartel in Michoacán, his native province. When the Milenio leader Ignacio Nacho Coronel died in 2010, El Mencho spotted a vacuum and seized his chance, linking up with the Sinaloa cartel to take control of drug trafficking in the area. From the Sinaloa cartel he leaned how to build and operate the laboratories necessary for transforming raw materials into drugs. The US authorities accused him of exporting tons of cocaine into the US. In mid-2015 the CJNG's grip on Guadalajara seemed to be strengthening; the battle between the CJNG and the police was not being won by the city's police force.

The economy

According to the United Nations Economic Commission for Latin America and the Caribbean, Mexico's GDP was expected to grow by an annual rate of 2.1 per cent in 2014, up from 1.4 per cent in 2013, mainly as a result of more vigorous growth in exports. The fiscal deficit was projected to bounce back to finish the year at a level equivalent to 1.5 per cent of gross domestic product (GDP), or by 3.5 per cent if investments by Petróleos Mexicanos (PEMEX) were included, compared to the 2.3 per cent seen in 2013. Annual inflation was forecast to be around 4.1 per cent at the close the year, slightly above the Banco de México (central bank)'s target range of 3 per cent, with a margin of one percentage point either side. The current account deficit was expected to be around 1.8 per cent of GDP, the same as in 2013, while the national average annual unemployment rate would remain stable at around 5.0 per cent of the economically active population.

According to ECLAC estimates, Mexico's GDP would grow at a rate of 3.2 per cent in 2015, spurred on by export growth and stronger public and private investment. How to boost domestic consumption remained a challenge because the wage bill is not rising quickly enough. The current account deficit would be around 2.0 per cent of GDP, while the fiscal deficit, including investments by PEMEX, would exceed 3 per cent of GDP for the second consecutive year. The slump in international oil prices would be partially offset by the ministry of finance and public credit's hedging of oil at US$76.40 per barrel, which will ensure steady oil revenues for the federal government.

ECLAC noted that the supporting legislation needed to implement the structural reforms agreed during President Enrique Peña Nieto's first year in office were adopted in 2014. Notable amongst these were planned changes in the following sectors: telecommunications, to pave the way for more competition and greater investment; energy, to open up greater leeway for private investment; finance, by setting up mechanisms for encouraging competition and improving access to credit; and education, with modifications designed to strengthen monitoring and evaluation mechanisms with a view to improving the quality of education. Successful implementation of these reforms was expected to boost Mexico's future economic performance.

The reform of the energy sector had, according to ECLAC, led to the establishment of the Mexican Petroleum Fund for Stabilisation and Development (FMP), which from January 2015 became responsible for collecting, managing and disbursing all non-tax revenue that the Mexican State receives from oil and natural gas exploration and extraction activities. The fund's mission was to bring greater stability to public finances by establishing a long-term savings fund to enable implementation of counter-cyclical measures, to channel resources into a universal pension system and to invest in areas such as science and technology and infrastructure.

ECLAC noted that Mexico's fiscal policy was expansionary in 2014, with the government running the largest budget deficit in more than a decade with a view to stimulating economic activity. Total public sector spending jumped by 8.5 per cent year-on-year in real terms in the first nine months of 2014, up from 0.4 per cent in the same period of 2013. Spending on social development rose by 5.7 per cent in real terms, while spending on economic development surged by 10.3 per cent. Public-sector budgetary revenues grew by 2 per cent year-on-year in real terms between January and September 2014. Oil revenue declined by 2.2 per cent year-on-year in real terms as production volume and the price of Mexico's crude oil mix both fell (See Energy below). Non-oil tax revenues, meanwhile, saw growth of 6.1 per cent. The value-added tax take was up (by 16.9 per cent in real terms), driven by the approval of a rate increase from 11 per cent to 16 per cent in the border region and increased receipts from windfall taxes on production and services (49.1 per cent), largely thanks to the introduction of a new levy of 5 per cent on the sale and importation of high-calorie, non-staple foods. Receipts from the set of income taxes were down by 2.6 per cent in real terms in 2014 because the extraordinary receipts from the tax debt regularisation programme implemented in 2013 were a one-time gain that was not repeated in 2014.

The federal public sector's net debt stood at 37.5 per cent of GDP at the end of September 2014, compared to 35.0 per cent at the end of 2013. Although public debt remained within sustainable limits and was below the average for Organisation for Economic Co-operation and Development (OECD) member countries, it had grown significantly in recent years and is something that would, in the opinion of ECLAC, have to be watched closely over the short and medium term. Another fiscal issue in need of attention was the low multiplier effect of public spending, since the increased public deficit had failed to have the desired effect on economic activity. In June 2014 the central bank cut its benchmark interest rate by 50 basis points to 3 per cent, given the sluggish performance of the economy and the fact that inflation had remained within its target range. This rate has since remained unchanged. Against this backdrop, nominal yields on treasury certificates (CETES) reached their lowest-ever levels (rates on 28-day certificates stood at 2.9 per cent at the end of October), with negative rates in real terms throughout the year (-1.3 per cent at the end of October). In February 2014, Moody's Investors Service upgraded its rating of Mexico's sovereign bonds by one notch, from Baa1 to A3, with an optimistically stable outlook in view of the country's greater growth potential following its approval of the structural reforms. Bank lending to the private sector grew by 8.5 per cent year-on-year in nominal terms (and by 4.1 per cent in real terms) in the first nine months of 2014, down from a nominal 10.5 per cent in the same period of 2013 (6.8 per cent in real terms). Consumer credit and lending for services both showed notable year-on-year expansions (8.6 per cent and 15.4 per cent, respectively). Between September and November 2014, the strength of the dollar on international markets put upward pressure on the exchange rate. The interbank exchange rate thus stood at 13.7 pesos to the dollar at the end of November 2014, representing a nominal depreciation of 4.1 per cent in respect of the end of 2013. The real bilateral exchange rate depreciated by 1.2 per cent over the first nine months of the year.

International reserves stood at US$192.72 billion at the end of November 2014, a nominal increase of 9.1 per cent on figures at the close of 2013. Mexico also continued to have access to a flexible credit line of US$73 billion with the International Monetary Fund (IMF). Once the structural reforms and the supporting legislation had been adopted, two of the items at the top of the current administration's agenda until its term of office ends in 2018 would be reinvigorating economic activity and combating public insecurity. Negotiations for a free-trade agreement between Panama and Mexico concluded in March 2014. Mexico also continued to participate in the Trans-Pacific Partnership negotiation rounds.

Exports, according to ECLAC, grew by 4.6 per cent year-on-year in the first nine months of 2014 compared to 2.5 per cent in the same period of 2013, driven by an expansion in non-oil exports (6.7 per cent) that was in turn partially offset by an 8.7 per cent decline in oil exports owing to falling crude production volume and lower international prices. Growth in manufacturing exports picked up (6.4 per cent) after a modest expansion in 2013. Automotive industry and professional and scientific equipment exports surged (by 10.6 per cent and 14.3 per cent, respectively). Imports increased by 4.1 per cent in the first nine months of 2014, up from 2.8 per cent in the same period of 2013. The highest rate of year-on-year expansion was in intermediate goods imports (5.3 per cent); capital goods imports saw lacklustre growth (1.3 per cent). Imports of consumer goods contracted (by 0.12 per cent). The deficit in the balance of trade in goods narrowed to a cumulative US$1.762 billion in September (against a US$2.99 billion deficit in the same period of 2013).

Income from family remittances over the first ten months of 2014 came to US$19.629 billion, which represented year-on-year growth of 7.2 per cent and a continuation of the recovery that began in the second half of 2013. Foreign direct investment (FDI), meanwhile, stood at US$15.310 billion in the first nine months of the year, a long way short of the US$28.234 billion posted in the same period of 2013. This change was due in part to a one-time transaction in the second quarter of 2014 (Mexican investors purchased a stake in América Móvil, involving an FDI outflow of US$4.495 billion) and to the acquisition in 2013 of the beer maker Grupo Modelo by the Belgian-owned multinational AB InBev for a net US$13.25 billion.

Economic activity in the first half of 2014 (with a year-on-year expansion of 1.7 per cent) was not as buoyant as had been expected. Growth forecasts for the year as a whole had needed to be trimmed. The third quarter saw a slight acceleration with GDP rising by an annual 2.2 per cent. Primary activities expanded by 3.9 per cent in the first nine months of the year as a result of dynamic growth in agriculture. Secondary activities grew at a rate of 1.6 per cent, driven by manufacturing, while tertiary activities increased by 2.0 per cent. In the first half of the year, private consumption grew 1.4 per cent year-on-year in real terms. Gross fixed capital formation fell by 0.6 per cent. Following a rise in inflation in January 2014, monthly variations between March and July remained within the central bank's target range (3 per cent, with a margin of one percentage point either side), but inflation picked up again from August, driven by price rises in agricultural goods and energy, to reach 4.3 per cent at the end of October 2014.

The average unemployment rate between January and September 2014 held at 5 per cent, unchanged on the level seen in the first nine months of 2013, against a backdrop of falling employment and participation rates. By the end of October 2014, the number of new formal-sector workers registered with the Mexican Social Security Institute (IMSS) had risen by 700,000 permanent workers, 4.2 per cent more than at the same point in 2013. The real minimum wage fell by 0.3 per cent year-on-year between October 2013 and October 2014; the real average wage rose by 0.3 per cent.

Energy

Announcing the launch of the new Fondo Mexicano del Petróleo (FMP) (Petroleum Stabilisation and Development Fund) to take effect from January 2015, the Banco de México governor Agustín Carstens advised that surplus petroleum funds would be channelled into a long-term savings plan for future generations. Modelled on the Norwegian Sovereign Wealth Fund (the world's largest, holding around US$850 billion), the new oil fund would finance oil and gas exploration and production, as well as infrastructure, pensions and research and other development projects. Mr Carstens noted that similar funds had proven successful in over 25 other countries. Previously, Mexico's government had used oil revenue exclusively for budgetary purposes and not for investment. Once the fund reached 3 per cent of GDP, any surplus would be divided, with at least 40 per cent remaining in the oil fund and at least 10 per cent remaining in the universal pension fund. A further 10 per cent would be invested in science and technology projects and another 10 per cent in scholarships and industry connectivity and development projects. Officials described the fund as a 'tool for transparency', enabling Mexicans to see 'the origin and destination of the oil and gas revenues' managed by the fund. The fund would issue quarterly financial statements.

According to figures produced by the US government Energy Information Administration (EIA) Mexico is one of the 10 largest oil producers in the world, the third-largest in the Americas after the United States and Canada and an important partner in the US energy trade. However, the EIA noted that Mexico's oil production had steadily decreased since 2005 as a result of natural production declines from Cantarell and other large offshore fields. The rate of total production decline had however abated in the previous several years. In December 2013, in an effort to address the declines of its domestic oil production, the Mexican government enacted constitutional reforms that ended the 75-year monopoly of PEMEX, the state-owned oil company. The oil sector generated 13 per cent of Mexico's export earnings in 2013, a proportion that had declined over the previous decade, according to Mexico's central bank. More significantly, earnings from the oil industry (including taxes and direct payments from PEMEX) accounted for about 32 per cent of total government revenues in 2013. Declines in oil production and falls in the price of oil have a direct impact on Mexico's economic output and on the government's fiscal health, particularly as refined product consumption and import needs grow.

Mexico produced an average of 2.9 million barrels per day (bpd) of total oil liquids during 2013. Crude oil accounted for 2.5 million bpd, or 87 per cent of total output, with the remainder attributable to lease condensate, natural gas liquids and refinery processing gain. Mexico's total oil production had been declining substantially, by 22 per cent from its height in 2004 to 2009, but the decline thereafter had remained at less than an annual one per cent. Crude oil production in 2013 was at its lowest since 1995 and had continued to decline into 2014. Mexico is a significant exporter, the third largest in the Americas, but a declining net crude exporter. Mexico is also a net importer of refined petroleum products. Its largest trading partner is the United States, which is the destination for most of its crude oil exports and the source of most of its refined product imports. According to the *Oil & Gas Journal* (OGJ), Mexico had 10 billion barrels of proved oil reserves as of the end of 2013. Most reserves consist of heavy crude oil varieties, with the largest concentration occurring offshore of the southern part of the country, particularly the Campeche Basin. There are also sizeable reserves in onshore basins in the northern parts of the country.

Mexico nationalised its oil sector in 1938, when PEMEX was created as the sole oil operator in the country. In 2014 PEMEX was still the largest company in Mexico and one of the largest oil companies in the world. The energy sector is regulated by the Secretaría de Energía (SENER) and the Comisión Nacional de Hidrocárburos (CNH) provides additional oversight of PEMEX and its oil and gas activities. After years of declining production, in December 2013 Mexico instituted its most significant energy reforms to date. These ended PEMEX's monopoly on the oil and gas sector, opening it to greater foreign investment. The reforms allowed for new exploration and production contract models: licences, production-sharing, profit-sharing and service contracts. PEMEX was to remain state-owned but would be given more budgetary and administrative autonomy and would have to compete for bids with other firms on new projects. As stipulated by the reforms, PEMEX was allowed first refusal of its current oil and gas holdings and had submitted to the energy ministry its intention to retain and develop deepwater oil fields in the Perdido Fold Belt and offshore Lakach gas fields. Mexico now needed to develop and approve secondary legislation detailing the fiscal regime and contract terms for the models. While reform proponents overcame the major obstacle of constitutional change, the remaining legislation still faced significant opposition.

Most of Mexico's oil production occurs off the eastern coast in the Bay of Campeche of the Gulf of Mexico, near the states of Veracruz, Tabasco and Campeche. The two main production centres in the area are Cantarell and Ku-Maloob-Zaap (KMZ). In total, approximately 1.9 million bpd – or three-quarters – of Mexico's crude oil is produced offshore in the Bay of Campeche. Because of the concentration of Mexico's oil production offshore, tropical storms or hurricanes passing through the area can disrupt oil operations.

Offshore & onshore…

Over half of Mexico's oil production comes from two offshore fields in the north-eastern region of the Bay of Campeche – KMZ and Cantarell. Another important source of oil production is south-west in the same bay, offshore Tabasco state. Cantarell was once one of the largest oil fields in the world, but its output has been declining significantly for almost a decade. Meanwhile, KMZ, which is adjacent to Cantarell, emerged as Mexico's most prolific field. Production nearly tripled between 2004 and 2013, when it reached 864,000bpd, Views differ about whether the KMZ complex has already reached peak production. Onshore fields accounted for 25 per cent of Mexico's total crude oil production in 2013. Most of this production consisted of light or extra-light crude oil in the southern part of the country, accounting for 77 per cent of Mexico's onshore production. The largest oilfield in the south is Samaria-Luna, which produced about 173,000bpd in 2013.

Mexican authorities report that the country exported 1.19 million bpd of crude oil in 2013, a decline that had occurred since 2010. The United States received approximately 71 per cent of Mexico's oil exports. Mexico was typically among the top three exporters of oil to the United States. In 2013, the United States imported 850,000bpd of crude oil from Mexico, behind Canada and Saudi Arabia. Mexico's crude oil exports to the United States had risen steadily through the 1980s and 1990s, before peaking in 2004 at 1.6 million bpd. In 2013, Mexico exported 182,000bpd of refined petroleum products. The United States imported 68,000bpd of that total, most of which was residual fuel oil, naphtha and pentanes plus. As with crude oil, US imports of refined petroleum products from Mexico have declined in recent years, from a high of 132,000bpd in 2010.

Natural gas

Mexico has considerable natural gas resources, but its production is modest relative to other North American countries. The development of its shale gas resources is proceeding slowly. Mexico's import needs are rising as domestic production stagnates and demand increases, particularly in the electricity sector. Consequently, Mexico will rely on increased pipeline imports of natural gas from the United States and liquefied natural gas (LNG) from other countries. According to the OGJ, Mexico had 17 trillion cubic feet (tcf) of proved natural gas reserves at year-end 2013. While the southern region of the country contains the largest share of proved reserves, the northern region has the potential to be the centre of growth in future, as it contains almost 10 times as much probable and possible natural gas reserves. Mexico has one of the world's largest shale gas resource bases, which could support increased natural gas reserves and production. According to the EIA, Mexico has an estimated 545tcf of technically recoverable shale gas resources – the sixth largest of any country examined in the study.

Risk assessment

Economy	Fair
Politics	Fair/poor
Regional stability	Good
Corruption	Poor

People to watch

Jaime Rodríguez, (also known as 'El Bronco') elected governor of Nueva León in June 2015.

Andrés Manuel López Obrador (twice a presidential candidate), leader of the left wing Partido de la Revolución Democrática (PRD) (Democratic Revolution Party)

COUNTRY PROFILE

The Olmecs inhabited the country around 3,500 years ago, their civilisation reaching its peak about 1200 BC. By AD 500–600, the Mayas had risen to prominence and Teotihuacan (where Mexico City now stands) was thriving, with 200,000 inhabitants.

1519 The Spanish, and Hernan Cortés, arrived. The Aztecs were the dominant culture.

1810–21 The Spanish colony became independent. Conflicts with the US and France ensued.

1876–1910 The Porfirio Díaz dictatorship, known as the *Porfiriato*, led to a series of revolutions and coups.

1910 The Epic Revolution, led by Emiliano Zapata, began

1911 Porfirio Diaz was overthrown. Francisco Madero, a liberal and one of the revolutionary leaders, became president. He introduced land reform and labour legislation. Political unrest continued with Zapata leading a peasant revolt in the south.

1913 Madero was assassinated. Victoriano Huerta seized power.

1914 Huerta resigned. He had been viewed with suspicion by the United States for his alleged pro-German sympathies. Huerta is succeeded by General Venustiano Carranza, preventing the re-emergence of the *Porfiriato*.

1917 Mexico's modern liberal constitution was adopted, enshrining land reform and labour rights.

1920 Carranza was assassinated. Civil war broke out.

1929 President Plutarco Elías Calles created the Partido Nacional Revolucionario (PNR) (National Revolutionary Party), a multi-class party that developed institutionalised mechanisms which enabled and controlled popular participation in government.

1934 General Lázaro Cárdenas became president and restructured the PNR, renaming it the Partido de la Revolución Mexicana (PRM) (Party of the Mexican Revolution). He also created official unions for workers and peasants, which were controlled by the official party.

1939 Disenchanted middle-class conservatives launched the Partido de Acción Nacional (PAN) (National Action Party).

1940 Leon Trotsky was assassinated in Mexico.

1946 Miguel Alemán became president and renamed the ruling party the Partido Revolucionario Institucional (PRI) (Institutional Revolutionary Party), signifying the final transition from the ideals of the revolution to liberal capitalism and a corporatist state.

1968 Growing disenchantment with authoritarian politics and rising urban poverty led to a series of mass demonstrations, culminating in a massacre of several hundred peaceful demonstrators, most of them young students.

1970 Luis Echeverría Alvarez became president, seeking to calm political turbulence through increased state spending and bolstering the power of trade unions.

1976 José López Portillo was appointed president. Oil revenues were used to borrow additional capital to initiate a rapid transition towards industrial development.

1982 A debt crisis was sparked by an economic recession in the US which left Mexico unable to obtain enough loans to service existing debts. A programme of economic stabilisation and structural adjustment was initiated under the administration of President Miguel de la Madrid.

1988 The PRI split. The left-wing *corriente democrática* joined a coalition of minor parties to back the presidential candidacy of Cuauhtémoc Cárdenas, son of former president, Lázaro Cárdenas. Despite massive electoral fraud, Cárdenas still managed to come second behind the PRI's Carlos Salinas de Gortari.

1992 As part of Mexico's commitments in the run-up to the signing of the North American Free Trade Agreement (Nafta), Salinas effectively repealed Article 27 of the Mexican Constitution which had guaranteed land reform.

1994 The Zapatistas led an uprising in Chiapas state in response to the treatment of indigenous peasants and neo-liberal economic policy. The Zapatistas attracted worldwide sympathy and attention was fixed on the effects of Mexico's economic policy and Nafta on the growing number of Mexican poor. The PRI's presidential candidate, Luis Donaldo Colosio, was murdered; many believed the killing was carried out by members of his own party.

1994 Ernesto Zedillo of the PRI won the presidential election amid accusations of dirty tricks and vote buying.

2000 PAN won parliamentary elections, the PRI lost the presidency and its majority in the Senate, as well as its status as the party with the largest number of seats in the lower house. The break with PRI rule was historic, as the party, including its previous incarnations, had enjoyed continuous office since 1929.

2001 The Senate unanimously approved a constitutional bill granting autonomy to indigenous people.

2002 Roberto Madrazo won the elections for the leadership of PRI.

2005 Six prison officers were murdered and all high security jails were put on alert, following an escalation of tension between the authorities and drug gangs.

2006 Felipe de Jesús Calderón Hinojosa (PAN) narrowly won the presidential election. The president declared war on drug cartels, with a new federal police force and thousands of troops deployed to the western state of Michoacán.

2007 Over 75,000 people protested in Mexico City and more in other locations, at the rapid rise in prices of basic foodstuffs. Tortillas, the staple food particularly among the poor, had risen by 40 per cent in the previous months and at a rate far faster than inflation in general. The price increases were largely due to the cost of maize imports from the US where such produce has been redirected for use in bio-fuel.

2008 There were 1,400 deaths due to organised drug cartels recorded in the first five months, bringing to 4,000 the number of drug trafficking related deaths since the beginning of the police crackdown in 2006. The navy seized a makeshift submarine smuggling almost six tonnes of cocaine to the US, while the army seized 12 tonnes of marijuana in Tijuana.

2009 The first case of a worldwide flu virus (H1N1) epidemic, characterised as a 'mild' strain, was reported in Mexico. The virus rapidly infected over 1,500 people in 20 countries and killed 26 people. The PRI made impressive gains by winning 241 seats in elections for the Chamber of Deputies, and became the leading political party in the coalition government.

2010 Amid an upsurge in drug-related gang violence gubernatorial and mayoral elections were held in 14 out of the 31 states of Mexico. The PRI won the majority of states in contention.
2011 In January the governorship election in Guerrero was won by Angel Aguirre of the left wing Partido de la Revolución Democrática (PRD (Democratic Revolutionary Party); Manuel Añorve of the opposition PRI was runner-up. Thousands of demonstrators joined marches in over 20 cities around the country in April to protest against drug related violence since President Calderón began deploying the army to fight the cartels in 2006. The PRI retained the governorship of Mexico State in the July election. General elections were set for 2012. A drought, the worst since the 1930s, left lakes and reservoirs low by the end of 2011. Agricultural output was affected as communities and farms became dangerously low on water, with the risk of food insecurity for many of the most vulnerable in Mexico. In a speech in December, President Calderón declared that organised crime posed an 'open threat' to Mexico's democracy, as drug gangs were attempting to manipulate political elections, with reports of intimidation of voters and candidates by armed thugs.
2012 On 1 May parliament unanimously voted approval for the provision of compensation for victims of organised crime. A new national body will record crimes such as kidnapping and forced disappearances and oversee the legal, medical and financial support of the victims and families. Since 2006 an estimated 50,000 people have died from drug-related organised crime. Presidential and parliamentary elections took place on 1 July. Enrique Peña Neito (PRI) was declared the winner although Andrés Manuel López Obrador (PRD) his closest rival did not concede defeat. On 3 July, Lopez Obrador challenged the early results saying the voting had been 'plagued by irregularities'. Results of the presidential election were finally released on 13 July following a recount in around two-thirds of all polling stations. Enrique Peña Neito (PRI) won 39.1 per cent of the vote, Andrés Manuel López Obrador (PRD) won 32.43 per cent. In September, the results of the Chamber of Deputies (Camara de Diputados) election showed that the PRI had won 207 seats (out of 500), PAN 114 and PRD 100. In the Senate (Camara de Senadores) PRI won 52 seats (out of 128), PAN 38 and PRD 22. On 1 November, a new 25km metro line was opened linking Tlahuag (a semi-rural terminal) to Mexico City. The US$1.8 billion Line 12 (Golden line) interchanges with four other metro lines. Enrique Peña Nieto was inaugurated as president on 1 December, with a promise to boost the economy and deal with drug related violence.
2013 Congress passed a bill aimed at making the telecommunications industry more competitive on 30 April. The reform is expected to challenge America Movil company (owned by Carlos Slim, said to be the world's richest man), which controls two-thirds of the phone market. On 15 July the government reported that Miguel Angel Trevino Morales, head of the brutal Zetas drug cartel, had been captured. In August President Nieto put forward proposals for reforms to the oil industry, opening up the sector to private investment. Pemex can no longer fund the exploration and development needed to maintain current levels of production and it is hoped that the reforms would attract both domestic and foreign investment.
2014 In July President Nieto successfully negotiated legislation ending Pemex's monopoly of the oil and gas industry. In September the president revealed the buget for a new airport for Mexico City.
2015 Elections to the Chamber of Deputies were held on 7 June. The ruling Partido Revolucionario Institucional (PRI) (Institutional Revolutionary Party) won 29.18 per cent and 203 seats (out of 500), Partido Acción Nacional (PAN) (National Action Party) 21.01 per cent and 108 seats were second.

Political structure

Constitution

The political system established by the 1917 constitution emphasises presidential power.
Mexico is a federal republic of 31 states and one federal district (Mexico City). States are divided into municipalities. State governors are directly elected every six years. Deputies of state legislatures hold office for three years. The states are empowered to raise taxes and introduce and enforce state laws.
In order to register for federal elections, political parties must have a total of at least 65,000 party members and must have 3,000 supporters per state in at least 16 states or 300 party members per constituency in at least half of the constituencies which return deputies elected by majority vote. Alternatively, a party may be allowed conditional registration if it has been active for four years. This conditional registration can be converted to official registration if the party then obtains at least 1.5 per cent of the vote. In 1989, a law was adopted giving a party obtaining 35 per cent of the vote in a general election an absolute majority in the chamber of deputies.

Form of state

Federal presidential democratic republic

The executive

The president is directly elected by majority vote for a period of six years and takes office on 1 December of the election year, but is unable to stand for a second term. The president is assisted by a cabinet (usually 19 members), one of whom is the governor of the Federal District (the administrative area which includes the capital, Mexico City), the attorney general for the country as a whole and the attorney general for the Federal District. The cabinet is appointed by the president.
The president also appoints the judges of the supreme court and higher courts of justice, the senior officers of the armed forces and diplomats, but these appointments are subject to approval by the Senate.

National legislature

The Congreso de la Union (Congress (of the Union)) is a bicameral legislature comprising the Cámara de Diputados (Chamber of Deputies) and the Senado de la República (Senate). Membership of the Chamber of Deputies is per 200,000 citizens and in 2009 there were 500 *diputado federal* (federal deputies), of which 300 are directly elected in single-seat districts. The remainder are elected by proportional representation from party lists and not tied to districts. All members of the Chamber of Deputies are elected for only one three-year term.
The Senate (upper chamber) has 128 members. Each state (31) and the federal district elects senators by relative majority (64 in number) based on a winning vote; an additional 32 senators are elected as runners up in the vote and a further 32 seats are divided among the parties in proportion to their share of the national vote. All members of the Senate are elected for only one six-year term.
In 2013 the Pacto por México (Pact for Mexico) set out a number of electoral reforms, including shortening the length of time between the election of a president (July) and the inauguration (December) to an inauguration date of 15 September. A bill sent to Congress by then President Felipe Calderón in 2009 which would reduce the number of members of both chambers had still not been passed by 2013.

Legal system

Under the 1917 constitution, the judiciary is independent of the executive and legislative bodies, but in practice the judiciary tends not to oppose the president.
The judicial system is divided into federal and state judiciaries.
The federal system has both ordinary and constitutional jurisdiction. It consists of the 21-member supreme court (which deals

with penal, administrative, civil and labour cases), collegiate circuit courts (cases regarding an individual's constitutional rights) and unitary circuit courts (appeals). There are 12 collegiate circuits and nine unitary circuits. There are 68 district courts.

Last elections

1 July 2012 (senate and presidential) and 7 June 2015 (chamber of deputies)

Results: Chamber of Deputies: Partido Revolucionario Institucional (PRI) (Institutional Revolutionary Party) won 29.18 per cent and 203 seats (out of 500), Partido Acción Nacional (PAN) (National Action Party) 21.01 per cent and 108 seats, Partido de la Revolución Democrática (PRD) (Party of the Democratic Revolution) won 10.87 per cent and 56 seats, Movimiento Regeneración Nacional (MORENA) (National Regeneration Movement) 8.39 per cent and 35 seats, Partido Verde Ecologista de México (PVEM) (Ecological Green Party of Mexico) 6.91 per cent and 47 seats, Movimiento Ciudadano (MC) (Citizens' Movement) 6.09 and 26 seats, Partido Nueva Alianza (PNA) (New Alliance Party) 3.72 per cent and 9 seats, Partido Encuentro Social (PES) (Social Encounter Party) 3.32 per cent and 8 seats, Partido del Trabajo (PT) (Labour Party) 2.84 per cent and 6 seats. Independent won the last remaining seat.
Senate (2012): PRI 57 seats (out of 128) PAN 38, PRD 23, PVEM four, PT four, PNA two, MC one. Turnout was 62.3 per cent.
Presidential: Enrique Peña Neito (PRI) won 39.1 per cent of the vote, Andrés Manuel López Obrador (PRD) 32.43 per cent, Josefina Vázquez Mota (PAN) 26.04 per cent, Gabriel Quadri de la Torre (Partido Neuva Alianza (PNA) (New Alliance Party)) 2.36 per cent. Turnout was 63.1 per cent.

Next elections

2018 (presidential and parliamentary)

Political parties

Ruling party

Three party coalition led by Partido Revolucionario Institucional (PRI). Other parties are Partido Verde Ecologista de México (PVEM) and Partido Nueva Alianza (PNA) (from 7 June 2015)

Main opposition party

Partido Acción Nacional (PAN)

About 35 per cent of the total population is under 15 years of age.

Population

118.40 million (2013) (112,336,538; 2010, census figure)

Last census: 12 June 2010: 112,336,538

Population density: 51 inhabitants per square km (2000). Urban population 78 per cent (2010 Unicef).

Annual growth rate: 1.5 per cent, 1990–2010 (Unicef).

Internally Displaced Persons (IDP)

10,000–12,000 (UNHCR 2004)

Ethnic make-up

Mestizo (mixed Indian-European) (55 per cent), Amerindian (29 per cent), European origin (16 per cent).

Religions

Roman Catholic (89 per cent), Protestant (6 per cent).

Education

Compulsory education is provided free of charge. Primary schooling lasts for six years; secondary education (which begins at age 12), is divided into two cycles of three years. Students either follow an academic or technical programme of education, which can lead on to higher education or specialised training.
In 1985, the government reorganised state education with priority given to literacy. A high proportion of spending has traditionally gone into higher education, with much of this devoted to adult literacy. While higher education has received relatively strong funding, the school system suffers from low teachers' pay, a consequent lack of teacher motivation and poor equipment. There is a high student drop-out rate from schools. Legal restrictions on religious education have reduced the willingness of the Catholic Church to provide education on a fee-paying basis. However, the falling birth rate has relieved some pressure on the school system. The student-teacher ratio, which reached a high point of 35.67 in 1964, improved during the 1980s and 1990s and was 27 by 2002.
At university level the private sector is active, although most Mexicans still attend state universities where fees are low. Standards are variable but often good. However, only a minority of students attending university complete their studies.

Literacy rate: 91 per cent adult rate; 97 per cent youth rate (15–24) (Unesco 2005).

Compulsory years: Six to 16

Enrolment rate: 106 per cent gross primary enrolment of relevant age group (including repeaters); 64 per cent gross secondary enrolment; 16 per cent in tertiary education (World Bank).

Pupils per teacher: 27 in primary schools (World Bank)

Health

Access to clean drinking water is available to over 80 per cent of the population. About half of the hospitals belong to the Instituto Mexicano del Seguro Social (IMSS) (Mexican Institute for Social Security).

HIV/Aids

HIV prevalence: 0.3 per cent aged 15–49 in 2003 (World Bank)

Life expectancy: 74 years, 2004 (WHO 2006)

Fertility rate/Maternal mortality rate: 2.3 births per woman, 2010 (Unicef)

Child (under 5 years) mortality rate (per 1,000): 16 per 1,000 live births (WHO 2012); about 7.5 per cent of children aged under five are malnourished (World Bank).

Welfare

Social welfare is administered primarily by the IMSS and financed by contributions from employees, employers and the government. Some institutions, such as Petróleos Mexicanos (Pemex) (Mexican Petroleum), the military and the Federal Electricity Commission, have their own systems. About half of the working population is covered by social security. There is no unemployment benefit.
Since 1997, Mexicans have been able to sign up with private pension fund administrators, bypassing the IMSS, notorious for its inefficiencies as a state operator. The previous government led by the Partido Revolucionario Institucional (PRI) (Institutional Revolutionary Party) transferred the pension system from a state-funded pay-as-you-go basis to a scheme where private fund administrators compete for workers' pension contributions.

Main cities

Mexico City (capital, estimated population 8.4 million in 2012, 2,240 metres above sea-level), Ecatepec (1.7m), Puebla (1.5m), Guadalajara (1.5m), Ciudad Juárez (1.4m), Tijuana (1.3m), León (1.3m), Zapopan (1.2m), Monterrey (1.1m), Nezahualcóyotl (1.1m).

Languages spoken

Native American languages spoken include Náhuati, Maya and Zapoteco. Some English is spoken in business centres.

Official language/s

Spanish

Media

The French-based Reporters Without Borders stated in 2008 that Mexico was the worst country in the Americas for violence against journalists reporting on organised crime. The authorities and the judiciary were considered hostile and unsupportive.

Press

With a population of over 100 million people the daily readership of newspapers is only around three million, which reviewers have ascribed to the politically biased nature of the press.

Dailies: In Spanish, the most influential newspapers include *Reforma* (www.reforma.com), *Excélsior* (www.exonline.com.mx), *La Jornada* (www.jornada.unam.mx) and *Diario de México* (www.diariodemexico.com.mx). The Organización Editortial Mexicana (www.oem.com.mx) publishes many newspapers throughout the country including *El Sol de Mexico*, *La Prensa* and one of the mass circulation newspapers on sport *Ovaciones*.

Weeklies: In Spanish, *Milenio* (www.milenio.com), *Proceso* (www.proceso.com.mx) and *Transición* (www.grupotransicion.com.mx) are influential political and analytical magazines. Other general interest magazines include *Siemprele* (www.siempre.com.mx) and *Vértigo* (www.revistavertigo.com).

In English, *Baja Times* (www.bajatimes.com), *Guadalajara Reporter* (http://guadalajarareporter.com), *Gringo Gazette* (www.gringogazettenorth.com) published in northern Mexico and from Mexico City *The News* (www.thenewsmexico.com).

Business: There are several publications available, which although carry a majority of business and financial news also cover more tabloid stories, including, in Spanish *El Economista* (http://eleconomista.com.mx), *Mundo Ejecutivo* (http://ejecutivo.mundoejecutivo.com.mx), *Expansion* (www.cnnexpansion.com), *Siglo 21* (www.siglo21.com.mx), *El Financiero* (www.elfinanciero.com.mx) and *Biz News* (www.biznews.com.mx) of North Mexico.

Periodicals: In Spanish, *Etcétera* (www.etcetera.com.mx) is a current affairs magazine.

Broadcasting

The huge, multinational, media group, Televisa (www.televisa.com.mx) was the first Latin American oligopoly producing Spanish language programmes for transmission worldwide. Since the introduction of modern media technology from satellite, internet and digital platforms Televisa's dominant hold has been broken.

Radio: There are well over 1,200 local radio stations, of which many are operated by the 35 regional networks in operation.

Grupo Radio Centro (http://radiocentro.com.mx) is one of the largest networks, broadcasting from Mexico City; Grupo ACIR (www.grupoacir.com.mx) is another, as is W Radio (www.wradio.com.mx) operated by the Televisa Group. Instituto Mexicano de la Radio (IMER) (www.imer.com.mx) is the state-run radio station, with an external service via short-wave.

Television: The popularity of watching television has become a leading pastime. There are over 400 television stations with a complex structure of interaction between regulators and TV providers, which critics have said has disadvantaged the interests of the masses.

Televisa (www.televisa.com.mx) a national network, with many affiliates, has the highest ratings. TV Azteca (www.tvazteca.com) is the seconded rated TV network. Public TV includes Once TV (http://oncetv-ipn.ne) is an educational channel and Televisión Metropolitana (Canal 22) (www.canal22.org.mx) is a cultural network.

Digital broadcasting began in 2004 and analogue television is expected to be closed down in 2022. Most TV stations broadcast via satellite providing hundreds of channels from which to choose.

National news agency: NTMX (Notimex)

Other news agencies: El Universal (in Spanish): www.agenciaeluniversal.com.mx Agencia Mexicana de Noticias (in Spanish): www.agenciamn.com

Economy

Mexico's economy is a diverse mixture of modern hi-tech, it has an interdependent manufacturing base that relies on trade with the US, and subsistence agriculture that is not part of the formal economy. Exports are the mainstay of the economy providing 32.7 per cent of GDP in 2014 with over 80 per cent of all commodities exported to the US. In return Mexico derives around 40 per cent of all foreign direct investment (FDI) from the US; total FDI reached a record of US$44.6 billion in 2013 before dropping to US$22.8 billion in 2014. The downturn in the US economy impacted Mexico in two ways – firstly, the US reduced its imports, and secondly, because 10 per cent of the population lives and works abroad, mostly in the US, remittances were low. Remittances from migrant workers, an important factor in Mexico's GDP, amounted to US$21.9 billion (1.8 per cent of GDP) in 2013, increasing by 7.8 per cent to US$23.6 billion in 2014.

As a member of the North American Free Trade Agreement (Nafta), Mexico's manufacturing base serves not only its large domestic market but also the huge US market and the Canadian market. A large number of the world's major companies are present in Mexico, using the cheaper labour market for manufacturing-based industries, driven by the initial growth of the *maquiladoras* (in-bond assembly lines) and the development of import-export business, particularly in the car and light manufacturing industries. Asian electronics companies, for instance, proliferate in the west coast state of Baja California, which is host to a multitude of operations run by companies based in the Far East.

Ironically the increase in Chinese exports directed to the US has begun to have an adverse effect on Mexican exports.

Due to the global economic crisis, Mexico dropped into a harsh recession in 2009 of -6.3 per cent. However, thanks to expanding world trade the economy rebounded to strong growth of 5.1 per cent in 2010. This was largely maintained until 2013 when growth slowed down to 1.4 per cent before increasing slightly to 2.1 per cent in 2014.

Although the economy is expected to experience stronger growth in 2015 as a result of increased investment and stronger demand for Mexican exports, growth is predicted to remain below potential for reasons of inefficiencies, with a large portion of the economy and workforce in the informal sector, and corruption. The aggregate Mexican drug industry is estimated to generate between US$6.6 billion to over US$30 billion annually through trafficking of cocaine, marijuana, heroin and crystal meth into North America. The enormous profits made by trafficking illegal drugs into North America is not exploited by the Mexican government and they are simply bypassed as what could constitute a major part of the economy. Furthermore, the amount of government money spent on damage limitation from the violence and crime that comes with illegal drug trafficking (drug cartels) is extortionate and it is largely wasted. Due to the seemingly limitless power that drug cartels have over the Mexican government, they have cemented their position in Mexican politics by investing approximately US$500 million per year in bribery and the capturing of substantial elements of the state apparatus. Mexico, like Colombia, is a narco-state and there seems to be no sign of significant change. While there is demand in North America, there will be supply.

Economic reforms were undertaken by the Partido Acción Nacional (PAN) government in 2010 to reduce external public debt. Unemployment in the formal sector had remained fairly constant at around 3.5 per cent since 2004, but as the recession struck unemployment rose to 4 per cent in 2008 and higher to 5.5 per cent in 2009 and then 5.4 in 2010. Unemployment fell to around 4 per cent in 2014.

Proven oil reserves were 11.1 billion barrels at the end of 2014, however without new oil finds, production is falling – production fell by 3.3 per cent in 2014 to 2.78 million barrels per day (bpd). Proven natural gas reserves were 300 billion cubic metres (cum) at the end of 2014, with production of 58.1 billion cum. However, consumption in the same period was 85.8

billion cum with the shortfall made up by imports.

External trade

Mexico is a member of the North American Free Trade Agreement (Nafta), with the United States and Canada. Mexico has also signed free trade agreements with the European Union, the Central American Free Trade Agreement (DR-Cafta) and Japan.

The economy is heavily dependent on trade, and foreign trade accounts for around 32.7 per cent of GDP, of which over 80 per cent is carried out with the US. There are free economic zones, *maquiladoras*, where semi-manufactured and duty-free goods are assembled and shipped directly to the US. A leading *maquiladoras* product was finished garments but heavy competition from Asian manufacturers has resulted in a drop in production since 2005.

Mexico is a leading world exporter of many minerals and agricultural products as well as petroleum and natural gas.

Imports

Principal imports are metalworking machines, steel mill products, agricultural machinery, electrical equipment, capital machinery for car assembly and aircraft building and parts.

Main sources: US (48.8 per cent of total in 2014), China (16.6 per cent), Japan (4.4 per cent)

Exports

Principal exports are manufactured foods, oil and oil products, silver, fruits, vegetables, coffee and cotton.

Main destinations: US (80.2 per cent of total in 2014), Canada (2.7 per cent), China (1.5 per cent)

Agriculture

Farming

Approximately 3.5 per cent of Mexico's total GDP is attributable to the agricultural sector. Despite this relatively low percentage contribution to GDP, the labour intensive nature of the agricultural sector ensures that it employs around 13 per cent of the total workforce.

Farming is small-scale and frequently inefficient. About 50 per cent of total cultivatable land (estimated at 19 million hectares) is held by *ejidos*, rural communities farming on small individual/collective lots. There are few large commercial farms except in export-oriented vegetable-producing regions of the north-west.

The principal food crops are maize (over 50 per cent of harvested area and 60 per cent of total grain production), sorghum, wheat, rice, barley, potatoes, soya beans and dry beans. The production of basic foodstuffs can be severely affected by drought, insufficient irrigation (less than 30 per cent of cultivated land is irrigated) and underdeveloped marketing and infrastructural back-up. Supplies of food grain in particular have not kept up with the demands imposed by rapid population growth. Principal export crops are coffee, cotton, fresh fruit, honey, sugar, tobacco and tomatoes. Exports of cattle are also important.

Mexico's membership of the North American Free Trade Agreement (Nafta) has affected the farming sector, with the US dominating trade.

A drought, the worst since the 1930s, left lakes and reservoirs low by the end of 2011. Agricultural output was affected as communities and farms became dangerously low on water, with the risk of food insecurity for many of the most vulnerable in Mexico. In 2015 the drought was still affecting large parts of Mexico and was estimated to have cut agricultural production by 40 per cent since 2011.

Fishing

Mexico's level of fish production is relatively high, with demand being met almost entirely by domestic production. Imports represent less than 10 per cent of total seafood consumption.

Shrimps, tuna, mackerel, bass, perch, bonito, shark, and oysters have risen in importance in the Mexican fishing sector. The leading fish producing states Sinaloa, Sonora, Baja California, Veracruz and Baja California Sur contribute to approximately 65.2 per cent of the country's total catch. Annually 70 per cent of the total catch comes from the Pacific Ocean compared to 30 per cent from the Gulf of Mexico, Caribbean and non-coastal states.

Forestry

Approximately a third of Mexico's total landmass is covered by forests and the country is endowed with vast resources of soft and hard woods. Around 4 per cent of the country's total forested area is protected.

Most forestry products are produced for domestic consumption, mainly softwood, sawnwood and wood-based panels.

Industry and manufacturing

The industrial sector accounted for 34.8 per cent of GDP in 2014 and employed just over 20 per cent of the workforce; it accounts for a growing proportion of exports. Mexico's manufacturing sector has continued to grow even when other major Latin American economy's manufacturing sectors have been slumping. This is largely due to Mexico's integration and dependence on the US market.

Most public sector firms are in strategic industries such as base metal manufacture, construction materials, paper and paper products, chemicals and petrochemicals, textiles and apparel, food processing, beverages, motor vehicles, domestic electrical appliances, machinery and equipment.

The *maquiladoras* (in-bond manufacturers) make, assemble or process components and raw materials brought in 'in-bond' from the US, and then re-export them duty-free. The growing importance of *maquiladora* exports to the US has made the Mexican economy more exposed to US volatility.

The weak peso is making the already attractive labour market of Mexico more enticing to US and other foreign companies, the automotive sector, in particular is booming. On 30 March 2012, Ford Motor Company (of the US) announced that it would be investing US$1.3 billion in a new production plant in Hermosillo, creating around 1,000 jobs. The new assembly line should meet the growing demand for the Ford Fusion (hybrid car) and Lincoln MKZ (luxury car) models. German automotive company BMW announced in July 2014 it would be investing US$1 billion in a plant in San Luis Potoso, one that will provide employment to 1,500 workers and with a capacity of 150,000 units per year. In April 2015, the tire and rubber company, Goodyear announced it would be investing US$550 million in a new plant in Central Mexico.

Tourism

Mexico was the home of two pre-European civilisations, as well as being one of the first European settlements in the Americas. As a result there is a wealth of archaeological and historic sites included on Unesco's World Heritage List. Mexico is also a top destination for visitors from South and North America who wish to enjoy beach resort holidays, particularly Mexico's premier resort of Cancun.

The introduction of niche marketing has had a threefold advantage of spreading the development of tourist facilities, extending the season of tourists visiting and providing greater value-added holidays. The specific recommendations include ecotourism (sightseeing, marine life and wildlife), culture (cuisine and wines, carnivals and history) and others, such as sports, family holidays and wedding venues.

There were 29.0 million visitors in 2014 (a growth of 20.5 per cent on 2013), making it the second largest travel destination in the Americas.

Travel and tourism contributed an average 14.4 per cent of GDP over 2006–09, falling to 13 per cent in 2010 as the effects of the global economic recession impacted on tourism but recovered to 14.8 per cent by 2014. Employment in the industry matched the downturn with an average 16.9 per cent (7.36 million jobs) of total employment (2006–09) falling to 14.2 per cent (6.53 million jobs) in 2010 and 13.7 per cent (6.35 million) in 2011, before increasing to 15.7 per cent of total employment (7,857,000 jobs) in 2014.

Environment

In November 2007, the worst flooding in recorded history struck in the southern state of Tabasco affecting more that two million people and trapping around 300,000 in their homes. With 70 per cent of the state underwater it was estimated that the entire state's crop production was lost. Dozen of people were killed in neighbouring Chiapas State where the rain caused mud slides and buried a village. When foreign aid began to arrive distribution was found to be particularly difficult as the roads were unusable.

Mining

Mining is an important industry in Mexico and the country is a major producer of gold, silver and base metals. Mexico accounts for approximately 17 per cent of total world production of silver, 38 per cent of celestite production and 29 per cent of bismuth production. The mining sector continues to attract significant foreign investment, the vast majority of which comes from the US and Canada.

There are four major domestic producers: Industrias Peñoles, Grupo Industrial Menera Mexico, Empresas Frisco and Luismin. The main mining states are Sonora, Coahuila, Zacatecas, Chihuahua, Baja California Sur, San Luis Potosí, Durango and Guanajuato.

Mexico gold mining companies are plagued by robberies and kidnappings directed at their refineries. In April 2015, McEwan Mining Inc. became the third victim of the year when armed robbers looted approximately US$8.4 million worth of gold. This incident happened a month after another gold mining company, Goldcorp Inc., had four employees go missing, only one of whom survived.

Hydrocarbons

Proven oil reserves were 11.1 billion barrels in 2014, with production at 2.78 million barrels per day (bpd). Mexico is a significant oil producer and the oil sector is vital to the country's economy, providing around 40 per cent of government revenue. However, production is slowly declining with production in 2014 falling by 3.3 per cent form the 2013 figure. Without new sources of oil, not only will the economy be adversely affected but Mexico will become a net importer of oil by 2020.

The state-owned Petróleos Mexicanos (Pemex) is one of the world's largest multinational oil corporations. It has exclusive rights to oil exploration and production and is the sole supplier of petroleum products in Mexico. The majority of oil exports are taken by the US, supplied either by pipeline or tanker.

Although Mexico is not a member of the Organisation of the Petroleum Exporting Countries (Opec), government policy has often been to cut production in line with OPEC targets in an effort to increase world prices.

Mexico has the eleventh-largest refining capacity in the world, which has improved the country's export potential, with six refineries and a total capacity of 1.6 million bpd in 2014. Despite government plans to increase refinery capacity by 350,000bpd, hurricane damage has led to unscheduled shut-downs and static annual capacity.

In February 2012, the US and Mexico signed an agreement to co-operate on developing the deep-water oil and gas fields that straddle their mutual border in the Gulf of Mexico.

In August 2013 President Nieto put forward proposals for reforms to the oil industry, opening up the sector to private investment. Pemex can no longer fund the exploration and development needed to maintain current levels of production and it is hoped that the reforms will attract both domestic and foreign investment.

In June 2015, Pemex announced its discovery of four oil fields in the southern Gulf of Mexico. The fields could have up to 350 million barrels of oil between them, and it is estimated that they could produce 200,000 bpd by 2018.

Proven gas reserves were 300 billion cubic metres (cum) in 2014, with production at 58.1 billion cum. However, consumption was 85.8 billion cum and Mexico had to import the difference, either by natural gas pipelines from Canada and the US or by liquefied natural gas (LNG) from Egypt, Trinidad and Tobago or Nigeria of which it imported 7.8 billion cum in 2013.

Most gas production is associated with oil extraction. Although Pemex dominates the upstream gas industry, the downstream sector has undergone liberalisation which has allowed private companies to participate in gas transportation, storage and distribution. There are two LNG re-gasification plants in operation with another under construction and more, smaller facilities planned. In June 2011, TransCanada Corporation completed the Guadalajara Pipeline, to carry up to 14.2 million cubic metres of natural gas 310 kilometres from the LNG regasification terminal near Manzanillo (Colima State) to the city of Guadalajara (Jalisco State). The gas is used primarily to run a series of gas-fired electricity generators in the city.

On 22nd June 2015, Mexico's Federal Electricity Commission (ECF) announced it would be going ahead with 24 new energy infrastructure projects totalling US$10 billion, including a US$3 billion underwater pipeline bringing US natural gas from Texas to Tuxpan, Veracruz.

Mexico had proven coal reserves of 1.21 billion tonnes at the end of 2014, mostly located in Coahuila in the north-east. Over 850 million tonnes are made up of anthracite, mainly used for steel production, with around 350 million tonnes in electricity generation.

Energy

Total installed generating capacity was 53.5 gigawatts in 2013, generating 296 billion kilowatt hours (kWh). Around 80 per cent of total electricity generated comes from conventional thermal sources, in particular from natural gas, with coal providing 11.5 per cent; hydropower accounts for around 10 per cent, while fuel oil and diesel have fallen in use. Alternative sources of energy, such as wind, solar and biomass, make up the remainder.

Independent power producers (IPPs) have become a major source of investment in the Mexican electricity sector.

Mexico exports electricity to the US and is a participant of the Sistema de Interconexion Electrica para America Central (Siepac) to connect power grids with Guatemala and Belize and an integrated Central American electric power market.

Financial markets

Stock exchange

Bolsa Mexicana de Valores (BMV) (Mexico Stock Exchange)

Commodity exchange

Mercado Mexicano de Derivados (Mexican Derivatives Exchange) (MexDer)

Banking and insurance

Mexico's banking and financial services sector is now well established, following privatisation in 1990. The sector had previously been nationalised in 1982. There are three main types of account held in Mexican banks; peso denominated checking accounts, US dollar checking accounts and certificates of deposit

Banco de México issues currency, controls monetary policy and is responsible for exchange rates and national reserves. Participation of the private sector is encouraged in a capital market involving leasing, mutual funds, insurance and brokerage. The banking crisis of 1995 caused by the turmoil of peso devaluation, resulted in the closure of several banks. The government was forced to inject huge amounts of emergency capital into the system. Mexico had 44 banks, 13 of which were government-owned.

Banamex is the country's largest bank, and comprises the operations of Citigroup and Banacci, which merged in August 2001.

Central bank

Banco de México

Main financial centre

Mexico City

Time

Central Mexico: GMT minus six hours (daylight saving, minus five hours)
Northern Mexico: GMT minus seven hours (daylight saving, minus six hours)
Sonora State: GMT minus seven hours (no daylight saving)
Baja State: GMT minus eight hours (daylight saving minus seven hours)

Geography

Mexico has a northern frontier of 2,400km with the US and a southern frontier of 885km with Guatemala and Belize. It has a coastline of 2,780km on the Gulf of Mexico and the Caribbean and of 7,360km on the Pacific and the Gulf of California.

Mexico comprises a great variety of terrain, ranging from swamp to desert, from tropical lowland jungle to high alpine vegetation and from thin, arid soils to others so rich that they can support three crops a year. More than half the country is at an altitude of over 1,000 metres and much is over 2,000 metres.

The centre is flanked by an eastern and a western range of mountains running roughly parallel to the coasts. The northern part of the plateau is low, arid and thinly populated. The southern section of the central plateau is crossed by a volcanic range of mountains. The mountainous southern end of the plateau, the heart of Mexico, has ample rainfall and although comprising only 14 per cent of the land, it holds nearly half the country's population. Mexico City lies in a small high basin measuring 50 square km.

Hemisphere

Northern

Climate

Varies with altitude. Tropical southern region and coastlands are hot and wet, while the highlands of the central plateau are temperate. Temperature in Mexico City ranges from 5–25 degrees Celsius (C) with occasional sharp frosts in winter (December–February).

Climate and vegetation depend on altitude. The *tierra caliente* (hot area) takes in the coastal and plateau lands below 750 metres. The *tierra fria* (cold zone) is from 2,000 metres upwards. The climate of the inland highlands is mostly mild, but with sharp changes of temperature between day and night, sunshine and shade.

Generally, winter is the dry season and summer the wet season. There are only two areas where sufficient rain falls all year round. The first lies south of Tampico, the capital of Tamaulipas state, along the lower slopes of the Sierra Madre Oriental and across the isthmus of Tehuantepec into Tabasco state, and the second along the Pacific coast state of Chiapas. The two areas represent about 12 per cent of the total surface area. Apart from these favoured regions, the rest of Mexico is arid.

Dress codes

People generally dress smartly in Mexico City. Shorts are worn only at holiday resorts. Dress codes for business and leisure are usually the same as those of Europe. There is little central heating and moderately warm clothing is needed in the winter, particularly at night. The capital, Mexico City, is 2,240 metres above sea level. At lower altitudes temperatures can be very high and lightweight clothing is essential.

Entry requirements

Requirements for Mexico are complex and comprehensive guidance should be obtained from consular sections of local embassies before departure, any infringement of regulations can result in fines and expulsion.

Passports

Required for all.

Visa

The regulations for entry into Mexico are complex and visitors are advised to confirm all aspects of visa requirements before travelling. Visas are not required by those using a tourist card, which are issued only to tourists and are valid for 30 days. All other visitors require visas. Business visas are divided into two, 'lucrative' and 'non-lucrative', and applications must be accompanied by a business letter of accreditation stating the nature of business, proof of sufficient funds for length of stay and a full itinerary, plus an invitation from a local company. See www.inm.gov.mx and follow the links, in English, to *I would like to visit Mexico* for full details, or www.mexonline.com for more general information.

Currency advice/regulations

The import and export of local currency is unrestricted up to the equivalent amount of US$10,000; amounts greater than this must be declared. The import of foreign currency is unlimited but must be declared as export is limited to the amount declared on arrival. The export of gold coins is prohibited.

Many establishments in cities or tourist areas accept payment in US dollars.

Travellers cheques in US dollars are readily accepted in most banks, hotels and commercial outlets.

Customs

There are sometimes rigorous searches for drugs, firearms or large sums of currency, and expensive jewellery or electronic equipment may attract attention and demands for customs duty. There are restrictions on the import of motor vehicles.

Prohibited imports

Fresh meat, particularly pork, fish, fruit, vegetables, flowers and seeds are prohibited unless a permit is obtained before travelling. Firearms and ammunition require an import licence.

Archaeological artifacts may not be exported.

Health (for visitors)

Mandatory precautions

A yellow fever vaccination certificate is required if arriving from an infected area.

Advisable precautions

Diphtheria, tuberculosis, hepatitis A and B, typhoid, tetanus and polio vaccinations. Malaria risk exists in some rural areas – prophylaxis recommended. There is a rabies risk. Dengue fever is endemic in northern regions.

Bottled water and water supplied from taps marked 'drinking/sterilised water' in hotels can be drunk without precautions. All other water should be regarded as potentially contaminated.

Mexico City is at 2.250 metres (7,400ft), and visitors may take some time to acclimatise to the altitude. The levels of pollution in Mexico City are extremely high and cab be a health threat.

Health insurance is advised. Medical facilities are good and pharmacies are permitted to diagnose and treat minor ailments.

Hotels

There are six classified types of hotels, of five stars and an additional *Gran Turismo*, with maximum rates set by the government.

Mexico City is one of the biggest cities in the world, so location is very important. The main hotels are in the business, financial and commercial area along Reforma Avenue. It is advisable to book in advance expecially during the high season and to confirm the booking in writing. There is a levy of 15 per cent VAT and 2 per cent accommodation tax added to bills – unless the visitor is from overseas travelling for meetings and conventions and fairs, who have confirmed their migatory status, use a credit card and make their arrangements through the event's organisers then VAT is exempt. Tipping is usually 10 per cent.

Credit cards
Visa and Mastercard are readily accepted, however there is a government tax of 6 per cent on transaction. ATMs are widely available.

Public holidays (national)
Fixed dates

1 Jan (New Year's Day), 5 Feb (Constitution Day), 21 Mar (Birthday of Benito Juárez), 1 May (Primero de Mayo), 5 May (Battle of Puebla Day), 1 June (Navy Day), 20 Nov (Revolution Day), 25 Dec (Christmas Day).

Religious holidays are celebrated by adherents.

Variable dates

Carnival (Jan/Feb, five days)

Working hours
Hours of business in Mexico City are variable and hours in other parts of the country vary considerably according to the climate and local custom.

Banking

Mon–Fri: 0900–1600; larger branches in Mexico city may opened Mon–Fri: 0800–1900; Sat 0800–1200. Small town branches may only open Mon–Fri 0800–1330.

Business

Mon–Fri: 0800–1800; lunch is taken anywhere between 1300–1500, for up to two hours.

Government

Mon–Fri: 0800–1500.

Shops

Mon–Sat: 1000–1800/1900.

Telecommunications
Mobile/cell phones

GSM 900 and 1900 services are available in highly populated areas only.

Electricity supply
120V AC, 60 cycles. Two-pin flat plugs (as in USA) are used.

Social customs/useful tips
During the working day moderate punctuality is appreciated although some lateness is tolerated. It is acceptable to arrive late for evening social occasions which often continue well into the night.

Mexicans are patient, courteous and hospitable and will often treat visiting foreigners with polite reserve. An effort to speak Spanish is much appreciated. Otherwise it is advisable not to presume too much until you know the people concerned fairly well.

Tipping in hotels, restaurants and bars is expected since service charges are not added to the bill. A normal tip is 15 per cent. If service has been very good, 20 per cent should be given.

Security
It is unwise to carry large sums of money or valuables in Mexico City, where the number of assaults is rising.

Visitors should be wary of walking through neighbourhood streets during festivities. Many Mexicans own guns and they tend to fire them in the air to celebrate, especially towards evening.

Armed robbery in urban areas is a risk. Short-term opportunistic kidnapping is common. Visitors should exercise care when using ATMs.

Getting there
Air

National airline: Aeroméxico (AM) and Mexicana (MX)

International airport/s: Mexico City-Benito Juárez (MEX), 13km south of city; duty-free shops, restaurants, bank, *bureau de change*, 24-hour refreshments, chemist, tourist information, 24-hour left luggage, post office, first aid (with vaccinations for cholera and yellow fever available) car hire.

A taxi to the city takes about 45 minutes. Prepaid taxi tickets are available from the 'Authorised Taxi Service' booth in baggage reclaim; authorised taxis are white and mustard yellow with an aeroplane logo. Travellers are strongly advised to take an authorised, prepaid taxi and to always lock taxi doors when inside.

Major hotels run shuttle minibuses from the airport. There is also a train and regular airport bus to the city centre.

Other airport/s: Acapulco (ACA) 26km from city; Guadalajara (GDL) 20km from city; Monterrey (MTY) 24km from city. All include restaurant, bank and car hire facilities; and access by taxi and bus.

Airport tax: Approximately US$21, which may be included in the ticket price, transit passengers are exempt.

Surface

Road: There are roads into Mexico from the US, Belize and Guatemala. Drivers should note that permission is required to bring a car into Mexico for longer than 72 hours.

Rail: Connections with Mexico can be made from any city in the US or Canada. All trains are provided with pullman sleepers, restaurant cars and club cars and most are air conditioned.

Water: Regular passenger ships run from the US and South America. There are also riverboat services from Flores and Tikal (Guatemala) to Palenque, Chiapas in Mexico. Enquire locally for further details.

Main port/s: Gulf of Mexico coast: Altamira, Cd del Carmen, Coatzacoalcos, Pto Madero, Tampico, Veracruz; Pacific coast: Acapulco, Ensenada, La Paz, Lázaro Cardenas, Mazatlán, Manzanillo, Puerto Vallarta, Salina Cruz, Santa Rosalia.

Getting about
National transport

Air: There is a comprehensive network of daily scheduled services between main commercial centres.

Road: There are 95,000km of paved roads, about half of which are operated by the federal government, and the other half by the state governments. There are also more than 5,600km of toll roads, which are operated by private companies. Mexico's roads carry more than 85 per cent of the nation's overland freight and almost all intercity passengers.

Buses: There are three kinds, first- and second-class and local. It is advisable to book seats in advance in Baja California. Buses with odd numbers run north-south, while even numbered run east-west. Peribus services circulate Mexico City.

Rail: Rail services include special first-class, regular first-class and second-class. Routes include Guadalajara to Mexico City; Monterrey to Mexico City; Mexico City to Veracruz to Tapachula; Cuidad Juárez to Chihuahua. Services are slower than buses but electrification is in progress. There are sleeper services between Mexico City and Guadalajara, Monterrey, Veracruz, Ciudad Juárez, Chihuahua, Mérida. It is advisable to book well in advance.

Water: There are regular ferries from the mainland at Quaymas in Sonora, to Santa Rosalía in Baja California Sur. There are services to the Caribbean Islands of Isla Mujeres and Cozumel.

City transport

Taxis: Taxis are usually fitted with meters, but these are often not used. Agree fare in advance. No tip is necessary.

Fixed route taxis can be identified by lime-green colour, rank taxis by coral and those with no fixed route by yellow. There are around 17 fixed routes. The number of fingers held out of a taxi window indicates the number of seats left.

Special tourist taxis, *turismo*, have English-speaking drivers.

The safest means of transport is a *taxi de sitio* – dial-a-cab services which charge about double the metered street taxi rates, but which are still cheap by international standards. These can be found outside every hotel.

It is best to carry a map of Mexico City as taxi drivers cannot be relied on to know their way around the huge city.

Buses, trams & metro: The Mexico City Metro, with eight lines, is excellent, but often crowded. Runs 0500–0000 Mon–Sat; opens 0700 (Sun). Maps are not displayed at all stations, but can be obtained at Insurgentes station.

There is also a small tramway network, and extensive bus and trolley bus services. The latter system has been modernised, and also has a flat fare. There is a state-run bus and trolley bus service in Guadalajara, with trolley buses running in tunnels, and also extensive private bus services.
The Monterrey City metro system (called *Metrorrey*) has two lines with 25 stations, with more under construction, which runs from Sun–Sat: 0500–2400.

Car hire

Car hire is widely available, with or without a driver, but often expensive. A foreign licence is acceptable. Car hire is not recommended for business travellers or tourists because of excessive traffic, aggressive drivers, and counter-pollution measures which mean that on certain days of the week, driving is off limits.

BUSINESS DIRECTORY

The addresses listed below are a selection only. While World of Information makes every endeavour to check these addresses, we cannot guarantee that changes have not been made, especially to telephone numbers and area codes. We would welcome any corrections.

Telephone area codes

The international direct dialling (IDD) code for Mexico is +52, followed by area code and subscriber's number:

Acapulco	744	Mexico City	55
Chihuahua	614	Monterrey	81
Ciudad Juárez	656	Oaxaca	951
Durango	618	Puebla	222
Guardalajara	33	Tampico	833
León	477	Torreón	817
Mérida	999	Veracruz	229

Useful telephone numbers

Police: 060
Fire/ambulance: 078
Highway emergency: 078
Locatel (service to locate missing persons or stolen cars): (55) 5658-1111.
Sectur (24-hour help to tourists in trouble): (55) 5250-0123

Chambers of Commerce

American Chamber of Commerce Mexico, Lucerna 78, Colonia Juarez, 06600 México, DF (tel: 5141-3800; fax: 5703-3908; e-mail: amchammx@amcham.com.mx).

British Chamber of Commerce in Mexico, 30 Río de la Plata, 6500 México, DF (tel: 5256-0901; fax: 5211-5451; e-mail: britchamexico@britchamexico.com).

Chihuahua Cámara Nacional de Comercio, Servicios y Turismo, 1800 Avenida Cuauhtemoc, 31020 Chihuahua (tel: 416-0000; fax: 415-1928; e-mail: cfn@infosel.net.mx).

Confederación de Cámaras Nacionales de Comercio, Servicios y Turismo, 144 Balderas, Colonia Centro, 06079 México, DF (tel/fax: 5722-9300; e-mail: sistemas@concanacored.com).

Guadalajara Cámara Nacional de Comercio, Servicios y Turismo, 4095 Avenida Vallarta, Fraccionamiento Camino Real, 45000 Guadalajara (tel: 3880-9090; fax: 3880-9097; e-mail: direccion@canacogdl.com.mx).

Juarez Cámara Nacional de Comercio, Servicios y Turismo, 4505 Avenida Henry Dunant y Avenida M Diaz, 32315 Ciudad Juarez (tel: 113-707; fax: 112-674; e-mail: canacojr@hotmail.com).

Mexico City Cámara Nacional de Comercio, 42 Paseo de la Reforma, Colonia Centro, 06048 México, DF (tel: 535-2502; fax: 703-2958; e-mail: presidencia1@ccmexico.com.mx).

Puebla Cámara Nacional de Comercio, Servicios y Turismo, 2704 Avenida Reforma, 72160 Puebla (tel: 480-705; fax: 480-800; e-mail: canacopu@axtel.net.mx).

Banking

Banamex, Actuario Robero Medellin 800, Colonia Santa Fé, 01219 México, DF (tel: 1226-2639; tel: 5999-2888).

Bancomer, Montes Urales 620,Colonia Lomas de Chapultepec, 11000 México, DF (tel: 5201-2264; fax: 5238-7790).

Banorte, Periférico Sur 4355, Colonia Jardines en la Montaña, 14210 México, DF (tel: 5169-9300; fax: 5169-9460).

Bital, Paseo de la Reforma 156, Juarez, 06600 México DF (tel: 5721-5715; fax: 5721-3846).

Santander Mexicano, Prolongación Paseo de la Reforma 500, Colonia Lomas de Santa Fé, 01210 México, D F (tel: 5257-8000; fax: 5629-4742).

Scotiabank Inverlat, Manuel Avila Camacho 1, 11009 México, DF (tel: 5229-2053; fax: 5395-9050).

Central bank

Banco de México, Avenida 5 de Mayo 1, Colonia Centro, Delegación Cuauhtémoc, 06059 (tel: 5237-2000; fax: 5237-2070; e-mail: sidaoui@banxico.org.mx).

Stock exchange

Bolsa Mexicana de Valores (BMV) (Mexico Stock Exchange), www.bmv.com.mx

Commodity exchange

Mercado Mexicano de Derivados (Mexican Derivatives Exchange) (MexDer), www.mexder.com

Travel information

Benito Juárez International Airport, Av Capitán Carlos León s/n Col Peñón de los Baños Del Venustiano Carranza, México, DF CP 15620 (tel: 5571-3600; fax: 5726-0107).

Fondo Nacional de Fomento al Turismo (FONATUR) 22nd Floor, Insurgentes Sur 800, Colonia del Valle, 03100 México DF (tel: 5687-0567/8; fax: 5687-5058, 5682-5058; email: ibotas@fonatur.gob.mx; internet: www.fonatur.gob.mx).

Infotour, Zona Rosa, Amberes 54, Mexico City (tel: 5525-9380).

Ministry of tourism

Secretaría de Turismo (SECTUR) Presidente Mazaryck 172, Colonia Polanco, 11570 México DF (tel: 5250-8555; fax: 5250-4406 (general enquiries), 5254-0942 (marketing), email: correspondencia@mexico-travel.com; internet: www.mexico-travel.com).

National tourist organisation offices

Consejo de Promoción Turística de México, Mariano Escobedo 550, 11580 Mexico DF (tel: 5258-1090/2; email: cptmex@infosel.net.mx; internet: www.visitmexico.com).

Ministries

Ministry of Agrarian Reform (SRA), Tepozteco 36, 1er Piso, Col Vertiz Narvarte, 03020 Mexico (tel: 5579-6094; fax: 5579-3767).

Ministry of Agriculture, Rural Development and Livestock (SAGAR), Av Insurgentes Sur 476, 50. piso, Col Roma Sur, 06700 Mexico (tel: 5584-0808; fax: 5584-1177).

Ministry of Communication and Transport (SCT), Xola y Av Universidad, Cuerpo C, PB, Col Narvarte, 03028 Mexico (tel: 5538-5148; fax: 5519-9748).

Ministry of Defence (SEDENA), Blvd Manuel Avila Camacho y Av Industria Militar, Col Lomas de Sotelo, 11600 Mexico (tel: 5395-6766; fax: 5557-1370).

Ministry of Education (SEP), Brasil 31, PB oficina 115, Col Centro, 06029 Mexico (tel: 5329-6827; fax: 5329-6822).

Ministry of Energy (SE), Av Insurgentes Sur 552, 1er. Piso, Col Roma Sur, 06769 Mexico (tel: 5584-4304; fax: 5564-9782).

Ministry of Finance and Public Credit (SHCP), República de El Salvador 47, PA, Col Centro, 06080 Mexico (tel: 5709-6675; fax: 5709-3272).

Ministry of Fishing, Environment and Natural Resources (SEMARNAP), Anillo Periférico Sur 4209, 3er Piso, Col Jardines en la Montaña, 14210 Mexico (tel: 5628-0891; fax: 5628-0780).

Ministry of Foreign Affairs (SRE), Eje Central Lázaro Cardenas 257, ala 'A', 1er Nivel, Col Guerrero, 09600 Mexico (tel: 5782-3660; fax: 5327-3025).

Ministry of Health (SSA), Lieja 8, 50 piso, Col Juárez, 06600 Mexico (tel: 5553-7670; fax: 5286-5497).

Ministry of the Interior (SG), Abraham Gonzalez 48, PB, Col Juárez, 06699, Mexico (tel: 5535-2718; fax: 5535-9952).

Ministry of Labour and Social Welfare (STPS), Periférico Sur 4271, Edificio A, 1er Nivel, Col Fuentes del Pedregal, 14149, Mixico (tel/fax: 5645-3715).

Ministry of Naval Affairs (SM), Eje 2 Oriente 861, Tramo Heroica Escuela Naval Militar, Col Los Cipreses, Coyoacan, 04830 Mexico (tel: 5684-8188; fax: 5679-6411).

Ministry of Social Development (SEDESOL), Av Constituyentes 947-B, PB, Col Belén de las Flores, 01110 Mexico (tel: 5515-4508; fax: 5272-0118).

Ministry of Trade and Industry (SECOFI), Av Alfonso Reyes 30, 20 piso, Col Condesa, 06140 Mexico (tel: 5729-9193; fax: 5729-9314).

Other useful addresses

Asociación Nacional de importadores y Exportadores de la República Mexicana, Monterrey 130, Col Roma Sur, 06700, Mexico, DF (tel: 5564-9379; fax: 5584-5317).

Asociación Nacional para el Fomento de las Exportaciones Mexicanas, Ed de las Instituciones 702, Ocampo 250 Poncente Apartado 64100, Monterrey NL (tel: 5428-010, 422-143, 422-154; fax: 528-207).

Asociación de Personal Técnico para Conferencias Internacionales AC, Universidad 1855-502, Mexico 20, DF (tel: 5550-0170).

British Embassy, Lerma 71, Col. Cuauhtemoc, 06500 Mexico City (207-2569, 207-2089/2149; fax: 5207-2593, 207-7672).

Comptroller General (SECOGEF), Av Insurgentes Sur 1735, PB Ala Norte, Oficina 39, Col Guadalupe Inn, 01020 Mexico (tel: 5662-2762; fax: 5662-4511).

Confederación de Cámaras Industriales de los Estados Unidos Mexicanos, Manuel Maria Contreras 133, 8, Cuauhtemoc, 06597, Mexico DF (tel: 5546-9053; fax: 5535-6871).

Consejo Nacional de Comercio Exterior, Tiaxcala 177 Desp 803, Apartado 06100, Mexico DF (tel: 5286-8744, 286-8798; fax: 5211-8465).

Dirección General de Telecommunicaciones, Lázaro Cárdenas 567 11 Piso Ala Norte, Col Navarate, 03020 Mexico, DF (tel: 5519-4049, 530-3492, 519-0908; fax: 5559-9812).

Instituto de Intérpretes y Traductores SA, Rio Rhin 40, 06500 Mexico 5, DF (tel: 5566-7722, 566-8312).

Instituto Mexicano del Petróleo, Avenida Eje Central Lázaro Cardenas 152, 07730 Apartado 14-805, Mexico 14, DF (tel: 5567-6600).

International Telegraph Office, Balderas 14-18 Colon, Mexico DF.

Mexican Embassy (USA), 1911 Pennsylvania Avenue, NW, Washington DC 20006 (tel: (+1-202) 728-1600; fax: (+1-202) 728-1698; e-mail: mexembusa@aol.com).

Mexican Investment Board MIB, Paseo de la Reforma No. 915, Lomas de Chapultepec, 11000 Mexico (tel: 5202-7804; fax: 5328-9930).

Mexican Stock Exchange, Paseo de la Reforma 255, Colonia Cuauhtemoc, 06500 Mexico (tel: 5726-6600; fax: 5726-6805).

Pemex (Petróleos Mexicanos), Avenida Marina Nacional 329, Mexico 17, DF (tel: 5250-2611, 254-2044).

Public Telex Office, Vallejo y Norte 45, Mexico 2, DF/San Bartolo Naucaplan, Mexico 16, DF.

Secretariat of State for Commerce and Industrial Development, Alfonso Reyes 30, Mexico, DF (tel: 5286-1823, 211- 0036; fax: 5286-0804).

Secretariat of State for Energy, Mines and Federal Industry, Insurgentes Sur 552, 3, 06769 Mexico, DF (tel: 5564-9790; fax: 5574-3396).

Secretariat of State for Finance and Public Credit, Palacio Nacional, 1 Patio Mariano, 06066 Piso ofna 3045, Mexico, DF (tel: 5518-5420; fax: 5542-2821).

US Embassy, PO Box 3087, Paseo de la Reforma 305, Colonia Cuauhtemoc, 06500 Mexico City, DF (tel: 5211-0042; fax: 5207-8938).

National news agency: NTMX (Notimex), Morena 110, Col del Valle, Delg. Benito Juárez CP 03100 México DF (internet: www.notimex.com.mx).

El Universal (in Spanish): www.agenciaeluniversal.com.mx

Agencia Mexicana de Noticias (in Spanish): www.agenciamn.com

Internet sites

Communicación Mass Media de Mexico (Spanish): http://www.mexnews.com

Comprehensive information site: http://www.mexonline.com

Central bank http://www.banxico.org.mx

El Heraldo newspaper http://www.heraldo.com.mx

General directory http://www.mexicoweb.com.mx

General guide http://www.mexconnect.com

Mexicana: airline http://www.mexicana.com

Mexican government agencies, chambers of commerce and other trade institutions (English) http://www.mexicosi.com

Statistics: http://www.inegi.gob.mx

Stock exchange http://www.bmv.com.mx

Travel & tourism information http://www.go2mexico.org.mx

Travel & tourism information http://www.visitmexico.com

Federated States of Micronesia

COUNTRY PROFILE

The Federated States of Micronesia (FSM) comprises four island states – the capital state of Pohnpei (formerly Ponape), Chuuk (known until 1990 as Truk), Yap and Kosrae. These were formerly Japanese League of Nations mandated islands.
1947 The islands became part of the UN's Trust Territory of the Pacific Islands (TTPI), administered by the US under a UN mandate.
1978 The FSM gained sovereignty following a constitutional convention and referendum.
1979 On implementing the FSM constitution, former districts became States of the Federation.
1982 FSM signed a 15-year Compact of Free Association (CFA, referred to as the Contract) with the US, which would retain responsibility for foreign affairs and defence.
1986 The Contract was implemented.
1990 The US Trusteeship was ended by the UN Security Council.
1991 FSM joined the UN.
1999 Talks on the relationship between the US and FSM following the ending of the Contract began.
2001 The Contract was extended for a further two years
2002 The super-typhoon Chata'an devastated the island of Chuuk, killing 37 people and destroying homes and crops. US federal funds were provided to help recovery and rebuilding.
2003 In FSM congressional elections, Joseph J Urusemal was elected.. A US$3.5 billion, 15-year, Contract was signed with the US.
2004 The super-typhoon Sudel devastated the island of Yap destroying 1,500 homes and utility facilities.
2006 China pledged around US$3.0 million in grant assistance to FSM. The first project to be undertaken with the funds is the Pohnpei State Administration building.
2007 FSM and the US Peace Corps celebrated 40 years of partnership in regional development. Parliamentary elections were held and congress elected Manny Mori as president.
2008 The Australian conman, Peter Foster, was jailed in Brisbane, Australia for money laundering and defrauding the Bank of FSM of around US$580,000.
2009 Foreign donations provided a photovoltaic (solar)-powered groundwater supply system and desalination units.
2010 FSM mourned the loss of two eminent persons: Chief Justice Andon L Amaraich, a founding father of the nation and an influential negotiator for the Compact of Free Association with the US, and Mau Piailug, a native navigator who taught how to navigate the vast Pacific Ocean using traditional knowledge and naturally occurring elements, such as tides, winds, stars, bird migrations and the position of the moon. The Chinese government granted FSM a concessionary loan of US$22 million, for use in refurbishing the main ports and adding facilities to include fish processing plants.
2011 In parliamentary elections held in March, 14 non-partisan candidates were elected. Parliament re-elected Manny Mori unopposed as president in May. A grant from the European Union began construction of the Pohnpei State Emergency Operations Centre on 2 May. Legislation allowing for a controversial hotel and casino resort to be built on Pohnpei was passed in May.
2012 The government commissioned a survey of migration of FSM nationals (undertaken between February and July). It showed that more FSM citizens were leaving Guam and Hawaii for better economic prospects on the US mainland. From 2007–12 Guam received 375 new immigrants per year and Hawaii 450 migrants from FSM; in the same period, the US mainland received 1,200 FSM migrants per year, of which one third were arriving from Guam and Hawaii (these figures do not include births to FSM nationals in Guam, Hawaii and the US mainland).
2013 The FSM Office of Statistics, Budget and Economic Management, Overseas Development Assistance and Compact Management published the Compact Trust Fund Committee's report on fiscal year 2012 in April. It was sent to President Manny Mori and FSM Congress Speaker Isaac Figir on 6 May. The report showed a 30 per cent increase in net asset value to US$257.3 million, largely as a result of strong performances in US and international public equity markets.
2014 In March the state governments saw an increase in their respective shares

KEY FACTS

Official name: Federated States of Micronesia

Head of State: President Peter Christian (from 11 May 2015)

Head of government: President Peter Christian (from 11 May 2015)

Ruling party: All parliamentary members sit as independents

Area: 607 Volcanic islands and coral atolls with land area of just over 700 square km

Population: 104,000 (2014)* (102,624; 2010, census figure)

Capital: Palikir (in Pohnpei state)

Official language: English (nationwide); each state has its own official language including Pohnpeian, Ulithian, Woleaian, Yapese, Kosraean and Chuukese.

Currency: US dollar (US$) = 100 cents

Exchange rate: US$1.00 per US$ (fixed)

GDP per capita: US$3,041 (2014)*

GDP real growth: 0.08% (2014)*

GDP: US$315.00 million (2014)*

Inflation: 0.67% (2014)*

Balance of trade: -US$131.10 million (2013)

Foreign debt: US$87.00 million (2012)

* estimated figure

under the Compact sector grants when the national government put into effect a new grant distribution that reduces its 10 per cent share to only 5 per cent pursuant to Public Law 18-12. On 22 September agreed the fiscal year 2015 revenue projection made available by President Manny Mori. The committee recommended the revenue projection of US$66,886,705 in domestic revenue be used as provided by the FY 2015 budget book.

2015 Elections were held on 3 March in three of the four states for the 14 seats in the nineteenth Congress. 14 non-partisan candidates were elected. The referendum on Chuukese independence was postponed.

Political structure

Constitution

The constitution was promulgated in 1979, it guarantees fundamental human rights and established a separation of powers. Each state has a constitutional government with an elected governor and lieutenant governor. The US is responsible for defence and security issues.

Each state has its own constitution with an elected legislature, governor and power for implementing its own budget.

Form of state

Federal presidential republic

The executive

The president and vice president are elected from a group of four senators, one nominated from each state, for a four-year term. The president is Head of State and Head of Government but does not exercise executive power, which is retained by the congress.

The president appoints a cabinet of supporters and technocrats.

National legislature

The unicameral congress has 14 non-partisan members; 10 members are elected in single seats constituencies for two-year terms (five from Chuuk, three from Pohnpei, one from Yap and one from Kosrae), four members are elected by proportional representation, one from each state, for four-year terms – these members provide the pool from which a president and vice president are chosen by congress members.

The congress exercises executive and legislative power.

Last elections

3 March 2015 (parliamentary); 11 May 2015 (presidential, in congress).

Results: Parliamentary: 14 non-partisan candidates were elected.

Presidential: Peter Christian was elected by parliament unopposed.

Next elections

2019 (parliamentary and presidential, in congress).

Political parties

There are no political parties; political allegiances follow family and island-related dynamics.

Ruling party

All parliamentary members sit as independents

Political situation

In an effort to find other revenue streams and reduce the reliance of FSM on the funding by the Compact of Free Association (with the US), President Mori set up a National Trade Facilitation Committee (NTFC) in 2008. One of the committee's first objectives was to formulate a comprehensive trade police to be used when FSM participates in international trade negotiations. Mori is also targeting FSM's need for foreign direct investment and China is rapidly become the country's high-profile donor. Self sustaining development would also include the world's most productive tuna resources and tourism. Construction of an extension to the airport runway in Pohnpei, should boost tourist numbers as larger jet aircraft, particularly from Japan, are able to land.

The project for an underwater, telecommunications optic cable had, by early 2008, secured the US$15 million necessary for phase one of the project. At the same time Mori has his eye on making FSM the agricultural centre of the region, not only to feed the growing domestic population but also the US military bases in Guam. The plans include investment in infrastructure and education with the re-opening of an abandoned agricultural and technical college on Pohnpei.

There is a high emigration rate, 21 per 1,000 population.

Population

103,000 (2012)* (102,624; 2010, census figure)

Last census: 4 April 2010: 102,624

Population density: 154 inhabitants per square km (2010). Urban population 23 per cent (2010 Unicef).

Annual growth rate: 0.7 per cent, 1990–2010 (Unicef).

Ethnic make-up

The population is composed of nine Micronesian and Polynesian groups.

Religions

Roman Catholic (50 per cent), Protestant (47 per cent).

Education

The education system is modelled after the US educational system. Over 30 per cent of the population attend secondary schools. Private elementary and secondary schools also exist, sponsored by religious groups. Although the College of Micronesia-FSM provides two- and three-year programmes, most students prefer to enrol in US tertiary educational institutions.

The Micronesia Maritime and Fisheries Academy in the State of Yap was set up to provide effective training in maritime and fisheries technologies, to cater for the growing demand for trained personnel in the expanding fishing industry.

Compulsory years: 6 to 14.

Enrolment rate: 142 per cent gross primary enrolment, of relevant age groups (including repeaters) (World Bank 2003).

Health

There are inadequate primary health care facilities, with little secondary and tertiary-level treatment facilities. In some states there are shortages of essential medical supplies including contraceptives. As a result patients have little choice but to travel to health facilities overseas. Government funds are channelled towards curative services rather than preventative and primary health care. The Asian Development Bank has granted loans for training health workers, improving medical supplies and extending a limited health insurance scheme to provide broader and universal coverage.

The number of cases of leprosy has increased; 124 new cases were reported in 2008.

Life expectancy: 70 years, 2004 (WHO 2006)

Fertility rate/Maternal mortality rate: 3.5 births per woman, 2010 (Unicef)

Birth rate/Death rate: 25.1 births per 1,000 population; 4.9 deaths per 1,000 population (2005).

Child (under 5 years) mortality rate (per 1,000): 39 per 1,000 live births (WHO 2012)

Welfare

Although the FSM does not produce a poverty profile as such, recent household income and expenditure surveys suggest that around 40 per cent of households could be considered as low income. Despite some remittances from overseas migrants, the number of low income households is still high. The lowest income households are on the outer islands where opportunities for formal sector employment and commercial activities are few.

Main cities

Palikir (capital, in Pohnpei State, estimated population 7,747 in 2012), Weno (on Chuuk) (12,935), Kitti (7,743), Nett (6,375), Madolenihmw (6,293), Tol (on Chuuk) (5,654), Kolonia (4,396), Fefen (4,024), Tonoas (3,762).

Languages spoken

English is the *lingua franca* of the country. Yap has four languages: Yapese, Ulithian, Woleaian, and Satawalese; Pohnpei languages are Pohnpeian, Nukuoroan and Kapingamarangian, Chuukese in Chuuk and Kosraean in Kosrae. Other spoken languages include: Pingelapese, Ngatikese, Mokilese, Puluwatese and Mokilese.

Official language/s

English (nationwide); each state has its own official language including Pohnpeian, Ulithian, Woleaian, Yapese, Kosraean and Chuukese.

Media

Press

There are no daily newspapers but various weeklies, the *Pohnpei Business News*, *The Island Tribune* and *Micronesia Weekly* cover a range of subjects. The federal government publishes *The National Union*, with information bulletins, every fortnight, while state governments produce their own newsletters.

Broadcasting

Radio: There is a radio stations in each state, operated by both the government and a religious organisation through FSM Telecommunications (www.fm/radio.htm). Broadcasts are transmitted in English and the main local dialects.

Television: The government runs the only TV coverage on the islands KPON TV (on Pohnpei), TTKK TV (on Chuuk) and WAAB TV (on Colonia).

Other news agencies: ABC Pacific Beat: www.radioaustralia.net.au/pacbeat
Pacific Magazine:
www.pacificmagazine.net
Pacific Islands New Association (Pina):
www.pina.com.fj

Economy

Fishing and subsistence farming are the main economic activities. Marine products generate almost all export revenues. Tourism is being developed, but the remoteness of the islands and the lack of air access hinder development.

The economy is dependent on US financial support, provided through the Compact of Free Association (CFA), which provided FSM with US$1.3 billion from 1986–2001. This was modified in 2003 under a new agreement whereby both the US and FSM governments contribute to a trust fund annually until 2023. All earnings from the trust fund will remain untouched until 2023 and thereafter will provide for FSM through pay-outs from the trust fund. However, the International Monetary Fund (IMF) has advised that if FSM were to avoid a large revenue gap from 2024 then the government must increase its savings substantially, as well as the contributions to the trust fund. These payments should be achieved through tax reforms, expenditure cuts and improved governance and structural reforms to support the private sector.

The economy had been in recession in 2007–08, but improved in 2009 with GDP growth of 0.4 per cent. The progress continued in 2010 with GDP growth of 3.1 per cent; however the economy slowed down in 2012 to 1.4 per cent, which reflected the IMF's warning that activity in the private sector remained weak with the economy dependent on public sector infrastructure projects for growth. The IMF was also concerned that emigration in the near to medium-term could cause future contraction in the economy as active members of the community are lost. Capital investment in people, the infrastructure and telecommunications and IT were suggested as a means for FSM to provide long-term prosperity. The economy dropped into recession again in 2013, recording a contraction in GDP of -4.0 per cent. Positive growth was achieved in 2014, however, only 0.1 per cent.

In 2014, the UN Human Development Index (HDI) ranked FSM 124 (out of 187) for national development in health, education and income.

Economic growth is predicted to slow in the near term, as private sector activities are yet to offset a decline in public sector investments, caused by the scheduled reduction in financing from the Compact of Free Associations. While the fisheries sector is expected to continue its healthy expansion, limited wholesale and retail activities pose a challenge to continued private sector growth. Despite this, the upgrading of the US military base in Guam and an accelerated release of Compact infrastructure grants present export opportunities.

External trade

The FSM is a member of the South Pacific Regional Trade and Economic Co-operation Agreement (Sparteca) along with 12 other regional nations, which allows products duty free access by Pacific Island Forum members to Australian and New Zealand markets (subject to the country of origin restrictions).

FSM has an exclusive economic zone of almost 3 million square km of the Pacific Ocean and fish exports account for 80 per cent of export trade, mainly to Japan; it also has a bilateral trade agreement with the European Union regarding tuna fisheries.

Imports

Principal imports are petroleum, food, manufactured goods, machinery, equipment and beverages. Imports are approximately three times larger than exports.

Main sources: US (37 per cent of total in 2013), Guam (22.1 per cent), Japan (6.7 per cent)

Exports

Principal exports are fish, garments, bananas and black pepper. Some beef, fruit and vegetables are also exported.

Copra was formerly Yap's principal export, but this has been overtaken by betel nut and pepper leaf, traditionally, used in chewing. A 'chew' consists of a betel nut wrapped in pepper leaf with a touch of lime powder made from burned coral; the combination stains teeth red and betel nut is described as mildly narcotic.

Main destinations: Guam (11.8 per cent of total in 2013), Northern Mariana Islands (4.8 per cent), US (2.7 per cent)

Agriculture

Farming

The agricultural sector contributes approximately 28 per cent to GDP. Subsistence farming is the main occupation and provides most of the food consumed in the territory.

Fishing

Fishing is the mainstay of the economy and generates most of the country's export revenues. International fishing fleets pay to fish in FSM's rich territorial waters, including one of the world's best tuna grounds. However, the sector is dominated by foreign owned companies operating offshore and so employs few local people.

The Pohnpei State government expanded its local fishing industry, using vessels that had been donated by the government of the Republic of Korea.

Fishing provides a primary source of protein for the local population.

FSM also typically harvests 150,000 pearls annually.

On 12 April 2011, a summit of the Parties to the Nauru Agreement (PNA) concluded its strategy for a policy of sustainable fishing in the Pacific. The PNA treaty, which was established in 1989 and expired in 2012, is seen as in need of an overhaul. As a collective region the PNA (FSM, Kiribati, Marshall Islands, Nauru, Palau, PNG, Solomon Islands and Tuvalu) controls around 25–30 per cent of world stocks of tuna. Only 5 per cent of sales revenue is returned to the PNA and ministers called for specific changes, including an increased share of profits, PNA crews on-board purse seine vessels (minimum 10 per cent), conservation and management measures including a limit to fish trapping (fish aggregating devices (FADs)), net mesh rules and the establishment of an observer agency and fisheries information management system. The PNA met in May 2012 to discuss even stronger management measures to ensure even more sustainable tuna fisheries and minimise environmental damage. Many of the ideas put forward were implemented in January 2013, for example observation and monitoring of catches and environmental damage by 100 per cent independent bodies.

Industry and manufacturing

Small-scale industries include handicrafts, fish processing, bottling, copra processing, bakeries and boat building. The Pohnpei Agricultural and Trade School runs a small coconut products plant, which makes 'Oil of Ponape' toiletries.
Most private sector activity is in retail and wholesale trade which are dependent on demand generated by government spending.

Tourism

FSM is particularly attractive to divers as the region's most spectacular scenery is underwater. The island of Chuuk has an underwater-wreck-museum where more than 60 Japanese ships, as well as planes, that were sunk during the Second World War are open to divers to view.
The annual number of arrivals to FSM is steadily on the rise, and in 2014 there was a total of 42,000 international tourists visiting.
Tourism could provide a greater component of GDP, but the remoteness of the islands and the lack of direct flights limit the potential for growth.

Environment

In May 2011, the Federated State of Micronesia (FSM) challenged Czech Republic government plans to expand its coal-fired Prunerov Two power plant, Europe's second-largest. Low-lying FSM is threatened by submersion as global warming adds to rising sea levels. It feels this expansion, and its resulting increase in carbon dioxide output could exacerbate its problems. FSM will use a legal instrument of the UN Convention on Environmental Impact Assessment in a Transboundary Context (known as the EIA convention) in Czech Republic courts and if successful will challenge similar projects in other signatory countries where the EIA convention applies.

Mining

Small mineral deposits exist, but there are doubts about the economic viability of commercial exploitation, which would be hampered by a shortage of land to accommodate any displaced population.
The FSM, Solomon Islands and Papua New Guinea submitted a joint proposal to the United Nations in 2009 to develop the Ontong Java Plateau, which is part of their extended continental shelf, for mineral prospecting. The proposal was updated in 2014, however by 2015 no permission had been granted.

Hydrocarbons

There are no known hydrocarbon reserves; all petroleum products are imported to meet domestic needs.

Energy

Each state has its own generating authority including the Chuuk Public Utility Corporation, Kosrae Utility Authority, Pohnpei Utility Corporation and the Yap State Public Service Corporation, which are responsible for electricity generation and supply.

Banking and insurance

There are three commercial banks which serve the four states: Bank of the Federated States of Micronesia, Bank of Guam and the Bank of Hawaii. A government chartered FSM Development Bank is the main financial institution used to foster the growth of new business ventures and private sector development.

Central bank

The FSM does not have a central bank.

Time

GMT plus 12 hours

Geography

The Federated States of Micronesia (FSM), together with Palau, form the archipelago of the Caroline Islands, about 800km east of the Philippines. It is a group of 608 small islands, only four large islands are inhabited, in an area over 2.5 million square kilometres of Pacific Ocean.
Most of the islands are little more than sandy coral outcrops, while others are high rise volcanic peaks covered with forests, or mangroves along shorelines and lagoons.

Hemisphere

Northern

Climate

Warm and humid, temperatures 23–30 degrees Celsius with humidity around 80 per cent. Rainfall is variable, but the minimum is generally 250mm per annum.
Hurricanes are possible.

Entry requirements

Passports

Required by all except US citizens with proof of citizenship. Passports must be valid for 120 days beyond date of entry.

Visa

Not required by US citizens with proof of adequate funds. Entry permits granted to all others with proof of return/onward passage and adequate funds for stays up to 30 days. Business visits need an entry permit, (see www.visit-fsm.org/visitors/permit.pdf).

Currency advice/regulations

No restrictions on import and export of local or foreign currency.
Travellers cheques and credit/charge cards are accepted in visitor orientated businesses.

Health (for visitors)

Mandatory precautions

Vaccination certificates required for yellow fever if travelling from infected area.

Advisable precautions

Vaccinations for diphtheria, tuberculosis, hepatitis A and B, polio, TB, tetanus, typhoid and paratyphoid are advisable.
Leprosy has been endemic for generations.
Water precautions are necessary. There is a cholera risk due to lack of access to safe water.
There is a rabies risk.

Hotels

Hotels tend to be low rise, resort style. There is no star ratings. There is a 6 per cent accommodation tax on Pohnpei and 10 per cent on Yap; Chuuk and Kosrae do not levy a tax.

Credit cards

Limited to certain businesses and hotels in the state centres.

Public holidays (national)

Fixed dates

1 Jan (New Year's Day), 10 May (FSM Constitution Day), 24 Oct (United Nations Day), 3 Nov (National Day), 25 Dec (Christmas Day).

Variable dates

Good Friday (Mar/Apr)

Working hours

Banking

Mon–Thurs: 0930–1430; Fri: 0930–1600.

Business

Mon–Fri: 0800–1700.

Government

Mon–Fri: 0800–1700.

Shops

Mon–Sat: 0800–2000; Sun 0900–1030.

Telecommunications

Mobile/cell phones

A GSM 900 service exists on the inhabited islands.

Electricity supply

110 volt and US type outlets are used.

Social customs/useful tips

Tips are neither expected nor encouraged.

Getting there

Air

National airline: None but the US owned Continental Micronesia Airlines operates throughout Micronesia with connections to Hawaii and Guam.
International airport/s: Pohnpei (PNI), 5km south of Kolonia Town.
Other airport/s: Chuuk (TKK), Yap (YAP), Kosrae (KSA).
Airport tax: Departure tax: Pohnpei US$10, Chuuk US$15, Kosrae US$10, Yap none.

Getting about

National transport

A trip to the outer islands can be complicated and arrangements should be made at least several months in advance.

Air: Pacific Missionary Aviation (PMA) in Yap State and in Pohnpei State provide domestic air services. There are airstrips in the outer islands of Ulul and Ta in Chuuk State.

Road: The road network has been upgraded in many areas through a resurfacing programme begun in the late 1990s.

Taxis: Inexpensive and readily available in most centres.

Water: Passenger and freight services between the islands and atolls are provided by state-owned vessels. The frequency of inter-island services is governed by weather conditions; it is best to contact the FSM visitor's board for current information (www.visit-fsm.org).

BUSINESS DIRECTORY

The addresses listed below are a selection only. While World of Information makes every endeavour to check these addresses, we cannot guarantee that changes have not been made, especially to telephone numbers and area codes. We would welcome any corrections.

Telephone area codes

The international direct dialling (IDD) code for the FSM is +691, followed by area code and subscriber's number:

Chuuk	330	Pohnpei	320
Kosrae	370	Yap	350

Useful telephone numbers

Pohnpei
Police: 320-2221
Fire: 320-2223
Ambulance: 320-2213
Chuuk
Police: 330-2223
Fire: 330-2222
Ambulance: 330-2444
Kosrae
Police: 911
Fire: 370-3333
Ambulance: 370-3012
Yap
Police: 911
Fire: 350-2415
Ambulance: 350-3446

Chambers of Commerce

Chuuk Chamber of Commerce, PO Box 700, Weno, Chuuk 96942 (tel: 330-2318; fax: 330-2314).

Kosrae Chamber of Commerce, PO Box 1075, Tofol, Kosrae 96944 (tel: 370-2044; fax: 370-2066; e-mail: kosraecci@mail.fm).

Pohnpei Chamber of Commerce, PO Box 405, Kolonia, Pohnpei 96941 (tel: 320-2452; fax: 320-5277).

Banking

Bank of the Federated States of Micronesia, PO Box BF, Tofol, Kosrae, 96944 (tel: 320-2850; fax: 370-3568; email: bofsmhq@mail.fm).

FSM Development Bank, Box M, Kolonia, Pohnpei State, 96941 (tel: 320-2840; fax: 320-2842)

Bank of Guam, Chuuk Office (tel: 330-2567; fax: 330-2640).

Bank of Hawaii, Kosrae Office (tel: 370-3230; fax: 370-2027).

Travel information

Chief of Immigration, Office of the Attorney General, Palikir, Pohnpei 96941 (tel: 320-5844; fax: 320-2234).

Pohnpei International Airport, PO Box 1150, Kolonia Town, Pohnpei 96941 (tel: 320-2682/2793/3999; fax: 320-2798).

National tourist organisation offices

National Visitors Board, PO Box PS-12, Palikir, Pohnpei, 96941 (tel: 320-5133; fax: 320-3251; email: fsminfo@visit-fsm.org; internet: www.visit-fsm.org).

Ministries

Department of Foreign Affairs and Trade, Pacific Islands Branch, R G Casey Building, John McEwan Crescent, Barton ACT 0221, Australia (fax: (+62-2) 6261-2332).

Secretary for Foreign Affairs, Pohnpei (tel: 320-2641; fax: 320-2933).

Secretary for Economic Affairs, Pohnpei (tel: 320-2646; fax: 320-5854).

Other useful addresses

British Embassy, PO Box No 61, Bairiki Tarawa (tel: 21-327; fax: 21-488).

Chuuk State Government, Weno, Chuuk State, 96942.

FSM Embassy (US), 1725 North Street, NW Washington 20036 (tel: (+1-202) 223-4383; fax: (+1-202) 223-4391; email: fsmamb@aol.com).

FSM Public Information Office, FSM Government, Box P.S. 34, Palikir, Pohnpei, 96941.

Kosrae State Government, Tofol, Kosrae, 96944.

Office of the Governor, Yap State Government, PO Box 39, Colonia, Yap, 96943.

Pohnpei State Government, Kolonia, Pohnpei, 96941.

The Secretary of Finance, PO Box P.S. 158, Palikir, Pohnpei, 96941 (tel: 320-2640; fax: 320-2380).

ABC Pacific Beat: www.radioaustralia.net.au/pacbeat

Pacific Magazine: www.pacificmagazine.net

Pacific Islands New Association (Pina): www.pina.com.fj

Internet sites

FSM Telecom: http://www.telecom.fm

Government website: http://www.fm.org

Tourist information: http://www.visit.micronesia.fm

US Office of Insular affairs: http://www.doi.gov/oia

Moldova

KEY FACTS

Official name: Republica Moldoveneasca (Republic of Moldova)

Head of State: President Nicolae Timofti (from 16 Mar 2012)

Head of government: Prime Minister Valeriu Strelet (from 30 July 2015)

Ruling party: Coalition: Alliance for European Integration (AEI), led by Liberal Democrat din Moldova (PLDM) (Liberal Democratic Party of Moldova), with Partidul Democrat din Moldova (PDM) (Democratic Party of Moldova) and Partidul Liberal (PL) (Liberal Party) (from 2009; re-elected 30 Nov 2014, despite losing ground)

Area: 33,700 square km

Population: 3.56 million (2014)*

Capital: Chisinau (Kishinev)

Official language: Moldovan (in latin script)

Currency: Leu (L) = 100 bani

Exchange rate: L19.25 per US$ (Sep 2015)

GDP per capita: US$2,233 (2014)*

GDP real growth: 4.60% (2014)*

GDP: US$7.94 billion (2014)*

Labour force: 1.20 million (2012)*

Unemployment: 4.00% (2014)*

Inflation: 5.06% (2014)*

Balance of trade: -US$3.10 billion (2014)

* estimated figure

In Moldova's mid-June 2015 local elections, the pro-European and pro-Russian parties took roughly equal shares of the vote. This flew in the face of most of the poll predictions, which had suggested that the pro-Moscow camp would secure a big-win. In the capital Chisinau, neither the incumbent mayor, pro-European Dorin Chirtoaca, nor pro-Russian candidate Zinaida Greceanii gained the 50 per cent of votes required for a win. A second round was held two weeks later with Dorin Chirtoaca being a comfortale winner. The biggest electoral surprise was in the town of Orhei, which elected Ilan Shor as mayor with just over 60 per cent of the votes. Mr Shor was elected while under house arrest for fraud (see below).

Political splits

Politics in Moldova are, sadly, never dull. The local elections were held two days after the pro-European Prime Minister Chiril Gaburici resigned. He had only been prime minister since February. In June 2015 Reuters reported that a criminal investigation was to be undertaken into whether Mr Gaburici, had forged his school record. This announcement coincided with Mr Gaburici's attack on the judiciary for failing to find the US$1 billion or so that had apparently been stolen from three of the country's banks. Moldova's politics had been in a politically febrile state since the theft, corresponding to about one eighth of annual gross domestic product (GDP), had been uncovered.

Gheorghe Brega became acting prime minister on 30 October and at the time of going to press in November was still holding the post.

The beleaguered, pro-European Mr Gaburici, had only been in office for four months. Not tainted personally by the scandal, he had called for the resignations of a number of senior civil servants, including the director of the prosecutor's office. Tit for tat, (in a rather lop-sided way) the prosecutors' office had come up with the investigation into whether a signature and a stamp had been forged on two of his secondary school documents.

In advance of the June elections, the polls had been predicting a strong performance by the pro-Moscow opposition Socialists. The political fault line in Moldova – quite apart from the huge problem of the Transdniestr breakaway republic, is between the pro-Russian socialist supporters and the pro (West) European liberal voters. Both sides accused the other of corruption during their periods in power.

Moldova had acquired a higher profile in 2014 following Russia's invasion of Ukraine's Crimea peninsula. Some 1,500 Russian troops have occupied a chunk of Moldovan territory since the end of the Soviet Union, supposedly protecting the separatist – and pro Moscow – Transdniestr territory. In 2014 Moldova ratified a political and trade agreement with the EU, prompting Russia to prohibit the import of wine, vegetables and meat from agricultural Moldova.

Big Brother – but no airport

Responding to the Russian pressure, Ukraine and Moldova appeared to take their time before restricting Russian military access to Transdniestr, where in 2015, Russia maintained a force of about 1,500 troops. Radio Free Europe (RFE) reported that around 1,000 of these are pure and simple Russian troops, without Moldova's blessing. The other 500 or so are legitimate 'peacekeepers', a hangover from the 1994 civil war between the opposing Moldovan factions and regulated by the Joint Control Commission, which is represented by Moldova, Transdnistra and… Russia.

When the Ukrainian parliament finally got around to suspending military co-operation with Russia, the latter was no longer able to use Ukrainian territory to supply its troops in Transdniestr. According to RFE, Russian officials announced that Russia was 'left with no other option than to supply Russian forces with all the necessities by air bridge, with military-transport aircraft.' Adding that 'The Russian contingent will be supplied under any circumstances.'

The Russian newspaper *Kommersant* also reported that Moldova had been detaining and even arresting and deporting any Russian soldiers not in the peacekeeping mission who tried to reach Transdniestr via Moldova. Ordinary Russian troops were required to give a month's notice that they will be travelling via Moldova. It was reported that 'hundreds' of Russian soldiers had been simply sent back. Transdniestr only has borders with Ukraine and Moldova and has no useable airports. Neither country is prepared to assist Russia's military presence. It was rumoured that Russia might be planning to reopen the long-abandoned airport in Tiraspol, the *de facto* capital of the separatist territory.

Shor of himself

Moldova risked entering the Guinness Book of Records in 2015 – for all the wrong reasons. The sudden insolvency of three banks – Banca de Economii (among Moldova's biggest lenders), Banca Sociala and Unibank was related to an alleged fraud adding up to some US$750 million by one of the Banca Economii's shareholders, one Ilan Shor, a self described Moldovan 'oligarch'. The apparent theft, by means of a web of bank loans between the three banks added up to around 12 per cent of Moldovan GDP. The 28 year-old Mr Shor was considered to be one of Moldova's richest citizens; as a candidate in the 2015 elections, Mr Shor was protected from prosecution, but not from house arrest. In late November, according to a report in the *New York Times* quoting a report prepared for the Moldovan government by the US Kroll company, Mr Shor had transferred around US$800 million to a number of offshore accounts, in a number of cases via accounts held by banks in Latvia. Moldova's then prime minister, Chiril Gaburici, was quoted as saying that he did not believe Mr Shor was solely responsible for the missing money.

Corruption is considered to be rife in Moldova, which ranked a lowly 103 on the Transparency International 2014 *Corruption Perceptions Index*. According to the results of another survey by Transparency International, in Moldova half the population consider the judiciary to be the most corrupt state body.

The odds on Prime Minister Gaburici walking the plank had steadily increased following the 2014 parliamentary elections. His coalition government was paradoxically dependent for support on Moldova's Partidul Comunistilor din Moldova (PCM) (Party of Communists of Moldova), which in blunt terms meant that the new government might collapse at any time – and that could trigger yet another national parliamentary election and further erode public enthusiasm for democracy. Moscow's attitude to Moldova seemed strangely uncertain. Although anxious to counter the Chisinau government's pro-European stance, it was reluctant to commit to additional expenditure and further international opprobrium. Rather like his counterpart in Ukraine, Petro Poroshenko, the 38 year old Mr Gaburici had precious little political experience. Ironically and paradoxically, having failed to reach agreement, the three pro-Western parties couldn't form a government. The Partidul Liberal Democrat din Moldova (PLDM) (Liberal Democratic Party of Moldova) simply walked out of the discussions and refused to vote for the Gaburici government. The former prime minister Iurie Leanca – probably Moldova's most popular politician – whose efforts to form a government had been rejected by the Communists, also refused to vote for the minority government on the grounds that a coalition between the liberal parties and the Communists was not feasible. Moldova's liberal parties had called the electoral shots since 2008; however, what they had failed to do was to carry the electorate with them in their support of a pro-EU agenda. The next political hurdle would be the election of a new president in 2016. This requires 61 of the 101 members of parliament. A failure to elect a president would also trigger early parliamentary elections.

The economy: shocks and struggles

Prime Minister Gaburici, although only four months in power, had become associated with the loss of spending power as the Moldovan leu suffered a *de-facto* devaluation of 35 per cent in value against the dollar in the first few months of 2015. Moldova's economy, which grew by 4.6 per cent in 2014, was forecast by the government to contract by 2 per cent in 2015.

Moldova continues to be among the poorest countries in Europe. The Moldovan economy is small. It is vulnerable to external shocks due to its major dependence on external power resources, particularly on natural gas imported from Russia. It is also dependent on its agrarian sector, which is poorly protected against weather shocks; and its wine industry on whether or not Russia has banned imports or not. It is further dependent on the

KEY INDICATORS — Moldova

	Unit	2011	2012	2013	2014	**2015
Population	m	3.56	3.56	3.56	*3.56	*3.56
Gross domestic product (GDP)	US$bn	7.00	7.28	7.99	*7.94	*0.61
GDP per capita	US$	1,969	2,046	2,243	*2,233	*1,726
GDP real growth	%	6.4	-0.7	9.4	*4.6	*-1.0
Inflation	%	7.7	4.6	4.6	*5.1	*7.5
Unemployment	%	9.4	5.6	5.1	*4.0	*4.5
Exports (fob) (goods)	US$m	1,749.0	1,697.2	1,902.3	1,769.7	0.0
Imports (fob) (goods)	US$m	4,715.4	4,738.2	5,016.5	4,867.0	0.0
Balance of trade	US$m	-2,966.4	-3,041.0	-3,114.2	-3,097.4	0.0
Current account	US$m	-868.9	-440.0	-399.0	*-435.0	*-277.0
Total reserves minus gold	US$m	1,988.1	2,511.1	2,817.8	2,153.8	0.0
Foreign exchange	US$m	1,987.3	2,509.4	2,811.3	0.0	0.0
Exchange rate	per US$	11.80	12.26	13.02	15.61	0.00

* estimated figure ** forecast figure

annual growth of about 7 to 8 per cent. That is 7.1 per cent in 2010, 6.7 per cent in 2011 and 8.9 per cent in 2013. In 2012, GDP declined by 0.7 per cent as a result of the financial crisis and of weather unfavourable to farming.

In its December 2014 assessment of the Moldovan economy, the International Monetary Fund (IMF) noted that the political calendar has affected economic policies and generated uncertainty about Moldova's outlook.

In June 2014, Moldova had signed an Association Agreement with the European Union (EU) which included provisions establishing a so-called Deep and Comprehensive Free Trade Area (DCFTA). The DCFTA envisioned an immediate elimination of both sides' export duties. On import duties, the process was to be 'asymmetric': while EU import tariffs on most imports from Moldova were lifted immediately, those on key EU products entering Moldova will be removed over five to ten years. Russia had introduced several restrictions on import of Moldovan products. In September, Moldova also signed a free trade agreement with Turkey, which was expected to enter into effect in 2015.

Russia's restrictions on imports, especially wine, from Moldova were expected to exacerbate the nascent slowdown in activity. While economic activity indicators in the first half of 2014 were slightly better than expected, reflecting the good performance of the agriculture sector, a more pronounced decline in growth in key trading partners, moderating agricultural output and Russia's additional restrictions on imports of Moldovan food products were holding back economic activity in the second half of 2014. In 2014, GDP was projected to grow by 2 per cent, compared to 8.9 per cent in 2013. Over the medium term, activity was projected to recover with the implementation of free trade agreements with both the EU and Turkey. In 2014, despite the expected easing of food price pressures, inflation was projected to remain within the Banca Nationala a Moldovei (BNM) (National Bank of Moldova) (central bank) target range of 5 per cent plus or minus (±) 1.5 percentage points. However, inflation was projected to pick up in 2015, reflecting overdue utility tariff increases after mid-year local elections. While there was a collapse in wine exports to Russia during the first half of 2014, agricultural producers had been able to find new markets for their products in the EU and other CIS countries. Also, foreign remittances had remained stronger than anticipated in 2014. However, the uncertainties related to geopolitical tensions had triggered capital outflows and holdings of foreign currencies, culminating in the depreciation of the leu by about 12.5 per cent vis-à-vis the US dollar since the end of 2013. Moldova's international reserves had declined to US$2.7 billion, but in the view of the IMF, remained adequate. The current account deficit was projected to widen to 7.25 per cent in 2015, reflecting a projected decline in remittances growth and a recovery in imports, as economic and political uncertainties subsided. In the view of the IMF, the risks to the economic outlook are tilted to the downside. The main risks related to serious vulnerabilities and governance problems in the banking system, a protracted economic activity slowdown in key trading partners, further intensification of geopolitical tensions in the region and additional policy slippages in the run up to the elections.

In the view of the IMF, Moldova's economy and external stability were highly vulnerable to the continuing regional geopolitical tensions. Although a re-orientation of exports was under way, Moldovan producers were still in the process of adopting EU standards and therefore additional exports to the EU were unlikely to be sufficient to fully match the slowdown in exports to Russia in the near term.

The economy – EBRD sees volatile performance

In its 2014 *Transition Report* assessment of the Moldovan economy, the European Bank for Reconstruction and Development (EBRD) noted that following the 'drought-induced' recession of 2012, the Moldovan economy grew by an impressive 8.9 per cent in 2013. This was not only the highest rate of growth since independence, it was reportedly the highest growth rate of any European country. In the first half of 2014, according to the EBRD, the economy slowed down to an annual growth rate of 3.9 per cent. In the view of the EBRD, the volatility of the growth rate reflected the economy's narrow base, dependent for the most part on agriculture (12.5 per cent of GDP) and foreign remittances (24 per cent). The EBRD also reported that Moldova's investment activity had 'remained subdued'. This was seen in lower foreign direct investment (FDI), wary of the unfavourable business environment and what the EBRD described as 'significant governance problems in the banking sector.' Net FDI inflows had fallen from over 10 per cent of GDP before the global financial crisis to just over 2 per cent. The growth of remittances also fell in the first half of 2014, reflecting the slow-down in the Russian economy. As already noted, inflation remained within the central bank's target range of 5 per cent plus or minus 1.5 per cent.

According to the EBRD, Moldova's current account deficit shrank sharply in the 12 month period up to June 2014, down from 11.2 per cent of GDP in 2011 to a respectable 2.5 per cent in the first half of 2014. Reserves covered some five months of imports and external debt repayments were low. The leu had steadily depreciated against the US dollar, by some 15 per cent since the beginning of 2013. The fiscal discipline seen in the first half of 2014 had been cast aside as the elections and their spending commitments had approached.

Despite 2013's strong performance, growth was expected to weaken in 2014 owing in some measure to the crisis in neighbouring Ukraine, the trade restrictions imposed by Russia and the general slowdown of the Russian economy which in turn caused remittances by Moldovans from Russia to fall away. The EBRD noted that Moldova's dependence on the remittances from Russia left Moldova vulnerable to any tightening of Russian migration and labour laws. Investment activity looked unlikely to pick up due to the challenges facing the banking sector and the forthcoming elections. Signing into law the DCFTA was not itself enough. Moldova's longer-term growth prospects would rest on the ability of the government to implement the necessary structural reforms and, crucially, to attract investment.

On the economic front, it was hoped that the enhanced contractual relationship with the EU would facilitate the free movement of goods, capital, services and people between Moldova and the EU member states. In addition, any greater approximation and convergence with the EU's globally recognised technical norms and standards might open up new commercial opportunities beyond the EU. The association also entailed an increase in development assistance to Moldova, including a so-called 'multi-faceted institutional capacity-building effort.' While the EU expected the DCFTA to boost Moldova's GDP by 5.4 per cent in the long term, the overall positive effect might be even bigger if Moldova's reforms were ever completed. In May 2014 the EU liberalised the visa regime for Moldova, to enhance mobility opportunities and could diversify – with a view to increasing – migrant remittances. The EBRD also noted that challenges were still evident in the banking sector. It was feared that Moldova's banking sector might be exposed to risks of intermeshed political party lending and money laundering, with adverse consequences for financial and macro-economic stability. An inability to tackle these issues decisively and in a timely manner had compromised the central bank's independence and credibility. The EBRD reported that in October 2013 Moldova's Constitutional Court had issued a ruling that authorised any Moldovan court to suspend decisions of the NBM. In December 2013 parliament had partially restored the NBM's authority. In 2014 the government made some progress in addressing banking sector challenges.

In July 2014 the cabinet had adopted a series of tighter legislative measures aimed at preventing 'opaque' transactions: (i) the threshold on transactions with shares was lowered from 5 per cent to 1 per cent, above which the NMB's approval was required for new shareholders/buyers; (ii) shares held by shareholders acting in concert could be sold only to NBM-approved buyers; (iii) bank shares could not be used as collateral (unless approved by the NBM); and (iv) the rules governing the criminal liability of bank managers were tightened.

At the beginning of 2014, the government had postponed the privatisation of key state-owned enterprises in the tobacco, alcohol, energy and telecommunication industries, giving as a reason its failure to secure a transparent and effective process. The privatisation of small and medium-sized enterprises had continued in 2014.

The construction of the Iasi-Ungheni gas pipeline connecting Romania and Moldova's gas transport systems was completed at the end of August 2014, enabling Moldova to receive gas supplies from the EU. This should promote energy diversification for Moldova and help to foster competition in the local gas market, although, due to capacity constraints, the pipeline could only supply the region around the town of Ungheni, which consumed between 3–5 per cent of the Moldova's annual gas consumption. A feasibility study was under way for the construction of another pipeline between Ungheni and Chisinau. If supplemented with a new gas compression station in Romania, the pipeline would provide much larger diversification benefits.

In July 2013 Moldova had set up an economic council to improve the business climate. The council, which became operational in late 2013, was chaired by the prime minister and brought together policy-makers as well as domestic and foreign investors. The council identified key obstacles to doing business and has been instrumental in reducing a number of minor trade barriers. New state aid and competition legislation have been approved by parliament and new powers have been attributed to the competition authority. In late 2013 parliament also adopted legislation aimed at combating corruption in the courts. It envisaged, among other things, salary increases for judges, mandatory polygraph tests for candidates applying for the position of judge and increased financial liability for illegal enrichment activities.

Risk assessment

Economy	Fair
Politics	Poor
Regional stability	Fair

COUNTRY PROFILE

1940 The Moldovan Soviet Socialist Republic (SSR) was established within the Soviet Union. The Moldovan SSR included land annexed from Romania and the Ukraine, providing much of the basis for the inter-communal strife.

1989 Achieved *de facto* independence from the former Soviet Union.

1990 Moldova's attempts to become an independent republic were hindered by the country's economic weaknesses and its strained relations with Russia. Ethnic Russians proclaimed the Transdniestr Republic on the left bank of the Dniestr River.

1991 Civil war erupted between the Transdniestr separatists and Moldova. Russian troops were deployed in Moldova to oversee a cease-fire agreed between the warring factions. Moldova formally declared its independence, with Mercea Snegur as the country's first president; it joined the Commonwealth of Independent States (CIS).

1992 Moldova was recognised by the UN. The Partidul Popular Crestin-Democrat (PPCD) (Christian-Democrat People's Party) resigned in favour of a new coalition government.

1994 Moldova pursued a pro-Western policy and joined NATO's Partnership for Peace (PfP) programme. The extreme left Partidul Democrat Agrar din Moldova (PDAM) (Agrarian-Democratic Party of Moldova) won elections. A new constitution was introduced.

1996 Petru Lucinschi won the presidential elections.

1998 The Partidul Comunistilor din Moldova (PCM) (Communist Party of Moldova) won the biggest share of the vote in the parliamentary elections, but was unable to form a government as it was short of an absolute majority in the Parlamentul (Parliament). Right-wing parties, which had finished behind the PCM in the elections, joined together and formed a coalition government, led by Ion Ciubuc.

1999 There were three governments in one year as coalitions collapsed. A non-affiliated government emerged, led by Dumitru Braghis.

2000 Against President Lucinschi's wishes, Moldova was transformed into a parliamentary republic – giving the parliament the opportunity to elect the president instead of election by popular vote. Parliament failed to elect a new president when neither candidate received the 61 votes required for outright victory.

2001 The PCM won elections and Vasile Tarlev was appointed prime minister. Vladimir Voronin, leader of the PCM, was elected president by parliament. An Organisation for Security and Co-operation in Europe (OSCE) sponsored agreement committed Russia to removing troops from Moldova by 2002. Moldova joined the World Trade Organisation (WTO). Igor Smirnov was re-elected as self-styled president of the breakaway Transdniestr region.

2002 The announcement of plans to make Russian an official language and compulsory in schools sparked months of mass protests which ended only when the scheme was shelved. The OSCE deadline for Russian troops to withdraw from Transdniestr was extended until the end of 2003, then 2004.

2004 Moldova imposed economic sanctions on Transdniestr (the Russian and Ukrainian-speaking autonomous territory) after it closed several schools using the Moldovan language and Latin instead of Cyrillic script.

2005 Vasile Tarlev's ruling PCM and President Voronin were re-elected. During the winter Gazprom doubled the price of gas and temporarily cut off supplies when Moldova refused to pay.

2006 The halted gas supplies also affected the flow through Moldova to Germany. An agreement was reached with phased price increases. Transdniestr reacted badly to a new law that all goods entering Ukraine through Transdniestr must have Moldovan custom stamps, to foil smuggling. In reprisal, Russia suspended imports of Moldovan meat and

wine, claiming a lack of quality, but lifted the ban after Moldova threatened to block Russia's bid for membership of the WTO. A referendum in Transdniestr voted for independence from Moldova and eventually to become a region of Russia.
2008 Vasile Tarlev resigned as prime minister; Zinaida Greceanîi, became the first Moldovan woman prime minister.
2009 PCM won parliamentary elections; it nominated Zinaida Greceanîi as president but parliament twice failed to give her the minimum 61 votes necessary to take office. This automatically triggered a rerun of parliamentary elections, which were won by a coalition, called the Alianta Pentru Integrare Europeana (APIE) (Alliance for European Integration) (comprising Partidul Liberal Democrat din Moldova (PLDM) (Liberal Democrats (of Moldova)), Partidul Liberal (PL) (Liberal Party) and Partidul Alianta Moldova Noastra (PAMN) (Our Moldova Alliance)) with a combined 53 seats (out of 101), which outnumber the PCM's 48 seats. President Vladimir Voronin resigned and Mihai Ghimpu became acting president; he nominated and parliament endorsed, Vlad Filat (PLDM) as prime minister. Parliament failed to elect Filat's nomination of Marian Lupu as president and a new presidential election was postponed until 2010.
2010 There was overwhelming support in a referendum to amend the constitution and return presidents to being directly elected by popular vote (87.83 per cent favour of the proposals). However, there was an insufficient turnout of just 30.29 per cent so the motion failed. After months of legal wrangling and the failure of parliament to elect a new president, the Constitutional Court ordered fresh parliamentary elections. The APIE won 59 seats (out of 101) and the PCM 42. The result was once again a stalemate with neither side winning the required 61 votes necessary to elect their candidate as president. Parliament appointed Marian Lupu (PLDM) as acting president, who in turn re-appointed Vlad Filat (PLDM) as prime minister.
2011 In January, Prime Minister Filat offered two cabinet posts to the opposition PCM in return for two votes to break the political deadlock and formally accept Marian Lupu as president. In February, the Constitutional Court ruled that only parliament could decide when new presidential elections should take place. The current government could therefore prolong its sitting by not setting a date for presidential elections. In July the EU agreed to provide around €200 million (US$281 million) in financial assistance, to be used in the energy sector, strengthening institutional capacities, measures to mitigate conflict in Transdniestr, legal reforms and support for the government's budget. In December, the national parliament held elections for a new president. However, the result was disputed and the Constitutional Court later ruled it was invalid due to violations in secret voting procedures. In Transdniestr presidential elections were held: Yevgeny Shevchuk (independent) won 38.6 per cent of the vote, Anatoly Kaminsky (Obnovleniye (Renewal)) 26.3 per cent, and incumbent Igor Smirnov (independent) 24.7 per cent; three other candidates each won less than 6 per cent. Turnout was 60 per cent. As no candidate won over 50 per cent, a runoff was held on 25 December, in which Shevchuk won 73.88 per cent of the vote; Kaminski 19.67 per cent.
2012 On 12 January, the Constitutional Court cancelled the presidential election scheduled for 15 January. In Transdniestr, President Shevchuk nominated Pyotr Stepanov as the first occupant of the new post of prime minister; the nomination was endorsed by the Transdniestr parliament on 18 January. On 16 March parliament voted by 62 votes out of 101 for Nicolae Timofti (independent) as president; he took office on 23 March.
2013 The government lost a vote of no-confidence on 5 March after the PDM voted with the Communists. Prime Minister Filat refused to resign. Elections are due in 2014. On 5 October the Communist Party held rallies across the country, demanding the pro-Europe government resign. Iurie Leanca (PLDM) became prime minister on 31 May.
2014 Parliamentary elections were held on 30 November.
2015 On 14 February President Timofti asked Chiril Gaburici (Partidul Liberal Democrat din Moldova (PLDM) (Liberal Democratic Party)) to become prime minister, following on from Iurie Leanca; his government was approved by Parliament on 18 February. However, he resigned on 12 June after prosecutors questioned the authenticity of his school-leaving certificate. He remained in office until Natalia Gherman was briefly installed as acting prime minister on 22 June; she was replaced by Valeriu Strele as acting prime minister on 30 July until a vote of no-confidence on 29 October. Gheorghe Brega became acting prime minister on 30 October.

Political structure

Constitution

The 1977 constitution was replaced in August 1994, establishing the country as a 'presidential, parliamentary republic' based on political pluralism and 'the preservation, development and expression of ethnic and linguistic identity'. The constitution enforces the separation of judicial, legislative and executive powers. Moldova's independence and neutrality are enshrined in the constitution, as are the rights of all ethnic minorities.
For administrative purposes Moldova is divided into 40 districts (*raioane*) and 10 cities. Gagauz-Yeri and Transdniestr are guarenteed autonomous status, although the unrecognised separatist government of Transdniestr also claims outright independence.

Independence date

27 August 1991

Form of state

Parliamentary democratic republic

The executive

Executive power is held by the president of the republic, who must approve legislation and may also propose it. The president nominates the prime minister and government.
Candidates for the presidency must be over 35 years of age, resident in the country for at least 10 years and speakers of the national language. The president is elected for a term of four years by the parliament. The president is limited to two consecutive terms of office.

National legislature

The unicameral Parlamentul (parliament) has 101-members elected by proportional representation for a term of four years. The legislative body appoints the president. It can also approve or reject presidential nominations for the prime minister and government. The government must be appointed within 30 days of parliamentary elections or fresh elections must be called.

Legal system

The legal system is based on civil law. The Constitutional Court is the highest legal authority. It reviews the legality of legislative acts and must validate the election of the president and all members of parliament. Its independence is guaranteed by the constitution and judges, once selected, cannot be removed without their consent. The Constitutional Court consists of six judges, two each appointed by the president, parliament and Higher Council of Magistrates, all for a six-year term.
The rest of the justice system is administered by the Supreme Court, Appeals Court and lesser courts. Following recommendation by the Higher Council of Justice, the judges of the Supreme Court are appointed by parliament, and those of all lesser courts by the president of the republic, all for a renewable term of five years.
The Higher Council of Magistrates consists of 11 members, of which five (the minister of justice, the president of the Supreme Court, the president of the Court of Appeal, the president of the Court of

Business Audit and the prosecutor general) are automatic members, a further three are judges appointed by the Supreme Court and three are academic lawyers appointed by parliament.

Last elections

30 November 2014 (parliamentary); 16 March 2012 (presidential, indirect)

Results: Parliamentary (early): Partidul Socialistilor din Republica Moldova (PSRM) (Party of Socialists of the Republic of Moldova) (previously known as Partidul Socialistilor din Moldova 'Patria-Rodina' (PSMPR) (Party of Socialists of Moldova 'Motherland') 20.51 per cent (25 seats, out of 101), Partidul Liberal Democrat din Moldova (PLDM) (Liberal Democratic Party of Moldova) 20.16 per cent (23), Partidul Comunistilor din Moldova (PCM) (Party of Communists of Moldova) 17.48 per cent (23), Partidul Democrat din Moldova (PDM) (Democratic Party of Moldova) 15.80 per cent (13), Partidul Liberal (PL) (Liberal Party) 9.97 per cent (13). No other party won the minimum of 5 per cent necessary to win seats under the party-list proportional representation system. Turnout was 55.85 per cent. Presidential: Nicolae Timofti won 61.4 per cent of the vote.

Next elections

2018 (parliamentary); 2016 (presidential)

Political parties

Ruling party

Coalition: Alliance for European Integration (AEI), led by Liberal Democrat din Moldova (PLDM) (Liberal Democratic Party of Moldova), with Partidul Democrat din Moldova (PDM) (Democratic Party of Moldova) and Partidul Liberal (PL) (Liberal Party) (from 2009; re-elected 30 Nov 2014, despite losing ground)

Main opposition party

Partidul Socialistilor din Republica Moldova (Party of Socialists of the Republic of Moldova) (PSMPR)

The population is declining owing to low birth rates, low life expectancy and high emigration.

Population

3.56 million (2013)

Last census: October 2004: 3,388,071 (provisional)

Population density: At 132 people per square km. Urban population 47 per cent (2010 Unicef).

Annual growth rate: -1.0 per cent, 1990–2010 (Unicef).

Internally Displaced Persons (IDP)

1,000 (UNHCR 2004)

Ethnic make-up

The high number of ethnic Ukrainians and Russians in Moldova stems from the former Soviet Union's forced emigration policies in an attempt to dilute the ethnic Moldovan population. There are internal disputes with ethnic Russians and Ukrainians in the separatist Transdniestr region and with Gagauz Turks in the south. Ethnic groups in Moldova include: Moldovan/Romanian (64.5 per cent); Ukrainian (13.8 per cent); Russian (13 per cent); Gagauz (3.5 per cent); Bulgarian (2 per cent); and others (3.2 per cent).

Religions

Christianity is the majority religion in Moldova, the principal denomination being the Eastern Orthodox Church (98.5 per cent). The Gagauz also adhere to Orthodox Christianity despite their Turkic roots. There are Romanian and Turkish liturgies in Moldova, but the Russian Orthodox Church (Moscow Patriarchy) has jurisdiction.

Although there are an estimated 20,000 Roman Catholics in Moldova, the Moldovan branch of the Roman Catholic Church, founded in 1848, has few active congregations. Approximately 1.5 per cent of the population is Jewish.

Education

Primary education lasts for four years, at aged 10 students move on to secondary school for seven or eight years. This is divided into five years of lower secondary school and may be followed by two or three years of upper secondary school, following either technical or academic programmes, leading to either higher education or further training. Lessons may be given in either Romanian or Russian. There are several private higher education institutions.

Before the collapse of the Soviet Union, Moldova's education system was completely integrated into the Soviet system. This meant that most teaching was in the Russian language. Since independence, the curriculum has become much more focussed on Moldovan history and culture. The Moldovan government has restored the Romanian language in schools and added courses in Romanian literature and history to the curriculum. The governments of Romania and Moldova established strong ties between their education systems. Several thousand Moldovan students have attended school in Romania, and the Romanian government has donated textbooks to replace Soviet-era books.

The government's decision to introduce Russian in primary schools as a mandatory subject in 2002 was a cause of much controversy, later however, the government announced that the Russian language lessons would be optional.

Literacy rate: 99 per cent adult rate; 100 per cent youth rate (15–24) (Unesco 2005).

Compulsory years: 6 to 15.

Enrolment rate: 97 per cent total primary enrolment of the relevant age group (including repetition rates); 81 per cent secondary enrolment (World Bank).

Pupils per teacher: 23 in primary schools.

Health

HIV/Aids

HIV prevalence: 0.2 per cent aged 15–49 in 2003 (World Bank)

Life expectancy: 67 years, 2004 (WHO 2006)

Fertility rate/Maternal mortality rate: 1.5 births per woman, 2010 (Unicef)

Birth rate/Death rate: 15.27 births and 12.79 deaths per 1,000 people (2005 estimates)

Child (under 5 years) mortality rate (per 1,000): 18 per 1,000 live births (WHO 2012)

Head of population per physician: 2.64 physicians per 1,000 people, 2003 (WHO 2006)

Welfare

A social insurance system covers old age pensions, worker's disability, survivors, sickness and maternity benefit and family allowance, plus unemployment payments. Contributions are obtained from workers at 1 per cent of earnings (23 per cent for self-employed); 29–30 per cent employer's payroll, dependent on industry or enterprise; central government pays *ad hoc* flat-rate payments; regional (Republics), local authorities and employers can also provide supplementary benefits, from their own budgets, for specific needs.

Moldova remains one of the poorest countries in the region and pensioners remain particularly disadvantaged, accounting for 20 per cent of the population. The government intends to introduce private pensions to supplement the current state pension system. In 1999, legislation on private pensions allowed for the establishment of both open and closed pension funds based on voluntary contributions.

Pensions

The minimum retirement age is 62 years with a full pension dependent on 32 years of insurance cover.

Main cities

Chisinau (Kishinev) (capital, estimated population 554,585 in 2012), Tiraspol (132,105), Balti (97,237), Tighina (90,627), Rybnica (46,997).

Languages spoken

The 1994 constitution states that Moldovan is the country's official language, although it allows for the use of other languages in the country's ethnic minority areas. Officially known as 'limba moldoveneasca' (language of Moldova), Moldovan is a dialect of Romanian.

Russian is the first language of about one-third of the population, and is more universally spoken than Moldovan. Most people are bilingual.
The government attempted to introduce a language law in 1989 which would force government officials to speak both Moldovan and Russian. Since many Russian-speakers could not speak Moldovan and needed time to learn the language, the parliament decided in 1994 to postpone the law indefinitely. The law was a major factor in accelerating the separatist movements of the Russian-speaking Transdniestr region and of the Gagauz-Yeri minority who speak Gagauz (a Turkish dialect). Other minority languages include Ukrainian and Bulgarian.
The government's decision, although later annulled, to introduce Russian in primary schools as a mandatory subject in 2002 was the cause of much controversy.

Official language/s

Moldovan (in latin script)

Media

Despite freedom of the press guaranteed under the constitution, press laws and a penal code can be used by the state to curb the reporting powers of the press. There is little real independence, particularly within the state-owned media. Editorial interference in privately or publicly owned media by political and business interests is commonplace.

Press

Dailies: In Moldovan Romanian, top newspapers include *Timpul* (www.timpul.mdl.net), *Moldova Suverana* (www.moldova-suverana.md) and *Jurnal de Chisinau* (www.jurnal.md), while *Flux* (www.flux.md) is an influential publication. In Russian, *Nezavisimaya Moldova* (www.nm.md) is a government publication, *Moldavskie Vedomosti* (www.vedomosti.md) is a conservative newspaper.
In Transdniestr, in Moldovan Romanian *Ziarul de Garda*, with an online English edition (http://garda.com.md/english/), is funded by the US government.
Weeklies: In Moldovan Romanian, *Saptamina* is a centrist publication. In Transdniestr, in English, *The Tiraspol Times* (www.tiraspoltimes.com) is a news review magazine.
Business: In Russian, publications include *Delovaya Gazeta* and *Ekonomicheskoe Obozrenie* (http://logos.press.md) and in Romanian *Observator Economic*.
Periodicals: In Moldovan Romanian, the arts magazine *Sud-Est* (www.sud-est.md) is published monthly.

Broadcasting

Teleradio Moldova (TRM) (www.trm.md) is the national broadcaster.
Radio: TRM (www.trm.md) operates Radio Moldova, which includes an international station. Other, private stations include Fresh FM (www.freshfm.md), which is a national network, Radio Noroc (www.radionoroc.md), Radio 7 (www.radio7.md), Russkoye Radio (www.rusradio.md) in Russian and Vocea Basarabiei (www.voceabasarabiei.net) a Christian content station.
Television: TRM (www.trm.md) operates Moldova One and TV Moldova International. Other, private digital channels include Pro TV (www.protv.md), TV7 (www.tv7.md) and Perviy Kanal Moldova (www.prime.md) which re-broadcasts the Russian federal channel from Moscow.
Other news agencies: Basa-press: www.basa.md
Infotag: www.infotag.md
Interlic: http://en.interlic.md
Moldpres: www.moldpres.md

Economy

Agriculture plays a large role in the economy, although its share of GDP has decreased from 17 per cent in 2005–06 to 13.8 per cent in 2013. Moldova's long established viniculture sector typically provides 30 per cent of all exports. Now that foreign direct investment (FDI) and international economic aid is being applied, Moldova has embraced a free market economy. In 2013, Moldova increased its ranking from 99 to 78 (out of 183) on the World Bank's *Ease of Doing Business* survey. FDI was US$712.7 million in 2008 which plummeted to US$127.8 million in 2009, before increasing to a modest US$194.3 million in 2010 and then further to US$251 million in 2013 and US$207 million in 2014.
GDP growth has fallen from a steady 7.5 in 2004–05 to an average of 3.9 per cent in 2006–07 due to a year-long ban that was imposed by Russia on Moldavian wine imports and then a major drought in 2007 that severely reduced agricultural production. Despite a recovery of GDP growth in 2008 to 7.8 per cent, the economy fell into recession of -6.0 per cent in 2009 as Moldova was affected by the global economic downturn, as remittances declined and FDI dropped off sharply. GDP growth rebounded to a rate of 7.1 per cent in 2010, which fell back into recession at -0.7 per cent in 2012 before improving to 9.4 per cent in 2013 and 4.6 per cent in 2014.
Moldova is one of the poorest countries in Europe, with an economy that was under-developed during the period of the Soviet Union's centrally planned economic control. In 2013, the UN Human Development Index (HDI) ranked Moldova 114 (out of 187) for national development in health, education and income. Since 2000, Moldova's progress has strengthened but has not matched the improvement of other countries in Europe and Central Asia. In 2013, 38.8 per cent of the population experienced at least one indicator of poverty.
Emigration is around 14 per cent per annum, with over 85 per cent of migrants working in Europe. Remittances from migrant workers amounted to US$1.4 billion (23.2 per cent of GDP) in 2010 and was estimated to have reached US$2 billion in 2013 (25 per cent of GDP).
Inflation had been in double digits since before 2004, averaging 12 per cent, but in 2009 a sharp increase in imported natural gas and higher food prices cut domestic spending so that inflation fell to 0.0 per cent. It rose to 7.4 per cent as world trade began to pick up in 2010 but had dropped to 4.7 per cent by 2013, it has once again increased to 12.2 per cent in August 2015.

External trade

Moldova has a free trade agreement with the Central European Free Trade Agreement (Cefta). It has traditional ties with Russia which were, following the break-up of the Soviet Union, formalised through the Commonwealth of Independent States (CIS).
On 19 October 2011, Russia signed a free trade agreement (FTA) with seven of its former Soviet republics: Armenia, Belarus, Kazakhstan, Kyrgyzstan, Moldova and Tajikistan.

Imports

Mineral products and fuel, machinery and equipment, chemicals and textiles.
Main sources: Romania (15.2 per cent of total in 2014), Russia (13.5 per cent), Ukraine (10.3 per cent), China (9.1 per cent) and Germany (8.1 per cent).

Exports

Foodstuffs, textiles and machinery.
Main destinations: Romania (18.9 per cent of total in 2014), Russia (18.4 per cent), Italy (10.6 per cent), Germany (6 per cent) and Belarus (5.9 per cent).

Agriculture

Farming

Agriculture remains a key sector of the national economy. The sector contributes around a fifth of GDP and is a considerable source of export revenue. It employs over 40 per cent of the working population. Moldova's main resources are its climate and the rich black *chernozem* soil covering 75 per cent of the land, making it ideal for growing wine grapes, tobacco, sugar beet and for raising dairy cattle. Grains, vegetables and fruits are also important. The animal husbandry sector specialises in the breeding of livestock, pigs and poultry.

The majority of production continues to be from state farms and co-operatives, although as the land reform programme progresses this is expected to change. Agro-industrial complexes are dominant in meat and dairy production. Pork is the main domestic protein source. A quarter of total meat production is exported. There are around 150 wineries in Moldova and 170,000 hectares (ha) of vineyards. The wine making industry has attracted foreign investment and is dependent upon markets in the CIS. The majority of annual sugar exports go to former Soviet republics. Moldova is also a major tobacco producer.

Fishing

Only 20 fish species, including crucian carp, perch, bream and soodak, are of any commercial importance. Most of the fish resources are concentrated in natural and artificial lakes devoted to fish breeding.

Forestry

Agriculture remains a key sector of the national economy. The sector contributed around 14 per cent of GDP in 2013 and is a considerable source of export revenue. It employs over 25 per cent of the working population. Moldova's main resources are its climate and the rich black *chernozem* soil covering 75 per cent of the land, making it ideal for growing wine grapes, tobacco, sugar beet and for raising dairy cattle. Grains, vegetables and fruits are also important. The animal husbandry sector specialises in the breeding of livestock, pigs and poultry.

The majority of production continues to be from state farms and co-operatives, although as the land reform programme progresses this is expected to change. Agro-industrial complexes are dominant in meat and dairy production. Pork is the main domestic protein source. A quarter of total meat production is exported. There are around 150 wineries in Moldova and 170,000 hectares (ha) of vineyards. The wine making industry has attracted foreign investment and is dependent upon markets in the CIS. The majority of annual sugar exports go to former Soviet republics. Moldova is also a major tobacco producer.

Industry and manufacturing

Industry accounts for approximately 35 per cent of GDP. A quarter of industrial production is located in the disputed Transdniestr region, where most of Moldova's electricity, metallurgy and metallurgical equipment are produced.

The agro-industrial sector is at the heart of the economy, carrying out the production, transportation, processing, storage and sale of agricultural products. Other industries are diverse and include electronics, machine tools, tractors, agricultural engineering, building materials, chemicals and furniture manufacture.

Industrial production increased by 9 per cent in 2003.

Tourism

Moldova has a rich and diverse tradition in wine making and attracts many visitors to experience its viniculture. Visitors have also been drawn to its rural villages, remote monasteries and natural landscapes.

Tourism in Moldova is an underdeveloped industry that has suffered from a lack of tourist infrastructure, as well as an economy that has struggled since the global economic crisis struck in 2008, which pushed up prices and cut visitor numbers. In 2013, 12,000 foreign visitors arrived, the majority of which were from Romania, Turkey, Ukraine and Russia, up from 8,956 in 2010.

Travel and tourism contributed 2.6 per cent of GDP in 2013 (US$200 million, down form US$300 million in 2007). Employment in the industry fell from 4.1 per cent of total employment (66,800 jobs) in 2007 to 2.8 per cent (32,300 jobs) in 2010 and further to 2.2 per cent (27,000 jobs) in 2013.

Hydrocarbons

There were no commercially exploited oil or gas reserves by 2013. Consumption of oil was 19,660 barrels per day in 2013, all of which were imported. The potential for oil and gas is high, as Moldova has contiguous geology with known deposits of oil in neighbouring Ukraine. However, exploration is still hampered by limited foreign investment.

A new, US$38 million, oil terminal was opened in 2007 in the south of Moldova at Giurgiulesti, on the Danube, reducing Moldova's overall reliance on Russian oil.

Natural gas imports were 2.1 billion cubic metres (cum) in 2012, all of which was imported from Russia. Although breakaway Transdniestr has only 15 per cent of Moldova's population it consumes around 50 per cent of total natural gas imports for industrial production. The monopoly domestic gas distributor Moldovagaz, is heavily indebted to Russian gas monopoly Gazprom. Following the loss of a court case in Russia in 2008, it was decided that Moldovagaz was responsible for debts accrued by the Transdniestr's gas distributor Tiraspoltransgaz, which owes US$1.46 billion of the total debt.

Exploration for natural gas reserves is ongoing, with Gazprom leading the way.

There are an estimated 10 million tonnes of bituminous coal; however production is only around 100,000 tonnes per annum.

Energy

Total installed generating capacity was 552MW in 2012, producing over 5.8 billion-kilowatt hours. The majority of energy is produced in three power stations. However, most capacity is produced in the disputed province of Transdniestr.

Hydropower produces around 60MW of energy. Moldova is trying to conserve energy and to develop alternative power sources – solar, wind and geothermal.

Financial markets

Stock exchange

Bursei de Valori a Moldavie (Moldova Stock Exchange) (MSE)

Banking and insurance

Central bank

Banca Nationala a Moldovei (BNM) (National Bank of Moldova)

Time

GMT plus two hours (daylight saving, late March to late October, GMT plus three hours)

Geography

Moldova is a landlocked country in south-eastern Europe, bordered to the north, east and south by Ukraine and to the west by Romania. Most of the country consists of flat plains with low hills. Approximately 11 per cent of Moldova is forested.

Moldova is a fertile plain with small areas of hill country in the centre and north. The main rivers are the Dniestr, which flows through the eastern regions and on into the Black Sea, and the Prut, which marks the western border with Romania and which joins the Danube at the southern tip of Moldova.

The separatist Republic of Transdniestr (not officially recognised) lies between the eastern Ukrainian border and the Dniestr River.

Hemisphere

Northern

Climate

With a temperate, continental climate Moldova has long hot summers and chilly winters. Average temperatures vary between minus 2 degrees Celsius (C) and 22 degrees C. Extremes of temperature can reach 35 degrees C during summer and minus 25 degrees C (with a good deal of ice and snow) in the winter. Average annual rainfall is 500–550mm in the northern and central areas and 450mm in the south.

Dress codes

Business dress is usually quite conservative, but not excessively formal.

Entry requirements

Passports

Required by all. Passports must be valid for at least six months after the date of departure.

Visa

Required by all except CIS nationals. Visit www.consularassistance.com/consular.html for the requirements and a visa application form, to be submitted to the nearest consulate for processing. Limited stay visas can be obtained at Chisinau airport and some major road crossings from Romania; however, these cost more than those organised in advance. Arrival by train requires a visa before travelling.

Currency advice/regulations

The import and export of local currency is unlimited; the import of foreign currency is unlimited but the amount must be declared and export is limited to the amount declared.

Travellers cheques are not in general use, although some banks may exchange them.

Customs

A small amount of personal goods are allowed in duty-free. On arrival declare all valuable items such as jewellery, cameras, computers and musical instruments.

Health (for visitors)

Mandatory precautions

Vaccination certificates for cholera and yellow fever are mandatory if travelling from an infected area. Any person applying for a visa for a stay of more than three months must present a certificate showing that the individual is HIV negative. Only tests performed at clinics approved by the Moldovan government are accepted.

Advisable precautions

It is advisable to be in date for the following immunisations: diphtheria, polio and tetanus (within 10 years), typhoid fever, hepatitis A (moderate risk only), hepatitis B, tuberculosis and tick-borne encephalitis. Healthcare is free in Moldova (although medicines must be purchased). There are chemists where you can buy basic drugs (aspirin, etc), but it is wise to take a supply of frequently used medicines with you, including precautionary antibiotics if travelling outside main urban areas. A travel kit, including disposable syringes, is a reasonable precaution. There is a rabies risk. Water precautions are recommended and water purification tablets may be useful.

Credit cards

Credit cards are not in general use, some banks may accept them.

Public holidays (national)

Fixed dates

1 Jan (New Year's Day), 8 Mar (Women's Day), 1 May (Labour Day), 9 May (Victory Day), 27 Aug (Independence Day), 31 Aug (Limba Noastra/National Language Day), 14 Oct (Chisinau City Day).

Variable dates

Religious holidays are celebrated by adherents (Orthodox Christmas and Easter).

Working hours

Banking

Mon–Sat: 0930–1730 for banks; 0900–1800 for *bureau de change*.

Business

Mon–Fri: 0900–1800.

Government

Mon–Fri: 0900–1800.

Shops

Mon: 0800–1700, Tue–Sat: 0800–2100.

Telecommunications

Mobile/cell phones

GSM 900 services available throughout most of the country.

Electricity supply

220V AC 50 Hz.

Weights and measures

Metric system

Social customs/useful tips

Business appointments are essential and punctuality appreciated. Business cards are usually exchanged. There are many customs and traditions to be understood. Gratuities are becoming more customary, particularly in international hotels.

Take flowers if invited to someone's home and leave shoes at the door.

Security

Although safer than many Western cities, the streets of Chisinau have become more dangerous since independence, particularly after dark. Care should be taken to avoid unlit areas, even in the city centre. There are few embassies in Chisinau (no British Embassy, for instance). Before departure to Moldova, visitors are advised to check with their own ministry of foreign affairs for information on who to contact in the case of an emergency. The British Foreign & Commonwealth Office (FCO), for example, advises its nationals to contact the British Embassy in Bucharest in Romania.

Avoid all travel in the eastern region of Transdniestr.

Getting there

Air

National airline: Air Moldova; services are not extensive with international flights to Europe only.

International airport/s: Chisinau International (KIV), 13km south-east of the city with duty-free and bank. Taxis and a regular bus service are available to the city (travel time 15–25 minutes).

Airport tax: Departure tax: US$12.

Surface

Road: The principal route runs from Odessa in the Crimea into Moldova through Tiraspol, north to Chisinau, Bel'tsy and then back into Ukraine. Buses run to Chisinau from Bucharest, Romania.

Rail: The Moldovan rail network is connected to that of Ukraine, Romania and Russia. The principal rail routes connect Chisinau with Tiraspol and Ukraine to the east, and Lasi in Romania to the west. The journey time to Bucharest is approximately 11.5 hours, to Moscow 22 hours and Sofia 23 hours. First-class sleeping carriages, booked in advance from Chisinau station, are recommended.

Water: The Dniestr River flows into the Black Sea in Ukraine, near the port of Odessa. It is used more for industrial transportation than for passengers.

Getting about

National transport

Road: The road network, although extensive, is in need of significant investment and repair. The main routes run from Kagul to Chisinau via Komrat and from Chisinau to Lipkany via Bel'tsy. Roads from Tiraspol in Transdniestr to Chisinau and other destinations in the rest of Moldova may be subject to closure due to conflict in the breakaway region.

Buses: There are buses between larger towns.

Taxis: Can be hired by the hour, prices should be negotiated before travelling.

Rail: Most larger towns are connected by rail. Lines run north-south from Kagul and the southern border with Ukraine to Lipkany and the northern border with Ukraine. Owing to the Transdniestr conflict, routes from Chisinau and Kagul to Tiraspol and Bendery are liable to disruption.

Water: The Dniestr River runs parallel to Moldova's eastern border, and is extensively used, although mostly for industrial rather than passenger transport.

City transport

The names of streets are in both Moldovan and Russian.

Taxis: Taxis are widely available and can be picked up at stands or hailed anywhere in the city.

Car hire

Vehicles with a driver or for self-drive are readily available; an international driving permit is required.

BUSINESS DIRECTORY

The addresses listed below are a selection only. While World of Information makes every endeavour to check these addresses, we cannot guarantee that changes have not been made, especially to telephone numbers and area codes. We would welcome any corrections.

Telephone area codes

The international direct dialling (IDD) code for Moldova is +373, followed by the area code and subscriber's number:

Chisinau	22	Bendery	282
Bel'tsy	231	Tiraspol	284

Useful telephone numbers

Ambulance: 903
Fire: 901
Police: 902
Operator assistance for international telephone calls: 071

Chambers of Commerce

American Chamber of Commerce in Moldova, Joly Alon Hotel, 37 Maria Cebotari Street, Chisinau 2012.

Moldova Chamber of Commerce and Industry, 151 Stefan cel Mare Street, Chisinau 2004 (tel: 221-552; fax: 234-425; e-mail: president@chamber.md).

Banking

Banca Comerciala Romana SA Sucursala, 32A Tricolorului Street, Chisinau 2012 (tel: 220-549; fax: 223-509; email: bcr@cni.md).

Banca Sociala, 61 Banulescu-Bodoni Street, Chisinau 2006 (tel: 221-481; fax: 224-230).

BTR Moldova, 18 Renasterii Street, Chisinau 2005 (tel: 201-100; fax: 201-101; e-mail: office@btr.md).

Businessbanca, 9 Alexandru cel Bun Street, Chisinau 2012 (tel: 223-338; fax: 222-370).

Chisinau Municipal Bank, 83 Stefan cel Mare Avenue, Chisinau 2012 (tel/fax: 228-090).

Comertbank, 63 Columna Street, Chisinau 2001 (tel: 541-356; fax: 543-151; e-mail: combank@chmoldpac.md).

Energbank, 78 Vasile Alexandri Street, Chisinau 2012 (tel: 544-377; fax: 253-409).

Export - Import, 6 Stefan cel Mare Avenue, Chisinau 2001 (tel: 272-583; fax: 546-234; e-mail: exim@eximbank.com).

Finance and Trade Bank, 26 Pushkin Street, Chisinau 2012 (tel: 227-435; fax: 228-253; e-mail: fincom@fcb.mldnet.com).

International Commercial Bank (Moldova), 108 Mitropolit Dosoftei Street, Chisnau 2012 (tel: 226-025; fax: 225-053; e-mail: info@icbsb.md).

Investprivatbank, 34 Sciusev Street, Chisinau 2001 (tel: 274-386; fax: 540-510; email: bnc@ipb.mldnet.com).

Mobiasbanca, 65 Tighina Street, Chisinau 2001 (tel/fax: 541-974; email: info@bcmobias.moldova.su).

Moldindconbank, 38 Armeneasca Street, Chisinau 2012. (tel: 225-521: fax: 279-195; email: computer@micb.net.md).

Moldova - Agroindbank, 9 Cosmonautilor Street, Chisinau 2006 (tel: 222-770; fax: 242-454).

PetrolBANK, 33 Ismail Street, Chisinau 2001 (tel: 500-101; fax: 548-827; email: juri@petrolbank.com).

Savings Bank, 115 Columna Street, Chisinau 2012 (tel: 244-722; fax: 244-731; email: bem@cni.md).

Unibank, 26 Pushkin Street, Chisinau 2012 (tel: 225-586; fax: 220-530).

Universalbank, 180 Stefan cel Mare Avenue, Chisinau 2004 (tel: 246-406; fax: 246-489; email:stabil@mail.universalbank.md).

Victoriabank, 141 August 31 Street, Chisinau 2004 (tel: 233-065; fax: 233-933; email: mail@victoriabank.md).

Central bank

Banca Nationala a Moldovei, 7 Renasterii Avenue, Chisinau 2006 (tel: 221-679; fax: 220-591; e-mail: webmaster@bnm.org).

Stock exchange

Bursei de Valori a Moldavie (Moldova Stock Exchange) (MSE), www.moldse.md

Travel information

Air Moldova, Aeroportul Chisinau, MD 2026, Chisinau (tel: 529-356; fax: 525-064; internet: www.mdv.md).

Ministry of tourism

Ministry of Culture and Tourism, Piata Marii Adunari 1, MD-2033, Chisinau (tel: 227-620; fax: 232-388).

National tourist organisation offices

National Tourism Agency, 180 Stefan cel Mare Street, Office 901 Chisinau MD 2004, (tel: 210 774; internet www.turism.md).

Ministries

Ministry of Agriculture and Food Industry, 162 Stefan cel Mare Boulevard, Chisinau (tel: 233-427; fax: 232-368).

Ministry of Culture, 1 Piata Marii Adunari Nationale, Chisinau (tel: 227-620; fax: 232-388).

Ministry of Defence, 84 Vasile Alexandri Street, Chisinau (tel: 781-156; fax: 233-507).

Ministry of Economy and Reforms, Piata Marii Adunari Nationale 1, 277033 Chisinau (tel: 221-133; fax: 234-064).

Ministry of Education, 1 Piata Marii Adunari Nationale (tel: 233-151; fax: 233-474).

Ministry of Finance, Cosmonautilor Street, 277012 Chisinau (tel: 233-575; fax: 228-610).

Ministry of Foreign Affairs, 1 Piata Marii Adunari Nationale, Chisinau (tel: 233-940; fax: 232-302).

Ministry of Foreign Economic Relations, Piata Marii Adunari Nationale 1, Chisinau 277033 (tel/fax: 234-628).

Ministry of Health, 1 Vasile Alexandri Street, Chisinau (tel: 721-010; fax: 738-781).

Ministry of Industry and Trade, 69 Stefan cel Mare Boulevard, Chisinau (tel: 233-556; fax: 227-346).

Ministry of Internal Affairs, 75 Stefan cel Mare Boulevard, Chisinau (tel: 221-201; fax: 222-723).

Ministry of Justice, 82, 31 August Street, Chisinau (tel: 233-340; fax: 234-797).

Ministry of Labour, Social Protection and Family, 1 Vasile Alexandri Street, Chisinau (tel: 737-572; fax: 723-000).

Ministry of National Security, 166 Stefan cel Mare Boulevard, Chisinau (tel: 239-454; fax: 242-018).

Ministry of Privatisation and State Property Administration, 26 Puskin Street, Chisinau (tel: 234-350; fax: 234-336; internet site: http://privatization.md).

Ministry of Territorial Development, Public Utilities and Construction, 3 Gheorghe Tudor Street, Chisinau (tel: 259-111; fax: 259-499).

Ministry of Telecommunications and Informatics, 134 Stefan cel Mare Boulevard, Chisinau (tel: 221-001; fax: 241-553).

Ministry of Transport and Road Construction, 12/A Bucuriei Street, Chisinau (tel: 629-450; fax: 624-875).

Other useful addresses

British Embassy (there is no British representative in Moldova but the British Embassy in Moscow has some responsibility), Commercial Department, Kutuzovsky Prospeckt 7/4, Moscow 121248 (tel: 956-7477; fax: 956-7480).

Business Centre of Moldova Ltd., Stefan cel Mare 180, Room 303, 277004 Chisinau (tel: 247-914; fax: 247-915).

Department of Civil Protection and Exceptional Situations, 69 Cheorghe Asachi Street, Chisinau (tel: 233-430; fax: 233-430).

Department of Customs Control, 65 Columna Street, Chisinau (tel: 549-460; fax: 263-061).

Department of Energy Resources and Fuel, 50 Eminescu Street, Chisinau (tel: 221-010; fax: 222-264).

Department of Environmental Protection, 73 Stefan cel Mare Boulevard, Chisinau (tel: 226-161; fax: 233-806).

Department of National Relations, 109/1, Alexei Mateevici Street, Chisinau (tel: 240-292; fax: 243-610).

Department of Publishing, Polygraphy and Trade of Books, 180 Stefan cel Mare Boulevard, Chisinau (tel: 246-525).

Department of Standards, Metrology and Technical Control, 48 Serghei Lazo Street, Chisinau (tel: 247-991; fax: 222-321).

Department of Statistics, 124 Stefan cel Mare Avenue, Chisinau 227001 (tel: 233-549; fax: 545-162).

MoldEnergo, 78 Vasile Alexandri Str, 277012 Chisinau (tel: 221-065; fax: 253-142).

Moldexpo International Exhibition Centre, 1 Ghioceilor, 277008 Chisinau (tel: 627-416; fax: 627-420).

Moldovan Foreign Trade Organisation, ul Sadovaya 65, 277018 Chisinau (tel: 244-436; fax: 223-226).

Moldova-Gaz, 38 Albisoara Str, 277005 Chisinau (tel: 256-778; fax: 240-014).

Moldova Stock Exchange, 73 Stefan cel Mare, 277001 Chisinau (tel: 265-554; fax: 228-969).

Moldovan Embassy (USA), 2101 S Street, NW, Washington DC 20008 (tel: (+1-202) 667-1130; fax: (+1-202) 667-120-4; e-mail: moldova@dgs.dgsys.com).

Moldsilva (Forestry Association), 124 Stefan cel Mare Blvd, 277012 Chisinau (tel: 262-256; fax: 223-251).

National Association of Banks, 7 Renasterii Str, 277006 Chisinau (tel: 225-177; fax: 229-382).

National Foreign Trade Company (Moldova-EXIM), 65 Mateevici Str, 277012 Chisinau (tel: 223-226; fax: 244-436).

National Fuel Association, 90 Columna Str, 277001 Chisinau (tel: 223-078; fax: 240-509).

State Company Teleradio Moldova National TV and Radio, 64 Hincesti Highway, 277028 Chisinau (tel: 721-077, 721-863).

Basa-press: www.basa.md

Infotag: www.infotag.md

Interlic: http://en.interlic.md

Moldpres: www.moldpres.md

Internet sites

Business information: http://www.infomarket.md

Business network: http://www.mbinet.md

Chamber of Commerce: http://www:chamber.md

Freezone and export processing: http://www:moldova-freezone.com

General information (in Moldovan - Romanian): http://www.moldova.md

General government and economy: http://www.moldova.org

IMF Moldova office: http://www.imf.md

Internet resources directory: http://www.ournet.md

Ministry of Economy - Trade department: http://www.trade.moldova

Moldovan parliament: http://www.parlament.md

National Bank rates: http://www.mldnet.com

Monaco

COUNTRY PROFILE

1297 Francois Grimaldi, at the time in exile from Genoa, led a group of partisans into Monaco, which has been ruled by the family ever since.
Honore II signed a treaty of friendship with France, guaranteeing the independence of the principality.
1524–1641 The Grimaldi family was allied with Spain and Monaco came under Spanish protection.
1793 After the French Revolution the Grimaldis were deposed and Monaco was unified with France.
1814 The principality was re-established after its abolition during the French Revolution.
1861 Its independence was guaranteed under French protection. The first constitution was introduced.
1918 Louis, the heir to the throne, was a bachelor and the next male in line to succeed if Louis died without an heir was a German prince, the Duke of Urach. France would not countenance a German monarch and therefore imposed a constitutional provision that only the monarch's own children could inherit the throne.
1949 Prince Rainier III succeeded to the throne.
1956 Prince Rainier married the American actress, Grace Kelly.
1962 A constitution was enacted that allowed for sharing of legislative powers between the monarch and elected national council; principle of divine right was abolished.
1982 Princess Grace was killed in a car accident.
1988 The Union Nationale et Démocratique (UND) (National and Democratic Union) won the elections.
1993 The UND was defeated by two lists of candidates, known as Liste Campora and Liste Medecin.
1993 Monaco was admitted to the UN.
1998 UND won the elections.
2000 France threatened to take legislative measures against Monaco unless it clamped down on money laundering activities.
2001 France and Monaco reached an agreement on money laundering. Monaco agreed to work more closely with the Financial Oversight Commission (FOC) to revise rules governing investment management companies.
2002 Monaco adopted the euro as its official currency. Parliament changed the 1918 law of succession, allowing succession through the female line (distaff side) if Prince Albert died without a legitimate heir. Liechtenstein concluded an agreement with Monaco over the prevention of money laundering and terrorist financing.
2003 The Union pour Monaco (UPM) (Union for Monaco) alliance, led by Stephané Valeri, won a landslide majority in the parliamentary elections, ending the 40-year rule of the UND.
2004 Prince Rainier was diagnosed with heart problems.
2005 Prince Rainier III died. He had been the longest serving monarch in Europe. Prince Albert II was enthroned and Jean-Paul Proust was appointed as minister of state.
2008 In parliamentary elections, the ruling Union pour Monaco (Union for Monaco) coalition won 21 out of 24 seats, the Rassemblement et Enjeux pour Monaco (REM) (Rally and Issues of Monaco) won three seats and the Monaco Ensemble (Monaco Together) failed to win any. Turnout was 76.9 per cent.
2009 The Organisation for Economic Co-operation and Development (OECD) removed Monaco from its list of non-co-operative tax havens, after Monaco declared that it would comply with OECD requirements.
2011 Prince Albert married Charlene Wittstock (a South African Olympic swimmer) in June.
2012 On 12 July the government revived the proposal for the St Portier Quarter land reclamation project, but on a smaller scale of no more than five hectares. A new political party was founded in November, called Renaissance. It was formed by employees of the Société des Bains Mer (SBM) (leisure industry), largely to fight for better employment prospects.
2013 In October MEPs urged the European Commission to allow the three micro-states of Andorra, Monaco and San Marino to join the European Economic Area (EEA).
2015 The twin daughters of Prince Albert II and Princess Charlene were baptised at Monaco Cathedral on 10 May.

KEY FACTS

Official name: Principauté de Monaco (The Principality of Monaco)

Head of State: Prince Albert II (acceded to the throne 6 Apr 2005)

Head of government: Minister of State Michel Roger (took office 29 Mar 2010)

Ruling party: Horizon Monaco, a right-leaning coalition

Area: 2 square km

Population: 36,000 (2011)*

Capital: Monaco-Ville

Official language: French and Monégasque

Currency: Euro (€) = 100 cents

Exchange rate: €0.89 per US$ (Sep 2015)

GDP per capita: US$172,676 (2009)*

GDP real growth: -2.60% (2009)*

GDP: US$6.11 billion (2009)

Inflation: 0.50% (2009)*

* estimated figure

Political structure

Constitution

Under the 1962 constitution, Monaco is governed under the authority of the monarch, a minister of state and a unicameral National Council.

Only Monégasques may vote.

In 2002, parliament passed a change to the 1918 law of succession. Princesses Caroline or Stephanie may inherit if Prince Albert dies without a legitimate heir. The line of succession will pass down through the line of whichever Princess assumes the title. An agreement with France allows Monaco to remain an independent country in the event of a lack of heir to succeed to the Principality.

Form of state

Parliamentary democratic monarchy

The executive

The monarch is the head of state. The monarch nominates the minister of state from a list of three French diplomats submitted by the French government. As head of the Council of Government (three members appointed by the monarch), the minister of state exercises executive power under the monarch.

The laws are initiated by the monarch; the Council of Government prepares draft legislation in his name; the National Council passes laws and the national budget (in public session); the monarch alone promulgates laws which are then published in the *Journal de Monaco*.

The government is assisted by two consultative bodies: the Council of State and the Economic Council.

National legislature

The unicameral Conseil National (national council) has 24-members, elected from lists to serve for five years. The national council has no power to topple the government, although it may act independently of the monarch.

Legal system

Although judicial authority is vested in the monarch, it is delegated to the courts and tribunals, which dispense justice in the monarch's name, but completely independently (there is no minister of justice in the Principality).

Last elections

10 February 2013 (parliamentary)

Results: Parliamentary: Horizon Monaco won 50.34 per cent and 20 seats (out of 24), Union Monégasque 38.99 per cent and 3 seats, Renaissance 10.67 per cent and 1 seat. Turnout was 74.55 per cent.

Next elections

2018 (parliamentary)

Political parties

Ruling party

Horizon Monaco, a right-leaning coalition

Main opposition party

Union Monégasque, a centrist coalition

Political situation

There was a landslide majority for the UPM alliance, led by Stephané Valeri, in the 203 parliamentary elections that ended the 40-year rule of the UND. The UND, which had held all the seats in the previous parliament, only managed to hold on to three seats. The swing in favour of the UPM was largely due to the increasing unpopularity of the UND leader, Jean-Louis Campora, who had served as parliamentary speaker for 30 years. Campora lost his seat in the election. Turnout was 80 per cent, but only around 20 per cent of the total population is eligible to vote due to the constitutional nationality requirements.

Population

36,000 (2011)*

Last census: June 2000: 32,017 (provisional)

Population density: 16,410 inhabitants per sq km. Urban population 100 per cent (2010 Unicef).

Annual growth rate: 0.7 per cent, 1990–2010 (Unicef).

Ethnic make-up

According to the 2000 census, around 7,000 of the total population are Monégasques, 11,000 French, 7,000 Italian and some 2,000 British.

Religions

The state religion is Catholicism, but religious freedom is guaranteed by the constitution. Other religions practised are Anglicanism, Baha'i, Judaism, Protestantism.

Health

Life expectancy: 82 years, 2004 (WHO 2006)

Fertility rate/Maternal mortality rate: 1.8 births per woman, 2004 (WHO 2006)

Child (under 5 years) mortality rate (per 1,000): 4 per 1,000 live births (WHO 2012)

Main cities

Monaco-Ville (capital, estimated population 912 in 2003), Monte Carlo (16,631), La Condamine (12,064), Fontvieille (4,814).

Languages spoken

Italian and English are widely spoken and understood. The traditional Monégasque language is spoken by the older generation of Monégasques and is taught in schools. Ligurian and Occitan are also spoken.

Official language/s

French and Monégasque

Media

Press

The official *Journal de Monaco* is a journal published weekly by the ministry of state,

The independent, Mediterraneum Editions (www.mediterra.com), publishes newspapers in several languages, including the in-house publications, in English *The Monaco Times* (www.mctimes.com) in Italian, *Il Corriere di Monaco* (www.corrieremonaco.com) and in German *Monaco Zeitung*. In French, *Monaco Hebdo* covers current affairs. Regional newspapers with sections devoted to Monaco include *Nice-Matin, Gazette Monaco-Côte d'Azur, Monaco Actualité* and *Monte Carlo Méditerranée*.

Broadcasting

The influence of Monaco on media broadcasting is high due, not only to its extensive radio network, but also as host to one of the oldest television awards festival.

Radio: Radio Monte Carlo (RMC) (www.rmc.fr) broadcasts throughout France and northern Italy with external services in 12 languages. The service it began, transmitting to the Arab world, Monte Carlo Doualiva, was taken over by Radio France Internationale. Riviera Radio (www.rivieraradio.mc), based in RMC studios, broadcasts in English 24 hours per day. Evangelical programmes are broadcast by shortwave in numerous foreign languages by Trans World Radio (www.twr.org).

There are also a number of private, commercial FM stations including Nostalgie (www.nostalgie.fr), Radio Monaco (www.radio-monaco.com) and Radio Classique (www.radioclassique.fr).

Television: The commercial station TMC Monte Carlo (www.tmc.tv) broadcasts popular imported films and shows as well as local news programmes. The government also operates a localised TV station, Monaco Info, showing cultural and magazine style programmes, for a limited number of hours each week.

Economy

Monaco enjoys a small, open and diversified economy based on tourism, the convention business, banking and insurance, but with a significant industrial sector. Income tax is low and Monaco attracts a number of wealthy tax 'exiles' as residents. The government does not publish primary economic information and such information typically comes from secondary sources. Government revenue is derived from value added tax (VAT) levied on hotel, banking and commercial services (55 per cent) and state monopolies such as telecommunications, the post office and tobacco industry (16 per cent);

gambling revenue accounts for 4 per cent. It is thought that financial services account for 25 per cent of GDP. The service sector contributes just under 90 per cent to GDP.

In 2009, Monaco's GDP plummeted by 11.5 per cent as the euro-zone crisis lead to a sharp drop in tourism. Monaco's economy recovered moderately in 2010 and accelerated in 2011, posting an expansion in GDP of 7.0 per cent. After dropping to 1.2 per cent in 2012, GDP growth accelerated even further reaching 9.3 per cent in 2013.

Although Monaco is not a member of the EU, France's membership gives it access to the European marketplace. Monaco adopted the euro as its official currency at the same time as France.

The base of the local economy was broadened notably through the Fontvieille development of 22 hectares of reclaimed land to the west of the old town, which is now a centre for light industry and low-cost housing. Monaco's total area was increased by one-tenth by this project.

Monaco is diversifying into the knowledge-based industry, aiming to become a European leader in multimedia, the Internet and telecommunications.

Monaco and France have a joint economic and customs union to regulate customs, postal services, telecommunications and the banking sector.

External trade

Monaco has a free trade and customs union with France, which operates within the European Union and, by extension, effects Monaco. France collects and rebates Monegasque trade duties. Virtually all foreign trade is within the service sector including financial, commercial and tourism. Many companies are registered, for tax reasons, in Monaco, which does not publish official statistics.

Imports

Fuels, food, vehicles and consumer goods.

Exports

Financial services.

Agriculture

Farming

There is no commercial agriculture in Monaco.

Industry and manufacturing

Around 200 firms employing 4,000 people typically account for about 10 per cent of GDP. Main products are cosmetics, healthcare, pharmaceuticals, precision instruments, glass, plastics, electrical goods, electronics, textiles and food processing. Also important are construction and public works.

Tourism

Known as the 'rich man's playground', Monaco (also called Monte Carlo) has venues for conferences and private functions. It has an open border with France and many of its attractions are contiguous with the coastline of Nice and Cannes. There are plenty of three- to five-star hotels available but Monaco is so small that day-trippers greatly outnumber overnight visitors.

The annual Monaco Grand Prix has been run since 1929 (suspended 1939–45) and is one of the most prestigious automobile races in the world. Formula One cars use the streets of Monaco as the circuit. Hundreds of thousands of spectators line the route to watch the event, which demands great skill.

Tourism is a vital component of the economy and contributes anywhere between 15–25 per cent of GDP (national accounts are not made public).

Hydrocarbons

There are no known hydrocarbon reserves. All oil, natural gas and coal imports are provided through France.

Energy

Monaco is entirely reliant on imports from France to meet its energy requirements. The Société Monégasque de l'Electricité et du Gaz is responsible for distribution and has a contract for electricity supply with Electricité de France (EDF).

Banking and insurance

There are nearly 50 banks and around 20 other financial institutions catering to 130,000 clients worth US$78 billion. In addition to commercial and retail services, Monaco has in recent decades increasingly provided private banking and wealth management services. Monaco's banking system operates under French banking law and is subject to regulation by the Banque de France.

Monaco's reputation as a tax haven with a secretive banking system has made enemies in other jurisdictions, which accuse Monaco of abetting money-laundering and tax evasion. Monaco has been resistant to pressure to be more be more rigorous and transparent in its dealings, but does take action against money-laundering under existing legislation. In addition, mutual assistance agreements to exchange information on money-laundering have been concluded since 2001 with several countries, including France, Spain, Belgium, and Switzerland .

Monaco was obliged to accede to the EU Savings Tax Directive, which took effect in July 2005. Under the withholding tax option, Monaco's banks and financial institutions will automatically deduct tax, initially 15 per cent rising to 35 per cent by 2011, from income earned on interest and other savings of EU citizens and transfer it to the national tax departments. Monaco will be able to retain its banking secrecy by being allowed to withhold information on non-residents' savings. Monaco has also agreed to supply information on tax fraud, for criminal or civil trials, and notify EU member states about additional malpractices.

Central bank

European Central Bank

Monaco does not have a central bank, but monetary links to France have included acceptance of French currency and subsequently the euro as legal tender, while financial institutions located in Monaco have access to the Banque de France on the similar terms to French banks.

Main financial centre

Monaco-Ville

Time

GMT plus one hour (daylight saving, late March to late September, GMT plus two hours)

Geography

The Principality of Monaco is a small enclave in south-eastern France, close to the French-Italian frontier. It comprises a narrow, 4km stretch of Mediterranean coastline with an area of 1.9 square km, situated at the foot of the Alpes Maritimes, which gives it a rocky aspect on the landward side. The highest point is Mont Agel, which reaches 140m.

Monaco is divided into four main localities: the old fortified town of Monaco-Ville, where the palace and cathedral are located; La Condamine, the harbour and business area; Monte Carlo, the resort and main residential area; and Fontvieille, an area of 0.33 square km recovered from the sea in recent years for light industry and residential development.

Hemisphere

Northern

Climate

The climate is Mediterranean with mild winters and warm summers. The hottest months are July and August, with average temperatures of 25 degrees Celsius.

Entry requirements

Passports

Required by all, except nationals of EU/EEAcountries, Switzerland, Andorra and San Marino, valid for three months beyond date of departure.

Visa

Not required for visits up to three months provided visitors arrive from France and adhere to French entry requirements. French visas are required by all, except citizens of EU, North America, Australasia and Japan, for stays up to three months;

this includes business trips by representatives of foreign entities with an invitation from a local company or organisation. Proof of adequate funds for stay, an itinerary, a guarantee of repatriation if necessary and return/onward ticket are also required.

Currency advice/regulations
There are no restrictions on the import or export of local and foreign currencies.

Health (for visitors)
Mandatory precautions
None
Advisable precautions
Up-to-date tetanus and polio immunisations.

Hotels
Classified into one- to four-star and predominantly four-star/luxury categories. Monaco has around 2,500 hotel rooms, most of which are four-star. The occupancy rate is around 50 per cent.

Credit cards
All credit cards are accepted.

Public holidays (national)
Fixed dates
1 Jan (New Year's Day), 26–27 Jan (Feast of St Dévote), 1 May (Labour Day), 31 May (Prince Albert Day),15 Aug (Assumption Day), 1 Nov (All Saints' Day), 19 Nov (National Day/ Fête du Prince), 8 Dec (Immaculate Conception), 25 Dec (Christmas Day).
Variable dates
Easter Monday, Ascension Day, Whit Monday, Corpus Christ (May/Jun).

Working hours
Banking
Mon–Sat: 0900–1200 and 1400–1630 (except Saturday afternoons preceding Bank Holidays). Banque Franco-Portugaise, Monte Carlo, is open on Saturdays.
Business
Mon–Fri: 0900–1200 and 1400–1700.
Government
Mon–Fri: 0930–1230 and 1330–1700.
Shops
Mon–Sat: 0900–1230 and 1500–1830.

Telecommunications
Mobile/cell phones
GSM 900 serivice is available throughout the territory with a 3G service planned.

Security
Monaco has relatively low rates of crime. Pickpockets operate in train stations and subways.

Getting there
Air
The nearest international airport is at Nice (NCE) in France, 22km from Monaco. There is a heliport in Monte Carlo (MCM), from which Heli-Air Monaco and Monacair operate.

Airport tax: None.
Surface
Road: There are good road links between Monaco and France. No formalities are required to cross the border.
Rail: Monaco is well-served by rail links between and to cities in France, Italy and Switzerland. Daily and over-night through trains transit the Principality. The *TGV Méditeranée* operates between Monaco and Paris
Water: Harbours at Condamine (Hercule port) and Fontvieille can accommodate yachts. Larger vessels can anchor in the bay of Monaco.

Getting about
National transport
There are around 50km of roads and 1.6km of railways (operated by Société Nationale des Chemins de Fer Français).
Buses: There are regular bus services within Monaco, as well as to neighbouring French centres. A direct service is available from Nice Airport to Monaco, stopping at a number of hotels.
City transport
Taxis: Taxis are available around the clock in the Avenue de Monte Carlo and from the railway station. There are taxi ranks at Fontvieille, Place des Moulins, Avenue de la Costa and Beach Plaza.
Buses, trams & metro: Buses operate every five minutes from Monaco-Ville to the casino and every 10 minutes to the railway station and the beaches.

BUSINESS DIRECTORY
The addresses listed below are a selection only. While World of Information makes every endeavour to check these addresses, we cannot guarantee that changes have not been made, especially to telephone numbers and area codes. We would welcome any corrections.

Telephone area codes
The international direct dialling (IDD) code for Monaco is +377, followed by an eight-digit number.

Useful telephone numbers
Police (emergencies):17 (switchboard): 9315-3015
Ambulance/Fire services (emergencies): 18 (switchboard):9330-1945
Medical/paramedic team/ambulance: 9375-2525
Doctor or chemist on duty:9325-3325
Princess Grace General Hospital, Av Pasteur (emergencies): 9325-9869; (switchboard): 9325-9900.
Main Post Office, Palais de la Scala: 9325-1111.
Car pound (Parking des Ecoles car park), Av des Guelfes, Monte Carlo: 9315-3084.

Chambers of Commerce
Monaco Economic Development Chamber, 11 Rue du Gabian, BP 653, MC 98013 Monaco (tel: 9798-6868; fax: 9798-6869; e-mail: info@cde.mc).

Banking
Banque Franco Portugaise (BFP), 5 Av Princesse Alice, MC 98000 (tel: 9350-1115; fax: 9350-1921).

Banque Générale du Commerce, 2 Av des Spélugues, Monte Carlo (tel: 9350-1762).

Banque Internationale de Monaco, Sporting d'Hiver, 2 Av Princesse Alice, Monte Carlo (tel: 9216-5757; fax: 9216-5750).

Barclays Bank plc, 31 Av de la Costa, Monte Carlo (tel: 9315-3535; fax: 9325-1568).

Crédit Foncier de Monaco, 11 Bd Albert 1er, MC98000 (tel: 9310-2000; fax: 9310-2350).

Société Générale, 16 Ave de la Costa (tel: 9315-5700); also at 17 Bd Albert 1er (tel: 9350-8692).

Société Monégasque de Banque Privée, 9 Boulevard d'Italie, MC 98000 (tel: 9315-2323).

Central bank
European Central Bank (ECB), Kaiserstrasse 29, D-60311 Frankfurt am Main, Germany (tel: +49(69)13-440; fax: +49(69)1344-6000; e-mail: info@ecb.int).

Travel information
Automobile Club of Monaco, 23 Boulevard Albert 1er, Monaco (tel: 9315-2600; fax: 9325-8008; e-mail: info@acm.mc).

Gare de Monaco, 26 Avenue Prince Pierre, Monaco (tel: 9310-6015; e-mail: info@monaco-gare.com).

Heli-Air Monaco, Héliport de Monaco, Quartier de Fontvieille, Monaco (tel: 9205-0050; fax: 9205-0051; e-mail: helico@heliairmonaco.com).

Monacair, Héliport de Monaco, Quartier de Fontvieille, Monaco (tel: 9797-3900; fax: 9797-3909; e-mail: accueil@monacair.mc).

Compagnie des Autobus de Monaco (CAM), 3 Avenue Président J F Kennedy, Monaco (tel: 9770-2222; fax: 9770-2223).

Service de la Marine, Direction des Ports, 6 Quai Antoine, PO Box 468, Monaco (tel: 9315-8678; fax: 9315-3715; e-mail: marine@gouv.mc).

National tourist organisation offices
Direction du Tourisme et des Congrès, 2a Boulevard des Moulins, Monaco (tel: 9216-6116; fax: 9216-6000; e-mail: dtc@monaco-tourisme.com).

Other useful addresses

Centre de Congrès, Bd Louis II, Monaco (tel: 9310-8400).

Centre d'Informations Administratives, 23 Av Prince Héréditaire Albert, Monaco (tel: 9315-4026).

Centre de Presse, 4 Rue des Iris, Monte Carlo (tel: 9330-4227).

Centre de Rencontres Internationales, Ave d'Ostende, Monaco (tel: 9310-8600).

Comité des Fêtes, Monaco-ville (tel: 9330-8004).

Direction de l'Expansion Economique, 'Le Concorde', 11 Rue du Gabian, PO Box 665, Monaco (tel: 9798-6868; fax: 9798-6869; e-mail: info@cde.mc).

Directorate of Fiscal Services, 57 Rue Grimaldi, MC98000 (tel: 9315-8122; fax: 9205-8155).

Douanes, 7 Av Président JF Kennedy, Monaco (tel: 9330-2600).

Mairie de Monaco, Monaco-ville (tel: 9315-2863).

Ministère d'Etat, Monaco-ville (tel: 9315-8000).

Monte Carlo Casino, Place du Casino, Monaco (tel: 9216-2000; fax: 9216-3862; e-mail: mrk.jeux@sbm.mc).

Monte Carlo Main Post, Square Beaumarchais (Palais de la Scala) (tel: 9350-6987).

Radio Monte Carlo (RMC), 16 Bd Princesse Charlotte, Monte Carlo (tel: 9315-1617).

Service du Contrôle Technique et de la Circulation (traffic control service), 23 Av Prince Héréditaire Albert, Monaco (tel: 9315-8000).

Service de l'Urbanisme et de la Construction, 23 Av Prince Hérditaire Albert, Monaco (tel: 9315-8000).

Télé Monte Carlo, 16 Bd Princesse Charlotte, Monaco (tel: 9315-1415).

Internet sites

Banking and investment advice: www.cmb.mc

Monaco online: www.monaco.mc/

Monte Carlo web directory: http://monte-carlo.mc/

Mongolia

KEY FACTS

Official name: Mongol Uls (The State of Mongolia)

Head of State: President Tsakhiagiyn Elbegdorj (since 18 Jun 2009, re-elected 26 Jun 2013)

Head of government: Prime Minister Chimed Saikhanbileg (since 21 November 2014), he replaced Norov Altankhuyag who was removed from his post following a no-confidence vote on 5 November 2014.

Ruling party: Coalition led by Ardchilsan Nam (Democratic Party) (DP) with Shudarga Yos Evsel (Justice Coalition) (JC) and Irgenii Zorig-Nogoon Nam (Civil Will-Green Party) (CWGP) (from 10 Aug 2012)

Area: 1,565,000 square km

Population: 2.92 million (2014)*

Capital: Ulaanbaatar (Ulan Bator) (formerly Urga)

Official language: Khalkha Mongolian

Currency: Tugrik (Tug)

Exchange rate: Tug1,989.00 per US$ (Jul 2014)

GDP per capita: US$4,096 (2014)*

GDP real growth: 7.82% (2014)*

GDP: US$11.98 billion (2014)*

Unemployment: 8.77% (2014)*

Inflation: 12.91% (2014)

Balance of trade: -US$1.31 billion (2013)*

Aid flow: US$700.00 million (2009)

Annual FDI: US$4.71 billion (2011)

* estimated figure

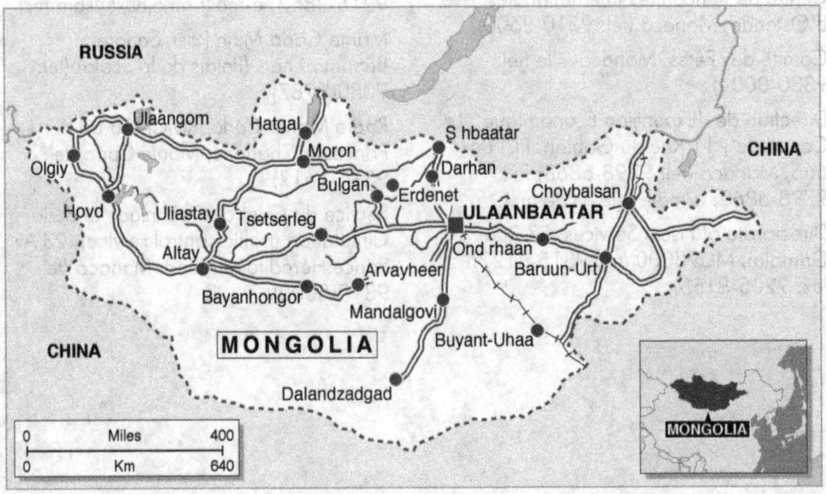

There is a Mongolian saying that states that 'A donkey would not know if there is gold or water in his ears.' The land-locked country, almost entirely dependent on a small number of mineral resources and commodity prices, needed, in the view of most independent analysts, to effect a number of structural changes to its economy, carry out greater economic diversification and acquire the flexibility to respond to sudden changes in the external environment.

Those resource rich countries who have managed to achieve this – Mongolian officials and businessmen had visited countries such as Norway and Chile – had first established funds to manage changes. If the prices turned out to be higher than expected, the extra revenue was accumulated in a special fund, such as a national fund or a sustainability fund. When the commodity prices are lower than envisioned, the fund was used to make up for the deficit, which protected the economy from price fluctuations. Despite Mongolia's first hand experience of how other countries managed their economies, nothing seemed to have been written down and duly digested. Mongolia was failing to use mining income to develop other industries, encourage the activities of the private sector, support market competition, build required infrastructure, prepare the domestic workforce or help businesses enter the international market.

To make matters worse, Mongolia had acquired more loans than it c0uld handle. The government therefore needed to decide how these loans might be repaid and how accumulated reserve funds might be created. An independent analysis was needed of where the capital raised by previous bonds had gone and how – if at all – their repayment prospects stacked up. On the Transparency International 2014 *Corruption Perceptions Index*, Mongolia had ranked 80 out of the 175 countries surveyed. However, in 2015 the Mongolian government appeared to be doing nothing to address how and when, or whether, the loans should be repaid. In a self preservation effort, Mongolia's politicians were soon to pass a law to grant amnesty to those of their associates who were under investigation for corruption charges. Although President Tsakhiagiyn Elbegdorj had partially vetoed the proposed law, the politicians involved were still expected to oppose the veto.

Chinese uplift

In 2014 the Mongolian economy remained in a weak position, hit by plunging commodity prices and a seriously rapid decline in foreign direct investment (FDI). Thus it was that when in August 2014 the Chinese President Xi Jinping made the first visit to Ulaanbaatar by a Chinese president in eleven years, Mongolian hopes for some good economic years were high. President Xi did not disappoint, proposing the expansion of bilateral trade with Mongolia to US$10 billion a year by 2020 Mongolia appeared almost over-enthusiastic to agree to new deals on transport, energy and mining investment with its dominant trading partner. During President Xi's visit the two countries signed a joint declaration upgrading their relationship to that of 'comprehensive strategic partnership'. They also signed agreements to co-operate further in a number of areas such as economics, energy, mining and finance.

According to Reuters (relaying announcements by China's Xinhua state news agency) Mr Xi proposed to expand China-Mongolia trade to US$10 billion by 2020. The bi-lateral trade was worth US$324 million in 2002 but rose to US$6 billion in 2013, accounting for more than half of Mongolia's total foreign trade. China and Mongolia signed 26 new deals on railroads, mining and power generation during Chinese President Xi Jinping's state visit. The closer economic relations with China were possibly Mongolia's answer to recent economic woes. Mongolia had seen a 70 per cent fall in FDI in the first half of 2014, but with its southern neighbour aiming for an expansion of trade, hopes were raised. However, with a slightly negative slant, the Mongolian foreign affairs ministry and the Mongolian president's press secretary both said there was at present no available figure for the value of the deals.

The IMF sees long-term promise

In its April 2015 assessment of the Mongolian economy the International Monetary Fund (IMF) expressed the view that the medium- to long-term prospects were promising, taking into account Mongolia's extensive natural resources. In the near term, however, the Fund noted that Mongolia continued to face balance-of-payments (BOP) pressures on account of low levels of FDI and weak commodity prices, as well as expansionary macro-economic policies. Imports had begun to taper off and, with the first phase of the Oyu Tolgoi copper and gold mine now in operation, exports had picked up. The trade balance had improved, but with FDI and other financial-account flows still depressed, the overall BOP in the view of the IMF, remained weak. In addition, public debt had risen sharply and the banking sector needed to be watched closely in the wake of the rapid credit expansion over the previous two years. Barring a change in policies and/or major new developments in the 'real' economy, these trends were likely to continue. According to the IMF, the risks were on the downside and related to possible difficulties in securing agreement on major investment projects, as well as to the possibilities of a further slowdown in China or a surge in global financial market volatility.

Recognising these challenges, the new government had already taken some policy action. It had implemented a Comprehensive Macro Adjustment Plan which targeted a substantial reduction in the fiscal deficit, phased out some of the Bank of Mongolia (central bank)'s unconventional easing programmes and introduced a number of structural measures to boost exports and substitutes for imports. However, additional measures – under discussion in 2015 – were needed to underpin the fiscal deficit targets, strengthen monetary and banking-sector policies and ensure that the most vulnerable were protected from the impact of the necessary macro adjustment.

Going into more detailed analysis, the Asian Development Bank (ADB) observed that despite a substantial increase in mining output, gross domestic product (GDP) growth slowed to 7.8 per cent in 2014 from 11.6 per cent in 2013. FDI continued to fall and the sizeable monetary stimulus that kept growth high in the previous year became increasingly difficult to maintain in the light of pressures from inflation and the BOP. As value added in mining increased by 24.2 per cent, reflecting the first full year of production at the vast Oyu Tolgoi copper and gold mine, industrial production expanded by 16.1 per cent and contributed 4.8 percentage points to GDP growth. This came despite a 16.3 per cent drop in coal production. Agriculture remained a driver of growth, rising by 14.4 per cent with favourable weather. Growth in services slowed to 4.8 per cent, however, as plunging mine investment took its toll. Agriculture and services each contributed 1.5 percentage points to GDP growth, while the contribution from industry other than mining was negligible.

FDI dropped by 80.7 per cent following the completion of the first phase of Oyu Tolgoi and reflecting uncertainty over the economic viability of projects in the light of lower commodity prices, as well as over the broader investment climate. Gross capital formation contracted by 33.5 per cent, dragging GDP growth down by 18.4 percentage points. Domestic consumption increased by 8.6 per cent and contributed 6.0 percentage points to GDP growth, with private consumption accounting for nearly all of the increase. As exports grew by 51.4 per cent in real terms and imports by only 4.9 per cent, the trade deficit shrank by 82.7 per cent and the contribution of net exports to GDP growth expanded to 20.3 percentage points.

Oyu Tolgoi's contribution to GDP growth thus continued to shift from investment to net exports. The current account deficit narrowed significantly to 8.2 per cent of GDP from 25.4 per cent in 2013 as the trade deficit crossed into surplus. Merchandise exports grew by 35.3 per cent as higher exports of copper concentrates more than compensated for a decline in other exports. Merchandise imports fell by 14.4 per cent, largely reflecting a sharp drop in investment-related material and equipment, as well as lower

KEY INDICATORS — Mongolia

	Unit	2011	2012	2013	2014	**2015
Population	m	*2.80	*2.84	2.88	*2.92	*2.97
Gross domestic product (GDP)	US$bn	8.50	10.32	12.55	*11.98	*12.46
GDP per capita	US$	3,042	3,635	4,353	*4,096	*4,195
GDP real growth	%	17.3	12.4	11.6	*7.8	*4.4
Inflation	%	9.5	15.0	10.4	12.9	*9.2
Unemployment	%	7.7	8.2	10.4	*8.8	*9.1
Exports (fob) (goods)	US$m	4,816.4	4,281.5	4,267.7	–	–
Imports (fob) (goods)	US$m	5,806.6	5,933.4	5,574.0	–	–
Balance of trade	US$m	-990.1	-1,552.0	-1,306.3	–	–
Current account	US$m	-2,760.4	-3,362.0	-3,192.0	*-985.0	*-1,379.0
Total reserves minus gold	US$m	2,285.5	3,930.3	2,095.8	1,540.4	–
Foreign exchange	US$m	2,210.9	3,862.3	2,029.1	–	–
Exchange rate	per US$	1,241.86	1,393.20	1,668.50	1,887.45	–

* estimated figure ** forecast figure

fuel prices. The services deficit stabilised at US$1.3 billion, equal to 11.2 per cent of GDP. Declining capital inflows generated a BOP deficit equal to 3.9 per cent of GDP despite nearly US$700 million in government-guaranteed borrowing by the Development Bank of Mongolia.

Gross international reserves fell to US$1.6 billion – cover for 2.9 months of imports – from US$4.1 billion in 2012 and are increasingly financed by short-term foreign liabilities, including a three-year currency swap arrangement with the People's Republic of China (central bank). Raising the currency swap ceiling in August 2014 to 15 billion Chinese yuan (equal to 20 per cent of GDP) provided a liquidity buffer, but withdrawals would eventually need to be repaid or renewed. Public and publicly guaranteed external debt including the foreign liabilities of the Bank of Mongolia, stood at 57.3 per cent of GDP at the year-end, having more than doubled in 4 years and approaching the US$1.5 billion raised through the US dollar-denominated sovereign Chinggis bond. As capital inflows ebbed, the Mongolian tugrik (or tögrög) depreciated by 13.8 per cent against the US dollar, having already depreciated by 19.2 per cent in 2013. Meanwhile, rouble depreciation caused the tugrik to appreciate in nominal effective terms by 2.3 per cent and by 11.0 per cent in real terms because of comparatively high inflation in Mongolia.

The government continued its highly pro-cyclical fiscal policy in 2014 and the structural deficit reached 3.7 per cent, breaching the 2 per cent ceiling under the Fiscal Stability Law (FSL). Budgetary expenditure remained constant at 32.2 per cent of GDP. However, revenue fell to 28.1 per cent of GDP from 31.3 per cent in 2013 as receipts increased by only 2.6 per cent, falling short of the highly optimistic budget partly because of falling commodity prices. On the positive side, the Glass Account Law (the key features of which are that it obliges all government agencies and legal entities with state involvement to make information on budgets and financial matters, including the utilisation of financing and other government indebtedness, available to the public) will improve the transparency of the procurement, budgets and finances of government agencies and legal entities with state involvement.

The ratio of public debt to GDP rose in net present value terms to 54.7 per cent in 2014 (breaching the 40 per cent ceiling of the FSL) and to 77.4 per cent in nominal terms including the central bank's foreign liabilities. Interest payments reached 7.1 per cent of government expenditures in 2014. Debt sustainability is further affected by the rising share of commercial borrowing since 2012 and the uncertain economic returns of some public investment projects.

Expansionary monetary and fiscal policies and currency depreciation drove consumer price inflation to a peak in July 2014 of 14.9 per cent year on year. Facing inflationary and BOP pressures, the central bank raised the policy rate from 10.5 per cent to 12.0 per cent in July 2014 and 13.0 per cent in January 2015. Despite starting corporate lending worth 1.6 per cent of GDP, the central bank's total quasi-fiscal loans – mainly for housing and construction at subsidised rates – were reduced to 18.7 per cent of GDP from 23.7 per cent in 2013, largely by channelling substantial expenditures off-budget through the Development Bank of Mongolia and financing them with the proceeds of the Chinggis bond and government-guaranteed external borrowing. The consolidated fiscal deficit, which included off-budget spending, rose to 11.5 per cent of GDP from 9.8 per cent in 2013. Excluding off-budget spending, the cash deficit expanded to 4.1 per cent of GDP from 0.9 per cent in 2013.

Growth in domestic lending slowed markedly to 16.1 per cent, holding broad money growth to 12.5 per cent. Inflation moderated to 11.0 per cent in December 2014, having averaged 12.8 per cent for the year. The quality of bank assets was under pressure in the light of the banks' rapid expansion in recent years and slowing economic growth. While commercial banks' stock of non-performing loans grew by 48.5 per cent, the ratio of such loans rose only slightly to 3.1 per cent of all loans outstanding. However, loan growth was slowing rapidly and the stock of loans past due – a leading indicator – more than doubled by the end of 2014 to 2.2 per cent of all loans. Moreover, sizeable policy loan programmes pointed to supervisory forbearance and increased exposure to the cyclical construction and housing sector. In the view of the ADB, Mongolia's banks needed bolstering by closer monitoring of asset quality and liquidity buffers, stronger supervision of risk, the adoption of international capital standards, improved corporate governance and forward-looking provisioning. Some positive steps from January 2015 – introducing a one per cent provisioning ratio for new loans and imposing higher risk weights on new foreign currency loans to unhedged borrowers – should perhaps be gradually extended to existing loans.

Summarising the situation, the ADB considered that despite the robust growth expected in agriculture and expanded extraction at Oyu Tolgoi (albeit less than in 2014), Mongolia's GDP growth was forecast to slow to 3.0 per cent in 2015 as falling prices for exports were felt and as monetary and fiscal policies were tightened to contain inflationary and BOP pressures. Industrial production was expected to grow more slowly than in 2014 as a credit squeeze affects construction and real estate and as lower export prices pressured mine operators. Services were projected to grow only marginally as other economic activity slowed. Assuming a stable external environment and the resumption of major investment in mining in 2015, economic growth was likely to recover to 5.0 per cent in 2016 even with the continuation of restrictive fiscal and monetary policies.

Risk assessment

Politics	Fair/poor
Economy	Fair
Regional stability	Good

COUNTRY PROFILE

1206-63 Mongol tribes were unified under the leadership of Temujin, later called Genghis Khan. With his cavalry army, he invaded China and occupied Peking and built the largest land empire ever. His offspring increased the empire by invading much of Russia and defeating the armies of most of Eastern Europe, including Hungary and Poland. The onslaught stopped just 40 miles short of Venice when the Mongol commander Subutai was ordered to return home.

1368 The Mongols were forced out of Peking by Chinese troops as the Mongol empire collapsed.

1380 The Golden Horde (troops of Genghis Khan's oldest son, Juchi) was defeated by the Russian, Prince Dmitriy Donskoy, in Russia. Chinese troops destroyed Karakorum, the Mongol capital.

1636 Inner Mongolia was formed by the conquest of the southern Mongols by the Chinese Manchu Empire.

1691 Outer Mongolia was formed when the Manchu empire offered protection to the northern Mongols.

1911 Following the republican revolution, Mongolian princes declared the province's independence.

1921 The Mongolian People's Party was founded and a Provisional People's government was established.

1924 The Mongolian People's Republic was proclaimed.
1928–1960 The Soviet Union (USSR) influenced the governing of Mongolia as ideological and repressive communist rule was instigated. Historical and cultural heritage were undermined, family names were prohibited, monasteries destroyed and lamas murdered.
1961 Mongolia became a member of the UN, and was accorded diplomatic recognition by West European states.
1987 Mongolia was finally granted diplomatic recognition by the US.
1991 Mongolia's main backer, the USSR, disintegrated, ending decades of economic and political support for the country.
1992 A new constitution was introduced, establishing Mongolia as a democratic parliamentary state. Mongolia's official title became the State of Mongolia.
1997 Natsagiin Bagabandi of the Mongol Ardyn Khuv'sgalt Nam (Mongolian People's Revolutionary Party) (MPRP) (formerly the Mongolian People's Party), was elected president.
1999 Rinchinnyamiyn Amarjargal became prime minister.
2000 The MPRP won the parliamentary elections and Nambariin Enkhbayar (MPRP), was elected prime minister.
2001 The incumbent president, Natsagiin Bagabandi of the MPRP, was re-elected.
2002 Prime Minister Mikhail Kayanov of Russia visited Mongolia to boost economic co-operation between the two countries.
2004 The World Bank endorsed a new Country Assistance Strategy (CAS) and US$18 million urban water credit. Parliament elected Tsakhiagiyn Elbegdorj (Ekh Oron-Ardchilan (Motherland Democratic Coalition) (MDC)) as prime minister and parliament approved his cabinet.
2005 Nambaryn Enkhbayar (MPRP) won the presidential elections.
2006 Ten ministers, members of the MPRP, resigned accusing the coalition government of not doing enough to counter corruption and poverty. Parliament voted to dissolve the coalition government. Miyeegombo Enkhbold (MPRP) was endorsed by parliament as the new prime minister.
2007 Parliament elected Sanjaagiin Bayar as prime minister.
2008 A new voting system was used in parliamentary elections. The ruling MPRP won 46 seats (out of 76) and Prime Minister Bayar remained in office. The elections were widely contested and although election observers reported no major problems the results sparked violent protests over claims that they had been rigged. After four deaths and hundreds injured, a four-day state of emergency was imposed. At the opening of parliament, the 27 Democrat members staged a walkout and brought the session to a halt.
2009 In presidential elections opposition leader, Tsakhiagiyn Elbegdorj (Ardchilsan Nam) (Democratic Party) (DP) (formerly the MDC), won 51.2 per cent of the vote on a campaign of anti-corruption and proposed use of revenue from the country's rich resources. Incumbent Nambaryn Enkhbayar (MPRP) won 47.4 per cent and said he would abide by the result. Mongolia and Russia signed a five-year agreement that transferred the management of Mongolia's railways to Russia – they had previously been jointly managed. Prime Minister Bayar resigned due to ill health and Batbold Sukhbaatar (MPRP) replaced him.
2010 A number of privatisations of Mongolia's extensive mineral assets began. The minister for mineral resources and energy, Dashdorj Zorigt, said that the government would welcome investment 'from our neighbours and third neighbours'. It is hoped these 'third neighbours' would balance the Chinese and Russian partners that are currently dominant. Parliament unanimously approved the building of a 5,000km east–west railway. The plans involve six lines, with construction of 1,800km beginning immediately, and completion by 2015. The MPRP was renamed the Mongol Ardyn Nam (Mongolian People's Party) (MPP).
2011 In March the government announced plans to send 1,500 troops to be a part of the UN peacekeeping force to Côte d'Ivoire (UNOCI); however this did not take place. In May Russia, which supplies over 90 per cent of all oil to Mongolia, increased its export duty on oil by 40 per cent, citing domestic shortages; the imposition quickly caused shortages as prices doubled overnight. The government later announced plans to stockpile petrol reserves and construct the country's first modern oil refinery to mitigate future energy shocks. In June, Unesco added the 12,000-year-old petroglyphs (rock carvings) of the Altai Mountains to its list of world heritage sites.
2012 On 5 January the death penalty was abolished (a moratorium had been introduced in 2010). On 13 April, former president Nambar Enkhbayer was arrested by the Independent Authority Against Corruption (IAAC), on charges of corruption and misusing state assets while he was in power. He began a hunger strike at the beginning of May and was released on bail for medical treatment on 14 May. Parliamentary elections were held on 28 June, amid widespread allegations of corruption, particularly associated with the mining concessions to foreign companies. The opposition DP won 31 seats (out of 76) and the ruling MPP won 25 (down 20 seats from the 2008 elections). As no party achieved 39 seats for a majority in parliament, the DP began coalition talks with the new, anti-foreign mining party, Shudarga Yos Evsel (Justice Coalition) (JC), led by former president Nambaryn Enkhbayar. On 3 August, former president Enkhbayar was convicted and jailed for four yearsfor corruption. On 10 August a coalition government of DP, JC and Irgenii Zorig-Nogoon Nam (Civil Will-Green Party) (CWGP) was sworn into office; Norov Altankhuyag (DP) became prime minister.
2013 Presidential elections were held on 29 June. The result was a second win for Tsakhiagiyn Elbegdorj (DP) with 50.89 per cent of the vote. Runner up was Badmaanyambuugiin Bat-Erden with 42.52 per cent, while Natsagiin Udval came a distant third with 6.58 per cent; turnout was 66.50 per cent.
2014 On 5 November parliament voted to dismiss Prime Minister Norov Altankhuyag, accusing him of economic mismanagement, corruption and nepotism. The vote was 36 to 30, with some members of his own party voting against him. Deputy prime minister, Dendev Terbishdagva, was named as temporary prime minister; under the constitution he has to form a new government within 14 days.

Political structure

Constitution

The constitution entered into force on 12 February 1992. A January 1998 constitutional amendment stated that legislators were eligible to serve concurrently as prime minister or as other ministers. The January amendment was later effectively nullified by the Constitutional Court ruling of 24 November 1998 that prohibited members of the People's Great Hural from holding cabinet posts. On 15 March 2000, the Constitutional Court cancelled amendments to the 1992 constitution, which had been approved by the People's Great Hural, and later vetoed by the president.

Independence date

11 July 1921

Form of state

Parliamentary republic

The executive

The Head of State is the president, nominated by political parties in the People's Great Hural, and directly elected by simple majority popular vote for a four-year term (eligible for a second term). Following legislative elections, the leader of the majority party or majority coalition is usually elected prime minister by the State Great Hural.

National legislature
The unicameral Ulsyn Ikh Khural (State Great Khural or Hural (Assembly)) has 76 seats of which 48 members are directly elected in 26 multi-seat constituencies by simple majority vote and 28 members are directly elected in multi-seat constituencies by proportional representation vote. Members serve for four-year terms. The Assembly elects the prime minister and appoints a cabinet, in consultation with the president.
Legal system
A mixture of Russian, German and US law.
Last elections
28 June 2012 (parliamentary); 26 June 2013 (presidential)
Results: 28 June 2012 (parliamentary); Parliamentary: Ardchilsan Nam (Democratic Party) (DP) won 31 seats (out of 76), Mongol Ardyn Nam (Mongolian People's Party) (MPP) 25, Shudarga Yos Evsel (Justice Coalition) (JC) 11, Irgenii Zorig-Nogoon Nam (Civil Will-Green Party) (CWGP) two, independents three; *the results of four seats were to be decided*. Turnout was 65.24 per cent.
Presidential: Tsakhiagiyn Elbegdorj (DP) won 50.89 per cent of the vote, Badmaanyambuugiin Bat-Erden 42.52 per cent, Natsagiin Udval 6.58 per cent; turnout was 66.50 per cent.
Next elections
June 2016 (parliamentary); June 2017 (presidential)

Political parties
Ruling party
Coalition led by Ardchilsan Nam (Democratic Party) (DP) with Shudarga Yos Evsel (Justice Coalition) (JC) and Irgenii Zorig-Nogoon Nam (Civil Will-Green Party) (CWGP) (from 10 Aug 2012)
Main opposition party
Mongol Ardyn Nam (Mongolian People's Party) (MPP)
Approximately 70 per cent of the population is under 30 years of age.
The population is small. Approximately 1.2 million live in towns, with over 600,000 in the capital. About half of the population of Ulaanbaatar live in yurts, the traditional tent-like home of the nomadic Mongolian people.

Population
2.92 million (2014)*
Last census: January 2000: 2,373,493
Population density: Two inhabitants per square km, one of the lowest densities in the world (2010). Urban population 62 per cent (2010 Unicef).
Annual growth rate: 1.1 per cent, 1990–2010 (Unicef).

Religions
Tibetan Buddhist Lamaism and Shamanism, Islam (4 per cent) – there is no state religion.

Education
Primary schooling lasts for four years until aged 12. Secondary education is divided into four years compulsory lower secondary schooling for students aged 12–16 years and two years upper secondary for those aged 16–18 years. Only students of upper secondary schools progress to higher education. Technical and vocational schools admit graduates of both lower and upper secondary schools. Government and private institutions provide higher education and offer BA, MA and PhD degrees.
Public expenditure on education typically amounts to 5.7 per cent of annual gross national income.
Literacy rate: 98 per cent adult rate; 98 per cent youth rate (15–24) (Unesco 2005).
Compulsory years: Eight to 16.
Enrolment rate: 88 per cent gross primary enrolment, of relevant age group (including repeaters); 56 per cent gross secondary enrolment (World Bank).
Pupils per teacher: 31 in primary schools.

Health
About 98 per cent of infants aged less than one year are immunised against measles.
HIV/Aids
HIV prevalence: 0.1 per cent aged 15–49 in 2003 (World Bank)
Life expectancy: 65 years, 2004 (WHO 2006)
Fertility rate/Maternal mortality rate: 2.5 births per woman, 2010 (Unicef); maternal mortality 150 per 100,000 live births (World Bank).
Child (under 5 years) mortality rate (per 1,000): 28 per 1,000 live births (WHO 2012); 12.5 per cent children under aged five were malnourished (World Bank).
Head of population per physician: 2.63 physicians per 1,000 people, 2002 (WHO 2006)

Welfare
Growing unemployment and a weak social safety net remain the country's prime concern. About 36 per cent of Mongolia's population still live below the official poverty line. Many poor are unable to work and rely on social security to meet their basic needs. In 2001, the Asian Development Bank (ADB) granted two loans totalling US$12 million to strengthen Mongolia's social security services. The first loan of US$8 million supported policy and legal reforms to enhance the delivery of social welfare services and strengthen social insurance schemes. A second ADB loan of US$4 million invested in projects such as nursing homes, services for the disabled and day care centers. The government aimed to replace the large centralised institutions with smaller community-based nursing homes and day care centers. The Government provided co-financing of US$2 million. ADB also provided a US$600,000 technical assistance grant financed by the Japanese Government.
More than 100,000 people are registered as disabled by Mongolia's Ministry of Social Welfare and Labor. About 40,000 disabled people, who are capable of working, remain jobless.

Main cities
Ulaanbaatar (which translates as 'Red Hero') (Ulan Bator) (formerly Urga) (capital, estimated population 885,140 in 2012), Erdenèt (79,550), Darhan (76,616), Cojbalsan (48,578), Olgij (32,677), Zuunharaa (31,699).

Languages spoken
Russian is the principal foreign language, although English is being encouraged. Kazak is also spoken in western Mongolia.
Official language/s
Khalkha Mongolian

Media
Although media is generally free to criticise, journalists are still governed by laws of defamation and state security.
Press
The newspapers with the largest circulations are the government *Odriyn Sonin*, successor to the state-owned *Ardyn Erh* (established in 1990) and *Zasgiyn Gazryn Medee* (weekly), *Nügel Buyan* (police) and *Ulaanbaatar* (local government). The party newspapers *Ardchilal* (MNDP), *Ug* (MSDP) and *Unen* (MPRP) appear less frequently.
English-language weekly newspapers include the *Mongol Messenger* and the on-line publication *Mongolia This Week* (http://www.mongoliathisweek.mn).
Broadcasting
The Mongolian National Broadcaster (MNB) (www.mnb.mn) is the only national, public network via satellite transmissions.
Radio: Radio services are important to the large nomad community. MNB (www.mnb.mn) operates the Voice of Mongolia, transmitting in Chinese, English, Russian and Japanese. Other, private radio stations include Radio Ulaanbaator, New Century 107FM and Info Radio.
Television: MNB (www.mnb.mn) broadcasts locally produced and imported programmes. There are several private and international TV services provided by

both satellite and cable, including TV5 (www.tv5.mn), TV9 (www.tv9.mn) and TM Television.

Most newspapers are owned by the government or political parties. Dailies include, in Mongolian, *Odriyn Sonin* (*Daily news*) (www.dailynews.mn), *Unen* (*Truth*) (www.unen.mn), *Zuuny Medee* (www.zuuniimedee.mn) and *Onoodor*. Weeklies include, in English, *Mongol Messenger* (www.mongolmessenger.mn), *The UB Post* (http://ubpost.mongolnews.mn).

National news agency: Montsame Agency

Economy

Mongolia not only has extensive deposits of minerals that include gold, copper, coal, tin, tungsten and molybdenum, it also has huge unspoiled areas of land. In the western region around 30 per cent of the national livestock herd, which is being raised in traditional methods, could supply meat to most of Central Asia, as well niche markets for organic meat in the West. Mongolia's enormous reserves of mineral deposits have transformed their economy, which traditionally has been dependent on herding and agriculture.

Mongolia's copper, gold, coal, molybdenum, fluorspar, uranium, tin and tungsten deposits have attracted foreign direct investment (FDI). FDI was US$508 million in 2014 down from a huge US$2.1 billion in 2013.

The industrial sector constituted about 35 per cent of GDP in 2014, of which manufacturing comprised 5 per cent, with the service sector accounting for 52.8 per cent. Agriculture accounted for 12.2 per cent of GDP and employed about 29 per cent of the population.

In 2014, the UN Human Development Index (HDI) ranked Mongolia 103 (out of 187) for national development in health, education and income, which was 7 positions better than the country's ranking in 2011. Since 2000, Mongolia's progress has improved to parallel the improvement of other countries in East Asia and the Pacific. In 2010, 38.7 per cent of the population fell below the national poverty line, and by 2013 this had dropped below 25 per cent. Remittances in 2014 amounted to about US$265.3 million (0.8 per cent of GDP), thereby providing a significant proportion of foreign exchange earnings, along with international aid.

The new government that took power in 2013 has aimed to restore investor trust and revive the economy. It will be challenged to unwind the monetary and fiscal stimulus programs in use since 2013 to counteract the fall in FDI. In December 2014, the government awarded a deal to develop the massive Tavan Tolgoi coal field to a consortium comprising Energy Resources/MCS (Mongolia), Shenhua (China), and Sumitomo (Japan); talks continue to hammer out the financing and operating details. A Mongolian negotiator recently announced that the US$4 billion deal is unlikely to go through, as China's economic growth has slowed.

Mongolia has done much to embrace the practices of a free-market economy by privatising state-owned enterprises, but it also has a substantial grey economy, estimated to be as much as 50 per cent of GDP. The authorities have much more to do to bring this into the financial system, at a time of growing concern regarding money laundering through its banking system.

Mongolia still has close ties with China and the Russian Federation, established when it was a dependent state of the former Soviet Union, and both still have an influence on the economy. Mongolia buys around 80 per cent of its petroleum needs from Russia while China is Mongolia's principal export partner. China receives some 95 per cent of Mongolia's exports and supplies Mongolia with more than one-third of its imports. The economic dependence on China and Russia is unhealthy and they are vulnerable to volatility in their markets and their energy prices.

GDP growth in 2007 was 10.2 per cent, falling to 8.9 per cent in 2008 before moving into recession in 2009 with -1.3 per cent as the global economic crisis cut trade and foreign exchange fell. Growth picked up and registered 6.4 per cent in 2010, before surging to an estimated 17.3 per cent in 2011. Growth fell in 2012 to 12.4 per cent and again in 2013 to 11.7 per cent. GDP growth has stabilised at 7.8 per cent in 2014.

Inflation escalated from 8.2 per cent in 2007 to 26.8 per cent in 2008 as food imports and energy reached a record high. A fall in imports and consumer spending in 2009 meant that inflation fell back to around 6.3 per cent in 2009, before rising to 10.2 per cent in 2010. By 2013 inflation had dropped to an estimated 9.6 per cent before increasing to 12.9 per cent in 2014.

External trade

Mongolia belongs to the World Trade Organisation (WTO), but does not belong to any regional trade community; it has bilateral agreements with India, Russia and the US.

The economy is underpinned by sales in primary products, in particular copper, gold, molybdenum, tin and tungsten, which together represent 20 per cent of GDP.

Imports

Main imports are machinery and equipment, fuel, cars, food products, industrial consumer goods, chemicals, building materials, cigarettes & tobacco, appliances, soap and detergent.

Main sources: China (41.5 per cent of total in 2014), Russia (27.4 per cent), South Korea (6.5 per cent) and Japan (6.1 per cent).

Exports

The main export products are copper, apparel, livestock, animal products, cashmere, wool, hides, fluorspar, other nonferrous metals, coal and crude oil.

Main destinations: China (95.3 per cent of total in 2014).

Agriculture

Farming

Major crops include barley, potatoes and wheat. Primary meat products include beef and veal, chicken, horse, camel, lamb and pork. The major agricultural exports are carded hair, wool sheepskins, beef and fine animal hair.

Following a severe winter in 2009–10, when 15 out of 21 provinces were declared disaster zones, around 20 per cent (over 8.5 million head of livestock) of the national herd died through hunger or by freezing to death in -45 degrees Celsius temperatures and heavy snows. Those that survived the winter were left weak, threatening the nomadic nature of herders in Mongolia, who were in some part forced to relinquish their lifestyle. The brutal winter, called a *zhud*, was blamed on climate change. The UN called on donor countries to provide US$21 million to help clean up and re-build the lives of the nomads, while analysts pointed out that an increase in animal numbers and inexperienced herders contributed to the poor winter's outcome.

Industry and manufacturing

The industrial sector contributed 33 per cent to GDP in 2013 and typically employs 12 per cent of the workforce. Industrial activity is centred on Ulaanbaatar and other main cities and is based mainly on agricultural products and mining. Products include bricks, cement, lime, sawn timber, scoured wool, felt, felt boots, woollen fabric, leather footwear, soap, flour, garments, matches, bakery goods, confectionery, meat products, beer and vodka.

Tourism

Mongolia does not have a modern history of tourism.

Mongolia lacks modern hotels and other tourist amenities, which can both inhibit and attract foreign visitors. It offers the experience of its culture and people, so far unspoiled by insensitive over-development. Eco-tourism and activity holidays such as mountaineering and pony and camel trekking are being marketed for the adventurous visitor, with sightseeing tours for the less daring. Mongolia has three natural and historic sites on Unesco's World Heritage List.

Travel and tourism contributed 5 per cent of GDP in 2014. The travel and tourism industry provided 4.4 per cent of total employment (56,000 jobs). To date, China has been the main market for tourism but in 2011 a new, official tourism website (www.mongoliatourism.gov.mn) was established with information and suggestions for visits offered in English and Russian. This has made Mongolia more accessible to Russian and English speaking tourists.

Construction of the new Khushigtiin Khundii international airport (in the north-east of the central region) is expected to be finished by 2016. It is being financed by a Japanese loan of US$28 billion.

Mining

Mineral products account for around 40 per cent of the country's total exports. Almost all of Mongolia's copper concentrates are exported to Russia and China. Since 2004 mining has become the major component of the Mongolian economy. In 2014 the sector contributed 20 per cent of GDP.

The Erdenet copper-molybdenum complex, an open-pit mining and concentrating development 340km from Ulaanbaatar, accounts for a large proportion of exports by value. Copper reserves are large enough for another 60 years. The government signed a number of agreements with multinational mining companies to develop Mongolia's large copper deposits 80km from its border with China. When fully expanded the copper mining sector could provide around one-third of government revenue. The estimate is that deposits could produce 450,000 tonnes of copper ore by 2018.

An agreement was reached in 2015 between the Mongolian government and the Anglo-American company, Rio Tinto to develop one of the world's largest copper and gold mines at Oyu Tolgoi. The development of the mine is expected to trigger a rush to exploit $1 trillion worth of mineral resources. The development is so large that it has the potential to bring Mongolia's mainly agrarian society into the modern age. The majority of the mine's copper production will ultimately head to China where demand for the metal is expected to rise significantly over the next decade.

Other mines include fluorspar at Bor-Ondör and gold at Ih-altat.

A law passed in 1995 permits full foreign ownership of mining ventures in Mongolia, including those involving precious metals. Gold producers are no longer forced to sell to the Mongolian central bank at prices below the prevailing international price. Gold mining has increased significantly since 1990. Mongolia has approximately 2,000 tonnes of gold reserves. Major gold-producing areas are Naran, Tolgoi and Zamar. The first foreign investment gold mine, Boroo Gold, opened in 2004 and immediately pushed up Mongolia's output by 40 per cent.

Other minerals present include iron, zinc, silver, tungsten, tin, lead and graphite, but production levels are limited by inefficient extraction methods.

In December 2014, the government awarded a deal to develop the massive Tavan Tolgoi coal field to a consortium comprising Energy Resources/MCS (Mongolia), Shenhua (China), and Sumitomo (Japan); talks continue to hammer out the financing and operating details. A Mongolian negotiator recently announced that the US$4 billion deal is unlikely to go through, as China's economic growth has slowed.

Hydrocarbons

Introduction (All pubs)

There are only small reserves of oil that have been identified, and no known natural gas reserves. There is very little production of oil, most of which is exported to China. However, international oil companies are interested in investing in Mongolia as a country with no drilling history and contiguous geological features, which have produced hydrocarbon reserves in neighbouring countries.

The Swiss company, Manas Petroleum Corporation, signed a production deal with the Petroleum Authority of Mongolia (PAM) in April 2009 to explore in licensed blocks in the south. The US company, Canoil International Energy Limited, signed a production deal with the PAM in May 2009 to explore in south-eastern Mongolia in the East Gobi basin, close to China's currently productive oil field in the Erlian basin. In 2012, the Manas Petroleum Corporation drilled two wells in Mongolia.

There are sizeable deposits of coal reserves most of which is lignite. Production was almost 50 million tonnes in 2014 and this will likely more than double by 2025 to over 100 million tonnes and then increase to 125 million tonnes by 2030. Coal accounts for around 80 per cent of primary energy consumption. The Mineral Resources Authority of Mongolia (MRAM) is responsible for policymaking and managing national coal assets.

In December 2014, the government awarded a deal to develop the massive Tavan Tolgoi coal field to a consortium comprising Energy Resources/MCS (Mongolia), Shenhua (China), and Sumitomo (Japan); talks continue to hammer out the financing and operating details. A Mongolian negotiator recently announced that the US$4 billion deal is unlikely to go through, as China's economic growth has slowed. The mine has a total estimated resource of 6.4 billion tonnes, one quarter of which is high quality coking coal.

Energy

Total installed generating capacity was 1050 MW in 2014 of which only 728 MW is available due to losses from ageing plants and transmission. The energy sector is almost entirely fossil fuel based and is dominated by coal. There has been virtually no investment in new power generation since 1985, however, in recent years, driven by the economic boom, domestic consumption has been increasing rapidly and demand will be need to be met. The financial viability of Mongolia's electricity providers is being threatened by the increasing price of Russian electricity, inefficient infrastructure and the low cost of electricity for consumers.

An Engie-led group of companies has agreed with Mongolia on a Power Purchase Agreement for a $1.4 billion power station in Ulaanbaatar, a project that could help reduce smog plaguing the nation's capital. Engie, Sojitz Corp of Japan, Posco Energy Corp of South Korea and Mongolia's Newcom Group signed the PPA in 2015. The 450MW combined heat and power facility will help meet the capital's growing electricity needs amid an economic expansion driven by coal and copper mining.

Financial markets

Stock exchange

Mongolyn Khöröngiin Birj (Mongolian Stock Exchange) (MSE)

Banking and insurance

There is a two-tier banking system. Mongolia's first private commercial bank, the Central Asia Bank (CAB), established in 1992, collapsed in 1996 due to bad debt and poor management. The Reconstruction Bank of Mongolia was established as a universal commercial bank in 1997. Two domestic banks were sold to international interests, the AG Bank to the Japanese-based H S Securities for US$6.9 million, following a three-year restructuring programme and the Trade and Development Bank of Mongolia, sold for US$12.23 million, to the Swiss-based Banca Commerciale Lugano and US-based Gerald Metals.

Central bank
Bank of Mongolia
Main financial centre
Ulaanbaatar

Time
GMT plus eight hours

Geography
Mongolia is a landlocked country in central Asia, with Russia to the north and the People's Republic of China to the south, east and west.
The land consists of a plateau that rises to between 914–1,524 metres with mountain ranges running from the west to north-east. The tallest mountains are the Altai Mountains in the south-west, which rise to 4,267 metres. The large, flat plains of the centre, east and south-east include untracked Steppes and the arid Gobi desert. The largest rivers are the Selenge Mörön and its tributary, the Orhon Gol, which crosses the border into Russia in the north.
Hemisphere
Northern

Climate
Summers are warm and wet, and winters extremely cold. In Ulaanbaatar, winter temperatures range from minus 4 degrees Celsius (C) to minus 50 degrees C, with an average of minus 26 degrees C in January; in summer temperatures range from 0–40 degrees C, with an average of 17 degrees C in July. Relative humidity ranges from 65 per cent (July–August) to 75 per cent (November–February). Rainfall is low, with an average of 233mm per year in Ulaanbaatar (two-thirds of which falls June–August) and 116–344mm per year elsewhere. On average, there are 250 cloudless days a year.

Entry requirements
Passports
Required by all and must have six months validity from the date of entry to Mongolia.
Visa
Required by all, with some exceptions see: www.un.int/mongolia and follow the link to *visa and travel* for further information.
Business and tourist visitors staying for more than 30 days are referred to as temporary residents and apply with a non-tourist visa; a local contact or business partner will increase the chance of visa approval. When granted, visitors must register with the Foreign Citizens Bureau in Ulaanbaatar within seven days of arrival. Visitors who need to register must de-register before leaving Mongolia, at the Office of Immigration, Naturalization and Foreign Citizens. After de-registering, an 'exit visa' from the consular department of the Mongolian Ministry of Foreign Affairs will be issued.
Contact the nearest consulate for further advice and to confirm all aspects of visa requirements before travelling.
Currency advice/regulations
The import of local currency is limited to Tug815 and must be declared. The import of foreign currency is limited to US$2,000 or its equivalent. The export of local and foreign currency is limited the amount declared on arrival.
Travellers cheques have limited use in the capital, cheques in US dollars are easiest to exchange.
Customs
Importation of pornography and export of valuable antiques is strictly prohibited. Customs regulations are enforced by strict examinations. Firearms for sporting purposes require a licence. Import allowances included 200 cigarettes and two litres of alcohol.

Health (for visitors)
Mandatory precautions
No vaccination certificates are required.
Advisable precautions
Immunisations for typhoid, TB, hepatitis A and B are necessary while tetanus, diphtheria and polio vaccinations should be up-to-date. Rabies is a risk, particularly in rural areas.
There is a shortage of routine medications and visitors should take all necessary medicines with them. A first aid kit that includes disposable syringes, is a reasonable precaution. Use only bottled or boiled water for drinks, washing teeth and making ice. Eat only well cooked meals, preferably served hot; vegetables should be cooked and fruit peeled. Dairy products are unpasteurised and should be avoided, unless cooked.
Healthcare is not to Western standards and medical insurance, including emergency evacuation, is necessary.

Hotels
There are a number of suitable hotels for foreign visitors in Ulaanbaatar, but in the provinces facilities are basic.

Credit cards
International credit and charge cards are accepted in major city centres.

Public holidays (national)
Fixed dates
1 Jan (New Year's Day), 8 Mar (Women's Day), 1 Jun (Mothers' and Childrens' Day), 11–13 Jul (Naadam), 26 Nov (Independence Day).
Variable dates
Bituum and Tsagaan Sar (Lunar New Year) (Jan/Feb/Mar, three days)

Working hours
Banking
Mon–Fri: 0930–1230; 1400–1500.
Business
Mon–Fri: 0900–1800.
Government
Mon–Fri: 0900–1800.
Shops
Mon–Sat: 1000–1800 (some food shops stay open later). Some open Sunday.

Telecommunications
Mobile/cell phones
GSM 900 services are available in large urban areas only.

Electricity supply
240V AC, 50Hz

Weights and measures
Metric system.

Getting there
Air
National airline: MIAT (Mongolian Airlines)
International airport/s: Ulaanbaatar Buyant-Ukhaa (ULN), 15km from city, facilities include duty-free shops, bank, restaurant and car hire. Taxis and buses provide access to the city, travel time 15–30 minutes.
Airport tax: Departure tax of US$12
Surface
Road: While there are many roads that cross the borders from China and Russia only a few are designated for international visitors and permission must be obtained from Mongolian authorities to cross, before travelling.
The Regional Road Corridor Improvement Project, estimated at US$18 billion, to improve Central Asian roads, airports, railway lines and seaports and provide a vital transit route between Europe and Asia was agreed, on 3 November 2007. Six new transit corridors, between Afghanistan, Azerbaijan, China, Kazakhstan, Kyrgyzstan, Mongolia, Tajikistan and Uzbekistan, of mainly roads and rail links, will be constructed, or existing resources upgraded, by 2013. Half the costs with be provided by the Asian Development Bank and other multilateral organisations and the other half by participating countries.
Rail: Ulaanbaatar is served by the Trans-Mongolian Railway connecting Moscow and Beijing, with an express train that runs once a week. International trains have restaurant and sleeping cars.
There are frequent delays on the routes to Beijing and Siberia. Trains operate on summer and winter schedules, alternating in May and October.

Getting about
National transport
Air: MIAT operates an extensive domestic network. Regular air services provide the only feasible means of long-distance internal travel, although delays and cancellations are frequent. There are officially

21 airports, but only eight have paved runways.

Road: There are 46,700km of roads and tracks. Only 3 per cent of roads are paved (mainly around the cities). Many of the unpaved roads and cross-country tracks are impassable during the summer, because of flooding or waterlogging. The poor railway network dictates that roads provide the only access routes to 16 of Mongolia's 21 provinces.

Buses: Inter-urban bus services are available, with many long-distance bus routes, but their use is unfeasible due to the distances involved.

Rail: In addition to the cities served by the Trans-Mongolian Railway (Sühbaatar, Darhan, Ulaanbaatar, Dzamyn-Uüd and Saynshand), there are branch lines to various industrial centres and mining towns, including Erdenet, Baganuur and Bor-Ondör. Total network 1,815km.

City transport

Taxis: Taxis are available for journeys from the airport to the city centre, with a journey time of 15 minutes.

Buses, trams & metro: There are trolley-buses and buses. Service 11 operates 0600–2200 from airport to city centre, journey time 30 minutes.

Car hire

A hire car with driver is the only option as local knowledge of conditions is vital; hires can be arranged by most hotels or tourist organisations in Ulaanbaatar. Rates vary from fixed hourly, daily, weekly or monthly hire.

Off-road vehicles can be hired from specialist suppliers but a local licence is required, this can be obtained, for a fee, using a valid national or international licence.

BUSINESS DIRECTORY

The addresses listed below are a selection only. While World of Information makes every endeavour to check these addresses, we cannot guarantee that changes have not been made, especially to telephone numbers and area codes. We would welcome any corrections.

Telephone area codes

The international direct dialling code (IDD) for Mongolia is +976, followed by area code and subscriber's number:

Ulaanbataar 11

Useful telephone numbers

Police: 102
Fire: 101
Ambulance: 103
Car hire
Ulaanbaatar
Car Base: (tel: 379-965).

Chambers of Commerce

Mongolian National Chamber of Commerce & Industry, 11 J Sambuu Street, Ulaanbaatar 38 (tel: 312-501; fax: 324-620; e-mail: info@mongolchamber.mn).

Ulaanbaatar Chamber of Commerce, Box 254, Ulaanbaatar 210136 (tel; 329-912; fax: 311-385; e-mail: ubcc@ magicnet.mn).

Banking

Agricultural Bank, PO Box 185, Peace Avenue, Ulaanbaatar (tel: 457-880; fax: 458-670); e-mail: haab@magicnet.mn).

Anod Bank of Mongolia, PO Box 361, 18 Commerce Street, Chingeltei, Ulaanbaatar (tel: 327-566; fax: 313-070); e-mail: anod@magicnet.mn).

The Bank of Mongolia, Baga Toiruu-9, Ulaanbaatar (tel: 322-166; fax: 311-471).

Credit Bank, Suknbaatar Square, 20A, Ulaanbaatar (tel: 321-897; fax: 321-897).

Erelbank Ltd, Chingis Avenue, Khan-uul District, Ulaanbaatar (tel: 343-387; fax: 343-567).

Golomt Bank of Mongolia, PO Box 22, 4th Floor, Sukhbaatar Square 3, Central Place of Culture, Ulaanbaatar (tel: 311-530; fax: 312-307).

Mongol Post Bank, PO Box 874, Kholboochdiin Street 4, Ulaanbaatar (tel: 310-301; fax: 328-501).

Savings Bank, 6 Commerce Street, Ulaanbaatar (tel: 327-467; fax: 327-467).

Trade & Development Bank of Mongolia, 7 Commerce Street, Ulaanbaatar (tel: 327-020; fax: 312-418).

Ulaanbaater City Bank, PO Box 370, Baga toiruu 15, Ulaanbaatar (tel: 312-155; fax: 311-067).

Zoos Bank, 6 Choimbalin, Chingeltei, Ulaanbaatar (tel: 329-537; fax: 329-537).

Central bank

Bank of Mongolia, Baga Toiruu 9, Ulaanbaatar 46 (tel: 310-392; fax: 311-417; email: feprmd@mongolbank.mn).

Stock exchange

Mongolyn Khöröngiin Birj (Mongolian Stock Exchange) (MSE), www.mse.mn

Travel information

Flight information (0800-2200 hours) (tel: 119).

Juulchin, Ulaanbaatar (tel: 320-246, 328-428).

MIAT Head Office, MIAT Building, Buyant-Ukhaa 45, Ulaanbaatar 210134 (tel: 379-935, 984-070; fax: 379-919; email: contact@miat.com; internet: www.miat.com).

Ulaanbaatar Buyant-Ukhaa Airport, Ulaanbaatar 34 (tel: 379-986; fax: 379-744).

National tourist organisation offices

Mongolian Tourism Association, Room 318, Trade Union Building, Sukhbaatar Square 11, Ulaanbaatar 38 (tel/fax: 327-820; internet: www. travelmongolia.org)

Ministries

Ministry of Finance, Ulaanbaatar 46.

Ministry of Foreign Relations, Ulaanbaatar 11.

Ministry of Trade and Industry, 11 Sambuu St, Ulaanbaatar 46 (tel: 706-146; fax: 326-325).

Other useful addresses

Mongol An Corporation, Baigal Ordon, Ulaanbaatar 38 (tel/fax: 360-067).

Mongolian Business Development Agency (MBDA), U Barsbold (fax: 311-092; email: mbda@magicnet.mn).

Mongolian Embassy (US), 2833 M Street, NW, Washington DC 20007 (tel: (+1-202) 333-7117; fax: (+1-202) 298-9227; email: monemb@aol.com).

Mongolian Stock Exchange, Sukhbaatar Square 14, Ulaanbaatar (tel: 310-501; fax: 325-170; email: msebatj@magicnet.mn).

The Permanent Mission of Mongolia to the United Nations, 6 East 77th street, New York, NY10021-1704 (tel: (+1-212) 861-9460; fax: (+1-212) 861-9464; email: mongolia@un.int).

School of Economic Studies (Economic Institute), National University of Mongolia (fax: 325-349; email: suvd@magicnet.mn).

State Statistical Board, Ulaanbaatar 11 (fax: 324-518).

National news agency: Montsame Agency, PO Box 1514, 8 Jigiidjav Street, Ulaanbaatar (tel: 314-507; fax: 327-857; internet: www.montsame.mn).

Internet sites

Mongolian Stock Exchange:
http://mse.com.mn

Parliament of Mongolia:
http://www.parl.gov.mn/english.htm

School of Economic Studies:
http://www.ses.edu.mn

State Property Committee:
http://www.spc.gov.mn

Montenegro

Montenegro's prime minister Milo Đukanovic could, in 2015, be excused for looking smug. The Koalicija za Evropsku Crnu Goru (KECG) (Coalition for European Montenegro), led by Mr Đukanovic (who liked to style himself 'Europe's most successful statesman') had won the October 2012 parliamentary elections, although with 45.6 per cent of the votes it did not have an absolute majority. The ruling coalition was made up of the Demokratska Partija Socijalista (DPS) (Democratic Party of Socialists), Socijaldemokratska Partija (SDP) (Social Democratic Party) and Lberalna Partija Crne Gore (LPCG) (Liberal Party of Montenegro). With 39 of the 81 seats in Parliament, the coalition had fallen two seats short of a majority. The turnout was an impressive 70.56 per cent, with 514,055 voters.

There were, however, one or two flies in the Montenegrin political ointment. Just when Mr Đukanovic could think things were really going his way, the tide seemed to turn. European Union (EU) officials had made it clear that Montenegro's levels of corruption and crime were simply unacceptable. This challenge was echoed by Montenegro's parliament which was also beginning to flex its democratic muscles. Mr Đukanovic's position had not been helped by the leak of a tape recording allegedly of discussions between the prime minister and his associates as to how forthcoming presidential elections might be 'fixed'. In the event, the opposition candidate Miodrag Lekic, came close to taking the presidency away from Filip Vujanovic, who was 'supported' by Mr Đukanovic. Mr Lekic's followers alleged that the vote had been rigged, which in view of the leaked tape recording was not beyond the pale. The opposition also claimed that Mr Vujanovic was no longer a legitimate president since the constitution did not permit him to run for a third term in office.

Montenegro had begun European accession talks in 2012. Following Croatia's membership, it was fair to assume that in normal circumstances Montenegro was next in the accession 'queue'. One issue with the accession talks had been the EU's concern at Montenegro's levels of crime and corruption. On the 2014 Transparency International *Corruption Perceptions Index*, Montenegro ranked 76 out of the 175 countries surveyed; two places ahead of Serbia, but well behind every EU member state.

The economy – the IMF…

In October 2015 the International Monetary Fund (IMF) presented a thorough assessment of the Montenegrin economy. The IMF concluded that the strong growth apparent in 2015 looked set to continue into the medium term, driven by the authorities' plans to boost development and transport linkages. Although infrastructure development was clearly needed, the emphasis on large investment projects in the view of the IMF, carried risks, notably to the public finances. The authorities intended to mitigate those risks through the use of concessions and public private partnerships. The IMF noted that the economy had rebounded strongly. Tourism arrivals had seen double digit growth. Industrial production had recovered, largely driven by increased manufacturing. The IMF projected growth of around 4 per cent in 2015, well up on the 1.75 per cent seen in 2014.The IMF expected growth to continue over the medium term, driven by foreign-financed capital investment projects. Low inflation in the euro-zone was expected to help restrain price pressures.

The IMF noted that the Montenegrin authorities had taken steps to contain underlying fiscal stresses and were committed to managing debt vulnerabilities in the period ahead. However, the IMF considered that some recent measures raised questions about the ability to sustain fiscal discipline. The crisis tax had been cut, new social spending measures had been introduced; overall the intention to contain expenditure in the medium term lacked specifics. The IMF expected public debt to continue to increase further and then to fall gradually. Fiscal deficits would increase with highway spending; based on current policies, public debt was expected by the IMF to peak at around 77 per cent of GDP over the following three to four years, from 70 per

KEY FACTS

Official name: Republika Crna Gora (Republic of Montenegro) (ROM)

Head of State: President Filip Vujanovic (from 22 May 2003, re-elected 2013)

Head of government: Prime Minister Milo Đukanovic (KECG) (from 9 Nov 2012)

Ruling party: Koalicija za Evropsku Crnu Goru (KECG) (Coalition for European Montenegro, comprising Demokratska Partija Socijalista (DPS) (Democratic Party of Socialists), Socijaldemokratska Partija (SDP) (Social Democratic Party) and Lberalna Partija Crne Gore (LPCG) (Liberal Party of Montenegro) (from 2006; re-elected 2012)

Area: 14,026 square km

Population: 624,000 (2014)* (620,029; 2011, census figure (preliminary)

Capital: Podgorica (administrative); Cetinje (cultural)

Official language: Montenegro Serbian (Lekavian dialect)

Currency: Euro (€) = 100 cents (from 1 Jan 2002; previous currency Deutsche mark, locked at DM1.96 per euro)

Exchange rate: €0.89 per US$ (Sep 2015)

GDP per capita: US$7,149 (2014)*

GDP real growth: 1.13% (2014)

GDP: US$4.46 billion (2014)

Labour force: 194,000 (2010)

Unemployment: 17.20% (2011)*

Inflation: -0.73% (2014)

Balance of trade: -US$1.83 billion (2014)

Annual FDI: US$558.05 million (2011)

* estimated figure

cent in 2015, decreasing to around 73 per cent of GDP in 2020.

The IMF estimated that if these additional measures, forecast at 1.5 percentage points of GDP, could be sustained up to 2025, they would bring debt below the Maastricht threshold of 60 per cent of GDP by the end of the period. Measures that could rapidly yield returns included increasing tourism taxes, unwinding VAT exemptions and temporarily freezing public wages and pensions.

The IMF also noted that Montenegro's financial conditions were slowly improving. Its banks are highly liquid and average capital ratios exceeded regulatory minimums, albeit with some variation. Profitability for most banks had increased, but remained weak despite high interest margins and declining non-performing loans (NPL). Credit to the private sector had increased, after shrinking for a sustained period, although not as fast as might be expected given high liquidity and the rebound in growth. This reflected persistent problems with non-performing loans, weak accounting and reporting practices and slow collateral execution.

The IMF's recent Financial Sector Assessment Programme for Montenegro identified a number of steps to mitigate risks to the financial system. These included improving the management of non-performing assets and liquidity risk and reducing operational, funding and credit concentration risks. Decisive actions to deal with weaker banks were important for preserving financial stability. Improved labour productivity and economic flexibility were crucial to complement the authorities' investment-led growth strategy. The high level of long-term unemployed remained a pressing concern; the IMF considered that the Montenegrin government should consider using funds directed at subsidising the hiring of university graduates for retraining, which could be used to help the long-term unemployed re-enter the labour force, reduce pressures on the pension system from those taking early retirement and alleviate pressures on social spending.

... and the EBRD

In its 2014 *Transition Report*, the European Bank for Reconstruction and Development (EBRD) noted that growth returned to positive territory in 2013, with real GDP rising by 3.5 per cent, following the 2012 recession (when GDP fell by 2.5 per cent). While an increase in external demand was the main growth driver over the previous year – largely due to higher exports in electricity and a strong tourism season – domestic demand remained subdued. As a result, Montenegro's economic recovery in 2013 had a limited impact on the labour market and the unemployment rate had remained high at 19.5 per cent. Subdued domestic demand ultimately led to a period of deflation, as the average price level showed a year-on-year decline from the beginning of 2014. Montenegro's current account deficit continued to decline due to a narrowing trade deficit and a rise in revenue from tourism and remittances. Despite this, the current account remained one of the highest in the region at close to 15 per cent of GDP. However, as Montenegro entered a new investment cycle, with several major projects in tourism, energy and infrastructure in the pipeline, the declining current account trend was likely to reverse.

According to the EBRD Montenegro's public finances had been under pressure. The activation of state loan guarantees for the aluminium producer, KAP, had weakened the government's fiscal position and elevated the government deficit to an unplanned 3.2 per cent of GDP. Under the 2014 budget law, Montenegro planned to cut its deficit to below two per cent of GDP. This was to be achieved by a combination of higher budget revenue from continued GDP growth, a one-year extension on the so-called crisis tax (the 15 per cent tax introduced in early 2013 on above-average salaries) and a freeze on wages and pensions until the end of 2014. However, risks persisted from the activation of further state loan guarantees, equivalent to 9.4 per cent of GDP. This deteriorating fiscal situation contributed to public debt rising to just below 60 per cent of GDP, a 10 percentage point increase relative to 2011. In line with the latest negative developments, the Montenegrin parliament had endorsed a law on fiscal responsibility, which regulated budget execution and the issuance of state guarantees and set a three per cent GDP limit for the budget deficit and a 60 per cent GDP limit for public debt. This, in the view of the EBRD, was an important step towards improving the standards of public finance management in Montenegro. However, the EBRD noted that 'sticking to these rules will be a serious challenge, especially in light of the launch of a major highway construction project.'

As a small and open economy, Montenegro was, in the view of the EBRD, highly vulnerable to external shocks, such as the crisis in Ukraine. Diversification of the economy remained a challenge for building sustainable growth in the medium term, but the visible progress in the EU accession process should help to attract further foreign direct investment (FDI) and, together with major investment projects currently in the pipeline, ultimately boost growth prospects. Joining the IMF, the EBRD also noted that Montenegro was making good progress in the EU accession negotiations. These had begun in June 2012 and, by August 2014, Montenegro had opened 12 negotiating chapters (out of 35) and had provisionally closed two: science and research and education and culture. The more recently opened chapters included those relating to free movement of capital, intellectual

KEY INDICATORS — Montenegro

	Unit	2011	2012	2013	2014	**2015
Population	m	0.62	*0.62	0.62	*0.62	*0.63
Gross domestic product (GDP)	US$bn	4.50	4.05	4.42	4.46	*4.24
GDP per capita	US$	7,317	6,511	7,093	*7,149	*6,778
GDP real growth	%	2.5	-2.5	3.3	1.1	*4.7
Inflation	%	3.1	3.6	2.2	-0.7	*0.5
Unemployment	%	17.2	–	–	–	–
Exports (fob) (goods)	US$m	654.2	498.6	525.2	473.1	–
Imports (fob) (goods)	US$m	2,464.8	2,273.4	2,289.4	2,300.8	–
Balance of trade	US$m	-1,810.6	-1,774.8	-1,764.1	-1,827.7	–
Current account	US$m	-882.0	-755.0	-646.0	-793.0	*-873.0
Total reserves minus gold	US$m	546.0	458.7	584.0	661.4	–
Foreign exchange	US$m	493.6	408.2	533.3	–	–
Exchange rate	per US$	0.71	0.77	0.73	0.82	–

* estimated figure ** forecast figure

property, foreign security and defence policy and financial control. Under the new enlargement rules, Montenegro had also started negotiations on the two most challenging chapters relating to judiciary and fundamental rights (chapter 23) and justice, freedom and security (chapter 24).

Montenegro's large-scale privatisation was advancing, albeit with some setbacks. The privatisation council's plan for 2014 had included preparing tenders for privatisation of a number of assets, including the rail cargo operator, Montecargo, the national airline, Montenegro Airlines, the tobacco company, Novi Duvanski Kombinat Podgorica, the Igalo Health Institute and the hotel and tourism operators, Budvanska Rivijera and Ulcinjska Rivijera. Public-private partnership contracts were also to be sought for 32 companies – including the postal operator, Posta Crne Gore – as well as a number of tourism companies and locations, such as Ada Bojana and Velika Plaza. However, offers of sale of many of these companies had failed over the years. A tender for a majority stake in the Bijela shipyard attracted just one bid by the April 2014 deadline, the fourth failed attempt at privatising the company. In March 2014 the government reclaimed its stake in Marina Bar from the Latvian owner and cancelled its 30-year concession deal for port operations, on the grounds that the company had acted against the terms of the privatisation contract. However, the government managed to sell the Container Terminal and General Cargo Company in the Montenegrin port of Bar to a Turkish company, Global Ports. Between 2006 and 2008 Montenegro had reported annual credit growth rates of over 100 per cent. Since the global financial crisis there had been an annual credit contraction, which finally reversed in 2013. The financial sector reported strong earnings in the first half of 2014 but credit contraction returned in the same period, reflecting conservative lending policies and a lack of attractive projects. The banking sector continued to be characterised by a high level of non-performing loans, approximately 17 per cent of total loans in mid-2014. At the end of 2013, a total of 11 banks were active in the country and another one was opened in mid-2014. At the end of 2014 foreign owned banks controlled 90 per cent of Montenegro's banking assets.

Risk assessment

Economy	Fair/good
Politics	Good
Regional stability	Good

Muslims in Montenegro

% of population	18.5
Sunni (% of Muslims)	99
Shi'a (% of Muslims)	0

COUNTRY PROFILE

1878 Following the collapse of the Ottoman Empire, of which Montenegro had been an autonomous region, the independence of the principality of Montenegro was recognised under international treaties.

1910 Prince Nikola became king and helped lead the Balkan forces that pushed the European boundaries of the Ottoman Empire back to north of Constantinople.

1914–18 As a supporter of the Allies (*Entente* Powers), Montenegro was occupied by Austro-Hungarian troops.

1918 The defeat of the Austro-Hungarian empire during the First World War saw the creation of the Kingdom of the Serbs, Croats and Slovenes, encompassing Bosnia and Hercegovina (BiH), Croatia, parts of Dalmatia and Macedonia, Montenegro, Serbia, Slavonia and Slovenia. King Nikola was deposed when, during the Podgorica People's Assembly, Montenegro voted for a union with the Kingdom of Serbia.

1919 The Kingdom of Serbs, Croats and Slovenes became a semi-autonomous region of Hungary.

1929 Following disputes between Serbs and Croats, King Alexander assumed dictatorial powers and the country was renamed Yugoslavia.

1941–45 During the Second World War parts of Yugoslavia were occupied by the Germans, Italians, Hungarians and Bulgarians.

1945–46 Following the end of the war, Serbia and Montenegro became two of the constituent republics of a federated Yugoslavia. The other republics were Bosnia and Hercegovina (BiH), Croatia, Macedonia, Slovenia and the two autonomous regions of Vojvodina and Kosovo. As the leader of the Yugoslav Communist Party (YCP), Josip Broz Tito became head of state and a Soviet-style constitution was adopted. The Serbian state and Belgrade, as the federation's capital, were the primary focus of economic and political control and the majority of the officers of the Yugoslav military were from Serbia and Montenegro.

1980 Tito died. A system of collective (rotating) presidency was adopted; ethnic tensions began to re-surface.

1989 The Serbian nationalist, Slobodan Milosevic, became president of the Republic of Serbia.

1991 Slovenia and Croatia and later Macedonia declared their independence from Yugoslavia.

1992 BiH declared its independence. Bosnian Serbs (who made up 30 per cent of the population) backed by the remaining Yugoslav federation, declared their own independence from BiH, claiming 65 per cent of the territory. The degree of inter-ethnic violence that followed, including 'ethnic cleansing', had not been seen in Europe since the Second World War. The UN imposed economic sanctions against Serbia and Montenegro, the only two Yugoslavian republics remaining.

1997 Milo Djukanovic (prime minister of Montenegro since 1994) became president of Montenegro, after defeating a pro-Milosevic candidate. Milosevic was named president of what remained of Yugoslavia.

1998 NATO began air-strikes against military targets. NATO peace-keepers moved into Kosovo.

1999 NATO extended air-strikes to include mainly Serbian infrastructure. Politically, Montenegro began to distance itself from Serbia declaring it was not a party to the conflict in Kosovo.

2002 Demokratska Lista za Evropsku Crnu Goru (DLECG) (Democratic List for a European Montenegro) coalition, led by the Demokratska Partua Socualista Crne Gore (DPS) (Democratic Socialist Party), won the parliamentary elections. Milo Djukanovic (DPS) resigned from the presidency to become prime minister while former prime minister, Filip Vujanovic, took over as acting president. The euro was adopted as the official currency.

2003 Yugoslavia was abolished and replaced with a looser federation of its two member states, Serbia and Montenegro. Yugoslav President Kostunica stepped down and was replaced as Head of the State of Serbia and Montenegro by Svetozar Marovic, a Montenegrin. Filip Vujanovic was elected president of Montenegro.

2006 In a referendum on independence, 55 per cent voted to sever ties with Serbia. Montenegro formally declared itself an independent state and also became a member of the United Nations. In the first independent parliamentary elections the ruling coalition claimed victory. Prime Minister Djukanovic resigned and Zeljko Sturanovic (DPS) was appointed as his replacement. Montenegro joined NATO.

2007 A Stabilisation and Association Agreement (SAA) between the European Union and Montenegro, the first step in the process for accession to the EU, was signed. The agreement required constitutional and judicial reforms to comply with EU membership.

2008 Prime Minister Sturanovic resigned due to ill health; Milo Đukanovic took over. In presidential elections, incumbent Filip Vujanovic (DPS) won 51.89 per cent of the vote, while his nearest rival Andrija Mandic (Serb List) polled 19.55 per cent.
2009 In early parliamentary elections, incumbent KECG won 51.94 per cent of the vote (48 seats (out of 81)); Prime Minister Đukanovic continued in office. The EU approved Montenegro's application to become a candidate for membership. Visa-free travel for all citizens of Montenegro within the EU's Schengen area became operable.
2010 Montenegro was designated as .me on internet domain sites. A government-backed Eurobond of €200 million (US$254.9 million) was issued, in a measure to cover the public deficit and avoid borrowing the amount from the International Monetary Fund (IMF). The Montenegrin bond, the first issued since independence, was set at ten years with a fixed interest rate of 7.85 per cent. Prime Minister Milo Đukanovic resigned and Igor Lukšic (DPS) became prime minister.
2011 A national census took place between 1–15 April, with preliminary results published in July. The population was 625,266, of which 44.98 per cent were designated Montenegrins, 28.73 Serbian, and 11.96 per cent Bosniaks (Bosnian Muslims). On 21 June, EU officials announced that Montenegro could apply for EU membership by the end of the year.
2012 Montenegro joined the World Trade Organisation (WTO) on 29 April, after seven years of negotiations. Parliamentary elections were held early, on 14 October, and won by the ruling KECG with 46.3 per cent of the vote (39 seats out of 81). However this was not enough to rule alone and coalition talks began immediately. Igor Lukšic (DPS) remained in post as caretaker prime minister. On 9 November, President Vujanovic asked Milo Đukanovic to form a new government. This time the coalition consisted of the DPS, Socijaldemokratska Partija (SDP) (Social Democratic Party) and Lberalna Partija Crne Gore (LPCG) (Liberal Party of Montenegro). Milo Đukanovic became prime minister.
2013 The presidential elections held on 7 April were won by Filip Vujanovic with 51.21 per cent. Miodrag Lekic of the Democratic Front was close on his heels with 48.79 per cent.
2014 The dispute with Croatia over the Prevlaka peninsula, south of Dubrovnik flared again in November when opposition leader, Nebojsa Medojevic accused the government of handing over vital territorial waters to Croatia.
2015 There were violent demonstrations outside parliament on 24 October demanding the resignation of Prime Minister Milo Djukanovic. Protesters chanted 'Milo, thief!' and called for fair elections to be organised by a transitional government ahead of those scheduled for 2016.

Political structure

Constitution

Passed in 1992.

The constitution may be amended if 10,000 voters, not less than 25 deputies or the president and prime minister submit a proposal, which is subsequently agreed by two-thirds of the Assembly members.

Montenegro became independent from Serbia in 2006.

Independence date

3 June 2006 (from Serbia); 27 April 1992 (from Yugoslavia)

Form of state

Republic

The executive

The president of the republic is elected by universal suffrage for a term of five years. A president is limited to two terms in office.

The president has the right to refer adopted laws back to the Assembly for review; if the new legislation is passed for a second time the president must promulgate the law. The president names a successor if a prime minister loses the confidence of the Assembly.

A new law governing presidential elections was enacted in December 2007. All candidates must collect signatures from 1.5 per cent of registered voters to achieve a place in the ballot.

National legislature

The unicameral Skupština Republike Crne Gore (Parliament of Montenegro) has 81 members elected by proportional representation through party lists, to serve for four-year terms. The total number of deputies may vary dependent on population numbers of one deputy elected per 6,000 votes.

The president nominates the prime minister and parliament confirms the appointment, plus the proposed cabinet. All government policies and laws must be agreed by parliament; without agreement the prime minister must resign and be replaced by another candidate.

Legal system

The rule of law is mandated in the constitution.

The legal system is independent and autonomous. The law is administered by a judge and jury in public, where citizens have the right to legal assistance. The Supreme Court is the highest court of law. Capital punishment is reserved for the most serious offences.

Last elections

7 April 2013 (presidential); 14 October 2012 (parliamentary)

Results: Presidential (2013): Filip Vujanovic (DPS) won 51.21 per cent of the vote, Miodrag Lekic (DF) 48.91 per cent. Turnout was 63.90 per cent.

Parliamentary: Koalicija za Evropsku Crnu Goru (KECG) (Coalition for European Montenegro) led by the Demokratska Partija Socijalista (DPS) (Democratic Party of Socialists), won 46.3 per cent of the vote and 39 seats (out of 81), The Demokratski Front (DF) (Democratic Front) (a coalition of two parties) 23.2 per cent and 20 seats, Socijalisticka Narodna Partija Crne Gore (SNP) (Socialist People's Party (of Montenegro) 11.2 per cent and 9 seats, Pozitivna Crna Gora (PCG) (Positive Montenegro) 8.4 per cent and 7 seats, Bošnjacka Stranka (BS) (Bosniak Party) 4.2 per cent and 3 seats. 8 other parties won 1 seat or less. Turnout was 70.56 per cent.

Next elections

2018 (presidential); October 2016 (parliamentary)

Political parties

Ruling party

Koalicija za Evropsku Crnu Goru (KECG) (Coalition for European Montenegro, comprising Demokratska Partija Socijalista (DPS) (Democratic Party of Socialists), Socijaldemokratska Partija (SDP) (Social Democratic Party) and Lberalna Partija Crne Gore (LPCG) (Liberal Party of Montenegro) (from 2006; re-elected 2012)

Main opposition party

Demokratski Front (Democratic Front) (DF)

Population

622,000 (2012)* (620,029; 2011, census figure (preliminary)

Last census: 1–15 April 2011: 620,029 (preliminary)

Population density: Urban population 61 per cent (2010 Unicef).

Annual growth rate: 0.2 per cent, 1990–2010 (Unicef).

Ethnic make-up

Montenegrin (43.2 per cent), Serbian (32.0 per cent), Bosniak (7.7 per cent), Albanian (5.3 per cent), Croats (1.1 per cent) all others (10.7 per cent).

Religions

Orthodox Christian, Muslim and Roman Catholic.

Education

Compulsory education is provided free by the state. Lessons are taught in Serbian and Albanian, although under the constitution lessons may be taught in the language of any ethnic group.

Cyrillic and Latin text have equal standing under the constitution.

Secondary education may continue from three–four years and culminates in a *matura* graduation certificate, which allows acceptance at a university. There is only one university, in Podgorica, that provides higher education and post-graduate education.

Compulsory years: 7 to 16

Health

Healthcare is publicly financed for children, expectant mothers and the elderly, under the constitution.

Since 1992, the extent and quality of healthcare provision has sharply deteriorated. However, a well-developed private healthcare system has emerged for the better-off. Largely free at the point of delivery and funded by a universal social insurance tax levied on all employees and employers, public healthcare provision require all kinds of charges, most notably for imported medications.

HIV/Aids

There have been few cases of HIV/Aids recorded since the first case was diagnosed in Montenegro in 1989. Nevertheless, the Global Fund to Fight Aids provided US$2.9 million, for a national strategy to combat the disease including prevention measures and diagnostic and antiretroviral treatment for the years 2006–2010.

Fertility rate/Maternal mortality rate: 1.7 births per woman, 2010 (Unicef)

Child (under 5 years) mortality rate (per 1,000): 6 per 1,000 live births (WHO 2012)

Welfare

The constitution declared that a mandatory insurance scheme provides all employees and their family all forms of social security. The state is required to provide for the old, infirm and incapable.

Main cities

Podgorica (capital, 149,228 in 2012), Nikšic (58,644), Pljevlja (20,979), Bar (15, 861), Bijelo Polje (15,084), Budva (14,342), Cetinje (14,263), Herceg Novi (13,663).

Languages spoken

Serbian and Albanian

Official language/s

Montenegro Serbian (Lekavian dialect)

Media

Press freedom is guaranteed in law.

Press

Dailies: There are several newspapers published in Montenegro Serbian including *Pobjeda* (www.pobjeda.co.me) *Vijesti* (www.vijesti.cg.me), *Dan* (www.dan.cg.me) and *Republika* (www.republika.cg.me); *Monitor* (www.monitor.cg.me) is a weekly publication. Newspapers in other languages include *The Montenegro Times* (www.themontenegrotimes.com) in English and *Koha Javore* (www.kohajavore.cg.me) in Albanian.

Broadcasting

Media laws allowed the transformation of the state-funded broadcaster Radio Televizija CRNE Gore (RTCG) (www.rtcg.cg.me) into an independent commercial public broadcaster in 2002.

Radio: Most radio stations operate from Podgorica. RTCG (www.rtcg.cg.me) operates Radio Crne Gore with two stations. Other, private stations include Radio Antena M (www.antenam.net), Corona Radio (www.corona-radio.com) and City Radio (www.cityradio.fm).

Television: RTCG (www.rtcg.cg.yu) operates two, national, terrestrial channels and a satellite channel, broadcasting domestic and imported programmes. Other private channels include TV IN (www.rtvin.com), ntv Montena (www.montena.cg.yu), Elmag RTV and TV Pink M (www.rtvpink.com) a relay from a Serbian station. There are small local TV channels located in larger cities.

National news agency: Mina (MNNews): http://mnnews.net

Other news agencies: Media Club: www.mediaclub.cg.me

Economy

Since disengaging from Serbia in 2005, the economy has strengthened as Montenegro adopted a fully open market economy and joined the European Monetary Union (EMU) hence adopting the euro as its currency. Despite joining the EMU, it is not an official member of the Euro-Zone. In January 2007, Montenegro joined the World Bank and IMF, and in December 2011, the World Trade Organization. It has opened talks with the EC in 2012 to join the EU, but first it needs to make significant steps in fighting corruption and organized crime. In 2009, over 85 per cent of state-owned commercial entities were privatised, while the banking, telecommunications and oil import and distribution sectors were also fully privatised. This was achieved mainly through a steady increase in foreign direct investment (FDI), so that by 2009 FDI had reached US$1.5 billion (over 10 times the amount of FDI in 2004. FDI began to weaken in the aftermath of the global economic recession and was down to US$760 million in 2010. FDI in Montenegro has continued to decrease at US$620 million in 2012 before stabilising at US$447 million in 2013 and US$497 million in 2014. The biggest foreign investors in Montenegro are Italy, Norway, Austria, Russia, Hungary and Great Britain, its investment per capita still remains as one of the highest in Europe.

Tourism brings in twice as many visitors as Montenegro's total population every year and therefore, several new luxury tourism complexes are in various stages of development along the coast and a number are being offered in connection with nearby boating and yachting facilities. Montenegro is currently planning major overhauls of its road, rail and air transportation systems. In 2014, the government selected two Chinese companies to construct a 41 km-long section of the country's highway system costing around $1.1 billion.

To encourage domestic spending the government decreased personal tax to a flat rate of 9 per cent in 2010. GDP growth in 2008 was 6.9 per cent; however the global economic crisis quickly turned the budget surplus into a large deficit and the economy fell into recession in 2009 with a negative growth of -5.7 per cent, which caused a rapid rise in public debt. Government revenue fell by around 10 per cent and didn't return until global trade picked up in 2010 and GDP growth grew by 2.5 per cent. GDP growth has since fluctuated going into recession at -2.5 per cent in 2012 before rebounding to 3.3 per cent growth in 2013. GDP growth stabilised at 1.1 per cent in 2014.

High unemployment, typically in double digits, is still characteristic of an earlier economic regime when Montenegro was integrated with Serbia. However, unemployment has steadily fallen from 19.7 per cent in 2005 to 15.1 per cent in 2008 and 14 per cent in 2009 before rising to 16.5 per cent in 2010. Unfortunately, the earlier decrease in the unemployment rate has culminated in an unhealthy 18.5 per cent of the working population in 2014.

External trade

Montenegro has bilateral free trade agreements with the EU, European Free Trade Association (Efta), Russia and countries of Central and South-Eastern Europe (Cefta). Montenegro has joined the World Trade Organisation (WTO), the IMF and the World Bank as a full member.

Montenegro will be able to join the EU once it has met the requirements which is to reduce corruption and organized crime.

While Montenegro has an established industrial sector based on bauxite mining and aluminium production, tourism has become the principal foreign exchange earner.

Imports

Main imports include petroleum and lubricants, vehicles and machinery, capital machinery, manufactured goods, chemicals, food and live animals and raw materials.

Main sources: Serbia (26.9 per cent of total in 2014), Greece (8.1 per cent) and China (7.4 per cent).

Exports

Principal exports include aluminium, manufactured goods, food and live animals and raw materials.

Main destinations: Serbia (23.7 per cent of total in 2014), Italy (10.3 per cent) and Belarus (9.8 per cent).

Agriculture

Farming

5.3 per cent of the workforce is employed in the farming industry and it constitutes 8.3 per cent of GDP. Main agricultural products are potatoes, citrus fruits, grapes, sheep, olives and tobacco. Significant money is made from exporting high value crops including tobacco and olives.

Fishing

Less than one per cent of the workforce is employed in the fishing industry. Fishing is virtually non-existent in Montenegro, the sector only occupies 0.5 per cent of GDP as of 2014. It is estimated that only 400 people are engaged in the business. It would be a good time for country to expand its fleet because after joining the EU it will not be possible, due to the policy of preserving fish resources.

Forestry

Montenegro, when it committed itself to eco-friendly development in its 1992 constitution has made it so that forests had not been plundered during eras of autocracy so that a largely pristine ecosystem is available for sustainable development including tourism and timber production. Forest and woodland cover over half the total area of land – 743,609 hectares (ha), of which forest cover is 620,872ha. The majority of forests are state-owned – 500,041ha – while 243,568ha are privately owned. There is an estimated 72.1 million square metres of standing stock, of which conifers amount to 30 million square metres.

State ownership protects forests from over-exploitation, with sustainable objectives for timber production.

Industry and manufacturing

The manufacturing industry is one of the largest employers, followed by retail and transport.

The state-owned and bankrupt, Niksic Steel Plant, one of the country's largest firms, was put up for sale on 5 January 2012, as part of the government's privatisation plans. The sale was expected to return €30 million (US$39.4 million) to the state treasury. However, despite interest being shown by investors from six other countries the only confirmed offer came from Niksic's former Dutch owners.

Tourism

Montenegro's constitution proclaims the country as an 'ecological state' and as such it promotes itself as a destination for visitors who love the outdoors. The country has been largely unspoilt by intensive development along the Adriatic coast and its interior retains historic and cultural landscapes as well as national parks and some of Europe's most rugged mountains. Winter sports are popular, as well as water sports, especially along the Tara River Canyon.

Travel and tourism is important to the economy of Montenegro. In 2008, just before the global economic crisis struck, tourism contributed 26.4 per cent (US$1.2 billion) of GDP; however this has fallen steadily so that by 2011 it contributed 15.4 per cent (US$728 million) of GDP. In 2014 tourism contributed 20 per cent to GDP (US$733.2 million) which represents a slight improvement on the numbers in 2011. The sector is predicted to contribute 21 per cent to GDP in 2015. Tourism provided employment for 18.5 per cent of the workforce (32,000 jobs) in 2014. By 2025, travel and tourism is forecast to support 55,000 jobs (almost 30 per cent of total employment). In 2015, it is predicted that 1,378,000 international tourists will visit Montenegro.

Environment

The constitution mandates that the environment is protected from exploitation.

Mining

There are large deposits of bauxite; aluminium accounts for around 25 per cent of Montenegro's industrial output and almost 75 per cent of export earnings. The first and largest bauxite mines are in Nikšic, employing about 1,400 workers. There are coal mines in Plijevlja but they are chronically underfunded and in need of investment to increase production.

There are shale deposits but Montenegro does not have the technology to exploit them.

Hydrocarbons

There are no known oil and gas reserves; oil consumption is typically over 11,640 barrels per day, all of which is imported. Natural gas is not produced; any consumption is commercially negligible.

In February 2012, the government signed an agreement to join the multinational, South Stream Transport group, which is in the process of organising the building a natural gas pipeline off- and onshore, to transport Russian gas to Western and Central Europe bypassing Ukraine. The expected start date for construction was announced as December 2012.

Consumption of lignite coal is some 1.30 million tonnes for domestic and industrial needs and an additional 1.38 million tonnes for electricity generation.

Coalmines, containing lignite, are mainly based in Plijevlja and have been chronically underfunded and in need of investment to increase production. There are shale deposits but Montenegro does not have the technology to exploit them.

Energy

Total installed generating capacity was 885,500 kW in 2013. The energy market has been privatised and the once state-owned Elektroprivreda Crne Gore (EPCG) was broken up. In May 2009, Italy's energy company A2A bought a 15 per cent share in the utility. Although EPCG is responsible for generation, distribution and supply of electricity, it no longer has a monopoly and transmission has been unbundled into a separate company. It runs the two hydroelectric power stations of Piva and Perucica with capacities of 342MW and 302MW respectively, plus the coal-fired power station at Plievlja, producing 210MW.

The Djerdap (Iron Gate) Gorge, located on the Danube, provided 2,532MW shared between Serbia, Montenegro and Romania, but since Montenegro split with Serbia the supply of electricity is subject to international commercial considerations.

Montenegro has the potential to be a major exporter of electricity to neighbours and beyond the Balkans from its hydropower reserves. It is currently constructing new hydroelectric dams, including a controversial plan in the world heritage site of the Tara Gorge.

75 per cent of total installed capacity is garnered from hydroelectric plants while 24.6 per cent is from fossil fuels.

Financial markets

Stock exchange

Montenegro Berza (Montenegro Stock Exchange) (MSE)

Banking and insurance

Central bank

Centralna Banka Crne Gore

Main financial centre

Podgorica

Time

GMT plus two hours, (daylight saving GMT plus one hour, end March to end of October).

Geography

Montenegro is somewhat diamond in shape with a tiny, 25km, border with Croatia in the west. It has a much longer, 225km, border with Bosnia and Herzegovina from the west to the north. Serbia has a 203km border on its east to south east and Albania has a 172km border along the south. Lastly, it has a

294km coastline along the Adriatic Sea from the south west to west.
The name Montenegro (*Crne Gora*) means black mountain and, from the sea, must seem like a solid rock formation. High limestone mountains overshadow the shoreline, rising sharply from the narrow coastal plain (no wider than 10km), which is dotted with many bays and coves. The mountains form a tableland that lacks the soil to sustain much life as rainwater is quickly drained through porous rocks. At 2,522m the highest peak is Bobotov Kuk, in the north west of the country, in high mountains, that stretch along the border with Bosnia and Hercegovina. A matching mountain range lies along the Albanian border. These mountain ranges generally rise to over 2,000m in height, but then 60 per cent of the country is above 1,000m, nevertheless the northern region is futile pasturelands. Over 80 per cent of the country is forest, much of it primeval.
There are three main rivers running north/south – Piva, Tara and Lim – added to which are 40 lakes, the largest of which is Skadar, which spans the border with Albania. The river Tara has a 82km long, 1300m deep canyon, which is the world's second deepest chasm (after the US Grand Canyon).

Hemisphere
Northern

Climate
The climate is dictated by the geography. Mediterranean climate allows coastal summer temperatures to reach 26 degrees Celsius (C), falling to 12 degrees C in winter. The tableland has a continental climate, when summer temperatures can reach 40 degrees C and drop during winter as low as 5 degrees C. In the alpine, snowcapped northern mountains winters are cold, temperatures can fall to minus 7 degrees C and summers cool at 20 degrees C.

Entry requirements
Passports
Required by all

Visa
Requirements for Montenegro have yet to be published – the following were appropriate for the union of Serbia and Montenegro and should only be considered as guidelines. Contact a Montenegro Consulate for further information.
Visas are required by all, with the exception of most European, North American and Australasian visitors for both business and tourist reasons. Visitors arriving via Serbia require a visa.
Those visitors that require visas should contact the nearest embassy or consulate for an application form. Business travellers in this category will require a letter of invitation from a local company giving the nature of business, duration of visit and a full itinerary, plus a letter from the employing company confirming details; and proof of sufficient funds for living expenses and medical insurance.

Currency advice/regulations
The import of local and foreign currency is unlimited but must be declared; export is limited to the declared amount.

Hotels
There are a wide range of hotels ranging from luxury to family-run *pensions*. The ministry of tourism began a system of star rating, but by August 2006 had not completed the process.
Hotel reservations should be made in advance, especially during summer.

Credit cards
Major international credit and charge cards are accepted.

Public holidays (national)
Fixed dates
1 Jan (New Year), 1 May (Labour Day), 9 May (Victory Day), 13 Jul (National Day), 29 Nov (Republic Day).

Variable dates
Orthodox: Christmas (three days), and Easter (two days); Bayram (Feast of the Sacrifice, first day of Ramadam)
These religious holidays are based on the lunar calendar.

Working hours
Banking
Mon–Fri: 0830–1630

Business
Mon–Fri: 0800–1500.

Government
Mon–Fri: 0730–1530.

Shops
Mon–Fri: generally in larger towns: 0800–2000 (some shops may close between 1200–1700); Sat: 0800–1500.

Telecommunications
Mobile/cell phones
There are GSM 900/1800 services that cover almost all of the country.

Electricity supply
220V, 50Hz with European flat and round, two-pin plugs.

Weights and measures
Metric system

Getting there
Air
National airline: Montenegro Airlines
International airport/s: Podgorica International airport (TGD), 12km from the city. A new terminal, opened in May 2006, includes *bureau de change*, restaurant, shops and an information centre. Taxis and buses are available to the city.
Other airport/s: Tivat Airport, on the Adriatic Coast, caters largely for tourist flights from Europe.
Airport tax: Departure tax: eur16, in cash.

Surface
Road: There are border crossings from Croatia at Debeli and Brijeg, from Albania at Bozaj, several from Bosnia and Hercegovina at Vilusi, Vracenovici, Scepan Polje and Metaljka and from Serbia at Bijelo Polje.
Vehicle owners must pay a toll on entering Montenegro.
Rail: There are links to Serbia via Belgrade and Albania via Skadar.
Water: There are regular ferry services from Italy.

Main port/s: Bar, Kotor and Zelenika

Getting about
National transport
Road: There are over 5,000km of roads but only 60 per cent are paved and are not maintained to a high standard. Two major roads that provide access around the country are the Adriatic Highway which runs along the coast from Ulcinj to Igalo and the motorway, with tolls, from Petrovac to the Serbian border at Bijelo Polje, via Podgorica.
Buses: Bus services link most towns and cities.
Rail: There are almost 250km of railways, with most lines running from the coast in the south west to the Serbian border in the north east. All lines run into Podgorica, of which one rail link terminates at Nikšic.

City transport
There are bus services in Podgorica.
Taxis: City taxis have meters, although if not in use negotiate a price before travelling.

Car hire
There are several local and international car hire firms in Montenegro, with cars available at the airport and in large towns.
An international driving licence is necessary, along with insurance. Traffic drives on the right, with speed limits at 120kph on motorways, 100kph on other main roads. Road signs are likely to be in Cyrillic script.

BUSINESS DIRECTORY
The addresses listed below are a selection only. While World of Information makes every endeavour to check these addresses, we cannot guarantee that changes have not been made, especially to telephone numbers and area codes. We would welcome any corrections.

Telephone area codes
The international direct dialling (IDD) code is +381, followed by area code and subscriber's number:

Podgorica 81

Useful telephone numbers
Ambulance: 94
Fire: 93
Police: 92

Chambers of Commerce
Montenegro Chamber of Economy, 29 Novaka Miloseva, 81000 Podgorica (tel: 230-545; fax: 230-943; e-mail: pkcg@cg.me).

Banking
Atlasmont Banka, 4 Stanka Dragojevica St, Podgorica (tel: 407-200; fax: 665-451; e-mail: office@atlasmont.cg.me).

Crnogorska Komercijalna Banka (Commercial Bank of Montenegro), Moskovska bb, 81000 Podgorica (tel: 404-232; fax: 404-277: email: info@ckb.cg.me).

NLB Montenegrobanka, 46 Bulevar Stanka Gragojevica, 81000 Podgorica (tel: 402-212; fax: 402-212; e-mail: info@montenegro-banka.com).

Podgoricka Banka, 8a Novaka Miloseva Street, 81000 Podgorica (tel: 224-555; fax: 405-100; email: pgbanka@cg.me).

Central bank
Centralna Banka Crne Gore (CBCG) (Central Bank of Montenegro), Bulevar Svetog Petra Cetinjskog 7, Podgorica (tel: 403-191; fax: 664-140; e-mail: info@cb-cg.org).

Stock exchange
Montenegro Berza (Montenegro Stock Exchange) (MSE), www.montenegroberza.com

Nova Berza Hartija od Vrijednosti Crne Gore (New Securities Exchange of Montenegro) (NEX Montenegro), www.nex.cg.yu

Travel information
Automobile Association of Montenegro, Podgorica (AMSCG), (tel: 225-493, 224-467).

Montenegro Airlines, Slobode 23, Podgorica (tel: 664-411/433/455; email: office.podgorica@mgx.cg.me).

National Tourist Organization of Montenegro, Omladinskih Brigada 7, 81000 Podgorica (tel: 230-959; fax: 230-979; e-mail: tourism@cg.me)

Zeljeznica Crne Gore (Montenegro railways), Trg Golootockih Zrtava 13, 81000 Podgorica (tel: 441-302; fax: 633-957; email: zcg-uprava@cg.me).

Tivat Airport, PP24, 85320 Tivat (tel: 670-960; fax: 670-950; internet: www.aptivat.com).

Ministry of tourism
Ministry of Tourism, Rimski trg 46, Kancelarija br 8 Podgorica (tel: 482-145; e-mail: ministarstvo.turizma@mn.me; internet: www.mturizma.cg.me; www.visit-montenegro.org).

National tourist organisation offices
National Tourism Organisation, Omladinskih Brigada 7, 81000 Podgorica (tel: 230-959, 230-981; fax: 230-979; email: tourism@cg.me; internet: www.visit-montenegro.com

Ministries
Ministry of Agriculture, Forestry and Water Management, Podgorica (tel: 482-109; fax: 234-306; email: milanm@mn.me).

Ministry of Culture and Media, Podgorica (tel: 231-561; fax: 231-540; email: marinko_vorgic@min-kulture.mn.me).

Ministry of Economics, Podgorica (tel: 242-104, 482-112; fax: 242-028; email: minprivrede@mn.me).

Ministry of Education and Science, Podgorica (tel: 405-301; fax: 405-334; email: mpin@cg.me).

Ministry of Environmental Protection and Physical Planning, Podgorica (tel: 482-220; fax: 34-131; email: milenaz@mn.me).

Ministry of Finance, Stanka Dragojevica br 2, Podgorica (tel: 242-835; fax: 224-450; email: mf@mn.me).

Ministry of Foreign Affairs, Stanka Dragojevica 2, Podgorica (tel: 246-357, 201-530; fax: 224-670; email: mip.ministar@mn.me).

Ministry of Health, 46 Romas Square, Podgorica (tel: 234-056, 482-346; fax: 242-762; email: tijanak@mn.me).

Ministry of Interior, Podgorica (tel: 241-252, 349-000; email: mup.kabinet@cg.me).

Ministry for International Economic Relations, Stanka Dragojevica br 2, 81000 Podgorica (tel: 225-568; 225-591; email: mierei@mn.me).

Ministry of Justice, Vuka Karadzica 3, 81000 Podgorica (tel: 507-552; fax: 407-522; email: pravda@cg.me).

Ministry of Labour and Social Welfare, Podgorica (tel: 234-252; fax: 482-443).

Ministry of Maritime Affairs and Transportation, Rimski trg 46, 81000 Podgorica (tel: 234-179; fax: 234-331; email: mps@mn.me).

Ministry of Minority Protection, Podgorica (tel: 482-126; fax: 234-198; email: min.manj@cg.me).

Other useful addresses
Agency of Montenegro for Economic Restructuring and Foreign Investment, Jovana Tomasevica bb, 81000 Podgorica, Montenegro (tel: 242-640; fax: 245-756; email: anaz@mn.me).

Aluminium Industry of Montenegro (tel: 620-616; fax: 620-955; e-mail: kap.board@cg.me).

Vektra Montenegro (management, transportation, storage, international trade), Vuka karadzica 10, 81000 Podgorica (tel: 624-500; fax: 625-335; e-mail: office@vektra.cg.me; internet: www.vektra.cg.me).

Directorate for Construction of Highways in Montenegro, Podgorica (tel: 625-110, 625-102; fax: 624-353).

Montenegro Development Fund, Bulevar Rvolucije 9, 81000 Podgorica (tel: 245-973; email: fzcrg@cg.me; internet: www.fzrcg.cg.me).

Montenegrin Investment Promotion Agency (MIPA), Podgorica (e-mail: info@mipa.cg.me; internet: www.mipa.cg.me).

Montenegro Stock Exchange, Cetinjski put 2a (Zgrada Vektre) 81000 Podgorica (tel: 205-940, 205-960; fax: 205-920; internet: www.montenegroberza.com).

Statistical Office of Montenegro (MONSTAT), IV Proleterske 2,20 000 Podgorica (tel: 230-811; fax: 230-814; email: statistika@t-com.me; contact@monstat.org).

New Securities Exchange Montenegro (NEX Montenegro), Miljana Vukova bb, 81000 Podgorica (tel: 230-670, 230-690, 210-170; fax: 230-640; internet: www.nex.cg.me).

National news agency: Mina (MNNews): http://mnnews.net

Media Club: www.mediaclub.cg.me

Internet sites
Customs Administration: www.djp.gc.me

Government of Montenegro: www.vlada.cg.me/eng

Official Gazette: www.sllrcg.cg.me

Montenegro tourism: www.visit-montenegro.com

Montenegro Business Alliance: www.visit-mba.org

Montserrat

Montserrat has just one constituency, down from the nine there were before the massive volcanic eruption of 1997 left the southern half of the island uninhabitable and destroyed the capital Plymouth, the airport and the port. So many people fled the island that it was no-longer feasible to have so many constituencies. When the 11 September 2014 elections were held, to elect the nine members of the Legislative Council (LegCo) each voter had nine votes.

The campaign lasted four months and the result was a resounding win for the newly formed People's Democratic Movement (PDM), lead by former opposition leader, Donaldson Romeo. Mr Donaldson was sworn in as premier on 12 September.

'I'm very thankful that God has spoken through the people of Montserrat' he said. 'I am glad the people have responded to our agenda and I must say thanks to those who supported our campaign. I'm thankful to the honourable premier who gave such a respectful concessionary statement,' Romeo went on, after former premier Reuben Meade had conceded the election live on Radio Montserrat early the following day. The results showed that only he and minister Joseph Farrell of the former ruling Movement for Change and Prosperity (MCAP) had made it into the top nine candidates that will make up the Legislative Assembly, the other seven having been won by PDM candidates.

Following a brief ceremony at Government House on 12 September, officiated by Governor Adrian Davis, the new premier said this was 'a victorious moment for the people of Montserrat at home and abroad. The quest to build permanent jobs, build proper housing, revitalise the private sector, practice good governance, value gender equity, take care of our youth, the vulnerable and the elderly are expectations that I take seriously.'

Romeo said these initiatives which his party championed during the campaign constitute the plan of action to turn Montserrat into a self-sufficient state. He called on all residents to 'affirm each other's gift and talents and work together,' adding that the principles of compassion, forgiveness and positive thinking should be their guide.

The PDM was formed earlier in 2014 with a team of senior civil servants, which included two women who became part of the incoming government. Deputy party leader Delmaude Ryan is a human resource specialist was sixth in the polls; popular local doctor, Dr Ingrid Buffonge, was second, closely behind Romeo.

Mr Romeo said the challenge would be to maintain the unity and the team spirit of his party. 'It is going to take 10 to 20 years for Montserrat to get where it needs to go and this party must last beyond this to get the job done.'

Prior to the September election Mr Meade had announced at a Caribbean Community (Caricom) heads of government meeting in July that Montserrat intended to accede to the Revised Treaty of Chaguaramas and to participate in the Caricom Single Market and Economy (CSME).

Montserrat's economy was still recovering in 2014 from the effects of the volcanic explosion, and of a number of hurricanes, which had destroyed much of the island's infrastucture, as well as drastically reduced its population. As a result Montserrat has been heavily reliant on transfers from the UK, which have been reduced in recent years and lead in delays or cancellations of public works projects. Never-the-less, economic development plans and the associated construction in the tourism sector, will give a boost to the overall economy in the medium to long term.

A report from the respected *Latin America Monitor* in May 2014 expected real GDP growth in Montserrat to remain relatively tepid in the coming quarters, at 1.5 per cent in 2014, up from an estimated 0.0 per cent in 2013.

Risk assessment

Politics	Good
Economy	Fair
Regional stability	Good

COUNTRY PROFILE

1493 Montserrat was first sighted by Columbus.

KEY FACTS

Official name: Montserrat

Head of State: Queen Elizabeth II; represented by Governor Elizabeth Carriere (from 5 Aug 2015)

Head of government: Premier Donaldson Romeo (sworn in 12 Sep 2014)

Ruling party: People's Democratic Movement (PDM) (from 11 Sep 2014)

Area: 102 square km

Population: 4,922 (2011; census figure) (An estimated 8,000 citizens left the island when volcanic eruptions began in 1995; numbers have yet to return to former levels).

Capital: Plymouth – destroyed by volcano in 1997; temporary headquarters at Brades while Little Bay is being developed as the new capital.

Official language: English

Currency: East Caribbean dollar (EC$) = 100 cents

Exchange rate: EC$2.70 per US$ (fixed)

GDP: US$60.37 million (2012)*

Balance of trade: -US$30.17 million (2012)*

* estimated figure

1632 Britain gained possession of the island and English and Irish Catholic settlers from the Protestant island of St Kitts and Nevis colonised Montserrat.
1648 There were some 1,000 Irish families on the island.
1651 The first slaves were brought to the island to work in the sugar-based economy.
1871–1956 Montserrat was part of the Leeward Islands, and then became a British Dependent Territory.
1958–62 Montserrat was part of the Federation of the West Indies. From 1960 the island had its own administrator (the title was changed to governor in 1971).
1990 A new constitution was adopted.
1995 The Soufriere Hills volcano began to erupt.
1997 Massive volcanic eruptions destroyed the capital Plymouth, the airport and the port, and left the southern half of the island uninhabitable. Nineteen people were killed, thousands were left homeless and the population fell to around 4,000 as many fled to Britain and nearby Caribbean islands. David Brandt replaced Bertrand Osborne as chief minister.
1998 Reconstruction work began under the UK's Sustainable Development Plan.
1999 The UK government announced volcanic activity had dropped to safe levels. Evacuees began to return. With the loss of four and a half of the original seven constituencies, new election rules were introduced, and all national legislature seats became single-seat, first-pass-the-post constituencies.
2000 The growth of a new lava dome at the Soufriere Hills volcano once again threatened the island.
2002 A constitutional review was begun.
2003 There was another major eruption at the Soufriere Hills volcano.
2004 Deborah Barnes-Jones was sworn in as governor. The US Department of Homeland Security removed the temporary protected status of US-based Montserratians.
2005 The new airport was opened allowing access for international visitors.
2006 Although the Movement for Change and Prosperity (MCAP) won most seats In parliamentary elections, it did not win enough for an outright majority. The New People's Liberation Movement (NPLM) and the Montserrat Democratic Party (MDP) coalition formed the government. Lowell Lewis (MDP) was elected chief minister by his coalition colleagues.
2007 Peter Waterworth was sworn in as governor.
2008 The Soufriere Hills volcano exploded again without warning, scattering ash and debris over an area of many kilometres. Gerald's Airport was renamed John A Osborne Airport, in honour of the long-standing chief minister.
2009 Government plans to rebuild the capital were published. Early general elections were called. The UK extended conditional aid, with the proviso that the government agreed to the reform of public service pensions; the enactment of legislation for integrity in public office; the demonstration of good governance; and the appointment of a co-ordinator to oversee improved transport services. The agreement also required the government to provide plans to reduce public expenditure; reduce the size of the public service; and increase revenues to the treasury by 2012. The MCAP won six seats (out of nine) in parliamentary elections, independents won three; Reuben Meade (MCAP) took office as Chief Minister; he also became finance minister.
2010 The Office of Chief Minister became Office of Premier.
2011 In March Premier Meade announced that after five years of discussion, the new constitution would come into effect in September. In April Adrian Davis was sworn in as governor. In July Premier Meade was appointed annual chairman of the Monetary Council of the Eastern Caribbean Central Bank (ECCB). In September, Reuben Meade was sworn in to the Office of Premier.
2012 In July, the government unveiled its new capital and administrative centre, Little Bay on the north west of the island, although Brades continues as the *de facto* capital. On 17 October an agreement was signed with the Icelandic engineering company Jardboranir for exploratory geothermal drilling in Montserrat.
2013 On 1 May Montserrat, along with Anguilla, Bermuda, the British Virgin Islands, the Cayman Islands, and the Turks and Caicos Islands, signed a tax sharing agreement with the tax authorities of France, Germany, Italy, Spain and the UK.
2014 Overseas Territory representatives from the British Virgin Islands, Bermuda, Montserrat, the Cayman Islands and Anguilla met with United Kingdom business networking specialists, CaribDirect International Business Network (CIBN) in May. CIBN is an agency designed to facilitate and connect entrepreneurs and business people in the UK with Caribbean government and business representatives for trade and investment. On 4 July Reuben Meade, announced at a meeting of heads of government of the Caribbean Community (CARICOM) that Montserrat intends to accede to the Revised Treaty of Chaguaramas (RTC) and to join the CARICOM Single Market and Economy (CSME). Mr Meade said that it was his government's intention to bring the RTC Bill to parliament for its first reading before September 2014 and he anticipated the enactment of the Bill by the end of the year. Parliamentary elections were held on 11 September. The result was a win for the newly formed People's Democratic Movement (PDM) with seven seats (out of nine); the Movement for Change and Prosperity (MCAP) won 2 seats. Montserrat has just one constituency, with the top nine candidates winning a seat. Donaldson Romeo was sworn in as prime minister on 14 September and the Cabinet on 22 September.
2015 On 24 March Prime Minister Romeo presented a budget of EC$170.8 million (US$63.23 million) for 2015/16 to the Montserrat Legislative Assembly.

Political structure

Constitution

The 1989 Constitution sets out the legal framework for all executive and legislative power, which came into force in 1990. Montserrat is an internally self-governing British Overseas Territory. In 2011, the Legislative Council was abolished and replaced with the Legislative Assembly.

Form of state

British self-governing dependency

The executive

The British monarch is Head of State and is represented by a governor, who is responsible for defence, internal security (including the police force), external affairs, the public service and international financial services.
The governor chairs meetings of the Executive Council (ExCo), which consists of the governor, attorney general, financial secretary, chief minister and three other ministers, elected from the Assembly.

National legislature

The Legislative Assembly has nine members, elected for a five-year term in one constituency (since the eruption of the Soufriere volcano in 1997 which destroyed much of the island and lead to the departure of a large number of residents). Each voter now has nine votes.

Last elections

11 September 2014 (parliamentary)
Results: Parliamentary: People's Democratic Movement (PDM) won 50.02 per cent of the vote and 7 seats (out of 9), Movement for Change and Prosperity (MCAP) won 35.36 per cent and 2 seats. Independents and independent alliances got the remaining 15 per cent, but failed to gain any seats. Montserrat has just one constituency, with the top nine candidates winning a seat.

Next elections

2019 (parliamentary)

Political parties

Ruling party

People's Democratic Movement (PDM) (from 11 Sep 2014)

Main opposition party

Opposition members sit as independents

Population

During 1996–97 an estimated 8,000 people left the island as volcanic eruptions left much of the island uninhabitable. Evacuees began to return from early 1999.

Last census: 21 May 2011: 4,922

Population density: 94.1 inhabitants per square km, prior to the volcanic eruptions in 1995.

Annual growth rate: 4.2 per cent (2003)

Ethnic make-up

Afro-Caribbean (95 per cent), white (5 per cent).

Religions

Anglican, Methodist, Roman Catholic, Pentecostal, Seventh-Day Adventist.

Education

Montserrat has a high level of literacy. Primary education formally begins at the age of five and continues until the age of 11. The state provides for a full five-year secondary education. Secondary schools offer programmes for academic entry courses to higher education and technical, vocational skills training. The University of the West Indies School of Continuing Studies offers university level courses.

The Montserrat Community College project, which is jointly funded by the EU and the UK-based Department for International Development (DfID), will cost EC$6 million (US$1.8 million). The new college will include classrooms, laboratories, library and offices.

Compulsory years: 2 to 16.

Health

Periodic volcanic eruption has wreaked havoc with health service maintenance, record keeping, and the overall collection of information. The immunisation programme continued to operate well throughout the volcanic emergency.

Life expectancy: 78 years (estimate 2003)

Fertility rate/Maternal mortality rate: 1.8 births per woman (2003)

Birth rate/Death rate: 17.6 births per 1,000 population; 7.3 deaths per 1,000 population (2003).

Child (under 5 years) mortality rate (per 1,000): 7.8 per 1,000 live births (2003)

Welfare

Montserrat remains dependent on the British government for budgetary aid and to finance its capital programmes. Previous Public Sector Investment Programmes were aimed at developing critical infrastructure in the habitable North. The emphasis was on accommodating the displaced population on the island and providing housing for a number of migrant workers from neighbouring Caribbean islands.

The Social Welfare System in Montserrat has developed a comprehensive Poverty Protection Programme providing various forms of assistance to its people.

Main cities

Brades (new capital, estimated population 1,308 in 2012), St Peter's (796), St John's (Old Norwood) (729), Salem (553).

Government buildings have been built at Brades, in the Carr's Bay/ Little Bay vicinity at the north-west end of Montserrat.

Plymouth (estimated population 3,500 before being evacuated in 1996 (due to volcanic activity), by the end of 1997, the city had been destroyed by volcanic eruptions).

Languages spoken

Official language/s

English

Media

Press

The only newspaper is the weekly *The Montserrat Reporter* (www.themontserratreporter.com).

Broadcasting

Radio: The public radio service ZJB (www.zjb.gov.ms) has a full range of programmes with news, music and regular reports on volcanic activities.

Television: There are two private, cable TV channels, both operated by foreign services.

Other news agencies: Caribbean Net News: www.caribbeannetnews.com

Economy

Volcanic activity between 1995–97 left around half of the island uninhabitable as two-thirds of the population fled and the economy fell into ruin. Intensive reconstruction efforts have helped pull the island out of a deep and prolonged recession, aided by US$33 million in funds from the UK Department for International Development (DfID).

GDP growth registers typically in reconstruction work to replace or relocate infrastructure, and new construction of facilities for the recovering and strengthening tourism sector, including completion of the new airport, support for private sector development, tourism, housing, improvements to the road network and developing Little Bay as the new capital.

The Montserrat Development Corporation (MDC) was formed in 2007 to facilitate the building of a new central town at Little Bay, in the north of the island. The MDC forms partnerships with private and public sector organisations to redevelop the island, the first being the new capital. Local businesses are relocating to Little Bay and what began as temporary accommodation has become permanent. On 4 August 2012, the first sod of the social security offices was turned; the offices opened in 2013.

Local seismic predictions stated in 2008 that, in the short-term, further eruptions from the still active volcano are likely to remain localised and relatively small. For a decade the value of land has been depressed but local residents are beginning to notice that foreign visitors are buying up land for redevelopment as holiday homes and worrying that if this trend continues those in exile will never be able to return home.

In January 2013 the European Union (EU) announced an aid package of US$55.2 million to boost Montserrat's economy.

On 4 July 2014 Reuben Meade, announced at a meeting of heads of government of the Caribbean Community (Caricom) that Montserrat intends to accede to the Revised Treaty of Chaguaramas (RTC) and to join the Caricom Single Market and Economy (CSME). Mr Meade said that it was his government's intention to bring the RTC Bill to parliament for its first reading before September 2014 and he anticipated the enactment of the Bill by the end of the year.

In September 2014 Montserrat was given a BBB-/A-3 rating on its long- and short-term foreign and local currency issuer standing by Standard & Poor's. The outlook was given as stable.

External trade

As a British Overseas Territory, Montserrat is a member of the association of overseas countries and territories (OCTs) with formal relations with the European Union, which provides, among other things, investment in economic and sustainable development.

Remittances and tourism provide the majority of foreign earnings. There is, however, a large trade deficit, caused by the need to import most basic commodities.

Imports

Main imports include petroleum, lubricants and related materials, machinery and vehicles, foodstuffs and manufactured goods.

Main sources: US, UK, Trinidad and Tobago.

Exports

Commodity exports include light manufactures, agricultural produce and quarried stone.

Main destinations: US, Antigua and Barbuda, UK.

Agriculture

Farming

The agricultural sector was declining prior to the volcanic eruptions (1995–97), when approximately 25 per cent of land area was cultivated. There was a further setback when the Soufriere Hills volcano erupted again in 2004, covering 95 per cent of planted crops with ash. Agriculture used to contributed around 4 per cent to GDP, employing 5 per cent of the labour force. The main crops have traditionally been potatoes, tomatoes, carrots, cabbages, cucumbers, sweet potatoes and string beans.

Output in the agricultural sector has been reduced to merely producing goods for domestic consumption. With the south of the island destroyed by the volcano, land has become a precious commodity. Much of the land in the north is unsuitable for farming. Development efforts now focus on high-yield crops and restoring self-sufficiency in vegetables and livestock. In 2012 agriculture contributed only 1.6 per cent to GDP.

Fishing

The typical total annual fish catch is 50t.

Industry and manufacturing

The industrial sector used to account for around 19 per cent of GDP and 10 per cent of employment and included rum, textiles and electronic appliances. After the electronic component assembly plant and the rice milling factory were forced to close due to the volcanic eruptions, the manufacturing sector's share of GDP fell from 5.9 per cent to less than 1 per cent. Manufacturing output is concentrated on two small furniture businesses.

Construction is the largest sector of the economy – mainly due to the demand for housing and basic infrastructure. This has been bolstered by substantial grants from the British government.

In 2012 industry contributed 23.2 per cent to GDP.

Tourism

Although over 50 per cent of the island is excluded from use due to the Soufriere Hills volcano (which in late 2013 was showing little signs of being active) and the damage the 1995 eruption caused to the island, tourism is still one of the few industries that bring in foreign exchange.

The main objective of the tourist board is to diversify the tourism experience, to appeal to a wider market than the pre-1995 clientele. Capital investment is vital, with emphasis on activities such as volcano adventures, with viewing sites for the amateur volcanologist, festivals, water sports and the flora and fauna.

Tourist numbers have increased from the low of the post-volcano eruption but following the global economic crisis in 2008 the number of arrivals in 2009 fell by 14.3 per cent (from 2008), to 6,300. However, by 2011 numbers had increased again to 7,392 and increased a further 34 per cent in 2012 to 9,905.

Hydrocarbons

There are no known hydrocarbon reserves. Consumption of oil was 600 barrels per day (bpd) in 2013, all of which was imported.

Any natural gas or coal used is commercially insignificant

Energy

The state-owned Montserrat Utilities Limited (MUL) is responsible for electricity and water supplies. While currently all generation is produced by diesel turbines renewable energy sources are being considered. Two geothermal wells have been successfully tested by the Iceland Drilling Company Ltd, which was appointed by the government in October 2012 to assess the possibility of geothermal energy leading to sustainable investment opportunities.

Installed capacity was 10MW in 2011.

Financial markets

Stock exchange

Eastern Caribbean Securities Exchange (ECSE)

Banking and insurance

The banking sector was severely effected by the volcano eruption, which destroyed the buildings of the country's main banks. Barclays Bank pulled out of the island while the Royal Bank of Canada reduced its range of services. The locally-owned Bank of Montserrat continues to operate.

The seven members of the Organisation of Eastern Caribbean States (OECS), Antigua and Barbuda, Dominica, Grenada, Montserrat, St Kitts and Nevis, St Lucia and St Vincent and the Grenadines, share a common currency (the East Caribbean dollar (EC$)) and central bank. The British Virgin Islands and Anguilla are associate members.

Montserrat has implemented the EU tax directive, introduced in July 2005, as a British Caribbean Dependency. Details of all EU nationals' deposits will be forwarded to the tax department of the relevant EU country, allowing tax to be levied in their home country.

Montserrat has also agreed to supply information on tax fraud, for criminal or civil trials, and notify EU member states about additional malpractices.

On 1 May 2013 Montserrat, along with Anguilla, Bermuda, the British Virgin Islands, the Cayman Islands, and the Turks and Caicos Islands, signed a tax sharing agreement with the tax authorities of France, Germany, Italy, Spain and the UK.

Central bank

The Eastern Caribbean Central Bank, St Kitts & Nevis

Offshore facilities

The government is trying to promote offshore banking on the island.

Time

GMT minus four hours

Geography

Montserrat is one of the Leeward Islands in the West Indies. It is a mountainous, volcanic island, which lies about 55km (35 miles) north of Basse Terre, Guadeloupe, and about 43km (27 miles) south-west of Antigua.

Hemisphere

Northern

Climate

The island has tropical weather with a mean temperature of 30 degrees Celsius and low humidity due to tradewinds. There is little variation throughout the year. The wettest months are from September–November, and the driest from February–June.

Dress codes

Casual lightweight clothing, and during the winter months a light jacket or sweater for the late evening is advisable.

Entry requirements

Passports

Required by all and valid for six months.

Visa

Required by all, except nationals of most EU and Commonwealth countries, North America, Japan and a number of other countries and territories. An onward/return ticket, proof of accommodation and sufficient funds for the stay are required.

Currency advice/regulations

There are no restrictions on import and export of local or foreign currencies, subject to declaration on arrival and limited to declared amount on departure.

Health (for visitors)

Mandatory precautions

Yellow fever vaccination certificate if arriving within six months from an infected area.

Those arriving from areas of known epidemics, including cholera must have vaccination certificates.

Advisable precautions

Typhoid and polio vaccinations are recommended. Tap water is considered safe.

Credit cards

Few shops, hotels or restaurants accept credit cards.

Public holidays (national)

Fixed dates

1 Jan (New Year's Day), 17 Mar (St Patrick's Day), 25–26 Dec (Christmas), 31 Dec (Festival Day).

Variable dates

Good Friday, Easter Monday, Labour Day (first Mon in May), Whit Monday, August Monday (first Mon in Aug).

Working hours

Banking

Bank of Montserrat: Mon, Tue, Thurs: 0800–1400; Wed 0800–1300; Fri: 0800–1500.
Royal Bank of Canada: Mon–Thurs: 0800–1400; Fri 0800–1500.

Business

Mon–Fri: 0800–1200, 1300–1600. Some businesses close early Wed: 0800–1200, and some open Sat: 0800–1230.

Government

Mon–Fri: 0800—1600.

Shops

0800–1600. Most shops close early in the afternoon on Wednesday and Saturday.

Telecommunications

Telephone/fax

A 100 per cent automatic system.

Mobile/cell phones

There is a GSM 850 services available throughout the country.

Electricity supply

220V AC, 60 cycles; also 400V, three-phase.

Social customs/useful tips

A tip of 10 per cent, in hotels and restaurants, is usual.

Getting there

Air

International airport/s: John A Osborne Airport (MNI/TRPG), (formerly Gerald's Airport), 2km from Little Bay; restaurant, shop, car hire.
Airport tax: Caricom nationals US$13; other nationals US$21.

Surface

Water: The ferry service between Montserrat and Antigua was discontinued following the opening of Gerald's Airport in July 2005.

Getting about

National transport

Due to volcanic activity, much of the south of the island is designated as an Exclusion Zone, to which entry is banned. Maps of affected areas are available on arrival.
Road: Before the eruption of Soufriere Hills volcano in 1995, there were 269km of roads, of which 203km were paved. The roads in the Exclusion Zone in the south were ruined and many in the rest of the island suffered considerable damage.
Buses: Buses are privately owned and readily available.

City transport

Taxis: Readily available. Legal fixed-rate system.

Car hire

Temporary licences can be obtained on production of national licence. Traffic drives on the left.

BUSINESS DIRECTORY

The addresses listed below are a selection only. While World of Information makes every endeavour to check these addresses, we cannot guarantee that changes have not been made, especially to telephone numbers and area codes. We would welcome any corrections.

Telephone area codes

The international direct dialling code (IDD) for Montserrat is +1 664, followed by subscriber's number.

Chambers of Commerce

Montserrat Chamber of Commerce and Industry, PO Box 384, Brades (tel: 491-3640; fax: 491-3639; e-mail: chamber@candw.ag).

Banking

Bank of Montserrat, PO Box 10, St Peters (tel: 491-3843; fax: 491-3163; e-mail: bom@candw.ag).

Royal Bank of Canada, PO Box 222, Brades (tel: 491-2426; fax: 491-3391; e-mail: rbcmont@candw.ag).

Central bank

Eastern Caribbean Central Bank, Agency Office, PO Box 484, 2 Farara Plaza, Brades (tel: 491-6877; fax: 491-6878; e-mail: eccbmni@candw.ms).

Stock exchange

Eastern Caribbean Securities Exchange (ECSE), www.ecseonline.com

Travel information

Carib Aviation, VC Bird International Airport, PO Box 318, St Johns, Antigua (tel: (+1-268) 481-2401; fax: (+1-268) 481-2405; email: operationsmanager@carib-aviation.com).

Carib World Travel, Redcliffe Street, PO Box W122, Antigua (tel: (+1-268) 460-6103; fax: 480-2995; email: info@carib-world.com).

Montserrat Aviation Services, PO Box 257, Brades (tel: 491-2533; fax: 491-7186; email: monair@candw.ms).

National tourist organisation offices

Montserrat Tourist Board, 7 Farara Plaza, Buildings B&C: PO Box 7, Brades (tel: 491-2230 fax: 491-7430; e-mail: info@montserrattourism.ms).

Ministries

Governor's Office Lancaster House, Olveston (tel: 491-2688/9; fax: 491-8867; e-mail: govoff@cnadw.ag).

Ministry of Finance, Government Headquarters, Brades (tel: 491-2356; fax: 491-2367; e-mail: minfin@candw.ag).

Other useful addresses

British High Commission, 11 Old Parham Road, Box 483, St John's, Antigua (tel: (+1-268) 462-0008; fax: (+1-268) 562-2124; e-mail: britishh@candw.ag).

Development Unit, Government Headquarters, Brades (tel: 491-2066/2557; fax: 491-4632; e-mail: devunit@candw.ag).

Financial Services Commission, Phoenix House, PO Box 188, Brades (tel: 491-6887/8; fax: 491-9888; e-mail: fscmrat@candw.ag).

Montserrat government in UK, 7 Portland Place, London W1B 1PP. (tel: (+44-(0)20) 7031-0317; fax: (+44-(0)20) 7031-0318; e-mail: j.panton@montserratgov.co.uk).

National Development Foundation Montserrat Ltd, PO Box 337, Davy Hill (tel: 491-3070; fax: 491-6566; e-mail: mon;ndf@candw.ag).

Caribbean Net News: www.caribbeannetnews.com

Internet sites

Montserrat info: http://www.volcano-island.com.

Montserrat Volcano Observatory (MVO): http://www.mvo.ms

KEY FACTS

Official name: Al Mamlaka al Maghrebia (The Kingdom of Morocco)

Head of State: King Mohammed VI (since 30 July 1999)

Head of government: Prime Minister Abdelilah Benkirane (appointed 29 Nov 2011)

Ruling party: Coalition, led by Parti de la Justice et du Développement (PJD) (Hizb al Adala wa at Tanmia) (Justice and Development Party) with Parti du Progrès et du Socialisme (PPS) (Party of Progress and Socialism) and Mouvement Populaire (MP) (Popular Movement) (from 3 Jan 2012)

Area: 711,000 square km

Population: 33.18 million (2014)*

Capital: Rabat (official, diplomatic) Casablanca (commercial centre)

Official language: Arabic and Amazigh (the Berber language)

Currency: Dirham (Dh) = 100 centimes

Exchange rate: Dh9.73 per US$ (Sep 2015)

GDP per capita: US$3,291 (2014)*

GDP real growth: 2.92% (2014)*

GDP: US$109.20 billion (2014)*

Labour force: 11.82 million (2014)*

Unemployment: 9.14% (2014)*

Inflation: 0.44% (2014)*

Balance of trade: -US$21.59 billion (2013)*

Annual FDI: US$2.52 billion (2011)

* estimated figure

Morocco

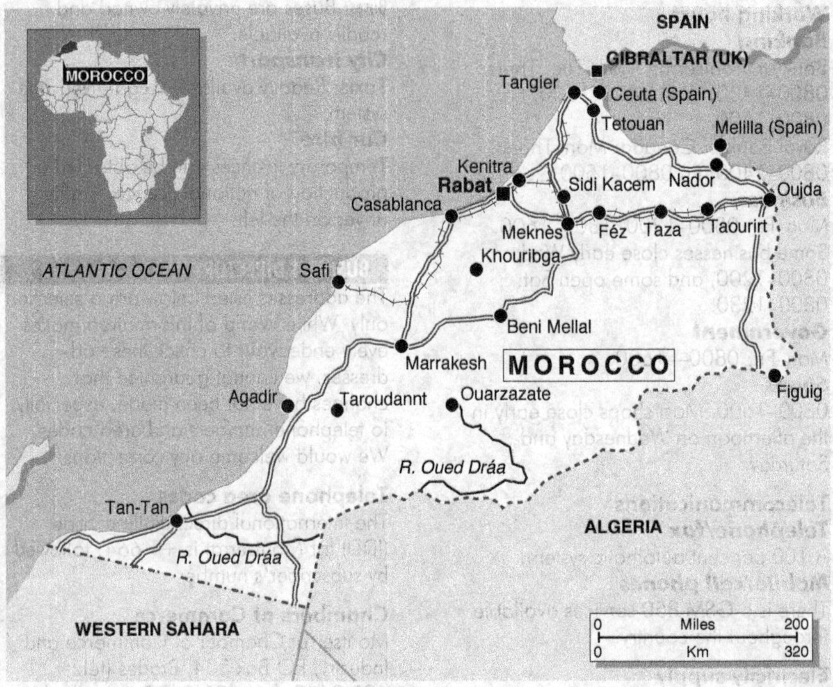

According to the Arab Labour Organisation 'The average unemployment rate for the age group 15–24 years in the group of Arab countries reaches to 30 per cent, compared with an average world rate of 14.4 per cent'. 'Problem [sic] of high unemployment rates among the educated graduates from universities and colleges, which reaches to 26.8 per cent in Morocco and 19.3 per cent in Algeria.'

In Morocco's November local elections, the ruling Parti de la Justice et du Développement (PJD) (Hizb al Adala wa at Tanmia) (Justice and Development Party) managed to win most of the country's key cities. This represented a quantum extension of the PJD's grip on Moroccan politics, following four years of a national coalition government during which it had at least undertaken a number of major fiscal reforms. The PJD had come to power on an anti-corruption platform in 2011, harnessing where it could the perceived popular enthusiasm for greater liberty and obliging King Mohammed to start to devolve some royal powers. Meanwhile, the PJD had long seen itself as a lone fighter against the old guard (which, curiously, included the Royal Family) that had controlled Morocco's politics and economy since it gained independence from France in 1956.

The PJD grows

In the November elections, for the first time in its history, the PJD had made a clean sweep of all Morocco's major cities including the capital Rabat, Casablanca, Tangier, Fez, Marrakesh and Agadir. The election results indicated that the PJD had won 5,021 local or 174 regional assembly seats just behind its closest rivals, the Authenticity and Modernity Party (PAM), with 6,655 local but only 132 regional assembly seats, and the more conservative Independence Party, with 5,106 local and 119 regional seats. The electoral turnout was 53.67 per cent, almost the same as that seen in the previous local elections, in 2009.

Among their notable gains, the Islamists managed to take Fez, long perceived to be a bastion of the Hizb al Istiqlal (Istiqlal) (Independence Party) and its populist leader Hamid Chabat, who had left the ruling coalition in 2013 to contest the PJD's economic policies.

To its credit, during its years in power following the 2011 election victory, the PJD-led coalition had made structural reform, in particular in the public finance sector, a priority, reducing Morocco's budget deficit, embarking on the reform of an unwieldy (and probably counter-productive) subsidy system and freezing the number of public sector jobs.

In 2011, when pro-democracy uprisings erupted across much of the Arab world, Morocco had managed to calm down the protests by carrying out a number of limited, often simply cosmetic, reforms. However, in the political pecking order, the royal palace still retained the ultimate authority. The PJD's other partners in the coalition, such as the centre-right Rassemblement National des Indépendents (RNI) (National Rally of Independent) and the Mouvement Populaire (Popular Movement), were closer to the royal establishment, which was manifestly ill at ease at sharing power with Islamists.

As was the case with several Arab authoritarian rulers in the wave of protests that took place in 2011, in Morocco King Mohamed VI rapidly passed a new constitution and rather predictably promised reforms. Having swallowed a bitter pill and invited the PJD, the main Islamist party into government, the King seemed to take his foot off the gas, as the majority of Morocco's putative new laws remained just that. In fact, the gesture was more evident than the action: Morocco's press continued to be censored, its fledgling human-rights groups closely monitored and often harassed by the police or government inspired thugs.

What little opposition to the King that ever saw the light of day appeared to have faded away, despite the fact that Morocco was not a happy country. Superficially, the economy appeared to be doing well, with growth of 4.6 per cent forecast for 2015, but unemployment – particularly youth unemployment at over 25 per cent – and the lack of opportunities threatened to undermine any economic progress. The Moroccan economy was expected to grow by 4.6 per cent in 2015. This macro-figure looked good on paper, but in the world of the micro-economy, in the bars of Marrakesh or the coffee shops of Casablanca and in the villages of the Atlas mountains, at grass roots levels things were dire. In 2014, according to one report, only 21,000 new jobs were created; so Morocco, with a population of over 33 million, was going backwards. Unemployment inevitably generates social unrest, as the gap between those in and out of work widens, as does the gap between urban professional workers and the rural agricultural workers. King Mohammed had observed that Morocco could not have 'a two-speed system in which the poor are excluded from the development process.' Easier said than done, however. To create more jobs, more demand is needed. And Morocco still needed to address the burning issue of corruption: in 2014 it ranked 80 out of the 175 countries surveyed by Transparency International in its annual *Corruption Perceptions Index*, level with Benin and Mongolia, but one place behind Tunisia. It goes without saying that Morocco needs to fight corruption. But that could not be simply legislated for. The body least likely to approve any serious anti-corruption measures was the Royal Family itself. For the palace to encourage fairness and openness would mean it abandoning many of its privileges and much of its power. However, the low oil prices had at least made it easier to reduce fuel subsidies. Worsening regional problems, such as terrorism and illegal immigration, had actually given Morocco greater leverage with the European Union (EU), which needed its co-operation more than ever.

Time to go, time to stay

In June 2015 the Moroccan government announced that it was setting the country's official time back by an hour during the month of Ramadan to synchronise better the timing during what would be the abnormally long days of Ramadan in the summer period. The clocks would go back until late July so that sunset would be an hour earlier. In short, sunset, the hour in which the daily Ramadan fast was broken, would be at 2000 hours instead of 2100. Whether the government had realised that the number of daylight hours – during which fasting was required – would remain exactly the same, was not altogether clear. The government's thinking seemed to rest on the fact that the timing of dawn was less important because millions of Moroccans were still sleeping at that time, in contrast to the keenly awaited sunset when the fast could be broken. During the daylight hours, Muslims who had passed the age of puberty are forbidden to drink, eat, smoke or have sexual relations. Only the chronically ill and pregnant women are exempt from Ramadan's restrictions.

Morocco was the Arab country with the longest daylight hours. In 2015 the average length of daylight (and therefore of fasting) was 16 hours 10 minutes, although it later transpired that in neighbouring Algeria the daylight hours were even longer, 16 hours 44 minutes according to the www.arabiaweather.com website. The website had published a 'fasting map' which showed that in Somalia daily fasting only lasted 13 hours 30 minutes, whereas in addition to Morocco and Algeria, Tunisia, Libya, Syria and Lebanon all had more than 16 hungry hours to contend with.

The economy

In its November 2015 annual assessment of the Moroccan economy, the

KEY INDICATORS — Morocco

	Unit	2011	2012	2013	2014	**2015
Population	m	*32.19	32.52	32.85	*33.18	*33.50
Gross domestic product (GDP)	US$bn	99.20	95.98	103.84	*109.20	*102.04
GDP per capita	US$	3,083	2,951	3,161	*3,291	*3,046
GDP real growth	%	4.3	2.7	4.4	*2.9	*4.4
Inflation	%	0.9	1.3	1.9	*0.4	*1.5
Unemployment	%	8.9	9.0	9.2	*9.1	*9.0
Exports (fob) (goods)	US$m	15,945.8	16,992.0	18,261.8	–	–
Imports (fob) (goods)	US$m	37,333.1	38,877.0	39,853.6	–	–
Balance of trade	US$m	-21,387.3	-21,885.0	-21,591.9	–	–
Current account	US$m	-8,336.9	-9,346.0	-7,872.0	*-6,384.0	*-3,486.0
Total reserves minus gold	US$m	22,872.8	16,356.0	18,404.0	19,555.0	–
Foreign exchange	US$m	22,005.0	15,812.0	17,918.0	–	–
Exchange rate	per US$	8.03	8.56	8.22	9.06	–

* estimated figure ** forecast figure

KEY FACTS

Official name: Western Sahara (The legal status of the territory and the issue of sovereignty are unresolved; they are contested by Morocco and the Polisario, which in Feb 1976, formally proclaimed a government-in-exile of the Sahrawi Arab Democratic Republic (SADR))

Head of State: President Mohammed Abdelazziz (Frente Polisario) (since 1982) (based in Tindouf Refugee camp, Algeria)

Head of government: Prime Minister Abdelkader Taleb Oumar (from Oct 2004) (based in Tindouf Refugee camp, Algeria)

Ruling party: Independence movement – Frente para la Liberación de Saguia al Hamra y Río de Oro (Polisario) (Popular Front for the Liberation of Saguia al Hamra and Río de Oro) (based in Tindouf Refugee camp, Algeria)

Area: 266,000 square km

Population: 491,519 (2010)*

Capital: Laayoune (El Aaiún)

Official language: Arabic and Spanish

Currency: Moroccan dirham (Dh) = 100 centimes; the currency used in the Occupied Zone

Exchange rate: Dh9.73 per US$ (Sep 2015); (roughly pegged at Dh10 per euro, which circulates widely)

Labour force: 12,000 (2005)*

Aid flow: US$10.00 million (annually)*

* estimated figure

International Monetary Fund (IMF) noted that the country's 'prudent economic policies and sustained structural reforms had served it well over the previous few years. In the view of the IMF, growth was recovering and expected by the IMF to reach 4.7 per cent at the end of 2015, due in part to a good agricultural season. However, the recovery in non-agricultural activity remained sluggish, because the European recovery was slower than expected. Inflation was low and credit had remained subdued. The current account deficit had narrowed further in 2014 to a projected -1.5 per cent of GDP and international reserves had improved to 6.5 month of imports. This performance reflected in part the reduced fuel and food import bill, as well as the sustained growth in automobile exports and remittances. The fiscal deficit had also continued to improve due to measures taken by the government, in particular subsidy reforms. Poverty rates, unemployment and inequality had declined over the decade, but much remained to be done to promote a more inclusive growth. In particular, continued efforts were needed to reduce social and regional disparities, increase female labour force participation and to improve the quality of education and medical coverage.

Growth was expected to slow to 3 per cent in 2016, as agricultural activity returned to normal and was expected to strengthen gradually in the medium term to close to 5 per cent. However, the risks from lower growth in advanced and emerging countries, any increase in world energy prices resulting from geopolitical tensions in the region and a surge in global financial market volatility remained substantial.

In the view of the IMF, fiscal developments up until the end of September had been positive and in line with the deficit target of 4.3 per cent of GDP in 2015. The efforts to further strengthen public finances, as reflected in the 2016 draft budget that targeted a deficit of 3.5 per cent of GDP, were welcome. In the medium term, fiscal reforms ought to continue to increase the economy's resilience to shocks and to provide more room for investment in infrastructure, health, education and social protection, which were crucial to raise the economy's potential and inclusiveness. In that respect, the progress achieved in reforming the subsidy system and in strengthening the fiscal framework was considered commendable by the IMF. Other priorities were to make the tax system more efficient and equitable. Reforming the pension system was also urgent to secure its viability. These reforms would help place public debt on a downward path. Indeed, in the view of the IMF, public debt remained sustainable and resilient to various shocks, but it needed to be reduced in order to create further fiscal space.

On the external front, the improved current account position and robust capital flows had helped strengthen international reserves. Efforts to improve the business environment, transparency and governance would be essential to enhance external competitiveness. The IMF supported the authorities' efforts to improve financial inclusion and access to credit, especially for very small, small and medium enterprises. In addition, the IMF welcomed the authorities' intention to move to a more flexible exchange rate regime, which would facilitate the further diversification of the economy and enhance its international integration and its capacity to absorb external shocks.

According to the European Bank for Reconstruction and Development (EBRD) in its annual Transition Report, Morocco's economic output weakened significantly in the first quarter of 2014, on the back of contracting agricultural production and weaker non-agricultural output. After registering an expansion of 4.4 per cent in 2013, annual growth slowed to just 1.7 per cent in the first quarter of 2014. Agricultural output shrank by 1.6 per cent, compared to growth of 20 per cent in 2013. At the same time, non-agricultural output grew modestly by 2.1 per cent, due to sluggish industrial activity and stagnation in the construction sector. Continued weaknesses in these sectors pushed unemployment up to 9.8 per cent in the first half of 2014 from 9.2 per cent in 2013. Meanwhile, inflation remained low (the lowest in the southern and eastern Mediterranean region), averaging 1.9 per cent in 2013 and declining to 0 per cent year-on-year in August 2014.

Morocco's current account deficit narrowed to 7.6 per cent in 2013 from 10 per cent in 2012, owing to lower fuel and food imports. The strategies implemented by the government to target the development of high value-added exports contributed to strong export growth in motor vehicles (21 per cent), aerospace (13 per cent) and electronics (12 per cent) in 2013. The impressive performance of these sectors continued through the first half of 2014, with exports of motor vehicles and electronics accelerating on average by 40 per cent year-on-year and 17 per cent year-on-year, respectively. Meanwhile, net foreign direct investment (FDI) jumped by 27 per cent (after a modest rise of 3.6 per cent in 2012) and inched up again in the first quarter of 2014, while international reserves stabilised at above four months of import cover.

According to the EBRD, Morocco's fiscal deficit declined from 7.3 per cent of GDP in 2012 to 5.4 per cent of GDP in 2013, driven by a reduction in subsidies and wage bills. The trend of year-on-year improvement continued into the first quarter of 2014, partly due to the removal and reduction of a number of energy subsidies in January. On the financing front, Morocco sold €1 billion (US$1.35 billion) worth of 10-year bonds to international investors.

Morocco's liquidity conditions were, in the view of the EBRD, improving thanks to a number of interventions by the Bank al Maghrib (central bank). These interventions included injecting liquidity primarily through seven-day advances and introducing a programme that provided banks with liquidity using loans made to small- and medium-sized enterprises (SMEs) as collateral. In addition, the required reserve ratio had been reduced from 4 per cent to 2 per cent in March 2014. As a result, liquidity conditions were improving and interventions by the central bank had receded. In fact, seven-day advances had declined by 25 per cent (quarter-over-quarter) in the quarter ending June 2014. The slow-down in agricultural output had been seen as limiting growth in 2014. The EBRD expected a moderation of growth to 4.2 per cent in 2014 (from 5.5 per cent in 2013), predominantly due to the slow-down in agricultural growth following the strong recovery in the sector in 2013. The performance of the non-agricultural sector would be closely linked to euro-zone stability. Consequently, the outlook was subject to downside risks associated with any deterioration in euro-zone conditions that might adversely affect Morocco via trade, tourism and remittance linkages. The World Bank *Doing Business 2015* report ranked Morocco at 71 (out of 189 countries) for ease of doing business, an improvement of 23 places between 2011 and 2014. This was largely due to a number of improvements in the procedures for starting a business, such as the ease of registering property and paying taxes. A law strengthening the autonomy of Morocco's Competition Council was adopted in February 2014 – another positive development with respect to the business environment. In the autumn of 2014, the implementation of a new procurement law was also in the pipeline and efforts were under way to create a structured legal framework for the identification and development of public-private partnership projects. However, important gaps in the reform programme needed to be addressed in order to improve the business environment, particularly for SMEs. The legal and institutional frameworks that support lending to SMEs also needed improvement.

Some steps had been taken to address structural fiscal issues, but implementation challenges remained. In February 2014 all the remaining subsidies on petrol (gasoline) and industrial fuels were removed, following on from a price indexation system set up in 2013. In parallel, measures had been taken to limit the effect of price hikes on vulnerable low-income groups and on the cost of public transport. Progress on other reforms (such as broader subsidy reform and the adoption of a new organic budget law) had been slower, owing to their politically sensitive nature and the difficulty of achieving consensus. One of the most crucial fiscal topics to be addressed was pension reform. The government had submitted draft proposals – which included measures to lift the retirement age, increase employee contributions and decrease annuities – to the relevant parliamentary council. Talks between the government and labour unions had been due to resume in September 2014.

Reforms aimed at deepening and safeguarding the financial sector have continued. These advocated fostering the development of alternative financial products, increasing access to finance and strengthening macro-prudential supervision. On the alternative products front, efforts are under way to develop a framework for Islamic finance in Morocco, which would cover equities, deposits and Islamic bonds (*sukuk*). In terms of access to finance, microfinance, financial literacy and risk management initiatives were continuing. Reviews of the statutes of Bank Al Maghrib and the Banking Act also continued, with technical assistance provided by the IMF to better monitor systemic risks to the financial sector. This was especially important in light of the cross-border expansion of Moroccan banks, particularly into sub-Saharan Africa, which would complicate banking supervision and increase the need to monitor risks related to branches or subsidiaries.

Regulations governing the capital markets have been strengthened. A new securitisation law had been adopted in 2013 and a draft law was being prepared to establish a regulated market for the trading of derivatives. A draft law was also being prepared to introduce a framework for asset-backed securities and in particular covered bonds, as banks had expressed a willingness to issue mortgage-backed bonds. In foreign exchange markets, the central bank had announced plans to gradually allow greater flexibility of the exchange rate over the next three years, in order to reduce external vulnerabilities and strengthen competitiveness.

Risk assessment

Economy	Good/fair
Politics	Fair/poor
Regional stability	Good/fair

Muslims in Morocco

% of population	99.9
Sunni (% of Muslims)	99
Shi'a (% of Muslims)	1

COUNTRY PROFILE

1777 Morocco was the first country to recognise the newly sovereign USA. The Treaty of Peace and Friendship between the two countries (negotiated in 1787) is the longest unbroken US treaty relationship.

1860 Spain declared war in a dispute over the Ceuta enclave and temporarily occupied Tetuán (later relinquished) and won an enlarged Melilla and Ceuta.

1884 Spain created a protectorate in coastal areas of Morocco.

1904 France and Spain agreed on respective zones of influence in the country.

1912 Morocco became a French protectorate under the Treaty of Fez. Spain continued to operate its coastal protectorate.

1923 France, Spain and Britain set up the international zone of Tangier.

1921–26 A rebellion in the Rif Mountains, led by Abdel Krim, was eventually quelled by French and Spanish troops.

1943 The Istiqlal (Parti de l'Istiqlal) (Independence Party) was founded and an independence struggle began.

1956–57 Independence was granted by France and Spain. Tangier became Moroccan once more. Spain kept its two coastal enclaves. Sultan Sidi Mohammed ben Youssef adopted the title of King Mohammed V and established an hereditary monarchy.

1961 Mohammed V died and was succeeded by King Hassan II. He introduced political liberalisation.

1963 The first general elections were held.

1965 Following student riots and civil unrest, the King declared a state of emergency and suspended parliament.
1971 There was a failed attempt to depose the King and to establish a republic.
1972 A constitution was adopted.
1973–76 The Frente Popular para la Liberación de Saguia el Hamra y Río de Oro (Polisario) (Popular Front for the Liberation of Saguia el Hamra y Río de Oro), formed with Algerian support, aimed at an independent state in Spanish Sahara, a territory south of Morocco, controlled by Spain. King Hassan ordered a 350,000-strong Green March into the territory, attempting to annex it for Morocco. Spain agreed to withdraw from the region (later to become Western Sahara) and to transfer it to joint Moroccan-Mauritanian control. Polisario announced the formation of the Saharawi Arab Democratic Republic (SADR) and formed a government-in-exile. Western Sahara was divided between Morocco and Mauritania. Fighting continued between Moroccan military and Polisario forces.
1977 Morocco left the Organisation of African Unity (OAU) in protest at the SADR's admission to the body.
1983 Relations between Morocco and Algeria improve.
1988 Full diplomatic relations with Algeria were resumed.
1991 A UN-monitored cease-fire began in Western Sahara.
1998 The moderate Union Socialiste des Forces Populaires (USFP) (Socialist Union of Popular Forces) won the elections and formed a government.
1999 King Hassan II died suddenly and his son, Mohammed VI acceded to the throne.
2000 King Mohammed VI began a process of modest political liberalisation.
2002 King Mohammed married Salma Bennani, a 24-year-old computer engineer; the marriage to a commoner was a break with Royal Moroccan tradition. Morocco occupied the tiny, uninhabited island of Leila or Isla del Perejil (Parsley Island) off its coast and owned by Spain, prompting an international spat. After the general election, the two main parties – the USFP and Istiqlal – formed a coalition government. Driss Jettou was appointed prime minister.
2003 Senegal and Morocco signed agreements on closer co-operation. There were suicide bombings in Casablanca killing 41 and injuring many more. Anti-terrorism laws were enacted and a campaign against extremists undertaken. Crown Prince Moulay Hassan was born.
2004 An earthquake in the north killed over 500 people. A free trade agreement was signed with the US after Morocco had been designated a major non-NATO ally.
2005 Prime Minister Jettou announced a proposal for a TGV (French high-speed train) service, from Tangier to Casablanca (by 2015). Hundreds of migrants from sub-Saharan Africa attempted to force their entry into the Spanish enclaves of Melilla and Ceuta. Once repelled they were later deported from Morocco. An official commission reported that human rights abuses during the rule of King Hassan II included almost 600 deaths.
2007 Morocco proposed the Sahara autonomy plan, which would allow Morocco and the Polisario to discuss the future of Western Sahara without pre-conditions, but later failed to achieve agreement. In parliamentary elections, 33 parties and 6,600 candidates participated; the Istiqlal won most votes, to retain power and become the governing coalition party. Its partner in the outgoing government, the USFP lost 12 seats. The turnout, at 37 per cent, was the lowest in Morocco's history.
2009 Christopher Ross was named as the UN's Special Envoy in mediation talks over the future of Western Sahara. Over US$10.3 billion was committed to modernising the energy sector, including 11 wind-generated electricity turbines. The tourism minister announced the government would invest US$37.3 million in its tourist industry.
2010 New talks with Polisario, concerning the future of Western Sahara, began. The minister of transport announced that the motorway network will total 1,417km by 2011 following US$3.4 billion in investment. In Western Sahara, 11 people were killed and hundreds reported missing in an operation by Moroccan security forces to clear the Gadaym Izik, Frente Polisario, protest camp close to Laayoune. Morocco defended its security forces, saying police had intervened in a peaceful manner and that they only defended themselves.
2011 In April a remote controlled bomb in a café in Djemaa el Fna square, Marrakesh, killed 15 people, including a number of tourists. King Mohammed VI announced proposed constitutional amendments in June, to be put to a referendum on 1 July. The amendments included giving the prime minister more executive authority, reducing the powers of the monarch, making Berger an official language and boosting the independence of the judiciary; the King would remain supreme commander of the armed forces. There was scepticism within the opposition who said the reforms did not go far enough. However, 98.49 per cent of voters were in favour; turnout was 72.65 per cent. In May, Morocco was invited to join the political and economic union, Co-operation Council for the Arab States of the Gulf (CCASG) (known as Gulf Co-operation Council (GCC)). Although no timetable for integration was set. The recorded unemployment rate was 8.7 per cent by 30 June. Unemployment for those aged under 34 was 30.2 per cent. On 29 September King Mohammed and French President Sarkozy jointly launched the 350km high-speed railway project between the cities of Rabat and Casablanca in the south. The joint Moroccan-French, US$4.1 billion, Tangiers-Casablanca line development is due for completion in 2015, with a journey time cut from over six hours to two. The French engineering company Alstom will provide 14 high-speed trains for the new line. Early general elections were held on 25 November. The moderate Islamist, Hizb al Adala wa at Tanmia (Parti de la Justice et du Développement) (PJD) (Justice and Development Party) won the single largest block of seats of 107 (out of 395), while the pro-monarchy, Alliance pour la Démocratie (Coalition for Democracy), an eight party bloc, won 159 seats and Koutla, an alliance of three parties led by Istiqlal, won 117 seats. On 29 November, King Mohammed appointed Abdelilah Benkirane (PJD) to be prime minister. The PJD began coalition talks with Koutla.
2012 On 3 January PJD agreed to a coalition with Parti du Progrès et du Socialisme (PPS) (Party of Progress and Socialism) and Mouvement Populaire (MP) (Popular Movement). A report from the UN Secretary General concerning Western Sahara was published in April, with a complaint that the UN force had been 'unable to exercise fully its peacekeeping monitoring, observation and reporting functions' due to Moroccan interference. The report detailed the positions of both sides, which remain the unchanged, namely that Morocco claims Western Sahara is a self-governing territory within its country and Polisario argues that not only is it not a self-governing territory, but also that it claims the right to self-determination. On 22 May, opponents of the TGV organised protests in several cities objecting to the cost of the project, estimated at Bh25 billion (US$2.9 billion) that they said would be better spent on social programmes.
2013 On 9 July five ministers from the secular centre-right Istiqlal party, the second largest party in parliament, resigned from the government. A Spanish paedophile who was freed by royal decree along with 47 other imprisoned Spaniards was rearrested in Spain a day later after protests Rabat had lead the King to rescind the pardon. The release of the 48 had been requested by King Juan Carlos of Spain. King Mohammed IV ordered an investigation.

2014 On 11 November Morocco confirmed that it would not host the Africa Cup of Nations scheduled for 17 January–8 February 2015 after the Confederation of African Football (CAF) had refused a request to postpone the competition until the Ebola outbreak across West Africa had been contained.
2015 Former Guantánamo Bay inmate, Younis Chekkouri, arrived back in Morocco on 16 September.

Political structure

Constitution

Adopted 10 March 1972; amended 1992 and 1996.
The Constitution prohibits a one-party political system.
The King is *Amir al Moumineen* (Commander of the Faithful), hereditary Head of State and supreme commander of the armed forces.
A Constitutional referendum held on 1 July 2011 was approved by 98.49 per cent of voters. The changes included: requiring the King to name a prime minister from the largest political party in parliament; transferring some rights of government from the King to prime minister (including the dissolution of parliament); allowing parliament to grant amnesties (a privilege previously held by the King alone); promoting Berber to be an official language of Morocco.

Independence date

1956

Form of state

Constitutional monarchy

The executive

The King holds executive power, which is delegated to the prime minister and cabinet.
The Council of Ministers is chosen by the prime minister in consultation with Parliament and appointed by the monarch from the majority party following legislative elections.

National legislature

The bicameral Barlaman (parliament) consists of the Chamber of Advisors which has 90-120 seats of which members are indirectly elected by an electoral college of local councils, professional organizations, and labour unions. Members serve six-year terms.
The Chamber of Representatives has 395 seats of which 305 members are directly elected in multi-seat constituencies by proportional representation vote and 90 are directly elected in a single nationwide constituency by proportional representation vote. In the national constituency, 60 seats are reserved for women and 30 reserved for young people. Members serve five-year terms.
(The lower house debates legislation presented to it by the government; approved legislation is automatically promulgated after one month. The upper house has the power to caution or censure the government, which if successful requires the government to resign.

Legal system

The legal system is based on Islamic law and a combination of French and Spanish civil law codes. The Supreme Court is responsible for reviewing government legislation.

Last elections

1 July 2011 (constitutional referendum); 3 October 2009 (parliamentary – Chamber of Advisors) 25 November 2011 (parliamentary – Chamber of Representatives)
Results: Referendum: approval was given by 98.49 per cent of voters, 1.5 per cent opposed; turnout was 72.65 per cent.
Parliamentary: (Hizb al Adala wa at Tanmia) (Parti de la Justice et du Développement) (PJD) (Justice and Development Party) won 107 seats (out of 395), Hizb al Istiqlal (Istiqlal) (Independence Party) 60, Rassemblement National des Indépendents (National Rally of Independent) 52, Parti Authenticité et Modernité (PAM) (Authenticity and Modernity Party) 47, Union Socialiste des Forces Populaires) (Socialist Union of Popular Forces) 39, Mouvement Populaire (Popular Movement) 32, Union Constitutionelle (Constitutional Union) 23, Parti du Progrès et du Socialisme (Party of Progress and Socialism) 18, Parti Travailliste (Labour Parti) four; four other political parties each won two seats and five other parties each won one seat. 13 other parties fail to win any seats. Turnout was 45.4 per cent.

Next elections

Late 2015 (Parliamentary - Chamber of Advisors); 2016 (parliamentary – Chamber of Representatives).

Political parties

Ruling party

Coalition, led by Parti de la Justice et du Développement (PJD) (Hizb al Adala wa at Tanmia) (Justice and Development Party) with Parti du Progrès et du Socialisme (PPS) (Party of Progress and Socialism) and Mouvement Populaire (MP) (Popular Movement) (from 3 Jan 2012)

Main opposition party

Alliance pour la Démocratie (Coalition for Democracy), an eight party bloc, led by Mouvement Populaire (Popular Movement).

Population

33.18 million (2014)* Around 70 per cent of the population is under 25 years of age.
Last census: September 2004: 29,680,069
Population density: 68 inhabitants per square km. Urban population 58 per cent (2010 Unicef).
Annual growth rate: 1.3 per cent, 1990–2010 (Unicef).

Ethnic make-up

Mostly Berbers and Arabs. There is a small Jewish minority and an estimated 60,000 foreign residents, mainly of French, Spanish and Italian origin.

Religions

Islam is the state religion. Sunni Muslim (98 per cent). There are small minority Jewish and Roman Catholic communities.

Education

The illiteracy rate is as high as 83 per cent among women in rural areas. The government aims to increase the literacy to 76 per cent by 2010. Public expenditure on education is about 5 per cent of annual Gross National Income (GNI) and includes subsidies to private education at all levels.
Primary, or first stage education lasts until the age of 12, then students move onto second stage until aged 15, when they choose between an academic general secondary school or a technical secondary school for three years. At aged 18 the academic students undertake the Baccalauréat for progression to higher education. Technical students may undertake a further two years study in their specialised skill.
Higher education is provided by 13 universities, specialised schools and institutes under the supervision of the National Ministry of Education. Besides a traditional system of higher education, there are 28 executive training institutes (Etablissements de Formation des Cadres), which provide specialised training under the direct control of ministerial departments. There are also eight Grandes Ecoles d'Ingénieurs (engineering schools). A private university opened in September 1994. Universities are mainly public institutions with budgetary autonomy.
In 2003, schools began to teach Tamazight, the Berber language which predates Arabic in north Africa; children will have to learn using Arabic, Latin and Berber scripts.
Literacy rate: 51 per cent adult rate; 70 per cent youth rate (15–24) (Unesco 2005).
Compulsory years: 7 to 14.
Enrolment rate: 86 per cent gross primary enrolment of relevant age group (including repeaters); 39 per cent gross secondary enrolment (World Bank).
Pupils per teacher: 28 in primary schools.

Health

It is estimated that less than 20 per cent of Moroccans have access to healthcare.

Public hospitals are free, but patients must buy medicine and pay for certain services, such as X-rays. Medical fees are reimbursed only for children. There are basic health services in rural areas, including local dispensaries, rural hospitals and provincial hospitals. Government policy specifically targets the reduction of infant deaths, the provision of family planning services, nutrition awareness programmes and campaigns against malaria and tuberculosis.

HIV/Aids

HIV prevalence: 0.1 per cent aged 15–49 in 2003 (World Bank)

Life expectancy: 71 years, 2004 (WHO 2006)

Fertility rate/Maternal mortality rate: 2.3 births per woman, 2010 (Unicef); maternal mortality 230 per 100,000 live births (World Bank).

Birth rate/Death rate: Seven deaths and 25 births per 1,000 head of population (World Bank).

Child (under 5 years) mortality rate (per 1,000): 31 per 1,000 live births (WHO 2012)

Head of population per physician: 0.51 physicians per 1,000 people, 2004 (WHO 2006)

Welfare

There is a stark contrast between the living standards of the rural and urban population. In 2004, 19 per cent of the population lived below the poverty line. In rural areas over a third of the population are classified as poor.

Morocco's social security system is based on the Caisse Nationale de la Sécurité Sociale (CNSS) (National Social Security Fund), which is funded by subscribers' contributions and interest on investments. All salaried workers in industry, commerce and services must belong to the CNSS. Civil servants belong to a similar scheme, run by the Caisse Nationale des Organismes de Prévoyance Sociale (CNOPS).

In cases of illness or accident, an employee can receive 50 per cent of salary after the eighth day. The employee can claim this benefit for up to 52 weeks every two years. Maternity benefit, equal to 50 per cent of salary, is paid for up to 10 weeks. The invalidity pension is equal to 50 per cent of salary for someone who has worked between five and 15 years. If a worker dies, the family is entitled to a payment equal to two months' salary. Old age pensions, equal to 50 per cent of salary, are payable to employees who have contributed for at least 15 years. The retirement age is 60. A pension is paid to the family of a deceased retired worker, provided they had worked for more than 15 years.

Main cities

Rabat (capital, estimated population 1.9 million (m) in 2012), Casablanca (commercial centre, 3.4m), Fez (1.1m), Marrakesh (953,305), Tangier (793,776), Meknès (616,110), Agadir (600,177), Oujda (435,378), Kenitra (418,222).

Languages spoken

Business literature and correspondence should be in French or Arabic.

Arabic is spoken in general. French is taught in school and is more commonly spoken in government, business and among the Moroccans elite.

There are three main dialects of Tamazight (the Berber language) spoken all over the country. Tamazight belongs to the Afro-Asiatic family and is related to ancient Egyptian and Ethiopian.

Berber groups and their dialects: Shleuh (Ishalhiyan), in the High Atlas, Tashalhit dialect; Imazighen (Imazighen), Middle Atlas/Eastern High Atlas, Tamazight dialect; Rifans (Irifiyan), Northern Morocco, Tarifit dialect.

In the north, Spanish is widely spoken, while in the bigger cities like Casablanca, English is very common.

Official language/s

Arabic and Amazigh (the Berber language)

Media

The government has a continued interest in the countries media with a participating role in newspapers, television and radio. Through a degree of liberalisation the private press has an expanded remit to report on previously prohibited topics. However there remains a stringent press code that could be used to curb journalist, who still exercise self-censorship.

In November 2008 the Ministry of Information banned the French *L'Express International* magazine, which was deemed to have insulted Islam and was in breach of the country's press code. The magazine had discussed the relationship between the Christian and Muslim faiths, ahead of the meeting of scholars and officials being held in the Vatican.

Press

Dailies: In Arabic, *Al Anbaa* is an official publication, other private newspapers include *Al Alam* (www.alalam.ma), *Assabah* (www.assabah.press.ma) and *Bayane al Yaoume* (www.bayanealyaoume.ma). In French, *Libération* (http://liberation.press.ma), *Maroc Hebdo* (www.maroc-hebdo.press.ma) and *Aujourd'hui Le Maroc* (www.aujourdhui.ma). In English, *Morocco Today* (www.moroccotoday.net).

Weeklies: In French *Telquel* (www.telquel-online.com), *La Gazette du Maroc* (www.lagazettedumaroc.com) and *La Nouvelle Tribune* (www.lanouvelletribune.com) report on news and current affairs.

Business: There are several publications, in French, including *l'Economiste* (www.leconomiste.com) *Finances News Hebdo* (http://menara.ma/fr/Finance), *La Vie Éco* (www.lavieeco.com). Daily newspapers also have financial news sections.

Broadcasting

The national public broadcaster is Société Nationale de Radiodiffusion et de Télévision (SNRT) (www.snrt.ma) and is state-run.

Radio: SNRT (www.snrt.ma) has five stations which broadcast news, religious and regional programmes. The national, commercial broadcaster 2M (www.2m.ma) is partly government owned and operates Radio 2M (www.radio2m.ma), and Hit Maroc (www.hitmaroc.com). Other stations include the bilingual French and Arabic Medi 1 Radio (www.medi1.com), Chada FM and Radio Atlantic.

Television: SNRT (www.snrt.ma) has several channels that provide programmes of news, culture, sport and entertainment. 2M (www.2m.ma) is the second national, commercial network with a range of imported and domestic news programmes. Cable and satellite TV has grown in popularity with many overseas broadcasters reaching Morocco.

National news agency: Maghreb Arabe Presse (MAP)

Other news agencies: APA (African Press Agency): www.apanews.net

Reuters Africa: http://africa.reuters.com

Economy

The economy has been steadily liberalised since the early 1990s, with many state-owned entities privatised through government policies of diversification. Morocco is the world's third largest producer of phosphorous (after China and the US) and mining and industry provides around 25 per cent of GDP, agriculture (including fish and seafood) around 14 per cent and the service sector 61 per cent, of which tourism is the major component. Industrial development strategies and infrastructure improvements, most visibly illustrated by a new port and free trade zone near Tangier are improving Morocco's competitiveness. It also seeks to expand its renewable energy capacity with a goal of making renewables more than 40 per cent of electricity output by 2020. Despite Morocco's economic progress the country suffers from high unemployment (9.1 per cent in 2014), poverty, and illiteracy, particularly in rural areas. In 2014, Morocco ended subsidies on diesel, gasoline, and fuel oil, which has improved its budget deficit. However, subsidies on sugar, butane gas, and flour remain. Their current account deficit has also benefited from the fall in oil prices. Key economic challenges for Morocco include reforming the education system and the judiciary, while increasing the competitiveness of the private sector.

GDP growth in 2008 was 5.8 per cent, following a bumper harvest of cereals, before falling to 4.9 per cent in 2009 as global trade slumped. Growth in 2010 was 3.7 per cent, which rose to an estimated 4.3 per cent in 2011. GDP growth in Morocco has slowed significantly posting a rate of 2.7 per cent in 2012 before rebounding to 4.4 per cent in 2013 and then falling back to a lowly rate of 2.9 per cent in 2014.

In 2008, the Department of Tourism launched its *2010 Vision and Future*, to attract 10 million visitors by 2010, with a strategy to expand the sector from 160,000 beds to 230,000 beds and create 600,000 new jobs. However, despite a good start in 2008 when eight million visitors arrived, primarily from France and Spain, (over three million visitors were expatriates returning home on vacation), the downturn in the global economy reduced the number of visitors to 7.7 million in 2009. The numbers in 2010 reached 9.3 million, however the disruption throughout Arab North Africa in 2011 caused visitors to switch to other destinations and Morocco's visitor numbers fell. Since the economic recession, tourist numbers have rebounded and Morocco finally achieved its ambition of attracting 10 million visitors in 2014, just four years later than anticipated. By 2025, it is estimated that tourist arrivals will total 13.2 million.

Remittances represent a significant share of Moroccan GDP. It was a record US$6.4 billion in 2010 (6.86 per cent of GDP), which rose to an estimated US$7.1 billion in 2011. Since 2011, remittances have stabilised at $US6.8 billion in 2012 and $US6.6 billion in 2013.

The Islamic Development Bank (IDB) and the World Bank announced in 2010, that they were setting up a regional initiative of up to US$1 billion to help close the infrastructure gap in the Middle East and North Africa (Mena) and help boost economic growth. The World Bank considers that the Mena region requires US$75–100 billion per year to sustain the growth of recent years and boost economic competitiveness. Private sector investment is limited and although it was hoped the new initiative would help address this shortfall in investment through both Shari'a-compliant and conventional investment, the unrest that began in the Mahgreb at the end of 2010 has proved difficult to overcome.

In 2014, the UN Human Development Index (HDI) ranked Morocco 129 (out of 187) for national development in health, education and income down very slightly from 130 in 2011. Since 2000, Morocco's progress has grown steadily but has not matched the improvement of other Arab states.

External trade

Morocco is a member of the Greater Arab Free Trade Area (Gafta) along with 16 other countries, within an Arab economic bloc. A customs union was established whereby tariffs on locally produced items within Gafta are zero. It is also a signatory of the Euro-Mediterranean Partnership agreement, which provides for the introduction of free trade between the EU and 10 Mediterranean countries.

Morocco belongs to the Arab Maghreb Union (AMU) with Algeria, Libya, Mauritania and Tunisia. However internal disputes have hampered the implementation of a free trade or customs union. It also has a free trade agreement with the US.

Imports

Principal imports are crude petroleum, textile fabric, telecommunications equipment, wheat, gas and electricity, transistors and plastics.

Main sources: Spain (13.4 per cent of total in 2014), France (13.3 per cent), China (7.6 per cent), US (7.0 per cent)

Exports

Principal exports are clothing and textiles, automobiles, electric components, inorganic chemicals, transistors, crude minerals, fertilizers (including phosphates), petroleum products, citrus fruits, vegetables and fish.

Main destinations: Spain (22 per cent of total in 2014), France (20.7 per cent), Brazil (4.6 per cent), Italy (4.3 per cent)

Agriculture

Farming

Total agricultural land is 44.6 million hectares (ha), of which 47.1 per cent is pasture and 18 per cent arable land, cultivated mainly by subsistent farmers. Agriculture constitutes 14 per cent of GDP and it employs 39 per cent of the workforce.

Principal crops are wheat, barley, maize (grown in the rain-fed areas), citrus fruits, grapes, beans, chick peas and other pulses, tomatoes (mainly for export), potatoes, wine, livestock, olives and oilseeds. Important export crops are sugar cane, sugar beet (the production of which is being developed to cut down on sugar imports) and cotton.

Livestock productivity and crop yields have remained low and regular food imports of grain are necessary to meet domestic cereal requirements. Agricultural development has also been hampered by the small size of the majority of holdings and restricted access to EU markets. Many long-term government projects are under way, including irrigation schemes, development of new techniques and financial incentives to farmers.

As the increasing population puts pressure on available resources, access to water will become more difficult. The World Bank has estimated that Morocco will become a water deficit country by 2020.

Morocco has a number of well-intended programmes including the National Initiate for Human Development, which has the potential to ensure food and nutrition security for everyone. There has already been significant progress made in reducing disparities across regions, however, necessary infrastructure has hindered its full dissemination. Morocco's 'Green Plan' was also developed to boost the agriculture sector and it should be implemented equally across all regions through effective consultation with local populations and improved coordination services.

Some 32,500 tonnes of cannabis is grown annually in the deprived north of Morocco for the European market. King Mohammed has made developing the north a priority in government policy in order to combat illicit crop cultivation.

Fishing

The fishing sector offers considerable potential, although export markets for the main catch, sardines, are restricted by strong competition from Spain, Portugal and France. The total catch is estimated at around one million tonnes a year, of which 150,000 tonnes is shellfish and 930,000 tonnes is marine fish.

Morocco's fleet fishes in both Atlantic and Mediterranean waters and has an agreement to fish in the Gulf of Guinea. As well as its own ports, some of Morocco's catch is landed in Portugal. Fish frozen at sea is landed at Agadir and Tan-Tan.

The government is modernising the fishing fleet and ports to exploit the rich potential of local fishing grounds. The EU donated US$22.2 million to build four new fishing villages on Morocco's Mediterranean coast. A US$13 million expansion programme at Sidi Ifni fishing port, enabled catches in excess of 50,000 tonnes per annum.

Morocco has signed a protocol with the EU in July 2014 to issue fishing licenses to European vessels from 11 EU member states; Spain, Portugal, Italy, France, Germany, Lithuania, Latvia, the Netherlands, Ireland, Poland and the United Kingdom. The new fisheries protocol, which is in effect for four years, seeks to develop economic cooperation between Moroccan and European operators in the fishing industry in Morocco. The package includes payment of 40 million Euros per year provided by the EU as part of its budget to develop the Moroccan fishery sector and

10 million Euros paid by ship owners for the payment of licenses fees.

Forestry

Only 9 per cent of land area is forested and most of Morocco's wood needs are imported.

Industry and manufacturing

The industrial sector accounts for 30–35 per cent of GDP and employs 37 per cent of the workforce. Most activity is concentrated in the Casablanca area.

The main industry is the processing of phosphates into phosphoric acid and fertilisers. Food processing is another major industry. Other significant industries include oil refining, steel, cement, chemicals, pharmaceuticals, toiletries, metallurgy, textiles, leather, paper and timber, metals, rubber, plastics and vehicle assembly. The textile and leather industries employ one quarter of the industrial workforce, and export successfully.

Industrial development has switched in recent years away from import substitution and towards encouraging the manufacture of goods for export, support for small- and medium-sized producers, devolution of spending powers to local authorities and investment in other areas of the country away from Casablanca.

The French car manufacturer, Renault, opened the largest automotive factory in North Africa – inside the Tangiers Free Zone – on 9 February 2012. The plant has a capacity to produce 147,000 cars per year with a current workforce of 2,000; it could also indirectly account for up to 35,000 jobs. Renault invested US$1.5 billion on the industrial assembly line and expects to market low price cars to Bric and other emerging economic countries.

Tourism

Morocco has a variety of destinations that include historic cities, the Sahara desert, the Atlas Mountains and the Atlantic coast, all attracting a wide assortment of visitors. The tourist industry is well established and diverse enough to cater for not only differing pockets but also culturally different clientele. There are eight sites on Unesco's World Heritage List, including archaeological sites, several historic Medinas and the ksar of Ait Ben Haddou (traditional earthen buildings of the Sahara) in southern Morocco.

Morocco was not unduly affected by the unsettled political situation of the 2011 Arab Spring. In fact, visitor numbers grew 3 per cent from January–September 2011, over the same period in 2010, when 9.3 million visitors, mostly from Europe arrived, due in large part to the 'open sky' agreement with the EU that allows any Moroccan-EU private airline operator to fly into and out of each other's territories.

Travel and tourism contributed 17.9 per cent of GDP and US$16.5 billion in 2014. This is expected to increase to US$29 billion by 2025. The industry also provides jobs for 1,740,500 workers (16 per cent of the workforce), the industry is expected to provide jobs for 2,114,000 workers by 2025. Capital investment in the industry absorbed 12.1 per cent of total national investment in 2014 and is forecast to absorb 12.4 per cent in 2025. Travel and tourism is expected to have attracted capital investment of US$3.5 billion in 2014.

Mining

Government policy has been to open up the mining sector to investments by both minor and major mining companies.

There are more than 90 mining companies producing 20 different mineral products. The sector contributes approximately 15 per cent to GDP and employs 4 per cent of the workforce.

Although phosphates account for 92 per cent of mineral production, smaller quantities of other minerals are produced, including 500,000 tonnes of anthracite.

Morocco has large deposits of lead, zinc, copper, iron, fluorine, silver, manganese, cobalt, antimony, barytine, salt and other minerals.

Phosphate mining and the production of phosphoric acid are of vital importance to the Moroccan economy, although a large proportion of reserves is located in the disputed Western Sahara area occupied by Morocco since 1975. The sector is controlled by the state through the country's largest company, Office Chérifien des Phosphates (OCP). OCP is the world's largest exporter of phosphate rock. With reserves of approximately 50 billion tonnes, Morocco contains the world's largest reserve of phosphate, however, it only produces 30 tonnes a year in contrast with China, which produces 100 tonnes a year (and a reserve of 3.7 billion tonnes).

Iron ore deposits in the northern Rif region, 25km from the port of Beni Eznar, include 18.2 million tonnes of magnetite ore, which could bring in 700,000–800,000 tonnes of ore per year. Silver, copper, zinc and lead are also mined.

The European Bank for Reconstruction and Development started investing in Morocco in 2012; it has invested EUR400 million in 18 projects across the country, in addition to EUR130 million of trade facilitation credit lines with small banks. It has also provided technical assistance to more than 175 local small and medium-sized enterprises. Its most recent provision has been a $6 million loan to Maya Gold & Silver Inc, a Canadian mining company operating in Morocco, to help finance the expansion of the Zgounder Silver Mine. It will support the modernisation of the mine, as well as finance exploration and development works and the introduction of silver separation flotation units. These units will bring energy efficiency and environmental improvements to its operations.

Hydrocarbons

Proven oil reserves were 680,000 barrels in 2014, with production at 5,500 barrels per day (bpd) from Morocco's Sidi Rhelem oil field. With total consumption of around 209,400bpd, the country is heavily reliant on imported oil. Oil accounts for over 80 per cent of total energy requirements, mainly imported from Saudi Arabia. Exploration projects are under way onshore, mainly in the southwest and northeast, as well as offshore.

Morocco has two oil refineries, Samir and Sidi Kacem, with a combined capacity of 155,000bpd.

Although Morocco contains only limited natural gas reserves at 1.4 billion cubic metres (cum) in 2014, the country is a major transit centre for Algerian gas exports to Europe. The Maghreb-Europe pipeline transports Algerian gas to Spain via Morocco and the Straits of Gibraltar. Ultimately it is planned to carry 20 billion cum of gas per year to Europe via Spain. Natural gas consumption is approximately 1 billion cum per year and imports represent all of that.

Although there is one coal mine, at Jerada, with 91 million tonnes of reserves no production is undertaken and all coal is imported from South Africa and Poland.

Energy

Total installed electricity generating capacity was 7,892 MW in 2014, producing 27,781 GWh. 11.5 per cent of generation came from renewable sources (mainly hydro, then wind and others), while 38 per cent was based on coal, 18.4 per cent on natural gas and 14.3 per cent on oil. Morocco depends on imports for 91 per cent of energy supply; dependency is particularly serious for oil, which still dominates the country's energy mix. Most of its oil comes from Saudi Arabia while most of its natural gas comes from Algeria. Electricity imports from Spain have also increased sharply over the last decade.

Almost 100 per cent of the population has access to electricity, a huge improvement from 1995 where only 18 per cent has access. The Programme d'Electrification Rural Global (PERG) (global rural electrification programme) has been extremely successful and through the use of distribution lines or

photovoltaic panels most rural homes and villages have access to electricity. Around 10 per cent of homes are powered by solar energy.
To avoid blackouts and government expenditure the private sector is increasing its market share of electricity generation. The Office National de l'Electicité (ONE) is solely responsible for electricity transmission and distribution. The entire energy sector is in the process of being liberalised and observers consider the state's share of electricity generation will decline to around 40 per cent by 2020.

Financial markets

Stock exchange

Borse de Casablanca (Casablanca Stock Exchange) (CSE)

Banking and insurance

The Banque Marocaine du Commerce Extérieur (BMCE) was the first Moroccan bank and has grown steadily since 1995. It has broadened its international shareholder base and opened new branches throughout Morocco and abroad. At 8 per cent it has the largest capitalisations on the stock exchange, and around 25 per cent of that of the banking sector.
The Banque Commerciale du Maroc (BCM) holds the sector's best return on equity. It has a bad debt reduction strategy, and lower levels of bad debts than its competitors.
The Banque Centrale Populaire (BCP), the Banque Nationale pour le Développement Economique (BNDE) and the Crédit Immobilier et Hôtelier (CIH) are scheduled for privatisation. They are criticised for being burdened with high levels of bad debt and may need radical restructuring if they are to survive and compete in an adverse economic climate.

Central bank

Bank al Maghrib

Main financial centre

Casablanca

Time

GMT

Geography

Morocco is situated in the extreme north-west of Africa. It has a long coastline on the shores of the Atlantic Ocean and, east of the Strait of Gibraltar, on the Mediterranean Sea, facing southern Spain. Morocco's eastern frontier is with Algeria, while to the south lies the disputed territory of Western Sahara.
There are four distinct geographical regions, from the low-lying arid Saharan desert in the south to the Rif mountains in the north. A wide, fertile, coastal plain runs in an arc along the western seaboard and around to the Mediterranean Coast, bounded by the Rif and Atlas mountains. The Atlas mountains bisect the country from south-west to north-east and contain the highest peak in North Africa, Jebel Toubkal (4,165 metres) in the main range called the Great Atlas. The two main rivers, the Moulouya flows into the Mediterranean sea and the Sebou flows into the Atlantic.
Western Sahara is typical semiarid Sahel (an Arab word to describe a border or margin) of savannah and scrubland with low hills in the north and south.

Hemisphere

Northern

Climate

Varies widely with area; while Mediterranean on the coast, it is hotter and drier inland and Alpine in the High Atlas, yet Saharan in the south. Summer is from May–October. It is dry and hot, with temperatures between 23–28 degrees Celsius (C) on the coast, 30–45 degrees C inland. Winter runs from November–April, with light rain on the coast, average temperature 15–21 degrees C, and dry inland with temperatures between 20–30 degrees C.

Dress codes

Lightweight suits are best for formal wear. Women should dress modestly. Some visitors adopt the traditional *jellaba*, which is more comfortable in both hot and cool weather and is usually worn by men. It can get cool quickly after dark, so a light overcoat or wrap is advised.

Entry requirements

Passports

Required by all. Passports must be valid for at least six months from the date of entry.

Visa

Required by all, except citizens of EU, North America and Australasia, for visits including business trips up to three months, for further exceptions and information see: www.maec.gov.ma and follow link from *Consular* to *Formalities and procedures for international visitors*.

Currency advice/regulations

The import and export of local currency is prohibited. The import and export of foreign currency is unlimited but all amounts over Dh15,000 must be declared.
Up to half (and a greater percentage for visits of less than 48 hours) of the Moroccan dirham purchased by a visitor may be re-exchanged for foreign currency, on the production of bank sales vouchers, when departing.
Travellers cheques are accepted in banks and to avoid additional exchange fees, cheques in US dollars and pounds sterling are best.

Prohibited imports

Import restrictions apply to firearms and ammunition, permits must be obtained before travelling.

Health (for visitors)

Mandatory precautions

Vaccinations against yellow fever are required if arriving from an infected area.

Advisable precautions

Typhoid, tetanus and polio vaccinations are recommended. Anti-malaria precautions should be taken. Water may be contaminated. Milk is unpasteurised and should be boiled.

Hotels

Inexpensive and widely available. Two main types: graded hotels (which are given a one- to five-star rating by the Tourist Board) and small (and usually old) unlisted hotels. A service charge and local tax is normally added to bill.

Credit cards

Major credit cards widely accepted. ATMs can be found in cities and large towns.

Public holidays (national)

Fixed dates

1 Jan (New Year's Day), 11 Jan (Independence Day), 1 May (Labour Day), 30 Jul (Feast of the Throne), 14 Aug (Oued Eddahab Allegiance Day), 20 Aug (The King and the People's Revolution Day), 21 Aug (King Mohammed's Birthday), 6 Nov (Anniversary of the Green March), 18 Nov (Independence Day).
Holidays that fall at the weekend are not transferred to another day.

Variable dates

Eid al Adha (two days), Islamic New Year, Birth of the Prophet (two days), Eid al Fitr (two days).
Islamic year 1437 (15 Oct 2015–2 Oct 2016):: The Islamic year contains 354 or 355 days, with the result that Muslim feasts advance by 10–12 days against the Gregorian calendar. Dates of feasts vary according to the sighting of the new moon, so cannot be forecast exactly.

Working hours

Banking

Mon–Thu: 0815–1215 and 1415–1715, Fri: 0815–1115 and 1430–1730; Sat 0900–1300. Ramadan: Mon–Fri: 0900–1530.

Business

Winter: Mon–Fri: 0800–1200 and 1400–1800/2000. Summer hours vary, some work Mon–Fri: 0800–1500/1600, others revert to winter hours. Ramadan: Mon–Fri: 0900–1500/1600.

Government

Winter: Mon–Fri: 0800–1200 and 1430–1800. Summer: Mon–Sat: 0800–1600. Ramadan: Mon–Sat: 0900–1500.

Shops
Shops are usually open between 0800 and 1800, often closing for a few hours in the middle of the day.

Telecommunications
Mobile/cell phones
GSM 900 services are available for most of Morocco and northern Western Sahara.

Electricity supply
220V AC, 50 cycles; sockets are typically the European two-pronged variety.

Social customs/useful tips
Business visits during the Muslim month of Ramadan are best avoided, as many businesses close during part or all of this period. During Ramadan, visitors should respect Muslim traditions and avoid drinking, eating and smoking in public during daylight hours.
Pork and alcohol are forbidden to Muslims at all times, so these should not be offered, although in practice alcohol is widely available and its consumption not considered an insult to Islam.
Business practices in most respects are similar to those in France and Spain.
Tipping is common for most services, including hotel porters, cinema usherettes, cloakroom attendants, railway porters, and so on. In hotels and restaurants a service charge is normally added to the bill.
Taxi drivers (in *grand* taxis only) will expect a 10 per cent tip.

Security
Street crime is a problem, especially in the larger cities where petty theft is rife.
Women may also encounter sexual harassment on the streets at any time, especially when walking alone.

Getting there
Air
National airline: Royal Air Maroc
International airport/s: Casablanca-Mohammed V (CMN), 30km south of the city, duty-free shops, restaurant, bank, post office, car hire and business centre. There are taxis to Casablanca and a rail link to Rabat.
Tangier-Boukhalef Souahel (TNG), 11km from city, with duty-free shops, restaurant, bank, post office, shops, car hire.
Other airport/s: Agadir-Inezgane (AGA), 6.5km south of city, bar, buffet, bank, car hire; Fez-Sais (FEZ), 10km from city; Rabat-Salé (RBA), 10km from city, restaurant, bank, car hire; Marrakesh (RAK), 6km from city.
Airport tax: None
Surface
Road: Road access is possible from Algeria via Oujda.
Rail: There are good rail connections to Tunisia, France and Spain (via rail-ferry link). The international rail link is via Oujda. In 2002, rail links to Algeria were suspended.
Water: Regular car ferry and hydrofoil services connect Spain, France and Gibraltar with Tangier and the Spanish administered ports of Ceuta and Melilla.
Main port/s: Agadir, Casablanca (major freight port), Jorf Lasfar, Kenitra, Mohammedia, Nador, Safi, Tangier (main passenger port).

Getting about
National transport
Air: Royal Air Maroc operates domestic services to main centres. Regional Airlines is another domestic carrrier.
Road: Morocco has approximately 30,000km of surfaced roads. The links between main centres are generally good. Some of the 30,000km country roads need care and/or local knowledge.
The Atlas Mountains may be impassable in winter.
Buses: There are frequent, cheap services between towns. Long-distance services include: Tangier-Oujda, Fez-Marrakesh; Agadir-Casablanca and Tangier-Casablanca. It is advisable to book in advance.
Rail: A limited (1,893km) but efficient network is operated by Office National des Chemins de Fer (ONCF). Fares are cheap. Three classes are available. Air-conditioning, air-conditioned sleeping cars – couchettes and restaurant cars are available; supplements may be payable. Routes include: Oujda-Fez-Rabat-Casablanca, Marrakesh-Casablanca-Rabat and Casablanca-Rabat-Tangier.
City transport
Taxis: The *grand* taxis (Moroccan bus-taxis), seating up to six persons, operate along specific routes and can be arranged at hotel receptions, or can be found outside bus and train stations and the airport. They are cheaper than a conventional taxi for long journeys and more comfortable and convenient than a bus.
The *petit* taxis are metered and operate within cities. Fares vary considerably; drivers prefer to set fares in advance, rather than use the meter, so each journey is preceded by a negotiation. A 10 per cent tip is usual.
Buses, trams & metro: Agadir, Casablanca, Tangier and other main towns have good bus services. Tickets can be bought in advance of journeys. There is a shuttle bus service from the Casablanca rail station to the CTM Gare Routière (bus station) which takes at least 45 minutes, depending on traffic.
Trains: Train service every 30 minutes connects Casablanca's Mohammed V Airport with the city's main railway stations, Voyageurs and Port.

Car hire
Car hire is widely available but expensive. Major hire companies operate from Agadir, Casablanca and Tangier. National or international driving licences are accepted. Driving is on the right.

BUSINESS DIRECTORY
The addresses listed below are a selection only. While World of Information makes every endeavour to check these addresses, we cannot guarantee that changes have not been made, especially to telephone numbers and area codes. We would welcome any corrections.

Telephone area codes
The international dialling code (IDD) for Morocco is +212, followed by area code and subscriber's number:

Agadir	48	Mohammedia	232
Casablanca	22	Rabat	37
Fes	55	Tangier	39
Marrakech	44		

Chambers of Commerce
American Chamber of Commerce in Morocco, Hyatt Regency Casablanca, Place des Nations Unies, Casablanca (tel: 293-028; fax: 481-597; email: amcham@amcham-morocco.com).

British Chamber of Commerce for Morocco, 65 Avenue Hassan Seghir, Casablanca (tel: 448-860; fax: 448-868; email: britcham@casanet.net.ma).

Casablanca Chambre de Commerce, d'Industrie et des Services, 98 Boulevard Mohammed V,PO Box 423, Casablanca (tel: 264-327; fax: 268-436; email: ccisc@cciscx.gov.ma).

Chambre de Commerce Internationale, Boulevard de Bordeaux, Casablanca (tel: 225-111; fax: 225-119; email: icc@casanet.net.ma).

French Chambre de Commerce et d'Industrie du Maroc,15 Avenue Mers Sultan, PO Box 15810, Casablanca (tel: 209-090; fax: 200-130; email: cfcim@cfcim.org).

Marrakech Chambre de Commerce, d'Industrie et de Services, Djnan El Harti Gueliz, Marrakech (tel: 431-951; fax: 430-950; email: ccismar@iam.net.ma).

Morocco Fédération des Chambres de Commerce et d'Industrie, 6 Rue Erfoud, Rabat (tel: 766-108; fax: 767-076; e-mail: fccjsm@maghrebnet.net.ma).

Rabat Chambre de Commerce, d'Industrie et de Services, 6 Rue Ghandi, PO Box 131, Rabat (tel: 703-185; fax: 703-166; email: ccisrs@ccisrs.org.ma).

Tangiers Chambre de Commerce, d'Industrie et de Services, Angle Rue Ibn Taymia et Rue El Hariri, Tangier (tel:

946-026; fax: 942-954; email: cciswtg@iam.net.ma).

Banking

ABN Amro Bank (Maroc) SA, PO Box 13478, 47 Rue Allal Ben Abellah, Casablanca 20000 (tel: 266-027; fax: 222-514).

Banque Centrale Populaire, 101 Boulevard Mohamed Zerktouni, Casablanca (tel: 222-589; fax: 222-699; e-mail: aslamti@cpm.co.ma).

Banque Commerciale du Maroc, 2 Boulevard Moulay Youssef, Casablanca (tel: 224-169; fax: 469-916).

Banque Marocaine du Commerce Extérieur SA, PO Box 13.425, 140 Avenue Hassan II, Casablanca 01 (tel: 220-0325, 220-0467; fax: 220-0005, 220-0060).

Crédit du Maroc SA, PO Box 13579, 48-58 Boulevard Mohammed V, Casablanca 20000 (tel: 477-000; fax: 277-127, 206-076/77).

Crédit Immobilier et Hôtelier, 187 Avenue Hassan II, Casablanca 20000 (tel: 222-7863; fax: 248-7537, 227-8631).

Groupement Professionel des Banques du Maroc (Moroccan Banking Association), 71 Avenue des Forces Armées Royales, Casablanca (tel: 311-624; fax: 311-911).

Société Marocaine de Dépôt et de Crédit, 79 Avenue Hassan II, Casablanca (tel: 224-114; fax: 271-590).

Wafabank, 163 Avenue Hassan II, Casablanca (tel: 220-0200, 227-1091, 226-5151, 222-4105; fax: 226-3621).

Central bank

Bank al Maghrib, PO Box 445, 277 Avenue Mohammed V, Rabat (tel: 702-626; fax:706-677).

Stock exchange

Borse de Casablanca (Casablanca Stock Exchange) (CSE), www.casablanca-bourse.com

Travel information

Casablana Airport, Office National des Aéroports, Casa-Oasis, BP 8101 Casablanca (tel: 539-040, 539-140; fax: 539-051, 539-901; internet: www.ondo.org.ma).

Office National des Chemins de Fer (ONCF) Tourist Office, 98 Boulevard Mohammed V, Casablanca (tel: 221-524).

Royal Air Maroc, 44 Avenue des Forces Armées Royales, Casablanca (tel: 311-122; fax: 442-409).

Ministry of tourism

Ministry of Economy, Finance and Tourism, Quartier Administratif, Chellah, Rabat (tel: 760-147; 760-509; fax: 761-575; e-mail: ministre@mfie.gov.ma; internet site: http://www.tourisme-marocain.com/frame/infos.htm).

National tourist organisation offices

Morocco National Tourist Board (ONMT), Rue Oued Fes, Angle Avenue Al Abtal, Agdal, Rabat (tel: 681-531; fax: 777-437; e-mail: visitemorocco@mbox.azure.net).

Ministries

Prime Minister's Office, Palais Royal, Le Méchouar, Rabat (tel: 762-709; fax: 769-995).

Ministry of Agriculture and Rural Development, Place Abdallah Chefchaouni, Quartier Administratif, Rabat (tel: 760-933; fax: 763-378).

Ministry of Communication, 10 Rue de Béni Mellal, Place de la Grande Poste, Avenue Mohammed V, Rabat (tel: 766-016; fax: 766-908; internet site: www.mincom.gov.ma).

Ministry of Economic Forecasts and Planning, Avenue Al Haj Cherkaoui, Agdal, Rabat (tel: 761-415; fax: 760-771).

Ministry of Economy, Finance and Tourism, Quartier Administratif, Chellah, Rabat (tel: 760-147; 760-509; fax: 761-575; email: ministre@mfie.gov.ma; internet site: www.finances.gov.ma).

Ministry of Education, Bab Rouah, Rabat (tel: 771-822; fax: 772-042).

Minister of Employment, Vocational Training, Social Development and Solidarity (tel: 760-695; fax: 766-633).

Ministry of Equipment, Quartier Administratif, Chellah, Rabat (tel: 762-811; fax: 765-505).

Ministry of Foreign Affairs and Co-operation, Avenue Roosevelt, Rabat (tel: 762-841; fax: 764-679; email: mail@maec.gov.ma; internet site: www.maec.gov.ma).

Minister of Habous and Islamic Affairs, Le Méchouar, Rabat (tel: 766-801; fax: 765-257; e-mail: webmaster@habous.gov.ma).

Ministry of Health, 335 Boulevard Mohammed V, Rabat (tel: 761-121; fax: 768-401; e-mail: webmaster@sante.gov.ma).

Ministry of Higher Education and Scientific Research, Charia Bouregreg, Rabat (tel: 707-496; fax: 737-236).

Ministry of Human Rights (tel: 673-131; fax: 671-967).

Ministry of Industry, Commerce, Energy, and Mines, Quartier Administratif, Chellah, Rabat (tel: 761-868; fax: 766-265; email: ministre@mcinet).

Ministry of Interior, Quartier Administratif, Rabat (tel: 761-861; fax: 762-056).

Ministry of Justice, Place Mamounia, Rabat (tel: 732-941; fax: 730-772).

Minister of Land Management, Urban Affairs, Housing and the Environment (tel: 763-539; fax: 763-510).

Ministry of Parliamentary Relations, Quartier Administratif, Agdal, Rabat (tel: 775-170; fax: 775-468).

Ministry of Public Service and Administrative Reform (770-894; fax: 775-690).

Ministry of Public Sector and Privatisation (internet site: www.minpriv.gov.ma).

Ministry of Sea Fisheries, Quartier Administratif, Rabat (tel: 770-154; fax: 778-540).

Ministry of Transport and Merchant Marine (tel: 774-266; fax: 779-525).

Ministry of Youth and Sport, Boulevard Ibn Sina, Agdal, Rabat, (tel: 680-045; fax: 680-916).

Other useful addresses

Bourse de Casablanca (Stock Exchange), Avenue de l'Armée Royale, Casablanca (tel: 452-626; fax: 452-625; email: contact@casablanca-bourse.com).

British Consulate-General, 43 Boulevard d'Anfa, Casablanca (tel: 221-653; fax: 265-779; email: british. consulate@casanet.net.ma).

British Embassy, 17 Boulevard de la Tour Hassan, Rabat (tel: 729-696; fax: 704-531; email: britemb@mtds.com).

Confédération Générale des Enterprises du Maroc (CGEM), Angle Avenue des Forces Armées Royales et Rue Mohamed Errachid, Casablanca (tel: 252-696; fax: 253-839).

Fédération des Industries Chimiques et Parachimiques (FICP), 36 Rue Chaouia, Casablanca (tel: 229-215; fax:225-613).

Fédération des Industries de la Conserve des Produits Agricoles du Maroc (FICOPAM), 77 Rue Mohamed Smiha, Casablanca (tel: 303-953; fax: 303-534).

Fédération des Industries Métallurgiques, Mécaniques, Electriques et Electroniques (FIMME), 147 Rue Mohamed Smiha, Casablanca (tel: 301-683; fax: 940-587).

Moroccan Centre for Export Promotion, 23 Rue Bnou Majed El Bahar, Casablanca (tel: 522 302 210; fax: 522 301-793; email: info@marocexport.ma).

Moroccan Embassy (USA), 1601 21st Street, NW, Washington DC 20009 (tel: (+1-202) 462-7979; fax: (+1-202) 265-0161; email: sifarausa@erols.com).

National Telecommunications Regulatory Agency (ANRT), Boulevard Ennakhil, Rabat (tel: 717-312; email: webmaster@anrt.net.ma).

Office pour le Développement Industriel (ODI), 10 Rue Ghandi, Rabat (tel: 708-460; fax: 707-695).

ONAREP (national oil company), 34 Avenue Al Fadila, Rabat (tel: 281-616; fax: 281-634; email: benkhadr@onarep.com).

United States Embassy, 2 Avenue de Mohamed El Fassi, Rabat (tel: 762-265; fax: 765-661).

National news agency: Maghreb Arabe Presse (MAP), BP1049, 122 Ave Allal Ben Abdellah, Rabat (tel: 764-083; email: webmap@map.co.ma; internet: www.map.ma/eng).

APA (African Press Agency): www.apanews.net

Reuters Africa: http://africa.reuters.com

Internet sites

Africa Business Network: www.ifc.org/abn

AllAfrica.com: http://allafrica.com

African Development Bank: www.afdb.org

Information on Morocco – historical events, cities, economy, culture and media: www.dsg.ki.se/maroc/

Mbendi AfroPaedia (information on companies, countries, industries and stock exchanges in Africa): http://mbendi.co.za

Menara Yellow Pages (in French): www.menara.co.ma/pagejauneHome.asp

Mozambique

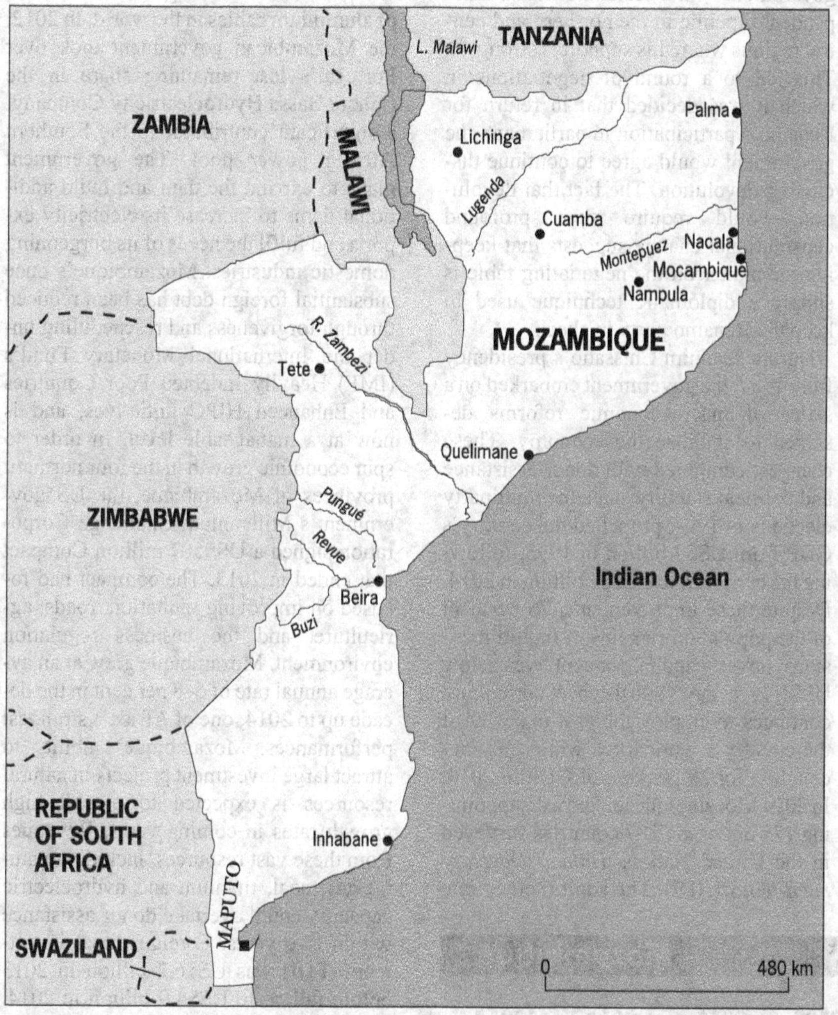

Mozambique had been a Portuguese colony for five centuries before its independence in 1975. Subsequently, large-scale emigration, economic dependence on South Africa, a severe drought, and a prolonged civil war hindered the country's development until the mid-1990s. The conflict between the two main parties in Mozambique – Front for the Liberation of Mozambique party (Frelimo) and Mozambique National Resistance (Renamo) resulted in an estimated one million deaths. The ruling Frelimo formally abandoned Marxism in 1989, and a new constitution the following year provided for multiparty elections and a free market economy. Marxism had been an important component of Mozambican politics prior to the constitutional changes, the star on its flag represents the famous international theory. Just like Marxism had failed to work in Soviet Russia, it did not result in success for Mozambique either. A UN-negotiated peace agreement between Frelimo and the rebel group, Renamo ended the fighting in 1992.

President Joaquim had became the leader of Mozambique in 1987 and he continued to rule for 18 years before stepping down in December 2004, prompting Mozambique to undertake a delicate

KEY FACTS

Official name: República de Moçambique (Republic of Mozambique)

Head of State: President Filipe Nyusi (Frelimo) (from 15 Oct 2014, sworn in 15 Jan 2015)

Head of government: Prime Minister Carlos Agostinho do Rosario (from 17 Jan 2015)

Ruling party: Frente de Libertação de Moçambique (Frelimo) (Front for the Liberation of Mozambique) (since 1975; re-elected 15 Oct 2014)

Area: 799,380 square km

Population: 26.49 million (2014)*

Capital: Maputo

Official language: Portuguese

Currency: Metical (MT) = 100 centavos (New notes were issued in 2006 as part of a reform of the currency, which dropped three zeros).

Exchange rate: MT42.90 per US$ (Sep 2015)

GDP per capita: US$630 (2014)*

GDP real growth: 7.37% (2014)*

GDP: US$16.68 billion (2014)*

Inflation: 2.29% (2014)

Balance of trade: -US$4.36 billion (2013)*

Annual FDI: US$2.08 billion (2011)

* estimated figure

transition. Chissano's elected successor, Armando Guebuza, promised to continue the sound economic policies that had encouraged foreign investment. President Guebuza was re-elected for a second term in October 2009, however, the elections were flawed by voter fraud, questionable disqualification of candidates, and Frelimo use of government resources during the campaign.

On 15 October 2014, Mozambique held another general election in which the Frelimo candidate, Filipe Nyusi, won the presidential race, the first northerner to do so, with 57 per cent of the vote, ahead of Renamo's Afonso Dhlakama who won 37 per cent of the vote. Inevitably, the Renamo party disputed the election results saying that they were riddled with irregularities. On the night of the election results, there were sporadic bouts of violence at counting centres in some parts of the country, with police using tear gas to disperse rioting youths. Mr Dhlakama had come out of hiding to run for the presidency, his last-minute entry making this the most fiercely contested election since independence. Frelimo's tally of parliamentary seats dropped from 191 to 144, while Renamo increased its representation in parliament from 51 to 89. This lies in stark contrast with the presidential results where solid gains by the opposition as a whole, came nowhere near challenging the outright majority enjoyed by Frelimo and by its candidate. This mismatch between the presidential and parliamentary results demonstrates the ambivalence that led a substantial number of people to split their vote. Renamo and the other main opposition party, Mozambique Democratic Movement (MDM), both benefit from a long-held sentiment in central and northern Mozambique because those regions have been neglected by successive southern-dominated governments.

Dhlakama's rejection of the election results led him to threaten the Mozambican government with a declaration of an independent republic in the northern and central regions where his support is strongest. This led to a round of negotiations in which it was decided that in return for Renamo's participation in parliament, the government would agree to continue discussing devolution. The fact that devolution would require such profound constitutional change suggests that keeping the matter on the negotiating table is simply a diplomatic technique used to keep the Renamo party in check.

During Joaquim Chissano's presidency from 1987, the government embarked on a series of macroeconomic reforms designed to stabilise the economy. These changes, combined with donor assistance and political stability since the multiparty elections in 1994, propelled the country's GDP from US$4 billion in 1993, following the civil war, to US$31 billion in 2014. Despite these improvements, 70 per cent of the population remains in multidimensional poverty and 60 per cent lives below US$1.25 a day. Subsistence agriculture continues to employ the vast majority of the country's work force while only accounting for 29 per cent of GDP in 2014. In 2014 Mozambique ranked a disappointing 178 out of the 187 countries surveyed in the United Nations *Human Development Index* (HDI). The adult literacy rate was only 51 per cent and average life expectancy at birth was a mere 50 years.

A substantial trade imbalance persists although aluminium production from the Mozal smelter has significantly boosted export earnings especially since 2013 as Mozal signed an agreement under which it would supply 50,000 tonnes of aluminium to Midal, one of the largest manufactures of aluminium cables in the world. In 2012, the Mozambican government took over Portugal's last remaining share in the Cahora Bassa Hydroelectricity Company, a significant contributor to the Southern African power pool. The government plans to expand the dam and build additional dams to increase its electricity exports and fulfil the needs of its burgeoning domestic industries. Mozambique's once substantial foreign debt has been reduced through forgiveness and rescheduling under the International Monetary Fund's (IMF) Heavily Indebted Poor Countries and Enhanced HIPC initiatives, and is now at a manageable level. In order to spur economic growth in the four northern provinces of Mozambique, the US government's Millennium Challenge Corporation signed a US$507 million Compact that ended in 2013. The compact had focused on improving sanitation, roads, agriculture, and the business regulation environment. Mozambique grew at an average annual rate of 6–8 per cent in the decade up to 2014, one of Africa's strongest performances. Mozambique's ability to attract large investment projects in natural resources is expected to extend high growth rates in coming years. Revenues from these vast resources, including natural gas, coal, titanium and hydroelectric capacity, could overtake donor assistance within five years. Foreign direct investment (FDI) was US$6.2 billion in 2013 before falling to US$4.9 billion in 2014. Despite the decrease in foreign investment, it still remains very high. The main sectors benefitting from FDI are construction, services to enterprises, transport and communications, and the financial sector.

In spite of lower than expected coal production, the extractive sector is a key economic driver. The government has completely revised the legal and fiscal framework for the mining and hydrocarbons sector, aimed at increasing revenues and enlarging domestic participation in the sector. A concession contract for a local liquefied natural gas (LNG) plant was negotiated, however, the current depression in the international oil markets could delay the final investment decision and implementation. In conjunction with the

KEY INDICATORS Mozambique

	Unit	2011	2012	2013	2014	**2015
Population	m	*22.02	*25.23	25.83	*26.49	*27.12
Gross domestic product (GDP)	US$bn	12.80	14.29	15.66	*16.68	*16.92
GDP per capita	US$	583	567	605	*630	*624
GDP real growth	%	7.1	7.2	7.4	*7.4	*6.5
Inflation	%	10.4	2.1	4.2	2.3	*5.0
Exports (fob) (goods)	US$m	3,118.3	3,469.8	4,122.6	–	–
Imports (fob) (goods)	US$m	5,367.6	6,167.8	8,479.5	–	–
Balance of trade	US$m	-2,249.3	-2,698.0	-4,356.9	–	–
Current account	US$m	-2,438.3	-6,517.0	-6,253.0	*-5,797.0	*-6,960.0
Total reserves minus gold	US$m	2,352.4	2,770.2	3,142.3	3,010.0	–
Foreign exchange	US$m	2,179.3	2,607.3	2,982.0	–	–
Exchange rate	per US$	30.88	29.52	29.95	33.99	–

* estimated figure ** forecast figure

possibility for a new LNG plant, a fifth international tender has been launched for the exploration of new oil and gas fields, opening up new prospects for further hydrocarbon discoveries. Proven reserves of natural gas was 2.8 trillion cum in 2014, the fourteenth largest in the world. Production of natural gas was only 4.3 billion cum in 2013, the 53rd most productive in the world. This significant difference between reserves and production of natural gas needs to narrow in order for Mozambique to properly exploit their rich natural gas resources. Of the natural gas produced, 95 per cent of it is exported in the form of electricity while approximately 191 million cum is consumed locally. Electricity is exported mainly to South Africa. The Mozambican government will initially invest more than US$30 billion in Mozambique's natural gas sector to build capacity to produce 20 million tonnes per year of LNG with the first exports due to start in 2018.

The discovery of natural gas in Mozambique is not all positive as thousands of people face resettlement to make way for planned gas projects. Unless sharp improvements are made to reduce unemployment and improve education and social welfare, poor Mozambicans are still likely to seek out whatever petro-dollars they can get. This could involve prostitution or selling drugs, there will be a plethora of illegal activities available to poor citizens once the petro-dollars start rolling in. The government has already shown signs of reckless spending and it is somewhat likely that an increase in political violence will occur. A controversial US$850 million bond was launched in 2012 to start state tuna-fishing company Ematum, which has intensified fears that the government is not ready to handle windfalls. Around US$500 million of the proceeds turned out to be for defence spending and, so far, no details have been provided on where exactly the money went.

Mozambique might become the latest African country to suffer the 'resource curse', in which an injection of petro-dollars suffocates the rest of the economy which encourages corruption and stirs unrest. President Nyusi promises to use the money collected from energy and mining to diversify the economy and provide work for the poor. This may well represent an empty promise based on similar examples in other African countries. In countries such as Angola and Nigeria, decades of oil and gas wealth have enriched a local elite and given foreign energy firms enormous profits while doing very little for the millions of poor people, stoking deadly periods of civil unrest. Standard Bank forecasts that the LNG projects themselves will create 15,000 jobs plus another 200,000 indirectly, but with many of these short-term positions and 350,000 Mozambicans joining the job market every year, they will not solve mass poverty. The most serious negative consequence that could result from the gas boom is the potential for conflict. Signs of political upheaval have already reared their ugly heads and it is likely that they will intensify when gas spoils increase.

The mining sector in Mozambique is dominated by coal. High quality hard coking coal (metallurgical coal) is mined in the western and landlocked Tete province. According to the African Development Bank's *African Economic Outlook 2015* (AEO), mining and quarrying accounted for 1.6 per cent of GDP in 2009 before increasing to 3.6 per cent of GDP in 2013. The coal sector is the predominant creditor for this growth. Moreover, the extractive sector was the fastest growing part of the Mozambican economy in 2014, at 22 per cent. Mozambican coal production in 2013 was 7.5 million tonnes, representing a 4.8 million tonne increase over the 2012 figure. However, the coal sector has been afflicted by infrastructural inadequacies, particularly in port and especially railway capacity. Furthermore, global coal prices have fallen by half since 2007. As of November 2014, the Mozambican government had granted, for Tete province, 124 exploration licences and approved 11 mining concessions but only four operating licences had been issued. The AEO 2015 reported that all coal mines in Mozambique are currently losing money. Coal mining in Tete is largely the preserve of big international corporations with long-term plans and lots of money. The majority of mining companies that work in Mozambique do so to export coal and make a profit from that. Ncondezi Energy hopes to exploit the 15 per cent annual increase in Mozambique's power demand. The company is focused on mining thermal coal and instead of exporting it, it seeks to turn that coal into electricity and sell that. The company plans to build an integrated mine and power station, which will be developed in stages, from 300MW in the first stage to 1,800MW in the final stage. The electricity will be sold to national power utility Electricdade de Mocambique (EdM). Currently, the plan is to commission the mine and plant in 2017 and start commercial operations in 2018.

Poaching

The unsustainable levels of poverty in Mozambique have led more Mozambicans than ever to poach elephants and rhinoceroses. The police arrested 434 people for poaching between 2014 and November 2015. The latest census of elephants showed that between 2009 and 2014, Mozambique lost 48 per cent of its elephants, with numbers falling from around 20,000 to 10,300. There were 158 poachers arrested in 2014, while 276 poachers have been arrested so far in 2015. Poaching is motivated by the large sums paid by those who order the crime. The poachers often use large calibre weapons, including military weapons, such as AK-47 rifles, often with faked documents and altered registration numbers. The authorities have seized 5,110 snares and 55 firearms so far in 2015, used to catch and kill elephants and rhinos. Currently in 2015, the authorities seized 1,124 kilos of ivory, and 75 kilos of rhinoceros horns. Since both species of African rhinoceros, the black and white, are believed to be extinct in Mozambique, these horns probably came from animals poached in South Africa's Kruger National Park.

Risk assessment

Politics	Poor/fair
EconomyFair	
Regional stability	Fair/good

People to watch

Daviz Simango, leader of the Movimento Democrático de Moçambique (MDM) (Mozambique Democratic Movement) the third largest political party.

Afonso Dhlakama leader of the Resistência Nacional Moçambicana (Renamo) the largest opposition party

COUNTRY PROFILE

1498 Portuguese explorer Vasco da Gama landed on the shores of what is now Mozambique.

Portuguese settlements were quickly established, but full-scale colonisation did not begin until the seventeenth century. In the eighteenth and nineteenth centuries, Mozambique served as a major slave-trading centre.

1842 Portugal abolished the slave trade, although the practice continued.

1891 Mozambique's southern and western borders were defined by the British and Portuguese.
1932 Portugal broke up the land-owning companies that controlled trade and imposed direct rule over Mozambique.
1962 The Frente de Libertação de Moçambique (Frelimo) (Front for the Liberation of Mozambique) was established and launched a military campaign for independence.
1975 Mozambique gained independence. A one-party system was implemented with Frelimo as the sole legal party. Mozambican support for the independence war in Rhodesia (Zimbabwe) and the African National Congress (ANC) in South Africa led to frequent reprisals from the governments of those countries. Independence was followed by 16 years of civil war against the rebels of the Resistencia Nacional de Moçambique (Renamo) (Mozambique National Resistance), a guerrilla army supported first by Rhodesia and later by South Africa and the US.
1977 Frelimo adopted Marxism-Leninism as its official doctrine.
1984 Frelimo reached a deal with South Africa in which it would halt its support for the ANC in return for an end to South Africa's aid to Renamo.
1986 President Machel was killed in an airplane crash; Joaquim Chissano became president.
1989 Frelimo formally abandoned Marxism-Leninism in favour of democratic socialism and a market economy. Renamo's support faltered as the civil war was already turning in the government's favour.
1990 A new constitution was promulgated to allow for a multi-party electoral system.
1992 A cease-fire was agreed, followed by a full peace agreement.
1994 In the first multi-party elections, Frelimo won an absolute parliamentary majority. Joaquim Chissano was re-elected president.
1995 Mozambique joined the Commonwealth, the only member not to have been a British colony.
1998 Low turnout for local elections, which were boycotted by Renamo, due to flaws in voter registration, prompted the government to overhaul the voting procedures for the national elections.
1999 Joaquim Chissano was re-elected president and Frelimo increased its parliamentary majority.
2000/01 Mozambique was devastated by a tropical cyclone and severe flooding. There was rioting over Renamo allegations that the 1999 elections were rigged; international observers claimed the elections were free and fair.
2003 Cyclones Delfina and Japhet caused extensive damage.
2004 Armando Guebuza won the presidential elections and Frelimo was re-elected in parliamentary elections.
2005 Guebuza (Frelimo) became president. A new bridge spanning the Zambezi between Sofala and Zambezia provinces began construction.
2006 The World Bank cancelled most of Mozambique's foreign debt. New bank notes bearing the face of independence leader and first president Samora Machel were issued as part of a reform of the currency, which dropped three zeros. The government announced a 13 per cent increase in the minimum wage for industry and services.
2007 Severe flooding in the Zambezi valley, caused by 340mm of rain falling within 24 hours, displaced over 50,000 people and more than 3,500 people had to seek shelter in government accommodation centres in the provincial city of Quelimane.
2008 Violence in South Africa towards foreign workers forced thousands of Mozambican workers to return home.
2009 According to the UN, 350,000 people were at risk of hunger due to meagre rains and poor harvests. In presidential and parliamentary elections, incumbents President Guebuza and Frelimo were returned to office.
2010 The president appointed Aires Ali as prime minister. The cashew nut crop was the largest since 2007, at over 95,000 tonnes, due to favourable weather conditions. A new bridge, called the Samora Machel Bridge (in Mozambique) across the Ruvuma River in the north was inaugurated by the presidents of Mozambique and Tanzania. The US$35 million investment in the bridge is shared between the two countries and will link new roads already either constructed or under construction. Another new bridge spanning the Zambezi River at the city of Tete was opened. Food riots broke out as bread prices increased by 30 per cent. US diplomatic communiqués published by *Wikileaks*, accused two senior businessmen of being drug-traffickers and that they were being protected by President Guebuza. The leaks also stated that Mozambique had become a major African hub for drugs from South Asia.
2011 In February, the US-exploration company Anadarko Petroleum Corporation announced that it had found large quantities of 'high quality' natural gas offshore of Northern Mozambique.
2012 On 2 October, the German government granted €28.5 million (US$36.7 million) to fund expansion of financial services for small- and medium-sized enterprises (SMEs). On 3 October, the Chinese contractor completed and handed over the new domestic terminal of Maputo International Airport to its owner-operator Mozambique Airports Company. On 8 October President Guebuza dismissed Aires Ali as prime minister and appointed Alberto Vaquina as his replacement.
2013 In April floods following cyclone Haruna in February and locusts two months later threatened food security in the south-western province of Tulear, one of Mozambique's poorest regions. The bush camp of a group of some 300 Renamo rebels was attacked by the government on 21 October. Their leader, Afonso Dhlakama, escaped. A spokesman was reported as saying that this would end the peace accord signed in 1992. The government said that at least five people had been killed in a Renamo attack on a police post in April and accused Renamo of dragging the country back to war.
2014 Presidential and general elections were held on 15 October. Although Frelimo again won both, the margin of success was down on previous years. Incumbent President Armando Guebuza could not stand again after his two presidential terms, and he was succeeded by Filipe Nyusi who won with 57.03 per cent of the vote, ahead of Afonso Dhlakama (36.6 per cent). Frelimo won the general election with 55.93 per cent of the vote (144 seats out of 259), followed by Renamo with 32.46 per cent (89 seats). Frelimo still has a solid majority, but with 44 fewer seats than before; Renamo was up by 38 seats and the MDM by nine.
2015 On 10 January, Afonso Dhlakama, the Renamo leader, announced he would form an autonomous region in the gas-rich nouthern and central regions where his support lies; he would rule as president. At the time Renamo were still disputing the result of the October 2014 election, delaying the formation of the government. Filipe Nyusi was sworn in as President on 15 January after winning the 2014 presidential election. Mr Nyusi is the first northerner to hold the position (much of Mozambique's gas is found in the north). On 17 January Carlos Agostinho do Rosario was named as Prime Minister, leading a slimmed down cabinet.

Political structure

Constitution

The 1975 independence Constitution was replaced by the 1990 Constitution, which provides for a multi-party system, direct elections and a free market economy.

Form of state

Unitary republic

The executive

The Head of State is the president, directly elected by absolute majority popular vote in 2 rounds if needed for a five-year term (eligible for two consecutive terms), and who governs with his appointed prime minister and Council of Ministers.

National legislature
The unicameral Assembleia de la República (Assembly of the Republic) has 250 seats of which its members are directly elected in single- and multi-seat constituencies by proportional representation from party lists. Two members represent Mozambicans abroad. Members serve for five-year terms.

Legal system
Based on Portuguese/Roman law and the 1990 constitution. Since 1996, there has been a Law Reform Commission which has the responsibility for revising legislation.

Last elections
15 October 2014 (presidential and parliamentary)
Results: Presidential: Filipe Nyusi (Frelimo) won 57.03 per cent of the vote, Afonso Dhlakama (Renamo) 36.61 per cent, Daviz Simango (Movimento Democrático de Moçambique (MDM) (Democratic Movement of Mozambique)) 6.36 per cent. Turnout was 48.6 per cent.
Parliamentary: Frelimo won 55.93 per cent of the votes cast (144 seats (out of 250)), Renamo 32.46 per cent (89), MDM 8.35 per cent (17). Turnout was 48.5 per cent.

Next elections
October 2019 (presidential and parliamentary)

Political parties

Ruling party
Frente de Libertação de Moçambique (Frelimo) (Front for the Liberation of Mozambique) (since 1975; re-elected 15 Oct 2014)

Main opposition party
Resistencia Nacional de Moçambique (Renamo) (Mozambique National Resistance)

Population
25.86 million (2013)* Approximately 46 per cent of the population are under 14 years of age.
About 38 per cent of the urban population and 9 per cent of the rural population have access to clean water.
Last census: 1 August 2007: 20,530,714 (provisional)
Population density: 22 inhabitants per square km. Urban population 38 per cent (2010 Unicef).
Annual growth rate: 2.7 per cent, 1990–2010 (Unicef).

Ethnic make-up
Indigenous tribal groups, including Ronga, Shangaan, Chokwe, Manyika, Sena and Makua (99 per cent); European (1 per cent).

Religions
Some 300 registered religions, including traditional beliefs (50 per cent), Christianity (majority Roman Catholic) (30 per cent), Muslim (20 per cent).

Education
Primary education lasts until the aged 13. At this point students attend either a general or technical secondary school. The general school lasts for five years when students graduate for progression into higher education. Technical secondary school lasts for three years with a further two years for advanced courses.
The war devastated the education sector. However, by the end of the 1990s, the primary school network had recovered to levels seen in 1983. In 1999, there were 6,600 first-level primary schools (first to fifth years) attended by 2.1 million children. A third of primary school children attend schools that are so crowded that classes are oversubscribed by over 300 per cent. Educational provision is far worse in the second-level primary schools (sixth and seventh years), with only 440 operating in the entire country. The secondary school sector consists of 81 schools, with fewer than 64,000 students receiving basic secondary education.
There are around 7,000 students enrolled in Mozambique's six university-level institutions and 15,000 in vocational colleges.
Literacy rate: 47 per cent adult rate; 63 per cent youth rate (15–24) (Unesco 2005).
Compulsory years: 6 to 13
Enrolment rate: 60 per cent gross primary enrolment, 7 per cent gross secondary enrolment; of relevant age group (including repeaters) (World Bank).
Pupils per teacher: 58 in primary schools

Health
With resources targetted at the growing problem of HIV/Aids, other healthcare needs are increasingly neglected. Moreover, the IMF forced the government to abandon its commitment to free healthcare provision and it is estimated that rural Mozambicans must walk an average of 46km to reach the nearest doctor. While modern health services reach around 40 per cent of the population the maternal mortality rate is high, and cholera has been rampant due to poor sanitation. However, mobile medical brigades have formed the backbone of the government's inoculation campaign, with polio virtually eradicated.

HIV/Aids
Mozambique has been one of the countries worst affected by the Aids pandemic which is sweeping Africa. Central provinces are more affected than southern and northern provinces with infection trends following the major transport routes and areas bordering Zimbabwe, Malawi and Zambia. In the cities of Chimoio and Tete, HIV seroprevalence in pregnant women is over 20 per cent.
HIV prevalence: 12.2 per cent aged 15–49 in 2003 (World Bank)
Life expectancy: 45 years, 2004 (WHO 2006)
Fertility rate/Maternal mortality rate: 4.9 births per woman, 2010 (Unicef); maternal mortality 1,100 per 100,000 live births (World Bank).
Birth rate/Death rate: 20 deaths and 40 births per 1,000 head of population (World Bank 2002).
Child (under 5 years) mortality rate (per 1,000): 90 per 1,000 live births (WHO 2012)
Head of population per physician: 0.03 physicians per 1,000 people, 2004 (WHO 2006)

Welfare
World Bank figures show 69 per cent of the population live in poverty.
Economic liberalisation, hailed as the driving force behind Mozambique's high growth levels, has also removed the safety nets that existed under the command economy. The minimum wage of US$30 per month is paltry and in many companies even the minimum is not paid and workers often receive their wages weeks or months late. There is no longer a basic ration of subsidised food, leaving many in the growing informal economy with little to eat.

Main cities
Maputo (capital, estimated population 1.1 million in 2012), Matola (817,008), Nampula (575,587), Beira (441,723), Chimoio 272,875), Nacala (230,229), Quelimane (212,519).

Languages spoken
Portuguese is spoken by less than 30 per cent of the population. English is widely spoken in business circles.
There are three main African language groups: Tsonga, Sena-Nyanja, Makua-Lomwe.

Official language/s
Portuguese

Media
Freedom of the press is guaranteed under the constitution; however there are libel laws that result in penalties under criminal law which may encourage self-censorship.

Press
Dailies: In Portuguese, from Muputo *Noticias* (www.jornalnoticias.co.mz) with the largest circulation and, from Beira, *Diario de Mozambique* are both government supported. The cost of printing severely hampers distribution of newspapers

and has resulted in a limit of two dailies published in different cities. Privately owned newspapers have resorted to faxing copies of newssheets around the country or via the internet; as such these newspapers arrive in an A4 format. MediaCoop, which owns the successful *Mediafax*, operates in this method to hundreds of direct subscribers.

Weeklies: In Portuguese *Fim de Semana* (www.fimdesemana.co.mz), *Savana*, *Domingo*, *Folha Universal* and *Demos* are independent magazines.

Periodicals: In English, the fortnightly *Mozambique Inview* is an independent publication.

Broadcasting

Radio: Radio services, particularly through community radio, are the main medium of mass communication and sources of news and information for most of the rural population.

The state-owned, Rádio Moçambique operates the Antena Nacional (www.rm.co.mz) network with stations throughout the country, with programmes in Portuguese, English and local languages. Other, private stations include Radio 99FM (www.99fm.co.mz) and Radio Maria Mozambique (www.radiomaria.org.mz) operated by the Catholic Church. Foreign services are provided by the South African TWR (www.twrafrica.org), the Portuguese RTP (http://tv.rtp.pt) and the French FRI (www.rfi.fr).

Television: The state-owned Televisão de Moçambique (TVM) (www.tvm.co.mz) is the only national network with one, commercial channel. Private TV stations include Radio televisão Klint (RTK), Soico Televisão (www.stv.co.mz) and TV Miramar (www.redemiramar.co.mz). Transmission coverage outside the region surrounding Maputo is poor, but there are moves to improve the situation.

National news agency: Agência de Informação de Moçambique (AIM)

Other news agencies: APA (African Press Agency): www.apanews.net

Reuters Africa: http://africa.reuters.com

Economy

Mozambique was one of the world's poorest countries in 1975 because of social mismanagement and a brutal civil war. Since then, a series of macroeconomic reforms combined with donor assistance and political stability has increased the country's GDP from US$4 billion in 1993 to US$30.9 billion in 2014. Despite these gains, more than half the population remains below the poverty line and subsistence agriculture still employs the vast majority of the country's workforce. A substantial trade imbalance persists although aluminium production from the Mozal smelter has significantly boosted export earning in recent years. Mozambique's GDP grew at an average annual rate of 6-8 per cent in the decade up to 2014, one of Africa's strongest performances. Its ability to attract large investment projects in natural resources is expected to extend high growth rates in coming years. Revenues from these vast resources, including natural gas, coal, titanium and hydroelectricity, could overtake donor assistance within five years.

The main agricultural cash crops include sugar, cotton and tea although these products face significant struggles in competing on the international market. Other agricultural products include cashew nuts, cassava, corn, coconuts, citrus and tropical fruits, potatoes, sunflowers; beef and poultry. The agriculture sector employs 81 per cent of the population and represents only 29 per cent of GDP.

The industry sector employs just 6 per cent of the population, mainly in aluminium, petroleum products, chemicals (fertilizer, soap, and paints), textiles, cement, glass, asbestos, tobacco, food and beverages. Heavy industrial production includes mega-projects (those that attract large foreign direct investment) such as the Mozal aluminium smelter, the 900km Sasol pipeline from Beira, the Maputo Corridor project (to develop infrastructure between southern Mozambique and South Africa) and the Chibuto heavy sand project. The industrial production growth rate was 9 per cent in 2014.

GDP growth was 6.8 per cent in 2008, falling marginally to 6.3 per cent in 2009 and returning to 6.8 per cent in 2010, despite the cut in world trade as the global economy slowed. GDP growth has since stabilised at a healthy 7.1 per cent in 2012 before increasing to 7.4 per cent in both 2013 and 2014. GDP per capita has reflected the rate of growth although it is still minimal, it steadily rose from US$362 in 2006 to a high of US$479 in 2008, before falling back to US$439 in 2010. Since then it has increased to US$1000 in 2012 before increasing to US$1100 in 2013 and then US$1200 in 2014. The inflation rate was 4.2 per cent in 2013 before falling to 2.3 per cent in 2014.

In 2014, the UN Human Development Index (HDI) ranked Mozambique as 178 (out of 187) for national development in health, education and income, a fall of 6 places from 184 in 2011. Since 2000, Mozambique's progress has strengthened steadily but has not matched the improvement of other countries in sub-Saharan Africa. In 2010, 64.6 per cent of the population experienced at least one indicator of poverty, while 60 per cent lived on less than the equivalent of US$1.25 per day; the headcount poverty rate was 79.3 per cent of the population (2000–10). Remittances from migrant workers amounted to US$132 million (1.2 per cent of GDP) in 2010 and were estimated to have remained constant in 2011.

On 2 October 2012, the German government, via the KfW Entwicklungsbank, granted EUR28.5 million (US$36.7 million) to fund, in large part, the expansion of financial services for small- and medium-sized enterprises (SMEs). The government will use the money to provide lines of microcredit, promote banking services, provide savings guarantees, support for the Gabinete Apoio a Pequena Indústria (GAPI) (Office for the Promotion of Small Businesses) as well as provide promotions to educate the public in financial matters.

Mozambique's government also took over Portugal's last remaining share in the Cahora Bassa Hydroelectricity Company (HCB) in 2012 which represents a significant contributor to the Southern African Power Pool.

External trade

Mozambique was one of the founding members of the Common Market of Eastern and Southern Africa (Comesa), but withdrew to concentrate on commercial opportunities with membership in the Southern African Development Community (SADC), the objectives of which include reducing trade barriers, achieving regional development and economic growth and evolving common systems and institutions. A free trade agreement is operation between 12 of the 14 members.

Mozambique provides a major transit route for landlocked areas and countries in southern Africa. Its ports and transfer services provide a significant amount of foreign earnings. An aluminium smelter processes local bauxite using domestically produced electricity.

Imports

Principal imports machinery and equipment, vehicles, chemicals, metal products, foodstuffs and textiles.

Main sources: South Africa (26.5 per cent of total in 2014), China (17.4 per cent) and India (16.6 per cent).

Exports

Principal exports are aluminium, prawns, cashews, cotton, sugar, citrus, timber and bulk electricity.

Main destinations: China (28.8 per cent of total in 2014), South Africa (20 per cent), Italy (7.7 per cent), Belgium (5.9 per cent), India (5.7 per cent) and Spain (5.2 per cent).

Agriculture

Farming

The agricultural sector is the mainstay of the economy, employing 80 per cent of the workforce, mainly engaged in subsistence farming, and accounting for 29 per cent of GDP. The main cash crops are cashew nuts, tea, sugar and cotton while other products include sunflowers, beef, poultry, copra, tobacco, oil seeds and some citrus and tropical fruits. Maize is the main subsistence crop, but cassava, millet, sorghum, groundnuts, beans and rice are also grown.

Some 45 per cent of the land area is considered suitable for agriculture, but only 4 per cent of that is under cultivation. Most production is carried out through rain-fed farming in the north, and much continues to be done by hand, with only 7 per cent of farmers using traction (animal or mechanical) and only 2 per cent using fertilisers and pesticides. The agricultural sector is dominated by peasant family smallholdings, which occupy 90 per cent of the total cultivated area. Only 5 per cent of cultivated land is used by commercial operations, which grow cash or export crops. There is significantly large potential for foreign investment in the agriculture sector due to the fertility and availability of unused cultivatable land.

Peace, good rains and an increase in the area under cultivation have resolved the chronic food deficit seen in the 1980s. However, food stocks are low and most families do not produce enough to build up a reserve of food and money that would see them through a bad harvest. Therefore, the sector is in need of ongoing structural improvement particularly in the fragile marketing systems and poor infrastructure. The state marketing body intervenes in the market in order to pay farmers for crops they have been unable to sell, either due to low prices on the open market or because the transport infrastructure is too poor. However, with bank credit scarce and with a reluctance of international financial institutions to support marketing boards, the state has been unable to fulfil its role completely. This has encouraged the growth of unscrupulous middlemen who demand lower farm gate prices.

On 3 October 2012, the International Fund for Agricultural Development (IFAD) granted a loan of US$16.3 million to fund agriculture, in three particular areas of development: irrigated horticulture, cassava cultivation and red meat production. Over 20,000 vulnerable rural households are expected to benefit from the projects.

Fishing

Fishing is of increasing importance. Prawns have become one of the sector's main exports. Mozambique's sustainable fish catch is estimated at 250,000 tonnes of which the majority is anchovy. The sustainable catch of prawns is estimated at 14,000 tonnes. Inland fish farming, especially of prawns, expanded.

Mozambique gets an estimated annual revenue of US$80 million (1 per cent of GDP) from exporting fish. Mozambican fisheries production has remained relatively stable and the role played by the government has been to promote strengthening of domestic supply without losing sight of international markets. Over-fishing, particularly in the shallow coastal waters, has left the majority small-scale fishermen, who do not have the boats or engines for deep-water fishing, without an income. Large international fishing boats mostly cause the over-fishing.

In a meeting of African ministers in Namibia, held in 2009, members discussed illegal and unregulated fishing, which is estimated to cost Africa US$1 billion per annum in lost revenue and the threat to stocks and local artisan fishing. A five-day meeting, organised with the UN Food and Agriculture Organization (FAO) aimed to address regional fish stocks, over-fishing, and sustainable management in 2014.

Forestry

There is an important forestry sector, based on the exploitation of hardwoods from Zambezia, Sofala, Nampula, Manica and Niassa provinces. Almost 50 per cent of land is categorised as other wooded land. Wood fuel comprises almost 80 per cent of the country's energy needs. A wide variety of non-wood forest products includes grass, bamboo, medicinal plants and other wild edible plants. Forestry resources are exploited on a more systematic basis than previously and the government compels timber concerns to initiate reforestation programmes. The government-owned Industrias Florestais de Manica (Ifloma), which manages 20,000ha of forest, has established a sawmill and particle-board factory with Swedish government and Arab fund assistance.

An independent company valued the forestry sector in Mozambique as having a net present value of US$161 million, based on businesses having 11 concessions covering 280,000 hectares in 2014. Obtala Resources PLC is set to complete the acquisition of 50-year leases for two new timber concessions totalling 35,000 hectares in Mozambique bringing the total forestry area to 315,000 hectares. The company has predicted that sales over the 10 year period beginning in 2014 will be US$395 million.

Industry and manufacturing

During the 1980s and 1990s, government policy emphasised the production of consumer goods, especially food, beverages and textiles, where supplies can be locally sourced, in an attempt to reduce import dependency and strengthen the market for peasant farmers producing cash crops. However, industry suffered from capital shortages, poor infrastructure and the high cost of credit. Manufacturers rely largely on internal funding from operating profits or owner savings. Recent metallurgical investments promise a dramatic departure from Mozambique's import substituting industrialisation strategy.

The greatest problems have occurred in the food processing industry, with cashew nut and sugar production particularly affected. Cashew nut prices have plummeted due to increased output in India, where production is more cost-effective and tree-planting has increased. India intends to become self-sufficient in cashew nuts, which is dealing a big blow to this important sector in Mozambique. The situation has been exacerbated by the damaging policy of trade liberalisation demanded by the World Bank, which had originally advised Mozambique to stop processing cashew nuts domestically, close down the processing factories and export unshelled nuts to India.

Sugar refining is another industry which was in the doldrums. Mozambican sugar mills were severely affected by the civil war, which virtually wiped out the industry. Foreign investment, mostly from South African companies such as Illovo, has been the driving force behind the rehabilitation of the sector.

Limak Holding has started the construction of its 2 million tons per year cement plant in Maputo, the plant is scheduled to come into operation in 2016. Its initial investment was worth US$40 million and it is prepared to increase their investment to US$150 million if required. A second cement plant is also set to begin operation instigated by Cimentos da Beira in November 2015, it will have annual production capacity of 800,000 tons and it will employ 70 workers. US$45 million was invested from the UK and South Africa.

By far the most important industrial project in Mozambique is the Mozal aluminium smelter. The plant is owned by BHP-Billiton (the leading shareholder), Mitsubishi, South Africa's Industrial Development Corporation (IDC) and the Mozambican government. The US$1.2 billion smelter is one of the largest industrial projects in sub-Saharan Africa and began production in June 2000, six months ahead of schedule. The US$1 billion second phase of the project has seen capacity rise to 506,000 tonnes of aluminium per annum. Mozal is the world's cheapest producer of aluminium, and costs will continue to fall as capacity is increased. The completion of the project has led to around US$800 million in aluminium exports per year, increasing total exports by over 300 per cent of 2000 levels and adding up to 20 per cent to GDP. However, most of the profits from the smelter has been repatriated by its foreign investors and since it is highly capital intensive, it will not have a significant impact on employment. Although Mozal appears as a success story for Mozambique's development, it has had a limited long-term role in alleviating poverty and generating growth in other sectors.

Tourism

Mozambique has the potential to be a great tourist destination with its varied terrain, including wetlands, forests and the Limpopo River, as well as game and nature reserves. However, it lacks the infrastructure to provide the deep penetration of visitors into the country, nor when they arrive the accommodation necessary. The capital city Maputo has the only international airport, which again limits the potential for expansion, and contains around half the total number of hotels available (around 4,000 hotels) within the country. The contribution of travel and tourism was 7 per cent of total GDP in 2014 (US$819 million). This is set to increase to US$1.6 billion by 2025. Employment in the sector constitutes 6 per cent of total employment (720,500 jobs), the industry is forecast to support 940,000 jobs by 2025. National investment in the industry is forecast to be 4.3 per cent in 2015. The sector has attracted capital investment of US$131 million in 2014.

Environment

Unexpectedly high rainfall caused severe flooding in January 2008, forcing around 100,000 people living along the Zambezi River to be displaced. By February when waters had begun to receed the authorities for the Kariba Dam in Zambia announced that for safety reasons they had to release more water. The overflow was estimated to have displaced another 40,000 people as the water from the upper reaches of the river arrived downstream.

Mining

Mining is limited to gold in Manica province, pegmatites, ilmenite, zircon, rutile, monazite, tantalum, copper, marble and semi-precious stones. The sector is small and contributed 3.6 per cent of GDP in 2013. The large increase from the 1.6 per cent in 2009 can be largely attributed to the coal sector. Coal production in 2013 was 7.5 million tons a year representing a 4.8 million ton increase over the 2012 figure. In order to make coal mining profitable, infrastructure needs to be greatly improved because currently it is inadequate.

There are around 50,000 artisanal miners who concentrate their operations on gold and gemstone extraction. Kenmare Resources has two gold licences in Niassa, with reserves of 200,000 ounces. Kenmare also has a licence for the titanium reserves at Congolone, which is considered one of the most valuable undeveloped titanium mines in the world. The titanium reserves near Xai-Xai, about 250km north of Maputo, have the potential to develop a second large mineral smelter project in the region.

Xtract Resources has formed a partnership with Mineral Technologies International Ltd in 2015 to explore an alluvial gold concession in the province of Manica, Mozambique. The companies hope that the partnership will annually extract 32,000 ounces of gold, in addition to gold from an open pit mine. Xtract Resources already acquired a gold mining license in Manica from Auroch Minerals, an Austrlaian mining company, for US$10 million.

There are considerable secondary mineral resources, including iron, graphite, fluorites, mica, lime clays, tin, nickel and bauxite. There has been little foreign interest in developing these resources.

A Dutch based mining firm, Advanced Metallurgical Group has secured funding to develop its graphite mine and processing plant at Ancuabe in the northern Mozambican province of Cabo Delgado. The US$9.4 million funding will come from a German Investment and Development Corporation, DEG. Mining will begin in 2016 with an expected initial production of 6,000 tonnes of graphite per year.

Hydrocarbons

There are no known reserves of oil. Mozambique relies entirely on refined oil imports, mainly from South Africa, with consumption of 24,000 barrels of oil per day.

There are substantial reserves of gas, estimated at 2.8 trillion cubic metres (cum) in 2015, with production at 4.4 billion cum. Mozambique is becoming a major gas producer in the region, with an 865km pipeline exporting natural gas to South Africa. Mozambique consumes 755 million cum annually, and therefore, it is fully self-sufficient in natural gas.

Mozambique is set to experience positive gas consumption growth as the government looks to increase the use of natural gas in domestic power generation. For example, Investec Power has begun a Kuvaninga project in Mozambique to construct and operate a 40.3 MW gas-fired power plant near the town of Chokwé. The plant will be located alongside the natural gas pipeline, co-owned by petroleum company Sasol and Mozambique's government. The gas will be converted into power and supplied to the regional electricity grid – EDM.

Unfortunately, the lower price environment for both oil and natural gas means that companies will have to secure more off-take agreements before reach final investment decisions. Furthermore, it is unclear whether these projects in developing the natural gas market in Mozambique will be economically viable at current pricing levels, and given expectations for a slow recovery in oil prices over the coming years.

However, in 2015, India's third largest oil refining company is negotiating the purchase of natural gas to be extracted in Mozambique to supply a future terminal in Gujarat. The natural liquefied gas port in the port of Chhara with a capacity of 5 million tons should be operational in 2019 following an estimated investment of US$850 million.

Proven coal reserves are approximately six billion tonnes, mined at Moatize in Tete province. The 670km Sena Railway line, running from the coal-rich mines of northern Moatize to the Indian Ocean port of Kacala, will be restored by 2015, following an agreement for funding by the Dutch and Danish governments and the EU in October 2009. Although the line was cleared of unexploded ordnance in 2006, it was unserviceable and the port silted up. When fully modernised the line will become a regional transhipment route. Coal production in 2013 was 6.8 million tonnes a year representing a 4.4 million tonnes increase over the 2012 figure. In order to make coal mining profitable, infrastructure needs to be greatly improved because currently it is inadequate.

Energy

Total installed generating capacity was 2.43 gigawatts in 2013, 90 per cent of which comes from hydroelectric plants and 10 per cent of which comes from fossil fuels. Mozambique is one of the largest energy producers in the Southern African Development Community (SADC) and a member of the Southern African Power Pool (Sapp), set up to provide reliable and economical energy supplies to all 12 member countries in the region.

The state-owned Electricidade de Moçambique (EDM) is responsible for generation, transmission and distribution. A Mozambique energy company

Hidroelectrica de Cahora Bassa, owns the biggest hydroelectric scheme in Southern Africa, which exports electricity to South Africa from the Cahora Bassa hydroelectric dam. The government has plans to expand the dam and build additional dams to increase its electricity exports and fulfil the needs of its burgeoning domestic industries.

There are a number of ongoing proposals to increase output based on the considerable potential in hydroelectric power and thermal power stations. These include the Moatize thermal power station (1,000MW) and a 2,000MW coal-fired power station, which is planned in conjunction with a new coalmine at Moatize, to be built by the Brazilian Companhia Vale do Rio Doce (CVRD), mining company.

Investec Power has begun a Kuvaninga project in Mozambique which is to construct and operate a 40.3 MW gas-fired power plant near the town of Chokwé. The plant will be located alongside the natural gas pipeline, co-owned by petroleum company Sasol and Mozambique's government. The gas will be converted into power and supplied to the regional electricity grid – EDM.

Financial markets

The listing of enterprises has seen slow and modest growth, although the privatisation programme will provide potential for growth.

Stock exchange

The Bolsa de Valores de Moçambique (BVM) (Mozambique Stock Exchange) opened in October 1999.

Banking and insurance

All banks in Mozambique are privately owned, with more foreign competition entering the sector with the completion of the bank privatisation process in 2002 when Banco Austral was sold to Absa.

On 2 October 2012, the German government, via the KfW Entwicklungsbank, granted €28.5 million (US$36.7 million) to fund, in large part, the expansion of financial services for small- and medium-sized enterprises (SMEs). The government will use the money to provide lines of microcredit, promote banking services, provide savings guarantees, support for the Gabinete Apoio a Pequena Indústria (GAPI) (Office for the Promotion of Small Businesses) as well as provide promotions to educate the public in financial matters.

Central bank

Banco de Moçambique, with branches throughout the country.

Main financial centre

Maputo

Time

GMT plus two hours

Geography

Mozambique lies on the east coast of Africa, south of the equator. It is bordered by Tanzania to the north; Malawi, Zambia and Zimbabwe to the west; South Africa and Swaziland to the south and south-west; and by the Indian Ocean to the east (2,470km of coastline).

The country is divided into the coastal lowlands and plateaux (200–600 metres over most of the central region and north, reaching 1,000 metres in the north-west). The country is crossed by a large number of rivers, including the Zambezi (navigable for 460km), the Limpopo and the Save.

Hemisphere

Southern

Climate

Mozambique has two main seasons: a hot, normally wet season from October to March and a cooler, mostly dry season from April to September.

In the extreme south the mean annual temperature is around 23 degrees Celsius (C), with a difference of about 8 degrees C between the hottest and coldest months. In the north the mean annual temperature is about 25 degrees C. The temperature in Maputo is influenced by the direction of the wind and wide variations are experienced, especially during the cool season. Temperatures in Maputo can reach as high as 45 degrees C.

Most rain falls in the second half of the hot season. Northern regions receive 640–1,280mm and southern regions may receive 260–1,540mm. The average is 770mm.

Dress codes

During the hot wet season (October–March) light cotton clothes are advisable. During the temperate dry season (April–September) light or medium weight clothing should suffice. Warmer clothing is required for frequent cold spells.

Entry requirements

Passports

Required by all, valid for a minimum of six months beyond the intended date of departure.

Visa

Required by all. A proposed tourist *univisa* (a single visa to visit all 15-member states of SADC: Angola, Botswana, DRC, Lesotho, Madagascar, Malawi, Mauritius, Mozambique, Namibia, South Africa, Seychelles, Swaziland, Tanzania, Zambia and Zimbabwe) is expected to be in use by 2013. Visitors should check with the appropriate consulates to confirm start of *univisas* and their scope before beginning a tour of southern Africa.

Business visas require a letter from the visitor's company and should include an itinerary.

Currency advice/regulations

The import and export of local currency is prohibited. Unlimited import of foreign currency is allowed, subject to declaration on arrival; export of foreign currency is limited to the amount declared on arrival. It is advisable to take travellers cheques or currency in sterling, US dollars or South African rands. Travellers entering Mozambique have to fill out a statement detailing the amount of currency in bank notes, cheques and travellers cheques being brought into the country. The declaration is passed over to the Exchange Control Office at the point of entry.

A new 'family' of bank notes came into circulation on 1 July 2006. This was part of wider currency reforms which also dropped three zeros, making 50,000 old meticais 50 meticais. The new notes (1,000, 500, 200, 100, 50 and 20 meticais) all bear the face of Samora Machel, who was Mozambique's first president after independence.

Prohibited imports

Illegal drugs and pornography. A permit is required for firearms.

Health (for visitors)

Mandatory precautions

Yellow fever certificate if arriving from an infected area.

Advisable precautions

Typhoid, polio, tetanus and hepatitis A and B vaccinations are recommended. Malaria prophylaxis is essential as risk exists throughout the country, and cerebral malaria occurs in some places. There is a risk of rabies.

Water precautions are advisable, especially in the rural areas where bilharzia is present. Some milk is unpasteurised and should be boiled. Avoid dairy products and only eat well-cooked hot meat and fish. Vegetables must be cooked and fruit peeled.

Medical facilities are minimal and many medicines are not available. Basic medical supplies, medicines and sterile syringes should be carried. Full medical insurance is essential. Insurance cover which provides for medical evacuation by air to South Africa is advisable.

Hotels

Good accommodation is available in Maputo and Beira, but of lower quality elsewhere. Bills must be paid in hard currency, travellers cheques or credit cards.

Public holidays (national)

Fixed dates

1 Jan (New Year's Day), 3 Feb (Heroes' Day), 7 Apr (Women's Day), 1 May (Workers' Day), 25 Jun (Independence

Day), 7 Sep (Victory Day), 25 Sep (Armed Forces' Day), 25 Dec (National Family/Christmas Day).

Working hours

Banking

Mon–Fri: 0745–1130.

Business

Mon–Thu: 0730–1230, 1400–1730; Fri: 0730–1230, 1400–1700.

Government

Mon–Thu: 0730–1230, 1400–1730; Fri: 0730–1230, 1400–1700.

Shops

Mon–Fri: 0800–1230; 1400–1800; Sat: 0800–1330.

Electricity supply

220 V AC, 50 cycles.

Social customs/useful tips

The courtesies and modes of address customary in Portugal and other Latin countries are still observed. Visitors are normally addressed as O *Senhor*. Occasionally *camarada* (comrade) is used, but this is not correct outside the circles of the ruling party, Frente de Libertaçao de Moçambique (Frelimo), and is discouraged.

Security

Street crime is an increasingly serious problem, with armed robbery prevalent in Maputo. Visitors should not carry or display cash or jewellery, and are advised not to venture outside well-lit, busy streets. Female visitors should not walk unaccompanied along any beaches in Mozambique.

Visitors should check conditions with the local authorities before travelling outside major urban areas and should be aware that Mozambique has a severe problem with landmines left over from the conflict between Frelimo and Renamo.

Identity documents should be carried at all times.

Getting there

Air

National airline: Linhas Aéreas de Moçambique (LAM) (Mozambique Airlines)

International airport/s: Mavalane International (MPM), 3km north of Maputo; bank, restaurant, bar, car hire and post office. Beira (BEW), 13km from the city; restaurant, shops, car hire and post office.

Airport tax: US$20 destinations outside Africa; US$10 destinations within Africa.

Surface

Road: Road access is possible from all neighbouring countries except Tanzania; there are good paved roads from South Africa and Zimbabwe. The condition of roads in Mozambique is poor and banditry along major highways threatens the safety of road travellers. Travel outside Maputo often requires four-wheel drive vehicles.

Rail: Rail services can be unreliable. A daily service runs from Johannesburg to the border at Komatipoort where there is a connection to Maputo. There is also an overnight train from Durban to Maputo. A service runs from Harare to Beira. There are connections from Malawi to Beira but the border has to be crossed on foot.

Water: There are no regular passenger services.

Main port/s: Beira, Maputo, Nacala and Quelimane.

Getting about

National transport

Mozambique acts as a corridor between the ports of the Indian Ocean and the landlocked countries of the African hinterland with both rail and road tending to run east-west, with very few north-south connections.

Air: Travel between cities within Mozambique is best by air. LAM and Air Corridor operate domestic service to main towns. Local and charter flights can also be arranged with companies with offices at Maputo Airport.

Road: There are around 30,000km of roads in Mozambique. Good roads connect Maputo to main centres. Many roads are unpaved and are impassable in the rainy season (November–April).

In July 2010 the government announced plans to build a new bridge across the Zambezi river to improve access to Tete province and the coal deposits there. There are also plans to construct a forth deep water port to ease traffic on Maputo, Beira and Nacala.

Buses: There are services covering most parts of the country but are restricted by the state of the roads.

Rail: There are three separate networks: in the south (Maputo to Swaziland, South Africa and Zimbabwe), in the centre (Beira to Zimbabwe and Malawi) and in the north (Nacala to Malawi and to Lichinga). There is no link between Maputo and Beira. There are some branch lines (Xai-Xai to Manjacase; Inhambane to Inharrime; and Quelimane to Mocuba). Services are unreliable. In 2009 the government announced it had funding to build a new line to link the port of Nacala with mines in the north by 2015.

Water: There are plans to construct a forth deep water port to ease traffic on Maputo, Beira and Nacala.

City transport

Taxis: Available in cities, taxis are metered but for long journeys fares should be negotiated. A 10 per cent tip is usual.

Car hire

Car rental is available at airports and hotels. Only hard currency will be accepted. International licence required. Traffic drives on the left. Driving after dark can be hazardous due to other vehicles travelling without headlights.

BUSINESS DIRECTORY

The addresses listed below are a selection only. While World of Information makes every endeavour to check these addresses, we cannot guarantee that changes have not been made, especially to telephone numbers and area codes. We would welcome any corrections.

Telephone area codes

The international dialling code (IDD) for Mozambique is +258 followed by the area code and subscriber's number. New area codes came into operation 1 August 2005.

Beira	23	Maputo	21
Chokwe	221	Nampula	26

Chambers of Commerce

American-Mozambique Chamber of Commerce, Rua Mateus Sansão Muthemba 452, Maputo (tel: 492-904; fax: 492-779; e-mail: mail@mail.ccmusa.co.mz).

Mozambique Camara de Comercio, Rua Mateus Sansão Muthemba 452, Maputo (tel: 491-970; fax: 492-211).

Portugal-Mozambique Chamber of Commerce, Hotel Rovuma Centro de Escritórios, Rua da Sé 114, Maputo (tel: 300-229; fax: 300-232; e-mail: ccpmoc@teledata.mz).

South Africa-Mozambique Chamber of Commerce, FACIM, Avenida 10 de Novembro, Maputo (tel/fax: 431-621).

Banking

Banco Comercial do Moçambique, PO Box 865, Av 25 de Setembro 1800, Maputo (tel: 307-533, 307-471, 307-532; fax: 307-564/557/543).

Banco Internacional de Moçambique SARL, Av Zedequias Manganhela 478, Maputo (tel: 429-390/3; fax: 429-389).

Banco Standard Totta de Moçambique SARL, PO Box 2086, Praça 25 de Junho Nr 1, Maputo (tel: 423-041/5, 424-405, 301-616; fax: 426-967, 423-029).

Banco de Fomento SARL; Av. Julius Nyerere 1016, Maputo (tel. 494-010/1; fax: 494-401).

Banco de Moçambique, PO Box 423, Av 25 de Setembro 1679, Maputo (tel: 428-150/9; fax: 429-721).

BIM Investimento SARL, Av Kim Il Sung 961, Maputo (tel: 490-085/7; fax: 490-212; e-mail: bimi@vircom.com).

BNP Nedbank (Mocambique) SARL, PO Box 1445, Prédio 33 Andares; Av 25 de Setembro 1230, Maputo (tel: 306-700;

fax: 306-305; e-mail: bnpnebank@bnpnedbank.co.mz).

Novo Banco SARL, Av.do Trabalho, 750-Sede, Maputo (tel: 407-755/6, 408-209; fax: 407-755/6, 408-210; e-mail: novobanco@teledata.mz).

Uniao Comercial de Bancos (Moçambique) SARL, Av. Fredrich Engels 400, Maputo (tel: 499-900, 495-221-5 fax: 498-675; e-mail: banque_fc@teledata.mz).

Central bank

Banco de Moçambique, Avenida 25 de Setembro 1695, PO Box 423, Maputo (tel: 318-001; fax: 323-712; e-mail: cdi@bancomoc.mz).

Stock exchange

The Bolsa de Valores de Moçambique (BVM) (Mozambique Stock Exchange) opened in October 1999.

Travel information

Empresa Nacional de Turismo (ENT) (Mozambique National Tourism Company), PO Box 2446, Avenida 25 de Setembro 1203, Maputo (tel: 420-324; fax: 421-795).

Linhas Aereas de Moçambique, Avenida Karl Marx 220, PO Box 2060, Maputo (tel: 326-001; fax: 496-105; e-mail: commercial@lam.co.mz).

Ministry of tourism

Ministry of Tourism, Avenida 25 de Setembro 1018, PO Box 4101, Maputo (tel: 313-755; fax: 306-212; e-mail: info@turismo.imoz.com).

National tourist organisation offices

Fundo Nacional do Turismo-FUTURA, Avenida de 25 Setembro 1203, PO Box 4758, Maputo (tel: 307-320; fax: 307-324; e-mail: info@futur.org.mz).

Ministries

Ministry of Commerce, Industry and Tourism, Praça do 25 Junho 37, Maputo (tel: 426-091/7).

Ministry of Finance and Planning, Praça da Marinha Popular, CP 272, Maputo (tel: 420-648; fax: 425-240).

Ministry of Industry and Energy, Avenida 25 de Setembro, PO Box 2904, 1502 Maputo (tel: 420-963, 492-011).

Ministry of Trade, PO Box 1831, Maputo (tel: 426-091/7; fax: 421-305).

Other useful addresses

Agência de Informação de Moçambique (AIM), CP 896, Maputo (tel: 430-795).

Agência Nacional de Frete e Navegação (ANFRENA) (main national shipping agency), Rua Consiglieri Pedroson 366, CP 1430, Maputo (tel: 427-064, 428-111).

BP Mozambique, PO Box 854, Maputo (tel: 425-021/5; fax: 426-042).

British Council, Travessa da Catembe 21 (corner of Av Martires de Inhaminga 1421), CP 4178, Maputo (tel: 421-571; fax: 421-577).

British Embassy, Av Vladimir I Lenine 310, CP 55, Maputo (tel: 420-111/2/5/6/7; fax: 421-666).

Commonwealth Development Corporation, Maputo (tel: 421-325; fax: 422-150).

Direcção Nacional Portos e Caminhos de Ferro (railways), PO Box 276, Maputo (tel: 420-748, 424-133, 430-151).

Empresa Nacional de Minas, PO Box 1152, Maputo (tel: 423-933).

Empresa Nacional de Portos e Caminhos de Ferro de Moçambique, Maputo (tel: 427-173).

Empresa Nacional Petroleos de Moçambique (Petromoc), PO Box 417, Maputo (tel: 427-191/7).

FACIM, PO Box 1761, Maputo (tel: 423-713, 427-151/2; fax: 427-129) (annual international trade fair).

Hidroelectrica de Cabora Bassa (HCB) (operators of Cabora Bassa power complex), Head Office, CP 263, Songo, Tete (tel: 82-221/4; fax: 82-364); PO Box 4120, Maputo (tel: 400-551, 400-647, 491-346, 492-976).

Imprensa Nacional de Moçambique (publishes statistical bulletins, census information etc), PO Box 275, Maputo.

Maputo Development Corridor, Maputo (tel: 426-359; fax: 430-159).

Mozambique Embassy (USA), Suite 570, 1990 M Street, NW, Washington DC 20036 (tel: (+1-202)-293-7146; fax: (+1-202)-835-0245; e-mail: embamoc@aol.com).

Mozambique Institute of Export Promotion (IPEX) (Government agency for export promotion), Av 25 de Setembro 1008, PO Box 4487, Maputo (tel: 423-343).

Office for Foreign Investment Promotion (GPIE), Av 25 de Setembro 2049, 2 andar, PO Box 2049, Maputo (tel: 422-456/7; fax: 422-459).

Radio Moçambique, PO Box 2000, Maputo (tel: 434-041/5, 432-591; fax: 421-816).

Technical Unit for Enterprise Restructuring (UTRE) (information on company tenders for privatisation and investment opportunities), Ministry of Planning and Finance, Rua da Imprensa No 256, 7th Floor, Suites 704-708, PO Box 4350, Maputo (tel: 426-514/6; fax: 421-541).

Televisão de Moçambique, Av Julius Nyerere 942, PO Box 2675, Maputo (tel: 491-198).

World Bank, Maputo (tel: 492-841; fax: 492-893).

National news agency: Agência de Informação de Moçambique (AIM)

APA (African Press Agency): www.apanews.net

Reuters Africa: http://africa.reuters.com

Internet sites

Africa Business Network: http://www.ifc.org/abn

AllAfrica.com: http://allafrica.com

African Development Bank: http://www.afdb.org

Africa Online: http://www.africaonline.com

Mbendi AfroPaedia (information on companies, countries, industries and stock exchanges in Africa): http://mbendi.co.za

Myanmar

KEY FACTS

Official name: Myanmar Naingngandaw (The Union of Myanmar)

Head of State: President Thein Sein (from 4 Feb 2011)

Head of government: President Thein Sein

Ruling party: Union Solidarity and Development Party (USDP) (from 7 Nov 2010)

Area: 676,552 square km

Population: 51.42 million (2014)*

Capital: Naypyidaw (Abode of Kings) (from 2005)

Official language: Myanmar (Burmese)

Currency: Kyat (Kt) = 100 pyas; from 2 April 2012 the kyat became a managed floating currency starting at K818 per US dollar.

Exchange rate: Kt1,288.00 per US$ (Sep 2015)

GDP per capita: US$1,221 (2014)*

GDP real growth: 7.69% (2014)

GDP: US$62.80 billion (2014)

Unemployment: 4.00% (2014)*

Inflation: 5.94% (2014)

Natural gas production: 16.80 billion cum (2014)

Balance of trade: -US$439.90 million (2013)

Annual FDI: US$1.00 billion (2011)

* estimated figure

Nota

Myanmar's official national accounts data are available only on an annual basis with a two-year lag and they show considerably higher rates of GDP growth that are inconsistent with correlates of growth such as energy use..

If Myanmar were to mint a post election commemorative coin at the end of 2015, there was every likelihood that it would bear the image of the hugely popular figure of Aung San Suu Kyi. In the run up to the 8 November 2015 election, observers expected her either to be about to become president, or, despite massive popularity, a gerrymandered election to have enabled Myanmar's ex-military politicians to have engineered her exclusion from power. As noted by Martin Woolacott in the London *Guardian* newspaper, 'if she is not given the opportunity to stand for the presidency, which is an indirectly elected position, the democratic new start the regime has promised will be deeply flawed.'

For some time in mid-2015 it was by no means clear whether 'Daw Suu' (Aung San Suu Kyi's popular nickname – which translates as 'The Lady') would actually get to stand for president. There had been some speculation that the opposition National League for Democracy (NLD) party, which looked to be a dead cert for a considerable number of seats in both houses of parliament, might boycott the election. However, parliament's decision to bar her from the presidency for the obscure reason that her two sons hold British passports, appeared to stiffen the sinews of the NLD as, with the support of Aung San Suu Kyi, it decided to contest the elections.

If, as expected and as it turned out, there were no amendments, Aung San Suu Kyi had said her party 'had several plans in mind.' One of these plans presumably included constitutional changes that would enable her to become president. She was also known to have asked Myanmar's President Thein Sein to take up proposals for talks on the transition to democracy that had been on the table for two years.

In the event the NLD achieved a landslide victory and by 13 November it was confirmed that the NLD had won the two-thirds of seats they needed to control both houses of parliament and choose the next president. The Union Solidarity Development Party (USDP) of the military won only some 40 seats. The change-over in government will not happen until February 2016. Aung San Suu Kyi, who is currently barred from becoming president under the constitution, will wield power behind the scenes as NLD leader, and has asked President Thein Sein, parliamentary speaker Shwe Mann and military chief Min Aung Hlaing to hold talks aimed at a smooth transition of power.

Rohingyas

Aung San Suu Kyi's voice has been curiously absent from the debate on Myanmar's treatment of its Rohingya population. Many Rohingyas had been treated like common criminals by the Myanmar authorities, rounded up from their villages (many of which were subsequently destroyed) and herded into camps, allegedly for their own protection. Myanmar had firmly rejected United Nations (UN) allegations that it was this treatment that had caused so many Rohingya to flee the country – many aimlessly drifting around the Bay of Bengal and the Andaman Sea on inadequate craft after paying traffickers large sums of money to get them out of Myanmar. The Rohingyas have, with some justification, been called one of the most persecuted minorities in the world, unable to claim citizenship in Myanmar (where an estimated 1.1 million of them were living in the Western Rakhine). Their social and political exclusion worsened in 2012, following the rape and murder of a Rakhine woman. In protest Rakhine mobs ran amok, killing an estimated 200 people. Subsequently, almost 150,000 Rohingyas were forced into the camps, denied schooling and medical attention. As Myanmar's November 2015 elections approached, the International Organisation for Migration (IOM) called for the 'root causes' of the exodus and the virtual imprisonment of Rohingyas to be addressed.

But those root causes lay very, very, deep; a small Muslim community had lived in Rakhine since the eighth century. In the nineteenth century, under British (Indian) administration, the Rakhine area saw an influx of Muslim Bengalis, which created social and religious tensions with the region's Buddhist natives who called the Rohingyas simply Bengalis, thereby

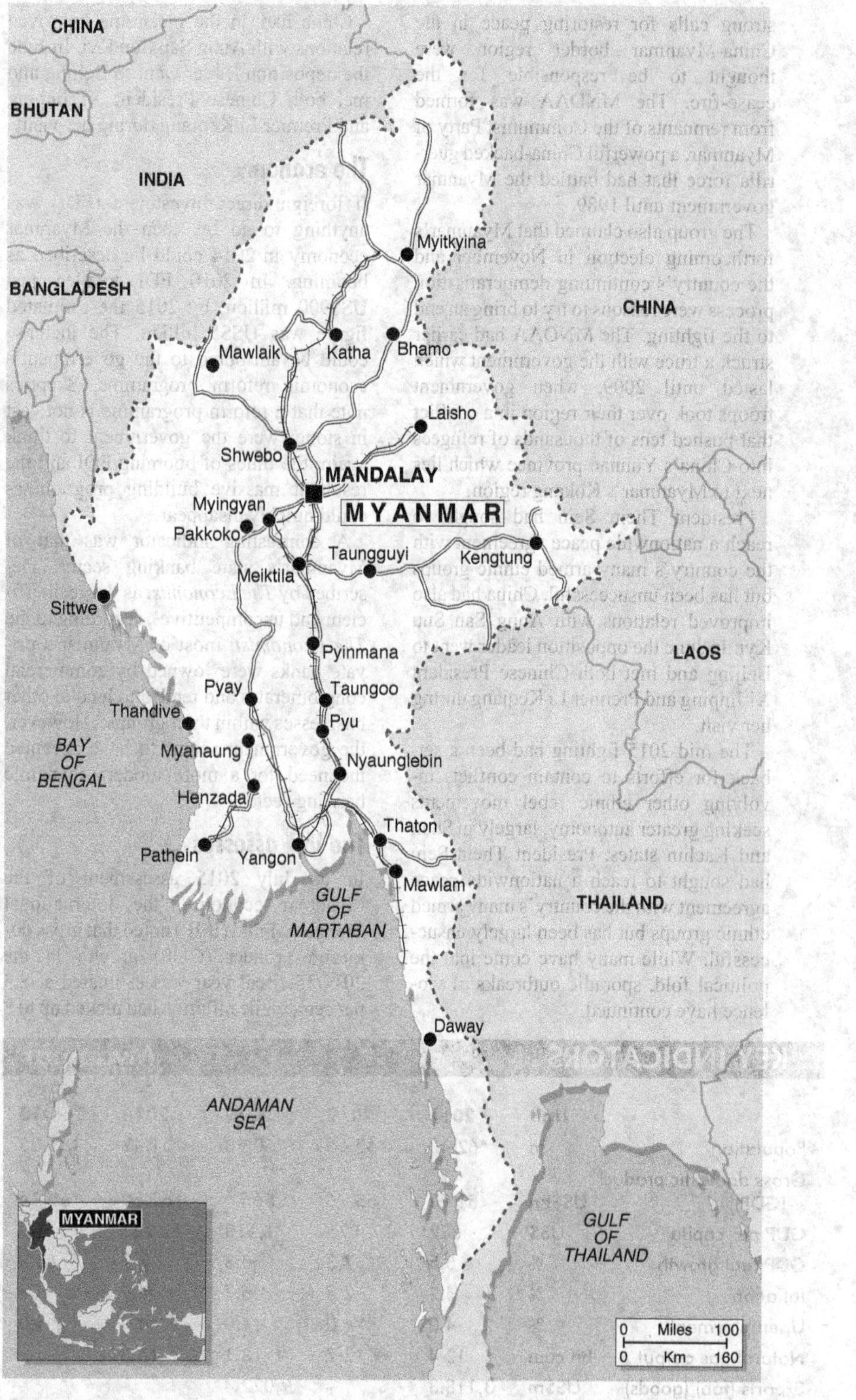

underlining their different origins. An extended article in the London *Economist* described the Rohingyas as 'the most persecuted people on earth.' The religious divide was one factor, as was the ethnic factor. But there were others. During the Second World War the Rohingyas had lent support to the Japanese and after the war Burmese military governments refrained from granting any sort of recognition to the Rohingyas.

Representatives of the International State Crime Initiative (ISCI) at the University of London quoted by the *Economist*, had claimed that the ethnic cleansing in 2012 of the Rohingyas was a stage in 'the process of genocide.' The ISCI had identified 'five stages of genocide', the first four of which had already been experienced by the Rohingyas. The final stage, that of mass annihilation, still awaited them unless the international community found a way of intervening. Aung San Suu Kyi's silence was shared by virtually every Myanmar politician; for them, Buddhist votes seemed to be more important.

Ethnic discord

While a mesmerised world watched events in Ukraine, something similar was happening in Myanmar, which entered 2015 with its military in charge of most of those eastern states bordering China. The Kokang 'special region' area had been evacuated as troops took over, accompanied by the occasional sound of heavy artillery.

The roots of this issue date back to the 1980s when ethnic Chinese attempted to break away from the heavy hand of the (then) Rangoon, now Yangon, government. A so-called special administrative region (SAR) was created which the Rangoon government allowed ethnic Chinese to control. The SAR soon became a hub for drug production and smuggling.

February 2015 saw fighting between the ethnic Chinese and the military increase in the Kokang region, causing some 10,000 ethnic Chinese to flee into China. The dispute reflected the faultline in Myanmar's relationship with its more powerful neighbour. Three separate groups of ethnic Chinese were confronting the Myanmar military, allegedly receiving support from Chinese officials. President Thein Sein had handed power in the area over to the military and imposed a three-month period of martial law. The leader of the Myanmar National Democratic Alliance Army (MNDAA), Pheung Kya-shin (Péng Jiasheng in Burmese) returned to Myanmar after five years in exile in China.

In June 2015 one of the ethnic Chinese rebel groups that had been battling the Myanmar military on the border with China announced a unilateral ceasefire, after reportedly coming under pressure from Beijing to end four months of intense fighting. The MNDAA led by Péng Jiasheng, (its political wing is the Kokang Democracy Party (KDP) headed by Yang Mao-liang) announced that it had agreed the ceasefire with government forces. The MNDAA is not to be confused with the National Democratic Alliance Army (NDAA). The Chinese government's strong calls for restoring peace in the China-Myanmar border region were thought to be responsible for the cease-fire. The MNDAA was formed from remnants of the Communist Party of Myanmar, a powerful China-backed guerrilla force that had battled the Myanmar government until 1989.

The group also claimed that Myanmar's forthcoming election in November and the country's continuing democratisation process were reasons to try to bring an end to the fighting. The MNDAA had earlier struck a truce with the government which lasted until 2009, when government troops took over their region in a conflict that pushed tens of thousands of refugees into China's Yunnan province which lies next to Myanmar's Kokang region.

President Thein Sein had sought to reach a nationwide peace agreement with the country's many armed ethnic groups but has been unsuccessful. China had also improved relations with Aung San Suu Kyi. In June the opposition leader went to Beijing and met both Chinese President Xi Jinping and Premier Li Keqiang during her visit.

The mid-2015 fighting had been a setback for efforts to contain conflicts involving other ethnic rebel movements seeking greater autonomy, largely in Shan and Kachin states. President Thein Sein had sought to reach a nationwide peace agreement with the country's many armed ethnic groups but has been largely unsuccessful. While many have come into the political fold, sporadic outbreaks of violence have continued.

China had, in the meantime improved relations with Aung San Suu Kyi. In June the opposition leader went to Beijing and met both Chinese President Xi Jinping and Premier Li Keqiang during her visit.

The economy

If foreign direct investment (FDI) was anything to go by, then the Myanmar economy in 2014 could be described as booming. In 2010 FDI totalled just US$900 million; by 2015 the estimated figure was US$5 billion. The increase could be attributed to the government's economic reform programme. Skeptics note that a reform programme is not cast in stone; were the government to think again, the times of booming FDI and the resultant massive building programmes could quickly disappear.

A contrasting indicator was that of Myanmar's state banking sector. Described by *The Economist* as 'large, inefficient and uncompetitive', according to the *The Economist*, most of Myanmar's private banks were 'owned by commercial conglomerates and tended to lend to other businesses within their groups.' However, the government seems to have accepted the need for a more modern, dynamic banking sector.

The IMF assesses...

In its July 2015 assessment of the Myanmar economy, the International Monetary Fund (IMF) noted that gross domestic product (GDP) growth in the 2014/15 fiscal year was estimated at 8.5 per cent, while inflation had picked up to 8 per cent by May 2015. Credit to the private sector was growing rapidly, at 36 per cent (year on year) in the 2014/15 year. For the same period, according to the IMF, the fiscal deficit stood at 3 per cent of GDP, but the underlying deficit was estimated at 5.5 per cent of GDP once one-off telecommunications and natural gas revenues were excluded. The current account deficit widened further to about 6 per cent of GDP, largely driven by strong import growth. With lower-than-expected FDI inflows, the foreign reserves held by the Central Bank of Myanmar (CBM) remained below 3 months of imports. The kyat had depreciated notably although in real effective terms it has remained largely unchanged.

Economic growth was expected by the IMF to remain strong in 2015/16, at 8.5 per cent, led by strong domestic demand. The increased fiscal deficit in the 2015/16 budget and continued monetisation of the deficit would contribute to strong demand and credit growth. Inflation might rise further in 2015/16 and Myanmar's external current account deficit was expected to widen further.

In the view of the IMF, the Myanmar economy was facing some downside risks. The persistent strength of the dollar and low natural gas prices (see 'Energy' below) could further weaken Myanmar's fiscal and external positions. Vulnerabilities from rapid credit growth, an expansionary budget and a widening trade deficit might also pose risks to price and external stability. Moreover, the rapid liberalisation of the financial sector should be carefully managed despite its overall benefits. These potential risks could affect the economy given weak capacity and thin policy buffers.

The IMF also suggested that a tightening of monetary and fiscal policies might be required to contain inflationary pressure and anchor exchange rate expectations. This policy move would need to be supported by the prompt introduction and the vigorous enforcement of prudential standards in the banking sector to slow credit expansion and reduce financial sector risks.

The IMF stressed the need to tighten monetary policy to curb credit growth. The central bank would need to scale up deposit auctions to mop up excess liquidity and implement a prompt transition to the newly calibrated reserve requirement for banks. The IMF also considered that the fiscal deficit for 2015/16 should be reduced through greater efforts on revenue mobilisation and expenditure

KEY INDICATORS — **Myanmar**

	Unit	2011	2012	2013	2014	**2015
Population	m	*62.42	*63.66	*50.98	*51.42	*51.85
Gross domestic product (GDP)	US$bn	51.90	55.76	56.76	62.80	*69.14
GDP per capita	US$	832	876	*1,113	*1,221	*1,334
GDP real growth	%	5.5	7.3	8.3	7.7	*8.3
Inflation	%	4.2	2.8	5.7	5.9	*8.4
Unemployment	%	4.0	4.0	*4.0	*4.0	*4.0
Natural gas output	bn cum	12.4	12.7	13.1	16.8	–
Exports (fob) (goods)	US$m	3,118.3	–	9,022.4	–	–
Imports (fob) (goods)	US$m	5,367.6	–	9,462.2	–	–
Balance of trade	US$m	-2,249.3	–	-439.9	–	–
Current account	US$m	-1,331.0	-2,438.0	-2,888.0	*-4,509.0	*-4,832.0
Total reserves minus gold	US$m	–	9,694.0	–	–	–
Foreign exchange	US$m	–	6,963.5	–	–	–
Exchange rate	per US$	5.38	850.25	982.00	1,026.00	–

* estimated figure ** forecast figure

're-prioritisation'. Myanmar could substantially increase its tax revenue by minimising tax incentives, strengthening tax compliance and promptly implementing the commercial tax on telecommunication services. Tighter monetary and fiscal policies were essential to stabilise exchange rate expectations. At the same time, a more flexible central bank interest rate structure that reflected market conditions and closed the gap between the bank's reference rate and the 'parallel' market rates would help contain demand and bring back the supply of foreign exchange to the market. The IMF concluded by observing that maintaining macro-economic stability was critical in managing the continuing process of economic and social transition. Meanwhile, sustained reforms would be needed to create the fiscal space needed to boost public investment, strengthen banking regulation and supervision to maintain financial stability and to improve the business environment to support inclusive growth. Building the institutional capacity for macro-economic management was, in the view of the IMF, key to addressing Myanmar's huge development challenges.

... the ADB concurs

According to the Asian Development Bank (ADB) Myanmar's GDP growth was estimated at 7.7 per cent in the 2014 fiscal year (Myanmar's national accounts end on the 31 March each year), reflecting strong expansion in construction, manufacturing and the services sector. The government's ambitious structural reform programme had underpinned Myanmar's strong growth performance in recent years. The construction sector was driven by government investment in infrastructure and by property development in Yangon and Mandalay. Manufacturing benefitted from increasing flows of foreign direct investment, with more than one new garment factory opening per week on average in 2014. The ADB noted that the growth in the services sector was bolstered by a surge in tourist arrivals from 2.0 million in 2013 to an estimated 3.1 million in 2014. The natural gas industry continued to expand, as reflected in a US$400 million increase in gas exports to US$2.1 billion in the first half of 2014. However, growth in agriculture slowed. Generally, agriculture provides 30 per cent of GDP and more than 60 per cent of employment. A 10 per cent increase in business registrations in the first nine months of 2014 indicated that business confidence remained robust.

The Directorate of Investment and Company Administration streamlined procedures to slash from 72 days to 3 days the time it takes to register a company. Growth in credit to the private sector continued to grow rapidly at 36 per cent year on year in November 2014. FDI approvals totalled US$6.6 billion between April and December 2014, up from US$4.0 billion for all of 2013. Telecommunications attracted almost a third, followed by oil and gas at 24 per cent, real estate at 18 per cent, hotels at 13 per cent and manufacturing (primarily garments) at 8 per cent. Less than 1 per cent was for agriculture.

Inflation picked up toward the end of FY2014, partly because of rising food prices and higher prices for imports owing to depreciation of the Myanmar kyat. The kyat weakened from MK965 to the US dollar at the start of the 2014 fiscal year to MK1,042 by the end, largely the result of a widening current account deficit and a stronger US dollar. Inflation averaged an estimated 5.9 per cent. Strong demand for capital equipment and liberalised import and foreign exchange restrictions drove a surge in merchandise imports that outpaced exports, widening the current account deficit to an estimated 7.1 per cent of GDP in FY2014. Gross official reserves looked set to total US$4.8 billion at the end of the fiscal year, which was cover for 2.7 months of imports, down from 3.0 months in FY2013.

The government increased spending in the 2014 fiscal year, while revenue from sales of telecommunications licences declined from 2013, widening the fiscal deficit to an estimated 4.3 per cent of GDP. Treasury bill auctions introduced in January 2015 broadened options for funding the deficit and strengthened the capacity of the Central Bank of Myanmar to follow an independent monetary policy. Total external debt as a ratio to GDP fell slightly to 17.6 per cent. Debt sustainability analysis by the IMF in October 2014 found Myanmar at low risk of external debt distress after clearing its arrears with Paris Club creditors in 2013.

After moderating in 2014, growth was forecast to accelerate to 8.3 per cent in 2015 and remain close to this pace in 2016 as it is propelled by investment stimulated by structural reforms, an improved business environment and Myanmar's gradual integration into the neighbouring sub-region. Better prospects in neighbouring India and Thailand – and further afield in the major industrial economies – supported the broadly positive outlook for Myanmar, but were partly offset by a slowdown in the People's Republic of China. Fiscal policy was expected to provide additional stimulus in 2015. Increases in government spending and higher civil service salaries could sharply widen the fiscal deficit to 6.3 per cent of GDP. This raised concerns because a prudent fiscal policy was particularly important to macro-economic stability when monetary policy tools are limited. Maintaining fiscal discipline ahead of the national elections in November 2015 was a challenge.

Higher fiscal spending and expected higher wages would add to domestic demand such that inflation was projected to accelerate to 8.4 per cent in 2015 before easing in 2016. Strong economic growth would drive up imports, though lower global oil prices will counteract some of the impact on the trade balance. The current account deficit was seen as narrowing through the forecast period. Eventually, however, low oil prices could drag down natural gas prices, dampening export earnings and government revenue. This vulnerability in fiscal and external accounts intensified the need to build gross official reserves up to more comfortable levels.

External debt was projected by the ADB to rise to US$12.5 billion in FY2015, or 18 per cent of GDP. Myanmar's risk of debt distress was expected to remain low as significant concessional funding became available. In addition, a new public debt law and debt management office would strengthen the management of debt, both external and domestic. After four years of significant economic reform, in the view of the ADB, many development challenges remained: improving infrastructure, strengthening governance and public sector capacity, developing human capital, building a dynamic private sector and revitalising agriculture. Poverty reduction was imperative. The United Nations Development Programme (UNDP) in 2014 ranked Myanmar 150 of the 187 countries surveyed in its human development index, with 26 per cent of the population below the poverty line. On the 2014 Transparency International *Corruption Perceptions Index* Myanmar ranked an embarrassingly low 156 out of the 175 countries surveyed, level with fellow Association of Southeast Asian Nations (Asean) member Cambodia, and Zimbabwe.

Energy – oil

The fact that Myanmar is a major natural gas producer in South-east Asia is often overlooked. Possibly because its upstream hydrocarbons sector still remained severely underdeveloped in 2015. The financial constraints imposed by Myanmar's national oil company, Myanma Oil and Gas Enterprise (MOGE), a lack of technical capacity, opaque regulatory policy, insufficient investment by foreign companies and international sanctions have all taken their toll on Myanmar's efforts to develop and begin to realise its oil and natural gas production potential. Alongside this underdevelopment, these factors have also hampered the development of the necessary energy infrastructure. However, US and European Union sanctions were eased or suspended in 2012 and 2013 following the government's economic reforms and this should allow an increase in international investment.

The US government's Energy Information Administration (EIA) has noted that following the suspension of sanctions, more international companies have begun oil and natural gas exploration efforts in Myanmar. The government is understandably keen to attract foreign investment and technical assistance and has been issuing production-sharing contracts through direct negotiations or the licensing rounds which began in 2011. As part of its most recent bidding rounds initiated in 2013, Myanmar had awarded 16 onshore and 20 offshore blocks to several foreign and domestic companies. The EIA reported that the government had decided to delay launching the next offshore bidding round until at least 2017.

Myanmar produces a minimal amount of crude oil and condensates from the onshore Salin basin and offshore Yetagun field. Total liquid fuels production has gradually increased over the past decade from 13,000 barrels per day (bpd) in 2000 to 21,000bpd in 2014. Myanmar's petroleum consumption is also small, estimated at 29,000bpd in 2014. However, Myanmar's limited production and refining capacity are still insufficient to cope with domestic consumption for crude oil and petroleum products, making oil imports essential.

As noted above, Myanmar's economy is beginning to expand following the lifting of sanctions and energy sector reforms. More petroleum products will be required to meet growing transportation and industrial needs.

According to the EIA, Myanmar had less than 50,000bpd of refining capacity in 2015 and utilisation rates are lower than 40 per cent as a result of the ageing infrastructure. The government and foreign companies, including China's Guangdong Zhenrong Energy Company, have announced proposals for constructing refineries, although these facilities are in the preliminary stages of development.

Natural gas

Myanmar's natural gas production has increased substantially, rising from 61 billion cubic feet (bcf) in 1999 to 463bcf by 2013. The natural gas output mostly came from the offshore Yadana and Yetagun fields in the Moattama basin, but has been forecast to rise further as a result of new projects coming online. Natural gas consumption has historically lagged behind production levels, but economic development is increasing its consumption, which reached a peak of 162bcf in 2013. In anticipation of greater local gas demand for the power, fertiliser and transportation industries, Myanmar imposed a domestic obligation to retain 25 per cent of the production from any new projects for the domestic market and is in the process of negotiating contracts.

Most of Burma's natural gas production was initially exported to Thailand and, more recently, to China. Natural gas exports to Thailand, which accounted for an average of 70 per cent, or 304 bcf/y in 2014, of Burma's natural gas output over the past decade, came solely from the Yetagun and Yadan fields. Thailand's national oil company launched commercial operations in the Zawtika gas project in the second half of 2014 and expected to produce 110bcf/y or 300 million cubic feet per day (MMcf/d) at the field's peak. This project is expected to increase natural gas exports to Thailand and also to serve Myanmar's domestic market.

Meanwhile, the EIA reported that natural gas exports to China commenced in mid-2013 with the development of the first phase of the Shwe natural gas project in the Rakhine Basin. Peak production capacity from phase one of this project is anticipated to be 183bcf/y (500 MMcf/d). In 2014, Myanmar exported about 108bcf of natural gas to China.

Myanmar and China have constructed twin crude oil and gas pipelines running from Myanmar's port of Kyaukphyu to Kunming in south-western China. A consortium of Asian oil companies, including the China National Petroleum Corporation, commissioned the onshore natural gas pipeline with a capacity of 424bcf/y in 2013 to carry exported gas from the Shwe gas project to China. The crude oil pipeline, holding a capacity of 440,000bpd, is designed to allow China to diversify transit routes for its crude oil imports from the Middle East and Africa, which have traditionally passed through the Strait of Malacca. This pipeline commenced operations in January 2015 and most of the crude oil was expected to serve the Yunnan refinery project in China. However, the refinery was not expected to be operational before 2016, which could limit the amount of oil transiting the pipeline in the short term.

Risk assessment

Economy	Fair/good
Politics	Poor
Regional stability	Fair/poor

People to watch

Shwe Mann –Speaker of the lower house, former general and member of the ruling Junta. Likely to make a bid for the Presidency in 2015.

COUNTRY PROFILE

Burma was annexed to British India in the nineteenth century.

1824–26 Burma ceded the Arakan coastal strip (Chittagong to Cape Negrais) to the British at the end of the first Anglo-Burmese war.

1852 At the end of the second Anglo-Burmese war Britain annexed lower Burma, including Rangoon.

1885–86 Britain captured Mandalay after a brief battle; Burma became a province of British India.

1937 Burma became a separate British dependency, with limited self-government.

1942 Japan invaded and occupied the country. The Burma Independence Army sided with the Japanese although it later transformed itself into the Anti-Fascist People's Freedom League (AFPFL) and fought against the invaders. A Provisional Administration was set up led by Dr Ba Maw.

1945 The AFPFL nationalists, led by Aung San, helped Allied forces to re-occupy the country.

1947 Aung San and six members of his interim government were assassinated. U Nu, foreign minister in Ba Maw's government, was asked to head the AFPFL and the government.

1948 The Union of Burma became independent outside the Commonwealth, with U Nu as the first prime minister.

1960 The ruling AFPFL party split and a caretaker government was formed, lead by army Chief of Staff General Ne Win.

1962 U Nu was overthrown in a coup led by Ne Win. The Revolutionary Council suspended the constitution and instituted authoritarian control through the Burma

Socialist Programme Party (BSPP). Under the 'Burmese Way to Socialism' the economy was nationalised, the BSPP became the single political party and independent newspapers were banned.
1964 Political parties were outlawed.
1973 A new constitution was approved. BSPP became the only authorised political party and the country's name was changed to the Socialist Republic of the Union of Burma.
1974 The revolutionary council was dissolved and Ne Win was elected president by the state council. Secretary General of the UN, U Thant died and was buried in Rangoon without official state recognition.
1978 An election gave Ne Win the mandate for four more years in power.
1988 A military government, the State Law and Order Restoration Council (SLORC), took power in September, ending months of unrest. It took over the function of the former ruling party, the BSPP, and the parliament (Pyithu Hluttaw).
1989 Burma was renamed Myanmar.
1990 The government fulfilled its promise to hold multi-party elections, but said a new constitution must be brought into effect before power could be transferred to the victorious National League for Democracy (NLD), led by Aung San Suu Kyi (daughter of Aung San, who had lead the AFPFL).
1992 General Than Shwe became SLORC chairman, prime minister and defence minister, replacing Saw Maung.
1996 The law and order situation deteriorated and open conflict erupted. SLORC closed the universities and detained protesters.
1997 Bomb attacks were aimed at leading SLORC figures. Several thousand Karen National Union (KNU) ethnic minority refugees were forced across the Thai border leading to international protests when refugees were killed by SLORC forces. The US imposed economic sanctions, banning investments by US companies. The Association of Southeast Asian Nations (Asean) admitted Myanmar as a full member of the Association. A governing military *junta*, formed by the top four SLORC leaders, was named the State Peace and Development Council (SPDC).
1998 The SPDC detained some 110 leading members of the NLD.
1999 Madame Aung San Suu Kyi was put under house arrest and isolated from the world. The authorities refused her dying husband a visa to come and visit her for the last time. The International Labour Organisation (ILO) banned Myanmar from its activities until it ceased using forced labour.
2001 The military *junta* approached Aung San Suu Kyi to arrange talks – the first contact in five years. President Jiang Zemin of China visited – the first Chinese head of state to visit since the military *junta* seized power in 1988.
2002 Aung San Suu Kyi (NLD) was released from house arrest. Former president, military leader and BSPP chairman, Ne Win died. He was considered to have had *sub rosa* influence on national political machinations for decades.
2003 Aung San Suu Kyi was re-arrested and Japan suspended aid in protest. General Khin Nyunt was appointed prime minister.
2004 The government and the Karen National Union, the most significant ethnic insurgency group, agreed to end hostilities. A constitutional convention began, despite a boycott by the NLD. General Khin Nyunt resigned and was replaced by Lt General Soe Win. An earthquake off the island of Sumatra caused a *tsunami* that damaged coastal areas, particularly in the Irrawaddy Delta. The final official estimate for Myanmar's dead was 90 and 5,000 displaced. However others estimated the death toll was up to 600 and 30,000 displaced.
2006 The military *junta* renewed Aung San Suu Kyi's detention order. Her plight was the first case submitted to the newly established UN Human Rights Council. Thousands of ethnic Karens fled to Thailand in the face of the construction of the new capital, Naypyidaw, which had forced them from their homes.
2007 Russia agreed to provide the technology and train technicians to build and operate a 10MW light-water nuclear reactor to power Pyinmana. The International Committee of the Red Cross formally accused the government of abusing the rights of its citizens. A major civil rights protest developed, led by Buddhist monks, calling for a return to democratic rule. The protest was sparked by an increase in the price of domestic fuel. As demonstrations grew the government retaliated by arresting hundreds of monks and firing on protesters; internet and mobile telephone connections were cut by the authorities to prevent pictures and details of the demonstrations being sent to media outlets overseas. Scores of monks were forced to flee from Yangoon as thousands of civilians including three prominent activists were arrested. A UN special envoy met General Than Shwe in an effort to stem the repression. Prime Minister Soe Win died and was succeeded by Thein Sein. The government began to release detained protesters at the end of the year, as monks again marched, although in fewer numbers.
2008 Cyclone Nargis struck the southern region of the Irrawaddy Delta; relief efforts were hampered by the seeming indifference and obstruction of authorities to accept and distribute the huge international aid on offer to Myanmar. Despite disruption from the national disaster the constitutional referendum was held and within five days the government claimed 92 per cent of voters had approved the constitutional changes. Aung San Suu Kyi's house arrest was extended for another year. An official estimate put 84,500 deaths following Cyclone Nargis with hundreds of thousands of people at risk from disease, homelessness, lack of food and clean water. UN President Ban Ki-moon criticised President General Than Shwe, who had refused to meet him to discuss the crisis. It was estimated by the UN and Asean that relief and reconstruction work following Cyclone Nargis would cost over US$1 billion, for food, agricultural and housing needs. They also estimated that as many as 134,000 had died during the cyclone.
2009 The UN stated that international and domestic law was being flouted by the military regime in the continued detention of Aung San Suu Kyi. She was formally arrested again for 'violating the terms of her house arrest', following an incident when an uninvited US citizen swam across a lake to her residence. Suu Kyi was convicted and sentenced to a further 18 month's house arrest; as a result she was unable to campaign in the 2010 elections. Despite the ruling, Suu Kyi had diplomatic meetings with representatives of the UK, Australia and the US, focussing on sanctions imposed by Western nations on Myanmar. The government removed a ban on the use of mobile telephones in the capital, Naypyidaw. At the Asean summit, Prime Minister Thein Sein was quoted as saying Aung San Suu Kyi could contribute to an unspecified 'process of national reconciliation'. The supreme court agreed that it would hear an appeal into Suu Kyi's sentence of a further 18 month's house arrest.
2010 Tin Oo, vice president of the NLD opposition party led by Suu Kyi was released, after serving six years under house arrest. New election laws were introduced banning candidates with criminal records from standing in elections; the law drew international condemnation. Suu Kyi's political party (NLD) announced it would not expel Suu Kyi as leader nor register for the parliamentary elections, declaring the law 'unjust'. The NLD was disbanded after the election registration deadline expired. The *junta* carried out a military reshuffle ahead of the elections. 37 political parties took part in elections for the two houses of parliament, plus 14 regional state assembly elections. However, due to the boycott by, and deregistration of, the NLD, plus the high fee for entering the contest, virtually all parties taking part

were proxy parties for the ruling military *junta*, in particular the Union Solidarity and Development Party (USDP), which contested all 1,157 seats nationally, and the National Unity Party (NUP), which contested 990. The National Democratic Force (a splinter of NLD) contested 163. As predicted the USDP won an overwhelming majority in both houses of parliament. The government released Aung San Suu Kyi. The UN human rights committee condemned the elections as being neither free nor fair.

2011 In January, following an Asean meeting of foreign ministers, a call was made to drop all international sanctions against the military regime in Myanmar. This was in line with a similar declaration from five of the ethnic minority groups within Myanmar, urging an end to sanctions, which they said disadvantaged their people disproportionately. The first legislative session to be held since 1988 was opened in January, in the newly built parliament in Naypyidaw. A presidential election was held in February, with three nominated candidates, all drawn from the military-backed political party; President General Than Shwe did not stand for the post. Former prime minister, Thein Sein, was elected as Myanmar's first civilian president (albeit a retired military officer) by parliament with 408 votes (out of 659). In March the military government was officially dissolved after the new president of a civilian-led parliament was sworn in, the first civilian government since 1962. Than Shwe retired, having ruled Myanmar since 1992. The ethnic Kachin Independence Army (KIA) attacked the area close to the site of a hydroelectric power plant being built by the Chinese in northern Myanmar in June. The government responded by mounting a military offensive against the rebels. A truce, which had been in place before the attack, had been broken when the KIA refused to become state border guards. In August, President Thein Sein invited home Myanmar's diaspora that fled after the 2008 uprising. However following the speech, he was also quoted saying that those who had 'committed a crime' during the demonstrations would still be punished. The government issued an invitation to Aung San Suu Kyi to visit Naypyidaw, where she met President Thein Sein in August. The government set up a National Human Rights Commission (NHRC) in September, to investigate reported abuses within the country. In October, the government unexpectedly suspended further construction of the Chinese-funded hydroelectric power plant on the Irrawaddy River; no reason was given. In October, 200 political prisoners were freed as part of a government sanctioned general amnesty. Two prominent detainees, the Buddhist monk who had led the 2007 civil unrest and a popular comedian and dissident called Zarganar, plus other monks, minority ethnic group activists and journalists were among the released. In November the NLD, led by Aung San Suu Kyi, agreed to register and contest the upcoming parliamentary by-elections. The NLD had boycotted all electoral processes since 1990 when, although it had won the elections, it was denied power by the military.

2012 The government signed a ceasefire with the Karen National Union on 12 January; bringing to an end six decades of insurgency by the ethnic rebel group. In January, Aung San Suu Kyi began campaigning for the upcoming parliamentary by-elections. As thousands turned out to see her, a major rally on 3–4 February, in Mandalay, had to be postponed when the venue was judged too small. On 1 April by-elections were held in 45 constituencies – 43 were won by candidates of the NLD, including Aung San Suu Kyi. On 2 April, the central bank adopted a managed float of the currency (kyat) and dropped the fixed exchange rate that had been in operation since 1977. The daily rate of 818 kyat per US dollar on 2 April (close to the black market rate), which replaced the 6.2 kyat per US dollar of 1 April. The UK's prime minister, David Cameron, visited Myanmar on 13 April and met President Thein Sein in Naypyidaw and Aung San Suu Kyi in Yangoon. Cameron stated that in recognition of the improved political situation in Myanmar sanctions against the regime should be suspended. The US, EU, and Australia, among others, later announced that most sanctions would be lifted, although with the proviso that democratic improvements continue. On 30 April, following a meeting with President Thein Sein, the UN chief, Ban Ki-moon urged other nations to ease sanctions against Myanmar to encourage reforms. Aung San Suu Kyi and other members of the NLD were sworn in as members of parliament on 2 May. The NLD had originally refused to take the oath, which called on them to 'protect the constitution'. They finally accepted the oath, so that they could participate in parliament. Indian Prime Minister Singh visited Myanma in May, the first Indian prime minister to do so since 1987. He had meetings with both President Thein Sein and opposition leader Aung San Suu Kyi. A state of emergency was declared in the western province of Rakhine, following a week of violence between Buddhists and Muslims, over attacks on members of their communities. The Press Scrutiny and Registration Department (PSRD) announced that from 20 August journalistic material would no long be censored before publication. On 6 September, parliament voted to impeach the entire bench of the Constitutional Tribunal of Myanmar (CTM) (nine in total) and force them from office. However in a pre-emptive move, the justices all resigned. A political row between the government and parliament over political reforms had begun in March when the CTM had issued an order limiting the powers of parliamentary committees and commissions, denying them the rights, among other things, to summon government ministers for questioning. On 28 October, an estimated 22,000 people had been displaced by communal violence between the majority ethnic Rakhine Buddhists and the minority Muslim Rohingya, in Rakhine State (western coast). A UN report, published on 31 October, reported that opium production had increased year-on-year since 2006, despite eradication efforts. Some 51,000 hectares of land are given over to cultivation. Myanmar is the world's second largest opium producer, after Afghanistan.

2013 The European Union lifted the last of its trade, economic and individual sanctions on 22 April; they had been temporarily lifted in 2012. This was despite the continuing violence being committed against the Muslims by Buddhists, including monks. In May UNHCR reported that there were more than 1.2 million stateless people nationwide. Human rights groups have been calling for a review of Myanmar's citizenship law to help alleviate the problem. President Thein Sein visited the US in May, the first state visit since 1966. The government and rebels from the ethnic Wa guerrilla group reached a peace deal in July, reported state media. The agreement comes as the government reaches out to ethnic groups, with the 30,000 strong United Wa State Army (UWSA) estimated to be the largest guerrilla group in the country. On his first visit to Britain, in July, President Sein announced that all 'prisoners of conscience' would be released 'by the end of the year'. Public commemorations took place on 8 August to mark the 25th anniversary of the uprisings which launched the country's pro-democracy movement. Five Muslims were killed during a visit by President Thein Sein to Rakhine state, where Bhuddists have been attacking Muslims. On 10 October, after three days of talks, a preliminary peace agreement with ethnic Kachin rebels in the north was signed. An exposion in the prestigious Traders Hotel in Rangoon on 15 October injured one guest; it was thought to have been a bomb and was the latest in a series of blasts across the country in the previous three days.

2014 The building of factories set to move into the Thilawa Special Economic Zone (SEZ) in 2015 began at the end of October. Some 22 companies have agreed to set up; when fully operational it is expected that as many as 70,000 people will be employed in the zone. A government official announced in late October that the next election would be held in late 2015. The President held roundtable talks with the opposition, military and ethnic groups on 31 October. A spokesman said the talks had included discussions on amendments to the constitution but gave no details. On 5 November opposition leader Aung San Suu Kyi said that reforms have 'stalled' and warned against 'over optimism'.

2015 Ashin Wirathu, a Buddhist nationalist monk, was condemned by the UN for sexist comments he made related to South Korean envoy Yanghee Lee, who was in Myanmar in January to address the plight of its Muslim minority. On October 15 a peace agreement was signed between the government and eight of 15 rebel groups with whom they had been negotiating for the last two years. Several of the main groups, including the United Wa State Army (UWSA), and the Kachin Independence Organisation (KIO), were among those who did not sign the agreement. The seven groups that signed have been removed from the government's list of 'unlawful associations'.

Political structure

Constitution

Since 1997, the principal organs of power are the State Peace and Development Council (SPDC), headed by a chairman, and the 40-strong military-dominated cabinet.

Politically, Myanmar is spread over seven divisions where the ethnic Burmans are in the majority, and seven states where the non-Burmans, the ethnic minority groups, are in the majority.

A constitutional referendum was held on 10 May 2008 in advance of multi-party elections scheduled for 2010. Among the articles to change were: the military commander in chief will assume full executive, legislative and judicial powers in the event of a state of emergency, including the power to suspend the constitution if they see fit; a guarantee of 25 per cent of parliamentary seats for the military; the military would be fully in control of the Ministry of Home Affairs; Myanmar citizens married to foreigners will be barred from the presidency; the military to be immune from prosecution for past crimes.

According to the military junta which drew up the amended constitution it will ensure the creation of a 'discipline-flourishing democracy'.

Despite this, the 2010 elections were widely considered fraudulent and unfair.

Independence date

4 January 1948

Form of state

Republic

National legislature

The bicameral national legislature, as constituted in 2010, consists of the Amyotha Hluttaw (Nationalities Assembly (upper house)) with 224 members (of which 56 are reserved for military officers as members) and the Pyithu Hluttaw (People's Assembly (lower house)) with 440 members (of which 110 are reserved for military officers).

Although under the pretence of democracy, the Myanmar political system still remains heavily controlled by the military with their 25 per cent allocated seats in both houses – what the generals call 'disciplined democracy'. Before 2010 the most recent elections had been twenty years previously. Aung San Suu Kyi's National League for Democracy party won with 59 per cent of the national vote. However, the election was not recognised by the military and was placed under house arrest and was detained until November 2010.

Last elections

8 November 2015 (parliamentary); 10 May 2008 (referendum on constitution); 4 February 2011 (president, indirect)

Results: Parliamentary (2010) (Upper house): Union Solidarity and Development Party (USDP) won 129 seats (out of 168), Rakhine Nationalities Development Party (RNDP) seven, National Unity Party (NUP) five, Shan Nationalities Democratic Party (SNDP) three; two other political parties failed to win any seats.

Lower house: USDP 259 seats (out of 330), SNDP 18, NUP 12, RNDP nine; two other political parties failed to win any seats.

Referendum on constitution (2008): government announcement declared 92 per cent of voters had approved the changes to introduce a bicameral parliament.

President(2011): Thein Sein won 408 votes (out of 659), Tin Aung Myint Oo 171, Sai Mauk Kham 75 (four votes unaccounted).

Next elections

2020

Political parties

Ruling party

Union Solidarity and Development Party (USDP) (from 7 Nov 2010)

Main opposition party

National League for Democracy (NLD)

Population

63.67 million (2012)*

Last census: March 1983: 35,307,913

Population density: 89 inhabitants per square km (2010). Urban population 34 per cent (2010 Unicef).

Annual growth rate: 1.0 per cent, 1990–2010 (Unicef).

Internally Displaced Persons (IDP)

600,000–1.0 million (UNHCR 2004)

Ethnic make-up

The indigenous population is Mongoloid. More than two-thirds are Burmans, racially akin to the Tibetans and the Chinese. There are also several indigenous minorities with their own language and culture – the Karen, Shan, Mon, Chin and Kachin; each group has its own state. The population includes immigrant minorities from India and China.

Religions

Theravada Buddhism (88 per cent), Christianity (7 per cent), Islam (3 per cent), Hinduism (0.5 per cent).

Education

Schooling begins in kindergarten for one year, then on to junior school for four years.

Secondary education is not compulsory and is divided into two phases: middle school, for four years, where all students undertake a general programme of learning; then upper secondary school where they elect to undertake either an academic course leading to higher education, or technical school, each lasting for two years. Technical education prepares students for admission to the government technical institutes or trade schools, or advancement on to university engineering courses.

All universities and colleges are financed by the state, although a nominal fee is charged for studies.

Literacy rate: 85 per cent adult rate; 91 per cent youth rate (15–24) (Unesco 2005).

Compulsory years: Five to 10.

Enrolment rate: 121 per cent gross primary enrolment of the relevant age group (including repetition rates); 30 per cent gross secondary enrolment (World Bank).

Pupils per teacher: 46 in primary schools.

Health

Each year an estimated 150,000 children aged less than five die of malaria, acute respiratory infections and diarrhoea.

Access to clean drinking water is available to over 68 per cent of the population.

Malaria and Tuberculosis are widespread.

HIV/Aids

Stories of emigrant Burmese labour in Thailand uniformly infected with hepatitis and/or HIV/Aids are commonplace. Foreign estimates place some 2 per cent of the population as HIV positive. The proportion is many times higher in the army and areas crossed by the 'needle trail' of heroin exports into Manipur, India, and Yunnan, China, among others. This is a clear legacy of neglect of basic human development under the *junta*, in favour of internal and external security expenditures, and will be a dangerous and pressing cost to the Burmese economy over the long term, possibly on a sub-Saharan African level.

Without official statistics published, it can only be estimated by aid workers that there are over 660,000 people with HIV/Aids, making Myanmar the centre of one of south-east Asia's worst epidemics. In August 2005 the Global Fund to Fight Aids, Tuberculosis and Malaria announced that is was withdrawing from its US$98 million health programme due to government restrictions on health workers in the country. The HIV/Aids epidemic is one of the worst in Asia.

HIV prevalence: 1.2 per cent aged 15–49 in 2003 (World Bank)

Life expectancy: 59 years, 2004 (WHO 2006)

Fertility rate/Maternal mortality rate: 2.0 births per woman, 2010 (Unicef); maternal mortality 230 per 100,000 live births (World Bank).

Birth rate/Death rate: 10 deaths to 26 births per 1,000 people (World Bank).

Child (under 5 years) mortality rate (per 1,000): 52 per 1,000 live births (WHO 2012)

Head of population per physician: 0.36 physicians per 1,000 people, 2004 (WHO 2006)

Welfare

The department of social welfare (DSW) under the ministry of social welfare, relief and resettlement implements social welfare services in eight different areas of social needs by both direct and indirect means covering the aged, children, youths and women welfare services. There is provision for the rehabilitation of ex-drug addicts and the disabled. It provides grants-in-aids to voluntary organisations. In Myanmar, all government servants retire at the age of 60, and are entitled to gratuity and pension.

There are approximately 45 homes for the aged throughout the country, which provide food, clothing, shelter and healthcare services to the aged. The traditional family structures also provide ample care for the aged. Several religious organisations donate large sums of money towards social welfare.

Main cities

Naypyidaw (new official capital, estimated population 925,000 in 2009). Yangon (formerly Rangoon) (former capital, estimated population 4.9 million in 2012), Mandalay (1.6 million), Mawla Myaing (formerly Moulmein, 542,017), Bago (278,622), Pathein (formerly Bassein, 277,382), Meiktila (244,768), Sittwe (formerly Akyab, 205,059).

Languages spoken

English is used in business circles.

Official language/s

Myanmar (Burmese)

Media

In 2008, Freedom House, the US human rights watchdog, assessed Myanmar as not free and has the most tightly restricted media environment in the world. The government is the only broadcaster allowed and owns all daily newspapers. Private weekly and monthly printed material is subject to censorship. Self-censorship by journalists is widespread.

The Press Scrutiny and Registration Department (PSRD) announced that from 20 August 2012 journalistic material would no long be censored before publication.

Press

In Burmese, with online editions in English, official publications include the daily *Kyehmon (The Mirror)* (www.myanmar.gov.mm), *Myanmar Alin* (www.mrtv3.net.mm), *The New Light of Myanmar* (www.myanmar.com/nim) is government owned and reports officially sanctioned news, *Pyaw Pyaw Shwin Shwin* is a humorous magazine and, in English, the *Myanmar Times* (www.myanmar.com/myanmartimes) is a weekly.

Dailies: In Yangon, *The New Light of Myanmar*, the multi-language official daily newspaper of the military junta was previously called *The Working People's Daily*. Other newspapers in Myanmar include *Burma Daily*, *Loktha Pyithu Nesin*, *Kyemon* (The Mirror), *Myotaw* (evening tabloid) and *Yadanabon* (Mandalay).

Periodicals: *Burma Focus* is a bi-monthly newsletter.

Broadcasting

Broadcasting is strictly controlled by the government. Due to the high level of illiteracy and the poor circulation of newspapers, radio and television are the main medium of mass communication and sources of news and information for most of the population. Listeners to foreign radio and television stations are subject to arrest.

Radio: The state-run stations include Radio Myanmar and City FM, which offers entertainment.

Popular, broadcasts that provide independent news include the Voice of America, Radio Free Asia and, from Norway, The Democratic Voice of Burma (http://english.dvb.no) which is run by Burmese exiles who provide unfettered and objective news, plus a platform for public opinion and political debate.

Television: TV Myanmar broadcasts in nine local languages plus English. MRTV-3 (www.mrtv3.net.mm) is the state-owned international service. Myawady TV is a military network and TV5 is the first, pay-to-view TV service in a joint state-private venture.

Other news agencies: Mizzima News (by Burmese exiles): www.mizzima.com

Economy

In 2011, Myanmar adopted a democratic government and reforms to its economy, which has led to it attracting foreign investment and reintegration into the global economy. Reforms have included floating the Burmese kyat in 2012, re-writing the Foreign Investment Law in 2012 to allow more foreign investment participation, Central Bank operation independence in July 2013, enacting a new anti-corruption law in September 2013 and authorizing a small number of foreign banks to open branch offices for limited operations beginning in 2015. FDI has doubled from US$4.1 billion in 2013 to US$8.1 billion in 2014. China is the biggest investor, predominately in energy projects, followed by Hong Kong and Thailand. Despite these positive reforms, more than one-third of the country's 51 million people live in poverty. The previous government has left Burma with poor infrastructure, endemic corruption, and underdeveloped human resources and inadequate access to capital, which will require a major commitment to reverse. In order for sustained growth to occur, the financial sector needs opening up and modernising, there must be increased budget allocation for social services and agricultural and land reforms must be accelerated.

Myanmar has rich natural resources including forestry, minerals and fresh water and marine reserves as well a young labour force and proximity to some of Asia's most powerful and dynamic economies. This has led to significant investment in the energy sector, garment industry, information technology, and food and beverages.

Proven natural gas reserves were 283.2 billion cubic metres (cum) in 2014, with annual production of 13.1 billion cum, of which about 70 per cent is exported to Thailand and the majority of the rest to China.

Agriculture provided 37 per cent of GDP in 2014, the majority of exports are rice, pulses and beans but sesame, groundnuts, sugarcane, fish, fish products and hardwood are also produced for export. 35 per cent of the labour force is occupied by agriculture.

In 2014, the UN Human Development Index (HDI) ranked Myanmar 150 (out of

187) for national development in health, education and income. Since 2000, Myanmar's progress has strengthened but has not matched the improvement of other countries in East Asia and the Pacific. In 2014, a third of the population remained in poverty.

Remittances from migrant workers amounted to US$275 million (less than 1 per cent of GDP) in 2012, which is much less than the average amount in neighbouring countries. Burmese migrant workers do not trust their banks, and look for more informal ways of sending money home. In 2013, remittances from migrant workers fell to just US$229 million.

In February 2014, the finance ministry revealed that Myanmar's foreign debt was US$2.5 billion, a significant decrease from the US$11 billion debt in 2012. Between 1962–88, when the debt grew to US$6.4 billion, Japan was Myanmar's biggest creditor, followed by the World Bank, the Asian Development Bank and Germany; since 1988 China has lent Myanmar US$2.13 billion.

External trade

Myanmar belongs to the Association of Southeast Asian Nations (Asean) Free Trade Area (Afta) and maintains a list of goods that have preferential import duties between members. All of the member countries have agreed to enact zero tariff rates on virtually all imports.

Most imports and exports originate with trade corporations and state boards.

Trade is handled by the Myanmar Export Import Services using the Myanmar Five Star Line for shipping. The picture of external trade presented by official statistics does not reflect the considerable amount of smuggling and black market trading that is present in the country. Myanmar is a major hub for the production of illegal heroin, estimated at around 2,000 tonnes annually, and amphetamines. Heroin is by far the largest export commodity.

Imports

Principal imports are fabric, petroleum products, fertilizer, plastics, machinery, transport equipment; cement, construction materials, crude oil; food products and edible oil.

Main sources: China (42.4 per cent of total in 2014), Thailand (19 per cent), Singapore (10.9 per cent) and Japan (5.4 per cent).

Exports

Principal exports are natural gas, wood products, pulses, beans, fish, rice, clothing, jade and gems.

Main destinations: China (63 per cent of total in 2014), Thailand (15.8 per cent) and India (5.7 per cent).

Agriculture

Farming

Agriculture accounted for 37 per cent of GDP in 2014 and it provided around 35 per cent of employment. About 15 per cent of the total land area is cultivated. Myanmar is usually self-sufficient in rice, although adverse weather conditions and an under-invested farming sector can cause shortages. Other main crops are sugar cane, wheat, maize, jute, cotton, beans, wheat and vegetables. Cattle, pigs, buffaloes, sheep, goats and poultry are raised for domestic consumption. Oil palm and rubber plantations are replacing forest in some areas.

Myanmar is a major hub for the production of illegal heroin, estimated at around 2,000 tonnes annually, and amphetamines. Heroin is by far the largest export commodity. It is the world's second largest producer of illicit opium, after Afghanistan. The country's drug export trade is said to be worth between US$1 and US$2 billion per year.

Fishing

Fishing is a large contributor to Myanmar's food production, with over 300 species in the country's fresh waters including several endemic species.

Forestry

Around 50 per cent of the land area is forest (32 million ha), containing about 75 per cent of the world's teak resources. Heavy logging is carried out, mostly of export hardwoods, bamboo and fuel, leading to fears of rapid deforestation.

Plantation forests form a total of 676 ha (2.1 per cent) where there are key species for export including teak (46 per cent), pyinkado (8 per cent), pine (3 per cent) and padauk (2 per cent). In 2012, Roundwood exports amounted to over 2 million cubic metres, it is likely that there is a high prevalence of illegal logic and wood smuggling within Myanmar's forests. From 2001-13, Myanmar's government only authorized timber harvests equal to 53 per cent of recorded global imports of Myanmar logs. This suggests that the illegal logging trade in Myanmar supplied at least 47 per cent of all exported timber products. Not only does this mean that the government has not been receiving the full revenues from the forestry sector but it has also led to unsustainable deforestation with annual rates of 1.4 per cent. The illegal export of logs via the Myanmar-China land border alone is valued at more than US$200 million per year.

On April 1 2014, Myanmar began implementing its first log export ban, making it one of the last of its neighbouring countries to do so. The hope is that it will dramatically raise revenue from sales of finished wood products, draw higher tax receipts, and provide more benefits to the Myanmar people.

Industry and manufacturing

The industrial sector accounts for around 20 per cent of GDP and employs around 10 per cent of the population.

Small enterprises predominate.

Manufacturing industries include food processing (sugar, tobacco, palm oil, rice), cement, textiles, beverages, cigarettes, aluminium products, paper and nails, steel, cotton yarn, soap, pharmaceuticals and fertilisers. Textile and jute production is being expanded.

There are 20 industrial zones.

Tourism

After years of neglect by the government and with tourists discouraged, the tourism sector was in the doldrums until early 2011. The beauties of Myanmar, its wealth of Buddhist temples, former royal palaces and spectacular landscapes, including the culturally important Irrawaddy River ('the road to Mandalay') are, however, becoming more accessible. According to government statistics the number of tourist arrivals were over 1 million in 2014, of which the largest number were from Thailand (16 per cent), followed by China (12 per cent) and then Japan (8 per cent). The Asian Development Bank (ADB) said that tourism should be a 'pillar' of the economy and in May 2013, a tourism master plan, funded by Norway, was unveiled, including 38 projects costing some US$487 million.

The tourist and travel sector contributed 4.8 per cent to GDP (US$2.4 billion) and employed 1,134,500 people in 2014 (4 per cent of total employment).

Although Myanmar has no sites currently listed on Unesco's World Heritage List there are a number being considered, including bio-diverse natural sites of conservation, the ancient cities of the Mon (the first known people to inhabit Myanmar) and the archaeological remains of the lost Pyu people (later inhabitants, with a language closely related to the current Burmese and who were living when Buddhism was introduced into the region).

Mining

Mining accounts for around 4 per cent of GDP and employs around 3 per cent of the workforce.

Minerals mined include ores of zinc, lead, tin and copper, silver, gypsum, limestone and gems such as rubies, sapphires and jade.

International sales of precious gems earn around US$300 million in foreign exchange annually. Myanmar supplies around 90 per cent of the world's rubies and 98 per cent of jade. Burma's famous 'Valley of Rubies' is the mountainous

Mogok area which lies 200 km north of Mandalay. It is noted for its rare pigeon's blood rubies and blue sapphires. While many sanctions placed on the former regime were eased or lifted in 2012, the US has left restrictions on importing rubies and jade from Myanmar intact.

Hydrocarbons

Myanmar Oil and Gas Enterprise (Moge) is the 100 per cent state owned enterprise and is responsible for the upstream petroleum sub-sector.

The Chinese state-owned oil company, China Natural Petroleum Corporation (CNPC), finished construction of a 2,520km pipeline linking Myanmar and China in early 2013. The pipeline became operational in July 2013 and in its first year supplied China with 1.87 billion cubic meters (cum) of natural gas.

Myanmar has minimal crude oil reserves of 50 million barrels, however, its consumption is only 28,000 bpd and, therefore, it just needs to import 5000 barrels per day. Its refined petroleum production is 19,000 bpd.

Proven reserves of natural gas was 283 billion cum in 2014 and production was 11.8 billion cum. Consumption was 3.3 billion cum and, therefore, it is fully self-sufficient in natural gas. It exports 8.5 billion cum each year.

Any use of coal is negligible. However, by 2030, Myanmar wants a third of electricity to be powered by coal and officials have commissioned 10 coal plants. In April, the Thai engineering company Toyo-Thai Company limited and Myanmar's power ministry signed an MOU on the construction of a US$2.8 billion plant in the eastern state of Mon. The planned coal-fired station will have a generation capacity of 1.3 GW, nearly as much as the country's total capacity of 1.7 GW. The proposed coal plant will use 4 million tonnes a year when it comes online in 2019.

Energy

Total generating capacity was 1,713MW in 2013, producing 5.96 billion kilowatt hours (kWh). Myanmar is seeking to develop its considerable hydroelectric generating potential, but is constrained by the cost factor. Electricity services are not available for much of the population, who rely on traditional methods of cooking, lighting and power. In 2013, only 30 per cent of the population had access to electricity. 74 per cent of total installed capacity is received from hydroelectric plants while 26 per cent comes from fossil fuels. By 2030, Myanmar wants a third of electricity to be powered by coal, 38 per cent from hydro and 20 per cent from gas. They are also aiming for 7.2 million new grid connections, to meet future energy requirements, estimated to be eight times higher than 2015 levels, officials have commissioned 10 coal plants. In April, the Thai engineering company Toyo-Thai Company limited and Myanmar's power ministry signed an MOU on the construction of a US$2.8 billion plant in the eastern state of Mon. The planned coal-fired station will have a generation capacity of 1.3 GW, nearly as much as the country's total capacity of 1.7 GW. The proposed coal plant will use 4 million tonnes a year when it comes online in 2019.

Financial markets

Stock exchange

The Myanmar Securities Exchange Centre opened in 1996.

Banking and insurance

Since 1995, the government has allowed foreign banks to operate in Myanmar which have opened representative offices, to set up joint ventures with private local banks.

Myanmar is on the Organisation for Economic Co-operation and Development (OECD) Financial Action Task Force (FATF) list of non-co-operative countries on money laundering.

In early 2003, there was trouble in the financial sector with the collapse of some private finance companies, which had taken deposits from the public. The problem spread to some private banks and large amounts of cash were withdrawn by depositors. A stronger regulatory framework for the banking system and a strategy to identify and resolve the problem banks are necessary to restore confidence in the sector.

Central bank

Central Bank of Myanmar

Time

GMT plus 6.5 hours

Geography

Myanmar lies in the north-west region of south-east Asia between the Tibetan plateau and the Malay peninsula. It is bordered by Bangladesh and India to the north-west, the People's Republic of China and Laos to the north-east and by Thailand to the south-east.

Myanmar covers an area of 676,552 square km. It is dominated by mountains, rivers and forests. The Ayeyarwady (Irrawaddy) river, which rises in Tibet, flows southwards through the country, dividing it in two, and opening out into a vast delta region. The system is extremely fertile. Other important rivers are the Chindwin and Sittaung. There are several high mountain ranges ringing the country and providing almost impassable barriers against neighbouring countries. These and other interior mountains make land travel difficult within Myanmar. The highest point in the country and in south-east Asia is Mount Hkakabo Razi, which reaches 5,881m. Much of the country is covered in thick, tropical forests.

Hemisphere

Northern

Climate

There are three seasons: the rainy season May/June–October with high humidity and monsoon rains; the hot season February/March–May with likely temperatures of 37 degrees Celsius (C) (coastal and delta areas) to 40 degrees C (central region); and the cool, dry season November–February with temperatures of 16 degrees C (central region) to 21 degrees C (coastal and delta areas). Average rainfall varies from 5,000mm (northern hills and coastal areas) to 2,500mm (delta areas) to 750mm (central region).

Dress codes

Revealing or sloppy clothing is not advisable on any occasion. There are no strict rules regarding business attire.

Entry requirements

Passports

Required by all, valid for six months beyond date of departure.

Visa

Required by all. Tourist and business visas, applied for well in advance of arrival, are valid for 28 days; they may be extended. For a business visa a letter of introduction and an invitation are required, with a full itinerary.

Currency advice/regulations

The import and export of local currency is not allowed. There are no restrictions on the import of foreign currency, subject to declaration; export is restricted to the amount declared on arrival. Exchange controls are strictly enforced and all foreign exchange receipts should be safeguarded.

Customs

Personal effects are allowed duty-free, but customs regulations are restrictive and it is best to travel light. Jewellery, cameras and electric goods must be declared on entry. Video cameras are not allowed into the country.

Health (for visitors)

Mandatory precautions

Yellow fever certificate if arriving from infected area.

Advisable precautions

It is advisable to be in date for polio (within 10 years), tetanus (within 10 years), hepatitis A and B, rabies (within one to three years, depending on exposure to risk), Japanese B encephalitis (within three years if travelling June to September), tuberculosis (children should be immunised at any age, although it is less important for adults), diphtheria (within 10 years). Dengue fever occurs intermittently, especially in the northern Mandalay division.

If travelling through the country it is advisable to be vaccinated against cholera. Only Yangon (Rangoon) city and areas above 1,000m are malaria free; if in doubt, take malaria prophylaxis.

It is advisable to carry a pack of sterilised needles, and to take any medicines required – they can be in short supply.

Water should be boiled and filtered before drinking. It is advisable to drink bottled water.

There is a rabies risk.

Hotels

Accommodation has been described as 'decrepit almost to the extent of charm'. There is no official rating system. Main Yangon (Rangoon) hotels can arrange an interpreter or translation services if necessary. Some Yangon hotels require payment in foreign currency. A 10 per cent service charge and a 10 per cent government tax are included in the bill.

Credit cards

American Express, Diners Club, Master, Visa, JCB are accepted at airlines, major hotels and supermarkets.

Public holidays (national)

Fixed dates

4 Jan (Independence Day), 12 Feb (Union Day), 2 Mar (Peasants' Day), 27 Mar (Armed Forces Day), 13–16 Apr (Maha Thingyan/Water Festival), 17 Apr (Myanmar New Year), 1 May (May Day), 19 Jul (Martyrs' Day), 25 Dec (Christmas Day).

Variable dates

Eid al Adha, Full Moon of Tabaung (Feb/Mar), Full Moon of Kasone (Apr/May), Full Moon of Waso/Beginning of Buddhist Lent (Jul/Aug), Full Moon of Thadingyut/End of Buddhist Lent (Oct), Diwali/Deepavali (Oct/Nov), Tazaungdaing Full Moon Day (Nov), National Day (Dec), Kayin New Year (Dec).

In general, Hindu and Buddhist festivals are declared according to local astronomical observations.

Working hours

Banking

Mon–Fri: 1000–1400.

Business

Mon–Fri: 0930–1630.

Government

Mon–Fri: 0930–1630.

Shops

Mon–Sun: 0600–2200.

Telecommunications

Mobile/cell phones

In 2012 only some 9 per cent of the population had mobile phones. The government announced on 26 June 2013 that it had awarded mobile licences to Telenor (Norway) and Ooredoo (Qatar).

Electricity supply

230V AC, 50 cycles single-phase; five or 15 amp plugs with three round pins for power.

Weights and measures

Imperial system (the metric system and local units are also in use).

Social customs/useful tips

Shoes and socks must be removed before entering any religious building, and visitors should not wear shorts.

The title 'U' (pronounced 'oo') is the equivalent of 'Mr' in English. When addressing people always use the appropriate prefix and family name. Many people do not have a first name.

The head is considered the temple of the body and should not be touched by other people. It is also considered the ultimate in bad manners to put one's feet on the table or cross one's legs so that the sole of the shoe points at someone. This is because the feet are considered to be the least clean part of the body.

The code of standard behaviour is referred to as *bamahsan chin*. According to this mode of conduct, people are expected to respect elders, exhibit discretion in dealing with the opposite sex, be aware of Buddhist sayings and have an ability to recite some Buddhist verses. Additionally, one should maintain a reserved and indirect approach to another person and not be direct at all. This can lead to misunderstandings, especially in business dealings.

Getting there

Air

National airline: Myanmar Airways International .

International airport/s: Yangon International (RGN), 19km from city centre; duty-free shop, bar, restaurant, buffet, bank, post office and hotel reservations. Mandalay International (MDL), 25km from city; post office, bank, duty-free shop, car rental.

Airport tax: US$10, payable in Foreign Exchange Certificates (FEC).

Surface

Road: There are overland entry points on the borders with China and Thailand. A border pass is required for entry.

Water: Cruise vessels stop at Yangon.

Main port/s: Yangon.

Getting about

Not all parts of the country are open to visitors, and some are subject to guerrilla or bandit activity.

National transport

Tourists are required to keep to officially designated tourist areas and all arrangements for internal travel must be made well in advance via Myanmar Travel and Tours. Travel outside Yangon (Rangoon) is difficult to arrange. No attempt should be made to travel to restricted areas.

Air: Flying is the best and generally only permitted method of traversing the country and visiting tourist destinations. Flight schedules are restricted and subject to change without warning.

Road: There is a large network of roads all over the country, which are being upgraded, and new roads are being built.

Buses: There are a number of privately-owned bus companies which operate air-conditioned coaches between main centres. The main routes are from Yangon to Meiktila, Pyay, Mandalay and Taunggyi.

Rail: There is an extensive rail network. Myanmar Railways operates services to main centres. The Yangon-Mandalay express service runs four trains daily, with a branch line to Shwenyaung and Taunggyi. A service from Yangon to Bagan runs every other day.There are services from Mandalay to Lashio, Monywa and Bagan. Standards of equipment, service and safety are not high.

Water: There is extensive river and coastal traffic. Trips can only be made as part of an organised tour.

City transport

Taxis: In Yangon the government operates blue taxis with standard fares; otherwise, fares are by negotiation. Taxis can be shared or hired on a time basis.

Buses, trams & metro: There are antiquated and overcrowded bus services in all cities; they are not recommended for visitors. Yangon has a circular rail system.

Car hire

Tourists are not permitted to drive. Cars are hired with driver.

BUSINESS DIRECTORY

The addresses listed below are a selection only. While World of Information makes every endeavour to check these addresses, we cannot guarantee that changes have not been made, especially to telephone numbers and area codes. We would welcome any corrections.

Telephone area codes

The international direct dialling (IDD) code for Myanmar is +95 followed by area code:

Bassein	42	Moulmein	32
Mandalay	2	Naypyidaw	67
Monywa	71	Prome	53
		Yangon	1

Useful telephone numbers

Ambulance: 192, 71-111
Red Cross: 295-133
Police (emergency): 199
(headquarters): 282-541, 284-764
Telephone enquiries: 100

Booking (inland): 101
Booking (overseas): 130, 131, 667-444, 667-555, 667-601/2
Airport Security: 662-677
Customs: 284-533
Immigration: 286-434

Chambers of Commerce

Myanmar Federation of Chambers of Commerce & Industry, 504 Merchant Street, Kyauktada Township, Yangon (tel: 243-150; fax: 248-177; e-mail: ird@umfcci.com.mm).

Banking

Asia Wealth Bank, Ahlone, River View Housing Project, Olympic Tower II, Yangon (tel: 212-701; fax: 212-704).

First Private Bank Ltd, 619-621 Merchant Street, Pabedan T/S, Yangon (tel: 251-748; fax: 242-320).

Innwa Bank Ltd; 554-556 Corner of Merchant Street & 35th Street, Yangon (tel: 254-641, 254-647; fax: 254-431).

Kanbawza Bank Ltd; 1st Floor, Lanmadaw Condo Centre, No. 02/06, 02/07 Lanmadaw Street, Latha T/S, Yangon (tel: 212-780; fax: 212-778).

Myanmar Agricultural Development Bank, No. 1/7 Corner of Latha St & Kanna Rd, Latha T/S, Yangon (tel: 253-180, 250-569; fax: 245-119).

Myanmar Economic Bank, 1-19 Sule Pagoda Rd, Pabedan T/S, Yangon (tel: 289-329; fax: 283-679).

Myanmar Foreign Trade Bank, PO Box 203, 80-86 Maha Bandoola Garden Street, Kyauktada T/S, Yangon (tel: 284-911; fax: 289-585, 254-585).

Myanmar Industrial Development Bank Ltd, 26/42 Pansodan Street, Kyauktada T/S, Yangon (tel: 249-536; fax: 249-529).

Myanmar Investment and Commercial Bank, 170/176 Bo Aung Kyaw Street, Botataung Township, Yangon (tel: 250-509; fax: 281-775).

Myanmar Livestock & Fisheries Development Bank Ltd, 654-666 Corner of Merchant Street & Shwe Bon Tha Street, Pabedan T/S, Yangon (tel: 249-620; fax: 243-240).

Myanmar Citizens Bank Ltd, 383 Maha Bandoola St, Kyauktada T/S, Yangon (tel: 283-209, 283-719; fax: 245-932).

Myanmar May Flower Bank Ltd, Yadana Housing Project, 9 Mile, Pyay Rd, Mayangon T/S, Yangon (tel: 661-261; fax: 661-262).

Myanmar Oriental Bank Ltd, 166-168 Pansodan Street, Yangon (tel: 246-596; fax: 251-831).

Myanmar Universal Bank Ltd, 81 Theinbyu Rd, Botataung T/S, Yangon (tel: 297-337; fax: 245-449).

Yoma Bank Ltd, 1 Kun Gyan Road, Mingalar Taung Nyunt Township, Yangon (tel: 703-493; fax: 246-548).

Central bank

Central Bank of Myanmar, PO Box 184, 26(A) Sethmin Road, Yankin Tsp, Yangon (tel: 543-751; fax: 543-621; e-mail: cbm.ygn@mptmail.net.mm).

Stock exchange

The Myanmar Securities Exchange Centre opened in 1996.

Travel information

Myanmar Airways International , Sakura Toer, 339 Bogyoke Aung San Road, Yangon (tel: 255-260; fax: 255-305; e-mail: management@maiair.com).

Myanmar Tourism Promotion Board, Traders Hotel, 223 Sule Pagoda Road, Yangon (tel: 242-828; fax: 242-800; e-mail: mtpb@mptmail.net.mm).

Ministry of tourism

Ministry of Hotels and Tourism, 77-91 Sule Pagoda Road, Kyauktada Tsp, Yangon (tel: 285-689; fax: 289-588; e-mail: mtt.mht@mptmail.net).

National tourist organisation offices

Myanmar Travels and Tours, 77-91 Sule Pagoda Road, PO Box 559, Yangon (tel: 382-243; fax: 254-417; e-mail: mtt.mht@mptmail.net.mm).

Ministries

Ministry of Agriculture and Irrigation, Thiri Mingala Lane, Kaba Aye Pagoda Road, Yankin Tsp, Yangon (tel: 665-587; fax: 664-493).

Ministry of Commerce, 228-240 Strand Road, Pabedan Tsp, Yangon (tel: 289-660; fax: 289-578).

Ministry of Communications, Post and Telecommunications, 80 Corner of Merchant St & Theinbyu Street, Botahtaung Tsp, Yangon (tel: 292-019).

Ministry of Construction, 39 Nawaday Street, Botahtaung Tsp, Yangon (tel: 283-938).

Ministry of Co-operatives, 259-263 Bogyoke Aung San Street, Kyauktada Tsp, Yangon (tel: 277-096, 280-280; fax: 287-919).

Ministry of Culture, 26-42 Pansodan Street, Kyauktada Tsp, Yangon (tel: 243-235).

Ministry of Defence, Ahlanpya Phaya Street, Yangon (tel: 281-611).

Ministry of Education, Theinbyu Street, Botahtaung Tsp, Yangon (tel: 285-588).

Ministry of Energy, 23 Pyay Road, Yangon (tel: 221-060; fax: 222-964).

Ministry of Finance and Revenue, 26 Setmu Road, Kyauktada Tsp, Yangon (tel: 284-763).

Ministry of Foreign Affairs, Pyay Road, Dagon Tsp, Yangon (tel: 222-844; fax: 222-950).

Ministry of Forestry, Thirimingala Lane, Kabe Aye Pagoda Road, Mayangon Tsp, Yangon (tel: 289-184; fax: 664-459).

Ministry of Health, Theinbyu Street, Botahtaung Tsp, Yangon (tel: 277-334; fax: 282-834).

Ministry of Home Affairs, Corner of Saya San Street & No 1 Industrial Street, Yankin Tsp, Yangon (tel: 549-208).

Ministry of Immigration & Population, Theinbyu Street, Botahtaung Tsp, Yangon (tel: 249-215).

Ministry of Industry (I), 192 Kaba Aye Pagoda Road Yangon (tel: 566-066).

Ministry of Industry (II), 56 Kaba Aye Pagoda Road, Yangon (tel: 661-140; fax: 667-156).

Ministry of Information, 365-367 Bo Aung Kyaw Street, Kyauktada Tsp, Yangon (tel: 245-631; fax: 289-274).

Ministry of Labour, Theinbyu Street, Botahtaung Tsp, Yangon (tel: 278-320; fax: 256-185).

Ministry of Livestock Breeding and Fisheries, Theinbyu Street, Botahtaung Tsp, Yangon (tel: 280-398; fax: 289-711).

Ministry of Mines, 90 Kanbe Road, Yankin Tsp, Yangon (tel: 577-316).

Ministry of National Planning and Economic Development, Theinbyu Street, Botahtaung Tsp, Yangon (tel: 280-816; fax: 282-101).

Ministry of Development of Border Areas and National Races and Development Affairs, Theinbyu Street, Botahtaung Tsp, Yangon (tel: 280-032; fax: 285-257).

Ministry of Rail Transport, 88 Theinbyu Street, Botahtaung Tsp, Yangon (tel: 292-769).

Ministry of Religious Affairs, Kaba Aye Pagoda Precinct, Mayangon Tsp, Yangon (tel: 665-620; fax: 665-728).

Ministry of Science and Technology, 6 Kaba Aye Pagoda Road, Yangon (tel: 665-686).

Ministry of Social Welfare, Relief & Resettlement, Theinbyu Street, Botahtaung Tsp, Yangon (tel: 282-610).

Ministry of Sports, Office of the Ministers, Yangon (tel: 553-958).

Ministry of Transport, 363/421 Merchant Street, Yangon (tel: 296-815; fax: 296-824).

Office of the Prime Minister, Minister's Office, Yangon (tel: 283-742).

Other useful addresses

ASEAN Investment Promotion Agency, 653/691 Merchant Street, Pabedan, Yangon (tel: 372-855; fax: 254-660; e-mail: dica.nped@mptmail.net.mm).

British Embassy, Commercial Section, 80 Strand Road, Box No 638, Yangon (tel: 281-700; fax: 289-566).

Central Statistical Organisation, New Secretariat, Yangon (tel: 270-578; e-mail: cso.stat@mptmail.net.mm).

Livestock Foodstuff & Milk Products Enterprise, Pyay Road, 10th Mile, Mayangon Tsp, Yangon (tel: 664-244; fax: 240-109).

Myanmar Embassy (US), 2300 S Street, NW, Washington DC 20008 (tel: (+1-202)-332-9044; fax: (+1-202)-332-9046; e-mail: thuriya@aol.com).

Myanmar Export and Import Services, 622-624 Merchant Street, Yangon (tel: 280-260; fax: 289-587).

Myanmar Fisheries Enterprise, 654 Merchant Street, Latha Tsp, Yangon (tel: 20-710; fax: 222-951).

Myanmar General Industries, 192 Kaba Aye Pagoda Road, Yankin Tsp, Yangon (tel: 660-521; fax: 56-066).

Myanmar Investment Commisssion, 653/691 Merchant Road, Yangon (tel: 272-912; fax: 282-101).

Myanmar Oil and Gas Enterprise, 604 Merchant Street, Pabedan Tsp, Yangon (tel: 282-121; fax: 222-964).

Myanmar Petrochemical Enterprise, 23 Pyay Road, Lanmadaw Tsp, Yangon (tel: 222-816; fax: 222-960).

Myanmar Ports Authority, 10 Pansodan Street, Yangon (tel: 283-122).

Myanmar Post & Telecommunications, 43 Bo Aung Gyaw Street, Kyauktada Tsp, Yangon (tel: 285-840; fax: 290-429).

Myanmar Railways, Bogyoke Aung San Street, Pabedan Tsp, Yangon (tel: 274-027; fax: 282-267).

Myanmar Textile Industries, 192 Kaba Aye Pagoda Road, Yankin Tsp, Yangon (tel: 566-320; fax: 566-053).

Post & Telecommunications Department, 125 Pansodan Street, Kyauktada Tsp, Yangon (tel: 283-737; fax: 286-365).

US Embassy, 581 Merchant Street, Yangon (tel: 282-055; fax: 280-409).

Mizzima News (by Burmese exiles): www.mizzima.com

Internet sites

Myanmar Resources: http://www.myanmars.net

Official Website of Myanmar: http://www.myanmar.com

Myanmar Business Information: http://www.myanmarpyi.com

Radio Free Myanmar: http://users.imagiware.com/wtongue/dvb2.html

Namibia

KEY FACTS

Official name: Republic of Namibia

Head of State: President Hage Geingob (since 21 March 2015)

Head of government: President Hage Geingob (since 21 March 2015)

Ruling party: South West African People's Organisation (SWAPO)

Area: 824,269 square km

Population: 2.19 million (2014)*

Capital: Windhoek

Official language: English

Currency: Namibian dollar (N$) = 100 cents; at par with the South African commercial Rand

Exchange rate: N$13.79 per US$ (Sep 2015)

GDP per capita: US$6,095 (2014)*

GDP real growth: 5.30% (2014)*

GDP: US$13.35 billion (2014)*

Inflation: 5.35% (2014)*

Balance of trade: -US$2.15 billion (2013)

Annual FDI: US$968.87 million (2011)

* estimated figure

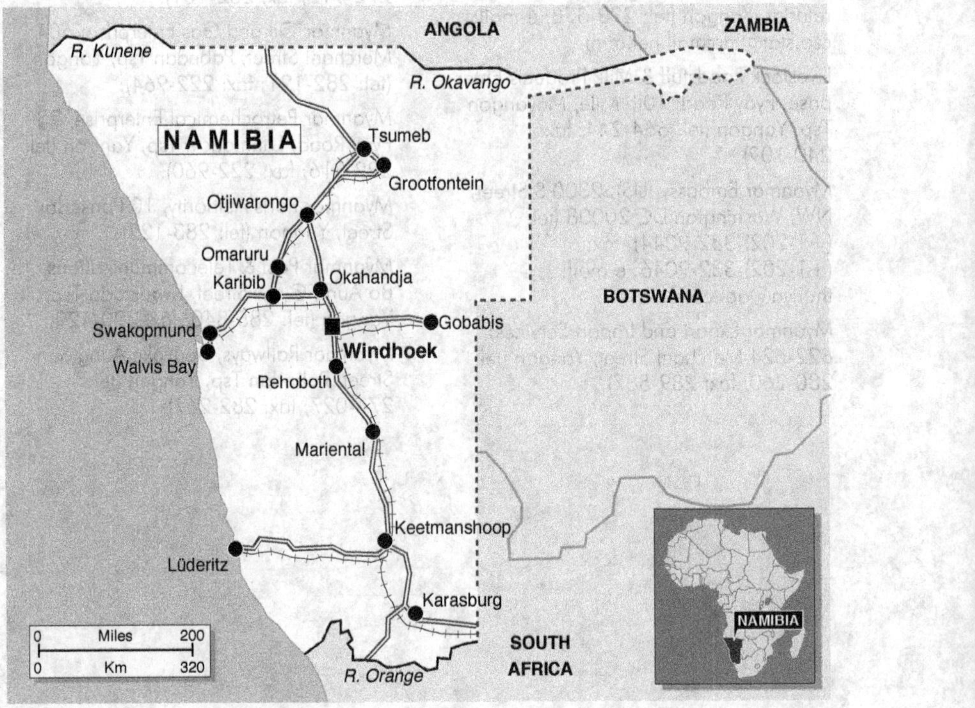

Violence was a part of the experience of Namibia for many years. During the forty years of German imperial conquest, the Namibian people were forcibly dispossessed of their land and cattle and 80,000 of them died as a result. South Africa then occupied the German colony of South-West Africa during First World War and administered it as a mandate until after the Second World War, when it annexed the territory. In 1966 the Marxist South West African People's Organisation (Swapo) launched a war of independence for the area that was soon named Namibia, but it was not until 1988 that South Africa agreed to end its administration in accordance with a United Nations' peace plan for the entire region. Namibia won its independence in 1990 and has been governed by Swapo since.

Given the relatively conservative nature of Namibian politics, it is not the country from which surprises would normally be expected. But, as Alexander O'Riordan of the South African Civil Society Information Service reported on AllAfrica.com, in 2014 a quietly unique gender revolution never before seen in southern Africa was committed to filling half of the seats in parliament with women. Namibia is also committed to what it calls a 'zebra system', whereby if a minister is a woman, the deputy minister will be a man, and vice versa.

Even more ambitiously, the implication was that the roles will be switched in successive elections. What this meant was that if Namibia was appointing a man to the presidency in 2014, it would be committed to appoint a woman to the presidency in 2019.

According to Mr O'Riordan, in 2014 Swapo was already moving to put this commitment to gender equality into operation. The group had initially agreed in 2002 to pursue greater gender equality, in calling for 50 per cent of leadership positions in parliament, government and state-owned enterprises to be occupied by women. At the last Swapo conference held before the election, it was agreed that this policy would be put into operation in the elections in November 2014. Though 50 per cent was not quite achieved,

Namibia is tenth in the world for female representation in parliament, with the lower house being composed 41.3 per cent by women and 23.1 per cent in the upper house.

The Namibian government executive had taken the first steps towards expanding the number of seats in parliament's national assembly to 100 members in May 2014. The issue was discussed in cabinet at the time, with the press reporting that a bill was being prepared. The meeting was chaired by the prime minister, Hage Geingob, suggesting that Swapo was taking the matter seriously. However, Mr O'Riordan claimed that in Namibia, as was the case in South Africa, a growing urban, black middle class masked endemic and entrenched rural poverty, widening inequality and structural impediments that undermined social mobility. As in South Africa, a rural education combined with a first-world economy meant that if your parents did not have the resources to augment the second-rate government education system your children would remain in poverty. The Achilles heel of Namibia's political system was that the system was increasingly seen to voice the interests of only a vested few, and with that vested few rapidly greying, it was only a matter of time before they retired or died.

In the 27–28 November 2014 general elections, which saw the first use of electronic voting on the African continent, Swapo, who have been in power since Namibia gained independence in 1990, again experienced huge successes at the voting stations securing 86.7 per cent of the popular vote and another five years in power. The presidential election held at the same time was a convincing win for Hage Geingob of the Swapo with 86.7 per cent of the vote, followed by McHenry Venaani (Democratic Turnhalle Alliance) with 5 per cent.

The economy

Namibia is heavily dependent on the extraction and processing of minerals for export. Mining directly accounted for 13 per cent of gross domestic product (GDP) in 2014. It is a primary source for gem-quality diamonds, which are mined and marketed in partnership with De Beers. The capital intensive, highly mechanised mining sector employs only three per cent of the workforce. A high per capita GDP hides a great inequality of income distribution. Unemployment has remained extremely high for decades and was estimated at 28.1 per cent in 2014. Namibia was ranked 127 out of the 187 countries surveyed in the 2013 United Nations Human Development Report.

The African Development Bank (AfDB) in its 2015 *Economic Outlook* observed that the Namibian economy had recovered from the global economic crisis. Growth of GDP remained robust at 5.3 per cent in 2014, up from 4.2 per cent in 2013, despite the persistent global economic turbulence, helped by the continued expansion of construction activities related to new projects such as the government's launch of a massive housing project, the beginning of the expansion of the container terminal at Walvis Bay and large investment projects in mining. The lack of an independent monetary tool has led to the active use of fiscal policy as a major counter-cyclical tool to sustain economic growth in the aftermath of the global economic crisis. The budget deficit for 2013/14 was estimated to be lower than expected on account of lower spending than budgeted, a recovery in the Southern African Customs Union (SACU) revenues and increased revenue collection associated with higher domestic economic growth and initiatives to improve the tax-administration regime. Nonetheless for 2014/15, total expenditure was estimated to have expanded to 42.6 per cent of GDP from 38 per cent of GDP in 2013/14, leaving the overall fiscal deficit at 5.5 per cent of GDP.

Inflationary pressures eased in 2013. Year-on-year inflation slowed down to 4.4 per cent in November 2013, but had increased slightly to 5.4 per cent in 2014. In the view of the AfDB, key risks to medium-term growth included weak global demand for mineral exports that would result in lower export earnings, adverse weather-related shocks that would further weaken growth in agriculture, delays in construction projects, and lower SACU revenues due to the economic slowdown in South Africa. Namibia's growth prospects continued to be clouded by the country's massive challenges of poverty, high unemployment and inequality.

The International Monetary Fund (IMF) noted that Namibia's positive growth record over the years had raised overall incomes and led to positive economic outcomes. However, growth had not translated into sufficient job creation contributing to persistently high unemployment and income inequality.

In 2014 Namibia agreed to sign the Economic Partnership Agreement (EPA) with the EU after terms of the agreement were negotiated and finalised between the European Commission and the Southern African Development Community (SADC). This agreement was welcomed by the fish and meat markets which rely heavily on exports to the EU for their livelihoods. However, given the peg to the South African rand, the IMF considered it important to return to fiscal prudence through greater expenditure control. With an uncertain external environment, the Namibian authorities were recommended to pursue a 'growth-friendly' fiscal consolidation, reining in unproductive current spending, while protecting growth-promoting capital spending. The IMF welcomed efforts by the government to look into ways to steer a gradual reduction of the wage bill, which would improve labour market outcomes. Measures to

KEY INDICATORS **Namibia**

	Unit	2011	2012	2013	2014	**2015
Population	m	*2.14	*2.16	*2.17	*2.19	*2.21
Gross domestic product (GDP)	US$bn	12.50	13.07	13.12	*13.35	*12.57
GDP per capita	US$	5,828	6,064	6,039	*6,095	*5,691
GDP real growth	%	3.6	5.0	5.1	*5.3	*5.6
Inflation	%	5.8	6.5	5.6	*5.3	*5.1
Exports (fob) (goods)	US$m	4,373.0	4,368.8	4,614.4	–	–
Imports (fob) (goods)	US$m	5,585.5	6,523.4	6,523.4	–	–
Balance of trade	US$m	-1,212.4	-2,154.6	-2,154.6	–	–
Current account	US$m	-584.7	-337.0	-538.0	*-883.0	*-1,240.0
Total reserves minus gold	US$m	1,820.5	1,745.9	1,511.2	1,208.7	–
Foreign exchange	US$m	1,611.7	1,737.9	1,503.3	–	–
Exchange rate	per US$	6.89	8.69	10.66	11.57	–

* estimated figure ** forecast figure

enhance domestic revenue mobilisation would also help balance the fiscal consolidation strategy. Although the level of household indebtedness had stabilised, it remains elevated.

Risk assessment

Politics	Fair
Economy	Fair
Regional stability	Fair

COUNTRY PROFILE

1884 Declared a German territory (except Walvis Bay, which was occupied in 1878 by the British).
1920 Mandated to South Africa by the League of Nations.
1946 There was stalemate when the United Nations (UN) refused to allow South Africa to annex South West Africa (SWA) and South Africa refused to place SWA under UN trusteeship.
1958 The Ovamboland People's Congress, which later became the South West Africa People's Organisation (Swapo), was created by Herman Toivo Ya Toivo and others in the anti-contract labour movement.
1960 The Ovamboland People's Congress becomes Swapo.
1968 South West Africa officially renamed Namibia by UN General Assembly.
1966 South Africa introduced apartheid laws, the UN terminated its mandate and Swapo launched an armed struggle for independence.
1972 The UN General Assembly recognised Swapo as the 'sole legitimate representative of Namibian people'.
1977 The UN declared South Africa's decision to annex Walvis Bay as 'illegal, null and void and an act of colonial expansion'.
1985 South Africa established the Transitional Government (TG), an un-elected black majority government consisting of members of six different tribal parties, instructing it to draw up a constitution.
1988 South Africa turned down the TG's constitutional draft but eventually agreed, along with Angola, Cuba, (the then) USSR and USA, Namibian independence in exchange for removal of Cuban troops from Angola.
1989 Free and fair elections were held under the auspices of the UN. South Africa withdrew its forces. The Swapo leader, Sam Nujoma, formed a transitional ministerial team.
1990 Independence was granted and Nujoma became Namibia's first president.
1994 Walvis Bay and 12 offshore Penguin Islands were formally transferred from South African to Namibian sovereignty. In Namibia's first post independence presidential and National Assembly elections in December, Swapo and Nujoma defeated the Democratic Turnhalle Alliance party of Mishake Muyongo.
1998 Namibia, Angola and Zimbabwe sent troops to the Democratic Republic of Congo to support President Laurent Kabila against rebels.
1999 President Sam Nujoma and the ruling Swapo won the presidential and legislative elections.
2001 President Nujoma said he would not stand in the 2004 presidential election although he would remain as leader of Swapo until at least 2007.
2002 President Sam Nujoma dismissed his prime minister, Hage Geingob and replaced him with Theo-Ben Gurirab, the former foreign minister
2003 Flood waters from the Zambezi River affected 10,000 villagers in the eastern Caprivi.
2004 Germany expressed regret for the colonial-era killing of tens of thousands of ethnic Hereros. Hifikepunye Lucas Pohamba was chosen by Swapo to run in the presidential election and won with 76.4 per cent of the vote. In National Assembly elections, Swapo won 76.1 per cent of the vote (55 out of 72 seats).
2005 President Hifikepunye Pohamba appointed Nahas Angula as prime minister. The ministry of lands and resettlement announced that it would cost N$3.7 billion (US$555 million) over 15 years to implement the land reforms proposed by the government. While 33 million hectares of communal land will be converted to small-scale farming, controversially one aspect of the reforms is the expropriation of white farmer-owned lands.
2007 A rich deposit of uranium was found in the Erongo region. Sam Nujoma resigned as president of Swapo; he had led the party for 47 years. A joint dam and hydroelectric power station project was agreed between Angola and Namibia. A new political party, the Rally for Democracy and Progress (RDP), was formed.
2008 The location of a 500-year-old sunken treasure ship off the coast of Namibia was announced by the diamond company Namdeb during exploration operations. The finds included gold coins and tonnes of elephant tusks.
2009 Incumbents, Hifikepunye Pohamba and Swapo won presidential and parliamentary elections
2010 A landmark court case began, concerning the forced sterilisation of HIV positive women since the mid-1990s (the case involved as many as 230 women litigants and lasted into 2011). Travel restrictions on people living with HIV/Aids and other contagious diseases were lifted. Nine members of parliament ended their boycott of parliament, imposed after the Supreme Court struck down the case brought by opposition parties contesting the last parliamentary elections on a technicality.
2011 In March, a state of emergency was declared in the north of the country around the town of Oshakati after serious flooding following heavy seasonal rains. Over 20 people were drowned and around 10,000 people displaced, as well as damage to crops and livestock and roads washed away. In July, mining and energy minister, Isak Katali announced that an estimated 11 billion barrels of oil had been found offshore in Namibian waters, with initial production scheduled for 2015.
2012 In January, China's state-owned Guangdong Nuclear Power Holding Corporation (CGNPC) (nuclear energy producer) acquired a 42 per cent share in Kalahari Minerals , which has rights to mine uranium in Namibia. This followed its offer of US$1.2 billion for the mining company in 2011. On 30 July, a ruling in the forced sterilisation case, brought by HIV sufferers, was won by three victims, although it was decided that their status as HIV-positive was not a factor. In August a consignment of African animals from Namibia arrived in Cuba to become part of Havana's zoo, prompting international concern at the removal of 146 wild animals and their future lives in captivity. On 30 September, tribal leaders took possession of the remains of the nine Herero and 11 Nama people, returned to Namibia by German museums. On 4 December, Hage Geingob was named as prime minister. A vast aquifer that could supply the north of Namibia for the next 400 years at the current rate of consumption was discovered in July. It could have a major impact on development in the driest country in sub-Saharan Africa.
2013 Drought throughout the country, but especially in the north-east, affected some 780,000 people, a third of the population. The government declared a state of emergency in May and started handing out maize meal to those most affected. There are concerns that the wildlife vital to the tourist industry as well as farm stock will suffer.
2014 Presidential and parliamentary elections were held on 28 November, Africa's first electonic ballot. The result of the presidential election was a convincing win for Hage Geingob of the South West African People's Organisation (Swapo) with 86.7 per cent of the vote, followed by McHenry Venaani (Democratic Turnhalle Alliance) with 5 per cent; the general election was also a convincing win for

Swapo with 80 per cent of the vote (77 seats out of 96).
2015 On 29 October President Geingob was urged to reconsider the appointment of justice minister, Albert Kawana, after he was reported as having referred to opposition parties as 'mosquitoes and frogs'.

Political structure

Constitution

In 1999 the Constitution was altered to allow President Nujoma to serve a third term.

On the 28 August 2014, the Third Constitutional Amendment Bill was passed which has increased the number of seats in the National Council from 26 to 42 and in the National Assembly from 72 to 96. It also saw the appointment of a vice president and it has increased the number of presidential appointments in the National Assembly from six to eight.

Independence date

1990

Form of state

Multi-party republic

The executive

Executive power rests with the president, who is Head of State and Head of Government, elected by absolute majority popular vote in two rounds if needed for a five-year term (eligible for a second term).

National legislature

Legislative power is vested in a bicameral parliament comprised of a 104 seat National Assembly of which 96 members are directly elected in multi-seat constituencies by proportional representation vote and 8 non-voting members appointed by the president. Members serve five-year terms. It is also comprised of a National Council which is made up of 42 seats of which members are indirectly elected by the regional councils to serve five-year terms.

Last elections

27–28 November 2014 (presidential and parliamentary)

Results: Presidential: Hage Geingob South West African People's Organisation (SWAPO) won 86.7 per cent of the vote, McHenry Venaani (Democratic Turnhalle Alliance) 5 per cent, Hidipo Hamutenya 3.4 per cent; six other candidates won less than two per cent each. Turnout was 71.8 per cent.

Parliamentary: SWAPO won 80 per cent of the vote (77 seats out of 96), Democratic Turnhalle Alliance 4.8 per cent (5); eight other political parties shared the remaining 14 seats with none wining more than three, six other parties failed to win any seats. Turnout was 72 per cent.

Next elections

2019 (presidential and parliamentary)

Political parties

Ruling party

South West African People's Organisation (SWAPO)

Main opposition party

Democratic Turnhalle Alliance (DTA)

Population

2.19 million (2014)* Over 70 per cent of the population is under 29 years.

Two-thirds of the predominantly rural population live in the north: Ovamboland (now four non-tribal regions), Okavango and Caprivi.

Last census: August 2001: 1,830,330

Population density: Two inhabitants per square km. Urban population 38 per cent (2010 Unicef).

Annual growth rate: 2.4 per cent, 1990–2010 (Unicef).

Ethnic make-up

87.5 per cent black, 6.5 per cent mixed race (coloured) and 6.0 per cent white.

Religions

Christianity (approximately 80 per cent), traditional beliefs (20 per cent).

Education

Primary schooling is compulsory and lasts for seven years. Secondary education is divided into two stages, junior secondary between the ages of 12 and 15 and senior secondary level lasting for another two years. A final two-year school course may be undertaken for the pre-university certificate, until aged 19.

The country has a serious lack of secondary school teachers and because of the remoteness of villages many older children are unable to complete high school.

Public expenditure on education amounts to approximately 4 per cent of annual GDP.

Literacy rate: 83 per cent adult rate; 92 per cent youth rate (15–24) (Unesco 2005).

Compulsory years: Five to 21

Enrolment rate: 131 per cent gross primary enrolment, 62 per cent gross secondary enrolment; of relevant age group (including repeaters) (World Bank).

Health

As a result of HIV/Aids, the annual cost of public healthcare has risen steadily.

Over 68 per cent of infants aged less than one year are immunised against measles.

Access to clean drinking water is available to over 77 per cent of the population.

An outbreak of polio in 2006 prompted three mass immunisation campaigns 178 people were reported to have died of the disease. An international alert has increased vigilance in Namibia's border region with Botswana and Angola.

There were cases of polio reported to the World Health Organisation – Global Polio Eradication Initiative in 2006; the country had previously been free of the disease and its re-emergence was due to infected travellers.

HIV/Aids

Namibia has one of the highest rates of HIV infection in the world. If the trend continues, the number of individuals living with the disease will rise to 400,000 by 2006. Aids is the main single cause of death for all age groups. UNAIDS estimates that the annual loss to GDP per capita growth will be 1.5 per cent by 2010.

HIV prevalence: 21.3 per cent aged 15–49 in 2003 (World Bank)

Life expectancy: 54 years, 2004 (WHO 2006)

Fertility rate/Maternal mortality rate: 3.2 births per woman, 2010 (Unicef); maternal mortality 230 per 100,000 live births (World Bank).

Child (under 5 years) mortality rate (per 1,000): 39 per 1,000 live births (WHO 2012)

Head of population per physician: 0.3 physicians per 1,000 people, 2004 (WHO 2006)

Welfare

The social pension scheme (from 1949) has massive anti-poverty objectives. Surveys in Namibia have shown that pension-dependent households are better off than small farmers. The scheme offers a non-contributory social pension for its elderly citizens. Namibia's 85,000 social pensioners receive a much lower amount each month compared to South Africa and Botswana. The social pension also supports unemployed adults, young grandchildren and other relatives. Increasingly, the pension is providing vital support to relatives of those suffering from HIV/Aids, with many elderly people fostering Aids orphans. The social pension costs the Namibian government an average of 4.8 per cent of total government expenditure.

Rape constitutes a massive problem in society. It is estimated that as many as 15,000 people a year could be victims of rape or attempted rape with only one in every 20 rapes being reported to the police.

Main cities

Windhoek (capital, estimated population 334,580 in 2012), Rundu (96,915), Walvis Bay (74,062), Swakopmund (35,675), Oshakati (35,144), Katima Mulilo (28,699), Okahandja (27,335).

Languages spoken

English is the first language of only 7 per cent of the population. All documents, notices and directional signs are in English. German and Afrikaans are widely used throughout the country.

There are six main African languages: Oshiwambo, Herero, Nama-Damara, Kwangali (Okavango region), Lozi (Caprivi region) and Tswana.

Official language/s

English

Media

The constitution guarantees freedom of the press, which is respected by the authorities.

Press

Dailies: In English and Oshiwambo, *The Namibia* (www.namibian.com.na) has the highest circulation; *New Era* (www.newera.com.na) is government owned; in Africaans *Die Republikein* (www.republikein.com.na) and in German *Allgemeine Zeitung* (www.az.com.na) all cover general news and current affairs.

Weeklies: In English, *Namibia Plus* (www.namibiaplus.com), *Windhoek Observer* and *The Southern Times* (www.southerntimesafrica.com) is published on Sunday.

Business: In English, the weekly *Namibia Economist* (www.economist.com.na) covers financial and economic news.

Periodicals: In English, *Insight Namibia* (www.insight.com.na) covers current affairs.

Broadcasting

The national public broadcaster is the Namibian Broadcasting Corporation (NBC) (www.nbc.com.na).

Radio: NBC (www.nbc.com.na) operates nine services over FM, medium wave and short wave in English, Afrikaans, German and seven local languages. There are many private, radio stations providing national networks including Radiowave (www.radiowave.com.na) and Omulunga Radio (www.omulunga.com) and Kanal 7 (www.k7.com.na).

Television: NBC (www.nbc.com.na) operates one channel, broadcasting locally produced and imported programmes in English. The private station Desert TV is located in Windhoek.

National news agency: Nampa (Namibia Press Agency)

Other news agencies: APA (African Press Agency): www.apanews.net

Reuters Africa: http://africa.reuters.com

Economy

The economy is dominated by primary industry, in particular mining of diamonds and uranium, as well as farming and fishing. For historic and trade reasons, the economy is heavily integrated with neighbouring South Africa; the Namibian dollar is pegged at one-to-one with the South African rand, which is legal tender in Namibia, and the majority of imports and exports are generated by South Africa.

There is a pool of skilled workers and professional managers that are employed in capital-intensive industries. Tourism has become a major industry since the mid-1990s, with the fastest growth of all sectors and which unlike other sectors has registered continued growth over the past five years. In 2014, the service sector constituted 63.3 per cent of GDP, industry 29.6 per cent, of which manufacturing amounted to 14 per cent, and agriculture 7.1 per cent.

GDP growth was 3.4 per cent in 2008, but in 2009 as the global economic crisis cut world trade, especially in exports of minerals, the economy fell into recession of -0.4 per cent. As world trade picked up in 2010 GDP growth bounced back to 6.6 per cent; the economy weakened in 2011 with growth estimated at 3.6 per cent but had bounced back to 5.3 per cent by 2014 as the diamond industry flourished again. Mining now contributes 11.5 per cent to GDP but accounts for over 50 per cent of foreign exchange earnings, making it vulnerable to global market trends, but rising mining costs have diminished profit margins.

Foreign direct investment net inflow stood at US$903 million, moderating slightly from the FDI figure of 2009 (US$1.1 billion).

Revenue from the Southern African Customs Union (Sacu) tariff pool was some US$1.01 billion in 2009, the largest single contribution to government income. However, as a result of the global financial crisis, in 2010 Namibia's share of the pool was significantly lower at US$853 million. Namibia is also required to repay excess Sacu transfers of N$5.2 billion (US$710 million). Finance minister Saara Kuukongelwa-Amadhila was reported in 2010 as saying she would not raise taxes, which may have led to a cut in social spending, but the government continued to stimulate the economy by spending money on infrastructure and other projects designed to attract investment and generate employment.

The government is attempting to diversify economic activities. Namibia offers relatively low labour costs, and, at Walvis Bay, a strategic location for sea exports from the southern African region. The government is targeting manufacturing, trans-shipment and energy as prime sectors for new business.

Unemployment continues to be a major problem with a rate of 28.1 per cent in 2014, this is, however, down from 50 per cent in 2009. The government is attempting to address this issue by, among other actions, a land re-allocation programme. Much will depend on the training opportunities for local farmers who are typically engaged in subsistence farming and herding.

Income inequality in Namibia is one of the largest in the world. In 2014, the UN Human Development Index (HDI) ranked Namibia 127 (out of 187) for development in health, education and income. In 2014, 31.9 per cent of the population lived on less than US$1.25 a day.

Under Namibia's millennium goal initiatives, the high rates of HIV/Aids had been reduced to 13.3 per cent of the adult population in 2014; with around 80 per cent of HIV positive Namibians were receiving antiretroviral (ARV) treatment.

External trade

Namibia is a member of the Southern African Customs Union (Sacu), with South Africa, Lesotho, Swaziland and Botswana. Sacu sets customs duties for commodities passing between member states and members share the common pool of customs and excise revenue on all external trade. It is also a member of the Southern African Development Community (SADC), the objectives of which include reducing trade barriers, achieving regional development and economic growth and evolving common systems and institutions. The bulk of imports originate in South Africa.

Imports

Principal imports are foodstuffs, petroleum products and fuel, manufactured goods, machinery, equipment, chemicals and construction materials.

Main sources: South Africa (61.8 per cent of total in 2013), Switzerland (5.8 per cent), Marshall Islands (4.1 per cent).

Exports

Principal exports are diamonds, copper, gold, zinc, lead, uranium and agricultural produce including cattle, processed fish and sheep (karakul) skins and wool.

Main destinations: South Africa (26.7 per cent of total in 2013), Botswana (13.7 per cent), Switzerland (8.8 per cent).

Agriculture

Farming

The agricultural sector contributed around 7.1 per cent to GDP in 2014 and employed 16.3 per cent of the workforce.

Only half the country is suitable for farming. In the north, yields remain low on average due to overgrazing.

Commercial farming is dominated by livestock ranching – cattle in the north-central districts, sheep (karakul and mutton) and ostriches in the south – and accounts for 80 per cent of total agricultural output.

Namibia normally produces some 40 per cent of its maize requirements from commercial farms and is generally self-sufficient in millet, the main food crop grown in the north by communal farmers. Beef is the most high-value product and exports go to the EU with an annual quota of 60,000 tonnes.

The government is pursuing a land reform programme to redistribute lands owned by white farmers. While initially the policy was to be implemented on a voluntary basis, expropriation orders began to be issued in 2005 against reluctant farmers.

Fishing

The south-east Atlantic is a rich fishing ground, with sardines, hake and mackerel being the main species.

The government declared a 370km exclusive economic zone and banned unlicensed foreign trawlers after independence. A new fishing policy designed to maximise shore-based processing, and long-term concessions to 159 operators (including 54 new ones) were granted. Namibia has a 300-strong fishing fleet and foreign trawlers operate under charter. 60,000 tonnes of fish are caught annually, 90 per cent of which is exported. The industry employs 40,000 people and accounts for 8 per cent of GDP.

In a meeting of African ministers in Namibia, held on 2 July 2009, members discussed illegal and unregulated fishing, which is estimated to cost Africa US$1 billion per annum in lost revenue and the threat to stocks and local artisan fishing.

Industry and manufacturing

The industrial sector contributes around 29.6 per cent of GDP and employs 22.4 per cent of the workforce.

There is a small and highly specialised manufacturing sector, concentrated in Windhoek and Walvis Bay, with food processing (meat, agronomic products, fish) and beverages (beer and soft drinks) predominant. Other activities include structural metal products, non-metal mineral products, wood furniture, leather goods. An export processing zone (EPZ) regime was established in 1995; it provides incentives to investors in manufacturing plants producing goods mainly for export, including a zero income tax liability for an unlimited period.

Tourism

Namibia has some extreme environments, including the Namib desert with its huge sand dunes and the Skeleton Coast with its eerie ship wrecks (the environment here is so fragile that special permits must be obtained before visiting). Air and balloon rides are a popular method of seeing these sites. Namibia is home to an array of typical African animals, such as the desert elephant and free-roaming black rhino, that have adapted to the dry conditions,.

The Twyfelfontein included on Unesco's World Heritage List has the largest concentration of rock art (petroglyphs, engravings) in Africa.

Travel and tourism is a vital component of the economy and has a direct contribution of 3 per cent (2014), and a total contribution of 14.9 per cent and is expected to rise to 20.5 per cent in 2015. The industry also provides a total employment of 19.2 per cent of the workforce (around 102,500 jobs), which is expected to rise by 4.7 per cent in 2015. Tourism is also responsible for 11.7 per cent of total investment in Namibia.

Mining

The mining sector is the traditional backbone of the economy, contributing around 11.5 per cent to GDP in 2014. Around 25 per cent of government revenues and 50 per cent of the country's foreign exchange earnings come from diamonds. Namdeb Diamond Corporation (50 per cent owned by De Beers and 50 per cent owned by the Namibian government) mines the world's richest source of high quality gem diamonds onshore north of Oranjemund, while offshore diamond recoveries by De Beers Marine have expanded significantly since commercial mining began in 1991.

The Skorpion zinc mining complex is one of the largest zinc producers in the world. Costs of extraction at Skorpion are low at around US$0.40 per kg, compared to the industry average of around US$0.70 per kg. This puts it in a good position to compete in tough markets.

Primary gold production started in 1989 and significant quantities of copper, lead, pyrite, salt and zinc are also produced while there are large unexploited deposits of base, precious and industrial minerals. Marble, granite and semi-precious stones such as rose quartz, tourmaline, amethyst and blue-lace agate are also mined; the government is seeking to promote local value by adding processing. Larger mines are mainly owned by foreign multinationals from South Africa and the UK.

Namibia is also the worlds fifth largest producer of uranium.

Hydrocarbons

There are no known oil reserves in Namibia but exploration is ongoing; prospects are considered good in the offshore Lüderitz Basin. Namibia and Angola have agreed to explore blocks in the Namibe Basin, adjoining Angola's deepwater oil fields.

There is no refinery capacity and Namibia relies on imported petroleum products, which amounted to 27,000 barrels per day in 2013. Dependence on South Africa for oil products has been reduced with supplies also coming from Angola and other overseas refineries.

Natural gas reserves totalled around 62.3 billion cubic metres in 2014. The Kudu offshore gas field, in the south, contained some 36.8 billion cubic metres of natural gas. Production has, however, not yet begun.

Coal is not produced and only a small amount is imported from neighbouring countries to meet energy demands.

Energy

Total installed generating capacity was 1000MW in 2013, production 1.33 billion kilowatt hours. Namibia and Angola have had plans to build a hydroelectric dam, to be located at Baynes, on the Kunene River, along the border with Angola since 2007. Another plan, for the 400MW Epupa hydroelectric plant, was given the go-ahead in April 2009. The US$7 billion project is scheduled to be completed by 2017. All new dam projects have attracted international pressure not to be built, especially across the Kunene River, one of only six perennial rivers in Africa, at a time of increased droughts. However Namibia's energy shortage is just as pressing and despite the potential for electricity generated from domestically produced natural gas and solar power projects, the dam is still favoured by government policy makers.

NamPower is the national electricity company responsible for generation, transmission and supply of electricity. It is a member of the Southern African Power Pool (Sapp); set up to provide reliable and economical energy supplies to all 12-member countries.

A power line from Victoria Falls in Zambia to Katima Mulilo in Namibia was commissioned by Presidents Mwanawasa and Pohamba in 2008. The 231km line will allow Zambia to supply 220 kilovolts of power to Namibia; it will form part of the Zimbabwe-Zambia-Botswana-Namibia (Zizabona) agreement, which will link the four country's power grids.

Financial markets

Stock exchange

Namibian Stock Exchange (NSE)

Banking and insurance

The banking sector is small, with four private commercial banks. The ratio of non-performing loans is relatively low, making the sector stable and financially sound.

Central bank

Bank of Namibia

Main financial centre

Windhoek

Time

GMT plus two hours

Geography

Namibia lies in south-western Africa, with South Africa to the south and south-east, Botswana to the east and Angola to the north. The country has a long coastline on the Atlantic Ocean. The narrow Caprivi

Strip, between Angola and Botswana in the north-east, extends Namibia to the Zambezi river, giving it a border with Zambia. The arid Namib Desert stretches along the west coast, while the easternmost area is part of the Kalahari Desert.

Hemisphere

Southern

Climate

Namibia has one of the driest climates in the world. Sub-tropical, the hottest months are January–February (20–29 degrees Celsius (C)) and the coldest are June–July (6–18 degrees C).

Entry requirements

Passports

Required by all and must be valid for six months after intended departure date.

Visa

Required by all, except tourist visitors, for up to 90 days, from North America, Australasia, most of Europe, and some Asian countries, for a full list of exceptions see www.mfa.gov.na. A proposed tourist *univisa* (a single visa to visit all 15-member states of SADC: Angola, Botswana, DRC, Lesotho, Madagascar, Malawi, Mauritius, Mozambique, Namibia, South Africa, Seychelles, Swaziland, Tanzania, Zambia and Zimbabwe) is expected to be in use by 2013. Visitors should check with the appropriate consulates to confirm start of *univisas* and their scope before beginning a tour of southern Africa.

Business visas require a letter of invitation or a full list and addresses of business contacts to be visited in Namibia. A certified copy of the return ticket should also be submitted. For a multiple entry visa, application should be made to the Ministry of Home Affairs on arrival in Windhoek.

Currency advice/regulations

The import and export of local currency is limited to N$50,000. The import of foreign currency is unrestricted but must be declared on arrival, and export is allowed up to declared amount.

Customs

Personal items are duty-free. Hunting rifles require a permit that can be issued by customs on arrival; handguns are prohibited.

Health (for visitors)

Mandatory precautions

Yellow fever vaccination certificate required if arriving from an infected area.

Advisable precautions

Visitors should take precautions against all tropical diseases. Vaccinations for diphtheria, tetanus, hepatitis A and typhoid and polio are recommended. Hepatitis B vaccinations may be recommended. Malaria risk exists in most areas in the north. Water in all main towns is purified and safe to drink. There is a risk of rabies. To avoid the risk of bilharzia, only use well maintained, chlorinated swimming pools.

Tap water must be treated as unsafe unless boiled and filtered (bottled water is available in the main cities). Eat only well cooked meals, preferably served hot; vegetables should be cooked and fruit peeled. Dairy products are unpasteurised and should be avoided

A first aid kit that includes disposable syringes, is a reasonable precaution. Medical insurance is essential, including emergency evacuation, and an adequate supply of personal medicines is necessary.

Hotels

Classified from one to four stars. Accommodation in towns outside Windhoek is limited apart from Swakopmund so should always be booked well in advance. Luxury lodges or bungalow accommodation is available at Etosha and other national parks; there is also an expanding range of desert lodges and guest farms.

Credit cards

International cards are widely accepted throughout the country.

Public holidays (national)

Fixed dates

1 Jan (New Year's Day), 21 Mar (Independence Day), 1 May (Workers' Day), 4 May (Cassinga Day), 25 May (Africa Day), 26 Aug (Heroes' Day), 10 Dec (International Human Rights Day), 25 Dec (Christmas Day), 26 Dec (Family Day).

Variable dates

Good Friday, Easter Holiday (Mar/Apr), Ascension Day (Apr/May).

Working hours

Banking

Mon–Fri: 0900–1530; Sat: 0830–1100.

Business

Mon–Fri: 0800–1700.

Government

Mon–Fri: 0800–1700.

Shops

Mon–Sat 0800–1800.

Telecommunications

Mobile/cell phones

There are GSM 900/1800 networks that cover most populated areas.

Electricity supply

220 V AC

Getting there

Air

National airline: Air Namibia

International airport/s: Windhoek Airport (WDH), 40km from city. Facilities include restaurant, bars, duty-free shops, post office, *bureau de change* and car hire. Taxis, minivans and buses are available to the city.

Airport tax: None

Surface

Road: Tarred highways link the South African border via Keetmanshoop to Windhoek then Oshakati and the northern border with Angola, and between Windhoek and Swakopmund-Walvis Bay. The new Trans-Kalahari highway from Botswana via Ghanzi, along with the Trans-Caprivi tarred highway, provide direct road links between Walvis Bay and central Africa.

A road bridge across the River Zambezi, between the Caprivi Strip (Namibia) and Zambia, opened in 2004.

Rail: Main line runs from South African border via Keetmanshoop and Windhoek to Swakopmund, Walvis Bay, and via Otavi to Tsumeb and Grootfontein, the northern railheads.

Main port/s: Walvis Bay is a modern, deep-water harbour, Lüderitz is older and smaller.

Getting about

National transport

Air: Flying is the most efficient way of connecting with all main towns, either using the extensive scheduled services or charter flights.

Road: Roads are generally well maintained. There are 64,799km of road, of which 7,841km are tarred, while the rest are gravel and earth. The former Owambo region in the north of the country is inhabited by about 44 per cent of the population, yet is served by only 5 per cent of the total road network.

The Trans-Kalahari and Trans-Caprivi highway provide the backbone of a network serving rural areas as well as connecting landlocked countries with the coast.

Buses: A luxury bus service exists between Windhoek and all major towns.

Rail: The main rail routes in Namibia are Windhoek-Keetmanshoop-De Aar, Walvis Bay-Swakopmund-Windhoek-Tsumeb and Lüderitz-Keetmanshoop. First- and second-class carriages are available on these routes. Light refreshments are offered on some services. On overnight services, seats in first-class compartments convert to four couchettes and those in second-class to six couchettes.

City transport

Taxis: Available in main towns; 10 per cent tip is usual.

Buses, trams & metro: Bus services are not well developed and there is generally no transport except taxis.

Car hire

Available in Windhoek city centre, international airport, Walvis Bay.

Although roads between major towns are generally of a good standard, the distances involved can be prohibitive;

four-wheel drive is advisable if going off the main routes.
International driving licence is required. Traffic drives on the left. The general speed limit is 60kph in built-up areas and 120kph on open roads. Safety belts must be used at all times.

BUSINESS DIRECTORY

The addresses listed below are a selection only. While World of Information makes every endeavour to check these addresses, we cannot guarantee that changes have not been made, especially to telephone numbers and area codes. We would welcome any corrections.

Telephone area codes

The international dialling code (IDD) for Namibia is +264 followed by the area code and subscriber's number:

Keetmanshoop	631	Swakopmund	641
Luderitz	6331	Tsumeb	671
Mariental	661	Windhoek	61

Chambers of Commerce

Namibia Chamber of Commerce and Industry, 2 Jenner Street, PO Box 9355, Windhoek (tel/fax: 228-009; e-mail: nccihq@iwwn.com.na).

Windhoek Chamber of Commerce and Industries, 315 Swa Building, 7 Post Street Mall, PO Box 191, Windhoek (tel: 222-000; fax: 233-690; e-mail: whkchamber@namib.com).

Banking

Bank of Windhoek, 262 Independence Avenue, PO Box 15, Windhoek (tel: 299-1229; fax: 299-1285).

City Savings and Investment Bank, PO Box 63, FGI Building, Post St Mall, Windhoek (tel: 221-262; fax: 221-555).

Commercial Bank of Namibia, 12-20 Bulow Street, PO Box 1, Windhoek (tel: 295-9111, 295-2014; fax: 295-2046; e-mail: cbon@iwwn.com.na).

First National Bank Namibia, 209 Independence Avenue, PO Box 195, Windhoek (tel: 229-610; fax: 225-994).

Standard Bank Namibia, Mutual Platz Building, Post Street Mall, PO Box 3327, Windhoek (tel: 294-2283; fax: 294-2583).

Central bank

Bank of Namibia, PO Box 2882, 71 Robert Mugabe Avenue, Windhoek (tel: 283-5111; fax: 283-5067; e-mail: general.inquiries@bon.com.na).

Stock exchange

Namibian Stock Exchange (NSE), www.nsx.com.na

Travel information

Air Namibia, PO Box 731, Transnamib Building, Bahnhofstreet, Windhoek 9000; (tel: 299-6000; fax: 299-6168); Town Office (tel: 229-6444; fax: 299-6168); internet: www.airnamibia.com.na).

Automobile Association, PO Box 61, Windhoek (tel: 224-201).

Etosha Northern Tourism and Publicity Association, PO Box 779, Tsumeb (tel: 220-728; fax: 220-916).

Lodge and Guest Farm Reservations, PO Box 21783, Windhoek (tel: 226-979; fax: 226-999).

Namibia Resorts International, PO Box 2862, Windhoek (tel: 233-145; fax: 234-512).

Southern Tourism Forum, Private Bag 2125, Keetmanshoop (tel: 2095; fax: 3818).

Tour and Safari Association of Namibia, PO Box 5144, Windhoek (tel: 232-748; fax: 228-461).

National tourist organisation offices

Namibia Tourism Board, Independence Avenue, Private Bag 13346, Windhoek (tel: 290-6000; fax: 254-848; email: tourism@mweb.com.na; internet: www.namibiatourism.com.na).

Ministries

Ministry of Agriculture, Water and Rural Development, Private Bag 13184, Windhoek (tel: 202-9111; fax: 229-961).

Ministry of Basic Education and Culture, Private Bag 13186, Windhoek (tel: 293-9411; fax: 224-277).

Ministry of the Environment and Tourism, Private Bag 13346, Swabour Building, Independence Avenue, Windhoek (tel: 284-2111; fax: 229-936).

Ministry of Finance, Private Bag 13295, Windhoek (tel: 209-9111; fax: 236-454).

Ministry of Fisheries and Marine Resources, Private Bag 13355, Windhoek (tel: 205-3911; fax: 233-286).

Ministry of Foreign Affairs, Private Bag 13347, Windhoek (tel: 282-9111; fax: 223-937).

Ministry of Higher Education, Vocational Training, Science & Technology, Private Bag 13391, Windhoek (tel: 253-670; fax: 253-671).

Ministry of Information and Broadcasting, Private Bag 13344, Windhoek (tel: 283-911; fax: 222-343).

Ministry of Mines and Energy, 1 Aviation Road, Private Bag 13297, Windhoek (tel: 284-8111; fax: 283-643; email: info@mme.gov.na).

Ministry of Trade and Industry, Private Bag 13340, Windhoek (tel: 283-7111; fax: 220-148).

Ministry of Works Transport and Communication, Private Bag 13341, Windhoek (tel: 208-9111; fax: 228-560).

President's Office, State House, Private Bag 13339, Windhoek (tel: 220-010; fax: 221-770).

Prime Minister's Office, Private Bag 13338, Windhoek (tel: 287-9111; fax: 226-189).

Other useful addresses

Investment Centre, Private Bag 13340, Windhoek (tel: 283-7335; fax: 22-0278).

Meat Board of Namibia, PO Box 38, Windhoek (tel: 233-280; fax: 228-310).

Namibia Crafts Centre, 40 Talstreet, Windhoek (tel: 222-236).

Namibia Development Corporation, Private Bag 13252, Windhoek (tel: 206-9111; fax: 23-3943).

Namibia Power Corporation, PO Box 2864, Windhoek (tel: 205-4111; fax: 23-2805).

Namibian Embassy (USA), 1605 New Hampshire Avenue, NW, Washington DC 2009 (tel: (+1-202) 986-0540; fax: (+1-202) 986-0443; e-mail: embnamibia@aol.com).

Namibian Ports Authority, PO Box 361, Walvis Bay (tel: 20-8201; fax: 20-8242).

National Planning Commission (NPC), Office of the President, Private Bag 13356, Windhoek (tel: 222-549; fax: 226-501).

Offshore Development Company, Private Bag 13397, Windhoek (tel: 239-032; fax: 231-001).

Ombudsman's Office, Private Bag 13211, Windhoek (tel: 225-998; fax: 226-838).

Telecom Namibia, PO Box 297, Windhoek (tel: 201-2221; fax: 223-323).

TransNamib Ltd, Private Bag 13204, Windhoek (tel: 298-1111; fax: 298-2053).

US Embassy, Private Bag 12029, 14 Lossen Street, Ausspannplatz, Windhoek (tel: 221-601; fax: 229-792).

National news agency: Nampa (Namibia Press Agency), PO Box 26185, Windhoek (tel: 374-000; fax: 221-713; internet: www.nampa.org).

APA (African Press Agency): www.apanews.net

Reuters Africa: http://africa.reuters.com

Internet sites

Africa Business Network: www.ifc.org/abn

AllAfrica.com: http://allafrica.com

African Development Bank: www.afdb.org

Office of Prime Minister: http://opm.gov.na

Nauru

KEY FACTS

Official name: Republic of Nauru

Head of State: President Baron Divavesi Waqa (from 11 Jun 2013)

Head of government: President Baron Divavesi Waqa (from 11 Jun 2013)

Ruling party: There is no formal party system; parliament is traditionally dominated by independents that form factions.

Area: 21 square km

Population: 9,454 (July 2013)*

Capital: Owing to its small size and absence of urban development, Nauru has no capital. Yaren is the main town.

Official language: Nauruan

Currency: Australian dollar (A$) = 100 cents

Exchange rate: A$1.43 per US$ (Sep 2015)

GDP per capita: US$5,632 (2009)

GDP real growth: 4.90% (2012)

GDP: US$55.00 million (2009)

Inflation: -0.50% (2012)*

Foreign debt: US$63.00 million (2010)

* estimated figure

Although an independent republic, Nauru, with a population of around 10,000, is largely dependent on Australia for its existence. A review of Australia's official development assistance (ODA) published in 2012 acknowledged the limited growth prospects for very small Pacific countries, such as Nauru. A planned increase in ODA, to offset the lack of private sector activity, is likely to be delivered through programme based approaches. This will require improvements to the country's public financial management strategies in order to efficiently absorb and manage higher ODA levels and translate this into economic growth.

Nevertheless, growth in FY2011 (ending 30 June 2011) was a respectable 4.0 per cent, largely because phosphate exports increased by more than 20 per cent. . Recently improved phosphate-loading facilities are expected to further increase phosphate exports to 450,000 tons in FY2012 from 350,000 tons in FY2011, taking economic growth to 4.8 per cent in FY2012 and 4.2 per cent in FY2013.

The *Asian Development Bank Economic Outlook 2012* reports that Nauru has been experiencing deflation for the last few years and in FY2011 the consumer price index declined by 3.5 per cent, in part because of appreciation of the Australian dollar (which Nauru uses as its official currency). Government revenue in FY2012 is expected to be A$31.6 million (US$) and expenditure A$32.5 million, yielding a small deficit of A$0.9 million. Cash reserves brought forward from FY2011 will, however, result in a small surplus.

Good, bad and ugly

Tony Abbott's 2013 Australian election victory has seen a nationwide clampdown on immigration. As such the Nauru detention facility, run by the Australian government in the form of Wilson Security, has become one of Australia's foremost immigrant holding centres and, international controversy.

Reports of sexual harassment, Abu Ghraib style abuse, torture and rape have streamed out of Nauru in waves of increasingly incriminating governmental reports and independent investigations. First hand accounts of handcuffing children 'as a joke', 'zipping' (where a person is attached to a bed before its dropped on their back) and waterboarding have led to growing calls to immediately ship women and children away to Australia and suspend practices at the site indefinitely.

For Nauruans, the centre provides a critical source of employment and calls for its closure has thus far been muted.

COUNTRY PROFILE

1798 Sighted by the British and named Pleasant Island.
1887 Nauru became a German protectorate.
1888 Became part of the (German) Marshall Islands.
1900 Phosphate was discovered.
1906 Mining began under an agreement signed by the Australian Pacific Phosphate Company and the German government.
1914 Nauru was captured by Australian forces.
1919 After Germany's defeat, the island was placed under the joint administration of the UK, Australia and New Zealand. The three countries formed the British Phosphate Commission in order to share phosphate-mining revenues.
1942 Nauru was invaded by the Japanese.
1945 At the end of the Second World War, Nauru was made a UN Trust Territory under Australian Administration.
1968 The adoption of the Nauru constitution established it as the world's smallest republic with a parliamentary system of government. Hammer DeRoburt was Nauru's first head of state.
1970 Nauru took control of its phosphate industry. Nauru's per capita income became one the world's highest.
1976 Parliament unseated DeRoburt after objections to his autocratic style.
1978 DeRoburt was re-elected.
1989 Bernard Dowiyogo was elected president, defeating DeRoburt by 10 votes.
1995 Lagumot Harris defeated Dowiyogo.
1996 Harris resigned and Dowiyogo returned to power. Dowiyogo was ousted in parliament and Kennan Adeang became

president; he in turn was replaced by Reuben Kun.
1997 Kinza Clodumar won the presidential election, backed by Bernard Dowiyogo.
1998 Dowiyogo replaced Clodumar as president.
1999 Dowiyogo was defeated in parliament and René Harris, a former president of the Nauru Phosphate Corporation, was elected president.
2000 René Harris resigned and Dowiyogo was re-elected president.
2001 Nauru agreed to Australia's proposal to house its asylum-seekers, refugees and illegal immigrants in Nauru for a fee. Parliament ousted Dowiyogo and re-elected former president, Lagumot Harris. The Financial Action Task Force (FATF) (established by the G-7 Summit of 1989) on money laundering blacklisted Nauru for not implementing appropriate legislation to curb money laundering, especially by the Russian mafia.
2002 Over 400 asylum-seekers bound for Australia were rescued from a sinking ship in the Indian Ocean and 293 were sent to Nauru which housed around 1,000 in detention.
2003 Bernard Dowiyogo ousted René Harris and became president. When Dowiyogo died of a heart attack Derog Gioura was appointed acting president. The US threatened to impose sanctions if Nauru did not halt the sale of passports and close down its banking sector, both allegedly used by the terrorist group al Qaeda. Ludwig Scotty won presidential elections. Scotty lost a no-confidence vote and was replaced by René Harris.
2004 Nauru defaulted on loan payments to Australia and had its assets seized when foreign debts were over US$165 million. Although René Harris organised a restructured loan he lost a vote of no confidence in parliament and Scotty was re-appointed president. Australia installed officials in Nauru to handle state finances. Scotty declared a state of emergency and dissolved parliament after it failed to pass a reform budget. In parliamentary elections supporters of Scotty won.
2005 Ties were severed with China and links re-established with Taiwan. Nauru was removed from the FATF blacklist of countries lacking restrictions on international money laundering; the US also lifted its 2003 sanctions.
2007 In parliamentary elections, supporters of Ludwig Scotty won 14 seats out of 18. Scotty was re-elected president beating Marcus Stephen. President Scotty lost a vote of no confidence in parliament and Marcus Stephen was appointed in his place.
2008 The Australian offshore processing centre for asylum seekers was closed when the remaining 21 Sri Lankans, who had been granted refugee status, were flown to Australia. This brought to an end the controversial 'Pacific Solution' that Australia had instituted in 2002. The centre is said to have contributed around 20 per cent of Nauru's GDP, and employed about 100 people. President Stephen called a snap election after declaring a state of emergency, following political stalemate since he took office. President Stephen won most support with 12 members (out of 18) of his grouping elected; the remainder were either opposition or independent members. Former president, René Harris died.
2009 The Organisation for Economic Co-operation and Development (OECD) published a list of countries that had not implemented international tax information exchange standards, of which Nauru was one, despite signing a co-operation agreement in 2003.
2010 In a constitutional referendum, 66.96 per cent of voters rejected changes that included a directly elected president and a distribution of power and a strengthening human rights legislation. The President dissolved parliament and scheduled elections, one year earlier than planned, as a series of no-confidence motions in parliament had undermined his position and had stalled the budget. The elections had no clear majority for or opposed to President Marcus Stephen. In another round the result was nine pro-Stephen, eight opposed and one independent. A state of emergency was imposed and government business carried on under presidential decree. The Supreme Court rejected the oppositions' challenge to the president's imposition of a state of emergency and a deal was forged whereby Ludwig Scotty became Speaker of the House and, following an indirect presidential ballot, Marcus Stephen was re-elected president, beating Milton Dube by 11 votes to six.
2011 Nauru signed the UN Refugee Convention in June, which precludes refugees being forcibly returned to their country of origin. On 10 November, President Marcus Stephen resigned and Fredrick Pitcher was elected by parliament (nine votes to eight for Milton Dube) as president. However, on 15 November parliament changed its decision and Pitcher was deposed (by nine votes to eight) and replaced by Sprent Dabwido.
2012 On 14 August the Nauru Detention Centre was reopened on behalf of the Australian government and the first irregular maritime arrivals (IMAs) (asylum seekers and unauthorised migrants). When fully operational the centre will house up to 1,500 people, including families. However, the camp is a makeshift tent city and by 2 November, 170 (out of 400) IMAs were on hunger strike in protest about the conditions and their prospects.
2013 On 18 March the elections scheduled for 6 April were cancelled by the Supreme Court. President Sprent Dabwido withdrew his notice, submitted to the speaker of Parliament on the 1 March, advising that parliament be dissolved, on 15 April. Elections were rescheduled for 22 June. However, the President declared a state of emergency and brought the date forward to 8 June. Supporters of Baron Waqa won 14 seats and those of Roland Kun 5 seats. Baron Waqa was elected President.
2014 In late September Nauru's finance minister, David Adeang, reported that the country was rapidly running out of money and that services would soon be shutting down. Government bank accounts were frozen after the government refused to comply with a court order to pay A$30 million (US$26 million) on bonds owned by Firebird Global Master Fund; the bonds had been issued on the Japanese stock exchange in the 1980s.
2015 On 7 October Australian lawyers began their arguements before the high court that the detention centres on Nauru breach the Australian constitution.

Political structure

Constitution

Republic
Voting is compulsory for all over the age of 20.

Independence date

31 January (anniversary of independence from Australia in 1968).

The executive

The president is head of state and head of government. The president, elected by parliament, governs for a three-year term, with the assistance of a cabinet of four or five ministers appointed from within parliament.

National legislature

Legislative power is vested in an 18-member unicameral parliament, elected for a three-year term in multi-seat constituencies.

Last elections

8 June 2013 (parliamentary)
Results: Parliamentary: 14 'non-partisan' supporters of President Baron Waqa and five 'non-partisan' supporters of Roland Kun were elected.

Next elections

2016 (parliamentary and presidential).

Political parties

Informal alliances and personal links rather than formal, strong party discipline.

Ruling party

There is no formal party system; parliament is traditionally dominated by independents that form factions.

Political situation
Government business became fraught in 2010 as parliament ground to a halt following the political stand-off between President Marcus Stephen and the opposition. President Stephen survived a series of no-confidence motions in parliament, while the opposition held up the budget, until in April when Stephen called a snap election to break the deadlock. However, the electorate did not look favourably on either camp and returned the same members of parliament; this happened twice. The Speaker was sacked by the president and in June and President Stephen declared a state of emergency. The opposition retaliated by challenging the legitimacy of the caretaker government in the Supreme Court in October 2010. However, the Supreme Court threw out the motion saying the president had every right to call a state of emergency, under the circumstances.
Parliament now has to find some consensus and bipartisan support for constitutional changes that will stop such deadlock in the future.

Population
9,454 (July 2013)*
Last census: April 1992: 9,919
Population density: 475 inhabitants per square km (2010). Urban population 100 per cent (2010 Unicef).
Annual growth rate: 0.6 per cent, 1990–2010 (Unicef).
Ethnic make-up
Nauruan (58 per cent), other Pacific islanders (26 per cent), Chinese (8 per cent), European (8 per cent). The indigenous population is of Micronesian descent.
Religions
Protestant (66 per cent), Roman Catholic (33 per cent).

Education
Schooling is provided free and is compulsory from aged 4–16. 10 per cent of schoolchildren are expected to complete secondary education. The government has backed the 'one laptop per child' programme (OLPC).
Scholarships are available for higher education overseas.

Health
The population's general health is not good; Nauru has a high rate of type two diabetes, with one-third of adults suffering from the disease due to the consumption of large amounts of processed food. In May 2004, a report ranked Nauruans as the most obese people in the world. A new diabetes centre has been set up as a focal point to provide multi-faceted treatment and education.
The World Health Organisation (WHO) released statistics in January 2011 that ranked Nauru's population with the world's highest level of obesity, with 97 per cent of men and 93 per cent of women overweight or obese. Associated chronic diseases, such as diabetes, heart disease and cancer are responsible for around 75 per cent of all deaths. A diet of processed foods, which are high in sugar and fat, have replaced the traditional diet of fish, coconuts and root vegetables and is held responsible for the condition of most people. Cultural values, which equate size with prosperity, also contribute to the condition.
Life expectancy: 61 years, 2004 (WHO 2006)
Fertility rate/Maternal mortality rate: 3.8 births per woman, 2004 (WHO 2006)
Birth rate/Death rate: 26 births per 1,000 population; seven deaths per 1,000 population (2003).
Child (under 5 years) mortality rate (per 1,000): 37 per 1,000 live births (WHO 2012)

Main cities
Owing to its small size and absence of urban development, Nauru has no capital. Yaren is the main town (estimated population 4,859 in 2012).

Languages spoken
Nauruan and English, which is widely spoken and used for most government and commercial purposes.
Official language/s
Nauruan

Media
Press
The government-owned, weekly *Nauru Bulletin*, publishes in Nauruan and English. Other newspapers include the fortnightly *Central Star News* published on Saturdays and *Nauru Chronicle*.
Broadcasting
The Nauru Broadcasting Service operates public radio and TV.
Radio: Radio Nauru operated two services on AM and FM, in English and Nauruan, with imported material from Radio Australia and the BBC.
Television: Nauru Television (NTV) moved its operation to New Zealand in 1991 and broadcasts via satellite and on video-tapes.
Other news agencies: ABC Pacific Beat: www.radioaustralia.net.au/pacbeat
Pacific Magazine:
www.pacificmagazine.net

Economy
The economy, which once relied almost solely on phosphate mining to give the islanders in the 1960s the highest per capita income in the world, has virtually collapsed so that by 2009 the island was dependent on fishing rights and international grants and development funding and aid (particularly from Australia) to survive. The resumption of limited phosphate mining and its export by the Australian company Incitec Pivot, which invested A$6 million (US$7.9 million) in a government backed revitalisation of the industry, has shown small profits but can only provide limited respite. After phosphate reserves looked to be almost gone in 2007, mining companies began to look deeper into the earth to find reserves. According to the Asian Development Bank (ADB), secondary phosphate reserves could last another 30 years.
With the help of the Pacific Island Forum the government is undertaking a strategic development programme to create a new sustainable economic framework for the future.
GDP growth plunged into recession in 2007 with negative growth of -27.3 per cent, before rallying to 1 per cent in 2008. It remained static for the next two years at 0 per cent, until 2011 when the economy registered estimated GDP growth of 4 per cent, a figure which increased to 4.9 per cent in 2012 (latest figures). Inflation typically runs at around 3–4 per cent and the government often has difficulty in balancing the budget with poor agricultural productivity and little prospect for industrial expansion. In 2009 inflation spiked at 21.2 per cent following the collapse in international trade due to the global economic crisis and the high prices of imports of food and fuel. In 2010–11, as domestic and government spending reacted to sharp rises in costs, an average -2 per cent deflation rate was recorded. In 2012 Nauru had inflation of -0.5 per cent which had dropped further to -2.1 per cent in 2013 (latest figures).
Unemployment in 2011 (latest figures) was 23.5 per cent.
Phosphate mining is one of the only resources which the island possesses, and it provided some 10-15 per cent of the national budget in 2014/5.

External trade
Nauru is a member of the South Pacific Regional Trade and Economic Co-operation Agreement (Sparteca) along with 12 other regional nations, which allows products duty free access by Pacific Island Forum members to Australian and New Zealand markets (subject to the country of origin restrictions).
Imports
Imports include food, fuel, consumer goods, building materials, vehicles and machinery.

Main sources: Australia (92.1 per cent of total in 2013 (latest figures)), New Zealand (1.4 per cent), Fiji (1.0 per cent).

Exports

Phosphates, besides financial services, are the sole export.

Main destinations: Phosphates, besides financial services, are the sole export.

Agriculture

Farming

Arable land is confined to a strip 150–300 metres between the beach and the cliff, surrounding a vast crater caused by the phosphate mine.

Artisanal vessels (canoes and aluminium dinghies) supply fish for local consumption. Most food is imported.

There are long-term plans to rehabilitate former mining land into agricultural land with funds from the Australian government.

Fishing

The total fish catch is typically 400 tonnes per annum.

On 12 April 2011, a summit of the Parties to the Nauru Agreement (PNA) concluded its strategy for a policy of sustainable fishing in the Pacific. The PNA treaty, which was established in 1989 and expired in 2012, is seen as in need of an overhaul. As a collective region the PNA (FSM, Kiribati, Marshall Islands, Nauru, Palau, PNG, Solomon Islands and Tuvalu) controls around 25–30 per cent of world stocks of tuna. Only 5 per cent of sales revenue is returned to the PNA and ministers called for specific changes, including an increased share of profits, PNA crews on-board purse seine vessels (minimum 10 per cent), conservation and management measures including a limit to fish trapping (fish aggregating devices (FADs)), net mesh rules and the establishment of an observer agency and fisheries information management system. The PNA met in May 2012 to discuss even stronger management measures to ensure even more sustainable tuna fisheries and minimise environmental damage. Many of the ideas put forward were implemented in January 2013, for example, observation and monitoring of catches and environmental damage by 100 per cent independent bodies. The area involved stretches from Palau and Papua New Guinea in the west to Kiribati in the east, from the Marshall Islands in the north to Tuvalu in the south; it holds an estimated 25 per cent of the world's tuna supply.

Industry and manufacturing

Phosphate processing is the only industry.

Tourism

Nauru offers the quintessential white sandy beaches fringed by palms that make up the image of a tropical paradise, and is particularly suited to those visitors who want to get away from a frenetic lifestyle. The island has little in the way of tourist development with only two hotels and two lodges and activities limited to sea sports (fishing, diving and swimming). Trips to Nauru involve a flight from Brisbane (Australia), which are limited to two flights a week.

The Nauru Tourism Department has a new, interactive website (www.discovernauru.com) that offers advice, a range of accommodation and all activities available.

Environment

Rehabilitation of the island is necessary after decades of phosphate mining. Nauru was one of the first countries to sign the Framework Convention on Climate Change. Rising sea levels related to global warming mean that in the future habitable low-lying land areas will be at risk from tidal surges and flooding.

Mining

Nauru's phosphate reserves, the legacy of a millennia of fossilised bird excreta, represented the highest-grade phosphate ore in the world. There are plans to reach deeper sources via boring coral, in a more involved secondary mining process.

Hydrocarbons

There are no known hydrocarbon reserves. Consumption of oil was 1,000 barrels per day (bpd) in 2013 (latest figures), all of which was imported.

Energy

Total installed generating capacity was 10MW in 2011 (latest figures), producing 3 million kilowatt hours. The Nauru Utilities Authority (NUA) is responsible for electricity generation. It is participating in the Pacific Islands review of renewable energies, specifically wind power, sponsored by the European Union.

Banking and insurance

There are no reliable commercial banking services in Nauru. Setting up a viable domestic banking system will be a major task to be addressed in the government's economic reform programme.

Central bank

The Bank of Nauru is insolvent and operates on a very limited basis.

Offshore facilities

Nauru is in the process of closing down its offshore banking sector, and thereby closing off access of criminal money laundering. The 2004/05 budget set aside funds for the establishment of a financial investigations unit to support the implementation process. The Organisation for Economic Co-operation and Development (OECD) published a list on 2 April 2009 of countries that had not implemented international tax information exchange standards, of which Nauru was one, despite signing a co-operation agreement in 2003.

Time

GMT plus 12 hours

Geography

Nauru is a small island in the central Pacific Ocean, lying about 40km (25 miles) south of the Equator and about 4,000km (2,500 miles) north-east of Sydney, Australia. Banaba (Ocean Island), in Kiribati, is about 300km (185 miles) to the east.

It is oval-shaped and was one of the Pacific's largest phosphate-rock islands (the phosphate has since been depleted), ringed by a wide coral reef that gives no natural harbour or anchorage. Sandy beaches fringe a fertile belt between the shore and a coral cliff that rises to a central plateau up to 60 metres above sea level. There are no rivers or large lakes and the populations' main source of fresh water is either the often brackish water of the 300 acre Buada lagoon, or rainwater; there is an underground lake in the south-east in the Moqua Cave.

Hemisphere

Southern

Climate

Tropical, tempered by sea breezes, but humid (80 per cent) with variable rainfall. Temperatures range from 24–34 degrees Celsius in the shade. Monsoon season from November–February; average annual rainfall is 2,060mm. Between May–October is the best time to visit.

Entry requirements

Passports

Required by all.

Visa

Required by all, except nationals of New Zealand for visits up to three months and South Korea for 14 days. Tourist visas, for up to 30 days, may be obtained on arrival by nationals of US, Canada, UK and Caribbean Commonwealth countries with proof of sufficient funds, accommodation and return/onward passage.

Business and visitors' visas from all other countries must be obtained in advance directly from the Department of Foreign Affairs in Nauru (details in Ministry Addresses).

Currency advice/regulations

The import of local and foreign currencies is unlimited but must be declared on arrival. Export of local currency is limited to the equivalent of A$2,500; amounts greater then this must be authorised by the Bank of Nauru. The export of foreign currency is unlimited.

Travellers cheques are readily accepted.

Customs

Personal property is duty-free.

Traditional artifacts of Nauru require an export licence.

Prohibited imports

Firearms, ammunition, pornography and illegal drugs.

Health (for visitors)

Mandatory precautions

Cholera vaccination certificate if arriving from or via an infected area within five days. Yellow fever vaccination certificate if arriving from an infected area.

Advisable precautions

Vaccination for diphtheria, tuberculosis, hepatitis A and B, polio, tetanus, typhoid. There is a rabies risk. Main water is chlorinated but may cause mild stomach upset. Local water may be contaminated. There are no medical specialists, and serious cases are sent to Australia so medical insurance, including emergency evacuation, is necessary.

Hotels

There are two hotels on the island the Menen and the Od-N-Aiwo.

Credit cards

All major credit and charge cards are accepted. ATMs are not available.

Public holidays (national)

Fixed dates

1 Jan (New Year's Day), 31 Jan (Independence Day), 17 May (Constitution Day), 25 Sep (Youth Day), 26 Oct (Angam Day), 25–26 Dec (Christmas).

Variable dates

Good Friday, Easter Monday and Tuesday.

Working hours

Banking

Mon–Thu: 0900–1600; Fri: 0900–1630.

Business

Mon–Fri: 0800–1200, 1330–1630.

Government

Mon–Fri: 0900–1700.

Shops

Mon–Fri 0800–1800. Some food shops are open for longer hours and at the weekend.

Telecommunications

There is an automatic island and international radio communications system in operation.

Electricity supply

110/240V AC, 50Hz

Weights and measures

Metric system

Social customs/useful tips

In business an informal attitude prevails, shirts and smart trousers or skirts are acceptable and only on very special occasions is more formal wear advisable. It is customary to shake hands on meeting and taking leave.

Gratuities are not customary. The minimum drinking age is 21 years.

Getting there

Air

National airline: Our Airline (formerly Air Nauru), with limited services to Brisbane (Australia), Kiribati and the Marshall Islands.

International airport/s: Nauru Island International (INU), there are few facilities; buses run to Yaren after each arriving plane and there is a courtesy bus provided by the Menen Hotel.

Airport tax: Departures tax: A$25.

Surface

Water: The main sealinks are with Australia, New Zealand and Japan. Without a natural harbour most commercial vessels moor offshore, in what are reputedly some of the world's deepest permanent anchorages, and passengers and cargo have to be ferried ashore.

Getting about

National transport

Road: A main road (19.3km) circles the island, and all residential areas are linked by surfaced roads. A regular local bus service operates around the island. Buada and the former phosphate areas are linked by an inland road.

Car hire

Car hire can be arranged locally. Traffic drives on the left. A national driving licence should suffice.

BUSINESS DIRECTORY

The addresses listed below are a selection only. While World of Information makes every endeavour to check these addresses, we cannot guarantee that changes have not been made, especially to telephone numbers and area codes. We would welcome any corrections.

Telephone area codes

The international direct dialling (IDD) code for Nauru is +674 followed by subscriber's number.

Useful telephone numbers

Police: 110

Fire: 119

Ambulance: 118 or 117

Banking

Central bank

Bank of Nauru, PO Box 289, Civic Centre, Aiwo District (tel: 444-3238/3267; fax: 444-3203; e-mail:bon@cenpac.net.nr).

Travel information

Air Nauru, Government Building, Yaren District (tel: 444-3141, 444-3418; fax: 444-3170).

Nauru International Airport, PO Box 40, Nauru Air Corporation (tel: 444-3754/3141; fax: 444-3282-3705).

Pacific Island Travel, Herengracht 495, 1017 BT Amsterdam, The Netherlands (tel: (+31) 020-626-1325; fax (+31) 020-623-0008; internet: www.pacificislandtravel.com).

National tourist organisation offices

National Tourist Office, c/o Special Project Officer (Culture and Tourism), Department of Island Development and Industry, Government Offices, Aiwo District (tel: 444-3191; fax: 444-3791).

Ministries

Address for all Government Offices: Government Offices, Yaren District.

Chief Secretary, Secretary to Cabinet, Public Service Commissioner and Registrar of Births, Deaths and Marriages (tel: 444-3133; fax: 444-3110).

Department of Foreign Affairs (tel: 444-3133; fax: 444-3105).

Secretary for Education (tel: 444-3130; fax: 444-3718).

Secretary for External Affairs (tel: 444-3191, 444-3701; fax: 444-3105).

Secretary for Finance (tel: 444-3285, 444-3287; fax: 444-3125).

Secretary for Health (tel: 444-3702; fax: 444-3106).

Secretary for Island Development and Industry (tel: 444-3281; fax: 444-3705) (economic development and privatisation and foreign investment).

Secretary for Justice (tel: 444-3747, 444-3160; fax: 444-3108).

Secretary for Works and Community Services (tel: 444-3703; fax: 444-3718).

Other useful addresses

Directorate of Telecommunications, Private Bag, Yaren (tel: 444-3132; fax: 444-3111).

Nauru Finance Corporation, PO Box 306, Yaren (tel: 3390; fax: 3345) (responsible for promoting economic diversification, including offshore banking).

Nauru Permanent Mission to the UN, 800 Second Ave, Suite 400D, New York, NY-10017 (tel: (+1-212) 937-0074; internet: www.un.int/nauru).

ABC Pacific Beat: www.radioaustralia.net.au/pacbeat

Pacific Magazine: www.pacificmagazine.net

Internet sites

Nauru International Airport: www.airnauru.com.au

Nauru website: www.nauruwire.org

Nepal

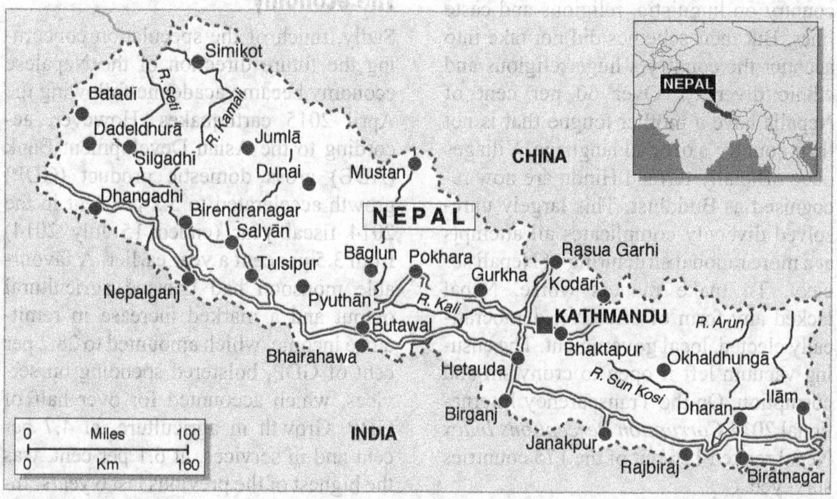

Nepal will remember the earthquake that struck on 25 April 2015 for years to come. Not that it was exactly a terrestrial paradise before the earthquake struck just before noon. Nepal is one of Asia's poorest countries, with cast and ethnic divisions creating a fragmented society, where a ten-year long civil war (from 1996 to 2006) failed to bring harmony.

Picking up the pieces

The April 2015 disaster was the worst to hit Nepal on record. In fact there were two earthquakes, the first registered 7.8 on the Richter scale, killing over 8,000 and destroying over half a million homes. The second earthquake, registering 7.3 on the scale, struck two weeks later, some 75 kilometres to the east of the capital Kathmandu. One report put the total death toll from the two earthquakes at 8,583. The previous deadliest earthquake to strike the country – in 1934 – killed at least 8,519.

In early 2015 Nepal's politicians, who for the most part seemed incapable of agreeing on anything, had through their inertia already frittered away whatever peace dividend there might have been after the civil war. It remained to be seen whether the April catastrophe would bring them to their senses, or whether the pressure exerted by international organisations and non-governmental organisations (NGOs) would expose the weaknesses of a largely unrepresentative government that had been shown to be both inefficient and corrupt.

One month after the earthquake, there were an estimated one million homeless Nepalese. Entire villages needed to be rebuilt or relocated before the annual rainy season. In the relatively thinly populated Gorkha district (home of the legendary Gurkha mercenaries that have long served with both the British and Indian armies), twenty-two villages needed to be abandoned and initial estimates put the number of houses that would need to be rebuilt at 2,314. In Katmandu, one month after the earthquake 1,500 buildings needed to be demolished immediately. Buddhist organisations reported that two hundred monks had died following the destruction of some 1,000 monasteries.

Political damage

The often violent political divisions within Nepalese society inevitably made matters worse. Less than a decade earlier, over 80 per cent of the country was dominated by the Maoist rebellion. The peace agreement, negotiated by India, established a democratic, federal and secular republic. However, it took seven years of debate (and, some might say, an earthquake) before Nepal's politicians had

KEY FACTS

Official name: Sanghiya Loktantrik Ganatantra Nepal (Federal Democratic Republic of Nepal)

Head of State: President Ram Baran Yadav (Nepali Congress) (from 23 Jul 2008)

Head of government: Prime Minister Khadga Prasad Oli (elected by parliament 11 Oct 2015)

Ruling party: Communist Party of Nepal (Unified Marxist–Leninist) (CPN-UML)

Area: 147,181 square km

Population: 28.11 million (2014)* (26,620,809; 2011, census figure)

Capital: Kathmandu

Official language: Nepali (Devnagari script)

Currency: Rupee (NRs) = 100 paisa (the NRs is pegged to the Indian rupee – NRs 160 = Rs100) (Notes with the King's image became illegal tender on 17 March 2011)

Exchange rate: NRs106.47 per US$ (Sep 2015)

GDP per capita: US$699 (2014)*

GDP real growth: 5.48% (2014)

GDP: US$19.64 billion (2014)

Labour force: 18.00 million (2009)*

Inflation: 9.04% (2014)

Balance of trade: -US$5.51 billion (2013)

Annual FDI: US$94.02 million (2011)

* estimated figure

finally approved a new constitution which came into effect on 20 September 2015. The sticking point had, perhaps surprisingly, been the federal re-organisation of the country which in theory was designed to benefit the native Nepalis (the *janajatis*) from the mountainous regions more than those from the plains (the *madhesis*), many of whom were immigrants from India. Those minorities traditionally excluded from Nepali society, notably the low castes and the Muslim community, could see little benefit from federalisation. For most Nepalis on all sides of the divide, there was little perceived benefit from federalisation; former (until October 2015) prime minister Sushil Koirala, came from a well-established political family – no less than three of his cousins had been prime minister before him. The President, Ram Baran Yadav was a madhesi. All of them were members of the generally 'pro-Indian' ruling Congress Party.

Two weeks before the earthquake, the Maoist opposition Unified Communist Party – which had been in power for a short period from 2008 to 2009 – had paralised the country by calling a general strike in protest at the government's decision to approve a new draft constitution by consensus rather than by majority vote. The Maoist and Muslim communities had wanted the new plans to be based on ethnic-lingustic divisions (as was the case in India) rather than the purely administrative divisions preferred by the political 'élite' who saw this as a more effective way of retaining power. Since the eighteenth century, the two higher Indian *varnas*, or caste division, the Brahmins and the Kshatriyas, had endeavoured to unify Nepal's varied collection of valleys into some sort of recognisable structure. The two castes hold down some 80 per cent of public posts and the professions, so that Nepal's doctors, lawyers, civil servants and military all had similar appearances, quite different from those of – for example – a Sherpa.

For some three centuries, the Nepalese monarchy had attempted to unify the country on linguistic, religious and caste lines. But their schemes did not take into account the country's huge religious and ethnic diversity. Over 60 per cent of Nepalis have a mother tongue that is not their country's official language. Villages once officially termed Hindu are now recognised as Buddhist. This largely unresolved diversity complicates all attempts at a more rational structuring of Nepali society. To make matters worse, Nepal lacked any form of effective, democratically elected, local government. The ensuing vacuum left it open to cronyism and corruption. On the Transparency International 2014 *Corruption Perceptions Index* Nepal ranked 126 out of the 175 countries surveyed.

Political paralysis

The 2015 political paralysis arose from the opposition's insistence that no local elections could be held until the draft constitution had been approved. What had not been foreseen were the drastic effects the political paralysis would have on the rescue operations following the earthquake. Instead of seeing it as an opportunity for consolidating their apparent popularity, the Maoists opted to continue their political warfare. International NGOs often found that their aid efforts and supplies were blocked by local wrangling and intrigue. Nepal's lack of basic democracy meant that its caste system remained a serious obstacle in social and political development. Much more so than in India – where the caste system had originated – where the steady encroachment of local and regional democracy meant that caste divisions had become less important than was the case in Nepal.

The economy

Sadly, much of the speculation concerning the future direction of the Nepalese economy became academic following the April 2015 earthquakes. However, according to the Asian Development Bank (ADB) gross domestic product (GDP) growth accelerated to 5.2 per cent in the 2014 fiscal year (ended 15 July 2014) from 3.5 per cent a year earlier. A favourable monsoon had boosted agricultural output and a marked increase in remittance income, which amounted to 28.2 per cent of GDP, bolstered spending on services, which accounted for over half of GDP. Growth in agriculture, at 4.7 per cent and in services, at 6.1 per cent, was the highest of the previous last 6 years. Industry again advanced only marginally, at 2.7 per cent, as long hours of power outages and other supply-side constraints continued to stunt manufacturing and divert to imports consumer spending on finished goods.

Inflation stayed high at an average of 9.1 per cent in 2014, moderating little from 9.9 per cent a year earlier as stubbornly rising food prices offset gains from falling prices for other expenditures. Despite a better harvest, food price inflation averaged 11.6 per cent, up from 8.6 per cent a year earlier, as transport costs rose, supply-side bottlenecks persisted and food inflation worsened in India, an important supplier. In the first half of the 2015 fiscal year, year-on-year inflation fell to 6.8 per cent by January 2015, reflecting several downward adjustments to domestic fuel prices that have helped to ease non-food inflation, though food inflation remains elevated.

Despite the timely adoption of the 2014 budget, actual expenditure amounted to just 82.4 per cent of budget allocations, which held spending to 20.9 per cent of GDP, only slightly improved from the previous year's depressed level. Budget execution shortfalls reflect long-standing procedural and procurement inefficiencies that constrain investment spending and development. Higher tax collections from a surge in imports and efficiency gains in revenue administration allowed revenue, including grants, to expand by

KEY INDICATORS — **Nepal**

	Unit	2011	2012	2013	2014	**2015
Population	m	26.62	*27.47	*27.79	*28.11	*28.43
Gross domestic product (GDP)	US$bn	18.60	18.96	19.24	19.64	*21.69
GDP per capita	US$	653	690	692	*699	*763
GDP real growth	%	3.5	4.9	3.9	5.5	*5.0
Inflation	%	9.6	8.3	9.9	9.0	*7.1
Exports (fob) (goods)	US$m	999.0	1,004.3	991.5	–	–
Imports (fob) (goods)	US$m	5,665.1	5,951.1	6,502.1	–	–
Balance of trade	US$m	-4,666.1	-4,946.8	-5,510.6	–	–
Current account	US$m	49.0	909.0	635.0	908.0	*88.0
Total reserves minus gold	US$m	–	4,306.6	5,293.5	6,027.1	–
Exchange rate	per US$	71.86	86.58	99.53	100.99	–

* estimated figure ** forecast figure

21.3 per cent, pushing it to a record 20.8 per cent of GDP. The budget balance turned into a deficit of 0.1 per cent of GDP, much less than the target deficit of 2.4 per cent, but an improvement on the unintended surplus in the previous year. Monetary conditions remained highly accommodative in FY2014. The increase in remittance inflows boosted deposits and bank liquidity and financial institutions struggled to find bankable projects immediately ready for investment.

The interbank rate hovered at close to zero and weighted average rates for deposits and loans continued to ease, leaving real lending rates positive and deposit rates negative. Growth in credit to the private sector was, at 18.3 per cent, more contained than the 20.2 per cent expansion recorded in FY2013. While the central bank has sought to channel credit to productive investment and so foster growth, monetary policy cannot compensate for inadequate infrastructure, political uncertainty and other supply side constraints that might inhibit productive business activity.

The current account surplus expanded to 4.7 per cent of GDP on large remittance inflows despite an ever-widening trade deficit. Exports reversed a decline in FY2013 to increase by 5.1 per cent with the help of a marked deprecation of the Nepalese rupee, which is pegged to the Indian currency. Imports grew by 13.9 per cent, mainly because imports other than oil expanded sharply as disposable income rose, though imports of petroleum products, about 20 per cent of the total, also recorded a double-digit increase. The trade deficit widened to 30.9 per cent of GDP. Remittance inflows grew by 11.9 per cent, reaching a record 28.2 per cent of GDP. The balance of payments surplus climbed to US$1.3 billion and gross foreign exchange reserves hit US$6.9 billion, equivalent to 10.2 months of imports of goods and services.

The economic outlook was less favourable than in 2014 because agricultural output was crimped by a weak monsoon and the political situation was fluid. The Constituent Assembly, the second of which was elected in November 2013, failed yet again to write a new constitution, this time by the 22 January 2015 deadline that had been agreed by all political parties.

The weak monsoon and such natural disasters as floods and landslides would affect the output of paddy, maize and millet. Industry might see better conditions in the medium term following the government's strong commitment under the 2015 budget to ease business regulations by introducing updated policies and legislation, although a downside risk was that the unsettled political environment would derail legislative action. Nevertheless, news from the power sector had bolstered business and investor confidence. The government concluded project development agreements in the first half of the 2015 fiscal year for two 900-megawatt hydroelectricity projects promoted by Indian investors.

Considering the unfavourable monsoon (but not, of course, the impact of the earthquake) and the lingering political uncertainty, GDP growth was projected to slow to 4.6 per cent in FY2015, less than the government's revised target of 5.0 per cent. The ministry of agricultural development had projected rice output to drop by 5.1 per cent and maize by 6.0 per cent. Almost half of growth had been expected to come from the services sector, particularly robust growth in wholesale and retail trade, tourism and transport and communications. The reform-oriented budget had called for higher capital expenditure and for total planned spending to increase to 23.7 per cent of GDP, up by 5 percentage points. This would have helped to underpin growth, especially in construction, even if capital spending fell modestly short. Assuming (which with the election of the new prime minister, Khadga Prasad Sharma Oli on 11 October is possible) a stable political situation, a normal monsoon, a timely budget and its effective execution and strong remittance inflows, GDP growth was expected to rebound to 5.1 per cent in 2016. Despite the expected agricultural shortfall – and an increase in civil service salaries and allowances for a second consecutive year – average inflation had been expected to continue to slow to 7.7 per cent, lower than the target set by the Nepal Rastra Bank (central bank) in its 2015 monetary policy, as neighbouring India experiences markedly lower inflation and the drop in international oil prices was passed through in the form of lower administered fuel prices. Food inflation was expected to ease somewhat but would remain elevated owing to the smaller domestic harvest. Inflation had been projected to edge lower in 2016, to 7.3 per cent reflecting a better harvest, broadly stable oil and commodity prices and the central bank's progress in efforts to rein in excess bank liquidity.

The external position had been expected to weaken in 2015 with lower surpluses in the current account and the overall balance of payments. Although export growth had been expected to stay at 5.0 per cent and import growth to slow to 10.0 per cent on lower prices for petroleum imports, the improvement in the trade deficit had been expected to be offset by some slowing in remittance inflows, narrowing the current account surplus to 2.7 per cent of GDP. A pickup in export growth, strong remittance inflows and tourism receipts and continued low global oil prices had also been expected to boost the current account surplus to 3.5 per cent of GDP in 2016.

Capital spending in Nepal had been persistently weak, with both planned and actual spending languishing far below what is required to close the infrastructure deficit, which had been estimated to require capital spending equal to between 8.2 per cent and 11.8 per cent of GDP per year until 2020. Raising the amount and quality of capital expenditure was one of the country's most pressing challenges. Accelerated capital spending was needed to scale up infrastructure investments and thereby attract the private investment needed for Nepal to attain higher economic growth that was both sustainable and inclusive.

In its provision and quality of infrastructure, Nepal has been rated one of the least competitive countries in the world, ranked 132 out of 147. Selecting aspects of infrastructure, Nepal's rankings on the quality of electricity supply was 136, on air transport infrastructure 129 and on roads 115. These dismal figures indicated that Nepal needed more and better investment to foster innovation, make the economy competitive and enhance the efficiency of markets for goods, labour and finance. Gross fixed capital investment had to be raised to at least 30 per cent of GDP from the current 22 per cent to support higher economic growth. Higher public capital spending was crucial, as it was the catalyst for private capital investment.

Risk assessment

Economy	Fair
Politics	Poor
Regional stability	Good

COUNTRY PROFILE

Modern Nepal began its formation in the second half of the eighteenth century, when the kingdom of Gorkha, led by Prithivi Narayan Shah, began to expand. 1769 Shah conquered Kathmandu and completed the unification of what is today's Nepal, laying the foundation of a dynasty that was to last until 2008 when parliament voted on 28 December 2007 to abolish the monarchy.

1792 Nepal's expansion was halted by Chinese armies in Tibet.
1816 Nepal became a British protectorate after the Anglo-Nepalese war. The treaty also established the boundaries as they are today.
1846 Jang Bahadur Rana extracted a decree from the monarch that transferred sovereign powers to the family of Ranas, who ruled as hereditary prime ministers for 104 years.
1923 Nepal's independence was recognised by Britain, although it retained control of the country's foreign affairs.
1950–59 King Tribhuvan fled to India, intensifying the revolt led by the Nepali Congress party (NC) against the Ranas. It ended with an agreement brokered by India which recognised the role of the monarch, legalised political parties and established a constitutional monarchy. In the eight years that followed, the King ruled the country while political parties took shape.
1953 Edmund Hillary of New Zealand and Nepal's Sherpa Tenzing Norgay were the first climbers to reach the summit of Mount Everest (known as Sagarmatha in Nepal).
1955 Nepal became a member of the United Nations. King Tribhuwan died and King Mahendra ascended the throne.
1959 The first, multi-party, election under a new constitution was won by the NC. B P Koirala became prime minister.
1960 King Mahendra seized control and suspended parliament and politics.
1962 He introduced a new constitution establishing a party-less Panchayat system which banned political competition and parties. The King retained absolute powers.
1972 King Mahendra died in 1972 and was succeeded by his son, King Birendra, who continued his father's policies.
1979 After a series of protests against the Panchayat system, the King ordered a national referendum: the choice was between a 'reformed' Panchayat, or a multi-party democracy. A narrow majority voted in favour of the Panchayat, with reforms allowing direct elections – but still on a non-party basis.
1985 The NC began a campaign of civil disobedience for the restoration of the multi-party system.
1986 Elections were boycotted by the NC.
1990 Pro-democracy protests were staged by the NC and leftist groups which resulted in killings and mass arrests by the police. The King bowed to pressure and agreed a new democratic constitution.
1991 The NC won the elections and Girija Prasad Koirala became prime minister.
1994 Koirala's government was toppled due to party infighting. The Communist Party of Nepal-United Marxist-Leninist (CPN-UML) emerged as the largest single party in the elections and formed a minority government.
1995 The CPN-UML government was toppled, making way for a number of coalition and minority governments, until another round of elections was held in 1999.
1996 While the mainstream parties jostled for power in the centre, the Maoists launched their 'people's war'.
1998 The CPN-UML suffered a major blow when a faction of the party broke away.
1999 The NC won the general elections; Krishna Prasad Bhattarai became prime minister.
2000 Bhattarai was forced to step down due to party infighting. Koirala became prime minister again. The NC remained effectively divided between the supporters of Koirala and Bhattarai.
2001 Crown Prince Dipendra killed his closest family members, including King Birendra and Queen Aishwarya, in a drunken shooting spree, before committing suicide. Gyanendra Bir Bikram Shah Deva became king. The Maoists increased their violent campaign of opposition. Koirala resigned and Sher Bahadur Deuba (NC) became prime minister. A truce was agreed between the rebels and the government but when peace talks failed the insurgency resumed.
2002 Maoists rebels successfully staged a five-day general strike after more than 500 people were killed in clashes with government forces. King Gyanendra dissolved parliament and called for fresh general elections; the ruling NC suspended Deuba from the party for advising the King to do so. King Gyanendra dismissed Deuba, abolished the Council of Ministers and assumed executive powers. The King appointed Lokendra Bahadur Chand as prime minister.
2003 Maoist rebels and the government agreed to a cease-fire. King Gyanendra appointed Surya Bahadur Thapa of the Rastriya Prajatantra Party (RPP) as prime minister. Maoists ended the truce. Violence and political stalemate marked the end of the year.
2004 Nepal joined the World Trade Organisation (WTO). Prime Minister Thapa resigned after weeks of civil protest. Former prime minister, Sher Bahadur Deuba, was re-appointed.
2005 King Gyanendra dismissed Deuba and assumed absolute power, citing the need to defeat the Maoists. A royal anti-graft commission sentenced former prime minister Deuba to two years imprisonment for corruption. The rebels declared a unilateral cease-fire. Maoists and opposition parties agreed a strategy to restore democracy.
2006 Nepal, Bhutan, Bangladesh, India, Maldives, Pakistan and Sri Lanka signed the South Asia Free Trade Agreement (SAFTA). A seven-party alliance led by former prime minister Girija Prasad Koirala (leader of NC), in opposition to the King, called mass pro-democracy demonstrations. Riots broke out in the capital, leaving several police and demonstrators dead. International calls urged the King to negotiate with his opponents and in the face of so much opposition the King reinstated parliament and was removed as head of the armed forces. Parliament restricted the powers of the King as executive rule was passed to the Council of Ministers. A peace agreement was signed between the government and Maoist insurgents, formally ending 10 years of internal conflict. Maoists rebels disarmed, monitored by the United Nations.
2007 The two chambers of parliament were replaced by a unicameral interim legislature, with Maoists holding 83 out of 330 seats, under the terms of the temporary constitution. An interim multi-party cabinet, including Maoists, was formed to prepare the way for legislative elections. The special assembly was charged with writing a new constitution, including deciding on the future of the monarchy. Three bombs exploded in Kathmandu, the first terrorist attacks since the peace agreement in 2006. Maoist members of the interim government resigned in protest at the continued existence of the monarchy. General elections were postponed due to a deadlock between Maoist and ruling parties over the abolition of the monarchy and the adoption of proportional representation. Parliament voted to abolish the monarchy and five Maoists joined the cabinet in a number of key positions, including communication and information, which gave the Maoists control over the state-run media.
2008 In parliamentary elections the Communist Party of Nepal (Maoists), won 220 seats (out of 601), the Nepali Congress party 110 seats, the CPN-UML 103 seats, the Madhesi Jana Adhikar Forum 52 seats, the Tarai-Madhesh Loktantrik Party 20 seats; 20 other parties shared the remaining seats with none holding more than eight. The Constituent Assembly voted by 560–4 to declare the country a republic and depose King Gyanendra. Ex-King Gyanendra and his wife, Komal, took up temporary residence outside Kathmandu, becoming known as Mr Shah. Within days his former palace was turned into a museum; among the treasures are the royal throne and the priceless crown and sceptre. Interim Prime Minister Koirala announced he would

resign if the candidate he supported for president, Ram Raja Prasad Singh, was defeated. In the presidential election no candidate won the necessary 298 votes for victory and a second round had to be scheduled, in which Ram Baran Yadav (NC) won 308 votes, beating Ram Raja Prasad Singh (nominated by the Maoists). Baran was sworn in as the first president of Nepal. Interim Prime Minister Koirala resigned after Baran took office; parliament elected Maoist leader, Prachandra (also known as Pushpa Kamal Dahal) as prime minister. The collapse of the Koshi dam, in the south-east of Nepal, lead to severe flooding which forced over 50,000 people to flee their homes.
2009 The prime minister ordered the General Chief of Staff, Rookmangud Katawal, to integrate ex-Maoist rebel fighters into the army. When he refused he was dismissed and a political crisis followed when the president revoked the dismissal. Prime Minister Prachanda resigned in protest. A 22-party coalition, led by the NC and the CPN-UML formed the government. Madhav Kumar Nepal (CPN-UML) was sworn in as prime minister. Following years of campaigning, the UK granted full residency in Britain to Gurkha veterans with at least four years' service. Chairman of Nepal Constituent Assembly (NCA), Subash Nemwang, announced that the draft of the new constitution would be ready by the deadline of May 2010. A series of demonstrations and blockades in Kathmandu turned violent as Maoist activists protested against the governing coalition and called for a parliamentary debate over the power of the president.
2010 Nepal and China agreed the height of Mount Everest to be 8,848m, the snow height. China had previously argued that it should be 4m lower, at the rock height. The ruling coalition proposed extending the mandate of the NCA for one year, in an effort to complete work on the new constitution. However the majority Maoist party refused to extend it without Prime Minister Kumar stepping down. Kumar resigned. However parliament failed seven times to elect his replacement and Kumar remained in office as acting-prime minister.
2011 In January, the only prime ministerial candidate, Ram Chandra Poudel, withdrew and further attempts to elect a prime minister were cancelled. The mandate for the UN peacekeeping mission, established in 2007, expired in January. The government and Maoists agreed to continue arms monitoring arrangements. After seven months of deadlock and 16 attempted votes, Jhala Nath Khanal (CPN-UML) was elected prime minister in February, following the Maoist's withdrawal of their own candidate and their support given to Khanal. Bank notes carrying an image of the King of Nepal ceased to be legal tender in March; the central bank estimated that as much as Rp10 billion (US$135 million) was left un-exchanged. Mount Everest replaced the King's image. At the end of May members of parliament announced that parliament would be extended by three months so that details of the new constitution could be finalised. In June, in a ceremony to mark the occasion, Prime Minister Khanal detonated the explosion that destroyed the last landmine and to finally clear all unexploded ordnance (UXO) from Nepal. In July, Nepal said it had commissioned a new survey to determine the exact height of Mount Everest in an effort to lay to rest the 'confusion' with China which, despite a 2010 agreement, continued to use the rock (rather than the snowline) height during border talks. The generally accepted height of 8,848 metres had been recorded by an Indian survey in 1955; a US GPS survey recorded 8,850 metres in 1999, although this figure has not been accepted by either Nepal or China. In August Prime Minister Khanal resigned, saying he was unable to forge a political consensus with other parties in order to form a government. Parliament elected Baburam Bhattarai (Maoist) as prime minister, with 340 votes against Ram Chandra Poudel (CPN) with 235. An earthquake of magnitude 6.9 struck in September in the Himalayan regions of India, Nepal and Tibet.
2012 Demobilisation of over 7,000 Maoist rebels began in February; they were given a cash payment to return to civilian life. A further 9,000 elected to join the national army, despite the limit on recruitment of 6,500 new soldiers. The result left the government in dispute with the opposition NCP. On 24 May the Supreme Court rejected the government's proposal for a three-month extension for the Constitutional Assembly (CA) to agree a new post-conflict constitution. On 28 May, parliamentary elections were called following years of political deadlock. Despite the electoral commission setting the date for April or May 2013, they were were first postponed until 22 November, and then into 2013 at a date to be decided, and when the weather allows. In May the CA was disolved, leaving in place a caretaker government led by Maoist Prime Minister Baburam Bhattarai.
2013 Mr Bhattarai stepped down in March and, in a controversial move, Supreme Court Chief Justice Khilraj Regmi became the head of government being sworn in on 14 March. The tiger population of Nepal reached 198 in July, a rise of 63 per cent since 2009. Mr Regmi announced 19 November as parliamentary election date. Some 56 national and international organisations registered to observe the election. The election was a win for the Nepali Congress with a total of 196 seats (out of 595) (105 (out of 240) first passed the post + 91 (out of 355) proportional), followed by the Communist Party of Nepal (Unified Marxist-Leninist) with 175 (91 + 84) and the Unified Communist Party of Nepal (Maoist) with 80 (26 + 54). The Rastriya Prajatantra Party Nepal won 24 proportional seats but no first passed the post seats. No other parties won over 5 per cent of votes and the remaining 144 seats were won by 26 parties).
2014 Sushil Koirala was elected prime minister by the parliament on 10 February; he was inaugurated on 11 February. A particularly severe blizzard in October lead to the deaths of some 39 tourists and guides on the Annapurna Trail. By October monsoon rains had triggered over 35 floods and landslides, killing over 200 people and displacing many thousands.
2015 New, heavily refuced, rates for climbing the Himalaya range in Nepal came into effect on 1 January. The rate for Mount Everest is US$10,000, down from US$25,000. An earthquake measuring 7.8 struck on 25 April. There were over 8,000 deaths. A second earthquake, measuring 7.3, followed on 12 May. Parliament elected Khadga Prasad Oli as prime minister on 11 October by a margin of 338 votes out of 597. He is the first prime minister to be elected under the new constitution. Previous prime minister, Sushil Koirala, was the runner up.

Political structure

Constitution

An interim constitution came into effect on 15 January 2007, the constitution for the State of Nepal replaced the previous constitution of the Kingdom of Nepal.
An amendment passed in March 2007 changed the country to a federal state from a unitary one. It also increased the number of constituencies in the south to 50 per cent of the seats in parliament.

Form of state

Federal parliamentary republic

The executive

The president is the Head of State. Under an amendment to the interim constitution (January 2007) the president, vice president, prime minister and constituent assembly chairman and vice chairman would be elected based on a 'political understanding' or failing that by a simple majority vote.
Members of the Nepalese Constituent Assembly (NCA) provide the executive which makes up the government. The 26 seats of the NCA are divided among nine

political parties, proportional to the popular vote received.

National legislature

The Nepal Constituent Assembly has 601 members, of which 240 are directly elected, 335 are elected by proportional representation and 26 members are nominated. The assembly will re-write the constitution and govern the country until an elected government can be decided. The assembly has a mandate until 2010. In August 2009 Nepal Constituent Assembly chairman Subash Nemwang expressed confidence that the draft of the new constitution would be ready by the deadline of May 2010. In the event the Constituent Assembly was dissolved in May 2012 and after several delays elections were held on 19 May 2013.

Legal system

Independent judiciary

Last elections

19 November 2013 (parliamentary); 19 and 21 July 2008 (presidential, first and second round).

Results: Parliamentary: Nepali Congress Party won a total of 196 seats (out of 595) (105 (out of 240) first passed the post + 91 (out of 355) proportional), followed by the Communist Party of Nepal (Unified Marxist-Leninist) (UML) with 175 (91 + 84) and the Unified Communist Party of Nepal (Maoist) with 80 (26 + 54). The Rastriya Prajatantra Party Nepal won 24 proportional seats but no first passed the post seats. No other parties won over 5 per cent of votes and the remaining 144 seats were shared by 26 parties. Turnout was 78.34 per cent.

Presidential: (first round) Ram Baran Yadav (Nepali Congress) won 283 votes, Ram Raja Prasad Singh (Maoist) 270. (Second round): Yadav won 308 votes beating Singh who got 282.

Paramananda Jha (Madhesi Jana Adhikar Forum (MJF) (Madhesi People's Rights Forum) was elected vice president with 305 votes; Shanta Shrestha (Maoist) won 243.

Next elections

2018 (parliament)

Political parties

Ruling party

Coalition of the Nepali Congress Party and the Communist Party of Nepal (CPN-UML)

Main opposition party

United Communist Party of Nepal (Maoist)

Population

27.92 million (2013)*

Last census: 22 June 2011: 26,620,809

Population density: 191 inhabitants per square km (2010). Urban population 19 per cent (2010 Unicef).

Annual growth rate: 2.3 per cent, 1990–2010 (Unicef).

Internally Displaced Persons (IDP)

100,000–200,000 (UNHCR 2004)

Ethnic make-up

Nepal has a mixture of Indo-Caucasian and Tibeto-Mongoloid people and a number of Tibetan refugees. There are 61 different ethnic and caste groups and many have their own language and dialect.

Religions

Hinduism (90 per cent), Tibetan Buddhism (5.3 per cent), Islam (2.7 per cent). Nepal is a Hindu kingdom, but it allows other religions to practise their faiths. It is illegal to proselytise. The Kumari Devi is revered by both Hindus and Buddhists in Nepal as a 'living Goddess'.

Education

The education system is based on the Chinese model. A non-compulsory pre-school education can begin at aged three. Primary schooling lasts for five years at the end of which students are separated into academic and technical programmes.

The academic programme is divided into lower secondary, upper secondary and higher secondary schooling in a cycle of three, two and two years until the age of 18 when, if they have been successful, students may access higher education courses at university or other institutions. The three-year lower secondary schools are of two types: general and Sanskrit. Upon completing the second stage, exams undertaken by students allows advancement to the higher secondary school or graduation with a school leaving certificate.

The Tribhuvan University, Mahendra Sanskrit University, Kathmandu University and Purbanchal University and B P Korala Institute of Health Science mainly provide higher education.

The technical programme is divided into cycles of either four and two, or four and four, years and students graduate with either a craftsman's certificate at age 16 or a technical certificate at aged 18.

Literacy rate: 44 per cent adult rate; 63 per cent youth rate (15–24) (Unesco 2005).

Compulsory years: Six to 16.

Enrolment rate: 113 per cent gross primary enrolment of the relevant age group (including repeaters); 42 per cent gross secondary enrolment (World Bank).

Pupils per teacher: 39 in primary schools.

Health

National morbidity patterns show ailments related to inadequate water and sanitation account for more than 70 per cent of all sickness reported. Furthermore, around 10,000 people die from cancer after a long-term exposure of arsenic compounds in drinking water.

There were cases of polio reported t the World Health Organisation – Global Polio Eradication Initiative in 2006; the country had previously been free of the disease and its re-emergence was due to infected travellers.

HIV/Aids

The UN estimated 60,000 people are living with HIV/Aids in 2003, which represents 0.25 per cent of the total population.

HIV prevalence: 0.5 per cent aged 15–49 in 2003 (World Bank)

Life expectancy: 61 years, 2004 (WHO 2006)

Fertility rate/Maternal mortality rate: 2.7 births per woman, 2010 (Unicef)

Child (under 5 years) mortality rate (per 1,000): 42 per 1,000 live births (WHO 2012); 48 per cent of children aged under five are malnourished (World Bank).

Head of population per physician: 0.21 physicians per 1,000 people, 2004 (WHO 2006)

Welfare

The government of Nepal and the Asian Development Bank (ADB) signed a partnership agreement aiming to reduce the incidence of poverty from over 40 per cent of the population to less than 10 per cent by 2017. The problems related to rural poverty are being tackled by improving access to impoverished areas. Several non-government organisations have stepped up their aid to tackle poverty and disease in the country.

It is estimated that more than 10 out of 100 people in Nepal suffer from one or the other form of disability. The government does not have concrete programmes to address the problems facing the disabled.

Main cities

Kathmandu (capital, estimated population 997,911 in 2012), Pokhara (250,902), Lalitpur (230,022), Biratnagar (217,482), Birgañj (184,418), Bharatpur (147,395), Dharan (138,987), Butwal (130,735).

Languages spoken

Maithili, Bhojpuri, Hindi, Bengali and Newari are some other languages spoken. English is spoken, mainly in urban centres.

Official language/s

Nepali (Devnagari script)

Media

Press freedom and journalists were under pressure from the former royal regime and from within Maoist-held territories. Since the change in government all anti-media laws were struck down and the interim constitution guaranteed the freedom of the press.

Press

Dailies: Most newspapers are published in either Nepalese or English. The government owned *Gorkhapatra* (in English, *The Rising Nepal*) (www.gorkhapatra.org.np) is the oldest published daily; private newspapers include *Kantipur* (www.kantipuronline.com) which also publishes *The Kathmandu Post*. Other independents include *Nepal Samacharpatra* (www.newsofnepal.com) and *Rajdhani*.

Weeklies: News magazines include, *Nepali Times* (www.nepalitimes.com.np), *Spotlight* (www.nepalnews.com.np) and from the same publisher *The Weekly Telegraph* and the *People's Review* (www.peoplesreview.com.np).

Business: The monthly magazines *New Business Age* (www.nepalnews.com/new_businessage.php) is published by Mercantile Communications, which owns over a dozen other publications in Nepal.

Periodicals: Monthly magazines, in English, include *ECS* (www.ecs.com.np) on culture, *Wave* (www.wavemag.com.np), a gossip magazine and *Himal Southasian* (www.himalmag.com) has regional reviews. In Nepalese, *Himal Khabarpatrika* (www.himalkhabar.com) is a fortnightly news magazine.

Broadcasting

Radio: The state-run Radio Nepal (www.radionepal.org) reaches all areas and is listen to by up to 80 per cent of the population. Its national and regional programmes cover a wide range of shows in information, education and entertainment. There are many, private, commercial stations located regionally, which include Maitri FM (http://maitrifm.org), Annapurna FM (www.annapurnafm.com.np), Kantipur FM (www.kfm961.com) and Janakpur FM (www.janakifm.org.np).

Television: The state-run, commercial, Nepal Television (NTV) (www.nepaltelevision.com.np) broadcasts nationally and internationally via satellite. Other private TV stations include Avenues TV, a news channel, Channel Nepal (www.channelnepal.com), Image Channel TV (www.imagechannels.com) and Kantipur TV (www.kantipuronline.com).

National news agency: Rastriya Samachar Samiti (RSS)

Other news agencies: Nepalnews: www.nepalnews.com

Economy

Nepal is a largely underdeveloped country with a subsistence agricultural economy producing a surplus of rice and wheat, used for export to India. However, it is subject to adverse external factors, such as variable monsoon rains, that can influence economic growth.

The structure of the economy indicates a semi-agrarian society with an agricultural sector that constituted around 35.1 per cent of GDP in 2014, after the service sector that accounted for 49.2 per cent; industry accounted for some 15.7 per cent, of which manufacturing was around half. Around 70 per cent of manufacturing is made up of export-destined carpets and garments.

Due to its limited integration in world financial markets, Nepal was not subject to many of the pressures of the global economic crisis, although inflation spiked at 12.6 per cent in 2009 as global trade was cut and remained high in 2014 at 8.4 per cent. Although political uncertainties in 2012 and early 2013 delayed the final budget, a good agriculture harvest and robust services sector made sure GDP growth continued to remain strong. It was 4.5 per cent in 2012, it decreased to 3.7 per cent in 2013 before rebounding back to the strong growth rate of 5.5 per cent in 2014.

The government encouraged external assistance from India, the UK, the US, Japan, Germany, the Scandinavian countries and several multilateral organisations. Such aid accounts for over 50 per cent of the country's development budget.

In 2014, the UN Human Development Index (HDI) ranked Nepal 145 (out of 187) for national development in health, education and income. Since 2000, Nepal's progress has grown but has not matched the improvement of other countries in South Asia. In 2014, 41.44 per cent of the population experienced at least one indicator of poverty, while almost three quarters of the population live on less than the equivalent of US$1.25 per day.

Remittances from migrant workers reached US$5.6 billion in 2013 (around 29 per cent of GDP) and were expected to have grown further in 2014.

Nepal has abundant prospects for hydroelectricity production and plans to export surplus power. Its prospects depend largely on a stable government and improved infrastructure. There is scope for the tourism sector, based on the country's mountainous terrain offering climbing and trekking holidays, to become a healthy foreign exchange earner as well as employment provider.

In April 2015, a devastating earthquake struck Nepal, killing 9,000 people and injuring 23,000 more. Following the earthquake there was concern that there would be losses to harvests, as people affected would have very little time to plant crops before the onset of the monsoon season. As one of Asia's poorest countries, Nepal has little power to fund a major reconstruction project on its own. Even before the earthquake struck, the Asian Development Bank stated that Nepal would need to spend four times as much on infrastructure than it already does in order to attract foreign investments by 2020.

External trade

Nepal is a member of South Asia Association for Regional Co-operation, which operates a preferential trading arrangement (Sapta) that covers 6,000 products. In 2004 the South Asia Free Trade Area was agreed by Sapta, and was implemented between the member states (India, Pakistan, Bhutan, Nepal, Bangladesh, Sri Lanka and Maldives) in 2011.

Remittances represent around 30 per cent of GDP and are a major source of foreign exchange.

Hand woven carpets and valuable cashmere pashmina fabric (for couture clothing) are manufactured for export.

Imports

The principal imports are petroleum products, machinery and equipment, gold, electrical goods and medicine.

Main sources: India (57 per cent of total in 2014) and China (29.6 per cent).

Exports

The principal exports are clothing, pulses, carpets, textiles, juice and jute goods.

Main destinations: India (59.7 per cent of total in 2013), US (8.6 per cent), China (4.6 per cent)

Agriculture

Farming

Agriculture accounts for around 35.1 per cent of GDP, providing most foreign exchange earnings and 80 per cent of employment. Only about 25 per cent of the total land area is cultivable; another 33 per cent is forested and most of the rest is mountainous. The lowland Terai region produces an agricultural surplus, part of which supplies the food-deficient hill areas.

Major food crops are rice, maize, wheat, barley and millet. The principal cash crops are sugar cane, soya beans, oilseeds, tobacco, potato and jute. Cattle, buffaloes, goats, sheep, pigs, yaks and poultry are also raised. River fish are an important source of protein.

Much of the agriculture is rain-fed and is carried out in the narrow strip of plains in the south along the border with India. Agricultural land is highly fragmented. Production is extremely vulnerable to adverse weather conditions, with little irrigation. Deforested plains and lower hilltops are terraced for rice production. Severe soil erosion is becoming a problem.

Nepal has removed all subsidies on fertilisers, which makes it difficult for Nepali produce to compete with highly subsidised

Indian agro-products. There are some transport subsidies for taking fertilisers to remote districts.

Forestry

Forests occupy around 33 per cent of Nepal's land area. The canopy cover in the mid-hills is growing thicker as a result of the government's successful policy of handing over forests to local communities. Deforestation is still high in the government-managed forests of the plains, coupled with timber that is smuggled into India.

Industry and manufacturing

Industry accounts for around 15 per cent of GDP. The sector consists mainly of manufacturing low-end consumer goods – principally carpets, garments and handicrafts. The development of this sector is constrained by poor infrastructure, a small local market, high industrial factor costs and lack of access to the sea.

Nepal offers duty concessions on raw material imports and start-up tax holidays for new industry, but foreign direct investment flows have remained slow.

Tourism

The foothills of the Himalayan Mountains occupy most of Nepal, which is able to offer activity holidays for the athletic traveller, particularly to see the world's first and second highest (Everest and Annapurna) mountains. The less able visitor may use vehicles to reach some worthwhile sites such as temples and the Kathmandu Valley, which along with Lumbini (birthplace of the Lord Buddha) is included on Unesco's World Heritage List as places of cultural importance.

Travel and tourism contributed 8.9 per cent of GDP in 2014. Employment in the industry has fallen from 9.3 per cent of the workforce employed in the sector in 2009 to 7.5 per cent (1.1 million jobs) in 2014.

Environment

The Sagarmatha (Mount Everest) Pollution Control Committee (SPCC), set up in 1991, spends US$15,000 cleaning up the Sagarmatha National Park every year. The government charges a minimum of US$50,000 for each expedition to Mount Everest, and ploughs back 30–40 per cent of this and other tourist fees to support the SPCC's work. Since the old trekking routes pose serious problems to the indigenous communities already, there are many opposing voices among the environmentalists in Kathmandu.

Mining

Mining and quarrying accounts for less than 1 per cent of GDP.

Among the major known mineral reserves only limestone has been extracted for commercial use in considerable volumes. Nepal also has deposits of lead, zinc, marble, iron ore and magnesite.

Hydrocarbons

There are no known oil or natural gas reserves, although exploration is ongoing. Consumption of oil was around 20,000 barrels per day in 2014, all of which was imported. Any use of natural gas is commercially insignificant.

Nepal has a small coal industry with reserves of around two million tonnes. Annual output meets less than 5 per cent of domestic demand and about 531,000 tonnes of coal are imported.

Energy

Total installed generating capacity was 721MW in 2013, mostly supplied by hydropower, but with around 10 per cent from thermal plants. Electricity supplies only 1 per cent of Nepal's energy mix; wood fuel accounts for around 75 per cent, with agricultural waste providing most of the rest.

Hydropower offers the greatest potential, not only for sustainable energy with an estimated economically viable capacity of 43,000MW, but also a valuable component of GDP and foreign earnings in the export of surplus electricity. However, plans for hydropower expansions have been met with much opposition from the public and so far plans have struggled to take off. Nevertheless, the government is seeking investment in more projects.

There are currently 6 hydropower stations under construction, including one in Upper Tamakoshi that will have a capacity of 456MW.

Financial markets

Stock exchange

Nepal Stock Exchange (Nepse)

Banking and insurance

Central bank

Nepal Rastra Bank

Main financial centre

Kathmandu

Time

GMT plus five hours and forty-five minutes

Geography

Nepal is a landlocked, roughly rectangular country located south of the Himalayan mountain range. It is about 885km long (east to west) and an average non-uniform, north-south width of 193km. The country is divided into five development regions and 75 districts. Ecologically, Nepal is divided into three regions – mountain, hill and terai (plains). India borders Nepal in the east, south and west. China borders Nepal in the north. The topography is rugged and harsh and with a vertical distance of less than 200km, the altitude changes from sea level to the highest point on earth – the 8,848m Mount Everest.

Hemisphere

Northern

Climate

The climate is generally temperate but harsh and cold at high altitudes. The low-lying plains are hot in summer and warm during the winters. The high mountains are permanently covered with snow (above 4,800 metres). High temperatures range between 17–30 degrees Celsius (C) and lows are in the range of 0–17 C. May–September is the monsoon season; July is the wettest month and also the hottest.

Dress codes

If travelling outside Kathmandu, it is respectable and practical to wear casual trousers and full-sleeved shirts and jackets. Shorts may be acceptable only in urban centres.

Entry requirements

Passports

Required by all except nationals of India. Entry may be refused, and airlines may not carry passengers holding passports with less than six months validity.

Visa

Required by all, except nationals of India with a valid national ID card. Tourist visas are issued on arrival. Overnight visas are issued free of cost.

Business visas are only issued to those who have been officially recognised as either a) the official representative (of a commercial entity that has obtained a licence to invest in the Kingdom of Nepal in a business or industrial enterprise) or b) an individual who has obtained a licence to invest in Nepal in export trade. Applications for multiple-entry business visas (one or five years) need to be made in advance. Applications should be made to the Director General, Department of Immigration, Kathmandu (www.immi.gov.np). An authorisation from the relevant Nepalese ministry is needed, as are photocopies of the relevant pages of the visitor's passport. The applicant will be sent application forms which must be returned fully completed. If accepted, the visa will be stamped on the visitor's passport at Kathmandu airport.

The Nepal Tourism Board website (www.welcomenepal.com) provides updated information on changes in related policies and rules.

Currency advice/regulations

The import of local and Indian currency is prohibited. On arrival, all foreign currency must be declared, export is limited to the amount declared. Foreign currency exchange receipts must be retained as only 10 per cent of local currency will be

reconverted on departure. Export of local currency is prohibited. Currency can be exchanged at banks or authorised foreign exchange dealers and at major hotels.
Only Indian and Nepalese nationals may carry Indian currency; possession of Indian Rs500 bills is illegal in Nepal.
Travellers cheques are accepted in banks and large hotels.

Customs

Personal effects may be imported duty-free. Items such as cameras, laptop computers, portable music systems and 15 reels of film are permitted as long as they are re-exported.
Exports of antiques and religious artefacts must be certified and cleared by the Department of Archaeology. It is illegal to export goods which are over 100 years old, or endangered wildlife.

Prohibited imports

Narcotics, beef and beef products.
Firearms, ammunition and explosives, wireless radio transmitters and precious metals require special licences.

Health (for visitors)

Mandatory precautions

Vaccination certificate for yellow fever if travelling from an infected area.

Advisable precautions

Vaccinations that are necessary include: cholera, diphtheria, tetanus, hepatitis A, polio and typhoid. Vaccinations that may be advised include: hepatitis B, tuberculosis, Japanese B encephalitis and rabies.
Anti-malarial precautions should be taken; the use of mosquito nets and repellents and covering up the body after dark can help avoid malaria, hepatitis B and encephalitis.
Use only bottled or boiled water for drinks, washing teeth and making ice. Eat only well cooked meals, preferably served hot; vegetables should be cooked and fruit peeled; avoid dairy products. A first-aid kit, including disposable syringes, would be useful.
Full medical insurance including emergency repatriation is strongly recommended.

Hotels

Nepal has about 100 tourist-class hotels, ranging from up-market five-star deluxe to those with one-star ratings. Other accommodation includes over 750 non-star-rated, but affordable and safe, speciality establishments.
Hotels may be full during the tourist season and it is advisable to book in advance.
Payment is required in foreign currency.

Credit cards

All major credit and charge cards are accepted by banks, tourist hotels and shops. ATMs can be found in Kathmandu.

Public holidays (national)

Fixed dates

11 Jan (National Unity Day – cancelled in 2007), 29 Jan (Martyrs' Day), 19 Feb (National Democracy Day), 8 Mar (Women's Day), 14 Apr (Nepali New Year), 9 Nov (Constitution Day), 29 Dec (King Birendra's Birthday).

Variable dates

Vasant Panchami (Jan/Feb), Shivaratri (Feb/Mar), Ghode Jatra (Festival of Horses) (Mar), Holi (Mar), Chaite Dashain (Mar/Apr), Ram Nawami (Birthday of Lord Ram) (Mar/Apr), Lord Buddha's Birthday (Apr/May), Rakshya Bandhan (Janai Purnima) (Aug), Gai Jatra/Procession of Cows (Aug/Sep), Krishna Asthami (Birthday of Lord Krishna) (Aug/Sep), Teej (Festival of Women) (Sep), Dasain (Durga Puja Festival) (Oct), Diwali/Deepawali (Oct/Nov), Indra Jatra/Festival of Rain God (Oct/Nov).
In general, Hindu and Buddhist festivals are declared according to local astronomical observations.

Working hours

Banking

Sun–Thu: 1000–1500, Fri: 1000–1200; Kathmandu Valley, Mon–Fri: 0900–1530. Some banks open at weekends.

Business

Sun–Fri: 1000–1700; Kathmandu Valley, Mon–Fri: 0900–1700

Government

Mon–Fri: 0900–1700 (summer); Mon–Fri: 0900–1600 (winter, mid-Nov–mid-Feb).

Shops

Sun–Fri: 1000–1900 (some shops also open on Saturdays).

Telecommunications

Mobile/cell phones

GSM 900 and 1800 services are available in populated areas.

Weights and measures

Metric system (local measures are also used).

Social customs/useful tips

The traditional form of greeting is called *namaste* – performed by placing the palms together at chest height and bowing slightly; it means 'I celebrate the divinity in you'. Some Nepali women may prefer not to shake hands with a man. Always use the right hand to eat or pass anything on. Remove shoes before entering temples and homes.
Do not take photographs before asking permission.

Security

Internal terrorist activities have seen indiscriminate attacks in and around the capital as well as tourist areas, visitors are advised to exercise extra vigilance and also take care to respect any local curfews.

Getting there

Air

National airline: Royal Nepal Airlines (all flights must be paid for in hard currencies).
International airport/s: Kathmandu Tribhuwan International (KTM), 6km from the city. Facilities include bank, *bureau de change*, duty free, post office and tourist information.
Airport tax: Departure tax to regional neighbours (excluding China): NRs1,356; departure tax to all other destinations NRs1,695.

Surface

Road: There are many access routes from India and Tibet, however visitors must use official crossings, which are open 24 hours. Visitors driving their own vehicle must possess a *international carnet*.
Rail: There are two lines in India that run to the border of Nepal at Birgani/Sunauli and at Jaynagar, but neither cross the border.

Getting about

National transport

Air: The only way to reach many parts of Nepal is by air. Nepal has 44 domestic airports and 120 helicopter landing strips. Royal Nepal Airlines and private airline companies have flights to and from these airports. Special helicopter charters can also be arranged. Flights may be delayed during the rainy months; otherwise, they are an efficient means of getting around.
Road: There is a road network of over 13,000km. Kathmandu, Pokhara and Biratnagar are linked by surfaced road. Transport is difficult outside main centres. The Mahendra Highway makes west Nepal accessible throughout the year. The mountainous nature of the country means that many of its roads are unusable, especially during the winter and the monsoon.
Buses: Long distance day or night bus services operate from Kathmandu to all cities of Nepal.
Rail: The only line serves Jaynagar to Janakpur and Bizalpura.

City transport

Taxis: Metered taxis can be hailed in Kathmandu. Private taxis are also available at the hotels, but they may cost more.
Buses, trams & metro: The airport bus to the city centre takes 35 minutes.

Car hire

Driving is on the left. An international driving permit is required. Local authorities also issue a local permit upon presentation of a national licence.
Chauffeur-driven car hire is available.

BUSINESS DIRECTORY

The addresses listed below are a selection only. While World of Information makes every endeavour to check these addresses, we cannot guarantee that changes have not been made, especially to telephone numbers and area codes. We would welcome any corrections.

Telephone area codes

The international direct dialling (IDD) code for Nepal is +977, followed by area code and subscriber's number:

Bhairawa	71	Janakpur	41
Bhaktapur	1	Kathmandu	1
Birgunj	51	Nepalgunj	81
Biratnagar	21	Patan	1
Dhangadhi	91	Pokhara	61

Useful telephone numbers

Police: 100

Directory enquiries: 197

Chambers of Commerce

Federation of Nepalese Chambers of Commerce and Industry, Shahid Shukra FNCCI Milan Marg, Teku, Kathmandu (tel: 426-2061; fax: 426-2007; email: fncci@mos.com.np).

Nepal Britain Chamber of Commerce and Industry, British Embassy Premises, Lainchaur, PO Box 106, Kathmandu (tel: 441-0583; fax: 441-8137; email: info@nbcci.org).

Nepal Chamber of Commerce, Chamber Bhawan, Kantipath, PO Box 198, Kathmandu (tel: 422-2890; fax: 422-9998; email: chamber@wlink.com.np).

Nepal-US Chamber of Commerce and Industry, TNT Building, Tinkune, Koteshwor, PO Box 2769, Kathmandu (tel: 447-8020; fax: 447-4508; email: nusacci@vishnu.ccsl.com.np).

Banking

Agricultural Development Bank, Ramshahpath, Kathmandu (tel: 421-1744, 421-1802/3; fax: 422-5329).

Himalayan Bank Ltd, PO Box 20590, Karmachari Sanchaya Kosh Building, Tridevi Marg, Thamel, Kathmandu (tel: 422-7749, 425-0201; fax: 422-2800).

Nepal Arab Bank Ltd (Nabil Bank), PO Box 3729, Kantipath, Kathmandu (tel: 421-1784/6; fax: 422-6905).

Nepal Bangladesh Bank Ltd, PO Box 9062, Bijuli Bazar, Naya Baneshwor, Kathmandu (tel: 490-767/70; fax: 490-824, 493-259) .

Nepal Bank Ltd, Dharmapath, Kathmandu (tel: 422-1185, 422-4337; fax: 422-6905).

Nepal Grindlays Bank Ltd, PO Box 3990, Naya Baneswor, Kathmandu (tel: 421-2683/6; fax: 422-6762).

Nepal Indosuez Bank Ltd, PO BOx 3412, Durbar Marg, Kathmandu (tel: 422-8229; fax: 422-6349).

Rastriya Banijya Bank, Singha Durbar Plaza, Kathmandu (tel: 425-2595, 426-8409, 425-1982; fax: 425-2931).

Citibank, PO Box 2826, c/o Hotel Yak & Yeti, Durbar Marg, Kathmandu (tel: 422-8884; fax: 422-7884).

Standard Chartered Bank, PO Box 1526, Durbar, PO Box 1526, Durbar, Marg, Kathmandu (tel/fax: 422-0129).

Central bank

Nepal Rastra Bank, PO Box 73, Baluwatar, Kathmandu (tel: 422-1763; fax: 425-4170; e-mail: nrb@mos.com.np).

Stock exchange

Nepal Stock Exchange (Nepse), www.nepalstock.com

Travel information

Automobile Association of Nepal, c/o Traffic Police Office, Kathmandu (tel: 421-1093).

Everest Air, Durbar Marg, Kathmandu (tel: 422-4188; fax: 422-6795).

Himalayan Helicopters PVT Ltd, Durbar Marg, Kathmandu (tel: 421-7236; fax: 422-5150).

Kathmandu Tribhuvan International Airport, Air Traffic Controller, Gauchar (tel: 472-258 or 473-985, ext 486; fax: 474-180; e-mail: tiao@mod.com.mp).

Nepal Mountaineering Association, 16/53 Ramshah Path, PO Box 1435, Kathmandu (tel: 421-1596).

Royal Nepal Airlines, PO Box 401, RNAC Building, Kantipath, Kathmandu 711000 (tel: 421-4511; fax: 422-5348).

Tourist Information Centre, Basantpur, Kathmandu; Tribhuwan International Airport, Kathmandu (tel: 470-537).

Ministry of tourism

Ministry of Culture, Tourism and Civil Aviation, Bhrikutimandap, Kathmandu (tel: 425-6231/2, 425-6228; fax; 422-7281; email: tourism@mail.com.np).

National tourist organisation offices

Nepal Tourism Board, Tourist Service Centre, Bhrikutimandap, PO Bix 11018, Kathmandu (tel: 425-6909, 425-6229; fax: 425-6910; email: info@ntb.org.np; internet: www.welcomenepal.com).

Ministries

Ministry of Commerce, Babar Mahal, Kathmandu (tel: 223-489, 224-805; fax: 225-594).

Ministry of Finance, Hari Bhawan, Kathmandu (tel: 224-527, 227-367; fax: 227-529).

Ministry of Industry, Tripureshwor, Kathmandu (tel: 213-880, 213-838; fax: 226-112).

Ministry of Interior, Dept of Immigration, Bhrikutimandap, Kathmandu (tel: 422-3590, 422-1996; fax: 422-3127; email: deptimi@net.np; internet: www.immi.gov.np).

Office of the Prime Minister, Singh Durbar, Kathmandu (tel: 421-000; email: info@opmcm.gov.np).

Other useful addresses

Asian Development Bank (ADB), Nepal Resident Mission, Srikunj Kamaladi Ward No 31, Block 2597, Ka.Na.Pa. Kathmandu; Postal address: PO Box 5017 K.D.P.O., Kathmandu (tel: 422-7779; fax: 422-5063; email: adbnrm@mail.asiandevbank.org; internet: www.adb.org/).

Department of Commerce, Kathmandu (tel: 422-7364, 422-7404).

Director General, Department of Immigration, Kathmandu (tel: 422-3681).

National Planning Commission, PO Box 1284, Singha Dubar, Kathmandu (tel: 421-5000).

Nepal Economic and Commerce Research Centre, PO Box 285, 7/358 Kohity Bahal, Kathmandu (tel: 421-5336).

Nepal Industrial Development Corporation (NIDC), NIDC Building, PO Box 10, Durba Marg, Kathmandu (tel: 411-211, 411-225).

Royal Nepalese Embassy (USA), 2131 Leroy Place, NW, Washington DC 20008 (tel: (+1-202) 667-4550; fax: (+1-202) 667-5534; e-mail: info@nepalembassyusa.org).

Trade Promotion Centre, Kathmandu (tel: 524-771, 524-772; fax: 521-637).

United Nations Development Programme, United Nations Building, Pulchowk, PO Box 7, Kathmandu (tel: 523-200; fax: 523-991).

National news agency: Rastriya Samachar Samiti (RSS), PO Box 222; Central Office, Bhadrakali Plaza, Kathmandu (tel: 426-2912; fax: 426-2744; internet: www.rss.com.np)

Nepalnews: www.nepalnews.com

Internet sites

Government of Nepal: www.nepalgov.np

Market information: www.feer.com

News portal: www.nepalnews.com

Nepalese tourism: www.visitnepal.com

The Netherlands

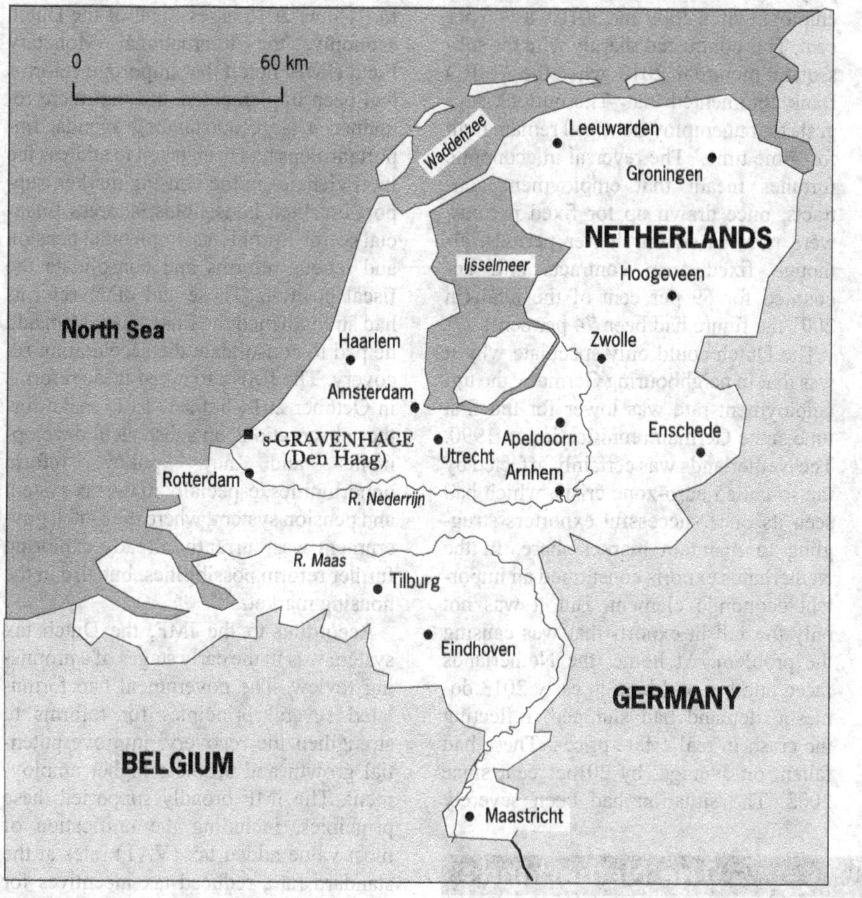

The Netherlands' March 2015 provincial assembly elections were something of a psephologist's nightmare. The importance of the provincial elections is that the provincial assemblies choose the country's senate. But a curious trend emerged from the election, as the six largest parties each obtained between 10 per cent and 16 per cent of the vote. The fragmentation of the vote might eventually make it virtually impossible for any centrist government to achieve much. The Dutch electorate appeared to be looking for new avenues of political expression and abandoning their country's rather tired traditional parties of power.

So Dutch psephologists were understandably confused. Voters may not like the old established parties that much, but it was not clear what their preferences were, or stood for. Government in the Netherlands has always been a matter of consensus grouped, if anything, around what might best be described as a loosely centrist political ideology. Government was a matter of concessions and alliances. The net result was one of general dissatisfaction all round. The right of centre considered their government to be too leftist and those on the left felt it was too right-wing. Not for Holland any bold political direction or inspiration – more the feeling of an under-performing parliament atop an equally under-performing economy and unacceptably high unemployment.

The results of the March 2015 provincial elections meant that the Partij van de Arbeid (PvDA) (Labour Party) lost six seats in the senate, leaving it with only

KEY FACTS

Official name: Koninkrijk der Nederlanden (The Kingdom of The Netherlands)

Head of State: King Willem-Alexander (crowned 30 April 2013)

Head of government: Prime Minister Mark Rutte (VVD) (from 2010; re-elected 12 Sep 2012)

Ruling party: Coalition, led by Volkspartij voor Vrijheid en Democratie (VVD) (People's Party for Freedom and Democracy) with Partij van de Arbeid (PvdA) (Labour Party) (from 2010; re-elected Sep 2012)

Area: 41,473 square km

Population: 16.86 million (2014)

Capital: The Hague (seat of government); Amsterdam (legal and cultural)

Official language: Dutch and Frisian

Currency: Euro (€) = 100 cents (from 1 Jan 2002; previous currency guilder, locked at f2.20 per euro)

Exchange rate: €0.89 per US$ (Sep 2015)

GDP per capita: US$51,373 (2014)

GDP real growth: 0.88% (2014)

GDP: US$866.35 billion (2014)

Labour force: 8.90 million (2014)*

Unemployment: 7.40% (2014)

Inflation: 0.32% (2014)

Natural gas production: 55.80 billion cum (2014)

Balance of trade: US$105.25 billion (2014)*

Annual FDI: US$15.60 billion (2011)

* estimated figure

eight. The Liberale Partij (LP) (Liberal Party) fared a bit better, losing only three seats to end up with 13, but still leaving them as the biggest party in the Dutch parliament. The parties that did best were the Christen-Democratische Partij (CDP) (Christian Democrats), which had 12 seats, and the left-wing D66 (aka Democrats66) party which doubled its seats from 5 to 10. Geert Wilders' Partij voor de Vrijheid (PVV) (Party for Freedom) only lost one seat, ending up with nine, the same number of seats as the Socialistische Partij (SP) (Socialist Party).

On the job

For most of the EU member countries, in 2013 an unemployment rate of 6.5 per cent would be considered a major achievement. Not so in the Netherlands, where the figure gave considerable cause for concern, not to mention serious cold shivers. While the actual rate was still relatively low, in the Netherlands it was growing with a worrying speed. In 2011 the unemployment rate was only 4.1 per cent according to Eurostat. However according to the more rigorous national calculations the rate was nudging 8 per cent as it included people employed for less than 12 hours per month although still seeking employment. The Netherlands' Central Planning Office has forecast the 2014 unemployment number at 635,000, the highest since 1995. The sad conclusion was that the Netherlands' flexible labour legislation had proved unable to create enough jobs. Comparisons with Germany gave little comfort.

The Dutch labour market had held up well in the earlier stages of the financial crisis. Despite the sharp drop in gross domestic product (GDP) that had followed the fall of Lehman Brothers, for the most part Dutch companies retained their employment levels. The highest level of unemployment in 2009 and 2010 was 4.6 per cent. This contrasted sharply with the subsequent picture in 2013, when the AMRO Bank commented that 'The outlook suggests that unemployment will remain high for some time.' The reversal in economic fortunes meant that employment contracts, once drawn up for fixed periods, were now based on shorter periods, although fixed term contracts still accounted for 69 per cent of the total (in 2001 the figure had been 74 per cent).

The Dutch could only speculate why it was that in neighbouring Germany the unemployment rate was lower for the first time since German reunification in 1990. The Netherlands was certainly affected by the so-called euro-zone crisis, which had seen its once successful exporters struggling to maintain market share. In the Netherlands exports constituted an important economic element. But it was not only the fall in exports that was causing the problem. At home, the Netherlands faced another problem: in early 2013 domestic demand had slumped, reflecting the crash in real estate prices. These had fallen, on average, by 20 per cent since 2008. The situation had been severely aggravated by the fiscal changes made in the late 1990 when mortgage rates had fallen and interest-only mortgages had become common. As property prices fell, so house-owners discovered that real estate investments were less certain than they had anticipated.

KEY INDICATORS — The Netherlands

	Unit	2011	2012	2013	2014	**2015
Population	m	*16.69	16.75	16.80	16.86	*16.93
Gross domestic product (GDP)	US$bn	840.40	770.49	853.81	866.35	*749.37
GDP per capita	US$	50,355	45,989	50,810	51,373	*44,249
GDP real growth	%	1.3	-1.2	-0.7	0.9	*1.6
Inflation	%	2.5	2.8	2.6	0.3	*-0.1
Unemployment	%	5.3	5.3	7.3	7.4	*7.2
Natural gas output	bn cum	64.2	63.9	68.7	55.8	–
Exports (fob) (goods)	US$m	544,175.0	533,189.0	550,893.0	574,673.0	–
Imports (fob) (goods)	US$m	480,578.0	472,170.0	484,489.0	469,423.0	–
Balance of trade	US$m	63,597.0	61,019.0	66,404.0	105,250.0	–
Current account	US$m	81,323.0	72,632.0	87,089.0	89,656.0	76,090.0
Total reserves minus gold	US$m	20,707.0	22,050.0	22,591.0	19,307.0	–
Foreign exchange	US$m	9,654.0	10,803.0	11,688.0	–	–
Exchange rate	per US$	0.75	0.77	0.73	0.83	–

* estimated figure ** forecast figure

Reform

In its June 2015 assessment of the Dutch economy, the International Monetary Fund (IMF) noted that important reforms had been implemented, but that there remained a large outstanding agenda. Important steps had been taken to address the inefficiencies in the housing market, support indebted households, address financial sector's problems, implement pension and labour reforms and consolidate the fiscal position. These and other reforms had strengthened the financial system and helped to consolidate the accelerating recovery. The IMF had noted these reforms in October 2014 but saw fit to make further observations on subsequent developments and new policy reform opportunities, especially in the tax system and pension system, where the Dutch government was currently already exploring further reform possibilities, but also in the housing market.

According to the IMF, the Dutch tax system was in the early stages of a promising review. The government had formulated several principles for reforms to strengthen the recovery, improve potential growth and promote higher employment. The IMF broadly supported these principles, including the unification of most value added tax (VAT) rates at the standard rate, reduced tax incentives for real estate and a reduction in labour taxes. These and other reforms could potentially increase the efficiency of the tax system and promote higher employment. A substantial tax reform package could also be the vehicle to simplify areas of taxation that had become complicated and burdensome for both tax administration and taxpayers.

The IMF also noted that the Dutch pension system had many virtues, but was now facing new challenges. The existing second pillar of the system had provided a funded system with wide coverage and high replacement rates. However, changing demographics and labour market developments were straining the system with an increasing dependency ratio and an increasing number of self-employed or employees outside the pension system. In this context, a review of how to adapt the pension system to these changing realities was welcome, including considerations of how to ensure sustainability, increase inter-generational equity and bring into the pension system those currently on its margins. The increasing numbers of the self-employed also raised broader questions about how to ensure equitable treatment of the self-employed and others in the tax, health and disability systems.

However, the government's immediate priority seemed to be reforming the tax system and structures. Both the Labour and the Liberal parties wanted to encourage the work ethic by cutting the Netherlands' high income tax rates, which, according to the London *Economist* magazine reached 42 per cent for those earning €33,589 ($35,900) per year and 52 per cent for those making €57,585 (US$64,700) or more. But it is hard to see how the government can put together a majority in the senate. Mark Rutte, the prime minister, optimistically predicted that the splintering of the senate meant that 'every party must take responsibility' for helping to pass legislation. But both D66 and the Christian Democrats were in a position to call the shots, able to block any legislation they disapproved of.

The economy

According to the Paris-based Organisation for Economic Co-operation and Development (OECD) in its 2014 Economic Survey of the Netherlands, the country was gradually emerging from a protracted recession. The Dutch authorities had implemented, or were going to put in place, significant structural reforms in the labour market, health care and the pension system to ease the reallocation of resources and help the economy to recover. Significant fiscal consolidation had, in the view of the OECD, also been achieved and the budget deficit lowered to below 3 per cent of GDP. However, the Netherlands' banking sector was large and remained vulnerable to high household indebtedness. Small and medium-sized enterprises (SMEs) also faced major credit constraints.

The Netherlands government's fiscal policy had accomplished a major structural adjustment and long-term fiscal sustainability had been strengthened by reducing ageing-related pressures on public budgets. The fiscal framework was considered by the OECD to be robust, but Dutch commitments to the European Union (EU) had led to a suspension of automatic stabilisation on the revenue side, induced frequent revisions of consolidation plans and made fiscal policy pro-cyclical. A specific international tax issue was the tax planning strategies of foreign multinational firms.

The Dutch banking sector was considered large compared to the size of the country and remained vulnerable to domestic risks. The number of non-performing loans not covered by loan loss provisions was high in relation to bank capital, reported the OECD. Dutch banks' dependence on international capital markets was extensive and they were highly exposed to the property market. Some structural reforms had been implemented to improve the housing market. Nominal house prices had dropped by 20 per cent since their 2008 peak and around 40 per cent of households with mortgage debt had negative home equity. Moreover, the majority of the mortgage portfolio was not amortised regularly. Households had significant assets on average, but their composition and distribution suggest that they might not be available to repay the full principal once it falls due.

The OECD also noted that SMEs played an important role in the Dutch economy, but had been hit hard by the global financial crisis. Dutch banks had been tightening credit conditions and few alternative sources of financing were available. At the same time, not all public guarantees for loans were being used. Restrictive labour regulations were another barrier for the development of dynamic SMEs and could also raise the incidence of last-resort self-employment. The authorities intended to increase the protection of employees on temporary contracts and simultaneously both reduce the protection of those on permanent contracts and restrict access to unemployment benefits. The number of SMEs engaging in collaboration on innovation was comparatively low. In the view of the OECD, tax policies could have encouraged the growth of self-employment. Regulatory barriers to entrepreneurship were low, but the licence and permits system was stricter and some compliance costs were higher than in the best performing OECD countries.

Energy

Although not a significant producer of liquid fuels, according to the US government's Energy Information Administration (EIA), the Netherlands plays an important role as a European liquid fuels transportation and processing hub. It is also the second-largest producer and exporter of natural gas in Europe, behind Norway; the Netherlands is also home to Europe's largest natural gas trading hub in terms of spot volumes. The Netherlands is, as well, a major petroleum liquids refining and storage centre. In January 2015, the Netherlands had 1.2 million barrels per day (bpd) of crude oil refining capacity, according to the *Oil and Gas Journal* (OGJ). At the beginning of 2014, the country had more than 210 million barrels of storage capacity, with the majority (more than 170 million barrels) located in Rotterdam. Additionally, the Port of Amsterdam served as a major hub for gasoline storage, blending and trans-shipment.

The Netherlands produced just over 3.0 trillion cubic feet (tcf) of natural gas in 2013. Most of its natural gas fields are located offshore in the North Sea, although a number of them are located onshore, including Groningen, one of the ten largest natural gas fields in the world. The government has capped annual natural gas production at the Groningen field as part of a policy to encourage production from smaller fields and to prolong the life of the field. This field acts as a swing producer to help balance the high seasonal fluctuations in demand in northern Europe. To help meet the increased winter demand for natural gas in the Netherlands and in north-west Europe, gas production from the Groningen field in January was generally around double the output in July. In both January 2014 and December 2014, the Netherlands' government reduced the annual cap on production from the Groningen field because of concerns over an increase in the frequency and intensity of earthquakes in the area. The government production cap was 1.5tcf for 2014, more than 20 per cent lower than the nearly 1.9tcf produced from Groningen in 2013. In December 2014, the Dutch government set the cap for 2015 at 1.4tcf, but in February 2015, the government further reduced the cap for the first half of 2015 to just 0.6tcf.

Natural gas produced in the Netherlands is shipped via an extensive domestic and export pipeline system, which directly connects the country with the United Kingdom, Germany and Belgium and indirectly connects it to most of Europe. In addition to pipeline natural gas, the Netherlands serves as a transport hub for liquefied natural gas (LNG). The Gas Access to Europe (GATE) LNG terminal became operational in September 2011. While initially designed to unload, store and re-gasify LNG and deliver the gas into the pipeline system, the terminal can also act as a break-bulk and re-export facility, loading LNG onto trucks or small ships for distribution in north-west Europe, or reloading LNG onto large ocean-going tankers for re-export throughout the world. The Netherlands is also home to the Title Transfer Facility (TTF) natural gas hub, the largest and most liquid natural gas hub in continental Europe. TTF has also been the fastest-growing natural gas hub in Europe and in 2014, TTF surpassed the United Kingdom's National Balancing Point hub in terms of spot volumes traded.

Risk assessment

Economy	Good
Politics	Good
Regional stability	Goo

Muslims in The Netherlands

% of population	5.5
Sunni (% of Muslims)	95
Shi'a (% of Muslims)	5

COUNTRY PROFILE

1579 The Protestant majority in the Netherlands rebelled against the Catholic Habsburg Empire and declared independence, with William of Orange crowned Prince William I of Holland and Zeeland. In the seventeenth century, the Netherlands became a powerful trading nation with an empire in the East Indies (modern day Indonesia) and the Caribbean. In the 1650s, the Dutch fought several wars against the English, mainly due to colonial rivalry.
1688 William of Orange (the grandson of William I) acceded to the English throne as William III, ending conflict between the two countries.
1704–06 The English army under John Churchill helped to defeat attempts by the combined armies of Austria and France to invade the Netherlands.
1804 The Netherlands was occupied by the French under Napoleon.
1812 The Netherlands was liberated by British and Prussian armies.
1815 A renewed invasion attempt by Napoleon was defeated at the Battle of Waterloo. Attempts to unify Catholic Belgium with the Netherlands at the Vienna Conference failed, and the two countries remained separate.
1914–18 The country remained neutral in the First World War.
1922 Women were given the vote.
1940–45 The Netherlands declared its neutrality but was occupied by Nazi Germany during the Second World War. The royal family was exiled in the UK.
1945 The Netherlands became a charter member of the United Nations.
1949 The policy of neutrality was abandoned and the Netherlands became a founder member of NATO. The Dutch East Indies became independent.
1958 The Netherlands was a founding member of the European Economic Community (EEC).
1980 Queen Juliana abdicated in favour of her eldest daughter Princess Beatrix. Prince Willem-Alexander became heir apparent.
1989 The Christen Democratisch Appèl (CDA) (Christian Democratic Appeal) and Volkspartij voor Vrijheid en Democratie (VVD) (People's Party for Freedom and Democracy) government fell when VVD refused to support proposals for a 20-year environmental protection programme. A centre-left cabinet was formed by CDA and the Partij van de Arbeid (PvdA) (Labour Party), with Ruud Lubbers as prime minister.
1992–93 Ruud Lubbers' government was discredited by a serious economic recession.
1994 A three-party coalition, headed by Wim Kok (PvdA), and including VVD and Democraten 66 (D66) (Democrats 66) won elections. The CDA was frozen out of power for the first time since the First World War.
1999 The Netherlands was a founder member of European Economic and Monetary Union (Emu).
2000 Ruud Lubbers was chosen to head the UN High Commission on Refugees (UNHCR). After 25 years of debating, a bill to legalise euthanasia was approved.
2002 The euro currency replaced the guilder. Wim Kok resigned following a report that criticised Dutch troops in (former) Yugoslavia who had failed to stop the massacre of as many as 8,000 Muslims by Bosnian Serbs in Srebrenica in 1995. Pim Fortuyn, leader of the far-right, anti-immigration, Lijst Pim Fortuyn (LPF) (List Pim Fortuyn) party, was shot dead during election campaigning. CDA won elections and Jan Peter Balkenende became prime minister of a fragile coalition, which later collapsed and Balkenende resigned. Prince Claus von Amsberg, husband of Queen Beatrix, died.
2003 After early parliamentary elections, Jan Peter Balkenende was reinstated as prime minister to head a coalition government, led by the CDA, and including the VVD and the D66.
2004 Former Queen (1948–80) Juliana died. Prominent filmmaker Theo van Gogh was murdered by an Islamist radical; tit-for-tat attacks on Dutch mosques and churches ensued.
2005 The Netherlands rejected the proposed constitution of the EU. Parliament introduced a test of the Dutch language and culture for would-be immigrants.
2006 Prime Minister Balkenende resigned, following a row with D66 about immigration policies. Balkenende reformed the coalition government without the D66. In parliamentary elections, the ruling CDA won 41 seats (out of 150). The Socialistische Partij,
(SP) (Socialist Party) increased its seat numbers to 25. The new right-wing Partij voor de Vrijheid (PvdV) (Party for Freedom) won nine seats, while the LPF failed to win any.
2007 Negotiations began between The Netherlands and Caribbean islands of Bonaire, Saba and St Eustatius (three of the five islands of the Netherlands Antilles) due to become city-states within the Kingdom of The Netherlands as the Netherlands Antilles ceases to exist as an entity. A coalition government was formed with the CDA, PvdV and Christen Unie (CU) (Christian Union), with Jan Peter Balkenende as prime minister. Relatives of victims of the Srebrenica massacre in Bosnia in 1995 filed a case against the UN and the Netherlands state, claiming negligence in allowing the massacre to take place.
2008 A ban on tobacco smoking in public places was introduced; no ban was introduced for smoking marijuana in designated coffee shops.
2010 The coalition government collapsed, following a disagreement over extending troop deployment to Afghanistan as part of NATO's forces. In new parliamentary elections for the Tweede Kamer (second chamber), the centre-right VVD won 20.4 per cent of the vote and the right to form a coalition government. Dutch troops, who had been in Afghanistan since 2006, withdrew; although there had been less than 2,000 troops, they were praised for their effectiveness in Uruzgan province. A coalition government of VVD with CDA, and including the PvdV, was formed, led by Mark Rutte (VVD) as prime minister.
2011 In June, The Netherlands announced that it would veto the EU decision (taken in June), to admit Bulgaria and Romania into the Schengen area for passport-free travel of citizens and goods. The Netherlands imposed a one-year delay in view of the turmoil in the Middle East and its potential for Arab migration to the EU in 2011–12, as well as the failure by Romania and Bulgaria to fight corruption and organised crime. Geert Wilders, of the far-right PvdV, who had been arrested in 2009 for inciting hatred against Muslims by making a film that linked radical Islamist actions to the Quran, was acquitted of all charges in June. Parliament voted to ban the killing of animals for halal meat.
2012 On 1 March, Prime Minister Rutte announced that The Netherlands' Schengen veto on Bulgaria and Romania

would be reconsidered by September if the expected June EU report gave a 'reasonably positive' opinion of their progress. On 23 April the coalition government of Mark Rutte resigned following the withdrawal from talks by the PVV over budget cuts. On 26 April tough budget cuts were agreed between three opposition political parties (D66, GL and CU) and the two ruling parties of the caretaker government, thereby allowing the government to implement measures to cut the deficit to 3 per cent of GDP in 2013. The vote came just before the EU deadline of 30 April. Early general elections (by two years) were scheduled for June; initially postponed, they finally took place on 12 September. The main focus of all parties was on the economy and austerity measures to reduce the national deficit. The VVD won a greater share of the vote than in 2010 and with more seats continued to lead a coalition government. Mark Rutte remained in post as prime minister. A meeting of the EU Justice and Home Affairs Council scheduled for 19–20 September, to discuss Bulgaria and Romania's admittance to the Schengen Area treaty, was postponed to 25–26 October.

2013 After announcing on 28 January in a live television broadcast that she was abdicating, Queen Beatrix signed the instrument of abdication in Amsterdam on 30 April, handing the throne to her son Prince Willem-Alexander. He is the country's first king since 1890. Queen Beatrix will in future be known as Princess Beatrix.

2015 Provincial elections were held in March.

Political structure

Constitution

Under the constitution of 1983, The Netherlands is divided into 12 administrative provinces. Each province is run by a royal commissioner and an elected Provinciale Staten (regional parliamentary assembly). Each regional assembly elects its own governing executive (Gedeputeerde Staten) from among its members. Both council and executive are presided over by a royal commissioner, who is appointed by the crown.

The 672 municipalities, including the major cities, each have an elected council which in turn elects aldermen to sit on the municipal executive along with a mayor, who is appointed by the crown.

The constitution guarantees equality and freedom from discrimination on the grounds of religion, political opinion, race, or sex. The constitution is unique in placing upon the government a duty to promote environmental protection both domestically and internationally.

Where there is no adult successor to the throne or the serving monarch is unable to exercise royal prerogative, the national legislature has the power to appoint a temporary regent.

On 10 October 2010, the Caribbean islands of Curaçao and St Maarten joined Aruba (1986) as semi-autonomous countries within the Kingdom of the Netherlands; at the same time the Caribbean islands of Bonaire, St Eustatius and Saba became Bijzondere Gemeenten (special municipalities) of the Netherlands.

Form of state

Parliamentary democratic monarchy

The executive

The monarch is the head of state but has few executive powers. The monarch has the power to appoint the prime minister, to dissolve the national assembly and call new elections – all on the recommendation of the national assembly.

The principle executive functions are carried out by the prime minister, who is selected by the national assembly and appoints a council of ministers from both inside and outside the assembly. State ministers are not allowed to continue to sit as members of parliament.

National legislature

Legislative power is vested in the Staten Generaal (States General), a bicameral national assembly.

The 150-member Tweede Kamer (Second Chamber or lower house), is directly elected by the *d'Hondt* system of proportional representation (a system invented in The Netherlands which takes account of the country's provincial units) for a four-year term. It is empowered to review the actions of the cabinet, debate bills and pass approved measures to the Eerste Kamer (First Chamber or upper house), for enactment.

The First Chamber has 75 members who are indirectly elected by the 12 provincial councils, for a period of four years. The First Chamber does not initiate legislation, but is responsible for approving or rejecting bills presented by the Second Chamber. The First Chamber cannot amend legislation directly, but acts which it rejects are likely to be amended in the Second Chamber and represented for approval.

Legal system

The Supreme Court is the highest legal body in the country and it hears appeals arising from cases previously heard in the lower courts. It also has the power of cassation over legislation deemed to conflict with the constitution.

There are five Appeal Courts at lower levels. Most cases are heard either at the 19 Provincial Courts of Justice or at the 62 Municipal Courts. Judges are nominated by the crown and serve for life.

Last elections

(Tweede Kamer)

Results: Parliamentary (Tweede Kamer): Volkspartij voor Vrijheid en Democratie (VVD) (People's Party for Freedom and Democracy) won 26.6 per cent of the vote (41 seats out of 150), Partij van de Arbeid (PvdA) (Labour Party) 24.8 per cent (38), Partij voor de Vrijheid (PvdV) (Party for Freedom) 10.1 per cent (15), Socialistische Partij (SP) (Socialist Party) 9.7 per cent (15); Christen-Democratisch Appèl (CDA) (Christian Democratic Appeal) 8.5 per cent (13), Democraten 66 (D66) (Democrats 66) 8.0 per cent (12), Christen Unie (CU) (Christian Union) 3.1 per cent (five); Groen Links (GL) (Green Left) 2.3 per cent (four), Staatkundig Gereformeerde Partij (SGP) (Reformed Political Party) 2.1 per cent (three), Partij voor de Dieren (PvdD) (Animal Rights Party) 1.9 per cent (two), 50Plus (50+) 1.9 per cent (two); 10 other political parties won less than 1 per cent each and failed to win any seats. Turnout was 75 per cent.

First Chamber (membership by appointment only): CDA (23 seats); PvdA (19 seats); VVD (15 seats); SP (four seats); LPF (one seat); GL (five seats); D66 (three seats); CU (two seats); SGP (two seats); Onafhankelijke Senaatsfractie-Fryske Nasjonale Partij (FNP) (Frisian National Party) (one seat).

Next elections

No later than 17 March 2017

Political parties

Ruling party

Coalition, led by Volkspartij voor Vrijheid en Democratie (VVD) (People's Party for Freedom and Democracy) with Partij van de Arbeid (PvdA) (Labour Party) (from 2010; re-elected Sep 2012)

Main opposition party

With multiple parties in parliament no one party forms an official opposition.

Population

16.75 million (2012)* The population is concentrated in the major conurbations around Amsterdam, Rotterdam, The Hague and Utrecht, which form the Randstad or Ring Cities. Population density is much lower in the north and east.

Last census: January 2002: 16,105,285

Population density: 469 inhabitants per square kilometre. Urban population 83 per cent (2010 Unicef).

Annual growth rate: 0.5 per cent, 1990–2010 (Unicef).

Ethnic make-up

Dutch (96 per cent); others, predominantly Afro-Caribbean (Surinamese), Indonesian, Moroccan and Turkish (4 per cent).

Religions

Catholic (34 per cent), Protestant (28 per cent), Muslim (3 per cent), Jewish (1 per cent).

Education
Primary schooling may begin at aged four, and continue until aged 12. At aged 12, pupils are channelled into secondary schools with courses designed for their aptitude. The length of time in these schools varies dependent on the courses undertaken; mixed general and vocational courses last for four years and pre-university courses last six years. Schools are either publicly maintained by government, state or municipal authorities, (attended by 28 per cent of children), or private schools, mostly denominational (attended by 72 per cent of children). Total public expenditure on education is equivalent to approximately 5 per cent of annual GNP.
Compulsory years: 5 to 16.
Enrolment rate: 109 per cent and 106 per cent, male and female gross enrolment rates respectively, of relevant age groups for primary schools, (including repeaters); 126 per cent and 122 per cent, male and female gross enrolment rates respectively, of relevant age groups for secondary schools, (including repeaters), 1997–2000 (Unicef 2004).
Pupils per teacher: 14 in primary schools.

Health
The private sector is important in the supply of healthcare in the Netherlands and private health insurance is compulsory for most wage earners.
HIV/Aids
HIV prevalence: 0.2 per cent aged 15–49 in 2003 (World Bank)
Life expectancy: 79 years, 2004 (WHO 2006)
Fertility rate/Maternal mortality rate: 1.8 births per woman, 2010 (Unicef); maternal mortality 7 per 100,000 live births (World Bank).
Child (under 5 years) mortality rate (per 1,000): 4 per 1,000 live births (WHO 2012)
Head of population per physician: 3.15 physicians per 1,000 people, 2003 (WHO 2006)

Welfare
The Netherlands provides generous income support linked to the minimum wage. However, following a government drive to limit the growth of social security spending, the criteria for eligibility for benefits has been narrowed and earnings-related benefits have been reduced from 80 to 70 per cent of previous income.
As in many EU countries, the ageing population is threatening to make the funding of state pensions an unsustainable burden on public finances over the next 30 years. In 2000, expenditure on pensions was some 5.7 per cent of GDP, but this is projected to rise to the equivalent of 8.4 per cent by 2020 and 11.2 per cent by 2030.

Main cities
Amsterdam (cultural capital, estimated population 776,226 in 2012), Rotterdam (576,302), The Hague (seat of government, 490,282), Utrecht (311,171), Eindhoven (225,421), Almere (216,369), Tilburg (209,542), Groningen (183,147), Breda (181,887).

Languages spoken
English, German and French are widely spoken. About 2.9 per cent of the population speak Frisian, mostly in the province of Friesland in the north-east. Turkish and Arabic are also spoken.
Official language/s
Dutch and Frisian

Media
Press
A free press is guaranteed under the constitution
Dailies: There are around 50 daily newspapers. Leading national dailies include *De Telegraaf* (www.telegraaf.nl), *NRC Handelsblad* (www.nrc.nl), *Metro* (www.metronieuws.nl) (tabloid), *Nederlands Dagblad, Trouw* (www.trouw.nl), *Algemeen Dagblad* (www.ad.nl), *De Volkskrant* (www.volkskrant.nl), *Het Parool* (www.parool.nl) (tabloid).
Weeklies: A number of daily newspapers publish weekend editions including *De Telegraaf Weekeinde, NRC Handelsblad* and *De Volkskrant.* Magazines include *Vrij Nederland* (www.vn.nl) for general news; in English a newsletter Dutch News (www.dutchnews.nl) is published online, with political and general news.
Business: In Dutch, (with some online English translations), publications include the daily *Het Financieele Dagblad* (www.fd.nl), periodicals include *Intermediair* (www.intermediair.nl), with the biggest circulation figure *Management Team* (www.mt.nl), (fortnightly) is a major publication, *Elseviers Weekblad* (www.elsevier.nl) (weekly), *Bizz* (www.bizz.nl) (monthly) and *De Zaak* (www.dezaak.nl) (fortnightly); *Ondernemen* (www.mkb.nl) (monthly) for entrepreneurs and *Beleggers Belangen* (www.beleggersbelangen.nl) for investors.
Periodicals: Official government publications are provided by Overheid (www.overheid.nl) the state-owned press.
Broadcasting
Domestic, public broadcasting allocates broadcasting time by proportional representation. Programmes can be made by any group, political, religious or civil and airtime is allocated based on the number of member they have.
The Netherlands has the largest take-up of cable television and consequently viewers have access to an ample range of domestic and foreign channels. The Netherlands Public Broadcasting (Omroep) operates three national TV channels and seven radio stations plus a website (http://portal.omroep.nl) with video access.
Radio: In addition to the seven national channels including an external service (Radio Netherlands, in several languages, www.radionetherlands.nl), and special interest radio, there are 10 regional stations and approximately 180 local channels. There are over 3,000 local and regional commercial radio stations catering for all styles of music and information, some of the largest include Sky Radio (www.skyradio.nl) with continuous music, Radio 538 (www.radio538.nl). BNR Nieuwsradio (www.bnr.nl) is a business radio station (in Dutch).
Television: All analogue TV broadcasting was discontinued in December 2006; broadcasts are now digital and by 2008 between 80–85 per cent of all transmissions will be in high definition (HD). Omroep operates channels Netherlands 1, 2 and 3 (Ned 1, 2, 3) and the children's channel ZapTV; each province has at least one local channel. BVN (www.bvn.nl) broadcasts an external service worldwide.
TV programmes are broadcast in their original languages – often English – with Dutch subtitles.
Other news agencies: ANP (Netherlands National News Agency): www.anp.nl

Economy
Not only does the Netherlands have a mature history of hydrocarbon sales, particularly natural gas sold to the European Union, it is also a major European transport hub, with Rotterdam as the world's fourth largest port and Europe's largest, handling over twice as much as Europe's next largest port (Antwerp, Belgium); in 2014 it processed 444.7 million tonnes of freight and over 34,000 sea-going vessels and 133,000 inland vessels. Manufacturing of machinery and equipment, chemicals and foodstuffs all contribute to strong foreign trade, which is the backbone of the Dutch economy, accounting for 73 per cent of gross domestic product (GDP) in 2013. It is the World's fifth largest exporter of goods.
When the economy fell into recession in the fourth quarter; in 2009 the rate was -4.0 per cent. The crisis prompted the government to launch three economic stimulation packages from 2008–10, totalling over US$34.5 billion. The packages were needed to shore up the financial sector, including nationalising

ABN Amro/Fortis Bank and aiding the ING insurance company, both of which carried significant US mortgage-backed securities (toxic debt) as recorded assets. The economy returned to positive growth of 1.6 per cent, as world trade strengthened in 2010, and a 1.7 per cent growth in 2011. Growth was recorded at 0.9 per cent in 2014.

In 2010 the trade balance returned to its pre-crisis level of US$57.2 billion. Since then vast improvements in exports has seen this figure rise to US$85.6 billion in 2014.

The Netherlands may only produce a small quantity of crude oil, but it is a relatively large producer and supplier of natural gas. It is the European Union's largest natural gas producer (taking over from the UK in 2009), with pipelines to Germany, France, Italy, the UK and Belgium. Proven natural gas reserves were 32 trillion cubic feet at the end of 2013, with production of 3052 billion cubic feet, of which 2376 billion was exported in 2013.

External trade

As a member of the European Union, The Netherlands operates within a community-wide free trade area, with tariffs set as a whole. Internationally, the EU has free trade agreements with a number of nations and trading blocs worldwide.

The economy is open to foreign trade with 60 per cent of agricultural produce exported, and the majority of foreign earnings provided by services including international transport and distribution, banking and insurance. Industrial production includes processed foods, petrochemicals and plastics, machinery and vehicle assembly.

Imports

Main imports include machinery and vehicles, chemicals, fuels, consumer goods, foodstuffs and clothing.

Main sources: Germany (14.2 per cent of total in 2014), China (12.8 per cent), Belgium (8.3 per cent).

Exports

Major exports include petroleum and natural gas, organic chemicals, agricultural products and foodstuffs, machinery, electronics and vehicles.

Main destinations: Germany (22.2 per cent of total in 2014), Belgium (12.2 per cent), United Kingdom (8.2 per cent).

Agriculture

Farming

The agricultural sector employs around 4 per cent of the workforce and contributes 3 per cent to annual GDP, accounting for 25 per cent of total exports.

Despite a high population density in the Netherlands, approximately 70 per cent of all land area is under cultivation. Population growth and wider commercial land use, combined with rising water levels, are placing considerable pressure on land resources. Given the Netherlands' small surface area and high population density, farming is generally highly concentrated, specialised and efficient. Dairy farming is the most substantial activity, involving over a third of the country's farmers.

Overall, Dutch farms tend to be larger than those in other EU member states, with only 25 per cent of farms smaller than five hectares, compared to an EU norm of 50 per cent. Productivity rates are consequently higher than the EU average, and the Netherlands is a net contributor to the EU's Common Agricultural Policy (CAP) budget. Fundamental reform to the CAP was introduced throughout most of the EU in 2005. The subsidies paid on farm output, which tended to benefit large farms and encourage overproduction, were replaced by single farm payments not conditional on production. This is expected to reward farms that provide and maintain a healthy environment, food safety and animal welfare standards. The changes are also intended to encourage market conscious production and cut the cost of CAP to the EU taxpayer. Dutch farmers are one of the world's most prolific consumers of pesticides, using 19,000 tonnes of active chemical ingredients per annum (an average 10 kilograms per hectare), with potatoes and flower bulbs the most intensively sprayed crops. Traditional Dutch horticulture, in particular the production of flowers and bulbs, is the highest value-added sector. The Netherlands typically has over 24,000 hectares (ha) of land dedicated to open floriculture, and a further 7,000ha of floriculture under glass.

Fishing

The typical Dutch fish catch is over 500,000 tonnes per annum, of which approximately 450,000mt is seafood. Around 20 per cent of the fish catch is exported, generating annual revenues of approximately US$250 million.

Forestry

Total forest area is 339,000 hectares (ha) or approximately 10 per cent of total land area. Almost all timber needs are imported, but The Netherlands is a major re-exporter of forest products.

Industry and manufacturing

The Netherlands has a broad industrial base. In 2004, manufacturing contributed 36 per cent to GDP and employ over 20 per cent of the labour force. Due to the small home market, Dutch industry is heavily dependent on foreign trade. It is also reliant upon imports of raw materials as industrial inputs.

As in most Western European countries, the industrial sector is increasingly focussed on high value-added manufacturing, where technological and skills advantages counteract the lower labour and production costs in emerging industrial economies. The Netherlands' lack of natural resources has increased its dependency on its manufacturing sector and imported materials.

Owing to rapid growth and the need for efficient land use, the construction industry is also significant and often pioneering in the field of space-saving design work.

Manufacturing accounts for 15.1 per cent of GDP and construction for a further 5.2 per cent.

Industrial production growth for the Netherlands was estimated at 0.8 per cent for 2004.

Tourism

The Netherlands has a long tradition as a tourist destination, not only for its quaint historic windmills, with the rows of fields full of variously coloured tulips and long flat roads that lead from one town to the next, but also for the sophisticated city centres of adult entertainment. The major cities have museums to showcase Dutch artists such as Rembrandt and Van Gogh. There are nine sites included on Unesco's World Heritage.

Travel and tourism accounted for around 6 per cent of GDP in 2014. The total contribution to employment was 9.8 per cent of total employment (709,000 people).

On 27 April 2012, a law was enacted whereby foreign visitors were banned from entering cannabis cafes. The law was enforced in three southern provinces in May and nationwide in December.

Hydrocarbons

The hydrocarbons sector accounts for approximately 9 per cent of GDP and employs 4 per cent of the workforce.

The Netherlands produces around 28 per cent of its oil needs domestically, with almost 70 per cent of production coming from offshore deposits. Total reserves stand at around 106 million barrels and consumption runs at around 950,000 barrels per day (bpd). Onshore deposits of oil were first discovered in the late 1930s near The Hague, but attention shifted in the 1940s to better deposits in the Schoonebeek region. Offshore oil, by comparison, is a relatively recent discovery. Average oil production in has fallen over recent years as a result of diminishing reserves in a number of oil fields in the Dutch sector of the North Sea.

Proven natural gas reserves were 32 trillion cubic feet (cuf) at the end of 2014, with annual production of 3052billion cuf in 2014. The largest onshore gas field is at Groningen, first discovered in the 1960s. This was the main source of gas

until the discovery of offshore deposits. Although it is expected that gas reserves will be depleted by 2030, the rate of new discoveries is sufficiently high that Dutch gas production is expected to continue beyond that time. The Netherlands is a substantial net exporter of gas because it has one of the biggest operations drilling for offshore natural gas in the North Sea – 62 wells – The Netherlands is one of western Europe's major natural gas suppliers,, importing only 8 per cent of total supplies and exporting approximately 48 per cent of domestic production. The first liquefied natural gas (LNG) terminal, Gas Access to Europe (Gate), began operations in the port of Rotterdam in September 2011. Gate cost €800 million (US$1.1 billion) and when fully operational will process 8.8 million tonnes of LNG per year. Rotterdam is a key link in Western Europe's energy supply chain, home to a number of refineries and ancillary industries.
With proven low quality coal reserves of 500 million tonnes coupled with high labour costs and falling demand the last coal pit was closed in 1970. Approximately 320 million tonnes of coal were imported in 2007, of which over 90 per cent was consumed by domestic thermal power stations.

Energy
The Netherlands has an electricity capacity of 20 million kilowatts (KW). Natural gas provides over 50 per cent of electric power needs and oil around 20 per cent. Nuclear power supplies around 4.5 per cent and the remainder by other material such as coal. The long-term emphasis is on developing sustainable energy sources such as solar and wind power.

Financial markets
Stock exchange
Euronext NV Amsterdam (AEX)
Commodity exchange
Liffe Connect

Banking and insurance
Banking supervision remains the responsibility of De Nederlandsche Bank (DNB). The oversight of currency transactions was in the hands of DNB until 2002, when it was assumed by the European Central Bank (ECB). Foreign banks operating in the Netherlands face no special restrictions.
The Dutch banking sector is dominated by three banking conglomerates, ABN Amro, ING Bank and Rabobank Nederland, which together control approximately 75 per cent of total domestic lending. Including Bank Nederlandse Gemeeten and the joint Belgian/Dutch banking group Fortis, these banks are estimated to hold almost 90 per cent of domestic banking assets, loans and deposits.
In 1995, ING bought Britain's Baring Bank for £1 when Baring was on the verge of collapse after the activities of employee and 'rogue trader' Nick Leeson. ING sold at a profit its remaining Baring division in November 2004.
Central bank
De Nederlandsche Bank (DNB); European Central Bank (ECB).
Main financial centre
Amsterdam

Time
GMT plus one hour (daylight saving, late March to late October, GMT plus two hours)

Geography
The Netherlands is situated in Western Europe, bordered to the east by Germany and to the south by Belgium. The North Sea lies to the north and west, giving the country a coastline of over 450km.
Except for small areas in the east of the country, the Netherlands' topography is dominated by river plains and flatlands which provide excellent growing conditions for agriculture. The major rivers are the Neder-Rijn and the Waal.
More than a third of the country is below sea level and made up of *polder*, land reclaimed from the sea by the construction of successive sea-walls over the years, but especially since the 1930s.
In the south-west of the country, the major cities of Amsterdam, Rotterdam, The Hague and Utrecht form a heavily urbanised area known as the Randstad or ring city. The flat character of the land, population density and intensive land use have heightened awareness of environmental issues such as air, soil and water pollution and the threat of rising sea levels caused by global warming.
Hemisphere
Northern

Climate
The country has an equitable north European climate, with warm though often damp summers and occasionally severe winters. Average temperatures peak in July and August at around 17 degrees Celsius (C), but manage barely 2 degrees C in January and February before picking up sharply in April and May. Rainfall is heaviest in March and April, when on average 76mm and 81mm respectively are recorded. July and August, by comparison, are the driest months with 41mm and 43mm of rainfall respectively.

Dress codes
Formal dress is usual for business; otherwise, no special restrictions apply. Warm clothing is recommended in winter, especially in coastal regions.

Entry requirements
Passports
Required by all, except nationals of countries which are signatories of the Schengen Accords, which includes most EU/EEA member states, who may visit on national IDs.
Visa
Required by all, except nationals of EU and Schengen Accord signatory countries; North America, Australasia and Japan. For further exceptions contact the nearest consulate. Schengen visas cover all entry needs; for business trips, an original invitation from a business contact in The Netherlands is necessary when applying. A Schengen visa application (offered in several languages) can be downloaded from http://europa.eu/abc/travel/ see 'documents you will need'.
Currency advice/regulations
There are no restrictions on the import or export of local and foreign currencies. Travellers' cheques are widely accepted.
Customs
Personal items are duty-free. There are no duties levied on alcohol and tobacco between EU member states, providing amounts imported are for personal consumption.
Prohibited imports
Illegal drugs and firearms

Health (for visitors)
Nationals of the European Economic Area (EEA) countries and Switzerland can access reduced cost and sometimes free medical treatment using a European Health Insurance Card (EHIC) while visiting the EEA. Exceptions include nationals of the 10 countries, which joined the EU in 2004, whose EHIC is not valid in Switzerland. Applications for the EHIC should be made before travelling.

Hotels
Classified from one- to five-star by Netherlands Board of Tourism, the Royal Dutch Touring Club and the Royal Netherlands Automobile Club. Accommodation may be booked through the Netherlands Reservation Centre in Leidschendam (tel: (070) 202-500). It is advisable to book well in advance during spring and summer. Foreign nationals must present passports before booking in, and are automatically registered with local police.

Credit cards
All major credit cards are accepted.

Public holidays (national)
Fixed dates
1 Jan (New Year's Day), 30 Apr (Queen's Day), 4 May (Remembrance Day), 5 May (Liberation Day), 25–26 Dec (Christmas). Holidays that fall on the weekend are not taken *in lieu*.

Variable dates
Easter Monday (Mar/Apr), Whitsun (May/Jun), Ascension Day (Aug).

Working hours
Banking
Mon–Fri: 0900–1600, some open Sat and on late shopping evenings.
Business
Mon–Fri: 0830–1730.
Government
Mon–Fri: 0830–1700.
Shops
0830/0900–1730/1800 (half-day closing usually Mon or Wed). Main shops open Sat and Thu/Fri evening.

Telecommunications
Mobile/cell phones
There is comprehensive GSM coverage throughout the country

Electricity supply
220V AC.

Social customs/useful tips
Appointments are necessary and business cards are exchanged, although the business climate is less formal than in some Western European countries and cordiality and consensus at business meetings are highly valued. The best months for business visits are considered to be March to May and September to November. When invited to a meal in a Dutch home it is usual to bring flowers or a small gift.
On 27 April 2012, a law was enacted whereby foreign visitors were banned from entering cannabis cafes. The law was enforced in three southern provinces in May and nationwide in December.

Security
There are no special problems with security in the Netherlands, although increased caution against petty theft is advised in the heavily populated areas of Rotterdam and Amsterdam.

Getting there
Air
National airline: KLM (Koninklijke Luchtvaart Maatschappij – Royal Dutch Airlines)
Air France acquired KLM in 2004.
International airport/s: Amsterdam Schiphol (AMS), 15km south-west of city; facilities include restaurants, duty-free shops, banks, showers, a business centre, conference rooms and car hire. There are regular, scheduled train and bus routes into the city, travel time 15–30 minutes. Taxis are numerous.
A direct, express train connects Schiphol with main cities in Holland, and some cities in Belgium.
A limited range of international flight destinations also originate from Eindhoven (EIN), 8km north of city; Maastricht (MST), 7km from city; Rotterdam (RTM), 8km north-west of city.
Airport tax: None
Surface
Road: Major routes from the rest of Europe are by a good network of motorways, well signposted with green 'E' symbols, indicating international highways.
Water: There are good connections between all major European ports. Boat trains operate to the Hook of Holland from many European countries.
The Netherlands is a leading international maritime shipper with extensive port facilities.
Main port/s: Ferries berth at Vlissingen, Rotterdam and Hook of Holland (Hoek van Holland).

Getting about
National transport
Air: Groningen (GRQ) in the north has connecting flights to the international airports. Den Helder (DHR), in the west is one of the largest heliports in Europe providing access to offshore oil and gas fields; charter planes are also available. Other internal services link Amsterdam, Eindhoven, Rotterdam and Maastricht.
Road: Roadways include high speed expressways, limited access motorways, dual highways and secondary roads. All roads are well signposted with red 'A's indicating national highways, and smaller routes indicated by yellow 'N's.
Buses: Most bus services run between 0600–2330. The Interliner is a service used for longer distances and has very few stops. The Connexxion bus company serves the major part of Holland including the provinces of Noord and Zuid Holland, Gelderland, Overijssel and Zeeland.
Rail: There is an hourly service, running 24 hours, between Utrecht, Amsterdam, Schiphol, The Hague and Rotterdam. The Netherlands Railways operate an Intercity (IC) network connecting large cities. IC trains only stop at the major stations. Local trains provide transportation to smaller cities. Tickets can be purchased from railway stations prior to travelling.
Water: There is an extensive network of inland waterways. Scheduled boat services operate from Enkhuizen to Urk and Staveren and between the mainland and the islands in the north.
City transport
The country is divided into zones with set tariffs. A *strippenkaart*, containing 15 strip tickets, is valid throughout the country for travel on buses, trams and subways, including trips within cities. To travel within one zone costs two strips. An extra strip is charged for each subsequent zone. A time limit, notated on the back of the card, allows interchange with other transport systems within the same zone.
Taxis: Taxis have blue licence plates with black letters and figures. Taxis can be booked in advance or, in some larger cities, hailed on the street. Prices may vary between regions and are sometimes open to negotiation.
A *treintaxi* (train-taxi) is a publicly shared taxi, offering shared costs.
Buses, trams & metro: Amsterdam has an intergrated public transport service that runs between 0600–0030 daily throughout the city; night buses run between 0030– 0730. Tickets (*strippenkaart*) can be purchased from a tobacconist, post office or railway station. They should be franked when boarding, for each trip. Elsewhere, city buses run within the boundaries of larger towns. A metro runs in Rotterdam, as well as trams, which also run in The Hague. They typically run between 0600–0000. The metro and trams are usually faster than city buses.
Trains: The train to the city centre from Schiphol is an efficient mode of transport. Inter-city train tickets are not interchangeable with local passenger services.
Ferry: There are ferries running on the canals of Amsterdam and Rotterdam, although these services are more for tourist purposes than for convenience.
Car hire
Car hire is widely available, the minimum age is dependent on insurance usually 21 years. An international driving license is necessary for all non-EU drivers. Traffic drives on the right. Speed limits: urban areas 50kph, normal roads 80kph, motorways 120kph. The wearing of seat belts is compulsory. It is illegal to use a handheld mobile phone while driving (including times when vehicle is stationary in traffic). Do not ignore parking fees as failure can result in a fine and if not paid within 24 hours, the car will be towed away when the cost of retrieval becomes very high.

BUSINESS DIRECTORY
The addresses listed below are a selection only. While World of Information makes every endeavour to check these addresses, we cannot guarantee that changes have not been made, especially to telephone numbers and area codes. We would welcome any corrections.

Telephone area codes
The international direct dialling (IDD) code for The Netherlands is +31, followed by area code and subscriber's number:

Amersfoort	33	The Hague	70
Amsterdam	20	Leiden	71
Breda	76	Rotterdam	10
Eindhoven	40	Tiel	344
Haarlem	23	Utrecht	30

Useful telephone numbers
Directory enquiries: 068-008 (national), 060-418 (international)
Operator: 060-410
Police/fire: 0611
National public transport information service: 0900-9292

Chambers of Commerce

American Chamber of Commerce in The Netherlands, 58 Scheveningseweg, 2517 KW The Hague (tel: 365-9808; fax: 364-6992; email: office@amcham.nl).

Amsterdam Chamber of Commerce, 5 De Ruyterkade, 1013AA Amsterdam (tel: 531-4000; fax: 531-4799; email: post@amsterdam.kvk.nl).

Arnhem Chamber of Commerce, 525 Kronenburginsel, 6800 KZ Arnhem (tel: 353-8888; fax: 353-8999; email: info@arnhem.kvk.nl).

British-Netherlands Chamber of Commerce, Oxford House, 328L Nieuwezijds Voorburgwal, 1012 RW Amsterdam (tel: 421-7040; fax: 421-7003; email: info@nbcc.co.uk).

Maastricht Chamber of Commerce, 5 Pierre de Coubertinweg, 6225 XT Maastricht (tel: 350-6666; fax; 350-6660; email: info@maastricht.kvk.nl).

Netherlands Federation of Chambers of Commerce, 1 Watermolenlaan, 3440 AG Woerden (tel: 426-911; fax: 426-216; email: site@vvk.kvk.nl).

Rotterdam Chamber of Commerce, 40 Blaak, 3000 AL Rotterdam (tel: 402-7777; fax: 414-5754; email: dvergeer@rotterdam.kvk.nl).

The Hague Chamber of Commerce, 30 Koningskade, 2502 LS The Hague (tel: 328-7100; fax: 326-2010; email: info@denhaag.kvk.nl).

Tilburg Chamber of Commerce, 1 Reitseplein, 5000 LG Tilburg, (tel: 594-4122; fax: 468-6215; email: info@tilburg.kvk.nl).

Utrecht Chamber of Commerce, 50 Kroonstraat, 3500 AA Utrecht (tel: 326-3211; fax: 231-2804; email: servicecenter@utrecht.kvk.nl).

Zwolle Chamber of Commerce, 1 Govert Flinckstrasse, 8021 ET Zwolle (tel: 455-3800; fax: 453-7424; email: info@zwolle.kvk.nl).

Banking

ABN Amro Bank, 10 Gustav Mahlerlaan, 1082 PP Amsterdam (tel: 628-9393; fax: 628-7637; e-mail: postbox@abnamro.com).

ASN Bank, 28 Alexanderstraat, 2514 JM The Hague (tel: 0800-0380; fax: 361-7948; e-mail: informatie@asnbank.nl).

NIB Capital Bank, 4 Carnegieplein, 2517 KJ The Hague (tel: 342-5425; fax: 363-5425).

ING Bank, De Amsterdamse Poort, 1102 MG Amsterdam (tel: 563-9111; fax: 563-5700; e-mail: info@ingbank.com).

Postbank NV, 506 Haarlemmerweg , 1014 BL Amsterdam (tel: 584-9111; fax: 584-6600; e-mail: postbank@postbank.nl).

Rabobank Nederland, 18 Croeselaan, 3521 CB Utrecht (tel: 216-0000; fax: 216-2672; e-mail: info@rabobank.nl).

Central bank

De Nederlandsche Bank, Head office, Postbus 98 1000 AB Amsterdam; 1 Westeinde, 1017 ZN Amsterdam (tel: 524-9111; fax: 524-2500; email: info@dnb.nl).

European Central Bank (ECB), Kaiserstrasse 29, D-60311 Frankfurt am Main, Germany (tel: (+49-69) 13-440; fax: (+49-69) 1344-6000; email: info@ecb.int).

Stock exchange

Euronext NV Amsterdam (AEX), www.euronext.com
Chi-X, www.chi-x.com

Commodity exchange

Liffe Connect, www.nyse.com/nyseeuronext
Climex, www.climex.com

Travel information

Algemene Nederlandse Vereniging van VVs (ANVV) (association of tourist information offices), 25 Hogeweg, 3814 CC Amersfoort (tel: 33-756-060; fax: 33-723-146; e-mail: anvv@euronet.nl).

Amsterdam Schiphol Airport, 202 Evert van der Beekstraat, Schiphol-Centrum, Haarlemmermeer (tel: 601-9111; fax: 604-1475; e-mail: info@schiphol.nl).

Amsterdam Tourist Office (VVV), 10 Stationplein, 1012 AB Amsterdam (tel: 551-2512; fax: 625-2869; e-mail: info@amsterdamtourist.nl).

KLM Royal Dutch Airlines, 55 Amsterdamseweg, Schiphol Airport, 1182 GP Amstelveen (tel: 20-649-9123; fax: 20-649-300; e-mail: info@klm.nl).

Netherlands Reservation Centre, 1 Nieuwe Gouw, 1442 LE Purmerend (tel: 299-689-144; fax: 299-689-154; e-mail: info@hotelres.nl).

National tourist organisation offices

Netherlands Board of Tourism and Conventions, (head office) Postbus 458; Vlietweg 15, Leidschendam (tel: 370-5705; fax: 320-1654; email: info@holland.com; internet: www.nbtc.nl and www.holland.com).

Ministries

Ministry of Agriculture, Nature Management and Fisheries, 73 Bezuidenhoutseweg, 2594 AC The Hague (tel: 378-6868; fax: 378-6100; email: info@minlnv.nl).

Ministry of Defence, 38 Kalvermarkt, 2511 CB The Hague (tel: 318-8802; fax: 318-8320; email: defensie.voorlichting@co.dnet.mindef.nl).

Ministry of Economic Affairs, 30 Bezuidenhoutseweg, 2594 AV The Hague (tel: 308-1986; fax: 347-4081; email: ezinfo@postbus51.nl).

Ministry of Education, Culture and Science, 4 Europaweg, 2711 AH Zoetermeer (tel: 323-2323; fax: 323-2320; email: info@minocw.nl).

Ministry of Finance, 7 Korte Voorhout, 2511 CW The Hague (tel: 342-7540; fax: 342-7900; internet: www.minfin.nl).

Ministry of Foreign Affairs, 67 Bezuidenhoutseweg, 2594 AC The Hague (tel: 348-6486; fax: 348-4848; email: dvl-info@minbuza.nl).

Ministry of General Affairs, 20 Binnenhof, 2513 AA The Hague (tel: 356-4100; fax: 356-4683).

Ministry of Health, Welfare and Sport, 5 Parnassusplein, 2511 VX The Hague (tel: 340-7911; fax: 340-7890; email: info@minvws.nl).

Ministry of Housing, Spatial Planning and the Environment, Rijnstraat 8, 2515 XP The Hague (tel: 339-3939; fax: 339-1352; email: info@minvrom.nl).

Ministry of the Interior and Kingdom Relations, Schedeldoekshaven 200, 2511 EZ The Hague (tel: 426-6426; fax: 363-9153; email: info@minbzk.nl).

Ministry of Justice, Schedeldoekshaven 100, 2511 EX The Hague 9 (tel: 370-6850; fax: 370-7594; email: voorlichting@minjus.nl).

Ministry of Social Affairs and Employment, 4 Anna van Hannoverstraat, 2595 BJ The Hague (tel: 333-4444; fax: 333-4033; email: info@minszw.nl).

Ministry of Transport, Public Works and Water Management, 1-6 Plesmanweg, 2597 JG The Hague (tel: 351-6171; fax: 351-7895; email: info@minvenw.nl).

Other useful addresses

Algemeen Nederlands Persbureau (national news agency), 49 Handelskade, 2288 BA Rijswick (tel: 70-414-1414; fax: 70-414-1401; e-mail: nieuwsdienst@anp.nl).

American Embassy, 102 Lange Voorhout, 2514 EJ The Hague (tel: 310-9209; fax: 361-4688; email: usemb@usemb.nl).

British Embassy, 10 Lange Voorhout, 2514 ED The Hague (tel: 427-0427; fax: 427-0345).

Congrestolken (conference interpreters), 11 Jan van Goyenkade, 1075 HP Amsterdam (tel: 625-2535; fax: 626-5642; e-mail: interpreters@conferenceinterpreters.com).

Euronext Amsterdam (stock exchange), Beursplein 5, 1012 JW Amsterdam (tel: 550-4444; fax: 550-4900; email: info@euronext.nl).

Federation for Dutch Export (Fenedex), 14 Raamweg 2596 HL The Hague (tel: 330-5600; fax: 330-5656; email: info@fenedex.nl).

Netherlands Convention Bureau, 166 Amsteldijk, 1079 LH Amsterdam (tel: 646-2580; fax: 644-5935; email: info@nlcongress.nl).

Netherlands Council for Trade Promotions (NCH), 181 Bezuidenhoutseweg, 2594 AH The Hague (tel: 344-1544; fax: 385-3531; e-mail: info@nchnl.nl).

Netherlands Development Finance Company, Anna van Saksenlaan 71, 2593 HW The Hague (tel: 314-9696; fax: 324-6187).

Netherlands Embassy (USA), 4200 Linnean Avenue, NW, Washington DC (tel: (+1-202) 244-5300; fax: (+1-202) 362-3430; email: webmaster@netherlands-embassy.org).

Netherlands Foreign Investment Agency (CBIN), 2 Bezuidenhoutseweg, 2594 AV The Hague (tel: 379-8818; fax: 379-6322; email: info@nfia.nl; internet: www.nfia.com).

Netherlands Foreign Trade Agency (EVD), 181 Bezuidenhoutseweg, 2594 AG The Hague (tel: 778-8888; fax: 778-8889; email: eic@info.evd.nl; internet: www2.holland.com/trade/).

Statistics Netherlands (CBS), 428 Prinses Beatrixlaan, 2273 XZ Voorburg (tel: 70-337-3800; fax: 70-387-7429; email: infoserve@cbs.nl; internet: (in Dutch): www.cbs.nl/enindex.htm).

ANP (Netherlands National News Agency): www.anp.nl

Internet sites

Dutch Tourist Board: www.visitholland.com

Dutch yellow pages www.markt.nl./dyp/index-en.html

Netherlands web directory: www:nl-menu.nl

Tourist information: www:holland.com

Tourist information: www: nbt.nl

Hotel information: www:hotelsinholland.com

Statistics: www: cbs.nl:

Netherlands Embassy in the USA: www: netherlands-embassy.org

Dutch Railways: www: ns.nl

Ministry of Foreign Affairs: www: minbuza.nl

Dutch Parliament: www:parlement.nl

Ministry of Finance: www:minfin.nl

New Caledonia

KEY FACTS

Official name: Nouvelle Calédonie (New Caledonia)

Head of State: President of France François Hollande (PS) (from 15 May 2012), represented by High Commissioner Vincent Bouvier (from 23 Jul 2014)

Head of government: President of the Congress of New Caledonia, Philippe Germain (from 1 Apr 2015)

Ruling party: Grand Coalition (government posts are allocated in proportion to electoral victory and support of head of government) lead by L'Avenir Ensemble (Future Together) (from 11 May 2014)

Area: 18,575 square km – Grande Terre island: 16,600 square km

Population: 264,022 (July 2013)*

Capital: Nouméa (on Grande Terre)

Official language: French

Currency: Change Franc Pacifique franc (CFPf) = 100 centimes

Exchange rate: CFPf106.68 per US$ (Sept 2015); (pegged CFPf119.25 per euro)

GDP per capita: US$41,646 (2011)*

GDP real growth: 1.90% (2011)*

GDP: US$10.60 billion (2011)*

Inflation: 2.40% (2011)*

* estimated figure

COUNTRY PROFILE

1766 First sighted by Europeans.
1774 Captain James Cook named the island after the Latin name for Scotland.
1853 New Caledonia became a French colony.
1863 Nickel deposits were discovered. The displacement of villages, which stood on new mine sites, and the encroachment of settlers' cattle on Kanak (indigenous Melanesians) land provoked several rebellions, all of which were suppressed by the French authorities.
1864–97 The island grew as a penal colony.
1878 A Kanak revolt led to over a 1,000 deaths.
1942 New Caledonia was transformed into a US military base during the Second World War.
1946 The colony became a French territory.
1980s Tensions increased between the Kanaks and European settlers, principally over land.
1988 Jean-Marie Tijbaou, leader of the Front de Libération Nationale Kanak et Socialiste (FLNKS) (Kanak and Socialist National Liberation Front), signed the Martignon Accord which divided New Caledonia into three distinct regions. It also proposed an end to rule from Paris and agreed a vote on independence in 1998.
1989 Tijbaou was assassinated.
1998 The referendum agreed in 1988 was postponed after the signing, between the government of France and FLNKS and Rassemblement pour la Calédonie dans la République (RPCR), of the Nouméa Accord on 5 May, giving increased autonomy and a referendum on independence to be held sometime between 1914–20.
1999 The French Loi Organique of 19 March agreed changes to the constitution, changing the national assembly into a more autonomous congress and restricting voting rights to those who have been resident for a minimum of five years.
2001 The territory's president, Jean Lèques, (RPCR), resigned. Pierre Frogier (RPCR) replaced him.
2002 Negotiations started on the future adoption of the euro. Land disputes caused ethnic clashes between native Kanaks and Wallisian immigrants.
2004 Parliamentary elections resulted in a four-party coalition government. Marie-Noëlle Thémereau (Avénir Ensemble (AE) (Future Together)) was elected president.
2005 Michel Mathieu was appointed High Commissioner.
2006 The French parliament voted on constitutional amendments to restrict the voting rights of settlers, who must be resident for 10 years before eligibility to vote.
2007 Marie-Noëlle Thémereau resigned and Harold Martin was elected President of the Congress. High Commissioner Mathieu resigned and was replaced by Yves Dassonville.
2008 Despite scientific claims that the rich coral lagoon in Goro would not be damaged by the release of liquid mining effluent, residents remained unconvinced and warned the authorities that they would keep a watch on the surrounding environment.
2009 A five-month epidemic of dengue fever, which intensified during the summer heat wave, killed two and infected over 3,000. Around 100,000 litres of toxic sulphuric acid spilled into North Bay Creek, killing thousands of fish and crustaceans in Prony Bay in the Southern Province. The Worldwide Fund for Nature called for the licence of the Vale-Inco Nickel plant in Goro to be suspended pending plant monitoring and emergency measures being brought up to specification. A fine of US$5,000 was imposed in 2012. In Territorial Congress elections, anti-independence parties won 36 seats out of 54 and nationalists 10. Parliament elected Philippe Gomès as president of the Congress.
2010 President Gomes was indicted on suspicion of bribery, that his company had won a US$1.3 million contract to supply electrical units to Vale-Inco to the Brazilian mining company, which in turn had been granted an operating licence when Gomes was president of the South Province in 2005–06. Albert Dupuy was appointed as high commissioner.
2011 The government of President Gomés collapsed after ministers belonging to Union Calédonienne (UC) (Caledonian Union) resigned from the cabinet in February. In March, parliament elected a new government and Harold Martin was chosen as president. However, Martin's

government collapsed on the same day following the resignation of one of its members. Harold Martin was re-elected as president on 17 March but again his government collapsed within the day after the resignations of some of his cabinet. Parliament re-elected Harold Martin as President of Congress in June.
2012 Almost 80 containers of nickel oxide were shipped to South Korea and China on 6 April, the first shipment of finished product from the Vale-Inco Nickel (in Goro). The French presidential election was held on 22 April, with a runoff on 6 May. The runoff was won by François Hollande (Parti Socialiste (PS) (Socialist Party)) with 51.63 per cent of the vote; turnout was 80.35 per cent. On 15 May François Hollande took office as president and Head of State. The official opening of the Vale-Inco Nickel plant (in Goro) was delayed in June following serious damage to the plant in May, estimated at US$4 billion.
2013 Cook Islands premier, Henry Puna, visited in July as part of his assignment as the head of a Pacific Islands Forum delegation monitoring progress in self-determination efforts in New Caledonia.
2014 Legislative elections were held on 11 May. The result was L'Avenir Ensemble (Future Together) with 13 (out of 54) seats, Caledonian Union–FLINKS nine seats, Front for Unity seven seats, Union for Caledonia in France, Build Our Rainbow Nation and National Union for Independence six seats each. Six other parties won the remaining seven seats. Turnout was 69.95 per cent. The election of the provincial presidents followed on 16 May. Gaël Yanno was elected as the new president of the Congress of New Caledonia on 23 May, and on 5 June Cynthia Ligeard was elected president of the government of New Caledonia with nine out of eleven votes. High Commissioner Jean-Jacques Brot unexpectedly resigned on 22 July at the time of the visit of French overseas minister, George Pau-Langevin. He was replaced by Vincent Bouvier on 23 July.
2015 A proposed law mandating that only indigenous Kanaks and persons enrolled in 1998 will be automatically eligible to vote in the 2018 independence referendum, approved by both the French Supreme Court and the Senate, was was by July making its way through the French National Assembly. The bill has upset the anti-independence majority in the New Caledonian Congress, who insist that the law is discriminatory against non-Kanaks born after 1998.

Political structure

Constitution

Under the Nouméa Accord of 1998, New Caledonia has a special status within the French constitution. The local government, elected by universal suffrage, has wider degrees of autonomy regarding legislative issues. Up until 2010, France will retain power only over justice, public order, currency, defence and foreign affairs outside the South Pacific region.
France is also obliged to conduct up to three referenda on independence between 2013–18. Until then, the High Commissioner has overall responsibility for the territory while the president of the Territorial Congress is the head of local government.
New Caledonia is represented in the French parliament by two deputies and two senators
The territory is divided into three provinces, each with its own assembly and local executive. There is an economic and social committee, which has an advisory role, and a Custom Senate, which advises the government on matters affecting the indigenous Kanak community.

Form of state

Self-governing territory of France

The executive

Executive power is exercised by the High Commissioner, with delegated power, for local administration, from France. The president of Congress advises the High Commissioner on matters of local jurisdiction.
The Congress elects the president who represents the congress and directs administrative services aided by an 11-member executive council drawn from Congress members (with at least one member from all political parties represented).

National legislature

Under the Loi Organique (Organic Act, 1999) the Congrès de la Nouvelle-Calédonie (Congress of New Caledonia) has enhanced powers to elect the government and enact legislation, separately from France. It has 54-members elected by proportional representation from the provinces of New Caledonia (32 from the South Province, 15 from the Northern Province and 7 from the Province des Iles Loyauté). All members serve for five-year terms.
To be eligible to vote for congress members, voters must have been resident for 10 years and resident for 20 years to vote in referenda scheduled in 2015–20.

Last elections

11 May 2014 (parliamentary)
Results: Parliamentary: Avenir Ensemble (Future Together) won 13 (out of 54) seats, Front de Libération Nationale Kanak et Socialiste (FLNKS) (Kanak and Socialist National Liberation Front) 9, Rassemblement pour une Calédonie dans la République (Le Rassemblement-UMP) (The Rally-UMP) 7, Union for Caledonia in France 6, Build Our Rainbow Nation 6, Union Nationale pour l'Indépendance (UNI) (National Union for Independence) 6, One Province for All 2, Parti Travailliste (Labour Party) 1, four other parties won one seat each.
Turnout was 69.95 per cent.

Next elections

2019 (parliamentary)

Political parties

Ruling party

Grand Coalition (government posts are allocated in proportion to electoral victory and support of head of government) lead by L'Avenir Ensemble (Future Together) (from 11 May 2014)

Main opposition party

Front de Libération Nationale Kanak et Socialiste (FLNKS) (Kanak and Socialist National Liberation Front) alliance

Population

264,022 (July 2013)* More than 70 per cent of the total population live in the south of La Grand-Terre Island.
Last census: August 2004: 230,789
Population density: 11 inhabitants per square km.
Annual growth rate: 1.8 per cent (2003)

Ethnic make-up

Of the total population, 45 per cent are Melanesian Kanaks, 34 per cent Europeans (mainly French), 20 per cent are Wallisians and the remainder are mainly Tahitian, Indonesian and Vietnamese.
The wealthy southern province is mainly inhabited by Europeans and the remainder of the country is mostly populated by the poorer ethnic Kanak community.

Education

Education is provided free for the compulsory years. Primary education covers ages six to 11 years and secondary education from aged 12 to a maximum of 18 years. There is a major shortage in the supply of trained secondary school teachers.
Public expenditure on education is typically 7 per cent of GNP. Nearly US$30 million was allocated, up to 2005, to implement the government's policy of equity funding for the early childhood education sector. The government also doubled funding for adult literacy, setting aside US$18 million to fund the Adult Literacy Strategy. More emphasis has been given to Mäori and Pacific children with special educational needs.
Compulsory years: Six to 15
Enrolment rate: 101 per cent gross primary enrolment of the relevant age group (including repeaters) (World Bank 2003).

Pupils per teacher: 18 in primary schools.

Health

Life expectancy: 74 years (estimate 2003)

Fertility rate/Maternal mortality rate: 2.5 births per woman (World Bank)

Child (under 5 years) mortality rate (per 1,000): Seven deaths per 1,000 live births.

Main cities

Nouméa (capital, on Grande Terre, estimated population 106,105 in 2012); Le Mont Dore (27,909), Dumbéa (24,852), Païta (17,483), Wé (10,616).

Languages spoken

Thirty Canaque languages are spoken. English is often understood.

Official language/s

French

Media

Press

In French, the only dailies newspaper is *Les Nouvelles Calédoniennes* (www.info.lnc.nc), weeklies include *Télé 7 Jours, Les Nouvelles Hebdo, L'Echo Calédonien, Dimanche Patinane and Femmes*, which is a women's magazine.

Broadcasting

The French overseas broadcaster RFO (www.rfo.fr) provides locally produced radio and television news and imported French programmes, as well as internet TV services.

Radio: RFO operates Radio France Internationale (http://www.rfi.fr). Private local radio services operate 24 hours a day; stations include NRJ (www.nrj.nc) and Radio Djiido (www.radiodjiido.nc).

Television: From France, RFO Nouvelle-Calédonie (http://nouvellecaledonie.rfo.fr) offers a fully range of programmes. Pay-to-view TV is also available.

Other news agencies: ABC Pacific Beat: www.radioaustralia.net.au/pacbeat Pacific Magazine: www.pacificmagazine.net

Economy

There is a lack of economic diversity; however as New Caledonia has large deposits of nickel ore, around 25 per cent of world deposits, its economy is largely buoyed by sales of ore, from smelting enterprises, such as the development of the Koniambo deposit, and financial transfers from France, which amount to some US$1.5 billion per annum (14 per cent of GDP). Nickel production accounts for around 7 per cent of GDP. The new and improved infrastructure made necessary by building the nickel plants will also benefit other sectors of the economy, such as tourism, education and health. Other activities include manufacturing of consumer goods and intermediate products such as electrical components and capital goods including mechanical and electrical automotive parts. Other components of the economy include financial transfers from France and foreign aid. Agriculture includes production of premium coffee, meat and other food processing, while aquaculture includes fish processing and packaging.

The territory's other big source of foreign exchange is its tourist sector, which had been rising steadily since the 1990s, with cruise arrivals increasing. However, by 2009 tourist numbers had slumped to a 15-year low with just 99,379 arrivals; numbers increased slightly to 108,000 in 2013 (latest figures).

Citizens of New Caledonia have one of the highest per capita incomes in the Pacific region (after Australia and New Zealand), rising to an estimated US$38,800 in 2012 (latest figures). GDP growth in 2007 was 0.5 per cent which remained constant until 2011 when it rose to 1.9 per cent, when global trade strengthened and economic nickel exports increased. Since then New caledonia had seen stable growth at around 3 per cent, sitting at 2.8 per cent in 2014.

Although the French military presence in New Caledonia has been a source of internal tension, it also makes a significant contribution to the local economy. France contributes around 14 per cent of GDP, 80 per cent of which covers healthcare, education and public sector wages.

Economic prospects for the future look bright for New Caledonia as two major new nickel plants have been opened as well as the global nickel prices rising again. On top of this, due to a ban on the export of nickel ore in Indonesia, New Caledonia is set to make up China's nickel shortfall in 2015.

New Caledonia uses the euro-pegged Comptoirs Français du Pacifique franc (CFPf) as its currency. The government began negotiations in 2002 over the adoption of the euro, which would boost the territory's chances of attracting investment and tourism, but has been unsuccessful in overcoming the objections of pro-independence groups.

External trade

As a *collectivité sui generis* of France, New Caledonia is a Special Territory of the European Union and applies its rulings and trade agreements.

Imports

Main imports are machinery and equipment, fuels, chemicals and foodstuffs.

Main sources: France (22.3 per cent of total in 2014), Singapore (17.5 per cent), Australia (8.9 per cent).

Exports

Main exports are processed nickel ore and processed nickel, mechanical and electrical components and fish.

Main destinations: China (19.1 per cent of total in 2014), Japan (15.3 per cent), Australia (11.7 per cent).

Agriculture

Farming

The agricultural sector typically accounts for as little as 1.5 per cent of GDP. Although the soil is fertile, only 10 per cent of the land area is cultivated. There is a ratio of around 50:50 for locally grown to imported foods. The number of farmers has fallen by almost 50 per cent since the early 1990s, with the greatest percentage loss in the northern province.

About one-third of the main island's land area is devoted to cattle raising, chiefly on the central and north-west coasts.

Fishing

Tropical shrimp farming has been developed, although the farms are fragile as there is always the risk of disease. Fishing is both for local consumption and for export, mainly to Japan.

Annual fish production typically includes 2,800 tonnes (t) marine fish, 1,900t other seafood and 343,000 units of pearls and shells.

Forestry

Domestic forests supply about 35 per cent of timber demand, with some reforestation undertaken.

Industry and manufacturing

The industrial sector typically contributes 20 per cent to GDP. Main industries include nickel processing, domestic equipment, clothing, foodstuffs and beer.

Tourism

New Caledonia combines a traditional Melanesian culture overlaid with a French flavour. As such, it attracts many French visitors, fleeing a bleak Northern Hemisphere winter. The seas around the islands are popular sites for water sports including diving and fishing. The lagoons which include mangroves and the barrier reef, are listed as World Heritage Sites by Unesco. Inland the diverse terrain also offers a variety of activities.

Visitor numbers fell below 100,000 in 2011, after being relatively constant at above this. Numbers picked up again to 108,000 in 2013 (latest figures). The government has instigated measures to offer value-added holidays, including festivals held on different islands each year and a proposal for tourists to stay with local people and experience the culture first hand by fishing, working in 'gardens' (smallholder plots) and exploring the islands. There is a range of accommodation, from hotels to bungalows to traditional huts. Infrastructure to enhance the market is still being constructed in the Northern Province, whereas in the Southern Province there are more amenities and internationally branded hotel chains.

Mining

New Caledonia holds between 25–40 per cent of known world nickel deposits and is one of the world's largest producers.
There are several mines in New Caledonia, the principal ones are located at Koniambo, Tiebaghi, Thio, Kouaoua, Nepoui-Kopeto and Etoile du Nord.
The potential production capacity of the seven main nickel mining operators making up Société Le Nickel (SLN) has been estimated at 830,000 tonnes a year, with reserves expected to last until 2012. SLN is 60 per cent owned by France's Eramet and 30 per cent by the Société Minière de Sud Pacific (SMSP), which is owned by ethnic Kanak groups.
Nickel and ferronickel production accounts for up to 10 per cent of GDP and contributes 80 per cent of foreign earnings.
Chrome extraction is undertaken. There are also deposits of iron ore, copper, manganese, lead and zinc.
SLN is expanding its smelting plant in Nouméa, and in order to supply enough ore for the plant's increased capacity, it is increasing production at one of its mines from 250,000 tonnes to one million tonnes a year, creating around 200 new jobs. The project is to be completed in 2006.
Production in the new Goro Nickel plant was scheduled to be 20,000 tonnes by December 2012. The nickel ore is processed into nickel oxide locally before being exported to a refinery in Canada, also owned by the Brazilian mining company, Vale SA, which owns the Goro Nickel mine.

Hydrocarbons

There are no known natural gas or oil reserves. Consumption of oil was 14,350 barrels per day (bpd) in 2013 (latest figures), all of which was imported.
Imported coal was 300,000 tonnes in 2013 (latest figures), all of which was used in power generation.

Energy

Total installed generating capacity was 500MW in 2013 (latest figures), producing over 2 billion kilowatt hours. Électricité et Eau de Caledonie and Enercal are responsible for electricity generation and supply. Around 80 per cent of electricity generation is produced by thermal generators. Renewable sources of energy, including hydroelectricity and wind generation, are growing in importance. The nickel extraction and smelting sectors consume around 75 per cent of electricity output.

Banking and insurance

Central bank

The Paris-based Institut d'Emission d'Outre-Mer (IEOM) provides all central banking services except foreign exchange reserves.

Main financial centre

Nouméa

Time

GMT plus 10 hours

Geography

New Caledonia comprises one large island and several smaller ones, situated in the south Pacific Ocean, about 1,500km (930 miles) east of Queensland, Australia. The main island is La Grand-Terre, it is long and narrow. Rugged mountains divide the west of the island from the east, and there is little flat land. The nearby Loyalty Islands and a third group of islands, the uninhabited Chesterfield Islands, lie about 400km north-west of the main island.

Hemisphere

Southern

Climate

Hot (average temperature 26 degrees Celsius (C)), with occasional tropical depressions and cyclones, from mid-November to mid-April; and cool (average temperature 23 degrees C), with moderate rains, from mid-May to mid-September. Rainfall is quite irregular and can be extremely heavy. The east coast (at about two metres per annum) has twice the rainfall of the west; the wettest months are January, February and March.

Entry requirements

Passports

Required by all, except certain French nationals; all passports must have at least six months validity from the date of visit.

Visa

Required by all, except citizens of EU, North America, Australasia and Japan, for stays up to one month; this includes business trips by representatives of foreign entities with an invitation from a local company or organisation. Proof of adequate funds for stay, an itinerary, a guarantee of repatriation if necessary and return/onward ticket are also required.
For further exceptions, full details and a copy of the application form visit www.diplomatie.gouv.fr/thema/dossier.gb.asp and follow the path (going to France) to the database.

Currency advice/regulations

The import and export of local and foreign currencies are unristricted but amounts over CFPf 900,000 must be declared.

Customs

Personal effects are allowed entry duty-free. Duty is not payable on goods of EU origin, although all imported goods are subject to a general tax, and an increasing number of goods require import licences. Expensive items, such as laptop computers, may require proof of ownership when departing.

Prohibited imports

Parrots, parakeets, pigeons, turtle-doves and non-domestic mammals; plants and seeds require a health certificate.
Export of birds of paradise and objects of ethnographic interest are prohibited.

Health (for visitors)

Mandatory precautions

Vaccination certificate required for yellow fever if travelling from infected area.

Advisable precautions

Vaccination for diphtheria, tuberculosis, hepatitis A and B, polio, TB, tetanus, typhoid. There is a rabies risk.
There has been an increased risk of dengue fever, visitors are advised to use mosquito repellent, a mosquito net at night, and wear protective clothing at dawn and dusk, to reduce the risk.

Hotels

Tourist hotels are classified by category and size on the five-star system. Hotel tax is levied, the amount varying according to classification. Details of rural or tribal lodgings in some Melanesian villages and areas are available from tourist information offices. Upper-end bungalow accommodation is growing.

Credit cards

Most major credit cards are accepted.

Public holidays (national)

Fixed dates

1 Jan (New Year), 1 May (Labour Day), 8 May (1945 Victory Day), 14 Jul (Bastille Day), 15 Aug (Assumption Day), 24 Sep (New Caledonia Day), 1 Nov (All Saints' Day), 11 Nov (Armistice Day), 25 Dec (Christmas Day).

Variable dates

Easter Monday (Mar–Apr), Ascension Day (Apr–May).

Working hours

Banking

Mon–Fri: 0730–1545.

Business

Mon–Fri: 0730–1130, 1330–1730. Sat: 0730–1130.

Government

Mon–Fri: 0730–1130, 1215–1600.

Shops

Mon–Fri: 0730–1100, 1400–1800.
Half-day Sat and Sun.

Telecommunications

Mobile/cell phones

There is a GSM 900 service that covers the coastal regions of Grand Terre and surrounding islands.

Electricity supply

220V AC, with two-pin plug fittings.

Weights and measures

Metric system

Social customs/useful tips

Tipping is not customary. Islanders find it offensive when women sunbathe topless.

Getting there

Air

National airline: Aircalin

International airport/s: Nouméa La Tontouta International (NOU), 48km from Nouméa; duty-free shop, bar, restaurant, bank, shops, car hire.

Airport tax: None

Surface

There are regular shipping services from Australasia, Europe, Japan and South East Asia.

Getting about

National transport

Air: Air Calédonie operates regular flights from Nouméa's domestic airport, Magenta, to the east and west coasts of Grande-Terre island and daily flights to the Ile des Pins, Maré, Tiga, Lifou and Ouvea. Charter and tour airplanes and helicopters are available.

Road: Grande-Terre, the main island, has a total road network of approximately 5,000km, about 71 per cent sealed in municipal areas and a considerable length of track suitable for four-wheel drive and similar vehicles. Exercise care driving along the west and east coasts, as some roads are not sealed. The Canala-Thio main road is one-way only, with direction of traffic changing at scheduled times.

Buses: Regular bus services operate on Grande-Terre.

Water: There is a high-speed catamaran link between Grande-Terre and Ile des Pins, and Loyalty Islands. Small trading vessels also sail to nearby islands.

City transport

Taxis: Taxis are available in the central square (Place des Cocotiers), with some operating 24 hours. Charges are for time and distance. There is a surcharge after 1900 and on Sundays.

Buses, trams & metro: Buses from the airport to city centre usually take about 60 minutes.

Car hire

Self-drive car hire is available in Nouméa. A current valid driving licence is required. Driving is on the right-hand side of the road.

BUSINESS DIRECTORY

The addresses listed below are a selection only. While World of Information makes every endeavour to check these addresses, we cannot guarantee that changes have not been made, especially to telephone numbers and area codes. We would welcome any corrections.

Telephone area codes

The international dialling code (IDD) for New Caledonia is +687 followed by subscriber's number.

Useful telephone numbers

Fire station: 18

Police: 17

Ambulance (Nouméa): 252-100

Banking

Bank of Hawaii-Nouvelle Calédonie, BP L3, 25 Avenue de la Victoire, Avenue Henri Lafleur, 98849 Nouméa Cedex (tel: 257-400; fax: 274-147).

Banque Calédonienne d'Investissement, BP K5, 50 Avenue de la Victore, 98849 Nouméa (tel: 256-565; fax: 274-035).

Banque Nationale de Paris Nouvelle Calédonie, BP K3, 37 Ave Henri Lafleur, 98800 Nouméa (tel: 258-400; fax: 258-459) .

Société Générale Calédonienne de Banque; 44 rue de l'Alma, Siége et Agence Principale, 98848 Nouméa (tel: 256-300; fax: 276-245).

Central bank

Institut d'Emission d'Outre-Mer (IEOM), 5 rue Roland Barthes, 75598 Paris Cedex 12, France (tel : (+33-1) 5344-4141; fax : (+33-1) 4347-5134; email: contact@ieom.fr).

European Central Bank, Kaiserstrasse 29, D-60311 Frankfurt am Main, Germany (tel: (+49-69) 13-440; fax: (+49-69) 1344-6000; e-mail: info@ecb.int).

Travel information

Air Caledonia, BP 98845 Nouméa (tel: 252-339; (bookings tel: 252-177); internet: www.air-caledonie.nc).

Aircalin, 8 rue Frederic Surleau, BP 3736, Nouméa (tel: 265-500; fax: 265-651; internet: www.aircalin.nc).

Destination Nouvelle Calédonie, 39-41 rue de Verdun, PO Box 688, Nouméa (tel: 272-632; fax: 274-623).

Nouméa La Tontouta International Airport, BP2, Tontouta 98840 (tel: 352-500; fax: 352-535; e-mail: ccita@cci.nc).

Nouméa Tourist Office, 24 rue Anotole France, BP 2828, Nouméa 98.800 (tel: 287-580; fax: 287-585).

National tourist organisation offices

New Caledonian Tourism Promotion Board (internet site: http://www.nouvelle-caledonie-tourisme.nc).

Other useful addresses

Institut Territorial de la Statistique et des Etudes Economiques, PO Box 823, 5 rue Gallieni, Nouméa (tel: 275-481, 283-156; fax: 288-148).

South Pacific Commission, PO Box D5 Cedex, Nouméa (tel: 262-000; fax: 261-844).

ABC Pacific Beat:
www.radioaustralia.net.au/pacbeat

Pacific Magazine:
www.pacificmagazine.net

Internet sites

South Pacific Tourism Organisation:
www.tcsp.com/new_caledonia/index.html

New Caledonia tourism:
www.nctps.com/home.cfm

New Caledonia tourism:
www.newcaledonia.com.au

New Caledonia website (in French):
www.yahoue.com

Travel information:
http://perso.wanadoo.fr/caledonie/indexe.htm

New Zealand

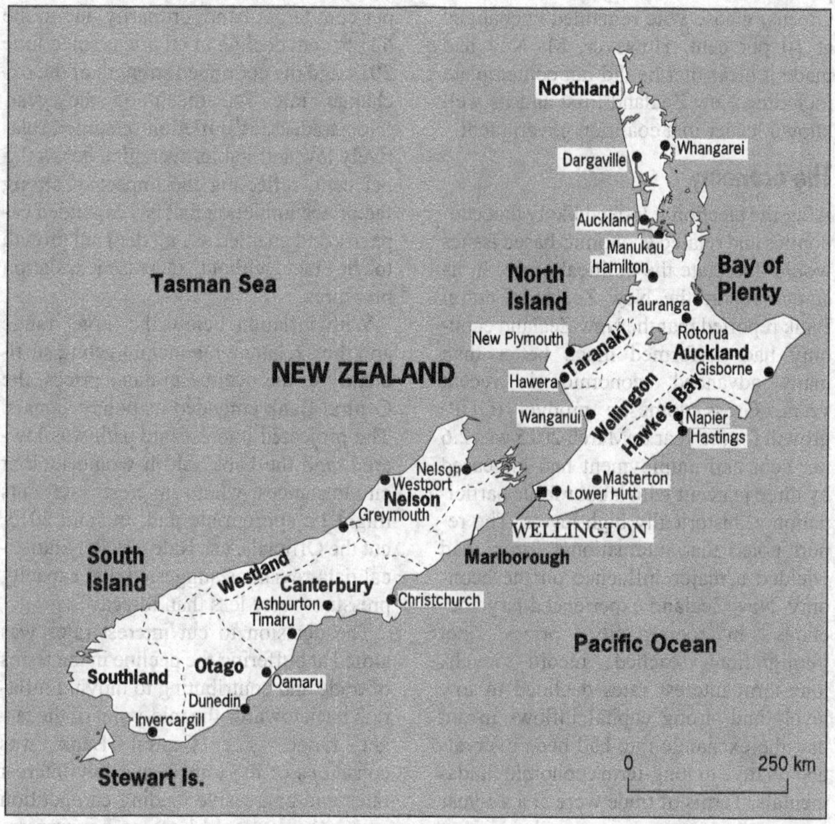

New Zealand entered 2015 with the government headed by John Key backed by a substantially increased majority after the roller coaster of an election in October 2014. Elections in New Zealand were normally tranquil affairs, but the 2014 poll had more to do with Las Vegas than Queenstown, more in common with Caracas than Christchurch.

The elections...

The entry into New Zealand politics of the reportedly billionaire and fugitive internet entrepreneur Kim Dotcom, who is fighting extradition to the US, was as much a surprise as a mystery. The portly German's electoral platform appeared to be based on the idea of turning New Zealand into a safe haven for those on the run from the judiciaries of their countries of residence. This group were headed up by Messrs Julian Assange (boxed up in London's Ecuadorean embassy) and Edward Snowden (currently a guest of the Russian government in Moscow). Mr Dotcom (born Kim Schmitz) was said to have invested over US$1.5 million in his Internet party's electoral campaign. This was more than all the other parties put together.

The incumbent prime minister, John Key had begun his electoral campaign as the clear favourite. However, a series of scandals eroded both his reputation and the image of his party. The first allegation was that a senior member of Mr Key's team had been using a right-wing blogger to publish derogatory articles about his rivals in New Zealand's press. Next to fall was the National Party's justice minister, Judith Collins, who fell on her sword following allegations that she was involved in an attempt to defame the head of the Serious Fraud Office. The allegations came

KEY FACTS

Official name: The Dominion of New Zealand

Head of State: Queen Elizabeth II, represented by Governor General Sir Jeremiah (Jerry) Mateparae (from 31 Aug 2011)

Head of government: Prime Minister John Key (Nationals) (from 2008; re-elected 26 Nov 2011, 20 Sept 2014)

Ruling party: Coalition led by the National Party, with ACT New Zealand (ACT), United Future (UF) and the Maori Party (from 20 Sept 2014)

Area: 268,676 square km: North Island (115,690 square km); South Island (152,356 square km)

Population: 4.52 million (2014)

Capital: Wellington

Official language: English, Māori

Currency: New Zealand dollar (NZ$) = 100 cents

Exchange rate: NZ$1.58 per US$ (Sep 2015)

GDP per capita: US$43,837 (2014)*

GDP real growth: 3.24% (2014)*

GDP: US$198.12 billion (2014)*

Labour force: 2.50 million (2014)*

Unemployment: 5.37% (2014)

Inflation: 1.23% (2014)

Natural gas production: 4.30 billion (2011)

Balance of trade: US$960.40 million (2014)

Annual FDI: US$3.58 billion (2011)

* estimated figure

shortly after John Banks, a former Mayor of Auckland, was obliged to resign following a conviction for a breach of the rules involving political donations and Mr Dotcom. As the election approached, New Zealanders could only wonder if this was the end of their country's years in the image of Tunbridge Wells. And wonder whether in future the outcome of their elections would be determined by who spent the most, rather than who had the best policies.

... and the results

In the event, Prime Minister John Key's National Party won a significant victory, with 61 seats in the New Zealand parliament and more than 48 per cent of votes – an increase on his 2011 winning margin. It was therefore down to Mr Key to form the next coalition government consisting of the National Party, with ACT New Zealand (ACT), United Future (UF) and the Maori Party. Meanwhile Labour leader, David Cunliffe, had to try and pick up the pieces after his party's apparent implosion, winning less than 25 per cent of the votes. Rather forlornly, Mr Cunliffe announced that he wanted to continue as Labour leader and defeat the National Party in three years' time. The Mana Party's leader, Hone Harawira, losing his stronghold of Te Tai Tokerau. Some analysts saw this as the beginning of the end for the Mana Party.

Perhaps predictably, Kim Dotcom's Internet party, which had set its sights on a victory in the Harawira constituency, obtained no seats at all. This raised doubts about the party's future and was greeted with a sense of relief by many New Zealanders. The Conservatives also failed to win any seats in parliament after obtaining less than 5 per cent of the vote. In contrast Winston Peters' New Zealand First party did better than expected, winning almost 9 per cent of the vote, just short of the Greens, whose vote remained unchanged at 10 per cent. However, Mr Key had made it clear that he did not contemplate including New Zealand First and its well known leader in a coalition government.

The economy

After the election it looked likely that economics and related economic-based issues would dominate the political arena. In its annual report the New Zealand Central Bank reported that the New Zealand economy had performed much better than many advanced economies in recent years. Gross domestic product (GDP) growth for the year to March 2015 was 2.6 per cent and employment had increased by three per cent with labour force participation at historically high levels. The report noted that international forces had wielded a major influence on the economy. New Zealand experienced large declines in commodity prices, net immigration reached record levels, long-term interest rates declined to low levels and strong capital inflows meant that the exchange rate had been overvalued relative to long-term economic fundamentals. Terms of trade were at a 40-year high in June 2014 but, as at August 2015, global dairy prices had fallen by 65 per cent since February 2014.

Like most of the advanced economies, headline and underlying inflation had been lower than the Central Bank would have wished. Since the December quarter of 2014, annual Consumer Price Index (CPI) inflation had been below the 1 to 3 per cent target band, primarily due to the 52 per cent decline in oil prices since June 2014 and the continued strength of the exchange rate for much of the year. 'Non-tradeables' inflation remained relatively low and stable, averaging below 2.5 per cent, reflecting the impact of strong factor accumulation that has expanded capacity and enabled strong demand growth to be met without increased inflation pressures.

With inflation below the target range and the exchange rate not adjusting sufficiently to the decline in dairy prices, the Central Bank amended its policy signals. The projected interest rate path was lowered, and the bank said it would look at circumstances where interest rate cuts might be appropriate and, in June 2015, cut the Official Cash Rate (OCR). Statistical data revisions suggested that capacity pressures were less than forecast.

The decision to cut interest rates was aimed at buffering the decline in the terms of trade and contributing to moving inflation back towards the mid-point of the target range. The Central Bank was conscious of the impact that low interest rates and aggressive lending competition among banks could have on housing demand and its potential to feed into house price inflation. The Bank also expressed concern about the financial stability risks and risks to the broader economy that would be associated with a major correction in Auckland house prices. Although a strong supply response over several years was needed to address Auckland's housing imbalance, the Bank felt that macro-prudential policy could help to reduce the financial stability risks arising from pressures in the Auckland housing market. The proposed loan-to-value ratio (LVR) measures and the government's policy initiatives that had been announced in the 2015 Budget should, in the view of the Bank, begin to ease the impact of heightened investor activity and help lower the financial and economic risks while important regulatory and infrastructure issues were addressed and additional investment in new housing took place. The Central Bank's May 2015 Financial Stability Report (FSR) also focussed on

KEY INDICATORS — New Zealand

	Unit	2011	2012	2013	2014	**2015
Population	m	*4.42	4.44	4.45	4.52	*4.56
Gross domestic product (GDP)	US$bn	616.90	170.41	184.75	*198.12	*19.17
GDP per capita	US$	36,648	38,385	41,490	*43,837	42,017
GDP real growth	%	1.4	2.6	2.2	*3.2	*2.9
Inflation	%	4.0	1.1	1.1	1.2	*0.8
Unemployment	%	6.6	6.9	6.2	5.4	*5.3
Coal output	mtoe	3.1	3.1	2.8	2.5	–
Exports (fob) (goods)	US$m	38,344.5	37,866.5	39,944.7	41,961.2	–
Imports (fob) (goods)	US$m	35,605.7	37,042.3	38,807.8	40,999.9	–
Balance of trade	US$m	2,738.8	824.2	1,136.9	960.4	–
Current account	US$m	-6,762.6	-7,013.0	-5,906.0	*-6,972.0	*-9,298.0
Total reserves minus gold	US$m	19,805.3	17,583.0	16,318.0	15,861.0	–
Foreign exchange	US$m	18,059.0	15,778.0	14,409.0	–	–
Exchange rate	per US$	1.27	1.21	1.22	1.28	–

* estimated figure ** forecast figure

the imbalances in the housing market, the implications of recent developments in the dairy sector for farmer indebtedness and loose global financial conditions. These would, said the Central Bank, be important themes in the months ahead.

For its part, in its June 2015 Economic Survey of New Zealand the Paris-based Organisation for Economic Co-operation and Development (OECD) took the view that New Zealand's economic growth had been faster than in most other OECD countries in recent years. Inflation and inflation expectations were well anchored, but the current account had been in sizeable deficit for some time. Strong fiscal and monetary policy frameworks and a healthy financial sector had, in the view of the OECD, yielded macro-economic stability, underpinning growth. Employment was high, in large part thanks to flexible labour markets and ample immigration, business investment was robust and households and firms were optimistic. Well-being was high, although a considerable income gap with the top half of the OECD remained.

However, bottlenecks in housing, urban infrastructure and skills, inequalities in living standards and rising environmental pressures all pose risks for sustaining growth. The government was moving to deal with these weaknesses. Businesses had reported increasing difficulties in finding skilled labour. However, wage pressures remained subdued thanks to immigration, policies to improve labour market matching (eg the Canterbury Skills and Employment Hub which has matched demand and labour supply in the post-earthquake rebuild) and skills training. Rapid population growth and a low responsiveness of supply had led to housing and urban infrastructure constraints. In particular, the OECD noted, house prices had risen sharply in Auckland, the largest city, eroding affordability and raising financial-stability risks. Efforts to speed the housing supply had been made, although community resistance to rezoning and densification might limit development. Environmental regulations also appeared to the OECD to be relatively burdensome for economic activity, including for residential investment. Finally, the foreign debt position, which reflected low private saving, had been large for some time and was an ongoing vulnerability. It called for a continued solid fiscal position, as New Zealand faced potentially large macro-economic shocks and longer-run pension and health spending pressures.

Words of warning

The views of both the Central Bank and the OECD were summed up in an article published in *Forbes* magazine by Jesse Colombo in which he painted a rather gloomy scenario, describing the New Zealand economy as 'heading for a crisis caused in the first place by consistently low interest rates for a five year period, a phenomenon it shared with the United Kingdom and a number of European countries. Low interest rates, in Mr Colombo's view, were responsible for the 85 per cent appreciation of the New Zealand dollar against the US dollar. To combat this 'export harming' factor, the Central Bank had reduced its short term interest rates to all time lows.

According to Mr Colombo, property prices in New Zealand, (especially in Auckland, as noted by the Central Bank) had in many cases doubled, in the previous decade, creating a property bubble. This had meant that property prices had overtaken household income and rent growth, making the New Zealand property market the third most overvalued in the world, behind Canada and – somewhat improbably – Belgium. New Zealand's mortgages had grown from NZ$70 billion (US$44.3 billion) in 2002 to NZ$186 billion (US$117.7 billion) in 2013, an increase of 165 per cent. The mortgage debt-to-GDP ratio had grown from 57 per cent to 85 per cent. According to Mr Colombo, half of New Zealand's mortgages were on a floating interest basis, leaving mortgagees vulnerable to interest rate rises. In consequence, by 2014 mortgages accounted for half of New Zealand's bank loan portfolios.

The balance of the New Zealand economy had changed fundamentally. By 2014 agriculture accounted for only 5.1 per cent of GDP, whereas the financial sector accounted for 28.8 per cent. New Zealand's banks accounted for 80 per cent of the assets of the financial sector. However, the banking system was dominated by four Australian owned banks. This left New Zealand vulnerable to the weaknesses of the Australian economy. Both Australia and by extension New Zealand, had become exposed to any sudden downturn in the Chinese economy.

Mr Colombo also noted that New Zealand's household debt to income ratio rose from 100 per cent in the early 2000s to almost 150 per cent in 2014. At the same time, the New Zealand government had trebled its overseas borrowings. In summary, Mr Colombo considered that the bubble was likely to burst when interest rates began to rise. In his sombre view, the 'popping' of the Australian, or even the Chinese, property bubbles would have a high probability of bursting the New Zealand bubble.

Risk assessment

Economy	Fair
Politics	Good
Regional stability	Good

COUNTRY PROFILE

Migrants from Polynesia arrived in New Zealand and colonised it between 800–1000AD.

1642 Dutch explorer Abel Tasman was the first European to sight New Zealand.

1769 and 1779 British explorer James Cook charted the islands of New Zealand. After his second voyage, British and other European settlers began to arrive.

1815 The first British missionaries arrived in New Zealand.

1840 European settlers and the Mäori tribes signed the *Treaty of Waitangi*, under which European settlers agreed to respect Mäori land rights in return for recognition of British rule. The Treaty is generally considered to be the founding document of the nation.

1845–47 Mäoris revolted against land loss.

1852 New Zealand became a self-governing British colony.

1858 A series of major Mäori revolts began in response to encroachments by Europeans on to Mäori land.

1860–72 Mäoris revolted again. The conflict was resolved after the Europeans promised to abide by the *Treaty of Waitangi*.

1893 New Zealand became the first country to give women the right to vote.

1898 The government introduced old age pensions.

1907 New Zealand became an independent dominion within the British Empire.

1914–18 New Zealand fought alongside the UK during the First World War and suffered heavy casualties in the Gallipoli campaign in Turkey in 1915.

1931 The Westminster Declaration established the concept of a Commonwealth between the UK, New Zealand and several other former British colonies.

1939–45 New Zealand fought alongside the UK during the Second World War.

1947 Dominion status began to be phased out and replaced by the Commonwealth.

1951 New Zealand formed the ANZUS military pact with Australia and the US.

1963 New Zealand agreed to provide a military presence in Vietnam – initially with military advisors.
1965 Under increasing US pressure for the commitment of troops in Vietnam, a non-combative engineering force was augmented by a field artillery battery of around 120 men.
1972 The last New Zealand troops were withdrawn from Vietnam.
1975 A legal tribunal ruled that there should be an investigation into whether Mäori land rights under the *Treaty of Waitangi* had been systematically ignored. This led to a vast number of lawsuits under which Mäori tribes demanded financial reparations for the illegal confiscation of their lands.
1984 Prime Minister David Lange declared New Zealand (NZ) a 'nuclear free zone' and forbade nuclear-powered vessels to dock at NZ ports.
1985 French secret agents bombed and destroyed the Greenpeace ship *Rainbow Warrior* in Auckland Harbour, killing one person.
1986 US suspended ANZUS obligations towards New Zealand.
1989 Lange resigned and was replaced by Geoffrey Palmer.
1990 The National Party (Nationals) won its first election victory for 10 years, with Jim Bolger becoming prime minister.
1993 The Nationals won the general elections. A referendum on electoral reform showed a majority in favour of proportional representation.
1996 New Zealand adopted a new parliamentary electoral system called Mixed Member Proportional (MMP) representation, which was designed to give better representation for smaller parties and the Mäori community.
1997 Bolger resigned rather than face a leadership challenge from cabinet minister Jenny Shipley, who went on to become New Zealand's first woman prime minister.
1998 The NP-led coalition collapsed, leaving the NP as a minority government reliant on support from independent MPs.
1999 New Zealand sent troops to join UN peace-keeping forces in East Timor. The opposition New Zealand Labour Party (NZLP) won general elections.
2001 The government re-nationalised Air New Zealand 12 years after it had been privatised.
2004 Official contact with Israel was suspended after two Israelis were jailed for attempting to obtain New Zealand passports for Mossad agents. A law was passed making all of the coastline public property; Mäori opposition claimed the law infringed the *Treaty of Waitangi*.
2005 Former prime minister David Lange died. Prime Minister Helen Clark formed a coalition government following an indecisive general election.
2006 Anand Satyanand became governor general. Te Arikinui Dame Te Atairangikaahu, the Great Chief of the Mäori population died, her eldest son Tuheitia Paki, became her successor.
2008 The Nationals won parliamentary elections; John Key (Nationals) became prime minister.
2009 The economy recorded its worst official figures since the early 1990s as a recession was declared after growth fell for five consecutive quarters. Unemployment rose to 6 per cent in the second quarter (from a low of 3.5 per cent in the fourth quarter of 2007).
2010 Fiji and New Zealand re-established diplomatic relations which had been broken in 2008. A settlement was reached between the government and Mäori negotiators, which allowed Mäoris the rights of 'customary title' to coastlines they have occupied since the *Treaty of Waitangi* (1840).
2011 In February an earthquake struck NZ's second city Christchurch, around mid-day, flattening some and damaging many buildings, including the spire of the iconic Christchurch Cathedral. Following all efforts and hope that anyone else could be rescued alive, 163 people had been killed and over 300 people were still missing. The national census was postponed from February and re-scheduled for March 2013, due to the disruption caused by the earthquake. The estimate of damage was US$15 billion (NZ$20 billion); the government provided an initial support package of NZ$120 million to pay people unable to work due to the loss of business and workplaces. Engineers declared that over 30 per cent of all buildings in the centre of the city would have to be demolished and that hundreds of suburban homes may also need to be razed. The estimated cost of the damage had doubled by August, to US$5.759 billion. Lieutenant-General Sir Jerry Mataparae was appointed as governor general, taking up his post on 31 August; he is the first Mäori to be appointed to the position. During the Commonwealth Heads of Government summit, in October, the 16 countries in which the British monarch is Head of State unanimously agreed to change the royal line of succession from that of first born son to the first born child (regardless of its gender). The change will be enacted after the succession of Prince William (currently second in line to the throne, after his father Charles, Prince of Wales). Parliamentary elections were held in November, in which the ruling Nationals won 48 per cent of the vote and increased its seats to 60 out of 121, the opposition Labour Party won 27.1 per cent, winning 34 seats. Prime Minister Key's coalition government gained the strength and backing to control parliamentary business with the aid of one other parliamentarian. A referendum was also held in November with the proposition should NZ keep the mixed member proportional (MMP) voting system; 53.74 per cent voted yes and 42.62 per cent voted no. The NP formed a coalition government with ACT and the UF on 5 December.
2012 On 30 July Australia and NZ agreed to restore full diplomatic relations with Fiji as it moved towards democratic elections in 2014. On 19 November, plans for a new Mäori unit based within the Ministry of Business were announced. The Mäori Economic Development Panel will drive government programmes to lift Mäori economic performance, centred on education, job training and providing mentoring and evaluating plans and strategies.
2013 Fonterra, New Zealand's largest company and co-operatively owned by 95 per cent of New Zealand's dairy farmers, suffered a scare over contaminated food products in August. The dairy industry is vital to New Zealand's economy, contributing some 7 per cent of GDP and accounting for almost 25 per cent of exports. The discovery of bacteria that could cause botulism in a whey product used in infant formula lead China to ban some products and for other countries to ban all New Zealand dairy products. The government announced a ministerial-level inquiry on 12 August. Another inquiry was announced by the ministry for primary industries and Fonterra itself said it was conducting two internal inquiries. A cardboard cathedral which will seat some 700 worshippers was dedicated on 15 August in Christchurch. The structure, which took less than a year to construct, could last as long as 50 years, until a new permanent cathedral can replace the one destroyed in the February 2011 earthquake. Two earthquakes shook Wellington on 16 August; although there were power cuts and traffic delays there was no major damage to buildings. On 28 August the government said that the Fonterra products did not, in fact, contain botulism-causing bacteria. The ministry for primary industries reported that there were bacteria, but not those that could cause botulism.
2014 A general election was held on 20 September. Prime Minister John Key's New Zealand National Party won a total of 60 seats (out of 121), followed by the New Zealand Labour Party with 32 seats, the Green Party of Aotearoa New Zealand with 14 seats and New Zealand First with 11 seats. The remaining three seats were won by the Maori Party (2), ACT

New Zealand (1) and United Future New Zealand (1). Turnout was 76.95 per cent.
2015 In November New Zealanders received their voting papers to chose an alternative flag that may replace the current flag. In this first stage voters are shown five flags to choose the one that will go forward to the second round in March 2016 when voters will be asked whether the current flag should be replaced.

Political structure

Constitution

New Zealand has no written constitution. Its constitutional history dates back to the signing of the *Treaty of Waitangi* in 1840, when the indigenous Mäori people ceded sovereignty over New Zealand to the British monarch. The Constitution Act 1986 brought together the most important constitutional provisions.
New Zealand is an independent parliamentary democracy and member of the Commonwealth. Government is based on the Westminster (United Kingdom) model.

Form of state

Constitutional monarchy

The executive

The head of state is the British sovereign, represented by a governor general who acts on the advice of the cabinet. The governor general is appointed by the sovereign on the advice of the New Zealand government.
The prime minister and cabinet are responsible to the legislature and are appointed by the governor general acting upon its advice. The prime minister and cabinet must be chosen from among elected members of parliament.
The Executive Council is a formal body made up of the cabinet and the governor general, who acts on the cabinet's advice. The cabinet consists of the prime minister and ministers, who must be chosen from among elected members of parliament.

National legislature

The unicameral parliament (the House of Representatives) typically has 120 members. Of which 70 are directly elected in 70 electorates (constituencies) with roughly the same number of voters. However as the South Island has a smaller population it has 16 guaranteed seats; elsewhere the voter numbers are divided by 16 to determine electorate boundaries, which may lead to a fluctuation in the total number of representatives elected.
Seven seats are reserved for Mäori representatives. There are an additional 50 members elected in national seats determined by proportional representation from party lists to reflect the overall share of votes cast. All members serve for up to three years.
Authority for raising revenue by taxation and for public expenditure must be granted by parliament. It also controls the government through its power to pass a resolution of no confidence.

Legal system

The law consists of common law, New Zealand statutes and some British statutes. The judiciary is independent from the executive. High Court judges, who also sit on the Court of Appeal, are appointed by the governor general and cannot be removed from office except by the sovereign or the governor general.

Last elections

20 September 2014
Results: Parliamentary (2014): National Party (Nationals) 47.04 per cent of the vote (60 seats of 121), the Labour Party 25.13 per cent (32), the Green Party of Aotearoa New Zealand 10.7 per cent (14), New Zealand First 6.8 per cent (11), the Maori Party 1.32 per cent (2), ACT New Zealand 0.79 per cent (1), United Future 0.22 per cent (1). Turnout was 76.95 per cent.

Next elections

2017 (parliamentary)

Political parties

Ruling party

Coalition led by the National Party, with ACT New Zealand (ACT), United Future (UF) and the Maori Party (from 20 Sept 2014)

Main opposition party

The Labour Party

Population

4.48 million (2013)* Around 75 per cent of the population live on North Island. There is a growing imbalance between the South Island and the North Island.
Last census: 7 March 2006: 4,143,282
Population density: 14 inhabitants per square km. Urban population 86 per cent (2010 Unicef).
Annual growth rate: 1.3 per cent, 1990–2010 (Unicef).

Ethnic make-up

Approximately 77.3 per cent of the population is of European origin, with Mäoris representing another 14.5 per cent, Pacific Islanders 5.6 per cent and others 2.6 per cent. Pacific Islanders are attracted by job opportunities and a higher standard of living. However, socio-economic problems plague the Mäoris and Pacific Islanders.

Religions

Anglican (25 per cent), Presbyterian (18 per cent), Roman Catholic (15 per cent), Methodist (5 per cent), Baptist (2 per cent) and other Christian religions (34 per cent).

Education

Education is free and secondary admission is non-selective. Primary education covers ages five to 12 years and secondary education ages 13 to 16 years. A one-year sixth form follows and leads to a one-year pre-university course.
Public expenditure on education is typically 7 per cent of GNP. Nearly NZ$30 million (US$14.5 million) was allocated to implement the government's policy of equity funding for the early childhood education sector and funding for adult literacy was doubled, to NZ$18 million (US$8.7 million) as part of the Adult Literacy Strategy.
A campaign was launched that targets the Mäori community called *Te Mana*, with a specific objective of providing education from a Mäori perspective to youths, parents, life-long learners and teachers. It uses television, IT and a magazine, which has expanded to include study guides and a website, with relevent, current and contemporary tutoring.
Literacy rate: 99 per cent, adult rate
Compulsory years: Six to 17
Enrolment rate: 101 per cent gross primary enrolment of the relevant age group (including repeaters); 113 per cent gross secondary enrolment (World Bank).
Pupils per teacher: 18 in primary schools

Health

The health system is made up of the public, private and voluntary sectors. The public sector provides free treatment at hospitals for immediate and major medical problems as well as chronic complaints, some continuing care and maternity and geriatric care. It also provides health benefits and subsidises pharmaceutical benefits and laboratory tests. The provision of mental health services is largely the responsibility of the public sector (with a small voluntary sector contribution) caring for both acute and chronic cases. It also provides free dental health treatment for school-age children. The public sector meets more than three-quarters of the total cost of healthcare and subsidises healthcare provided by general practitioners and specialists in private practice.
Private healthcare includes services provided by general practitioners, dentists, pharmacists and therapists in both public and private hospitals. The state subsidises many of these services although the main feature of this sector is the steady and rapid growth of private health and medical insurance.

HIV/Aids

HIV prevalence: 0.1 per cent aged 15–49 in 2003 (World Bank)
Life expectancy: 80 years, 2004 (WHO 2006)
Fertility rate/Maternal mortality rate: 2.2 births per woman, 2010 (Unicef);

maternal mortality 15 per 100,000 live births (World Bank)
Birth rate/Death rate: 15 births and Seven deaths per 1,000 people (World Bank)
Child (under 5 years) mortality rate (per 1,000): 6 per 1,000 live births (WHO 2012)
Head of population per physician: 2.37 physicians per 1,000 people, 2001 (WHO 2006)

Welfare
New Zealand Superannuation (NZS), which is a universal, publicly provided pension, is at the core of its retirement income system provided to everyone over the age of 64 years and who meet certain residential qualifications. It is estimated that more than 92 per cent of older people receive NZS.
The government has tried to develop the welfare system, which actively works with beneficiaries to boost their skills. In 2002/03, a NZ$3 million (US$1.4 million) pilot programme was initiated to encourage sickness and invalids benefit recipients to participate in paid work and community-based activities.

Main cities
North Island: Wellington (capital, estimated population 193,525 in 2012); Auckland (434,699), North Shore (280,323), Waitakere (213,184), Hamilton (172,429), Tauranga (125,477).
South Island: Manukau (430,144), Christchurch (385,663), Dunedin (112,470), Invercargill (45,816), Nelson (44,112).

Languages spoken
Some Polynesian dialects are spoken and a variety of other languages, reflecting the diverse origins of New Zealand's immigrant population.

Official language/s
English, Māori

Media
There is a free press although media content is subject to libel and contempt of court rulings. Media groups are privately owned by mostly international corporations.

Press
Ownership of the print media is dominated by Fairfax New Zealand and APN News and Media.
Dailies: There is no genuinely nationally circulated daily although, from Auckland, *The New Zealand Herald* (www.nzherald.co.nz) which has the largest circulation and from Wellington the *Dominion Post* (www.stuff.co.nz/dominionpost), can be purchased outside their core regions. Other city based newspapers include, from Christchurch *The Press* (www.thepress.co.nz) with the largest circulation in the South Island and *Otago Daily Times* (www.odt.co.nz) from Dunedin. There are a number of regional, daily newspapers which delivers up to date news covering local issues.
Weeklies: There are numerous magazines which cater for all interests. Many local newspapers are published once a week, including *Sunday Star Times* (www.sstlive.co.nz) and *Sunday News* (www.sundaynews.co.nz) is a tabloid along with *New Zealand Truth* (http://truth.co.nz). The *New Zealand Listener* (www.listener.co.nz) is a respected current affairs magazine. A publications for young women is *Indigo* (www.indigomag.co.nz), and *New Zealand Women's Weekly* (www.nzww.co.nz) for older women.
Business: There are several publications on offer including the daily *Businessday* (www.businessday.co.nz), the weekly *National Business Review* (www.nbr.co.nz) and the monthly *NZ Business* (www.nzbusiness.co.nz) and *Business to Business* (www.btob.co.nz). The monthly *University of Auckland Business Review* (www.uabr.auckland.ac.nz) and *Unlimited* (www.unlimited.co.nz) are journals reporting on emerging business issues, while *Her Business Magazine* (www.herbusinessmagazine.com) targets businesswomen.
Periodicals: The majority of local magazines and community newsletters are published monthly, including those which provide news in the Maori-language, such as the bi-monthly *Mana* covering Maori current affairs, and other languages of the Pacific communities such as Niuean, Tongan and Samoan. In English, popular monthly magazines include *Investigate* (www.investigatemagazine.com) on current affairs, *Metro* (www.metrolive.co.nz) on lifestyle and the annual *Jet Magazine* (www.jetmag.co.nz) a free-issue publication aimed at a youth market with articles on careers, education and training.

Broadcasting
Radio: Radio New Zealand (RNZ) (www.radionz.co.nz), it the national, public station with three networks: National Radio, Concert FM and AM Network. RNZ also operates an international service broadcasting mostly to the South Pacific via shortwave. There are numerous, private, commercial stations throughout the islands including Newstalk ZB (www.newstalkzb.co.nz) from Auckland, The Rock (www.therock.net.nz) from Wellington, Radio Live (www.radiolive.co.nz) from Christchurch and More FM (http://dunedin.morefm.co.nz) from Dunedin.
There are several government-funded and privately-owned radio stations broadcasting in the Maori-language.
Television: Analogue signals are expected to be replaced by digital services by no later than 2013. There are almost a dozen free-to-air channels, including those provided through digital signals. Pay-to-view TV is available via satellite and cable distribution.
The state-owned Television New Zealand (TVNZ) is funded by advertising revenue and is in competition for ratings with commercial TV networks, including TV3 (www.tv3.co.nz) and Prime TV (www.primetv.co.nz). There are local TV stations located in major towns and cities with minority interests such as the Chinese-language CTV8 (www.wtv.co.nz) or horse and dog racing TAB Trackside (www.trackside.co.nz) or music and live performance such as C4 (www.c4tv.co.nz). Maori Television (www.maoritelevision.com) is a public channel.
Other news agencies: New Zealand Press Association: www.nzpa-online.co.nz
Scoop: www.scoop.co.nz

Economy
New Zealand, a once agrarian economy with more head-of-sheep than people, has since moved to become a fully industrialised nation with a market economy trading freely with its international partners. It has a historical tie with Australia, its largest single trading partner, there is an agreement between them whereby goods and services are traded freely, forming a single market. Agricultural produce including meat (particularly lamb) and live animals, dairy, wool, wine, fruit and vegetables are still the primary exports. Total merchandise exports accounted for NZ$50,074 million (US$34,067 million) in 2014. Other important industries include financial services, tourism, education, information technology and telecommunications.
GDP growth was 2.8 per cent in 2007, but as the global economic crisis struck in 2008 the economy slipped into recession with a GDP rate of -0.1 per cent, which deepened to -2.1 per cent in 2009 as trading partners cut their imports of New Zealand goods and services, making this the longest recession in New Zealand's history. The economy grew out of recession with GDP growth of 1.2 per cent in 2010. This was allowed to happen because in line with global peers, the central bank cut interest rates aggressively and the government developed fiscal stimulus measures. GDP growth reached 3.2 per cent in 2014, a significant improvement from the previous year in which it was 2.2 per cent. Despite the fact that economic

growth has improved, key trade sectors remain vulnerable to weak external demand and lower commodity prices.

The earthquake in Christchurch on 22 February 2011 was expected to have an adverse impact on production and government spending. The GDP growth rate was expected to decline in 2011, even though the Rugby World Cup, which was held in September and October 2011, had been forecast to boost the economy by some US$1.2 billion. In actual fact, the economy grew 1.4 per cent, which was an improvement on 2010. In the aftermath of the Canterbury earthquakes, the government has continued to expand export markets, develop capital markets, invest in innovation, raise productivity growth, and develop infrastructure, while easing its fiscal austerity.

Inflation, which had been 2.4 per cent in 2007, jumped to 4.0 per cent in 2008, but fell back again in 2009 to 2.1 per cent due to weak economic activity and a drop in global oil prices. Inflation decreased further to 1.1 per cent in 2013 before increasing slightly to 1.2 per cent in 2014. Unemployment grew steadily from 4.5 per cent in 2008 to 6.4 per cent in 2009 and remained steady at 6.7 per cent in 2010. Since the end of the global recession, the unemployment rate continued at a relatively high rate at 6.2 per cent in 2013 before decreasing to 5.4 per cent in 2014. As a result, GDP per capita income fell from US$31,063 in 2007 to US$30,777 in 2008 and further still to US$27,293 in 2009; it rebounded to US$32,130 in 2010. Following this, GDP per capita matched the economic recovery and increased to US$34,000 in 2013 and further to US$35,200 in 2014.

External trade

New Zealand (NZ) is a member of the South Pacific Regional Trade and Economic Co-operation Agreement (Sparteca) along with 13 regional nations, which allows products duty free access by Pacific Island Forum members to Australian and NZ markets (subject to the country of origin restrictions). Australia and NZ have formed a single market under their Closer Economic Relations (CER) agreement, which allows free trade in goods and many services. NZ is a member of the Trans-Pacific Strategic Economic Partnership (TPP) to liberalise trade in goods and services between Chile, Brunei and, if negotiations begun in 2008 are successful, the US. NZ has a number of bilateral free trade agreements (BFTA), notably with Thailand, China and Malaysia. Negotiations are underway for BFTAs with Japan and South Korea.

Exports contributed over 29.2 per cent of GDP in 2013, of which around 50 per cent is provided by agricultural produce. NZ supplies almost 40 per cent of mutton and lamb exports worldwide.

Imports

Main imports include vehicles, machinery and equipment, vehicles and aircraft, petroleum, electronics, textiles and plastics.

Main sources: China (17 per cent of total in 2014), Australia (12.3 per cent), US (11.7 per cent) and Japan (6.7 per cent)

Exports

Main exports include dairy products, meat and edible offal, logs and wood articles, fruit, crude oil and wine.

Main destinations: China (20 per cent of total in 2014), Australia (17.5 per cent), US (9.3 per cent) and Japan (5.9 per cent)

Agriculture

Farming

The New Zealand (NZ) agricultural sector is almost unique among its developed nation competitors for being virtually free of subsidies, with farming produce being forced to compete against that produced in countries that do provide subsidies and incentives to their farmers. With a level of producer support estimate of 1 per cent (the OECD average is around 31 per cent) the agricultural industry still provides around 29 per cent of export earnings.

The removal of subsidies was both a burden and a boon to the NZ industry. Farmers contended with a fluctuating international market, which was dependent on the state of the general economy and specifically the value of the NZ dollar, while reorganising and diversifying. To compete, the industry shed obsolete equipment and old practices in favour of reinvestment and embracing market economies. The industry also adopted the latest research and development findings, applying biotechnology and information technology to improve productivity.

Of the total area of New Zealand (26.8 million hectares), 14.3 million hectares is farming land (2013) of which grassland is 10.5 million hectares, plantations are 1.6 million hectares and other land is 2.1 million hectares. 44 per cent of farming is dedicated to beef and sheep; they have been the mainstay of the country's agricultural sector for over a century. Since subsidies were withdrawn in 1982, these sectors have been rationalised and have seen a fall in the number of farms and animals. Productivity in meat and wool has increased since 1994 with 14 per cent more lambs born to 32 per cent fewer ewes. Weight gain of the average lamb at slaughter and lamb meat production have increased.

Dairy farming, particularly in the South Island, has increased with the addition of 1,650 new farms since 1994; the number of dairy cows rose by 52 per cent to 5.24 million. In mid-2013 Fonterra, New Zealand's largest company and co-operatively owned by 95 per cent of New Zealand's dairy farmers, suffered a scare over contaminated food products. The dairy industry is important to New Zealand's economy, contributing some 7 per cent of GDP and accounting for almost 25 per cent of exports. The discovery of bacteria that could cause botulism in a product lead China to ban some products and for other countries to ban all New Zealand dairy products. Dairy farming constituted 21 per cent of total farms in 2012.

The agriculture, fishing and forestry sectors together account for approximately 7–8 per cent of GDP and provide employment for over 11 per cent of the workforce. Of the total land area, grazing accounts for almost 12 million hectares (ha), horticulture over 100,000ha and planted forests 1.9 million ha.

Deer farming has led to a rapid growth in venison exports, and goats are reared for mohair. Wheat production is sufficient to meet national demand, as are crops including barley, maize and fresh vegetables. Other products include apples, pears, stone and berry fruits, citrus and sub-tropical fruits.

Fishing

The seafood industry is one of New Zealand's top five export earners. The total seafood harvest including aquaculture was 600,000 tonnes in 2013, of which 69 per cent was produced through marine fishing. Total volume of exported fish was 291,302 tonnes in 2013 of which rock lobster, hoki, mussels, tuna, squid, salmon, jack mackerel, ling, paua (sea snails) and orange roughy made up the majority of them.

Following the annual meeting of the Commission for the Conservation of Southern Bluefin Tuna (CCSBT), held on Cheju Island, South Korea, all members agreed to a 20 per cut in the roughly 17,000 tonnes in 2009 bluefin tuna catches from 2010. Scientists had warned that without a cut fish stocks could crash as numbers had become dangerously low.

Forestry

Forests cover about 9.5 million hectares of New Zealand's land area. Of this, around 7.8 million ha are indigenous forest and 1.75 million ha are plantations. The majority of plantations, cultivating exotic species, are in the central region of North Island. Some 95 per cent of plantations grow exotic softwoods, of which 80 per cent were radiata pine, 10 per cent Douglas Fir and 10 per cent other species. The state owns 55 per cent of the exotic resource, with forestry companies,

Māori incorporates, local authorities and individuals owning the remainder. Chile is New Zealand's major competitor in the market for radiata pine. The planting of exotic species began on a large scale in 1923; there was a second major planting in the 1960s and these trees are now reaching maturity, which will boost the supply of mature trees over the medium-term. In the long term a vibrant log processing industry, comparable to that of the southern US, could be developed.
Forestry was the third highest industry contributor to GDP after meat, wool and dairy in 2014. 46,001 ha were harvested in 2014. 3,500 ha were newly panted and 40,867 ha were restocked. Total employment for the forestry and first stage processing sector was 17,495.

Industry and manufacturing
Industry constitutes 26.6 per cent of GDP and it employs 19 per cent of the working population. US$1.43 billion of New Zealand's exports are from high-tech manufacturing and the sector employs 26,550 employees as of 2014. 80 countries buy aviation product and service solutions from New Zealand.
New Zealand has developed one of the world's most efficient, profitable and innovative aviation systems and it represents an important part of the economy. The aviation industry annually exports NZ$3.8 billion (US$2.6 billion) of products and services and contributes 6.9 per cent of overall GDP. Thirty percent growth is projected over the next five years in light aircraft design and manufacture.

Tourism
New Zealand is promoted as a destination for nature lovers and visitors who wish to experience a clean, largely unspoilt environment with an urban culture that is small and relaxed. There are three sites of natural wonder on Unesco's World Heritage List (including the NZ sub-Antarctic Islands). The principal cities, Auckland and Christchurch have amenities to rival other modern cities.
The Māori community has an enthusiastic commitment to allow access to its culture through festivals and community centres.
The country is expected to attract 2,863,000 international tourist arrivals in 2015. This number is set to increase to 5,085,000 by 2025.
Travel and tourism has contributed over 14 per cent of GDP since 2008, and has remained stable even during the global economic crisis that cut visitor numbers in world travel. The reason is largely due to the strength of domestic tourism spending compared to foreign receipts of US$6.4 billion in 2011, local spending was US$11.3 billion in the same period. Visitor numbers have typically remained above 2.4 million people (2007–11). Employment in the industry averaged 16.9 per cent of the workforce (370,000 jobs) (2007–11). Travel and tourism generated 100,000 jobs directly in 2014 (4.4 per cent of total employment), this is forecast to grow by 0.7 per cent in 2015 to 100,500. The total contribution of tourism to employment including the wider effects from investment and the supply chain was 354,000 jobs in 2014 (15.5 per cent of total employment).
In 2011, 133,200 foreign visitors arrived for the Rugby World Cup tournament hosted by New Zealand. The earthquake in Christchurch in 2011 caused disruption to visitors to the area and has had a continued effect as reconstruction gets underway. The direct contribution of travel and tourism to GDP is 2014 was NZD9.0 billion (3.9 per cent of GDP). This is forecast to rise by 2.2 per cent to NZD9.2 billion in 2015.

Mining
The mining sector accounted for 2.6 per cent of GDP in 2013 and employs 1.5 per cent of the workforce. Gold, silver, ironsand, clays, sand and aggregates are the main minerals mined. Ironsand is used to produce steel and is exported to Japan. Other metals include tungsten, manganese, copper, lead, zinc, tin, mercury (as cinnabar), platinum, titanium and aluminium (as bauxite). Non-metallic minerals include aggregates for roads; clays for ceramics and fillers; bentonite for bonding and drilling; limestone for agriculture and cement; and dolomite, serpentine, silica sand, sulphur, diatomite, mica, pumice and feldspar.

Hydrocarbons
Proven oil reserves were 81.4 million barrels in 2014, with production at 117,600 barrels per day (bpd) in 2012. However, consumption is around 152,800bpd and New Zealand has to import petroleum products to meet its domestic demand. Refinery capacity is 107,000bpd.
Hydrocarbon fields are located onshore in the Taranaki Basin, yielding oil and gas-condensates and offshore in the Maui natural gas-condensate field as well as the Kupe and Pohokura gas discoveries.
Proven natural gas reserves were 29.4 billion cubic metres (cum) in 2014, with production at 4.7 billion cum and consumption of 4.7 billion cum. There is a 3,100km network of transmission pipelines and a 7,900km network of natural gas pipelines throughout North Island, allowing a deregulated market with a number of competing energy companies ready to supply gas to customers, using the network. Natural gas supplies are not available in South Island.
Proven coal reserves are 571 million tonnes in 2014, and production was 2.5 million tonnes of oil equivalent (mtoe) - a fall of -13.6 per cent on the 2013 figure of 2.8mtoe. Coal exports to Japan, India, South Africa, South America, Europe and China account for 2.2 million tonnes of output, with the remainder used in domestic power generation.

Energy
Total installed generating capacity was 9.7GW in 2013, producing 42.91 billion kilowatt hours. Around 74 per cent of generated electricity is produced from renewable sources, in particular hydropower (54 per cent of total installed capacity) and geothermal power. 30.9 per cent of total installed capacity still comes from fossil fuels.
The Huntly Power Station, situated close to Auckland, is the largest thermal power station in the country, producing up to 17 per cent of primary energy. Despite two upgrades, with the addition of new gas-fired turbine plants allowing production of 1,485MW, the station is destined to be closed by 2015, due to New Zealand's agreement on reducing its carbon dioxide emissions. However, decommissioning may be delayed if an alternative energy provider is not found to accommodate the annual growth in energy consumption, particularly in the Auckland area.

Financial markets
Stock exchange
New Zealand Stock Exchange (NZX)

Banking and insurance
Banking has been opened up to international competition, but domestic demand for credit remains weak. All but one of New Zealand's 18 banks are foreign-owned.
Central bank
The Reserve Bank of New Zealand (RBNZ) formulates and implements monetary policy and is the supervisory authority for New Zealand's registered banks.
Main financial centre
Wellington

Time
GMT plus 13 hours October–March; GMT plus 12 hours March–October.

Geography
New Zealand is in the south-west Pacific, 1,600km south-east of Australia, separated from it by the Tasman Sea, and has no continental neighbours to the east before South America. Its combined length is over 1,600km and it is about 450km across at its widest point. Mount Cook in the Southern Alps is its highest point at 3,764 metres – one of more than 230 named peaks above 2,300 metres.

It consists of two main islands (North Island and South Island – usually referred to by locals as the mainland, as it is the larger of the two islands) and other outlying islands, the Stewart Island, off the southern tip of South Island and the Chatham Islands, 800km east of the South Island.

Geologically speaking, New Zealand is one of the youngest countries in the world, with a topography that is still being shaped by earthquakes, active volcanoes and glaciers.

The North Island has low-lying, rolling hills that rise to around 1,700 metres and form the heart of the area, with rich farmland on all sides. Lake Taupo, the largest in the North Island, is almost in the centre of the range, which is dominated by a volcanic plateau at Rotorua.

The South Island is much more rugged, with the Southern Alps that rise to over 3,000 metres running the length of the island. West of the Alps are rainforests and to the east farmland and the alluvial plains formed by rivers flowing down from the mountains. The Southern Alps contain glaciers, the largest of which is the Tasman glacier.

Stewart Island is largely low rolling hills which, unlike the two main islands, retains almost all of its native vegetation.

Hemisphere

Southern

Climate

New Zealand is a temperate country with a variable and unpredictable climate, generally drier and warmer on North Island than on South Island, particularly in winter. Rainfall averages 600–1,500mm annually and strong winds are common. On North Island, January temperatures average 18 degrees Celsius (C) and in winter 4 degrees C. It is 3 to 5 degrees C colder on South Island.

Dress codes

Visitors should take warm clothing during the winter months, from May to October. Even in the summer, from December to early March, a light sweater is an essential travelling item. Suits are worn for business meetings. For leisure, smart casual clothes are acceptable.

Entry requirements

Passports

Passports are required by all and must be valid for three months beyond the intended length of stay.

Visa

Required by all, except visitors from visa free countries. For a full list see www.immigration.govt.nz. Business visas may not be required for company representatives, a visitors visa is sufficient for stays up to three months. However proof of onward/return tickets and sufficient funds are required.

Currency advice/regulations

There are no restrictions on the import and export of local or foreign currencies.

Customs

Equipment used with animals, camping equipment, golf clubs and used bicycles must be declared.

Personal effects are allowed duty-free: 200 cigarettes, 4.5 litres of wine/beer, or goods up to the value of NZ$700 (or equivalent) are permitted.

Visitors arriving from countries suffering from certain diseases affecting livestock and plants may have items of clothing and produce disinfected.

Prohibited imports

Illegal drugs, plants or plant material, animals or by-products (these include any fruit, vegetables or meat – cooked or raw), biological specimens, artifacts made from endangered wildlife and weapons, such as flick knives, are prohibited. Firearms and ammunition require a permit.

Health (for visitors)

A reciprocal health agreement for urgent medical treatment exists with the United Kingdom. Some proof of UK residence will be required.

Mandatory precautions

There are no compulsory vaccinations.

Advisable precautions

Travellers are advised to have up-to-date tetanus and polio immunisations.

Hotels

Motel, serviced-unit accommodation is widespread. Neither a service charge nor tipping is customary. Advance booking is advisable for major hotels in urban centres.

Credit cards

All major credit cards are accepted.

Public holidays (national)

Fixed dates

1–2 Jan (New Year), 6 Feb (Waitangi Day), 25 Apr (Anzac Day), 25–26 Dec (Christmas).

Variable dates

Easter Holiday, Queen's Official Birthday (first Mon in Jun), Labour Day (Oct).

Working hours

Mid-December to mid-February is the summer holiday season during which the majority of New Zealanders take most of their annual leave.

Banking

Mon–Fri: 0900–1630.

Business

Mon–Fri: 0900–1700.

Government

Mon–Fri: 0800–1630.

Shops

Mon–Thu: 0900–1730; Fri: 0900–2100; Sat: 0900–1230. Some shops open on Sundays.

Telecommunications

Postal services

The government agreed in October 2013 that the current six-day-a-week deliveries in urban areas may drop to three days starting in June 2015. Rural areas, where customers tend to rely more on mail, will be maintained at five days. The move is a result of the increasing use of electronic communications.

Mobile/cell phones

GSM 900, 1800 and 3G services are available throughout most of the country.

Electricity supply

230/240V AC, 50 hertz, with three-pin flat plug fittings, most hotels supply 110V AC sockets for razors.

Weights and measures

Metric system

Social customs/useful tips

In general, be polite and patient. New Zealanders appreciate frankness and like prompt timekeeping for business meetings. Business can also be discussed over lunch and dinner. Late night life can be sparse. People tend to go to bed early and start work early.

Should a visitor be invited to a formal Mäori occasion the *hongi* (pressing of noses) is common.

Tipping is acceptable but is not particularly sought after and there is sometimes a built-in service charge at hotels and restaurants. There is a smoking ban in restaurants and pubs.

Same sex marriages became legal on 19 August 2013.

Security

The cities are safe, even at night.

Getting there

Air

National airline: Air New Zealand

International airport/s: Auckland International, Mangere (AKL), 22km south of Auckland; Christchurch International (CHC), 10km of the city; Wellington International (WLG), 8km south-east of the city; all with duty-free shop, bar, restaurant, bank, hotel reservations, post office, shops, car hire and office facilities. Taxi journeys from Auckland International Airport to the city centre take 35 minutes; from Christchurch Airport to city centre 15 minutes; from Wellington Airport to city centre 20 minutes.

Airport tax: Departures and security tax: up to NZ$30, depending on the airport; transit passengers up to 24 hours are exempt.

Surface

Water: Apart from cruise ships there are no regular passenger ships sailing to New Zealand. International shipping lines that maintain contacts with New Zealand may provide passenger services on cargo ships.

Main port/s: Auckland (containers), Dunedin, Lyttelton (containers), Tauranga, Wellington (containers), Port Chalmers (containers), Picton, Opua.

Getting about

National transport

Air: There are good regular air services between the four major cities (Wellington, Auckland, Christchurch and Dunedin) with links to smaller, regional towns and tourist centres. Internal air services serve around 30 airports.

Road: The road network includes over 11,000km of state highways. The main routes are surfaced, and roads are generally well-maintained.

On 1 August 2011, the minimum aged of a driver was raised from 15 to 16 years.

Buses: Luxury coach services link the main centres. Advance booking for these is advisable, especially during the main holiday periods (December–February and Easter).

Rail: The rail network operates over 4,300km of track linking cities and main towns with express services that have buffet cars.

Water: Interisland Lines operates a regular ferry service between Wellington and Picton several times a day. Advance booking is advisable, especially during the main holiday periods.

City transport

Taxis: Taxis may be hired from ranks or by telephone 24 hours a day, although there is an extra charge for telephone booking. Fares are generally charged per km, but rates vary throughout the country and are generally higher at night and on weekends. Tipping is not customary.

Buses, trams & metro: Auckland's integrated transport system, in the city centre, is connected by the Britomart rail network that handles suburban and intercity trains, to buses and ferries. Wellington has a rail-metro with five lines terminating in the city centre. Christchurch has a comprehensive bus-metro.

There are good, privately operated, local buses in all urban areas.

Car hire

Car hire is available throughout the country; drivers must be over 21 years with either a national licence or international driving permit. It is advisable to book ahead at motels when touring. Driving is on the left-hand side of the road. Parking can be a problem in larger cities. Outside the major centres there is little traffic as country areas are sparsely populated.

BUSINESS DIRECTORY

The addresses listed below are a selection only. While World of Information makes every endeavour to check these addresses, we cannot guarantee that changes have not been made, especially to telephone numbers and area codes. We would welcome any corrections.

Telephone area codes

The international direct dialling code (IDD) for New Zealand is +64, followed by area code and subscriber's number:

Auckland	9	Nelson	3
Bay of Plenty	7	New Plymouth	6
Christchurch	3	Palmerston N	6
Dunedin	3	Rotorua	7
Gisborne	6	Tauranga	7
Hamilton	7	The South Island	3
Hastings	6	Timaru	3
Invercargil	3	Wanganui	6
Manawatu	6	Wellington	4
Napier	6	Whangarei	9

Useful telephone numbers

Emergency (all services): 111

Chambers of Commerce

American Chamber of Commerce in New Zealand, Affco House, 12-26 Swanson Street, PO Box 106002, Auckland Central 1001 (tel: 309-9140; fax: 309-1090; e-mail: amcham@amcham.co.nz).

Auckland Chamber of Commerce, 100 Mayoral Drive, PO Box 47, Auckland (tel: 309-6100; fax: 309-0081; e-mail: akl@chamber.co.nz).

British New Zealand Trade Council, PO Box 37162, Parnell, Auckland (tel/fax: 522-0526; e-mail: info@bnztc.co.nz).

Canterbury Employers Chamber of Commerce, 57 Kilmore Street, PO Box 359, Christchurch (tel: 366-5096; fax: 379-5454; e-mail: info@cecc.org.nz).

New Zealand Chambers of Commerce & Industry, 109 Featherston Street, PO Box 11043, Wellington (tel: 472-3376; fax: 471-1767).

Otago Chamber of Commerce & Industry, WestpacTrust Building, 106 George Street, Dunedin (tel: 479-0181; fax: 477-0341; e-mail: office@otagochamber.co.nz).

Wellington Regional Chamber of Commerce, 109 Featherston Street, PO Box 1590, Wellington 6015 (tel: 914-6500; fax: 914-6524; e-mail: info@wgtn-chamber.co.nz).

Banking

ANZ Banking Group (New Zealand) Limited, PO Box 1492, ANZ Tower, Level 9, 215-229 Lambton Quay, Wellington (tel: 496-6938; fax: 496-6934).

ASB Bank Ltd, 198-204 Lambton Quay, Wellington (tel: 499-0864; fax: 495-2102).

Bank of New Zealand, PO Box 2392, State Insurance Centre, 1 Willis Street, Wellington (tel: 474-6999; fax: 474-6861).

BNZ Finance Ltd; PO Box 401, Level 24, BNZ Centre, 1 Willis Street, Wellington (tel: 495-3630; fax: 495-3632).

National Bank of New Zealand Ltd, PO Box 1791, 1 Victoria Street, Wellington 6000 (tel: 498-6020; fax: 494-4023).

Reserve Bank of New Zealand, PO Box 2498, 2 The Terrace, Wellington (tel: 472-2029; fax: 473-8554).

Westpac Banking Corporation, PO Box 691, 157 Lambton Quay, Wellington (tel: 381-1430; fax: 470-8202).

Central bank

Reserve Bank of New Zealand, 2 The Terrace, PO Box 2498, Wellington (tel: 472-2029; fax: 473-8554; e-mail: rbnz-info@rbnz.govt.nz).

Stock exchange

New Zealand Stock Exchange (NZX), www.nzx.com

Travel information

Air New Zealand, Customer Support, Private Bag 92007, Auckland 1020 (tel: 255-8758; fax: 256-3531; internet site: www.airnz.co.nz/).

Intercity Coachlines (InterCity Group (NZ)), PO Box 26 601, Epsom, Auckland (tel: 623-1503; email: info@intercitygroup.co.nz; internet site: www.intercitycoach.co.nz).

Interislander (ferry service) (Ticket Office) PO Box 2085, Wellington (tel: 498-3302; fax: 498-3090; email: info@interislander.co.nz; internet site: www.interislander.co.nz).

Trains: tel (outside NZ): (+64-4) 495-0775; fax: (+64-4) 4728903; tel inside NZ: 0800-872-467; email: bookings@tranzscenic.co.nz; internet: www.transcenic.co.nz).

National tourist organisation offices

New Zealand Tourism Board, level 16, 80 The Terrace, PO Box 95, Wellington (tel: 917-5400; fax: 915-3817; internet: www.purenz.com).

Ministries

Ministry of Agriculture and Fisheries, PO Box 2526, Wellington (tel: 474-4100; fax: 474-4111).

Ministry of Civil Defence, PO Box 5010, Wellington (tel: 473-7363; fax: 473-7369).

Ministry of Commerce, PO Box 1473, Wellington (tel: 472-0030; fax: 473-4638).

Ministry of Consumer Affairs, PO Box 1473, Wellington (tel: 474-2750; fax: 473-9400).

Ministry of Defence, PO Box 5347, Wellington (tel: 496-0999; fax: 496-0859).

Ministry of Education, Private Bag 1666, Wellington (tel: 473-5544; fax: 499-1327).

Ministry for the Environment, PO Box 10362, Wellington (tel: 473-4090; fax: 471-0195).

Ministry of Foreign Affairs and Trade, Private Bag 18-901, Parliament Bldgs, Wellington (tel: 472-8877; fax: 472-9596).

Ministry of Forestry, PO Box 1610, Wellington (tel: 472-1569; fax: 472-2314).

Ministry of Health, PO Box 5013, Wellington (tel: 496-2000; fax: 496-2340).

Ministry of Māori Development, PO Box 3943, Wellington (tel: 494-7100; fax: 494-7010).

Ministry of Pacific Island Affairs, PO Box 833, Wellington (tel: 473-4493; fax: 473-4301).

Ministry of Research, Science and Technology, PO Box 5336, Wellington (tel: 472-6400; fax: 471-1284).

Ministry of Transport, PO Box 3175, Wellington (tel: 472-1253; fax: 473-3697).

Ministry of Women's Affairs, PO Box 10049, Wellington (tel: 473-4112; fax: 472-0961).

Ministry of Youth Affairs, PO Box 10300, Wellington (tel: 471-2158; fax: 471-2233).

Prime Minister and Cabinet Department, Executive Wing, Parliament Bldgs, Wellington (tel: 471-9700; fax: 473-2508).

Other useful addresses

Airways Corporation of New Zealand, 44-48 Willis Street, PO Box 294, Wellington (tel: 471-1888; fax: 471-0395; internet: www.airways.co.nz/).

British High Commission, PO Box 1812, 44 Hill Street, Wellington 1 (tel: 472-6049; fax: 471-1974).

British/New Zealand Trade Council Inc, 22 Newton Road, Newton, Auckland (tel: 378-9066; fax: 378-0539).

Central Region Health Authority, PO Box 10097, 155 The Terrace, Wellington (tel: 472-7633; fax: 472-7639).

Coal Corporation of New Zealand Ltd, PO Box 439, Wellington (tel: 474-3600; fax: 474-3601).

Commerce Commission, PO Box 2351, Wellington (tel: 471-0180; fax: 471-0771).

Conservation Department, PO Box 10420, Wellington (tel: 471-0726; fax: 471-1082).

Customs Department, PO Box 2218, Whitmore Street, Wellington (tel: 473-6099; fax: 473-7370).

Earthquake Commission, PO Box 311, Wellington (tel: 499-0045; fax: 499-0046).

Electricity Corporation of New Zealand, PO Box 930, Wellington (tel: 472-3550; fax: 473-7091).

Hillary Commission for Sport, Fitness and Leisure, PO Box 2251, Wellington (tel: 472-8058; fax: 471-0813).

Housing Corporation of New Zealand, PO Box 5009, Wellington (tel: 495-1045; fax: 472-3152).

Human Rights Commission, PO Box 6751, Wellesley Street, Auckland (tel: 309-0874; fax: 377-3593).

Inland Revenue Department, PO Box 2198, Wellington (tel: 472-1032; fax: 499-0806).

Internal Affairs Department, PO Box 805, Wellington (tel: 495-7200; fax: 495-7222).

Justice Department, PO Box 180, Wellington (tel: 472-5980; fax: 499-2295).

Labour Department, PO Box 3705, Wellington (tel: 473-7800; fax: 495-4009).

Land Corporation Ltd, PO Box 5349, Wellington (tel: 471-0400; fax: 473-4966).

New Zealand Embassy (USA), 37 Observatory Circle, NW, Washington DC 20008 (tel: (+1-202) 328-4800; fax: (+1-202) 667-5227; e-mail: nz@nzemb.org).

New Zealand Manufacturers' Federation, 3–9 Church Street, PO Box 11543, Wellington (tel: 473-3000; fax: 473-3004).

New Zealand Minerals Industry Association, Druids Building, 188 Lambton Quay, PO Box 5039, Wellington (tel: 499-9871; fax: 499-9873; email: nzmia@xtra.co.nz).

New Zealand Stock Exchange, Caltex Tower, 286-292 Lambton Quay, PO Box 2959, Wellington (tel: 472-7599; fax: 473-1470).

New Zealand Trade Development Board (TRADENZ), Pastoral House, 25 The Terrace, PO Box 10341, Wellington (tel: 499-2244; fax: 473-3193).

Overseas Investment Commission, 2 The Terrace, PO Box 2498, Wellington (tel: 471-3838; fax: 471-3655).

Race Relations Office, PO Box 12411, Thorndon, Wellington (tel: 499-5885; fax: 499-5998).

Radio New Zealand, PO Box 2092, Wellington (tel: 474-1555; fax: 474-1712).

Statistics Department, 85 Molesworth Street, PO Box 2922, Wellington (tel: 495-4600; fax: 472-9135).

Survey and Land Information Department, Private Box 170, Charles Ferguson Building, Wellington (tel: 473-5022; fax: 472-2244).

Telecom New Zealand, PO Box 1473, Christchurch (tel: 374-0253; internet: www.telecom.co.nz).

Television New Zealand Ltd, PO Box 3819, Auckland (tel: 377-0630; fax: 375-0828).

Tranz Rail Ltd, Private Bag, Wellington (tel: 498-3095; fax: 498-3322).

Treasury Department, PO Box 3724, Wellington (tel: 472-2733; fax: 473-0982).

Works and Development Services Corporation Ltd, PO Box 12041, Wellington (tel: 496-1300; fax: 471-0224).

New Zealand Press Association: www.nzpa-online.co.nz

Scoop: www.scoop.co.nz

Internet sites

AA Travel: www.aatravel.co.nz

Air New Zealand: www:airnz.com

Asia Pacific Economic Co-operation (APEC): www.apecsec.org.sg

Auckland Airport: www:auckland-airport.co.nz

Destination New Zealand (gateway site): www.destinationnz.co.nz

Economic & Trade Development Agency: www:nzte.govt.nz

General Information: www:nz.com

Immigration: www:immigration.govt.nz

Ministry of Foreign Affairs and Trade: www:mft.govt.nz

New Zealand Government: www.govt.nz

New Zealand Herald newspaper: www:nzherald.co.nz

Parliament: www:parliament.govt.nz

Reserve Bank: www:rbnz.govt.nz

Statistics: www:stats.govt.nz

Stock exchange: www:nzse.co.nz

Treasury: www:treasury.govt.nz

Tourism: www:purenz.com

White Pages: www:whitepages.co.nz

Nicaragua

KEY FACTS

Official name: República de Nicaragua (Republic of Nicaragua)

Head of State: President Jose Daniel Ortega (from 2007; re-elected 6 Nov 2011)

Head of government: President Jose Daniel Ortega (from 2007; re-elected 6 Nov 2011)

Ruling party: Frente Sandinista de Liberación Nacional (FSLN) (Sandinista National Liberation Front) (from 2007; re-elected 6 Nov 2011)

Area: 147,950 square km

Population: 6.22 million (2014)*

Capital: Managua

Official language: Spanish

Currency: Córdoba de oro (gold córdoba) (C) = 100 centavos

Exchange rate: C27.51 per US$ (Sep 2015)

GDP per capita: US$1,881 (2014)*

GDP real growth: 4.54% (2014)*

GDP: US$11.71 billion (2014)*

Unemployment: 4.83% (2014)*

Inflation: 6.04% (2014)

Balance of trade: -US$2.40 billion (2014)

Annual FDI: US$967.90 million (2011)

* estimated figure

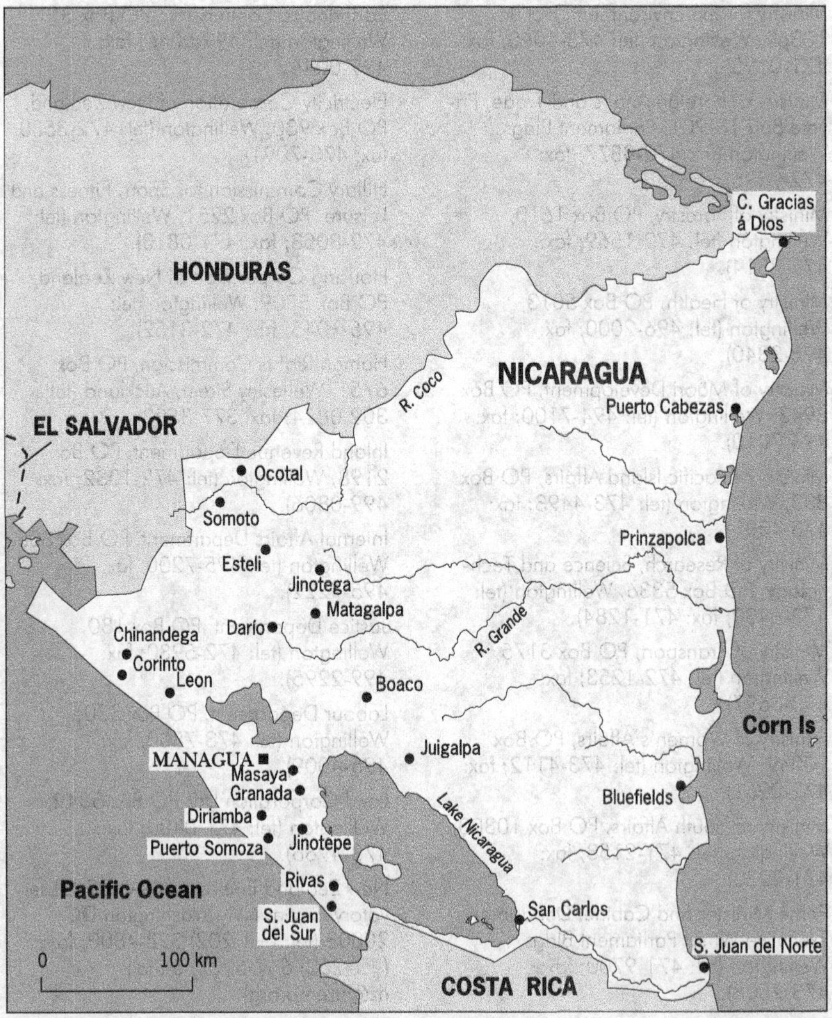

In mid-2014 it was announced that a representative of the Nicaraguan government would be travelling to London to present his country's plans to resurrect a 100-year-old scheme to dig a canal across the country from the Pacific to the Atlantic to compete with the Panama Canal. Preparatory work began on the Chinese-financed project in December 2014. The Nicaraguan canal would reduce by 800 kilometres the maritime distance from New York to Los Angeles. In the late nineteenth century, the United States government had favoured building the canal in Nicaragua which was seen as a less volatile country. The plans shifted largely after French engineer Philippe-Jean Bunau-Varilla, effectively using photographs of the active volcano Mount Momotombo, convinced US legislators to opt for Panama.

The twenty-first century Nicaraguan project, called the 'Gran Canal de Nicaragua' proposed linking the Pacific with the Caribbean, via a canal with a railway, an oleo duct, two deep-water ports, two airports and two free zones. Controversially, the canal would traverse Lake Nicaragua. The total investment, according to initial Nicaraguan government estimates, would be in the order of US$50 billion. The head concession for 50 years, with a 50 year extension, had been granted to the HKND Group, a Chinese-backed infrastructure development firm incorporated in the Cayman Islands. HKND was fully owned by the Hong Kong-based HK Nicaragua Canal Development Investment Company, linked to Mr Wang Jing, the president of Xinwei Telecom Enterprise Group, a Chinese telecommunications group with interests in Nicaragua.

According to the HKND website, the company has entrusted the China Railway Construction Corporation (CRCC) to undertake technical feasibility studies, McKinsey & Company (US) to provide fact based data and analysis and Environmental Resource Management (ERM – UK) to undertake social and environmental evaluations and impact assessments. HKND has also invited XCMG (construction machinery – China), SBE (civil engineers – Belgium) and MEC Mining from Australia, to help with the project. The proposed US$50 billion (most of which, it seemed, still had to be raised) canal could hardly be termed uncontroversial. It would be the largest civil engineering project of its kind in the world and before anything much had actually been signed its very mention had already led to street protests in Managua. The Nicaraguan constitutional court was also reviewing a challenge to the project by indigenous and creole groups, who claimed that their autonomy would be violated. According to the Hong Kong daily, the *South China Morning Post*, 'such was US sensitivity to any major Chinese activity in its back yard' that some US commentators had already dismissed the project as Beijing's 'back-door' plan to make Nicaragua, currently an ally of Taiwan, switch allegiance to the mainland. The Chinese company's ambitious plan was to have the new canal open and functioning by December 2019. Allegations that the whole project was in fact being funded and master-minded by the Chinese government were strenuously denied by both contractors and the Nicaraguan government. However, it did seem strange that senior Nicaraguan politicians had been invited to visit China – although the country's diplomatic links were with Taiwan.

The Nicaraguan government claimed that the canal could boost the economy significantly, creating some 25,000 jobs for Nicaraguans and would finally lift Nicaragua out of poverty; figures referred to by the canal's supporters and contractors suggested the creation of 250,000 jobs. However, representatives of Germany's Konstanz University, which had been monitoring the Nicaraguan environment for a period of 30 years, described the canal's construction plans as a 'shattering environmental disaster'. The University's researchers had confirmed in the respected journal, *Nature*, that the canal's construction plans included the creation of industrial centres, airports, oil pipelines and a railway system. One endangered area was the island of Ometepe on Lake Nicaragua which depended on the lake for its water supply. According to the University of Konstanz the first environmental studies were not begun until after the canal's construction was under way. The Lake Nicaragua section of the canal project would involve not only dredging, but also underwater excavation using explosives, projected by the lake's fishing communities to endanger, or even eliminate, the region's fish resources. Lake Nicaragua is the largest freshwater lake in Central America.

ECLAC – macro-development

In its report on the Nicaraguan economy in 2014, the United Nations Economic Commission for Latin America and the Caribbean (ECAC/CEPAL) expected Nicaragua's economy, as measured by its gross domestic product (GDP), to have continued growing faster than the regional average in 2014, expanding by 4.5 per cent, compared with 4.6 per cent in 2013. Two main factors were responsible for the slowdown: the earthquake and aftershocks in April 2014, which forced the closure of most production facilities and the *El Niño* phenomenon, which had a negative impact on agricultural production.

In ECLAC's view, the process of fiscal consolidation looked set to continue thanks to the tax reforms introduced in January 2013. As a result, the central government deficit before grants was expected to be around 0.7 per cent of GDP at the end of 2014. Meanwhile, year-on-year inflation would be around 6.5 per cent, almost one percentage point higher than the 5.7 per cent recorded at the end of 2013. The balance-of-payments current account deficit could reach 11 per cent of GDP (compared with 11.3 per cent in 2013).

Growth of around 4.5 per cent was expected by ECLAC for 2014 overall, on the back of rising external demand as the United States economy expanded, as well as an increase in domestic demand – both factors that had mitigated the economic impact from the April earthquakes and the drought. During the year discussions continued on the inter-oceanic canal mega-project, which would involve an investment in infrastructure equivalent to nearly four times Nicaragua's GDP. The first findings of the environmental impact study were presented in early November. The government continued to support the scheme, which could be the region's largest infrastructure project if it came to fruition.

In September 2014 total central government revenue expanded by 15.5 per cent, while spending rose by 18.2 per cent, both in nominal terms over the same period in 2013. The more progressive tax structure contributed to the higher revenues: 39 per

KEY INDICATORS **Nicaragua**

	Unit	2011	2012	2013	2014	**2015
Population	m	*5.89	6.06	*6.15	*6.22	*6.30
Gross domestic product (GDP)	US$bn	7.30	10.51	10.84	*11.71	*12.30
GDP per capita	US$	1,243	1,733	1,764	*1,881	*1,952
GDP real growth	%	4.7	5.2	4.4	*4.5	*4.6
Inflation	%	11.1	7.2	7.1	6.0	*5.4
Unemployment	%	7.8	5.9	5.9	*4.8	*3.6
Exports (fob) (goods)	US$m	3,655.1	4,157.1	4,122.5	3,621.8	–
Imports (fob) (goods)	US$m	5,835.9	6,449.9	6,401.9	6,023.5	–
Balance of trade	US$m	-2,180.9	-2,292.8	-2,279.4	-2,401.7	–
Current account	US$m	-1,302.1	-1,350.0	-960.0	*-729.0	*-832.0
Total reserves minus gold	US$m	1,771.5	1,887.2	1,993.0	2,276.2	–
Foreign exchange	US$m	1,597.2	1,724.1	1,846.1	–	–
Exchange rate	per US$	22.20	23.98	25.34	26.60	–

* estimated figure ** forecast figure

cent of revenues came from direct taxes, compared with 37 per cent for the same date in 2013. The rising share of income tax was the result of the full implementation of the Tax Co-ordination Act, which led to administrative improvements and tighter surveillance. At the end of the third quarter, value added tax revenues were 25 per cent higher than the year-earlier period. ECLAC noted that the Nicaraguan authorities continued to maintain a contractionary monetary policy, stepping up the volume of open market operations in order to avert pressures on the external sector and the exchange rate and to hold nominal local currency depreciation to the target rate of 5 per cent per annum. The government shored up this policy by increasing its deposits in the Banco Central de Nicaragua (BCN) (central bank), as part of a co-ordinated fiscal and monetary policy. This monetary policy stance led to slightly lower growth in credit to the private sector: up by 20.9 per cent at the end of the third quarter, compared with 22.6 per cent in September 2013. The largest loan volumes went to the livestock, commerce, industry and construction sectors.

What ECLAC described as the 'implicit' bank lending rate remained virtually unchanged, standing at 12.65 per cent in September 2014, compared with 12.63 per cent in December 2013. Meanwhile, at the end of the third quarter of 2014 financial system profitability stood at 2.22 per cent in terms of return on assets (compared with 2.20 per cent in September 2013), while return on equity stayed at 21.5 per cent. A 20 per cent year-on-year increase in credit was expected by the end of the year, in line with the central bank's financial stability objective. Monetary policy actions and inflows of resources from external loans and grants, as well as the improvement in the trade balance, pushed net international reserves up by US$31.7 million. Gross international reserves totalled US$2.170 billion, which was equivalent to 2.87 times the monetary base and more than four months of imports.

In 2014, official external co-operation remained the third largest source of external resources in Nicaragua, after exports of goods and services and remittances. Total co-operation to June mounted to US$528 million, of which US$345.6 million went to the private sector and US$182.4 million to the public sector. Venezuela remained the primary source of international co-operation, although its grants decreased slightly owing to the drop in oil prices. Total external debt as a percentage of GDP stood at 39.7 per cent at the end of the third quarter of 2014.

The export sector continued to perform robustly. Exports of goods and services increased by 9.7 per cent year-on-year to September, while imports grew at a moderate, cumulative rate of 1 per cent. Ten products accounted for 76 per cent of the value of exports, the top five of which were coffee, beef, gold, sugar and milk. The top five destinations captured 67.8 per cent of exports. The largest markets remain the United States, Central America, Venezuela and Canada. Central America as a whole received 20 per cent of exports, confirming the importance of sub-region to the Nicaraguan economy.

With respect to imports, the main increase was seen in consumer goods, while capital goods fell by 2.1 per cent year-on-year in September, with the largest contractions for purchases of telecommunications equipment and transport equipment. The balance-of-payments current account deficit was expected by ECLAC to be around 11 per cent of GDP at the end of 2014.Cumulative remittances to August totalled US$740 million. By the end of December inflows were expected to be at least 7 per cent higher than in 2013 and to represent about 9 per cent of GDP. The largest source of remittances to Nicaragua remains the United States (accounting for 54 per cent), followed by Costa Rica (with 20 per cent). In the case of remittances from the United States, the monthly average is US$205 per sender. Foreign direct investment (FDI) also continued to play an important role in foreign-exchange inflows to Nicaragua. At the end of 2014 net FDI inflows were expected by ECLAC to total US$780 million (compared with US$850 million in 2013). These resources were directed primarily at the energy, free zone and construction sectors. The principal incentives continued to be public safety, favourable free zone conditions and wage competitiveness compared with elsewhere in the region.

The IMF: (more) Macro-Development

In its May 2014 assessment of the Nicaraguan economy, the International Monetary Fund (IMF) noted that during the previous few years, Nicaragua's economy had grown at relatively high rates and macro-economic stability had strengthened. In 2013, the real growth of GDP was 4.6 per cent and inflation was 5.7 per cent. In spite of a slowdown in tax revenue collections, the consolidated public sector deficit after grants was in line with the budget (1.4 per cent of GDP) and the public debt ratio had declined. At the same time, the external current account deficit, while large, narrowed and the coverage of gross international reserves remained stable at 3.7 months of imports (excluding imports of export processing zones). In 2013, growth in private sector credit remained elevated (at 20 per cent) while the capitalisation of the banking system remained above the regulatory requirements.

In the view of the IMF, Nicaragua's economic outlook remained favourable. For 2014, the IMF projected GDP growth of 4.3 per cent, inflation of about 7 per cent and a public sector deficit below 2 per cent of GDP. Private sector credit growth was expected to decline to levels consistent with the growth in the deposits of commercial banks. The external current account deficit was likely to increase somewhat, but the coverage of gross international reserves was expected to remain stable. The main risks to these projections stemmed from potential changes to the external environment, such as a result of a slowdown in global economic activity or changes in the availability of external financing.

The IMF stressed that to maintain this favourable economic outlook it would be necessary to strengthen further public finances, continue modernising the functioning of the financial system and implementing additional improvements to the electricity generation matrix. The fiscal outlook had strengthened as a result of the parametric changes introduced to the pension system. In the view of the IMF, improvements in public finance management could be achieved through rationalising public spending and improving the presentation of fiscal and quasi-fiscal operations in conformity with international standards. In addition, the financial system would benefit from a strengthening of the payments system, the development of the domestic bond market and further enhancements in monetary and inter-bank operations.

Social failures

The Nicaraguan government claims that Nicaragua was advancing on a broad front, which included the population's social development, were subject to doubt. Nicaragua's 6.1 million population continued to be the second poorest in the Americas, after Haiti. Half of its two million school-aged children lived in poverty, according to the United Nations Educational, Scientific and Cultural

Organisation (UNESCO). Depressingly, the United Nations' children's agency, Unicef, estimated that half a million Nicaraguan children aged between three to 17 were not in the educational system at all. A national child labour survey, published in 2005, reported almost 240,000 child workers aged between five and 17.

Despite this bleak picture, Nicaraguan officials had informed the Inter America Commission of Human Rights (IACHR/CIDH), that the ending of child labour was somehow a governmental priority. In 2014 Nicaragua had also signed up to the International Labour Organisation's (ILO) 'road map', which sought to eradicate the 'worst forms' of child labour by 2016 and all child labour by 2020. Despite the government's professed good intentions, Nicaragua was the last country in the region to sign up. A report by the London based British Broadcasting Corporation (BBC) concluded that the government's claims that it was reducing child labour were not supported by any published evidence. On the contrary, businesses estimated that there were between 250,000 and 320,000 child workers in Nicaragua, one third aged less than 14. Nicaraguan law allowed children to begin working at 14, among the youngest in the region, but not in hazardous environments like sugar cane, mines or quarries.

According to the ILO, in Nicaragua children were only obliged to attend school until 12. Only 72 per cent of children finished primary school in 2009 and only 65 per cent of children from the poorest 20 per cent of families completed primary school, compared to 98 per cent from the richer homes. Scope for improvement.

Risk assessment

Economy	Fair/good
Politics	Fair
Regional stability	Good

COUNTRY PROFILE

1821 The Central American provinces (Costa Rica, Guatemala, Honduras, Nicaragua and El Salvador) declared independence from Spain.
1822 Central American provinces annexed themselves to the Mexican Empire, under General Agustín de Iturbde, later Emporer Agustín I.
1823 Agustín I was overthrown and Mexico became a republic. The Central American states formed the United Provinces of Central America.
1825 Costa Rica, Guatemala, Honduras, Nicaragua and El Salvador formed the Central American Federation (CAF).
1838 The CAF was dissolved and Nicaragua became a fully independent republic.
1856–57 Nicaragua was ruled by a US buccaneer, William Walker, who proclaimed himself president and was overthrown in 1857 following intervention by a Central American coalition.
1860 British ceded control over the Caribbean coast to Nicaragua.
1893 General José Santos Zelaya, a liberal, seized power and established a dictatorship.
1909 Zelaya was driven from office following a US-backed coup. Nicaragua allowed the US to run its customs and excise (raising money to pay the foreign debt), the national bank and the railway.
1912–25 The US established a number of military bases.
1929–33 Guerrillas led by Augusto César Sandino campaigned against the US military presence.
1934 Sandino was assassinated on the orders of the National Guard commander, General Anastasio 'Tacho' Somoza García. The US marines left with Somoza in power as a puppet dictator.
1956 General Somoza was assassinated; his son, Luis Somoza Debayle became president
1961 The Frente Sandinista de Liberación Nacional (FSLN) (Sandinista National Liberation Front) was founded. The Central American Common Market (CACM) was formed, comprising Nicaragua, Costa Rica, El Salvador, Honduras and Guatemala.
1967 Anastasio Somoza Debayle was officially elected president, succeeding his brother Luis.
1969 CACM collapsed following the 'soccer war' between El Salvador and Honduras.
1978 Prominent opposition leader and editor of *La Prensa* newspaper, Pedro Joaquín Chamorro was assassinated, leading to a general strike and consolidation within the opposition.
1979 The Somoza dynasty was overthrown by a cross-party junta, known as the Junta de Gobierno de Reconstrucción Nacional (Junta of National Reconstruction) led by the FSLN under Daniel Ortega. The new government seized land and private businesses owned by Somoza and his allies, who had fled the country.
1981 The US broke off diplomatic links with Nicaragua claiming it was part of a communist 'evil empire'. A number of opposition leaders fled to Costa Rica and Honduras where they established guerrilla groups known as counter-revolutionaries or Contras.
1982 The US began the Contra war against Nicaragua, arming Contra supporters of the former Somoza regime and using bases in Honduras.
1984 Daniel Ortega, leader of the nine ruling *comandantes*, was elected president (the only opposition candidate withdrew). The US mined Nicaragua's harbours. Nicaragua began legal action against the US in the World Court for violating international law.
1986 The Nicaraguan government closed *La Prensa* after it began receiving funds from the CIA. The US was found to have given aid to the Contras, funded by arms sales from the US to Iran in what became known as the Iran-Contra Affair. The World Court found the US guilty of violating international law and ordered reparations. The US ignored the judgement.
1988 The government and the Contras agreed a cease-fire.
1990 The US-backed Unión Nacional Opositora (UNO) assumed office after elections in which it defeated the FSLN. The presidential opposition candidate, Violeta Chamorro, wife of the founding publisher of *La Prensa*, won presidential elections.
1994 Following defections from the UNO coalition, the *de facto* ruling coalition became a centrist block in alliance with the FSLN.
1997 President Alemán's right-wing Alianza Liberal Nicaragüense (ALN) (Nicaraguan Liberal Alliance), dominated by the Partido Liberal Constitucionalista (PLC) (Constitutionalist Liberal Party), became the largest single group in the National Assembly.
1998 Hurricane Mitch devastated large parts of Nicaragua.
1999 The FSLN and the AL entered into a pact in order to force through controversial laws that worked against the emergence of a 'third force' in Nicaraguan politics.
2000 The FSLN made significant gains in the municipal elections, winning the major cities including the capital, Managua.
2001 PLC and Enrique Bolaños (PLC) won office.
2003 The FSLN re-elected Daniel Ortega as party leader.
2004 Over 70 per cent of Nicaragua's debt to the World Bank was waived. An agreement was reached with Russia to cancel Nicaragua's huge debt with the former Soviet Union.
2005 Violent street protests erupted following fuel price rises. The government and an alliance of opposition parties in Congress began a power struggle over constitutional reforms but later agreed to delay reforms. The eighth national census recorded a population of 4,357,099.
2006 Daniel Ortega was elected president and the FSLN won 38 of the 90 seats in parliamentary elections. Tough laws that banned legal abortions, including

those for women whose lives were at risk, were approved.
2007 Ortega was inaugurated as president. After eight years of conflict, the International Court of Justice (ICJ) ruled on a new maritime boundary between Honduras and Nicaragua which resulted in both countries having equal access to the rich fishing grounds and oil and gas exploration waters in the area.
2008 Nicaragua recognised the independence of Abkhazia and South Ossetia and agreed with Russia's position of support, while criticising Georgia for its attempts to regain control of its breakaway regions.
2009 Ousted president of Honduras, Manuel Zelaya, was forced to land in Managua following an abortive attempt to return home. Japan donated US$7.5 million for projects including road improvements. The Supreme Court amended the constitution to allow consecutive presidential terms in office.
2010 Daniel Ortega's way to a third term in office was cleared when a ruling by magistrates that over-turned the ban on re-elections was upheld by the Supreme Court. This was despite the fact that he had failed to persuade the national assembly to repeal the constitutional limit of two non-consecutive terms.
2011 A border dispute that had flared in 2010 when Costa Rica complained to the ICJ that Nicaragua had sent troops and engineers illegally into its territory to dredge part of the San Juan River was dampened following a court ruling in March that each country must remove their troops from the disputed river border. Both sides welcomed the ruling. In parliamentary and presidential elections held on 6 November, the ruling party FSLN won 60.93 per cent of the vote and its leader Daniel Ortega won 62.45 per cent.
2012 Tomás Borge, the last surviving founder to the Sandinista (FSLN) movement died on 30 April, aged 81 years. On 5 September the San Cristóbal Volcano erupted; 3,000 people were evacuated from the surrounding areas. On 19 November, the ICJ rejected Nicaragua's claim to ownership of a group of disputed islets in the Caribbean and awarded them to Colombia. However, the maritime border was redrawn and more sea (and its fishing grounds) was awarded to Nicaragua. President Ortega welcomed the decision.
2013 In August President Ortega announced the government had allocated blocks for exploration in the search for oil and gas in the territories demarcated as Nicaraguan in 2012. Initial drilling, by Noble Energy of the US, is expected to take place about 168km offshore. In September Nicaragua asked the court to rule on the exact boundaries agreed in 2012.
2014 On 29 January the National Assembly approved changes to the constitution to allow President Ortega to run for a third successive term in 2016. The changes remove limits to the number of terms Nicaraguan presidents can serve.
2015 In October it emerged that Wang Jing, the Chinese telecoms tycoon involved in the US$50 billion 'Gran Canal de Nicaragua' project had lost some 85 per cent of his US$10.2 billion fortune on the Chinese stock market crisis. Analysts reported that this could affect his HKND company's participation in the giant project.

Political structure

In addition to their unicameral national parliaments, El Salvador, Guatemala, Honduras, Nicaragua, Panama and Dominican Republic also return directly-elected deputies to the supranational Central American Parliament.

Constitution

The National Assembly approved constitutional reforms in January 2000 which provide outgoing presidents and vice presidents with a lifelong seat in the legislature. Other constitutional reforms included a reduction of the percentage of votes required to elect a president without the need for a run-off election, from 45 per cent to 35 per cent of the total, and the restructuring of the judiciary, the electoral authorities and the comptroller general's office, giving the two main parties a bigger share of the posts.
On 29 January 2014, constitutional changes were approved by the Nicaraguan National Assembly that scraps limits to the number of terms Nicaraguan presidents can serve. In essence, Daniel Ortega will be able to run for a third successive term in 2016.
The country comprises 16 departments which are divided into two zones: the Pacific zone and the Atlantic zone.
The minimum voting age is 16 years.

Form of state

Presidential democratic republic

The executive

Power is vested in the president who is Head of State and commander-in-chief of the armed forces, elected for a period of five years by simple majority popular vote (for unlimited terms). The president appoints a cabinet of ministers.

National legislature

The unicameral Asamblea Nacional (National Assembly) has 92 seats of which 70 members in multi-seat constituencies and 20 members in a single nationwide constituency are directly elected by proportional representation vote, the two remaining seats are reserved for the previous president and the runner-up candidate in the previous presidential election. Members serve five-year terms.

Legal system

The Nicaraguan legal system comprises civil and military courts. The highest court is the Supreme Court, which administers the judicial system and nominates all appellate and lower court judges. The Supreme Court consists of 12 magistrates elected for seven-year terms by the National Assembly.

Last elections

November 6 2011 (presidential and parliamentary)
Results: Parliamentary: Frente Sandinista de Liberación Nacional (FSLN) (Sandinista National Liberation Front) won 60.9 per cent of the vote (63 seats out of 92), Partido Liberal Independiente (PLI) (Independent Liberal Party) 31.6 per cent (27), Partido Liberal Constitucionalista (PLC) (Constitutionalist Liberal Party) 6.4 per cent (2); two other parties each won less than 1 per cent of the vote and failed to gain any seats.
Presidential (results as of 6 November 2011): Daniel Ortega (FSLN) won 62.5 per cent, Fabio Gadea (PLI) 31 per cent, Arnoldo Alemán (PLC) 5.9 per cent. The remaining two presidential candidates each won less than 0.5 per cent of the vote.

Next elections

November 2016 (presidential and parliamentary)

Political parties

Ruling party

Frente Sandinista de Liberación Nacional (FSLN) (Sandinista National Liberation Front) (from 2007; re-elected 6 Nov 2011)

Main opposition party

Partido Liberal Independiente (PLI) (Independent Liberal Party)

Population

6.22 million (2014)* Some 65 per cent of the total population is under 25 years.
Last census: 25 April 2005: 4,357,099
Population density: 41 inhabitants per square km. Urban population 57 per cent (2010 Unicef).
Annual growth rate: 1.7 per cent, 1990–2010 (Unicef).

Ethnic make-up

Mestizo (mixed indigenous-European) (69 per cent), European (17 per cent), black (9 per cent) and indigenous people (5 per cent).
Creole and Indian peoples live in the eastern region of the country on the Atlantic coast. The Creoles number some 26,000, the Miskitos 182,000 and the Sumus 9,000. There are also two very

small indigenous groups – the Ramas and the Garifunos.

Religions

The majority of the population is Catholic, although mainstream Protestant and evangelical groups make up 20 per cent of the population. The majority of the Atlantic coast population is Moravian. There is no official religion.

Education

Nicaragua has been slowly moving towards universal primary enrolment despite severe setbacks resulting from Hurricane Mitch in 1998.

Primary education is free for six years although a report issued by the Nicaraguan Office of the Advocate for Children and Youth revealed that 80 per cent of children in primary and secondary state schools were required to pay a minimum fee per month, including voluntary contributions to teachers' salaries and payments for examinations, in violation of the constitutional right to free education for children.

Secondary education runs in two cycles of three and two years and leads to higher education, or in a cycle of two and three years leading to a technical qualification.

There are both state universities and private universities. The Consejo Nacional de Universidades is responsible for all higher education planning. Nicaragua's major institutions of higher education are the Jesuit-run Central American University, Managua (UCA), the public National Autonomous Universities in Managua and León (Unan) and the private, Harvard-affiliated Central American Institute of Business Administration (Incae) outside Managua.

Spending on primary education amounts to less than US$10 per capita.

Literacy rate: 77 per cent adult rate; 86 per cent youth rate (15–24) (Unesco 2005).

Compulsory years: 6 to 12.

Enrolment rate: 102 per cent gross primary enrolment of the relevant age group (including repeaters); 55 per cent gross secondary enrolment (World Bank).

Pupils per teacher: 36 in primary schools.

Health

Although public health improved during the 1990s, access to medical facilities continues to be uneven and many of the country's poor, particularly in rural areas and on the Atlantic coast, are experiencing inadequate healthcare due to government cutbacks in 2002/03. A growing market of private services exists, but the ministry of health continues to be the main provider of services for the Nicaraguan population as a whole.

Government spending emphasises primary healthcare with priority given to improving local healthcare systems, through national, departmental, regional and municipal co-ordination. The World Bank's International Development Association (IDA) funded the rehabilitation of healthcare centres, nutrition centres for children, and schools for training nurses and other healthcare workers, and the provision of social services.

HIV/Aids

HIV prevalence: 0.2 per cent aged 15–49 in 2003 (World Bank)

Life expectancy: 69 years, 2004 (WHO 2006)

Fertility rate/Maternal mortality rate: 2.6 births per woman, 2010 (Unicef); maternal mortality 150 per 100,000 live births (World Bank).

Child (under 5 years) mortality rate (per 1,000): 24 per 1,000 live births (WHO 2012); 12.2 per cent of children under aged five are malnourished (World Bank).

Head of population per physician: 0.37 physicians per 1,000 people, 2003 (WHO 2006)

Welfare

Under the presidency of Arnoldo Alemán (1997—2001), welfare expenditure was squeezed as a result of the government's IMF-dictated austerity measures and high levels of debt servicing. Funds for social protection remain decentralised and the responsibility for resource management lies with local authorities. There are no clear regulations about the amount of money that can be allocated or is necessary for the municipalities. An increasing number of self-employed people do not have access to social protection mechanisms.

Nicaragua's welfare programme combines a traditional cash transfer programme with financial incentives for families to obtain preventive healthcare and education and to participate in other government-sponsored welfare-related programmes.

In 2001, the government initiated a welfare reform programme under the auspices of a three-year Poverty Reduction and Growth Facility (PRGF) arrangement with the IMF. Pension reform is central to the structural adjustment programme. A pension system of privately managed individual accounts was introduced in the last quarter of 2001. Under the pension reform, the country changed from a pay-as-you-go pension system to a defined contribution system in which contributions are safeguarded. The reform was designed to contain the fiscal deficit created by the previous system, broaden the base of contributors and contribute to the development of domestic financial markets.

The Nicaraguan Institute for Social Security and Welfare (INSSBI) operates nursing homes for the elderly and rehabilitation centres for the physically and mentally handicapped, for prostitutes, drug addicts and alcoholics.

Main cities

Managua (capital, estimated population 928,621 in 2012), León (147,199), Estelí (102,851), Tipitapa (98,453), Matagalpa (96,090), Masaya (92,745), Chinandega (92,222), Granada (93,042).

Languages spoken

Some business people speak English. In the Bluefields (Atlantic) region, English is particularly widely spoken.

Many names of towns, medicines, foods, flora and fauna are in the Nahuate language.

On the Atlantic Coast, Indian towns and ethnic communities still preserve their language and cultural traditions. Autonomous law guarantees bilingual education in the Miskito, Creole, English, Sumus, Ramas and Garifuna dialects.

Official language/s

Spanish

Media

The constitution guarantees freedom of speech and there is no censorship.

Press

Dailies: In Spanish, the handful of newspapers include *La Prensa* (www-usa.laprensa.com.ni), which is conservative in tone, *El Nuevo Diario* (www.elnuevodiario.com.ni) a left-wing pro-Sandinista publication, *Bolsa de Noticias* (www.grupoese.com.ni) *Trinchera de la Noticia* (www.trinchera.com.ni) and the independent *Semanario Hoy* (www.semanahoydigital.com)

Weeklies: In Spanish, *Confidencial* (www.confidencial.com.ni) gives political analysis, *Semana Cómica* is a left-wing satirical magazine, *7 Días* (www.7dias.com.ni) is a family publication. In English, the bi-weekly *The Nicaraguan Post* (www.nicaraguanpost.com) covers general interest and news.

Business: The monthly *El Observador Economico* (www.elobservadoreconomico.com) is a magazine with a comprehensive review of national and international financial news.

Periodicals: In Spanish, the quarterly *El Pez y la Serviente* (www.elpezylaserpiente.com.ni) reviews culture, monthly magazines include *Envio*, the left-wing *Pensamiento Propio*, and the bi-monthly, *Crítica* and *La Avispa* are pro-Sandinista publications.

Broadcasting
Television and particularly radio are popular source of news and information.
Radio: Radio is an important source of news and information and has been the target of opposing forces at times of unrest.
There are over 100 radio stations, most of which are located around the capital. The government-owned Radio Nicaragua (www.radionicaragua.com.ni) is a national service. Other, private, commercial stations include Radio La Primerisima (www.radiolaprimerisima.com), Radio Corporación (www.radio-corporacion.com) and Radio Sandino (www.lasandino.net) a news channel.
Television: There are over 10 national television stations and about the same number of local stations, most of which are private and commercial. Larger stations include Televicentro (www.canal2tv.com), Canal 10 (www.canal10nicaragua.com) Nicavisión and CDNN 23.
Other news agencies: Prensa Latina: www.plenglish.com

Economy
The Nicaraguan economy is one of the weakest and least competitive in the Americas (second only to Haiti), but has the potential for improvement based on its natural resources of geothermal power, gold, timber and other agricultural products. The country is stable but underdeveloped and Nicaragua remains plagued by poverty.
In 2014, the UN Human Development Index (HDI) ranked Nicaragua 132 (out of 187) for development in health, education and income.
The Nicaraguan economy continues to register relatively high growth rates in the context of macroeconomic stability. In 2014, real GDP grew by 4.5 percent, while inflation was 6.5 percent. For 2015, real GDP is projected to grow by 4.6 percent, while inflation is expected to decline to 6 percent.
Since 2000, Nicaragua's progress has improved but has not matched the growth of other countries in Latin America and the Caribbean. In 2010, 45.7 per cent of the population experienced at least one indicator of poverty, while 15.8 per cent lived on less than the equivalent of US$1.25 per day; the headcount poverty rate was 28 per cent of the population (2000–10).
Around 20 per cent of the population live and work abroad sending home remittances, which amounted to US$1,140,200,000 in 2014. This amount has been steadily increasing year on year; remittances totalled US$913,600,000 in 2011 and US$1,081,300,000 in 2013.
Nicaragua is in need of foreign direct investment (FDI), which by 2014 reached US$840 million (a rise from the US$815.5 million in 2013). FDI is hindered predominantly because of its history of military dictatorships replaced by a Communist government and followed by a civil war, plus a series of natural disasters and poor prices for its main commodity exports, particularly coffee. In 2008 Iran began investing in Nicaragua, funding among other projects the US$230 million Bodoke hydroelectric dam in Jinotega Province, a farm equipment assembly plant and two piers in the Pacific port of Corinto. In exchange Nicaragua exports coffee, meat and bananas to Iran. In 2010 the construction of the US$697 million, 220MW, Tumarin hydroelectric power plant was, initiated. As of yet (2015), the project is still under appraisal.

External trade
Nicaragua is a member of the Central America Free Trade Agreement (Cafta-DR), which includes the Dominican Republic, Costa Rica, El Salvador, Guatemala and the US; it is working to remove all tariffs and barriers between members by 2024. It is also a member of the Central American Common Market (CACM), along with El Salvador, Guatemala and Honduras, which has removed duties on most products between members and unified external tariffs.
The Grand Inter-Oceanic Canal, An audacious US$50 billion plan to cross Central America and challenge the Panama Canal, threatens the livelihood of Nicaragua as a trading route. There are still many doubts that this project will ever be completed however.
The US is Nicaragua's largest trading partner, accounting for just under a fifth of the country's imports and receiving some 50 per cent of its exports. As Nicaragua has developed its manufacturing base, imports of services, intermediate goods and capital goods have all risen, while imports of consumer goods have diminished.
Imports
Principal imports include petroleum, consumer goods, machinery and equipment and raw materials.
Main sources: US (16.2 per cent of total in 2014), Venezuela (15.9 per cent), Mexico (13.6 per cent), China (9.1 per cent), Guatemala (8.2 per cent) and Costa Rica (8 per cent).
Exports
Principal exports include coffee, beef, gold, sugar, peanuts, shrimp and lobster, tobacco, cigars, automobile wiring harnesses, textiles, apparel and cotton.
Main destinations: US (52.3 per cent total in 2014), Mexico (11.8 per cent), Venezuela (6.8 per cent) and Canada (5.9 per cent).

Agriculture
Farming
Agriculture plays a very significant role in the economy of Nicaragua, contributing about a quarter of the country's total GDP. The sector also employs up to 30 per cent of the total workforce.
The principal export crop is coffee, which represents around a fifth of total export earnings. Meat, cotton, bananas and sugar are the other main agricultural exports. Maize, rice, beans and sorghum are also grown. Timber, tobacco, sugar cane and rubber are geared towards Nicaragua's agro-industrial sector.
The Nicaraguan government is actively engaged in the agricultural sector although it is estimated that upwards of 60 per cent of cultivated land is in the hands of private smallholders. Despite continuous agrarian reform, food production has not kept up with demand owing mainly to poor weather, war damage and shortages of vital inputs.
Fishing
Nicaragua's typical annual fish catch is over 28,000mt, 16,500mt of which is shellfish. The main seafood exports are shellfish, particularly shrimp and lobster. Offshore fishing consists mainly of tuna, bass and mackerel. The government follows an export subsidy policy, providing tax rebates on every kilogramme of trawled shrimp and farmed shrimp exported.
Forestry
Some 3.2 million hectares (ha) of Nicaragua is covered by forests and woodland, which amounts to 60 per cent of the country's total landmass. Nicaragua has some of the largest humid tropical rainforests concentrated in the north and east, in the Caribbean lowlands. Forests are principally in the southern Atlantic coastal region. Species include pine, cedar and other hardwoods covering four million hectares. The government is keen to develop plans for self-sustaining exploitation of the forests. The Food and Agriculture Organisation (FAO) has estimated timber reserves at 33 million cubic metres.
The forestry industry thrives on sawnwood production, most of which is exported. Nicaragua imports moderate quantities of paper and wood-based panels. Most of the forest wood is used for fuel consumption.

Industry and manufacturing
Industrial Production in Nicaragua increased by 15.40 per cent in July 2014 over the same month in the previous year. Industrial Production growth in Nicaragua

averaged 4.30 percent from 1995 until 2014, reaching an all-time high of 41.30 percent in March of 2014 and a record low of -24 percent in August of 1997.

During the 1980s the national government of Nicaragua launched an unsuccessful policy of industrial development, premised on the promotion of joint public and-private enterprises, in a bid to provide basic consumer goods at prices accessible to most people.

Unfortunately, one unforeseen consequence of this policy was the lowering of economic efficiency as a result of subsidies on state-produced goods. By the end of the decade, many private producers had been forced to close their factories, sell out to the state or scale down activities.

However, there has been significant growth in the non-traditional *maquiladora* (assembly line) sector, which has made use of the Free Trade Zones (FTZs). Concentrated mainly on textiles, particularly clothing for the US market, the *maquiladora* sector has rapidly become a major sub-sector in Nicaraguan industry. Low labour costs and minimal labour regulation has made it both an attractive opportunity for foreign investors and a target for trade unions and labour rights activists.

Its strategic geographic location at the center of the Americas and preferential access to the world's most important markets, has made Nicaragua an ideal exporting platform.

The most important projects undertaken in recent years have reflected a renewed priority placed on large-scale agro-industrial production, which had been neglected by the government in the early 1990s. The two biggest projects carried out have been the Timal sugar refinery and the Sebaco food processing complex. The Timal sugar refinery, located north of Managua in the Tipitapa-Malacatoya lowlands, cost US$200 million and was financed through loans and donations from a consortium of 14 countries, including Cuba, France, Spain and Canada, as well as from the Central American Bank for Economic Integration (CABEI). The refinery was designed by Cuban engineers and is capable of producing 7.55 tonnes of refined sugar daily. It also produces energy from the sugar cane refuse. The Sebaco food processing complex is engaged in canning, dehydration and frozen food processing for export markets. A new industrial free zone law was approved by Congress in the mid-1990s, with a total area of 48,000 square km (30,000 square miles).

Investment in Nicaragua's fledgling manufacturing sector is crucial to ensure that the structural reforms needed to make the sector more competitive and efficient are carried out. In the past, investment resources were often diverted to the defence sector, while factories closed as result of non-availability of replacement parts and basic inputs. At the moment, most of Nicaragua's income derives from remittances.

Tourism

Nicaragua has lush interior rainforests (including Bosawas, the largest rainforest in Nicaragua, north of the Amazon) with rich biodiversity that are marketed for their ecotourism potential. Other, successful tourist destinations include rural communities that offer a chance to visit coffee farms (the major export commodity).

There are also a number of volcanoes to visit with outdoor activities including sand skiing or surfing.

The cultural and historic sites of León Viejo, the oldest Spanish colonial settlements in the Americas, and the León Cathedral are both included on Unesco's World Heritage List.

The travel and tourism sector accounted for 9.9 per cent of GDP in 2014, and is forecast to rise by 2.9 per cent in 2015. The total contribution to employment was 212,000 jobs in the same year.

Travel and tourism investment in 2014 was 3.2 per cent of total investment. It is forecast to increase by around 4.1 per cent per annum over the next ten years.

Environment

The deforestation and cultivation of marginal lands in Nicaragua contributed to the mudslides after Hurricane Mitch hit the country in late 1998, while flooding was made worse due to a lack of watershed management.

Mining

Nicaragua is endowed with deposits of both gold and silver. The country also has mineral deposits, including copper, zinc, platinum, iron, magnesium, chrome, titanium, tungsten, lead, cadmium, bismuth, bentonite, marble, clay, masonry stone, limestone and gypsum.

Gold and silver are mined intensively in Siuna and Bonanza, inland from the northern Atlantic coast region. More modest mining activity takes place in Chontales and Nueva Segovia. Geological studies of the region have identified the existence of a reserve of gold in the area of La Libertad, which could have a productive lifetime of 70 years. The reserves are estimated at 3.8 million ounces of gold and 4.9 million ounces of silver.

All natural resources are state property and exploitation rights are leased on a long-term basis. Since huge portions of the central areas of Nicaragua's mineral reserves have already been leased, the scope for investment remains limited. The decline in global gold prices has affected the fortunes of foreign companies and the value of exports have, consequently diminished.

The Toronto-based Black Hawk international mining and exploration company owns the El Limon mine through its 95 per cent-owned subsidiary Triton Minera SA. The mine, located 140km north of Managua, has been in continuous production for more than 50 years, gaining from both open pit and underground operations. Mill capacity is 1,000 tonnes per day and gold recoveries exceed 80 per cent.

Mining has become one of the country's most dynamic economic sectors. Gold exports alone totaled US$436 million in 2013. In 2014, Nicaragua produced 205 600 oz of gold and 254 860 oz of silver. With a territorial reach of more than 130 000 km, Nicaragua is a country with vast natural resources. It offers more than 34 868 km of potential for mining activities.

Hydrocarbons

Oil consumption in 2013 was 34,000 barrels per day (bpd), all of which was imported, primarily from Mexico and Venezuela under the San José pact. Refinery capacity was 20,000bpd. Under a previous administration, Petronic contracted all rights to downstream facilities to the Swiss oil company Glencore in exchange for annual royalties.

There are no proven natural gas reserves and use of gas is negligible. An existing gas pipeline from Mexico to Guatemala could be extended to Nicaragua as part of a wider Central American gas pipeline network. There is also the possibility of a pipeline from Colombia's northern offshore fields to Panama with connections to Nicaragua, but no plans have been formally agreed.

Coal is not produced and any amounts imported and consumed are commercially negligible.

The companies Statoil and Petronic won four contracts for exploration and exploitation of oil in a total area of 16 thousand square kilometers in the Nicaraguan Pacific in 2015. Costa Rica, however, noted that the signing of a contract to explore for hydrocarbons was made on disputed maritime areas.

Energy

Total installed generating capacity was 648MW in 2007, producing over 3.0 billion kilowatt hours (kWh). Consumption was 2.41 billion kWh and the excess generation was exported.

A major objective of the government remains the electrification of rural areas. A World Bank loan helped to fund the National Rural Electrification Program, which

aims at bringing electric power to 90 per cent of rural areas by 2012.
The energy mix includes two hydroelectric plants, one geothermal plant, two diesel plants and five thermoelectric plants. The country will need to increase generating capacity to satisfy its 6 per cent annual growth and a new US$350 million, 180MW Tumarín hydroelectric power station was awaiting approval by the national assembly in June 2009.
The Empresa Nicaragüense de Electricidad (Enel) (Nicaraguan Electricity Company) is responsible for generation and distribution of electricity, while the Empresa Nacional de Transmisión Eléctrica (Entresa) (National Electric Transmission Company) is responsible for transmission.

Financial markets

Stock exchange

Bolsa de Valores de Nicaragua (BVDN) (Stock Exchange of Nicaragua)

Banking and insurance

In recent years the banking and financial services sector of Nicaragua has undergone a degree of stabilisation, which in turn has resulted in increasing deposit levels. However, the sector still remains fragile and vocal critics have accused the regulatory authorities of failing to tackle the state banking system's overdue debt which has contributed to a feeling of pessimism in some quarters.
Moreover, the government's bail-out of the country's third largest bank – Interbank – in 2000 amid reports of widespread corruption did nothing to reassure foreign investors and donors of the legitimacy of the country's banking system. The failure of the Banco Nicaraguense de Industria y Comercio (Banic) to resolve its debt led to another government intervention in the banking sector in August 2001. Banic's assets and liabilities were subsequently auctioned off to Banpro, which had already absorbed Interbank in October 2000.
The chaos in the banking sector led to a shake-up of the regulatory system. In 2003, the government introduced a new, rigorous framework to bring the legal framework in line with the Basel Core Principles.
Although foreign banks were permitted to remain in Nicaragua when the banking system was nationalised in 1979, they were no longer permitted to accept local deposits. The branches of US, British and Canadian commercial banks continue to operate non-deposit business.

Central bank

Banco Central de Nicaragua (BCN)

Main financial centre

Managua

Time

GMT minus six hours

Geography

Nicaragua is in the central American isthmus, with the Pacific Ocean to the west and the Caribbean Sea to the east. Honduras is to the north and Costa Rica to the south. The Pacific plateau is noted for its rich lands, and is where the larger farms which grow crops for export are to be found, particularly in the northern area of Chinandega. The Atlantic plateau, occupying fully half of the national territory, is largely pasture savannah; small gold and silver mines are also found in this area. The lands along the Rio Coco (forming the border with Honduras) are a rich banana-growing area, and are worked largely by the Miskito Indians. Tropical rainforest predominates in the southern Atlantic coast adjacent to Costa Rica. Corn Island, in the Caribbean Sea, is home to a fishing community.

Hemisphere

Northern

Climate

Nicaragua has a semi-tropical climate; the hottest month is May (27–32 degrees Celsius (C) in Managua) and the coldest is January (23–30 degrees C in Managua). Temperatures may be up to 10 degrees C lower in the mountain range that runs the length of the country. The rainy season (May–December) is referred to as 'winter'; and the dry season (December–April) as 'summer'.

Dress codes

On the most formal of occasions Nicaraguan men traditionally wear the Caribbean-style *guayabera*, in white, although an increasing number of men today prefer to wear a suit and tie.

Entry requirements

Passports

Required by all and must be valid for at least six months from the date of entry, with onward/return tickets and proof of sufficient funds for length of stay.
Passports and entry cards must be carried at all times.

Visa

Most visitors may not need a visa; contact the nearest Nicaraguan consulate for details of requirements. Many visitors may visit with a tourist card that is issued on arrival, for a fee of US$10, paid in US dollars for either up to 30 or 90 days. A valid entry stamp is necessary to exit the country, therefore any extension must be applied for locally; failure to do so will result in a fine.
Visitors who are admitted using a tourist card for business trips must provide a letter of introduction from their employer or an invitation from a Nicaraguan company.

Currency advice/regulations

The import and export of local and foreign currency is unlimited, but amounts over the equivalent of US$10,000 must be declared.

Customs

Personal items, including cameras, personal music players and laptop computers to the value of US$500 are duty-free.

Prohibited imports

Fresh and canned meat and diary products. Firearms require a licence.
The export of archaeological artefacts and gold are prohibited.

Health (for visitors)

Mandatory precautions

Yellow fever vaccination certificate if arriving within six months from an infected area.

Advisable precautions

Inoculations and booster should be current for tetanus, hepatitis A and typhoid. There may be a need for vaccinations for diphtheria, tuberculosis, hepatitis B. Use malaria prophylaxis if travelling outside urban areas. Malaria, hepatitis B and dengue fever are caused by mosquitoes, precautions including mosquito repellents, nets and clothing covering the body after dark should be used. There is a risk of rabies in rural areas.
There is a shortage of routine medications and visitors should take all necessary medicines with them. A first aid kit that includes disposable syringes, is a reasonable precaution. Outside the main hoteld use only bottled or boiled water for drinks, washing teeth and making ice. Eat only well cooked meals, preferably served hot; vegetables should be cooked and fruit peeled. Dairy products are unpasteurised and should be avoided, unless cooked. Healthcare is not to Western standards and medical insurance, including emergency evacuation, is necessary.

Hotels

Availability is limited but there are a few good hotels in Managua, the main coastal towns and along the Pan-American Highway. Bills are subject to 15 per cent sales tax, and must usually be paid in dollars. A 10 per cent tip is usual.

Credit cards

International credit and debit cards are accepted in banks in large towns.

Public holidays (national)

Fixed dates

1 Jan (New Year's Day), 1 May (Labour Day), 19 Jul (Liberation Day), 14 Sep (Battle of Jacinto), 15 Sep (Independence Day), 25 Dec (Christmas Day).

Variable dates

Maundy Thursday, Good Friday.

Working hours

Banking

Mon–Fri: 0830–1830; Sat: 0830–1230. Some banks close may close for an hour at lunch time.

Business

Mon–Fri: 0800–1700; Sat: 0800–1300.

Government

Mon–Fri: 0800–1700.

Telecommunications

Mobile/cell phones

There are GSM 1900 services available in most west-coast cities and a few east coast urban areas. A GSM 850 service is planned.

Electricity supply

110V AC, 60 cycles

Social customs/useful tips

It is helpful to know something of the political background and affiliations of those you are meeting.

Men and women shake hands in Nicaragua and social kisses on one cheek are also exchanged. The use of titles, such as Doctor, Arquitecto, Licenciado, Profesora, is widespread and it is courteous to learn and use the correct titles for both men and women.

Do not immediately launch into a business conversation. It is considered polite to first get to know the person to whom you are talking.

A small gift for the host or hostess is always appreciated.

Late-night parties, with dinner served at 2200 or 2300, are common. Guests need not plan to arrive on time for a large social gathering as being up to two hours late is acceptable. For smaller gatherings, arrival about 30 minutes later than the specified time is considered appropriate.

Security

Nicaragua had a low rate of violent crime compared to other Central American countries and armed groups involved in the civil war were demobilised however street crime is rising and visitors are advised not to walk alone at night.

Getting there

Air

National airline: Nicaragüenses de Aviación (Nica Airlines)

International airport/s: Managua-Augusto César Sandino (MGA), 9km from city; duty-free shop, bar, restaurant, post office, shops (restricted hours in some instances), banks.

Airport tax: Departure tax: US$35 (may be included in the price of a ticket); excluding transit passengers.

Surface

Road: The Pan-American Highway is well maintained and runs from Honduras, through Managua, to Costa Rica.

Water: Shipping lines from North and South America and Europe regularly visit Nicaragua.

Main port/s: Bluefields, Corinto, Puerto Cabezas, Puerto Sandino, San Juan de Sur, Puerto Arlen Siu.

Getting about

National transport

Air: Nicaragüenses de Aviación (Nica Airlines) runs regional, passenger and cargo services.

Road: The western region is provided with most sealed roads connecting the more populated areas of the country. There is only one major road to the Caribbean side and this stops, before the coast, at Rama.

Buses: Services are regular and connect main towns served by the road system (eg Managua-Rama, Managua-León, Chinandega, Corinto), however they are not advised for foreign travellers.

Water: A boat service links Rama and Bluefields port on the Caribbean coast.

City transport

Taxis: Taxis are the best way to get around most cities; fares should be negotiated in advance of journeys and tipping is not necessary.

Buses, trams & metro: City buses are cheap but crowded.

Car hire

Foreign licences are acceptable for short stays (up to 30 days). Due to poor public transport, hired cars may often be the best way to get around in Managua. However roads are often in poor repair and need a skilled driver to avoid mishap. Drivers in accidents are always arrested even if they are insured and appear to be blameless. Licensed drivers can be hired, through local car rentals, who are familiar with local roads and conditions and, in the case of a traffic accident, will be taken into custody, in accordance with the law.

BUSINESS DIRECTORY

The addresses listed below are a selection only. While World of Information makes every endeavour to check these addresses, we cannot guarantee that changes have not been made, especially to telephone numbers and area codes. We would welcome any corrections.

Telephone area codes

The international dialling code (IDD) for Nicaragua is +505, followed by area code and subscriber's number:
León311Managua2

Chambers of Commerce

American Chamber of Commerce of Nicaragua, Centro Finarca, PO Box 2720, Managua (tel: 67-3098; fax: 67-3099; e-mail: amcham@amchamnic.org.ni).

Nicaraguan Cámara de Comercio, Rotonda Gueguense, PO Box 135, Managua (tel: 68-3505; fax: 68-3600; e-mail: comercio@ibw.com.ni).

Banking

Banco de América Central (BAC), Apdo 2304 Managua (tel: 670-220; fax: 670-224).

Banco de Crédito Centroamericano (Bancentro), Edificio Bancentro, KM. 4-1/2 Carretera Masaya (tel: 782-777; fax: 786-001).

Banco de Exportación (Banexpo), Centro Comercial Metrocentro, Managua.

Banco de la Producción (Banpro), Plaza Libertad, Contiguo a Metrocentro, Apdo 2309, Managua (tel: 782-508/783-278/784-188; fax: 784-113).

Banco de Préstamos (Banpres), Esquina Opuesta Hotel Intercontinental, Managua (tel: 23-046/223-048; fax: 23-057).

Banco Europeo de Centro América SA (BECA), Apdo 188, Managua (fax: 783-827).

Banco Mercantil, Gerente General Oscar Martín Aguado A., Plaza Banco Mercantil, Managua (tel 668-228/668-231; fax: 668-024).

Banco Nacional de Desarrollo (Banades), Apdo 328-1447, Managua (tel: 671-334; fax: 670-869).

Central bank

Banco Central de Nicaragua, Km 7 carretera sur, PO Box 2252, Managua (tel: 65-0500; fax: 65-0561; e-mail: bcn@bcn.gob.ni).

Stock exchange

Bolsa de Valores de Nicaragua (BVDN) (Stock Exchange of Nicaragua) www.bolsanic.com

Travel information

Aerolíneas Nicaragüenses (AERONICA), Contiguo Aeropuerto Internacional August C Sandino, Apdo 3688, Managua, JR (tel: 31-801).

Instituto Nicaragüense de Turismo, Avenida Bolivar Sur, Apdo 122, Managua (tel: 25-436; fax: 25-314).

Ministry of tourism

Ministry of Tourism, Residencial Bolonia, Hotel Intercontinental, 1c. al Oeste 1c. al Sur, Managua (tel: 226-610, 222-6617; fax: 226-618).

Ministries

Ministry of Agriculture and Livestock, Km 8 1/2, Carretera a Masaya, Managua (tel: 76-0200; fax: 76-0256).

Ministry of Construction and Transport, Frente Al Estadio Nacional, Managua (tel: 22-5111; fax: 22-6429).

Ministry of Economy and Development, Carretera a Masaya, Km 6 1/2 Frente a Centro Comercial Camino de Oriente, Managua (tel: 67-0161; fax: 78-4590).

Ministry of Education, Centro Cívico Camilo Ortega, Managua (tel: 65-0046; fax: 65-0715).

Ministry of the Environment and Natural Resources, Carretera Norte, Km 12 1/2, Managua (tel: 63-1343; fax: 63-2833).

Ministry of External Co-operation, Casa Ricardo Morales Aviles, Managua (tel: 28-5002; fax: 28-2026).

Ministry of Finance, Frente a la Asamblea Nacional, Managua (tel: 22-7231; fax: 78-5984).

Ministry of Foreign Affairs, Barrío Altagracia, Frente a Restaurante Los Ranchos, Managua (tel: 66-6222; fax: 66-2572).

Ministry of Health, Complejo Concepción Palacios, Managua (tel: 89-7554; fax: 89-7997).

Ministry of Industry and Commerce, Km 6, Carretera Masaya, Apdo 2412, Managua.

Ministry of the Interior, Barrio 19 de Julio, Edif Silvio Mayorga, Managua (tel: 85-005; fax: 627-910).

Ministry of Labour, Estadio Nacional, 300 vs. al Norte, Managua (tel: 28-1168; fax: 28-2028).

Ministry of the Presidency, Avenida Bolivar, Detrás de la Asamblea Nacional, Managua (tel: 78-5299; fax: 22-3448).

Ministry of Social Action, Pista de Resistencia ENEL Central, 150vs. al Sur, Managua (tel: 67-2907; fax: 67-0768).

Ministry of Tourism, Residencial Bolonia, Hotel Intercontinental, 1c. al Oeste 1c. al Sur, Managua (tel: 22-6610, 22-6617; fax: 22-6618).

Ministry of Transport and Construction, Frente al Estadio Nacional, Managua (tel: 283-698, 282-061, 225-954; fax: 282-161).

Ministry of Works, Estadio Nacional, 400 Metros Al Norte, Managua (tel: 226-002, 222-115, 226-677; fax: 622-103).

Other useful addresses

Association of Nicaraguan Producers and Exporters of Non-Traditional Products (APENN), Del Restaurante Terraza 1/2 C Al Norte (tel: 668-276, 668-279).

Bank of Central American Economic Intergration (BCIE), Edificio BCIE, 2do, piso, Plaza España, Managua (tel: 66-4120; fax: 66-4125).

British Embassy, El Reparto Los Robles 1, entrada principal de la Primera Etapa, Los Robles, Managua (tel: 780-014, 780-887, 674-050; fax: 784-085).

Central American Institute of Business Administration (INCAE), Carretera Sur Km 15 1/2, Managua.

Centre of Export and Investments, Hotel Intercontinental, 1c, abajo 3 1/2c al Sur, Managua (tel: 68-1063; fax: 66-4476; e-mail: cei@cei.lbw.com.ni).

Development Bank (BID), Carretera a Masaya, Km 4 1/2, Managua (tel: 67-0831; fax: 67-3469).

Dirección General de Promoción de Exportaciones, Km 6, Carretera a Masaya, Apdo 2412, Managua, JR.

Empresa Nicaragüense de Promoción de Exportaciones, Apdo 1449, Managua.

Exports of the Handicraft Industry, S.A., Centro de Feria la Pinata (tel: 670-358; fax: 670-192).

Institute of Local Governments, Los Arcos, Entrada principal, 20 varas al Sur, Managua (tel: 66-6050; fax: 44-4567).

Institute of National Technology, Centro Cívico, Managua (tel: 65-0049; fax: 65-1976).

Institute of Nicaraguan Insurance and Reinsurance, Carretera Sur, Km 4 1/2, Managua (tel: 68-0239; fax: 68-0265).

Institute of Nicaraguan Social Security (NSS), Semáforos del Hotel Intercontinental, 2c abajo, 1c al lago, Contiguo a Policlínica Central, Managua (tel: 22-7445; fax: 22-7454).

Institute of Statistics and Censors, Frente Hospital Lenin Fonséca, Managua (tel: 66-7663; fax: 66-7872).

International Development Agency (AID), Semáforos Centroamérica, 400 mts al Oeste, Managua (tel: 67-3909; fax: 77-0210).

Nicaraguan Electricity, Frente Entrada a Colegio Rigoberto López, Pérez, Managua (tel: 77-4159; fax: 67-1700).

Nicaraguan Centre of Technological Information (CENIT), Sandy's 11/2 C. Arriba (tel: 675-325).

Nicaraguan Canals and Irrigation Authority, Carretera Sur Km 5, Managua (tel: 66-7863; fax: 66-7872).

Nicaraguan Development Fund, AP 2598, Managua (tel: 666-077, 666-066).

Nicaraguan Embassy (USA), 1627 New Hampshire Avenue, NW, Washington DC 20009 (tel: (+1-202) 939-6531; fax: (+1-202) 939-6532; ofemb@embanic.org).

Nicaraguan Institute for Economic and Social Investigations (INIES), del Hospital Alejandro Davila Bolanas, 3 c. al Lago, Managua.

Nicaraguan Investment Fund (of Central Bank), Shell de Colonia Centroamericana, Media al Lago, Managua.

Nicaraguan Telephone Company, Residencial Villa Fontana, Edificio Ville Fontana, Managua (tel: 28-5280; fax: 28-4628).

Port Authority, Residencial Bolonia, Optica Nicaragüense, 1c al Lago, 1c abajo, Managua (tel: 66-3274; fax: 66-4622).

Superior Council of Private Enterprise (COSEP), del Restaurante Terraza, Media cuadra al lago, Managua.

UN High Commission for Relief (ACNUR), Residencial Bolonia, Contiguo a Viajes Atlantida, Managua (tel/fax: 68-0476).

US Embassy, Apdo 327, Managua (tel: 666-010).

World Bank, Plaza España, Edificio Málaga, Modulos No A 1/A 22, Managua (tel: 26-0562; fax: 661-000).

Prensa Latina: www.plenglish.com

Internet sites

Banco Central de Nicaragua: www.bcn.gob.ni

Nicaraguan Centre for Exports and Investments (CEI): www.cei.org.ni

Organisation of American States: www.oas.org

Ministry of Foreign Affairs: www.cancilleria.gob.ni

Nicaraguan stock exchange: http://bolsanic.com

Nicaraguan Solidarity Campaign: www.nicaraguasc.org.uk

Nicaragua Network: www.nicanet.org

La Prensa: www.laprensa.com.ni

El Nuevo Diario: www.elnuevodiario.com.ni

La Noticia: www.lanoticia.com.ni

Niger

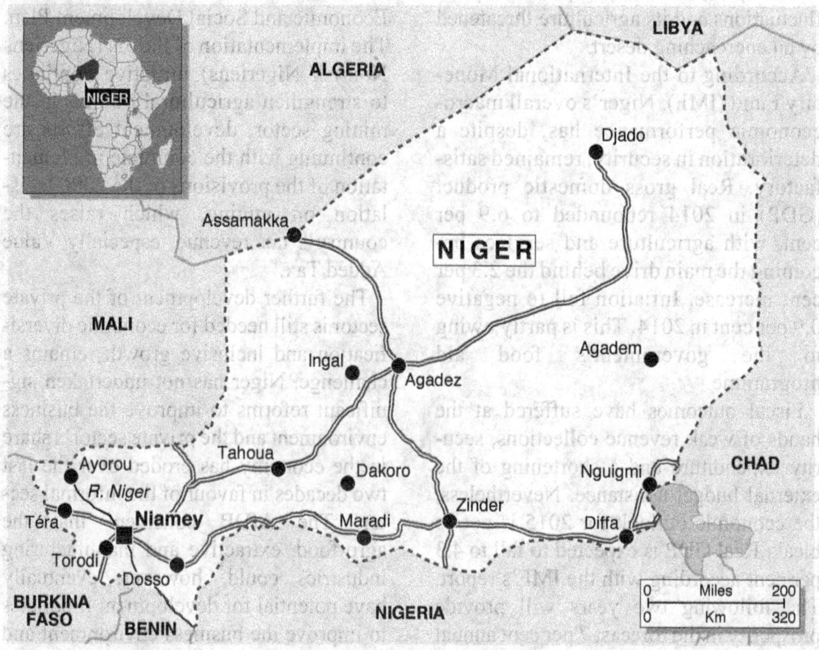

A vast state situated on the border of the Sahara desert, Niger has endured military rule for much of the time since it's post-dependence from France in 1960. The first democratic government arrived in 1993 after public pressure ensured that multi-party elections could take place. Political fighting brought the government to a standstill and in 1996 a *coup* occurred, lead by Colonel Ibrahim Baré Maïnassara, who became president after winning (with around 52 per cent) a widely disputed election in July. Three years later, in 1999, another *coup* took place, unsettling Colonel Baré and restoring democratic rule to the country. The elected president Mamadou Tandja was re-elected in 2004 and 2009, and led a constitutional amendment that would enable him to extend his term. He was deposed in 2010, following another military *coup*. Mahamadou Issoufou emerged victorious in April 2011, and remains in office today.

The United Nations (UN) rates Niger as one of the most poverty-stricken nations in the world. Minimal provision of government services, poor funding, and the disruption caused by extended droughts common to the Sahel region mean that sustainable growth is difficult. The Mouvement des Nigériens pour la Justice (MNJ) (Nigerien Movement for Justice), a predominantly Tuareg rebel group, emerged in 2007. They attacked several military targets in the north. The rebellion was largely squashed by the government in 2009. However, increasingly worrying security issues are commonplace with the advent of the terrorist organisation Boko Haram and external threats from Libya and Mali.

Niger found itself being steadily swept into the world of international terrorism in 2014. In October 2014 French forces that were deployed in Niger destroyed a convoy transporting weapons from Libya to Mali and captured fighters linked to al Qaeda. A reconnaissance aircraft was purchased in October, a significant investment for Niger, costing US$13.5 million. No details were given on the type of aircraft, except that it was to be operated by Niger's intelligence service, the General Direction of Documentation and External Security.

Boko Haram's close proximity to the south of Niger poses a new threat to the

KEY FACTS

Official name: République du Niger (Republic of Niger)

Head of State: President Issoufou Mahamadou (from 7 Apr 2011)

Head of government: Prime Minister Brigi Rafini (from 7 Apr 2011)

Ruling party: Coalition led by Parti Nigerien pour la Démocratie et le Socialisme (PNDS) (Niger Party for Democracy and Socialism) and independents (from 7 April 2011)

Area: 1,267,000 square km

Population: 17.12 million (2014)*

Capital: Niamey

Official language: French; Hausa is the major *lingua franca* especially for trade

Currency: CFA franc (CFAf) = 100 centimes (Communauté Financière Africaine (African Financial Community) franc). New notes have been issued; old notes cease to be legal tender from Jan 2005.

Exchange rate: CFAf586.44 per US$ (Sep 2015)

GDP per capita: US$469 (2014)*

GDP real growth: 6.90% (2014)*

GDP: US$8.03 billion (2014)*

Inflation: -0.94% (2014)

Balance of trade: -US$549.60 million (2012)

Annual FDI: US$1.01 billion (2011)

* estimated figure

country. The Islamist militant group killed dozens of Nigeriens in June 2015 – following the first attack in February of the same year. The government claimed it had repulsed the first attack and taken the lives of over a 100 insurgent fighters. A US funded multinational force has been deployed with the aim of countering the insurgency.

The United States already operates unarmed surveillance drones in Niger, following a French-led military operation in 2013 which destroyed an allegedly al Qaeda enclave in neighbouring Mali. Supported by some 120 US military personnel, the drones operate from a base outside Niamey. It was reported that the Pentagon was considering moving the operation to Agadez, 750km north-east of Niamey. Additionally some of the 3,000 French troops operating in the region are based in Niger. The principal objective is to police the 'Sahel band', thereby limiting the effectiveness of the Islamist groups operating in the region.

Niger has lengthy – and largely unmonitored – borders, not only with Mali, but also with Libya, Nigeria, Burkina Faso, Algeria, Benin and Chad. A 2013 ruling by the International Court of Justice stated that the West African nations of Niger and Burkina Faso, needed to redefine their shared 620 miles of border and exchange territory. Implementation of this ruling only really began in May 2015, as agreement was reached in the exchange of 18 towns between the two nations, ending years of litigation.

The economy

At the beginning of the 1980s, some observers had seen Niger having a rosy economic future. Its enormous potential as a uranium producer lead them to think that Niger would benefit as the developed world sought alternatives to oil. However, over a quarter of a century has passed with little sign of the economic boom once forecast. Niger is a drought-prone country that often struggles to feed its people. Its main export, uranium, is prone to price fluctuations and its agriculture threatened by an encroaching desert.

According to the International Monetary Fund (IMF), Niger's overall macroeconomic performance has, despite a deterioration in security, remained satisfactory. Real gross domestic product (GDP) in 2014 rebounded to 6.9 per cent, with agriculture and services becoming the main drive behind the 2.3 per cent increase. Inflation fell to negative 0.9 per cent in 2014. This is partly owing to the government's food aid programme.

Fiscal outcomes have suffered at the hands of weak revenue collections, security expenditure and a shortening of the external budget assistance. Nevertheless, the economic outlook for 2015 is not so bleak. Real GDP is expected to fall to 4.3 per cent according with the IMF's report. The following two years will provide prosperity in the forecast 7 per cent annual growth 2016–18. This will mainly arise due to greater utilisation of the extraction industry.

The African Development Bank (AfDB) reported Niger's growth in 2014 to be slightly higher at 7.1 per cent. To consolidate its gains and speed up economic and social progress, the government and its technical and financial partners developed a programme to improve performance in the implementation of the Economic and Social Development Plan (Programme d'amélioration de la Performance pour la mise en oeuvre du Plan de Développement Économique et Social (PAPMO-PDES)). The programme aims to tackle the constraints hampering achievement of the aims of the 2012–15 Economic and Social Development Plan. The implementation of the 3N (Nigeriens Nourish Nigeriens) initiative continues to strengthen agricultural output. In the mining sector, development efforts are continuing with the complete implementation of the provisions of the 2006 legislation on mining, which raises the country's tax revenue, especially Value Added Tax.

The further development of the private sector is still needed for economic diversification and inclusive growth remains a challenge. Niger has not undertaken significant reforms to improve the business environment and the private sector's share in the economy has eroded over the last two decades in favour of the informal sector. The AfDB considers that the agro-food, extractive and manufacturing industries could, however, eventually have potential for development if policies to improve the business environment and promote greater links between economic sectors were introduced, particularly between the mining sector and the rest of the economy.

Niger is a landlocked country with two-thirds of the mass of land uninhabitable desert. The population is heavily concentrated in a narrow strip in the south. It is doubling every 18 years, as birth control is low and high birth rates are an entrenched part of the culture. As a result, challenges for food security, education, healthcare, employment and social protection are strained. Niger has a low quality of life, with a Human Development Index (HDI) of 0.337 for 2014. This ranking places it 187 out of 187 on the scale. Between 1980 and 2013, Niger's HDI value increased from 0.191 to 0.337. The World Bank reports GDP per capita to be at a measly US$415.40.

KEY INDICATORS — Niger

	Unit	2011	2012	2013	2014	**2015
Population	m	*15.09	*16.10	*16.60	*17.12	*17.65
Gross domestic product (GDP)	US$bn	6.02	6.69	7.50	*8.03	*7.27
GDP per capita	US$	374	416	*452	*469	*412
GDP real growth	%	2.3	11.1	4.6	*6.9	*4.6
Inflation	%	3.6	0.5	2.3	-0.9	*1.4
Exports (fob) (goods)	US$m	1,172.8	1,353.3	–	–	–
Imports (fob) (goods)	US$m	2,192.4	1,903.0	–	–	–
Balance of trade	US$m	-1,019.6	-549.6	–	–	–
Current account	US$m	-1,556.0	-1,030.0	*-1,150.0	*-1,448.0	*-1,974.0
Total reserves minus gold	US$m	610.3	1,014.5	1,166.6	1,281.5	–
Foreign exchange	US$m	527.0	917.8	1,069.8	–	–
Exchange rate	per US$	466.82	505.65	480.26	542.07	–

* estimated figure ** forecast figure

Risk assessment

Politics	Poor
Economy	Fair
Regional stability	Poor

Muslims in Niger

% of population	98.3
Sunni (% of Muslims)	99
Shi'a (% of Muslims)	1

COUNTRY PROFILE

1800s The British were the first Europeans to explore the area.
1891–1911 France colonised the region, although it did not gain full control until much later and even then resistance movements continued.
1960 Niger gained independence from France under the presidency of Hamani Diori.
1974 Diori was overthrown and replaced by Lieutenant Colonel Seyni Kountche.
1987 Kountche died and was replaced by Brigadier Ali Saibou.
1989 Civilian rule was re-introduced with a new constitution, under a one-party system. Ali Saibou was re-elected president.
1990 The Tuareg people in the north began a rebellion.
1991 Saibou lost power to a transitional government led by Andre Salifou.
1992 A referendum overwhelmingly approved a new multi-party constitution
1993 Multi-party elections resulted in Mahamane Ousmane being elected president; his coalition, the Alliance of the Forces of Change (AFC), won most seats in parliament.
1995 A peace accord was signed between the government and the Tuareg.
1996 Ousmane was toppled in a coup and replaced by Ibrahim Maïnassara Baré. A military-backed civilian government was formed. Colonel Ibrahim Baré Maïnassara became president after winning around 52 per cent in a widely discredited election held on 7–8 July.
1997 A peace accord with the last Tuareg rebel group was signed.
1999 President Maïnassara was assassinated and Major Daouda Mallam Wanké assumed power. A new constitution was approved, which balanced the power between the president, prime minister and the National Assembly. Mamadou Tandja won the presidential election.
2000 Droughts caused widespread food shortages.
2001 After another poor harvest, food prices escalated and famine ensued.
2002 The EU granted US$319.5 million for Niger's poverty reduction effort.
2003 The US claimed Iraq had attempted to purchase uranium from Niger, in violation of UN sanctions. The claim was rejected by the government. Slavery was made illegal.
2004 The World Bank and the IMF supported a US$1.20 billion debt relief programme. Incumbent Tandja was re-elected president and the ruling Mouvement National pour la Société du Développement (MNSD) (National Movement for the Society of Development) won the parliamentary elections.
2005 Hama Amadou became prime minister. Taxes were increased by 20 per cent and sparked widespread protests. The UN warned that three million faced starvation due to a severe drought after locusts had damaged crops.
2006 The government began repatriating Mahamid Arab settlers to Chad.
2007 Niger assumed control of the island of Lete and other islands in the river Niger in accordance with an International Court of Justice ruling settling a border dispute with Benin. Opponents accused the government of embezzling US$9 million from foreign donor funds for education, between 2002–06. Prime Minister Hama Amadou lost four votes of no confidence in parliament and the president appointed Seyni Oumarou as prime minister.
2008 New satellite images released showed that extensive tree planting has transformed once deforested areas.
2009 The constitutional court ruled that President Tandja's plan to hold a referendum to extend his time in office by a third term was illegal. Opposition parties and civil society groups formed a coalition, La Co-ordination des Forces Démocratiques pour la République (CFDR) (Co-ordination of Democratic Forces for the Republic) to resist his proposal. President Tandja dissolved parliament and suspended the constitution, and assumed power by presidential decree. Opposition leaders described the action as a *coup d'état*. Despite a call by the opposition to boycott the referendum on extending Presidential Tandja's term in office, according to official statistics, 92.5 per cent voted in favour of the proposition, with a turnout of 68.26 per cent. CFDR claimed the turnout was less than 7 per cent. President Tandja appointed Ali Badjo Gamatié as prime minister. In parliamentary elections, boycotted by the opposition, the ruling MNSD won a majority with 76 seats (out of 113). The Economic Community of West African States (Ecowas) announced that it did not recognise the legitimacy of Mamadou Tandja's presidency.
2010 Colonel Salou Djibo mounted a *coup d'état* that toppled President Tandja and installed a military junta, the Conseil Suprême pour la Restauration de la Démocratie (CSRD) (Supreme Council for the Restoration of Democracy), by which Colonel Djibo was proclaimed president. Both the AU and France condemned the actions. The CSRD appointed Mahamadou Danda as caretaker prime minister. The military government announced that a constitutional referendum would be held, followed by a presidential election, with a run-off in January 2011, if no clear winner was chosen. The World Food Programme (UN-WFP) declared that Niger was facing its worst ever food crisis, with around 7.3 million people (almost half the population) in desperate need of food, following crop failures after a drought in 2009. Heavy rains broke the prolonged drought but were too late to save harvests and bought flooding that damaged homes and stored grain instead. In a constitutional referendum 90.18 per cent voted in favour of changes to give immunity to the February coup leaders and requiring a transition of power by April 2011.
2011 Parliamentary elections, postponed from December 2010 were held in January. Parti Nigerien pour la Democratie et le Socialisme-Tarayya (PNDS) (Nigerien Party for Democracy and Socialism-Tarayya) won 39 seats out of 113 and the MNSD 26 seats. In the first round of presidential elections held at the same time, of the four candidates standing Mahamadou Issoufou (PNDS) won 36.1 per cent, Seyni Oumarou (MNSD) 23.2 per cent of the vote. In the run-off, held on 12 March, Issoufou won 57.95 per cent and Oumarou 42.05 per cent; turnout was 48.2 per cent. Oumarou conceded defeat on 17 March. The president and government took office on 7 April, when Mahamadou Issoufou immediately appointed Brigi Rafini (an ethnic Tuareg) as prime minister, plus forming a coalition government with most members drawn from the PNDS and other posts given to independent members of parliament (MP). In April, the International Organisation for Migration stated that Niger was providing emergency relief and accommodation to over 54,000 people fleeing the conflict in Libya. Ten people were arrested in August accused of a coup attempt in July, while a further suspect was reported to be on the run. Officials confirmed in September that Saadi Qadafi, one of fugitive Libyan leader Col Muammar Qadafi's sons had arrived in Niamey and had been granted refuge.
2012 Malian refugees crossed into the northern Tillabéry region, straining local resources, and requiring food aid from Red Cross Niger. Heavy rains in July added to Niger's woes. The southern Dosso region was worst affected, with over 10,000 homes destroyed according to the UN. Niamey was hit when the River Niger burst its banks, flooding the city's suburbs.
On 29 October China and Niger signed two aid agreements for the provision of a US$25.6 million, 500-bed, national referral hospital (to be located in Niamey) and the purchase of 30 attendant vehicles, valued at US$1.9 million.
2013 On 4 Feb President Mahamadou Issoufou confirmed that French troops were involved in guarding the Arlit mine, one of Niger's largest uranium mines. A military camp and a French-run uranium mine were attacked in May by a group

lead by Algerian Mokhtar Belmokhtar's Al Mulathameen (Masked Men Brigade) and the Mali-based Movement for Oneness and Jihad in West Africa (Mojwa), killing 25 people.

2014 History was made in June when the first person in Niger to be convicted of slavery was sent to jail for four years for having purchased a 'fifth' wife. Slavery has been illegal in Niger since 2003. According to Anti-Slavery International there are reckoned still to be 40,000 slaves in Niger. Many are born into slavery because their mother was a slave. They grow up under the direct or indirect control of slave-owning 'noble' families or 'masters', who make them herd animals, control their nomadic migrations, and arrange their marriages without their consent. They are unpaid. The practice of taking a 'fifth' wife is common throughout the country and in northern Nigeria, where Muslims may legally take four wives.

2015 In an effort to curtail the activities of Boko Haram in Chad and Niger the two countries launched a ground and air offensive against the militant group in north-eastern Nigeria on 8 March.

Political structure

Constitution

A referendum was held on 4 August 2009 to agree a new Constitution which includes: an extension to President Tanja's mandate until 2012, during which time a new Constitution will be drafted and proposed; the system of government will change from semi-presidential to full presidential; no limit to the term in office for a president; a new bicameral parliament would include a senate.

The constitution adopted in October 2010 requires the government to publish all mining contracts and information on the revenues generated under these contracts. It also mandates that revenue from natural resources be shared between the central and regional governments, and that funds be set aside for public investments in agriculture and livestock farming, health and education.

The constitution was amended in November 2010 to give immunity to the February 2010 *coup d'état* leaders and require that a transition of power be made by 6 April 2011.

Form of state

Presidential, unitary, multiparty republic.

The executive

The directly elected president by absolute majority vote in 2 rounds if needed is the Head of State, elected for a five-year term, renewable only once.

The president, shares power with the prime minister but has final responsibility for co-ordinating the actions of the executive branch of government. The president names the prime minister, from a list of three candidates, who become Head of government and is accountable to parliament.

National legislature

The unicameral Assemblée Nationale (National Assembly) has 113 members elected for a maximum five-year term of which 105 members are directly elected in multi-seat constituencies by proportional representation vote and eight directly elected in special single-seat constituencies for minorities by simple majority vote.

Legal system

Based on French civil law system and customary law.

Last elections

4 August 2009 (constitutional amendment); 31 January 2011 (parliament), 31 January and 12 March 2011 (presidential, first round and runoff)

Results: Referendum: 90.18 per cent voted in favour of changes.

Parliamentary: Parti Nigerien pour la Démocratie et le Socialisme (PNDS) (Niger Party for Democracy and Socialism) won 39 seats (out of 113), Mouvement National de la Société de Développement (MNSD) (National Movement for a Developing Society) 26, Mouvement Démocratique Nigérien pour une Fédération Africaine (Moden-FA) (Nigerien Democratic Movement for an African Federation) 24, Alliance Nigérienne pour la Démocratie et le Progrès (ANDP) (Nigerien Alliance for Democracy and Progress) eight, Rassemblement pour la Démocratie et le Progrès (RDP) (Party for Democracy and Progress) seven, Union pour la République (UPR) (Union for the Republic) six, Convention Démocratique et Sociale (CDS) (Democratic and Social Convention) two; one seat undeclared. Turnout was 52.8 per cent.

Presidential, first round: Mahamadou Issoufou (PNDS) won 36.1 per cent of the vote, Seyni Oumarou MNSD 23.2 per cent, Hama Amadou (Moden-FA) 19.8 per cent, Mahamane Ousmane (CDS) 8.4 per cent. Turnout was 50.4 per cent

Runoff: Issoufou won 57.95 per cent of the vote, Oumarou 42.05 per cent; turnout was 48.2 per cent.

Next elections

2016 (parliamentary and presidential).

Political parties

Ruling party

Coalition led by Parti Nigerien pour la Démocratie et le Socialisme (PNDS) (Niger Party for Democracy and Socialism) and independents (from 7 April 2011)

Main opposition party

Mouvement National pour la Société du Développement (MNSD) (National Movement for the Society of Development)

Population

17.12 million (2014)* Niger's population lives mostly in the southern and more fertile part of the country. Around 400,000 Tuareg Berbers live in Niger. the Institute for National Statistics (INS) has warned that unless there is more information on contraception the population of Niger is likely to be as high as 56 million by 2050.

Last census: May 2001: 10,790,352 (provisional)

Population density: Eight inhabitants per square km. Urban population 17 per cent (2010 Unicef).

Annual growth rate: 3.4 per cent, 1990–2010 (Unicef).

Ethnic make-up

Hausa (56 per cent), Djerma (22 per cent), Tuareg (8 per cent).

Religions

Islam (85 per cent), traditional beliefs (14.5 per cent), Christianity (0.5 per cent).

Education

Public expenditure on education is around 2 per cent of GDP.

Primary education is free and compulsory and lasts until aged 12. Secondary schooling is divided, beginning with the first cycle secondary school from aged 12 to 16, then second cycle secondary school from aged 16 to 19, when students are expected to graduate with a Baccalauréat. Alternatively, at aged 16 students may elect to undertake a three year technical course. All education is conducted in French.

Literacy rate: 17 per cent adult rate; 25 per cent youth rate (15–24) (Unesco 2005).

Compulsory years: 6 to 12

Enrolment rate: 29 per cent gross primary enrolment, 7 per cent gross secondary enrolment; of relevant age groups (including repeaters) (World Bank).

Pupils per teacher: 41 in primary schools

Health

A report by the charity Save the Children (STC) was published in May 2012 that described Niger as the worst country in which to be a mother. STC compared conditions and ranked 165 countries in categories that included health, education, economic status and nutrition. Due to the severe food crisis in the Sahel region, mothers in Niger in 2011–12 are particularly vulnerable and likely to to produce underweight and weak babies.

HIV/Aids

There are an estimated 64,000 people living with HIV/Aids, of which 36,000 are women. In addition there are 5,900 children (0–17) HIV positive and 24,000 orphans. In 2003 there were 4,800 deaths due to Aids, although Niger has so far escaped much of the African pandemic. However, with 25–35 per cent of sex workers testing positive, there is a chance that increased population mobility and a lack of condom use could make Niger vulnerable.

HIV prevalence: 1.2 per cent aged 15–49 in 2003 (World Bank)

Life expectancy: 41 years, 2004 (WHO 2006)

Fertility rate/Maternal mortality rate: 7.1 births per woman, 2010 (Unicef); maternal mortality 590 per 100,000 live births (World Bank).

Child (under 5 years) mortality rate (per 1,000): 114 per 1,000 live births (WHO 2012); 40 per cent of children aged under five are malnourished (World Bank).

Head of population per physician: 0.03 physicians per 1,000 people, 2004 (WHO 2006)

Welfare

Around 61.4 per cent of the population live on less than US$1 per day and 85.3 per cent live on less than US$2 per day. The distribution of wealth is highly unequal with a Gini index of 50.5 and the richest 20 per cent of the population owning 53.3 per cent of the total wealth.

Main cities

Niamey (capital, estimated population 1.1 million in 2012), Zinder (253,766), Maradi (188,008), Arlit (built for the uranium industry) (128,807), Agadez (118,647), Tahoua (110,046), Dosso (71,643).

Languages spoken

The distribution of languages is dependent on the ethnic groups within Niger. The Hausa are the largest group and their language is recognised as a national language, as is Songhai-Zarma (Djerma) the next largest language group. Tamashek, which is spoken by the Tuareg, is related to Berber. Others languages in daily use include Fulani, Arabic, Kanauri, Courmantché and Toubou.

Official language/s

French; Hausa is the major *lingua franca* especially for trade

Media

Despite laws which provide for freedom of the press there are government restrictions and journalists are subject to intimidation so that self-censorship is practiced.

Press

With low literacy levels there are few publications on offer. In French, *Le Sahel* is the government daily; weeklies include the weekend *Sahel Dimanche* and *Le Républicain Niger* (www.republicain-niger.com), which is an independent magazine. Tam Tam (www.tamtaminfo.com) is an online publication in French.

Broadcasting

The national, state-run broadcaster is the Office de Radiodiffusion Télévision du Niger (ORTN) (www.ortn.ne).

Radio: Due to the low literacy rate radio services are the main medium of mass communication and sources of news and information.

ORTN (www.ortn.ne) operates the only national radio station called La Voix du Sahel (www.ortn.ne) with programmes in French, Arabic, Hausa and local languages. There are several private radio stations which target specific audiences with programmes of social development, health, education and the interests of women, such as Anfani FM and Tambara FM. Entertainment radio includes Radio et Musique, Horizon FM and Tenere FM.

Television: ORTN (www.ortn.ne) operates two channels. TV Sahel is the national network using satellite technology and Tal TV is a digital service for the capital and its environs. A private stations Tenere TV and the pay-to-view Telestar are based in the capital.

Other news agencies: APA (African Press Agency): www.apanews.net
Reuters Africa: http://africa.reuters.com

Economy

As one of the least developed countries in the world, Niger's economy is dominated by agriculture and the export of uranium from the world's largest deposits situated in the north of the country. In 2013, the UN Human Development Index (HDI) ranked Niger at 187 out of 187 for its development in health, education and income. In 2013 89.81 per cent of the population experienced multidimensional poverty and 43.62 per cent were living on an equivalent of US$1.25 per day. Per capita income was estimated at US$441 in 2014 with most of the population sustained by subsistence agriculture, which is the main source of income for most households; livestock production is mostly exported to neighbouring countries, particularly Nigeria. Remittances in 2010 and 2011 were US$823 million (1.9 per cent of GDP in 2010) (latest published figures in 2015).

GDP growth was 3.4 per cent in 2007, growing to 8.7 per cent in 2008, due to an excellent harvest that increased agricultural production by 25 per cent; the industrial sector also grew through the increase in electricity production, telecommunications and transport which reflected the expansion in public and private investment, particularly in mining and infrastructure construction. However, by 2009 the economy had slipped into recession with negative growth of -0.9 per cent. GDP growth was 8 per cent as global trade picked up in 2010, but weakened in 2011 to a projected 2.3 per cent. However, in 2014 GDP growth rose to 4.1 per cent as farmers experienced favourable weather and the agricultural sector boosted the economy.

Uranium exports provide the largest proportion of foreign exchange. Government revenue is around 17.5 per of GDP, of which mining receipts accounted for over 60 per cent. Uranium exports require special licences which are only granted to registered buyers, particularly in France and Japan. In the long-term, Niger hopes to move away from its dependence on uranium through the exploitation of other mineral resources, such as gold and oil. The Samira Hill gold mine, operated by a Moroccan-Canadian consortium, with a 20 per cent Niger stake, has been in production since 2004. Two new gold seams were found in 2008, close to the current operation.

External trade

It is a member of the Economic Community of West African States (Ecowas), which was set up to promote economic integration among members. Niger is also a member of the West African Economic and Monetary Union (WAEMU) using the common currency, the CFA franc.

Along with uranium exports, live animal exports, primarily to Nigeria, are also very important to the economy.

A weak industrial and manufacturing sector typically requires domestic needs to be met by imports.

Imports

Principal imports are foodstuffs, consumer goods, machinery, vehicles and parts, petroleum and cereals.

Main sources: France (13.7 per cent of total in 2013), China (11.6 per cent), US (9.1 per cent).

Exports

Principal exports are uranium ore, gold, livestock, cow-peas and onions.

Main destinations: Nigeria (54.2 per cent of total in 2013), South Korea (26.2 per cent), Ghana (6.7 per cent).

Agriculture

Farming

Subsistence farming and stock rearing contribute 37.7 per cent to GDP and employ 70 per cent of the workforce.

Less than 3 per cent of the total land area is cultivated.

Hides and skins and cotton account for around 20 per cent of export earnings.

The government is encouraging market gardening – galmi onions are an important cash crop.

Production of the two principal food crops, millet and sorghum, is generally insufficient to satisfy domestic needs, even in times of good rains, and is supplemented by food aid. Other food crops include rice, cowpeas and green beans. Recurrent drought and desertification have had a serious impact on livestock rearing and have led to significant food shortages with disastrous consequences. The government is investing heavily in anti-desertification schemes and is encouraging animal husbandry.

Industry and manufacturing

The industrial sector is small-scale, contributing around 7 per cent to GDP and employing 5 per cent of the workforce. Manufacturing is concentrated on the processing of agricultural commodities such as sugar refining, brewing, cotton ginning, tanning and flour/rice milling.
Other activities include small-scale production of cement and metals, textiles, plastics, soft drinks and construction materials.
Industrial development is handicapped by the shortage of capital and skilled labour and by the country's weak infrastructure.

Tourism

Niger's tourist industry is close to being paralysed due to the Tuareg insurgency in the north, and Islamic militancy throughout the country. As a result Western governments have issued warnings to their citizens to avoid the north entirely and only allow essential travel to the capital and the western region.
Tourism accounts for less than 5 per cent of GDP and around 4 per cent of total employment.
Before the country became dangerous for visitors Niger had been using travel and tourism to help build the economy by providing extra income in rural communities. Niger is home to the highly endangered West African Giraffe, in a protected area in Kouré region. Ecotourism provides employment as guides for local people, so that the giraffe is looked on as an asset to the community, thereby encouraging its protection. Reforestation of the habitat of the giraffe, which had been damaged through clearing for agriculture, is slowly being extended through the introduction of tiger bush nurseries (mixed vegetation of low and tall plant that form stripes, as seen from the air).

Environment

In June 2010 the African Union backed a proposal to build the 'Great Green Wall' project, of a 15km wide, 7,775km long, continuous belt of trees from Senegal in the west to Djibouti in the east (traversing 11 countries) in an effort to halt the advance of the Sahara Desert. The trees to be used would be drought-adapted, preferably native to the area from a list of 37 possible species, and should help to slow soil erosion and filter rain water.

Mining

The mining sector accounts for around 11 per cent of GDP and employs 5 per cent of the workforce.
Niger is the third-largest exporter of uranium and it has been the country's principal export since early 1970s. Proven reserves total 280,000 tonnes with extraction undertaken mainly at two opencast mines, at Arlit and Akouta. Production stagnated at 3,000–3,200 tonnes due to a world slump in the demand for uranium. Production has increased in recent years, but depressed prices on the world market have seen the value of uranium exports fall. The major export markets are France, Japan, Spain, Germany and Egypt. On 6 January 2009, Niger licensed the French nuclear energy group Areva to operate the Imouraren mine. The mine will become the largest in Africa and the second largest in the world, it is expected to begin production of uranium in 2012, producing 5,000 tonnes per year. Areva will invest US$1.51 billion, over 60 per cent of the initial investment and will take a two-thirds stake in the mine, with the government owning the remainder.
Other minerals exploited are the tin-bearing ore cassiterite, phosphates, molybdenum, salt and coal. There are also known reserves of iron ore.
The Samira gold mine in Niamey, in the Koma Bangou concession in west Niger, produces around 5,000 ounces of gold annually and, before 2011, is expected to produce three tonnes and earn US$28 billion. The government owns 20 per cent and two Canadian mining companies the other 80 per cent of the mine. Gold prospecting agreements have been reached with three other Canadian companies for further research in the region.
Imperial Metals is drilling for diamonds on the M'Banga concession.

Hydrocarbons

Though Niger has a history of oil exploration, dating back to the 1970s, it was not until 2011 that the oil industry took off with the opening of the Soraz refinery and the Agadem oil field. In 2014 Niger had proven reserves of some 150 million barrels though it is thought that there could be up to 1 billion barrels. If this is the case then Niger hopes to begin producing 80,000 barrels per day (bpd), compared to 20,000 now.
In July 2009, Algeria, Niger and Nigeria signed an agreement to build a 2,580km trans-Sahara gas pipeline (TSGP) traversing all three countries, which is estimated will cost US$13 billion and transport up to 30 billion cum of natural gas, destined for Europe. Three foreign energy companies also expressed an interest in investing in the project, Russia's Gazprom, France's Total and the Anglo-Dutch Shell.
There are small coal reserves at Tchirozerine (1,000km north of the capital). These reserves stand at around 780,000 tonnes. Annual production is typically 200,000 tonnes of bituminous (brown coal) used in power generation. There is negligible domestic demand, although this may be set to rise. There has been a further discovery of coal reserves in Takanamat, in central Niger.
Natural gas is neither produced nor consumed.

Energy

Total installed generating capacity was 105MW in 2007, producing around 200 million kilowatt hours; only 12 per cent of the population has access to mains electricity. Niger has an estimated hydroelectric potential of 250MW, but an agreement with Nigeria whereby 45MW of electricity is guaranteed from Nigeria in return for the uninterrupted flow of water along the Niger River inhibits Niger's ability to dam the river in its territory. There are small-scale, isolated diesel generators providing the majority of the country's community needs. The majority of the population relies on non-commercial biomass, mostly fuel wood, for cooking, lighting and power.
It may be possible to use the 1.3 million tonnes of agricultural waste to produce biogas, but no plans exist for its exploitation. Solar panels are being introduced by private individuals.

Financial markets

Stock exchange

Afribourse (Bourse Régionale des Valeurs Moblières) (BRVM)

Banking and insurance

Central bank

Banque Centrale des Etats de l'Afrique de l'Ouest

Main financial centre

Niamey

Time

GMT plus one hour

Geography

Niger is a landlocked country in western Africa, with Algeria and Libya to the north, Nigeria and Benin to the south, Mali and Burkina Faso to the west and Chad to the east. It is 80 per cent desert, in the north, and 20 per cent savannah in the south. In the central north there is a volcanic mountain range, Aïr Massif, which includes Mount Gréboun, the tallest peak at a height of 1,944 metres. The Niger river flows from Mali to Nigeria through Niger in the south west for about 563km and a small portion of Lake Chad occupies the south-eastern corner of Niger.

Hemisphere

Northern

Climate

Niger is very hot with temperatures ranging from 28–44 degrees Celsius. There is rain mainly in the south from June–September. Frequent Sahara dust storms occur from November–January. The dry season is from October–May.

Entry requirements

Passports

Required by all and must have at least six month validity left; nationals of certain African countries may visit with national ID cards.

At each overnight stay passports must be presented to the police. As passports are stamped each time, they will require enough blank pages for the visit. Travel by any other route than that stamped in the passport by the police is forbidden.

Visa

Required by all, except citizens of some African countries close to Niger. Contact the nearest Niger embassy for further details and an application form. Visitors are required to supply proof of return/onward passage and funds, for living expenses of US$500. All documents require a French translation.

An exit permit will be required for all visitors that required an entry visa, from the Immigration Department in Niamey, before departure.

Currency advice/regulations

The import of local currency is unlimited; export is limited to CFAf25,000. Import and export of foreign currency is unlimited.

Travellers cheques are accepted in hotels and banks; to avoid extra exchange charges cheques in euros are recommended.

Health (for visitors)

Mandatory precautions

A yellow fever and cholera vaccination certificate is required if arriving from an infected area.

Advisable precautions

Inoculations and booster should be current for tetanus, hepatitis A, diphtheria, typhoid and yellow fever. There may be a need for vaccinations for tuberculosis, hepatitis B and meningitis and cholera.

Anti-mosquito measures including mosquito repellents, nets and clothing covering the body should be used for protection against hepatitis B and yellow fever. There is a risk of rabies.

There is a shortage of routine medications and visitors should take all necessary medicines with them. A first aid kit that includes disposable syringes is a reasonable precaution. Use only bottled or boiled water for drinks, washing teeth and making ice. Eat only well cooked meals, preferably served hot; vegetables should be cooked and fruit peeled. Dairy products are unpasteurised and should be avoided, unless cooked.

Medical insurance is essential, including emergency evacuation, and an adequate supply of personal medicines is necessary.

Hotels

There are good hotels in Niamey. A 5 per cent service charge is usually added to bills.

Credit cards

International credit and debit cards are accepted in a limited number of places.

Public holidays (national)

Fixed dates

1 Jan (New Year's Day), 24 Apr (National Concord Day), 1 May (Labour Day), 3 Aug (Independence Day), 18 Dec (Republic Day), 25 Dec (Christmas Day).

Variable dates

Islamic New Year (two days), Easter Monday (Mar/Apr), Eid al Adha (two days), Birth of the Prophet (two days), Eid al Fitr (four days).

Islamic year 1437 (15 Oct 2015–2 Oct 2016):: The Islamic year contains 354 or 355 days, with the result that Muslim feasts advance by 10–12 days against the Gregorian calendar. Dates of feasts vary according to the sighting of the new moon, so cannot be forecast exactly.

Working hours

Banking

Mon–Fri: 0800–1100 and 1600–1700.

Business

Winter: Mon–Fri: 0730–1230, 1500–1800; Sat: 0730–1230.

Summer: Mon–Fri: 0730–1230, 1530–1830; Sat: 0730–1230.

Government

Oct–Feb: Mon–Fri: 0730–1230 and 1500–1800; Mar–Sep: Mon–Fri: 0730–1230 and 1530–1830.

Shops

Mon–Fri: 0800–1200, 1600–1900; Sat: 0800–1200.

Telecommunications

Mobile/cell phones

There are 900 GSM services available in larger town in the south.

Electricity supply

220/380V AC, 50 cycles

Getting there

Air

International airport/s: Niamey International (NIM), 12km south-east of city; bar, currency exchange, post office, shops, car hire, hotel courtesy coaches.

Airport tax: None

Surface

Road: There are road connections and border crossings with all neighbouring countries. Access from Algeria and Mali is difficult, but a surfaced road connects Benin with Niamey. Access from Chad may be restricted.

Water: Ferries on the Niger River coming from Mali are dependent on the water level.

Getting about

National transport

Air: Charter flights are available in Niamey.

Road: Main highways link Tillabery with N'guigmi, Tahoua and Arlit, however not all roads are open to visitors without a permit. Petrol is not always available. Best months for road travel December–March. Visitors must report to police on arrival at main centres.

Buses: Services operate from Niamey to Zinder, Agadez, and other towns.

City transport

Taxis: Fixed rates apply for long-distance and urban services. Taxis in Niamey are cheap and widely available. Tipping is optional.

Journey time from airport to city centre 10 minutes.

Car hire

Self-drive or chauffeur-driven cars are available in Niamey. Chauffeurs are compulsory outside the capital. International driving licence required. Petrol and spares are in short supply and there are no recovery services.

BUSINESS DIRECTORY

The addresses listed below are a selection only. While World of Information makes every endeavour to check these addresses, we cannot guarantee that changes have not been made, especially to telephone numbers and area codes. We would welcome any corrections.

Telephone area codes

The international direct dialling code (IDD) for Niger is +227, followed by subscriber's number.

Useful telephone numbers

Police: 17

Fire: 18

Chambers of Commerce

Maradi Chamber of Commerce and Agriculture, PO Box 79, Maradi (tel: 410-366; fax: 410-451).

Niger Chamber of Commerce, Agriculture, Industriy and Handicrafts, Place de la Concertation, PO Box 209, Niamey (tel: 732-210; fax: 734-668; e-mail: cham209n@intnet.ne).

Zinder Chambre of Commerce and Agriculture, PO Box 83, Zinder (tel: 510-087; fax: 510-217).

Banking

Bank of Africa (Niger, Head Office); BP 10 973, Immeuble Sonara II, Niamey (tel: 733-620, 733-621; fax: 733-818).

Banque Centrale des Etats de l'Afrique de l'Ouest (Agency); BP 487, Rond Point de la Poste, Niamey (tel: 722-491/92; fax: 734-743).

Banque Commerciale du Niger (Head Office); BP 11 363, Rond Point Maourey, Niamey (tel: 733-915, 733-331; fax: 732-163).

Banque Internationale pour l'Afrique au Niger (Head Office); BP 10350, Avenue de la Mairie, Niamey (tel: 733-101; fax: 733-595; e-mail: bia@intnet.ne).

Banque Islamique du Niger pour le Commerce et l'industrie (BINCI), BP 12754, Immeuble El-Nasr, Niamey (tel: 732-730, 732-740; fax: 734-735).

Caisse de Prêts aux Collectivités Territoriale, BP 730, Route Torodi, Rive droite, Niamey (tel: 723-412, 723-080).

Caisse Nationale d'Epargne, Avenue du Niger, BP 11778 Niamey (tel: 732-498, 732-499; fax: 735-812)

Crédit du Niger, BP 213, Blvd de la République, Niamey (tel: 722-701, 722-702; fax: 722-390).

Ecobank-Niger, BP 13804, Niamey (tel: 737-181, 901-052; fax: 737-204, 737-203).

Société Nigérienne de Banque, BP 891, Ave de la Mairie, Niamey (tel: 734-569, 734-643; fax: 734-693).

Central bank

Banque Centrale des Etats de l'Afrique de l'Ouest, Direction Nationale, Rue de l'Uranium, PO Box 487, Niamey (tel: 722-491; fax: 734-743).

Stock exchange

Afribourse (Bourse Régionale des Valeurs Moblières) (BRVM), www.brvm.org

Travel information

Niamey International Airport, ASECNA, BP 1096, Niamey (tel: 732-517/518/519, 732-381/382; fax: 735-512).

Ministry of tourism

Ministère du Tourisme et d'Artisanat BP 12710, Niamey, Niger (tel: 736 522; fax: 732 387).

National tourist organisation offices

Office du Tourisme du Niger, BP 612, Niamey.

Other useful addresses

Centre for Investment Promotion, BP 12129, Niamey (tel: 736-836; fax: 736-772).

Conseil National de Développement, c/o Ministry of Planning, Niamey (tel: 722-233).

Direction des Statistiques, c/o Ministry of Planning, Niamey (tel: 722-799).

Embassy of the Republic of Niger, 154 rue du Longchamp, 75116 Paris, France (tel: (+33-1) 4504 8060; fax: (+33-1) 4504 7973).

Niger Embassy (US), 2204 R Street, NW, Washington DC 20008 (tel: (+1-202) 483-4224; fax: (+1-202) 483-3169; e-mail: ambassadeniger@hotmail.com).

Office Nationale des Ressources Minières (Onarem), BP 210, Niamey (tel: 723-935).

Société Nationale de Commerce et de Production du Niger, BP 615, Niamey.

Société Nigérienne de Produits Pétroliers (Sonidep), BP 2735, Niamey (tel: 733-335).

Sonhotel (Société Nigerienne de Gestion des Hôtels de l'Etat) (tel: 732-387).

Syndicat des Commerçants, Importateurs et Exportateurs du Niger, BP 535, Niamey.

APA (African Press Agency): www.apanews.net

Reuters Africa: http://africa.reuters.com

Internet sites

Africa Business Network: www.ifc.org/abn

AllAfrica.com: http://allafrica.com

African Development Bank: www.afdb.org

Africa Online: www.africaonline.com

Mbendi AfroPaedia (information on companies, countries, industries and stock exchanges in Africa): http://mbendi.co.za

Nigeria

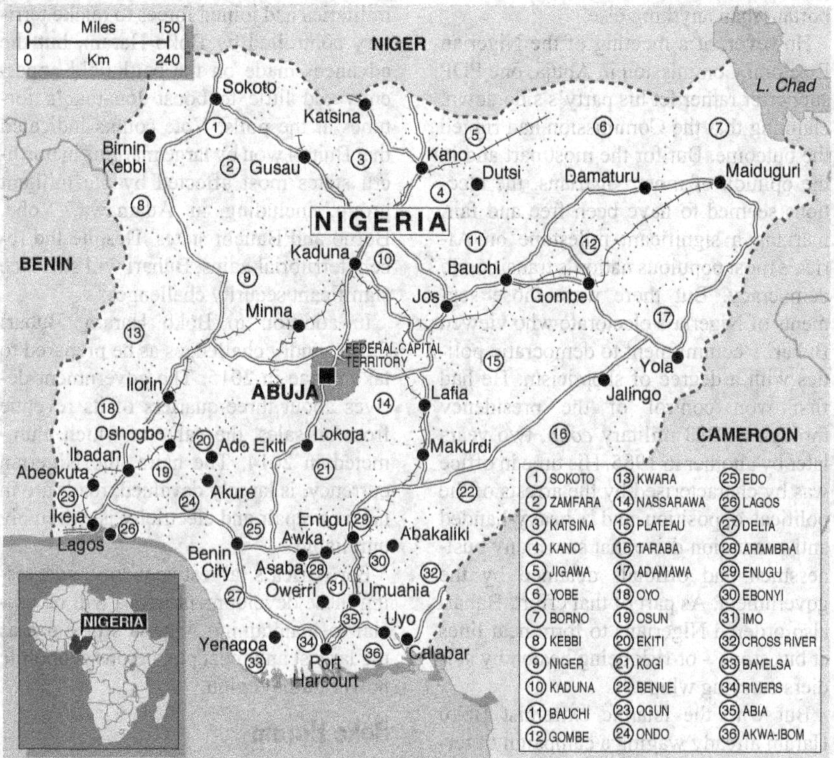

It had been described as 'one of the most divisive election campaigns in recent African history'. It was between two seasoned politicians, the challenger – Mohammadu Buhari aged 72 – 15 years older than the other – Goodluck Jonathan, a sprightly 52. One from the south, a Christian, the other a Muslim northerner. Mr Buhari's critics accused him of being past it, of being senile and worse still, poorly educated. In the way of African elections, Mr Buhari had even been described as a collaborator of the Boko Haram Islamic extremists. Mr Jonathan had come into office almost by accident. He had been chosen to run as vice president with President Umaru Yar'Adua, but he had died in office. Mr Buhari had been the military head of state in the early 1980s, famous for his zero tolerance approach to crime and for his 'war on indiscipline' where drug dealers were executed and members of Nigeria's business community, as well as its politicians, often found themselves behind bars.

Election success

The elections had been initially scheduled for mid-February 2015, but were postponed until the end of March after officials claimed many citizens were lacking voter ID cards. Moreover, the deteriorating security situation in the north raised questions about whether the army would be able to provide adequate security on election day. After long wait times and glitches with reading voter ID cards, polling was extended by a day. The new electoral system made it possible for results to be declared as they came in.

In his fourth democratic bid for Nigeria's presidency, on 28 March, former military ruler Muhammadu Buhari finally claimed victory, beating the incumbent Goodluck Jonathan by more than 2.5 million votes. By the time that Nigeria's National Electoral Commission (NEC)

KEY FACTS

Official name: Federal Republic of Nigeria

Head of State: Muhammadu Buhari (APC) (sworn in 29 May 2015)

Head of government: Muhammadu Buhari (APC) (sworn in 29 May 2015)

Ruling party: All Progressives Congress (APC) (elected Mar 2015)

Area: 923,768 square km

Population: 173.94 million (2014)*

Capital: Abuja – federal capital since 1991; Lagos – commercial capital.

Official language: English

Currency: Naira (N) = 100 kobo

Exchange rate: N199.05 per US$ (Sep 2015)

GDP per capita: US$3,298 (2014)*

GDP real growth: 6.31% (2014)

GDP: US$573.65 billion (2014)

Inflation: 8.06% (2014)

Oil production: 2.36 million bpd (2014)

Natural gas production: 38.60 billion cum (2014)

Balance of trade: US$42.32 billion (2012)*

Annual FDI: US$8.84 billion (2011)

* estimated figure

announced the results 'President' Buhari had already announced his win and the misnamed 'Goodluck' Jonathan had reportedly called his rival and conceded defeat. The result was not only a success for General Buhari's All Progressives Congress, but also for Nigeria's new biometric voting system. The system had been introduced as a means of countering the fraud that had characterised earlier elections. The responsibility of the NEC, the innovation had been heavily criticised by members of the ruling People's Democratic Party (PDP) although it was suspected that the motivation for the criticism was the ruling part's inability to 'manage' the result. It did seem as though the tenor of Nigerian political debate had moved up a notch or two. The outgoing Jonathan had been widely congratulated for his willingness to accept his loss and in a statement said that he 'promised the country free and fair elections' and that he had kept his word.

The election saw a number of 'firsts'. It marked the first time since Nigeria's 1999 transition from military rule that the PDP had lost the country's presidency and the first time that an incumbent had been democratically ousted from office. Unsurprisingly, representatives of the PDP had claimed that the election had seen widespread fraud in certain states, raising fears that Jonathan's supporters might lapse into violence. Precedents existed: when in 2011, Buhari lost to Jonathan, his supporters went on the rampage, carrying out violent attacks that resulted in the inevitable reprisals, leaving a death toll of over 800 in Nigeria's northern states, which had long been a stronghold of the former military ruler. In public at any rate, Jonathan appeared to be magnanimous and anxious to avoid any violence. 'As I have always affirmed, nobody's ambition is worth the blood of any Nigerian. The unity, stability and progress of our dear country is more important than anything else.'

However, at a meeting of the Nigerian Electoral Commission in Abuja, one PDP supporter rather let his party's side down, claiming that the Commission had rigged the outcome. But for the most part and in the opinion of most Nigerians, the elections seemed to have been free and fair, marking a significant milestone on Africa's most populous nation's transition to democracy. But there were those segments of Nigeria's electorate who viewed Buhari's commitment to democratic politics with a degree of skepticism. He had first won control of the presidency through a 1983 military *coup*, two years later by another in 1985. His time in office was by characterised by the arrests of the political opposition and a heavy-handed anti-corruption drive that saw many businessmen and officials detained by the government. As part of that effort, Buhari also ordered Nigerians to form neat lines at bus stops – or risk being beaten by soldiers carrying whips.

But with the Islamic extremist Boko Haram already waging a campaign of terror, kidnappings and suicide bombings, Nigerians appear to have opted for Buhari's heavy-handed past over Jonathan's more lackadaisical approach to the presidency. On President Jonathan's watch Boko Haram had consolidated its control over large parts of Nigeria's north-east, seizing major towns and army bases, killing more than 7,400 civilians in a single year and launching deadly suicide attacks in major cities.

In response, a coalition of West African militaries had joined forces to retake territory controlled by Boko Haram, but the advances made on the battlefield apparently did little to boost Jonathan's fortunes at the polls. Vote counts indicated that Buhari won by large margins in northern states most affected by the militant group, including in Adamawa, Yobe, Borno and Bauchi states. Despite the recent territorial gains, Buhari will still face significant security challenges.

In addition to Boko Haram, Buhari faced sundry challenges as he prepared to take office in 2015. The government derives about three-quarters of its revenue from oil sales, the value of which plummeted in 2014. The naira, the Nigerian currency, is largely devalued, roads are in need of repair and electricity is extremely unreliable.

For Africa's largest economy, addressing these development issues will be crucial to maintaining Nigeria's position as the largest and most prosperous economic power in the region.

Boko Haram

By 2015 the Islamic State franchise Boko Haram had overtaken its parent organisation as the world's most deadly terrorist organisation, according to a report published in the third edition of the *Global Terrorism Index*, produced by the Institute for Economics and Peace (IEP) which is based on data from the Global Terrorism Database (GTD) which is prepared at the University of Maryland based in Baltimore, US. The Nigerian-based terror group, now also known as Islamic State's West's Africa Province (ISWAP), was responsible for 6,644 deaths in 2014. The (so-called) Islamic State (IS) itself was believed to have killed 6,073 people in the same period. Boko Haram had pledged allegiance to IS in March 2015.

Boko Haram had carried out most of its attacks in Northern Africa, although Nigeria had witnessed a 300 per cent rise in fatalities from terror acts to 7,512 in 2014. This was the largest increase in terrorist-caused deaths ever recorded by any country and was predominantly due to Boko Haram's apparent expansion. In 2013, Nigeria had ranked fifth in terms of

KEY INDICATORS — Nigeria

	Unit	2011	2012	2013	2014	**2015
Population	m	*160.34	164.75	*169.28	*173.94	*178.72
Gross domestic product (GDP)	US$bn	238.90	264.20	521.81	573.65	*515.43
GDP per capita	US$	1,490	1,604	3,082	*3,298	*2,884
GDP real growth	%	7.2	6.6	5.4	6.3	*4.8
Inflation	%	10.8	12.2	8.5	8.1	*9.6
Oil output	'000 bpd	2,457.0	2,417.0	2,322.0	2,361.0	–
Natural gas output	bn cum	39.9	43.2	36.1	38.6	–
Exports (fob) (goods)	US$m	92,503.9	95,676.6	–	–	–
Imports (fob) (goods)	US$m	61,652.8	53,358.8	–	–	–
Balance of trade	US$m	30,851.1	42,317.8	–	–	–
Current account	US$m	8,689.1	20,443.0	20,148.0	*12,674.0	*3,483.0
Total reserves minus gold	US$m	35,768.4	46,405.0	–	36,669.0	–
Foreign exchange	US$m	33,107.2	43,830.0	–	–	–
Exchange rate	per US$	152.98	155.24	158.53	183.00	–

* estimated figure ** forecast figure

the highest levels of deaths, but had moved to second place in 2014, the year in which it expanded rapidly into Chad and Cameroon, staging 46 attacks and claiming 520 lives.

Most Boko Haram attacks are carried out using machine guns. Nigeria's security agency have claimed major breakthroughs in the fight against Boko Haram, reportedly arresting 20 senior members of the group who were accused of orchestrating its attacks. Since his election victory, former President Buhari had made halting Boko Haram's six-year-old insurgency a priority. Buhari had also been working with neighbouring states to set up an 8,700-strong regional military task force to fight the insurgency.

However, a Reuters survey indicated that the militants had killed more than 700 people in Nigeria in bomb attacks and shootings since he came to office at the end of May 2015.

Boko Haram's violent campaign to create a state adhering to strict Islamic law in the north-east of Nigeria had not only left thousands dead. It had also forced around 1.5 million people to flee their homes since 2009.

The insurgents had scattered in early 2015 after an army counter-offensive, but have since returned to a strategy of selective attacks in which they have bombed or fired on targets in public places such as markets and places of worship.

Nevertheless, Nigeria has made some progress against the Islamic insurgents. In 2012–13 Boko Haram had managed to occupy an area of north-eastern Nigeria about the size of the Netherlands. Government offensives had pushed the rebels back into an area based on the Sambisa forest bordering Cameroon. Nigeria's soldiers were no better equipped and better trained. A rehabilitation and rebuilding programme has been started, but progress has been slow. The extent to which towns and villages have actually been retaken and are being restored is also a mater of debate. Boko Haram attacks continue to take lives and agricultural workers are often hesitant about returning to their fields. An estimate quoted in the London *Economist* put the total number of Nigerians displaced by Boko Haram as high as 2.15 million.

The economy

For Africa's largest economy, consolidating on the election result and addressing these development issues will be key to maintaining Nigeria's position as the largest and most prosperous economic power in the region. In its March 2015 annual overview of the Nigerian economy, the International Monetary Fund (IMF) noted that Nigeria had a large and diverse economy that had achieved a decade of strong growth, averaging 6.8 per cent a year. However, Nigeria still lagged behind its peers in critical infrastructure and had high rates of poverty and income inequality. The sharp decline in oil prices in the second half of 2014 underscored the challenging but compelling need to address remaining development challenges.

In 2015, oil exports were projected to decline by 6 percentage points of GDP and oil revenue by 2.4 per cent of GDP from their 2014 levels, with a reduction in the current account balance and loss in international reserves. A sharp contraction in public investment and domestic demand was projected to reduce growth to 4.75 per cent, with inflation increasing to 11.5 per cent from the effects of exchange rate depreciation. These developments also increased the risks to the banking sector, given its significant exposure to the oil industry and the potential for capital outflows. The outlook was subject to significant risks, both external (changes in oil market developments and investor sentiment) and domestic (uncertainty over the new government's policies and the security situation).

In the view of the IMF, the Nigerian authorities had adopted bold policy actions in November 2014 – an adjustment in the official foreign exchange rate and band, the tightening of monetary policy rates and spending cuts totalling 1.7 per cent of GDP in the proposed 2015 budget. As the oil price fall appeared to be more permanent than temporary, additional policies would be needed, including greater flexibility in the exchange rate and further fiscal adjustment, particularly in state and local governments. The IMF considered that it would be essential to ensure that fiscal adjustment was achieved without endangering the delivery of critical public services.

The (outgoing) Nigerian authorities had drawn up a comprehensive economic transformation agenda, designed to boost growth, create new job opportunities and reduce poverty. With recent oil market developments, however, non-oil revenue mobilisation (including an increase in the value added tax (VAT) rate) was more urgent than ever and was critical for creating the fiscal space necessary to implement the transformation agenda. Furthermore, the national infrastructure investment plan needed careful prioritisation, as financing the entire plan would be a challenge, even with more supportive financial conditions and good progress in financial inclusion.

In its 2015 *Economic Outlook* for Nigeria, the African Development Bank (AfDB) noted that the Nigerian economy had enjoyed sustained economic growth for a decade, with annual gross domestic product (GDP) increasing by around 7 per cent; the figure was 6.3 per cent in 2014. The non-oil sector had been the main driver of growth, with services contributing about 57 per cent, while manufacturing and agriculture, respectively contributed about 9 per cent and 21 per cent. The economy was thus diversifying and was becoming more services-oriented, in particular through retail and wholesale trade, real estate, information and communications.

In the view of the AfDB, the 2015 outlook was for moderate growth of 5 per cent, due to vulnerability to slow global economic recovery, oil-price volatility and global financial developments. The low oil price was expected to lead to a sharp decline in fiscal revenues. However, the overall impact on non-oil sector GDP would be relatively muted. The sector was, thus, expected to remain the main driver of growth over the medium term and, in the light of the recent macro-economic challenges, the government had adopted an adjustment strategy that hinged on tightening government spending and shoring up non-oil revenues to compensate for dwindling oil revenues.

Addressing security issues remained a key challenge. The Boko haram insurgency in the north-east and other parts of the country had negative implications for investment; it also might hamper the fight against poverty as well as increase crime. An increased number of both internally displaced persons and refugees in neighbouring Cameroon and Niger had, in he view of the AfDB, created a grave humanitarian situation. However, the current regional coalition force against Boko Haram appeared to be making headway in subduing the insurgency.

Overcoming geographical and socio-economic barriers was central to achieving inclusive growth and sustainable development. Addressing rural-urban differences to ensure more balanced development through job creation and societal transformation would also be critical for Nigeria's future. This would need to be done within all the six geopolitical zones, in addition to addressing inequalities across these zones. Though there had been several policy initiatives aimed at territorial development in Nigeria, limited success had been achieved in addressing the fundamental causes of unevenness. The problem often lay with a structure of governance that gave room for developmental policy implementation at the federal, state and local levels of governance but not at the regional level.

Energy

Nigeria is the largest oil producer in Africa and is among the world's top five exporters of LNG. Despite the relatively large volumes of oil it produces, Nigeria's oil production has been hampered by instability and supply disruptions, while the natural gas sector is restricted by the lack of infrastructure to monetise natural gas that is currently burned off. The long delayed Petroleum Industry Bill (PIB), which was initially proposed in 2008, was expected by the US government Energy Information Administration to change the organisational structure and fiscal terms governing the oil and natural gas industry when it eventually becomes law. However, further delays are expected after incoming President Buhari sacked the entire board of the Nigerian National Petroleum Company (NNPC) in June, less than a month after he was inaugurated on 29 May. International oil companies (IOCs) are concerned that proposed changes to fiscal terms might make some projects commercially unviable, particularly deep-water projects that involve greater capital spending.

Nigeria has the second largest amount of proven crude oil reserves in Africa, but reserve estimates have been stagnant as exploration activity has been low. Rising security problems coupled with regulatory uncertainty have contributed to decreased exploration activity.

Crude oil production in Nigeria reached its peak of 2.44 million barrels per day (bpd) in 2005, before it began to decline significantly as violence from militant groups surged, forcing many companies to withdraw staff and shut down production. Oil production recovered somewhat after 2009 but still remained lower than its peak level because of continuing supply disruptions. The instability in the Niger Delta has resulted in significant amounts of shut-in production at onshore and shallow offshore fields, forcing companies to frequently declare *force majeure* contractual problems on oil shipments.

Risk assessment

Economy	Good/fair
Politics	Fair/good
Regional stability	Fair

Muslims in Nigeria

% of population	47.9
Sunni (% of Muslims)	94
Shi'a (% of Muslims)	5

COUNTRY PROFILE

Between the eleventh and fourteenth centuries, a number of Islamic Hausa kingdoms flourished in the area of modern-day Nigeria, while in the fourteenth and fifteenth centuries the Yoruba Empire developed into a regional power in the south. The Ibo (Igbo), with a diffuse political structure, lived in the east. The Yoruba first made contact with Europeans (Portuguese) in the fifteenth century, who, along with other European nations, began trading in slaves from West Africa.

Mid-1800s There were several civil wars in Yorubaland and in the 1850s the British established themselves in Lagos.

1914 The Colony and Protectorate of Nigeria, the territory that is now Nigeria, was governed by the British through local leaders.

1919 A post-war League of Nations mandate gave some four-fifths of what was then Kamerun to France, and the remainder, bordering Nigeria, to Britain. It became part of Nigeria.

1922 A legislative council was set up. Much local power was left in the hands of traditional chiefs.

1947 A constitution established a federal system of government which attempted to take into account the interests of the three main regions of the colony – the northern and mainly Muslim Hausa and Fulanis, the predominantly Catholic Ibo in the south-east and the mixed Anglican and Muslim Yoruba in the south and west.

1960 Nigeria became independent. Sir Abubakar Tafawa Balewa became prime minister of a coalition government.

1963 The Federal Republic of Nigeria was proclaimed.

1966 In January Sir Abubakar Tafawa Balewa was killed in a coup lead by Major General Johnson Aguiyi-Ironsi. In July Ironsi was killed in a counter-coup lead by Lieutenant-Colonel Yakubu Gowon.

1967 Three eastern, Ibo, states attempted to secede, starting the Biafran Civil War, which was to become one of Africa's most bloody eras. Estimates for the death toll during the war range between 500,000 and two million.

1970 The Civil War ended with the surrender of the Biafran leaders, lead by Colonel Emeka Ojukwu, who went into exile in Côte d'Ivoire.

1970s The Opec-led doubling of the price of oil in October 1973 and again in 1974, led to Nigeria becoming one of Africa's wealthiest states. Nigeria experienced a construction and consumer boom until the price of oil plummeted in the early 1980s.

1975 Yakubu Gowon was overthrown by Brigadier Murtala Ramat Mohammed.

1976 In an attempted coup Murtala Mohammed was assassinated and replaced by Lieutenant-General Olusegun Obasanjo, who had been his deputy. Obasanjo was instrumental in introducing an American-style presidential constitution, which called for elections for the hand over of by the military.

1979 The first elections under the new constitution saw Alhaji Shehu Shagari, a northerner, become president.

1983 Shagari was re-elected in the August elections, which were widely held to be unfair. In December Major-General Muhammad Buhari seized power in bloodless coup.

1985 General Ibrahim Babangida seized power in another bloodless coup. He was widely supported by intellectuals, the press, some former politicians and the business community. The General pledged to return Nigeria to civilian rule, but the hand-over date was repeatedly postponed.

1993 Elections were held, but were later annulled when it appeared that Chief Moshood Abiola was about to win. Babangida stepped down from office. General Sani Abacha seized power in a *coup d'état*. He began to suppress all opposition.

1994 Abiola declared himself president, but was promptly arrested.

1995 Ken Saro-Wiwa, Nigerian writer and advocate of the Ogoni people in eastern Nigeria, and eight other minority rights activists, were executed. There was international outrage against both the government and Shell Oil Company, which had allegedly polluted Ogoni land. Nigeria was suspended from the Commonwealth and the EU imposed sanctions.

1998 Abacha died and General Abdulsalami Abubaker became Head of State. Chief Abiola died while still in custody.

1999 State legislative, National Assembly and presidential elections were held. Olusegun Obasanjo was declared president.

2000 *Sharia* (Islamic law) was adopted in several northern states despite opposition by the Christian minority. Religious and ethnic tensions grew and hundreds of deaths resulted from clashes between Muslims and Christians. Equatorial Guinea and Nigeria signed a treaty agreeing the demarcation of their maritime border.

2001 The heads of Nigeria's army, navy and air force were asked to retire.

President Obasanjo set up a National Security Commission in an attempt to halt the communal violence, sparked mainly by religious differences, which had resulted in thousands of deaths.
2002 Nigeria rejected the International Court of Justice (ICJ) ruling that gave sovereignty of the oil-rich Bakassi peninsula to Cameroon. Clashes in Lagos between northern Hausas and southern Yorubas lead to some 100 deaths.
2003 The People's Democratic Party (PDP) won legislative elections with large majorities in the Lower House and the Senate. Olusegun Obasanjo (PDP) won the presidential election with over 60 per cent of the vote. EU observers said the elections were marred by 'serious irregularities'.
2004 The UN brokered talks between Nigeria and Cameroon concerning their disputed border and both countries agreed to start joint security patrols. Religious clashes in the central Plateau State resulted in a local state of emergency; clashes between gangs in the oil city of Port Harcourt lead to as many as 500 deaths, according to Amnesty International. Swiss authorities said that they would unfreeze most of the US$500 million deposited in Switzerland by the ex-dictator Sani Abacha.
2005 Two-thirds of Nigeria's US$30 billion foreign debt was written off by Paris Club lenders.
2006 The Central Bank of Nigeria (CBN) announced that 13 banks faced liquidation for failing to meet the N25 billion capitalisation targets. Nigeria ceded the Bakassi Peninsula to Cameroon in accordance with the 2002 ICJ ruling. Foreign workers were kidnapped in the Niger Delta area, and pipelines damaged, by militants demanding more control of the oil revenues. Nigeria was able to pay off the remainder of its Paris Club debt after record oil prices.
2007 Umaru Yar'Adua (PDP) was elected president. The Movement for the Emancipation of the Niger Delta (Mend) threatened to resume attacks on oil facilities and to abduct foreign workers in pursuit of their aims to gain more oil revenue for their region. The agreement to hand over parts of the Bakassi Peninsula to Cameroon was rejected by the Senate.
2008 Two leaders of Mend were extradited from Angola. Yar'Adua was confirmed as president following challenges to the elections which were dismissed by a tribunal. Nigeria finally handed over to Cameroon the disputed maritime territory off the Bakassi Peninsula.
2009 Islamist extremist groups, known as Boko Haram (roughly meaning 'Western education is forbidden' in Hausa), established in 2002, began its terrorist actions when it attacked and killed over 140 people across four northern states. The violence was ended after the army shelled the compound in Maiduguri in which many militants were entrenched. The leader of Boko Haram, Mohammed Yusuf, died later in police custody. Hundreds of combatants of Mend surrendered their weapons to the government in an amnesty ceremony. A small faction of Mend said it would continue to resist the oil industry in the Delta region. President Yar'Adua flew to Saudi Arabia for treatment for a heart condition. He left under 'mysterious' circumstances and without informing parliament.
2010 President Yar'Adua died, aged 58 years. Acting-President Goodluck Jonathan was sworn in as president. Namadi Sambo, governor of Kaduna State, was confirmed as vice president by both houses of parliament on 18 May. The CBN extended loans of US$3.3 billion to Nigerian Eagle Airlines, which had been at risk of bankruptcy. The bank had already loaned five other Nigerian airlines amounts totalling over US$2 billion. An agreement was signed for the China State Construction Engineering Corporation (CSCEC) to build a US$8 billion oil refinery in the Lekki free trade zone in Lagos, with three refineries in total; the refineries should go some way to relieving Nigeria's shortage of refined fuel. In an effort to clean up the Nigerian Stock Exchange, the Securities and Exchange Commission sacked its director general, Ndi Okereke-Onyuike, and suspended its chairman. President Jonathan announced he would stand in the 2011 presidential elections, breaking an unwritten agreement within his party that presidential candidates would rotate between the north (typically Muslim) and the south (typically Christian). A car bomb exploded in Abuja as Nigeria celebrated 50 years of independence. At least 12 people were killed by the explosion. Atiku Abubakar emerged as a consensus candidate from the north to challenge President Jonathan in the ruling party primaries.
2011 President Jonathan won party primaries held in January. Parliamentary elections were held in April; 360 members of the House of Representatives and 109 senatorial seats were in contention, 74 million registered voters chose between 54 political parties. Presidential elections were also held in April, in which incumbent Goodluck Jonathan won a convincing majority with 58.89 per cent of the vote, his closest rival, Muhammadu Buhari (CPC), won 31.98 per cent. Riots broke out in northern states after the results were announced and the Red Cross reported that 'tens of thousands' of people had fled their homes as over 200 people were killed and hundreds arrested. Results of the parliamentary elections were not announced for several weeks. By the end of June a preliminary announcement was that the ruling PDP had won 123 seats and ACN 47 in the house of representatives (HR) and 45 and 13 seats in the Senate respectively. Logistical problems in 15 senatorial and 48 HR constituencies held elections that had been postponed. In July, the Independent National Electoral Commission (INEC) said it was postponing its announcement of a definitive account of parliamentary elections and requested continued patience from all parties. President Jonathan announced that he would ask parliament to amend the constitution so that a presidential term in office would be extended, but limited to one term only. In August, the Dutch-owned oil company Shell admitted full liability for environmental damage done to the Niger Delta from two massive oil spills originating from its oil wells. The UN estimated an initial US$1 billion for the cost of the clean-up, which could take up to 30 years. Boko Haram was held responsible for an attack on a Christian church close to Abuja, on Christmas day, killing 40 people.
2012 By the beginning of the year, Nigerian estimates showed Boko Haram had been responsible for some 900 deaths and the attacks and bombings of Christian churches, the police, government buildings and the UN office in Abuja. The parliamentary election results were finally published in April, showing that the PDP had won an unassailable 54.48 per cent of the vote, 152 seats (out of 279) in the house of representatives, and 62.35 per cent (53 seats out of 109) in the senate. On 2 May Chadian President Idriss Déby called for, as a matter of urgency, the creation of a regional force to counter the threat of Boko Haram. A number of West African governments had become concerned by the spread, and increased frequency, of attacks attributed to the group, and its possible connection with Al Qaeda senior leadership, most likely through Al Qaeda in the lands of the Islamic Maghreb. On 16 October, Boko Haram bombed the city of Maiduguri; the army killed 24 militants. On 6 November, over 100 Nigerians were charged with treason for their protest calling for independence in Biafra.
2013 On 6 July least 29 pupils and a teacher were killed in a pre-dawn attack by suspected Islamists on a school in the north-eastern state of Yobe. Bars in Kano suffered a series of explosions on 29 July; at least 28 are people were killed. Similar attacks continued, culminating in an attack killing at least 44 worshippers in a mosque in the north-eastern state of

Borno on 12 August; Boko Haram militants were suspected. The military announced that it had killed Boko Haram's second in command, Momodu Bama early in August. On 19 August at least 35 people were killed in Demba in the north-east; the Boko Haram were suspected. President Jonathan sacked nine cabinet ministers on 11 September. Up to 50 students were shot dead in their dormitory at the College of Agriculture in Yobe state on 29 September. Boko Haram claimed responsibility. The US designated Boko Haram and Ansaru militant groups as foreign 'terrorist' organisations. US regulatory agencies will in future block business and financial transactions with the groups.
2014 A bomb blast in the capital Abuja on 14 April killed 71 people and injured over 120. Although the Boko Haram were blamed there was no confirmation from the rebels that they had caused the blast. It is estimated that by April some 1,500 persons had been killed by the Boko Haram since January. Some 250 students were kidnapped from a girl's school in Chibok in the north-east on 15 April. The girls were driven away into a forested region of Borno state, making rescue extremely difficult. The exact number was not confirmed until 2 May when the Nigerian police announced that of the 276 originally kidnapped 53 had escaped. The President made his first public comments on 3 May when he confirmed that the government would accept assistance from the international community, including the US, UK and France. On 5 May a video statement by Abubakar Shekau, Boko Haram leader, confirmed that the group held the girls and were threatening to 'sell' them as 'slaves' accross the borders into Chad and Cameroon. A video released on 12 May showed some 130 of the abducted girls. On 2 June police banned protests in Abuja demanding the release of the girls. Former central bank governor and prominent government critic, Lamido Sanusi, was named as the new emir of Kano on 9 June. His predecessor, al-Haji Ado Bayero, died on 6 June. He had survived an attack on his convoy on 6 February 2013. A Nigerian finance ministry statement confirmed that 'Nigeria will on 25 June 2014 receive the sum of euros 167 million (US$227 million) from the government of the principality of Liechtenstein, part of looted funds recovered from the Abacha family.' Deaths from the Ebola virus in Nigeria up to 29 October were said, by WHO, to be 8 (out of a total for West Africa of 4,951). The army re-took the town of Chibok four days after it was captured by the Boko Haram on 13 November. Kano's Central Mosque was attacked on 28 November; more than 100 people were reported to have been killed. On 10 December a suicide bomber killed 49 students and injured 86 others at a boys school in Potiskum; two days later a female suicide bomber kill at least three, and injured many others, at a college in Kontangora town. A nation-wide strike by the two main oil workers' unions began on 15 December. Finance minister, Ngozi Okonjo-Iweala, revised the government's growth forecast down to 5.5 per cent for the year, from 6.4 per cent. A new budget was also published in mid-December, based on an oil price of US$65 a barrel.
2015 The Abuja Peace Accord, to resist violence before, during and after the general elections, was signed by President Jonathan, Muhammadu Buhari and other 12 presidential candidates on 10 January. On 20 January a video was seen in which Boko Haram leader Abubakar Shekau claimed his group had been responsible for the attacks on Baga and Doron Baga in the far north-east. Amnesty International satellite pictures showed widespread destruction in the area; there were reports of as many as 2,000 deaths, although the government said the figure was nearer 150. On 30 January the AU backed plans for a West African task force of 7,500 troops to fight Boko Haram militants. The army reported it had repelled a second attack in a week on Maiduguri on 1 February. On 7 February the election commission announced that the 14 February presidential election would be postponed until 28 March for security reasons. On 23 February three suicide bombs (one in Kano and two in Potiskum) killed over 30 people in what was considered a move by Boko Haram to disrupt the election and demonstate that despite the military's recent activity it is still a force to be reckoned with. A pledge of allegiance to Islamic State leader Abu Bakr al-Baghda was posted on line by Boko Haram leader Abubakar Shekau on 6 March. He also called on all Muslims to swear loyalty to IS. Presidential elections were held on 28 March with an extra day after technical problems with the biometric card readers had caused delays. The result was a win for northerner Muhammadu Buhari (APC) with 15,424,921 votes (53.96 per cent) from incumbent Goodluck Jonathan (PDP) with 12,853,162 votes (44.96 per cent). The third placed contestant won just 53,537 votes (0.19 per cent). Turn out was 42.76 per cent. Mr Buhari will take office on 29 May. Mr Jonathan publically conceded defeat and conveyed his 'best wishes' to the president-elect as soon as it became clear that Mr Buhari would be the winner; observers suggest that this will have enabled a peaceful transition and congratulated Mr Jonathan on his move. The military announced on 27 April that they had rescued nearly 300 women and girls from Boko Haram camps in the Sambisa Forest. Although the Chibok girls were thought at one stage to be held in the same area, the military said than they were not among those rescued. On 1 and 2 July suspected Boko Haram Islamist militants were involved in two incidents in Borno State in the north-east. Nearly 150 persons were murdered in two villages. On 10 August President Buhari announced he had appointed a seven-member Presidential Advisory Committee on Anti-Corruption, mostly made up of academics. He is said to beilieve that as much as US$150 billion has been stolen by government officials since 2005. On 25 September the WHO announced that there had been no new cases of polio for a year and that they were removing Nigeria from the list of polio endemic countries. President Buhari submitted his list cabinet members to the Senate president on September 30. It is reported that he will remain in charge of the oil ministry himself, where he has vowed to trace and recover the 'mind-boggling' amount of money that has gone 'missing' from the ministry.

Political structure

Constitution

The 1979 Constitution was amended in 1999, when significant powers were devolved to the 36 states.
The political system is divided into three tiers: the federal or central level, the state level and local government.
Under a presidential system, the president, who is also the commander-in-chief of the armed forces, is vested with executive powers under the Constitution of the federal republic. The president and his ministers form the federal executive council with the president as the chairman.
A similar structure exists in the states where the governor and his commissioners form the state executive councils. Each state has a legislature, executive and judiciary, although their legislative arm is unicameral.

Form of state

Federal republic comprising 36 states and the Federal Capital Territory (FCT, Abuja).

The executive

The Federal Executive Council is headed by an elected president who serves no more than two four-year terms. To win a candidate needs more than 50 per cent of the national vote and at least 25 per cent of the votes in two-thirds of Nigeria's 36 states.
Minimum voting age is 18.
The president is both Head of State and Head of government, initiating the

policies and programmes of the government and ensuring that they are implemented after they have been passed into law by the legislature. The success or failure of any government depends largely on the incumbent president who combines the roles of the chief executive with those of the ceremonial Head of State. The president is directly elected by 'qualified' majority popular vote and must win at least 25 per cent of the votes cast in 24 of Nigeria's 36 states. The president is elected for a four-year term (eligible for a second term).

Despite his wide-ranging power, the president has restrictions, which include ratification of all his major appointments by the National Assembly. The president is excluded from membership of both houses of the National Assembly.

Although he is empowered to conduct foreign affairs, all treaties require the ratification of the Senate. Only the National Assembly can declare war and peace.

While he appoints members of the judiciary, he cannot remove them.

National legislature

The federal, bicameral National Assembly consists of the House of Representatives (lower house), with 360 members elected in single-seat constituencies by simple majority vote, and the Senate (upper house) with 109 members; three elected from each of the 36 states and one from the federal capital territory (FCT). Members are directly elected in single-seat constituencies by simple majority vote. All members of the National Assembly serve for four-year terms.

Each of the states of the federation has a unicameral legislature.

Legal system

Nigeria's legal system is based on English common law, Nigerian customs and tradition, and *Sharia* (Islamic law). *Sharia* predominates in the northern Islamic states.

Last elections

28 March 2015 (presidential); 28 March 2015 (parliamentary).

Results: Presidential: Muhammadu Buhari (All Progressives Congress) (APC) won 15,424,921 votes (53.96 per cent), Goodluck Jonathan (People's Democratic Party) (PDP) 12,853,162 votes (44.96 per cent), 12 other candidates each won less than 0.20 per cent of the vote. Turnout was 43.65 per cent.

Parliamentary (house of representatives): All Progressives Congress (APC) won 225 (out of 360) seats, People's Democratic Party (PDP) 125 seats, the remaining 10 seats were won by other parties.

Parliamentary (Senate): All Progressives Congress (APC) won 60 (out of 109) seats, People's Democratic Party (PDP) 40 seats,Presidential: Muhammadu Buhari (All Progressives Congress) (APC) won 15,424,921 votes (53.96 per cent), Goodluck Jonathan (People's Democratic Party) (PDP) 12,853,162 votes (44.96 per cent), 12 other candidates each won less than 0.20 per cent of the vote. Turnout was 43.65 per cent.

Parliamentary (House of Representatives): All Progressives Congress (APC) won 225 (out of 360) seats, People's Democratic Party (PDP) 125 seats, the remaining 10 seats were won by other parties.

Parliamentary (Senate): All Progressives Congress (APC) won 60 (out of 109) seats, People's Democratic Party (PDP) 40 seats.

Next elections

February 2019 (presidential and parliamentary)

Political parties

Ruling party

All Progressives Congress (APC) (elected Mar 2015)

Main opposition party

Action Congress of Nigeria (ACN)

Population

169.28 million (2013)* The population is expected to reach 278.8 million by 2050. About 52 per cent of the population is male and 48 per cent female. Approximately 47 per cent of the total population is under 15 years of age.

Much of the population is concentrated in the southern part of the country as well and Kano in the north. There has been an expansion of a number of cities, spurred by development and rural–urban migration.

Last census: 21 March 2006: 140,003,542 (provisional)

Population density: 128 inhabitants per square km. Urban population 50 per cent (2010 Unicef).

Annual growth rate: 2.4 per cent, 1990–2010 (Unicef).

Internally Displaced Persons (IDP)

250,000 (UNHCR 2004)

Ethnic make-up

Hausas (21 per cent), Yorubas (20 per cent), Ibos (17 per cent) and Fulani (9 per cent) comprise the four major tribes.

Religions

Islam (about 50 per cent), Christianity (about 40 per cent), traditional beliefs (about 10 per cent).

Education

Primary schooling lasts for six years. Admittance to secondary schooling is through examination. Junior secondary school lasts for three years until age 15 with progress on to senior secondary school until age 18. Some students may undertake technical, vocational schooling from age 12 and can undertake academic and specialised subjects and graduate at age 18.

Around 7 per cent of the government's budget is allocated to education.

Literacy rate: 67 per cent adult rate; 89 per cent youth rate (15–24) (Unesco 2005).

Compulsory years: Six to 15

Enrolment rate: 98 per cent gross primary enrolment of relevant age group (including repeaters); 33 per cent gross secondary enrolment (World Bank).

Pupils per teacher: 34 in primary schools

Health

The Federal Ministry of Health (FMOH) provides policy and technical guidance to the states and the federal capital territory (Abuja), co-ordinating state efforts towards the goals set by the national health policy. Annual health expenditure stands at around 3–4 per cent of GDP, of which government spending is approximately 23 per cent and foreign spending about 7 per cent.

The primary healthcare network has seriously declined with low level coverage of services such as immunisation and supply of essential drugs. The Health System Fund is a major project implemented by the state and federal ministries of health aimed at institutional development, training and an essential drug programme.

Nigeria has a growing problem of HIV/Aids as well as a significant rise of other non-communicable diseases, however, with 65 per cent of the population living below the poverty line, health measures can provide only short-term solutions to systemic problems.

Nigeria in 2012 was one of only three remaining countries (with Pakistan and Afghanistan) where polio is endemic. The UN announced that an outbreak of polio had recurred in Northern Nigeria with 53 cases reported by November 2011, compared to a total of 11 in 2010. There has been a history of mistrust by local people to immunisation and the WHO plans to target the population with more health benefits by combining the polio vaccinations with anti-malaria treatments and integrated healthcare. Some 30 million children were vaccinated against polio during 2009, sponsored by the UN Children's fund, the World Health Organisation and the Nigerian health ministry. Nine vaccinators were shot dead in Kano in 2013. However, rather than scare away the parents of children needing vaccinations, it galvanised support at every level. On 25 September 2015 the WHO announced that there had been no new cases of polio for a year and that they were removing Nigeria from the list of polio endemic countries. There needs to be three years without a new case before the country can be declared free of polio.

Improved water sources are available to 39 per cent of the population.

HIV/Aids

An estimated 3.5 million adults and children are living with HIV/Aids and there are over one million orphans due to Aids. In March 2004 it was disclosed, by Dr Chindo Bissala, the co-ordinator of the State Action Committee against Aids (SACA), that 254,000 persons living in Niger State were confirmed as HIV positive. Dr Bissala was not optimistic that much was being done to check the spread of the disease and that generally people failed to recognise the problem.

In 2003, the government allocated US$157 million for prevention and control activities.

HIV prevalence: 5.4 per cent aged 15–49 in 2003 (World Bank)

Life expectancy: 46 years, 2004 (WHO 2006)

Fertility rate/Maternal mortality rate: 5.5 births per woman, 2010 (Unicef); maternal mortality 800 per 100,000 live births (World Bank).

Birth rate/Death rate: 39.6 births and 13.9 deaths per 1,000 people

Child (under 5 years) mortality rate (per 1,000): 124 per 1,000 live births (WHO 2012); 28.7 per cent of children aged under five-years suffer malnutrition (World Bank).

Head of population per physician: 0.28 physicians per 1,000 people, 2003 (WHO 2006)

Welfare

The Nigerian public service schemes, the private sector self-administered and insured scheme, the National Provident Fund (NPF) and the Nigeria Social Insurance Trust Fund (NSITF) schemes, provide for old age, survivorship, invalidity and industrial injury benefits, gratuity and pension. The Workmen's Compensation Act provides for industrial injury benefits. Despite the existence of these bodies, the social security system is virtually non-existent in Nigeria.

The pensions fund management is divided into two categories: government schemes and occupational schemes. The government scheme provides basic social benefits that are not earnings-related, and earnings-related pension provisions. Such schemes are funded mainly through contributions from the government, with minimal contributions from the scheme members. The government policy allows individuals in self-employment to claim premiums paid to any insurance company, provided such premiums do not exceed 10 per cent of the individuals total income. This is in addition to any relief claimed in respect of life assurance policies. The occupational pension schemes consists of private companies' schemes, which are employment related and financed jointly by the employers and employees.

Main cities

Abuja (Federal Capital Territory in central Nigeria – estimated population 1.6 million (m) in 2012). Lagos (former capital; estimated population 10.4m). State capitals: Ibadan (Oyo) (5.5m), Benin City (Edo) (2.6m), Kano (Kano) (2.4m), Port Harcourt (Rivers) (2.3m), Kaduna (Kaduna) (2.2m). Other populous cities: Aba (1.7m), Maiduguri (Borno) (1.2m), Ilorin (Kogi – formerly Kwara) (1.2m), Warri (1.1m), Onitsha (990,712).

Languages spoken

English is used in business and public life. Hausa, Yoruba and Ibo are widely spoken.

Official language/s

English

Media

The constitution guarantees freedom of the press. However the intimidate of journalists and editors by security forces has resulted in beatings and detentions. State authorities have also charged editors and owners with sedition or security implications for articles with which they have take exception.

Libel is a criminal offence, with the onus of truth of opinion or valued judgement placed on the defendant, so that self-censorship is not unknown.

Press

Dailies: There are over a dozen newspapers published in both the morning and evening, although not all are nationally distributed. Three evening papers are published in Lagos and one in Ibadan.

In English, government-owned newspapers include *Daily Times of Nigeria* (www.dailytimes-nigeria.com), *New Nigerian* (www.newnigeriannews.com) and *Daily Independent* (www.independentng.com). Independent newspapers include *The Guardian* (www.ngrguardiannews.com), *Daily Vanguard* (www.vanguardngr.com), *Punch* (www.punchng.com) and the *Daily Sun* (www.sunnewsonline.com), which is a tabloid.

Weeklies: There are several news magazines published including *Newswatch* (www.newswatchngr.com) and *Tell* (www.tellng.com).

Business: In English, several publications are available, *Business Day* (www.businessdayonline.com) and *Financial Standard* (www.financialstandardnews.com) are dailies, other journals include *Business Eye* (www.businesseyeng.com), and *Business Life* (www.thenigeriabusiness.com).

Periodicals: Monthly magazines include *The President* for current affairs, *Ovation* (www.ovationinternational.com) for society and lifestyles and *Genevieve* for young women.

Broadcasting

Both federal and state governments operate radio stations and most operate television services, in English and local languages.

Radio: Due to the low literacy rate radio services are the main medium of mass communication and sources of news and information. Radio station must be licensed to operate.

The Federal Radio Corporation of Nigeria (FRCN) operates Radio Nigeria (www.radionigeriaonline.com) a national network which includes regional programming and the external service Voice of Nigeria (www.voiceofnigeria.org) broadcasting in English, French and Arabic as well as five local languages. There are many other, private stations including Brilla FM (http://brila-fm.the11sow.com) from Lagos, Aso Radio from Abuja and Cosmo FM (www.cosmofm.com) from Enugu.

Television: Licensing rules require locally made content to amount to around 60 per cent which places additional costs on private broadcasters, plus insufficient advertising revenues limits the potential for free-to-air services; pay-to-view TV is growing in popularity.

The national, state-owned broadcaster is the Nigerian Television Authority (NTA) (www.ntaplus.com) operates a number of regional stations to make up a comprehensive network. Other private, regional TV stations include AIT (www.daarnews.com) from Lagos and Abuja, Silverbird TV (www.silverbirdgroup.com) from Lagos and Port Harcourt and Channels TV (www.channelstv.com).

National news agency: NAN (News Agency of Nigeria)

Other news agencies: APA (African Press Agency): www.apanews.net Reuters Africa: http://africa.reuters.com

Economy

Following an April 2014 statistical 'rebasing' exercise, Nigeria emerged as Africa's largest economy, with 2014 GDP estimated at US$479 billion. Oil has been a dominant source of government revenues since the 1970s, however, diversification in agriculture, telecommunications, and services has allowed the Nigerian economy to continue to grow at a rapid rate of 6–8 per cent per annum despite the fall in oil prices. Economic diversification and strong growth have not translated into a significant decline in poverty levels – over 62 per cent of

Nigeria's population live in extreme poverty. Former President Goodluck Jonathon established an economic team which aimed to increase transparency, continue to diversify production, and further improve fiscal management. The government is working to develop stronger public/private partnerships for roads, agriculture, and power. Nigeria still lacks an adequate power supply and infrastructure, it has a slow and ineffective judicial system, unreliable dispute resolution mechanisms, insecurity and pervasive corruption.

Nigeria has vast wealth in petroleum reserves; however as the most populous country in Africa, with 178.3 million inhabitants its per capita income in 2014 was just US$3,150. It has Africa's second largest oil reserves (after Libya) at 37 billion barrels at the end of 2014; with production at 2.4 million barrels per day; it is Africa's biggest petroleum exporter. There were natural gas reserves of 5.1 trillion cubic metres (cum) at the end of 2014, with production of 38.6 billion cum in 2014 and a target of 35 billion cum in 2015. Of the 27 billion cum exported in 2014, approximately 9 million cum was exported via the new West African Gas Pipeline (WAGP) to Ghana and the remainder converted to liquefied natural gas (LNG) and exported to Asia, Europe and North America.

The exploitation of Nigeria's oil reserves has created political and economic turmoil and has not benefited the majority of its population in tangible ways. There has been a huge loss of oil revenues due to fraud and embezzlement by the ruling elite, as well as wastage and the 'diversion' of oil for illegal sales. High levels of inflation (8.1 per cent in 2014) and a lack of investment in non-oil sectors have also contributed to Nigeria's economic woes.

The structure of the economy in 2014 reflects the influence of the hydrocarbon sector but also the successful diversification in the economy, with industry accounting for some 26 per cent of GDP, agriculture 21 per cent and a huge increase in services of 54 per cent.

The International Monetary Fund (IMF) considered that Nigeria had weathered the global economic crisis better than other oil-based economies in 2008, due in large part to economic reforms undertaken before 2008. GDP growth was 6.0 per cent in 2008, increasing to 7 per cent in 2009 and higher still to 8 per cent in 2010, reflecting the marked increase in exports of natural gas; the economy weakened to an estimated 7.2 per cent in 2011. High inflation is a long-term problem, averaging 15 per cent between 2000–05 but falling to 8.2 per cent in 2006 and further still to 5.4 per cent in 2007; it sprang back to 11.6 per cent in 2008 due to higher food and local fuel prices and continued to grow, to 12.5 per cent, in 2009 and as world trade weakened further to 13.7 per cent in 2010. Inflation has since decreased to 8.5 per cent in 2013 and 8.1 per cent in 2014. GDP growth has continued to remain strong at a rate of 4.3 per cent in 2012 and 5.4 per cent in 2013 before increasing to a healthy rate of 6.3 per cent in 2014.

In 2010, a new bank was founded, the Asset Management Corporation of Nigeria (Amcon), specifically to siphon off toxic debts owned by domestic banks. This followed a US$4 billion bailout of nine of the biggest banks in Nigeria in 2009. The bad debts were replaced with government-guaranteed bonds to re-invigorate the banking sector as a whole and make it attractive to new investors. The high global prices for oil in 2008 boosted Nigeria's current account, which increased from US$31.2 billion in 2007 to US$42.3 billion in 2008, and gave it the cushion necessary for the external shock of capital outflows of foreign investor equities.

In 2014, the UN Human Development Index (HDI) ranked Nigeria as 152 (out of 187) for development in health, education and income and in 2014, 60 per cent of the population live in extreme poverty. The inequality and poverty that has caused ethnic tensions and resulted in violence and death between residents, newcomers and migrant workers, as seen in 2014, may continue until the economy can generate and maintain an income for the majority of the population. Remittances amounted to US$21 billion in 2014 (4 per cent of GDP).

External trade

Nigeria is a member of the Economic Community of West African States (Ecowas), which was set up to promote economic integration among members. It is a member of the Anglophone, West African Monetary Zone (WAMZ), which plans to introduce a common currency. WAMZ will eventually be merged with the Francophone-members' currency to produce a single currency (the eco) for the region.

The oil sector is vital to the economy as it provides US$77 billion and 14 per cent of GDP and 92 per cent of foreign earnings.

As Africa's most populous nation, Nigeria is required to import food and goods.

Imports

Principal imports include machinery, chemicals, transport equipment, manufactured foods, food and live animals.

Main sources: China (25.3 per cent of total in 2014), US (9.7 per cent) and India (4.7 per cent).

Exports

Principal exports are petroleum and petroleum products (typically 95 per cent of total), cocoa, rubber, timber and manufactured goods.

Main destinations: India (15.4 per cent of total in 2014), Brazil (10.2 per cent), Netherlands (8.5 per cent), Spain (8.5 per cent), South Africa (5.5 per cent) and France (5.4 per cent).

Agriculture

Farming

The sector has suffered a relative decline because of the dominance of oil in the economy, but it is still the dominant area of employment, employing around half of the workforce in 2014.

Land suitable for arable production has been put at 25 per cent of the total area, of which about 12 per cent is cultivated. The country suffers from soil degradation, deforestation and water pollution.

Key government policies include food self-sufficiency and boosting non-food crops to meet demand from the agri-processing sector. The sector is still dominated by unproductive smallholders raising subsistence crops such as sorghum, maize, cassava, yams, millet, rice and increasing quantities of wheat – up to 70 per cent of which is for private consumption. Nigeria is a leading world producer of cassava and the second largest producer of ginger.

Plantations, sometimes owned by, or in partnership with, multinational corporations, are gaining ground in producing raw materials for commercial use, for example grain for breweries. Irrigation schemes, higher producer prices, the expansion of credit and improvements in the rural infrastructure are beginning to show positive results.

Cash crops include cocoa, rubber (nearly all exported), coffee, cotton, peanuts and palm kernels. Cocoa is Nigeria's largest foreign exchange earner after oil. The palm oil sector is being redeveloped. Livestock farming is important, while poultry farming is rapidly increasing.

In 2013 a sharp decline was reported in Northern Nigeria's grain trade, which supplies almost half of the Sahel's cereals. Abnormally high prices of staple grains across the Sahel were causing serious food security concerns in northern Nigeria, northern Benin and south-eastern and central Niger. The widespread flooding of 2012 as well as the Boko Haram insurgency which has disrupted farming, have contributed to the shortage.

Fishing

Over N30 billion (US$238 million) is spent annually on fish imports despite the country's large fishing potential.

There is extensive fishing in the Niger River network and along the south coast.

Forestry

Nigeria has 15 per cent forest cover and an additional 54 per cent of other wooded land comprising mainly savannah. There are growing forestry operations in the tropical zones in southern Nigeria and north of Port Harcourt. The extensive network of national parks and reserves protect around 5 per cent of its forests.

Nigeria is one of the largest wood producers in Africa showing an annual harvest of more than 100 million cubic metres, most of which is used for fuel consumption. The large-scale industrial forestry sector produces sawn timber, plywood, particleboard and paper mostly to meet local demands.

Northern Nigeria is most threatened by deforestation and government concerns over desertification led to urgent action plans including a US$44.5 million National Tree Nursery Programme. However, the National Forest Conservation Council of Nigeria (NFCCN) reported that of the 50 million seedlings planted each year in the 11 northern states, 37.5 million died within two months. The remaining 12.5 million seedlings are insufficient to create a deforestation-reforestation equilibrium. An estimated 40.5 million tonnes is used as firewood in the north annually.

Industry and manufacturing

Production costs in industry are considerably increased by a lack of basic infrastructure, which compels every factory to have its own standby electricity plant and sometimes a water borehole. Companies also find it difficult to source vital components from abroad with uncertain supplies of foreign exchange, but this situation is gradually improving thanks to the liberalisation of the economy.

The most promising sub-sector is the textile industry, which has taken advantage of the country's production of raw materials, such as cotton. With growth in textiles, there has been substantial consolidation in the sector with many small operations being swallowed up by larger firms. However, the liberalisation of trade threatens the sector.

The manufacturing sector in Nigeria has suffered as much neglect as have agriculture, health and education. There is a total absence of hi-tech industrial complex, which causes the country to be absolutely import-dependent for technological hard and soft ware. An example of Nigeria's weak manufacturing sector is that 151 million Nigerians own mobile phones and every single one of them is imported into the country along with their spare parts and accessories. Developed countries like South Korea, Germany and the US make huge amounts of money from supplying high quality ICT devices to Nigeria's enormous market.

The steel industry in Nigeria is also suffering because of a recent influx of foreign steel. Apart from the job losses likely to result, a country's steel sector is at the hearts of its industrial revolution, an area where Nigeria is grossly lacking both in capacity and efficiency. It is estimated that 7000 people in the employment of Africa Foundries limited and an estimated 13,000 other employees in other steel producing companies across the country are threatened.

In order to save the manufacturing sector in Nigeria, the government needs to invest a huge amount of money into the industry to create jobs and reduce dependence on foreign imports.

Tourism

Nigeria is not only one of Africa's largest countries, it is the most populous, roughly divided into the Muslim north and Christian south with different cultural features to attract visitors. The north of the country is a dry, savannah terrain with domestic browsing animals alongside African wildlife. The south has lush forests that fringe the coastline with mangrove swamps.

There are two sites included on Unesco's World Heritage List.

Despite the government's recognition of the potential for ecotourism to the economy, few large forest animals have survived. The African species that draw visitors – elephants, lions and hippopotami – have dwindled in numbers and are isolated in scattered localities. Without a co-ordinated strategy to save their habitat most of these species, located in the south, are likely to die out.

The contribution of travel and tourism to the economy averaged 3.8 per cent over 2007–11. The contribution of the tourism sector to the economy was 4.1 per cent in 2014 (US$19 billion). Employment in the industry remains low with an average 3.3 per cent (1.9 million jobs) (2007–11). Employment in the sector was 3.6 per cent of the total employment (2,198,500 jobs). Domestic spending on travel and tourism was US$12.8 billion, far outstripping foreign receipts of US$582 million in 2014.

Nigeria has the potential to be a major tourist destination but it is currently underdeveloped and while there are sites of excellence, in hotels, animal reservations and individual tourist attractions, the infrastructure that should link or support them are woefully inadequate. Major capital investment in the country is necessary before the country could benefit from the trade and foreign exchange that tourism could provide.

In 2012 Western governments began to warn their citizens of the risk posed by the terrorist Islamic group Boko Haram, not only from bombings but also the possible kidnapping of tourists. In 2014, civilians are still not advised to visit Nigeria, it is only the hardiest of tourists that will venture out to the country.

Environment

Drilling operations in the Niger Delta region have created huge pollution problems from oil spills and explosions. Oil exploitation has been a fact of life for many people living in the Delta, particularly the Ogoni people.

Nigeria's pollution problems are exacerbated by the fact that the country does not have a pollution control policy. Analysts have reported that during oil production, Nigeria flares more natural gas than any other country in the world, contributing to global warming. The government hopes to end gas flaring by 2008.

In June 2010 the African Union backed a proposal to build the 'Great Green Wall' project, of a 15km wide, 7,775km long, continuous belt of trees from Senegal in the west to Djibouti in the east (traversing 11 countries) in an effort to halt the advance of the Sahara Desert. The trees to be used would be drought-adapted, preferably native to the area from a list of 37 possible species, and should help to slow soil erosion and filter rain water.

Mining

In 2014, mining only contributed 0.3 per cent to Nigeria's GDP.

Nigeria used to be one of the world's largest producers of tin, with production based around the highland district of Jos. It is now the smallest of the Association of Tin Producing Countries (ATPC). The country's only tin smelter is at Makeri. Tin reserves are estimated at 16,000 tonnes.

Independent estimates place iron ore reserves at 800 million tonnes, averaging 37 per cent metal content.

Deposits of uranium, lead, zinc, tungsten and gold have not yet been exploited.

There are 65 sites in Nigeria where gold has been located. The Iperindo gold project in Oshun State has a resource of some 400,000 ounces of gold.

Nigeria Mining Corp has taken up a number of projects including gold, tantalum and tin with the aim of attracting more capital in anticipation of increased private sector involvement.

Work on a new mine began in May 2009, which has become the world's second-largest uranium mine, producing

5,000 tonnes per annum. The French-based Areva provided the majority of the investment of US$1.5 billion and will take a majority share in its profits. The mine is located in the north in the traditional region of the Tuareg people.

Hydrocarbons

Proven oil reserves were 37 billion barrels in 2014, with production at 2.4 billion barrels per day (bpd); Nigeria is the world's thirteenth and Africa's largest producer of crude oil. The economy is heavily dependent on the petroleum sector, which accounts for 92 per cent of export earnings and around 85 per cent of government revenue. The Nigerian National Petroleum Corporation (NNPC) is the commercial entity through which the government Department of Petroleum Resources (DPR) participates in the oil industry. The NNPC is responsible for all upstream and downstream developments, including exploration, production and distribution activities within the sector. It also regulates and supervises the oil industry.

Under the constitution, all hydrocarbon reserves are the legal property of the federal government, therefore all oil companies in production have a portion of their revenue, appropriated by the government; typically this amounts to almost 60 per cent of all revenue generated by the industry.

Refinery capacity was 445,000 bpd in 2015, however, Nigeria only refined 57,000 bpd. Nigeria exported 2.1 million bpd of crude oil in 2015. It is a net exporter of crude oil.

In February 2012, the principal foreign oil company operating in Nigeria, Shell, estimated that up to 150,000bpd of oil (5 per cent of total production) was being stolen from pipelines each year. In Shell's opinion, theft has reduced the interest of foreign oil companies in further exploration. This was confirmed by a report published by the London-based think-tank Chatham House in September 2013 which said Nigeria's oil was being looted on an 'industrial' scale and that the proceeds were being laundered in world financial centres. The report also estimated that as much as 5 per cent of Nigeria's oil is looted.

The industry has been traditionally located in the south-eastern Niger River Delta, which has become a battleground for indigenous peoples, with militants of the Movement for the Emancipation of the Niger Delta (Mend) demanding more control and redistribution of profits from oil production. Supplies of oil and gas have been targeted with pipeline vandalism and oil siphoning – which has resulted in a number of major explosions with hundreds of deaths each year. The government estimates that around 300,000bpd of oil is sold illegally on to the black market – with militant take-overs of facilities and foreign workers kidnapped. Such attacks have hampered production, down as low as 1.8 billion bpd in 2008, and forced some oil companies to shut-in (suspend) production. Corruption has been blamed for much of the squandering of the billions of US dollars in oil revenue earned since the 1960s, so much so that of the 20 million people in 3,000 communities living in the Niger River Delta, 70 per cent are reckoned to live on less than US$1 per day.

Proven gas reserves were 5.1 trillion cubic metres (cum) in 2014, with production targeted at 35 billion cum in 2015, Nigeria is the world's twenty-seventh largest and Africa's third largest producer (after Algeria and Egypt) of natural gas, however, its reserves are the ninth largest in the world. Nigeria would like to use gas as its principle source of domestic energy, however capital investment has not been forthcoming for the necessary infrastructure projects to collect, process and distribute natural gas. Much of the associated natural gas is flared at source (at oil-heads), losing an estimated US$1.46 billion per annum in revenue for NNPC, as well as meaning that less is available domestically for energy purposes. The majority of natural gas production is used in exports of liquefied natural gas (LNG), 25.9 billion cum in 2011 and Spain was the single largest recipient with 6.6 billion cum. Nigeria has a long way to go before it can exploit its large natural gas reserves properly. Its infrastructure is lacking and corruption is rife.

The West African Gas Pipeline (WAGP), funded by US oil company Chevron Texaco and the governments of Nigeria, Ghana, Togo and Benin, began pumping natural gas to Ghana in 2008, providing 120 million cum per annum. Togo and Benin are supplied with substantially smaller amounts. Chevron Texaco will manage the pipeline, for a fixed fee, until 2016.

Coal reserves are plentiful, although production only supplies a tiny percentage of domestic energy requirements. Coal exports are negligible, due to obsolete equipment and a lack of investment following years when the coal sector was a government monopoly.

Energy

Total installed generating capacity was 6,953MW in 2013, producing over 22.1 billion kilowatt hours, of which 67 per cent was produced by oil and natural gas while 33 per cent was produced from by hydroelectric power.

The state-owned Power Holding Company of Nigeria (PHCN) is responsible for generating, transmission, distribution and sale of electricity in Nigeria. However it is a poorly functioning company and lack of capacity and outages are commonplace. The government is in the process of privatising it, by unbundling aspects of the business.

Over 50 per cent of the population is not connected to electricity supplies and the population, mainly rural, relies on biomass (wood fuel, kerosene and charcoal) for energy, which has led to considerable deforestation. The Egbin thermal power station, outside Lagos, is the country's largest electricity plant, fuelled by oil. Other thermal and hydroelectric stations have also been neglected. It is common for international companies setting up in business in Nigeria to provide their own power, as do many individuals who generate electricity for their own domestic and commercial use.

Financial markets

Stock exchange

Nigerian Stock Exchange (NSE). Plans to de-mutalise the NSE were at an early stage in August 2010.

Banking and insurance

Nigeria's banking sector is the second-largest in Africa behind South Africa, but it has experienced difficulties in recent years. Since the late 1990s, the Central Bank of Nigeria (CBN) has worked towards cleaning up the banking sector.

The end of military rule in 1999 saw international banks return to Nigeria, although they concentrate their operations in Lagos and Abuja supplying services for big businesses and Nigerian expatriates. The CBN does not differentiate between licensing of commercial and merchant banks, which enables merchant banks to issue cheques and allows them to access the CBN's clearing house.

In 2005 the CBN began restructuring the banking sector by setting a minimum capital requirement that has forced banks into consolidation. The IMF is advising the CBN on the banking reform programme.

A persistent obstacle to the banking sector's development is Nigeria's culture of fraud; the CBN has been keen to address, the advance fee fraud scams, run by criminal gangs. A Financial Intelligence Unit monitors the banking environment to strengthen the anti-money laundering framework that is under way.

Other problems include the federal and state governments' borrowing from domestic banks, which has severely restricted liquidity in the banking sector.

It was announced in March 2005 that the introduction of the shared currency, the Eco, in Nigeria, Ghana, Guinea, Sierra

Leone and The Gambia, which was due in July 2005, would be postponed. The currency was proposed to facilitate trade and growth with an ultimate plan to merge it with the CFA franc.
On 1 January 2006 the CBN announced that 13 banks faced liquidation for failing to meet its N25 billion capitalisation target.

Central bank
Central Bank of Nigeria (CBN)

Main financial centre
Lagos

Offshore facilities
Nigeria is on the Organisation for Economic Co-operation and Development (OECD) Financial Action Task Force (FATF) list of non-co-operative countries on money laundering.

Time
GMT plus one hour

Geography
Nigeria is bordered to the west by Benin, to the north by Niger, to the north-east by Chad, to the east by Cameroon and to the south by the Bight of Benin (Atlantic Ocean). The main rivers, the Niger and Benue, merge in the centre of the country, dividing it into three main regions of north, south and east. The north consists of dry savannah, the south of jungle, with mangrove swamps nearer the coast, and the east of a plateau leading into the country's only major mountain range along the Cameroon border.

Hemisphere
Northern

Climate
The climate varies from tropical on the coast to sub-tropical in the north. There are two main seasons, the rainy season from April to October and the dry season from November to March, which is characterised by a cool dust haze from the Sahara known as the *harmattan*.
Average temperatures remain fairly constant throughout the year at 29 degrees Celsius (C) in the south. The average daytime temperature in the north is 42 degrees C, but the temperature can drop to as low as 6 degrees C at night.
Humidity is high in the south, with a maximum varying from 100 per cent to 80 per cent. Rainfall is heavy on the coast, ranging from about 180cm a year in the south-west to 430cm in the south-east.
Near-temperate conditions are common on the central plateau and along the hilly north-eastern border with Cameroon.

Dress codes
Suits or traditional dress are worn for business meetings, but otherwise dress is informal. Women are advised to dress modestly, especially in the Islamic north. For social occasions, dress as for a business meeting.

Entry requirements
Passports
Required by all and must be valid for six months beyond the date of departure.

Visa
Required by all; some exceptions are made for citizens of countries located close to Nigeria. Visas should be obtained before arrival, contact the nearest consular office, or see www.nigeriabusinessinfo.com/visas.htm for details.
Business visitors will require a letter of invitation, from an organisation or individual, addressed to the Visa Section of the High Commission or Embassy. A declaration of full compliance of all entry requirements or proof of sufficient funds for expenses (such as traveller's cheques to be cashed in Nigeria), must be lodged.
Any individual inviting a visitor must attach photocopies of the first five pages of his/her own passport, while a resident must enclose a copy of his/her residence permit.

Currency advice/regulations
The import and export of local currency is limited to N20. The import of foreign currency is unlimited but must be declared, its export is limited to N100. Visitors are advised not to use unauthorised currency exchange methods, which are illegal.
Travellers cheques have limited use in cities and larger towns.

Customs
Laws against exporting Nigerian antiquities are strictly enforced.

Prohibited imports
Sparkling wines and beer, fruits and vegetables, eggs and cereals, precious metals and textiles including mosquito netting.

Health (for visitors)
Mandatory precautions
Yellow fever vaccination certificate required if coming from an infected area.

Advisable precautions
Inoculations and booster should be current for tetanus, polio, hepatitis A, diphtheria, typhoid and yellow fever. There may be a need for vaccinations for tuberculosis, hepatitis B and meningitis and cholera. Use malaria prophylaxis (which will also provide protection for hepatitis B and yellow fever) including mosquito repellents, nets and clothing that fully cover the body after dark. There is a risk of rabies.
Other diseases that require preventative measures are HIV/Aids, hepatitis C and E; to avoid bilharzia, use only well-maintained and chlorinated swimming pools.
Use only bottled or boiled water for drinks, washing teeth and making ice. Eat only well cooked meals, preferably served hot; vegetables should be cooked and fruit peeled. Dairy products are unpasteurised and should be avoided, unless cooked.
Walking in bare feet, or even open sandals, can attract parasites, notably jikkers.
Visitors should seek advice before accepting treatment involving hypodermic needles or blood transfusions. Medical insurance is essential, including emergency evacuation, and an adequate supply of personal medicines is necessary.

Hotels
There is a wide range of hotels available, though rooms are difficult to obtain and expensive in Lagos. Bills must be paid for in foreign currency and a high deposit in advance is required to cover the estimated length of stay. Most major hotels are air-conditioned.

Credit cards
Credit cards are not widely used.

Public holidays (national)
Fixed dates
1 Jan (New Year's Day), 1 May (Workers' Day), 29 May (Democracy Day), 1 Oct (National Day), 25–26 Dec (Christmas).

Variable dates
Easter (Mar/Apr), Eid al Adha, Birth of the Prophet, National Day (first Mon in Oct), Eid al Fitr.
Holidays that fall at the weekend may be taken on Monday.
Islamic year 1437 (15 Oct 2015–2 Oct 2016):: The Islamic year contains 354 or 355 days, with the result that Muslim feasts advance by 10–12 days against the Gregorian calendar. Dates of feasts vary according to the sighting of the new moon, so cannot be forecast exactly.

Working hours
Banking
Mon: 0800–1500; Tue–Fri: 0800–1330 (some banks work until 1600 or 1700); Sat, some banks only: 1000–1500.

Business
Mon–Fri: 0800–1230 and 1400–1630. Some offices also Sat: 0800–1200.

Government
Mon–Fri: 0730–1530, some states also Sat: 0800–1300.

Shops
Mon–Fri: 0800–1200 and 1430–1800; Sat: 0800–1300.

Telecommunications
Mobile/cell phones
There are GSM roaming facilities available, with coverage throughout most of the country. As of June 2014 it was estimated that there were almost 166 million mobile subscribers in Nigeria.

Electricity supply
230V AC, 50 cycles

Social customs/useful tips
Because of the prodigious traffic jams, called 'go-slows', which often grip Lagos, it is hard to be punctual, so both Nigerians and expatriates are generally tolerant of latecomers.
Appointments with government officials should be made in advance. With business executives, a more informal attitude prevails. Business cards are exchanged after introduction and business is mostly conducted in English. Meetings can be long and they are less formal than in Europe. It is customary to shake hands on meeting and taking leave.
Confirm the business organisation's status with the Chamber of Commerce, Corporate Affairs Commission, Abuja and the Federal Ministry of Commerce and Tourism, Abuja, before entering into a firm contract.
Local customs and conventions should be adhered to, particularly in Muslim areas in the northern states. Women should not wear trousers.
Gifts are welcomed but not essential, unless hospitality extends to accommodation and/or meals, in which case gifts are expected on departure.
Gratuities are around 10 per cent. A service charge is usually added to restaurant and hotel bills. Tips are not expected by taxi drivers. Giving *dash* or gratuities for other commercial services is widespread, although officially discouraged .

Security
Security remains a serious problem in several Nigerian cities, but chiefly in Lagos. The biggest threat comes from armed robbers. They either attack houses at night or, more frequently, stop cars at gunpoint on urban or country expressways and order the driver to hand over the keys. Petty theft is also common; moneybelts are advisable.
During outbreaks of violence, the capital is likely to be dotted with checkpoints manned by armed police, where visitors should remain calm and courteous. It is not necessary to offer a bribe at these roadblocks.

Getting there
Air
International airport/s: Abuja Nnamdi Azikiwe (ABV), 35km from city; Kano-Mallam-Aminu Kano (KAN), 8km from city; Lagos-Murtala Muhammed (LOS), 22km from city. All airport facilities include duty-free shop, restaurant, bar, bank, post office, car hire.
It is advisable to be met at Lagos airport by someone you know, or someone who can prove their identity. Also make sure you do not give your passport to anyone but the immigration officer. Check in early for flights as overbooking is common.
Airport tax: None
Surface
Road: There are good roads linking Niger (Maradi, Zinder, Agadez, Niamey) to Kano, and from Benin; there are all-weather roads from Cameroon (Maroua, Mokolo) and Chad (N'Djamna). The southern road from Cameroon (Mamfe) to Enugu is not generally recommended.
Water: Nigeria has the biggest port facilities and international sailings in the region.
Main port/s: Apapa (Lagos), Port Harcourt, Calabar and the Delta Port complex including Warri, Sapele and Koko.

Getting about
National transport
Air: There is a number of local airlines providing intercity services. Routes and airlines frequently change.
Road: A national road network system of 113,000km links all main centres. Principal main roads connect Lagos and Port Harcourt in the south with Kano and Katsina in the north. The motorway running from Lagos-Ibadan is often congested. There are often long delays in major towns.
Some secondary roads can become impassable during rainy season.
Buses: Scheduled coach services include: Kaduna-Jos; Lagos-Umuahia.
Rail: There are some 3,500km of railway, mostly single track.
Rail travel is cheap, but slow. There are two classes. Some trains have restaurant cars and buffet facilities and some have air-conditioning.
There are two main rail lines: Lagos-Kano Express (via Ibadan and Minna) with branches to Baro, Kaura Namoda and Nguru, Plateau Express (Lagos-Jos); and Port Harcourt-Kano with branch to Jos and Maiduguri.
Water: There are over 8,575 km of waterways including the Niger and Benue rivers, with ferry services on these and along the southern coast.
City transport
Taxis: Taxis are widely available in Lagos and other main towns. The traditional taxis are usually yellow Peugeots in Lagos (these charge by distance), other colours elsewhere. Also numerous cars belonging to car hire companies. Taxi ranks are mainly found at the big hotels. Fare and tip should be agreed before starting journey. All drivers should have an Identity Card.
Journey time from Lagos Murtala Mohammed Airport to city centre is around 40 minutes, but can take several hours if the traffic is heavy.
Car hire
Available in most of the large towns through the main hotels. International driving licence and two passport-sized photographs required; chauffeur-driven services generally recommended.
Be aware that in Lagos the Lagos State Traffic Management Authority (Lastma) has wide powers and frequently stops and seizes vehicles for minor, alleged, offences. On the spot 'fines' are frequently suggested. Owners of vehicles that are impounded have to pay a daily charge to recover them.

BUSINESS DIRECTORY
The addresses listed below are a selection only. While World of Information makes every endeavour to check these addresses, we cannot guarantee that changes have not been made, especially to telephone numbers and area codes. We would welcome any corrections.

Telephone area codes
The international direct dialling code (IDD) for Nigeria is +234, followed by area code and subscriber's number:

Abuja	9	Katsina	65
Akure	34	Lagos	1
Bauchi	77	Maiduguri	76
Calabar	87	Makurdi	44
Enugu	42	Minna	66
Ibadan	22	Owerri	83
Ikeja	1	Oyo	38
Ilorin	31	Port Harcourt	84
Jos	73	Sokoto	60
Kaduna	62	Yola	75
Kano	64	Zaria	69

Useful telephone numbers
Police: 199
Fire and ambulance: 999

Chambers of Commerce
Abuja Chamber of Commerce and Industry, International Trade Fair Centre, Airport Road, PO Box 86, Abuja (tel: 523-0453; fax: 523-6231; e-mail: anmgbemere@hotmail.com).

British-Nigerian Chamber of Commerce, Ebani House, 149 Broad Street, Lagos (tel: 264-1266; fax: 266-0298; e-mail: hq@n-bcc.org).

Enugu Chamber of Commerce, Industry, Mines and Agriculture, International Trade Fair Complex, Abakaliki Road, PO Box 734, Enugu (tel: 250-575; fax: 252-186; e-mail: eccima@infoweb.abs.net).

Ibadan Chamber of Commerce and Industry, Commerce House, Ring Road, PO Box 5168, Ibadan (tel: 317-223; fax: 311-647; e-mail: icci@infoweb.abs.net).

Kaduna Chamber of Commerce, Industry, Mines and Agriculture, Kaduna-Zaria Road, Rigachikun, PO Box 728, Kaduna (tel: 318-794; fax: 318-795; e-mail: kadccima@inet-global.com).

Kano Chamber of Commerce and Industry, Trade Fair Complex, Zoo Road, PO Box 10, Kano (tel: 666-936; fax: 667-138; e-mail: kaccima@hotmail.com).

Lagos Chamber of Commerce and Industry, 1 Idowu Taylor Street, Victoria Island, PO Box 109, Lagos (tel: 774-6617; fax: 262-3665; e-mail: inform@lagoschamber.com).

National Association of Chambers of Commerce, Industry and Agriculture, 15A Ikorodu Road, Maryland, PO Box 12816, Lagos (tel: 496-4727, 496-4737; e-mail: naccima@pinet.com.ng).

Port Harcourt Chamber of Commerce, Industry, Mines and Agriculture, 169 Aba Road, PO Box 71, Port Harcourt (tel: 330-394; fax: 243-307; e-mail: phccima@hotmail.com).

Banking

Nigerian Industrial Development Bank Ltd (NIMB), PMB 205, 1st Floor, NIMB Building, 4th Avenue, Plot 207, Cadastral Zone AO, Off Herbert Macaulay Way, Central Business District, Abuja (tel: 234-6579; fax: 234-6578).

Commercial Bank (Crédit Lyonnais Nigeria) Ltd, PMB 12829, Plot 146B Ligali Ayorinde, Victoria Island Annex, Lagos (tel: 262-5700; fax: 262-5699).

Ecobank Nigeria plc, 2 Ajose Adeogun St, Victoria Island, Lagos (tel: 262-0910/4; fax: 261-6568, 262-0920).

Investment Banking & Trust Co Ltd (IBTC), PMB 71707, IBTC Place, Walter Carrington Crescent, Victoria Island, Lagos (tel: 262-6520/40; fax: 262-6541/2; e-mail: IBTC@IBTCLagos.com; internet site: http://www.IBTCLagos.com).

Lion Bank of Nigeria plc, PMB 12852, 121/125 Broad St, Lagos (tel: 266-914, 266-7735).

Nigerian Industrial Development Bank Ltd (NIDB), PMB 2357, NIDB House, 63/71 Broad St, Lagos (tel: 266-3495, 266-1545; fax: 266-7074, 266-6733).

Central bank

Central Bank of Nigeria, Central Business District, Cadastral Zone, PO Box 0187, Garki, Abuja (tel: 234-3191; fax: 234-3137; email: info@cenbank.org).

Stock exchange

Nigerian Stock Exchange (NSE). www.nigerianstockexchange.com.

Travel information

ADC Airlines (tel: 271-4020; reservations: 496-1942; internet: www.adcairlines.com).

Virgin Nigeria, Head Office, 3rd Floor, Ark Towers, Plot 17, Ligali Ayorinde Street, Victoria Island Extension, Lagos (tel: 460-0505, 271-1111; internet: www.virginnigeria.com).

Ministry of tourism

Federal Ministry of Culture and Tourism, Area 1 Secretariat Complex, Garki, Abuja (tel: 234-2727).

National tourist organisation offices

Nigerian Tourism Developemnt Corporation, Old Secretariat, Area 1, Garki, PMB 167, Abuja (tel: 234-2764; fax: 234-2775; e-mail: information@nigeriatourism.net).

Ministries

Federal Ministry of Agriculture and Rural Development, Area 1 Secretariat Complex, Garki, Abuja (tel: 314-1185).

Federal Ministry of Aviation, New Federal Secretariat Complex, Shehu Shagari Way, Abuja (tel: 523-2112).

Federal Ministry of Commerce, Area 1 Secretariat Complex, Garki, Abuja (tel: 234-1884).

Federal Ministry of Communications, New Federal Secretariat Complex, Shehu Shagari Way, Abuja (tel: 523-7183).

Federal Ministry of Culture and Tourism, Area 1 Secretariat Complex, Garki, Abuja (tel: 234-2727).

Federal Ministry of Defence, Ship House, Central Area, Abuja (tel: 234-0534).

Federal Ministry of Education, New Federal Secretariat Complex, Shehu Shagari Way, Abuja (tel: 523-2800).

Federal Ministry for Federal Capital Territory, Area 11, Garki, Abuja (tel: 523-4014).

Federal Ministry of Finance, Garki, Abuja (tel: 234-4686).

Federal Ministry of Foreign Affairs, Maputo Street, Zone 3 Wuse District, Abuja (tel: 523-0576).

Federal Ministry of Health, New Federal Secretariat Complex, Shehu Shagari Way, Abuja, (tel: 523-0576).

Federal Ministry of Industries, Area 1 Secretariat Complex, Garki, Abuja (tel: 523-0576).

Federal Ministry of Information, Radio House, Herbert Macaulay Way, Garki, Abuja (tel: 234-6350).

Federal Ministry of Internal Affairs, Area 1 Secretariat Complex, Garki, Abuja (tel: 234-6884).

Federal Ministry of Justice, New Federal Secretariat Complex, Shehu Shagari Way, Abuja (tel: 523-5194).

Federal Ministry of Labour and Productivity, New Federal Secretariat Complex, Shehu Shagari Way, Abuja (tel: 523-5980).

Federal Ministry of Police Affairs, New Federal Secretariat Complex, Shehu Shagari Way, Abuja (tel: 523-0549).

Federal Ministry of Power and Steel, New Federal Secretariat Complex, Shehu Shagari Way, Abuja (tel: 523-7064).

Federal Ministry of Science and Technology, New Federal Secretariat Complex, Shehu Shagari Way, Abuja (tel: 523-3397).

Federal Ministry of Solid Minerals Development, New Federal Secretariat Complex, Shehu Shagari Way, Abuja (tel: 523-5830; fax: 523,6518; e-mail: minsolmindev@linkserve.com).

Federal Ministry of Sports and Social Development, New Federal Secretariat Complex, Shehu Shagari Way, Abuja (tel: 523-5905).

Federal Ministry of Transport, National Maritime Agency Building, Central Area, Abuja (tel: 523-7053).

Federal Ministry of Water Resources, Area 1 Secretariat Complex, Garki, Abuja (tel: 234-2376).

Federal Ministry of Women's Affairs and Youth Development, New Federal Secretariat Complex, Shehu Shegari Way, Abuja (tel: 523-7051).

Federal Ministry of Works and Housing, Mabushi Districti, Abuja (tel: 521-1622).

Other useful addresses

African Petroleum plc, AP House, 54-56 Broad Street, PO Box 512, Lagos (tel: 260-0050/9, 260-0145/9; fax: 263-5290).

Bureau of Public Enterprises, 1 Osun Crescent, Off Ibrahim Babangida Way, Maitama, Abuja (tel: 413-4673; fax: 413-4674; internet: www.bpeng.org).

British High Commission, Dangote House, Aguyi Ironsi Street, Maitama District, Abuja (tel 413-4559–64 (6 lines); fax: 413-4565, 413-3888; email: visa.enquiries.abuja@fco.gov.uk).

Britain Nigeria Business Council, 2 Vincent Street, London, SW1P 4LD (tel: (+44-20) 7828-9661; fax: (+44-20) 7828-9779; email: bnbc-uk@btconnect.com)

Chevron Nigeria Ltd, 2 Chevron Drive, Lekki Peninsular, PMB 12825, Lagos.

Economic Community of West African States (Ecowas), 6 King George V Road, Lagos (tel: 260-0720/5).

Manufacturers' Association of Nigeria, 12th Floor, Unity House, 37 Marina, PO Box 3835, Lagos.

National Council on Privatisation, Secretariat, Bureau of Public Enterprises, 1 Osun Crescent, Off Ibrahim Babangida Way, Maitama District, PMB 442, Garki, Abuja (tel: 413-4660/4670/4673; fax: 413-4671/4672/4674; e-mail: bpegen@micro.com.ng).

National Maritime Authority, 4 Burma Road, Apapa, Lagos.

National Planning Commission, Federal Secretariat, Shehu Shagari Way, Abuja (tel: 523-6628; fax: 523-6625).

National Science & Technology Development Agency, PO Box 12695, Lagos.

Nigerian Communications Commission, 72 Ahmadu Bello Way, Benue Plaza, Abuja (tel: 234-2327, 234-4590/2; fax: 234-4593; email: ncc@cyberspace.net.ng; internet site: www.ncc.gov.ng).

Nigeria Export Processing Zone Authority, 4th Floor, Radio House, Herbert Macauley Way (South), PMB 037, Garki Abuja (tel: 234-3060; fax: 234-3061).

Nigerian Embassy (USA), 1333 16th Street, NW, Washington DC 20036 (tel: (+1-202) 986-8400; fax: (+1-202) 462-7124).

Nigeria-São Tomé and Príncipe Joint Development Authority, Plot 1101 Aminu Kano Crescent, Wuse II, Abuja (tel: 524-1069; fax: 524-1052; e-mail: enquiries@nigeriasaotomejda.com; internet site: www.nigeriasaotomejda.com).

Ports Sector Reforms, Bureau of Public Enterprises, 1 Osun Crescent, Off Ibrahim Babangida Way, Maitama, PMB 442, Garki, Abuja (tel: 413-4634/46; fax: 413-4671/2/4; email: husmanbpeng.org).

National news agency: NAN (News Agency of Nigeria)

APA (African Press Agency): www.apanews.net

Reuters Africa: http://africa.reuters.com

Internet sites

Portal site: www.nigerianation.com

Africa Business Network: http://www.ifc.org/abn

AllAfrica.com: http://allafrica.com

African Development Bank: http://www.afdb.org

Africa News Online: http://www.allafrica.com

Africa Online: http://www.africaonline.com

Mbendi AfroPaedia (information on companies, countries, industries and stock exchanges in Africa): http://mbendi.co.za

Movement for the Survival of the Ogoni People (MOSOP): http://www.mosopcanada.org/index1.html

Niue

KEY FACTS

Official name: Republic of Niue

Head of State: Queen Elizabeth II, represented by the Governor General of New Zealand and High Commissioner Sir Jerry Mateparae (from 31 Aug 2011)

Head of government: Prime Minister Toke Talagi (elected by parliament 2008; re-elected 7 May 2011 and 12 Apr 2014)

Ruling party: There are no political parties; parliamentarians sit as independents

Area: 256 square km

Population: 1,229 (July 2013)*; over 20,000 Niueans reside in New Zealand.

Capital: Alofi is the main town.

Official language: English, Niuean

Currency: New Zealand dollar (NZ$) = 100 cents

Exchange rate: NZ$1.58 per US$ (Sep 2015)

GDP per capita: US$10,277 (2009)

GDP real growth: 0.10% (2009)

GDP: US$15.80 million (2009)

Inflation: 5.40% (2010)

Aid flow: US$2.60 million (annually)

* estimated figure

COUNTRY PROFILE

The first inhabitants arrived from Tonga, Samoa and Fiji between AD600 and AD1000.
1774 Visited by Captain James Cook and given the name, Savage Island
1846 Conversion to Christianity commenced by the London Missionary Society.
1900 Niue became a British protectorate.
1901 Niue was formally annexed to New Zealand, as part of the Cook Islands.
1960 The first Niue Assembly was established.
1974 Niue was granted 'self-government in free association with New Zealand'. It became the smallest self-governing state with that status.
1982 Robert Rex was elected prime minister.
1992 Robert Rex died. He was succeeded by Young Vivian.
1993 Frank Lui won the election and became prime minister.
1996 Lui was re-elected.
1999 Sani Elia Lakatani of the Niue People's Party (NPP) was elected prime minister.
2001 The US imposed trading sanctions on Niue due its tax haven status. A census recorded 1,799 people.
2002 All 20 members of the Niue Assembly were re-elected and Young Vivian (NPP) was elected prime minister.
2003 The NPP was dissolved, despite which the coalition government continued.
2004 A 300km per hour cyclone, Heta, devastated Niue.
2005 A census recorded that the population figure was 1,600, a drop of almost 200 people, with the village of North Alofi losing 113 of its 256 residents. There are some 20,000 Niueans living abroad, mostly in New Zealand; the government is trying to encourage them to return. Young Vivian retained his parliamentary seat unopposed and was re-elected prime minister.
2006 Niue had been suffering from frequent power failures when one of its generators was damaged causing further problems in pumping water from the reservoir. The island's electricity network was over 30 years old and due for upgrading; a new replacement, five tonne generator was flown in from New Zealand at short notice.
2008 20 independent members were elected (nine unopposed) to parliamentary. Toke Talagi became prime minister. 500 educational laptops were distributed among all school children, allowing them to web-surf via existing wireless internet services.
2009 The Organisation for Economic Co-operation and Development (OECD) published a list of countries that had not implemented international tax information exchange standards, of which Niue was one despite signing a co-operation agreement in 2002.
2010 Air New Zealand began a direct weekly flight between Auckland and Niue. New Zealand appointed Mark Blumsky as high commissioner.
2011 In parliamentary elections, held in May, 20 non-partisan candidates were elected. Toke Talagi was re-elected as prime minister (with 12 votes). In July, the New Zealand government announced it would committed US$12.65 million (NZ$15 million) to help Niue develop into a 'boutique tourism destination', building on Niue's natural beauty and environment as the main attraction for adventure holidays.
2012 On 14 March, a new shipping registry was launched and expected to receive revenue of US$100,000 in its first year of operation and double this in the second. Such registries for countries without a fleet of their own (including Niue) are known as 'flags of convenience'. On 4 October, Niue signed an agreement under which they will receive US$4 million from the Pacific Environment Community (PEC) to install photovoltaic cells to replace fossil fuel electrical generation for public use. The solar power should provide savings of US320,000 per annum and around 300 tonnes in fuel.
2013 Two new Nuie US$2 coins were minted in 2013 - the Great Horned Owl and the Osprey. The sale of coins is an important source of revenue.
2014 Elections were held on 12 April. Twelve of the successful candidates are supporters of Prime Minister Toke Talagi In August Mr Talagi said he was frustrated by a lack of financial support for the Smaller Island States Unit of the Pacific Islands Forum (PIF) and was considering leaving the sub-group.

2015 On May 15 Niue became the 195th state recognised by Tokyo. Japan and China are both courting Pacific islands. Niue is one of only two (the other being Cook Islands) recognised by the United Nations as neither members nor permanent observers of its General Assembly. Both, however, are members of UN specialised agencies (such as UNESCO or the ILO), whose memberships are only open to sovereign states.

Political structure

Constitution

Under the 1974 constitution, New Zealand remains responsible for defence and foreign affairs and is ready to provide necessary economic and administrative assistance. Niueans are New Zealand citizens.

The head of state, the British monarch, is represented in Niue by the Governor General of New Zealand.

Village affairs are handled by 14 village councils of three to five members, elected to three-year terms in conjunction with the Community Affairs Office.

Form of state

Self-governing state, in free association with New Zealand.

The executive

The four-member executive cabinet is headed by a prime minister elected by the Legislative Assembly, who in turn appoints three ministers.

National legislature

The island is governed by the 20-member Niue Assembly – 14 elected from village constituencies and six from the common roll – elected by popular vote for a three-year term.

Last elections

12 April 2014 (parliamentary)

Results: Parliamentary: 20 non-partisan candidates were elected, half of whom were elected unopposed. Twelve are supporters of Prime Minister Toke Talagi.

Next elections

2017 (parliamentary)

Political parties

The Niue political system is not based on formal political organisations. Until 2003, two loose groupings existed: the Niue People's Party (NPP) and the Alliance of Independents. The NPP was dissolved in July 2003 and all candidates since then have run as independents.

Ruling party

There are no political parties; parliamentarians sit as independents

Population

1,229 (July 2013)*; over 20,000 Niueans reside in New Zealand.

There is considerable migration to New Zealand, as people from Niue are New Zealand citizens. The government is running a campaign to repopulate the island by persuading some of the 18,000 expatriates to return. Pensions in Niue are much lower than those in New Zealand, so restrictions on the proportion of New Zealand pensions they could bring with them remain a problem.

In September 2003, Niue invited Tuvaluans to migrate to their island to boost the dwindling population.

Last census: 9 September 2006: 1,625

Population density: 8 inhabitants per square km. Urban population 38 per cent (2010 Unicef).

Annual growth rate: -2.3 per cent, 1990–2010 (Unicef).

Ethnic make-up

The population is mainly of Polynesian (Tongan) descent, with some New Zealand elements.

Religions

Predominantly Christian.

Education

The education system is modelled on New Zealand's with services provided free until aged 14. For the first four years teaching may be in either Niuean or English. In 2004, the schools increased the content of Niuean language in the curriculum.

The government has backed the 'one laptop per child' programme (OLPC).

Compulsory years: Five to 14

Health

Life expectancy: 71 years, 2004 (WHO 2006)

Fertility rate/Maternal mortality rate: 2.8 births per woman, 2004 (WHO 2006)

Child (under 5 years) mortality rate (per 1,000): 25 per 1,000 live births (WHO 2012)

Main cities

Alofi (largest settlement) (estimated population 554 in 2012); Avatele (212), Hakupu (181).

Languages spoken

English is widely understood. The people who live in the north speak a Polynesian dialect which differs from the dialect of the people living on the rest of the island who speak a language closer to Tongan.

Official language/s

English, Niuean

Media

There is limited media availability.

Press

The weekly *Niue Star* is a private newspaper published in English and Niue. A fortnightly newspaper *Niuean* (www.niuean.com) is published in Australia. An online news round-up is *Niue Business News* (www.webpost.net/nb/nbn).

Broadcasting

The Broadcasting Corporation of Niue operates the only radio (Radio Sunshine) and television station, which broadcasts in English and Niue in the evenings only.

Radio: Radio Sunshine broadcasts are transmitted on AM594/FM91 six days/week during limited hours.

Television: Television Niue broadcasts in English and Niue in the evenings only, usually 1730–2200.

Other news agencies: ABC Pacific Beat: www.radioaustralia.net.au/pacbeat

Pacific Magazine: www.pacificmagazine.net

Economy

Niue's economy is wholly dependent on financial assistance from New Zealand, which contributes around 40 per cent of GDP. Per capita income at over US$10,277 (2009 – latest published figures in 2015) is one of the highest of the Pacific islands and kept artificially high by New Zealand's aid.

The local economy is based on government employment and subsistence farming, raising vegetables, fruit, pigs and poultry for family consumption. Industry is limited to agricultural production, although some small building and joinery operations have been started. Sales of postage stamps and remittances from Niuean workers overseas are important sources of revenue.

In order to boost Niue's meagre income, the government leases international telephone codes for use by foreign companies and has built a quarantine station for alpaca – a wool-bearing llama-like South American mammal – *en route* to Australia. Marketing of the '.nu' Internet domain name has been a controversial income source. The government is also hoping to gain revenue from investment partnerships in fishing and organic products and is seeking interest in developing tourism.

External trade

Niue is a member of the South Pacific Regional Trade and Economic Co-operation Agreement (Sparteca) along with 12 other regional nations, which allows products duty free access by Pacific Island Forum members to Australian and New Zealand markets (subject to the country of origin restrictions).

In March 2012, the Niue Ship Registry was set up. Such registries for countries without a fleet of their own (including Niue) are known as 'flags of convenience'.

Imports

Main imports are food, live animals, construction materials, manufactured goods, vehicles, fuels and medicines.

Main sources: New Zealand (95.5 per cent in 2008), Japan (2.7 per cent), China (1 per cent).

Exports

Agricultural products – fish, taro, copra, honey, vanilla, passion fruit, paw paws, root crops and limes, financial and telecommunication services.

Main destinations: Principally to New Zealand, Fiji, Cook Islands, Australia

Agriculture

Farming

Development of agriculture has been hindered by the limited amount of fertile or cultivable land, lack of surface water and susceptibility to drought conditions. Only 20 per cent of land can be used for agriculture. Cyclones are a major problem. Alienation of land is forbidden, but leases may be granted for a maximum term of 66 years.

Limes and passion fruit are grown for export. Goats have been introduced on a trial basis.

Fishing

Annual fishing production typically includes 200 tonnes (t) marine fish. A fish plant employs 30 people.

Forestry

About 20 per cent of the land area is forest with millable timber. Logging serves local demand.

Industry and manufacturing

The Office of Economic Affairs is responsible for planning and financing productive ventures relating to agriculture, tourism and industry. Niue Handicrafts handles production and marketing of objects plaited from pandanus and coconut palm leaves.

Small-scale industries include honey extraction and bottling, saw milling, joinery, furniture and handicrafts.

Investment has been made in the vanilla and forestry industries.

Tourism

Niue offers all the traditional tropical island features, with water activities and ecotourism as important elements of the experience. Tourism is an important component of the economy, although Niue's one flight per week from New Zealand hampers the growth in the market for those wishing to stay for shorter periods. New Zealand agreed to invest NZ$15 million (US$18 million) (2011–14) on essential infrastructure and management systems to develop Niue as a 'boutique tourism destination'. Previous investment has included a new visitor centre and redevelopment of the Matavai Resort (Alofi) with an increase in the number of rooms from 24 to 44, which was completed in 2012.

Hydrocarbons

There are no known hydrocarbon reserves. Consumption of oil was around 20 barrels per day (bpd) in 2013, all of which was imported.

Energy

Total installed generating capacity was 3MW in 2011. The Niue Power Corporation is responsible for electricity generation and supply. The majority of the population relies on non-commercial biomass, mostly fuel wood for cooking, lighting and power.

In October 2012, Niue signed an agreement under which they will receive US$4 million from the Pacific Environment Community (PEC) to install photovoltaic cells to replace fossil fuel electrical generation for public use. The solar power should provide savings of US$320,000 per annum and around 300 tonnes in fuel.

Banking and insurance

Central bank

Reserve Bank of New Zealand

Offshore facilities

In 2002, the introduction of US sanctions on banking activities was a major blow to Niue. The US accused Niue of having connections to Latin American tax haven operations.

Niue licensed six offshore banks operating in Australia, which the Organisation for Economic Co-operation and Development (OECD) wanted to close down. In 2002, the Niue Legislative Assembly repealed the legislation which authorised the issuing of banking licences and Niue was removed from the OECD Financial Action Task Force (FATF) blacklist of places associated with money laundering. The OECD published a list on 2 April 2009 of countries that had not implemented international tax information exchange standards, of which Nuie was one, despite signing the co-operation agreement in 2002.

Time

GMT minus eleven hours

Geography

Niue is a coral island in the Pacific Ocean about 480km (300 miles) east of Tonga and 930km (580 miles) west of the southern Cook Islands. It rises to only 65 metres, as an outcrop, from the sea, with a steep and jagged coastline. The land has many caves and fissures and although is has no rivers there are plenty of wells to keep the topsoil fertile. It is also known as the 'The Rock of Polynesia' and is the world's largest coral island.

Hemisphere

Southern

Climate

Subtropical and humid, with temperature 25–30 degrees Celsius and average rainfall of nearly 200cm per annum.

Entry requirements

Passports

Required by all.

Visa

Not required by tourist visitors staying less than 30 days. Visitors are required to have return/onward tickets and all necessary entry documentation for the next destination, as well as sufficient funds for length of stay and suitable accommodation. Visitors may extend their stay by applying to the Immigration officials upon arrival, an extension permit of three months (cost of NZ$30) is usually granted.

Visas are required by all visitors for stays of over 30 days. Further information may be obtained from the Immigration Department, PO Box 69, Alofi, Niue Island (email: immigrationniue@mail.gov.nu).

Currency advice/regulations

The import of local currency is unlimited; export is limited to NZ$10,000. The import of foreign currency must be declared; export is limited to the amount declared.

Customs

Personal items are duty free, only one personal electronic item, camera or binoculars are allowed.

The export of native artifacts, coral and rare shells is prohibited.

Prohibited imports

Firearms and ammunition require a permit from the Chief of Police in Alofi.

Health (for visitors)

Mandatory precautions

Vaccination certificates for yellow fever are required if travelling from infected area.

Advisable precautions

Vaccinations for diphtheria, TB, hepatitis A and B, polio, tetanus and typhoid are all recommended. There is a rabies risk. It is advisable to take water precautions.

Public holidays (national)

Fixed dates

1 Jan (New Year's Day), 4 Jan (Takai Commission Holiday), 6 Feb (Waitangi Day), 25 Apr (Anzac Day), 16–19 Oct (Constitution Celebrations), 17 Oct (Peniamina's Day), 25–26 Dec (Christmas).

Holidays that fall on the weekend are taken *in lieu* on the following Monday/Tuesday.

Variable dates

Good Friday (Mar/Apr), Easter Monday (Mar/Apr), Queen's Official Birthday (first Mon in Jun).

Working hours
Banking
Mon–Thur: 0900–1500; Fri: 0830–1500.
Business
Mon–Fri: 0730–1530.
Shops
Mon–Fri: 0830–1600; Sat: 0830–1500.

Telecommunications
Mobile/cell phones
The Harris Cellular Network provides fixed and mobile coverage.

Social customs/useful tips
It is customary to shake hands on meeting and taking leave. Gratuities are not encouraged.

Getting there
Air
There are limited connections from Auckland, New Zealand; Sydney, Australia; Samoa; Fiji and Los Angeles, US.
International airport/s: Hanan (IUE), 7km north of Alofi.
Airport tax: Departure tax: NZ$25
Surface
There are no port facilities. Ships anchor off Alofi and barges transfer cargo.

Getting about
National transport
Road: There are approximately 130km of all-weather road and 96km bush track negotiable by heavy trucks and four-wheel drive vehicles. A 60km road circles the island and roads link main centres.
Car hire
Visitors with an foreign driver's licence must obtain a local licence from the Niue police department before driving a hired vehicle. It is advisable to reserve hire vehicles before arrival.
Driving is on the left.

BUSINESS DIRECTORY

The addresses listed below are a selection only. While World of Information makes every endeavour to check these addresses, we cannot guarantee that changes have not been made, especially to telephone numbers and area codes. We would welcome any corrections.

Telephone area codes
The international direct dialling code (IDD) for Niue is +683 followed by subscriber's number.

Useful telephone numbers
Police, fire and ambulance:999/4000
Hospital:998.

Chambers of Commerce
Niue Chamber of Commerce and Industry, PO Box 160, Alofi (tel: 43-99; fax: 40-17; e-mail: chamber@sin.net.nu).

Banking
Westpac Banking Corporation, PO Box 76, Alofi (tel: 4221; fax: 4043).
Central bank
The Reserve Bank of New Zealand, PO Box 2498, Wellington, New Zealand (tel: (+64-4) 472-2029; fax: (+64-4) 473-8554).
Travel information
Air Nauru, Government Building, Yaren District, Republic of Nauru (tel: (+674) 3141, 3418; fax: (+674) 3170).

Matavai Resort (hotel), PO Box 133, Alofi (tel: 4360, email: matavai@niue.nu).

Niue International Airport (Hanan), PO Box 83, Alofi (tel: 4020, 4133, 4096; fax: 4010).

National tourist organisation offices
Niue Tourism Office, PO Box 42, Alofi (tel: 4224; fax: 4225; internet site: http://www.niueisland.com).

Other useful addresses
Broadcasting Corporation of Niue, PO Box 26, Alofi (tel: 4026; fax: 4217).

Business Advisory Service, Alofi (tel: 4228).

Department of Immigration, PO Box, Alofi (tel: 4349, 4333; fax: 4336; email: immigrationniue@mail.gov.nu).

Office of Economic Affairs, PO Box 42, Alofi (tel: 4126).

Office of the Prime Minister. PO Box 40, Alofi (tel: 4200; fax: 4206, 4232).

Office of the Secretary to Government, PO Box 67, Alofi (tel: 4017; fax: 4232).

ABC Pacific Beat: www.radioaustralia.net.au/pacbeat

Pacific Magazine: www.pacificmagazine.net

Internet sites
Niue government website: http://www.gov.nu

Niue website: http://www.niueisland.nu

South Pacific Tourism Organisation: http://www.tcsp.com/niue/index.html

KEY FACTS

Official name: Norfolk Island

Head of State: Queen Elizabeth II of Australia; represented by Administrator (appointed by Governor General of Australia) Gary Douglas Hardgrave (from 1 Jul 2014)

Head of government: As of June 2015 self-government has been abolished. Martin Turnbull, Australian Prime Minister, assumed office on 14 Sep 2015.

Ruling party: None, legislative assembly members sit as independents

Area: 35 square km

Population: 2,196 (July 2013)* (2011; census figure)

Capital: Kingston

Official language: English

Currency: Australian dollar (A$) = 100 cents

Exchange rate: A$1.43 per US$ (Sep 2015)

Visitor numbers: 40,000 (annually)

* estimated figure

Norfolk Island

The Norfolk Islanders are an independent people who consider their state to predate that of the Commonwealth of Australia, the country to which they were tied by a British administration in 1897.

The Australian government published its *Norfolk Island Road Map* on 2 March 2011, outlining its plans for change to its funding for the territory. It identified three pillars that were fundamental in underpinning the changes: providing economic diversity for sustained growth; providing social cohesion; and resilience and protecting the island's unique heritage and environment.

Visitor numbers have been declining since 2000 and the economy has become unsustainable in its current form, so much so that the island's government is unable to operate without cash injections from the commonwealth government. The Road Map said that reforms in governance and economic development must be undertaken or the prospects for Norfolk Island will remain unchanged and that the infrastructure had declined and there is little prospect of improvement without change.

Seven, specific proposals were submitted for discussion, the most controversial of which for the islanders were the imposition of Australian management, which would include paying all national and state taxes in operation in Australia, an opening up the economy to foreign investment and allowing immigration from the mainland. The Road Map was quick to unite any negative proposal with its corresponding benefit and emphasised that the changes would be undertaken in partnership with the people's wishes. Nevertheless, the opening remarks that the status quo could not be maintained requires the population to find accommodation for these changes in someway, before any implicit threat or sanctions were used to force the issue.

COUNTRY PROFILE

1774 First European sighting of Norfolk Island by Captain James Cook. He named the island in honour of the Ninth Duchess of Norfolk.

1788 Norfolk Island was occupied by the British.

1790 A settlement was established to supply the New South Wales penal colony.

1814 The settlement was abandoned.

1825 The island was re-settled as a penal colony.

1856 The British authorities moved the 193 descendants of the *Bounty* mutineers from Pitcairn Island to Norfolk Island.

1858 16 Pitcairners returned to Pitcairn Island after a dispute with the British about land ownership. Other Pitcairners followed.

1897 Norfolk Island became a dependency of New South Wales.

1914 Norfolk Island became a Territory under the authority of the Commonwealth of Australia.

1979 The Norfolk Island Act conferred a measure of self-government.

1992 Norfolk Islanders became entitled to vote in elections for the Australian parliament.

2000 Norfolk Islanders signed a deal with genetic researchers to study the population for genes that predispose people to high blood pressure or migraines.

2001 A census recorded a total population of 2,601 including 564 tourists and visitors.

2002 The killing of an Australian tourist, Janelle Patton, was the first murder to take place on the island since the 1850s.

2004 Deputy Chief Minister Ivens Buffett was shot dead; his son was later acquitted of his murder.

2006 A census recorded a total population of 2,523 including 660 tourists and visitors. The Australian government published its Commonwealth Grants Commission report on the financial capacity of Norfolk Island.

2007 A branch of the Australian Labor Party (ALP) was established to work to reform the political system. A New Zealander, Glenn McNeill was convicted of the murder of Janelle Patton. In legislative assembly elections André Nobbs won most votes and was elected chief minister.

2010 Island council elections were held in which the nine candidates (out of 28 in total) that won most votes were elected. David Buffett became chief minister. The Australian national parliament imposed more accountability and rules of good governance on Norfolk Island public

spending. Norfolk Island was chosen to be the first country worldwide to pilot a personal carbon-trading programme. The inhabitants were encouraged to sign up for the scheme whereby they receive carbon credits to be exchanged for energy or petrol, when they take actions against obesity and climate change.
2011 In March the Australian government published the *Norfolk Island Road Map*, outlining its plans for changes to its funding for the territory. It identified the need for change to the status of the island as a semi-autonomous, self-governing territory to one under more direct control from Canberra. The Australian Regional Development and Local government body undertook a 'community survey' of the population and economic conditions of Norfolk Island to determine the long-term needs of both. The Australian government agreed to provide A$14.1 million (US$14,778 million) in emergency financial assistance in September, through a funding agreement for 2011/12.
2012 On 2 March, Air New Zealand won an open tender to provide regular services between Norfolk Island and Australia. In March it was confirmed that Norfolk Island was insolvent, largely due to the collapse of the tourist industry; the island's own air service, Norfolk Air had been grounded through lack of funds. The Department of Regional Australia showed that the Commonwealth emergency funding had pumped over A$37 million (US$39 million) into the economy to maintain services. The federal government warned islanders that the situation was critical and that reforms should be initiated, assets sold and the tax system fully integrated into the Australian system.
2013 Lisle Denis Snell was elected Chief Minister by 14th Legislative Assembly on 20 March. Norfolk Islanders were quite excited when Kevin Rudd became Prime Minister of Australia in June – he was, afterall, reckoned to be a descendant of a Norfolk Island convict, and surely he would do something special for them. However, his premiership didn't last too long and he lost the election called for 7 September. That left the Islanders with a failing tourism industry (26,000 visitors in 2012, down from 100,000) and an Australia reluctant to bail them out yet again.
2014 A report tabled by the Australian National Audit Office on 27 March showed Norfolk Island as being officially insolvent. Gary Douglas Hardgrave was appointed Administrator by the Governor General from 1 Jul 2014).
2015 A letter dated 19 March from Australian assistant minister for infrastructure and regional development, Jamie Briggs, announced plans to present legislation to parliament to dismantle the Norfolk Island legislative assembly by amending the Norfolk Island Act 1979 (Cth) to transition the Norfolk Island Legislative Assembly (NILA) to a Norfolk Island Regional Council.. This would mean the islanders would have access to Australian health and welfare payments, but at the same they would have to pay income and company tax to Australia. The New South Wales government would provide essential services on behalf of the Commonwealth of Australia. On 24 March the NILA met to consider a Matter of Public Importance in relation to the announcement.

Political structure

Constitution

The Norfolk Island Act of 1979 provides for an administrator (appointed by the Governor General of Australia and responsible to the Australian government), a Legislative Assembly and Executive Council. The Act provides that proposed laws passed by the legislative assembly must be presented to the administrator for assent. Both the legislative assembly and Executive Council are presided over by the president of the legislative assembly.
Since 1992, Norfolk Islanders are entitled to vote in elections for the Australian parliament.
The Norfolk Island Legislation Amendment Bill was passed by the Australian government on 14 May 2015. Despite an earlier Norfolk Island referendum stressing the native public's desire to remain independent, crippling debts necessitated an abandonment of self-government and tax-free status in return for Australian political control and welfare system benefits.

Form of state

Territory of Australia

The executive

The Executive Council is made up of five members of the legislative assembly; each member holds the position of minister, with one or more portfolios.

National legislature

The unicameral, Norfolk Legislative Assembly has nine members, elected from a list of candidates, to serve for a three-year term. By 2016, the Legislative Assembly will be officially abolished and Norfolk Island will instead send elected representatives to the New South Wales council in Australia.

Legal system

The judicial system consists of a Supreme Court and a Court of Petty Sessions.

Last elections

13 March 2013 (parliamentary)

Results: Parliamentary: nine non-partisan candidates were elected; André Nobbs received most votes. Turnout was 91.2 per cent.

Next elections

From 1 July 2016, legislative duties will be passed to the New South Wales council of Australia

Political parties

There are no political parties in the legislative assembly; all members sit as independents.

Ruling party

None, legislative assembly members sit as independents

Population

2,196 (July 2013)*

Last census: 8 August 2011: 2,302 (of which 22 per cent were visitors); 80 per cent were Australian citizens; 13 per cent were New Zealanders. 38 per cent are decended from Pitcairn Islanders.

Population density: 50.2 inhabitants per sq km.

Annual growth rate: -1.8 per cent (2006–11)

Ethnic make-up

Approximately 37 per cent of the permanent population were born on Norfolk Island (of which 47 per cent are of Pitcairn descent), 31 per cent were born on the Australian mainland and 23 per cent were born in New Zealand.

Religions

Anglicans (34 per cent), Roman Catholics (12 per cent), Uniting Church of Australia (13 per cent) and Seventh-Day Adventist (3 per cent).

Education

Infant, primary and secondary schooling is provided by the Norfolk Island Government. Education is free until the age of 15.

Compulsory years: six to 15

Main cities

Burnt Pine, Kingston (estimated population 910 in 2012).

Languages spoken

English is spoken in business circles. Norfolk, a dialect derived from the language evolved by the *Bounty* mutineers and their Tahitian wives (a mixture of mainly English and Tahitian) and brought by settlers from Pitcairn Island in the nineteenth century, is also in use.

Official language/s

English

Media

Press

There are two local weekly newspapers *The Norfolk Islander* and the *Norfolk Window*. National newspapers from Australia and New Zealand are available.

Broadcasting

Radio: The Norfolk Island Government Broadcasting Services operates the radio station. Radio Norfolk broadcasts on AM and FM for 10 hours per day during the

week and for six to seven hours during the weekend.
Television: The privately owned TVN station broadcasts local material. Satellite services relay TV programmes from Australian.
Other news agencies: Norfolk Online: www.norfolkonline.nlk.nf

Economy
Norfolk Island's economy is based largely on its tourist industry, catering mainly to visitors from Australia (around 80 per cent of total) and New Zealand. It receives indirect funding from Australia through Australian federal agencies (of between A$3–4 million (US$3.8–5 million) per year) and grants provided to offshore Australian communities. Australia has also restored a number of historic buildings and provides certain technical services for public works on the island.
In addition to importing most of its requirements, Norfolk Island has developed a re-export industry geared to its tourist industry.
Sales of Norfolk Island postage stamps contribute to the island's revenue.
In March 2015 the government announced that some reforms would be undertaken. Under these reforms the Legislative Assembly will be replaced with a regional council. On top of this, the residents of the island will have to pay income tax for the first time but under this plan they will receive access to Australian welfare and healthcare. The reforms will see the island become a part of the Australian commonwealth. The reforms will be put in place by June 2016.

External trade
As a self-governing territory of Australia, Norfolk Island maintains strong links with the mainland but not an open market; taxes are levied on imports to provide government revenue. Exports to Australia are duty free, subject to the country of origin restrictions.
Imports
Main imports are petroleum, food, consumer goods, alcohol, building materials, footwear and clothing.
Main sources: Australia, New Zealand, neighbouring Pacific islands, Asia and EU
Exports
Main commodity exports are seeds from the Norfolk Island pine, gerbera and kentia palm, avocados and small quantities of timber, ceramics and local crafts and postage stamps.
Main destinations: Australia, neighbouring Pacific islands, New Zealand and the European Union.

Agriculture
Farming
Only 12 per cent of land is cultivatable so production is constrained by poor terrain, porous soil, a low water table and fragmented holdings. Many farms are run on a part-time basis. Crops tend to be seasonal, and provide cereals, vegetables and fruit. There is a successful commercial hydroponic vegetable garden. Livestock is limited to cattle and poultry and the island is self-sufficient in beef, poultry and eggs.
Fishing
The lack of a harbour restricts fisheries development, and catches serve local consumption only.
Forestry
The Norfolk Island pine and kentia palm seeds are an important export and some hardwood afforestation is being undertaken.

Industry and manufacturing
The island produces its own handicrafts, chocolates, beers, liqueurs (including an 'aromatised whiskey' called *Convict's Curse*) and arabica coffee. Grapes are grown for the small wine industry.

Tourism
Since the mid-1960s, tourism has been the mainstay of the island's economy. The Norfolk Island Government Tourist Bureau promotes Norfolk Island in Australia and New Zealand - the island's primary markets. 22,700 tourists visited Norfolk Island in 2013, down form 25,100 in 2012.
It is a sub-tropical island with world-class scuba diving and fishing. There are areas of sub-tropical rainforest, much of it protected in national parks, with a network of tracks which is ideal for walking, birdwatching, cycling or horse riding. Norfolk Island is included on Unesco's World Heritage List (under Australian Convict Sites), as part of Britain's legacy of penal colonies in Australia.

Hydrocarbons
There are unexploited offshore oil and gas fields. All petroleum products are imported from Singapore refineries via New Caledonia and Fiji, around 33 per cent of the price of oil is transport, handling and insurance costs.

Energy
The Norfolk Island Administration operates six 1MW 16-cylinder diesel engines, producing 7 million kilowatt hours per annum. Anywhere between 10–20 per cent of total energy generated is used in refrigeration plants. A past study has determined that any move to use renewable energy will likely be a wind/diesel combination system.

Banking and insurance
There are branches of the Commonwealth Bank of Australia (which has an ATM) and Westpac Banking Corporation on the island.

Time
GMT plus eleven and a half hours.

Geography
Norfolk Island lies off the eastern coast of Australia about 1,400km east of Brisbane, to the south of New Caledonia and 640km north of New Zealand. Norfolk Island is hilly and fertile, with a coastline of cliffs. It is about 8km long and 4.8km wide. The territory also includes uninhabited Phillip Island 7km south of the main island.
Hemisphere
Southern

Climate
The island has a sub-tropical climate. Temperatures can range from 11–27 degrees Celsius, with an average rainfall of 1,346mm per year. November tends to be the driest month and the wetter months are May to August. Most rain falls at night. Average morning humidity is around 80 per cent.

Dress codes
Clothing should be comfortable and casual to suit the subtropical climate. A sweater is advisable on winter nights. A hat and sunscreen are necessary in summer.

Entry requirements
Passports
Required for all.
Visa
Required by all, except Australian and New Zealand citizens.
Any visitor who is in possession of an Australian visa may stay for up to 30 days, with travel insurance and confirmed accommodation obtained prior to arrival.
Most citizens of EU and North America can apply for an Australian Electronic Travel Authority (ETA), issued by a travel agent or airline, or online. See www.eta.immi.gov.au for details of those eligible, and follow links to the application site. ETA-eligible business visitors may stay for up to three months without additional documentation.
Those not eligible for an ETA must apply using form 456, through the nearest embassy or mission. Business visas will require a letter of invitation from a local company or organisation, a business letter from an employer stating purpose of trip and details of employee's function, proof of sufficient funds, and a full itinerary.
Further details and application form can be obtained at www.immi.gov.au/allforms.

Currency advice/regulations
There are no restrictions on import and export of local and foreign currency.
Customs
Some medications may be restricted and visitors should declare all prescription drugs.
Prohibited imports
Illicit drugs, dangerous weapons, fruit, vegetables, flowers and seeds; pork and poultry from New Zealand are also prohibited. Firearms require a permit.

Health (for visitors)
Mandatory precautions
Vaccination certificates required for yellow fever if travelling from an infected area.
Advisable precautions
Vaccination for diphtheria, TB, hepatitis A and B, polio, tetanus, typhoid. Rabies is a risk.

Public holidays (national)
Fixed dates
1 Jan (New Year's Day), 26 Jan (Australia Day), 6 Mar (Foundation Day), 25 Apr (Anzac Day), 8 Jun (Bounty Day), 25–26 Dec (Christmas).
If Christmas Day or New Year's Day falls on a Saturday, the next Monday is given as a holiday.
Variable dates
Good Friday and Easter Monday (Mar/Apr), Queen's Official Birthday (second Mon in Jun), Show Day, Thanksgiving Day (last Wed in Nov).

Working hours
Banking
Mon–Thu: 0930–1600; Fri: 0930–1700.
Business
Mon, Tue and Thu, Fri: 0900–1700; Wed and Sat: 0900–1200.
Government
Mon–Fri: 0800–1630.
Shops
Mon–Tues, Thu–Fri: 0900–1700; Wed/Sat: 0900–1230. Some shops open on Sun.
Supermarket, Mon–Sat: 0800–1800; Sun: 0900–1800.

Telecommunications
Mobile/cell phones
In 2002, the Norfolk Island residents voted against allowing a mobile phone service on the Island.

Electricity supply
Diesel generated 240V 50 cycles.

Social customs/useful tips
Tipping is not expected. It is customary to shake hands on meeting and taking leave. Punctuality on social occasions is appreciated.

Getting there
Air
The only air connections are provided by OzJet and Air New Zealand which fly from the east coast of Australia and New Zealand.
International airport/s: Norfolk (NLK).
Airport tax: A$30 for international departures, payable at the airport when leaving or at the Visitor Information Centre prior to departure.
Surface
Water: Ships anchor offshore.

Getting about
National transport
Road: The entire road network amounts to 200km.
Buses: There is no public transport system on the island, but tour buses are available for tourists.
City transport
Taxis: There is a limited taxi service.
Car hire
Arrangements may be made locally for hiring cars, motorcycles and bicycles.

BUSINESS DIRECTORY

The addresses listed below are a selection only. While World of Information makes every endeavour to check these addresses, we cannot guarantee that changes have not been made, especially to telephone numbers and area codes. We would welcome any corrections.

Telephone area codes
The international direct dialling (IDD) code for Norfolk Island is +672, followed by area code 3 and subscriber's number.

Useful telephone numbers
Police: 922
Fire: 955
Ambulance: 911
Telephone exchange: 22-244

Banking
Commonwealth Bank of Australia, Burnt Pine (tel: 22-144).

Westpac Banking Corporation, Burnt Pine (tel: 22-120).

Travel information
Norfolk Island Airport, P.O.Box 149, Norfolk Island (tel: 22-445; fax: 23-201; email (manager): grobinson@airport.gov.nf).

The Travel Centre, PO Box 172, Norfolk Island (tel: 22-502; fax: 23-205; email: travel@travelcentre.nf).

National tourist organisation offices
Norfolk Island Government Tourist Bureau, PO Box 211, Norfolk Island (tel: 22-147; fax: 23-109; email: info@norfolkisland.com.au).

Other useful addresses
Postal services for Norfolk Island have an Australian postal code – NSW 2899, Australia – to be added to the end of an address.

Customs House, Taylors Road, Norfolk Island (tel: 22-899; fax: 23-260; email customs@admin.gov.nf; internet: www.customs.gov.nf).

Legislative Assembly, Old Military Barracks, Quality Row, Kingston, Norfolk Island (tel:22-003; fax: 22-624; email: clerk@assembly.gov.nf).

Norfolk Online: www.norfolkonline.nlk.nf

Internet sites
Australian Government (see territories of Australia): www.ag.gov.au

Norfolk Island website: www.norfolk.gov.nf

Northern Marianas

KEY FACTS

Official name: Commonwealth of the Northern Mariana Islands

Head of State: President of the United States of America Barack Obama (from 20 Jan 2009)

Head of government: Governor Eloy Songao Inos (Covenant) (from 20 Feb 2013)

Ruling party: Republican Party (since 2007; re-elected 7 Nov 2009)

Area: 471 square km (14 islands) – Saipan (122 square km); Tinian (101 square km)

Population: 51,170 (July 2013)* (53,883; 2010, census figure)

Capital: Garapan (Saipan)

Official language: English

Currency: US dollar (US$) = 100 cents

* estimated figure

COUNTRY PROFILE

Ancestors of the native Chamorros settled on the islands in about 2000 BC.

1521 Magellan claimed the islands for Spain.

1698 The native population was transferred to Guam.

1899 The Germans bought the islands from the Spaniards.

1914 The Japanese seized the islands from the Germans.

1947 Northern Marianas was the first Japanese territory in the Western Pacific to be invaded by the US; it became a part of the Trust Territory of the Pacific Islands (TTPI), administered by the US, under a mandate granted by the UN.

1975 In a referendum islanders voted to become an unincorporated territory of the United States under a covenant.

1977 A new local constitution was adopted.

1978 The Commonwealth of Northern Mariana Islands (CNMI) was created, as the TTPI was dissolved.

1980s Tourism and clothing manufacture became major industries, leading to foreign contract workers outnumbering local residents.

1984 Many US civil and political rights were made available to the islands' residents.

1986 Following the end of the UN mandate, the islands, under the *Covenant to Establish a Commonwealth of the Northern Mariana Islands (CNMI) in Political Union with the United States*, acquired US Commonwealth status and residents were granted US citizenship

1990 The UN Security Council formally terminated its Trusteeship. Under the covenant, the US has responsibility for foreign affairs and defence but CNMI is exempt from customs and labour laws.

2001 The Republican Party was re-elected and Juan Babauta (Rep) was elected governor.

2003 The Covenant Party won the parliamentary elections.

2004 Anatahan's active volcano had a small eruption. Northern Marianas and Guam were struck by super-typhoon Chaba.

2005 Numerous (over 500) small earthquakes were recorded on three uninhabited islands. Anatahan volcano continued erupting, with the largest eruption sending ash up to a height of 15,000 metres. In gubernatorial elections, Benigno Fitial won 28.1 per cent and unseated the incumbent, Juan Babouta.

2006 The CNMI revised its agreement with the US for increased environmental protection on the US missile testing range on Kwajalein Atoll. Two extra seats were added to the House of Representatives.

2007 In parliamentary elections the Covenant party lost much of its support as the Republicans won 12 seats (out of 20), the Covenant Party four, independents three and the Democrats one, in the House of Representatives. In the Senate, of the three seats in contention, independents won two and the Covenant Party one.

2008 The Northern Mariana Islands Delegate Act (immigration, security and labour act) was passed by the US Congress.

2009 The US announced the establishment of a protective marine zone around the Pacific islands it was responsible for, totalling 500,000 square km of sea and sea floor. Mining and commercial fishing, out to 50 nautical miles (54.26km) from shore, was banned. Lieutenant Governor Timothy Villagomez resigned, following his conviction on corruption charges including conspiracy, theft of US government funds, bribery and wire fraud; Eloy S Inos replaced him. Responsibility for immigration was taken out of the hands of CNMI officials and given to a US federal government agency, which now applies the same visa regulations as the mainland US. Tourism was the first industry to be hit by the changed rules, as the process of visiting became more difficult and time consuming. However, the handover controls access to the vital US naval base while applying curbs to illegal activity of multinational criminal gangs from China and Japan. In the gubernatorial election neither of the leading candidates won sufficient votes for an outright win; the runoff was won by incumbent Governor Fitial. In parliamentary elections, the Republican Party won the single largest number of seats (nine out of 20) and won four seats out of nine in the Senate.

2010 The resident population took part in the United States census of 1 April, which, after personal details, included questions on race, housing and internet and mobile phone access. The Northern Marianas College (NMC) was given notice by the

US-based Western Association of Schools and Colleges (WASC) to show 10 specific improvements in administration or risk losing accreditation. Over 700 students at the only college in CNMI receive a total of US$2.6 million from the Pell Scholarship fund, which would be withdrawn without a college to attend. Gregorio Sablan (independent) won re-election as Delegate to the US Congress.

2011 In January the legislature passed a ban on shark fishing within the territorial waters of CNMI. Acting Governor Inos declared a state of emergency on 22 July, due to 'an imminent threat of disruption of the delivery of critical healthcare services… due to a severe cash shortage'. The health care system was operating with a US$3 million debt and with a lack of vital medical laboratory supplies. The result of the census showed a population fall of 22.7 per cent, from 62,392 in 2000 to 48,220 in 2010. In October, CNMI offered to lease several of its uninhabited islands to China, specifically for recreational and industrial purposes only, in a move designed to alleviate CNMI's desperate need for foreign exchange. However, the move was not looked on with favour by the US, which does not want a greater Chinese presence in the region.

2012 On 29 June, Saipan Air announced that it was ceasing operations and filing for bankruptcy. The NMC was given accreditation by WASC in time for the start of the academic year.

2013 Governor Fitial was succeeded by Eloy Songao Inos on 20 February. Russian visitors to the Marianas jumped from 688 in March 2012 to 1,648 in March 2013. As a result the Marianas Visitors Authority (MVA) proposed opening a tourism offive there.

2014 Elections will be held on 4 November, a year later than originally scheduled in order to move future elections to even years. Governor Inos will stand for re-election as a member of the Republican Party, having switched from the Covenant Party in 2013.

2015 On 5 August President Obama declared a major disaster in the Commonwealth of Northern Mariana Islands and ordered federal aid to supplement commonwealth and local recovery efforts in the area affected by Typhoon Soudelor over 1–3 August. The President's action makes federal funding available to affected individuals on the island of Saipan.

Political structure

Constitution

The 1978 constitution was fully effective until 1986. It provides for an executive governor and a bicameral legislature. It also obligates the people of the Northern Mariana Islands to adopt a Commonwealth Constitution providing for a republican form of government which contains a bill of rights.

CNMI citizens have US citizenship and have a degree of autonomy and are exempt from some US federal laws concerning employment and immigration. CNMI defers to the US for foreign policy and defence and CNMI citizens do not vote in US presidential elections. There is one resident representative present in the US Congress and federal government.

Form of state

Democratic, self-governing commonwealth (but politically linked to the US)

The executive

An executive governor and lieutenant governor are elected every four years by universal suffrage.

National legislature

A bicameral legislature consisting of a 20-member House of Representatives and a nine-member Senate (with staggered terms); all elected in single-seat constituencies for two-year terms.

Legal system

The system is based on US jurisprudence but is exempt from US laws for customs, wages, immigration and taxation.

Last elections

4 November 2014 (gubernatorial and parliamentary), 21 November (gubernatorial run-off)

Results: Parliamentary: (House of Representatives) Democratic Party four (out of 17), Republican Party three seats, independents 10. Senate: (seven seats up for election) Republican Party won two seats (out of nine), (Democratic Party one seat, independents four .

Gubernatorial (first round): Eloy Songao Inos (Republican Party) won 45.96 per cent of the vote, Heinz Hofschneider (Independent) 32.62 per cent, Juan Nekai Babauta (Independent) 17.50 per cent, Edward Masga Deleon (Democratic) 3.92 per cent. Runoff: Inos won 56.96 per cent, Hofschneider 43.04 per cent.

Next elections

November 2018 (parliamentary and gubernatorial)

Political parties

Ruling party

The party with the most seats is the Democratic Party (four seats), however Independents are in the majority.

Main opposition party

Republican Party

Political situation

In 2007 the US Senate took a long hard look at the state of the CNMI Covenant Implementation Act, and its exemption from immigration and employment laws. The US federal government proposed a federalisation bill to bring the immigration system under its control. It was seen that CNMI authorities were unable to provide a fully comprehensive screening process for all visitors and migrant workers to the islands. US concerns regarding this did not only cover security – the CNMI was seen as a backdoor route to the US – but also problems of human trafficking, particularly of girls for the sex-trade and inappropriate migrant workers' visas. A federal minimum wage bill was also included in the federalisation bill.

Further study questioned why there were so many migrant workers, and concluded there was a historical legacy following the collapse of the garment manufacturing industry and the general downturn in tourism.

The CNMI federalisation bill came into force in November 2009.

In March 2011, the Republican controlled US-Congress voted to rescind the voting rites of representations of CNMI, effectively disenfranchising their electorate in policies that directly affect them.

Population

51,170 (July 2013)* The high growth rate is largely accounted for by the recruitment of large numbers of foreign workers, particularly in the garment and tourism sectors.

Last census: 1 April 2010: 53,883

Population density: 143 inhabitants per square km.

Annual growth rate: 3.3 per cent (2003)

Ethnic make-up

There are tensions between the resident population and people from other countries – Philippines, Republic of Korea, Thailand and China. Approximately 75 per cent of the native population is Chamorro, the rest are Carolinian.

Religions

Roman Catholic and indigenous beliefs.

Education

Education is based on the US system. There are several private schools available to cater for the international community.

Literacy rate: 97 per cent, adult rate.

Compulsory years: Six to 16

Health

The major medical needs of the population are met by the Commonwealth Health Centre (CHC). The CHC operates inpatient and outpatient services. There is 24-hour emergency care available provided by a team of emergency nurses, emergency physicians and support staff. In addition to the CHC, there are several private health clinics. All medical services are required to meet US standards, although the cost of medical care is much cheaper than in the US.

Main cities
Garapan/Susupe (Saipan) (capital, estimated population 4,360 in 2012), Dandan (7,426), San Antonio (6,920), San Vicente (6,719), Tanapag (6,307), Kagman (4,230).

Main islands
Six islands, including the three largest (Saipan, Tinian and Rota) are inhabited.

Languages spoken
Chamorro and Carolinian are the native tongues and are widely spoken. Japanese and Korean are also spoken.

Official language/s
English

Media

Press
The daily newspaper *Saipan Tribune* (www.saipantribune.com) has the largest circulation, while *Marianas Variety* (www.mvariety.com) has news covering from other Micronesian islands.

Broadcasting
Radio: There are several radio stations including the public KRNM (www.krnm.org), commercial KRSI (www.pacificnewscenter.com), KPXP (www.radiopacific.com/p99) and KWAW (www.magic100radio.com). Religious stations include KFBS (www.febc.org) and KYOI.
Television: The TV station WSZE 10 transmits via cable and satellite.
Other news agencies: ABC Pacific Beat: www.radioaustralia.net.au/pacbeat
Pacific Magazine: www.pacificmagazine.net

Economy
The economy of the islands is small and has few natural resources. Bilateral aid from the US remains an important source of income, particularly aid directed towards improving the inadequate infrastructure. In 2006 an unfunded government liability of US$500 million in the Defined Pension Plan was identified and prompted new legislation in 2007, for the introduction of a new pension system designed to be self-sustaining through employee's contributions. However, by 2009 the government had suspended pension payments as the national pension fund was in imminent danger of bankruptcy. A US court had ruled in June that full restitution of lost investment payments should be paid by the CNMI government to the CNMI employees' pension fund. In February 2012, the government had yet to pay US$325 million, as ordered in 2009, and was planning to issue 10-year government bonds (pension obligation bond (POB)), to raise US$300 million to cover the financial void. In April 2012, the pension fund declared bankruptcy as they anticipated the loss of funding by 2014. Following this, in August 2012, Governor Fitial was impeached as he was held responsible for withholding payments to the pension fund.
Tourism is the mainstay of the economy, employing around 25 per cent of the workforce and contributing some 25 per cent to GDP. The tourist industry has experienced good growth, registering double figure growth in 2013 from 2012.
The economy is heavily dependent on financial assistance from the US, in 2013 federal grants from the US accounted for some 35 per cent of GDP.
In 2009 the former chief justice said that restrictive land laws as enshrined in the constitution made foreign investors reluctant to do business in CNMI as leased land could only be held by non-CNMI people for up to 40 years and 55 years for public and private land respectively.
The constitution regarding land ownership was reconsidered in 2011, but after due consideration was rejected by the islands' senate in 2012.
The textile sector, which has been in decline since the US halted its Multi-Fibre Agreement (MFA), lost US$518.4 million in export revenue between 2004–07; nevertheless garment manufacturing is still the largest export, with the bulk of production going to the US.

External trade
As a self-governing territory of the US, CNMI has an open market with the US. Tourism is the main provider of foreign exchange. The textile sector, which is in decline due to the US halting its Multi-Fibre Agreement (MFA), lost US$518.4 million in export revenue between 2004–07; nevertheless garment manufacturing still provides the highest export revenue, with the bulk of production going to the US.

Imports
Principal imports are food, construction equipment and materials, petroleum products and consumer goods.
Main sources: US, Japan

Exports
The principal export is garments; minor exports include livestock, tuna fish, fruit and vegetables.
Main destinations: Mainly to US

Agriculture

Farming
The agricultural sector contributes approximately 1.7 per cent to annual GDP. Cultivable land is rich and volcanic.
Vegetables such as coconuts, breadfruit, tomatoes, melons and cucumbers are widely grown on smallholdings. Livestock is reared for export. The copra industry is also important.

Fishing
The fishing sector has revived following a blanket ban in some areas, introduced in 2000, due to over-fishing. Stocks include black-tip sharks, tuna, emperor fish and bonito. Tuna is transshipped en route to the US via the canneries at Pago Pago (Fagatogo) in American Samoa.

Industry and manufacturing
Until 2004 industrial sector contributed approximately 19 per cent to annual GDP while the garment industry flourished under the Multi-Fibre Agreement (MFA). However, when this ended in 2004 exports to the US were threatened by even cheaper exports from China and a number of factories closed, putting some 2,000 workers out of their jobs. CMNI is also expected to have the same minimum wage as in the USA by 2015 and this is also likely to affect the garment industry as costs continue to rise.
Other industrial activity consists of construction, small-scale fish processing and handicrafts manufacture.

Tourism
Tourism is the mainstay of the economy, employing around 25 per cent of the workforce and contributing some 25 per cent to GDP. The tourist industry has experienced good growth, registering double figure growth in 2013 from 2012.
A report to the US Department of Commerce in December 2011 noted that CNMI has a pristine and safe natural environment, and along with its close affiliation to the US offers scope for growth in educational and eco-tourism. Both could be combined to offer sustainable development

Hydrocarbons
There are no known hydrocarbon reserves and all petroleum needs are met by imports.

Energy
With the rise in global oil prices, which has impacted on the price of energy production, there has been an expansion in the use of renewable energy, such as solar-photovoltaic panels for water heaters and lighting and wind turbines.

Banking and insurance

Central bank
US Federal Reserve (Washington DC)

Time
GMT plus 10 hours

Geography
The Northern Marianas Islands comprises 16 islands across 640km of the western Pacific Ocean, about 5,300km (3,300 miles) west of Hawaii. The islands are part of the chain of Mariana Islands. The ones in the south are formed of limestone terraces, and those in the north are volcanic, several of which are still active. The largest volcano, Agrihan, is also the tallest

peak in the islands at 965 metres. Saipan is a fertile island with lagoons and rolling hills. Rota has dense rain forests and is largely undeveloped.

Climate
The climate is tropical marine.

Entry requirements
Passports
Passports required by all except US citizens with proof of citizenship; (all US nationals require a passport for re-entry to the US from January 2007).
Visa
Required by all. There are a few exceptions for visits up to 30 days. See www.cnmiago.gov.mp or www.mymarianas.com for a full list and details or contact the Division of Immigration for further information. All applications must be made at least four weeks before intended departure.
Prohibited entry
See www.mymarianas.com for a full list and details, contact the Division of Immigration for further information.
Currency advice/regulations
The US dollar is the official currency. There are no restrictions on import and export of local and foreign currency, however all amounts over US$10,000 (or foreign equivalent) must be declared.
Prohibited imports
Fruits, vegetables, plants and soils, meat and meat products, live animals and animal products.
Firearms and ammunition require a permit, obtained in advance. For more information see: www.cnmiago.gov.mp.

Health (for visitors)
Mandatory precautions
Vaccination certificate required for yellow fever if travelling from an infected area.
Advisable precautions
Vaccination for diphtheria, TB, hepatitis A and B, polio, tetanus, typhoid. Rabies risk. Water from the mains is usually chlorinated and although safe to drink, may cause mild abdominal upsets. Drinking water outside the main cities and towns may be contaminated. Sterilisation by boiling is thus advisable.
Full medical facilities are available, although they are not free of charge. Health insurance is advisable.

Hotels
There is a 10 per cent hotel tax. A tip of 10–15 per cent is usual.

Credit cards
Major credit cards are accepted on Saipan and at car rental agencies on Rota.

Working hours
Banking
Mon–Thu: 0900–1500, Fri: 1000–1800.
Business
Mon–Fri: 0800–1200, 1300–1700.
Government
Mon–Fri: 0730–1130, 1230–1630.
Shops
Mon–Sat: 0800–2000, Sun: 0800–1800.

Telecommunications
Mobile/cell phones
A 1900 GSM service is available.

Electricity supply
220/240V, 50Hz

Weights and measures
Imperial

Getting there
Air
International airport/s: Saipan International (SPN), 13km south-east of Garapan, with duty-free shops, bar, restaurant, currency exchange, shops and car hire. Taxis are available to the centre of town.
Airport tax: None
Surface
Main port/s: Saipan, Tinian, Rota.

Getting about
National transport
Air: There are several daily flights between Saipan and Tinian and between Rota and Saipan.
Road: Roads are good on the main islands, particularly around the main centres. Driving is on the right-hand side.
Buses: There is no public bus system on Saipan, although shuttle buses run between the major towns.
Water: There are sea links between the islands.
City transport
Taxis: A taxi service is available on Saipan. Taxis are metered and privately owned.
Buses, trams & metro: Tour bus from airport to city centre, journey time is about 15 minutes.

BUSINESS DIRECTORY
The addresses listed below are a selection only. While World of Information makes every endeavour to check these addresses, we cannot guarantee that changes have not been made, especially to telephone numbers and area codes. We would welcome any corrections.

Telephone area codes
The international direct dialling (IDD) code for Northern Marianas is +1 670, followed by the subscriber's number.

Useful telephone numbers
Police, fire, ambulance: 911

Chambers of Commerce
Saipan Chamber of Commerce, PO Box 500806, Saipan MP 96950 (tel: 233-7150; fax: 233-7151; e-mail: saipanchamber@saipan.com).

Banking
Central bank
Bank of Saipan, PO Box 500690, Saipan MP 96950 (tel: 235-6260; fax: 235-1802; email: bankofsaipan@saipan.com).

Federal Reserve System, 20th Street and Constitution Avenue, NW, Washington DC 20551 (tel: (202) 452-3000; fax: (202) 452-3819).

Travel information
Continental Micronesia, PO Box 138CK, Saipan (tel: 234-8223; fax: 234-8358).

Pacific Island Travel, Herengracht 495, 1017 BT Amsterdam, The Netherlands (tel: (+31-20) 626-1325; fax (+31-20) 623-0008; internet: www.pacificislandtravel.com).

Saipan International Airport, PO Box 1055, Saipan (tel: 664-3500/01; fax: 234-5962; e-mail: cpa.admin@saipan.com).

Travel Bureau, PO Box 503 Rota (tel: 532-3561; fax: 532-3562).

National tourist organisation offices
Marianas Visitors Authority, P O Box 500861, Saipan, (tel: 664-3200/3201; fax: 664-3237; internet: www.mymarianas.com).

Other useful addresses
All Northern Marianas postal addresses have the US zip code: MP 96950, USA

Commonwealth of the Northern Mariana Islands, Caller Box 10,007, Saipan, (tel: 664-2200; internet: www.gov.mp).

Division of Immigration, Office of the Attorney General, Afetna Square Bld, San Antonio Village, PO Box 10007, Saipan (tel: 236-0922, 236-0923; fax: 664-3190; internet: www.cnmiago.gov.mp).

ABC Pacific Beat: www.radioaustralia.net.au/pacbeat

Pacific Magazine: www.pacificmagazine.net

Internet sites
Commonwealth of the Northern Marianas General Information: www.gov.mp

Marianas Variety, newspaper: www.mvariety.com

Saipan Tribune: www.saipantribune.com

US Office of Insular affairs: www.doi.gov/oia

KEY FACTS

Official name: Kongeriket Norge (Kingdom of Norway)

Head of State: King Harald V (since 17 Jan 1991)

Head of government: Prime Minister Erna Solberg (Høyre) (from 9 Sep 2013)

Ruling party: Coalition lead by Høyre (Right) and including Fremskrittspartiet (FrP) (Progress Party), Kristelig Folkeparti (KrF) (Christian Democrats) and the Venstre (V) (Liberal Party) (from 9 Sep 2013)

Area: 323,985 square km

Population: 5.16 million (2014)

Capital: Oslo

Official language: Norwegian

Currency: Norwegian krone (Nkr) = 100 ore

Exchange rate: Nkr8.25 per US$ (Sep 2015)

GDP per capita: US$97,013 (2014)

GDP real growth: 2.23% (2014)

GDP: US$500.24 billion (2014)

Labour force: 2.75 million (2014)*

Unemployment: 3.53% (2014)

Inflation: 2.03% (2014)

Oil production: 1.90 million bpd (2014)

Natural gas production: 108.80 billion cum (2014)

Balance of trade: US$60.51 billion (2013)*

Annual FDI: -US$796.10 million (2011)

* estimated figure

Norway

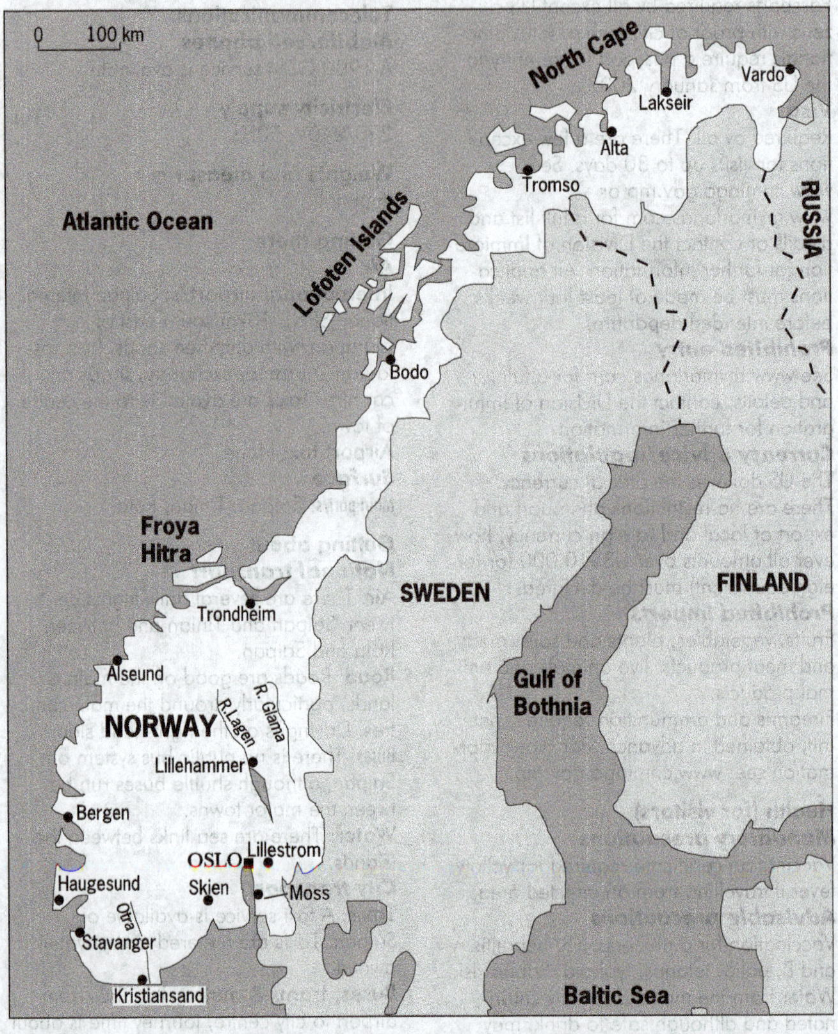

A study published in 2006 had suggested that Norway was the place to emigrate to for the lazy of this world. Norwegians, it seems, work less hours per year – an estimated average of some 1,337– than any other developed country in the world. At the other end of the spectrum was South Korea, whose citizens worked an average of 2,390 hours each year. The survey omitted to mention that Norway was one of the world's most expensive – and cold – countries.

Iron Erna

Norwegian politics had shifted noticeably in September 2013 when, following her party's election victory, the leader of the Høyre (Conservative) party, Erna Solberg became prime minister. Ms Solberg was Norway's second female to hold the position, bringing to an end eight years of Arbeiderparti (AP) (Labour Party)-led coalitions under the left wing leader Jens Stoltenberg. Mr Stoltenberg had not, by any means, been an unpopular leader, but the tragic events of 2011 when 77 people were massacred by Anders Breivik not only damaged Mr Stoltenberg's credibility, but also illuminated security weaknesses for which, technically, the Stoltenberg administration could be held responsible. Much of these criticisms were felt rather than enumerated, but the net effect was that Norwegians – anxious to draw a line under a sorry national episode – sought change. Mrs Solberg – also known, a la Merkel, as 'Iron Erna' – faced a large initial challenge in putting her coalition together. Unable to do any deal with Norway's more moderate right-wing parties, she was thrown back on to some sort of deal with the anti-immigrant Fremskrittspartiet (FrP) (Progress Party). The Høyre and other right-wing parties took 96 out of the 169 seats as the left ended up with only 73.

There was no general hysteria in Norway over the issue of security. Amazingly, by North American standards, even after the Breivik murders no armed bodyguard was to be seen anywhere near the prime minister. Norway had impressed the world, not only with its dignified mourning, but also because of the country's clear recognition of democracy and for the graceful way its people handled Breivik's trial and his outbursts in court. Norwegian opinion polls even indicated that the Norwegians' faith in democracy had grown since the attacks. If there were cracks in this image of a tolerant and humane Norway, they focussed on the right-wing so-called Progress Party. What place could the FrP's extremist views play in a Norway of tolerance and compassion? Did the fact that 20 per cent of the Norwegian electorate had cast their votes for the right-wing FrP mean that Norway, had changed irrevocably?

For a while Anders Behring Breivik had been a member of the FrP youth organisation. Since 2000 the FrP had seen its fortunes rise again. One poll showed it with more than 22 per cent of support among voters – almost twice FrP's showing in the local elections held just weeks after the attacks. However, the Norwegian political panorama had been altered, at least in terms of perception, by the emergence of an immigrant Roma community. This had sparked racist outbursts on Norwegian Internet forums, where the Roma were insulted and threatened. Local residents had also been hostile to the nomadic groups, who mostly originated from Romania.The leader of the FrP, Siv Jensen, had even called for the Roma to be deported.

In a heart-searching newspaper editorial, former Norwegian prime minister, Thorbjørn Jagland (October 1996–October 1997) expressed the view that regardless of the decision made by the courts over whether or not Mr Breivik was sane, the question had to be raised as to whether there existed a cultural explanation for all the hate and prejudices that were now rising up against the Roma, 'namely that we have become so rich and content in this country' that people have lost focus of the things that really matter. If they are unable to suppress the rising levels of poverty, then people will quickly turn it into something 'repulsive and criminal' in order to sustain their own self-image. One commentator observed that Norwegians needed to learn how to have opposing opinions and argue without hatred. If this was the challenge, the response was none too encouraging. In mid-2012 the trend seemed to be in the opposite direction, as the FrP recovered from the dip in popularity it experienced following Breivik's terror attacks. Mr Stoltenberg's Labour Party had also slumped back to its pre-Breivik popularity level. Stoltenberg, who had been considered somewhat stiff in manner, had become something of a father to the country after the attacks. His poll ratings reaching as high as 90 per cent. He managed to comfort his people, partly because he too was personally affected, having lost colleagues in what was also an attack on his party. But even the prime minister couldn't hold on to that, as an increasing number of Norwegians now supported a change in government leadership. In the June 2012 opinion polls, the head of the Conservative Party, Erna Solberg, was – for the first time – more popular than Stoltenberg.

The economy

In 2013 Norway's new government had taken over responsibility for a prosperous, well-managed economy, where people were generally happy – indicators of both material and non-material welfare were at high levels. Intelligent use of wealth from petroleum resources and active use of monetary policy within the flexible inflation-targeting framework had insulated Norway from the worst of the financial crisis-induced recession and supported the recovery. Flexible inflation targeting worked well in the face of the financial turmoil of the past decade. More recently, the authorities have been rightly concerned about rising house prices and the vulnerability of highly-geared households. Policy interest rates have been somewhat higher than would have otherwise been warranted because of this. Signs of a cooling housing market may be due to guidance on loan-to-value ratios and perhaps also to anticipation of tighter capital requirement for banks. Norway has adopted a counter-cyclical buffer, to strengthen the banking system in case of severe shocks, before others. Its operation will involve some learning by doing and, while not being concerned with fine tuning, should also give the central bank a little more room for manoeuvre in its use of policy rates.

The new government continued to follow the cross-party consensus on keeping the structural non-petroleum budget deficit to 4 per cent of the value of the government Pension Fund Global (GPFG) over the business cycle; a structural non-petroleum deficit of around 3 per cent of the

KEY INDICATORS — Norway

	Unit	2011	2012	2013	2014	**2015
Population	m	*4.97	5.04	5.10	5.16	*5.21
Gross domestic product (GDP)	US$bn	483.70	500.03	522.35	500.24	*420.96
GDP per capita	US$	97,255	99,249	102,496	97,013	*80,749
GDP real growth	%	1.7	2.8	0.7	2.2	*1.0
Inflation	%	1.3	0.7	2.1	2.0	*2.3
Unemployment	%	3.2	3.2	3.5	3.5	*3.8
Oil output	'000 bpd	2,039.0	1,916.0	1,837.0	1,895.0	–
Natural gas output	bn cum	101.4	114.9	108.7	108.8	–
Exports (fob) (goods)	US$m	159,209.0	165,999.0	153,521.0	–	–
Imports (fob) (goods)	US$m	89,101.0	89,046.0	93,015.0	–	–
Balance of trade	US$m	70,108.0	76,953.0	60,506.0	–	–
Current account	US$m	62,705.0	71,716.0	52,379.0	42,328.0	*31,949.0
Total reserves minus gold	US$m	54,413.9	51,856.4	58,283.1	64,800.7	–
Foreign exchange	US$m	50,931.5	47,999.5	54,587.8	–	–
Exchange rate	per US$	5.56	5.68	6.13	7.48	–

* estimated figure ** forecast figure

GPFG had been budgeted for 2014. The real return on the assets of the GPFG has often been less than 4 per cent. Despite the benefit of petroleum revenues, overall taxation levels in Norway are quite high. A reduction in Norway's relatively high taxation, beyond the steps taken in the 2014 budget, with concomitantly lower public spending growth, could increase economic dynamism. With greater attention to prioritisation and spending efficiency, there would still be room for increasing public expenditure in some areas. Full transparency in public finances was important for maintaining consensus and effective planning.

In August 2014 in its annual assessment of the Norwegian economy the International Monetary Fund (IMF) noted that the rate of growth in the economy slowed in 2013 with both mainland (ie non-oil) and offshore growth below the 2012 pace. Mainland growth moderated to 2.1 per cent in part due to weak private consumption and mainland investment, while Norway's lower oil production kept offshore growth down. The unemployment rate remained low, at around 3.5 per cent, in spite of a growing labour force due to immigration. Norwegian house prices stabilised in mid-2013, although at high levels and the housing market showed signs of cooling. Inflation rose to about the inflation target, 2.5 per cent, partly due to the exchange rate depreciation seen in 2013. The structural non-oil deficit was 3.1 per cent of GPFG assets and 5.1 per cent of trend mainland gross domestic product (GDP). This was below the deficit permitted under the authorities' fiscal policy rule, but it still implied a positive fiscal impulse due to the strong growth in GPFG assets. The overall current account surplus remained high, at 14 per cent of mainland GDP, but declined in 2013 partly due to weaker petroleum exports.

The IMF noted that Norwegian banks' profitability had improved and capital ratios had strengthened. The banks continued to rely on wholesale funding, mostly in the form of covered bonds and many banks still had some way to go before meeting the Liquidity Coverage Ratio (LCR) requirement. Norway's financial system is part of a tightly integrated Nordic-Baltic system; inward links are mainly from Swedish and Danish banks with a combined market share of a quarter to a third. Outward links are relatively modest and concentrated in the Nordic and Baltic countries and the shipping industry.

In the view of the IMF, Norway's near-term outlook remained stable with moderate growth and inflation. However, the medium and longer term presented new challenges and uncertainties, particularly because of the expected slowdown in oil and gas investment. Steadily increasing oil and gas investment over the previous decade had culminated in a 17 per cent growth rate in 2013. With this investment expected to flatten out in 2014–15 before beginning a slow decline, new sources of growth were needed. The IMF's overall forecast was for a continuation of growth with only a modest rise in unemployment in the next few years with inflation gradually rising back towards the target. However, this was based on a scenario in which the sources of growth shifted away from supplying the oil and gas sectors and towards other sectors of the economy or exports of oil-related goods and services.

However, the IMF considered that there were risks to this scenario. A substantial decline in oil and gas prices could undercut growth through a reduction in demand for mainland goods and services and through a reduction in private demand due to confidence and income effects. Any significant reduction in housing prices could possibly reduce household consumption with adverse consequences for retail trade, construction and commercial real estate and lenders to those sectors. Also, a more difficult transition to a growth model less dependent on supplying the oil and gas sector could result in slower growth and higher unemployment during the shift.

Hydrocarbons

According to the US government Energy Information Administration (EIA), Norway, the largest holder of oil and natural gas reserves in Europe, provides much of the oil and natural gas consumed on the continent. The EIA estimates that Norway was the third largest exporter of natural gas in the world after Russia and Qatar and the twelfth largest net exporter of oil in 2013. In 2012, crude oil, natural gas and pipeline transport services accounted for 52 per cent of Norway's exports revenues, 23 per cent of GDP and 30 per cent of government revenues, according to the Norwegian Petroleum Directorate (NPD). Norway's oil production peaked in 2001 at 3.4 million barrels per day (bpd) and declined to 1.8 million bpd in 2013. Natural gas production, on the other hand, has increased nearly every year since 1993. Norway experienced a slight decline in natural gas production in 2013 to 3.97 trillion cubic feet (tcf) from 4.16tcf in 2012.

2011 had seen the ratification of an historic agreement between Norway and Russia, which defined their maritime boundaries in the Barents and Arctic Seas and resolved their 40-year old dispute. The ratification meant that the Agreement could take effect in July 2011. This had been good news for Norway; as a result of the agreement, Norway gained an additional 54,000 square miles of continental shelf, according to the Norwegian Petroleum Directorate (NPD). The agreement required the two countries jointly to develop the oil and gas deposits that crossed over their boundaries, a 109,360 square mile maritime area that straddled their economic zones in the Barents and Arctic Seas.

According to the *Oil & Gas Journal* (OGJ), Norway had 5.83 billion barrels of proven crude oil reserves in January 2015, the largest oil reserves in Western Europe. All of Norway's oil reserves are located offshore on the Norwegian Continental Shelf (NCS), which is divided into three sections: the North Sea, the Norwegian Sea and the Barents Sea. The bulk of Norway's oil production occurs in the North Sea, with smaller amounts in the Norwegian Sea. New exploration and production activity was continuing in the Barents Sea.

The EIA estimated that in 2014, Norway produced 1.895 million barrels per day (bpd) of petroleum and other liquids. Norway's petroleum production had gradually declined since 2001 as oil fields began to mature. The NPD expected production to continue to decline slowly over the next few years and that in the longer term the number and size of new discoveries would be a critical factor in maintaining production levels. The NPD estimated that the three largest producing oil fields in 2013 were Troll (122,000bpd), Ekofisk (110,000bpd) and Grane (95,000bpd). According to Statistics Norway, total investments in oil and gas extraction and pipeline transport in 2013 were US$34.6 billion, US$0.6 billion higher than in 2012.

According to Statistics Norway, Norway exported an estimated 1.19 million bpd of crude oil in 2013, of which 92 per cent went to Organisation for Economic Co-operation and Development (OECD) member countries. The top five importers of Norwegian crude in 2013 were the United Kingdom (42 per cent), the Netherlands (21 per cent), Germany (10 per cent), Sweden (6 per cent) and the United States (5 per cent).

Natural gas

According to the *BP Statistical Review of World Energy* of June 2015, Norway had 67.9 trillion cubic feet (tcf) of proven natural gas reserves in December 2014. Despite maturing major natural gas fields in the North Sea, Norway has been able to sustain increases nearly every year in total natural gas production since 1993 by continuing to develop new fields. The BP Review estimated that Norway produced 108.8 billion cubic metres (bcm) of dry natural gas in 2014, down from 117.7bcm in 2012. This was the second time natural gas production has declined year-over-year since 1993. The first decline occurred in 2011 as a result of what the NPD assessed to be largely market-driven forces.

The EIA estimated that Norway exported an estimated 3.8tcf of natural gas in 2013, 96 per cent of its production. Most of the natural gas was transported to other European countries via its extensive export pipeline infrastructure and a small fraction was exported via LNG tanker. Norway is the second largest supplier of natural gas to the European Union, behind Russia, supplying about 21 per cent of Europe's total gas demand in 2013. According to data from Statistics Norway, the largest importers of Norway's natural gas exports in 2013 were the United Kingdom, Germany, France, the Netherlands, Belgium and Italy.

Risk assessment

Politics	Good
Economy	Good
Regional stability	Good

COUNTRY PROFILE

1397 Under the Kalmar Union, the Kingdom of Norway ceased to exist as a separate nation and was ruled by Danish governors.
1720 Norway, a dominion of Denmark, was lost to Sweden following the Great Nordic War.
1814 An *Act of Union* with Sweden recognised Norway as an independent Kingdom with its own constitution and parliament.
1905 The Norwegian parliament dissolved the *Act of Union* with Sweden. A plebiscite voted for full independence and a return to a monarchy. Denmark's Prince Frederick VIII became Norway's King Haakon VII.
1911 Norwegian Roald Amundsen was the first person to reach the South Pole, 35 days before Englishman Robert Scott.
1914–18 Norway adopted a policy of neutrality in the First World War.
1920 An international agreement on the Svalbard Arctic archipelago gave full sovereignty to Norway.
1940 Despite its neutrality, Norway was invaded and occupied by the Germans in the Second World War. There was active resistance to the Nazi puppet government of Vidkun Quisling.
1945 Norway abandoned its policy of neutrality and lent troops to take part in the Allied war effort.
1949 Norway became a member of NATO.
1935–65 With the exception of the years of German occupation Arbeiderparti (AP) (Labour Party) held continuous office.
1952 Norway joined the Nordic Council, set up to promote co-operation between Nordic parliaments.
1959 Norway was a founding member of the European Free Trade Association (Efta).
1957 King Olav V came to the throne.
1965 Centre-right coalition unseated the AP government.
1960–80s From the late 1960s to early 1980s oil and gas were discovered in the Norwegian sector of the North Sea and within a decade their exploitation accounted for one-third of Norway's GDP.
1972 Norwegians rejected a proposal for membership of the European Community (EC).
1973–1981 Minority AP government held power.
1981–86 The first majority conservative government since 1928 came to power. Following labour disputes, the government was defeated on its austerity programme.
1986 Minority AP government was elected with Harlem Brundtland as Norway's first female prime minister.
1989 The election was won by a coalition of conservative, Christian democrat and centre parties.
1991 King Olav V died; he was succeeded by his son Harald V.
1992 Norway withdrew from the International Whaling Treaty, provoking international controversy.
1994 In a referendum, membership of the European Union (EU) was rejected by 52.2 per cent of voters (turnout was 88.6 per cent).
1993 Norway brokered secret negotiations for a peace deal between Israel and the Palestinian Liberation Organisation that led to the *Oslo Accords*.
1997 Kjell Magne Bondevik led a minority centrist coalition government.
2000 The government fell after Bondevik was defeated in a vote of no-confidence over controversial plans to build new gas-fired power plants. Jens Stoltenberg led a AP government.
2001 Norway and Australia became embroiled in a diplomatic row following the attempt by a Norwegian-registered cargo ship to land Afghan refugees it had rescued at sea ashore in Australia. Parliamentary elections were inconclusive and Bondevik returned as prime minister, leading a centre-right coalition.
2003 Norway took the lead in trying to broker a peace deal in Sri Lanka.
2004 The government intervened to end a strike by oil workers seeking better pension rights and job security.
2005 In Parliamentary elections a coalition of socialist parties led by AP won 87 out of 169 parliament seats. Stoltenberg became prime minister for the second time. Norway became embroiled in two diplomatic rows, one with Russia, the other with Spain, over fishing rights off the Norwegian island of Svalbard.
2006 A law came into effect making it mandatory for all private companies to allocate 40 per cent of all board of director positions to women. The Statoil and Norsk Hydro companies announced the merger of their offshore operations.
2007 A referendum was passed which amended the constitution, abolishing the bicameral division of Storting (parliament) after the next elections.
2008 State income from the petroleum sector was a record high of net Nk356 billion (US$61.19 billion), representing around 32 per cent of total government income and equating to some Nk80,000 (US$13,750) for each citizen),
2009 In parliamentary elections the ruling AP-led coalition won 86 seats (out of 169); Prime Minister Jens Stoltenberg remained in office. The bicameral division of the Storting was abolished following the general elections, as agreed in the constitutional changes of 2007.
2010 An agreement on the Arctic border between Norway and Russia in the Barents Sea, which cuts across an oil and natural gas rich region, was finally resolved after several decades of discussions.
2011 Anders Behring Breivik confessed to the mass-murder of 76 people in two atrocities carried out in July. Breivik gunned down around 70 people on Utøya Island in Lake Tyrifjorden (40km west of Oslo), where a youth summer-camp for members of the ruling AP was underway, having earlier exploded a car-bomb in the government district of Oslo. Breivik was identified with extreme, nationalist ideologies following a 1,500 page manifesto posted on the internet just hours before the outrages. In August, Norway withdrew from the air attacks on Libya by a NATO-led coalition. The

Norwegian air force took part in 583 missions, out of a total 6,498 missions flown by NATO since a no-fly-zone was imposed over Libya in March.

2012 On 24 August, despite psychiatric opinion that Anders Behring Breivik was a paranoid schizophrenic, the final judgement against him was that he was sane and must serve 21 years in prison for terrorism and premeditated murder. In an annual survey on e-commerce, published on 26 November, 89 per cent of people aged over 18 shop online for tickets, small electronic items and books. The ease of shopping was quoted at the primary reason for the popularity of e-commerce.

2013 General elections were held on 9 September, resulting in a change of government. Although the leader of the previous coalition, the Det Norske Arbeiderparti (DNA) (Norwegian Labour Party), again won the highest vote with 30.8 per cent (55of 169 seats), it was the centre-right who were able to form a governing coalition of Høyre (Right) 26.8 per cent (48), Fremskrittspartiet (FrP) (Progress Party) 16.3 per cent (29), Kristelig Folkeparti (KrF) (Christian Democrats) 5.6 per cent (10) and the Venstre (V) (Liberal Party) 5.2 per cent (9).

2014 Despite Western sanctions imposed on Russia, on 18 August Norwegian oil company Statoil announced an agreement with Russian state energy giant Rosneft to search for oil in the Arctic.

2015 Provincial elections were held in March. The right wing FrP was the biggest looser.

Political structure

Constitution

Norway has the oldest constitution in Europe and the second oldest worldwide (after the US) still in operation. The constitution dates from 17 May 1814 and is grouped into five areas of interest, the form of government, executive power, rights of the citizen and legislative power, judicial power and general provisions.

Any amendment to the constitution requires majority support in both the Storting and approval in a referendum.

Form of state

Parliamentary democratic monarchy

The executive

Executive power (nominally held by the monarch) is exercised by the Statsråd (Council of State), which is led by the prime minister, who is responsible to the Storting (parliament).

The Council of State is appointed by the monarch, with the approval of parliament. Following parliamentary elections, the leader of the majority party or the leader of the majority coalition is usually appointed as prime minister by the monarch, with the approval of the parliament.

National legislature

A referendum held in 2007 approved changes to the constitution whereby the previous bicameral parliament became unicameral.

Legislative power is vested in a unicameral Storting (parliament) comprising 169 members elected by proportional representation in 19 multi-seat constituencies for four-year terms. There is no constitutional mechanism for dissolving the Storting between elections.

Legal system

The legal system is a mixture of customary law, civil law, and common law traditions. The Hoyesterett (Supreme Court) renders advisory opinions to the legislature, when asked. Justices are appointed by the monarch. Norway accepts compulsory International Court of Justice (ICJ) jurisdiction, although with reservations.

Last elections

9 September 2013 (parliamentary)

Results: Parliamentary: Det Norske Arbeiderparti (DNA) (Norwegian Labour Party), won 30.8 per cent of the vote (55 of 169 seats), Høyre (Right) 26.8 per cent (48), Fremskrittspartiet (FrP) (Progress Party) 16.3 per cent (29), Kristelig Folkeparti (KrF) (Christian Democrats) 5.6 per cent (10), Senterpartiet (SP) (Centre Party) 5.5 per cent (10), Venstre (V) (Liberal Party) 5.2 per cent (9), Sosialistisk Venstreparti (SV) (Socialist Left Party) 4.1 per cent (7), Miljøpartiet De Grønne (Green Party) 2.8 per cent (1). Turnout was 78.3 per cent.

Next elections

September 2017 (parliamentary)

Political parties

Ruling party

Coalition lead by Høyre (Right) and including Fremskrittspartiet (FrP) (Progress Party), Kristelig Folkeparti (KrF) (Christian Democrats) and the Venstre (V) (Liberal Party) (from 9 Sep 2013)

Main opposition party

Red-Green coalition of Det Norske Arbeiderparti (DNA) (Norwegian Labour Party), Senterpartiet (SP) (Centre Party) and Sosialistisk Venstreparti (SV) (Socialist Left Party).

Population

5.04 million (2012)

Last census: November 2001: 4,520,947

Population density: 15 inhabitants per square km. Urban population 79 per cent (2010 Unicef).

Annual growth rate: 0.7 per cent, 1990–2010 (Unicef).

Ethnic make-up

Predominantly Norwegian. In addition, there are about 60,000 Sami (Lapps), mainly in the north of the country, although there are substantial Sami communities in larger cities.

Religions

More than 90 per cent of all Norwegians belong to the Church of Norway, an Evangelical Lutheran denomination. There are also small Roman Catholic, Jewish and Muslim communities.

Education

All public education in Norway is free. Primary education lasts for seven years; lower secondary education and upper secondary education, which is not compulsory, last for three years, from 13 to 16 and 16 to 19 respectively. On completion of a three-year course at an upper secondary school, students can apply to university. Alternatively, students may, at aged 16, undertake either technical training at vocational schools or practical training at apprenticeship schools; for three years.

Primary and lower secondary education is founded on the principle of every individual having a statutory right to primary, lower secondary and upper secondary education in a unified school system that provides equal education for all on the basis of a single national curriculum.

The right to upper secondary education has been in force since 2000, while the right to primary and lower secondary education was implemented from August 2002.

Higher education in Norway is mainly offered at state institutions, notably four universities, six university colleges, 26 state colleges and two art colleges. A degree candidate may combine studies from universities and colleges, as the courses offered are at the same academic level. The 26 colleges primarily offer shorter courses of a more vocational nature than those offered by the universities.

Compulsory years: Six to 16

Enrolment rate: 100 per cent gross primary enrolment of the relevant age group (including repeaters); 119 gross secondary enrolment (World Bank).

Pupils per teacher: Seven in primary schools

Health

A national health insurance scheme covers medical treatment in hospitals and the reimbursement of costs for medical attention and medicines for certain chronic diseases. Sickness benefit is paid for short-term illness, while chronic or long-term illness is covered by a disability allowance. A small sum is charged for medicine and primary care. The majority of hospitals are state-run.

HIV/Aids

HIV prevalence: 0.1 per cent aged 15–49 in 2003 (World Bank)

Life expectancy: 80 years, 2004 (WHO 2006)
Fertility rate/Maternal mortality rate: 1.9 births per woman, 2010 (Unicef); maternal mortality 6 per 100,000 live births (World Bank).
Birth rate/Death rate: 13 births and 10 deaths per 1,000 population (World Bank).
Child (under 5 years) mortality rate (per 1,000): 3 per 1,000 live births (WHO 2012)
Head of population per physician: 3.13 physicians per 1,000 people, 2003 (WHO 2006)

Welfare

The extensive welfare system has greatly reduced the gap between rich and poor. Social security legislation stipulates that everyone has the right to employment, housing, education, welfare and healthcare. The main general social insurance schemes are the National Insurance Scheme (NIS) and the Family Allowance Scheme. The NIS is a compulsory insurance and pension system and covers pensions, unemployment pay and healthcare for all Norwegians.
A basic retirement pension, adjusted annually, is guaranteed for all Norwegians of 67 years and older regardless of assets or previous income.
Non-pensioners whose income falls below a certain minimum qualify for supplementary benefits. These may include loans or other financial assistance from the local municipality. All families with children under 16 receive a family allowance according to the number of children.
The government subsidises low-cost housing through loans with low rates of interest and easy repayment terms. Families living in housing financed by a state bank can receive an allowance for housing costs should they have difficulties meeting their living expenses.

Main cities

Oslo (capital, estimated population 932,533 in 2012), Bergen (239,249), Stavanger (206,309), Trondheim (170,851), Fredrikstad (100,458), Drammen (94,901).

Languages spoken

Norwegian has two main dialects: Bokmål and Nynorsk. Finnish and Sámi are also spoken. English is widely understood and spoken, especially in urban areas.

Official language/s

Norwegian

Media

Press

Freedom of the press is guaranteed by the constitution. The majority of the press is privately-owned and explicitly partisan. Since the early 1990s only three media owners have accounted for 55–60 per cent of the total sales of newspapers – Schibsted, Orkla and A-Pressen, all of which are Norwegian companies. There are over 200 newspaper titles, Norway has the world's highest level of newspaper readership. Activity is concentrated in south-eastern Norway, especially around Oslo where the majority of papers are published, while local papers tend to dominate each particular region.
Dailies: In Norwegian, two newspapers dominate the national press, *VG* (www.vg.no) and *Dagbladet* (www.dagbladet.no). Other newspapers include *Aftenposten* (www.aftenposten.no), which stopped its online English publication in 2008; *Dagsavisen* (www.dagsavisen.no) and *Nardlys* (www.nordlys.no). Some regional newspapers publish daily such as *Stavanger Aftenblad* (www.aftenbladet.no) and *Bergens Tidende* (www.bt.no). In English, *The Norway Post* (www.norwaypost.no) provides general and international news.
Weeklies: A number of daily newspapers publish weekend editions. In Norwegian, *Se og Hør* and *Her og Hå* vie with one another for readership, with popular articles on celebrities and royal news. Others magazines include *Allers*, for the older woman, *Norsk Ukeblad* for younger women and *Vi Menn* for young men.
Business: A large number of business publications cover various aspects of trade and industry. In Norwegian, the leading daily financial newspaper, in tabloid form is *Dagens Naeringsliv* (DN) (www.dn.no), it is owned by Norge Handels og Sjøfartstidende (www.nhst.no) media conglomerate, which also publishes other trade papers. Hegnar Media (www.hegnar.no) publishes several business publications including *Kapital*, a comprehensive financial magazine and *Finansavisen*. Other, weekly publications include *Handelsbladet FK* (www.handelsbladetfk.no) a retail trade magazine, *Fiskeribladet Fiskaren* (www.fiskeribladetfiskaren.no), a magazine for the fishing industry and *Bondebladet* (www.bondebladet.no), an agricultural newspaper.
Periodicals: A large number of general and special interest magazines exist. Those aimed at women of all ages have the largest circulations, including, in Norwegian, the monthly magazines *Eva* for women, the bi-monthly *Tigue* (www.tique.no) is aimed at young women and *Henne* (www.henne.no) for women's fashion and style. The popular magazine *Mann* is aimed at young men. The quarterly *Vinduet* (www.vinduet.no) is a literary publication.

Broadcasting

The Norwegian Broadcasting Corporation's (NRK) (www.nrk.no) is the national, public broadcaster providing domestically produced programmes for radio, television and digital services, which is funded by a licence fee.
Radio: There are many radio stations broadcasting, with a wide variety of programming. NRK Radio (www.nrk.no) operates three national networks P1, P2 and P3 (Petre), along with several regional and local stations. It also runs an overseas, shortwave service, Radio Norway International. Other, private, commercial stations that comprise networks are NRJ (www.nrj.no), Radio Modum (www.radiomodum.no) and Radio 1 (www.radio1.no).
Television: The switch over from analogue television to digital services is expected to be completed by December 2009.
NRK (www.nrk.no) operates two TV channels. The main, commercial channel is TV2 (www.tv2.no), which broadcasts a combination of local and imported programmes. TV Norge (www.tvnorge.no) provides commercial TV via satellite.
There are other, interest-led TV stations such as Rikstoto Direkte (www.rikstoto.no), a horse-racing channel or Visjon Norge (www.visjonnorge.no) a Christian content channel.
There are over a dozen different European channels broadcasting via satellite or cable, including several pan-Scandinavian channels.
National news agency: NTB (Norsk Telegrambyrå)
Other news agencies: NW (Nyhetsbyrået Newswire): www.newswire.no

Economy

The population of Norway has one of the highest per capita incomes in the world at US$97,363 in 2014. The economy is unique among Western European countries for its large and dominant offshore oil sector. It also has one of the world's largest and most modern maritime fleets, which supports its metalworking and shipbuilding skills. Other industrial sectors include timber, pulp and paper products, chemicals and fishing.
Norway had proven oil reserves of 5.5 billion barrels in 2015, with production of 1904 thousand barrels per day in 2014. Proven natural gas reserves were 1.9 trillion cubic metres (cum) at the end of 2014, with production of 108 billion cum, of which 96 billion cum was exported. Oil and gas extraction accounted 64 per cent of exports in 2014. Since the 1980s the economy has experienced a major structural change, becoming increasingly

focussed on service industries, which accounts for about 60 per cent of GDP. The manufacturing sector is important, particularly in metals and chemicals. Traditional primary sectors, like agriculture, forestry and fishing, have declined; forestry and forest products account for around 0.6 per cent of GDP, farming accounts for 0.5 per cent and fishing 0.4 per cent of GDP; an increasing amount of foodstuffs have to be imported. However, Norway has a thriving aquaculture industry, farming salmon, cod, halibut and shellfish, of which salmon accounts for 85 per cent of total farmed and sold, and typically accounts for around 5 per cent of total export revenue.

The Norwegian economy grew steadily in 2014 at 2.2 per cent, an improvement of 1.5 per cent from the previous year. This is despite the sharp fall in oil prices towards the end of the year. Inflation remained relatively stable and house prices rose by around 7 per cent in the first quarter of 2015. However, growth is forecasted to fall to 1.4 per cent in 2015 due to the volatile nature of oil prices which have been so low so far in 2015.

A key challenge for the government was the tight nature of its labour market, especially in the construction and health sectors. Norwegian firms have had to look abroad to fill vacancies, as the unemployment rate is relatively low at 3.5 per cent in 2010 and 4.1 per cent in 2015. A shortage in the labour market in the recent past has caused high wage growth, leading to a loss of competitiveness in Norwegian exports.

External trade

Norway is a member of the European Economic Area (EEA) which maintains an internal market with, but without joining, the EU. The EU consults EEA members before making its decisions on community legislation. The EEA agreement allows freedom of movement of goods (excluding, to a significant degree, agriculture and fisheries), persons, services and capital.

Norway is the third largest exporter of oil and gas worldwide and that, along with shipping, provides the county's principal foreign exchange earnings.

Norway has a thriving aquaculture industry, farming salmon, cod, halibut and shellfish, of which salmon accounts for 85 per cent of total farmed and which is sold mostly to the EU, accounting for 4.5 per cent of total export revenue.

Imports

Main imports include machinery, vehicles and equipment, consumer goods, chemicals, metals and foodstuffs.

Main sources: Sweden (12.3 per cent of total in 2014), Germany (11.9 per cent), China (9.5 per cent).

Exports

Principal exports are crude oil and petroleum products, natural gas, machinery and equipment, metals, chemicals, ships, manufactured items, primary goods such as timber, ore, fish and foodstuffs.

Main destinations: UK (22.9 per cent total in 2014), Germany (16.9 per cent), Netherlands (12.8 per cent).

Agriculture

Farming

The agricultural sector typically accounts for 1.7 per cent of GDP and employs around 6 per cent of the workforce.

Grain and fodder are grown predominantly from lowland crops whilst mountain farms mainly raise livestock and grow fodder. Grain production is increasing, especially barley and oats, although wheat and rye are increasing in importance. The main grain-growing districts are in southern and central Norway. Coarse fodder, mostly hay and silage, can be cultivated at high altitudes and in the far north.

Other crops include potatoes, other roots, berries and fruits. Crop yields per hectare have risen consistently over the last three decades. Some dairy produce is exported and there is self-sufficiency in meat, milk, cheese, butter, fish and potatoes.

Norway's agricultural policy has two main aims. The first is to promote a high degree of self-sufficiency in animal products and secondly to ensure an adequate livelihood for the country's 120,000 farmers and smallholders. In many regions, agriculture and related activities are the main sources of income. Farm prices are set annually by agreement between the government and agricultural organisations.

Almost all farmland is privately owned and farms tend to be small. Produce is bought and distributed by large co-operative purchasing and sales organisations.

The total cultivated area is just over 868,500 hectares (ha), only 3 per cent of the mainland area. Agricultural production is hampered by difficult topographical conditions and an unfavourable climate. However, Norwegian agriculture is generally efficient, with a high degree of mechanisation and emphasis on training and research.

Fishing

Fishing is a significant industry in the northern and western regions. Fish, including farmed fish, is Norway's second largest export group, accounting for 20 per cent of all exports. Mackerel, cod and capelin are the main species caught, but catches have been falling because of overfishing. The typical annual export value of fish is between Nkr 25–30 billion (US$3.3– 4 billion) and as a whole the fishing industry provides work for 23,000 people.

Fish farms produce mainly salmon and trout, although some are experimenting with other fish, such as halibut. Norway has the world's largest farmed salmon industry, producing about half the total supplies of Atlantic salmon. Demand for farmed salmon has increased by 20–30 per cent annually, but production normally exceeds demand. The emerging new markets in southern Europe are seen as a useful outlet for the surplus, even though salmon exports are in competition with EU production and the EU sets a minimum price requirement for sales from Norway. Salmon comprises 31 per cent of Norway's fish exports.

In October 2008, Norway was forced to undertake the decontamination of infected rivers by culling fish to kill off a deadly parasite (*Gyrodactylus Salaris* (Gs)). After the rivers were purged of fish, dry of replacement stocks, particularly Atlantic salmon, were re-introduced.

Forestry

Forest cover is estimated at 8.8 million hectares (ha). Most forests are situated in southern and central Norway. Spruce, used for making pulp and paper, makes up about 50 per cent of the forest. Pines account for about 30 per cent and broad-leafed trees for around 15 per cent. Mechanisation and automation have allowed logging in previously inaccessible forest land.

About 85 per cent of forest land is privately owned by farmers. The forestry sector has a well-developed co-operative sales apparatus. Forest-owner organisations have become more active in processing. The forestry and the forest-products industry, contributes heavily to local economies. Norway exports nearly 90 per cent of the paper and paperboard production and nearly a quarter of the pulp production. Imports of roundwood and sawnwood, mainly from Sweden, have increased considerably. Per capita consumption of forest products is among the highest in Europe.

Industry and manufacturing

The industrial sector typically accounts for 38 per cent of GDP, employing around 20 per cent of the workforce. Manufacturing accounts for 8 per cent of GDP and has developed relatively slowly in comparison with other industrialised nations.

The goals of Norway's industrial policy has been to maximise employment and the quality of production, maintain the rural population, promote a just and equitable distribution of wealth and income, and keep control over natural resources. Secondary goals have been to control

inflation, protect the environment and achieve a healthy trade balance.
The state channels financial resources to industry on concessionary terms through its Industry Fund and via the state banks. Enterprises in depressed or uncompetitive markets are also provided with loans through the state run District Development Fund. The government aims for around 2 per cent of GDP to be invested in research and development (R&D). Priorities for R&D spending are biotechnology, communications, electronics, metallurgical technology and aquaculture.
Most enterprises are privately owned but subject to strict regulations, especially with regard to safety conditions at the workplace and environmental controls. The government owns and operates a number of key corporations.
Industrial expansion from 1945 to the 1970s was based on inexpensive hydroelectric power. Since the mid-1970s, hydrocarbons have dominated the economy, pushing up labour costs and eroding the competitiveness of manufacturing.

Tourism
Norway is marketed for its landscape and history. Its famous fjords provide spectacular locations for hotels and cruises that travel along the coast. Resorts and communities provide centres in the mountains for winter sports and summer hiking.
Tourists may visit some of the nature reserves on Svalbard, Norway's most northerly territory, which lies within the Arctic Circle or other places of interest, including cultural centres such as historic Viking settlements and Norwegian cities.
Travel and tourism is an important component of the economy, averaging 6.74 per cent of GDP over 2007–11. The sector was adversely affected by the downturn in the global economy, so that in 2010–11 growth fell by 6.75 per cent. In response, the government backed a comprehensive package of promotion, which coincided with the expansion of low-cost airline operations in Norway in 2010. The total contribution to GDP in 2014 was 7.1 per cent of GDP. The contribution to employment was 10.1 per cent of employment, or 266,500 jobs. Investment in the same year equated to 3.8 per cent of total investment.

Environment
With the highest environmental standards in the world, sulphur emissions have plummeted by over 80 per cent since 1980. Pollution is kept low by the country's extensive hydroelectric production, although per capita nitrogen oxide emissions are among the highest in the world. In December 2001, environmentalists accused Norway December 2001of undermining the spirit of the Kyoto Protocol for announcing plans to triple coal production in Svalbard.

Mining
Norway has a highly skilled workforce, experienced in mining, quarrying and processing.
Activity is confined to small-scale mining of iron ore, copper, titanium, coal (on Spitsbergen), zinc, lead and pyrites. Most of these ores and concentrates are exported.
The mining sector has been progressively contracting, causing many problems in areas where there is no alternative employment. However, the country's mining potential has yet to be fully explored and it is believed that Norway has the capacity to develop super-quarries.
On the south coast, near Lillesand, feldspars and quartz are found. Graphite, with differing carbon content and quality, is produced on the island of Senja and research is being carried out to upgrade the quality. Large dimension stones like granite, marbles and quartzites, are available in large quantities. Larvikite is one of the most predominant stones, there are also exclusive marbles, including Norwegian Rose, to be found in the north. From the quarries in northern and central Norway high quality quartzite and phullite-slate are processed. Rock aggregate is found along the coast, in both large sizes and quantities, making transportation very easy.
Norway is the world's seventh largest producer of crude oil and the third largest net oil exporter after Saudi Arabia and Russia. Around two-thirds of exports go to European markets and smaller quantities to the USA and Canada. Oil production doubled in the 1990s as improved recovery techniques were introduced and new wells came on stream. The high level of reserves ensures that production can carry on for several more decades.
Norway has created a sovereign wealth fund to manage the oil revenue and invest the surplus income for future generations. The industry accounts for around 19 per cent of GDP and employs 1.2 per cent of the workforce
Natural gas reserves stand at around 2.50 trillion cubic metres (cum) with production of around 74 billion cum per year. Norway is the seventh-largest gas producer in the world and exports its output to other European countries, with Germany and France as the major customers. Norwegian gas accounts for 14 per cent of consumption in Europe.
Norway's coal comes from the island of Spitsbergen, off the country's north-eastern coast inside the Arctic Circle, where the country's only coal-fired power plant is also located. Around 1.73 million tonnes of coal is produced.
Electricity output exceeds demand, with some of the surplus being exported to Sweden and Denmark. Hydro-electric plants supply 99 per cent of output. Plans for new gas-fired power plants in Kollsnes and Karst have failed in the face of strong opposition by environmentalists. Statoil, the forestry group Norske Skog and the Elkem industrial group have extended the time scale on plans to build an 800MW gas-fired power station in Skogn, to be fully operational by late 2006.

Hydrocarbons
Proven oil reserves were 6.5 billion barrels in 2014, with production at 1895 thousand barrels per day (bpd).
Norway is the world's third largest net oil exporter after Saudi Arabia and Russia and is also a major non-Opec (Organisation of Petroleum Exporting Countries) member and is not bound by cartel export limits. All of its reserves are located offshore in three sites, the North Sea (where most production takes place), the Norwegian Sea (where production is smaller) and the Barents Sea (where no production takes place but reserves are considered to be extensive).
Statoil (71 per cent owned by the government) controls 60 per cent of all oil and gas production and administers subsidiaries in concomitant industries.
Pipelines link offshore platforms with onshore terminals through an extensive sub-sea network. One pipeline links the Ekofisk system in the North Sea to the north-east of England, supplying 900,000bpd of oil.
Proven natural gas reserves were 1.9 trillion cubic metres (cum) in 2014, with production of 108.8 billion cum. There has been a steady increase in not only production from 46 billion cum in 1998, but also an increase in reserves from 1.48 trillion cum as new fields were started up. Norway's composition of production is relatively high at 3.1 per cent in the world.
The only coal reserves in production come from Spitsbergen, on the Svalbard Islands, off the country's northern coast, which provides for the only coal-fired power plant in operation.

Energy
Total installed generating capacity was 28 gigawatts (GW) in 2007, producing over 135 billion kilowatt hours, which typically exceeds domestic demand; all surplus is exported to Sweden and Denmark.
The electricity industry is deregulated, but state-owned entities remain active within the sector, particularly in generation and distribution. Statkraft, the largest publicly owned utility, controls over 30 per cent of

total generating capacity and is increasing its market share by acquiring interests in regional power companies.

Hydroelectric plants supply 99 per cent of total output, but seasonal weather conditions may impact on output, requiring imports to meet needs at such times; Norway is connected to the Scandinavian power grid.

The government has encouraged diversification in the energy market and licences have been issued for gas-fired power plants and wind farms.

Financial markets

Stock exchange

Oslo Børs (Oslo Stock Exchange)

Banking and insurance

Central bank

Norges Bank (Bank of Norway)

Main financial centre

Oslo

Time

GMT plus one hour (daylight saving, late March to late October, GMT plus two hours)

Geography

Norway lies on the west side of the Scandinavian peninsula, in north-west Europe. Its extended coastline faces the North Sea and the North Atlantic Ocean. It is the fifth-largest country in Europe and it has the third-lowest population density in Europe after Greenland and Iceland. The coastline measures 28,000km if fjords and inlets are included, 2,650km if they are not.

The capital, Oslo, in the south, lies on the same latitude as Greenland and Alaska, while Hammerfest on the northern tip of the Norwegian mainland, is the most northerly town in the world. The Svalbard Arctic archipelago is part of Norway, and sovereignty is also exercised over Jan Mayen island and the uninhabited island dependencies of Bouvet and Peter I. In Antartica, Queen Maud Land is a Norwegian dependency.

Norway shares a 1,619km land border with Sweden, and within the Arctic Circle, a 716km frontier with Finland and a 196km border with Russia.

The terrain mostly consists of high plateaux, deep fjords and mountains. More than 70 per cent of the mainland consists of mountains, glaciers, lakes, forest and moorland. The highest peak is Galdhoepiggen in the south which reaches 2,469 metres above sea level.

Only 2.8 per cent of the land area is cultivable soil, while another 20 per cent is productive forest.

Hemisphere

Northern

Climate

Influenced by the Atlantic Gulf Stream and westerly winds, the climate is much warmer than that of other countries on the same latitude. The temperature varies little from north to south, but there is a big contrast between the inland and coastal regions. In winter, while the interior freezes hard, most fjords and harbours remain ice-free. The average annual temperature is 8 degrees Celsius (C) along the west coast, and minus 2 degrees C in the northernmost county, Finnmark. January and February are the coldest months, while July and August are the warmest. The average annual rainfall is 1,960mm in Bergen and 740mm in Oslo. Northern Norway is popularly known as the 'Land of the Midnight Sun'. In Finnmark the midnight sun is visible from mid-May to late-July, and the period of darkness lasts from mid-November to late-January.

Dress codes

Clothing to suit the climate is vital because of the extremes in weather; heavy coats, warm boots, gloves and ear protection are required in winter and light clothing in summer. Normal European business attire, otherwise dress is generally casual.

Entry requirements

Passports

Passports are required by all and must be valid for three months beyond the date of stay. Nationals of countries which are signatories of the Schengen Agreement may visit on national IDs.

Visa

Visas are not required by nationals of most European countries, US, Canada, Australasia, Japan or transit passengers. For further exceptions, contact the nearest embassy. AA Schengen visa application (offered in several languages) can be downloaded from http://europa.eu/abc/travel/ see 'documents you will need'.

Business visitors require a letter of invitation from a Norwegian entity, giving the nature and duration of the stay, with proof of accommodation.

Currency advice/regulations

The import and export of local currency is limited to Nkr25,000. The export of foreign currency is unlimited if proof of import or conversion from another currency can be produced.

Travellers cheque are widely accepted.

Customs

Personal effects duty-free, plus duty-free allowance. Imported products from certain countries such as Japan, South Korea and some East European countries require a licence. Imported cars are heavily taxed.

Prohibited imports

Illegal drugs, firearms.

Health (for visitors)

Nationals of the European Economic Area (EEA) countries and Switzerland can access reduced cost and sometimes free medical treatment using a European Health Insurance Card (EHIC) while visiting the EEA. Exceptions include nationals of the 10 countries which joined the EU in 2004 whose EHIC is not valid in Switzerland. Applications for the EHIC should be made before travelling.

Mandatory precautions

None

Hotels

There is a wide range of hotels available in most towns. There is no official rating system in operation. Private accommodation can be obtained through local tourist offices or accommodation offices in central railway stations. There is a service charge of 15 per cent included in the bill, but tipping is also expected.

Credit cards

Major credit and charge cards are accepted. ATMs are widely accepted.

Public holidays (national)

Fixed dates

31 Dec–1 Jan (New Year, from midday 31 Dec), 1 May (Labour Day), 17 May (Constitution Day), 24 Dec (Christmas Eve, afternoon only), 25–26 Dec (Christmas).

Variable dates

Maundy Thursday, Good Friday, Easter Monday, Ascension Day, Whit Monday.

Working hours

Banking

Mon–Thu: 0900–1600; Fri: 0900–1700; Sat: 0900–1200.

Business

Mon–Fri: 0900–1600.

Government

Mon–Fri: 0830–1600.

Shops

Mon–Wed: 0900–1700; Thu: 0900–1900; Sat: 0830–1300.

Many shops are increasingly introducing longer opening hours, and some are open on Sundays.

Telecommunications

Mobile/cell phones

GSM 3G, 900 and 1800 services are available in inhabited areas.

Electricity supply

220V AC

Social customs/useful tips

Punctuality is expected. Shake hands on meeting. Business lunches are rare. The main meal of the day is generally taken at home at 1700 hours, though people will expect to eat later if invited out.

Security
Serious crime is not a big problem. It is usually safe to walk at night in major cities, such as Oslo and Bergen, although some neighbourhoods are less safe than others. Car theft, on the other hand, is fairly common, especially in the major cities.

Getting there

Air

National airline: SAS Braathens
International airport/s: Oslo International Airport (OSL) (Gardermoen) 47km north of city. Facilities include duty-free shops, banks/*bureaux de change*, restaurants, car hire and dry cleaning. Business lounge including Internet facilities.
Other airport/s: Bergen (BGO), 19km from city; Stavanger (SVG), 14.5km south-west of city.
Airport tax: None

Surface

Road: The are several routes across the border from Sweden in the east and Finland in the north. These roads may be closed in winter.
Rail: There are daily train connections between Stockholm-Oslo-Trondheim. There are also train connections between Oslo-Gothenburg-Copenhagen-Helsingborg.
Water: There are frequent ferry services to Denmark, UK and Germany.
Main port/s: Oslo, Kristiansand, Bergen and Larvik.

Getting about

National transport

Air: Efficient services, operated by various carriers, link all major and many smaller towns. Charter sea and land planes are widely available.
Road: The road network is extensive; main highways are kept open although certain roads in the mountainous areas could be closed in winter and spring.
Buses: There is an extensive bus network. The main bus company is the Nor-Way Bussekspress with routes connecting every main city. Tickets can be purchased on the buses.
Rail: Norway has a good, though somewhat limited, national rail system. All railway lines are operated by the Norwegian State Railways (Norges Statsbaner or NSB). From Oslo, the main lines go to Stavanger, Bergen, Åndalsnes, Bodø and Sweden.
Water: There are regular and efficient motor ship services visiting all the major ports. There are also numerous local ferry, hydrofoil and catamaran services.

City transport

Taxis: Taxis are available in most cities. They can be obtained at ranks or by telephone (Oslo 388-090, Bergen 900-990, Stavanger 526-040). Telephone numbers of taxi stands are listed in the directory under *Drosjer*. Meters are compulsory. It is not expected that the tip will be more than small change.
In addition to regular taxis, there are airport taxis, cheaper taxis which must be ordered in advance by groups of up to three people, and wheelchair taxis.
Buses, trams & metro: There are eight tram lines and five metro lines in Oslo, plus numerous bus services. Public transport runs from 0530–2400 everyday. Tickets are best pre-purchased and self-cancelled, there is one hour's free transfer between any of the modes. (www.trafikanten.no can offer more information). Buses serving the airport take about 45 minutes and there is also a new regional bus station for services further afield.
Trains: A high-speed airport express train leaves every 10 minutes to and from Oslo's central station (20 minutes).
Ferry: Ferries from Oslo to Bygdøy leave from Rådhusbrygge, while ferries to the island in Oslofjord leave from Vippetangen.

Car hire

Available from airports and major towns. For travel between towns public transport tends to be quicker and much cheaper. Studded or winter tyres are recommended during winter. There are strict laws against drinking and driving and wearing seatbelts is compulsory. The speed limit in built-up areas is 50kph and 80kph on highways.

BUSINESS DIRECTORY

The addresses listed below are a selection only. While World of Information makes every endeavour to check these addresses, we cannot guarantee that changes have not been made, especially to telephone numbers and area codes. We would welcome any corrections.

Telephone area codes
The international direct dialling (IDD) code for Norway is +47, followed by subscriber's number.

Chambers of Commerce
American Chamber of Commerce in Norway, 20C Drammesveien, PO Box 2604 Solli, 0203 Oslo (tel: 2254-6040; fax: 2254-6720; fax: amcham@amcham.no).

Bergen Chamber of Commerce and Industry, 11 Olav Kyrresgt, 5014 Bergen (tel: 5555-3900; fax: 5555-3901; email: firmapost@bergen-chamber.no).

British-Norwegian Chamber of Commerce, 1 Dronning Maudsgate, 0250 Oslo (tel: 2311-1790; fax: 2283-4120; email: bncc@c21.net).

Kristiansand Chamber of Commerce, PO Box 269, 4663 Kristiansand (tel: 3812-3970; fax: 3812-3979; email: post@kristiansand-chamber.no).

Oslo Chamber of Commerce, 30 Drammensveien, PO Box 2874 Solli, 0230 Oslo (tel: 2212-9400; fax: 2212-9401; email: mail@chamber.no).

Stavanger Chamber of Commerce, 1 Rosenkildetorget, PO Box 182, 4001 Stavanger (tel: 5151-0880; fax: 5151-0881; email: post@stavanger-chamber.no).

Trondheim Chamber of Commerce, PO Box 778 Sentrum, 7408 Trondheim (tel: 7388-3110; fax: 7388-3111; email: firmapost@trondheim-chamber.no).

Tromsø Chamber of Commerce and Industry, 83 Grønnegata, PO Box 464, 9255 Tromsø (tel: 7766-5230; fax: 7766-5253; email: firmapost@tromso-chamber.no).

Banking
Christiania Bank og Kreditkasse, PO Box 1166, N-0107 Oslo (tel: 2248-5000; fax: 2248-4749).

Den norske Bank, Stranden 21, Aker Brygge, N-0021 Oslo (tel.: 2248-1050; fax: 2248-1870; internet: www.dnb.no; email: dnb@dnb.no).

Fokus Bank A/S, Vestre Rosten 77, PO Box 6090, N-7466 Trondheim (tel: 7288-2011; fax: 7288-2061).

Postbanken, Akersgata 68, N-0180 Oslo (tel: 2297-6000; fax: 2297-7665; internet: www.postbanken.no).

Central bank
Norges Bank, Bankplassen 2, PO Box 1179, Sentrum, 0107 Oslo (tel: 2231-6000; fax: 2241-3105; email: central.bank@norges-bank.no).

Stock exchange
Oslo Børs (Oslo Stock Exchange), www.oslobors.no

Travel information
Noges Automobilforbund (NAF), Storgata 2, N-0155 Oslo (tel: 2234-1400).

Nor-Way Bussekspress, Karl Johans gate 2; NO-0154 Oslo (tel: 8154-4444; fax: 2200-1631; email: administrasjon@nor-way.no; internet: www.nbe.no).

Road User Information Centre (tel: 2265-4040).

SAS Braathens, Oksenøyveien 3, Fornebu; PO Box 0080, Oslo (tel: 9150-54000; internet: www.sasbraathens.no).

National tourist organisation offices
Norwegian Tourist Board, Stortorvet 10, N-0155 Oslo; PO Box 722 Sentrum, N-0105 Oslo (tel: 2414-4600; fax: 2414-4601; e-mail: norway@ntr.no; internet: www.visitnorway.com).

Ministries
Department of Transport and Communications, Akersgaten 59, PO Box 8010 Dep, N-0030 Oslo (tel: 2224-9090; fax: 2224-9571).

Ministry of Agriculture, PO Box 8007 Dep, N-0032 Oslo (tel: 2224-9090; fax: 2224- 9555).

Ministry of Finance (Finansdepartementet), Akersgaten 40 (Blokk G), PO Box 8008 Dep, N-0030 Oslo (tel: 2224- 9090; fax: 2224-9510; internet: www.finans.dep.no).

Ministry of Foreign Affairs, 7 Juni-Plassen/Victoria Terrasse, PO Box 8114 Dep, N-0032 Oslo (tel: 2224-3600; fax: 2224-9580/81).

Ministry of Industry and Trade, Grubbegt 8, PO Box 8148 Dep, N-0033 Oslo (tel: 2224-9090; fax: 2224-9565).

Ministry of Petroleum and Energy, Einar Gerhardsens Plass 1, PO Box 8148 Dep, N-0033 Oslo (tel: 2224-6107; fax: 2224-9525).

Other useful addresses
Directorate of Immigration, PO Box 8108 Dep, N-0032 Oslo (tel: 2335-1500; fax: 2335-1504).

Næringslivets Hovedorganisasjon (Confederation of Norwegian Business and Industry), Middelthuns Gate 27, Pb 5250 Majorstua, N-0303 Oslo (tel: 2296-5000; fax: 2296-5593).

Norges Eksportrad (Export Council of Norway), Drammensveien 40, N-0243 Oslo (tel: 2292-6300: fax: 2292-6400).

Norges Varemesse (the Norwegian Trade Fair Foundation), PO Box 75, NO-2001 Lillestrøm (tel: 6693-9100: fax: 6693-9101; internet: www.messe.no).

Norinform, Norwegian Information Service, PO Box 241 Sentrum, N-0103 Oslo (tel: 2211-4685; fax: 2242-4887).

Norwegian Trade Council, N-0243 Oslo (tel: 2292-6300; fax: 2292-6400).

Oslo Bors (stock exchange), Tollbugaten 2, Box 460, Sentrum, 0105 Oslo (tel: 2234-1700; fax: 2234-1925; email: info@ose.no; internet: www.oslobors.no).

Royal Norwegian Embassy (US), 2729 34th Street, NW, Washington DC 20008 (tel: (+1-202) 333-6000; fax: (+1-202) 337-0870; email: emb.washington@mfa.no).

Statistics Norway, PO Box 8131 Dep, N-0033 Oslo 1 (tel: 2109-0000; fax: 2109-4973; internet: (English section) www.ssb.no//www-open/english/).

National news agency: NTB (Norsk Telegrambyrå), PO Box 6817, St Olavs Plass, N-0130 Oslo (tel: 2203-4400; email: marked@ntb.no).

NW (Nyhetsbyrået Newswire): www.newswire.no

Internet sites
National bus company: www.nbe.no

National railway company: www.nsb.no

Nordic Pages: www.markovits.com/nordic

Yellow Pages: www.gulesider.no

Oman

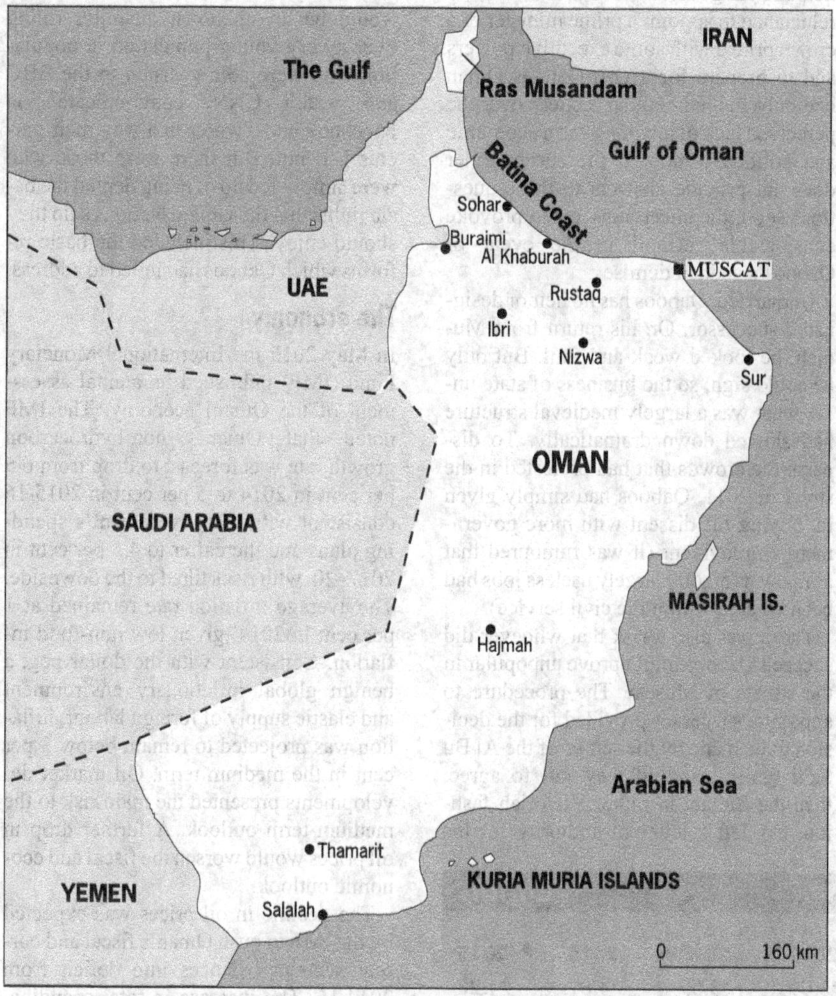

For eight months beginning in July 2014 Oman's solitary ruler Sultan Qaboos, aged 74, received treatment for an undisclosed illness in Munich. He had ruled for 45 years, had no heir and held every important portfolio in government. As no-one had any idea who his successor might be, it was hardly surprising that a climate of uncertainty prevailed. Oman's next ruler was certain to find himself dealing with a young, media savvy, citizenry articulating demands for reform. A report in the London *Economist* observed that stability abroad – in Yemen, Syria, Iraq and other Arab states – might not be the new sultan's (whoever he turned out to be) highest priority or even his biggest challenge. As the *Economist* warned, the greatest threat to Omani stability might well come from within the country.

The uncertain health of the Sultan of Oman had certainly heightened concern about the future of the country probably most, Omanis had long identified their country with its ruler. After a shaky start, the Beethoven loving Sultan Qaboos bin Said Al Said had managed to gain their respect and loyalty by creating a state and a national identity simply centred on himself, or at least centred on the image they had of him. However, following the Arab Spring events of 2011, mounting popular frustration and even criticism of Sultan

KEY FACTS

Official name: Sultanatu Oman (Saltanat Uman) (Sultanate of Oman)

Head of State: Sultan Qaboos bin Said (from 1970)

Head of government: Sultan Qaboos bin Said (from 1970)

Ruling party: Political parties are not permitted.

Area: 320,000 square km (including Kuria Muria Islands)

Population: 4.09 million (2014)* (2,694,094; 2010, census figure)

Capital: Muscat (Masqat)

Official language: Arabic

Currency: Omani rial (RO) = 1,000 baiza

Exchange rate: RO0.39 per US$ (Sep 2015)

GDP per capita: US$19,002 (2014)*

GDP real growth: 2.95% (2014)*

GDP: US$77.75 billion (2014)*

Inflation: 1.01% (2014)

Oil production: 943,000 bpd (2014)

Natural gas production: 29.00 billion cum (2014)

Balance of trade: US$24.59 billion (2013)*

Annual FDI: US$788.04 million (2011)

* estimated figure

Qaboos had emerged, probably connected to fears over what was likely to occur should their ruler of over 40 years die.

Although the Omani model of political legitimacy was closely linked to Sultan Qaboos, elements of the country's young population had for some time felt less in awe of their ruler. Oman's increasingly vocal civil society had been complaining about deep-seated flaws existing in the body of the state he built after taking power in 1970. In 2011 and 2012, most major towns saw peaceful protests by Omanis demanding higher salaries, better living conditions, substantial political reforms and the end of corruption. The régime responded with a combination of economic gestures, the dismissal of some top officials and the detention of peaceful activists. However, since 2012, repressive measures have become more prominent, with new investments in the security sector and crackdowns on dissonant voices. Political parties are prohibited in Oman and, despite the odd cosmetic reform, nearly all power remains with the monarch.

Qaboos

Although the protests had not initially targeted the Sultan, criticism of Qaboos and his management practices had become more widespread. Protesters were not unreasonably worried about the future of the country and were beginning to voice their concerns. Oman's leaders were, for the most part, out of touch with their country. Younger Omanis would not be likely to grant the next ruler the same degree of authority that their parents and grandparents had granted Qaboos. Instead, Qaboos' successor was quite likely to face renewed demands for reform.

Rather than dismissing alternative voices, the régime needed to encourage civil society organisations, the first step towards allowing a degree of public participation in government. But the régime's reluctance to appoint a prime minister or a crown prince with some executive powers and to prepare for a post-Qaboos Oman had only fuelled popular anxiety over the perceived lack of any long-term economic and political vision. If the current ruler does not provide answers to these questions soon, the uncertainty could provoke considerable turmoil in the event of Qaboos's sudden demise.

Unmarried, Qaboos has no heir or designated successor. On his return from Munich, he looked weak and frail. But only he could sign; so the business of state under what was a largely medieval structure had slowed down dramatically. To disperse the crowds that had protested in the street in 2011, Qaboos had simply given in, buying off dissent with more government employment (it was rumoured that as many as 50,000 largely useless jobs had been created within the civil service).

There was also a risk that whoever did succeed Qaboos might prove unpopular in the streets of Muscat. The procedure to appoint a successor provided for the decision to be made by the scions of the Al Bu Said family. Should they fail to agree, then the Sultan, in rather Victorian fashion, has left a letter of authority for his choice to prevail. The betting was on one of the Sultan's three cousins Assad, Shihab and Haithem bin Tariq al Said. Little is known about them by the public.

Whatever discontent was expressed by a minority of the population, there was still little popular pressure for political change. The fear of the unknown created enough uncertainty. However, the new ruler would be an unknown quantity, ruling over a very young population, a population who were able to listen to the BBC and watch CNN, communicate via Facebook and Twitter in a way their parents had not. But there were those who were simply fed up of being denied the basic rights that the United Nations said they should enjoy. This included the basic reforms which Qaboos had failed to address.

The economy

In May 2015 the International Monetary Fund (IMF) published its annual assessment of the Omani economy. The IMF noted that Oman's non-hydrocarbon growth rate was forecast to drop from 6.5 per cent in 2014 to 5 per cent in 2015/16 consistent with the government's spending plans and thereafter to 4.5 per cent in 2017–20, with risks tilted to the downside. The average inflation rate remained at 1 per cent in 2014, given low non-food inflation. Consistent with the dollar peg, a benign global inflationary environment and elastic supply of foreign labour, inflation was projected to remain below 3 per cent in the medium term. Oil market developments presented the main risk to the medium-term outlook. A further drop in oil prices would worsen the fiscal and economic outlook.

The decline in oil prices was expected by the IMF to push Oman's fiscal and current account balances into deficit from 2014/15. The increase in total spending, particularly during 2010–14, mainly in response to social demands, had pushed the breakeven oil price to US$108 per barrel in 2014. Ongoing efforts to pursue economic diversification were becoming more critical in the lower oil price environment.

The overall fiscal deficit was projected by the IMF at 14.8 per cent of GDP in 2015 and would remain in double digits over the medium-term in the absence of fiscal reforms. Without further fiscal adjustment, financing the projected cumulative fiscal deficit between 2015 and 2020 would exhaust fiscal buffers and raise debt to about 25 per cent of GDP, or increase government debt to over 70 per cent of GDP by 2020 if buffers were to be preserved.

KEY INDICATORS — Oman

	Unit	2011	2012	2013	2014	**2015
Population	m	*3.08	*3.09	*3.59	*4.09	*4.23
Gross domestic product (GDP)	US$bn	71.90	78.29	76.98	*77.75	*62.94
GDP per capita	US$	23,315	25,356	21,417	*19,002	*14,887
GDP real growth	%	5.5	5.0	4.7	*2.9	*4.6
Inflation	%	4.0	2.9	1.2	1.0	*1.0
Oil output	'000 bpd	891.0	922.0	942.0	943.0	–
Natural gas output	bn cum	26.5	29.0	30.9	29.0	–
Exports (fob) (goods)	US$m	47,092.3	52,137.8	56,429.1	–	–
Imports (fob) (goods)	US$m	21,498.0	25,628.1	31,841.8	–	–
Balance of trade	US$m	25,594.3	26,509.8	24,587.3	–	–
Current account	US$m	10,262.7	9,052.0	5,116.0	*1,679.0	*-9,462.0
Total reserves minus gold	US$m	12,128.9	14,400.1	15,950.3	16,323.7	–
Foreign exchange	US$m	11,742.5	1,401.4	15,552.5	–	–
Exchange rate	per US$	0.38	0.38	0.39	0.39	–

* estimated figure ** forecast figure

The capital adequacy ratio of banks stood high at 15.1 per cent, supported by low net non-performing loans and high provisioning ratios of 0.6 per cent and 136 per cent, respectively, at end-September 2014. Stress tests suggested that under a combination of interest rate and market shocks, the solvency of the banking system would be preserved, although some banks would be required to raise capital to meet the central bank's regulatory capital requirement. The banks' liquidity situation augured well for meeting emerging private sector credit demand and for further financial deepening.

Efforts to establish fiscal sustainability should, in the view of the IMF, be underpinned by reforms to modernise the current budget system. There was a need for integrating the dual budget, establishing a medium-term budget framework that was integrated with the medium-term macro-economic framework and improving the public financial management system. Strengthening the macro-fiscal unit would provide expertise in some of these areas.

Oman's banking system was considered resilient by the IMF, but the Central Bank of Oman (CBO) needed to remain vigilant in monitoring and managing evolving risks. The central bank also needed to consider measures to enhance capital cushions to equip banks to face potential further oil price declines, including strengthening banks' risk management capacity. A sudden sharp withdrawal of government deposits would induce liquidity pressures in banks. Avoiding such a situation warranted close co-ordination between the CBO and the government and would require the CBO to inject temporary liquidity into the system, if the need arose.

Efforts toward economic diversification also needed to be strengthened, to reduce dependence on oil and to generate jobs for nationals. Oman needed to improve the business environment by removing impediments to physical, legal and business infrastructure. Although the government was making serious efforts to develop the small- and medium-sized (SME) segment, greater co-ordination between the agencies involved would be beneficial. Developing domestic debt markets would strengthen the diversification process and reduce concentration risks of banks.

Hydrocarbons

Oman is the largest oil and natural gas producer in the Middle East that is not a member of the Organisation of the Petroleum Exporting Countries (OPEC). In 2012, Oman's hydrocarbons sector accounted for 86 per cent of government revenues, according to the country's ministry of finance. Revenues from oil and natural gas accounted for approximately 50 per cent of Oman's gross domestic product (GDP) in 2013, according to the Central Bank of Oman. Oman's fiscal breakeven price for oil in 2014 was approximately US$105 per barrel, according to the ministry of oil and gas, meaning that Oman's government needed the export price of oil to remain at or above that level to secure sufficient revenues. In 2013, the price for Omani crude averaged US$105.50, 3.7 per cent lower than the previous year. The average price per barrel had fallen well below the US$100.00 mark in 2015 and looked set to stay there.

According to the OGJ, Oman had 5.2 billion barrels of estimated proved oil reserves in December 2014. Oman's 5.2 billion barrels of proved oil reserves rank seventh in the Middle East and 23rd in the world. A report published by the US Geological Survey in 2012 stated that the estimated mean undiscovered energy resources in the South Oman Salt Basin – located in the southern part of the country – totalled more than 370 million barrels of oil, 315 billion cubic feet (bcf) of natural gas and more than 40 million barrels of natural gas liquids (NGL). With rising production levels, a growing petrochemical sector – which relied on liquefied petroleum gases (LPG) and NGL – and additional potential resources, the country was unlikely to significantly alter its dependence on hydrocarbons in the short term.

According to the US government Energy Information Administration (EIA), Oman's average annual crude oil production and lease condensate peaked in 2000 at 970,000 barrels per day (bpd), but dropped to 710,000bpd in 2007. Oman successfully reversed that decline and annual crude oil and lease condensate production rose each of the next five years, averaging 945,000bpd in 2013. To increase oil production, enhanced oil recovery techniques, such as steam injection and miscible injection, have been the key driver of Oman's oil production. Oman's only export crude stream is the Oman blend, which is a medium-light and sour (high sulfur) crude. Oman is an important crude oil exporter, particularly to Asian markets. In 2013, Oman exported an estimated 833,400bpd of crude oil and condensate, of which nearly 60 per cent went to China.

Natural gas

Petroleum Development Oman (PDO) has an even greater presence in the natural gas sector than it does in the oil sector, accounting for nearly all of Oman's natural gas supply along with smaller contributions from Occidental Petroleum, Oman's largest independent oil producer, and Thailand's PTTEP. The Oman Gas Company (OGC) directs the country's natural gas transmission and distribution systems. The OGC is a joint venture between the Omani ministry of oil and gas (80 per cent) and Oman Oil Company (OOC) (20 per cent). Oman Liquefied Natural Gas (OLNG) – owned by a consortium including the government, Shell and Total – operates all LNG activities in Oman through its three liquefaction trains in Qalhat near Sur.

Oman held 30 trillion cubic feet (tcf) of proved natural gas reserves as of January 2014, according to the *Oil & Gas Journal*. In 2012, the country was the fifth largest dry natural gas producer in the Middle East and the 26th largest producer worldwide. Oman's natural gas sector grew in importance over the past two decades, largely the result of the opening of the country's two LNG facilities, in 2000 and 2005. Prior to 2000, Oman produced small quantities of dry natural gas, averaging just 154 billion cubic feet (bcf) per year between 1990 and 1999. In 2013, Oman produced 1.1tcf of dry natural gas, exporting almost 410bcf in the form of LNG and consuming the remainder in the domestic market.

Oman is a member of the Gas Exporting Countries Forum (GECF) and exports natural gas as LNG through its liquefaction facilities near Sur, in the Gulf of Oman. In 2013, Oman exported approximately 410bcf of natural gas, which is roughly 63 per cent of the country's total capacity. Nearly all of Oman's natural gas exports go to Japan and South Korea, although in 2013 a small amount went to Spain.

Risk assessment

Economy	Good
Politics	Poor
Regional stability	Good/fair

Muslims in Oman

% of population	87.7
Sunni (% of Muslims)	
Shi'a (% of Muslims)	

COUNTRY PROFILE

Ibadite imams of the Ibadiyah Islamic sect, both hereditary and elected, first began to rule the area in the 800s.

1507–1650 The Portuguese occupied Muscat and established a garrison there until they were expelled by Imam Sultan bin Saif.
1737–49 The Persians invaded and after they were driven out, the Al bin Said dynasty came to power, which still rules the country today.
1798 The first treaty of friendship was signed between Oman and Britain.
1800s The Omani empire expanded to include Zanzibar and Mombasa and parts of the Indian subcontinent. When Sultan Said bin Sultan (known as Said the Great) died in 1856, his empire was divided: one son became Sultan of Zanzibar and the other the Sultan of Muscat and Oman.
1913 After an uprising against the Sultan, control of Oman split, with the interior being ruled by Ibadit imams and the coast by the Sultan.
1932 Said bin Taimur became Sultan.
1959 The Sultan regained control of the interior from the Ibadit imams.
1965–75 A rebellion in the southern region of Dhofar, led by the Popular Front for the Liberation of Oman (PFLO), was put down with the help of soldiers from India, Iran, Jordan, Pakistan, Saudi Arabia, the Trucial States and Britain.
1964 Oil was discovered.
1967 Oil extraction began.
1970 Qaboos bin Said, aged 30, overthrew his father, Said bin Taimur. Sultan Qaboos started to open up the country and, using money from oil, built roads, schools and hospitals and gave homes to people and boats to fishermen. He set in place strict environmental laws.
1971 Oman joined the Arab League.
1978 Sultan Qaboos was active in helping implement the Camp David Accords, signed by Israel and Egypt.
1981 The political and economic union, Co-operation Council for the Arab States of the Gulf (CCASG) (known as Gulf Co-operation Council (GCC)) was formed by Bahrain, Kuwait, Oman, Qatar, Saudi Arabia and the United Arab Emirates (UAE).
1985 Oman established full diplomatic relations with the Soviet Union for the first time.
1991 During the Gulf War, Oman was used as a base for forces fighting Iraq. Sultan Qaboos established the Majlis al Shura (Consultative Council).
1996 Sultan Qaboos promulgated the Basic Statute of the State, or Basic Law, the Gulf's first written constitution. A new bicameral parliament was inaugurated, consisting of an upper chamber or Majlis al Dawla (Council of State) (41 members appointed by the monarch) and a transformed lower chamber (Majlis al Shura) (Consultative Assembly), with 83 members elected by limited suffrage. The Assembly and the Council of Ministers meet once a year at which Cabinet members present their departments' plans. Majlis al Shura power is limited to proposing and reviewing legislation and, although it can affect policy on minor issues, it remains relatively powerless as executive power remains with the Sultan.
1997 The Sultan issued a decree allowing women to stand for election to, and vote for, the Majlis al Shura; two women were elected.
1999 Oman and the UAE signed a border agreement, defining their common frontier.
2000 Majlis al Shura elections took place, involving just 25 per cent of the adult population; no political parties were allowed and all candidates were hand-picked by the Sultan. Oman joined the World Trade Organisation (WTO).
2001 Oman became an important base for international military operations against the Taliban government in Afghanistan.
2002 Voting rights were extended to all citizens over the age of 21.
2003 The 83-seat Majlis al Shura was freely elected for the first time.
2004 Sultan Qaboos appointed Oman's first female minister with a portfolio (in higher education).
2005 A state security court convicted 31 people of plotting to overthrow the Sultan and install an Islamist government.
2006 Oman signed a free trade agreement with the US.
2007 The Arabian Oryx sanctuary became the first site to be removed from Unesco's World Heritage list, as Oryx numbers dwindled and the park was reduced in size by 90 per cent.
2008 A common market was created by the GCC. Citizens of these countries are now allowed to travel between and live in any of the six states, where they may find employment, buy properties and businesses and use the educational and health facilities freely.
2009 The Information Technology Authority was re-branded as e.oman (www.ita.gov.om). The website, in English and Arabic, provides information on all government departments and services.
2010 Investment of US$1.3 billion in new power plants was contracted out to a consortium of South Korean and German companies in September. Two thermal electricity generating plants producing up to 750MW will be built to the north-west of Muscat in 2013.
2011 Demonstrations in the second city of Sohar, led to a number of concessions, including promises of jobs and benefits being made by the Sultan. In August plans were announced to build a factory to make electric cars. The cars were designed by Sultan al Amri, and a production is expected to begin in January 2014. On 13 October Sultan Qaboos decreed that the parliament would be granted oversight powers. In elections for the consultative assembly, held on 15 October, 1,300 candidates took part (77 of whom were women); 84 candidates were elected as independent members of the assembly.
2012 On 18 July Amnesty International condemned the trials of dozens of activists 'exercising their rights to freedom of expression'. On 9 September, six activists who took part in 2011 demonstrations, were convicted on defamation charges for insulting the Sultan, undermining the status of the state and using the internet to publish defamatory materials.
2013 *The Week* was suspended on 3 September after publishing an article suggesting Oman was more tolerant of homosexuality than other Gulf states, despite printing a full page apology. Omani foreign minister, Youssef bin Alawi, told an audience at the International Institute for Strategic Studies Manama Dialogue Forum (held in December) that Oman was still not in favour of a closer union of the GCC. Saudi Arabia had previously proposed the union in 2011.

Political structure

Constitution

In November 1996, Sultan Qaboos bin Said promulgated the 'Basic Statute of the State', or Basic Law, the Gulf's first written constitution, that clarified the royal succession, provided for a legislature and guaranteed basic civil liberties for Omani citizens within a framework of Islamic and traditional law.

The country is divided into 59 *wilayat* (regions), each under the authority of a wali (governor). There are special governates for the cities of Muscat and Salalah, with Muscat consisting of six separate *wilayat*.

Independence date

18 November 1970.

Form of state

Absolute monarchy

The executive

Executive, judiciary and legislative power lies with Sultan Qaboos bin Said, who appoints the Council of Ministers and other officials and promulgates laws by decree.

National legislature

The bicameral parliament consists of the Majlis al Shura (Consultative Assembly) (lower house) with 84 members elected by majority vote, to serve for four-year terms in an entirely consultative capacity and the Majlis al Dawla (Council of State) (upper house) with 59 members appointed by the Sultan; this house enacts not only laws it recommends but also those submitted by the lower house, with the exception of specific laws that must be referred to the Sultan. It also administers other state councils and committees.

Legal system

The legal system is mainly the preserve of Sharia courts, which apply Islamic law. The local courts are administered by *qadis* (Islamic judges) appointed by the minister of justice. Appeals from local courts are heard at the Court of Appeal in Muscat.

Last elections

15 October 2011 (consultative assembly)

Results: Consultative assembly: of the 1,300 candidates taking part (77 of whom were women); 84 candidates were elected as independent members of the assembly.

Next elections

2015 (consultative council)

Political parties

Ruling party

Political parties are not permitted.

Main opposition party

There is no legal opposition.

Population

3.09 million (2012)* (2,694,094; 2010, census figure)

Last census: 16 May 2010: 2,694,094

Population density: 11 people per square km. Urban population 73 per cent (2010 Unicef).

Annual growth rate: 2.0 per cent, 1990–2010 (Unicef).

Ethnic make-up

Predominantly Arab, with non-Arab pockets in long-established Baluchi, Iranian and Gujarati communities. Many Omanis are of Zanzibari descendancy (prior to 1964, Zanzibar had been part of the Sultanate of Oman).

Religions

Islam is the official religion. The majority are Ibadi Muslims with about one-quarter being Sunnis. There is a small concentration of Shi'ite Muslims in Muscat.

Education

The government sponsors literacy centres in an attempt to improve the literacy rate. Primary education lasts from aged six to 12. Secondary education consists of two stages: first the preparatory school for three years then the secondary school for a further three years. Islamic Institute secondary schools accept students who have completed their preparatory study in a mosque. It teaches the same subjects as secondary schools but with an emphasis on Islam and the Arabic language.

Literacy rate: 74 per cent adult rate; 99 per cent youth rate (15–24) (Unesco 2005).

Compulsory years: None.

Enrolment rate: 76 per cent gross primary enrolment of relevant age group (including repeaters); 67 per cent gross secondary enrolment (World Bank).

Pupils per teacher: 26 in primary schools.

Health

Free medical care is available throughout the Sultanate for all Omani citizens.

HIV/Aids

HIV prevalence: 0.1 per cent aged 15–49 in 2003 (World Bank)

Life expectancy: 74 years, 2004 (WHO 2006)

Fertility rate/Maternal mortality rate: 2.3 births per woman, 2010 (Unicef); maternal mortality 19 per 100,000 live births (World Bank).

Birth rate/Death rate: 28 births and 3 deaths per 1,000 people respectively (World Bank).

Child (under 5 years) mortality rate (per 1,000): 12 per 1,000 live births (WHO 2012)

Head of population per physician: 1.32 physicians per 1,000 people, 2004 (WHO 2006)

Welfare

Most Omanis depend on the extended family for financial support. Since 1984 the Ministry of Social Affairs has run a scheme of monthly welfare payments for eight categories of Omani citizens, provided that they can prove indigence. The categories are: orphans, divorcees, people unable to work, refugees, widows, spinsters, people over 60 years of age and the families of prisoners.

The Sultanate of Oman has extended social security benefits for workers in the private sector. Since the issue of the Social Insurance law in 1992, the Public Authority for Social Insurance (PASI) has registered companies and establishments in the private sector including workers and their families, who are entitled to receive sickness, injury and disability benefits, pension and death compensation.

The Association for the Welfare of Handicapped Children, a charitable organisation, supplements the work of the ministry of social affairs, labour and vocational training with centres at Al-Khoudh, Quriyat and Bilad Banu Bu Hassan. The government has made donations towards women's training centres and nurseries for childcare. Special attention is given to the needs of the disabled, particularly young people who are encouraged to join the training centre at Al-Khoudh. The centre also cares for severely disabled children between 3—14 years of age. The ministry has developed sport facilities as part of the disabled welfare programme. The Oman Charitable Organisation (OCO), a non-governmental body, has co-operated with the ministry to build 45 shelters at a cost of RO58,500 (US$152,161) for the Bedu living in remote areas of the country and assisted with programmes for the disabled.

Main cities

Muscat (Masqat) (capital, estimated population 24,721 in 2012), Seeb (338,436), Bawshar (224,652), Salalah (203,776), Matrah (165,459), Sohar (132,702), as Suwayq (132,549), Ibri (113,164), Saham (107,051), al Buraymi (101,385).

Languages spoken

English is spoken in business circles. KiSwahili is often spoken among the older generation and those of Zanzibari descent. Given the size of the immigrant population, Farsi, Urdu and Baluchi are common languages.

Official language/s

Arabic

Media

Press

Government censorship is applied to political and cultural items and due to the law that requires all publications and journalists be licensed by the Ministry of Information, with stiff penalties for transgressions, has resulted in widespread journalistic self-censorship.

Dailies: In English, the *Oman Daily Observer* (www.omanobserver.com) is government-owned, while the Times of Oman (www.timesofoman.com) and *Oman Tribune* (www.omantribune.com), *and Week* (www.freetheweek.com) are independent. In Arabic, *Oman Daily* (www.omandaily.com), *Al Shabiba* (www.shabiba.com), *Alquds Newspaper* and the independent daily *Al-Watan* (www.alwatan.com).

Business: In English, *Business Today*, *Zawya* a business directory; multiply publications (by www.apexstuff.com) include *Oman 2day* and the free publication *The Week*.

Periodicals: In English, the monthly *Oman Today* (www.apexstuff.com) is a lifestyle publication.

Broadcasting

Radio: Radio Oman (www.oman-radio.gov.om/rdeng) is government-run, while Hala FM (www.ohigroup.com/ohigroup/news2.asp) , which opened in May 2007, is privately owned. Presentations are in both English and Arabic.

Television: Oman has two government-run television channels (www.oman-tv.gov.om/tveng) and domestic satellite dishes allow programmes from Saudi Arabia, Yemen and the UAE to be received.

Oman News Agency (ONA)

National news agency: PO Box 3659, 112, Ruwi, Oman (tel: 2460-5659;

email: editorarabic@omannews.com; internet: www.omannews.com).

Economy

With a population of less than three million and a relatively high per capita income, Oman is classed as a high-income country by the World Bank. It relies principally on the export of its hydrocarbon natural resources for its income. At the end of 2014 Oman had reserves of 5.2 billion barrels of oil, with production of 943,000 barrels per day. Oman also has reserves of 700 billion cubic metres of natural gas, with production at 29 billion cum per year, of which 10.9 billion cum was exported in liquefied natural gas form and shipped mainly to South Korea and Japan. Oman's heavy dependence on its dwindling oil resources, which generates 77 per cent of government revenue is unsustainable despite its enhanced oil recovery techniques to boost production. An effort to pursue a development plan that focuses on diversification, industrialization, and privatization, with the objective of reducing the oil sector's contribution to GDP from 46 per cent to 9 per cent has been targeted by 2020. More jobs also need to be created in order for this project to work, tourism and gas-based industries are key components of the government's diversification strategy. The project has come under pressure particularly since the Arab Spring as there have been increases in the already very high social welfare benefits. Oman's authorities are comfortable with short-term budget deficits and have approved an expansionary 2015 budget.

GDP growth was 12.9 per cent in 2008 at a time of record high oil prices, before dropping to 1.1 per cent in 2009 as world trade was impacted by the global economic crisis. However as world trade picked up so did GDP growth, which registered 4.0 per cent in 2010 and an estimated 5.5 per cent in 2011. GDP growth increased further to 5.8 per cent in 2012 before decreasing to 4.7 per cent in 2013. Following this strong period of growth, it has almost been halved to just 2.9 per cent in 2014, which is reflective of the unsustainable nature of Oman's economic growth.

Inflation, which had been relatively low, hit a high of 12.6 in 2008, caused by a weakened petrocurrency, the US dollar, which pushed up the price of imports and increased the trade deficit, before falling back to 3.5 per cent in 2009 as weaker domestic spending cut imports. In 2010 inflation returned to the 2006 level of 3.3 per cent and increased to an estimated 4 per cent in 2011. Inflation decreased to just 1.2 per cent in 2013 before rebounding to 2.8 per cent in 2014.

Oman did not suffer unduly during the global economic crisis as its banks are tightly controlled and well capitalised. The banking sector continued to be profitable, albeit at a lower level than previous years.

External trade

In 2005 the Greater Arab Free Trade Area (Gafta) was ratified by 17 members, including Oman, creating an Arab economic bloc. A customs union was established whereby tariffs within Gafta will be reduced by a percentage each year, until none remain. In 2009, Oman was considering the viability of introducing value added tax (VAT) if it joined the Gafta customs union. A US-Oman free trade agreement (OFTA) became operational in 2009.

Imports

Principal imports are machinery and transport equipment, manufactured goods, food, livestock and lubricants.

Main sources: UAE (32.5 per cent of total in 2014), Japan (12.2 per cent), China (4.8 per cent), India (4.3 per cent), US (4.3 per cent) and Saudi Arabia (4.1 per cent)

Exports

Petroleum, liquefied natural gas (LNG), re-exports, fish, processed copper, metals, textiles and dates.

Main destinations: China (43 per cent of total in 2014), UAE (10.3 per cent) and South Korea (8.2 per cent)

Agriculture

Farming

Agriculture accounts for around 1.3 per cent of GDP and employs around 200,000 people. Agriculture and fisheries account for an average 35 per cent per annum of Oman's main non-oil exports. Main agricultural exports include dates, limes, bananas, alfalfa, vegetables; camels and cattle.

The shortage of water and pasture and the salinity of the soil are the main constraints on agricultural development. The emphasis of government investment in this sector has been on digging wells, repairing old irrigation systems and building dams to trap rainwater, which previously ran off into the sea. Irrigation studies show potential arable land to be twice that under cultivation, but agriculture already uses over 90 per cent of the available water. Apart from a narrow coastal strip (the Batinah coastline), most of Oman is either mountain or desert.

A network of collection and distribution centres is run by the Public Authority for Marketing Agricultural Produce (Pamap). Pamap exports fruit and vegetables, particularly bananas, and operates a banana ripening and packing factory at Salalah and a handling centre at al Suwaiq.

Fishing

The fishing industry is well developed and has helped to diversify the economy. After oil, fish is the number one earner of foreign currency in Oman. Stocks include between 15,000 and 27,000 tonnes of kingfish, 50,000 tonnes of tuna and 2,000 tonnes of shellfish. The total fish catch in 2014 was 200,000 tonnes. Fish and shellfish exports totalled US$960 million in 2014.

Oman Fisheries Co SAOG is the largest fishing company in the country. It undertakes processing and marketing of fish and fishery products, which are approved for export to European countries. Exports include fresh fish, frozen fish and seafood (prawns, crabs and lobsters). The Gulf Co-operation Council (GCC) states are the destination for almost half of Omani fish exports.

Oman plans to more than double its fishery production to 480,000 tonnes per year, increasing industry revenues to US$1.9 billion. The new investment will see Oman build nine new fishery harbours, to bring the total number of ports to 30. The Omani fisheries industry currently provides direct or indirect employment to around 40,000 Omanis, and the new investment will aim to create another 20,000 jobs by 2020. Along with the new ports, Oman will also be investing in its fishing fleet, processing facilities and aquaculture industry.

Forestry

There is very little forest or woodland in Oman with forest cover estimated at 1,000 hectares, mainly composed of scattered areas of Juniperus forest in the Hajar Mountains. About 10 million date palms are grown along the northern Batinah coastal strip. Although some wood is used for domestic consumption, there is no significant commercial exploitation. Much of the demand for wood and paper products is met through imports.

In Dhofar, south Oman, it is one of the only places in the world where aromatic Frankincense trees live and thrive in the wild. The fragrant oil extracted from the trees is a rare commodity and somewhat sought after by countries around the world. Oman is one of the few countries to sell it in relative abundance.

Industry and manufacturing

The government is acutely aware that oil reserves are dropping and the population is growing significantly with a high proportion of young people. As a result, government policy aims to promote growth and employment through encouraging private sector investment in industry. This has been done by offering incentives such as tax exemptions, customs protection, soft or interest-free loans and by providing infrastructure, usually in the form of industrial estates. It favours small- to medium-sized industries that are import-substituting, use local raw materials, have a relative advantage in export markets or employ a high ratio of Omanis.

An effort to pursue a development plan that focuses on diversification, industrialization, and privatization, with the objective of reducing the oil sector's contribution to GDP from 46 per cent to 9 per cent has been targeted by 2020. More jobs also need to be created in order for this project to work, tourism and gas-based industries are key components of the government's diversification strategy. The project has come under pressure particularly since the Arab Spring as there have been increases in the already very high social welfare benefits. Oman's authorities are comfortable with short-term budget deficits and have approved an expansionary 2015 budget. Oman has expanded efforts to support the development of small and medium-size enterprises and entrepreneurship. Government agencies and large oligarchic group companies have announced new initiatives to spin off non-essential functions to entrepreneurs, incubate new businesses, train and mentor up and coming business people, and provide financing for start-ups.

Tourism

The government of Oman has been encouraging tourism as part of the diversification of the economy. Attractions include towns of traditional and impressive public buildings, such as the Sultan Qaboos Grand Mosque, natural vistas of desert and the Arabian Sea. There are several tourist resorts that cater for foreign and domestic visitors and activities that include diving, shopping in the Arab souk and tours into the desert. There are archaeological sites included on Unesco's World Heritage List, such as Bat, al Khutm and al Ayn and the ancient city of Galhat.

Travel and tourism indirectly contributed 5.7 per cent of GDP in 2014; this figure is expected to reach 7.3 per cent by 2025. The tourism sector directly contributed 2.6 per cent of GDP in 2014. Direct employment in the industry was 44,500 jobs (2.8 per cent of total employment) and this is forecast to grow by 11 per cent in 2015 to 49,500 (2.9 per cent of total employment). The total indirect contribution of the sector to employment was 90,500 jobs in 2014 (5.7 per cent of total employment).

In April 2012 the minister of tourism announced that the government intended to operate as the main developer of core projects to attract tourists, while encouraging the private sector to undertake complementary projects. Domestic, family-oriented tourism was emphasised as a part of sustainable growth. Capital investment in travel and tourism has grown from a ten-year low of 4.6 per cent of total investment in 2009 to 5.9 per cent in 2011 and it was 3.5 per cent in 2014. The new strategy for tourist promotion is to target business people, the wealthy and visitors from the Gulf States and those from Bric countries.

Mining

Mining typically contributes around 1 per cent to annual GDP and employs around 3 per cent of the workforce.

Oman has large resources of industrial rocks and minerals, some of which are already being exploited. They include silica sand, dolomite, limestone, gypsum, ornamental stone, clays, rockwool, iron oxides, heavy sands, wollastonite, celestite, asbestos, aggregate, laterite and barite. These non-metallic minerals are in huge quantities and most of it is exported.

Mineral deposits of copper, manganese, lead, iron, zinc, chrome, phosphates, gold, silver and nickel exist, many of them in inaccessible areas.

Government policy is to exploit raw materials wherever commercially feasible and diversify the development of its mineral resources. As in other sectors of the economy, the government aims for self-sufficiency and the mineral-based industry is expected to contribute significantly to the growth of GDP in coming years. The indigenous mineral-based industries include cement, limestone, ceramics and construction and the production of processed marble, gold ore, chromite, industrial and edible salt and clays. The government has encouraged the processing of ores within Oman rather than exporting them untreated.

Investors are exploring the 700 km long and nearly 150 km wide mountains in Oman where they are extracting copper, gold, silver, chromite, lead and zinc. Studies show that Yanqul alone holds out 25 million tonnes of copper reserves and separate study estimated Oman's coal reserves at 122 million tonnes.

In the late 1990s, the Japan International Corporation discovered new gold and copper deposits at Ghuzayn and Daris, which led to the development of potential areas for copper and gold mineralisation. The government-owned Oman Mining Company (OMCO) mines copper and chromite near Sohar. Saudi Arabia is the main market for cathode copper production. There are probable copper ore reserves of 15.2 million tonnes at Rakah and Hayl al Safil in.Chromite reserves are put at two million tonnes and annual production is around 6,000 tonnes. Chromite is exported to Japan and China. Gold and silver are produced from the copper oxide deposits by the OMCO processing plant.

The contribution of Oman's mining and quarrying activities to GDP in 2013 reach OMR107.7 million (US$279.7 million), growing faster than the economy at a rate of 23 per cent over the decade. Production of rocks and minerals increased more than eight-fold between 1996 and 2013. The formation of the Public Authority for Mining in 2014 also established a dedicated organisation to guide Oman's mining operations and also bring the industry in line with international standards. Oman is also attracting considerable investment from Canada and India. In 2013, London-based Savannah Resources announced its US$6.3 million investment in the Sultanate, which will fund expansion into Oman's highly prospective copper belt.

Hydrocarbons

Proven oil reserves were 5.2 billion barrels in 2014, with production at 943,000 barrels per day (bpd), an increase of 0.4 per cent on the previous year. Although Oman is an oil exporter, it is not a member of the Organisation of Petroleum Exporting Countries (Opec). The oil sector is a major provider of revenue for the economy, at around 75 per cent of all export earnings and 40 per cent to GDP.

Oman's oil reserves are declining and production falling, however the government has invested in enhanced oil recovery projects and production techniques on existing oil fields and new exploration, while at the same time continuing to diversify the economy away from the oil sector.

Proven natural gas reserves were 700 billion cubic metres (cum) in 2014, with production at 29 billion cum. Domestic consumption has grown steadily and the export of liquefied natural gas (LNG) has become a significant element in Oman's export revenue with 10.9 billion cum, going mostly to the Far East, in 2014.

Coal represents one of many energy sources that the Omani government is looking at as part of a long-term Strategic National Energy Policy covering the period through to 2040. With the advent and advancement of clean coal technologies, coupled with carbon capture and sequestration, coal is being increasingly seen as an alternative to natural gas and other fossil fuels for energy generation.

Energy

Total installed electricity generating capacity was around 4.3GW in 2013, all of which was provided by conventional thermal power stations. Demand is growing rapidly at 5 per cent per annum.

The 280MW Al Kamil power plant, built by International Power plc, the 430MW Barka power plant, owned by AES, the 240MW integrated power plant, owned by PSEG and supplying the Dhofar region, and the 140MW plant at Qarn Alam, owned by Bharat Heavy Electricals, are all run on natural gas.

A new 2,000MW combined cycle power plant in Sur is Oman's largest electricity generating station when completed.

Oman is setting out tenders for up to three new power plants, as they seek to boost generating capacity to 5GW. The new plants will come on line by 2017-18 in order to meet a growing demand for power in the country.

Oman Power and Water Procurement Co (OPWP) it set to find a new location for a new 200MW-300MW power plant in Duqm. The country has added two new 744MW gas power plants to its generation fleet as it continues to build out capacity.

Completion of a new, US$1 billion, desalination plant in the Dhofar Governorate, capable of producing around 70 million litres per day, was announced in May 2012. The plant will also produce 445MW for the region and will stop water from being syphoned off from ground water in Salalah, Taqah and Mirbat.

A Gulf Co-operation Council (GCC) project to link the six member states (Saudi Arabia, Qatar, Bahrain, Kuwait, Oman and the United Arab Emirates) to an integrated power-grid began in 2005. The first phase of the GCC power grid was completed in July 2009 at a cost of US$1,095 million, linking Saudi Arabia, Bahrain, Kuwait and Qatar through 800km of transmission lines. Kuwait and Saudi Arabia will each receive an extra 1,200MW of power capacity and later, the UAE will receive 900MW, Qatar 750MW, Bahrain 600MW and Oman 400MW. In the first phase, a 400kV overhead line links Kuwait's Al Zour power station with Doha, and a 400kV submarine line to Saudi Arabia with Bahrain. The second phase will link the UAE with Oman. The resulting two mega-grids will be joined in the final phase.

Financial markets

Stock exchange

Muscat Securities Market (MSM)

Banking and insurance

Oman has a robust banking sector both foreign and domestic with two specialised banks subsidised by the government – the Oman Housing Bank and the Oman Bank for Industrial Development. However, experts believe the sector is over-banked and have called for mergers to consolidate the sector.

A royal decree was issued in May 2011 allowing for a new, stand-alone Islamic bank based in Oman, called the Bank Nizwa. Operations may not begin until 2012 or until the Central Bank of Oman develops and adopts the regulatory and supervisory regime to enable Islamic banking. In July, further details were released. The CBO had overseen the set-up of a panel to organise the Islamic-compliance of the new bank and organisers were planning on opening Bank Nizwa either at the end of 2011 or the beginning of 2012 in Muscat. With assets of RO150 million (US$390 million), of which 40 per cent will be raised through an initial offer of public shares, the bank will be the first to offer Sharia-compliant financial products to the local market, using exclusive accounts.

Central bank

Central Bank of Oman

Main financial centre

Muttrah Business District

Time

GMT plus four hours

Geography

Oman lies at the south-eastern tip of the Arabian peninsula, bordering Yemen, Saudi Arabia and the United Arab Emirates (UAE). The Musandam Peninsula in the far north is separated from the rest of Oman by UAE territory. The coastline is 1,700km long.

There are two distinct areas of population, centred on the Hajar mountains, with a narrow, fertile strip along the coast, in the north and the Batinah plain and its hinterland in the south. Between them lies 800km of virtually uninhabited gravel plain.

Hemisphere

Northern

Climate

Most of the country is hot and arid, with noon temperatures in summer exceeding 40 degrees Celsius (C) and annual rainfall of around 100mm. There is a higher rainfall over the mountains. The southern region, however, has a tropical climate, with noon temperatures between 27 and 33 degrees C all year round and a rainy season from June to August.

Dress codes

Formal clothing is recommended for public places and in general the body should be fully covered. Businessmen should wear suits and ties to appointments, but the jacket can be carried. Shorts are not allowed, except for sports. Women are advised to dress modestly. Swimwear should be worn only at hotel pools and on the beach.

Entry requirements

Passports

Required by all, except citizens of some neighbouring countries. Passports must be valid for six months beyond the date of visit.

Visa

Required by all. Details for tourist or business visitors listed at www.destinationoman.com, follow link to *Plan your trip*, then *Getting there*. Visas may be obtained at a point of entry (all land and sea ports, but only at Seeb International airport if arriving by air).

Those who do not appear on the list of eligibility should contact the nearest Omani Embassy and apply for a visa as required.

Oman has a joint visa agreement with the Emirate of Dubai – visitors with a visa for either country may cross to the other without a further visa, however the term of visit is a maximum of three weeks.

A new visa system (similar to the European Schengen agreement) allowing multiple entry for foreigners to the six Gulf Co-operation Council (GCC) countries was introduced in November 2012.

Prohibited entry

Holders of Israeli passports

Currency advice/regulations

The import and export of local and foreign currency is unlimited; Israeli currency is prohibited.

Travellers cheques are widely available.

Customs

Personal effects and one bottle of alcohol per non-muslim adult are duty-free.

Prohibited imports

Firearms, ammunition, narcotics and pornography. Certain food items and plant materials may be quarantined. Clothing bearing Koranic inscriptions is banned.

Although goods of Israeli origin and imports from Israel are no longer illegal in Oman, goods produced by companies boycotted by the Arab League are prohibited.

Health (for visitors)

Mandatory precautions

Vaccination certificate against yellow fever if travelling from infected area.

Advisable precautions

Health facilities in the city are good but expensive for foreigners; health insurance is therefore recommended for visitors. All visitors should carry a list of their generic medication and if necessary their own hypodermic needles.

Inoculations and boosters should be current for tetanus, hepatitis A, and typhoid. There may be a need for vaccinations for tuberculosis, diphtheria, polio hepatitis B.

Use malaria prophylaxis for visits to the far north of the country, including Musandam province, which will also provide protection for hepatitis B, these

include mosquito repellents, nets and clothing that covers the body after dark. There is a risk of rabies. Avoid bathing in freshwater, use only well-maintained and chlorinated swimming pools.
Milk is unpasteurised and should be boiled or avoided. Meat, fish and vegetables should be served cooked and fruit peeled before consumption.
Between April and October the sun is very strong and sunscreens, protective clothing, sunglasses and hats are necessary.

Hotels
There are several five-star hotels in Muscat/Muttrah/Ruwi Capital Area. There is a lack of hotels in provincial towns, although a programme of expansion is underway.
A service charge of 10 per cent is included in all bills.
Dhofar coast beaches are the main tourist area.

Credit cards
Major credit cards are widely accepted. ATMs are available in largerly bank branches.

Public holidays (national)
Fixed dates
1 Jan (New Year's Day), 18 Nov (National Day), 19 Nov (Sultan's Birthday), 31 Dec (Bank Holiday).
Variable dates
Islamic New Year, Eid al Adha (four days), Eid Milad Nnabi (birth of prophet), Ascension of Mohammed, Eid al Fitr (three days), Birth of the Prophet (two days).
Islamic year 1437 (15 Oct 2015–2 Oct 2016):: The Islamic year has 354 or 355 days, with the result that Muslim feasts advance by 10–12 days against the Gregorian calendar each year. Dates of the Muslim feasts vary according to sightings of the new moon, so cannot be forecast exactly.

Working hours
Work hours are affected by Ramadan, the Muslim holy month of fasting during daylight hours.
Banking
Sat–Wed: 0800–1200.
Business
Sat–Wed: 0800–1300, 1400–1900; Thu: 0800–1300.
Government
Sat–Wed: 0730–1430.
Shops
Sat–Thu: 0900–1300, 1400–2100. Supermarkets and shopping malls: 0900–2200, with short lunch breaks.

Telecommunications
Mobile/cell phones
GSM 900 services are available in inhabited areas.

Electricity supply
220/240V AC, with two or three-pin round, or three-pin flat types, plug fittings.

Weights and measures
Metric.

Social customs/useful tips
Handshaking is the normal form of greeting and business cards are exchanged at business meetings. Appointments are required for business meetings.
It is discourteous to eat, drink or smoke in front of Muslims in daylight hours during Ramadan. It is polite to accept the refreshments customarily offered to visitors.
Alcohol is available in hotel bars and restaurants. Non-Muslims with liquor permits from the Omani police can buy alcoholic drinks at special stores for consumption at home.
The government regularly issues strong-worded ordinances designed to keep the country clean and tidy. It is an offence, for example, to drive a dirty car or hang out washing in view of main roads. Foreigners should take care to observe these regulations, although the police rarely enforce them.

Security
Visitors should keep in touch with developments in the Middle East as any increase in regional tension might affect travel advice. Oman is the most stable country in the Arabian peninsula. Even levels of petty crime are minimal.

Getting there
Air
National airline: Oman Air (regional airline); Oman is a shareholder of Gulf Air (international airline).
International airport/s: Seeb International Airport (MCT), 40km from Muscat, with duty-free shops and a restaurant; Salalah International Airport, near the southern city of Salalah.
Airport tax: None
Surface
Road: The Yemen border is not open to travellers, but there are road links with the United Arab Emirates, including regular bus services between Muscat and Dubai.
Water: There are some ferry services into Muscat from other Gulf States.

Getting about
National transport
Air: There are six civil airports. Oman Air operates scheduled flights to Salalah Airport, Fahud and Marmul. There are also flights to the Musandam Peninsula, Buraimi, Sur and the island of Masirah. All flights should be booked well in advance and confirmed on the day before travelling.
Road: An excellent asphalt road system links all the main centres. A 780km highway links Dhofar with the north and the national network.
There are over 9,000km of paved roads (550km of dual carriageway) and over 22,000km of unpaved track roads. Improvements and the widening of existing highways is on-going, as are linking roads between towns and villages of the interior.
Buses: The Oman National Transport Company (ONTC) operates national bus services and local services in the capital area.
Taxis: There is an excellent network of minibuses which operate as service taxis linking up the major centres of population.
Water: There are regular ferry services from Muscat to Khasab on the Musandam Peninsular.
City transport
Taxis: Taxis are expensive by Gulf standards; they should have a scale of charges, but it is advisable to negotiate fares in advance (there are no meters). Tipping is not usual. Some hotels offer a courtesy pick-up service; others offer the service but charge.
Buses, trams & metro: An urban bus service operates in Muscat, but is not recommended for visitors.
Car hire
It is necessary to hold an international driving licence when hiring a car in Oman. Check licence rules in advance. Speed limits are 120kph and driving is on the right-hand side of the road. Most hotels have self-drive car hire facilities.

BUSINESS DIRECTORY

The addresses listed below are a selection only. While World of Information makes every endeavour to check these addresses, we cannot guarantee that changes have not been made, especially to telephone numbers and area codes. We would welcome any corrections.

Telephone area codes
The international direct dialling (IDD) code for Oman is +968, followed by subscriber's number.

Useful telephone numbers
Capital area
Police: 560-099
Fire: 999
International operator: 195
International enquiries: 197
Directory enquiries: 198
Operator: 190

Chambers of Commerce
Oman Chamber of Commerce and Industry, PO Box 1400, Ruwi 112 (tel: 2470-7674; fax: 2470-8497; email: occi@chamberoman.com).

Banking

Bank Dhofar, PO Box 1507, Ruwi 112 (tel: 2479-0466; fax: 2479-7246; email: info@bankdhofar.com).

BankMuscat, PO Box 1708, 112 Ruwi (tel: 2445-6365; fax: 2445-6077; email: info@bankmuscat.com).

Industrial Bank of Oman, PO Box 2613, Ruwi 112 (tel: 2470-6786; fax: 2470-6986; email: indlbank@omantel.net.om).

Majan International Bank, PO Box 2717, Ruwi 112 (tel: 2478-0388; fax: 2478-0643; email: majanbk@omantel.net.om).

National Bank of Oman, PO Box 2613, 112 Ruwi (tel: 2470-6786 fax: 2470-6986; email: ask@nbo.om).

Oman Arab Bank, PO Box 2010, Ruwi 112 (tel: 2470-6265; fax: 2479-7736; email: mktoab@omantel.net.om).

Oman Development Bank, PO Box 309, Muscat 113 (tel: 2473-8021; fax: 2473-8026; email: odebe@omantel.net.om).

Oman Housing Bank, PO Box 2555, Muscat 112 (tel: 24704-444; email: i-ohb@i-ohb.com.om).

Oman International Bank, PO Box 1216, P C 112 Ruwi (tel: 2457-6039, 2457-6618; fax: 2457-6040; email: omintbnk@omantel.net.om).

Central bank

Central Bank of Oman, PO Box 1161, Ruwi 112 (tel: 2470-6175; fax: 2470-5961; email: markazi@omantel.net.com).

Stock exchange

Muscat Securities Market (MSM), www.msm.gov.om

Travel information

Seeb International Airport, PO Box 58, Muscat 111 (tel: 2451-9285; fax: 2451-0805).

Gulf Air, PO Box 1444, Ruwi 112 (tel: 2470-3222; fax: 2479-3381).

Oman Air, PO Box 58, Seeb International Airport, Muscat 111 (tel: 2451-9953; fax: 2452-1075).

Oman Automobile Association, PO Box 2874, Muscat 111 (tel: 2451-0239; fax: 2451-0276; email: omanauto@omantel.net.om).

Oman Aviation Services, PO Box 58, Muscat 111 (tel: 2451-9237; fax: 2451-0805).

Oman National Transport Company, PO Box 620, Muscat 113 (tel: 2459-0046, 2459-0603; email: ontc01@omantel.net.om).

Ministry of tourism

Directorate General of Tourism, Ministry of Commerce and Industry, PO Box 550, Muscat 113 (tel: 2477-16527; fax: 2477-14213; e-mail: dgt@mocioman.org; internet: omantourism.gov.om).

Ministries

Ministry of Agriculture and Fisheries, PO Box 467, Muscat 113 (tel: 2469-6300; fax: 2460-5304).

Ministry of Awqaf and Religious Affairs, PO Box 3232, Ruwi 112 (tel: 2469-6870; fax: 2460-1109).

Ministry of Civil Service, PO Box 3994, Ruwi 112 (tel: 2469-6000; fax: 2460-1771).

Ministry of Commerce and Industry, PO Box 550, Muscat 113 (tel: 2477-13500; fax: 2477-17239).

Ministry of Defence, PO Box 113, Muscat 113 (tel: 2431-2605; fax: 2470-2521).

Ministry of Education, PO Box 3, Muscat 113 (tel: 2477-5209; fax: 2470-8485).

Ministry of Foreign Affairs, PO Box 252, Muscat 113 (tel: 2469-9500; fax: 2469-6641).

Ministry of Health, PO Box 393, Muscat 113 (tel: 2460-2177; fax: 2460-2647).

Ministry of Higher Education, PO Box 82, Ruwi 112 (tel: 24695330; fax: 2469-4481)

Ministry of Housing, Electricity & Water, PO Box 1491, Ruwi 112 (tel: 2460-3800; fax: 2469-9180).

Ministry of Information, PO Box 600, Muscat 113 (tel: 2460-3222; fax: 2460-1638; internet: www.omanet.com).

Ministry of Interior, PO Box 127, Ruwi 112 (tel: 2460-2244; fax: 2466-0644).

Ministry of Justice, PO Box 354, Ruwi 112 (tel: 2469-7699; fax: 2460-2725).

Ministry of Legal Affairs, PO Box 578, Ruwi 112 (tel: 2460-5802; fax: 2460-5697).

Ministry of National Economy, PO Box 506, Muscat 113 (tel: 2473-8201; fax: 2473-7068).

Ministry of National Heritage & Culture, PO Box 668, Muscat 113 (tel: 2460-2555; fax: 2469-7060).

Ministry of Oil and Gas, PO Box 551, Muscat 113 (tel: 2460-3333; fax: 2469-6972).

Ministry of Regional Municipalities, Environment and Water Resources, PO Box 323, Muscat 113 (tel: 2469-2550; fax: 2469-3995).

Ministry of Social Development, [PO Box 560, Muscat 113 (tel: 2460-2444; fax: 2469-9357).

Ministry of Transport and Telecommunications, PO Box 338, Ruwi 112 (tel: 2469-7888; fax: 24696817).

Other useful addresses

British Embassy, PO Box 300, 185 Mina al Fahral, Muscat 113 (tel: 2469-3086; fax: 2469-3088; email: becomu@omantel.net).

Capital Market Authority, PO Box 3265, Ruwi 112 (tel: 2482 3600; fax: 2481 6260).

Development Council, PO Box 881, Muscat 113 (tel: 2469-8900; fax: 2469-6285).

High Commitee for Conferences, PO Box 891, Muscat 113 (tel: 2469-8221; fax: 2460-7497).

Muscat Securities Market, PO Box 3265, Ruwi 112 (tel: 2482-3600; fax: 2481 5776).

Oman International Trade and Exhibitions (OITE), PO Box 112, Ruwi 112 (tel: 2456-4303; fax: 2456-5165; email: oitex@omantel.net.om).

Oman Oil Company, PO Box 261, Qurm 118 (tel: 2456-7392; fax: 2456-7386; email: oman-oil@omantel.net.om).

Omani Centre for Investment Promotion and Export Development, PO Box 25, Wadi Kabir 117 (tel: 2481-2344; fax: 2481-0890; email: info@ociped.com).

Omani Embassy (USA), 2535 Belmont Road NW, Washington DC 20008 (tel: (+1-202) 387-1980; fax: (+1-202) 745-4933; email: emboman@erols.com).

Petroleum Development Oman (PDO), PO Box 81, Muscat 113 (tel: 2467-8111; fax: 2467-7106).

Salalah Port Services Company, PO Box 105, Muscat 118 (tel: 2456-7188; fax: 2456-7166).

US Embassy, PO Box 202, Medinat Al Sultan Qaboos, Muscat 115 (tel: 2469-8989; fax: 2469-9189; email: aemctcns@gto.net).

National news agency: PO Box 3659, 112, Ruwi, Oman (tel: 2460-5659; email: editorarabic@omannews.com; internet: www.omannews.com).

Internet sites

Arab net: www.arab.net

Arabia on-line: www.arabia.com

Gulf business explorer: www.igulf.com

Official tourist site: www.destinationoman.com

Oman online archives of political, economic and business news: www.newsbriefsoman.info

Times of Oman: http://omantimes.com/

Pakistan

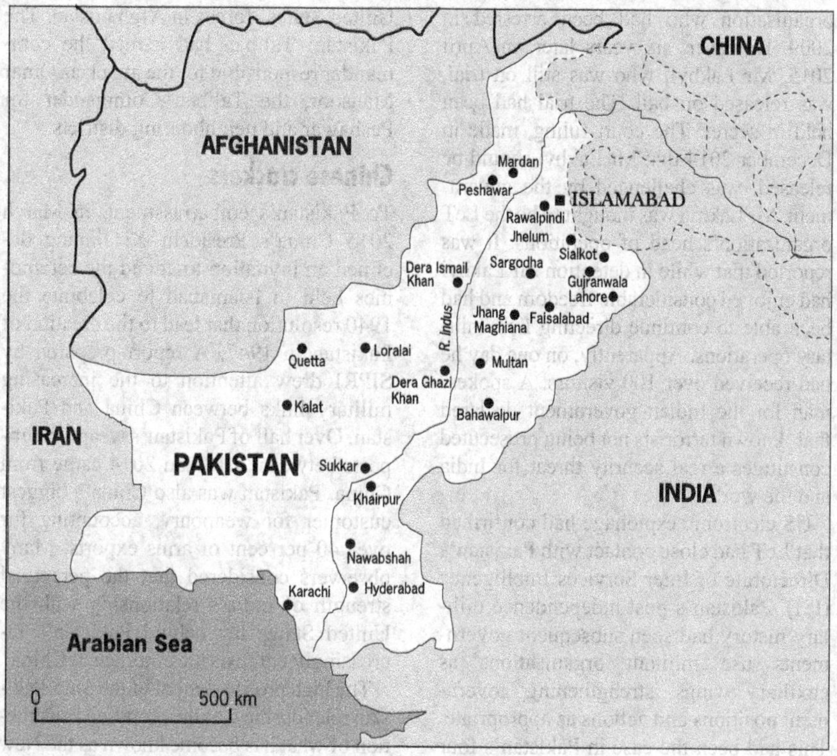

Described by one foreign correspondent as surviving on a 'cycle of aid dependency and corruption', in 2015 Pakistan certainly seemed to lack the commercial and entrepreneurial drive of India, its neighbour to the east. Pakistan's foreign policy, as interpreted by its powerful military, is ultimately based on the goal of controlling events in Afghanistan as a riposte to the increasing power and success of India. Pakistan's other riposte is to feverishly pursue the development of its nuclear arsenal. A report dating back to 2012 prepared by the British American Security Information Council noted that Pakistan was developing nuclear weapons for 'war fighting roles and in military planning.' In similar vein, the Stockholm International Peace research Institute (SIPRI) described Pakistan's nuclear development programme as the most rapid nuclear proliferation in the world. Estimates put the number of nuclear weapons held by Pakistan at over 100. SIPRI considered that Pakistan was 'in danger of losing control of part of its nuclear arsenal' to terrorists.

East is east – but what about the West?

Almost seventy years after the partition of India and the establishment of Pakistan as an independent state, it is sometimes difficult to remember that India and Pakistan were once the same country – or colony. In the twenty-first century, the prevailing impression is that Pakistan is more similar to its neighbour in the west (Afghanistan) than that in the east (India), the country with which it shares much of its history. Successive military and political élites have stamped an official Islamic seal on the country in initiatives to differentiate it from India. Pakistan's history textbooks describe the sub-continent's Hindus and Muslims – for centuries intermingling – as 'two nations'. Because Pakistan has disowned and attempted to disguise elements of its past it has become easier to

KEY FACTS

Official name: Islami Jamhuriya e Pakistan (Islamic Republic of Pakistan)

Head of State: President Mamnoon Hussain (from 9 Sep 2013)

Head of government: Prime Minister Nawaz Sharif (PML-N) (from 9 Jun 2013)

Ruling party: Coalition led by Pakistan Muslim League-Nawaz (PML-N) and 19 Independents (elected 11 May 2013)

Area: 803,943 square km

Population: 186.29 million (2014)*

Capital: Islamabad

Official language: Urdu (national language) and English

Currency: Rupee (Rp) = 100 paisa

Exchange rate: Rp104.28 per US$ (Sep 2015)

GDP per capita: US$1,343 (2014)*

GDP real growth: 4.14% (2014)

GDP: US$250.14 billion (2014)

Labour force: 53.78 million (2009)

Unemployment: 6.75% (2014)* (plus additional underemployment)

Inflation: 7.36% (2014)

Natural gas production: 42.00 billion cum (2014)

Balance of trade: -US$17.77 billion (2014)

Annual FDI: US$1.31 billion (2011)

* estimated figure

describe it purely in terms of its recent struggle with international terrorism.

Sadly, there are no lack of opportunities for this method of interpretation to be deployed. In mid-December 2014 148 pupils at Peshawar's Army Public School (APS) were killed in an attack which lasted seven hours. The killing was orchestrated by the Tehreek-e-Taliban Pakistan (TTP); although Pakistan had become to some extent inured to the constant threat of bomb attacks on its cities, the APS massacre was unprecedented. Assertions that 'this time it was different' abounded. But what most Pakistanis knew was that however different, the military establishment with its links to many, if not all, terrorist groups would continue to call and control the government's ability to deal with the terrorists within its borders. The London *Guardian* reported that at the funeral of one of the victims, circulating among the mourners were members of the Falah-e-Insaniyat Foundation, the so-called welfare wing of the Jamaat-ud-Dawa, a group close to the Lashkar-e-Taiba organisation responsible for the 2008 terrorist attacks in Mumbai (India).

Reflecting his country's anger at the school massacre, Pakistan's Prime Minister Nawaz Sharif lifted the moratorium on the death penalty for terrorist related cases. The Prime Minister also announced that there would 'no longer be any differentiation between 'good' and 'bad' terrorists.' This was a direct reference to the Pakistani intelligence services' often overt support for those militant organisations it considered to run parallel to its own 'strategic' (ie anti-Indian) objectives. One such organisation was the Lashkar-e-Taiba (LeT), which had claimed responsibility for the 2008 Mumbai hotel killings in which 164 people died. The organisation's commander for the operation, one Kaki-ur-Rehman Lakhvi had been arrested, along with six other members of the organisation who had been arrested in 2009. However, six years later, in April 2015, Mr Lakhvi, who was still on trial, was released on bail. The trial had been held in secret. The court ruling, made in December 2014 that Mr Lakhvi should be released, was challenged by the government. Mr Lakhvi was thought to be the LeT organisation's head of operations. It was reported that while in detention Mr Lakhvi had enjoyed considerable freedom and had been able to continue directing LeT military operations. Apparently, on one day he had received over 100 visitors. A spokesman for the Indian government declared that 'known terrorists not being prosecuted constitutes a real security threat for India and the world.'

US electronic espionage had confirmed that LeT had close contact with Pakistan's Directorate of Inter Services Intelligence (ISI). Pakistan's post independence military history had seen subsequent governments use militant organisations as auxiliary wings, strengthening government positions and actions as appropriate. This had been the case in Pakistan's four wars with India and in Kashmir.

While accepting that its own intelligence operation may have been aware of the imminent attacks, the perpetrators of the Peshawar APS attack were thought to be in Afghanistan. Senior generals were despatched to Kabul for meetings with President Ashraf Ghani and also General John Campbell, the commander of North Atlantic Treaty Organisation (NATO) and United States' forces in Afghanistan. The Pakistani Taliban had named the commander responsible for the attack as Omar Mansoor, the Taliban Commander for Peshawar and neighbouring districts.

Chinese crackers

To Pakistan's embarrassment, in March 2015 China's President Xi Jinping declined an invitation to attend the ceremonies held in Islamabad to celebrate the 1940 resolution that lead to the creation of Pakistan in 1947. A report prepared by SIPRI drew attention to the increasing military links between China and Pakistan. Over half of Pakistan's weapons' imports between 2010 and 2014 came from China. Pakistan was also China's biggest customer for weaponry, accounting for over 40 per cent of arms exports. Many observers considered that the perceived strength of India's relationship with the United States lay behind Pakistan's increasingly enthusiastic embrace of China.

The high profile symbol of the Sino-Pakistan relationship was the proposed construction of what has become known as the New Silk Road, a 3,000 kilometre rail and road route connecting Kashgar in China's Xinjiang province to Karachi and the southern coastal city of Gwadar, which would become China's gateway to the Indian Ocean. The project would take twenty-five years to complete and would cost a reported US$46 billion. For the Chinese the underlying objective was to counteract the growing regional influence if India.

Andrew Small, the author of *The China-Pakistan Axis: Asia's New Geopolitics*, states that China was trying to stabilise its closest partner, Pakistan, which had in recent years given Beijing cause for concern. For China, the Silk Road project also had a security objective. According to Mr Small 'China was also concerned by the side effects of the US withdrawal from Afghanistan and the resultant increased terrorist threat. China saw increased and improved economic links as the best way of countering this threat.'

Since the 1970s, Pakistan's military and political elite have chosen religious fundamentalism over a democratic plurality. However, in his August 1947, address to the

KEY INDICATORS — Pakistan

	Unit	2011	2012	2013	2014	**2015
Population	m	*175.31	178.91	182.59	*186.29	*190.01
Gross domestic product (GDP)	US$bn	*210.60	225.56	232.76	250.14	–
GDP per capita	US$	*1,201	1,261	1,248	*1,343	*4
GDP real growth	%	*2.4	4.4	3.7	4.1	–
Inflation	%	*13.7	11.0	7.4	8.6	*4.7
Unemployment	%	6.0	6.5	7.2	*6.8	*6.5
Natural gas output	bn cum	39.2	41.5	38.6	42.0	–
Coal output	mtoe	1.4	1.2	1.5	1.4	–
Exports (fob) (goods)	US$m	26,308.3	*24,705.7	25,180.0	24,798.0	–
Imports (fob) (goods)	US$m	38,851.8	*40,073.8	40,995.0	42,565.0	–
Balance of trade	US$m	-12,543.5	*-15,368.1	-15,815.0	-17,767.0	–
Current account	US$m	214.0	-4,658.0	-2,496.0	-3,096.0	–
Total reserves minus gold	US$m	16,798.0	*10,242.0	5,156.0	11,807.0	–
Foreign exchange	US$m	15,609.0	*9,320.0	4,306.0	–	–
Exchange rate	per US$	85.48	*96.28	105.51	100.53	–

* estimated figure ** forecast figure

Constituent Assembly, Pakistan's founder Muhammad Ali Jinnah had made it clear that he intended it to be a country for Muslims that welcomed all religions, not an Islamic country. Today, his vision has given way to a harsh, one-dimensional reality – to a country better known for harbouring bin Laden than anything else. The establishment has emphasised a Sunni Muslim identity at the exclusion of all other ethnic, religious and sectarian identities.

Fragility

On the Fund for Peace's *Fragile States Index* Pakistan comes within the 'High Alert' category, ranked 13, one place above Iraq. Much of Pakistan is run by a military obsessed with – and, for decades, invested in – the conflict, or the phony war, with India and by a civilian elite notorious for stealing what it can and for evading taxes where possible. The fundamental cause of the problem, according to one report, would seem to be the artificiality of Pakistan itself. A territory once dreamt up by the East India Company to account for the area between India and Central Asia that had since 1947 divided what the British Empire once ruled as a single, 'indivisible' subcontinent. However, Pakistan, which is deemed to be simply a 'problem' country, but one which probably gives American policymakers more headaches than any other country, does actually have some geographical logic. The vision of Pakistan's founder, Muhammad Ali Jinnah, in the 1940s did not add up to some form of Unilateral Declaration of Independence, a clumsy power grab at the expense of India's Hindu-dominated Congress party. There was much history and geography behind his drive to create a separate Muslim state anchored in the subcontinent's northwest, abutting southern Central Asia. Understanding this legacy properly ends up with a troubling scenario about where Pakistan – and by extension, Afghanistan and India – might now be heading for. Pakistan's present and future, for better or worse, are still best understood through its geography. Rather than a fake modern creation, Pakistan has acquired a symbolic significance as the embodiment of all the Muslim invasions that have swept down into India throughout its history. Importantly, Pakistan's south-west was the sub-continental region first occupied by Muslim Arabs invading from the Middle East.

Yet, for centuries, in periods when empire did not rule both the entire Indus and the entire Ganges, the southern and eastern parts of Afghanistan, most of Pakistan and north-western India were all governed as one political unit. And the rich and populous Indus Valley, as close to the wild and woolly Central Asian frontier as it was, formed the imperial centre of that unit.

AfPak

Pakistan may not be a failed state, but it is not too far from it. It may, in principle, be historically and geographically well founded, but the past alone is never a justification for statehood. The region's past was not always a world of fixed borders, but often one formed by varying spheres of control by different armies. But the boundaries, such as they are or were – comprised vague and somewhat different forms, lines and shapes – all of which means Pakistan cannot claim its borders are legitimate by history alone. And what in the twenty-first century it lacks is glaringly obvious: the respectability and legitimacy that comes with good governance and strong institutions. On the 2014 *Corruption Perceptions Index* published by the Berlin based NGO, Transparency International, Pakistan ranked a lowly 126 out of the 175 countries surveyed. India did better, ranking 85 out of 125. In the 2013 survey, Pakistan had ranked one place lower, 127 out of 177 countries surveyed. As things stand, the region made up by Afghanistan and Pakistan – AfPak – for short, is certainly a borderline case. The AfPak nomenclature was coined by Richard Holbrooke, lumping together Afghanistan and Pakistan where borders are as porous as they are unclear, tribal (often cross border) loyalties are paramount. The term AfPak is, it seems, a reference to two conjoined failed states – otherwise, they would share a strong border and would not have to be described by one word. This is a world where ethnic boundaries do not configure with national ones. The tribal jigsaw takes no account of political geography: Pashtunistan and Baluchistan overlap with Afghanistan and also with Iran. Roughly half of the world's 40-plus million Pashtuns live on the Pakistani side of the border, the rest in neighbouring Afghanistan and Iran.

The economy

According to the Asian Development Bank (ADB), in its end 2014 assessment, a strong revival in Pakistan's construction sector and steady expansion in manufacturing and services pushed gross domestic product (GDP) growth up to a provisional estimate of 4.1 per cent in the fiscal year 2014 (ended 30 June 2014) from 3.7 per cent in the previous year. Agriculture growth decelerated to 2.1 per cent as a fall in the production of minor crops and slow growth in livestock offset rising output in most major crops. Construction expanded in double digits on larger government development expenditure, providing most of the lift to industry. Large scale manufacturing, which contributed 80 per cent of manufacturing output grew by 3.9 per cent in 2014, little changed from 2013. Energy shortages continued to suppress manufacturing output despite efforts to improve energy supply and management. Textiles (21 per cent of manufacturing), food, petroleum products, automobiles and cement expanded at a slightly slower pace, but leather products saw strong gains, as did fertiliser with the improved supply of natural gas for the sector. The expansion in the services sector, which makes up nearly 60 per cent of GDP, slowed to 4.3 per cent in 2014 from 4.9 per cent in the previous year. Weaker growth in transport and government services offset rapid growth in wholesale and retail trade.

According to the ADB, increased remittances and the growth in rural and small business income markedly boosted private consumption expenditure and, alongside government consumption, essentially accounted for all the rise in domestic demand. Investment remained stagnant and contributed only 0.2 percentage points to GDP growth despite the improved availability of credit to the private sector. Fixed investment as a share of GDP declined from 12.6 per cent to 12.4 per cent in FY2014. Net exports turned negative, reflecting higher import growth.

GDP growth was projected by the ADB at 4.2 per cent in 2015 and 4.5 per cent in 2016, underpinned by low international oil prices and the expected rise in economic growth in advanced economies. These projections assumed steady progress in macro-economic and structural reforms, manageable political and security challenges and normal weather. Growth in 2016 might be higher if economic reform proceeds at a faster pace. The government has made some progress in implementing macro-economic and structural reforms to strengthen its fiscal position, alleviate energy shortages and restructure and privatise loss-making public enterprises.

Headline inflation, according to the ADB, rose to 8.6 per cent in 2014 from 7.4 per cent the year before. The surge was led by food price acceleration reflecting short supply, rising utility prices and an increase in the general sales tax by one percentage point. The depreciation of the Pakistan rupee against the US dollar raised prices for imports. To control inflation, the State Bank of Pakistan, the central bank, had raised its policy rate by 50 basis points in September and again in November 2013, to 10 per cent.

The consolidated budget deficit narrowed to 5.5 per cent from 8.2 per cent in 2013. Revenues rose by 22 per cent with strong growth for the second year in a row in non-tax revenues, reflecting sharp increases in central bank profits, inflows under the Coalition Support Fund and the Pakistan Development Fund, proceeds from the auction of 3G/4G spectrum licences and the utilisation of the Universal Support Fund. Despite 16.7 per cent growth in tax collection by the Federal Board of Revenue, the ADB noted that the target set in the budget was missed, as in previous years. Improving the low ratio of tax to GDP (10.1 per cent in 2014) continued to be a key policy challenge.

Total expenditure grew by 9.2 per cent in 2014 over the previous year as provincial expenditure fell short and subsidies declined. Subsidies contracted by 16.8 per cent in FY2014 as those to the power sector were contained by an increase in electricity tariffs. Subsidies still remained above the budget target, totalling PRs309 billion or 1.2 per cent of GDP. The exclusion of power sector arrears for 2014, estimated at 0.9 per cent of GDP, helped lower accounted expenditures. Interest payments and defence expenditures each increased by over 15 per cent. Consolidated development spending expanded by 46.2 per cent, reflecting an enlarged public sector development programme, but spending was below target by 14.4 per cent.

The smaller budget deficit was financed with increased foreign inflows in the second half of 2014. Government borrowing from domestic banks fell significantly to Rps323 billion (US$3.10 billion) from Rps1.4 trillion (US$0.13 trillion) in the previous year. This left funds for better provision of credit to private firms in food, textiles, telecoms and energy for working capital, fixed investment and trade finance – allowing credit to the private sector to balloon to Rps298 billion (US$2.86 billion) from PRs17 billion in 2013 (US$0.16 billion). Consumer financing doubled in 2014 from a small base. Public debt decreased as a share of GDP by 0.6 percentage points to 64.8 per cent in 2014. The government's domestic debt stock increased only marginally, by 0.4 percentage points to 43.2 per cent of GDP. The maturity profile of domestic debt improved with an increased share of long-term debt largely comprising 3-year investment bonds. Public external debt and liabilities increased to 22.1 per cent of GDP from 21.9 per cent in 2013. To guide policy, the government produced the country's first medium-term debt-management strategy, which assesses different financing strategies and their associated costs and risks under alternative scenarios for interest and exchange rates.

The ADB also noted that the current account deficit widened slightly to 1.3 per cent of GDP in 2014 from 1.1 per cent a year earlier, as import growth picked up while exports rose only modestly. Remittances were robust, growing at 13.7 per cent. The services deficit widened because Coalition Support Fund inflows fell to US$1.0 billion from US$1.8 billion in FY2013. Financing the current account deficit were strong foreign inflows through eurobond placements, the one-off receipt of a US$1.5 billion external grant, further revenue from the sale of 3G/4G spectrum licences and disbursements by multilateral agencies.

Reflecting the large external inflows, net foreign exchange reserves rose to US$9.1 billion at the end of June 2014 and the Pakistan rupee, which had come under depreciating pressure during the first half of 2014, rebounded to Rps98.9 to the US dollar in the last quarter, for overall appreciation of 0.9 per cent in 2014. Appreciation in real effective terms was by 5.6 per cent, with likely adverse implications for export competitiveness.

GDP growth was projected by the ADB at 4.2 per cent in 2015 and 4.5 per cent in 2016, underpinned by low international oil prices and the expected rise in economic growth in advanced economies. The projections assumed steady progress in macro-economic and structural reforms, manageable political and security challenges and normal weather. Growth in 2016 could be higher if economic reform proceeds at a faster pace. The government has made some progress in implementing macro-economic and structural reforms to strengthen its fiscal position, alleviate energy shortages and restructure and privatise loss-making public enterprises. However, progress remained slow in a challenging political and security environment.

Risk assessment

Economy	Poor
Politics	Poor
Regional stability	Poor

Muslims in Pakistan

% of population	96.4
Sunni (% of Muslims)	80
Shi'a (% of Muslims)	18

COUNTRY PROFILE

1906 The Muslim League was founded to promote Indian Muslim separatism.
1940 The Muslim League endorsed the idea of a separate nation for Indian Muslims.
1947 Pakistan (including East Pakistan or what is now Bangladesh) was granted independence as a British Dominion following the partition of the British Indian Empire. The partition of the sub-continent into mainly Hindu India and the Muslim-majority state of Pakistan led to the death of hundreds of thousands as up to 15 million people moved from across the new border. The ruler of the Muslim-majority states of Jammu and Kashmir joined secular India rather than Islamic Pakistan. India and Pakistan have disputed Kashmir ever since.
1948 Muhammed Ali Jinnah, the first governor general of Pakistan, died. Pakistan and India fought over the disputed territory of Kashmir.
1951 Liaquat Ali Khan, Jinnah's successor, was assassinated.
1956 The Islamic Republic of Pakistan was proclaimed.
1958 Martial law was declared and General Ayub Khan took power.
1960 Ayub Khan became president.
1965 Pakistan and India fought over Kashmir.
1969 General Yahya Khan took control when Ayub Khan resigned.
1970 Tensions between East and West Pakistan escalated following the separatist Awami League's success in the general elections.
1971 A civil war broke out when East Pakistan attempted to secede. India intervened in support of East Pakistan, which broke away to become Bangladesh.
1972 The Simla peace agreement set a new line of control (LoC) in Kashmir; India and Pakistan agreed to settle the dispute through peaceful and mutual means.
1973 Zulfiqar Ali Bhutto became prime minister.
1977 Allegations that Bhutto's party, the Pakistan People's Party (PPP), had won the general elections due to vote-rigging sparked widespread civil disturbances. General Zia ul Haq led a military coup *d'état* and deposed Bhutto.
1978 General Zia became president.
1979 The deposed prime minister Zulfiqar Ali Bhutto was hanged, having been convicted of murdering a political rival. His trial was widely condemned as unfair.

1980 The US pledged military assistance to Pakistan in order to strengthen the Islamist opposition to the Soviet occupation in Afghanistan.
1985 After nearly eight years of martial law, parliamentary democracy with a civilian prime minister was reintroduced.
1986 Benazir Bhutto, (the daughter of former prime minister Bhutto), returned from exile to lead the PPP.
1988 Former military dictator and president, Zia ul Haq, remained pre-eminent until he died with the US ambassador and top Pakistani army officers in a mysterious air crash. General elections on a party basis were finally allowed and were won by the PPP; Benazir Bhutto became Pakistan's first woman prime minister.
1990 President Ghulam Ishaq Khan dismissed Bhutto on charges of incompetence and corruption; Nawaz Sharif (Pakistan Muslim League (PML)) was elected prime minister.
1991 Sharif began a programme of economic liberalisation and incorporated *Sharia* (Islamic law) into the legal code.
1993 President Khan dismissed Prime Minister Sharif (for corruption); the supreme court quashed the presidential order and Sharif was reinstated. However, both president and prime minister were forced to resign later. In the elections that followed, Farooq Ahmad Khan Leghari was elected president and Benazir Bhutto returned to power and formed a government by allying with a number of smaller parties.
1996 President Leghari dismissed Bhutto's government for corruption.
1997 The Pakistan Muslim League (PML) won the elections and Nawaz Sharif returned to power as prime minister.
1998 Muhammad Rafiq Tarar became president. Both India and Pakistan conducted underground nuclear tests, leading to widespread international condemnation and US sanctions.
1999 Benazir Bhutto and her husband were convicted of corruption and given jail sentences *in absentia*; they remained in exile. Over 1,000 people died in clashes between Pakistani and Indian forces around Kargil in Kashmir. General Pervez Musharraf led a military coup that deposed Sharif. Pakistan was expelled from the Commonwealth.
2000 US President Bill Clinton visited and urged a return to democracy. Sharif was sentenced to life imprisonment on hijacking and terrorism charges, but was later pardoned and sent into exile in Saudi Arabia.
2001 General Musharraf assumed the presidency (dismissing the incumbent President Tarar) and dissolved parliament. Musharraf backed the US war on terrorism in Afghanistan, which led to the US lifting some of the sanctions imposed after the 1998 nuclear testing.
2002 A referendum approved Musharraf's presidency for a further five years. Mir Zafarullah Khan Jamali was elected prime minister. Tension between India and Pakistan increased and only intense diplomatic efforts prevented war.
2003 A cease-fire began across the LoC – the first formal cease-fire since the insurgency began in 1989. After a two-year ban, Pakistan and India agreed to resume direct air links and allow over-flights. President Musharraf survived an assassination attempt.
2004 Prime Minister Vajpayee of India visited Pakistan for a summit meeting. Pakistan was re-admitted to the Commonwealth. Prime Minister Jamali resigned; Shaukat Aziz replaced him.
2005 The first bus-link for 57 years between divided India- and Pakistan-held Kashmir commenced. Pakistan, Bhutan, Bangladesh, India, Maldives, Nepal and Sri Lanka signed the South Asia Free Trade Agreement (Safta). In October an earthquake with its epicentre in Kashmir kills tens of thousands of people.
2006 A third bus link between Pakistan and India was launched – the service (Lahore-Amritsar) became the first direct link across divided Punjab since partition in 1947. Pakistan test-fired several nuclear-capable short-range ballistic missiles.
2007 The US reported the Al Qaeda leadership was hiding in Pakistan; the government denied this. President Musharraf suspended chief justice Iftikhar Chaudhary; the move lead to protests across the country. He was reinstated by the Supreme Court in July. The leader of the Muttahida Majlis e Amal (MMA), Pakistan's biggest Islamic party, resigned in protest against moves to allow President Musharraf to stand for a second term in office. The Supreme Court revoked the exile order of former president Nawaz Sharif but he was initially denied entry when he attempted to return to stand for president. Musharraf won the October presidential election in parliament although the supreme court refused to declare him winner until after it ruled whether he had been eligible to stand while still army chief. Musharraf declared a state of emergency in November, allowing him to purge the supreme court. He resigned from the army and was declared president. Mohammad Mian Soomro was sworn in as interim prime minister of a care-taker government. Commonwealth leaders suspended Pakistan's membership, declaring that the state of emergency was 'unreasonable and unjustified'. The state of emergency was lifted. Former prime minister Benazir Bhutto returned from exile in October, but did not stand for president; she was assassinated on 27 December while campaigning in Rawalpindi. Following the reading of her will, her son Bilawal Bhutto Zardari was appointed as leader of the PPP, with day-to-day control held by her widower, Asif Ali Zardari. Al Qaeda was accused of her murder. Parliamentary elections were postponed by one month to allow for another leader of PPP to be chosen.
2008 In parliamentary elections the opposition parties PPP and PML-N together gained more seats (171 seats out of 342) than PML-QA (51 seats), which backed the president. The PPP and PML-N agreed to form a coalition along with other political parties including the Awami National Party (ANP). Parliament elected Makhdoom Syed Yousaf Raza Gilani (PPP) as prime minister. President Musharraf resigned, following parliamentary threats of impeachment and Mohammad Mian Soomro became interim president. The government banned the Taliban militant group, Tehreek e Taliban Pakistan (TPP). The ruling coalition collapsed when the PML-N split over a dispute about reinstating the judges previously dismissed by Musharraf. Parliament elected Asif Ali Zardari as president.
2009 The government agreed to the enforcement of *Sharia* (Islamic law) in the Swat valley in the north-east in return for a cease-fire by the Taliban. The move was criticised as an abrogation of responsibility by the government. The Taliban attacked a police academy in Lahore, killing 18 and injuring 95 in an eight-hour battle, which prompted army retaliation and a full-scale assault on Taliban strongholds. The presidents of Afghanistan and Pakistan agreed to increase military co-operation against Islamic extremists operating from strongholds in their shared border areas. Around two million people fled fighting in the north-east and sought refuge in camps elsewhere in Pakistan. After weeks of fighting, the Swat valley was declared safe for civilians and thousands of displaced peoples began to return home. The Supreme Court acquitted opposition leader, Nawaz Sharif, on hijacking charges, allowing him to stand for public office. A UN inquiry team began work into the assassination of Benazir Bhutto. In a ruling the Supreme Court abolished the amnesty that protected senior politicians, including President Zardari, from prosecution. Ahmed Mukhtar, the defence minister, became the first politician to face charges of corruption.
2010 A UN report into the assassination of Benazir Bhutto in 2008 concluded that her death could have been prevented. The report criticised the Pakistani criminal

investigation that followed, which had not pursued those who had organised the killing and that the country's politicised intelligence agencies had hampered the UN's investigation. Landmark legislation was enacted to limit the powers of the president so that the office became a titular position and the executive could no longer dismiss an elected government. The Northwest Frontier Province (NWFP) was renamed the Khyber Pakhtunkhwa. Monsoon rains were so severe that an estimated 14 million people were affected by flood waters, which were registered as the worst flooding in Pakistan's recorded history. Over 1,600 people died as violent waters washed away whole villages, as well as a substantial amount of the country's infrastructure. Water borne infections quickly became a public health issue as hundreds of thousands of people were left homeless and without food and drinking water. The estimated cost of rebuilding roads was US$59 million with a further US$30 million for the power infrastructure. Some 557,000 hectares of cropland were flooded. Around 20 million people were affected and the homes of seven million people destroyed, mostly along the Indus Valley.

2011 Unicef reported in January that in the southern province of Sindh 23 per cent of the population were malnourished following the flood of 2010. Agricultural land was damaged from sand deposited on top of fertile soil during the flood, hampering annual crop planting. The cabinet resigned in February. Prime Minister Gilani announced the move live on television, as part of a plan to reduce the number of ministers by a third and to cut government spending. The government's only Christian cabinet member, Shahbaz Bhatti, was murdered in March, reportedly by the Taliban, over his stance against blasphemy laws, which he considered were used exclusively against minority groups. India's cricket team beat Pakistan in a World Cup semi-final played in the Indian city of Mohali. Indian Prime Minister Manmohan Singh and Prime Minister Yousuf Raza Gilani watched the match together. In discussions the two premiers pledged to 'normalise relations'. Osama Bin Laden, the leader of al Qaeda, was shot dead by US military Special Forces in his fortified hideout, on the outskirts of Abbottabad in north-west Pakistan in May. The body of Bin Laden was flown first to Afghanistan and then buried at sea. In July, the US announced a cut of US$800 million in its military aid for Pakistan. The US Joint Chief of Staff, Admiral Mullens, stated to a US Senate inquiry in September that the militant Islamist Haqqani Network (allied to the Taliban) acts as an arm of Pakistan's Inter-Services Intelligence Agency' (ISIA). He referred to two terrorist attacks, one on coalition troops and the other on the US embassy, both in Kabul and in September, of which, he said the Haqqani Network had support from the ISIA.

2012 On 2 February, the Supreme Court ruled that Prime Minister Gilani must appear before it on 13 February to face contempt of court charges for refusing to reopen a corruption investigation into President Zardari on behalf of Swiss officials; Gilani had said that the president, as head of state, had immunity. Prime Minister Gilani pleaded not guilty. On 26 February, the compound of Osama bin Laden in Abbottabad was demolished by security forces. On 8 March the Supreme Court ordered the government to request that Swiss officials reopen the corruption investigation into President Zardari. It also set a date of 21 March for a compliance report to be filed with the court. On 26 April Prime Minister Gilani was found guilty of contempt of court and released; sentencing was deferred. He was later dismissed by the Supreme Court for refusing to pursue corruption charges against President Zardari. The PPP's preferred candidate to replace Mr Gilani as prime minister, Makhdoom Shahabuddin, had an arrest warrant issued against him; Raja Pervez Ashraf was chosen in his stead. On 19 June, the Supreme Court disqualified Prime Minister Gilani from holding office and attending parliament. President Zardari asked parliament to elect a new prime minister. Parliament voted in Raja Pervez Ashraf (PPP) as prime minister on 22 June. On 5 July, Pakistan re-opened its borders to NATO supply trucks, allowing them to transport materials to Afghanistan. The closed borders had lasted eight months following the NATO air strike on a Pakistan-Afghanistan border checkpoint that killed 24 Pakistani troops. On 29 October, a Taliban gunman shot Malala Yousafzai a 14-year old campaigner for girls' rights to education. The Taliban claimed she was targeted because she 'promoted secularism'. Following initial emergency medical treatment in Pakistan, Miss Yousafzai was flown to the UK for extensive recuperative treatment. In November, a series of suicide bombings by the Taliban killed over 90 people at holy sites during the holy month of Muharram.

2013 Former military ruler, Pervez Musharraf, returned to Pakistan in March. He planned to lead his PML-N party in the May general elections but his candidacy in four seats, including Chitral, was refused. While in the Islamabad High Court on 18 April, seeking to extend bail, the judges issued an order for his arrest. He fled the court for his property outside Islamabad. On 20 April he returned to court and was remanded in custody for two weeks. On 7 May the leader of the Pakistan Tehreek-e-Insaf (PTI) (Movement for Justice) party, Imran Khan, was injured in a fall while campaigning in the Punjab for general election. A general election was held on 11 May. The PML-N won 166 seats (out of 342), just 6 seats short of a majority, Pakistan People's Party (PPP) won 42 seats and the Pakistan Tehreek-e-Insaf (PTI) (Pakistan Movement for Justice) of Imran Khan won 35 seats. Turnout was 55.02 per cent. PML-N leader Nawaz Sharif immediately set about forming a coalition and on 19 May announced 19 of the 27 independents who had won seats would give him their support. A government report leaked to Al Jazira on 9 July said that incompetence and negligence allowed Osama Bin Laden to live in Abbottabad undetected for almost a decade. The Abbottabad Commission described the lack of intelligence as 'government implosion syndrome'. It also criticised the US Navy Seal raid in 2011 that killed bin Laden as an 'American act of war'. Taliban militants freed 248 prisoners in an armed assault on a prison in north-west Pakistan on 29 July. Mamnoon Hussain was elected president on 30 July by parliament and the four provincial assemblies. He will replace President Zadari on 9 September. Mr Hussain is a member of the ruling PML-N party and is said to be close to Prime Minister Sharif. The US ordered non-essential personnel to leave its consulate general in Lahore on 8 August. The government warned of a 'credible threat', and also issued a travel warning to US citizens not to travel to Pakistan. On 18 August ex-President Pervez Musharraf was charged with murder, criminal conspiracy to murder and facilitation of murder of Benezir Bhutto in 2007. On 8 September Asif Ali Zardari stepped down at the end of his five-year term in office, the first democratically elected president to finish a full tenure in office. In a move supported by the Afghan government Mullah Abdul Ghani Baradar, co-founder of the Afghan Taliban, was released from prison by Pakistan on 21 September. At least 80 people were killed in a double suicide bomb attack on a church in Peshawar on 22 September, the worst ever such attack. An earthquake of 7.7 magnitude hit Balochistan in the south-west on 23 September. There were over 400 deaths. An island some 80 metres long and 65 metres high appeared about a kilometre off-shore. A second quake struck on 26 September. Mr Musharraf wasarrested on 10 October over a 2007 mosque raid, a day after the country's supreme court granted him bail in another case. Latif Mehsud, a Pakistan Taliban leader and

said to be a 'terrorist leader' wanted by the Americans for the Times Square bombing in 2010, was captured on the border with Afghanistan in early October. Leader of the Taliban in Pakistan, Hakimullah Mehsud, was killed in a US drone attack on 1 November. There was anger in the government at what was considered an invasion of Pakistani territory. 'Every aspect of Pakistan's co-operation and relations with Washington will be reviewed following the situation created after Mehsud's killing, said Chaudry Nisar Ali Khan, interior minister. Mullah Fazlullah was named as Taliban leader on 7 November; he has said he would not be entering peace talks with the government. Mr Musharraf was released from house arrest on 7 November.
2014 The Taliban claimed they were behind an attack on Karachi's international airport on 9 June. Some 28 people were killed before the army regained control. Late monsoon rains in September hit the mountainous areas of Gilgit-Balitstan and Pakistani-administered Kashmir, unleashing a torrent of water flowing into Punjab's agricultural heartlands. Swollen rivers breached flood defences, sweeping away thousands of villages as the 'super-flood' surged south, wreaking havoc throughout Punjab, the country's most populous province. By mid-September the National Disaster Management Authority (NDMA) reported that 312 people had died, with 2,275,000 affected and nearly 1.7 million acres (687,965 hectares) of crops lost. A state of emergency was declared in Punjab Province. A bomb blast on the Pakistan side of the one road border crossing with India killed as many as 50 and injured over 100 on 2 November.
2015 The ruling party won a closely contested by-election in Punjab on 11 October. Ayaz Sadiq, who had originally won the 2013 election but who's win was voided, won by a narrow margin.

Political structure

Constitution

The federal constitution comprises four semi-autonomous provinces – Punjab, Sindh, Khyber Paktoonkhwa (previously North West Frontier Province) and Baluchistan – as well as federally administered tribal areas (FATAs) and the federal capital area (FCA) of Islamabad. The constitution is an amended version of one promulgated in 1973.
In October 2002, parliament and regional assemblies were elected for the first time since they were suspended following the military take-over led by General Pervez Musharraf in October 1999. Everyone over the age of 18 years and who is not deemed insane is allowed to vote. The president is chosen by the four provinces and the two chambers of parliament.
In April 2010 the National Assembly (lower house) unanimously approved constitutional changes limiting the powers of the president. The changes will come into law once the Senate (upper house) has signed the bill. These will be the first amendments to the constitution since 1973. The measures will reduce the powers of the president, making the prime minister the most powerful person in the country. The amendments include: removing the president's power to dismiss elected governments, appoint the chief election commissioner and impose emergency rule in the provinces; judges will be appointed by a judicial commission; elections of the prime minister and chief ministers of the provinces will no longer be by secret ballot; and prime ministers may stand for more than two terms. The North West Frontier Province becomes Khyber Paktoonkhwa ('Khyber side of the land of the Pjakhtuns').

Independence date

14 August 1947

Form of state

Federal Islamic republic

The executive

The president is elected by an electoral college, consisting of members of the senate and national assembly, as well as members of provincial assemblies. The presidential term of office is five years, for a maximum two-terms. The president must be a Muslim, as per the state religion, Islam.
Legislation, enacted in April 2010, limited the powers of the president to that of a titular Head of State, with ceremonial duties only.

National legislature

The bicameral Majlis i Shura (parliament) comprises the National Assembly (lower house) and Senate (upper house). National Assembly has 342 members in total, of which 272 are directly elected in single-seat constituencies. An additional 10 seats are reserved for religious minorities and 60 seats for female members, filled by proportional representation among parties that win over 5 per cent of the vote. All members are elected for five-year terms. The lower house has the responsibility to review the budget.
The Senate has 100 members elected by the provincial assemblies and allocated according to the four provinces and Federal Capital Area (FCA). The president may not dissolve the senate.

Legal system

The Supreme Court is the highest court of justice. Each of the four provinces has a High Court. The Federal *Sharia* (Islamic) Court hears appeals against the decisions of lower courts under Islamic laws in force concurrently with ordinary laws, and its decisions can be appealed before a *Sharia* Appellate Bench of the Supreme Court.
Each province is divided into a number of districts, each of which is under the judicial jurisdiction, both civil and criminal, of a principal court presided over by a district or sessions judge. Subordinate civil judges and magistrates dispense justice at lower levels of the judicial hierarchy.
Following the coup of 12 October 1999, the army declined to adopt martial law. Therefore, the judicial system continues to operate.

Last elections

11 May 2013 (parliamentary)
Results: Parliamentary 2013: PML-N 166 seats (out of 342) (32.77 per cent), Pakistan Tehreek-e-Insaf (PTI) (Pakistan Movement for Justice) 35 (16.92 per cent), PPP 42 (15.32 per cent), Muttahida Qaumi Movement (MQM) 23 (5.41 per cent), Jamiat Ulema-e-Islam-Fazal-ur-Rehman Group (JUI-F) 15 (3.22 per cent), Pakistan Muslim League (Quaid e Azam Group) (PML-Q) 2 (2.11 per cent), Pakistan Muslim League (F) (PML-F) 6 (2.36 per cent), Jamaat-e-Islami 4 (2.12 per cent), Awami National Party 1 (1 per cent), minor parties with less than 500,000 votes won 14 seats, Independents 27. Turnout was 55.02 per cent. A number of seats held by-elections on 22 August.
Parliament voted Mamnoon Hussain as president on 30 July and he was sworn in on 8 September 2013.

Next elections

2018 (parliamentary and presidential)

Political parties

Ruling party

Coalition led by Pakistan Muslim League-Nawaz (PML-N) and 19 Independents (elected 11 May 2013)

Main opposition party

There is no official opposition party in Pakistan, but Tehrik-e-Insaf (PTI), lead by former cricketer, Imran Khan, is one of a number of parties opposed to the PPP.

Population

178.91 million (2012)*
Last census: March 1998: 130,579,571
Population density: 209 inhabitants per square km (2010). Urban population 36 per cent (2010 Unicef).
Annual growth rate: 2.2 per cent, 1990–2010 (Unicef).

Internally Displaced Persons (IDP)

45,000 (UNHCR 2004)

Ethnic make-up

Punjabi, Sindhi, Pashtun, Baluchi and others including Mohajirs (Muslim emigrés from India). The populations are relatively homogeneous in Punjab, Baluchistan and

North Western Frontier Province (NWFP) (predominantly Pashtun), but Sindh is more diverse, with many non-Sindhi communities in the cities of Karachi and Hyderbad. Precise ethnicity statistics are unobtainable, but a regional population breakdown can be used as an approximate estimate of ethnic proportions in the country as a whole. The most recent figures are as follows: Punjab (56 per cent), Sindh (23 per cent), NWFP (13 per cent) and Baluchistan (5 per cent).
Pakistan is home to millions of Afghan refugees and to one million illegal immigrants from Bangladesh, Sri Lanka, Iran, Iraq and India.

Religions

Islam 97 per cent, Christianity 1.5 per cent, Hinduism 1.5 per cent.

Education

More than 200,000 extra teachers have been recruited since 2001, most under US donor funding estimated at US$10 million.
The government proposes to establish an international centre of computer science in collaboration with the European Centre of Nuclear Physics. Free internet connections have been extended to public sector universities. A nationwide network of schools called the National Centres for the Rehabilitation of Child Labour (NCRCL) has been set up with 33 schools in areas where child labour is rampant.
Literacy rate: 42 per cent adult rate; 54 per cent youth rate (15–24) (Unesco 2005).
Compulsory years: Five to 15
Enrolment rate: 40 per cent in secondary schools.
Pupils per teacher: 40 in primary schools.

Health

Many in poorer rural areas have limited access to healthcare facilities. Although there have been improvements in provision, facilities remain relatively poor, and there are still fewer than 1,000 hospitals for the entire country, providing less than one hospital bed for every 1,000 people. Pakistani authorities have made some efforts to provide increased preventive health care. Particular attention has been given to the provision of safe drinking water supplies, and the government claims that about 88 per cent of the Pakistani population have access to safe drinking water. The World Bank estimates that this is accurate for urban areas only, and the figure among the rural population is thought to be lower, with only about 50 per cent having access to proper sanitation.
Access to immunisation and family planning services hve improved. Low government expenditure and the poor quality of private health care continue to be a problem. One quarter of the national budget is spent on the military, compared with less than 7 per cent on health.
Pakistan in 2012 was one of only three remaining countries (with Afghanistan and Nigeria) where polio is endemic. The World Health Organisation – Global Polio Eradication Initiative (WHO – Polio Eradication) said that improvements in vaccination programmes could only be successful when the central government and the Federally Administered Tribal Areas (FATA) region of North West Frontier Province (NWFP) in particular were fully engaged with the problem. Pakistan liaises with Afghanistan concerning the shared corridor of transmission in the NWFP and southern Afghanistan. In August 2011, Unicef reported there had been an increased number of polio cases since the beginning of the year, with the majority of cases from the western, and largest, state of Baluchistan. The UN said Pakistan was the 'last polio reservoir worldwide', which was standing in the way of total eradication of the disease. A new vaccination campaign for 16.5 million children in districts of highest risk was held on 19–21 September 2011. In 2012 a number of aid and health workers involved in polio vaccinations were murdered by militants who have targeted polio vaccination programmes after rumours that the vaccine would was a steralising agent.

HIV/Aids

HIV prevalence: 0.1 per cent aged 15–49 in 2003 (World Bank)
Life expectancy: 62 years, 2004 (WHO 2006)
Fertility rate/Maternal mortality rate: 3.4 births per woman, 2010 (Unicef)
Birth rate/Death rate: 9.51 deaths to 32.11 births per 1,000 people (World Bank).
Child (under 5 years) mortality rate (per 1,000): 86 per 1,000 live births (WHO 2012); 38 per cent of children aged under five are malnourished (World Bank).
Head of population per physician: 0.74 physician per 1,000 people, 2004 (WHO 2006)

Welfare

A Poverty Alleviation Programme includes pension, death and marriage grants, and a policy formulated for the elimination of bonded and child labour. An estimated 40 per cent of the urban population lives in slums or other poor housing areas.

Main cities

Islamabad (capital, estimated population 1.1 million (m) in 2012), Karachi (11.1m), Lahore (6.7m), Faisalabad (formerly called Lyallpur) (2.6m), Rawalpindi (1.8m), Multan (1.6m), Gujranwala (1.5m), Hyderabad (1.4m), Peshawar (1.3m), Quetta (842,410).

Languages spoken

There are 69 other languages, including Punjabi, Sindhi, Pashtu, Baluchi, Seraiki.

Official language/s

Urdu (national language) and English

Media

Press

Legislation gives the government powers to close media and Internet outlets. Foreign correspondents are allowed to move freely in Pakistan, but are barred from some border areas.
Dailies: There are over 100 national and regional daily newspapers representing all local languages with around 25 published either in English or as an English version of a local language.
In English, *Dawn* (www.dawn.com) is the leading newspaper; others include *Daily Times* (www.dailytimes.com.pk), *Nation* (www.nation.com.pk), *Post* (www.thepost.com.pk), *Karachi News* (www.kashmirnews.com), *Daily Mail* (http://dailymailnews.com), *Statesman* (www.statesman.com.pk) and *Pakistan Observer* (www.pakobserver.net).
In Urdu, the leading newspaper is *Daily Jang* (www.jang.com.pk), others include *Daily Khabrain* (www.khabrain.com), *Daily Nawa i Waqt* (www.nawaiwaqt.com.pk), *Daily Al Akbar* (www.alakhbar.com.pk), *Daily Ausaf* (www.dailyausaf.com), *Daily Millat* (www.millat.com) and *Daily Asas* (www.dailyasas.com.pk). In Sindh, the largest circulation is *Daily Kawish* (www.dailykawish.com) and the *Daily Ibrat* (www.dailyibrat.com).
Weeklies: In English, *The Friday Times* (www.thefridaytimes.com) is an independent newspaper; magazines include the *Herald* (www.dawn.com/herald), *Newline* (www.newsline.com.pk) and *Weekly Cutting Edge* (www.weeklycuttingedge.com). In Urdo, *Akhbar e Jehan* (www.akhbar-e-jehan.com).
Business: In English, two publications, based in Karachi, include *Pakistan and Gulf Economist* (www.pakistaneconomist.com), (international magazine) and *Business Recorder* (www.brecorder.com), with industry specific news.
Periodicals: Almost all major foreign magazines are available in Pakistan, although specific issues may be banned from time to time if they carry material deemed offensive to Islam or critical of Pakistan.

Broadcasting

The Pakistan Electronic Regulatory Authority (Pemra) (www.pemra.gov.pk) is the official organisation that regulates broadcast operations. There are state controlled and privately operated radio and television stations.

Only a Pakistani national or permanent resident may own and operate a broadcast company.

Radio: The state-run Pakistan Broadcasting Corporation (PBC) (www.radio.gov.pk) operates a nationwide service as well as regional and local services. It also operates a range of external services in 15 languages.

Television: The Pakistan Television Corporation (PTV) (www.ptv.com.pk) provides national as well as regional services. In 2002 the first private satellite TV station licenses were issued, by 2007, 20 had been granted and were operational. DawnNews is an English language news channel. ATV (terrestrial); Aaj TV, Indus TV and Ary Digital are satellite stations.

Films shown on television are censored to meet conservative Islamic standards of morality.

In June 2008 the authorities in UAE, asked Geo TV news channel to suspend transmission of two talk shows that were critical of President Musharraf. It is assumed that Pakistan put pressure on the UAE. Geo TV announced that rather than stop transmissions of 'objective and unbiased' information to millions of Urdu-speaking people worldwide it might move its operations to either the UK or Hong Kong.

National news agency: Associated Press of Pakistan (APP)

Other news agencies: The News Network International (NNI) www.nni-news.com.pk

Pahel www.pehel.com

Economy

Pakistan is characterised as an emerging economy, it has a service sector that constituted 53.6 per cent of GDP in 2014 while industry made up 21.3 per cent, of which manufacturing was about 15 per cent, and agriculture was still an important constituent at 25.1 per cent of GDP. Agriculture, typically subsistence farming, provides 45 per cent of all employment. Over 10 million bales of cotton are produced per annum, which are either channelled into Pakistan's textile industries, which export 60 per cent of their production, or exported raw. Pakistan is the world's second largest producer of chickpeas and a major producer and exporter of other agricultural products such as fruit, sugar cane, rice and wheat. Heavy industry includes mining, hydrocarbon extraction, petroleum refining and chemical production. With such a mixed economy the country should be able to maintain a steady increase in economic growth, however it is subject to internal and external pressures and natural and manmade shocks.

Pakistan has suffered from increasing internal insurgency, as well as fighting along its border with Afghanistan. This has led to the breakdown of civil order in several provinces. The economy in such regions cannot be productive and may have an effect on long-term development. The military requires a higher proportion of GDP than would be expected during a period of peace. Although the US provides funds for military aid, money that could be used for development is allocated elsewhere. Remittances from migrant workers amounted to US$14.6 billion (6.3 per cent of GDP) in 2013 and grew to US$17.1 billion (6.9 per cent of GDP) in 2014.

GDP growth was 3.7 per cent in 2008 as the global economic crisis began to impact on the economy and output in manufacturing slowed and exports fell. However a bumper crop of wheat in 2008 and a fall in imports as well as increased remittances from the seven million overseas workers, plus international aid (much through military spending by the US) maintained growth. Pakistan did not experience a recession, although GDP growth in 2009 fell to 1.7 per cent, before rebounding with growth of 3.8 per cent in 2010 as global trade picked up. The economy could have expected a higher growth rate, as experienced by other low-income countries in the region, but it was struck by widespread destruction from severe flooding in 2010, which displaced millions of residents along the Indus valley, caused a humanitarian disaster and overwhelmed the civil administration. The loss of crops was estimated at US$5 billion and livestock at US$106 million, while 20 per cent of the cotton crop was lost. In 2014 thousands were still homeless and production in much of the flooded areas had not returned to pre-2010 levels. Growth in GDP was 2.7 per cent in 2011 and has been steadily increasing since, reaching 5.4 per cent by 2014.

Inflation has been a long-term problem, although typically remaining below 10 per cent. Since 2007 the Pakistani rupee has depreciated by 40 per cent as a result of the macroeconomic instability. In 2013 inflation was 7.4 per cent, rising to 8.6 per cent in 2014.

In 2014, the UN Human Development Index (HDI) ranked Pakistan 146 (out of 187) for development in health, education and income. Pakistan's progress has strengthened but has not matched the improvement of other countries in South Asia. In 2014, 21.0 per cent of the population were living on less than US$1.25 a day, and 57 per cent were on less than US$2 a day.

External trade

Pakistan is a member of South Asia Association for Regional Co-operation, which operates a preferential trading arrangement that covers 6,000 products. The South Asia Free Trade Area (Safta) agreement was signed in January 2004 and custom duties on all traded goods will be zero between the seven member states (Bangladesh, Bhutan, India, Maldives, Nepal, Pakistan and Sri Lanka) in 2016.

In February 2012, the European Union waived import duties on 75 products, including textiles, until 2014. The waiver was granted on humanitarian grounds following the damage caused to manufacturing by the 2010 floods. The value of the goods affected by the waiver is expected to be around €900 million (US$1.2 billion), almost 27 per cent of Pakistan's total exports to the EU.

In December 2013, the EU granted Pakistan GSP Plus status until 2017. This grants the country the ability to export 20 per cent of its goods with zero tariff, and 70 per cent at preferential rates to the EU market.

Foreign exchange revenue comes from textiles and garment production, remittances and thirdly cotton (Pakistan is the fourth largest producer, worldwide). Combined with shipping and industrial manufacturing foreign trade accounts for about 35 per cent of GDP.

In August 2012, restrictions on foreign direct investment (FDI) by Pakistani citizens in the Indian economy (excluding defence, space and atomic energy sectors) were lifted, and came into effect in September 2012.

Imports

Main imports include petroleum and derivatives, capital machinery, plastics, vehicles, edible oils, paper products, iron, steel and tea.

Main sources: China (24.5 per cent of total in 2014), Saudi Arabia (11.1 per cent), UAE (11.0 per cent)

Exports

Main exports include textiles (garments, bed linen, cotton cloth and yarn), cotton, rice, leather goods, sports goods, chemicals, carpets and rugs, oil, natural gas and fertilisers.

Main destinations: US (12.4 per cent of total in 2014), China (9.3 per cent), UAE (8.6 per cent)

Agriculture

Farming

Agriculture represents around a fourth of GDP, supplies work to approximately 44 per cent of the population and is the driver of the economy, supplying food and raw materials for the manufacturing sector. Sustainable economic development requires long-term growth in agriculture. Main food crops include wheat, rice, maize, barley, millet, sorghum, sugar cane, tobacco, groundnuts, pulses, potatoes, onions, mangoes and citrus fruit. Cotton is the main cash crop and the largest foreign exchange earner, with productivity rising as greater use is made of insecticides. Rice is also an important export. Livestock production includes goats, sheep, cattle, buffaloes, pigs, donkeys, horses, mules, camels and poultry, and accounts for around 7.5 per cent of GDP, providing meat, eggs, dairy products, leather and wool, as well as draught power and fertiliser for cultivation. There are around 27 million hectares available for agriculture. Typically 26 per cent of agricultural land is given over to arable crops, while 6.25 per cent is permanent pasture. There are grazing difficulties in border regions, where Afghan refugees have brought about three million head of cattle with them.

The agricultural policies pursued by successive governments have traditionally been geared towards attaining self-sufficiency in the production of foodstuffs, increasing cash crop production and maximising foreign exchange earnings from the export of agricultural commodities such as cotton and rice.

Owing to a shortage of unused cultivatable land, planners have concentrated on increased yields per hectare rather than an expansion of planted acreage. The government announced support for procurement prices for all major crops before sowing, and has encouraged farmers to adopt modern cultivation practices by providing them with subsidised inputs such as chemical fertilisers, pesticides and improved seed varieties. As the use of these inputs has become more popular and the government's budgetary constraints have become more pressing, these subsidies are gradually being phased out, but farmers are being compensated through rising crop prices.

The extended use of pesticides and fertilisers has been accompanied by a selective mechanisation of farm operations, facilitated by a liberal import policy for farm machinery and an expansion of domestic manufacturing capacity for the production of agricultural equipment. Mechanisation has become a routine operation for small farmers, who hire harvesters from richer farmers, and gain a higher yield in return.

Farmers have called on the government to address the problems constraining the agricultural sector by allowing them a three-year remission period on their debts, deregulation, improving irrigation and water use and waiving tax and loan recovery in the areas worst hit by drought.

Special attention is being given to the problems of small farmers who suffer mainly from a lack of finance. To alleviate this problem, the government has traditionally adopted a liberal stance towards the provision of rural credit, which is disbursed by the state-run Agricultural Development Bank of Pakistan (ADBP), commercial banks and co-operatives.

Fishing

Pakistan is largely self-sufficient in freshwater fish and seafood, with an active fishing fleet operating out of Karachi and on the Indus River. The Karachi Fish Harbor handles about 90 per cent of fish and seafood catch and 95 per cent of exports.

Forestry

Forests cover only 17,000 square kilometres, equivalent to 3 per cent of the country's land area. A higher level of forestation is needed to improve the quality of the environment, reducing the severity of flooding and the impact of strong winds and sandstorms. The authorities have encouraged a growth in forests, with forest cover increasing by an average of about 2 per cent per annum.

Around 90 per cent of Pakistan's wood production is used for fuel. Wood and wood-based products contribute little to external trade.

Industry and manufacturing

The industrial sector contributed 21.3 per cent GDP in 2014, of which around 15 per cent was derived from manufacturing. The manufacturing industry employs around 17 per cent of the labour force. General Musharraf's economic revival plan (ERP) envisages the establishment of a corporate and industrial restructuring corporation for the revitalisation of underperforming units.

Manufactured and semi-manufactured goods account for about 72 per cent of Pakistan's exports by value, of which 64 per cent is attained by textiles. The manufacturing sector depends on the agricultural sector for most of its raw materials: cotton for weaving, spinning and processing industries, leather and wool for handicrafts and carpet weaving. There is a growing emphasis on private sector development, with approximately 85 per cent of manufacturing output taking place in the private sector.

Pakistan is the fourth largest producer of cotton (after the US, China and India), which accounts for over half of the country's exports. In 2014 Pakistan produced over 2 million tonnes of cotton.

Cotton farming and textile manufacture are interdependent, if the textile sector maintains its viability in the face of stiff competition from mainly Chinese rivals, then cotton production will benefit.

Tourism

Pakistan has a rich history and a diverse and often spectacular landscape. The Indus River (one of Asia's major waterways) runs the length of the country, from the high Himalayan Mountains where it crosses into Pakistan through the rugged mountainous Khyber Pakhtunkhwa, a draw for the active tourist. The river flows out into the Arabian Sea and provides water for the World's largest irrigated farmland. There are major man-made attractions that include ancient ruins with historical links to the Buddhist, Sikh and Hindu religions as well as other historic sites built through the ages. Modern cities include cultural centres and amenities.

Travel and tourism contributed 6.9 per cent to GDP in 2014 and was predicted to rise by 5.2 per cent in 2015. Employment in the industry was 6.0 per cent (3.5 million jobs), projected to rise to 3.6 million in 2015.

The political situation in Pakistan has prompted Western governments to warn their citizens that not all regions of Pakistan are safe and that terrorists have committed atrocities in urban areas.

Rehabilitation of the damaged areas, caused by the Indus valley flooding of 2010, is still on going and may impede travellers who wish to travel overland by road.

Environment

In its efforts to improve living standards for its citizens Pakistan has compromised environmental standards in favour of economic development. Hazardous chemicals, including agricultural run-off, industrial activity and vehicle emissions all add to pollution in general and water contamination in particular.

Mining

Pakistan has deposits of a wide range of minerals, including uranium, rock phosphate, gypsum, iron ore, copper, gold, silver, magnesium, chromite, antimony, barite, rock salt, sulphur, porcelain, china clays and gemstones.

The government is seeking to enhance the role of the mining sector, which has historically played a negligible role in the Pakistan economy. In the past, priority has been given to the further development of rock phosphate mining at Kakul in the North West Frontier Province and the establishment of copper and iron ore mines at Saindak and Nokundi in Baluchistan. These projects have been delayed by insufficient investment, economic unviability and the poor quality of reserves.

Pakistan typically produces nine million tonnes of limestone, 800,000 tonnes of rock salt, 300,000 tonnes of argonite and marble, 30,000 tonnes of barytes, 30,000 tonnes of soap stone, 15,000 tonnes of sulphur, 2–3,000 tonnes of bauxite and 23 tonnes of uranium per annum.

Hydrocarbons

Punjab and Sindh provinces provide all of Pakistan's oil output. However production only provides for about 27 per cent of consumption, with the shortfall made up of imports. The government wants to reduce dependency on imports and has encouraged foreign investment to boost production and raise domestic capacity. Exploration is taking place both onshore and offshore. Pakistan has a total refinery capacity of 513,000bpd. The majority state-owned Pakistan Petroleum is the largest oil and gas exploration and production company.

Plans for a pipeline supplying liquefied natural gas (LNG) from Iran to Pakistan were revived in 2004, however, following a series of extensions and controversies had not been completed by 2015.

The government has set up the Gas Regulatory Authority (GRA) and Petroleum Regulatory Board (PRB) to separate out government functions from state-owned entities that as of 2015 were still in the process of being privatised.

Much of the coal mined in the country is of relatively poor quality and is used primarily for domestic heating and for brick making.

Energy

Total installed generating capacity was 22.3 gigawatts (GW) in 2013.

Hydropower accounts for about 30 per cent of production with thermal power plants providing almost 65 per cent, and nuclear energy providing 4 per cent. There are plans to increase the share of alternative energy sources, such as solar and wind, to 10 per cent of the energy mix. Over 30 per cent of the population are not connected to the national grid and significant growth in demand is expected in the long-term.

Crippling power shortages that had sparked riots across Pakistan in 2009–10 resulted in government measures to reduce demand. As from April 2010 the weekend has been extended from one to two days and street markets are to close earlier, while government offices had their power cut by 50 per cent. As of 2013 the long-standing electricity shortages continued. In the years building up to 2013, energy generation dropped by 50 per cent due to an over-reliance on fossil fuels.

Much of the energy sector is owned by the state and dominated by two parastatal utility companies: the Water and Power Development Authority (Wapda) and the Karachi Electricity Supply Company (KESC), plus a number of small, independent power producers. KESC was sold to foreign investors in 2005, but with the government retaining a 26 per cent share in the company. Plans to privatise Wapda will follow its division into three generating and eight distribution companies and one transmission entity. In early 2014 protests were held by the Hydro Electric Central Labour Union (Heclu) and All Pakistan Employees Coordination Council (Apecc) against the privatisation of Wapda.

Financial markets

Stock exchange

Karachi Stock Exchange (KSE)

Commodity exchange

National Commodities Exchange Limited (NCEL)

Banking and insurance

The banking sector is dominated by state-owned banks: the United Bank Ltd (UBL), Habib Bank Ltd (HBL) and the National Bank of Pakistan (NBP).

In June 2002, the Islamic bench of Pakistan's Supreme Court reversed a decision made in 1999 to outlaw charging interest on bank transactions as un-Islamic. The move came less than a week ahead of a deadline by which all financial institutions had to conform to an Islamic system of banking, which prohibits fixed rates of interest. If the measures had gone ahead, Pakistan would have become the first country to adopt a pure Islamic system. Banks had argued that full Islamicisation of the banking system would create chaos, leading to a possible collapse of the financial sector. Foreign banks were prepared to quit Pakistan if interest charging was abolished. International lenders were also wary of the changes, jeopardising Pakistan's ability to secure foreign loans.

Instead of converting to a fully Islamic financial system, Pakistan has effectively had to accept, at least in the medium-term, a dual system which allows Islamic and conventional banks to coexist. The problem facing Pakistan is the high level of non-performing loans (NPLs) in the banking system caused mainly by economic mismanagement in the past.

In September 2010 Moody's credit rating agency warned that there was a danger of a sharp increase in the number of non-performing loans after the flood crisis. Rural areas were initially hit, but with so many businesses affected it was felt that the formal economy could be undermined and impact onto the banking sector.

Central bank

State Bank of Pakistan

Main financial centre

Karachi

Time

GMT plus five hours

Geography

Pakistan is a wedge-shaped country bordering India to the east, China to the north-east, Afghanistan to the north and Iran to the west. Its southern boundary is the shore of the Arabian Sea.

Pakistan has some of the hottest deserts and highest mountains in the world. The areas north of the capital Islamabad are mountainous, with a temperate climate. The world's second-highest mountain, K-2 (8,611 metres), also known as Mount Godwin Austen, is located in the Karakoram Range, where the Himalayas meet the Hindu Kush.

The plains of the Punjab and Sindh, irrigated by the Indus river and its tributaries, are the main agricultural areas. Apart from its temperate Makran coast on the Arabian Sea, Baluchistan is a vast and mostly empty area of deserts and low bare hills.

Hemisphere

Northern

Climate

The terrain ranges from mountainous to desert, and the climate varies accordingly. It is cool in the mountains and foothills, with rain in summer and snow in winter, and hot in summer and cool in winter in plateau regions, with some rain in winter. The Indus valley experiences year-round heat, with extreme heat and dry winds in summer. Temperatures vary from an average of 15 degrees Celsius (C) in January to an average of 37 degrees C in May–July. Summer temperatures can rise as high as 50 degrees C in northern Sindh and eastern Baluchistan. The monsoon season lasts from mid-July–September when the average monthly rainfall amounts to 16cm. The best time for tourists to visit is between October and April.

Dress codes

Pakistan is an Islamic country where modesty in dress is the rule. The widely worn national dress is the *salwaar kameez*, a unisex combination of baggy shirt and trousers completely covering the arms and legs. Western-style suits are seen only in big cities. Tourists are advised to dress modestly, especially when outside cities like Karachi, Lahore and Islamabad. Women are expected to dress soberly and act discreetly and a headscarf is essential when visiting holy places.

Entry requirements

Passports

Required by all and must be valid for six months beyond date of visit.

Visa

Required by all. Business travellers must provide, an invitation or sponsorship from a local company or organisation; a business letter of intention from an employer;

a full itinerary; proof of financial guarantee of maintenance and emergency repatriation and proof of return/onward passage, with their application form. See www.mofa.gov.pk and follow link to consular services for full details and embassy locations worldwide.

Visitors staying over 30 days must register with the District Foreigners Registration Office within 30 days of arrival; over-staying the visa allowance can be treated as a criminal offence. Indian and Afghan visitors must register within 24 hours of arrival.

Prohibited entry

Israeli passport holders.

Currency advice/regulations

The import and export of local currency is limited to Rp100, in denominations up to Rp10 only. The import and export of foreign currency is unlimited; on departure, only amounts up to Rp500 may be reconverted into foreign currency and only with official exchange receipts.

Travellers cheques, in US dollars or pound sterling, are accepted in banks and major shops and hotels (all other currencies may attract higher exchange rates.

Customs

Personal effects are allowed duty-free. Visitors are not permitted to import alcohol. Motor vehicles may be imported duty-free for a period of up to three months. Export of certain antiques may require a permit.

Prohibited imports

Firearms and ammunition (without a permit), obscene and subversive publications. Fruit and plants may be destroyed to prevent agricultural diseases entering the country.

Health (for visitors)

Mandatory precautions

A vaccination certificate is required for yellow fever and cholera, if travelling from an infected area.

Advisable precautions

Inoculations and booster shots should be current for cholera, tetanus, hepatitis A, diphtheria, and typhoid. There may be a need for vaccinations for polio, tuberculosis, hepatitis B, Japanese B encephalitis and meningitis.

Use malaria prophylaxis (which will also provide protection for hepatitis B and encephalitis) including mosquito repellents, sleeping nets and clothing that cover the body after dark. There is a risk of rabies.

Use only bottled or boiled water for drinks, washing teeth and making ice. Eat only well cooked meals, preferably served hot; vegetables should be cooked and fruit peeled. Avoid uncooked dairy products and salad, and food from street vendors. Healthcare facilities outside Islamabad and Karachi are limited, medical insurance is essential including emergency evacuation. A supply of any regular medicines required should be taken, with their prescription details and a full first-aid kit would be useful.

Credit cards

Major credit cards are accepted in limited outlets. ATMs are found in city centres and at airports.

Public holidays (national)

Fixed dates

23 Mar (Pakistan Day), 1 May (May Day), 14 Aug (Independence Day), 9 Nov (Iqbal Day), 25 Dec (Birthday of Qaid-i-Azam/Christmas).

Variable dates

Eid al Adha (two days), Eid al Fitr (three days), Islamic New Year, Ashura (two days), Birth of the Prophet.

Islamic year 1437 (15 Oct 2015–2 Oct 2016):: The Islamic year contains 354 or 355 days, with the result that Muslim feasts advance by 10–12 days against the Gregorian calendar. Dates of feasts vary according to the sightings of the new moon, so cannot be forecast exactly.

Working hours

As from April 2010 the weekend was extended from one to two days and street markets closed earlier.

Banking

Mon–Thu and Sat: 0900–1330; Fri: 0900–1230.

Business

Mon–Thu and Sat: 0900–1700; Fri: 0900–1230, 1430–1700.

Government

Mon–Thu and Sat: 0900–1700; Fri: 0900–1230.

Shops

Sat–Thu: 0800/0900–1800/1900.

Electricity supply

220–240V AC, with two or three-pin round plug fittings.

Weights and measures

Metric system (local units are also in use).

Social customs/useful tips

It is customary to shake hands on meeting and taking leave; business cards are exchanged after introductions. Business appointments should be made in advance. The attitude to punctuality is variable. Visits during Ramadan should be avoided. Visitors should make themselves familiar with local customs and care should be taken to respect Muslim conventions. For instance, only use the right hand when shaking hands and passing or receiving anything.

Security

Visitors should keep in touch with regional conditions as any increase in political tensions might affect travel advice. Personal security arrangements should be thoroughly considered throughout a visit. There is a risk from indiscriminate attacks and sectarian violence, including tribal killings, armed car-jacking, robbery, kidnap, murder and bombings in public places such as markets, offices and public transport. Although these may not be aimed at foreigners, there is always a risk of being caught up in such attacks. Large-scale demonstrations that become violent can occur, throughout Pakistan, at short notice. Visitors should monitor local media and avoid any demonstrations announced or gatherings encountered. There is also a threat of criminal violence, including theft, burglary and the kidnapping of businessmen, especially in Karachi. Visitors of visibly western origin should not linger in public places. In major towns, especially Karachi, visitors should confine themselves to business areas, and avoid the back streets and bazaars.

Avoid long road journeys (except between major cities), cross-country journeys, and non-essential travel to the border areas of Afghanistan and India (Kashmir province). If visitors must travel to these regions, contact with Pakistani authorities should be made in advance. Police protection may be arranged, as necessary; advice about a No Objection Certificate (issued by the Pakistani Ministry of Foreign Affairs) can also be obtained.

Getting there

Air

National airline: Pakistan International Airlines (PIA)

International airport/s: Karachi International (Jinnah International) Airport (KHI), 12km north-east of Karachi; duty-free and tax-free shops, bar, restaurant, buffet, bank, hotel reservations, post office, shops.

Other airport/s: Lahore (LHE), 3km south-east of Lahore; restaurant, bank, post office, shops, car hire; Peshawar (PEW), 4km from Peshawar; Islamabad International (ISB), 8km from Islamabad; restaurant, car hire, banks, post office.

Airport tax: Departure tax: Rp400–800 (cash only), amount depends on airport; transit passengers are exempt.

Surface

Road: Generally in poor condition. There is access via India (Amritsar-Lahore) and China (the 805km Karakoram Highway serving Sinkiang Province-Islamabad and Rawalpindi via the Khunjerab Pass), plus road connections to Iran. The route from China is open to foreigners, but not to most Pakistanis.

Routes from Afghanistan (via Qandhar-Chaman-Quetta or

Kabul-Peshawar), are closed following the fighting in that country.
Rail: A line runs from Iran (Zahedan-Naukundi-Quetta).
The train service between Pakistan and India was restored in 2004 – one train a week between Lahore in Pakistan and Attari in India.
Water: There are some ferry services from Bombay, although these are not widely used.
Main port/s: Karachi and Bin Qasim (south-east of Karachi).

Getting about

National transport

Air: Four carriers operate daily flights to 37 cities, providing better access than other forms of travel.
Road: The 800km Karakoram Highway permits entry to northern areas. The only multi-lane road is a two-lane highway linking Karachi and Peshawar. Although a new network of highways has greatly facilitated inter-city road travel, it can still be long, hot and harrowing. Avoid travelling at night on mountain roads in northern areas.
Buses: The air-conditioned Flying Coach national buses running between main centres (hourly between Lahore and Rawalpindi) are recommended over the local buses, which are colourful but not very reliable. Seats should be booked in advance.
Rail: There is an extensive rail network with over 8,775km of track, but it is slow and somewhat dilapidated. It is not suited to the business traveller working to a tight timetable. The main route runs Karachi-Lahore-Rawalpindi-Peshawar, with three classes. Certain services include air-conditioning, restaurant cars, sleeping cars, ice containers and women only accommodation. Advance booking is generally advisable, and is essential for some services.
Water: Although the Indus is unnavigable in many places, there are some passenger boats operating on certain stretches, which are recommended more for tourism than commercial travel.

City transport

Business travellers are advised to avoid arriving in Karachi at night and to ensure they are met at the airport.
Taxis: Taxis can be hired at all big hotels, and provide the most practical way for visitors to travel in cities. It is advisable to keep the taxi for the return trip as taxis do not usually cruise looking for passengers and there are not many taxi stands. Waiting costs are low, especially when compared to the time and trouble the traveller would face in looking for another taxi. Hotel taxi drivers are more likely to speak at least some English than those from taxi stands. Metered taxis are painted black and yellow, although the meter may not be used. Tipping normally 10 per cent.

Car hire

Self-drive and chauffeur-driven car hire is available, and minibuses may be hired. Driving is on the left-hand side of the road. National licence and international driving permit required.

BUSINESS DIRECTORY

The addresses listed below are a selection only. While World of Information makes every endeavour to check these addresses, we cannot guarantee that changes have not been made, especially to telephone numbers and area codes. We would welcome any corrections.

Telephone area codes

The international direct dialling (IDD) code for Pakistan is +92 followed by area code and subscriber's number:

Faisalabad	41	Multan	61
Gujranwala	431	Peshawar	91
Hyderabad	221	Quetta	81
Islamabad	51	Rawalpindi	51
Karachi	21	Sialkot	432
Lahore	42	Sukkur	71

Useful telephone numbers

Karachi
Police: 222-222/224-400
Fire: 74-891
Ambulance: 73-259/70-600
International calls: 0102
Calls to India, Bangladesh, China: 102
To check on booked call: 0104
Islamabad
Police: 23-333
Fire: 27-222
International call: 109
To check on booked call: 103
All places
Directory enquiries: 17

Chambers of Commerce

Federation of Pakistan Chambers of Commerce and Industries, Federation House, Sharea Firdousi, Main Clifton Road, Karachi 75600 (tel: 587-3691; fax: 587-4332; email: info@fpcci.com.pk).

Hyderabad Chamber of Commerce and Industry, PO Box 99, Aiwan-e-Tijarat, Saddar, Hyderabad (email: hcci@paknet3.ptc.pk).

Islamabad Chamber of Commerce and Industry, Aiwan-e-Sanat-o-Tijarat, Islamabad (tel: 225-0526; fax: 225-2950; email: icci@brain.net.pk).

Karachi Chamber of Commerce and Industry, PO Box 4158, Aiwan-e-Tijarat, Karachi 74000 (tel: 241-6091; fax: 241-6095; email: info@karachichamber.com).

Lahore Chamber of Commerce and Industry, 11 Sharah-e-Aiwan-eTijarat, Lahore (tel: 630-5538; fax: 636-8854; email: sect@lcci.org.pk).

Quetta Chamber of Commerce and Industry, PO Box 117, Zarghoon Road, Quetta (tel: 824-857; fax: 821-948; email: qcci@hotmail.com).

Rawalpindi Chamber of Commerce and Industry, Chamber House, 108 Adamjee Road, Rawalpindi (tel: 556-6238; fax: 558-6849; email: chamber@rcci.org.pk).

Overseas Investors Chamber of Commerce and Industry, Chamber of Commerce Building, Talpur Rd, Karachi (tel: 241-0814; fax: 242-7313; email: oicci@global.net.pk).

Banking

Allied Bank of Pakistan, Khayaban-e-Iqbal, Main Clifton Road, Bath Island, Karachi (tel: 567-8155; fax: 568-3312, 568-0134).

Federal Bank for Co-operative, 85-W, Rizwan Centre, Blue Area, PO Box 1218, Islamabad (tel: 81-2469).

Faysal Bank, PO Box 472, 11/13 Trade Centre, I. I. Chundrigar Road, Karachi (tel: 263-8011-20; fax: 263-7975).

Habib Bank, Habib Bank Plaza, 1.1 Chundrigar Road, Karachi (tel: 241-8000/8034; fax: 241-4191).

Industrial Development Bank of Pakistan, State Life Building 2, Off 1.1. Chundrigar Road, Wallace Road, Karachi (tel: 241-9160/9168; fax: 241-1990).

Metropolitan Bank, PO Box 1289, Spencer's Building, I.I. Chundrigar Road, Karachi (tel: 263-6740; fax: 263-0404/5).

Muslim Commercial Bank, Adamjee House, 1.1 Chundrigar Road, Karachi 74000 (tel: 241-4090/9, 241-4110/9; fax: 241-3116).

National Bank of Pakistan, 1.1 Chundrigar Rd, Karachi (tel: 241-6789; fax: 241-6769).

United Bank, 1.1 Chundrigar Road, PO Box 4306, Karachi (tel: 2417100; fax: 243-7068).

Central bank

State Bank of Pakistan, PO Box 4456, I.I Chundrigar Road, Karachi 74000 (tel: 111-727-111; fax: 921-2440; email: info@sbp.org.pk).

Stock exchange

Karachi Stock Exchange (KSE), www.kse.com.pk
Lahore Stock Exchange, www.lahorestock.com

Islamabad Stock Exchange (ISE), www.ise.com.pk

Commodity exchange
National Commodities Exchange Limited (NCEL), www.ncel.com.pk

Travel information
Automobile Association of West Pakistan, 8 Multan Rd, PO Box 76, Lahore.

Karachi Automobile Association (KAA), Standard Insurance House, 1 Chundrigar Rd, Karachi 0226 (tel: 232-173).

Pakistan International Airlines (PIA), PIA Bldg, Quaid-e-Azam International Airport, Karachi 75200 (tel: 412-011; fax: 772-7727, 457-0419).

Ministry of tourism
Ministry of Culture and Tourism, 13-T/U, Comm Area, F-7/2, Islamabad (tel: 27-023).

National tourist organisation offices
Pakistan Tourism Development Corporation, House 2, St 61, F-7/4, PO Box 1465, Islamabad 44000 (tel: 811-001/2/3/4; fax: 824-173).

Ministries
Ministry of Commerce, Industry and Production, Block A, Pakistan Secretariat, Islamabad (tel: 921-0277; fax: 920-5241; email: mincom@meganet.com.pk).

Ministry of Communications and Railways, Block D, Pakistan Secretariat, Islamabad (tel: 920-1252; fax: 920-6171).

Ministry of Culture, Sports, Minority Affairs and Youth, College Road, Shalimar 7/2, Islamabad (tel: 921-3121; fax: 922-1863).

Ministry of Defence, Pakistan Secretariat No II, Rawalpindi 46000 (tel: 927-1114; fax: 927-1115).

Ministry of Education, Block D, Pakistan Secretariat, Islamabad (tel: 920-1401; fax: 920-2851; email: pak@yahoo.com).

Ministry of the Environment, Local Government, Rural Development, Labour, Manpower and Overseas Pakistanis, Islamabad (tel: 922-4579; fax: 920-2211; email: envir@isb.compol.com).

Ministry of Finance, Revenues, Economic Affairs, Planning and Development, and Statistics,Block Q, Pakistan Secretariat, Islamabad (tel:920-3687; fax: 921-3780; email: finance@isb.paknet.com.pk).

Ministry of Food, Agriculture & Livestock, Block B, Pakistan Secretariat, Islamabad (tel: 920-3307; fax: 922-1246).

Ministry of Foreign Affairs, Constitution Avenue, Islamabad (tel: 921-0335; fax: 920-4205; email: pak.fm@usa.net).

Ministry of Health, Block C, Pakistan Secretariat, Islamabad (tel: 921-1622; fax: 920-5481; email: sehat@apollo.net.pk).

Ministry of Information and Ministry Development, Cabinet Block, Pakistan Secretariat, Islamabad (tel: 920-7314; fax: 920-2448; email: dgep@isb.comsats.net.pk)

Ministry of the Interior, Block R, Pakistan Secretariat, Islamabad (tel: 921-0086; fax: 920-1472).

Ministry of Kashmir Affairs, Northern Affairs, States and Frontier Region, Housing and Works, Block R, Pakistan Secretariat, Islamabad (tel: 920-3032; fax: 920-2494; email: safron@isb.perd.net.pk).

Ministry of Law, Justice, Human Rights and Parliamentary Affairs, Islamabad (tel: 921-0062; fax: 920-2628; email: molaw@comsats.net.pk).

Ministry of Petroleum and Natural Resources, Block A, Pakistan Secretariat, Islamabad (tel: 921-1220; fax: 920-1770; email: info@mpnr.gov.pk).

Ministry of Religious Affairs, Zakat and Usher, Plot 20, Ramna-6, Islamabad (tel: 920-1909; fax: 920-1646; email: mara@paknet.ptc.pk).

Ministry of Science and Technology, Shaheed-e-Millat Secretariat, Islamabad (tel: 920-8026; fax: 920-2603; email: minister@most.gov.pk).

Office of the President, Constitution Avenue, Islamabad (tel: 922-0136; fax: 920-3938; email: psecyp@isb.paknet.com.pk).

Office of the Chief Executive, Islamabad (tel: 922-2666; fax: 920-4632).

Other useful addresses
All-Pakistan Textile Mills Association, 44-A Lalazar, Off MT Khan Rd, PO Box 5446, Karachi (tel: 552-296).

Asian Development Bank, Pakistan Resident Mission, Overseas Pakistani Foundation (OPF) Building, Sharah-e-Jamhuriyat, G-52, Islamabad (tel: 825-011; fax: 823-324; email: adbpim@mail.asiandevbank.org).

Board of Investment, Saudi Pak Tower, 61-A Jinnah Ave, PO BOx 3100, Islamabad (tel: 817-165/2, 218-267/6; fax: 217-665, 215-554, 263-9580).

British Deputy High Commission, York Place, Clifton, Karachi 6 (tel: 532-041/6; fax: 587-4014).

British Trade Office, 65 Mozang Road, PO Box 1679, Lahore (tel: 631-6589/90; fax: 631-6591).

Export Promotion Bureau, Government of Pakistan, Block A, Finance & Trade Centre, Sharea Faisal, Karachi (tel: 566-0305/9; fax: 566-0300, 568-0422/4010).

Institute of Marketing Management, 68-B Block 2, PECHS, Karachi (tel: 455-8365).

Islamabad Stock Exchange (tel: 215-047/50).

Karachi Cotton Association, Cotton Exchange Bldg, 1.1 Chundrigar Rd, Karachi (tel: 241-0336/2570).

Karachi Stock Exchange (Guarantee) Ltd, Stock Exchange Bldg, Stock Exchange Rd, Karachi 2 (tel: 242-5501/2/3/4/5; fax: 241-0825).

Lahore Stock Exchange (tel: 636-8000, 636-8333).

Pakistan Art Silk Fabrics & Garments Exporters Association, 204 Amber Estate, Shahrah-e-Faisal, Karachi (tel: 360-919, 368-488).

Pakistan Cotton Association, 5 Amber Court, Shaheed-e-Millat Rd, Karachi (tel: 438-461).

Pakistan Embassy (USA), 2315 Massachusetts Avenue, NW, Washington DC 20008 (tel: (+1-202) 939-6200; fax: (+1-202) 387-0484; email: parepwashington@erols.com).

Pakistan Fruit & Vegetables Exporters, Importers & Manufacturers Association, 8 New Onion & Potato Market, University Rd, Karachi (tel: 493-7126, 493-125).

Pakistan Handicrafts Manufacturers & Exporters Association, MA Jinnah Rd, Karachi (tel: 772-8121).

Pakistan Shipowners Association, Ralli Brothers Bldg, Talpur Rd, Karachi (tel: 242-7154).

Privatisation Commission, Government of Pakistan, 5A Constitution Avenue, EAC Building, Islamabad (tel: 920-5146; fax: 920-3076, 921-1692; email: info@privatisation.gov.pk).

Sindh Coal Authority, F-158/A-I, Block 5, Clifton, Karachi (tel: 583-3549, 583-3550; fax: 587-4708).

National news agency: Associated Press of Pakistan (APP), 18 Mauve Area, G-7/1, Islamabad (Tel: 220-3064–67; email: news@app.com.pk; internet: www.app.com.pk) (state run).

The News Network International (NNI) www.nni-news.com.pk

Pahel www.pehel.com

Internet sites
Karachi Airport: www.karachiairport.com

Pakistan argricultural information: www.pakissan.com

Pakistan Government Homepage: www.pak.gov.pk

Trade index of Pakistan: www.PakistanBiz.com

Palau

COUNTRY PROFILE

1686 Spain claimed the Caroline Islands, including Palau.
1783 A British landing on Palau inaugurated a century of trading links.
1885 The Spanish claim to the Caroline Islands was upheld by the Pope.
1899 Spain sold the islands to Germany.
1914 Japan occupied the islands.
1947 Palau became part of the Trust Territory of the Pacific Islands, administered by the US under an UN trusteeship mandate.
1978 Palau voted against becoming a part of the Federated States of Micronesia.
1980 Palau adopted its own constitution in July.
1981 Palau became the Republic of Palau with Haruo Remeliik as its first president.
1982 A Compact of Free Association with the US (CFA) was signed.
1985 President Remeliik was assassinated in June. Lazarus Salii was elected president in September.
1987 Palau voted to amend its constitution to allow approval of the CFA by a simple majority.
1988 The Palau Supreme Court ruled the constitutional change invalid on procedural grounds. President Salii committed suicide in August. Ngiratkel Etpiison elected president in November.
1989 Agreements with the US provided aid for paying off foreign debt and funds for new development.
1992 Kuniwo Nakamura became president.
1993 Palau voted in a referendum to adopt the CFA.
1994 Palau became an independent republic under the CFA.
1996 President Kuniwo Nakamura was re-elected.
2000 Tommy Remengesau became president.
2003 A new airport terminal, costing US$16 million, was completed.
2004 Incumbent Tommy Remengesau was re-elected president.
2006 The government began relocation to the new capital of Melekeok, on Babeldaob Island. Some departments such as the police, immigration and customs remained on Koror, still the largest settlement. The Pacific Savings Bank (PSB) collapsed. Following an independent investigation criminal charges were brought against all of the PSB's board of directors and senior managers. US$1.5 million was lost from pension deposits in the uninsured PSB.
2007 Convictions were achieved in Palau's first case of human trafficking.
2008 In parliamentary elections all candidates stood as independents. In presidential elections Johnson Toribiong was elected as incumbent Tommy Remengesau was required to stand down.
2009 An agreement between the US and Palau resulted in 17 ethnic Uighurs, originally from China and held in the US-detention prison in Guantanamo Military Base as suspected Islamist terrorists, were resettled in Palau.
2010 A new airline, Pacific Flier, began operations with a direct air link between Palau and Brisbane, Australia. The first resident US ambassador to Palau, Helen Reed-Rowe, was appointed.
2011 By March, Palau had received a total of US$12.6 million in grants from the US, UN, South Korea and Taiwan, to be used in road and civic projects, health services and programmes, a tourist rest centre and the Palau Congress Project. A state of emergency was declared at the end of September due to the lack of fresh water for its residents. The New Zealand Red Cross and Australian authorities responded by delivering personnel and supplies. In November electricity was rationed, with households limited to eight hours per day, due to fire-damage of a power generator at Aimeliik in Koror State. A state of emergency was imposed as hospitals, schools and the airport were threatened with power cuts.
2012 President Johnson Toribiong was brought to court charged with misuse of funds provided by the US to resettle Uighur detainees released from Guantanamo Bay in 2009. It was alleged that he had authorised spending US$250,000 on the renovation of a family property to house the six Uighurs. President Toribiong said the property had the best security on offer and that the court case was politically motivated. On 17 April 25 Chinese nationals were deported for being illegally present in Palau waters. They had been picked up aboard three small, fast boats after they had incinerated

KEY FACTS

Official name: Belu'u era Belau (Republic of Palau)

Head of State: President Tommy Remengesau (Junior) (from 15 Jan 2013)

Head of government: President Tommy Remengesau (from 15 Jan 2013)

Ruling party: Members of the national congress sit as independents

Area: 380 square km

Population: 18,000 (2014)*

Capital: Melekeok, on Ngerekebesand Island, since 2006 (Koror: commercial centre)

Official language: English on all islands; there are four officially recognised dialects (Palauan, Sonsoralese, Tobi, Angaur – on Angaur, Japanese is also included as official)

Currency: US dollar (US$) = 100 cents

GDP per capita: US$15,210 (2014)*

GDP real growth: 7.95% (2014)*

GDP: US$269.00 million (2014)*

Inflation: 4.00% (2014)

Balance of trade: -US$132.13 million (2013)

Foreign debt: US$80.00 million (2012)

* estimated figure

their 'mother ship'. Presidential elections held on 6 November, were won by opposition leader Tommy Remengesau (Jr) with 49.1 per cent of the vote.
2013 In March President Tommy Remengesau announced that since Palau's revenue from fishing was negligible (US$5million), the Islanders would be better off banning all commercial fishing in Palau's waters and creating one of the world's largest marine reserves, covering an area roughly the size of France, so as to attract more tourists. The reserve would be within Palau's exclusive economic zone (EEZ), which is 630,000 square kilometres.
2014 The new British ambassador to Palau, Asif Ahmad, presented his credentials on 30 May. From 8 September overseas birth and death registrations of British Citizens will nolonger take place at the British Consulate and will be carried out instead in a central registration unit in the UK.
2015 Japan's Emperor Akihito and Empress Michiko made their first visit to Palau on 10 April to mark the 70th anniversary of the end of World War II. Palau, one-time colony of Japan, is the site of one of the Second World War's fiercest battles in the Pacific. Some 10,000 Japanese solders and 1,700 Americans were killed during a two-month fight in 1944 on Palau's Peleliu island. The Presidents of the Marshall Islands and the Federated States of Micronesia also met the Emperor and Empress.

Political structure

Constitution

The constitution was promulgated in January 1981.
Each state has a governor.
A council of chiefs advises the government on matters of traditional law and custom.
Voting: universal suffrage over 18 years.

Form of state

Republic, in free association with the US.

The executive

The president is head of state and head of government, elected for a four-year term by popular vote. Presidents may stand for only two terms.

National legislature

The bicameral Olbiil Era Kelulau (OEK) (National Congress) comprises a nine-seat Senate (upper chamber) and a 16-member House of Delegates (lower chamber); both elected by popular vote for four-year terms.

Legal system

The legal system is based on Trust Territory laws, acts of the legislature, municipal, common and customary laws.

Last elections

6 November 2012 (presidential and parliamentary)
Results: Presidential: Tommy Remengesau (Junior) won 49.1 per cent of the vote, Johnson Toribiong, 33 per cent, Sandra Pierantozzi 18 per cent. Parliamentary: non-partisans were elected – no political parties exist.

Next elections

2016 (presidential and parliamentary)

Political parties

There are no political parties.

Ruling party

Members of the National Congress sit as independents

Political situation

Palau's largest foreign earnings come from tourism, remittances and revenue from the Compact of Free Association (commonly referred to as the Compact) which Palau has with the US. And while the Compact brings in a regular income each year, it is capped and extra income from the other two are subject to the mercy of external pressures and vagaries. Added to which frequent disasters caused by hurricanes snap up any reserves that may be around. No matter how detailed Palau's economic plans are, they are always prone to external disruption and as such the government has poor a track record for steady fiscal management.
In 2010, former president, Tommy Remengesau, declared the Palau was over governed, with one national and 16 state governments for 20,000 people. Perhaps this is why the aid package of US$250 million offered by the US for 2010–25 was rejected by Palau in July 2010. In exchange for the aid, the US insisted in more input in Palauan economic matters. This was rejected by Palau negotiators, saying the US wanted to micromanage Palauan affairs and didn't acknowledge the Palau was a sovereign nation.
Palau is divided between those that call for complete independence and accepting the country's debt liabilities, and those content to stay with the *status quo*, even if that means losing a little more independence to the US.

Population

21,108 (July 2012)* Nearly 70 per cent of the population lives on the island of Koror while the island of Babeldaob is nearly empty.
Last census: 1 April 2006: 19,907
Population density: 45 inhabitants per square km (2010). Urban population 83 per cent (2010 Unicef).
Annual growth rate: 1.5 per cent, 1990–2010 (Unicef).

Ethnic make-up

Palauan (Micronesian with Malayan and Melanesian mixtures) 70 per cent; Asian (Filipinos, Chinese, Taiwanese and Vietnamese) 28 per cent; white 2 per cent.

Religions

Predominantly Christian, although one third of the population practise an indigenous religion known as Modekngei.

Education

The school system of Palau follows that of the US. Education is compulsory until the age of 14. Palauian and English are taught in schools, but English has gradually become the main instruction medium. There were 22 elementary schools, one high school, seven private schools and one community college. Around 94 per cent of school-aged children attend school and 97 per cent complete elementary school. The completion rate for high school students is 78 per cent.

Health

Only around 75 per cent of the population have access to medical facilities.
Life expectancy: 68 years, 2004 (WHO 2006)
Fertility rate/Maternal mortality rate: 1.4 births per woman, 2004 (WHO 2006)
Child (under 5 years) mortality rate (per 1,000): 21 per 1,000 live births (WHO 2012)

Welfare

There is no social welfare system.

Main cities

Koror (capital, population 8,895 in 2012), Airai (1,285), Meyuns (1,056), Kloulklubed (818).

Languages spoken

Local languages and Japanese spoken in some states.

Official language/s

English on all islands; there are four officially recognised dialects (Palauan, Sonsoralese, Tobi, Angaur – on Angaur, Japanese is also included as official)

Media

Press

The Government Media Office publishes the *Palau Gazette* monthly.
Dailies: In English *Marianas Variety* and the *Independent* published abroad but read in Palau. Regional online newspaper *Pacific Magazine* (www.pacificmagazine.net).
Weeklies: In English *Tia Belau*, *Palau Horizon*; in Palau *Roureur Belau*. These are independent local publications. Regional, online *Inside Oceania* (www.insideoceania.com)

Broadcasting

Radio: In Palau and English, Eco Paradise FM, is government-operated; T8AA radio station, WWFM and KRFM, and a Christian religious broadcaster (High Adventure Ministries), are independent.

Television: Over 90 per cent of households have cable television, there are no local or regional TV broadcasts. Island Cable Television ((www.palaunet.com/CableTV.asp) is the only cable provider.

Palau National Communications Corporation (PNCC), PO Box 99, Koror, Palau 96940 (tel: 587-9900; email: edcarter@palaunet.com; internet: www.palaunet.com)

Other news agencies: ABC Pacific Beat: www.radioaustralia.net.au/pacbeat

Pacific Magazine: www.pacificmagazine.net

Economy

Palau has one of the highest standards of living in the Pacific and is classified as a middle-income country, with a high human development ranking and a per capita GDP of US$11,880 in 2014.

Since the end of Japanese occupation in 1945, the US has retained control over defence and foreign policy matters in return for several hundred million dollars in aid over 15 years (1994–2009). Of the US$630 million guaranteed under the Compact of Free Association (COFA) with the US, US$70 million was placed in an investment fund, to provide a US$5 million boost to the annual budget. A decision to extend the COFA agreement for a further 15 years was introduced in the 2013–14 Congress.

The economy is based on agriculture and fishing, with a growing tourism sector focused on sailing, scuba diving and sports-fishing. GDP growth fell to a low of -2.0 per cent in 2013 following a period of positive growth ending on 4.6 per cent in 2012. However, due to development of tourism and related industries such as communications, wholesale and retail trade, and financial intermediation, GDP grew by 8.0 per cent in 2014.

Foreign fishing vessels (mainly from Japan and Taiwan) pay royalties to fish in Palau's Exclusive Economic Zone. The government is investigating alleged use of the territory for money laundering activities.

A two-lane highway, Compact Road, around the main island, Babeldaob, is an important addition to Palau's infrastructure and basis for economic growth. With the road's completion, all Palau's major public infrastructure projects that started after the signing of the Compact in 1994 were concluded.

External trade

Palau is a member of the South Pacific Regional Trade and Economic Co-operation Agreement (Sparteca) along with 12 other regional nations, which allows products duty free access by Pacific Island Forum members to Australian and New Zealand markets (subject to country of origin restrictions). Palau has become a major investment destination for Chinese entrepreneurs wishing to benefit from its unlimited access to US markets.

Commercial fishing licences for foreign trawlers have become an important source of foreign earnings.

Imports

Principal imports are machinery and equipment, manufactured goods, fuels, metals, live animals and foodstuffs.

Main sources: US (33.2 per cent of total in 2014), Singapore (19.7 per cent), Japan (12.2 per cent), Philippines (5.4 per cent) and Guam (4.9 per cent).

Exports

Main exports include shellfish, tuna, copra and garments, which have become a major export following investment by Chinese firms, eager to take advantage of Palau's access to the US market.

Main destinations: Japan (40.6 per cent of total in 2014), United States (38.3 per cent) and Guam (2.5 per cent).

Agriculture

Farming

Agriculture accounts for around 1 per cent of GDP, with farming accounting for around 0.5 per cent. Subsistence farming of taro, bananas, sweet potatoes, tapioca and vegetables, with pig and poultry raising, is the main occupation. Commercial farming is practised where climate and soils are favourable. Land is parcelled into an estimated 20,000 holdings; a Land Commission maintains a register to provide security of land tenure for Palauan citizens.

Fishing

Fishing supplies the principal source of protein and export revenues. Fishing revenue is valuable because of the sale of fishing licences to large foreign fleets, permitting them to fish within Palau's Exclusive Economic Zone.

On 12 April 2011, a summit of the Parties to the Nauru Agreement (PNA) concluded its strategy for a policy of sustainable fishing in the Pacific. The PNA treaty, which was established in 1989 and expired in 2012, was seen as in need of an overhaul. As a collective region, the PNA (FSM, Kiribati, Marshall Islands, Nauru, Palau, PNG, Solomon Islands and Tuvalu) controls around 25–30 per cent of world stocks of tuna. Only 5 per cent of sales revenue is returned to the PNA and ministers called for specific changes, including an increased share of profits, PNA crews on-board purse seine vessels (minimum 10 per cent), conservation and management measures including a limit to fish trapping (fish aggregating devices (FADs)), net mesh rules and the establishment of an observer agency and fisheries information management system. The PNA met in May 2012 to discuss even stronger management measures to ensure even more sustainable tuna fisheries and minimise environmental damage. Many of the ideas put forward were implemented in January 2013, for example observation and monitoring of catches and environmental damage by 100 per cent independent bodies.

Industry and manufacturing

Small-scale industries include handicrafts, garments, fish processing, bottling, bakeries and boat building. Industry typically represents around 7–9 per cent of GDP, but has been boosted by on-going activity in the construction industry to around 15 per cent.

Tourism

The tropical beauty of Palau and its pristine marine environment attracts a variety of visitors from Asia (35 per cent from Taiwan, 30 per cent from Japan and 15 per cent from South Korea) and the US (5 per cent). The number of visitors in 2012 was 119,000, up from 109,000 in 2011, a number that by 2014 had grown even further to a record 141,000.

Tourism (combined with its associated infrastructure) is the top industry for economic growth in Palau – revenue from hotels and restaurants alone contributes 10 per cent of GDP.

In July 2012, the Rock Islands Southern Lagoon was added to Unesco's World Heritage List.

Hydrocarbons

Fossil fuel makes up for around 85 per cent of Palau's energy requirements. Currently, Palau relies on the import of hydrocarbons from the US to meet its requirements.

Energy

Installed generating capacity was 28MW in 2012 (latest available), produced mainly from hydropower, providing 30 million kilowatt hours per year. Diesel-fired generators also provide electricity. The Palau Utilities Corporation (PUC) is responsible for generation and supply of electricity

Long term considerations include ocean thermal energy conversion (otec) exchanges, proposed by the World Energy Council, to produce around 3,000kW of electricity, rising to 30,000kW as the project expands. However, overseas sponsorship, necessary to develop the exchange plant, remains unavailable.

Banking and insurance
Palau has a well-developed banking sector with 12 commercial banks in operation and one development bank, several of which are representative offices of US or Asian corporations. US banks are dominant, holding around 80 per cent of deposits. The main banks are the Bank of Guam and the Bank of Hawaii.

Time
GMT plus ten hours

Geography
Palau consists of more than 200 islands in a chain about 650km (400 miles) long, lying about 7,150km (4,450 miles) south-west of Hawaii and about 1,160km (720 miles) south of Guam. Together with the Federated States of Micronesia, Palau forms the archipelago of the Caroline Islands.
Babeldaob is the largest island in Palau, and in the centre of its east coast is the new site for the capital, Melekeok, (relocation began on 7 October 2006) and is home to Lake Ngardok, the largest body of freshwater (5 square km) in Palau; Meyuns, the second largest settlement, is also located on the northern shore, and the international airport is in the south.
Koror Island (still with the largest settlement, Koror) is connected to Malakal Island (location of Koror's port) by two land bridges and a man-made bridge to Babeldaob Island.
The islands are composed largely of volcanic and limestone rock with coral reefs encircling the inhabited islands. The tallest peaks are on Babeldaob and Koror, with elevations of 217 metres (m) and 628m, respectively.

Hemisphere
Northern

Climate
Warm and humid, with temperatures between 23–30 degrees Celsius and humidity around 80 per cent. Rainfall (variable, minimum 250 mm/year), can occur in downpours. Typhoons are possible.

Entry requirements
Passports
Required by all. US citizens may visit with photo ID, however all US nationals require a passport for re-entry to the US from January 2007).

Visa
Required by all and issued by travel agent or airline for visits up to 30 days with proof of return/onward passage and adequate funds for maintenance. Extended entry permits are issued on application to Chief of Immigration, Bureau of Legal Affairs, Ministry of Justice, PO Box 100, Koror, Palau 96940.
Special regulations may apply to some non-tourist destinations within the islands.

Currency advice/regulations
No restrictions on import and export of local and foreign currency. Foreign currency over US$5,000 must be declared.

Prohibited imports
Illegal drugs and weapons

Health (for visitors)
Mandatory precautions
Cholera and yellow fever immunisations are required for those arriving from infected areas.

Advisable precautions
Vaccination for diphtheria, TB, hepatitis A and B, polio, tetanus and typhoid are recommended. There is a rabies risk.
Hospitals often expect immediate cash payment for medical treatment.

Hotels
There are hotels and guest-houses in Melekeok, Koror, Peliliu and Angaur.

Credit cards
Major credit cards are widely accepted at main visitor facilities.

Public holidays (national)
Fixed dates
1 Jan (New Year's Day), 15 Mar (Youth Day), 5 May (Senior Citizens' Day), 1 Jun (President's Day), 9 Jul (Constitution Day), 1 Oct (Independence Day), 24 Oct (United Nations Day), 25 Dec (Christmas Day).

Variable dates
Labour Day (first Mon in Sep), Thanksgiving Day (last Thu in Nov).

Working hours
Banking
Mon–Thu: 1000–1500, Fri: 1000–1800.

Business
Mon–Fri: 0900–1700.

Government
Mon–Fri: 0900–1700.

Shops
Mon–Sat: 0800–2000; Sun 0800–1800.

Telecommunications
Telephone/fax
Palau National Communications Corporation provides all modern public and private telecommunications facilities, including phone cards, international calls and mobile phones.

Mobile/cell phones
There are 900/1800 GSM services available.

Electricity supply
115V AC 60Hz, with flat, two or three pin plugs.

Social customs/useful tips
An informal attitude prevails in business. Business cards are sometimes exchanged. Business is usually conducted in English. Visitors should familiarise themselves with local customs. Permission should be sought before photographing people. Gratuities are optional.

Getting there
Air
National airline: A new carrier, Pacific Flier, began operations with a direct air link between Palau and Brisbane, Australia in April 2010. Other destinations include The Philippines and Guam.
International airport/s: Koror Babeldaob (ROR), 19km north-east of Airai, on Babeldaob. Unmetered taxis, with fixed fares, are available, travel time to Koror 30 minutes. Hotel shuttle buses are available if requested when making bookings.
Airport tax: US$20

Surface
Water: Malakal Harbour is the main commercial port facility in Palau. Cargo ships that carry passengers visit occasionally.

Getting about
National transport
Road: Outside administrative areas, the road network may consist of tracks not passable to ordinary vehicles. Ngiwal, Melekeok and Ngaremlengui each have road systems which link up with the main hamlets.
Driving is on the right with 40km per hour as the maximum allowable speed. Passing is prohibited anywhere in Palau.
In July 2005, Japan awarded almost US$20 million in grants to improve Palau's roads.
Water: The islands of Peleliu and Anguar are served by municipal boats. Other inter-island services rely on privately operated boats.

City transport
Taxis: Although taxis are not metered all fares are fixed, enquire before travelling.

BUSINESS DIRECTORY
The addresses listed below are a selection only. While World of Information makes every endeavour to check these addresses, we cannot guarantee that changes have not been made, especially to telephone numbers and area codes. We would welcome any corrections.

Telephone area codes
The international direct dialling code (IDD) for Palau is +680, followed by subscriber's number.

Useful telephone numbers
Ambulance: 488-1411
Police: 911

Chambers of Commerce
Palau Chamber of Commerce, PO Box 1742, Koror 96940 (tel: 488-3400; fax: 488-3401; e-mail: pcoc@palaunet.com).

Banking

Bank of Guam, PO Box 338, Koror 96940 (tel: 488-1648/2696/2697; fax: 488-1384).

Bank of Hawaii, PO Box 340, Koror 96940 (tel: 488-2602/2428; fax: 488-2427).

Bank Pacific, PO Box 1000, Koror 96940 (tel: 488-5635; fax: 488-4752).

Pacific Savings Bank, PO Box 399, Koror 96940 (tel: 488-1859/1860; fax: 488-1858; email: bank@palaunet.com).

First Commercial Banking, PDC Building; PO Box 1605, Koror 96940 (tel: 488-6297/8/9; fax: 488-6295).

Central bank

National Bank of Palau, PO Box 816, Koror 96940 (tel: 488-2578; fax: 488-2579; internet: ndbp.com).

Travel information

Continental Micronesia, PO Box 138CK, Saipan MP 96950, Northern Mariana Islands (tel: (+1-670) 234-8223; fax: (+1-670) 234-8358).

National tourist organisation offices

Palau Visitors' Authority, PO Box 256, Koror, ROP 96940 (tel: 488-2793/1930; fax: 488-1453; internet site: http://www.visit-palau.com).

Ministries

Bureau of Commercial Development, PO Box 1471, Koror, 96940 (tel: 488-2502).

Bureau of Education, PO Box 189, Koror 96940 (tel: 488-1464; fax: 488-1465; email: moe@palaugov.net).

Bureau of National Treasure (tel: 488-2501; email: bnt@palaugov.net).

Other useful addresses

British High Commissioner (for information on Palau), Victoria House, 47 Gladstone Rd; PO Box 1355, Suva, Fiji (tel: (+679) 322-9100).

Office of the President, PO Box 100, Koror, ROP 96940 (tel: 488-2403/2828; fax: 488-2424/1662).

Palau Embassy (USA), Suite 400, 1700 Pennsylvania Ave, NW Washington, DC 20006 (tel (+1-202) 452-6814; fax (+1-202) 452-6281; internet: www.palauembassy.com).

Palau Liaison Office (Hawaii), 1441 Kapiolani Blvd, Suite 1120, Honolulu, Hawaii 96814 (tel: (+1-808) 941-0988/89; fax: (+1-808) 943-1689).

Palau Liaison Office (Guam) ITC Bldg, Suite 615, PO Box 9457, Tamuning, Guam 96911 (tel: (+1-671) 646-9281/81).

ABC Pacific Beat: www.radioaustralia.net.au/pacbeat

Pacific Magazine: www.pacificmagazine.net

Internet sites

Government of Palau: www.palaugov.net

Destination Micronesia, Palau: www.destmic.com/palau.html

US Office of Insular affairs: www.doi.gov/oia

Yellow Pages: http://directory.palaunet.com/yellowpages

Palestine

KEY FACTS

Official name: Palestine (State of)

Head of State: Mahmoud Abbas (Fatah) *pro tem president until national elections can be held* (from 2005)

Head of government: Prime Minister Rami Hamdallah (sworn in 18 Sept 2013, and 24 June 2014 as Prime Minister)

Ruling party: There is no ruling party – the Government of the State of Palestine was sworn in by President Abbas on 2 June 2014. It controls the Gaza Strip and part of the West Bank Gaza. Strip only: Harakat al Muqawama al Islamia (Hamas) (Islamic Resistance Movement). West Bank only; Harakat al Tahir al Watani al Falistin (Fatah) (Movement for the National Liberation of Palestine) and independents

Area: 6,257 square km

Population: 4.17 million (2011); (Around three million Palestinians live in Jordan)

Official language: Arabic

Currency: Egypt pound; New Israeli shekel; Jordanian dinar ((LE; NIS; JD)) = 100 piastres / = 100 agorot / = 100 fils

Exchange rate: (LE; NIS; JD)7.83 per US$ (LE); 3.91 (NIS); 0.71 (JD) (Nov 2015)

GDP per capita: US$2,186 (2010)

GDP: US$8.33 billion (2010)

Labour force: 745,600 (2010)

Unemployment: 28.40% (2011)

Inflation: 3.80% (2010)*

Balance of trade: -US$4.63 billion (2011)

* estimated figure

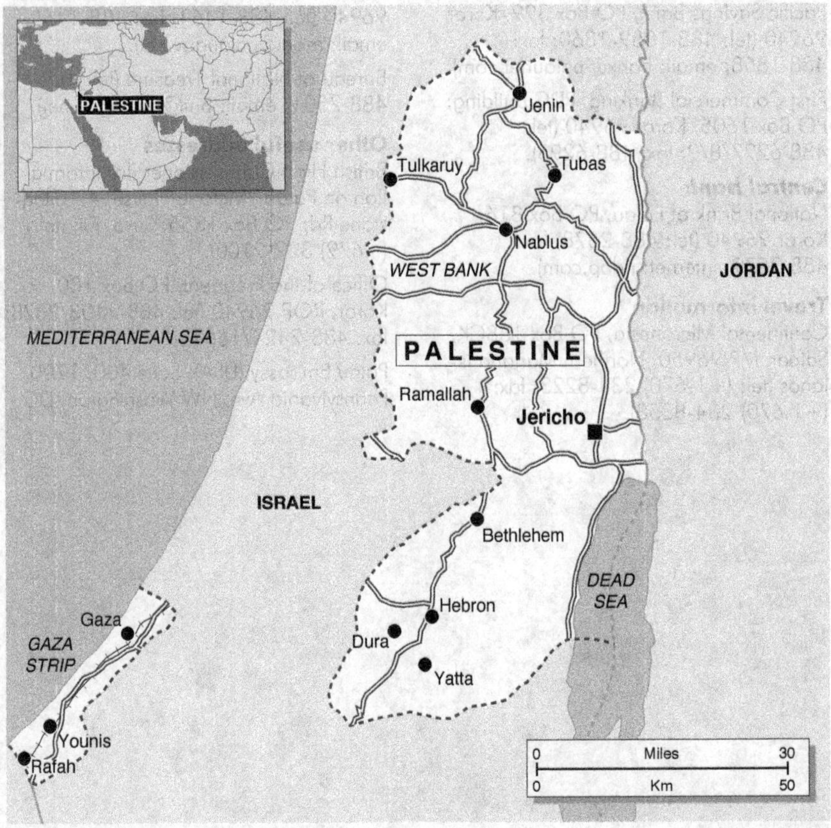

It was Robert Frost who wrote that 'Good fences make good neighbours'. Palestinians could be forgiven for disagreeing. Fenced in by Israel, with no dialogue taking place over their future, Palestinians could also be forgiven for feeling that violence, be it *Intifada* or unco-ordinated acts of desperation, was their only recourse. Over the years, too often the words hopes, dreams and aspirations feature in any discussion of the current state of affairs in Palestine; this is no exception.

Hopes dashed

Any hopes that might have been inspired by the cooling of relations between President Obama and the newly re-elected (March 2015) Benjamin Netanyahu had soon faded. However, the US government and an exasperated Secretary of State John Kerry, had none the less appeared to tolerate the unpredictable behaviour of Israel's prime minister. The baggage that came with that behaviour was heavy: it represented the Israeli government's ambition to place the prospect of an independent Palestinian state beyond reach. Whether this would provide one iota more of collective Israeli happiness was at best doubtful. That it would condemn Palestinians to living in a fenced in world where they could neither participate nor exercise control, was certain. And the neighbours, the Jordanians, the Lebanese, the Iranians and eventually the Syrians, would continue to harbour resentment.

In the run-up to Israel's 17 March 2015 elections, Mr Netanyahu had revealed his true colours when he called on Israeli Jews to vote in response to the votes of 'droves of Israeli Arabs who would be rushing to the polls.' The fact that this was a reference by Israel's head of government to one fifth of his country's population did not appear to be of significance.

Mr Netanyahu's pre-election dismissal of a two state solution was also seen as a vote-winner in a close run election. After the election Mr Netanyahu apologised for his remarks, but the damage had been done.

Palestinian politicians considered Mr Netanyahu's remarks to vindicate their unilateral strategy of pursuing statehood outside the rather tired US formula of fruitless discussions and frequent failures to even get round the same table. Omar Baghouti of Palestine's Boycott movement announced that 'the mask has fallen' from Mr Netanyahu's overt position, adding that 'The rift between the White House and Israel is opening up space for criticism of Israel that was not there before.'

In April 2015, there were rumours that some EU countries, lead by Sweden, were planning to table a UN Resolution that would still feature a two states solution – Israel alongside an independent Palestine based on the territory that Israel had won in the 1967 Arab-Israeli war. In October 2014 Sweden took the decision to become the first EU member state to formally recognise Palestine. Sweden's newly (October 2014) elected Prime Minister Stefan Löfven went so far as to make a specific reference to Palestine in his parliamentary investiture, saying that 'The conflict between Israel and Palestine can only be resolved by a two-state solution.' Despite its rejection by Israel and the United States in November 2012 Palestine was granted, by a substantial majority, non-member observer status at the United Nations. This was generally perceived as a *de-facto* recognition. Although there were already seven member countries that 'officially' recognised Palestine, this was an inheritance from the days of Soviet hegemony.

Mr Löfven did not spell out the timing of the Swedish recognition of Palestine, but no parliamentary move would be necessary. His predecessor, the ex-prime minister, Fredrik Reiner, had adhered to what had long been the European Union (EU) attitude to Palestinian recognition. This pointed out that the Palestinian authorities did not control the territory in question. Sweden's change of heart represented something of a boost for Palestine. Sweden was known as an international mediator and carried some weight within the EU. Israel's riposte to the arguments for Palestinian independence was that any decision on Palestinian independence, or even on its recognition, cannot simply be taken unilaterally. It should be, according to Israel, the result of negotiations between the two parties. While Palestine's representative in Sweden welcomed the decision, in Israel there was 'no comment'.

The next steps for the Obama administration on Palestine – if there are to be any – were unclear. In 2014 the US had blocked a draft UN Security Council resolution that called for a Palestinian state within three years. In the game of chess that the negotiations, or the lack of them, represented, a putative timetable had become an important component. Without it and knowing that the Obama administration was approaching election year, Mr Netanyahu could sit and watch from the side-lines knowing that neither the Democratic Party nor, even less so, its Republican counterpart, whichever candidate they ultimately elected, would risk jeopardising the all important Jewish vote.

Palestinian divisions

Mid-June 2015 saw Palestine's President Mahmud Abbas announce the 'definitive' dissolution of the unity government between his Al Fatah nationalist movement and the Hamas Islamists. In 2014 the two factions had managed to put together a government consisting of 18 technocrats headed by Rami Hamdallah as prime minister.

Despite the existence of this government, Hamas had continued to control the Gaza strip alone. The strip was home to 1.8 million Palestinians and since its *coup* in 2007, Hamas had been in charge. In mid-June 2015, Mr Hamdallah tendered his resignation to President Abbas, although the latter was thought to have it in mind to ask him to form another coalition government in which the ministers would once again be politicians and which would count on support from a number of political factions including Hamas.

At the same time, in late June, the Middle East's rumour mill was buzzing with stories of contacts and meetings between Hamas and Israeli representatives. The apparent objective was a long term truce in exchange for some sort of economic regularisation of the Gaza Strip. Writing on the website *Al-Monitor* Uri Savir noted that there had been no denial of the stories by the Israeli government. The rumours apparently reflected Israeli government leaks and media rumours about the negotiations. The former foreign minister, Avigdor Liberman, had accused the Israeli Prime Minister Benjamin Netanyahu on a number of occasions of 'surrendering to terror'.

Truce deal?

In June 2015 a source reportedly close to Mr Netanyahu had told *Al Monitor* (on condition of anonymity) that proposals for a truce deal were being circulated between the Israeli prime minister and defence minister's offices and the Hamas leadership in Gaza, via the Egyptian intelligence services, but also directly between Israeli and Palestinian security forces on the ground. Additionally, the topic had also been raised in the late June 2015 talks between Turkish and Israeli officials in Rome.

It seemed, however, that the talks might falter over practicalities rather than principles. An official in the Palestinian Authority had said that Hamas wanted the establishment of a Gaza international airport, as well as a harbour, that the frontier crossings between Gaza and Israel and between Egypt and Gaza be open for 24 hours and that there be free movement of goods with Egypt. It was hardly surprising that in the early stages of negotiation there existed major differences. The discussion of missile disarmament and the halting of tunnel construction (between Egypt and Gaza) was not on the table. As a *quid pro quo* for the return of the bodies of the two Israel Defence Force soldiers who died during the 2014 Gaza war, Hamas demanded a wider ranging prisoner exchange. On the practicalities, Israel would only agree to a floating harbour that would be established offshore and to a more limited opening of the crossings. Israel also required the return of the remains of the two soldiers.

While the gaps between the two parties were apparently substantial, the picture that emerged was nevertheless one of a curious convergence of interests between Israel and Hamas. In 2015 Hamas found itself fighting – in two cases literally – on three fronts. Its three 'enemies' were Israel, the so-called Islamic State (IS) and, even closer to home, the Fatah West Bank Palestinian Authority. Hamas was obviously interested in reconstructing Gaza economically, if only to improve its legitimacy among Gazans. Hamas also saw a truce deal and the restoration of the Gazan economy as something of a trump card to play against the more orthodox President Abbas and the Fatah movement. It was also in Hamas' interest to resuscitate the dormant European aid programme with a view to generating interest in investing in the economic development of Gaza. A truce with Israel might improve things in this respect.

As for Mr Netanyahu, whatever he had said about Hamas, it remained in his interest to avoid regular military conflicts with Hamas and the continued – if largely ineffective – missile attacks on Israeli cities. It was thought by Gaza's Hamas politicians that, on a divide and rule principle, Mr Netanyahu would probably opt for a strengthening of Hamas at the expense of President Abbas. For Israel, resolving some of its issues with Gaza might mean containing Gaza's politicians and preventing the establishment of what he had referred to as a 'Hamastan' on the West Bank.

Meanwhile, the Egyptian government appeared to have softened its position on Gaza, probably in the light of apparently closer relations between Hamas and Shi'a Iran. Cairo had insisted that Hamas end its support for terror acts in the Sinai desert against Egyptian troops, in return for the re-opening of the Rafah crossing.

Whither Hamas?

Hamas had come to power after winning the 2006 parliamentary elections. Paradoxically, although it has fought three wars against Israel, it has on occasion shown itself prepared to negotiate with Israel. This, however, rendered it a target for miscellaneous groupings of Salafists, ultraconservative Muslims who see Hamas as too secular and too soft on Israel. The extremists had targeted Hamas members and even bombed Internet cafes and video stores that were deemed to be 'immoral'. In 2009, when the leader of the al Qaeda-linked Jund Ansar Allah group declared an 'Islamic emirate' in the southern city of Rafah, Hamas gunmen promptly stormed his mosque, killing him and dozens of supporters. Other Salafi groups got the message and the violence subsided. Hamas' officials described this as a problem of *takfiri*, a term used to describe extremists who accuse other Muslims of apostasy. This was, none the less, a generational problem within Hamas. Its younger members considered it 'soft' on Israel, but the older militants who had been round this particular block several times, knew better.

For roughly six months, following the 2014 war with Israel, Salafi extremists waged a campaign of bombings and assassinations in Gaza. Although their numbers were small and casualties had been low, the campaign threatened to jeopardise the fragile cease-fire with Israel. None the less, the new radical groups had found a degree of support from within Hamas itself. The militants had for the most part turned out to be former members of the al Qassam Brigades, the armed wing of Hamas. Defections to more militant groups risked fracturing Hamas, already divided about whether to return to war with Israel. Especially as Hamas' relatively moderate political leadership was (see above) rumoured to be discussing a long-term truce with Israel. Eighty per cent of those joining the extremist groups were thought to have defected from one of the Hamas resistance factions, angry that the war had not been continued. Collectively, they shared the idea that there should be no agreements between Hamas and Israel.

The economy suffers, the restrictions remain

Re-opening the Rafah crossing had, for those living in Gaza a symbolic as well as a practical significance. According to the World Bank, even prior to the conflict, growth had slowed from 6 per cent in 2012 to about 2 per cent in 2013 as a result of political uncertainty, a reduction in aid, the ongoing restrictions on the movement of people and goods and the collapse of tunnel activity between Gaza and Egypt. The 2014 conflict in July-August 2014 caused an estimated US$2.8 billion in damages. The World Bank had described Gaza's economy as 'on the verge of collapse'.

The Gaza economy had contracted by nearly 15 per cent as a result of the conflict, whereas the economy in the West Bank had grown by 4.5 per cent in 2014, but the growth was driven primarily by new building construction. Overall, in 2014 the Palestinian economy contracted and entered recession. Continued negative growth in Gaza had a severe effect on unemployment, causing it to go up to 43 per cent. Youth unemployment in Gaza was estimated by the World Bank to be a 'staggering' 60 per cent. Taken together, unemployment in the West Bank and Gaza increased in 2014 to 27 per cent. Donors' aid for budget support had been uneven since its peak in 2008 and the fiscal adjustments put in place to mitigate the dropping aid flows had not been commensurate. The Palestinian Authority (PA)'s already difficult fiscal position had been exacerbated by the Gaza conflict. The fiscal pressures threatened the provision of public services and any institutional development gains made by the PA. The World Bank noted that this state of decline could be reversed in an environment where sustainable, private sector-led growth was fostered, coupled with a greater commitment of ongoing financial support from the international community. A dynamic private sector could, in the view of the World Bank, generate the sustainable growth needed. However, the World Bank also noted that restrictions put in place by the government of Israel continued to stand in the way of potential private investment. Access to Gaza remained highly controlled and much of Area C, which makes up 60 per cent of the West Bank, was inaccessible to Palestinians.

According to The Israeli Information Centre for Human Rights in the Occupied Territories (B'Tselem), Israel maintained almost complete control of this area, including on security matters and all land-related civil matters, including land allocation, planning and construction and infrastructure. Which doesn't leave very much. The PA was responsible for providing education and medical services to Area C's Palestinian population. Critically, however, construction and maintenance of the infrastructure necessary for these services remained in Israel's hands. Civil matters remained under Israeli control in Area C and were the responsibility of the Civil Administration. B'Tselem noted that Israel prohibited Palestinian construction and development on some 70 per cent of Area C territory, 'arguing various rationales, such as being 'state lands' or 'firing zones'. According to B'Tselem Israel's planning and construction policy 'virtually ignores the needs of the local population: it refuses to recognise most of the villages in the area or draw up plans for them, prevents the expansion and development of Palestinian communities, demolishes homes and does not allow the communities to hook up to infrastructure.' Thus, thousands of inhabitants live under the constant threat of expulsion. In addition, Israel had taken over most of the water sources in Area C and had restricted Palestinian access to them.

In January 2015 the International Monetary Fund (IMF) conducted its annual assessment of the Palestinian economy. The IMF also noted that economic activity had contracted in 2014, following the war in Gaza in the summer and the mounting political tensions in the West Bank and East Jerusalem. The IMF estimated that gross domestic product (GDP) fell by nearly one per cent, the first contraction since 2006, with GDP declining by as much as 15 per cent in Gaza but rising by 4.5 per cent in the West Bank, with a sharp slowdown in the third quarter. Unemployment rates remained at high levels, reaching an estimated 41 per cent in Gaza and 19 per cent in the West Bank. Despite the difficult economic and political situation of 2014, the PA had maintained its efforts to keep the fiscal deficit in check, helped by strong revenue performance.

However, in the view of the IMF, a high degree of uncertainty and various headwinds were likely to prevent a strong economic recovery in 2015. The most notable factor was what the IMF described as the 'non-transfer to the PA' of clearance revenues collected by Israel on goods imported into the West Bank and Gaza. These represented about two-thirds of net revenues and were essential to the PA's budget and to the Palestinian economy. Reduced wage payments and other public spending cuts necessitated by the suspension of clearance revenues in the presence of financing constraints were likely to cause a sharp reduction in private consumption and investment. In addition, the reconstruction of Gaza after the war was proceeding more slowly than expected, reflecting insufficient progress on national reconciliation and unfulfilled donor pledges. The IMF expected GDP in 2015 to rise only modestly, with a possible pickup in Gaza from a low base and a drop of nearly 2 per cent in the West Bank, although the sharp fall in oil prices provided some relief to energy consumers. Medium-term growth would remain modest, unless there was an improvement in the political climate that would lead to a lifting of restrictions in the West Bank and of the blockade in Gaza.

However, the IMF noted that the continuing fiscal crisis exacerbated by the withholding of clearance revenue could deepen. The absence of clearance revenue would inevitably lead to a curtailment of wages and allowances, cuts in non-wage spending, further borrowing from the banking system, or additional arrears accumulation. In this context, reduced salary payments should be differentiated so as to minimise the impact on lower income earners. Assistance from donors was needed to provide bridge financing in the absence of the clearance revenues. For 2015 as a whole, even assuming a resumption of clearance revenue transfers, the IMF projected a large financing gap that called for a prudent fiscal stance, with strict restraint on public sector wages. Taking into account the humanitarian consequences, the IMF recommended safeguarding transfers to the poor and to vulnerable households and social assistance in Gaza, where the humanitarian situation was particularly dire. Moreover, the IMF considered that contingency measures should be in place in case the suspension of clearance revenue extended beyond a few months.

In this volatile environment, the IMF also considered safeguarding financial stability to remain a priority. The Palestine Monetary Authority (central bank) has made considerable progress in risk-based supervision and enhancing crisis preparedness. While the financial system was sound and well capitalised, the high exposure of the banking system to the PA and its employees 'called for vigilance', especially given the clearance revenue suspension.

The IMF concluded by pointing out that efforts by the PA could only contain the crisis for a few months. The situation could become untenable, with a growing risk of social unrest and strikes that could lead to political instability. These serious risks could be mitigated if Israel quickly resumed transfers of clearance revenue.

The water question

Access to water has for some time been an issue in Palestine. Israel began controlling Palestinian water resources as long ago as 1948, initially by restricting the development of wells and water springs as well as developing existing resources for use by settlements and for agricultural purposes often at the expense of the Palestinians. In the mid-1960s, Israel also began to exploit the water of the Jordan River basin that feeds the Dead Sea, diverting the water to settlements in Negev and to settlements south of Palestine through the National Water Carrier System. Lake Hula in northern Palestine was also drained. After the occupation of the Golan Heights, the West Bank and the Gaza Strip in 1967, Israeli control over water resources increased. A passive, but effective, administration of water developed whereby drilling was controlled through drilling permissions, diverting springs and the tight regulation of licences until some 90 per cent of Palestinian water resources were subject to civil and military orders and legislation. The water issue was moved to final-status negotiations within the framework of the Oslo Accord due to its importance and complexity. However, demographics in both Palestine and Israel suggest that the future of water in Palestine is not encouraging. This was especially the case within the Gaza Strip, where it had been reported that 97 per cent of the coastal aquifer water was unfit for human use because of seawater intrusion and leakage of sewage water. By 2017 there would probably no longer be usable water in Gaza. Some experts expected the aquifer to be exhausted by 2020.

According to the Palestinian Water Authority (PWA), only 5.8 per cent of Palestinian families in the Gaza Strip considered their water to be drinkable. By contrast, 73.5 per cent of Palestinian families in the West Bank said that their water was drinkable. Overall, 48.8 per cent of all Palestinian families in both the West Bank and the Gaza Strip consider their water to be good enough to drink. Quoted on *Al Monitor*, Abdul Rahman al Tamimi, the president of the Water Committee of the Economic and Social Commission for Western Asia (ESCWA) had said that 'Nothing is left of Palestinian water rights. The Palestinians have become customers for the Israeli Mekorot Water Company. Instead of demanding our rights back, we are now seeking to buy larger quantities of water from the Israelis. We now depend on the Israeli Mekorot Company.' Mr Ghoneim said the West Bank alone consumed 104 million cubic meters of drinking water yearly, of which 22 million cubic meters are pumped from the PWA's wells, 32 million cubic meters are pumped from the municipalities and 50 million cubic meters are purchased from Israel for approximately US$50 million per year.

The ICC answer?

On 1 April 2015 Palestine became a member of the International Criminal Court (ICC) in The Hague. Israel, which is not a member, had opposed Palestinian membership and had announced that it had no plans to co-operate with the courts investigators looking into possible war crimes committed by both sides during the 2014 war in Gaza. Membership of the ICC was considered to be the most significant and the most controversial step in Palestine's recently developed strategy of eventually obtaining full statehood through the membership of respected international bodies such as the ICC. Legal experts considered it unlikely that there would ever be any trial on the war crimes issue, as some degree of prior certainty would first be necessary but unlikely in the case of the Gaza conflict. None the less, Palestine's membership of the ICC represented a serious irritation for Israel. In addition Israel risked being called to account over its continued construction of settlements in the occupied West Bank. On joining the ICC, the Palestinian foreign minister, Riad al Malki, declared that 'the world is a step closer to ending a long era of impunity and injustice.'

Although Palestinian membership in the court did not ensure any ICC investigation, let alone indictments, any report produced by the ICC's senior prosecutor, Fatou Bensouda, was likely to be bad news for Israel, even though it might *inter alia* find that Palestine had also offended. Palestine's ICC membership, the recent Gaza conflict and Israel's election result have all increased the possibility of a confrontation between Israel's leaders and the international court. There was even a small but real chance that the ICC could end up indicting senior Israeli officials.

The war crimes allegations against Israel had focussed on its military actions in the Gaza Strip in mid-2014, which resulted in over 1,800 Palestinian deaths, the majority of them civilians. Human rights groups had criticised Israel for employing excessive force and targeting civilian buildings and homes. For their part, Israeli officials insisted they conducted the war as carefully as possible given Hamas's policy of mingling with and sheltering behind the civilian population.

However, Israel had an important line of defence, namely that it was already investigating its own conduct. Not long after the fighting began, the Israeli Defence Forces (IDF) had initiated an internal investigation of civilian deaths and possible violations of humanitarian law. As the ICC's rules require it to defer to genuine national investigations, any indictments against Israel based on the Gaza fighting are unlikely. The Palestinians could not claim that any similar self-investigation process was under way or ever likely to be. From a legal point of view the most sensitive issue for Israel was not so much its behaviour during the Gaza war, but the well documented illegal settlements in the West Bank. The ICC's statutes were wide ranging, listing as a war crime 'the transfer, directly or indirectly, by the Occupying Power of parts of its own civilian population into the territory it occupies.' Israeli lines of legal defence had been based on the uncertainties surrounding exactly who was sovereign in Palestine before the occupation.

Much of the ICC's weight was in Palestine's favour as far as initiating any action against Israel went. The ICC statute gave the United Nations Security Council the power to delay an investigation for up to a year. Given the strained relations between President Obama and Prime Minister Netanyahu, it was no longer certain that the US would opt for delaying. However, were it to do so, it would need to secure the support of the other four veto-wielding members as well as several non-permanent members. This support was by no means certain. Even if it were, the council could only delay a court investigation for a year and would then have to renew the deferral annually.

Although Israel has an active, respected and independent judiciary, the supreme Israeli court has repeatedly avoided the question of whether Israeli settlements in the West Bank are legal. In a series of cases, the Supreme Court has fudged the issue, deciding that settlements are a political question that should be resolved through international negotiations.

Passing judgement on settlements would place Israel's Supreme Court into its most sensitive position ever. But Palestine's membership of the ICC began to narrow the options. Were the settlements policy to be declared illegal, it would obviously be better for Israelis to hear it from Jerusalem than from The Hague.

Risk assessment

Politics	Poor
Economy	Catastrophic
Regional stability	None

Muslims in Palestine

% of population	85
Sunni (% of Muslims)	99
Shi'a (% of Muslims)	1

COUNTRY PROFILE

1915 Palestinians accepted the McMahon-Hussein Agreement in October 1915. Under the Agreement the British promised that after the First World War, land previously held by the Turks would be returned to the Arab nationals who lived in that land.

1916 In May two diplomats, Sir Mark Sykes (British) and Georges Picot (French), concluded a secret agreement covering the partition of the Ottoman Empire after the First World War. Officially the Asia Minor Agreement, it is more commonly known as the Sykes-Picot Agreement. In essence the Agreement gave governmental and administrative control of Syria, Lebanon and Turkish Cilicia to the French, and Palestine, Jordan and areas around the Persian Gulf and Baghdad to the British. The Agreement differed from the McMahon Agreement of 1915, and with statements made by T E Lawrence to the Arabs who had expected to be allowed to govern their own regions after helping the Allies fight the Turks during First World War. The Agreement (which remained secret until released by the Russians after the 1917 Boshevik Revolution) was never completely fulfilled, and lead to deep mistrust of the British and French governments.

1917 The Balfour Declaration suggested the establishment in Palestine of a national home for the Jewish people.

1922 The Council of the League of Nations assigned to Britain a mandate for the Ottoman Arab territory of Palestine, a region that covered present-day Israel and Jordan, plus the Golan Heights region (claimed by Syria). The British divided the mandate into two parts, designating all lands west of the Jordan River as Palestine and those easts of the river as Transjordan. The League of Nations mandate also addressed the goal of restoring a Jewish homeland in Palestine.

1929 Riots in Jerusalem between Arab Palestinians and Jews were sparked by a dispute over the use of the western wall of the Al Aqsa Mosque (the site is sacred to Muslims, and Jews claim it as part of their temple).

1936–39 The Arab Higher Committee opposed Jewish immigration to Palestine and the Peel Commission concluded that the mandate was unworkable. Legislation limiting the number of Jewish immigrants was introduced by the British government.

1945 Many of the Jews who had survived the Nazi German Holocaust arrived and Jewish extremists began to oppose Britain's immigration legislation.

1946 Transjordan became independent and was later re-named Jordan.

1947 Britain decided to leave. The UN adopted Resolution 181, which called for the establishment of both Jewish and Arab states within Palestine and a partition plan was drawn up, based solely on population, with Jerusalem as an international zone under UN jurisdiction. The Jews agreed to the partition; the Arabs did not.

1948 Conflict ensued between Arabs and Jews. Jewish leaders announced the formation of the State of Israel, open to the immigration of Jews from all countries. Egypt, Iraq, Lebanon, Syria and Jordan joined Palestinian and other Arab guerrillas and invaded Israel. The armistice agreements extended the territory under Israel's control beyond the UN partition boundaries. Many Arabs became refugees in surrounding Arab countries, ending the Arab majority in the new Jewish state. Palestinians refer to this period as *al Nakkba*, the catastrophe.

1957 Harakat al Tahir al Watani al Falistin (Al Fatah) (Movement for the National Liberation of Palestine) was formed by Arab students, including Yasser Arafat – an Egyptian Palestinian, who grew up in the Gaza Strip.

1964 The Palestine Liberation Organisation (PLO) was founded in Egypt as a Palestinian nationalist umbrella organisation dedicated to the establishment of an

independent Palestinian state; later, it operated from Lebanon.
1967 Israel launched and won the Six Day War against Egypt, Jordan and Syria, taking control of the Sinai peninsular and the Gaza Strip, which had been Egyptian territory, together with the Golan Heights, formerly claimed by Syria. Around 300,000 Palestinian Arabs fled to Jordan. After the Six-Day War, control of the PLO devolved to the leadership of the various fedayeen militia groups, the most dominant of which was Yasser Arafat's Al Fatah. Israel's settlement policy started; it occupied the Sinai peninsular (returned to Egypt in 1982), the Golan Heights, the Gaza Strip and the West Bank, including East Jerusalem; the Jews transferred to these areas became known as settlers.
1969 Arafat was appointed chairman of the PLO's Executive Committee.
1970 Civil war (Black September) between the Jordanian army and Palestinians followed airplane hijackings by a Palestinian resistance group. The PLO was forcefully expelled from its bases in Jordan and moved to Lebanon.
1973 Lebanon was used by the Palestinians as a base for activities against Israel. In retaliation, Israeli commandos raided Beirut, killing three associates of Yasser Arafat. Arab states officially recognised the PLO as the representative of the Palestinians.
1981 Israel annexed East Jerusalem.
1982–85 Israel invaded Lebanon to prevent the PLO from carrying out armed resistance to its rule in the occupied territories of the Gaza Strip and the West Bank. A Western multinational force monitored the evacuation of the PLO; it relocated to Tunis, where it stayed until it moved to the Palestinian autonomous areas (Gaza and Jericho) in 1994.
1987 The Palestinians launched an *intifida* (uprising) against the Israelis. The Harakat al Muqawama al Islamia (Hamas) (Islamic Resistance Movement) was formed in the Gaza Strip, with two objectives: armed resistance to Israeli rule in the West Bank and the Gaza Strip and the establishment of a sovereign, independent state located in historic Palestine (present-day Israel, the West Bank, and the Gaza Strip). There was an upsurge in violence as large numbers of Jews from the Soviet Union began to settle in the West Bank and the Gaza Strip.
1988 The State of Palestine was declared, as outlined in the UN partition plan 181, the new state being recognised only by states that did not recognise Israel.
1993–95 The Oslo Peace Accords laid the basis for transfer of authority from the Israeli military administration to the PLO in the Gaza Strip and an undefined area around the town of Jericho in the West Bank. A follow-up treaty, Oslo II, was signed, which envisaged Palestinian autonomy with Israeli troop units withdrawing from the West Bank.
1996 Yasser Arafat was elected president of the Palestinian Legislative Council (PLC), the assembly of the Palestinian Authority (PA).
1998 The Wye peace agreement between the Israelis and the Palestinians, brokered by the US, ended 19 months of deadlock in the peace process.
2000 Israel agreed to allow the PA to control 39.8 per cent of the West Bank. However, after Israel's right-wing opposition leader, Ariel Sharon, visited the Temple Mount in Jerusalem and reiterated Israel's claims to Muslim holy places in the city, a second *intifada* was launched and a total blockade was imposed by Israel on the West Bank and Gaza.
2001 Israel declared the PA to be a terrorist-supporting organisation and launched Operation 'Defensive Shield', invading the PA-controlled West Bank and Gaza, attacking its institutions and besieging Arafat's headquarters. Deaths in Israel by Palestinian suicide bombers increased.
2002 Saudi Arabia proposed a peace initiative and a UN Security Council resolution endorsed a Palestinian state and called for the cessation of hostilities. Israel besieged Arafat's compound in Ramallah and reoccupied most of the West Bank. For five weeks the Israeli army surrounded militants and civilians taking sanctuary in the Church of the Nativity in Bethlehem; it ended when 13 militants were sent into exile. Israel began building a wall as a barrier between it and Gaza claiming it was the only way to control infiltration of militant terrorists.
2003 The US proposed a *Road Map to Peace*, with a cease-fire and end to Jewish settlements in the occupied territories and the creation of an independent Palestinian state by 2005. Ahmed Qureia became prime minister.
2004 Israel's Sharon, declared he would remove all Jewish settlements in Gaza. President Yasser Arafat became ill and died in Paris.
2005 Mahmoud Abbas was elected president of the Palestinian Authority by an overwhelming majority. He persuaded Hamas and Islamic Jihad to agree an unofficial cease-fire. At the Sharm el Sheikh summit in Egypt, a truce was signed by Sharon and Abbas, ending four years of violence between Israel and Palestine. President Abbas and the Israeli cabinet approved the removal of Jewish settlers from Gaza and parts of the West Bank.
2006 Parliamentary elections were won convincingly by Hamas with a majority of 74 seats. Ismail Haniya was appointed prime minister and the new Hamas-dominated parliament revoked legislation passed by the previous Fatah-dominated parliament, which had given increased powers to the president, including the right to allocate key administrative posts to Fatah members. Hamas refused to recognise Israel, renounce violence or accept previous agreements made by Fatah. International sanctions were imposed, which caused financial hardship as government benefits and wages went unpaid and supplies to hospitals ran out. The president undertook negotiations with Israel and Hamas in an attempt to broker an accommodation and allow financial aid to resume.
2007 Rival Hamas and Fatah gunmen began a deadly power struggle in the Gaza Strip, killing over 20 people. A new government of unity was announced by President Abbas and Prime Minister Haniya. A new cabinet was approved by the legislative council (83:3). The US and EU continued to withhold recognition of the unity government until it recognised the state of Israel and renounced violence. Violence erupted again and a power struggle resulted in Hamas gaining control of Gaza while local Hamas leaders fled to Egypt. The president, based in the West Bank, dismissed Prime Minister Haniya and appointed Salam Fayyad while announcing that he would rule by presidential decrees; Hamas officials rejected this decision. The president swore in his new cabinet in Ramallah and outlawed a Hamas paramilitary force (the Executive Force) and other allied militia. However presidential rule was not enforced in Gaza. The US signed an agreement to give the PA US$80 million towards reforming their security services. Israel imposed an economic embargo on Gaza after Hamas gained control of the territory and restricted Gaza Strip entry and exit. The number of humanitarian convoys for Gaza halved from 3,000 to 1,500. Israel imposed further Gaza sanctions on fuel and energy supplies in retaliation for rockets fired into Israel. Palestinian leaders claimed this amounted to collective punishment (a war crime under the Geneva Convention). The Israeli Supreme Court agreed that cutbacks in fuel were legal but that a cut-back in electricity supplies had to be delayed. A US$7 billion foreign aid package was agreed by donor countries, to help underpin a viable Palestinian state and avoid bankruptcy. Hamas, which did not attend the conference, rejected the measures and although money was designated for Gaza the territory did not benefit from the aid. The World Bank warned that unless Israel lifted its system of restrictions on the movement of goods, finance and

Palestinian people the measures could not rebuild the economy.
2008 Following an Israeli army operation against Hamas forces in Gaza, 200 rockets were fired into Israel and in response, Israel imposed power cuts on Gaza. Petrol for vehicles and fuel for the Hamas-run power plant in the Gaza Strip were reduced. Within days the UNHCR called the situation in Gaza desperate; adding that electricity provided by generators in hospitals was only able to power equipment and could not provide the heating necessary during winter. Following international disquiet Israel eased the blockade of energy supplies while Palestinian militants exploded holes in the border wall near the Rafah crossing between Gaza and Egypt allowing thousands of people to cross and stock up on essential supplies. Israel demanded that the border be closed to prevent the restocking of militant's armouries. Egypt rejected the demand, allowing access on humanitarian grounds. George Habbash, founder of the radical Popular Front for the Liberation of Palestine (PFLP), died. Egypt closed the Rafah border, but other openings elsewhere were made and hundreds more Palestinians continued to cross into Egypt. Hamas and Egyptian officials reached an agreement, whereby all Palestinians would return to Gaza, except those seeking medical treatment in Egypt and those travelling to a third country. Following a speech by US President Bush, President Abbas accused the US of bias towards Israel, as Bush said that the Arab world had to reform and the US was Israel's closest ally. Mahmoud Darwish, Palestine's respected poet and author of its 1988 declaration of independence, died. President Abbas extended his term in office until 2010. Israel began a bombardment of and then an offensive on the Gaza Strip.
2009 Over 1,000 Palestinians were estimated to have been killed and 4,700 wounded in Israel's offensive, with an estimated 35,000 people displaced. UN and EU representatives called for a halt to the military action and for the supply of humanitarian aid to be allowed. Israel agreed to a daily aid convoy during a three-hour cease-fire. After Israel declared a cease-fire, Hamas announced that it would stop launching missiles into Israel. The UN estimated that rebuilding in the Gaza Strip would cost around US$1.9 billion. A large stockpile of 7,000kg of unexploded ordnance (UXO), gathered up and held under the supervision of Gaza-Hamas officials, was stolen. Included in the stockpile were white phosphorus shells and 2,000 pound and 500 pound bombs. The US announced that it would donate US$900 million in aid towards the recovery of the Gaza Strip; the money would not be given to Hamas, but rather to non-governmental organisations (NGOs) and the PA. By the time of a cease-fire, 90 per cent of Gaza's residents had only intermittent electricity and 50,000 people were without mains water. The border with Israel was closed to all but essential supplies while peace negotiations continued. At an international donor conference held to support the rebuilding of the Gaza Strip, US$4.5 billion was pledged. The money was offered to the PA and not Hamas. Following an investigation by the UN Human Rights Council, the legality of Israel's three-week offensive in Gaza was questioned. The Council determined that there had been a disproportionate use of force by Israel – the overall ratio of deaths was 1,434 in Gaza (the Palestinian authorities broke the numbers down as 960 civilians, 239 uniformed police and 235 'fighters') to 13 in Israel. Israel accused the Council of seeking to 'demonise' it and later challenged the number of dead as 1,166, of which 709 were 'terror operatives'. The UN appointed Richard Goldstone, a South African judge and former war crimes prosecutor, as its investigator into alleged violations of international law during Israel's conflict in the Gaza Strip. The UN inquiry into attacks on UN property during the Israeli Gaza offensive accused the Israeli army of six incidents of taking 'inadequate' precautions to protect the premises and causing deaths and injuries of people sheltering inside. Hamas was accused of one attack. The exiled leader of the Palestinian Hamas in Gaza, Khaled Meshaal, rejected the terms for a Palestinian state as proposed by Israeli Prime Minister Netanyahu. Conditions for the state included demilitarisation and recognition of Israel as a Jewish state. Meshaal said this was 'merely self-governance under the name of a country'.
The International Red Cross reported that 1.5 million people living in Gaza were unable to rebuild their lives as they had no access to building materials and the water supply and sanitation system are near to collapse. Poverty was described as at an 'alarming' level and medical treatment was limited. President Abbas, whose tenure as President officially came to an end on 9 January, announced that presidential and parliamentary elections in all Palestinian territories were scheduled for 2010. Hamas rejected this saying that any ruling by what it saw as an unconstitutionally sitting president could not be legitimate. The elections were postponed. In Gaza Aziz Duwaik, as speaker of the PLC, is considered by many in the Gaza Strip to be the acting President of the Palestinian National Authority.
2010 After Israel added the Tomb of the Patriarchs in Hebron to their list of national heritage sites the Palestinian cabinet met in Hebron as a sign of protest. The first commercial and privately-organised convoy of goods (clothes and shoes) since 2005 was allowed into the Gaza Strip, following pressure on the Israeli government by both the UN and EU to lift its blockade. Nine activists were killed by Israeli security forces when they stormed a ship in international waters; it had been attempting to break the blockade of Gaza. The attack led to UN condemnation. Israel announced that it would ease the Gaza Strip blockade and allow more civilian items into the territory. Palestine and Israel agreed to resume peace talks after a two year gap, which began between Israeli Prime Minister Netanyahu and President Mohmoud Abbas in Washington, hosted by President Obama and chaired by US Secretary of State, Hillary Clinton. The negotiations began with a dinner at the White House, which President Mubarak of Egypt and King Abdullah of Jordan also attended.
2011 In March, thousands joined matching demonstrations of unity in Gaza City and Ramallah (West Bank), calling for an end to the political deadlock between Hamas and Fatah. A group of 21 prominent Israelis signed an open letter in May calling on the international community to recognise a Palestinian state in Jerusalem, the West Bank and Gaza. From May the Egyptian government relaxed restrictions at the Rafah border crossing with the Gaza Strip, allowing women, children and men over 40 to pass freely. Men aged between 18 and 40 still require a permit, and trade is prohibited. An agreement was reached between Fatah and Hamas in May, aimed at ending their division. A UN report, published in June, put unemployment in Gaza at 45.2 per cent, one of the world's highest rates. In August, President Abbas announced that in September the Palestinian territories would submit an application to the UN for international recognition of statehood. The recognition would as an independent, sovereign state as the West Bank, Gaza Strip and East Jerusalem. Despite pressure from other members, including US President Obama, President Abbas formally applied for membership of the UN. In October the board of the cultural agency Unesco agreed to put forward to its member states Palestine's bid for full membership. A prisoner swap deal between the Hamas and the Israeli government involving the young Israeli soldier, Gilad Shalit, and 'hundreds' of Palestinian prisoners was agreed in the Israeli parliament by 26–3 votes in October. Sergeant Shalit had been held for five years. In

November, Hamas and Fatah agreed to parliamentary elections, to be held in May 2012, following power-sharing talks held in Egypt. Members of opposing factions will be released by either side before preparations for the elections are undertaken.
2012 An agreement between the ruling factions of Hamas (Gaza Strip) and Fatah (West Bank) was achieved on 7 February, in which President Abbas would lead a government of unity, ahead of elections in both regions. The first exports of goods from the Gaza Strip since 2007 began on 5 March. The shipment of 13 lorry loads of date bars to the West Bank was deemed a 'one-off pilot project' by the Israeli Army that maintains a blockade of Gaza. On 23 March the US announced it was releasing US$88.6 million in development aid for the Palestinians that had been frozen for over six months. Local elections were held in May in the West Bank, but not in Gaza where the electoral commission was unable to operate. On 16 May, in Ramallah, President Abbas swore in a new cabinet for the PA, with Salam Fayyad remaining in post as prime minister. However, the expected government of unity, which combined members of the rival Fatah and Hamas factions failed to be formed. A Hamas spokesman considered the makeup of the new cabinet as a 'big error'. On 28 August, a murder inquiry into the death of Palestine and Fatah leader, Yasser Arafat, was opened by French investigators. Arafat had died in a French military hospital and his family claimed the poison polonium-210 had been used to kill him. On 23 October, the Emir of Qatar, Sheikh Hamad bin Khalifa al Thani, was the first head of state to visit the Gaza Strip since 2007 when Hamas took power. The Emir urged unity talks between Hamas and Fatah and pledged US$400 million on building projects in Gaza. On 1 November, an account by a former (and deceased) Israeli commando admitted that he had killed Abu Jihad (real name Khalil al Wazir) in Tunisia in 1988. Abu Jihad was Yasser Arafat's deputy and together they had set up the PLO. Hamas launched missiles at Israel on 4 November, Israel retaliated with air and artillery weapons on Gaza on 13 November, aimed at the Hamas leadership and weapons dumps. A ceasefire was agreed on 21 November. The body of Yasser Arafat was exhumed on 27 November for forensic analysis by French, Swiss and Russian experts, looking for evidence of radioactive polonium-120 poisoning. On 29 November, following a vote in the general assembly, the UN granted Palestine non-member observer status.
2013 Prime Minister Salam Fayyad resigned in April; he was replaced by Rami Hamdallah, who himself offered his resignation on 20 June, just two weeks after taking office. Although Mr Abbas accepted his resignation he immediately asked him to stay on as a caretaker premier. Six weeks later, he asked him to form a new government and on 18 September Mr Hamdallah and his 24-member cabinet were sworn in. On 22 July Mr Netanyahu said he would put any future peace deal with the Palestinians to a referendum. After months of shuttle diplomacy by US secretary of state John Kerry, Israeli and Palestinian negotiators resumed stalled (since 2010) peace talks about talks in Washington. As part of the deal the Israeli cabinet approved (by 13 votes to seven) the release of some 104 long-term Palestinian prisoners. The prisoners will be released in four stages over a number of months and will be linked to progress in the talks. The second of four groups of Palestinians, 26 who had served 19-28 years in prison, was freed on 30 October. On the same day Israel announced approval for the construction of 1,500 housing units at Ramat Shlomo. In November experts at the Vaudois University Hospital Centre (CHUV) in Lausanne said that samples taken from the exhumed body of Yaser Arafat contained 'unexpectedly high' amounts of polonium-210. They could not, however, confirm it had caused his death.
2014 A government of national consensus between Gaza and the West Bank was formed in early June. Gaza prime minister, Ismail Haniyeh, stepped down on 14 June to allow Rami Hamdallah to become the national consensus government prime minister.. In June Israel accused Hamas of the kidnapping and killing of three young Israelis, leading to a crackdown on Hamas in the West Bank. In a seeming revenge killing, on 2 July a young Palestinian was killed in Jerusalem. Six Israels were arrested. On 7 July Hamas admitted to firing rockets into Israel after Israel initiated a series or arial attacks on Gaza, killing several members of Hamas. There was an escalation of violence between the two sides and by 14 August the UN estimated that 1,973 Palestinians had been killed in Gaza, 70 per cent of whom were civilians, many of them children. In Israel, three civilians had been killed and 64 soldiers. The UN also estimated that since the Israel offensive had begun on 8 July there had been over 4,760 air strikes on Gaza and 3,488 rockets had been fired at Israel. Israel's protective rocket shield, Iron Dome, together with an extensive system of bomb shelters, were very effective in protecting its population and buildings, while the Gaza strip was severly damaged, including the distruction of the power plant that supplied power to most of the Strip.
Talks in Cairo were largely unproductive until an Egyptian proposal for a three-day truce was agreed on 4 August. Israel withdrew its troops and took up 'defensive positions' after destroying the tunnels that had been dug under the border. A surprise second three-day ceasefire was agreed on 10 August and Israeli negotiators arrived in Cairo for discussions with the Palestinan delegation. A further, five-day ceasefire, ending at midnight on 18 August, was agreed as the three-day ceasefire ended. The indirect talks in Cairo resumed on 18 August as the end of the five-day ceasefire approached. The peace talks are made difficult by Egypt's distrust of Hamas, and the US's refusal to talk with Hamas which they consider a terrorist group. The five-day ceasefire was extended by 24 hours to enable talks in Cairo to continue. The government of national consensus met in Gaza on 10 October, the first meeting it had held since its formation in June. The main item on the agenda was the arrangements for the reconstruction of Gaza, including co-ordination between government agencies and civil and international agencies. On 13 October the British parliament voted by 274 to 12 in favour of recognising Palestine as a state alongside Israel. The newly elected (3 October) centre-left government of Sweden led by Prime Minister Stefan Lofven also said that it would 'recognise the state of Palestine'. Israel sealed off the Al-Aqsa Mosque (Temple Mount) on 30 October, after an attack on a Jewish activist the previous day. Mahmoud Abbas said the closure was tantamount to a declaration of war. Jordan submitted a draft resolution to the UNSC on 17 December, setting out a timetable for a Palestinian peace deal with Israel. The document calls for a deal within one year and Israeli withdrawal from occupied territories by the end of 2017.
2015 On 17 November the Israeli government banned the Islamic Movement (IM). The IM is the main religious, political and social movement representing Palestinians in Israel. Palestinians make up some 20 per cent of the population of Israel, many of whom support the IM.

Political structure

Constitution

A provisional framework for the Palestinian state was approved by the Palestinian Legislative Council in a 1996 Draft Basic Law. This law will be fully endorsed when a permanent settlement is achieved.

Independence date

13 September 1993

Form of state
Parliamentary Democracy
The executive
Executive power is vested in the head of the Palestinian National Authority (PNA – also known as the Palestinian Authority (PA)), who is president, elected by direct universal suffrage for up to two four-year terms, and Head of State.
The president is head of armed and security forces, is responsible for initiating and proposing laws and foreign policy. The president appoints a prime minister, who forms a cabinet.
There have been no presidential elections in ten years, which renders Palestine undemocratic. Hamas rules the majority of the West Bank whilst the supposed Palestinian government and the President control the Gaza Strip. No common ground has been formed and in its current situation, Palestine is far being from a state in its own right.
National legislature
The schism between the Hamas-led Gaza Strip and the Fatah-led West Bank has resulted in two independently operating administrations, with Hamas operating without a Fatah elected executive and Fatah rejecting the authority of the Hamas dominated legislative council.
The unicameral Palestinian Legislative Council (PLC) was established in 1994 and is composed of 132 members plus the president as an *ex officio* member.
The PLC's members are elected in 16 multi-seat constituencies for 5-year terms.
The current situation in the State of Palestine renders its national legislature meaningless. No elections have been held to form a new parliament in nine years. The continued divide between Hamas and Fatah means that the State of Palestine does not even really exist.
Legal system
The Basic Law provides for an independent judiciary.
The High Judicial Council oversees the administration of a hierarchy of courts beginning with the magistrate courts, Courts of first Instance, Courts of Appeal and The Supreme Court.
Last elections
25 January 2006 (parliamentary); 9 January 2005 (presidential).
Results: Presidential: Mahmoud Abbas, also known as Abu Mazen, candidate of the mainstream Fatah, was elected president of the Palestinian council with 62.3 per cent of the vote against independent candidate, Mustafa Barghouti, 19.8 per cent. Turnout was 70 per cent.
Parliamentary: Hamas won 74 seats (out of 132); Fatah won 45 seats. The Popular Front for the Liberation of Palestine (PFLP) won 3 seats. Three groupings (The Alternative, Independent Palestine and Third Way) won 2 seats each. Independents won the 4 remaining seats. Turnout was 78.2 per cent.
Next elections
A Palestinian general election was scheduled to be held in Palestine less than 6 months from April 2014, in accordance with the Fatah-Hamas Gaza Agreement of April 2014. However, the elections have been delayed indefinitely. A unity government was formed between Fatah and Hamas which formed on 2 June 2014, however, it has since collapsed.

Political parties
Ruling party
There is no ruling party – the Government of the State of Palestine was sworn in by President Abbas on 2 June 2014. It controls the Gaza Strip and part of the West Bank Gaza. Strip only: Harakat al Muqawama al Islamia (Hamas) (Islamic Resistance Movement). West Bank only; Harakat al Tahir al Watani al Falistin (Fatah) (Movement for the National Liberation of Palestine) and independents

Population
4.17 million (2011); (Around three million Palestinians live in Jordan)
Last census: 1 December 2007: 3,761,646
Population density: 489 inhabitants per square km. Urban population 74 per cent (2010 Unicef).
Annual growth rate: 3.3 per cent, 1990–2010 (Unicef).
Ethnic make-up
Gaza: Palestinians and other Arabs (99.4 per cent), Israelis (0.6 per cent).
West Bank: Palestinians and other Arabs (83 per cent), Israelis (17 per cent).
Religions
The majority of the population is Muslim (mainly Sunni); also Jewish and Christian minorities.

Education
Formal basic education is provided to the majority of those who are of primary school age (94.7 per cent), although the quality of education does not correspond to the rising demand.
The education sector has suffered tremendous decline since the Israeli occupation. Most of the schools in the Gaza Strip are overcrowded and run two to three shifts per day. It is estimated that there are 1,175 schools of which 995 are in the West Bank and 180 in the Gaza Strip.
The education ministry in its five-year reform project (2000–05) is keen on developing a Palestinian curriculum emphasising studies in Palestinian identity and has invested in providing textbooks and improving the teaching methods in schools. It will also encourage the private sector to invest in vocational training, which otherwise concentrates on building and running cultural centres.
There are six universities in the West Bank and two in the Gaza Strip. West Bank Universities include Birzeit, Al Najah, Bethlehem, Al Quds University, Hebron University and Al Quds Open University.
The UN began distributing laptop computers to thousands of children attending school in the Gaza Strip in April 2010, in a measure to improve education in the region's disrupted school system. The laptops include textbooks used in primary school curriculum and teaching aids.

Health
The Israeli occupation has almost paralysed the provision of healthcare to the civilian population. Most hospitals and clinics are unable to operate and as a result 73 per cent of Palestinians in rural areas are deprived of medical treatment.
Vaccinations among children have been largely hindered spreading the fear of epidemics. Moreover, elderly people with chronic diseases suffer from acute shortages of medicine.
A hospital in Gaza, funded by the EU, is largely unworkable as staff, patients and supplies are denied access by Israeli authorities during times of trouble.
Life expectancy: 72.8 years (estimate 2010)
Fertility rate/Maternal mortality rate: 4.5 births per woman, 2010 (Unicef)
Birth rate/Death rate: 37.5 births per 1,000 population; 4.1 deaths per 1,000 population (2003).
Child (under 5 years) mortality rate (per 1,000): 23 per 1,000 live births (WHO 2012)

Welfare
The UN World Food Programme (WFP) aims to provide basic food support to 500,000 non-refugee Palestinians, in the West Bank and Gaza Strip. It targets those who have been classified as 'social hardship cases' (360,000 people according to latest estimates) and are eligible for welfare assistance from the PNA. In Jerusalem, an Emergency Food Crisis Group, chaired by WFP, has been established with the help of other UN agencies, non-governmental organisations and donors.
The Israeli occupation has forced the poverty level higher than ever before. While unemployment stands at 30 per cent, an estimated 40 per cent of Palestinian households have a monthly income that is less than US$200 per month. The percentage is 45 per cent in Gaza and 37 per cent in the West Bank.
Estimates show that 38 per cent of refugees live in the Palestinian territories; 15.8 per cent in the West Bank and 21.9 per cent in the Gaza Strip. The PNA along

with other international non-government organisations have been struggling to rehabilitate the housing conditions of people in the refugee camps such as Jenin and Nablus. The Palestinian Housing Council has been active in providing low cost housing. More than 400,000 Palestinians are deprived of electricity and running water.

Main cities

Gaza Strip: Gaza (also called Gaza City) (estimated population 42,185 in 2012), Abasan al Kabira (42,185), Han Yunis (46,070), Rafah (133,701).
West Bank: East Jerusalem (135,506), Jericho (19,806), Ramallah (32,713), Nablus (137,043), Hebron (183,538).

Languages spoken

Arabic. Hebrew is spoken by Israeli settlers. English is widely understood.

Official language/s

Arabic

Media

Press

A number of Palestinian newspapers are based in Nazareth, outside the PNA.
Dailies: In Arabic *Al Quds*, *Al Hayat al Jadedah*, Al Ayyam Daily Newspaper. In English, *Palestine Times* and *Bethlehem News*.
Weeklies: Weeklies include *Kul-Alarab*, *Assabeel Weekly*, *Filsteen Almoslima* and *Akhbar Alnaqab*.
Periodicals: In Arabic, *Al Ayyam*.

Broadcasting

The Palestinian Broadcasting Corporation broadcasts from Ramallah.
Radio: In Arabic, the Voice of Palestine, run by Hamas, and Gaza FM.
Television: The official Palestinian Broadcasting Corporation broadcasts televisions programmes from Ramallah as well as a satellite channel.
In English, Arabic, WAFA Palestine News Agency (http://english.wafa.ps), Ma'an News Agency (www.maannews.net/en), Ramattan (www.ramattan.com/default-en.asp).

Economy

Although the West Bank and Gaza Strip make up the combined territory of Palestine, each region has worked autonomously since 2007, following the Hamas victory in parliamentary elections. After violent clashes with Fatah, Hamas took control of the Gaza Strip and a political and economic schism occurred between the two territories. Hamas refused to acknowledge Israel as a legitimate state and renounce violence as a means of opposition to Israel and was subsequently shunned by most foreign governments.
The West Bank, home of the rival, Fatah-led president, began negotiations to work with the international community and has since been rewarded with international aid and improved trade relations.

Economic statistics for Gaza are limited; however the UNHCR published a report in 2009/10 (*Investing in Human Security for a Future State*), which included some statistics, dated up to 2008. The report concluded that Gaza's economy was severely limited and, due to the destruction incurred during Israel's military action in 2008–09, 'further decline is inevitable'. The composition of the economy in Gaza, which had once been focused on small-scale industries and agriculture, has become driven by 'government and private consumption of donor aid and remittances respectively' and that 'investments have fallen to dangerously low levels, leaving little productive base for a self-sustaining economy.' Remittances from Palestinian migrant workers have averaged US$1.1 billion (2009–11) and play a major part in sustaining family budgets. The ongoing conflict between Israel and Palestine, and the bombing of Palestine in July 2014, has meant that Palestine's economy has remained unstable and with little structure.
Until 2011, the black economy in Gaza had been centred on the more than 1,200 smuggler's tunnels that lead into Sinai around Rafah and transport goods from Egypt to sustain the population. In August 2012, a Gaza-based economist estimated that the 'trade volume between Gaza and Egypt through the tunnels is up to US$700 million a year' and that 10,000 workers are employed in the tunnels. Along with vehicles, fuel and people that are smuggled daily, the Israelis also claim that weapons used to target its citizens come unimpeded across the border. However, the largest trade goods that are smuggled in are construction materials, as Israel still imposes firm restrictions on its legitimate trade. During the Israel-Palestine conflict in 2014 many of these tunnels were closed and destroyed by Israeli forces. However, the full extent of the effects on the black economy is not yet known.
At an international donor conference held in 2009, to support the rebuilding of the Gaza Strip, US$4.5 billion was pledged by international governments and organisations. However the money was offered to the Palestinian Authority based in the West Bank and not Hamas.
The UN complained, in 2010, that Israel was blocking 26 of its building projects including homes, schools and health clinics by denying permission for materials to pass through their border controls. Economic activity in the Gaza Strip is almost non-existent. The UN estimated that the economic cost following the 2008–09 Israeli incursion, for rebuilding in the Gaza Strip, would be around US$1.9 billion, as over 50,000 people were made homeless and around 400,000 people were without running water. In 2014 the Israeli trade embargo on Palestine was in part responsible for the outbreak of the conflict in July, which took the lives of over 1,000 Palestinians. The economic costs of the conflict are not yet fully known.
The International Monetary Fund (IMF) estimated that the GDP growth of Palestine shrank to 0.5 per cent in 2007 and would reach only 0.8 per cent in 2008, figures much lower than the estimated 3.5 per cent that it could have achieved had the Israeli blockade been fully lifted from the Gaza Strip. Since 2010, supplies limited to food and consumer goods were allowed entry to Gaza. The economy of the West Bank has improved as tourists have returned to Bethlehem and freight transport has grown, leading to an increased average daily wage and a fall in unemployment.
In July 2012, the World Bank reported that the economy of the Palestinian territories was 'unsustainable' because it was too heavily reliant on foreign aid, which only provided growth in government services, real estate and the service sector and failed to provide growth in manufacturing and agriculture. It was stated that it was critically necessary to spur private sector growth and increase trade. The report also said that although the PA was in the process of establishing state institutions for Palestine's future viability, without GDP growth its economy would be too weak to support the state bodies.
In the summer of 2014 the tensions between Palestine and Israel continued, culminating in missiles being launched by extremists from Gaza. Israel retaliated with a military campaign targeted at rocket launching sites, and also destroyed Gaza's only power station, exacerbating an already present issue of water supply, sewage treatment and power supplies to medical facilities. The conflict ended in an uneasy ceasefire in August 2014.
The World Bank estimated GDP growth in 2013 to have been -4.4 per cent.

External trade

Palestine has no operational ports or airports to ship goods directly to markets other than Israel. Since Hamas took control of the Gaza Strip and Israel closed the border, manufacturing has all but collapsed, as 80 per cent of businesses have closed in this region.
All import and export information refers to the West Bank territory only.

Imports
Food, consumer goods and construction materials.
Main sources: Israel and Egypt
Exports
Citrus fruit, flowers, olives, fruit, vegetables, furniture and limestone.
Main destinations: Israel, Egypt, Jordan

Agriculture
Farming
The sector has been badly damaged by the Israeli-Palestinian conflict since 2000 when agriculture contributed 7 per cent to GDP and employed about 25 per cent of the workforce. In 2012, only 15 per cent of the workforce were employed in agriculture, however, 90 per cent are employed informally by agriculture.
Before the second *intifida* and the Israeli invasion of the West Bank and Gaza, about a quarter of the land area was cultivated and smallholdings of five hectares (ha) or less dominated. Crops, including olives, grapes and almonds, took up 60 per cent of cultivated rain-fed areas and field crops (mainly cereals) about 30 per cent. Olive growing accounted for more than 50 per cent of cultivated land.
The Separation Barrier (constructed by Israel between the two countries) has led to confiscation and levelling of Palestinian lands and by mid-2004 around 260 square kilometres, or 15 per cent of agricultural land had been lost to production.
Trade embargoes imposed on Palestine have caused serious damage to the agricultural sector.
Fishing
Forestry

Industry and manufacturing
There are proposals by a US-led syndicate to invest US$500 million in industry and manufacturing after the withdrawal of Israeli troops from Gaza, but only if Israel allows free access of goods through its territory to overseas markets.
A UN report, published in June 2011, put unemployment in Gaza at 45.2 per cent, one of the world's highest rates.

Tourism
The only region open to tourists is the West Bank, which includes parts of Jerusalem and the eastern region of Israel.
The Gaza Strip is closed to foreign visitors. The West Bank has many towns that date back to biblical times, such as Jericho, Bethlehem and Nablus. The Qumran National Park, site of the location of the Dead Seas Scrolls is close to the Palestinian section of the Dead Sea (the lowest land-point in the world).
Jerusalem is a major world city for culture and religion, with an unbroken link back into antiquity. It has historical buildings that represent all of the invaders that have colonised the city.
Access to the West Bank is via Israel.
On 29 June 2012, the Church of the Nativity in Bethlehem, among the holiest sites for Christians, was added to Unesco's World Heritage List.

Hydrocarbons
Extensive gas reserves were located off the Gaza Strip coastline in 2000. However the on-going hostilities between Palestine and Israel have hampered any exploitation. A proposal by Israel to pump natural gas from the only two wells in the Gaza Strip's gas field (which contain 33 billion cubic metres of natural gas), to the Israeli terminal at Ashkelon was put on hold when the major UK operator withdrew from negotiations in 2007. By 2015 these gas reserves had still not been exploited and worsening relations between Israel and Palestine means they are not likely to be in the near future.
All hydrocarbons must be delivered to the Gaza Strip through Israeli borders and are subject to embargo. In 2013 Palestine consumed 23,260 barrels per day of oil, all of which was imported.

Energy
The Gaza Strip had only one power station, until it was destroyed in an intense airstrike from Israel in July 2014. Over 100 people were also killed in the airstrike that exacerbated Palestine's already present issues of water supply, sewage treatment and power supply to medical facilities.
In 2013 Palestine consumed 4.57 billion Kwh, almost all of which was imported.

Financial markets
The second mobile (cell) operator, Wataniya Palestine Mobile Telecommunications Company began trading on 9 January 2011 on the Palestine Stock Exchange
Stock exchange
Palestine Stock Exchange (PEX)
Commodity exchange
Palestine Securities Exchange (PSE)

Banking and insurance
Central bank
The Palestine Monetary Authority (PMA), was established in 1995, with responsibilty for licensing, supervising and inspecting banks; determining the liquidity requirements on all deposits held by banks operating in the self-rule areas; managing foreign exchange reserves and foreign currency transactions. The PMA also has the power to regulate and supervise capital activities in the self-rule areas including the licensing of capital market institutions, finance companies and investment funds.

Main financial centre
Ramallah

Time
GMT plus two hours (daylight saving GMT plus three hours)

Geography
Palestine consists of the Gaza Strip and the West Bank, which together measure 6,020 square km. The Gaza Strip is level, fertile, coastal land of only 5–12km wide and 45km long to the south-west of Israel and on the Mediterranean sea. It is almost entirely surrounded by Israel but has a short border with Egypt in the south.
The West Bank is 5,655 square km within the demarcation line set up in 1949. It is an area west of the Jordan River, including much of Jerusalem and areas north and south of the city, the borders of which have been in dispute since the 1967 *Six Day War*. Jordan lies to the east and in the south-east the border runs through the Dead Sea, the lowest lying land on earth at 399 metres below sea level.
The land is generally fertile, although arid.
Hemisphere
Northern

Climate
Summer (Apr–Oct): temperatures range from 23 degrees Celsius (C) to 31 degrees C; humidity 70–75 per cent. Winter (Nov–Mar): temperatures range from 15–20 degrees C. Rainfall: Nov–Mar in periodic downpours.

Entry requirements
Passports
Required by all. The only routes to the Palestinian territories are through Israel and visitors must comply with Israeli requirements before access is allowed to the West Bank or Gaza Strip. Israel imposes tight restrictions and passport holders are advised to contact Israeli authorities for written permission to cross into the Gaza Strip in advance of travelling. At the border crossing it can take at least five working days for the documentation to be verified.
The Israeli Ministry of the Interior insists that Palestinian citizens holding dual nationality must enter and leave Israel on a Palestinian passport; they are required to obtain travel documents to depart.
NB An Israeli stamp, or exit stamp from any of the neighbouring countries, will mean entry is barred to almost any other Arab country. It is possible to request that the passport should not be stamped and a separate form is stamped instead and attached to the passport; the form can be removed when exiting the country.
Visa
Egypt and Jordan have open borders with Palestine, access was via the Allenby

bridge (West Bank-Jordan) or the border crossing at Rafah (Gaza-Egypt). However, since Israel commands these access points and limits admission, practical entry can only be gained through Israel. Israel has agreements with 65 countries for visa-free travel, including most citizens from Europe, the Americas, Australasia and some Asian countries (visa applications can be downloaded from: www.mfa.gov.il/mfa and follow link from *About the ministry* to *Consular affairs*, then *Services for foreign nationals only*). Travel within the West Bank and Gaza usually involves passing through multiple Israeli military checkpoints.

Currency advice/regulations

Most places accept US dollars, Israeli shekels and Jordanian dinars.

Customs

Video cameras and other electronic items must be declared to customs at Israeli points of entry.

Prohibited imports

Fresh meat and fruit and vegetables from Africa are prohibited by Israel.

Hotels

There is a lack of good hotels in the West Bank and Gaza.

Public holidays (national)

Fixed dates

14 Nov (National Day)

Variable dates

Eid al Adha, Islamic New Year, Birth of the Prophet, Ascent of the Prophet, Eid al Fitr.

Islamic year 1437 (15 Oct 2015–2 Oct 2016):: The Islamic year contains 354 or 355 days, with the result that Muslim feasts advance by 10–12 days against the Gregorian calendar. Dates of feasts vary according to the sighting of the new moon, so cannot be forecast exactly.

Working hours

The official weekend is Friday, and the working week varies, to accommodate Muslim, Christian or Jewish religious schedules.

Banking

Sat–Thu: 0800–1230. Some larger bank branches re-open Mon–Thu: 1500–1700.

Business

Sat–Thu: 0800–1430.

Government

Sat–Thu: 0800–1430.

Shops

Sat–Thu: 0800–1900. Christian owned shops open on Friday and close on Sunday.

Telecommunications

Mobile/cell phones

There is a 900 GSM service available throughout the territories.

Security

Foreign nationals are warned not to travel to the West Bank and Gaza Strip, which are subject to terrorist and military activity.

Getting there

Air

International airport/s: Dahaniya Gaza International Airport is not in operation. It is located south of Gaza City near the Egyptian border.

Surface

Gaza is accessible from the Rafah border with Egypt in the south; only women, children and men over 40 to pass freely. Men aged between 18 and 40 require a permit, and trade is prohibited. The Allenby Bridge crossing from the West Bank into Jordan is controlled by Israel.

Road: Private vehicles cannot cross from Israel into the Gaza Strip and may be stopped at checkpoints entering or leaving the West Bank.

The border crossing from Egypt, at Rafah, for foot-traffic, opens from 0900–2100, Saturday–Thursday (excluding public holidays).

Main port/s: An internationally funded port was opened in the late 1990s, with the aim of reducing the need for Palestinian trade to go through Israel before reaching the outside world. However, access to and from the port has become restricted due to the Israeli occupation of the West Bank and Gaza Strip in early 2002. All access to Gaza is via the port of Haifa.

Getting about

National transport

Road: Gaza Strip has a small, poorly developed road network.

West Bank has 4,500km of roads, of which 2,700km are paved; Israel developed many highways to service their settlements.

Buses: Buses run from East Jerusalem to Nablus and between Tel Aviv and Ramallah.

Taxis: Collective taxis regularly commute between Gaza and Ramallah, Jerusalem or Hebron.

City transport

Taxis: Taxis operate in the main cities.

Car hire

Palestinian licence plates are either green or blue, whereas Israeli number plates are yellow. Visitors are advised not to drive vehicles with yellow licence plates in the West Bank or Gaza Strip.

BUSINESS DIRECTORY

The addresses listed below are a selection only. While World of Information makes every endeavour to check these addresses, we cannot guarantee that changes have not been made, especially to telephone numbers and area codes. We would welcome any corrections.

Telephone area codes

The international direct dialling code (IDD) for Palestine is +970, followed by area code and subscriber's number:

Bethlehem	2	Jericho	2
Gaza	7	Jerusalem	2
Hebron	2	Nablus	9
Jenin	6	Ramallah	2

Chambers of Commerce

Bethlehem Chamber of Commerce and Industry, PO Box 59, Bethlehem (tel: 274-2742; fax: 276-4402; e-mail: bcham@palnet.com).

European Palestinian Chamber of Commerce, 19 Nablus Road, PO Box 20185, Jerusalem (tel: 626-4883; fax: 626-4975; e-mail: epcc@palnet.com).

Federation of Palestinian Chambers of Commerce, Industry and Agriculture, Al-Rashid Street, PO Box 54107, Jerusalem (tel: 628-0727; fax: 628-0644; email: fpccia@palnet.com).

Gaza Palestinian Chamber of Commerce, PO Box 33, Gaza (tel: 282-1172; fax: 286-4588; e-mail: gazacham@palnet.com).

Hebron Chamber of Commerce and Industry, King Faisal Street, PO Box 272, Hebron, West Bank (tel: 222-8218; fax: 222-7490; e-mail: hebcham@hebronet.com).

Jenin Chamber of Commerce, Industry and Agriculture, City Centre, Jenin (tel: 250-1107; fax: 250-3388; e-mail: jencham@hally.net).

Jericho Commercial, Industrial and Agricultural Arab Chamber, PO Box 91, Jericho (tel: 232-3313; fax: 232-2394; e-mail: jercom@palnet.com).

Jerusalem Arab Chamber of Commerce, Al-Rashid Street, PO Box 19151, Jerusalem 91191 (tel: 628-2351; fax: 627-2615; e-mail: chamber@alqudsnet.com).

Nablus Chamber of Commerce and Industry, PO Box 35, Nablus (tel: 238-0335; fax: 237-7605; e-mail: nablus@palnet.com).

Qalqilya Chamber of Commerce, Industry and Agriculture, PO Box 13, Qalqilya (tel: 294-1473; fax: 294-0164; e-mail: chamberq@hally.net).

Ramallah and Albeireh Chamber of Commerce and Industry, PO Box 256, Ramallah (tel: 295-6043; fax: 298-4691; e-mail: ramcom@palnet.com).

Tulkarm Chamber of Commerce and Industry, PO Box 51, Tulkarm (tel: 267-1010; fax: 267-5623; e-mail: tulkarm@palnet.com).

Banking
Al-Ahli Jordan Bank, Al-Quds Street, PO Box 550, Ramallah (tel: 998-6370; fax: 998-6372).

Al-Ittihad Bank for Saving and Investment, Commercial Centre, Al-Barid Street, PO Box 1557, Ramallah (tel: 298-6412/5; fax: 298-6416).

ANZ Grindlays, PO Box 19390, East Jerusalem (tel: 626-3444; fax: 626-3311).

Arab Bank, Al-Harajeh, PO Box 1476, Ramallah (tel: 298-2456; fax: 298-2444).

Arab Land Bank, PO Box 565, Jerusalem/Ramallah Road, Ramallah (tel: 298-5958; fax: 295-8426/5).

Arab Palestinian Investment Bank, Regional Headquarters, Al-Harajeh Building, PO Box 1268, Ramallah (tel: 298-7126; fax: 298-7125).

Bank of Jordan, Al-Quds Street, PO Box 1328, Ramallah (tel: 295-2696; fax: 295-2705).

Bank of Palestine, Al-Rimal Quarter, Omar El-Mukhtar Street, PO Box 50, Gaza (tel: 286-5676; fax: 282-8974).

British Bank of the Middle East, PO Box 2067, Al-Quds Street, Ramallah (tel: 298-7802, 298-1551; fax: 298-7804).

Cairo Amman Bank, Wadi El-Tuffah Street, PO Box 665, Hebron (tel: 993-6768; fax: 993-6770).

Cairo Amman Bank, El-Hussein Circle, Nablus (tel: 238-1301; fax: 238-0188).

Commercial Bank of Palestine, Al-Awdah Street, PO Box 1799, Ramallah (tel: 295-4102; fax: 295-3888).

Jordan Gulf Bank, Al-Sa'ah Circle, Ramallah (tel: 998-7680; fax: 998-7682).

Jordan Housing Bank, Rukab Street, PO Box 1473, Ramallah (tel: 998-6255; fax: 998-6275).

Jordan Kuwait Bank, Commercial Centre, Sufian Street, PO Box 33, Nablus (tel: 237-7223; fax: 237-7181).

Palestinian Construction Bank, Al-Bireh, Al-Silwadi Building, Ramallah (tel: 995-4796; fax: 995-4797).

Palestinian International Bank, PO Box 1244, Gaza (tel: 282-7360; fax: 282-5269).

Palestinian Investment Bank, Midan Al-Nahda, Al-Hilal Street, PO Box 3675, Ramallah (tel: 998-7880; fax: 998-7881).

Palestinian Islamic Bank, PO Box 1244, Al-Rimal Quarter, Omar El-Mukhtar Street, Gaza (tel: 282-7360; fax: 282-5269).

Central bank
Palestine Monetary Authority, Nablus Road; PO Box 452,, Ramallah (tel: 240-9920/1; fax: 240-9922/24; e-mail: info@pma.gov.ps).

Stock exchange
Palestine Stock Exchange (PEX)

Commodity exchange
Palestine Securities Exchange (PSE), www.p-s-e.com

Travel information
The Higher Council for the Arab Tourist Industry, PO Box 19850, East Jerusalem (tel: 628-1805; fax: 628-7981).

Ministry of tourism
Ministry of Tourism and Antiquities, Manger Street; PO Box 534, Bethlehem (tel: 274-1581/2/3; fax: 274-3753; email: mota@pl.org; internet site: www.visit-palestine.com).

Ministries
Ministry of Agriculture, Abu Khadrah Building, Gaza (tel: 286-5990; fax: 286-3926).

Ministry of Economy and Trade, PO Box 1629, Ramallah, West Bank (tel: 298-1214/5; fax: 298-4011).

Ministry of Finance, Omer El-Mokhtar Street, Government Departments Complex, Gaza (tel: 282-4368; fax: 282-3356).

Ministry of Housing, PO Box 4034, Omer El-Mokhtar Street, Government Departments Complex, Gaza (tel: 282-2233/4; fax: 282-2235).

Ministry of Industry, PO Box 1629, Ramallah, West Bank (tel: 298-7641/2; fax: 298-7440).

Ministry of Planning and International Co-operation, PO Box 4017, Omer El-Mokhtar Street, Government Departments Complex, Gaza (tel: 282-9260; fax: 282-4090).

Ministry of Telecommunications, Gaza (tel: 282-5612; fax: 282-4555).

Other useful addresses
Arab Medical Professions College, Al-Bireh (tel: 995-5611).

Birzeit University, Ramallah (tel: 995-7650; fax: 995-7656).

College of Islamic Studies, PO Box 21402, Beit Hanina (tel: 585-3918).

Fine Arts Institute, Ramallah (tel: 995-5974).

Girls' Arts College, PO Box 19377, Jerusalem (tel: 627-3477; fax: 627-3477).

Hebron Polytechnic College, Hebron (tel: 992-8912; fax: 993-8912).

Hebron University, Hebron (tel: 992-0995).

Higher Council for the Arab Tourist Industry, PO Box 19850, East Jerusalem (tel: 628-1805; fax: 628-3981, 628-7981).

Ibrahimieh Community College PO Box 19014, Jerusalem (tel: 626-4216; fax: 628-2925).

Jerusalem Open University, PO Box 51800, Jerusalem (tel: 581-7237; fax: 581-6734).

Khaduri College, PO Box 7, Tulkarem (tel: 671-026; fax: 672-7733).

Palestine Agricultural Relief Committee (PARC), PO Box 25128, Jerusalem (tel: 583-1897, 583-3818; fax: 582-1898).

Palestinian Economic Council for Development and Reconstruction (PECDAR), PO Box 1629, Dahyet El-Bareed, West Bank (tel: 574-7040; fax: 574-9032).

Palestine Securities Exchange, PO Box 128, Nablus, West Bank (tel: 237-5946; fax: 237-5945).

Palestinian Standards Institute, PO Box 1648, Nablus, West Bank (tel: 238-5721; fax: 237-5745).

Palestine Telecommunications Company Ltd (Patel), PO Box 1570, Al-Adel Street, Nablus (tel: 237-6225; fax: 237-6227; e-mail: paltel@palnet.com).

Internet sites
Palestine and Holy Land Tourism Guide: www.palguide.com

Palestinian National Authority (links to other sites): www.palestine-net.com

Palestinian News Agency: http://english.wafa.ps

The Electronic Intifada: http://electronicintifada.net

Panama

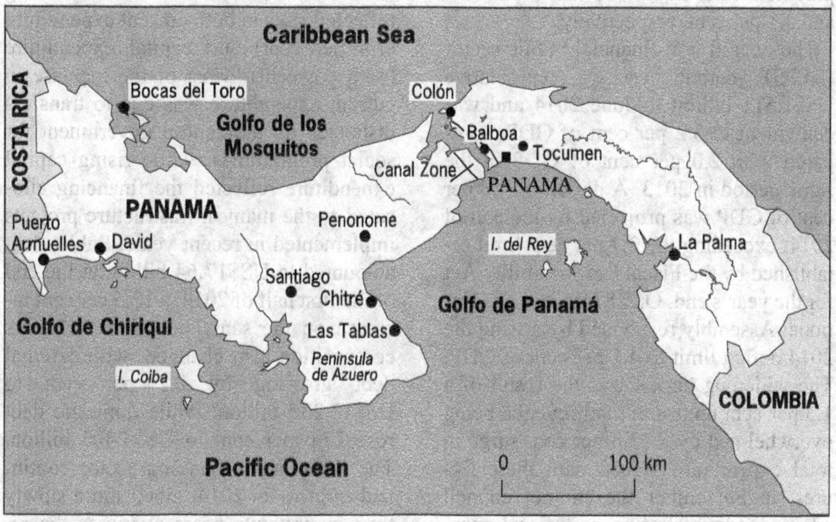

On the first of July 2014 Juan Carlos Varela had assumed the Presidency of Panama. President Varela promised to launch a campaign against corruption and organised crime and illegal speculation, particularly in the manipulation of basic food prices. In his 25 minute speech – short by Latin American standards – to thousands of Panamanians gathered in the capital's football stadium, the new President referred to the alleged harm that democracy in Panama had suffered in recent years, announcing the beginning of a 'new era' which would restore the 'strength and credibility' of Panama's institutions. 'The process of repairing our democracy begins today and we will realise it at the same time as we work to fulfil the agenda of our government' said Varela, a political ally of the outgoing President Ricardo Martinelli. Sr Varela had previously been appointed as vice president of Panama with the 'assistance' of Martinelli, but in August 2011 Varela had distanced himself from the President amid allegations of corruption.

New broom?

Corruption was 'not to be tolerated' and over the next five years the state's resources would be used 'only to serve the people' said the new president, reaffirming that he would confront crime with 'an iron fist'. (On Transparency International's 2014 *Corruption Perceptions Index* Panama ranked 94 out of the 175 countries surveyed – level with neighbouring Colombia) The presidency, Mr Varela said, would lend its full support to Panama's 15,000 strong police force, but would not neglect the country's programmes of social integration and the development of culture and sport. The president invited the 200 gangs that operated in Panama to lay down their arms in a month long amnesty, during which they would be able to return to a more normal civilian lifestyle.

The president, whose background was not only in politics – he also owned a drinks business – claimed that he was allergic to speculation with food prices and announced that on his first day in office he had already signed a decree controlling the prices of 22 basic foodstuffs. This had been one key element of his electoral campaign and ranged across types of meat, vegetables, rice, eggs and milk. He noted that the measure would allow 'thousands of families to buy at fair prices and thereby improve their standard of living. In his investiture speech the flamboyant president exhorted Panama's farmers to go back to their land 'to sow' and 'produce'. He added yet another reassurance that they would have 'all his backing' to

KEY FACTS

Official name: República de Panamá (Republic of Panama)

Head of State: President Juan Carlos Varela (since 1 July 2014)

Head of government: President Juan Carlos Varela (since 1 July 2014)

Ruling party: Cambio Democrático (Democratic Change)

Area: 77,082 square km

Population: 3.93 million (2014)* (3,405,813; 2010, census figure)

Capital: Panama City

Official language: Spanish

Currency: Balboa (B and US$) and US dollar = 100 cents

Exchange rate: B and US$1.00 per US$ (fixed peg)

GDP per capita: US$11,147 (2014)*

GDP real growth: 6.20% (2014)

GDP: US$43.78 billion (2014)

Labour force: 1.65 million (2010)

Unemployment: 4.10% (2014)*

Inflation: 2.63% (2014)

Balance of trade: -US$8.13 billion (2014)

Annual FDI: US$3.26 billion (2011)

* estimated figure

increase agricultural production and guarantee Panama's food security. Varela also promised to increase foreign direct investment (FDI), tourism and to strengthen the judiciary. The investment ceremony was attended by all the region's great and good, presidents, vice presidents and heads of government. Before the ceremony President Varela had a meeting with the US Secretary of State John Kerry.

The president's position in parliament was by no means secure, even if his term of office as president was to last three years. His party, the Partido Panameñista (PPa) (Panameñista Party) had joined forces with the alarmingly named opposition Partido Revolucionario Democrático (PRD) (Revolutionary Democratic Party), which held 20 seats.

The economy.

On assuming the presidency in July 2015, the president had taken on a Panama that had been a regional leader in gross domestic product (GDP) growth rates in recent years, with growth exceeding 10 per cent in 2011 and 2012 and 8.5 per cent in 2013. Growth for 2014 had been expected to be around 6 per cent. In its assessment of the Panamanian economy, the United Nations Economic Commission for Latin America and the Caribbean (ECLAC/CEPAL) said Panama was projected to achieve growth of 6.0 per cent in 2014, retaining its position as one of the fastest-growing economies in the region. The non-financial public-sector deficit stood at 3.2 per cent of GDP in June 2014, while the cumulative balance-of-payments current account deficit in that month was US$2.294 billion, down 4.4 per cent on the same period in 2013. Public debt totalled US$17.64 billion at the end of the first half of the year, up 12.5 per cent year on year in nominal terms. The consumer price index posted a year-on-year increase of 2.1 per cent up to October 2014, while in March 2014 the jobless and open unemployment rates had stood at 4.3 per cent and 3.1 per cent, respectively.

The overall non-financial public sector (NFPS) deficit was a cumulative US$1.511 billion in June 2014 and was equivalent to 3.2 per cent of GDP, compared with 2.0 per cent of GDP in the same period in 2013. A deficit of 4.0 per cent of GDP was projected by the end of 2014, exceeding the 2.7 per cent limit established by the Fiscal Responsibility Act for the year's end. On 28 October, the National Assembly responded by raising the 2014 deficit limit to 4.1 per cent of GDP. The widening deficit was the result of a 1.5 per cent upturn in total revenue being overwhelmed by a 13.6 per cent surge in total expenditure. Faced with these figures, in September the cabinet council adopted administrative and fiscal measures to rein in spending by US$549 million.

Tax revenues up to June 2014 amounted to US$2.36 billion, down 0.9 per cent on the figure for the same period in 2013, as a 5.6 per cent increase in indirect tax revenues was fully neutralised by a 6.4 per cent fall in direct tax revenues. In view of the weak revenue generation of the preceding months, the new administration that took office in July 2014 granted an amnesty on the payment of overdue taxes, which would be exempt from surcharges, fines or interest. The amnesty period was due to expire at the end of 2014.

Non-tax revenues totalled US$770.9 million in June 2014, a year-on-year increase of 38.5 per cent driven by non-recurring income from the renewal of telecommunications and casino concessions. The surge in overall NFPS spending reflected rises in both current expenditure (7.4 per cent) and capital expenditure (13.3 per cent). Most of the increase in current expenditure was due to transfers disbursed by the central government for social programmes, while rising capital expenditure reflected the financing allocated to the many infrastructure projects implemented in recent years. Public debt amounted to US$17.64 billion at the end of the first half of 2014, a 12.5 per cent increase on the same period in 2013. Its composition also changed, with external debt growing by 8.2 per cent to US$13.236 billion, while domestic debt rose 27.6 per cent to US$4.403 billion. The Panamanian banking sector continued to grow in 2014, albeit more slowly than in previous years owing to the reduced level of economic activity. In July 2014, the local credit portfolio stood at US$39.014 billion, a nominal increase of 8.6 per cent year on year (compared with a 13.6 per cent year-on-year increase in July 2013). Public debt amounted to US$17.64 billion at the end of the first half of 2014, a 12.5 per cent increase on the same period in 2013. Its composition also changed, with external debt growing by 8.2 per cent to US$13.236 billion, while domestic debt rose 27.6 per cent to US$4.403 billion. Mortgage lending expanded by 13.2 per cent in nominal terms on the back of a positive performance in residential and commercial construction. Lending to the commerce sector, however, recorded only 0.9 per cent nominal growth, largely owing to the continued decline in exports from the Colón Free Zone to Panama's main trading partners. Consumer credit expanded at a nominal rate of 11.2 per cent, thanks to low interest rates and the extension of debt repayment deadlines, especially on loans for new vehicle purchases. Credit for the construction sector grew by 12.7 per cent.

The current account deficit was US$2.294 billion as of June 2014, compared with US$2.401 billion in the same period in 2013. The narrower deficit reflected a US$642 million increase in the surplus on the services account, partially offset by increases of US$250 million and US$224 million on the goods trade deficit

KEY INDICATORS — Panama

	Unit	2011	2012	2013	2014	**2015
Population	m	*3.59	*3.65	3.85	*3.93	*4.01
Gross domestic product (GDP)	US$bn	30.60	35.94	40.39	43.78	*47.48
GDP per capita	US$	8,514	9,833	10,490	*11,147	*11,851
GDP real growth	%	10.6	10.8	8.4	6.2	*6.1
Inflation	%	5.9	5.7	4.0	2.6	*0.9
Unemployment	%	4.2	4.2	4.1	*4.1	*4.1
Exports (fob) (goods)	US$m	16,925.7	18,877.8	17,501.8	15,337.6	–
Imports (fob) (goods)	US$m	22,941.5	24,613.6	24,245.1	23,467.5	–
Balance of trade	US$m	-6,015.8	-5,735.8	-6,743.3	-8,129.9	–
Current account	US$m	-3,873.6	-3,816.0	-4,918.0	-5,257.0	*-4,941.0
Total reserves minus gold	US$m	2,891.4	2,466.3	2,848.0	4,032.2	–
Foreign exchange	US$m	2,604.7	2,185.4	2,566.6	–	–
Exchange rate	per US$	1.00	1.00	1.00	1.00	–

* estimated figure ** forecast figure

and the income account deficit, respectively. The services surplus increased owing to higher income from exports in the travel, air transport and sea transport categories, while the higher goods trade deficit was due to a drop in the surplus posted by the Colón Free Zone coupled with a sharper contraction in the country's exports (down 12.4 per cent) than in its imports (down 6.6 per cent). Lastly, the deficit on income transfers between residents and non-residents totalled US$1.719 billion, up 15.0 per cent on the figure reported in June 2013. FDI amounted to US$2.575 billion, a 26.0 per cent increase on the June 2013 figure, thanks to reinvestment of earnings totalling US$1.644 billion and equity purchases totalling US$780 million.

Panama's economy continued to grow briskly during the first half of 2014, albeit more slowly than in 2013. The construction sector posted year-on-year growth of 15.5 per cent in June 2014 (compared with 25.9 per cent in June 2013) on the back of home building and non-residential infrastructure projects. The mining sector grew by 12.0 per cent amid strong demand for non-metallic minerals from the construction sector. The transport, storage and telecommunications sector remained buoyant, with growth of 7.7 per cent reflecting a 6.8 per cent increase in the volume of commercial cargo shipped though the Panama canal and a 12.6 year on-year rise in air transport, with a total of 3.5 million passengers travelling up to June 2014. After contracting for several years, the fisheries sector grew by 36.0 per cent, a rally driven by increased shrimp exports and an upturn in non-industrial fishing. The commerce sector expanded by 3.3 per cent in the period to June 2014 (compared with 1.0 per cent to September 2013), spurred by faster growth in retail trade, which more than compensated for the continued decline in activity at the Colón Free Zone, where sales continued to drop over the year, with a 12-month decline of 13.4 per cent in the period to June. This pattern reflects falling exports to Panama's main trading partners, including Venezuela (down 36.1 per cent), Puerto Rico (down 27.5 per cent), Ecuador (down 10.8 per cent) and Guatemala (down 7.8 per cent).

In October 2014, the consumer price index (CPI) posted an increase of 2.1 per cent year on year, thereby continuing the downward trend in inflation observed since mid-2012. The jobless rate stood at 4.3 per cent and the open unemployment rate at 3.1 per cent in March 2014, broadly in line with the year-earlier figures. Where job quality is concerned, a rise of 5.3 per cent in formal employment was accounted for mainly by specific task contracts. The average wage as of June 2014 was US$1,013.90, which was 7.9 per cent higher than in the first half of 2013.

Canal news

One hundred and one years ago the Panama Canal opened, in August 1914, allowing shipping to cut across the Isthmus of Panama and so saving them a 13,000km trip around Cape Horn. The journey through the canal – from Limón Bay to the Gulf of Panama – takes ships roughly eight hours, negotiating the six massive locks that take them from sea level up some 25 metres. It costs ship-owners as much as US$450,000 for a fully laden container ship (or cruise liner with 2,500 passengers) to cross the canal.

Bigger – and better...

The Canal's anniversary year saw the introduction of new locks costing some US$5.5 billion. These locks will allow ships up to 1,200 feet long (the accepted unit of measurement for the so-called Panamax dimensions, is the foot) (366 metres) and 160 feet (49 metres) wide to cross through the Canal, an increase from the original 965 feet (294 metres) long and 106 feet (32 metres) wide. However the water depth in the lock chambers can vary; the shallowest depth – 41.2 feet (12.56 metres) – is in the Pedro Miguel Locks. Depth limitations are determined by the water level in the Miraflores Lake, the par figure for which should be 54 ft 6 in (16.61 metres). The height limiting factor is that of the Bridge of the Americas at Balboa. The exact figure depends on the lake's water level – for which a three week forecast is made available to shipping.

The Canal improvements have been a massive undertaking, involving removing an estimated 200 million cubic metres of rock to create the necessary water saving basins and deeper channels. The initial works involved digging a hole 1.6km long, over 100 metres wide and 30 metres deep. The Canal's previous capacity was roughly 35 ships per day – a figure which will increase by an estimated 15 ships per day when the new dimensions come in to play in 2015. The widened 'New Panamax' canal will be able to cope with ships that are up to 25 per cent longer and 50 per cent wider carrying cargoes which are more than double the current limits. Strategically, the new Canal may offer shippers a more attractive, safer and more predictable alternative to the Suez Canal.

Widening the Canal had come into sharper focus for the administration of President Ricardo Martinelli in 2013 when both Nicaragua and Guatemala claimed to have plans for the construction of inter-oceanic links. Nicaragua said it had signed contracts worth US$2 billion to build a canal that would compete with Panama. More puzzlingly, Guatemala announced the construction of an inter-oceanic 'dry corridor' for US$6,000 million.

Both the Nicaraguan and Guatemalan projects were designed to compete with the Panama Canal. However, the Panama Canal is a mere 80km long and there already exists in Panama an inter-oceanic motorway. The Guatemalan link would be 372km long and the Nicaraguan Canal would be 290km. Panamanian officials dismissed the threats, pointing out that similar projects were mooted in both Honduras and El Salvador. It was pointed out that the Guatemalan link would require extremely expensive loading and unloading facilities which alone would cost more than a Panama Canal crossing. It looked likely that even with the new links, the Panama Canal would still be the quickest and cheapest crossing. For the time being it was also likely to be the safest and most secure way of linking the two oceans.

... and later

The Canal widening project has not been without its difficulties. The building consortium led by Sacyr of Spain had been enmeshed in a lengthy dispute over cost overruns that had not just delayed, but actually endangered the completion of the multi-billion-dollar project. Agreement was finally reached in May 2014 when the Grupo Unido por el Canal (GUPC) consortium, announced that under the new agreement – which had a lot of loose ends – a revised deadline of December 2015 was set, six months later than earlier 2014 estimates. The delays have had serious implications for owners of the new generation of large container ships and liquefied gas tankers. At the heart of the dispute were cost overruns that added up to US$1.6 billion, roughly 25 per cent of the originally forecast total. With 70 per cent of the project completed, the contractors and the Canal Authority had each blamed the other for the increased costs. Accusatory fingers had been pointed at the lead contractor for the project, (Sacyr), which was considered by many to have bitten off more than it could chew – the Canal projected represented 25 per cent of all its international revenue. When news of the original disagreement was made public, Sacyr's shares fell by some 8 per cent reflecting investors' concerns that the already vulnerable company could be forced to pull out of the project.

Under the new agreement, the Panama Canal Authority (PCA) and the contracting consortium were each to contribute US$100 million to get the work re-started and the PCA would extend a moratorium on the refund of advance payments until 2018, freeing up funds to complete the work, the consortium said. Any, claims relating to unexpected costs would be resolved in international arbitration courts. Just when all seemed to be, finally, sweetness and light the proposed schedule for completing the project by the end of 2015 was thrown into doubt as construction workers had gone on strike in pursuit of further pay increases, bringing work to a halt for the second time in 2014.

Election surprises

The five years' presidency of Ricardo Martinelli ended in June 2014. The dynamic former businessman had found plenty to busy himself with and spend on, during his time in power with the US$5.5 billion (the actual costs have been difficult to pin down) (see: Bigger… and better' above) expansion of the canal at the top of the list. An article in the London *Economist* pointed out that the total public expenditure of US$19 billion – which included the construction of the first public underground railway system in Central America – was not far short of Panama's total GDP of US$24 billion when Mr Martinelli took office as president in 2009. However, the outgoing president could point to an average annual growth rate of 8 per cent during his five years in office.

So it came as something of a surprise – not least to Mr Martinelli – when his chosen successor, José Domingo Arias, had come home second in the election. If that wasn't enough, the victor Juan Carlos Varela, himself a former vice president, was known to have had a parting of the ways with Mr Martinelli. However, the many Panamanians who looked upon the election as a test of their country's democratic systems could take considerable comfort from the outcome. On the day Mr Varela, whom no opinion poll had tipped to win, took 39 per cent of the vote compared with 31 per cent for José Domingo Arias. Mr Varela had sought to depict his rival as the president's puppet. Concerns were rightly expressed that Mr Martinelli was hoping, somehow, to keep in control. This was certainly the case at the parliamentary level where Mr Martinelli's ruling coalition – with 30 seats in the National Assembly – held sway.

Risk assessment

Economy	Good
Politics	Good/fair
Regional stability	Good

People to watch

Juan Carlos Varela – elected President, May 2014.

COUNTRY PROFILE

1502 European explorers first visited Panama.
1519 Panama became part of the Vice-royalty of New Andalucia.
1821 Following independence from Spanish rule Panama joined the union of Central American provinces and became part of the confederacy of Gran Colombia (Gran Colombia collapsed in 1830 and Panama became part of Colombia).
1846 The US signed a treaty with Colombia to build a railway across the isthmus.
1880 A canal, to link the Atlantic and Pacific oceans, was begun by Ferdinand de Lesseps, (who had previously built the Suez Canal), with French backing. Tropical disease killed thousands of workers; financial difficulties halted the project.
1903 After Colombian parliamentarians refused to endorse a treaty with the US to build a canal the US encouraged the Panamanians to rebel and declare independence. The new rulers signed a treaty with the US that gave rights for the building and independent operation of a canal and surrounding area called the Canal Zone. The treaty was granted in perpetuity.
1914 The Panama Canal was completed.
1939 Panama ceased to be a US protectorate.
1941–68 Panama was mostly ruled by presidents representing the landowners, traders and building companies. Arnulfo Arias, although ousted in 1941, was an unpredictable populist orator, much loved by the crowds. He was in and out of office between 1949–68.
1968 Omar Torrijos became president.
1977 President Omar Torrijos and US president Jimmy Carter signed a treaty under which the US would hand back control of the canal to Panama and withdraw its troops by the end of 1999.
1981 Torrijos, president since 1968, died in a plane crash.
1983 General Manuel Antonio Noriega became commander of the National Guard. He increased his own power and that of the guard, which he renamed the Panama Defence Forces and assumed *de facto* rule of Panama.
1988 The US accused Noriega of drug trafficking. Noriega declared a state of emergency.
1989 The opposition, Alianza Democrática de Oposición Civilista (Civil Democratic Opposition Alliance) and its presidential candidate Guillermo Endara, won the elections. Noriega declared the results invalid. The US increased diplomatic pressure and threats until Noriega declared a 'state of war'. The US invaded and removed Noriega from power. He was taken to the US to stand trial on charges of drug smuggling. Endara became president.
1990 Noriega was sentenced to 20 years in prison in the US.
1991 Constitutional changes adopted included the abolition of a standing army.
1992 Noriega was found guilty of drug offences and sentenced to 30 years in a US prison.
1994 Ernest Pérez Balladares won the presidential election.
1999 Mireya Elisa Moscoso Rodríguez of the Partido Arnulfista (PA) (Arnulfista Party) won the presidential elections, becoming Panama's first female president.
2000 Under the Torrijos-Carter treaty ownership and control of the Panama Zone was handed back to Panama on 1 January. President Moscoso set up a tribunal to investigate crimes and human rights abuses during the military rule of 1968–89. The PA lost control of the National Assembly and an alliance led by the Partido Revolucionario Democrático (PRD) (Democratic Revolutionary Party) formed a majority.
2002 Panama signed a framework trade agreement with its five Central American neighbours to boost trade in the region. The PA gained from the defections of three members of the opposition PRD when they voted to approve Moscoso's appointees for the Supreme Court.
2003 Panama's first free trade agreement (FTA) was established with El Salvador.
2004 Martín Torrijos won the presidential election. The PRD won parliamentary elections and formed a coalition government. The Panama Canal made record profits of US$1 billion during the financial year.
2006 Parliament approved a US$5.25 billion programme to widen the Panama Canal. A referendum approved the project, beginning in 2008, scheduled to be completed by 2014.
2007 Work began to widen the Panama Canal with an additional series of locks.
2009 The US agreed to extradite former president Noriega to France on money-laundering charges, following his early release from jail (for good

behaviour) in 2007. In parliamentary elections the political bloc which supported the president, including Cambio Democrático (CD) (Democratic Change), supported by Partido Unión Patriotica (PUP) (Patriotic Union Party), Partido Panameñista (PP) (Panameñista Party) and Movimiento Liberal Republicano Nacionalista (Molirena) (Nationalist Republican Liberal Movement) won 42 seats in the national assembly, the PRD won 26 seats. In the presidential election, also held in May, Ricardo Martinelli (CD) won 61 per cent, Balbina Herrera, supported by the incumbent PRD, won 37 per cent.

2010 Former dictator, Manuel Noriega, was extradicted to France where a court had convicted him *in absentia* of laundering US$7 million in drug money and sentenced him to seven years in prison in France.

2011 In October, a trade agreement with the US was finally agreed by both houses of the US congress. In December, France extradited Manuel Noriega to Panama to serve a prison sentence for murder, embezzlement and corruption. He arrived on 12 December and was immediately escorted to El Renacer jail, south-east of Panama City.

2012 On 16 March, Panama and Dominica agreed to establish diplomatic and ambassador level relations with one another. On 27 June the Portobelo-San Lorenzo group of historic military fortifications, already on Unesco's World Heritage List, was placed on its register of endangered sites, due to the lack of maintenance and uncontrolled urban development along Panama's Caribbean coastline. A new law allowing the sale of state owned land in Colon free trade zone (FTZ) to private investors, was repealed after nine days, on 28 October, following large and violent opposition by those that feared the sale would damage employment prospects and push down wages. Colon is the largest FTZ in Latin America, sited at the Caribbean end of the Panama Canal.

2013 On 15 July President Martinelli reported that a North Korean-flagged ship en route from Cuba had been searched and 'undeclared military cargo' found. North Korea is banned under UN sanctions from exporting or importing most weapons. Dino Bouterse, the son of Suriname President Desi Bouterse, was extradited from Panama by the US in August. He was charged on 8 November with attempting to provide material support to a foreign terrorist organisation. He had allegedly been paid to provide a base and weapons by Hezbollah Shi'a militants who were said to be planning attacks on the US and the Netherlands.

2014 The first metro/subway in Central America was opened in Panama in April. Presidential and general elections were held on 3 May. The presidential election was won by Juan Carlos Varela with 39.09 per cent of the vote, followed by José Domingo Arias with 31.38 per cent. Mr Varela took office on 1 July. The parliamentary elections were won by the Cambio Democrático (CD) (Democratic Change) with 31 seats (out of 71), followed by Partido Revolucionario Democrático (PRD) (Democratic Revolutionary Party) 25 and the new president's party, Partido Panameñista (PP) (Panameñista Party) 12.

2015 In May it was reported the former dictator Manuell Noriega, already serving a 60-year jail sentence, would face yet another trial, this time charged with the murder in 1970 of Heliodoro Portugal, a prominent leftist leader and political opponent. Although the new trial will violate the terms under which France had allowed his extradition in 2011, it appears the trial will start on 21 May. On 11 October the government of Paraguay ordered former prime minister, Ricardo Martinelli, to leave immediately; he faces 11 different criminal charges in Panama, including human rights violations.

Political structure

In addition to their unicameral national parliaments, El Salvador, Guatemala, Honduras, Nicaragua, Panama and Dominican Republic also return directly-elected deputies to the supranational Central American Parliament.

Constitution

Panama's constitution dates from 1972 and was reformed in 1983 and 1994.

Form of state

Presidential democratic republic

The executive

The president is both head of state and head of government, elected for a period of five years by universal adult suffrage. The Cabinet is appointed by the president.

National legislature

The unicameral Asamblea Legislativa (National Assembly) has 71 seats of which 45 are members directly elected in multi-seat constituencies by proportional representation vote and 26 members directly elected in single-seat constituencies (outlying rural districts) by plurality vote. Members serve for five-year terms.

Legal system

The Corte Suprema de Justicia (Supreme Court of Justice) has nine judges appointed for 10-year terms. There are five superior courts and three courts of appeal.

Last elections

4 May 2014 (presidential and parliamentary)

Results: Presidential: Juan Carlos Varela (Partido Panameñista (PP) (Panameñista Party)) won 39.09 per cent of the vote, José Domingo Arias (Cambio Democratico (CD) (Democratic Exchange) 31.38 per cent, Juan Carlos Navarro (Partido Revolucionario Democrático (PRD) (Democratic Revolutionary Party) 28.1 per cent; the remaining four candidates won less than one per cent between them. Turnout was 76.8 per cent.

Parliamentary: Cambio Democrático (CD) (Democratic Change) won 33.7 per cent of the vote (30 seats out of 71), Partido Revolucionario Democrático (PRD) (Democratic Revolutionary Party) won 31.5 per cent (25), Partido Panameñista (PP) (Panameñista Party) won 20.2 per cent (12), Movimiento Liberal Republicano Nacionalista (Molirena) (Nationalist Republican Liberal Movement) won 7.2 per cent (2), Partido Popular (People's Party) won 3.3 per cent (1), Independents won 3 per cent between them (1); turnout was 75.19 per cent.

Next elections

May 2019 (presidential and parliamentary)

Political parties

Ruling party

Cambio Democrático (Democratic Change)

Main opposition party

Partido Revolucionario Democrático (PRD) (Democratic Revolutionary Party)

Population

3.93 million (2014)* (3,405,813; 2010, census figure)

Last census: 16 May 2010: 3,405,813

Population density: 36 inhabitants per square km. Urban population 75 per cent (2010 Unicef).

Annual growth rate: 1.9 per cent, 1990–2010 (Unicef).

Ethnic make-up

The population is predominantly mestizo, a mingling of indigenous Indian groups, Spanish and African (65 per cent), and Afro-Caribbean (14 per cent). Indians make up approximately 6 per cent of the total population. There are also descendants of North Americans, Chinese, French, Italians, Greeks and Asians (15 per cent).

The most numerous of Panama's indigenous groups are the Guaymi Indians who live primarily in the western provinces of Chiriqui, Bocas del Toro and Veraguas. The next most populous indigenous group is the Cuna, who live mainly in the San Blas Islands and along the nearby coast. The Choco is another indigenous group.

Religions

Traditionally the population is about 90 per cent Roman Catholic, with Protestants, Muslims, Baha'i and Hindus accounting for 5 per cent.

Education

Schooling lasts for 12 years, six years each in an elementary and a secondary school. Education is free up to university level. University education lasts for six years. There are three universities and nearly one in three of the relevant age group attends them.

Higher education is mainly provided by universities, schools and institutes. There are both public and private universities. State universities are autonomous. The University of Panama is responsible for establishing the guidelines relating to the universities in the country.

Literacy rate: 92 per cent adult rate; 97 per cent youth rate (15–24) (Unesco 2005). The 2007 Move Throughout Panama literacy programme was being revived in 2014 with Cuban Assistance. The government aims to reduce the 5.5 per cent illiteracy rate to 3 per cent by 2020.

Compulsory years: Six to 15

Enrolment rate: 106 per cent gross primary enrolment of relevant age group (including repeaters); 69 per cent gross secondary enrolment (World Bank).

Health

Panama has both a free public health care system and a private system that are generally served by the same professionals. Panama's hospitals, clinics and insurance plans are scrambling to meet the healthcare needs of wealthier Panamanians, many of whom are retired US civil servants. The cost of healthcare in Panama is lower than in the US and is often of better quality. This is fuelling 'healthcare tourism', with US citizens visiting Panama for medical and surgical treatment.

HIV/Aids

HIV prevalence: 0.9 per cent aged 15–49 in 2003 (World Bank)

Life expectancy: 76 years, 2004 (WHO 2006)

Fertility rate/Maternal mortality rate: 2.5 births per woman, 2010 (Unicef)

Child (under 5 years) mortality rate (per 1,000): 19 per 1,000 live births (WHO 2012)

Welfare

There is a large difference between welfare levels in the cities and in the countryside in Panama. While the percentage of the population below the poverty line is 15 per cent in urban areas, it rises to 65 per cent in rural areas. The national average is 37 per cent.

Panama's social security system is financed through a 6.75 per cent contribution from individual incomes and a 2.75 per cent contribution from company payrolls. Retirement ages are 62 for men and 57 for women. Medical services are provided through the Social Insurance Fund. Sick workers can claim 70 per cent of their average earnings from the last two months for a maximum period of 52 weeks.

Main cities

Panama City (capital, estimated population 441,014 in 2012), San Miguelito (355,313), Las Cumbres (suburb of Panama City) (112,992), Tocumen (107,625), Columbus (82,282), David (91,592), Arraiján (77,120).

Languages spoken

English is widely used, so much so that Panama should be considered bilingual. English is particularly spoken along the Caribbean coast and in the capital. Three distinct indigenous groups, the Cuna, Guaymi and Choco, also speak either Cuna, Movere or Embera.

Official language/s

Spanish

Media

Press

Dailies: In Spanish, *La Prensa* (www.prensa.com), *El Heraldo* (www.elheraldo.com.co), *La Crítica Libre* (www.critica.com.pa), *La Estrella de Panamá* (www.estrelladepanama.com) and *El Siglo* (www.elsiglo.com), and *La República* (evening). Online newspapers *El Panama America* (www.pa-digital.com.pa).

Weeklies: In English, *The Panama News* (www.thopanamanews.com) and *The News Herald* (www.newsherald.com) in Panama City.

Business: In Spanish, *Revista Centro Financiero* (www.asociacionbancaria.com) published by the central bank, *FOB Zona Libre De Colón* (www.colonfreezone.com) (trade directory) and *Capital Financiero* (www.capitalfinanciero.com).

Periodicals: There are some periodicals featuring travel and holiday news.

Broadcasting

The vast majority of television and radio broadcasting is in Spanish. There are 82 AM and 31 FM radio stations and six television stations.

Radio: In English, Panama FM (http://panamafm.com) regional station. In Spanish, RPC Radio (www.rpcradio.com), Meto 103.5 (www.meto103-5.com), Super Q (www.superqpanama.com), Omega Stereo (www.omegastereo.com) and KW Continente (http://kwcontinente.net).

There are a number of local, commercial radio stations.

Television: Commercial stations, in Spanish, RPC TV (www.rpctv.com), Telemetro (www.telemetro.com) and Televisora Nacional (TVN) (www.tvn-2.com). FETV (www.fetv.org) is an educational channel.

Economy

Panama has few primary resources; it relies instead on the ownership and management of the Panama Canal, which links the Pacific and Atlantic Oceans, and is a strategic component of world trade. Opened in 1914 it was initially under the control of the United States, then a joint US-Panama administration from 1979 until 31 December 1999 when the Panama Canal Authority took command. Work began in 2007 at a total cost of US$5.2 billion to widen the Canal to allow passage of larger super tankers; the work is scheduled for completion by the end of 2015. As of July 2015, 91 per cent of the project has been completed.

The country has developed a strong service sector, not only to international trade but also insurance and banking, which contributes around 75 per cent of GDP. The Canal, container ports and the Cólon Free Zone, which offers duty-free storage and redistribution to over 1,000 foreign companies, contribute around 15 per cent of GDP alone. Other service industries include tourism and flagship registration. The service sector accounts for more than three-quarters of GDP. The United States and China are the top users of the Canal. Panama also constructed a metro system in Panama City, valued at US$1.2 billion. It was inaugurated in April 2014.

Unlike other Central American countries, Panama does not have to rely on primary industries for GDP growth as its services sector helps protect it from the consequences of adverse weather conditions on the agricultural sector and of low global commodity prices, which have affected neighbouring economies. The service sector in 2012 constituted 74.7 per cent of GDP, while industry represented 14.1 per cent; manufacturing provided 0.2 per cent in 2014; and agriculture 2.9 per cent of GDP in 2014.

GDP growth was 10.1 per cent in 2008, before dropping sharply to 3.2 per cent in 2009 as the global economic crisis cut world trade, and impacted on revenues from the Canal. In 2010, as international trade picked up the economy rebounded with growth of 7.6 per cent and remained high at 6.2 per cent in 2014. Inflation was relatively stable at 2.6 per cent in 2014.

Despite its economic strength, Panama has an unequal income distribution, and since the mid-1990s it has been addressing the issues of poverty. In 2014, the UN Human Development Index (HDI) ranked Panama at 65 (out of 187) in the High Human Development category for development in health, education and income. The HDI ranking showed Panama's development trend was higher than the average for other countries within Latin America and the Caribbean. The poverty rate has been reduced from 37.3 per cent in 1997 to 24 per cent in 2012 and extreme poverty reduced from 18.8 per cent in 1997 to 14.2 per cent in 2008. By 2012, 4 per cent of the population lived on less than the equivalent of US$1.25 per day.

External trade

Panama does not belong to any regional trade or economic bloc but it does have bilateral free trade agreements with Chile, El Salvador, Singapore, Taiwan and all Central American countries, excluding Mexico.

Panama has on of the world's largest merchant fleet due to flagship registration, of around 7,000 ships. In 2014 the Panama Canal provided passage for 11,947 ships between the Pacific Ocean and the Caribbean Sea.

The Colón Free Zone (CFZ) provides the focus for foreign investment in a duty-free manufacturing zone, which is dominated by electronics, watches, pharmaceuticals, toiletries, clothing and jewellery, food processing, sugar refining and garment manufacturing.

Imports

Principal imports are fuels, machinery, vehicles, iron and steel rods and pharmaceuticals.

Main sources: US (25 per cent of total in 2043), China (8.1 per cent) and Mexico (4.2 per cent)

Exports

Fruit and nuts, fish, iron, wood and steel waste.

Main destinations: United States (19.8 per cent of total in 2014), Germany (10.7 per cent) and China (8.5 per cent).

Re-exports

Petroleum (to the US).

Agriculture

Farming

Panama's principal cash crops include bananas, sugar cane and coffee. Approximately 60 per cent of the country's total landmass is in agricultural use. About 16 per cent is cultivated while the remainder is natural pasture and forest. Food production does not meet domestic demand and consequently food imports are supplied by the US in order to meet the shortfall.

Panama's trading regime has been liberalised to reduce the average tariff level to 15 per cent for agricultural goods, regarded as one of the lowest in Latin America. The tariff rate was 6.1 per cent on all products in 2013.

The agricultural sector is ailing and has experienced difficulties resulting both from meteorological factors and poor demand for products. The strengthening of the agricultural sector is a government priority and includes upgrading irrigation systems and equipment. Problems include the decline in the price of coffee on international markets, which threatens to deepen rural poverty.

Fishing

The vast majority of Panama's annual fish catch is exported to the US- approximately 80 per cent- with the EU being the second biggest buyer of Panamanian fish.

Deep-sea shrimp fishing is the predominant activity in the sector and this type of fishing increased in increased in importance after the improvement to the port and fishing terminal at Vacamonte which was completed in 1994.

Freshwater fishing and marine products have increased in production steadily since the 1990s. Lobster exports rose by 39 per cent and there were also increases in the sales of fresh and frozen fish. The exception was shrimp exports, which dropped by 50 per cent.

Forestry

The majority of Panama's forested area has semi-deciduous tropical moist vegetation, while plantation forest comprises mainly pine. Approximately 40 per cent of the country's total landmass is covered by forests.

Panama has a large network of protected forest areas. However, large-scale deforestation has led to an annual average loss of 1.65 per cent, the equivalent of 52,000ha of forest cover.

The forest industry produces modest quantities of industrial roundwood, which is used for manufacturing sawnwood and panels. Some amount of forest products particularly paper is imported.

Industry and manufacturing

Panama's industrial sector remains relatively small scale, contributing around 12 per cent to total GDP and employing 16 per cent of the total workforce. The sector is predominantly geared toward domestic consumption.

The main industrial centres are Panama City and Colón, inclusive of food processing (about a third of the gross value of manufacturing output), textiles and clothing, footwear and leather goods, chemicals, plastics, paper, beverages, cigarettes, construction materials and petroleum products from the Las Minas refinery near Colón (capacity 100,000bpd).

The emphasis is on encouraging foreign investment in labour-intensive, light assembly, export-based industries.

Tourism

In addition to the Canal, there are a variety of inland and coastal destinations, particularly conducive to ecotourism and heritage attractions, including three national parks and the cultural, historic district of Panamá and Portobelo San Lorenzo, all of which are on Unesco's World Heritage List.

The tourist industry is recognised as an important component of the economy and contributed around 17.5 per cent of GDP (2014), in total contributions. Travel and tourism investment totalled 7.1 per cent of total investments in 2014 with forecasts for this to rise by 5.3 per cent per annum over the next ten years.

The Panama Tourism Authority took positive action in 2011. It launched a marketing campaign with a target of two million visitors from the US and other Latin American countries. It negotiated an agreement with Mexico to increase the frequency of existing flights into Panama and formed an association with a Russian travel operator to open up Panama as a new market.

The expansion of Tocumen International Airport, was completed in January 2012. The new, US$100 million, North Concourse has 12 additional gates to allow a 50 per cent increase in passenger traffic. Cruise ship visits are being encouraged and account for a growing proportion of arrivals.

Tourism was not a major focus for Panama before the early 1990s. As American involvement in Panama waned and as Panama's leaders began to exert greater control domestically, political and economic instability ensued, making Panama less attractive for tourists. Subsequently in 1981, the famed dictator, Manuel Noriega emerged after Omar Torrijos died in a mysterious plane crash. Noriega's tenure saw relations between Panama and the US turn hostile and escalated into a military confrontation, which led to his capture by US troops. Fortunately democratic elections took place thereafter and brought new emphasis on accountability and economic growth. Over the past decade, tourism has bloomed into a major services sector for Panama.

The World Economic Forum placed Panama at 34 out of 141 in its 'Travel and Tourism Competitiveness Index Ranking' in 2015.

Environment

Deforestation continues at an alarming rate, even in National parks and the Canal watershed. About 80 per cent of

Panama's coral reefs have been destroyed. Soil erosion is becoming a serious problem in many areas, and Panama's desert in the province of Los Santos (the legacy of slash and burn ranching activities) is expanding.
Illegal gold mining by Colombian immigrants is also contaminating rivers and local water supplies in the Darien and Portobello National parks.
There is serious pollution in the Bay of Panama.

Mining
At present, the mining sector of the Panamanian economy contributes very little to GDP and accounts for a small section of the total labour force. Approximately 0.1 per cent of GDP is generated by the sector and 0.2 per cent of total employment is accounted for by it. However, the mining sector in Panama is, at present, severely underdeveloped. It is estimated that, if properly developed, the sector could grow to contribute as much as 15 per cent of total GDP and directly employ up to 4,000 people.
Mining has become one of the fastest growing sectors in the economy, and it is expected to grow even quicker than initially thought as the government identified mineral reserves estimated at US$200 billion in 2014. Mining related activities increased by 25 per cent in 2013. The ongoing construction of a US$6.2 billion copper, gold, silver and molybdenum Cobre Panama mine should help to expand the industry by a third.
Despite its important mineral reserves, Panama has not experienced a mining boom. There is only one operating mine in the country, the Molejon Gold mine. The government is keen on promoting exploration of gold and copper deposits. Tax concessions and other benefits are available to foreign companies interested in developing the resources. However, proposals for new mines often face strong local opposition.
Copper reserves in Panama are considered to be relatively large with significant deposits in Cerro Colorado and Petaquilla, although the development of the mines has been slow. It is estimated that copper reserves at Cerro Colorado are one billion tonnes, making it one of the world's largest deposits. The Petaquilla studies show copper reserves of 1.1 billion tonnes and significant quantities of gold and molybdenum.
There are also known reserves of manganese, and limited extraction of limestone, clays, gravel and sea salt. Cement is produced by Empresa Estatal de Cemento Bayano at a plant with a capacity of 300,000 tonnes per year (tpy).

Hydrocarbons
There are no hydrocarbon reserves; all energy needs must be met by imports. Consumption of oil was 92,000 barrels per day (bpd) in 2007. There were two separate proposals in 2007, by multinational consortiums, for oil refineries producing two million bpd in one case and processing 350,000bpd of crude oil in the other and which would have turned Panama into a petrochemical hub. But by 2008 the first had been shelved as the global economic crisis worsened and the latter was still subject to determining its viability.
The Panama Canal is a major transit centre and Panama is very important to the hydrocarbon industry. Petroleum, at 15 per cent of total canal shipments, is the largest single commodity (by tonnage) to pass through the canal, around two-thirds from the Atlantic to the Pacific. A US$100 million contract for construction of the second phase of the Trans-Panama Pipeline, including expansion of terminal facilities (for 5.4 billion barrels of oil) and the oil pipeline from Chiriqui Grande on the Atlantic coast to Puerto Armuelles on the Pacific coast, was signed on 15 October 2009. The pipeline will be used to transport African and Atlantic regional oil speedily to the Pacific coast for onward shipment to the US West Coast.
Although there have been some discoveries of oil and gas deposits these have not been in commercially viable quantities. There are coal deposits in the provinces of Colón and Chiriquí but are not used.

Energy
Total installed generating capacity was 1.49GW in 2006. Around 80 per cent of electricity is generated by hydropower. The remaining 20 per cent of capacity is provided by conventional thermal power by the Panama Canal Authority. Consumption is growing at 4 per cent per annum and growth in capacity is expected to increase by 1,000MW between 2009–12, as hydroelectric plants come online at Los Algarrobos and Los Planetas in 2009 and Dos Mares in 2010 and the largest, Changuinola in 2012; other smaller plants will also become operational.

Financial markets
Stock exchange
Bolsa de Valores de Panamá (Panama Stock Exchange)

Banking and insurance
The banking and financial services sector is regulated by the Comisión Bancaria Nacional. The central bank carries out retail and commercial transactions and development banking, it is government-owned and operates as a depository of public funds. Only coins are minted locally, the notes in circulation being US dollars. Interest rates follow US dollar rates.
Panama banking was rated as top for tier one capital, among banks in Central America, as recently as 2004. The Panamanian banking sector is expected to benefit from growth in Central America rather than trying to compete against Brazil, Mexico or Argentina. Before the overall liberalisation of the banking sector in Latin America, banks had used Panama as a base to target markets in the rest of the region; those same banks can now target other Latin American markets directly.
Although it does not have the same size of assets in its banking sector, Panama has always seen its main competitors as the Cayman Islands and the Bahamas. Panama requests all banks to have a physical presence in the country.

Central bank
Banco Nacional de Panamá

Main financial centre
Panama City

Time
GMT minus five hours

Geography
Panama is a narrow country situated at the southern end of the isthmus separating North and South America. To the west is Costa Rica and to the east is Colombia in South America. The Caribbean Sea lies to the north and the Pacific Ocean to the south.
The eastern section of the country, adjoining Colombia, is thinly populated. The western section of the country, near the Costa Rican border, is the richest agricultural area.

Hemisphere
Northern

Climate
For its relatively small area, the geography of Panama's 'S'-shaped isthmus is quite varied and consists of three distinct areas.
The largest, which accounts for approximately 85 per cent of the land area, is lowland coastal areas, with a tropical rainy climate. Here the temperature ranges from 21 degrees Centigrade (C) to 31 degrees C. The rainy season is approximately April–December, with the heaviest rains falling in November (about 570mm). Rainfall is significantly heavier on the Pacific coast than on the Caribbean. The driest season is January—April.
About 10 per cent of the land area lies between 700 metres and 1,490 metres and has a temperate climate.
The remaining 5 per cent of the land is at an altitude of about 1,520 metres and is cold.

Dress codes
Like most of Central America, Panama remains fairly conservative and formal in respect of dress. Although Panama City is cosmopolitan, it is not considered proper for adults to wear shorts in the city, regardless of the heat. It is also considered inappropriate for women to wear shorts in public, either in the city or countryside. A certain amount of leniency is allowed to foreigners, who are thought not to know any better.
For business appointments, men should wear suits and women should wear dresses. A man may wear a *panabrisa,* a loose fitting, short sleeved shirt, which is not tucked into the trousers. However, these are not generally worn by top officials or businessmen during formal business meetings.

Entry requirements
Passports
Required by all, valid for six months.
Visa
Required by all, except nationals of EU/EEA and most Latin American countries, Israel, Singapore and North and South Korea. For latest information, see http://panama.embassy.uk.com.
Currency advice/regulations
There are no restrictions on the import and export of local or foreign currencies. Local currency exists only as coins and is interchangeable with US currency of the same denomination.

Health (for visitors)
Mandatory precautions
Cholera vaccination certificate if arriving from an infected area. Yellow fever vaccination certificate may be required for visits to certain regions.
Advisable precautions
A yellow fever vaccination certificate is required only for those who are going to visit the provinces of Bocas del Toro and Darien. Typhoid and polio vaccinations are advisable. Malaria risk exists in rural areas – prophylaxis recommended (in some places malaria is reported to be resistant to chloroquine). Water precautions should be taken, especially outside cities. Rabies is endemic.
Medical insurance is necessary as medical charges are high.

Hotels
There is a wide variety of hotels available. It is advisable to book in advance, particularly between December and May. There is a 10 per cent government surcharge on bills.

Credit cards
Major credit cards are accepted.

Public holidays (national)
Fixed dates
1 Jan (New Year), 9 Jan (Martyrs' Day), 1 May (Labour Day), 15 Aug (Panama City Day/Assumption Day), 3 Nov (Independence from Colombia Day), 4 Nov (Flag Day), 5 Nov (Colón City Independence Day, Colón City only), 10 Nov (First Call for Independence from Spain), 28 Nov (Independence from Spain Day,), 24 Dec (Christmas Eve), 25 Dec (Christmas Day), 31 Dec (New Year's Eve).
For public holidays falling on a Sunday, the following Monday is observed as a holiday.
Variable dates
Carnival (two days, Feb), Ash Wednesday, Maundy Thursday, Good Friday.

Working hours
Banking
Mon–Sat: 0800–1300.
Business
Mon–Fri: 0800–1200, 1400–1700; Sat: 0800–1200.
Government
Mon–Fri: 0900–1700.
Shops
Mon–Sat: 0800–1200, 1400–1800/1900.

Electricity supply
110V AC, 60 cycles (domestic), 220V AC (industrial).

Social customs/useful tips
The use of titles, such as Doctor, Arquitecto, Licenciado, Profesora, is widespread, and it is courteous to learn and use the correct titles for both men and women. Do not immediately launch into a business conversation. It is considered polite to first get to know the person to whom you are talking.
Men and women shake hands in Panama and social kisses on one cheek are also exchanged. At a large social gathering do not expect your host or hostess to introduce you to every individual. Feel free to circulate and introduce yourself. A small gift for the host or hostess is always appreciated.
Late night parties with dinner served at 2200 or 2300 are common. It is accepted to be up to two hours late for a large social gathering, 30 minutes for smaller gatherings.
Panama is an eclectic country, with a ready acceptance of immigrants from all over the world. Public celebrations therefore express the hybrid nature of its diverse cultures. Although once part of Colombia, Panamanian culture and traditions are uniquely its own and show Caribbean rather than South American influence. However, there is little interchange between different social and ethnic groups.
Do not take photos without permission, especially of Indians. Be prepared to pay for them if permission is given.

Security
Common street crime has always been prevalent in Panama City and Colón, but poverty as a result of the disrupted economy has worsened the situation. Visitors are warned specifically to avoid the San Miguelito squatter section of Panama City.
The Judicial Technical Police (PTJ) is responsible for the struggle against the still prevalent narcotics traffic. The PTJ, which is supposed to work jointly with the Customs Service, is composed of former Panamanian Defence Force members and is widely reported to be corrupt.

Getting there
Air
National airline: Copa Airlines (Compañía Panameña de Aviación)
International airport/s: Panama City-Tocumen (PTY), 27km from city; duty-free shop, restaurant, buffet, bank, post office, car hire.
Airport tax: US$20.
Surface
Road: The Pan-American Highway is the main route into Panama from Costa Rica. The border with Colombia is forested and unsafe.
Rail: Panama has no rail connections with neighbouring countries.
Water: Cruise ships call at the ports of Colon on the Atlantic coast and Panama city on the Pacific coast.
Main port/s: Balboa (Pacific), Cristóbal (Atlantic).

Getting about
National transport
Air: Several domestic airlines link Panama City with all parts of the country.
Road: The road system is generally good, but sections can be unpassable in the rainy season (Apr–Dec). The Panama section of Pan-American Highway connects Chepo and Panama City with the Costa Rican border. The Trans-Isthmian Highway links Panama City and Colón.
Buses: Regional buses link most towns. Ticabus run modern air-conditioned service to main centres; it is advisable to book in advance.
Rail: The Panama Canal Railway Company operates trains daily (Mon–Fri) between Panama City and Colón.
City transport
Taxis: Travel by taxi is inexpensive. Taxis are readily available and can be ordered by telephone. Taxis are not metered, fares being regulated and fixed according to the number of zones traversed. The drivers carry a map of the zones for consultation. Fares should be agreed beforehand.

Car hire
Available in main towns and at the airport. International licence required. After 90 days a local permit is required.

BUSINESS DIRECTORY

The addresses listed below are a selection only. While World of Information makes every endeavour to check these addresses, we cannot guarantee that changes have not been made, especially to telephone numbers and area codes. We would welcome any corrections.

Telephone area codes
The international direct dialling (IDD) code for Panama is +507, followed by the customer's number.

Chambers of Commerce
American Chamber of Commerce and Industry of Panama, PO Box 168, Balboa Ancon, Panama (tel: 269-3881; fax: 223-3508; e-mail: amcham@panamcham.com).

Colón Cámara de Comercio, Agricultura e Industrias, Calle 6, Avenida Amador Guerrero 322, Colón (tel: 441-7223; fax: 441-7281; e-mail: camcolon@pananet.com).

Panama Cámara de Comercio, Industria y Agricultura, Avenidas Cuba y Ecuador 33A, PO Box 74, Zona 1, Panama (tel: 225-1233; fax: 227-4186; e-mail: infocciap@panacamara.com).

Panama Federacion de Cámaras de Comercio e Industria, Avenida Cuba, Zona 1, Panama (tel: 225-4615; fax: 227-4186).

Banking
Asociación Bancaria de Panamá, Apartado 4554, zona 5, Panama (tel: 263-7044).

Banco Comercial de Panamá SA (BANCOMER), PO Box 7659, Panama (tel: 263-6800; fax: 263-8033).

Banco Continental de Panamá SA, PO Box 135, Via España, Panama 9A (tel: 263-5955; fax: 263-7646).

Banco Disa, PO Box 7201, Panama 5 (tel: 263-5933; fax: 264-1084).

Banco de Latinoamérica SA (BANCOLAT), PO Box 4401, Panama 5 (tel: 264-0466; fax: 263-7368).

Banco del Istmo SA, PO Box 6-3823, El Dorado, Panama (tel: 269-5555; fax: 269-5168).

Banco del Pacífico SA, PO Box 6-3100, El Dorado, Panama (tel: 263-5833; fax: 263-7481).

Banco General SA, PO Box 4592, Panama 5 (tel: 227-3200; fax: 227-3427).

Banco Internacional de Costa Rica SA (BICSA), PO Box 600, Panama 1 (tel: 263-6822; fax: 263-6393).

Banco Internacional de Panamá SA (BIPAN), PO Box 11181, Panama 6 (tel: 263-9000; fax: 263-9514).

Banco Latinoamericano de Exportaciones SA (BLADEX), PO Box 6-1497, El Dorado, Panama (tel: 263-6766; fax: 269-6333).

Banco Nacional de Panamá, International Operations Department, PO Box 5220, Panama 5 (tel: 263-8292).

Banco Panamericano SA (PANABANK), PO Box 1828, Panama 1 (tel: 262-0881; fax: 269-1537).

Comisión Bancaria Nacional, Piso 12, Edificio de Boston, Viá Espana, Panama (tel: 223-2855; fax: 223-2864).

Central bank
Banco Nacional de Panamá, Via España 120, Torre Banco Nacional, PO Box 5220, Panama 5 (tel: 205-2000; fax: 205-2150; e-mail:mercador@banconal.com.pa).

Stock exchange
Bolsa de Valores de Panamá (Panama Stock Exchange), www.panabolsa.com

Travel information
Copa Airlines, Avenida Justo Arosemena y Calle 39, Apartado 1572, Panama (tel: 227-5232; fax: 227-1952).

National tourist organisation offices
Instituto Panameño de Turismo, Centro de Convenciones Atlapa, PO Box 4421, Zona 5, Panama (tel: 226-7000; fax: 226-4002; e-mail: infotur@ns.ipat.gob.pa).

Ministries
Ministry of the Canal (tel: 263-4545; fax: 263-4355).

Ministry of Commerce and Industry, Edificio de la Loteria, Piso 21, Ave Cuba, Apartado 9658, Zona 4, Panama (tel: 227-4177; fax: 227-3927).

Ministry of Development and Agriculture, Edificio 576, Altos de Curundu, Avenida Frangipany, Panama (tel: 232-5041; fax: 232-5044).

Ministry of Education, Apartado 2440, Zona 3, Panama (tel: 262-2000; fax: 262-9087).

Ministry of Employment and Social Welfare, Apartado 2441, Zona 3, Panama (tel: 225-7503; fax: 225-4529).

Ministry of Finance and Treasury, Calle 35 y 36 entre Ave, Perú y Cuba, Apdo 5245, Zona 5, Panama (tel: 227-4879; fax: 227-2357).

Ministry of Foreign Affairs, Amador, Edificio, Panama 4 (tel: 228-2815; fax: 227-2716).

Ministry of Government and Justice, Calle 1 a, San Felipe, Apartado 1628, Zona 1, Panama (tel: 212-0287; fax: 212-0372).

Ministry of Health, Calle 36 y Ave Cuba, Apartado 2048, Zona 1, Panama (tel: 225-6080; fax: 227-5276).

Ministry of Housing, Ave México y calle 12 de octubre, Apartado 5228, Zona 5, Panama (tel: 262-4358; fax: 262-9250).

Ministry of Labour and Social Welfare, Avenida Balboa, Edif de Diego, 7 Piso, Apdo 2441, Zona 3 (tel: 225-7503; fax: 225-4529).

Ministry of Planning and Economic Policy, Via España, Edif OGAWA, Apartado 2694, Zona 3, Panama (tel: 269-2810; fax: 264-7755).

Ministry of the President, Palacio Presidencial, San Felipe, Panama (tel: 227-9662; fax: 227-4119).

Ministry of Property and Finance, Calle 35 y 36, entre Ave Perú Ave Cuba, Panama (tel: 227-3992; fax: 227-2357).

Ministry of Public Works, Curundu Edif 1019, Apartado 1632, Zona 1, Panama (tel: 232-5333; fax: 232-5776).

Other useful addresses
ARI Promotion and Marketing Department, PO Box 2097, Balboa Ancón, Panama (tel: 228-8037/5668; fax: 228-1698/7488; e-mail: ari@sinfo.net).

Asociación Panameña de Radiodifusión SA, Avenida 11 y Calle 28, Apdo 1795, Panama City (tel: 225-0160).

British Embassy, Commercial Section, Torre Swiss Bank, 4, Urb Marbella, Calle 53, Apdo 889, Panama 1 (tel: 269-0866; fax: 223-0730).

Central Post Office, Plaza Catedral, Calle 6, Panama City.

Colón Free Zone, Avenida Roosevelt, Apdo 1118, Colón (tel: 441-5794, 441-5114, 445-1033, 445-1559; fax: 445-2165).

Consejo Nacional de Inversiones (CNI), Edif Banco Nacional de Panamá, Apdo 2350, Panama (tel: 647-211).

Consular and Maritime Affairs, PO Box 5245, 50th Street and 69th Street, Plaza Guadalupe, San Francisco, Panama 5 (tel: 270-0166, 277-0326; fax: 270-0716).

Corporación Azucarera La Victoria, Apartado 1228,, zona 1, Panama (tel: 229-4797; fax: 229-4806).

Dirección Nacional de Medios de Comunicación Social (Panamanian Media Authority), Ministerio de Gobierno y Justicia, Apartado 1628, zona 1, Panama (tel: 262-3197/3166; fax: 262-1490).

Empleos y Servicios de Oficina SA (translator Service), Avenida 4, Panama City (tel: 225-0527).

Instituto de Recursos Hidráulicos y Electrificación (IRHE), Edif Poli, Avenida Justo Arosemanay 26 Este, Apdo 5285, Panama 5 (tel: 262-6272).

Instituto Panameño de Comercio Exterior, Avenida Manuel Icaza, Apdo 1897, El Dorado 6, Panama.

Panama Stock Exchange, Calle Elvira Mendez y Calle 52, Edificio Vallarino, Panama (tel: 269-1966; fax: 269-2457).

Panamanian Embassy (USA), 2862 McGill Terrace, NW, Washington DC 20008 (tel: (+1-202)-483-1407; fax: (+1-202)-483-8413: e-mail: panaemb@erols.com).

ProPrivat, Ave Perú y Calle 35, Apartado Postal 1464-Paitilla, Panama (tel: 225-0123/6172/4387/0630; fax: 227-4620).

Sindicato de Industriales de Panamá, Apdo 952, Panama City (tel: 230-0619).

US Embassy, Avenida Balboa entre Calle 37 y 38, Apdo 6959, Panama 5 (tel: 227-1777; fax: 203-9470).

Internet sites

Daily internet newspaper: *El Siglo*: http://www.elsiglo.com

General information on doing business in Panama: http://www.infonetsa.com/infonetsa/incorp/buss1.htm

Papua New Guinea

KEY FACTS

Official name: The Independent State of Papua New Guinea (PNG)

Head of State: Queen Elizabeth II; represented by Governor General Sir Michael Ogio (from 25 Feb 2011)

Head of government: Prime Minister Peter O'Neill (PNC) (from 2011; re-elected 3 Aug 2012)

Ruling party: Coalition led by the People's National Congress (PNC) (from 3 Aug 2012)

Area: 462,840 square km

Population: 7.53 million (2014)*

Capital: Port Moresby

Official language: English, Tok Pisin, Motu

Currency: Kina (K) = 100 toea

Exchange rate: K2.80 per US$ (Sep 2015)

GDP per capita: US$2,133 (2014)*

GDP real growth: 5.84% (2014)*

GDP: US$16.06 billion (2014)*

Inflation: 5.31% (2014)*

Balance of trade: US$1.57 billion (2013)

Foreign debt: US$1.26 billion (2012)

Annual FDI: -US$309.20 million (2011)

* estimated figure

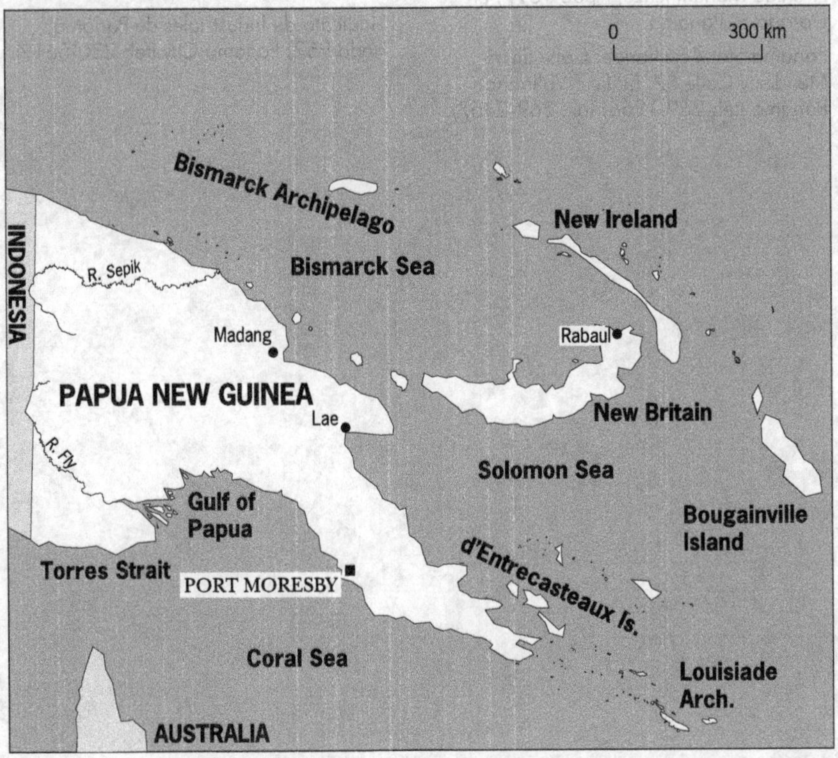

Given the often volatile characteristics of politics in Papua New Guinea (PNG), it came as no surprise when the organisers of the July 2015 Pacific Games, held in Port Moresby, announced that in the run-up to the opening ceremony, they had faced a 'campaign' to discredit the readiness of the stadium venues. The comments came after Papua New Guinea (PNG) opposition leader Don Polye called for an independent engineer to declare the facilities safe, claiming that the work had been rushed to completion. However, the Pacific Games Organising Committee chief executive Peter Stewart dismissed the claims, announcing that the committee had 'every confidence that these venues are being built to world-class standards.' During the two weeks of the games, Port Moresby hosted more than 20 Pacific countries – including Australia and New Zealand – for the games. Mr Polye had long expressed his disapproval of the preparations and in March called for the opening ceremony to be delayed. In the event, the games were a great success, to the extent that in his closing address, governor-general Sir Michael Ogio announced that Papua New Guinea was planning to bid for the 2026 Commonwealth Games.

Calm before…

In June 2014 Papua New Guinea's politics had seemed to be calm enough, even quiet. Prime Minister O'Neill's ruling coalition controlled around 100 votes in the 111-seat parliament, leaving him unconcerned about losing votes. He was also basking in the reflected (gas) glory of PNG's first shipments of liquid natural gas to Asia. One week later and all was anything but calm. Mr O'Neill found himself on the wrong end of corruption allegations. Worse still, under the PNG criminal code corruption allegations automatically trigger an arrest warrant. The accusations did little more than confirm, in the minds of most Papua New Guineans, the perception that in their country there was no such thing as an honest politician. The corruption charges related to payments of AUS$28 million (US$19.6 million) to lawyers for work done for the government between 2003 and 2006. This was well before Mr O'Neill took power in 2011, but the government still had not paid the bills and payment was finally authorised in 2012. Exactly who authorised the payments was a crucial, moot point. A copy of a January 2012 letter apparently bearing Mr O'Neill's signature had emerged, instructing the finance ministry to make the payment. Mr O'Neill said it was a forgery. Maintaining the colourful flow of events, the PM's chief lawyer – the formidable Tiffany Twivey Nongorr successfully argued that it was improper to pursue Mr O'Neill for allegedly authorising the payment of bills that were still technically considered valid.

Rumours have long surrounded Mr O'Neill's business and political connections. Many of these – which are only rumours – relate to the PNG prime minister's connections with the Israeli LR Group. There are persistent rumours that during a trip to Israel in 2013 Mr O'Neill arranged an arms and support deal worth approximately US$500 million – which included giving the LR Group a contract in PNG intelligence activities. It was reported that PNG and Australian sources had confirmed that the prime minister had already asked Australia to remove the Australian Federal Police operating in PNG. Communications monitoring equipment and expertise were allegedly part of the deal signed between the two prime ministers. Some sources suggested that the Israeli contractors would also have access to the banking system, including private banks and the Bank of Papua New Guinea (central bank), the Investment Promotion Authority and the Internal Revenue Commission. Perhaps with some paranoia, it was also reported that they would report direct to the prime minister.

The economy

According to the Asian Development Bank (ADB), economic growth in Papua New Guinea (PNG) rose to 8.0 per cent in 2014 following the start of liquefied natural gas (LNG) exports. Growth in other sectors of the economy remained modest. Construction output fell by 6.4 per cent in 2014 and this spilled over into the broader economy, stalling wholesale and retail trade growth at 5.5 per cent and slowing utilities from 9.0 per cent growth in 2013 to 6.0 per cent in 2014. Long-term declines continued at a number of older mining operations, but rising output from a new nickel project meant mining and quarrying as a whole expanded by 5.9 per cent.

Agriculture, forestry and fishery growth picked up to 3.9 per cent in 2014 as the weather improved, enabling greater production and exports of cocoa, coffee and oil palm. However, much of this growth was recovery from weak growth in previous years. The sector continued to be hampered by low global commodity prices, declining yields from ageing plantations, inadequate pest control and poor transport infrastructure. In the view of the ADB, PNG's fiscal policy remained expansionary, with the government achieving its planned budget deficit of 5.9 per cent of GDP in 2014.

However, with revenue growth lower than expected and a number of unplanned expenditures, hitting the target required an expenditure slowdown toward the end of the year and K1 billion (US$0.36 billion) (nearly 5 per cent of domestic revenue) reapportioned from unspent project trust funds back into the central government account. Despite the slowdown, government spending grew by 20 per cent in 2014, continuing 4 years of rapid fiscal expansion that had seen expenditure grow by an average of 25 per cent annually.

PNG's rapid spending growth over the three years had required a significant increase in government borrowing, some 70 per cent of which was from local capital markets. This has the potential to crowd out finance for local investment and has begun to push up local interest rates. Government borrowing costs for long-term domestic debt reached 14 per cent per annum in 2014. While government debt remained modest by regional standards, the cost of servicing it was rising sharply, from 5.5 per cent of domestic revenue in 2013 to an expected 9.2 per cent in 2015.

Aggregate demand eased following the completion of LNG project construction and global commodity prices declines, exerting downward pressure on inflation during 2014. However, these pressures were more than offset by government spending and price rises for imports caused by a depreciating currency. The rise in the consumer price index accelerated in 2014 and reached a high of 8.3 per cent in December, averaging 5.9 per cent for the whole year.

In June 2014, the Bank of Papua New Guinea attempted to stem the kina depreciation by placing a trading band on an official rate. That the official rate valued the kina 20–30 per cent higher than prevailing market rates triggered a shortage of foreign exchange as residents and businesses moved currency offshore.

Although the kina was allowed to depreciate slowly in the latter half of the year, foreign currency shortages continued, with all the commercial banks reporting order backlogs. The central bank's continuing intervention in the currency market had drained foreign exchange reserves during 2014. By the end of the year, they were sufficient to cover only 4.6 months of imports, down from 9 months at the end of 2013 and a peak of 10.5 months at the end of 2011.

The PNG current account balance strengthened significantly in 2014, recording a deficit equal to 11.4 per cent of GDP, or half of the 22.6 per cent deficit in

KEY INDICATORS — Papua New Guinea

	Unit	2011	2012	2013	2014	**2015
Population	m	*6.66	*6.83	*7.35	*7.53	*7.72
Gross domestic product (GDP)	US$bn	12.70	15.13	15.41	*16.06	*20.04
GDP per capita	US$	1,900	2,217	*2,098	*2,133	*2,597
GDP real growth	%	8.9	8.1	4.5	*5.8	*19.3
Inflation	%	8.4	2.2	5.0	*5.3	*4.8
Exports (fob) (goods)	US$m	5,744.7	6,332.7	–	–	–
Imports (fob) (goods)	US$m	3,528.9	4,766.6	–	–	–
Balance of trade	US$m	2,215.8	1,566.1	–	–	–
Current account	US$m	-269.0	-7,717.0	-4,750.0	*1,947.0	*2,053.0
Total reserves minus gold	US$m	3,054.7	3,930.3	2,774.7	2,253.5	–
Foreign exchange	US$m	3,038.2	3,915.2	2,759.7	–	–
Exchange rate	per US$	2.52	2.09	2.52	2.59	–

* estimated figure ** forecast figure

2013. This improvement reflected growing surpluses in the goods balance driven by the onset of LNG exports and strengthened agricultural exports, partly offsetting large deficits in services and income.

GDP growth was forecast at 15.0 per cent in 2015, slowing to 5.0 per cent in 2016. Leading this growth is the oil and gas sector, as 2015 will be the first full year of LNG production. While near a record high, current growth projections for 2015 are significantly below the 21.0 per cent forecast in the ADB's *Asian Development Outlook 2014*. This largely reflects the early commencement of LNG production in 2014, which raised the base in 2014 and the delay of peak production until 2016, which lowers projected production this year. A rebound in the mining and quarrying sector was expected as operations at a new nickel mine continued to expand, more than offsetting declines at a number of older operations. Real growth in the sector was expected to reach 12.0 per cent in 2015, falling back to 3.0 per cent in 2016. In contrast with mining and petroleum, activity in the rest of the economy was expected to remain modest, with non-mineral growth forecast at 4.0 per cent in 2015 and 2016.

Risk assessment

Economy	Good
Politics	Fair
Regional stability	Good

COUNTRY PROFILE

1526 Islanders first traded with ships from China and the Malay Empire. Portuguese sailor Jorge de Meneses is the first European visitor. He names one of the islands 'ilhas dos Papuas' ('land of fuzzy-haired people)'.
1546 The Spanish explorer Inigo Ortiz de Retes named the other main island New Guinea because the islanders looked like the people of Guinea in Africa.
1768 French explorer Louis-Antoine de Bougainville landed on the islands during his circumnavigation of the world.
1873 Port Moresby was named after one of several English explorers to lay claim to the island for Great Britain.
1942–45 Parts of both territories were occupied by Japanese forces during the Second World War.
1949 A joint administration for the two territories was established by Australia. The union was named the Territory of Papua and New Guinea.
1971 The territory was renamed Papua and New Guinea.
1975 Became independent as Papua New Guinea.
1988 Conflict on Bougainville Island began when a number of locals, unhappy with the level of royalties they were receiving from the Panguna copper mine and concerned about its environmental impact, began to protest. The islanders' opposition organised itself into the Bougainville Revolutionary Army (BRA) and full-scale war began.
1989 Panguna mine was closed down by protesters.
1997 Prime Minister Julius Chan attempted to hire UK-based mercenaries to quell the nine-year Bougainville uprising, prompting intervention by the Australian navy and the resignation of Chan. Bill Skate, a reformist, was elected prime minister of a government largely dominated by politicians from the previously ousted government.
1998 The government signed a truce with the secessionist group, the Bougainville Reconciliation Government (BRG), seeking to end the nine-year rebellion on the island of Bougainville, in which up to 20,000 are believed to have been killed. The People's Progress Party (PPP) left the ruling coalition, joining opposition parties and groups in an attempt to oust Skate's government. The prime minister announced the suspension of parliament.
1999 The interim BRG held its first sitting. Skate resigned from the PNG premiership and was replaced by Mekere Morauta of the People's Democratic Movement (PDM).
2000 Morauta was forced to adjourn parliament after a bid to limit inter-party defections threatened to trigger a vote of no confidence in his government. Local landowners brought a suit against Rio Tinto in the US courts, for environmental and social damage at Panguna.
2001 The government signed the Bougainville Peace Agreement with the BRG. PNG accepted Australian aid in return for taking asylum-seekers who sought to settle in Australia.
2002 The National Alliance Party (NAP) won parliamentary elections. Michael Somare became prime minister.
2003 A new heads of agreement was signed for the proposed US$6 billion PNG gas pipeline to Queensland, Australia. The Supreme Court ruled that the election of Albert Kipalan as governor general was invalid. Pato Kakaraya was elected governor general. PNG signed an agreement to introduce more Australian involvement in areas of law and order and public administration PNG.
2004 The Supreme Court ruled the election of Pato Kakaraya as governor general null and void and ordered a new election. Prime Minister Somare dismissed the People's National Congress (PNC) ministers from the cabinet. Talks began to finalise the constitution for the autonomous government of Bougainville province. Paulias Matane was sworn in as governor general of PNG.
2005 Joseph Kabui (Bougainville People's Congress) won presidential elections of the Bougainville Autonomous Government. Rebel leader of the Bougainville secessionists, Francis Ona, died.
2006 Continuous, heavy rains early in the year caused destruction and food shortages in several provinces.
2007 A new system of voting was introduced; majority voting was replaced by limited preferential voting (of three most preferred candidates). Prime Minister Michael Somare was re-elected by parliament with 86 votes to 21 for Julius Chan.
2008 The president of Bougainville, Joseph Kabui, died; vice president John Tabinaman became acting president. A huge king tidal wave flooded villages and towns along 500km of the northern coastline around Wewak, affecting over 50,000 people and making over 500 people homeless.
2009 James Tanis took office as president of Bougainville. Two new highlands region provinces were approved by parliament. Hela and Jiwaka will be formed from the existing Southern and Western Highlands provinces.
2010 John Momis was elected as president of Bougainville. Paulias Matane was reappointed governor general.. The Supreme Court ruled as unconstitutional the re-election by parliament of Governor General Sir Paulias Matane and removed him from office. Jeffery Nape became acting governor general. Prime Minister Somare voluntarily stepped down in order to clear his name, following accusations of failing to submit full annual financial statements in the 1990s. Foreign minister Sam Abal stood in as prime minister. Governor General Nape resigned without explanation.
2011 In January, parliament elected Michael Ogio as governor general, beating the opposition candidate Sir Pato Kakaraya (by 65 votes to 23). After five weeks out of office on leave-of-absence while awaiting an investigation into the non-submission of financial records, and following legal advice that a prime minister could not step aside temporarily, Prime Minister Somare resumed his premiership on 17 January. As parliament had already adjourned until 10 May it was unable to question his behaviour. Sir Michael Ogio was sworn into office in February. In March, Prime Minister Somare was found guilty of 13 counts of not filing, or late filing or incomplete filing of financial annual returns to the country's Ombudsman Commission, by a leadership tribunal. The public prosecutor called for Somare's

dismissal from office. The leadership tribunal decided to suspend Somare from office for two weeks. He was suspended in April and Sam Abal became acting prime minister. Somare did not return to office and in April announced that he was taking indefinite medical leave; he was later admitted to hospital for heart surgery in Singapore. Disgruntled NAP members of parliament, seeing no end to Somare's absence, as he remained in intensive care in hospital, joined with opposition members and voted to declare the office of prime minister vacant and elected Peter O'Neill (PNC) (70-24) as prime minister in August. Arthur Somare (son of the former prime minister), who had been charged with the same offence as his father, lost his appeal in August, to delay his trial until leadership of the NAP was concluded. The courts rejected an appeal that O'Neill's election was unconstitutional. Prime Minister O'Neill announced an investigation would begin into allegations of corruption by a government department and the loss of US$883.9 million in public funds. Nineteen MPs, of the NAP were expelled from the party in September for supporting the opposition in deposing Michael Somare and electing Peter O'Neill as prime minister. They also supported disqualification of Somare from parliament due to his continued absenteeism. During the Commonwealth Heads of Government summit, on 28 October, the 16 countries in which the British monarch is Head of State unanimously agreed to change the royal line of succession from that of first born son to the first born child (regardless of its gender). The change will be enacted after the succession of Prince William (currently second in line to the throne, after his father Prince Charles). In December, the Supreme Court ruled that the removal of Michael Somare as prime minister in August was unconstitutional, despite retrospective legislation passed by parliament earlier in the day to legalise his unseating. From this time a political schism developed whereby two rival governments claimed authority and the offices of state. Former governor general Matane supported the legal ruling and swore Somare back into office; Peter O'Neill refused to step down as prime minister. On 14 December Paulias Matane swore in Somare's government. However parliament voted to suspend Ogio and appointed Jeffery Nape as Acting Governor General; he then swore in Peter O'Neill and his government. The military refused to take sides. On 15 December, the rival attorney generals agreed to discuss a possible solution to the political crisis of two prime ministers vying for power. On 19 December, the chief of the public service in PNG said that the administration recognised O'Neill as prime minister, because he had control of the cabinet and parliament.

2012 On 8 February, the supreme court directed the rival contenders to the offices of state, and heads of defence and police forces, to appear before it to resolve the leadership impasse. On 6 March, Chief Justice Salamo Injia was arrested and charged with attempting to obstruct a police investigation into mismanagement of a deceased judge's estate. The timing of his arrest and his history with the government of Prime Minister O'Neill led to accusations of political motivation into Injia's arrest. On 13 March parliament passed a new law that allowed it to suspend judges for misconduct in office. On 5 April the government postponed the general elections by six months from mid- to late-2012. On 12 April the Supreme Court issued a stay order to prevent the use of the new 'misconduct in office' law, effectively reinstating Chief Justice Injia, and another judge, Nicholas Kirriwon, who had also been suspended. On 23 May the Supreme Court again ruled that the government of Prime Minister O'Neill was unconstitutional and that Michael Somare should be reinstated. On 24 May parliamentary elections were announced for 23 June On 24 May the Chief Justice Salamo Injia (whose ruling was in favour of Somare) was arrested for sedition and on 28 May a second judge, Nicholas Kirriwom, was also arrested on the same charge. On 25 May parliament was recalled to nullify the ruling of the Supreme Court. Although parliament agreed the ruling, the deputy speaker declared that as Somare had missed three sittings of the house the office of the prime minister was vacant and O'Neill was re-elected unopposed (56 votes out of 109 MPs), and sworn in as prime minister by Speaker Jeffery Nape (acting for the absent Governor General Michael Ogio) on 30 May. Parliamentary elections, scheduled to take 14 days to complete, began on 24 June. Following months of intense political rivalry between the two main political parties and their respective leaders 3,500 candidates contested the 111 parliamentary seats in contention. After weeks of vote-counting the results were declared. The PNC had won 27 seats (out of 111) and the Triumph Heritage Empowerment Party (THEP) had won 12 seats. On 25 July, PNC's leader, Peter O'Neill, announced that he would form a coalition government with his erstwhile rival, former prime minister Michael Somare (NAP). On 3 August, parliament elected Peter O'Neill as prime minister, winning 94 votes against his rival, Michael Somare's 12 votes. Peter O'Neill was sworn into office on the same day and a coalition government formed which included many of the newly elected MPs. On 20 August, the PNG government agreed to reopen the Manus Regional Asylum processing centre (on Manus Island), to screen irregular maritime arrivals (IMAs) (asylum seekers and unauthorised migrants) before they could land in Australia. The facility will be funded by the Australian government. The first IMA's were interned in the camp on 21 November.

2013 A long trail of foreign visitors, including the prime ministers of Australia, Thailand and Fiji, culminated in the Japanese vice foreign Minister Minoru Kuichi in June. The visits were largely the result of PNG's current political stability and economic progress. Japan has made a number of investments, the latest of which is PNG's first LNG project, scheduled to start in late 2014.

2015 The Pacific Games were held in Port Moresby in July.

Political structure

Constitution

The political structure is that of a unicameral parliamentary democracy. The present constitution came into effect in 1975 when the country became independent within the Commonwealth.

The 1975 constitution provided for the decentralisation of power to 20 provincial governments. Since then, Papua New Guinea (PNG) has been developing a system of local government.

An amendment to the constitution in 1977 led to the formation of 20 elected provincial governments which enjoy limited legislative and administrative powers and are funded mainly by central government.

Administrative divisions:

Bougainville	Milne Bay
Central	Morobe
Chimbu	National Capital
Eastern Highlands	New Ireland
East New Britain	Northern
East Sepik	Sandaun
Enga	Southern Highlands
Gulf	Western
Madang	Western Highlands
Manus	West New Britain
Hela	
Jiwaka	

Bougainville became an autonomous region in 2005, with PNG's federal government retaining control over defence and the economy.

Independence date

16 September 1975

Form of state

Sovereign independent state; it is a member of the Commonwealth.

The executive

The British monarch is the head of state and is represented by the governor general whose normal term of office is six years. Effective power resides with the prime minister and his cabinet, the National Executive Council. The governor general is appointed on the recommendation of the National Executive Council and on the basis of a simple majority vote in parliament. The prime minister is appointed by the head of state on the proposal of parliament.

National legislature

The unicameral National Parliament has 111 members, of which 89 are elected by limited preferential voting in open electorates and 20 from provincial electorates. All members are elected for five-year terms. Parliament votes for the prime minister (typically the leader of the largest party), the speaker and deputy speaker (the latter may not hold ministerial posts).

Legal system

The legal system is based on English common law. The national judicial system comprises the Supreme Court, the national court and subsidiary courts. The Supreme Court is responsible for all matters concerning the interpretation of the constitution and is the final court of appeal. The Chief Justice is appointed by the head of state and the judiciary is formally independent of other branches of government.

Last elections

24 June–8 July 2012 (parliamentary); 21 May 2010 (Bougainville presidential).

Results: Parliamentary: People's National Congress (PNC) won 24.32 per cent (27 seats out of 111), independents (combined totals) 14.41 per cent (16), Triumph Heritage Empowerment Party (THEP) 10.81 per cent (12), PNG Party (PNGP) 7.21 per cent (eight), National Alliance Party (NAP) 6.31 per cent (seven), United Resources Party (URP) 6.31 per cent (seven); 16 other political parties each won less than 6 per cent of the vote and won 34 seats among them.

Bougainville presidential: John Momis beat six other candidates with 52.35 per cent of the vote.

Next elections

June/July 2017 (parliamentary)

Political parties

Papua New Guinea has no real party system and most members of parliament function as independents, although they have various party labels.

Ruling party

Coalition led by the People's National Congress (PNC) (from 3 Aug 2012)

Main opposition party

People's Democratic Movement (PDM)

Over 39 per cent of the population is under 15 years of age.

The population is scattered, with highest concentrations in the Highland regions.

Population

6.83 million (2012)*

Last census: July 2000: 5,190,786

Population density: 15 inhabitants per square km (2010). Urban population 13 per cent (2010 Unicef).

Annual growth rate: 2.5 per cent, 1990–2010 (Unicef).

Ethnic make-up

Most of the population is Melanesian. There are numerous other ethnic groups in Papua New Guinea's 20 provinces, including those of Papuan, Polynesian and Micronesian descent. There is a sizeable minority of Australians, some Europeans and a small Chinese community in the country's limited commercial centre.

Religions

The indigenous population is mainly pantheistic, although a significant proportion has adopted Christianity. There are more than 10 different Christian religious groups in the country, including a substantial Roman Catholic congregation (22 per cent of the population) and various Protestant congregations (44 per cent). Indigenous beliefs account for 34 per cent of the population.

Education

Education standards before independence were poor, reflected in low literacy levels in the workforce. School fees have to be paid although these are subsidised by the government. Staff shortages remain an acute problem at secondary level. Lack of materials and up to date curricula are further burdens for the education system.

The government has backed the 'one laptop per child' programme (OLPC).

Despite these disadvantages, there has been some development, made possible by help from the Australian government, through AusAid. AusAid has improved the condition of student housing and provided science laboratories in several schools.

In March 2009 the European Union warned the government that a grant of US$53 million, to improve teacher training and to purchase school text and library books would be withdrawn following the government's failure to provide detailed plans for the money's allocation.

Literacy rate: 66 per cent, adult rates (2003).

Enrolment rate: 80 per cent gross primary enrolment of relevant age group (including repeaters); 47 per cent gross secondary enrolment (World Bank).

Pupils per teacher: 38 in primary schools.

Health

The death toll from a three-fold disease of cholera, flu and dysentery killed over 400 people, prompting the WHO to issue a warning to the government, which declared a state of emergency in 2009 and provided medical aid to Morobe Province, as the disease was spreading into the Eastern Highlands and Gulf Province. By April 2010 the disease had spread along the north coast and reached Port Moresby, initially killing three people.

Fears grew that the poor living conditions in the city's squatter settlements would provide ample victims for an epidemic.

The population suffers from poor health. The government provides hospitals and other health care facilities, but while hospital treatment is available in all major centres, they have varying levels of service and efficiency. A charge on the basis of ability to pay is levied for health services, although most people are treated free or make only a small contribution.

In 2004, health authorities stated that the maternal death rate in PNG was greater than in any other Pacific island; over 1,000 women per annum, die of complications. In 2010, due to worryingly high maternal mortality figures (one in seven chance of death) in remote communities, prompted the government to train village health volunteers to provide basic medical treatment. An Australian charity will issue birthing kits, which include some of the basic equipment needed during a delivery.

PNG is to receive US$20 million to fight malaria from the Global Fund, set up to fight malaria, Aids and tuberculosis. Insecticide impregnated anti-malaria nets have been provided by the World Health Organistion and Australian aid to increased numbers of children and reduced the incidence of the desease, acknowledged as the number one killer of children in PNG.

An agreement of employment between the governments of PNG and Cuba in 2006, allowed 20 Cuban doctors to work in rural areas of PNG to overcome an acute shortage.

HIV/Aids

There is a serious AIDS epidemic in PNG, which has the largest number of HIV positive citizens in the Pacific region. While the prevalence rate is only 2 per cent, for those at most risk the rate is 16 per cent. In 2002, 15,000 people had the disease, by 2005 the reported number was over 40,000, however screening of 3,000 A&E patients at the Port Moresby General Hospital found 18 per cent were HIV positive; other evidence indicates the current prevalence rate is doubling each year. In 2004 a survey found that 1 per cent of expectant mothers were testing positive for HIV and fears are that PNG has reached the trigger point for a widespread epidemic of Aids.

In 2005 220 new HIV/Aids cases were being reported monthly, the overall number of HIV/Aids cases was 60,000. In 2006, the health minister reported that the infection rate in some remote parts of

the country was over 10 per cent and nationwide the rate was rising by 30 per cent per annum.
HIV prevalence: 2 per cent aged 15–49 in 2005
Life expectancy: 60 years, 2004 (WHO 2006)
Fertility rate/Maternal mortality rate: 4.0 births per woman, 2010 (Unicef)
Birth rate/Death rate: 31 births per 1,000 population; 7.6 deaths per 1,000 population (2003).
Child (under 5 years) mortality rate (per 1,000): 63 per 1,000 live births (WHO 2012)

Welfare

A number of defined-contribution provident funds provide limited social benefits. A National Provident Fund (NPF) provides social benefits for employees of private-sector companies with 20 or more personnel, while the Public Officers' Superannuation Fund (POSF) provides a similar facility for public servants.

Main cities

Port Moresby (capital, estimated population 317,374 in 2012), Lae (100,677), Mendi (51,391), Popondetta (46,375), Mount Hagen (44,644), Arawa (38,100), Kokopo (37,573), Madang (29,216), Kimbe (26,039).

Languages spoken

Tok Pisin or Pidgin is the lingua franca of the islands. It is derived from Melanesian Pidgin and includes German and English words. English is spoken by only 1–2 per cent of the population but is the language of government and business, however in parliamentary sessions, Pidgin is used. Motu is spoken by Motuan villagers and has been modified into Police Motu which is spoken widely in the southern region. There are 715 indigenous languages.

Official language/s

English, Tok Pisin, Motu

Media

Press

There are numerous newspapers and magazines published in English, Tok Pisin and vernacular languages.
Dailies: In English, the two main daily newspapers are *The National* (www.thenational.com.pg) and *Papua New Guinea Post-Courier* (www.postcourier.com.pg) published Monday to Friday.
Weeklies: *Times of Papua New Guinea* is a well-regarded weekly publication in English.

Broadcasting

Radio: The government-owned National Broadcasting Commission (NBC-PNG) (www.nbc.com.pg) operates two AM networks and a FM commercial station broadcasting in English, Tok Pisin and various other local languages. Two other independent, national commercial radio stations are in operation, Nau FM and Yumi FM; plus broadcasts are received from Australia.
Television: Fiji Television Limited owns PNG's only television station EMTV, which has an estimated 2.5 million audience and about 38 per cent of the advertising market. The Media council monitors the output for local content and community initiatives in broadcasting.

Economy

Papua New Guinea (PNG) has a variety of natural resources, including gold, timber, hydrocarbons, fish and copper. Its mining sector provided record revenue in 2008 as global prices for minerals surged. However the industry has to contend with poor communications, a lack of infrastructure and tough terrain that means extraction and transport is laborious and expensive. Mineral extractions, including oil and gas, are exploited mainly by foreign interests and account for nearly three-quarters of all exports. A project to supply liquefied national gas (LNG) was agreed in 2009 with initial investment of US$100 million, with production at 6.9 million tonnes a year. In 2014 PNG started to export LNG to China, as well as to Japan and South Korea. In contrast to the period prior to the recent decade-long boom, the resources sector has exhibited remarkable resilience with an optimistic future. Until the end of 2014, the downturn in the mining sector was barely reflected in the petroleum sector. The first shipments of liquefied natural gas commenced in 2014.
Industry dominates the economy and contributed 34.8 per cent to GDP in 2014, with agriculture the second most important sector at 26.3 per cent; services provide 34.8 per cent.
Growth was expected to be strong in 2009, however high energy costs and imports depressed the economy, so that growth remained relatively static at 6.1 per cent, even though world trade weakened. Growth rebounded in 2010 to 7.6 per cent and has fluctuated in the intermittent period to a more stable 5.8 per cent in 2014.
In 2014, the UN Human Development Index (HDI) ranked PNG 157 (out of 187) for development in health, education and income. The majority of the population live outside the narrow organised economic activity – 85 per cent of the population depend on subsistence farming for their livelihood. Around 38 per cent of the population survive on less than US$1.25 per day. Only around 2 per cent of the land is suitable for agriculture, mainly in coastal areas and upland plateaux. Some cash crops, such as coffee, palm oil and tea, are nevertheless grown and exported. The World Bank ranks PNG as a lower middle income country, with a GNI per capita of US$2,010, which means loans with concessions and low interest rates can be granted by international investment banks.

External trade

Papua New Guinea is a member of the South Pacific Regional Trade and Economic Co-operation Agreement (Sparteca) along with 12 other regional nations, which allows products duty free access by Pacific Island Forum members to Australian and New Zealand markets (subject to the country of origin restrictions). It is also a member of the Melanesian Spearhead Group (with Fiji, Solomon Islands and Vanuatu) as a sub-regional trade group, whereby customs tariffs have been harmonised under the Melanesian free trade agreement (MFTA).

Imports

Principal imports are machinery and transport equipment, manufactured goods, food, fuels and chemicals.
Main sources: Australia (26.5 per cent of total in 2014), Algeria (23.2 per cent), Singapore (11.4 per cent), China (8.7 per cent) and Malaysia (5.9 per cent).

Exports

Principle exports are oil, gold, copper ore, logs, palm oil, coffee, cocoa, crayfish and prawns.
Main destinations: Australia (23.6 per cent of total in 2014), Japan (15.6 per cent) and China (9.1 per cent).

Agriculture

Farming

Agriculture accounted for around 26.38 per cent of GDP in 2014. More than 70 per cent of the population depend on agriculture for their livelihoods. Approximately 2 per cent of land area is cultivated, arable land, which is restricted by dense rain forests and mountainous terrain.
Coconuts, coffee, cocoa, palm oil, rubber and tea are grown as cash crops on plantations, employing around one-third of those engaged in agriculture.
Processing, quality control and pricing for main crops are the concern of the Coffee Marketing Board and the Copra Marketing Board, which operate stabilisation funds for these products and for cocoa. Smallholdings produce 70 per cent of all coffee for export, in addition to subsistence crops of yams, sago, cassava, bananas, pineapples, vegetables, sweet potatoes, tea, natural rubber, groundnuts, sorghum and rice, with some raising of pigs, goats and poultry. Food production has kept pace with the population growth.

Fishing

One considerable resource Papua New Guinea has yet to exploit is its fishing grounds, probably the world's richest. The total annual fish catch in 2014 was 580,000 tonnes, yet the country's waters have been estimated to be capable of supplying up to one million tonnes of fish a year. PNG's waters are home to more than 1,800 different species of fish. Activity in the sector is largely centred on domestic fleets tapping the country's 2.4 million square kilometres exclusive fishing zone. Foreign fleets have been excluded from the zone. PNG has become one of the biggest players in the Western tuna fish industry. The growth of the industry has been encouraged by favourable government policies such as the removal of export duties on fisheries products.

More than 60 per cent of the world's tuna is caught in the Pacific by vessels from distant water fishing nations such as China, Japan, Taiwan South Korea, Spain, North and South America. The PNG fisheries zone of 2.4 million square kilometers is the largest in the South Pacific, and between 10 per cent and 20 per cent of the world's tuna catch is caught in PNG waters.

On 12 April 2011, a summit of the Parties to the Nauru Agreement (PNA) concluded its strategy for a policy of sustainable fishing in the Pacific. The PNA treaty, which was established in 1989 and expired in 2012, is seen as in need of an overhaul. As a collective regions the PNA (FSM, Kiribati, Marshall Islands, Nauru, Palau, PNG, Solomon Islands and Tuvalu) control around 25–30 per cent of world stocks of tuna. Only 5 per cent of sales revenue is returned to the PNA and ministers called for specific changes, including an increased share of profits, PNA crews on-board purse seine vessels (minimum 10 per cent), conservation and management measures including a limit to fish trapping (fish aggregating devices (FADs)), net mesh rules and the establishment of an observer agency and fisheries information management system. The PNA met in May 2012 to discuss even stronger management measures to ensure even more sustainable tuna fisheries and minimise environmental damage. Many of the ideas put forward were implemented in January 2013, for example observation and monitoring of catches and environmental damage by 100 per cent independent bodies.

The PNA members have agreed to increase the fishing day price to US$8,000 for 2015 from the previous US$6,000. This should generate and increase greater economic benefit from the tuna fisheries in the country.

Forestry

The economy benefits from huge exports of tropical logs, while the sawn timber industry caters to domestic demands. Forests and woodlands cover around 63 per cent of land area, but are subject to deforestation for tropical timber exports and to pollution from mining projects. The government is seeking to regain control of an industry which seems to have operated outside existing regulations and in which political corruption has played an important part. There has been little monitoring of commercial operations and reforestation is inadequate. PNG has a relatively small plantation estate.

PNG has an established presence in the Asian log market and exports around one million cubic metres of logs annually to South Korea, as well as around 400,000 cubic metres to Japan.

In July 2011, landowners in the Western Province won a landmark legal case against the Malaysian logging company, Concord Pacific Limited, which was ordered to pay US$97 million for environmental damage due to its illegal logging.

In 2011 PNG became the world's second largest exporter of tropical logs, according to the organisation that represents logging companies. This is despite a public outcry and a government inquiry which announced a moratorium on new leases for logging; exports for these leases reached 650,000 cubic metres in 2011 and are expected to remain high until 2017–18.

In 2015, mainland PNG had the world's third largest intact tropical rainforest; however, since 2000, 11 per cent of the island has been leased for 99 years under 'special agricultural and business leases' (SABL). Many of these leases were approved without the knowledge or permission of indigenous landowners and legal disputes have ensued.

At least seventy-five per cent of its original forest cover is still standing, occupying vast, biologically rich tracts over 100,000 square miles in all. Its forests provide the habitat for about 200 species of mammals, 20,000 species of plants, 1,500 species of trees and 750 species of birds, half of which are endemic to the island.

Industry and manufacturing

The industrial sector, including mining, accounts for around 30 per cent of GDP and employs around 10 per cent of the workforce. Manufacturing accounts for around 10 per cent of GDP.

Industry is focused on mining (gold, silver, copper), crude oil and processing Papua New Guinea's main agricultural products. Copra crushing, palm and coconut oil processing, sugar processing, brewing, meat production, plywood production and wood chip production are prominent.

Government policy, through the Industrial Centres Development Corporation (ICDC), aims to promote non-mining sectors, particularly import substitution and export-oriented industries such as manufacturing and downstream processing.

Main activities include boat-building, steel fabrication and manufacture of cement, paper products, soap, matches, chemicals, paint, sawn timber, furniture, plywood, bottles and cigarettes.

Tourism

Tourism is an underdeveloped industry although PNG has the potential because it is a great destination for eco-tourists, with unspoiled rainforests, indigenous people living in traditional villages and a spectacular array of wildlife. The Kokoda Trail is a popular destination for Australian visitors who walk all or part of the trail used by Anzac forces during World War Two. Diving in the waters around the coast is also popular, as well as the surfing and sailing.

Travel and tourism accounts for less than 2.5 per cent of GDP and only employs around 2.1 per cent of the workforce (around 63,000 jobs). Travel and tourism investment totalled 3.8 per cent of total investment in 2014.

Unesco added the Kuk Early Agricultural Site to its World Heritage List in 2008.

Environment

Papua New Guinea, Philippines, Indonesia, Australia and Solomon Islands are the countries with the most coral reef fish species.

An Asian Development Bank (ADB) study (*Economics of Climate Change in the Pacific*) published in November 2013 projected that the most significant losses as a result of climate change would be felt in Papua New Guinea (PNG), where severe failures in sweet potato crops and other agricultural products and the increased economic burdens of cooling, mortality and land depletion, could trigger a loss of up to 15.2 per cent of its GDP by 2100.

Mining

Mining contributes around 8 per cent of GDP. Copper and gold are the most important export minerals. Most mineral resources are too difficult and costly to extract.

PNG, the Federated States of Micronesia and the Solomon Islands will submit a joint proposal to the United Nations in 2009 to develop the Ontong Java Plateau, which is part of their extended continental shelf, for mineral prospecting.

2014 saw the completion of a large LNG plant, which is expected to boost overall GDP growth to 15 per cent in 2015. However, growth of the non-resource economy has slowed since 2012, mainly a result of the PNG-LNG project moving from construction to production. While exports from LNG will eventually provide revenue to the state, they are unlikely to be felt in the short term.

There was much speculation in 2002 that much of PNG's resource sector was doomed for closure. However, the situation is vastly different today as mine-life extension programs have ensured that the OK Tedi copper-gold mine continues production until at least 2025. Porgera gold mine continues to produce half a million ounces of gold per annum. The most challenging problem to the sector is the longer-life Lihir gold mine; whilst still remaining PNG's largest gold producer, it has experienced numerous technical issues in recent times.

In 2010, sediment from the gold mine that washed down the Watut River destroyed the river system and surrounding area, taking the livelihood of thousands of villagers. The Australian-based Newcrest Mining accepted responsibility and paid compensation.

The government granted a 20-year mining lease in January 2011 to the Canadian company, Nautilus Minerals to mine, among other ores, gold and copper from the seabed in the Bismarck Sea, which is in PNG territorial waters. This will be the world's first commercial seabed mining operation and is expected to produce in total around 1.3 million tonnes of ore annually (80,000 tonnes of copper, 150,000–200,000 ounces of gold), with the operation fully underway by June 2014. The PNG government negotiated to invest up to 30 per cent of the operations, (US$103 million) over 2011–14.

Hydrocarbons

Proven oil reserves are negligible, however there is active exploration for oil both onshore and offshore. PNG has substantial untapped reserves of natural gas, but the rugged terrain and the problems of inaccessibility are major obstacles to extraction. There can also be problems in gaining permission to exploit tribal lands.

The government created Petromin (PNG) Holdings, to manage state interests in the energy and mining commodities sectors. It works with foreign partners to explore, develop and produce oil, gas and mining ores. Under legislation, the state could acquire up to 22.5 per cent interest in all petroleum development projects.

Proven natural gas reserves were 5.5 trillion cubic feet (cum) in 2014, domestic consumption is negligible and any production is due for use in liquefied natural gas (LNG) projects. In 2009, InterOil Corp reported that, in total, it had discovered a further 280 billion cum of natural gas onshore. The field will be used to supply natural gas to the proposed US$11 billion Liquid Niugini Gas project, near Port Moresby, where it will be turned into LNG, at an estimated rate of nine million tonnes per annum. Landowners of the LNG site claimed, in 2009, that they had not been compensated for its use, just as the royalties from the project were being allocated. The National Court ordered that any agreement regarding the proposed LNG project could not be legally binding unless proper procedures stipulated by PNG laws were reached. Landowners who had taken legal action for compensation must be included in any later agreements. France's Total SA and InterOil Corp. of the US agreed a deal worth up to US$3.6 billion to develop two PNG natural gas fields in 2013. Elk and Antelope are among the largest natural-gas discoveries in Asia in the past two decades. The estimated amount of natural gas is likely to be at 8 trillion cubic feet.

A 20-year agreement for 36.3 million tonnes of PNG LNG to be sold to China was signed in 2009 and exports began in 2014.

Coal is neither produced nor imported.

Energy

Total installed generating capacity was 700MW in 2012. Hydropower produces 220MW, with another 513MW under construction and 11MW planned. The major hydroelectric schemes are located at Port Moresby, Ramu River and the Gazelle Peninsula. The energy mix also includes oil-turbines with natural gas-turbines in the region of Kutubu supplying 42MW to the local Porgera gold mine. Geothermal power is in operation on the island of Lihir supplying 56MW of electricity to the local gold mine.

Plans for a new hydroelectric power plant in PNG to supply electricity to northern Queensland were announced in September 2010. The Australian power company Origin Energy and PNG's Energy Developments will build the power plant, with the first phase generating 1,800MW to be supplied via an undersea cable to Townsville by about 2020. Environmentalists have condemned the proposals.

Financial markets

Stock exchange

Port Moresby Stock Exchange (PoMSOX)

Banking and insurance

In July 2012 the PNG-based Bank of the South Pacific (BSP) announced that it was targeting the 80 per cent of Papuans in rural areas that did not have access to banking facilities. Between 2010–12 the bank had signed up 30,000 new customers, who are served through portable banking systems.

On 11 July 2011, Standard & Poor's upgraded BSP credit rating from B to B+ for its strong business and domestic market position and sound profitability.

Central bank

Bank of Papua New Guinea

Main financial centre

Port Moresby

Time

GMT plus 10 hours

Geography

Papua New Guinea (PNG) has only one land border with Indonesia, which lies at the west end of the island of New Guinea. PNG lies across the Torres Stait, north of the north-eastern extremity of Australia. Although the bulk of the country's land area is formed by the mainland, PNG includes many smaller islands, principally the Bismark Archipelago, which largely comprises New Britain, New Ireland and Manus, and the North Solomon Islands of which Bougainville and Buka are the largest. PNG has coastlines extending for a total of 5,152km; its highest point is Mount Wilhelm, at 4,509 metres.

The country is a land of great geographic diversity. The coast is low-lying swamp, the central core has a massive system of mountain ranges but there is also an extensive range of foothills as well as volcanoes (PNG forms a constituent part of the Pacific 'Rim of Fire' – a line of tectonic activity, which produces many volcanoes in a string that stretches from New Zealand in the south-east and circles the Pacific up to the Aleutian Islands and down along the US west coast). The country has substantial mineral wealth and good agricultural potential with fertile soil and abundant rainfall. There are large expanses of tropical forest and good fishery stocks.

Hemisphere

Southern

Climate

Papua New Guinea has a tropical climate with an average maximum temperature of 33 degrees Celsius (C) and an average minimum of 22 degrees C. Temperature and humidity are fairly constant throughout the year. The Highlands region has a more temperate climate than the rest of the country. Papua New Guinea also has seasonal monsoons, varying considerably between regions. Rainfall totals up to 4,600mm per year in some areas.

Dress codes

As Papua New Guinea is in the tropics, light clothes are worn at all times, although travellers to the Highlands may require sweaters for the evening. Business wear is usually lightweight trousers and a short sleeved shirt. The Australian sartorial influence can be seen in the wearing of shorts and long socks by males even in administrative positions. Jackets are not normally required but safari suits are often worn. Formal evening wear is seldom required but sometimes tropical formal wear is stipulated on invitations and this would mean a long sleeved shirt and tie for men and a cocktail dress for women.

Entry requirements

Passports

Required by all. Passports must be valid for 12 months from the date of entry.

Visa

Required by all. Contact the nearest PNG Consulate for visa details and application form.

All travellers should be in possession of sufficient funds for onward or return flight before the expiry date of their visa.

Visa conditions are liable to change and should be checked before travelling.

Currency advice/regulations

The import of local and foreign currency is unlimited. Export of local currency is limited to K200; foreign currency is limited to K10,000 (equivalent), amounts greater require approval from the Central Bank.

Travellers cheques are readily accepted; to avoid additional exchange charges cheques should be in Australian or US dollars or pound sterling.

Customs

The export of items of ethnographic interest is banned.

Health (for visitors)

Mandatory precautions

Vaccination certificates for yellow fever if travelling from an infected area.

Advisable precautions

Vaccinations that are necessary include typhoid, tetanus, and hepatitis A. Vaccinations that may be advised include diphtheria, hepatitis B, tuberculosis, Japanese B encephalitis and rabies. Anti-malarial precautions must be taken when visiting all but the central highlands; the use of mosquito nets and repellents and covering up the body after dark can help avoid malaria, hepatitis B, dengue fever and encephalitis (which is a risk in remote regions only). There is a very high prevalence of HIV/Aids.

Use only bottled or boiled water for drinks, washing teeth and making ice. Eat only well cooked meals, preferably served hot; vegetables should be cooked and fruit peeled. Eating grouper, snapper, amberjack, and barracuda reef fish can frequently result in ciguatera poisoning; the toxin remains active even when the fish is well cooked.

A full, first-aid kit would be useful. Visitors should seek advice before accepting treatment involving hypodermic needles or blood transfusions. Medical insurance is essential, including emergency evacuation, and an adequate supply of personal medicines is necessary.

Hotels

In addition to Western-style hotels, the Tourist Board operates a scheme of village-style guest-houses run by nationals. Tipping is not usual.

Public holidays (national)

Fixed dates

1 Jan (New Year's Day), 13 Jun (Queen's Birthday), 16 Sep (Independence Day), 25–26 Dec (Christmas).

Days *in lieu* are given for holidays that occur at the weekend, usually at the beginning of the following week.

Variable dates

Good Friday and Easter Monday (Mar/Apr), Anzac Remembrance Day.

Working hours

Banking

Mon–Thu: 0845–1500; Fri: 0845–1600.

Business

Mon–Fri: 0800–1630.

Government

Mon–Fri: 0800–1600.

Shops

Mon–Fri: 0900–1630/1700; Sat: 0900–1200. Markets open all daylight hours.

Telecommunications

Mobile/cell phones

There is a 900 GSM service available in the capital and six of the larger towns.

Electricity supply

240/415V AC, 50 cycles; plugs are three-pin Australian type.

Weights and measures

Metric system

Social customs/useful tips

The use of first names is common in business, reflecting the tendency (of Australian origin) towards informality. The Papua New Guineans have a relaxed attitude to punctuality and this can make it difficult for the foreign visitor to keep to a schedule of appointments or to make business arrangements.

The belief in magic and sorcery is still widespread. There is little interest in national issues but local group and tribal sympathies are strong. Pressure from the provinces has resulted in the formation of a separate and tribal level of provincial government.

The traditional (custom) land tenure system promotes social stability and equal access to land within clans. Land disputes are endemic.

Tipping is not practised or encouraged.

Security

It has been advised that visitors to Papua New Guinea (PNG) should take care and ensure their personal safety at all times. PNG is characterised by regionalism and tribalism, with widespread corruption and prevalent violent crime bordering on anarchy. Law and order remain very weak in Port Moresby and Lae, reflecting the rising level of unemployment in the urban areas and a breakdown in the customary lines of authority. Criminal gangs of so-called 'rascals' have become a serious problem, and particularly worrying is a growing tendency in some areas in the use of firearms. Robbery, vehicle hijacks, assaults and random shootings are all common. Violent incidents can occur without warning and while foreigners are not necessarily the target they are visible and can be engulfed by them. Outside urban areas the situation is better, although sporadic tribal fighting is common and areas where it is reported, such as the Southern Highlands Province, is a particularly dangerous area and should be avoided.

Getting there

Air

National airline: Air Niugini

International airport/s: Port Moresby Jacksons International (POM), 11km south of the city; duty-free shop, bar, bank, hotel reservations and car hire. Buses and taxis are available to the city, journey time 20–60 minutes.

Airport tax: Departure tax K30; transit passengers are exempt.

Surface

Water: Cruise ships call, and passenger accommodation is sometimes available on cargo ships from Australia, the Far East, Europe and the west coast of the US.

Main port/s: Port Moresby, Lae and Madang; Rabaul (on New Britain).

Getting about

National transport

Air: Domestic air services provide the only realistically efficient and speedy way of accessing all areas in PNG. Air Niugini, AirLink and Islands Nationair, operate scheduled and charter flights. Some flights may use light aircraft or helicopters to the hundreds of smaller air strips in remote locations.

Road: There are over 19,000km of roads; only around 5,000km are paved. The highland interior is still underdeveloped; most of the road systems form coastal networks with little connection between individual provinces.

Water: Inland waterways total 10,940km but there are no public transport systems using them. Ferries to other PNG islands and river transport may be available on an *ad hoc* basis.

City transport

Taxis: Metered taxi services are available in main centres, but are scarce and expensive. Negotiate fares wherever possible.

Buses, trams & metro: PMVs (public motor vehicles), usually light buses or covered trucks, operate within and between main centres from bus shelters in towns (or they can be hailed elsewhere).

Car hire

It is not recommended that visitors drive into the interior where the roads are rugged, unpredictable and without rescue service. A number of international car hire companies operate in the cities. A national driving licence is required.

BUSINESS DIRECTORY

The addresses listed below are a selection only. While World of Information makes every endeavour to check these addresses, we cannot guarantee that changes have not been made, especially to telephone numbers and area codes. We would welcome any corrections.

Telephone area codes

The international direct dialling (IDD) code for Papua New Guinea is +675 followed by subscriber's number.

Useful telephone numbers

Police, fire and ambulance: 000

Chambers of Commerce

Lae Chamber of Commerce and Industry, PO Box 265, Lae, Morobe Province (tel: 472-2340; fax: 472-6038; e-mail: lcci@global.net.pg.

Papua New Guinea Chamber of Commerce and Industry, PO Box 1621, Trukai Building, Lawes Road, Konebadu, Port Moresby, NCD (tel: 321-3057; fax: 321-0566; e-mail: pngcci@global.net.pg).

Port Moresby Chamber of Commerce and Industry, PO Box 1764, Monian Tower, Douglas Street, Port Moresby (tel: 321-3077; fax: 321-4203; e-mail: info@pomcci.org.pg).

Banking

ANZ Banking Group (PNG), 3rd Floor, Defens Haus, Cnr Champion Parade and Hunter St, Port Moresby (tel: 322-3333; fax: 322-3306).

Bank South Pacific Limited (BSP), PO Box 173, Douglas Street, Port Moresby 121 NCD (tel: 321-2444; fax: 321-7302).

Indosuez Niugini Bank Limited, PO Box 1390, Burns Haus, Champion Parade, Port Moresby (tel: 321-3533; fax: 321-3115).

Maybank (PNG) Limited, PO Box 882, Waigani Drive, Waigani (tel: 325-0101; fax: 325-6128).

Central bank

Bank of Papua New Guinea, PO Box 121, ToRobert Haus; Crn Douglas Street, Port Moresby 111 (tel: 322-7200; fax: 321-1617; e-mail: webmaster@bankpng.gov.pg).

Stock exchange

Port Moresby Stock Exchange (PoMSOX), www.pomsox.com.pg

Travel information

Airlink Ltd, PO Box 1208, Madang Province, 511 (tel: 852-2933; fax: 852-2725; email: info@airlink.com.pg).

Air Niugini, PO Box 7186, Boroko 111 (tel: 325-9000; fax: 327-3482).

East New Britain Tourist Bureau, PO Box 385, Rabaul 611 (tel: 982-8697; fax: 982-8634).

Islands Nationair, PO Box 488, Boroko 111 (tel: 325-4055; fax: 325-5059).

Melanesian Tourist Services, PO Box 707, Madang 511 (tel: 854-1300; fax: 852-3543; internet: www.meltours.com).

Port Moresby Jacksons International Airport, PO Box 684, Boroko, Port Moresby (tel: 324-4400, 324-4755; fax: 325-0833).

National tourist organisation offices

PNG Tourism Promotion Authority, 2nd Floor, Pacific MMI Building, Champion Parade; PO Box 1291, Port Moresby 121 (tel: 320-0211; fax: 320-0223; internet: www.pngtourism.org.pg).

Ministries

Ministry of Agriculture and Livestock, PO Box 417, Konedobu NCD (tel: 325-9544; fax: 325-9722).

Ministry of Bougainville Affairs, House Tisa (2nd Floor), PO Box 343, Waigani NCD (tel: 325-2977; fax: 325-8038).

Ministry of Churches, Family Affairs, & NGO's, National Parliament, PO Parliament, Port Moresby NCD (tel: 327-7350; fax: 320-0903).

Ministry of Civil Aviation, PO Box 684, Boroko NCD (tel: 323-6185; fax: 325-1919).

Ministry of Commerce and Industry, PO Box 375, Waigani NCD (tel: 327-6621; fax: 323-3050).

Ministry of Defence, Murray Barracks, Free Mail Bag Service, Boroko NCD (tel: 327-346; fax: 327-7480).

Ministry of Education, Culture and Science, PSA Haus, PO Box 446, Waigani NCD (tel: 323-3944; fax: 327-7480).

Ministry of Employment and Youth, PO Box 5644, Boroko NCD (tel: 327-7578; fax: 327-7480).

Ministry of Environment, PO Box 6601, Boroko NCD (tel: 325-0174; fax: 325-0182).

Ministry of Finance and Internal Revenue, PO Box 777, Port Moresby NCD (tel: 322-6613; fax: 322-6856).

Ministry of Fisheries, Investment Haus (8th Floor), PO Box 2016, Port Moresby NCD (tel: 321-3443; fax: 320-3024).

Ministry of Foreign Affairs and Trade, PO Box 422, Waigani NCD (tel: 327-7545; fax: 325-4467).

Ministry of Forests, PO Box 1550, Boroko NCD (tel: 327-7591; fax: 327-7589).

Ministry of Health, Aopi Centre (5th Floor), PO Box 807, Boroko NCD (tel: 301-3605; fax: 301-3604).

Ministry of Justice, Po Box 591, Waigani NCD (tel: 323-0138; fax: 323-0241).

Ministry of Lands, Aopi Centre (4th Floor), PO Box 5665, Boroko NCD (tel: 301-3102; fax: 301-3205).

Ministry of Mining and Energy, NIC Building (1st Floor), Private Mail Bag, Port Moresby NCD (tel: 327-7350; fax: 320-0903).

Ministry of Petroleum and Gas, Parliament House, Waigani NCD (tel: 327-7752; fax: 327-7753).

Ministry of Police and Correctional Institution Services, PO Box 5097, Boroko NCD (tel: 327-7519; fax: 327-7528).

Ministry of Provincial and Local level Government Affairs, PO Box 1287, Boroko NCD (tel: 301-1000; fax: 325-0553).

Ministry of Public Enterprises, Communications and Assisting Prime Minister on Infrastructure and Public Investment Program Matters, PO Parliament, Waigani NCD (tel: 327-7366; fax: 327-7387).

Ministry of Public Service, Morauta House, (2nd Floor, PO Box 519, Waigani NCD (tel: 327-6440; fax: 323-3050).

Ministry of Rural Development, PO Box 639, Waigani NCD (tel: 327-6767; fax: 327-6349).

Ministry of Transport, PO Box 1489, Port moresby NCD (tel: 321-1866; fax: 320-0556).

Ministry of Treasury and Corporate Affairs, Vulupindi Haus (4th Floor), PO Box 710, Waigani NCD (tel: 328-8460; fax: 328-8433).

Office of the Prime Minister, Parliament House (4th Floor), National Parliament, Waigan NCD (tel: 327-7489; fax: 327-7497).

Other useful addresses

British High Commission, Kiroki Street, Waigani, PO Box 4778, Boroko, Port Moresby (tel: 321-1677; fax: 325-3547).

Bureau of Customs, PO Box 932, Port Moresby NCD (tel: 321-2488; fax: 321-3004).

Department of Industrial Development, PO Box 5644, Goroko (tel: 327-2286).

Electricity Commission of PNG, PO Box 1105, Boroko NCD (tel: 324-3200; fax: 325-0072).

Forest Research Institute, PO Box 314, LAE, Morobe Province (tel: 342-4188; fax: 432-4357).

Investment Promotion Authority, PO Box 5053, Boroko NCD (tel: 321-7311; fax: 321-2819).

National Curltural Commission, PO Box 7144, Boroko NCD (tel: 325-3288; fax: 325-9119).

National Housing Corporation, PO Box 1550, Boroko NCD (tel: 324-7200; fax: 325-9918).

National Institute of Standards and Industrial Technology, PO Box 3042, Boroko NCD (tel: 327-2102; fax: 325-2403).

National Statistical Office, PO Wardstrip, Waigani NCD (tel: 327-1499; fax: 325-1869).

Papua New Guinea Embassy (US), Suite 805, 1779 Massachusetts Avenue, NW, Washington DC 20036 (tel: (+1-202) 745-3680; fax: (+1-202) 745-3679; e-mail: kunduwash@aol.com).

Papua New Guinea Investment Corporation, PO Box 155, Port Moresby (tel: 321-2855; fax: 321-1240).

Post and Telecommunication Corporation, PO Box 1349, Boroko NCD (tel: 300-4000; fax: 300-4098).

Small Business Development Corporation, PO Box 481, Port Moresby NCD (tel: 325-0100; fax: 325-3725).

US Embassy, PO Box 1492, Port Moresby (tel: 321-1455; fax: 321-3423).

Internet sites

Asian Development Bank: www.adb.org

Government departments: www.pngonline.gov.pg

Investment promotion authority: www.ipa.gov.pg

PNG Business listings: www.pngbd.com

Tourism Council of the South Pacific: www.tcsp.com

Paraguay

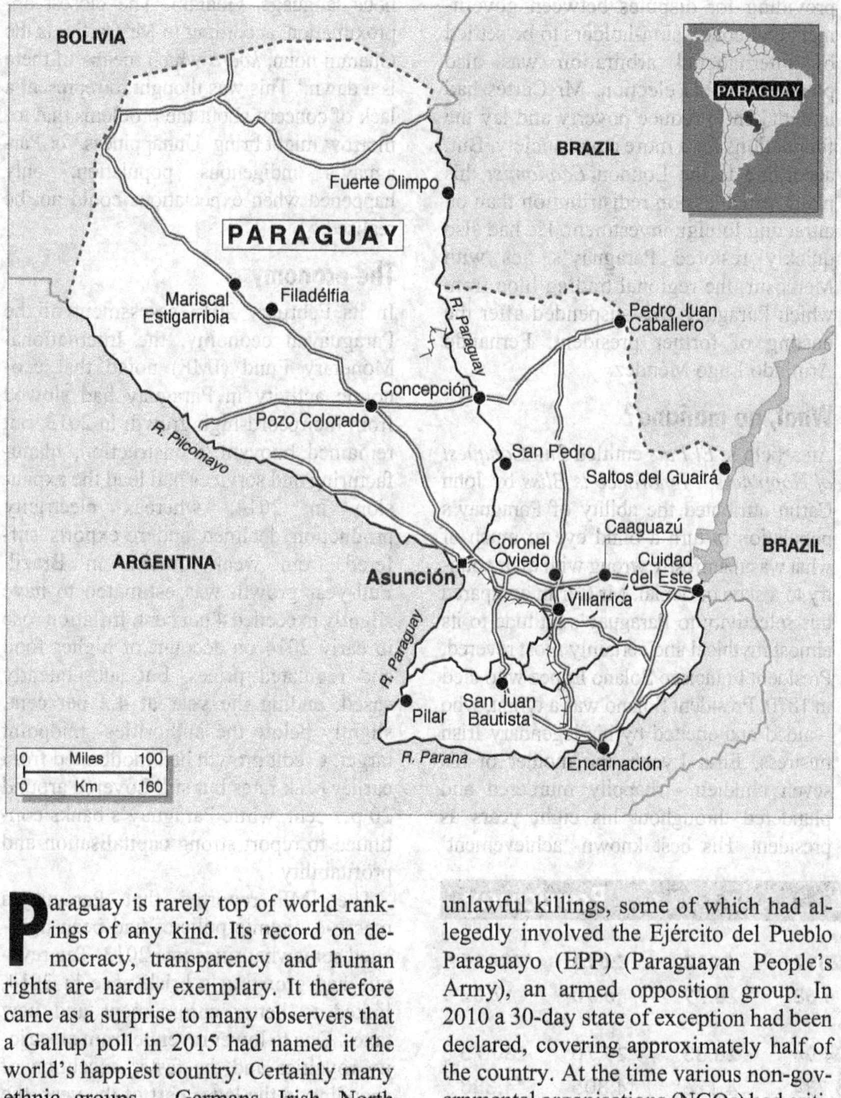

Paraguay is rarely top of world rankings of any kind. Its record on democracy, transparency and human rights are hardly exemplary. It therefore came as a surprise to many observers that a Gallup poll in 2015 had named it the world's happiest country. Certainly many ethnic groups – Germans, Irish, North Americans – had made their way to the land locked country in search of happiness. But not all had necessarily found it.

Heaven on earth?

On the 2014 Transparency International *Corruption Perceptions Index* Paraguay ranked 150 out of the 175 countries surveyed, level with the Central African Republic. The only Latin American country that had a lower ranking was Venezuela (161). A number of violent incidents had been reported by Amnesty International since 2010, including kidnapping and unlawful killings, some of which had allegedly involved the Ejército del Pueblo Paraguayo (EPP) (Paraguayan People's Army), an armed opposition group. In 2010 a 30-day state of exception had been declared, covering approximately half of the country. At the time various non-governmental organisations (NGOs) had criticised the vague definition of 'terrorism' contained in the anti-terrorism legislation introduced during the state of exception.

In 2010 the UN Special Rapporteur on the right to education expressed concerns regarding the poor quality of education in Paraguay, the lack of resources, inadequate infrastructure and the lack of viable options for rural populations seeking higher education in Paraguay. Amnesty International was concerned with the rights of Paraguay's Indigenous Peoples. 'The organisation alleged that abuses had been committed by police and security forces, as

KEY FACTS

Official name: República del Paraguay (Republic of Paraguay)

Head of State: President Horacio Cartes (from 15 Aug 2013)

Head of government: President Horacio Cartes (from 15 Aug 2013)

Ruling party: Asociación Nacional Republicana-Partido Colorado (National Republican Association (Colorado Party)

Area: 406,752 square km

Population: 6.90 million (2014)*

Capital: Asunción

Official language: Spanish and Guaraní

Currency: Guaraní (G) = 100 pesos

Exchange rate: G5,401.66 per US$ (Sep 2015)

GDP per capita: US$4,305 (2014)*

GDP real growth: 4.39% (2014)*

GDP: US$29.70 billion (2014)*

Unemployment: 5.50% (2014)*

Inflation: 5.04% (2014)*

Balance of trade: US$1.58 billion (2013)

Annual FDI: US$411.97 million (2011)

* estimated figure

well as acts of violence against women and girls and human rights defenders. Efforts to redress the social and ethnic imbalance in Paraguay's land distribution had failed to live up to expectations. An Amnesty report showed that in the two years since 2008 indigenous peoples had been given title to only 26,119 hectares of land, taking the total extent of titled territory to 55,970 hectares; the target set by the authorities had been to recognise indigenous title to 279,850 hectares of land by 2013. Equality does not feature pre-eminently in Paraguayan politics.

In his inaugural speech in August 2013 President Horacio Cartés, had promised to wage war on poverty – a fairly safe objective in that Paraguay continued to be one of the poorest countries in South America. The most refreshing aspect of the president was that he was a political newcomer, who, reportedly, had not even voted before 2008. Another plus for many Paraguayans was the departure from previous practices when Mr Cartés chose a cabinet of technocrats and business people rather than selecting a band of the party faithful. The Asociación Nacional Republicana-Partido Colorado (National Republican Association-Colorado Party) certainly knew something about governing Paraguay – for better or for worse – having been in power for some 60 years most of which (from 1954 to 1989) had seen the military rule of discredited General Alfredo Stroessner.

Mr Cartés struck a positive note with the electorate when he passed a fiscal-responsibility law limiting budget growth to 4 per cent above inflation and the deficit to no more than 1.5 per cent of GDP. He also introduced a new law that would allow the executive to auction infrastructure concessions without having to get approval from Congress, where the Colorado old guard still held sway. Proposals were also afoot to auction off waterway concessions. For landlocked Paraguay water transport was essential for delivering its soya and beef exports to market. A law providing for disputes between government and concession-holders to be settled by international arbitration was also planned. On his election, Mr Cartés had undertaken to reduce poverty and lay the foundations for a more equal society. But, according to the London *Economist*, his plans relied less on redistribution than on attracting foreign investment. He had also quickly restored Paraguay's ties with Mercosur, the regional trading bloc from which Paraguay was suspended after the ousting of former president, Fernando Armindo Lugo Méndez.

What, no mañana?

An article in *El Pais* entitled *The Conquest of Happiness – Ignorance is Bliss* by John Carlin attributed the ability of Paraguay's population to turn a blind eye to much of what was manifestly wrong with their country to a state of denial. Mr Carlin compared this selectivity to Paraguay's attitude to its almost mythical and certainly most revered, President Francisco Solano López who died in 1870. President Solano was a tyrant, who – aided and abetted by his legendary Irish mistress, Elisa Lynch, the mother of his seven children – happily murdered and plundered throughout his eight years as president. His best known 'achievement' was to declare war not only on Argentina, but simultaneously on Brazil and Uruguay. The war wiped out an estimated 85 per cent of Paraguay's population, leaving it almost without males of working age. None the less, Solano's birthday remains Paraguay's biggest national celebration. Mr Carlin's theory is confirmed by the absence of a word for 'tomorrow' in Paraguay's indigenous language, Guaraní. The closest approximation, according to Mr Carlin, is the Guaraní noun, *koera* which means 'if there is a dawn.' This was thought to represent a lack of concern about the problems that tomorrow might bring. Unhappiness, for Paraguay's indigenous population, only happened when expectations could not be realised.

The economy

In its February 2015 assessment of the Paraguayan economy, the International Monetary Fund (IMF) noted that economic activity in Paraguay had slowed from the record-high growth in 2013, but remained buoyant. Construction, manufacturing and services had lead the expansion in 2014, whereas electricity production declined and re-exports suffered from weak growth in Brazil. Full-year growth was estimated to have slightly exceeded 4 per cent. Inflation rose in early 2014 on account of higher food and regulated prices, but subsequently eased, ending the year at 4.2 per cent, slightly below the authorities' midpoint target. Credit growth had moderated from earlier peak rates but still hovered around 20 per cent, while Paraguay's banks continued to report strong capitalisation and profitability.

The IMF reported that Paraguay's macro-economic policies had been tightened somewhat since late 2013. Tax revenue had grown at a brisk pace in 2014, linked to better enforcement and new taxes. Due to lower revenue from electricity royalties and the faster execution of spending in the latter part of the year, the headline deficit increased slightly relative to 2013. None the less, estimates pointed to a modest contractionary impulse. Monetary policy had been on hold since the Banco Central de Paraguay (BCP) (central bank) raised the official bank rate by 125 basis points, to 6.75 per cent, between December 2013 and February 2014.

Gross domestic product (GDP) was projected to remain close to 4 per cent in 2015. Weak trading partner growth and lower export prices had clouded the outlook and agricultural production was projected to rise only marginally above the

KEY INDICATORS **Paraguay**

	Unit	2011	2012	2013	2014	**2015
Population	m	*6.53	6.68	6.79	*6.90	*7.02
Gross domestic product (GDP)	US$bn	21.20	24.94	28.33	*29.70	*30.75
GDP per capita	US$	3,252	3,734	4,176	*4,305	*4,383
GDP real growth	%	3.8	-1.2	14.2	*4.4	*4.0
Inflation	%	6.6	3.7	2.7	*5.0	*3.6
Unemployment	%	5.6	5.8	5.4	*5.5	*5.5
Exports (fob) (goods)	US$m	10,620.8	11,903.9	13,444.3	–	–
Imports (fob) (goods)	US$m	12,014.2	11,056.1	11,861.0	–	–
Balance of trade	US$m	-1,393.3	847.7	1,583.3	–	–
Current account	US$m	-270.2	-238.0	622.0	*150.0	*-531.0
Total reserves minus gold	US$m	4,943.1	45,566.1	5,555.6	6,668.9	–
Foreign exchange	US$m	4,732.1	4,353.6	5,352.1	–	–
Exchange rate	per US$	4,152.85	4,377.10	4,605.21	4,635.73	–

* estimated figure ** forecast figure

high level seen in 2014. However, positive impulses were expected to come from the projected rebound in electricity generation, the lower oil price and the launch of new infrastructure projects. Paraguay's external current account was projected to fall from a small surplus in 2014 to a moderate deficit in 2015, reflecting weaker terms of trade.

The risks around the outlook were broadly balanced. On the one hand, worsening terms of trade could affect domestic spending more than anticipated, while further rouble depreciation might hurt exports to Russia. On the other hand, looser-than-expected macro-economic policies and efforts to exploit a recently discovered hydrocarbon resource could create upside surprises. Inflation was expected to hover around the 4.5 per cent target in 2015, as recent guaraní depreciation and a small positive output gap offset the impact of lower commodity prices.

Broadly agreeing with the IMF's conclusions, the United Nations Economic Commission for Latin America and the Caribbean (ECLAC/CEPAL) estimated that Paraguay's GDP would expand by 4.0 per cent in 2014 (it turned out to be 4.4 per cent), outpacing the average growth rate for the Latin America and Caribbean region. Arable agriculture was again the engine of growth, but a strong performance was also rendered by the production of edible oils, livestock and the meat and dairy industries. Thanks to the reforms of 2012 and 2013, tax revenues had risen, while the public accounts were expected to show a deficit of approximately 1.8 per cent of GDP, a narrow improvement on the 2 per cent posted in 2013. Bond issues on the international market financed part of this deficit, with the proceeds also likely to be invested in infrastructure improvements. Following the central bank interventions early in 2014, the year-on-year variation in the consumer price index to October 2014 (3.5 per cent) remained below the midpoint of the target range set by the BCP (5 per cent, with a margin of 2 percentage points on either side). In the external sector, the current account surplus was projected to be modest, as a result of lower soybean and electricity exports. Economic growth in 2015 was expected to be similar to that of 2014. The ministry of finance had forecast that current income and expenditure trends could yield a fiscal deficit of 1.8 per cent of GDP at the close of the year – close to the 1.5 per cent target for 2015 established under the Fiscal Responsibility Act. This result would be an improvement on 2013, when the deficit stood at 2 per cent of GDP and would be similar to the 2012 figure, when expansionary fiscal policies led to the first deficit on the public accounts after eight years of surplus. A fiscal reform had been adopted in 2013 to expand the tax base, introducing value added tax for agricultural products and a new agricultural income tax. The impact of these reforms was seen in 2014: by September, tax revenues were 18.4 per cent higher than in the same period the previous year. Another positive factor was the personal income tax penalty, which had taken effect in August 2012 and had a favourable impact on the formalisation of economy. However, in September 2014 total revenues had shown a more modest increase.

Paraguay's ministry of finance had forecast that current income and expenditure trends could yield a fiscal deficit of 1.8 per cent of GDP at the close of the year – close to the 1.5 per cent target for 2015 established under the Fiscal Act. This result would be an improvement on 2013, when the deficit stood at 2 per cent of GDP and would be similar to the 2012 figure, when expansionary fiscal policies led to the first deficit on the public accounts after eight years of surplus. A fiscal reform was adopted in 2013 to expand the tax base, introducing value added tax for agricultural products and a new agricultural income tax. The impact of these reforms was seen in 2014: by September, tax revenues were 8.4 per cent higher than in the same period the previous year. Another positive factor was the personal income tax penalty, which took effect in August 2012 and had a favourable impact on the economy. However, in September 2014 total revenues showed a more modest increase (14 per cent) – largely owing to the drop in revenue from binational enterprises – while total central government spending swelled by 16.3 per cent on the back of a 31.4 per cent rise in capital expenditure. The nominal exchange rate of the guaraní against the dollar fell by 6.5 per cent (appreciation) between January and September 2014, largely as a result of the trade balance surplus. The real exchange rate also fell against the dollar, as the guaraní appreciated by 6.4 per cent between January and September 2014. The currency also strengthened against the euro (by 14.4 per cent) and the Brazilian real (7.7 per cent), though it weakened against the Argentine peso (by 3.6 per cent). The current account posted a surplus of 1.4 per cent of GDP in the second quarter of 2014. The trade balance reversed the trend in the second half of the year and was expected to end 2014 with a surplus of about 1.1 per cent of GDP. In October 2014, the value of exports posted a year-on-year increase of 3.6 per cent, mainly on the strength of soybean exports, which accounted for 27 per cent of total export value. Imports suffered a negative year-on-year variation (of 0.1 per cent), as capital goods imports diminished (by 10 per cent), especially goods for re-export that were affected by the slowdown of the Brazilian economy. It was also thought that the depreciation of the Argentine peso had provided an incentive for unregistered imports.

The Paraguayan economy was projected to expand by 4 per cent during 2014. This percentage was lower than the extraordinary growth of 13 per cent that was witnessed in 2013 as the farming sector bounced back after contracting in 2012 owing to a drought. Economic activity in 2014 was notable for extremely positive results in crop-farming, livestock and the agricultural production chain overall. There was also an upturn in construction and related sectors such as mining and the production of construction materials. Conversely, the binational hydropower sector shrank in 2014, mainly as a result of operational factors at the hydroelectric facilities.

Year-on-year inflation rose by 3.5 per cent in the period up to October 2014, thus remaining below the midpoint of the target range set by the central bank (of 5 per cent, plus or minus 2 per cent). This was largely due to deflationary pressures from June 2014 onwards, since year-on-year inflation had been 7 per cent in May. Consumer prices remained stable as lower food prices offset rises in other categories.

According to the findings of Paraguay's continuous employment survey, unemployment was 7.9 per cent in the second quarter of 2014, slightly down on the rate recorded in the year-earlier period (8.1 per cent). However, while the male unemployment rate dropped from 7.4 per cent to 6.0 per cent, female unemployment climbed from 8.8 per cent to 10.3 per cent. The central bank's wage and salary index posted a year-on-year variation of 6.4 per cent in June 2014.

Risk assessment

Economy	Good/fair
Politics	Fair
Regional stability	Good

COUNTRY PROFILE

1537 The Spanish began colonising the plains of Paraguay.

1811 Paraguay gained independence from Spain.
1864–70 A disastrous war against Argentina, Brazil and Uruguay was lost. It halved Paraguay's population and stripped it of 155,400 square km of land.
1870 Occupation forces set up a provisional government with a liberal-democratic constitution, although the constitution was never put into practice.
1874 The Partido Colorado (PC) (Colorado Party) (also known as the Red Party), representing the land-owning elite, was formed.
1887 The Liberal party, who advocated a minimal state and representative government, was formed.
1883 A Colorado government began driving peasants off the land and selling it to foreign investors.
1904 After a revolution the Liberal party seized power and introduced political and economic changes.
1932–35 The Chaco War with Bolivia over disputed territory.
1936 The army, which held the government responsible for loosing the Chaco War, overthrew the government of President Eusobio Ayala (Liberal) in February and installed war hero Rafael Franco as president, an act that virtually destroyed the Liberals as a political force. The Partido Revolucionario Febrerista (PRF) (*Febrerista* Revolutionary Party) government was a mix of political ideologies, including Communists and Fascists. It implemented land re-distribution and workers rights. Franco's government had popular support but its policies were hastily devised and led to protests when Decree Law 152, promising a 'totalitarian transformation', was announced. The divergent political opinions within the government finally pulled it apart, although Franco continued to hold power with a new party, the Unión Nacional Revolucionaria (Revolutionary National Union). He was unable to provide more land to his peasant supporters and was undermined by Liberal party supporters in the army.
1937 Franco lost support of the army when he withdrew troops from the territories won in Chaco in 1935. The army revolted and returned the Liberal party to power.
1938 A treaty was signed between Bolivia and Paraguay following an international peace conference. It returned most of the disputed land to Bolivia.
1940 The military regime installed Higinio Morínigo, a follower of Nazi Germany's Adolf Hitler, as president.
1946 Following the defeat of Germany and Japan, Paraguay's chief trading partners, Morínigo legalised liberal, communist and *Febrerista* parties.
1947 Paraguay descended into civil war, following the emergence of political divisions within the army.
1948 The PC deposed Morínigo, leading to a series of coups and short-lived regimes.
1949 Federico Chaves became president.
1954 General Alfredo Stroessner led a *coup d'état* that deposed Chaves. Stroessner was re-elected seven times under the constitutional 'state-of-siege' provision. His dictatorship was ruthless against all opposition.
1967 A new constitution endorsed Stroessner's dictatorship. Paraguay was isolated within the world community.
1989 Stroessner was deposed in a bloodless coup by General Antonio Rodríguez who later won the presidential election. However the military-backed National Republican Association-PC won the parliamentary elections.
1993 Juan Carlos Wasmosy was elected president and the PC won a majority of parliamentary seats in the first free presidential and multi-party elections.
1998 Raúl Cubas Grau (PC) won the presidential election, despite allegations of fraud.
1999 Cubas resigned, following the assassination of his vice president, Luís Argaña. Luis González Macchi was appointed as interim president.
2000 Supporters of dissident Colorado leader, General Lino Oviedo, staged an unsuccessful coup. Oviedo fled and was found by Brazilian police at a Brazilian border hideout.
2001 Paraguay asked for, but was denied, Oviedo's extradition.
2002 President Macchi was accused of corruption. Violent street protestors demanded his resignation. He was impeached by congress.
2003 President Macchi survived his impeachment trial; the Senate voted 25–18 against him, short of the two-thirds majority (30 votes) necessary to remove him from power. Nicanor Duarte Frutos won presidential elections. Macchi was again charged with corruption and put on trial.
2004 Former military commander, General Oviedo, was arrested after returning from exile in Brazil. An estimated 464 shoppers were killed in a fire in a three storey supermarket, it was the worst fire in Latin American history. The daughter of former president, Raúl Cubas, was kidnapped.
2005 The body of Cecilia Cubas was found in a shallow grave. President Nicanor ordered a crackdown on organised crime, blamed for widespread kidnapping and murder. Paraguay hosted the world's first conference of landlocked nations, which was attended by 30 states.
2006 A new socialist movement, Tekojoja (Equality), was launched to contest the 2008 presidential elections with the former Bishop Fernando Lugo as candidate.
2008 In presidential elections, Fernando Armindo Lugo Méndez (Partido Demócrata Cristiano) (PDC) (Christian Democratic Party) won 41 per cent of the vote, ending the rule (since 1948) of the PC, whose candidate Blanca Ovelar won 31 per cent, Lino Oviedo (Unión Nacional de Ciudadanos Éticos) (National Union of Ethical Citizens) (Unace) won 22 per cent. In elections for the Chamber of Deputies the ruling Colorado Party won 29 seats and the opposition Partido Liberal Radical Auténtico (PLRA) (Authentic Radical Liberal Party) won 26 seats, the Unión Nacional de Ciudadanos Éticos (UNCE) (National Union of Ethical Citizens) won 16 seats; all other political parties won less than five seats.
2009 An agreement was signed by the presidents of Bolivia and Paraguay settling a border dispute, which had led to the Chaco Wars in the 1930s. The accord leads the way to more development of oil and gas fields in the Chaco region. Brazil agreed to triple its payment to Paraguay for the operation of the Itaipú hydroelectric power station on their shared border. Paraguay also gained permission to sell excess electricity to a third-party from 2023.
2010 Security forces mounted a large operation against left-wing insurgents in the north, blamed for a series of violent incidents.
2011 An experimental titanium oxide extraction plant was opened in August in Minga Pora, east of Asunción. According to the operators of the plant the titanium deposits could be the largest in the world. A referendum was held in October, in which 80 per cent voted in favour of giving voting rights to expatriate nationals.
2012 The congress enacted the extension of voting rights for expatriate nationals, who will be able to vote in the next presidential elections. On 15 June around 150 farmers in the province of Canindeyu clashed with 300 police officers when eviction notices were served on the farmers for occupying land they had previously been evicted from during the 1954–89 Stroessner dictatorship and given to his allies. At least nine farmers and seven police officers were killed, some by firearms. Nine farmers were later arrested on murder charges. On 20 June President Lugo announced he would open an investigation into the circumstances of the conflict. On 21 June the opposition-led lower house of parliament voted to impeach the president over his handling of the evictions (for the motion 73, against one). The impeachment trial was held on 22 June in

the Senate, which, following a vote (for the motion 39, against four), removed Lugo from the presidency. On 23 June Fernando Lugo accepted the decision and stepped down from the presidency but the next day he denounced his dismissal as a 'parliamentary coup' and called for a 'peaceful strike'. Federico Franco was sworn in as the new president. Mercosur suspended Paraguay from its trade organisation due to the impeachment of former president Lugo. No sanctions were imposed and membership will be reviewed following the scheduled presidential elections in 2013. On 21 August, the electoral court announced that the next presidential and parliamentary elections will be held on 12 April 2013. On 2 December, Vidal Vega, the leader of the landless peasant movement was shot dead. Vega had been negotiating with an official inquiry into the killing of evicted farmers, before his planned appearance at the inquiry.

2013 The 21 April presidential election was won by Horacio Cartés with 48.38 per cent, ahead of Efraí Alegre with 39.05 per cent. No other candidate won over 10 per cent. The Senate election was won by the Colorado Party with 19 seats, ahead if the ARLP with 13 seats. the Chamber of Deputies was also won by the Colorado Party with 44 seats to the ARLP's 27 seats. The new President moved quickly to secure extra powers after attacks in the north of the country, attributed to the Ejército del Pueblo Paraguayo (EPP) (Paraguayan People's Army) nationalist guerilla movement. The powers allow the president to deploy the military to tackle unrest in the country, without first declaring a state of emergency. On 11 October the government ordered former Panama prime minister, Ricardo Martinelli, to leave immediately; he faces 11 different criminal charges in Panama, including human rights violations.

2015 On 7 September Paraguay's three branches of government agreed that Asuncion bears no obligation to repay US$85 million borrowed by Gustavo Gramont Berres, a confidant of Alfredo Stroessner, during the last years of the 1954–89 military regime. Mr Gramont held the post of Paraguayan consul in Geneva, but had no legal authority to borrow on behalf of the government.

Political structure

Constitution

Paraguay became an independent republic in 1811. Under the dictatorship of Alfredo Stroessner (1954–89) a new Constitution was introduced in 1967 which granted strong powers to the executive, entrenching political control in the hands of the ruling Partido Colorado (PC) (Colorado Party). In 1992, a new Constitution was enacted.

There are 19 departments and 213 municipalities each with their own directly elected administration.

In 1990, a new electoral law was passed. Among its provisions were the introduction of proportional representation, provision for a second round in the event that no candidate secures an absolute majority in presidential elections, the prohibition of compulsory deductions from salaries of public-sector workers for political parties, the selection of party authorities by the direct vote of all members, a ban on party affiliation by members of the armed forces and the police and the lifting of a previous ban on electoral alliances by political parties.

Form of state

Presidential democratic republic

The executive

Under the constitution executive power is exercised by the president of the republic, who must be a Roman Catholic. The president is elected directly by popular vote for five years and formulates and enacts legislation. Executive power rests with the president who appoints a council of 11 ministers. The president has powers to rule by decree when congress is in recess. The president cannot be re-elected.

National legislature

The bicameral Congreso Nacional (National Congress), consists of the Cámara de Diputados (Chamber of Deputies) (lower house) with 80 members directly elected in 18 multi-seat constituencies corresponding to the country's seventeen departments and capital city by proportional representation vote. The Cámara de Senadores (Chamber of Senators) (upper house) has 45 seats Members of which members are directly elected in a single nationwide constituency by proportional representation vote. Members from both legislative bodies serve five-year terms.

Legal system

At the apex of the judiciary is the Supreme Court which has the power to declare legislation unconstitutional. The five members of the Supreme Court are appointed by the president and their tenure of office coincides with that of the presidency. There are appeal courts and lower level criminal and civil courts.

Last elections

21 April 2013 (parliamentary and presidential)

Results: Presidential: Horacio Cartes (Colardo Party) won 48.5 per cent, Efraín Alegre (PC) won 39 per cent, Mario Ferreiro (Avanza País (Forward Country)) won 6.2 per cent. The remaining eight presidential candidates each won less than 3.5 per cent of the vote. Turnout was 68.5 per cent.

Parliament (Chamber of Deputies): the Asociación Nacional Republicana-Partido Colorado (National Republican Association-Colorado Party) (Colorado Party) won 44 seats (out of 80), the Partido Liberal Radical Auténtico (PLRA) (Authentic Radical Liberal Party) won 27 seats, the Unión Nacional de Ciudadanos Éticos (UNCE) (National Union of Ethical Citizens) won 2 seats; all other political parties won two or fewer seats. Turnout was 68.2 per cent. (Senate) the Colorado Party won 19 seats (out of 45), the PLRA won 13 seats, the Frente Guasú (Guasú Front) won 5 seats, Partido Democrático Progresista (Democratic Progressive Party) 3 seats, the Avanza País (Forward Country) 2 seats and the UNCE 2 seats. Turnout was 68.5 per cent.

Impeachment (chamber of deputies): for the motion 73, against one. Senate: for the motion 39, against four.

Next elections

April 2018 (parliamentary and presidential)

Political parties

Ruling party

Asociación Nacional Republicana-Partido Colorado (National Republican Association (Colorado Party)

Main opposition party

Partido Liberal Radical Auténtico (PLRA) (Authentic Radical Liberal Party)

About 22 per cent of the urban population live in Asunción.

Population

6.90 million (2014)*

Last census: August 2002: 5,163,198

Population density: 12 inhabitants per square km. Urban population 61 per cent (2010 Unicef).

Annual growth rate: 2.1 per cent, 1990–2010 (Unicef).

Ethnic make-up

Over 95 per cent of the population is of Spanish-Guaraní origin. There are approximately 40,000 indigenous people in the country, most of whom live in the Chaco region.

In addition, there are large Korean, German and Japanese immigrant communities, along with small Italian and Polish communities, and some communities of people originating from Lebanon, Taiwan and Hong Kong.

Religions

Roman Catholicism is the state religion and is practised by 90 per cent of the population, the remainder are mostly Protestants.

Education

There are just over 4,300 primary schools and an estimated 92 per cent of the

relevant age group attends primary school. Secondary education begins aged 13 years and comprises two cycles of three years each.
Paraguay has two universities – the National and the Catholic. The state-run Universidad Nacional de Asunción has a student enrolment of around 20,000. It comprises 11 faculties, law and social sciences, medicine, economics, chemistry, dentistry, philosophy, agriculture, veterinary science, fine arts, architecture and engineering. It also has six Institutes and six Higher Schools.
Literacy rate: 92 per cent adult rate; 96 per cent youth rate (15–24) (Unesco 2005).
Compulsory years: Seven to 13
Enrolment rate: 111 per cent gross primary enrolment of relevant age group (including repeaters); 47 per cent gross secondary enrolment (World Bank).
Pupils per teacher: 21 in primary schools

Health
HIV/Aids
HIV prevalence: 0.5 per cent aged 15–49 in 2003 (World Bank)
Life expectancy: 72 years, 2004 (WHO 2006)
Fertility rate/Maternal mortality rate: 3.0 births per woman, 2010 (Unicef); maternal mortality 190 per 100,000 live births (World Bank).
Child (under 5 years) mortality rate (per 1,000): 22 per 1,000 live births (WHO 2012)
Head of population per physician: 1.11 physicians per 1,000 people, 2002 (WHO 2006)

Welfare
The Social Security Institute was formed by Decree Law 17071 in 1948, and is regulated by Decree Law 1860 of 1950. The laws refer to health, medical care and sickness benefits. Workers, their wives and children up to 16 have the right to receive medical, surgical and dental attention, medicine and hospitalisation, as well as cash subsidies for temporary illnesses, maternity and death. Old age pensions are paid to those who have made the necessary contributions. The social security system is in disarray and in 2001 the IMF urged the government to stop lending money to the system.
Women must not work for three weeks before or six weeks after childbirth. During these periods a woman receives a cash subsidy from the Social Security Institute. The worker has the right to receive an allowance equal to 5 per cent of the legal minimum wage for each child under 17 for whose maintenance and education he is responsible. This allowance is wholly the employer's expense and is discontinued once the worker's wage reaches 200 per cent more than the legal minimum.

Main cities
Asunción (capital, estimated population 544,309 in 2012), Cuidad del Este (396,091) (on the Brazilian border), Capiatá (366,998), Luque (361,662), San Lorenzo (320,878), Limpio (201,245), Ñemby (192,224), Lambaré (151,484), Itauguá (148,721), Fernando de la Mora (143,524).

Languages spoken
Guaraní, the aboriginal Indian tongue is widely spoken. In some rural districts, the less educated speak little or no Spanish.
Official language/s
Spanish and Guaraní

Media
Press
Dailies: In Spanish, the main national dailies and Sunday newspapers are *ABC Color* (www.abc.com.py), *Diario Popular* (www.diariopopular.com.py), *Ultima Hora* (www.ultimahora.com), *La Nacion* (www.lanacion.com.py), and *Viva Paraguay* (www.vivaparaguay.com).
Weeklies: In Spanish, *Paraguay Ahora* (www.paraquayahora.com), La Síntesis Económic (http://kaavo.pol.com.py).
Periodicals: Itacom (www.itacom.com.py), Neike (www.neike.com.py), PPN (Portal Paraguayo de Noticias) (www.ppn.com.py), Paraguay Aldia (www.paraguayaldia.com), Paraguay News (www.paraguaynews.com.py), Zeta Revista (www.revistazeta.com.py), regional publications, International Action (www.accion.org), UnMundo Améruca Latina (www.un-mundo.org, in English: http://amlat.oneworld.net).
Broadcasting
Radio: The government-owned Radio Nacional del Paraguay (www.rnpy.com), broadcasts on AM and FM; there are several private radio stations. Radio Cardinal (www.cardinal.com.py), Radio Nanduti (www.nanduti.com.py), Radio Venus (www.venus.com.py), Radio Venus (www.fmradiocity.com), Radio Canal 100 (www.canal100.com.py).
Television: There are several television channels, all privately owned with broadcasts in Spanish – Sistema Nacional de Televisión (SNT, Canal 9) (www.snt.com.py), RED Guarani (Canal 2) (www.redguarani.com.py), Telefuturo (Canal 4) (www.telefuturo.com.py), Red Privada de Televisión (El Trece, Canal 13) (www.rpc.com.py), Paravision (Canal 5) (www.canal5paravision.com). These broadcasters syndicate their programmes around the country and on cable TV.
None are based in Paraguay but Mercopress (www.mercopress.com) specialises in news from Latin America countries within Mercosur and the Falkland Islands.

Economy
Paraguay has evolved into a modern service sector driven economy, with services constituting 50.3 per cent of GDP in 2014. Agriculture is still important, comprising 20.9 of GDP, with industry at 28.8 per cent, of which manufacturing was 12 per cent. Agricultural products account for the majority of export items, especially soya beans, cotton, cattle, timber and sugar. International trade is an important aspect of the economy with goods purchased from Japan and the US and re-exported (around 50 per cent of all imported goods are re-exported at a profit with little or no changes made to them). Although there are few mineral resources and little heavy industry, Paraguay operates the world's largest, single, hydroelectric power station, Itaipú on the River Paraná, which generates up to US$360 million per year from the sale of electricity to Brazil.
GDP growth in 2014 was 4.4 per cent. Paraguay's economy has recently experienced large output swings due to various exogenous events such as harvests. This has led to questions over what exactly Paraguay's potential output could be.
In 2014, the UN Human Development Index (HDI) ranked Paraguay 111 (out of 187) for development in health, education and income.
In 2010, 48.5 per cent of the population experienced deprivation in at least one indicator of poverty and 5.1 per cent of the population were living on the equivalent of US$1.25 per day. Paraguay is subject to a widespread informal economy with smuggling to and from neighbouring countries a problem for government revenue collection.
Remittances in 2013 had grown to US$591 million, a reduction from US$634 million in 2012.

External trade
As a member of Mercosur, the world's fourth largest free-trade zone, Paraguay (along with Argentina, Brazil and Uruguay), has access to a market of over 200 million consumers. Paraguay is also an associate member of the Andean Community (AC), since Mercosur negotiated a free trade area with AC.
Paraguay's economy is predominately agricultural, which constitutes 20.9 per cent of GDP in 2014 and exports represent a large portion of this. The world's largest single hydroelectric generating facility at the Itaipú Dam, is jointly owned and operated by Paraguay and Brazil; US$360

million per year of electricity is exported to Brazil.

Imports

Main imports include road vehicles, consumer goods, tobacco, petroleum products, electrical machinery, tractors, chemicals and vehicle parts.

Main sources: Brazil (28 per cent of total in 2014), China (25.5 per cent), Argentina (14.6 per cent) and the US (7.9 per cent).

Exports

Soybeans, livestock feed, cotton, meat, edible oils, wood and leather.

Main destinations: Brazil (30.8 per cent of total in 2014), Russia (10.8 per cent), Argentina (7.4 per cent), Chile (6.9 per cent) and the Netherlands (4.5 per cent).

Re-exports

The country re-exports significant amounts of US products to regional neighbours. Around 50 per cent of all imported goods are re-exported at a profit with little or no changes made to them. There is evidence of trade through informal channels such as smuggling.

Agriculture

Farming

The agricultural sector remains an important sector of the country's economy. The sector employs approximately 30 per cent of the labour force and contributed 20.9 per cent of total GDP in 2014.

Agricultural products account for more than 90 per cent of exports, of which cotton and soya beans together account for more than two-thirds of export earnings. Sawn timber, meat products and, to a lesser extent, fruit, vegetables and hides are also exported. Sugar cane, wheat, tobacco and various new specialist crops for industrial use are expanding as more land comes under cultivation. Paraguay has nearly achieved self-sufficiency in basic foodstuffs (rice, maize, wheat, beans). Approximately 5 per cent of total land area is arable land or under permanent crops, pasture constitutes 35 per cent of the land and 50 per cent is woodland/forest. While the fertile eastern region is ideal for arable farming and cattle grazing the rich soil has been subject to erosion since the 1970s. There are extensive forests with a variety of timbers. The potential of the Chaco region to the west is still to be realised, dependent as it is upon the exploitation of its known groundwater resources for irrigated farming.

Agricultural production fluctuates from year to year owing to climatic conditions (both flooding and drought) and widespread smuggling (particularly livestock and soya beans).

Fishing

Despite its landlocked geographical status, Paraguay's annual fish catch amounts to approximately 10,000 tonnes. The illegal trade of fishery products remains a problem despite attempts by the authorities to bring it under control.

Forestry

Paraguay has a significant area of forested land, accounting for approximately 30 per cent of the country's total landmass. The majority of the forested areas are to the east of the Paraguay River. Historically, deforestation has been a problem in Paraguay. The country lost on average 0.51 per cent of forest cover each year during the 1990-2000 period. This amounted to a decrease of 123,000 hectares year on year.

Local forest resources produce moderate volumes of sawn timber and panels, most of which is usually exported. Domestic demand for paper is usually met by imports. Consumption of wood fuel is significant.

Industry and manufacturing

In a typical year for the economy of Paraguay the industrial sector accounts for approximately a quarter of total GDP. Although Paraguay is South America's least industrialised country, the sector does account for just under 20 per cent of the total workforce.

Manufacturing is small-scale and geared to the processing of primary products with agro-industry representing about 70 per cent of total industrial production. Construction contributes approximately 6 per cent of GDP. Manufacturing is centred on the processing of agricultural products, particularly textiles, cotton yarn, wood products, beef products, and industrial and edible oils. The country is self-sufficient in cement and there is an oil refinery (capacity 10,000 barrels per day (bpd)) and steel works (150,000 tonnes per year).

Contrasting with other Latin American countries, which have undergone a process of industrialisation based on import-substitution, development strategy in Paraguay has emphasised export-led growth. This involved minimal protection for domestic industry, whose growth problems have been compounded by the small size of the home market, high freight costs for imported products and the effects of extensive smuggling of a wide range of consumer goods from neighbouring countries.

Tourism

Tourist amenities are modest in general, so Paraguay has made a virtue out of its character and offers urban visitors the chance to experience its rural charms. It offers activity holidays on *estrancias* (ranches) in its eastern region, as well as some ecotourism in its western region. National parks provide unspoiled habitats for a range of Latin American animals and vegetation.

Travel and tourism contributes around 4 per cent of GDP and accounts for around 3.4 per cent of employment (around 113,500 jobs). Investment in travel and tourism in 2014 totalled 1.4 per cent of total investment.

Environment

In 2004, USAID reported that indiscriminate exploitation threatened the country's natural resources. In the eastern border region, which had been largely uncultivated until the 1970s, the rich topsoil was severely eroded and unmanaged use of land was jeopardising the largest underground water aquifer on the continent.

Mining

Paraguay's mining sector is negligible, contributing just 0.5 per cent to GDP in a typical year. The national government has attempted to introduce a programme of financial incentives in order to promote exploration for petroleum, lead and uranium. It has also encouraged mineral prospecting by granting tax concessions. However, few commercial reserves have been discovered and the sector employs just 0.3 per cent of the country's total workforce.

Studies commissioned by the Dirección General de Recursos Minerales (DGRM), with the support of the United Nations Development Programme (UNDP), have revealed that opportunities exist for the commercial extraction of marble, pyrophyllite, granite, slate, talc, gypsum and lignite.

Paraguay has limited proven mineral reserves and at present mining is concentrated on the extraction of salt, gypsum, limestone, kaolin and other clays. Prospecting has revealed the existence of uranium and bauxite, manganese, iron ore and copper. From the 1990s, none have been found in large enough quantities to overcome the high extraction costs involved.

According to CIC Resources mining company, the deposits at an experimental titanium oxide extraction plant that it operates in Minga Pora, east of Asunción, could be the largest in the world. The plant opened on 5 August 2011.

Hydrocarbons

There are no proven oil reserves in Paraguay; consumption of imported oil (refined oil, lubricants and aviation fuel) was 27,000 barrels per day (bpd) in 2013. Oil exploration continues but has failed to find reserves of commercial value. Oil deposits in the border regions of Formosa (Argentina) and Chaco (Bolivia) exist and the prospects of finding oil in Paraguay are thought to be promising. The

state-owned Petropar refinery near Asunción can produce 7,500bpd of refined oil.
There are no reserves of natural gas and consumption is negligible, although were there to be discoveries of commercially viable natural gas in the north-western Chaco region, it is anticipated that gas use would grow. There are discussions about constructing an 850km pipeline to the capital Asunción from southern Bolivia, which would also mean demand for natural gas in Paraguay would increase, along with the country becoming an important transit centre for Bolivian natural gas.
Coal is neither produced nor imported.

Energy
Total installed generating capacity was 10.1 gigawatts (GW) in 2008, producing around 92 billion kilowatt hours (kWh). Paraguay's electricity needs are almost entirely met by hydropower and it is a net exporter of electricity, mostly to Brazil and Argentina.
The bulk of electricity supplies come mainly from the world's largest hydroelectric plant, Itaipú on the River Paraná, which produces 13.3GW and is jointly run by Brazil and Paraguay. Brazil financed the Itaipú construction using Paraguay's resources; all excess electricity produced by Itaipú is sold to Brazil. In May 2009 a review of the contractual agreement was discussed at ministerial level as Paraguay maintained that the price paid by Brazil for its electricity had not increased since Itaipú became operational in 1973; Brazil considered Paraguay must take into account the investment Brazil originally made. Other hydroelectric plants include the 3.1GW Yacyretá plant and 2.8GW Corpus Christi on the Paraná, co-owned with Argentina, and the wholly owned Acaray of 210MW. The government has plans to increase the use of biofuels and the production of ethanol from sugar cane. Although rural communities still use wood fuel, solar energy sources are being introduced.

Financial markets
Stock exchange
Bolsa de Valores y Productos de Asunción (BVPASA) (Asunción Stock Exchange)

Banking and insurance
Paraguay's banking and financial services sector has suffered from numerous crises and bad loans. The sector has undergone slow reform and the government has persisted in its policy of propping up ailing banking houses over recent years.
A new Bank of the South, with a headquarters in Venezuela, will be launched in 2008 to provide an alternative source of development funding for the participating countries. Assets of US$7 billion will underpin its operations.
Central bank
Banco Central del Paraguay.

Time
GMT minus four hours (daylight saving, Otober–March, GMT minus three hours)

Geography
Paraguay is a landlocked country in central South America. Bolivia lies to the north, Brazil to the east, and Argentina to the south and west. The River Paraguay effectively splits the country in two, with an area known as the Chaco to the west, which comprises 61 per cent (246,950 square km) of the country's land area, but only 3 per cent of the national population. In contrast, the eastern region is a much richer area in which most of the population is concentrated. This region is divided into two by a high ridge of hills. East of the hills lies the Paraná Plateau which is 300–600 metres high, and in the west lies a fertile, treeless pampas that floods once a year and stretches to the River Paraguay.
The Chaco is scrub forest used mostly for cattle. Much of the area is a national park, with jaguars, tapirs, puma and wild hog found here.
Hemisphere
Southern

Climate
The climate is subtropical with an average annual temperature of 23 degrees Celsius (C). The hot season is October–March and the average temperature rises to 32 degrees C. The temperate season is from April to September when the average temperature is 15 degrees C. The heaviest rains take place during this period, and the average annual rainfall is 1,500mm. In spring and autumn the arrival of cold fronts from the south can cause temperatures to fall suddenly by 10–20 degrees C within a few hours.

Dress codes
In the cities, businessmen wear European-style clothing; shorts are normally worn only for recreation.

Entry requirements
Passports
Required by all, except tourists from the Mercado Común del Sur (Mercosur) (Common Market of the South).
Visa
Required by all except citizens, visiting as tourists, from countries included on the list found at www.paraguayembassy.co.uk/exemptlist.htm. All visits must commence within 90 days of visa issue. Business travellers should either contact the nearest consular section to request an application form. An invitation from a local company or organisation, provision of adequate funds for stay and proof of return/onward passage are necessary.
Currency advice/regulations
There are no restrictions on the import and export of foreign or local currency. Travellers cheques have limited acceptance.

Health (for visitors)
Mandatory precautions
Yellow fever vaccination certificates are required if arriving from an infected area.
Advisable precautions
Inoculations and booster should be current for tetanus, hepatitis A and typhoid. There may be a need for vaccinations for tuberculosis, diphtheria, yellow fever and hepatitis B. The use of malaria prophylaxis (including mosquito repellents, nets and clothing that cover the body after dark) will also provide protection for hepatitis B and yellow fever. There is a risk of rabies. Mains water is usually safe to drink in Asunción and other major towns. Elsewhere precautions should be taken. Bottled water is advisable for the first few weeks of any stay. Milk is unpasteurised and should be boiled. Dairy products likely to have been made from local milk should be avoided, and meat and fish should be well cooked.
Medical insurance is essential, including emergency evacuation; an adequate supply of personal medicines is necessary.

Credit cards
International credit cards are widely accepted. ATMs are found in most towns.

Public holidays (national)
Fixed dates
1 Jan (New Year's Day), 1 Mar (Heroes' Day), 1 May (Labour Day), 15 May (Independence Day), 12 Jun (Peace of Chaco), 15 Aug (Foundation of Asunción), 29 Sep (Battle of Boquerón), 8 Dec (Immaculate Conception), 25 Dec (Christmas Day).
Variable dates
Maundy Thursday, Good Friday.

Working hours
Banking
Mon–Fri: 0845–1500.
Business
Mon–Fri: 0800–1200 and 1430–1900; Sat: 0800–1200.
Government
Mon–Fri: 0700–1300.
Shops
Mon–Sat: 0900–2100. Some shops open 0730–2000.

Telecommunications
Mobile/cell phones
There are limited 850/1900 GSM services located in the capital and towns close by.

Electricity supply
220V AC, 50 cycles

Social customs/useful tips
Business people are punctual and expect appointments to be kept. Business cards are exchanged on visits and it is usual to shake hands when arriving or leaving an office or home. The best time to visit is between May and September
While most businessmen may speak English, it is advantageous to have some knowledge of Spanish. It is important to use the correct mode of address in writing or in speech.
Most businessmen do not wear a jacket and tie during office hours, but visitors, including businesswomen, are advised to wear lightweight business suits.
A 10–15 per cent tip is usually included on hotel and bar bills.

Security
Normal precautions apply. The level of street crime is much lower than other countries in Latin America.

Getting there
Air
National airline: Transportes Aéreo del Mercosur (TAM Mercusor).
International airport/s: Asunción-Silvio Pettirossi International Airport (ASU), 16km from city; *bureau de change*, duty-free shops, restaurants and car hire. Travel time to city centre by taxi or bus is 20 minutes.
Airport tax: International departures US$25; 24-hour transit passengers exempt.
Domestic departures from Asunción Pettirossi International Airport (ASU) US$4.
Surface
Road: There are paved roads from Brazil (Rio de Janeiro-Asunción; length 1,700km) and from Argentina (Buenos Aires-Asunción, length 1,450km) which are considered good, less so the access from Bolivia.
Rail: A regular service by means of a train-ferry runs from Concepión to Posadas (Argentina), where a connection can be made to Buenos Aires. Services are slow.
Water: There are ferry links with Argentina, Bolivia and Brazil. For journeys to Buenos Aires check the route chosen is the most direct. From Brazil, boats connect Corumba with Asunción.
Main port/s: Asunción (on River Paraguay) is approximately 1,500km from the sea; Concepción, in suitable conditions, is accessible by ocean-going ships.

Getting about
National transport
Air: There are six carriers operating scheduled services to most parts of the country. Planes can be chartered and seats booked on air taxis for many destinations. Flights are frequently affected by weather.
Road: Around 10 per cent of the total network is surfaced, those serving main centres are in good condition. The main route is triangular, linking Asunción, Encarnación and Ciudad del Este. The Trans-Chaco Highway runs to the Bolivian border, but is paved for only half the distance. Some unsurfaced roads are closed in bad weather; service stations etc may be widely spaced.
Buses: There are frequent express services linking major towns; for longer distances it is advisable to make advance bookings (eg Asunción-Encarnación; Asunción-Ciudad del Este).
Rail: The main route is Asunción-Villarrica-Encarnación but the service is slow.
Water: The river Paraná is a major access route from the Atlantic coast. Asunción-Concepción service is not frequent and takes 24 hours, Asunción-Pilar 20 hours, and Asunción-Encarnación nine hours.
City transport
Taxis: In Asunción metered taxis operate with a minimum fare system; they can be hired on a time basis; a 10 per cent tip is optional.
Buses, trams & metro: Private companies operate bus and minibus services in the capital. Two tram routes also operate.
Car hire
Foreign or international licences are acceptable. Chauffeur and self-drive cars are available at reasonable rates.

BUSINESS DIRECTORY
The addresses listed below are a selection only. While World of Information makes every endeavour to check these addresses, we cannot guarantee that changes have not been made, especially to telephone numbers and area codes. We would welcome any corrections.

Telephone area codes
The internatioanl direct dialling (IDD) code for Paraguay is +595, followed by area code:

Asunción	21	Encarnación	71
Ciudad Del Este	61	Pilar	86
Concepción	31	Villarrica	541
Coronel Oviedo	521		

Chambers of Commerce
American-Paraguayan Chamber of Commerce, General Diaz 521, Edificio El Faro Internacional, Piso 4, Asunción (tel: 442-136; fax: 442-135; e-mail: pamchamb@conexion.com.py).

British–Paraguayan Chamber of Commerce, Gral Diaz 521, Edificio Internacional Faro, Piso 2, Asunción (tel/fax: 498-274; e-mail: britcham@infonet.com.py).

Paraguay Cámara Nacional de Comercio y Servicios, Estrella 540-550, Asunción (tel: 493-321; fax: 440-817; e-mail: info@ccparaguay.com.py).

Banking
Private Banking Association (ABP), Juan O'Leary y Estrella, 30 Piso Asunción (tel: 491-450; fax: 491-450).

Banco Alemán Paraguayo, Estrella No 505 y 14 de mayo, Zona Postal 1428, Asunción (tel: 490-166/9, 444-714/6; fax: 447-645).

Banco Comercial Paraguayo, Av Mariscal López 780, Zona Postal 2350, Asunción (tel: 207-251/7, 440-504; fax: 207-259).

Banco Continental, Estrella No 621, Apartado postal 2260, Asunción (tel: 446-915/18; fax: 442-001, 441-377).

Banco de Asunción, Palma Esquina 14 de mayo, Asunción Central (tel: 493-191/8; fax: 493-190).

Banco de Inversiones del Paraguay, Palma No 202, Esquina Nuestra Señora de la Asunción, Apartado postal 702, Asunción (tel: 449-550, 498-593/94; fax: 443-749).

Banco de la Nación Argentina, Chile y Palma, Apartado postal 064, Asunción (tel: 447-433, 449-463; fax: 444-365).

Banco del Paraná, Yegros y 25 de mayo, Apartado postal 2298, Asunción (tel: 446-827, 446-691/5; fax: 498-909).

Banco do Brasil, Oliva y Nuestra Señora de la Asunción, Apartado postal 667, Asunción (tel: 90-121, 90-126; fax: 448-761).

Banco do Estado de São Paulo, Ind Nacional, Esquina Fulgencio R Moreno, Apartado postal 2211, Asunción (tel: 494-981/3; fax: 494-985).

Banco Exterior, Yegros y 25 de mayo, Apartado postal 824, Asunción (tel: 492-072/9; fax: 448-103).

Banco Finamerica, Chile y Oliva, Apartado postal 824, Asunción (tel: 491-021/025; fax: 445-159, 445-604).

Banco General, Chile y Haedo, Apartado postal 3202, Asunción (tel: 496-815/9; fax: 496-822).

Banco Holandés Unido, E V Haedo 103, Esquina Independencia Nacional, Apartado postal 1180, Asunción (tel: 490-001; fax: 491-734).

Banco Nacional de Fomento, Independencia Nacional y Cerro Cora, Asunción (tel: 444-440/1/2/3; fax: 446-053).

Banco Paraguayo Oriental de Inversión y Fomento, Azara 197 Esquina Yegros, Apartado postal 1496, Asunción (tel: 444-212 al 16; fax: 446-820).

Banco Real del Paraguay, Calle Estrella y Alberdi, Apartado postal 1442, Asunción (tel: 493-171/80; fax: 443-664).

Banco Sudameris Paraguay, Independencia Nacional y Cerro Cora, Apartado postal 1433, Asunción (tel: 494-542/8, 444-172/3).

Citibank, Chile, Esquina Estrella, Apartado postal 1174, Asunción (tel: 494-951/9; fax: 444-820).

Inter-American Development Bank (IDB), Edif. Aurora 1-3 pisos, Caballero esq Eligio Ayala, Casilla 1209, Asunción (tel: 492-061; fax: 446-537).

Interbanco, 14 de mayo 339, Apartado postal 392, Asunción (tel: 494-992/5; fax: 448-587).

ING Bank (Internationale Nederlanden Bank), Av España y San Rafael, Apartado postal, 10007 Asunción (tel: 606-423; fax: 606-437).

Lloyds Bank, Palma Esq Juan E O'Leary, Casilla Postal 696, Asunción (tel: 443-580; fax: 443-569).

Central bank

Banco Central del Paraguay, Federación Rusa y Sargento Marecos, Asunción (tel: 619-2061; fax: 610-088; e-mail: ccs@bcp.gov.py).

Stock exchange

Bolsa de Valores y Productos de Asunción (BVPASA) (Asunción Stock Exchange), www.bvpasa.com.py

Travel information

Dirección Nacional de Turismo, Palma 468, Alberdi/Oliva, Asunción (tel: 441-530; fax: 491-230).

Transportes Aéreo Marilia (TAM), Oliva 467, Asunción (tel: 91-041; fax: 96-484).

National tourist organisation offices

Secretaría Nacional de Turismo, Palma 468, Casi 14 de Mayo, Edificio Central, Asunción (tel: 494-110; internet: www.senatur.gov.py).

Ministries

Ministry of Agriculture and Livestock, Presidente Franco 479, Asunción (tel: 443-791, 449-614; fax: 441-036).

Ministry of Defence, Avenids Mcal López y Vice Pte Sánchez, Asunción (tel: 204-771; fax: 211-583).

Ministry of Education and Culture, Chile 898 c/ Humaitá, Asunción (tel: 443-078; fax: 443-919).

Ministry of Exterior Relations, Presidente Franco c/ O'Leary, Asunción (tel: 493-872; fax: 493-910).

Ministry of Finance, Chile 128 esq Palmas, Asunción (tel: 440-010; fax: 448-283).

Ministry of Foreign Affairs, Juan E O'Leary y Pte, Franco, Asunción (tel: 494-593, 493-872; fax: 493-910).

Ministry of Health and Public Welfare, Av Petirrossi y Brasil, Asunción (tel: 207-328; fax: 206-700).

Ministry of Housing, Chile 128 c/ Palma, Asunción (tel: 440-010; fax: 448-283).

Ministry of Industry and Commerce, Avenida España 323, Asunción (tel: 204-638; fax: 213-529; internet site: www.mic.gov.py).

Ministry of the Interior, Chile c/ Manduvirá, Asunción (tel: 493-661; fax: 448-446).

Ministry of Justice and Labour, Avda Dr Gaspar Rodriguez de Francia c/ EE UU, Asunción (tel: 447-196, 491-555; fax: 440-066).

Ministry of Public Health and Social Welfare, Av Pettirossi c/Brasil, Asunción (tel: 207-328; fax: 206-700).

Ministry of Public Works and Communications, Olivia c/ Alberdi, Asunción (tel: 444-411, 496-666; fax: 443-625).

Other useful addresses

Administración Nacional de Electricidad (ANDE) (National Electricity Board), España el Padre Caroloto 360, Asunción (tel: 22-713/719).

Administración Nacional de Telecom (Antelco – Telecommunications Authority), Alberdi, esq General Diaz, Asunción (tel: 44-001).

Agencia Publicitaria Visión, 25 de Mayo, 966, Asunción (tel: 24-796).

Asociación Paraguaya de Cias de Seguros, 15 de Agosto esq Lugano, Casilla 1435, Asunción (tel: 446-474; fax: 444-343).

British Airways, Azara 192, Asunción (tel: 490-020).

British Embassy, Av. Boggiani 5848, C/R16 Boquerón, Casilla 404, Asunción (tel: 595-21 612 611; fax: 595-21 605 007).

Association of Cotton Ginners, CADELPA, Av Boggiani 4744, Asunción (tel: 595 21 609-272; fax: 595 21 600-739).

Customs Office, Colón c/ Plaza Isabel La Católica, Asunción (tel: 492-202, 495-086; fax: 445-085).

Dirección General de Estadísticas y Censos (National Statistics Office), Dr Miguel Torres, Asunción (tel: 610-331, 663-489).

Federation of Agroindustrial Exporters (FEDEXA), Brasilia 840 c/Sgto Gauto, Asunción (tel: 208-855, 205-749; fax: 213-971).

Federation of Industrial and Commercial Production (FEPRINCO), Palma 751 c/ Ayolas, Edif Unión Club, Piso 3, Asunción (tel: 444-963; fax: 446-638).

Importers Association (Centro de Importadores), Montevideo 671, Montevideo 671 c/ E V Haedo, Asunción (tel: 441-295, 490-291; fax: 441-295).

Industrial Union of Paraguay (UIP), Cerro Corá 1038 Casilla 782, Asunción (tel: 212-556; fax: 312-260).

Municipality of Asunción, Mariscal López y Cap. Villamayor Bloque A, 1er Piso Asunción (tel: 610-576, 610-577; fax: 610-578).

Paraguayan Embassy (USA), 2400 Massachusetts Avenue, NW, Washington DC 20008 (tel: (+1-202) 483-6960; fax: (+1-202) 234-4508; e-mail: embapar@erols.com).

Petróleos Paraguayos (Petropar), Oliva 299, 4er Piso, Casilla 571, Asunción (tel: 95-117).

Planning Office, Pdte Franco c/ Ayolas, Edif Ayfra, Piso 3, Asunción (tel: 491-159, 448-366; fax: 496-510).

Pro Paraguay (Promotion of Exporters and Importers), Padre Cardozo 469 c/ España, Asunción (tel: 208-276, 208-641; fax: 200-425).

Rural Association of Paraguay (ARP), Ruta Transchaco Km 14, Mariano Roque Alonso (tel: 291-036, 291-061; fax: 291-061).

Siderurgia Paraguaya (Sidepar), Azara 197, 6er Piso, esq Yegros, Casilla 2441, Asunción (tel: 95-963).

Soybean Exporters Association (CAPECO), Av Brasilia 840, Asunción (tel: 208-855; fax: 595 21 213 971).

US Embassy, Avenida Mcal Lopez 1776, Casilla 402, Asunción (tel: 213-715; fax: 213-728).

Water Authority (Corporación de Obras Sanitarias Corposana), JoséBerges: e/Brasil y San José, Asunción (tel: 25-001/003).

Internet sites

Noticias (newspaper): www.diarionoticias.com.py

Office of the President: www.presidencia.gov.py

The Congress of Paraguay: www.camdip.gov.py

Peru

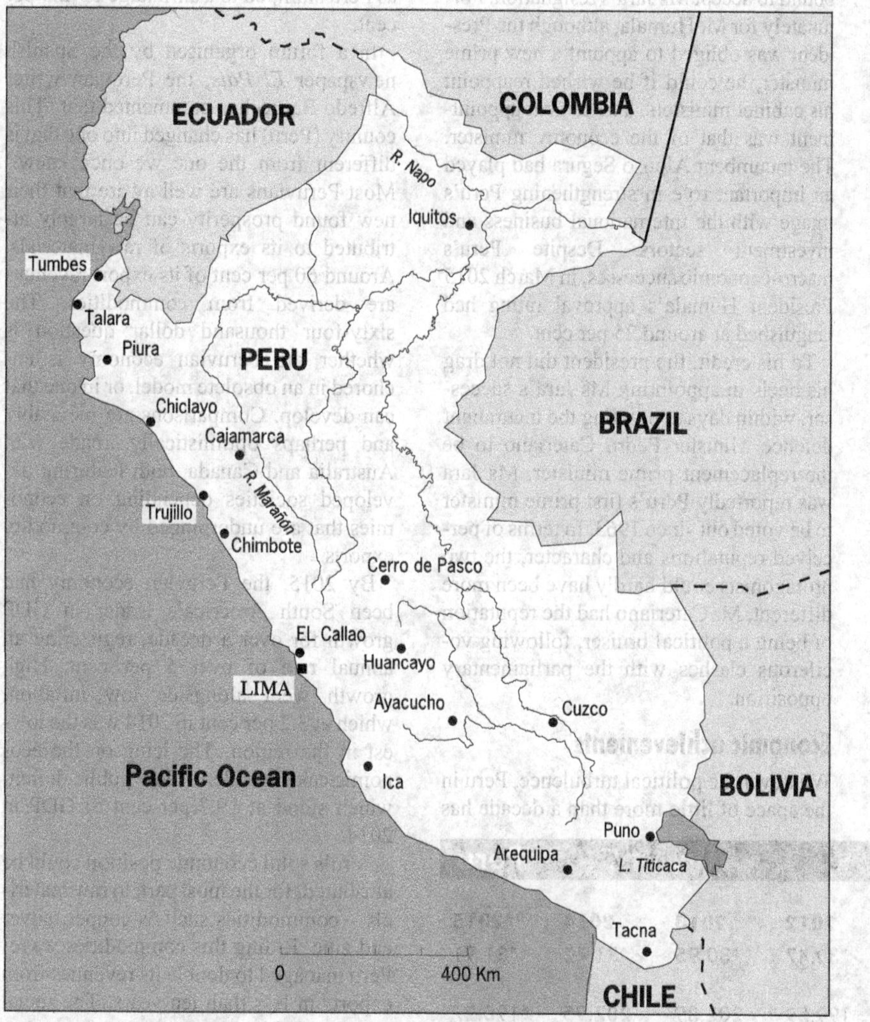

In July 2015 Peru's Confederación General de Trabajadores del Perú (CGTP) (General Workers Confederation) organised a day of protest mobilising its supporters against the economic policies of President Ollanta Humala. Protestors took to the streets and roads were blocked. The protests were significant, if not massive. Some 4,000 protestors walked from Lima's Plaza Dos de Mayo to the city's Parque Universitario. From there a delegation made its way to Congress to submit a document listing their demands.

The president of the CGTP, Carmela Sifuentes, told the Spanish news agency EFE that the demands included an increase in the minimum wage (currently a monthly US$235) as well as greater respect for collective wage negotiation. The protests' organisers claimed that 25,000 people had turned out across Peru in their support. The CTGP vice president, Juan José Gorriti, announced that the purpose of the protests was to draw attention to the 'defects' of the Peruvian government's policies.

The CTGP rejected the government's *Servir* programme which sought to integrate Peru's trades unions into the state apparatus. The protestors were also opposed to the government's privatisation programmes. Mr Gorriti asserted that 'we

KEY FACTS

Official name: República Peruana (Peruvian Republic)

Head of State: President Ollanta Moisés Humala Tasso (from 28 Jul 2011)

Head of government: Prime Minister Pedro Álvaro Cateriano Bellido (from 2 Apr 2015)

Ruling party: Coalition named Alianza Gana Perú (Win Peru) (from 28 Jul 2011) including the Partido Nacionalista Peruano (Peruvian Nationalist Party), Partido Socialista (Socialist Party), Partido Comunista Peruano (Peruvian Communist Party), Partido Socialista Revolucionario (Revolutionary Socialist Party) and the Movimento Político Voz Socialista (Political Movement Socialist Voice).

Area: 1,285,216 square km

Population: 31.42 million (2014)*

Capital: Lima

Official language: Spanish, Quechua and Aymara

Currency: Nuevo sol (S/) = 100 centimos

Exchange rate: S/3.23 per US$ (Sep 2015)

GDP per capita: US$6,458 (2014)*

GDP real growth: 2.35% (2014)

GDP: US$202.95 billion (2014)

Labour force: 4.70 billion (2010)

Unemployment: 6.00% (2014) (plus additional underemployment)

Inflation: 3.25% (2014)

Oil production: 110,000 bpd (2014)

Natural gas production: 12.90 billion cum (2014)

Balance of trade: US$612.90 million (2013)

Annual FDI: US$8.23 billion (2011)

* estimated figure

need to pass from a commodities and raw materials economic model to one that develops the country's industry and generates more dignified employment for Peruvians.'

The protestors blocked numerous roads including the Interoceánica, which links Peru with Brazil. The Peruvian government had been granted special powers to legislate on a series of economic reforms designed to increase private investment. It was expected that in his end July 2015 (and final) Message to the Nation, President Humala would detail the economic reforms envisaged.

Elections loom

Peruvians were well aware in 2015 that in 2016 the country would be holding presidential elections. Leonidas Cuenca, of the *Apoyo Consultoría*, poignantly observed that on current form 20 per cent of the electorate would make their choice one week before the election and 23 per cent on the day of the election. 'Politics has always been a problem, noted Mr Cuenca. Others considered that until that ceased to be the case, Peru would have found its future.

In the short term, however, that prospect looked a little distant, with the resignation in March 2015 of Ana Jara, Peru's prime minister, after losing a confidence vote in Congress. The prime minister had been accused of spying on her opponents. It was not only Ms Jara who had to step down – all her ministers also resigned, meaning that President Ollanta Humala would have to form another new government. This augured badly for Peru's image – Ms Jara was the seventh prime minister during the Humala presidency. The vote of confidence – or rather the lack of it – was conclusive. Seventy-two deputies voted against Ms Jara, with only 42 supporting her. The president was constitutionally bound to accept Ms Jara's resignation. Fortunately for Mr Humala, although the President was obliged to appoint a new prime minister, he could if he wished reappoint his cabinet ministers. The critical appointment was that of the economy minister. The incumbent Alonso Segura had played an important role in strengthening Peru's image with the international business and investment sectors. Despite Peru's macro-economic successes, in March 2015 President Humala's approval rating had languished at around 25 per cent.

To his credit, the president did not drag his heels in appointing Ms Jara's successor, within days appointing the incumbent defence Minister Pedro Cateriano to be the replacement prime minister. Ms Jara was reportedly Peru's first prime minister to be voted out since 1963. In terms of perceived reputations and character, the two protagonists could hardly have been more different. Mr Cateriano had the reputation of being a political bruiser, following vociferous clashes with the parliamentary opposition.

Economic achievements

Whatever the political turbulence, Peru in the space of little more than a decade has become a flagship Latin American economy. In 2010 and 2011, two of the worst years for most European economies, in economic terms Peru had two of its most impressive years ever, recording gross domestic product (GDP) growth levels of 8.5 per cent and 6.5 per cent respectively. 2014, however, was a year best ignored, as Peru slumped to a shrinkage of -2.4 per cent.

In a forum organised by the Spanish newspaper *El País*, the Peruvian writer Alfredo Barnechea commented that 'This country (Peru) has changed into one that is different from the one we once knew.' Most Peruvians are well aware that their new found prosperity can be largely attributed to its exports of raw materials. Around 60 per cent of its export revenues are derived from commodities. The sixty-four thousand dollar question is whether the Peruvian economy is anchored in an obsolete model, or in one that can develop. Comparisons are inevitably and perhaps optimistically, made with Australia and Canada, both featuring developed societies depending on economies that are underpinned by commodity exports.

By 2015, the Peruvian economy had been South America's leader in GDP growth for over a decade, registering an annual rate of over 5 per cent. High growth went alongside low inflation, which at 3.2 per cent in 2014 was the lowest in the region. The icing on the economic cake was Peru's low public deficit, which stood at 19.7 per cent of GDP in 2014.

Peru's solid economic position could be attributed, for the most part, to raw materials – commodities such as copper, silver and zinc. Riding this commodities wave' Peru managed to double its revenues from exports in less than ten years. The social impact of this unprecedented boom has been significant – Peru has seen its middle class grow by as much as 45 per cent. Peru's present may be in its mining, its future is in a wider spread of activities which could include less obvious activities such as archaeological tourism and gastronomy. But for this future objective to be fulfilled requires the development of the country's infrastructure, particularly the transport system. In mid-2015 there were no less than 31 transport infrastructure projects under way, representing an investment of US$13.75 billion. And for the following two years another US$19.2 billion has been allocated to public works. This was only the tip of the iceberg – according to economists a total of US$80

KEY INDICATORS — Peru

	Unit	2011	2012	2013	2014	**2015
Population	m	*30.01	*30.47	*30.95	*31.42	*31.91
Gross domestic product (GDP)	US$bn	173.50	199.59	202.39	202.95	*190.27
GDP per capita	US$	5,782	6,550	6,504	*6,458	*5,962
GDP real growth	%	6.9	6.3	5.8	2.4	*3.8
Inflation	%	3.4	3.7	2.8	3.2	*2.5
Unemployment	%	7.7	6.8	7.5	6.0	*6.0
Oil output	'000 bpd	153.0	107.0	104.0	110.0	–
Natural gas output	bn cum	11.4	12.9	12.2	12.9	–
Exports (fob) (goods)	US$m	46,268.5	45,933.4	42,176.8	–	–
Imports (fob) (goods)	US$m	36,264.0	40,374.0	41,563.9	–	–
Balance of trade	US$m	10,004.5	5,559.4	612.9	–	–
Current account	US$m	-3,340.7	-6,842.0	-8,829.0	-8,234.0	*-8,706.0
Total reserves minus gold	US$m	44,448.1	62,300.3	64,423.2	61,185.3	–
Foreign exchange	US$m	43,346.1	61,167.8	63,247.3	–	–
Exchange rate	per US$	2.78	2.58	2.80	2.98	–

* estimated figure ** forecast figure

billion would be required to eliminate Peru's infrastructural deficit and create a modern communications network.

Social development has been encouraging. In a ten year period some 9 million Peruvians (about one third of the population) were taken out of poverty. The number of Peruvians with access to drinking water increased from 67 per cent of the population in 2004 to 84 per cent in 2014. Despite this impressive progress, unofficial estimates put the number still living in poverty at around seven million. The World Bank considered that the government's priority areas should be its basic services, education and health, both of which underpinned the access of those in poverty to improvement. The challenge existed of reducing social inequality, of reducing – if not eliminating – the gap between the rural and urban populations and convincing Peruvians that their country offered the same opportunities to all its citizens. One idea under study has been the creation of a network of medium sized cities that would amplify and stabilise growth.

The Banco Central de Reserva del Perú (BCRP) (central bank) has sought to maintain this degree of stability by keeping inflation under control and accumulating significant reserves – roughly corresponding to 30 per cent of Peru's national wealth – one of the world's highest ratios. This has permitted the Peruvian authorities to deal with the contraction felt in the economy since 2012. Growth forecasts for 2015 ranged between 3.6 per cent and 3.9 per cent, well down on the 5.4 per cent that had pertained for a decade or so. The International Monetary Fund (IMF – see below) has forecast a growth level of 3.8 per cent for 2015 and an ambitious 5 per cent for 2016.

What was a certainty was that with mineral exports cooling off, Peru would become more dependent on alternative, more competitive exports. The Humala administration hads endeavoured to avoid populist economic remedies, instead opting for a more orthodox Keynesian solution. Corruption remains a problem in Peru, as evidenced by the riots of 2014. The negative effect on the national image could easily deter investors. In reducing corruption Peru still has a long way to go. In the 2014 Transparency International *Corruption Perceptions Index*, Peru ranked 85 out of the 175 countries surveyed. On most international comparisons Peru fares badly, whether in education or health or on levels of infrastructure.

IMF endorsement

In its May 2015 assessment of the Peruvian economy the IMF confirmed the perception that Peru remained one of the best performing economies in Latin America, with 'solid macro-economic fundamentals, strong policy frameworks and visible gains in poverty reduction.' None the less, the IMF noted that like most of the region, Peru had faced a challenging external environment in 2014. External shocks had been compounded by domestic supply disruptions and a drop in sub-national public investment; the IMF also reported that GDP growth had decelerated sharply. Inflation was slightly above the upper band of the BCRP's target range due to supply shocks, but expectations remained well anchored.

According to the IMF, the external current account deficit declined slightly despite weaker external conditions. Growth was expected to recover in 2015 and over the medium term, contingent on production at new mines approaching capacity, priority infrastructure projects advancing and shocks to terms of trade fading. However, the downside risks dominated. Externally, these included a surge in global financial volatility, further dollar appreciation, or lower commodity prices and external demand. The domestic downside risks included weaker investment, the growing uncertainties surrounding the 2016 presidential elections and persistent social conflicts. A faster unwinding of supply shocks or a more complete pass- through of lower food and fuel global prices constituted upside risks.

Peru's policy mix was considered by the IMF to be broadly adequate to support the recovery and maintain macro-economic stability. Peru's immediate priority was expediting public investment in line with government plans, while avoiding increases in non-priority current spending. Monetary policy should remain responsive to inflation expectations and external developments. Exchange rate flexibility should be the main line of defence against any additional external pressures. The timely use of macro-prudential tools and on-going de-dollarisation efforts should further solidify financial stability.

Anticipating the end of the commodity boom, the IMF considered that a push to deepen structural reforms would be necessary to sustain potential growth and diversify the economy. Revenue losses would need to be offset to finance structural reforms, investment and inclusion along a gradual fiscal consolidation path. Streamlining legal requirements and red tape was, in the view of the IMF, a recommended government reform priority and the Peruvian government's ambitious education reform and inclusion polices should stay their course within the framework of fiscal discipline. Persevering with labour market reform also remains important.

Energy

According to the United States government Energy Information Administration (EIA), Peru is the eighth largest crude oil reserve holder in Central and South America, with 1.6 thousand million barrels of proved reserves, as of December 2014, according to the *Oil and Gas Journal* (OGJ). Much of Peru's proved oil reserves are located onshore in the Amazon region. Proved natural gas reserves in Peru were 15.4 trillion cubic feet in 2014, the third largest in Central and South America, behind Venezuela and Mexico.

Crude oil production in Peru has been declining since the mid-1990s, but the country's total liquid fuels production has been bolstered by increased output of natural gas liquids (NGLs). As a result, total liquid fuels production has steadily increased over the past decade to average 175,000 barrels per day (bpd) in 2013, of which nearly 60 per cent was NGLs.

Petroleum consumption in Peru averaged 171,000bpd in 2013. Peru imports crude oil and refined products to satisfy both domestic demand and export commitments. The country imports most of its crude oil from Ecuador, with smaller amounts from other countries in South America and West Africa.

The vast majority of Peru's refined product imports come from the United States and its reliance on US imports has been growing. Peru imported 63,000bpd of petroleum products from the United States in 2013, increasing 142 per cent since 2008. Nearly 80 per cent of its product imports were distillate fuel oil.

Peru has six oil refineries with a total crude distillation capacity of almost 199,000bpd. Repsol YPF operates the largest refinery in the country, the 108,000bpd La Pampilla refinery located in Lima. Most of the other refineries are owned by the state-owned company, Petroperú (not to be confused with Perúpetro, which negotiates and administers hydrocarbon contracts with companies). In addition to refining, Petroperú is heavily engaged in the production, transport and distribution of oil.

Risk assessment

Economy	Good
Politics	Fair/good
Regional stability	Good

COUNTRY PROFILE

1500s The Inca empire stretched from the Pacific Ocean east to the sources of the Paraguay and Amazon rivers and from the region of modern Quito in Ecuador south to the Maule River in Chile.

1532 Francisco Pizarro of Spain led an armed expedition into the region. Weakened by a civil war over succession to the throne, the Inca Empire was easily overturned by the Spanish.

1542 The vice-royalty of Peru was established with Lima as its capital.

1569 Francisco de Toledo was appointed by the Spanish crown to administer the colony. He established a harsh, repressive system of government that ensured political stability by co-opting indigenous people as low-level officials. The system of government lasted for almost 200 years.

1820 José de San Martín led an invasion army into Peru with the support of rebel Chilean troops in a regional war against Spanish imperial rule.

1821 Peru became independent from Spain after San Martín's forces captured Lima.

1824 Simón Bolívar (who later led Bolivia to independence) became head of state of a centralised state, which included a unicameral legislature.

1826 Bolívar left Peru, which was subsequently ruled by a series of military commanders.

1845 Ramón Castilla became president, ensuring a period of stability and economic development.

1860 Peru adopted a liberal constitution for the first time.

1864 Peru went to war with Spain over control of the guano-rich Chincha Islands. Aided by Ecuador, Bolivia and Chile, Peru defeated the Spanish.

1879–84 Peru backed Bolivia in the War of the Pacific with Chile, but Chile invaded Peru and occupied Lima.

1884 The Treaty of Ancón was signed with Chile. Peru's nitrate-rich province of Tarapacá was handed over to Chile, which also occupied the provinces of Tacna and Arica. The poor state of the nation's economy, weakened by war and the loss of resource-rich regions, undermined governments for the next 30 years.

1895 Civilian rule began, although it was tainted by corruption and economic mismanagement.

1919 President Augusto Leguía launched an *autogolpe* (self-coup), against his own government in order to abolish democratic rule and establish a dictatorship.

1924 The Alianza Popular Revolucionaria Americana (APRA) (American Revolutionary People's Alliance), the country's first mass-based political party, was formed and led by Haya de la Torre.

1930 Leguía was overthrown by a group, including the military, the ruling oligarchy and APRA. A tripartite system of government was formed between the three groups; APRA soon left the alliance to lead a series of popular uprisings. In the early 1930s, APRA was banned.

1933 Luis Miguel Sánchez Cerro, president since 1931, was assassinated. The Congress appointed General Benavides as president.

1939 Manuel Prado y Ugarteche (a moderate) was elected president; he relaxed the government's attitude to APRA.

1945 Free elections took place and José Luís Bustamente y Rivero won the presidency.

1948 General Manuel Odría, staged a *coup d'état*. His military *junta* banned the APRA.

1962 The APRA became the largest party in congress, but fell short of the one-third required to form a government. It entered into a coalition with former military leader Manuel Odría and his supporters. The military seized power and called new elections.

1963 The election of Fernando Belaúnde Terry as president marked the beginning of a brief period of genuine democracy in Peru.

1968 Belaúnde nationalised Standard Oil's Peruvian subsidiary, the International Petroleum Company (IPC). General Juan Velasco Alvarado led a palace coup that removed Belaúnde from office. The military *docenio* (12-year rule) began.

1970s The Maoist *Sendero Luminoso* (Shining Path) terrorist group was formed by Abimael Guzman.

1975 Velasco was removed from office by General Franscisco Morales Bermúdez.

1978 A Constituent Assembly was elected, with leftist parties winning an unprecedented 36 per cent of the vote, although APRA won most of the seats.

1979 A new constitution was promulgated, which provided for free elections to be held every five years.

1981 Belaúnde returned to power after fresh elections enabled by the new constitution. The Peruvian economy was in a weak state, aggravated by the guerrilla group, Shining Path, which attacked rural areas and imposed its rule on villages. Military efforts to eliminate Shining Path were ineffectual. It is estimated that over 70,000 people were killed during the insurgency led by Shining Path. Debt repayment was suspended and Peru was denied further international loans.

1985 Alan García Pérez (APRA) won the presidential election. He campaigned to remove the military and police 'old guard'.

1987 Peru faced bankruptcy; writer Mario Vargas Llosa and his New Libertad movement blocked plans to nationalise banks.

1990 Alberto Fujimori won the presidential election. Under international pressure he introduced a programme of sweeping economic reforms by removing state subsidies, privatising state-owned assets and reducing state involvement in virtually all aspects of the economy. These measures reduced inflation and increased growth.

1992 Guzman, the leader of the Shining Path, was captured. Fujimori instigated an *autogolpe*. He suspended the constitution, dismissed the National Assembly and assumed wide emergency powers, appointing ministers to a new, smaller, unicameral chamber. The economy had begun to recover but regional disparity had increased.

1993 The constitution was reinstated with some amendments.

1995 President Fujimori was elected for a second term. Several setbacks undermined his position including the collapse of foreign direct investment due to the worldwide effects of the Asian financial crisis, and the damage to agriculture from *El Niño*.

2000 Fujimori was sworn in for a third presidential term – after much-criticised elections – without a controlling majority in the National Congress. Fraud tainted his presidency and a bribery scandal prompted him to flee to Japan, from where he resigned. Valentin Paniagua became caretaker president.

2001 Alejandro Toledo won the presidential election and his party, Perú Posible (PP), won the congressional elections.

2002 Power was devolved with the election of 25 regional presidents. The centre-left APRA, led by former president Alan García Pérez, took 12 of the 25 regional presidencies.

2003 Toledo's presidency lost its popular support. He dismissed Beatriz Merino as prime minister and appointed Carlos Ferrero Costa.

2004 President Toledo reshuffled his cabinet for the fifth time since coming to power.

2005 Prime Minister Carlos Ferrero. Pedro Pablo Kuczynski became prime minister. Former President Fujimori was arrested in Chile.

2006 Alan García Pérez (APRA) won a second (not-consecutive) presidential election. An APRA-led coalition government was formed. Abimael Guzman, (Shining Path), was retried for terrorism and sentenced to life imprisonment. An earthquake struck south of Lima, killing

hundreds and demolishing many buildings along the coast near the epicentre.
2008 The entire cabinet resigned following an oil scandal, when audio tapes implicated ministers in bribe taking. President García appointed Yehude Simon Munaro, a popular left-wing regional governor, as prime minister.
2009 A free trade agreement (FTA) with the US was ratified. Negotiations for the FTA had been completed in 2006 but ratification was held up over US concerns about labour-rights and Peruvian government environmental policies regarding risks to the Amazon rain forest. Following protests and a month-long blockade of roads, rivers and fuel pipelines, which culminated in violence between indigenous Amazonians and police in which 34 people were killed, the national congress repealed land laws that had allowed logging, oil and natural gas exploration and other developments in the Amazon rainforests. Prime Minister Yehude Simon resigned; Javier Velásquez Quesquén was appointed as prime minister.
2010 A new political party, to represent the interests of the indigenous Amazon Indians, was launched. The objectives of the Alianza para una Alternativa para la Humanidad (APHU) (Alliance for an Alternative for Humanity) is to campaign to protect both the rights of the aboriginal inhabitants and their rainforest home in the Andes Mountains and Amazon region. President García appointed José Antonio Chang as prime minister. Coca farmers overran the power plant in the regional capital, Pucallpa, for several hours, in protest at plans to destroy their coca crops. The UN estimated that cultivation of Peruvian coca rivals that of Colombia, the farmers (*cocaleros*) claim the leaves of the coca plant have been chewed by indigenous people for many centuries.
2011 In March Prime Minister José Chang resigned and Rosario Fernández was sworn in as prime minister. The conservative, Partido Nacionalista Peruano (PNP) (Peruvian Nationalist Party) formed a coalition to contest the elections, under the name Gana Perú (Peru Wins). Elections for the congress were held in April, in which the Gana Perú coalition (of two parties) won 25.27 per cent of the votes (47 seats out of 130) and Fuerza 2011 (Fuerza) (Force 2011) coalition (of two parties) won 22.96 per cent (37 seats). Ten candidates contested the presidential election held at the same time. Former army officer, Ollanta Humala Tasso (Gana Perú) won 31.7 per cent of the vote, his closest rival Keiko Fujimori Higuchi (daughter of disgraced ex-leader Alberto Fujimori) (Fuerza) 23.5 per cent. However, as no candidate won the minimum 50 per cent of votes a run-off took place in June, in which Humala won 51.49 per cent and Fujimori 48.51 per cent. Humala was sworn-in in July; he appointed Salomón Lerner (independent) as prime minister. In August, Brazilian authorities feared that a remote indigenous tribe, photographed for the first time in the Amazon in 2008, had had their land and village 'invaded and looted' by 'Peruvian drug traffickers' and many killed. Prime Minister Salomon Lerner resigned in December, following a week of street protests objecting to a huge, open-cast gold and copper mine in the northern, Cajamarca region. The violence resulted in a state of emergency as the demonstrations hindered Peru's biggest project that had attracted US$4.8 billion alone in foreign direct investment (FDI). President Humala appointed Óscar Valdés as prime minister.
2012 Shining Path leader, Florindo Eleuterio Flores, known as Comrade Artemio, was captured in early February and brought to Lima. He had been badly wounded following a skirmish with the national army in the Alto Huallaga valley, a hotspot for rebel activity and a centre of cocaine production. In late February, the suspected new leader, Walter Diaz, was captured. On 23 July Prime Minister Valdés resigned and the president appointed Juan Jiménez as his head of government. On 13 November the US returned the last of the artefacts found by US archaeologist Hiram Bingham in Machu Picchu in 1911 and taken to the US. An agreement for the return of the artefacts had been signed in 2010.
2013 On 6 June former Shining Path leader, Florindo Flores (Comrade Artemio), was found guilty of terrorism, drug trafficking and money laundering. He was jailed for life and ordered to pay a fine of US$183 million. Peru came the top producer of coca leaves in 2013, ousting Colombia.
2014 Alonso Segura was named as economy and finance minister on 14 September after the dismissal of Luis Miguel Castilla who had been minister for three years.
2015 Prime Minister Ana Jara and her entire government resigned after loosing a confidence vote on 31 March. she was replaced by Pedro Álvaro Cateriano Bellido on 2 April.

Political structure

Constitution

Peru's Constitution dates from 29 December 1993. The country is divided into 25 regions which each elect a president once every five years. Regions are divided into provinces, which in turn are divided into districts governed by mayors elected by direct popular vote every three years. The voting age is 18 years.

Form of state

Presidential democratic republic

The executive

Executive power is vested in the president, who is elected by absolute majority vote in two rounds if needed for a five-year term by universal adult suffrage (eligible for non-consecutive terms). The president governs with the assistance of a prime minister and an appointed Council of Ministers. The prime minister is president of the Council of Ministers and appointed by the president. The prime minister does not serve has the head of government since Peru has a presidential system of government whereby the president serves as both head of state and head of government. The prime minister does not exercise any executive power.

National legislature

The unicameral Congreso de la República (Congress of the Republic) has 130 seats of which members are directly elected in multi-seat constituencies by proportional representation vote to serve five-year terms. Voting is compulsory for those aged 18–70.

Legal system

The judiciary consists of a 16-member Supreme Court, the ministry of justice and the nine-member Constitutional Court. By constitutional right the judiciary is entitled to at least 2 per cent of the central government budget. Members of the Supreme Court are appointed by the president. The posts are permanent, but members of the court must be aged over 50 and retire at 70.

Last elections

10 April 2011 (parliamentary); 10 April and 5 June 2011 presidential, first round and runoff)

Results: Parliamentary: Gana Perú (Peru Wins) won 25.27 per cent of the votes (47 seats out of 130), Fuerza 2011 (Fuerza) (Force 2011) 22.96 per cent (37), Alianza Electoral Perú Posible (AEPP) (Electoral Alliance for a Possible Peru) 14.83 per cent (21), Alianza por el Gran Cambio (AGC) (Alliance for a Great Change) 14.41 (12), Alianza Solidaridad Nacional (ASN) (National Solidarity Alliance) 10.21 (nine), Alianza Popular Revolucionaria Americana (Apra) (Popular American Revolutionary Party) 6.42 per cent (four); seven other political parties each won less than 2 per cent and fail to win any seats.
Presidential, first round: Ollanta Humala Tasso (Gana Perú) won 31.7 per cent of the vote, Keiko Fujimori (Fuerza 2001) 23.5 per cent of the vote, Pedro Pablo Kuczynski (PPK) 18.5 per cent, Alejandro Toledo (Perú Posible) 15.6 per cent, and Luis Castañeda (Solidaridad Nacional) 9.8 per cent; five other candidates each won less than 1 per cent. Second round:

Humala won 51.49 per cent, Fujimori 48.51 per cent.

Next elections

10 April 2016 (presidential and parliamentary)

Political parties

Ruling party

Coalition named Alianza Gana Perú (Win Peru) (from 28 Jul 2011) including the Partido Nacionalista Peruano (Peruvian Nationalist Party), Partido Socialista (Socialist Party), Partido Comunista Peruano (Peruvian Communist Party), Partido Socialista Revolucionario (Revolutionary Socialist Party) and the Movimento Político Voz Socialista (Political Movement Socialist Voice).

Main opposition party

Fuerza 2011 (Fuerza) (Force 2011)

Conditions are very poor for Peru's highland farmers, but tend to be better in most urban areas.

Population

31.42 million (2014)*

Last census: 21 October 2007: 27,412,640

Population density: 20 inhabitants per square km. Urban population 77 per cent (2010 Unicef).

Annual growth rate: 1.5 per cent, 1990–2010 (Unicef).

Internally Displaced Persons (IDP)

60,000 (UNHCR 2004)

Ethnic make-up

45 per cent indigenous, 37 per cent *mestizo*, 15 per cent white, 3 per cent black, Asian or other.

Religions

Catholic (95 per cent), others (5 per cent).

Education

Adult literacy is relatively high in Peru. The 9 per cent difference in male and female litracy reflects the gender division in education provision.

The government provides free education for children up to the age of 15. Primary education lasts for six years, with secondary education divided into two stages of three and two years each. In rural areas, 40 per cent of the children traditionally help in the fields, with all but a few abandoning their schooling.

Literacy rate: 85 per cent adult rate; 97 per cent youth rate (15–24) (Unesco 2005).

Compulsory years: Six to 15

Enrolment rate: 123 per cent gross primary enrolment of the relevant age group (including repeaters); 73 per cent gross secondary enrolment (World Bank).

Pupils per teacher: 27 in primary schools

Health

About three million people are in the pension and health schemes administered by the state-owned Peruvian Institute of Social Security (IPSS). Salaried workers are obliged to contribute to the scheme, which provides free health care.

The health ministry budget covers health care for those outside the IPSS system. A small charge is made for treatment under this service.

HIV/Aids

HIV prevalence: 0.5 per cent aged 15–49 in 2003 (World Bank)

Life expectancy: 71 years, 2004 (WHO 2006)

Fertility rate/Maternal mortality rate: 2.5 births per woman, 2010 (Unicef)

Child (under 5 years) mortality rate (per 1,000): 18 per 1,000 live births (WHO 2012); 8 per cent of children aged under five are malnourished (World Bank).

Welfare

Peru reformed its pension system in 1993, allowing the investment of individual accounts in real assets and introducing private pension funds to replace state pensions. In addition, the system provides disability and survivors' benefits administered by insurance companies, and old-age pensions.

Employees are required to pay social security taxes equivalent to 13 per cent of their gross income into the public Oficina de Normalización Provisional (ONP) pension fund. Alternatively, employees may opt to pay 11.4 per cent of their salary into a private pension scheme. Workers are allowed to continue joining the old pay-as-you-go system, although the new system urges employers to pay more per worker into the private system than they were paying under the old system. One major challenge for the pension system in Peru is that as much as 51 per cent of the workforce is in the informal economy, covered by neither the old nor the new system.

Main cities

Lima (capital, estimated population 8.1 million in 2012), Arequipa (959,763), Trujillo (892,175), Chiclayo (540,706), Piura (407,109), Iquitos (405,511), Cusco (371,448), Chimbote (335,141), Huancayo (330,373), Sullana (326,888).

Languages spoken

English is spoken in the main tourist regions.

Official language/s

Spanish, Quechua and Aymara

Media

Press

Dailies: Most national dailies and Sunday newspapers are published in Lima, in Spanish, including *El Comercio* (www.elcomercio.com.pe) *El Mundo*, *Expreso* (http://www.expreso.com.pe), *La Tribuna* (www.le-tribuna.org), *Ojo* (www.ojo.com.pe) – the largest selling newpaper, *El Peruano* (www.elperuano.com.pe) – the official State Gazette, *Horas Libre* (www.24horaslibre.com), *La República* (www.larepublica.com.pe) and *Correo* (www.correoperu.com.pe). There are also local publications for regional cities.

Weeklies: In Spanish *Caretas* (www.caretas.com.pe), *Gatopardo* (www.gatopardo.com), *Sí* (www.rcp.net.pe), *Crónica Viva* (www.cronicaviva.com.pe). In English, *Peru Finance*.

Online, in English, Lima Post (www.limapost.com) and Inside America-Peru (www.insideperu.com).

Business: In Spanish, *Business* (www.businessperu.com.pe), and *Punto de Equilibrio* (www.puntodeequilibrio.com.pe), *Gestión* (www.diariogestion.com.pe) and *Nuevo Oiga* (www.peru.com/revistas/oiga/index.asp).

Broadcasting

Radio: In Spanish, Radio Programas de Peru (RPP) (www.rpp.com.pe), Panamericana Radio (www.radiopanamericana.com), CPN Radio (www.cpnradio.com.pe), Radio Nacional (www.radionacional.com.pe) (government operated). Other regional and local radio stations, mainly commercial, broadcast in AM and FM throughout Peru.

Television: In Spanish, Panamericana Televisión (www.pantel.com.pe), Frecuencia Latina (www.frecuencialatina.com.pe), Andina de Radiodifusión (ATV) (www.atv.com.pe), América TV (www.americatv.com.pe), Uranio 15 (www.uranio15.com) and the state-owned Televisión Nacional de Perú, TVPerú (www.tvperu.gob.pe).

Andina (Agencia Peruana de Noticias), Ave Alfonso Ugarte 873, Lima 1 (tel: 315-0400; email: andina@editoraperu.com.pe; internet: www.andina.com.pe).

Economy

Peru has experienced an evolution in its economic fortunes. It has become one of the fastest growing economies in the world, experiencing above average growth since 2000, due to its embrace of an open, market-oriented economy with a high level of foreign trade. The government has implemented macroeconomic policies, advocated by leading economists, such as prudent spending, debt reduction, fiscal surpluses, high international reserve accumulation and achieving investment grade status. Between 2002 and 2013, the average growth rate was 6.1 per cent in a context of an average inflation rate of 2.6 per cent.

There are large deposits of gold, silver, copper and other metals. With these mineral resources, in great demand in 2008 when world prices were at a premium, GDP growth was at a five-year high of 9.8 per cent (more than double the figure of 4.0 per cent in 2003). As a result Peru has had one of the world's highest GDP growth rates of over 6 per cent since 2005 and although it plummeted to 0.9 per cent in 2009, it did not experience recession during the global economic crisis. The government increased domestic spending by 13.1 per cent (US$28.34 billion) in its 2010 budget, which energised the economy and helped it bounce back with growth of 8.8 per cent, as world trade picked up. Growth weakened to an estimated 6.9 per cent in 2011 along with the worldwide general trend. GDP growth fell from 5.8 per cent in 2013 to 2.4 in 2014. Lower demand for trading partners and reduced metal prices proved detrimental to growth in the recent period.

The service sector was the biggest component of GDP in 2014, at 56.2 per cent, with industry constituting 36.7 per cent, of which manufacturing was around 15 per cent, and agriculture 7.1 per cent. Remittances from migrant workers (around 50 per cent of which are sent from expatriate workers in the US) amounted to US$2.7 billion (1.6 per cent of GDP) in 2013.

In November 2011, the UK-based Fitch rating agency upgraded its issuer default rating (IDR) from BBB- to BBB+ due to 'significant and sustained strengthening of the sovereign's external and fiscal balance sheet.' This was reaffirmed in 2014.

In 2014, the UN Human Development Index (HDI) ranked Peru 82 (out of 187) for national development in health, education and income. In 2014, around 10 per cent of the population experienced multi-dimensional poverty, while around 6 per cent lived on the equivalent of US$1.25 a day or less. The poverty and unemployment rate has steadily fallen as Peru has addressed articles of the Millennium Development Goals (MDG).

Proven oil reserves were 1.6 billion barrels at the end of 2014, with production of 110,000 barrels per day (bpd), however as consumption was 231,000bpd in 2014, imports are necessary to cover the shortfall. Proven natural gas reserves were 400 billion cubic metres (cum) at the end of 2014, with production of 12.9 billion cum. Consumption in 2014 rose to 7.2 billion cum; the remainder was exported as liquefied natural gas to North America, Europe and Asia.

External trade

Peru is a member of the Asia-Pacific Economic Co-operation (Apec) forum and the Andean Community, which with Mercado Común del Sur (Mercorsur) (Southern Common Market) formed the South American free trade area (Safta).

Principal manufacturing includes textiles, consumer goods, processed food and fish products, and cement. Mining production includes silver (Peru is the world's second-largest producer), gold (it is the world's sixth-largest producer) and copper, with zinc and lead.

Imports

Principal imports are petroleum and petroleum products, plastics, machinery, vehicles, iron and steel, wheat, foodstuffs and processed food.

Main sources: China (21.2 per cent of total in 2014), US (20.9 per cent), Brazil (4.7 per cent)

Exports

Main exports include minerals (typically 40 per cent of total), crude oil and petroleum products, and coffee, agricultural products and foodstuffs.

Main destinations: China (18.3 per cent of total in 2014), US (16.2 per cent), Switzerland (6.9 per cent)

Agriculture

Farming

The agricultural sector employs approximately 28 per cent of the population and contributes 7.5 per cent to GDP. Less than 3 per cent of Peru's land area is devoted to arable production and permanent crops. Subsistence farming predominates and productivity is low due to drainage and salinity problems, although productivity increased during the 1990s.

The government has given priority to farming as part of its programme to channel resources to the poorer regions and increase self-sufficiency. The highest priority sectors include rice, corn and wheat. By reviving traditional irrigation and terracing methods the government hopes to extend cultivation through the use of marginal land, while also promoting modern farming techniques.

Production has increasingly begun to focus on the winter export markets of the EU and the US. It is along the northern coast of Peru where export crops such as oranges, mangoes, asparagus, passion fruit and limes are grown, together with cotton, rice and sugar for the domestic market.

Animal husbandry (sheep, poultry and cattle) is important in southern regions.

As part of a move to encourage the development of cash crops to replace coca (the raw ingredient for cocaine), coffee production has received considerable support from the US Agency for International Development (USAID), the United Nations Development Programme (UNDP) and GTZ, the German technical co-operation agency. Nevertheless Peru's cultivation of coca rose for a sixth consecutive year in 2011, the UN Office on Drugs and Crime (UNODC) reported in September 2012. However, the cultivation of coca, is down some 17.5 per cent in Peru, according to the 2013 national coca crop monitoring survey.

Fishing

One of the world's largest suppliers of fishmeal, Peru is also a major producer of canned, frozen and salted fish.

The shrimp industry has traditionally been a source of local employment, mainly in the northern coastal departments of Tumbes and Piura. Large quantities of shrimp are exported to the US, Canada, Spain and Taiwan. The shrimp industry is investing in improving the water quality of ponds and it is also importing genetically treated baby shrimps to prevent white spot virus attacks in the future, which had caused production to decline.

Forestry

Around half of the country's total land mass is covered by forests, most of which are located in the montaña region.

The northern Pacific coast has areas of dry forests and savannas. The state owns all natural forests. There are significant numbers of privately owned plantations, primarily consisting of eucalyptus. Estimates in 2012 showed that forest cover was about 676,920 square kilometres.

Peru produces a variety of woods including cedar, mahogany, dyewoods and other products, such as rubber and raw quinine from the Amazon Basin. Most production is geared towards sawn timber and panels with some quantities of bagasse pulp and solid wood products.

Industry and manufacturing

The industrial sector typically contributes 36.7 per cent to GDP and employs 15 per cent of the workforce. Manufacturing contributes around 15 per cent to GDP. Manufacturing activity, centred in Lima and Callao, includes food processing, beverages, fishmeal, chemicals, petrochemicals, rubber, plastics, basic metallurgy, metal products, cement, textiles, footwear, paper products, machinery and motor vehicle assembly. Large firms dominate.

Tourism

Peru has much to offer the visitor, from those that wish to experience a city-based holiday, to beach resorts, to those who want to visit the rainforest interior. There are archaeological sites to visit and cultural tours on offer to all of the 11 sites on Unesco's World Heritage List, including the world famous Inca city of Machu

Picchu, which has limited access to 2,500 people per day, supervised by the tourist authorities.
Domestic tourism is an important market, with coastal holidays a popular pastime. The number of visitors has grown steadily, from 1.9 million in 2007 to 3.1 million in 2013. The contribution of travel and tourism to the economy grew from US$16.27 billion in 2013 to US$17.5 billion in 2014. The industry also provides employment for 7.9 per cent of the workforce (around 1.27 million jobs).
The sector has a problem with unregulated activities and amenities, with around 70 per cent of accommodation venues uncategorised and lacking a set of standards of service or provision. These problems, along with unregulated and unsafe vehicles, could affect Peru's long-term reputation if they are not addressed as a priority.

Mining

Peru's mining sector contributes approximately 15 per cent to total GDP. The country remains one of the world's largest producers of silver, copper, zinc and lead. The mining sector as a whole accounts for around 8 per cent of total employment in Peru. In recent years, the mining sector has generated on average 58 per cent of total exports and 16 per cent of fiscal income.
Copper dominates the economy, not only as the main export earner, but also as a major source of employment. Export revenue is set to rise as new investments come on stream. Southern Peru Copper Corporation, controlled by US-based Asarco, remains the largest copper producer with an annual output of around 340,000 tonnes of fine copper content from its mining operations at Toquepala and the open pit Cuajone mine. Minera Yanacocha gold mine is the largest private gold producer in Peru, producing 40 per cent of the country's gold production. Other important minerals include tin, iron and steel.
Between 2003 and 2012, the mining GDP grew at an average annual rate of 2.7% driven by the increase in the production of metallic and non-metallic mining and of the greater flow of mining investments.
Between 1998 and 2012, copper production has more than doubled, growing at an average annual rate of 8 per cent; gold production has grown close to 88 per cent at an average rate of 5 per cent; silver production has increased by 89 per cent at an average rate of 5 per cent; Barrick Gold's Lagunas Norte gold deposit exploration during 2002 resulted in an increase in its estimated resource from 3.5 million to 7.3 million ounces of gold.

Hydrocarbons

Petroperu, founded in 1969, is the state-owned company engaged in production, transport, refining and distribution of petroleum. Perúpetro oversees all exploration and production activities, including licences.
Proven oil reserves were 1.6 billion barrels in 2014; production was 110,000 barrels per day (bpd), a steady decrease from previous years. With oil consumption at nearly 231,000bpd, Peru needs to import oil, mainly from Colombia, Ecuador and Venezuela. Peru awarded 13 exploration contracts to international oil companies in 2009, valued at US$650 million; these contracts brought the total number of exploration licences to 92.
However, Energy Minister Eleodoro Mayorga Alba announced in 2014 that oil and gas companies planning to explore by conducting seismic tests will be exempt from the EIA process in an attempt to increase exploration in the area.
Proven natural gas reserves were 400 billion cubic metres (cum) in 2014, with production of 12.9 billion cum. The largest gas reserves are located in Camisea in the Amazon basin. Construction of the first liquefied natural gas (LNG) plant in South America began in 2010. The US$3.8 billion, Melchorita plant produced 5.1 billion cum of LNG in 2011, for sales worldwide. A consortium of four companies (one Peruvian and three foreign) built and operate the plant. The gas pipeline company, Transportadora de Gas del Perú, provides the gas supplied to the domestic market.
Peru produces a small amount of coal, although it is almost entirely reliant on imports to meet domestic consumption levels. In a typical year, it produces 20,750 tonnes, and imports 1,230,000 tonnes, of coal.

Energy

Total installed generating capacity was 6,100MW in 2007, of which around 50 per cent is provided by hydropower and the remainder by conventional thermal power. However around 80 per cent of electricity is derived from hydroelectric stations while thermal power plants only operated during peak periods or when lack of rain suppresses hydroelectric output.
Following the partial privatisation of the energy market, begun in the 1990s, investment in gas-fired power stations has grown. Around 80 per cent of the population had access to electricity in 2007, although rural areas are typically still without electricity.
By 2008 there were 38 generation, 6 transmission and 22 distribution companies operating in Peru, all of which were created out of publicly owned entities and are overseen by government agencies responsible for national strategy, policy, environment and renewable energies.
The SNMPE (Sociedad Nacional de Minería, Petróleo y Energía) (National Society for Mining, Petroleum and Energy), whose members contribute 95 per cent of all power generated, announced in 2008 that there were plans to develop a number of new power stations. These included a hydroelectric power station in El Platanal that will generate 220MW, an additional gas-turbine at the Chilca I thermoelectric power station to generate a further 193.5MW, a gas-turbine to generate 192MW at the Kallpa power station and another gas-turbine to be installed at the Edegel project to produce 164.5 MW. Together these will increase Peru's electricity generating capacity by 770MW. All gas will be supplied from the Camisea gas field.

Financial markets

Stock exchange

Bolsa de Valores de Lima (BVL) (Lima Stock Exchange)

Banking and insurance

Peru's banking and financial services sector has suffered a series of external shocks in recent years, with the Asian crisis, *El Niño* and turmoil in Brazil and Russia affecting confidence in emerging markets. Restoring confidence in Peru is widely considered to be just a matter of time, with the country's regulatory system among the most effective in the region. Moreover, the presence of foreign competition (foreign banks account for four of the country's top five banks), a tough provisioning system and a federal programme to facilitate commercial debt restructuring, meant that in 2002 the Peruvian banking sector was less affected by external crises than many in the region.
Peru's banking sector includes over 25 commercial banks and a number of local savings banks, with the four largest groups accounting for over 60 per cent of the systems assets, loans and deposits.

Central bank

Banco Central de Reserva del Perú

Main financial centre

Lima

Time

GMT minus five hours

Geography

The geography of Peru, the third-largest country in South America, ranges from Andean peaks almost 7,000 metres high to tropical Amazonian rain forests and burning coastal deserts.
Peru is bordered by Ecuador and Colombia to the north, Brazil and Bolivia to the east, Chile to the south and the Pacific Ocean to the west.

Almost half the population lives in a narrow coastal strip which covers about 10 per cent of the country's total area. The coastal zone, running 3,079km from Ecuador to Chile, is a desert cut by rivers and oases which are fed by melting snow from the Andes.
The Andes cover around 30 per cent of Peru and form a plateau averaging 3,000 metres high studded with towering peaks. The highest summit is Huascaran at 6,768 metres. In the Andes there are many fertile valleys, such as those of Cuzco and Cajamarca. Lake Titicaca in the south, at an altitude of 3,815 metres, is the highest navigable lake in the world. East of the Andes, around 60 per cent of Peru's area is covered by the jungle of the Amazon basin. Ecuador claims a large section of the northern Amazonian territory. The area is flat and very low. Iquitos, the main town in the area, is about 4,000km from the mouth of the Amazon but only 106 metres above sea level.

Hemisphere

Southern

Climate

Although Peru lies between the equator and the tropic of Capricorn, only the Amazonian jungle has a typically tropical climate, with high rainfall and humidity and little seasonal change in temperatures.
The effects of altitude in the Andes and the cold Humboldt current flowing up from the south moderates the climate in the central and coastal sections.
Temperatures in the capital, Lima, vary only slightly throughout the year due to the cold Humboldt current. They rarely rise above 28 degrees Celsius (C) in summer or dip below 12C in winter. Although Lima is set in a coastal desert, with annual rainfall around 48mm, the sky is overcast with a thick sea mist from June to September. This can be so dense as to resemble light drizzle and requires the use of a raincoat. In the Andes, the rainy season lasts from December to March and makes some road travel hazardous. About three-quarters of Cuzco's average annual rainfall of 80cm falls in this period.

Dress codes

Peruvians dress relatively informally, especially in the summer months from January to March when many government officials and other professionals go to work in casual loose-fitting clothes. In winter, jackets and ties for men and skirts for women are more common.

Entry requirements

Passports

Required by all.

Visa

Tourist visas are not required by nationals of EU/EEA countries, the Americas, Australasia and the Pacific, Asia and South Africa, for visits of up to 90 days. Business visas, valid for 90 days, are required by nationals of all countries. Applications must include a letter of introduction from the employer or, where self-employed, the local chamber of commerce, detailing the purpose of the visit and length of stay, together with proof of adequate funds and return/onward passage.
For further information see http://peru.embassyhomepage.com.

Currency advice/regulations

There are no restrictions on the import and export of local currency or on the import of foreign currency, the export of which is restricted to the amount imported.

Health (for visitors)

Mandatory precautions

A yellow fever vaccination certificate is required if arriving from an infected area.

Advisable precautions

Yellow fever vaccination is recommended (essential for visits to some rural areas). Diphtheria, TB, typhoid, polio, tetanus and hepatitis A and B vaccinations are also advisable.
Malaria risk exists in some rural areas – prophylaxis is recommended.
Water precautions should be taken – it is advisable to drink only bottled water.

Hotels

In main centres hotels are classified by stars (maximum five) according to available facilities. In smaller towns, the best accommodation is often the government-run *Hoteles Turistas*. Hotel bills include a 10 per cent service charge; for stays of less than 60 days, foreign visitors are exempted from the 19 per cent government sales tax on presentation of travel documents.
Visitors arriving in Lima are well advised to inform their hotel of their arrival flight number and time. Most major hotels operate a free courtesy coach service to Jorge Chávez airport and will meet arriving guests.

Public holidays (national)

Fixed dates

1 Jan (New Year's Day), 1 May (Labour Day), 24 Jun (Inti Raymi), 29 Jun (St Peter and St Paul's Day), 28–29 Jul (Independence Day Celebrations), 30 Aug (St Rose of Lima Day), 8 Oct (Battle of Angamos Day), 1 Nov (All Saints' Day), 8 Dec (Immaculate Conception), 24–25 Dec (Christmas).

Variable dates

Maundy Thursday, Good Friday.

Working hours

Banking

Mon–Fri, Jan–Mar: 0815–1130.
Mon—Fri, Apr–Dec: 0915–1245. Some banks may open afternooons.

Business

Mon–Fri: 0900–1300 and 1430–1630.

Government

Mon–Fri: 0900–1300 and 1430–1630.

Shops

Mon–Sat: 1000–1300 and 1600–1900.

Telecommunications

Mobile/cell phones

GSM 1900 service available around the largest cities and towns.

Electricity supply

Generally 220V AC, 60 cycles. Exceptions include Arequipa (220V AC, 50 cycles) and Iquitos (110V AC, 60 cycles).

Social customs/useful tips

It is customary to shake hands on meeting and taking leave. Professional titles should be used and although most people have two family names, only the first is used.
The style of business is generally relaxed and the informal *tu* form is commonly used with younger Spanish-speaking business visitors. Meetings should be arranged in advance and reconfirmed.
Visiting cards are used. While Peruvians are sometimes inclined to be late for appointments, visitors are expected to be punctual.
Never point the soles of your feet at anyone; it is considered highly insulting.

Security

Internal terrorist groups no longer pose a threat to security in most regions, but *Sendero Luminoso* (Shining Path) terrorists are still active in the remoter areas of central Peru Apurimac. There is a risk of armed robbery and hijacking of buses and cars on the road between Lima and Cuzco.
It is not considered safe to walk around the centre of Lima at night. There is a high level of street crime particularly in the city centre. Extreme caution should be taken on all streets, especially in pedestrian precincts. Visitors should be careful not to display valuables – especially at bus stations, railways and airports. Travellers should never journey outside the principal cities after dark and as a general rule are advised to use air travel wherever possible.
If you are robbed, report immediately to the nearest police station and ensure you receive a certified copy of the official statement.

Getting there

Air

National airline: LAN Perú.

International airport/s: Lima, Jorge Chávez International (LIM), 16km west of city; duty-free shop, bar, restaurant, bank, post office, shops, car hire.
Airport tax: US$30.25.

Surface

Road: There is road access and bus services from neighbouring countries. The Pan-American Highway passes through Peru, from Ecuador in the north to Chile in the south.

In January 2011 a road from Nazca on the Peruvian coast, across the Andes cordillera to Cusco and on to Inapari on the border with Brazil was officially opened by some 30 racing drivers. The road is expected to increase trade between the two countries, especially Brazilian exports to Asia. There are, however, fears for the ecology of region as the road opens up the area to miners with heavy equipment to replace the old panners. Migration too is having an effect as miners move from the Andes to the Amazon. The 2,589km road took five years to build.

Main port/s: Callao, San Martin, Matarani.

Getting about

National transport

Visitors are advised to contact the tourist police or the South American Explorers' Club in Lima for up-to-date information on travel to the interior of the country.

Air: There are regular services between Lima and all main towns, provided by several operators, including Aerocóndor Perú, LAN Perú, Star Perú and Taca Perú. There are 19 airports which receive domestic flights; another 22 airports operate charter and support services.

Due to weather conditions flights may be delayed or cancelled. It is essential to reconfirm bookings as flights are often overbooked.

Road: The Pan-American Highway, paved over most of the distance, runs north to south along the coast from the Ecuador border to the Chilean border (with a north-east arm into the Sierra, through Arequipa and on to the Bolivian frontier). The Trans-Andean Highway runs from Lima to Pucallpa, via La Oroya and Huanuco. The Central Highway connects Lima with La Oroya, Huancayo, Huancavelica, Ayacucho, Cuzco and Puno (linking with the Pan-American Highway spur from Arequipa).

In the rainy season (Dec–Apr) landslides are frequent, causing blockages and delays.

Buses: Cheap but fairly uncomfortable services are available on the Pan-American Highway north to Ecuador, south to Chile and on the highway to Callejon de Huaylas in northern Andes. Yellow city buses and mini-buses connect Lima with Callao and the residential suburbs.

Rail: There are regular rail services between Lima and La Oroya with branches to Cerro de Pasco, Huancayo and Huancavelica. The Southern Railway of Peru operates between Arequipa and Puno (on Lake Titicaca) with one weekly connection (Wed) by steamer across the lake to Bolivia. Also regular rail connections from Puno to Cuzco. A short line runs from Tacna to Arica in Chile. Railways have separate summer and winter schedules.

City transport

Taxis: Taxis are the best means of travel in the main cities. For safety reasons, radio-controlled taxis and, in Lima, yellow registered taxis should be used rather than unlicensed or cruising taxis. The passenger should avoid taxis containing anyone other than the driver and always lock the rear doors and close the rear windows if possible.

Recognised taxi ranks (*estaciones*) are found at hotels and airports. Taxis are not metered and fares should be agreed in advance.

Car hire

Major international companies operate in Lima and other main centres. Chauffeur and self-drive cars available. International licence preferred and credit cards essential. Cost includes basic insurance cover. Traffic is congested in Lima.

BUSINESS DIRECTORY

The addresses listed below are a selection only. While World of Information makes every endeavour to check these addresses, we cannot guarantee that changes have not been made, especially to telephone numbers and area codes. We would welcome any corrections.

Telephone area codes

The international dialling code (IDD) for Peru is +51 followed by area code and subscriber's number:

Amazonas	41	Junin	64
Ayacucho	66	Lima	1
Cajamarca	76	Loreto	65
Cuzco	84	San Martin	42

Useful telephone numbers

Police: 105
Fire: 116
Ambulance: 117

Chambers of Commerce

American Chamber of Commerce of Peru, Avenida Ricardo Palma 836, Lima 18 (tel: 241-0708; fax: 241-0709; e-mail: amcham@amcham.org.pe).

British-Peruvian Chamber of Commerce, Avenida José Larco 1301, Lima 18 (tel: 617-3090; fax: 617-3095; e-mail: bpcc@bpcc.org.pe).

Lima Cámara de Comercio, Avenida Gregorio Escobedo 398, Lima 11 (tel: 463-8080; fax: 463-2837; e-mail: presidencia@camaralima.org.pe).

Trujillo Cámara de Comercio y Producción de la Libertad, Jirón Junín 454, PO Box 729m Trujillo (tel: 231-114; fax 242-888; e-mail: camara@camaratru.org.pe).

Banking

Banco Banex, Av República de Panamá 3680, San Isidro, Lima 27 (tel: 210-0071; fax: 440-3298).

Banco Continental, Av República de Panamá 3073, 27 Lima (tel: 421-7272; fax: 441-8922).

Banco de Comercio, Jr Lampa 560, Piso 2, Lima 1 (tel: 428-9400; fax: 426-8454).

Banco de Crédito del Perú, Av Huarochiri y Calle Centenario, 156 URB Las Ladera de Melgarejo, Lima 12 (tel: 349-0304; fax: 349-0548).

Banco de Desarrollo, Jr Camaná 700, Lima 1 (tel: 428-6360; fax: 427-7665).

Banco Exterior de Los Andes y de España, Extebandes, Av Canaval Y Moreyra 454, Lima 27 (tel: 442-2121; fax: 440-4572).

Banco Financiero Del Perú, Avenue Ricardo Palma 229, Lima 18 (tel: 241-0324; fax: 447-8766).

Banco Interamericano de Desarrollo, Paseo de la República 3245, 14th Floor, PO Box 270154, San Isidro, Lima 27 (tel: 442-3400).

Banco Interamericano de Finanzas (BIF), Ricardo Rivera Navarrete 543, Lima 27 (tel: 221-2888; fax: 221-2489).

Banco Interandino Saema, Augusto Tamayo 120, Lima 27 (tel: 471-7777; fax: 441-1404).

Banco Internacional Del Perú (Interbanc), Jr De La Unión 600, Lima 1 (tel: 427-2000; fax: 426-2630).

Banco Latino, Av Paseo de la República 3505, Lima 27 (tel: 422-1290; fax: 442-6200).

Banco del Libertador, Av P De la República 3245, San Isidro, Lima 27 (tel: 442-1661; fax: 441-4908).

Banco de Lima, Esquina Puno y Carabaya 698, Lima 1 (tel: 426-8676; fax: 426-2356).

Banco Mercantil del Peru SA, Av Rivera Navarrete 641, Lima 27 (tel: 442-1290; fax: 442-5277).

Banco de la Nación (national bank), Av Nicolas de Piérola, Lima 1 (tel: 426-2000; fax: 426-1133).

Banco del Nuevo Mundo, Av Paseo de la República 3033, 27 Lima (tel: 472-5121; fax: 440-2940).

Banco del Progreso - Probank, Av Javier Prado Este 595, 27 Lima (tel: 421-2800; fax: 441-1058).

Banco Regional del Norte (Norbank), Av Emancipación 199, Lima 1 (tel: 422-3589; fax: 442-2703).

Banco República, Jr Camaná 700, Lima 1 (tel: 444-3214; fax: 444-3774).

Banco Santander, A Tamayo 120, San Isidro, Lima 27 (tel: 221-5000; fax: 221-5001).

Banco Solventa, Av Aviación 2401, Piso 11, San Borja (tel: 225-0505; fax: 225-0505).

Banco Sudamericano SA, Av Camino Real 815, Lima 27 (tel: 221-1111; fax: 442-3392).

Banco del Sur del Perú (Bancosur), Chinchón 986, San Isidro, Lima 27 (tel: 442-1170; fax: 442-1178).

Banco del Trabajo, Av Paseo de La República 3587, San Isidro, Lima 27 (tel: 421-9000; fax: 421-2521).

Citibank NA, Av Camino Real 456, Torre Real, Piso 5TO, Lima 27 (tel: 421-400; fax: 440-9044).

Central bank

Banco Central de Reserva del Perú, Miroquesada 441, Lima (tel: 613-2000; fax: 427-5880; e-mail: webmaster@bcrp.gob.pe).

Stock exchange

Bolsa de Valores de Lima (BVL) (Lima Stock Exchange), , Pasaje Acuna 191, Lima (tel: 286-280; fax: 337-650).www.bvl.com.pe

Travel information

South American Explorers Club, Cale Piura 135, Miraflores, Lima (tel: 445-3306; e-mail: limaclub@saexplorers.org).

Tourist Bureau of Complaints, PO Box 1596, Lima (tel: 224-7888; e-mail: postmaster@indecopi.gob.pe).

Tourist Police (speak several languages; wear white belts over their green dress uniforms), Lima (tel: 225-8698; fax: 476-7708); toll-free number for tourists outside Lima: 0800-42579).

Ministry of tourism

Ministry of International Trade and Tourism, Calle 1 Oeste No 50, Urbani Córpac, Edificio Mincetur, San Isidro, Lima (tel: 224-3347; fax: 224-3264; e-mail: informa@mincetur.gob.pe).

National tourist organisation offices

PromPerú, Calle 1 Oeste No 50, Urbanización Córpac, Edificio Mincetur, San Isidro, Lima (tel: 224-3131; Fax: 224-7134; e-mail: postmaster@promperu.gob.pe).

Ministries

Ministry of Agriculture, Avenida Salaverry s/n, Jesús Maria, Lima (tel: 433-3034; fax: 432-9098).

Ministry of Defence, Avenida Arequipa 291, Lince, Lima (tel: 435-9567; fax: 433-5150).

Ministry of Economy and Finance, Jr Junín 339, Lima (tel: 427-3930; fax: 431-7836).

Ministry of Education, Avenida San Develde 160, San Borja, Lima (tel: 436-1240; fax: 433-0230).

Ministry of Energy and Mines, Avenida Las Artes s/n, San Borja, Lima (tel: 475-0206; fax: 475-0689).

Ministry of Fisheries, Calle Uno Oeste s/n, Urbanización Corpac, San Isidro, Lima (tel: 224-3336; fax: 224-3233).

Ministry of Foreign Affairs, Palacio de Torre Tagle, Jr. Ucayali 363, Lima (tel: 427-3860; fax: 426-3266).

Ministry of Health, Avenida Salaverry Cdra 8, Jesús María, Lima (tel: 432-3535; fax: 431-3671).

Ministry of the Interior, Plaza 30 de Agosto 150, San Isidro, Lima (tel: 475-2995; fax: 441-5128).

Ministry of Justice, Scipión e Llona 350, Miraflores, Lima (tel: 441-7320; fax: 440-4407).

Ministry of Labour and Social Promotion, Avenida Salaverry 655, Jesús Maria, Lima (tel: 433-2512; fax: 433-8126).

Ministry of the Presidency, Avenida Paseo de la República 4297, Lima (tel: 446-5886; fax: 447-0379).

Ministry of Transport, Communications, Housing and Construction, Avenida 28 de Julio 800, Lima 1 (tel: 433-1212; fax: 433-9378).

Ministry for Women's Promotion and Human Development, Avenida Emancipación 235 o Esquina Jr Camaná 616, Lima 1 (tel: 426-4336).

Other useful addresses

Adex (export association), Javier Prado Este No 2875, San Borja, Lima (tel: 346-2530; fax: 346-1879; e-mail: postmast@adex.org.pe).

Andean Group, Avda Paseo de la República, Casilla Postal 3237, Lima.

Asociación de Bancos del Perú (Bank Association), Av Antonio Miro Quesada 247 of 409, Lima 1 (tel: 428-8850, 427-6378, 428-5136).

Centromin (Empresa Minera del Centro del Perú SA), Avda Javier Prado Este 2175, San Borja, Apdo 2412, Lima 34 (tel: 365-924; fax: 358-782).

Cepri (Electroperú Privatisation), Avda Pedro Miotta s/n, Lima 29 (tel: 661-844; fax: 661-899).

Cofide (Corporación Financiera de Desarrollo), Camino Real 390, San Isidro, Lima 27 (tel: 422-550; fax: 423-384).

Conaco (Confederación Nacional de Comerciantes) (National Federation of Commerce), Avenida Abancay 210, Lima (tel: 273-528, 286-026).

Conite (National Commission for Investments and Foreign Technology), Avenida Abancay 500, Piso 6 (MEF), Lima 1.

Copri (Private Investment Promotion Committee), Comité Especial de Minero Perú SA, Bernardo Monteagudo No 222, Piso 12, Lima 17 (tel: 461-4300; fax: 462-7049).

Corpac (Corporación Peruana de Aeropuertos y Aviación Comercial), Aeropuerto Internacional Jorge Chávez, Avenida Faucett s/n, Callao (tel: 529-570).

Electroperú, Centro Cívico, Paseo de la República 144, Lima 1 (tel: 310-664).

Empresa Nacional de Ferrocarriles del Perú, Ancash 207, Apdo 1379, Lima (tel: 289-440).

Enapu SA (National Port Company), Avenida Guardia Chalaca s/n, Callao (tel: 299-210).

Hierroperú(State Iron Company of Peru), Avenida Paseo de la República 3587, Lima (tel: 410-636).

International Translation Service, Avenida Arequipa 3200, San Isidro, PO Box 6046, Lima (tel: 411-396).

Lima Stock Exchange

Mineroperú (State Mining Company of Peru), Avenida Bernardo Monteagudo Orrantia 222, Magdalena del Mar, Lima (tel: 620-740; fax: 627-049).

Peruvian Embassy (USA), 1700 Massachusetts Avenue, NW, Washington DC (tel: (+1-202) 833-9860; fax: (+1-202) 659-8124; e-mail: peru@peruemb.org).

PetroPerú (State Petroleum Company), Paseo de la República 3361, San Isidro, Lima 27 (tel: 411-919).

PromPerú, Comisión de Promoción del Perú (investment promotion), Edificio Mitinci, Piso 13, calle 1 Oeste S/N, Lima 27 (tel: 224-3125/3271/3279; fax: 224-3323; e-mail: perunet@promperu.gob.pe).

Sociedad de Industrias (Society of Industries), Los Laureles 365, San Isidro, Lima 27 (tel: 408-700).

Internet sites

ADEX, Asociacion de Exportadores: http://www.adexperu.org.p

Philippines

KEY FACTS

Official name: Republika ng Pilipinas (Republic of the Philippines)

Head of State: President Benigno Aquino III (LP) (since 30 June 2010)

Head of government: President Benigno Aquino III (LP) (since 30 June 2010)

Ruling party: Partido Liberal (Liberal Party) (coalition with Kalapian ng mga Kaibigan sa Kaunlaran (KKK) (Friends Of Development – City of Hagonoy) (from 29 Jun 2010)

Area: 300,439 square km (7,107 islands)

Population: 99.43 million (2014) (92,337,852; 2010, census figure)

Capital: Manila (on Luzon)

Official language: Filipino (based on Tagalog)

Currency: Peso (P) = 100 centavos

Exchange rate: P46.96 per US$ (Sep 2015)

GDP per capita: US$2,865 (2014)

GDP real growth: 6.10% (2014)

GDP: US$284.93 billion (2014)

Labour force: 41.32 million (2014)*

Unemployment: 6.80% (2014)

Inflation: 4.17% (2014)

Balance of trade: -US$15.85 billion (2014)

Annual FDI: US$1.87 billion (2011)

* estimated figure

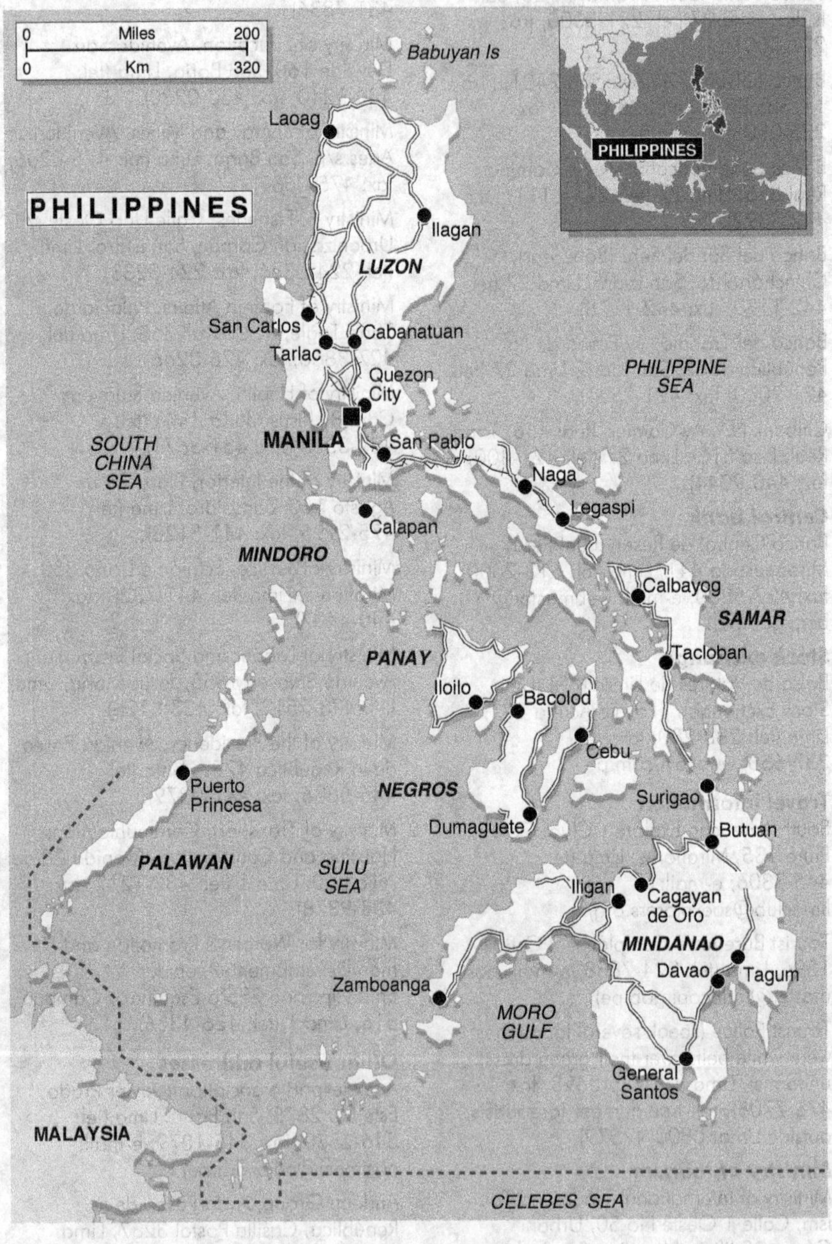

In early 2015 there were, for the first time, reports in Manila of rallies calling for the resignation of the Philippines President Benigno 'Noynoy' Aquino. In his last yer as President, Aquino had been attempting to revive the stalled peace process with Muslim insurgents, endeavouring to persuade his government to grant greater autonomy to the country's restive Bangsamoro southern region while he could.

Progress?

In March 2014 the Moro Islamic Liberation Front (MILF) had handed in a token 75 weapons. The MILF, which is the largest Muslim rebel group in the Philippines, had also agreed to disband its guerrilla force and surrender 15,000 weapons in exchange for control of their economy, culture and politics. However, progress in getting the so-called Bangsamoro Basic Law (BBL) on to the statute book had stalled after fighting on the island of Mindanao in January 2015 had killed 44 policemen and 18 rebels. The Mindanao massacres – not only of the police commandos but also of civilians – had become President Aquino's greatest political crisis, with unprecedented calls for him to resign.

The Mindanao conflict, which rarely breaks into the world's headlines, dates back 45 years, during which time an estimated 120,000 people had died and a further two million had been displaced. To conclude a genuine peace deal before the end of his term in office (in 2016) would be a feather in Aquino's cap.

In what was seen as a significant first step, the MILF weapons were handed over to a group of independent monitors, in return for 25,000 pesos (US$555) each to 145 former combatants to enable them to begin a new life as farmers.

For their part, the rebels feared that the Philippines Congress, which suspended work on the BBL after the January killings, would try to dilute Aquino's proposed law. Some observers saw the decommissioning ceremony as no more than a propaganda effort in an attempt to convince both politicians and the Philippine population to lend it their support. It remained an uphill struggle – surveys suggested that only 23 per cent of the population supported the BBL initiative. Many politicians considered Aquino to be a lame duck president, for whom they were not prepared to risk re-election.

The unprecedented calls for President Aquino's resignation had followed a Philippine senate inquiry, that placed the blame on the President for intervening in the affair by breaking the chain of command and allowing a suspended police chief to launch an anti-terror operation in which 44 police officers died. The president had allegedly ordered an already suspended National Police commander, one Alan Purisima, to launch operation Oplan Exodus, a manhunt for wanted Malaysian bombmaker Zulkifli Bin Hir, alias Marwan. The operation went wrong and in January a military skirmish had claimed the lives of five civilians and 18 Filipino-Muslim rebels.

According to the senate report, neither the armed forces chief of staff, nor the interior and defence secretaries were told about the campaign. It emerged that the president was aware that Alan Purisima had been suspended by the Philippino Ombudsman in December 2014. An earlier report by the Philippine Nationak Police Board of Inquiry had blamed the President for the January bloodbath. The opinion polls showed that the Philippine president's popularity rating went down from 59 per cent in November 2014 to 38 per cent in March 2015, his lowest rating since his election in 2010.

Islands in the sun

If to most of the world the Scarborough Shoal, The Paracels and the South Spratleys sounded more like football teams than strategic locations in the South China Sea, in Manila this is not the case. If Mindanao was the principal item on the domestic agenda, China's behaviour in the South China Sea had become the preoccupation of the day in terms of foreign affairs. At a May 2015 conference in Singapore, the US Defence Secretary Ashton Carter had made it clear that the United States would continue to monitor and counter Chinese efforts to assert sovereignty in the South China Sea, largely by boosting military support to its regional allies. The new US policy was called the Southeast Asia Maritime Security Initiative, with a budget of some US$425 million for maritime capacity-building efforts in the region.

However, for the Philippines, unquestionably – and traditionally – Washington's strongest ally in the region, the new initiative was seen as being too little, too late. The Philippines military had come to see themselves as having walk on parts in a larger drama featuring the United States and China and were left wondering how to secure their own interests in the area. In a May 2015 meeting at Camp Aguinaldo, the Philippines' Manila military headquarters, Philippine officials sought to demonstrate that if not stopped, Chinese aggression in the South China Sea, would represent a serious threat to the security of the Philippines.

In January 2013, under the UN Convention of the Law of the Sea, the Philippines brought a case for international arbitration against China, seeking clarification on Beijing's so-called 'nine-dash-line' claim and on whether the areas in the South China Sea over which Beijing is asserting control qualified as actual islands – and were eligible for their own distinct exclusive economic zones. Beijing refused to participate in the arbitration proceedings, but in December 2014 did submit a paper setting out its arguments. Of the land features China occupied, three were within the Philippines' exclusive economic zone, officials in the Philippines claim: Johnson South, McKennan and Mischief Reefs.

The most serious issue for the Philippines officials is the status of the 58-square-mile Scarborough Shoal (or Bajo de Masinloc) which it was claimed by Manila had long been an integral part of the Philippines. Historical records, the Filipinos argued, showed that it was considered part of the outlying islands of the Philippines, which were ceded by Spain to the United States at the conclusion of the Spanish-American War under the Treaty of Washington in 1900.

KEY INDICATORS — Philippines

	Unit	2011	2012	2013	2014	**2015
Population	m	*95.86	95.80	97.48	99.43	*101.42
Gross domestic product (GDP)	US$bn	213.10	250.18	272.07	284.93	*308.03
GDP per capita	US$	2,223	2,612	2,791	2,865	*3,037
GDP real growth	%	3.7	6.8	7.2	6.1	*6.7
Inflation	%	4.8	3.2	2.9	4.2	*2.1
Unemployment	%	7.4	7.0	7.1	6.8	*6.2
Exports (fob) (goods)	US$m	38,890.0	46,284.0	44,736.0	47,758.0	–
Imports (fob) (goods)	US$m	55,412.0	61,489.0	63,261.3	63,609.0	–
Balance of trade	US$m	-16,522.0	-15,205.0	-18,525.3	-15,851.0	–
Current account	US$m	6,988.0	7,177.0	11,384.0	12,645.0	*16,954.0
Total reserves minus gold	US$m	59,385.8	73,478.0	75,689.0	72,057.0	–
Foreign exchange	US$m	57,863.0	71,656.0	73,792.0	–	–
Exchange rate	per US$	43.42	41.19	44.45	44.78	–

* estimated figure ** forecast figure

As the South China Sea tensions grew, the United States had begun re-engaging militarily with the Philippines, most notably through the 2014 Enhanced Defence Co-operation agreement. Washington had allocated around US$50 million in military aid to Manila for 2014 and US$40 million for 2015, up from US$25.5 million in 2013. In addition, the United States contributed an annual US$50 million to assist with military training and intelligence operations for counter-terrorism operations.

The economy

According to the Asian Development Bank (ADB) the Philippines economy expanded by 6.1 per cent in 2014, fuelled by sustained increases in private consumption, higher fixed investment and recovery in exports. The pace of growth decelerated by almost 1 percentage point from the average of the previous 2 years, largely reflecting the slowdown in government expenditure.

Private consumption generated more than 60 per cent of the gross domestic product (GDP) growth in 2014. Consumer spending grew by 5.4 per cent, benefitting from a 2.8 per cent rise in employment, modest inflation and higher remittances from overseas Filipinos, which reached US$27.0 billion after climbing in 2014 by 6.3 per cent, or by 10.9 per cent in Philippine peso terms.

Government consumption contracted through the first 3 quarters of 2014, reflecting in part a Supreme Court ruling against certain government funds that slowed disbursements. In the fourth quarter of 2014, the government accelerated spending so that outlays for the year edged up by 1.8 per cent, compared with the much bigger increase of 7.7 per cent seen in 2013.

Fixed investment rose by 8.6 per cent, also decelerating from the previous year largely due to the slowdown in government spending. Private construction rose at a double-digit pace, driven by demand for offices, retail space and housing. Investment in machinery and transport equipment expanded as well. However, public construction fell by 1.5 per cent, though it started to recover in the fourth quarter. Exports of goods and services rebounded in volume terms from contraction in 2013. Imports rose in volume terms at a slower pace, which generated a significant contribution to GDP growth from net external demand.

From the production side, services contributed nearly 60 per cent of GDP growth and manufacturing one-third. Comprising about half the economy, services grew by 6.0 per cent, led by wholesale and retail trading, business process outsourcing, tourism, finance and real estate. Manufacturing grew by 8.1 per cent, close to its recent annual average rate of increase. Buoyant domestic demand and rising export orders for manufactured products underpinned this growth. The damage inflicted by Super Typhoon Haiyan late in 2013 and other storms in 2014 hurt agricultural production for much of last year, but fisheries output and crops recovered to lift full-year agricultural production by 1.9 per cent over 2013.

Nevertheless, poor harvests and supply bottlenecks pushed inflation to 4.9 per cent year on year by August 2013, the highest for 3 years. Supply bottlenecks included a Manila city ordinance restricting cargo trucks, which disrupted deliveries. After August, better harvests, additional rice supplies from imports and plunging global oil prices brought inflation down and put the average for 2014 at 4.1 per cent.

Inflation in the first 3 quarters of 2014 prompted Bangko Sentral ng Pilipinas, the central bank, to raise policy interest rates by 50 basis points between July and September 2014, to 4.0 per cent for the overnight borrowing rate and 6.0 per cent for the overnight lending rate. The central bank raised the reserve requirement for banks by 2 percentage points to mitigate risk from the rapid expansion of domestic liquidity and it increased the interest rate on its special deposit account. Consequently, growth in broad money (M3) decelerated to 11.3 per cent in December.

Subdued government spending, as well as higher revenue, cut the fiscal deficit to 0.6 per cent of GDP in 2014, well under the ceiling of 2.0 per cent and narrower than the deficit of 1.4 per cent recorded in 2013. Revenue rose by 11.2 per cent, helped by more stringent tax administration, while expenditure excluding interest increased by 6.7 per cent. Merchandise exports rebounded to shrink the trade deficit. Exports rose in US dollar terms by an estimated 9.0 per cent on higher shipments of machinery and transport equipment, furniture, garments, fruit and vegetables and minerals. Exports of electronics, mainly semiconductors, recovered from a slump in 2013. A modest 2.4 per cent increase in merchandise imports in US dollars reflected increases in capital and consumer goods tempered by falling oil prices in the second half of the year.

After accounting for higher inflows of remittances and earnings from business process outsourcing, the current account surplus was estimated at 3.6 per cent of GDP. The balance of payments was in deficit, however, on net outflows in the financial account, mainly of portfolio investment. Gross international reserves at US$81.3 billion in February 2014 provided a high 10.4 months of cover for imports of goods and services and income payments. The peso depreciated by 0.5 per cent against the US dollar between the end of 2013 and the end of 2014. Strong GDP growth was projected for 2015 and 2016 based on buoyant private consumption, a solid outlook for investment and exports and recovery in government expenditure. GDP is projected to increase by 6.4 per cent in 2015 and 6.3 per cent in 2016.

The factors that powered private consumption in 2014 – growth in employment, modest inflation and higher inflows of remittances – were projected to continue through the forecast period. One million new jobs were generated in the 12 months to January 2015, mostly in services, and the unemployment rate fell to 6.6 per cent from 7.5 per cent in January 2014. Lower fuel prices were benefiting consumers and businesses alike. Surveys conducted by the central bank showed positive consumer and business sentiment. Upgrades to the country's credit rating supported investor sentiment. After lifting its rating for the Philippines to investment grade in 2013, Moody's upgraded it again in December 2014 by one notch to Baa2.

Energy – high hopes

The Philippines is a net energy importer in spite of its low consumption levels when compared to its south-east Asian neighbours. The country produces modest volumes of oil, natural gas and coal. However, geothermal, hydropower and other renewable sources constitute a significant share of electricity generation.

According to the United States Energy Information Administration (EIA), in 2011 total primary energy consumption in the Philippines was roughly 1.3 quadrillion British thermal units (Btu). Oil constituted roughly 41 per cent of total consumption, coal made up 22 per cent, biomass made up 19 per cent and the remainder came from natural gas and various renewable sources.

In 2013, total oil production was 26,000 barrels per day (bpd) while the country consumed 299,000bpd. In May 2014, the government invited tenders for 11 oil and gas blocks in the Palawan Basin and nearby areas, including one in the South China Sea, according to Reuters. In the view of the EIA, this exploration bid round could push oil production up to 39,000bpd by 2019.

Two of the blocks being launched for exploration licensing are located close to the Spratly Islands (of which – see above 'Islands in the Sun') a portion are claimed by the Philippines), which are areas under territorial dispute with China. EIA estimates the South China Sea contains approximately 11 billion barrels of oil and 190 trillion cubic feet of natural gas in proved and probable reserves.

The Philippines imported roughly 270,000bpd of crude oil and petroleum products in 2013, with 35 per cent of crude oil imports coming from Saudi Arabia and Russia. The Philippines possess the capacity to refine 290,000bpd. Shell Philippines – a subsidiary of Shell – and Otto Energy play significant roles in the upstream sector, while Petron Corporation operates the largest refinery in the country, supplying nearly 40 per cent of the country's oil needs. The Philippines exports nearly all the crude oil it produces.

Risk assessment

Economy	Good
Politics	Good
Regional stability	Fair

Muslims in Philippines

% of population	5.1
Sunni (% of Muslims)	99
Shi'a (% of Muslims)	1

COUNTRY PROFILE

1898 During the Spanish-American War, the independence of the Philippines was declared by General Emilio Aguinaldo, leader of the revolutionary movement, with the support of the US. Spain ceded the islands to the US under the Treaty of Paris.

1935 A constitution was ratified by plebiscite, giving the Philippines internal self-government and providing independence after 10 years.

1946 The islands were occupied by Japanese forces from 1942–45. US rule was restored at the end of the Second World War, and the Philippines became an independent republic with Manuel Roxas as its first president.

1965 After a succession of presidents, under the control of US economic interests and the Filipino land-owning class, Ferdinand Marcos won elections.

1972 Martial law was imposed by the President, in order to deal with subversive activity and to introduce drastic reforms.

1973 A new constitution was ratified by President Marcos. Transitional provisions gave the president the combined authority of the presidency and the premiership without any fixed term of office.

1981 Martial law was lifted.

1986 Ferdinand Marcos claimed to have defeated his challenger, Corazon Aquino, in the general election. However, it was so blatantly rigged that the result triggered a popular revolt. Marcos and associates fled the country and Aquino took over.

1987 A plebiscite ratified a new constitution with Aquino as president. Congressional elections confirmed her popular support.

1992 In the presidential and legislative elections, Aquino's chosen successor, Fidel Ramos, succeeded her as president, although his supporters failed to achieve an overall majority in the legislature.

1994 President Ramos' Lakas ng Edsa (Lakas-NUCD) (National Union of Christian Democrats) party formed an electoral pact with the Laban ng Makabayang Masang Pilipino (LaMMP) (Struggle of the Nationalist Filipino Masses).

1995 Candidates representing the Lakas-NUCD/LDP alliance secured the bulk of the seats contested in the mid-term elections.

1996 A peace agreement was reached with Mindanao's Muslim rebels, the Moro Islamic Liberation Front (MILF).

1998 Joseph Estrada easily won the presidential elections. Estrada replaced Ramos, who during his six years in power had built up a reputation for ensuring the political stability and economic growth urgently required after the Marcos era.

2000 President Estrada was impeached by the lower house of the legislature after allegations that he had accepted bribes and diverted taxes for personal use.

2001 Estrada was stripped of his powers by a Supreme Court ruling, paving the way for the inauguration of Vice President Gloria Macapagal Arroyo as president. Supporters of President Arroyo won control of the Senate in the legislative elections. The government's offer of enhanced autonomy to Mindanao, instead of independence, was turned down by the MILF.

2002 Filipino and US military forces launched joint exercises near to the stronghold of Abu Sayyaf, the high-profile Islamist rebel group, believed to have links with the al Qaeda terrorist group. Tensions in southern Philippines increased following a declaration made by exiled Filipino Muslim leader Nur Misuari for an independent Muslim state. Indonesia, Malaysia and the Philippines signed a pact to counter terrorism and to stop a network that is believed to be bent on turning all three into a single Islamic state.

2004 Gloria Arroyo was elected president, defeating her nearest rival, actor Fernando Poe. A typhoon and powerful storms caused major floods and mudslides that killed hundreds of people.

2005 The two-year cease-fire with the MILF was broken when heavy fighting broke out between government troops and the MILF.

2006 The death penalty was abolished

2007 The body of Khaddafy Janjalani, the leader of Abu Sayyaf, was found; the army stated he had been killed during fighting in 2006. Former president, Joseph Estada, was found guilty of corruption and embezzlement of an estimated US$84 million; he was sentenced to life imprisonment. An agreement was reached between the government and the MILF, the main separatist group, on a boundary for a Muslim homeland in the southern region of Mindanao.

2008 In a negotiated settlement the government and the MILF agreed to an enlarged autonomous region in the south of the country for the Muslim rebel separatist group. Critics said the deal effectively established an independent state within the Philippines, contrary to the constitution. The Supreme Court blocked the territorial aspect of the agreement, forcing the government to break the deal. Fierce fighting broke out as militants, led by the MILF, attacked towns and villages in the previously designated border area. The government estimated 100,000 people had been killed and hundreds of thousands had been displaced since the insurrection began in the 1970s.

2009 The Philippines was removed from an OECD blacklist of secretive tax havens and placed on a grey list of countries that have agreed to adhere to tax disclosure standards, although without legislation enacting it. Former president Corazon Aquino died.

2010 The ruling Lakas-Kampi-CMD coalition won 38.1 per cent (105 seats out of 228) in parliamentary elections held in May. Nine candidates took part in presidential elections held at the same time. Benigno Aquino III (LP) was elected with 42.1 per cent of the vote, while his closest rival, former president Joseph Estrada (Pwersa ng Masang Pilipino) (Force of the Filipino Masses) (FFM) won 26.3 per cent. GDP growth of 7.9 per cent for the first two quarters was the strongest growth recorded since the late 1980s.

2011 The Philippines suffered a series of floods and mudslides through January, caused by severe rains, which killed 51 and affected 1.6 million people in total. Four years after losing the vote and a long legal battle to achieve a recount,

Aquilino Pimentel was finally declared a winner and took his seat as a senator in August. Extensive and severe flooding in northern Philippines caused widespread destruction in the central Luson region north of Manila, following typhoons on 27 September and 1 October. Hundreds of thousands of people had to be evacuated, with an initial death toll of 60 people and 30 missing. On 18 November, former president, Gloria Arroyo, was arrested for electoral fraud during the 2007 presidential elections. Devastating flash floods and landslides killed over 650 people, with another 900 missing, on the southern island of Mindanao following tropical storm Washi.

2012 Further severe flooding throughout the country in February, July and August caused widespread damage to life, property and production. On 6 October, the police arrested former president Gloria Arroyo on charges of corruption. She was alleged to have misused US$8.8 million in state lottery funds. On 7 October, a peace agreement was reached between the government and the MILF, which provides for a new autonomous Muslim homeland in the southern region of Mindanao. An official signing was scheduled for 15 October. Typhoon Bopha, which struck the south on 5–6 December, killed over 1,000 people, with over 850 people missing and damaged crops and infrastructure in the Compostela Valley Province, the worst affected area.

2013 Typhoon Haiyan struck on 6 November. It was reported as one of the most powerful storms ever recorded on land. It hit the coastal Philippine provinces of Leyte and Samar and swept through six central Philippine islands. Initial reports were of 10,000 deaths in Tacloban alone; this figure was later revised down, but the full death count is not expected for some time. Cesar Purisma, finance minister, told the BBC that the devastation caused by the typhoon could reduce growth by one percentage point in 2014. The worst affected region accounts for 12.5 per cent of the Philippines economy.

2014 President Aquino and leaders of the MILF signed a peace agreement in Manila on 27 March. The agreement brings to an end some 40 years of conflict. Amongst othe moves it will allow mostly Muslim areas of Mindanao to have more autonomy. The deal was brokered by Malaysia, whose prime minister, Najib Razak, attended the signing ceremony.

2015 Military chief, Gen Gregorio Catapang, announced on a visit to Pagasa (known internationally as Thitu and in China as Zhong Ye Dao) on 12 May that the government intended to develop the nine islands Spratly Islands claimed by the Philippines into a tourist attraction.

Political structure

Constitution

Between January 1987 and February 1988, the Philippines adopted a new constitution, elected a newly created two-tier congress, and voted in provincial governors, and town and city councils around the country. The written constitution provides for a presidential system of government with separation of powers and was ratified by national referendum in February 1987. The drafting of the constitution was designed to prevent the emergence of another dictator.

Its principal provisions are that sovereignty resides in the people, and all government authority emanates from them; war is renounced as an instrument of national policy; and civilian authority is supreme over military authority. It has wide powers to check the presidency, including presidential impeachment, the right to lift any imposition of martial law, veto of presidential appointments and human rights protection. These steps completed the rebuilding of democratic structures after two decades of martial law and dictatorial rule by Ferdinand Marcos, whose presidency was ended in the near-bloodless revolution of February 1986.

Suffrage is granted to all citizens over 18 years of age who have resided for at least one year previously in the Philippines, and for at least six months in their voting district. Voting is by secret ballot.

Local government is vested in 13 regions, with provincial, city and municipal councils.

Independence date

12 June 1898

Form of state

Republic

The executive

Executive power is vested in the directly elected president and an appointed cabinet.

The constitution allows the president a single six-year term and prevents any vice president from serving for more than two successive terms.

The president is head of state, chief executive of the republic and commander-in-chief of the armed forces. The vice president is elected on a separate ticket and may represent a different political party.

National legislature

The bicameral legislative congress consists of the Kapulungán ng mgá Kinatawán (House of Representatives, commonly referred to as the Congress) and the Senado (Senate). Congress has no more than 250 members, unless otherwise fixed by law, who shall be directly elected in single-seat constituencies by simple majority vote. The party-list representatives must constitute 20 per cent of the total number of representatives including those under the party list. Members serve for three-year terms. The Senate has 24 seats of which members are directly elected in multi-seat constituencies by majority vote to serve for six years. All senators must be aged over 35 years and have been born in the Philippines. An alternate 50 per cent of the senate are elected every three years.

All financial legislation and powers to check the presidency, including impeachment, the right to lift any imposition of martial law, veto of presidential appointments and human rights protection is exclusively the responsible of Congress, while the senate is exclusively responsible for ratifying treaties.

Legal system

Based on Spanish and Anglo-American law.

There is a formal separation of powers between legislative, executive and judiciary. There are also the following courts: the Supreme Court, the court of appeals (formerly the intermediate apellate court), regional trial courts, metropolitan trial courts, municipal trial courts and municipal circuit trial courts. Other laws have created special courts such as the Sandiganbayan (with an anti-corruption brief), and the Sharia courts (for matters involving Muslims). The Supreme Court comprises a chief justice and 14 associate judges, 10 of whom are required to declare on constitutional matters.

Last elections

10 May 2010 (House of Representatives and half Senate and presidential)

Results: Parliamentary (House of Representatives): Lakas ng Edsa (Lakas), Kabalikat ng Mamamayang Pilipino (Kampi) Christian Muslim Democrats Party CMD (coalition of five political parties) won 38.1 per cent (106 seats out of 228), Partido Liberal (Liberal Party) (coalition of three political parties), 20.3 per cent (45), Nacionalista Party (NP) (National Party) (coalition of four political parties) 11.4 per cent (31), seven independent candidates won a total of 2.43 per cent (seven) (Pwersa ng Masang Pilipino (PMP) (Force of the Filipino Masses) (coalition of two political parties and seven independents) 2.8 per cent (six). The remaining seats were won between 16 political parties that each won less than 1 per cent of the vote; the remaining 57 seats were determined by proportional representative votes by party lists. Turnout was 78.95 per cent.

Presidential: Benigno Aquino III (LP) won 42.1 per cent of the vote, Joseph Estrada (PMP) 26.3 per cent, Manuel Villar (NP) 15.4 per cent, and Gilberto Teodoro

(Lakas) 11.3 per cent; five other candidates each won less than 4 per cent.

Next elections

9 May 2016 (presidential and parliamentary)

Political parties

Ruling party

Partido Liberal (Liberal Party) (coalition with Kalapian ng mga Kaibigan sa Kaunlaran (KKK) (Friends Of Development – City of Hagonoy) (from 29 Jun 2010)

Main opposition party

Lakas ng Edsa (Lakas), Kabalikat ng Mamamayang Pilipino (Kampi) Christian Muslim Democrats Party CMD (coalition of five political parties)

Population

99.43 million (2014) (92,337,852; 2010, census figure)

Last census: 1 May 2010: 92,337,852

Population density: 313 inhabitants per square km (2010). Urban population 49 per cent (2010 Unicef).

Annual growth rate: 2.1 per cent, 1990–2010 (Unicef).

Internally Displaced Persons (IDP)

More than 75,000 (UNHCR 2004)

Ethnic make-up

Filipinos are of Malayan descent with Chinese and Spanish ancestries. There are around six million tribal Filipinos – 60 ethnological groups – comprising approximately 8 per cent of the total population, mainly around North Luzon, central Luzon and western Mindanao and the Sulu Islands.

Religions

The Philippines is the only country in Asia with a Christian majority. About 85 per cent of the population are baptised Roman Catholics; a sect, the Philippine Independent Church which, since 1902, has not recognised the authority of the Holy See, (4 per cent). There is a strong Muslim presence (5 per cent) especially on Mindanao and a Protestant minority (4 per cent). Buddhism and other beliefs (2 per cent) account for the remainder.

Education

Primary education lasts for four years followed by two years of intermediate and four years of secondary education. Instruction is in both English and Filipino at elementary level, while English is the usual language at secondary level and beyond. However, a curriculum for secondary schools, introduced in 1989, made Filipino (Tagalog) the language of instruction for all subjects except mathematics and the sciences.

Both public and private universities offer higher education. Estimates in 2001 showed that 72 per cent of all students were enrolled in private higher education institutions. Public expenditure on education typically amounted to 3.4 per cent of annual gross national income between 1994–1997.

Literacy rate: 93 per cent adult rate; 95 per cent youth rate (15–24) (Unesco 2005).

Compulsory years: 6 to 12

Enrolment rate: 117 per cent gross primary enrolment of relevant age group (including repeaters); 78 per cent gross secondary enrolment (World Bank).

Pupils per teacher: 35 in primary schools

Health

HIV/Aids

HIV prevalence: 0.1 per cent aged 15–49 in 2003 (World Bank)

Life expectancy: 68 years, 2004 (WHO 2006)

Fertility rate/Maternal mortality rate: 3.1 births per woman, 2010 (Unicef); maternal mortality 170 per 100,000 live births (World Bank).

Child (under 5 years) mortality rate (per 1,000): 30 per 1,000 live births (WHO 2012); 32 per cent of children aged under five are malnourished (World Bank).

Welfare

The government runs a comprehensive social security scheme, providing a retirement fund, hospital coverage, funeral grants, sickness and disability leave and maternity benefits. Three separate and complementary social security programmes are operated by the state. The first is the basic scheme, providing a pension plan and illness, disability and maternity leave. The second is employee compensation covering disability or work related death and the third is medical care, providing for hospital coverage. Despite government intentions, only a small proportion of the population benefit from these schemes. Income disparities are extreme, with approximately one out of every four residents in Manila a squatter. Two-thirds of the population live below the national poverty line, with the richest 20 per cent typically receiving more than half of the country's income. At least five million families are estimated to be in extreme poverty or severely malnourished.

Main cities

Manila (on Luzon) (capital, estimated population – including Caloocan and Quezon cities – 12.6 million (m) in 2012). Davao City, on Mindanao (1.4m), Cebu, on Visayas, (818,924), Antipolo (765,260), Zamboanga (722,308), Dasmariñas (713,595), Dadiangas (613,988), Cagayan de Oro (598,526).

Languages spoken

English is widely understood and generally used in government and commerce.

There are altogether 11 long-established cultural and racial groups, each with their own language. The major linguistic groups are Tagalog, Ilocano, Cebuano, Hiligaynon, Bicolana, Waray, Pampanago and Pangasinense. Other languages include Leytenhon-Samarnon, Maranao, Tausog and highland ethnic languages. Based on a survey by the national census and statistics office, a representative population of 8.6 million Filipinos showed that 2.5 million speak Tagalog as a mother language and 2.1 million speak Cebuano. The rest of the surveyed population speak one of the more than 80 other dialects in the country. Arabic and Chinese dialects are spoken by a minority of the population.

Official language/s

Filipino (based on Tagalog)

Media

Press

Dailies: Others are *The Daily Tribune* (www.tribune.net.ph), *Malaya* (www.malaya.com.ph), *Manila Standard* (online: www.manilastandardtoday.com) *The Manila Times* (www.manilatimes.net) and the *Manila Bulletin* (www.mb.com.ph) with a large circulation, *Philippines Daily Inquirer* (www.inquirer.net). Major regional dailies, in English, include *Sun Star Sebu* (www.sunstar.com.ph/cebu), *Mindanao Times* (www.mindanaotimes.com.ph), Davao Today (www.davaotoday.com) and *Minda News* (www.mindanews.com). In Tagalog, *Abante* (www.abante.com.ph), *Ang Pilipino Star Ngayon* (www.philstar.com) and *Taliba* (www.journal.com.ph).

English language newspapers with Online editions updated regularly include the *Philippine Star* (www.philstar.com) and *Philippine Daily Inquirer* and *Philippines News.Net* (www.philippinesnews.net).

English language newspapers with Online editions updated regularly include the *Philippine Star* (www.philstar.com) and *Philippine Daily Inquirer* and *Philippines News.Net* (www.philippinesnews.net)

Weeklies: The leading magazines, in English, are *Cosmopolitan Philippines* (www.cosmomagazine.com.ph) for women, *Candy* (www.candymag.com) for teenagers, *FHM Philippines* (www.fhm.com.ph) for men and *Bayani Magazine* (http://bayanimagazine.com) on general interest. In Tagalog, *Pinoy Weekly* (www.pinoyweekly.org).

Business: In English, national and Manila based *Business World* (www.bworldonline.com), *Business Mirror* (www.businessmirror.com.ph). Agricultural and agribusiness publications are issued by the Philippine Council for Agriculture, Forestry and Natural Resources Research and Development.

Periodicals: Periodicals include the women's quarterly *Attitude*.

Broadcasting

Radio: There are 350 local radio stations, of which around 10 per cent are either government-owned, non-commercial religious or educational stations, the remaining 90 per cent are commercial broadcasters. National radio networks include Bombo Radyo (www.bomboradyo.com), FEBC (Far East Broadcasting Company) (www.febc.org), MBC Radio (www.mbcradio.net), Radio Philippines (www.radiophilippines.com). and the state-owned PBS (Philippine Broadcasting Service). In Tagalog, RMN Networks (www.rmn.com.ph).

Television: In English, ABS-CBN (www.abs-cbnnews.com), GMA Network (www.gmanews.tv). Online television services in English and Tagalog, iGMA TV (www.igma.tv) and Filamvision TV (www.filamvision.tv).

There are over 50 originating television stations around the country, five of them in Manila, and about 30 relay stations.

Philippines News Agency (PNA), 2nd Floor, National Media Center, Visayas Ave, Diliman, Quezon City, Metro Manila (tel: 920-6551–65; internet: www.pna.gov.ph).

Economy

The Philippines has a variety of thriving sectors. Agriculture is an important component of the economy accounting for 11.3 per cent of GDP and employing 30 per cent of the workforce.

The Philippines' other important primary industry, mining, is a leading source of export revenue. There are reserves of gold, copper, chromite and nickel ore, as well as oil, natural gas and coal; but the largest components of the Philippines' mining sector are stone quarrying and salt farms (around 40 per cent and 20 per cent of total respectively). There is a successful high-tech industry of manufactured electronic components and automotive parts as well as service industries including call centre facilities – the Philippines being second largest in Asia (after India).

In 2009, high prices for fuel and food helped slow the economy so that when the global economic crisis was at its deepest GDP growth fell to 1.1 per cent as world trade was severely weakened. However, in 2010 as the world economy picked up GDP growth reached 7.6 per cent. Inflation, which had been 2.8 per cent in 2007 rose sharply to 8.2 per cent in 2008, before falling back to 4.2 per cent in 2009 and further still to 3.8 per cent in 2010. Growth remained at a high rate of 6.1 per cent in 2014, whilst inflation increased by 1.1 per cent to 4.1 per cent in the same year.

Around eight million Filipinos work overseas – remittances in 2013 were US$26.7 billion and grew to US$28.4 billion in 2014.

The benefits of this source of revenue are offset by the structural consequences to the economy on account of continued loss of professional, skilled and unskilled workers. The growth rate in remittances in 2009 was 5.61 per cent, of which sea-based remittances rose by 12.06 per cent – Philippine seamen are considered skilled operatives, with years of crewing experience. The global recession had an impact on the number of migrant workers overseas as factories closed or reduced their workforces and foreign workers were the first to be laid off; thousands of Philippine migrant workers have been forced to return home. Typically, over 80 per cent of all migrants are female, working in domestic situations.

In 2014, the UN Human Development Index (HDI) ranked the Philippines 117 (out of 187) for national development in health, education and income. In 2010, 47.4 per cent of the population experienced deprivation in at least one indicator for poverty, while 22.6 per cent lived on the equivalent of US$1.25 per day.

External trade

The Philippines is a member of the Association of Southeast Asian Nations (Asean) Free Trade Area (Afta) and maintains a list of goods that have preferential import duties between members and a programme of tariff reductions due to be introduced in the next few years.

The country has some of the world's highest levels of mineral reserves, including copper, gold and zinc; most deposits have yet to be exploited. There is an extensive heavy industrial sector as well as a manufacturing sector with commodities dominated by electronic goods which represents around 60 per cent of exports. Foreign trade accounts for 95 per cent of GDP and remittances are an important source of foreign revenue.

Imports

Principal imports are petroleum and oil products, transport equipment, capital machinery, plastics, ores and scrap metal, telecommunication equipment, consumer goods and food.

Main sources: China (15.0 per cent of total in 2014), US (8.7 per cent), Japan (8 per cent)

Exports

Principal exports are semiconductors, electrical and electronic equipment, vehicles, garments, optical and medical instruments, petroleum products, gold, copper concentrates and chemicals, processed foods, fruits and nuts, garments and textiles.

Main destinations: Japan (22.5 per cent of total in 2014), US (14.1 per cent), China (13 per cent)

Agriculture

Farming

Agriculture, once the main contributor to GDP, has lost its position to the services sector. It accounts for 11.3 per cent of GDP and employs about 30 per cent of the labour force.

Some 35 per cent of the total land area is used to cultivate food crops, mostly on smallholdings.

About one-third of the population depends on coconuts, the major export crop. Other commercial crops include sugar cane, hemp, bananas, coffee, tobacco, peanuts and various fruits. Rice and maize production is sufficient to meet domestic demand and other crops include sweet potatoes, cassava, plantains, pineapples, mangoes and cocoa.

The Asian Development Bank highlighted the need for further reforms to stimulate rural development, to improve irrigation systems, which cover only 42 per cent of irrigatable areas, and to improve the yield and production of paddy rice.

Livestock reared for local consumption include cattle, goats, pigs and poultry.

A record rice harvest of 7.57 million tonnes was recorded in the first half of 2011, a 14.4 per cent year-on-year increase compared to 2010. The wheat harvest was also up by 37 per cent year-on-year at 3.3 million tonnes. The Department of Agriculture put the increase down to irrigated farmland and sufficient rainwater for all farming.

The Philippines' department of agriculture reported in 2014 that the country's farm sector would grow at 3 per cent due to sustained good performance in the livestock and fisheries sector.

Fishing

The fishing industry is a big export earner for the Philippines. During the mid-1990s, the annual net trade surplus in fish products amounted to almost US$100 million. In recent years, thousands of hectares, estimated at 40 per cent of former sugar lands, have been converted into shrimp aquaculture ponds. The southern Philippines has traditionally been bountiful for tuna fishermen, but the tuna catch decreased during the 1990s. There is massive overcapacity at Philippine canneries and fishing companies blame years of unrestrained plunder, rising imports and the destruction of the habitat for the slump in the annual catch.

Since the government initiated a reef development plan to create artificial fish

spawning grounds, production of fish has increased dramatically, and the Philippines now boasts the largest area of developed estuarine fishponds in south-east Asia.
Following the annual meeting of the Commission for the Conservation of Southern Bluefin Tuna (CCSBT), held on Cheju Island, South Korea, all members agreed to a 20 per cut in the roughly 17,000 tonnes in 2009 bluefin tuna catches from 2010. Scientists had warned that without a cut fish stocks could crash as numbers had become dangerously low.

Forestry

Woodland and forests cover 51 per cent of the land area and contains an estimated 1.45 billion cubic metres of hardwood. Exports of logs were phased out to assist the local timber processing industries. The reafforestation programme is markedly behind schedule, but is being accelerated.

Industry and manufacturing

The industrial sector accounts for around a third of GDP and employs 16 per cent of the workforce.
Food and beverage processing is the main manufacturing activity, including sugar, meat, fruit and vegetables, fish and shrimp processing, soft drinks and alcoholic beverages. Electronics (semiconductors, circuit boards etc) has been the fastest growing sector of the economy. Production of computers and computer parts is principally carried out by Japanese, US, South Korean and Taiwanese companies. Other major industries include petroleum and coal products, chemicals and chemical products. Main light industrial products, which are often produced from imported materials or components, are cotton and textiles, vehicles, chemicals, machine tools and electrical and consumer goods such as refrigerators, radios, TVs, freezers, air-conditioning equipment, sewing machines and watches.

Tourism

The Philippines has many islands offering a wide variety of experiences but most tourist activity is centred on the sandy beach-lined island of Boracay and metropolitan Cebu (second largest city). The scope for ecotourism is wide as there are unspoiled rainforests and marine environments to explore.
There are five sites on Unesco's World Heritage List, including historic buildings and national parks. The Tubbataha Reefs National Park is a unique and pristine atoll reef that has a high density of marine species. The Puerto Princesa Subterranean River National Park became one of the 'New7Wonders of Nature' in January 2012.
Travel and tourism accounts for 11.2 per cent of GDP (US$30.5 billion) and provides employment for 11.1 per cent of the workforce (4.2 million jobs). Foreign visitor numbers have fluctuated as the global economic crisis curbed discretionary spending on holidays. Arrivals in 2010 were 3.5 million which has steadily increased to 4.8 million in 2014.
Government backs the tourism management plan that provides a framework for tourist development and its related infrastructure. Currently the Philippines lacks adequate tourist accommodation away from resort areas. There are few international airports outside Manila necessary to allow growth in tourism from North America and Europe. Domestic transport, which lacks an integrated, scheduled service between many of the islands, has also been identified as a problem inhibiting growth. Internal travel costs are comparatively high.

Environment

Tree felling in the 1980s caused erosion and soil degradation, and in 1989 deforestation was prohibited by law. In April 2012, two new species of frogs were identified in the country's fast-disappearing forests. The forests have been identified, by the US-based Conservation International, as one the world's top 'biodiversity hotspots'.
New mining regulations introduced after copper leakages into river systems in the mid-1990s, stipulate that companies must allocate 10 per cent of initial costs for environmental improvements, and set aside a further 3–5 per cent of mining and milling costs for an environmental protection programme, to be audited annually.
Fishing methods using dynamite and cyanide to stun tropical fish in the coral reefs have poisoned the reef and killed other sea creatures living there. Philippines, Indonesia, Australia, Papua New Guinea and Solomon Islands are the countries with the most coral reef fish species.

Mining

The mining sector accounts for 1 per cent of GDP and a similar proportion of the workforce.
The Philippines is the second largest gold producer in Asia (after Indonesia) and one of the top 20 producers in the world. It also produces large quantities of silver. There are copper reserves estimated at 3.6 billion tonnes.
The Philippines holds the second largest reserve of gold in the world. Applications from foreign mining firms are piling up to tap into these reserves and the other abundant reserves in the nation. Access to the US$1.4 trillion mining sector has been impeded by various environmental, land and regulatory issues.
Nickel (fourth-largest reserves in the world after Cuba, New Caledonia and Indonesia), chromium, manganese, zinc, mercury, sand, gravel and rock asphalt are also mined. Other metal and mineral resources include iron ore (reserves, mainly laterite, 1.3 billion tonnes), molybdenum, lead, platinum, palladium, cadmium, cobalt, uranium, phosphate, guano, sulphur, pyrites, limestone, shale, gypsum, clay, kaolin, feldspar and silica sand.
Large mineral resources, scattered throughout the archipelago, remain unmeasured and untouched.

Hydrocarbons

Proven oil reserves were 139 billion barrels and production was 23,000 barrels per day (bpd). The Philippines is still heavily reliant on imports of crude oil and petroleum products, although the high cost of oil has made investment in exploration appear reasonable and a number of major oil companies had started either exploring or drilling for oil in 2008.
The Philippines, along with China, Taiwan, Brunei, Malaysia and Vietnam, claims the potentially oil-rich Spratly Islands.
Proven natural gas reserves were 3.5 trillion cubic feet in 2014. Natural gas is being used to replace oil for electricity generation. The US$4.5 billion development of the Malampaya offshore field, containing up to 73.2 billion cum of gas, is one of the country's largest investments ever seen. The field is being developed by an international consortium, including operator Shell Philippines Exploration (SPEX) (45 per cent), Texaco (45 per cent) and the Philippine National Oil Company (PNOC) (10 per cent).
The Philippines has around 264 million tonnes of recoverable coal reserves and produces around two million tonnes per year (tpy), which satisfies around 25 per cent of annual domestic consumption. The remaining 75 per cent is imported, primarily from Indonesia, China and Australia. The sector has been affected by the increasing use of natural gas.

Energy

Total installed generating capacity is 15.5 gigawatts (GW), of which 68 per cent is thermal (gas, oil, coal and solid fuel), 15 per cent hydroelectric and 17 per cent other, mostly geothermal. The country is spearheading the development of environmentally friendly electricity generation.
The Philippines has the potential for self-sufficiency in electricity generation thanks to its vast geothermal energy reserves. The first merchant power plant of 49.37MW became operational in 2007 and there are plans for two more such

power plants to come online by 2011.
The government has proposed plans for a further 70 hydropower plants with a potential capacity of 2.6GW.
The government also plans to complete the restructuring process that involves privatisation of the energy market and full electrification of the archipelago.

Financial markets

Stock exchange

Pamilihang Sapi ng Pilipinas (Philippine Stock Exchange) (PSE)

Banking and insurance

The government made its first step to liberalise the banking sector in 2000 when it introduced a general banking law, allowing foreign banks to gradually take over domestic banks. However, the government continues to intervene in the sector, bailing out banks that experience difficulties.
Philippines was removed from the OECD Financial Action Task Force (FATF) list of non-co-operative countries on money laundering in 2005.

Central bank

Bangko Sentral ng Pilipinas (Central Bank of the Philippines).

Main financial centre

Manila, Makati

Time

GMT plus eight hours

Geography

The Philippines is an archipelago of 7,107 islands, some large and some only islets, stretching more than 1,700km north to south. Fewer than 5,000 of the islands have names, and less than 2,000 are inhabited.
The nearest neighbours are Indonesia and parts of Malaysia to the south and Taiwan to the north. To the west, across the South China Sea, are Vietnam and peninsular Malaysia. The Pacific Ocean is to the east. The Philippines is situated in the centre of the Asia Pacific region – Japan, South Korea, Hong Kong, Thailand, Malaysia, Singapore and Indonesia can all be reached within two to four hours flying time.
Nearly 95 per cent of the population live on the 11 largest islands. These are mostly mountainous, except for coastal areas and the central plain on Luzon, the largest island (104,683 square km). The second largest island is Mindanao (94,596 square km) in the south, followed by Palawan (14,896 square km), Panay (12,327 square km) and Mindoro (10,245 square km).
There are some 40 active volcanoes (including Balusan and Mayon, both of which erupted in 2006) scattered across the country, and 21 less active ones.

Hemisphere

Northern

Climate

The climate is tropical, with an average temperature of 27 degrees Celsius. Tropical storms and typhoons are common between July–October and they can hit any part of the country. The Philippines is vulnerable to the *El Niño* phenomenon, which has severely affected agricultural output. The climate is drier and more comfortable between October–February, and can be very pleasant at the higher elevations.

Dress codes

National dress, often worn by men in the office or at any formal occasion, is the *barong* or embroidered native shirt worn outside the trousers. Reflecting US influence, business suits are almost as prevalent. National dress for women, a scoop-necked dress with ballooning short sleeves, is worn at formal social occasions, not for work. Leisure wear tends to be 'smart casual'.

Entry requirements

Passports

Required by all, valid for six months beyond date of departure.

Visa

Visas are not required by nationals of most countries, including business travellers, for visits of up to 21 days, with valid passports and proof of return/onward passage. For details see www.gov.ph/faqs/visa.asp.

Currency advice/regulations

Import and export of local currency up to P10,000 is allowed; amounts exceeding this figure require authorisation from the Central Bank of the Philippines. There are no restrictions on the import and export of foreign currency, subject to declaration of amounts over P10,000.
Travellers cheques and major foreign currencies may be cashed in large commercial banks and by central bank dealers in Manila, and they are also accepted in most hotels, restaurants and shops. Always use authorised money changers or banks. Outside the capital, it is advisable to carry a sufficient amount of local currency when travelling to provinces, as there is a shortage of exchange facilities.

Customs

Personal effects are allowed duty-free. Visitors may import motorcycles and boats duty-free for stays of up to one month; longer stays require a bond guaranteeing re-export.

Health (for visitors)

Mandatory precautions

Vaccination certificate required for yellow fever if travelling from an infected area.

Advisable precautions

Vaccinations for diphtheria, tuberculosis, hepatitis A and B, Japanese B encephalitis, polio, tetanus and typhoid are advisable. Anti-malaria precautions should be taken if travelling outside urban areas. There is a rabies risk. Tap water is generally clean and safe to drink in the towns.

Hotels

A service charge of 13 per cent and a government tax of 10 per cent are usually added to hotel bills, and gratuities are not necessary, although it is customary to leave small change.

Credit cards

International credit cards are widely accepted in major establishments throughout big cities.

Public holidays (national)

Fixed dates

1 Jan (New Year), 9 Apr (Bataan and Corregidor Heroes Day), 1 May (Labour Day), 12 Jun (Independence Day), 1 Nov (All Saints' Day), 30 Nov (Bonifacio Day), 25 Dec (Christmas Day), 30 Dec (Rizal Day), 31 Dec (New Year's Eve).

Variable dates

Easter, National Heroes Day (last Sun in Aug), Eid al Fitr.
Easter is a major holiday in the Philippines and travel may be disrupted.

Working hours

Working hours vary. Some banks and offices open for a half day on Saturday and, in the Manila area, many shops open for a half day on Sunday.

Banking

Mon–Fri: 0900–1600. Automated banking systems exist (24 hours).

Business

Mon–Fri: 0800–1200/1300, 1300/1400–1700; Sat: 0830–1200.

Government

Mon–Fri: 0730–1130, 1230–1630 or 0800–1200, 1300–1700.

Shops

Mon–Sat: 0930–2030. Most tourist shops open on Sundays.

Electricity supply

220 or 110V AC, 60 cycles with flat and round two-pin plug fittings.

Weights and measures

Metric system, with some local units still in use.

Social customs/useful tips

It is customary to shake hands on meeting and taking leave. If people have an academic or professional title (eg doctor, director) they should be addressed by their title. Senior citizens should be treated with particular respect. Shoes should be removed before entering someone's home.

Central to Filipino values is the concept of maintaining 'face'. Anything which appears to constitute a slight to a Filipino can have serious consequences. Criticism, however mild, of anyone present is to be avoided. New ideas need to be carefully introduced. A strong personal element to relationships, including those of business and state, makes refusal of frequently proffered hospitality offensive. It can be common to receive a positive answer to a question when the appropriate answer is negative. Reciprocity of hospitality is also required. Despite the appearance of extensive westernisation, conservative values usually apply.

Religious matters are taken seriously, but so is superstition to the extent that no building displays a thirteenth floor. Belief in witches happily co-exists alongside more mainstream religions.

Punctuality is aimed at, but not always achieved. Tips of about 10 per cent for most services are considered standard.

Gift-giving, on the smallest pretext, is widely practised, although the gift itself may be inexpensive.

Old-style chivalry towards women reigns supreme, disguising the extent to which women's dominance at home translates into effective control of the Filipino male. Male visitors will be offered companions as a matter of course, but should not extend this apparent availability into loose behaviour with women outside the bounds of the sex industry.

The most important tradition is that of *utang na loob*, or a lifelong debt of gratitude. This is not just a matter of mutual back-scratching. It is a deeply felt belief that even small favours can never be fully repaid, so that complex networks of loyalties develop, providing a hidden structure to relationships.

Another important tradition is that of *pakikisama*, or co-operating with the team view. Group identification is all-important, reaching back to one's class at school, or to one's village of origin. Approval of the group is often needed before any serious decision is reached. In this context, the supreme importance of family links can be seen, and the paramount significance of family honour understood.

Security

Widespread poverty makes robbery the most common crime. Changing money at a black-market operator will probably deliver you into the hands of pickpockets outside. Foreigners are rarely targetted for more violent crimes.

Getting there

Air

National airline: Philippine Airlines (PAL)
International airport/s: Ninoy Aquino International Airport (MNL) is 12km south of Manila; facilities include bank, duty-free shop, restauraunts, post office and car hire. Mactan-Cebu International Airport (CEB), on Mactan Island, is 9km from Cebu City and 45km from Manila.
Airport tax: P550.

Surface

Water: It may be possible to find a freight ship which will carry passengers from nearby Malaysian or Indonesian ports, but schedules are unreliable. Cruise ships stop in Manila Bay. There is danger from smugglers and pirates operating between Borneo and Mindanao.
Main port/s: Manila, Batangas City, Cebu, Davao, Iloilo, Zamboanga, Cagayan de Oro, Subic Bay Freeport.

Getting about

National transport

Air: Philippine Airlines (PAL), Cebu Pacific Air, and Air Philippines are the main operators of relatively inexpensive domestic flights.
Road: The network of highways is mainly confined to coastal areas. The Maharlika Highway runs from Luzon to Mindanao, with connecting ferry services.
Buses: There are bus services between Manila and the rest of the country. Air-conditioned buses are available. There is no central bus terminal in Manila, each company having its own terminal.
Rail: The only railway line is on Luzon island, running south from Manila to Legazpi. A line from Manila to San Fernando and San Jose in the north is not open. Both lines are single track and narrow gauge. Train services are slow; some have restaurant cars and air-conditioning.
Water: Inter-island services are operated by several companies, some with air-conditioned cabins and dining rooms. There are numerous public and private ports, many serving coastal shipping traffic.

City transport

If travelling by road, allow extra travel time between appointments – there are many traffic jams. Tricycles (motorbikes with sidecars) and trishaws are a cheap alternative for shorter distances around towns.
Taxis: Taxis are plentiful and cheap, but not easy to hail. Because traffic is heavy, drivers will often refuse to go beyond the local district. It may be worthwhile retaining a driver for the day. Taxis are metered, but passengers need to ensure that the drivers switch them on; if they make excuses, they should not be engaged. Tipping taxi drivers is not customary.
Buses, trams & metro: Numerous inexpensive bus services operate in and around main centres, but they can be crowded, and knowledge of the area is recommended before travelling by bus.
Jeepneys are shared taxis, which ply regular routes and are cheap.
The Metrorail Light Rail Transit (LRT) is an overhead railway which runs from north to south Manila.

Car hire

Self-drive and chauffeur-driven car hire is available. It is advisable to hire a car and driver. Local driving habits make traffic conditions extremely difficult. International driving licences are acceptable. Driving is on the right-hand side of the road.

BUSINESS DIRECTORY

The addresses listed below are a selection only. While World of Information makes every endeavour to check these addresses, we cannot guarantee that changes have not been made, especially to telephone numbers and area codes. We would welcome any corrections.

Telephone area codes

The international dialling code (IDD) for the Philippines is +63, followed by the area code and subscriber's number:

Bacolod	34	Iloilo	33
Cebu	32	Manila	2
Dagupan	75	San Pablo	49
Davao	82		

Useful telephone numbers

Manila
Police: 599-011
Fire: 581-176

Chambers of Commerce

American Chamber of Commerce of the Philippines, Corinthian Plaza, Paseo de Roxas, Legazpi Village, PO Box 2562, Makati, Manila (tel: 818-7911; fax: 811-3081; e-mail: info@amchamphilippines.com).

British Chamber of Commerce of the Philippines, c/o British Embassy, 6752 Ayala Avenue corner Makati Avenue, Makati, Manila (tel: 580-8359; fax: 893-9073; e-mail: administrator@bccphil.com).

Cebu Chamber of Commerce and Industry, CCCI Center, Corner 11th and 13th Avenues, North Reclamation Area, Cebu City (tel: 232-1421; fax: 232-1422; e-mail: ccci@gsilink.com).

Davao City Chamber of Commerce and Industry, DCCII Building, JP Laurel Avenue, Davao City (tel: 221-4148; fax: 226-4433; e-mail: dccii@skynet.net).

European Chamber of Commerce of the Philippines, Axa Life Center, Sen Gil Puyat Avenue corner Tindalo Street, Makati, Manila (tel: 845-1324; fax: 845-1395; e-mail: info@eccp.com).

Philippine Chamber of Commerce and Industry, Salcedo Towers, 169 HV dela Costa Street, Salcedo Village, Makati, Manila (tel: 844-5713; fax: 843-4102; e-mail: pcci@philcham.com).

Banking

Allied Banking Corp, Allied Bank Centre, 6754 Ayala Avenue corner Legaspi Street, Makati, Manila (tel: 816-331; fax: 816-0921).

Bank of the Philippine Islands, PO Box 1827 MCC, BPI Bldg, Ayala Avenue, corner Paseo de Roxas, Makati City (tel: 818-5541; fax: 815-9434).

Development Bank of the Philippines, DBP Building, Makati Avenue corner Sen Gil Puyat Avenue, Makati, Manila (tel: 818-9511; fax: 818-6699).

Equitable PCI Bank, Equitable PCI Bank Tower 1, Makati Avenue corner HV Dela Costa Street, Makati, Manila (tel: 817-7330; fax: 817-6984).

Land Bank of the Philippines, 319 Sen Gil Puyat Avenue, Makati, Manila (tel/fax: 814-0179).

Metrobank, Metrobank Plaza Building, Sen Gil Puyat Avenue, Makati, Manila (tel: 810-3311; fax: 817-6248; e-mail: metrobank@metrobank.com.ph).

Philippine National Bank, Cacho-Gonzales Bldg, cor Aguirre & Transierra Sts, Legaspi Village, Makati City 1229 (tel: 892-8780; fax: 840-3039).

Rizal Commercial Banking Corporation, RCBC Building, 333 Sen Gil Puyat Avenue, Makati, Manila (tel: 819-3061; fax: 891-0775).

Security Bank Corporation, SBTC Building, 6776 Ayala Avenue, Makati, Manila (tel: 888-7340; fax: 893-2563; e-mail: inquiry@securitybank.com.ph).

Union Bank of the Philippines, SSS (Makati) Building, Ayala Avenue corner Herrera Street, Makati, Manila (tel: 892-0011; fax: 840-0168).

Central bank

Bangko Sentral ng Pilipinas, A Mabini Street, Corner Pablo Ocampo Street, Malate, Manila 1004 (tel: 524-7011; fax: 523-6210; e-mail: bspmail@bsp.gov.ph).

Stock exchange

Pamilihang Sapi ng Pilipinas (Philippines Stock Exchange) (PSE), www.pse.org.ph

Philippine Dealing Exchange (PDEx), www.pdex.com.ph

Travel information

Automobile Association Philippines, PO Box 999, 683 Aurora Boulevard, Quezon, Manila (tel: 723-0808; fax: 726-5878; e-mail: aaphils@greendot.com.ph).

Cebu Pacific Air, Robinsons Equitable Building, Ortigas Centre, Pasig, Manila (tel: 702-0888; fax: 637-9170; e-mail: feedback@cebupacificair.com).

Hotel and Restaurant Association of the Philippines, Regina Building, Legazpi Village, Makati, Manila (tel: 815-4659; fax: 815-4663; e-mail: hrap@mnl.sequelnet).

Manila Ninoy Aquino International Airport, NAIA Complex, Pascay, Manila (tel: 877-1109; fax: 833-1180; e-mail: info@miaa.gov.ph).

Philippine Airlines (PAL), PO Box 954, Philippine Airlines Centre, Legazpi Street, Makati, Manila (tel: 818-0111; fax: 818-3298; e-mail: webmgr@pal.com.ph).

Philippine Travel and Tourism Council, 1102 City and Land Mega Plaza, Ortigas Centre, Pasig, Manila (tel: 687-4812; fax: 931-8307; e-mail: info@philippinetourism.org).

Ministry of tourism

Department of Tourism, Kalaw Street, Rizal Park, Manila (tel:525-2000; fax: 521-7374; e-mail: webmaster@tourism.gov.ph).

National tourist organisation offices

Philippine Tourism Authority, Kalaw Street, Ermita, PO Box 1813, Manila (tel: 524-7141; fax: 521-8113; e-mail: info@philtourism.gov.ph).

Ministries

Office of the President, Malacanang Palace , JP Laurel Street, San Miguel, Manila (tel: 564-1451; fax: 742-1641).

Department of Agrarian Reform, Elliptical Road, Diliman, Quezon City (tel: 928-3979; fax: 929-3088).

Department of Agriculture, Elliptical Road, Diliman, Quezon City (tel: 920-4358; fax: 920-3986).

Department of Budget and Mangement, General Solano Street, San Miguel, Manila (tel: 735-4929; fax: 735-4927).

Department of Defence, Camp Aguinaldo, Quezon City (tel: 911-6193; fax: 911-6213).

Department of Education, Culture and Sports, Meralco Avenue, Pasig, Manila (tel: 634-2925; fax: 636-4876).

Department of Energy, PNCP Complex, Meritt Road, Fort Bonifacio, Makati, Manila (tel: 844-2850; fax: 817-8603).

Department of Environment and Natural Resources, Visayas Avenue, Diliman, Quezon City (tel: 929-6633; fax: 920-4352).

Department of Finance, Vito Cruz corner Mabini Street, Malate, Manila (tel: 523-4255; fax: 521-9495).

Department of Foreign Affairs, 2330 Roxas Boulevard, Pasay, Manila (tel: 831-8955; fax: 832-1597).

Department of Health, Rizal Avenue, Santa Cruz, Manila (tel: 743-8301; fax: 711-6055).

Department of the Interior and Local Government, EDSA corner Reliance Street, Mandaluyong, Manila (tel: 631-8777; fax: 631-8831).

Department of Justice, Padre Faura Street, Ermita, Manila (tel: 521-8344; fax: 521-1614).

Department of Labour and Employment, San Jose Street, Intramuros, Manila (tel: 527-2118; fax: 527-3499).

Department of Public Works and Highways, Bonifacio Drive, Port Area, Manila (tel: 527-4111; fax: 527-5635).

Department of Science and Technology, General Santos Avenue, Bicutan, Taguig, Manila (tel: 837-2939; fax: 837-2937).

Department of Social Welfare and Development, Constitution Hills, Quezon City, Manila (tel: 931-8101; fax: 931-8191).

Department of Tourism, Kalaw Street, Rizal Park, Manila (tel:524-1751; fax: 521-7374).

Department of Trade and Industry, 385 Sen Gil Puyat Avenue, Makati, Manila (tel: 895-3515; fax: 896-1166).

Department of Transportation and Communications, Ortigas Avenue, Pasig, Manila (tel: 726-7106; fax: 632-9985).

National Economic and Development Authority, Amber Avenue, Pasig, Manila (tel: 631-3716; fax: 631-3747).

Other useful addresses

ASEAN Investment Promotion Agency, Board of Investments (BOI), Industry and Investments Building, 385 Sen Gil J Puyat Avenue, Makati, Manila (tel: 890-1332; fax: 895-3512).

ASEAN Secretariat, 70 Jl Sisingamangaraja, Jakarta 12110, Indonesia (tel: 62 (21) 726-2991; fax: 739-8234; e-mail: termsak@asean.or.id).

Asian Development Bank, 6 ADB Avenue, Mandaluyong, Manila (tel: 632-4444; fax: 636-2444; e-mail: information@adb.org).

Board of Investments, Industry and Investments Building, 385 Sen Gil Puyat Avenue, Makati, Manila (tel: 897-6682; fax: 895-3521; e-mail: mis@boi.gov.ph).

British Embassy, L V Locsin Building, 6752 Ayala Avenue corner Makati Avenue, Makati, Manila (tel: 816-7116; fax: 819-7206).

Bureau of Export Trade Promotion, New Solid Building, 357 Sen Gil Puyat Avenue, Makati, Manila (tel: 899-0133; fax: 890-4707; e-mail: betpod@dti.gov.ph).

National Economic Development Authority, NEDA Building, Blessed Joseph Maria Escriva Drive, Pasig, Manila (tel: 631-0945; fax: 633-6011; internet site: http://www.neda.gov.ph).

Petroleum Association of the Philippines, c/o 7/F Basic Petroleum Building, C. Palanca Jr Street, Legaspi Village, Makati, Manila (tel: 817-3329; fax: 817-0191).

Philippine Convention and Visitors Corporation, Legazpi Towers, 300 Roxas Boulevard, Pasay City, Manila (tel: 525-9318; fax: 521-6165; e-mail: pcvcnet@info.com.ph).

Philippine Electronics & Telecommunications Federation, 7/F PS Bank Building, Tindalo Street corner Sen.Gil Puyat Avenue, Makati, Manila (tel/fax: 813-6397).

Philippine Exporters Confederation, Roxas Boulevard corner Sen Gil Puyat Avenue, Pasay City, Manila (tel: 833-2531; fax: 831-2132; e-mail: philxprt@I-next.net; internet site: http://www.philexport.org/launch/index.htm).

Philippines Embassy (US), 1600 Massachusetts Avenue, NW, Washington DC 20036 (tel: (+1-202)-467-9300; fax: (+1-202)-467-9417; e-mail: uswashpe@aol.com).

Philippines Food Processors and Exporters Organisation, Suite 304, JS Contractor Building, 423 Magallanes Street, Intramuros, Manila (tel: 527-5540; fax: 527-5539).

Philippine Information Agency, PIA Building, 1100 Visayas Avenue, Quezon City, Manila (tel: 921-7941; fax: 920-4394; e-mail: odg@pia.gov.ph).

Philippine Iron and Steel Traders Association, 700 Aurora Boulevard, Quezon City, Manila (tel: 722-0536; fax: 721-3599).

Philippine International Trading Corporation, Philippines International Centre, 46 Sen Gil Puyat Avenue, Makati, Manila (tel: 845-4376; fax: 845-4363; e-mail: pitc@info.com.ph).

Philippine Stock Exchange, Exchange Road, Ortigas Centre, Pasig, Manila (tel: 636-0122; fax: 634-5920; e-mail: write@pse.org.ph).

Subic Bay Metropolitan Authority, Building 229, Waterfront Road, Subic Bay Freeport Zone, Olongapo City (tel: 252-4365; fax: 252-3014; e-mail: bgroup@sbma.com).

Textile Producers Association of the Philippines, Room 513, Downtown Center Building, 516 Quintin Paredes Street, Binondo, Manila (tel: 241-1144; fax: 241-1162).

US Embassy, 1201 Roxas Boulevard, Ermita, Manila (tel: 523-1001; fax: 522-4361).

Internet sites

Philippine Consulate General Toronto (gateway site): http://www.philcongen-toronto.com/links.htm

Philippine National Statistics Offices: http://www.census.gov.ph/

Tanikalang Ginto (small gateway site): http://www.filipinolinks.com/business/businformation.html

Pitcairn Island

KEY FACTS

Official name: Pitcairn, Henderson, Ducie and Oeno Islands (Pitcairn Island)

Head of State: Queen Elizabeth II, represented by UK High Commissioner to New Zealand and Governor (non-resident) of the Pitcairn Islands Mr Jonathan Sinclair (since August 2014)

Head of government: Mayor Shawn Christian (from 1 January 2014)

Ruling party: All candidates are non-partisan

Area: 27 square km (four islands)

Population: 48 (2012)*; (66, 1 Jul 2008, census figure)

Capital: Adamstown

Official language: English

Currency: Pound sterling (£) (£=100 pence); New Zealand dollar (NZ$=100 cents)

Exchange rate: £0.65 per US$ (Sep 2015)

* estimated figure

Perhaps inevitably, in the twenty-first century Pitcairn Island (officially Pitcairn, Henderson, Ducie and Oeno Islands, but only Pitcairn is inhabited) seemed to stagger, blinded, into the limelight, its long spell of obscurity transforming to one of notoriety. The rest of the world – or at least those bits of it that were even aware of the islands' existence – began to take a disconcerting degree of interest – curiosity tinged with occasional prurience.

Lost paradise?

As described in Kathy Mark's excellent book, *Lost Paradise*, in 2000 Pitcairn became the scene of a tragi-comedy when its long-boats brought not fish, but – improbably – Gail Cox, a Kent police constable to be stationed temporarily on Pitcairn. Ms Cox was the first British officer ever posted to the remote (but not quite the most remote, a claim held by the UK's Antarctic Research Stations) British territory. PC Cox came to investigate an allegation of the rape of a fifteen-year-old girl, only to uncover the systematic abuse of young girls that dated back at least 40 years. She found herself generally less than welcome on the three square miles that is Pitcairn, faced with the task of interviewing almost all of Pitcairn's women to find out quite what had been going on in the island's close-knit community. No easy task as the abuse accusations stretched back three generations. Virtually every family (not that there are that many families) appeared to host either 'an offender, or a victim, or both.' The very future of the island, dependent on its men and their prowess in the longboats, appeared at risk. The islanders were understandably resentful – towards the Kent police and toward the distant, but awkward British authorities who would rather have not had to bother about these troublesome islanders. For their part, the islanders regarded the British authorities as meddlesome colonialists.

Having investigated the allegations of rape and child abuse, the British authorities eventually decided that there was a substantial case to be answered. In 2004 there descended, in a manner more reminiscent of a Gilbert and Sullivan opera than the Old Bailey, not only New Zealand policemen, but judges, court officials and sundry journalists. One of the half a dozen journalists to cover the trials, Kathy Marks, lived on Pitcairn for six weeks, with the accused men as her neighbours. She had regular encounters with the islanders, not all of them civil, and was able to record how the islanders responded to events. The whole legal process was an anachronism within an illogicality.

At the conclusion of the trial, five male islanders, including the island's mayor, Steve Christian, were found guilty. The sixth, Dennis Christian, had already entered a guilty plea; one of the accused, Jay Warren, was cleared of indecently assaulting a young girl. A total of 31 men had been named as abusers by women who had grown up in Pitcairn, a number of which were now living in New Zealand, Australia, Norfolk Island and England. Seven women testified by video link from Auckland, and the three New Zealand judges believed them. The witnesses had resisted years of family and community pressure to withdraw their complaints. They also vindicated the work of the Kent Police. One of the convicted, Steve Christian had assumed the role of ambassador at large for Pitcairn, globetrotting to promote (with little apparent success) the island. With charges pending, he had addressed the UN committee on decolonisation.

The defendants' relatives had claimed that the island was likely to implode if the convicted men, amounting to a large proportion of the community, were jailed. Other islanders considered the trials as marking the closure of an unsatisfactory episode in Pitcairn history.

Immigrants please

A report funded in 2014 by the British government suggested that Pitcairn was on the brink of 'social collapse' – an already diminishing population confronted by the reality that only one or two of its female population were capable of childbearing. Pitcairn's population had peaked in the 1930s when there were some 250 islanders. But by 2014 the population profile was sadly geriatric, facing the prospect of 'emigrating' to New Zealand, a mere 5,500 kilometres away. The so called *Solomon Study* also considered that there were not enough young people to do the 'essential work'.

Wellington consultant Rob Solomon, who produced the report, warned that '... Pitcairn is too isolated and it will never pay its own way.' He says a survey of 33 Pitkerners living mostly in New Zealand showed only three had any interest in returning. Most spoke of being ashamed of their heritage because of its sex scandal. In August 2014 Auckland based Deputy Governor of Pitcairn Kevin Lynch told the New Zealand based *Sunday Star-Times* that '... whilst there have been many enquiries, serious interest in migrating to Pitcairn has been minimal.' In fact, it appears that not a single person has shown up.

COUNTRY PROFILE

1767 Pitcairn's island (as it was originally called, after the young seaman on the *Swallow* who first spotted it) was sighted and its position recorded, although the longitude was incorrect. The island was uninhabited.

1790 Pitcairn's inaccessibility made it a perfect hideaway for the survivors of the mutinous crew of the British *HMS Bounty*, led by the Master's Mate, Fletcher Christian, and their Tahitian consorts when they arrived in January. Because the island's longitude had been incorrectly recorded in 1767 (it was in fact some 200 miles from its recorded position), it was 18 years before an American whaler, the *Topaz* next found the island.

1808 The community of descendants of Christian's original 27-strong group of settlers was discovered by a group of American whalers.

1838 Pitcairn Island was constituted a British colony when Captain R Elliot of *HMS Fly* gave the Pitcairners formal authority to elect 'a magistrate or elder to be periodically chosen among themselves and answerable for their proceedings to Her Majesty's government'.

1855 The prison on Norfolk Island was decreed to be shut down, but because of increased whaling activity and other traffic in the South Pacific it was considered by the British government to be prudent to colonise the island on a permanent basis. As the resources of Pitcairn Island were by now deemed to be insufficient for the islanders it was suggested that the Pitcairners might relocate to Norfolk Island, a similarly isolated island.

1856 The British offer of Norfolk Island was accepted and all 193 islanders were moved on the *Morayshire*, with their material possessions, including animals, tools, relics and documents, arriving on 8 June.

1858 16 of the original Pitcairners left Norfolk Island and returned to Pitcairn Island after a land ownership dispute; the second Pitcairn settlement was established. They were followed by other disenchanted groups over the next decade.

1998 Pitcairn became a member of the Secretariat of the Pacific Community.

1999 British economic aid to the island was withdrawn, including subsidised electricity and the cost of bringing in goods.

2000 British police began investigating allegations of child molestation by islanders.

2003 A scientific diving expedition began studying marine life surrounding the islands. Thirteen men went on trial accused of sex crimes. Islanders warned that if the men were jailed their society would collapse through lack of manpower. The UK dismissed Pitcairn Island commissioner, Leon Salt, amid claims that he had obstructed the pursuit of the alleged child rapists. The first child since 1986 was born.

2004 The Supreme Court of Pitcairn Island (sitting in New Zealand) found six men, including the mayor, Steve Christian, guilty of sex crimes; four were sentenced to between two and six years in prison and two to community service. Jay Warren, who had been cleared of indecent assault, was elected mayor. Leslie Jacques was appointed Commissioner of Pitcairn by the British government. A UK fund of US$15.3 million was set up to aid development on the island.

2005 The Supreme Court rejected the appeal of the men convicted of sexual assault, and confirmed Britain's sovereignty and jurisdiction over the islands.

2006 The UK Privy Council turned down the last appeal by the defendants convicted of sex offences. The first full-time policeman was appointed.

2007 A new silver enamelled coin was issued, with an engraving of a rat to coincide with the Chinese year of the rat. Although the face value has NZ$2 the coins retail for NZ$79 (US$70). The second child since 1986 was born on the island.

2009 Mike Warren was elected mayor for a three-year term. The 200-year-plus ban on alcohol was lifted, although the ban remains operative for crew members of the two longboats that transfer supplies from passing ships to the island.

2010 Governor George Fergusson visited the island to officially proclaim and sign the new Pitcairn Island constitution. Consultation with the islanders had resulted in a document that enshrined basic human rights and education up to the age of 15, as well as reasserting the constitutional arrangements for the island in respect to the UK. Victoria Treadell became Governor of Pitcairn Island.

2011 The British, Royal Society of Protection of Birds (RSPB) launched a programme to eradicate rodents on Henderson Island (a World Heritage-listed site), in a bid to protect the Henderson petrel. The rodents had been introduced by settlers.

2012 In June, the UK government published a White Paper on its overseas territories that considered a range of measures to improve the sustainability of the economic development of Pitcairn Island through immigration.

2013 A DfID project to build a wind farm, started in 2006, was cancelled in April after the Australian contractors took the money but failed to build any turbines. Thomas Coleman Christian, long-time radio officer and community leader of Pitcairn Island, died on 7 July aged 77. He was a direct descendant of Fletcher Christian, masters' mate on HMS Bounty.

2014 During the year plans were made for the symbolic hand-over of the Bible taken from Captain Bligh's cabin during the mutiny on the *Bounty* on 28 April 1789. Maurice Bligh, 70, the great-great-great-grandson of Captain William Bligh, will travel from Kent in England to Tahiti to meet Jacqui Christian, 44, from Pitcairn whose great-great-great-great grandfather Fletcher Christian was the leader of the mutiny. She will bring the stolen Bible with her and hand it to Mr Bligh, who, in an act of friendship, will return it to the Islanders, thereby, he says 'publicly ending the silly fictionalised feud between the Blighs and the Christians'. A report commissioned by the British government and produced by Wellington consultant Rob Solomon warned that '... Pitcairn is too isolated and it will never pay its own way.'

2015 In march the UK it will establish the largest, continuous marine reserve in the world, around the Pitcairn Islands. According to a report by the BBC the Pacific zone will cover 834,000 sq km (322,000 sq miles) - more than twice the land area of the British Isles. The intention is to protect the wealth of ocean life from illegal fishing activities. Somewhat ironically, considering the sex scandal of a few years ago, a new law came into effect of 15 May allowing same-sex marriage, even though it has no gay couples wanting to wed, or even gay couples.

Political structure

Constitution

The Pitcairn Order of 1970 and the Pitcairn Royal Instructions provide for the constitution. It established the office of governor, who is appointed by the British monarch.

The governor has full legislative authority and has the power to create laws, subject to approval by the monarch. The UK government has the power to legislate directly for Pitcairn Island.

A new constitution was declared in March 2010, following consultation with the islanders. It enshrines basic human rights and the provision of education up to the age of 15, as well as reasserting the constitutional arrangements for the island in respect to the UK.

Form of state

British dependent territory

The executive

The mayor, in conjunction with the Island Council, wields executive authority.

The non-resident commissioner of Pitcairn serves as liaison between the governor and the Island Council.

National legislature

The unicameral Island Council has 10 members. Five are directly elected, two spaces are left for the Mayor and Deputy Mayor. The Queen's representative appoints two members, one of which is the Island Secretary. The tenth council member is a commissioner who liaises between the governor and council. The council deals with internal matters and decisions made are implemented by an internal committee. The chairman and councillors are elected on 24 December each year. The Island Council also doubles as a court making it one of the few legislative bodies in the world to also hold judicial authority.

Legal system

The Island Court is presided over by the Island Magistrate elected every three years.

Last elections

12 November 2013 (general and mayoral)

Results: Mayoral: Shawn Christian defeated Simon Young after the third round of voting with 20 votes to 19.

Island Council: Charlene Warren, Darralyn Griffiths, David Brown, Michele Christian and Leslie Jacques were all elected

Next elections

2015 (mayoral and island council)

Political parties

There are no political parties.

Ruling party

All candidates are non-partisan

Political situation

The community has begun to rebuild both physically and metaphorically since the convictions of six men for sex offences in 2004. With the celebration of Bounty Day on 20 January 2008, which included families re-united and the women verses men tug-of-war (the women won), plus the UK government funded development to give the islanders more contact with the outside world with the construction of a slipway to allow boats to land, for which a scheduled boat services is planned, running from Mangareva in French Polynesia, six time per year, it is intended that the island's unhealthy isolation will be ended.

The population totalled 233 in 1937 but annual emigration, primarily to New Zealand, has reduced the figure to below 48. The population is ageing. All native islanders are related; other residents include a school teacher, a doctor, a religious minister and a seconded policeman.

Population

48 (2015)*

Last census: 1 July 2008: 66

Annual growth rate: Declined by 1.32 per cent in 2002.

Ethnic make-up

The inhabitants are mostly descendants of mutineers from the *Bounty*, and Tahitian women, who settled in Pitcairn in 1790.

Religions

Christian (Seventh-day Adventist).

Education

Island children go to school in New Zealand when they are 16 and few return.

Languages spoken

Pitkern (Pitcairn dialect – a mixture of English and Polynesian) uses many eighteenth century expressions.

Official language/s

English

Media

Press

The Pitcairn Islands Study Centre (PISC) publishes *Pitcairn Log* and the Online *Pitcairn News Page* (http://library.puc.edu/pitcairn/index.shtml), covering key news stories. The Pitcairn Islands Study Group (PISG) publishes a *UK Log* newsletter. With an English edition, the German *Mare* magazine publishes regular columns including items about Pitcairn.

Periodicals: The *Pitcairn Miscellany* (www.miscellany.pn), started in 1959, publishes monthly, with a circulation of over 3,000 sent to subscribers worldwide. The *Pitcairn Postcard Magazine* is an occasional publication illustrating Pitcairn Island postcards, for collectors and people interested in Pitcairn.

Economy

The inhabitants of this tiny isolated economy exist on fishing, subsistence farming, handicrafts and postage stamps. The fertile soil of the valleys produces a wide variety of agricultural products including citrus, sugarcane, watermelons, bananas, yams, and beans. The major sources of revenue are the sale of postage stamps to collectors and the sale of handicrafts to passing ships.

The major sources of public revenue are the sale of postage stamps. First introduced in 1940 to collectors. However following the global economic crisis there was a downturn in the market, which led to financial reserves being exhausted. Other possible sources of revenue include the sale of handicrafts to passing ships and the lease of the internet suffix '.pn'. A limited amount of honey is exported and, while Pitcairn's isolation means that the honey produced is pure and disease free, its distance from most markets limits its potential. The islanders have set up the Pitcairn Island Producer's Co-operative (PIPCO) to promote honey production.

Except for minor licences, there is no formal taxation – every person between the ages of 15–65 is required to perform public work each month, in lieu of taxation. Allowances and wages are paid to members of the community who participate in local government activities and who perform communal services. Local expenditure is estimated and controlled by the Island Council. The financial administration for Pitcairn Island is vested in the governor.

There is no price index maintained on the island and there are no statistics relating to external trade, GDP, trade balance etc. There is no retail trading except for a small co-operative store which was established on the island in 1967. Bartering is an important part of the economy. Modest and simple banking facilities are proposed, to allow islanders access to funds through the treasurer's office and made available for purchases in New Zealand.

External trade

Imports

The principal imports are fuel oil, machinery, building materials, textiles, flour, sugar and other foodstuffs.

Exports

The main exports are postage stamps, handicrafts, woodcarvings, basketry and honey. Fruit and vegetables are sold to visiting ships.

Agriculture

Farming

The island has highly fertile volcanic soil and rainfall is adequate. Main crops include a wide variety of fruits and vegetables, including citrus, sugar cane, watermelons, bananas, yams, beans and honey; which is said to have become a favourite of Queen Elizabeth II. Taro and coconuts are also grown. There is some goat and poultry rearing.

Fishing

Fish is caught for the islanders' own consumption.

Industry and manufacturing

The predominant industries include postage stamps, handicrafts, beekeeping and honey.

Tourism

The scope for tourism is limited as any visitor must arrive by sea and all transfers to land are via small boats which pull up a stone jetty – rough seas can impede landings.

Local residents have rooms to let and although there is one metalled road through the town, most people walk to their various destinations.

The islands are an important site for birdlife, with several groups of seabirds, wading birds and resident island birds, including the unique, flightless Henderson Crake.

Environment

Deforestation is a problem, caused by historic slash-and-burn agriculture and settlement.

Mining

Manganese, iron, copper, gold, silver, and zinc have been discovered offshore.

Hydrocarbons

There are no known hydrocarbon reserves and all petroleum needs are met by imports.

Energy

Electricity is produced by diesel generators, allowing 10 hours of electricity per day.

Time

GMT minus nine hours

Geography

The islands consist of Pitcairn Island and three uninhabited islands, Henderson, Ducie and Oeno. Pitcairn is situated about midway between Peru and New Zealand. The island is volcanic in formation and has a rocky coastline with cliffs. Pawala Valley Ridge, 347 metres, is the highest point.

Hemisphere

Southern

Climate

Subtropical and humid, with temperatures ranging from 13–30 degrees Celsius (C), averaging 18 degrees C in August and 24 degrees C in February. There are south-east trade winds. The rainy season runs from November to March with a possibility of typhoons. Rainfall varies, but can exceed 2,000mm per year.

Entry requirements

Passports

Required by all, valid for six months beyond the intended length of stay.

Visa

Required by all; referred to as a Licence to Land and Reside. This should be applied for, from the governor (Pitcairn Island Administration Office in Auckland), for visits up to six months. The application must include a certificate of good health, proof of return/onward passage, US$300 per week for maintenance and health insurance (including emergency repatriation). See http://www.government.pn/noticapp.htm for the full list of requirements.

Health (for visitors)

Mandatory precautions

Vaccination certificates are required for yellow fever if travelling from an infected area.

Advisable precautions

Vaccination is recommended for diphtheria, tuberculosis, hepatitis A and B, polio, tetanus and typhoid. There is a risk of rabies.

Public holidays (national)

Fixed dates

New Year's Day (1 Jan), Bounty Day (28 Apr), Christmas Day (25 Dec), Family Day (26 Dec).

Variable dates

Good Friday, Easter Monday, Early May Bank Holiday, Queen's Birthday (second Sat in Jun).

Telecommunications

External contacts used to be by SSB, wireless telegraphy, radio telephone and one satellite phone; some islanders are amateur radio enthusiasts. Since 2006 however, every home on the island has a telephone with broadband internet access, and live television broadcasts.

Getting there

Air

Pitcairn Island is not accessible by air. The nearest airstrip is on Mangareva, in French Polynesia, which is served weekly by Air Tahiti. Boats may be chartered to sail to Pitcairn.

Surface

Water: Cruise ships make brief stopovers and yachts may be chartered from Mangareva and Tahiti. Otherwise, the only shipping services are occasional supply and mail ships from New Zealand, which will accept passengers for Pitcairn. As there are no port facilities for large vessels, longboats are used to pick up mail, passengers, etc, and, consequently, contact and therefore landing may be prevented by adverse weather conditions.

Getting about

National transport

Road: There is only one paved road. The Hill of Difficulty from the Botany Bay jetty to Adamstown was formerly a dirt track, which became impassable in bad weather. It was surfaced in 2005. Other routes are still dirt tracks. Walking and all-terrain bikes are the principal means of getting about.

Water: In Bounty Bay, on the north side of the island, there is a slip for launching the islanders' longboats.

BUSINESS DIRECTORY

The addresses listed below are a selection only. While World of Information makes every endeavour to check these addresses, we cannot guarantee that changes have not been made, especially to telephone numbers and area codes. We would welcome any corrections.

Telephone area codes

The international direct dialling (IDD) code for Pitcairn Island is +124 followed by the subscriber's number.

Ministries

Pitcairn Islands Administration, PO Box 105-696, Auckland, New Zealand (tel: (+64-9)-366-0186; fax: (+64-9)-366-0187; e-mail: admin@pitcairn.gov.pn).

Other useful addresses

Pitcairn Islands Philatelic Bureau, PO Box 17184, Karori, Wellington, New Zealand (tel: (+64-4) 476-9507; fax: (+64-4) 476-9506; e-mail: stamps@pitcairn.gov.pn).

Pitcairn Island Producers Co-operative (PIPCO), PO Box 69, Adamstown, Pitcairn Island (Fax: (+872) 7612-24116).

Pitcairn Island Study Center, Pacific Union College, 1 Angwin Avenue, Angwin, CA 94508, USA (tel: (+1-202) 707-965-6625; fax: (+1-202) 707-965-6504; e-mail: hford@puc.edu).

Pitcairn Log, Editor Dr Everett L Parker, 719 Moosehead Lake Road, Greenville, ME 04441 9727, USA (e-mail: eparker@midmaine.com).

Internet sites

Pitcairn Island Study Centre: http://library.puc.edu/pitcairn/index.shtml

Pitcairn Island Web Site: http://www.lareau.org/pitc.html

Pitcairn Islands Office: http://www.pitcairn.pn

Pitcairn Islands Study Group: http://www.pisg.org

Pitcairn News: http://www.pitcairnnews.co.nz

Poland

KEY FACTS

Official name: Rzeczpospolita Polska (Republic of Poland)

Head of State: President Andrzej Sebastian Duda (Independent) (assumed office 6 Aug 2015)

Head of government: Prime Minister Designate Beata Szydlo (PO) (from 25 Oct 2015)

Ruling party: Prawo i Sprawiedliwosc (PiS) (Law and Justice Party) (elected 25 Oct 2015)

Area: 312,683 square km

Population: 38.02 million (2014)* (38,501,000; 2011, census figure)

Capital: Warsaw

Official language: Polish

Currency: Zloty (Zl) = 100 groszy

Exchange rate: Zl3.78 per US$ (Nov 2015)

GDP per capita: US$14,379 (2014)*

GDP real growth: 3.30% (2014)*

GDP: US$546.64 billion (2014)*

Labour force: 17.43 million (2012)*

Unemployment: 8.99% (2014)*

Inflation: -0.03% (2014)*

Natural gas production: 4.20 billion cum (2014)

Balance of trade: -US$6.87 billion (2012)

Annual FDI: US$15.30 billion (2011)

* estimated figure

In the run-up to Poland's October 2015 legislative elections, the principal interest in the May presidential elections lay in whatever clues they gave to the likely outcome in October. The front-runner in the presidential election was the incumbent Bronislaw Komorowski. The polls placed Mr Komorowski in first place, with 42 per cent of the vote, well ahead of his rival for the second, final round, the nationalist Andrzej Duda. Whereas the incumbent Komorowski advocated closer links with Europe and stiff resistance to the perceived threats emanating from Russia, Mr Duda appeared to hark back to a rose-tinted vision of a semi-soviet Poland where retirement ages would be lowered and benefits approved. Mr Duda's closest political model was Hungary's Viktor Orbán. Mr Duda, who had been snatched from anonymity earlier in 2015 by the authoritative leader of the Prawo i Sprawiedliwosc (PiS) (Law and Justice), Jaroslaw Kaczynski claiming to offer 'acceptable change' rather than any rejection of more liberal policies. However, many Poles could see through the smoke and mirrors to the same old 'anti-European' nationalism adopted by Mr Kacynski's government between 2005 and 2007. The 'dream team' of Mr Duda as president and Mr Kacynski as head of government had sent shivers down the spines of many Poles. On the PiS agenda was the repeal of the 'liberal' legislation that had allegedly brought Poland to its knees and further investigation into the alleged attack on the aircraft carrying Mr Kacynski's brother to Russia. Also to be addressed was the banning of abortions, the prohibition of homosexual partnerships and prison sentences for those carrying out in-vitro fertilisation.

What next?

The electoral victory of the PiS with 39.1 per cent of the vote, was more of a shock than a surprise. Some extreme responses hailed it as 'Polish Putinism' or 'The Orbánisation of the Vistula'. The British commentator, Timothy Garton Ash, noted that Poland was probably the European Union's biggest success in Eastern Europe, as well as the most powerful country east of Germany. The PiS party had won the parliamentary elections, according to Mr Garton Ash, for two reasons. The first could be put down to the time-honoured 'it's time for a change' slogan. The outgoing Platforma Obywatelska (PO) (Civic Platform), a liberal-conservative, Christian democratic party, had served Poland well for eight years, notching up an annual gross domestic product (GDP) growth rate of four per cent. However, in 2015, the PO administration had the appearance of a 'tired' government. The writing was on the wall when Andrezj Duda of the PiS defeated the government's presidential candidate, the incumbent Bronislaw Komorowski.

Secondly, the PiS had run a well organised and arresting electoral campaign prominently featuring their candidate (and later prime minister) Beata Szydlo. The real leader of the Pis party, Jaroslaw Kaczynski had decided not to run. In opinion polls he came across as 'old school', carrying the image of a disconnected politician. Ms Szydlo knew that her party had the support of Poland's rural communities – her campaign had focussed more on winning the votes of Poland's urban poor, many of whom found the PiS populist agenda chimed with their disgruntled political views. The PiS party had learnt from its short spell in government from 2005–07, when , under Mr Kaczynski as prime minister and his twin brother Lech as president, it managed to antagonise and irritate Poles from across the political spectrum. Lech Kaczynski was killed in a mysterious aircraft accident in 2010. The PiS advocated traditional values, as well as adhering to conservative views on sexuality (no abortion, or test-tube babies), as well as promoting an alarming xenophobia (no Muslim refugees).

The PiS election majority meant that it would be able to form a single party government, the first in Poland's 25 years of post communist history. The PiS had won 235 out of the 460 seats in the Senate or Sejm. The PiS gathered 37.6 per cent of the vote, the PO fell to 24.1 per cent. It remained to see whether it would be able to stick to its populist electoral promises. It's social welfare programme would certainly drain government coffers. One Polish economist had calculated that the proposed plan would lower GDP growth to around 0.5 per cent annually. The PiS' nearest thing to soul-mates in the European Parliament were the British Conservatives, or at least those of them who went so far as to share the PiS' rather extremist views. Quoted in the London *Economist*, a Polish political scientist advised that it was a mistake to call the PiS party 'conservative' – the party did not advocate 'small government', quite the opposite.

The economy

In its July 2015 assessment of the Polish Economy, the International Monetary Find (IMF) noted that the economy had recovered from its 2012–13 slowdown, supported by sound policies and improving external conditions. The outlook was for robust growth and subdued inflation but risks, although moderating, were tilted to the downside. In the view of the IMF, further structural reforms and stronger policy buffers would mitigate risks and ensure that the recovery was durable and balanced. Poland's strong interconnectedness with Europe through both trade and financial linkages had facilitated growth and income convergence and reduced inequality. However, it also exposed Poland to external shocks that could propagate through substantial foreign participation in the government bond market and in the banking system.

The IMF considered that Poland's recent policy interest rate cuts should help gradually return inflation to its target. However, the Monetary Policy Council (MPC) should be ready to further ease monetary policy if inflation expectations were to disappoint. The IMF considered that the financial sector remained profitable, well-capitalised and liquid. Credit growth was picking up. Addressing legacy vulnerabilities and completing financial sector reforms would further strengthen financial stability and support continued healthy credit expansion. Gradual fiscal consolidation should continue to build policy buffers and address long-term age-related contingent liabilities. The Polish authorities should, in the view of the IMF, also identify measures to underpin their fiscal plans. Over the previous two decades, Poland had succeeded in closing a quarter of its per capita income gap with the European Union (EU) average. Further boosting income levels and living standards requires structural reforms to move up the value-added chain and facilitate labour mobility to higher productivity sectors.

In the view of the European Bank for Reconstruction and Development (EBRD) the Polish economy was likely to continue to expand after the slow-down that was registered in 2013, although the turbulent external environment might, in the view of the EBRD, slow the pace of

KEY INDICATORS **Poland**

	Unit	2011	2012	2013	2014	**2015
Population	m	38.50	38.54	38.06	*38.02	*38.02
Gross domestic product (GDP)	US$bn	513.80	489.78	526.03	*546.64	*491.24
GDP per capita	US$	13,540	12,709	13,820	*14,379	*12,921
GDP real growth	%	4.4	1.9	1.7	*3.3	*3.5
Inflation	%	4.3	3.7	0.9	*0.0	*-0.8
Unemployment	%	12.8	10.1	10.3	*9.0	*8.0
Natural gas output	bn cum	4.3	4.2	4.2	4.2	–
Coal output	mtoe	56.6	58.8	57.6	55.0	–
Exports (fob) (goods)	US$m	195,209.0	188,408.0	197,787.0	–	–
Imports (fob) (goods)	US$m	209,245.0	195,276.0	196,954.0	–	–
Balance of trade	US$m	-14,036.0	-6,868.0	833.0	–	–
Current account	US$m	-25,023.0	-17,169.0	-6,988.0	*-6,675.0	*-8,861.0
Total reserves minus gold	US$m	100,929.3	103,396.2	102,235.9	964,615.0	–
Foreign exchange	US$m	98,325.9	100,316.9	99,336.9	–	–
Exchange rate	per US$	2.82	3.17	3.05	3.54	–

* estimated figure ** forecast figure

recovery. After relatively slow growth of 1.6 per cent in 2013, real GDP growth accelerated to 3.4 per cent in annual terms in the first half of 2014. However, the beginning of the third quarter brought some signs of deceleration, as evident in industrial production and retail sales, both of which started to lose momentum. Domestic demand was gradually becoming a more prominent driver of economic growth. Gross fixed capital investments picked up substantially in the first half of 2014 and were expected by the EBRD to strengthen further as the government moved into the new 2014–20 phase of European Union structural funds. An additional contribution might come from long-term investment projects. Low inflation rates and improved labour market conditions should also increase private consumption. Real GDP growth was forecast to average 3 per cent and 3.3 per cent in 2014 and 2015, respectively.

A key downside risk for the economy in 2015 was Russia's food import ban. Poland's export volumes to non-EU countries in emerging Europe had already shrunk in the first half of 2014. This trend was expected to be amplified by Russia's ban on food imports from the West, which came into effect in August 2014. Polish exports to Ukraine had declined by more than 25 per cent, while sales to Russia had dropped by 11 per cent over the first half of 2014. These two countries represented about 8.3 per cent of Poland's overall exports; foodstuffs banned by Russia accounted for only 0.5 per cent of total exports. However, the agribusiness sector was highly exposed (20 per cent of fruit and vegetable exports were destined for Russia) and confidence indicators had already deteriorated.

Stronger-than-expected growth, the transfer of certain pension assets and reduced contributions to private pension funds should benefit public finances. With the transfer of pension assets into the state-run social security system in February 2014, public debt was reduced by an estimated 8.6 per cent of GDP. As the government had, in the process, taken on additional pension liabilities, the overall effect on long-term public finances was unclear. Despite the positive windfall in the short term, Poland remained under the EU Excessive Deficit Procedure (EDP). However, an expected reduction in the deficit below 3 per cent of GDP in 2015 might allow Poland to exit the EDP.

The reform of Poland's pension system, which was first announced in September 2013, had been carried through. While this was of considerable benefit to the still-stretched public finances, the role of local institutional investors in providing long-term capital has been curtailed. Poland's 13 privately managed pension funds (OFEs) had transferred 51.5 per cent of their assets, consisting mainly of treasury bonds and treasury-guaranteed bonds, to the state-run Zaklad Ubezpieczen Spolecznych (ZUS) (Social Insurance Institution) in early February 2014. OFEs had been banned from investing in domestic or foreign government bonds. Nevertheless, they face fewer restrictions on their share of equity holdings. To continue diverting their social security contributions to the privately managed pension funds, some 16 million OFE members had to re-enrol in the system. However, by the end of July 2014, when this option came to an end, only about 15.4 per cent of members had done so. In addition, those approaching retirement within 10 years would gradually shift accumulated assets into the state-run system. The diminished contribution and gradual redemption therefore implied that in the coming years, the OFEs would be a net drain on Polish capital markets.

Most firms in Poland suffer from weak innovation performance, which was evident from the relatively low expenditures (0.9 per cent of GDP) in research and development (R&D), compared with the EU average of more than 2 per cent. In the EU's Innovation Union Scoreboard 2014, Poland ranked 25th (out of 28 EU member states) in terms of overall innovation performance. In Poland the state funds the major part of research expenditures and just over one-third comes from enterprises, compared with the EU average, where more than 63 per cent of total R&D expenditures comes from enterprises. Consequently, innovation may be poorly matched to the demands of businesses. Against this background the government had adopted an operational programme under the new phase of the EU structural and cohesion funds, roughly €10 billion (US$11.24 billion) of which was allocated to innovation over the following seven years and aimed to support national and regional innovation programmes.

Infrastructure investments were still expected by the EBRD to pick up. The government initiative of 2012 to stimulate investment through two state-backed entities had had a slow start, although it appeared to be taking off as the number of signed projects had grown since May 2013. The programme aimed to provide funding to viable infrastructure projects and in the process, catalyse long-term private capital without impairing public finances. The two pillars were Polskie Inwestycje Rozwojowe (PIR) (Polish Investment and Development SA), which were responsible for preparing and implementing infrastructure projects and the state development bank (Bank Gospodarstwa Krajowego (BGK)), which would enable an increase in the volume of new loans and guarantees up to Zl40 billion (approximately US$10.58 billion). PIR and BGK would both be gradually capitalised by shares of up to Zl10 billion (US$2.65 billion). At the same time, PIR, which operated on commercial terms, signed its first public-private partnership for oil exploration in the Baltic Sea in August 2014. Over 60 projects had been analysed, of which five were at an advanced stage. Recently, government officials had voiced scepticism over the efficacy of PIR in stimulating investment and might consider further institutional changes. The second package on professional deregulation was approved in May 2014. The package, which lowered barriers for 82 technical professionals (such as architects and building engineers) and financial market professionals (accountants, tax advisers, insurance agents, brokers and actuaries), would affect some 200,000 professionals. This deregulation formed part of the government's drive to accelerate structural reforms through cutting red tape and reducing legal barriers that grant monopolistic privileges to incumbents. Poland has the highest number of regulated professions in Europe. New shale gas regulations had been adopted based on expectations that exploration will speed up. The main aim of the new regulations was to attract investment in exploration in order to assess the potential of shale gas production in Poland in the long term (subject to environmental concerns and economic viability). The regulation was designed to encourage investors by cutting red tape and reducing regulatory hurdles. Therefore, the so-called special taxes in this sector (totalling up to 40 per cent of gross profits) would not be charged until 2020 and only a single type of concession for exploration and production was created, simplifying the three different forms previously available. The pace of shale gas exploration in Poland had slowed in 2013 with only half as many wells drilled compared with the previous year. This was mostly due to concerns over poor exploration results and regulations that had prompted some international companies to leave (including ExxonMobil,

Marathon Oil and Talisman). Poland was also striving to cut back its energy sector's reliance on Russia through a new liquefied natural gas terminal in Swinoujscie, originally scheduled for completion by mid-2015. This terminal would have a capacity of 5 billion cubic metres per year (one-third of Poland's annual consumption of natural gas). Poland's first nuclear power plant was expected to become operational by 2024. The government had adopted a national nuclear power programme that involved the construction of two nuclear power plants, each capable of producing 3GW of electricity. The first block was expected to be completed within ten years and the whole project was due to be finished by 2030. The investment would cost an estimated €12 billion (US$13.5 billion) and the work was expected to be done by a consortium of Polish energy companies led by the state controlled Polish company PGE. Coal still accounts for more than 80 per cent of Poland's primary energy supply and the nuclear power plants are seen as the most cost-effective ways of meeting the ambitious EU energy and climate goals.

Risk assessment

Economy	Good
Politics	Good
Regional security	Good

People to watch

Foreign Minister Radoslaw Sikorski

COUNTRY PROFILE

Poland's geographical position between east and west Europe has put it at the mercy of the great European powers.

1918 An independent republic was declared at the end of the First World War.

1919–21 The Polish-Russian War broke out in February 1919. After the Poles defeated the Russians during the Battle of Warsaw in August 1920, a peace treaty was eventually signed in April 1921.

1939 The Second World War began as Germany, with military assistance from the Soviet Union, invaded Poland. German forces occupied Poland until 1945, when the Soviet Union, now on the side of the Allies, liberated the country.

1945 After the end of the Second World War, Poland came under the Soviet Union's sphere of influence and it annexed Poland's eastern provinces. The Soviet Union established a puppet government in Poland, comprised mostly of communists of the Polskiej Partii Robotniczej (PPR) (Polish Workers' Party) and Polskiej Partii Socjalistycznej (PPS) (Polish Socialist Party). Communist rule did not end until 1989.

1948 The PPR and PPS merged to form the Polska Zjednoczona Partia Robotnicza (PZPR) (Polish United Workers' Party) to cement Poland's one-party political system.

1956 Riots due to food shortages resulted in the reinstatement of Wladyslaw Gomulka as the first secretary of the PZRP. Gomulka had been distrusted as too liberal in 1948. Liberalisation and some economic reform ensued.

1970 Food price strikes brought about the resignation of Gomulka, who was succeeded by Edward Gierek.

1980–82 The rise of the trade union, *Solidarnosc* (Solidarity), under Lech Walesa, followed strikes at the Gdansk, Gdynia and Szczecin shipyards. The right to form independent unions was recognised by the government. General Wojcieck Jaruzelski succeeded Gierek as PZPR leader. Serious unrest continued during the 1980s, including a period of martial law, the imprisonment of *Solidarnosc* leaders and the abolition of independent unions.

1987 Government plans for rapid economic reform necessitating further hardship were rejected in a referendum, but political reform was approved.

1988 A series of politically motivated strikes kept up pressure on the government for change.

1989 As the rule of communism ebbed semi-free elections for the national assembly were held. Seats for the Sejm were allocated one-third to communists, one-third to existing communist coalition partners and one-third were free-to-vote, the majority of which were won by supporters of *Solidarnosc*. Poland's Third Republic was declared on 19 July.

1990 Lech Walesa became Poland's first democratically elected president.

1991 The first completely free parliamentary elections were held, resulting in the election of a new centre-right government under Prime Minister Jan Olszewski. He was succeeded by Waldemar Pawlak, who was unable to form a government.

1992 Hanna Suchocka became prime minister (Poland's fifth prime minister since the end of communist rule in 1989).

1993 Suchocka resigned and elections, under the new 5 per cent threshold rule (parties not reaching this level of the vote are not eligible for parliamentary representation), reduced the number of parties in parliament. Voters opted for a slowdown in the pace of market-led economic reforms by bringing back the former communists – the Sojusz Lewicy Demokratycznej (SLD) (Democratic Left Alliance). A coalition government of the SLD and the Polskie Stronnictwo Ludowe (PSL) (Polish People's Party) was formed. Waldemar Pawlak of the PSL became prime minister.

1995 Aleksander Kwasniewski (SLD) was elected president.

1996 Poland became a member of the Organisation for Economic Co-operation and Development (OECD). A political wing of *Solidarnosc* was founded as the Akcja Wyborcza Solidarnosc (AWS) (Solidarity Electoral Action)

1997 A new constitution strengthened the powers of parliament. The AWS formed a centre-right coalition government with Unia Wolnosci (UW) (Freedom Union) after the election.

1999 Poland joined NATO.

2000 UW withdrew from the coalition government in order to slow pace of reform. Kwasniewski was re-elected president.

2001 After parliamentary elections, Leszek Miller, leader of the centre-left SLD, formed a left-wing coalition government with the Unia Pracy (UP) (Labour Union) and the PSL.

2003 The coalition split when the PSL was ejected from government after it refused to vote in favour of government legalisation. The SLD and UP carried on as a minority government.

2004 Poland joined the EU.

2005 The referendum on the EU constitution was postponed indefinitely. The Prawo i Sprawiedliwosc (PiS) (Law and Justice) party won 28 per cent of the vote. Lech Kaczynski was elected president and a new PiS minority government was formed with eight non-partisan members of parliament providing support; Kazimierz Marcinkiewicz became prime minister.

2006 The PiS party established a new ruling coalition with Samoobrona Rzeczypospolitej Polskiej (SRP) (Self-Defence of the Polish Republic) and Liga Polskich Rodzin (LPR) (League of Polish Families). Kazimierz Marcinkiewicz resigned as prime minister and was replaced by the president's twin brother, Jaroslaw Kaczynski. A new lustration law was introduced designed to purge ex-communist and communist collaborators from current positions of power.

2007 The Bishop of Warsaw resigned as Archbishop just hours after being appointed, following revelations that he had collaborated with the Polish communist secret police. The coalition government broke down, but a minority government remained in power. In snap parliamentary elections the opposition Platforma Obywatelska (PO) (Civic Platform) won. It immediately began talks to form a coalition and Donald Tusk became prime minister. Poland became a member of the European Union Schengen area whereby

all travellers may cross borders without a passport or visa.
2008 Prime Minister Donald Tusk announced that Poland aimed to join the euro-zone by 2011. Former Communist leader General Jaruzelski was put on trial for the imposition of martial law in 1981.
2009 Poland marked the anniversary of the doomed Warsaw uprising in 1944 when an estimated 250,000 civilians, 18,000 Polish fighters, and 17,000 Nazi troops were killed during two months of fighting. The city was virtually destroyed and around 500,000 residents were expelled by the occupying Nazi force.
2010 President Lech Kaczynski was killed in an aeroplane crash in Smolensk (Russia), along with all other passengers. He had been on his was to attend a memorial service for the Polish victims of the Katyn massacre in 1940. Bronislaw Komorowski was appointed acting president. After two rounds, Acting President, Bronislaw Komorowski (PO) won 52.63 per cent of the vote, Jaroslaw Kaczynski (PiS) 47.37 per cent. The European Commission reported that Poland had been the largest recipient of EU funds in 2009, receiving €6.5 billion (US$9.1 billion). The Russian Duma passed a resolution confirming that Josef Stalin had, according to papers kept in a secret archive, given the direct order for the massacre of 22,000 Polish officers in the Katyn massacre.
2011 An official report released in July, into the death of former president Lech Kaczynski, in the April 2010 plane crash in Russia, concluded that incorrect and confusing Russian instructions were as much to blame for the accident as Polish officials who applied undue pressure on the Polish pilots, even though they had insufficient experience in flying the Tupolev 154 airplane. In parliamentary elections, held in October, all 460 Sejm seats and all 100 Senate seats were in contention and for the first time the Senate was chosen by the first-past-the-post electoral system. The PO was returned to power with 39.18 per cent of the vote (206 seats out of 460) and the opposition Prawo i Sprawiedliwosc (PiS) (Law and Justice) won 32.11 per cent (158). Prime Minister Tusk remained in office.
2012 On 17 September the sale of liquor from the Czech Republic was banned, following a series of poisoning from bootleg liquor and the death of four; beer and wine was excluded from the ban.
2013 Four days of protests against propposted labour law changes ended on 14 September. The protesters were demanding a higher minimum wage and greater job security, as well as a repeal of the law raising the retirement age to 67.
2014 At an extraordinary EU Council meeting held on 30 August it was announced that Prime Minister Tusk would become the next President of the European Council. He resigned on 9 September and was succeeded by Ewa Kopacz on 22 September.
2015 In the first round of the 2015 presidential election held on 10 May Andrzej Sebastian Duda (PiS) came first with 34.76 per cent (5,179,092 votes) to 33.77 per cent (5,031,060) for incumbent Bronislaw Komorowski (Independent/PO) and 20.80 per cent (3,099,079) for Pawel Kukiz (Independent). In the second round held on 24 May Mr Duda won 51.55 per cent against the 48.45 per cent for Bronislaw Komorowski. Mr Duda resigned his party membership (of PiS) on 26 May and assumed office on 6 August. In the parliamentary elections held on 25 October the opposition Prawo i Sprawiedliwosc (PiS) (Law and Justice Party) won with 39.1 per cent, followed by the previous governing party, Platforma Obywatelsk (PO) (Civic Platform), with 23.4 per cent. Beata Szydlo was designated prime minister.

Political structure

Constitution

The 1952 constitution was amended in 1989 and 1990. Poland is divided into 49 regional *vovoids* (administrations).

Independence date

11 November 1918

Form of state

Parliamentary democratic republic

The executive

The president is head of state, directly elected by universal suffrage for a five-year term. The president has the power to dissolve parliament and nominates the prime minister. Supreme executive power is vested in the Council of Ministers, headed by the prime minister, responsible to the Sejm.

National legislature

The bicameral Zgromadzenie Narodowe (National Assembly) consists of the Sejm (lower house) with 460 members elected by proportional representation in multi-seat constituencies, and the Senat (Senate) with 100 members elected in 40, multi-seats constituencies. Members of both houses serve for four-year terms

Legal system

The apex of the legal structure is the Supreme Court, whose judges are elected by the State Council for five years. The Council also appoints a prosecutor general. Below the Supreme Court are district and special courts. Family courts deal with cases involving divorce and domestic relations.

Last elections

25 October 2015 (parliamentary); 10 and 24 May 2015 (presidential: first round and runoff)

Results: Parliamentary (Sejm) 2015: Prawo i Sprawiedliwosc (PiS) (Law and Justice Party) 37.6 per cent, Platforma Obywatelska (PO) (Civic Platform) 24.1 per cent.
Presidential: in the first round held on 10 May 2015 Andrzej Duda won 34.76 per cent of the vote, followed by incumbent President Bronislaw Komorowski with 33.77 per cent and independent Pawel Kukiz with 20.80 per cent. As no candidate achieved 45 per cent, a run off was held on 24 May between Mr Duda and President Komorowski. The result was a win for Mr Duda with 51.5 per cent to Mr Komorowski's 48.5 per cent.

Next elections

2020 (presidential); October 2019 (parliamentary)

Political parties

Ruling party

Coalition government led by Platforma Obywatelska (PO) (Civic Platform) (since 2007; re-elected 9 Oct 2011)

Main opposition party

Platforma Obywatelska (PO) (Civic Platform) (from October 2015)

Population

38.53 million (2013) (38,501,000
Last census: 31 March 2011: 38,501,000
Population density: 127 inhabitants per square km. Urban population 61 per cent (2010 Unicef).
Annual growth rate: 0.0 per cent, 1990–2010 (Unicef).

Ethnic make-up

Poland is one of the most ethnically uniform countries in Europe. The non-Polish population, including Ukrainians, Germans and Russians, accounts for only 1.3 per cent of the total population.

Religions

The population is predominantly Roman Catholic. There are small communities of Protestants, Orthodox Christians and Jews.

Education

Public expenditure on education is typically equivalent to 7.5 per cent of annual GNP, including subsidies to private education at the primary, secondary and tertiary levels.
Education is provided free of charge; primary schooling lasts for eight years followed by secondary, academic and technical or vocational qualifications. Under the former communist state, technical education was biased towards heavy industries and the decline of these industries has left large sections of the mature workforce in need of retraining. Current government aims are to improve education and information technology skills as part of its long-term growth programme.

Students attending Poland's most prestigious universities must pass a tough entrance exam. Since 1990, over 280 private universities have opened, providing an extra 50,000 graduates for the employment market. Typical fees for private universities can vary from US$530 (the average monthly wage), up to US$1,855 per annum, for high cost subjects like medicine.

Compulsory years: 7 to 14

Enrolment rate: 96 per cent gross primary enrolment,98 per cent gross secondary enrolment, of relevant age groups (including repeaters) (World Bank).

Pupils per teacher: 15 in primary schools.

Health

Primary healthcare is provided by a network of healthcare centres and specialist physicians. Initial reforms during the 1990s started with the decentralisation of healthcare (mostly primary care) and the introduction of new payment mechanisms to doctors. This led to a range of publicly subsidised private providers.

The concept of primary healthcare is now based on family medicine. Clinics are run by family practitioners who provide a wide range of healthcare services, or make referals to contracted specialists. Development according to this model has signalled movement towards the privatisation of state-owned primary healthcare. Private healthcare services are provided to eligible individuals via contracts with sickness funds.

A common form of mobile healthcare delivery is the non-public clinic (*npzoz*), which typically employs two or more doctors. The high investment cost has limited the number of private hospitals to gynaecological and surgical clinics.

HIV/Aids

HIV prevalence: 0.1 per cent aged 15–49 in 2003 (World Bank)

Life expectancy: 75 years, 2004 (WHO 2006)

Fertility rate/Maternal mortality rate: 1.4 births per woman, 2010 (Unicef); maternal mortality 8 per 100,000 live births (World Bank).

Child (under 5 years) mortality rate (per 1,000): 5 per 1,000 live births (WHO 2012)

Head of population per physician: 2.47 physicians per 1,000 people, 2003 (WHO 2006)

Welfare

Poland has operated a dual state-run social insurance system and a mandatory private insurance system since 1999. The system, for those under the age of 30, who are obliged to join, consists of a modified social insurance and individual accounts.

Social insurance covers employees, members of co-operatives, self-employed artisans, homeworkers, lawyers and clergy. Special systems exist for independent farmers.

Poland is unique among the former Soviet bloc countries in creating Kasa Rolniczego Ubezpiecznia Spolecznego (KRUS) (Office of Rural Social Insurance), a farmers' social security system, distinct and separate from the workers' system.

Main cities

Warsaw (capital, estimated population 1.7 million in 2012), Krakow (754,095), Lodz (725,658), Wroclaw (627,562), Poznan (549,403), Gdansk (449,794), Szczecin (401,343), Bydgoszcz (351,345), Lublin (347,159).

Languages spoken

There is a small German-speaking community and German is widely understood and spoken. Kashubian, Ukrainian and Belarusian are also spoken. English and French are used in business circles.

Official language/s

Polish

Media

Press

Dailies: In Polish, the leading newspapers are *Rzeczpospolita* (www.rzeczpospolita.pl), *Gazetta Wyborcza* (www.gazetawyborcza.pl), with English online version and *Trybuna Slaska* (www.trybuna.com.pl). Other, mainly tabloids, include *Super Express*, (www.se.com.pl), *Dziennik* (www.dziennik.pl), *Fakt* (http://efakt.pl) and regional newspapers including *Gazeta Krakowie* (www.gk.pl) Krokaw, *Glos Wielkopolski* (www.glos.com) Pozan, *Kurier Szczecinski* (www.kurier.szczecin.pl) Szczecin, *Dziennik Baltycki* (www.dziennikbaltycki.pl) Gdansk, and *Zycie Warszawy* (*Life*) (www.zw.com.pl) Warsaw.

Weeklies: In Polish, the most influential weeklies are *Polityka* (polityka.onet.pl), *Wprost* (*News*) (www.wprost.pl), *Gazeta Polska* (www.gazetapolska.pl) and *Newsweek Polska* (www.newsweek.pl). Others include *Nie* (satirical), *Przyjaciolka* (womens' magazine), *Poradnik Domowy* (home ideas). Sports magazines, TV/radio guides and youth magazines are also widely available.

Business: In Polish, newspapers include *Parkiet* (www.parkiet.com) and *Puls Biznesu* (www.pb.pl). The most influential periodicals are *Gazeta Bankowa* (*Bankers' Weekly*) (www.gazetabankowa.pl), *Zycie Gospodarcze* (www.nzq.pl) (economic weekly), *Rynki Zagraniczne* (www.rynkizagraniczne.pl) (three per week; foreign trade), *Gazeta Prawna* (*Legal Gazette*) and *Handel Zagraniczny* (*Foreign Trade*). In English, *The Warsaw Voice* (www.warsawvoice.pl), *Polish Market* (http://polishmarket.com.pl) and *Warsaw Business Journal* (www.wbj.pl).

Broadcasting

Radio: There are many public and commercial radio stations. The public broadcaster, Polskie Radio, operates six nationally channels including an external service broadcasting in several languages including English (www.polskieradio.pl/zagranica/gb).

There are around six commercial radio networks broadcasting locally and nationally in FM and AM.

Television: The national broadcasting corporation is Telewizja Polska Spólka Akcyjna (TVP SA, known as PTV), with three commercial channels, broadcasting general programmes with an additional four speciality channels. International, satellite and pay-for-TV networks are also available.

Polska Agencja Prasowa (PAP), ul. Bracka 6/8, 00502 Warsaw, (tel: 628-001, 628-0710; internet: www.pap.pl).

Economy

Poland has a long tradition of heavy industry in coal, iron and steel, including shipbuilding, petrochemicals and vehicle assembly as well as textiles. Its service industries include information technologies and accounting centres for international companies. It also exports meat, dairy produce, fruit, vegetables and processed foods, including confectioneries.

The Polish economy was the eighth largest in the EU in 2014. It maintained economic growth throughout the global economic crisis and avoided going into recession. Poland had the highest growth rates in Europe in the period 2005–2014, at around 46 per cent. Growth was maintained in 2011 at 4.4 per cent. The following years showed a second shrink in growth, at 1.9 per cent in 2012 and a further decrease to 1.7 per cent in 2013. Growth rebounded in 2014 as the economy achieved a growth rate of 3.4 per cent.

Poland will reach the highest average growth rate among all big EU economies until 2050. The real average annual GDP growth in Poland by that time will likely reach some 2.7 per cent or 2.9 per capita. However, this consistent growth is not an accurate indication of some of the aspects of its economy. Poland suffers from chronic high unemployment, low wages (highest percentage of population working for national minimum wage in the EU) and a massive flight of educated population abroad.

The structure of the economy is dominated by the service sector at 63.5 per cent of GDP, with industry providing 31.2

per cent, of which manufacturing accounts for 18 per cent, and agriculture at 4 per cent.

Economic reforms, beginning in the 1990s, have resulted in a comprehensive move from the previously centrally planned economy to a market orientated economy, with the sale of small-and medium-sized state entities. However, the government kept control of what it considered strategic industries, such as energy and the railways, as well as those unattractive to a potential buyer through privatisation.

Investment and restructuring, encouraged by foreign direct investment (FDI) (US$12 million net inflow in 2013), has improved the steel and energy sectors, although problems still remain in turning around other sectors.

External trade

As a member of the EU, Poland operates within a community-wide free trade area, with tariffs set as a whole. Internationally, the EU has free trade agreements with a number of nations and trading blocs worldwide.

Manufacturing represents around 19 per cent of GDP, of which almost 75 per cent is foreign trade. Recent predominant imports have been capital goods for industrial retooling. Poland's industrial sector produces vehicles, machinery, telecommunications, building supplies and processed food.

Imports

Main imports include machinery and transport equipment, petroleum and lubricants, intermediate manufactured goods and raw materials, chemicals, minerals and related materials.

Main sources: Germany (21.7 per cent of total in 2014), Russia (10.8 per cent), China (10.6 per cent)

Exports

Main exports include machinery and transport equipment, intermediate manufactured goods, miscellaneous manufactured goods, food and live animals.

Main destinations: Germany (25.9 per cent of total in 2014), UK (6.4 per cent), Czech Republic (6.3 per cent)

Agriculture

Farming

Poland's large agricultural sector remains handicapped by structural problems, surplus labour, small farms and a lack of investment. There are about 2 million small private farms averaging eight hectares in size. Production is concentrated in livestock farming (dairy and pigs), cereals, potatoes, sugar beet and oilseed. Pork and poultry output has increased considerably. The agricultural sector contributes around 4 per cent to GDP and employs around a quarter of the workforce.

The agricultural sector is subject to the reformed Common Agricultural Policy (CAP), whereby subsidies are no longer paid on farm output, which tended to benefit large farms and encourage overproduction, but rather on single farm payments not conditional on production.

The agricultural sector employs around 27 per cent of the workforce and contributes around 6 per cent to GDP. The government's agricultural policy was largely dictated by the need to join the EU's Common Agricultural Policy (CAP) over a 10-year transition period. Poland is a net importer of food and its membership of the CAP is likely to have a positive impact on EU finances. However, there is deep resentment among Polish farmers that they will not receive the same level of subsidies as their Western counterparts on entry to the EU.

Poland is a major exporter of meat, dairy produce, fruit, vegetables and processed foods, including confectioneries.

In 2013, Poland exported US$27 billion of agriculture products, which was an increase of 11.5 per cent on 2012. Growth has risen by a further 10 per cent in 2014. Only US$19 billion of agriculture products were imported, leaving the sector with a healthy trade balance of US$8 billion. Growth in 2015 will be an estimated 10 per cent.

Fishing

Poland has no immediate access to oceanic fishing grounds, but it has its own deep-sea fleet, which has been granted an EU export licence. It has about 44 fish processing plants regulated by EU requirements.

There is a very low level of fish consumption in Poland; only an estimated 3 per cent of household spending is spent on seafood and fresh water fish.

Forestry

Forests account for less than 33 per cent of Poland's land area. Over 90 per cent of forested land is available for wood supply and the most common species are coniferous, mostly Scots pine. Pollution and insect infestation has degraded much of the forestry resources, although the government has attempted to repair the damage by placing most of the forests under protection. Only the Bialowieza primeval forest is excluded from harvesting.

Industry and manufacturing

The industrial and manufacturing sectors form the mainstay of the economy, accounting for just over a third of GDP.

Heavy export-based industries dominate, such as shipbuilding, metallurgy (particularly steel), chemicals, motor vehicles and cement. The 1990s saw growth in sectors such as electronics and light industries, while food processing, glass, beverages, textile and forestry industries are also significant. The Polish car market is the sixth largest in Europe behind Germany, Italy, France, UK and Spain. The best investment opportunities are considered to be in food, textiles, timber, paper, mechanical engineering and furniture.

The steel sector was the focus of early restructuring plans in preparation for entry to the EU. Progress has been slow due to opposition from trade unions.

Industrial production grew by 3.5 per cent in 2014.

Tourism

Tourist development in Poland has improved steadily, with its many varied attractions to encourage visitors. Not only do large numbers visit Warsaw, Cracow (the former capital of Poland) and other cities, the Baltic Sea and Tatra Mountains, there are specialist destinations such as the historic, late medieval timber board and shingle churches of southern (Lesser) Poland, royal palaces and monuments to the destruction suffered during World War Two, particularly Auschwitz-Birkenau state Museum. Visitor numbers averaged around 15 million in 2014.

Travel and tourism experienced negative growth averaging -2.4 per cent over the period 2008–10. In 2008, the sector accounted for 5.2 per cent of GDP, which fell to 5 per cent in 2009. Since then it has steadily risen, reaching 4.4 per cent in 2014, supplying work to 4.3 per cent of the population (669,500 jobs) in the same year. Investment was 3.7 per cent of total investment in 2014.

Environment

Cutting pollution was a condition for Poland's entry into the EU.

While industry has tackled its pollution domestic consumers burn coal in boilers and fires, and more people are buying cars to add to the growing traffic jams on Poland's roads (motor vehicle population is expanding at 30 per cent a year).

Mining

Rich mineral resources include the largest deposits of copper ore in Europe and substantial deposits of coal, zinc-lead ores, sulphur and salt. Lesser deposits include nickel and precious metals such as silver.

Poland's oil reserves are small and it relies on crude oil imports for some 98 per cent of its domestic demands, mostly from Russia. Total proven oil reserves stood at 100 million barrels as of 2014.

Total natural gas reserves stood at 3 trillion cubic feet (cum) in 2014 and production was 219 billion cubic feet in 2013. Gas production meets around 30 per cent of local needs.

Poland also has reserves of sulphur, copper, lead and zinc.

Hydrocarbons
The state-owned Polskie Górnictwo Naftowe i Gazownictwo (PGNiG) is responsible for all aspects of hydrocarbons including exploration, production, import and storage. It owns around 16,400km of transmission pipelines. PGNiG operates the few, small onshore oil fields that Poland has, and also the B3 Oil Field 80km off the Polish coastal town Rozewie in the Baltic Sea.
Construction of a liquefied natural gas (LNG) regasification terminal at Swinoujscie began in 2011. The project developed by Gaz-System is predicted to be completed by the end of 2014 and will initially have a capacity of 5 billion cubic metres (cum). There are plans to build a third tank after completion, extending capacity to 7.5 billion cum, supplying 50 per cent of Poland's annual gas demands.

In October 2010, an agreement was reached with Russia's Gazprom for the supply of 10 billion cum of gas a year from 2012–22. There are concerns that this will make Poland over-dependent on Russia.
Kompania Weglowa is one of the largest coal mining companies in Europe, operating 23 mines. The majority of Poland's coal is the commercially valuable anthracite and exports, mostly to Europe, are a major source of foreign exchange. At 97 per cent of the country's primary energy production and 65 per cent of electricity generation, coal is the dominant source of energy.
Though the Polish coal industry has been in decline for the last two decades it still generates about 65 per cent of Polish electricity and employs over 100,000 people. Prime Minister Donald Trusk proposed a 'rehabilitation of coal' in 2014.The pledge aimed at promoting and protecting Polish coal. This attempt is to reduce the European Union's dependence on Russian exports.

Energy
Total installed electricity capacity is 33 gigawatts (GW), with peak-demand at around 24GW. Coal-fired power pants are located at mine heads, where the country's entire lignite (brown coal) production is used to generate electricity. Poland exports over 16 billion kilowatt hours (kWh) to neighbouring countries. In 2013 the government expected to raise as much as US$913 million by selling a 34.2 per cent share in Energa, a state owned power generator. The sale of shares will leave the government with a 50 per cent share in the company.

Financial markets
Stock exchange
Gielda Papierów Wartosciowych w Warszawie (Warsaw Stock Exchange) (WSE)
Commodity exchange
Warszawska Gielda Towarown (WGT) (Warsaw Commodity Exchange)

Banking and insurance
Banks are moving into new areas, such as investment banking, retail banking and asset management. Foreign banks have increased their involvement in the sector – over 70 per cent of Polish banking assets are administered by foreign companies. In the period 2000–05 the banking sector expanded by 14 per cent per annum as foreign competition increased and banking services attracted more customers.
Central bank
Narodowy Bank Polski (NBP) (National Bank of Poland)
Main financial centre
Warsaw

Time
GMT plus one hour (daylight saving, late March to late October, GMT plus two hours)

Geography
Poland is situated to the north of Central Europe, with Germany to the west, the Czech Republic to the south-west, Slovakia to the south and the Russian Federation enclave around Kaliningrad on the Baltic coast to the north. There is a short border with Lithuania to the north-east and Belarus lies beyond the northern part of the eastern border and Ukraine the southern. Poland has a 520km coastline along the Baltic Sea to the north-west. The country's borders are marked by the Odra and Neisse rivers in the west, the River Bug in the east, the Sudetic Mountains in the south-west and the Carpathian range of mountains in the south-east.
The highest point in the country is 2,499 metres at Rysy on the border with Slovakia. The two major rivers are the Odra and the Vistula which rise in the Sudetic and Carpathian mountains respectively, along the southern borders, and flow into the Baltic Sea.
Hemisphere
Northern

Climate
Poland has a continental climate with cold winters and warm summers. The mountainous regions of the south have a long, cold winter and a relatively short summer. Areas around the Baltic are warmer, with an average temperature of minus one degree Celsius (C) in January and 18 degrees C in July. Southern Poland has annual rainfall of more than 1,500mm, while the rest of the country experiences moderate rainfall of 500–650mm per year. The Vistula and Odra rivers are usually frozen for about two months each year.

Dress codes
Dress codes are generally similar to western European. Lightweight clothing is required from June to August, medium to heavyweight for the rest of year, plus a heavy topcoat in winter.

Entry requirements
Visitors are required to possess sufficient funds for stay, Zl100 per day (or foreign equivalent) and Zl300 per day for medical expenses (or valid insurance).
Passports
Required by all, except members of the EU, EEA and Switzerland who may use a valid national ID card. Passports must be valid for at least three months from date of arrival.
Visa
Required by all, except nationals of EU and Schengen area signatory countries, North America, Australasia and Japan. For further exceptions contact the nearest embassy. A Schengen visa application (offered in several languages) can be downloaded from http://europa.eu/abc/travel/ see 'documents you will need'. For details of those who must apply for a visa see www.polandembassy.org and follow link from *consular services* to *visas for Poland*. Contact the nearest embassy consular section for further information and application form.
Those business people who require a visa should have a formal invitation from a local company or organisation giving specific details regarding the purpose and duration of the intended trip. Also required are a company letter from the applicant's employer regarding his/her status, proof of financial means and receipt of payment for full board accommodation, and return/onward passage.
Currency advice/regulations
The import or export of local currency is limited to the equivalent of eur10,000. The import and export of foreign currency is unlimited, although all amounts must be declared on entry.
Travellers cheques are accepted in larger bank branches only.
Customs
Personal items, including one example of electronic items, are duty-free. There are no duties levied on alcohol and tobacco between EU member states, providing amounts imported are for personal consumption.
Artistic items dated before 1945 should have customs clearance before export.

Prohibited imports
Illegal drugs, poisons and explosives. Plants and animals are restricted. Firearms and ammunition require a permit.

Health (for visitors)
Nationals of the European Economic Area (EEA) countries and Switzerland can access reduced cost and sometimes free medical treatment using a European Health Insurance Card (EHIC) while visiting the EEA. Exceptions include nationals of the 10 countries, which joined the EU in 2004, whose EHIC is not valid in Switzerland. Applications for the EHIC should be made before travelling.

Mandatory precautions
None.

Advisable precautions
Hepatitis A, tetanus and polio immunisations. Rabies is a health risk.

Hotels
Most locally run hotels belong to the Orbis hotel chain and are classified one- to four-star. Internationally run chains include the Intercontinental, Holiday Inn and Novotel. Accommodation can be scarce in all main towns, so it is advisable to book well in advance. In an emergency a large travel agency or airline may be able to provide a hotel room. Bills include a 10 per cent service charge; tipping around 10 per cent is customary.

Credit cards
International credit cards are accepted where displayed signs are shown.

Public holidays (national)
Fixed dates
1 Jan (New Year's Day), 1 May (Labour Day), 3 May (National Day), 15 Aug (Assumption Day), 1 Nov (All Saints' Day), 11 Nov (Independence Day), 25–26 Dec (Christmas).

Variable dates
Easter Monday (Mar/Apr), Corpus Christi (May/Jun).

Working hours
Banking
Mon–Fri: 0800–1800.
Polski Bank Kredytowy, Warsaw Okecie airport Mon–Fri: 0730–1700, Sat: 0730–1130. Banks at Katowice Pyrzowice airport Mon–Fri: 0830–1500.

Business
Mon–Fri: 0800–1600.

Government
Mon–Fri: 0800/0900–1500/1600.
Post Offices, Mon–Fri: 0800–2000.

Shops
Mon–Fri: 1100–1900; Sat: 1000–1500, general shops.
Mon–Fri: 0600/0700–1800/1900, food shops.
Commercial companies and shops, other than food shops, close on 'Free Saturdays' which vary between businesses, but usually three per month (one for shops).

Telecommunications
Mobile/cell phones
There are GSM 900/1800 and a 3G services available throughout country with more 3G services planned.

Electricity supply
Domestic 220V AC, 50 cycles; adaptor need for continental-type, round two-pin sockets.

Weights and measures
Metric system

Social customs/useful tips
Organisations do not stop for lunch in the middle of the day. The main meal *obiad* is taken from 1500. Formal address in the Polish language is expected. Polite small talk is appreciated as a prelude to talking business.

Security
Poland has no particular problem with security and street crime, although since the collapse of communism, street crime has increased. Normal precautions should be followed.

Getting there
Air
National airline: LOT Airlines (Polskie Linie Lotnicze)
International airport/s: Warsaw-Okecie (WAW), 10km south-west of the city (20–40 minutes by bus; 20–30 minutes by taxi); duty-free shops, post office, banks and *bureaux de change*, bars and restaurants, left-luggage, tourist information and car hire.
Other airport/s: Kraków-Balice (John Paul II International) (KRK), 11km from the city. Wroclaw-Strachowice (WRO), 10 km from the city. Katowice International (KTW), 34km from the city. Gdansk-Trojmaaaiasto (GDN), 10km from the city.
Airport tax: None

Surface
Road: Access is best through Germany and the Czech Republic. All vehicle documentation should include car registration, driver's national driving licence and valid Green Card motor insurance. An International Driving Permit is also required.
Rail: EuroCity rail services from Western Europe pass through Germany (from Berlin, travelling time is approximately 80 minutes), the Czech Republic or the Slovia Republic. Main lines also link Warsaw with Cologne, Vienna, Budapest and Prague. There are car-sleeper services from the Hook of Holland to Poznan/Warsaw.
Water: Pol Ferries operates between Poland and Sweden, Denmark and Finland.

Getting about
National transport
Air: LOT operates regular services connecting all major cities.
Road: Approximately 154,000km surfaced roads, of which 80 per cent are main roads.
The motorways include a north-south expressway, the Polish section of the Helsinki-Warsaw highway, known as the Via Baltica, and an expressway from Golonice to Opole.
Buses: Extensive bus and coach services are operated by Polish Motor Communications (PKS) and Polski Express.
Rail: There are approximately 30,000km of track. Some lines are narrow-gauge, and some are steam-hauled. Diesel is typical with only 33 per cent of the lines electrified. Regular services are operated by Polskie Koleje Panstwowe (PKP) (Polish State Railways), connecting major towns. Intercity express trains are inexpensive and reliable.
Polrailpass tickets valid for between 8–30 days are available from travel agents and railway offices, both locally and internationally. For an additional sum tickets for sleeping berths are available.
Water: About 4,000km of navigable inland waterways, including about 400km of canals. Ferries and hydrofoils link Baltic resorts in summer.

City transport
Taxis: Metered taxis are available in all main towns; they can be hired from ranks or ordered by phone. Payment in hard currency may be required; tipping is usual. A surcharge is imposed for journies between 2300–0500, out of town, and at weekends.
Buses, trams & metro: Regular public transport operates 0530–2300. Good bus services in all towns, also trams in some. Tickets for Warsaw can be bought at RUCH kiosks and used indiscriminately. In Warsaw seven-day tram tourist tickets can be bought at 37 Senatorska Street (entrance E) (Mon–Wed: 0730–1700, Thu–Fri: 0730–1400).
A metro is in operation in Warsaw.

Car hire
A hirer must be over 21 and have held a full licence for a year. Rental firms are available in all main towns through Orbis. International driving licence and insurance cover recommended. Minimum renting period is 24 hours. Payment is by cash or credit card. Speed limits: built-up areas 60kph, normal roads 90kph, motorways 100kph.

BUSINESS DIRECTORY
The addresses listed below are a selection only. While World of Information makes every endeavour to check these addresses, we cannot guarantee that

changes have not been made, especially to telephone numbers and area codes. We would welcome any corrections.

Telephone area codes

The international direct dialling code (IDD) for Poland is +48, followed by area code and subscriber's number:

Bialystok	85	Lódz	42
Bydgoszcz	52	Lublin	81
Gdansk	58	Poznan	61
Katowice	32	Szczecin	91
Kraków	12	Warsaw	22
Leszno	65	Wroclaw	71

Useful telephone numbers

Ambulance: 999
Police emergency service: 997
Fire Brigade: 998
Customs information: 694-5596
Central Tourist Information Office: 270-000
Intercity directory assistance: 912
Local directory assistance: 911/913
Radiotaxi: 919 (complaints 224-444)

Chambers of Commerce

American Chamber of Commerce in Poland, Warsaw Financial Centre, 53 ulica Emilii Plater, 00-113 Warsaw (tel: 520-5999; fax: 520-5998; e-mail: office@amcham.com.pl).

British-Polish Chamber of Commerce, 2 ulica Zimna, 100-138 Warsaw (tel: 654-5971; fax: 621-1937; e-mail: bpcc@bpcc.org.pl).

Banking

AmerBank, Marszalkowska 115, 00-102 Warsaw.

American Express Bank, ul Krakowskie Przedmiescie 11, 00-068 Warsaw.

Bank Gospodarki Zywnosciowej (commercial bank), ul Grzybowska 4, 00-131 Warsaw.

Bank Polska Kasa Opieki SA (Grupa Pekao), Grzybowska 53/57, PO Box 1008, 00-950 Warsaw (tel: 656-0000; fax: 656-0004; e-mail: info@pekao.com.pl).

Bank Przemyslowo-Handlowy (Bank BPH), ul Na Zjezdzie 11, 30-527 Krakow.

Bank Rozwoju Eksportu SA (export development bank), PO Box 728, Bankowy 2, 00-950 Warsaw (tel: 829-0000; fax: 829-0081).

Bank Zachodni we Wroclawiu (Western Bank in Wroclaw), 41–43 Ofiar Oswiecimskich St, 50-850 Wroclaw.

Bre Bank SA, ul Senatorska 18, PO Box 728, PL 00-950 Warsaw (tel: 829-0000; fax: 829-0033).

Citibank, ul. Senatorska 12, 00-082 Warsaw (tel: 657-7200).

Creditanstalt, ul Prosta 69, 00-838 Warsaw (tel: 637-9000; fax: 637-9099).

ING Bank, ul. Emilii Plater 28 pietro 7, 00-950 Warsaw (tel: 630-5695).

Lodzi Bank Rozwoju SA, PO Box 465, ul Piotrkowska 173, 90-950 Lodz.

National Credit Bank, Nowy Swiat 6–12, 00-950 Warsaw (tel: 210-321; fax: 296-988).

Polski Bank Rozwoju SA (Polish development bank), ul Zurawia 47–49, 00-680 Warsaw (tel: 628-0490, 628-0790; fax: 628-6164; (Saturday 2120-828); satellite phone and fax: (39) 120-828, 120-844).

Powszechny Bank Gospodarczy w Lodzi, Pilsudskieo 12, 90-950 Lodz (tel: 361-470, 362-886; fax: 362-870).

Powszechna Kasa Oszczednosci Bank Panstwowy (state savings bank), ul Swietokrzyska 11–21, 00-950 Warsaw (tel: 220-0321, 226-3839; fax: 226-3863).

WBK (Wielkopolski Bank Kredytowy SA), 60-967 Posnan Place, Wolnosci 16 (tel: 56-4900; fax: 52-1113).

Central bank

Narodowy Bank Polski, ul Swietokrzyska 11/21; PO Box 1011, 00-919 Warsaw (tel: 653-1000; fax: 620-8518; e-mail: nbp@nbp.pl).

Stock exchange

Gielda Papierów Wartosciowych w Warszawie (Warsaw Stock Exchange) (WSE), www.gpw.pl

Commodity exchange

Warszawska Gielda Towarown (WGT) (Warsaw Commodity Exchange), www.wgt.com.pl

Travel information

Central Bus Station, Warszawa Zachodnia Aleje Jerozolimskie 144 (tel: 236-394/6).

Central Railway Station, Warszawa Centralna 54 Aleje Jerozolimskie (tel: 255-001, 255-000).

Foundation for Tourism Development, Ul Mazowiecka 7, 00059 Warsaw (tel: 269-238; fax: 269-695).

International train connections – information (tel: 204512); local train connections – information (tel: 200-361).

LOT, Aleje Jerozolmskie 6579, 00-697 Warsaw (reservations in Poland, tel: 0801-703-703; fax: 630-5229); airport information in Warsaw (tel: 650-4220); internet: www.lot.com).

Lufthansa Warsaw Airport Office (tel: 650-4510); town office, Al Jerozolimskie 56c, Warsaw (tel: 630-2555; fax: 630-2535); Katowice Airport Office (tel: 184-5045); town office Al Korfantego 51, Katowice (tel: 106-2443; fax: 106-2444).

Orbis, 16 Bracka Street, 00-028 Warsaw (tel: 829-3939; fax: 827-3301).

State Sports and Tourism Administration, Swietokrzyska 12, 00916 Warsaw (fax: 694-5176).

Warsavawfie Centrum Informacji Gurwstycznej (Warsaw Tourist Information Centre), Zankowy Square 1/13, 00-262 Warsaw (tel: 635-1881).

Ministry of tourism

National Administration of Tourism and Physical Culture, ul. Swietokrzyska 12, 00-916 Warsaw (tel: 694-5555; fax: 826-2172).

Ministries

Ministry of Agriculture and Rural Development, ul Wspólna 30, 00-930 Warsaw (tel: 623-1000; fax: 623-2750; e-mail: kancelaria@minrol.gov.pl).

Ministry of Culture and National Heritage, Ul Krakowskie Przedmiescie 15/17, 00-071 Warsaw (tel: 620-0231; fax: 826-7533).

Ministry of Defence, ul Klonowa 1, 00-909 Warsaw (tel: 845-0441; e-mail: bpimon@wp.mil.pl).

Ministry of Education, Al Szucha 25, 00-918 Warsaw (tel: 628-0461; fax: 628-0461; e-mail: minister@men.waw.pl).

Ministry of the Environment, ul Wawelska 52/54, 02-922 Warsaw (tel: 825-0001; fax: 253-332; e-mail: info@mos.gov.pl).

Ministry of Foreign Affairs, Al Szucha 23, 00-580 Warsaw (tel: 523-9000; fax: 629-0287; e-mail: poland@mfa.gov.pl; internet: www.msz.gov.pl).

Ministry of Health, ul Miodowa 15, 00-923 Warsaw (tel: 831-3441; fax: 831-1553; e-mail: rzecznik@mzios.gov.pl).

Ministry of Internal Affairs and Administration, ul Batorego 5, 02-514 Warsaw (tel: 621-0251; fax: 628-9983; e-mail: wp@mswia.gov.pl).

Ministry of Justice, Al Ujazdowskie 11, 00-950 Warsaw (tel: 521-2808; fax: 628-1692; nagorska@ms.gov.pl).

Ministry of Labour and Social Policy, ul Nowogrodzka 1/3/5, 00-513 Warsaw (tel: 661-0100; fax: 628-4048; e-mail: bip@mpips.gov.pl).

Ministry of Post and Telecommunications, pl Malachowskiego 2, 00-940 Warsaw (tel: 656-5000; fax: 826-4840; e-mail: rzecznik@ml.gov.pl).

Ministry of Transport and Maritime Economy, ul Chalubinskiego 4/6, 00-928 Warsaw (tel: 624-4000; fax: 628-5365).

Ministry of the Treasury, ul Krucza 36, 00-522 Warsaw (tel: 695-9000; fax: 625-1114; e-mail: minister@mst.gov.pl).

President's Office, ul Wiejska 10, 00-902 Warsaw (tel: 695-2900; fax: 695-3819; e-mail: listy@prezydent.pl).

Prime Minister's Office, Al Ujazdowskie 1/3, 00-583 Warsaw (tel: 694-66983; fax: 625-2637; e-mail: cirinfo@kprm.gov.pol).

Other useful addresses

British Consul (Szczecin), Ul Starego Wiarusa 32, 71-206 Szczecin (tel: 487-0302; fax: 487-3697).

British Embassy, Corporate Centre, 2nd Floor, Emilii Plater 28, Warsaw 00-688 (tel: 625-3030; fax: 625-3472); Aleja Roz 1, 00-556 Warsaw (tel: 628-1001/5; fax: 621-7161).

Central Board of Customs, Swietokrzyska 12, 00-916 Warsaw (tel: 694-5555). Press Office (tel: 694-5882; fax: 827-3427).

Central Statistical Office, International Co-operation Division, Al Niepodleglosci 208, 00-925 Warsaw (tel: 608-3113; fax: 608-3870; e-mail: j.szczerbinska@gus.stsp.gov.pl).

Co-operation Fund, Ul Zurawia 4a, 00-503 Warsaw (tel: 693-5165/827/868; fax: 693-5815/365).

Energy Restructuring Group, Ministry of Industry and Trade, 2 Mysia Street, 00926 Warsaw 63 (tel: 625-6280; fax: 625-6305, 628-0970).

Euro Information Centre Network/Correspondence Centre, Ul Zurawia 6/12, 00-503 Warsaw (tel: 625-1319; fax: 625-1290).

European Integration Committee, Aleje Ujazdowskie 9, 00-583 Warsaw (tel: 694-7354; fax: 629-4888).

Foreign Trade Research Institute Market Information Center of Foreign Trade, Krucza 38/42, 00-512 Warsaw (tel: 629-1222; fax: 628-8680).

Foundation for Privatisation, 36 Ul Krucza, 00525 Warsaw (tel: 628-2198/99; fax: 625-1114); external department (tel: 693-5419, 693-5818; fax: 693-5300).

Government Centre for Strategic Studies, Wspolna 4, 00-926 Warsaw (tel: 661-8111); Press Office (tel: 661-8664; fax: 629-1619).

Government Information Department, Ul. Wiejska 4/6, 00-902 Warsaw (tel: 694-2500; fax: 694-1911).

Housing and Urban Development Office, ul. Wspolna 2, 00-926 Warsaw (tel: 661-8111; fax: 628-5887).

Industrial Development Agency, ul Wspolna 4, 00-930 Warsaw (tel: 628-7954, 628-0934; fax: 628-2363).

Main Post Office (open 24 hours), 31–33 Swietokrzyska Street, Warsaw.

National Administration of Tourism and Physical Culture, ul. Swietokrzyska 12, 00-916 Warsaw (tel: 694-5555; fax: 826-2172).

Parliament, Sajm RP, ul. Wiejska 4/6/8, 00-902 Warsaw (tel: 694-2500; fax: 694-2215).

Polcargo (cargo experts and supervisors), Zeromskiego 32, Box 223, 81963 Gdynia (tel: 213-921/957).

Polish Agency for Foreign Investment (PAIZ), Al Roz 2, 00-556 Warsaw (tel: 621-6261; fax: 621-8427).

Polish Chartering Agents (Polfracht), Ul Pulaskiego 8, Box 206, 81368 Gdynia (tel: 214-991).

Polish Corporation of Trade Fairs and Economic Exhibition Organisers, Ul Glogowska 26, 60-734 Poznan (tel: 661-532, 692-245; fax: 661-053; e-mail: korptarg@soho-online.com).

Polish Embassy (USA), 2640 16th Street, NW, Washington DC 20009 (tel: (+1-202) 234-3800; fax: (+1-202) 328-6271; e-mail: information@ioip.com).

Polish Foundation for Promotion and Development of SMEs, Ul Zurawia 4a, 00-503 Warsaw (tel: 693-5868/18/27; fax: 693-5815/365).

Polish State Railways (PKP), Ul Chalubinskiego 4/6, 00-928 Warsaw (tel: 628-4909, 293-596; fax: 244-039, 621-9557, 244-870).

Polska Agencja Interpress (Polish information agency), Ul Bagatela 12, 00-585 Warsaw (tel: 628-2221; fax: 628-4651).

Polska Agencja Prasowa (Polish press agency), Ul Jerozolimskie 7, 00-950 Warsaw (tel: 628-0001).

Polskie Linie Oceaniczne (Polish Ocean Lines), Ul 10 Lutego 24, 81-364 Gdynia (tel: 201-901).

Poznan International Fair Co Ltd, Ul Glogowska 14, 60-734 Poznan (tel: 869-2000; fax: 866-5827; e-mail: info@mtp.com.pl); Department of Services (tel: 668-320, 692-547; fax: 660-642); Department of Employment (contracts out exhibition stall personnel) (tel: 666-721, 692-250; fax: 665-827).

State Committee of Science and Technology, ul, Wspolna 1/3, 00-529 Warsaw (tel: 628-4071; fax: 628-0922).

Technology Agency, Krucza 38/42, 00-512 Warsaw (tel: 661-8610; fax: 628-3611).

Telekomunikacja Polska SA, Special Projects Department, Ul Obrzezna 7, 02-691 Warsaw (tel: 275-037; fax: 276-789); External Department, Telephony Polskie Fundacja (Polish Telephone Foundation), Al Stanow Zjednoczonych 24, 03-964 Warsaw (tel/fax: 136-833; fax: 120-544).

Universal SA (foreign trading company), Al Jerozolimskie 44, 00-950 Warsaw (tel: 8144-3135, 693-6091/92; fax: 278-312).

Internet sites

Official Website of Poland: http://poland.pl

Business Directory: www.polish-bus.com/anghome.html

Business Polska: www.polska.net

Polish company directory: www.teleadreson.com.pl

Polish Embassy, London: http://home.btclick.com/polishembassy

Polish Tourism: www.poland-tourism.pl

Warsaw Business Journal: www.wbj.pl

Portugal

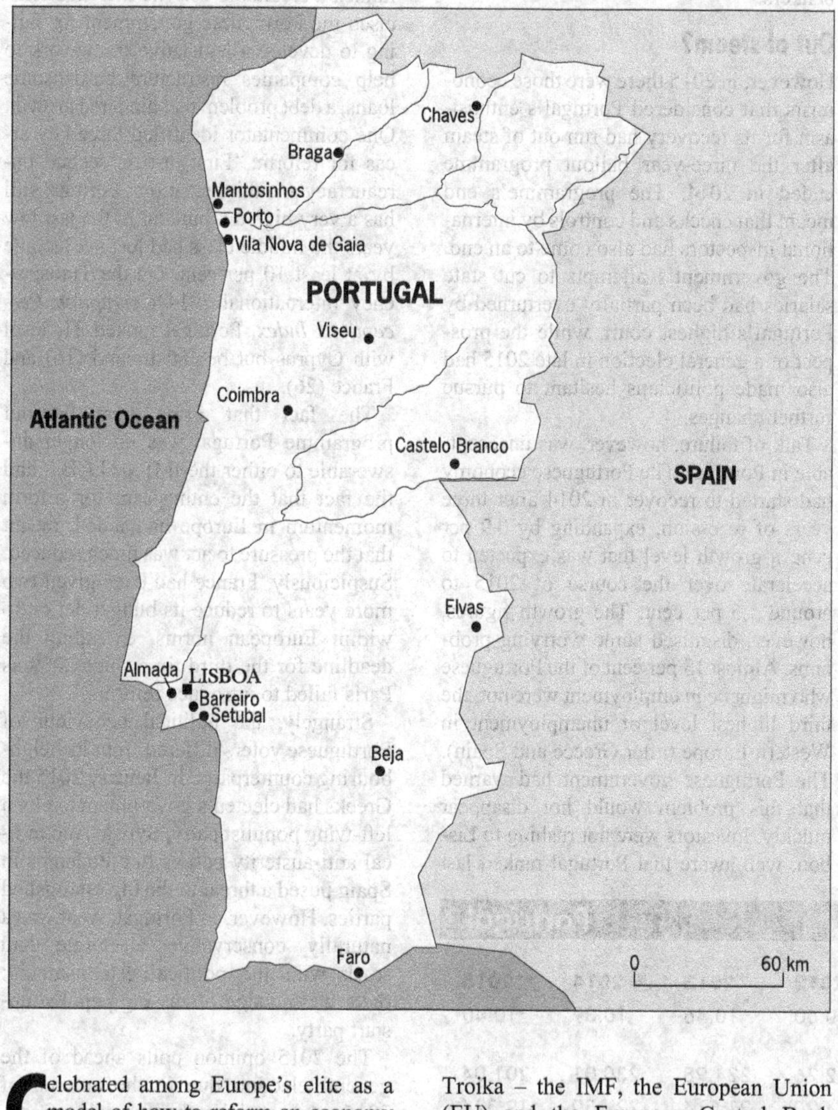

Celebrated among Europe's elite as a model of how to reform an economy after a debt binge, Portugal's enthusiasm for change has waned as Europe loses its appetite for further belt-tightening. None the less, Portugal could be excused for feeling a little smug in mid-2015. If Greece was the miscreant pupil, Portugal – alongside Ireland – could be seen as the teacher's favourite. Portugal was the country held up to Greece's government as the model they should – belatedly – have followed.

Taking the medicine

Since 2011, when Portugal requested a €78 billion (US$) loan from the so-called Troika – the IMF, the European Union (EU) and the European Central Bank (ECB) – Portugal had not hesitated to apply the cuts to public expenditure that the Troika had recommended. At the same time taxes were increased, meaning that the burden on Portugal's taxpayers rose from 33.4 per cent in 2009 to 37.1 per cent in 2014. Pay rises for civil servants and pensioners were ruled out. Pay levels also fell while taxation increased; value added tax (VAT) rose to as high as 23 per cent.

In this four year period, counter intuitively, unemployment fell from 17 per cent to13 per cent. The budget deficit was reduced by half, exports increased,

KEY FACTS

Official name: República Portuguesa (Portuguese Republic)

Head of State: President Aníbal Cavaco Silva (PSD) (from 2006; re-elected 23 Jan 2011)

Head of government: Prime Minister, Pedro Passos Coelho (PSD) (from 21 Jun 2011)

Ruling party: Coalition led by Partido Social Democrata (PSD) (Social Democratic Party), with the Centro Democrático e Social-Partido Popular (CDS-PP) (Democratic and Social Centre-Popular Party) (from 21 Jun 2011)

Area: 92,072 square km

Population: 10.39 million (2014) (10,561,614; 2011, census figure)

Capital: Lisbon

Official language: Portuguese

Currency: Euro (€) = 100 cents (from 1 Jan 2002; previous currency escudo, locked at esc200.48 per euro)

Exchange rate: €0.89 per US$ (Jul 2014)

GDP per capita: US$22,130 (2014)

GDP real growth: 0.90% (2014)

GDP: US$230.01 billion (2014)

Labour force: 5.19 million (2014)*

Unemployment: 13.89% (2014)

Inflation: -0.16% (2014)

Balance of trade: -US$11.89 billion (2014)*

Annual FDI: US$13.07 billion (2011)

* estimated figure

tourism receipts rose and gross domestic product (GDP) rose at an annual rate of 1.5 per cent. That was the good news. Less good was the realisation that the country's public deficit had risen from €173,000 (US$) million to €234,000 (US$).

It was therefore understandable that the Portuguese took exception to the remarks made by the volatile Greek finance minister, Yanis Varoufakis, when he asked: 'Who will be next? Portugal?' The Portuguese could take some satisfaction from the support of the German President, Joachim Gluck, who had suggested that 'Portugal was a good example of successful reforms.' Meanwhile, the managing director of the International Monetary Fund, Christine Lagarde suggested that 'all the Greek political parties take some inspiration from the example of Portugal and Ireland.' Initially sympathetic towards the Greek plight, the constant comparisons with Portugal had become an understandable irritant for most Portuguese. None the less, many Portuguese were aware of the possibility that were Greece to leave the euro-zone, the international markets might consider Portugal as their next 'weak' target.

Hoping to minimalise the effects of a Grexit, Europe's policy-makers were putting a positive spin on all the economic news coming out of Portugal and to a lesser extent out of the other countries that had been bailed out. Thus Portugal was seen as a success story. 'Recovery is now on the way,' announced José Manuel Barroso the former president of the European Commission and once prime minister of Portugal. The European Central Bank President Mario Draghi added his support, praising Portugal for getting on with reform and making difficult changes to the country's long established structures. 'A great deal has been achieved and we have praised progress where it has taken place, including here in Portugal,' Mr Draghi told a meeting of central bankers.

Out of steam?

However, in 2015 there were those economists that considered Portugal's enthusiasm for its recovery had run out of steam after the three-year bailout programme ended in 2014. The programme's end meant that checks and controls by international inspectors had also come to an end. The government's attempts to cut state salaries had been partially overturned by Portugal's highest court, while the prospect of a general election in late 2015 had also made politicians hesitant to pursue further changes.

Talk of failure, however, was unacceptable in Portugal. The Portuguese economy had started to recover in 2014 after three years of recession, expanding by 0.9 per cent, a growth level that was expected to accelerate over the course of 2015 to around 1.5 per cent. The growth figures, however, disguised some worrying problems. Almost 13 per cent of the Portuguese who might be in employment were not, the third highest level of unemployment in Western Europe (after Greece and Spain). The Portuguese government had warned that this problem would not disappear quickly. Investors were not rushing to Lisbon, well aware that Portugal ranked last on a list of euro-zone countries for labour productivity, well behind Spain, Italy and France. On an international ranking of countries by 'ease of doing business', Portugal ranked mid-way (25) down the list, behind Ireland, but ahead of France (31), Italy (56) and Greece (61). Significantly, in the 'Starting a Business' category, Portugal ranked a creditable 10. The IMF had criticised the Portuguese government for failing to develop a legislative framework to help companies restructure burdensome loans, a debt problem that hindered growth. One commentator identified three key areas for reform: 'First justice, second bureaucracy and third taxation.' Portugal still has a very high tax burden. In the last few years the middle class had lost net income by at least 10 per cent. On the Transparency International 2014 *Corruption Perceptions Index*, Portugal ranked 31, level with Cyprus but behind Ireland (16) and France (26).

The fact that in a post bail-out programme Portugal was no longer answerable to either the IMF or ECB – and the fact that the enthusiasm for reform momentum in Europe had faded, meant that the pressure to act was much reduced. Suspiciously, France had been given two more years to reduce its budget deficit to within European norms, extending the deadline for the third time since 2009 as Paris failed to introduce reforms.

Strangely, the political behaviour of Portuguese voters differed from its neighbouring counterparts. In January 2015 the Greeks had elected a government led by a left-wing populist party, Syrisa. And radical anti-austerity parties like Podemos in Spain posed a threat to the big established parties. However, in Portugal, what was a naturally conservative electorate had stuck with the political establishment: there was no sign of any big populist upstart party.

The 2015 opinion polls ahead of the general election due in the autumn of 2015, suggested that the two right-of-centre ruling parties that had presided over four years of austerity were running level with the main opposition centre-left Partido Socialista (PS) (Socialist Party). One poll placed the centre-right Partido Social Democrata (PSD) (Social Democratic Party) of Pedro Passos Coelho, the prime minister and his smaller coalition partners, the Centro Democrático e Social-Partido Popular (CDS-PP) (Democratic and Social Centre-Popular Party) just a tenth of a point behind the PS.

Many analysts expected the anti-austerity PS to be running ahead and the

KEY INDICATORS — Portugal

	Unit	2011	2012	2013	2014	**2015
Population	m	10.56	10.60	10.46	10.39	*10.40
Gross domestic product (GDP)	US$bn	238.90	212.26	224.98	230.01	*201.04
GDP per capita	US$	22,413	20,020	21,514	22,130	*19,324
GDP real growth	%	-1.5	-3.2	-1.6	0.9	*1.6
Inflation	%	3.6	2.8	0.4	-0.2	*0.6
Unemployment	%	11.3	15.7	16.2	13.9	*13.1
Exports (fob) (goods)	US$m	59,248.8	58,238.1	62,980.6	62,916.2	–
Imports (fob) (goods)	US$m	77,710.7	69,483.0	72,626.3	74,804.6	–
Balance of trade	US$m	-18,461.8	-11,244.8	-9,645.7	-11,889.8	–
Current account	US$m	-15,539.4	-4,283.0	3,192.0	1,388.0	*2,866.0
Total reserves minus gold	US$m	2,684.0	2,196.0	2,778.0	4,869.0	–
Foreign exchange	US$m	984.0	559.0	1,138.0	–	–
Exchange rate	per US$	0.75	0.77	0.73	0.82	–

* estimated figure ** forecast figure

unpopular ruling coalition to be falling apart. However, the opposite seemed to be the case. The coalition, which two years earlier had almost collapsed in a dispute over austerity, had managed to be more united than ever. With a politician's eye on the Greek situation, Mr Passos Coelho asked the Portuguese: 'Do we want to build something positive on what we have already achieved, or do we want to return to the days of debt and uncertainty?'

The Prime Minister was speaking at celebrations to mark the first anniversary of the country's exit from its three-year euro bail-out. The current account had moved from a deficit of 12 per cent of GDP into a surplus. The government says the budget deficit this year will fall below 3 per cent of GDP for the first time in 15 years. The economy has been growing for four quarters in a row; it should expand by 1.7 per cent this year. Alongside Ireland, Portugal was held up as proof that 'austerity works.'

The Socialist party leader, António Costa (a former mayor of Lisbon, who took over as the PS leader in November 2014), had undertaken to 'turn the page on austerity', claiming that it had produced 'nothing but poverty'. Mr Costa noted that Portugal's public debt had risen to 130 per cent of GDP, a level that many economists saw as unsustainable. Mr Costa's overt plan was to stimulate growth along predictably socialist lines, by putting more money into circulation, reversing public-sector wage cuts, reducing taxes and even lowering workers' social-security contributions from 11 per cent to 7 per cent of pay. Tacitly, however, observers wondered to what extent Mr Costa seriously contemplated embarking on his stated objectives.

Just as predictably, Prime Minister Passos Coelho dismissed this approach as 'reckless'. But the detail of the PS programme represented a toning down of its previous rhetoric. However, as the Greek Syrisa party leadership bravely tried to fly in the face of reason, the Portuguese socialists decided to shift to the centre ground. The PS, like most Portuguese voters, was quietly moving to the centre – in anticipation of an election in which it would have to attract a reasonable proportion of middle class voters.

What is being Portuguese?

The Portuguese are a patriotic nation. Parliamentary debates may be ferocious, pitting Communists against Conservatives, but the session always ends with a full blooded rendering of the national anthem. Patriotism, in Portugal, is not the monopoly of any particular politics. In 2015 a private television channel opened a debate with the question: 'What is being Portuguese?' The idea of all members singing the anthem and the citizens discussing their national identity would, in neighbouring Spain, for example, be unthinkable. In the Portuguese debate some of the answers were both light-heated and inevitable – 'A love of cod' – or simply surprising – 'Being happy.' No respondent connected the country with its major companies; unsurprisingly the debate coincided with the privatisation of the emblematic national airline, TAP, the only European airline still to be 100 per cent state owned. The government had overcome the strikes, the opposition of many sections of Portuguese society, statements by the PS that it would reverse the decision if elected, to sell TAP to foreign interests – in this case Brazilian.

The privatisation programme had altered the commercial complexion of Portugal. The Redes Energéticas Nacionais (National Electrical Gri) had been purchased by Chinese interests, as had the remnants of the once all powerful Banco Espírito Santo. More surprisingly Angolan companies had assumed a controlling interest in communication companies, banks and the GALP oil company. Portugal Telecom ended up in the hands of France's Altice. Despite the serious opposition to the TAP privatisation, many Portuguese failed to see why, when they had to pay 100 euros for a visit to hospital, the government was prepared to pay over €1,000 million (US$1,123 million) to keep TAP afloat. Portugal's main ruling PSD took a further hit in an opinion poll of voting intentions before the autumn election, falling far behind the opposition Socialists after the prime minister came under fire for failing to pay taxes on time.

Ruling parties rarely fare well in the run up to elections. The London *Economist* reported that a survey, conducted by Eurosondagempollsters for *Expresso* newspaper and SIC television, in June 2015 showed Prime Minister Pedro Passos Coelho's party slumping 2.6 percentage points from a previous poll only two weeks earlier, to 25.2 per cent. The same poll showed the PS rising 1.6 points to 38.1 per cent, still short of a parliamentary majority. CDS-PP, the smaller partner in the centre-right ruling coalition, nudged up fractionally, by 0.4 points to 8.1 per cent, which placed the coalition partners almost 5 points behind the PS. Two weeks earlier, the coalition had been some 3 points behind, a figure that was considered to be inside the statistical margin of error. Embarassingly for the prime minister, newspaper reports that he had failed to make tax and social security contributions on time turned out to be accurate, forcing him to acknowledge and apologise for his 'mistakes'. Mr Passos Coelho, it seemed, had incurred fines and run up debts with the Portuguese tax authorities, but claimed that he had always paid what he owed, attributing his delayed payments to a lapse of memory or ignorance. Although some Socialist deputies demanded his resignation, the *Economist* noted that Mr Costa had remarked that it was better left to the voters to decide.

The economy – the IMF view....

In May 2015, the International Monetary Fund (IMF) assessed the Portuguese economy, noting that Portugal's 'significant flow imbalances' had largely been corrected in the wake of the global financial crisis, with employment increasing, output expanding and the current account balance posting surpluses for the first time in decades. Nevertheless, the weaknesses that had accumulated over the years – most notably public and non-financial corporate debt and a large negative international investment position – in the view of the IMF also remained pronounced.

The IMF reported that the Portuguese economy had expanded at close to 1 per cent per year on average since early 2013, with growth driven largely by consumption. The 2014 fiscal deficit objective of 4.0 per cent of GDP had been achieved, implying a structural primary adjustment of one per cent. The trend of downward inflation pressures, exacerbated by falling energy prices, appeared to have been arrested. The banking system was reducing its reliance on Eurosystem financing, although it remained unprofitable and saddled with a rising number of non-performing loans.

The IMF considered that Portugal's short-term outlook was benefiting from the triple effect of record low interest rates, a weakening euro and low oil prices. Output was expected to increase by 1.6 per cent in 2015 and by 1.5 per cent in 2016, with the outlook for inflation improving as well. As the boost from short-term factors faded, however, growth was projected to moderate over the medium term, as Portugal continued to lag behind its peers in key structural indicators. Nevertheless, the outlook was largely positive, as the impact of the ECB's expanded asset purchase programme looked likely to turn out to be stronger than anticipated. At the same time, there were low-probability but potentially disruptive downside possibilities, most notably the possible volatility associated with turmoil at the euro-zone level.

... and the OECD View

In the view of the Paris based Organisation for Economic Co-operation and Development (OECD), the Portuguese recovery was projected to strengthen in 2015 on the back of strong external demand, a weaker euro and lower oil prices. The OECD noted that after having contracted for three years, domestic demand had started to rise and business investment was projected to pick up further in 2016. However, the OECD expected considerable economic slack to remain, as the unemployment rate would only continue to fall moderately.

As the Portuguese recovery remained fragile, the more moderate pace of fiscal consolidation was to be welcomed. Further tax reforms, suggested the OECD, such as an additional, revenue-neutral, reduction in the effective corporate tax rate might strengthen business investment. Further reductions of the high unemployment rate would help to reduce income inequality. Despite progress, the competitiveness of Portugal's tradable sectors was held back by the weak competition prevailing in upstream services sectors, which the OECD considered could be addressed through further structural reforms in the electricity and gas sectors and by curbing unnecessary restrictions in professional services. Notwithstanding some progress in deleveraging, reducing still high private sector indebtedness, including through an assessment of the performance of new insolvency procedures, remained a priority for raising bank credit and investment.

Investment fell by nearly 35 per cent between 2007 and 2014, more than twice the decline in the European Union (EU) as a whole. Business investment had started to increase again, driven by stronger prospects for internal and external demand, higher capacity utilisation and the need to renew depleted capital stock. Still, the pick-up in investment observed in key euro-zone economies had yet to materialise in Portugal. Public and residential investment would continue to stay subdued, reflecting fiscal consolidation needs and high leverage ratios of households and firms in the construction sector.

In an earlier (October 2014) Economic Survey of Portugal, the OECD had considered that 'a successful rebalancing of the economy was underway, noting that 'competitiveness had improved and export performance had risen.' Further progress was needed, but was held back by weak competition in the services sectors, including electricity, and by wage bargaining mechanisms that hampered market entry. An overburdened judicial system and a high tax burden, in particular for large firms, curbed productivity in exporting sectors. Portugal's innovation performance, such as it was, suffered from the lack of any effective connection between research in universities and the private sector, while the complex structure of tax credits for research and development was also a barrier to market entry.

Inequality

In the view of the IMF, Portugal has one of the most unequal income distributions in Europe and its poverty levels are high. The economic crisis had halted the gradual long-term decline in both inequality and poverty and the number of poor households was rising, with children and youths being particularly affected. Recent tax reforms had probably increased the progressivity of taxes, but transfer payments were biased towards older workers, which was not the most efficient tool to reduce inequality and poverty. Conversely, benefit levels in the minimum income support scheme were low and the coverage of unemployment benefits was narrow. Overall, transfer programmes suffered from overlaps and insufficient targeting. In the education system, high drop-out rates were associated with frequent grade-repetition, also increasing inequality as the children of disadvantaged families were more likely to drop out. Vocational courses and adult education were being developed, but did not yet play a major role in Portugal, although they could lead to a more equitable distribution of income.

Risk assessment

Economy	Fair
Politics	Fair
Regional stability	Good

COUNTRY PROFILE

1383 The seventh Portuguese King, Fernando I, died. The Spanish Castilians invaded Portugal in an attempt to claim the country's throne.
1385 João I of Avis defeated the Castilians and became King.
1400s Portugal expanded its trading routes by colonising parts of Africa, Asia and the Americas.
1558 Portugal tried to colonise Morocco. After Portugal was defeated, the country went into economic and imperial decline.
1580 King Phillip II of Spain invaded Portugal. It remained under Spanish rule until a revolt in 1640.
1600s Portugal colonised Brazil and became a major gold exporter. Portugal became a major trading partner to Britain.
1793–1801 Portuguese and Spanish troops invaded France, but were defeated. Portugal was forced to temporarily break relations with Britain as part of a peace settlement with France.
1807–10 Portugal re-established relations with Britain and declared its neutrality. France and Spain invaded Portugal three times after it had refused to break relations with Britain. A joint Anglo-Portuguese Army eventually expelled the occupation forces.
1822–24 Brazil declared its independence in 1822. An attempt to introduce a new constitution in Portugal failed. Royalists refused to accept the constitution, which would have separated the powers of the monarchy, government and judiciary, and launched uprisings against the government. Power remained in the hands of the monarchy.
1828–51 Liberals rebelled against the Royalist government. Despite splitting into moderate and radical elements, the Liberals eventually gained control of the government.
1907–08 The Republicans, who were gaining support among the population, failed in an attempt to overthrow the government of João Franco.
1908 Republican extremists assassinated King Carlos I. His son, Manuel II succeeded him, becoming Portugal's last king.
1910 The army overthrew the monarchy forcing the King to abdicate. A Republican government was installed and Portugal was declared a republic. Teófilo Braga was appointed as Portugal's first president.
1911 A new constitution was introduced confirming Portugal's republican status and introducing a bicameral legislature.
1914–18 Portugal fought alongside Britain and France in the First World War.
1926 A military *coup d'état* overthrew the government and replaced it with a *junta*. The coup leader, General Gomes da Costa, was temporarily appointed head of the *junta* before General Óscar Fragoso Carmona replaced him.
1928 General Carmona was appointed president and Colonel José Vicente de Freitas became prime minister.
1932 A civilian academic, António de Oliveira Salazar, was appointed prime minister. Salazar introduced a new

constitution consolidating authoritarian government.
1939–45 Portugal was neutral during the Second World War, but allowed the Allies to establish military bases in the Azores.
1955 After initially being blocked by the Soviet Union, Portugal was allowed to join the UN.
1968 Marcello José das Neves Caetano succeeded Salazar who had suffered a stroke and was in a coma.
1970 António de Oliveira Salazar died.
1974 A group of army officers of the Movimento das Forças Armadasa (MFA) (Armed Forces Movement), and led by General António de Spínola staged a *coup d'état* and overthrew Caetano's government. A provisional coalition government restored civil liberties and freedom of the press, abolished the secret police and freed political prisoners.
1975 Portugal granted independence to its African territories, where wars against nationalist forces had long been a drain on the economy; military spending had absorbed about 40 per cent of GDP per annum. Portugal also withdrew from Timor-Leste. Many expatriates returned from former colonies. In the first free parliamentary elections victory went to the Partido Socialista (PS) (Socialist Party). Mário Lopes Soares became prime minister and General Antonio Ramalho Eanes won the presidency. Banks and many industries were nationalised.
1976 A new constitution was introduced, officially establishing Portugal as a parliamentary democracy. The constitution was later amended in 1982, 1989, 1992 and 1997.
1977–86 A period of political instability with 17 left-wing coalition governments in power.
1986 Portugal joined the forerunner of the EU, the European Community (EC). Former prime minister Mário Soares became the first civilian president for 60 years.
1987 In the general election, Partido Social Democrata (PSD) (Social Democratic Party) became the first majority party in parliament since the 1974 revolution. Anibal Cavaco Silva was elected prime minister.
1991 Mário Soares was re-elected president and PSD won re-election. Portugal took Australia to the International Court of Justice (ICJ), on behalf of then Timor-Leste, a former colony, alleging Australia had failed to observe the rights of the Timorese to national self-determination, when it recognised Indonesia's occupation of Timor-Leste in 1975.
1995 PSD lost to the PS in the general election. António Guterres became prime minister. The ICJ ruled it did not have jurisdiction in the matter of Australia actions concerning Timor-Leste.
1996 The presidential election was won by the PS's Jorge Sampaio.
1998 Portuguese voters narrowly rejected in a referendum a proposal to legalise abortion.
1999 António Guterres and the PS were re-elected. Macau, Portugal's last colonial territory was returned to China. Portugal joined the EU single currency unit.
2001 Jorge Sampaio was re-elected as president for a second five-year term. Guterres resigned, as prime minister after the PS was defeated in local elections.
2002 Euro currency replaced the escudos. José Manuel Durão Barroso (PSD) formed a coalition government comprising PSD and Partido Popular (PP) (Popular Party).
2003 The last extension on the Via Infante motorway Lisbon-Algarve-Spain (known as the A22) was opened.
2004 Prime Minister Barroso resigned; he assumed the presidency of the European Commission.
2005 The opposition PS won parliamentary elections and José Sócrates (PS) became prime minister. Portugal's constitutional court ruled against the government's decision to hold a referendum on relaxing the country's abortion laws. The country's economic rating was downgraded, by Standard and Poor's, from AA to -AA, as a result of the deterioration in public finances and the lack of fiscal reforms necessary to boost fiscal dynamics. The government introduced a radical budget designed to cut public spending in an attempt to revive the economy and cut a deficit that was twice the level permitted under EU monetary rules.
2006 Aníbal Cavaco Silva won the presidency.
2007 Mass demonstrations protested the government's austerity measures. A new law permitting abortion within the first ten-weeks of pregnancy was introduced in alignment with most other EU countries.
2008 Official approval of Portuguese spelling in line with Brazilian practice was given by parliament.
2009 Portugal signed a loan agreement with São Tomé and Príncipe, to allow its former colony's currency, the dobra, to be anchored to the euro. In parliamentary elections, the ruling PS won 37.7 per cent of the vote (96 seats of 230) and the opposition PSD 30 per cent (78); Prime Minister José Sócrates (PS) remained in office.
2010 Torrential rain caused severe flooding on the island of Madeira, resulting in the death of 42 people; the flooding later caused landslides, further endangering islanders. Value added tax (VAT) was increased to 21 per cent and income tax raised, along with higher corporation taxes, as part of the government's latest austerity measures to cut the budget deficit. A heat wave resulted in massive forest fires across northern Portugal.
2011 Presidential elections were held in January, in which three candidates took part. Incumbent Aníbal Cavaco Silva (PDS) won 52.9 per cent and his closest rival, Manuel Alegre (PS), won 19.8 per cent. The turnout was low at 46.6 per cent. The government resigned in March following parliament's rejection of its third austerity budget. Socrates remained in office as caretaker prime minister until an early general election was called. Portugal became the third euro-zone state to request financial aid. The European Central Bank (ECB) and the International Monetary Fund (IMF) agreed in May to offer Portugal €78 billion (US$116 billion) in financial assistance. Caretaker Prime Minister Socrates, assured both parties that the deficit would be cut by 5.9 per cent in 2011/12, by 4.5 per cent in 2012/13 and 3 per cent in 2013/14. In parliamentary elections held in June, the ruling PS lost power, wining only 28.05 per cent of the vote. The opposition Partido Social Democrata (PSD) (Social Democratic Party) won 38.63 per cent (105 seats out of 230). Pedro Passos Coelho (PSD) became prime minister in June leading a coalition of PSD and the Centro Democrático e Social-Partido Popular (CDS-PP) (Democratic and Social Centre-Popular Party). In July Portugal's debt was downgraded to junk status by credit ratings agency Moody's.
2012 On 9 May, as part of the government's austerity measures, four public holidays (two religious and two secular) will be suspended (2013–18). With the removal of these holidays, the total number was reduced to 10 days. On 15 October a new draft budget was published for 2013, which was described as one of the harshest in Portugal's history. Average income tax will rise from 9.8 per cent in 2012 to 13.2 per cent and public spending will be cut by US$2.7 billion. The budget is designed to cut the deficit by 4.5 per cent and allow the country's spending to be below the 3 per cent of GDP as required under EU targets.
2013 Vitor Gaspar, finance minister, resigned on 1 July, followed the next day by Paulo Portas, foreign minister. Both pointed to unsustainable austerity measures as the reason. Prime Minister Coelho said he would not be standing down.
On 5 July Mr Coelho presented President Silva with what he called an agreed 'deal' to keep his coalition intact. He said that his centre-right governing partner, the CDS-PP, lead by Cavaco Silva, had pledged to continue supporting his PSD

party in government. The deal was approved by the president who also rejected opposition parties' demands for an early election. He said that 'The current government has all the authority to exercise its functions...' and urged the main parties to reach a compromise so as to prevent Portugal from asking for a second international bailout.
2014 The Portuguese navy escorted a Russian oceanic research vessel away from Portugal's coastal economic zone on 5 November.
2015 The 4 October general election the Portugal à Frente (PàF) (Portugal Ahead) coalition of Partido Social Democrata (PSD) (Social Democratic Party), with the Centro Democrático e Social-Partido Popular (CDS-PP) (Democratic and Social Centre-Popular Party) won 44.35 per cent of the vote (102 seats out of 230), loosing their overall majority.

Political structure

Constitution

The constitution was promulgated in 1976 and amended in 1982, 1989, 1992 and 1999. Voting is by direct universal suffrage. Voting age: 18 years.

Form of state

Parliamentary democratic republic

The executive

The president, who is directly elected for a maximum of two consecutive terms of five years, appoints a prime minister, and, on his recommendation, the rest of the government. The president can dissolve parliament, call elections and is supreme commander of the armed forces. The president can dissolve parliament, call elections and is supreme commander of the armed forces.
The principal organ of executive power within the government is the Council of Ministers which is responsible to parliament.

National legislature

The unicameral Assembléia da República (Assembly of the Republic) has 230 members elected for four-year terms by proportional representation. There is a fixed number of representatives, two, for each autonomous region of the Azores and Madeira, Portuguese nationals living in Europe and Portuguese nationals living elsewhere in the world. The size of the electorate determines the number of representatives for all other mainland Portuguese constituencies.

Legal system

The legal system is based on the 1976 constitution.

Last elections

23 January 2011 (presidential); 4 October 2015 (parliamentary)
Results: Presidential (2011): Aníbal Cavaco Silva (PSD) won 52.9 per cent, Manuel Alegre (PS) 19.8 per cent, Fernando Nobre (independent) 14.1 per cent, Francisco Lopes (Partido Comunista Português (PCP) (Portuguese Communist Party)) 7.1 per cent; turnout was 46.63 per cent.
Parliamentary (2015): the Portugal à Frente (PàF) (Portugal Ahead) coalition of Partido Social Democrata (PSD) (Social Democratic Party), with the Centro Democrático e Social-Partido Popular (CDS-PP) (Democratic and Social Centre-Popular Party) won 44.35 per cent of the vote (102 seats out of 230), Partido Socialista (PS) (Socialist Party) 32.32 per cent (86), Bloco de Esquerda (BE) (Left Block) 10.19 per cent (19); Coligação Democrática Unitária (CDU) (Democratic Unity Coalition (alliance of the Partido Comunista dos Trabalhadores (Communist Party) and Partido Ecologista (Os Verdes) (Ecologist Party (The Greens)) 8.25 per cent (17); Social Democratic Party Partido Social Democrata (Social Democratic Party) 1.49 per cent (2), Pessoas-Animais-Natureza (PAN) (People-Animals-Nature) 1.39 per cent (1); 15 other political parties failed to win any seats. Turnout was 55.84 per cent.

Next elections

January/February 2016 (presidential); 2019 (parliamentary)

Political parties

Ruling party

Coalition led by Partido Social Democrata (PSD) (Social Democratic Party), with the Centro Democrático e Social-Partido Popular (CDS-PP) (Democratic and Social Centre-Popular Party) (from 21 Jun 2011, re-elected Oct 2015 but without overall majority)

Main opposition party

Partido Socialista (PS) (Socialist Party)

Population

10.39 million (2014) (10,561,614
Last census: 21 March 2011: 10,561,614
Population density: 109 inhabitants per square km. Urban population 61 per cent (2010 Unicef).
Annual growth rate: 0.4 per cent, 1990–2010 (Unicef).

Ethnic make-up

Predominantly Portuguese. There are immigrant groups from former African colonies – Cape Verde, Mozambique, Angola, Guinea-Bissau and São Tomé. Also from East Timor and Chinese from Macao. There were 200,000 members of ethnic minorities in Portugal in 2000 (1.8 per cent of the total population).

Religions

Roman Catholic (97 per cent), Protestant denominations (1 per cent).

Education

Basic education is undertaken between the ages of six and 15. Secondary education is optional and is undertaken over three years. Higher education is divided into two sub-systems: university education and non-university higher education and it is provided in autonomous public universities, private universities, polytechnic institutions and private higher education institutions of other types. The two systems of higher education are linked and it is possible to transfer from one to the other. It is also possible to transfer from a public institution to a private one and vice versa.
Literacy rate: 94 per cent male, 89 per cent female; adult rates (World Bank).
Enrolment rate: 128 per cent gross primary enrolment of the relevant age group (including repeaters); 98 per cent gross secondary enrolment (World Bank).
Pupils per teacher: 12 in primary schools.

Health

Health care is delivered under a national health service, which is accessible to all Portuguese citizens and to citizens of member states of the EU.

HIV/Aids

HIV prevalence: 0.4 per cent aged 15–49 in 2003 (World Bank)
Life expectancy: 78 years, 2004 (WHO 2006)
Fertility rate/Maternal mortality rate: 1.3 births per woman, 2010 (Unicef); maternal mortality 8.0 per 100,000 live births (World Bank).
Birth rate/Death rate: 11 deaths to 12 births per 1,000 people (World Bank).
Child (under 5 years) mortality rate (per 1,000): 4 per 1,000 live births (WHO 2012)
Head of population per physician: 3.42 physicians per 1,000 people, 2003 (WHO 2006)

Welfare

Portugal's social security system is characterised by a general contributory scheme covering all workers and their families, with special arrangements for self-employed persons and a non-contributory protection scheme for people facing social or economic problems. Benefits available under the general scheme include sickness (cash benefits), birth/adoption, accidents at work and occupational diseases, invalidity, old age and death, unemployment and dependants.
Self-employed persons are entitled to a compulsory insurance scheme and there is an opt-in extended benefits scheme relating to sickness, occupational diseases and dependants. Membership of the general scheme is compulsory. In addition, there is a voluntary social security scheme for

those not in work or who are in work but are not covered by the general scheme. As a rule, the employer pays the contributions and deducts the employee's social security contribution from his or her pay. Employers are also responsible for full financing of the protection of employees against accidents at work and occupational diseases.

Main cities

Lisbon (capital, estimated population 475,353 in 2012), Oporto (219,099), Amadora (162,875), Braga (132,823), Queluz (130,895), Setúbal (121,506), Agualva-Cacém (115,577), Coimbra (106,824), Algueirão-Mem Martins (98,563).

Languages spoken

Business languages include English, Spanish and French.

Official language/s

Portuguese

Media

Press

Dailies: In Portugese, *Jornal de Noticias* (http://dn.sapo.pt) is the largest daily.. Others include *Diario de Noticias* (http://dn.sapo.pt), *Record*, *Correio da Manha* and *Público* (ww2.publico.clix.pt), *Destak* (www.destak.pt), government announcements and politics in *Diário da República* (www.dre.pt), and *Correio da Manha* (www.correiomanha.pt). On Madeira *Diário de Notícias* (www.dnoticias.pt), the *Tribuna da Madeira* (www.tribunadamadeira.pt) and *Jornal da Madeira (www.jornaldamadeira.pt); in English, The Madeira Times* (www.themadeiratimes.com), In the Azores, *O Açoriano Oriental* (http://acorianooriental.sapo.pt) and Diario Insular (www.diarioinsular.com).

Weeklies: Major weeklies are published in Lisbon. The most widely circulated is *Expresso* (http://expresso.clix.pt), others include *O Independente* (www.oindependente.pt) and *Sol* (http://sol.sapo.pt/). Political and news publications include *Courrier Internacional* (http://clix.courrierinternacional.com.pt), *Focus* (http://html.impala.pt) and *Sábado* (www.sabado.xl.pt). Women's magazines include *Mulher Moderna* (www.mulhermoderna.com), *Exame* and *Activa* are both imprints of (www.edipresse.com).*Máxima* (www.maxima.xl.pt), *Guia*, *Maria* and *Marie Claire* are also popular. *Sojornal* is a general interest weekly. *The News* is Portugal's national weekend newspaper. *Visão* (http://aeiou.visao.pt). In English, with news and current affairs are *The Portugal News* (www.the-news.net), *The Resident* (www.portugalresident.com) and *Euro Weekly News* (www.euroweeklynews.com).

Business: In Portuguese, the most influential business newspapers are *Diário Económico* (http://diarioeconomico.sapo.pt), *Jornal de Negócios* (www.jornaldenegocios.pt), *Oje* (www.oje.pt), and *Vida Económica* (weekly) (www.centroatl.pt). Many newspapers have economic sections.

Broadcasting

The national public broadcaster is Radio e Televisão de Portugal (RTP) (www.rtp.pt), which runs television, radio, teletext and online, transmits national and regional programmes including services to the Madeira Islands and the Azores.

Radio: There are over 280 radio stations, almost all of which are commercial, RTP runs Antena 1–3, and an external service broadcasting to Africa. The Roman Catholic Church operates Radio Renascença, the only private national radio station. The major commercial stations are Radio Comercial (radiocomercial.clix.pt), TSF (http://tsf.sapo.pt) and Radio Clube Portugues (http://radioclube.clix.pt)

Television: RTP operates two channels on the mainline and regional services to the Azores and Madeira and the external services RTP Africa and RTP Internacional. SIC (http://sic.sapo.pt) and TVI (www.tvi.iol.pt), which has close ties with the Roman Catholic church in Portugal, are private stations. There are satellite TV broadcasts from several international sources.

National news agency: Lusa News Press Agency

Other news agencies: Photonews (Agência Noticiosa) (www.photonews.com.pt)

Economy

Portugal has a small mixed economy with a heavy dependence on foreign trade and few natural resources. The service sector, which comprises tourism, government services, retail and recreation, is the largest component of GDP at 75 per cent; it employs 68 per cent of the workforce. The industrial sector and an export-oriented manufacturing sector accounts for almost 22 per cent of GDP. It includes a globally recognised dye and mould making industry for automobile assembly and one of Europe's largest electricity operators, EDP (Energias de Portugal), as well as textiles, clothing and footwear, cork and wood products, wine and port, porcelain and glass. Agriculture and fishing accounts for only 3 per cent of GDP; its world-renowned fortified wine is named after its second city Porto (port wine). Pedro Coelho's government has passed legislation aimed at reducing labour market rigidity, and this, along with fiscal discipline could make Portugal more attractive to foreign direct investment. FDI has increased drastically from US$2.2 billion in 2013 to US$8.8 billion in 2014. The government has also reduced the budget deficit from 11.2 per cent of GDP in 2010 to 4.8 per cent in 2014, still 0.8 per cent higher than the EU-IMF target. The government has pledged to lower the deficit to less than 3 per cent of GDP in 2015 in order to comply with EU fiscal obligations.

The global economic crisis caused a deep recession in Portugal in 2008 as GDP growth fell from 2.4 per cent in 2007 to 0.0 per cent, before falling into a recessionary -2.9 per cent as the banking sector came under financial strain and a credit squeeze began affecting the private sector and domestic spending. In 2009 the international ratings agency Standard and Poor's lowered Portugal's long-term credit rating from 'stable' to 'negative'. It gave a pessimistic outlook concerning the country's structural weaknesses, with its poor competitiveness hampering growth and Portugal's capacity to strengthen its public finances and reduce debt. The unemployment rate was 13.9 per cent in 2014.

In 2010 GDP growth returned at 1.4 per cent, although the economy had not fully recovered. The economy was classed as underperforming, having one of the lowest GDP per capita rates (US$22,997) in Western Europe. Portugal's 10-year cost of borrowing reached a peak of almost 8 per cent of GDP on 2 March 2010, when it was required to borrow US$1.38 billion through a Treasury bill sale. An austerity budget was announced later in March 2010, designed to cut the public deficit to 8.3 per cent of GDP (down from 9.3 per cent in 2009) and return the country's spending to the EU mandated 3 per cent of GDP by 2013. The measures planned included a public workers' pay freeze and cuts in pensions. Another austerity budget passed in November 2010.

However in March 2011 when Prime Minister Socrates could not convince his government to back his fourth austerity budget, he resigned, although remained as care taker prime minister until the June elections. The European Central Bank (ECB) and the International Monetary Fund (IMF) agreed on 3 May 2012 to offer Portugal EUR78 billion (US$116 billion) in financial assistance. The three-year loan agreement should allow Portugal to reach its budget deficit targets without a run on its economy. Caretaker Prime Minister Socrates assured both parties that the deficit would be cut by 5.9 per cent in 2011/12, by 4.5 per cent in 2012/13 and 3 per cent in 2013/14. Clearly this has not been achieved.

Fresh elections were held in June 2011 and a new coalition government was formed and introduced its own austerity budget. In July 2011, Portugal's sovereign debt rating was downgraded to junk status by credit ratings agency Moody's. GDP growth in 2011 was estimated as a recessionary -1.5 per cent, and predicted to deepen to -3.3 per cent in 2012 as unemployment rose to around 15 per cent. The government estimated that the deficit for 2011 was close to 4 per cent of GDP, well below the official target of 5.9 per cent, as it cut 27 per cent of all managerial positions within central government and forced other cuts on public sector workers. In October another austerity budget was submitted to parliament, which prompted hundreds of thousands of protestors to strike before the budget was passed in November.
In September 2012, the EU, IMF and European Central Bank granted Portugal another year in which to bring its deficit to below the EU target of 3 per cent of GDP. On 22 September, the government agreed to reconsider its proposed increase in social security contributions (due in 2013) from 11 per cent to 18 per cent, as set out in Portugal's conditions for a US$101 billion EU-IMF, three-year, financial rescue plan (offered in May 2012). On 15 October 2012 a new draft budget was published for 2013, which was described as one of the harshest in Portugal's history. Average income tax will rise from 9.8 per cent in 2012 to 13.2 per cent and public spending will be cut by US$2.7 billion. The budget is designed to cut the deficit by 4.5 per cent and allow the country's spending to be below the 3 per cent of GDP as required under EU targets.
GDP growth was -4 per cent in 2012, worse than the prediction of -3.3 per cent before improving slightly to -1.6 per cent in 2013 and finally recording positive growth of 0.9 per cent in 2014. The modest recovery began in 2013 and gathered steam in 2014 due to strong export performance and a rebound in private consumption. The austerity measures, which were instituted to reduce the global deficit, contributed to record unemployment and a wave of emigration not seen since the 1960s. A continued reduction in private and public sector debt could weigh on consumption and investment in 2015, holding back a stronger recovery. Legislative elections in 2015 could increase the risk of fiscal slippage and undermine investment confidence in Portugal's economy, which has improved over the course of the EU-IMF programme.

External trade
As a member of the European Union, Portugal operates within a community-wide free trade area, with tariffs sets as a whole. Internationally, the EU has free trade agreements with a number of nations and trading blocs worldwide.
Around 70 per cent of GDP is provided through foreign trade, of which 80 per cent is with other EU members. The modern manufacturing sector provides a major input of mould-making items for Europe's automotive industry. Important export products include marble, wine, especially port, and cork as well as mineral ores.

Imports
Main imports are machinery and transport equipment, chemicals, petroleum, textiles and agricultural products.
Main sources: Spain (32.6 per cent of total in 2014), Germany (12.4 per cent), France (7.1 per cent), Italy (5.3 per cent) and the Netherlands (5.1 per cent).

Exports
Main exports include clothing and footwear, wine, machinery, chemicals, cork and paper products and hides, port and sherry.
Main destinations: Spain (23.7 per cent of total in 2014), Germany (11.8 per cent), France (11.8 per cent), Angola (6.1 per cent), UK (6.1 per cent), US (4.2 per cent) and the Netherlands (4 per cent).

Agriculture

Farming
About 34 per cent of the land area is arable, 9 per cent is under pasture and 32 per cent is used for forestry or is woodland. Farming is the most backward sector of the economy and crop yields and animal productivity are well below the EU average due to a legacy of low agricultural investment, minimal machinery, little use of fertiliser, poor soil quality and a fragmented land tenure system.
The agricultural sector is subject to the reformed Common Agricultural Policy (CAP), whereby subsidies are no longer paid on farm output, which tended to benefit large farms and encourage overproduction, but rather on single farm payments not conditional on production.
Portugal is the world's largest exporter of tomato paste and a leading exporter of wine. Its principal agricultural imports are wheat and meat.
The main crops grown in Portugal are cereals (wheat, barley, corn and rice), potatoes, grapes, olives and tomatoes. Other agricultural products include sheep, cattle, oats, pigs, poultry, dairy products and fish.

Fishing
The waters around Portugal are rich fishing grounds. Sardines, anchovies and tuna are caught near the coast and deep-sea trawlers in the North Atlantic catch species such as cod.
Portugal's territorial waters were ceded to the EU on its accession. This stimulated investment of the fishing sector and helped modernise the industry.

Forestry
Portugal's forests are a major natural resource. More than one-third of the country's total continental territory (3.1 million hectares out of a total of 8.9 million hectares) is forested, notably with pine, cork oak and eucalyptus. More than 90 per cent of forested land is privately owned, the highest proportion in the EU.
Portugal's cork production supplies around 52 per cent of the world market. Cork forests are declining and being replaced by eucalyptus plantations as plastic corks become more popular in wine bottles. Eucalyptus trees are contributing to desertification, as they require large amounts of water to grow.

Industry and manufacturing
Although it contributes around 38 per cent to GDP and employs 32 per cent of the workforce, industry remains relatively underdeveloped and dependent on imported energy and materials.
Portugal faces a difficult transition from traditional industries – clothing, textiles and footwear – afflicted by low value-added products, inefficient management and outmoded technology, to a diversified industrial base.
Important industries include processed cork, paper, cement, fertilisers, steel and glassware. High-growth sectors include vehicle manufacture, semiconductors, electronics, plastics, food processing and franchising.
Industrial production increased by 1.5 per cent in 2003 and an estimated 1.1 per cent in 2004.

Tourism
Portugal is said to have an Atlantic front and Mediterranean heart. Its history is interwoven with world events, as its pioneering explorers opened up sea routes to start an empire spanning three continents. Portugal has 13 sites on the UN World Heritage list, including prehistoric rock art, the historic centre of Oporto, the landscape of Sintra and the largest surviving laurel forest (on the island of Medeira). Its lush northern lands produce the grapes necessary for its famous ports (fortified wines) and its sun-bathed southern regions attract many tourists from Northern Europe in particular.
Travel and tourism is an important component of the economy and accounted for 16 per cent of GDP (US$30.1 billion) and employed 18 per cent of the workforce (858,000 jobs) in 2014. The global

economic crisis impacted on the sector with visitor revenue falling from a high of US$14 billion in 2008 to US$12.3 billion in 2009; in 2010 spending increased marginally to US$12.9 billion and further still to an anticipated US$13.3 billion in 2011. Visitor revenue is set to increase by 5 per cent from 2014 to US$15.1 billion in 2015.

Capital investment in travel and tourism has included the increased use of broadband internet connections to boost bookings. The travel and tourism sector attracted capital investment of US$2.8 billion in 2014 set to increase by 1.2 per cent in 2015.

Mining

The mining sector contributes around 1 per cent of GDP and employs a similar fraction of the workforce. Although there is considerable mineral wealth, deposits are scattered and not easily exploitable on a large scale. The most important mineral resources include non-metallic ores such as rock salt, pyrites (the reserves in the Alentejo region make up nearly 23 per cent of total worldwide reserves) and excellent quality marble. Large reserves of uranium are also available. Small-scale mining of tin, copper, tungsten concentrates, marble, stone and iron pyrites takes place.

Hydrocarbons

Portugal had proven oil reserves of 538,100 barrels in 2014 and production of 0 bpd due to the unfeasibility of extracting such a tiny amount of oil.

The state-owned Galp Energia (Petróleos e Gás de Portugal) is responsible for oil and gas businesses. It controls the only refining company Petrogal, which operates two oil refineries with a total capacity of 304,174 barrels per day (bpd) and its distribution operation, plus GDP which is responsible for natural gas imports, transport and distributions. It also has foreign energy interests, including exploration and production and energy generation. Portugal consumed 244,200 bpd and refined 285,300 bpd in 2014. It exported 168,000 bpd in 2013 and imported 86,720 bpd.

Portugal has no proven reserves of natural gas, however, consumption of natural gas has grown considerably from 116 million cubic metres (cum) in 1997 to 4 billion cum in 2014. In March 2009 the Algerian state-owned Sonatrach which had been supplying 2.5 billion cum, was given a licence to sell its natural gas directly to Portuguese consumers, to be supplied via the Maghreb-Europe gas pipeline, and assuring Portugal's long-term energy supply.

A liquid natural gas (LNG) re-gasification terminal has been built at the port of Setubal, south of Lisbon, connected by a pipeline extended along the Atlantic coast to the northern town of Braga. The pipeline is linked to the European natural gas network via Spain, providing an alternative source of supply for Europe. LNG is imported from Algeria and Nigeria.

Portugal imports all of its natural gas, which amounted to 4.1 billion cum in 2014.

Reserves of coal are scarce and of poor quality, production ceased in 1994. Any use of coal is commercially insignificant.

Energy

Total installed generating capacity was 19.6 gigawatts (GW) in 2013.

Portugal built its first offshore wind turbine on June 16 2012 and it is floating, the first offshore wind turbine to be installed without the use of any heavy lift vessels or piling equipment at sea. It has a turbine capable of producing enough electricity for 1,300 households. On April 27 2015, the EU granted approval for a 25 MW floating farm demonstration project to be developed off the coast of Portugal. It will contribute to increasing Portugal's share of renewable energy by developing new generation technologies. Floating wind turbines are unique because they have the ability to be deployed in much deeper waters than is feasible for traditional offshore wind farms that require columns affixed to the seafloor.

42.4 per cent of total installed capacity is derived from fossil fuels while 28.2 per cent is produced from hydroelectric plants and 29.4 per cent from other renewable sources.

Energias de Portugal (EdP) is the national power utility and one of the largest energy companies in Europe. Portugal and Spain's electricity grids are integrated.

Financial markets

Stock exchange

Euronext NV Lisbon

Commodity exchange

Liffe Connect

Banking and insurance

In November 2008 the government announced it was going to nationalise Banco Portugues de Negócios after the bank ran up losses of almost US$900 million.

Central bank

Banco de Portugal (Bank of Portugal); European Central Bank (ECB).

Main financial centre

Lisbon

Time

GMT (daylight saving, late March to late October, GMT plus one hour)

Geography

Mainland Portugal lies on the west side of the Iberian peninsula with the furthermost point of western Europe jutting into the Atlantic Ocean. The 837km coastline runs down along the west and south coast. Spain borders Portugal in the north and east. There are two archipelagos in the Atlantic Ocean – the Azores and the Madeira Islands.

All inclusive, Portugal is 92,080 square km in size. There are six major rivers, three of which rise in Spain and flow into the Atlantic Ocean. The Duoro in the mountainous north runs east-west across the country and used to provide an important shipping route. It flows through the city of Oporto. The longest river, the Tagus, has a large estuary, on which the capital, Lisbon, sits and is navigable for over 100km by seagoing ships. The Guadiana in the south, forms part of the border with Spain. The tallest peaks at 1,991 meters (m) are in the Serra da Estrela, in central Portugal. In the south the land is rolling hills and plains.

Lying south-west of the European mainland, the Azores consist of three scattered groups of nine inhabited islands and several uninhabitable ones, and include 12 active volcanoes. The Madeira archipelago is west of North Africa and has only two inhabited islands. The Azores and Madeira are volcanic in origin with steep topographies, the tallest – and youngest due to the continued lava flows that add to its mass – is located on Pico (Azores), at 2,321m high.

Hemisphere

Northern

Climate

Situated in the middle of the northern hemisphere, Portugal has a mild welcoming climate. However, the difference between the north/south and coast/inland weather is marked. Inland areas have more variable weather than coastal regions. To the south of the Tagus river the Mediterranean influences are clear. Long, hot, humid summers and dry, short, relatively mild winters. May–October dry and warm, November–April cool with rain in north, mild in south (though often wet and windy January–March). Temperatures vary between 8–28 Celsius.

Dress codes

Business people dress conservatively in dark blue or grey suits and ties.

Entry requirements

Passports

Required by all, except members of the EU, EEA and Switzerland who may use a valid national ID card. Passports must be valid for at least three months from date of arrival.

Visa
Required by all, except nationals of EU and Schengen Accord signatory countries, North America, Australasia and Japan. For further exceptions contact the nearest Portuguese consulate or a travel agent. Schengen visas cover all entry needs..For business trips, an original invitation from a business contact in Portugal is necessary, plus proof of accommodation booking and a letter from an employer giving the purpose and duration of the visit, when applying. A Schengen visa application (offered in several languages) can be downloaded from http://europa.eu/abc/travel/ see 'documents you will need'.

Currency advice/regulations
The import of local and foreign currency is unlimited but amounts over eur5,000 should be declared on entry. Export of local currency is limited to eur5,000 and an equivalent amount in foreign currency may require currency exchange receipts to be produced.
Travellers cheques are readily accepted.

Customs
Personal items are duty-free. There are no duties levied on alcohol and tobacco between EU member states, providing amounts imported are for personal consumption only. The export of luxury goods, such as gold, silver and jewellery, is limited to the value of eur150, without special permission.

Health (for visitors)
Nationals of the European Economic Area (EEA) countries and Switzerland can access reduced cost and sometimes free medical treatment using a European Health Insurance Card (EHIC) while visiting the EEA. Exceptions include nationals of the 10 countries, which joined the EU in 2004, whose EHIC is not valid in Switzerland. Applications for the EHIC should be made before travelling.

Mandatory precautions
Yellow fever vaccination certificate required for Azores and Madeira only if arriving from infected areas.

Advisable precautions
Immunisations that may be recommended is for hepatitis A and tuberculosis (although not for a short duration stay).

Hotels
A full range of hotels are available throughout the country, and are classified from one- to five-star. There is a 10 per cent service charge but a tip is also expected.

Credit cards
All usual credit cards are widely accepted. ATMs are readily available.

Public holidays (national)

Fixed dates
1 Jan (New Year's Day), 25 Apr (Liberty Day), 1 May (Labour Day), 10 Jun (Portugal Day), 15 Aug (Assumption Day), 5 Oct (Republic Day), 1 Nov (All Saints' Day), 1 Dec (Restoration of Independence Day), 8 Dec (Immaculate Conception), 25 Dec (Christmas).

Variable dates
Carnival (Feb), Good Friday (Mar/Apr), Corpus Christi (May/Jun).
From 2013–18, public holidays on 1 Nov (All Saints' Day), 5 Oct (Republic Day), 1 Dec (Restoration of Independence) and Corpus Christi will be suspended.

Working hours

Banking
Mon–Fri: 0830–1500. Some banks in Lisbon open until 1800.

Business
Mon–Fri: 0900–1300 and 1500–1900.

Government
Mon–Fri: 0930–1200 and 1430–1800, closed 1730 on Mon and Tue.

Shops
Mon–Fri: 0900–1300, 1500–1900; Sat: 0900/1000–1300 general shops.
Mon–Sun: 1000–2300/2400 shopping centres/malls.

Telecommunications

Mobile/cell phones
There are 900/1800 and 3G GSM services available throughout the country.

Electricity supply
220V AC, with two round-pin plugs.

Social customs/useful tips
The Portuguese like to entertain. Lunch usually takes place between 1200 and 1400, dinner between 1900 and 2200. The Portuguese are extremely courteous, helpful and open to foreigners. Men always shake hands when they meet strangers or male friends. Women often kiss each other or their male friends once on each cheek.
It is impolite to refuse an offer of coffee. Tips should be given to anyone who carries out a service for you. There is no set rule on how much to tip.

Getting there

Air
National airline: TAP-Air Portugal.
International airport/s: Lisbon (LIS), 7km north of capital. Facilities include 24-hour *bureau de change*, banks, tourist information, post office, duty-free shops and car hire.
A special *aerobus* departs for the city centre every 20 minutes. Other express buses run to the railway station and other destinations around the country. Taxis are available, with a surcharge after 2200hrs.
Other airport/s: Oporto (OPO), 11km from city, Faro (FAO), 4km from city; Funchal (FNC) on Maderia; and Santa Maria (SMA) in the Azores, 3.2km from Vila do Porto.
Airport tax: None

Surface
Road: There are only road connections with Spain, of which the principle are motorways (with tolls), these in turn connect to the trans-European road network. Smaller cross-border roads maintain traditional routes.
Rail: There are four cross-border railway lines from Spain via either Salamanca, Santiago de Compostela, Badajoz or Madrid, which is the hub for lines to France.
Water: There are car ferry services from Plymouth or Portsmouth (UK) to Santander or Bilbao (northern Spain) respectively, from March–December.
The islands of Madeira and Azores have regular ferry services to the mainland of Spain and Portugal as well as to Grand Canary and Cape Verde.
Main port/s: The three most important ports are Lisbon, Leixes (Oporto) and Sines (south of Lisbon).

Getting about

National transport
Air: TAP and domestic charter airlines operate scheduled flights between most major cities, Madeira and the Azores.
Road: The Lisbon-Oporto, Lisbon-Algarve and Lisbon-Badajoz roads are national highway, toll roads. The road network has been upgraded in recent years and while local roads can often be narrow they link all rural communities with provincial roads.
Buses: Regular coach services, *Expresso* are inter-city and *Rápidas* link major regional towns, they can provide a quicker alternative service than by rail, although with a relatively higher priced ticket.
Rail: Caminhos de Ferro Portugueses (CP) operates about 3,600km of track, of which 500km are electrified. The *Alfa Pendular* provides a high-speed service between Oporto-Faro via Lisbon (journey time around six hours) reservations must be made and bookings can be made online. Regional services are available between cities and main towns.
Water: The 800km of inland waterways are only rarely used. Some coastal shipping operates, including services to Madeira and the Azores.

City transport
Taxis: Lisbon taxis are green and black. They are relatively cheap and offer an efficient service. A tip of 15 per cent is expected. Taxis may be scarce during rush-hours.
Buses, trams & metro: Lisbon has some steep climbs and there are three

elevadors (funiculars – cable cars) from Baixa to the Bairro Alto neighbourhood and the Santa Justa. Buses run throughout the city.

The metro (from 0630–0100) provides four lines within the city and links to five suburban lines. the remaining services for the city.

Other cities and towns have public bus services.

Ferry: There are two ferry companies operating in Lisbon on the river Tagus. CP provides links from the city centre to Barreiro, on the south shore, which connects with the railway line to the Algarve. Transtejo provides services to Montijo, Seixal and Cacilhas.

Car hire

Self-drive and chauffeur-driven cars are available throughout the country.

An international driving licence or full national licence is required, as well as an international insurance Green Card. The wearing of seat belts is compulsory and all vehicles must carry a warning red triangle and warning waistcoats (fluorescent jackets) when leaving a vehicle during a breakdown or emergency.

Detailed motoring information is available from Automovel Clube de Portugal in Lisbon.

Driving in Portugal can be hazardous. In proportion to the number of vehicles, the country has one of the highest death and accident rates in Europe.

BUSINESS DIRECTORY

The addresses listed below are a selection only. While World of Information makes every endeavour to check these addresses, we cannot guarantee that changes have not been made, especially to telephone numbers and area codes. We would welcome any corrections.

Telephone area codes

The international dialling code (IDD) for Portugal is +351, followed by area code and subscriber's number:

Beja	284	Faro	289
Braga	253	Lisbon	21
Braganca	273	Madeira	291
Coimbra	239	Oporto	22
Covilha	275	Ponta Delgado	296

Chambers of Commerce

American Chamber of Commerce in Portugal, 155 Rua D Estefânia, 1000-154 Lisbon (tel: 357-2561; fax: 357-2580; e-mail: nop37676@mail.telepac.pt).

British-Portuguese Chamber of Commerce, 8 Rua da Estrela, 1200-669 Lisbon (tel: 394-2020; fax: 394-2029; e-mail: info@bpcc.pt).

Coimbra Chamber of Commerce and Industry, Rua Coronel Júlio Veiga Simão, Edificio Novotecna, 3020-260 Coimbra (tel: 497-160; fax: 494-066; e-mail: geral@cec.org.pt).

Madeira Chamber of Commerce and Industry, 41 Avenida Arriaga, 9004-507 Funchal (tel: 206-800; fax: 206-868; e-mail: geral@acif-ccim.pt).

Oporto Chamber of Commerce and Industry, Rua Ferreira Borges, Palácio da Bolsa, 4050-253 Oporto (tel: 399-000; fax: 399-090; e-mail: cciporto@mail.telepac.pt).

Ponta Delgada Chamber of Commerce and Industry, 13 Rua Ernsto do Canto, 9504-531 Ponta Delgada, Azores (tel: 305-000; fax: 305-050; e-mail: ccipd@ccipd.pt).

Portuguese Chamber of Commerce and Industry, 89 Rua das Portas de Santo Antão, 1169-022 Lisbon (tel: 322-4050; fax: 322-4051; e-mail: geral@port-chambers.com).

Banking

ABN AMRO Bank NV, Av da Liberdade 131, 5, Lisbon (tel: 321-1800; fax: 321-1900).

Associação Portuguesa de Bancos (Portuguese Bankers' Association), 35 Avenida da República, Lisbon (tel: 357-9804; fax: 357-9533, 352-9682).

Banco BPI SA, Rua do Comércio 132, Lisbon (tel: 887-4801, 887-3161, 311-1000; fax: 346-7308).

Banco Comercial Português SA, International Division, Rua Augusta 62—74, Lisbon (tel: 321-1780, 312-5936; fax: 321-1789; e-mail: dint@bcp.pt); Investor Relations Division (tel: 321-1080; e-mail: investors@bcp.pt).

Banco Espírito Santo e Com de Lisbon, Avenida da Liberdade 195, Lisbon (tel: 315-8331; fax: 353-2931, 350-8977).

Banco Internacional de Crédito, Avenida Fontes Pereira de Melo 27, Lisbon (tel/fax: 315-7135).

Banco Mello, Av José Malhoa, Lote 1682, Lisbon (tel: 720-1500; fax: 720-1766, 720-1599; e-mail: investor@bancomello.pt).

Banco Nacional Ultramarino (commercial bank), Av 5 de Outubro 175, Lisbon (tel: 793-3223, 793-0112; fax: (International Department) 793-8952).

Banco Pinto e Sotto Mayor (commercial bank), Rua do Ouro 28, Lisbon (tel: 340-3000, 347-6261; fax: (International Department) 357-3973).

Banco Português do Atlântico SA, Tagus Park, Edif Serv 1, Piso 2, Oeiras (tel: 422-4000; fax: 422-4489).

Banco Santander Portugal SA, Praça Marquês de Pombal 2, Lisbon (tel: 310-7000; fax: 315-4963).

Banco Totta & Açores SA (commercial bank), Rua do Ouro 88, Lisbon (tel: 321-3000; fax: 321-1582).

Caixa Geral de Depósitos (savings bank), International Department, Largo do Calhariz, Lisbon (tel: 790-5018; fax: 790-5068).

Central Banco de Investimento SA, Rua Castilho 233-4, Lisbon (tel: 386-4097; fax: 387-3208).

Credito Predial Português, Rua Augusta 237, Lisbon (tel: 321-4200; fax: (International Department) 313-7438).

Finibanco, Av de Berna, 10-1064, Lisbon (tel: 790-2800; fax: 790-2801).

Central bank

Banco de Portugal, 27 Rua do Ouro 1100-150 Lisbon (tel: 321-3200; fax: 346-4843; email: info@bportugal.pt).

European Central Bank (ECB), Kaiserstrasse 29, D-60311 Frankfurt am Main, Germany (tel: (+49-69) 13-440; fax: (+49-69) 1344-6000; email: info@ecb.int).

Stock exchange

Euronext NV Lisbon, www.euronext.com

Chi-X, www.chi-x.com

Commodity exchange

Liffe Connect, www.nyse.com/nyseeuronext

Travel information

Comissão Municipal de Turismo de Lisboa, Pavilhao Carlos Lopes, Parque Eduardo VII, 1070 Lisbon (tel: 315-1915/6/7/8; fax: 352-1472).

Comissão Municipal de Turismo do Oporto, Rua Clube dos Fenianos 25, 4000 Oporto (tel: 323-303, 312-543; fax: 208-4548).

Costa Verde Tourism Office, Praça D Joao I 43, 4000 Oporto (tel: 317-514).

Lisbon Airport Tourism Office, 1700 Lisbon (tel: 849-4323/3689; fax: 848-5974).

Lisbon Tourist Office, Palácio Foz, Praça dos Restauradores, 1200 Lisbon (tel: 346-3314/3643; fax: 346-8772).

Madeira Tourism Office, Avenida Arriaga 18, 9000 Funchal (tel: (+091) 229-057, 225-658; fax: (+091) 232-151; internet: www.madeiraguide.com).

Pousadas of Portugal, Rua Soares de Passos, 3 Alto de Santo Amaro, 1300-314 Lisbon (tel: 844-2001; fax: 844-2085; internet: www.pousadas.pt).

Regiao de Turismo da Planicie Dourada, Praca da Republica 12, 7800 Beja (tel: 321-369; fax: 326-332).

National tourist organisation offices
Portuguese Tourism Board (ITP), Rua Ivone Silva, Lote 6, 1050-124 Lisbon (tel: 781-0000; fax: 793-7537; email: info@iturismo.pt; internet: www.iturismo.pt).

Ministries
Ministry of Agriculture, Food and Fisheries, Praça do Comércio, 1149-010 Lisbon (tel: 346-3151; fax: 347-7890).

Ministry of Culture, Palácio Nacional da Ajuda, 1349-003 Lisbon (tel: 361-4500; fax: 364-9999).

Ministry of Defence, Avenida Ilha da Madeira, 1400-204 Lisbon (tel: 303-4500; fax: 303-4525).

Ministry of Economy, Rua da Horta Seca 15, 1200-221 Lisbon (tel: 322-8600; fax: 322-8741).

Ministry of Education, Avenida 5 de Outubro 107-13, 1069-018 Lisbon (tel: 795-0330; fax: 793-3618).

Ministry for Employment, Praça de Londres 2-14, 1049-056 Lisbon (tel: 844-1700; fax: 847-0027).

Ministry of the Environment, Rua do Século 51-2, 1200-433 Lisbon (tel: 3223-2500; fax: 323-2531).

Ministry of Finance, Avenida Infante D Henriques 5, 1149-009 Lisbon (tel: 888-4675; fax: 886-0032).

Ministry of Foreign Affairs, Largo do Rilvas, 11399-030 Lisbon (tel: 394-6000; fax: 390-9708).

Ministry of Health, Avenida João Crisóstomo 9-6, 1049-062 Lisbon (tel: 354-4560; fax: 354-0302).

Ministry of Home Affairs, Praça do Comércio, 1149-015 Lisbon (tel: 323-3000; fax: 342-7372).

Ministry of Industry and Energy, Rua da Horta Seca 15, 1200 Lisbon (tel: 346-3091/6091; fax: 347-5901).

Ministry of Justice, Praça do Comércio, 1149-019 Lisbon (322-2300; fax: 347-9208).

Ministry of Planning, Public Works and Territorial Administration, Palacio Penafiel, Rua de S Mamede ao Caldas 21, 1149-050 Lisbon (tel: 886-1119; fax: 886-3827).

Ministry of Science and Technology, Praça do Comércio - Ala Oriental, 1149-003 Lisbon (tel: 881-2000; fax: 888-2434).

Ministry of Social Security, Rua Rosa Araújo 43, 1250-194 Lisbon (tel: 353-0049; fax: 353-0074).

Prime Minister's Office, Rua da Imprensa a Estrela 2, 1200 Lisbon (tel: 397-4091; fax: 395-1616).

Other useful addresses
Agencia de Informação LUSA (news agency), Rua Dr João Couto, Lote C, Lisbon (tel: 714-4099).

Associação Industrial Portuguesa, Apt 5200, Praça das Indústrias, 1301 Lisbon (tel: 360-1500).

Associação Industrial Portuense, Avenida da Boavista 2671, Oporto (tel: 615-8500; fax: 617-6840).

Bolsa de Valores de Lisboa (Lisbon Stock Exchange), Edificio da Bolsa, Rua Soeiro Pereira Gomes, Lisbon (tel: 790-0000; fax: 795-2021; e-mail: Infomktg@bvl.pt; internet site: www.bvl.pt/).

Comissão Co-ordenação Regiao (CCR) Norte, Rua Rainha D Estefania 251, Oporto (tel: 695-236/7/8/9/0; fax: 600-2040).

CCR Algarve, Praça da Liberdade 2, Faro (tel: 802-401; fax: 803-591).

CCR Lisboa e Vale do Tejo, Rua Artilharia Um 33, Lisbon (tel: 387-5541; fax: 691-292).

Instituto de Apoio às Pequenas e Médias Empresas Industriais (IAPMEI), Rua Rodrigo da Fonseca 73, Lisbon (tel: 562-211).

Instituto Nacional de Estatistica (INE), Av António José de Almeida 2, Lisbon (tel: 847-0050; fax: 848-9480; internet site: www.ine.pt).

Investimentos Comércio e Turismo de Portugal (ICEP), (e-mail: icepdiesnar@mail.telepac.pt; internet: www.icep.pt).

Portugal Telecom (PT), Investor Relations, Lisbon (tel: 500-1701, 500-8739; e-mail: manuel.j.castela@telecom.pt).

Portuguese Embassy (USA), 2125 Kalorama Road, NW, Washington DC 20008 (tel: (+1-202) 328-8610; fax: (+1-202) 462-3726; e-mail: embportwash@mindspring.com).

Privatisation Office, c/o Ministério das Finanças – Commissão de Acompanhamento das Privatizacões (c/o Ministry of Finance – Commission for the Accompaniment of Privatisations), Av Infante D Henrique 5, Lisbon (tel: 618-0057).

Radiotelevisão Portuguesa – RTP (Portugal's radio/television broadcaster), 197 Avenida 5 de Outubro, Lisbon (tel: 793-1774; fax: 796-6227).

Sociedade de Desenvolvimento da Madeira SA (SDM), 1st Floor, 9 Rua da Mouraria; PO Box 4164, Funchal, Madeira (tel: (351-291) 201-333; fax: (351-291) 201-399; email: sdm@sdm.pt; internet site: www.sdmadeira.pt).

Sociedade Independente de Comunicação – SIC (independent broadcasting company), 119 Estrada da Outurela, Carnaxide, Linda a Velha (tel: 417-3138; fax: 417-3118).

Televisão Independente – TVI (independent television broadcasting), Pt16-s 603-B Rua 3, Matinha, Lisbon (tel: 858-7968; fax: 858-2319).

National news agency: Lusa News Press Agency, Rua Dr Joao Couto, Lote C P 1503-809 Lisbon (tel: 711-6500; email: agencialusa@lusa.pt; internet:www.lusa.pt).

Photonews (Agência Noticiosa) (www.photonews.com.pt)

Internet sites
Guide to business: www.portugaloffer.pt

Icep Portugal (business promotion): www.portugalinbusiness.com

Portugal portal: www.portugal.org

Lisbon Airport: www.ana-aeroportos.pt

Tourist portal: www.portugalvisitor.com

Yellow Pages: www.paginasamarelas.pt

Puerto Rico

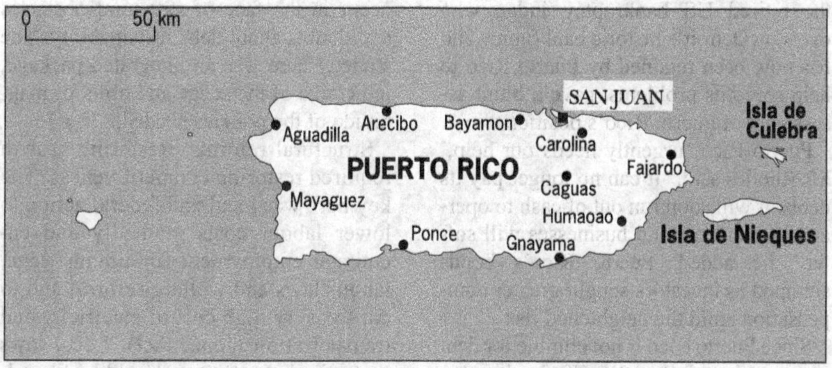

According to Puerto Rico's Institute of Statistics, between 2000 and 2010, 288,000 Puerto Ricans left the island for the US. And it seems that since then the rate of emigration has accelerated. The annual emigration rate averaged 54,000 in 2011 and 2012 – out of a population of some 3.6 million. Although Puerto Ricans have had what is described as a form of US citizenship since 1917, they cannot, for example, vote in Presidential elections. Under the Jones Shafrot Act they are granted special immigrant status. They can travel freely, they can join the military, they can vote in local elections and they are eligible for some federal benefits. But that's as far as it goes. After almost six centuries of absent administration, first by Spain and – since 1898 – by the US, Puerto Ricans still had difficulty in managing their own affairs. But rarely with such difficulty as that which faced them in mid-2015.

From Puerto Rico to Puerto Pobre

Unquestionably, Puerto Rico had entered 2015 facing a very tight situation. Its debt of 70 billion dollars had brought about a number of downgrades in its credit rating, which (in February 2015) hovered just above 'junk' status. Investors had reached the point where they could no longer see Puerto Rico paying its debts. The emigration level was the highest since the decade of the 1950s, when an estimated 470,000 Puerto Ricans had left for the United States. Then, the emigrants consisted mostly of rural farm workers who left to work on the farms and in the factories of a booming US. The Puerto Rican government encouraged them to depart, aware that the island's economy simply could not generate enough jobs.

By 2015, those emigrating were for the most part young, qualified professionals, that the government (having invested in their training and formation) would rather see stay. According to the Statistics Institute, in 2011 they were made up of 2,700 in the catering sector, teachers (2,000) and lawyers (280). Florida was the most popular destination, followed by the states of New York and Texas. The combination of this exodus and reduced levels of fertility meant that the population had fallen from 3.83 million in 2004 (its highest ever level) to 3.62 million in 2013. The US Census Bureau forecast a level of 2.98 million by 2050, the same level as that seen in 1975.

With unemployment entrenched at 14.7 per cent, economists can see that the government's revenues risk declining dramatically. Optimists hope that a number of those who left for the US would return, better qualified and competent to start new businesses that would re-invigorate the economy. Swimming against the tide, Governor Alejandro García Padilla, had been talking up the island's attractiveness for businesses, claiming that since his taking office in January 2013, over 25,000 jobs had been created. He had set a target of 50,000 new jobs by mid-2016. The Governor's cabinet director, Ingrid Vila Biaggi, stated that 'Our people have already been faced with serious problems and has always overcome them.'

KEY FACTS

Official name: Estado Libre Asociado de Puerto Rico (Commonwealth of Puerto Rico)

Head of State: US President Barack Obama

Head of government: Governor Alejandro Javier Garcia Padilla (PPD) (from 2 Jan 2013)

Ruling party: Partido Popular Democrático (PPD) (Popular Democratic Party) (from 2 Jan 2013)

Area: 8,897 square km (Puerto Rico comprises the main island plus two smaller islands (Vieques and Culebra) and numerous smaller islets.)

Population: 3.71 million (2011); (3,725,789; 2010, census figure)

Capital: San Juan

Official language: Spanish, English

Currency: US dollar (US$) = 100 cents

Exchange rate: US$1.00 per US$ (fixed rate)

GDP per capita: US$17,687 (2011)*

GDP real growth: -1.70% (2011)*

GDP: US$65.40 billion (2011)*

Unemployment: 15.90% (2012)*

Inflation: 3.60% (2011)*

Balance of trade: US$20.16 billion (2009)*

* estimated figure

It's the math(s)

Pointedly speaking in Spanish, the Governor of Puerto Rico announced in a televised address in late June 2015 that the island could not pay back more than US$70 billion in debt, thereby triggering an unprecedented financial crisis that would rock the municipal bond market and lead to higher borrowing costs for governments across the United States. This is not about politics,' said the governor, 'It's about math.' Mr Garcia Padilla said that the island territory needed to postpone for several years its debt payments. 'The first step is to revive economic growth...We will never get out of this vicious cycle,' said Garcia Padilla. 'But we need to do more – much more – to return to riches and to become more competitive and have an expansion in the private market.' Quite how 'much more' was going to be done by much less people, much less qualified people, was not made clear.

The Puerto Rican default also raised questions about the traditionally conservative municipal bond market, which states and cities of the US had long relied on to pay upfront costs for public improvements such as roads, parks and hospitals. For decades, those bonds had been considered safe investments – although some of those assumptions had been recalibrated in recent years as a number of US municipalities, notably Detroit, but also Stockton and Vallejo in California, had declared bankruptcy. Those defaults at least offered investors the protection provided by Chapter 9 of the US bankruptcy code, which set out an orderly process by which investors could recoup at least some of their money. However, Puerto Rico is treated as a state rather than a municipality and is therefore not permitted to file for bankruptcy. Any failure to thrash out some sort of an agreement with creditors could ignite an unwieldy, uncharted and long-lasting process to sort out the island's financial obligations.

To make matters worse, with as much as US$73 billion in debt, the island's debt obligation is four times that of Detroit, which had been the largest US city to file for bankruptcy in 2012. The implications were serious for Americans outside Puerto Rico largely because many held island bonds in mutual funds. At one point in 2013, an estimated three out of four municipal bond mutual funds held Puerto Rican bonds, which were attractive because of their high yields and exemption from federal, state and local taxes.

The Caribbean island has been struggling to relieve a US$73 billion debt burden. It came to a crunch point at the end of June 2015 – ironically at the same time as it did for debt-laden Greece – after a dire report on its stability by former International Monetary Fund economists was released in June 2015, ahead of key deadlines to repay debt. Steven Rhodes, the retired US bankruptcy judge who oversaw Detroit's historic bankruptcy and has now been retained by Puerto Rico to help solve its problems, gave a blunt assessment of Puerto Rico's position.

Puerto Rico 'urgently needs our help,' Mr Rhodes said. 'It can no longer pay its debts, it will soon run out of cash to operate, its residents and businesses will suffer,' he added. Puerto Rico's bonds slumped as investors sought greater compensation amid the heightened risk.

Since Puerto Rico is not eligible for debt restructuring under the US bankruptcy code because it is not a municipality, Mr Rhodes said that the island's future hinged on gaining eligibility for debt restructuring, while stressing that bankruptcy would not be a 'bailout'.

Governor Garcia Padilla called for Washington to grant the US territory the ability to file for bankruptcy in a televised address, as he said that his goal was to come up with a negotiated moratorium with bondholders to postpone debt payments for a number of years.

Backing up the default announcement was the simultaneous publication of a report commissioned by the governor and by Puerto Rico's government Development Bank, which analysed the island's finances. The report was written by the former World Bank chief economist and former deputy director of the IMF, Anne Krueger, and the economists Ranjit Teja and Andrew Wolfe. The report's authors acknowledged that Puerto Rico faced hard times. Structural problems, economic shocks and weak public finances had yielded a decade of stagnation, emigration ('outmigration') and debt. The financial markets had once overlooked these realities but had since cut off the Commonwealth from normal market access. A crisis loomed. For its part, the administration had worked hard to stave off a financing crisis with important measures since 2013, including higher taxes, pension reforms and spending cuts. However, as much as these were needed, much remained to be done to build on this progress. Given the economic downdrafts, the coming years would be difficult. But it was within the power of this government, which has repeatedly demonstrated a willingness to act, to set the economy on a sustainable path.

PuertoRico, in the authors' view, had advantages it could parlay (convert) into market confidence and durable growth if decades-old policy failings were fully addressed. The debt could not be made sustainable without growth, nor could growth occur in the face of structural obstacles and doubts about debt sustainability. The strategy here was an integrated package, indicative of the scope and order of magnitude of the policies needed:

Structural reforms: Restoring growth required restoring competitiveness. The key here was local and federal action to lower labour costs gradually and encourage employment (minimum wage, labour laws and welfare reform) and to cut the very high cost of electricity and transportation (Jones Act). Local laws that raised input costs should be liberalised and obstacles to the ease of doing business removed. Public enterprise reform was also crucial.

Fiscal reform and public debt. Probably the most startling finding in the report would be that the true fiscal deficit was much larger than had been assumed. Even a major fiscal effort would leave residual financing gaps in the coming years, which could be bridged by debt restructuring (a voluntary exchange of existing bonds for new ones with a longer/lower debt service profile). Public enterprises also faced financial challenges and were in discussions with their creditors. Despite legal complexities, all discussions with creditors should be co-ordinated.

Institutional credibility. The legacy of weak budget execution and opaque data – our fiscal analysis entailed many iterations – needed to be overcome. Priorities included legislative approval of a multi-year fiscal adjustment plan, legislative rules on deficits, a fiscal oversight board and more reliable and timely data. The report's authors also acknowledged that this was a daunting agenda politically, legally and organisationally. It was also an urgent one: the government's cash balances could evaporate in the face of delays, reducing the room for manoeuvre and intensifying the crisis.

Mr Garcia Padilla warned that citizens might face cuts in services as the government reduced spending. Anne Kreuger said that 'The situation is dire and I mean really dire, the needed measures may face political resistance but failure to address the issues would affect even more the people of Puerto Rico.'

The citizens of Puerto Rico faced tough measures such as fewer teachers, higher property taxes and the suspension of the minimum wage if Puerto Rico followed the report's recommendations of debt restructuring and austerity measures. However, Mr Garcia Padilla said he would not support cuts to the minimum wage.

It was reported that the US government seemed unlikely to get involved, despite months of talks between Puerto Rico and the US Treasury about options to seek financial help. A White House spokesman confirmed that 'There's no one in the administration or in Washington DC that's contemplating a federal bailout of Puerto Rico.'

Risk assessment

Economy	Poor/Catastrophic
Politics	Poor
Regional stability	Good

COUNTRY PROFILE

1493 The island was inhabited by some 100,000 Taíno Indians (an Arawak culture that also occupied most of Hispaniola and part of Cuba) at the time of the first European sighting by Columbus.
1508 Juan Ponce de Léon landed from Hispaniola and took control of the island. He named it San Juan.
1898 The island was ceded to the US by Spain at the end of the Spanish-American war. The US ruled it as an unincorporated territory.
1917 Puerto Ricans became citizens of the US.
1948 Puerto Rico elected Luis Muñoz Marín as its first governor.
1952 A new constitution designated Puerto Rico a self-governing commonwealth within the US.
1967 A plebiscite rejected the option of becoming a state of the US.
1993 The statehood option was rejected for a second time in a national referendum.
1998 The option of statehood was narrowly rejected in favour of maintaining the constitutional *status quo*.
2000 Sila Maria Calderón Serra became the first female governor. Partido Popular Democrático (PPD) (Popular Democratic Party) won the parliamentary elections.
2001 The Blue Riband Commission was empanelled to review large transactions made by the previous (Rosselló) administration.
2003 Closure of the US navy base on Vieques lost Puerto Rico an estimated US$300 million per year in revenues.
2004 Aníbal Acevedo Vilá won gubernatorial elections.
2005 Although a referendum approved the proposal that the Senate and House of Representatives be replaced by a unicameral legislature, the House of Representatives allowed the legislation to lapse.
2006 The US Supreme Court turned down an appeal to give Puerto Ricans voting rights in presidential elections.
2008 Governor Acevedo called on the UN to back Puerto Rico's right of self-determination. In gubernatorial elections, Luis Fortuño (Partido Nuevo Progresista (PNP) (New Progressive Party)) won 52.8 per cent of the vote.
2009 Luis Fortuño (PNP) was inaugurated as governor in January.
2010 A census for the United States, including Puerto Rico took part. Existing birth certificates were declared invalid and all citizens had to be issued with new ones in an effort to combat identity theft. Criminal organisations had targeted Puerto Rico where nationals have rights to US passports. The US State Department had discovered that around 40 per cent of fraudulent US passport applications were using birth certificates from Puerto Rico. US banking regulators shut down three Puerto Rican banks and sold their deposits to other financial institutions. The move cost the Federal Deposit Insurance Corporation (FDIC) US$5.3 billion as the banks were insolvent and unable to trade due to large numbers of unsustainable loans. The US pharmaceutical company, Pfizer, closed its chemical plant in Puerto Rico with the loss of 6,000 jobs at a time of high unemployment.
2011 In March, the Republican controlled Congress voted to rescind the voting rights of representatives of among others, Puerto Rico, effectively disenfranchising its electorate in policies that directly affect them.
2012 On 19 August, in a referendum to amend the constitution, voters rejected the (cost cutting) proposal to reduce the number of seats in the legislature. An earthquake, of magnitude 7.6, struck in the Nicoya Peninsula (140km from San José) on 5 September; damage was not considered serious. General elections, and a referendum on the political status of Puerto Rico, were held on 6 November. The opposition PPD won 28 seats (out of 51) in the House of Representatives and the PNP 23; four other political parties failed to win any seats. In senate elections, the PPD won 18 seats (out of 27), the PNP eight and the Partido Independentista Puertorriqueño (PIP) (Puerto Rican Independence Party) one. In gubernatorial elections, Alejandro Garcia Padilla (PPD) won 47.9 per cent of the vote, incumbent Luis Fortuño (PNP) 47 per cent. Garcia takes office on 2 January 2013. Two questions were posed in the referendum: should Puerto Rica continue is territorial status and (without regard for the answer to the first question) what should the alternative be. Three non-territorial alternatives to the current status were proposed – statehood, complete independency or nationhood in free association with the US. A majority of voters rejected continuing the current status and the majority favoured joining the US as a state of the union.
2014 The government announced in October that it is looking for a major international port operator to partner with it on the development of the Port of the Americas, located in Ponce, on the southern coast of the island. The Port of the Americas site sits on over 300 acres, located just five miles from Mercedita Airport.
2015 The Municipality of San Juan has agreed to make substantial upgrades to its storm sewer systems by spending some US$180 million on upgrades and related cleaning activities. These will be aimed at eliminating or minimising daily discharges of large volumes of raw sewage and will minimise discharges of other pollutants into nearby water bodies, including the San Juan Bay Estuary and the Martin Peña Canal. On 5 November a march took place to demand the US help bail out Puerto Rico. New York Governor Andrew Cuomo, NYC Mayor Bill de Blasio, NYC Speaker Melissa Mark-Viverito, Congresswoman Nydia Velázquez and Bronx Borough President Rubén Díaz, Jr were among those who flew in for te event. Puerto Rico has a deficit of US$72 billion, which so far the US government has refused to help with. An alternative would be for the island to declare itself bankrupt.

Political structure

Constitution

The local government consists of executive, legislative and judicial branches. Puerto Rico has 78 municipal governments.

Detailed laws governing the status and relationship of the Commonwealth of Puerto Rico with the US cover, among other aspects: military conscription, tax and trade, social security, citizenship, constitutional changes and internal autonomy.

There is universal suffrage from aged 18 years.

Form of state

Puerto Rico is an overseas commonwealth territory and freely associated state of the US.

Both the constitution of Puerto Rico and the US constitution are applicable. Puerto Rican nationals are US citizens but do not vote in US presidential elections.

The executive

The Head of State is the president of the US.

Executive power is exercised by the governor, elected by popular vote every four years, who leads a cabinet of 15 ministers.

National legislature

The bicameral Asamblea Legislativa (Legislative Assembly) includes the Cámara de Representantes (Chamber of Representatives), with 51 members, elected for four-year terms, 40 elected in single-seat constituencies and 11 by proportional representation from a national list. Up to an additional three seats can be allocated to allow the opposition to have one-third of the seats.

The Senado (Senate) has 27 members, elected for four-year terms – 16 members elected in two-seat constituencies and 11 by proportional representation from a national list and one additional seat to allow the opposition to have one-third of the seats.

Legal system

The civil and commercial codes; penal, procedural, public (including constitutional) laws are fashioned after US models.

Last elections

6 November 2012 (parliamentary, gubernatorial and referendum)

Results: House of Representatives: Partido Popular Democrático (PPD) (Popular Democratic Party) won 28 seats out (out of 51) and the Partido Nuevo Progresista (PNP) (New Progressive Party) 23; four other political parties failed to win any seats.

Senate: PPD won 18 seats (out of 27), the PNP eight and the Partido Independentista Puertorriqueño (PIP) (Puerto Rican Independence Party) one; three other political parties failed to win any seats.

Gubernatorial: Alejandro Garcia Padilla (PPD) won 47.9 per cent of the vote, Luis Fortuño (PNP) 47 per cent, Juan Dalmau Ramírez (PIP) 2.5 per cent; all other candidates each won less than 1 per cent.

Referendum: two questions were posed (1) should PR continue with its current territorial status and (2) (without regard for the answer to the first question), choose between three non-territorial alternatives to the current status, either: statehood; complete independency; or nationhood in free association with the US. Question one 54 per cent voted no; question two, 61.1 per cent favoured statehood, 33.3 per cent for sovereign free association state (with the US) and 5.5 per cent for independence.

Next elections

November 2016 (gubernatorial and parliamentary)

Political parties

Ruling party

Partido Popular Democrático (PPD) (Popular Democratic Party) (from 2 Jan 2013)

Main opposition party

Partido Nuevo Progresista (PNP) (New Progressive Party)

Around three million Puerto Ricans live in the US.

The population is forecast to reach 4.5 million by 2025.

Population

3.71 million (2011); (3,725,789; 2010, census figure)

Last census: 1 April 2010: 3,725,789

Population density: 436 inhabitants per square km. Urban population: 76 per cent (World Bank 2002).

Annual growth rate: 0.9 per cent (2003); projected 0.7 per cent 2002–15.

Ethnic make-up

There is a fusion of three main cultures: native Indian, European and African.

The Spanish *conquistadores* initially came to the New World without wives or family and married into the native population, producing the *mestizo* (Spanish and Taío) and the *mulatto* (Spanish and African) groups.

The Spanish settlers brought in African slaves to work in the sugar cane plantations. When migration restrictions were relaxed, more Spanish came, together with a large contingent of Corsicans and a small number of Irish.

Thousands of mainland Americans have established themselves in Puerto Rico and migrants have also come from the Dominican Republic, Canada, Europe, Asia, Cuba and South and Central America.

Religions

99 per cent of the population are Christians (85 per cent Roman Catholic). Religion has traditionally played an important role in the island's history. The religious groups have been instrumental in fostering community co-operation and providing health and educational services.

Education

Six years of elementary (primary) school are followed by three years of junior high school and three years of senior high school. All teaching is conducted in Spanish, although English is a compulsory subject at all levels. There are 34 post-school educational institutions, both government and private. The State University has three main campuses and six colleges. Special training programmes are provided in technical and vocational schools, as well as on-the-job training for labour skills for which a workforce does not exist.

Literacy rate: 93.7 per cent male, 94 per cent female; adult rates (World Bank).

Compulsory years: Six to 16

Health

HIV/Aids

It is estimated that there are 7,397 people living with HIV/Aids.

Life expectancy: 79 (estimate 2005)

Birth rate/Death rate: 12.88 births and 7.54 deaths per 1,000 population (2005)

Child (under 5 years) mortality rate (per 1,000): 9.28 per 1,000 live births (2005)

Welfare

The US social security system is in operation, together with Puerto Rico's own health, unemployment, and workers' compensation schemes. Employer contributions to the unemployment and social security funds are compulsory. Despite a high per capita national income, about 60 per cent of the population were recorded as living below the official US poverty line, and 45 per cent of the population received federal food stamps. Federal medical aid is also provided. These provide an important cushion against the effects of unemployment, to which a further safety valve is supplied by emigration. There are more Puerto Ricans living in New York than in San Juan.

Main cities

San Juan (capital, population estimated at 402,141 in 2012), Bayamón (194,115), Carolina (166,579), Ponce (142,317), Guaynabo (81,400), Caguas (79,550).

Languages spoken

Spanish is the primary language of the vast majority of Puerto Ricans. English as an important second language is taught in public and private schools from first grade through to tertiary institutions. Government affairs are conducted in Spanish while English is the language of commerce.

Official language/s

Spanish, English

Media

Press

Dailies: The three main dailies widely circulated include *El Vocero de Puerto Rico* (www.vocero.com), *El Nuevo Día* (www.elnuevodia.com) and *Primera Hora* (www.primerahora.com). Other regional dailies and those published from San Juan are *El Impacto* (www.elimpacto.com) and *El Vocero* (www.vocero.com).

In English *San Juan Star* (www.thesanjuanstar.com) *Puerto Rico Herald* (www.puertorico-herald.org) (published by the statehood campaign) and *Caribbean Business* (http://pal.prwow.com).

Weeklies: *Caribbean Business*.

Business: A multilingual, regional publication *América Economía* (www.americaeconomia.com) is the leading magazine.

Periodicals: In Spanish *La Estrella de Puerto Rico* (www.periodicolaestrella.com), *El Expresso* (www.elexpresso.com), *La Esquina* (www.laesquina.com), *El Periódico* (www.elperiodico.com), Bilingual (Spanish and English) publications include *El Boricua* (www.elboricua.com) featuring people and culture, *An(with a wavy line ontop)il* (www.plazaboricua.com).

Broadcasting

Radio: There are over 20 public and commercial radio stations, broadcasting news, music and special interest programmes. Spanish is the typical broadcast language including Radio Puerto Rico (www.radiopr740.com) and Sistema102 (www.sistema102.com); there is one local radio station broadcasting in English, WOSO (www.woso.com).

Television: The public broadcast service TUTV (www.tutv.puertorico.pr) transmits educational and international material. Other, commercial stations, Telemundo (http://tv.telemundo.yahoo.com), Televincento (www.wapa.tv) and Univision (http://univision.centennialpr.net) broadcast a wide variety of programmes in Spanish.

Around 115 national commercial radio stations and nine television stations broadcast. There are satellite TV broadcasts from several international sources.

Economy

The economy of Puerto Rico is influenced and affected by the US economy, from which it derives much of its commercial investment and federal aid. Around 48.5 per cent of GDP was generated by the industrial sector in 2014, mainly deriving from manufacturing, much of which is hi-tech industries, including capital-intensive industries and knowledge intensive industries, such as pharmaceuticals, electronics and biotechnology. The service sector, which generated 50.8 per cent of GDP in 2014 is dominated by financial services (15 per cent of GDP alone) and includes construction, transport, communications, utilities and public services. Agriculture contributed only 0.7 per cent to GDP (2014). Over three million visitors arrived in 2013, with the tourist industry contributing 7 per cent to GDP (US$7 billion). Tourism employs 6.1 per cent of the work force (64,000 jobs).

Major improvements to Puerto Rico's business environment has included the slashing of capital gains taxes and lowering operating costs for manufacturing plants. Puerto Ricans do not pay federal income taxes, and the local authorities have discretion to design tax incentives to attract foreign direct investment (FDI). The government has lobbied for permanent tax exemption status, saying this would be the best way to secure the Commonwealth's fiscal autonomy from the US federal government. With approximately 50 per cent of the economy supported by special exemptions for foreign firms, the repeal of tax incentives would severely undermine Puerto Rico's ability to compete with its Caribbean neighbours, prompting concern that the economy would collapse. Regional agreements such as the North American Free Trade Agreement (Nafta) made countries such as Mexico attractive low wage, tariff free alternatives to Puerto Rico.

Despite once having one of the most dynamic economies in the Caribbean, Puerto Rico has not posted a year of positive growth since 2006. This downturn was a result of the removal of tax preferences that attracted investment from US firms as well as a steep-rise in the price of oil – Puerto Rico is heavily dependant on imports, particularly petroleum products. The economy shrunk to -2.8 per cent in 2012 before increasing slightly to a rate of -0.6 per cent in 2013.

External trade

As an overseas commonwealth territory of the United States, the US has authority over interstate trade, commerce and customs administration. Puerto Rico is part of the North American Free Trade Agreement (Nafta).

Since Nafta was signed, the level of exported manufactured goods has fallen as Mexico, with its lower unit costs, has become the major supplier to the US and Canada. However, while low paid jobs were lost to Mexico there was an increase in pharmaceutical and hi-tech manufacturing in Puerto Rico.

The US accounts for over 45 per cent of imports and exports. Most trade is in intra-company shipments, as parts from US companies are imported and finished goods are exported in return. This flow of materials and products creates profits for private companies and jobs for workers in Puerto Rico and the US.

With few natural resources the balance of payments is still reliant on US federal aid and tax incentives.

Imports

Principal imports include petroleum and derivatives, chemicals, capital machinery and electronic components, textiles and yarns, raw and processed foodstuff, building materials and manufacturing raw materials.

Main sources: US (47.2 per cent of total in 2014), Ireland (20 per cent), Nigeria (5 per cent).

Exports

Principal exports include chemicals, pharmaceuticals, medical products and equipment, finished goods, electronics, clothing, tuna and other fish products, beverages, tropical fruit, dairy and meat.

Main destinations: US (69.6 per cent of total in 2014), Germany (5 per cent), The Netherlands (3 per cent).

Agriculture

Farming

The agricultural sector is small-scale and contributed only 0.7 per cent to GDP in 2014 while employing 2 per cent of the workforce. Only 10 per cent of land is suitable for agriculture. An additional 25 per cent of the island is composed of uplands, partially suited for agricultural purposes. Dairy and livestock farming is of increasing importance.

Farming on the island has changed considerably since the 1940s and 1950s, when traditional small-scale farming methods prevailed and sugar cane, coffee and tobacco were the dominant crops. Of these, only coffee has survived, but it lags behind milk and poultry production. Milk production accounts for 34 per cent of total gross farm income. Changes in consumer preferences are slowly taking place as the population ages.

Around 90 per cent of food requirements are met by imports. Almost all of Puerto Rico's farm output is consumed locally, although small quantities of coffee are exported to Europe and Japan. Some fruit and vegetables, mangoes, tomatoes and onions also go to Europe.

Agriculture has been traditionally based on sugar, coffee, pineapples, plantains, bananas, livestock products and poultry. Sugar production declined during the 1980s, partly due to the closure of the Central Cambalache sugar mill in 1982. Coffee production meets only three-quarters of local demand but half of production is exported. Livestock production has not displayed the same rate of decline as arable agriculture, but is still insufficient to meet local demand. The cost of imported food represents a major constraint on development.

Fishing

Although fishing is conducted on a relatively small scale, it is nevertheless important. Puerto Rico used to be a major tuna supplier to the USA but in recent times has faced a number of problems such as increased competition from Southeast Asia. The annual production of processed fish is around 4,000 tonnes.

Industry and manufacturing

The industrial sector forms the mainstay of the economy, contributing approximately 49 per cent to GDP and employing 14 per cent of the workforce. Most of the island's manufacturing output is shipped to mainland US.

Industrialisation has been the focus of government economic policy since the late 1940s when a programme known as 'Operation Bootstrap' was launched. In 1950, there were 82 industrial plants in Puerto Rico, but by 1965 there were around 1,000. Since then industrial development has tended to be more capital intensive and dependent upon highly skilled labour.

Production is centred on food processing, textiles, petrochemicals, rum distilling, pharmaceuticals, metal fabrication and assembly of electrical/electronic components.

Most of the assembly industries are US-owned and are heavily dependent on the US market. Manufacturers exporting goods to the US benefit from being within the US Customs zone, with the US dollar as the local currency, and US legal protection of intellectual property – particularly useful for IT industries.

The US Commerce Department's Foreign Trade Zones Board has approved the conversion of all the island's industrial parks into free trade zones (FTZs). This, together with Puerto Rico's generous incentives package and skilled workforce has in the past made the island a prime destination for companies looking to expand or relocate. However, competition, from Mexico in particular, has had an adverse effect.

The island's agricultural industry makes an important contribution to the economy through the food industry services of prepared food and retail sales.

The pharmaceutical industry is crucial to Puerto Rico; over half of the top 20 pharmaceutical drugs in the US are manufactured in Puerto Rico and all the leading US manufacturers are represented, some with major investments. There is heavy investment by US computer and electronics companies, footwear and rubber goods manufacturers. The K-Mart Corporation, the US retailing group, is well represented in Puerto Rico.

Tourism

The tourist board guides visitors towards niche market activities, including adventure, beach resorts, culture and ecotourism. There are many outdoor activities and natural wonders including zip lines (face-down, horizontal rappelling) over the forest canopy, scuba diving, horse riding and kayaking. There are several tourist resorts that include a range of hotels, some with amenities such as casinos. The historic district of Ponce has over 1,000 restored buildings.

Visitor arrivals in 2013 were over 3.1 million people and travel and tourism contributed 7.3 per cent of GDP in 2014. The sector provides employment to around 6.3 per cent of the workforce (64,000 jobs), the level of which is closely aligned with the number of visitor arrivals. In 2014, 931 new hotel rooms were added in Puerto Rico and the country posted an average occupancy of 70 per cent.

Mining

Activity in this area is extremely small – production is centred on non-metals such as stone, sand, salt and clay.

There are small unquantified reserves of copper, nickel, cobalt, iron, chromium, lead, gold and silver.

Hydrocarbons

There are no known hydrocarbon reserves and all needs are met by imports. Oil imports were 135,330 barrels per day (bpd) in 2013. Production stood at 67,000bpd from an oil refinery, operated by Caribbean Petroleum (GulfPR), sited in Bayamón and able to process a maximum of 73,000bpd.

Liquefied natural gas (LNG) imports were 1.36 billion cubic metres (cum) in 2012, mainly from Trinidad and Tobago. A re-gasification terminal and power plant in Punta Guayanilla, Peñuelas, are owned and operated by the independent energy company EcoEléctrica.

All coal imports are used in the coal-fired power plant in Guayama. Consumption of coal increased markedly after its completion in 2002 and production of electricity reached full power.

Energy

Total installed generating capacity was 5.6 gigawatts in 2013. The Puerto Rico Electric Power Authority (Prepa) is responsible for generating, transmitting and distributing practically all electricity used. It is the second-largest municipally-owned US utility. Over 90 per cent of all energy is produced from petroleum sources. The independent energy company EcoEléctrica provides electricity from its liquefied natural gas (LNG) fired power plant to the power grid. Over 85MW is provided by hydropower. Many companies still maintain their own generators as essential back-up.

Banking and insurance

The Puerto Rican commercial banking system had comprised about 17 banks with around 300 branches in 2009. On 30 April 2010, US banking regulators shut down three Puerto Rican banks and sold their deposits to other financial institutions. The move cost the Federal Deposit Insurance Corporation (FDIC) US$5.3 billion as the banks were insolvent and unable to trade due to large numbers of unsustainable loans.

Major US banks include Citibank, Chase Manhattan and First National Bank of Boston. Foreign banks include Royal Bank of Canada, Bank of Nova Scotia, Banco Central de Madrid, Banco Bilbao Vizcaya and Banco de Santander.

Banco Popular de Puerto Rico, Puerto Rico's largest bank, continues to expand into US Hispanic markets.

Central bank

There is no central bank.

Such functions as fiscal agent for the Commonwealth of Puerto Rico and its public entities, and the provision of development loans to the public as well as the private sector, are undertaken by the Government Development Bank for Puerto Rico (GDB).

Time

GMT minus four hours

Geography

Puerto Rico comprises the main island, together with the small offshore islands of Vieques and Culebra and many other smaller islets, lying about 80km (50 miles) east of Hispaniola (Haiti and the Dominican Republic) in the Caribbean Sea. Roughly 160km long by 48km wide, Puerto Rico is the smallest and most westerly of the Greater Antilles. The centre of the island is composed of dead volcanoes, the highest of which, the Cordillera Central, has an elevation of 1,325 metres. To the north of the mountains lies a belt of broken limestone country, and then a fertile coastal plain. The whole island is well supplied with rivers. Only about 1 per cent of the country remains forested and is largely reserved.

Hemisphere

Northern

Climate

Tropical with extremes of heat tempered by constant sea winds. Temperatures are 28–30 degrees Celsius (C) in summer, and 21–26 degrees C in winter. Rainfall is heaviest in the second half of the year, especially June–October. Puerto Rico lies in the 'hurricane belt'.

Dress codes

Suits and ties are customary for businessmen since almost all offices are air conditioned. A jacket and tie may be required in first class restaurants. The Hispanic Caribbean *guayabera*, a long decorated shirt, is worn increasingly commonly.

Entry requirements

US entry requirements apply.

Passports

Required by all, valid for six months from date of entry.

Visa

Required by all, except nationals of Canada and Visa Waiver Scheme countries in possession of machine-readable passports; otherwise, visas must be applied for. Visits, for both tourism and business, and visas are valid for up to 90 days. A return/onward ticket is also required. Further information can be found at http://travel.state.gov.

Currency advice/regulations

There are no restrictions on the import or export of local and foreign currencies, subject to declaration of amounts in excess of US$10,000.

Health (for visitors)

The standard of health care in both government and private hospitals is high, but expensive.

Mandatory precautions

None

Advisable precautions

Hepatitis A occurs in the northern Caribbean. There is also a risk of rabies. Travellers should consider vaccination before travelling. Dengue fever, transmitted by mosquitoes, is endemic in rural areas. Its initial symptoms may be similar to influenza. Bilharzia parasites may be present in rivers.

No special precautions are necessary for food and drink.

Hotels

There are several modern business hotels in San Juan. There are also *paradores*, government-owned inns, that are of a reasonable standard. Fifteen per cent tip usual.

Public holidays (national)

Fixed dates

1 Jan (New Year's Day), 6 Jan (Epiphany), 10 Jan (Eugenio Maria De Hostos' Birthday), 22 Mar (Emancipation Day), 4 Jul (US Independence Day), 25 Jul (Constitution Day), 26 Jul (José Celso Barbosa's Birthday), 11 Nov (Veterans' Day), 19 Nov (Discovery of Puerty Rico Day), 25 Dec (Christmas Day).

Each town celebrates a festival or fiesta in honour of a local patron saint. These can last up to 10 days.

Variable dates

Eugenio Maria de Hostos' Birthday (second Mon in Jan), Martin Luther King's Birthday (third Mon in Jan), Washington's Birthday (third Mon in Feb), Good Friday, José de Diego Day (Apr), Memorial Day (last Mon in May), Luis Muñoz Rivera's Day (Jul), Labour Day (first Mon in Sep), Columbus Day (second Mon in Oct), Thanksgiving Day (fourth Thu in Nov).

Working hours

Banking

Mon–Fri: 0830–1430. (Some banks 0830–1700; some banks open Sat.)

Business

Mon–Fri: 0800–1700.

Government

Mon–Fri: 0800–1630.

Telecommunications

Puerto Rico's telecommunications system is fully integrated with that of the US.

Telephone/fax

Direct dialling and fax facilities are available at all main hotels.

Mobile/cell phones

The main providers of mobile phone services are Centennial, Cingular, MoviStar, Suncom, Verizon and Sprint PCS.

Electricity supply

120V AC

Social customs/useful tips

Despite links with the US and the almost universal ability in the business community to understand English, the use of Spanish by the visitor is appreciated.

Hotel and restaurant staff, and taxi drivers, may expect tips of 15–20 per cent. Service charges are rarely included in restaurant bills.

Puerto Rico combines the lifestyle and social customs of the modern US and the traditional Spanish-speaking Caribbean.

Security

Poverty and unemployment have helped to contribute to a growing crime rate, particularly in San Juan. As in all cities, it is unwise to leave articles unattended in parked cars or hotel rooms.

Getting there

Air

There are direct flights from Europe. Latin American countries are connected via Miami. There are also numerous other connections via New York. Other US cities are also well connected to Puerto Rico.

International airport/s: Luis Muñoz Marín (SJU), 14km east of San Juan; duty-free shop, restaurants, bank, post office, shops, car hire.

Airport tax: None

Surface

Main port/s: San Juan, Ponce and Mayagüez.

Getting about

National transport

Air: Several local airlines operate flights within Puerto Rico, as well as island-hopping trips. Charter services are available.

Road: An extensive network of modern roads and highways link all main centres.

Buses: Regular bus (*guagua*) services operates in San Juan from central terminal at Plaza Colón.

Buses are scarce after 2100.

Taxis: Officially regulated, independently owned *públicos* (publicly shared) taxis have 'P' or 'PD' at the of end a licence plate and run regular routes from established points, picking up and dropping off passengers along the way. They are an inexpensive way of reaching urban areas and provincial towns less accessible by public transport.

Water: There is a ferry service linking the islands of Culebra and Vieques to the port of Fajardo, on the east coast of Puerto Rico.

City transport

Taxis: Special tourist taxis (*Taxi Turístico*) operate between the airport and main tourist areas around San Juan. They operate on a zonal basis and charge set fares. Commercial taxis are metered and can be hired by the hour.

Buses, trams & metro: There are good bus services (*guaguas*) in San Juan. Services outside the capital are less reliable. A metro system *Tren Urbano* (Urban Train) provides regular services running through the San Juan metropolitan area.

Car hire

The major car hire companies are represented. Parking is in short supply.

BUSINESS DIRECTORY

The addresses listed below are a selection only. While World of Information makes every endeavour to check these addresses, we cannot guarantee that changes have not been made, especially to telephone numbers and area codes. We would welcome any corrections.

Telephone area codes

The international dialling code (IDD) for Puerto Rico is +1, followed by area code (787) and subscriber's number.

Chambers of Commerce

Puerto Rico Chamber of Commerce, PO Box 9024033, San Juan 00902 (tel: 721-6060; fax: 723-1891; e-mail: camarapr@camarapr.net).

West of Puerto Rico Chamber of Commerce, PO Box 9, Mayagüez 00681 (tel: 832-3749; fax: 832-4287).

Banking

Banco Comercial de Mayagüez, Mayagüez 00708 (tel: 834-3717).

Banco de Ponce, Plaza Degetau, Ponce 00731 (tel: 842-8000).

Banco Popular, M. Rivera Avenue and Bolivia Street, Hato Rey, San Juan (tel: 765-9800; fax: 764-1706).

Banco Santander de Puerto Rico, 207 Ponce de León Avenue, Hato Rey, San Juan (tel: 759-7070; fax: 751-3639).

Government Development Bank for Puerto Rico, PO Box 42001, San Juan 00940-2001 (tel: 726-2525).

Central bank

Government Development Bank for Puerto Rico, PO Box 42001, San Juan 00940-2001 (tel: 722-2525; fax: 721-5496; e-mail: gdbcomm@bgf.gobierno.pr).

Federal Reserve System, 20th Street and Constitution Avenue, NW, Washington DC 20551 (tel: (+1-202) 452-3000; fax: (+1-202) 452-3819).

Travel information

National tourist organisation offices

Puerto Rico Tourism Company, La Princesa Building, 2 Paseo La Princesa, PO Box 902-3060, Old San Juan 00902 (tel: 721-2400; fax: 725-4417).

Ministries

Department of Agriculture, PO Box 10163, San Juan (tel: 721-2120; fax: 723-9747).

Department of Economic Development and Commerce, F.D. Roosevelt Ave 355, 4th Floor, Hato Rey, 00918 (tel: 764-1175 fax: 765-7709).

Department of Education, PO Box 190759, 00919 (tel: 758-4949; fax: 250-0275).

Department of Justice, PO Box 191, 00912 (tel: 721-2900; fax: 724-4770).

Department of Labour and Human Resources, 505 Munoz Rivera Avenue, 00918 (tel: 754-5353; fax: 753-9550).

Department of Natural and Environmental Resources, PO Box 5887, 00906 (tel: 724-8774; fax: 723-4255).

Department of the State, PO Box 3271, 00902 (tel: 722-2121; fax: 725-7303).

Department of the Treasury, PO Box 4515, 00902 (tel: 721-2020; fax: 723-6213).

Department of Transportation and Public works, PO Box 41269, 00940 (tel: 722-2929; fax: 728-8963).

Government of Puerto Rico Economic Development Administration, PO Box 362350, San Juan 00936 (tel: 758-4747; fax: 764-1415).

Office of the Governor, La Fortaleza, 00901 (tel: 721-7000; fax: 721-7483).

Other useful addresses

Caribbean Development Programme, Puerto Rico Department of State, PO Box 3271, San Juan, 00912 (tel: 721-1751; fax: 723-3304).

Legislative Assembly, Capitol Building, 00901 (tel: 724-5200; fax: 724-2428).

Puerto Rico Bankers' Association, 820 Banco Popular Center, San Juan, 00918 (tel: 753-8630; fax: 754-6077).

Puerto Rico Industrial Development Company (FOMENTO), FD Roosevelt Ave, Hato Rey, San Juan, 00918; PO Box 362350, San Juan, PR 00936-2350 (tel: 758-4747; fax: 754-9640; internet site: http://www.pridco.com).

Puerto Rico Manufacturers' Association, PO Box 192410, San Juan, 00919 (tel: 759-9445; fax: 756-7670).

Puerto Rico Ports Authority, PO Box 362829, San Juan (tel: 723-2260; fax: 724-6444).

San Juan Convention Bureau, Ashford Avenue 1110, San Turce, 00907 (tel: 725-2110).

Supreme Court, Supreme Court Building, 00901 (tel: 723-6033; fax: 725-4910).

Internet sites

Puerto Rico Tourism Company: http://www.gotopuertorico.com

Urban transit: http://www.urbanrail.net

Welcome to Puerto Rico: http://www.topuertorico.com

Yellow and White Pages: http://www.escapetopuertorico.com/ypages

Qatar

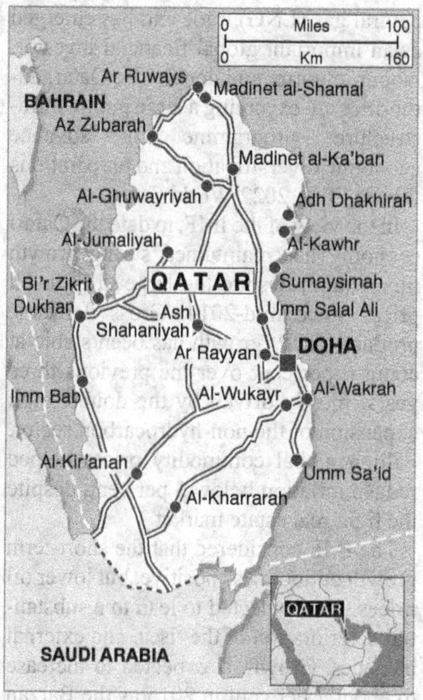

It would be fair to assume that in 2015 Qatar had decided to draw in its horns and seek to adopt a lower international profile than had been the case for the previous few years. In Gulf terms, Qatar – a member of the Gulf Co-operation Council (GCC), had come to be seen as the 'new kid on the block'. Its often hyperactive participation in world events – in Egypt (where it had been hugger mugger with the Muslim Brotherhood), in Syria (where it had been funding some very doubtful allies), in Libya (where it had enthusiastically backed the North Atlantic Treaty Organisation (NATO) intervention) in the Gulf itself (where it had managed to antagonise Saudi Arabia) and in the world of sport, where its 'successful' bid to host the World Football Cup in 2022 had become something of a public relations disaster. Allegations of vote rigging and bribery surrounded the successful World Cup bid. The very idea of holding a summer football tournament in Qatar steadily assumed the proportions of a rather sad joke.

Friends and neighbours?

Qatar had also taken it upon itself to become an international broker, arranging meetings between the Taliban and Western officials. Quoted in the *New York Review of Books* in June 2011, a Wiki-leaked state department document observed that: 'Egypt is determined to thwart every single initiative Qatar proposes during its current term as President of the Arab League.' Resentment towards Qatar had, at one time or another, been expressed by six Arab League States over the coverage it received from the al Jazeera broadcasting service, based in Qatar and funded by the Qatari government. In the same *New York Review* article, the author Hugh Eakin listed the countries that had, at one time or another, withdrawn their ambassadors from Doha. To cap it all and perhaps the most ironic disparity of all, was that while providing facilities for the headquarters of the US military's Central Command (CENTCOM) Qatar was also giving support to Hamas. According to Mr Eakin, as long ago as 2009 the US Secretary of State John Kerry had complained that 'Qatar can't continue to be an American ally on Monday that sends money to Hamas on Tuesday.'

World Cup worries

When first aware of his country's 2010 bid to host the FIFA World Cup, Qatar's UK educated (Sherborne School) Ruler Sheikh Tamim Bin Hamad al Thani probably thought it an excellent idea. At the time he was still ruler in waiting, although he had reportedly been closely involved with the bid-negotiations. By 2015 the game had changed: surrounded by allegations of corruption and human rights abuses. None the less, in mid-2015 Qatar still seemed determined to go ahead with its expensive preparations for hosting the World Cup in 2022. However, following the arraignment of numerous FIFA officials on charges of bribery, money-laundering and embezzlement by both the US and Swiss authorities, there was a real possibility that the Emirate might lose the tournament.

Calls for a boycott of the tournament had circulated for some time, based on documented revelations of the conditions that pertained in Qatar for migrant

KEY FACTS

Official name: Dawlat Qatar (State of Qatar)

Head of State: Emir Sheikh Tamim bin Hamad Al Thani (since 25 Jun 2013)

Head of government: Prime Minister Abdullah bin Nasser bin Khalifa Al Thani (since 25 June 2013)

Ruling party: Political parties are not permitted.

Area: 11,437 square km

Population: 2.23 million (2014) (1,699,435; 2010, census figure)

Capital: Doha

Official language: Arabic

Currency: Rial (QR) = 100 dirhams

Exchange rate: QR3.64 per US$ (fixed)

GDP per capita: US$93,965 (2014)*

GDP real growth: 6.14% (2014)*

GDP: US$210.00 billion (2014)*

Inflation: 3.04% (2014)

Oil production: 1.98 million bpd (2014)

Natural gas production: 177.20 billion cum (2014)

Balance of trade: US$100.57 billion (2014)

Annual FDI: -US$86.76 million (2011)

* estimated figure

workers were less than satisfactory. The London based international organisation Amnesty International had published a report in May 2015 drawing attention to what it described as the 'rampant abuse of migrant workers' rights.' On top of the conditions experienced by migrant workers, there were concerns for the football players. Summer temperatures in Qatar, when the tournament was originally scheduled, can reach into the 40 degree Celsius range. Thus, the dates for the tournament were re-scheduled, from June and July to November, which was not welcomed by many of the European football leagues as it interrupted a long-established timetable tradition.

To counter the criticism and allegations of corruption, the Qatari government could only resort to one measure – that of money. Following in the footsteps of its Arabian Gulf neighbour Dubai (with which Qatar has a long tradition of friendship and alliance), it purchased a majority shareholding in the French Paris Saint-Germain club and funded the purchase of top league players. It also signed a sponsorship deal with Spanish champions Barcelona and invited a number of high ranking European clubs to Qatar for training and exhibition matches. The Italian Super-Cup, traditionally held at the beginning of the season was inexplicably played in Doha in August 2014, rendering it virtually impossible for supporters of the two clubs involved to see the fixture except on television.

Those opposed to the Qatari involvement have tabled requests for a fresh vote and in mid-2015 the Swiss authorities were investigating bribery allegations surrounding the Qatari 'fixer' Mohammed bin Hamman, who the London *Sunday Times* claimed had bribed FIFA officials from the Caribbean. Qatar could at least afford to hire competent lawyers to defend attempts to remove the tournament, but as a public relations exercise the World Cup, some seven years away, has already proved disastrous.

Wider woes

Three quarters of Qatar's two million population are immigrants of one sort or another. Those working on building sites allocated to the World Cup come from impoverished countries such as Nepal or Bangladesh. Amnesty International reports have suggested that weekly working hours may be as long as 60 hours or more, with no paid overtime. Other local reports have put the construction death toll at a scandalous 1,200, roughly one death per working day. The International Trade Union Confederation (ITUC) has estimated that if the current casualty rate persists, over 4,000 workers will have died before the cup festivities begin. The ITUC has suggested that FIFA hold a minute's silence for every dead worker; that however, at current rates, would mean an hour's silence before each event. To put the scale of the Qatari deaths in context, in all the six previous winter and summer Olympic Games sites' construction – both summer and winter – there had been a total of 80 deaths during construction. Nothing to be proud of, perhaps. But 4,000?

KEY INDICATORS — Qatar

	Unit	2011	2012	2013	2014	**2015
Population	m	*1.77	1.84	2.04	2.23	*2.41
Gross domestic product (GDP)	US$bn	173.80	192.40	203.24	*210.00	*196.96
GDP per capita	US$	98,329	104,756	99,370	*93,965	*81,603
GDP real growth	%	18.8	6.2	6.3	*6.1	*7.1
Inflation	%	2.0	1.9	3.1	3.0	*1.8
Oil output	'000 bpd	1,723.0	1,966.0	1,995.0	1,982.0	–
Natural gas output	bn cum	146.8	157.0	158.5	177.2	–
Exports (fob) (goods)	US$m	114,298.6	132,967.9	136,936.8	131,715.9	–
Imports (fob) (goods)	US$m	26,925.9	30,787.2	31,474.7	31,145.3	–
Balance of trade	US$m	87,372.7	102,180.7	105,462.1	100,570.6	–
Current account	US$m	51,977.9	62,335.0	62,587.0	*52,790.0	*16,464.0
Total reserves minus gold	US$m	23,136.5	32,521.0	41,601.5	42,734.1	–
Foreign exchange	US$m	22,583.4	31,956.5	41,021.6	–	–
Exchange rate	per US$	3.64	3.64	3.64	3.64	–

* estimated figure ** forecast figure

We're in the money

In its April 2015 assessment of the Qatari economy, the International Monetary Fund (IMF) noted that Qatar was implementing an ambitious diversification strategy, while retaining its systemic role in the global natural gas market. Qatar accounts for one-third of global liquefied natural gas (LNG) trade and has emerged as an important global financial investor, labour importer and donor. The Qatari authorities are executing a large public infrastructure programme to advance economic diversification and preparations for the FIFA 2022 World Cup.

In the view of the IMF, to date the Qatari economy has maintained strong growth momentum, despite the large drop in oil prices since mid-2014. Gross domestic product (GDP) growth has been stable at about 6 per cent over the previous three years, mostly driven by the double-digit expansion of the non-hydrocarbon sector. Falling global commodity prices helped reduce inflation below 3 per cent, despite the tight real estate market.

The IMF considered that the short-term growth outlook was positive, but lower oil prices were expected to lead to a substantial deterioration of the fiscal and external balances. Growth is expected to increase to about 7 per cent in 2015 as the Barzan natural gas field has started production and the authorities continue implementing the public investment programme. Falling import prices are also expected to continue keeping inflationary pressures in check. However, the government budget might fall into deficit from 2016 onwards and external surpluses could shrink substantially. Growth is expected to slow over the medium term as public investment growth tapers and the private sector offsets the decline only partially. The main risks to the macro-economic outlook are the possibility of lower-than-expected oil and natural gas prices.

Hydrocarbons

Like most Gulf states, Qatar relies heavily on its energy sector to support its economy. According to the Qatar National Bank (QNB) (central bank), Qatar's earnings from its hydrocarbon sector accounted for 49 per cent of total government revenues in 2014, a figure that has declined over the past four years. According to the US government Energy Information Administration (EIA), Qatar earned n estimated US$38 billion from net oil exports in 2014.

In 2013 Qatar was the world's fourth-largest dry natural gas producer (behind only the US, Russia and Iran). It has been the world's leading liquefied natural gas (LNG) exporter since 2006, with 31 per cent of market share in 2014. Qatar is also at the forefront of gas-to-liquids (GTL) production and is home to the world's largest GTL facility. The growth in Qatar's natural gas production, particularly since 2000, has also increased Qatar's total liquids production, as lease condensates, natural gas plant liquids and other petroleum liquids are a significant (and valuable) by product of natural gas production.

Qatar produced 2.1 million barrels per day (bpd) of petroleum and other liquids in 2014, of which 1.5 million bpd was crude oil and the remainder was non-crude liquids. Although Qatar is a member of the Organisation of the Petroleum Exporting Countries (Opec), it is the second-smallest crude oil producer among the 12-member group. Natural gas meets most of Qatar's domestic energy demand, so most of its liquid fuels production is exported. Given its small population, Qatar's energy needs are met almost entirely by domestic sources.

Qatar's fiscal year 2014/15 budget had assumed an oil price of US$65 per barrel, which when the budget was being prepared had seemed a reasonable enough estimate. However, in the period up until mid-2015 the price per barrel stayed firmly below the estimate. In the wake of declining oil and natural gas prices, the state-owned Qatar Petroleum (QP) announced a restructuring programme in June 2015 aimed at cutting costs and increasing efficiency.

QP controls all aspects of Qatar's upstream and downstream oil and natural gas sectors, including exploration, production, transport, storage, marketing and sale of crude oil, natural gas, natural gas liquids, liquefied natural gas, gas-to-liquids (GTL), refined products and petrochemicals and fertilisers. Qatar generally focuses its natural gas development on integrated, large-scale projects linked to LNG exports or downstream industries that use natural gas as a feedstock. These projects normally include investment from international oil companies (IOCs).

With proved reserves of crude oil estimated at 25.2 billion barrels by the *Oil & Gas Journal* (in January 2015), Qatar holds the 9th largest reserves in Opec and 13th largest in the world. Qatar's crude oil and lease condensate production ranks 17th in the world, with most of the country's production sent abroad as exports.

In 2012, Qatar's non-crude liquids production surpassed its crude oil production for the first time. Recent growth in non-crude liquids is the result of the country's robust natural gas production, which produces many heavier hydrocarbons in addition to natural gas. With high levels of natural gas production expected to continue, Qatar's non-crude liquids supply is also likely to remain high. Meanwhile, production of crude oil has declined in recent years as mature oil fields experienced natural decline. Crude oil represented 35 per cent of petroleum and other liquid production in Qatar in 2014, down from 44 per cent in 2010.

Oil exploration activity in Qatar continues, although not to the degree seen in other oil-producing countries. The latest major discovery in Qatar came in 1994 (the Al Rayyan field) and any supply growth in the near term is likely to come from increased output at Qatar's existing fields, particularly through the use of enhanced oil recovery (EOR) techniques.

In 2015 a previous government crude oil production capacity target of 1.2 million bpd no longer appeared feasible, although investment from IOCs could also help boost, or at least maintain, crude oil production levels. QP's development plan to increase crude oil production seems to have steadied output somewhat; however, further investment in crude oil projects is uneconomic in the current price environment.

Qatar's non-crude liquids production has grown significantly over the past several years largely as a result of increased natural gas production in the country. According to the QNB, non-crude oil liquids (condensate and NGLs) accounted for 65 per cent of Qatar's total petroleum and other liquids supply in 2014, a figure which is expected to grow as crude production declines and condensate production continues to grow. QNB reported in August 2013 that Qatar held condensate reserves of more than 22 billion barrels, although it is unclear under what economic and technological conditions those reserves would be considered economically viable.

According to the Opec Annual Statistical Bulletin 2015, Qatar exported 595,000bpd of crude oil and 522,000bpd of refined petroleum products in 2014. In 2014, Qatar sent all of its crude oil refined product exports to Asian countries, according to Opec estimates. Most of Qatar's refined products (60 per cent or more) go to Japan.

Natural gas

In January 2015, Qatar had the third-largest proved reserves of natural gas in the world, at 872 trillion cubic feet (tcf), according to the *Oil & Gas Journal*. Nearly all of the reserves are in Qatar's North Field. There is currently a moratorium on new projects in the North Field while operators continue to examine ways of sustaining high levels of output over the longer term. As a result, natural gas production has levelled out and could begin to decline soon.

In 2013, according to the EIA, Qatar was the second-largest dry natural producer in the Middle East and the fourth-largest producer in the world. Qatar's natural gas production has increased its output of condensates and natural gas plant liquids, which are valuable by-products of natural gas production. Qatar's condensate production is approximately 700,000bpd with exports of about 500,000bpd, making it the largest condensate exporter in the world.

Qatar is the world's second-largest exporter of natural gas, exporting nearly 4.3tcf in 2014 and the country was again the world's largest LNG exporter, as it has

FIFA World Cup and human rights abuses

When Sepp Blatter, former president of FIFA, announced to the world on 2 December 2010 that Qatar – a nation of 1.7 million people – had secured the 2022 FIFA World Cup, there was widespread astonishment and then soon after, inquest. Commonly alleged to have been the result of extensive FIFA corruption and Qatari bribes, the awarding of the 2022 World Cup has revealed to the world more than just the depth of Qatar's pockets.

According to independent commission, Fair Play Qatar, 'more than 62 workers will die for each game played during the 2022 tournament'. It is a terrifying abuse of basic human rights and evidence enough to revoke FIFA's 2022 decision. However, given FIFA's own chequered history under Blatter, the alliance between dirty money and grand sporting events will likely outweigh that of the human cost.

been since 2006, accounting for 32 per cent of global natural gas exports. Most of Qatar's exports go to markets in Asia in the form of LNG, while the country sends a small amount of natural gas via the Dolphin Pipeline to the UAE and Oman. Qatar's LNG export capacity is the highest in the world at 77 million tons per year (MMt/y).

Risk assessment

Economy	Good
Politics	Poor
Regional stability	Fair

Muslims in Qatar

% of population	77.5
Sunni (% of Muslims)	90
Shi'a (% of Muslims)	10

COUNTRY PROFILE

632 Advent of Islam.
1700s Mining and pearl fishing settlements were established along the coast.
1868 Qatar's first Al Thani Emir, Sheikh Mohammed bin Thani, signed a treaty with Britain.
1871–1916 A treaty with the Turks allowed them to place a garrison in Doha. After Turkey entered the First World War on the side of Germany, the Turkish forces were expelled by the British.
1916 Qatar became a British protectorate with Sheikh Abdullah bin Jassim al Thani as ruler.
1930 The collapse of the pearl trade devastated the economy.
1939 Oil was discovered, but the Second World War delayed exploitation.
1949 Qatar began exporting oil.
1950s Qatar's infrastructure was modernised and extended, using oil revenues.
1968 Britain announced its intention to withdraw from the Gulf by 1971.
1971 Qatar became independent. Land disputes with Bahrain ensued.
1972 Sheikh Khalifa bin Hamad al Thani became Emir after deposing his uncle.
1980s and 1990s Qatar had territorial disputes with Bahrain and Saudi Arabia.
1981 The political and economic union, the Co-operation Council for the Arab States of the Gulf (CCASG) (known as Gulf Co-operation Council (GCC)) was formed by Bahrain, Kuwait, Oman, Qatar, Saudi Arabia and the United Arab Emirates (UAE).
1990 After Iraq invaded Kuwait, Qatar allowed foreign forces into the country and Qatari troops took part in the liberation of Kuwait.
1995 In a bloodless coup, Sheikh Hamad bin Khalifa al Thani, replaced his father Sheikh Khalifa.
1996 Qatar began exporting liquefied natural gas. Based in Qatar and funded by the Emir, the pan-Arab Al Jazeera satellite TV station was launched.
1999 A democratisation programme began when male citizens over the age of 18 were allowed to vote in municipal council elections. Only half the 40,000 eligible to vote actually registered.
2000 The Emir's cousin and 32 others were jailed for life for planning a coup, in 1996, which was foiled.
2001 The International Court of Justice settled a land dispute between Qatar and Bahrain, awarding Zubarah town and the shallows surrounding the islet of Fasht el Dibal to Qatar. A border dispute with Saudi Arabia was also settled. WTO trade talks, held in Doha, called for the US, EU and Japan to open their markets and remove agricultural export subsidies.
2002 The Al Udeid air base was redeveloped in preparation for the Iraq War when it became the HQ for the US Central Command.
2003 A referendum approved a new constitution, which guarantees equal rights and a 45-member parliament. The Emir named his younger son, Prince Tamim, as crown prince, replacing his elder son Prince Jassim.
2004 The exiled former Chechen president, Zelimkhan Yanderbiyev, was assassinated in Doha; two Russian agents were convicted of the murder. Around six thousand members of the Al Ghfran clan, a sub-set of one of Qatar's largest tribes, had their citizenship revoked on the grounds that they held dual nationality with Saudi Arabia.
2005 A suicide bombing in Doha injured 12 and killed one Briton; it was the first major terrorist attack in Qatar. The new constitution was implemented. Work began on building the world's largest liquefied natural gas plant, with joint US-Qatar investment of US$14 billion.
2007 Sheikh Abdullah bin Khalifa resigned as prime minister and was replaced by Sheikh Hamad bin Jassem.
2008 A common market was created by Bahrain, Kuwait, Oman, Qatar, Saudi Arabia and UAE, the six wealthiest Gulf states. Citizens of these countries are now allowed to travel between and live in any of the six states, where they may find employment, buy properties and businesses and use the educational and health facilities freely. Qatar, Iran and Russia formed a technical committee to lead an Opec-style, international exporting organisation for natural gas.
2009 Qatar (the only Arab Gulf state with trade agreements) cut trade ties with Israel following Israel's offensive in Palestine.
2010 Elections for the legislative assembly were postponed when the Emir extended its term in office until 2013. The Gulf's second largest stock exchange, by market value, in Qatar, set up a new trading system, in a bid to become the primary bourse among Gulf states. Electronic trading went live using the NYSE Euronext's universal trading platform (UTP) technology.
2011 In February the Qatar Red Crescent (QRC) was one of the first humanitarian organisations to provide food aid to Somalia during its episode of famine. As part of the *National Development strategy 2011–2016*, expatriates may be offered permanent residency if they meet 'pre-determined criteria'. The policy was aimed at attracting and retaining Qatar's high skilled workforce. The policy also reviewed and revised the current sponsorship system, in which employers had full control over residence and the work undertaken, as well as permission of entry and exit. Qatar played a leading role in providing support for Libya's rebels, with funds and projects such as setting up Libya TV, to counter pro-Gadafi propaganda. It has helped market Libya's oil and is well placed to assist in further development of Libya's natural gas reserves.
2012 On 12 August, a US$406.4 million contract was agreed for engineering services to build a metro in Doha, in preparation for its hosting of the 2022 football (soccer) World Cup. On 25 September, in a speech to the UN General Assembly (UNGA), the Emir Sheikh Hamad bin Khalifa al Thani said that Arab countries should intervene in Syria, to provide national, humanitarian, political and military leadership, in the face of UN inaction and to stop the bloodshed. He suggested that bypassing the UNGA would enable a peaceful transition of power in Syria, while criticising the UNGA for failing 'to reach an effective position'. On 20 November, the annual World Innovation Summit for Education (Wise) was held in Doha, to discuss the Educate a Child project (to provide basic education to around 61 million children in Africa, Asia and the Middle East). Attendees included a mix of politicians, business leaders, head of NGOs, academics and social activists.
2013 On 24 June the Emir, Sheikh Hamad bin Khalifa Al Thani, handed power to Crown Prince Sheikh Tamim bin Hamad Al Thani. Sheikh Hamad had named Sheikh Tamin as his heir in 2003. In August Greg Dyke, the newly installed chairman of the English Football Association, said that it would be 'impossible' to hold the 2022 Football World Cup in summer. Qatar's World Cup organising committee has said it would be prepared to move the event to winter. Hassan al-Thawadi, head of the Qatar 2022 World Cup, said that any call to move the games to another country would be rejected.

2014 In February the Qatar 2022 World Cup organisers announced a Workers' Charter to protect the rights of immigrant workers. The Charter was developed with the International Labour Organisation (ILO) after it was reported that as many as 185 workers had died, and many more been injured, in 2013 as a result of unsafe working practices. The Charter also requires employers, among other conditions, to provide healthy working and living conditions and to pay employees on time.

Political structure

Constitution

A new, written constitution came into effect on 8 June 2005. It provides for the hereditary rule of the al Thani family. A new unicamal, legislative authority was inaugurated.

Independence date

3 September 1971

Form of state

Constitutional Emirate

The executive

Executive power is vested in the Emir, who is the Head of State. He appoints a prime minister and ministers. He also appoints 15 members of the Majlis al Shura. The Emir is the supreme commander of the armed and security forces.

National legislature

In 2009, the unicameral Majlis al Shura (Consultative Assembly) had 35 appointed members who, as an Advisory Council, was consulted by the Emir.

From 2010, 30 members of the Consultative Assembly will be directly elected by universal suffrage (aged over 18 years); 15 members will be appointed by the Emir. The Assembly will be responsible for approving the budget (but not drafting it), reviewing the performance of ministers and drafting and voting on proposed legislation; all legislation must by endorsed by the executive authority.

Legal system

Two former court systems – civil and *Sharia* (Islamic law) – were merged under a higher court, the Court of Cassation, established for appeals, under a new judiciary law issued in 2003.

Last elections

None

Next elections

The first legislative elections were scheduled for 2013, but were postponed in June of the same year. Proposals have been made for 2016, but that may also prove unlikely.

Political parties

Ruling party

Political parties are not permitted.

The indigenous Qatari population is characterised by its youth (about 50 per cent under the age of 15) and high birth rate. Approximately 80 per cent of the population live in or around Doha.

Population

2.02 million (2013)* (1,699,435; 2010, census figure)

Last census: 21 April 2010: 1,699,435

Population density: 51 inhabitants per sq km. Urban population 96 per cent (2010 Unicef).

Annual growth rate: 6.6 per cent, 1990–2010 (Unicef).

Ethnic make-up

Arab (40 per cent), Pakistani (18 per cent), Indian (18 per cent), Iranian (10 per cent), others (14 per cent).

Expatriates comprise about 80 per cent of the total population. Some foreign nationals have been resident in Qatar for many years and come largely from the Indian sub-continent, other Arab countries and south-east Asia. The number of non-national children is high, indicating a trend among non-nationals to settle in the country.

Religions

Islam is the state religion. Most Qataris (95 per cent) are Sunni Muslims of the strict Wahhabi sect, known as *muwahhidun* (unitarians); they shun the veneration of saints and shrines. The small Hindu and Christian communities do not have formal places of worship.

Education

Primary education begins at aged six and lasts until aged 12. From aged 12 to 15 students attend a preparatory school and if they pass their promotional examination go forward to secondary school. There are three different types of secondary schools: academic, commercial and technical, and each offer three-year courses. However, girls are only allowed to attend the academic secondary schools.

In 2004, Qatar announced that it would spend US$900 million on a huge new medical teaching hospital to be built on the outskirts of Doha; it is expected to be completed by 2008. An endowment of US$8 billion will also be provided to carry out research. The hospital's teaching programme will be run in partnership with the US Cornell University, and have US$200 million per annum to spend on research, initially concentrating on women's health and paediatric medicine. The emphasis on research is a new direction for medical facilities in the region.

Literacy rate: 83 per cent, adult rate (2003)

Compulsory years: None.

Health

All residents have access to free medical services.

Life expectancy: 76 years, 2004 (WHO 2006)

Fertility rate/Maternal mortality rate: 2.3 births per woman, 2010 (Unicef)

Birth rate/Death rate: 16 births per 1,000 population; 4.4 deaths per 1,000 population (2003).

Child (under 5 years) mortality rate (per 1,000): 7 per 1,000 live births (WHO 2012)

Head of population per physician: 2.22 physicians per 1,000 people, 2001 (WHO 2006)

Welfare

The state provides generous welfare services for indigenous Qataris.

Main cities

Doha (capital, estimated population 437,639 in 2012), ar Rayyan (4307267), Umm Salal (47,314), al Wakrah (34,482), Khor (33,600), as Dahirah (26,054).

Languages spoken

English is widely spoken in business circles. Correspondence with government organisations is normally conducted in Arabic.

Official language/s

Arabic

Media

Press

The government formally lifted censorship of the media in 1995 and since then government interference has remained limited although censorship is implicit and self-censorship by editors common.

Dailies: The main daily newspapers in Arabic are *al Sharq (The East)* (www.al-sharq.com), *al Raya (The Banner)* (www.raya.com), *al Watan (The Homeland)* (www.al-watan.com) and the regional publication *al Arab* (www.alarabonline.org) of political matters.

In English, *Qatar Post* (www.qatarpost.com), *Qatar Journal* (www.qatarjournal.com) and *The Peninsula* (www.thepeninsulaqatar.com) is the leading English newspaper. A regional publication is *The Gulf Times* (www.gulf-times.com).

Weeklies: The *Gulf Times* is published in English.

Periodicals: In Arabic, the monthly *al Sehah Magazine* publishes items on health. In English, *This is Qatar* is a tourist magazine, *Qatar Falcon* (http://www.qatar-falcon.com) is a lifestyle publication aimed at male readers, while *Zawya* (www.zawya.com) is an online business magazine, with news and features.

Broadcasting

Isreal began a boycott of al Jazeera on 12 March 2008 in reaction to what it claimed was al Jazeera's bias when it reported on the conflict in Gaza – Israeli action in bombing the territory was not matched by reports of missiles fired on the city of Ashkelon.

Radio: Radio broadcasts are in Arabic, with other services in English, French and Urdu also available. The government run, Qatar Broadcasting Service broadcasts nationally. A few local radio stations also broadcast in FM and AM.

Television: Although privately funded, al Jazeera (www.aljazeera.com) has grown in size and reputation from a regional TV Channel, to an international broadcaster with an English language service that was launched in 2006 and video streaming supplied over the Internet. The state television runs three channels, including one for the Koran channel and two others in Arabic and English channel. Cable satellite TV is also available throughout Qatar and offers some 20 channels.

National news agency: Qatar News Agency

Economy

The economy is dominated by the production of, and revenue from, Qatar's hydrocarbon sector. Although GDP growth has been largely driven by the oil and gas industry, there has been significant improvement in the manufacturing, construction, and financial services sector which have pushed the non-oil component to just over half of Qatar's nominal GDP for the first time since 2000. Economic policy is focused on diversifying the economy by increasing private and foreign investment in non-energy sectors, however, oil and gas still account for approximately 92 per cent of export earnings, and 62 per cent of government revenues. Qatar has the highest GDP per capita in the world (US$143,400 in 2014) and the lowest unemployment (0.4 per cent in 2014).

Qatar's successful 2022 World Cup bid is accelerating large-scale infrastructure projects such as Qatar's metro system, light rail system, the construction of a new port, roads, stadiums and related sporting infrastructure. The new Hamad International Airport opened in 2014 with an initial passenger capacity of 24 million and with a projected 50 million when complete.

Oil and gas reserves were 25.2 billion barrels of oil and 25 trillion cubic metres (cum) of natural gas at the end of 2014. Between them, they provide over 50 per cent of GDP. Production of oil was 2.0 million barrels per day (bpd) in 2014; production of natural gas was 158.5 billion cum per annum. Qatar has the world's third largest deposits of natural gas (13 per cent of the world's total) and has been the world's largest exporter of liquefied natural gas (LNG) since 2006. Japan, India and South Korea each imported over 10 billion cum of Qatar LNG in 2012; Qatar also exported 48 million cum per day by gas pipeline to the UAE.

Qatar was not affected by the global economic crisis in 2008 as its banks are tightly regulated and well capitalised.

Since 2004, GDP growth has remained in the mid-teens, with only one dip below 10 per cent, in 2005, due to a fall in global oil prices. GDP growth in 2007 was 18.0 per cent, falling to 17.7 per cent in 2008, despite the expansion of hydrocarbon production and a strong performance in manufacturing, construction and financial services. As global trade slumped GDP growth also fell, to 12.0 per cent in 2009 before rebounding to 16.6 per cent in 2010 and higher still to an estimated 18.8 per cent in 2011. However, growth dropped considerably in 2012 to 6 per cent, and this dip was maintained in 2013 at 6.3 per cent. In 2014 GDP growth has stabilised at a healthy rate of 6.1 per cent.

Inflation remained high, peaking at 15.0 per cent in 2008 due to high prices for imported food and housing rents. By 2012 inflation had dropped steadily to 1.9 per cent, but increased to 3.1 per cent in 2013. The inflation rate has since stabilised at 3 per cent in 2014.

Per capita income reached a record US$79,409 in 2008, before falling to US$59,545 in 2009 and recovering in 2010 to US$74,901. By 2013, GDP per capita reached US$135,100 making Qatar's population the wealthiest in the world. In 2014, GDP per capita increased even further to US$143,400.

External trade

In 2005 the Greater Arab Free Trade Area (Gafta) was ratified by 17 members (including Qatar), creating an Arab economic bloc. A customs union was established whereby tariffs within Gafta will be reduced by a percentage each year, until none remain.

Qatar is the world's largest exporter of liquefied natural gas (LNG) and operates the biggest processing facility, which can process over 30 billion cubic metres (cum) of natural gas. It has other heavy industrial processing sites producing fertilisers and petrochemicals and a steel plant.

Imports

Principal imports are machinery and transport equipment, food and chemicals.

Main sources: US (11.5 per cent of total in 2014), China (10.6 per cent), UAE (8.2 per cent), Germany (7.1 per cent) and Japan (6.4 per cent)

Exports

Exports are dominated by liquefied natural gas (LNG), crude oil, petroleum products, fertilisers and steel.

Main destinations: Japan (25.3 per cent of total in 2014), South Korea (18.8 per cent), India (12.7 per cent), China (7.7 per cent) and Singapore (6.2 per cent)

Agriculture

Farming

The agriculture sector only contributes 0.1 per cent to GDP and it employs just 1 per cent of the workforce. Nevertheless the country is 70 per cent self-sufficient in summer vegetables and 40 per cent in winter vegetables, 25 per cent in dairy produce and 10 per cent in cereals. Other crops include fruit, dates, fodder crops and cereals.

The government owns all agricultural land in Qatar, which is keen to support and encourage agricultural production. However, this is limited by the scarcity of water and the unfavourable terrain. A new industrial project began in Ras Laffan, providing desalinated water as part of a plan for further irrigation. Only about 8,000 hectares of the estimated 65,000 hectares of cultivable land (5.7 per cent of the total land area) is farmed.

The Qatar National Food Security Programme (QNFSP) has outlined ambitious plans to make Qatar as close as possible to self-sufficiency in food by the year 2023. Due to the environmental factors of Qatar, unconventional methods of farming such as vertical (agriculture in skyscrapers) or hydroponics have been considered.

Major emphasis is placed on educating the population in agricultural techniques, experimenting with new methods of cultivation and developing better marketing structures.

Fishing

Due to polluted water, the fishing industry is declining in Qatar. The Ministry of Municipal Affairs and Urban Planning (MMUP) is taking steps to boost the industry by developing fishing harbours to help improve business for fishermen.

Industry and manufacturing

The industrial sector contributes 72.4 per cent of GDP; it employs around 50 per cent of the working population.

The government offers incentives to encourage private sector development of light industry. Industries include the production of intermediate building materials (cement, concrete, moulded aluminium, marble tiles and paving stone), food processing, freezing and packaging, paper products, batteries, paint, plastics, detergents, lubricants, household utensils and furniture.

Qatar is considered one of the main players in diversifying national income and bringing dependence away from hydrocarbon industries.

Tourism
Qatar has begun to market itself as a hub for the business traveller. In 2014, Doha was voted as the world's leading business travel destination, with dedicated meetings, incentives, conference and exhibitions (MICE) venues. Qatar is also planning to build 77 new hotels and 42 hotel apartments to expand its accommodation portfolio in advance of the FIFA World Cup football competition in 2022. Ahead of the 2022 FIFA World Cup, Qatar plans to invest US$45 billion in the tourism industry. This is part of a bid to almost double the industry's direct contribution to GDP from 2.6 per cent in 2013 to 5.1 per cent by 2030. Strategies include setting up eight new satellite offices in key outbound markets on top of the existing offices in London and Paris. In 2014, Qatar had 2.9 million visitors mainly from neighbour countries, however, by 2030, the country hopes to have 7 million visitors per annum.
In 2014, the tourism and travel industry contributed in total 5.1 per cent of GDP (US$11 billion), which is forecast to rise by 6.6 per cent in 2015. The industry provided employment to 6.1 per cent of the total work force (105,000 jobs).

Environment
Among the proposals to meet the country's water shortage are the construction of a 700km pipeline from the Karun River in northern Iran to Qatar, as well as the development of more desalination plants.

Hydrocarbons
In order to support its economy, Qatar relies heavily on its energy sector – like many of its neighbours. In 2014, the hydrocarbons sector contributed around 50 per cent to GDP. The largest oil field is onshore at Dukhan, along the west coast, which produces around half of Qatar's total oil output. There are six other oil fields and if the country's production levels remained constant reserves will last until 2070. The state-run Qatar Petroleum (QP) has overall control of all aspects of the industry, not only holding the rights to all petroleum resources but also including operational exploration, production, refining, transport and storage of hydrocarbons. QP entered into a number of production sharing agreements (PSAs) with companies such as ExxonMobil, Chevron, Total and BP Amoco after the oil sector was opened up to foreign investment. However no onshore discoveries of oil have been made since the 1990s and only the offshore Al Shaheen field, operated by the Danish-based Maersk Oil and Gas, is being developed. The largest percentage of crude oil is exported to Japan.
There are three export terminals; two primarily for the export of oil and the other, at the Ras Laffan Industrial City, is mainly for the export of liquefied natural gas (LNG).
Qatar has the third largest reserves of natural gas (behind Russia and Iran), possessing around13 per cent of the world's reserves, concentrated largely in the massive North Field, off the north-east coast, which is the largest known non-associated gas field in the world. There is a natural gas pipeline to the United Arab Emirates and Oman as part of the Dolphin Project to connect to these countries natural gas networks.

Energy
Total installed generation capacity was 4,893MW in 2013. Natural gas is the source of energy for all public power plants and provides 79 per cent of all electricity generation, the remainder is provided by oil.
As a result of steadily rising demand, the government has embarked on a process of restructuring the electricity sector with an emphasis on attracting foreign investment through independent power projects (IPPs). Nevertheless, the partially state-owned General Electricity and Water Corporation (QEWC, known as Kahramaa) keeps control of transmission and distribution activities, while retaining a monopoly as sole purchaser of all generated electricity.
The Ras Abu Fontas power station has been re-furbished with an increased generating capacity of 1,030MW. An additional 2,250MW generating capacity has been added in 2015 with the completion of a new power plant. A Gulf Co-operation Council (GCC) project to link the six member states (Saudi Arabia, Qatar, Bahrain, Kuwait, Oman and the United Arab Emirates) to an integrated power-grid began in 2005. The first phase of the GCC power grid was completed in July 2009 at a cost of US$1,095 million, linking Saudi Arabia, Bahrain, Kuwait and Qatar through 800km of transmission lines. Kuwait and Saudi Arabia will each receive an extra 1,200MW of power capacity and later, the UAE will receive 900MW, Qatar 750MW, Bahrain 600MW and Oman 400MW. In the first phase, a 400kV overhead line links Kuwait's Al Zour power station with Doha, and a 400kV submarine line to Saudi Arabia with Bahrain. The second phase will link the UAE with Oman. The resulting two mega-grids will be joined in the final phase.

Financial markets
A regional financial services centre provides Qatar-based projects with financing, bond insurance and asset management to financial institutions which allows them to enter the liquefied natural gas (LNG) markets. A regulator was appointed to oversee the operations.
The Qatar Exchange announced on 17 January 2012 that the technical and regulatory infrastructure necessary to launch trading in small and medium enterprises (SMEs), the QE Venture Market, was ready and was inviting companies to participate.

Stock exchange
Doha Securities Market (DSM)

Banking and insurance
The banking sector consists of 15 commercial banks, including seven locally owned banks. There are 12 insurance companies, the majority of which are foreign-owned; the largest is the locally-owned Qatar Insurance Company.
An agreement was reached between Saudi Arabia, Kuwait, Bahrain and Qatar to establish the Gulf Co-operation Council (GCC) Monetary Council to be established (originally in 2009), marking plans to set up a regional central bank, to be based in Riyadh (Saudi Arabia). The GCC Monetary Council will oversee the introduction of a monetary union, due to be in operation by 2013.
In February 2011, the Central Bank of Qatar ordered all non-Islamic lenders to stop offering Islamic banking services or to restructure them into conventional loans or sell them to Islamic financial operators by the end of 2011. The move was seen to benefit purely Islamic operators in Qatar, at the expense of foreign (non-Islamic) banks and financial institutions. However, within a week, the chief executive of the Doha Bank declared that while no Islamic accounts would be closed no new business would be undertaken and indicated a relaxation in the original direction.
In April 2012 the Qatar National Bank announced that it had purchased a 49 per cent stake in a private in Libya, the Bank of Commerce and Development.

Central bank
The Qatar Central Bank (QCB)

Main financial centre
Doha

Time
GMT plus three hours

Geography
Qatar occupies a peninsula, projecting northwards from the Arabian mainland, on the west coast of the Gulf. It is bordered, to the south by Saudi Arabia and the United Arab Emirates. The archipelago of Bahrain lies to the north-west. On the opposite side of the Gulf lies Iran. The terrain consists primarily of sand dunes laid over flat rocky areas or salt flats, with some limestone outcrops,

particularly in the west around Dukhan and in the north around Fuwairit.

Hemisphere

Northern

Climate

Desert climate with extremely hot and humid summers, when temperatures can reach 44 degrees Celsius from July–September, and mild winters with occasional rainfall.

Entry requirements

Passports

Required by all.

Visa

Required by all; except nationals of neighbouring countries.

For all others, requirements are subject to change and it is advisable to contact an embassy of Qatar for up-to-date information. Business and tourist visas (valid for 21 days) may be obtained on arrival. However, obtaining a visa in advance will save time.

A new visa system (similar to the European Schengen agreement) allowing multiply entry for foreigners to the six Gulf Co-operation Council (GCC) countries was introduced in November.

Prohibited entry

Holders of passports issued by Israel.

Currency advice/regulations

There are no exchange restrictions. Israeli currency is prohibited.

Customs

Personal effects are duty-free. Certain goods (firearms, ammunition, drugs and alcohol) may only be imported under licence.

Import of pork and pork products, cultured pearls, and obscene or seditious literature is forbidden.

Importers must register with the Controller of Companies and appear on the Chamber of Commerce's register of importers. All foodstuffs must be labelled in Arabic.

Prohibited imports

Alcohol, even for personal consumption.

Health (for visitors)

Mandatory precautions

Vaccination certificate against yellow fever if travelling from infected area.

Advisable precautions

Inoculations and boosters should be current for tetanus, polio, typhoid and hepatitis A. There may be a need for vaccinations for tuberculosis, diphtheria and hepatitis B. In border areas with Saudi Arabia rabies is considered high risk and therefore any animal or bat bites should be assessed carefully.

A supply of any regular medicines required should be taken, with their prescription details; medical insurance, which includes emergency evacuation, is recommended.

Hotels

There is a large selection of first-class hotels. Tax of 15 per cent is added to the bill.

Credit cards

Major credit cards are accepted.

Public holidays (national)

Fixed dates

27 Jun (Accession of the Emir), 3 Sep (Independence Day), 31 Dec (banks only).

Variable dates

Eid al Adha (five days), Islamic New Year, Eid al Fitr (four days),

Islamic year 1437 (15 Oct 2015–2 Oct 2016):: The Islamic year has 354 or 355 days, with the result that Muslim feasts advance by 10–12 days against the Gregorian calendar each year. Dates of the Muslim feasts vary according to sightings of the new moon, so cannot be forecast exactly.

Working hours

Friday is the official weekend holiday. During Ramadan, the Muslim holy month of fasting during daylight hours, most officials work 0900–1300.

Banking

Sat–Wed: 0730–1330.

Business

Sat–Thu: 0800–1200, 1600–1900.

Government

Sat–Thu: 0700–1400.

Shops

Sat–Thu: 0830–1230, 1630–2030; Fri: most shops are closed, although some supermarkets are open.

Telecommunications

Mobile/cell phones

There is a 900/1800 GSM service available throughout the country.

Electricity supply

220/240V AC, with three-pin flat plug fittings most common.

Weights and measures

Metric system; other weights are still in use, however.

Social customs/useful tips

Correspondence and technical literature is acceptable in English.

At business meetings it is not uncommon for several people to be present. While in negotiations be careful about committing yourself orally. In a traditional Muslim Sharia Court, oral evidence carries far more weight than written. You should also be aware that you will be held to the letter of any agreement.

Keep contracts as simple as possible; the main part should be couched in easily translated terms with detailed ramifications of the deal relegated to annexes. Amendments should be avoided as they are considered dishonourable.

Increasingly, be prepared to consider contracts under local law – with the provision of neutral (ie Swiss, Dutch) arbitration.

In public places, women should dress modestly.

Refrain from taking photographs without permission.

Pork should not be eaten in the presence of Muslims. It is polite to avoid eating, drinking or smoking in front of Muslims, during daylight hours in the month of Ramadan (when such consumption in public is illegal).

The purchase of alcohol is restricted to expatriate residents with a special liquor permit (not available to Muslims) and its consumption is confined to their private homes. Alcohol is a particularly sensitive subject in Qatar and the utmost discretion must be shown at all times by those permitted to consume it.

Getting there

Air

National airline: Qatar Airways

International airport/s: Doha International (DOH), 8km from city, with restaurant, bank, hotel reservations, shops, car hire.

A taxi from the airport to the city centre takes about 15 minutes. The larger hotels will send transport to the airport to collect their guests.

Airport tax: None

Surface

Road: Tarmac roads link all towns and villages in Qatar with Saudi Arabia. It is also possible to enter by good roads from the UAE.

Main port/s: Passenger services through Mina Salman, Mina Manama and Mina Muharroq, with ferries to Iran and Bahrain.

Getting about

National transport

Road: There are more than 1,000km of good roads (some dual carriageway), with a ring road system around Doha.

The Trans-Arabian Highway which links Doha with Saudi Arabia provides a continuous land connection between Qatar and Europe. Another highway which was build in conjunction with the UAE, links Qatar with the Gulf countries' network.

Buses: Doha's public bus service provides transport to and from the neighbouring towns. There is no public transport within the city.

City transport

Taxis: Taxis are orange and white and have black-on-yellow number plates, with metered fares.

Two-tier (day and night) fare system applies within the Doha city limits. They can be hired on a time basis, with a set hourly rate.

Some hotels offer a courtesy pick-up service; others offer the service but charge. A limousine can be booked through the hotel.

Car hire

If hiring for more than seven days, it is necessary to obtain a 30-day local licence – international or foreign licences are not acceptable. For this, a foreign or international licence, a letter from a local sponsor and passport must be produced within a week of arrival, and a test on road signs may be required. Third-party insurance is compulsory.

Speed limits are 60kph in cities and 100kph on highways. Traffic drives on the right.

Air-conditioned cars are available for hire, with a driver, and can be delivered to the airport or hotel.

BUSINESS DIRECTORY

The addresses listed below are a selection only. While World of Information makes every endeavour to check these addresses, we cannot guarantee that changes have not been made, especially to telephone numbers and area codes. We would welcome any corrections.

Telephone area codes

The international dialling code (IDD) for Qatar is +974, followed by subscriber's number.

Useful telephone numbers

Emergency (all services): 999
International operator: 150
Directory enquiries: 180
International enquiries: 190
Telegram service: 130
Speaking clock (English): 140
Ship to shore: 864-444

Chambers of Commerce

Qatar Chamber of Commerce and Industry, PO Box 402, Doha, (tel: 455-9111; fax: 466-1693; email: infor@qcci.org; internet: www.qcci.org).

Banking

Al Ahli Bank of Qatar, PO Box 2309, Doha (tel: 4326-611; fax: 4444-652).

Al Mashriq, PO Box 173, Doha (tel: 4413-213; fax: 4413-880).

Arab Bank Ltd., PO Box 172, Doha (tel: 4437-979; fax: 4410-774).

Bank Saderat Iran, PO Box 2256, Doha (tel: 4414-646; fax: 4428-077).

Banque Paribas, PO Box 2636, Doha (tel: 4433-844; fax: 4410-861).

Bank Sederat Iran, PO Box 2256, Doha (tel: 4414-646; fax: 4430-121).

Bank of Oman Ltd., PO Box 173, Doha (tel: 4413-213; fax: 4413-800).

Commercial Bank of Qatar Ltd, PO Box 3232, Doha (tel: 4490-222; fax: 4438-182).

Doha Bank, PO Box 3818, Doha (tel: 4456-660; fax: 4416-631).

Grindlays Qatar Bank, PO Box 2001, Doha (tel: 4425-466; fax: 4428-077).

HSBC Bank of the Middle East, PO Box 57, 810 Abdulla bin Jassim Street, Doha (tel: 4438-2100; fax: 4416-353).

Qatar Industrial Development Bank, PO Box 22789, Doha (tel: 4421-600; fax: 4416-631).

Qatar International Islamic Bank, PO Box 664, Doha (tel: 4409-409; fax: 4444-101).

Qatar Islamic Bank, PO Box 559, Doha (tel: 4438-000; fax: 4412-700).

Qatar National Bank, PO Box 1000, Doha (tel: 4407-407; fax: 4413-753; e-mail: webmaster@qatarbank.com).

Standard Chartered Bank, PO Box 29, Doha (tel: 4414-252; fax: 4413-739).

United Bank Ltd, PO Box 242, Doha (tel: 4438-666; fax: 4424-600).

Central bank

Qatar Central Bank, Corniche Street; PO Box 1234, Doha (tel: 445-6456; email: webmaster@qcb.gov.qa; internet: www.qcb.gov.qa).

Stock exchange

Doha Securities Market (DSM), www2.dsm.com.qa

Travel information

Doha International Airport information (tel: 4438-111).

Gulf Air, PO Box 138, Manama, Bahrain (tel: (+973) 322-200; fax: (+973) 440-466).

Qatar Airways, Almana Tower, PO Box 22550, Doha (tel: 4430-707; fax: 4352-433).

Qatar National Hotels Co, PO Box 2977, Doha (tel: 4426-414; fax: 4431-223).

National tourist organisation offices

Qatar Tourism Authority, P.O. Box 24624, Doha (tel: 441-1555; fax: 437-2993; email: info@experienceqatar.com; internet: http://experienceqatar.com)

Ministries

Ministry of Amiri Diwan Affairs, PO Box 923, Doha (tel: 4468-333; fax: 4412-617).

Ministry of Communications and Transport, PO Box 3416, Doha (tel: 4464-000; fax: 4413-886).

Ministry of Defence, PO Box 37, Doha (tel: 4604-111; fax: 4608-366).

Ministry of Education, PO Box 80, Doha (tel: 4333-444; fax: 4413-954).

Ministry of Electricity and Water, Department of Electricity, PO Box 41, Doha (tel: 4326-622; fax: 4426-608).

Ministry of Endowments and Islamic Affairs, PO Box 232, Doha (tel: 4452-222).

Ministry of Finance, PO Box 83, Doha (tel: 446-1444; fax: 441-3617).

Ministry of Foreign Affairs, PO Box 250, Doha (tel: 4334-334; fax: 4442-777).

Ministry of Information and Culture, PO Box 1836, Doha (tel: 4831-333; fax: 4831-518).

Ministry of Interior, PO Box 920, Doha (tel: 4430-000; fax: 44330-168); Passport and Immigration Division, PO Box 122, Doha (tel: 4443-300); Police Headquarters, PO Box 920, Doha (tel: 4330-000); Police Traffic Division, PO Box 8989, Doha (tel: 4868-000; fax: 4872-624); Residence Permits, PO Box 122, Doha (tel: 4325-588); Visa Section, PO Box 122, Doha (tel: 4328-129).

Ministry of Justice, PO Box 2377, Doha (tel: 4435-777; fax: 4832-868).

Ministry of Labour, Social Affairs and Housing, PO Box 201, Doha (tel: 4321-955; fax: 4432-929).

Ministry of Municipal and Agricultural Affairs, PO Box 2727, Doha (tel: 4336-336; fax: 4430-239).

Ministry of Public Health, PO Box 42, Doha (tel: 4441-555; fax: 4429-565).

National Oil Distribution Company (NODCO), PO Box 50033, Mesaieed (tel: 4776-555; fax: 4771-232).

Other useful addresses

Broadcasting and Television Corporation, PO Box 1836, Doha (tel: 4831-333; fax: 4831-518).

Central Tenders Committee, PO Box 1968, Doha (tel: 4413-089; fax: 4439-360).

Department of Civil Aviation, PO Box 3000, Doha (tel: 4426-262; fax: 4429-070).

Department of Commercial Affairs, PO Box 22355, Doha (tel: 4432-103; fax: 4431-412).

Department of Customs, PO Box 81, Doha (tel: 4457-457; fax: 4414-959).

Department of Economic Affairs, PO Box 1968, Doha (tel: 4416-234; fax: 4415-731).

Department of Environmental Affairs, PO Box 7634, Doha (tel: 4320-825; fax: 4415-246).

Department of Financial Affairs, PO Box 83, Doha (tel: 4461-444; fax: 4413-617).

Department of Industrial Development, PO Box 2599, Doha (tel: 4832-121; fax: 4832-024).

Department of Museum and Antiquities, PO Box 2777, Doha (tel: 4438-123).

Department of Post, PO Box 713, Doha (tel: 4835-555; fax: 4837-777).

Department of Safety, Quality and Environment, PO Box 47, Doha (tel: 4402-538; fax: 4402-207).

Department of Water, PO Box 162, Doha (tel: 4494-444).

Doha Securities Market, PO Box 22114, Doha (tel: 4328-025; fax: 4326-497).

Exhibitions Department, PO Box 1968, Doha (tel: 4834-450; fax: 4834-480).

Exploration and Development of New Ventures Department, PO Box 3212, Doha (tel: 4491-288; fax: 4831-850).

Government House, jPO Box 83, Doha (tel: 4461-444).

HH the Emir's Doha Palace, PO Box 923 (tel: 4415-888).

Information and Computer Services Department, PO Box 47, Doha (tel: 4402-240; fax: 4413-629).

Al Jazeera Satellite Channel, PO Box 23123, Doha (tel: 4890-890; fax: 4885-333).

Legal Affairs and Contracts Department, PO Box 3212, Doha (tel: 4491-467; fax: 4831-752).

Materials Department, PO Box 47, Doha (tel: 4332-222; fax: 4343-458).

Petroleum Engineering Department, PO Box 47, Doha (tel: 4402-440; fax: 4402-215).

Pharmaceuticals and Medicines Control Department, PO Box 1919, Doha (tel: 4447-828; fax: 4425-399).

Qatar Broadcasting Services, PO Box 3939, Doha (tel: 4894-4444; fax: 4894-202).

Qatari Business Association, PO Box 24475, Doha (435-3120; fax:435-3834).

Qatar Clean Energy Company (QACENCO), PO Box 22074, Doha (tel: 4415-556; fax: 4415-640).

Qatar Embassy (USA), 4200 Wisconsin Avenue, NW, Washington DC 20016 (tel: (+1-202) 274-1603; fax: (+1-202) 237-0061; email: washington@mofa.gov.qa).

Qatar Fertiliser Company (QAFCO), PO Box 50001, Doha (tel: 4770-252; fax: 4771-655).

Qatar Fuel Additives Company (QAFAC), PO Box 22700, Doha (tel: 4433-700; fax: 4433-766).

Qatar General Petroleum Corporation, Headquarters: PO Box 3212, Doha (tel: 4491-491; fax: 4836-999; internet: www.qgpc.com.qa); Oil and Gas Operations: PO Box 47, Doha (tel: 4402-000).

Qatar Liquefied Gas Company (QATARGAS), PO Box 22666, Doha (tel: 4739-400; fax: 4739-423).

Qatar National Cement Company, PO Box 1333, Doha (tel: 4350-800).

Qatar Petrochemical Company (QAPCO), PO Box 756, Doha (tel: 4321-105; fax: 4324-700).

Qatar Public Telecommunications Corp, PO Box 217, Doha (tel: 4400-333; fax: 4413-904).

Qatar Steel Company Ltd, PO Box 50090, Doha (tel: 4770-011; fax: 4771-424).

Qatar Television, PO Box 1944, Doha (tel: 4894-444; fax: 4438-316).

Ras Laffan Liquefied Natural Gas Company, PO Box 2400, Doha (tel: 4859-400; fax: 4833-855).

State Audit Bureau, PO Box 2466, Doha (tel: 4441-000; fax: 4412-101).

Qatar Financial Centre, PO Box 23245, Doha (tel: 4945-508; fax: 4830-928; email: info@qfc.com.qa, website: www.qfc.com.qa).

Qatar Financial Centre Regulatory Authority, PO Box 22989, Doha (tel: 4945-433; fax: 4835-031; email: info@qfcra.com.qa, website: www.qfcra.com.qa).

National news agency: Qatar News Agency, PO Box 3299, Doha (tel: 445-0319; email: info@qnaol.com; internet: www.qnaol.com).

Internet sites

Arab net: www.arab.net/welcome.html

Arabia on line: www.arabia.com

Gulf business explorer: www.igulf.com/main.htm

Qatar Investment Promotion Department: www.investinqatar.com.qa

Qatar website: www.dib-qatar.com

Qatar yellow pages: www.qatar-yellowpages.com

Réunion

COUNTRY PROFILE

The island was uninhabited until the beginning of the seventeenth century when Arab explorers called it Diva Margabin. The Portuguese renamed it Ilha Santa Apolonia and the French settlers called it l'Île Bourbon. After the French Revolution it was given its current name, La Réunion.
1642 The island was first occupied by France and was ruled as a colony.
1946 La Réunion became a French Département d'Outre-Mer (DOM) (Overseas Department).
1973 France established the headquarters of its military forces in the Indian Ocean on the island.
1974 La Réunion was further incorporated into the French political system and granted the status of region of France.
1983 France granted autonomy in the administration of La Réunion through devolution, establishing a Regional Council.
1992 A contentious newcomer to local politics, Camille Sudre, the owner of a pirate television station, created the Free-DOM party, which won the largest block of seats in the Regional Council. The result was annulled when Sudre's TV broadcasts for his party were deemed to have been political propaganda.
1993 The Free-DOM party led by Camille Sudre's wife, Marguerite, won the elections with a reduced majority.
1996 Unemployment reached 40 per cent.
1998 Paul Vergés was elected head of the regional council.
2001 Gonthier Friederici became *préfet*.
2002 La Réunion adopted the euro as its official currency.
2004 Dominique Vian took office as *préfet*.
2005 Laurent Cayrel was appointed *préfet*.
2006 Pierre-Henry Maccioni was appointed *préfet*. An estimated one-third of the population were afflicted by the mosquito-borne chikungunya disease which killed several hundred; the tourist industry suffered a sharp downturn and French army sanitisation crews were drafted in to spray insecticide.
2008 In local elections Nassimah Dindar was re-elected Conseil Général. She organised a broad spectrum political coalition including the Mouvement Démocrate (MoDem) (Democratic Movement) with Parti Socialiste (PS) (Socialist Party), Parti Communiste de Réunion (PCR) (Réunion Communist Party), Union pour un Mouvement Populaire (UMP) (Popular Movement Union) and other various small, right-wing groupings.
2009 A new metalled road, Route 17, connecting the north and south of the island, was opened by François Fillon (Etats Généraux (Overseas Estates General)).
2010 Growth in tourist numbers from the EU, in the first half of the year, was up 23 per cent. Didier Robert was elected president of the Regional Council. Three areas of outstanding natural beauty and biodiversity, pitons, cirques and remparts, in the central region of the Réunion National Park were added to the Unesco World Heritage list.
2012 The second and final round of the French presidential elections, on 6 May, were won by the socialist candidate, François Hollande, with 51.63 per cent of the vote against incumbent Nicolas Sarkozy with 48.37 per cent; turnout was 80.35 per cent. On 15 May François Hollande took office as president and head of state. On 27 August Jean-Luc Marx took office as *Préfet* (high commissioner).
2013 Cyclone Dumile hit the island in January. Air traffic and shipping came to a standstill and power was cut to some 60,000 homes. A teenage girl was killed by a shark while swimming off the west coast on 16 July. The incident was unusual since it was only a few metres off-shore. It was the second fatal attack in 2013, the first being a surfer further off-shore.
2014 Cyclone Bejisa swept through Réunion in early January, claiming at least one life, leaving 15 injured, and cutting off water and electricity for hundreds of thousands.

Political structure
Constitution
The Constitution of Réunion is the French Constitution of 28 September 1958 (French Fifth Republic).
Under the 1946 constitution of the French Fourth Republic, La Réunion became a Département d'Outre-Mer (DOM) (Overseas Department) of France. In 1974, it was granted additional status as a region of France.

KEY FACTS

Official name: La Réunion

Head of State: President of France François Hollande (PS) (from 15 May 2012), represented by *Préfet* Dominique Sorain (appointed 30 July 2014).

Head of government: President of the Conseil Général Nassimah Dindar (since 2004; re-elected March 2008); President of the Conseil Régional Didier Robert (from 26 Mar 2010).

Ruling party: Supporters of Didier Robert (from Mar 2010)

Area: 2,512 square km

Population: 765,000 (2010)*

Capital: Saint Denis

Official language: French

Currency: Euro (€) = 100 cents

Exchange rate: €0.89 per US$ (Sep 2015)

* estimated figure

La Réunion is represented in the French National Assembly in Paris by five directly elected deputies, for five-year terms, and in the Senate by four indirectly elected senators for nine-year terms.
Since 1983, following the French government's policy of decentralisation, regional councils have been elected with powers similar to those of the mainland French regions.
Administration is by a préfét appointed by the government in Paris.

Form of state

Democratic, presidential republic Département d'Outre-Mer (DOM) (Overseas Department) of France, with additional status as a région (region) of France.

The executive

The Conseil Général (General Council) is indirectly elected by the regional council and has powers to raise a budget.
The préfet, appointed from Paris, oversees financial probity, judicial integrity and the official functions of the state. The préfet also plays a role in managing funding awarded from the EU, and has become a representative of the EU in Réunion.
Réunion also elects three Senators to the French Senate for six-year terms.

National legislature

The unicameral Conseil Régional (Regional Council) has 45 members elected by proportional representation for terms of six years. Its duties include determining the demand for, among other things, investment, education, training, transport, infrastructure, tourism and the environment, by liaising with local communes and departments.

Legal system

French legal system

Last elections

March 2010 (Conseil Régional)
Results: Conseil Régional: supporters of Didier Robert won 27 seats (out of 45), Parti Communiste de Réunion (PCR) (Réunion Communist Party) 12, Parti Socialiste (PS) (Socialist Party) six; turnout was 57.33 per cent.

Next elections

2014 (Conseil Régional)

Political parties

Free-DOM (right-wing group); Parti Communiste de Réunion (PCR) (Réunion Communist Party); Rassemblement pour la République (RPR) (Gaullist Rally for the Republic); two factions of the Parti Socialiste (PS) (Socialist Party); Union pour la France (UPF) (Union for France); Union pour la Démocratie Française-Centre Démocratique Sociale (UDF-CDS) (Union for French Democracy-Social Democratic Centre).

Ruling party

Supporters of Didier Robert (from Mar 2010)

Population

765,000 (2010)*
Last census: 1 January 2006: 781,962
Population density: 262 inhabitants per square km. Urban population: 69 per cent.
Annual growth rate: 1.8 per cent (2003)

Ethnic make-up

African (64 per cent), Indian (28 per cent), European (2.2 per cent) and Chinese (2.2 per cent) descent.

Religions

The majority of the population is Roman Catholic (86 per cent); there are also groups of Hindus, Muslims and Buddhists.

Education

Literacy rate: 89 per cent, adult rate (2003)

Health

Health services comply with French standards, there are some 1,270 doctors, 275 pharmacies and 17 hospitals, including clinics.
Life expectancy: 73.4 years (estimate 2003)
Fertility rate/Maternal mortality rate: 2.5 births per woman (2003)
Birth rate/Death rate: 20 births per 1,000 population; 5.5 deaths per 1,000 population (2003).
Child (under 5 years) mortality rate (per 1,000): Eight per 1,000 live births (2003)

Main cities

Saint Denis (capital, estimated population 137,687 in 2012), Saint Paul (110,309), Saint Pierre (83,451), Le Tampon (79,930), Saint André (54,174), Saint Louis (51,335), Le Port (41,982).

Languages spoken

As well as French, Creole is commonly spoken.

Official language/s

French

Media

Press

In French, *Le Journal de l'Ile de la Réunion* (www.clicanoo.com) and *Temoignages* (www.temoignages.re) are published daily in St Denis. Regional publications, in English, include *APA* (www.apanews.net) and *Panapress* (www.panapress.com).

Broadcasting

RFO Réunion (http://reunion.rfo.fr) is the public broadcasting network providing radio and television programmes originating from France. The private TV station Antenne Réunion Télévision (www.antennereunion.fr) provides a range of local news and international programmes. All broadcasts are in French.
Other news agencies: Imaz Press Réunion, (tel: 200-656; email: fax: 200-549; email: ipr@ipreunion.com; internet: www.ipreunion.com).

Economy

La Réunion is dependent on France for around three quarters of its GNP.
The service sector typically accounts for 73 per cent of GDP, of which trade, transport, telecommunications and health and social services have become the most important components; tourism is also an important contributor to the economy (7.8 per cent to GDP in 2014) and has become increasingly so as the government is pushing development of the industry in order to deal with high unemployment.
Sugar cane production (once representing over 50 per cent of available arable land) has fallen by up to one-third of the amount grown in 1980s, and been replaced by crops for domestic consumption. As of 2015, harvested land accounted for 19 per cent of total landmass in La Réunion. The fishing industry has three differing categories, small-scale, long line and industrial fishing (which is regulated by quotas and an electronically monitored exclusion zone).
Although social indicators are good, unemployment is a pressing problem affecting around 40 per cent and is particularly bad amongst the 16-25 age group. There is a large income and social divide between the majority of the population, which is impoverished and largely black, and the rich minority, which is white or Indian. The extremely large gap between the well off and those in poverty gives rise to persistent social tensions. There is a history of anti-governmental riots, which most recently broke into violence in March 2009 when there were protests at rising food prices.
The island is plagued by regular cyclone devastation. In January 2013 Cyclone Dumile hit the island causing air traffic and shipping to come to a standstill. Power was cut to some 60,000 homes as well. In January 2014 Cyclone Bejisa claimed at least one life and left 15 people injured. La Réunion is also home to one of the most active volcanoes in the world – Piton de la Fournaise.

External trade

As a département d'outre-mer (DOM) of France, Réunion is integrated as an outermost region of the European Union and adopts all EU trade agreements.

Imports

The main imports are manufactured goods, food, beverages, tobacco,

machinery and transportation equipment, raw materials, and petroleum products.
Main sources: France (typically over 60 per cent), Bahrain (3.0 per cent), Germany (3.0 per cent), Italy (3.0 per cent).
Exports
The main export is sugar (over 60 per cent), rum and molasses, perfume essences and lobster.
Main destinations: France (typically over 70 per cent), Japan (6.0 per cent), Comoros (4.0 per cent).

Agriculture
Farming
Sugar cane, the main crop, was grown on over 26,000 hectares in 2014, producing about 200,000 tonnes of sugar. Cash crops include tea and tobacco.
Ylang-ylang, vetiver and geraniums are used as components of aromatic essences.
The agriculture sector contributes about 8 per cent to GDP and employs approximately 13 per cent of the workforce.
Around 19 per cent of the land is cultivated. Much of the island's food supply is imported.
Fishing
Typical annual fish catches are over 4,000mt and crustacean catches are over 15mt.

Industry and manufacturing
The industrial sector contributes about 19 per cent to GDP and employs some 12 per cent of the workforce.
The production of processed sugar and rum accounts for most industrial activity.
The Ecopipe steel pipe mill (funded by the French government and South African private capital) started operations in 1997 at Le Port, on the west coast of Réunion. It has the capacity to produce 15,000 tonnes a year and employs 80 people.

Tourism
Tourism is now the principal economic activity. As a former French colony Réunion, on the Indian Ocean, offers a tropical holiday with a flavour of France and an infusion of African and Indian cultures. As a *department de outré mer* of France, the majority of visitors tend to be French.
Réunion's coast has one of the highest rates of shark attacks in the world, a location also very popular with surfers. In the 2011–15 period, 17 shark attacks were recorded, 7 of which were fatal. The government has had to move focus towards land based tourism as potential tourists have begun to think of La Réunion's seas as dangerous.
The Réunion National Park, which covers around 40 per cent of the island, is included on Unesco's World Heritage List, for its volcanic peaks and natural ramparts.
Travel and tourism contributed US$1.46 billion to GDP in 2014 (7.8 per cent of GDP) and provided employment to 7.9 per cent of the workforce (around 20,500 jobs).

Mining
There are no significant mineral resources.

Hydrocarbons
There are no hydrocarbon reserves.
Réunion relies entirely on imported petroleum products, provided from France, although commercial oil companies carry out fuel distribution and marketing.
Natural gas is neither produced nor consumed.

Energy
Total installed generating capacity is some 47MW, approximately 60 per cent of which is provided by hydropower.
Réunion has one thermal power plant that runs on imported coal. This produces around 39 per cent of Réunion's electricity needs.
In April 2015, the French renewable energies company Albomia acquired 14 photovoltaic power plants in La Réunion with a combined generating capacity of 3MW.

Banking and insurance
Central bank
Banque de France; European Central Bank (ECB).

Time
GMT plus four hours

Geography
Réunion is an island in the Indian Ocean, lying about 800km (500 miles) east of Madagascar. It is a volcanic, mountainous island.
Hemisphere
Southern

Climate
The climate varies greatly according to altitude: at sea-level, it is tropical, with average temperatures between 20 and 28 degrees Celsius (C); in the uplands, it is much cooler, with average temperatures between 8 and 19 degrees C. From July to November, the temperature in high altitude places can drop to 10 degrees C during the day and to 6 degrees C at night.
Rainfall is abundant; the cyclone season lasts from December to April.
Summer runs from November to April with an average temperature of 27 degrees C. Winter stretches from May to October with an average temperature of 23 degrees C.

Dress codes
Generally light summer clothes are required, with some woollen garments for chilly evenings.

Entry requirements
Passports
Required by all, except nationals of EU/EEA countries, Monaco, Switzerland with national identity cards; passports must be valid for three months beyond date of departure,
Visa
Required by all, except nationals of EU/EEA countries, North America, Australasia, Japan, Israel and some other countries for stays up to three months.
Nationals of the US, Canada and several other countries need a visa if they receive a salary. Nationals of EU/EEA countries, the Vatican, Liechtenstein and Monaco do not require long-term visas issued for stays in excess of three months. Proof of adequate funds for stay, an itinerary, a guarantee of repatriation if necessary, return/onward ticket and, for business travellers, an invitation from a local company or organisation are also required.
Currency advice/regulations
There are no restrictions on the import or export of local and foreign currency, subject to declaration of amounts over eur7,600.

Health (for visitors)
There are no compulsory vaccinations.
Passengers from endemic countries should be inoculated against yellow fever.
Advisable precautions
Vaccinations for diphtheria, tetanus, typhoid fever, hepatitis A and tuberculosis are advisable, and precautions should be taken against malaria. Malaria and chikungunya are caused by mosquitoes, precautions including mosquito repellents, nets and clothing covering the body should be used.

Credit cards
Major credit cards are accepted.

Public holidays (national)
Fixed dates
1 Jan (New Year's Day), 1 May (Labour Day), 8 May (1945 Victory Day), 14 Jul (Bastille Day), 15 Aug (Assumption Day), 1 Nov (All Saints' Day), 11 Nov (Armistice Day), 20 Dec (Abolition of Slavery Day), 25 Dec (Christmas Day).
Variable dates
Good Friday, Easter Monday, Ascension Day, Whit Monday.

Working hours
Banking
Mon–Fri: 0800–1600.
Business
Mon–Fri: 0800–1200; 1400–1800.

Government
Mon–Fri: 0800–1900; Sat: 0900–1400.
Shops
Mon–Sat: 0830–1200; 1430–1800.
Some food stores are open on Sunday.

Telecommunications
Telephone/fax
The telephone network is entirely automatic and is linked to metropolitan France and the rest of the world via satellite.
Mobile/cell phones
There are GSM 900 and 1800 services available.

Electricity supply
220V

Weights and measures
The metric system is in use.

Social customs/useful tips
Maloya dance music, once banned by the French as being a threat to the French state, in 2012 was being played on French radio and spreading around the world.

Getting there
Air
National airline: Air Austral.
International airport/s: Roland-Garros Airport (RUN), 8km from Saint Denis; post office, restaraunts, duty free shop, car hire.
Other airport/s: Pierrefonds Airport (ZSE), 5km from Saint Pierre.
Airport tax: None.
Surface
Water: There are limited passenger services to Réunion. A cruise liner from Mauritius visits regularly.
Main port/s: Port Réunion.

Getting about
National transport
Road: A *route nationale* circles the island, following the coast and linking all the main towns, and another crosses the island from south-west to north-east linking Saint Pierre and Saint Benoît. There are 370km of main roads, 754km of secondary roads and nearly 1,600km of smaller secondary roads, all in good condition.
Buses: A comfortable bus service (*cars jaunes*), links most towns.
Car hire
A French or international driver's licence is required. The highway code is the same as for France. Driving is on the right.

BUSINESS DIRECTORY

The addresses listed below are a selection only. While World of Information makes every endeavour to check these addresses, we cannot guarantee that changes have not been made, especially to telephone numbers and area codes. We would welcome any corrections.

Telephone area codes
The international dialling code (IDD) for Réunion is +262; this is followed by another 262 and then the subscriber's number.

Useful telephone numbers
Available services for visiting cell phone users:
Emergency calls: (free)112
Telephone enquiries: (call SFR for information)222
Suberscriber services: (local rate)900

Chambers of Commerce
Réunion Chamber of Commerce Industry, 13 Rue Pasteur, PO Box 120, 97463 Saint-Denis cedex (tel: 942-100; fax: 942-290; e-mail: sg.dir@reunion.cci.fr).

Banking
Banque de la Réunion, 27 rue Jean Chatel, 97711 Saint Denis, Cedex 9 (tel: 400-157; fax: 400-060).

Banque Nationale de Paris Intercontinentale (BNPI), 67 rue Juliette-Dodu, Saint Denis (tel: 403-030).

Banque Régionale d'Escompte et de Depot (BRED), 33 rue Victor-Mac-Auliffe, Saint Denis (tel: 901-560).

Caisse d'Epargne Ecureuil, 55 rue de Paris, Saint Denis (tel: 948-000).

Crédit Agricole, 18 rue Félix-Guyon, Saint Denis (tel: 909-100).

Banque Française Commerciale (BFC'OI'), 60 rue Alexis-de-Villeneuve, Saint Denis (tel: 405-555).

Central bank
Banque de France, 1 rue la Vrillière, 75001 Paris, Dept 75, France (tel: (+33-1) 4292-4292; fax: (+33-1) 4292-4500)

European Central Bank (ECB), Kaiserstrasse 29, D-60311 Frankfurt am Main, Germany (tel: (+49-69) 13-440; fax: (+49-69) 1344-6000).

Travel information
Air Austral, PO Box 611, 4 Rue de Nice, 97473 Saint Denis Cedex (tel: 909-090; fax: 909-09; e-mail: reservation@air-austral.com).

Air France, PO Box 845, 7 Avenue de la Victoire, 97477 Saint Denis Cedex (tel: 403-800; fax: 403-840; e-mail: mail.runsh@airfrance.fr).

Fédération Réunionnaise du Tourisme, Résidence Sainte Anne, 18 rue Sainte Anne, 97400 Saint Denis (tel : 413-967; fax : 943-180; e-mail: fr-pat@wanadoo.fr).

Maison de la Montagne, 5 rue Rontaunay, 97400 Saint-Denis (tel: 907-878; fax : 418-429; e-mail : resa@reunion-nature.com).

Ministry of tourism
Delegation Régionale au Commerce, à l'Artisanat et Tourisme, Préfecture de la Réunion, 31 rue de Paris, 97400 Saint-Denis (tel: 319-999; fax: 316-666; e-mail: DRT974@tourisme.gouv.fr).

National tourist organisation offices
Comité du Tourisme de la Réunion, PO Box 615, Place du 20 Décembre 1848, 97472 Saint Denis Cedex (tel: 210-041; fax: 210-021; e-mail: ctr@la-reunion-tourisme.com).

Ministries
Direction Départementale des Affaires Sanitaires et Sociales, Rue Georges Brassens, BP 199, 97490 Sainte-Clothilde (tel: 486-060; fax: 486-008).

Direction Départementale du Travail et de l'Emploi, 24 Rue Maréchal Leclerc, 97488 Saint Denis Cedex (tel: 486-600; fax: 486-666).

Direction Régionale des Affaires Culturelles, 31 Rue Amiral Lacaze 97400 Saint Denis (tel: 219-171; fax: 416-193).

Direction Régionale de la Jeunesse et des Sports, 14 Allée des Saphirs, BP 297, 97487 Saint Denis Cedex (tel: 901-616; fax: 213-864).

Other useful addresses
Agence Nationale pour l'Emploi 10 Rue Champ Fleury, 97490 Sainte Clothilde (tel: 219-236; fax: 417-383).

Association pour le Développement Industriel de la Réunion, 18 Rue Milius, 97468 Saint Denis Cedex (tel: 214-269; fax: 203-757).

British Consul, 94b Avenue Leconte Delisle, 97490 Sainte Clotilde (tel: 291-491; fax: 293-991).

Civil Aviation Management, 11 Avenue de la Victoire, 97489 Saint Denis Cedex (tel: 930-000; fax: 211-331).

Compagnie Générale Maritime (CGM), 2 Rue de l'Est, BP 2010, 97822 Le Port Cedex (tel: 420-088; fax: 432-304).

Conseil Economique et Social de la Réunion, PO Box 7191, 10 Rue du Béarn, 97719 Saint Denis (tel: 979-630; fax: 979-631; e-mail: webmaster@cesr-reunion.fr).

Conseil Général, Hôtel du Département, 2 Rue Source, 97400 Saint Denis (tel: 903-030; fax: 903-999).

Conseil Régional, Hôtel de la Région, Avenue René Cassin, Le Moufia, 97494 Sainte Clothilde Cedex (tel: 487-000; fax: 487-071).

Institut National de la Statistique et des Etudes Economiques, Service Régional de la Réunion, 15 Rue de l'Ecole, 97490 Sainte Clotilde (tel: 295-157).

Palais du Justice, 166 Rue Juliette Dodu, 97488 Saint Denis (tel: 405-858; fax: 219-532).

Rectorat de la Réunion, 24 Avenue Georges, Brassens, 97702 Saint Denis, Messagerie Cedex 9 (tel: 481-010; fax: 481-366).

Société de Développement Economique de la Réunion (SODERE), 26 Rue Labourdonnais, 97469 Saint Denis (tel: 200-168; fax: 200-507).

Imaz Press Réunion, (tel: 200-656; email: fax: 200-549; email: ipr@ipreunion.com; internet: www.ipreunion.com).

Internet sites

Africa Business Network: http://www.ifc.org/abn

African Development Bank: http://www.afdb.org

Mbendi AfroPaedia (information on companies, countries, industries and stock exchanges in Africa): http://mbendi.co.za

Romania

KEY FACTS

Official name: Romania

Head of State: President Klaus Iohannis (from 21 December 2014).

Head of government: Prime Minister Victor-Viorel Ponta (PSD) (from 7 May 2012; elected 9 Dec 2012).

Ruling party: Uniunea Social Liberala (USL) (Social Liberal Union) (coalition of four political parties) led by Partidul Social Democrat-Partidul Conservator (Alianta PSD+PC) (Social Democratic Party-Conservative Party) (appointed Apr 2012; elected 9 Dec 2012)

Area: 237,500 square km

Population: 19.93 million (2014) (19,042,936; 2011, census figure)

Capital: Bucharest

Official language: Romanian

Currency: New leu (plural lei) (Nleu) = 100 ban

Exchange rate: Nleu3.96 per US$ (Sep 2015)

GDP per capita: US$10,035 (2014)

GDP real growth: 2.90% (2014)

GDP: US$20.00 billion (2014)

Labour force: 4.24 billion (2010)

Unemployment: 6.78% (2014)

Inflation: 1.08% (2014)

Oil production: 85,000 bpd (2014)

Natural gas production: 11.40 billion cum (2014)

Balance of trade: -US$7.14 billion (2014)

Annual FDI: US$2.56 billion (2011)

Romania has the embarrassing position of being one of the European Union's most corrupt countries. On the Transparency International 2014 *Corruption Perceptions Index* Romania ranked 69 out of the 175 countries surveyed, level with neighbouring Bulgaria, Greece and Italy. The Directia Nationala Anticoruptie (DNA) (National Anti-Corruption Directorate) appeared to have made some progress, convicting over 1,000 officials of corruption in 2014. Inevitably for the most part those convicted were low level officials, (according to a report in the London *Economist*, 24 were mayors, five were members of parliament, two were ex-ministers and one – Adrian Nastase – was a former prime minister.

The bigger fish

The DNA (described by one cynical observer as 'having entered Romania's bloodstream') was not overawed by rank. It was headed up by a chief prosecutor, Laura Codruta Kovesi, a former national basketball player. Early 2015 had seen the conviction of Elena Udrea, a former tourism minister, for laundering millions of dollars accumulated by her former husband Dorin Cocos, money made from over-invoicing on government software and computer contracts.

Having collected Ms Udrea's scalp, in June 2015 Ms Kovesi went on to bring charges against Prime Minister Victor Ponta on money-laundering, tax evasion and forgery charges. Mr Ponta's fortunes had ebbed somewhat since his defeat by Klaus Iohannis in the November 2014 presidential election. The charges levelled at him were not the only embarrassment. Similar charges had also been brought by the DNA against his finance minister and other political cronies. Unsurprisingly, both the DNA and Ms Kovesi had found themselves subjected to charges of witch-hunting and allegations of political motivation. The DNA's success had made waves outside Romania, both in Brussels and in Washington following the visit of Secretary of State John Kerry.

Mr Ponta was forced to blow hot and cold on the DNA's successes. Initially negative, the DNA's successes had become a major positive in Romania's international image. Having initially supported the ruling coalition's moves to pass laws protecting members of parliament from prosecution, publically Mr Ponta had to voice his support for the DNA. Mr Ponta had, one day before the DNA pressed charges against him, resigned as leader of the ruling coalition's leading Partidul Social Democrat (PSD) (Social Democratic Party). He was succeeded as leader by the interim party leader Liviu Dragnea, himself on the wrong end of a one-year suspended sentence for trying to fix a referendum in 2012. Romania's next general election is due in late 2016.

On the political back-foot, Mr Ponta had sought to introduce significant tax cuts that would win votes. However, both the Banca Nationala a Romaniei (BNR) (National Bank of Romania) (central bank) and the International Monetary Fund (IMF) (see below) had criticised the move. The Romanian Parliament was due to vote on the tax changes in August 2015.

The economy

In its March 2015 assessment of the Romanian economy, the IMF noted that Romania's economic recovery had 'become more entrenched and broad-based', with 'private consumption picking up on the back of rising real disposable income.' The IMF also noted that Romania's level of inflation had fallen substantially in the previous two years and that a negative output gap persisted. A positive factor was the reduction of non-performing loans, although according to the IMF they remained high. Private sector credit had fallen since 2013.

The IMF expected gross domestic product (GDP) growth to remain strong in a low inflation environment. However, Romania's progress towards income convergence with the European Union (EU) had been slow, youth unemployment remained high and the weak public infrastructure had emerged as a bottleneck for faster growth. In the view of the IMF, increased volatility in the external environment and any failure to implement a much needed infrastructure upgrade, presented downside risks to the overall outlook.

In the view of the IMF, Romania had in large part addressed its internal and external imbalances thanks to a significant reduction in the fiscal deficit as well as prudent monetary and financial sector policies. However, the IMF considered that Romania's structural reform momentum had slowed reflecting the high levels of political uncertainty. The country's sound macro-economic policies needed to be combined with measures that boosted the efficiency of public spending, re-invigorated delayed state-owned enterprise reforms and further strengthened the financial sector.

The IMF concluded its summary assessment by recommending that increased growth prospects over the longer term required a continuity of sustainable macro-economic policies, underpinned by stronger fiscal and regulatory institutions and a more stable and predictable business environment which was crucial for investor confidence. According to the European Bank for Reconstruction and Development (EBRD) in its 2014 *Transition Report*, Romania's economy had been on a solid recovery path in 2013. Economic activity had picked up, as GDP growth rose to 3.5 per cent above market expectations, on the back of a strong export performance and higher agricultural production. This, in the view of the EBRD was a major improvement on 2012 when GDP had risen by only 0.6 per cent. In the first quarter of 2014 the EBRD noted that growth had been strong at an impressive 3.8 per cent. However, by the second quarter of 2014 growth registered a fall to 1.4 per cent. Inflation had returned to the central bank's target range of 1.5–3.5 per cent in 2013, with a drop below the bottom range in January 2014 (down to 1.2 per cent), staying at around one per cent in the first half of the year.

The EBRD noted that there had been substantial fiscal adjustment since the start of the financal crisis, which had brought the budget deficit down from over 7 per cent of GDP in 2009 to an estimated 2.5 per cent of GDP by 2013. Impressively, Romania was rated at investment grade by the three main ratings agencies. None the less, the expenditure reductions were being achieved partly through cuts to public investment which could adversely affect long-term development if funding for high-quality projects were to be lowered. By regional standards public debt was low at around 39 per cent of GDP. The current account was almost in balance. The IMF programme had posited further fiscal adjustment in both 2014 and 2015, which was expected to bring the deficit down to below two per cent of GDP. However, completion of the IMF's third review had been delayed and complicated by the Romanian parliament's decision in September 2014 to introduce a 5 per cent cut in employment taxes. This measure, which is designed to promote job creation, took effect from October 2014. Growth was expected to remain between 2 and 3 per cent in 2014 and 2015, aided by further export growth and a recovery in domestic demand. However, the high level of non performing loans (NPL) and uncertainties in Ukraine might, in the view of the IMF, affect growth prospects. The EBRD considered that Romania's medium-term prospects were favourable, reflecting its diversified economy, large population base and the scope for what the EBRD termed 'catch-up' in a country

KEY INDICATORS — Romania

	Unit	2011	2012	2013	2014	**2015
Population	m	19.04	21.34	21.29	19.93	*19.83
Gross domestic product (GDP)	US$bn	189.80	169.18	191.50	20.00	*189.75
GDP per capita	US$	8,863	7,929	9,001	10,035	*9,570
GDP real growth	%	2.5	0.7	3.4	2.9	*2.7
Inflation	%	5.8	3.3	4.0	1.1	*1.0
Unemployment	%	5.8	7.0	7.3	6.8	*6.7
Oil output	'000 bpd	88.0	86.0	87.0	85.0	–
Natural gas output	bn cum	11.0	10.9	11.0	11.4	–
Coal output	mtoe	6.7	6.4	4.6	4.4	–
Exports (fob) (goods)	US$m	55,614.0	51,291.0	58,292.0	62,132.0	–
Imports (fob) (goods)	US$m	68,190.0	62,749.0	65,578.0	69,273.3	–
Balance of trade	US$m	-12,576.0	-11,458.0	-7,286.0	-7,140.7	–
Current account	US$m	-8,541.0	-7,512.0	-1,551.0	*-921.0	*-2,112.0
Total reserves minus gold	US$m	46,684.0	41,162.0	44,811.0	39,165.0	–
Foreign exchange	US$m	45,823.0	41,012.0	44,773.0	–	–
Exchange rate	per US$	2.98	3.49	3.29	3.71	–

* estimated figure ** forecast figure

where GDP per capita was only 53 per cent of the EU average, according to Eurostat estimates. This meant that annual growth rates of 4 to 5 per cent were feasible provided that the pace of structural reforms was accelerated and increased investment was attracted. The adoption of the euro as the national currency was now envisaged for 2019. Romania had, in the view of the EBRD, made progress in many areas under the EU's Co-operation and Verification Mechanism (CVM), but there were some lingering concerns. In its January 2014 report on the CVM, the European Commission (EC) had concluded that Romania had made progress in many areas of judicial reform and the fight against corruption, particularly in non-partisan investigation and prosecutions in high-level corruption cases. However, the EC drew attention to the weaknesses in the functioning of the judicial system.

The EBRD also drew attention to Romania's relatively poor scores when compared with other EU countries on business environment indicators. Although some improvements to the business environment had been made over the previous year, Romania ranked lower than most of its regional peers for ease of doing business. In the World Bank *Doing Business 2015* report, Romania ranked 48 out of 189 countries, up two positions from the previous year. One big improvement was the jump of 76 places under the paying taxes rubric, although this was from the very low position of 128.

In the view of the EBRD, the quality of Romania's transport infrastructure remains poor by EU standards. Although private sector participation in road sector projects was encouraged officially and although some public-private partnership contracts had been awarded, Romania has so far failed to achieve a structure in line with good industry practice. The government had drafted a master plan for transport, which was under public consultation. In the railway sector, the collapse of the privatisation of state-owned freight company, CFR Marfa, in October 2013 was a serious setback for the industry, which continued to rely on large, non-transparent budget allocations for its survival. CFR Marfa has been undergoing restructuring, including a reduction in personnel costs and the privatisation process has resumed.

Energy

Romania's electricity prices have been raised several times in line with the energy price liberalisation road map and there is now a functioning competitive electricity market for non-residential consumers. Gas price liberalisation for this segment has also continued, with price increases in October 2013 and January 2014 in accordance with the liberalisation road map, but the process has not yet been completed. Meanwhile, gas price liberalisation for households has been delayed. The price of gas for end-consumers is still regulated by the Romanian Energy Regulatory Authority, ANRE and there remains a degree of cross-subsidisation between different categories of consumers

However, a major success was the sale, in November 2013, of a minority 15 per cent stake in the natural gas producer, Romgaz, for 1.7 billion lei (US$438 million) through an international IPO. The launch of an IPO for 51 per cent of the shares of the electricity distribution company, Electrica, in June 2014 was another landmark deal for Romania. However, other privatisations were proving more challenging. In February 2014 the Appeals Court returned the hydropower generator, Hidroelectrica, to insolvency until the legal claims of energy traders against the company were resolved. The IPO was to be launched as soon as the company exited insolvency, which was expected for mid-2015.

According to the US government Energy Information Administration (EIA) Romania's energy strategy is to secure supply through both fuel imports and domestic supplies and maintain a balanced energy resource portfolio by promoting clean coal technologies, nuclear energy, renewable energy expansion and shale gas development. Romania has nine crude oil refineries with a total capacity of 467,642 barrels per day (bpd) according to the *Oil & Gas Journal* (OGJ), among the largest refining capacities in Eastern Europe. Although Romania's refineries operate below capacity, refinery output exceeds domestic consumption allowing the export of surplus petroleum products. Romania consumed 215,000bpd of petroleum in 2013.

The EIA noted that oil production in Romania had steadily declined over time. Total crude oil and other liquids production in Romania was 104,000bpd in 2013, down from around 134,000bpd in 2003. Romania had the fourth-largest crude oil reserves in Europe with 600 million barrels of proved reserves as of 1January 2014, according to OGJ estimates.

Dry natural gas production has declined steadily over the past three decades, from its peak of 1.4 trillion cubic feet (tcf) in 1983 to 375 billion cubic feet (bcf) in 2012. Romania has the fifth-largest natural gas reserves in Europe with 3.7tcf of proved reserves as of 1 January 2014. Romania is looking to develop a shale gas industry and reduce its reliance on Russian natural gas supplies. According to Eurogas, imports of natural gas from Russia accounted for 24 per cent of the natural gas Romania consumed and for 100 per cent of the natural gas Romania imported in 2012.

Risk assessment

Economy	Good
Politics	Fair
Regional stability	Good

People to watch

Laura Codruta Kovesi: Former national basketball player and Chief Prosecutor of the National Anti-Corruption Directorate (DNA).

COUNTRY PROFILE

1881 After surviving numerous invasions and regional upheavals, Romania became an independent country headed by a monarchy.

1918 Romania supported the Allies during the First World War and gained territory close to its borders.

1919 Hungary attacked Romania in retaliation for lost territory. The Romanians quickly defeated Hungary and briefly occupied parts of the country.

1920 Romania gained further parts of Hungarian territory through the Treaty of Trianon.

1929–34 Romania's agricultural sector was severely affected by a collapse in international grain prices. With the country in recession, the fascist and German-funded Iron Guard movement increased in popularity. In 1933, the organisation assassinated the prime minister, Ion Duca.

1938 King Carol, the head of state, declared Romania a royalist dictatorship and appointed a right-wing government. Carol ordered the arrest and execution of members of the Iron Guard.

1940 Military officers, helped by the Iron Guard, seized power. General Ion Antonescu forced Carol to abdicate. Carol's son, Michel V, replaced him as King. German troops were deployed in Romania and the country joined the Axis powers.

1941 The Iron Guard attempted to rebel against the Romanian government after they were ordered to disarm. A joint Romanian and German operation crushed the Iron Guard's rebellion.

1943 The Soviet Union invaded Romania.
1944 Antonescu's government was overthrown and replaced by a Communist coalition government.
1947–48 The monarchy was deposed and the Communist government declared the Romanian People's Republic.
1965 Nicolae Ceausescu took the position of first secretary of the Partidul Comunist Roman (RCP) (Romanian Communist Party).
1974 Ceausescu became president.
1985–86 An austerity programme lead to food shortages and widespread power cuts.
1987 The army occupied power plants and crushed workers' demonstrations in Brasov.
1989 Riots in the city of Timisoara ignited a nationwide revolt. Parts of the army joined the revolutionaries, forming the Frontul Salvarii Nationale (FSN) (National Salvation Front). Ceausescu and his wife, Elena, were summarily executed by a military tribunal and nearly 45 years of Communist dictatorship came to an abrupt and bloody end.
1990 Ion Iliescu was elected president, winning 85 per cent of the vote as the FSN candidate. Petre Roman formed a new government.
1991 Roman resigned as prime minister and was replaced by Teodro Stolojan after his reform programme led to civil unrest. Stolojan successfully guided Romania's new constitution through a referendum and parliamentary vote.
1992 Presidential elections were again won by Iliescu, who had formed his own political party, the Frontul Democrat al Salvarii Nationale (FDSN) (Democratic National Salvation Front), following a split within the FSN.
1996 Iliescu stood again for the presidency and was defeated by Emil Constantinescu of the Conventia Democrata Romana (CDR) (Romanian Democratic Convention) coalition. Victor Ciorbea (of the ruling CDR coalition). The FSN re-named itself the Partidul Democratiei Sociale din Romania (PDSR) (Democratic Social Party of Romania).
1998 Ciorbea resigned and was replaced by Radu Vasile.
1999 After relations with his cabinet collapsed, Vasile was replaced as prime minister by Mugur Isarescu.
2000 Cyanide leaked from a mine in northern Romania and polluted rivers in Hungary and Yugoslavia. Ion Iliescu won the presidency in the second round of voting. After parliamentary elections Adrian Nastase became prime minister, heading a coalition government, comprising the PDSR, Partidul Social Democrat Romania (PSDR) (Romanian Social Democratic Party) and the Partidul Umanist din Romania (PUR) (Humanist Party of Romania).
2001 Iliescu's PDSR merged with the PSDR to become the Partidul Social Democrat (PSD) (Social Democratic Party).
2003 In a referendum, 90 per cent of voters approved constitutional amendments to bring Romanian law in line with EU law.
2004 Romania joined NATO. Bucharest mayor (he later resigned as required by the constitution), Traian Basescu of the Partidul Democrat-Liberal (PD-L) (Democratic Liberal Party), won the runoff presidential election. Basescu appointed Calin Popescu Tariceanu (PNL) as prime minister.
2005 Romania approved the EU accession treaty. The currency was re-valued at the rate of 10,000 old lei to one new leu. Prime Minister Tariceanu resigned, but after severe flooding killed 20 people, he retracted his resignation in order to focus on the reconstruction of the country.
2006 The EU officially agreed Romania's membership providing strong curbs were imposed on organised crime and corruption.
2007 Romania joined the EU. Parliament impeached President Basescu on charges of unconstitutional conduct during months of dispute between the president and prime minister. A later referendum on impeachment failed. The Constitutional Court reinstated Basescu's presidency.
2008 In new elections the Partidul Social Democrat-Partidul Conservator (Alianta PSD+PC) (Social Democratic Party-Conservative Party) alliance won by a tiny majority, 33.09 per cent (114 seats) in the vote in the Chamber of Deputies; the PD-L with 32.4 per cent (115), won most seats for a single party. The PSD and PD-L formed a ruling coalition and President Basescu appointed Emil Boc (PD-L) as prime minister.
2009 The International Court of Justice ruled on a maritime boundary dispute between Romania and Ukraine. A new border settled a 40-year disagreement (over an area of the Black Sea) by extending a line offshore from the land border, giving Romania and Ukraine a segment each of what is thought to contain rich fields of hydrocarbons. The PSD withdrew from the coalition government in protest at the sacking of the PSD interior minister, who had implied potential fraud in the upcoming presidential elections. The ruling PD-L continued as a minority government until it later lost a vote of no-confidence in parliament and was forced to resign. President Basescu nominated firstly Lucian Croitoru and later Liviu Negoita as prime minister, but the PSD majority in parliament insisted that Klaus Iohannis should by prime minister; a stalemate followed as neither side backed down. A referendum agreed to abolish the senate and reduce the number of parliamentarians to a maximum of 300. In a runoff presidential election, incumbent Traian Basescu won 50.33 per cent of the vote, Mircea Geoana (PSD) 49.66 per cent. Breaking the deadlock, parliament agreed to President Basescu's nomination of Emil Boc as prime minister.
2010 In a move condemned by the the EU and human rights groups, French authorities repatriated to Romania foreign-born Roma people living without permits in camps around France. The government announced a package of austerity measures, including large-scale cuts. The constitutional court ruled against the proposed 15 per cent cut in state pensions; the government increased the rate of VAT to 24 per cent instead. Further austerity measures included a 25 per cent cut in public sector wages. Romania's high level of corruption became an issue when the EU called on Romania to take urgent action to tackle crime and corruption, and France and Germany blocked Romania's membership of the Schengen passport-free zone, saying it still needed to make 'irreversible progress' against corruption and organised crime.
2012 In January, nine EU members (Belgium, Germany, Ireland, France, Luxembourg, The Netherlands, Austria, the United Kingdom and Malta, and to a limited extent, Spain) extended their restrictions on work permits for Romanians until 2014. On 30 January former prime minister, Adrian Nastase (2000–04), was sentenced to two years in prison for corruption and siphoning-off state funds of around US$2.1 million to fund his 2004 re-election campaign. On 5 February Emil Boc resigned as prime minister, to 'diffuse social tensions' in the face of protests at extended austerity budgets presented by his government and accusations of corruption and incompetence. The president nominated Mihai-Razvan Ungureanu (independent) as prime minister, which was ratified by parliament on 9 February. However, the opposition PSD boycotted the vote saying it would contest the decision to form a new government in the constitutional court. On 27 April, the government of Mihai Razvan Ungureanu resigned following parliament's vote of no confidence in its administration. The unpopularity of Ungureanu's austerity policies, which had cut salaries and raised taxes, allowed the opposition Alianta PSD+PC to seize the initiative and power. President Basescu appointed Victor Ponta (PSD) as acting prime minister until parliamentary elections, due to be held on 9 December, decides an outcome. On 6 July parliament voted to suspend President

Basescu for 30 days, during which time a referendum would be held to decide whether to remove him from office. Crin Antonescu became acting president. President Basescu survived the impeachment vote on 29 July, due to a low voter turnout (46.13 per cent), although 87.5 per cent of those who voted were in favour of impeachment. Basescu resumed office on 28 August. On 25–26 October, at a meeting of the EU Justice and Home Affairs Council, it was agreed to postpone consideration of Romania's admittance to the Schengen Area treaty until March 2013. Parliamentary elections were held on 9 December, in which the Uniunea Social Liberala (USL) (Social Liberal Union) (coalition of four political parties) led by the ruling Partidul Social Democrat-Partidul Conservator (Alianta PSD+PC) (Social Democratic Party-Conservative Party) won 273 seats out of 412. Prime Minister Ponta remained in office.

2013 In July the EU suspended aid payments after the government had failed to get to grips with corruption. On 13 September a four year old boy was killed by stray dogs. Within days parliament had passed a law ordering stray dogs to be euthanised within 14 days if an owned wasn't found.

2014 The first round of the presidential elections was held on 2 November.

2015 A fire in a night club on 31 October killed at least 60 people. Protestors took to the streets under the slogan *Coruptia Ucide* (Corruption kills) demanding resignations and prosecutions, and for good measure, a cut in the number of lawmakers, new anti-corruption laws, and higher pay for officials to reduce the temptation to accept bribes. Prime Minister Ponta resigned on 4 November. He was succeeded by Sorin Cîmpeanu as acting prime minister until 17 November when Dacian Julien Ciolos assumed office.

Political structure

Constitution

The 1991 Constitution proclaimed a democratic, pluralist system of government in which citizens' freedom and rights are guaranteed, although there are no specific measures protecting minority rights. It also stipulated the separation of the three public authorities – legislative, executive and judicial.

In 2003, the Constitution was changed to bring it in line with EU law, in which private property is guaranteed, the police is demilitarised and the justice system is independent; ethnic minorities may use their mother tongue when dealing with the state and foreigners are permitted to buy land in Romania.

Both parliament and the president are elected by universal vote every four years. The president may not remain a member of any political party, and is limited to a maximum two terms in office. The minimum voting age is 18 years.

Romania is divided into 40 administrative counties, with Bucharest divided into administrative sectors. Each county, town and village has its own local authority headed by an elected, executive mayor and an elected council. Local government is based on the principle of local autonomy and decentralisation of public services, with locally elected mayors, city and county councils. A prefect for each county is appointed by central government as the ultimate authority for that region.

Form of state

Parliamentary democratic republic

The executive

The president nominates the prime minister and the government on the basis of a vote of confidence from parliament and is the commander-in-chief of the armed forces. The president's term of office is four years, renewable once only.

National legislature

The bicameral Parliament consists of the Senate which has 176 seats of which 137 members are directly elected by absolute majority vote and 39 members are directly elected by proportional representation vote. Members serve four year terms. The Chamber of Deputies consists of 412 seats of which 315 members are directly elected by absolute majority vote and 97 members are directly elected by proportional representation vote. Members also serve four year terms. In the Chamber of Deputies, seats are reserved for minority parties that receive at least 10 percent of total valid votes cast.

Legal system

The legal system is based on the Napolenic Code and the 1991 constitution. There is an independent judiciary, although judges are appointed by the president and parliament. The Supreme Court comprises judges appointed by the president for a term of six years. It administers law, but cannot undertake judicial review. This is undertaken by the Constitutional Court, which comprises nine judges appointed by the president and parliament for a period of nine years.

Last elections

9 December 2012 (parliamentary); 2 (first round) and 16 November (runoff) 2014 (presidential).

Results: Parliamentary (chamber of deputies): Uniunea Social Liberala (USL) (Social Liberal Union) (coalition of four political parties) won 58.6 per cent of the vote (273 seats out of 412), Alianta România Dreapta (ARD) (Right Romania Alliance) (coalition of three political parties) 16.5 per cent (56), Partidul Poporului-Dan Diaconescu (PP-DD) 13.9 per cent (47), Uniunea Democrata Maghiara din România (UDMR) (Democratic Union of Hungarians in Romania) 5.2 per cent (18); 18 other political parties each won one seat. Turnout was 41.72 per cent.

Senate: USL won 60.1 per cent (122 seats out of 176), ARD 16.7 per cent (24), PP-DD 14.6 per cent (21), UDMR 5.3 per cent (nine); turnout 41.7 per cent.

Presidential (first round): Victor Ponta (PSD–UNPR–PC Alliance) won 40.44 per cent of the vote, Klaus Johannis (PNL) 30.37 per cent, Calin Popescu-Tariceanu (Independent) 5.36 per cent; Elena Udrea (PMP–PNTCD Alliance) 5.2 per cent; of the 10 other candidates none won more than 5.0 per cent. Turnout was 53.17 per cent.

Runoff: Klaus Iohannis won 54.4 per cent of the vote and Victor Ponta won 45.6 per cent of the vote. Turnout was 64.1 per cent.

Next elections

2018 (presidential); 2016 (parliamentary)

Political parties

Ruling party

Uniunea Social Liberala (USL) (Social Liberal Union) (coalition of four political parties) led by Partidul Social Democrat-Partidul Conservator (Alianta PSD+PC) (Social Democratic Party-Conservative Party) (appointed Apr 2012; elected 9 Dec 2012)

Main opposition party

Partidul Social Democrat-Partidul Conservator (Alianta PSD+PC) (Social Democratic Party-Conservative Party alliance)

Population

19.93 million (2014)

Last census: 20 October 2011: 19,042,936

Population density: 98 inhabitants per square km. Urban population 57 per cent (2010 Unicef).

Annual growth rate: -0.4 per cent, 1990–2010 (Unicef).

Ethnic make-up

Romanian (89 per cent), Hungarian (9 per cent), German (0.4 per cent), Ukrainian, Serb, Croat, Russian Turk and Gypsy (1.6 per cent). The Hungarian minority live principally in the Transylvania region. Around half of the then resident ethnic Germans returned to Germany in 1990 and many of the remainder have followed in recent years. Other small ethnic groups include Jews and a number of Greeks and Armenians.

Religions

Romanian Orthodox (70 per cent), Roman Catholic (6 per cent, of which 3 per cent are Uniate), Protestant (6 per cent), and unaffiliated (18 per cent). Since the revolution of 1989 there has been complete religious freedom. The dominant religion is Romanian Orthodox, with over 18 million believers, headed by a Patriarch based in Bucharest. The Roman Catholic Church has approximately 1.35 million members, and includes adherents of the Armenian, Latin and Romanian (Byzantine) rites. The Hungarian and German minorities are predominantly Protestant, and there are communities of the Old-Rite Christian Church (an Orthodox sect) and the Armenian-Gregorian Church. Despite emigration there is still a small Jewish community.

Education

Romania's transition to a market economy made a comprehensive reform of the education sector necessary. The World Bank has supported three reform projects with loan contributions amounting to US$170 million. The centralised education system, with a standard curriculum and ineffective student evaluation system, has been replaced by a flexible curriculum framework, alternative textbooks and a modern evaluation system. Improvements in teacher training, financing and management are under way.

Primary education begins at age seven and lasts until age 11. Lower secondary education lasts for four years until age 15. Upper secondary courses take another four years to complete. Romania's five types of secondary schools specialise in different areas of education, including general secondary schools, vocational and art schools, those specialising in physical education and teacher training. Minority language schooling is available, mainly in Hungarian and German. Higher education is offered in both public and private institutions.

Public expenditure on education typically amounts to 3.6 per cent of annual gross national income.

Literacy rate: 97 per cent adult rate; 98 per cent youth rate (15–24) (Unesco 2005).

Compulsory years: Seven to 15.

Enrolment rate: 104 per cent gross primary enrolment of relevant age group (including repeaters); 78 per cent gross secondary enrolment (World Bank).

Pupils per teacher: 20 in primary schools.

Health

As primary healthcare units suffer due to financial shortage, there is over-concentration of already scarce resources on hospitals. Outbreaks of infectious diseases, often contracted in hospitals, are common.

HIV/Aids

HIV prevalence: 0.1 per cent aged 15–49 in 2003 (World Bank)

Life expectancy: 72 years, 2004 (WHO 2006)

Fertility rate/Maternal mortality rate: 1.4 births per woman, 2010 (Unicef)

Birth rate/Death rate: 10.8 births per 1,000 population; 12.3 deaths per 1,000 population (2003).

Child (under 5 years) mortality rate (per 1,000): 12 per 1,000 live births (WHO 2012)

Head of population per physician: 1.9 physicians per 1,000 people, 2003 (WHO 2006)

Welfare

The comprehensive state insurance scheme, with premiums paid by enterprises and institutions on behalf of employees, provides free health care and benefits for all Romanian citizens. An unemployment allowance was created in 1991 and there are also funds allocated to sickness benefits, children's allowance and pensions. Employers make social security contributions of 28—38 per cent, unemployment fund contributions of 5 per cent and disabled fund contributions of 1 per cent on gross salaries. Employees pay 3 per cent of gross salaries to the supplementary pension fund and 1 per cent to the unemployment insurance fund.

There is high unemployment in Romania and there has been a 40 per cent fall in real wages since 1989. Survival is partly due to the fact that most Romanians do not pay rent or have a mortgage, since over 90 per cent were able to buy their homes for the equivalent of a few months rent after the revolution. Many also have small plots of farm land for subsistence farming. It is expected that there will be a housing crisis for future generations, with many houses too small to be occupied by more than one family. Mortgages to buy houses are very expensive and are almost impossible to obtain. The government's housing programme aims to complete the tower blocks and apartments that were left unfinished after the revolution, and then allocate funds to social housing.

There is wide variation between urban and rural infrastructure, with less than 10 per cent of country dwellers living in houses with running water and sewerage.

Main cities

Bucharest (capital, estimated population 1.9 million in 2012), Craiova (295,336), Cluj-Napoca (294,882), Galati (294,074), Constanta (293,310), Iasi (279,404), Timisoara (277,415), Brasov (274,404), Ploiesti (233,065).

Languages spoken

The most significant minority language is Hungarian. German and English are spoken in tourist regions. Romanian, although a Romance language developed from Latin, has influences from Slavic languages as well as Hungarian, French and Turkish.

Official language/s

Romanian

Media

Press

The press is highly regionalised and includes publications in minority languages such as Hungarian, German and Serbian. Over 60 per cent of the population read one or more newspapers a day. There are around 10 national dailies, as well as dailies and weeklies published in the main cities. Newspapers tend to be independent, governmental or published by a political party.

Dailies: The most important independent national dailies in Romanian are *Evenimental Zilei* (www.evz.ro) is a mass-market newspaper, *Adevarul* (www.adevarul.ro), *Cronica Romana* (www.cronicaromana.ro), *Curierul National* (www.curierulnational.ro), *Libertatea* (www.libertatea.ro) and *Romania Libera* (www.romanialibera.ro). In English, *Nine O'Clock* (www.nineoclock.ro), *Jurnalul National* (www.jurnalul.ro) and *Evenimentul* (www.evenimentul.ro) have English online editions. In German, *Allgemeine Zeitung für Rumanien* is published five times a week and *Hermannstadter Zeitung* (www.hermannstaedter.ro); in Turkish *Zaman* (www.zaman.ro) and in Hungarian, *Uj Magyar Szo* (www.maszol.ro) *Háromszék* (www.3szek.ro) and *Krónika* (www.kronika.ro).

Regional dailies include *Azi* (www.azi.ro/) *Gardianul* (www.gardianul.ro), *Ieseanul* (www.ieseanul.ro) and *Observator de Constanta* (www.observator.ro).

Weeklies: The Sunday newspapers include *Adevarul*, *Cronica Romana*, *Curierul National*, *Nine O'Clock* (English) and *Azi*.

Business: In Romanian, *Bursa* (www.bursa.ro) reports on the stock exchange, *Capital* (www.capital.ro), *Sàptàmàna Financiarà* (www.sfin.ro) and *Ziarul Financiar* (www.zf.ro) deal with financial news. In English, *Bucharest Business Week* (www.bbw.ro) and *The Diplomat* (www.thediplomat.ro) is publish weekly.

Periodicals: Many special interest and business publications are published, mostly by independent companies.

Broadcasting

Radio: There are several domestic stations with the state-owned Radio Romania (www.srr.ro) providing four nationwide networks, featuring news, music and cultural shows, plus an international channel in English and 11 other languages. Commercial radio stations include Europa FM (www.europafm.ro), Kiss FM

(www.mykiss.ro), Pro FM (www.profm.ro) and Radio 21 (www.radio21.ro).
Television: The state-owned television, Televiziunea Romana (TVR) (www.tvr.ro) operates two channels – Romania 1 and TVR2. Commercial networks include Antena 1 (www.antena1.ro), Prima TV (www.primatv.ro), Acasa TV (www.acasatv.ro) and Realitatea TV (www.realitatea.net) showing domestic and international programmes.
National news agency: Rompres
Other news agencies: Mediafax (www.mediafax.ro)

Economy

The economy is diverse with a wide range of productive sectors. Romania has a substantial industrial base, accounting for over 25 per cent of GDP, primarily in mining of iron ore. Around 20 per cent of industrial production includes a wide range of manufacturing enterprises, such as construction materials, chemicals, food processing, textiles and clothing. The service sector accounts for over 65 per cent of GDP; agriculture accounts for just over 5 per cent of GDP but employs around 30 per cent of the workforce. The country has a broad range of energy resources; including oil, natural gas and coal, as well as electricity produced from hydro- and nuclear-power stations, the output of which can be utilised locally and the excess exported.

The economy grew at an average rate of 6.2 per cent over 2005–08, but was badly affected by the global economic crisis which firstly damaged the construction industry and then real estate, with a knock-on effect to the financial sector. As a result growth fell to a recessionary -6.6 per cent in 2009. The IMF agreed to a bailout loan of US$17.5 billion in 2009, to stabilise the economy, while the European Central Bank (ECB) agreed to provide US$28 billion in multilateral financial assistance, including five direct payments over three-years amounting to US$7 billion. In the short-term this had the effect of slowing the negative growth to -1.6 per cent in 2010, at a time when the strength of the euro-zone weakened, despite a pick-up in world trade. The implementation of a bold package of macro-stabilization and structural measures, supported by a multilateral program with the World Bank, International Monetary Fund (IMF), and the European Commission (EC), helped the country overcome the effects of the global crisis by restoring macroeconomic balances and reviving economic growth. Economic activity picked up in 2013, with growth estimated at 3.5 per cent, whilst growth remained at a stable rate of 1.8 per cent in 2014.

Inflation remains low at around 1 per cent for 2014. This is expected to aid in ensuring robust growth within the Romanian economy. It has decelerated substantially over the past two years, falling by 3 per cent since 2012.

Unemployment in Romania is one of the highest rates in the EU; it has remained relatively steady, with growth from 7 per cent in 2011 and 2012 increased to 7.1 per cent in 2013. Estimates for 2014 show a reduction to 6.4 per cent, due primarily to increased consumption owing to increased domestic disposable income.

An important source of domestic revenue is the amount of remittances sent by migrant workers living abroad. In 2008, a record US$9.38 billion was sent to families in Romania, which fell to US$4.93 billion in 2009 and down to an estimated US$3.95 billion in 2011. Since this, relative increases have seen this figure increase to US$5.46 billion in 2013.

The down side of this departure of large numbers of workers to countries offering higher wages, which had accelerated entry into the EU, is that it left Romania with a labour shortage, which has impeded its own economic expansion. It has also been forecast by the Demographic Research Centre of the National Institute for Economic Research (INCE) of the Romanian Academy that by 2050 the population could decrease by almost 23 per cent (from 21 million in 2008 to 17 million in 2050) if the falling birth and rising death rates continue and citizens are lost through emigration).

On 27 April 2012, the government of Mihai Razvan Ungureanu resigned following parliament's vote of no confidence in its administration. The unpopularity of Ungureanu's austerity policies, which had cut salaries and raised taxes allowed the opposition Alianta PSD+PC to seize the initiative. President Basescu appointed Victor Ponta (PSD) as acting prime minister until parliamentary elections, which were held in November 2014. Klaus Iohannis won the largest share of the vote and replaced Ponta in order to become Romania's head of state.

External trade

As a member of the European Union, Romania operates within a communitywide free trade area, with tariffs set as a whole. Internationally, the EU has free trade agreements with a number of nations and trading blocs worldwide.

Foreign trade represented 85 per cent of GDP and is expected to rise further since entry to the EU. Over 30 per cent of trade is with the EU while Russia supplies the majority of Romania's energy imports.

Imports

Main imports include machinery and equipment, fuels and minerals, chemicals, textile and products, basic metals and agricultural products.
Main sources: Germany (19.1 per cent of total in 2014), Italy (10.8 per cent), Hungary (7.9 per cent).

Exports

Main exports include clothing and footwear, metals and metal products, machinery and equipment, minerals and fuels, chemicals and agricultural products.
Main destinations: Germany (19.3 per cent of total in 2014), Italy (11.9 per cent), France (6.8 per cent).

Agriculture

Farming

The agricultural sector accounts for 5.5 per cent of GDP and employs 27 per cent of the workforce. The total agricultural area is 147,900 square km, of which 94,100 square km is arable. Arable land, pastures and hayfields cover 59.5 per cent of Romania, forests 26.7 per cent and vineyards 2.5 per cent.

Romania is Central Europe's most important agricultural producer, after Poland. Important agricultural produce includes grapes (the leading European producer), corn, wheat, maize, rye, sugar beet, oilseed, potatoes, plums, apples and meat. Although there has been progress in restructuring the sector, it has been slower than international financial institutions would like. Moreover, concerns have also been expressed at the re-introduction of import barriers and subsidies to protect the sector from Hungarian wheat and flour exports.

The restitution and privatisation of land has – in comparison with enterprise privatisation – advanced at a rapid pace, with over 85 per cent of agricultural land in private ownership. Land restitution was highly politicised, with arguments surrounding the amount of land that was returned to claimants. Claims exceeded by a third the amount of land held in state hands, and delays in the process held up investment in the sector. Although land restitution was a major step forward, problems facing the sector include the small size of farms, no functioning land market, very few rural credit and investment schemes, and an extremely limited distribution and marketing infrastructure.

The agricultural sector is subject to the reformed Common Agricultural Policy (CAP), whereby subsidies are no longer paid on farm output, which tended to benefit large farms and encourage overproduction, but rather on single farm payments not conditional on production. Full implementation of CAP was completed in 2013.

Fishing
Romania's fishing sector has declined in the past decade, making little contribution to GDP. National consumption is falling too. Fisheries in the Black Sea have been spoilt by eutrophication and overfishing. Carp, mackerel and sardines are the principal catches. European spratt and anchovy are also plentiful. There are an estimated 10,000 persons working in the fishing industry.
Fish farming, including primary processing, packaging and trade will be improved through major investment projects.

Forestry
Forest and other wooded land accounts for less than one-third of the land area, with forest cover estimated at 6.4 million hectares (ha). Most of the forest area is located in the Carpathian mountainous region in the centre and west of the country. About nine-tenths of the forest is available for wood supply and is largely semi-natural. The growing stock consists of Norway spruce as the principal coniferous species, with beech and oak the main deciduous varieties. Although most of the forest is owned by the state, claims for restitution have increased private ownership.
Forests provide sufficient raw materials for the domestic industry to meet internal demands and also product for exports. Romania has a well developed timber and wood processing industry, concentrated in the northern regions of Moldavia and Transylvania. Substantial investments have been made to modernise older mills so as to improve its existing export base. Over half of the sawnwood production is exported, while more value-added products such as parquet, solid wood panels and furniture are obtained from hardwoods. Most of the paper demand is met by imports.

Industry and manufacturing
The industrial sector accounts for 26.2 per cent of GDP with manufacturing accounting for 21.8 per cent of GDP.
The main industries are textiles and footwear, light machinery and auto assembly. Mining, timber, construction materials, chemicals, food processing and petroleum refining are all also significant sectors.
In June 2012 the US Ford Motor Company's first automated car plant in Craiova produced its first car, a B-Max model, which was purchased by the president. In full production, the plant is capable of producing 250,000 vehicles per year.

Tourism
Romania has historic buildings, six of which are included on Unesco's World Heritage List. However it is Romania's rugged Carpathian Mountains that attract many tourists who enjoy outdoor activities, such as skiing in winter and hiking in summer. The Blue Danube Delta, on the Black Sea, is one of Europe's biggest and best preserved deltas. It attracts amateur anglers who can fish for specific species during certain seasons. Tours to sites associated with Vlad Tepes, the inspiration for the fictional Count Dracula, are popular and include Sighisoara (Transylvania), his birthplace, and others in the south in Walachia.
Travel and tourism contributed 4.8 per cent of GDP in 2014. Employment, including jobs indirectly supported by the industry, was 5.5 per cent of total employment, totalling 467,000 jobs in 2014. Visitor exports generated 2.5 per cent of total exports in the same year.
The tourist sector has had to work hard, to both revitalise a moribund sector and initiate extensive development, to enhance the reputation and image of Romania as a worthwhile destination for tourists. An EU Regional Operational Programme was implemented from 2007–13 to provide funds for regional development, including plans to improve tourism infrastructure.

Mining
Taken together, the mining and hydrocarbons sectors account for around 13 per cent of GDP and employ 8 per cent of the workforce. Output dramatically declined in the 1990s, reflecting prolonged restructuring. Romania's mining industry is well developed, although it suffers from outdated technology and a lack of investment.
Mineral deposits include salt, lignite, iron ore, bauxite, manganese and small quantities of gold, zinc, uranium, tin and copper.
Romania aims to exploit domestic resources instead of relying on imports, even if the initial cost is high. Annual zinc output is around 28,000 tonnes, aluminium output around 150,000 tonnes and copper output around 30,000 tonnes. Minvest, privatised in 1999, accounts for 60 per cent of Romania's copper production.
The government opened the gold mining sector to foreign exploration in 1999. Gabriel Resources, a Canadian company, are behind a US $400 million project to create Europe's largest open-pit gold mine in the Rosia Montana valley. The International Finance Corporation (IFC) has refused financial backing to the proposal, which would displace 2,000 residents and produce high levels of hazardous cyanide.

Hydrocarbons
Proven oil reserves were 600 million barrels in 2014. Consumption was 188,000 barrels per day (bpd) in 2014. Idle oil wells are being re-opened following the liberalisation of state prices and rising world prices.
The industry is independent with government owning shares in oil companies. Petrom is the largest oil and gas group, involved in exploration and production; public ownership is just 20.64 per cent of shares. Rompetrol is the second largest and an important multinational oil company in the EU. Russia's Lukoil is a major player in the downstream sector, owning the third-largest, and modernised, refinery in Romania. Other refinery owners have also sought external links, although the Romanian government is in general wary of Russian interests expanding into the domestic industry. Romania was instrumental in launching the Pan-European Oil Pipeline (PEOP) project, which will transport Caspian oil through Romania, Serbia, Croatia, and Slovenia to the Italian port of Trieste.
Proven natural gas reserves were at 10.4 billion cubic metres (cum) in 2014. Even though Romania is Central and Eastern Europe's largest natural gas producer, production has fallen from 17.4 billion cum in 1997 to 10.4 billion cum in 2014, whilst consumption was 13.8 billion cum; the shortfall was made up solely of Russian gas imported by pipeline through Ukraine. Romania is looking for not just alternative sources of natural gas but a security in its sources. Russian gas supplies have been disrupted in two consecutive winters (2008/09) by disputes between Russia and Ukraine, when supplies were suspended. Bulgaria, Italy and Russia are building a southern European gas pipeline (South Stream) that avoids traversing Ukraine and in 2009 Russia invited Romania to join the project.
Romgaz operates the national gas distribution system and is entirely owned by the state.
Proven coal reserves were 291 million tonnes in 2011, of which the majority is brown coal, typically used in power plants. Production was 6.7 million tonnes of oil equivalent in 2011.
Although the government has backed plans for restructuring and reinvesting in the industry, since 2000 the number of mines and miners has fallen, despite coal being planned to take a larger part of the energy mix until 2020.

Energy
Total installed generating capacity was 20.3 gigawatts (GW) in 2006. Romania has an energy mix that included coal (41.5 per cent), natural gas (16.7 per cent), oil and derivatives (0.7 per cent), hydro (32.0 per cent) and nuclear (9.2 per cent) in 2006. By 2008, nuclear energy was contributing around 20 per cent

of electricity following the opening of the Cernavoda-1 nuclear power plant, which became operational in 2007. The potential for renewable energy is great but by 2009 any contribution to national electricity production was negligible.
In December 2011, three state-owned energy companies and the coal mines of Societatea Nationala a Lignitului, were merged in preparation for public sale in mid-2012. The thermal power stations were Complexul Energetic Craiova, Complexul Energetic Rovinari and Complexul Energetic Turceni; the new merged entity will be called Complexul Energetic Oltenia.

Financial markets
Stock exchange
Bursa de Valori Bucuresti (Bucharest Stock Exchange)
Commodity exchange
Bursa Monetar Financiară si de Mărfuri Sibiu (BMFMS) (Sibiu Monetary Financial and Commodities Exchange)

Banking and insurance
Since the early 1990s, the banking sector has undergone major restructuring and privatisation, although some areas of the banking, insurance, legal and financial sectors require upgrading. About 55 per cent of the banking system is foreign owned. Privatisation of Romania's largest bank, Banca Comerciala Romana (BCR), is scheduled for completion in 2006.
When both BCR and Casa de Economii si Consemnatiuni (CEC) are privatised, the banking sector will be 90 per cent foreign owned and highly competitive.
Central bank
Banca Nationala a Romaniei (BNR) (National Bank of Romania)
Main financial centre
Bucharest

Time
GMT plus two hours (daylight saving, late March to late October, GMT plus three hours)

Geography
Romania is situated in south-eastern Europe in the lower Danube basin bordering the Black Sea to the south-west (250km of coastline). Much of the country forms part of the Balkan Peninsula. Romania is the largest of the Balkan states. Ukraine is to the north, Moldova to the north-east, Hungary to the north-west, Serbia and Montenegro and Macedonia to the south-west and Bulgaria to the south.
Romania is divided into four geographical areas. Moldavia and Transylvania (forest and mountains) make up the northern half, which is divided by the Carpathian Mountains. South of the Carpathians is the Danube plain of Walachia (including Bucharest), with the lower Danube marking the border with Bulgaria. Romania's Black Sea coastline incorporates the Danube delta and the port of Constanta.
Hemisphere
Northern

Climate
Romania has a moderate, continental temperate climate with long hot summers and cold winters. Snow falls throughout the country, although winters are coldest in the Carpathian mountains with snow between December and April, and mildest on the Black Sea coast. Mean temperatures in Bucharest are minus 2 degrees Celsius (C) in January and 23 degrees C in July. The coldest month is January with a mean temperature of minus 7 degrees C, rising to a peak of 30 degrees C in July. Temperatures can differ by 5–10 degrees C from the plains to the mountains. The wettest month is June with approximately 85mm of rain; the driest September with 30mm. The Black Sea water temperatures are 20-28 degrees C in July and August.

Dress codes
The business dress code is usually informal, with ties, sports jackets or blazers acceptable for meetings.
Clothing should be medium-weight, plus a heavy topcoat and overshoes for winter. Lightweight clothing and a light raincoat are advisable for summer.

Entry requirements
Passports
Required by all, valid for six months from date of arrival.
Visa
Required by all, except nationals of EU/EEA countries, USA, Canada, Japan, Israel and some other countries. Transit visas are required by nationals of some countries. For full details of countries affected by all visa requirements, see www.roembus.org. An application form can also be downloaded. Business visitors, when required to apply for visas, should provide an employer's letter certifying purpose of visit, an invitation from a local company, proof of sufficient funds, travel insurance and return/onward passage.
Currency advice/regulations
The import and export of local currency is prohibited. There are no restrictions on the import of foreign currency, subject to declaration over eur10,000 (or foreign equivalent); export of foreign currency is limited to the unused amount, subject to presentation of exchange receipts.
Changing money at private exchange offices is often better than at banks. Kiosks are required to advertise an official rate, but ask if they can offer a better deal.
Romania is largely a cash-only economy. In Bucharest and main centres, major credit cards may be accepted at large hotels, car hire firms and stores; travellers cheques can be changed at banks and hotels. US dollars are the preferred hard currency.
Customs
Personal effects, 200 cigarettes and two litres of alcoholic beverages and small gifts are permitted duty-free. Banned imports include ammunition, explosives, narcotics and pornography.

Health (for visitors)
Hospital emergency rooms provide free first aid, but charge for all other medical services.
Mandatory precautions
There are no special requirements.
Advisable precautions
Typhoid, diphtheria and both hepatitis A and B inoculations are recommended, as well as inoculation against tick-borne encephalitis. It is advisable to boil water or drink bottled water where possible, although water in mountainous regions is supplied from local springs and is safe. Rabies is a health risk.
Basic medical supplies are limited, especially outside major cities, so always travel with sufficient medication.

Hotels
Classified as de luxe, A and B. Accommodation outside Bucharest is generally cheaper. Advisable to purchase pre-paid vouchers for accommodation through travel agents, as a confirmed reservation, if not pre-paid, is not a guarantee of accommodation.

Credit cards
Credit cards are not widely used but are accepted in most major hotels. American Express, Visa and Eurocard are preferred. Credit card transactions are charged at a worse rate than that offered by exchange bureaux

Public holidays (national)
Fixed dates
1–2 Jan (New Year's Day), 1 May (Labour Day), 1 Dec (National Day), 25–26 Dec (Christmas).
Variable dates
Orthodox Easter Sunday, Orthodox Easter Monday

Working hours
Banking
Mon–Fri: 0900–1200 and 1300–1500. Creditbank, Bucharest Otopeni airport, open 1000–1800 daily.
Business
Mon–Fri: 0800–1700, lunch usually 1230–1300. Business hours can be haphazard with many offices closing on Friday afternoons.

Government
Mon–Fri: 0800–1700, lunch usually 1230–1300.
Shops
Mon–Fri: 0900–1800; Sat: 0900–1400.

Telecommunications
Telephone/fax
There are only basic telephone services.
Mobile/cell phones
There is widespread coverage, particularly in the major cities.

Social customs/useful tips
Traditional Central European courtesies with a measure of Latin informality are expected. Punctuality is observed to a degree. Shaking hands is the traditional form of greeting. Accepting hospitality from and giving social invitations to officials is normal, usually taking place in restaurants or hotels.
Smoking is prohibited on public transport and in cinemas and theatres, although many Romanians smoke and Western cigarettes are greatly appreciated.
Tips are expected by porters, chambermaids and taxi drivers.
Anyone photographing demonstrations risks arrest.
It is advisable to avoid the many stray dogs in and around Bucharest.

Security
Crimes against tourists are a growing problem in Romania. Money exchange schemes targetting travellers are becoming increasingly common. Bogus policemen are an increasing hazard for the unwary business traveller. Their technique is to demand to see proof of identification, and then make off with a visitor's wallet. Keep passports separate from other valuables.
Extreme caution must be taken with unofficial change vendors: they are illegal and often fraudulent.

Getting there
Air
National airline: Tarom (Transporturile Aeriene Romane) (Romanian Air Transport)
International airport/s: Henry Coanda International Airport (OTP), 16km north of Bucharest; bank, post office, duty-free shop, car hire
Airport tax: None
Surface
Road: International roads connect Romania with Hungary. The E64 from Budapest goes through Arad, Brasov, Campina and Ploiesti to Bucharest. From Germany, the E60 goes via northern Hungary before going through Oradea. The route from Bucharest to Ukraine goes north through Bacau and to Chernovtsy in southern Ukraine. From Moldova, take the road from the border to the town of Husi. The better road links are via Germany, Austria and Hungary.
Rail: There are good rail connections with all neighbouring countries.
Water: Ships provide regular passenger services and cruises on the Danube, starting at Passau in Germany, through Austria, Slovakia, Hungary, Serbia, to Giurgiu (48km from Bucharest), and finally Constanta on the Black Sea.
Main port/s: Black Sea ports: Constanta, Mangalia and Sulina.
Danube ports: Orsova, Drobeta-Turnu Severin, Turnu Magurele, Giurgiu, Oltenita, Calaras, Cernavoda. Braila, Galati and Tulcea are both river and sea ports. The Danube is used heavily for freight transport since the opening of the canal link with the Black Sea.

Getting about
National transport
Air: Tarom and Carpatair operate regular internal services to main centres in Romania.
Road: Romania has around 78,000km of roads, of which 14,500km are national roads; 4,680km of the national roads are included within the European Road Network ('E' roads).
In July 2012, 50km of new roads were opened, extending two highways. One segment of the A2 (Autostrada Soarelui (Sun Motorway)), links Bucharest with Constanta, a port on the Black Sea. The other new road is part of the A3 connecting Bucharest with the city of Ploiesti (on the route into the Carpathian Mountains).
Buses: There are regular inter-city connections and local services to most towns and villages.
Rail: There is an extensive rail network. Efficient and cheap services operate between all main cities and towns. In addition to slower local services, there are express and inter-city services with dining and sleeping cars. Bucharest's principal station is the *Gara de Nord*.
Water: The principal navigable waterway is the Danube, on which cruises are available.
City transport
Taxis: Taxis are readily available in main centres and are inexpensive. Authorised taxis are identified by a 'Taxi' sign on the roof. Metered taxis should be used, although drivers may need to be reminded to switch them on. While a taxi may be hailed in the street, it is advisable to arrange a taxi by telephone, preferably from a company. A 10 per cent tip is normal. Informal operators at the main hotels and the airport overcharge and should be avoided.
Buses, trams & metro: It is easy to get around by bus, both within towns and cities and cross-country, but they are often slow, over-crowded and uncomfortable. Trams and trollies also run in many centres. Tickets are purchased from booths and in some hotels; they should be punched immediately upon entering the vehicle. There is a metro system in Bucharest.
Car hire
Self-drive and chauffeur-driven cars are available from international and local companies in the main cities and airports. International or national driving licences are required. Traffic drives on the right, although Romanian driving can be very unpredictable. Speed limits are 120km per hour on highways, 90km per hour on other roads and 50km per hour in built-up areas.

BUSINESS DIRECTORY

The addresses listed below are a selection only. While World of Information makes every endeavour to check these addresses, we cannot guarantee that changes have not been made, especially to telephone numbers and area codes. We would welcome any corrections.

Telephone area codes
The international dialling code (IDD) for Romania is +40, followed by area code and subscriber's number:

Braila	239	Gaesti	245
Brasov	268	Oradea	259
Bucharest	21	Ploiesti	244
Cluj-Napoca	264	Sibiu	269
Constanta	241	Timisoara	256

Useful telephone numbers
Fire brigade: 981
Police: 955
Ambulance: 961
Special ambulance service (pregnant women or women with small children): 969
Emergency hospital: 679-4310
Special information: 951
Time: 958
Railway information: 952
Weather report: 959
Enquiries: 930, 931, 932

Chambers of Commerce
American Chamber of Commerce in Romania, Union International Centre, 11 Ion Cimpineanu Street, Sector 1, 78664 Bucharest (tel: 315-8694; fax: 312-4851; e-mail: amcham@amcham.ro).

Brasov Chamber of Commerce and Industry, 18-20 M Kogalniceanu Street, 2200 Brasov (tel: 412-357; fax: 477-333; e-mail: ccibv@ccibv.ro).

Constanta Chamber of Commerce, Industry, Shipping and Agriculture, 84 Mircea cel Batran Street, bl MF1, Constanta tel: 619-854; fax: 619-454; e-mail: office@ccina.ro)

Prahova Chamber of Commerce and Industry, 8 Cuza Voda Street, Ploiesti (tel: 513-122; fax: 516-666; e-mail: office@cciph.ro).

Romania and Bucharest Chamber of Commerce and Industry, 2 Octavian Goga Boulevard, Sector 3, Bucharest (tel: 322-9535; fax: 322-9542; e-mail: ccir@ccir.ro).

Sibiu Chamber of Commerce, Industry and Agriculture, 1 Telefoanelor Street, 2400 Sibliu (tel: 210-503; fax: 211-831; e-mail: cciasb@cciasb.ro).

Timisoara Chamber of Commerce, Industry and Agriculture, 3 Piata Victoriei, 300030 Timisoara (tel: 490-766; fax: 490-311; e-mail: cciat@cciat.ro).

Banking

Banca Agricola, B-dul Voda, Sector 3, Bucharest (tel/fax: 323-6027).

Banco Comerciala Romana, B-dul Regina Elisabeta 5, Sector 3, Bucharest (tel: 312-6185; fax: 312-0056).

Bankco-op, 13 Ion Ghica St, Bucharest (614-3900; fax: 312-0037).

Romanian Bank for Development, 4 Doamnei St, Bucharest (tel: 613-3200, 615-9600; fax: 615-7603).

Romanian Commercial Bank, 14 Republicii Ave, Bucharest (tel: 614-5680, 615-7560; fax: 614-3213).

Central bank

National Bank of Romania, 25 Lipscani Street, Bucharest (tel: 313-0410; fax: 312-3831; e-mail: bnr@bnro.ro).

Stock exchange

Bursa de Valori Bucuresti (Bucharest Stock Exchange), www.bvb.ro

Sibex (Bursa Monetar Financiara Si De Marfuri Sibiu), www.sibex.ro

Commodity exchange

Bursa Monetar Financiară si de Mărfuri Sibiu (BMFMS) (Sibiu Monetary Financial and Commodities Exchange), www.bmfms.ro

Travel information

Association of Ecotourism in Romania, Gabroveni Street 2, Sector 3, Bucharest (tel: 319-742; fax: 828-721; e-mail: roving@deltanet.ro).

Henri Coanda International Airport, 224E Bucharest Road, Otopeni (tel: 204-1200; fax:201-4990; e-mail: otp@otp-airport.ro).

Romanian Automobile Club (Automobil Clubul Roman), 27 Tache Ionescu Street, 010353 Bucharest (tel: 317-8253; fax: 317-3964; e-mail: acr@acr.ro).

Tarom (Airline), Victoria Sq., 59 Buzesti Street, Bucharest (tel: 204-6464; fax: 204-6427; e-mail: agvictoria@tarom.ro).

Ministry of tourism

Ministry of Transport, Construction and Tourism, Bulevardul Dinicu Golescu 38, 010873 Bucharest 1 (tel: 319-6112; fax: 319-6204; e-mail: relpub@mt.ro).

National tourist organisation offices

Autoritatea Nationala Pentru Turism, Bulevardul Dinicu Golescu 38, 010873 Bucharest 1 (tel: 314-9957 fax: 314-9964; ie-mail: promovare@mturism.ro).

Ministries

Ministry of Agriculture, Blvd Carol I 24, 70312 Bucharest (tel: 614-4020; fax: 312-4410).

Ministry of Communications and Information Technology, 14 Libertatii Blvd, 76106 Bucharest 5 (tel: 400-1100, 312-0017; fax: 400-1329; internet site: http://www.mcti.ro).

Ministry of Culture, Piata Presei 1, Bucharest 71341 (tel: 223-1516; fax: 223-4951).

Ministry of Defence, Str Izvor 1-3, 70642 Bucharest (tel: 410-4040; fax: 312-0863).

Ministry of Foreign Affairs, Aleea Modrogan 14, 71274 Bucharest (tel: 212-2160; fax: 230-7489).

Ministry of Health, Str Ministerului 1-3, 70109 Bucharest (tel: 222-3850; fax: 312-4916).

Ministry of the Interior, Str Mihai Voda 3-5, 070622 Bucharest (tel: 311-2021; fax: 614-0909).

Ministry of Justice, Bd Mihail Kogalniceanu 33, 70602 Bucharest (tel: 614-4400; fax: 323-6179).

Ministry of Labour and Social Protection, Str Dem I Dobrescu 2, 70119 Bucharest (tel: 222-3850; fax: 312-2768).

Ministry of National Education, Str Gen Berthelot 28-30, 70749 Bucharest (tel: 614-4588; fax: 312-4719).

Ministry of Privatisation, Str Ministerului 2-4, 70109 Bucharest (tel: 222-3850; fax: 312-0809).

Ministry of Public Finance, Str Apolodor 17, 70663 Bucharest (tel: 410-3400; fax: 312-2077).

Ministry of Public Works and Land Use Planning, Str Apollodor 15-17, Sector 6, 70663 Bucharest (tel: 410-1933; fax: 411-1138).

Ministry of Youth and Sports, Str Vasile Conta 16, 70139 Bucharest (tel: 211-5550; fax: 211-1710).

Office of the Prime Minister, Piata Victoriei 1, 71201 Bucharest (tel: 212-1660; fax: 222-5814).

Presidency of Republic, Building Geniului 1 Cotroceni Palace, Bucharest 76238 (tel: 410-0581; fax: 312-1247).

Other useful addresses

Administration of Sulina Free Trade Zone, Dr Marcovici Str 2, Ground Floor, Bucharest (tel: 613-8733).

Agency for Restructuring, 152 Calea Victoriei, Sector 1, Bucharest (tel: 212-2424; fax: 212-1176).

Asigurara Romaneasca SA (Asirom), Str Smirdan 5, 70406 Bucharest (tel: 312-5020; fax: 312-4819).

British Embassy, Str Jules Michelot 24, 70154 Bucharest (tel: 312-0303; fax: 312-9741).

Centrul Roman pentru Dezvoltarea Intreprinderilor Mici si Mijlocii (Crimm)-PMU, 20 Ion Campineanu Str, Sector 1, 70709 Bucharest (tel: 311-1995/6/7; fax: 312-6966).

Chamber of Deputies, 1 Parlamentului Str, Bucharest (tel: 335-0111; fax: 312-0827).

Constanta South Free Zone Administration, Ferry Boat Terminal Building Agigea, code 8711, Jud Constanta (tel: 741-378, 618-718, 619-100 (ext 2118, 2162); fax: 639-000, 619-729, 693-913).

Council for Reform, Piata Victoriei 1, 71201 Bucharest (tel: 222-3687; fax: 222-4686).

Council for Economic Co-ordination, Strategy and Reform, Piaja Victorei 1, 71201 Bucharest (tel: 222-3687, 312-4767; fax: 222-4686).

Department for European Integration (tel: 312-6928; fax: 312-6929).

Department of Public Information (tel: 222-3619; fax: 222-6088).

Department for Selective Restructuring of the State Ownership Fund, 6-10, Callea Grivitei, Sector 1, Bucharest (tel: 650-4822; 659-7693).

Economic Reform and Strategy and Co-ordination Council, 1 Victoriei Sq, Bucharest (tel: 617-7977; fax: 312-4686).

Fiman Fund PMU, 6-8 Povernei Str, Bucharest (tel: 212-2912; fax: 211-1937).

Insurance and Reinsurance Company SA (Aatra), Str Smirdan 5, 79118 Bucharest (tel: 150-986; fax: 139-306).

Land Reclamation Agriculture Department, Sos Oltenitei 35-37, 75501 Bucharest (tel: 634-5020; fax: 312-3712).

Lignite Public Authority, Str Tudor Vladimirescu 2, 1400 Târgu-Jiu (tel: 321-2513; fax: 321-664).

National Administration of Roads, Blvd Dinicu Golescu 38, 77113 Bucharest (tel: 312-8496).

National Agency for Privatisation, Str Ministerului 2-4, 4th Floor, Bucharest sector 1 (tel: 615-8558, 614-9495, 312-3030, 614-7854; fax: 312-0809/3030, 613-6136).

National Committee for Statistics, 16 Libertatii Str, Sector 5, Bucharest (tel: 312-4875; fax: 312-4873).

National Council for Environmental Protection, Piata Victorei 1, Bucharest (tel: 143-400).

Navrom (Romanian Shipping Company), 8700 Constanta (tel: 615-821; fax: 618-413).

Nord-Est Press (Independent news agency), Str Smirdan 5, 6600 Iasi (tel/fax: 144-776).

Petrotel SA, Str Mihai Bravu 235, Jud Prahova, 2000 Ploiesti (tel: 146-671; fax: 142-408).

Project Implementation Unit within the Authority for Privatisation and Management of the State Ownership, Bucharest (tel: 303-6417; fax: 303-6416).

Radiodifuziuna Romana, Str Gral Berthelot 61-62, PO Box 63-1200, Bucharest (tel: 633-4710; fax: 312-3640).

Radioteleviziuna Romana (Romanian Radio and Television), Calea Dorobantilor 191, PO Box 63-1200, Bucharest (tel: 334-710; fax: 337-544).

Radio Nord-Est, Str Smirdan 5, 6600 Iasi (tel: 145-530; fax: 146-363).

Rafo SA, Str Cauciucului 2, Jud Bacau, Onesti (tel: 324-786; fax: 323-267).

Research Institute for Foreign Trade, Str Apollodor 17, 5 Bucharest (tel: 312-3652, 631-1293; fax: 312-5652).

Romanian Agency for Energy Conservation, Splaiul Independentei 202A, 77208 Bucharest (tel: 650-6470; fax: 312-3197).

Romanian Commodity Exchange, 71341 Bucharest 1, Presei Libere Sq, Bucharest (tel: 01-617-2231; fax: 01-312-2167).

Romanian Development Agency (RDA), Boulevard Magheru 7, Bucharest 1 (tel: 615-6686, 312-3311; fax: 613-2415).

Romanian Embassy (USA), 1607 23rd Street, Washington DC 20008 (tel: (+1-202)-332-4846; fax: (+1-202)-232-4748; e-mail: info@roembus.org).

Romanian Government, 1 Victoriei Sq, Bucharest (tel: 222-3677; fax: 222-6088).

Romanian National Commission for Unesco, Str Anton Cehov 8, 71292 Bucharest (tel: 633-3223; fax: 312-763).

Romanian Parliament, Calea 13, Septembrie 1, 76117 Bucharest (tel: 335-0111).

Romanian Post Office, 14 Libertatii Avenue, 70106 Bucharest 5 (tel: 400-1102; fax: 400-1515).

Romanian State Railways (SNCFR), Blvd 38 Dinicu Golescu, Sector 1-Cod 78123 Bucharest (tel: 617-0148).

Romexpo SA (Trade fairs and exhibitions). Bd Marasti 65-67, 71331 Bucharest (tel: 618-1160; fax: 618 3725).

Rompres (Romanian News Agency), Piata Presei Libere I, 71341 Bucharest (tel: 618-2878; fax: 617-0487).

Secretariat for the Privatisation and Restructuring Programmes within the Council for Co-ordination, Strategy and Economic Reform, 1 Piata Victoriei, Sector 1, Bucharest (tel: 312-8445, 222-8335; fax: 312-6932).

Senate of Romania, 1 Revolutiei Sq, Bucharest (tel: 615-0200, 617-0160; fax: 312-1752).

Societatea Nationala a Cailor Ferate, State Ownership Fund, CA Rosetti Str 21, Bucharest (tel: 611-4943).

State Ownership Fund, RDA Business Centre, World Trade Plaza, 2 Expozitiei Avenue, Ground Floor, Bucharest (tel: 230-0760).

Supreme Court of Justice, 4 Rahovei Str, Bucharest (312-0920; fax: 613-0882).

Prosecutor General's under the Supreme Court of Justice, 2-4 Unirii Ave, Bucharest (tel: 631-1750, 781-3065; fax: 781-6210).

Televiziuna Romana – Telecentrul Bucuresti, Calea Dorobantilor 191, PO Box 63-1200, Bucharest (tel: 633-4710; fax: 633-7544).

USA Embassy, Str Tudor Arghezi 7-9, Bucharest (tel: 312-4042; fax: 312-0395).

National news agency: Rompres

Address: Piata Presei Libere 1, Sector 1, Bucharest 013701 (tel: 207-6110; fax: 317-0707; email: rompers@rompres.ro; internet: www.rompres.ro).

Mediafax (www.mediafax.ro)

Internet sites

Association of Ecotourism in Romania: www.eco-romania.ro

Yellow Pages: www.romanianyellowpages.com/~mozaic

Romanian Home Page: www.ici.ro/romania

Romanian National Tourist Office: www.romaniantourism.com

Russia

KEY FACTS

Official name: Rossiiskaya Federatsiya (Russian Federation)

Head of State: President Vladimir Putin (from 7 May 2012)

Head of government: Prime Minister Dmitry Medvedev (from 7 May 2012)

Ruling party: Yedinaya Rossiya (YR) (United Russia) (from 2003; re-elected 4 Dec 2011)

Area: 17,075,000 square km

Population: 143.70 million (2014)*

Capital: Moscow

Official language: Russian

Currency: Rouble (R) = 100 kopeks

Exchange rate: R68.26 per US$ (Sep 2015)

GDP per capita: US$12,926 (2014)*

GDP real growth: 0.62% (2014)*

GDP: US$1,857.46 billion (2014)*

Labour force: 75.60 million (2014)*

Unemployment: 7.82% (2014)* (with additional underemployment)

Inflation: 7.82% (2014)

Oil production: 10.84 million bpd (2014)

Natural gas production: 578.70 billion cum (2014)

Balance of trade: US$189.74 billion (2014)

Annual FDI: US$52.88 billion (2011)

* estimated figure

Understanding Russia in the twenty-first century has essentially meant understanding one man. By mid-2015 Vladimir Putin's Russia appeared to be in a state of frozen, and impoverished, anarchy. There was no certainty how the Ukrainian adventure would end, international sanctions – despite Mr Putin's bold dismissals, continued to bite steadily harder. Russia, and Putin, had traditionally taken the view that 'might was right'. The prevalent perception in Moscow was that an already weak North Atlantic Treaty Organisation (NATO)had yet again fallen asleep at the wheel. The first instance of this was over Russia's Georgia incursion in 2008, now seen to be a dress rehearsal for the Crimea and Ukrainian adventures.

It's all about Putin

An analysis of Mr Putin's character broadcast by the British Broadcasting Corporation (BBC) in early 2015 provided an interesting insight into Russian political thinking. The BBC noted that the former German Democratic Republic (DDR) – 'East' Germany – was where Vladimir Putin, a native of St Petersburg (then Leningrad), was trained by the Russian security force, the former KGB. Mr Putin arrived in Dresden in the mid-1980s to take up a not particularly important post, not even in the DDR's capital, Berlin. Putin, it seems, was no James Bond , 'more involved with table seating plans and low level espionage.' However, according to the records of the Stasi, the DDR's secret police, Mr Putin did have direct contact with senior Stasi officials in his role as liaison officer. In provincial East Germany Mr Putin had a good social life – a relatively smart apartment and a fondness for Western gadgets and creature comforts. The BBC suggested that Putin came to perceive the DDR as an ideal society – relatively good living standards – modest consumerism alongside tight political control. Something to be emulated later?

However, 1989 saw the DDR transform from (the Russian view) being a socialist paradise to being the equivalent of hell. Putin and other KGB officials must have found it hard to comprehend. Hours were spent in KGB buildings burning compromising documents. Despite DDR requests for USSR intervention, as the situation went out of control the Gorbachev regime in Moscow did not respond. Many DDR officials (as well as their Russian –confreres) went into a state of shock – this was the collapse of their world. For Mr Putin the message was that this could happen elsewhere – low level street protests gaining strength and popularity until the political system simply failed.

Meanwhile, Mr Putin had missed out on the transformation that was taking place in the USSR. He no longer recognised his own country and he did not like what he saw. However, Putin and his KGB colleagues were well placed to exploit that transformation commercially and financially.

Eminences grises

Photos from his DDR days show Putin alongside some of his future cronies, of which one, Nikolai Tokarev, had by 2010 become a wealthy Russian businessman, president of the pipeline (monopoly) company Transneft. He was reportedly a KGB officer in East Germany when he first met KGB officer Putin. He later held a post with the Presidential Property Management Department in 1996 and 1999 – deputy director: Vladimir Putin. If connections like these were important, so – probably more so – were connections to Russia's west, where lay the markets for one of its few export commodities, gas.

The German connection was prominent in a number of President Putin's post KGB relationships. The most visible of these has been his apparent friendship with former chancellor Gerhard Schröder. But the Russian president also maintained close connections with other Germans. Reportedly, the *primus inter pares* German businessman who has the trust of the Russian president is one Matthias Warnig. Mr Warnig has meetings with the Russian president more often than former chancellor Schröder. As often as 'every three weeks', according to one Moscow report.

The two mens' paths first crossed in the 1990s; as Mr Putin rose to the centre of

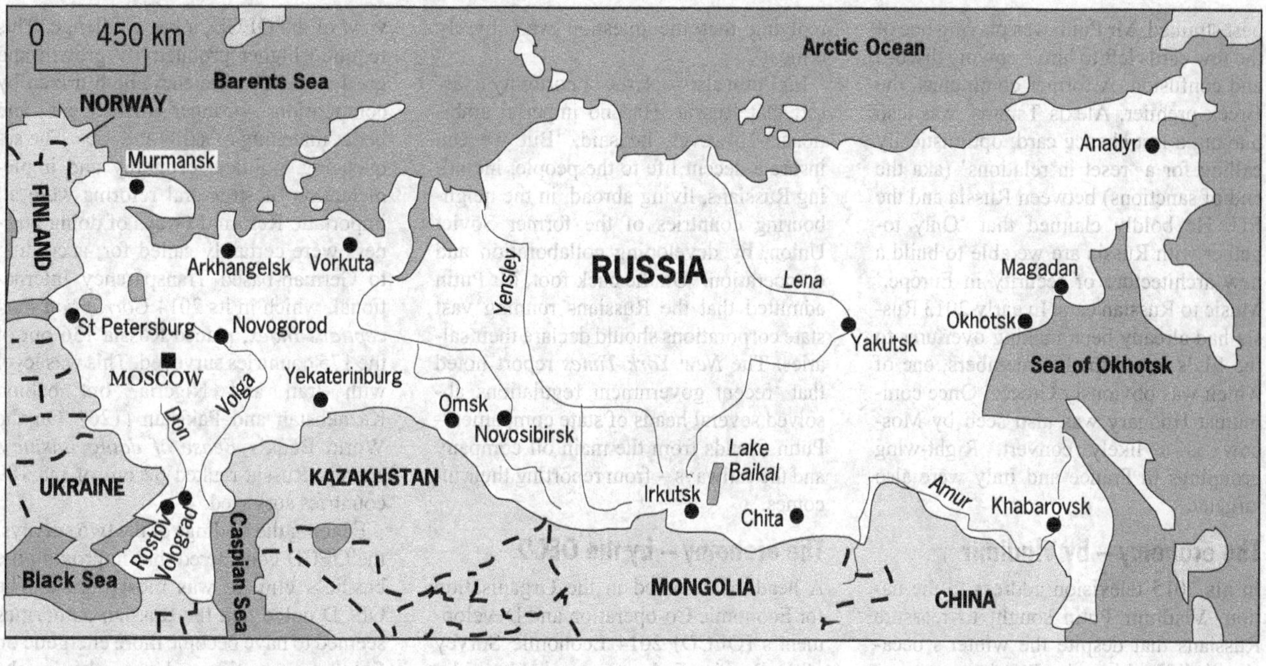

power, so 'coincidentally' did Mr Warnig. A report in the London *Guardian* tracked Mr Warnig's rise. His first break was when, as a member of the DDR's Stasi based in West Germany he was introduced to Wolfgang Röller, the chairman of the board of the Dresdner Bank. Mr Röller knew that his bank would need qualified personnel for the bank's expansion in Eastern Europe when the moment came. So it was that Mr Warnig left the Stasi and in May 1990 began his job with the Dresdner Bank, handling East German privatisations. A further fortunate coincidence was that his immediate boss was Bernhard Walter, the Dresdner board member responsible for the former DDR and the Warsaw pact countries. Mr Walter became Mr Röller's successor and sent his protégé to London for an apprenticeship in banking.

Mr Warnig was then sent to Russia, to oversee the Dresdner Bank's establishment there. According to the *Guardian* report, his boss, Mr Walter, unwittingly gave him the *carte blanche* to make new contacts. So Mr Warnig became the director of the first Dresdner bank office in Russia, in St Petersburg. Opening the bank required official approval, from a Vladimir Putin, then a middle ranking civil servant in charge of foreign trade. The *Guardian* reported that after an unpromising start, the two men became friendly.

Mr Putin regularly invited Mr Warnig to his *dacha*. Their career paths and their personal circumstances had been remarkably similar. After a car-crash, Mr Warnig arranged for Lyudmila Putin (from whom Mr Putin divorced in 2013) to be flown to Germany for surgery. The expenses were paid for by the Dresdner Bank. Mr Putin was indebted to Warnig and to the Dresdner Bank.

Fast forward to 2013 and jowever close the Russo-German business link, its beneficiaries had failed to take into account the importance and strength of one person: Angela Merkel was no pushover. The German business community had lobbied hard against sanctions, but unsuccessfully. The personal ties between Germany and Russia may be strong, but the political ties between Germany and the European Union (EU) and even between Berlin and Washington, had proved to be stronger.

Might is right

Russia has always viewed might as right. The Georgia 2008 incursion had been something of a dress rehearsal for that of the Crimea and eastern Ukraine. But since then, military expenditure had been vastly increased and the army re-equipped with improved weaponry and logistical equipment. In the early months of 2015, it seemed that the violence in eastern Ukraine was still not contained, spreading randomly rather than dying down. To the bewilderment of neutral observers, the elephant in the room was the simple realisation that the so-called 'Minsk-II' agreement on Ukraine, risked collapsing completely. Armchair pundits advocated increasing the supply of 'defensive' arms to Ukraine's inefficient army. But reflecting the Obama administration's hesitant foreign policy, the US made no statements. President Obama was no interventionist, understandably perhaps – he had seen many military assessments prove to be both simplistic and optimistic. The US strategy appeared to be one of exhorting NATO members to pick up the cudgels. The logic may have been well-founded, but asking Estonia's 6,000 strong military to take a proactive anti-Russian stance was at best naïve.

In the US, senior military officials had indeed begun to favour providing Kiev with more, improved, arms and equipment. This had caused President Obama to announce that he was considering 'all options' should diplomatic negotiations fail. The conundrum for President Obama and his advisors was the extent to which the mere threat of arms supply to Ukraine would be enough to cause a Russian re-think. Unlike Russia, the US could still deploy a plethora of non-military measures, closing down the Russian banking system and denying its industry raw materials. The Russian people might rise to the occasion of a military threat, but to see their savings locked up and their credit cards unusable might have a greater effect. At the end of the day, the Kremlin had to accept that confronting the US was a different kettle of fish than leaning on Latvia or Estonia.

Greece greased

Meanwhile, an impoverished Russia had invited the prime minister of bankrupt Greece to discussions. By doing so when Greece's relations with the EU were at best strained, Mr Putin was playing one of the few cards left to him – sowing discord and confusion. A former communist, the Greek premier, Alexis Tsipras, was also playing a last chance card, optimistically calling for a 'reset in relations' (aka the end of sanctions) between Russia and the EU. He boldly claimed that 'Only together with Russia are we able to build a new architecture of security in Europe.' Music to Russian ears. In early 2013 Russia had already been making overtures to the EU's less orthodox members, one of which was obviously Greece. Once communist Hungary was also seen by Moscow as a likely convert. Right-wing groupings in France and Italy were also targeted.

The economy – by Vladimir

In his 2015 television address to the nation, Vladimir Putin sought to reassure Russians that despite the winter's occasional difficulties, the Russian economy was performing well. Mr Putin claimed that the rouble had stabilised, even if inflation was over 11 per cent. 'Experts see we have passed the peak of the problems, nothing burst and everything works.' Reportedly, over half the three million questions submitted were about the economy. Some of the questions came from the television studio – one went so far as to suggest that Mr Putin's principle policy was one of waiting for the oil price to increase. The *New York Times* quoted Mr Putin as replying that the question was 'overly critical'.

Mr Putin also took the opportunity to assert that Russia 'Had no imperial ambitions.' However, he said, 'But we can insure a decent life to the people, including Russians, living abroad, in the neighbouring countries of the former Soviet Union, by developing collaboration and co-operation.' On the back foot, Mr Putin admitted that the Russians running vast state corporations should declare their salaries. The *New York Times* report noted that 'recent government regulations absolved several heads of state companies – Putin friends from the main oil company and the railways – from reporting their incomes.'

The economy – by the OECD

A headline featured in the Organisation for Economic Co-operation and Development's (OECD) 2014 Economic Survey of the Russian Federation probably said it all: 'The economy is too dependent on natural resources.' The survey went on to note that structural reforms to improve the business climate were key to raising potential growth and economic resilience. As energy prices stagnated and labour and capital became fully utilised, Russia's gross domestic product (GDP) growth was falling behind pre-crisis rates. Making the economy stronger, more balanced and less dependent on volatile rents from natural resource extraction was, in the view of the OECD, a key challenge. This required higher productivity growth and greater energy efficiency, both driven by competition, stronger investment and better matching of skills and jobs. The sequencing, political economy and implementation of structural reforms were all important. Reform to ways of doing business were certainly called for, according to German-based Transparency International, which in its 2014 *Corruption Perceptions Index*, placed Russia 136 out of the 175 countries surveyed. This was level with Iran and Nigeria, but behind Kazakhstan and Pakistan (126). On the World Bank's *Eease of doing Business* survey, Russia ranked 62 out of the 189 countries surveyed.

Echoing the findings of the two surveys, the OECD considered that improving the business climate was most urgent. The OECD noted that the Russian authorities seemed to have become more energetic on fighting corruption and strengthening the legal protection of businesses. However, capital outflows and the low market valuation of Russian companies suggested that the business community was not fully convinced. Law enforcement appeared to be uneven, whistle-blower protection was weak and civil society organisations and non-aligned media faced constraints. Red tape had been reduced and new federal initiatives tackled many administrative barriers. However, there had been less progress on the regional level. The governance standards of state-owned enterprises had improved somewhat, but privatisation plans had been downsized. Notwithstanding Russia's World Trade Organisation (WTO) accession in 2012, market opening was meeting resistance. Transport system bottlenecks also posed barriers to more geographically balanced growth.

The economy – by the IMF

In its May 2015 assessment of the Russian economy, the International Monetary Fund (IMF) adopted a largely negative view, stating that the Russian economy was in recession due to lower oil prices and sanctions. In addition, according to the IMF, long-term growth remained low due to structural bottlenecks. The authorities' macro-economic policies had helped stabilise the situation, but there remained significant uncertainties regarding oil prices and geopolitical risks. Given these risks, Russia's macro-economic policy needed to be prudent. Thus, Russia's monetary policy normalisation needed to continue at a pace commensurate with the

KEY INDICATORS — Russia

	Unit	2011	2012	2013	2014	**2015
Population	m	142.41	143.00	143.70	*143.70	*143.70
Gross domestic product (GDP)	US$bn	1,850.40	2,004.25	2,079.13	*1,857.46	*1,176.00
GDP per capita	US$	12,993	14,016	14,469	*12,926	*8,184
GDP real growth	%	4.3	3.4	1.3	*0.6	*-3.8
Inflation	%	8.4	5.1	6.8	7.8	*17.9
Unemployment	%	7.1	5.5	5.5	*7.8	*6.5
Oil output –	'000 bpd	10,280.0	10,643.0	10,788,000.0	10,838.0	
Natural gas output	bn cum	607.0	592.3	604.8	578.7	–
Coal output	mtoe	157.3	168.1	165.1	170.9	–
Exports (fob) (goods)	US$m	512,872.0	528,005.0	523,275.0	497,763.0	–
Imports (fob) (goods)	US$m	315,758.0	335,709.0	341,337.0	308,026.0	–
Balance of trade	US$m	197,115.0	192,296.0	181,939.0	189,737.0	–
Current account	US$m	98,834.0	72,015.0	34,141.0	57,412.0	*63,258.0
Total reserves minus gold	US$m	490,248.5	486,576.8	469,602.7	339,370.0	–
Foreign exchange	US$m	477,855.0	473,110.4	456,446.9	–	–
Exchange rate	per US$	28.52	31.08	33.11	58.57	–

decline in underlying inflation and inflation expectations. Fiscal policy rightly allowed for a limited stimulus in 2015, but a medium-term consolidation programme was necessary to adjust to permanently lower oil prices. The banking system recapitalisation programme should be better tailored and targeted to ensure that public funds were used efficiently. Finally, re-invigorating the structural reform agenda and avoiding 'de-integration' from the world economy remained crucial to lift potential growth.

The IMF expected a recession in 2015 followed by a mild recovery in 2016. Gross domestic product (GDP) was expected to decline by 3.4 per cent in 2015 driven by a contraction in domestic demand weighed down by falling real wages, higher cost of capital and weakened confidence. The rouble depreciation compared to 2014 was expected to boost net exports, with the current account surplus increasing to around 4 per cent of GDP, although it would not be enough to avert a contraction in output. The external position would remain challenging due to deleveraging in the face of limited market access. Inflation was expected to fall to 12.5 per cent by the end of the year. Due to the authorities' policy response and the expected higher oil prices, the IMF expected growth to resume in 2016 while inflation was expected to decline further to single digits. However, the recovery was unlikely to be strong as the limiting factors behind decelerating potential growth would take time to be addressed, leading to medium-term growth of 1.5 per cent per year.

Persistently low oil prices or an increase in geopolitical tensions could further weaken the economic outlook and increase balance of payment pressures. However, in the near-term, sizeable buffers, including high international reserves, low public debt and a positive net international investment position should help safeguard external sustainability.

The Russian authorities response to balance of payment pressures in the fourth quarter of 2014, which included the adoption of a fully flexible exchange rate, a tightening of monetary policy, the announcement of a bank recapitalisation programme and the introduction of foreign exchange (FX) facilities, were broadly appropriate to stabilise confidence. In view of the continuing external uncertainties, policies should in the view of the IMF, continue to be prudent and aim at a careful use of the existing buffers to maintain macro-economic stability.

The measures recommended by the IMF included monetary policy normalisation at a pace commensurate with the decline in underlying inflation and inflation expectations. The acceleration in inflation up to March 2015 reflected the one-off impact of rouble depreciation and counter-sanctions. The economic slowdown, recent rouble appreciation and the partial wage indexation in the 2015 budget would support deflation. However, the pace of easing needed to be balanced against uncertainties over the external outlook, the potential for second-round effects and the Central Bank of the Russian Federation (Bank of Russia)'s need to build credibility under the recently introduced inflation targeting regime.

The IMF thought that the central bank could consider limiting further the FX allocations to ensure that the facilities remained sufficient for emergency purposes. The announced programme of FX purchases to build precautionary buffers was welcome. The general government non-oil deficit was expected to deteriorate to about 13 per cent of GDP in 2015. This was justifiable given cyclical considerations and the available fiscal space. However, the use of off-budget measures – investment by the National Wealth Fund and issuance of guarantees – should be co-ordinated to avoid an overly stimulative fiscal stance.

Although Russia's projected non-oil deficits were expected to improve over time, they would remain relatively large, considerably depleting the Reserve Fund. Moreover, fiscal consolidation efforts could be undermined by the implementation of the current fiscal rule and the full indexation of pension benefits, especially in 2016. The needed fiscal adjustment should safeguard productive spending, such as public investment and education and be anchored by revisiting the fiscal rule. In addition, in the view of the IMF, it should be accompanied by permanent fiscal measures which could include (i) pension reform, (ii) reducing energy subsidies and (iii) better targeting social transfers.

The IMF considered that the medium term growth outlook was mediocre due to low potential growth. Boosting growth required re-invigorating the reform agenda. In that context, avoiding deflation contagion from the world economy, coupled with less regulation and a reduction of the government's role in the economy remained crucial to foster efficiency, confidence and investment. Specific reforms could include (i) improving the protection of property rights, (ii) enhancing customs administration and reducing trade barriers and (iii) empowering the Federal Antimonopoly Service (FAS) to eliminate entry barriers to several sectors/markets. In addition, to improve labour force dynamics in the face of negative demographic trends, pension reform should be a priority. Finally, reducing banking sector fragmentation by continuing the ongoing intensification of supervision, tightening capital standards through the implementation of Basel III and further strengthening the role of credit bureaus and collateral registries, would help improve capital allocation, thereby enhancing potential growth.

Energy

According to the United States Energy Information Administration (EIA), Russia is the second-largest producer of dry natural gas and the third-largest liquid fuels producer in the world. Despite its significant reserves of coal, it produces only modest amount of coal. The economy is highly dependent on its hydrocarbons and oil and gas revenues account for more than 50 per cent of the federal budget revenues.

In recession, what growth there is in the economy continues to be driven by energy exports; Russia may have high levels of oil and gas production, but as the oil price has fallen, so have oil and gas revenues. In 2012 oil and gas revenues had accounted for 52 per cent of federal budget revenues and over 70 per cent of total exports, according to PFC Energy. According to the EIA, Russia was the world's third-largest producer of oil (after Saudi Arabia and the United States). Data for 2013 showed that Russia was still the third-ranked producer of total liquids, with average production at 10.5 million barrels per day (bpd) in September 2013. Russia was the second-largest producer of natural gas in 2012 (second to the United States). Russia is also the third-largest generator of nuclear power in the world and the fourth-largest in terms of installed capacity. Russia consumed 32.77 quadrillion British thermal units (Btu) of energy in 2011, the majority of which was in the form of natural gas (56 per cent). Petroleum and coal accounted for 19 per cent and 14 per cent, respectively.

Reserves and production

Russia's oil reserves were put at 103.2 billion barrels in December 2014 by the *BP Statistical Review of World Energy* of June 2015 (BP15 Review). Most of Russia's resources are located in Western Siberia and in the Volga-Urals region, extending into the Caspian Sea. Eastern Siberia holds some reserves, but the region has had little exploration. In 2014, Russia produced an estimated 10.8 million bpd of total liguids and it consumed roughly 3.2 million bpd. Russia exported over 7 million bpd in 2012, including roughly 5 million bpd of crude oil and the remainder in products. Russia's pipeline oil exports fall under the jurisdiction of Transneft, the state-owned pipeline monopoly.

Most of Russia's oil production continues to originate in Western Siberia, notably from the Priobskoye and Samotlor fields. The Sakhalin group of fields in the Far East only contributes about 3 per cent of Russia's total production, although it has yet to realise hopes and expectations that it would contribute significantly to Russia's total oil production. In the longer term, however, Sakhalin, along with the untapped oil reserves in Eastern Siberia and the Russian Arctic, may play a larger role. Several international oil companies are actively working in this area. The Russian sector of the Caspian Sea and the undeveloped areas of Timan-Pechora in northern Russia also may hold large hydrocarbon reserves.

A number of new projects are in development, but these new projects may only offset declining output from ageing fields and not result in significant output growth. The use of more advanced technologies and the application of improved recovery techniques have resulted in increased oil output. Production in the region is dominated by Russian firms.

Most of Russia's production remains dominated by domestic firms. Following the collapse of the Soviet Union, Russia initially privatised its oil industry, but Russia's oil and gas sector has largely reverted to state control in the past few years. In the late 1990s, a few privately-owned companies drove growth in the sector and, a number of international oil companies attempted to enter the market, with varying success. However, by 2015, the state-run Rosneft had emerged as Russia's top producer following the liquidation of Yukos assets, which Rosneft acquired. LUKoil, a privately-held company, is the second-largest holder of oil reserves and producer in Russia, second only to Rosneft. LUKoil holds an extensive portfolio of both upstream and downstream assets.

Exports

In 2012, Russia exported approximately 7.4 million bpd of total liquid fuels, with 5 million bpd of crude oil and 2.4 million bpd of petroleum products. The majority (79 per cent) of Russia's crude oil exports went to European countries (including Eastern Europe), particularly Germany, the Netherlands and Poland. Around 18 per cent of Russia's crude oil exports were destined for Asia, while the remainder went mostly to the Americas. Russia's crude oil exports to North America and South America have been largely displaced by increases in crude oil production in the United States, Canada and, to a lesser extent, in Brazil, Colombia and other countries on the continent. More than 80 per cent of Russia's oil is exported via the Transneft pipeline system and the remainder is shipped via rail and on vessels that load at independently-owned terminals.

Natural gas

According to the the 2015 BP Review, in December 2014 Russia held the world's second largest (behind Iran) natural gas reserves, with 1,152 trillion cubic feet (tcf). Russia's reserves accounted for about a quarter of the world's total reserves. The majority of these reserves are located in Siberia, while other significant deposits are located in northern Russia. The state-run Gazprom dominates Russia's upstream management, producing about 74 per cent of Russia's total natural gas output. Gazprom also controls most of Russia's gas reserves, with more than 65 per cent of reserves under its control and additional reserves controlled by Gazprom in joint ventures with other companies.

While independent producers have gained importance, with producers such as Novatek and LUKoil contributing increasing volumes to Russia's production, upstream opportunities remain fairly limited for independent producers and other companies, including Russian oil majors. Gazprom's position is further cemented by its legal monopoly on Russian gas exports, although this monopoly may be ending. Russia's government had announced that it intended to liberalise liquefied natural gas (LNG) exports in January 2014, breaking Gazprom's absolute export monopoly. Russia sends about 76 per cent of its natural gas exports to customers in Western Europe, with Germany, Turkey, Italy, France and the UK receiving the bulk of these volumes.

Coal

Russia held the world's second-largest recoverable coal reserves, behind the United States, of roughly 157,010 million tonnes at the end of 2014. Russia produced 389 million short tons in 2012, according to Eastern Bloc Energy, of which about 80 per cent was steam coal and 20 per cent was coking coal. Most of Russia's coal (66 per cent) was produced using the open cast mining method. Following a restructuring of the sector, nearly all domestic coal production now comes from independent producers.

In conclusion

The 'frozen anarchy' referred to in the opening paragraph is a symptom of Mr Putin's isolation. However much he may play down the importance of sanctions, or dismiss the significance or likely duration of low oil and gas prices, these are all problems beyond his control. In 2015 Russia risked sinking into an isolation caused by the creation of a new iron curtain. The timing of Russia's massive military expenditure now seemed unfortunate when civil service salaries were behind schedule. The exclusion of Russia from international fora and the prohibition of travel on the part of so many of its business leaders all added up to embarrassingly unwelcome inconveniences. But what could be done to change things? Answer came there not.

Risk assessment

Economy	Poor
Politics	Poor
Regional stability	Poor

Muslims in Russia

% of population	11.7
Sunni (% of Muslims)	88
Shi'a (% of Muslims)	10

People to watch

Lena Nemirovskaya of the Moscow School for Political Studies.

Pavel Durov, founder of the principal Russian internet social platform, Vkontakte.

Mikhail B Khodorosvky: Former oligarch and former political prisoner now public opponent of Putin. Founder of the Open Russia organisation.

Alexei Navalny: High profile blogger and political opponent of Putin.

COUNTRY PROFILE

The first monarchic dynasty ruled from the ninth century and built Kiev as its capital. It was overthrown by the Mongol invasion in the thirteenth century.

In the fifteenth century, the Grand Prince of Moscow, Ivan III, annexed the rival

principalities of Russia and became its first national sovereign.
Ivan IV (Ivan the Terrible) further expanded Russia's frontiers and became the first holder of the title of Tsar.
1613 Michael Romanov was elected tsar, establishing the Romanov dynasty, which ruled Russia until the 1917 revolution.
Peter the Great (1682–1725) and Catherine the Great (1762–96) consolidated the regime.
1772 Russia started expanding its territory. It acquired the Crimea and over the next 40 years parts of Poland, Ukraine, Belarus, Moldova and Georgia.
1812 The French invasion of Russia ended when France was driven out.
In the mid-nineteenth century, most of Siberia was annexed and expansion to the south and east continued until 1905.
1914–16 After initial success in the First Would War against Germany and Austria, military defeats weakened the position of the Tsar as personal head of the army and increased political and economy tensions.
1917 In February Tsar Nicholas II was forced to abdicate. The liberal government was overthrown in a Bolshevik coup, under the leadership of Lenin.
1918–20 A civil war raged between the communist Bolsheviks and anti-Bolsheviks, the right-wing white army. The Tsar and his family, captives of the Bolsheviks, were executed by their jailers on 17 July 1918, to prevent them from being liberated by Tsarist forces. The civil war ended in defeat for the white army, despite assistance from Britain, France, Japan and the US.
1922 The Union of Soviet Socialist Republics (USSR) was formed by Russia, Ukraine, Belarus and the Transcaucasus region.
1924 Following Lenin's death, Josef Stalin took over the leadership of the USSR as the general secretary of the Communist Party of the Soviet Union (CPSU) and a period of industrialisation, collectivisation of agriculture and purges of Stalin's opponents began. Key leadership rival Leon Trotsky was exiled in 1927 and assassinated in 1940.
1939 The USSR signed a non-aggression pact, the *Molotov-Ribbentrop Treaty*, with Nazi Germany. Soviet forces assisted the German invasion of Poland. The USSR also invaded Finland but was forced to respect Finnish independence in a 1940 peace agreement.
1940 Stalin ordered the execution of up to 22,000 captured Polish army officers at Katyn, near Smolensk in Russia.
1941 After the USSR was invaded by Germany, it joined the Allies and declared war on the Axis powers.
1944–45 The USSR liberated parts of Eastern Europe and Eastern Germany, these being pulled into its sphere of influence after the Second World War. Western Europe, meanwhile, fell under the sphere of influence of the US, marking the start of the Cold War.
1949 The USSR became the world's second nuclear power (after the US), when it exploded its first atomic bomb.
1953 Following Stalin's death, Nikita Krushchev took over the leadership of the USSR.
1955 The Warsaw Pact was established by the USSR and its satellite Eastern European states as a security apparatus to defend the region against NATO.
1962 The USSR's deployment of nuclear missiles in Cuba, within striking distance of the US, led to the 14-day missile crisis between the US and the USSR.
1964 After Krushchev's fall from power the USSR was led by Leonid Brezhnev.
1979 Soviet forces invaded Afghanistan to prop up the communist Afghan government.
1982 After Brezhnev's death, Yuri Andropov became leader of the USSR.
1984 Konstantin Chernenko replaced Andropov, following his death.
1985 Chernenko died. His successor, Mikhail Gorbachev, instigated a programme of social, political and economic reforms, centred on *perestroika* (restructuring) and *glasnost* (openness).
1989 The USSR withdrew from Afghanistan. Communist rule ended in most of Eastern and Central Europe.
1991 Gorbachev survived a coup attempt by communist hard-liners, but lost power; he dissolved the CPSU, the communist central committee. In the ensuing power vacuum Boris Yeltsin emerged as a leader when he prevented a military takeover in Moscow. He was elected Russia's president. The USSR ceased to exist on 31 December and the Commonwealth of Independent States (CIS) was formed by 11 of the former USSR republics, including Russia. Dzhokhar Dudayev won presidential elections in Chechnya and proclaimed independence from Russia. The remains of the last Tsar and his family, found in 1989, were identified after two years of forensic and DNA tests.
1992 Yeltsin appointed Yegor Gaidar acting prime minister. Yeltsin appointed Viktor Chernomyrdin prime minister.
1993 Yeltsin ordered the army to crush an anti-government uprising in Moscow and end a parliamentary sit-in. The Federal Assembly, comprising the State Duma and the Federation Council replaced the Supreme Soviet. A referendum approved a new constitution that gave the president sweeping powers.
1994 Russian troops invaded Chechnya, which is *de facto* independent, but *de jure* part of Russia. Uzbekistan and Russia signed an economic integration treaty.
1995 In Duma elections, the reformed Kommunisticheskaya Partiya Rossiiskoi Federatsii (KPRF) (Communist Party of the Russian Federation) won the largest vote. Chechen rebels seized hundreds of hostages during a raid on the southern Russian town of Budennovsk. More than 100 are killed in the ensuing violence.
1996 Yeltsin was re-elected president. Russia joined in G7 discussions on nuclear security. Chechen rebels seized thousands of hostages in the Russian town of Kizlyar. Chechen President Dudayev was killed by the Russian air force; he was succeeded by Zelimkhan Yandarbiyev. A peace treaty was signed between Russia and Chechen separatists, temporarily ending the conflict. Chechen forces drove the Russian army out of the capital, Grozny.
1997 Yeltsin and the Belarusian president, Aleksander Lukashenko, signed the Treaty on the Union of Belarus and Russia. The treaty aimed at increasing political and economic co-operation between the two states. Yeltsin and the new Chechen president, Aslan Maskhadov, signed a formal peace agreement.
1998 The Russian rouble collapsed, sending Russia into temporary economic crisis as it defaulted on foreign debts. The bodies of the last Russian Tsar and his family were interred in the Cathedral of Saints Peter and Paul in St Petersburg.
1999 An Islamist separatist group declared the Russian republic of Dagestan to be independent. Chechen fighters under the command of the former prime minister of Chechnya, Shamil Basayev, invaded Dagestan in support of the separatists. Yeltsin appointed Vladimir Putin as prime minister. A series of bomb explosions in Russian cities were blamed on Chechen separatists and Russia launched a second invasion of Chechnya. Yeltsin resigned before the official end of his term. Putin became acting president.
2000 Vladimir Putin was elected president. The presidents of Belarus, Kazakhstan, Kyrgyzstan, Russia and Tajikistan (formerly the Customs Five) established the Eurasian Economic Community (EEC). Mikhail Kasyanov became prime minister.
2001 The Russian army started a gradual withdrawal of troops from Chechnya. The main pro-Putin parties created the Yedinaya Rossiya (YR) (United Russia) party by merging the ruling Mezhregional'noye Dvishenie Yedinstvo (Medved) (Inter-Regional Movement Unity) and the Otechestvo-Vsya Rossiya (OVR) (Fatherland-All Russia). Tajikistan, China, Russia, Kazakhstan, Kyrgyzstan and Uzbekistan formed the Shanghai

Co-operation Organisation (SCO) and agreed to fight ethnic and religious militancy, while promoting investment and trade.
2002 The US and Russia agreed to cut 70 per cent of their nuclear arsenals. Chechen Prime Minister Ilyasov resigned and was appointed by President Putin as Russia's federal minister of Chechnya affairs. Akhmed Kadyrov, appointed Mikhail Babich as prime minister of Chechnya. Chechnya's leading rebel warlord, Shamil Basayev, claimed responsibility for the Moscow theatre siege, during which 119 hostages died.
2003 Kadyrov appointed Anatoly Popov as Chechen prime minister. Russia, Ukraine, Kazakhstan and Belarus signed an economic union treaty. The YR won parliamentary elections.
2004 President Putin dismissed Prime Minister Kasyanov and appointed Mikhail Fradkov, in his place. Putin was re-elected president.
In Chechnya, Sergei Abramov was confirmed as prime minister of a pro-Moscow government. The president, Akhmad Kadyrov, was killed in an explosion and Abramov won the presidential elections. At least 330 people died in the Beslan school massacre when Russian troops stormed the school held by Chechen terrorists, in an attempt to free the hostage schoolchildren and teachers.
2005 Russian special forces killed the Chechen rebel leader, Maskhadov. Russia gave asylum to exiled President Askar Akayev of Tajikistan. State control was tightened through media and electoral laws. A diplomatic row developed when Ukraine refused to pay a four-fold increase in the price of gas and Gazprom cut off supplies. The row escalated and antagonised the EU when supplies to some of its member states were also cut by default. Germany and Russia signed an agreement to build a gas pipeline beneath the Baltic Sea and secure Russian natural gas for Western Europe.
2006 The rouble was made fully convertible against foreign currencies. President Abdul-Khalim Sadulayev of Chechnya was killed by Russian forces. Russia denied it was responsible for the death in the UK of outspoken critic of Putin's regime and former security service officer, Aleksandr Litvinenko, by radioactive poison. Belarus became the latest former Soviet-satellite country to be given an ultimatum to pay the market price for Russian gas or be denied supplies.
2007 The transit oil pipeline through Belarus was shut-down after Belarus attempted to impose a transit tax on the oil; Russia accused Belarus of siphoning off oil. President Putin dismissed Chechen president, Alu Alkhanov and appointed Ramzan Kadyrov in his place. The Russians planted their flag below the North Pole using two mini-submarines in an action laying claim to the potential oil and minerals below the seabed. The US and Canada both criticised the claim and launched competing claims. The North Pole (administered by the International Seabed Authority) was regarded as being not subject to any one country's claim. The remains of the last two missing children of Tsar Nicholas II, including his son Alexei, were found near Ekaterinburg. In parliamentary elections YR won over 64.3 per cent of the vote (315 seats out of 450); the KPRF party 11.6 per cent (57). The OSCE declared the election to be 'not fair and failed to meet many… commitments and standards for democratic elections'.
2008 The number of members of the Federal Assembly was reduced to 168. In the presidential elections, Dmitry Medvedev won with 70.3 per cent of the vote. International observers criticised the election campaign for not allowing candidates equal access to the media. After President Medvedev was sworn into office he appointed Vladimir Putin (YR), as prime minister. Russia backed South Ossetia when Georgia attacked separatist forces in its break-away territory. Russian forces ejected Georgian troops and later recognised the independence of the Russian enclaves, South Ossetia and Abkhazia. Winner of the Nobel Prize for Literature in 1970, Alexander Solzhenitsyn, died. The international global financial crisis caused the Moscow stock exchange to fall sharply; the government instituted a US$68 billion package to stabilise its banking system.
2009 A three-week international row between Russia and Ukraine, in which several European countries lost their gas supply as Gazprom shut-down its supplies, was resolved, but only after EU officials advised national gas suppliers to sue Russia and Ukraine for the break in supplies. US President Obama visited Moscow; talks included limiting nuclear weapons. The Russian rights activist Nataliya Estemirova was murdered in Chechnya and her body dumped in Ingushetia.
2010 The new Severo-Kavkazsky federalny okrug (North Caucasian federal district) was created by presidential decree; it was formed by a split in the South Caucasian federal district, in the extreme south-west of Russia. It has an area of 170,700 square kilometres, with a population of over 10 million; its administrative capital is Pyatigorsk. The Verkhny Lars-Kazbegi border checkpoint between Georgia and Russia, which had been closed in 2006, was reopened. The US and Russia signed another nuclear disarmament treaty in Prague (Czech Republic). The treaty limits the number of warheads and launchers each country may possess. The signing took place only after the US scrapped previous plans for a 'missile shield' based in Eastern Europe, which Russia considered provocative. An agreement on the Arctic border between Norway and Russia in the Barents Sea, which cuts across an oil and natural gas rich region, was finally resolved after several decades in dispute and considered 'good and balanced' by President Medvedev. A customs union between Russia, Belarus and Kazakhstan became fully operational. After a prolonged drought a temporary ban on the export of wheat was imposed. Wild fires, caused by a severe heat wave, covered over 170,000 hectares in the south and west of the country; over 40 people were killed, around 2,000 homes were engulfed within the many individual fires and about one-third of the grain harvest was destroyed. The Duma passed a resolution confirming that Josef Stalin had, according to papers kept in a secret archive, given the direct order for the massacre of 22,000 Polish officers at Katyn in 1940. President Medvedev said, a video blog, that 'if a political opposition doesn't stand the slightest chance of winning a fair election, then it degrades and becomes marginalised' and 'if the ruling party never has to worry about losing an election anywhere, then it too degrades' the process and ultimately leads to stagnation.
2011 In January, the upper house of the Duma approved the nuclear disarmament agreement with the US, signed in 2010. The New Start (Strategic Arms Reduction Treaty), replaced the 1991 disarmament treaty, which had lapsed in 2009. New Start cuts warheads by 30 per cent from the previous limit and allows verifiable inspection of each other's capabilities. In June the Central Election Commission announced it had refused to register Partiya Narodnoi Svobodi (Parnas) (People's Freedom Party) a new, liberal, political party. The party leaders included four prominent opposition figures. The justice ministry said the party failed to meet several legal requirements and all members will be barred from standing in the next general elections. The Nord Stream pipeline carrying Russian gas direct to Germany and the rest of Europe was opened in September. The pipeline is the first to bypass Ukraine and other central European countries. Vatentina Matviyenko, former governor of St Petersburg, was elected Speaker of the upper house in September. She is a supporter of Putin and replaces Sergei Mironov of the Spravedlivaya Rossiya (SR) (A Just Russia)

who was ousted in May. In November, the presidents of Russia, Belarus and Kazakhstan signed an agreement to set targets for setting up an internal market, the Eurasian Union, by 2015. Elections for the lower house (Duma) of parliament were held on 4 December, in which the four political parties that had been present in the last session in parliament, plus seven other political parties that had been granted registration, took part. As expected YR won a majority with 49.29 per cent (238 seats, out of 450), but its result was down from the 315 seats in the 2007 elections. The KPRF won 92 seats and the new party won SR 64 and LDPR won 56 seats; turnout was 60.2 per cent. Thousands of protestors took to the streets of Moscow and other cities on 5–7 December, defying a ban on rallies. Hundreds were arrested. On 7 December former president Mikhail Gorbachev (of the USSR), declared 'the authorities must admit that numerous instances of vote-rigging and fraud have taken place, and the announced results do not reflect the voters' wishes', and 'the current authorities should make only one decision – annul the election results, and hold a new poll.' The Central Election Commission stated that 'recorded violations were insignificant…' On 8 December, Prime Minister Putin accused US authorities of inciting opposition protests to the election results. The official US response to the results had been of 'serious concerns', with US Secretary of State Hillary Clinton saying that they were neither free not fair.

2012 On 1 January a Eurasian Commission began overseeing the integration of a Eurasian Union. As agreed by parliament in 2008, future presidential terms in office will be six years (extended from four years). On 8 February the Supreme Court backed the CEC in banning opposition candidate Grigory Yavlinsky (Russian United Democratic Party (Yabloko)) from contesting the 2012 presidential elections. Yavlinsky claimed the ban was politically motivated. Presidential elections were held on 4 March, Vladimir Putin won 63.64 per cent, his closest rival Gennady Zyuganov (KPRF) won 17.18 per cent; turnout was 65.25 per cent. The leaders of the Bric countries (Brazil, Russia, India and China) met in Delhi on 29 March to discuss their position regarding the control the US and Europe has on the World Bank and the IMF. Prime Minister Manmohan Singh (India) said 'The Brics countries have agreed to examine in greater detail a proposal to set up a South-South development bank, funded and managed by the Brics and other developing countries.' On 7 May Vladimir Putin was inaugurated as president for his third term in office. As one of his first acts, President Putin appointed former president Medvedev as prime minister. On 6 June, parliament backed a new law that introduced stringent controls and large fines for unauthorised protest gatherings and any injury and damage caused. However, before the final vote, a faction, in opposition to the new measures, attempted a philibuster, the first time in the Duma's modern history that such a strategy was employed. On 11 June the new law on rallies and protests came into force and the homes of several prominent anti-government rally organisers were searched by police. On 16 June, the opposition (to Putin's rule) political parties, Parnas and Respublikanskaya Partiya Rossii (RPR) (Republican Party of Russia) merged to form RPR-Parnas. On 10 July the Duma voted 238 to 208 to pass the bill ratifying Russia's membership of the WTO. On 4 September, the European Commission (EC) opened antitrust proceedings against Gazprom, which were quickly rejected by the energy giant, claiming it was 'outside the jurisdiction of the EC' as it was a state-owned gas producer (as defined by Russian law). The EC said it was investigating three instances of anticompetitive practices of unfair pricing and market segmentation in eight EU countries. Gazprom supplies around 25 per cent of all European natural gas needs. On 14 November treason laws were redefined so that any Russian working for any foreign organisation that passes on what are deemed to be state secrets is criminally liable. Even those that provide consultancy or 'other assistance' to a foreign entity may be liable and can incur greater penalty if surveillance equipment is employed. Civil rights campaigners claim that this could seriously undermine their ability to monitor the government and scare Russians into cutting ties with Western non-governmental organisations (NGOs). On 5 December, the Congress passed the 'Maginitsky Bill' that targets Russian officials who have allegedly committed human rights violations and were involved in the death in custody of Sergei Maginitsky, a Russian lawyer employed by foreign entities, who had alleged large-scale systematic theft by public officials of Russian government funds. On 7 December Russia warned it would respond in kind.

2013 On 6 June Russian Vladimir Putin and his wife Lyudmila said their marriage was over. It was unclear whether they had actually divorced or not. The Popular Front for Russia, a pro-Putin movement, was launched on 12 June, with President Putin himself as leader. Analysts see the movement as a means of boosting support for Putin as the ruling United Russia party looses support. On 1 August the American Edward Snowden, who had been sheltering in Sheremetyevo Airport since 23 June, was granted a one year passport with permission to stay. The Americans expressed annoyance that asylum was granted to a man who had been charged with leaking documents showing the extent of US government snooping and said they were 'reconsidering' a meeting scheduled for September between President Obama and President Putin at the G20 economic talks to be held in St Petersberg. The meeting was cancelled on 7 August and the Russians expressed 'disappointment'. Sergei Sobyanin, an ally of President Putin, narrowly won the election to continue as mayor of Moscow. Turnout was under 30 per cent. In an article published in the *New York Times* on 11 September President Putin made an appeal to the American people over the Syrian crisis the day before a scheduled meeting between Russian and US officials on Syria's chemical weapons. In an 'opinion' article he said that millions of people see the US not as a model of democracy but as relying on brute force. After being criticised over a new law banning 'homosexual propaganda', and with international threats to boycott the Winter Olympics being held in Sochi in 2014, President Putin said in October that gay and lesbian athletes would have nothing to fear. At the end of October President Putin was named the world's most powerful person by *Forbes* magazine, pushing President Obama into second place.

2014 On 29 July US President Obama announced further economic sanctions against Russia. The sanctions, co-ordinated with the EU, include banning US citizens from banking with three Russian banks, either in the US or in Russia. In retaliation to the sanctions imposed by the West, on 8 August Russia announced a ban on the import of agriculture products. In a move the central bank hoped would ease the fall in the value of the rouble against the US dollar it raised its key interest rate from 10.5 per cent to 17 per cent on 15 December. It followed a 1 per cent rise made on 11 December.

2015 On 29 January the EU agreed to extend the sanctions currently in place until September. Opposition politician Boris Nemtsov was shot dead on 27 February. Five ethnic Chechens were arrested, including Zaur Dadayev, who is said to have close links with the Chechen president, Ramzan Kadyrov, who in turn is said to be a supporter of Mr Putin. Dadayev is alleged to have confessed to shooting Mr Nemtsov, but later retracted it, saying he had been tortured. On 27 April Russia unveiled a new-generation battle tank called Armata T-14, in time for World

War Two Victory Day celebrations on 9 May. Direct flights between Ukraine and Russia were stopped from 25 October as new sanctions initiated by Kiev come into effect.

Political structure

Constitution

The constitution was adopted in December 1993. The Russian Federation consists of 89 republics and regions, including the federal cities of Moscow and St Petersburg.

If the ruling party has over two thirds of the Duma seats it has enough power to amend the constitution unchallenged.

Electoral system: universal direct suffrage over the age of 18.

Parliament voted in 2008 to increase a president's term in office from four years to six, from 2012.

Form of state

Federal state with a republican form of government

The executive

Executive power is held by the president, who has the right to veto parliamentary legislation, while issuing decrees on which the Federal Assembly may advise but not veto. The president is elected for a four-year term.

The cabinet is appointed by the prime minister, who is appointed by the president.

The State Council of the Russian Federation, which has consultative functions only, was formed in 2000. It advises the president on issues concerning the relationship between the central administration and the regions.

In 2008 parliament voted to increase a president's term in office from four years to six, from 2012.

National legislature

The 1993 constitution created a bicameral Federal'noye Sobraniye (Federal Assembly), comprising the Gosudarstvennaya Duma (State Duma, commonly called Gosduma, lower house) with 450 seats elected by proportional representative from party lists, and the Sovet Federatsii (Federation Council, upper house) with 168 seats of two deputies from each of Russia's 84 republics and regions, appointed by regional legislatures; all serve for four year terms.

Legal system

The legal system is based on civil law. There is judicial review of legislative acts. The top levels of the judicial branch consist of: the Constitutional Court, which reviews the constitutionality of federal legislation; the Supreme Court, which is the highest civil and criminal judiciary body; and the Supreme Arbitration Court, which resolves economic disputes between subjects of the Federation. The Supreme Court and Supreme Arbitration Court preside over a federal system of lower criminal and civil courts.

Last elections

4 December 2011 (parliamentary); 4 March 2012 (presidential)

Results: Parliamentary: Yedinaya Rossiya (YR) (United Russia) 49.29 per cent (238 seats, out of 450 (down from 315 in the 2007 elections), Kommunisticheskaya Partiya Rossiiskoi Federatsii (KPRF) (Communist Party of the Russian Federation) 19.2 per cent (92), Spravedlivaya Rossiya (SR) (A Just Russia) 13.25 per cent (64), Liberal'no-Demokraticheskaya Partiya Rossii (LDPR) (Russia's Liberal Democratic Party) 11.68 per cent (56); no other political party won enough votes to win seats. Turnout was 60.2 per cent.

Presidential: Vladimir Putin (YR) won 63.64 per cent of the vote, Gennady Zyuganov (KPRF) 17.18 per cent, Mikhail Prokhorov (independent) 7.94 per cent, Vladimir Zhirinovsky (LDPR) 6.22 per cent, Sergey Mironov (Spravedlivaya Rossiya (SR) (A Just Russia)) 3.85 per cent. Turnout was 65.25 per cent.

Next elections

2016 (parliamentary); 2018 (presidential)

Political parties

Ruling party

Yedinaya Rossiya (YR) (United Russia) (from 2003; re-elected 4 Dec 2011)

Main opposition party

With such an overwhelming majority in parliament for the ruling YR, to achieve any semblance of parliamentary debate an opposition had to be appointed by the government, which has come to be called a 'systemic opposition' by opponents of the process. Despite this, the Communist Party (second largest in parliament) garnered 19.2% of the vote and A Just Russia (third largest) attained 13.2%.

Population

141.92 million (2012)

Last census: March 2002: 145,537,200

Population density: Nine inhabitants per square km. Urban population 73 per cent (2010 Unicef).

Annual growth rate: -0.2 per cent, 1990–2010 (Unicef).

Internally Displaced Persons (IDP)

330,000 (UNHCR 2004)

Ethnic make-up

Russian (82 per cent), Tatars (4 per cent) and Ukrainians (3 per cent).

Religions

The majority of the population is Christian, mainly Russian Orthodox. Religion, while not actually forbidden under communism, was officially discouraged. Religious observance and interest is growing steeply with the relaxation of state restrictions. Russian Orthodox Christmas was made an official holiday for the first time in 1991.

Russia also has sizeable Muslim (12 million) and Jewish (700,000) minorities.

Education

After compulsory education at age 15, secondary (complete) general education begins. Students may also enter vocational schools or non-university level higher education institutions. Initial vocational schools offer one-and-a-half to two years of vocational education. Secondary (complete) general education continues for two years and ends when students are aged 17–18 years.

Higher education is provided by 553 public and 260 non-public accredited higher education institutions. Education in public higher education is free of charge. There are three levels of higher educational institutions including those lasting between two to four years and an advanced level lasting between five and six years. The government aims to diversify higher education courses and boost the private sector. In addition to universities in the public and private sector, there are 3,000 non-university institutions in Russia.

Literacy rate: 100 per cent adult rate; 100 per cent youth rate (15–24) (Unesco 2005).

Compulsory years: Six to 15 years.

Enrolment rate: 107 per cent total primary enrolment of the relevant age group (including repeaters) (World Bank).

Pupils per teacher: 20 in primary schools.

Health

In 2006 President Putin announced government sponsored health measures to reduce the falling birth rate, low life expectancy and unusually high male mortality rate. Child benefits were increased and one-off payments made to mothers to encourage fertility. Nevertheless, Russia has one of the highest rates of abortion in the world, with 66 terminations for every 100 pregnancies. Fertility rates fell from 2.19 births per woman in 1986–87 to 1.34 in 2003 and is still below the 2.1 births necessary to sustain population growth.

In every hour there is only one birth for 77 deaths and Russia has been warned that its population could crash by 2050 if the trend is not reversed. Mortality rates have ballooned for a wide number of reasons including poor diet, disease, alcoholism and risky activities – Russia has twice as many road accident fatalities as any other G8 country.

HIV/Aids

HIV/Aids has spread in Russia at a time when infection rates have been steady and declining for a number of years in Europe and North America.

In the first six months of 2012 the number of HIV cases was 12 per cent higher than in the same period of 2011. Official data shows that in the first 10 months, 703,781 Russians had the virus, of whom 90,396 died.
Russian health officials blame the high number of HIV/Aids cases on intravenous drug use rather than sexual activity.
HIV prevalence: 1.1 per cent aged 15–49 in 2003 (World Bank)
Life expectancy: 65 years, 2004 (WHO 2006)
Fertility rate/Maternal mortality rate: 1.5 births per woman, 2010 (Unicef)
Birth rate/Death rate: 10 births per 1,000 population; 14 deaths per 1,000 population (2003).
Child (under 5 years) mortality rate (per 1,000): 10 per 1,000 live births (WHO 2012)
Head of population per physician: 4.25 physicians per 1,000 people, 2003 (WHO 2006)

Welfare
In January 2005, widespread demonstrations forced Vladimir Putin to amend newly instigated reforms to the benefits system after they were introduced. The plan to offer cash payments in exchange for what had been free services such as medicines, transport and subsidised housing continued but the amounts were increased and pension payments brought by a month. About 34 million pensioners, infirm and war veterans are estimated to be affected by the changes, with the lowest payments at just US$7.5 per month. Critics said that the implimentation of the change was mishandled and the calculations sloppy, whereas the government believes that 'monetising' benefits was the only option to streamline social benefits and generate considerable cost savings. This set-back is thought, by some, to risk Putin's reform agenda.
Given budgetary constraints, reforms are targetted at increasing the transparency and efficiency of Russia's main social funds and eliminating unproductive social programmes. There have been massive increases in health service funding, especially to reduce infant mortality rates and bring healthcare up to world standards. Maternity benefits are being enhanced in order to induce women to stay at home for two or three years.
The tax code has been used to unify and reduce the different social security contributions but, despite recent tax cuts, average real incomes remain low.
Unemployment benefits based on past earnings remain very low due to high inflation. Income inequality levels have consequently been increasing and it is estimated that about 20.4 per cent of the population live below the minimum subsistence level laid down by the state.

Main cities
Moscow (capital, estimated population 10.5 million (m) in 2012); St Petersburg (4.5m), Novosibirsk (1.4m), Yekaterinburg (formerly Sverdlovsk) (1.3m), Nizhny Novgorod (formerly Gorki, 1.2m), Kazan (capital of the sovereign republic Tatarstan) (1.1m), Omsk (1.1m), Samara (formerly Kuybyshev) (1.1), Cheljabinsk (1.1m), Rostov-on-Don (1.0m).

Languages spoken
There are as many as 100 local ethnic languages, some of the larger groupings include Baskin, Chuvash Tatar and Yakut. Russian is spoken throughout the country. Russian and most local languages are written in variants of the Cyrillic alphabet, which was devised by the ninth century saints, Cyril and Methodius. In September 2000, the Tatarstan republic (population four million, a large minority of whom are Russian) began a 10-year transition period for the switch in schools from Cyrillic to the Latin alphabet for the local Turkic language. Russian is the second language spoken in Tatarstan. However, Russian MPs voted in June 2002 to make the use of the Cyrillic alphabet mandatory throughout the country.
On 5 Feb 2003, the State Duma passed a law making Russian the official state language, prohibiting the use in public documents of foreign words or expressions that have Russian-language equivalents).
Ukrainian, Mordvin and Chechen are also spoken.

Official language/s
Russian

Media
In February 2008 the worldwide human right's campaigning organisation, Amnesty International, stated that freedom of speech was 'shrinking alarmingly' with intimidation and arbitrary laws to curb outspoken media outlets and NGOs, while others alleged the extrajudicial killing of journalists.

Press
Dailies: There are many national and regional newspapers, most of which publish in Russian with a few in minority languages, as well as English. Some regional news is published over the Internet only while others are published (see www.wps.ru, monitoring – regional press). Major nationals in Russian are *Izvestia* (www.izvestia.ru) owned by Gazprom and *Rossiyskaya Gazeta* (www.rg.ru) is government owned. The *Komsomolskaya Pravda* (www.kp.ru) is a mass-circulation paper while *Nezavisimaya Gazeta* is an influential privately owned daily. *Kommersant* (www.kommersant.ru) is business orientated while *Trud* (www.trud.ru), is a socialist minded paper. In English, *The Moscow Times* (www.themoscowtimes.com) and its companion newspaper the *St Petersburg Times* (ww.sptimes.ru) report, among other things, on politics and business.
Weeklies: In Russian, the most popular publication is *Argumenty i Facty (Arguments & Facts)* (www.aif.ru) containing in-depth analysis of political and economic events. Others include *Itogi* (www.itogi.ru), *Ogonyok* (www.ogoniok.com) and *Profil* (www.profile.ru) and the *Moskovskie Novosti* (www.mn.ru) is a weekly international socio-political newspaper. In English, *Russia Profile* (www.russiaprofile.org) is published 10 times per year, the *Moscow News Weekly* (www.mnweekly.ru) and *The Russia Journal* (www.russiajournal.com) contain weekly news, analysis, and political opinion.
Business: *Moscow Times* is an English-language business publication.
Periodicals: In English, *Russia Profile* (www.russiaprofile.org) is published 10 times per year, and *Vladivostok News* (http://vn.vladnews.ru) both cover political and business information.

Broadcasting
Russian authorities pressured all radio stations to stopped broadcasting the BBC's Russian services in 2007.
Radio: There are two national state-run radio networks, Radio Russia (www.radiorus.ru) and Radio Mayak (www.radiomayak.ru). There are many commercial radio stations broadcasting in regional markets, Russkoye Radio (www.rusradio.ru) and Moscow Echo (www.echo.msk.ru) are the two most important.
The Voice of Russia (http://ruvr.ru) broadcasts programmes in 33 languages to 160 countries worldwide.
Television: Since 2001 the independence of Russian television has been circumscribed by government regulations that restricted majority foreign ownership and banned some stations, particularly those critical of the government.
The state-run Russia TV Channel (www.rutv.ru) network, the state part-owned Channel One (www.1tv.ru) and the Gazprom-owned NTV (www.ntv.ru), broadcast nationally. Fully commercial stations include Centre TV (www.tvc.ru) and Ren TV (www.ren-tv.com). Russia Today (www.russiatoday.ru) with news programming is state-funded and broadcasts in English, by satellite and cable.
National news agency: Itar-Tass News Agency

Other news agencies: RIA Novosti, 4 Zubovsky Blvd, Moscow 119031 (tel: 637-2424; internet: http://en.rian.ru). Interfax, 2 Pervaya Tverskaya-Yamskaya Ul, Building 1, Moscow 127006 (tel: 250-9840; fax: 250-9727; internet: www.interfax.ru).

Economy

With a vast territory that spans 11 time zones it isn't surprising that the Russian Federation has a diverse economy that ranges from its high-tech space programme, which can provide tourist jaunts into space for the (immensely) rich, to primary industries such as agriculture – with over 50 per cent of all farms and garden plots privately owned – and all technological and service industries in between. However, dominating all of its many productive sectors the extraction and supply of hydrocarbons has become Russia's foremost wealth creating industry, so much so that exports and access to further supplies has become an instrument of state policy. Russia is also a top exporter of metals such as steel and primary aluminium. Russia's manufacturing sector is generally uncompetitive on world markets and is geared toward domestic consumption, its reliance on commodity exports makes it vulnerable to boom and bust cycles that follow the volatile swing in global prices.

The Russian economy, which had averaged 7 per cent growth during 1998-2008 as oil prices rose rapidly, was one of the hardest hit by 2008-09 global economic crisis as oil prices plummeted and the foreign credits that Russian banks and firms relied on dried up. In 2014, Russia forcibly violated Ukraine's sovereignty and territorial integrity by illegally annexing the Crimea. It declared independence from Ukraine on March 11 2014 and voters overwhelmingly approved accession into Russia in a controversial March 16 referendum. As a result of this, foreign sanctions have been imposed upon Russia from the EU and the US. The ruble also lost half its value in the second half of 2014 which contributed to increased capital outflows that reached US$152 billion in 2014. Declining oil prices, lack of economic reforms, and the imposition of foreign sanctions have contributed to the downturn and created wide expectations that the economy will continue to slump.

GDP growth in Russia since the global economic crisis has been slow, however, it reached a relatively high rate of 3.4 per cent in 2012. Since then, the economy has contracted to 1.3 per cent growth in 2013 and 0.6 per cent growth in 2014. In April 2015, the Russian Ministry of Economic Development predicted that the economy will contract by 3 per cent in 2015, and average only 2.5 growth through 2030. The inflation rate increased from 6.8 per cent in 2013 to an extremely high level of 11.4 per cent in 2014. GDP per capita has remained stable but low at US$24,300 in 2012, US$24,700 in 2013 and US$24,800 in 2014. This is aligned with a relatively high unemployment rate of 5.1 per cent in 2014.

Russia has large reserves of oil – 80 billion barrels in 2014, which was 5.4 per cent of the world's total. Production of crude oil in 2014 was10 million bpd and production of refined petroleum was 4.8 million bpd and with consumption of just 3.3 million bpd, it is the world's second largest oil exporter (10.5 per cent of total crude oil exports) after Saudi Arabia. Russia exports 4.6 million bpd of crude oil and 3 million bpd of refined petroleum. Russia also has the largest reserve of natural gas in the world – 47.8 trillion cubic metres (cum) (26 per cent of the world's total) in 2014, with production of 668 billion cum, of which 196 billion cum is exported via gas pipelines to Europe and CIS countries and exported as liquefied natural gas to Asia. There are major reserves of coal and electricity generation from hydro- and nuclear-power stations which constitutes enough energy to meet domestic demands.

External trade

The Russian Federation leads the Commonwealth of Independent States (CIS), of former republics of the defunct Soviet Union, which promotes trade, cultural and legal ties amongst its members, however, it does not operate a free trade zone due to differences in economic objectives, degrees of reforms and economic development. Russia became a member of the World Trade Organisation on 16 December 2011, having begun negotiations to join in 1993.

A bilateral trade agreement with the EU was signed on 7 December 2010. The agreement paved the way for Russia's membership of the WTO in 2011; Russia is the last major economy to become a member of the WTO.

On 18 October 2011, Russia signed a free trade agreement (FTA) with seven of its former Soviet republics: Armenia, Belarus, Kazakhstan, Georgia, Kyrgyzstan, Moldova, Tajikistan and Ukraine.

On 18 November 2011, the presidents of Russia, Belarus and Kazakhstan signed an agreement to set targets for setting up an internal market, the Eurasian Union, by 2015. A Eurasian Commission began an overseeing role for integration on 1 January 2012.

Russia has immense mineral deposits of diamonds, precious metals and coal as well as timber and is a leading world supplier of oil and natural gas, which represents around 80 per cent of its exports. Foreign trade amounts to over 55 per cent of GDP. Investment in industry, manufacturing and infrastructure has been low and hampers progress.

Imports

Principal imports include machinery, vehicles, pharmaceutical products, plastic, semi-finished metal products, meat, fruits and nuts, optical and medical instruments, iron and steel.

Main sources: China (17.8 per cent of total in 2014), Germany (11.5 per cent), US (6.6 per cent), Italy (4.5 per cent) and Belarus (4.1 per cent).

Exports

Principal exports include petroleum and petroleum products, natural gas, metals, wood and wood products, chemicals and a wide variety of civilian and military manufactures.

Main destinations: The Netherlands (13.7 per cent of total in 2014), China (7.5 per cent), Germany (7.5 per cent), Italy (7.2 per cent) and Turkey (5 per cent).

Agriculture

Farming

Production in the agricultural sector in Russia has fallen since reforms began in 1992, following the substantial reduction in large state subsidies. The livestock sector contracted by about half. Progress has been particularly slow in land reform, and Russia still lacks a free market in agricultural land. Agricultural production contributes only 4 per cent of GDP, with 133 million hectares (ha) of arable land, and a large agrarian workforce constituting nearly 10 per cent of the total. Agricultural products include grain, sugar beets, sunflower seeds, vegetables, fruits; beef and milk.

The sector has suffered due to incomplete agriculture-specific and economy-wide institutional reform, such as price and trade reform, as well as privatisation. Russia has the potential to increase grain exports significantly if such reforms are implemented. Wheat and barley are the most significant crops produced in Russia that are widely traded on world markets.

Fishing

There has been a very noticeable drop in recorded fish production in Russia, since the end of the Soviet era. Production shortfalls have resulted in rising prices and steadily increasing imports of fish and fishery products.

In addition to the consequences of major economic and political changes, aquaculture and inland capture fisheries continue to face problems from environmental impacts on water resources affecting living aquatic resources. The environmental degradation of inland waters through industrial, urban and agrochemical pollution, and the damming of major rivers has had significant local impacts on fish stocks. As a result of the large-scale uptake of water for irrigation, the original fish fauna of Russia has been significantly modified.

Production from subsistence and recreational fisheries is seldom accurately reflected in the official statistics, and it is likely that production from these sectors plays an important role for food supply in the country. However, capture fisheries in many inland waters of the region, including, in particular, reservoirs and lakes, continue to depend heavily on stocking of fry and fingerlings produced in hatcheries, lake farms and artificial spawning grounds, or by other types of enhancement measures.

In order to attempt to bring fish production in Russia back to what it used to be, 1 million hectares of water bodies have become potential development areas for freshwater aquaculture. The National Project on Agricultural Sector Development has set a target for 2020 for 1.4 million tonnes of freshwater aquaculture and 400 thousand tonnes of mariculture. The federal government is considering a subsidy of two-thirds the capital needed to construct the new facilities.

Forestry

Russia has by far the largest forested area of any country in the world with forest and other wooded land constituting more than half of its land area estimated at 851.3 million hectares (ha) or almost 55 per cent of the total land area. Russia accounts for more than 20 per cent of global forest resources, more than 35 per cent of temperate/boreal forests in terms of area and 45 per cent in terms of growing stock. The area of forest is fairly stable, showing a marginal average annual increase of 0.02 per cent, or the equivalent of 135,000ha of forest cover. The importance of Russia's forests as a regulator of the global carbon balance, and mitigation of climate change, is difficult to overestimate.

The predominant coniferous species are larch and spruce. The deciduous species are represented mainly by birch, aspen and oaks (either European or Mongolian), and hornbeam, ash, maple and elm to a lesser degree. Mature and over-mature stands, situated mainly in the Asian part of Russia, prevail and about two-thirds of the forest is available for wood supply.

Russia is one of the largest producers and exporters of industrial roundwood in the world market. Significant volumes of sawn wood, plywood and pulp and paper are exported. The forest industry is almost completely privatised, although the forests and the roundwood production remain under state control.

Industry and manufacturing

The industrial sector accounts for 36 per cent of GDP and provides employment for 28 per cent of the working population.

The industrial production growth rate was just 0.6 per cent in 2014.

Factors that continue to dog efficiency include wasteful consumption of fuel and raw materials, antiquated machinery, poor technology and management and overstaffing. Early on in the reform process emphasis was placed on individual enterprise and factory production decisions, resulting in anarchic management practices.

Major production bottlenecks in the 1990s included steel, construction inputs (such as cement) and consumer and light industry products (such as television sets, robots and computers).

Emphasis during the 1990s was on light industry, modernisation and computerisation. The sector is reliant on large- and medium-sized firms to increase production and stimulate growth, particularly in engineering and metallurgy working.

The dominant industries in Russia are mining and extractive industries producing coal, oil, gas, chemicals, and metals, all forms of machine building as well as shipbuilding; road and rail transportation equipment; communications equipment; agricultural machinery, tractors and construction equipment.

Tourism

Russia has a vast land area that can offer visitors a range of holidays to suit any requirement. Its tourist infrastructure is centred on traditional resorts and facilities that cater for the large domestic market, and a newer market for foreign travellers. Some 80 per cent of foreign visitors specifically visit the imperial sites of St Petersburg and Moscow. Domestic travel and tourism represents over three times the amount to the economy than foreign visitors.

Travel and tourism constituted 6 per cent of GDP in 2014 (US$70 billion) set to increase to US$89 billion in 2015. 5.6 per cent of employment was related to the industry (3,961,000 jobs) set to increase slightly to 3,977,000 jobs in 2015.

Mining

Russia is the world's ninth largest producer of iron ore producing 105 million tonnes in 2014. It is also an important producer of asbestos, manganese ore, nickel, chromite, platinum group metals and potassium salts, and the third-largest producer of gold and fourth-largest producer of lead and phosphate ores. There are vast reserves, but extraction has been held back due to rising production costs, labour shortages and a shortage of technology.

Major foreign exchange earners include gold and diamonds. Estimated annual production of diamonds is 12,000 tonnes.

There are large deposits of antimony, beryllium, cadmium, mercury, molybdenum, tin and vanadium plus workable deposits of all rare earth metals.

Large-scale investment in the sector is improving extraction and processing techniques, while reducing wastage and controlling production costs. Gold production in 2013 totalled 254,241 tonnes, much of which originates in Russia's Sakha Republic (formerly Yakutia). This represents an increase in production of 12.6 per cent from 2008.

Hydrocarbons

Russia has large reserves of oil – 80 billion barrels in 2014, which was 5.4 per cent of the world's total. Production of crude oil in 2014 was10 million bpd and production of refined petroleum was 4.8 million bpd and with consumption of just 3.3 million bpd, it is the world's second largest oil exporter (10.5 per cent of total crude oil exports) after Saudi Arabia. Russia exports 4.6 million bpd of crude oil and 3 million bpd of refined petroleum.

Russia has 41 refineries with a total capacity of 5.5 million bpd, which require further development and investment to increase production, due to their inefficiency and ageing. Most exports of Russian oil are in the form of fuel oil and diesel and as domestic refineries concentrate on production for export, there is a shortfall of around 50 per cent in high-octane petroleum which must be imported.

The oil pipeline network bringing oil to markets in Europe and the Far East has grown significantly. The network began under the Soviet regime, running to CIS states and former Soviet states, but new markets have required an expansion and modernisation. Before the global financial crisis Russia was the principal shareholder in all pipeline projects but by 2008 when oil prices had fallen and money markets were not investing it was forced to barter oil for investment in new pipelines

In 2013, the world's second largest oil producing company, Lukoil, announced that its proven hydrocarbon reserves, as of 31 December 2012, were 17.3 billion barrels of oil equivalent, of which 13.4 billion barrels were oil with 656.6 million cubic metres of natural gas. Lukoil has ongoing projects in five other countries than Russia, however 90.6 per cent of the company's proven reserves are in Russia.

Russia's natural gas industry is dominated by Gazprom, which controls more than 95 per cent of Russia's gas production. Gazprom oversees eight production associations, operates Russia's 141,000km gas pipeline grid, runs trading houses and marketing joint ventures in many European countries and controls one-fifth of the world's natural gas reserves.

Russia also has the largest reserve of natural gas in the world – 47.8 trillion cubic metres (cum) (26 per cent of the world's total) in 2014, with production of 668 billion cum, of which 196 billion cum is exported via gas pipelines to Europe and CIS countries and exported as liquefied natural gas to Asia. There are major reserves of coal and electricity generation from hydro- and nuclear-power stations which constitutes enough energy to meet domestic demands.

Russia's share of global proven coal reserves was 18.2 per cent in 2013 which totals 157 billion tonnes, comprising sub-bituminous and lignite grade coal reserves of 108 billion tonnes and bituminous reserves of 49 billion tonnes. At current production levels, coal reserves in Russia could help support its coal needs for around 443 years. 84 per cent of coal reserves are spread across eastern Siberia and the far east of Russia. Russia is the world's sixth largest coal producer after China, the US, India, Australia and Indonesia

Energy

Russia is the fourth-largest generator of electricity in the world and the largest in Europe, with total installed capacity of 239GW in 2013. In the same year output was about 997 billion kWh, of which about 69 per cent is produced thermally, 21 per cent by hydropower and 11 per cent nuclear generation. Government policy is to expand nuclear generation and hydropower to allow greater exports of hydrocarbons. At current production levels coal reserves will last another 443 years.

Russia announced it will build 40 nuclear reactors by 2020 to prevent an energy crisis and, by July 2014, eight nuclear power plants were under construction, all destined to be operational between 2014–18.

Russia exports electricity to CIS states as well as China, Poland, Turkey and Finland.

Financial markets

Stock exchange

Moscow Interbank Currency Exchange (Micex)

Banking and insurance

Most major banks are located in Moscow. The majority of Russian banks suffer from being undercapitalised and the high rate of inflation has constantly eroded their reserves. This is not surprising given the high degree of fragmentation in the sector. The system has been criticised for having too many owner-operators; this is a situation with potential for abuse. The retail banking sector is still in its infancy and branch networking is not particularly common.

Foreign banks are not permitted to open their own branches in Russia and instead must rely upon subsidiaries, which drives up their costs. President Putin reiterated his opposition to direct foreign entry in December 2005. The US has protested this decision and has pointed out that Russia's desire to join the WTO will require banking liberalisation.

In June 2003, Russia was removed from the Organisation for Economic Co-operation and Development (OECD) black list of havens for money laundering.

Beginning 29 July 2004, the Central Bank revoked the licences for operations of three Moscow banks: the Commercial Bank of Savings, the Industrial Export-Import Bank and the Investment and Commercial Moscow Housing Construction Bank.

Central bank

Central Bank of the Russian Federation (Bank of Russia)

Main financial centre

Moscow

Time

The Russian Federation covers nine time zones, from GMT plus three hours to GMT plus 12 hours. The previous 11 time zones were reduced to nine in March 2010. Daylight saving was abolished from March 2011 (ie the last use of daylight saving was in March 2010). Domestically, Russia refers to Moscow standard time (MST).

Kaliningrad Oblast: GMT plus three hours (MST minus one).

Moscow and Samara: GMT plus four hours (MST)

Yekaterinburg: GMT plus six hours (MST plus two).

Tomsk and Novosibirsk: GMT plus seven hours (MST plus three).

Krasnoyarsk: GMT plus eight hours (MST plus four).

Irkutsk: GMT plus nine hours (MST plus five).

Yakutsk: GMT plus 10 hours (MST plus six).

Valdivostok and Sakhalin: GMT plus 11 hours (MST plus seven).

Magadan and Kamchatka Peninsula: GMT plus 12 hours (MST plus eight).

Geography

The Russian Federation is the largest country in the world at 17.07 million square km. Even European Russia (west of the Ural Mountains), which is only a quarter of the total landmass, dwarfs all other European countries. Major cities and towns are concentrated in western Russia, with the population thinning out to the far north and east.

Norway lies to the far north-west of Russia, with Finland, Estonia, and Latvia to the north. Belarus and Ukraine lie to the south-west of European Russia, the southern borders of which are with the Trans-Caucasian states of Georgia and Azerbaijan, and with Kazakhstan. In the north-west, near St Petersburg, there is a short coastline where there is access to the Baltic Sea via the gulf of Finland. Towards the south, European Russia has a coastline on the Black Sea in the south-west, with the Caspian Sea to the east. Beyond the Ural Mountains, the Siberian and Far Eastern regions have southern frontiers with the People's Republic of China, Mongolia, and in the south-east, North Korea. The eastern coastline is on the Sea of Japan, the Sea of Okhotsk, the Pacific Ocean and the Barents Sea. The northern coastline is on the Arctic Ocean. The region around Kaliningrad on the Baltic Sea is separated from the rest of the Russian Federation by Lithuania to the north and east, and has a coastline on the Baltic Sea.

The territory includes a wide variety of physical features. European Russia and western Siberia form a vast plain. Between the Black and Caspian Seas in the south, the land is more undulating, until it reaches the foothills of the Caucasus mountain range in the far south. The northern regions of both Asian and European Russia are inhospitable areas, much of the territory being covered by permafrost.

Europe's highest mountain, Elbrus (at 5,642 metres), is just on the Russian side of the Georgian border. Russia has Europe's longest river, the 3,690km Volga which rises north-west of Moscow and flows east before turning south to the Caspian Sea. The two largest lakes in Europe are also in Russia. Lake Ladoga (18,390 square km) and Lake Onega (9,600 square km) are both north-east of St Petersburg. Lake Baikal, located in the south-east in Siberia, at over 31,000 square km is the world's deepest and largest (by volume) freshwater lake, containing 20 per cent of the planet's liquid freshwater.

Hemisphere

Northern

Climate

The climate in Russia is extremely varied. The north is arctic, with an extensive zone of permafrost, but there are a few subtropical zones in the southern region of the country. The majority of the land mass is continental or moderate continental.

The Russian winter is deservedly famous: winter snow cover lasts as long as 160 days in St Petersburg.

Moscow has a warm spring with an average temperature of 18 degrees Celsius (C) in the period April to May. It is often hot in summer (June to August 20–30 degrees C), mild in autumn (September to October 10–15 degrees C) and freezing (down to minus 30 degrees C) for the rest of the year. Average annual rainfall is 575mm.

Average temperatures in the southern Siberian town of Irkutsk range from minus 21 degrees C in January to 18 degrees C in July. Average annual rainfall is 458mm, most of which falls in the summer. In the far north of Siberia, the average January temperature is minus 47 degrees C.

The far eastern region combines the extreme temperatures of Siberia with monsoon-type conditions common elsewhere in Asia. The mean temperature in January in the eastern port of Vladivostok is minus 14 degrees C; in August the average is 21 degrees C.

In the more moderate western portion of Russia, the average January temperature is slightly below zero. Summer is very hot in some areas. The snow in European Russia begins to melt in March and the muddy transition period demands waterproof footwear.

Dress codes

Dress well as business people are judged by their attire. Warm outer clothes, hats, gloves and footwear are essential in winter, although interiors are well heated.

The most important factor is neatness. Shoes should be polished and clothes pressed. Russians themselves do not always wear a suit and tie at business meetings, but it is wise to err on the safe side. Dark suits, white shirts and conservative ties are the norm, with business suits for women. Formal evening wear is not normally necessary. Summer dress is modest.

Entry requirements

Passports

Required by all.

Visa

Required by all. See www.rusemblon.org/ and follow link to application forms to download a visa form. US citizens should see www.russianembassy.org for further information. All travellers should check the general information links to see if the additional requirements affect them. All applications should be submitted to the closest Russian consulate.

Visitors must register their visas within three working days of arrival in Russia with the local branch of the ministry of the interior. Most major hotels will do this for their guests automatically. All visas are issued with an exit visa included.

Business travellers must include, with their application, a letter of invitation from the Russian foreign ministry or its regional representatives or ministry of the interior or its local offices. The letter must contain the official seal and legal address of the agency, a document registration number, date of registration, the signature and name of official authorised to issue invitations, and a travel itinerary with dates of stay and names of persons involved. A letter from an employer (or own letter if self-employed) giving personal details, a full itinerary, purpose of visit and a guarantee accepting full responsibility for any expenses incurred must also to be included. The right to request the submission of all original documents is reserved by the embassy, and multiple entry visas require original letters of invitation in all cases.

Currency advice/regulations

The import and export of local currency is prohibited. The import of foreign currency is unlimited up to US$10,000 (or equivalent), but amounts over US$3,000 must be declared. Export of foreign currency is limited to the amount declared on arrival.

It is illegal to exchange money anywhere except official exchange facilities; shops, hotels and restaurants may advertise dollar prices, but bills must be paid in roubles. It is advisable to retain all exchange receipts.

Travellers cheques have limited acceptance. Unmarked US dollar bills in good condition should be used for travel to more remote regions.

Customs

The customs declaration made on entry must be retained for exit, this allows for personal items, such as jewellery, cameras, computers and musical instruments to remain duty-free.

Retain all shop receipts and certificates of money exchange for customs formalities on exit.

In 2006, 250g caviar per person was allowed for export, with proof of purchase from licensed purveyors.

Prohibited imports

Firearms, ammunition, illegal drugs, precious metals and furs, radio, electrical items, fruit and vegetables, sturgeon and sturgeon products and photographic and printed material that vilifies the Russian Federation.

Live animals, antiques and works of art require permits.

Health (for visitors)

Advisable precautions

Inoculations and boosters should be current for tetanus, hepatitis A and diphtheria. There may be a need for vaccinations for typhoid, tuberculosis, hepatitis B and meningitis (Moscow only).

Visitors to Asian and far-eastern provinces may need vaccinations for Japanese B encephalitis and cholera. There is a risk of rabies.

Water precautions outside main cities are recommended (purification tablets may be useful or use bottled or boiled water for drinks, washing teeth and making ice – especially in St Petersburg, where the water supply may be infected by giardia).

Mosquito repellents and long clothing will help avoid hepatitis B and Japanese B encephalitis; there is a risk of HIV/Aids.

Russian medical care is not up to Western standards and medical insurance, including emergency evacuation, is necessary. A travel kit including a disposable syringe is a reasonable precaution. A supply of any regular medicines required should be taken, with their prescription details and it could be wise to have precautionary antibiotics if going outside major urban centres.

Hotels

Moscow has an increasing number of Western-run hotels. Accommodation is difficult to obtain in Moscow at short notice. It is crucial to make bookings in advance as hotels refuse to check in a guest without a reservation. First-class and tourist class are available, with all prices fixed by Intourist. Main hotels have foreign currency restaurants and bars. Tipping is increasingly common, typically 10 per cent.

Credit cards

Credit cards are not widely accepted outside Moscow and St Petersburg. ATMs are widely available.

Public holidays (national)

Fixed dates

1–10 Jan (New Year Holidays), 23 Feb (Defender's Day), 8 Mar (Women's Day), 1 May (Labour Day), 9 May (Victory Day), 12 Jun (Russia Day), 4 Nov (National Unity Day).

Days *in lieu* are given for holidays that occur at the weekend, usually at the beginning of the following week.

Variable dates

Russian Orthodox Christmas

Working hours

Banking

Mon–Fri: 0930–1730.

Business

Mon–Fri: 0900–1800 (appointments best between 0900–1000).

Shops

Mon–Sat: 0900–1900.

Telecommunications

Mobile/cell phones

There are limited 900, 1800, 900/1800 GSM services available in Moscow, St Petersburg and other major cities.

Electricity supply

220V AC

Social customs/useful tips

A firm handshake is important as is negotiating an agenda at the beginning of the meeting. Smoking in meetings is very common. Ask permission before lighting a cigarette and offer cigarettes generously.
Written communications are particularly important with large bureaucracies. Address the recipient formally and keep a copy of everything.
It is customary to take a small gift on a business or social visit. Offering basic food is considered insulting. Offer little luxuries.
It is impolite to take along people who are not invited to a social function. If you are offered a second helping of caviar, resist the temptation and refuse. The offer will be made again, but it is polite to refuse the first time.
Many Russians take certain superstitions somewhat seriously. Do not give an even number of flowers, for example, as this is for funerals only; do not greet people in a doorway – it is considered unlucky.
Although homosexuality was decriminalised in Russia in 1993, anti-gay sentiment remained high in 2013. A law passed by the Duma on 11 June 2013 means that private individuals promoting 'homosexual behaviour among minors' could face fines of up to 5,000 roubles (US$155), officials could be fined 10 times that amount and businesses and schools up to 500,000 roubles.

Security

The normal precautions should be taken when visiting Russia – avoid showing large amounts of cash or expensive personal belongings. Avoid travelling alone at night in Moscow and St Petersburg, particularly on the metro.

Getting there

Air

National airline: Aeroflot – Russian Airlines

International airport/s: Moscow-Sheremetyevo International (SVO), 29km north-west of city centre; St Petersburg-Pulkovo (LED), 17km from city. Both airports have duty-free shops, banks, *bureau de change*, restaurants.
Taxis, to Moscow city centre (journey time 30–40 minutes) and fixed route and buses are available. There are scheduled express coaches and trains to other destinations.
There are taxis to St Petersburg (journey time 10 minutes) as well as buses.

Airport tax: None

Surface

Road: Major European highways connect Moscow via Kiev (Ukraine), Minsk (Belarus), Riga (Latvia), Warsaw (Poland) and Scandinavia to St Petersburg via Helsinki (Finland). The Verkhny Lars-Kazbegi border checkpoint between Georgia and Russia, which had been closed in July 2006, was reopened in March 2010.

Rail: The Russian/CIS rail network (around 87,079km) extends to all Russian Federation countries. The main European rail services are through Germany including a sleeper service from Cologne to Moscow and the *Mockva Express* via Berlin-Warsaw-Moscow.
Through-trains are also available from other Western and Eastern European cities and from Turkey, Iran, and the *Trans-Siberian Express* from Mongolia and China.

Water: There are sea links from Finland, Norway, Sweden and Germany and from the Ukraine in the west. In the east, a weekly ferry runs between Vladivostok and Niigata-Fushiki in Japan.

Main port/s: Vladivostok, Magadan, Nakhodka, St Petersburg and Kaliningrad. Links to the Atlantic are provided by the Murmansk (Arctic Ocean) and Archangelisk ports (during summer months only).

Getting about

National transport

Air: There is an extensive internal air service which provides the only viable option for travelling between cities. Domestic services are operated by Aeroflot and Transaero (due to a small fleet, flights are more often delayed than those of Aeroflot). Sky Express, a budget airline, began operations in early 2007. It will initially fly between Moscow and Sochi on the Black Sea, charging US$19, compared to Aeroflot's rate of US$120.
The internal air network centres around Moscow. Domestic airports include Vnukovo (VKO), 29km south-west of city; Domodedovo (DME), 40km south-east of city and Irkutsk (IRK), 7km from city.

Road: Distances between major cities are extensive: Moscow to St Petersburg 692km (432 miles); Moscow to Odessa 1,347km (837 miles). Approximately 60 per cent of the road network needs to be rehabilitated or upgraded. In general the few roads connecting with Siberia are impassable during winter. Secondary roads are often untarred.

Buses: Long-distance coach services operate.

Rail: Rail is the major means of transport. There is a cheap and efficient service to all major towns. There is an extensive network of commuter and inter-city services, most offering first and second class seats or accommodation.
The rolling stock needs modernising and trains are typically over-crowded and over-booked. Food is often available on inter-city services but, because of the generally poor quality, most passengers bring their own. Many carriages have a samovar which produces hot water for drinks.
Security can be a problem, especially on overnight services. The famous Trans-Siberian railway stretches from Moscow to Vladivostok.
The railways are wide gauge. Almost all the rail network is electrified. Sleepers should be booked well in advance.

Water: Rivers play an important role in transport; in summer it is possible to travel great distances either by cruises or river passenger boats. Routes include: St Petersberg-Astrakhan on the Caspian sea, and St Petersberg-Rostov-on-Don on the Black Sea. These routes may include detours via Moscow.
The largest inland waterway is the River Volga. There are a number of inland ports and canals.

City transport

Taxis: Use only officially marked taxis and do not share them with strangers. Taxis are yellow with a checkerboard stripe and a green light at the top right hand corner of the windscreen indicating availability; they can be hired at taxi ranks or by booking in advance. Beware of illegal taxi touts operating at both the airport and city centre.
Tariffs for foreigners are often subject to negotiation and may be charged in hard currency.
It is possible to find a reliable taxi firm in the airport arrivals section at Moscow airport. Payment is by credit card though fares may have to be negotiated with the driver as the fare shown on the meter may not correspond with the fare asked. Arrangements to be met at the airport in advance can be made by contacting Intourist, or telephoning Moscow Taxi (tel: 238-1001).

Buses, trams & metro: Cheap and reliable, though often crowded, available from 0600–0100. Bus services 5817 and 551 from Moscow airport to the city centre operate between 0500–2359 every 10 minutes, with a journey time of 30–45 minutes. Long distance coach services operate.

Trains: An express train service from Moscow airport to the city centre operates every 30 minutes.

Car hire

Available in major towns. International driving licence required with Russian translation of details. Notification of route

to be taken should be given if travelling outside main cities.
Visitors travelling in private cars should be in possession of their passport and visa, and an itinerary card complete with visitor's name and citizenship and car registration number.
Traffic drives on the right. Speeds are limited to 60kph (37mph) in built-up areas and 90kph (55mph) elsewhere. Cars are required to display registration plates and stickers denoting the country of registration.

BUSINESS DIRECTORY

The addresses listed below are a selection only. While World of Information makes every endeavour to check these addresses, we cannot guarantee that changes have not been made, especially to telephone numbers and area codes. We would welcome any corrections.

Telephone area codes

The international direct dialling code (IDD) for Russia is +7, followed by the area code and subscriber's number:

Chelyabinsk	3512	St Petersburg	812
Ekaterinberg	3432	Smolensk	481
Kaliningrad	401	Tula	487
Moscow	495	Vladivostok	4232
Nizhny Novgorod	8312	Yakutsk	41122

Useful telephone numbers

International operator: (English-speaking operator): 8196
General enquiries (Moscow area): 09
Police: 02
Fire: 01
Ambulance: 03

Chambers of Commerce

American Chamber of Commerce in Russia, 7 Dolgorukovskaya Street, Moscow 127006 (tel: 961-2141; fax: 961-2142; e-mail: info@amcham.ru).

Moscow Chamber of Commerce and Industry, 22 Akademika Pilyugina Street, Moscow 117393 (tel: 132-7510; fax: 132-0547; e-mail: mtpp@mtpp.org).

Nizhny Novgorod Region Chamber of Commerce and Industry, 1 Oktyabrskaya Square, Nizhny Novgorod 603005 (tel: 194-210; fax:194-009; e-mail: tpp@rda.nnov.ru).

Russian Federation Chamber of Commerce and Industry, 6 Ilyinka Street, Moscow 109012 (tel: 929-0009; fax: 929-0360; e-mail: tpprf@tpprf.ru).

St Petersburg Chamber of Commerce and Industry, 46-48 Chaikovsky Street, St Petersburg 191194 (tel: 279-2833; fax: 272-6406; e-mail: spbcci@spbcci.ru).

South Ural Chamber of Commerce and Industrym 63 Vasenko Street, Chelyabinsk 454080 (tel: 661-816; fax: 665-223; e-mail: mail@tpp.chelreg.ru).

Smolensk Chamber of Commerce and Industry, 12 Karl Marx Street, Smolensk 214000 (tel: 554-142; fax: 237-450; e-mail: smolcci@keytown.com).

Tula Chamber of Commerce and Industry, 25 Krasnoarmeisky Prospekt, Tula 300600 (tel: 364-517; fax: 360-216; e-mail: tulacci@tula.net).

Banking

Agropromstraybank, Krasina Per, 123056 Moscow (tel: 254-4263; fax: 254-7081).
Gazprombank, Nametkina Str 16B, 117420 Moscow (tel: 719-1697/17; fax; 719-1763).

ING Bank Eurasia, ul Krasnaya Presnya 31, 125178 Moscow (tel: 755-5400; fax: 755-5459; fax: 755-5499).

Sberbank (savings bank), Vavilova Str 18, 117817 Moscow (tel: 971-4981, 957-5690, 957-5862; fax: 957-5731; internet site: http://www.sbrf.ru).

SDM Bank, 73 Volokolamskoe Shosse, 123424 Moscow (tel: 490-1545, 491-7572, 490-0703; fax: 490-6509).

United Export Import Bank (UNEXIM), 11 Masha Paryvaeva Street, PO Box 207, 107078 Moscow (tel: 232-3727; fax: 975-2205; e-mail: mailbox@mail.unexim.ru).

Vnesheconombank (Bank for Foreign Economic Affairs), Akademika Sakharova Prospekt 9, 107996 Moscow (tel: 207-1037).

Vneshtorgbank (Bank for Foreign Trade), Kuznetskiy Most Str 16, 103031 Moscow (tel: 929-8900; fax: 956-3727).

Central bank

Central Bank of the Russian Federation, 12 Neglinnaya Sreet, 107016 Moscow (tel: 771-9100; fax: 921-6465; e-mail: webmaster@www.cbr.ru).

Stock exchange

Moscow Interbank Currency Exchange (Micex), www.micex.com

Russian Trading System, www.rts.ru

Moscow Stock Exchange (MSE), www.mse.ru

St Petersburg Stock Exchange, www.spbex.ru

Travel information

Aeroflot, 37/9 Leningradsky Prospect, Moscow 125836 (tickets and enquiries, tel: 223-5555; fax: 186-2092; internet: www.aeroflot.ru/eng/).

Intourist, 150, Prospect Mira, Moscow 129366 (tel: 956-4207; fax: 730-1957; email: info@intourist.ru; internet: www.intourist.com/ENG/).

Russian National Group, Suite 214, 5/10 Chistoprudni Blvd, Moscow (tel: 980-8440; 980-8441; internet: www.russia-travel.com).

JSC Russian Railways (JSCo RZD), Novaya Basmannaya 2, 107174 Moscow (tel: 262-9901; email: info@rzd.ru; internet: www.eng.rzd.ru).

Ministries

Ministry of Agriculture and Food, 1-11 Orlikov Lane, Moscow 107139 (tel: 207-8000; fax: 207-8362, 288-9580).

Ministry of Atomic Energy, 24-26 Bolshaya Ordynka Str, Moscow 101100 (tel: 239-4753; fax: 233-4679).

Ministry for Civil Defence, Emergencies and Disaster Resources, 3 Teatralniy Pr-D, Moscow 103012 (tel: 926-3901; fax: 924-5683).

Ministry for Communications, 7 Tverskaya Str, Moscow 119332 (tel: 229-6966, 292-7070; fax: 292-7128).

Ministry of Construction, Comp 2, 8 Stroitelei Str, Moscow 117987 (tel: 930-1755; fax: 938-2202).

Ministry for Co-operation Between CIS Member Countries, 7 Varvarka Str, Moscow 103073 (tel: 206-1365; fax: 206-1084).

Ministry of Culture, 7 Kitaiskiy Pr-D, Moscow 103693 (tel: 925-1195; fax: 928-1791).

Ministry of Economics, 19 Noviy Arbat Str, Moscow 103025 (tel: 203-7534; fax: 203-7482).

Ministry of Education, 6 Chistoprudniy B-R, Moscow 101856 (tel: 927-0568; fax: 924-6989).

Ministry for Environmental Protection and Natural Resources, 4-6 B Gruzinskaya Str, Moscow 123812 (tel: 254-7683; fax: 254-8283).

Ministry of Finance, 9 Ilyinka str, Moscow 103097 (tel: 298-9101, 923-0967; fax: 925-0889).

Ministry of Foreign Affairs, 32-34 Smolenskaya-Sennaya Sq, Moscow 121200 (tel: 244-1606; fax: 230-2130).

Ministry for Foreign Economic Relations, 32-34 Smolenskaya-Sennaya Sq, Moscow 121200 (tel: 244-2450; fax: 244-3068/3981).

Ministry for Fuel and Power Development, 7 Kitaiskiy Pr, Moscow 103074 (tel: 220-5500; fax: 220-4818).

Ministry of the Interior, 16 Zhitnaya Str, Moscow 117049 (tel: 237-7585, 924-6572, 222-6669; fax: 925-2098).

Ministry of Justice, 4 Vorontsovo Pole Str, Moscow 109830 (tel: 209-6009/98; fax: 916-2903).

Ministry of Labour, 1 Birzhevaya Sq, Moscow 103706 (tel: 261-2030, 928-8208; fax: 230-2407).

Ministry for Nationalities and Regional Policy, 19 Trubnikovskiy Lane, Moscow 121819 (tel: 248-8635; fax: 202-4490).

Ministry of Public Health, 3 Rakhmanovskiy Lane, Moscow 103051 (tel: 928-4478; fax: 921-0128).

Ministry for Railways, 2 Novo-Basmannaya Str, Moscow 107174 (tel: 262-9901; fax: 262-9095).

Ministry for Science and Technology, 11 Tverskaya Str, Moscow 103905 (tel: 229-1192; fax: 230-2823).

Ministry for Social Protection, Bld 1, 4 Slavianskaya Sq, Moscow 103715 (tel: 220-9511/9384; fax: 924-3690).

Ministry of Transport, 10 Sadovo-Samotyochnaya Str, Moscow 101433 (tel: 200-0809; fax: 200-3356).

Other useful addresses

British Consulate, Sfoskaya Nberezhnaya 14, Moscow (tel: 956-7420; fax: 956-7420).

British Consulate, St Petersburg, Pl Proletarsky, Dikatury 5, 193124 St Petersburg (tel: 325-6036; fax: 325-6037; e-mail: uk.stpet@vmail.sprint.com).

British Consulate for Southern Russia, Petrak, 3a Fabrichnaya Street, Novorossisk (tel: 93-319; fax: 34-959).

British Embassy, Kutuzovsky Prospekt 7/4, Moscow 121248 (tel: 956-7200, 956-7477; fax: 956-7480, 956-7420; e-mail: uk.moscw@vmail.sprint.com).

British Trade Office, 4th Floor, 15a Gogol Street, Ekaterinburg 620151 (tel: 564-931; fax: 592-901; e-mail: uk.ekate@vmail.sprint.com).

BSCC British-Russian Business Centre, 42 Southwark Street, London SE1 1UN (tel: (+44-(0)171) 403-1706; fax: (+44-(0)171) 403-1245); 22/25 Bolshoi Strochenovskiy Pereulok, Moscow 113054 (tel: 230-6120; fax: 230-6124).

Delegation of the European Union (Office of), 2/10 Astakhovsky Pereulok, Moscow 109208 (tel: 956-3600; fax: 956-3615).

Expocentr, 1a Sokolnicheskiy val, Moscow 107113 (tel: 268-7083) (responsibility for organising, on a commercial basis, international and foreign exhibitions and symposia).

Foreign Investment Promotion Centre (FIPC), Ul Novy Arbat 19, 119898 Moscow (tel: 203-4863; internet site: www.fipc.ru/fipc/).

Foreign Trade Arbitration Commission, Moscow (tel: 205-6855).

Government of St. Petersburg, Smolny, 193060 St Petersburg (tel 576-4501; fax: 576-7827; internet: http://eng.gov.spb.ru).

Interstate Statistical Committee of the Commonwealth of Independent States, 39 Myasnitskaya Str, Moscow 103450 (tel: 207-4237/4802/4567; fax: 207-4592; e-mail: Statpro@Sovam.com).

Russian Federation Embassy (USA), 2650 Wisconsin Avenue, NW, Washington DC 2007 (tel: (+1-202) 298-5700; fax: (+1-202) 298-5735; e-mail: russ-amb@cerfnet.com).

Russian Federation Foreign Trade Organisation, Barrikabnaya Str Bld 8-5, 123242 Moscow (tel: 254-8090; fax: 253-9675).

Russian Information Telegraph Agency (ITAR-TASS) (news agency), Tverskoy bul 10, Moscow (tel: 3229-8053).

Russian Television and Radio, Corolov St 12, Moscow (tel: 217-7898; fax: 288-9508).

State Committee for Statistics, 39 Myasnitskaya Street, Moscow 103450 (tel: 207-4902; fax: 207-4640).

TACIS Technical Assistance Centre, 165 Nemirovicha-Danchenko, Novosibirsk 630087 (tel: 465-395, 464-836; fax: 464-426; e-mail: centre@tac.sib.ru).

US Consulate, St Petersburg (tel: 275-1701).

National news agency: Itar-Tass News Agency, 10–12 Tvershoy Blvd, Moscow 125993 (email: info@itar-tass.com; internet: www.tass-online.ru).

RIA Novosti, 4 Zubovsky Blvd, Moscow 119031 (tel: 637-2424; internet: http://en.rian.ru).

Interfax, 2 Pervaya Tverskaya-Yamskaya Ul, Building 1, Moscow 127006 (tel: 250-9840; fax: 250-9727; internet: www.interfax.ru).

Internet sites

Moscow Guide: www.moscow-guide.ru

Rusline (government information, company directories): www.rusline.com

Russian tourism: www.visitrussia.com

Russian travel: www.realrussia.com

Russian web portal: www.ru

Rwanda

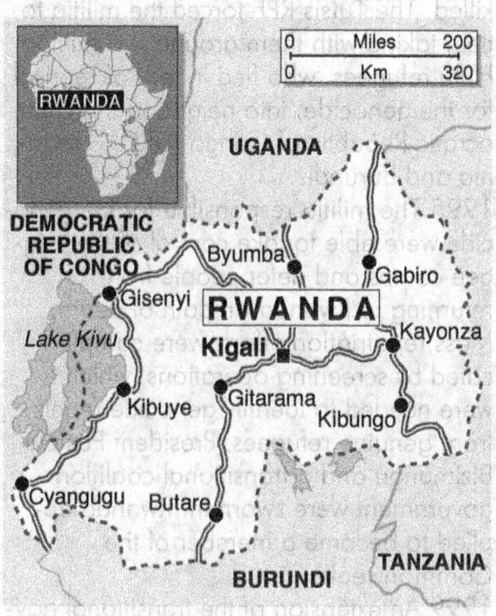

In October 2014 Rwanda suspended British Broadcasting Corporation (BBC) broadcasts in the Kinyarwanda language after a documentary was released questioning the official accounts of the 1994 genocide. By February 2015 this had escalated as Rwanda called for criminal and civil proceedings against the BBC. The British broadcaster rejected the inquiry's findings, and relations with Britain began to sharply deteriorate. In June 2015 the intelligence chief Karenzi Karake, was arrested in London on a Spanish warrant over genocide. The last hearings of the International Criminal Tribunal for Rwanda were held in April 2015, 10 years and 93 convictions after being opened.

Rwanda's impressive economic growth over the previous decade has imparted benefits beyond expectations to its people. Perhaps the most significant of these is that of life expectancy – doubling in the twenty years following 1994. The percentage of children dying before they even reached their fifth birthday was less than 55 per thousand in 2012 – in 1995 it had been 253 per 1,000. Sadly, in 2014 it had become clear that the future path that most educated Rwandans expected their country to follow – one in which their leader since the 1990s, Paul Kagame, stepped aside in favour of a democratically appointed successor, was not to be. Rumours abounded that Mr Kagame was – very much *à la Mode Africaine* – planning constitutional changes to permit him to stay in power for a further term. The likelihood seemed, at best, remote.

Never the less, major steps have been taken to further enhance political rights and civil liberties. Three new pieces of legislation were ratified to improve media regulation, promote transparency and encourage citizens' economic and political participation. Moreover, another political party was formally registered. Strong progress in human development continued to be registered. The infant mortality Millenium Development Goal (MDG) had been achieved and Rwanda was set to meet the targets for universal primary education, gender equality and under-five mortality. Poverty and income inequality had also all decreased.

Foreign, unfriendly, relations

If President Kagame's governmental style at home could be described as assertive, regionally it was seen by many as one of clumsy intervention. In 2012, a United Nations (UN) report had accused Mr Kagame's government of backing a rebel group in eastern Democratic Republic of Congo, prompting the West to halt some aid; economic growth took a hit. On top of this incident, Rwanda was also blamed for sending hit squads to assassinate opponents in South Africa, killing one of two alleged targets. Quoted by Reuters, a western diplomat said that 'It seems to me that they are getting less risk averse, the risk they run is sowing the seed for rupture with the international community.'

The economy

In its *African Economic Outlook* report, the African Development Bank (AfDB) noted that real GDP grew by 7.0 per cent in 2014, higher than the projected 6.0 per cent and the 4.7 per cent of 2013. This was despite a downturn in mining, manufacturing and construction which led to a slower growth in industry. The AfDB expects short- and medium- term growth to continue being driven by public and private investments, and a recovery in agriculture and services. A public investment programme targeted at transport and

KEY FACTS

Official name: Republika y'u Rwanda (Republic of Rwanda)

Head of State: President Paul Kagame (FPR) (elected 2000; re-elected Aug 2010)

Head of government: Prime Minister Anastase Murekezi (from 24 Jul 2014)

Ruling party: Coalition led by Front Patriotique Rwandais (FPR) (Rwandan Patriotic Front) (Tutsi-dominated) with six other political parties (elected 2003; re-elected Sep 2008 and Sep 2013)

Area: 26,338 square km

Population: 11.10 million (2014)*

Capital: Kigali

Official language: Kinyarwanda, French and English.

Currency: Rwanda franc (Rwf)

Exchange rate: Rwf729.08 per US$ (Sep 2015)

GDP per capita: US$722 (2014)*

GDP real growth: 7.01% (2014)

GDP: US$8.01 billion (2014)

Inflation: 1.78% (2014)

Balance of trade: -US$1.15 billion (2013)

Annual FDI: US$160.00 million (2011)

* estimated figure

energy infrastructure is in motion in order to ease bottlenecks and support economic growth.

The report mentioned that headline inflation is projected to converge around the Banque Nationale du Rwanda (central bank)'s medium term 5 per cent target over 2015 and 2016. Lower international food and oil prices will be an aid in achieving this and are expected to continue subduing inflationary pressures. Export earnings accounted for only 25 per cent of imports in both 2013 and 2014, meaning the current account deficit persists.

Rwanda has a highly rural population – 83.0 per cent live in rural areas. Almost three quarters of the population are still engaged in subsistence farming. The Economic Development and Poverty Reduction Strategy 2 (EDPRS 2) 2013–18, according to the AfDB, calls for expanding targeted economic zones and transferring Rwanda's logistics system in order to promote exports. The Kivu-Belt Tourism Master Plan is another measure in place to aid economic development. The report notes that progress has been made in promoting spatial inclusion, with most of rural households involved in integrated and economically viable planned settlements increasing from 37.5 per cent in 2012 to 53.0 per cent in 2014.

Risk assessment

Politics	Fair
Economy	Good/fair
Regional stability	Fair

COUNTRY PROFILE

1899 Rwanda, which for a long time had been an independent monarchy, was absorbed into German East Africa.

1916 It was taken over by Belgium, along with what is now Burundi.

1918 After the First World War ended, the two became Ruanda-Urundi, a Belgian-administered trust territory of the League of Nations (and later, the UN).

1950s Belgium had generally favoured the minority Tutsis as their Rwandan auxiliaries. They flourished and became more educated and prosperous than the majority Hutus. However, it was the Tutsis who agitated for independence after the Second World War and the Belgians switched their allegiance, promoting the Hutus, thereby laying the seeds of the genocide to follow. Belgian missionaries also encouraged the formation of a modern Hutu identity.

1959–63 Vengeful Hutus killed some 15,000 people, mainly Tutsis. Some 100,000 Tutsis fled, mainly to Uganda and Burundi.

1961 Rwanda's monarchy was abolished and a republic was proclaimed.

1962 Independence was granted. Belgium pulled out of the region.

1973 President Gregoire Kayibanda, was overthrown by Major General Juvenal Habyarimana. Habyarimana began a regime that stripped the Tutsis of their wealth and status; an estimated one million fled the country. The Front Patriotique Rwandais (Rwandan Patriotic Front) (RPF) was formed from this group, aiming to invade Rwanda and overthrow Habyarimana.

1990 Some 10,000 rebel Tutsi guerrillas the (RPF) invaded Rwanda from Uganda and occupied several towns.

1993 President Habyarimana signed a power-sharing agreement with the Tutsis (the Arusha Accord). A UN mission was sent to monitor the agreement.

1994 The death of Habyarimana when the plane in which he was travelling was shot down on 6 April (also killing Cyprien Ntaryamira, president of Burundi, who was travelling with him), triggered the breakdown of civil society. Extremist Hutu militia began the systematic murder of Tutsis. Within four months an estimated 800,000 Tutsis and moderate Hutus were killed. The Tutsis RPF forced the militia to flee, taking with them around two million Hutu refugees, who fled in fear of reprisal for the genocide, into neighbouring Democratic Republic of Congo (DRC), Tanzania and Burundi.

1995 The militia responsible for the genocide were able to take control of the refugee camps and deter people from returning to Rwanda on pain of death. Mass repatriation efforts were complicated by screening operations, which were needed to identify genocide rebels from genuine refugees. President Pasteur Bizimungu and a transitional coalition government were sworn in. Rwanda applied to become a member of the Commonwealth.

1999 An extension of the transitional government's term of office was approved.

2000 Pasteur Bizimungu resigned and Paul Kagame was officially elected president (the first Tutsi to hold presidential office since Rwanda's independence in 1961) in a joint vote of the Rwandan legislature and cabinet. Ethnic Hutu, Bernard Makuza, was appointed prime minister.

2001 A peace agreement was signed between Rwanda and Uganda. A new national flag, emblem and anthem were unveiled. *Gacaca*) courts, based on traditional courts, were set up to try those accused of involvement in the genocide. The accused were classified by four categories: planners, authors, perpetrators of human deaths and perpetrators of property theft. The *gacaca*) courts sat in mostly rural areas and tried local inhabitants accused of relatively low level crimes.

2002 Rwanda and DRC signed a peace agreement.

2003 In a referendum, voters approved a new, more democratic constitution. Incumbent Paul Kagame won the presidential elections and the ruling party, FPR, won the parliamentary elections.

2004 Kagame denied he ordered the attack on the president's plane in 1994 which had sparked the genocide. Former president Bizimungu was sentenced to 15 years imprisonment for embezzlement and inciting violence.

2005 The Forces Democratiques de Liberation du Rwanda (FDLR) (Democratic Liberation Forces of Rwanda) declared a cease-fire. A mass release of 36,000 prisoners took place as part of the process of

KEY INDICATORS — Rwanda

	Unit	2011	2012	2013	2014	**2015
Population	m	*10.21	10.42	*10.80	*11.10	*11.40
Gross domestic product (GDP)	US$bn	6.20	7.10	7.52	8.01	*8.76
GDP per capita	US$	605	682	696	*722	*769
GDP real growth	%	8.8	7.7	4.7	7.0	*7.0
Inflation	%	5.7	6.3	4.2	1.8	*2.9
Exports (fob) (goods)	US$m	464.2	590.7	703.0	–	–
Imports (fob) (goods)	US$m	1,578.9	1,967.0	1,851.5	–	–
Balance of trade	US$m	-1,114.7	-1,376.2	-1,148.4	–	–
Current account	US$m	-463.0	-813.0	-538.0	-964.0	*-922.0
Total reserves minus gold	US$m	752.4	847.8	1,070.5	–	–
Foreign exchange	US$m	619.1	721.1	945.3	–	–
Exchange rate	per US$	599.65	628.33	675.00	689.00	–

* estimated figure ** forecast figure

reconciliation; many had confessed to acts of genocide.
2006 The country's 12 administrative provinces were replaced by a larger number of ethnically-diverse districts. Roman Catholic priest, Fr Athanase Seromba, was convicted of involvement in the genocide by the International Criminal Tribunal for Rwanda (ICTR), and sentenced to 15 years imprisonment. Relations with France deteriorated as a French judge investigating the shooting down of President Juvénal Habyarimana's plane in 1994 and the killing of its French crew, accused President Kagame and nine top officials with involvement in the assassination. The president has immunity from prosecution as head of state and he strenuously denied the RPF were responsible for the death of the former president. A counter claim by Rwandan officials accused French authorities of attempting to divert international attention away from French collaboration in the Hutu regime responsible for the genocide. The Mouvement Démocratique Républicain (MDR) (Democratic Republican Movement) was banned following allegations that it promoted genocide ideology.
2007 The Communaute Economique des Pays des Grands Lacs (CEPGL) (Great Lakes Countries Economic Community) was re-launched by Burundi, DRC and Rwanda. CEPGL is intended to promote regional economic co-operation and integration. President Kagame pardoned former president Pasteur Bizimungu. The death penalty was repealed. The traditional *Gacaca* courts trying genocide suspects, had their mandate extended into 2007. Rwanda became a full member of the East African Community (EAC).
2008 Accusations and counter-accusations of who was responsible for the 1994 genocide broke out between Rwanda and France following the acquittal by a French Appeals court of two men said to have played crucial roles in the slaughter – one a former priest and the other a former provincial governor. At the same time arrest warrants were issued in France for senior aides to President Kagame, accused of responsibility for the aeroplane crash of former president Habyarimana. In parliamentary elections the ruling FPR (predominately ethnic Tutsi) won 78.8 per cent (42 seats out of 53 directly elected seats), the opposition (predominately ethnic Hutu) Parti Social Démocrate (Social Democratic Party) (SDP) won 13.1 per cent (7 seats); turnout was 96.5 per cent. The ICTR, convicted former army general Theoneste Bagosora of inciting the 1994 genocide and sentenced him to life in prison; Bagosora and two co-defendants had led a Hutu committee that organised the massacre of ethnic Tutsis. He had also set up the *Interahamwe* (gangs of Hutu extremists), which carried out much of the killings.
2009 Rwandan government troops crossed into DRC in a joint military operation to eliminate Rwandan Hutu militia, exiled in DRC since 1994 and causing widespread mayhem in DRC's eastern province, and generally destabilising the region. Former general and rebel leader Laurent Nkunda was arrested in Rwanda, having fled his stronghold in Bunagana (DRC). The Tanzanian-based ICTR, found Callixte Kalimanzira guilty of genocide and sentenced him to 30 years in jail. He had been interior minister and a close ally of then president, Bizimungu. The defence ministry announced that Rwanda was free of unexploded ordnance (UXO), after it completed a de-mining campaign ahead of the 2010 deadline set by the Ottawa Convention. Rwanda was admitted as a member of the Commonwealth of Nations.
2010 French President Nicolas Sarkozy made an historic visit to Rwanda and acknowledged that France had made 'serious errors of judgement' during the 1994 genocide; but he did not voice an apology. Transparency International, the Berlin-based anti-corruption watch-dog, included Rwanda in its East African bribery survey for the first time, where it scored best in East Africa with a prevalence of 6.6 per cent. Critics said this was because Rwanda was a police state. Four candidates took part in presidential elections. Incumbent Paul Kagame (FPR) won with 93.1 per cent of the vote while his closest rival, Jean Ntawukuriryayo (SDP), won 5.1 per cent; turnout was 97.5 per cent.
2011 Joseph Habineza, minister for youth and sport, resigned in February following allegations of improper behaviour after photographs taken in 2008 appeared on the internet. In May the ICTR, in Arusha found former army chief Augustin Bizimungu guilty of genocide and sentenced him to 30 years in prison. Augustin Ndindiliyimana was found guilty at the same time, but while Bizimungu was said to have been in 'complete' control of the men he commanded, Ndindiliyimana had only 'limited control' and was given a lesser prison sentence of 12 years. President Kagame appointed Bernard Makuza as a senator and replaced him as prime minister with Pierre Habumuremyi, who took office in October.
2012 On 28 May, the UN revealed evidence that Rwanda was supporting the rebellion in the eastern region of DRC through the training of troops in Rwanda and supplying some recruits (a number of which was deemed under-aged) to the insurgency. The government denied the charge. On 31 May the former youth minister; Callixte Nzabonimana, was convicted of genocide, conspiracy, incitement and extermination of Tutsis during the massacres of 1994. He was given a life sentence of imprisonment. The (*gacaca*) courts, set up in 2001 to administer community justice locally to those considered to be involved in the genocide, were terminated in June. Around 120,000 in total accused persons were tried by these courts. On 15 July the AU brokered an agreement between DRC and Rwanda to allow a neutral, international force to patrol their mutual border and tackle the militia forces active in the region. In November, Rwanda was voted as one of the top-ten destinations for adventure holidays in 2013, according to *Globe Spots* (an international travel guide).
2013 The RPF won a landslide victory of 76 per cent (40 out of 53 seats) in the directly elected portion of parliamentary elections held on 16 September.
2014 Augustin Ndindiliyimana, who had been found guilty of genocide by the ICTR in 2011, was acquited on appeal in February. The Court found he had only 'limited' control over his troops. Gen Bizimungu, who had also been found guilty in 2011 and sentenced to a heavier term of 30 years, still awaits the outcome of his appeal. A memorial service commemorating the 100 days of slaughter in which some 800,000 people were killed in 1984 took place in Kigali on 7 April. President Kagame lit a flame at the Amahoro Stadium, to last 100 days, after laying a wreath at the national genocide memorial.
2015 In July parliament voted in favour of changing the constitution to allow Mr Kagame to stay on for a third term. A constitutional commission was set up to debate the issue and on 28 October parliament voted to allow the constitutional change which will now have to be voted on in a national referendum.

Political structure

Constitution

A new 2003 constitution prevents a one-party dominance of the political system and bans incitement to racial hatred. It stipulates that no party can hold more than 50 per cent of the seats in cabinet, even if it secures an absolute majority in parliamentary elections.
It prevents a Tutsi or Hutu dominated government forming and restricts presidential terms to seven years.
The president, prime minister and president of the lower house cannot belong to the same party.

Form of state

Republic

The executive
The president is eligible for election for a maximum of two seven-year terms. Candidates must be Rwandan and over 35 years of age. Election is by universal suffrage with a simple majority of votes cast. The president effectively acts as both head of state and head of government and wields vast powers.
National legislature
The bicameral Inteko Ishinga Amategeko (Parlement) (parliament) consists of a lower and upper chambers. The Umutwe w'Abadepite (Chambre des Députés) (Chamber of Deputies) has 80 members, of which 53 are elected by proportional representation, 24 are female members elected by provincial councils, two are elected by the National Youth Council and one by the Federation of Associations of Disabled Persons. All deputies serve five-year terms.
The Umutwe wa Sena (Sénat) (senate) has 26 members, 12 of whom are elected, eight are appointed by the president, four are designated by the Forum of Political Organisations and two are appointed by the universities or institutions of higher learning. All serve eight-year terms. In addition, former heads of state may become members, providing they completed their terms in office or resigned voluntarily.
Last elections
16 September 2013 (parliamentary); 9 August 2010 (presidential).
Results: Parliamentary: Front Patriotique Rwandais (FPR) (Rwandan Patriotic Front) won 76.22 per cent and 41 seats (out of the 53 directly elected seats), Parti Social Démocrate (PSD) (Social Democratic Party) 13.03 per cent and 7 seats, Parti Libéral (PL) (Liberal Party) 9.29 per cent and 5 seats. Turnout was 98.80 per cent.
Presidential: Paul Kagame (RPF) won 93.08 per cent of the vote, Jean Ntawukuriryayo (PSD) 5.15 per cent, Prosper Higiro (PL) 1.37 per cent, Alvera Mukabaramba (PPC) 0.4 per cent; turnout was 97.5 per cent.
Next elections
2018 (chamber of deputies); 2017 (presidential).

Political parties
Ruling party
Coalition led by Front Patriotique Rwandais (FPR) (Rwandan Patriotic Front) (Tutsi-dominated) with six other political parties (elected 2003; re-elected Sep 2008 and Sep 2013)
Main opposition party
Social Democratic Party (SDP)

Population
10.64 million (2013)*
Last census: 16 August 2002: 8,128,553
Population density: 300 inhabitants per square km. Urban population 19 per cent (2010 Unicef).
Annual growth rate: 2.0 per cent, 1990–2010 (Unicef).
Ethnic make-up
There are three ethnic groups: the Hutu (90 per cent), the Tutsi (9 per cent) and the Twa (1 per cent).
Religions
Roman Catholic (56 per cent), Protestant (26 per cent), Adventist (11.1 per cent), Islam (4.6 per cent), indigenous beliefs (0.1 per cent).

Education
On completion of primary education, a competitive entrance examination allows students to progress to the first cycle secondary school for general education, from age 13 to 16. The second cycle secondary school covers either modern or classical humanities, from age 16 to 19.
Technical education is provided for students who have completed two to three years general secondary education, although some may begin straight from primary education joining four-year courses.
Education suffered badly as communities and the social infrastructure were devastated by the internal conflict of the early 1990s. This included the destruction of schools and educational institutions, as well as the loss of trained teachers. By 1998 it was estimated that approximately one-third of school-age children were not in school (having died or become refugees) and two-thirds of teachers were secondary school graduates with no teacher training (VSO 2003).
In October 2008 the government decided that all teaching classes would be undertaken using English instead of French. The decision will include every educational institution from nursery schools to universities. The decision was officially based on Rwanda joining the English-speaking East African Community (EAC) and the increasing use of English in business circles. However the political tension with France since 1994, when France was accused of supporting the Hutu Militia in genocide, has also added to the government's commitment to change.
Literacy rate: 69 per cent adult rate; 85 per cent youth rate (15–24) (Unesco 2005).
Compulsory years: Seven to 13.
Enrolment rate: 95.5 per cent net primary (World Bank).

Health
HIV/Aids
The average life expectancy of Rwandan citizens has reduced to under 40 due to the Aids epidemic. In 2003 there were 230,000 people HIV positive, of which 130,000 were women. There were also 22,000 children (0–17 years) with HIV/Aids and 160,000 orphans created by Aids. There has been evidence that national adult prevalence has fallen in Rwanda since reaching a peak in the mid-1990s (UNAID 2003).
HIV prevalence: 5.1 per cent aged 15–49 in 2003 (World Bank)
Life expectancy: 46 years, 2004 (WHO 2006)
Fertility rate/Maternal mortality rate: 5.4 births per woman, 2010 (Unicef)
Birth rate/Death rate: 40 births per 1,000 population; 21.7 deaths per 1000 population (2003).
Child (under 5 years) mortality rate (per 1,000): 55 per 1,000 live births (WHO 2012)
Head of population per physician: 0.05 physicians per 1,000 people, 2004 (WHO 2006)

Welfare
More than half the population live below the national poverty line. According to the 2002 UN Development Report, 84.6 per cent of the population exist on less than US$2 per day and 35.7 per cent on less than US$1 per day.

Main cities
Kigali (capital, estimated population 1.2 million in 2012), Ruhengeri (132,145), Gisenyi (127,587), Butare (115,704), Gitarama (86,741), Ruhango (84,836), Byumba (75,463), Cyangugu (69,992).

Languages spoken
KiSwahili is also used among traders.
Official language/s
Kinyarwanda, French and English.

Media
Press
There are only two domestically published newspapers, *La Nouvelle Relève* (www.orinfor.gov.rw), is government owned and printed in French, *The New Times* (www.newtimes.co.rw) is privately owned and printed in English.
A magazine, published regionally in French *Jeune Afrique* (www.jeuneafrique.com) covers news and interviews. Internet outlets in English include Inside Rwanda (www.insideworld.com/rwanda), and Rwanda Information Exchange (www.rwanda.net), and in French, Observatoire de l'Afrique Centrale (www.obsac.com).
Broadcasting
Radio: Most residents of Rwanda receive their news from radio broadcasts and the most listened to radio station is the government-owned, commercial Radio Rwanda (www.orinfor.gov.rw) broadcasting in KiSwahili, Kinyarwanda, French and English. There are six other private radio

stations, including Radio Maria with religious programmes.
BBC radio broadcasts in the Kinyarwanda language were suspended in April 2009 due to a bias concerning the 1994 genocide as detected by the government. The BBC reports were considered to deny the genocide, a claim the BBC rejected saying its reports only differed from the interpretation the government had of the genocide.
Television: Television Rwandaise (TVR) is the only television broadcasting company in the country.
Other news agencies: This is no national news agency but the African Press Agency (APA) (www.africanewsagency.org) and Panapress (www.panapress.com) report on news from Rwanda.

Economy

Rwanda has become one of the development success stories since the hundred day genocide of 1994 claimed the lives of 800,000 to 1,000,000 people, some 20 per cent of the population.
Rwanda has few natural resources. The country's economy is still largely based on agriculture, dominated by small family-run farms. The service sector constitutes 52.7 per cent of GDP (2014), agriculture around 32.5 per cent and industry almost 14.8 per cent, of which, manufacturing is around 5 per cent. Rwanda is the most densely populated country in Africa and suffers from land shortages with the average farm size at half a hectare, enough for subsistence farming only, of which around 70 per cent of the population relies. The land, with its steep mountain slopes, is not practical for most agribusiness purposes. Government land ownership has also increased pressure and reduced opportunities for development. Government aid and land reforms have been underway and are beginning to take shape as the percentage of the rural population living in integrated and economically viable planned settlements increasing form 37.5 per cent in 2012 to 53.0 per cent in 2013/14.
Agricultural production is led by exports of tea and coffee, plus pyrethrum (used in insect repellent), which together account for around 40 per cent of export earnings.
GDP growth spiked in 2008 at 11.2 per cent, due to aid and grants provided by donors, strong output in the service sector (tax revenue grew by 13.1 per cent during the fiscal year), as well as crop production (which fuelled exports). GDP growth slowed to 4.1 per cent in 2009 in the face of the global downturn, before strengthening in 2010 as world trade picked up with GDP growth of 7.5 per cent, which remained at 7.5 per cent in 2011. By 2013 GDP growth had dropped to a more stable 5 per cent before rising to 7 per cent in 2014, higher than the 6 per cent predicted.
The positive GDP growth was attributed to a robust expansion in agriculture facilitated by the government's crop-intensification programme (including providing seed and fertiliser to farmers and expanding harvest storage facilities) and good harvests. Growth in the Industrial sector has seen a slight reduction in growth due to a slight downturn in construction, mining, and manufacturing. According to the African Development Bank, total foreign direct investment rose by 9 million in 2014, reaching US$159 million, returning to 2012 levels.
Tourism, centred on the rare mountain gorillas and other upscale tourist venues, has grown in importance but still requires further investment to take full advantage of resources. In 2014 tourism had a total contribution, directly and indirectly, of 9.1 per cent of GDP, a figure that is expected to rise by 6.6 per cent in 2015.The industry also supports a total of 176,000 jobs (7.9 per cent of total employment).
In 2013, the UN Human Development Index (HDI) ranked Rwanda 151 (out of 187) for national development in health, education and income. In 2013, 70.8 per cent of the population experienced at least one indicator of poverty and 63.2 per cent were living on the equivalent of US$1.25 per day. However, since the depths of the genocide of the mid-1990s Rwanda has made continued improvement.

External trade

Rwanda is a member of the Common Market for Eastern and Southern Africa (Comesa), and operates within a free trade zone with 13 of the 19 member states. Around 35 per cent of all imports originate in Africa
Rwanda is a member of the East African Community (EAC) (with Burundi, Kenya, Tanzania and Uganda). The East African Community Common Market Protocol (EACMP) was launched on 1 July 2010, which will lead to the free movement of labour, capital, goods and services between member states as well as employment opportunities and easier flow of investment capital. The signed protocol now requires that legislation in all states must be harmonised to conform to its jurisdiction.
As a landlocked country, the infrastructure must be maintained to move any imports and exports from neighbouring countries, which increases shipping costs; there is no railway linking Rwanda to the Tanzanian rail system. Rwanda has few natural resources and imports its energy (beyond bio-fuels) as well as capital goods. Exports are limited to cash crops – tea represents 60 per cent – and pyrethrum, the extract of which is used in insect repellent.

Imports

Principal imports include foodstuffs, machinery and equipment, steel, petroleum products, cement and construction materials.
Main sources: China (18.7 per cent of total in 2014), Uganda (13.7 per cent), Kenya (9.2 per cent).

Exports

Principal exports are tea, coffee (in 2012 some 27 per cent of coffee exported was marketed as 'speciality' and commanded a higher price), pyrethrum, animal hides and tin ore.
Main destinations: Tanzania (27.8 per cent of total in 2014), Democratic Republic of Congo (23.5 per cent), Uganda (11.9 per cent)

Agriculture

Farming

The agricultural sector contributes about 32.5 per cent to GDP (2014) and employs some 75 per cent of the labour force, 70 per cent of the population is still engaged in subsistence farming. Approximately 30 per cent of the land area is cultivated arable land, 31 per cent pasture and 9 per cent forest; tree planting programmes are under way to combat deforestation.
The main food crops are beans (17 per cent of cultivated land), sweet potatoes (14 per cent), sorghum (7 per cent), plantains, bananas, potatoes, cassava and maize. Crop yields fluctuate due to drought, soil erosion and underinvestment.
The coffee industry was privatised in 2001. Coffee production fell so the government is encouraging the growth of speciality coffees that receive higher prices on the international market. If this move is successful, export revenues could be boosted, but if not, it is unlikely the failing coffee industry will recover swiftly.
Tea overtook coffee as the country's main export.
Food production was boosted in early 2008 when high-yielding seed varieties provided under the Crop Intensification Project proved successful.

Industry and manufacturing

The industrial sector contributed 14.8 per cent to GDP in 2014 and typically employs 6 per cent of the workforce. Industrial growth slowed in 2014 due to slight downturns in mining, manufacturing and construction.
Industries include brewing, food processing, cigarette production, soaps, plastics, tin smelting and textiles. Growth of the sector is limited by the small domestic

market, transport difficulties and irregular supply of imported fuels and raw materials which comprise 77 per cent of inputs.

Tourism

Rwanda is a hilly country with tea plantations, rainforests, savannahs and active volcanoes. The Congo Nile Trail of 227km was opened in November 2011, allowing visitors to hike between Gisenyi and Cyangugu-Kamembe. Eco-tourism, and in particular the mountain gorillas, has driven the tourist industry. Around one-third of all mountain gorillas are located in Rwanda and visitors are willing to pay high fees for the limited number of permits to see them in their natural habitat. The money earned from these permits is returned to provide funding for all national parks and conservation work.

Travel and tourism contributed a record 9.1 per cent of GDP in 2014, down slightly form 9.3 per cent in 2013. Employment in the industry has matched this trend as it fell from a record 9.2 per cent in 2008 to 7.9 per cent in 2014 (176,000 jobs). Rwanda had 1.1 million visitors in 2013 (latest figures).

Rwanda has been successful in attracting business and conference visitors, mainly from the Democratic Republic of Congo as well as other East African Community countries, for which hotels and restaurants have been provided.

In a move calculated to encourage tourists, Kenya, Rwanda and Uganda announced in November 2013 a joint visa scheme for tourists to take effect from 1 January 2014; the current cost per visa is US$50 each for Kenya and Uganda and US$30 for Rwanda. The single cross-border tourist visa for Rwanda, Kenya and Uganda was launched on 20 February 2014. The visa costs US$100 and is valid for 90 days (see http://www.visiteastafrica.org/visa/ for details). Tanzania and Burundi are expected to join in the future.

Environment

In February 2008 the governments of Democratic Republic of Congo, Rwanda and Uganda agreed to joint measures to protect the mountain gorillas found within their shared border regions. Tourists visiting the area to view the endangered great apes raise a combined US$5 million for the countries concerned. However, poaching and civil strife have dropped the numbers of gorillas to critically endangered levels, so that a 10-year conservation project which focuses of security and encouraging local people to preserve the animals and habitat is seen as the only hope for the gorilla's survival

Mining

The mining sector contributes 7 per cent to GDP and employs 1 per cent of the workforce.

Extraction of cassiterite (known reserves 90,000 tonnes) has been carried out since 1985, on an artisanal scale only.

Hydrocarbons

No significant reserves of hydrocarbons have been found in Rwanda, but oil exploration licences were issued in February 2009. All petroleum products must be imported, via Kenya/Uganda and Tanzania. Rwanda signed an agreement with Uganda in April 2008 to extend the proposed 320km Eldoret-Kampala (Kenya-Uganda) oil pipeline, construction of which began in April 2009, that was originally to be completed by 2012. However, in 2012 the contract was voided after progress was slow and as of May 2014 there are 14 companies bidding to continue the project. The proposed oil pipeline will benefit Rwanda through the lower costs of transportation of imported oil. Rwanda imported 5,270 barrel per day (bpd) in 2013 (latest figures).

There are around 56 billion cubic metres of methane gas in Lake Kivu, with a regenerative capacity of around 250 million cubic metres per annum. In 2009 Rwanda signed an agreement with the US company, Contour Global, to produce 100MW of energy from methane gas. Natural gas and coal are neither produced nor imported.

Energy

Total installed generating capacity was 57.3MW in 2013, using hydropower, conventional thermal power and solar. Over 15MW of electricity is imported from the Ruzizi hydropower station located in Democratic Republic of Congo (DRC).

The World Bank assisted Rwanda with funding for an urgent electricity rehabilitation project (2005–09), improving generation and the power system to alleviate the numerous power cuts including funds for a new thermal power station, which became operational in January 2009, producing an additional 20MW and designed to replace in part the country's extensive rented diesel generators. It also provided technical and administrative assistance as well as support in plans for future generation using renewable energies. The potential for geothermal generation was estimated at 170–300MW and a preliminary assessment confirmed the prospects for development.

The US company Contour Global will produce 100MW of energy from methane gas by 2034, according to a 2009 agreement with the government. The gas will be extracted from Lake Kivu, in the western province, for electricity generation.

The ministry of infrastructure is responsible for energy policy and the state-owned company, Electrogaz is responsible for generation, transmission and distribution of energy. Only 6 per cent of the population had access to electricity in 2008, with an increase to 16 per cent by 2012. The remainder of the population and the subsistence-farming sector in particular currently relies on wood and charcoal.

Financial markets

Stock exchange

Rwanda Stock Exchang (RSE), 1st Floor, Kigali City Tower, PO Box 3882, Kigali KN 81 ST (tel: 788516021; email:info@rse.rw; web: www.rse.rw).

Banking and insurance

Central bank

Banque Nationale du Rwanda

Main financial centre

Kigali

Time

GMT plus two hours

Geography

Rwanda is a landlocked country in central Africa, just south of the Equator, bounded by the Democratic Republic of Congo to the west, where Lake Kivu (one of the Great Lakes) provides the border; Uganda is to the north, Tanzania to the east and Burundi in the south.

Rwanda has rolling hill terrain for most of its eastern region. However, a chain of rugged, volcanic mountains runs from the north-west south to the border with Burundi in the south-west. The highest peak is Mount Karisimbi (4,532 metres). To the west of the mountain range Lake Kivu flows into the Congo River basin through the Ruzizi River valley, a section of Africa's Great Rift Valley. The south is swamp and savannah, which, in the south-east, peters out into desert.

Hemisphere

Southern

Climate

Warm, tempered by altitude. Rainfall is low and is concentrated in two seasons from mid-January to mid-May, and mid-October to mid-December. Temperatures in Kigali range from 12–14 degrees Celsius (C) at night to 28–32 degrees C during the day. Cooler in the highland areas.

Entry requirements

Passports

Required by all. Passports must be valid for six months from date of visit.

Visa

Are required by all, except nationals of US, Germany, Canada, Uganda, Tanzania, Kenya, Burundi and the DRC for visits up to 90 days; entry permits are issued on arrival, when visitors must provide evidence of sufficient funds for stay and return/onward passage.

Business travellers or tourists staying for longer must apply for a visa. A business visa requires a letter of introduction by an employer stating purpose of visit. Contact the nearest Rwanda Consulate for further details.

In a move calculated to encourage tourists, a single cross-border tourist visa for Rwanda, Kenya and Uganda was launched on 20 February 2014. The visa costs US$100 and is valid for 90 days (see http://www.visiteastafrica.org/visa/ for details).

Currency advice/regulations

Import and export of local currency is limited to a maximum Rwf5,000. Import of foreign currency is unlimited, but amounts should be declared; export is only allowed up to the amount declared.

Travellers cheques are not readily accepted.

Customs

Personal possessions are duty-free.

Export of game trophies require agreement from the relevant authority.

Health (for visitors)

Mandatory precautions

Yellow fever vaccination certificate is required by all.

Advisable precautions

Hepatitis A, tetanus, typhoid and polio vaccinations. Malaria prophylaxis is recommended. Water precautions should be taken. Aids is prevalent. There is a rabies risk.

Hotels

Tend to be expensive in Kigali; cheaper in Butare, Gisenyi and Ruhengeri. Advisable to book in advance.

Public holidays (national)

Fixed dates

1 Jan (New Year's Day), 28 Jan (Democracy Day), 7 Apr (Genocide Memorial Day), 1 May (Labour Day), 1 Jul (Independence Day), 4 Jul (Liberation Day), 15 Aug (Assumption Day), 25 Sep (Republic Day), 1 Nov (All Saints Day), 25–26 Dec (Christmas).

Variable dates

Good Friday and Easter Monday (Mar/Apr).

Working hours

Banking

Mon–Fri: 0800–1200, 1400–1800; Sat: 0800–1300.

Business

Mon–Fri: 0800–1230, 1330–1700.

Government

Mon–Fri: 0800–1230, 1330–1700.

Shops

Dawn to dusk.

Telecommunications

Mobile/cell phones

A GSM900 coverage exists.

Electricity supply

220V AC

Security

The threat of attack from rebel groups continues and despite the cease-fire and elections in neighbouring DRC, the border regions are volatile. Local advice should be sought by those proposing to visit such areas; a military escort may be necessary. Kigali and major towns in the east, such as Butare and Gitarma, can be visited, but precautions need to be taken. Cars should not be left unattended in the centre of town and walking after dark or carrying large amounts of money or valuables is ill-advised.

Getting there

Air

National airline: Rwandair Express

International airport/s: Kigali-Kanombe (KGL), 12km east of city; duty-free shop, bar, currency exchange, post office, shops, coach, taxi service.

Airport tax: None

Surface

Road: Roads from Uganda,Tanzania and Burundi are well-surfaced.

Water: Although landlocked there is a link on Lake Kivu, between the north and south.

Main port/s: Gisenyi, Cyangugu.

Getting about

National transport

Air: Rwandair Express operates a limited internal service.

Road: All cities are linked to Kigali by paved roads, and the roads Ruhengeri-Cyanika and Kayonza-Kagitumba are paved. Other roads are poor with many being impassable in bad weather.

Buses: Reliable regular bus services are available from Kigali to the main cities and between some cities themselves. Private minibuses (belonging to an association called ATRACO) also operate between Kigali and other cities.

Water: Services run between Gisenyi and Cyangugu, on Lake Kivu.

City transport

Taxis: They can be found in large towns; fares should be agreed at the start of journey and tipping is not necessary.

Car hire

Limited service is available in Kigali. International driving licence is required.

All-weather roads are sparse and in poor condition.

BUSINESS DIRECTORY

The addresses listed below are a selection only. While World of Information makes every endeavour to check these addresses, we cannot guarantee that changes have not been made, especially to telephone numbers and area codes. We would welcome any corrections.

Telephone area codes

The international dialling code (IDD) for Rwanda is +250, followed by subscriber's number.

Chambers of Commerce

Fédération Rwandaise du Secteur Privé, PO Box 319, Kigali (tel: 583-538/41; fax: 583-532; e-mail: frsp@rwanda1.com).

Banking

Banque à la Confiance d'Or, BP 2059, Kigali (tel: 575-780, 75-763; fax: 575-761).

Banque Commerciale du Rwanda, BP 354, Boulevard de la Revolution, Kigali (tel: 575-591, 576-117; fax: 573-395).

Banque Continentale Africaine (Rwanda) SA, BP 331, 20 Kigali, Boulevard de la Revolution, Kigali (tel: 574-456/7/8; fax: 573-486).

Banque de Commerce, de Developpement et d'Industrie, BP 3268, Kigali (tel: 574-143, 574-132, 74-427; fax: 573-790, 74-479).

Banque de Kigali, BP 175, 63 Avenue du Commerce, Kigali (tel: 576-931/2/3/4; fax: 573-461, 75-504).

Banque Nationale du Rwanda, BP 531, Kigali (tel: 574-282, 575-249; fax: 572-551).

Banque Rwandaise de Developpment, BP 1341, Kigali (tel: 575-079, 575-080; fax: 573-569).

Campagne Generale de Banque, BP 5230, Kigali (tel: 586-875; fax: 586-876).

Union des Banques Populaires du Rwanda, BP 1348, Kigali (tel: 573-564; fax: 573-579).

Central bank

Banque Nationale du Rwanda, Avenue Paul VI, BP 531, Kigali (tel: 574-282; fax: 572-551; e-mail: webmaster@bnr.rw).

Stock exchange

Rwanda Stock Exchang (RSE), 1st Floor, Kigali City Tower, PO Box 3882, Kigali KN 81 ST (tel: 788516021; email:info@rse.rw; web: www.rse.rw).

Travel information

Air France, BP 411, Kigali (tel: 575-566).

Rwandair Express, Ground & 2nd floor, Centenary House, Av de Revolution; BP 7275 Kigali (575-757, 503-687; fax: 503-686; internet: www.rwanda.com).

Office Rwandais du Tourisme et des Parcs Nationaux, BP 905, Kigali (tel:

576-514/5, 573-396; fax: 576-512; e-mail: Ortpn@rwandatel1.rwanda1.com).

Rwanda Travel Service, BP 140, Kigali (tel: 572-210).

Rwanda Explorations, BP 1514, Kigali (tel: 573-284).

Ministries

Ministry of Agriculture and Animal Resources, PO Box 621, Kigali (tel: 586-104; fax: 587-038; internet: www.minagri.gov.rw).

Ministry of Comerce, Industry, Investment, Promotion, Tourism and Co-operatives (tel: 574-725, 574-734; fax: 575-465; email: jnsengiyumva@minicom.gov.rw: internet: www.minicom.gov.rw).

Ministry of Education, Science, Technology and Scientific Research, BP 622 Kigali (tel: 583-051; fax: 582-161; email: info@mineduc.gov.rw).

Office of the Prime Minister, Kigali (tel: 585-444/5, 584-648; fax: 583-714; internet: www.primature.gov.rw).

Other useful addresses

Agence Rwandaise de Presse (ARP), 27 avenue du Commerce, BP 83, Kigali (tel: 575-665).

Economat Général (tobacco exports), BP 45, Ruhengeri.

L'Institut des Sciences Agronomiques du Rwanda, BP 138, Butare.

Office des Cafés, BP 104, Kigali (tel: 575-277).

Office du Pyrèthre au Rwanda, BP 79, Ruhengeri.

Office du Thé, BP 1344, Kigali (tel: 572-416).

Rwandan Embassy (USA), 1714 New Hampshire Avenue, NW, Washington DC 20009 (tel: (+1-202) 232-2882; fax: (+1-202) 232-4544; email: rwandemb@rwandemb.org).

This is no national news agency but the African Press Agency (APA) (www.africanewsagency.org) and Panapress (www.panapress.com) report on news from Rwanda.

Internet sites

General information: www.rwanda.net

Africa Business Network: www.ifc.org/abn

African Development Bank: www.afdb.org

Africa Online: www.africaonline.com

AllAfrica.com: http://allafrica.com

Mbendi AfroPaedia (information on companies, countries, industries and stock exchanges in Africa): http://mbendi.co.za

Official website of government of Rwanda: www.gov.rw

St Helena

COUNTRY PROFILE

1502 St Helena was sighted by Portuguese mariners on 21 May (St Helena's Day).
1513 The island was first settled.
1633 The Dutch claimed possession.
1659 The East India Company took possession of the uninhabited island.
1673 The island was briefly captured by the Dutch, before being regained by the East India Company.
1815 Napoleon Bonaparte was exiled to the island, where he died on 5 May 1821; his body was returned to France in 1840.
1834 The island passed under British control.
1981 The Nationality Act ended the islanders' British citizenship and right of abode, which they had held since 1673.
1992 The islanders established a Citizenship Commission, which began its case to regain full British citizenship.
2002 Full British citizenship was restored to the islanders.
2004 Michael Clancy became Governor and Commander-in-Chief.
2005 An environmental team from the UK conducted the first stage of investigations required to carry out an Environmental Impact Assessment (EIA) for the proposed new airport on Prosperous Bay Plain.
2007 Andrew Gurr took office as governor.
2008 The UK government's plans to sponsor construction of the airport were halted. A population census was undertaken; there were a total of 710 residents.
2009 The proposed new constitution was debated in the Executive Council (Exco), but failed to be passed. Governor Gurr, in an article printed in the *St Helena Herald*, said that it was 'inarguable that our progress as an island will be held back if we remain stuck in the time warp of the existing 1988 constitution'. He also said that the UK Parliamentary undersecretary of state at the foreign and commonwealth office would continue to consult with the elected members of the Exco, to ensure he had the most complete advice available before making a decision. Tristan da Cunha and Ascension Island have already voted in favour of the proposed changes. Elections for the Exco were held and the six candidates who won the most votes from both the East and West constituencies were elected.
2010 A Memorandum of Understanding (MoU) was signed between the UK's Department for International Development (DfID) and St Helena. The signing indicated that both parties agreed on what St Helena intended to do to implement the reforms needed in preparation for the new airport. It was a wide ranging document and included a series of undertakings to see through substantial improvements in organisation, legislation and performance to stimulate local and inward investment related to the airport and tourism.
2011 At the end of June the Exco signed a MoU with the UK 'to implement the reforms necessary to open the island's economy to inward investment and increased tourism'. The act will simplify the requirements for non-St Helenians to enter, settle and work on the island and acquire land. In September, Governor Gurr's term in office ended and Attorney General Ken Baddon was sworn in as acting governor on 24 September, until Mark Andrew Capes took up the post on 29 October.
2012 On 31 July the Executive Council unanimously approved a revised design for the external finish of the Airport Terminal. The Land Development Control Board said it represented a 'vast improvement' on the original 2008 version.
2013 St Helena raised its first ever flag on 11 May. It features the Ascension Island Crest, the Green Turtle, volcanic landscape, seabirds and endemic plants. Minimum wages of £2.30 for all employees over 18 years and £1.45 for all employees aged 16 and 17 years came into force on 1 June.
2014 Longwood House, where Napoleon died in 1821, has been restored as an attaction for tourists.
2015 With the airport finally due to open in early 2016 it has been announced that RMS St Helena will make its last vayage to the St Helena in March 2016.

Political structure

St Helena has an appointed governor assisted by an Executive Council (the chief secretary, the financial secretary, attorney general and committee chairmen) and also by a Legislative Council (made up of the same ex-officio members and 12 elected members). Restoration for the

KEY FACTS

Official name: St Helena Colony with Dependencies

Head of State: Queen Elizabeth II, represented by Governor and Commander-in-Chief Mark Andrew Capes (from 29 Oct 2011)

Head of government: Governor and Commander-in-Chief Mark Andrew Capes

Ruling party: All members of the legislative council stand as independents

Area: 122 square km

Population: 4,250 (2010)*

Capital: Jamestown

Official language: English

Currency: St Helena pound (StH£) = 100 pence

Exchange rate: StH£0.65 per US$ (Sep 2015)

Inflation: 100.00% (2nd quarter 2014, annual)

* estimated figure

islanders of full British citizenship was granted in May 2002.
The creation of a new overseas territories minister within the Foreign and Commonwealth Office (FCO) and the establishment of an Overseas Territories Consultative Council were both implemented in 1999, but responsibility for the British Overseas Territories, including St Helena, remains divided between the FCO and the Department for International Development.

Constitution
The 1988 St Helena Constitution Order came into force in February 1989. It sets out the separation of powers and the responsibilities of the executive, legislature and judiciary.
The proposed new constitution was debated in the Legislative Council (Legco) on 29 June 2009. The vote was four Elected Members in favour and four against; the Speaker voted against and the motion for change failed. Governor Gurr, in an article printed in the *St Helena Herald*, said that it was 'inarguable that our progress as an island will be held back if we remain stuck in the time warp of the existing 1988 constitution'. He also said that the UK Parliamentary under secretary of state at the foreign and commonwealth office would continue to consult with the Elected Members of the Legco, including the 4 members not present at the vote, to ensure he had the most complete advice available before making a decision. Tristan da Cunha and Ascension Island have already voted in favour of the proposed changes.

Form of state
As a British Overseas Territory, St Helena is a dependency of St Helena.

The executive
As a British Overseas Territory, St Helena has an appointed governor assisted by an Executive Council with three *ex-officio* appointments (the chief secretary, the financial secretary, attorney general and committee chairmen) and five elected members of the Legislative Council.
The creation of a new overseas territories minister within the Foreign and Commonwealth Office (FCO) and the establishment of an Overseas Territories Consultative Council were both implemented in 1999, but responsibility for the British Overseas Territories, including St Helena, remains divided between the FCO and the Department for International Development.

National legislature
The unicameral legislative assembly has 12 members elected for four-year terms. There are also three *ex-officio* appointments including the chief secretary, the financial secretary and the Attorney General.

Last elections
17 July 2013 (Legislative Council)
Results: Legislative Council: the six candidates who won the most votes in both the East and West constituencies (12 in total) were elected, with a turnout of 55 per cent (1,264 voters).

Next elections
2017 (Legislative Council)

Political parties
No parties exist.

Ruling party
All members of the legislative council stand as independents

Political situation
St Helena suffers from depopulation and dependency. As experienced by so many small communities, St Helena is losing too many of its young and potentially most valuable members to the outside world, even though families welcome the immediate value of remittances.
The goal of the UK government towards its dependency is self-sufficiency. In its 2008 *Sustainable Development Plan* (SDP) it outlined six objectives necessary for future sustainability: improved access – there is no air access and sea connections are slow and costly; improved standard of education; development of a sustainable and vibrant economy; and promote and develop a sustainable workforce; develop a healthy community in a safe environment and establish the democratic and human rights and self-determination of the people of St Helena.
However even as it published its SDP the UK government halted plans to build an airport on St Helena, closing off one avenue of economic growth. Better education is a long-term objective but in the meantime newly qualified students and possible entrepreneurs are leaving and depriving the island of most of its talent.
Whether St Helena can reverse the stance by the new UK administration remains to be seen.
4,250 (2010)*

Population
In addition to the island population, 1,250 St Helenians are employed elsewhere: Ascension Island (550), Falkland Islands (350), UK (250) and onboard the RMS *St Helena* (100).
10 Febuary 2008: 710
Population density: 43.8 inhabitants per square km.
Annual growth rate: -0.3 per cent (1998–2008)

Ethnic make-up
Black African (50 per cent), white (25 per cent), Chinese (25 per cent).

Religions
Anglican (majority), Baptist, Seventh-Day Adventist, Roman Catholic.

Health
Life expectancy: 74.5 years (estimate 2003)
Fertility rate/Maternal mortality rate: 1.5 births per woman (2003)
Birth rate/Death rate: 13 births per 1,000 population; 6.3 deaths per 1,000 population (2003).
Child (under 5 years) mortality rate (per 1,000): 21 per 1,000 live births (2003)

Main cities
Jamestown (capital, estimated population 429 in 2012), Half Tree Hollow (1,126), Longwood (473), Saint Pauls (444).

Languages spoken

Official language/s
English

Media

Press
Weeklies: The *St Helena Herald* (www.news.co.sh) is government funded while *The St Helena Independent* (www.saint.fm/Independent/) is independent.
Business: A publication, giving sailing, details of the Royal Mail Service (RMS) ship *St Helena* (www.albionshipping.co.uk), which has a regular service to the island from UK and Cape Town. The Gulf and South Atlantic Fisheries Foundation publishes a newsletter concerning fishery matters (www.gulfsouthfoundation.org/newsletters).
Periodicals: The St Helena News Bureau publishes the periodical *St Helena and South Atlantic News Review* and the monthly *The St Helena Catalogue*.

Broadcasting
Radio: The government-funded Radio St Helena (www.news.co.sh) operates on short wave (AM) daily, with relays of a number of BBC World Service programmes. Saint FM (www.saint.fm) features music, local events and information.
Television: There is no locally made television service. Cable & Wireless provides a two channel television service relaying selected programmes from BBC World, CNN, Supersport, Discovery Channel and MNET, a South African commercial service.

Economy
St Helena depends on aid from the UK for between 20–25 per cent of its recurrent public sector budget. In 2010 the Department for International Development (DfID) provided over £20 million (US$31 million) in budgetary aid, educational support and development programmes among others. The St Helena Development Agency (SHDA) is a government sponsored agency set up to attract inward

investment, help local business development, support start up schemes and encourage youth entrepreneurship.
Other means of income include fishing licence sales, local fishing catches, philatelic sales, coffee, livestock and timber, together with remittances from the estimated 1,700 offshore workers.
Andrew Weir Shipping Ltd manages the Royal Mail ship *RMS St Helena* which provides a regular re-supply service. Plans to build an airport were approved in a referendum held in 2002, but due to the rising cost planning was halted in 2008. Construction eventually began in 2012 and is expected to be completed by 2016. The project has seen a total investment of US$236.6 million which includes the cost of a wharf at St Rupert's bay to enable the unloading of construction machinery and materials, the building of the airport and airstrip, and 10 years of operation for the airport.
Minimum wages of £2.30 (US$3.58) for all employees over 18 years and £1.45 (US$2.26) for all employees aged 16 and 17 years came into force on 1 June 2013. Inflation has been low and stable for a number of years, rising slightly from 1.2 per cent in 2013 to 2.6 per cent in 2012.
Public expenditure rose from around £12 million (US$18.7 million) in 2006 to £28 million (US$43.6 million) in 2013 and in the same period the UK budgetary aid rose from £4.6 million (US$7.2 million) to £6.4 million (US$10.0 million). The private sector employs some 45 per cent of the population.
St Helena was originally developed as a re-victualling post for East India Company ships returning from the east. With the decline of sail from the 1870s, the island has struggled to find a basis for its economy. The production of New Zealand flax was started in 1874 and had some success during times of high world prices. However, St Helena's terrain is not suited to plantation cropping and the industry, heavily subsidised for most of its history, finally collapsed in 1966. The lack of employment opportunities for St Helenians has led to some 25 per cent of the workforce immigrating to find new possibilities, mainly to the Falkland Islands, Ascension Island, and the UK.

External trade

As a UK Overseas Territory St Helena is a part of the European Union's Association of Overseas Countries and Territories (OCT Association), and some EU laws apply.
The small quantity of coffee exported, three tonnes per year, produces one of the world's most expensive beverages. Fishing licences and frozen and canned tuna provide most foreign earnings.

Imports

Principal imports are foodstuffs, tobacco, petroleum, animal feed, building materials, vehicles and parts, machinery and parts.
Main sources: UK (typically over 50 per cent of total), South Africa (10 per cent), Spain (10 per cent).

Exports

Principal exports are fish (frozen, canned, and salt-dried skipjack, tuna), coffee and handicrafts.
Main destinations: Tanzania (typically over 35 per cent of total), US 15 per cent, Japan 15 per cent.

Agriculture

Farming

St Helena's volcanic origins, hills and deep valleys dominate the landscape. Semi-desert gives way to upland grasslands and lush valleys over a very short distance.
Arable and garden land is about 3 per cent of the total area, forest and woodland 5 per cent, pasture 11 per cent, barren and badland 53 per cent. New Zealand flax (hemp) was grown until the 1960s, but much of this land is now planted with trees. Principal crops include potatoes, coffee, bananas, vegetables, sweet potatoes.
Livestock raising is a main activity but there is no dairy production and all dairy products are imported.
Agricultural production does not meet demand. Seed potatoes, onions and eggs are all imported in quantity.

Fishing

In the past, the government of St Helena earned StH£1.0 million (US$1.4 million) per annum from fishing licence revenue, but fish stocks have declined.
There is a local fishery run by the St Helena Fisheries Corporation, which buys the fish from the local fishermen.
The fishing boats range from eight to 13 metres in size and fish on a daily basis. They meet EU standards and carry ice with them. All of the catch is landed within 12 hours.
St Helena has satellite surveillance, but no patrol boat to stop unlicensed boats fishing the waters.

Industry and manufacturing

Local fishermen sell their catch to the St Helena Fisheries Corporation (a government parastatal). St Helena Fisheries Corporation sells its product in frozen and smoked form primarily to the UK and South Africa and supplies the domestic market.
Working in partnership with the St Helena Fisheries Corporation, Argos Helena Ltd, a joint UK-Spanish owned company, runs a blast freezer and fish processing/canning facility. Locally caught high-quality tuna is processed for export to the European Union and the Far East. The Corporation's fish products have organic certification from the Soil Association in the UK.

Tourism

St Helena has few resources and a declining population. Tourism is seen as a means of rescuing the island's economy and future. There are three hotels on the island and some 3,923 visitors came to the island in 2014, up from 3,800 in 2013.
Until the airport is complete, the only means of reaching the island is by the RMS *St Helena*, which carries only 128 passengers on a round trip from UK (Portland) twice a year, and monthly from Cape Town to Walvis Bay (Namibia), St Helena and Ascension Island.
Tourism is a key target area in developing St Helena's economy. In June 2010 a Provisional Tourism Commission was appointed to oversee the future development of the tourist industry; in July a new Tourism Development Executive was appointed, as well as a sales and marketing executive, who will be based in the UK and liaise closely with Andrew Weir Shipping Ltd to increase traffic on the *St Helena*. In April 2013 a contract was awarded to Marine Maven (T&T) Ltd, to assess St Helena's needs to exploit its long and proud maritime tradition, including the potential for recreational tours, water sports, observation of local marine life and sports fishing.
In January 2013 a team of six from the Mantis Collection, a group of privately owned boutique hotels and eco-escapes across the globe, visited St Helena, which they have described as 'exceptional'. In August it was announced that St Helena would be an included feature on one of the 'boutique' cruises promoted by mantis.

Environment

St Helena's National Environmental Management Plan (NEMP) setting out a blueprint for delivery of National Goal 3, *Effective Management of the Environment* was officially launched on Tuesday 9 October 2012.

Hydrocarbons

St Helena does not have any hydrocarbon reserves and relies entirely on the import of petroleum products to meet energy needs, which were 80 barrels per day in 2013. St Helena does not import natural gas or coal.

Energy

The installation of a wind turbine in 2007, by the UK government, provided 240kW for the 1MW power grid, reducing the island's dependence on diesel fuel.

Time
GMT

Geography
St Helena is situated in the South Atlantic Ocean and is 1,950km (1,200 miles) due west from the south-west coast of Africa and 2,900km (1,800 miles) east of South America. The nearest land is one of its dependencies, Ascension Island, 1,130km (700 miles) to the north-west.

The island is of volcanic in origin. It is mountainous, presenting an almost continuous line of high, sheer cliffs, cut only by a few narrow and steep-sided valleys around its coastline. It is criss-crossed by deep valleys and slopes steeply from the central ridges to the sea. The highest point is Diana's Peak (820 metres above sea-level).

Hemisphere
Southern

Climate
Summer temperatures range from 21–29 degrees Celsius (C); winter 18–24 degrees C on coasts; inland temperatures may be five degrees lower; annual average rainfall in Jamestown is around 200mm, inland up to 950mm.

Entry requirements
Passports
Required by all.

Visa
All visiters must have the Administrator's written permission to land, before travelling. An *Ascension Island Entry Permit* form (valid for St Helena), to be completed, can be downloaded from www.ascension-island.gov.ac/visitors.htm. Entry is only granted with evidence of visitors full medical insurance policy, covering medical evacuation by air, when necessary.

Currency advice/regulations
Travllers cheques are accepted in the bank.

Prohibited imports
Obscene or pornographic materials are prohibited.

Firearms, ammunition, fruit, vegetables and plant materials require an import permit.

Health (for visitors)
There is one general hospital based in Jamestown and six health clinics on the island. The health service is not free and all St Helenians have to pay fees for medical treatment. UK Passport holders visiting the island pay local rates for medical treatment, while non-UK residents have to pay higher fees.

Mandatory precautions
None.

Hotels
There are three hotels on the island, reservations are necessary from December–March.

Credit cards
Major credit cards are accepted in a few locations.

Public holidays (national)
Fixed dates
1 Jan (New Year's Day), 21 May (St Helena Day), 25–26 Dec (Christmas).

Variable dates
Good Friday and Easter Monday (Mar/Apr), Pentecost (May/Jun), August Bank Holiday (last Mon in Aug).

Working hours
Banking
Mon–Sat: 0845/0900–1500/1600; except Thu: 0845–1200. Opening hours may be varied when a cruise ship is visiting.

Business
Mon–Fri: 0830–1230 and 1300–1600.

Government
Mon–Fri: 0830–1230, 1300–1600.

Shops
Mon–Sat: generally 0900–1700.

Getting there
Air
St Helena has no airport and can only be reached by sea. Wideawake Airfield on Ascension Island is the nearest airfield. It is a US military base, and will allow private air-charter access to Wakefield in 2007–08. Passengers for St Helena will need to transfer to a boat to reach the island.

Surface
Water: The *RMS St Helena* operates twice a year from the UK (Portland) and monthly from Cape Town to Walvis Bay (Namibia), St Helena and Ascension Island. The ship is operated under contract by Passenger Services Department, Andrew Weir Shipping Ltd (see travel information addresses).

Air connections can be made with the ship either through Cape Town, via commercial flights, or via military flights from Royal Air Force Brize Norton in Oxfordshire, UK to Ascension Island.

Main port/s: Jamestown

Getting about
National transport
Road: Road network of 80–85km classified as all-weather; at least further 60km surfaced and 25–30km suitable for dry-weather travel only. Roads are best described as steep and tortuous. Because most roads are single lane, motoring etiquette requires the driver coming down to make way for upcoming traffic.

BUSINESS DIRECTORY
The addresses listed below are a selection only. While World of Information makes every endeavour to check these addresses, we cannot guarantee that changes have not been made, especially to telephone numbers and area codes. We would welcome any corrections.

Telephone area codes
The international dialling code (IDD) for St Helena is +290 followed by subscriber's number.

Chambers of Commerce
St Helena Chamber of Commerce, c/o The Castle, Jamestown. (fax: tel: 22-58; fax: 25-98).

Banking
Bank of St. Helena, Post Office Building, Main Street, Jamestown STHL 1ZZ (tel: 2390; fax: 2553; internet: www.SaintHelenaBank.com).

Travel information
For air travel and bookings on the RMS St Helena:

Passenger Services Department, Andrew Weir Shipping Ltd, Dexter House, 2 Royal Mint Court, London EC N4XX, UK (tel: (+44-20) 575-6480; fax: (+44-20) 575-6200; e-mail: reservations@aws.co.uk).

St Helena Line, Andrew Weir Shipping (SA) Pty Ltd, 3rd Floor, BP Centre, Thibault Square, Cape Town, South Africa (tel: (+27-21) 425-1165; fax: (+27-21) 421-7485; e-mail: sthelenaline@mweb.co.za; internet site: www.aws.co.uk).

Miss Kerry Yon, Solomon and Co plc, Jamestown (tel: 2523; fax: 2423; e-mail: solco.shipping@helanta.sh).

National tourist organisation offices
St Helena Tourism, Jamestown (tel: 2158; fax: 2159; email: StHelena.Tourism @helanta.sh; internet: www.sthelenatourism.com).

Ministries
Governor's Office, The Castle, Jamestown (tel: 2555; fax: 2598; e-mail: OCS@helanta.sh).

Other useful addresses
Argos Atlantic Cold Stores, PO Box 151, Jamestown (tel: 2333; fax: 2334; e-mail: argos@argonaut.co.sh).

Cable & Wireless Fax Bureau, The Briars, Jamestown.

Director of Inward Investment, Office of the Chief Secretary, Government of St Helena, Jamestown (tel: 2470; fax: 2598; e-mail: DEPD@atlantis.co.ac).

Enterprise St Helena , 2 Main Street, Jamestown (tel: +290 2920).

Information Office, Broadway House, Jamestown (tel: 2612; fax: 2159; email: StHelena.Tourism@atlantis.co.ac).

Miles Apart (books, maps, videos on South Atlantic Islands), 5 Harraton House, Exning, Newmarket, Suffolk CB8 7HF, UK (tel: (+44-1638) 577-627: fax: (+44-1638) 577-874); 5929 Avon Drive, Bethesda, Maryland 20814, USA (tel/fax: (+1-301) 571-8942; e-mail: familycarter@msn.com).

The Postmistress, The Philatelic Bureau, The Post Office, Jamestown (fax: 2242).

St Helena Commercial Representative, Mr Wes Huxtable, 1 The Stables, Great Hyde Hall, Sawbridgeworth, Herts CM21 9JA, UK (tel: (+44-1279) 725-833; fax: (+44-1279) 724-894; e-mail: weston@huxtable.freeserve.co.uk).

St Helena Desk Officer, Foreign and Commonwealth Office, King Charles Street, London SW1A 2AH, UK (tel: (+44-20) 270-2695).

St Helena Development Agency, No 2 Main St, Jamestown (tel: 2920, fax: 2166, e-mail: shda@atlantis.co.uk).

The St Helena Link (cultural information), Trevor Hearl, 49 Noverton Lane, Prestbury, Cheltenham, Glos GL52 5DD, UK (tel/fax: +44 (0)1242-244-430).

St Helena Port Authority (formerly the Harbour Board)

Internet sites

East India Company (coffee): www.theeastindiacompany.com

St Helena Development Agency: www.shda.helanta.sh/

St Helena government: www.sainthelena.gov.sh

St Helena News: www.news.co.sh

St Helena web portal: www.sthelenaonline.com

St Kitts and Nevis

KEY FACTS

Official name: Federation of St Christopher and Nevis

Head of State: Queen Elizabeth II; represented by Governor General Samuel W.T. Seaton (since 2 September 2015)

Head of government: Prime Minister Timothy Harris (Team Unity) (sworn in 18 Feb 2015)

Ruling party: People's Action Movement (PAM) leading a coalition with the People's Labour Party (PLP) and the Concerned Citizens' Movement (CCM).

Area: 269 square km

Population: 60,000 (2014)* (54,841; 2010, census figure)

Capital: Basseterre (St Kitts)

Official language: English

Currency: East Caribbean dollar (EC$) = 100 cents

Exchange rate: EC$2.70 per US$ (fixed)

GDP per capita: US$14,102 (2014)*

GDP real growth: -2.79% (2014)*

GDP: US$841.00 million (2014)*

Inflation: 1.01% (2014)*

Balance of trade: -US$193.20 million (2013)

Annual FDI: US$114.06 million (2011)

* estimated figure

COUNTRY PROFILE

1623 Britain settled St Christopher (known as St Kitts), which became the first British colony in the West Indies.
1628 Nevis was settled by the British.
1816 Anguilla was joined to the territory.
1932 The St Kitts and Nevis Labour Party (SKNLP) was formed and campaigned for independence for the islands.
1958 St Christopher-Nevis-Anguilla became a member of the attempted West Indies Federation.
1962 The West Indies Federation was dissolved after the departure of Jamaica.
1967 St Christopher-Nevis-Anguilla, became a self-governing state in association with the UK. A House of Assembly replaced the Legislative Council, the administrator became governor and the chief minister became the state's first premier. The pro-independence SKNLP, became the ruling political party. The UK retained responsibility for defence and foreign relations.
1971 Anguilla reverted to being a British Dependent Territory after renouncing the rule of St Kitts.
1980 The SKNLP lost power to a coalition of the People's Action Movement (PAM) and the Nevis Reformation Party (NRP).
1983 Independence from Britain was attained.
1995 The SKNLP returned to power.
1997 The Nevis Island Assembly (NIA) elections were won by the Concerned Citizens' Movement (CCM).
1998 A referendum on independence for Nevis failed to achieve the two-thirds majority required for approval.
2000 The ruling SKNLP was re-elected and Denzil Douglas began a second term as prime minister.
2003 The largest hotel complex in the eastern Caribbean region opened at Frigate Bay.
2004 The NaturalSweet Corporation invested US$90 million for the cultivation and commercial development of stevia, a natural herbal plant. The ruling SKNLP won the parliamentary elections.
2005 The last harvest of sugar cane was delivered to the only remaining refinery, which ceased operations after the last run was made, and ended a centuries' old industry.
2006 The Nevis Reform Party (NRP) won NIA elections; Joseph Parry became prime minister of Nevis.
2008 Cotton lint from the first crop of Sea Island cotton since 2004 was ginned on Nevis. The total of 10,000kg was exported.
2009 An inquiry began into the governance of Nevis, particularly the financial instructions under which it was governed by the CCM party before 2006. A representative of the Japanese development fund visited Nevis and proposed financial assistance for an irrigation system in cotton production. Scheduled parliamentary elections were postponed until 2010. Basseterre was announced as the proposed headquarters of the Libyan Development Bank of the Eastern Caribbean.
2010 In general elections, the incumbent SKNLP won six seats out of 11 and continued in power; Prime Minister Douglas remained in office. Four electricity generators were delivered, two of which produced an additional 15.6MW of power for St Kitts. The US-based airline, American Eagle, began daily flights between Puerto Rico and Nevis.
2011 The NRP won NIA elections held in July; Joseph Parry remained in post as premier of Nevis. In August citizens of the Organisation of Eastern Caribbean States (OECS) – Antigua and Barbuda, Dominica, Grenada, St Kitts and Nevis, St Lucia and St Vincent and the Grenadines – were granted freedom of movement, allowing them to reside, work, establish businesses and provide services throughout the organisation. During the Commonwealth Heads of Government summit, in October, the 16 countries in which the British monarch is Head of State unanimously agreed to change the royal line of succession from that of first born son to the first born child (regardless of its gender). The change will be enacted after the succession of Prince William (currently second in line to the throne, after his father Prince Charles).
2012 On 27 August, the OECS Court of Appeal upheld the decision by the High Court that declared the 2011 elections on Nevis as null and void. On 10 November the NIA was dissolved ahead of new elections. St Kitts and Nevis and Kuwait established diplomatic relations on 16 November.

2013 Opposition coalition Team Unity leader Dr Timothy Harris came out some three points ahead of Prime Minister Denzil Douglas in an opinion poll held in June and July. In July the International Monetary Fund (IMF) reported that St Kitts and Nevis was showing signs of an economic recovery following a four-year contraction in economic activity.

2014 A steady improvement of the economy allowed the return of a US$40 million stand-by loan to the IMF in May. However, financial analyst Schneidman Warner said that the money would have been better spent repaying more expensive outstanding debts. In July the IMF completed its final review of St Kitts and Nevis' economic performance under its 36-month stand-by arrangement. This enables the authorities to draw an additional some US$4.5 million, bringing the total available to some US$7.9 million. The government has said that it will continue to treat the arrangement as precautionary. The government had hoped to make the constitutional amendment necessary to accept the Caribbean Court of Justice (CCJ) as the country's final appellate body in 2014. However, the opposition has said it will refuse to discuss the matter.

2015 As requested by Prime Minister Douglas, Governor General Sir Edmund Wickham Lawrence dissolved parliament on 16 January. An election date is yet to be announced. The dissolution was called just hours before an injunction was granted by the High Court on the same day restraining the government from proclaiming the constituency boundary changes, which had caused the initial dispute. On 20 January High Court Judge Marlene Carter ruled that a motion of no confidence should go ahead despite the fact it was filed after the dissolution since the opposition rights had been violated prior to the dissolution. On 27 January Justice Carter discharged the 16 January injunction granted to opposition MPs against the proclamation bringing the new boundary changes into law. Elections were announced for 16 February. However the boundary saga continued when on 31 January the Eastern Caribbean Supreme Court (ECSC) granted an interim injunction barring any action from being taken on new constituency boundaries, pending an appeal of a High Court ruling on 3 February. While the ECSC discharged the injunction, it at the same time granted leave to appeal its decision to the Privy Council in London, while allowing nominations to proceed from 6 February. The nominations were treated and remained as valid, whatever the Privy Council decision. The elections were held on 18 February and won by Team Unity with seven (out of the 11) elected seats, followed by St Kitts-Nevis Labour Party (three) and the Nevis Reformation Party (one). Dr Timothy Harris was sworn in, as the third prime minister of St Kitts and Nevis, on 18 February (followed by a public swearing-in ceremony on 22 February), after a delay until Governor General Sir Edmund Lawrence received official written confirmation of the result. Resident Judge Marlene Carter administered the Oath of Allegiance, Office and the Oath of Secrecy, while Governor General Lawrence presented the instrument of appointment. On 25 March the prime minster announced that as of 7 April VAT would not be charged on food, medicines and funeral expenses. The report by the OAS election observers was published in May. It reported first of all that the electoral office in St Kitts and Nevis should be staffed by professionals and not people with direct ties to political groups. This had lead to concerns related to the administrative and logistical aspects of the electoral process. It also noted problems with timeframes and deadlines of the electoral process, particularly the publication of the Voters' List, and noted the issue of the boundary changes should have been addressed earlier.

Political structure

Constitution

The constitution of 1983 gives the island of Nevis considerable autonomy within a federal framework.

Form of state

Independent parliamentary democratic state; it is a member of the Commonwealth with the British monarch as head of state, represented by a governor general, who exercises executive power.

Nevis has limited self-government.

The executive

The cabinet is appointed by the governor general in consultation with the prime minister.

The monarch is hereditary, the governor general is appointed by the monarch. Following legislative elections, the leader of the majority party or majority coalition is usually appointed prime minister by the governor general.

National legislature

The legislature is the unicameral National Assembly comprised of 14 seats of which 11 members are directly elected in single-seat constituencies by simple majority vote (eight from St Kitts, three from Nevis), plus three appointed members by the governor general. Members serve five-year terms.

Legal system

The legal system is based upon English common law. Appeals go to the Eastern Caribbean Supreme Court based on Saint Lucia. The final court of appeal is the Privy Council in the UK.

Last elections

16 February 2015 (National Assembly); 11 July 2011 (Nevis Island Assembly (NIA)

Results: National Assembly: Team Unity (Peoples' Action Movement (PAM) PLP, and CCM) won 39.3 per cent of the vote (four seats out of 11 constituency seats), St Kitts-Nevis Labour Party won 27.9 per cent (three), the Concerned Citizens' Movement won 13 per cent (two); the Nevis Reformation Party and the People's Labour Party won one seat each. Turnout was 72.2 per cent.

Next elections

February 2020 (National Assembly); 2016 (NIA)

KEY INDICATORS — St Kitts and Nevis

	Unit	2011	2012	2013	2014	**2015
Population	m	*0.06	*0.06	*0.06	*0.06	*0.06
Gross domestic product (GDP)	US$bn	0.71	0.73	0.77	*0.84	*0.89
GDP per capita	US$	13,364	12,790	*13,239	*14,102	*14,625
GDP real growth	%	-2.0	-0.9	3.8	*-2.8	*3.5
Inflation	%	5.4	1.4	0.7	*1.0	*2.0
Exports (fob) (goods)	US$m	54.3	62.8	58.0	–	–
Imports (fob) (goods)	US$m	218.3	227.7	251.3	–	–
Balance of trade	US$m	-164.0	-164.9	-193.2	–	–
Current account	US$m	-60.3	-87.0	-52.0	*-90.0	*-144.0
Total reserves minus gold	US$m	201.1	–	301.9	327.3	–
Foreign exchange	US$m	201.0	–	291.3	–	–
Exchange rate	per US$	2.70	2.70	2.70	2.70	–

* estimated figure ** forecast figure

Political parties

Ruling party

People's Action Movement (PAM) leading a coalition with the People's Labour Party (PLP) and the Concerned Citizens' Movement (CCM).

Main opposition party

Saint Kitts and Nevis Labour Party (SKNLP)

Political situation

St Kitts and Nevis has not avoided the economic pressures following the global economic downturn and despite record export sales to the US in the first half of 2010 – US$25.7 million, up from US$48.4 million in 2009 – it still has to contend with the introduction of several new taxes, including value added tax (VAT) of 17 per cent from 1 November 2010.

In May 2010 trade negotiators of the Organisation of Eastern Caribbean States (OECS), including those of St Kitts and Nevis, had to discuss how the organisation was going to prepare for the removal of government subsidies for export, typically used to attract foreign direct investment, which will be removed by 2015, in accordance with World Trade Organisation (WTO) requirements.

Population

60,000 (2014)* (54,841; 2010, census figure)

Approximately 30 per cent of the population is under 15 years.

People living on St Kitts are called Kittitians, while those on Nevis are called Nevisians.

May 2001: 45,841

Population density: 114 inhabitants per square km. Urban population 32 per cent (2010 Unicef).

Annual growth rate: 1.3 per cent, 1990–2010 (Unicef).

Ethnic make-up

Black African (91 per cent), mixed race (5 per cent), Asian (3 per cent), British, Portuguese and Lebanese descent (1 per cent).

Religions

Anglican (25 per cent), Methodist (25 per cent), Pentecostal (8 per cent), Moravian (7 per cent), other Protestant (12 per cent), Roman Catholic (7 per cent), Hindu (1 per cent).

Education

As part of an educational initiative, 2,400 laptops were delivered from Taiwan in August 2011, to be distributed to high school students (aged 14–16 years). Another batch of 2,400 is due in October–November for students aged 11–13 years.

Compulsory years: Five to 17

Enrolment rate: 101 per cent boys, 94 per cent girls gross primary enrolment of relevant age group (including repeaters) (Unicef 2004).

Health

Life expectancy: 71 years, 2004 (WHO 2006)

Fertility rate/Maternal mortality rate: 2.4 births per woman, 2004 (WHO 2006)

Birth rate/Death rate: 18.5 births per 1,000 population; nine deaths per 1,000 population (2003).

Child (under 5 years) mortality rate (per 1,000): 9 per 1,000 live births (WHO 2012)

Main cities

Basseterre (capital of St Kitts, estimated population 13,345 in 2012), St Paul's (1,364), Sadlers (1,056), Middle Island (899).

Charlestown (capital of Nevis, 2,294), Gingerland (612), Newcastle (611).

Languages spoken

Official language/s

English

Media

Press

There are no daily newspapers. Weekly publications include *The Democrat* (www.pamdemocrat.org), *The Leewards Times* (www.leewardstimes.com), Sun St Kitts Nevis (http://sunstkitts.com), *The St Kitts and Nevis Observer* and the bi-weekly *Labour Spokesman* (www.labourworksforme.com).

A regional online publication Caribbean Net News (www.caribbeannetnews.com) covers news from St Kitts and Nevis.

Broadcasting

The government-owned commercial radio and television station is ZIZ (www.zizonline.com).

Radio: There are ten radio stations, including two government-owned ZIZ and Big Wave. Commercial stations on St Kitts include Sugar City Rock (www.sugarcityrock.com) Kyss FM (kyssonline.com) and on Nevis, Voice of Nevis (VON) (www.vonradio.com), Choice FM (http://choicefm1053.com) and Radio Paradise in Nevis.

Television: There is ZIZ Television which airs on two free cable channels and Winn FM (www.winnfm.com).

Economy

St Kitts and Nevis is one of the world's most indebted countries, so it was welcome news that in April 2012, the government cleared around 45 per cent of the public debt by successfully concluding a deal with commercial creditors, ranging from commercial banks and bond holders, with an ultimate payment of just under US$500 million. This led to the Debt falling from 145 per cent of GDP in 2011 to 83 per cent in 2013. In May 2012, the government secured a stock-of-debt restructuring deal with the Paris Club of creditors. Multilateral restructuring was agreed of the entire debt, including arrears, which would be spaced out over a 20-year period, with a grace period on the principal repayments starting in 2019 and concessionary rates of interest applied to the rescheduling. The successful negotiations were based on the government's economic reforms, sound macroeconomic path and debt restructuring to date. The agreement should cancel over 60 per cent of the debt, from multilateral restructuring and other concessions.

The economy of the islands is largely based on tourism, manufacturing and agriculture. The tourism sector is a major source of foreign exchange. Tourist numbers fell between 2009-13, leading to the a fall in investment and a contraction of growth on the island. GDP growth in 2012 stood at -0.9 per cent before jumping to 3.8 per cent in 2013 and 3.5 in 2014. This improvement in the economy can be attributed to the improvement of the global economic climate, allowing visitor numbers to increase by around 20,000 from 2009 to some 107,000 in 2013. A new scheduled flight to St Kitts by British Airways also facilitated visitor numbers to rise higher than could have been expected given the downturn in the tourist sector world-wide. The flourishing of the tourist industry is vital for the Islands economy as, in 2014, tourism had a total contribution of 25.5 per cent to GDP and employed a total of 24.2 per cent of the workforce (6,000 jobs).

Traditional sugar cane cultivation ceased in 2005, with plantations being cleared for land development. As the agricultural sector is unable to feed the population imported food is a major drain on foreign reserves. Commercial agricultural production is led by tropical fruit and coconuts. The cultivation of cotton was re-introduced in 2008, after a gap of four years, after a trade agreement with japan was made.

St Kitts belongs to the East Caribbean Currency Union, under the supervision of the Eastern Caribbean Central Bank (which is based in Basseterre), with a common currency (the EC$) and shared resources and reserves pooled for economic stability. It offers offshore banking and financial services.

By 2014, with the tourist industry on the up, GDP growth was stable and positive at 3.5 per cent. Inflation has remained low over recent years, having not exceeded 2 per cent over the last three years, standing at 1.2 per cent in 2014.

External trade

As a member of the Caribbean Community and Common Market (Caricom), St Kitts and Nevis operates within the single market (Caribbean Single Market and Economy (CSME)), which became operational in 2006. Goods, services, businesses and money are free to move within the CSME without barriers and tariffs. It is also a member of the Eastern Caribbean Currency Union (ECCU) using the East Caribbean Dollar (EC$).

Since the closure of the sugar industry exports have fallen sharply so that light manufacturing and tourism provide foreign earnings. The cultivation of cotton was re-introduced in 2008, after a gap of four years, when a valuable contract of cotton lint for export to Japan was agreed.

Imports

Main imports are food, machinery, manufactured goods, petroleum and derivatives.

Main sources: US (27.1 per cent of total in 2013), Trinidad and Tobago (16.8 per cent), Germany (15.6 per cent).

Exports

Main exports are electrical appliances, electronic items and instrumentation, plastics, food and beverages and cotton.

Main destinations: US (49.6 per cent of total in 2013), Belgium (9.4 per cent), Canada (8.4 per cent).

Agriculture

Farming

The agricultural sector contributed around 1.5 per cent to GDP in 2014.

Historically, the most important crop had been sugar, however the sugar industry was closed down by the government and land re-deployed after the European Union ceased it's preferential pricing agreement under the Lomé Convention, although not necessarily for agricultural purposes.

Diversification into food crops has been encouraged to reduce dependence on imports.

The manufacture of cotton lint was re-introduced in 2008, after a gap of four years, when a valuable contract for over 3,200kg of cotton lint for export to Japan was agreed. Old, retired ginnery equipment was renovated with new parts before the work could begin. Processing raw cotton began in 2008, however the only supply available came from government owned farms, after the first year of cotton cultivation, but supplies from private sources are expected to maintain the volume of production in future. By 2011 Japan had more than doubled its purchases of Nevis cotton.

Fishing

Inshore fishing is a traditional occupation and a significant source of protein.

The fisheries management unit introduced new fishing methods resulting in a fish catch that increased over 40 per cent during the first year. Other improvements include a new fisheries complex, housing commercial storage and a fish market, constructed in Basseterre on St Kitts, while on Nevis the largest fishing facility includes a fish processing plant, walk-in freezers and market, is sited in Charlestown.

Industry and manufacturing

The industrial sector contributes around 23 per cent to GDP in 2014, with manufacturing contributing around 11 per cent.

Manufacturing activities have declined, with contraction in electrical and electronic components, due to poor US demand. The recession also led to a decline in domestic demand for locally produced manufactured goods.

Tourism

The two-island federation offers tourists a range of beach resorts that are not densely populated, but with leisure activities and quality dining. The industry is aimed at visitors from the US and Europe. However, in a move to open up its market base, it advertises regionally and in Asia and Australasia too.

Visitor numbers stood at 107,000 in 2013 (latest figure). Tourism contributed a total of 25.5 per cent to GDP in 2014 and 24.2 to total employment (6,000 jobs).

Visitors arriving by cruise liners make up around 80 per cent of all visitors, although air passengers stay for longer and use a greater variety of services and facilities.

Hydrocarbons

There are no known hydrocarbon reserves. Consumption was 1,740 barrels per day of oil in 2013, all of which was imported. In 2005, St Kitts and Nevis, plus a number of other Caribbean states, signed an agreement with Venezuela to establish PetroCaribe, a multi-national oil company, owned by the participating states. PetroCaribe buys low-priced Venezuelan crude oil under long-term payment plans.

St Kitts and Nevis imports no gas or coal.

Energy

Total installed generating capacity was 55MW in 2013 (latest figures), producing over 140 million kilowatt hours.. The Nevis Electricity Company (Nevlec) provides energy for both islands. Plans for the commercial development of a geothermal-fuelled power plant, developed by the Eastern Caribbean Geothermal Development Project (ECGDP) (or Geo-Caraïbes) which is estimated will provide 60–120MW overall, will be operated by the West Indies Power Limited (WIPL), which is owned by ECGDP countries. The government invested US$22 million in infrastructure and the purchase of four new 4MW electricity generators, delivered in 2010. Two were operational in Basseterre in November 2010 producing an additional 15.6MW of power for St Kitts and the remaining two became operational in 2011.

Energy from biomass is being considered. The sugar cane industry was closed down as uneconomical, but with the rise in hydrocarbon prices ethanol from sugar cane is seen as an alternative and a study to determine the viability of a limited revival of the sugar cane industry is underway.

Financial markets

Stock exchange

Eastern Caribbean Securities Exchange (ECSE)

Banking and insurance

The state-owned Development Bank provides credit to finance agriculture, industry, education and mortgages.

The seven members of the Organisation of Eastern Caribbean States (OECS), Antigua and Barbuda, Dominica, Grenada, Montserrat, St Kitts and Nevis, St Lucia and St Vincent and the Grenadines, share a common currency (the East Caribbean dollar (EC$)) and central bank. The British Virgin Islands and Anguilla are associate members.

Central bank

East Caribbean Central Bank (ECCB)

Main financial centre

Bassetterre

Offshore facilities

After St Kitts and Nevis was listed by the OECD as a tax haven which was unco-operative in fighting money laundering, the government passed the Money Laundering (Prevention) Bill, the Financial Services Intelligence Unit Bill and the Financial Services Commission Bill. The latter Bill established the Financial Services Commission as the main regulatory body for the offshore sector.

In 2002, St Kitts and Nevis was removed from the blacklist drawn up by the OECD.

Time

GMT minus four hours

Geography

St Kitts and Nevis is situated at the northern end of the Leeward Islands chain of the West Indies, with Saba and St Eustatius (both in the Netherlands Antilles) to the north-west, Barbuda to the north-east and Antigua to the south-east. Nevis lies about 3km (2 miles) to the south-east of St Kitts, separated by a narrow strait.

They are rugged volcanic islands covered with either original rich tropical rainforests or cultivated sugar cane plantations. St Kitts has a large crater, Mount Liamuiga, of 1,200 metres (m) high. In the south-east a peninsula stretches into the Caribbean Sea. Nevis is a circular island with a range of mountains. The highest peak, Mount Nevis, is 985m high.

Hemisphere

Northern

Climate

Tropical, tempered by trade winds, with an annual mean temperature of 27 degrees Celsius. December–April are the driest months. Rain can occur throughout the year, although generally wetter from May–October.

Entry requirements

Passports

Required by all except Canadian or US nationals with proof of identity (all US and Canadian nationals require a passport for re-entry to their country from January 2007). Passports must be valid for at least six months after date of entry.

Visa

Required by all with some exceptions; see www.gov.kn and follow link to *Information for non-citizens*, to view a list of those who require a visa and to download an application form. From May 2009 EU citizens may make a short-stay visit, for up to three months, without a visa.

Further information should be obtained from the nearest consulate.

Currency advice/regulations

The import of local and foreign currency is unlimited but must be declared; export of either is limited to the amount declared on arrival.

Travellers cheques in major currencies are widely accepted.

Health (for visitors)

Mandatory precautions

Vaccination certificates for yellow fever and cholera required when travelling from infected areas.

Advisable precautions

Typhoid, polio vaccinations. Water precautions.

Hotels

Advisable to book in advance. A 9 per cent room tax is added to bills and 10 per cent service charge usual.

Credit cards

Major credit and charge cards are widely accepted. ATMs are widely available.

Public holidays (national)

Fixed dates

1 Jan (New Year's Day), 2 Jan (Carnival Day), 1 May (Labour Day), 12 Jun (Queen's Birthday), 19 Sep (Independence Day), 25–26 Dec (Christmas).

Variable dates

Good Friday and Easter Monday (Mar/Apr), Whit Monday (May/June), Queen's Official Birthday (second Sat in Jun), August Monday (first Mon in Aug).

Working hours

Banking

Mon–Thu: 0800–1400; Fri: 0800–1600; Sat: 0830–1100.

Business

Mon–Fri: 0800–1200, 1300–1600/1630. Businesses generally close Thu afternoons and open Sat: 0800–1600.

Government

Mon–Fri: 0800–1200, 1300–1600/1630.

Telecommunications

Mobile/cell phones

There are 850/1900 and 900/1800 GSM services in operation.

Electricity supply

220V AC, 60 cycles. (Some hotel supplies are at 110V AC.)

Electricity is supplied from diesel engine generators and is available island-wide.

Getting there

Air

There are no direct intercontinental flights, only flights from regional hubs land in St Kitts or Nevis.

International airport/s: Robert Llewellyn Bradshaw International Airport (RLB), 3.2km from Basseterre, duty-free shop, restaurant, hotel reservations.

Taxis from the airport have regulated fares.

Other airport/s: Newcastle Airfield (NEV), 11km from Charlestown on Nevis.

Airport tax: Departure tax: EC$60

Surface

Water: There are regular ferry services between St Maarten and St Kitts. Cruise ships visit.

Main port/s: Basseterre (St Kitts) has a deep-water harbour, Charlestown (Nevis).

Getting about

National transport

Road: There is a 300km road network. Main routes cover perimeters of both islands.

In 2006 a new by-pass to reduce traffic congestion in Basseterre was opened. It was funded through a loan of US$7.56 million by the Caribbean Development Bank (CDB).

Buses: Privately operated buses provide a regular but unscheduled service.

Water: There are regular daily ferry services between the islands of St Kitts and Nevis.

City transport

Taxis: Serve both islands with set fare systems; 10 per cent tip usual.

Car hire

It is advisable to reserve a hire car well in advance. National licence required in order to obtain visitor's temporary licence. Traffic drives on the left.

BUSINESS DIRECTORY

The addresses listed below are a selection only. While World of Information makes every endeavour to check these addresses, we cannot guarantee that changes have not been made, especially to telephone numbers and area codes. We would welcome any corrections.

Telephone area codes

The international direct dialling code (IDD) for St Kitts and Nevis is +1 869, followed by subscriber's number.

Useful telephone numbers

Emergency: 911

Fire: 333

Air Ambulance: 465-2801

JNF General Hospital: 465-2551

Chambers of Commerce

St Kitts/Nevis Chamber of Industry and Commerce, South Independence Square, PO Box 332, Basseterre (tel: 465-2980; fax: 465-4490; e-mail: skchamber@caribsurf.com).

Banking

Bank of Nevis, The Main Street, Box 450, Charlestown, Nevis (tel: 469-5564/5796; fax: 469-5798).

Bank of Nova Scotia, Fort Street, Box 433, Basseterre, St Kitts (tel: 465-4141; fax: 465-8600).

Barclays Bank, The Circus, Box 42, Basseterre, St Kitts (tel: 465-2519/10/2449/1081/2264; fax: 465-1041).

Development Bank of St. Kitts & Nevis, Church Street, Box 249, Basseterre, St. Kitts (tel: 465-2288/2964/4041; fax: 465-4016).

National Bank, Central Street, Box 343, Basseterre, St Kitts (tel: 465-2204; fax: 465-1050).

Nevis Co-Op Banking Company, Chapel Street, Box 60, Charlestown, Nevis (tel: 469-5277/0113/4; fax: 469-1493).

Royal Bank of Canada, Cnr Bay Road & Fort Street, Box 91, Basseterre, St Kitts (tel: 465-2259/2409/2389/4374; fax: 465-1040).

Central bank

Eastern Caribbean Central Bank, Bird Rock Road, PO Box 89, Basseterre (tel: 465-2537; fax: 465-5615; email: info@eccb-centralbank.org).

Stock exchange

Eastern Caribbean Securities Exchange (ECSE), www.ecseonline.com

Travel information
Nevis Tourism Bureau, Charlestown, Nevis (tel: 469-1042; fax: 469-1066).

St Kitts-Nevis Hotel and Tourism Association, PO Box 438, Basseterre, St Kitts (tel: 465-5304; fax: 465-7746).

Ministry of tourism
Ministry of Trade, Industry and Tourism (National Development Corporation), Government Headquarters, Basseterre (tel: 465-2521, 465-4106; fax: 465-5202, 465-1778).

National tourist organisation offices
St Kitts-Nevis Department of Tourism, Pelican Mall, PO Box 132, Basseterre, St Kitts (tel: 465-2620; fax: 465-4040).

Ministries
Ministry of Agriculture, Lands, Housing and Development, Education, Youth and Community Affairs, Government Headquarters, PO Box 186, Basseterre (tel: 465-2521; fax: 465-9069).

Ministry of Finance, Marketing and Development Department, Rams Building, Liverpool Row, Basseterre, St Kitts (tel: 465-1153; fax: 465-1154).

Ministry of Health, Labour and Women's Affairs, Government Headquarters, Basseterre (tel: 465-2521; fax: 456-1316).

Office of The Prime Minister, Government Headquarters, PO Box 186, Basseterre (tel: 465-2103; fax: 465-1001).

Other useful addresses
Attorney General's Office, Government Headquarters, Basseterre (tel: 465-2521; fax: 465-5202).

Eastern Caribbean Securities Exchange, PO Box 94, Bird Rock, Basseterre (tel: 466-7192; fax: 465-3798; email: Info@ECSEonline.com).

Financial Services Department, PO Box 186, Basseterre (tel: 466-5048; fax: 466-5317; internet: www.fsd.gov.kn).

Government Offices, Administration Building, Charlestown (465-5521; fax: 465-5202).

Investment Promotion Agency, Bay Road, Basseterre (tel: 465-4106).

Embassy of St Kitts and Nevis (USA), OECS Bldg, 3216 New Mexico Ave, NW Washington DC 20016 (tel: (+1-202) 686-2636; fax: (+1-202) 686-5740).

St Kitts-Nevis Information Service, Government Headquarters, Church Street, Basseterre (tel: 465-2521; fax: 466-4504; email: skninfo@caribsurf.com; internet: www.gov.kn).

St Kitts-Nevis Manufacturers' Association, PO Box 392, Basseterre (tel: 465-6226).

Internet sites
Caribbean Export Development Agency: www.cartis.com/

Government website: www.gov.kn

Organisation of American States: www.oas.org

St Lucia

KEY FACTS

Official name: St Lucia

Head of State: Queen Elizabeth II; Governor General Dame Calliopa Pearlette Louisy (since 1997)

Head of government: Prime Minister Dr Kenneth (Kenny) Davis Anthony (SLP) (from 30 Nov 2011)

Ruling party: St Lucia Labour Party (SLP) (from 30 Nov 2011)

Area: 616 square km

Population: 170,000 (2014)* (166,526; 2010 census figure)

Capital: Castries

Official language: English

Currency: East Caribbean dollar (EC$) = 100 cents

Exchange rate: EC$2.70 per US$ (fixed)

GDP per capita: US$7,978 (2014)*

GDP real growth: -1.11% (2014)*

GDP: US$1.36 billion (2014)*

Inflation: 2.46% (2014)*

Balance of trade: -US$291.33 million (2013)

Annual FDI: US$80.98 million (2011)

* estimated figure

COUNTRY PROFILE

1605 Britain made an unsuccessful attempt to colonise the islands which were populated by a Carib people.
1642 France claimed sovereignty.
1814 After changing hands 14 times during the seventeenth and eighteenth centuries, St Lucia became a British colony. It formed part of the Windward Islands.
1924 A representative government was introduced.
1936 A constitution was provided with a legislative council of elected representatives.
1951 The first elections, under universal adult suffrage, were won by the St Lucia Labour Party (SLP).
1958 St Lucia joined the UK-sponsored West Indies Federation.
1962 The West Indies Federation was dissolved.
1964 Sugar cane production was abandoned.
1967 St Lucia became a self-governing associated state, with full autonomy over internal affairs. The UK retained control of foreign affairs and defence.
1979 St Lucia gained independence within the Commonwealth.
2002 Hurricane Lili destroyed around half of the annual banana crop.
2003 An amended constitution replaced the oath of allegiance to the British monarch with a pledge of loyalty to St Lucia. Julian Hunte, St Lucia's foreign minister, was elected president of the UN General Assembly's June session, the smallest country ever to lead the 191-member world body.
2004 The Caribbean Development Bank (CDB) approved a loan to help St Lucia build infrastructure against flooding in coastal cities.
2006 Air Jamaica introduced non-stop flights from New York. The opposition United Workers Party (UWP) won 11 seats (out of 17) in parliamentary elections, the incumbent SLP won six. Sir John Compton became prime minister.
2007 Diplomatic relations with Taiwan were re-established, after a 10-year break. Prime Minister Sir John Compton died and Stephenson King was elected prime minister by the ruling UWP.
2009 The EU signed an agreement with the government to provide financial assistance to fund a US$100 million general hospital, with a 122-bed facility. The first national forest inventory since the 1980s began, aimed at providing a current comprehensive survey of forest resources, including trees, animals and birds.
2011 In June, the World Bank agreed to a zero interest loan of US$5.6 million to fund an improved electricity distribution system and to diversify energy production (including renewable energy sources). In August citizens of the Organisation of Eastern Caribbean States (OECS) – Antigua and Barbuda, Dominica, Grenada, St Kitts and Nevis, St Lucia and St Vincent and the Grenadines – were granted freedom of movement, allowing them to reside, work, establish businesses and provide services throughout the organisation. During the Commonwealth Heads of Government summit, in October, the 16 countries in which the British monarch is Head of State unanimously agreed to change the royal line of succession from that of first born son to the first born child (regardless of its gender). The change will be enacted after the succession of Prince William (currently second in line to the throne, after his father Prince Charles). In parliamentary elections held on 28 November the opposition SLP won 11 seats, instead of the pre-election expectations of six, with 50.99 per cent of the vote, while the UWP won 46.96 per cent (six seats). Kenny Anthony (SLP) became prime minister.
2012 The government published its legislation for the introduction of a value added tax (VAT) on 14 September, with its introduction on 21 November.
2013 St Lucia become the ninth member of the La Alternativa Bolivariana para los Pueblos de Nuestra América (ALBA) (Bolivarian Alliance for the Peoples of Our Americas) in May. Under an agreement with Petrocaribé the members of ALBA pay a reduced rate for their oil imports from Venezuela.
2014 In March a water related emergency was announced for the north of the island as a result of a shortfall in annual rain. In July the Water and Sewage Company (WASCO) announced an extention of the emergency to cover the whole country as the drought became worse.
2015 Finance minister, Dr Kenny Anthony, presented the 2015/16 budget to parliament on 29 April. However the

opposition refused to open the customary debate on the estimates and the Speaker presented the motion for approval. No member of the House voted against the motion. A short-stay visa waiver agreement signed between the EU and a number of ACP countries on 28 May will allow citizens of St Lucia to travel visa free to the Schengen area.

Political structure

Constitution

Saint Lucia became independent of Great Britain on 22 February 1979. The Saint Lucia Constitution Order was first published on 20 December 1978. It achieved this upon its attainment of a fully responsible government. It has been revised a number of times since then.

Independence date

22 February 1979

Form of state

Parliamentary democracy

The executive

The British monarch is Head of State and represented by the governor general. The prime minister exercises executive power and is appointed by the governor general following legislative elections, usually the leader of the majority party or majority coalition. The Cabinet is appointed by the governor general on the advice of the prime minister.

National legislature

The bicameral parliament has a House of Assembly of 17 members (plus the Speaker) directly elected in single-member constituencies, for five-year terms. The Senate has 11 nominated members, six appointed by the prime minister, three by the leader of the opposition and two chosen by the governor general.

Universal age of suffrage 18.

Legal system

The legal system is a hybrid of English common law with a strong influence of French civil law.

Appeals are heard by the Eastern Caribbean Supreme Court. The final court of appeal is the Judicial Council of the Privy Council in the UK.

Last elections

28 November 2011 (parliamentary)

Results: Parliamentary: the St Lucia Labour Party (SLP) won 50.99 per cent (11 seats, out of 17), the United Workers Party (UWP) 46.96 per cent (six); three other political parties and independents failed to win enough votes to gain any seats.

Next elections

2016 (parliamentary)

Political parties

Ruling party

St Lucia Labour Party (SLP) (from 30 Nov 2011)

Main opposition party

United Workers Party (UWP); Lucian People's Movement (LPM); St Lucia Labour Party (SLP).

168,000 (2012)* (166,526; 2010 census figure)

Population

10 May 2010: 166,526

Population density: 253 inhabitants per square km. Urban population 28 per cent (2010 Unicef).

Annual growth rate: 1.2 per cent, 1990–2010 (Unicef).

Ethnic make-up

Black African (90 per cent), mixed race (6 per cent), East Indian (3 per cent).

Religions

Roman Catholic (90 per cent), Anglican (3 per cent) other Protestant (7 per cent).

Education

The education system is in great need of reform. Hampering the development of the island's education is the instructor-led method of learning but there has been little attempt to progress to a more learner-orientated approach.

The secondary education system will benefit from the construction of two new schools, with allocated funds of US$23 million, in 2005/06. The new facilities, one geared to the arts and the other towards agriculture and science will provide places for over 700 students. The government is aiming to achieve universal secondary education and has been aided by the World Bank Education Development Plan.

Compulsory years: 4 to 16.

Enrolment rate: 101 per cent primary and 85 per cent secondary enrolment; 111 per cent and 104 per cent enrolment respectively of boys and girls of relevant age group (including repeaters) (Unicef 2004).

Health

The provision of healthcare will be changed within 2005/06 when the environment levy will be replaced with a fixed tax on consumer goods of between 3.5–4 per cent and will be called the health and environment levy. It is expected to raise US$11 million to fund services for most of the population.

The government is concerned about the loss of medical personnel. Nurse migration, due to low pay, lack of opportunities and poor working conditions, has left Victoria Hospital the principal hospital facility chronically understaffed.

The European Commission has granted US$23 million in 2005 for a new hospital to replace Victoria Hospital, to be built on a new site. Construction is scheduled to begin in early 2006.

HIV/Aids

The Caribbean has the second highest rate of HIV/aids infection, after sub-Saharan Africa and the impact on the economy is already being felt with St Lucia losing around US$74 million since the mid-1980s. In February 2005 the Global Fund to Fight Aids approved a grant of US$10.1 million, over 2005–10, to help St Lucia fight the epidemic. The programme is targetting a 50 per cent reduction in HIV patients and HIV/Aids deaths as well as mother-to-infant transmission reduced from 30 per cent to less than 10 per cent.

Life expectancy: 74 years, 2004 (WHO 2006)

Fertility rate/Maternal mortality rate: 2.0 births per woman, 2010 (Unicef)

KEY INDICATORS — St Lucia

	Unit	2011	2012	2013	2014	**2015
Population	m	*0.17	0.17	*0.17	*0.17	*0.17
Gross domestic product (GDP)	US$bn	1.24	1.32	1.34	*1.36	*1.41
GDP per capita	US$	7,435	7,858	7,949	*7,978	*8,250
GDP real growth	%	0.2	-1.3	-0.5	*-1.1	*1.8
Inflation	%	2.8	4.2	1.5	*2.5	*2.4
Exports (fob) (goods)	US$m	179.8	212.4	205.3	–	–
Imports (fob) (goods)	US$m	616.0	566.4	496.7	–	–
Balance of trade	US$m	-436.2	-353.9	-291.3	–	–
Current account	US$m	-283.8	-169.0	-171.0	*-168.0	*-188.0
Total reserves minus gold	US$m	236.2	–	192.2	257.7	–
Foreign exchange	US$m	211.5	–	168.5	–	–
Exchange rate	per US$	2.70	2.70	2.70	2.70	–

* estimated figure ** forecast figure

Birth rate/Death rate: 21 births per 1,000 population; five deaths per 1,000 population (2003).

Child (under 5 years) mortality rate (per 1,000): 18 per 1,000 live births (WHO 2012)

Welfare

The social welfare system in St Lucia has been described as unfair, partial and out of touch with social realities and legislation is out of date. The Catholic Church run homes for the elderly and assistance is provided to the needy. There is no law protecting children born outside of marriage with regard to their property rights and no laws against sexual harassment.

Main cities

Castries (capital, estimated population 9,060 in 2012), Bexon (7,918), Babonneau (5,715), Ciceron (3,979), Dennery (3,853).

Languages spoken

English and French patois.

Official language/s

English

Media

Press

Weeklies: There are no daily newspapers, weeklies include *The Vanguard*, *The Voice of St Lucia* published on Wednesday and *The Crusader* and *The Star* (www.stluciastar.com), appear on Saturday. Online publications *Saint Lucia One Stop* (www.sluonestop.com) a local news service covering local news and business and *St Lucia Mirror* (www.stluciamirroronline.com) and *One Caribbean* (www.onecaribbeanmedia.net), based in Trinidad. Another regional online publication is Caribbean Net News (www.caribbeannetnews.com), which reports news from St Lucia.

The *Saint Lucia Nationwide*(www.stlucia.gov.lc – follow link from NTN) is published weekly by the Department of Information Services concerning government news and notices.

Broadcasting

Radio: In 2004 a radio service – Radio Caricom, the Voice of the Caribbean Community – was launched with St Lucia being one of the 'pilot states' in the project, which eventually will be available to all Caricom member states.

Commercial radio stations includes Radio Saint Lucia (RSL) (www.rslonline.com) is government-owned, Radio 100 (www.htsstlucia.com), affiliated to HTS, and Hot FM (www.caribbeanhotfm.com)

Television: The three networks are private, Daher Broadcasting service (DBS), Catholic Broadcasting (CBTN) and the commercial Helen Television Systems (HTS) (www.htsstlucia.com), which also runs a radio station. For a fee, there is cable television providing 40 channels of international and local viewing.

Economy

With an economy that is largely governed by the vagaries of the tourist industry, with tourism contributing a total of 39.5 per cent to GDP in 2014, St Lucia is vulnerable to external shocks. The spending capacity of foreign visitors, which may be limited by their domestic economy, plus internal problems such as hurricane damage or rising world commodity prices, can combine to make directing the economy more a reactive than a proactive process. Much of this has led to St Lucia having to battle with a significant external debt, which stood at 77 per cent of GDP in 2012 (latest figure).

Banana production was the other main contributor to GDP. Under the Cotonou agreement with the European Union banana exports preferential access measures. However, after a 15 year dispute with the World Trade Organisation (WTO), in 2009 the EU agreed to remove the import duties on all bananas imported into the EU, which lead to cheaper imports from large plantations. In 2010 the EU offered smaller Caribbean banana growers financial support packages to promote competitiveness and economic diversification but despite this St Lucia recorded record exports of bananas in 2014.

Other cash crops include mangoes and avocado pears; a lucrative deal was signed in 2005 to supply over 25 tonnes of cocoa beans to a leading US chocolate manufacturer. Other development projects focus on computer-driven information technology.

GDP growth has struggled in recent years due to St Lucia's reliance on external factors for the success of their economy. GDP growth has remained negative for a number of years standing at -1.2 per cent in 2012 before dropping further to -2.3 per cent in 2013. GDP growth improved slightly in 2014 to -1.1 per cent and as the global economic crisis improves it is hoped that positive growth will again soon take affect with an increase in visitor numbers and banana exports.

After inflation peaked at 5.6 per cent in 2008, due to world food and fuel prices, it has dropped again to a more sustainable and stable 1.5 per cent in 2013 and 1 per cent in 2014 as global commodity prices stabilised.

As public expenditure rose in 2009 the government introduced revenue enhancing measures such as increased petrol prices and a proposed value added tax (VAT) – which was implemented in 2012 at 15 per cent- making them the last eastern Carribean country to introduce a VAT.

External trade

As a member of the Caribbean Community and Common Market (Caricom), St Lucia operates within the single market (Caribbean Single Market and Economy (CSME)), which became operational in 2006. Goods, services, businesses and money are free to move within the CSME without barriers and tariffs. It is also a member of the Eastern Caribbean Currency Union (ECCU) using the East Caribbean Dollar (EC$).

Foreign earnings are principally generated by tourism, as Saint Lucia is a prime yachting centre and cruise destination, and remittances. The small manufacturing sector is diverse producing clothing, processed coconuts, electronic components and beverages.

Imports

Main imports are food, manufactured goods, machinery and transport equipment, chemicals and fuels.

Main sources: US (48.2 per cent of total in 2013), Trinidad and Tobago (20.5 per cent), Brazil (8.2 per cent).

Exports

Main exports are clothing, cocoa, vegetables, fruits and coconut oil.

Main destinations: Dominican Republic (25.5 per cent of total in 2013), US (10.2 per cent), Suriname (9.2 per cent).

Agriculture

Farming

The agricultural sector used to be the mainstay of the economy, but has been overtaken by tourism. Over 50 per cent of the total area is cultivated arable land. In 2014 agriculture contributed 3 per cent to GDP and employ some 21.7 per cent of the workforce.

The main export crop is bananas and St Lucia continues to be the leading Windward Island banana producer. However, the EU no longer offers preferential treatment for St Lucia exports and St Lucia will have to work hard to maintain export levels in the face of stiff competition from larger Central and South American plantations. Despite this St Lucia saw a record year for exports of bananas in 2014 as global economic conditions improved.

Diversification into other cash crops has been encouraged. A multimillion-dollar deal was signed between St Lucia and the World's Finest Chocolate Inc to supply 256,800 kilograms of cocoa beans a year. There has been an increase in non-banana agriculture production, in particular in copra cultivation, which has resulted in increased exports of coconut oil to Jamaica. Also grown are traditional fruits and vegetables for the domestic and regional markets, and tree crops, such as mangoes and avocados.

Fishing

The typical total annual fish catch is over 2,000 tonnes, shellfish, molluscs and cephalopods account for another 77t per annum.

Industry and manufacturing

The manufacturing sector is negligible and manufacturing activity is dominated by food and drinks production, electrical products and corrigated paper production.

Tourism

Tourism has become the most important sector generating most activity in St Lucia's economy. St Lucia is a relatively unspoilt island, offering tourists both beach and city activities. An aerial tram takes passengers into the Babonneau rainforest canopy.

Travel and tourism is a vital component of the economy, contributing a total of 39.5 per cent of GDP in 2014; it also provided employment to 44.1 per cent of the workforce (34,000 jobs) over the same period. Visitor numbers in 2014 stood at 338,000, up from 319,000 in 2013. Investment in the industry also accounted for 20.5 per cent of total investment (US$66.4 million).

Hydrocarbons

There are no known hydrocarbons reserves; all petroleum products must be imported.

In 2005, St Lucia, plus a number of other Caribbean states, signed an agreement with Venezuela to establish PetroCaribe, a multi-national oil company, owned by the participating states. PetroCaribe buys low-priced Venezuelan crude oil under long-term payment plans. However, it was not until 2014 that shipping fuel under the PetroCaribe agreement was in operation after detailed negotiations with other interested parties (Buckey, the operators of the storage facility; St Lucia Electricity Services Ltd; the Bureau of Standards; petroleum dealers and others involved in the distibution of fuel). St Lucia consumed 3,040 barrels per day of oil (bpd) in 2013, all of which was imported.

Energy

Total installed generating capacity was 76MW in 2013 (latest figures). St Lucia is committed to investment in renewable energy sources including a 4.25MW wind farm, 400KW biomass (methane), geothermal, solar and hybrid projects of any combination. Hydropower offers the greatest potential for energy with conventional technology and new ocean thermal energy conversion (otec).

Lucelec, the government-owned utility company is responsible for generation, transmission and distribution of electricity. The main power station is Cul de Sac, south of Castries with a hydroelectric dam in Roseau and a geothermal project in Soufrière.

On 20 June 2011, the World Bank agreed to a zero interest loan of US$5.6 million to fund an improved electricity distribution system and diversity of energy production (including renewable energy sources).

Financial markets

Stock exchange

Eastern Caribbean Securities Exchange (ECSE)

Banking and insurance

The seven members of the Organisation of Eastern Caribbean States (OECS), Antigua and Barbuda, Dominica, Grenada, Montserrat, St Kitts and Nevis, St Lucia and St Vincent and the Grenadines share a common currency (the East Caribbean dollar (EC$)) and central bank. The British Virgin Islands and Anguilla are associate members.

The Bankers Association of Saint Lucia (BA) announced in August 2014 that St Lucia's Foreign Financial Institutions (FFIs) had met the 1 July deadline for reporting requirements for United States clients which forms part of the Foreign Account Tax Compliance Act (FATCA).

Central bank

Eastern Caribbean Central Bank, St Kitts and Nevis

Offshore facilities

St Lucia is a relatively new entrant to the offshore financial sector. The Organisation for Economic Co-operation and Development (OECD) removed St Lucia from its blacklist of non-complainant government implementing anti-money laundering legislation after St Lucia introduced measures consistent with the OECD's call for transparency in the banking sector.

Time

GMT minus four hours

Geography

St Lucia is in the Windward Islands group of the West Indies, 40km (25 miles) to the south of Martinique and 32km (20 miles) to the north-east of St Vincent, in the Caribbean Sea. The island is volcanic, with spectacular mountain scenery.

Hemisphere

Northern

Climate

The mean annual temperature is 26 degrees Celsius. The island is cooled by the north-east trade winds. The weather is driest from January–April. The rainy season is from July–October.

Entry requirements

Passports

Required by all, except US, Canadian, French and UK citizens who possess valid identification, return tickets and are staying for less than eight days (all US and Canadian nationals require a passport for re-entry to their country from January 2007).

Visa

Requirements vary for citizens, country by country. See www.stlucia.gov.lc under *FAQ*, see *Do I need a Visa?* for a full list and procedures, plus an application form to be downloaded.

Currency advice/regulations

The import and export of local and foreign currency is unrestricted.

Travellers cheques, in US dollars, are widely accepted.

Health (for visitors)

Mandatory precautions

Yellow fever vaccination certificate required if arriving from an infected area.

Advisable precautions

Typhoid, polio vaccination. Medical services are limited. Travel insurance is essential, including cover for repatriation. Hospitalisation is costly and doctors often expect immediate cash payment before treatment begins.

Hotels

Bills include 8 per cent tax and usually a 10 per cent service charge.

Credit cards

Major credit and charge cards are accepted in large shopping areas. ATMs are widely available.

Public holidays (national)

Fixed dates

1–2 Jan (New Year), 22 Feb (Independence Day), 1 May (Labour Day), 1 Aug (Emancipation Day), 13 Dec (St Lucia Day), 25–26 Dec (Christmas).

Variable dates

Good Friday, Easter Monday, Whit Monday, Corpus Christi (May/Jun), Thanksgiving Day (first Mon in Oct).

Working hours

Banking

Mon–Thu: 0800–1400, Fri: 0800–1700. Banks are closed on weekends and public holidays. The Bank of Saint Lucia and First National Bank open Sat 0800–1200 at sub-branches in and around Rodney Bay.

Business

Mon–Fri: 0800–1230, 1330–1630.

Government

Mon–Fri: 0800–1230, 1330–1630.

Shops

In Castries (some shops may vary), Mon–Fri: 0830–1630, Sat: 0800–1230. In Sunny Acres, Mon–Sat: 0900–1900. In Rodney Bay, Mon–Thu: 0900–1900,

Fri–Sat: 0900–2000. All shops, except supermarkets, close Sunday.

Telecommunications

Mobile/cell phones

There are 850/900/1800/1900 GSM services operating throughout most of the territory.

Electricity supply

220V AC, 50 cycles; UK standard 3-pin plugs.

Weights and measures

The metric system was introduced in 2005 however the imperial system is still used unofficially.

Getting there

Air

National airline: LIAT (St Lucia is a major shareholder in this regional airline).

International airport/s: Hewanorra International Airport (UVF), 67km south of Castries, duty-free shop, bar, restaurant, shops, car hire, VIP business lounges. Caters for intercontinental flights. Transport from the airport includes taxis, buses and helicopter (by reservation).

Vigie (SLU), 3km from Castries, bar, restaurant, car hire. Caters for regional flights only.

Airport tax: Departure tax: EC$54

Surface

Main port/s: Castries, Vieux Fort, Soufrière.

Getting about

National transport

Road: All centres are served by a well maintained road network. Main roads constitute over half of 800km network.

Buses: Unscheduled local basic services are offered by independent drivers.

Water: Boats ply to various destinations.

City transport

Taxis: Taxis are relatively cheap and widely available. A fixed rate system operates but it is advisable to negotiate fares in advance, especially for long journeys. Tips are not expected.

Car hire

Available in Castries, Vieux Fort and Soufrière and through hotels. A national or international licence is acceptable. Traffic drives on the left.

BUSINESS DIRECTORY

The addresses listed below are a selection only. While World of Information makes every endeavour to check these addresses, we cannot guarantee that changes have not been made, especially to telephone numbers and area codes. We would welcome any corrections.

Telephone area codes

The international direct dialling code (IDD) for St Lucia is +1 758, followed by subscriber's number.

Useful telephone numbers

Emergencies: 911

Tourist Board: 452-5968, 453-0053

Chambers of Commerce

St Lucia Chamber of Commerce, Industry and Agriculture, Vide Bouteille, PO Box 482, Castries (tel: 452-3165; fax: 453-6907; e-mail: info@stluciachamber.org).

Banking

Bank of Nova Scotia, 6 Wm Peter Blvd, Box 301, Castries (tel: 452-2292, fax: 453-1051; e-mail: bns@candw.lc).

Barclays Bank, Bridge Street, Box 335, Castries (tel: 452-3306; fax: 452-6860).

CIBC Caribbean, Wm Peter Blvd, Box 350, Castries (tel: 452-3751; fax: 452-3735).

Caribbean Banking Corporation, Micoud Street, Box 1531, Castries (tel: 452-2265; fax: 452-1668, 451-7484).

First National Bank of St Lucia Ltd, 21 Bridge Street, Box 168, Castries (tel: 450-7000; fax: 453-1630).

National Commercial Bank of St Lucia, Waterfront Branch, Box 1031, Castries (tel: 452-2103/3562; fax: 453-1604, 451-7106; e-mail: ncbslu@candw.lc).

Royal Bank of Canada, Wm Peter Blvd, Box 280, Castries (tel: 452-2245, 451-6537; fax: 452-7855).

St Lucia Development Bank, National Insurance Bldg Block A, Waterfront, Box 368, Castries (tel: 452-3561/1493, 453-0236; fax: 453-6720).

Central bank

Eastern Caribbean Central Bank, Agency Office, PO Box 295; Ground Floor, Michael Chastnet's Colony House, John Compton Highway Castries (tel: 452-7449; fax: 453-6022; email: eccbslu@candw.lc).

Stock exchange

Eastern Caribbean Securities Exchange (ECSE), www.ecseonline.com

Travel information

St Lucia Helicopters, PO Box 2047, Gros Islet (tel: 453-6950; fax: 425-1553; internet: www.stluciahelicopters.com).

St Lucia Hotel and Tourism Association, Pointe Seraphine, PO Box 545, Castries (tel: 452-5978).

Ministry of tourism

Ministry of Commerce, Tourism, Investment and Consumer Affairs, 4th Floor, Heraldine Rock Building, Waterfront, Castries (tel: 468-4202, 468-4204; fax: 451-6986; email: mitandt@candw.lc).

National tourist organisation offices

St Lucia Tourist Board, PO Box 221; Sureline Building, Vide Boutielle, Castries (tel: 452-4094; fax: 453-1121; email: slutour@candw.lc; internet: www.stlucia.org).

Ministries

Ministry of Agriculture, Fisheries and Forestry, Stanislaus James Building, Waterfront, Castries (tel: 468-4210; fax: 453-6314; internet: www.slumaffe.org).

Ministry of Commerce, Tourism, Investment and Consumer Affairs, 4th Floor, Heraldine Rock Building, Waterfront, Castries (tel: 468-4202, 468-4204; fax: 451-6986; email: mitandt@candw.lc).

Ministry of Communications, works, Transport and Public Utilities, Union, Castries (tel: 468-4300; email: min_com@candw.lc).

Ministry of Education, Human Resources Development, Youth and Sorts, Francis Compton Building Waterfront, Castries (tel: 486-5203; fax: 453-2299; internet: www.education.gov.lc).

Ministry of External Affairs, International Trade and Civil Aviation, Conway Business Centre, Waterfront, Castries (tel: 468-4501/2; fax: 452-7427; email: foreign@candw.lc).

Ministry of Finance, International Financial Services and Economic Affairs, 2nd Floor, Bridge Street, Castries (tel: 468-5520; fax: 451-9231; email: minfin@gosl.gov.lc).

Ministry of Health, Human Services, Family Affairs and Gender Relations, Chaussee Road, Castries (tel: 452-2859; fax: 452-5655; email: health@candw.lc).

Ministry of Home Affairs and Internal Security, Erdistron's Place, Manoel Street, Castries (tel: 452-3772; fax: 453-6315).

Ministry of Labour, Public Service and Co operatives, 2nd Floor, Greaham Louisy Administrative Building, Waterfront, Castries (tel: 468-2202, 468-2205; fax: 453-1305; email: minpet@candw.lc).

Ministry of Physical Development, Housing and Environment, 3rd Floor, Greaham Louisy Administrative Building, Waterfront, Castries (tel: 568-4402; fax: 452-2506; email: econdept@candw.lc).

Ministry of Social Transformation, Culture and Local Government, 4th Floor, Greaham Louisy Administrative Building, Waterfront, Castries (tel: 468-5101, 468-5108; fax: 453-7921).

Other useful addresses

British High Commission, 24 Micoud St, Castries (tel: 452-2484; email: britishhc@candw.lc).

Cable & Wireless Public Telex Booth, Bridge Street, Castries (tel: 452-3301; fax: 452-2363).

Embassy of St Lucia 3216 New Mexico Avenue, NW, Washington, DC 20016,

USA (tel: (+1-202) 364-6792, fax: (+1-202) 364-6723; email: eofsaintlu@aol.com; internet: www.sluonestop.com).

Financial Centre Corporation, NIS Building, Ground Floor, The Waterfront, Castries (tel: 455-7700; fax: 455-7701; email: fcc@stluciaoffshore.com; internet: www.pinnaclestlucia.com).

National Development Corporation (NDC), PO Box 495, Monplaisir Building, Brazil Street, Castries (tel: 452-3614; fax: 452-1814; email: devcorp@candw.lc; internet: www.stluciandc.com).

National Research & Development Foundation (NTDF), PO Box 3067, La Clergy, Castries (tel: 452-4253; fax: 453-6389; email: ntdf@candw.lc).

Organisation of Eastern Caribbean States Natural Resources Management Unit (OECS NRMU), PO Box 1383, Morne Fortune, Castries.

Police Headquarters, Bridge Street, Castries (tel: 452-3854/5).

St Lucia Air and Sea Ports Authority, Micoud St, PO Box 651, Castries (tel: 452-2893; fax: 452-2062).

St Lucia Yacht Services Ltd, PO Box 188, Castries (tel: 452-5057).

Windward Islands Banana Growers' Association (WINBAN), Box 115, Compton Building, William Peter Boulevard, Castries (tel: 452-3975).

Internet sites

Government of St Lucia: www.stlucia.gov.lc

The Star Newspaper: www.stluciaStar.com

St Lucia Search Engine: www.stlucia.com

St Vincent and the Grenadines

KEY FACTS

Official name: Commonwealth of St Vincent and the Grenadines

Head of State: Queen Elizabeth II; Governor General Sir Frederick Ballantyne (since 2 September 2002)

Head of government: Prime Minister Ralph Gonsalves (ULP) (since 29 March 2001; re-elected 2010)

Ruling party: Unity Labour party (ULP) (from 2001; re-elected 2010)

Area: 388 square km

Population: 110,000 (2014)*

Capital: Kingstown

Official language: English

Currency: East Caribbean dollar (EC$) = 100 cents

Exchange rate: EC$2.70 per US$ (fixed)

GDP per capita: US$6,694 (2014)*

GDP real growth: 1.09% (2014)*

GDP: US$736.00 million (2014)*

Inflation: 0.20% (2014)*

Balance of trade: -US$280.11 million (2013)

Annual FDI: US$109.88 million (2011)

* estimated figure

Although the next elections are not scheduled until December 2015, leader of the opposition New Democratic Party (NDP), Arnhim Eustace, announced the 15 candidates who will stand. Mr Eustace said he thought Prime Minister Gonsalves could call early elections and after the one seat narrow defeat in 2010 he wanted the NDP to be ready.

The economy

After its visit to St Vincent and the Grenadines in October 2012 the International Monetary Fund (IM F) reported that economic indicators suggested a 'slow recovery may be underway' The IMF's visit was for the annual Article IV discussions on economic developments and macroeconomics policies.

The fund's mission was headed by Nita Thacker and met with Prime Minister Dr Ralph Gonsalves, Director General of the Ministry of Finance Maurice Edwards and other government and opposition officials, among others.

'Economic activity indicators suggest that a slow recovery may be underway, with some improvements in tourism and manufacturing,' Thacker said.

According to IMF data, real GDP increased by 2.1 per cent in 2013. Growth in St Vincent is expected to reach its 'potential level' of about 3 per cent over the medium term.

The slow recovery is being buoyed by some improvements in tourism and manufacturing, the fund said. 'Risks to the growth outlook are on the downside, especially if the recovery in advanced economies stalls,' she said. 'On a positive note, the decline in commodity prices, particularly fuel, has reduced pressure on inflation and on the balance of payments.'

The fund said the government's fiscal position was expected to improve as well in 2012, although revenues were lower than projected due to the slow recovery and an 'apparent decline in tax compliance.' However, it went on to say that 'Significant cuts to central government capital spending are projected to more than offset the lower revenues, leading to a reduction in the central government fiscal deficit,' Thacker said. 'Looking forward, the authorities agreed with the mission on the need to reduce current spending, strengthen tax compliance and administration and improve the operational efficiency of the central government and state-owned enterprises.'

Resulting savings, the fund said, could be applied to growth and employment-generating capital projects and social safety nets for the poor.

'Structural reforms should continue to aim to create a growth-friendly environment and stimulate private sector activity to ensure medium-term growth and generate employment, especially for the youth,' Thacker said. 'Achieving these goals will require vigorously implementing reforms, including easing access to credit and reducing its cost, enhancing labour skills, reducing energy costs and improving infrastructure.'

COUNTRY PROFILE

The country's first known inhabitants were Arawak Indians, who were later driven out by Carib Indians.

1498 The principal island was sighted by Columbus. No immediate European immigration followed this discovery.

1779 France occupied the island.

1783 Possession of the islands, as part of the Windward Islands, was passed from France to Britain under the Treaty of Versailles.

1795 Thousands of Carib Indians were deported to Belize, following an uprising.

1812 The volcano, La Soufrière, erupted and destroyed most of the island of St Vincent.

1834 After the emancipation of slaves by Britain, indentured labour from the East Indies and Portugal was brought in to remedy the labour shortage.

1958 St Vincent and the Grenadines became part of the UK-sponsored West Indies Federation.

1962 The West Indies Federation was dissolved.

1969 The territory gained internal self-government, the UK retained responsibility for foreign affairs and defence.

1979 St Vincent and the Grenadines gained independence within the Commonwealth.

1998 The New Democratic Party (NDP), led by Prime Minister James Mitchell, was re-elected.
2000 Prime Minister Mitchell stepped down and Arnhim Eustace became prime minister. Anti-government demonstrations forced the government to hold early elections.
2001 The Unity Labour Party (ULP) won early elections and Ralph Gonsalves became prime minister.
2002 Sir Charles James Antrobus, governor general since 1996, died; Sir Frederick Ballantyne became governor general.
2003 The leaders of the Organisation of the Eastern Caribbean States (OECS) agreed to an economic union and introduced a common passport for nationals of the member countries.
2005 Parliamentary elections were won by the ULP.
2006 Taiwan gave a grant of US$15 million and provided a loan of US$10 million, to assist in the construction of an international airport on St Vincent. Taiwan and St Vincent celebrated 25 years of diplomatic relations.
2009 The Millennium Bank, based in St Vincent, was accused by the US regulators of fraudulently selling certificates of deposit and of making 'blatant misrepresentations and glaring omissions' when selling products to US customers. The government put the Millennium Bank into receivership, with loses of US$68 million. A constitutional referendum was held to decide whether to abolish the monarchy (removing Queen Elizabeth II). The vote in favour was 43.13 per cent, short of the two-thirds in favour necessary for the proposal to succeed.
2010 In parliamentary elections, the ruling ULP won eight seats (out of 15), the New Democratic Party (NDP) won the remaining seven. Prime Minister Gonsalves remained in office.
2011 In August citizens of the Organisation of Eastern Caribbean States (OECS) – Antigua and Barbuda, Dominica, Grenada, St Kitts and Nevis, St Lucia and St Vincent and the Grenadines – were granted freedom of movement, allowing them to reside, work, establish businesses and provide services throughout the organisation. A memorandum of understanding (MOU), was signed on 16 August, with Armajaro Trading Limited to reintroduce cocoa cultivation. During the Commonwealth Heads of Government summit, in October, the 16 countries in which the British monarch is Head of State unanimously agreed to change the royal line of succession from that of first born son to the first born child (regardless of its gender). The change will be enacted after the succession of Prince William (currently second in line to the throne, after his father Prince Charles).
2012 On 14 November the government and the St Vincent and the Grenadines Tourism Authority announced plans to introduce a rating system and standards for the local hotel sector.
2013 In November Prime Minister Gonsalves asked parliament to increase the government's borrowing limit from US$35 million to US$50 million. The increase was approved.
2014 The Committee of Experts of the Follow-up Mechanism for the Implementation of the Inter-American Convention against Corruption (MESICIC) of the Organisation of American States (OAS) issued its report on St Vincent and the Grenadines in September. It made a number of recommendations to be considered, including establishing inter-institutional co-ordination mechanisms to assist and ensure that public agencies abide by their legal obligation of requesting the Office of the Attorney General's legal advice in a timely and correct fashion, particularly in matters involving acts of corruption.
2015 A short-stay visa waiver agreement signed between the EU and a number of ACP countries on 28 May will allow citizens of St Vincent and the Grenadines to travel visa free to the Schengen area.

Political structure

Constitution

The Saint Vincent and the Grenadines' Constitution was first published on 26 July 1979 prior to its independence from Great Britain on 27 October 1979.
Most recently, a constitutional referendum was held on 25 November 2009 asking voters whether they approved of a new constitution which would replace the existing one having been in force since 1979. The proposal was supported by only 43.7 per cent of voters well short of the two thirds required to bring the changes into play.

Independence date

27 October 1979

Form of state

Parliamentary democracy, within the Commonwealth.

The executive

The roles of both the Monarch and the Governor General are largely ceremonial functions.
The British monarch is Head of State and represented by the governor general. The prime minister exercises executive power and is appointed by the governor general following legislative elections, usually the leader of the majority party or majority coalition. The Cabinet is appointed by the governor general on the advice of the prime minister.

National legislature

The legislature is unicameral, with a House of Assembly of 23 members comprising 15 members elected at least every five years by universal adult suffrage (including Speaker and Attorney-General) and six senators appointed by the Governor-General (four on the advice of the Prime Minister and two on the leader of the Opposition). The parliamentary term of office is five years.

Legal system

The legal system is based on English common law with variations. Magisterial district courts exercise both civil and criminal jurisdiction up to a certain limit. The primary court of first instance is the High Court of Justice, from which appeal is made to the Eastern Caribbean Court of

KEY INDICATORS St Vincent and the Grenadines

	Unit	2011	2012	2013	2014	**2015
Population	m	*0.11	*0.11	*0.11	*0.11	*0.11
Gross domestic product (GDP)	US$bn	0.69	0.69	0.71	*0.74	*0.76
GDP per capita	US$	6,342	6,332	6,462	*6,694	*6,894
GDP real growth	%	-0.4	1.5	2.4	*1.1	*2.1
Inflation	%	3.2	2.6	0.9	*0.2	*0.2
Exports (fob) (goods)	US$m	43.0	47.8	53.4	–	–
Imports (fob) (goods)	US$m	294.5	315.0	333.5	–	–
Balance of trade	US$m	-251.5	-267.2	-280.1	–	–
Current account	US$m	-207.6	-193.0	-222.0	*-216.0	*-210.0
Total reserves minus gold	US$m	84.3	–	135.1	157.4	–
Foreign exchange	US$m	82.4	–	133.1	–	–
Exchange rate	per US$	2.70	2.70	2.70	2.70	–

* estimated figure ** forecast figure

Appeal. Final appeals go to the Privy Council in the UK.

Last elections

13 December 2010 (parliamentary)

Results: Parliamentary: Unity Labour Party (ULP) won eight seats (out of 15), the New Democratic Party (NDP) seven.

Next elections

December 2015 (parliamentary)

Political parties

Ruling party

Unity Labour party (ULP) (from 2001; re-elected 2010)

Main opposition party

New Democratic Party (NDP)

Political situation

Prime Minister Ralph Gonsalves called into question the leadership, in particular the political directorate, of the 15-member, regional grouping of the Caribbean Community (Caricom). After years of discussion it had not, by June 2010, achieved the level of progress he thought was possible and still had to introduce a fully functional Caricom single market and economy (CSME) by 2015, but which had suffered several setbacks in the progress towards the CSME.

Population

110,000 (2014)*

Approximately 35 per cent of the population is under 15 years. St Vincent has a high rate of emigration. With extremely high unemployment and underemployment, population growth remains a major problem.

Last Census: May 2001:109,202 (provisional)

Population density: 293 inhabitants per square km. Urban population 49 per cent (2010 Unicef).

Annual growth rate: 0.1 per cent, 1990–2010 (Unicef).

Ethnic make-up

Most of the population are the descendants of African slaves brought to the island to work on plantations. There are also a few white descendants of English colonists, as well as some East Indians, Carib Indians and a minority of mixed race.

Religions

Anglican (32 per cent), Methodist (18 per cent), Roman Catholic (10 per cent), Seventh-Day Adventist, Hindu, other Protestant (40 per cent).

Education

Education is not compulsory, but children are expected to attend school between the ages of five and 15. Public schooling is provided free of charge up to age 15, although books and equipment have to be supplied by parents. An estimated 95 per cent of the population attend school, but attendance may drop when family needs are pressing. There are 65 primary schools and 23 secondary schools. Around 10 per cent of the population have no formal education and are illiterate.

The emphasis on academic subjects in secondary schools has shifted to include more practical courses like carpentry and agricultural studies.

Health

Health care is free until the age of 17. There are six public hospitals in Kingstown and five other hospitals in rural areas. There is also a mental health institution and an old people's residence.

A national family planning policy has been in place since 1974 and as a result the fertility rate has dropped considerably.

Life expectancy: 69 years, 2004 (WHO 2006)

Fertility rate/Maternal mortality rate: 2.1 births per woman, 2010 (Unicef)

Birth rate/Death rate: 17 births per 1,000 population; six deaths per 1,000 population (2003).

Child (under 5 years) mortality rate (per 1,000): 23 per 1,000 live births (WHO 2012)

Welfare

The social welfare system is weak. There is no national health insurance, nor any pension allowance for the elderly. The infant mortality rate is high.

There is a limited framework for the protection of children and the number of child abuse cases that are reported is high.

The situation is generally difficult for disabled people, who seldom leave their homes. There is one institution that offers care and support to the elderly.

Main cities

Kingstown (capital on St Vincent, estimated population 16,416 in 2012), Georgetown (1,414), Byera (1,149), Biabou (884). Grenadines: Port Elizabeth (Isle Quatre) (760), Hamilton (570); Dovers (Baliceaux Island) (478).

Languages spoken

English, Vincentian Creole

Official language/s

English

Media

Press

Dailies: *The Daily Herald* was the first international daily newspaper published from Kingstown. A regional online publication Caribbean Net News (www.caribbeannetnews.com) covers news from the islands.

Weeklies: Publications include *The News*, *The Vincentian* (www.thevincentian.com) and *Searchlight* (www.searchlight.vc).

Broadcasting

Radio: There are five radio stations; the National Broadcasting Corporation (NBC) (www.nbcsvg.com) is the oldest and part government-owned network. Hitz FM (www.svgbc.com) is affiliated to SVGTV, We-FM (www.999wefm.com) is a private commercial service; Praise FM (www.praisefmsvg.com) is a Christian station; First FM and Hot 97 are local stations without internet access.

Television: The government-owned free-to-air SVGTV (www.svgbc.com) has six channels covering news, entertainment and sport. Cable TV provides US programmes for paying customers.

Economy

Tourism and agriculture are the principal sectors of the economy. Bananas dominate export commodities, while the Grenadines are a centre of high-end tourism, specialising in luxury hotels and Caribbean yachting.

Like many of the Caribbean Islands, St Vincent and the Grenadines is heavily dependent on external factors for their economy. Therefore, when the global economic crisis was under way the economy suffered and the island experienced negative growth for a number of years, peaking at -9.9 per cent growth in 2009 as visitor numbers dropped. Just as tourism began to recover, two natural disasters occurred – in 2010 Hurricane Tomas devastated 95 per cent of the banana harvest and a violent storm left widespread flooding and damage to infrastructure in north-central St Vincent in April 2011. By 2013 GDP growth had recovered slightly and stood at 2 per cent as revenue from tourism had grown again to near pre-recession levels. However, floods and mudslides caused by unseasonal rainfall caused significant damages, which the world bank put at around US$112 million, and growth fell to -0.5 per cent in 2014.

As growth weakened, domestic spending dropped in line with a fall in disposable incomes. Value added tax (VAT) was introduced in 2007, with a rate of 15 per cent on goods and services and 10 per cent on tourist accommodation; due to high world prices for food and petroleum inflation rose to a peak of 10.1 per cent in 2008. As domestic spending fell so inflation dropped to 0.4 per cent in 2009, remaining almost static at 0.8 per cent in 2010 but increased slightly to 1 per cent in 2013. By 2014, as the economy struggles slightly inflation rose to 5.4 per cent. Remittances in Traditionally amount to around US$30 million, standing at US$32 million in 2013, making up 4.4 per cent of GDP.

The governments ability to spend and invest in social programmes and projects is limited as the Island had a public debt of 67 per cent of GDP at the end of 2013. The banking sector, which is dominated by subsidiaries of Canadian banks, is well capitalised and had limited exposure to the distress experienced by other financial institutions worldwide. One exception was the Millennium Bank, based in St Vincent, which was accused by the US regulators in 2009, of fraudulently selling certificates of deposit and that it made 'blatant misrepresentations and glaring omissions' when selling products to US customers. The government put the Millennium Bank into receivership in 2009, with losses of US$68 million, and it was finally wound up in 2010. Since then the Island has moved to adopt international regulatory standards to attract more business.
St Vincent and the Grenadines is a member of the Caribbean Single Market and Economy (CSME), and the Eastern Caribbean Currency Union (ECCU) using the East Caribbean Dollar.

External trade

As a member of the Caribbean Community and Common Market (Caricom), St Vincent and the Grenadines operates within the single market (Caribbean Single Market and Economy (CSME)), which became operational on 1 January 2006. Goods, services, businesses and money are free to move within CSME without barriers and tariffs. It is also a member of the Eastern Caribbean Currency Union (ECCU) using the East Caribbean Dollar. Although the export of bananas produces around 50 per cent of all commodity sales, tourism is the principal foreign exchange earner as the Grenadines is a popular high-end tourist destination.

Imports

Main imports are machinery and telecommunication equipment and manufactured goods, foodstuffs, fertilisers and fuels.
Main sources: US (35.6 per cent of total in 2012 (most recent figures)), Trinidad & Tobago (26.8 per cent), Venezuela (5.6 per cent).

Exports

Main exports are bananas, taro and arrowroot starch.
Main destinations: St Lucia (25.6 per cent of total in 2016 (most recent figures)), Trinidad & Tobago (15.7 per cent), Barbados (14.3 per cent).

Agriculture

Farming

The agricultural sector is traditionally the mainstay of the economy, but its contribution to GDP, which stood at 40 per cent in 1960, had fallen to 8.5 per cent by 2014. Half of the total land area is arable with only a small proportion unused. St Vincent is the world's leading producer of arrowroot and an exporter of coconut oil. Carrots and plantains are also cash crops. The main food crops are sweet potatoes, tannias, yams, vegetables, and various fruits.
Bananas (grown mainly on small farms under the auspices of St Vincent Banana Growers Association) are the main export crop. The production of bananas, and earnings from their export, have declined in recent years. Unfavourable weather conditions, a sharp fall in the average domestic currency price received for fruit, and a reduction in the average green wholesale price of fruit have weakened the industry.
The EU phased out preferential treatment for banana producers from former colonies and the liberalisation of the banana trade has made it difficult for family-run businesses in St Vincent to compete on the world market. So, although bananas are still the main export, the industry is experiencing a decline.
A memorandum of understanding (MOU), was signed on 16 August 2011, with Armajaro Trading Limited to reintroduce cocoa cultivation. Armajaro Trading undertook to provide the seedlings and commercial loans for investment in tools and equipment and fertilizers, while the government will provide exclusivity in the sales and marketing of chocolate products to Armajaro Trading.
Floods and mudslides caused by unseasonal rainfall caused significant damages to crops and plantation, which the world bank put at around US$112 million.

Fishing

The typical total annual fish catch is over 45,800 tonnes. Shellfish, molluscs and cephalopods account for another 1,800t per annum.

Industry and manufacturing

The industrial sector contributes 20.9 per cent to GDP.
Activity is primarily based on agricultural processing. Units in operation include those producing cigarettes, tobacco products, coconut oil, textiles and clothing, soft drinks, fruit juices, milk, beer, rum, furniture, arrowroot starch, tyre retreading, concrete blocks and quarry products. A flour mill, serving all the Windward Islands, a box factory and a yacht building yard are the main export industries.

Tourism

St Vincent is a volcanic island with only one white sandy beach. There is only minimal scope for further expansion, limiting the industry. The Grenadines have more white sandy beaches, and the government has stepped up promotional work in the sector's main markets of the US, the UK, Canada and the rest of the Caribbean. The infrastructure has also been gradually upgraded.
Employment in the industry has been falling, in 2007 the total contribution of the tourist industry stood at 28.4 per cent of total employment (11,800 jobs) and by 2014 this had dropped to 18.2 per cent of total employment (8,000 jobs). In 2014 the industry contributed 19.9 per cent to GDP, down from 21.3 per cent in 2013. In 2013 (latest figures), there were 71,000 tourist arrivals.
A new tourism campaign under the logo of SVG, with a dedicated website (http://discoversvg.com/) was set up to promote all of the islands within the archipelago, along with their attractions.

Hydrocarbons

There are no known hydrocarbon resources. Consumption of oil was 2,000 barrels per day (bpd) in 2013 (latest figures), all of which was imported. In 2005, St Vincent and the Grenadines, plus a number of other Caribbean states, signed an agreement with Venezuela to establish PetroCaribe, a multi-national oil company, owned by the participating states. PetroCaribe buys low-priced Venezuelan crude oil under long-term payment plans. Any natural gas or coal used is commercially insignificant.

Energy

Total installed generating capacity was 47MW in 2013 (latest figures), of which 44 per cent is produced by hydropower. The government is exploring ways to tap the active (but dormant) volcano, La Sourière, for geothermal energy. Many people have private generators.

Financial markets

Stock exchange

Eastern Caribbean Securities Exchange (ECSE)

Banking and insurance

The banking sector contributes around 6 per cent of GDP.
The seven members of the Organisation of Eastern Caribbean States (OECS), Antigua and Barbuda, Dominica, Grenada, Montserrat, St Kitts and Nevis, St Lucia and St Vincent and the Grenadines, share a common currency (the East Caribbean dollar (EC$)) and central bank. The British Virgin Islands and Anguilla are associate members.The banking sector contributes around 6 per cent of GDP.
The seven members of the Organisation of Eastern Caribbean States (OECS), Antigua and Barbuda, Dominica, Grenada, Montserrat, St Kitts and Nevis, St Lucia and St Vincent and the Grenadines, share a common currency (the East Caribbean dollar (EC$)) and central bank. The

British Virgin Islands and Anguilla are associate members.

Central bank

Eastern Caribbean Central Bank, St Kitts and Nevis.

Offshore facilities

The offshore financial centre is an important element of the economy. The Exchange of Information Act, passed in 2002, attempts to increase financial transparency and accountability. An International Banks Act was also passed in 2002 that aims to strengthen the supervision of banking activities.

St Vincent and the Grenadines was removed from the OECD Financial Action Task Force (FATF) list of non-co-operative countries on money laundering in June 2003, after reforms had been implemented. The government, recognising the sector's importance to its diversification policy, responded by strengthening the regulatory and supervisory framework in line with international best practice. At end-2003, the former Offshore Finance Authority (OFA) was renamed the International Financial Services Authority of St Vincent and the Grenadines (IFSA).

In April 2004, the IFSA reported that in real terms 2004 had seen a growth in the registration of international business companies of 84 per cent over the same period in 2003.

Time

GMT minus four hours

Geography

St Vincent and the Grenadines is an archipelago of islands and cays (low-lying coral islets) in the Caribbean located in the Windward Islands group, approximately 160km west of Barbados in the West Indies. St Lucia is 34km to the north-east and Grenada is to the south. St Vincent, is a volcanic island, is 29km long and 18km wide and the most northerly of the chain. Of the Grenadines there are 32 islands and cays (not all inhabited) of which the principal islands of the group are Bequia, Canouan, Mustique, Mayreau, Isle D'Quatre and Union Island. St. Vincent has a mountainous centre with an inactive (since 1979) volcano, La Soufrière (1,220 metres (m)) at the north end of the island. The mountains are covered in rich rainforests with a 21m waterfall at Baleine.

Hemisphere

Northern

Climate

Tropical, tempered by trade winds, with temperature range 18–32 degrees Celsius. High levels of rainfall from May–November, especially in the north.

Entry requirements

Passports

Required by all. All visitors must have proof of a return/onward passage and enough funds for their stay.

Visa

Not required, except for nationals of the Dominican Republic, Jordan, Syria, Iran, Iraq, Lebanon and Nigeria who must apply to the Ministry of National Security in Kingstown (details in *Addresses* following).

Currency advice/regulations

The import of local and foreign currency is unlimited; export is limited to the amount declared on arrival.

Travellers cheques (in US dollars) are widely accepted.

Health (for visitors)

Mandatory precautions

Yellow fever vaccination certificate required if arriving from an infected area.

Advisable precautions

Typhoid, polio vaccination.

Hotels

Wide range of good hotels available at reasonable prices, except on the privately owned islands of Palm, Mustique and Petit St Vincent, where rates are higher. Seven per cent tax is added to room rates; 10 per cent tip is usual if service charge not included on bill.

Public holidays (national)

Fixed dates

1 Jan (New Year's Day), 14 Mar (National Heroes' Day), 1 May (Labour Day), 1 Aug (Emancipation Day), 27 Oct (Independence Day), 25–26 Dec (Christmas).

If a holiday falls on a Sunday, the following Monday is taken as a public holiday.

Variable dates

Good Friday, Easter Monday, Whit Monday, Carnival Monday (first Mon in Jul), Carnival Tuesday (first Tue in Jul).

Working hours

Banking

Mon–Fri: 0800–1300; also Fri: 1500–1700.

Business

Mon–Fri: 0800–1200, 1300–1600; Sat: 0800–1200.

Government

Mon–Fri: 0800–1615.

Shops

Mon–Fri: 0800–1200, 1300–1600; Sat: 0800–1200.

Telecommunications

Mobile/cell phones

There are 850, 900/1800, 900/1900 GSM services available throughout most of the territories.

Electricity supply

220/240V AC, 50 cycles with flat three-pin plugs.

Getting there

Air

National airline: LIAT (Leeward Islands Air Transport)

International airport/s: ET Joshua Airport (SVD) on St Vincent, 3km from Kingstown. Flights arrive from surrounding Caribbean islands only. Facilities include duty-free shops, restaurant and car hire.

Airport tax: Departure tax: EC$40.

Surface

Water: Cruise ships make regular stops. International shipping lines that maintain contacts with St Vincent may provide passenger services on cargo ships.

Main port/s: Kingstown (only deep-water harbour in country).

Getting about

National transport

Air: There are four local airports on Bequia, Mustique, Canouan and Union Island suitable for light aircraft only. LIAT, SVG Air, Mustique Airways provide scheduled services between Kingstown and most domestic islands.

Road: There is almost 600km of paved roads with the Leeward and Windward highways circling St Vincent. Interior roads are narrow with steep inclines.

Buses: Buses are fairly widespread. Stopping is on demand rather than at pre-specified points.

Water: There are regular, scheduled inter-island ferry services providing round trips between the large inhabited islands.

City transport

Taxis: The rate of fares are set by the government but taxis are unmetered and fares should be agreed at the start of a journey. Prices increase from late at night to early morning. Tipping is up to 10 per cent.

Car hire

Either an International Driving Permit must be stamped at the central police station, or a temporary driving licence can be obtained (for a fee) from the police station on Bay Street, or the Licensing Authority on Halifax Street (Kingstown, St Vincent), with the presentation of a valid overseas driving licence, is necessary.

Driving is on the left, road signs are limited and it is recommended drives should use the horn on sharp curves and turns.

BUSINESS DIRECTORY

The addresses listed below are a selection only. While World of Information makes every endeavour to check these addresses, we cannot guarantee that changes have not been made, especially to telephone numbers and area codes. We would welcome any corrections.

Telephone area codes

The international direct dialling code (IDD) for St Vincent is +1-784, followed by subscriber's number.

Useful telephone numbers
Local information: 118.
International information: 115.
Police: 457-1211.
Kingstown General Hospital: 456-1185.

Chambers of Commerce
St Vincent Chamber of Commerce and Industry, Corea's Building, Halifax Street, PO Box 134, Kingstown (tel: 457-1464; fax: 456-2994; e-mail: svgcic@caribsurf.com).

Banking
Bank of Nova Scotia, 76 Halifax Street, Box 237, Kingstown (tel: 457-1601; fax: 457-2623).

Barclays Bank, Halifax Street, PO Box 604, Kingstown (tel: 456-1706; fax: 457-2985).

CIBC Caribbean, Halifax Street, Box 212, Kingstown (tel: 457-1587; fax: 457-2873).

Canadian Imperial Bank of Commerce, Halifax Street, Box 212, Kingstown (tel: 457-1587/2873; fax: 457-2873).

Caribbean Banking Corporation, 81 South River Road, Box 118, Kingstown (tel: 456-1501; fax: 456-2141).

Development Corporation, Sharpe Street, Box 841, Kingstown (tel: 457-1358; 457-2838).

First St Vincent Bank, Lot 112 Granby Street, Box 154, Kingstown (tel: 456-1873; fax: 457-2675).

National Commercial Bank, Bedford Street, Box 880, Kingstown (tel: 457-1844; fax: 457-2612).

New Bank, Blue Caribbean Bldg Bay Street, Box 1628, Kingstown (tel: 457-1411, 456-2453; fax: 457-1357).

Owens Bank, Box 1045, Kingstown (tel: 457-1230; fax: 457-2610).

St. Vincent Co-operative Bank, Corner Long Lane Upper & South River Road, Box 886, Kingstown (tel: 456-1894).

Central bank
Eastern Caribbean Central Bank, Agency Office, PO Box 839, Granby Street, Kingstown (tel: 456-1413; fax: 456-1412).

Stock exchange
Eastern Caribbean Securities Exchange (ECSE), www.ecseonline.com

Travel information
Air Martinique (tel: 458-4528; fax: 458-4187).

LIAT Ltd, VC Bird International Airport, PO Box 819; Coolidge, Antigua (tel: (+1-268) 480-5634; fax: (+1-268) 480-5635; email: customerrelations@liatairline.com).

Mustique Airways, PO Box 1232, Arnos Vale (tel: 458-4380; fax: 456-4586).

St Vincent and The Grenadines Hotel and Tourism Association, PO Box 834, E T Joshua Int'l Airport, Kingstown, St Vincent (tel: 458-4379; fax: 456-4456; email: svghotels@caribsurf.com or office@svghotels.com; internet: www.svghotels.com).

SVG (airline), Arnos Vale (tel: 457-5124; fax: 457-5077; internet: www.svgair.com).

Ministry of tourism
Ministry of Tourism, Youth and Sports, Cruise Ship Terminal, Harbour Quay, St. Vincent (tel: 457-1502; fax: 451-2425).

National tourist organisation offices
Department of Tourism, Bay Street, PO Box 834, Kingstown (tel: 457-1502; fax: 451-2425; email: tourism@caribsurf.com; internet: www. svgtourism.com).

Ministries
Ministry of Agriculture and Labour, Administrative Building, Kingstown (tel: 456-1410; fax: 457-1688).

Ministry of Communications and Works, Administrative Building, Kingstown (tel: 456-1111; fax: 456-2168).

Ministry of Education, Youth and Women's Affairs, Administrative Building, Kingstown (tel: 457-2282; fax: 457-1114).

Ministry of Foreign Affairs and Tourism, Administrative Building, Kingstown (tel: 456-1111; fax: 456-2610).

Ministry of Health and the Environment, Administrative Building, Kingstown (tel: 457-1729; fax: 456-2610).

Ministry of Housing, Local Government and Community Development and Sports, Administrative Building, Kingstown (tel: 456-1111; fax: 456-2610).

Ministry of Legal Affairs and Information, Administrative Building, Kingstown (tel: 456-1111; fax: 457-2898).

Ministry of National Security, Halifax Street, Kingstown, St Vincent (tel: 451-2707; fax: 451-2820; email: office.natsec@mail.gov.vc).

Ministry of Trade, Industry and Consumer Affairs, Administrative Building, Kingstown (tel: 457-1223; fax: 457-2880).

Office of The Prime Minister, Administrative Building, Kingstown (tel: 456-1703; fax: 457-2152).

Other useful addresses
British High Commission PO Box 132, Granby Street, Kingstown (tel: 457 1701; fax: 456 2750; email: bhcsvg@caribsurf.com).

National Broadcasting Corporation, PO Box 705, Kingstown (tel: 457-1111).

Offshore Finance Authority, Kingstown (tel: 456-2577; fax: 457-2568; email: info@stvincentoffshore.com; internet: www.stvincentoffshore.com).

Radio St Vincent and the Grenadines, PO Box 705, Kingstown (tel: 456-1516).

Statistical Office, Central Planning Division, Ministry of Finance and Planning, Kingstown (fax: 457-2943).

St Vincent and the Grenadines Embassy (US), Suite 102, 1717 Massachusetts Avenue, Washington DC 20036 (tel: (+1-202) 462-7806).

St Vincent Development Corporation (DEVCO), PO Box 841, Granby Street, Kingstown (tel: 457-1358; fax: 457-2838).

Internet sites
Caribbean newspaper online: http://caribbeannetnews.com

Official government website: www.gov.vc

Samoa

KEY FACTS

Official name: Malotuto'atasi o Samoa (Independent State of Samoa) (dropped 'Western' 1997)

Head of State: O le Ao o le Malo, Tuiatua Tupua Tamasese Efi (from 2007; re-appointed 20 Jul 2012)

Head of government: Prime Minister Tuila'epa Sailele Malielegaoi (HRPP) (since 1998; re-elected Mar 2011)

Ruling party: Human Rights Protection Party (HRPP) (since 1982; re-elected Mar 2011)

Area: 2,840 square km (nine islands): Savai'i (1,708); Upolu (1,118)

Population: 192,000 (2014)*

Capital: Apia (on Upolu)

Official language: Samoan

Currency: Tala or Samoan dollar (S$) = 100 senes, or cents

Exchange rate: S$2.60 per US$ (Sep 2015)

GDP per capita: US$4,308 (2014)*

GDP real growth: 1.90% (2014)

GDP: US$826.00 million (2014)

Inflation: -1.20% (2014)

Balance of trade: -US$301.43 million (2013)

Foreign debt: US$278.00 million (2012)

Annual FDI: US$14.88 million (2011)

* estimated figure

COUNTRY PROFILE

The first Polynesians settled in the islands around 600BC. A former German protectorate, Samoa was governed by New Zealand from 1914 until its citizens voted for independence in 1961. The Independent State of Samoa was known as Western Samoa until 1997.

1722 The Dutch navigator, Jacob Roggeveen, was the first European to sight the islands.

1831 The London Missionary Society arrived in Samoa to convert native Samoans, establishing a British presence.

1889 The *Treaty of Berlin* between Britain, the US and Germany promised an independent Samoan government.

1899 The Berlin treaty was annulled by the *Tripartite Treaty*, which granted the US rights to all eastern islands of the Samoan group and gave Germany the remainder. In exchange for withdrawing its claim to Samoa, Britain gained control of Germany's rights in Tonga, Niue and the Solomon Islands (excluding Bougainville).

1914 New Zealand occupied Western Samoa during the First World War and continued to administer it after the War under a League of Nations' mandate.

1929 Eleven members of the Mau independence movement were killed by New Zealand authorities.

1946 After the Second World War, Western Samoa was administered as a UN Trust Territory by New Zealand.

1961 A UN-supervised plebiscite voted for independence.

1962 Western Samoa became the first Pacific island to declare independence.

1970 Western Samoa became a member of the Commonwealth.

1990 Voters approved universal suffrage and increased the legislature's term from three to five years.

1991 The general election employed universal suffrage for all those over 21.

1997 The constitution was amended and Western Samoa was re-named Samoa.

1998 The government imposed restrictions on the media.

2000 Samoa was one of the first to sign the Pacific Island Countries (free) Trade Agreement. Two former cabinet ministers, sentenced to death for a murder attempt on a fellow politician who could have exposed them for corruption, had their death sentences commuted to life imprisonment.

2001 Incumbent prime minister, Tuiaepa Sailele Malielegaoi (Human Rights' Protection Party (HRPP)) won a closely run election and retained control with the support of independent members.

2002 New Zealand formally apologised for its poor treatment of Samoan citizens in colonial times.

2004 The death penalty, which had not been used since the 1930s, was abolished.

2006 HRPP was re-elected, winning 36 of the 49 parliamentary seats.

2007 Susuga Malietoa Tanumafili II died aged 94. Tupua Tamasese Tupuola Tufuga Efi (known as Tuiatua Tupua Tamasese Efi) was appointed by parliament as O le Ao o le Malo (traditional head of state) Tupuola Efi.

2009 Following a Supreme Court ruling that Tautua Samoa (TS) had not been registered to participate in the general elections all nine members (forming the opposition) chose to sit in parliament as independents. However the speaker of parliament disqualified them, as the constitution required that they stand for re-election if they remained as a political party. The road code changed to introduce right-hand driving. An earthquake, of 8.3 magnitude, struck offshore in the Pacific Ocean and caused a devastating *tsunami* that swept over several Samoan islands, killing more than 140 people, including 25 in American Samoa. International aid was provided including emergency supplies.

2010 Daylight saving was introduced, moving GMT from minus 11 hours to GMT minus 10 hours.

2011 In parliamentary elections held in March, the ruling HRPP won 29 seats out of 49. Seven independent members also supported the HRPP. The opposition TS won 13 seats. Samoa's first period of daylight saving ended on 3 April. In May the Samoan government approved the International Date Line Act 2011 to change Samoa from being on the east of the International Dateline to being on the west, so that Samoa will be one of the first countries to begin the daily cycle and not the last to see the sun set; in effect it moves a day ahead in time and comes into line with its trading partners in

Oceania and Australasia. On Thursday 29 December at 11.59.59 Samoa lost one day and moved forward to Saturday 31 December at 00.00.
2012 On 20 July, parliament re-appointed, unopposed, Tuiatua Tupua Tamasese Efi as Head of State (O le Ao o le Malo). Bilateral discussions resumed on 11 October between Samoa and American Samoa covering joint concerns in health, telecommunications, customs and utilities. The last such meetings had been held in 2007.
2013 The Apia Export Fish Packers expressed concern in September when it was reported that the government was considering allowing China'sheavily subsidised vessels into its Exclusive Economic Zone. Chinese vessels are bigger and more efficient than local vessels and are likely to have a detrimental effect on fish stock.
2014 The Third International Conference on Small Island and Developing States was held in Apia in September. US$1.9 billion was pledged for sustainable development partnerships during the conference. From 8 September overseas birth and death registrations of British Citizens will nolonger take place at the British Consulate and will be carried out instead in a central registration unit in the UK.
2015 The Vth Commonwealth Youth Games took place on Samoa from 5–11 September.

Political structure

Constitution

The O le Ao O le Malo (Head of State) acts as a constitutional monarch with the power to dissolve the Fono (legislative assembly) and to appoint a prime minister with its recommendation. The constitution is based on the British parliamentary system and formally came into force in 1962.
A 1997 amendment changed the country's name from Western Samoa to Samoa.

Independence date

1962

The executive

Executive power rests with the prime minister who selects a 12-member cabinet. The Head of State (O le Ao o le Malo) does not play an active role in government. He appoints the prime minister on the Fono's recommendation and approves the laws passed by the Fono. The Head of State is elected for a five-year term.

National legislature

The unicameral Fono has 49-members, of which 47 are *matais* (traditional clan leaders) elected in six two-seat and 35 single constituencies. The remaining two members are elected by and represent non-ethnic Samoans. All members are elected for five-year terms.

Last elections

4 March 2011 (parliamentary)

Results: Parliamentary: the Human Rights Protection Party (HRPP) won 55.6 per cent and 29 seats (out of 49), Tautau Samoa (TS) 24.7 per cent and 13 seats, Independents (all were in support of HRPP) 19.7 per cent and 7 seats; turnout was 90 per cent.

Next elections

2016 (parliamentary)

Political parties

Ruling party

Human Rights Protection Party (HRPP) (since 1982; re-elected Mar 2011)

Main opposition party

Tautua Samoa (TSP)

Political situation

The devastating tsunami that killed more than 140 people, in 2009, left several islands in need of widespread reconstruction. In October 2010, the opposition Samoan Democratic United Party (SDUP) queried where the tsunami relief funds had been spent? A New Zealand TV3 documentary claimed that an amount of the aid monies had been misappropriated. The government strenuously denied the accusations saying that the money was budgeted to be spent over a four-year recovery period as pledges were paid.
Despite opposition by the National Council of Churches and the Tautua Somoa Party (TSP) a new casino legalisation bill was passed in October 2010. Prime Minister Tuila'epa expected the first casino to be in operation in mid-2011, although in the meantime, the Totalisator Agency Board would undertake research into what type of casino was best.

Population

200,000 (2012)*, One in four Samoans live outside Samoa. There is a high level of emigration to New Zealand.

Last census: 7 November 2011: 186,340

Population density: 64 inhabitants per square km (2010). Urban population 20 per cent (2010 Unicef).

Annual growth rate: 0.6 per cent, 1990–2010 (Unicef).

Ethnic make-up

Samoan (92.6 per cent); European and Polynesian mixed race (7 per cent); Europeans (0.4 per cent).

Religions

Christian

Education

The introduction of the bilingual, single curriculum in primary and secondary schools has increased the number of students successfully completing schooling. Teaching methods and teacher's tools, including dictionaries, grammars and workbooks for teachers, were re-oriented so that the focus became localised and seen as more relevant to the student's lives. The dual streaming of academic and non-academic students in secondary schools was discontinued and has improved the educational outcome of more students.

Literacy rate: 98.9 per cent, adult male rate; 98.4 per cent adult female rate (World Bank).

Compulsory years: Five to 13

Enrolment rate: 91.9 per cent net primary enrolment; 67.4 per cent net seconday enrolment (World Bank).

Health

Life expectancy: 68 years, 2004 (WHO 2006)

KEY INDICATORS — Samoa

	Unit	2011	2012	2013	2014	**2015
Population	m	0.19	*0.18	*0.19	*0.19	*0.19
Gross domestic product (GDP)	US$bn	0.63	0.69	0.79	0.83	*0.87
GDP per capita	US$	3,451	3,747	4,171	*4,308	*4,487
GDP real growth	%	2.1	2.9	-1.1	1.9	*2.8
Inflation	%	2.9	6.2	-0.2	-1.2	*3.0
Exports (fob) (goods)	US$m	11.4	31.2	23.9	–	–
Imports (fob) (goods)	US$m	318.7	308.4	325.4	–	–
Balance of trade	US$m	-307.3	-277.3	-301.4	–	–
Current account	US$m	-78.2	-63.0	3.0	*-31.0	*-59.0
Total reserves minus gold	US$m	179.7	–	170.8	140.7	–
Foreign exchange	US$m	158.4	–	150.3	–	–
Exchange rate	per US$	2.32	2.28	2.34	2.44	–

* estimated figure ** forecast figure

Fertility rate/Maternal mortality rate: 3.9 births per woman, 2010 (Unicef)
Birth rate/Death rate: 15 births per 1,000 population; six deaths per 1,000 population (2003).
Child (under 5 years) mortality rate (per 1,000): 18 per 1,000 live births (WHO 2012)

Main cities
Apia, on Upolu (capital, estimated population 35,841 in 2012), Vaitele (7,921), Faleasiu (4,026).

Languages spoken
English is widely spoken. The Samoan language has an equal status with English in schools.

Official language/s
Samoan

Media

Press
Publications are typically printed in both English and Samoan. Locally published newspapers include the *Samoa Observer*, a leading daily and *Samoa News* (www.samoalive.com) publishes every weekday. *Samoa Weekly* and *Talamua Magazine* are privately owned and *Savali* is a government-owned periodical.
Online news networks include Pacific Islands Report (www.eastwestcenter.org) and Samoa Live (www.samoalive.com). Several Samoan (and English) language publications are printed in New Zealand, including *Samoana Samoa Star* and *Samoa Sun*.
The monthly *Women's Times* became a weekly edition from July 2011.
Dailies: The *Samoa Observer* is a leading daily. *Samoa Live* (www.samoalive.com/samoanews.htm) is the leading local on-line network with regional Asia Pacific and international news links. Other regular publications include the *Samoa Times* and *South Seas Star*.
Weeklies: Local weekly publications include *Newsline*, *Le Samoa*, *Samoa Post* and *Samoa Weekly*.
Business: *Talanei News* (www.samoana.org/talanei) covers business news.
Periodicals: Periodicals include *Savali* and *Samoa Sports Monthly*.

Broadcasting
It is possible to pick up television and radio broadcasts from American Samoa.
Radio: There are three commercial FM stations and the Samoa Broadcasting Corporation operates commercial AM and FM radio stations.
Television: There are four TV stations the state-run SBC, and the private O Lau TV broadcasting 24 hours, TV3 broadcasting for 12 hours, and CCTV relays programmes from the Chinese state-run broadcaster.
Other news agencies: ABC Pacific Beat: www.radioaustralia.net.au/pacbeat
Pacific Magazine: www.pacificmagazine.net
Pacific Islands New Association (Pina): www.pina.com.fj

Economy
There are four main sources of income for the Samoan economy: development aid, tourism, agricultural exports and remittances. Agricultural exports provide over 90 per cent of export revenue. The structure of the economy in 2014 was 58.5 per cent services, 30.1 per cent industry, of which manufacturing comprised around 10 per cent, and 11.4 per cent agriculture. The agricultural sector employs around 60 per cent of the labour force in subsistence farming, while export products are centred on the coconut, with sales of copra and coconut oil and cream. The manufacturing sector is largely geared to fabricating vehicle parts for use in car assembly in Australia, under a market-access concession arrangement.
GDP growth was as high as 5.8 per cent in 2011, recovering from the negative growth of -4.8 per cent in 2009. In 2012 this figure dropped to 0.4 per cent and then even further in 2013 as the economy went back into recession, recording growth of -1.9 per cent. However, by 2014 positive growth had returned and the economy expanded by 1.2 per cent.
Since 2012, inflation has been falling, dropping from 2.0 per cent to 0.6 in 2013 before receding into deflation in 2014 at -0.4 per cent. Remittances in 2012 were US$157.8 million, remaining largely the same at US$158.0 million (19.9 per cent of GDP) in 2013.
The tourism sector is strong, providing around 25 per cent of GDP; it is however subject to volatility from climatic and other natural disasters. A *tsunami*, caused by an offshore earthquake, swept over much of the southern coast of Upolu in October 2009, devastating not only much of the tourist infrastructure, but also deterring many from visiting; eighteen resorts and family-run properties were destroyed and pristine beaches scarred and littered with debris. The *tsunami* also destroyed a huge portion of Samoa's staple food crop, taro. Visitor numbers are steadily beginning to rise again but are not at pre-*tsunami* levels in 2014.
Samoa was first included on the UN-list of least developed countries in 1971, but in 2007 it was agreed that Samoa should graduate to the status of developing county. On January 2014 the United Nations Office of the High Representative for the Least Developed Countries, Landlocked Developing Countries and Small Island Developing States (UN-OHRLLS) confirmed that Samoa had gained developing country economic status.

External trade
Samoa is a member of the South Pacific Regional Trade and Economic Co-operation Agreement (Sparteca) along with 12 other regional nations, which allows products duty free access by Pacific Island Forum members to Australian and New Zealand markets (subject to the country of origin restrictions).
Foreign trade underpins the economy in three major fields; agricultural produce, manufacturing and capital flows. Tourism, particularly by expatriates, and remittances (19.9 per cent of GDP) has covered Samoa's persistently large trade deficit for a number of years. Manufacturing is largely based on automotive components that are shipped to Australia. Agricultural products are mostly exported for processing except coconuts and their derivatives. Around 15 per cent of all exports are bound for European markets.
Samoa joined the World Trade Organisation (WTO), the 155th nation to do so, on 10 May 2012.

Imports
Principal imports are machinery and equipment, industrial supplies and foodstuffs.
Main sources: New Zealand (25.0 per cent of total in 2014), Singapore (24.8 per cent), China (12.6 per cent)

Exports
Although automotive parts (manufactured in Samoa's Foreign Trade Zone) are the major export items they are not included in government statistics on exports commodities as they are part of the market-access concession arrangement with Australia and are considered outside the domestic economy, only providing employment and peripheral trade. Agricultural produce constitutes 90 per cent of Samoan commodity exports, including (by volume) coconut oil, fresh fish, coconut cream, nonu fruit, spring water, beer, copra and taro.
Main destinations: Australia (57.9 per cent of total in 2014), New Zealand (19.1 per cent), American Samoa (6.3 per cent)

Agriculture

Farming
Agriculture, including fishing, accounted for 11.4 per cent of GDP in 2014 and employs some 65 per cent of the workforce with smallholdings producing surpluses in Samoa's fertile volcanic soil, enough for healthy export sales. Production of subsistence crops include cassava, breadfruit, maize and taro.
Export of nonu juice has in the past replaced fresh fish as Samoa's principal foreign exchange earner. Other produce

under development includes macadamia nuts, annatto (dye), timber and cattle.

A shipment of 43 sheep arrived from Fiji in 2004 where they had been specially bred to have a high meat content and to be suitable for tropical climates. By 2013 over 30 farmers were raising more than 800 sheep on Upolu and Savaii.

Fishing

Fishing is one of Samoa's major export earners. The typical annual fish catch is over 11,000 tonnes (an increase from 7,500t in 1998); there are concerns that overfishing is depleting fish stocks.

Forestry

Typical annual production includes 131,000 cubic metres (cum) round wood, 61,000cum industrial round wood, 21,000cum sawn wood, 58,000cum sawn logs and veneer logs, 70,000cum wood fuel.

Industry and manufacturing

The industrial sector typically accounts for over 25 per cent of GDP and employs approximately 6 per cent of the workforce. Small-scale manufacturing and industry has expanded. The government's industrial area of Vaitele (on Upolu) houses a brewery, a cigarette factory and a match factory.

Other industries include copra processing, food processing, light engineering, woodworking and manufacture of coconut oil, paint, concrete and construction materials, bottled gases, plastic bags, corned beef and garments. US food processors have expressed interest in investing in fish-processing capacity.

Tourism

Samoa is a popular tropical destination for regional tourists. The largest groups of visitors are from Australia and New Zealand. Total tourists in June 2013 were 12,229, an increase of 31.9 per cent on May, but 14.3 per cent down on June 2012. The total number of tourists in 2013 reached 132,000.

Ecotourism is a major component of the sector, with diving offshore and exploring the rainforest onshore, although most visitors simply relax and soak up the sun.

A new strategy to encourage visitors from further afield, which typically targets wealthier travellers, has resulted in a change of emphasis. From the current low-key accommodation and piecemeal development in tourism, in 2010 the US South Pacific Development Group signed a leasing contract with the government to develop the first major, oceanfront resort on Savai'i, to be called Sasina Village. The initial phase will include a hotel, time-share units, and sports and leisure centres, for completion by the end of 2015. The following phase will include additional hotels, private residences and a marina.

The International Date Line Act 2011 changed Samoa from being on the east of the International Date Line (IDL) to being on the west. This meant that Samoa went from being one of the last countries to see the sun set, to being one of the first to see it rise. It brought Samoa into line with its trading partners in Oceania and Australia, making it more possible to do business. The move also meant that neighbour American Samoa became a day behind.

Environment

An Asian Development Bank (ADB) study (*Economics of Climate Change in the Pacific*) published in November 2013 projected a potential 2°C rise in temperature, a pickup in extreme winds and tropical storms, and a possible sea level rise of up to 1.25 meters could cost Samoa's economy as much as 3.8 per cent of its annual GDP by 2100.

Hydrocarbons

As there are no hydrocarbon reserves, Samoa relies entirely on the import of petroleum products, of which refined oil makes up around 58 per cent of Samoa's energy consumption. Imports come from New Zealand, Australia, Fiji and the US, amounting to 1,100 barrels per day in 2013. Samoa does not import natural gas or coal.

Energy

Total installed generating capacity was 41MW in 2013. The autonomous government-owned, Electric Power Corporation (EPC) has sole responsibility to generate, transmit, distribute and sell electricity in Samoa with 95 per cent coverage.

Hydropower provides 50 per cent of all electricity from five hydro, several diesel- and a solar-powered plants operated by EPC. Plans are underway to develop renewable energy based on wind, solar, hydro and bio-fuels.

In January 2010 the government commissioned feasibility studies to determine the potential for the EPC to build five new hydroelectric plants, with two sites on Savaii and three on Upolu. Funds for an initial three plants will be forthcoming and the remaining two will be scheduled for implementation at a later date.

Banking and insurance

The government has increased its deposits in the banking system over the last few years, enabling commercial banks to lend and boosting private sector credit growth. Banks are strongly capitalised and earn good profits.

Central bank

Central Bank of Samoa

Time

GMT plus 13 hours; daylight saving, GMT plus 14 hours.

On 9 May 2011, the Samoan government decided that, from 29 December, the International Date Line would be shifted from west to east, so that Samoa will be one of the first countries to begin the daily cycle and not one that completes the cycle; in effect it moves a day ahead in time and comes into line with its trading partners in Oceania and Australasia. On Thursday 29 December at 11.59.59 Samoa will lose one day and move forward to Saturday 31 December at 00.00.

Geography

Samoa lies in the southern Pacific Ocean about 2,400km north-east of New Zealand and about 450km west of American Samoa. Samoa comprises two large islands – Savii and Upolu, separated by a 13km ocean channel – and seven small, mostly uninhabited islands. The total land area is 2,934 square km. Savii and Upolu are coral fringed, rugged volcanic mountains rising to 1,856 metres (m) and 1,115m respectively.

Hemisphere

Southern

Climate

Temperatures 24–30 degrees Celsius (hottest in March) and high humidity. Rainy season November–April, rainfall at least 5,000 mm/year, heaviest in January.

Entry requirements

Passports

Required by all and valid for six months beyond the date of departure. Proof of onward/return passage and visa documentation for following destination, booked accommodation and sufficient funds for stay are required.

Visa

Not required by tourists for a period not exceeding 60 days. American Samoan and US citizens resident in American Samoa may visit with a 14–30 days visitor permit.

Business visitors should apply for a temporary resident permit from the Samoan Immigrations Department. Requirements and application form can be found at www.samoaimmigration.gov.ws under *Permit Services*.

Currency advice/regulations

The import of local and foreign currency is unlimited. Export of local currency is prohibited and foreign currency is limited to the amount imported.

Travellers cheques are accepted in banks and larger hotels.

Customs

Personal effects allowed duty-free.

Prohibited imports

Firearms, ammunition, explosives, illegal drugs and pornography. Plants, seeds, soil and animals may be imported subject to approval from the Department of Agriculture.

Health (for visitors)

Mandatory precautions

Vaccination certificate for yellow fever if travelling from an infected area.

Advisable precautions

Vaccinations for diphtheria, tuberculosis, hepatitis A and B, polio, tetanus, typhoid. There is a rabies risk.

Hotels

Most hotels are located close to the capital. There are five standards available from deluxe and superior to budget.

Credit cards

Major credit cards are accepted; ATMs are available.

Public holidays (national)

Fixed dates

1–2 Jan (New Year), 25 Apr (Anzac Day), 10 May (Mothers-of-Samoa Day), 1 Jun (Independence Day), 3 Nov (Arbor Day), 25–26 Dec (Christmas).

Variable dates

Good Friday, Easter Monday, Labour Day (first Mon in Aug), *Lotu-a-Tamaiti* (second Mon in Oct, the day after White Sunday).

Working hours

Banking

Mon–Fri: 0900–1500. Larger branches are open Sat: 0900–1200.

Business

Mon–Fri: 0800–1200, 1300–1630.

Government

Mon–Fri: 0800–1200, 1300–1630.

Shops

Mon–Fri: 0800–1200, 1330–1630; Sat: 0800–1230.

Telecommunications

Telephone/fax

Samoa uses satellite communications and some domestic transmissions are conducted over microwave, generally in less densely populated areas, and between the islands of Upolu and Savaii. All can be adversely affected by bad weather.

Mobile/cell phones

A GSM 900 service is in operation.

Electricity supply

240V AC, with flat, three-pin plugs (Australian style).

Weights and measures

Imperial system, with metric systems in use.

Social customs/useful tips

Appointments should be made in advance. Ties need only be worn for formal meetings. English is used for business and commerce. Care should be taken to respect local customs and practices. Samoans do not like to disagree with someone in authority, or not give the anticipated reply, which can lead to misunderstandings by foreign visitors (a 'yes' can mean 'no'). Gratuities are optional and gifts for excellent service are appreciated. The minimum drinking age is 18 years.

Getting there

Air

National airline: Polynesian Airlines

International airport/s: Faleolo International (APW), 34km west of Apia, with banks, post office, duty-free and car hire. There are taxis and buses to the city.

Airport tax: Departures tax: S$40

Surface

Water: Ferry services operate from American Samoa; cargo ships also carry passengers from New Zealand, Australia, Japan and other Pacific islands, as well as Europe and the US.

Main port/s: Apia and Asau

Getting about

National transport

Air: Polynesian Airlines operates regular services between Faleolo (Upolu) and Maota (south-east Savii).

Buses: Scheduled bus services operate in and around Apia and Salelologa (Savai'i).

Water: Daily ferry services operate between Salelologa (Savai'i) and Mulianua (Upolu).

City transport

Taxis: Taxi service is available in Apia.

Car hire

International or national driving licence required. Traffic drives on the righ (from 6 September 2009).

BUSINESS DIRECTORY

The addresses listed below are a selection only. While World of Information makes every endeavour to check these addresses, we cannot guarantee that changes have not been made, especially to telephone numbers and area codes. We would welcome any corrections.

Telephone area codes

The international direct dialling (IDD) code for Samoa is +685 followed by subscriber's number.

Useful telephone numbers

Police, fire and ambulance: 999.

Chambers of Commerce

Samoa Chamber of Commerce and Industry, PO Box 2014, Lotemau Centre, Vaea Street, Apia (tel: 21-237; fax: 21-578; email: info@samoachamber.com).

Banking

ANZ Bank (Samoa) Ltd, PO Box L1855, Beach Road, Apia (tel: 22-422; fax: 24-595, 23-807).

Australia and New Zealand Banking Group Ltd, PO Box L1855, Apia (tel: 22-422; fax: 24-595).

Development Bank of Samoa, PO Box 1232, Apia (tel: 22-861; fax: 23-888).

International Business Bank Corp Ltd; Level 2, Chandra Hse, Convent St, Apia (tel: 22-393; fax: 23-253).

National Bank of Samoa Limited; PO Box L3047, Apia (tel: 23-077; fax: 23-085).

Pacific Commercial Bank Ltd, PO Box 1860, Beach Road, Apia (tel: 20-000; fax: 22-848).

Central bank

Central Bank of Samoa, Central Bank Building, Private Bag, Apia (tel: 34-100; fax: 20-293; e-mail: cbs@samoa.net; internet: www.cbs.gov.ws).

Travel information

Faleolo International Airport, Private Bag, Apia (tel: 23-201, 23-202, 42-050; fax; 24-281; e-mail: etuale@samoa.net).

Mulifanua Ferry Terminal Pier, PO Box 3267, Apia.

Polynesian Airlines, PO Box 599, Beech Road, Apia (tel: 21-261; fax: 20-023).

Samoa Shipping Corp, Shipping House, Matautu-tai; PO Bag, Apia (tel: 20-935/6; fax: 22-352; email: info@samoashipping.com).

Ministry of tourism

Samoa Tourism Authority, PO Box 2272, Apia (tel: 63-500; fax:20-886; email: info@visitsamoa.ws).

National tourist organisation offices

Samoa Visitors' Bureau, PO Box 862, Apia (tel: 20-878; fax: 20-886; e-mail: samoawsvb@pactok.peg.apc.org; internet site: http://www.visitsamoa.ws).

Ministries

Ministry of Agriculture, Quarantine Division, P O Box 1874, Apia (tel: 22-561; fax: 24-576; internet: www.samoaquarantine.gov.ws).

Ministry of Commerce, Industry and Labour, Level 4, ACB Building, Apia (tel: 20-441/2; internet: www.mcilsamoa.ws).

Ministry of Finance, Central Bank Bld, Matafele; Private Bag, Government of Samoa, Apia (tel: 34-333; fax: 21-321; internet: www.mof.gov.ws).

Ministry of Prime Minister and Cabinet, Samoa Immigration, Lever 2, Lober Bld; PO Box L1861, Apia (tel: 20-291/2; fax: 22-243; internet: www.samoaimmigration.gov.ws).

Other useful addresses

Asian Development Bank (ADB), South Pacific Regional Mission, La Casa di Andrea, Fr. Dr. W. H. Lini Highway; PO Box 127, Port Vila, Vanuatu (tel: (+678-2) 23-300; fax: (+678-2) 23-183; email: adbsprm@adb.org; internet: www.adb.org/SPRM).

Department of Statistics, PO Box 1151, Apia.

Department of Trade, Commerce and Industry, Chandra House, Trade Information Centre, PO Box 862, Apia (tel: 20-471; fax: 21-504; email: IPU@tci.gov.ws; internet: www.tradeinvestsamoa.ws).

Government of Samoa, PO Box L 1864, Apia (tel: 24-799, 63-115; fax: 21-742, 26-396; e-mail: contact@govt.ws).

Samoa Mission to the United Nations, 800 Second Avenue, Suite 400J, New York, NY 10017 (tel: (+1-212) 599 6196; fax: (+1-212) 599 0797).

ABC Pacific Beat: www.radioaustralia.net.au/pacbeat

Pacific Magazine: www.pacificmagazine.net

Pacific Islands New Association (Pina): www.pina.com.fj

Internet sites

Government of Samoa: www.govt.ws

Ministry of Commerce, Industry and Labour: www.mcil.gov.ws

Ministry of Finance: www.mof.gov.ws

Samoa Head of State: www.head-of-state-samoa.ws

Samoa Immigration: www.samoaimmigration.gov.ws

Samoa Industry of Manufacturers and Exporters: www.same.org.ws

Samoa International Finance Authority: www.sifa.ws

Samoa Live: www.samoalive.com

South Pacific Tourism Organisation: www.tcsp.com

San Marino

KEY FACTS

Official name: Serenissima Repubblica di San Marino (Most Serene Republic of San Marino)

Head of State: Two Capitani-Reggenti (Captains-Regent), elected for six month terms: Andrea Belluzi (PSD) and Roberto Venturini (PDCS) (from 1 April 2015)

Head of government: Two Capitani-Reggenti (Captains-Regent): Andrea Belluzi (PSD) and Roberto Venturini (PDCS) (from 1 April 2015)

Ruling party: San Marino Bene Comune (San Marino Common Good) coalition of three parties led by (Noi Sammarinesi (NS) (We Sammarinese), with Partito dei Socialisti e dei Democratici (PSD) (Party of Socialists and Democrats) and Alleanza Popolare (AP) (Popular Alliance) (from 11 Nov 2012)

Area: 61 square km

Population: 31,000 (2014)

Capital: San Marino

Official language: Italian

Currency: Euro (€) = 100 cents

Exchange rate: €0.89 per US$ (Sep 2015)

GDP per capita: US$56,820 (2014)*

GDP real growth: -1.00% (2014)*

GDP: US$1.79 billion (2014)*

Unemployment: 8.74% (2014)

Inflation: 1.10% (2014)

* estimated figure

COUNTRY PROFILE

San Marino is completely surrounded by Italy. It is the oldest surviving republic in the world, having been an independent republic since the year 301AD.

1600 The constitution was ratified.

1926 An additional electoral law was passed, which serves some of the functions of a constitution.

1988 San Marino joined the Council of Europe.

1990–92 A coalition of Partito Democratico Progressista (PDP) (Progressive Democratic Party) (ex-communists) and Partito Democratico Cristiano Sammarinese (PDCS) (San Marino Christian Democratic Party) took office.

1992 PDCS formed a coalition with the Partito Socialista Sammarinese (PSS) (San Marino Socialist Party). San Marino became a member of the UN.

1993 In the general election, the PDCS won 26 seats and the PSS 14 seats; the coalition continued.

1998 After general elections, the PDCS/PSS coalition continued.

2001 Differences within the PDCS/PSS coalition led to early parliamentary elections (originally scheduled for 2003), but resulted in a continuation of the coalition.

2002 San Marino, in line with Italy, replaced the lira with the euro currency.

2005 The Partito dei Socialisti e dei Democratici (PSD) (Party of Socialists and Democrats) was formed from the amalgamation of PSS and the Partito dei Democratici (PD) (Democratic Party).

2006 The PDCS won elections, but the PSD formed a coalition government with two other parties.

2008 In parliamentary elections the opposition, four-party centre-right Patto per San Marion (Pact for San Marino) coalition won 54.2 per cent of the vote (35 seats out of 60). Antonella Mularoni was appointed Secretary of State for Foreign and Political Affairs.

2009 Massimo Cenci (NPS) and Oscar Mina (PDCS) took office as captains-regent; six months later, Stefano Palmieri (AP) and Francesco Mussoni (PDCS) took over. An emergency census was conducted in response to the number of bogus residency claims filed by foreign residents in an effort to avoid paying tax in their own countries.

2010 Marco Conti (PDCS) and Glauco Sansovini (Alleanza Nazionale (AL) (National Alliance)) were elected as captains-regent. The Italian finance minister declared that San Marino was on Italy's blacklist for not agreeing to full transparency and to disclose details of bank deposits of Italian residents. San Marino's justice minister rejected the criticism saying that depositing money was not a crime and that rather than this being a matter of transparency it was one of San Marino's sovereignty.

2011 In April, Maria Luisa Berti (Noi Sammarinesi (NS) (We Sammarinese)) and Filippo Tamagnini (PDCS) took office as captains-regent; both are members of the Pact for San Marino ruling coalition. On 1 October Gabriele Gatti (PDCS), Matteo Fiorini (Alleanza Popolare (AP) took office as captains-regent.

2012 On 1 April, Italo Righi (PDCS) and Maurizio Rattini (NPS) became the captains-regent. On 23 July, the Fitch Ratings agency downgraded San Marino's long-term rating from A to BBB+, due to the deterioration of the financial sector and a weaker than expected outlook for the economy. On 1 October, Teodoro Lonfernini (PDCS) and Denise Bronzetti (PSD) took office as captains-regent. Parliamentary elections were held on 11 November, won by the San Marino Bene Comune (San Marino Common Good) a centrist coalition of three parties led by NS (with PSD and AP) with 50.7 per cent (35 seats out of 60). On 21 November, the first parliamentary session took place.

2013 In October MEPs urged the European Commission to allow the three micro-states of Andorra, Monaco and San Marino to join the European Economic Area.

2014 In April an IMF report commented that the exit of San Marino from Italy's tax black list should facilitate the process of recovery. It also said that the savings of about 1 per cent of GDP in the 2014 budget is an important first step towards putting debt on a sustainable path and stabilising the economy.

2015 The Council of Europe Commissioner for Human Rights, Nils Muižnieks, visited San Marino on 9 and 10 June for an inspection visit.

Political structure

Constitution

The constitution was ratified on 8 October 1600. An additional electoral law was passed in 1926, which serves some of the functions of a constitution.

The country is divided into nine *castelli* (municipalities), each governed by a Captain.

The executive

The Consiglio Grande e Generale (CGeG) (the Great and General Council) elects two members every six months to act as captains-regent, who functions jointly as heads of state and, together with a 10-member Congress of State (cabinet), exercise executive power. The secretary of state for foreign affairs has come to assume many of the prerogatives of a prime minister.

The Congress of State is elected by the CGeG for a five-year term.

National legislature

Legislative power is vested in the unicameral Consiglio Grande e Generale (CGeG) (Great and General Council), with 60 members elected by universal adult suffrage for five-year terms. It has the responsibility of electing the 10-member congress of state.

Last elections

11 November 2012 (parliamentary)

Results: Parliamentary: San Marino Bene Comune (San Marino Common Good) coalition of three parties won 50.7 per cent of the vote (35 seats out of 60), Intesa per il Paese (Agreement for the Country) coalition of three parties, 22.3 per cent (12), Cittadinanza Attiva (Active Citizenship) coalition of two parties 16.1 per cent (nine), Movimento Civico (Rete) (Civic Movement) (Network) 6.3 per cent (four); two other political parties failed to win any seats.

Next elections

November 2016 (parliamentary)

Political parties

Ruling party

San Marino Bene Comune (San Marino Common Good) coalition of three parties led by (Noi Sammarinesi (NS) (We Sammarinese), with Partito dei Socialisti e dei Democratici (PSD) (Party of Socialists and Democrats) and Alleanza Popolare (AP) (Popular Alliance) (from 11 Nov 2012)

Main opposition party

Riforme e Libertà (Reforms and Freedom) coalition comprising Partito dei Socialisti e dei Democratici (PSD) (Party of Socialists and Democrats), Sinistra Unita (SU) (United Left) and Democratici di Centro (DdC) (Centre Democrats).

Political situation

An emergency census got underway in September 2009, in response to the number of bogus residency claims filed by foreign residents in an effort to avoid paying tax in their own countries.

In May 2010 the Italian finance minister declared that San Marino was on Italy's blacklist for not agreeing to full transparency and disclosing details of bank deposits of Italian residents. So it was somewhat obtuse that the San Marino justice minister to rejected the criticism saying that depositing money was not a crime and that rather than this being a matter of transparency it was one of San Marino's sovereignty.

Population

31,738 (2011)

Last census: July 2000: 26,941

Population density: 433 inhabitants per sq km. Urban population 94 per cent (2010 Unicef).

Annual growth rate: 1.3 per cent, 1990–2010 (Unicef).

Ethnic make-up

The population includes Sammarinese and Italians.

Religions

Roman Catholic

Education

Schooling is free of charge and until aged 16. Primary schooling lasts until aged 11, then on to lower secondary education for three years, from ages 11 to 14, of general education, then the last two years of either technical or specialised academic study.

Higher secondary schools, from aged 16 to 19, provide two-year courses in preparation for higher education.

Higher education is provided by the Università degli Studi della Repùbblica di San Marino, and its Istituto di Cibernetica.

Compulsory years: 6 to 15.

Health

The age of the population has risen, reflecting a general trend in Western Europe.

Life expectancy: 82.2 years, 2006 (IMF 2012)

Fertility rate/Maternal mortality rate: 1.2 births per woman, 2004 (WHO 2006)

Birth rate/Death rate: 10.5 births per 1,000 population; eight deaths per 1,000 population (2003).

Child (under 5 years) mortality rate (per 1,000): 3 per 1,000 live births (WHO 2012)

Main cities

San Marino (capital, estimated population 4,454 in 2012); Serravalle/Dogano (9,936), Borgo Maggiore (6,054), Domagnano (2890), Fiorentino (2,252).

Languages spoken

Italian

Official language/s

Italian

Media

Press

In Italian, the two dailies published are *La Tribuna Sammarinese* (www.latribunasammarinese.net) and *San Marino Oggi*, with periodicals *San Marino* and *La Sportivo*. In Italian, L'Informazione di San Marino (www.libertas.sm) and San Marino Notizie (www.sanmarinonotizie.com) are online news outlets, while *Italica* (www.italica.sm) is in English.

Broadcasting

Radio: The government-controlled San Marino RTV (www.sanmarinortv.sm) broadcasts over several wavebands in FM. Some regional Italian stations can also be received.

Television: RTV operates the television station while some regional Italian broadcasts can also be received.

Economy

San Marino is closely linked with Italy, which surrounds it geographically. The economy is diverse, with tourism being the main source of revenue, providing around 50 per cent of GDP, including duty-free sales of goods to tourists. Traditional industries include quarrying for building stone, ceramics, leather goods, textiles, wine and food production and lately, electronics manufacturing. Sales of postage stamps and coins to collectors provide 10 per cent of the government's income. Italy compensates San Marino, in the form of an annual subsidy, for relinquishing certain rights.

Since the global economic crisis, San Marino has been in recession. GDP growth dropped from 3.5 per cent in 2007 to a low of -12.8 per cent in 2009 as tourist numbers from Italy also dropped. In 2012 the recession had slowed to -7.5 per cent, and even further to -4.5 per cent in 2013 before almost returning to positive growth in 2014 at -1.0 per cent. Rising unemployment (8.7 per cent in 2014) and stagnant wage growth have lead to a lack of confidence that contributed to falling private consumption, which has been a result of the prolonged recession.

While San Marino adopted the euro as its currency, it is not formally part of the euro-zone and is not a member of the European Central Bank. As such it did not have access to Euro-system liquidity when the global economic crisis struck in 2009 and its banking system came under stress as it only had indirect access to the EU payment system via Italian banks. Consequently, local banks were under greater credit risk and additional cost through cross-border transactions. Nevertheless, the banking system has contributed to high growth, despite the largest bank in San Marino facing financial difficulties in 2008/09 with accusations of money laundering levelled at senior bank officials.

On 23 July 2012, the Fitch Ratings agency downgraded San Marino's long-term rating from A to BBB+, due to the deterioration of the financial sector and a weaker than expected outlook for the economy. This rating was affirmed in June 2015 and the country was given 'Outlook Stable' status.

External trade

San Marino does not belong to the European Union but as it maintains a customs and currency union with Italy and uses the euro it has *de facto* ties with the EU. Italy accounts for 87 per cent of all external trade.

Imports

Imports predominantly consist of food and manufactured goods.

Exports

Important exports include financial services, building stone, lime, timber, hides and ceramics; foodstuffs, live animals, chestnuts, wheat, wine and baked goods.

Agriculture

Farming

The republic was formerly dependent on agriculture and forestry. The agricultural sector employs around 1 per cent of the workforce. Approximately 17 per cent of the land is arable. Principal crops include olives, grapes, wheat and corn.

Industry and manufacturing

Quarrying for building stone is a traditional industry.

Manufacturing employs 41 per cent of the workforce, construction 11 per cent, and services, transport and communications 19 per cent.

Tourism

Tourists en route from and to Italy often slip into San Marino as much for the duty free shopping as to visit the sites of the medieval old town. The structure of the historic centre and Mount Titano, on which it sits, is included in Unesco's World Heritage List.

Over 100,000 tourists visit San Marino each year and all must gain access through Italy. There are various classes of hotels situated within the old town, most of which include business, conference and training facilities.

Hydrocarbons

Banking and insurance

The banking sector is of strategic importance to San Marino's economy, making a sizeable contribution to the state revenue; its banks are profitable, well-provisioned and cost efficient. The Istituto di Credito Sammarinese (ICS) operates as a central bank, although it does not have an independent monetary policy.

San Marino is a signatory of a new EU tax agreement with non-EU countries. San Marino will impose a withholding tax, up to 35 per cent, to be passed to the tax department of an EU citizen's country, but retaining the anonymity of the saver.

San Marino has also agreed to supply information on tax fraud, for criminal or civil trials, and notify EU member states about additional malpractices.

Central bank

Banca Centrale della Repubblica di San Marino (Central Bank of the Republic of San Marino); European Central Bank (ECB).

Time

GMT plus one hour (daylight saving, late March to late October, GMT plus two hours)

Geography

San Marino is a landlocked country of 61.2 square kilometres, entirely surrounded by and located in central Italy. The Italian region of Emilia-Romagna borders to the north and east and the Marche to the south and west. The capital, also called San Marino has eight satellite villages. The geography is mountainous dominated by Mount Titano, the highest peak.

Hemisphere

Northern

Climate

San Marino enjoys a Mediterranean climate with warm summers and dry, cold winters. Temperatures can range between 0–30 degrees Celsius.

Dress codes

Lightweight clothing for summer, medium-weight and topcoat for winter.

Entry requirements

As per Italy

Passports

Required by all and passports must be valid for three months from arrival. Nationals of countries which are signatories of the Schengen Accords, which includes most EU/EEA member states, San Marino and Croatia, may visit on national IDs.

Visa

No visa requirements for citizens of most of Europe, the Americas, Australasia and some Asian countries, visiting for up to 90 days. For a full list, and further information for those citizens not included on the list of visa-free travel, visit www.ambwashingtondc.esteri.it and see *consular services*. A Schengen visa application (offered in several languages) can be downloaded from www.eurovisa.info/ApplicationForm.htm.

Business travellers who do not have visa-free arrangements must provide a letter from their employer guaranteeing travel expenses, including full itinerary and purpose of the trip. Letters of invitation from all Italian companies to be visited, and a current (not over 90 days) *Visura Camerale* issued by the Italian Chamber of Commerce should be attached; a return/onward ticket must be produced before collection of the passport and visa from the issuing consulate, which may request any additional documents at its discretion.

Within eight days of arrival in San Marion the visa traveller must appear before local police authorities to receive a Residency Permit and will also need to show proof of health insurance.

Prohibited entry

Visitors may be refused entry for public security or health reasons, or if not holding visible means of support and onward/return tickets and documents for their next destination.

Currency advice/regulations

The import and export of local or foreign currency up to eur10,300 is allowed. Any amount over this must be declared on Form V2 at customs on arrival.

Health (for visitors)

Mandatory precautions

None

Advisable precautions

Up-to-date tetanus and polio immunisations are recommended. Long-term visitors should consider hepatitis A immunisation.

Hotels

There are approximately 30 hotels of various standards.

Credit cards

Credit cards are widely accepted.

Public holidays (national)

Fixed dates

31 Dec–1 Jan (New Year), 6 Jan (Epiphany), 5 Feb (Liberation Day), 25 Mar (Arengo Day), 1 Apr (Captains Regent Investiture Day), 1 May (Labour Day), 28 Jul (Fall of Fascism Anniversary), 15 Aug (Assumption Day), 3 Sep (Republic Day), 1 Oct (Captains Regent Investiture Day), 1 Nov (All Saints' Day), 2 Nov (All Souls' Day), 8 Dec (Immaculate Conception), 24–26 Dec (Christmas).

Holidays which falls on a Sunday are observed on Monday.

Variable dates

Good Friday, Easter Monday, Corpus Christi (May/Jun).

Working hours

Banking

Mon–Fri: 0830–1330, 1530–1630.

Shops
Mon–Sat: 0830–1300, 1530–1930.

Telecommunications
Mobile/cell phones
Networks 900/1800 GSM are in operation.

Electricity supply
220V AC 50Hz

Getting there
Air
Closest international airports: Rimini (RMI) (Italy) 27km, or Bologna (BLQ) (Italy) 135km.

Surface
There are regular bus services, by highways, from Rimini or Bologna, Italy. The nearest railhead is at Rimini.

Getting about
National transport
The roads are good. A funicular (cable car) operates between Borgo Maggiore and the capital.

BUSINESS DIRECTORY
The addresses listed below are a selection only. While World of Information makes every endeavour to check these addresses, we cannot guarantee that changes have not been made, especially to telephone numbers and area codes. We would welcome any corrections.

Telephone area codes
The international direct dialling (IDD) code for San Marino is +378 followed by 0549 and subscriber's number.

Chambers of Commerce
Agency for Promotion and Development of the Economy, 33 Via G Giacomini, 47890 San Marino (tel: 914-001; fax: 913-473; e-mail: info@apse.sm).

Banking
Central bank
Banca Centrale della Repubblica di San Marino (Central Bank of the Republic of San Marino), 120 Via del Voltone, 47890 San Marino (tel: (+378) (0)549 882-325; fax: (+378) (0)549 882-328).

European Central Bank (ECB), Kaiserstrasse 29, D-60311 Frankfurt am Main, Germany (tel: (+49-69) 13-440; fax: (+49-69) 1344-6000).

Travel information
National tourist organisation offices
Ufficio di Stato per il Turismo (state tourist office), Contrada Omagnano 20, 47031, San Marino (tel: 882-998).

Other useful addresses
Azienda Autonoma di Stato Filatelica e Numismatica (AASFN) (stamps and coins), 5 Piazza Garibaldi, 47031 San Marino (tel: 882-370; fax: 882-363; e-mail: aasfn@omniway.sm).

British Consulate, 2 Lungarno Corsini, 1-50123 Florence, Italy (tel: (+39-055) 212-594; fax: (+39-055) 219-112).

Direzione Generale PPTT (post and telecommunications),17 Contrada Omerelli, San Marino (tel: 882-555; fax: 992-760).

Notizie de San Marino, Radiotelevisione Italiana, 14 Viale Mazzini, 1-00195 Rome, Italy (fax: (+39-06) 372-5680).

Office for Industry, Handicrafts and Trade, Palazzo Mercuri, San Marino (tel: 992-745, 991-385).

Secretariat of State for Finance and the Budget, Palazzo Begni, San Marino (tel: 992-345).

Internet sites
San Marino tourism authority: www.visitsanmarino.com

Web portal for trade: www.tradecenter.sm/index_e.htm

São Tomé and Príncipe

KEY FACTS

Official name: República Democrática de São Tomé e Príncipe (Democratic Republic of São Tomé and Príncipe)

Head of State: President Manuel Pinto da Costa (from 3 Sep 2011)

Head of government: Prime Minister Patrice Trovoada (from 25 Nov 2014)

Ruling party: Acção Democrática Independente (ADI) (Independent Democratic Action) (from Oct 2014)

Area: 964 square km

Population: 198,000 (2014)*

Capital: São Tomé

Official language: Portuguese

Currency: Dobra (Db) = 100 centavos

Exchange rate: Db21,900.00 per US$ (Sep 2015)

GDP per capita: US$1,725 (2014)*

GDP real growth: 4.50% (2014)*

GDP: US$341.00 million (2014)*

Unemployment: 13.47% (2014)*

Inflation: 6.99% (2014)

Balance of trade: -US$128.12 million (2014)

Annual FDI: US$35.00 million (2011)

* estimated figure

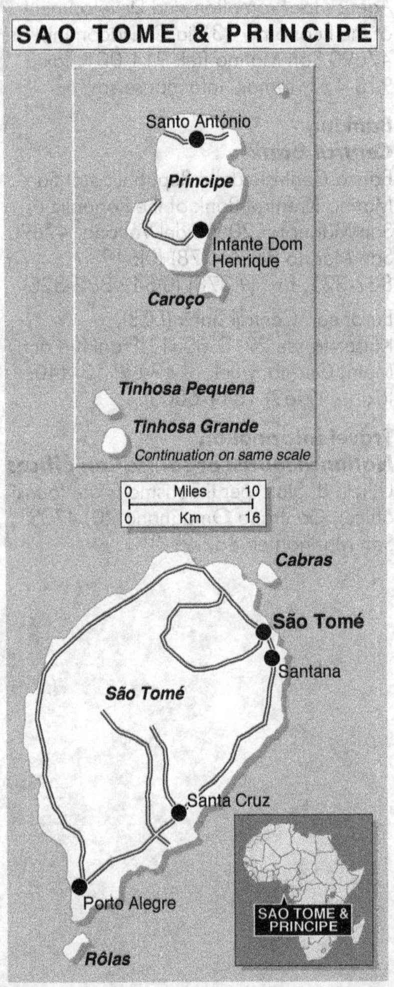

São Tomé and Príncipe, once a leading cocoa producer, is poised to profit from the commercial exploitation of large offshore reserves of oil. Arguments have arisen over how to spend the expected windfall, leading to political tensions amongst the framework of a unitary semi-presidential representative democratic republic.

Democratic reforms were only instituted in the late 1980s – almost a decade after São Tomé and Príncipe gained its independence from Portugal in 1975. Despite free elections being held in 1991, frequent internal and conflicting covets amongst the various political parties precipitated repeated changes in leadership and the following two failed *coup* attempts in 1995 and 2003. A coalition was created in 2012, when president Pinto da Costa dismissed Prime Minister Trovoada following a no confidence vote in the national assembly. Three opposition parties combined to form an inexperienced government. Two years later, in 2014 the opposition Acção Democrática Independente (ADI) (Independent Democratic Action) party won a parliamentary election with an outright majority.

The island consists of two archipelagos located around 87 miles apart. Both islands, São Tomé and Príncipe, are part of an extinct volcanic mountain range. The southern São Tomé island lies just north of the equator. The islands sugar-based economy gave way to coffee and cocoa in the nineteenth century, predominantly via the usage of slave labour. The nation is currently trying to shake off its dependence on the cocoa crop, as falls in production and prices have left the island state heavily reliant on foreign aid. The government has been encouraging economic diversification and is set to exploit the billions of barrels of oil which are thought to lie off the country's coast.

Commercial oil production had, for a period, been expected to begin within a few years. In 1997, a US company (Nigerian owned), named Environmental Remediation Holding Corporation, was awarded the country's first offshore oil exploration contract. In anticipation of increases in oil production, the magazine *Business Insider* optimistically forecast in 2013 that São Tomé and Príncipe would be the world's fastest-growing economy over the following five years. Mr Seibert, however, wisely noted that oil industry analysts had pointed out that there was no guarantee that even one drop of oil will be produced during the period. The article went on to note that in 1999, seismic surveys had revealed that there was a high probability of deep-sea oil reserves in São Tomé and Príncipe's territorial waters. This news was understandably welcomed by the elated, but impoverished country, which had seen its revenues from cocoa production dry up. São Tomé and Príncipe wasted no time in claiming its 200-mile Exclusive Economic Zone (EEZ) and signed agreements to recognise maritime borders with Gabon and (oil rich) Equatorial Guinea. When similar negotiations with Nigeria failed, according to *Foreign Affairs* magazine, the two countries solved the problem by establishing a Joint Development Zone (JDZ) in the disputed territorial waters. According to the treaty, which the two countries signed in 2001, they would share the income and expenditures of the JDZ, with 40 per cent going to São Tomé and Príncipe and 60 per cent going to Nigeria.

Figures circulating at the time estimated that the oil reserves of the 23 deep-water exploration blocks in the JDZ had about 14 billion barrels. Curiously, the US Energy Information Administration (EIA) makes scant comment on São Tome and Principe's oil reserve prospects. The excitement about the country's potential oil wealth reached its climax in October 2003 during the first licensing round for exploration blocks in the JDZ, when the highest bids submitted by oil companies for seven blocks reached US$500 million. Some analysts even speculated that the future oil revenues could soon turn the entire population of São Tomé and Príncipe into millionaires. Such speculations prompted the economist Jeffrey Sachs, director of the Earth Institute at Colombia University, to travel there with a self-styled advisory team to assist local authorities. The group hoped to help São Tomé and Príncipe avoid the oil curse by reinvesting its energy profits in socio-economic development projects that would benefit the entire population.

This euphoria, however, did not last long. The development of the country's oil sector was hit by delays and setbacks from the beginning. The greatest blow to São Tomé and Príncipe's oil expectations came in 2006, when Chevron announced that exploration drillings in JDZ Block 1 had not resulted in the discovery of commercially viable oil. In 2008, Mr Sachs's advisory team left the country unceremoniously; there has been little cause for optimism ever since. On the contrary, due to disappointing drilling results, in 2012, China's Sinopec and other oil companies abandoned JDZ Blocks 2, 3 and 4. Meanwhile, new hopes have been vested in JDZ Block 1, where France's Total carried out exploration drillings in 2012. *Foreign Affairs* reported that analysts have repeatedly revised and postponed predictions for the beginning of commercial oil production in São Tomé and Príncipe and it has become clear that nobody really knows if and when oil production will start.

The economy

According to the International Monetary Fund (IMF), economic activity in São Tomé and Príncipe remained strong in 2014. GDP growth was estimated to be at 4.5 per cent, predominantly driven through an inflow of high foreign direct investment (FDI). Inflation at end–2014 was at its lowest end year point, 6.4 per cent, for the past two decades. A domestic primary fiscal deficit of 3.6 per cent of GDP at the end of 2014 was higher than anticipated however.

The newly elected government remains committed to the maintenance of a fixed exchange rate regime and fiscal disciplines, enabling space to support public investment programmes. This may prove essential in the mitigation of São Tomé and Príncipe's future debts.

Despite the fertile soil and abundant rainfall, the country suffers from food insecurity and poverty. The African Development Bank (AfDB) reported in 2015 that over two-thirds of the population live in poverty, including over 71 per cent of women. Among small farmers, 68 per cent live below the poverty line. The AfDB announced that it would assist in tackling the issues associated with food security and poverty via a combined loan and grant of US$19.5 million. The US$16 million African Development Fund (ADF) soft loan and another US$5 million grant is being used to finance the second phase of the nation's Infrastructure Rehabilitation for Food and Nutrition Security Support Project (PRIASA II).The achievement of PRIASA II will mean that 16,000 farmers and 3,000 fisherman will be provided with basic infrastructure, new techniques involving quality improvements, conservation and marketing necessary to improve food and nutritional security.

Risk assessment

Politics	Fair
Economy	Fair
Regional stability	Good

COUNTRY PROFILE

1469–72 The islands were first sighted by Portuguese sailors.

1485 The town of São Tomé was founded; Príncipe was not settled until 15 years later. The islands quickly became the largest sugar producing area in the world, using slave labour.

1700–1800 Coffee and cocoa plantations were also set up using slave labour.

1875 Slavery was abolished, only to be replaced by a system of forced labour. The labour force consisted mainly of workers brought by the Portuguese from Angola, Mozambique and Cape Verde. On several occasions they launched rebellions against their colonial rulers which were brutally suppressed.

1951 The islands became an overseas province of Portugal.

1974 The end of fascist rule in Portugal marked the beginning of independence for its overseas colonies. A transitional government was established.

1975 The Democratic Republic of São Tomé and Príncipe gained independence from Portugal. The only legal party, the Movimiento de Libertação de São Tomé e Principe (MLSTP) (Movement for the Liberation of São Tomé), made a clean sweep

KEY INDICATORS — São Tomé and Príncipe

	Unit	2011	2012	2013	2014	**2015
Population	m	*0.17	*0.19	*0.19	*0.20	*0.20
Gross domestic product (GDP)	US$bn	0.26	0.26	0.30	*0.34	*0.39
GDP per capita	US$	1,473	1,404	1,568	*1,725	*1,912
GDP real growth	%	4.9	4.0	4.0	*4.5	*5.0
Inflation	%	14.3	10.6	8.1	7.0	*5.6
Unemployment	%	14.7	13.9	13.7	*13.5	*13.0
Exports (fob) (goods)	US$m	10.9	12.2	12.9	17.4	–
Imports (fob) (goods)	US$m	115.7	115.1	128.7	145.6	–
Balance of trade	US$m	-104.7	-103.0	-115.8	-128.1	–
Current account	US$m	-57.7	-54.0	-51.0	-71.0	*-48.0
Total reserves minus gold	US$m	–	51.6	63.8	63.4	–
Foreign direct investment (FDI)	US$bn	–	0.1	–	–	–
Exchange rate	per US$	17,435.57	18,893.00	17,378.00	20,108.62	–

in the general elections and its leader, Manuel Pinto da Costa became the first president. The economy was hard-hit when Portugal withdrew support. Most plantations were quickly nationalised and foreign investors and workers left; the islands developed strong links with Cuba. Under colonial administration there had been little investment in education or healthcare systems for the local population; at independence the literacy rate was 10 per cent and there was only one doctor in the entire country.
1980s A severe drought and a drop in world prices for cocoa crippled the economy. Pinto da Costa began a process of dropping economic ties with the Eastern Bloc in favour of a capitalist, market economy.
1989 Changes within MLSTP began; multi-party democracy was introduced as an objective.
1990 The MLSTP changed its name and adopted MLSTP-PSD (Social Democratic Party) to fight the next election. A multi-party constitution was approved by referendum, allowing direct and free elections for the presidency and legislature.
1991 The ruling MLSTP-PSD lost the country's first election, defeated by the Partido da Convergencia Democrática-Grupo de Reflexão (PCD-GR) (Democratic Convergence Party-Reflection Group). Miguel Trovoada, an independent candidate supported by the PCD-GR, was elected president. The currency was devalued by 40 per cent as part of stringent austerity measures, imposed by the International Monetary Fund (IMF) and the World Bank in exchange for economic assistance.
1994 The MLSTP-PSD won most seats in the National Assembly but fell short of an overall majority.
1995 Príncipe was granted autonomy; the MLSTP-PSD won most seats in its assembly. Strikes by public employees for promised pay rises destabilised the president and government. An abortive coup resulted in the formation of a coalition government which included members of the Ação Democrática Independente (ADI) (Independent Democratic Action), the Coligação Democrático da Oposição (CDO) (Democratic Opposition Coalition) and the Frente Democrática Crista (FDC) (Christian Democratic Front).
1996 Trovoada was re-elected president. Prime Minister Armindo Vaz d'Almeida was removed from office and his position was taken by Raw Wagner da Conceiçao Bragança Neto (MLSTP-PSD).
1998 Elections to the National Assembly resulted in a victory for the centre-left MLSTP-PSD.
2001 Fradique de Menezes won the presidential election.
2002 National Assembly elections were won by the MLSTP; Gabriel Costa became prime minister. He was dismissed by de Menezes in September and replaced in October by Maria das Neves, the country's first female prime minister.
2002 MLSTP won parliamentary elections; Maria das Neves, the country's first female prime minister replaced Gabriel Costa.
2003 The constitution was revised. A military coup staged by Major Fernando Pereira toppled the government while President de Menezes was out of the country. President de Menezes signed an accord with the coup leaders, which restored democratic rule and included an amnesty for the insurgents. Prime Minister das Neves resigned but was reappointed several days later. Bidding began for offshore oil blocs controlled by São Tomé and Príncipe and Nigeria.
2004 The president and prime minister clashed over control of oil deals. Maria das Neves was dismissed after a series of corruption scandals and Damião Vaz d'Almeida became prime minister.
2005 Maria do Carmo Silveira was nominated prime minister after Vaz d'Almeida's resigned.
2006 MLSTP was defeated in parliamentary elections, by a coalition led by the president's Movimento de Libertação de São Tomé e Príncipe-Partido Social Democrata (MLSTP/PSD) (Movement for the Liberation of São Tomé and Príncipe/Social Democratic Party). Tomé Vera Cruz became prime minister. Fradique de Menezes was re-elected president.
2008 Prime Minister Tomé Vera Cruz resigned, having failed in parliament to get the 2008 budget passed; Patrice Trovoada (ADI) was appointed as prime minister, but he lost a censure motion (30–23). The president appointed Joaquim Rafael Branco (MLSTP/PSD) as prime minister.
2009 A coup attempt was foiled; 36 of its perpetrators were arrested and a cache of arms were discovered in the home of opposition politician, Arlecio Costa. The requirement that European visitors must have a vaccination certificate for yellow fever was withdrawn, with the hope this would boost tourism. A government agreement was signed with the Spanish Aresa Group to provide a regular ferry service between the islands of São Tomé and Príncipe. Portugal signed a loan agreement with the government, to allow the dobra currency to be anchored to the euro.
2010 Postponed parliamentary elections were won by the Acção Democrática Independente (ADI) (Independent Democratic Action) won 26 seats (out of 55) and the ruling MLSTP-PSD won 21, with a turnout of 88 per cent.
2011 In the first round of presidential elections, held in July, 10 candidates took part but none won the required 50 per cent of the vote for outright victory. Manuel Pinto da Costa (independent), who had been leader of the MLSTP when São Tomé and Príncipe became independent in 1975 and was the country's first president, won most votes with 35.8 per cent. He duly won the run-off on 7 August with 52.88 per cent of the vote to 47.12 per cent for Evaristo Carvalho (Acção Democrática Independente) (ADI) (Independent Democratic Action), the speaker of parliament.
2012 On 23 September the government announced that the forecast food supply for 2013 had worsened and become 'pessimistic', due to the rise of international food prices. The government also said it could not keep basic commodity prices from rising. At the same time the government encouraged the population to cultivate more of their own food. On 26 November, the ADI had to choose a new leader following the resignation of Evaristo Carvalho. On 28 November parliament overwhelmingly moved a censure motion (29-0) against the government of Prime Minister Trovoada. On 4 December, President Pinto da Costa dismissed Prime Minister Trovoada and his cabinet. Arcanjo Ferreira Dacosta, a consensus builder, was appointed prime minister on 12 December. The assembly's second party MLSTP/PSD had nominated Mr Dacosta after the ADI had refused to put forward a candidate.
2013 President Manuel Pinto da Costa visited Portugal in late-September; on his return he passed through Angola, paying a visit to President José Eduardo dos Santos for discussions of bilateral and international interest.
2014 Parliamentary elections were held on 12 October. The main winners were the ADI with 38.01 per cent (33 seats, out of 55), followed by the MLSTP/PSD with 17.83 per cent (16).
2015 On 25 March, the minister of finance, Américo Ramos, announced a budget of US$150 million for the financial year 2015/16

Political structure

Constitution

The 5 November 1975 constitution was revised in September 1990, following a national referendum, which approved a multi-party constitution, allowing direct and free elections for the presidency and legislature. The constitution was revised again in January 2003.

The island of Príncipe was granted political and administrative autonomy in April 1995.

Form of state

Sovereign, unitary and democratic state.

The executive

The president is elected for a maximum of two five-year terms of office.

National legislature

The unicameral Assembleia Popular Nacional (National People's Assembly) 55 members elected by proportional representation in seven multi-seat constituencies (districts), to serve for four-year terms. There are six district assemblies on Sao Tomé and a seven-member regional assembly on the island of Príncipe.

Legal system

Portuguese legal system. The Supreme Court is appointed by the National Assembly.

Last elections

17 July and 7 August 2011 (presidential first round and runoff); 12 October 2014 (parliamentary)

Results: Parliamentary: Acção Democrática Independente (ADI) (Independent Democratic Action) won with 38.01 per cent (33 seats, out of 55), Movimento de Libertação de São Tomé e Príncipe-Partido Social Democrata (MLSTP-PSD) (Movement for the Liberation of São Tomé and Príncipe-Social Democratic Party) 17.83 per cent (16), Partido de Convergência Democrática-Grupa de Reflexão (PCD-GR) (Democratic Convergence Party-Reflection Group) 5 seats, União dos Democratas para Cidadania e Desenvolvimento (Union of Democrats for Citizenship and Development) 1 seat. 8 other parties failed to win a seat. Turnout was 74.91 per cent.

Presidential (first round): Manuel Pinto da Costa won (independent) 35.62 per cent of the vote, Evaristo Carvalho (ADI) 21.79 per cent, Maria das Neves (independent) 14.36 per cent, and Delfim Neves (four-party coalition of PCD-GR, MDFM-PL) 14.04 per cent; six other candidates each won less that 5 per cent. Turnout was 68.4 per cent. Runoff: Manuel Pinto da Costa 52.88 per cent, Evaristo Carvalho 47.12 per cent; turnout was 68.4 and 74.0 per cent respectively.

Next elections

2018 (parliamentary); 2016 (presidential)

Political parties

Ruling party

Coalition led by Acção Democrática Independente (ADI) (Independent Democratic Action) (from Aug 2010)

Main opposition party

Movimento Democrático das Forças da Mudança-Partido Liberal (MDFM-PL) (Force for Change Democratic Movement-Liberal Party)

Around 54 per cent of the population live below the national poverty line. About 94 per cent of the total population live on São Tomé; around 8,000 people live on Príncipe.

Population

191,000 (2013)*

Last census: August 2001: 137,599

Population density: 151 inhabitants per square km. Urban population 62 per cent (2010 Unicef).

Annual growth rate: 1.8 per cent, 1990–2010 (Unicef).

Ethnic make-up

There are five groups among the islands' inhabitants: the Filhos da Terra are the descendants of imported slaves and Europeans (mostly Portuguese); the Angolares are descendants of former castaway slaves from Angola, now primarily fishermen; the Forros are descendants of slaves freed when slavery was abolished in 1875; the Servicais are migrant labourers from Angola, Mozambique and Cape Verde, and the Tongas are their children, born on the islands.

Religions

Eighty per cent of the population are Roman Catholic, Evangelical Protestant or Seventh-Day Adventist.

Education

The literacy rate for the period 1995—2001 was estimated at 63 per cent.

Health

Life expectancy: 59 years, 2004 (WHO 2006)

Fertility rate/Maternal mortality rate: 3.7 births per woman, 2010 (Unicef)

Birth rate/Death rate: 42 births per 1,000 population; seven deaths per 1,000 population (2003).

Child (under 5 years) mortality rate (per 1,000): 53 per 1,000 live births (WHO 2012)

Head of population per physician: 0.49 physicians per 1,000 people, 2004 (WHO 2006)

Main cities

São Tomé (capital, estimated population 67,868 in 2012) Trinidade (8,392), Santo Amaro (8,339), Neves (7,548), Santana (7,410), Santo António, on Príncipe, (1,342).

Languages spoken

Portuguese is spoken by 95 per cent of the population; Lungwa Santomé is the main national dialect and Fôrro and Crioulo are also spoken.

Official language/s

Portuguese

Media

Press

In Portuguese, there are two weekly newspapers, *Diário da República* (www.cstome.net) and the official organ of Ministry of Information *Revolução*. The weekend newspaper and magazine is *Povo* and the sole independent periodical is *O Parvo*.

Jornal de São Tomé and Príncipe (www.jornal.st) is an online news outlet, in Portuguese.

Broadcasting

Radio: Radio Nacional de São Tomé e Príncipe broadcasts two FM services in Portuguese from Lisbon, Portugal. The French radio station RFI (www.rfi.fr), from neighbouring Cameroon, can also be picked up along with Voice of America (VoA).

Television: The state-run television service is Televisao Saotomense (TVS).

Economy

Agriculture is the mainstay of the economy, with cocoa being the major cash crop, representing around 80 per cent of total commodity exports. Foreign aid, most particularly from Portugal, is also an important factor, along with revenue from oil exploration companies prospecting for oil offshore in São Tomé and Príncipe's territorial waters in the Gulf of Guinea. Nigeria and São Tomé have a contract whereby joint development will result in 60 per cent of proceeds going to Nigeria and the remainder to São Tomé.

Although the dominant crop on São Tomé is cocoa, other export crops include copra, palm kernels, and coffee. Domestically, fishing and a small industrial sector processing local agricultural products and producing a few basic consumer goods provide an inadequate employment environment. However, the islands have potential for tourism, and the government is attempting to improve the undeveloped tourism infrastructure.

Since dropping from a GDP growth rate of 9.1 per cent in 2008 to 4.0 per cent in 2009 as a result of the global financial crisis forcing a decline in foreign investment, São Tomé e Príncipe has maintained a steady growth rate averaging 4.3 per cent from 2009—14 (4.2 per cent in 2014).

Inflation, which had been a long-term problem, peaked at 32 per cent in 2008, but in 2009, Portugal signed a loan agreement with the government, to allow the dobra currency to be anchored to the euro and stabilising the exchange rate. The fall in world food and oil prices meant inflation fell to 6.4 per cent by 2014.

Oil production is unlikely to come on-stream before 2016, when the enormous impact of oil receipts will be managed by an oil revenue management law, with a percentage of the profits channelled into a trust fund for future generations. There are estimated to be some 10 billion barrels of oil within São Tomé's borders. Revenue from oil is expected to pay debts and provide more government spending, particularly on poverty reduction schemes. There are already some benefits as construction and other activities increase to cater for the industry.

On 20 July 2012 the International Monetary Fund agreed to a three-year extended credit facility (ECF) of around US$3.9 million (with an immediate disbursement of about US$560,000) to maintain macroeconomic stability and accelerate structural reforms geared to the start of oil production in 2016.

In 2014, the UN Human Development Index (HDI) ranked São Tomé e Príncipe 142 (out of 187) for national development in health, education and income. Since 2005, São Tomé e Príncipe's progress has grown above the rate of other countries in sub-Saharan Africa. In 2013, 47.5 per cent of the population experienced at least one indicator of poverty.

External trade

São Tomé and Príncipe is a member of the Common Market for Eastern and Southern Africa (Comesa), and operates within a free trade zone with 13 of the 19 member states.

It is a mono-exporter with around 80 per cent of all commodity exports being cocoa that is shipped mainly to Europe. New found oil deposits are not expected to be in production until 2016, when it will radically increase foreign earnings.

Imports

Principal imports are machinery and electrical equipment, food products and petroleum products.

Main sources: Portugal (typically 56 per cent of total), Belgium (10 per cent), Japan (9 per cent).

Exports

Principal exports are cocoa, copra, coffee and palm oil.

Main destinations: Japan (typically 77 per cent of total), Belgium (8 per cent), The Netherlands (6 per cent).

Agriculture

Farming

Plantation agriculture forms the basis of the economy, but growth is slowing. Cocoa is the main crop, accounting for around 90 per cent of exports. Cocoa production, once the biggest in the world, has fallen over the years and now totals about 4,000 tonnes a year. The plantations were nationalised after independence to their detriment, but have since been privatised.

The second-largest export crop is coffee; other cash crops are copra, palm kernels, cinnamon, pepper and breadfruit. Priority is being given to the diversification of food crops in an effort to reduce the large food import bill.

Fishing

Fishing remains small-scale, but is being encouraged for local consumption and possible future export.

Forestry

Industry and manufacturing

The industrial sector is limited to small-scale manufacturing concerns such as soap, soft drinks, timber processing, palm oil, bricks and textiles. The development of oil fields in the Gulf of Guinea is likely to increase industrial activity associated with the sector, particularly construction. These will give incentives to investors, with tax breaks and free movement of goods. In 2013 industry and manufacturing contributed 19.5 per cent to GDP.

Tourism

Tourism plays an important role in the economy of the islands, but the infrastructure to provide for visitors' needs is underdeveloped. Almost 30 per cent of the country is rainforest with some unique flora and fauna. There are beach-fronted tourist resorts with individual accommodation units and combined amenities. Activities on offer are largely centred on water sports such as diving (to see the green sea turtles among other marine creatures), fishing and yachting.

Travel and tourism contributed over 14.0 per cent to GDP in 2014, and provided employment to some 13.1 per cent of the workforce (11,500 jobs).

Direct, international flights arrive six days a week (not Wednesday) into São Tomé, from Portugal. Flights from Angola have a 30-minute duration but only operate once per day and not daily.

Mining

São Tomé e Príncipe has no mineral resources.

Hydrocarbons

São Tomé and Príncipe has established a joint authority with Nigeria to manage offshore oil exploration and development in the oil-rich Gulf of Guinea. Under the accord, Nigeria will receive 60 per cent of revenues and São Tomé and Príncipe 40 per cent. Preliminary indications suggest that there may be substantial commercial reserves of oil in the area. Production is expected to begin in 2016.

In 2014 São Tomé and Príncipe was still dependent on imported refined oil products, which was around 1000 barrels per day. Oil-derived products supply 96 per cent of commercial energy requirements.

The World Bank estimated that oil imports consume 20–25 per cent of total export revenue. Distribution and marketing of fuels is carried out by the state-owned oil company, Empresa Nacional de Combustiveis e Oleos (Enco).

Energy

Installed electricity generating capacity is around 14MW, of which over 50 per cent is provided by hydro plants and the remainder by diesel generators. The national power grid is only operational in the densely populated area of north-east São Tomé. There is great need to increase capacity, by at least 3MW, just to meet demand; blackouts are frequent.

The state-owned monopoly, Empresa Nacional de Água e Electricidade (EMAE) (National Water and Electricity Enterprise) is responsible for generation, transmission and distribution of electricity. But the government is considering privatising the utility in an attempt to find investment and instil commercial principles.

The World Bank has stated that São Tomé and Príncipe has the potential to increase capacity, estimated up to a potential of 6,000MW, through development of major and minor hydroelectric power plants. However it also questioned São Tomé and Príncipe's ability to service the loan.

Banking and insurance

Central bank

Banco Central de São Tomé e Príncipe

Main financial centre

São Tomé.

Time

GMT.

Geography

The islands of the Republic of São Tomé and Príncipe, are located in the equatorial Atlantic Ocean, about 300–250km off the coast of Gabon, in the Gulf of Guinea. Both islands are remnants of an extinct volcanic mountain range. The tallest mountain is São Tomé Peak (2,024 metres) on the island of São Tomé. Príncipe's mountains have lush forests with swift streams flowing down to the sea. The country also includes the rocky islets of Caroço, Pedras and Tinhosas, off Príncipe, and Rôlas, off São Tomé.

Hemisphere

Northern

Climate

Equatorial with high temperatures and humidity. Average temperatures remain fairly constant throughout the year with a daily range from 20–32 degrees Celsius (C). Driest month July, wettest March.

Entry requirements

Passports

Required by all.

Visa
Required by all; apply well in advance. European visitors should contact the São Tomé e Príncipe consulate in Brussels; US visitors should contact the consulate in either New York or Atlanta; visitors from Canada and Australia should contact the Canadian embassy in Libreville in Gabon (See: Other useful addresses, for further information).

Currency advice/regulations
There are no restrictions on the import of local or foreign currency. Export is allowed up to the amount declared on entry.
Travellers cheques are not widely accepted. US dollars and euro are easily converted, other currencies may attract higher exchange fees.

Health (for visitors)
Mandatory precautions
Yellow fever vaccination certificate is required by all, except visitors from Europe (from April 2009).

Advisable precautions
Inoculations and boosters should be current for cholera, tetanus, yellow fever, hepatitis A, diphtheria, typhoid and polio. There may be a need for vaccinations for tuberculosis, hepatitis B and meningitis. Use malaria prophylaxis (which will also provide protection against yellow fever, dengue fever, hepatitis B and encephalitis) including mosquito repellents, sleeping nets and clothing that cover the body after dark. To avoid bilharzia, avoid exposure to fresh water and use only well-maintained, chlorinated swimming pools.
There is a risk of rabies.
Use only bottled or boiled water for drinks, washing teeth and making ice. Eat only well cooked meals, preferably served hot; vegetables should be cooked and fruit peeled. Dairy products are unpasteurised and should be avoided, unless cooked. There is a shortage of routine medications, including sun-screens, and visitors should take all necessary medicines with them. A first aid kit that includes disposable syringes, is a reasonable precaution.
Healthcare is not to Western standards and medical insurance, including emergency evacuation, is necessary.

Hotels
There is a limited number of reasonable hotels.

Public holidays (national)
Fixed dates
1 Jan (New Year's Day), 3 Feb (Heroes' Day), 1 May (Labour Day), 12 Jul (Independence Day), 6 Sep (Armed Forces Day), 30 Sep (Agricultural Reform Day), 26 Nov (Argel Accord Day), 21 Dec (São Tomé Day, Catholic), 25 Dec (Christmas Day).

Variable dates
Ash Wednesday, Good Friday.

Working hours
Banking
Mon–Fri: 0730–1130, 1430–1630.
Business
Mon–Fri: 0730–1200, 1430–1800.
Government
Mon–Fri: 0800–1200, 1500–1800; Sat: 0800–1300.
Shops
Mon–Sat: 0800–1200, 1500–1900.

Telecommunications
Mobile/cell phones
A 900 GSM service is available over most of the islands of São Tomé and Príncipe.

Electricity supply
220V AC

Weights and measures
Metric

Social customs/useful tips
Business is conducted in Portuguese. Many executives speak French, and some speak English.

Getting there
Air
The national airlines of Portugal (TAP) and Angola (TAAG), fly services to São Tomé.
National airline: Air São Tomé e Príncipe (KY), flies to Gabon only.
International airport/s: São Tomé (TMS), 5.5km from town. A minibus, taxi and buses provide transport to the centre of town.
Airport tax: Departure tax: US$21 or eur24, in cash.

Surface
Water: A high-speed ferry service between São Tomé and Cape Verde is planned by the ferry company Expresso LDA with a one-way journey taking five days. The ferry will have 400 berths and a capacity of 800 passengers. Although planning began in 2010, the service was still not operational in July 2011.
Main port/s: São Tomé, this is not a deep-water harbour so few international ships visit.

Getting about
National transport
Air: Restricted services link the two islands. Travellers should book their seats well in advance, to avoid being stranded.
Road: There are only about 300km of roads, of which about two-thirds are asphalted, but the network is being improved.
Buses: Frequent, efficient service on São Tomé. Limited bus service on Príncipe.

City transport
Taxis: On São Tomé a minivan or *collectivo* shared taxi can be taken to anywhere on the island. There are no fixed schedules and they leave only when they are full; this is no other public transport available.

BUSINESS DIRECTORY

The addresses listed below are a selection only. While World of Information makes every endeavour to check these addresses, we cannot guarantee that changes have not been made, especially to telephone numbers and area codes. We would welcome any corrections.

Telephone area codes
The international dialling code (IDD) for São Tomé and Príncipe is +239, followed by subscriber's number.

Chambers of Commerce
Camara de Comircio, Industria, Agricultura e Servicios, Avenida Marginal 12 de Julho, PO Box 527, Saõ Tomé (tel: 22-2723; fax: 22-1409; e-mail: ccias@cstome.net).

Banking
Banco Comercial do Equador, CP 361, Rua de Moçambique, São Tomé (tel: 22-3829; fax: 22-1989).

Banco Internacional de S Tomé e Príncipe, CP 536, Praça da Independência 3, São Tomé (tel: 22-1445; 22-5821; fax: 22-2427, 22-3462).

Central bank
Banco Central de São Tomé e Príncipe, CP 13, Praça da Independencia, São Tomé (tel: 22-1269, 22-1300; fax: 22-501, 22-2777; email: bcentral@cstome.net; internet: www.bcstp.st).

Travel information
TAP (Air Portugal), CP 414; Avenida Marginal 12 de Julho, São Tomé (tel: 22-2307, 22-1528).

National tourist organisation offices
Tourism Office, CP40, Avenue Marginal, 12 de Julho, São Tomé (tel: 221-542).

Ministries
Ministry of Commerce, Industry and Tourism, Largo das Alfândegas São Tomé; CP 201, São Tomé e Príncipe (tel: 22-4657, 22-4872, 22-4975).

Ministry of Foreign Affairs, Avenida 12 de Julho, São Tomé (tel: 22-2309; fax: 22-3237; email: popgender@sctome.net).

Ministry of Planning and Finance, Largo das Alfândegas São Tomé (tel: 22-4172/3; fax: 22-2182; email: fpublica@cstome.net).

Office of the President, Avenida da Independência, São Tomé (tel: 22-1143; fax: 22-1226).

Office of the Prime Minister, Rua do Município, São Tomé (tel: 22-3596, 22-4189; fax: 22-1670).

National Assembly, Palácio dos Congressos, São Tomé (tel: 22-1899, 22-2986; fax: 22-2835).

Other useful addresses

Canadian embassy, PO Box 4037 Libreville, Gabon (tel: (+241) 737-354; fax: 737-388; email: ibrve@dfait-maeci.gc.ca).

Directorate of Finance, Praça da Independência, São Tomé; CP 168, São Tomé and Príncipe (tel: 22-2372, 22-1484; fax: 22-1182; email: financas@cstome.net).

Nigeria-São Tomé and Príncipe Joint Development Authority, Plot 1101 Aminu Kano Crescent, Wuse II, Abuja, Nigeria (tel: (+234-9) 524-1069; fax: (234-9) 524-1052; e-mail: enquiries@nigeriasaotomejda.com; internet: www.nigeriasaotomejda.com).

São Tomé and Príncipe Embassy (USA), 7th Floor, 400 Park Avenue, New York 10044 (tel: (+1-212) 317-0533; fax 317-0580; email: stp1@attglobal.net; internet: www.saotome.org).

São Tomé and Príncipe Consulate (USA), Suite 305, 512 Means Street, Atlanta GA 30318, USA (tel: (+1-404) 221-0203; fax: (+1-404) 221-1006; e-mail: consul@saotome.org; internet: www.saotome.org).

São Tomé and Príncipe Embassy, Square Montgomery, 175 Avenue de Tervuren, 1150 Brussels, Belgium (tel: (+32-2) 734-9966; fax: (+32-2) 734-8815).

STP-Press, c/o Rádio Nacional de São Tomé e Príncipe, Avenida Marginal de 12 de Julho, CP 44, São Tomé (tel: 22-217).

São Tomé and Príncipe Telecom (CST), Av Marginal 12 de Julho, São Tomé; CP 141, São Tomé and Príncipe (tel: 22-2273; internt: www.cst.st).

Internet sites

AllAfrica information: http://allafrica.com/saotomeandprincipe

National Assembly (in Portuguese): www.parlamento.st

São Toméand Príncipe tourist site: www.saotome.st

São Tomé and Príncipe website: www.sao-tome.com

Saudi Arabia

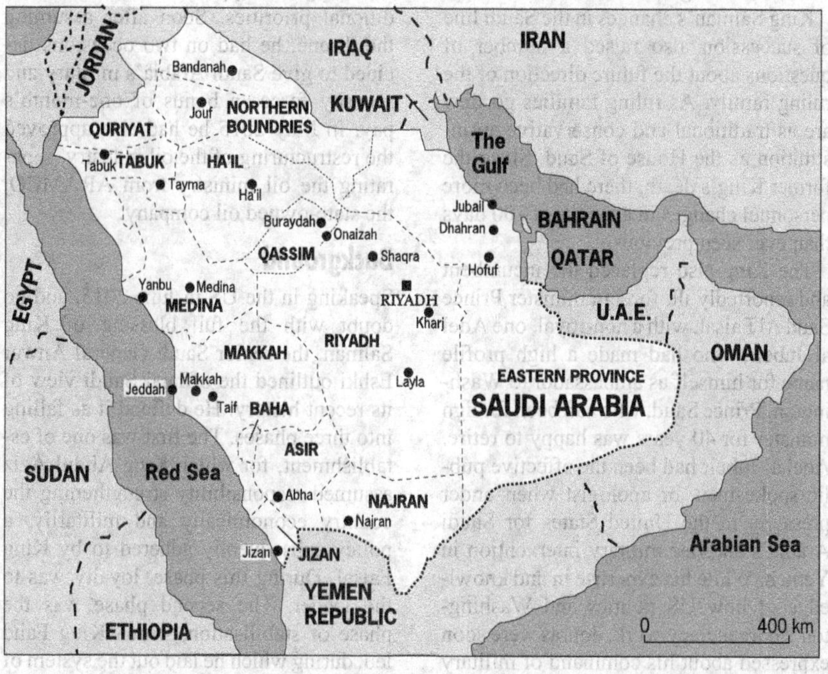

In January 2015 Saudi Arabia's long expected change of ruler took place. King Salman bin Abdul-Aziz Al Saud, 78, acceded to the throne in January after the death of his half-brother Abdullah bin Abdul Aziz. King Abdullah, who was thought to be aged about 90, had been on the throne since 2005 and had been Saudi Arabia's *de facto* leader for some 10 years before that. The new King faces several difficult issues, including adjusting to the fall in the price of oil (see Hydrocarbons) and the war in Yemen. And, perhaps most important of all, appointing a crown prince and new cabinet.

In April in what by any standards was an eventful week, King Salman announced a major cabinet reshuffle that puts in place a new generation to succeed him. Just four months into his reign, King Salman announced arrangements for the future of the al Saud dynasty. He appointed his nephew and third in the line of succession, the interior minister Prince Mohammed bin Nayef, as Crown Prince. The new crown prince, aged 55, is famous for defeating al Qaeda's violent attempt to overthrow the House of Saud at the turn of the century. He master-minded a four-year counter-terrorism campaign that saw off al Qaeda in the Kingdom and pushed its tattered remnants into Yemen. He has managed to survive at least four assassination plots.

Mohammed bin Nayef studied in the United States – for some reason in Oregon – and with the FBI in Washington DC and with Scotland Yard in London before joining the interior ministry. He also held the position of chairman of the Saudi security and political committee, which co-ordinates security issues. Human rights activists have been critical of his role as the nation's top policeman, but security experts have praised his record on counter-terrorism.

The King's son, Prince Mohammed bin Salman, was made deputy crown prince and defence minister. Following the March 2015 invasion of Yemen, Mohammed bin Salman soon became the (bearded) face of the Yemeni war. Television appearances, meetings with foreign statesmen and even popular songs made him the (slightly) more acceptable face of the Yemen invasion. Despite his apparent popularity, he had not convinced many of the King's cabinet to agree to send ground

KEY FACTS

Official name: Mamlaka al Arabiya as Sa'udiya (The Kingdom of Saudi Arabia)

Head of State: King Abdullah Salman bin Abdul Aziz al Sa'ud (since 23 January 2015)

Head of government: King Abdullah Salman bin Abdul Aziz al Sa'ud (since 23 January 2015)

Ruling party: None

Area: 2,149,690 square km (approximately)

Population: 30.77 million (2014)* (27,136,977; 2010, census figure)

Capital: Riyadh

Official language: Arabic

Currency: Saudi riyal (SR) = 100 halalas

Exchange rate: SR3.75 per US$ (fixed)(Jul 2014)*

GDP per capita: US$24,454 (2014)*

GDP real growth: 3.59% (2014)

GDP: US$752.46 billion (2014)

Unemployment: 5.55% (2014)

Inflation: 2.20% (May 2015)

Oil production: 11.51 million bpd (2014)

Natural gas production: 108.20 billion cum (2014)

Balance of trade: US$183.86 billion (2014)

Annual FDI: US$16.31 billion (2011)

* estimated figure

troops into Yemen. Some non-Saudi military advisers had questioned his military judgement. Mohammed bin Salman is considered ruthlessly ambitious and very close to his father. He had given up his position as chief of the royal court, but he would undoubtedly keep control of access to the King.

Not only did he lack experience, but unlike most Saudi princes, Mohammed bin Salman was not educated in the West. Instead, he studied law at King Saud University. There is also some doubt about his exact age; he is reputed to be anywhere from 29 to 34; officially his birthdate is 24 July 1980. He chairs a number of young people's organisations and seeks to portray himself as the leader of the next generation of Saudis. Two-thirds of Saudis are under 30. He also chairs the powerful development and economics committee, which co-ordinates economic policies, including oil pricing and supply.

When Prince Mohammed bin Salman was made deputy crown prince the foreign minister, Prince Saud al Faisal, found himself out of a job. The biggest loser, however, was the former Crown Prince and the King's half-brother, Muqrin bin Abdulaziz, who was left to make a public proclamation of his allegiance to the new broom. It was not altogether clear why he had been demoted – especially as he was not even kicked upstairs.

The speculation surrounding Muqrin's departure was at times feverish. Born to a Yemeni slave girl, he was a protege of the late Abdullah. He was not close to Salman's branch of the family, the Sudairis, who all share the same mother, Hassa bint Ahmad al Sudairi, the favourite wife of the kingdom's founder. Muqrin was allegedly worried that the cautious reforms seen under Abdullah would end under Salman, or that the war in Yemen risked becoming Saudi Arabia's Vietnam.

King Salman's changes in the Saudi line of succession also raised a number of questions about the future direction of the ruling family. As ruling families go, few are as traditional and conservative an institution as the House of Saud. Since the former King's death, there had been more personnel changes in a matter of 100 days than ever seen previously.

The King also replaced the incumbent and reportedly ill, foreign minister Prince Saud Al Faisal, with a non-royal, one Adel al Jubeir, who had made a high profile name for himself as ambassador to Washington. Prince Saud, who had been foreign minister for 40 years was happy to retire. Adel al Jubeir had been the effective public spokesman, or apologist when under pressure, in the United States for Saudi Arabia's surprise military intervention in Yemen. While his expertise in and knowledge of how US politics and Washington's bureaucracy work, doubts were soon expressed about his command of military strategy.

Among the other unexplained changes made by King Salman was the replacement of the only woman to ever hold a sub-cabinet position in Saudi Arabia. The feputy education minister for girls, Nura al Fayez, had been appointed by King Abdullah in 2009. She had possibly made the mistake of advocating girls' physical education, which Saudi Arabia's Wahhabi forcefully opposed. Despite his apparently modern and decisive outlook, the new King soon appeared to have more traditional priorities. Soon after assuming the throne, he had on two occasions decided to give Saudi Arabia's military and security forces a bonus of one-month's pay. In May 2015 he had also approved the restructuring of the oil industry, separating the oil ministry from ARAMCO, the state-owned oil company.

Background

Speaking in the US in June 2015, and no doubt with the full blessing of King Salman, the senior Saudi General Anwar Eshki outlined the official Saudi view of its recent history. He defined it as falling into three phases. The first was one of establishment, for which King Abdul Aziz assumed responsibility strengthening the country economically and militarily, a policy subsequently adhered to by King Faisal. During this phase, loyalty was to the leader. The second phase was the phase of stabilisation, which King Fahd led, during which he laid out the system of rule, transferred loyalty from the leader to the system and substituted nationalism in the place of pastoralism. The third phase was described as the phase of 'moving forward', (whatever that meant). This is the current phase wherein the Kingdom is moving toward positive work in the region. It had formed an alliance – which represented a sea change in Saudi policy – and laid down a strategic goal for the Arab world, which was Arab national security, starting with protecting Yemen (from what was seen as a possible takeover by pro-Tehran Shi'a rebels) and protecting the Gulf, eliminating conflicts and 'calming down' matters in the Middle East. In this period, during the reign of King Salman, Saudi Arabia – according to General Eshki – would transform more into a democracy 'with Islamic pillars'. In this phase, it has rebuilt its strategic alliance with the United States of America as well as its alliance with France, Pakistan, the United Kingdom, Turkey, with friends in China, Russia and other countries.

Quite how Saudi Arabia planned to transform itself more into a democracy was none too clear in mid-2015. By definition, an absolute monarchy is normally anti-democratic. By early March 2015,

KEY INDICATORS — Saudi Arabia

	Unit	2011	2012	2013	2014	**2015
Population	m	*28.17	*29.20	*29.99	*30.77	*31.39
Gross domestic product (GDP)	US$bn	577.60	733.96	744.34	752.46	*648.97
GDP per capita	US$	20,504	25,139	24,816	*24,454	*20,677
GDP real growth	%	6.8	5.8	2.7	3.6	*3.0
Inflation	%	5.0	2.9	3.5	2.7	*2.0
Unemployment	%	12.4	5.4	5.6	5.5	–
Oil output	'000 bpd	11,161.0	11,530.0	11,525.0	11,505.0	–
Natural gas output	bn cum	99.2	102.8	103.0	108.2	–
Exports (fob) (goods)	US$m	364,735.5	388,369.6	377,041.6	342,324.0	–
Imports (fob) (goods)	US$m	120,023.3	141,799.2	152,706.7	158,462.0	–
Balance of trade	US$m	244,712.2	246,570.4	224,334.9	183,862.0	–
Current account	US$m	158,459.2	164,693.0	132,640.0	*106,175.0	*-6,547.0
Total reserves minus gold	US$m	516,643.0	656,464.0	725,292.0	731,920.0	–
Foreign exchange	US$m	501,585.0	640,975.0	710,485.0	–	–
Exchange rate	per US$	3.75	3.75	3.75	3.75	–

* estimated figure ** forecast figure

according to Amnesty International, the Kingdom had executed no less than forty-four people in the year, an average of one per working day. A number of these were foreign nationals, hanged or beheaded for what in the US or Europe would be considered relatively minor drug-related charges. The Saudi press remained heavily censored, peaceful protests were banned and rights' advocates faced draconian sentences. Women in Saudi Arabia had the status of minors, unable to drive, travel or otherwise function as adults without the supervision of their fathers, husbands or sons. As elsewhere in the Gulf, menial jobs were done by migrant workers, who in many cases were little more than indentured labourers.

On the Transparency International 2014 *Corruption Perceptions Index* Saudi Arabia ranked a surprisingly high 55 out of the 175 countries surveyed, ahead of neighbours Kuwait (67) and Oman (64). Its 2014 position was an eight point improvement over the 63 it ranked in 2013. A joint letter signed by a number of respected non governmental organisations (NGOs) including Amnesty International and Human Rights Watch (HRW) observed that in Yemen 'the warring parties (led by Saudi Arabia) have committed serious violations of international humanitarian law and abuses of human rights. The Saudi-led coalition has conducted indiscriminate and disproportionate airstrikes that have killed and wounded scores of civilians and destroyed numerous civilian objects.'

Yemen

Quite what were the objectives – military and otherwise – of the Saudi led coalition were unclear. The overt opposition were the pro-Iranian Shi'ite Houthi rebels. Dubbing it Operation Decisive Storm the Saudi led coalition began to attack numerous Houthi related military objectives in late March 2015. If the 'Storm' did indeed prove 'Decisive' and Saudi Arabia could claim 'victory' in this campaign, the *de facto* control of Yemen that it had sought to hold in the previous few decades and that it had sought to maintain in the post-2011 revolution period, would be reinforced not so much by Restoring Hope (as the Saudis had dubbed phase two of the campaign) but more likely by the even greater belligerence and sense of entitlement that appeared to characterise the King Salman administration. There had already been references to a Saudi inspired (and funded) Yemen Marshall Plan (which one neutral military observer had dubbed) Operation 'Beginning Beheadings') and the prospect of allowing Yemen into the Gulf Co-operation Council (GCC) as the payback for the destruction of much of Yemen's infrastructure.

It was feared that the authoritarian system that Saudi Arabia had long supported and which it sought to salvage in the transition process would be entrenched in ways that former Yemeni President Saleh's regime never was. While the prospect of petrodollars and GCC jobs may sound alluring to a country that is starving and beaten by war, Operation Restore Hope was yet another reminder that Saudi Arabia had never really got to grips with events in Yemen, preferring to meddle on the sidelines of Yemen's internal struggles. Assuming, once again, a Saudi 'victory', Yemen might find itself confronting the consequences of replacing a largely unpopular, out of control rebel militia for an equally unpopular neighbouring imperial power that had long sought to weaken the Yemeni state.

The economy

For reasons unknown and unexplained, on the death of King Abdullah in January 2015, the International Monetary Fund's (IMF) Managing Director Christine Lagarde had described the late monarch as 'a strong advocate of women'. Adding, 'in a very discreet way.' A number of commentators asked what on earth Mme Lagarde was talking about. For all his minutely reforming ways, King Abdullah was not to make an appearance in the annals of female emancipation. More objectively, in its September 2015 annual assessment of the Saudi Arabian economy, the IMF noted that while activity had slowed in recent years, Saudi Arabia had been one of the strongest growing economies in the G-20. Over the previous decade, rising oil prices and production had resulted in large external and fiscal surpluses. The economy had benefited from strong government spending, boosting private sector activity, while government deposits in the banking system increased to nearly 56 per cent of GDP and government debt declined to about 1.5 per cent of GDP by the end of 2014. Inflation had been moderate and human and social development indicators had improved considerably.

With power transferred to King Salman, following the death of King Abdullah in January 2015, a reorganisation of government took place under which numerous committees were abolished and two ministries merged. Two new high-level councils were created to streamline policymaking – the Council of Economic and Development Affairs and the Council for Political and Security Affairs.

Managing the demographic pressures that emerge from a rapidly growing and young population is a key challenge for Saudi policymakers. The Saudi labour force had been growing annually by over 5 per cent in recent years. Within the labour market, Saudi nationals are employed primarily in the public sector, while the private sector relies on low-wage, low skilled expatriate labour. The provision of attractive private sector jobs for Saudi youth will, in the view of the IMF, require the diversification of the economy into high-productivity activities and ensuring that Saudi youth have the requisite skills for these positions.

The IMF noted that past episodes of large oil price declines had been associated with a strong impact on macro-economic and financial sector outcomes. Lower oil revenues had led to weaker fiscal and external positions, a drop in equity prices as markets anticipated the impact of lower oil prices on the corporate sector and generally slower government spending. In turn, slower government spending had led to weaker non-oil activity, tighter banking sector liquidity, lower credit growth and weaker bank balance sheets, with the drop in equity prices also having some wealth effects. The size and duration of the oil price declines had been important in determining their economic impact, as have the size of available buffers. So while in 2008–09, the government was able to maintain spending given the strong fiscal position, in 1998–99 it was not. And as the 1980s showed, even large buffers can be eroded if the price drop is sustained. Saudi Arabia's dependence on oil has remained high despite efforts at diversification – although there has been some progress in recent years in developing non-oil exports, these are concentrated in petrochemicals which are also exposed to oil price movements.

According to the IMF, the decline in oil prices since mid-2014 had substantially lowered export and fiscal revenues, resulting in a fiscal deficit and a narrowing of the current account surplus in 2014. Owing to the oil price decline, government revenues dropped, while government spending grew by 14.7 per cent in 2014. A central government deficit of 3.4 per cent of GDP was recorded in 2014, compared to a surplus of 5.8 per cent of GDP in 2013, while the general government balance also moved into deficit.

Nevertheless, government debt remained very low and deposits with the banking system stood at 56 per cent of GDP at end-2014. In the first quarter of 2015, the fiscal deficit widened owing to the impact of the fiscal packages that were announced in January and April (totalling about SR100 billion (US$26.67 billion) or 4.2 per cent of GDP) and financial assistance to neighbouring countries. The external position was also affected by the oil price (and petrochemical price) fall and the current account surplus declined from 18.2 per cent of GDP in 2013 to 10.9 per cent of GDP in 2014. Following a strong start, real GDP growth slowed during the course of 2014, reflecting a decline in oil production and weakening non-oil output growth. For the year as a whole, growth was 3.5 per cent, up from 2.7 per cent in 2013 with non-oil growth of 5 per cent, in part reflecting the continued strength in government spending. GDP growth in the first quarter of 2015 increased to an annual 2.4 per cent, up from 1.6 per cent in the final quarter of 2014 due to higher oil output, but remained much weaker than the 6.4 per cent growth in the first quarter of 2014. Inflation was 2.2 per cent in June 2015 compared to 2.7 per cent in May 2014, with the decline largely due to global food price trends and the effective appreciation of the exchange rate.

Employment growth was, according to the IMF, strong in 2014, but the unemployment rate for nationals remained high. Employment grew by 3.2 per cent in 2014, with Saudi employment growing by 4.4 per cent and non-Saudi by 2.2 per cent. Nevertheless, the unemployment rate for nationals stood at 11.7 per cent at the end of 2014, unchanged from a year earlier.

The decline in oil prices was expected to have a continuing impact on economic and financial developments. In particular the recent increase in oil production was expected to boost oil GDP growth to 2.4 per cent in 2015, before slowing down in 2016. Non-oil private sector growth was projected at 3.4 per cent in 2015 and 3.8 per cent in 2016. Over the medium-term, growth was expected to settle around 3 per cent. Oil GDP was projected to grow by around 1.5 per cent a year from 2017–20, driven by domestic consumption, while non-oil growth was expected to be around 4.25–4.5 per cent, lower than the average non-oil growth of close to 7 per cent during 2009–13. However, given the probable slowing of government spending, this outcome would depend on private sector growth becoming more self-sustaining as a result of the continuing reforms. Without a reform dividend, non-oil private sector growth could be about one percentage point a year lower because of weaker government spending, translating into lower overall growth of about 0.4 percentage points a year.

A large fiscal deficit was projected in 2015 and only a partial narrowing was expected over the medium-term. Government spending was projected by the IMF to increase by about 5 per cent in 2015 as some slowdown in capital spending offsets increased current expenditures, although the cost of military operations in Yemen was uncertain. Together with a large drop in revenues, this expenditure path was expected to result in a fiscal deficit of about 19.5 per cent of GDP in 2015, with the non-oil primary deficit increasing to 64.7 per cent of non-oil GDP. Over the medium term, government expenditure growth was expected to slow as the one-off spending in 2015 ended, a number of the large ongoing infrastructure projects were completed, some planned capital projects were postponed and spending on goods and services was more tightly controlled. With the partial recovery of oil prices, this expenditure path would result in the fiscal deficit narrowing to 9.5 per cent of GDP by 2020. Inflation is expected to pick up modestly as food prices start rising, but rent pressures may ease as housing supply increases and inflation is projected at just below 3 per cent in the medium-term. The current account is projected to move into a deficit of about 1 per cent of GDP in 2015 as export receipts fall, but should return to surplus during 2016–20.

Hydrocarbons

By mid-2015 it was something of a commonplace that oil prices had fallen by close to 50 per cent since mid-2014. In the view of the IMF, the price decline appeared to have been driven partly by demand weakness, but more importantly by supply factors (particularly rising oil production in the US and continued high levels of Organisation of the Petroleum Exporting Countries (Opec) output). In contrast to earlier periods of sharp oil price declines (1981–86, 1998–99 and 2008–09), Saudi Arabia has not cut its production. Indeed, production increased to 10.4 million barrels per day (bpd) in June.

According to the US Energy Information Administration (EIA) Saudi Arabia is the world's largest holder of crude oil proved reserves and was the largest exporter of total petroleum liquids in 2013. In 2013, Saudi Arabia was the world's second-largest petroleum liquids producer behind the United States and was the world's second-largest crude oil producer behind Russia. Saudi Arabia's economy inevitably remained heavily dependent on petroleum. Petroleum exports accounted for 85 per cent of total Saudi export revenues in 2013, according to the Opec's *Annual Statistical Bulletin 2014*.

According to the *Oil & Gas Journal* (OGJ), Saudi Arabia had approximately 267 billion barrels of proved oil reserves (in addition to 2.5 billion barrels in the Saudi-Kuwaiti shared Neutral Zone, half of the total reserves in the Neutral Zone) in December 2014, amounting to 16 per cent of proven world oil reserves. Although Saudi Arabia has about 100 major oil and gas fields, more than half of its oil reserves are contained in eight fields in the north-east portion of the country. The giant Ghawar field is the world's largest oil field in terms of production and total remaining reserves. The Ghawar field has estimated remaining proved oil reserves of 75 billion barrels, more than all but seven other countries. Saudi Arabia produced on average 11.6 million bpd of total petroleum liquids in 2014, of which 9.6 million bpd was crude oil production and 2 million bpd was non-crude liquids production. Saudi Arabia had decreased its crude oil production in 2013 to accommodate non- Opec production growth, mainly from the United States and, to a lesser extent, Canada.

Saudi Arabia also maintains the world's largest crude oil production capacity, estimated to reach about 12 million bpd at the end of 2014; production is, however, subject to Opec production quotas. Of this capacity, about 300,000bpd is Saudi Arabia's share of the production in the Neutral Zone. Non-crude liquids, which are not subject to Opec quotas or production targets, are produced at full capacity. There are currently no plans to increase oil production capacity.

The Saudi-Kuwait Neutral Zone (also called the Divided Zone) is an area of 2,230 square miles between the borders of Saudi Arabia and Kuwait. The Neutral Zone contains an estimated 5 billion barrels of total proved oil reserves that are divided equally between the two countries. According to the *Arab Oil and Gas Journal* (AOGJ), total crude oil production in the Neutral Zone is about 520,000bpd. Total crude oil production capacity in the Neutral Zone is estimated to be 600,000bpd.

According to the Global Trade Information Services (GTIS), Saudi Arabia exported an estimated 7.7 million bpd of crude oil in 2013. Asia received an estimated 68 per cent of Saudi Arabia's crude oil exports as well as most of its refined petroleum products. Saudi Arabia exported an average of 1.5 million bpd of total petroleum liquids to the United States in the first quarter of 2014, an increase of 0.4 million bpd from the first quarter of 2013. Since 2012, Saudi Arabia has been the second-largest petroleum exporter annually, after Canada, to the United States. In 2013, after the United States, the next four top importers of Saudi crude and petroleum products according to GTIS were Japan (1.2 million bpd), China (1.1 million bpd), South Korea (0.9 million bpd) and India (0.8 million bpd).

Saudi Arabia (including the Neutral Zone) had proved natural gas reserves of 291 trillion cubic feet (tcf) in January 2014, the fifth largest in the world behind Russia, Iran, Qatar and the United States, according to the OGJ. The majority of natural gas fields in Saudi Arabia are associated with petroleum deposits, or are found in the same wells as the crude oil and production increases of this type of gas remain linked to an increase in oil production. Saudi Arabia does not import or export natural gas, so all consumption must be met by domestic production. Saudi Arabia's dry natural gas production and consumption was 3.6tcf in 2013. As of 2011, more than 70 per cent of natural gas production consisted of associated gas from Ghawar, Safaniya and Zuluf fields. Associated gas produced at Ghawar oil field alone accounts for more than 60 per cent of total production.

Rapid reserve development is necessary for Saudi Arabia's plans to fuel the growth of the petrochemical sector, as well as for power generation and for water desalination. All current and future gas supplies (except NGLs) reportedly remain earmarked for domestic use, in part to minimise the use of crude oil for power generation. However, natural gas production remains limited, as soaring costs of production, exploration, processing and distribution of natural gas have squeezed supply. The National Oceanic and Atmospheric Administration (NOAA) and the World Bank Global Gas Flaring Reduction partnership estimate that in 2011, Saudi Arabia lost 131bcf of gas production to flaring.

Risk assessment

Politics	Poor
Economy	Good
Regional stability	Fair/poor

Muslims in Saudi Arabia

% of population	97.1
Sunni (% of Muslims)	85
Shi'a (% of Muslims)	15

COUNTRY PROFILE

1871 The Ottomans took the province of Al Ahsa.
1891 The Rashidi family seized control of Riyadh from the Sa'ud family, which was exiled to Kuwait.
1902 Abd al Aziz and other members of the deposed Sa'ud family regained control of Riyadh, expelling the Rashidis.
1913 Al Ahsa was taken back from the Ottomans by Abd al Aziz. The Anglo-Ottoman Convention established the 'Blue Line' as the eastern Arabian boundary between the Ottoman and British empires.
1914 Abd al Aziz signed a treaty with the Ottomans.
1915 The first Anglo-Saudi treaty provided recognition of Abd al Aziz.
1919–26 Between 1919 and 1925, Abd al Aziz defeated the four Arabian states of Hejaz, Asir, Ha'il and Jauf and incorporated them. Abd al Aziz took Makkah (Mecca) from King Ali of al Hejaz. In 1925, Medina, Yanbu and Jeddah surrendered to Abd al Aziz, and in 1926, Abd al Aziz was proclaimed King of Al Hejaz and Sultan of Najd and its dependencies.
1927 In the second Anglo-Saudi treaty, the British recognised the full independence of Abd al Aziz, while the Saudi leader acknowledged the British treaty relationships with the sheikhdoms of the Gulf.
1932 The Kingdom of Saudi Arabia was established when the two monarchies of Najd and Al Hejaz merged, with Abd al Aziz as King.
1933 Abd al Aziz's eldest son, Sa'ud, was named crown prince.
1938 Oil was discovered and production started under California Arabian Standard Oil Company (CASOC).
1944 CASOC changed its name to Arabian American Oil Company (Aramco).
1945 Oil exploration and exploitation increased after the Second World War and the country's infrastructure was modernised and developed with the growing oil revenues.
1953 King Abd al Aziz died and was succeeded by Crown Prince Sa'ud ibn Abdul Aziz al Sa'ud.
1960 Saudi Arabia was a founding member of the Organisation of Petroleum Exporting Countries (OPEC).
1964 King Sa'ud was deposed by his brother, Faisal ibn Abdul Aziz al Sa'ud, previously the crown prince and prime minister.
1972 Saudi Arabia gained control of 20 per cent of Aramco.
1973 Saudi Arabia lead an oil boycott against Western countries that had supported Israel in the 6 October War against Egypt and Syria. Oil prices subsequently quadrupled and the world economy went into depression.
1975 King Faisal was assassinated by one of his nephews and was succeeded by Khalid ibn Abdul Aziz al Sa'ud.
1979 Saudi Arabia cut off diplomatic relations with Egypt after the Egyptian-Israeli Peace Treaty was signed. The Grand Mosque of Makkah was seized by extemists; the government regained control and executed those captured.
1980 Saudi Arabia took over full control of Aramco.
1981 The political and economic union, Co-operation Council for the Arab States of the Gulf (CCASG) (known as the Gulf Co-operation Council (GCC)) was formed by Bahrain, Kuwait, Oman, Qatar, Saudi Arabia and the United Arab Emirates (UAE).
1982 King Khalid died and Fahd ibn Abdul Aziz al Sa'ud, his brother, became King.
1986 The King Fahd Causeway between Bahrain and Saudi Arabia was opened.
1987 Diplomatic relations with Egypt were resumed.
1991 Saudi Arabia was the launch pad for a US-led military operation to eject Iraqi forces that had occupied Kuwait in 1990.
1992 King Fahd announced that the country's Basic Law, which stipulated that the Quran was the country's constitution, and that he proposed setting up a *Majlis al Shura* (Consultative Council).
1993 King Fahd decreed the division of Saudi Arabia into thirteen administrative divisions. The *Majlis al Shura* was inaugurated in December, with 60 members nominated by the King, and a chairman.
1994 Osama bin Laden, who was later to become notorious as the leader of al Qaeda, a terrorist organisation, reportedly responsible for flying two aircraft into the World Trade Centre in New York in September 2001, was stripped of his Saudi nationality.
1995 King Fahd suffered a debilitating stroke and handed over *de facto* power to Crown Prince Abdullah.
1996 A bomb exploded at the US military complex near Dhahran.
1997 The *Majlis al Shura* membership was increased from 60 to 90.
1999 Women were allowed to attend a session of the *Majlis al Shura* for the first time.
2000 Yemen and Saudi Arabia signed a treaty resolving 65 years of dispute over land and sea boundaries.

2001 Saudi Arabia and Iran signed a security accord to combat terrorism, drug trafficking and organised crime. Out of 19 hijackers involved in the 11 September attacks in the US, 15 were Saudi nationals. King Fahd said that terrorism should be eradicated and that it is prohibited by Islam. Identity cards were issued to women for the first time.
2002 New criminal rights came into force banning torture and giving suspects legal representation. Crown Prince Abdullah proposed a peace initiative for Israel and Palestine, at the Beirut Summit of the Arab League. He suggested a settlement between Israel and the whole Arab world if Israel withdrew from all Palestinian territories it had occupied since 1967.
2003 Saudi Arabia denied US air bases and troops access to Iraq through its territory during the second invasion of Iraq. More than 300 Saudi intellectuals, including women, signed a petition calling for far-reaching political reforms and around 270 people were arrested when attending a rally in Riyadh, also calling for political reform. King Fahd granted wider powers to the *Majlis al Shura*, enabling it to initiate legislation without first seeking his permission.
2004 There was a stampede at the Haj pilgrimage in February, in which 251 people died. Security forces killed local al Qaeda leader, Abdul Aziz al Muqrin.
2005 Male Saudis voted in the first-ever nationwide municipal elections. King Fahd died and was succeeded by his half-brother, Crown Prince Abdullah bin Abdul Aziz. Saudi Arabia became a member of the World Trade Organisation.
2006 A committee of princes was created, under the Allegiance Institution Law, to ensure the orderly succession to the throne.
2008 A common market was created by Bahrain, Kuwait, Oman, Qatar, Saudi Arabia and the UAE, the six wealthiest Gulf States. Citizens of these countries are now allowed to travel between and live in any of the six states, where they may find employment, buy properties and businesses and use the educational and health facilities freely.
2009 Saudi Arabia awarded a key contract to build a new railway system between the major religious sites of Mecca, Mina, Arafat and Muzdalifah to the China Railway Company. The US$1.8 billion contract is expected to be completed by 2011. In a major re-organisation of his government, King Abdullah sacked two powerful religious officials – a senior judge, who said killing owners of satellite television stations that broadcast immoral programmes was permitted, and the head of the Commission for the Promotion of Virtue and the Prevention of Vice. The Commission was accused of using brutality to enforce Wahhabism, the conservative form of Islam practised in Saudi Arabia. The first female cabinet minister was appointed – for women's affairs – by King Abdullah. Hundreds of people were evacuated from 240 villages as security forces began enforcing a 10km buffer zone along the border with Yemen. The move was intended to prevent Yemeni rebels from taking shelter along the Saudi Arabian border while carrying on their insurgency in northern Yemen.
2010 BAE (British Aerospace Engineering) Systems was fined £285 million (US$452.9 million) for corruption and false accounting during the record al Yamamah arms deals begun in 1985. Use of the roaming internet receiver and email facilities in BlackBerry were temporarily blocked, due to the authority's inability to regulate the device's stored electronic data and instant messaging. A deal with the US worth US$60 billion was the largest arms contract either country had ever negotiated.
2011 Ex-president Zine al Abidine Ben Ali of Tunisia and his family found sanctuary in Saudi Arabia when they fled in January. After months of protests in Yemen, President Saleh was injured in June, during an attack on his Sana'a palace compound. Saleh left Yemen to receive medical treatment in Saudi Arabia. In August he left hospital but chose to remain in Saudi Arabia. King Abdullah condemned the escalating bloodshed in Syria and called on its leadership to 'stop the killing machine'. The Islamic Development Bank allocated US$2.2 million for food aid to famine victims in Somalia. In September King Abdullah announced that women will be given the right to vote and run in future municipal elections, as well as be appointed to the Shura Council. There were clashes between security forces and protesters in the eastern province of Qatif in October; 14 people were reported to be injured. The Saudi Press Association said there had been 'incitement from a foreign country that aims to undermine the nation's security and stability'. Crown Prince Sultan bin Abdulaziz al Saud died in October, after a long illness. Nayef bin Abdul Aziz al Saud was named crown prince of Saudi Arabia.
2012 Three contracts, worth in total US$8.6 billion, were signed on behalf of the Public Investment Fund on 28 January, for the construction of five railway stations, engine and carriage workshops, fuel supply stations, a communications centre, plus accommodation for technical support staff, for the north-south railway project. In February, the Saudi government informed the managing director of the IMF that in exchange for a contribution to the US$500 billion fund needed to fight the European debt crisis, Saudi Arabia expected to be given a greater share of voting rights within the IMF. On 16 June, Crown Prince Nayef bin Abdulaziz al Saud died, while in Switzerland seeking medical treatment. On 18 June, by royal decree, Salman bin Abdulaziz al Saud was named as the next crown prince. On 31 July a royal decree banning smoking in public places came into immediate effect. The areas affected were government buildings, restaurants, shops and commercial areas. The sale of tobacco to those aged less than 18 years was also banned. Almost four million Muslim pilgrims took part in the *Haj* in October. A new visa system (similar to the European Schengen agreement) allowing multiply entry for foreigners to the six Gulf Co-operation Council (GCC) countries was introduced in November.
2013 King Abdullsh named Prince Muqrin bin Abdulaziz al Saud, former head of Saudi intelligence, second deputy prime minister on 1 Feb 2013. Prince Muqrin becomes third in line to succeed King Abdullah, after Prince Salman. Heavy rain which began on 26 April lead to flash floods and a number of deaths, including in Riyadh. On 20 October Saudi Arabia turned down a seat on the UN Security Council. A foreign ministry spokesman was reported as accusing the world body of 'double standards' and that it had failed in its duties towards Syria as well as in other world conflicts. The amnesty introducing new employment rules expired on 3 November, leaving thousands of mostly Asian workers without permits. Under the *Nitaqat* law all companies must employ at least 10 per cent Saudi nationals, although in the case of construction work this may prove difficult.
2015 King Abdullah bin Abdul Aziz al Saud died on 23 January aged 90. He was succeeded by his half brother, Salman bin Abdulaziz al Saud. King Salman announced a major cabinet reshuffle on 29 January. He also named Muhammad Bin Nayef (a nephew) as crown prince and heir. Saudi authorities reported that the total death toll of the 24 October Haj crush was 769; foreign media reports and officials put the figure at over 1,200.

Political structure

Constitution

Saudi Arabia is an absolute monarchy. The country's 1992 Basic Law declares that the Quran is the country's Constitution.
A system of provincial government was introduced in 1993. Thirteen regional authorities, subdivided into 103 governorates, provide provincial services

alongside district councils and tribal and village councils. The 13 provinces are governed by princes or close relatives of the royal family and governors are appointed by the King.

Independence date

1927

Form of state

Absolute monarchy

The executive

The King (Custodian of the Two Holy Mosques), exercises absolute power as Head of State, Head of government and general commander of the armed forces. The 25-member Council of Ministers, an executive body appointed for a four-year term by the King, serves as an instrument of royal authority, passing legislation that becomes law once ratified by royal decree. The majority of the Council is comprised of members of the royal family, with the King as Council leader.

National legislature

There is no elected legislature. A Majlis al Shura (Consultative Council) was formed in 1993; it provides a forum for debate. There are 150 seats of which all the members appointed by the King, serving four-year terms. In 2003, wider powers were granted to the Majlis al Shura, enabling it to initiate legislation without first seeking the King's permission. In early 2013, the monarch granted women 30 seats on the Council.

Legal system

Saudi Arabia has judicial-Islamic courts of first instance and appeals based on *Sharia* (Islamic law) and the *Sunna* (practices or mode of life) of the Prophet Mohammed. Judges are appointed by the King on the recommendation of the Supreme Judicial Council, comprised of 12 senior jurists. Royal decrees and ministerial resolutions have been used to complement *Sharia* in modern Saudi Arabia and a dual system has developed. *Sharia* judgements generally override the judgements of non-*Sharia* tribunals. The King is the final court of appeal and has the power of sentencing or pardoning those found guilty of breaking the law.

In 2002, a new criminal justice system came into force, which included a ban on torture and the right of suspects to legal representation.

Next elections

There are no Consultative Council elections. Elections at municipal level were held for the first time in 2005 and on 29 September 2011. The next elections are to be held on 12 December 2015.

Political parties

Ruling party

None

Population

30.77 million (2014)* (27,136,977; 2010, census figure). The April 2010 census of people and dwellings recorded a population of 27,136,977, an increase of 20 per cent in the population since 2004, which was 22.678.262. Of the number of people recorded, Saudis numbered 18,707,576 (68.9 per cent of the population). Over 65 per cent of the population reside in four areas – the Riyadh, Mecca and Medina regions and the Eastern Province.

Last census: 28 April 2010: 27,136,977

Population density: Urban population 82 per cent (2010 Unicef).

Annual growth rate: 2.7 per cent, 1990–2010 (Unicef).

Ethnic make-up

The majority of Saudis originate in the peninsula and are of Arab extraction, but there is a sizeable minority of the population which has migrated mainly from central Asia and China. One-third of the population is non-Saudi. Most of these are from Yemen, Pakistan, Thailand and the Philippines as well as a significant number from Western Europe and North America.

Religions

The majority of the population is Wahhabi (Sunni) Muslim, with around 8 per cent Shi'a Muslim, the latter being mainly located in the Hasa (Eastern) Province. Sufism is practised throughout the Hejaz, and there is a Sunni Salafi opposition movement which, in particular, opposes the authoritarian rule of the clergy.

Islam's two holiest cities of Makkah (Mecca) and Medina are both in Saudi Arabia.

Despite Islam's recognition of Christians and Jews as People of the Book, public adherence to other faiths is forbidden in the Kingdom.

Education

Although education at all levels is free, it is not compulsory. Both primary and secondary education last for six years and begin at the ages of six and 12 years respectively. On average, boys receive an extra year of schooling (nine years) compared to girls and their education is completely segregated.

The educational system is geared to a future of high technology with computer science taught as a basic subject in secondary schools. However, the education system is widely recognised as being outdated and inefficient. There are over 22,700 schools and colleges, which are attended by about five million students. In 2010–11, around 120,000 students had their overseas graduate education and training funded by the state at a cost of US$6 billion. The funding was part of a larger spending programme, to increase the number of trained engineers, lawyers, medical personnel and information technologists in Saudi Arabia.

A ban was placed on all children of expatriate workers aged over eight years from attending state-run schools from the September 2012.

Literacy rate: 78 per cent adult rate; 97 per cent youth rate (15–24) (Unesco 2005).

Enrolment rate: 77 per cent boys; 75 per cent girls, total primary enrolment (including repetition rates) of the relevant age group between 1994–2000 (World Bank).

Pupils per teacher: 13 in primary schools.

Health

All medical care, including the cost of medicines, is provided free for Saudi citizens.

Saudi Arabia provides a two-tier health service plan. The first tier comprises a network of over 3,500 primary healthcare centres and clinics established throughout the country. These centres are supplemented by a fleet of mobile clinics that routinely visit the more remote villages and provide basic medical services. A network of over 300 advanced hospitals and specialised clinics spanning the urban areas constitute the second tier of health services with a capacity of almost 45,000 beds. The King Fahd Medical City in Riyadh is probably the largest medical facility in the Middle East.

Life expectancy: 71 years, 2004 (WHO 2006)

Fertility rate/Maternal mortality rate: 2.8 births per woman, 2010 (Unicef)

Birth rate/Death rate: 37 births per 1,000 population; six deaths per 1,000 population (2003).

Child (under 5 years) mortality rate (per 1,000): 9 per 1,000 live births (WHO 2012)

Head of population per physician: 1.37 physicians per 1,000 people, 2004 (WHO 2006)

Welfare

The General Organisation for Social Insurance (GOSI) administers programmes that support workers or their families in cases of disability, retirement and death and also covers occupational hazards for employees. Another major programme provides social security pensions, benefits and relief assistance to the disabled, the elderly, orphans and widows without income. The seventh Development Plan (2000—04) aims to expand national programmes for the rehabilitation and welfare of the handicapped, and immunisation of all children against infectious diseases.

Out of the 60 centres around the country that care for those with social, economic and physical problems, six specialise in rehabilitation of juvenile delinquents, nine in assisting the elderly and 14 in caring for orphans. A particularly important government policy has been to provide interest-free, easy-term loans towards low cost home construction for students and low-income employees.

Main cities

Riyadh (capital, estimated population 5.2 million (m) in 2012), Jeddah (3.4m), Mecca (Makkah) (1.5m), Medina (al Madinah) (1.2m), Dammam (961,808), Ta'if (600,590), Tabuk (567,902).

Languages spoken

Mainly Arabic, with English widely spoken in business and diplomatic circles.

Official language/s

Arabic

Media

Press

The press is closely monitored and subject to legal restrictions affecting freedom of expression, censorship is strict and criticism of the government is rare. Most newspapers are privately owned. There was a slight increase in press freedom after the accession of King Abdullah in 2005 although in August 2007 *al Hayat* was banned for a number of days after it had 'crossed a red line' by criticising the ministry of agriculture's handling of the death of over 2,000 camels from poisoning. In May 2010 Jamal Khashoggi, editor-in-chief of *al Watan*, resigned after the paper published an opinion piece on Salafism, a form of Islam at the heart of the Saudi state.

Dailies: Leading newspapers are regionally based. In Arabic, from Dammam *al Yaum Newspaper* (www.alyaum.com), from Riyadh *al Watan* (www.alwatan.com.sa), *al Jazirah* (www.al-jazirah.com), *al Sharq al Awsat* (www.asharqalawsat.com) and *al Riyadh* (www.alriyadh.com). From Jeddah, *Okaz* (www.okaz.com.sa) and *al Hayat* (www.daralhayat.com), also published in English as well as *Arab News* (www.arabnews.com) and *The Saudi Gazette* (www.saudigazette.com.sa). Many foreign publications can be found in the Kingdom.

Weeklies: There are a number of magazines and periodicals, including *al Yamama* and *Iqraa*. *Um al Qura* is the official weekly newspaper issued by the Saudi government.

Business: The leading business journal is the *Saudi Economic Survey* (weekly in English).

Periodicals: *Alnafetha*

Broadcasting

The Broadcasting Service of the Kingdom of Saudi Arabia (BSKSA) is responsible for all transmissions and no private radio or television networks are allowed to broadcast in Saudi Arabia but may operate from neighbouring countries.

Radio: Saudi Radio (www.saudiradio.net) is state-run, with regional programming and broadcasts in Arabic and English. It runs overseas services in Urdu, Indonesian, Persian, French, Somali and Swahili. Aramco Radio is a private amateur radio station from Dhahran broadcasting in English. Voice of America (VoA) can be received.

Television: BSKSA operates four TV networks including al Ikhbariya a news channel. The private and independent satellite broadcaster Arab Radio and Television Network (known as ART) (www.art-tv.net), based in Jeddah, operates 10 domestic and five international channels, by subscription. There are many satellite and cable TV stations operating from outside Saudi Arabia.

A new 24-hour international news channel, Alarab, is due to launch on 12 December 2012. The channel will be aimed at an Arabic-speaking audience worldwide.

National news agency: Saudi Press Agency (SPA)

Economy

With the world's largest reserves of oil at 16 per cent of the world's proven reserves and a leading member of the Organisation of the Petroleum Exporting Countries (Opec), Saudi Arabia's economy is dominated by oil and gas. Saudi Arabia ranks as the largest exporter of petroleum and the sector accounts for roughly 80 per cent of budget revenues, 45 per cent of GDP, and 90 per cent of export earnings.

Saudi Arabia is encouraging the growth of the private sector in order to diversify the economy, which constitutes focusing efforts on power generation, telecommunications, natural gas exploration, and petrochemical sectors. Over 6 million foreign workers play an important role in the Saudi economy while Riyadh is struggling to reduce unemployment among its own nationals. Saudi officials are particularly focused on employing its large youth population, which lacks the education and technical skills the private sector needs. In 2014, the Kingdom ran its first budget deficit and it will continue to face budget deficits for the foreseeable future because it requires an oil price greater than $100 per barrel to balance its budget. Saudi Arabia will need to begin to reduce capital spending if oil prices stay low through the next year, despite the existence of considerable foreign assets that it can draw from. FDI was US$8 billion in 2014, down from US$12 billion in 2012, likely due to the continued fall in oil prices.

Proven oil reserves in 2014 stood at 268 billion barrels of oil and 8.2 trillion cubic metres (cum) of natural gas. Oil production in 2014 was 11.6 million barrels per day (bpd) and natural gas production was 103.0 billion cum per annum. Hydrocarbon revenue provided around 80 per cent of government revenue in 2014, contributed to about 45 per cent of GDP and 90 per cent of export earnings.

After ten years of steadily increasing oil prices on the international markets, the sharp increase in 2008 pushed GDP growth up to 4.2 per cent, before falling sharply to 0.1 per cent in 2009 as the global economic crisis cut trade and production and the price of oil fell by 63 per cent within one year. The high oil prices had contributed to a trade balance of US$212.3 billion in 2008. As global markets fell sharply in 2009 and year-on-year oil sales slumped by 7.8 per cent, so the trade balance fell to US$105.4. It picked up in 2010 with a preliminary return to US$153.9 billion, as GDP growth rose to 4.6 per cent, before climbing higher to an estimated 6.8 per cent in 2011. Since 2011 it has been steadily falling, and in 2013 GDP growth was 2.7 per cent. In 2014, GDP growth had rebounded slightly to a modest 3.6 per cent.

Inflation jumped from 4.1 per cent in 2007 to 9.9 per cent in 2008 as imported food prices were at a record high; it fell to 5.1 per cent in 2009, and kept steady at 5.4 per cent in 2010. Since 2010, inflation has reduced and in 2013 was 3.5 per cent. In 2014, the inflation rate fell slightly to 2.7 per cent.

Saudi Arabia's industrial sector outside of hydrocarbons includes the mining of gold, silver, copper and zinc, phosphates, uranium, bauxite, tungsten, zinc, coal and iron. Saudi Arabia produces ammonia, industrial gases, sodium hydroxide, cement, fertilizer, plastics, metals, commercial ship repair, commercial aircraft repair and construction. The amount of arable land is comparatively small and agricultural production is limited; exported produce includes dates, grains, livestock, tomatoes, melons, citrus, eggs, milk and vegetables.

External trade

In 2005 the Greater Arab Free Trade Area (Gafta) was ratified by 17 members, including Saudi Arabia, creating an Arab economic bloc. Gafta includes a customs union in which tariffs are reduced by a percentage each year, until none remain. Saudi Arabia was a founder member of the Organisation of the Petroleum Exporting Countries (Opec), which organises oil

production policies of 13 member countries.
As a member of the WTO, Saudi Arabia has undertaken to liberalise its trade regime and accelerate its integration into the world economy.
Possessing one-sixth of the world total reserves of oil, crude oil, refined petroleum products and natural gas account for 90 per cent of total exports and 80 per cent of government revenues.

Imports
Main imports are machinery and equipment, foodstuffs, chemicals, motor vehicles and textiles.
Main sources: China (13.3 per cent of total in 2014), US (12.1 per cent), India (8.3 per cent), Germany (6.5 per cent) and South Korea (5.4 per cent).

Exports
Petroleum and petroleum products.
Main destinations: China (13.3 per cent of total in 2014), Japan (13 per cent), US (12.9 per cent), South Korea (10 per cent), India (8.9 per cent) and Singapore (4 per cent).

Agriculture

Farming
The sector contributed around 2 per cent to GDP in 2014 and employed 4 per cent of the labour force. Agricultural produce accounts for only around 5 per cent of non-oil exports.
Agricultural development projects have helped Saudi Arabia achieve self-sufficiency in wheat, eggs, some dairy products and vegetables. The development of water desalination plants is crucial to future development.
The role of agriculture in the overall economy is being re-valued. Subsidies have created large surpluses of wheat, while agricultural production has depleted scarce water supplies.
The agricultural sector is heavily subsidised and accounts for 90 per cent of Saudi Arabia's 14–16 billion cubic metres of annual water consumption. The policy of agricultural expansion has come under heavy criticism, as some 3,000 tonnes of water is required to produce one tonne of wheat, most of which is then exported. At present rates of depletion, fossil water sources are expected not to last more than 20 years. The importance of conservation and subsidy reduction to slow water demand is clear, but this needs to be balanced against the need to expand Saudi Arabia's agricultural output.
Main agriculture produce exported includes dates, grains, livestock, tomatoes, melons, citrus, eggs, milk and vegetables.
Most agricultural activity is north of Riyadh in Qasim, Hail and Al-Jauf areas and on a smaller scale in Wadi Dawasir and Abha. Despite significant growth in agricultural production, Saudi Arabia increasingly relies on imports to meet the demands of a rapidly growing population.

Fishing
Saudi Arabia has a small and developing fishing industry. The Saudi Fisheries Company (SFC) operates the fishing fleet, consisting of around 50 vessels. SFC operates four processing plants in Dammam, Jazan, Jeddah and Riyadh. Annual catch includes bream, barracuda, mackerel, sardine and tuna.

Forestry
Forest and wooded land accounts for only 1 per cent of Saudi Arabia's total land area. Most wood products are imported.

Industry and manufacturing

Saudi Arabia's economy is dominated by the oil industry, with the majority of manufactured goods imported and the services sector largely supporting the hydrocarbon sector. The industrial sector accounts for around 60 per cent of GDP value added, while manufacturing accounts for only 10 per cent.
Saudi Arabia's industrial sector outside of hydrocarbons includes the mining of gold, silver, copper and zinc, phosphates, uranium, bauxite, tungsten, zinc, coal and iron. Saudi Arabia produces ammonia, industrial gases, sodium hydroxide, cement, fertilizer, plastics, metals, commercial ship repair, commercial aircraft repair and construction.
The government has played a major role in the economy since an industrialisation programme was launched in the 1960s. Despite attempts to develop the private sector and withdraw the state from the economy, such attempts have not progressed very far. The government is highly involved in the economy, with the main sector, oil, dominated by the largest domestic oil company – 100 per cent state-owned Saudi Arabian Oil Company (Saudi Aramco). Upstream oil exploration and development, the country's most lucrative industry, is closed to foreign investment, with all activities undertaken by Saudi Aramco.
In an attempt to diversify its economy, the government is pumping a lot of money into the industry and manufacturing sector. It is investing more than US$70 billion in building up to six new 'economic cities' with modern infrastructure and business-friendly regulations. Mars (American confectioner) opened its first factory in one of them in December 2014. It is a sign of progress in their drive to create a more extensive and sophisticated manufacturing industry. Saudi Arabia is already strong in plastics and petrochemicals; SABIC (its largest public company) is one of the world's biggest producers of these. Saudi Aramco, the national oil company, is building a US$20 billion petrochemicals plant in a joint venture with an American giant, Dow Chemical. Several large aluminium producers have already set up shop, including Alcoa of America, since Saudi Arabia has two of the ingredients needed to produce the metal: bauxite ore and cheap electricity. The Saudi government wants to attract companies that will turn plastics into packaging, aluminium into car parts and basic foodstuffs into strong consumer food brands. Jaguar Land Rover has been in talks with the government since 2012, as yet without a result.
The state also intervenes in the price of domestic goods, with significant subsidies provided on a wide range of agricultural, utility and industrial products. As a result, the domestic economy rarely reflects international market prices.

Tourism

Previously, Saudi Arabia was almost exclusively the destination for devout Muslims participating in the annual *Haj* (religious pilgrimage) to Mekka and the site of the tomb of the prophet Mohammed at Medina. Both of these cities are exclusive to Muslims, with all non-believers prohibited from entry. Today, although pilgrims make up the majority of visitors (10–11 million annually) Saudi Arabia has begun to expand its tourist industry to attract Arab visitors not participating in the *Haj* and others, including non-Muslims, for business tourism. Riyadh is a modern city with extensive infrastructure necessary to offer itself as a centre for dedicated meetings, incentive travel, conferences and exhibitions (MICE). There are other sites of interest including classical, pre-Islamic Nabatean ruins and the late medieval citadel of at Turaif (as Dir'iyah).
Travel and tourism contributed 7.7 per cent of GDP in 2014 (US$58 billion) and it is predicted to increase to US$95 billion by 2025. The tourism sector provided employment for 11.1 per cent of the workforce (1,077,000 jobs) in 2014 and it is predicted to provide 1,691,000 jobs in 2025.
While Saudi Arabia is marketing itself as a tourist destination, visitors to hotel resorts must conform to Islamic traditions of modest dress, temperance and the social separation of men and single women.

Mining

The exploitation of mineral resources other than oil is the responsibility of the petroleum and minerals resources ministry.
The principal minerals are gold, silver, copper, zinc, lead, iron, magnesite, bauxite, phosphates, beryl, fluorite, magnesium, salt and sulphur and certain radioactive minerals. Other sought-after

minerals are those used for making cement and plaster such as granite, sandstone, coral stone and marble. Saudi Arabia is self-sufficient in these materials. Industrial minerals produced include limestone, gypsum, sulphur, marble, clay and salt. Much of the mineral deposits can be extracted by surface mining or quarrying. Saudi Arabia holds rich mineral resources such as tantalum, niobium, REE, quartz and iron ore among others that provide manufacturing opportunities to develop high value products for the growing demand of several advances industries such as automotive, aerospace, solar, oil and gas. Saudi Arabia also has significant phosphate reserves which coupled with low production cost could lead to a very profitable sector of the economy.
Saudi Arabia has hosted its first ever international mining and minerals conference and exhibition in a bid to boost a sector that offers US$19 billion worth of opportunities in upstream and downstream products. Upstream projects include extraction of resources and mining which constitutes US$4 billion of the investments while downstream projects include mineral and metal processing plants valued at US$15 billion.

Hydrocarbons

With 268 billion barrels of proven oil reserves in 2014 (with a further 5 billion barrels in the border neutral zone shared with Kuwait), Saudi Arabia has 16 per cent of the entire world's oil reserves and has maintained for many years the largest crude oil production of 11.6 million bpd in 2014. The state-owned Saudi Aramco is the world's largest oil corporation, with responsibility for exploration, production, marketing and shipping of the country's hydrocarbons. Saudi Arabia is a key player in Opec and manages its oil production in-line with Opec quotas and world prices.
There are five major oil fields both on- and off-shore, the largest of which is the Ghawar field in the eastern province, producing around 50 per cent of all production.
Saudi Arabia had a total refinery capacity of 3.7 million bpd in 2014. The new and refurbished Petro Rabigh petro-chemical refinery on the Red Sea that produces hundreds of thousands of barrels per day of polyethylene, polypropylene, monoethylene glycol and propylene oxide, has been enhanced following Saudi Aramco's signed agreement with Japan's Sumitomo Chemical Company to develop phase two of the Petro Rabigh refinery.
There are around 14,500km of oil pipelines, including the major East-West Crude Oil Pipeline (Petroline) supplying oil to the Red Sea terminals for shipment to Europe. Running parallel to this is the natural gas liquids (NGLs) pipeline.
The neutral zone along the border between Kuwait and Saudi Arabia contains approximately five billion barrels of proven oil reserves. Proposals to re-open an oil pipeline between Saudi Arabia and Iraq following the end of the 2003 Iraq War look unlikely to go ahead after state-owned Saudi Arabian Oil Company (Saudi Aramco) said that the pipeline was in a poor condition and would need major reconstruction because it had not been used since 1990.
Natural gas reserves were 8.2 trillion cubic metres (cum) in 2014 while natural gas production was 103.0 billion cum per annum. Saudi Arabia does not currently export any natural gas, it consumes 103.0 billion cum per annum and, therefore, it is fully self-sufficient and does not need to import any.
Saudi Arabia has no domestic coal production and any extraction is negligible.

Energy

Total installed generating capacity was 49.05GW in 2013, all of which is produced by conventional thermal power stations. The sector was a monopoly-controlled by the Saudi Electricity Company (SEC), which is a joint-stock company, 50 per cent owned by the Saudi government. However independent water and power projects (IWPP) have been introduced with schemes that allow private investment up to 60 per cent equity in IWPPs, with the remainder shared between the SEC and the Public Investment Fund (PIF). The first phase of the GCC power grid was completed in 2009 at a cost of US$1,095 million, linking Saudi Arabia, Bahrain, Kuwait and Qatar through 800km of transmission lines.
In 2012 Saudi Arabia revealed plans to become less reliant on hydrocarbons and increase production in the renewable energies sector. However, in 2014, the SEC claimed that the country would save itself 200 million barrels of oil per year by changing the turbines in its power stations to more efficient combined cycle turbines. By 2016 a planned 10 IWPPs will be launched, at a total cost of US$16 billion. Four of these projects alone will provide an addition 7,000MW. By 2020 the country plans to have a total installed generating capacity of 66GW.

Financial markets

In October 2012, the Investor for Securities Company (The Investor) launched Safa Investment Services, based in Riyadh, the first global Islamic asset management enterprise that provides Sharia compliant investments to Muslims worldwide.

Stock exchange

Tadawul (Saudi Stock Exchange)

Banking and insurance

Islamic banking rules are in force. The sector comprises 10 domestically-owned banks. Foreigners cannot own more than 49 per cent of domestic banks and foreign participation is mostly in the form of joint-ventures.
An agreement was reached between Saudi Arabia, Kuwait, Bahrain and Qatar to establish the Gulf Co-operation Council (GCC) Monetary Council to be established (originally in 2009), marking plans to set up a regional central bank, to be based in Riyadh (Saudi Arabia). The GCC Monetary Council will oversee the introduction of a monetary union, due to be in operation by 2013.

Central bank

Saudi Arabian Monetary Agency (SAMA)

Main financial centre

Riyadh

Time

GMT plus three hours

Geography

Saudi Arabia is bordered to the north by Egypt (the Sinai Peninsula), Jordan, Iraq and Kuwait; to the south by Yemen, Oman, the United Arab Emirates, Qatar and Bahrain (connected by a causeway); to the west by the Red Sea; and to the east by the Persian Gulf.
Saudi Arabia is a mainly barren land covering an area of 2.24 million square km. On the western coast is the Tihama plain, a hot region almost devoid of rainfall but with a humid coast. Inland from the Tihama rises a steep escarpment. In the centre of the Kingdom lies the Najd region and the Rub al-Khali (Empty Quarter) lies in the south-east. The eastern province, containing the oil fields, has an undulating topography with rocky outcrops.

Hemisphere

Northern

Climate

Average maximum temperatures are 38 degrees Celsius (C) in summer and the winter minimum is 13 degrees C. The summers are generally hot and dry (although humidity in some areas may reach 90 per cent) and the winters are cold. The coastal towns tend to be hot and humid all year. Rainfall in the Kingdom rarely exceeds 250mm a year, except in the extreme south-west.

Dress codes

A lightweight suit or jacket and trousers are advised. A tie and a long sleeved shirt should be worn at business meetings, but a jacket is not essential. Women should dress modestly, covering their arms and knees. Expatriate women often find it convenient to wear an *abaya*, a wrap-around shoulder cloak.

Entry requirements

Passports

Required by all, valid for six months from date of entry, except pilgrims with passes.

Visa

Required by all. Pilgrims should apply for visas through a visa agency accredited to an embassy of Saudi Arabia. During Haj and Umrah, pilgrims and visitors must have a valid certificate of vaccination against the ACWY strains of meningitis.

For business visas a letter of invitation from a Saudi company, endorsed by a Saudi Chamber of Commerce and Industry, must be faxed directly by the sponsor company to the Consulate to which the application is submitted. The original or copy of this invitation, together with an introductory letter from the employee's company addressed to the Embassy, should be submitted with the application form.

Women visitors are required to be met by their sponsor upon arrival. Women travelling alone, who are not met by sponsors, may experience delays before being allowed to enter or, if in transit, to continue their journey.

A new visa system (similar to the European Schengen agreement) allowing multiply entry for foreigners to the six Gulf Co-operation Council (GCC) countries was introduced in November 2012.

Prohibited entry

Travellers who arrive obviously inebriated are liable to arrest or deportation. Israeli nationals are barred from entering the Kingdom and an Israeli visa or stamp in a visitor's passport is likely to result in a ban on entry. Consultation with Saudi officials prior to departure is strongly recommended.

Currency advice/regulations

There are no restrictions on the import or export of local and foreign, except Israeli, currencies.

Customs

Personal effects are allowed duty-free. Duty is chargeable on many imported items, starting at 12 per cent but rising to 20 per cent for goods normally manufactured in the Kingdom; no duty on samples of low value.

Prohibited imports

The penalty for smuggling, promoting or circulating illegal drugs is capital punishment.

Other prohibitions include anything with an alcoholic content, certain foodstuffs (such as pork), pornography and censored literature. Prescription drugs should be carried only in small quantities in original containers. Dogs are banned, with the exception of guard dogs, hunting dogs and guide dogs.

Health (for visitors)

Mandatory precautions

A certificate of vaccination against yellow fever is required if travelling from an infected area.

During Haj and Umrah, pilgrims and visitors must have a valid certificate of vaccination against the ACWY strains of meningitis.

Advisable precautions

Vaccinations against cholera, typhoid and polio are recommended. Medical facilities in the Kingdom are excellent and there are few obvious health hazards.

Saudi Arabia is considered a high risk area for rabies, any animal or bat bites should be assessed carefully.

Hotels

There are many good hotels in the Kingdom. Alcoholic drinks are strictly prohibited.

Credit cards

All major credit cards are accepted.

Public holidays (national)

The Islamic year contains 354 or 355 days, with the result that Muslim feasts advance by 10–12 days against the Gregorian calendar. Dates of feasts vary according to the sighting of the new moon, so cannot be forecast exactly.

During the Haj, which immediately precedes Eid al Adha, government offices and some businesses close for 10 days. Work schedules may be seriously disrupted during the month of Ramadan, and businesses may take time off for other Islamic holidays.

Fixed dates

23 Sep (Saudi National Day)

For civil purposes, Saudi Arabia uses the Umm-ul-Qura calendar.

Variable dates

Eid al Adha (five days), Eid al Fitr (three days).

Islamic year 1437 (15 Oct 2015–2 Oct 2016):: The Islamic year contains 354 or 355 days, with the result that Muslim feasts advance by 10–12 days against the Gregorian calendar. Dates of feasts vary according to the sighting of the new moon, so cannot be forecast exactly.

Working hours

Banking

Sat–Wed: 0830–1200 and 1700–1900; Thu: 0830–1130; 1000–1330 during Ramadan.

Business

Sat–Wed: 0800–1200, 1630–2000 in Riyadh; 0900—1330, 1630–2000 in Jeddah; 0730–1200, 1430–1730 in Eastern Province (closed Thu afternoon and Fri).

Private business offices in other areas: 0800–1200; 1500–1800.

Government

0730–1430 (Sat–Wed); 1000–1430 during Ramadan.

Shops

0800/0830–1200 and 1600–2100/2200; closed Thursday and Friday and four times a day for prayer for up to half an hour.

Telecommunications

Telephone/fax

The Saudi telephone system is highly modernised and direct dialling is available to most of the world. The telephone, telex, telegraph and fax systems are operated by the Ministry of Posts, Telegraphs and Telecommunications (MOPTT).

The country's massive demand for telephone and fax connections has put the Kingdom's 2.3 million line capacity system under pressure. The telephone network is serviced by satellite and microwave systems as well as underground cables. The government, in a partnership with AT&T of the US, is embarking on a large scale telecommunications upgrade programme, Telephone Expansion Project 7 (TEP7), which will provide an additional four million lines by 2002.

Mobile/cell phones

Some Blackberry functions (such as instant messaging service) have been banned since August 2010.

Electricity supply

127V or 220V AC, 60 cycles, with two-pin European-type plugs and both bayonet and screw light fittings in use. 380V AC, 60 cycles is used by industry.

Social customs/useful tips

Punctuality is not always a Saudi virtue. While the foreign businessman will be expected to arrive at a meeting punctually, his Saudi counterpart may think nothing of being late or even of not showing up at all. Always shake hands (with your right hand) on meeting and leaving.

Take account of business hours and prayer times when making appointments; Saturday to Thursday is working week in Saudi Arabia.

Hospitality to the stranger lies at the heart of Arabian life. It is polite to accept at least one cup of tea or coffee when it is offered: oscillate the coffee cup when you do not want any more, otherwise the server will continue to fill it. Do not eat or drink with the left hand, as it is considered unclean; do not point the sole of your shoe at a Saudi at any time. You may ask after a man's children but not after his wife.

Saudi women are generally barred from public life. They do not drive and schools and universities are segregated.
The possession of alcohol is illegal. Although it is discreetly available it should not, in general, be offered to Saudis.
Some Blackberry functions (such as instant messaging service) were scheduled to be banned in August 2010.

Security
Visitors should keep in touch with developments in the Middle East as any increase in regional tension might affect travel advice.
The level of street crime has traditionally been far lower than in the west however, the influx of immigrant workers since the early 1970s has encouraged incidents of theft, although murder and violent crimes such as mugging and rape remain relatively rare.

Getting there
Air
National airline: Saudi Arabian Airlines (Saudia).
International airport/s: Jeddah-King Abdul Aziz International (JED), 18km north of city;, restaurant, bank, post office, shops, car hire and special pilgrimage facilities (during the annual pilgimages, the number of passengers using Jeddah airport can swell by 1.5m adding considerable delays to passport and visa controls); Riyadh-King Khaled International (RUH), 35km from the city; mosque, post office, bank, restaurant, shops, car hire.
Airport tax: SR50; not applicable to pilgrims.
Surface
Road: There are links to all countries sharing a common border with Saudi Arabia, as well as Bahrain via the causeway.
Main port/s: Dammam, Jeddah, Jizan, Jubail, Ras Tanura and Yanbu.

Getting about
National transport
Non-Muslims may not travel to the holy cities of Medina and Makkah (Makkah).
Air: Air travel is the most convenient way of getting around Saudi Arabia; there are numerous airports. Saudi Arabian Airlines operates a comprehensive schedule of domestic flights between Jeddah and Riyadh and other major centres. Always confirm flight bookings 24-hours before take-off, especially during the annual pilgrimage (Haj).
Road: The total length of the Saudi road network is over 156,000km, of which around 50,000km is asphalted and the remainder earth-surfaced. The main centres are linked by the Trans-Arabian Highway. Much of the network is of a high standard and undergoes regular maintenance and improvement.
Buses: Saudi Arabian Public Transport Company (SAPTCO) operates frequent bus services throughout the country on numerous local and national routes.
Travel by bus is comparatively cheap and an increasingly favoured means of seeing the country.
Rail: Daily rail service links Riyadh and Damman, with refreshments and air-conditioning available.
City transport
In July 2013 the government announced that it will spend US$22 billion on a metro system for the capital Riyadh. Work will start in 2014 and be finished in 2019.
Taxis: Taxis are yellow and should have a visible meter and taxi number in addition to normal registration. If using a taxi, it is adviable to agree the fare in advance.
Taxi drivers do not expect a tip.
White limousines are operated by a number of companies within the cities and especially to and from airports. Fixed fares for specific journeys are prominently displayed at airports and available from drivers.
Car hire
Available at airports and main hotels. Driving licence required. Valid licences from most countries will be accepted by car hire companies. Women are not allowed to drive (although in 2008 two Saudi Scholars said that there is nothing in Islamic law that forbids women drivers).
Driving is on the right-hand side of road at maximum 110kph on motorways and 40kph in cities. Insurance claims are not legally enforceable unless a police certification of the damage is obtained. Chauffeur-driven service is usually recommended.

BUSINESS DIRECTORY

The addresses listed below are a selection only. While World of Information makes every endeavour to check these addresses, we cannot guarantee that changes have not been made, especially to telephone numbers and area codes. We would welcome any corrections.

Telephone area codes
The international direct dialling (IDD) code for Saudi Arabia is +966, followed by area code and subscriber's number:

Jeddah	2	Medina	4
Hofuf	3	Qatif	3
Makkah	2	Riyadh	1

Useful telephone numbers
Emergency police: 999
Ambulance: 997
Traffic accidents: 993
Fire: 998
Directory enquiries: 905

Chambers of Commerce
Abha Chamber of Commerce & Industry, PO Box 722, Abha (tel: 227-1818; fax: 227-1919).

Al-Baha Chamber of Commerce & Industry, PO Box 311, Al-Baha (tel: 725-0476; fax: 727-0146).

American Business Association - Eastern Province, PO Box 1868, Al-Khobar 31952 (tel: 882-5288 ext 1253; fax: 882-5288 ext 1497; e-mail: abaep@al-bustinet.com).

American Businessmen's Group of Riyadh, PO Box 8273, 11482 Riyadh (tel: 478-2738; fax: 476-4363).

British Businessmen's Group - Jeddah, PO Box 393, Jeddah (tel: 622-5550; fax: 622-6249; e-mail: bbj@tri.net,sa).

Eastern Province Chamber of Commerce and Industry, PO Box 719, Dammam 31421 (tel: 857-1111; fax: 857-0607).

Jeddah Chamber of Commerce and Industry, PO Box 1264, Jeddah 21431 (tel: 651-5111; fax: 651-7373; e-mail: info@jcci.org.sa; website: www.jcci.org.sa).

Jizan Chamber of Commerce & Industry, PO Box 201, Jizan (tel: 322-5155; fax: 322-3635).

Makkah Chamber of Commerce and Industry, PO Box 1086, Makkah (tel: 534-3838; fax: 534-2904).

Medina Chamber of Commerce and Industry, PO Box 443, Medina (tel: 826-8961; fax: 826-8965).

Najran Chamber of Commerce & Industry, PO Box 1138, Najran (tel: 522-2216; fax: 522-3926).

Riyadh Chamber of Commerce and Industry, PO Box 596, Riyadh 11421 (tel: 404-0044; fax: 402-1103; website: www.riyadhchamber.com).

Tabuk Chamber of Commerce & Industry, PO Box 567, Tabuk (tel: 422-0464; fax: 422-7387).

Taif Chamber of Commerce and Industry, PO Box 1005, Taif (tel: 736-6800; Fax: 738-0040).

Yanbu Chamber of Commerce & Industry, PO Box 58, Yanbu (tel: 322-7722; fax: 322-6800).

Banking
Arab National Bank, PO Box 56921, Riyadh 11411 (tel: 402-9000; fax: 403-0052).

Al Bank al Saudi al Fransi, PO Box 56006, Riyadh 11421 (tel: 477-4770; fax: 404-2311).

Al Rajhi Banking & Investment Corporation, PO Box 28, Riyadh 11411 (tel: 405-4244; fax: 403-2969).

Bank al Jazira, PO Box 6277, Jeddah 21442 (tel: 660-8820; fax: 661-3044).

National Commercial Bank, PO Box 3555, Jeddah 21421 (tel: 644-6644; fax: 643-7670; internet site: http://www.alahli.com/islamic_banking).

Riyad Bank, PO Box 22622, Riyadh 11411 (tel: 401-0908; fax: 404-0090).

Saudi American Bank, PO Box 833, Riyadh 11421 (tel: 477-4770).

Saudi British Bank, PO Box 9084, Riyadh 11413 (tel: 405-0677; fax: 405-0660).

Saudi Hollandi Bank, PO Box 1467, Riyadh (tel: 406-7888; fax: 401-0968).

Saudi Investment Bank, PO Box 3533, Riyadh (tel: 477-8433; fax: 478-1557).

Central bank

Saudi Arabian Monetary Agency, PO Box 2992, Riyadh 11169 (tel: 463-3000; fax: 466-2936; e-mail: info@sama.gov.sa).

Stock exchange

Tadawul (Saudi Stock Exchange)

www.tadawul.com.sa

Capital Market Authority (CMA), www.cma.org.sa

Travel information

Saudi Arabian Airlines, PO Box 620, Jeddah 21231 (tel: 684-2000; fax: 686-4552; e-mail: webmaster@saudiairlines.com.sa).

National tourist organisation offices

Supreme Commission for Tourism, Kindi Center, PO Box 66680, Riyadh 11586 (tel: 480-8855; fax: 480-8844; e-mail: info@sctsaudi.com).

Ministries

Ministry of Agriculture & Water, PO Box 2639, Airport Road, Riyadh 11195 (tel: 401-6666; fax: 403-1415).

Ministry of Communication, PO Box 3813, Airport Road, Riyadh 11178 (tel: 404-3000; fax: 403-1401).

Ministry of Defence and Aviation, Airport Road, Riyadh 11165 (tel: 478-5900; fax: 401-1336).

Ministry of Education, Airport Road, Riyadh 11148 (tel: 404-2888; fax: 401-2365).

Ministry of Foreign Affairs, Nesseriya St. Riyadh 11124 (tel: 406-7777; fax: 403-0159; internet site: http://www.mofa.gov.sa).

Ministry of Health, PO Box 21217, Airport Road, Riyadh 11176 (tel: 401-2220; fax 402-9876).

Ministry of Higher Education, PO Box 1683, Riyadh 11153 (tel: 464-4444; fax: 441-9004).

Ministry of Information, PO Box 843, Nasseriya Street, Riyadh 11161 (tel: 401-4440; fax: 402-3570).

Ministry of Interior, PO Box 2933, Airport Road, Riyadh 11134 (tel: 401-1944; fax: 403-1185).

Ministry of Islamic Affairs, Endowments, Call and Guidance, Riyadh 11232 (tel: 473-0401).

Ministry of Labour & Social Affairs, PO Box 1182, Omar Ibn Al-Khatab Street, Riyadh 11157 (tel: 477-1480; fax: 477-7336).

Ministry of Justice, University Street, Riyadh 11137 (tel: 405-7777).

Ministry of Municipal and Rural Affairs, PO Box 5736, Nasseriya Street, Riyadh 11136 (tel: 441-5434; fax: 456-3196).

Ministry of Petroleum/Mineral Resources, PO Box 757, Airport Road, Riyadh 11189 (tel: 478-1661; fax: 479-3596).

Ministry of Pilgrimage, Omar Ibn Al-Khatab Street, Riyadh 11183 (tel:402-2200; fax: 402-2555).

Ministry of Post, Telegraphs & Telephones, Intercontinental Road, Riyadh 11112 (tel: 463-7225; fax: 405-2310).

Ministry of Public Works & Housing, Weshem Street, PO Box 56059, Riyadh 11151 (tel: 402-2268; fax: 402-2723 (public works), 406-7376 (housing)).

Other useful addresses

Arabian Oil Company, PO Box 256, Khafji 31971 (tel: 766-0555; fax: 766-2001).

Arab Petroleum Investments Corporation, PO Box 448, Dhahran Airport 31932 (tel: 864-7400; fax: 894-5076).

Arab Satellite Communiction Organisation, PO Box 1038, Riyadh 11431 (tel: 464-6666; fax: 465-6983).

Central Department of Statistics, PO Box 3735, Off Airport Road, Riyadh 11187 (tel:405-9638; fax: 405-9493).

Central Planning Organisation, Ministry of Planning, Riyadh.

Civil Defence, Airport Road, Riyadh 11174 (tel: 479-2828; fax: 478-0846).

Civil Service Commission, Washem Street, PO Box 18367, Riyadh 11114 (tel: 402-6900; fax: 403-4998).

Customs Department, PO Box 3483, Riyadh 11471 (tel: 401-3334; fax: 404-3412).

Dammam Seaport (King Abdul Aziz Sea Port) PO Box 28062, Dammam 31188 (tel: 833-2500; fax: 857-9223).

Dhahran International Expo, PO Box 7519, Dammam 31742 (tel: 833-7900; fax: 833-8010).

Director-General of Mineral Resources, PO Box 2880, Jeddah 21461 (tel: 631-0355; fax: 631-0357).

Directorate General of Zakat and Income Tax, Off Airport Road, Riyadh 11187 (tel: 404-1537; fax: 404-1495).

Federation of GCC Chambers, PO Box 2198, Dammam 31451 (tel: 826-5943; fax: 826-6794).

General Electricity Corp. (ELECTRICO), PO Box 1185, Riyadh 11431 (tel: 477-2772; fax: 477-5322).

General Organisation for Petroleum & Minerals (PETROMIN), PO Box 757, Riyadh 11189 (tel: 498-0995).

General Organisation for Social Insurance (GOSI), PO Box 2963, Riyadh 11461 (tel: 477-7735; fax: 477-9958).

General Organistion for Technical Education and Vocational Training, PO Box 7823, Riyadh 11472 (tel: 405-2770; fax: 406-5876).

General Ports Authority, PO Box 5162, Riyadh 11422 (tel: 476-0600).

General Presidency for Girls' Education, Television Street, Riyadh 11192 (tel: 402-9877; fax: 403-9570).

Grievances Court (Diwan-Al-Mazalem) Morabba-Nasseria Street, Riyadh 11138 (tel: 402-1724; fax: 403-4296).

Institute of Public Administration (IPA), PO Box 205, Riyadh 11411 (tel: 476-1600; fax: 479-2136).

International Airports Projects, PO Box 6326, Jeddah 21174 (tel: 685-4200).

Irish Embassy, Diplomatic Quarter, PO Box 94349, Riyadh 11693 (tel: 488-2300; fax: 488-0927; e-mail: irishembassy@awalnet,net.sa).

Jeddah Broadcasting Service, Broadcasting Station, Jeddah.

Jeddah Seaport, (Jeddah Islamic Port) PO Box 9285, Jeddah 21188 (tel: 643-2552).

King Abdul Aziz City for Science and Technology, PO Box 6068, Riyadh 11442 (tel: 478-8000; fax: 488-13756).

Meteorology and Environment Protection Agency, PO Box 1358, Jeddah 21431 (tel: 651-8887).

National Guard, PO Box 9799, Riyadh 11423 (tel: 491-2400; fax: 491-2824).

Presidency of Civil Aviation, Off Palestine Road East, PO Box 887, Jeddah 21421 (tel: 667-9000).

Real Estate Development Fund, PO Box 5591, Riyadh 11433 (tel: 477-5120; fax: 479-0148).

Royal Commission for Jubail and Yanbu, PO Box 5864, Riyadh 11432 (tel: 479-4444; fax: 477-5404).

Saline Water Conversion Corporation (SWCC), PO Box 5968, Riyadh 11432 (tel: 463-0501; fax: 463-1952).

Saudi Arabian Airlines Corporation, PO Box 620, Jeddah 21421 (tel: 684-2000; fax: 686-4552).

Saudi Arabian Embassy (USA), 601 New Hampshire Avenue, NW, Washington DC 20037 (tel: (+1-202 -342-3800; fax: (+1-202) 944-3140; e-mail: info@saudiembassy.net).

Saudi Arabian Oil Company (Saudi Aramco), PO Box 5000, Dhahran Airport 31311 (tel: 875-5229; fax: 876-6520).

Saudi Arabian Standards Organisation, PO Box 3437, Riyadh 11471 (tel: 479-3332; fax: 479-3063).

Saudi Aramco (Saudi Arabian Oil Company), PO Box 5000, Dhahran 31311 (tel: 875-4915; fax: 873-8490).

Saudi Basic Industries Corporation (SABIC), PO Box 5105, Riyadh 11422 (tel: 401-2033; fax: 401-2045).

Saudi Export Development Centre, PO Box 16683, Riyadh 11474 (tel: 405-3200; fax: 402-4747).

Saudi Fund for Development, PO Box 50483, Riyadh 11523 (tel: 464-0292; fax: 464-7450; e-mail: info@sfd.gov.sa; website: www.sfd.gov.sa).

Saudi National Shipping Company, Po Box 8931, Riyadh 11492 (tel: 478-5454; fax: 477-8036).

Saudi Ports Authority, Riyadh 11188 (tel: 405-0005; fax: 405-9974).

Saudi Public Transport Co, PO box 10667, Riyadh 11443 (tel: 454-5000; fax: 454-2100).

Saudi Railroad Organisation, PO Box 92, Dammam 31411 (tel: 871-2222; fax: 827-1130).

Saudi Red Crescent Association, al Dhabab Road, Riyadh 11129 (tel: 406-9072; fax: 405-1566).

Youth Welfare Organisation, PO Box 965, Riyadh 11421 (tel: 401-4576; fax: 401-0376).

National news agency: Saudi Press Agency (SPA), PO Box 7186, Riyadh 11171 (tel: 419-6422; fax: 419-4094; email: wass@spa.gov.sa; internet: www.spa.gov.sa).

Internet sites

Arab net: www.arab.net/welcome.html

Arabia on line: www.arabia.com

Saudi Arabia Information Resourse (in London): wwwsaudinf.com

Saudi Embassy, UK, with web links to other Saudi enterprises: www.saudiembassy.org.uk/index2.htm

Saudi Times: www.sauditimes.com

Senegal

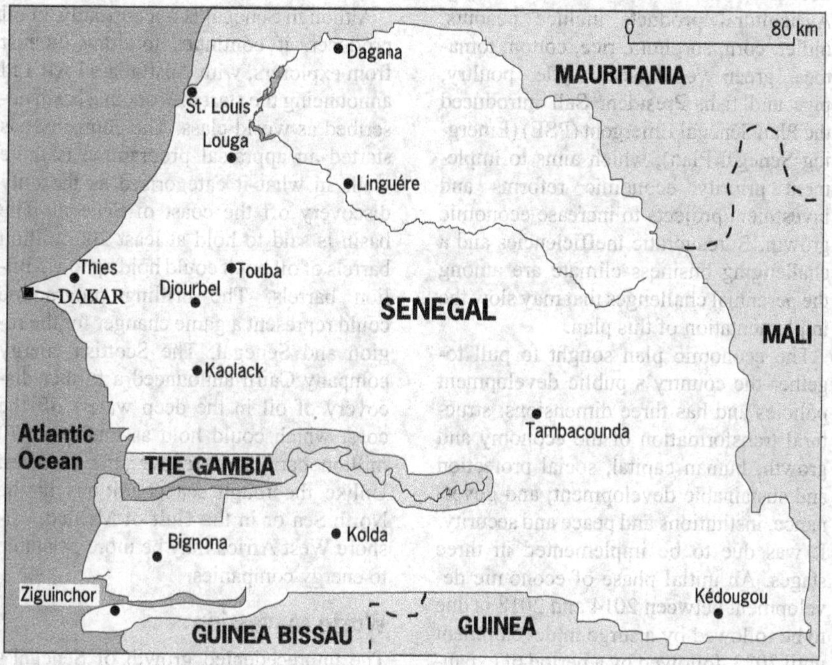

The French colony of Senegal gained independence from France in 1960 as part of the Federation of Mali, which almost immediately collapsed due to conflicts between the political leaders of the two territories (former French Soudan and Senegal). An independent Senegal was proclaimed under President Léopold Senghor, who remained in power for the next 20 years. He was the first African elected as a member of the Académie française.

Senegal and The Gambia formed the nominal confederation of Senegambia in 1982. However, the envisaged integration of the two countries was never fully implemented, and the union was dissolved in 1989. The Movement of Democratic Forces in the Casamance has led a low-level separatist insurgency in southern Senegal since the 1980s and several peace deals since have failed to resolve the conflict. Despite the conflict, Senegal remains one of the most stable democracies in Africa and has a long history of participating in international peacekeeping and regional mediation.

Unlike the British, whose chief imperial pre-occupations were the maintenance of peace so that trade could flourish, the French had a vision of their imperial purpose and destiny which was much more grandiose. Confident that French civilisation was the pinnacle of man's earthly achievements they sought to pass it on to the people they ruled. Nowhere was this more apparent than in Senegal, a country in which the arts and 'culture' have continued to enjoy greater importance than almost anywhere else on the African continent.

Senegal had been ruled by Parti Socialiste Sénégalais (PS) (Senegal Socialist Party) for 40 years until Abdoulaye Wade of the Parti Démocratique Sénégalais (PDS) (Senegalese Democratic Party) was elected president in 2000. Wade attempted to amend Senegal's constitution over a dozen times to increase executive power and weaken the opposition, however, his decision to run for a third term in 2012 sparked a large public backlash that led to his defeat in the March runoff election. Macky Sall, a former ally and prime minister took over his office. Since coming to power, President Sall has launched an economic reform

KEY FACTS

Official name: République du Sénégal (Republic of Senegal)

Head of State: President Macky Sall (APR) (from 2 Apr 2012)

Head of government: Prime Minister Mohammed Abdallah Boun Dionne (from 4 July 2014)

Ruling party: Unis pour un Même Espoir (UME) (United in Hope Coalition), led by Alliance pour la République (APR) (Alliance for the Republic)) (from 1 July 2012)

Area: 196,192 square km

Population: 14.54 million (2014)*

Capital: Dakar

Official language: French

Currency: CFA franc (CFAf) = 100 centimes (Communauté Financière Africaine (African Financial Community) franc).

Exchange rate: CFAf586.44 per US$ (Sep 2015)

GDP per capita: US$1,072 (2014)*

GDP real growth: 4.54% (2014)*

GDP: US$15.58 billion (2014)*

Inflation: -0.53% (2014)*

Balance of trade: -US$2.51 billion (2011)

Annual FDI: US$286.10 million (2011)

* estimated figure

programme aimed at boosting economic growth, and his administration has conducted corruption investigations against senior figures in Wade's government.

Ebola

Despite the basic precautions announced by the government, at the end of August 2014 Senegal confirmed its first case of Ebola, present in a Guinean national who had entered Senegal by road. To support the Senegalese government, the World Health Organisation (WHO) immediately responded with a risk assessment, the airlifting of adequate quantities of medical supplies and the deployment, within a day, of three of its most senior epidemiologists. Efforts at contact tracing were surprisingly successful. Numerous suspected cases were identified, tested and then discarded as all test results came back negative. Dakar further benefitted from the presence in the capital of an Institut Pasteur laboratory with its world-class diagnostic capacity. Up until late October, this first case remained Senegal's only one. The victim recovered completely and was eventually released from the hospital.

The WHO officially declared that the Ebola outbreak was over in Senegal on 17 October 2014. It commended the country on its diligence to end the transmission of the virus. The government's response plan included identifying and monitoring 74 close contacts of the patient, prompt testing of all suspected cases, stepped-up surveillance of the country's main entry points and nationwide public awareness campaigns.

The economy

Senegal's economy is driven by mining, construction, tourism, fisheries and agriculture, the primary source of employment in rural areas. The country's key export industries include phosphate mining, fertilizer production, agricultural production and commercial fishing. Agricultural products include peanuts, millet, corn, sorghum, rice, cotton, tomatoes, green vegetables; cattle, poultry, pigs and fish. President Sall introduced the Plan Sénégal Emergent (PSE) (Emerging Senegal Plan), which aims to implement priority economic reforms and investment projects to increase economic growth. Bureaucratic inefficiencies and a challenging business climate are among the perennial challenges that may slow the implementation of this plan.

The economic plan sought to pull together the country's public development policies and has three dimensions: structural transformation of the economy and growth; human capital, social protection and sustainable development; and governance, institutions and peace and security. It was due to be implemented in three stages. An initial phase of economic development between 2014 and 2018 is due to be followed by a surge in development until 2023, followed by a period of expansion until 2035.

According to the African Development Bank (AfDB) in its *2015 Economic Outlook* Senegal's economic recovery was confirmed in 2014 with a rate of growth estimated at 4.5 per cent, compared with 3.5 per cent in 2013. Growth was forecast to reach 4.6 per cent in 2015 and 5.0 per cent in 2016. This prospect depends on the implementation of the PSE, and its development strategy through to 2035. A third Decentralisation Act has been adopted to organise Senegal into territories that are viable, competitive and conducive to sustainable development, but its success will depend on improving the capacities of local actors.

Although Senegal is not currently an oil producer, it continues to draw interest from explorers, with Australia's FAR Ltd announcing the start of work in a basin described as world class. The company has started an appraisal programme is three wells in what it categorised as the only discovery off the coast of Senegal. The basin is said to hold at least 200 million barrels of oil but it could hold up to 1.5 billion barrels. The drilling programme could represent a game changer for the region and Senegal. The Scottish energy company Cairn announced a further discovery of oil in the deep waters off the coast which could hold as much as 670 million barrels of recoverable reserves. Unlike the tough sea conditions in the North Sea or in the Gulf of Mexico, offshore West Africa may be more palatable to energy companies.

Waste conversion

The unprecedented growth of Senegal's capital, Dakar to three million people in recent years has meant many homes in its vast suburbs are unconnected to sewage pipes, leaving residents vulnerable to diseases such as cholera, typhoid and hepatitis, particularly during the three-month rainy season. Many homes have no toilets and those that do pipe waste into septic tanks outside, which often flood during the rains. Sanitation trucks cannot often access many narrow alleys, meaning households must clean out tanks by hand or pay someone else to do it. Senegal's government aims to deal with this problem by installing new toilets that turn waste into compost or break down matter with worms in a bid to lower health risks. For the existing septic tanks, they are providing small portable pumps to allow sanitation teams to access the cramped backstreets to remove waste safely. Eventually, the project aims to use waste material collected in this way to power an electrical plant – using new technology to find a renewable means of tackling the problem of frequent blackouts in the port city. Initially, it will produce 1,000 megawatt hours of electricity a year – enough for 5,000 people – but project partners believe it can be scaled up as Dakar grows.

KEY INDICATORS — Senegal

	Unit	2011	2012	2013	2014	**2015
Population	m	*13.44	*13.72	*14.13	*14.54	*14.97
Gross domestic product (GDP)	US$bn	14.50	13.86	14.80	*15.58	*15.05
GDP per capita	US$	1,076	1,024	1,048	*1,072	*1,006
GDP real growth	%	2.6	3.5	3.5	*4.5	*4.6
Inflation	%	3.4	1.4	0.7	*-0.5	*1.5
Exports (fob) (goods)	US$m	2,621.0	–	–	–	–
Imports (fob) (goods)	US$m	5,129.4	–	–	–	–
Balance of trade	US$m	-2,508.4	–	–	–	–
Current account	US$m	-1,147.0	-1,454.0	-1,616.0	*-1,602.0	*-1,143.0
Total reserves minus gold	US$m	2,279.9	2,081.6	2,253.1	2,038.1	–
Foreign exchange	US$m	2,063.0	1,878.7	2,049.8	–	–
Exchange rate	per US$	466.82	505.65	480.26	542.07	–

* estimated figure ** forecast figure

The city's population is forecast to increase to 4.5 million by 2025.

Risk assessment

Politics	Good
Economy	Good
Regional stability	Fair

Muslims in Senegal

% of population	95.9
Sunni (% of Muslims)	98
Shi'a (% of Muslims)	1

COUNTRY PROFILE

1960 Senegal gained independence from France as part of the Federation of Mali, which almost immediately collapsed due to conflicts between the political leaders of the two territories (former French Soudan and Senegal). An independent Senegal was proclaimed under President Léopold Senghor.
1978 The first multi-party elections were held.
1980 President Senghor resigned.
1981 Abdou Diouf became president. Senegal and The Gambia signed an agreement on 12 December to form the Senegambia Confederation.
1982 The Senegambia Confederation came into being on 1 February, initially intended as a loose confederation between Senegal and The Gambia to promote cooperation between the two countries. Fighting began in Casamance between the Movement des Forces Démocratiques de Casamance (MFDC) (Democratic Forces of Casamance Movement), a separatist movement, and Senegalese government troops.
1983 The ruling Parti Socialiste Sénégalais (PS) (Senegal Socialist Party) returned to power with an overwhelming majority.
1989 The Senegambia Confederation was dissolved after The Gambia refused to move closer toward union.
1993 Diouf was re-elected.
1998 Parliamentary elections were won by the PS. The constitution was amended to include a second legislative chamber, the Senate, with the president appointing 20 per cent of the delegates and most of the rest chosen by an electoral college. The opposition boycotted the Senate elections and the PS won all the seats, later winning a majority in the elections for the expanded National Assembly.
1999 The government entered into a peace initiative with the secessionist MFDC, which resulted in a cease-fire later in the year.
2000 Presidential elections were won by Abdoulaye Wade, of the Parti Démocratique Sénégalais (PDS) (Democratic Party of Senegal). President Wade dissolved the Senate which removed the Senate leader who, under the constitution, would assume the presidency in the event the incumbent was incapacitated.
2001 A 90 per cent vote favoured the proposed new constitution that limited presidential power. President Wade's coalition won the parliamentary elections.
2002 The EU paid Senegal US$63 million for fishing rights to exploit Senegalese waters until 2006.
2003 The MFDC declared the Casamance secessionist war was over. President Wade and King Mohammed VI of Morocco agreed a mutual political and economic accord.
2004 The president and Father Diamacoune Senghor, leader of the MFDC, signed a peace deal.
2005 Travel between Senegal and The Gambia was blockaded in a dispute, which broke out over border ferry tariffs.
2006 Agreement was reached with Spain to promote a legal migration policy. Salif Sadio, leader of a breakaway faction of the MFDC refused to accept the 2004 peace agreement.
2007 Parliamentary elections were postponed following a legal challenge of gerrymandering. Abdoulaye Wade won the presidential election beating four other candidates. Later, in general elections the ruling Sopi alliance won 69.2 per cent of the vote (131 seats, out of 150). The opposition had boycotted the election. Cheikh Hadjibou Soumaré became prime minister. The Senate was reinstated, with elections for one-third of its members, while the president appointed the remaining two-thirds.
2009 Chinese President Hu Jintao agreed US$90 million in aid for Senegal. Prime Minister Cheikh Hadjibou Soumaré resigned and Souleymane Ndéné Ndiaye became prime minister. Parliament agreed to the creation of a new post of vice president, to be a presidential appointee. Observers considered the post had been created for Kirim Wade, the president's son, to be groomed as next president.
2010 The 50 years anniversary of independence celebrations began as Senegal closed all French military bases in the country. Eight days of national mourning was observed following the death of the Grand Marabout, El Hadji Serigne Mouhamadou Lamine Bara Mbacké, hereditary religious leader of the Islamic Mourides movement. The unusually high summer heat damaged the mango crop, with production falling by 70–80 per cent in Casamance. Insect infestation and groundwater salinity also contributed to a reduced harvest. The electoral law was changed with a mandatory requirement that candidate lists are comprised of an equal number of male and female candidates.
2011 A proposed constitutional change to reduce the proportion of votes needed to elect the president from 50 per cent to 25 per cent and avoid a run-off election was dropped in June after protests outside Dakar's parliament. President Wade had also wanted to create an elected post of vice president. Foreign Minister Madicke Niang announced in July that Senegal was suspending the repatriation of Chad's former president, Hissène Habré, on the grounds that he might be tortured. Habre had been sentenced *in absentia* for killing and torturing opponents 1982–90. In August the Islamic Development Bank (IDB) agreed to loan Senegal US$95 million to fund a 70MW electricity generator.
2012 On 27 January, the constitutional court ruled that President Wade was allowed to run for a third term in office, contrary to the current constitution. The court concluded that his first term in office began under the previous constitution and therefore did not count. The court also rejected the candidacy of popular singer-entertainer and activist, Youssou N'Dour, saying he did not have enough signatures for registration in the elections. Violent demonstrations erupted in protest in the capital following the announcements. A presidential election was held on 26 February with 14 candidates participating. Incumbent President Wade won 34.9 per cent of the vote and Alliance pour la République (APR) (Alliance for the Republic) leader,Macky Sall 26.6 per cent; a runoff was held on 25 March, in which Macky Sall won 65.8 per cent and Abdoulaye Wade 34.2 per cent. President Wade acknowledged his defeat after the voting had been counted and congratulated his one-time protégé, president-elect Macky Sall. President Macky Sall was sworn in on 2 April. He named Abdoul Mbaye as prime minister on 3 April. In a joint government and World Food Programme study, it was reported that 810,000 Senegalese were facing hunger following a reduced cereal harvest in 2011. The results of the study were not reported until 3 April, after the change of president. The new government requested international food aid to support 806,000 people until October and the next harvest. Parliamentary elections were held on 1 July, in which the coalition formed to support President Sall, Unis pour un Même Espoir (UME) (United in Hope Coalition), led by APR) won 119 seats (out of 150). Severe flooding in August caused widespread damage in many regions of the country, with Dakar particularly badly affected. On 28 August, President Sall proposed abolishing the senate and using the money used to support it (around US$15

million annually) to be spent on providing relief and building flood defences. On 19 September, in a joint session of parliament the senators were voted out of office and the senate abolished. The remaining congress then abolished the post of vice president, which had remained vacant since its inception in 2009 by then President Wade.

2013 Karim Wade, the son of former president, Abdoulaye Wade, was formally charged with corruption in connection with his vast fortune on 18 April. In April the government's anti-mines action centre, CNAMS, announced that over half of the mined land in the southern region of Casamance had been cleared. CNAMS said it is on track to reach the 2015 goal of the Ottawa treaty to eliminate such weapons. On 2 September President Macky replaced Abdoul Mbaye as prime minister with former justice minister Aminata Touré (APR). No reason was given for the change.

2014 On 4 July the President asked Prime Minister Touré to resign after the APR was defeated in the local elections. She was succeeded by Mohammed Dionne who was appointed by President Sall on 6 July.

2015 Former president of Chad, Hissene Habré, went on trial in Dakar on 21 July, accused of sanctioning killings and widespread torture during the 1980s.

Political structure

Constitution

The 2001 constitution allows for the formation of opposition parties, gives enhanced status to the prime minister and sets the length of the president's term of office at five years. It also gives the president power to dissolve the National Assembly after it has served for two years and call fresh parliamentary elections.

Form of state

Unitary republic

The executive

Executive power is vested in the president who is Head of State and commander-in-chief of the armed forces. The president is directly elected by absolute majority popular vote in two rounds if needed for a five-year term, renewable once.

The president appoints a prime minister who in turn appoints a Council of Ministers in consultation with the president.

In the event of the presidency falling vacant, the president of the National Assembly automatically becomes Head of State.

National legislature

The National Assembly of Senegal's parliament has passed laws to scrap the Senate, or upper house on September 13 2012. Its budget of $16 million would be used instead for dealing with the cyclical impact of deadly floods.

The subsequent unicameral Parlement du Sénégal (Parliament of Senegal) is comprised of the Assemblée Nationale (National Assembly) which has 150 directly elected members who serve five-year terms. 90 members are elected in single- and multi-seat constituencies by simple majority vote and 60 members are elected in single- and multi-seat constituencies by proportional representation vote.

Legal system

The members of the Supreme Court of Justice are appointed by the president, on the advice of the Superior Court of Magistrates, which determines the constitutionality of laws. The High Court of Justice is appointed by the National Assembly from its members; it has the power to impeach the president or members of the government.

Last elections

26 February; 25 March 2012 (presidential; runoff); 1 July 2012 (parliamentary)

Results: Presidential: Abdoulaye Wade won 34.9 per cent of the vote, Macky Sall 26.6 per cent, Moustapha Niasse 13.2 per cent; 11 other candidates shared 25.3 per cent. Turnout was 51.6 per cent.

Runoff : Sall won 65.8 per cent, Wade 34.2 per cent; turnout was 55 per cent.

Parliamentary: Unis pour un Même Espoir (UME) (United in Hope Coalition), led by Alliance pour la République (APR) (Alliance for the Republic) won 119 seats (out of 150), Parti Démocratique Sénégalais (PDS) (Senegalese Democratic Party) 12; 11 other political parties won the remaining 19 seats. Turnout was 36.8 per cent.

Next elections

2017 (parliamentary), 2019 (presidential)

Political parties

Ruling party

Unis pour un Même Espoir (UME) (United in Hope Coalition), led by Alliance pour la République (APR) (Alliance for the Republic)) (from 1 July 2012)

Main opposition party

Parti Socialiste Sénégalais (PS) (Socialist Party) (boycotted 2007 elections).

Around one-third of the population is estimated to live on less than US$1.25 a day.

Population

14.54 million (2014)*

Last census: December 2002: 9,956,202 (provisional)

Population density: 45 inhabitants per square km. Urban population 42 per cent (2010 Unicef).

Annual growth rate: 2.7 per cent, 1990–2010 (Unicef).

Internally Displaced Persons (IDP)

5,000 (UNHCR 2004)

Ethnic make-up

Wolof (43 per cent), Pular (24 per cent), Serer (15 per cent), Jola (4 per cent), Mandinka (3 per cent), Soninke 1 per cent), European and Lebanese (1 per cent).

Religions

Islam (94 per cent), Christian (mainly Roman Catholic) (5 per cent), indigenous beliefs (1 per cent).

Education

The investment in education amounts to 3.2 per cent of GDP. The government is pursuing a broad based programme to eliminate illiteracy by 2010.

Primary education is provided free of charge and is officially compulsory. However, attendance is low and on average approximately half the relevant age groups do not attend. School attendance rates in urban areas can be as high as 80 per cent, while those of rural areas can be as low as 30 per cent.

Secondary school lasts for seven years and is divided into two cycles of four- and three-years. The first cycle is middle school when all students undertake general education. At the age of 16, all those that pass an exam can choose between a general; short or long term technical; vocational or professional, upper secondary school. Only the general and professional schools culminate in a baccalauréat (at age 18) and students can continue to Dakar University or the smaller university at Sanar near Saint Louis. Vocational and technical secondary schools concentrate on applied subjects, particularly agriculture.

Literacy rate: 39 per cent adult rate; 53 per cent youth rate (15–24) (Unesco 2005).

Compulsory years: Six to 12.

Enrolment rate: 71 per cent gross primary enrolment of relevant age group (including repeaters); 16 per cent gross secondary enrolment (World Bank).

Pupils per teacher: 58 in primary schools.

Health

In 2008 pharmacists in a nationwide general strike protested at the illegal sale of fake drugs, worth an estimated US$23.7 million per year and centred openly in a compound in the capital, Dakar. There has been a rise in 'unknown' and 'inexplicable' medical cases which are being linked to the use of medicines brought from street vendors.

HIV/Aids

HIV prevalence: 0.8 per cent aged 15–49 in 2003 (World Bank)

Life expectancy: 55 years, 2004 (WHO 2006)

Fertility rate/Maternal mortality rate: 4.8 births per woman, 2010 (Unicef)

Birth rate/Death rate: 36 births per 1,000 population; 11 deaths per 1,000 population (2003).

Child (under 5 years) mortality rate (per 1,000): 60 per 1,000 live births (WHO 2012)
Head of population per physician: 0.06 physicians per 1,000 people, 2004 (WHO 2006)

Welfare
Most Senegalese are heavily indebted and poverty stricken. According to the World Bank, around 26 per cent of the population live below US$1 a day and around 68 per cent live on less than US$2 a day. There is a state medical service and workers receive some maternity and family benefits, but the welfare system is unable to provide sufficient economic security for Senegal's poor.

Main cities
Dakar (capital, estimated population 2.7 million in 2012), Thiès (282,256), Mbour (233,883), St Louis (183,838), Kaolack (181,745), Ziguinchor (168,605), Diourbel (108,580), Tambacounda (90,648).

Languages spoken
The main national languages are Jola-Fogny, Malinke, Mandinka, Pulaar, Serere-Sine, Soninke and Wolof. There are 36 spoken living languages. In business, it is essential to speak French. Very few executives speak English.

Official language/s
French

Media
Press
The press is subject to a *Code de la Presse*, adopted in March 1979, which stipulates that owners of national newspapers and magazines must be Senegalese. The same Code de la Presse provides for regulation and authorisation of journalists working in the national press, although there are no restrictions on the publication and distribution of the papers and magazines themselves. *cannot verify this, EM Nov 2007*
Dailies: In French national newspaper include *Le Soleil* (www.lesoleil.sn) is government-controlled, privately owned are *Sud quotidien* (www.sudonline.sn), *Le Quotidien* (www.lequotidien.sn) *Wal Fadjri L'Aurore* (www.walf.sn) and *L'Actuel* (www.lactuel.info), *Il est Midi* (www.ilestmidi.net), *Le Messager* (www.lemessager.sn), *L'Observateur* (www.lobservateur.sn), *L'Office* (www.loffice.sn) and *L'AS* (www.las.sn).
Periodicals: Various political parties and independent owners publish journals, mostly available in French. There are several satirical journals including *Le Cafard Libéré* and *Vive la République* (weeklies) and *Le Politicien* (fortnightly). Other monthly publications include *Afrique Tribune*, *Démocratie* and *Le Tournant*; *Le Journal de l'Economie* is a business magazine.

Broadcasting
Radiodiffusion-Télévision du Sénégal (ORTS) is the state-run broadcaster.
Radio: For most people radio is the main medium for news and information. ORTS operates regional, national, and international networks and an FM station in Dakar, broadcasting in French, Portuguese, Arabic, English and six African languages.
There are four private radio stations located mainly in Dakar, Sud FM (www.sudonline.sn) operated by the telecommunications company Groupe Sud, Sept FM, Walf FM (www.walf.sn) operated by Groupe Wal Fadjri, Radio Dunyaa and Radio Future Medias. The online portal www.seneweb.com provides access to several radio broadcasts and newspaper publications.
Television: ORTS has two television channel. Commercial satellite and cable TV are also available. There are many production companies operating out of Senegal for the West African market.
National news agency: Agence de Presse Senegalaise (APS)

Economy
In 2014, the service sector constituted 58.8 per cent of GDP, with tourism an important sector; industry was 24 per cent, of which manufacturing comprised 14 per cent; agriculture (typically subsistence farming) was 17.2 per cent, fishing is also a major component of the sector. There is a relatively advanced industrial sector that employs over 17 per cent of the population in energy production, phosphoric acid (used in fertilisers) and the manufacturing of construction materials. However, with a semi-arid terrain Senegal's population is largely rural and most of the workforce is employed (although not necessarily paid) in the production of groundnuts (peanuts). Agriculture is subject to a number of external pressures such as pest infestations and poor weather, which can adversely affect harvests. Erratic rainfall led to a disappointing harvest in 2014, with rain fed cereals production down 20 per cent in 2014.
GDP growth rose to 4.5 per cent in 2014, its highest rate since 2008. This is a vast improvement from the slow growth of 2.1 per cent in 2009. Senegal then avoided recession and as world trade picked up, GDP growth registered an increase to 4.1 per cent in 2010, although slowing down again to an estimated 2.6 per cent in 2011. Senegal was not directly hit be the global banking crisis, due to its relatively limited international integration, but non-performing loans increased in 2009 and several banks did not meet their targets for financial soundness.
The Senegalese economy is expected to accelerate in 2015; a rebound in agriculture, more favourable oil prices and the end to the Ebola epidemic are all expected to improve the economy. Real GDP is forecasted to increase slightly from the 4.5 per cent registered in 2014 to 4.8 per cent, only a slight improvement due to the negative fallout of Ebola upon the tourism industry.
Around 500,000 Senegalese work abroad (mainly in West Africa, France and Italy). Remittances from migrant workers amounted to US$1.6 billion (11 per cent of GDP) in 2011.
Unemployment remains one of Senegal's most prominent problems with only just over half the population in waged jobs; the majority of unemployed are the urban young. High unemployment rates hinder the reduction of poverty. In 2014, the UN Human Development Index (HDI) ranked Senegal 163 (out of 187) for national development in health, education and income. Poverty has remained high, with 46.7 per cent of the population left affected. The number of poor people within the country was 6.3 million in 2011.

External trade
Senegal is a member of the Economic Community of West African States (Ecowas), which was set up to promote economic integration among members, and is also a member of the West African Economic and Monetary Union (WAEMU) using the common currency, the CFA franc.
Foreign trade provides 74 per cent of GDP in 2014. Industrial production includes mining, energy production and construction materials. Manufacturing includes foreign-owned assembly production of vehicles and other consumer goods and food processing of domestic agricultural products.

Imports
Principal imports are food and beverages, petroleum, capital goods, fuels, semi-manufactured goods and vehicles.
Main sources: France (18.4 per cent of total in 2014), Nigeria (8.7 per cent), China (7.7 per cent), Netherlands (6.3 per cent), India (5.8 per cent), Turkey (4.6 per cent) and Belgium (4.3 per cent).

Exports
Principal exports are processed fish and groundnuts (peanuts), petroleum products, limestone, iron ore, gold and phosphates, cotton and textiles.
Main destinations: Mali (16 per cent of total in 2014), Switzerland (10.5 per cent), UAE (5.2 per cent) and France (4.6 per cent).

Agriculture

Farming

Agriculture contributes 17.2 per cent to GDP and employs 70 per cent of the working population. Farming is carried out almost exclusively on smallholdings and is relatively inefficient. Agricultural development has been hindered by poor transport infrastructure. The main subsistence crops are sorghum and millet, although production of rice is increasing. Agricultural output is increasing, supplying the domestic market and providing exports of out-of-season fruit and vegetables to European markets. Cash crops include groundnuts, cotton and sugar. Groundnut farming is crucial to the economy and employs a large percentage of the rural population.

Both groundnut and cotton output have been affected by the lack of farm credit and high levels of debt. The government established an agricultural development bank, the Caisse Nationale de Crédit Agricole and village co-operatives, which enjoyed greater autonomy. It also privatised the Société National de Commercialisation des Oléagineux de Sénégal (Sonacos), the national groundnut company. Sugar cane is the only sector with large plantations, which are operated by Compagnie Sucrière du Sénégal (CSS).

Cattle, sheep and goats are widely kept for domestic use. Poultry numbers are showing a long-term increase and there has been a marked increase in the sheep population since the mid-1980s.

Fishing

Fishing is important for the export revenues from the fish processing and canning industries, as well as licence revenues from foreign ships operating in Senegalese waters. Fish and fish products are typically the largest single item in export earnings. The fisheries sector is targeted for expansion, with assistance being given to artisanal fishermen, and the development of producer groups. Finance for this programme is partly derived from the foreign fishing licence revenues. The Senegalese government is supporting the development of marine fish farming (tuna, oysters, prawns and lobsters).

The Senegalese authorities raised the problem of overfishing and illegal methods employed by EU trawlers, which is causing fish stocks to plummet and has put Senegalese fishermen's livelihoods at risk; around 500,000 people in Senegal depend on the fishing industry for an income. Senegal's fisheries minister has said the country loses about US$312 million a year because of illegal fishing by foreign trawlers.

Forestry

Forest resources in Senegal are modest, although the country is well forested with 38 per cent forest cover estimated at 6.2 million hectares (ha) and an additional 30 per cent of other wooded land. Deforestation occurs at an average rate of 0.7 per cent per year. Desertification continues to be a major environmental problem in northern Senegal. The country has established significant areas of plantation forest to meet fuel and fodder needs. A programme of reforestation now under way aims to include the revival of gum arabic production.

Wood is mostly used for fuel consumption, while production of sawn timber and industrial roundwood caters to the domestic market. Some amount of wood and paper is also imported.

Industry and manufacturing

The industrial sector contributes around 24 per cent to GDP, with the manufacturing sector contributing 14 per cent of GDP. Most industry is located inside the Dakar area of the Cap Vert peninsula. There are heavy export industries; an oil refinery at Dakar-Mbao, a sulphuric/phosphoric acid plant at Darou Khoudou and a fertiliser complex (Industries Chimiques du Sénégal (ICS)) at Mbao. A power station in Kounoune began in 2012, whilst a coal fired power plant in Sendou was constructed in the same year.

The main industrial activity is light industry, transforming basic local commodities and import substitution goods to meet local demand. The government's industrial policy aims to make the economy more market-responsive and less centrally controlled. This entails a reduction in government participation in industry, price liberalisation and the encouragement of foreign investment (through a more favourable tax regime) and small businesses (through special incentives). It gives priority to high-value and export industries, especially chemicals, textiles, food processing and leather goods.

Light industry is mostly privately-owned and relies heavily on foreign capital and management skills. Most industrial enterprises are located in or around Dakar. Lack of adequate infrastructure has curtailed industrial development outside the capital.

Senegal's three major industries are food processing, textiles and chemicals. The food-processing sector and, to a lesser extent, textile manufacture, are influenced heavily by agricultural performance, as they rely mainly on locally-produced inputs. Therefore, industrial performance is affected by climatic conditions in a similar way to the agricultural sector.

Tourism

Senegal has been a popular destination for Europeans (particularly French and Belgian visitors) wishing to avoid the frigid rigors of a northern European winter. Senegal has attractive beaches and hotel resorts as well as a full range of hotels in Dakar. There are several sites incorporated in Unesco's World Heritage List, including, offshore, the island of Gorée, which was the largest slave-trading centre on the Africa coast and is currently part of the cultural trail of the African slave diaspora. In July 2012, the Fula and Bedik cultural landscapes, in the south-east of the country, were added to Unesco's World Heritage List.

Travel and tourism contributed a record 15.2 per cent of GDP in 2007, but this fell sharply in 2008 to 12.6 per cent, following the global economic crisis. The contribution has remained fairly constant at around 12 per cent since then. The total contribution to GDP was 11.3 per cent in 2014, and is expected to rise by 5.2 per cent in 2015 as the country recovers from the Ebola epidemic.

Tourism generated 132,500 jobs directly in 2014 (4.3 per cent of total employment) and this is forecast to grow by 2.9 per cent in 2015.

Leisure travel spending generated 50.8 per cent of direct tourism GDP, compared with 49.2 per cent for business travel spending.

Environment

In June 2010 the African Union backed a proposal to build the 'Great Green Wall' project, of a 15km wide, 7,775km long, continuous belt of trees from Senegal in the west to Djibouti in the east (traversing 11 countries) in an effort to halt the advance of the Sahara Desert. The trees to be used would be drought-adapted, preferably native to the area from a list of 37 possible species, and should help to slow soil erosion and filter rain water.

Mining

The mining sector contributes around 7 per cent to GDP and employs 3 per cent of the workforce.

Extraction of calcium and phosphates from open mines near Thiès are the most important mining activities. Workable deposits are estimated at around 130 million tonnes. Production (around 1.5 million tonnes per annum) is mainly for export, although it is also an important source of supply for the fertiliser complex at Mbao. Phosphates represent around 17 per cent of export earnings, although production declined by 30 per cent over the 1990s. The phosphate mine in the Matam area holds deposits of around 40.5 million tonnes.

Titanium, zircon and rutile are mined along the south coast of Cap Vert. The total available iron ore reserves at the Faleme iron ore project near the Mali border are estimated at 391 million tonnes, enough to sustain mining activities for over 30 years at the planned production rate of 12 million tonnes of marketable products per year. The Farangalia and Goto deposits hold estimated reserves of 250 million tonnes.

Despite holding a natural wealth of unexploited mineral deposits, Senegal is still not a highly coveted destination for foreign mining companies. In 2014, President Macky Sall cited the mining industry as one of the country's 'pillars for development'. Sall wants the resource industry to help Senegal's economy to expand by an average rate of 7 per cent for a decade.

Hydrocarbons

There are no known oil reserves although exploration offshore and along the coast has been ongoing since the early 2000s. All of Senegal's oil requirements are met by imports. Downstream, the Société Africaine de Raffinage (SAR) refinery has a nominal capacity of 17,000 barrels per day (bpd). Consumption is typically over 20,000bpd.

Natural gas reserves are estimated at 11 billion cubic metres (cum), primarily located offshore; consumption was 1.6 billion cubic feet in 2013. All natural gas is pumped directly to a gas-powered electricity generating plant.

Any use of coal is commercially insignificant.

Energy

Total installed electricity generating capacity was 600 million KW in 2012, producing 316 gigawatt hours (gWh).

Electricity is supplied from six thermal stations. Virtually all commercial energy requirements are imported.

Only one in three people in Senegal have access to electricity. In rural areas, wood fuel provides for most, with consequently serious deforestation. A programme of re-forestation is under way.

The government's 10-year energy plan aims to substitute 50 per cent of imported oil by local products, including oil/gas from the Dome Flore offshore field, peat deposits from Niayés and the expansion of hydropower from the Senegal and Gambia Rivers. It has been estimated that Senegal could produce 11 terrawatt hours (tWh) a year, given full exploitation of its hydro capacity.

The government has failed to divest the Société Nationale d'Electricité (Senelec), the state-owned electricity company, despite two attempts at privatisation.

Financial markets

Stock exchange

Afribourse (Bourse Régionale des Valeurs Moblières) (BRVM)

Banking and insurance

Eight commercial banks operate in Senegal, with the three largest banks holding approximately two-thirds of total deposits. The largest bank in Senegal is the Société Générale de Banques au Sénégal (SGBS). The SGBS faces strong competition from its main rival, the Banque International pour le Commerce et l'Industrie du Sénégal (BICIS).

The banking sector is overseen by the Banque Centrale des Etas de l'Afrique de l'Ouest (BCEAO), which sets policy throughout the Union Economique et Monetaire Ouest Africaine (UEMOA) (West African Economic and Monetary Union).

Central bank

Banque Centrale des Etats de l'Afrique de l'Ouest (BCEAO)

Main financial centre

Dakar

Time

GMT

Geography

Senegal lies on the west coast of Africa, bordered to the north by Mauritania, to the east by Mali, and to the south by Guinea and Guinea-Bissau. Senegal surrounds the small state of The Gambia, which straddles the River Gambia in the south-west of Senegal, and forms a narrow enclave extending some 320 kilometres (200 miles) inland.

The country is low-lying and flat, and is situated in the savannah grasslands. Apart from the River Gambia and the Senegal River, which forms the northern boundary, most rivers are seasonal and dry up in the arid winter months.

Hemisphere

Northern

Climate

The climate is tropical in the south (Casamance) and more temperate in the north.

The best time to visit is October—June, when it is cool and dry. The safest time to avoid the rain is mid November—April, but it is hot and humid during the day (cooler at night). During the rainy season, July—September, the humidity gets very high and the days very hot. In the southern part of the country, the rainy season can extend through October.

Dress codes

There is no restriction on clothing, although women are advised to dress modestly. In the dry season lightweight European clothing is suitable, and many government ministers wear lounge suits. Businessmen and other officials wear local dress – the *boubou*. Tropical clothing (not white) is necessary in the wet season.

Entry requirements

Passports

Required by all.

Visa

Required by all; except nationals of the EU, North America, Japan and many countries in the region for visits up to 90 days (for a full list of exceptions see www.senegalembassy.co.uk). Visitors should contact the nearest consulate to obtain an application form. Proof of return/onward passage is necessary.

Business travellers should include a letter of invitation, from a local company or organisation, and a business letter of intent, with their application form.

Currency advice/regulations

The import of local and foreign currency is unlimited. Export of local currency is only allowed to other African Financial Community countries and only up to CFAf20,000; export of foreign currency is limited to the equivalent of CFAf50,000. All foreign currency must be declared on arrival and departure.

Travellers cheques should be euro or US dollars to avoid additional exchange fees.

Customs

Alcoholic spirits are not duty-free.

Health (for visitors)

Mandatory precautions

A yellow fever certificate is required if arriving from an endemic area.

Advisable precautions

Inoculations and boosters should be current for tetanus, hepatitis A, diphtheria, typhoid and yellow fever. There may be a need for vaccinations for tuberculosis, hepatitis B and meningitis and cholera.

Anti-mosquito measures including mosquito repellents, nets and clothing covering the body should be used for protection against hepatitis B and yellow fever. Rabies is a risk. Bilharzia is present, visitors should avoid wadding in fresh water, only use well maintained, chlorinated swimming pools.

There is a shortage of routine medications and visitors should take all necessary medicines with them. A first aid kit that includes disposable syringes is a reasonable precaution. Use only bottled or boiled water for drinks, washing teeth and making ice. Eat only well cooked meals, preferably served hot; vegetables should be cooked and fruit peeled. Dairy products are unpasteurised and should be avoided, unless cooked.

Healthcare is not to Western standards and medical insurance, including emergency evacuation, is necessary.

Hotels

Air-conditioned hotels are available in Dakar, although they can be expensive. Hotel bills usually include service charges and local tax. Tipping is therefore optional.

Credit cards
Major credit cards are accepted; charge cards are not accepted. There are ATMs in Dakar.

Public holidays (national)
Fixed dates
1 Jan (New Year's Day), 4 Apr (Independence Day), 1 May (Labour Day), 15 Aug (Assumption Day), 1 Nov (All Saints' Day), 25 Dec (Christmas Day).
Variable dates
Eid al Adha, Islamic New Year, Birth of the Prophet, Easter Monday (Mar/Apr), Ascension Day, Whit Monday, Eid al Fitr.
Islamic year 1437 (15 Oct 2015–2 Oct 2016):: The Islamic year contains 354 or 355 days, with the result that Muslim feasts advance by 10–12 days against the Gregorian calendar. Dates of feasts vary according to the sighting of the new moon, so cannot be forecast exactly.

Working hours
Banking
Mon–Thu: 0730–1300, 1400–1630; Fri: 0730–1300, 1530–1730.
Business
Mon–Fri: 0800–1230, 1300–1600.
Government
Mon–Fri: 0800/ 0900–1200, 1500–1800; Sat: 0800/0900–1200.
Shops
Mon–Sat: 0800–1200, 1430–1800.

Telecommunications
Mobile/cell phones
There are GSM 900 services available over half of the country.

Electricity supply
127/220V AC, 50 cycles, with mainly round two-pin plugs.

Social customs/useful tips
Visitors should be punctual for appointments and visiting cards should be presented at business meetings. French-style formalities are observed. These include shaking hands when greeting and before departing.
Use the right hand when shaking hands and passing or receiving anything.
A service charge is normally added to the bill. Gratuities are not customary for taxis.
The minimum drinking age is 20 years.
Smoking is banned in some public places, including mosques.

Security
Purse snatching and pickpocketing is on the increase, particularly in the downtown area of Dakar. Avoid political gatherings and street demonstrations and maintain security awareness at all times.
The permission of the Senegalese authorities is required for travel to certain areas of the Casamance region where attacks from armed separatist rebels and bandits occur.

Getting there
Air
National airline: Air Sénégal
International airport/s: Dakar-Léopold Sédar Senghor (DKR), 17km north west of city; duty-free shop, bar, restaurant, bank, post office, car hire and taxis.
In March 2006 the ministry of tourism announced plans for a new international airport at Diass, 45km from Dakar. It will replace the existing Dakar airport and be named Aéroport International Blaise Diagne. The plans are for an initial capacity of three million passengers; it is anticipated it will relieve congestion around Dakar and encourage the creation of an economic development zone.
Airport tax: None
Surface
Road: Principal road routes are from the Gambia, Mali, Mauritania – those from Guinea are not generally recommended. A 720 metre bridge over the Mansoa river has improved the traffic flow on the trans-African coastal road between Bissau, Guinea-Bissau, and Senegal.
Rail: A rail service operates between Dakar and Bamako (Mali) via Kaolack and Tambacounda.
Water: Cargo ships carrying passengers have services from Spain, France, Morocco and the Canary Islands.
Main port/s: Dakar is the second-largest port in West Africa and serves Senegal, Mauritania and the Gambia. The port has extensive facilities for fishing vessels and fish processing.

Getting about
National transport
Air: Air Sénégal links Dakar with all the main towns. Small aircraft can be chartered from Amana Air Charters.
Road: Tarred roads are mainly near the coast; inland areas are served by roads of variable quality. Main highways: Dakar to St Louis, Rosso, Djourbel, Joal, Koalack and Ziguinchor.
Buses: Coach services Dakar-Ziguinchor; Tambacounda-Ziguinchor; Tambacounda-Gaoual are operated subject to demand.
Rail: The railway links Dakar with Tambacounda to the east, and with St Louis and Linguère to the north-east.
Water: The Senegal river in the north is only navigable for parts of the year: for three months as far as Kayes (Mali); for six months as far as Kaedi (Mauritania); and all year as far as Rosso and Podor. Other rivers include the Saloun and the Casamance.

City transport
Taxis: Taxis are plentiful in Dakar, all are fitted with meters. Rates are greater after midnight. Tipping is not customary.
Buses, trams & metro: Large green and yellow public buses operate a regular flat-fare service.
Car hire
An international or national driving licence, insurance and car registration document (*Carte Grise*) are required. Vehicles coming from the right always have right of way.

BUSINESS DIRECTORY

The addresses listed below are a selection only. While World of Information makes every endeavour to check these addresses, we cannot guarantee that changes have not been made, especially to telephone numbers and area codes. We would welcome any corrections.

Telephone area codes
The international dialling code (IDD) for Senegal is +221, followed by subscriber's number.

Useful telephone numbers
Police: 823-7149, 823-2529, 823-8383.

Chambers of Commerce
Union des Chambres de Commerce, d'Industrie et d'Agriculture de Senegal, 1 Place de l'Independence, PO Box 118, Dakar (tel: 823-7189; fax: 823-9363; e-mail: cciad@telecomplus-sn).

Dakar Chambre de Commerce, d'Industrie et d'Agriculture, 1 Place de l'Indépendance, PO Box 118, Dakar (tel: 823-7189; fax: 823-9363; e-mail: ccaid@telecomplus.sn).

Diourbel Chambre de Commerce, d'Industrie et d'Agriculture, PO Box 7, Diourbel (tel/fax: 971-1203; e-mail: ccdiour@cyg.sn).

Fatick Chambre de Commerce, d'Industrie et d'Agriculture, PO Box 66, Fatick (tel/fax: 949-1425).

Kaolack Chambre de Commerce, d'Industrie et d'Agriculture, Rue Noirot, PO Box 203, Kaolack (tel: 941-2050; fax: 941-2291; e-mail: cciak@visto.com).

Kolda Chambre de Commerce, d'Industrie et d'Agriculture, Quartier Escale, PO Box 23, Kolda (tel: 996-1230; fax: 996-1068; e-mail:cciakd@sentoo.sn).

Louga Chambre de Commerce, d'Industrie et d'Agriculture, 2 Rue Glozel, Quartier Thiokhma, PO Box 26 Louga (tel: 967-1114; fax: 967-4658; e-mail: ccial@sentoo.sn).

Saint Louis Chambre de Commerce, d'Industrie et d'Agriculture, 10 Rue Blanchot, PO Box 19, Saint Louis (tel: 961-1088; fax: 961-2980; e-mail: cciasl@tpsnet.sn).

Tambacounda Chambre de Commerce, d'Industrie et d'Agriculture, PO Box 27, Tambacounda (tel: 981-1014; fax: 981-2995).

Thies Chambre de Commerce, d'Industrie et d'Agriculture, 96 Avenue Lamine Gueye, PO Box 3020 Thies (tel: 951-1002; fax: 951-1397; e-mail: cciath@tpsnet.sn).

Ziguinchor Chambre de Commerce, d'Industrie et d'Agriculture, Rue de Général de Gaulle, PO Box 26, Ziguinchor (tel: 991-1310; fax: 991-2163).

Banking

Banque de l'Habitat du Sénégal, PO Box 229, 69 Boulevard Général de Gaulle, Dakar (tel: 8231-004; fax: 8238-043).

Banque Internationale pour le Commerce et l'Industrie du Sénégal SA, PO Box 392, 2 Avenue du Président L Senghor, Dakar (tel: 8390-390; fax: 8233-707).

Banque Islamique du Sénégal, PO Box 3381, Immeuble Abdallah Fayçal, Dakar (tel: 8496-262; fax: 8224-948) .

Banque Senegalo-Tunisienne (BST), PO Box 4111, Immeuble Kebe, 97 Avenue André Peytavin, Dakar (tel: 8237-576; fax: 8238-238).

Caisse Nationale de Crédit Agricole du Sénégal, PO Box 3890, 45 Avenue Albert Sarraut, Dakar (tel: 8222-300; fax: 8212-606).

Compagnie Bancaire de l'Afrique Occidentale, PO Box 129, 2 Place de l'Indépendance, Dakar (tel: 8231-000; fax: 8232-005).

Crédit Lyonnais Sénégal, PO Box 56, Boulevard El Hadji Djily Mbaye, Angle Rue Huart, Dakar (tel: 8231-008; fax: 8238-430).

Société Générale de Banques au Sénégal SA, PO Box 323, 19 Avenue du Président L Senghor, Dakar (tel: 8395-500; fax: 8219-119).

Central bank

Banque Centrale des Etats de l'Afrique de l'Ouest, Boulevard du Général de Gaulle, Angle Rue 11; PO Box 3159, Dakar (tel: 889-4545; fax: 823-5757).

Stock exchange

Afribourse (Bourse Régionale des Valeurs Moblières) (BRVM), www.brvm.org

Travel information

Air Sénégal International, 45 Albert Sarraut Ave, Dakar (tel: 842-4100, 823-4970; internet: www.air-senegal-international.com).

Amana Air Charters, 2 Rue Galandou Diouf, Dakar (tel: 842-2911/2933

Ministry of tourism

Ministry of Tourism and Air Transport, 23 Rue Calmette, BP 4049, Dakar (tel: 8229-226; fax: 8229-413; email: mtta@primature.sn; internet: www.tourisme.gouv.sn).

National tourist organisation offices

National Tourist Office, 23 Rue Calmette, PO Box 4049, Dakar (tel: 8229-226; fax: 8229-413).

Ministries

Ministry of Armed Forces, Batîment Administratif, Avenue Roume, Dakar (tel: 8231-216; fax: 8236-338).

Ministry of Commerce, Batîment Administratif, Avenue Roume, Dakar (tel: 8229-542; fax: 8219-132).

Ministry of the Habitat, Ex-Camp Lat-Dior, Dakar (tel: 8233-278; fax: 8236-245).

Ministry of the Interior, Place Washington, Dakar (tel: 8234-151; fax: 8210-542).

Ministry of Justice, Batîment Administratif, Avenue Roume, Dakar (tel: 8238-042; fax: 8232-727).

Ministry of Modernisation of the State, Rue Emile Zola, Dakar (tel: 8232-922; fax: 8229-764).

Ministry of National Education, Rue Calmette, Dakar (tel: 8224-123; fax: 8218-930).

Ministry of Tourism and Environment, 23 Rue Calmette, BP 4049, Dakar (tel: 8211-126; fax: 8229-413).

Ministry of Women, Children and the Family, Rue Beranger Ferraud, Dakar (tel: 8236-919; fax: 8236-673).

Prime Minister's Office, Batîment Administratif, Avenue Roume, Dakar (tel: 8224-917; fax: 8225-578).

Other useful addresses

British Embassy, 20 rue du Docteur Guillet, PO Box 6025, Dakar (tel: 8237-392, 8239-971; fax: 8232-766).

Direction de la Statistique, BP 116, Dakar (tel: 8230-881).

Foire Internationale de Dakar, route de l'Aéroport, BP 3329, Dakar (tel: 8231-011).

Port Autonome de Dakar, 35 boulevard de la Libération, Dakar (tel: 8224-545, 8227-421).

Senegalese Embassy (UK) 39 Marloes Road, London W8 6LA (tel: (+44-(0)20) 7937-7237, 7938-4048; fax: (+44-(0)20) 7938-2546; internet: www.senegalembassy.co.uk).

Senegalese Embassy (US), 2112 Wyoming Avenue, NW, Washington DC 20008 (tel: (+1-202) 234-0540; fax: (+1-202) 352-6315).

Société de Développement Agricole et Industriel du Sénégal, 23 avenue Roume, PO Box 222, Dakar (tel: 8251-818).

Société Nationale d'Etudes et de Promotion Industrielle, BP 100, derrière Residence Seydou Nourou Tall, Dakar (tel: 8252-130).

Société Nationale des Télécommunications du Sénégal (SONATEL), 6 rue Wagane Diouf, BP 62, Dakar (tel: 8231-023, 8214-242).

Société Nouvelle des Etudes de Développement en Afrique, 36 rue Calmette, PO Box 2084, Dakar (tel: 8234-231).

Syndicat des Commerçants, Importateurs et Exportateurs de l'Ouest Africaine (Scimpex), angle rue Parent et avenue Abdoulaye Fadiga, PO Box 806, Dakar (tel: 8213-662).

US Embassy, avenue Jean XXIII, PO Box 49, Dakar (tel: 8234-296; fax: 8222-991).

National news agency: Agence de Presse Senegalaise (APS), 58 Bld de la République; BP 117, Dakar (tel: 821-1427; fax: 822-0767; email: aps@aps.sn; internet: www.aps.sn).

Internet sites

Africa Business Network: www.ifc.org/abn

AllAfrica.com: http://allafrica.com

African Development Bank: www.afdb.org

Press agency (in French): www.aps.sn/

Web portal: www.au-senegal.com/

Serbia

KEY FACTS

Official name: Republika Srbije (Republic of Serbia) (ROS)

Head of State: President Tomislav Nikolic (since 11 June 2012)

Head of government: Prime Minister Aleksandar Vucic (since 22 April 2014)

Ruling party: Coalition of Srpska Napredna Stranka (SNS) (Serbian Progressive Party), with Socijaldemokratska partija Srbije (SDPS) (Social Democratic Party of Serbia), Nova Srbija (NS) (New Serbia), Srpski pokret obnove (Serbian Renewal Movement) and Pokret socijalista (PS) (Movement of Socialists).

Area: 77,474 square km

Population: 7.16 million (2014)* (7,120,666; 2011, census figure)

Capital: Belgrade

Official language: Serbian

Currency: Dinar (D) = 100 paras

Exchange rate: D107.64 per US$ (Sep 2015)

GDP per capita: US$6,123 (2014)*

GDP real growth: -1.81% (2014)

GDP: US$43.87 billion (2014)

Unemployment: 19.70% (2014)

Inflation: 2.08% (2014)

Balance of trade: -US$5.52 billion (2013)

Annual FDI: US$2.70 billion (2011)

* estimated figure

If the European Union (EU), or even the prospect of EU, membership was supposed to bring about sweetness and light among Europe's countries, then in mid-2015 – faced with Europe's migrant crisis – it appeared to have failed. Or at least it had certainly failed in the case of Serbia and its neighbour, Croatia. Whatever the new Europe looked like, the two countries' historical enmity quickly reared its head.

Migrant problems

Not surprisingly, the fifteen years of efforts at reconciliation that had seemingly drawn a veil over centuries of tribal, religious and cultural differences quickly fell away, as ministers from each country began a cross border slanging match. Sticks and stones and all that – the words were soon replaced by petty actions as each sought to deal with the widespread refugee crisis in ways which best served its own interests. Before long, Serbian registered vehicles – whether or not they contained refugees – were banned from entering Croatia. Similarly, Croatian trucks and goods were prohibited entry to Serbia.

At the heart of the dispute was Croatia's request to Serbia that it ceased sending literally tens of thousands of migrants bent on reaching the EU and most specifically, Germany, across its border. Croatia claimed that it did not have the resources to deal with the numbers. Truth was a quick casualty of the situation as the word on the streets of Belgrade was that Croatia, their country's former enemy, was refusing entry to Serbian citizens going about their legitimate business. A statement from Croatia's interior minister rather lamely attributed the 'misunderstanding' to a computer error, an explanation that Serbia refused to accept. Firing from the hip, the Serbian foreign ministry compared its neighbour's moves to the racial laws that were applied during Croatia's Second World War Nazi sympathising régime.

In the first half of 2015 the number of migrants who had officially sought asylum in Serbia was 37,391 according to the London *Economist* magazine. Virtually none of them actually wanted to stay in Serbia, but the asylum application gave them a precious 72 hours in which to traverse Serbia en route to either Hungary or Croatia. Notices posted at the station on Presevo on the Macedonia-Serbia border in Arabic and in English give details of trains that will take them to Subotica on the Hungarian border. In late September 2015 an estimated 50,000 migrants had crossed into Croatia from Serbia in a matter of days. By October the figure was estimated to have passed the 90,000 mark.

Matters were not helped any by Hungary's draconian closure of it's border with Serbia with a 100km long, 4 metre high metal fence. In self defence, the government in Zagreb had suggested that Serbia channel the refugees towards Hungary and Romania, as it closed seven of eight border crossings with Serbia, before finally deciding to halt all cargo traffic. A midnight deadline set by Serbia for Croatia to lift the blockade came and went, causing Belgrade to ban entry to all Croatian cargo vehicles and Croatian-made goods. In the true spirit of escalation, Croatia began to stop all Serbian-registered vehicles. Whether or not Serbian passport holders were in fact being turned back was almost immaterial; the rumours all added fuel to the fire. Confusion reigned as the Croatian interior minister announced that 'As far as people are concerned, they can enter Croatia.' Whether this meant that only those on foot could, or whether he was referring to their pet animals, was not quite clear. To further confuse the situation, on Twitter the Croatian government advised later that the vehicle ban applied to Serbian cars entering from Serbia, but not necessarily from Croatia's other neighbours, such as Bosnia. The 'necessarily' qualification was left unexplained.

Not content to let things calm down, the Serbian justice minister, Nikola Selakovic, said that Serbia had been 'brutally attacked by Croatia.' Local politics also loomed in the equation; the Croatian Prime Minister Zoran Milanovic, whose government faced a close run election fight with conservative opponents, announced that he would not allow Serbia 'to make fools out of us.'

Worries

In 2015 the majority of Serbs seemed to be as, or even more, worried about their jobs and the rising cost of living than about their democracy. Middle-class Belgraders, whose standard of living had risen in the years after the fall of Slobodan Milosevic in 2000, had begun to say that things had not been so tough for years. Understandably: unemployment stood at some 26 per cent. Gross domestic product (GDP) growth in 2014 had been estimated at a modest 1.3 per cent. Around a quarter of Serbia's workforce was unemployed and its public sector seen as over-inflated – with a mind-boggling 800,000 civil servants out of a population of only 7.1 million. Many civil servants owed their positions to political party connections.

Turnout was just over 40 per cent some three hours before the polling stations were due to close in the 16 March 2014 general election (which had been called earlier than necessary), slightly less than during the 2012 parliamentary election that brought the Srpska Napredna Stranka (SNS) (Serbian Progressive Party), former allies of late Serbian strongman Slobodan Milosevic, back to power in Serbia. This time it was a coalition of SNS, Socijaldemokratska partija Srbije (Social Democratic Party of Serbia) (SDPS), Nova Srbija (NS) (New Serbia) and Pokret socijalista (PS) (Movement of Socialists) won 48.4 per cent of the vote (158 seats out of 250),

The shift towards a more 'pro-EU' position was welcomed not only by Mr Vukic, but also by the EU authorities in Brussels. Within much of the international community Serbia was seen as an international pariah for its misbehaviour in the post-Yugloslav world. Despite its misdemeanours – especially in the Balkans in the 1990s – here was Serbia officially seeking entry into the EU while deep economic problems beset Serbian society at all levels. Serbia had opened membership talks with the EU in 2014 after finally signing an agreement that regularised its relationship with Kosovo.

Kosovo

The province of Kosovo is certainly still the elephant in the Serbian room. The name is hardly ever mentioned. The former southern Serbian province had officially declared its independence in 2008 and in 2014 was recognised by over 100 countries. Although Serbia does not recognise Kosovo as a sovereign state, the two countries have in fact signed several treaties in recent years. Serbia's motivation in signing was simple: EU entry.

KEY INDICATORS — Serbia

	Unit	2011	2012	2013	2014	**2015
Population	m	7.12	7.20	7.16	*7.16	*7.16
Gross domestic product (GDP)	US$bn	45.10	38.09	45.52	43.87	*40.66
GDP per capita	US$	6,081	5,292	6,354	*6,123	*5,676
GDP real growth	%	1.8	-1.5	2.6	-1.8	*-0.5
Inflation	%	11.2	7.3	7.7	2.1	*2.7
Unemployment	%	24.4	23.1	23.0	19.7	*20.7
Exports (fob) (goods)	US$m	11,748.1	11,334.8	14,010.3	–	–
Imports (fob) (goods)	US$m	19,123.7	18,270.8	19,527.9	–	–
Balance of trade	US$m	-7,375.7	-6,936.0	-5,517.6	–	–
Current account	US$m	-4,157.1	-4,086.0	-2,779.0	-2,648.0	*-1,926.0
Total reserves minus gold	US$m	13,795.2	13,584.8	14,802.9	11,371.9	–
Foreign exchange	US$m	13,795.0	13,310.1	14,618.4	–	–
Exchange rate	per US$	72.73	87.46	83.78	100.06	–

* estimated figure ** forecast figure

Recognising Kosovo was one of the most important requirements set by the European Union. In January 2014 the first intergovernmental conference between Serbia and the European Union had taken place, representing the first formal steps in Serbia's accession negotiations. By the end of July 2014, the screening reports for most of the chapters of the requisite *acquis* (the body of common rights and obligations that is binding on all the EU member states) had been completed and the first chapters were expected to be opened for negotiation by the end of 2014 or in the first half of 2015.

By October 2015 it looked as though Serbia's final accession talks with the EU might be on the point of getting under way. The announcement was made at a Vienna conference by the EU's enlargement commissioner. Serbia and Kosovo, it seemed, were acting to overcome decades of mutual animosity according to Johannes Hahn of the EU. The two countries had, under EU tutelage, signed energy and telecommunications agreements. Agreement had also been reached on granting the Serbs living in northern Kosovo greater rights and more devolved powers over education and local economic affairs. The Kosovo Serbs would also have access to funding from Belgrade. Serbia's EU membership aspirations had very much depended on an overall improvement of its relations with Kosovo. The former Serbian region declared independence in 2008 almost a decade after an insurgency in which North Atlantic Treaty Organisation (NATO) intervened with air strikes to stop killings and expulsions of Kosovo Albanian civilians by Serbian security forces

The economy

In its September 2015 annual assessment of the Serbian economy, the International Monetary Fund (IMF) noted that on the back of strong policies, Serbia had returned to positive economic growth, employment was rising and unemployment falling. Improved confidence had also helped Serbia avoid most adverse knock-on effects from developments in Greece or in other troubled markets in recent months. The IMF had revised upwards its gross domestic product (GDP) growth projection for 2015 to 0.5 per cent. In the view of the IMF, this somewhat improved economic outlook reflected the impact on domestic demand of lower oil prices and stronger-than-expected private sector wages, as well as an improved export performance. Inflation remained low, on account of low import prices, delays in administered price adjustments and economic activity still remaining below potential. Over the medium term, growth was expected to accelerate, depending on continued sound macro-economic policies and stepped-up structural reforms.

The IMF noted that the fiscal performance of Serbia in the first half of 2015 was strong. The general government deficit remained considerably lower than projected, mainly owing to improved revenue collection, but also due to a shortfall in public investment. While one-off revenues made sizeable contributions, stronger-than-projected tax collections were considered encouraging. The fiscal over-performance in 2015 was to be applied to debt reduction. The extent of permanent revenue gains and the scope for any potential additional spending in 2016 would be assessed in the context of the 2016 budget preparation.

Low inflation expectations and the sizeable fiscal consolidation had enabled the rebalancing of macro-economic policies. The IMF considered the recent easing of monetary policy to be appropriate and would support the economic recovery. Further policy rate cuts would still need to take into account inflation expectations, the external financing environment and the progress in fiscal consolidation. The IMF also welcomed substantial progress in the authorities' initiatives in the financial sector.

According to the European Bank for Reconstruction and Development (EBRD), the Serbian economy bounced back in 2013, growing by 2.5 per cent after the previous year's recession, when GDP fell by 1.5 per cent. The growth in 2013 was supported by strong exports, boosted by the revival of the car industry and a good agricultural harvest. However, growth in early 2014 was negative. Serbia suffered extensive flood-related damage (officially estimated at €1.5 billion (US$1.7 billion), or about 5 per cent of GDP) in late May 2014, which severely affected vital sectors such as energy, mining and agriculture. As a result of this damage, most observers, including the government, expected GDP to fall again in 2015; in fact, according to the IMF, GDP was positive in early 2015.

The EBRD noted that Serbia's inflationary pressures had subsided in 2013 and had subsequently stayed low. Inflation fell from its January 2013 peak of 12.8 per cent year-on-year to 2.2 per cent year-on-year in December 2013 and the low inflationary pressures continued through 2014, keeping the inflation rate below the lower band of the Narodna Banka Srbije (NBS) (National Bank of Serbia) (central bank)'s target range of 2.5–5.5 per cent. In response, the NBS had been able to loosen monetary policy and reduce the base interest rate, bringing it down in a succession of cuts from 11.75 per cent in April 2013 to 8.5 per cent in June 2014. Despite these rate cuts, the base rate remained high compared to peer countries.

In the view of the EBRD, Serbia's fiscal situation was increasingly serious. Public finances had, in the words of the Bank, 'reached a dire state'. The government deficit exceeded 5 per cent of GDP in 2013 and public debt had reached more than 65 per cent of GDP. The government's fiscal strategy, on the assumption that consolidation measures were implemented, envisaged an augmented budget deficit of 7.1 per cent of GDP in 2014, followed by fiscal adjustment, which would reduce the deficit to 5.2 per cent of GDP in 2015 and 3.2 per cent of GDP in 2016. Under this scenario, the level of public debt was expected to peak at around 70 per cent of GDP in 2015. Some fiscal adjustment was started in 2013 as the government announced new measures to reduce the deficit. However, these measures were insufficient to put the public finances back on a sustainable path and further cuts to public sector wages and pensions had been announced in October 2014. A return to positive but modest growth might, according to the EBRD, occur in 2015. Exports would continue to be the main growth driver. Meanwhile, consumption was expected to remain subdued, largely due to continued tightness in domestic credit markets and the necessary fiscal retrenchment. Nonetheless, medium-term prospects remained favourable if macro-economic and external stability was sustained and the economic reforms progressed, which would help restore the confidence of domestic and foreign investors.

In this context, the new privatisation law that was approved in July 2014, aimed to privatise 502 state or socially-owned (wholly or partially) companies that had been costing the government an estimated €300 million (US$337 million) each year. The new law envisaged that privatisation sales would take place through public tenders and auctions. In parallel, parliament had also approved amendments to the bankruptcy law, which will enable a more efficient bankruptcy process. The sale of 'socially-owned' companies was expected to be completed by the end of 2015.

Serbia's banking sector posted a loss in 2013 and annual credit growth was negative for the year as a whole. Year-on-year credit growth remained negative in the first few months of 2014, but it picked up from May when the government introduced a subsidised lending scheme (for dinar-denominated loans). Furthermore, non-performing loans (NPLs) were at 23 per cent of total loans as of the end of the second quarter of 2014, more than 10 percentage points above their level at the end of 2008. The high level of NPLs posed further risks to credit recovery in the near term, although these NPLs were well provisioned.

A new labour law was approved by parliament in July 2014, despite initial strong opposition from the unions. The law, which is broadly in line with EU legislation, contains a number of provisions designed to increase flexibility and strengthen incentives for firms to hire personnel. These included linking severance pay to the number of years of service with the current employer (rather than with all employers, current and previous) and allowing a longer duration of fixed-term contracts (of two years, or in some cases three), beyond the previous one-year limit. At the same time, a new pension law would gradually raise the retirement age for women from 60 to 65 by 2032. Revised laws on employment were part of a broader set of reforms aimed at reviving the country's economy and improving the business environment. Serbia ranked poorly on the World Bank *Doing Business 2015* report for ease of doing business – 91 out of the 189 surveyed – with particular problems in dealing with construction permits and paying taxes. Nor did Serbia do much better on the Transparency International Corruption Perceptions Index – 78 out of 175 and well behind Romania (69), generally considered to be the EU's most corrupt country.

Risk assessment

Economy	Fair
Politics	Good
Regional stability	Fair

Muslims in Serbia

% of population	3.7
Sunni (% of Muslims)	85
Shi'a (% of Muslims)	15

COUNTRY PROFILE

The Serbs are believed to be an ethnic Slavic clan that had settled in the Balkans by the eleventh century. A Serbian state was established in the twelfth century.

1389 The Turks defeated the Serbs at the Battle of Kosovo, and Serbia became an Ottoman subject state.

1860 Turkish troops left. Serbia signed a series of alliances with Montenegro, Romania and Greece. The Serbia-Greece pact assigned ownership of Bosnia and Hercegovina (BiH) to Serbia, with Thessaly and Epirus going to the Greeks.

1876 Serbia was again defeated by Turkey, although Austrian protection prevented the Serbs from falling under Turkish rule.

1878 Austria invaded Serbia. The Treaty of Berlin settled Serbian independence. Montenegro was also recognised as an independent state and doubled in size.

1913 The London Conference reduced the territory claimed by Albania after recognising its independence. Kosovo was granted to Serbia and Cameria (Chamouria) to Greece.

1914 Growing hostility in relations between the Serbs and the Habsburgs of Austro-Hungary came to a head with the assassination of the Austrian Archduke Frans Ferdinand by a Serbian nationalist, Gavrilo Princip. Austria and Germany declared war on Serbia, resulting in the First World War.

1918 The defeat of the Austro-Hungarian Empire during the World War One saw the creation of the Kingdom of the Serbs, Croats and Slovenes, encompassing Bosnia and Hercegovina (BiH), Croatia, parts of Dalmatia and Macedonia, Montenegro, Serbia, Slavonia and Slovenia.

1921 Prince Alexander, Regent of Serbia, became King.

1929 Following disputes between Serbs and Croats, King Alexander assumed dictatorial powers and the country was renamed Yugoslavia.

1934 King Alexander was assassinated in Marseilles while on a state visit to France.

1941 Parts of Yugoslavia were occupied by the Germans, Italians, Hungarians and Bulgarians.

1945–46 Following the end of the Second World War, Serbia and Montenegro became two of the constituent republics of the Federal People's Republic of Yugoslavia.

1948 Yugoslavia was expelled from the Communist Information Bureau (Cominform), responsible for co-ordinating Communist activities throughout the world.

1953 Tito was elected president in January. Constitutions adopted in 1953, 1963 and 1974 increased the autonomy extended to the country's constituent republics.

1955 After building a relationship with the West, Yugoslavia restored relations with the Soviet Union.

1960–70s To keep Yugoslavia out of the Cold War, President Tito pursued a policy of non-alignment and the country became one of the founder members of the Non-Alignment Movement (NAM). In 1963 the official name was changed to the Socialist Federal Republic of Yugoslavia.

1980 Tito died. A system of a collective (rotating) presidency was adopted.

1989 Differences and friction between the wealthier republics, Slovenia and Croatia, and the different ethnic groups intensified. Serbian and Montenegrin constitutions were inaugurated.

1990 Multi-party elections brought into power a government in Croatia which supported outright independence.

1991–92 The secession of Croatia, Slovenia and BiH led to invasions of these republics by the Jugoslovenska Narodna Armija (JNA) (Yugoslav National Army). In Slovenia, the JNA was promptly defeated. JNA units were eventually incorporated into the ethnic Serb armies in BiH and the Krajina region in Croatia. The reduced Yugoslav state, renamed the Federal Republic of Yugoslavia (FRY), comprised Serbia, Montenegro, Vojvodina and Kosovo; it was not internationally recognised and was deprived of its UN seat.

1993 Zoran Lilic was elected FRY president, replacing Dobrica Cosic, who had criticised the president of Serbia, Slobodan Milosevic.

1995 Milosevic was one of the signatories of the Dayton Peace Agreement, which ended the civil war in BiH.

1996 FRY and Croatia signed an agreement of mutual recognition, formally ending five years of hostility.

1997 Milosevic, for 10 years the president of Serbia, took over as the FRY president. A coalition government, led by Milosevic's Socialisticka Partija Srbije (SPS) (Socialist Party of Serbia), remained in power in Serbia, despite losing its parliamentary majority in elections. The first election for the presidency of Serbia was invalidated because less than half the electorate voted; Milan Milutinovic was elected president of Serbia at the end of the year.

1998 Since the 1980s, the Milosevic regime had been gradually reducing the civil rights of the ethnic Albanians in Kosovo. Opposition to this gathered momentum during the 1990s as the Ushtria Çlirimtare e Kosovës (UÇK) (Kosovo Liberation Army) began to carry out armed offensives and bombings against the Yugoslav authorities. By the beginning of the year, the UÇK controlled approximately half of the province of Kosovo. FRY

security forces launched a counter-offensive against the UÇK, destroying villages and displacing many thousands of Kosovans. Mirko Marjanovic (Montenegrin prime minister since 1994) was re-appointed in Montenegro.
1999 Vuk Draskovic resigned from the FRY government and took his party out of the coalition. After unsuccessful mediation and increased violence in Kosovo, NATO launched air strikes in March against FRY targets, centred primarily on Belgrade. In June, FRY forces withdrew entirely from Kosovo. NATO deployed peace-keeping troops in Kosovo, which became an international protectorate under UN control.
2000 Milosevic called early elections for the FRY presidency. Vojislav Kostunica of the Demokratska Opozicija Srbije (DOS) (Democratic Opposition of Serbia, a coalition formed to challenge Milosevic's rule) won the election but Milosevic remained in power (officially his term in office was to end in 2001). Street protests and workers strikes ensued until 5 October when the Radio Televizije Srbije (RTS) (Radio Television Serbia) broadcast offices were stormed and Milosevic was toppled. Kostunica became president of FRY. The DOS won FRY parliamentary elections, held in December. Local elections, held in Kosovo, were won by the Lidhja Demokratike e Kosovës (LDK) (Democratic League of Kosovo), led by Ibrahim Rugova. The Federal Republic of Yugoslavia (FRY) was allowed back into the UN after eight years of exclusion.
2001 Milo Djukanovic's Pobjeda je Crne Goru (PjCG) (Victory for Montenegro) coalition won the Montenegrin parliamentary elections. Slobodan Milosevic was extradited to stand trial at the International Criminal Tribunal for the former Yugoslavia (ICTY) in The Hague. The UN mission in Kosovo set up the Provisional Institutions of Self-Government (PISG), and included an assembly, mandated to elect a president and prime minister of the territory. The LDK won 46 per cent of the vote in the Assembly of Kosovo elections, but failed to get a majority.
2002 The Kosovo assembly elected Ibrahim Rugova as president; Bajram Rexhapi of the Partia Demokratike e Kosovës (PDK) (Democratic Party of Kosovo) was elected as prime minister of a power-sharing 10-member cabinet. Montenegrin President Milo Djukanovic's Demokratska Lista za Evropsku Crnu Goru (DLECG) (Democratic List for a European Montenegro) alliance won the Montenegro parliamentary elections. Parliamentary Speaker Natasa Micic was appointed Serbia's acting president after the results of three separate presidential elections were declared invalid due to insufficient voter turnout.
2003 The FRY state was reconstituted and renamed the State Union of Serbia and Montenegro; a looser federation of its two member states, Serbia and Montenegro and two autonomous provinces of Vojvodina (within Serbia) and Kosovo and Metohia (under UN administration). FRY President Kostunica stepped down and was replaced as head of state of Serbia and Montenegro by Svetozar Marovic, a Montenegrin. Serbian prime minister, Zoran Djindjic, was assassinated. In parliamentary elections an alliance of three political blocs headed by the Demokratska Stranka Srbije (DSS) (Democratic Party of Serbia), led by Zoran Zivkovic won. Later, the Srbije Demokratska Stranka (SDS) (Serbian Democratic Party) and the Narodna Demokratska Stranka (NDS) (People's Democratic Party) merged with the DSS.
2004 Boris Tadic, a pro-West liberal, was elected president of Serbia. Vojislav Kostunica replaced Zivkovic as leader of the DSS and became prime minister. In Kosovo, parliamentary and presidential elections took place; the LDK won the parliamentary elections and Ramush Haradinaj became prime minister. Incumbent President Ibrahim Rugova was re-elected
2005 The Kosovo prime minister Haradinaj resigned and Adem Salihaj replaced him. The US resumed aid to Serbia as a reward for improved co-operation with the ICTY. The European Union (EU) agreed to open talks with Serbia and Montenegro on a stabilisation and association agreement that could lead to EU membership. Five former Serbian policemen accused of taking part in the 1995 Srebrenica massacre went on trial in Belgrade.
2006 Kosovo president, Ibrahim Rugova, died; he had been considered a moderate Kosovo-Albanian leader and his death just as negotiations on the future of Kosovo were about to start, was considered a setback. He was succeeded by Fatmir Sejdiu. Agim Çeku became prime minister of Kosovo. Slobodan Milosevic was found dead of a heart attack in his cell in The Hague. The EU broke off membership talks with Serbia and Montenegro, citing failure by the authorities to arrest war crimes suspect Ratko Mladic. Montenegro formally declared independence from Serbia; Serbia declared itself the union's legal successor. Joachim Rucker took office as the head of the UN Interim Administration Mission in Kosovo. A referendum agreed by 51.5 per cent of the electorate (excluding ethnic Albanians from Kosovo) to constitutional changes. Among the articles promulgated was a ban on capital punishment and human cloning, guaranteed human rights and a degree of autonomy for the province of Vojvodina. Controversially, however, other articles claimed sovereignty over the UN-administered province of Kosovo and enshrined the Cyrillic alphabet (unused by ethnic minorities) as the official script.
2007 A coalition of the Demokratska Stranka (DS) (Democratic Party) – led by President Tadic – and the DSS won Serbian parliamentary elections with 112 seats (65 and 47 seats respectively). The far-right Srpska Radikalna Stranka (SRS) (Serbian Radical Party) was the largest single bloc with 81 seats. Such a large proportion of the electorate supporting the SRS, with a staunch nationalist agenda, was seen as an impediment to Serbia's EU membership aspirations. Serbia rejected the UN plan of self-rule, although not independence, for Kosovo. No agreement was reached during the first round of talks on the future of Kosovo: Serbian authorities offered broad autonomy but the province's ethnic Albanians demanded full independence. Kosovo parliamentary elections were won by the Democratic Party, led by Hashim Thaçi, the pro-independence candidate and former leader of the Kosovo Liberation Army (KLA). The UN proposed a multinational tribunal to include representatives from the EU, US, Russia and Serbian and Albanian Kosovas. Two camps developed with the US and Albanian Kosovas advocating a fully independent Kosovo, while Serbia and Russia staunchly opposed it. Albanian Kosovas threatened to declare a unilateral declaration of independence (UDI) if talks failed to find a negotiated peace. Hashim Thaçi became prime minister of the Assembly of Kosovo, as leader of a coalition led by the PDK and LDK.
2008 In Serbian presidential elections, Boris Tadic won 51.61 per cent of the vote. Thaçi became prime minister of Kosovo, which shortly after declared its independence. A riot broke out in Belgrade as many countries immediately recognised the newly independent Kosovo. Russia pledged its support for Serbia, while some EU countries with unresolved independence situations or historic sensibilities (Cyprus, Romania and Slovakia) also said they would not recognise the new state. Mobs attacked foreign embassies, targeting the US embassy in particular, until the EU threatened to suspend entry negotiation talks if the violence did not stop. Prime Minister Kostunica resigned following his inability to get his cabinet to reject closer ties to the EU, in protest at the EU's backing of Kosovo's independence. President Tadic called a snap general election. In parliamentary elections the coalition Za Evropsku Srbiju (ZES) (For a European Serbia) (five political parties, led by DS), led by Kostunica, won 78 seats out of

250, the Serbian Radical Party won 56. ZES won the right to form a government. a ruling coalition was formed with Ujedinjeni Regioni Srbije (URS) (United Regions of Serbia) (three parties led by G17 Plus) and SPS-JS (three parties led by Socijalisticka Partija Srbije (SPS) (Socialist Party of Serbia)), plus a number of other minority parties. As a last act of the outgoing government in Serbia the Serbian minister for Kosovo set up a new parliament in the divided city of Mitrovica (in Kosovo) for minority Serbs. Ethnic Serbs insisted that the new Kosovan constitution did not apply to them. The new Kosovan Serb Assembly in Mitrovica challenged the legitimacy of the Kosovan Assembly and the *de facto* partition of Kosovo. Parliament approved President Tadic's nomination of Mirko Cvetkovic as prime minister. The former Bosnian Serb leader Radovan Karadzic was arrested in Belgrade and extradited to stand at the UN War Crimes Tribunal in The Hague on charges of genocide. After months of obstruction, parliament ratified the pre-accession Stabilisation and Association Agreement with the EU. The agreement is subject to the arrest of the remaining two Serb war crimes suspects. The Montenegro ambassador was expelled following formal recognition of Kosovo by Montenegro.

2009 Kosovo's unilateral declaration of independence (UDI) came before the International Court of Justice (ICJ) as Serbia attempted to prevent further international recognition. Serbia maintained that the declaration was a 'flagrant violation' of international law while Kosovo contended that Serbia's brutality meant they had no right to rule. Serbia wanted to force Kosovo back into negotiations. The rail link between Belgrade and Sarajevo (Bosnia and Hercegovina), closed since the conflict in the 1990s, was re-opened.

2010. Parliament voted to offer an apology for the Srebrenica massacre in 1995 of 8,000 Bosniaks, perpetrated by Serb forces in Bosnia. However, the resolution failed to acknowledge the incident as an 'act of genocide' as recognised by the UN war crimes tribunal in The Hague. The ICJ ruled that Kosovo's UDI from Serbia did not violate international law. The ruling allows more countries to recognise Kosovo as a sovereign state. Croatia extradited Sretko Kalinic to Serbia; he had been convicted *in absentia* in 2003 for the assassination of Prime Minister Djindic. Serbia signed a protocol to jointly establish a new company, called Cargo 10, with Macedonia, Croatia and Slovenia, to incorporate their railway companies. EU foreign ministers agreed to pass Serbia's request for membership to the European Commission. This was a major step forward, only hampered by the outstanding arrest warrant on Ratko Mladic.

2011 Thousands congregated in front of parliament in February to protest at the poor condition of the economy. The opposition leader, Tomislav Nikolic (SRS), called on the government to hold early national elections or face further civil unrest. The first high-level talks between Serbia and Kosovo began in Brussels (Belgium) in March, sponsored by the EU. The focus of the meeting was daily, co-operative issues such as telecommunications and airspace. In April, at an anti-government protest in Belgrade, Tomislav Nikolic (Srpska Napredna Stranka (SNS) (Serbian Progressive Party)) said that he would go on hunger strike until the government agreed to elections. Ratko Mladic was arrested in a village north of Belgrade in May; despite an appeal against extradition he was flown to The Hague to await trial at the ICTY on charges including genocide. He appeared before the court in June, declining to plead against what he called 'obnoxious' charges. He then boycotted his next hearing in July when he was due to enter his pleas. Goran Hadzic, the last remaining fugitive war crimes suspect sought by the ICTY, was arrested in the Fruska Gora region north of Belgrade on 20 July; his extradition to The Hague to stand trial was quickly approved by a Serbian court. In October the EC recommended Serbia for EU candidate status, but said talks could only start after it normalised ties with Kosovo. In December, an EU-mediated the integrated border management (IBM) agreement was reached between Serbia and Kosovo to jointly manage and to 'gradually set up joint, integrated, single and secure posts at all their common crossing points.' The agreement moved Serbia into line for EU candidate status.

2012 On 24 February, Serbia and Kosovo reached an agreement whereby Kosovo can be represented at any regional forum without provoking a Serbian boycott. The complex formula has Kosovo registered under its name but with an addendum saying that giving the name and status does not prejudge UN Resolution 1244 and the ICJ opinion on Kosovo's UDI. This agreement concluded a technical protocol on the implementation of the IBM deal, reached in December 2011. The EU announced that Serbia had been accepted as a candidate for membership on 28 February. On 4 April, President Boris Tadic announced his resignation; Slavica Djukic Dejanovic became acting president on 5 April. The resignation of Tadic allowed for early presidential elections, in which he would stand. Parliamentary and presidential elections were held on 6 May. The Pokrenimo Srbiju coalition (PS) (Let's Get Serbia Moving), a newly formed coalition of 12 political parties, led by SNS, won 24.04 per cent of the vote (73 seats out of 250) in the parliamentary elections, and the newly formed Izbor za Bolji Život coalition (IBZ) (Choice for a Better Life), a coalition of six parties, led by Demokratska Stranka (DS) (Democratic Party) won 22.11 per cent (67). In the presidential elections, the leaders of the PS coalition, Tomislav Nikolic, and IBZ coalition, Boris Tadic, led the field and won 25.05 per cent and 25.31 per cent respectively in the first round. In the runoff, held on 20 May, Tomislav Nikolic won with 51.2 per cent against Boris Tadic's 48.8 per cent. President Nikolic took office on 31 May. Coalition talks to form a government began between various political parties – the new president initially granted a mandate to SNS, a member of the PS coalition. Boris Tadic, the defeated presidential candidate, also began to build a coalition with former allies, with which to challenge the SNS and PS coalitions. On 28 June, the president asked Ivica Dacic (SPS) to form a coalition government with the president's political party, SNS. On 10 July an agreement was reached between the SNS, the Socijalisticka Partija Srbije (SPS) (Socialist Party of Serbia) and the URS to form the next government, with Ivica Dacic as prime minister. On 27 July parliament endorsed the new government of Dacic. On 22 June, Istavn Pastor was elected president of the Autonomous Province of Vojvodina.

2013 In April the EC recommended the start of EU membership talks after agreement on relationships with Kosovo was reached on 19 April. On 28 June EU leaders agreed that negotiations for EU membership should begin by January 2014 at the latest. Former IMF managing director, Dominique Strauss-Kahn, become an economic advisor to the government in September; he is still being prosecuted in France on charges of pimping, which he denies. The government announced austerity measures on 8 October, including raising taxes, cutting subsidies to loss making companies and cutting public sector salaries by up to 25 per cent. Jovanka Broz, widow of former president, Josef Tito, died aged 88 on 21 October. Prime Minister Dacic said the country had lost 'one of the last most reliable witnesses of our former country's history'.

2014 Tensions in the coalition led by the SNS lead to early elections held on 16 March. The SNS lead coalition won a landslide victory with 48.35 per cent of the vote (158 seats, out of 250). The SPS (previous ruling coalition member) won

13.49 per cent (44 seats). Aleksandar Vucic becam prime minister on 27 April. 2015 Two Serbian diplomats were kidnapped in Libya on 24 November.

Political structure

Constitution

The Constitution was promulgated in 1990 and has articles that covers the sovereignty of state, the legal system and executive.

A referendum on constitutional amendments was held in October 2006 with over 100 new or amended articles agreed. It proposed a draft of the new Serbian constitution and it resulted in it being approved by the Serbian electorate. The constitution is Serbia's first as an independent state since the Kingdom of Serbia's 1903 constitution. 96.3 per cent of the electorate voted in favour of the draft constitution while just 2.7 per cent said no. Turnout was 54.9 per cent.

Form of state

Democratic republic

The executive

The president is the Head of State, directly elected for a term of five years; for two-terms only. The president nominates a prime minister, after conferring with the largest political party in the national assembly. Other powers include dissolving parliament, calling elections and vetoing legislature until it has been reconsidered. The government is comprised of the prime minister and cabinet ministers approved by the national assembly.

Kosovo has its own president and government which are responsible for the economy, education, health, agriculture and tourism, but requires UN approval to introduce or change any new legislation in these areas. The UNMIK representative also has the power to dissolve the Kosovo assembly and call new elections. The president is appointed by the Kosovan assembly for a period of three years.

National legislature

The national assembly (narodna skupstina) is unicameral, with 250 members, members directly elected in a single nationwide constituency by proportional representation vote. Members serve four-year terms.

It is the highest law making body in the country with the power to elect and dismiss the president, vice president, prime minister and any other person in a constitutionally mandated post.

Serbia has *de jure* sovereignty of Kosovo, however *de facto* government of the province is under the auspices of the UN Mission in Kosovo (UNMIK) and local Provisional Institutions of Self-Government (PISG).

Legal system

The legal system is based on the written constitution which states basic provisions and guarantees for a range of individual and collective rights, including civil laws. The court system is governed by the Supreme Court, the highest civil and criminal court in Serbia. The constitutional charter of Serbia was ratified in February 2003.

The Constitutional Court, which deals with the law and the constitution, comprises judges elected for a period of six years by the national assembly upon the recommendation of the Council of Ministers.

Last elections

16 March 2014 (early parliamentary election); 6 and 20 May 2012 (presidential, first round and runoff)

Results: Parliamentary: Coalition of SNS, SDPS, NS and PS won 48.4 per cent of the vote (158 seats out of 250), Coalition of SPS, PUPS and JS won 13.5 per cent (44 seats), a coalition of 5 parties won 6 per cent of the vote (19 seats) and a larger coalition of 6 parties won 5.7 per cent of the vote (18 seats); the remaining twenty-five parties each won less than 4.5 per cent of the vote and failed to win any seats. Turnout was 53.1 per cent.

Presidential (first round): Boris Tadic (DS) 25.3 per cent of the vote, Tomislav Nikolic (SNS) 25.1 per cent, Ivica Dacic (SPS) 14.2 per cent, Vojislav Koštunica (DSS) 7.4 per cent, Zoran Stankovic (URS) 6.6 per cent, Cedomir Jovanovic (Liberalno-Demokratska Partija (LDP) Liberal Democratic Party)) 5.03 per cent; six other candidates each won less that 4 per cent. Turnout was 57.8 per cent.

Runoff: Nikolic won 49.6 per cent, Tadic won 47.3 per cent. Turnout was 46.2 per cent.

Next elections

March 2018 (parliamentary), 2017 (presidential)

Political parties

Ruling party

Coalition of Srpska Napredna Stranka (SNS) (Serbian Progressive Party), with Socijaldemokratska partija Srbije (SDPS) (Social Democratic Party of Serbia), Nova Srbija (NS) (New Serbia), Srpski pokret obnove (Serbian Renewal Movement) and Pokret socijalista (PS) (Movement of Socialists).

Main opposition party

Coalition of Socijalisticka partija Srbije (SPS) (Socialist Party of Serbia), Partija ujedinjenih penzionera Srbije (PUPS) (Party of United Pensioners of Serbia) and Jedinstvena Srbija (United Serbia).

Population

7.16 million (2014)*. There are almost 40 different settled nationalities in Serbia. The population figure in Serbia has fallen since 1994 due to migration patterns and a drop in the fertility rate. In 2002, 46 per cent were designated migrant either local or regional.

Last census: 1 October 2011: 7,120,666

Population density: 104 inhabitants per square km. Urban population 56 per cent (2010 Unicef).

Annual growth rate: 0.1 per cent, 1990–2010 (Unicef).

Ethnic make-up

Serbian (63 per cent), Albanian (14 per cent), Montenegrin (6 per cent) and Hungarian (4 per cent).

Religions

Serbian Orthodox (65 per cent), Islam, Roman Catholic and Protestant

Education

With less developed education systems than Slovenia and Croatia during the Tito period, Serbia had an adult illiteracy rate of 10 per cent in 1990 (in Kosovo, the figure was then 17 per cent).

Primary education lasts for eight years from aged seven. Secondary education is provided in grammar, vocational and art schools with courses lasting up to four years. Higher education is provided in universities and colleges.

There are four universities in Serbia (Belgrade, Novi Sad, Nis and Kragujevac) and one in Kosovo (Pristina). However, graduate unemployment is high.

There was a major exodus of younger and more educated people abroad during the 1990s. In 1994 alone, around 100,000 people, or around 1 per cent of the population, may have emigrated.

During the lead-up to the conflict in Kosovo, education was a very controversial issue, with the majority Albanian population refusing to be taught in the Serbian language. Alternative or Albanian language education thus emerged in Kosovo.

Literacy rate: 99 per cent total; 97 per cent female; adult rates (Unicef 2004).

Compulsory years: 7 to 15

Enrolment rate: 66 per cent gross primary enrolment, 59 per cent gross secondary enrolment; of relevant age group (including repeaters) (Unesco).

Pupils per teacher: 20 primary; 14 secondary, (Unesco 2002)

Health

Since 1992, the extent and quality of healthcare provision has sharply deteriorated. However, a well-developed private healthcare system has emerged for the better-off. Largely free at the point of delivery and funded by a universal social insurance tax levied on all employees and employers, public healthcare provision now require all kinds of charges, most notably for imported medications.

HIV/Aids

HIV prevalence: 0.2 per cent aged 15–49 in 2003 (World Bank)

Life expectancy: 73 years, 2004 (WHO 2006)

Fertility rate/Maternal mortality rate: 1.6 births per woman, 2010 (Unicef)

Birth rate/Death rate: 12.7 births and 10.6 deaths per 1,000 population (2003)

Child (under 5 years) mortality rate (per 1,000): 7 per 1,000 live births (WHO 2012)

Head of population per physician: 2.06 physicians per 1,000 people, 2002 (WHO 2006)

Welfare

Welfare provision in Serbia was relatively generous during the Tito period, when retirement pensions were around 80 per cent of average monthly incomes. Since 2000, the World Bank has helped fund pensions and social benefits. A three-year Country Assistance Stratergy (CAS) includes reducing poverty levels through improved social protection.

Main cities

Belgrade (capital, estimated population 1.1 million in 2012), Novi Sad (202,389), Niš (171,385), Kragujevac (145,203), Subotica (99,395), Pancevo (79,634), Zrenjanin (78,433).

Languages spoken

Croatian, Bosnian, Hungarian, Slovak, Albanian (principally in Kosovo), Macedonian and Slovenian are all spoken. English is the most commonly used foreign business language. Other languages include German, Russian and Italian.

Official language/s

Serbian

Media

Press

Dailies: National publications in Serbian, include *Danas* (www.danas.co.yu), *Vecernje Novosti* (www.novosti.co.yu), *Politika* (www.politika.co.yu), *Glas Javnosti* (www.glas-javnosti.co.yu) and *Borba* (www.borba.co.yu). Regional papers in Serbian include *Dnevnik* (www.dnevnik.co.yu) from Novi Sad, *24 Sata* (www.24sata.co.yu) and *Kurir* (www.kurir-info.co.yu) are tabloids from Belgrade. In English *Blic* (www.blic.co.yu), *Balkan Web* (www.balkanweb.com/maineng.htm), *Kosovo Daily* (www.kosovodaily.com) and Belgrade News*www.belgradenews.com*.

Weeklies: In Serbian, *Nedeljne Telegraf* (www.nedeljnitelegraf.co.yu) is the largest weekly tabloid newspaper. *Vojvodina* (www.vojvodina.com) is an independent, open weekly newspaper about cultural, political, economic, agriculture and sports. Other significant weeklies are *NIN* (www.nin.co.yu), *Standard* (www.standardmagazin.com) and *Vreme* (www.vreme.com).

Business: The main magazine, in English, is *Ekonomist* (www.ekonomist.co.yu/eng).

Broadcasting

The Broadcasting Agency Council (BAC) oversees radio and television output and licenses operators.

Radio Televizije Srbije (RTS) (Radio Television Serbia) (www.rts.co.yu) is the national, public, state broadcaster, with two television channels and three radio stations with internet access and podcasts.

Radio: There are many private radio stations. B92 (www.b92.net) has a youthful audience; Medunarodni Radio Serbija (www.radioyu.org); Radio Index (www.indexradio.com) and Radio Pink (www.rtvpink.com). International radio stations from US, UK, France and Germany can be received.

Television: Independent networks include TV Pink (www.rtvpink.com) and TV-Avala (www.tv-avala.com) showing popular international programmes and local content shows.

National news agency: Tanjug

Other news agencies: Beta News Agency (www2.beta.co.yu); FoNet (www.fonet.co.yu), Tiker (www.tiker.co.yu).

Economy

Despite an economy largely dominated by the service industry, 54.9 per cent of GDP in 2014, Serbia also has an old, established industrial sector that constitutes 36.9 per cent of GDP. With large deposits of lead, zinc and coal (lignite) for energy generation, the extraction industry is an important element of the economy. The manufacturing sector includes furniture, clothes, pharmaceuticals and machinery and constitutes around 17 per cent of GDP. Agriculture has become less significant to the economy, contributing 8.2 per cent of GDP in 2014. The main crops are cereals such as corn (maize), which is also the leading agricultural export product (1.8 million tonnes in 2013, a record for Serbia), wheat, fruit, livestock, dairy products and alcohol.

Serbia's economy was adversely affected by its recent history. Its GDP growth in 1999 was -17.7 per cent due to the fighting between ethnic groupings and international sanctions. But from 2000 when it began to rebuild its infrastructure and introduce reforms, working towards a free-market economy, Serbia enjoyed mostly high GDP growth. However, following on from a two-year period of slow growth, in 2012 the economy dropped into its second recession caused by the global economic crisis, with a GDP contraction of 1.0 per cent. In 2013 the economy grew by 2.56 per cent before falling back into recession in 2014, posting a growth of -1.8 per cent.

Serbia's efforts to revive the economy are hampered by on going political and economic problems such as high unemployment and stagnant household incomes. Public debt as a percentage of GDP has more than doubled in between 2008 and 2014. In late 2014 the IMF and the Serbian government announced a precautionary loan worth approximately US$1 billion, which will see the government attempt to implement reforms targeting social spending and the large public sector.

External trade

Serbia is a candidate country for membership of the European Union (EU). Formal negotiations began in January 2014. Serbia is a member of the Central European free trade agreement (Cefta) which, by 2007, following the loss of those countries that had joined the European Union, had eight countries all located in the Balkans (apart from Moldova). It had duty-free access for agricultural products to the EU under the free trade measures until 2010, but with exceptions, including sugar, wine and young cattle for which quotas apply.

Foreign trade is underdeveloped and imports sustain a distorted balance of payments. Serbia has large deposits of minerals (coal, lead, zinc, copper and gold) but lack of investment has hampered development, which in turn hinders economic growth. Manufacturing includes foodstuffs, furniture and base metals. In 2015, Serbia was nearing the end of negotiations to become a member of the World Trade Organisation.

Imports

Main imports include machinery and vehicles, fuels and lubricants, consumer goods, chemicals, food and live animals and raw materials.

Main sources: Germany (12.0 per cent of total in 2014), Russia (11.3 per cent), Italy (11.3 per cent)

Exports

Principal exports include manufactured goods such as electrical machinery and appliances; wheat and corn (maize), fruit, wine, live animals, minerals and energy.

Main destinations: Italy (17.4 per cent of total in 2014), Germany (12.0 per cent), Bosnia and Hercegovina (8.8 per cent)

Agriculture

Farming

The main crops are wheat, maize, sugar beet and tobacco. There are extensive orchards and livestock is reared. Agricultural exports and imports are important for the whole economy. Animal husbandry

is still developing and is of minor importance.
About 80 per cent of the total agricultural area, which is the equivalent of 4.96 million hectares, is under mixed farming systems with elements of ecological farming. Most of the highly productive soil, located in the lowlands, receives small quantities of rainfall.
Serbia is the number two producer in both raspberries (second to Russia) and plums (second to China). It is also the world's 32nd producer of maize.
The agricultural sector in Serbia is hampered by shortages of industrial goods such as fertiliser, with an estimated US$44 million investment needed to ensure sufficient supplies of agri-chemicals annually. The country also suffers periodically from droughts, which reduces agriculture production and economic growth.

Fishing

Forestry

Forestry has experienced only slight falls in output, mainly because at times shortages of other fuels increase the demand for firewood locally.

Industry and manufacturing

Prior to the 1999 Kosovo War, Serbia and Montenegro had a diversified industrial base with major industries including metal processing, food production, textile and other manufacturing. The industrial sector accounted for almost US$1 billion of former Yugoslavia's exports. Much of the energy-dependent industry, including chemicals and iron and steel, collapsed because of shortages of energy and raw materials following the imposition of sanctions in 1999.
The damage done by the NATO bombing campaign to manufacturing was second only to the destruction to hydrocarbons and energy production. Total industrial production is thought to have fallen by 60 per cent, with whole sectors being wiped out. Its share of GDP consequently dropped from 45 per cent to 15–20 per cent. Previously, over 40 per cent of the labour force were employed in industry, but more than 100,000 jobs were lost immediately as a result of the industrial destruction. Since 2000, there has been a steady growth in industrial output, although it dropped to 0.5 per cent in 2003 demonstrating that industry has a long way to go to return to pre-1999 levels.
By 2014, the industrial sector had improved and its contribution to GDP was up to 36.9 per cent, including around 20 per cent from manufacturing. Industrial output is also rising, in July 2015 there was an 18.6 per cent increase on the output of the same period in 2014.

Tourism

Serbia has a northern region of flat, lowlands terrain and a southern mountainous region. The north, specifically the Autonomous Province of Vojvodina, has many historic sites dating back as far as the Neolithic age (4,200BC). There are several sites around Serbia included on Unesco's World Heritage List, such as the Roman Palace of Galerius and the medieval buildings of Stari Ras and the Studenica Monastery. Other historic sites include the first evidence of the Slavic settlement, the Habsburg administration and those of the recent Yugoslavian state.
There are four mountain ranges that provide destinations for active visitors and those interested in the native plants and animals. Festivals have become an important source of entertainment for visitors, including wine and beer festivals.
Travel and tourism has recorded steady growth from 2000, and in 2014 accounted for 6.1 per cent of GDP. This figure is predicted to rise by 1.1 per cent in 2015. Poor investment in the sector has been identified as a weakness, which may account for the lack of growth in jobs in travel and tourism, which had provided 6.4 per cent employment in 2014 (87,500 jobs).

Mining

Serbia has a significant mining sector. Lead and zinc are produced in substantial quantities. There is a large gold and silver mine at Bor in eastern Serbia. The fact that many of the most valuable non-ferrous metal mineral deposits are in Kosovo makes the area of great economic importance. In the longer-term, there is likely to be considerable foreign investor interest in Serbia's non-ferrous metal mineral ore resources, particularly copper and gold.

Hydrocarbons

In 2008 a trade and co-operation agreement was signed between Serbia and Russia, whereby Russia would underwrite the construction of a 400km section of the South Stream gas pipeline traversing Serbia, which will integrate Serbia into the large European infrastructure project and will give Serbia sustainable gas supplies in winter. Construction began in 2012. An underground gas storage facility has been constructed at Banatski Dvor to store excess Russian gas production, this will be linked to the South Stream pipeline. A controlling interest in the state-owned Nafta Industrija Srbije (NIS) was sold to the Russian Gazprom Neft, for EUR400 million (US$520 million), with a guaranteed investment of EUR500 million (US$651.2 million) to refurbish and modernise industrial facilities. NIS produces hydrocarbons in Serbia and Angola with production at one million tonnes per year. It owns oil refineries and a liquefied natural gas plant and downstream distribution outlets.
Serbia has an estimated 4.81 billion tonnes of oil shale, with up to 3.6 billion tonnes of recoverable reserves, however, this energy source is largely undeveloped. The 21 deposits are all located in the central-eastern part of the country.

Energy

Total installed generating capacity was 8.4GW in 2013. The energy market is state-owned and centralised under the Electric Power Industry of Serbia (EPS), which has a monopoly on generation and provision of electricity, and has a net capacity of 8,355MW which comprises 5,171MW coal-fired thermal plants, 2,831MW hydro plants and 353MW oil and natural gas-fired plants. There is also 89MW of installed capacity generated by geothermal power. Elektromreza Srbije (EMS) is responsible for transmission.

Financial markets

Stock exchange

Beogradska Berza (Belgrade Stock Exchange) (BSE)

Banking and insurance

Begradska Banka, Jugobanka, Investbanka and Beobanka, four of the country's old banking giants, were closed down in 2002. By 2006 Beobanka was merged with the Greek, Alpha Bank and the Hungarian OTP Bank bought almost 90 per cent of the provincial Niska Bank.

Central bank

Narodna Banka Srbije (NBS) (National Bank of Serbia).

Main financial centre

Belgrade

Time

GMT plus one hour (daylight saving, late March to late October, GMT plus two hours)

Geography

Landlocked and situated in the central Balkan Peninsula in south-eastern Europe, Serbia consists of two parts: the Great Danubian Plains of Vojvodina to the north, where the two main rivers are the Sava and the Danube, which meet at Belgrade; and the hilly and forested areas of inner (central) and southern Serbia, where the main rivers are the Drina, Morava and Vardar.
Serbia is bordered by Hungary to the north; Croatia, Bosnia and Hercegovina (BiH) and Montenegro to the west and south-west; Albania and Macedonia to the south and south-east; and Bulgaria and Romania to the east. Serbia has borders with Croatia and Romania along the River Danube. The River Drina marks the border between Serbia and BiH.

Hemisphere
Northern

Climate
The climate is largely continental. The summers are very hot and the winters bitterly cold. The average summer temperature in Belgrade is 22 degrees Celsius (C) and in winter the average temperature is zero degrees C. Precipitation is generally constant, with average annual rainfall in Belgrade of around 635mm. Snowfall is extensive in winter.

Entry requirements
Passports
Required by all.
Visa
Required by all, with the exception of nationals of most European countries, North America, Australasia and a number of other countries. A full list of exceptions and lengths of stay permitted will be found at www.mfa.gov.yu/Visas/f_without_visa.htm.
Currency advice/regulations
There are no restrictions on the import of local or foreign currencies. Local currency in excess of D120,000 must be declared and shown to have been acquired abroad. Foreign currency may be declared against a receipt which will allow re-export.
Customs
Various personal articles and goods are allowed duty-free.

Health (for visitors)
Mandatory precautions
None required
Advisable precautions
Hepatitis A and B, diphtheria, polio, TB, typhoid, tetanus vaccinations are recommended. There is a rabies risk.

Hotels
Hotels are classified into five categories: L (extra), A, B, C and D; boarding houses into three, I, II and III. There is a 10–20 per cent service charge. Visitors must also pay a residential tax, which varies between regions.

Credit cards
International credit cards are accepted in large hotels and businesses in Serbia.

Public holidays (national)
Fixed dates
1 Jan (New Year's Day), 7 Jan (Orthodox Christmas Day), 15 Feb (Serbia National day), 1–2 May (Labour Days), 9 May (Victory Day).
Variable dates
Orthodox Good Friday, Orthodox Easter Monday.

Working hours
Banking
Mon–Fri: 0700–1500; Sat: 0800–1400. Belgrade airport 0800–2000.
Business
Mon–Fri: 0800–1500.
Government
Mon–Fri: 0730–1530.
Shops
Mon–Fri: generally in larger towns: 0800–2000 (some shops closing between 1200 and 1700); Sat: 0800–1500.

Telecommunications
Mobile/cell phones
There are GSM 900/1800 services available throughout most of the country.

Electricity supply
220V, 50Hz with European flat and round, two-pin plugs.

Social customs/useful tips
Punctuality depends on the ethnic region: it is important in some, more casual in others. As elsewhere, it is customary to shake hands on meeting and taking leave.
Do carry some form of identity at all times. Appointments must be made in advance. Business cards should indicate academic/professional titles and are exchanged after introduction. Many executives speak a second language, including German, English, Italian or Russian. There are some restrictions on photography.

Security
Visitors are advised to avoid Kosovo unless absolutely necessary and should remain vigil if required. Armed conflict continues in parts of Kosovo, and the crime rate (including violent crime) is high. Any travel into these areas should only take place in organised groups after seeking advice from the local authorities before the journey is made.

Getting there
Air
National airline: JAT Airways
International airport/s: Belgrade Nikola Tesla Airport (LYBE), 18km west of Belgrade.
Airport tax: Around D1,200, but may be included in ticket price.
Surface
Road: There are border crossings from Hungary, Romania, Bulgaria, and Albania, Bosnia and Hercegovina, Croatia, Macedonia and Montenegro.
The E5 highway, part of the pan-European 'Corridor 10' road and rail project linking Germany to Greece, will traverse Serbia from the Hungarian to the Macedonian borders when completed. Construction of the southern part of the Serbian section of the highway has been held up due to lack of funding.
Rail: There are rail links with neighbouring countries. The newly reopened Belgrade and Sarajevo line takes six hours by train.
Water: Ships provide regular passenger services and cruises on the Danube from Germany, passing through Serbia. There are also links with the rivers Rhine and Main and the Black Sea.

Getting about
National transport
Air: JAT Airways flies several domestic routes and provides a charter service.
Road: There are some 48,423km of roads, including 374km of motorways. The main route links Belgrade with Subotica (via Novi Sad), Kragujevac and Nis. Road maintenance is often inadequate.
Buses: An extensive network of express buses links Serbia's cities, although fuel shortages can often restrict services. Multi-journey tickets are available and sold through tobacconists. In general, fares paid to the driver are usually double the price of pre-purchase tickets.
Rail: There are around 4,000km of track, of which over a quarter is electrified. Maintenance of track and stock has deteriorated in recent years. The services are often overcrowded, unpunctual and slow. International express trains link Belgrade with Subotica, Novi Sad, Kragujevac, Nis and Pristina.
Water: There is a well established inland waterways system, based on the Danube, Sava, Tizsa and Begej rivers.
City transport
Taxis: Good services operate in most large cities and towns. All taxis are metered. There are taxi stands in central locations, but they can also be hailed in the street. Taxis are cheaper in Belgrade if arranged by telephone.
Buses, trams & metro: All cities and towns are served by buses; trams only in the centre of Belgrade and in Subotica. The service is generally regular.
Car hire
Cars can be hired in most main towns through travel agencies. There is a speed limit of 120kph on motorways and 60kph in built-up areas. Drive on the right and give way to traffic from the right unless clearly marked otherwise. Seat belts are compulsory in front seats.
To be on the safe side, carry an international driver's licence as well as a national licence.

BUSINESS DIRECTORY
The addresses listed below are a selection only. While World of Information makes every endeavour to check these

addresses, we cannot guarantee that changes have not been made, especially to telephone numbers and area codes. We would welcome any corrections.

Telephone area codes

The international direct dialling (IDD) code is +381, followed by area code and subscriber's number:

Belgrade	11	Pec	39
Kragujevac	34	Podgorica	81
Krusevac	37	Pristina	38
Leskovac	16	Uzice	31
Novi Sad	21		

Useful telephone numbers

Police: 92
Fire: 93
Ambulance: 94

Chambers of Commerce

American Chamber of Commerce in Serbia, 30 Vlajkoviceva, 11000 Belgrade (tel: 334-5961; fax: 324-7771; e-mail: info@amcham.yu).

Belgrade Chamber of Economy , 12 Kneza Milosa, 11001 Belgrade (tel:264-1355; fax: 264-2029; e-mail: mmj@komberg.org.yu).

Kragujevac Chamber of Commerce and Industry, 10 Mose Pijade, 34000 Kragujevac (tel: 335-805; fax: 334-049; e-mail: rpkkg@eunet.yu).

Serbian Chamber of Commerce and Industry, 13-15 Resavska, 11000 Belgrade (tel: 324-0611; fax: 323-0949; e-mail: centar@pks.co.yu).

Uzice Regional Chamber of Commerce, 52 Dimirija Tucovica, 31000 Uzice (tel: 513-483; fax: 514-184; e-mail: office@rpk-uzice.co.yu).

Banking

Association of Serbian Banks (Udruzenje Banaka Srbije), Bulevar Kralja Aleksandra 86, 11000 Belgrade (tel: 302-0760; fax: 337-0179).

JIK Banka, Knez Mihailova 42, Belgrade (tel: 632-822; fax: 183-198).

Kreditna Banka Beograd, Lenjinov Bulevar 111, Belgrade (tel: 222-4428; fax: 144-923).

Panonska Banka, Bulevar Oslobodenja 76, Novi Sad (tel: 488-7100; e-mail: office@panban.co.yu).

PKB Banka, 29 Novembra 68a, Belgrade (tel: 753-366; fax: 750-932).

Privredna Banka, Brace Jugovica 17, Belgrade (tel: 623-272; fax: 627-247).

Vojvodjanska Banka, Trg Slobode 7, 21000 Novi Sad (tel: 621-277; fax: 021-624-940).

Central bank

Narodna Banka Srbije (NBS) (National Bank of Serbia), 12 Kralja Petra Street, 11000 Belgrade, (tel: 302-7100; fax: 302-7381; e-mail: gen.sec@nbs.yu).

Stock exchange

Beogradska Berza (Belgrade Stock Exchange) (BSE), www.belex.co.yu

Travel information

AutomobileAssociation of Serbia (AMSS), Kneginje Zorke 58, Belgrade (tel: 333-1100; fax: 245-1078; e-mail: info@amss.org.yu).

JAT Airways, Bulevar Umetnosti 16, 11070 Belgrade (tel: 311-4222; fax: 311-1082; e-mail: jatairways@jat.com).

Ministry of tourism

Ministry of Trade, Tourism and Services, Nemanjina Street 22-26, Belgrade (tel: 361-0579; fax: 361-0258; e-mail: kabinet@minttu.sr.gov.yu).

National tourist organisation offices

National Tourism Organization of Serbia, Decanska 8, 11000 Belgrade (tel: 323-0566; fax: 322-1068; e-mail: ntos@yubc.net).

Ministries

Ministry of Agriculture, Forestry and Water Management, 22-26 Nemanjina Street, Belgrade (tel: 306-5038; fax: 361-6272; e-mail: office@minpolj.sr.gov.yu).

Ministry of Capital Investment, 22-26 Nemanjina Street, Belgrade (tel: 361-6426; fax: 361-7486; e-mail: cabinet@mki.sr.gov.yu).

Ministry of Culture, 3 Vlajkoviceva Street, Belgrade (tel: 339-8404; fax: 339-8936; e-mail: kabinet@min-cul.sr.gov.yu).

Ministry of Diaspora, 42 Svetozara Markovica, Belgrade (tel: 263-8033; fax: 263-7624; e-mail: info@mzd.sr.gov.yu).

Ministry of Economy, 16 Kralja Milana Street, Belgrade (tel: 361-7599; fax: 361-7640; e-mail: officempriv@mpriv.sr.gov.yu).

Ministry of Education and Sport, 22-26 Nemanjina Street, Belgrade (tel: 361-6357; fax: 361-6491; e-mail: webmaster@mps.sr.gov.yu).

Ministry of Energy and Mining, 22-26 Nemanjina Street, Belgrade (tel: 334-6755; fax: 361- 6603; e-mail: kabinet@mem.sr.gov.yu).

Ministry of Finance, 20 Kneza Milosa Street, Belgrade (tel: 361-4972; fax: 361-8914; e-mail: informacije@mfin.sr.gov.yu).

Ministry of Foreign Affairs, 24-26 Kneza Milosa Street, Belgrade (tel: 361-6333; fax: 361-8366; e-mail: mfa@smip.sv.gov.yu).

Ministry of Health, 22-26 Nemanjina Street, Belgrade (tel: 361-6251; fax: 656-548; e-mail: kabinet.zdravlje@zdravlje.sr.gov.yu).

Ministry of the Interior, 101 Kneza Milosa Street, Belgrade (tel: 306-2000; fax: 361-7814; e-mail: mupr s@mup.sr.gov.yu).

Ministry of International Economic Relations, 10 Vlajkoviceva Street, Belgrade (tel: 361-7583; fax: 363-3142; e-mail: cabinet@mier.sr.gov.yu).

Ministry of Justice, 22-26 Nimanjina Street, Belgrade (tel: 361-6548; fax: 361-6419; e-mail: kabinet@mpravde.sr.gov.yu).

Ministry of Labour, Employment and Social Affairs, 22-26 Nemanjina Street, Belgrade (tel: 361-3734; fax: 363-1792; e-mail: kabinet@minrzs.sr.gov.yu).

Ministry of Public Administration and Local Self-Government, 6 Bircaninova Street, Belgrade (tel: 268-5387; fax: 268-5315; e-mail: info.mpalsg@mpalsg.sr.gov.yu).

Ministry of Religion, 11 Nemanjina Street, Belgrade (tel: 306-5960; fax: 363-3446; e-mail: kabinet.mv@mv.sr.gov.yu).

Ministry of Science and Environmental Protection, 22-26 Nemajina Street, Belgrade (tel: 268-8047; fax: 361-6516; e-mail: info@mntr.sr.gov.yu).

Ministry of Trade, Tourism and Services, Nemanjina Street 22-26, Belgrade (tel: 361-0579; fax: 361-0258; e-mail: kabinet@minttu.sr.gov.yu).

Other useful addresses

Kosovo Trust Agency, Ilir Konushevi 8, Pristina, Kosovo (tel: 500-400; fax: 248-076; e-mail: kta@eumik.org).

Novinska Agencija Tanjug (news agency), Obilicev Venac 2, Box 439, Belgrade 11001 (tel: 332-221).

Roads Directorate of the Republic of Serbia, Ljube Cupe 5, 11000 Belgrade (tel: 454-779; fax: 444-5557; e-mail: dzpnapl@eunet.yu).

Statistical Office of the Republic of Serbia, Milana Rakica 5, 11000 Belgrade (tel: 241-2922; fax: 240-1284; e-mail: stat@statserb.sr.gov.yu).

National news agency: Tanjug Obilicev Venac 2, Belgrade 11000 (tel: 328-8285; fax: 263-3550; email: direkcija@tanjug.co.yu; internet: www.tanjug.co.yu).

Beta News Agency (www2.beta.co.yu); FoNet (www.fonet.co.yu), Tiker (www.tiker.co.yu).

Internet sites

Belgrade News: www.belgradenews.com

European Commission/World Bank, Balkans reconstruction web site: www.seerecon.org

Seebiz (business portal): www.seebiz.eu

Seychelles

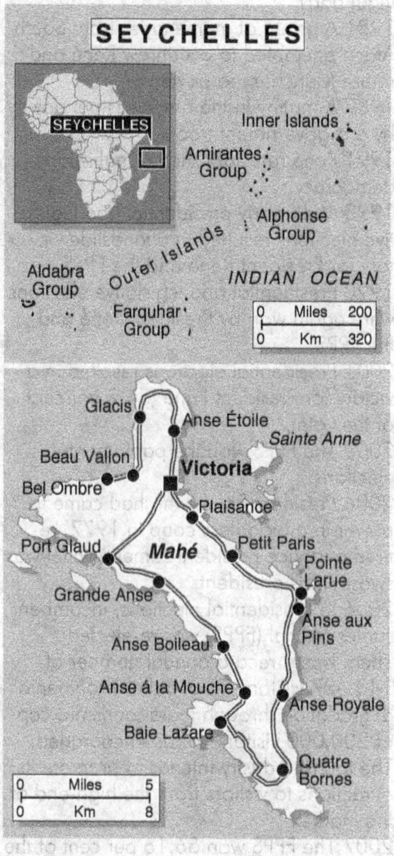

In 2015, the Seychelles earned the title of 'Country Destination of the Year', given by UK-based publication *Luxury Travel Guide*. The certificate was awarded to the nation after the publication's experts 'scoured the globe and travelled extensively in order to identify everything from the very best hotels, airlines and tour operators through to highlighting the most reputable transfer service companie'. Despite this 'honor for the Seychelles', the tourism industry did in fact experience a downturn in 2014 due to lack of demand from countries of origin. However, perhaps the *Luxury Travel Guide* has a committed reader-base as the International Monetary Fund (IMF)'s outlook for the Seychelles in 2016 was upgraded following the improvement of the tourism sector's performance in 2015.

The Indian Ocean nation, which declared independence from Britain in 1976, is a republic and member of the commonwealth. The country is comprised of approximately 115 islands, however, 90 per cent of the population is concentrated on one island, Mahe, which is also home to the country's capital, Victoria. The Seychelles People's Progressive Front (SPPF) has been the ruling party since 1977, when France Albert René came to power in a *coup*.

In February 2015 the credit rating agency Fitch ratings had affirmed the upgrade of the Seychelles' long-term foreign and local currency Issuer Default Ratings (IDRs) to 'B+' from 'B' and 'BB-' from 'B+' respectively. The outlook for the country was rated as stable. The issue ratings on Seychelles' unsecured foreign currency bonds have also been affirmed at 'B+'. The affirmation and the stable outlook reflected key rating drivers such as fairly high public debt burden, a large current account deficit and limited economic diversification against a high level of gross domestic product (GDP) per capita and standards of governance. The current account deficit worsened in 2014, reaching 22 per cent of GDP, from 15.5 per cent in 2013, a deficit primarily financed by foreign direct investment (FDI).

IMF Review

In June 2015 the IMF Executive board completed its second review under the Extended Fund Facility with Seychelles and approved a US$2.3 million disbursement, bringing the total disbursement to US$6.9 million. According to the review, the Seychelles' economy had been strengthened greatly by sound macroeconomic management. Near term growth outlook is positive and prospects in the tourism sector remain strong. Policies have been aimed at reinforcing economic stability, and have succeeded in keeping the country on track to achieve its target of reducing debt to below 50 per cent of GDP by 2018. Tight control of current expenditure will be needed in order to achieve this objective whilst addressing critical infrastructure issues. Further progress in building international reserves has ensured the Seychelles has a buffer against external pressures.

KEY FACTS

Official name: Republic of Seychelles

Head of State: President James Michel (Seychelles People's Progressive Front (SPPF) (from 2004; re-elected 19–21 May 2011)

Head of government: President James Michel

Ruling party: People's Party (Parti Lepep) (PP) (from 1993; re-elected 1 Oct 2011)

Area: 453 square km

Population: 94,000 (2014)* (90,945; 2010, census figure)

Capital: Victoria

Official language: Creole, English and French

Currency: Seychelle rupee (SR) = 100 cents

Exchange rate: SR13.17 per US$ (Sep 2015)

GDP per capita: US$15,115 (2014)*

GDP real growth: 2.94% (2014)*

GDP: US$1.42 billion (2014)*

Unemployment: 2.98% (2014)*

Inflation: 1.39% (2014)*

Balance of trade: -US$541.71 million (2014)

Visitor numbers: 174,529 (2010)

Annual FDI: US$138.75 million (2011)

* estimated figure

The IMF review suggested that the authorities should continue to improve the forward-looking elements of their monetary policy framework, including inflation and liquidity management. It was also suggested that structural reforms should aim to increase the role for the private sector in the economy and enhance competition in order to support sustained and inclusive growth. The exchange rate should also continue to be allowed to adjust freely to internal and external economic conditions.

AfDB Report

According to the African Development Bank (AfDB), the Seychelles grew by an estimated 3.8 per cent in 2014, down from 6.6 per cent in 2015. The main drivers of growth are tourism and manufacturing, and the lack of demand from tourist countries of origin can help to explain the deceleration. Manufacturing also slowed, and plant modernisation was undertaken in the main beverage sector. Private consumption remained strong as demand was aided by an increase in consumer credit. Growth is projected to remain moderate at around 3.6 per cent in 2015 and 2016. The continued growth of financial services and information and communications technology is expected to provide opportunities for economic diversification. In the latter half of 2014, the government tightened monetary policy in order to keep inflationary pressures at bay. As a result inflation was contained and remained within the target rate of less than 4 per cent a year.

The Seychelles is on its way to being the only African country to reach all of its Millennium Development Goals (MDGs) of which the deadline is the end of 2015. In its November 2013 MDG Status Report, the country indicated it had 'already achieved almost all of the MDGs, especially those relating to education, health and social development'. These targets that were adopted by the United Nations at the beginning of the millennium include achieving universal primary education, attaining gender equality and reducing child mortality. The deadline of the MDGs coincides with the medium-term national development strategy (NDS 2015–19), which the government approved in November 2014. The strategy includes four key areas: governance, economic development, social development and the environment.

Risk assessment

Politics	Good
Economy	Good
Regional stability	Good

COUNTRY PROFILE

1794 The islands were taken over by the British and administered from Mauritius.
1903 Seychelles became a separate colony.
1948 The first elections to the legislative assembly took place.
1964 The Seychelles' first political organisations were established – the Seychelles Democratic Party (SDP) led by James Mancham and the Front Progressiste du Peuple Seychellois (FPPS) (Seychelles People's Progressive Front) (formerly the SPUP) of France-Albert René.
1975 The Seychelles was granted internal self-government; the SDP and the FPPS formed a coalition government under the premiership of Mancham.
1976 Became an independent republic. James Mancham became president and René became prime minister.
1977 René seized power in an armed coup
1978 A new constitution established a one-party state with the FPPS as the sole legal party.
1981 A group of mercenaries from South Africa attempted to overthrow René and return Mancham to power.
1982 A mutiny in the army was put down by pro-government troops.
1991 René re-established a multi-party democracy.
1993 Multi-party presidential and legislative elections resulted in a landslide victory for President René and the FPPS.
1998 Presidential and legislative elections were again won by President René and the FPPS.
2001 Presidential elections resulted in a victory for President René (54.2 per cent of the vote).
2002 The FPPS won the parliamentary elections.
2004 President René, who had came to power in a bloodless coup in 1977, retired and Vice President James Michel was sworn in as president.
2006 In presidential elections, incumbent James Michel (FPPS) was re-elected. There was a record annual number of 140,627 visitors. To avoid environmental degradation through mass-tourism a cap of 200,000 visitors will be encouraged. The tourist industry intends to promote its attractions to visitors from the high-end of the market.
2007 The FPPS won 56.16 per cent of the vote in parliamentary elections; the Seychelles National Party (SNP) won 43.84 per cent. Seychelles was re-admitted to the Southern African Development Community (SADC).
2008 The global economic crisis had an adverse effect on the tourist industry; the International Monetary Fund agreed to extend a two-year US$26 million loan to the country. It also suggested moves to restructure the economy, including floating the Seychelles rupee, allowing citizens to hold foreign currencies and setting a minimum salary among other measures.
2009 The president called on international creditors to cancel around US$400 million in foreign debt. The ruling FPPS changed its name to the Parti Lepep (People's Party) (PP).
2010 Around 85 per cent of Seychelles' public debt was successfully reduced and rescheduled; external debt stock fell from 92 per cent of GDP in 2009 to 54 per cent. The government estimated that the Seychelles was losing 4 per cent of GDP

KEY INDICATORS — Seychelles

	Unit	2011	2012	2013	2014	**2015
Population	m	*0.09	*0.09	*0.09	*0.09	*0.10
Gross domestic product (GDP)	US$bn	1.01	1.13	1.41	*1.42	*1.38
GDP per capita	US$	11,170	12,290	15,187	*15,115	*14,500
GDP real growth	%	4.9	2.8	6.6	*2.9	*3.5
Inflation	%	2.6	7.1	4.3	*1.4	*4.0
Unemployment	%	4.1	3.7	3.3	*3.0	*2.7
Exports (fob) (goods)	US$m	477.9	559.1	629.2	538.9	–
Imports (fob) (goods)	US$m	879.6	1,028.6	1,074.7	1,080.6	–
Balance of trade	US$m	-401.4	-469.4	-445.4	-541.7	–
Current account	US$m	-226.3	-280.0	-215.0	*-139.0	*-266.0
Total reserves minus gold	US$m	257.4	318.7	425.9	465.0	–
Foreign exchange	US$m	245.4	308.0	415.6	–	–
Exchange rate	per US$	12.15	13.05	12.06	13.23	–

* estimated figure ** forecast figure

due to Somali piracy. A record number of tourists (174,529) visited the island, with most arriving from France, Italy, Germany and the UK.

2011 In February, the government negotiated with the Somali Transitional Federal Government and the breakaway governments of Somaliland and Puntland (Somalia) to form a four-party agreement on repatriation of convicted Somali pirates. Four candidates took part in presidential elections held on 19–21 May. Incumbent James Michel (FPPS) won with 55.46 per cent, opposition leader, Wavel Ramkalawan (SNP) won 41.43 per cent. It was almost an exact repeat of the 2006 election results, including the third placing of independent Philippe Boullé with 1.66 per cent; Ralph Volcere (New Democratic Party (NDP)) achieved 1.45 per cent. The September parliamentary elections were boycotted by the main opposition party, the SNP, in protest at the failure by the government to revise electoral laws and the amount of spending political parties were allowed for election campaigning. Voting began in outlying islands in September and the rest of the country in October. The PP won 88.6 per cent of the vote and all of the 31 seats available; 31.9 per cent of votes cast were spoiled.

2012 On 31 October the bidding process to license 30 oil and gas exploration blocks in the territorial waters of the Seychelles were postponed until 2013, while the government awaited recommendations by the International Monetary Fund on how best to run the bidding. On 4 November two Seychellois hostages were released by Somali pirates after a year in captivity.

2013 The Puntland government has signed piracy-transfer agreements with the governments of Seychelles, Mauritius and Maldives, to bring convicted Somali pirates to complete their prison sentences in Puntland prisons, Puntland Counter-Piracy Director Abdirizak Mohamed Dirir has said. The United Nations Office on Drugs and Crime has overseen a prison construction project in Bosaso and Garowe for the purpose of housing convicted pirates. Seychelles plans to transfer 11 convicted Somali pirates to Puntland in Ocober, to serve the remainder of their prison terms.

2014 The *Maersk Alabama*, made famous by a 2009 pirate hijacking that was portrayed in the Oscar-nominated movie *Captain Phillips*, hit the headlines again in February when two guards were found dead in their cabin while the ship was docked in the Seychelles.

Political structure

Constitution

In a June 1993 referendum, a new constitution was approved, institutionalising multi-party politics and providing for the establishment of a National Assembly. This represented a complete overhaul of the original 1979 document that restricted Seychelles to a one-party state.

An amendment in August 1996 created the office of vice-president.

Form of state

Republic

The executive

Executive power rests with the president, elected for a five-year term; renewable three times.

National legislature

The unicameral Assemblée Nationale (National Assembly) has 34 members, of which 25 are directly elected by majority vote in single-seat constituencies, the remaining nine are elected by proportional representation. All members serve for five-year terms.

Last elections

19–21 May 2011 (presidential); 29 September–1 October 2011 (parliamentary)

Results: Presidential: James Michel (FPPS) won 55 per cent of the vote, Wavel Ramkalawan (SNP) 41 per cent, Philippe Boullé (independent) 1.66 per cent, Ralph Volcere (New Democratic Party (NDP)) 1.45 per cent.

Parliamentary: the Parti Lepep (People's Party) (PP) won 88.6 per cent of the vote (all of the 31 seats available) the Mouvement Populaire Démocratique (Popular Democratic Movement) (PDM) 10.89 per cent (0). Turnout was 74.3 per cent, but 31.9 per cent of votes cast were spoiled. The two main opposition parties (Mouvement Populaire Démocratique (Popular Democratic Movement) (PDM) and Seychelles National Party (SNP)) boycotted the elections.

Next elections

2016 (parliamentary and presidential)

Political parties

Ruling party

People's Party (Parti Lepep) (PP) (from 1993; re-elected 1 Oct 2011)

Main opposition party

Seychelles National Party (SNP)

Population

92,000 (2012)* Approximately 34 per cent of the total population is under 15 years.

Last census: 26 August 2010: 90,945

Population density: 178 inhabitants per square km. Urban population 55 per cent (2010 Unicef).

Annual growth rate: 1.0 per cent, 1990–2010 (Unicef).

Ethnic make-up

The islanders have a variety of ethnic origins – African, French, Indian, Chinese and Arab.

Religions

Practically the whole population is Christian, with 87 per cent belonging to the Roman Catholic faith.

Education

The government provides free education. The school-going age population is largely concentrated on Mahe, the main island where most of the economic activities are concentrated. There are only two private schools as well as public schools. Total expenditure in public education has grown in real terms. The pupil per capita cost in (public) primary schools is typically US$910.

Literacy rate: 90 per cent (plus)

Compulsory years: 6 to 15

Pupils per teacher: 15 in primary schools (Unesco)

Health

The Victoria Hospital has about 445 beds and there are 56 in-patient admissions per bed per year. Health care is provided free of charge.

Life expectancy: 72 years, 2004 (WHO 2006)

Fertility rate/Maternal mortality rate: 2.3 births per woman, 2009 (FAO 2012)

Birth rate/Death rate: 17 births per 1,000 population; 6.5 deaths per 1,000 population (2003).

Child (under 5 years) mortality rate (per 1,000): 13 per 1,000 live births (WHO 2012)

Head of population per physician: 1.15 physicians per 1,000 people, 2004 (WHO 2006)

Welfare

The social security law requires employers and employees to contribute to a national pension programme that gives retirees a modest pension. Self-employed persons contribute by paying 15 per cent of gross earnings. The government also provides low-cost housing and housing loans. There is welfare provision for children and the disabled.

Main cities

Victoria, on Mahé island (capital, estimated population 21,184 in 2012).

Languages spoken

Creole is the local language, but English is used in business and government circles. French is also widely spoken.

Official language/s

Creole, English and French

Media

Freedom of speech has been improved since 1993 however tough libel laws are used by the government to contain opposition opinion.

Press

Dailies: The government-owned newspaper *Seychelles Nation* (www.nation.sc) is published from Monday to Saturday.
Weeklies: *The People* (www.thepeople.sc) is published by the FPPS political party, while *Le Nouveau Seychelles Weekly* (www.seychellesweekly.com), and *Regar* are FPPS-opposition.
Periodicals: *The People* is a monthly publication. A few periodicals are also published in English, French and Creole.

Broadcasting

The state-run, Seychelles Broadcasting Corporation (www.sbc.sc) (formerly known as Radio Television Seychelles) operates the only television network along with its radio services in Creole, English and French. Both mediums carry advertising. Reception is good on Mahé and the other main islands.
Radio: Along with Paradise FM, the SBC service, international broadcast from, RFI, BBC and VOA may be picked up on shortwave radios.
The African Press Agency (ww.apanews.net) and Panapress (www.panapress.com) provide information from the Seychelles.

Economy

The service sector, dominated by tourism, constituted over 83 per cent of GDP in 2014, with industry comprising 14.0 per cent, of which manufacturing was around 9 per cent and agriculture 3.0 per cent.
The Seychelles escaped recession in 2009 after the International Monetary Fund (IMF) agreed to a three-year US$31.1 million loan (2009–12) to support public finances and establish macroeconomic stability. By the end of this three-year period, global trade had improved and visitor numbers had grown, leading to a GDP expansion of 6.0 per cent in 2012. Growth accelerated further in 2013, reaching 6.6 per cent before dropping to 3.8 per cent in 2014, as the tourist industry was adversely affected by the lack of demand in countries of origin (mainly in Europe). Growth is expected to remain moderate in 2015–16 at 3.5–4%.
Inflation has greatly fallen since being as high as 37.0 per cent in 2008 and 31.7 per cent in 2009. In 2010 the figure plunged into deflation at -2.4 per cent, before reaching the more stable rate of 1.4 per cent by 2014. Despite the swings in the economy, the Seychelles still has one of the highest standards of living in Africa, with a per capita income of US$15,359 in 2014.
Although tourism provides vitally needed foreign exchange, the government has acknowledged that tourism also has inherent drawbacks such as damage to the environment, major foreign currency spending on food, goods and services, and fuel imports. The risk to the Seychelles is in becoming an economic monoculture, which would be at the mercy of external shocks and forces. The government is intent on developing other means of income such as the fishing industry, which is currently a major foreign currency earner, telecommunications, financial services, light industry and international conferences. However, this will require considerable foreign investment and the government will need to institute policies and adopt attitudes more compliant to investors. Foreign direct investment has grown steadily from US$85.8 million in 2005 to US$165.7 million in 2012, however it plummeted to US$57.3 million in 2013 before increasing to US$111.2 million in 2014.

External trade

The Seychelles is a member of the Common Market for Eastern and Southern Africa (Comesa), and it operates within a free trade zone with 13 of the 19 member states.
The visible trade deficit is partially offset by earnings from tourism, which is the main foreign exchange earner, plus foreign aid and investment, rental from a US satellite tracking station and a BBC relay station.
Preferential import tariffs are granted to goods from Indian Ocean Commission (IOC) member countries – Mauritius, Comoros, Madagascar, Réunion. In return, Seychelles receives preferential import tariffs from IOC countries.

Imports

Principal imports are machinery and equipment, foodstuffs, petroleum products and chemicals.
Main sources: Saudi Arabia (23.6 per cent of total in 2014), Spain (9.8 per cent), France (5.2 per cent) and South Africa (4.6 per cent).

Exports

Principal exports are canned tuna, fresh/frozen fish, petroleum products (re-exports), copra and various herbs and spices including vanilla, cinnamon, nutmeg and mace.
Main destinations: France (24.8 per cent of total in 2014), UK (18.6 per cent), Italy (11.9 per cent), Japan (9.2 per cent), Mauritius (6.2 per cent) and Spain (4.2 per cent).

Re-exports

Petroleum products.

Agriculture

Farming

With the expansion of the tourist industry, the overall importance of agriculture to the economy has declined, although it is still important as a source of foreign exchange and employment. There is a shortage of cultivable land and fertile soil. Approximately 6.5 per cent of the total land area is agricultural, much of which is used for the production of copra and cinnamon, which are the major export crops. Farming is traditionally organic and eco-friendly.
Small quantities of coconuts, vanilla, tea and limes are exported. Crops grown for local consumption include tropical fruits, cassava, sweet potatoes, yams, sugar cane, bananas, tea and vegetables; rice, the staple food crop, has to be imported. Seychelles is self-sufficient in pork, chicken, fish and some vegetables.
There are a number of large farms, 650 small farms and thousands of smallholdings, which the government hopes will reduce dependence on imported foods.
Government reforms include privatisation of state farms, while setting up smaller co-operatives, new marketing structures, upgrading infrastructure and irrigation facilities for farms. An animal feed factory has been established by the Seychelles Marketing Board (SMB) to support production of meat and eggs. Almost 100 per cent of milk is imported. The government is encouraging the production of bananas and mangoes.

Fishing

The fishing industry is an important source of income and foreign exchange, accounting for around 85 per cent of domestically-produced exports. It is being expanded as part of the government policy of economic diversification, with foreign companies being encouraged to become involved. HJ Heinz acquired a 60 per cent majority stake in the government-owned Indian Ocean Tuna processing factory. Heinz has invested nearly US$8 million in the plant, which operates in the country's International Trade Zone. France and Italy are the main importers of Seychelles tuna.
The Seychelles sells fishing licences in its exclusive 1.3 million square km economic zone. Despite the desire for a growth in capacity and productivity through the development of commercial fishing operations, small-scale artisanal fishing still represents about one-third of fishing exports.
Illegal fishing still costs Africa some US$1.3 billion annually.

Industry and manufacturing

The industrial sector, including mining, manufacturing, construction and power, accounted for 15.4 per cent of GDP in 2013.
There is a small-scale manufacturing sector. The main activities include the production of canned tuna, soft drinks, juices, jams, beer, cigarettes, paints, assembling

of television sets and processing of cinnamon and coconuts.
Emphasis is on private-sector investment. The government aims to expand light industry in other areas such as artisanal products, packaging, assembly and services.

Tourism

The numerous islands that make up the Seychelles offer tourists a relaxing, tropical experience. Attractions include coral beaches, water sports and local wildlife. The tourist industry has become the most important sector in the economy, constituting 56.9 per cent of GDP in 2014. Employment from tourism totalled 57.3 per cent of total employment (25,500 jobs), and investment in the industry accounted for 29.5 per cent of total investment.
The Seychelles National Assessment Report (2004–09) outlining government and industry planning has been steadily introduced. The Report included providing value for money tourism and value added holidays, improved training for tourism staff, improved access by air and sea, diverse attractions and activities and protection of the environment. In 2009, the Seychelles Tourism Board was privatised, to make it more responsive to the industry. Several large hotels were refurbished to attract a higher level of clientele.

Mining

Some granite is quarried. Offshore surveys have indicated the presence of certain metals on the seabed.

Hydrocarbons

The Seychelles has some known hydrocarbon deposits but due to their size and inaccessibility they have not yet been exploited. However in December 2008 licences were issued to two relatively small oil companies to begin exploration of offshore oil deposits. Some gas reserves have been found offshore, but they have not yet been exploited in 2015.
The parastatal Seychelles Petroleum Company (Sepec) is responsible for purchasing, supplying, transhipment and trading in petroleum. It operates ports and storage terminals, including an 880 tonne liquefied petroleum gas (LPG) storage and cylinder filling plant.
The parastatal Seychelles National Oil Company (Snoc) implements state policy on hydrocarbon exploration.
Seychelles imports all of its oil needs, which were 9,060 barrels per day in 2013.
Any use of natural gas or coal is commercially insignificant.

Energy

Total installed generating capacity was 89MW in 2013. Electricity is provided from liquefied petroleum gas (LPG) and diesel-fired turbines.

Banking and insurance

Central bank

Central Bank of Seychelles

Time

GMT plus four hours

Geography

There are around 115 islands and islets comprising the Seychelles, which cover more than 1.3 million square km in the Indian Ocean, North of Madagascar and over 1,500km from the coast of Kenya.
The major islands are a compact group of 41 granite islands, the largest of which includes Mahé, Praslin and La Digue. These islands have high central granite ridges, the highest of which is Morne Seychellois (905 metres) on Mahé. Other islands are composed of coral and are low-lying; many are sparcely populated and four are uninhabited bird sanctuaries. All major islands are lush with vegetation dependent on the surface composition – forests cover the granite islands and coconut palms the coral islands.

Hemisphere

Southern

Climate

Tropical and humid. Average daily temperature are 24–32 degrees Celsius throughout the year. Hottest months are December–May; the wettest are from December–March and cooler from June–November. The islands lie outside the cyclone belt.

Entry requirements

Passports

Required by all and must be valid for at least six months beyond length of stay.

Visa

A Visitor's Permit is issued on arrival, valid for four weeks (extensions are possible for three-month periods). From 2009 EU citizens may make a short-stay visit, for up to three months, without a visa. A proposed tourist *univisa* (a single visa to visit all 15-member states of SADC: Angola, Botswana, DRC, Lesotho, Madagascar, Malawi, Mauritius, Mozambique, Namibia, South Africa, Seychelles, Swaziland, Tanzania, Zambia and Zimbabwe) is expected to be in use by 2013. Visitors should check with the appropriate consulates to confirm start of *univisas* and their scope before beginning a tour of southern Africa.
All visitors must have confirmed accommodation and sufficient funds for the intended length of stay and hold onward/return tickets or pay a deposit equivalent to the value of a return ticket to the country of origin.

Currency advice/regulations

Unlimited import/export of foreign currency is permitted. Only legal to exchange foreign currencies for Seychelles Rupees through a bank.
Travellers may take or send out of Seychelles up to SR100 of domestic currency.

Customs

Personal items, including one video and one single frame camera, a musical instrument, an item of portable electronic equipment and personal music player. Video tapes must be declared. Animals and agricultural products require an entry permit.

Prohibited imports

Firearms, illegal drugs and spear-fishing equipment.

Health (for visitors)

Mandatory precautions

Yellow fever certificate if arriving from infected area.

Advisable precautions

Inoculations and boosters should be current for tetanus, hepatitis A and diphtheria. There may be a need for vaccinations for typhoid, tuberculosis, hepatitis B and cholera. Anti-mosquito measures including mosquito repellents, nets and clothing covering the body should be used for protection against dengue fever, hepatitis B and chikungunya fever, which include mosquito repellents and nets and clothing that covers the body after dark. There is a risk of rabies.
There is a shortage of routine medications and visitors should take all necessary medicines with them. A first aid kit that includes disposable syringe, is a reasonable precaution. Use only bottled or boiled water for drinks, washing teeth and making ice. Eat only well cooked meals, preferably served hot; vegetables should be cooked and fruit peeled. Dairy products are unpasteurised and should be avoided, unless cooked.
Healthcare is not to Western standards and medical insurance, including emergency evacuation, is necessary.

Hotels

Good standard and widely available. All the large hotels in Mahé are on the beach. Advisable to book and confirm reservation in advance, particularly at Christmas and during August. Government trades tax of 5 per cent is added to bill, and usually also a service charge. Tipping optional.

Credit cards

Major credit cards widely accepted.

Public holidays (national)

Fixed dates

1–2 Jan (New Year), 1 May (Labour Day), 5 Jun (Liberation Day), 18 Jun (National Day), 15 Aug (Assumption Day/La Digue

Festival), 1 Nov (All Saints' Day), 8 Dec (Immaculate Conception), 25 Dec (Christmas Day).

Variable dates

Good Friday (Mar/Apr), Corpus Christi (May/Jun).

Working hours

Banking

Mon–Fri: 0830–1300; Sat: 0800–1200.

Business

Mon–Fri: 0800–1200, 1300–1600.

Government

Mon–Fri: 0800–1200, 1300–1600.

Shops

Mon–Fri: 0800–1200, 1330–1700; Sat: 0800–1200; some open Sun morning.

Telecommunications

Mobile/cell phones

There are 900 and 1800 GSM services available throughout Mahé and surrounding islands. In September 2013 the Seychelles government agreed that Airtel Mobile Commerce (Seychelles) Limited should engage in a pilot programme to test the practical and technical aspects of mobile payment services in the country. The Central Bank of Seychelles and department of information communications technology (DICT) will have oversight of the payment system and technological aspects, respectively.

Electricity supply

240V AC, 50 cycles. Plugs are three-pin bayonet.

Getting there

Air

National airline: Air Seychelles

International airport/s: Seychelles International (SEZ), on Mahé Island, 10km from Victoria; duty-free shop, bar, restaurant, bank and car hire.

Airport tax: Included in ticket price

Surface

Water: International shipping lines that maintain contacts with Seychelles may provide passenger services on cargo ships.

Main port/s: Victoria, on Mahé island.

Getting about

National transport

Air: Air Seychelles operates regular services from Mahé to Praslin, Desroches, Fregate, Bird and Dennis islands.

Aircraft charters are available to Assumption, Farquhar and Poivre. Helicopter Seychelles provides services and charters from Mahé.

Road: Only three islands have metalled road, Mahé, La Digue and Praslin; all other roads are unpaved tracks.

Buses: The Seychelles Public Transport Corporation (SPTC) operate regular services on Mahé from Victoria and Praslin, between 0520–2130.

Water: There are regular ferry services; a catamaran, Cat Cocos, links Mahé-Praslin, traditional schooners link Praslin-La Digue and La Digue-Mahé.

City transport

Taxis: Taxis are available on Mahé and Praslin, they are privately operated, but with government controlled rates. On Praslin a surcharge is levied between 2200–0600.

Car hire

There are a limited number of hire cars available on Mahé and Praslin; reservations during peak seasons should be made well in advance. A foreign or international driving licence is required. Driving is on the left, the speed limit outside urban areas is 65kph and 40kph in towns.

BUSINESS DIRECTORY

The addresses listed below are a selection only. While World of Information makes every endeavour to check these addresses, we cannot guarantee that changes have not been made, especially to telephone numbers and area codes. We would welcome any corrections.

Telephone area codes

The international dialling code (IDD) for Seychelles is +248, followed by subscriber's number.

Chambers of Commerce

Seychelles Chamber of Commerce & Industry, Ebrahim Building, PO Box 1399, Victoria, Mahé (tel: 323-812; fax: 321-422; e-mail: scci@seychelles.net).

Banking

Barclays Bank (Seychelles), PO Box 167, Victoria (tel: 383-838; email: barclays@seychelles.net).

Bank of Baroda, PO Box 124, Victoria, (tel: 323-037/8; email: baroda@seychelles.net).

Habib Bank, PO Box 702, Victoria (tel: 224-371/2; email: habibsez@seychelles.net).

Mauritius Commercial Bank (Seychelles), PO Box 122, Victoria (tel: 284-555; email: contact@mcbseychelles.com).

Nouvobanq (Seychelles International Mercantile Banking Corporation), PO Box 241, Ground Floor, Victoria House, State House Avenue, Victoria (tel: 293-000; fax: 224-670; email: nvb@nouvobanqu.sc).

Seychelles Savings Bank Limited; PO Box 531, Independence Ave, Victoria (tel: 293-000; fax: 224-713; email: ssb.savingsbank.sc).

Central bank

Central Bank of Seychelles, Independence Avenue, PO Box 701, Victoria, Mahé (tel: 225-200; fax: 224-958; e-mail: cbs@seychelles.sc).

Travel information

Air Seychelles, Victoria House, PO Box 386, Victoria (tel: 225-300; fax: 225-159; internet: www.airseychelles.com).

Helicopter Seychelles, Providence Industrial Estate; PO Box 595, Victoria (tel: 385-858; fax: 373-055; internet: www.helicopterseychelles.com).

Island Development Co (charter flights), New Port; PO Box 638, Mahé (tel: 224-640; fax: 224-467; email: idc@seychelles.sc).

National Travel Agency, Kingsgate House, PO Box 611, Victoria (tel: 224-900; fax: 225-111).

Seychelles Tourist Office–La Digue, La Passes, La Digue (tel/fax: 234-393; email: stbladigue@seychelles.sc).

Seychelles Tourist Office–Praslin, Iles des Palmes Airport, Grand Anse, Praslin (tel: 233-346; fax: 233-571; email: praslin@seychelles.sc).

Travel Services (Seychelles) Ltd., Victoria House, PO Box 356, Victoria (tel: 322-414; fax: 325-010).

Ministry of tourism

Ministry of Tourism and Transport, Independence House, PO Box 92, Victoria (tel: 225-313; fax: 225-131).

National tourist organisation offices

Seychelles Tourist Board, Bel Ombre; PO Box 1262, Victoria, Mahé (tel: 671-300, fax: 620-620; internet: www.seychelles.com).

Ministries

Investment Development Advisory Services (IDEAS), c/o Ministry of Finance and Communication, 3rd Floor, Central Bank Building, Box 313, Victoria (tel: 225-252; fax: 225-265).

Ministry of Administration and Manpower, National House, PO Box 56, Victoria (tel: 383-000; fax: 224-936).

Ministry of Agriculture and Marine Resources, Independence House, PO Box 166, Victoria (tel: 224-030; fax: 225-245).

Ministry of Community Development, Independence House, PO Box 199, Victoria (tel: 224-030; fax: 225-287).

Ministry of Education and Culture, Mont Fleuri (tel: 224-777; fax: 224-859).

Ministry of Finance and Communication, 3rd Floor, Central Bank Building, PO Box 313, Victoria (tel: 225-252; fax: 225-265).

Ministry of Foreign Affairs, Planning and Environment, Mont Fleuri (tel: 224-688; fax: 224-845).

Ministry of Health, PO Box 52, Mont Fleuri (tel: 388-000; fax: 224-792).

Ministry of Industry, Maison du People, Victoria (tel: 224-030; fax: 225-086).

Ministry of Local Government Youth and Sports, Oceangate House, Victoria (tel: 225-477; fax: 225-262).

Other useful addresses

Island Development Company (IDC), PO Box 638, New Port, Victoria (tel: 224-640; fax: 224-467).

Public Utilities Corporation (PUC) (Electricity), PO Box 174, Victoria (tel: 322-444; fax: 321-020). (Water) Unity House, PO Box 34, Victoria (tel: 322-444; fax: 322-127).

RTS Radio, PO Box 321, Union Vale, Victoria (tel: 224-161).

RTS TV, PO Box 321, Hermitage, Mahé (tel: 224-161).

Seychelles Agricultural Development Company Ltd., PO Box 172, Victoria (tel: 276-618).

Seychelles Broadcasting Corporation, Hermitage, PO Box 321, Victoria (tel: 224-161; fax: 224-641).

Seychelles Embassy (USA), Suite 400C, 800 Second Avenue, New York, NW, 10017 (tel: (+1-202) 972-1785; fax: (+1-202) 972-1786; e-mail: seychelles@un.int).

Seychelles Fishing Authority (SFA), PO Box 449, Victoria (tel: 224-521; fax: 224-508).

Seychelles Industrial Development Corporation (SIDEC), PO Box 537, Victoria (tel: 224-941; fax: 225-121).

Seychelles International Business Authority (SIBA), PO Box 991, Central Bank Building, Victoria (tel: 225-402; fax: 225-851).

Seychelles Licensing Authority, PO Box 3, Francis Rachel Street, Victoria (tel: 224-314; fax: 224-256).

Seychelles Marketing Board, PO Box 516, Victoria (tel: 224-444).

Seychelles National Statistics Bureau, PO Box 206, Victoria, (internet: www.seychelles.net/misdstat).

Seychelles Timber Company, Grand Anse, Mahe (tel: 278-343).

State Assurance Corporation ofSeychelles, Pirate's Arms Building, PO Box 636, Victoria (tel: 225-000; fax: 224-495).

Internet sites

Africa Business Network: www.ifc.org/abn

AllAfrica.com: http://allafrica.com

African Development Bank: www.afdb.org

Africa Online: www.africaonline.com

Mbendi AfroPaedia (information on companies, countries, industries and stock exchanges in Africa): http://mbendi.co.za

Seychelles Nation online: www.nation.sc

Sierra Leone

KEY FACTS

Official name: Republic of Sierra Leone

Head of State: President Ernest Bai Koroma (APC) (from 2007; re-elected 17 Nov 2012)

Head of government: President Ernest Bai Koroma

Ruling party: All People's Congress (APC) (from 2007; re-elected 17 Nov 2012)

Area: 72,325 square km

Population: 6.23 million (2014)*

Capital: Freetown

Official language: English

Currency: Leone (Le) = 100 cents

Exchange rate: Le4,638.00 per US$ (Sep 2015)

GDP per capita: US$808 (2014)*

GDP real growth: 6.04% (2014)*

GDP: US$5.03 billion (2014)*

Inflation: 8.30% (2014)

Balance of trade: -US$2.90 million (2013)

Annual FDI: US$714.97 million (2011)

* estimated figure

The British first opened up a trading post near Freetown in the seventeenth century, originally involved with the trade of timber and ivory, but later it expanded into slaves. After the abolition of the slave trade in 1807, British crews delivered thousands of Africans liberated from illegal slave ships to Sierra Leone, particularly Freetown, which had been built by freed slaves from Nova Scotia in the 1790s. The colony gradually expanded inland during the course of the eighteenth century before independence was attained in 1961. Democracy is slowly being re-established after the civil war (1991–2002) that resulted in tens of thousands of deaths and the displacement of approximately one third of the population (two million people). The military, which took over full responsibility for security after the departure of the UN peacekeepers at the end of 2005, is increasingly developing as a guarantor of the country's stability. The military did not disrupt the 2007 or 2012 national elections, and deployed over 850 peacekeepers to the African Union Mission in Somalia. As of January 2014, Sierra Leone also fielded 122 staff for five UN peacekeeping missions. In March 2014, the closure of the UN Integrated Peacebuilding Office in Sierra Leone marked the end of more than 15 years of peacekeeping and political operations in the country. The government's priorities for the future are to further development – including recovering from the Ebola epidemic – creating jobs, and ending endemic corruption.

The last general election was held on 17 November 2012, the result was a victory for the incumbent President Ernest Bai Koroma of the All People's Congress (APC), who received 58.7 per cent of the vote. The APC also won 67 of the 112 elected seats in Parliament. Julius Maada Bio stood as the main opposition to Bai Koroma, receiving 37.4 per cent of the vote. If Bai Koroma had received less than 55 per cent of the vote, a second round would have been necessary. Once President Bai Koroma was sworn in for another term on 23 November 2012, he said that he would continue to attract investment and fight corruption. The President is not eligible for a third term unless he manages to change the constitution which he may aim to do towards the end of his second term. The next general election in Sierra Leone is set to be held in 2017.

The economy

Sierra Leone is extremely poor with 43 per cent of the working population engaged in subsistence agriculture. The country possesses substantial mineral, agricultural, and fishery resources, however, it is still recovering from the civil war that destroyed most institutions before it ended in 2002. Economic growth was 20 per cent in 2013 before slumping to just 6 per cent in 2014 (against an 11.3 per cent projection) caused by the rapid spread of the Ebola virus. The virus caused a contraction of economic activity in several areas, including transportation, health, and industrial production. Growth has been driven by mining – particularly iron ore, although its production dropped dramatically in 2014 due to low global prices and high costs, driven by the epidemic. A long-term slowdown of the industry would badly affect the economy since it supports thousands of jobs and contributes 20 per cent of gross domestic product (GDP). Prior to 2014, the government had relied on external assistance to support its budget, although it was gradually becoming more independent. The epidemic's disruption to economic activity has deterred private investment, and forced the government to increase expenditures on health care, straining the budget and restricting other public investment projects. An increase in international donor support will partially offset these fiscal constraints. Foreign direct investment (FDI) was at a low of just US$144 million in 2013 before more than doubling to US$440 million in 2014.

Sierra Leone's significant mining wealth, the absence of discrimination against foreign companies and the nonappearance of restrictions on the repatriation of profits, as well as the sale of assets (guaranteed by the new investment code) makes Sierra Leone attractive for FDI. However, the shortage in skilled labour, the lack of infrastructure, the slow legal system, the high level of corruption, political violence and serious social disorder due to social disparities are major obstacles to FDI. Sierra Leone ranked 140 out of 189 countries in the World Bank's 2015 *Doing Business Report*. The country's main investors are Belgium, Germany and the United States. China has also increased its presence in Sierra Leone and has helped finance a new airport, a hospital, a hydroelectric dam, a rubber production project spanning several thousand hectares (worth US$1.2 billion, financed by China Hainan Rubber Group) and rice cultivation (100,000 hectares).

According to the African Development Bank in its *African Economic Outlook 2015* (AEO), prior to the Ebola outbreak of May 2014, considerable progress had been made since the end of the civil conflict but the economic outlook in the medium term is now unfavourable. Economic growth is predicted to go as low as -2.5 per cent in 2015 before reaching 2.8 per cent in 2016. Inflation has been revised upwards from 8.8 per cent to 10 per cent for 2014 and is projected for 9.4 per cent and 8.3 per cent for 2015 and 2016, respectively. Infrastructure deficiencies post a serious threat to private-sector development although some progress had been made in improving the business environment prior to the outbreak of Ebola. Public debt levels (domestic and external) remain sustainable but historically, public finances have been stressed as total revenue has consistently been lower than public spending.

Regarding regional integration, challenges remain in the free movement of people and capital across the Economic Community of West African States (ECOWAS) countries, although the situation had been improving in recent years until the advent of the emergency restrictions imposed in the wake of the Ebola outbreak. The spatial nexus in Sierra Leone is such that the urban population has the vast majority of services, assets and earned income and is likely to bequeath more to successor generations compared to the rural population. There is no dedicated strategy for spatial inclusion in Sierra Leone, however, the essential elements of it are subsumed in the country's medium-term plan, the Agenda for Prosperity (2013–18).

Ebola

The World Health Organisation declared Sierra Leone free of Ebola on 6 November 2015, prompting nationwide celebrations tinged with sadness over the 3,589 lives the virus claimed (8,704 people were infected). The outbreak had lasted 17 months in Sierra Leone and although President Bai Koroma has ended the state of emergency declared during the outbreak, the country will now enter a 90-day period of heightened surveillance to make sure the virus does not return. The swabbing of dead bodies will be mandatory until June 2016 and the National Ebola Response Centre (NERC) will continue to operate until the end of 2015.

Ebola spread to Sierra Leone in May 2014, when two women were diagnosed as the country's first cases. Both had attended the funeral of a widely respected faith healer who had been attending to patients in a village a few hours' walk from Gueckedou in Guinea, where the outbreak began. At the peak of the outbreak in 2014, Sierra Leone was reporting hundreds of new cases a week, people queued for treatment at hospitals too full to cope and corpses were left on the streets.

Nearby Kenema district became the country's second major Ebola concentration. Luckily, Kenema government hospital already had a well-equipped isolation ward – in fact, the only Lassa fever isolation ward anywhere in the world. Initially, Sierra Leone's Lassa Fever Programme employed its contact-tracing staff and skills to try to contain the outbreak, but the capacity was simply overwhelmed. The triangular border area where the three countries – Guinea, Liberia and Sierra Leone – meet with each other was later identified as the cradle of the outbreak.

As in neighbouring Guinea, the virus spread quickly and widely, with a large proportion of doctors and nurses among the dead – severely depleting the response capacity (221 healthcare workers died during the outbreak). As in Guinea, the virus inevitably found its way to the capital city, Freetown, where it took advantage of overcrowded living conditions and fluid population movements to grow in explosive numbers. In July the head of Sierra Leone's Lassa Fever Programme, Dr Sheik Humarr Khan, a virologist and world-renowned expert on viral haemorrhagic fevers, died of Ebola aged only 39. Dr Khan had correctly identified the first case of Ebola, which had at first been wrongly diagnosed as Lassa. Although he wore a biohazard protective suit and all the accessories, it appeared that Dr Khan had simply succumbed to the rampant Ebola virus particles circulating in his

KEY INDICATORS — Sierra Leone

	Unit	2011	2012	2013	2014	**2015
Population	m	*6.00	5.98	*6.10	*6.23	*6.32
Gross domestic product (GDP)	US$bn	2.20	3.79	4.90	*5.03	*4.40
GDP per capita	US$	366	634	803	*808	0
GDP real growth	%	5.3	15.2	20.1	*6.0	*-12.8
GNP per capita	US$	0	0	0	0	*696
Inflation	%	18.5	13.8	9.8	8.3	*13.1
Exports (fob) (goods)	US$m	381.5	1,162.1	2,004.3	–	–
Imports (fob) (goods)	US$m	1,631.1	2,020.4	2,007.2	–	–
Balance of trade	US$m	-1,249.6	-858.3	-2.9	–	–
Current account	US$m	-1,531.0	-1,389.0	-512.0	*-382.0	*-582.0
Total reserves minus gold	US$m	421.1	478.0	532.5	600.8	–
Foreign exchange	US$m	231.4	306.1	367.4	–	–
Exchange rate	per US$	4,230.52	4,334.20	4,328.00	4,236.48	–

* estimated figure ** forecast figure

institute's air. Sierra Leone – and the international public health community – had lost one of its most respected and influential medical experts.

A breakthrough in the scientific understanding of Sierra Leone's outbreak came on 28 August, when the journal *Science* published the results of a major surveillance study of Ebola virus genomes, involving 99 complete virus sequences, that traced the start of the outbreak and its further spread. No such massive study had ever been undertaken before. The study confirmed the healer's funeral as a seminal event at the outbreak's explosive start, demonstrated that the virus's genome is changing fairly quickly and pinpointed 2004 as the year when the virus changed. The study also demonstrated a pattern of what was termed 'adaptive mutation'; the authors called for an urgent scaling up of control measures – lest the virus adapt to establish permanent residence in the affected areas. The study was not, however, designed to determine whether changes in the virus were linked to either the epidemiology or the severity of this outbreak. Nonetheless, understanding the outbreak appeared to be benefiting from the application of science, which could only contribute to response efforts in affected countries. Sadly and ironically, five co-authors of the study, who had contributed greatly to public health and research in Sierra Leone, contracted Ebola and died before the paper was published.

In September 2014 Sierra Leone's most urgent needs included opening up more Ebola care facilities – which meant more trained staff to meet a severe shortage. The British government despatched a Royal Navy vessel and a contingent of trained army medical staff to Freetown to assist the government as part of WHO and NGO operations. Controlling the spread of the disease will also require stronger district surveillance and epidemiology, contact tracing and burial teams.

Given Sierra Leone's violent recent history, it is both surprising and refreshing to discover that it is one of the few, possibly the only, countries where religious tolerance goes beyond a simple acceptance of a different theology. In Sierra Leone Christianity and Islam are not antagonistic; relations between the two are remarkably friendly. President Koroma, a Christian won the presidential election although 70 per cent of Sierra Leone's electorate is Muslim. The country's vice president, Samuel Sam-Sumana, is a Muslim. A May 2014 article in the London *Economist* pointed out that during the horrendous civil war of the 1990s religion was not on the agenda.

Given the delicate state of relations between President Koroma and Vice President Sumana, it is probably just as well that religion does not feature in Sierra Leone's political mix. Rumours and allegations of corruption have long circled around the presidential and vice presidential offices. Some international organisations have estimated that as a result of unsatisfactory mining negotiations and generous concessions, the government is set to lose revenues of US$131 million in the three years from 2014–16 from corporate income tax incentives granted to five mining companies – an average of US$43.7 million a year. Shockingly, if tax expenditure continues in its present trend, it is likely that Sierra Leone will also lose more than US$240 million a year from tax incentives in the near future. On Transparency International's 2014 *Corruption Perceptions Index* Sierra Leone ranked 119 out of the 174 countries surveyed. Its ranking position was the same as Mozambique, Belarus, Tanzania and Vietnam.

Risk assessment

Politics	Fair
Economy	Fair/good
Regional stability	Fair/good

COUNTRY PROFILE

1787 The state was founded by the British as a homeland for freed slaves.

1808 Freetown became a British colony. Over the following 60 years around 70,000 ex-slaves arrived in the country, mainly in the Freetown area. The colonial authorities appointed non-Indigenous Africans to the civil service and senior administrative positions, thus laying the foundation for future civil strife.

1954 Sierra Leone was allowed some degree of self-rule through a new local administration. Sir Milton Margai of the Sierra Leone People's Party (SLPP) was appointed the head of the newly-established administration.

1961 Sierra Leone gained independence from Britain in April, but remained part of the Commonwealth. Sir Milton Margai became the country's first prime minister.

1964 Following Sir Milton's death, his half-brother, Sir Albert Margai, was appointed prime minister.

1967 The All Peoples Congress (APC) won the parliamentary election, its leader, Siaka Stevens, was appointed prime minister. Sierra Leonean military officers staged a coup.

1968 After an army revolt, Stevens and the APC returned to government.

1971 Sierra Leone became a republic. Stevens was appointed as the country's first president.

1978 A new constitution established one-party rule with the APC as the only legal party.

1985 Stevens retired, Major General Joseph Momoh became president.

1991 Rebels opposed to the Momoh government – principally the Revolutionary United Front (RUF) led by Foday Sankoh – launched a series of attacks, which took much of the eastern part of the country. They were backed by Liberia.

1992 A coup brought Captain Valentine Strasser to power. He presided over a military government, which suspended the constitution and ruled by decree.

1996 Strasser was deposed by Brigadier Julius Bio. Multi-party elections ended four years of military rule. Ahmed Tejan Kabbah (SLPP) became president.

1997 Major Johnny-Paul Koroma led a coup and ousted Kabbah, who went into exile. The Armed Forces Revolutionary Council (ARFC) was installed, backed by the RUF. International sanctions were imposed. The Economic Community of West African States (Ecowas) dispatched a peace-keeping force – Ecowas Monitoring Group (Ecomog) – in order to reinstate the government of President Kabbah. A peace accord was reached in October.

1998 Ecomog launched a military offensive against the AFRC after Koroma showed no sign of implementing the 1997 agreement and stepping down from power. Ecomog ejected the AFRC from Freetown and Kabbah returned to Sierra Leone. The RUF remained in control of large areas outside the capital. The civilian population in rebel held territories were subjected to brutal treatment, with limb amputations meted out to victims of all ages.

1999 RUF rebels counter-attacked the capital and were finally driven off after weeks of fierce fighting. Liberia was accused of supporting the rebels and trading weapons for diamonds, mined in rebel territories. The government and the RUF signed a peace agreement, allowing for the deployment of UN peace-keeping forces.

2000 Foday Sankoh condemned the presence of UN forces in the country. The UN reported that civilians continued to be mutilated, raped and abducted in rebel held areas. RUF rebels clashed with UN troops when they were required to disarm. Over 13,000 UN troops held a limited peace in the south while British paratroopers trained government forces. Under a UK plan, several thousand British troops arrived to stabilise President Kabbah's regime. Sankoh was captured in Freetown where he had been hiding for weeks.

Within two months, Britain withdrew most of its forces leaving a contingent to continue training local government forces.
2001 Military operations continued to push into lawless regions of the country and restore civil society. Legislative and presidential elections were postponed due to the unstable security situation.
2002 The 11-year civil war was officially declared ended and state of emergency measures were lifted. Ahmad Tejan Kabbah (SLPP) won a landslide victory as president. The SLPP won the parliamentary elections.
2003 Agriculture production recovered to pre-war levels, as many people displaced during the civil war returned to their homes. Rebel leader Foday Sankoh died of natural causes while awaiting trial for war crimes.
2004 The first local elections in more than three decades were held. A war crimes court, staffed by senior US legal personnel, began taking evidence for a court mandated for three years and empowered to 'arrest, try and convict' those accused of war crimes.
2005 The UN agreed that Charles Taylor should be handed over to Sierra Leone to stand trial for war crimes perpetrated by Sierra Leone insurgents he had supported while he was Liberian president. The last UN-troops withdrew.
2006 Former Liberian president Charles Taylor was flown from his exile in Nigeria to Freetown, where he was wanted for war crimes and his alleged role in Sierra Leone's civil war. Taylor was transferred to stand trial in the International Court of Justice (ICJ) in The Hague (The Netherlands). The transfer was made possible after the UK agreed to provide detention facilities if Taylor was convicted. In a deal with creditors, around 90 per cent of Sierra Leone's debt, worth about US$1.64 billion, was written off following measures undertaken to stabilise the economy, tackle poverty and improve governance, with reforms in the economy, health, education and government administration. External debt was reduced to around US$110 million.
2007 The Paris Club of creditors forgave a further US$218 million of Sierra Leone's debt. The World Bank advised that the money which would have been spent on debt servicing should be spent on 'legitimate things for the people'. The vital Mano River Bridge, connecting Sierra Leone with Liberia, was officially re-opened in June. In general elections the opposition APC won 59 seats (out of 112), the SLPP 43. After two rounds in the presidential election, Ernest Bai Koroma (APC) won 54.6 per cent and Solomon Berewa (SLPP) won 45.5 per cent.
2009 A special international court (modelled on the Second World War Nuremberg tribunal) convicted three men of the RUF – 'Interim Leader' Issa Hassan Sesay, former commander Morris Kallon and Chief of Security Augustine Gbao – of war crimes including murder, rape, enforced recruiting of child soldiers, sexual slavery and the mutilating of limbs, which took place under their leadership during the civil war.
2010 Two senior officers of the defence ministry were indicted for corruption in the country's first major criminal case against corrupt officials. They were convicted, fined and imprisoned. The Sierra Leonean Human Rights Commission called for the uncut diamonds that Charles Taylor had given to fashion model Naomi Campbell at a party in South Africa and which she had given to aid the Nelson Mandela Children's Fund, to be returned to benefit the people of Sierra Leone. UN sanctions, including a ban on diamond exports and an arms embargo, imposed in 1998 were lifted. A new offshore oil field discovery was announced by the Spanish oil company, Repsol.
2011 Former junta leader (1996), Julius Maada Bio (Sierra Leone People's Party (SLPP)) declared his candidacy for the 2012 presidential elections.
2012 On 30 May the ICC sentenced Charles Taylor to 50 years in jail, to be served in the UK. The senior judge said Taylor 'aided and abetted' RUF rebels in prolonging a conflict where 'the lives of many more innocent civilians in Sierra Leone were lost or destroyed as a direct result of his actions.' A cholera outbreak that began early in the year had by 20 August killed 176 people and infected over 10,000. The presidential election took place on 17 November, in which nine candidates took part. Incumbent Ernest Bai Koroma (APC) won 58.7 per cent of the vote, his nearest rival, Julius Maada Bio (SLPP) won 37.4 per cent; no other candidate won over 1.5 per cent of the vote. In parliamentary elections held on the same day, the APC won 67 seats (out of 109 elected seats) and the SLPP won 42; seven other political parties and independents failed to win any seats. 12 hereditary chiefs were elected to parliament by their communities. The turnout was 87.3 per cent.
2013 On 7 August Ibrahim Bah, also known as Ibrahim Baldeh, a former ally of ex-President Charles Taylor, was deported to his home country of Senegal; he had been accused in a UN report as having supplied arms to the rebels during the 11-year civil war.
2014 Guinea announced an outbreak of the deadly Ebola virus in Conakry on 27 March; by July the total number of deaths across the region, including Sierra Leone, Liberia and Guinea, had reached over 670. Deaths in Sierra Leone from the Ebola virus up to 29 October were said, by WHO, to be 1,510 (out of a total for West Africa of 4,951).
2015 On 1 March Vice President Samuel Sam-Sumana said that he was putting himself into quarantine after one of his body guards died of Ebola. On 14 March he was reported to have gone into hiding and was seeking political asylum at the US embassy after troops withdrew his security detail; a government spokesperson, however, said the troops had been sent to strengthen the quarantine. Deaths in Sierra Leone since the ebola outbreak started in 2014 were reported by the WHO to be 3,904 (out of a total of 11,079 'probable, confirmed or suspected deaths') by 9 May. For the first time since the outbreak of ebola in May 2014 there were no new cases in the week ending 14 August.

Political structure

Constitution

The 1991 referendum, adopting a multi-party parliamentary system, based on the US model, was amended in 2002, and introduced the District Block System (DBS) for voting.

Independence date

27 April 1961

Form of state

Unitary republic

The executive

Executive power is vested in the president, who is both Head of State and head of government. The president is directly elected for up to two, five-year terms. The president appoints ministers, approved by parliament. The cabinet is composed of ministers who are answerable to the president.

National legislature

The unicameral Parliament (sometimes referred to as the House of Representatives) has 124 members, of which 112 are elected in multi-seat constituencies by proportional representation from party lists – with a threshold of 12.5 per cent necessary for any constituency. The remaining 12 members are indirectly elected paramount chiefs. All members serve for five-year terms.

Legal system

It is based on English law and is composed of a Supreme Court, Appeals Court and a High Court.
A special war crimes court, operating under Sierra Leonean law, was set up in 2004 to try those accused of heinous war crimes.

Last elections

17 November 2012 (parliamentary and presidential)

Results: Parliamentary: the All Peoples Congress (APC) won 53.67 per cent of the vote (59 seats out of 109 elected seats), the Sierra Leone People's Party (SLPP) 38.25 per cent (43), the People's Movement for Democratic Change (PMDC) 3.23 per cent (none; it lost 10 seats won in 2007), six other political parties and independents each won less than 1.5 per cent of the vote and failed to win any seats. 12 hereditary chiefs were elected to parliament by their communities.
Presidential: Ernest Bai Koroma (APC) won 58.7 per cent of the vote, Julius Maada Bio (SLPP) 37.4 per cent; seven other candidate each won less than 1.5 per cent of the vote. Turnout was 87.3 per cent.

Next elections

2017 (presidential and legislative)

Political parties

Ruling party

All People's Congress (APC) (from 2007; re-elected 17 Nov 2012)

Main opposition party

Sierra Leone People's Party (SLPP)

Population

6.16 million (2012)*
Last census: December 2004: 4,963,298 (provisional)
Population density: 66 inhabitants per square km. Urban population 38 per cent (2010 Unicef).
Annual growth rate: 1.9 per cent, 1990–2010 (Unicef).

Ethnic make-up

African groups: Temne (30 per cent), Mende (30 per cent), others (20 per cent)); Creole (Krio) (descendants of freed Jamaican slaves settled in the Freetown area in the late-18th century) (10 per cent); refugees from Liberia's civil war and small numbers of Europeans, Lebanese, Pakistanis and Indians.

Religions

Islam (60 per cent), indigenous beliefs (30 per cent), Christian (10 per cent).

Education

Government plans to increase primary school enrolment and to reduce the gender gap in education has only been under way since 2001 and while enrolment levels are rising the gender gap has also widened. The civil conflict has left about 50 per cent of primary schools functioning in inadequate accommodation. Unicef is assisting in the provision of teaching and learning materials and teacher training, it is also funding the Complementary Rapid Education for Primary Schools (CREPS) programme, designed to enable over-aged children to complete the primary school programme.
Primary education begins at aged six and lasts for six years. Junior secondary school lasts for three years. Students who are successfully may progress to the senior secondary school for a further three years and then onto university.
The University of Sierra Leone is the only institute of higher learning.
Literacy rate: 36 per cent (2004)
Compulsory years: Six to 12.
Enrolment rate: Primary school net enrolment/attendance was 69 per cent; 2005–09 (Unicef 2010).

Health

UN programmes aid the healthcare system to improve the country's ranking in the Human Development Index which is only one higher than Niger which, in 2005, is the lowest ranking. Around 70 per cent of the population lives below the poverty line.
Technical aid, rehabilitation and funding will be provided through a four-year programme (2004–07), including measures to improve water sources and sanitation and HIV/Aids education and prevention.
Donor support will have to be sustained over the long-term to cope with the ongoing rehabilitating of civil war amputees.
In April 2010, a new healthcare programme was launched providing treatment free of charge for pregnant women, breast-feeding mothers and children under the age of five years.

HIV/Aids

Aids has killed between two to three times more people than during the civil war, yet has received relatively little attention. Around 68,000 people are infected with HIV/Aids, 3,300 of them are under 15-years-old. Since the beginning of the epidemic, over 56,000 children have lost their mother or both parents. The spread of the disease is due to a low prevelance of condom use.
HIV prevalence: 0.9 per cent adult population (government statistic)
The Global Fund to Fight HIV/Aids, Tuberculosis and Malaria states government statistic significantly underestimates the prevalence rate and puts the figure closer to 3.4 per cent generally, and 5 per cent in Freetown. An international medical charity that undertook a study in Freetown in 2004 found a prevalence rate of 4.6 per cent among prenatal women, a typically non-risk group, which suggests the prevalence rate could be higher even than the Global Funds' estimation.
In February 2005 the government announced that it would undertake a nationwide survey to provide 'baseline information' about HIV/Aids in Sierra Leone.
Life expectancy: 39 years, 2004 (WHO 2006)
Fertility rate/Maternal mortality rate: 5.0 births per woman, 2010 (Unicef); maternal mortality, 1,800 per 100,000 live births (Unicef 2004).
Birth rate/Death rate: 44 births per 1,000 population; 20.7 deaths per 1,000 population (2003).
Child (under 5 years) mortality rate (per 1,000): 182 per 1,000 live births (WHO 2012)
Head of population per physician: 0.03 physicians per 1,000 people, 2004 (WHO 2006)

Main cities

Freetown (capital, estimated population 853,651 in 2012), Bo (233,684), Kenema (182,106), Makeni (109,125), Koidu (92,770), Lunsar (24,450), Port Koko (23,195).

Languages spoken

English is the main medium for business. Mende is spoken principally in the south, Temne in the north and Krio (English-based Creole) is spoken by 10 per cent of the population and understood by 95 per cent.

Official language/s

English

Media

Press

Dailies: In English, main newspapers are *Concord Times* (www.concordtimessl.com), *Standard Times Press* (http://standardtimespress.net) and Awoko (www.awoko.org), *Awareness Times* (http://awarenesstimes.com) and Christian Monitor (www.christian-monitor.org).
Weeklies: Weeklies include *New Sierra Leonean*, *Vision* and *Weekend Spark*.
Business: The Ministry of Information and Broadcasting publishes the quarterly *Sierra Leone Trade Journal*.

Broadcasting

Radio: The government-owned Sierra Leone Broadcasting Service (SLBS) broadcasts in English, French and local languages. There are several private stations operating in the Freetown area, including Sky FM, Kiss Fm, Radio Democracy (run by the UN) and Voice of the Handicapped (set up for the disabled, injured during the civil war, but attracting a wider audience). International broadcast from RFI and BBC can be received.
Television: There are two commercial TV stations (mainly received in Freetown area) operated by SLBS and ABC TV.
The African Press Agency (ww.apanews.net) and Panapress (www.panapress.com) provide information from Sierra Leone.

Economy

The economy is still dependent on its agricultural base, which although primarily subsistence farming, constituted 42.5 per cent of GDP in 2014; the services sector comprised 30.7 per cent and industry 26.8 per cent. The extraction industry consists of mining large quantities of alluvial diamonds, plus deposits of other valuable minerals such as rutile, bauxite, gold and iron ore. Sierra Leone's mining sector is of vital importance to bringing in foreign exchange. Before 1995 and the beginning of a series of civil wars, when its rutile (titanium ore) and bauxite operations closed down, the sector used to contribute around 20 per cent of GDP. In 2014, due to declining international market prices, lossmaking mines were closed down bringing the mining sector to a halt. Sierra Leone also has other natural resources such as timber, fresh water and offshore fishing grounds; its agricultural products include coffee, palm oil, cassava, rice and livestock

Since 2002, when the civil war ended, the economy has recovered, with GDP growth reaching as high as 15.2 per cent by 2012, and even further to 20.1 per cent in 2013. However, due to the break out of the Ebola virus and the closure of the mining sector, growth in 2014 fell to 6.0 per cent. Inflation has been historically high and long-term, but it has dropped below double digits in 2014 to 8.3 per cent from 10.3 per cent in 2013.

In 2014, the UN Human Development Index (HDI) ranked Sierra Leone183 (out of 187) for national development in health, education and income. In 2014, 72.7 per cent of the population lived in multidimensional poverty, while 51.7 per cent lived below the equivalent of US$1.25 per day. To promote growth and reduce poverty the government has focused on six key areas: state security, a sustainable fiscal position, raising domestic savings and investment, increasing infrastructure, agricultural and rural development and promoting the private sector.

Diamond exports are the largest foreign exchange earner, with annual production estimated at between US$250–300 million, despite losses through illegal smuggling activities. Around a quarter of taxes levied on diamond production is reinvested in mining communities to provide social assets such as schools and roads, as well as co-operatives to help miners market their finds.

The economy is broadly open with the government attempting to attract direct foreign investment (FDI) through the sale of state-owned financial, utility, commercial and transport entities. FDI was US$144 million in 2013, down from US$950 million in 2011. FDI has since increased to US$440 million in 2014. Because outright sale of national assets might be unpalatable to the majority of Sierra Leoneans, the government proposed incremental privatisation, with management contracts offered along with public/private partnerships. Sierra Leone has one of the worst rates of gross domestic savings in Africa and much remains to be done to encourage a reversal in this pattern.

External trade

Sierra Leone is a member of the Economic Community of West African States (Ecowas), which was set up to promote economic integration among members. It has a customs union with Liberia and Guinea.

Mining natural resources provides the majority of export earnings with gem-quality diamonds being paramount. Diamond exports, in the first half of 2015 however, had halved due to the devastation of the Ebola virus. Gold exports were also affected, falling to a third of the January figure by June 2015.

Cash crops, coffee, cocoa and palm oil, are exported to Europe.

Imports

Principal imports are foodstuffs (typically over 30 per cent of total value), machinery and vehicles, manufactured goods, fuels and lubricants, building materials, cloths and textiles.

Main sources: China (13.2 per cent of total in 2014), US (7.1 per cent), India (6.8 per cent)

Exports

Commodity exports include diamonds, rutile, bauxite, coffee, cocoa, fish and live animals.

Main destinations: China (80 per cent of total in 2014), Belgium (8.8 per cent)

Agriculture

Farming

The civil war seriously disrupted agricultural activity, destroying the homes and livelihood of many farming families. This will impact on food security for a number of years to come.

The agricultural sector contributed 42.5 per cent to GDP in 2014 and employs 65–75 per cent of labour force. Many young people have left rural areas since 2002 to find work in the cities.

Area under cultivation is approximately 25 per cent of the total land area. It is limited by a traditional land tenure system and is mostly in the hands of smallholders engaged in subsistence farming.

Major cash export crops are cocoa, coffee, palm kernels and ginger. Despite government efforts towards self-sufficiency, rice imports have risen. Other food crops include maize, cassava, sweet potatoes and sorghum.

Production has been hampered by poor infrastructure, a lack of incentives and a poor marketing and distribution system.

Fishing

The fishing sector has two distinct patterns. Coastal fishing, undertaken by men, is commercially driven with catches either sold fresh or preserved for transport inland. Inland fishing is performed by women and largely for private consumption.

While coastal fishing fleets have contracted over the 2000s production has risen.

The majority of vessels harvest shrimps.

Forestry

The majority of timber production is used as domestic fuel.

The Gola Forest Reserve, on the eastern border with Liberia, was designated as a national park. In 2008, the government re-imposed an export ban on timber. It accused foreign companies, in particular Chinese loggers, of plundering the country's timber assets and causing serious soil erosion. The ban will be lifted when a policy that benefits local communities and re-planting has been achieved.

Industry and manufacturing

The industrial sector accounts for around 30 per cent of GDP and employs 5 per cent of the workforce.

The sector is mainly limited to food processing and light manufacturing of consumer goods such as cigarettes, alcoholic beverages, plastic footwear, nails, paint and confectionery. Emphasis is placed on import substitution industries, but attempts to establish heavy industry have met with only limited success and have been undermined by political instability.

Expansion is limited by weak local demand, power shortages, foreign exchange shortages and low investment.

Tourism

A decade after the end of the civil war and Sierra Leone has made great strides to offer new attractions in ecotourism and modern accommodation. However, the breakout of the Ebola virus in 2014 has had large adverse affects on the tourism industry. Before this annual visitor numbers were rising, from 52,000 in 2011 to 81,000 in 2013.

Travel and tourism contributed 3.6 per cent to GDP in 2014 and provided employment to 4.0 per cent of the workforce (49,500 extended jobs) over the same period.

The government considers tourism as an important industry to promote growth and as such has been active in its campaign to secure greater foreign direct investment (FDI), to improve infrastructure and other tourism related facilities. In 2014, tourism attracted 4.6 per cent of total investment.

Mining

Gold and diamonds play an essential part in the economy. However, over the first half of 2015 gold exports reduced to a third of their January 2014 value, whilst diamond exports were reduced by a half.

The government, in an effort to bring artisanal mining into legal and regulated operation and minimise smuggling, has introduced a certification system for exporting diamonds and created a mining community development fund to return a percentage of the taxes back to the local population.

Sierra Leone has one of the world's largest deposits of rutile (a titanium ore). The Sierra Rutile mining operation was closed and damaged during the civil war. Bauxite mining is also an important sector with large reserves at Sieromco and Port Loko. Production was suspended due to the civil war. Foreign investment is necessary to begin a re-start operation.

Due to the decline in international market prices in 2014, there has been a mass closure of lossmaking mines, bringing the mining industry to a halt.

Hydrocarbons

All hydrocarbon needs are met by imports.

There are large deposits of oil and natural gas offshore within the West African region, which are not economically viable to extract currently.

In 2012, the US energy company Anadarko Petroleum announced that it had discovered its second offshore oil field in Sierra Leone's territorial waters. Chevron Corporation, the US-energy company and one of a three-company partnership in Sierra Leone, announced on 26 September 2012 that the government had awarded it two blocks with rights to deep-water exploration for hydrocarbons. The blocks are offshore, south-west of Freetown.

Energy

Total installed electricity generating capacity was 102MW in 2013, mostly from conventional oil-fired thermal power stations. Around 5 per cent of the population has access to electricity and blackouts are frequent due to the unstable power supply. The Sierra Leone Electricity Company (SLEC) oversees electricity generation and supply.

A 50MW Bumbuna hydroelectric project began construction on the Seli River in 1980s but was halted in the 1990s during the civil war. However, international loans of US$91.8 million, funnelled through the World Bank, allowed building to continue, so that by April 2009 water was being captured, prior to release for production. A stable supply of electricity and a reduction in the unit price of electricity will be the initial benefits of the project.

The government, in an effort to find renewable sources of energy, is considering biomass, of which 656,000 tonnes of crop waste is produced annually, which could produce 2,700 gigawatt hours (gWh); solar photovoltaic for lighting and water pumping; wind power to suit intermittent use and an increase in hydropower. It has been estimated that Sierra Leone could produce 11 terrawatt hours (tWh) a year, given full exploitation of its hydro capacity. There is an extra 50MW capacity by hydropower under construction with another 85MW planned.

The serious energy shortage has forced many citizens to buy personal diesel generators; the majority of the population uses biomass (wood fuel, kerosene and charcoal) for energy.

Banking and insurance

The banking sector has been weakened by war. However, the government has given the central bank power to tighten fiscal controls and prepare some for sale. The IMF is wary of donor funds that are distributed through local banks, bypassing the close scutiny and anti-corruption measures instituted by the central bank.

It was announced in March 2005 that the introduction of the shared currency, the eco, in Sierra Leone, Ghana, Guinea, Nigeria and The Gambia, which was due in July 2005, would be postponed. The currency was proposed to facilitate trade and growth with an ultimate plan to merge it with the CFA franc.

Central bank

Bank of Sierra Leone

Main financial centre

Freetown

Time

GMT

Geography

Sierra Leone – lion mountains, as named by an early Portuguese explorer – lies on the west coast of Africa; Guinea encircles it from the north-west around to the east and Liberia borders it to the south. There is a 400km Atlantic coastline in the west. The Guinea highlands cross the country from the south-east to the north. The tallest peak is Bintimani (1,948 metres) in the Loma Mountains of central Sierra Leone. There are a number of rivers, two of which have estuaries navigable by ocean-going ships, the Jong and the Rokel. The Freetown peninsular is heavily forested, mangrove swamps line the coast with savannah stretching to the once thickly forested central inland that has been largely cleared for agriculture.

Hemisphere

Northern

Climate

Is tropical, with high humidity and rainfall; the dry season is November–April. It is wet for the rest of year. The daily temperature range is 21–32 degrees Celsius, which remains fairly constant throughout the year.

Entry requirements

Passports

Required by all and must be valid for six months beyond date of entry.

Requirements may be subject to change at short notice; contact an embassy or consulate before departure.

Visa

Required by all, and must be obtained in advance. Citizens of Ecowas countries are exempt. Contact the nearest embassy for an application form. All visas require evidence of return/onward passage; tourists must provide evidence of hotel reservations.

Business visitors should include a letter of invitation from a local contact and a letter of introductory from their employer outlining the purpose of the trip, the nature of business and contacts in Sierra Leone. For new business, an applicant must provide evidence of commercial veracity and financial standing.

Currency advice/regulations

The import and export of local currency is limited to Le50,000. Import of foreign currency is unlimited however it must be declared and cash must not exceed US$5,000 (or equivalent); export is limited to the amount declared on arrival.

It is illegal to exchange money anywhere except official exchange facilities at banks and *bureau de change*.

Travellers cheques have very limited use.

Customs

All visitors must complete a customs declaration form on entering the country.

All gem stones require an export licence.

Prohibited imports

Illegal drugs, firearms and explosives, pornography and live animals.

It is illegal to export gold and historical artefacts, live animals, firearms and explosives.

Health (for visitors)

Mandatory precautions

Yellow fever, malaria and cholera vaccination certificates are required.

Advisable precautions

Hepatitis A, tetanus, polio, and typhoid vaccinations. Malaria prophylaxis should be taken. HIV/Aids is prevalent. Water precautions should be taken. There is a rabies risk. Use only well maintained, chlorinated swimming pools to avoid bilharzia. Lassa fever can be contracted in Kenema and the east; seek urgent medical advice for any fever not positively identified as malaria.

Visitors should carry basic medical supplies and any prescription medication necessary. Medical and emergency insurance (to include repatriation) is strongly recommended.

Hotels

Available in Freetown, especially at Lumley Beach, within easy taxi access of the centre of Freetown. Limited availability outside capital. Credit cards accepted only in major hotels and payment required in US dollars. A service charge is usually included in bill.

Credit cards

Not accepted. The government tourist organisation operates an international hotel reservation service that allows pre-payment of hotel accommodation by credit card (see: www.visitsierraleone.org/hotel-reservation.asp).

Public holidays (national)

Fixed dates

1 Jan (New Year's Day), 27 Apr (Independence Day), 25–26 Dec (Christmas).

Variable dates

Eid al Adha (Tabaski), Birth of the Prophet, Good Friday and Easter Monday (Mar/Apr), Eid al Fitr (Korité).

Islamic year 1437 (15 Oct 2015–2 Oct 2016):: The Islamic year contains 354 or 355 days, with the result that Muslim feasts advance by 10–12 days against the Gregorian calendar. Dates of feasts vary according to the sighting of the new moon, so cannot be forecast exactly.

Working hours

Banking

Mon–Thu: 0800–1330; Fri: 0800–1400.

Business

Mon–Fri: 0800–1200, 1400–1630.

Government

Mon–Fri: 0800–1230, 1330–1645; close 1500 on Fri.

Shops

Mon–Fri: 0800–1200, 1400–1630; shops open Sat.

Telecommunications

Mobile/cell phones

There are several GSM 900 and 900/1800 services available throughout most of the country.

Electricity supply

230/240V AC, 50 cycles. Voltage fluctuation and power cuts occur.

Social customs/useful tips

Carry some form of identification at all times.
Punctually and business cards are expected.

Security

Sierra Leone has begun to emerge from a brutal civil war and the security situation is improving. Visitors should take care travelling outside the capital at night, as much for the poor state of the roads as any criminal intent.

Getting there

Air

International airport/s: Freetown-Lungi International (FNA), 20km north of city; bar, currency exchange, post office, shops. The airport is on the opposite bank of the Sierra Leone River from Freetown which must be crossed either by helicopter, hovercraft or ferry.

Airport tax: Departure tax US$20, payable in hard currency; transit passengers are exempt.

Surface

Road: There are routes from Conaky (Guinea Republic). Access to Liberia requires a special permit to transit the border region in a private vehicle. The vital Mano River bridge connecting Sierre Leone with Liberia was officially reopened in June.

Water: Regional services run from Guinea and Liberia. International shipping lines that maintain contacts with Sierra Leone may provide passenger services on cargo ships.

Main port/s: Freetown

Getting about

National transport

Public transport is neither reliable nor safe. The heavy rainy season, which lasts for several months between May and November makes travel to outlying areas both difficult and hazardous.

Air: Internal air services were begun in 2006 by Eagle Air, which operates a 17 seat aircraft to Bo, Kenema and Yengema. Information is limited and visitors should contact local travel agents for further details.

Road: Most main roads in Freetown are paved but have potholes; unpaved side streets are generally poor. A major road resurfacing and repair programme in Freetown is slowly improving the quality of roads in the city. Most roads outside Freetown are unpaved. All roads are unlit and many in need of repair.

Buses: Buses in Freetown tend to be overcrowded and unreliable. Regular service Freetown-Kambia, Freetown-Pendembu, Freetown-Makeni-Kabala.

City transport

Public transport, when it exists, is unreliable.

Taxis: Available at the airport and in main towns; fares by negotiation; tipping is not usual. It is considered safer to use taxis that work in conjunction with an hotel.

Buses, trams & metro: There are buses from the airport to the city centre, but the services can be erratic.

Helicopter: Services operate between Freetown and Lungi airport – flight time five minutes.

Ferry: Links Lungi Airport with central Freetown and Lumley Beach area.

Car hire

Car hire is available at relatively high rates. International driving licence required.

BUSINESS DIRECTORY

The addresses listed below are a selection only. While World of Information makes every endeavour to check these addresses, we cannot guarantee that changes have not been made, especially to telephone numbers and area codes. We would welcome any corrections.

Telephone area codes

The international direct dialling code (IDD) for Sierra Leone is +232, followed by area code and subscriber's number: Freetown22Kenema32

Chambers of Commerce

Sierra Leone Chamber of Commerce, Guma Building, Lamina Sankoh Street, (tel: 226-305; fax: 220-696; e-mail: cocsl@sierratel.sl).

Banking

Bank of Sierra Leone, PO Box 30, Siaka Stevens Street, Freetown (tel: 226-501; fax: 224-764).

First Merchant Bank of Sierra Leone Ltd, Sparta Building, 12 Wilberforce Street, Freetown (tel: 228-493; fax: 228-318).

National Development Bank Ltd, 21/23 Siaka Stevens Street, Freetown (tel: 226-791/2; fax: 224-468).

Rokel Commercial Bank (Sierra Leone) Ltd, PO Box 12, 25-27 Stevens Street, Freetown (tel: 222-501; fax: 222-563).

Sierra Leone Commerical Bank Ltd, 29-31 Siaka Stevens Street, Freetown (tel: 225-264; fax: 225-292).

Standard Chartered Bank Sierra Leone Ltd, PO Box 1155, 9 -11 Lightfoot Boston Street, Freetown (tel: 226-220, 225-021; fax: 225-760).

Union Trust Bank Ltd, 2 Howe Street, Freetown (tel: 222-792, 226-954; fax: 226-214).

Central bank

Bank of Sierra Leone, Siaka Stevens Street, Freetown (tel: 226-501; fax: 224-764; e-mail: info@bankofsierraleone.org).

Travel information

Astraeus (charter flights) Astraeus House, Faraday Court, Faraday Road, Crawley, West Sussex, RH10 9PU (tel:

(+44) 1293-819800; fax: (+4 4) 1293-819832; internet: www.flyastraeus.com).

BMED (airline), Hetherington House, Bedfont Road, Heathrow Airport, Middlesex TW19 7NL (tel: (+44-20) 8630-4212; fax: (+44-20) 8630-4007; internet: www.flybmed.com).

Freetown International Airport, 15 Rawdon Street, Freetown (tel: 223-881; fax: 224-653; internet: www. freetownairport.org).

Ministry of tourism

Ministry of Tourism and Culture, Stadium Hostel, Syke Street, Freetown (tel: 241-256).

National tourist organisation offices

National Tourist Board of Sierra Leone, Room 100, Cape Sierra Hotel, Aberdeen; PO Box 1435

Freetown (tel: 236-620; fax: 236-621; email: info@welcometosierraleone.org or mailto:ntbslinfo@yahoo.com; internet: www.welcometosierraleone.org).

Ministries

Department of Finance, Secretariat Building, George Street, Freetown (tel: 26-911, 22-211; fax: 28-355).

Ministry of Information and Broadcasting, Youyi Building, Brookfields, Freetown.

Ministry of Tourism and Culture, Wallace Johnson Street, Freetown (tel: 26-345, 24-776).

Ministry of Trade and Industry, Ministerial Building, George Street, Freetown (tel: 26-045, 22-755, 22-706; fax: 28-373).

Other useful addresses

Central Statistics Office, Tower Hill, Freetown (tel: 223-897, 224-267).

National Trading Co, Howe Street, Freetown (tel: 223-986, 226-179).

Sierra Leone Embassy (USA), 1701 19th Street, NW, Washington DC 20009 (tel: (+1-202) 939-9261; fax: (+1-202) 483-1793; e-mail: fsec@embassyofsierraleone.org; internet: www.sierra-leone.org).

Sierra Leone Export Debelopment and Investment Corp, 18/20 Walpole Street; Private Mail Bag 6, Freetown (tel: 229-760, 227-604; fax: 229-097; email: info@sledic-sl.org; internet: sledic-sl.org).

SierraTel, Wallace Johnson Street, Freetown (tel: 222-801, 224-591).

Sierra Leone High Commission (UK), 245 Oxford Street, London W1D 2LX (tel: (+44-20) 7287-9884; fax: (+44-20) 7734-3822; e-mail: info@slhc-uk.org.uk; internet: www.slhc-uk.org.uk).

Sierra Leone Ports Authority, PO Box 386, Freetown.

The Chief Immigration Officer, Rawdon Street, Freetown (tel 227-174; fax: 224-761).

Internet sites

Africa Business Network: www.ifc.org/abn

African Development Bank: www.afdb.org

AllAfrica.com: http://allafrica.com

Africa Online: www.africaonline.com

Mbendi AfroPaedia (information on companies, countries, industries and stock exchanges in Africa): http://mbendi.co.za

Sierra Leone: www.sierra-leone.org

Sierra Leone government: www.sierraleone.gov.sl

Sierra Leone Investment and Export Promotion Agency (SLIEPA): www.sliepa.org

Singapore

The death of Singapore's father figure, Lee Kuan Yew, in March 2015 was an event marked by a mixture of sorrow and pride by most Singaporeans. LKY, as he was popularly known, was the architect of his country's independence from Malaysia in 1965. (Having, three years earlier, lead Singapore into a federation with (the then named) Malaya. Sadly, Mr Lee did not live to see the August 2015 fiftieth anniversary celebrations, at which he would undoubtedly have been the guest of honour. Although he had not been Prime Minister since 1990, such was his status and influence that almost until his death he was an almost *de facto* head of state.

Mourning and celebrating

On Lee Kuan Yew's death the tributes from heads of state and ministers all over the world were both warm-hearted and respectful. US President Barack Obama called Mr Lee 'a true giant of history'. According to the British Prime Minister David Cameron, his predecessor Margaret Thatcher the 'Iron Lady' (who died in 2013) had once said that there was no prime minister she admired more than Mr Lee for 'the strength of his convictions, the clarity of his views, the directness of his speech and his vision of the way ahead.' The LKY 'dynasty' has been prolonged, to a degree, by the presence of his son, Lee Hsien Loong, as prime minister. An article in the Washington based *Foreign Policy* quoted a Singaporean as saying: 'he gave us today and a chance for a better tomorrow.' The *Foreign Policy* article went on to say that the 'unwavering adoration for Lee is not as evident among the younger set of Singaporeans, those born after Singapore's independence from Malaysia in 1965, who have grown up in an affluent country that provides them with inexpensive health care and comfortable public housing.'

Authoritarian

One adjective featured in virtually every one of Mr Lee's obituaries. To describe his time in office as 'authoritarian' was probably not wide of the mark, but Mr Lee had witnessed – and learnt from – the chaos of a multi-cultural government in the post colonial Malaysian Federation. In 2011 (the year in which Mr Lee finally stepped down from government) Singapore held parliamentary elections, in which the People's Action Party (PAP), which he had co-founded in 1954, had its worst ever results – although in most of the world's nations the result would have been construed as a massively clear victory. The PAP, which had been dominant in Singapore since LKY took office in 1959, won 81 of 87 seats, with just over 60 per cent, well down from the 2006 election, where it won 67 per cent. Inevitably,

KEY FACTS

Official name: Repablik Singapura, Xinjiapo Gongheguo, Singapur Kutiyarasu, Republic of Singapore

Head of State: President Tony Tan Keng Yam (from 1 Sep 2011)

Head of government: Prime Minister Lee Hsien Loong (appointed 2004; re-elected 7 May 2011)

Ruling party: People's Action Party (PAP) (since 1965; re-elected 7 May 2011)

Area: 636 square km

Population: 5.47 million (2014)

Official language: English, Mandarin Chinese, Malay, Tamil.

Currency: Singapore dollar (S$) = 100 cents

Exchange rate: S$1.42 per US$ (Sep 2015)

GDP per capita: US$56,310 (2014)

GDP real growth: 2.92% (2014)

GDP: US$308.05 billion (2014)

Labour force: 3.41 million (2012)*

Unemployment: 1.95% (2014)

Inflation: 1.02% (2014)

Balance of trade: US$74.50 billion (2014)

Annual FDI: US$64.00 billion (2011)

* estimated figure

as his presence in cabinet diminished, so did his influence in the country. One or two of the legendary by-laws his government had introduced were relaxed: male hair length was not so closely watched, graffiti was not necessarily punished by a jail sentence. Chewing gum, however, remained strictly illegal. More serious crimes, such as drug smuggling and murder were no longer automatically punished by death. Whether the former leader's death would result in any further legal relaxations was not clear. Unlike his father, who had studied law in Cambridge, Lee Hsien Loong's formation was in the Singapore Army, where – in 1983 at the age of 31 – he became the youngest Brigadier General in Singapore. The likelihood of Singapore's Internal Security Act (which allowed political opponents to be arrested without trial) being repealed was probably remote, but Lee Hsien Loong could well consider relaxing media control or even recognising the demands for greater political freedom before the 2017 elections. The prime minister, like his late father, is very media savvy, well aware of the potential power of social media and its ability to by-pass traditional media. However, his own Facebook page does not reveal much about the Prime Minister's likes and dislikes.

In LKY's last memoir, published in 2013, he reflected on Singapore's future, to the extent of wondering if Singapore would still exist in a hundred years' time. Quoted in the London *Financial Times*, Mr Lee wrote that 'I am absolutely sure that if Singapore gets a dumb government, we are done for. The country will sink into nothingness.' The importance of the word 'dumb' was paramount here; whether it referred to providing greater educational opportunities for Singaporeans, or whether it was a reference to the increasingly predictable nature of its administration was unclear, however. Mr Lee may well have been predictable in some matters, but was anything but when it mattered. Camilla Cavendish noted that in 1998, when he learned that Singapore's prisons were full due to 'overcrowding, high re-offending rates and a recruitment crisis' the Singapore government was instructed to make prisons 'schools for life'. Ms Cavendish in her article did not exactly explain how, but 'Guards became teachers; drug addicts and those with mental health problems were given treatment; prisoners were helped to get jobs after their release.' According to the article, 'Within ten years re-offending rates fell from 44 per cent to 27 per cent. Staff morale boomed.' But Lee Kuan Yew didn't abandon his priorities, famously stating that 'poetry was a luxury Singapore could not afford.'

The Singapore city-state started life as a backwater trading post with no natural resources, insignificant when compared to its larger neighbours. For a swampy island the same size as the UK's Isle of Wight, or one fifth the size of Rhode Island, to become one of the wealthiest nations in the world is no mean achievement. Two men can take most of the credit for this: in the first instance, Sir Stamford Raffles who, in 1819, persuaded the Sultan of Johore to allow the East India Company to establish a trading post in Singapore. The other man was Lee Kuan Yew. On his watch, the island's gross domestic product (GDP) per capita grew to over US$55,000, a figure higher than that of the United States. So who needed poetry? LKY's vision and his 'authoritarian' laws and administration created the 'squeaky clean' city-state that was Singapore. Jokingly called 'the world's best-run company', Singapore had its perceived failings; the North American writer William Gibson dubbed it: 'Disneyland with the death penalty, a microcosm of conformity.'

KEY INDICATORS — Singapore

	Unit	2011	2012	2013	2014	**2015
Population	m	5.18	5.31	5.40	5.47	*5.52
Gross domestic product (GDP)	US$bn	259.80	284.30	302.25	308.05	*296.06
GDP per capita	US$	49,271	53,516	55,980	56,310	*53,604
GDP real growth	%	4.9	1.9	4.4	2.9	*3.0
Inflation	%	5.2	4.6	2.4	1.0	*0.0
Unemployment	%	2.7	2.0	1.9	2.0	*2.0
Exports (fob) (goods)	US$m	429,368.0	435,783.0	437,542.0	437,271.0	–
Imports (fob) (goods)	US$m	361,916.0	374,865.0	369,750.0	360,906.0	–
Balance of trade	US$m	67,453.0	60,917.0	67,792.0	74,501.0	–
Current account	US$m	65,323.0	49,385.0	54,084.0	58,806.0	*61,172.0
Total reserves minus gold	US$m	242,357.0	259,094.0	272,864.0	256,643.0	–
Foreign exchange	US$m	240,318.0	256,841.0	270,484.0	–	–
Exchange rate	per US$	1.25	1.22	1.27	1.33	–

* estimated figure ** forecast figure

The economy

In its July 2015 assessment of the Singaporean economy, the International Monetary Fund (IMF) noted that as Singapore prepared to celebrate its 50th anniversary in August 2015, its economy continued to perform well. This, despite the slow pace of the global recovery and a gradual decline in domestic credit growth and housing prices. The IMF considered that Singapore's projected economic growth of about 2.9 per cent in 2015 was consistent with full employment and price stability. Growth was projected to slow down in the medium term, consistent with a reduced reliance on foreign workers and rapid population ageing. The Singaporean authorities' new growth model took into account Singapore's physical resource limits and aimed to boost labour and land productivity. In the view of the IMF, Singapore's highly open economy was exposed to external shocks, most notably slower global growth and the side effects from volatility in global financial markets. Domestic vulnerabilities, including elevated private indebtedness, could amplify the impact of external shocks.

In January 2015, in response to a decline in expected inflation and a more uncertain outlook for growth, the Monetary Authority of Singapore (MAS) reduced the pace of appreciation of the nominal effective exchange rate (NEER) band. According to the IMF, the more benign near- to medium-term inflation outlook warranted the relative easing of monetary policy. Singapore's monetary policy framework was robust and flexible but rising domestic leverage and greater global interest rate and exchange rate volatility warranted heightened vigilance in assessing the balance of forces between the various channels of monetary policy. The IMF noted that Singapore continued to maintain high regulatory and supervisory standards. Recent macro-prudential measures had contributed to smoothing the cycle for credit and house prices. The budget's focus on boosting productivity, equality of opportunity and inclusiveness was laudable, while the fiscal impulse was opportune given cyclical conditions.

Building on Singapore's success and faced with high income inequality and the physical limits of a city state, the authorities had re-engineered the country's growth model to boost productivity while reducing reliance on foreign workers. This restructuring entailed lower steady state growth and a shift in the functional distribution of income toward labour. Incentives provided for firms to increase productivity-enhancing investments and for Singaporeans to upgrade their skills should help ensure a successful transition. But slower potential growth and a lower share of profits in income could, in the view of the IMF, affect those investments and gains in productivity could be realised only slowly. Flexibility in the application of foreign worker policies and the continued review of incentives were, according to the IMF, warranted. The authorities were recalibrating Singapore's fiscal policies with a view to dealing with rapid population ageing, enhancing inclusiveness and reducing inequality, while remaining true to the principles of individual responsibility and sound public finances.

There'll be some changes made

The IMF assessment of the Singaporean economy may have praised the government for Singapore's 'equality of opportunity and inclusiveness', but the perceived rebuff of the 2011 election had caused some heart-searching in government circles. The Singaporean government was not resting on its laurels. The budget announced in February 2015 was the most radical for some time. The single objective of higher GDP growth appeared to have been replaced by a refocussing towards expenditure on social welfare. The top income tax rate, paid by around 5 per cent of the population was increased from 20 per cent to 22 per cent. There was also a 30 per cent rise in healthcare expenditure to S$9.3 per cent. Infrastructure expenditure was expected to grow by 50 per cent, to around S$30 billion, some 6 per cent of GDP.

An article in the London *Financial Times* quoted one Singaporean: 'There's this perception that out of deference to him (LKY) certain changes have not been made, even though they may be necessary.' The Prime Minister and Lee Kuan Yew's son, Lee Hsien Loong was quoted as declaring that Singaporeans must not 'succumb to mediocrity.'

In its overview of the Singaporean economy, the Asian Development Bank (ADB) noted that GDP growth slowed to 2.9 per cent in 2014 from 4.4 per cent in 2013 as productivity gains remained weak for the third straight year. The service sector was the main driver of growth in 2014, expanding by 3.2 per cent and contributing 2.1 percentage points to GDP growth. Finance, insurance and business services were the best performers; their share of GDP increased to 25.6 per cent in 2014. Industry contributed 0.7 percentage points to growth, as biomedical and chemical output rose on strong external demand. Construction growth halved to 3.0 per cent on weak private sector activity. Quarrying rebounded, as did agriculture and fisheries as the government provided funds to farmers to increase their yield and productivity. On the demand side, net exports expanded further in 2014, contributing 1.7 percentage points to GDP growth as exports rose by 2.1 per cent in real terms, outpacing the 1.4 per cent rise in imports. Growth in domestic demand decelerated to 0.3 per cent because investment contracted and growth in government expenditure was weak, contributing only 0.01 percentage points to GDP growth. Investment for the construction of non-residential buildings fell and government expenditure rose by only 0.1 per cent, a tiny fraction of the 11.5 per cent expansion in 2013.

However, private consumption rose by 2.5 per cent and contributed a one percentage point to growth as wages continued to rise, reflecting the low unemployment rate and job vacancies outnumbering job seekers. With global commodity prices soft, inflation averaged 1.0 per cent in 2014, down from 2.4 per cent in 2013. Increases in prices for prepared food, recreation and health care were the main contributors to inflation, but transport and communication costs moderated as prices for automobiles and internet subscription fees declined. Core inflation, which excluded rent and private road transport, increased to 2.0 per cent in 2014 from 1.7 per cent in 2013.

The trade surplus expanded to equal 24.8 per cent of GDP in 2014, although exports and imports both declined in foreign currency terms. Exports were weighed down by falling exports of refined petroleum products and the continued slump in electronics, while merchandise imports shrank as oil imports fell by 1.7 per cent with the sharp drop in oil prices in the fourth quarter. Services exports have been recording robust growth in recent years and now make up over a quarter of the country's exports. However, net services registered a deficit amounting to 0.4 per cent of GDP in 2014 as insurance and financial payments exceeded maintenance, transport and insurance receipts. The current account surplus widened to 19.1 per cent of GDP, but the overall surplus in the balance of payments narrowed to 2.0 per cent of GDP, owing to large deficits in the capital and financial accounts.

The budget recorded a deficit of S$126 million (US$89 million) in the 2014 financial year (ending 31 March 2015), or 0.03 per cent of GDP, as government expenditure including special transfers rose by 16.1 per cent while revenue, including contributions from investment returns, grew by 7.0 per cent. Revenue growth reflected rising personal income tax and vehicle quota premiums paid to obtain certificates of entitlement, which are required for motor vehicle registration. The steep rise in government expenditure followed higher outlays on health care, culture, community and youth and special transfers.

The MAS maintained its policy of modest and gradual appreciation of the Singapore dollar in terms of its NEER – a policy that had served the country well by containing inflation both domestic and imported and by ensuring that inflation expectations remained anchored. The appreciating trend in the NEER and the real effective exchange rate continued in 2014, but at a slower pace than in 2013, with the NEER rising by 1.3 per cent and the real effective exchange rate by 0.1 per cent. The Singapore interbank offered rate increased by 0.03 basis points in 2014, dampening the growth of credit, which together with a substantial narrowing of the balance of payments surplus reduced the growth of money supply (M2) to 3.3 per cent from 4.3 per cent in 2013.

Influenced by diverging global economic developments and continued economic restructuring, the Singapore economy was forecast by the ADB to grow by 3.0 per cent in 2015 and 3.4 per cent in 2016, as the global recovery gathered momentum and the service sector continued to strengthen. Finance, insurance and business services were expected by the ADB to be the main drivers of growth again in 2015 and 2016, but growth in labour – intensive sectors such as construction, retail and food services could be constrained by the persistently tight labour market.

Domestic demand was expected to expand as public investment and government spending on public transportation and health-care infrastructure was expected to rise. Benefiting from higher government subsidies for education services and the enhancement of a low-income voucher scheme, private consumption should, in the view of the ADB, also rise in 2015. With moderate improvement in external demand in 2015 on the expected strengthening of its partner economies, Singapore should see exports grow modestly – although they may be also depressed by weakening exports of petroleum products, which fell by 33.3 per cent year on year in January 2015.

Energy

Singapore's strategic location between the Indian and Pacific Oceans and near the Strait of Malacca has allowed it to become one of Asia's major petrochemical and refining centres and oil trading hubs. According to the US government Energy Information Administration (EIA), Singapore has a world-class refining, storage and distribution infrastructure. Jurong Island on the southern edge of the country is the centre of Singapore's petrochemical industry. Singapore's government planned to promote long-term growth in refining capacity with a view to maintaining its market position as a refining and oil-trading leader.

Singapore has no indigenous hydrocarbon reserves and needs to import all its crude oil and natural gas. In 2014 Singapore's total primary energy consumption was made up of approximately 87 per cent from crude oil and petroleum products, 13 per cent from natural gas and less than 1 per cent from other fuel sources, according to the BP Statistical Review.

Singapore has a total crude refining capacity of about 1.5 million barrels per day (bpd) at three refineries, according to FACTS Global Energy. In 2014, Singapore imported approximately 950,000bpd of crude oil with more than two-thirds coming from the United Arab Emirates (UAE), Saudi Arabia and Qatar, according to the Singapore government. Imported crude oil is used mostly in the petrochemicals and refining sector. According to Global Trade Information Services, in 2014, Singapore was in the top ten exporters of refined oil products in Asia, with more than half of its exports going to Malaysia, Indonesia and Australia. Singapore is the world's largest consumer of bunker fuel oil. Nearly one fifth of worldwide fuel oil is consumed by Singapore.

Risk assessment

Economy	Good
Politics	Fair
Regional stability	Good

Muslims in Singapore

% of population	14.9
Sunni (% of Muslims)	98
Shi'a (% of Muslims)	1

COUNTRY PROFILE

The Republic of Singapore consists of Singapore Island, where Singapore City is located, and 57 smaller islands. One of these, Pedra Branca (Batu Putih), is claimed by Malaysia.

1819 Sir Stamford Raffles established a trading station in Singapore for the British East India Company. Singapore's free trade policy with no taxation attracted merchants from the entire region. The port captured much of the *entrepôt* trade of the East Indies. During the nineteenth century thousands of immigrant Chinese, Indians, Indonesians and Malays emigrated there.

1824 The Sultan of Johore allowed the British East India Company full control of the territory.

1826 Singapore, Malacca and Penang were incorporated into the Straits Settlements, part of the British East India Company.

1867 The Straits Settlements became a crown colony.

1942 During the Second World War, the island was captured and controlled by the Japanese.

1945 The British regained control of Singapore.

1946 The Straits Settlement dissolved. Penang and Malacca became part of Malaya while Singapore was made into a British Crown Colony.

1954 Lee Kuan Yew founded the People's Action Party (PAP). It attracted a strong following among the poor and the non-English speaking population.

1959 Singapore achieved internal self-government. The PAP won the election and Lee Kuan Yew became the first prime minister. Under his leadership, government opposition was suppressed and he attracted much international criticism for his authoritarian approach. Nevertheless, Singapore became a financial and industrial powerhouse.

1963 Singapore became a state of the Federation of Malaysia.

1965 The Republic of Singapore was legally declared an independent, sovereign state.

1967 Singapore was a founder member of the Association of Southeast Asian Nations (Asean).

1971 The last British troops were withdrawn from Singapore.

1984 For the first time in Singapore's political history, two opposition MPs were elected to parliament.

1990 Goh Chok Tong took over from Lee Kuan Yew as prime minister.

1993 In the first direct presidential election, Ong Teng Cheong (PAP), secured the post.

1999 Sellapan Ramanathan (S R Nathan) was elected president.

2001 A political rally by parliamentarian J B Jeyaretnam of the Workers' Party of Singapore (WPS) was allowed to take place – the first permitted outside an election period.

2003 The Sars virus infected 206 people and killed 31. A free trade agreement with the US came into effect.

2004 Lee Hsien Loong became prime minister following Goh Chok Tong's retirement.

2005 President S R Nathan was appointed to a second term after all other rivals were disqualified.

2006 The PAP was re-elected. The IMF and World Bank held their annual meeting in Singapore, which earned an unprecedented rebuke for seeking to prevent accredited activists from attending the meeting; Singapore was obliged to abide by its obligations as host nation.

2009 The economy contracted by 19.7 per cent in the first quarter, its highest since records began. New laws were enacted requiring all outdoor gatherings to have a police permit and banning the filming of police officers. The recession eased as the economy expanded at a 20.4 per cent annualised rate.

2010 The constitution was amended. A change to the electoral system increased the allowed number of Non-Constituency Members of Parliament (NCMP) from six to nine and gave admittance to parliament of the best-performing, losing parliamentary candidates. Nominated MPs (NMP) became a permanent component of parliament, to provide alternative, non-partisan views during debates. Tamasek, the government's sovereign wealth fund, showed an increase in value of 42 per cent as the economy improved following recovery from the global economic crisis. The government announced that investment in research and development would be increased by 20 per cent until 2015, by spending US$12 billion (1 per cent of GDP). Private industry was expected to match and double the amount.

2011 In parliamentary elections held in May the PAP won with 60.1 per cent of the vote (81 seats out of 87). The Workers' Party won 12.8 per cent (six) and although the number was low, it still marked a weakening of the supremacy of PAP in parliament. Rancour within PAP at the discordant election campaign led to former prime ministers, Lee Kuan Yew and Goh Chok Tong, retiring from active politics and giving up all government posts in May. In a joint statement they said it was time for 'a younger generation to carry Singapore forward in a more difficult and complex situation'. Both had won seats in the elections. In a closely run presidential election held in August, Tony Tan Keng Yam won with 35.19 per cent of the vote against Tan Cheng Bock with 34.85 per cent (turnout was 94.65 per cent). Tony Tan took office on 1 September.

2012 The government decided to change employment regulations for expatriate workers (not permanent residents) from 1 January. They must earn US$2,500 per month in their home country before they are eligible for an employment pass in Singapore. On 14 November the list of crimes that result in the mandatory death penalty was amended to exempt the mandatory aspect while boosting enforcement. Those that manufacture and traffic drugs can attract capital punishment, while those caught carrying drugs may not.

2014 On 25 May Former presidential candidate, Tan Jee Say, launched a new poltical party, Singaporeans First.

2015 Singapore's first prime minister (1959–90), Lee Kuan Yew, died on 23 March. On 25 August President Tan, on the advice of Prime Minister Lee Hsien Loong, called a general election for 11 September. The result was a comprehensive win for the PAP with 83 of the 89 seats. The WP won the remaining 6.

Political structure

Constitution

The 1959 constitution was amended in 1965, 1988, 1991 and 1996. Consequently, there are now 15 Group Representation Constituencies (GRCs) which elect teams of up to six members of parliament. At least one member of each team has to be of minority (non-Chinese) ethnic origin. The number of single member constituencies has been reduced from 21 to eight.

In the 1991 amendment, the position of president was modified to become a directly elected post with a six-year term. The responsibilities of the office were extended to include the safeguarding of Singapore's financial reserves, and the right to veto senior civil service and judicial appointments. Only those who have served as cabinet ministers, chief justice, senior civil servants or have headed a large company are eligible as presidential candidates.

The constitution was amended in April 2010. A change to the electoral system increased the allowed number of Non-Constituency Members of Parliament (NCMP) from six to nine and was intended to give admittance to parliament of the best-performing, losing parliamentary candidates. In July Nominated MPs (NMP) became a permanent component of parliament, to provide alternative, non-partisan views during debates.

There is a provision in the constitution for up to nine nominated MPs, appointed by the president for terms of 2.5 years to contribute non-partisan and independent views in parliament.

Elections must be held within three months of the dissolution of parliament.

There is full adult suffrage; voting is compulsory for all citizens aged 21 years and over.

Independence date

9 August 1965

Form of state

Republic

The executive

Executive power is vested in the cabinet, which is presided over by the prime minister and responsible to the unicameral parliament. The political hegemony of the People's Action Party (PAP) is absolute and parliamentary oversight of executive power is virtually non-existent. In 1995, a three-judge tribunal ruled that the president had no power to veto any bill that sought to restrict his existing powers.

National legislature

The unicameral Parliament of Singapore has elected and non-constituency (nominated) members (MPs) in single or group representation constituencies (GRCs). As of August 2015, there are a total 87 MPs directly elected, 9 nominated and 3 non-constituency members. All serve for a five-year term.

Political parties field a team of 3–6 candidates (of which one must belong to a minority race) to contest GRCs.

Legal system

Singaporean law is based on English common law.

The independence of the judiciary is safeguarded by the constitution. Judicial power is vested in Singapore's Supreme Court and in the Subordinate Courts. The Supreme Court consists of the High Court, the Court of Appeal and the Court of Criminal Appeal. The chief justice is appointed by the president, acting on the advice of the prime minister.

The Subordinate Courts consist of District Courts, Magistrates' Courts, Juvenile Courts, Coroners' Courts and Small Claims Tribunals. District judges, magistrates and coroners are appointed on the recommendation of the chief justice.

Although the constitution stipulates that the judiciary should act independently of government, it rarely does so in practice. Judges and judicial officials are appointed and dismissed by the president and judicial redress against abuses of executive power is therefore limited.

Sharia is the religious court with jurisdiction over Muslim law and domestic proceedings between Muslim parties.

Last elections

11 September 2015; 27 August 2011 (presidential)

Results: Parliamentary: the People's Action Party won 83 seats out of 87 (69.86 per cent of the vote), the Workers' Party (WP) six (12.48 per cent). No other parties won any seats. Turnout was 93.56 per cent.

Presidential: Tony Tan Keng Yam won 35.19 per cent of the vote, Tan Cheng Bock 34.85 per cent, Tan Jee Say 25.04 per cent, Tan Kin Lian 4.91 per cent; turnout was 94.65 per cent.

Next elections

May 2016 (presidential); 2020 (parliamentary)

Political parties

Ruling party

People's Action Party (PAP) (since 1965; re-elected 7 May 2011)

Main opposition party

Workers' Party (WP)

Population

5.41 million (2012)*. Population growth has slowed rapidly since the 1960s and the government is attempting to accelerate growth with financial incentives to parents.

Last census: June 2000: 4,017,700

Population density: 7,126 inhabitants per square km (2010), one of the world's highest population densities. Urban population 100 per cent (2010 Unicef).

Annual growth rate: 2.6 per cent, 1990–2010 (Unicef).

Ethnic make-up

Singapore is a multi-racial society. There are approximately 950,000 non-nationals. Chinese make up the majority of the population (77 per cent), and Malays (14 per cent), Indians (8 per cent), and other ethnic groups (1 per cent) make up the remainder.

Religions

Buddhism (32 per cent), Taoism (22 per cent), Islam (Sunni) (15 per cent), Christianity (13 per cent) and Hinduism (3 per cent) are the main religions. Other religions include Zoroastrianism (0.6 per cent) and Judaism. The constitution provides for freedom of worship.

Education

Primary school lasts for six years between the ages six and 12. Lower secondary education last for four years and students must attain good exam results to progress on to higher secondary school for a further three years, before advancing to higher education. There are three kinds of tertiary institutions: universities, polytechnics, and other centres of public and private training. The government almost wholly finances the National University of Singapore and the Nanyang Technological University. Many Singaporean students go abroad for their university education, increasingly to the US.

In October 2005, the UK's Warwick University pulled out of plans to set up a campus in Singapore, citing likely restrictions on academic freedom and reservations about the limitations on freedom of speech and assembly. Singapore probably was not too worried: already established are the campuses of many US universities – the University of Chicago, the Johns Hopkins University, the University of California and the Cornell and Stanford universities to name a few. In 2005 the prestigious Indian Institute of Management-Bangalore (IIM-B) opened a campus in the country and will initially offer a part-time course taught online.

Public expenditure on education typically amounts to 3 per cent of annual gross national income. In 2001 S$6,577 million was spent on education (Asian Development Bank 2004).

Literacy rate: 93 per cent adult rate; 100 per cent youth rate (15–24) (Unesco 2005).

Compulsory years: 6 to 12

Enrolment rate: 94 per cent gross primary enrolment of relevant age group (including repeaters); 74 per cent gross secondary enrolment (World Bank).

Pupils per teacher: 25 in primary schools

Health

Singapore has managed to create a developed country healthcare system at relatively little cost. The health care system has a mixture of private and public provision and shows radically improved healthcare indices.

The private sector provides over 60 per cent of primary healthcare through doctors in private practice. Hospital healthcare is mostly public sector, with only 20 per cent of beds in the private sector. The government provides public subsidies through a ward system in public hospitals. Basic healthcare is financed through Central Provident Fund (CPF) Medisave accounts. Between 6 and 8 per cent of a worker's monthly contribution to the CPF, depending on age, is set aside for Medisave, a mandatory national health programme which encourages individuals to pay for their own healthcare. An additional endowment fund, Medifund, is targetted at poor and indigent Singaporeans.

Government officials have warned that if Singapore's predominantly Chinese population age too quickly, this could lead to expensive healthcare problems. Official statistics show that the number of Singaporeans aged 64 and above will rise fourfold to make up 20 per cent of the total population by the year 2030, when the population is projected to decline after it has reached a 7.9 million peak.

HIV/Aids

HIV prevalence: 0.2 per cent aged 15–49 in 2003 (World Bank)

Life expectancy: 80 years, 2004 (WHO 2006)

Fertility rate/Maternal mortality rate: 1.3 births per woman, 2010 (Unicef)

Birth rate/Death rate: 12.8 births per 1,000 population; 4.3 deaths per 1,000 population (2003).

Child (under 5 years) mortality rate (per 1,000): 3 per 1,000 live births (WHO 2012)

Head of population per physician: 1.4 physicians per 1,000 people, 2001 (WHO 2006)

Welfare

The government discourages dependence on the state for social security; rather, all workers and employers contribute to the compulsory savings scheme, the CPF. The CPF has developed into a wide-ranging social security scheme covering retirement, home ownership and health needs. Members can withdraw their savings upon reaching 55 but must set aside a minimum amount to ensure they have enough money for their retirement. The minimum amount to be saved every year was capped at S$80,000 (US$43,618) in 2003. Employment assistance is provided free of charge by the Ministry of Manpower.

Some 85 per cent of the population is housed in accommodation built and developed by the Housing and Development Board (HDB), set up in 1960 as a statutory board of the Ministry of National Development to provide low-cost public housing.

Main cities

Singapore is a city-state (estimated population 6.1 million in 2012).

Languages spoken

English is the main administrative language and is almost universally understood. In parliamentary debates, members may speak in English, Malay, Mandarin Chinese or Tamil, and simultaneous translations are provided. Other dialects of Chinese, mostly Hokkien (Fukienese) and Cantonese, are also spoken.

Most Singaporeans are bi- or tri-lingual.

Official language/s

English, Mandarin Chinese, Malay, Tamil.

Media

Press

Newspapers and magazines are published only under government licence in a highly regulated market. The government has a reputation of litigation for defamation, which has led to widespread self-censorship.

Singapore Press Holdings (SPH) is one of the largest companies listed on the Singapore Exchange, controlling 15 newspapers, a number of regional magazines and a book distribution network.

Dailies: The two main Chinese-language dailies are *Lian He Zao Bao* (United Morning News) and *Lian He Wan Bao* (United Evening News). The major English-language dailes are *The Straits Times* and *Business Times*. *Berita Harian* (in Malay) and *Tamil Murasu* (in Tamil) have smaller circulations. International editions of foreign newspapers are also available.

Weeklies: Most daily newspapers have a Sunday edition with extended features.

Business: In Chinese, the highest circulation papers are *Lianhe Zaobao* (United Morning News) (www.zaobao.com) a major regional and international news gathering organ and *Lianhe Wanbao* (United Evening News). In English, *The Straits Times* (www.straitstimes.com), *Business Times* (www.businesstimes.com.sg), *The New Paper* (http://newpaper.asia1.com.sg) a tabloid and *Today* is a free issue. In Malay *Berita Harian* (http://cyberita.asia1.com.sg) and in Tamil, *Tamil Murasu* (http://tamilmurasu.tamil.sg) is a broadsheet.

Periodicals: In English, *The Executive* (www.executive.sg) is published monthly. The Singapore International Chamber of Commerce publishes a quarterly, *Business Minds* (www.sicc.com.sg) with business, corporate and personnel news. There are also numerous interest and trade publications, including *Singapore Business Federation* (www.sbf.org.sg).

Broadcasting

The government-owned MediaCorp operates the national television and radio stations.

Radio: MediaCorp operates 14 radio stations broadcasting in English, Mandarin, Malay and Tamil. There are a number of private, commercial stations.

Television: MediaCorp has a monopoly with six free-to-air TV channels, broadcasting in the four official languages. Private satellite dishes are banned however foreign broadcasts are available through cable TV.

Singapore Press Releases on the Internet (Sprinter) (www.sprinter.gov.sg), operated by Ministry of Information, Communications and the Arts, Singapore (tel: 6270-7988; internet: www.mica.gov.sg).

Economy

The economy is highly developed and integrated into global trade; it enjoys a remarkably open and corruption-free environment, stable prices, and a per capita GDP higher than that of most developed countries. Unemployment is also very low at just 2 per cent in 2014. The structure of the economy is dominated by the service sector, which accounted for 75 per cent of GDP in 2014, with financial services providing a major source of foreign exchange. Manufacturing, particularly of electronic components, pharmaceuticals and telecommunications equipment, produced by many multinational corporations sited in Singapore, accounted for 25 per cent of GDP in 2014. Industrial production includes oil refining and storage, shipbuilding and aircraft repairs and maintenance.

Singapore is less than 640 square kilometres in area and agriculture represents almost 0 per cent of GDP; it lacks any natural resources, but has capitalised upon its human resources and strategic location on the Straits of Malacca, where it has become a leading *entrepôt* and major shipping hub. Singapore is one of the world's leading destinations for FDI (US$67.5 billion in 2014). According to the World Bank, Singapore is the easiest country for doing business. Singapore has attracted major investments in pharmaceuticals and medical technology production and will continue efforts to strengthen its position as South-East Asia's leading financial and high-tech hub.

As Singapore has an economy that is dependent on foreign trade it was one of the first countries in Asia to be affected by the global economic recession when GDP growth dropped from 8.9 per cent in 2007 to 1.5 per cent in 2008, before falling into recession of -1.0 per cent in 2009 as world trade was at its weakest and exports fell and imports rose. In the 2009 financial year, the government introduced one of the largest (S$20.5 billion (US$29.3 billion), around 8 per cent of GDP) stimulus packages amongst advanced economies. To strengthen Singapore's long-term prospects the package focussed on employment, supporting companies, enhancing competitiveness, stimulating bank lending and supporting families. As a result, and when global trade picked up, GDP growth resurged in 2010 to 14.8 per cent, before weakening in 2011, in the face of the European currency crisis, when GDP growth was estimated at 4.9 per cent. The government is attempting to restructure Singapore's economy by weaning its dependence on foreign labour, addressing weak productivity, and increasing Singaporean wages. Since the resurgence of Singapore's economy, economic growth has stabilised at 3.4 per cent in 2012 before increasing slightly to 4.4 per cent in 2013 and then dropping to 2.9 per cent in 2014.

Inflation, which had been a low 2.1 per cent rose sharply to 6.6 per cent in 2008, before dropping to 0.6 per cent in 2009; it returned to 2.8 per cent in 2010. The Singapore dollar was allowed to rise against the US dollar in April 2010, in a measure to tackle inflation, increasing in value by 1.25 per cent. Inflation increased to 2.4 per cent in 2013 before falling to 1 per cent in 2014.

External trade

Singapore belongs to the Association of Southeast Asian Nations (Asean) Free Trade Area (Afta) and maintains a list of goods that have preferential import duties between members and a programme of tariff reductions due to be introduced in the next few years. It is also a member of the Asia-Pacific Economic Co-operation (Apec) forum, which is a group of 21 countries that border the Pacific. The objective of Apec is to facilitate trade, economic growth and investment in the region. In 2015, Singapore will form, with the other Asean members, the Asean Economic Community.

Foreign trade is a major function of the economy equalling 252 per cent of GDP in 2014. Many multinational corporations have manufacturing bases (accounting for around 65 per cent of total output) and direct export sales operations in Singapore. Of the major economic sectors, electronics represents 40 per cent of industrial production with petrochemicals 20 per cent. Singapore is only second to the Port of Shanghai as having the busiest port in the world.

Almost 50 per cent of exports are re-exports and, due to the lack of land for agricultural purposes, the majority of foodstuffs and fuel have to be imported.

Imports

Principal imports are machinery and equipment, mineral fuels, chemicals, foodstuffs and consumer goods.

Main sources: China (12.1 per cent of total in 2014), Malaysia (10.7 per cent), US (10.3 per cent), South Korea (5.9 per cent), Japan (5.5 per cent) and Indonesia (5.1 per cent)

Exports

Principal exports are machinery and equipment (including electronics and telecommunications), pharmaceuticals and other chemicals, refined petroleum products, foodstuffs and beverages.

Main destinations: China (12.6 per cent of total in 2014), Malaysia (12 per cent), Hong Kong (11 per cent), Indonesia (9.4 per cent), US (5.9 per cent) and Japan (4.1 per cent)

Agriculture

Farming

Only 1 per cent of Singapore's land area is used for agriculture of which 0.9 per cent is arable land and 0.1 per cent is for permanent crops. Singapore has some 2,000 licensed farms producing poultry, eggs, vegetables, fruit, orchids (both for domestic demand and export) and ornamental plants. Less than 6 per cent of fresh vegetables are produced locally, with the rest imported from Malaysia, Indonesia, China and Australia.

Although agriculture plays only a minor role in Singapore's economy, the Primary Production Department promotes intensive farming methods. Agri-technology parks have been developed on 554 hectares of land in Murai, Sungai Tengah, Nee Soon and Loyang.

Fishing

With limited agricultural and water resources, there is little scope for the development of Singapore's fisheries, although fish is an important component of the Singaporean diet. Singapore relies mainly on imports for domestic consumption. The government's priority is to increase imports through trade relations. The quality of Singapore's own catch is often described as poor. Rapid urbanisation and development have damaged natural habitats and caused the quality of inshore fish to deteriorate.

Forestry

Forests constitute only 3.3 per cent of the total land area of Singapore. There are three major forest reserves – Bukit Timah, Palau Ubin and Sungei Buloh. Singapore produces plywood and veneer and imports pulp and paper.

Industry and manufacturing

The industrial sector accounts for a quarter of GDP. Manufacturing employs 21 per cent of the workforce and construction employs a further 7 per cent. Electronics is the largest industry and typically contributes about 14 per cent to GDP, accounting for 70 per cent of non-oil exports. The second largest industry group encompasses life sciences, chemicals and petroleum refining. Other major industries include transport equipment, especially shipbuilding and related repair and conversion activities.

The UK manufacturer, Rolls-Royce Plc opened an engineering works, and manufacturing hub, in Singapore in February 2012, initially to build engines for the Airbus A380. The facility, built for US$562 million, will construct around 250 engines per year by 2020, and employ 1,600 people.

AbbVie (UK) has invested US$300 million into its first Asian manufacturing facility located in Singapore and it will support an emerging antibody-drug conjugate pipeline. The facility is set to come online in 2019 and will allow AbbVie to have biologic and potent small molecule manufacturing at one site. In less than seven years, Singapore has become home to nine biologics manufacturing facilities just like the one currently being built; they collectively represent approximately S$2.7 billion (US$1.9 billion) in total investments and employ close to 2000 people.

Tourism
For a small city-state, Singapore needs to pack in a variety of attractions to draw a diverse stream of visitors, which in 2015 will reach an expected 12.8 million people. Most visitors arriving for leisure go on shopping expeditions, followed by sightseeing and they account for 51 per cent of the sector. Business spending accounts for 49 per cent of the tourism sector.
Travel and tourism directly and indirectly contributed 10.1 per cent of GDP in 2014. The industry provided employment for 8.5 per cent (303,000 jobs) of the workforce in 2014, which is forecast to decrease to 7.7 per cent by 2025 (323,000 jobs). Singapore is a major trading centre and business spending was S$17.7 billion (US$12.7 billion) in 2014, while domestic travel and tourism spending was SGD17.8 billion; overall, visitor receipts in 2014 was US$30.4 billion.
Singapore is a major destination for medical and health services, as well as for business and conference venues.

Environment
The Singapore Green Plan (SGP), released in 1992, called for 5 per cent of the country's land to be classified as protected areas. Around S$3 billion (US$1.7 billion) was allocated towards the upgrade of sewage treatment, a refuse incineration plant and improvements to water sources in 2002.

Hydrocarbons
Singapore does not have any oil or natural gas reserves and is entirely reliant on imports. However, Singapore is one of Asia's principal oil refining centres, with 11 refineries and total oil refining capacity of around 1.4 million barrels per day (bpd). Along with Singapore's large refining industry there has been rapid growth of the petrochemical industry.
Demand for natural gas in Singapore is rising, due to the government's policy of cutting carbon emissions in power generation and the growing petrochemical industry. Singapore depends on Malaysia and Indonesia for a steady supply of natural gas for power generation. This includes 4.3 million cubic metres (cum) per day from Malaysia through the first Asian trans-national gas pipeline, and 9.9 million cum of gas per day via another pipeline from Indonesia.
Any use of coal is commercially insignificant.

Energy
Total installed electricity-generating capacity was 10.49 kW in 2011. 95.3 per cent of total installed capacity is from fossil fuels while 3.9 per cent is from renewable sources.

Financial markets
Stock exchange
Singapore Exchange (SGX)
Commodity exchange
Singapore Commodity Exchange (Sicom)

Banking and insurance
A bill amending income tax laws to comply with Organisation for Economic Co-operation and Development (OECD) standards was passed by parliament in October 2009. The bill, which allows the government to ask banks for client information, will move Singapore closer to being taken off the OECD's 'grey list' of countries considered to be unco-operative over tax. The banks hope this will make Singapore more attractive to clients from the Middle East and Europe.
Central bank
Monetary Authority of Singapore
Main financial centre
Singapore

Time
GMT plus eight hours

Geography
Singapore consists of the main island of Singapore and 58 smaller islands, more than 20 of them inhabited. Lying 137km north of the equator, it is linked to peninsular Malaysia in the north by a causeway carrying a road, railway and water pipeline across the narrow Straits of Johor, and separated from Indonesia to the south by the Straits of Singapore.
The island of Singapore itself is 42km long and 23km wide, with a coastline measuring 138km. It can be divided into three broad regions: a central hilly region, an area of hills and valleys in the west, and a relatively flat eastern region.
Hemisphere
Northern

Climate
The climate is equatorial, with uniformly high temperatures, high humidity and mean annual rainfall of 2,463mm with no defined wet or dry season. Mean daily temperatures range from a minimum 24 degrees Celsius (C) to a maximum 31 degrees C. The hottest month is May. The driest month is July, with an average rainfall of 70mm. November to January are generally the cooler and wetter months. Sometimes it rains for several days continuously and there may be serious flooding. Between monsoons, from April to November, there are regular pre-dawn thunderstorms, known as *Sumatras*. Singapore has an average of 180 lightning days a year.

Dress codes
Dress is generally informal, with light summer clothing the norm. A shirt and tie, or a safari suit, is the usual office dress for men, although jackets may be required in some restaurants for dinner; women should also dress smartly for business. Singapore's predominantly Chinese population follows Western fashion; a small section among the minority Indian and Malay communities wear traditional dress.

Entry requirements
Passports
Required by all, valid for six months beyond date of departure.
Visa
Visas are not required by nationals of most countries; a list of the countries whose nationals require visas is given on app.ica.gov.sg/travellers/entry/visa_requirements.asp. Social visit passes are issued on arrival to all other visitors by Immigration Officers, who determine the length of visit and grant social visit passes on the basis of sufficient funds for maintenance during the expected stay and confirmed return/onwards passage (including relevant visas for further destinations).
Prohibited entry
Singapore has tough laws against drug trafficking. The death penalty is mandatory for trafficking above certain prescribed levels.
Currency advice/regulations
There are no restrictions on the import or export of local or foreign currencies. Credit cards and travellers cheques are widely accepted.
Customs
1 litre each of spirits, wine and beer. Tobacco products are not duty-free and must be declared.
Prohibited imports
Include chewing gum, chewing tobacco and imitation tobacco products, cigarette lighters of pistol or revolver shape, controlled drugs and psychotropic substances, endangered species and by-products, firecrackers, obscene articles, publications, video tapes and software, reproduction of copyright publications, video tapes or disks, records or cassettes, or seditious and treasonable materials.

Health (for visitors)
Mandatory precautions
Yellow fever vaccination certificates for anyone who, within the preceding six days, has been to an infected area.

Advisable precautions

Vaccinations for diphtheria, tuberculosis, hepatitis A and B, polio, tetanus and typhoid are advisable. Tap water is safe.
All necessary medicines (especially sleeping pills, depressants, stimulants, etc) must have a physician's certification declaring their prescribed use.
The Singapore Medical Centre, on the sixth floor of Tanglin shopping centre, houses a large community of specialist doctors.

Hotels

There are numerous five-star international-class hotels with shopping arcades, bars and swimming pools. Tipping is discouraged. A 4 per cent tax and a 10 per cent service charge are generally added to the hotel bill.

Credit cards

All major credit cards are widely accepted.

Public holidays (national)

Owing to its multi-ethnic composition, Singapore celebrates a wide range of religious festivals and holidays in addition to those listed. Many festivals are based on a lunar calendar, while the dates of some are only finalised at the last minute.
Check with the Singapore Tourist Promotion Board for exact dates and locations affected.

Fixed dates

1 Jan (New Year's Day), 1 May (Labour Day), 9 Aug (National Day), 25 Dec (Christmas Day).

Variable dates

Chinese New Year (Jan/Feb), Good Friday, Vesak Day, Diwali (Oct/Nov), Eid al Adha, Eid al Fitr.

Working hours

During the Lunar New Year, many Chinese firms close for the whole week.

Banking

Mon–Fri: 1930–1500; Sat: 0930–1200; 0900–1500 (selected banks only).

Business

Mon–Fri: 0900–1300, 1400–1700.

Government

Mon–Fri: 0800–1300, 1400–1700.

Shops

Mon–Sat: 1930–2100. Some shops, particularly in tourist areas, open on Sundays.

Electricity supply

220—240V, 50 Hz, with three-pin (square) plug fittings.

Weights and measures

Metric system, with local variations.

Social customs/useful tips

Singaporeans are highly 'face' conscious and try to avoid self-embarrassment at all time.
Observe local etiquette – suit jackets remain off only as a concession to the climate, otherwise Western-style business formalities are in place.
Visiting cards are essential (although government officials do not use them). The cards should be presented with both hands. As a courtesy, it is a good idea to have cards printed in both Chinese and English. Cards should never be written on, put away before the meeting is over, or left behind.
When addressing Chinese persons, family or surname is mentioned first. When addressing Malay persons, the first of their two family names is used. Singaporean Indians use many different conventions.
Men and women should not touch each other. The heads of children should not be patted.
Tipping is not customary; it is not illegal, but is officially discouraged. In hotels and restaurants a 10 per cent service charge is included in the bill.
On-the-spot fines can be imposed for some offences. Smoking is not permitted in public buildings and restaurants, and is restricted in other public places.
Singapore celebrates the religious and cultural festivals of its four major communities, and therefore the year is punctuated by a series of colourful festivals.
Celebration of the Chinese New Year, the main event in the Chinese calendar, centres on traditional reunion dinners and visits to friends and relations. Business people should avoid visiting at Christmas, Easter, Chinese New Year, Islamic and Hindu religious holiday periods.

Security

Tourists can walk the streets without fear of being robbed or attacked.

Getting there

Air

National airline: Singapore Airlines.
International airport/s: Singapore-Changi International Airport (SIN), 20km north-east of city; bank, bureau de change, duty-free shop, post office, restaurants, shops, car rental. A third terminal is scheduled to open in 2008.
Airport tax: The departure tax of S$21 is usually included in the price of the air ticket.

Surface

Road: Road transport arrives via two causeways from Malaysia, with express bus services from Kuala Lumpur and Johor Bahru.
Rail: There are rail services to Kuala Lumpur and Bangkok.
Water: There are excellent sea links with other countries.

Getting about

National transport

Road: The road network comprises some 2,900km of roads, including about 100km of expressways. Vehicular access to the Central Business District (CBD) is restricted and there are charges for vehicles entering the area at certain times.
Buses: Timetables for the extensive and inexpensive bus network are widely available at news-stands. Fares to various destinations are displayed on a signboard on the front of the bus stop.
Rail: The light overland railway network reaches all districts of Singapore Island.
Water: Regular ferry services from the World Trade Centre operate to some of the islands; others may be reached by charter boats.

City transport

Taxis: Metered, air-conditioned taxis are widely available from taxi pick-up points and can be hailed in the street. Taxi companies are allowed to set their own fares. The basic meter fare is displayed on the window of the rear door and details of surcharges are displayed on the fare card in all taxis.Taxis can also be hired by the hour.
Buses, trams & metro: The easy-to-use bus service is extensive.
The Mass Rapid Transit system (MRT) is fast, clean and efficient. It comprises three lines running north/south, east/west and north/east with around 70 underground and elevated stations.

Car hire

An international driving licence is required for car hire. Driving is on the left. Coupons for use of the public car parks managed by the Urban Redevelopment Authority (URA) or Housing & Development Board (HBD) can be purchased at post offices, URA parking kiosks and some gas/petrol stations. Car hire companies are listed in the Yellow Pages of the telephone directory.

BUSINESS DIRECTORY

The addresses listed below are a selection only. While World of Information makes every endeavour to check these addresses, we cannot guarantee that changes have not been made, especially to telephone numbers and area codes. We would welcome any corrections.

Telephone area codes

The international direct dialling (IDD) code for Singapore is +65, followed by subscriber's number.

Useful telephone numbers

Police: 999
Fire/ambulance: 995
Directory enquiries: 103
International calls: 104
International enquiries: 162

Trunk calls to Malaysia: 109
Time of Day: 1711
Flight information: 6542-1234
Bus information: 6287-2727
AA road service (24 hrs): 6748-9911
Post Office information: 6533-0234, 6532-4536
Immigration Department: 6532-2877
Telecoms Customer Services Centres: 6734-3344, 6534-3111

Chambers of Commerce

American Chamber of Commerce in Singapore, Shaw Centre, 1 Scotts Road, Singapore 228208 (tel: 6235-0077; fax: 6732-5917; e-mail: info@amcham.org.sg).

British Chamber of Commerce Singapore, Cecil Court, 138 Cecil Street, Singapore 069538 (tel: 6222-3552; fax: 6222-3556; e-mail: info@britcham.org.sg).

Singapore Chinese Chamber of Commerce & Industry, SCCCI Building, 47 Hill Street, Singapore 179365 (tel: 6337-8381; fax: 6339-0605; e-mail: corporate@sccci.org.sg).

Singapore Indian Chamber of Commerce and Industry, Tong Eng Building, 101 Cecil Street, Singapore069533 (tel: 6222-2855; fax: 6223-1707; e-mail: sicci@sicci.com).

Singapore International Chamber of Commerce, John Hancock Tower, 6 Raffles Quay, Singapore 048580 (tel: 6224-1255; fax: 6224-2785; e-mail: general@sicc.com.sg).

Singapore Malay Chamber of Commerce, 72A Bussorah Street, Singapore 199485 (tel: 6297-9296; fax: 6392-4527; e-mail: smcci@singnet.com.sg).

Banking

ABN Amro Bank NV, 63 Chulia Street (tel: 6231-8888; fax: 6532-3108).

ABSA Bank Ltd, 7 Temasek Boulevard, Suntec Tower One (tel: 6333-1033; fax: 6333-1066).

Agricultural Bank of China, 80 Raffles Place, UOB Plaza 2 (tel: 6535-5255; fax: 6538-7960).

American Express Bank Ltd, 16 Collyer Quay, Hitachi Tower (tel: 6538-4833; fax: 6534-3022).

Arab Bank plc, 80 Raffles Place, UOB Plaza 2 (tel: 6533-0055; fax: 6532-2150).

Arab Banking Corporation (BSC), 35-01 Republic Plaza Singapore, 9 Raffles Place, 048619 (tel: 6535-9339; fax: 6532-6288).

Bangkok Bank plc, 180 Cecil Street (tel: 6221-9400; fax: 6225-5852).

Bank of America, National Association, 9 Raffles Place, Republic Plaza Tower 1 (tel: 6239-3888; fax: 6239-3068).

Bank of China, 4 Battery Road, Bank of China Building (tel: 6535-2411; fax: 6534-3401).

Bank of East Asia Ltd, 137 Market Street, Bank of East Asia Building (tel: 6224-1334; fax: 6225-1805).

Bank of India, 138 Robinson Road, Hong Leong Centre (tel: 6222-0011; fax: 6225-4407).

Bank of Montreal, 150 Beach Road, Gateway West (tel: 6296-3233; fax: 6296-5044).

Bank of New York, 1 Temasek Avenue, Millenia Tower (tel: 6432-0222; fax: 6337-4302).

Bank of Nova Scotia, 10 Collyer Quay, Ocean Building (tel: 6535-8688; fax: 6532-2440).

Bank of Singapore, Tong Eng Building, 101 Cecil Street 01-02, 0106 (tel: 6223-9266).

Bank of Tokyo-Mitsubishi Ltd, 9 Raffles Place, Republic Plaza (tel: 6538-3388; fax: 6538-8083).

Chase Manhattan Bank, Shell Tower, 50 Raffles Place, 048623 (tel: 6530-4135, 6224-2888; fax: 6530-4331).

Far Eastern Bank, 156 Cecil Street, Far Eastern Bank Building, PO Box 2950, 0106 (tel: 6221-9055).

Hongkong & Shanghai Banking Corp Ltd, 21 Collyer Quay, 19-00 Hongkong Bank Building (tel: 6530-5412; fax: 6225-0663).

Indian Overseas Bank, 64 Cecil Street, IOB Building (tel: 6225-1100; fax: 6224-4490).

Industrial and Commercial Bank, ICB Building, 2 Shenton Way, 0106 (tel: 6221-1711).

Overseas Chinese Banking Corporation, OCBC Centre, 65 Chulia Street, 0104 (tel: 6535-7222; fax: 6533-7891).

Overseas Union Bank, OUB Centre, 1 Raffles Place, 0104 (tel: 6533-8686; fax: 6533-2293).

Standard Chartered Bank, 6 Battery Road (tel: 6225-8888; fax: 6225-9136).

United Overseas Bank, UOB Plaza, 80 Raffles Place, 048624 (tel: 6533-9898; fax: 6534-2334).

Central bank

Monetary Authority of Singapore, MAS Building, 10 Shenton Way, Singapore 079117 (tel: 6225-5577; fax: 6229-9229; e-mail: webmaster@mas.gov.sg).

Stock exchange

Singapore Exchange (SGX), www.sgx.com

Commodity exchange

Singapore Commodity Exchange (Sicom), www.sicom.com.sg

Travel information

Automobile Association of Singapore, 336 River Valley Road, AA Centre, Singapore (tel: 6333-8811; fax: 6733-50944; e-mail: aasmail@aas.com.sg).

Singapore Airlines, Airline House, 25 Airline Road, Singapore 819829 (tel: 6541-4855; fax: 6542-3002).

Ministry of tourism

Ministry of Trade and Industry, 100 High Street, 09-01 The Treasury, Singapore 179434 (tel: 6225-9911; fax: 6332-7260; e-mail: mti_email@mti.gov.sg).

National tourist organisation offices

Singapore Tourism Board, Tourism Court, 1 Orchard Spring Lane, Singapore 247729 (tel: 6736-6622; fax: 6736-9423; e-mail: ms@stb.com.sg).

Ministries

Ministry of Communications, 39th Storey PSA Building, 460 Alexandra Road, Singapore 119963 (tel: 6270-7988; fax: 6279-9734).

Ministry of Defence, Gombak Drive (off Upper Bukit Timah Road), Mindef Building, Singapore 2366 (tel: 6760-8188; fax: 6762-0112).

Ministry of Development, c/o Meeting Planners Pte Ltd, 2nd Floor, Pico Centre, 20 Kallang Avenue, Singapore 1233 (tel: 6297-2822; fax: 6296-2670, 6292-7577).

Ministry of Environment, Sewerage Department, 14-00 Environmental Building, 40 Scotts Road, Singapore 228231 (tel: 6732-7733; fax: 6731-9699 (sewerage dept), 6731-9456 (general).

Ministry of Finance, 8 Shenton Way, 43rd, 45th, 46th and 50th Storey, Treasury Building, Singapore 0106 (tel: 6225-9911; fax: 6320-9435 (budget), 6320-9932 (PSD), 6224-6847 (revenue)).

Ministry of Foreign Affairs, 250 North Bridge Road, 07-00 Raffles City Tower, Singapore 0617 (tel: 6336-1177, 6330-5795 (after hours); fax: 6339-4330).

Ministry of Information, Communications and the Arts, Public Relations Department, 460 Alexandra Road 36-00, PSA Building, Singapore 0511 (tel: 6270-7988; fax: 6279-9765); Media Division, MITA Building, 140 Hill Street, 2nd Storey, Singapore 179369 (tel: 6837-9666).

Ministry of Manpower, 18 Havelock Road, Singapore 059764 (tel: 6438-5122; fax: 6534-4840; internet: www.mom.gov.sg).

Ministry of National Development, National Development Building, Maxwell Road, Singapore 0106 (tel: 6222-1211; fax: 6322-6254).

Ministry of Trade and Industry, 100 High Street, 09-01 The Treasury, Singapore 179434 (tel: 6225-9911; fax: 6332-7260; e-mail: mti_email@mti.gov.sg).

Other useful addresses

American Business Council, 10-12 Shaw House, 354 Orchard Road, Singapore 0923 (tel: 6235-00770).

ASEAN Investment Promotion Agency, Economic Development Board, 250 North Bridge Road, 24-00 Raffles City Tower, Singapore 0617 (tel: 6336-2288; 6338-8265).

ASEAN Secretariat, 70 A J1 Sisingamangaraja, Jakarta 12110, Indonesia (tel: (+62-21) 726-2991,) (+62-21) 724-3372; fax: (+62-21) 724-3504, (+62-21) 739-8234; e-mail: asean.or.id).

The Association of Banks in Singapore, 12-08 MAS Building, 10 Shenton Way, Singapore 0207 (tel: 6224-4300; fax: 6224-1785).

The Association of Small & Medium Enterprises, Blk 139 Kim Tain Road, Singapore 0316 (tel: 6271-2566; fax: 6271-1257).

British Business Association, 41 Duxton Road, Singapore 0208 (tel: 6227-7861; fax: 6227-7021).

British Businessmen's Association, 3rd Floor, Inchcape House, 450-452 Alexandra Road, Singapore 0511 (tel: 6475-4192).

British Council, 30 Napier Road, Singapore 1025 (tel: 6473-1111; fax: 6472-1010).

British High Commission, Tanglin Road, Singapore 912401 (tel: 6474-0461; fax; 6475-2320).

Civil Aviation Authority of Singapore, Singapore Airtropolis, Changi Airport (tel: 6542-1122; fax: 6545-6222).

Construction Industry Development Board, Annexe A, 3rd Storey, National Development Building, 9 Maxwell Road, Singapore 0106 (tel: 6225-6711; fax: 6225-7307).

Controller of Immigration, 95 South Bridge Road, Pidemco Centre, Singapore (tel: 6532-2877; fax: 6530-1840).

Customs & Excise Department, 03-01 & 10-01 World Trade Centre, 1 Maritime Square, Singapore 099253 (tel: 6272-8222; fax: 6375-2090).

Economic Development Board, 24-00 Raffles City Tower, 250 North Bridge Road, Singapore 0617 (tel: 6336-2288; fax: 6339-6077).

Export Credit Insurance Corporation of Singapore Ltd, 10 Shenton Way, 17-03 MAS Building, Singapore 0207 (tel: 6220-8344; fax: 6224-2887).

Housing and Development Board, 3451 Jalan Bukit Merah, HDB Centre, Singapore 0315 (tel: 6273-9090).

Immigration Department, 7th & 8th Storey, 08-26 Pidemco Centre, 95 South Bridge Road, Singapore 0105 (tel: 6532-2877; fax: 6530-1840).

Inland Revenue Authority of Singapore, Fullerton Building, B1-00 Fullerton Square, Singapore 049178 (tel: 6535-4244; fax: 6535-5393).

International Merchandise Mart PTE Ltd (IMM), Unit 04-01, 2 Jurong East Street 21, Singapore 609601 (tel: 6568-2000; fax: 6568-2500).

Jurong Town Corporation, Jurong Town Hall, 301 Jurong Town Hall Road, Singapore 609431 (tel: 6560-0056; fax: 6565-5301).

National Arts Council, Arts Division, MCD Building, 512 Thomson Road, Singapore 1129 (tel: 6258-9595; fax: 6350-6118).

National Productivity Board, 2 Bukit Merah, Central NPB Building, Singapore 0315 (tel: 6734-5534).

Port of Singapore Authority (PSA), PSA Building, 460 Alexandra Road, Singapore 119963 (tel: 6274-7111; fax: 6274-4677).

Public Utilities Board, PUB Building, 111 Somerset Way, Singapore 0207 (tel: 6235-8888; fax: 6731-3020).

Registry of Trade and Businesses, 05-01/15 International Plaza, 10 Anson Road, Singapore 0207 (tel: 6227-8551; fax: 6225-1676).

Singapore Confederation of Industries (formerly Singapore Manufacturers' Association), SMA House, 20 Orchard Road, Singapore 238830 (tel: 6338-8787; fax: 6339-3340).

Singapore Embassy (US), 3501 International Place, NW, Washington DC 20008 (tel: (+1-202)-537-3100; fax: (1-202)-537-0876; e-mail: singemb.dc@verizon.net).

Singapore Hotel Association, 11 Mount Sophia, Singapore 228461 (tel: 6339-9918; fax: 6339-3795).

Singapore Importers and Exporters Association, 2nd Floor, 76-C Robinson Road, Singapore 0106 (tel: 6222-3451).

Singapore Institute of Standards and Industrial Research (SISIR), 1 Science Park Drive, Singapore 0511 (tel: 6778-7777; fax: 6778-0086).

Singapore International Monetary Exchange (SIMEX), Square, 07-00 OUB Centre, Singapore 0104 (tel: 6535-7282; fax: 6535-7382).

Stock Exchange of Singapore, 26-01/08 The Exchange, 20 Cecil Street, Singapore 049705 (tel: 6535-3788; fax: 6535-0775).

Telecommunication Authority of Singapore, TAS Building, 35 Robinson Road, Singapore 068876 (tel: 6738-7788; fax: 6733-0073).

Trade Development Board, 07-00 Bugis Junction Office Tower, 230 Victoria Street, Singapore 188024 (tel: 6271-9388; fax: 6274-0770).

US Embassy, 30 Hill Street, Singapore 0617 (tel: 6338-0251; fax: 6338-8472).

Work Permit and Employment Department, Ministry of Labour, 18 Havelock Road, Singapore 059764 (tel: 6534-1511; fax: 6539-5344/5).

Internet sites

Singapore Connect: http://sgconnect.asia1.com.sg

Singapore Government: www.gov.sg

Singapore Statistical Office: www.singstat.gov.sg

Singapore Yellow Pages: www.yellowpages.com.sg

Sint Maarten

KEY FACTS

Official name: Sint Maarten (St Maarten)

Head of State: King William-Alexander of The Netherlands, represented by Governor Eugene Holiday (from 10 Oct 2010)

Head of government: Prime Minister Marcel Gumbs (UPP) (from 19 Dec 2014)

Ruling party: Coalition government led by United People's Party (UPP) (from Oct 2014)

Area: 34 square kilometres

Population: 37,249 (2010; census figure)

Capital: Philipsburg

Official language: Dutch and English (official)

Currency: US Dollar (US$) = 100 cents

GDP real growth: -0.10% (2011)*

GDP: US$851.00 million (2011)*

Unemployment: 12.00% (2011)*

Inflation: 3.70% (2011)*

Balance of trade: -US$747.50 million (2013)

* estimated figure

COUNTRY PROFILE

The islands of the Netherlands Antilles were first inhabited by Carib and Arawak Indians.

1493 Christopher Columbus was the first European to sight the islands.

1499 The Spanish explorer, Alonso de Ojedo, visited Curaçao but left without establishing a settlement.

1527 The islands were settled, mainly by Spanish and Portuguese Jews escaping persecution.

1634 The Dutch East India Company took over the islands, 'persuading' the settlers to depart, first from St Maarten and later from Aruba.

1642–46 Peter Stuyvesant was governor.

1816 After a number of changes in possession, the islands – Curaçao, Aruba and Bonaire (part of the Leeward Islands), St Eustatius, Saba and Sint Maarten (half of which is the French territory of St Martin) (which are part of the Windward Islands) – were confirmed as Dutch territory.

1863 Slavery was abolished.

1916 The first oil refinery was opened in Curaçao.

1954 Internal autonomy was granted as associated states within a federacy.

1986 Aruba separated from the other islands and became a self-governing member of the Kingdom of The Netherlands. The remaining islands became the Antilles of Five.

1998 A general election resulted in a six-party coalition government under Prime Minister Suzanne Camelia-Römer.

1999 The Partido Laboral Krusado Popular (PLKP) (Labour Party People's Crusade) left the coalition, to be replaced by the Partido Antiá Restrukturá (PAR) (Party for the Restructured Antilles), with Miguel Pourier becoming prime minister.

2000 In a referendum, St Maarten voted in favour of separate status within the Kingdom of The Netherlands and no longer to be a part of The Netherlands Antilles government.

2002 The ruling coalition was returned to power in the elections.

2004 The coalition government avoided collapse, caused by a corruption crisis, when support was offered by the Democratische Partij (DP) (Democratic Party) of Bonaire. However the collapse finally arrived when the National People's Party (PNP) withdrew citing its unwillingness to work with Justice Minster Ben Komproe. Prime Minister Louisa-Godett resigned and Etienne Ys became prime minister.

2005 The islanders of Curaçao voted to become an autonomous state within the Kingdom of The Netherlands and break with The Netherlands Antilles. The tiny neighbouring island, Sint Eustatius, decided to remain within the Antilles.

2006 Emily de Jongh-Elhage became prime minister, following parliamentary elections. The islands of Curaçao and St Maarten signed an agreement of independence with The Netherlands to become autonomous territories within the Kingdom of the Netherlands. At the same time Bonaire, Saba and St Eustatius will become city-states of the Kingdom of the Netherlands. When these changes are enacted the Netherlands Antilles will cease to exist. A new terminal at Curaçao International Airport was opened, designed to accommodate around 1.6 million passengers per year. The growth in tourism on the island and in the region is seen as a major industry and a phase two expansion is planned for when arrivals are expected to reach 2.5 million in 2031.

2007 Negotiations for a change in their status began between Bonaire, Saba and St Eustatius and The Netherlands.

2010 In the last general election to be held before The Netherlands Antilles ceased to exist as a country, the Partido Antiá Restrukturá (PAR) (Party for the Restructured Antilles) won six seats out of 22. In the first island council elections held the Democratische Partij Sint Eustatius (DPSE) (Democratic Party of Sint Eustatius) won 17 per cent of the vote (two seats out of 15), National Alliance (alliance of two parties) 46 per cent (seven), United People 36 per cent (six). A national census was undertaken in July that recorded a number of 37,249 people. Following coalition talks Sarah Westcot-Williams (DPSE) became prime minister of the independent St Maarten. On 10 October the Netherlands Antilles ceased to exist and Curaçao and St Maarten became semi-autonomous countries within the kingdom of The Netherlands. Bonaire, St Eustatius and Saba became Bijzondere Gemeenten (special municipalities).

2011 In April, new visa requirements were introduced that require visitors from Guyana and Jamaica obtain a visa in their home country before arriving in St Maarten. Puerto Rico's JetBlue Airways launched a daily, nonstop service from San Juan to St Maarten in mid-November.
2012 On 8 May the government led by Prime Minister Sarah Westcot-Williams resigned. On 21 May a new cabinet, headed by Sarah Wescot-Williams was sworn in. On 25 November the central bank announced that it would only allow a maximum growth of domestic private borrowing of 1 per cent until February 2013. The credit freeze, introduced in March, was extended to address the persistently high deficit on the current account. The fall in international reserves was halted and began to increase.
2013 In its September report the Royal Bank of Canada forecast growth in St Maarten at 1.1 per cent for 2013.
2014 On a visit to Barbados in April Governor Eugene Holiday expressed St Maarten's interest in developing closer bilateral ties with other Caribbean islands and becoming an associate member of the Caribbean Community (Caricom). In June the committee for the division of properties and debts (set up to formulate a balanced division of the properties and debts of the former Netherlands Antilles) announced that it would be able to present its findings in August. The chaiman announced that they still awaited reports from the Stichting Overheidsaccountantsbureau (SOAB) (the original accounting agency for the governments of the Netherlands Antilles and Curaçao) and accountants KPMG. Once these are received the final formula dividing the properties and debts between Curaçao, St Maarten and the BES islands will be presented to the governments of Curaçao, St Maarten and the minister of Kingdom relations in The Netherlands. The one sticking point appeared to have been the Saba Bank Resources Inc, which had been set up in the 1980s to exploit any potential oil found in the Saba Bank (in Saba territorial waters). Chairman Faroe Metry said that although no oil has so far been found, it is possible that with new techniques and 'some luck' it may be in the future, and in which case the islands should benefit. Elections to the Staten van Sint Maarten (Estates) were held on 29 August. The result was a win for the United People's party (UP) with 42.46 per cent of the vote (seven seats out of 15), followed by the National Alliance with 27.66 per cent (four), Democratische Partij Sint Maarten (DPSM) (Democratic Party Sint Maarten) 16.54 per cent (two), United Sint Maarten Party 11.28 per cent (2). Turnout was 69.43 per cent. On 6 October Governor Holiday asked in-coming prime minister, leader of UP, Theo Heyliger, to form a form a government. However, St Maarten newspaper, *Today*, reported that Dutch interior and kingdom relations minister, Ronald Plasterk, had instructed Governor Holiday not to ratify the appointments of the members of the new cabinet until an expanded vetting process has been completed.
2015 A decision was reached between the governments of The Netherlands, Aruba, Curaçao and St Maarten on 9 January whereby the four should work to agree a mechanism whereby future disagreements between the countries of the kingdom can be resolved. The result should be a proceedure to be followed to avoid disputes such as that between Aruba and the Netherlands over instructions as to its budget and St Maarten over problems with the reliability of politicians as candidates for ministerial posts. The government of Prime Minister Marcel Gumbs resigned after it lost a vote of no-confidence (by eight votes to seven) on 30 September.

Political structure

Constitution

A new constitution was formed in 2010 after the dissolution of the Netherlands Antilles.
Sint Maarten became a semi-autonomous country within the Kingdom of the Netherlands on 10 October 2010. The Netherlands government remains responsible for defence and foreign policy, and has oversight over Sint Maarten's finances under a debt relief agreement.

Independence date

10 October 2010.

Form of state

Parliamentary democratic monarchy.

The executive

Executive power is wielded by the Prime Minister and his appointed cabinet. The monarchy of the Netherlands holds purely ceremonial power.

National legislature

The parliament is known as the Estates of Sint Maarten (Estates). It has 15 members, elected by proportional representation for four-year terms.

Legal system

The legal system is based on Dutch civil law, with some English common law. Judges are appointed by the monarch. Rights of appeal exist from The Netherlands Antilles Court of Appeals to the Supreme Court of The Netherlands, in The Hague.

Last elections

29 August 2014 (Staten van Sint Maarten)
Results: Staten van Sint Maarten (Estates): United People's Party 42.46 per cent of the vote (seven seats out of 15), National Alliance (alliance of two parties) 27.66 per cent (four), Democratische Partij Sint Maarten (DPSM) (Democratic Party Sint Maarten) 16.54 per cent (two), United Sint Maarten Party 11.28 per cent (2). Turnout was 69.16 per cent.

Next elections

2018

Political parties

Ruling party

Coalition government led by United People's Party (UPP) (from Oct 2014)

Main opposition party

National Alliance

Population

37,249 (2010; census figure)

Ethnic make-up

African and mixed race (85 per cent), Carib Amerindian, white, East Asian.

Religions

Baptist, Roman Catholic, Protestant, Jewish, Seventh-Day Adventist and others.

Health

Curaçao has two general hospitals and one surgical hospital and receives patients from the other islands of the former Netherlands Antilles. Most health professionals receive training in The Netherlands.
It is estimated that around 30 per cent of the population of the former Netherlands Antilles suffer from hypertension; psychological problems are also highly prevalent among adults. The general standard of health among the Antilleans is poor, with poor nutrition and little or no exercise undertaken by the adult population. The Dutch government has assigned priority to encouraging the population to develop healthier lifestyles.

HIV/Aids

There is a national strategic action plan to halt the rapid spread of the disease. The drugs problem on the islands could prove to be a potent source of transmission.
Life expectancy: 76.3 years (estimate 2003)
Fertility rate/Maternal mortality rate: 2.1 births per woman (World Bank)
Birth rate/Death rate: 16 births per 1,000 population; 6.4 deaths per 1,000 population (2003).
Child (under 5 years) mortality rate (per 1,000): 11 per 1,000 live births (2003)

Welfare

A public insurance programme covers 100 per cent of health care costs for blue-collar workers. There is also an insurance fund for retired workers. Private companies also provide insurance plans for their employees. A social security fund covers employees of small private establishments.

Main cities

Philipsburg (capital, estimated population 1,669), Princess Quarter (16,516), Cul De Sac (10,717), Cole Bay (8,223), Little Bay (2,959).

Languages spoken

English is the most widely spoken, although with a strong local dialect. Dutch is typically used in official documents, particularly in the legal field. Spanish and French are also spoken.

Official language/s

Dutch and English (official)

Media

Press

Dailies: The only regional daily newspaper is *Amigoe* (www.amigoe.com), and the local *Daily Herald* (www.thedailyherald.com).

Broadcasting

There are several radio stations broadcasting, including Island 92 (www.island92.com), SXM radio (www.sxmradio.com), which offers a number of genres. The Leeward Broadcasting Corporation broadcasts in Sint Maarten. Channel 15 is the television station broadcasting, which belongs to the SXM network (www.sxmtv.15.com).

Economy

The former Netherlands Antilles economy, virtually devoid of natural resources, is heavily service-oriented, 84 per cent of GDP, and largely based on tourism with offshore financial services. In 2013, the country received 1.8 million visitors via cruise ship and roughly 500,000 arrivals through the international airport. These figures helped GDP growth to reach 4.1 per cent in 2013, before falling to 3.6 per cent in 2014.

St Maarten's economy is dominated by tourism. Agriculture accounts for only 1 per cent of GDP, producing aloes, sorghum, vegetables and tropical fruit. Dutch aid remains important to the economy. The unemployment rate remains high at over 15 per cent. The island has a higher per capita income and a well-developed infrastructure, compared with other countries in the region.

External trade

There is trade in high-quality jewelry, sold to tourist.

Imports

Foodstuffs, gold and other precious metals, gem stones, consumer goods, vehicles, household goods, petroleum products and energy.

Agriculture

Farming

The agricultural sector contributes 1 per cent to GDP and employs 5 per cent of the workforce.

About 8 per cent of total area is cultivated arable land. Soil is generally poor and rainfall inadequate for most crops.

Small amounts of fruit and vegetables are grown for local consumption.

Tourism

Tourism is the major industry and the majority of visitors are from the US (around 40 per cent of stay-over arrivals), followed by South America, the Netherlands, Canada and the Caribbean region. Most activities on offer to visitors are typically energetic and based around the sea and beach.

In 2013 there were 1.8 million visitors to the country that arrived via cruise ship, and a further 500,000 arrivals coming through the country's international airport.

Hydrocarbons

Banking and insurance

Under an EU tax directive introduced in 2005 in a number of associate and dependent EU countries, impose a withholding tax to be passed to the relevant EU country but typically retains the anonymity of the saver. Withholding taxes began at 15 per cent and will rise to 35 per cent by 2011.

The Netherlands Antillies has also agreed to supply information on tax fraud, for criminal or civil trials, and notify EU member states about additional malpractice.

Central bank

Centrale Bank van Curaçao en Sint Maarten (Central Bank of Curaçao and St Maarten) (CBCS)

Time

GMT minus five hours (minus six hours during summer daylight saving).

Geography

Sint Maarten is the southern 34 square kilometres of the island it shares with the French territory of Saint Martin (37square km), in the Windward islands located 250km north of the coast of Guadeloupe, in the Caribbean Sea.

The terrain is dry and volcanic, with little fresh water available and scant rainfall. There are several mountains, of which Pic Paradis is the largest (424 metres). There are two saltwater pans within Sint Maarten and a large one shared with St Martin. Tourists are drawn to the extensive white beaches and azure waters around the coasts on which its towns are built – the interior of the island is largely uninhabited.

Hemisphere

Northern

Climate

The average annual temperature is 27 degrees centegrade, the total average rainfall is 995mm. Along with all Caribbean islands St Maarten is subject to hurricans, typically between June–September.

Entry requirements

Passports

Required by all and must be valid for at least three months from date of departure.

Visa

Not required by nationals of countries which are signatories of the Schengen Accords, which includes most EU/EEA member states; North America and Australasia for visits up to three months.

Work permits must be obtained before arrival. See www.stmaarten-info.com (information page) for details.

All visitors must provide evidence of sufficient funds for their stay and a return/onward ticket.

Currency advice/regulations

There are no restrictions regarding the import and export of local or foreign currencies.

The US dollar is freely used and travellers cheques are widely accepted. ATM machines often accept international bank cards.

Prohibited imports

Include illegal drugs, weapons, ammunition, explosives and incendiary items, live animals and fresh foolstuffs, without permits.

It is illegal to export coral and marine shells from Sint Maarten.

Hotels

There are numerous hotels and of a range of qualities, all located near beaches. A government tax of 5 per cent and 10–15 per cent is added to the bill.

Credit cards

All major cards are accepted.

Public holidays (national)

Fixed dates

1 Jan (New Year's Day), 30 Apr (Queen's Birthday), 1 May (Labour Day), 11 Nov (St Maarten Day), 25–26 Dec (Christmas).

Variable dates

Good Friday and Easter Monday (Mar/Apr) Publis Day and Carnival (two day in Apr) Ascension Day (Aug), Kingdom Day (Dec).

Working hours

Banking

Mon–Fri: 0830–1200, 1330–1630.

Business

Mon–Fri: 0830–1200, 1330–1630.

Government

Mon–Fri: 0830–1200, 1330–1630.

Shops

Mon–Sat: 0800–1200, 1400–1800.

Tourist shops open on Sundays and public holidays and when cruise ships call.

Telecommunications

Mobile/cell phones

There are several 900, 900/1800 GSM services covering the island.

Electricity supply

110V with US style plugs and sockets.

Getting there

Air

National airline: Windward Islands Airways and AirStMaarten are both commercial organisations.

International airport/s: Princess Juliana International Airport (SXM); located 15km northwest of Philipsburg, with shops and restaurants. Intercontinental flights arrive during the main holiday seasons and inter-regional flights, particularly to other small Caribbean islands, throughout the year. Taxis, car hire and limousines, with chauffeur, are available.

Airport tax: All fees are included in the price of ticktes.

Surface

There are no road borders between the French north and Sint Maarten.

Water: There are ferries operating between Sint Maarten, Saint-Martin, St Eustatius and Saba.

Getting about

Car hire

Car and motorcycle hire is widely available. An international licence is required. Chauffeured limousines are also available, with daily rates.

BUSINESS DIRECTORY

Telephone area codes

The international dialling code (IDD) for St Maarten is + 599, followed by area code and subscriber's number.

Useful telephone numbers

Police emergency: 911
Fire: 919
Police and immigration department 542-2222
Lt. Governor's Office: 542-6085
Tourism office: 557-7966

Banking

Algemene Bank Nederland, Frontstraat, PO Box 295, Philipsburg, St Maarten (tel: 9542-7520).

Windward Islands Bank Ltd, Pondfill, Philipsburg, PO Box 220, St Maarten (tel: 542-2313; fax: 542-4761; internet: wib-bank.net).

Scotiabank, Backstreet 61, Philipsburg, PO Box 303, St Maarten (tel: 542-3317; fax: 542-2435; email: bns@stmaarten@scotiabank.com).

Central bank

Centrale Bank van Curaçao en Sint Maarten (Central Bank of Curaçao and St. Maarten) (CBCS), Walter Nisbeth Road 25, Pondfill, Philipsburg (tel: 42-3520; fax: 42-4307: email: info@centralbank.an).

Ministries

The Lieutenant Governor, Government Administration Bld, Clem Labega Sq, Philipsburg (tel: 542-6085; fax: 952-4884).

Office of the Minister Plenipotentiary of the Netherlands Antilles, Badhuisweg 175, 2597 JP The Hague, The Netherlands (tel: (+31-70) 351-2811; fax: (+31-70) 351-2722).

Other useful addresses

St. Maarten Medical Centre, Cay Hill, (tel: 543-1111).

Internet sites

Government of St Maarten: www.stmaarten-info.com

Princess Juliana International Airport: www.pjiae.com

St Maarten tourist information portal: www.st-maarten.com

Slovakia

KEY FACTS

Official name: Slovenská Republika (Slovak Republic)

Head of State: President Andrej Kiska (since 15 June 2014)

Head of government: Prime Minister Robert Fico (Smer-SD) (from 4 Apr 2012)

Ruling party: Strana Smer-Tretia Cesta-Sociálna Demokracia (Smer-SD) (Direction Party-Social Democrats) (from 10 Mar 2012)

Area: 49,035 square km

Population: 5.42 million (2014)*

Capital: Bratislava

Official language: Slovak

Currency: Euro (€) = 100 cents (from 1 Jan 2009; previous currency Slovak koruna, locked at Sk30.126 per euro)

Exchange rate: €0.89 per US$ (Sep 2015)

GDP per capita: US$18,454 (2014)*

GDP real growth: 2.41% (2014)

GDP: US$99.97 billion (2014)

Labour force: 2.74 million (2014)*

Unemployment: 13.22% (2014)

Inflation: -0.10% (2014)

Balance of trade: US$4.51 billion (2014)

Annual FDI: US$3.66 billion (2011)

* estimated figure

In 2015 Slovakia had become one of the European Union's 'tough' economic countries. In April Peter Kazimir, Slovakia's austere finance minister, had shown the door to the country's trade unions who were demanding an additional '13th month' additional pension payment. But Mr Kazimir did not only mete out his harsh treatment to the unions. One of the measures that had been introduced – presumably to incentivise ministers – was that which required a freeze on ministerial salaries when Slovakia's public debt rose above 53 per cent of GDP, a level it had attained in the two previous years. At least Slovakia was experiencing reasonable growth and declining budget deficits, perhaps understandably turning its ministers into zealous advocates of a growth-friendly austerity.

Good guys now

His country's improving economic performance had prompted Mr Kazimir to announce that 'Slovakia will no longer belong among the European sinners.' His remark did little justice to what was a largely impeccable European record. Slovakian members of the European Parliament (MEPs) had a well above average record of attending Brussels parliamentary votes and debates. While Slovakian MEPs could at least take some pride in showing up for almost 90 per cent of the parliament's votes – more than their counterparts from the Czech Republic and Poland (each at around 85 per cent) and Hungary (at 80 per cent). 'Showing up' often seemed more important than participating in parliamentary proceedings. The figures did not take into account the quality of their contributions to debates, nor indeed to the way in which they had actually voted.

Shocks and surprises in Bratislava

Of greater interest to the international community was not, however, what Slovakian deputies got up to in Brussels. There was much greater political excitement, surprise and interest back in Bratislava. Against all expectations, the incumbent Prime Minister Robert Fico managed to lose the presidential run-off election. Equally surprising was that his defeat was no wafer-thin affair – Fico could only garner 41 per cent of the votes, against his opponent, the independent Andrej Kiska's commanding 51 per cent. Mr Kiska was Slovakia's first president since independence not to have had any connections with the Communist Party. The election was hardly conducted to the highest standards – a political novice, the

51 year-old businessman Kiska had offered Slovakians an alternative – and apparently attractive – voice, leaving Mr Fico belatedly to resort to desperate electioneering tactics, one of which was to claim that his opponent had secret links to the Church of Scientology. Another charge levelled at the political outsider was that his wealth derived from unfairly high-interest loans.

His election tactics manifestly unsuccessful, Mr Fico was left to pick up the pieces of his presidential bid. The best laid plans had come to nought. Many observers considered that Mr Fico had lost – even thrown away – the election rather than perceiving Mr Kiska to have won it. Somehow, Mr Fico's success in turning around Slovakia's economy counted for little. Canny Slovakians were doubtful about any unbalanced concentration of political power in one party – in this case Mr Fico's Strana Smer-Tretia Cesta-Sociálna Demokracia (Smer-SD) (Direction Party-Social Democrats). Mr Kiska simply had to harvest the anti-Fico sentiments, principally among right-wing voters as well as the growing distrust of Slovakia's major political parties where corruption issues had surfaced. Slovakia ranked a middling 61 out of the 157 countries surveyed in Transparency International's 2014 *Corruption Perceptions Index*, only one place behind the Czech Republic, an improvement of 7 places over its 2013 ranking. International investors were increasingly conscious of the need to invest in countries where the rule of law actually meant something. Slovakia had succeeded in attracting major foreign manufacturers, which had helped maintain high growth levels. But the growth had not generated enough jobs (see Economy, below). There was, however, little to choose between Messrs Fico and Kiska on foreign policy, which meant that whatever else changed, Slovakia would probably continue with its pretty exemplary European policies. A report in the London *Economist* suggested that the independent Mr Kiska promised to correct the Smer-SD party's dominance 'and bring dignity to the office.' However, it remained to be seen whether the result of the presidential election was likely to prove 'a political turning point.'

The economy

Few Slovakians would have heard of the European Union's (EU) Excessive Deficit Procedure (EDP) and even fewer would have been aware that their country had been threatened with penalties for not adhering to the terms and conditions imposed by the EDP. So it was with some relief that the government greeted the news that in 2014 Slovakia, according to the EU's spring forecast, was likely to see its budget deficit drop below three per cent with growth set to reach 2.2 per cent in 2014 and an impressive 3.3 per cent in 2015.

In its November 2015 annual assessment of the Slovakian economy, the International Monetary Fund (IMF), confirmed that growth was picking up, as domestic demand strengthened further. Against a backdrop of accommodative monetary conditions and low oil prices, higher capacity utilisation and a concerted push to spend expiring EU Funds were boosting investment, while job creation and real wage growth were fuelling private consumption. Slovakia's export performance remained strong, but imports had managed to rise even faster, reflecting a healthy domestic demand. Growth was forecast by the IMF to reach 3.2 per cent in 2015 and 3.5 per cent in 2016–17 as further expansion of the automobile industry was expected, before settling at a little over three per cent in the medium term. Although inflation was expected to be near zero in 2015 due to falling energy costs, prices should rise in 2016 as the output gap closed.

Given Slovakia's comprehensive integration into the global economy, the strong outlook remained vulnerable to external risks. Resilience to shocks was strengthened by a sound and liquid banking sector, low private sector leverage and limited public debt. If, however, growth were to falter among its key trading partners such as Germany – whether due to weakness in the euro-zone itself, a slowdown in China or other emerging market economies, or tensions between Russia and Ukraine – Slovakia's important export sector would be affected. On the domestic side, rapid household credit growth could lead to financial sector risks, while high long-term unemployment could erode human capital, undermine growth and even exacerbate demographic challenges.

The IMF noted that high joblessness, especially long-term and among youth and among women, as well as sharp regional differences, remained key challenges. Rising growth had led to welcome job creation. Nonetheless, the unemployment rate remained in double digits and some groups were especially affected: more than 60 per cent of the unemployed had been jobless for longer than a year; youth unemployment had declined but remained near 25 per cent and the share of young people not in education, employment, or training was one of the highest in the EU; Slovakia also compared unfavourably with its European peers in terms of female labour force participation. Furthermore, substantial disparities in terms of income, employment and infrastructure remained obvious between Bratislava and Slovakia's other regions; there were few job opportunities in high unemployment areas.

Generating 'job-rich' growth in Slovakia's less dynamic regions while addressing longer-term labour market and demographic challenges called for a comprehensive approach. In the view of the

KEY INDICATORS — Slovakia

	Unit	2011	2012	2013	2014	**2015
Population	m	*5.45	5.40	5.41	*5.42	*5.42
Gross domestic product (GDP)	US$bn	96.10	91.40	97.74	99.97	*87.53
GDP per capita	US$	17,644	16,912	18,064	*18,454	*16,138
GDP real growth	%	3.3	1.8	1.4	2.4	*2.9
Inflation	%	4.1	3.7	1.5	-0.1	*0.0
Unemployment	%	13.6	14.0	14.3	13.2	*12.4
Exports (fob) (goods)	US$m	78,397.8	80,751.1	85,521.6	83,219.8	–
Imports (fob) (goods)	US$m	75,075.8	76,102.6	79,841.2	78,707.3	–
Balance of trade	US$m	3,322.0	4,648.5	5,680.4	4,512.6	–
Current account	US$m	-1,986.0	2,048.0	1,486.0	*161.0	*357.0
Total reserves minus gold	US$m	853.0	818.0	922.0	1,392.0	–
Foreign exchange	US$m	60.0	17.0	54.0	–	–
Exchange rate	per US$	0.75	0.77	0.73	0.82	–

* estimated figure ** forecast figure

IMF, this needed to include enhancing road and railway infrastructure, including making effective use of EU Funds, which would help promote investment in lagging regions, a priority recognised in recent government initiatives. Better transport links as well as a shift in budget resources toward rental housing programmes could also promote labour mobility. More broadly, strengthening the business climate (eg, improvements to the legal and procurement systems to address governance weaknesses) could encourage private investment.

The IMF also considered lowering the labour tax rate to be necessary, especially for low-wage or part-time workers, which would foster labour force participation and help reduce disincentives to hiring. In this spirit, the reduction in the health contribution allowance to offset the impact of the early 2015 minimum wage increase was a welcome step. The draft budget's moderate increase in the childcare allowance and funding for kindergarten facilities go in the right direction to raise female labour force participation.

Strengthening education and training would also allay the skill shortages and mismatches that were becoming more apparent. Effective implementation of the recently launched dual system for vocational education and job experience was essential to help meet workforce requirements. Efforts to improve elementary and secondary education, especially for marginalised populations such as the Roma (Gypsy) communities, where integration needs were still substantial should also be made a high priority.

Further fiscal consolidation was, in the view of the IMF, still needed to ensure room for policy manoeuvre. After a substantial narrowing of fiscal imbalances in 2013 to exit the EU's EDP, the deficit had remained between 2.5 and 3 per cent of GDP. While high unemployment, large infrastructure needs, subdued inflation and favourable borrowing conditions might argue for a supportive fiscal stance, the output gap was now closing rapidly. Moreover, there was limited room under a Fiscal Responsibility Act (FRA) debt brake that would require spending cuts and the FRA's thresholds were to be lowered by one percentage point per year starting in 2018, putting even more pressure on deficit targets in the medium term. To create the headroom necessary for fiscal policy to be able to play a counter-cyclical role in the event of shocks, a debt ratio safely below that of FRA debt brakes is necessary.

Broadening the tax base, enhancing revenue collection and achieving spending efficiencies would also help secure the required fiscal adjustment while funding key priorities. Improved revenue administration had anchored efforts to contain deficits in recent years, but there had also been cuts in investment spending and some reliance on temporary measures. An aggressive push to use EU Funds in 2015 might help fill some infrastructure gaps. Expenditure discipline would be needed in 2016 to offset costs from higher wages, a reduced VAT rate for basic foods and other social outlays. The IMF considered that fiscal policies should focus on enhancing revenue collection and broadening the tax base, improvements in VAT efficiency, the introduction of what the IMF described as a 'market value-based real estate tax' which would help achieve adjustment and create space for key priorities. It would also be important to ensure that the introduction of a reduced VAT rate did not undermine compliance.

Identifying spending efficiencies, potentially in health and public order and safety, was also deemed to be important by the IMF, as part of planned efforts to improve value-for-money in the budget and towards undertaking a comprehensive review of social benefits. Importance was also attached to funding priorities to address labour market challenges and regional disparities such as infrastructure investment (including by making effective use of EU Funds in the new programming period), a lower labour tax rate, education and training, childcare and kindergartens.

Consideration also ought to be given to using privatisation proceeds for debt reduction (eg the funds that had been realised from the sale of Slovak Telekom in May 2015), refraining from increasing public ownership of companies and undertaking the further privatisation of still sizeable state shareholdings.

Finally, the IMF stressed strengthening Slovakia's long-term finances. Going beyond recent pension reforms was likely to be necessary to address the rising retirement and healthcare costs due to population ageing, while the reopening of what was known as the second pension pillar had increased future government liabilities and undermined the development of institutional investors and domestic capital markets.

In its overview of the Slovakian economy, the European Bank for Reconstruction and Development (EBRD) broadly concurred with the IMF, noting that in 2013 economic growth had slumped to 0.9 per cent, dragged down by domestic demand, largely due to a 5 per cent drop (in annual terms) in gross fixed capital formation. By contrast, in the first half of 2014 the economy grew by 2.3 per cent, primarily on the back of a rebound in household consumption – the strongest since the pre-crisis peak in 2008 – and a robust increase in gross investments. Due to weaker growth in some key markets, exports slowed somewhat in the first half of 2014. Domestic demand was likely to become the main growth driver in 2014-15, supported by strong credit growth, especially as corporate credit growth turned positive in annual terms in March for the first time since May 2012. Following a significant expansion in 2013, export volumes began to stagnate in the second quarter of 2014. Exports to other EU countries had lost momentum in the first half of the year and exports to Russia had registered a drop of 7 per cent over the same period. However, exports to Russia represented only a small portion (less than 4 per cent of GDP) of total exports and the Slovak Republic remained virtually untouched by the ban on food imports imposed by Russia. As already mentioned, successful fiscal consolidation had enabled the Slovak Republic to exit the EU's EDP. After reaching eight per cent in 2009, the fiscal deficit narrowed to 2.8 per cent of GDP in 2013. The government's fiscal position had improved in the previous few years, in part due to measures such as an increase in corporate tax, the elimination of the flat tax on personal income and an earlier reduction in contributions to private pension funds. Nevertheless, public debt in 2013 had exceeded the 55 per cent threshold set under the 2011 Fiscal Responsibility Law, forcing the government to implement a partial freeze on spending. The labour market situation had also marginally improved. The unemployment rate had decreased somewhat, although at 13.8 per cent it remained high by regional standards. The labour force participation rate remained low and at 65.1 per cent, the employment rate was well below the EU-wide average of 68.4 per cent. The EBRD considered that Slovakia's economic growth should accelerate to 3 per cent in 2015. However, there were important downside risks. As a highly open economy, the Slovak Republic would always be significantly affected by weak performance in the euro-zone.

Risk assessment

Economy	Good
Politics	Good
Regional stability	Good

COUNTRY PROFILE

Slovakia, called Oberungarn (Upper Hungary) in some older maps, had politically been a part of the Hungarian kingdom for centuries, ever since the Moravian Kingdom had been destroyed in 902.

1536–1783 Bratislava, formerly Pressburg, was the capital of Hungary.

1867–1917 The Habsburg domains in central Europe were reconstituted as the dual monarchy of Austria-Hungary. Slovakia's struggle for independence suffered a setback when Hungary's parliament gained a large degree of political autonomy from the Austrian administration in Vienna. The policy of Magyarisation that the Hungarian administration strove to achieve – Hungarian was to be the exclusive language of administration, jurisdiction and education – was most disturbing to Slovakia.

1918 At the end of the First World War, Slovakia announced its independence from the Austro-Hungarian empire and incorporation into the new Republic of Czechoslovakia with Thomas Masaryk as the country's first president.

1938 Czechoslovakia ceded its German-speaking areas of Sudetenland to Germany.

1939–45 The country fell under German control until the end of the Second World War.

1946 The Czechoslovak Communist Party (CPCz) formed a power-sharing government following national elections.

1948 After mass protests and strikes orchestrated by the Communists, a government crisis left the CPCz with a majority in government.

1949–67 Stalinist-style rule, complete with party purges.

1968 Alexander Dubcek, the CPCz leader, introduced the policy of 'socialism with a human face', which ended with the crushing of the reformist movement by the Soviet army.

1969–88 There were on-going protests at occupation by the Soviet troops. Václav Havel and a group of dissidents called for the restoration of civil and political rights. Mass demonstrations in 1988 marked the anniversary of the 1968 invasion.

1989 The new spirit of *glasnost* was met with scepticism as the government initially resisted political and economic change. However, large public demonstrations in the major cities, the 'Velvet Revolution', led to the resignation of the Communist Party leadership. Václav Havel was elected president and a pluralistic political system and market economy were introduced.

1990 The country was renamed the Czech and Slovak Federative Republic. The first free elections since 1946 led to the establishment of a coalition government involving all major parties, with the exception of the CPCz, and Havel was re-elected president.

1991 The Soviet forces completed their withdrawal.

1992 In elections, the Czech voters backed the centre-right, while the Slovaks supported Slovak separatists and left-wing parties. Vladimir Meciar (a supporter of Slovak separatism) became Slovak prime minister. He opposed the rapid privatisation of the public sector proposed by the Czech prime minister, Václav Klaus. Neither was prepared to compromise and so agreed to the separation of Slovakia, despite President Havel's objections.

1993 Czechoslovakia divided into two independent countries, the Czech Republic (comprising the regions of Bohemia and Moravia) and the Slovak Republic (Slovakia). Michal Kovac became president of the Slovak Republic, with Vladimir Meciar continuing as prime minister.

1994 Meciar was voted out of office and was replaced by Jozef Moravcik. But following National Council elections Meciar was returned to power.

1998 Kovac's presidential term expired and Prime Minister Meciar assumed some presidential powers. Mikuláš Dzurinda became prime minister as opposition parties refused to co-operate with Meciar, despite his party, Hnutie Za Demokratické Slovensko (HZDS) (Movement for Democratic Slovakia), gaining most seats in the general elections.

1999 Rudolf Schuster was elected president.

2000 The Slovenská Demokratická a Krestanská Únia-Demokratická Strana (SDKÚ-DS) (Slovak Democratic and Christian Union-Democratic Party) backed Mikuláš Dzurinda in the next elections.

2002 The parliamentary elections were won by the SDKÚ-DS, which formed a coalition with the Hungarian Coalition Party (SMK), the Christian Democratic Movement (KDH) and the New Citizen Alliance (ANO). Nato invited Slovakia to join its alliance.

2003 Referendum voters approved European Union (EU) membership.

2004 Ivan Gasparovic won the presidency. Slovakia became an EU member.

2005 Slovakia entered the European Exchange Rate Mechanism (ERM II).

2006 The left-leaning Smer-Sociálna Demokracia (Smer) (Direction party-Social Democracy) won the general elections. Agreement between Smer, the Ludová Strana-Hnutie Za Demokratické Slovensko (LS-HZDS) (People's Party-Movement for a Democratic Slovakia), and the Slovenská Národná Strana (SNS) (Slovak National Party), created a coalition government. Robert Fico (Smer) became prime minister.

2007 Slovakia became a member of the EU Schengen area; all citizens may cross borders without a passport or visa.

2008 An agreement for visa-free visits of citizens to the US was signed.

2009 The national currency, the Koruna, was replaced by the euro. In presidential elections held in parliament, no candidate won over 50 per cent in the first round; in the runoff incumbent Ivan Gasparovic (candidate of the ruling coalition) won 55.5 per cent of the vote, Iveta Radicová (joint candidate of opposition parties) won 44.5 per cent. A new language law was introduced, making the use of minority languages (mainly Hungarian) in official government business a finable offence. The law was condemned by Hungary, which asked for EU support in condemning the law.

2010 In parliamentary elections the ruling Smer won 34.8 per cent of the vote (62 seats out of 150), the largest vote for a single party; a centre-right grouping won 79 seats. The president invited Prime Minister Fico (Smer) to form a new government. When Fico failed, the president asked Iveta Radicová to form a government. She became Slovakia's first woman prime minister, at the head of a centre-right, four-party coalition of SDKÚ-DS, SaS, KDH and Bridge.

2011 Slovakia voiced opposition to the second fiscal bailout of Greece by Euro-partners in July. As the second poorest nation (after Estonia) in the euro-zone it objected to its funds being used on a 'richer' country's debts. Along with Finland, Germany and The Netherlands it wanted more austerity and reforms from Greece as well as Greek state property used as collateral, plus private creditors to accept at least a US$43 billion share as their own liability. In October Parliament voted against the government's motion to support the EU-EMU bailout of weaker economies. An agreement was reached with the opposition whereby the EU ratification bill would be passed in exchange for early general elections. On 25 October, the government was reinstated in a caretaker function, but with reduced powers. Vaclav Havel, the first post-Communist president of Czechoslovakia (1989–93; 1993–2003 Czech Republic only) died on 18 December. He oversaw the transition to democracy of Czechoslovakia and its division when the Czech Republic and Slovakia were created.

2012 Early general elections (by two years and only two years after the last) were held on 10 March. The opposition Smer-Sociálna Demokracia (Smer-SD) won a decisive victory and gained a majority of seats in parliament, enough to

implement it's plans for a reduced public deficit with higher taxes for the rich. Robert Fico (Smer-SD) took office as prime minister on 4 April. On 28 November a national strike by teachers, protesting at their low pay and status, was ended after three days.
2013 The authorities of the eastern city of Kosice said they would take legal action to remove a wall separating Roma (Gypsy) families from majority Slovaks. The wall had been put up two months earlier. Kosice mayor Richard Rasi was responding to EU commissioner for culture Androulla Vassiliou who said the wall violated the EU's stand against racism.
2014 Presidential elections were held on 15 March with the run-off on 29 March. The result was a surprise defeat for former prime minister, Robert Fico, in the second round with 40.61 per cent compared to Andrej Kiska (Independent) with 59.38 per cent. Turnout was 50.48 per cent.
2015 On 19 May the sale of Slovak Telecom to Deutsche Telekom was agreed, for €900 million (US$1,011 million).

Political structure

Constitution

The Constitution was ratified in 1992. No new government can be formed until the president has accepted the resignation of the former one. Further amendments in January and February 2001 created an independent council, increasing the powers of the Constitutional court, and paved the way for reform of the public administration.
With reference to accession to EU and NATO, an amendment to the constitution was approved on 1 July 2001, which reclassified the relationship between national and international law, introduced judicial regulations and allowed for the creation of a second tier of self-administrative government in the regions.
Electoral system: Universal direct suffrage for party lists. All electoral coalitions have to win 5 per cent of the vote for every party they contain.
A referendum on 7 February 2015 was carried out asking three questions, one to support a ban on same sex marriage, one supporting a ban on LGBT adoption and on sex education. Although the results were unanimously in favour of each question, the referendum was deemed invalid due to low turnout, with just 21.4 per cent of eligible voters casting votes, far short of the 50 per cent required for the results to be legally binding

Independence date

1 January 1993

Form of state

Parliamentary democratic republic

The executive

Executive power lies with the prime minister and ministers, the former being nominated by the president. The prime minister is usually the leader of a majority party or a majority coalition are an election to the National Council of the Slovak Republic. The Cabinet is appointed by the president on recommendation of the prime minister but it must first gain a vote of confidence in the National Council.
The Head of State is the president, directly elected by the people for five years for a period of five years (eligible for a second term). A majority of three-fifths of all deputies' votes is required for the president to be elected. The presidency is largely a ceremonial office, but the president does exercise certain limited powers with absolute discretion.

National legislature

The unicameral Národná Rada (National Council) has 150 seats of which members directly elected in a single national constituency by proportional representation vote. Members serve four-year terms.

Legal system

Slovakia's legal system is partly based on the Czechslovakian system introduced before independence in 1993. The judiciary is independent of the government, although the president appoints judges to both the Constitutional Court and Supreme Court. The Constitutional Court is responsible for ensuring that legislation adheres to the constitution and 13 judges are appointed for a period of 12 years. Judges of the Supreme Court are appointed for an unlimited time period.
As part of the process toward accession to the EU, Slovakia has been attempting to harmonise its existing and new legislation with that of the organisation.

Last elections

15 March and 29 March 2014 (presidential and runoff); 10 March 2012 (parliamentary)
Results: Presidential: (first round): Robert Fico (Smer) 28 per cent, Andrej Kiska (Independent) 24 per cent, Radoslav Procházka (Independent) 21.2 per cent, Milan Knazko (Independent) 12.9 per cent, Gyula Bárdos (SMK–MKP) 5.1 per cent. No other candidate won over 5 per cent. Turnout was 43.4 per cent.
The second round was won convincingly by Andrej Kiska with 59.38 per cent to Robert Fico's 40.61 per cent. Turnout was 50.48 per cent.
Parliamentary: Strana Smer-Tretia Cesta-Sociálna Demokracia (Smer-SD) (Direction Party-Social Democrats) won 44.41 per cent of the vote (83 seats, out of 150), Krestansko-Demokratické Hnutie (KDH) (Christian Democratic Movement) 8.82 per cent (16), Obycajní Ludia a Nezávislé Osobnosti (Obycajní Ludia) (Ordinary People and Independent Personalities) (Ordinary People) 8.55 per cent (16), Most-Híd (Bridge) 6.89 per cent (13), Slovenská Demokratická a Krestanská Únia (SDKÚ) (Slovak Democratic and Christian Union) 6.09 per cent (11), Sloboda a Solidarita (SaS) (Freedom and Solidarity Party) 5.88 per cent (11); 20 other political parties each won less than 5 per cent of the vote and failed to win any seats. Turnout was 59.11 per cent.

Next elections

2019 (presidential); on or before March 2016 (parliamentary)

Political parties

Ruling party

Strana Smer-Tretia Cesta-Sociálna Demokracia (Smer-SD) (Direction Party-Social Democrats) (from 10 Mar 2012)

Main opposition party

Krestansko-Demokratické Hnutie (KDH) (Christian Democratic Movement)

Population

5.42 million (2014)*
Last census: May 2001: 5,379,455
Population density: 110.4 inhabitants per square km. Urban population 55 per cent (2010 Unicef).
Annual growth rate: 0.2 per cent, 1990–2010 (Unicef).

Ethnic make-up

The chief non-Roma minorities are Hungarians (10.8 per cent of the population), Czechs (3 per cent), Ruthenians, Ukrainians, Germans and Poles. Roma, although making up only 1.5 per cent of the overall population, make up a significant minority in some areas, and are growing faster than the national average.

Religions

Roman Catholic (60.3 per cent), Protestant (8.4 per cent), Orthodox (4.1 per cent).

Education

Slovakia has universal literacy and offers free education to all. Enrolment at all levels is high and there is no noticeable gender disparity. Languages of instruction are English and Slovak, although Hungarians may be taught in their own language.
In June 2004 the government failed, in a vote in parliament, to introduce student loans for teriary education.
Literacy rate: 100 per cent adult rate; 100 per cent youth rate (15–24) (Unesco 2005).
Compulsory years: 6 to 15
Enrolment rate: 102 per cent total primary enrolment, 94 per cent gross secondary enrolment; of the relevant age groups (including repeaters); (World Bank).

Pupils per teacher: 20 in primary schools

Health

There is a significant disparity between male and female life expectancy (9 years), partly due to the unbalanced diet and high cigarette and beer consumption by men, which the government is attempting to reduce.

HIV/Aids

HIV prevalence: 0.1 per cent aged 15–49 in 2003 (World Bank)

Life expectancy: 74 years, 2004 (WHO 2006)

Fertility rate/Maternal mortality rate: 1.3 births per woman, 2010 (Unicef)

Birth rate/Death rate: 10 births per and nine deaths per 1,000 population (2003).

Child (under 5 years) mortality rate (per 1,000): 8 per 1,000 live births (World Bank)

Head of population per physician: 3.18 physicians per 1,000 people, 2003 (WHO 2006)

Welfare

Slovakia has a 42.5 hour working week with a minimum wage set by the government. It has a well-developed social security system, including health, unemployment and pension benefits. Employees contribute 12 per cent of their wages to social security schemes and employers an additional 38 per cent.

Main cities

Bratislava (capital, estimated population 421,218 in 2012), Košice (233,346), Prešov (90,597), Žilina (85,528), Nitra (82,752), Banská Bystrica (79,265), Trnava (67,190), Martin (58,430).

Languages spoken

The Czech and Slovak languages are mutually comprehensible. Hungarian is widely spoken, especially in the south and east.

A large proportion of the population, particularly those engaged in industry and foreign trade, speaks German. Russian is also spoken by some executives. English is increasing, especially among the younger generation.

Official language/s

Slovak

Media

Press

Dailies: There are national and regional dailies, most published in Slovakian, including *Pravda* (www.pravda.sk), *Praca* (www.praca.sk), *Novy CAS* (www.bleskovky.sk),*SME* (www.sme.sk). In Hungarian, *Új Szó* (www.ujszo.com) and in English *Slovak Spectator* (www.slovakspectator.sk).

Regional publications in Slovakian includes, *Korzár* (www.cassovia.sk/korzar) from Kosice, *Presovsky Vecernik* (www.slovanet.sk/vecernik/pv) from Presov and *Nitrianske Noviny* (www.mynoviny.sk) from Nitra.

Weeklies: Magazines in Slovakian include *Plus 7 Dni* (www.plus7dni.sk), *Tyzden* (www.tyzden.sk) and in Hungarian *Vasárnap* (www.vasarnap.com).

Business: Magazines, in Slovakian, include *Profit* (http://profit.etrend.sk) and in English *Trend* (http://english.etrend.sk). Newspapers in Slovakian *Hospodarske Noviny* (www.hnonline.sk) and *Profini* (www.profini.sk).

Many dailies include sections on business news.

Periodicals: *Slovak Spectator*, an English-language newspaper, is published every second Wednesday.

Broadcasting

Radio: There are over 20 private, commercial radio stations. The public Slovensky Rozhlas (Slovak Radio) broadcasts nationwide as well as international programmes. Other major radio stations includes Radio Expres (www.expres.sk), Radio Viva (www.radioviva.sk), Radio Okey (www.okey.sk) and Fun Radio (www.funradio.sk).

Other European radio stations are available.

Television: There are several networks available including, TV Markiza (www.markiza.sk) which has the largest audience, Slovenská televízia (Slovak TV) (www.stv.sk) is the public channel, Joj TV (www.joj.sk) and the news channel TA3 (www.ta3.com), which broadcasts regional programmes via cable.

Reception of broadcasts from neighbouring countries allows greater variety.

TASR, Pribinova 23, 81928 Bratislava 111 (tel: 5921-0152; fax: 5296-3405; email: export@tasr.sk; internet: www.tasr.sk).

Sita (Slovak news agency) (www.sita.sk).

Economy

Since joining the European Union (EU) in 2004 Slovenia's economy has experienced a period of rapid growth, based on a vibrant export sector. With a population of 5.4 million the Slovak Republic has a small, open economy, with exports at around 92 per cent of GDP serving as the main driver of GDP growth. Slovakia has attracted a lot of FDI in recent years, because of its relatively low-cost, highly-skilled labour force, reasonable tax rates, and its geographic location in the heart of Central Europe. However, an ongoing problem with corruption potentially threatens the attractiveness of Slovakia to investors. In 2014 the World Bank ranked Slovakia at 37 (out of 189 countries) in the World Bank's annual *Ease of doing business*, a fall of 11 places on the 2012 ranking. FDI was at an astonishing US$3 billion in 2012 before stabilising at US$591 million in 2013 and US$479 million in 2014.

Following the economic recession, which hit the country hard due to its dependence on exports, Slovakia's recovery has been slow. The government introduced stimulus packages in late 2008 and early 2009, including tax reductions and subsidies and measures to increase liquidity in the corporate sector and incentives to speed up the use of EU funds. As world trade began to pick up Slovakia registered GDP growth at 1.6 per cent in 2012 before decreasing slightly to 1.4 per cent in 2013 and then rebounding to 2.4 per cent in 2014. The unemployment rate was 14.4 per cent in 2010 before decreasing slightly to 13.5 per cent in 2011 and then increasing once again back to 14.2 per cent in 2013 before stabilising at 13.2 per cent in 2014. The inflation rate was at 1.5 per cent in 2013 before hitting an extreme low of -0.1 per cent in 2014.

Heavy industries include automobiles; metal and metal products; gas, coke, oil, nuclear fuel, chemicals and machinery. Lighter industries include electricity, synthetic fibres, wood and pulp products, earthenware and ceramics; textiles; electric and optical apparatus; rubber products; food and beverages and pharmaceuticals. GDP in Slovakia is composed mainly by the service sector, which constituted 74.1 per cent of GDP in 2014 while industry contributed 22.5 per cent and agriculture just 3.4 per cent. Agricultural products include grains, potatoes, sugar beets, hops, fruit; pigs, cattle, poultry and forest products.

External trade

As a member of the European Union, Slovakia operates within a community-wide free trade area, with tariffs set as a whole. Internationally, the EU has free trade agreements with a number of nations and trading blocs worldwide.

Foreign trade represents 169 per cent of GDP, of which the greater part is automobile assembly. Traditional heavy industry is being replaced in importance by manufacturing of consumer goods, electronics and engineering and the petrochemical industry.

Natural resources, geared to exports, include mineral extraction (high-grade iron ore, copper, lead, and zinc) and forestry products.

Imports

Principal imports include machinery and electrical equipment (19 per cent), vehicles and related parts (13 per cent), nuclear reactors and furnaces (12 per cent) and fuel and mineral oils (11 per cent).

Main sources: Germany (19 per cent of total in 2014), Czech Republic (16.9 per cent), Austria (9.3 per cent), Russia (7.9 per cent), Poland (6.2 per cent)

Exports

Principal exports include vehicles and related parts (25 per cent), machinery and electric equipment (21 per cent), nuclear reactors and furnaces (12 per cent), iron and steel (5 per cent) and mineral oils and fuels (5 per cent).

Main destinations: Germany (23.3 per cent of total in 2014), Czech Republic (13.6 per cent), Poland (8.8 per cent), Hungary (6.6 per cent), Austria (6.5 per cent) and the UK (5.4 per cent)

Agriculture

Farming

The agricultural sector suffered from under-investment during the communist era. In an attempt to increase productivity, a land restitution act was adopted in 1990, under which all agricultural land taken by the state from 1948–55 was returned to its original owners. Agricultural land makes up 40.1 per cent of total area in Slovakia of which 28.9 per cent is arable, 10.8 per cent pasture and 0.4 per cent permanent crops.

Agriculture contributed around 3.4 per cent to GDP in 2014. Wheat, maize and barley are exported. Only 10 per cent of potato requirements are imported and about 20 per cent of raw sugar requirements. Slovakia is a net importer of oil crops, although the margin is very small, with equal amounts of rape and mustard seed imported and exported. Slovakia is mostly self-sufficient in meat, eggs and milk.

The agricultural sector is subject to the reformed Common Agricultural Policy (CAP), whereby subsidies are no longer paid on farm output, which tended to benefit large farms and encourage over-production, but rather on single farm payments not conditional on production.

The European Commission formally adopted the Slovak Rural Development Programme (RDP) on 13 February 2015. It aims to use EUR2.1 billion (US$2.4 billion) of public money that is available for the 7-year period 2014-2020. The programme is mainly focused on the increase of competitiveness of agriculture and forestry sectors aiming to support investments on 1250 farms and 400 food enterprises while ensuring the appropriate management of natural resources and encouraging climate friendly farming practices, with around 20 per cent of agricultural land managed to protect biodiversity, soil and water resources. The RDP also aims to boost the whole rural economy creating 2000 jobs.

Fishing

The fishing sector, based on inland fisheries and imported sea-fish, is not significant, producing around 2,500 tonnes a year..

Forestry

Forest and other wooded land account for 40.2 per cent of the land area, with forest cover estimated at 2.1 million hectares (ha). More than 80 per cent of the forest is available for wood supply and the rest is preserved. The ownership structure of forest areas has changed considerably since 1990 as a result of privatisation and restitution. Half of the forested area is state-owned.

The European Commission formally adopted the Slovak Rural Development Programme (RDP) on 13 February 2015. It aims to use EUR2.1 billion (US$2.4 billion) of public money that is available for the 7-year period 2014-2020. The competitiveness of the forestry sector will be increased by building or modernizing 250 km of forest roads, by investing in modern technologies including processing investments in 230 forestry holdings.

Consumption of forest products per capita is below the European average. Nearly all of the roundwood is processed in the country, using much of the hardwood and softwood species. Slovakia is a net exporter of forestry products and although the industry is in need of modernisation, it is a significant earner of foreign exchange. Over three-quarters of sawnwood produced is exported, mostly to Hungary. The pulp industry utilises half of the hardwood production, recovered paper and some non-wood fibre pulp. The bulk of exports also constitute paper and pulpboard.

Industry and manufacturing

Industry accounted for 22.5 per cent of GDP and 26 per cent of employment in 2014. Industrial production fell by approximately 20 per cent after the end of the Communist regime and privatisation has been unable to provide the necessary cash required for investment. Consequently, compared to neighbouring Hungary and Czech Republic, Slovak industry is marked by inefficiency, hidden bankruptcies and government subsidies.

The principal industries are the manufacture of machinery, chemicals and rubber, food and beverages, and iron metallurgy. Slovakian industry remains more vulnerable to the instability of Eastern European markets than its Czech neighbour. The long-term prospects for Slovakian industry depend on how successfully the country can recover from the dislocation of its traditional markets and find new ones for such key industries as steel. Half of all foreign direct investment (FDI) in Slovakia goes to the manufacturing sector.

Slovakia remains to be the world leader in car production per capita in 2015 and planned investments and the launch of new models mean it is likely to keep this position. Britain's Jaguar Land Rover is going to set up a new plant in Slovakia. The company is currently building at full capacity and, therefore, expansion into Slovakia is seemingly enticing. It is anticipated that the first cars will come off the production line in 2018. Slovakia produces 183 cars per 1000 citizens.

Slovakia's three carmakers – Kia Motors Slovakia, PSA Peugeot Citroen, and Volkswagen Slovakia made 973,370 cars in 2014, a decrease of 14,348 cars compared with 987,718 cars manufactured in 2013.

Tourism

Despite being a country of forests and mountains that feature rare animals and skiing in the winter, the capital, Bratislava is the single most visited place in Slovakia. In 2015 6.3 million foreign visitors are expected to arrive in Slovakia, of which the majority are from the Czech Republic, Poland and Germany.

Travel and tourism contributed 5.9 per cent to GDP in 2014 and this is expected to grow by 2.7 per cent in 2015. The tourism sector employed 5.8 per cent of the workforce in 2014 (136,000 jobs). Domestic spending has also fallen to 53.5 of overall GDP gains from the tourism sector as more Slovaks choose to spend their leisure time elsewhere.

Mining

Slovakia has workable deposits of antimony ore, mercury, iron ore, copper, lead, zinc, precious metals, limestone, dolomite, gravel, brick loam, ceramic materials and stone salt. In each case, except iron ores, only small quantities are actually mined.

Hydrocarbons

Slovakia has modest oil reserves of nine million barrels and produces about 9,522 barrels per day (bpd) of oil, a tiny contribution to the over 136,000 barrels per day Slovakia consumes. Imports make up the majority of all oil consumed. Oil imports come from Russia through two pipelines with a total capacity of 422,000bpd. Slovakia imports 303,500 bpd.

Natural gas reserves stand at around 14.6 billion cubic metres (cum) so that Slovakia also relies on the import of natural gas to meet demand. 5.1 billion cum are consumed per annum, all of which is imported, primarily from Russia. The country serves as an important transit route for gas, and around a quarter of gas consumed in Western Europe, and 70

per cent of Russia's total gas exports, transits Slovakia.
Coal is mined on a large scale. Reserves could last more than 40 years. Most is low quality brown coal (lignite) and looks likely to diminish as a key energy source due to the amount of pollution it causes.

Energy
Total installed electricity generating capacity was 8.1GW in 2013. Slovakia had five Chernobyl-style nuclear reactors in operation but an agreement with the EU saw the closure of three in 2008 and an upgrade in two. Before their shutdown nuclear energy supplied 57 per cent of electricity. Now electricity from nuclear fuels constitutes 24.9 per cent while fossil fuels provide 43.6 per cent of requirements and 31.5 per cent comes from hydroelectric plants and from other renewable sources.
The state-owned Slovenske Elektrarne (Slovak Electric) was partially sold off with 66 per cent purchased by the Italian Enel energy company. As a condition of the sale Enel agreed to invest EUR1.8 billion (US$2 billion) to increase generating capacity. Slovak Electric also operates thermal and hydroelectric plants.

Financial markets
Stock exchange
Burza Cennych Papierov v Bratislave (BSSE) (Bratislava Stock Exchange)

Banking and insurance
Slovakia's banking system has been reformed, although the sector has been plagued by bad debts coupled with massive losses affecting a third of banks. As a result, economic structuring has been essential to both macroeconomic stability and the integrity of the banking sector.
Many of the country's larger banks have been privatised. In early 2002, a 66.7 stake in Slovenska Poistovna (Slovak Insurance Bank) was sold to Germany's Allianz AG for US$142 million. Smaller banks have closed as the central bank has imposed a tough regulatory framework on commerce, with greater power given to creditors.
Central bank
Narodna Banka Slovenska (NBS) (National Bank of Slovakia)
Main financial centre
Bratislava

Time
GMT plus one hour (daylight saving, late March to late October, GMT plus two hours)

Geography
Slovakia is a landlocked, hilly country in the heart of Europe. Around 80 per cent of the country has an altitude of over 750 metres above sea level. The High Tatra Mountains in the north give way to large lowlands, broad valleys and meadows in the south.
Slovakia is bordered by the Czech Republic to the west (the border is 215km long), by Poland to the north (444km), Ukraine to the east (90km), Hungary to the south (515km) and Austria to the south-west (the border with Austria is only 15km from the capital, Bratislava).
The High Tatra Mountains are on the northern Polish border and the Low Tatras are in the centre and east of the country. The highest peak is Gerlach in the High Tatras (2,655 metres), with the lowest point the Bodrog river near Streda and Bodrogom (95 metres).
There are numerous rivers flowing south to the lowland areas, including the Váh, Nitra, Hron and Hornád. The River Danube marks part of the southern border. The lowland areas are in the south-west and south-east of the country.
Hemisphere
Northern

Climate
Slovakia has a continental climate (warm summers and cold winters). Summer maximum temperatures are 32 degrees Celsius (C) to 35 degrees C; July is the hottest month (average 30 degrees C). Minimum temperatures are minus 12 degrees C to minus 20 degrees C. January is the coldest month (average minus 8 degrees C). Long-term average rainfall is approximately 490mm.

Dress codes
Most people dress in standard casual wear. For winter, mediumweight clothing is required with a heavy coat. For summer, lightweight clothing is suitable. For business meetings, men should wear a suit and tie.

Entry requirements
Passports
Required by all. Passport must be valid for eight months from the date of issue of the visa.
Visa
Required by all, except nationals of EU and Schengen area signatory countries, North America, Australasia and Japan. For further exceptions contact the nearest embassy or see www.foreign.gov.sk (or www.slovakia.org and follow link through tourism to visa information). A Schengen visa application (offered in several languages) can be downloaded from http://europa.eu/abc/travel/ see 'documents you will need'.
Visitors are required to have onward/return passage.
Currency advice/regulations
Import of local currency is prohibited. There are no restrictions on import of foreign currency, but it must be declared on arrival.
Local currency up to Sk100 can be exported, and foreign currency up to the amount declared on entry.
Customs
Personal items are duty-free. There are no duties levied on alcohol and tobacco between EU member states, providing amounts imported are for personal consumption.
Items of value, such as cameras, should be declared.

Health (for visitors)
Nationals of the European Economic Area (EEA) countries and Switzerland can access reduced cost and sometimes free medical treatment using a European Health Insurance Card (EHIC) while visiting the EEA. Exceptions include nationals of the 10 countries, which joined the EU in 2004, whose EHIC is not valid in Switzerland. Applications for the EHIC should be made before travelling.
Mandatory precautions
Full medical insurance, covering the whole territory of the Slovak Republic, is required. Random checks at Slovak points of entry are carried out and entry can be refused if no medical insurance for the whole country can be produced.

Credit cards
Credit cards are generally accepted by major hotels and restaurants.

Public holidays (national)
Fixed dates
1 Jan (New Year's Day/Independence Day), 6 Jan (Epiphany), 1 May (Labour Day), 8 May (Liberation of the Republic), 5 Jul (Ss Cyril and Methodius Day), 29 Aug (Slovak National Uprising Day), 1 Sep (Constitution Day), 15 Sep (Our Lady of the Seven Sorrows Day), 1 Nov (All Saints' Day), 17 Nov (Freedom and Democracy Day), 24–26 Dec (Christmas).
Variable dates
Good Friday, Easter Monday.

Working hours
Banking
Mon–Fri: 0800–1700. There are also exchange offices in the main city centres, which operate seven days a week until 1900.
Business
Mon–Fri: 0800–1600.
Government
Mon–Fri: 0900–1700.
Shops
Mon–Fri: 0900–1800; Sat: 0900–1200; some shops remain open late on Thursday evenings.

Electricity supply
220V, 50 cycles AC

Weights and measures
Metric system. In addition, the following measures are used: quintal or metric hundredweight = 100 kg. Food is usually purchased by the decagramme and kilogram.

Social customs/useful tips
Appointments should be made in advance and punctuality is important. Shaking hands is customary when meeting people and on parting. Business is conducted in Slovak; many executives speak a second language – German, Russian or English. When drinks are served, it is considered polite to wait for everyone to be served and then wish each person *Nazdravi* ('to your health'). At meals it is usual to wait for everyone to be served before starting and to wish everyone *bon appetit* or *dobrou chut* just before eating. The terms *Pan* (Mr), *Pani* (Mrs) and *Slecna* (Miss) are used. *Slecna* is used for single women under 30 only; single women over 30 will usually be addressed as *Pani*.
Gratuities are between 5 and 10 per cent. The minimum drinking age is 18 years. When visiting private homes it is customary to take flowers for the hosts. Visitors also generally leave their shoes in the hallway, partly as a mark of respect and partly because of pollution in the streets. Men always take off their hats indoors. Illegally parked cars tend to be towed away by the police and it is advisable to park at attended car parks where the cost is relatively low.

Security
Street crime, especially in the towns, has become a problem since the 1989 revolution because the police tend to keep a low profile. Although the situation has improved, it is still advisable to carry as little in the way of valuables and cash as possible. Car vandalism and theft are also problems.

Getting there
Air
National airline: Slovak Airlines
International airport/s: MR Stefanik Airport (BTS), 9km from Bratislava; post office, bank, bureau de change, restaurants, duty free shop, car hire.
Airport tax: None
Surface
Slovakia is included in the Pan-European Corridor 5 scheme. The project has some 3,270km of railways, linking Kiev in the Ukraine with western Europe via Italy, and 2,850 of new and upgraded roads.
Road: There is ample road access from Czech Republic, Poland, Ukraine, Hungary and Austria. There is a motorway from Bratislava to Prague.
Rail: Slovakia has rail connections with Vienna, Hamburg, Berlin, Warsaw, Budapest, Moscow and St Petersburg.
Water: Ships provide regular passenger service and cruises on the Danube, from Passau and Regensburg (Germany) via Vienna (Austria). There are also links with the Rhine and Main rivers and the Black Sea.

Getting about
National transport
Air: There are internal connections provided by Slovak Airlines, SkyEurope Airlines and Air Slovakia.
Road: The road network is extensive and in good condition. The major route is from Bratislava to Presov and Kosice.
Buses: There is an extensive coach network.
Rail: Slovakia has a rail network of 3,665km, of which around 1,590km are electrified. There are frequent express services between Bratislava and the main centres and tourist destinations.
Water: The principal navigable waterway is the Danube, on which cruises are available.
City transport
Taxis: Taxis are available in all main towns and are relatively cheap. They are metered, but passengers should ensure that the driver switches them on before starting off.
Buses, trams & metro: Bratislava and other cities are well served by trams, trolley-buses and buses. Tickets can be purchased at news-stands or from dispensers at the queues.
Car hire
Car hire is available in major towns. Traffic drives on the right. There is an extensive network of roadside restaurants and petrol stations. Emergency telephones are located at half mile intervals on motorways and the emergency system is generally quick and reliable.

BUSINESS DIRECTORY
The addresses listed below are a selection only. While World of Information makes every endeavour to check these addresses, we cannot guarantee that changes have not been made, especially to telephone numbers and area codes. We would welcome any corrections.

Telephone area codes
The international direct dialling code (IDD) for Slovakia is +421, followed by area code and subscriber's number:

Banska Bystricá	48	Nitra	37
Bratislava	2	Presov	51
Kosice	55	Zilina	41
Liptoský Mikuláš	44		

Useful telephone numbers
Police: 158
Ambulance: 155
Fire: 150
Directory enquiries: 154

Chambers of Commerce
American Chamber of Commerce in the Slovak Republic, Hotel Danube, 1 Rybne namestie, 81338 Bratislava (tel: 5934-0508; fax: 5934-0556; e-mail: director@amcham.sk).

Banska Bystrica Regional Chamber of Commerce and Industry, 4 namestie S Moysesa, 97401 Banska Bystrica (tel: 412-5643; fax: 412-5636; e-mail: sopkrkbb@sopk.sk).

Bratislava Regional Chamber of Commerce and Industry, 6 Jasikova, 82673 Bratislava (tel: 4829-1257; fax: 4829-1260; e-mail: sopkrkbl@scci.sk).

British Chamber of Commerce in the Slovak Republic, 14 Cukrova, 81339 Bratislava (tel/fax: 5292-0371; e-mail: director@britcham.sk).

Kosice Regional Chamber of Commerce and Industry, 48/A Trieda SNP, 04011 Kosice (tel: 641-9477; fax: 641-9470; e-mail: sopkrkke@scci.sk).

Lucenec Regional Chamber of Commerce and Industry, 2 Vajanskeho, 98401 Lucenec (tel: 433-3939; fax: 433-3937; e-mail: sopkrklc@scci.sk).

Nitra Regional Chamber of Commerce and Industry, 4 Akademicka, 94901 Nitra (tel: 653-5466; fax: 733-6739; e-mail: sopkrknr@scci.sk).

Presov Regional Chamber of Commerce and Industry, 22 Masarykova, 08001 Presov (tel: 773-2818; fax: 773-2413; e-mail: sopkrkpo@scci.sk).

Slovak Chamber of Commerce and Industry, 9 Gorkeho, 81603 Bratislava (tel: 5443-3291; fax: 5413-1159; e-mail: sopkurad@sopk.sk).

Trencin Regional Chamber of Commerce and Industry, 2 Jilemnickeho, 91101 Trencin (tel: 652-3834; fax: 652-1023; e-mail: sopkrktn@scci.sk).

Trnava Regional Chamber of Commerce and Industry, 2 Trhova, 91701 Trnava (tel: 551-2588; fax: 551-2603; e-mail: sopkrktt@sopk.sk).

Zilina Regional Chamber of Commerce and Industry, 31 Halkova, 01001 Zilina (tel: 723-5101; fax: 723-5102; e-mail: sekrza@za.scci.sk).

Banking
Citibank (Slovakia),Mlynské nivy 43, 82501 Bratislava (tel: 5823-0224; fax: 5823-0211).

Consolidation Bank SFI, Cintorisíka 21, 81499 Bratislava (tel: 368-011; fax: 321-353).

Crédit Lyonnais Bank Slovakia, Medena 22, 811 02 Bratislava (tel: 325-320).

Deí1n Banka as, Frantiskánske nám 8, 81310 Bratislava (tel: 333-376; fax: 330-376).

General Credit Bank, Námestie SNP 19, 81856 Bratislava (tel: 531-7283; fax: 531-7020/05).

ING Bank, Kolarska 6, 811 06 Bratislava PO Box 123 (tel: 5346-111).

Investment and Development Bank, Stúrova 5, 81855 Bratislava (tel: 326-121; fax: 321-433).

Istrobanka as, Laurinská 1, 81101 Bratislava (tel: 539-7524; fax: 533-1744).

Konsolidacna Banka Bratislava, Cintorinska 21, 814 99 Bratislava (tel: 321-387; fax: 321-353).

Polnobanka as, Vajnorská 21, 83265 Bratislava (tel: 273-964; fax: 259-024).

Post Bank, PO Box 149, Gorkého 3, 81499 Bratislava (tel: 329-253; fax: 211-204).

Slovak Savings Bank, Námestie SNP 18, 81607 Bratislava (tel: 560-6580; fax: 560-6220).

TATRA Bank, Vajanského nábrezie 5, 81006 Bratislava (tel: 210-3519; fax: 324-760).

Volksbank, Námestie SNP 15, 81000 Bratislava (tel: 381-1140; fax: 364-847).

Central bank

Narodna banka Slovenska (National Bank of Slovakia), Imricha Karvasa 1, 81325 Bratislava (tel: 5787-1111; fax: 5787-1100; e-mail: webmaster@nbs.sk).

Stock exchange

Burza Cennych Papierov v Bratislave (BSSE) (Bratislava Stock Exchange) www.bsse.sk

Travel information

Air Slovakia BWJ, Pestovatelská ul c 2, 821 04 Bratislava (tel: 4342 2744; fax: 4342 2742; e-mail:

Association of Slovak Information Centres, Námestie Mieru 1, 03101 Liptoský Mikuláš (tel: 551-4541; fax: 551-4448; e-mail: info@airslovakia.sk)

Slovak Airlines, Ivanka Airport, Bratislava (tel: 4857-5170/1).

Slovak Association of Travel Agents, Bajkalská 2, 821 01 Bratislava 2, (tel: 5823-3385; fax: 5341-9058; email:sacka@ba.sknet.sk).

Slovak Republik Automobile Association (Autoklub SR), Údernicka 14, 85101 Bratislava (tel: 6383-4567; fax: 6383-4678; e-mail: autoklub@autoklubsr.sk).

Slovak Tourist Board (Bratislava branch), PO Box 97, Záhradnícka 153, 82005 Bratislava 25, (tel: 5070-0801; fax: 5557-1649; email: sacrba@sacr.sk).

Ministry of tourism

Ministry of Economy, Tourism Department, Mierova 19, 82715 Bratislava (tel: 4854-2315; fax: 4854-3321; e-mail: info@economy.gov.sk).

National tourist organisation offices

Slovak Tourist Board, Námestie L Štúra 1, PO Box 35, 974 05 Banská Bystrica, (tel: 413-6146-8; fax: 413-6149; email: sacr@sacr.sk).

Ministries

Ministry of Administration and Privatisation of National Property, Drienova 24, 82009 Bratislava (tel: 230-678; fax: 233-335).

Ministry of Agriculture, Dobrovicova 12, 81266 Bratislava (tel: 368-561, 456-111; fax: 3066-294).

Ministry of Construction and Public Works, Spitalska 8, 81644 Bratislava (tel: 536-1111; fax; 536-1203).

Ministry of Culture of the Slovak Republic, Dobrovicova 12, 81331 Bratislava (tel: 323-295; fax: 368-140).

Ministry of Defence, Kutuzovova 7, 83247 Bratislava (tel: 250-320; fax: 258-907).

Ministry of Economy of the Slovak Republic, Mierová 19, 82715 Bratislava (tel: 574-1407; fax: 237-827).

Ministry of Education and Sciences, Stromova 1, 81330 Bratislava (tel: 370-4111; fax: 370-4333).

Ministry of the Environment of the Slovak Republic, Namestie L Stura 1,, 81235 Bratislava (tel: 516-2458; fax: 516-2457).

Ministry of Finance of the Slovak Republic, Stefanovicova 5, 81308 Bratislava (tel: 518-2562; fax: 396-146).

Ministry of Foreign Affairs, Hlboka Cesta 3, 83336 Bratislava (tel: 438-1111; fax: 438-2005; internet: http://www.foreign.gov.sk).

Ministry of Health, Limbova 2, 83105 Bratislava (tel: 377-940; fax: 377-659).

Ministry of the Interior, Pribinova 2, 81272 Bratislava (tel: 546-1111; fax: 368-835).

Ministry of Justice, Zupné námestie 13, 81311 Bratislava (tel: 535-3111; fax: 531-5952).

Ministry of Labour, Social Welfare and Family of the Slovak Republic, Spitálska 4, 81643 Bratislava (tel: 338-2414; fax: 362-150).

Ministry of Transport and Communications, Nam Slobody 6, 81005 Bratislava (tel: 395-251; fax: 256-414).

Office of the Government, Nam Slobody 1, 84218 Bratislava (tel: 359-5111; fax: 397-595).

Office of the President, Stefanikova ul 1, 81104 Bratislava (tel: 531-7567; fax: 531-7065).

Other useful addresses

Bratislava International Commodity Exchange, Ruzinovská 1, 82102 Bratislava (tel: 522-6311; fax: 522-6318).

Bratislava Stock Exchange, Vysoká 17, 81499 Bratislava (tel: 386-121; fax: 386-103).

Federation of Employers' Unions and Associations of Slovak Republic, Information and Consulting Centre, Drienová 24, 82603 Bratislava (tel: 235-024; fax: 233-542).

National Agency for Development of Small and Medium Enterprises, Nevädzová 5, 82101 Bratislava (tel: 237-472/563, 231-873; fax: 522-2434); External Advisors (tel: 237-472; fax: 522-2434); BIC (Business Innovation Centre) (tel: 290-7417; fax: 522-2434, 290-7217).

National Property Fund PARP PMU, Drienova 27, 82656 Bratislava (tel: 561-1258, 561-1230, 561-1447, 235-280, 231-300, 231-531; fax: 561-1446, 235-280); external department (tel: 250-248; fax: 259-208).

Slovak National Agency for Foreign Investment and Development (SNAFID), Sládkovicova 7, 81106 Bratislava (tel: 533-5175; fax: 533-5022); Slovenska polnohospodarska a potravinarska komora, Krizna 52, 82108 Bratislava (tel: 566-2657, 526-1778; fax: 526-7336, 211-251).

Slovak Republic Embassy (USA), 3523 International Court, NW, Washington DC 20008 (tel: (+1-202) 237-1054; fax: (+1-202) 237-6438; e-mail: info@slovakembassy-us.org).

Statistical Office of the Slovak Republic, Mileticova 3, 82467 Bratislava (tel: 215-802; fax: 214-587).

Transport Department, Dept of European Integration, Namestie Slobody 6, 81370 Bratislava (tel: 499-766, 498-156 Ext. 331, 498-841, 495-251; fax: 499-761).

Internet sites

Slovakia Daily Surveyor: http://www.slovensko.com

Slovaks and Slovakia: http://www.slovak.com

Slovak Republic Government: http://www.government.gov.sk

Slovak Tourist Board: http://www.slovakiatourism.sk

Slovenia

KEY FACTS

Official name: Republika Slovenija (Republic of Slovenia)

Head of State: President Borut Pahor (from 22 Dec 2012)

Head of government: Prime Minister Miro Cerar Stranka Mira Cerarja (SMC) (Miro Cerar Party) (since 18 September 2014)

Ruling party: After his party's surprise win with 34.7% of the vote in the 13 July 2014 snap election Mr Cerar set about forming a new coalition government on 14 July. His party, Stranka Modernega Centra (SMC) (Modern Centre party) went into coalition with Demokraticna Stranka Upokojencev Slovenije (DeSUS) (Democratic Party of Pensioners of Slovenia), and Socialni Demokrati (SD) Social Democrats).

Area: 20,251 square km

Population: 2.06 million (2014)

Capital: Ljubljana

Official language: Slovene

Currency: Euro (€) = 100 cents (from 1 Jan 2007; previous currency tolar, locked at T239.64 per euro)

Exchange rate: €0.89 per US$ (Sep 2015)

GDP per capita: US$24,019 (2014)

GDP real growth: 2.64% (2014)

GDP: US$49.51 billion (2014)

Labour force: 921,000 (2014)*

Unemployment: 9.79% (2014)

Inflation: 0.21% (2014)

Balance of trade: US$1.73 billion (2014)

Annual FDI: US$817.99 million (2011)

* estimated figure

When the days of the former Yugoslavian republic finally came to an end, Slovenia was able to recover its national identity. Slovenia had, for years, been obliged to use Serbo-Croat as its official language, rather than its native Slovenian. The European Union (EU) eventually recognised Slovenia as an independent state in January 1992 and five months later, the United Nations accepted Slovenia as a member in May.

In the early days of independence, Slovenes could be forgiven for endeavouring to distance themselves from their Serbo-Croat neighbours to the south-east. Slovenia preferred to look towards its neighbours to the north, seeking closer economic links especially with Austria, but also with Germany. What was originally smugness faded into simple complacency as Slovenia became the first former Yugoslavian republic to complete the EU membership procedures in 2004. It almost seemed as though on entering the EU, Slovenes felt that they had done enough. Complacency was replaced by a generally comatose approach to local and national politics. These were considered to be matters for politicians, or for Brussels.

Dissatisfaction

Eventually, Slovenes became aware that not all was well. In November 2012 the tide turned as it became apparent that the wealth of senior politicians was not the fruit of their salary or their savings, but of simple corruption. Younger Slovenes took to the streets, prompting an ill-prepared police force to have recourse to tear gas, which only made matters worse.

Politicians resigned in disgrace, local administrations fell. Belatedly, Slovenia's politicians realised that they might be held to account by their once indifferent electorate. On the Transparency International *Corruption Perceptions Index* Slovenia ranked 39 out of the 175 countries surveyed. Not disgraceful, but nothing to be smug about. If that ranking could be achieved without public concern, it could only be hoped that greater public awareness would eventually have a beneficial effect.

New broom?

In mid-2014 the centre-left political upstart Miro Cerar led his eponymous party the Stranka Mira Cerarja (SMC) (Party of Miro Cerar) to victory in Slovenia's general election, promising to revisit the reform package already agreed by his predecessor, Alenka Bratusek, agreed with the EU in a an attempt to fix Slovenia's tattered finances. Mr Cerar, whose SMC had only come into existence some six weeks before the snap election, had expressed his opposition to a number of the privatisations (including the jewel in the crown Slovene Telekom and Lubljana Airport) that the EU and the IMF had insisted on as the answer to Slovenia's problems and the avoidance of an embarrassing bail-out.

The SMC had won 34.8 per cent of the vote, which corresponded to 36 seats in the 90-seat parliament. Although this was not an outright majority, it gave Mr Cerar a stronger hand than that held by earlier governments. The centre-right Slovenska Demokratska Stranka (SDS) (Slovenian Democratic Party) lead by Janez Jansa (himself subject to charges of corruption) was in second place with 20.6 per cent, followed by a cluster of smaller centre-left parties some of whom would end up in coalition with the SMC.

Assuming an eventual dilution of the privatisation programme, Mr Cerar and his government would have to find other ways to raise cash if the target agreed with the EU to reduce the budget deficit to three per cent of output by 2015 was to be met.

The economy

In its February 2015 overview of the Slovenian economy, the International Monetary Fund (IMF) noted that Slovenia had experienced a deep crisis, which had culminated in a bank bailout in late 2013. After being hit hard by the global crisis in 2009 through external trade and financing channels, the economy had experienced a modest recovery in 2010–11, only to fall back into recession in 2012. Domestic imbalances were largely at play in the relapse, with mounting losses in the highly-leveraged corporate sector leading to rising non-performing loans (NPLs) and a sharp contraction in credit, further fuelling the renewed recession. This raised concerns about the magnitude of bank losses and the sovereign's ability to address them. The state authorities managed to maintain market access after providing substantial support to the banks in 2013 following a bank asset-quality review and transferring part of their NPLs to the state-owned Bank Assets Management Company (BAMC).

According to the IMF, while growth had resumed, output remained below pre-crisis levels. Economic activity had expanded by 2.6 per cent (year-on-year) in the first three quarters of 2014 and high-frequency indicators pointed to continued improvement in the fourth quarter. The recovery had been driven largely by exports and EU-funded public investment. Private consumption was also showing signs of revival, as household balance sheets were relatively strong and confidence, employment and real wages were gradually rebounding. Private investment, however, remained weak, given that many firms were saddled with high debt. In all, output remained some 8 per cent below its pre-crisis peak – among the largest crisis-related losses in the region – and unemployment was still high, at 9.5 per cent (with youth unemployment at 16.5 per cent). Inflation had fallen sharply in 2014, driven by food and energy prices, averaging 0.2 per cent. The current account remained in surplus . The positive balance had reached 5.6 per cent of gross domestic product (GDP) in the first three quarters of 2014, slightly below its level over the same period a year earlier.

According to the European Bank for Reconstruction and Development (EBRD) in its 2014 Transition Report, growth had been better than expected in early 2014, but was likely to recede to 0.7 per cent. GDP grew by 2.1 per cent year-on-year in the first quarter of 2014 and by 2.9 per cent year-on-year in the second quarter. Strong export performance and investment activity had been the main drivers of growth, while political and economic uncertainties and subdued wages adversely affected consumption. Reforms undertaken in late 2013 and early 2014 also contributed to a higher growth rate in the second quarter by boosting market confidence, lowering Slovenia's country risk premium and reducing the sovereign's cost of funding. However, the prospective wave of corporate restructurings, were they to be pursued, was expected to weigh on employment and domestic demand in the short term, keeping GDP growth in 2014 at a modest 0.7 per cent, while at the same time improving medium-term growth prospects. Meanwhile, political uncertainties had contributed to S&P downgrading Slovenia's outlook from stable to negative, although the rating remained high at A-. Although the new SMC government had expressed its continued commitment to reforms and further privatisations, market sentiment would largely depend on whether this was confirmed in practice.

Slovenia's public debt rose sharply in 2013 due to banking sector recapitalisation. The budget deficit reached 14.9 per cent of GDP in 2013, with bank recapitalisation costs accounting for 10.3 percentage points, while the positive impact of higher value added tax rates and cuts to public wages and social benefits, were mainly offset by higher interest rates and pension expenditures. Consequently, public debt rose to above 70 per cent of GDP in 2013, from 54.4 per cent in 2012, owing to bank recapitalisations and the transfer of NPLs to the BAMC in December 2013, as well as negative output growth. The level of public debt was expected to deteriorate further, mainly due to additional cash transfers to the banking sector in the second half of 2014 and sustained moderate economic growth. According to the

KEY INDICATORS — Slovenia

	Unit	2011	2012	2013	2014	**2015
Population	m	*2.02	2.06	2.06	2.06	*2.06
Gross domestic product (GDP)	US$bn	49.60	45.41	48.01	49.51	*43.02
GDP per capita	US$	24,533	22,089	23,317	24,019	*20,850
GDP real growth	%	-0.2	-2.5	-1.0	2.6	*2.1
Inflation	%	1.8	2.6	1.8	0.2	*-0.4
Unemployment	%	12.1	8.9	10.1	9.8	*9.0
Exports (fob) (goods)	US$m	29,569.9	27,609.5	29,480.2	30,684.7	–
Imports (fob) (goods)	US$m	30,757.2	27,644.5	27,967.3	28,954.9	–
Balance of trade	US$m	-1,187.2	253.7	1,512.9	1,731.2	–
Current account	US$m	2,030.0	1,490.0	2,692.0	2,858.0	*3,033.0
Total reserves minus gold	US$m	989.8	782.2	799.3	893.4	–
Foreign exchange	US$m	480.4	271.1	291.5	–	–
Exchange rate	per US$	0.75	0.77	0.73	0.82	–

* estimated figure ** forecast figure

European Commission (EC), the debt to GDP ratio was expected to exceed 80 per cent of GDP by the end of 2014, more than double the ratio seen in 2010.

Growth was expected to remain subdued in 2015, with prospects improving over the medium term if reforms continued. While meaningful growth was crucial over the medium term, a wave of corporate restructurings would continue to weigh on domestic demand and subdue growth in 2015. Consequently, growth was expected to remain at one per cent over the following year and then pick up sustainably over the following few years. The medium-term growth outlook would, however, be challenged if the reform momentum, which had already slowed during the snap election cycle (as expected), did not accelerate with the new government that took over in September 2014. Other major risks to the forecast included the pace of recovery in the euro-zone – Slovenia's largest trading partner – as well as a change in market sentiment, which could lead to a rise in the risk premium if perceived fiscal consolidation does not remain on track.

Slovenia has significantly strengthened its reform agenda, although the momentum had slowed amid the snap elections. However, a number of positive developments had taken place in Slovenia during the previous government's term. Constitutional amendments passed in 2013, which limited the calling of referendums aimed at blocking individual reforms and budget laws, paved the way for rapid and much-needed reforms. A National Reform Programme, presented to the EC in May 2013, had progressed well in late 2013 and early 2014. Notably, parliament had approved the privatisation of 15 large companies, the authorities had completed a major bank recapitalisation and cleaned the banks' balance sheets and amendments to the insolvency law had been adopted. This boosted market confidence and enabled the government to borrow more easily and at lower costs, in the international markets. However, the government's resignation in May and the ensuing snap elections, slowed the reform momentum somewhat and fuelled concerns about future reforms amid still fragile growth prospects.

The major bank clean-up that took place in December 2013 followed stress tests and asset quality reviews. Tests and checks across all key banks had dispelled uncertainty about capital needs in Slovenia's banking sector. Completed in December 2013, assessments were carried out across all banks, including foreign-owned banks, using criteria set out by the European Central Bank (ECB) and the EC. Although capital needs for state-controlled banks could have been met by the government's liquid reserves, aggregate capital needs for all banks amounted to €4.8 billion (US$6.4 billion) (13 per cent of Slovenia's GDP). Immediate priority was given to preparing the two largest state-owned banks, Nova Ljubljanska Banka (NLB) and Nova Kreditna banka Maribor dd (NKBM), for restructuring and privatisation, as mandated by European Union state aid rules (the NKBM privatisation process was already under way as it featured among the 15 companies on the parliament-approved privatisation list). Slovenia had also announced its intention to merge Abanka with Banka Celje and privatise the joint entity.

Risk assessment

Economy	Fair
Politics	Fair/good
Regional stability	Good

COUNTRY PROFILE

In the thirteenth century, Slovenia became a hereditary possession of the House of Habsburg.

1867 The Slovenes fell under the jurisdiction of the Austrian Crown.

1918 After the downfall of the Austro-Hungarian Empire, Slovenia became a part of the new Kingdom of Serbs, Croats and Slovenes, encompassing Bosnia and Hercegovina (BiH), Croatia, parts of Dalmatia and Macedonia, Montenegro, Serbia, Slavonia and Slovenia.

1921 Prince Alexander, Regent of Serbia, became King.

1929 Following disputes between Serbs and Croats, King Alexander assumed dictatorial powers and the country was renamed Yugoslavia.

1934 King Alexander was assassinated in Marseilles while on a state visit to France.

1941 Yugoslavia was divided between Germany, Italy, Hungary and Bulgaria.

1945 Following the end of the Second World War, Slovenia became a constituent republic of the Yugoslav Federation. Josip Broz Tito assumed power, and a Soviet-style constitution was adopted. The other republics were: Bosnia and Hercegovina (BiH), Croatia, Macedonia, Montenegro and Serbia, and the two autonomous regions of Vojvodina and Kosovo.

1950-80s Constitutions adopted in 1953, 1963 and 1974 increased the autonomy of the constituent republics. The ruling Slovene Communists supported the Croats' demand for a confederate Yugoslavia during the 1960s and 1970s, although never to the point of provoking repression.

1980 Tito died. A system of a collective (rotating) presidency was adopted.

1986 Milan Kucan became the leader of the Slovene Communists.

1990 Kucan guided Slovenia towards independence following multi-party general elections, resulting in a six-party centre-right coalition, the Demokratska Opozicija Slovenije (DeMOS) (Democratic Opposition of Slovenia), under the leadership of Lozle Peterle.

1991 After a 10-day war against the Yugoslav army, Slovenia won independence. A border dispute began following the collapse of Yugoslavia between Croatia and as Slovenia. With such a small coastline (46km) Slovenia was intent on using the small Bay of Piran, on the Adriatic Sea, to give it access to international waters; Croatia also claimed the bay.

1992 Slovenia was admitted to the UN. Following the collapse of the DeMOS government, Janez Drnovšek took over as interim prime minister. In the parliamentary elections, the Liberal Democrats emerged as the largest party and Janez Drnovšek became prime minister at the head of a five-party coalition. Milan Kucan was elected president.

1994 The Liberal Democrats merged with the Democratic Party and the Ecologists to create the Liberalna Demokracija Slovenije (LDS) (Liberal Democracy of Slovenia).

1996 After the general elections, the LDS and its former opponent, Slovenska Ljudska Stranka (SLS) (Slovenian People's Party) formed a coalition with the Demokratièna Stranka Upokojencev Slovenije (DeSUS) (Democratic Party of Slovenian Pensioners). Drnovšek was re-elected prime minister.

1997 Kucan was re-elected president for a second and last consecutive five-year term.

2000 Withdrawal of the SLS from the government coalition prompted its collapse. A centre-right government, composed of the SLS and Slovenski Krsèanski Demokrati (SKD) (Slovenian Christian Democratic Party), together with the Socialdemokratska Stranka Slovenije (SDSS) (Social Democratic Party of Slovenia) was formed. The general election was won by the LDS, led by the former prime minister, Janez Drnovšek, who formed a coalition government.

2002 NATO invited Slovenia to join the alliance and the EU confirmed Slovenia's accession. Prime Minister Janez Drnovšek won the presidential run-off. Anton Rop of the LDS, the senior coalition party, was

elected prime minister with 63 votes for and 24 votes against (to be elected, Rop needed a minimum of 46 votes from the members of parliament).
2003 In a referendum, 89.6 per cent of Slovenes voted to join the EU and 66 per cent voted to join NATO.
2004 Slovenia joined NATO and the EU. Slovenska Demokratska Stranka (SDS) (Slovenian Democratic Party) won the parliamentary elections and Janez Jansa was elected prime minister by parliament.
2005 Parliament ratified the EU constitution.
2006 EU finance ministers gave final approval to Slovenia's application to adopt the euro currency.
2007 Slovenia joined the European Economic and Monetary Union (EMU) and introduced the euro as its official currency. Danilo Türk won presidential elections after two rounds. Slovenia became a member of the European Union Schengen area within which all travellers may cross borders without a passport or visa.
2008 Former president and prime minister, Janez Drnovšek died. In parliamentary elections the Socialni Demokrati (SD) (Social Democrats) won 30.5 per cent of the vote (29 seats, out of 90) and the ruling SDS 29.3 per cent (28); turnout was 62.3 per cent. A coalition was formed by SD, Zares-Nova Politika (Z-NP) (For Real-New Politics) and LDS. Later SD, LDS and DeSUS formed a government. Borut Pahor (SD) became prime minister.
2009 Slovenia vetoed Croatia's EU accession attempt, citing an on-going territorial dispute as the obstacle for agreement – Croatia wanted its border with Slovenia to be halfway through the Bay of Piran and submitted maps and documents to EU negotiators showing this. The biggest banking group, Nova Ljubljanska Banka (NLB) lost €23.6 million (US$33.1 million) as a bank and €86.8 million (US$121.7 million) as a group and had to resort to a public bailout; the bank denied accusations that it had made loans based on political connections.
2010 The Organisation for Economic Co-operation and Development (OECD) voted unanimously to admit Slovenia as a member. In a referendum, just 51.49 per cent of the vote was in favour of allowing international arbitration to resolve the border dispute concerning the Bay of Piran. A five-person panel, including one Slovene and one Croat, will settle the matter. Slovenia signed a protocol to jointly found a new company, Cargo 10, with Macedonia, Serbia and Croatia to incorporate their railway companies.
2011 In May, the panel to settle the Bay of Piran dispute submitted their arbitrated agreement to the UN for registration. A decision, binding on both parties, is expected to be given by the UN in 2014. A referendum was held in June, in which voters overwhelmingly rejected changes to counter the black economy. They also voted against opening up state security archives, and against amendments to the state pension system, which would have raised the age of retirement to 65. The failure of the proposals ran against government legislation introduced into parliament in December 2010. In September the government lost a vote of no-confidence in parliament. According to the constitution, a new prime minister had to be appointed within 30 days or a general election held. Early parliamentary elections were held on 4 December, in which the new party, Lista Zorana Jankovica-Pozitivna Slovenija (LZJ-PS) (Zoran Jankovic's Party-Positive Slovenia) won 28.5 per cent (29 seats out of 90) and the right to form a coalition government.
2012 On 5 January, Zoran Jankovic was designated as prime minister but parliament rejected his appointment when he failed to form a government. On 25 January a coalition government was agreed between the Slovenská Demokratska Stranka (SDS) (Slovenian Democratic Party), Državljanska lista Gregorja Viranta (DLGV) (Gregor Virant's Civic Party), Demokraticna Stranka Upokojencev Slovenije (DeSUS) (Democratic Party of Pensioners of Slovenia), Slovenska Ljudska Stranka (SLS) (Slovenian People's Party) and Nova Slovenija-Krščanska ljudska stranka (Nova Slovenija) (New Slovenia-Christian People's Party). Janez Janša (SDS) was designated as prime minister and parliament confirmed his appointment on 28 January. On 2 August, the credit ratings agency Moody's cut Slovenia's bonds rating from A2 to Baa2 (three levels and just two levels above 'junk' status), with a negative outlook. Moody's said the downgrading was due to bad loans in the banking sector worth billions of US dollars and the top three banks relied on public financial support. The first round of the presidential election was held on 11 November, in which Borut Pahor (independant) won 39.98 per cent of the vote, Danilo Türk (SD) 35.86 per cent and Milan Zver (Nova Slovenija) 24.16 per cent; turnout was 47.8 per cent. In the runoff, Pahor won 67.4 per cent and Türk 32.6 per cent; turnout was 42 per cent. President Borut Pahor took office on 22 December.
2013 On 23 Jan 2013 the DLGV withdrew from the coalition, leaving Prime Minister Janša without a majority. Janša himself was still on trial on corruption charges. On 27 February Mr Janša lost a no-confidence vote and Alenka Bratušek of Positive Slovenia formed a new government. Mr Janša was was found guilty of corruption and sentenced to two years imprisonment on 5 June.
2014 Ms Bratušek submitted her resignation on 5 May. Early elections were held on 13 July. These were won by the Stranka Mira Cerarja (SMC) (Miro Cerar Party), formed by Miro Cerar on 2 June, with 34.49 per cent of the vote (36 seats, out of 90), followed by SDS with 20.71 per cent (21) and DeSUS with 10.18 per cent (10). Mr Cerar submitted a coalition government of SMC, DeSUS and SDS, which the National Assembly approved by 54 votes to 25 on 18 September. Mr Cerar become prime minister on 18 September.
2015 In March Slovenia became the eleventh EU country to approve gay marriage when the parliament adopted by 51 to 28 votes a new law that authorises same-sex weddings. Deputies also voted in favour of legalising adoption by gay and lesbian couples.

Political structure

Constitution

The Slovenian constitution was adopted in December 1991 and amended in 1997 and 2000.

Form of state

Parliamentary democratic republic

The executive

The president, who is elected for a five-year term, by universal adult suffrage, is Head of State and commander-in-chief of the armed forces.
The president proposes a candidate for prime minister to the Skupscina Slovenije (Assembly of Slovenia) after consultation with parliamentary groups. The assembly has the final power of appointment of the prime minister and the government.

National legislature

The bicameral Parlament Slovenije (Slovenian Parliament), consists of the Drzavni Zbor (National Assembly) (lower house) with 90 seats of which 88 members are directly elected in single-seat constituencies by proportional representation vote and two directly elected in special constituencies for Italian and Hungarian ethnic minorities by simple majority vote. Members serve four-year terms.
The Drzavni Svet (National Council) (upper house) has 40 seats of which members are indirectly elected by an electoral college to serve five year terms. Two are nominated from interest groups; 22 represent local district interests, six represent non-commercial activities, four are employer representatives, four employee representatives and four represent artisans and professionals. The government is made up of members of the National

Assembly, and is answerable to that body. National Council members have a mainly advisory role, but may veto decisions of the National Assembly and must approve the composition of any government.

Legal system

The legal system is based on the 1991 constitution.

The judiciary is structurally independent from the government, with the Constitutional Court empowered to determine the conformity of national legislation with the constitution. All civil and criminal cases are dealt with by eight basic and four higher courts, and the Supreme Court is the final court of appeal. Prosecutions are the responsibility of the Public Prosecutor and to safeguard defendants rights there is also a Public Attorney. The Justice Ministry is the administrative authority of the Slovenian judiciary.

Last elections

13 July 2014 (parliamentary); 11 November and 2 December 2012 (presidential first round and runoff)

Results: Parliamentary: Stranka Mira Cerarja (SMC) (Miro Cerar Party) 34.49 per cent of the vote (36 seats, out of 90), Slovenská Demokratska Stranka (SDS) (Slovenian Democratic Party) 20.71 per cent (21), Demokraticna Stranka Upokojencev Slovenije (DeSUS) (Democratic Party of Pensioners of Slovenia) 10.18 per cent (10), Socialni Demokrati (SD) (Social Democrats) 5.98 per cent (6), Združena Levica (ZL) (United Left) 5.97 per cent (6), Nova Slovenija-Kršcanska ljudska stranka (NSi) (New Slovenia-Christian People's Party) 5.59 per cent (5), Zavezništvo Alenke Bratušek (ZaAB) (Alliance of Alenka Bratušek) 4.38 per cent (4), Hungarian and Italian minorities 1 each. Turnout was 51.73 per cent.

Presidential: (first round) Borut Pahor (independant) won 39.9 per cent of the vote, Danilo Türk (SD) 35.9 per cent, Milan Zver (Nova Slovenija) 24.2 per cent; turnout was 48.2 per cent.

Runoff: Pahor won 67.4 per cent, Türk 33.6 per cent; turnout was 42 per cent.

Next elections

2018 (parliamentary); 2017 (presidential)

Political parties

Ruling party

After his party's surprise win with 34.7% of the vote in the 13 July 2014 snap election Mr Cerar set about forming a new coalition government on 14 July. His party, Stranka Modernega Centra (SMC) (Modern Centre party) went into coalition with Demokraticna Stranka Upokojencev Slovenije (DeSUS) (Democratic Party of Pensioners of Slovenia), and Socialni Demokrati (SD) Social Democrats).

Main opposition party

Slovenska Demokratska Stranka (SDS) (Slovenian Democratic Party)

Population

2.06 million (2014)

Last census: March 2002: 1,964,036 (provisional)

Population density: 99 inhabitants per square km. Urban population 50 per cent (2010 Unicef).

Annual growth rate: 0.3 per cent, 1990–2010 (Unicef). Urban population 29 per cent (2010 Unicef).

Ethnic make-up

Around 88 per cent of the population are Slovenes, with small numbers of ethnic Serbs, Croats, Muslims, Albanians, Hungarians, Italians and Germans. Only the Italian and Hungarian communities are officially recognised minorities.

Religions

Roman Catholic (71 per cent), Lutheran (1 per cent), Islam (1 per cent).

Education

Unlike other parts of the former Yugoslavia, where adult illiteracy remains a major socioeconomic problem, Slovenia has always had a relatively highly educated society. Adult illiteracy is therefore virtually non-existent.

Primary and initial secondary schooling are combined in one school for nine-years. At aged 15 students are channelled onto one of three paths, general, technical or vocational. General and technical education lasts for four years, while vocational courses last for either two or three years.

As a critical determinant of future socioeconomic development, higher education experienced significant growth during the 1990s. Unesco estimates total gross enrolment rates for tertiary education at over 60 per cent. Law, business and economics remain popular courses, while further education institutions find it difficult to attract students to technical courses, resulting in a lack of skills in certain sectors of the workforce.

Literacy rate: 100 per cent adult rate; 100 per cent youth rate (15–24) (Unesco 2005).

Compulsory years: 6 to 15

Enrolment rate: 98 per cent gross primary enrolment, 92 per cent gross secondary enrolment; of relevant age groups (including repeaters) (World Bank).

Pupils per teacher: 12 in primary schools.

Health

Formerly entirely state controlled and funded, healthcare is now a growing private sector activity so that Slovenia is comparable with the EU for healthcare provision. In the long-term though, more funds will have to be directed towards it due to its ageing population. Healthcare provisions also includes a well-developed network of medicinal spas for all types of ailments. Lower healthcare charges attract paying customers from neighbouring countries.

Private health insurance is increasing rapidly and the government has encouraged additional forms of health insurance, and the preparation of national preventative programmes, that should reduce dependency on the state and bolster private sector provision.

HIV/Aids

HIV prevalence: 0.1 per cent aged 15–49 in 2003 (World Bank)

Life expectancy: 77 years, 2004 (WHO 2006)

Fertility rate/Maternal mortality rate: 1.4 births per woman, 2010 (Unicef)

Birth rate/Death rate: Nine births per 1,000 population; 10 deaths per 1,000 population (2003).

Child (under 5 years) mortality rate (per 1,000): 3 per 1,000 live births (WHO 2012)

Head of population per physician: 2.25 physicians per 1,000 people, 2002 (WHO 2006)

Welfare

The Pension and Disability Act, which significantly reformed the pension system, became effective from 2000 and consists of a reformed pay-as-you-go scheme, with a supplementary fund as part of waged contracts. The minimum age of retirement for women has gradually risen and the amount of full pensions reduced relative to the wage rate.

The government ensured better legal protection for workers by defining their rights at the minimum level, and strengthened investment in the area of labour, family and social welfare.

Main cities

Ljubljana (capital, estimated population 249,700 in 2012), Maribor (87,234), Celje (35,458), Kranj (33,704), Koper (26,305), Velenje (26,215), Novo Mesto (23,142).

Languages spoken

The main minority languages are Albanian, Hungarian and Italian, but Hungarian and Italian are officially recognised. Serbian, Croatian, German, English and French are also spoken.

Regional identities and dialects remain very strong.

Official language/s

Slovene

Media

Press

Dailies: A major publishing organisation *Delo* (www.delo.si) (with an English online edition) produces two dailies (including *Slovenske Novice* and *Ne Delo*), four magazines (including a free monthly magazine, *Delnicar*, with the highest circulation) and has three internet portals. Other national publications include *Dnevnik* (www.dnevnik.si), *Vecer* (www.vecer.si) and *Zurnal* (www.zurnal24.si). Major regional newspapers include *Direkt* (www.direkt.si) and *Ekipa-sport.so* both tabloids, from Ljubljana as does the *Slovenia Time* (www.sloveniatimes.com) published in English. From Celje *Novi Tednik* (www.novitednik.com) in Slovene, *Nepujsag* (www.nepujsag.net) is published in Hungarian in Lendava.

Weeklies: In Solvene, the variety includes *Demokracija* (www.demokracija.si) and *Dolenjski List* (www.dol-list.si), *Gorenjski Glas* (www.g-glas.si), *Jana*, *Kmecki Glas* (www.czd-kmeckiglas.si), *Mariborcan* (www.revijakapital.com/mariborcan), *Mladina* (www.mladina.si), *Primorske Novice* (www.primorske.si), and *Vestnik Murska Sobota* (www.p-inf.si) provide general information and local news. *Druzina* (www.druzina.si) is a Roman Catholic publication.

Based abroad, *TOL* reports on central European issues. The government publication *Sinfo* covering politics, business, culture can be accessed online (www.ukom.gov.si).

Business: In Slovene, the national publication *Podjetnik* (www.podjetnik.com) and the regional *Kapital* (www.revijakapital.com) are magazines, *Finance* (www.finance.si) is a regional newspaper. In English, *Slovenian Business Report* (www.sbr.si).

Periodicals: The free monthly newspaper, *Delnicar*, has the highest circulation.

Broadcasting

Radio: There are many commercial radio stations. RTV Slovenija (www.rtvslo.si) is the state-owned radio station which is the market leader with three national channels, of which one broadcasts in Italian, one in Hungarian and one in Slovene. During the tourist season, there are broadcasts in German and English each day covering: news, traffic news, local weather and tourist directions. Other major radio stations include Radio Hit (www.r-hit.si) and Radio City (www.radiocity.si).

Television: The state-owned Radio Televizija Slovenija (RTV) (www.rtvslo.si), broadcast in Slovene, Italian and Hungarian. The privately owned commerical TV stations Pop Tv (http://24ur.com) broadcasts foreign programmes. Both TV stations offer programmes online. Satellite and cable TV is also available, including TV Si21 (http://tv.si21.com).

STA (Slovenska Tiskovna Agencija), Cankarjeva 5, PO Box 145, 1101 Ljubljana, (tel: 241-0100; fax: 426-6050; email: desk@sta.si; internet: www.sta.si).

In Slovene, Morel (www.kabi.si).

Economy

Slovenia was one of the most prosperous regions of former Yugoslavia, and continued to be so after its independence. It has natural resources of coal, mercury and timber, which supply raw materials for the country's manufacturing sector, producing metal work, chemicals, paper, construction materials and furniture, household goods and electronic equipment, clothing and foodstuffs.

The service sector constituted 69.5 per cent of GDP in 2014. Agriculture contributes only 2.1 per cent of GDP, with the cultivation of crops and livestock.

The economy improved quickly following its adoption of the euro in 2007 with GDP growth of 6.9 per cent, before falling to 3.6 per cent in 2008 as energy and food costs rose to a record high. The global economic crisis caused a dramatic contraction in 2009 when Slovenia experienced the sharpest decline in the euro-zone, with a recessionary drop of -8.0 per cent, due to a significant cutback in external credit, which forced banks to curtail domestic credit and almost overnight ended construction and the housing boom. In 2010, as global trade picked up, so exports led a modest recovery, with growth of 1.2 per cent. Economic growth is still dependent on Germany, Slovenia's single largest trading partner. Slovenia entered recession in 2012, which lasted until 2014 when it returned to positive growth in GDP of 2.6 per cent.

Unemployment rose from 9.2 per cent in 2009 to 10.7 per cent in 2010, as thousands of workers were laid off; the minimum wage was cut and public sector worker's salaries were reduced. However, despite the improvement in economic performance in 2014, unemployment was high at 13.0 per cent.

Foreign direct investment (FDI) had reached a record US$1.94 billion in 2008, but fell to US$366.2 million in 2010, before rising to US$1.1 billion in 2011 as more state-owned entities were put up for sale. Along with the performance of the economy foreign direct investment jumped from US$95.1 million in 2013 to US$1.5 billion in 2014.

External trade

As a member of the European Union, Slovenia operates within a community-wide free trade union, with tariffs sets as a whole. Internationally, the EU has free trade agreements with a number of nations and trading blocs worldwide.

Foreign trade represents over 130 per cent of GDP, of which over 60 per cent is with the EU. The manufacturing sector is diversified with food processing, electrical equipment and electronics, textiles and timber products. Wine and animal husbandry are important agricultural exports, while industrial and mineral extraction represents around 30 per cent of GDP.

Imports

Main imports are vehicles, machinery, manufactured goods, chemicals, petroleum and derivatives and foodstuffs.

Main sources: Germany (16.2 per cent of total in 2014), Italy (14.4 per cent), Austria (10.3 per cent)

Exports

The principal exports are manufactured goods, machinery and transport equipment, chemicals and food.

Main destinations: Germany (19 per cent of total in 2014), Italy (11.2 per cent), Austria (8.7 per cent)

Agriculture

Farming

Agriculture accounts for 2.1 per cent of GDP and employs around 2 per cent of the workforce. Farming is generally carried out on smallholdings of less than 25 hectares (ha). There are also a number of large farms and co-operatives which produce most food exports as well as food consumed domestically. Agricultural production fell substantially after independence, but recovered quickly and is above pre-independence levels.

The restoration of farming land and forests to claimants continues, although agricultural development is still being held up. Several issues pertaining to rural development, including aid to underdeveloped regions and environmental programmes, are on the political agenda.

The agricultural sector is subject to the reformed Common Agricultural Policy (CAP), whereby subsidies are no longer paid on farm output, which tended to benefit large farms and encourage overproduction, but rather on single farm payments not conditional on production.

Fishing

The annual commercial catch of fish amounts to between 1,815 and 2,270 tonnes. This excludes the catches of private fishermen estimated between 182 and 272 tonnes. Another 136 tonnes of fish is obtained by mariculture. About 454 tonnes of freshwater fish is bred on fish farms. Slovenia imports about 7,258 tonnes of fish annually.

Slovenia's legislation on fisheries is largely oriented towards Europe, although more resources will be necessary to meet the requirements of the EU's Common Fisheries Policy (CFP). Slovenia has a fisheries agreement with Croatia and is also a member of the General Fisheries Commission for the Mediterranean.

Forestry
Slovenia has a significant forestry sector. Forest cover is estimated at 1.1 million hectares (ha). The sector has a long tradition of sustainable management and less than a third of the forest area is publicly owned. Only a small area of forest is available for wood supply. Forestry forms the basis of a number of key industrial sectors, notably furniture making, paper, pulp and construction materials. The industry includes both large and small saw mills, which rely on the domestic supply of raw materials. Paper is mainly exported to European countries. Per capita consumption of forest products remains around the European average.

Industry and manufacturing
Manufacturing accounts for 24 per cent of GDP and industry overall for 32 per cent.
The manufacture of capital goods has traditionally been the mainstay of Slovenia's industry, with iron and steel, metal working and machine-building accounting for a third of total manufactured added value. With intermediate goods accounting for 15 per cent and consumer goods for 55 per cent of manufactured added value, Slovenia has all the characteristics of an advanced industrial economy.
Slovenia is anxious to boost its exports to the EU. This strategic redirection of its industrial exports will require a complete restructuring of its entire industrial sector. The major structural problems are low levels of new investment, over-manning, technological backwardness and too many industrial enterprises for what is now a small domestic market with limited export potential. The newer and rising consumer goods industries, such as electrical products, are expected to become more capital intensive in order to compete internationally. High-technology industries based on computing and high added-value have yet to make a significant appearance.

Tourism
Slovenia has a diverse geography ranging from Alpine peaks and valleys to a small stretch of the Adriatic coast, which together offer a range of holidays for both the energetic and easy going visitor.
Travel and tourism contributed 12.7 per cent to GDP in 2014, forecast to rise by 2.5 per cent in 2015. The industry provided employment to 13.0 per cent of the workforce (103,500 jobs), forecast to rise by 0.9 per cent in 2015. Capital investment in the industry was 9.4 per cent of total investment in 2014.
Health spas and tourists staying in farm accommodation have increased in popularity, along with Slovenia as a destination for conferences and business meetings.

Hydrocarbons
Oil reserves have been exhausted and Slovenia relies entirely on imports of petroleum products. Consumption was 49,000 barrels per day (bpd) of oil in 2013. Nafta Lendava is the only refinery in the country, with a capacity of 35,000bpd.
Proven natural gas reserves are negligible and Slovenia relies entirely on Algerian and Russian gas imports of over 1.1 billion cubic metres per annum. The state-owned natural gas company, Geoplin, is responsible for transit, supply and sale of natural gas in Slovenia.
Slovenia has proven coal reserves, mainly lignite found in the Saleška Valley near Velenje, and sub-bituminous coal in several other parts of the country. Exploitable reserves at Velenje amount to 227 million tonnes; production could be sustained for 60 years. The sub-bituminous reserves are of low quality with high ash and sulphur content. Coal provides for one-quarter of the country's energy needs.

Energy
Slovenia has installed electricity capacity of 3.2GW, generated by thermal, hydropower and nuclear stations. The sole nuclear plant, sited at Krško, is jointly owned with Croatia. Slovenia is a net exporter of electricity.

Financial markets
Stock exchange
Ljubljanska Borza (Ljubljana Stock Exchange)

Banking and insurance
Slovenia has a well-developed banking sector. The central bank and the finance ministry are responsible for implementing EU banking directives.
Nova Ljubljanska Banka (NLB) and Nova Kreditna Banka Maribor, both state-owned, dominate the sector, together holding some 40 per cent of banking assets. The merger of the Abanka and Banka Vipa in December 2002 created a new bank, Abanka Vipa, which now has a major slice of the Slovenian banking sector.
Foreign banks own around 30 per cent of the banking sector. Approximately 96 per cent of SKB Banka was sold to France's Société Générale and a 34 per cent stake in NLB was sold to Belgium's KBC Bank.

Central bank
Banka Slovenije (BSI) (Bank of Slovenia)

Main financial centre
Ljubljana

Time
GMT plus one hour (daylight saving, late March to late October, GMT plus two hours)

Geography
Slovenia is bordered by Italy to the west, Austria to the north, Hungary to the east and Croatia to the south. There is a 46km coastal strip on the Gulf of Trieste in the Adriatic Sea, around the Istrian port of Koper.
An Alpine terrain covers over half Slovenia's area, stretching down from the north. This region is dominated by the Julian Alps in the north-west, where Mount Triglav (2,864 metres), the tallest peak, is located. The Slovene Alps are covered in forests, including some remnants of primeval forests, particularly around Kocevje in the south, and producing scores of rivers. The river Sava rises from two headstreams in the Julian Alps and flows down for 933km to the river Danube in Serbia.
The other half of the country is Mediterranean, one part of which, around the region of Karst, has a limestone landscape. A geological phenomenon where water has eaten into the rock has produced numerous sinkholes and cave networks and has given its name to a branch of science – karstology. The large Pannonian plain, in the east (around 20 per cent of the country) is fertile farmland and the source of thermal and mineral water springs.

Hemisphere
Northern

Climate
Ljubljana has an average summer temperature of 25 degrees Celsius (C) and in winter –3 degrees C. Precipitation is heavy, with an annual average rainfall of 1,407mm. Air pollution has had an adverse effect on the weather, notably in the Ljubljana Basin.
The north has an alpine climate with warm summers and cold winters, the west has Mediterranean weather with hot summers and mild winters and the east has a continental climate with hot summers and cold winters.

Dress codes
Formal dress is the norm for business and social meetings in Slovenia. Business visitors should be smartly dressed.

Entry requirements
Passports
Required by all except nationals of countries which are signatories of the Schengen Accords, which includes most EU/EEA member states, who may visit on national IDs. Passports must be valid for three months beyond the visit.

Visa
Required by all, except nationals of EU and Schengen area signatory countries, North America, Australasia and Japan. See www.mzz.gov.si and follow path to *Embassies, Diplomatic Missions and*

Consulates for a list of Slovene consulates and further information for other visitors regarding necessary documentation. A Schengen visa application (offered in several languages) can be downloaded from http://europa.eu/abc/travel/ see 'documents you will need'.

Currency advice/regulations

The import and export of local currency is unlimited, however amounts over T3 million (or foreign equivalent) must be declared. Slovenia will join the European Monetary Union on 1 January 2007 when the euro will become legal tender along side the tolar, which will be withdrawn after 14 days.
Travellers cheques are widely accepted.

Customs

Personal items are duty-free. There are no duties levied on alcohol and tobacco between EU member states, providing amounts imported are for personal consumption.
All items of cultural value, including artistic, archaeological, ethnographic, scientific and antiques over 100 years are prohibited from being exported.

Health (for visitors)

Nationals of the European Economic Area (EEA) countries and Switzerland can access reduced cost and sometimes free medical treatment using a European Health Insurance Card (EHIC) while visiting the EEA. Exceptions include nationals of the 10 countries which joined the EU in 2004 whose EHIC is not valid in Switzerland. Applications for the EHIC should be made before travelling.

Credit cards

International credit and charge cards are widely accepted. Credit cards can be used to get cash advances from banks.

Public holidays (national)

Fixed dates

1–2 Jan (New Year), 8 Feb (Preseren/Culture Day), 27 Apr (Resistance Day), 1–2 May (Labour Day), 25 Jun (National Day), 15 Aug (Assumption Day), 31 Oct (Reformation Day), 1 Nov (All Saints' Day), 25 Dec (Christmas Day), 26 Dec (Independence Day).
Holidays that fall at the weekend are not replaced.

Variable dates

Easter Monday

Working hours

Banking

Mon–Fri: 0730–1800; Sat: 0730–1200.

Business

Mon—Fri: 0800—1600.

Government

Mon–Fri: 0800–1600.

Shops

Mon–Fri: 0700–1900 or 0800–2000; some shops also open Sat: 0800–1300/1500, Sun: 0800–1200.

Telecommunications

Mobile/cell phones

GSM 900 and 1800 services available throughout most of the country.

Electricity supply

220V AC, with round two-pin plugs.

Weights and measures

Metric system

Social customs/useful tips

For business meetings, when appointments are made, visitors should be punctual. Business cards are essential.
Slovenia has a reputation for being efficient and reliable. Executives will generally have a good knowledge of German, English and sometimes Italian. There is a well-developed network of local agents, advisers, consultants and lawyers willing to act for foreign companies.
Slovenians are a rather reserved people with a tendency towards formality. As in Austria and Germany, titles are widely used. Informality on the part of a foreigner is not considered acceptable. It is not unusual for Slovenians to prefer to hold business discussions over lunch.
Athough smoking is generally accepted, it is restricted in many public places and buildings.
Visitors should carry some form of identity at all times.

Security

Slovenia has a low crime rate. Sometimes tourists are the targets of pickpockets and purse-snatchers, especially on the trains.

Getting there

Air

National airline: Adria Airways
International airport/s: Ljubljana (LJU), 27km from city centre, facilities include duty-free shops, bank, post office, restaurant, internet access and car hire. Buses provide access to Ljubljana (travel time 45 minutes). Taxis are available.
Other airport/s: Maribor (MBX) and Portoroz (POW) have European connections. They are open only during daylight hours.
Airport tax: None

Surface

Slovenia is included in the Pan-European Corridor 5 scheme. The project has some 3,270km of railways, linking Kiev in the Ukraine with western Europe via Italy, and 2,850km of new and upgraded roads.
Road: Most frontier posts are open for road traffic from Italy, Austria, Hungary and Croatia; almost all border crossings are open 24 hours.
Rail: Connections are available from major European cities. The Eurocity Mimara train connects Zagreb, Ljubljana, Munich and Leipzig. Direct trains to Slovenia are available from Italy (Rome, Milan, Venice and Trieste), Austria (Vienna and Villach) and Hungary (Budapest). Transport for cars may be available on some routes.
Water: A catamaran runs regular scheduled trips between Venice-Portoroz and Piran, between March–October.
Main port/s: Koper, Izola, Piran and Portoroz.

Getting about

National transport

Air: Domestic airports are situated at Maribor (MBX) in eastern Slovenia, with Potoroz (POW) on the Adriatic coast. There are regular services from the capital, Ljubljana.
Road: There is an extensive network of roads in Slovenia, many of which are in good condition. The main arterial road running south-west to north-east is a stretch of the Pan-European Corridor 5. The roads can be congested particularly during peak periods but have clear signposts, with rest and food facilities.
The following are toll motorways: Ljubljana-Razdrto, Arja vas-Hoce and Ljubljana-Kranj.
Buses: Good nationwide services operated by a number of companies.
Rail: There are good rail connections and rail travel is inexpensive. A high-speed train links Ljubljana-Maribor throughout the year and Ljubljana-Koper during the summer only. Intercity and Urban trains run to most regions

City transport

Taxis: Metered taxis are available in Ljubljana and other major towns. A tip of 10 per cent is expected.
Buses, trams & metro: Most city centres are served by trams, and the suburbs by buses. Service is inexpensive and regular, but radically reduced at night. Exact fares are required on the bus or tram, or tokens can be purchased from kiosks, post offices and in supermarkets beforehand.

Car hire

Many major car hire companies operate from the airport and capital. A full national driving licence and third party insurance for foreigners is compulsory. Speed limits are 130kph on motorways, 100kph on open highways, 90kph on urban roads outside residential areas and 50kph in cities and towns. Safety belts are compulsory and school buses must not be overtaken.
The AMZS (Automobile Association of Slovenia) provides a good emergency roadside service.
Much of the centre of Ljubljana has been pedestrianised and traffic is very congested. Finding parking spaces can be

very difficult; use of a car in the city on weekdays is not advisable.

BUSINESS DIRECTORY

The addresses listed below are a selection only. While World of Information makes every endeavour to check these addresses, we cannot guarantee that changes have not been made, especially to telephone numbers and area codes. We would welcome any corrections.

Telephone area codes

The international direct dialling code (IDD) for Slovenia is +386, followed by area code and subscriber's number:

Celje	3	Murska Sobota	02
Koper	5	Nova Gorica	5
Kranj	4	Novo Mesto	7
Krsko	7	Postojna	5
Ljubljana	1	Ravne	2
Maribor	2	Trbovlje	3

Useful telephone numbers

Emergency112

Chambers of Commerce

American Chamber of Commerce in Slovenia, 55 Pod Hribom, 1000 Ljubljana (tel: 581-6285; fax: 581-6111; e-mail: office@am-cham.si).

Koper Chamber of Commerce and Industry, 2 Ferrarska, 6000 Koper (tel: 639-5311; fax: 639-5316; e-mail: kozlovic@hg.gzs.si).

Ljubljana Chamber of Commerce and Industry, 9 Dimiceva, 1504 Ljubljana (tel: 230-1133; fax: 431-3040; e-mail: samardzija@hg.gzs.si).

Maribor Chamber of Commerce and Industry, 24 Talcev, 2000 Maribor (tel: 220-8700; fax: 252-2283; e-mail: breznik@hg.gzs.si).

Northern Primorska Chamber of Commerce and Industry, 3 Trg Edvarda Kardelja, 5000 Nova Gorica (tel: 330-6030; fax: 330-6031; e-mail: velikonja@hg.gzs.si).

Novo Mesto Chamber of Commerce and Industry, 5 Novi Trg, 8000 Novo Mesto (tel: 332-2182; fax: 332-2187; e-mail: goles@hg.gzs.si).

Postojna Chamber of Commerce and Industry, Cankarjeva 6, 6230 Postojna (tel: 720-0111; fax: 726-5344; e-mail: tiselj@hg.gzs.si).

Slovenia Chamber of Commerce and Industry, 13 Dimiceva, 1504 Ljubljana (tel: 589-8000; fax: 589-8100; e-mail: infolink@gzs.si).

Banking

Abanka Vipa dd, Slovenska 58, 1517 Ljubljana (tel: 471-8100; fax: 432-5165; email: info@abanka.si; internet site: www.abanka.si).

Bank Austria dd, Smartinska 140, 1000 Ljubljana (tel: 587-6600; fax: 587-6684; email: info@si.bacai.com).

Banka Celje dd, Vodnikova 2, 3000 Celje (tel: 543-1000 fax: 548-3511; email: info@banka-celje.si).

Banka Koper, Pristaniska 14, 6502 Koper (tel: 665-1100; fax: 639-7842; email: infor@banka-koper.si; internet site: www.banka-koper.si).

Factor Banka dd, Tivolska 48, 1000 Ljubljana (tel: 230-6600; fax: 230-7760; email: info@factorb.si).

Gorenjska Banka dd, Bleiweisova 1, 4000 Kranj (tel: 208-4000; fax: 202-1503; email: info@gbkr.si).

Hypo-Alpe-Adria Bank dd, Trv Osvobodine fronte 12, 1000 Ljubljana (tel: 300-4400; fax: 300-4401; email: hypo-banka@hypo.si).

Koroska Banka dd, Glavni trg 30, 2380 Slovenj Gradec (tel: 884-9111; fax: 884-2382).

Krekova Banka, Slomskov trg 18, 2000 Maribor (tel: 229-3100; fax: 252-2261; email: info@krekova-banka.si).

Nova Kreditna Banka Maribor, Vita Kraigherja 4, 2505 Maribor (tel: 229-2290; fax: 252-4333, 252-4371; email: info@nkbm.si).

Nova Ljubljanska Banka dd, Trg Republike 2, 1520 Ljubljana (tel: 425-0155; fax: 252-2422; email: info@nlb.si).

Postna Banka Slovenije dd, Vita Kraigherja 5, 2000 Maribor (tel: 228-8200; fax: 228-8210; email: info@pbs.si).

Probanka dd, Gosposka Ulica 23, 2000 Maribor (tel: 252-0500; fax: 252-5882; email: info@probanka.si).

SKB Banka dd, Ajdovscina 4, 1513 Ljubljana (tel: 433-213; fax: 231-4549: email: info@skb.si).

Slovenska Investicijska Banka dd, Copova 38, 1000 Ljubljana (tel: 242-0300; fax: 242-0521; email: sib@si-banka.si).

Slovenska Zadruzna Kmetijska Banka dd, Kolodvorska 9, 1000 Ljubljana (tel: 472-7100; fax: 472-7405); email: info@szkbanka.si).

Volksbank-Ljudska Banka dd, Dunajska 128a, 1101 Ljubljana (tel: 530-7400; fax: 520-7555; email: banka@volksbank.si).

Central bank

Banka Slovenije, Slovenska 35, 1505 Ljubljana (tel: 471-9000; fax: 251-5516; email: bsl@bsi.si; internet: www.bsi.si/en).

Stock exchange

Ljubljanska Borza (Ljubljana Stock Exchange), www.ljse.si

Travel information

Adria Airways, Kuzmiceva 7, 1000 Ljubljana (tel: 369-1000; fax: 230-1325; internet: www.adria.si).

Automobile Association of Slovenia, Dunajska 128a, SI-1000 Ljubljana (breakdown assistance tel: 530-5353; internet: www.amzs.si).

Ljubljana Airport, Zg Brnik 130a, 4210 Brnik (tel: 4-206-1981; fax: 4-202-1220; email: info@lju-airport.si; internet: www.lju-airport.si).

Slovenian Tourist Information Centre, Krekov trg 10, 1000 Ljubljana (tel: 306-4575/6; fax: 306-4580; email: stic@ljubljana-tourism.si; internet: www.ljubljana-tourism.si).

National tourist organisation offices

Slovenska Turisticna Organizacija (Slovenian Tourist Organisation), WTC, Dunajska 156, 1001 Ljubljana (tel: 589-1840; fax: 589-1841; e-mail: info@slovenia-tourism.si; internet: www.slovenia-tourism.si).

Ministries

Ministry of Agriculture, Forestry and Food, Dunajska 52, 1000 Ljubljana (tel: 478-9000; fax: 478-9021; email: janez.vertacnik@gov.si).

Ministry of Culture, Cankarjeva 5, 1000 Ljubljana (tel: 478-5900; fax: 478-5901; email: mkinfo@gov.si).

Ministry of Defence, Kardeljeva ploscad 25, 1000 Ljubljana (tel:471-2211; fax: 131-8164; email: darko.lubi@pub.mo-rs.si).

Ministry of the Economy, Kotnikova 5, 1000 Ljubljana (tel: 478-3600; fax: 478-3522; email: tatjana.zabasu@gov.si).

Ministry of Education, Science and Sport, Zupanèièeva 6, 1000 Ljubljana (tel: 478-5437; fax: 478-5669; email: info@mss.edus.si).

Ministry of Environment and Spatial Planning, Dunajska 48, 1000 Ljubljana (tel: 478-7400; fax: 478-7422; email: info.mop@gov.si).

Ministry of Finance, Zupanèièeva 3, 1502 Ljubljana (tel: 478-5211; fax: 478-5655; email: tilen.majnardi@mf-rs.si).

Ministry of Foreign Affairs, Presernova 25, 1000 Ljubljana (tel: 478-2000; fax: 478-2340; email: info.mzz@gov.si).

Ministry of Health, Stefanova 5, 1000 Ljubljana (tel: 478-6001; fax: 478-6058; email: ministrstvo.zdravsto@gov.si).

Ministry of the Information Society, Langusova 4, 1000 Ljubljana (tel: 478-8223; fax: 478-8142; email: mid@gov.si).

Ministry of the Interior, Stefanova 2, 1000 Ljubljana (tel: 472-5111; fax: 251-4330;email: jelka.smreka@mnz.si).

Ministry of Justice, Zupanèièeva 3, 1000 Ljubljana (tel: 478-5211; fax: 251-0200; email: stojan.klancar@gov.si).

Ministry of Labour, Family and Social Affairs, Kotnikova 5, 1000 Ljubljana (tel: 478-3450; fax: 478-3456; email: zmaga.grah@gov.si).

Ministry of Transport, Langusova 4, 1000 Ljubljana (tel: 478-8000; fax: 478-8139; email: mpz.info@gov.si).

Office for European Affairs, Subièeva 11, 1000 Ljubljana (tel: 478-24-47; fax: 478-2310; email: svez@gov.si).

President's Office, Erjavceva 17, 1000 Ljubljana (tel: 478-1205; fax: 478-1357).

Prime Minister's Office, Gregorèièeva 20, 1000 Ljubljana (tel: 478-1000; fax: 478-1607).

Other useful addresses

Agency of the Republic of Slovenia for Restructuring and Privatisation, Kotnikova Ulica 28, 1000 Ljubljana (tel: 131-2122; fax: 131-6011).

British Embassy, Fourth Floor, Trg Republike 3, 1000 Ljubljana (tel: 200-3910; fax: 425-0174; email: info@british-embassy.si).

Government Office for European Affairs, Subiceva 11, 1000 Ljubljana (tel: 478-2228; fax: 478-2310).

Government of the Republic of Slovenia, Gregorciceva 20, 1000 Ljubljana (tel: 478-1100; fax: 478-1607).

Government PR and Media Office, Slovenska 29, 1000 Ljubljana (tel: 478-2629; fax: 251-2312; internet: www.uvi.gov.si/eng).

Institute for Macroeconomic Analysis and Development, Gregorciceva 25, 1000 Ljubljana (tel: 478-2112; fax: 478-2070).

Ljubljana Stock Exchange, Trg Republike 3, 1000 Ljubljana (tel: 477-5500; fax: 477-5507, 477-5508).

Slovenian Embassy (USA), 1525 New Hampshire Avenue, NW, Washington DC 20036 (tel: (+1-202) 667-5363; fax: (+1-202) 667-4563; email: slovenia@embassy.org).

Small Business Development Centre, Dunajska 156, 1001 Ljubljana (tel: 189-1870; fax: 188-1178).

Statistical Office of the Republic of Slovenia, Vozarski Pot 12, 1000 Ljubljana (tel: 241-5300; fax: 241-5344).

Trade and Investment Promotion Office (TIPO), Kotnikova 28, 1000 Ljubljana (tel: 478-3557; fax: 478-3599; email: tipo@gov.si; internet site: www.investslovenia.org).

Internet sites

Republic of Slovenia website: www.sigov.si

Slovenske Zeleznice (Slovenian Railways): www.slo-zeleznice.si/en/home

Solomon Islands

KEY FACTS

Official name: Solomon Islands

Head of State: Queen Elizabeth II, represented by Governor General Frank Kabui (from 7 July 2009)

Head of government: Prime Minister Manasseh Sogavare (Independent) (from 9 December 2014)

Ruling party: Coalition led by Democratic Alliance Party (DAP) with Solomon Islands People First Party (SIPFP), Solomon Islands Party for Rural Advancement (SIPRA) and Peoples' Alliance Party (PAP).

Area: 27,556 square km – Guadalcanal: 5,302 square km

Population: 575,000 (2014)*

Capital: Honiara (on Guadalcanal)

Official language: English

Currency: Solomon Islands dollar (SI$) = 100 cents

Exchange rate: SI$7.97 per US$ (Sep 2015)

GDP per capita: US$2,009 (2014)*

GDP real growth: 1.49% (2014)*

GDP: US$1.16 billion (2014)*

Inflation: 5.08% (2014)*

Balance of trade: -US$16.45 million (2013)

Foreign debt: US$124.00 million (2012)

* estimated figure

There were 50 seats available in the Solomon Islands general election on 19 November 2014, 32 of which were won by independent candidates. Unexpectedly, one of those seats did not go to Prime Minister Gordon Darcy Lio. Under the islands' new legislation, only registered parties could form coalitions. However, only half of the 12 registered parties were actually successful in fielding candidates and therefore the MPs travelled to the capital, Honiara, in order to begin negotiations on a coalition government and also to elect the next prime minister. By December the results of the secret ballot had come through, and veteran politician Manasseh Sogavare had been elected and became prime minister for a third time.

Cooling down

The election was the country's first since the Australian-led peacekeeping mission (Regional Assistance Mission to Solomon Islands (RAMSI) had turned into a police-focussed mission the previous year. The military element of the mission ended as the Solomon Islands finally started showing signs of settling down following the often-violent conflict, which virtually brought the normally peaceful country to its knees between 1998 and 2003. The disparate geographical as well as ethnic nature of the islands (there are six main islands and literally hundreds of smaller islands) makes imposing standards of governance and social security something of a nightmare. Although an Australian orchestrated peace agreement was signed in 2000, it counted for little as the confrontations and violence continued, resulting in the arrival of Ramsi in 2003. At the core of the dispute were ethnic tensions reflecting the fundamental divide between Melanesians and Polynesians; the peace force arrested a number of so-called rebel leaders and collected large quantities of arms and ammunition.

Following Ramsi leaving the Solomon Islands in 2013, despite the apparent return to normality, prosperity remained elusive. The conflict virtually bankrupted the country, leaving hopes for a return to healthy growth rates resting on a resumption of palm oil production and gold mining. The World Bank says the Solomon Islands, one of the Pacific's poorest countries, has been hit by successive global food, fuel and financial crises.

According to the World Bank the Solomon Islands has a low population density with half a million people dispersed across the islands, 83 per cent of whom are rural and 40 per cent below the age of 14. It is also the poorest country in the Pacific on a per capita basis.

The economy

Although gold production has been brought to a halt in the Solomon Islands, according to the Asian Development Bank (ADB) exports in total rose by 5.3 per cent in the first half of 2015, thanks mainly to an increase in exports of bauxite and agricultural commodities.

The passage of the 2015 budget was delayed until April 2015, as the new coalition government needed time to prioritise expenses following the parliamentary elections in November 2014. The result was a budget with expenditure 11.8 per cent higher than the revised 2014 budget, due to increased need for food recovery. Total revenues and grants are also expected to rise by 3.3 per cent. The ADB projected fishing licence revenue to increase but not enough to counter the losses from the cessation of gold production. The government is planning on maintaining a deficit of 4.9 per cent of GDP for the second year running, and will draw down cash reserves to finance the deficit.

Inflation has fallen in 2015 as a result large flood-related consumer price rises from the previous year dissipating. The floods, the worst the islands have known, came after Cyclone Ita passed across the islands in April 2014 causing flash floods, killing as many as 16 people and leaving some 10,000 people homeless. On top of this, falling global food and fuel prices have contributed. Despite this, core inflation is still positive, implying headline inflation will rise in the latter part of 2015.

Inflation in 2016 is expected to pick up as the economic effects of the flood dissipate further. According to the ADB the current account deficit in 2014 was equal to 8.1 per cent of GDP as imports of equipment for post-flood reconstruction and rehabilitation were delayed. The deficit is expected to widen slightly in 2015 and much further in 2016 with the arrival of the delayed imports. The ADB expects development assistance flows and foreign direct investment (FDI) to help maintain foreign reserves above 8 months of import cover through 2015 and 2016.

Risk assessment

Politics	Fair
Economy	Fair/recovering
Regional stability	Good

COUNTRY PROFILE

The Solomon Islands were settled between 2,000–3,000BC by Austronesians, Neolithic people from south-east Asia.

1568 The Spanish explorer, Álvaro de Mendaña, first visited the islands. The islands were named after King Solomon as Mendana hoped that the islands were rich with gold.

The islands were left alone until the mid-nineteenth century when whaling ships stopped off for supplies.

1893 The central islands became a British protectorate.

1899 In the *Tripartite Treaty*, Britain gained control of the whole of the Solomon Islands in exchange for withdrawing its claim to Samoa.

1942–45 During the Second World War, Japanese occupied the islands and US troops fought one of the fiercest battles on Guadalcanal.

1945 Britain resumed the administration of the islands.

1946 An independence movement was founded to resist British rule.

1976 Self-government was granted.

1978 The Solomon Islands became fully independent.

1997 In the general election Bartholomew Ulufa'alu (Liberal Party) (a Mataita) won.

1999 Ethnic violence broke out on Guadalcanal as a native militia, the Isatabu Freedom Movement (IFM), tried to evict thousands of immigrant Malaitan. The Malaita Eagles Force (MEF) militia seized control of the capital, Honiara, claiming it was protecting Malaitan interests.

2000 Fighting broke out between the IFM and MEF. The MEF seized the parliament and forced Prime Minister Ulufa'alu to resign. The violence resulted in the breakdown in civil order with security and police forces often siding with one faction or another. The IFM and MEF signed *The Townsville Peace Agreement* in Australia. Unarmed peace-keepers were deployed.

2001 The IFM rebel leader, Selwyn Sake, was murdered. Sir Allan Kemakeza, (People's Alliance Party (PAP)), was elected prime minister by the new 50-member parliament.

2002 The economy began to collapse, as the government was unable to pay wages and fund services. Law and order began to disintegrate.

2003 A formal request to regional neighbours for international assistance to avert a spiral of anarchy led to the deployment of the Regional Assistance Mission of the Solomon Islands (Ramsi), including 300 police officers, which began to restore order and disarm militant groups. Infamous rebel leader, Harold Keke, viewed by many as a bandit warlord, particularly after he ordered the razing of two villages, surrendered to Ramsi forces. With peace restored Ramsi was scaled down.

2004 Nathaniel Waena became governor general. A constitution for a new federal system of government was drafted.

2005 The EU signed an agreement to provide US$13 million in aid. Keke was sentenced to life imprisonment for murder. The political party Solomon Islands Social Credit Party (Socreds) was founded. It advocated domestic control of the economy and full monetary and financial reform along social credit lines.

2006 Snyder Rini (an ethnic Chinese) (Association of Independent Members (AIM)) was elected prime minister, but rioting broke out following the announcement, with extensive damage caused to the commercial centre of Honiara, particularly to Chinese businesses, and he was forced to stand down within eight days. Manasseh Sogavare (Socreds) was elected prime minister. Julian Moti fled from Papua New Guinea, wanted by the Australian Federal Police on charges of sex tourism crimes.

2007 Prime Minister Sogavare appointed Julian Moti as the attorney general. Australian soldiers raided the prime minister's office in a search of Moti. The Sogavare government was defeated in a parliamentary vote of no confidence. Derek Sikua was elected prime minister by 32 to 15 votes for Patterson Oti. Moti was extradited to Australia.

2009 The SkyAirWorld carrier collapsed owing tens of millions of US dollars. The final report on the Commission of Inquiry into the 2006 Honiara riots said the riots had been orchestrated by criminals and that compensation to Chinese businesses that took the brunt of the violence would cause further anger against the Chinese community. The Inquiry also said that the Royal Solomon Islands Police (RSIP) force failed in its duty to protect persons and property and further that it was still unable to do its duty. A five-member panel to lead the nation's Truth and Reconciliation Commission (TRC) was announced. The TRC considered the cause and effect of the ethnic tensions and violence that struck the islands between 1998–2003. Parliament elected Frank Kabui as governor general.

2010 The Ownership, Unity and Responsibility Party (Our Party) was created, led by former prime minister Manasseh Sogavare. Six opposition political parties agreed to form an alliance to fight the general elections. Parliamentary elections were held and 509 candidates (including 25 women) and 12 new political parties took part. No political party achieved outright power and a coalition government was formed with Danny Philip (of the newly formed Reform Democratic Party (RDP)) was elected as prime minister, having gained support from 26 out of 50

KEY INDICATORS — Solomon Islands

	Unit	2011	2012	2013	2014	**2015
Population	m	*0.54	*0.55	*0.56	*0.57	*0.59
Gross domestic product (GDP)	US$bn	0.84	1.00	1.06	*1.16	*1.21
GDP per capita	US$	1,554	1,820	1,886	*2,009	*2,052
GDP real growth	%	9.3	4.9	3.0	*1.5	*3.3
Inflation	%	6.7	5.9	5.4	*5.1	*3.8
Exports (fob) (goods)	US$m	418.2	418.2	448.1	–	–
Imports (fob) (goods)	US$m	417.7	417.7	464.6	–	–
Balance of trade	US$m	0.6	-58.0	-16.4	–	–
Current account	US$m	52.0	2.0	-47.0	*-98.0	*-101.0
Total reserves minus gold	US$m	309.8	469.5	491.5	466.9	–
Foreign exchange	US$m	294.2	454.2	476.2	–	–
Exchange rate	per US$	7.89	7.35	7.19	7.63	–

* estimated figure ** forecast figure

elected members of parliament. The government's parliamentary majority was cut following the death of a sitting member and, later, the jailing of a cabinet minister, Jimmy Lusibaea, for unlawful wounding while a member of the MEF during ethnic violence in 2000. A government coalition was formed called the National Coalition for Reform and Advancement (NCRA), consisting of seven political parties and individuals: the Direct Development Party (DDP), the Independent Democratic Party (IDP), the Our Party, the Reform Democratic Party, the Rural and Urban Political Party (RUP), the Solomon Islands Party for Rural Advancement (SIPRA), and several independent members. Danny Philip (RDP) led the coalition.
2011 In January, Lusibaea was released from jail, having successfully argued that under the *The Townsville Peace Agreement* he should not have been prosecuted. Four cabinet ministers resigned in protest. The opposition first called on the prime minister to recall parliament, before asking the governor general to convene an emergency sitting of parliament to discuss the situation. Prime Minister Philip insisted that only he had the constitutional power to convene parliament and that he had enough support for his government to continue in office. Eventually five ministers had resigned and the opposition claimed two had joined the opposition. In April, Prime Minister Philip had regained control of parliament and remained in post. In June, the government re-valued the currency with an increase of 5 per cent, following advice from the central bank. The action intended to reduce the cost of living as imported goods fall in price. In July, approval was granted for three new overseas diplomatic missions for the Solomon Islands, to Cuba, New Zealand and Switzerland. In late July, the remote community of Ontong Java Atoll banned all government officials and the community's member of parliament (MP) from visiting their island, in protest at the lack of attention given by officials to the needs of the people concerning services, transport and traditional sources of food and income. During the Commonwealth Heads of Government summit, in October, the 16 countries in which the British monarch is Head of State unanimously agreed to change the royal line of succession from that of first born son to the first born child (regardless of its gender). The change will be enacted after the succession of Prince William (currently second in line to the throne, after his father Prince Charles). Prime Minister Danny Philip dismissed finance minister Gordon Darcy Lilo in November provoking an opposition-sponsored vote of no-confidence of his leadership. To avoid this, Prime Minister Philip resigned. However, the opposition could not agree on a candidate and of the six candidates nominated, Gordon Darcy Lilo (member of the ruling coalition) won 29 votes (out of 50); Milner Tozaka won 20. A riot broke out in Honiara between police and protestors opposed to Lilo's election.
2012 The International Monetary Fund (IMF) reported in April that the 2012 GDP had risen to an estimated US$979 billion (an increase from an estimated US$840 billion in 2011). On 1 June smoking was banned in schools, hospital workplaces and on public transport. On 31 October the Poha Bridge was opened connecting West Guadalcanal road to Honiara.
2013 In a speech celebrating the tenth anniversary or the setting up of Ramsi, New Zealand's Prime Minister John Key said that although New Zealand's military were withdrawing, a contingent of police would remain to contribute to the training and capacity building of the Royal Solomon Islands Police Force.
2014 Cyclone Ita hit the islands in April, causing flash John Kerry became the first US Secretary of State to visit the Solomon Islands when he made a brief stopover on 13 August. Mr Kerry visited a US war memorial in Guadalcanal island, laid a wreath at the Solomon Scouts and Coastwatchers Memorial to pay tribute to two men who rescued former US President John F Kennedy, and met with the prime minister to discuss the effects of climate change on the islands.
2015 An undersea quake of 6.9 magnitude hit near the Solomon Islands on 18 July. Although a tsumami *alert was put out, in fact it did not materialise.*

Political structure

Constitution

The Constitution of May 1978 delegates authority from the British monarch, through the governor general appointed on the recommendation of parliament. There are nine administrative areas each governed by elected provincial assemblies, and the tenth, Honiara, is administered by a town council.
A draft Constitution for a new federal system of government is expected to be ready by July 2009.

Independence date

1978

Form of state

Independent democracy, with British monarch as Head of State

The executive

The Head of State is the British Monarch, who is represented by the Governor General, who is chosen by the National Parliament, for a term of five years.
Executive power rests with the prime minister as Head of government. Parliament elects the prime minister from its membership; the prime minister appoints a cabinet of 18 ministers.
Every five years parliament votes in a governor general, a post that is largely ceremonial with few daily political functions.

National legislature

The unicameral, National Parliament has 50 seats of which members are directly elected in single-seat constituencies for four-year terms. A parliament may be dissolved by a majority of its members before the term expires.

Last elections

19 November 2014 (parliamentary); 15 June 2009 (governor general)
Results: Parliamentary: Democratic Alliance Party won seven seats (out of 50), United Democratic Party won five seats and the People's Alliance Party won three seats. Three more parties won a seat each and six others failed to win one. Independents won the majority of seats with 32 between them.
Governor general: in the fourth and final round, Frank Kabui (30 votes), Edmund Andresen (8) and Sir Nathaniel Waena (7).

Next elections

Unknown (governor general – chosen by parliament); 2018 (parliament)

Political parties

Ruling party

Coalition led by Democratic Alliance Party (DAP) with Solomon Islands People First Party (SIPFP), Solomon Islands Party for Rural Advancement (SIPRA) and Peoples' Alliance Party (PAP).

Main opposition party

United Democratic Party

Population

575,000 (2014)* Melanesians live mostly on the main islands, while Polynesians inhabit the outlying islands. In September 2011, the UN International Children's Emergency Fund (Unicef) launched a campaign to have all children's births registered, including a strategy to simplify the process. Birth registration is centralised in Honiara, however as 80 per cent of the population lives away from urban centres, in remote island communities, registration has been protracted and costly.
Last census: November 1999: 409,042
Population density: 18 inhabitants per square km (2010). Urban population 19 per cent (2010 Unicef).
Annual growth rate: 2.8 per cent, 1990–2010 (Unicef).

Internally Displaced Persons (IDP)

350 (UNHCR 2004)

Ethnic make-up

About 93 per cent Melanesian, 4 per cent Polynesian, 1.5 per cent Micronesian, European, Chinese and others. Many of the inhabitants of Western and Choiseul

Provinces in Malaita are from Papua New Guinea. Ethnic disputes have simmered since the end of the Second World War, as Malaitans have migrated to Guadalcanal for work.

Religions

Anglican (45 per cent), Roman Catholic (18 per cent), other Protestants (33 per cent). There are some native religions, especially on Malaita.

Education

Primary education last for six years. Lower secondary schooling lasts for three years and finishes at aged 15. Upper secondary school lasts for two years and is completed in a one-year sixth form. Students who have completed these years may attend a one-year's foundation programme to enter the University of the South Pacific; or enrol in a college of higher education. The Solomon Islands has one of the lowest literacy rates in the world and the government intends to tackle this with the aid that has been forthcoming since 2003 so that by 2005 free education was offered to all primary school aged children. The government has backed the 'one laptop per child' programme (OLPC).

Literacy rate: 64 per cent, adult rate (2003).

Compulsory years: Six to 15

Enrolment rate: 104 per cent boys, 90 per cent girls: gross primary enrolment (including repeaters); 21 per cent boys, 1 per cent girls: gross secondary enrolment (Unicef 2004).

Health

The Solomon Islands suffer from one of the highest malaria incidence rates in the world. It varies across the country with Honiara, Western Province and Choiseul Province the worst affected. Population growth and the mortality of mothers and children are one of the highest in the South Pacific due to endemic infectious diseases and low quality of rural health care.

Hospitals and pharmacies are limited, there are eight hospitals, the largest is the Central Hospital in Honiara. Church missions provide medical facilities on outlying islands. Serious health conditions usually require immediate medical evacuation to the nearest reliable medical facilities which are in Australia or New Zealand. Government statistics on infant mortality in 2010 showed that despite 20 years of sustained investment in healthcare the rate of child deaths had not fallen.

In May 2012, the Solomon Islands reached its leprosy elimination target (prevalence rate 0.14–0.34 per 10,000 people; 2005–11), according to the World Health Organisation. The disease is now confined to seven provinces, within the inner islands, with 129 new cases recorded between 2005–11.

Life expectancy: 68 years, 2004 (WHO 2006)

Fertility rate/Maternal mortality rate: 4.2 births per woman, 2010 (Unicef)

Birth rate/Death rate: 32.5 births per 1,000 population; four deaths per 1,000 population (2003).

Child (under 5 years) mortality rate (per 1,000): 31 per 1,000 live births (WHO 2012)

Welfare

Political instability and fighting have caused extensive damage requiring emergency rehabilitation of critical infrastructure. The Post-Conflict Emergency Rehabilitation Project entails restoration of government offices, roads, bridges, water supply and sanitation facilities, schools, and health facilities. The cost of restoration work on Guadalcanal and nearby provinces has been estimated at between US$30–35 million.

Main cities

Honiara, on Guadalcanal (capital, estimated population 66,168 in 2012), Auki (on Malaita) (7,448), Munda (5,064), Gizo (on Gizo Island) (4,340), Uruuru (3,433), Buala (2,862), Yandina (2,665), Kirakira (2,311).

Languages spoken

There is no main native language although nearly all the languages are distantly related to the Oceanic Austronesian language group. There are at least 12 different language groups containing 87 various languages and dialects. Melanesian pidgin is the *lingua franca*. It has evolved since the time of the first traders, whalers, missionaries and labour recruiters. The vocabulary is derived from English with Melanesian syntax and uses different intonations. English, as a first language, is spoken by 1–2 per cent of the population.

Official language/s

English

Media

Press

Dailies: In English, *Solomon Star* (www.solomonstarnews.com) is the only domestic newspaper. Online news is published by *Solomon Times Online* (www.solomontimes.com) and *People First* (www.peoplefirst.net.sb). Published abroad, other internet news outlets report on the Solomon Islands *Event Polynesia* (www.eventpolynesia.com), *Pacific Islands Report* (http://pidp.eastwestcenter.org) and *Pacific Beat* (www.radioaustralia.net.au/pacbeat) from Australia.

Periodicals: There are a number of publications, *Link* and *Solomon Nius* are government-owned, private monthlies include *Agrikalsa Nius* and *Citizen's Press*; *Mere Save* is a women's magazine.

Broadcasting

Radio: The public service broadcaster is SIBC (the Solomon Islands Broadcasting Corporation) (www.sibconline.com.sb), which produces radio programmes in English and Pidgin, transmitting on medium and short waves, plus FM, to local and overseas populations from Honiara, Gizo (in Western Province) and Lata.

Television: Terrestrial television services are not available, although satellite transmissions can be received.

Other news agencies: ABC Pacific Beat: www.radioaustralia.net.au/pacbeat
Pacific Magazine:
www.pacificmagazine.net
Pacific Islands New Association (Pina):
www.pina.com.fj

Economy

At the end of the ethnic struggles of 1999–2003, the country was bankrupt and had to rely on international aid and foreign investment to lead to a slow recovery, before national production could contribute significantly again. Primary products are mainly fish and timber (despite seriously denuded forests), although the growth of palm oil production is likely to outstrip both within the next decade. Most of the population live in rural areas and survive through subsistence farming. Guadalcanal Plains Palm Oil Limited (GPPOL), the Solomon Island's largest private employer, announced in 2010 that it planned to double in size by 2020 as its investments in plantations of palm oil grow. The Gold Ridge gold mine on Central Guadalcanal reopened in 2010. The rich seas around the islands offer opportunities for tuna fishing and canning for export markets.

As word trade picked up the Solomon Islands' economy recovered from recession in 2010, recording a growth in GDP of 7.0 per cent. However, since this peak, growth has been decelerating, falling from 4.7 per cent in 2012 to 3.0 per cent in 2013, and further to 1.5 per cent in 2014. Total exports in the first half of 2015 rose by 5.3 per cent on the same period in 2014, despite the cessation of gold production. Inflation has fallen from the record peak of 17.4 per cent in 2008, dropping to 6.7 per cent by 2013 and 5.1 per cent in 2014.

Prospects for the Solomon Islands are considered to be challenging. Although it avoided much of the banking crisis in 2008 it is still subject to external shocks and coupled with a lower logging output could see slower short-term growth.

The government re-valued the currency by 5 per cent on 16 June 2011, following advice from the Central Bank of the Solomon Islands. The action reduced the cost of living as imported goods fell in price.

External trade

The Solomon Islands is a member of the South Pacific Regional Trade and Economic Co-operation Agreement (Sparteca) along with 12 other regional nations, which allows products duty free access by Pacific Island Forum members to Australian and New Zealand markets (subject to the country of origin's restrictions). It is also a member of the Melanesian Spearhead Group (with Fiji, Papua New Guinea and Vanuatu), which is a sub-regional trade group, whereby customs tariffs have been harmonised under the Melanesian free trade agreement (MFTA).

A regular, once a month, cargo shipping service came into operation in September 2010, calling at Sikaiana; links to the six other remote islands began later in 2011. The service is supported by the government and the Asian Development Bank (ADB).

Imports

Principal imports are food, plant and equipment, manufactured goods, fuels and chemicals.

Main sources: Australia (27.6 per cent of total in 2014), Singapore (24.2 per cent), China (12.0 per cent).

Exports

Principal exports are timber, fish, copra, palm oil and cocoa.

Main destinations: China (57.5 per cent of total in 2014), Australia (10.6 per cent), United Kingdom (6.3 per cent).

Agriculture

Farming

Agriculture accounted for 51.9 per cent of GDP in 2014 and almost three-quarters of the workforce. About 25–30 per cent of total land area is suitable for intensive, non-traditional agriculture, mainly on Guadalcanal. Over 85 per cent of land is communally owned, which deters investment.

The islands are self-sufficient in beef and vegetables. Copra and cocoa are produced for market on smallholdings and private plantations.

The Government Shareholding Agency, in association with major plantations, has been encouraging new coconut and cocoa planting and extension of the palm oil plantations.

Fishing

Commercial fishing and fish processing around the islands is mainly of skipjack tuna. Fish exports account for about one-third of total export earnings. Domestic seafood demand is served by small, local operations.

On 12 April 2011, a summit of the Parties to the Nauru Agreement (PNA) concluded its strategy for a policy of sustainable fishing in the Pacific. The PNA treaty, which was established in 1989 and expired in 2012, was seen as in need of an overhaul. As a collective region, the PNA (FSM, Kiribati, Marshall Islands, Nauru, Palau, PNG, Solomon Islands and Tuvalu) control around 25–30 per cent of world stocks of tuna. Only 5 per cent of sales revenue is returned to the PNA and ministers called for specific changes, including an increased share of profits, PNA crews on-board purse seine vessels (minimum 10 per cent), conservation and management measures including a limit to fish trapping (fish aggregating devices (FADs)), net mesh rules and the establishment of an observer agency and fisheries information management system. The PNA met in May 2012 to discuss even stronger management measures to ensure even more sustainable tuna fisheries and minimise environmental damage. Many of the ideas put forward were implemented in January 2013, for example observation and monitoring of catches and environmental damage by 100 per cent independent bodies. The area involved stretches from Palau and Papua New Guinea in the west to Kiribati in the east, from the Marshall Islands in the north to Tuvalu in the south.

Forestry

Logging is one of the country's main economic lifelines, contributing around 18 per cent of GDP. The forests contain some 170,000 hectares of exploitable land having 13 million cubic metres of commercial timber. However, instead of the 250,000cum recommended by environmentalists as sustainable felling, felling described as 'unsustainable' by the Asian Development Bank, accelerated as logging companies increased production ahead of new legislation aimed at curbing exploitation of the natural forests.

In June 2011, a successful export order from India was granted to local landowning farmers of plantation teak trees (grown since the late-1990s) ready for harvesting.

Industry and manufacturing

The industrial sector accounts for 6.8 per cent of GDP and employs some 5 per cent of the workforce.

Manufacturing activities include palm oil, rice milling, fish smoking, canning and freezing, saw milling, copra drying, food processing, tobacco, soft drinks, production of nails, detergents and soaps, wood and rattan furniture, fibreglass articles, boats, clothing, handicrafts, shell jewellery, buttons.

Most timber is exported as logs, but an increasing proportion is being sawn; the government hopes to develop wood processing to enable profitable marketing of sawn timber and veneers.

Tourism

The six main islands offer a base for a range of holiday interests. Lake Tenggano (Rennel Island) is included on Unesco's World Heritage List and the Marovo Lagoon and tropical rainforest, with its unique bird species and marine life surrounded by three large volcanic islands, are at the forefront of the island's ecotourism. There is a range of accommodation, from hotels in the capital Honiara or along the coast in secluded cabins, to stays with local communities.

Travel and tourism contributed 10.7 per cent to GDP over 2014. The industry provided employment for 9.4 per cent of the workforce (18,000 jobs), over the same period. The number of visitors grew from 14,000 in 2007 to 24,000 in 2013.

The islands also attract visitors with an interest in the World War Two battles that took place on Guadalcanal.

Environment

The Solomon Islands is ranked second, after Indonesia, for coral reef fish species and the range and variety of its corals.

The main environmental problems are deforestation, soil erosion and major, possibly irreversible, destruction to coral reefs There is a lack of resources to control the activities of the logging companies.

An Asian Development Bank (ADB) study (*Economics of Climate Change in the Pacific*) published in November 2013 projected that agriculture, fisheries and other sectors of the economy will take a severe hit in the face of more extreme temperatures and other climate change-linked events, triggering economic losses of up to 4.7 per cent of annual GDP in Solomon Islands by 2100.

Hydrocarbons

There are no hydrocarbon reserves and imported petroleum products are required to meet all domestic demand, which was 1,870 barrels per day in 2013.

Energy

Total installed generating capacity was 36MW in 2013. The state-owned Solomon Islands Electricity Authority (SIEA) is responsible for generation, transmission, distribution and sale of electricity.

A feasibility study for a new hydroelectric power plant on the Tina River, 30km south-east of Honiara, was completed in September 2010. Solomon Islands' electricity charges are among the most expensive in the world and the new power plant would reduce them and slash Honiara's carbon emissions by up to 70 per cent.

Locally grown and produced bio-fuel (coconut oil) is replacing motor oil in outboard motors on boats and small fishing craft.

Banking and insurance

The ADB considers the banking sector to employ limited competition with strong participation by Australian financial institutions.

Central bank

Central Bank of Solomon Islands

Main financial centre

Honiara, on Guadalcanal Island

Time

GMT plus 11 hours

Geography

The Solomon Islands lie in the south-western Pacific Ocean, to the north-east of Australia and Papua New Guinea, its closest neighbour, and north of Vanuatu. The country comprises hundreds of mainly small islands, extending over an area of around 28,500sq kilometres. There are six main islands: Guadalcanal, where the capital, Honiara, is located, Choiseul, San Cristobal, Makira, New Georgia and Malaita. The islands are mountainous and forested, with active as well as dormant volcanoes.

Hemisphere

Southern

Climate

Warm and humid, equatorial with average temperatures from 22 degrees Celsius (C) (mountainous areas inland) to 28 degrees C (coastal areas). Rainfall averages about 3,500mm per annum, but varies greatly according to location and mostly falls Nov–Apr, when cyclones may occur as well.

Entry requirements

Passports

Required by all, valid for at least six months.

Visa

Visas required by all except nationals of most EU countries, North America, Australasia and some other countries. (For a list of countries for which prior approval is required, see www.commerce.gov.sb/Divisions/Immigration/Immigration_Requirements.htm.) Travellers with onward passage and adequate funds are issued on arrival with a visitor's permit for up to three months.

Currency advice/regulations

There are no restrictions on the import of local currency, but export is limited to SI$250, or on the import of foreign currencies, subject to declaration; re-export is limited to the amount imported.

Customs

Personal effects (including an allowance of alcoholic beverages and tobacco) are allowed duty-free up to SI$500. Import licences are required for most goods and specific licences are required for fruit, vegetables and animal products.

Prohibited imports

Weapons without a police permit, narcotics and pornography.

Health (for visitors)

Mandatory precautions

Vaccination certificate required for yellow fever if travelling from an infected zone.

Advisable precautions

Vaccination for diphtheria, tuberculosis, hepatitis A and B, polio, tetanus, typhoid. Malaria is a problem, especially in Honiara, and prophylaxis should be taken. Hookworm is endemic and any itchy rash should be checked by a physician. There is a rabies risk.

Hotels

There are over 60 hotels. Visitors are advised to book well in advance. Hotel tax of 10 per cent is added to bill. In addition to Honiara's three hotels, there are resorts, guesthouses and government resthouses of varying standards and quality scattered throughout the islands. Tipping is not customary or encouraged.

Public holidays (national)

Fixed dates

1 Jan (New Year's Day), 7 Jul (Independence Day), 25 Dec (Christmas Day), 26 Dec (National Day of Thanksgiving). Each province celebrates their own public national holiday: 25 Feb (Choiseul), 2 Jun (Isable), 8 Jun (Temotu), 29 Jun (Central Island), 20 Jul (Rennell), 1 Aug (Guadalcanal), 3 Aug (Makira/Ulawa), 15 Aug (Malaita), 7 Dec (Western Province).

Variable dates

Good Friday, Easter Monday, Queen's Official Birthday (second Fri in Jun).

Working hours

Banking

Mon–Fri: 0830–1500.

Business

Mon–Fri: 0730/0800–1200, 1300–1630/1700; Sat: 0730/0800–1200.

Government

Mon–Fri: 0800–1200, 1300–1630.

Shops

Mon–Fri: 0800–1700; 0800–1200; Sat: 0800–1200. Many shops open Sat afternoon and Sun; Chinese stores often open at other times. There are several 24-hour stores in Honiara.

Telecommunications

Telephone/fax

Automatic telephone service available in Honiara, Auki, Gizo, Noro, Munda, Buala, Lata and Tulagi. International services available 24 hours via TELECOM (Solomon Islands) satellite and cable links. Specialised systems such as private leased circuits and data links can be provided.

Postal services

There is no local delivery system.

Mobile/cell phones

A second mobile/cell network, Bemobile, came into operation in the urban area of Honiara in August 2010, with SMS services, interconnect and data services.

Electricity supply

240/220V AC with flat three-pin plug fittings and bayonet-type sockets, typical of Australia.

Weights and measures

Officially, the metric system is in use.

Social customs/useful tips

Tipping is not customary, and visitors are strongly advised to refrain from the practice. Women should avoid wearing shorts and make sure their legs are adequately covered to avoid giving offence. The social structure of the Solomon Islands is extremely complex, with traditions, culture and even language varying from island to island and among villages on the same island.

Security

The security situation has improved since 2003, however resources are still limited and response times to calls for assistance may be slow. Attacks on foreign nationals are rare however personal security precausions should be taken if visiting the island of Malaita and rural Guadalcanal. Swearing is a crime and can lead to large civil fines and even jail.

Getting there

Air

National airline: Solomon Airlines.

International airport/s: Henderson International (HIR), 13km from Honiara; bank, duty free shop and car hire.

Airport tax: SI$40.

Surface

Water: Regular shipping links with Australia, New Zealand, Hong Kong, Japan, UK and Europe.

Getting about

National transport

Air: Solomon Airlines fly regular services from Henderson Airport to main islands and towns. Charter flights are available.

Road: Surfaced roads are concentrated on Guadalcanal and Malaita and few are properly maintained. Other roads, mostly in the rural areas, are coral or gravel surfaced, supplemented by dirt tracks. Terrain can be difficult.

Buses: Bus services operate in and around Honiara.

Water: Inter-island shipping services are operated by the government and also by private companies and missionaries. There are large passenger boats, and cargo vessels also carry passengers in varying degrees of comfort.

City transport

Taxis: Taxis are available in Honiara and Auki and can be booked in advance or hailed in the street. As they are not metered, it is advisable to agree the fare before the journey starts.

Car hire

Car hire is available in Honiara. Driving is on the left.

BUSINESS DIRECTORY

The addresses listed below are a selection only. While World of Information makes every endeavour to check these addresses, we cannot guarantee that changes have not been made, especially to telephone numbers and area codes. We would welcome any corrections.

Telephone area codes

Dialling code for Solomon Islands, IDD access code +677 followed by subscriber's number.

Useful telephone numbers

Police and fire: 23-666
Fire: 999
Ambulance: 25-566
Marine emergency: 21-535
Emergencies outside Honiara: 111
Directory enquiries: 101
Overseas operator: 102
Shipping and time: 107
Operator assistance: 100
Customs: 22-301
Immigration: 22-243

Chambers of Commerce

Solomon Islands Chamber of Commerce and Employers, PO Box 70, Honiara (tel: 23-342; fax: 21-851; e-mail: chamberc@solomon.com.sb).

Banking

Australia and New Zealand Banking Group Ltd (ANZ), PO Box 10, Honiara (tel: 21-111; fax: 26-937; e-mail: solomons@anz.com).

Development Bank of Solomon Islands, PO Box 911, Honiara (tel: 21-595; fax: 23-715; e-mail: dbsi@welkam.solomon.com.sb).

National Bank of Solomon Islands, PO Box 37, Honiara (tel: 21-874; fax: 23-478; e-mail: nbsi@welkam.solomon.com.sb).

Westpac Banking Corporation, 721 Mendana Avenue, PO Box 466, Honiara (tel: 21-222; fax: 24-957).

Central bank

Central Bank of Solomon Islands, PO Box 634, Honiara (tel: 21-791 fax: 23-513; e-mail: info@cbsi.com.sb).

Travel information

Guadalcanal Travel Service, Mendana Avenue, PO Box 114, Honiara (tel: 22-586; fax: 26-184; e-mail: gts@welkem.solomon.com.sb).

Henderson International Airport, PO Box G8, Honiara (tel: 36-720; fax: 36-775; e-mail: civilair@welkam.solomon.com.sb).

Solomon Islands Airlines, PO Box 23, Mendana Avenue, Honiara (tel: 20-031; fax: 20-232; e-mail: solair@welkam.solomon.com.sb).

Western Province Tourism Association, PO Box 56, Gizo (tel: 30-254; fax: 39-240)

Ministry of tourism

Ministry of Culture and Tourism, PO Box G26, Honiara (tel: 28-603; fax: 27-587; e-mail: commerce@commerce.gov.sb).

National tourist organisation offices

Solomon Islands Visitors Bureau, P.O.Box 321, Medana Avenue, Honiara (tel: 22-442; fax: 23-986; e-mail: info@sivb.com.sb).

Ministries

Ministry of Agriculture and Fisheries, PO Box G13, Honiara (tel: 21-327; fax: 21-955).

Ministry of Commerce, Industries and Employment, PO Box G26, Honiara (tel: 21-849; fax: 25-084).

Ministry of Education and Human Resources Development, PO Box G28, Honiara (tel: 23-900; fax: 20-485).

Ministry of Finance, PO Box 26, Honiara (tel: 23-700; fax: 20-392).

Ministry of Foreign Affairs, PO Box G10, Honiara (tel: 21-250; fax: 20-351).

Ministry of Forest Environment and Conservation, PO Box G24, Honiara (tel: 25-848; fax: 21-245).

Ministry of Health and Medical Services, PO Box 349, Honiara (tel: 20-830; fax: 20-085).

Ministry of Home Affairs, PO Box G11, Honiara (tel: 21-621; fax: 22-606).

Ministry of Justice and Legal Affairs, PO Box 404, Honiara (tel: 21-181; fax: 25-610).

Ministry of Lands and Housing, PO Box G38, Honiara (tel: 21-430; fax: 20-094).

Ministry of Mines and Energy, PO Box G37, Honiara (tel: 21-521; fax: 25-811).

Ministry of National Planning and Development, PO Box G30, Honiara (tel: 25-063; fax: 25-138).

Ministry of Police and National Security, PO Box G4, Honiara (tel: 22-208; fax: 25-949).

Ministry of Post and Telecommunication, PO Box G25, Honiara (tel: 21-821; fax: 21-472).

Ministry of Provincial Government and Rural Development, PO Box G35, Honiara (tel: 21-140; fax: 21-289).

Ministry of Transport, Works and Utilities, PO Box G8, Honara (tel: 26-560; fax: 26-458; e-mail: sidapp@pipolfastaem.gov.sb).

Ministry of Youth, Women, Sports and Recreation, PO Box G39, Honiara (tel: 25-490; fax: 25-686).

Office of the Prime Minister, PO Box G1, Honiara (tel: 22-202, 21-863; fax: 21-608, 25-470).

Other useful addresses

Controller of Customs and Excise, Customs and Excise Division, Ministry of National Planning and Development, PO Box G30, Honiara.

Foreign Investment Board, Ministry of Commerce, Industries and Employment, PO Box G26, Honiara (tel: 21-849; fax: 25-084).

Governor General, PO Box 252, Honiara (tel: 22-222, 21-777; fax: 23-335).

Investment Corporation of Solomon Islands Ltd, PO Box 570, Honiara (tel: 22-511; fax: 21-263).

Solomon Islands Ports Authority, PO Box 307, Honiara (tel: 22-646; fax: 23-994).

Solomon Islands Statistics Office, PO Box G6, Honiara (tel: 23-700).

Telekom Office, Mendana Avenue, Honiara (tel: 21-576; fax: 23-110).

Trading Co (Solomons) Ltd, Mendana Avenue, PO Box 114, Honiara (tel: 22-588).

ABC Pacific Beat:
www.radioaustralia.net.au/pacbeat

Pacific Magazine:
www.pacificmagazine.net

Pacific Islands New Association (Pina):
www.pina.com.fj

Internet sites

Asia Business Connection (gateway site):
http://asiabiz.com

Somalia

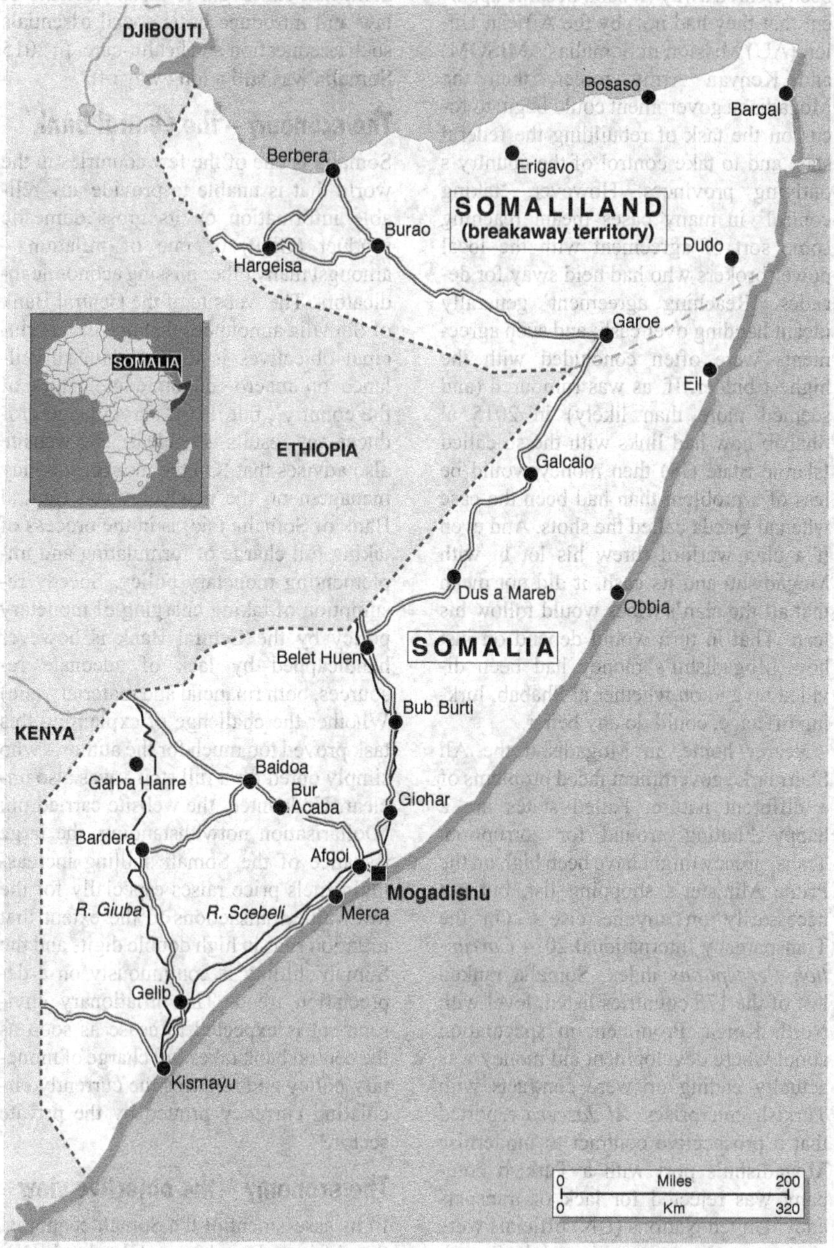

Since independence in 1956, Somalia has had eighteen prime ministers. The latest in this impossible role is Omar Abdirashid Ali Sharmarke, who having already held the post in 2009–10 returned from his position as ambassador in Washington to assume the premiership in December 2014, heading up the latest in a line of short-lived administrations since the fall of the left-leaning, Soviet influenced and discredited Siad Barre dictatorship in 1989.

Efforts by successive governments to restore some semblance of peace and civil order have largely failed, earning Somalia the embarrassing sobriquet of being

KEY FACTS

Official name: Jamhuriyadda ee Soomaaliya (Republic of Somalia)

Head of State: President Hassan Sheikh Mohamud (from 10 Sep 2012)

Head of government: Prime Minister Omar Abdirashid Ali Sharmarke (from 24 December 2014)

Ruling party: None

Area: 738,000 square km

Population: 51.20 million (2012)*

Capital: Mogadishu

Official language: Somali

Currency: Somali shilling (SoSh) = 100 centesimi

Exchange rate: SoSh614.00 per US$ (Sep 2015)

GDP per capita: US$600 (2009, PPP)*

GDP real growth: 6.00% (2013)*

GDP: US$5.80 billion (2010)*

Labour force: 3.45 million (2007)

Inflation: 30.00% (2007)

* estimated figure

Somaliland

Head of State: President Ahmed Mohamed Mohamoud (from10 Jul 2010)

Area : 137,600 square kilometres

Population : 3.5 million

Capital: Hargeisa

Official languages: Principally Somali; Arabic and English are also official languages

Currency: Somaliland shilling (SlSh)

Main exports: Livestock

Somaliland announced its unilateral declaration of independence (UDI) in May 1991. Although Somaliland has its own currency and an established and functioning democracy, no foreign government has recognised it as a legitimate entity.

Puntland

Head of government: Abdiweli Mohamed Ali (from 8 Jan 2014)

Area : 212,510 square kilometres

Population : 2.4 million

Capital: Garowe (administrative); Bosasso (commercial)

Official languages: Somali, Arabic

Currency: Somali shilling (SoSh)

Main exports: Livestock

Although a self-governing autonomous state since 1998, Puntland has no plans for independence from Somalia.

Africa's 'leading' failed state. When, in 2012–13 civil order was claimed to have been restored, that had been a brief interval of euphoria in Somalia. (NB The present analysis does not apply to the northern provinces of Somalia, aka 'Puntland' as it occupies the Horn Of Africa – see Box).

If the al Shabab guerrillas had indeed been cleared away (it soon became apparent that they had not) by the African Union (AU) Mission in Somalia (AMISOM) and Kenyan Army forces, then the Mogadishu government could begin to focus on the task of rebuilding the federal state and to take control of the country's outlying provinces. However, 'taking control' in many cases meant reaching some sort of agreement with the local power brokers who had held sway for decades. 'Reaching agreement' generally meant handing over cash; and such agreements were often concluded with the highest bidder. If, as was rumoured (and seemed more than likely) in 2015 al Shabab now had links with the so-called Islamic State (IS) then money would be less of a problem than had been the case when al Qaeda called the shots. And even if a clan warlord threw his lot in with Mogadishu and its cash, it did not mean that all the clan's tribes would follow his lead. That in turn would depend on just how Mogadishu's money had been divided up and on whether al Shabab, lurking offstage, could do any better.

Nearer home, in Mogadishu the Ali Sharmarke government faced problems of a different nature. Failed states are a happy hunting ground for corruption. Transparency might have been high on the Prime Minister's shopping list, but not necessarily on anyone else's. On the Transparency International 2014 *Corruption Perceptions* index, Somalia ranked last of the 175 countries listed, level with North Korea. Prominent in speculation about where development aid money was actually ending up were contracts with Turkish enterprises. *Al Jazeera* reported that a prospective contract to modernise Mogadishu's port with a Turkish company was rejected for lack of transparency. United Nations (UN) officials were also reported to have criticised the Somali government for striking up secret contracts and co-operation agreements. This finally led to a review of major international contracts by the newly installed Finance Governance Committee, a watchdog with an IMF and World Bank presence.

Mr Sharmarke's government faced, on all fronts – political, military, economic, social – a seemingly impossible task. After more than two decades of anarchic warlord rule and an intermittent al Shabab regime, Somalia's population ('long suffering' barely expresses what they have been through) could have little confidence or faith in any government. For that trust to develop required a non-pareil government that can begin to install the rule of law and introduce basic social essentials such as education and health-care. In 2015 Somalia was still a long way off.

The economy – the Central Bank

Somalia is one of the few countries in the world that is unable to provide any reliable information on its gross domestic product (GDP) or rate of inflation – amongst many other missing economic indicators. The website of the Central Bank of Somalia announces that one of its principal objectives is to 'maintain surveillance on macro-economic indicators of the country', but if that surveillance produces any results is unclear. The website also advises that 'On the monetary policy management, the newly revived Central Bank of Somalia (sic) is in the process of taking full charge of formulating and implementing monetary policy. Speedy resumption of taking charging of monetary policy by the Central Bank is however handicapped by lack of adequate resources, both financial and material.' (sic) Whether the challenge of explaining this task proved too much for the author – who simply opted for a full stop – was also unclear. Undaunted, the website carried on: 'Dollarisation notwithstanding, the large issuance of the Somali shilling increasingly fuels price raises especially for the low value transactions to the extent that inflation runs in high double digits and the Somali shilling is continuously on a depreciation trend. The inflationary environment is expected to cease as soon as the central bank takes full charge of monetary policy and replaces the currently circulating currency printed by the private sector.'

The economy – the objective view

In its assessment of the Somali economy, the African Development bank (AfDB) could only resort to generalisations. It noted that the demographic base of the economy was narrow because the majority of the population continued to be nomadic and highly dependent on livestock and livestock exports for its livelihood. A lack of internal revenue and weak public financial management are also serious constraints on the national budget, leaving the country almost totally dependent on foreign assistance. AMISOM and the Somali National Army have succeeded in recovering many areas from al Shabaab control and what the AfDB describes as 'capacity development' was continuing, but insecurity in most parts of the country, weak institutional capacity and political instability remain the main obstacles to reconstruction and development.

According to the AfDB, the socio-economic indicators of Somalia remained – unsurprisingly – very low. Somalia continued to be highly dependent on livestock production and exports, most of which went to Saudi Arabia. This reflected the country's narrow economic base and consequent high vulnerability to external shocks. Somalia's narrow economic base remained a serious constraint on the federal government's capacity to generate sufficient revenues to support reconstruction and development in an unstable macro-economic environment.

A new income tax law had been prepared and submitted to parliament for approval. The new income tax legislation is part of a broader Revenue Mobilisation Strategy aimed at increasing fiscal sustainability by raising adequate resources for financing fiscal recurrent expenditures. This strategy would initially focus on inland revenue with new or restored taxes and increasing citizen awareness, accountability and legitimacy through improved tax administration. However, security concerns and political instability still had a significant impact on economic development and the provision of social services.

In 2015 Somalia had its third prime minister in two years. On the security front, government security forces and the strengthened AU Mission have registered some progress. Donor co-ordination remained a significant challenge in Somalia due to the government's weak institutional capacity, the diverse roles of various regional entities (Federal government, Puntland and Somaliland) in managing aid and the challenging security environment, which had forced most donors to operate from the Kenyan capital, Nairobi. In order to manage donor aid, the main active donors in Somalia had been co-ordinating their work programmes under the Somalia Development Partners Forum (DPF), whose membership included the UN agencies, the multilateral development banks (MDBs), about 30 bilateral African and non-African representatives and the NGO Consortium. The AfDB was also playing a lead role in supporting the international re-engagement of Somalia, particularly in the Arrears Clearance/ Debt Relief process with the World Bank and IMF. The Bank would also continue its lead role in the areas of public financial management, notably through its representation and involvement in the Financial Governance Committee (FGC) established in 2014 and

'We're different – Somaliland...

Once a British Protectorate, the northern area of Somalia known as Somaliland has a working political system, government institutions, a police force and its own currency. The conquest of what was once known as 'British Somaliland' in 1940 was Italy's only victory without the co-operation of German troops in World War Two. In 1941 it was the first overseas British territory to be freed from Axis rule following defeat by a British expeditionary force.

Although the population is only one million (or thereabouts – there is no exact figure; the government of Somaliland had 3.5 million in 2012) the territory has lobbied hard to persuade international opinion that it should be a sovereign state. Amazingly, the territory has managed to avoid the chaos and violence that have beset Somalia. In the early tears of the twenty-first century attacks on Western aid workers had suggested that Islamic militants were present, but subsequently the attacks had subsided.

Somaliland was independent for a few days in 1960, between the end of British colonial rule and its union with the former Italian colony of Somalia. More than 40 years later voters in the territory overwhelmingly backed its self-declared independence in a 2001 referendum. Although there is a thriving private business sector, poverty and unemployment are widespread. The economy is highly dependent on money sent home by members of the diaspora.

Duties from Berbera, a port used by landlocked Ethiopia, and livestock exports are the territory's principal sources of revenue. As soon as Somalia fell into civil war, the Isaaqs clan of Somaliland had distanced themselves, proudly declaring themselves to be an independent country.

Despite not being recognised by any sovereign countries Somaliland has managed to strengthen its economy and its domestic politics, creating a separate monetary system and a relatively stable, markedly more secure living environment. The president, Ahmed Mohamed Mohamoud, is from the Isaaq clan, which grants him a significant allegiance and gives Somaliland's a much stabler political environment than Somalia or neighbouring Puntland (see below). The Isaaqs, unlike most Somali clans, are for the most part concentrated in one area, allowing Somaliland to be a more homogenous body politic. Importantly and unlike other Somali clans, the Isaaqs are generally perceived to be more liberal by nature and less fanatical by faith. This characteristic has allowed them to attract modest amounts of foreign investment and to a more inclusive society. Despite their apparent level-headeness, there is no love lost between the Isaaqs of Somaliland and the Darods of neighbouring Puntland.

... And so are we – but a different sort of difference – Puntland'

Puntland presents a rather more confusing picture. It considers itself to be an autonomous (or at least semi-autonomous) region, part of the Mogadishu-Somalia body politic, but in reality – at least geographically – working as a totally independent country. It has a government of its own, with all the necessary ministries and pays little attention to the government (if it may be called such) in Mogadishu under President Hassan Sheikh Mohamud, whose rule is entirely ineffective in Puntland. Puntland is composed primarily of members of the Darod tribe. Despite almost total autonomy from Mogadishu, the Puntlanders always emphasise their affinities with the south. The official name for the territory is 'Puntland, Somalia', not just 'Puntland'.

comprising government and donor representatives to deliberate on contracts, concessions and the recovery of national assets overseas.

Risk assessment

Politics	Poor
Economy	Poor – or worse
Regional stability	Poor

Muslims in Somalia

% of population	98.6
Sunni (% of Muslims)	99
Shi'a (% of Muslims)	1

COUNTRY PROFILE

1900 Somalia was controlled by the British in the north (British Somaliland Protectorate), and Italy in the south (Italian Somaliland).
1950–60 Italian Somaliland was a UN Trust Territory, under Italian administration.
1960 The northern and southern regions were united when granted independence from the UK and Italy. Aden Abdullah Osman Daar was elected president.
1967 Abdi Rashid Ali Shermarke won the presidential election.
1969 President Shermarke was assassinated in a *coup d'état* and the military leader, Mohammed Siad Barre, became president. The country was renamed the Somali Democratic Republic, political parties were banned and the National Assembly dissolved.
1970 Barre declared Somalia a socialist and one-party state under the Somali Revolutionary Socialist Party.
1974–75 Major droughts affected thousands and caused widespread starvation.
1977 Ethnic Somalis in the Ogaden rebelled against Ethiopian control and war began when Somali troops invaded the territory.
1978 Abdullahi Yusuf Ahmed led a failed military coup against Barre.
1980s There were devastating droughts that caused widespread starvation throughout most of the decade.
1981 The president appointed members of his own Marehan clan to government posts, at the expense of other, Mijertyn and Isaq, clans.
1982 Disaffected clans, with Ethiopian military support, attacked government positions. Although the government repulsed the rebels, clashes continued throughout the 1980s.
1988 A peace agreement with Ethiopia ended the Ogaden war but civil tensions increased.
1989 As the security situation worsened, Barre offered to resign and hold free elections in 1990.
1991 President Barre fled after rebels entered Mogadishu and the state of Somalia collapsed. Numerous international efforts were made to resolve the situation but effective central government was lacking for almost a decade. Warlords controlled territories through violence and clan allegiances as civil society degenerate into fiefdoms of factional fighting. The self-styled Republic of Somaliland (in the north), headed by Mohammed Ibrahim Egal, broke away from war-torn Somalia.
1992 After a period of intense conflict between the numerous clans, the US sent a force to protect the UN humanitarian aid effort and help restore order.
1993 The Addis Ababa Accords were signed. The UN began peace-keeping operations, taking over from US Marines. US Task Force Rangers launched a military offensive (later known as the Battle of Mogadishu) against General Aideed and the Somali National Alliance (SNA). Eighteen US troops, and up to 1,000 Somalis, were killed.
1994 The US withdrew all of its forces from Somalia.
1995 The remainder of the UN peace-keeping force withdrew.
1996 General Aideed died from gunshot wounds. His son, Hussein Aideed, replaced him as head of the clan-based gang.
1997 Twenty-six of Somalia's 28 factions signed the Cairo Declaration peace accord.
1998 The leaders of the northeastern region of Puntland, including Abdullahi Yusuf Ahmed, declared the region autonomous.
1999 Inter-clan violence continued in central and southern Somalia. President Guelleh of Djibouti announced an international peace plan based on the participation of Islamic and civil groups rather than warlords.
2000 A four-month reconciliation conference in Djibouti ended when the transitional national government (TNG) elected a civilian as the country's first president since 1990 – Abd al Qasim Salad Hassan. Hussein Aideed, and other warlords, in Somalia, and Abdullahi Yusuf, president of Puntland, opposed the TNG.
2001 Militia loyal to Aideed attacked TNG forces. Jama Ali Jama deposed Abdullahi Yusuf as president of Puntland but was later overthrown by Abdullahi Yusuf who recaptured the presidency, with the help of Ethiopian forces. The president of Somaliland, Muhammad Haji Ibrahim Egal, died and was succeeded by Dahir Riyale Kahin.
2002 A cease-fire was agreed between 21 warring factions and the TNG.
2003 Dahir Riyale Kahin of the ruling United People's Party (UDUB) (Somaliland), won presidential and parliamentary elections. A peace conference, the Somali National Reconciliation Conference, was set up in Kenya
2004 At peace talks, warlords and politicians signed a deal to set up a new parliament; the Transitional National Assembly (TNA) was inaugurated and for security reasons continued to be held in Kenya. Abdullahi Yusuf, (president of Puntland), won the TNA presidential elections held. Abdullahi appointed Mohammed Ali Ghedi as prime minister. Hundreds of deaths were caused by the south-Asian *tsunami* that hit the coastline of Puntland.
2005 Authority within the country was maintained by rival warlords who controlled various tribal lands.
2006 Fighting broke out between forces of the Islamic Courts Union (ICU), which had restored some order to parts of the capital through the use of *Sharia* (Islamic law), and warlord militias. The ICU gained full control in the capital and most of central and southern Somalia. Sheikh Hassan Dihir Aweys was appointed head of the ICU, which was renamed Midowga Maxkamadaha Islaamiga (Supreme Islamic Courts Council) (SICC). Mogadishu's international airport and seaport were reopened. Peace talks failed between the transitional government and the SICC and fighting resumed. Ethiopian ground and air forces entered Somalia in support of the transitional government. The SICC was routed and the transitional government took control of Mogadishu.
2007 Fighting in the capital erupted as factions supporting the president and prime minister clashed over interests in oil exploration contracts. The head of the World Food Programme UN humanitarian agency was kidnapped in Mogadishu. The main market in Mogadishu, which provided trade of essential goods for around 85 per cent of residents and traders throughout the country, was destroyed by fire. The UN reported that 400,000 people had fled from Mogadishu. Mohammed Ali Ghedi resigned as prime minister and Nur 'Adde' Hassan Hussein was appointed in his place. The prime minister announced that he would be replacing the 30-member cabinet with a much smaller cabinet.
2008 Twice, the UN Security Council extended the African Union (AU)-led mission to Somalia by six months. Representatives of the Transitional Federal Government (TFG) and the Alliance for the Re-liberation of Somalia (The Alliance) signed an agreement, to cease hostilities, the result of several months of talks in Djibouti. By the end of the year Islamist forces not only controlled northern regions, but also took over much of the south. Ethiopia

announced its troops would leave and would not be replaced by AU peacekeepers as had been expected. The government of Somalia was left without military support and over 80 per cent of the country's army and police force had deserted, in some cases taking weapons, uniforms and vehicles with them. Prime Minister Hussein and his government were sacked for failing to bring security to the country. However, Hussein rejected presidential power to replace him. The president appointed Muhammad Mahmud Guled Gamadhere as prime minister. In parliament, the required one-third vote to impeach the president was achieved. Charges against him included nepotism, illegally printing money, being autocratic and failing to foster the peace process. The AU agreed to extend its military mission. President Abdullahi Yusuf Ahmed lost a vote of confidence in parliament and resigned and Adan Mohamed Nuur (also known as Adan Madobe) became acting president.

2009 Ethiopia withdrew its troops. Islamist insurgents seized the government's capital city of Baidoa, (just hours after Ethiopian troops had withdrawn) and imposed *Sharia* (Islamic law). Sheikh Sharif Ahmed, a moderate Islamist, was elected president by parliament. Omar Abdirashid Ali Sharmarke, nominated by the president, was approved by parliament and was sworn into office as prime minister. The president, endorsed by the government, announced the introduction of *Sharia* (Islamic law) nationwide, in an agreement with religious leaders and rival political factions. Islamist forces attacked Mogadishu; the president declared a state of emergency following the killing of the security minister and over 20 others in a suicide bombing, as violence intensified. An appeal was made for troops from neighbouring countries to intervene during battles between government and Islamist troops. Ethiopia decided that it would only intervene if the fighting threatened its national security. Hundreds of politicians fled the country, leaving the national assembly membership dangerously close to the 250 needed to make up a quorum.

In Puntland, parliament elected Abdirahman Mohamed Farole as president.

In the secessionist Republic of Somaliland the upper house of parliament extended the term of office for President Dahir Riyale Kahin.

2010 The World Food Programme (WFP) organisation pulled out of southern Somalia after threats from Islamist groups. The UN Food and Agriculture Organisation (FAO) reported that some two million Somalis still needed emergency food supplies. This was despite a good harvest of sorghum and maize after better than average rains. Horn Afrik and GBC radio stations were raided by militants from Al Shabab and Hizbul Islam. The US banned all cargo from Somalia. Omar Sharmarke resigned as prime minister. He was criticised for failing to defeat Al Shabab (militant Islamist militia). Once again feuding within the transitional government left the country without a functioning government. Mohamed Abdullahi Mohamed was appointed prime minister.

Following a two-year delay due to security worries, a presidential election was held in Somaliland, in which three candidates took part. Ahmed Silanyo won 49.59 per cent of the vote, incumbent Dahir Kahin won 33.23 per cent. Ahmed Mahamoud Silanyo became president.

Somaliland and Puntland, once-warring territories in northern Somalia, rather surprisingly agreed in principle to work together to tackle common security threats.

2011 In February, parliament extended its mandate until 2014, following approval by the AU, despite failing to enact a new constitution or preparations for organising national elections by August 2011. In March, the General Service Union of the Kenyan police force crossed into Somalia at the border town of Liboi, to confront the militant forces of the Al Shabab. It was the first time that Kenyan forces had directly fought Al Shabab, which was accused of raids into Kenya. On 28 March the government itself extended its mandate by another year, despite criticism from donors and attacks by Islamist extremists. In June, rival leaders within government agreed to postpone parliamentary elections until August 2012; the president and speaker of parliament retain their posts. The aid agency Save the Children reported in June that some 1,300 people, including at least 800 children, were arriving daily at the Dadaab refugee camp in Kenya. They had been driven to make the arduous journey by a combination of severe drought, the on-going conflict and rising food prices. The Dadaab refugee camp had a population of over 350,000 in mid-2011. Prime Minister Mohamed Abdullahi Mohamed announced his resignation in June and Abdiweli Mohamed Ali was appointed as his replacement. A crisis in malnutrition that developed over months as a two-year drought caused widespread failure in crop and animal production caused tens of thousands of vulnerable people to seek food in neighbouring Kenya while also fleeing the internal conflict. The UN estimated that 10 million people in the Horn of Africa were affected by drought and food insecurity. The Islamist group Al Shabab announced in July that it had lifted its ban (imposed in 2009) on foreign aid agencies providing relief in the territories under its control. However the UN and US demanded further safety guarantees from armed groups before they allowed their staff to enter the areas in need. On 20 July, the UN officially declared a famine in Bakool and Lower Shabelle in southern Somalia, while other areas were considered at extreme risk. The area experienced the worst drought for over 50 years. It was estimated that US$300 million was needed to provide aid for 8–10 weeks from the middle of July. Prime Minister Ali announced the creation of a special force to protect convoys delivering famine aid. Al Shabab militants withdrew from Mogadishu in August, as the first shipment of food aid reached the city. The AU called for another 1,000 troops to protect the food aid and to secure and consolidate military gains in Mogadishu. Turkey's Prime Minister Erdogan and his family visited Mogadishu in August. Another state (the Bay region) was declared a famine zone by the UN on 5 September, with around 750,000 people at risk of starvation. In September, Mohamed Ibrahim was appointed as deputy prime minister. Two major telecommunications companies and a major money transfer firm were temporarily banned at the end of September after Al Shabab demanded the companies pay *zikat*, a form of charity paid by Muslims. Aid agencies said that if Al Shabab persisted in their demands there would be a severe knock-on effect for the poor of Somalia who relied in remittances from abroad during a time of famine in particular. The UN's Secretary General Ban Ki-moon visited Mogadishu in December and met the prime minister. Mr Ban was visiting at a time when UN-backed AU forces were in deadly battle with Al Shabab in and around the city. His agenda included not only the famine in the south of Somalia, but also the UN's impatience at the apparent corruption and divided political leadership. Mr Ban said that unless serious progress towards a new constitution and a reformed parliament was accomplished by August 2012, then funding from the UN would be curtailed.

2012 For several months Al Shabab forces had targeted and kidnapped Western tourists in Kenya and transported them to Somalia for ransom. On 25 January the Kenyan army crossed into Somalia to attack Al Shabab forces, in an effort to deter the criminal activity that was threatening Kenya's tourist industry. The EU began training Somali forces of the transitional government to become defenders of Mogadishu in the battle with Islamist insurgents. The UN announced on 3 February that the famine in Somalia had ended, six months after it had been declared, following a good harvest and international aid, which had alleviated the situation. On 10 February, Al Shabab and Al Qaeda announce that the two groups had merged, at a time when Al Shabab had been under concerted attack from AU, Kenyan and Ethiopian military forces, as well as offshore international forces. AU forces attacked the central city of Baidoa, an Islamic militant stronghold on 15 February. The heavy fighting around Mogadishu, in the Afgoye corridor, caused thousands of internally displaced persons (IDPs) to flee to relative safety in the city. An agreement was reached among Somali leaders on 19 February to reform the political system by reducing the number of members of parliament to 225, of which 30 per cent would be made up of women (proposed by 'respected women') with MPs drawn from traditional regions and reflecting the national clans. A bicameral parliament was to be created with the addition of an upper chamber for 54 'elders'. Also agreed was the establishment of a civil society. The meeting took place in Puntland, but did not include all Somali leaders or factions. On 22 February, the UN Security Council voted to increase the AU force in Somalia (Amison) by up to 18,000. On 6 March, Turkish Airlines became the first major commercial airline to fly to Mogadishu from outside East Africa since the 1990s. Twice weekly flights from Istanbul, via Khartoum (Sudan) will begin before the end of the year. Al Shabab fighters attacked an Ethiopian base near Yurkut village (central Geddo), close to Baidoa, on 10 March, killing an unverifiable number of fighters from both sides. The attack had quickly followed-on from an announcement that Ethiopian troops were to be withdrawn from the area by the end of April and replaced with AU troops. The national theatre in Mogadishu reopened on 19 March and its first performance since the early 1990s was presented to President Sharif Ahmed and other guests. The programme included traditional music, a play and comedy performances. On 23 March, the EU approved a change to operational tactics against Somali pirates, enabling EU warships to target boats and fuel dumps on land and within Somali national waters. This marked a significant increase in the naval operations that support commercial shipping off the Horn of Africa and in the Indian Ocean. On 5 April, an Al Shabab suicide bomber killed up to six people when blowing up the national theatre. On 11 April President Farole (of Puntland) said that forces of Al Shabab had been pushed out of central Somalia and had moved into the semi-autonomous state of Puntland. Two MPs were killed and several injured in a suicide bombing in Dusa Mareb (central Somalia) on 1 May. Around 20 politicians had travelled to Dusa Mareb to promote reconciliation, but were targeted by Al Shabab, which had been under pressure from opposing forces in the south and west of Somalia. On 31 May Turkey played host to a two-day 'reconciliation conference' of Somali politicians, 135-traditional elders (representing their clans), business leaders and civil society groups, in an attempt to provide a new political framework for when the TSC's UN-backed mandate ended on 20 August. On 25 July, a newly convened National Constituent Assembly (NCA), a body of 825-members drawn from Somali clans, began work to construct a provisional constitution, which would provide the legal framework to govern the workings of the new Somali Federal Institutions – following the dissolution of the TFG. On 1 August, the NCA supported a newly drafted constitution and elections to be held on 20 August. The new constitution included, among other clauses, a bill of rights with everyone declared equal regardless of their clan or religion; a federal system; Islam as the state religion; all to have a right to basic education, and the establishment of a Truth and Reconciliation Commission. The gathering of traditional leaders (first established during the Turkey 'reconciliation conference') began to propose nominees (from their respective clans) to become members of parliament. Names of nominees were scrutinised by the Technical Selection Committee (TSC), which weeded out those that had criminal records, were accused of being a war lord and those with too little education. On 9 August, the TSC announced an extension to the deadline (8 August) for receiving lists of proposed candidates, who would ultimately elect a president and ratify the constitutional document before it could be enacted and put to a referendum. Women's groups called on the traditional elders to ensure that they were properly represented in parliament; even so some clans failed to nominate any female representatives. On 20 August the Federal Parliament of Somalia was inaugurated as 225 selected members (out of a total 275 members) were sworn in as MPs; around 15 per cent of the membership was female. The TSC said a 225-membership was sufficient to elect a speaker of parliament and president (both by secret ballot). Around 24 candidates took part in the election.On 10 September, parliament voted for a new president. There were 25 candidates taking part, but in the first round no candidate won the necessary two-thirds majority and a runoff was held between Hassan Sheikh Mohamud (Xisbiga Nabadda Iyo Horumarka (Peace and Development Party) (PDP), a social democratic party, who won 190 votes in the first round and former president Sharif Sheikh Ahmed who had won 79 votes. Hassan Sheikh Mohamud won the runoff vote unopposed. President Mohamud took office on 16 September. Somalia became the 160th member of the Anti-Personnel Mine Ban Convention on 4 October. It is the last of the sub-Saharan African countries to commit to the treaty. The president appointed Abdi Farah Shirdon Saaid as prime minister on 6 October. Parliament ratified the appointment of Prime Minister Shirdon on 17 October.

2013 On 7 May British premier, David Cameron, hosted an international conference in London to help Somalia rebuild itself. Also in May Barclays Bank announced it would stop supporting transfers to remittance to companies in Somalia, where up to half the population relies on remittances from the Somali diaspora. Barclays is concerned that it will be accused of money-laundering. Some US$130 million was pledged by international donors. On 14 August Medecins Sans Frontieres (MSF) said it would be closing after a number of attacks on its staff. The agency first set up in Somalia in 1991. At a conference held in Mogadishu in early September on tackling extremism some 160 Islamic scholars issued a fatwa against al Shabab, saying it had no place in Islam. A conference held in Brussels in September pledged €1.8 billion (US$2.4 billion) as part of a 'New Deal' which focuses on peace and state-building. On 1 October Barclays Bank announced a further short delay until 16 October before closing the account of leading Somali money-transfer operator Dahabshiil after Dahabshiil had launched a court action to prevent Barclays from closing the account. Dahabshiil won an injunction preventing Barclays from halting its money transfer services for the foreseeable future. A ban on slaughtering animals anywhere except at the revamped Mogadishu Slaughterhous came into force in Mogadishu on 12 November. The move is part of an attempt to improve hygiene.

2014 Al-Shabab fighters attacked the presidential compound on 8 July. They were beaten back by AU and government forces, but not before three of the attackers had been killed and one captured. As a result the chiefs of police and intelligence were sacked. The information minister, Mustaf Sheikh Ali Dhuhulow, announced that from 9 October a system to deliver letters from abroad was reintroduced. Post codes to all 18 regions of Somalia have also been allocated. Somalia

has had no postal service since 1991.
Omar Abdirashid Ali Sharmarke was appointed prime minister and took office on 24 December.
2015 A car bomb outside a restaurant frequently used by politicians killed 11 people on 20 April.

Political structure

The self-styled republics of Somaliland and Puntland have their own elected governments (but are unrecognised internationally).

Constitution

The Somali National Reconciliation Conference, held in Mbagathi, Nairobi, Kenya, began in 2003 and the Leaders Committee agreed that Somalia should adopt a federal system of government, with selection of the MPs being carried out by the signatories (political leaders) to the Declaration of Cessation of Hostilities signed in Eldoret, Kenya, in 2002, and by certain politicians, who were officially invited.
If the government fails to complete the process of federalism throughout Somalia within a period of two-and-a-half years, parliament should withdraw its vote of confidence, necessitating the formation of a new transitional government to complete the process of federalism within one year.

Form of state

Federal republic

The executive

The president is indirectly elected by the Federal Parliament by two-thirds majority vote in two rounds if needed for a single 4-year term. The prime minister is appointed by the president and approved by the Federal Parliament.

National legislature

In November 2008, in UN-backed reconciliation negotiations, parliament agreed to increase the number of members of parliament from 275 to 550. Apart from the existing arrangement of 61 seats each allocated to four main tribal groupings and 31 seats divided between the remaining small tribal groupings, 200 more seats will be allocated to opposition representatives and 75 reserved for civil society groups. However, Islamist groups that control much of Somalia were not party to the agreement.
The National Parliament will become bicameral in 2016 with the formation of an upper house that will consist of 54 seats with members indirectly elected by regional governing councils to serve four-year terms.

Legal system

At independence in 1960, Somalia had four legal systems: English common law, Italian law, Islamic Sharia and Somali customary law. In 1973, the Siad Barre regime introduced a unified civil code. There is no national judicial system.

Last elections

20 August 2012, members of the Federal Parliament of Somalia were appointed and senior political posts were elected by the Transitional Federal Parliament (TFP).
10 September 2012: presidential. Elected by members of the Federal Parliament.
11 January 2009 (Puntland, presidential); 26 June 2009 (Somaliland, presidential)
Results: Puntland: parliament elected Abdirahman Mohamed Farole as president.
Somaliland, presidential: Ahmed Mahamoud Silanyo (Kulmiye Nabad, Midnimo iyo horumar iyo (Peace, Unity and Development Party) (PUDP)) won 49.59 per cent of the vote, Dahir Riyale Kahin (Ururka Dimuqraadiga Ummadda Bahawday (United People's Democratic Party) (UPDP)) 33.23 per cent, Faysal Cali Warabe (Ururka Caddaalada iyo Daryeelka (For Justice and Development) (FJD)) 17.18 per cent.
Somali presidential (10 September): 2nd round Hassan Sheikh Mohamud 190 votes, Sheikh Sharif Sheikh Ahmed 79 votes.

Next elections

September 2016 (presidential and parliamentary)

Political parties

There are no formal political parties. Warlords and their supporters wield most of the power. Political organisation largely reflects membership of clans and sub-clans.

Ruling party

None

Population

51.20 million (2012)* In 2010, 44.8 per cent of the population were aged 0–14 years and 4.6 per cent were aged over 65 years (FAO Yearbook 2012).
Last census: February 1987: 7,114,431
Population density: 15 inhabitants per square km. Urban population 37 per cent (2010 Unicef).
Annual growth rate: 1.7 per cent, 1990–2010 (Unicef).

Internally Displaced Persons (IDP)

375,000 (UNHCR 2004)

Ethnic make-up

Somali (85 per cent), Bantu, Arabs and others (15 per cent).

Religions

Islam is the state religion (majority Sunni Muslims) (98 per cent), Christian minority (2 per cent).

Education

The UN Children's Fund (Unicef) supports 352 primary schools in central and southern Somalia, out of 418 that are operational. Additionally, Unicef has rehabilitated 35 schools, trained 2,300 teachers and initiated a school improvement programme. Several non-government organisations have concentrated on adult literacy programmes and civic education. Private education has recently been re-established in Somali, although school fees are proving to be out of reach of the ordinary Somali family.
Somaliland expatriates residing in the United Arab Emirates (UAE) have initiated efforts to raise funds for the Amoud University. The University, established in 1997 in Boroma, is essentially a community project. In June 2003, Somalia opened its first medical college, the Benadir University Medical College (BUMC), since 1991. BUMC will be funded by donations from Somali physicians and by tuition fees.
The education sector received only 12 per cent funding in the Consolidated Appeals Process (CAP), 2003. About 40 per cent of all teachers are unqualified and many have not completed their primary school education.
Literacy rate: 17.1 per cent, adult rate: 35 per cent, adult rate for the urban population; 10 per cent for rural and nomadic populations (2003).
Female adult literacy is estimated to be 52 per cent of the male rate.
Compulsory years: Six to 14.
Enrolment rate: Primary school enrolment increased by 29 per cent in 2002, compared to 2001, and there were 30 per cent more teachers. In 2003, one out of six children received formal primary education. Female primary school enrolment was 53 per cent of the male rate.

Health

The country's health services collapsed during the war and access to healthcare depends mostly on external assistance.
Unicef remains the key provider of essential medical services and supplies to 123 maternal and child health centres, 174 health posts, and 16 hospitals.
Surveys in areas with high concentrations of displaced families show malnutrition rates as high as 40 per cent. Only 1.5 per cent of one to two years old are vaccinated. In addition, Somalia has the highest incidence of tuberculosis in the world, while cholera is endemic in most areas. In 2004, Somalia was removed from the UN list of countries with endemic polio.
It is estimated that 31 per cent of the population have access to improved water facilities.
Life expectancy: 44 years, 2004 (WHO 2006)
Fertility rate/Maternal mortality rate: 6.3 births per woman, 2010 (Unicef)

Birth rate/Death rate: 46.4 births per 1,000 population; 17.6 deaths per 1,000 population (2003).
Child (under 5 years) mortality rate (per 1,000): 133 per 1,000 live births (World Bank)

Welfare
Insecurity continues to be the greatest threat to the lives and welfare of the population, who are highly dependent on external assistance. International aid is jeopardised by widespread factional fighting, the kidnapping of aid workers and also by the mining of all major roads in Northern Gedo, the area most in need of food aid. An estimated 400,000 Somalis are internally displaced.
Although the World Food Programme (WFP) supports the repatriation of refugees with a nine-month food supply or cash equivalent, more than 10 per cent of the population require emergency food assistance. In May 2003, the WFP distributed 1,355 tonnes of food around Somalia.

Main cities
Somalia: Mogadishu (capital, estimated population 1.6 million in 2012), Beledweyne (94,157), Kismayu (57,321), Baydhabo (76,839), Baidoa (76,839), Galkayo (76,149).
Somaliland: Hargeisa (478,514), Burao (155,832), Berbera (78,047), Lasanod (42,674), Garowe (32,523), Erigavo (27,007).
Puntland: Bosaso (107,326), Qardho (27,476).

Languages spoken
Somali is one of the major languages of Africa and belongs to a set of languages called lowland Eastern Cushitic. It did not have a written form until the Latin script was adopted in 1972. Arabic, Italian and English (mainly for business) are also in use.
Arabic and English are to be the second official languages of the Transitional Federal Government of Somalia, as agreed on 5 July 2003 at the Somali National Reconciliation Conference.

Official language/s
Somali

Media
Press
Dailies: In Somalia, newspapers include *Xog-Ogaal Qaran News* (www.qarannews.com), *Codka xoriyadda* and *Ayaamaha*.
Dhambaal News (www.dhambaalnews.com) and *Jamhuuriya* (www.jamhuuriya.info) are based in Somaliland. In English, *Somaliland Times* (www.somalilandtimes.net) and the Awdal New Network (www.awdalnews.com) gives online news from Somaliland.
There are a number of internet news outlets aimed at the Somali diaspora including www.luuliyo.com, www.waagacusub.com, www.hiiraan.com, www.hormoodnews.com and www.banadir.com (with articles in English).
Weeklies: Publications include *Dadka*, *Panorama*, *Republican* (Hargeisa), *Sanca* and *Xurmo*.
Periodicals: Monthly publications include *Ayaamaha* and *Himilo*.

Broadcasting
Radio: In June 2007 the government ordered the closure of the three main radio stations in the capital (Shabelle Media Network, Horn Afrik and IQK). The order was rescinded four days later, reportedly after pressure from the US ambassador to Kenya.
The governments in the breakaway provinces of Somaliland and Puntland maintain a tight control on broadcasting in their areas. The Transitional Federal Government closed the Shabelle Media Network, Banadir Radio and Radio Simba on 12/13 November 2007, without explanation. The information minister said the stations had been 'carrying false reports and misrepresenting the activities of the security forces'. Critics claimed the government was closing down independent news outlets that did not report pro-government news.
There is no national, domestic broadcaster however the many independent radio stations provide the principal source of news for the population. Radio Magadishu is government-run with coverage limited to the capital. The FM stations Radio HornAfrk (www.hornafrik.com), Radio Shabelle (www.shabelle.net) and Radio Banaadir (www.radiobanadir.com) all broadcast in the capital. Radio Hargeisa (www.radiohargeysa.net) is Somaliland government-owned; the privately owned Radio Galkayo (www.radiogaalkacyo.com) and Voice of Peace broadcast in Puntland.
Television: Two private TV networks exist, Somali Telemedia Network (STN) and HornAfrk TV (www.hornafrik.com), broadcast international produced programmes. Somaliland National TV (SLNTV) is government-owned. Somali Broadcasting Corporation (SBC) is a private station in Puntland.
There is no official agency but APA and Panapress report on Somali matters.

Economy
The state of Somalia has few natural resources with the greater proportion of the population relying on subsistence farming (although there are commercial banana plantations in the south), and remittances from abroad. On top of this, Somalia has experienced decades of civil war, disastrous governance and misfortune.
A famine was officially declared in Bakool and Lower Shabelle, in southern Somalia, on 20 July 2011 in an area experiencing the worst drought for over 50 years. Millions experienced significant food insecurity and hundreds of thousands fled across the borders into neighbouring countries, especially Kenya. In January 2012 there were concerted efforts by forces of the African Union (AU), Kenya and Ethiopia to dislodge the militant Islamist militia, al Shabab, from their strongholds in Mogadishu and around the port of Kismayo. The heavy fighting around Mogadishu, in the Afgoye corridor, caused thousands of internally displaced persons (IDPs) to flee to relative safety in the city. The UN announced on 3 February 2012 that the famine had ended, six months after it had been declared, following a good harvest and international aid, which had alleviated the situation. As al Shabab was forced into defensive positions an agreement was reached among Somali leaders on 19 February to reform the political system and construct a new, provisional constitution. A National Constituent Assembly (NCA) organised elections of nominees, who worked to produce the legal governing framework of the new Somali Federal Institutions, which took office as a new parliament on 1 August 2012, following the dissolution of the Transitional Federal Government (TFG). Around 24 candidates were in competition for the position of president, and Hassan Sheikh Mohamud was voted into the post as president on 10 August.
The informal economy has been a mainstay for the population, based mainly on ownership of livestock and land. The traditional trade in exports of livestock to Arab Gulf states has been periodically suspended due to animal health concerns. International economic agencies are reluctant to invest in the country until it can achieve a measure of peace and the rule of law. Even so, a Coca-Cola bottling plant opened in 2004, becoming the largest investment the country had received since 1991.
The UN Human Development Index (HDI) is unable to rank Somalia, given its lack of verifiable ministry statistics for national development in health, education and income. In 2014, however, based on work by non-governmental agencies, it was able to determine that 63.6 per cent of the population experienced at least one indicator of poverty; the headcount poverty rate was 81.8 per cent of the population.

The overall political situation is complicated further by the break-away Republic of Somaliland, which has become an autonomous zone with its own currency and government. Somaliland represents the strongest local economy and has undergone something of a boom since it declared independence in 1991. The autonomous region has undergone a modest transformation with infrastructural improvements and an emerging business elite. Without international recognition, however, Somaliland cannot access funds from the IMF or World Bank or develop trade relations. Around 70 per cent of the population receive help in the form of remittances from family members abroad.
Another autonomous region, the Puntland State of Somalia, has its own chaotic economic policy, where many Somalis wish to remain part of Somalia. Puntland faces many of the problems faced by Somalia, including factional fighting and almost complete economic collapse.
Somali pirates have become the scourge of the Somalia coast and further into the Indian Ocean. Ships are routinely hijacked and held for ransom for millions of dollars, paid by ship owners and insurance companies. In 2008 there were 111 acts of piracy (out of a total 293 worldwide) undertaken by Somali pirates; double the number in 2007. In 2009 214 attacks took place. The piracy has become a business in which wealthy Somalis (including some members of the Diaspora) purchase, finance and outfit skiffs, mother-ships and crews, enabling gangs to select targets and intercept laden cargo ships, oil tankers and private yachts. International maritime protection includes military naval vessels on patrol but the sheer enormity of the area limits their effectiveness. In 2013 the US Office of Naval Intelligence reported that only 9 vessels had been subject to Somali pirate hijackings and none of them had been successful. This 90 per cent drop in pirate activity on 2012 was attributed to better management practices by vessel owners, armed on board security, significant naval presence and development of onshore security forces.

External trade

While Somalia belongs to the African, Caribbean and Pacific Group of States (ACP Group) which has a trade agreement with the European Union, it does not have a central government authority that can provide evidence of conformity of international and official regulations. Nevertheless, less formal trade is undertaken with regional neighbours, while remittances provide the majority of foreign earnings.
The continuing need for the large-scale import of fuels and food results in an ongoing negative balance of trade. There is a tradition of livestock exports to the Arab Gulf states.
There is an illegal trade in *qat* (called *jaad* in Somalia), an additive, mild hallucinogen) between Somalia, Ethiopia and Yemen.

Imports

Principal imports are manufactures, petroleum products, foodstuffs and construction materials.
Main sources: Djibouti (19.8 per cent of total in 2014), India (14.7 per cent) and Oman (9.1 per cent).

Exports

Principal exports are livestock, bananas, hides, fish, charcoal and scrap metal.
Main destinations: UAE (44.4 per cent of total in 2014), Yemen (19.1 per cent) and Oman (15.4 per cent).

Agriculture

Farming

Agriculture is the most important sector of the economy. It contributes about 60 per cent to GDP and employs 65 per cent of the working population. It is often badly affected by drought, as well as by the chaos of recent years.
Livestock, particularly camels, is the principal foreign exchange earner, accounting for 40 per cent of GDP. Exports are mainly to Arabian Gulf states and formerly to Saudi Arabia. A Saudi ban on the import of allegedly diseased Somali livestock has damaged the trade.
Much of the land is desert or semi-desert and only 13 per cent is cultivated, making food security a constant concern. Some crops are grown on the fertile land in the Juba and Scebali valleys, but the farmers have been displaced by nomads.
A famine was officially declared in Bakool and Lower Shabelle, in southern Somalia, on 20 July 2011 in an area experiencing the worst drought for over 50 years. Millions experienced significant food insecurity and hundreds of thousands fled across the borders into neighbouring countries, especially Kenya. The UN announced on 3 February 2012 that the famine had ended, six months after it had been declared, following a good harvest and international aid, which had alleviated the situation.
Subsistence farmers grow maize and sorghum whilst wheat and rice are imported. The most important cash crops are bananas, cotton and frankincense.

Fishing

Forestry

In 2006, the Supreme Islamic Courts Council (SICC) issued a directive to halt the production of charcoal. Somalia lost 1.2 million hectares, or 14 per cent of its forest cover from 1990–2005 and it has had a detrimental effect upon the environment. The principal export of charcoal is to the Gulf States, where wood from mango trees is highly favoured and a bag of charcoal can cost as much as US$15 each.
In between 2010 and 2013 forest loss was much slower at an average of 0.1 per cent a year. In 2013 10.3 per cent of the land mass was covered in forest.

Industry and manufacturing

The industrial sector is small, contributing about 5 per cent to GDP and employing 8 per cent of the working population.
The principal industries are meat and fish processing, sugar refining, fruit and vegetable canning, textiles and leather goods. Many factories are idle, because foreign exchange shortages have cut off foreign inputs.

Tourism

There is a general warning for all foreigners not to visit Somalia due to its political instability and lack of security. However there are scheduled flights from Turkey, Ethiopia and Kenya.
It is possible to visit Somaliland, in the north. A visa is obtainable from Liaison Offices in the US, UK and in Addis Ababa (Ethiopia); see: www.visitsomaliland.org for more information.

Mining

There are significant mineral resources, but they have not yet been commercially exploited. The most important regions include an area extending from the Ethiopian border to beyond Berbera in Somaliland and west of the River Scebali near Mogadishu. The former contains reserves of copper, gold, molybdenum and bismuth, while the latter contains iron, gold and apatite.
The country also contains reserves of uranium, marble, manganese, tin, beryl and columbite. Salt and gypsum were extracted commercially before the civil war began.

Hydrocarbons

Although there are no proven oil reserves, the potential for oil and gas is high. Major Western oil companies ceased exploration after the outbreak of the civil war in 1991. In 2007 a Kuwait and Indonesian consortium was created to undertake further exploration under a preliminary agreement of partnership with a newly formed state company, Somalia Petroleum Corporation. Downstream, Somalia has a single oil refinery with a capacity of 10,000 barrels per day (bpd), although it has not been in use for some years and is in a state of disrepair.
The breakaway region of Somaliland (also called Puntland), in the north, undertook

oil exploration under its own offices, sparking clan warfare in March 2009 over ownership of land being investigated.
The Nogal and Dharoor basins are considered to have a high probability of oil and gas.
Somalia relies heavily on imports of oil for its fuel needs.
Total proved natural gas reserves are around 5.6 billion cubic metres located in one gas field, although political and economic chaos has prevented exploitation. Currently, there is no production or import of natural gas.
Coal is neither produced nor imported.
Puntland: The Canadian company Africa Oil announced that it would begin drilling for oil in its leased sites in the Nugaal and Dharoor Valley in Puntland from mid-2010.

Energy
Total installed generating capacity is 80MW, all of which is provided by diesel-fired generators. The state-owned Ente Nazionale Energia Elettrica (ENEE) has a monopoly of generation, transmission and distribution and supply. Much of the energy infrastructure has been damaged or destroyed and the unstable state of the country hinders re-development.
Somalia has been identified as a prime location for wind farms but until the country has some degree of stability no development is likely.

Banking and insurance
In July 2013 Barclays Bank of the UK announced it would be withdrawing banking services from over 250 money-transfer companies. NGOs and rights activists and academics said the move risked severing an essential lifeline for millions of people in Somalia who depend on remittances from relatives in the UK. Barclays said it was a matter of compliance with international financial regulations, and the potential risk to the bank in terms of reputation and possible legal penalties from the US and other jurisdictions.
The UN's top humanitarian official in Somalia, Philippe Lazzarini, said that 'It is not an overstatement to say this move will cut a lifeline for essential services in Somalia… since a huge number of Somalis rely on remittances, which are estimated to be as much as US$1.2 billion every year – more than the entire humanitarian operation in the country.'

Central bank
Central Bank of Somalia

Main financial centre
Mogadishu

Time
GMT plus three hours

Geography
Somalia lies on the east coast of Africa, with Ethiopia to the north-west and Kenya to the west. There is a short frontier with Djibouti in the north-east. Somalia has a long coastline of 3,200km on the Indian Ocean and the Gulf of Aden, forming the Horn of Africa.
The country is shaped like the number 7 with the northern top stretching west along the coast of the Gulf of Aden. Here the land is a desert plain that rises to the Ogo and Migiurtinia mountains fringing the coastline, – of which the highest peak is Surud Ad at 2,408 metres (m). Southwards, the land becomes more fertile savannah which eventually runs into an arid and extensive region of sand dunes and rugged plateau. There are few rivers, the largest are in the central and southern regions, the Webi Guiba and Webi Scebeli rise in Ethiopia and flow into the Indian Ocean. The north has no permanently flowing rivers, the Daror and the Nugaaleed are intermittent streams.

Hemisphere
Northern

Climate
Tropical. Humid on coast, drier in north. Average temperatures 27–32 degrees Celsius (C) throughout year, but can reach 42 degrees C on coast. Dry seasons from January–February and August–September. Rainy seasons from March–June and October–December.

Dress codes
Lightweight clothes are required. Women should dress modestly.

Entry requirements
Passports
Required by all.

Visa
The civil war has disrupted consular services worldwide. Visas are required by the break-away territories of Somiland and Puntland and can be obtained at the port of entry. Travellers should contact their own ministry of foreign affairs for advice about local conditions and travelling to Somalia and breakaway provinces.

Currency advice/regulations
Import/export of only small amounts of local currency is allowed. Import of foreign currency is unlimited, but it must be declared on a form for which a small charge may be made. Currency transactions should be recorded at each exchange. Export of foreign currency is limited to the amount declared on arrival.
The Somali shilling is the unit of currency, except in Somaliland, which uses the Somaliland shilling. US dollars are accepted everywhere.

Health (for visitors)
Mandatory precautions
Yellow fever and cholera certificates if arriving from an infected area.

Advisable precautions
Hepatitis A and E are widespread and hepatitis B is hyper-endemic. Vacinations for meningococcal meningitis, yellow fever, cholera, typhoid and polio vaccinations are advisable. Malaria prophylaxis should be taken as risk exists throughout the country (two types of prophylaxis are recommended); anti-mosquito measures include mosquito repellents, nets and clothing covering the body, these offer protection against hepatitis B. Tap water must be treated as unsafe unless boiled and filtered. Eat only well cooked meals, preferably served hot; vegetables should be cooked and fruit peeled. Dairy products are unpasteurised and should be avoided.
A comprehensive medical pack and all medication is essential for the traveller as there is little to be found in the country. Medical insurance is essential, including emergency evacuation.

Hotels
Available in principal towns. Service charge of 10 per cent added to bills.

Credit cards
Credit cards are not accepted in Somalia.

Public holidays (national)
Fixed dates
1 Jan (New Year's Day), 1 May (Labour Day), 26 Jun (Independence Day), 1 Jul (Foundation Day).

Variable dates
Eid al Adha, Ashura, Birth of the Prophet, Eid al Fitr (three days).
Islamic year 1437 (15 Oct 2015–2 Oct 2016):: The Islamic year contains 354 or 355 days, with the result that Muslim feasts advance by 10–12 days against the Gregorian calendar. Dates of feasts vary according to the sighting of the new moon, so cannot be forecast exactly.

Working hours
Banking
Sat–Thu: 0800–1130.

Business
Sat–Thu: 0800–1230, 1630–1900.

Government
Sat–Thu: 0800–1400.

Shops
Sat–Thu: 0900–1300, 1600–2000.

Telecommunications
Mobile/cell phones
There are several GSM 900 and 900/1800 services available.

Electricity supply
220V AC, 50 cycles. The electricity system is poor.

Social customs/useful tips

Islamic customs should be respected. It is the convention to use the right hand when shaking hands and passing or receiving anything. Muslims are not permitted to drink alcohol or eat pork. Do not smoke or drink in public during Ramadan. Refusal of offered refreshment is considered discourteous. Shoes should be removed on entry to mosques.

Khat was banned by the Islamists in November 2006. It is a stimulant and commonly chewed by men, inducing a state of calm and sometimes causing aggressive behavior. It is grown in much of the Horn of Africa, including Kenya, and exported to Yemen.

In January 2011 hand-shaking between men and women who are not related was banned by al Shabab in the town of Jowhar, which they control. They are also barred from chatting or walking together in public; punishment will be according to Sharia.

Security

Any visit to Somalia should be undertaken only after a risk assessment has been carefully weighed; terrorism is a constant threat. Armed robbery and kidnapping by numerous bands of militia is endemic. Hargeisa, capital of the self-declared Republic of Somaliland is the only place that may offer a relatively secure environment in the country. Foreign nationals should register their presence with their respective diplomatic representatives.

Getting there

Air

National airline: Damal Airlines (based in the UAE) operates scheduled regional flights from eight airports in Somalia. In 2012, Turkish Airlines plans to begin twice weekly flights from Istanbul, via Khartoum (Sudan) into Mogadishu.

International airport/s: Mogadishu International (MGQ), 6.4km from city. This airport was re-opened on 15 July 2006.

Surface

Road: There are road links with Kenya in the south and Djibouti in the north. Four-wheel drive vehicles are recommended.

Main port/s: El Ma'an, Bassasso, Kismayu, Merca, Mogadishu.

Berbera is the economic lifeline for the self-declared Somaliland Republic.

Getting about

National transport

Air: Damal Airlines flies to nine towns throughout the country, including Mogadishu.

Road: Travel may be restricted and local enquiries should be made. There were good roads from Mogadishu to Kismayu (via Merca) and Baidoa in the southern part of the country, and to Hargeisa and Berbera in the north. However, since the civil strife began conditions have deteriorated. Most other routes are mainly tracks and gravel roads. Driving is on the right.

Water: Coastal shipping of both freight and passengers is extensive. The number of incidents of piracy off the Somali coast has increased sharply in the last few years.

City transport

Taxis: Fares are by negotiation and tipping is not usual. Taxis can be hired on a time basis.

Car hire

Car hire is available in Mogadishu although foreign visitor should avoid driving alone until the politicial situation in Somalia improves.

There are no traffic lights in the country except in Hargeisa in Somaliland. The condition of the roads makes driving difficult and night driving is dangerous due to the absence of lighting.

BUSINESS DIRECTORY

The addresses listed below are a selection only. While World of Information makes every endeavour to check these addresses, we cannot guarantee that changes have not been made, especially to telephone numbers and area codes. We would welcome any corrections.

Telephone area codes

It is unlikely that all landlines quoted are working.

The international direct dialling (IDD) code for Somalia is +252, followed by area code and subscriber's number:

Mogadishu1 Hargeisa2

Chambers of Commerce

Somalia Chamber of Commerce, Industry and Agriculture, PO Box 27, Via Asha, Mogadishu (tel: 281-866).

Somaliland Chamber of Commerce, Hargeisa (tel: 523-143; email: hargcham@yahoo.com; internet: www.somalilandchamberofcommerce.com).

Banking

Commercial and Savings Bank of Somalia, PO Box 203, Juley Street 1st, Mogadishu (tel: 22-861, 22-959).

Central bank

Central Bank of Somalia, PO Box 11, Corso Somalia 55, Mogadishu, Somalia (tel: 215-241).

Travel information

Daallo Airlines, # 30 Street, Baraka Market, Mogadishu (tel: 215-301; fax: 216-248; email: daallo@globalsom.com; internet: www.daallo.com).

Damalair, PO Box 27449, Dubai UAE (tel :+ (+971-4) 271-5005; fax: (+971-4) 272-0890; email: airdamal@emirates.net.ae; internet: www.damalair.co.ae).

Somali Airlines (operations suspended), PO Box 726, Via Medina, Mogadishu.

Other useful addresses

Agricultural Development Corporation, PO Box 930, Mogadishu.

Livestock Development Agency of Somalia, PO Box 1759, Mogadishu.

National Petroleum Agency of Somalia, PO Box 573, Mogadishu.

Somali Broadcasting Service, Ministry of Information and National Guidance, Private Bag, Mogadishu (tel: 2455).

Statistical Department, PO Box 1742, Mogadishu (tel: 80-385).

Internet sites

Africa Business Network: www.ifc.org/abn

African Development Bank: www.afdb.org

Africa Online: www.africaonline.com

AllAfrica.com: http://allafrica.com

Puntland State of Somalia: http://members.tripod.com/~Puntland/

Somalia News: www.somalianews.com

Somaliland official website: www.somalilandgov.com

United Nations Somalia: www.unsomalia.org

Wakiil Business Centre: www.wakiil.com

South Africa

KEY FACTS

Official name: Republic of South Africa

Head of State: President Jacob Gedleyihlekisa Zuma (ANZ) (from 9 May 2009; re-elected 21 May 2014)

Head of government: President Jacob Zuma (ANZ) (from 7 May 2009; re-elected 21 May 2014)

Ruling party: African National Congress (ANC) (since 1994; re-elected 7 May 2014)

Area: 1,127,200 square km

Population: 54.00 million (2014)

Capital: Cape Town (legislative); Johannesburg (financial); Pretoria (to be renamed Tshwane) (administrative); Bloemfontein (judicial)

Official language: Afrikaans, English, Ndebele, Sesotho, Northern Sotho, SiSwati, Tsonga, Tswana, Venda, Xhosa, Zulu.

Currency: Rand (R) = 100 cents

Exchange rate: R13.79 per US$ (Sep 2015)

GDP per capita: US$6,483 (2014)

GDP real growth: 1.53% (2014)

GDP: US$350.08 billion (2014)

Labour force: 20.23 million (2014)*

Unemployment: 25.10% (2014)

Inflation: 6.07% (2014)

Balance of trade: -US$6.37 billion (2014)

Annual FDI: US$5.72 billion (2011)

* estimated figure

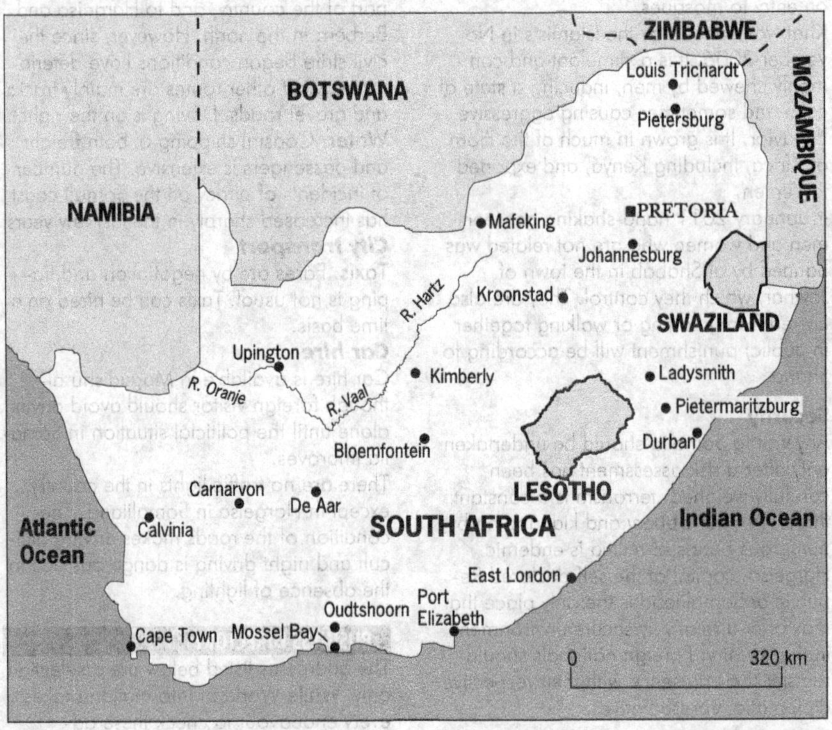

One of the problems facing South Africa in 2015 was the fact that Nelson Mandela's legacy was proving impossible to live up to. The moral power of a quiet man who had spent 27 years in prison for what he believed in was such that on his release he could negotiate with those who had put him in jail. However, if Nelson Mandela was a statesman, those politicians that followed him were of lesser stature. Writing in the *International Herald Tribunel*, back in 2012, the American journalist Bill Keller noted that in its 18 years of power the ANC [African National Congress] had managed to create a substantial black middle class. It had not, however, 'significantly narrowed the gulf between the shack-dwelling underclass and everyone else.' 'Inequality' wrote Mr Keller, 'breeds serious resentment, violent protests, strikes, fatalism.'

Corruption

According to the independent Corruption Watch (CW) – a non-profit organisation working to fight corruption in South Africa – corruption was growing faster than ever in South Africa. Corruption Watch was demanding a change in mentality – not just from politicians and officials, but also the public because 'you get the government you deserve.' The organisation noted that 'even before the end of apartheid, people fought hard for democratic elections and a new constitution. So how is it possible that their new, democratically-elected leaders are engaged in nepotism and self-enrichment?' The organisation's director, David Lewis, was quoted as saying that 'We fell asleep at the wheel in 1994 [the year the ANC came to power]. After winning the struggle for democracy, we thought everything would come naturally. Clearly we were mistaken, because whether you live in Sweden or South Africa, you have to keep a watchful eye on the government and be demanding.'

According to CW, corruption was rooted in South Africa at all levels of public administration. 'The president pays for his villa with taxpayers' money, police look the other way for a small fee and teachers give good grades in exchange for sex. The result is that the public has completely lost confidence in the government.' In the view of CW a change in mentality was needed to fight corruption and restore confidence in the public sector. That applied to government officials, who must realise that their misbehaviour will not go unpunished, but also for citizens, who ought to demand that such misconduct be penalised.

One less publicised area of corruption that CW was focussing on was that of corruption in the educational system, where there were many reports. Corruption at this level could mean an education department clerk offering jobs to friends and family, to learners at a no-fees school being forced to give teachers money, or a drunken principal embezzling funds.

CW's actions had saved several whistleblowers from prosecution, forced corrupt officials to resign, made the Johannesburg police department revise its policies and had been hugely amplified through traditional and social media.

Nkandla

On South Africa's corruption league table, one scandal consistently scored the highest. The name Nkandla had, by 2015, become synonymous with 'corruption.' The allegations maintained that President Zuma's private residence in the province had benefited from US$22 million in upgrades paid for with taxpayers money. The matter had been investigated by the Public Prosecutor's Office which recommended (rather than ordered) that he pay back some of the money. The 'Nkandlagate' affair had, in the eyes of many South Africans, come to symbolise the corrupt practices embraced not only by their president, but also by those around him. One of President Zuma's sons-in law – Lonwabo Sambudla – came into this category. Reports in the *Saturday Dispatch* newspaper alleged that a company, Syneza Group, with links to Mr Sambudla had been awarded a US$53 million contract for building – improbably enough – 66,000 toilets in the Eastern Cape province.

Most South Africans could only gasp in amazement over the money that had been spent on their president's residence. But the gasps were just as loud when they learned that in belt-tightening times, it had cost the South African taxpayer R54.6-million (US$4 million) to support the country's four first ladies during President Jacob Zuma's first term in office. President Zuma had been married six times (one wife divorced him, another committed suicide) and allegedly fathered 20 children. In comparison, the average annual cost of the Presidential Spousal Support Unit for the last four years of former president Thabo Mbeki's administration, from 2005 to 2008, was R7.1 million (US$0.5 million). In President Zuma's first term, the average rose to R10.9 million (US$0.8 million) a year – an increase of R3.8 million (US$0.28 million). A spokesman for the president, Mac Maharaj, said the unit cost R7.877 million (US$0.57 million) in 2010–11; R11.165 million (US$0.81 million) in 2011–12; R7.068 million (US$0.56 million) in 2012–13 and R13.019 million (US$0.94 million) in 2013–14. The last time information was made publicly available on the unit was in February 2010 when the Presidency revealed in response to a parliamentary question that during Zuma's first year in office, 2009 to 2010, the unit cost R15.517 million (US$1.13 million).

It was not only the cost of the support for the Spousal Support Unit that had drawn such political outrage. The President's promiscuity flew in the face of governmental efforts to control HIV/Aids and develop responsible sexual education. The opposition Democratic Alliance called for 'a special presidential handbook to introduce a strict regulatory framework for spending on the spousal office' in the light of the increases under President Zuma. The Economic Freedom Fighters referred to the unit in its 2014 election manifesto, saying that an EFF government would 'remove all presidential spousal support'.

Protests

For a decade or so the waves of protest that had shown themselves in South Africa had been seen as no more than a means of pressurising the ruling African National Congress (ANC) into delivering better services. However, as the protests became more widespread and occasionally more violent, their motivation had been called into question. Were they single issue protests, or did they represent a further reaching challenge for South Africa's government and politicians.

Some South African academics had argued that the protests were of such a scale and intensity that they represented a broader 'rebellion of the poor', a challenge to the state, its political system and its economic system – capitalism. Others interpreted the protests as being a means of calling the ANC to account, while remaining supportive of its broad political direction and the existing social order more generally. Those holding this view did not consider the protests to be a challenge to the system, nor a significant shift away from the ANC.

For the ANC to have side-stepped the widespread political scandals that swirled around it was in itself no mean achievement. To fly in the face of mounting allegations of corruption was quite another. South Africa ranked 67 on the Transparency International 2014 *Corruption*

KEY INDICATORS — South Africa

	Unit	2011	2012	2013	2014	**2015
Population	m	*50.59	*52.27	53.16	54.00	*54.86
Gross domestic product (GDP)	US$bn	408.10	382.34	366.24	350.08	*323.81
GDP per capita	US$	8,066	7,314	6,890	6,483	*5,902
GDP real growth	%	3.1	2.5	2.2	1.5	*2.0
Inflation	%	5.0	5.7	5.8	6.1	*4.5
Unemployment	%	25.4	24.9	24.7	25.1	*25.1
Coal output	mtoe	143.8	146.6	144.7	147.7	–
Exports (fob) (goods)	US$m	102,857.6	93,480.5	94,917.8	92,478.2	–
Imports (fob) (goods)	US$m	100,402.9	102,624.9	102,588.2	98,848.1	–
Balance of trade	US$m	2,454.7	-9,144.5	-7,670.4	-6,369.9	–
Current account	US$m	-13,682.7	-20,043.0	-21,116.0	*-19,055.0	*-14,792.0
Total reserves minus gold	US$m	43,611.0	43,995.0	44,864.0	44,267.0	–
Foreign exchange	US$m	40,749.0	41,183.0	41,943.0	–	–
Exchange rate	per US$	6.89	8.69	10.66	11.55	–

* estimated figure ** forecast figure

Perceptions Index, an improvement of 5 places over 2013 (when it ranked 72), but still not very impressive. Economic discontent was certainly increasing – and fuelling corruption.

Surprisingly, in the 2014 election the ANC had held on to a 62.2 per cent share of the vote, only slightly down from the 65.9 per cent it won in 2009. *Inter alia, the result guaranteed a second five-year term for Mr Zuma. The Democratic Alliance share was up: the party said it gained 1.1 million new voters, including 700,000 votes from black South Africans. This was its best ever result, topping 4 million votes, although its growth still failed to meet some expectations*

The hopes carried by South Africa's two new parties had met with sharply contrasting fates. On the plus side was that of the Economic Freedom Fighters, led by Julius Malema, the 32 year-old founder. The EFF had only been founded in July 2013 following Mr Malema's expulsion from the ANC in April. Just one year late the EFF won more than one million votes to come in third on 6.3 per cent. Although the ANC's rather cosy grip on political power in South Africa had not been seriously challenged in the election, it did seem a little less secure. President Zuma remains the ANC leader, but at the age of 71 he was increasingly perceived to lack the necessary vitality – and honesty.

But the electoral fortunes of Mamphela Ramphele, a former soulmate of the black consciousness (and later murdered) founder Steve Biko, imploded dismally. Her party, Agang SA, had also been launched in 2013, promising to restore South African dreams; but it could only muster a fraction of a percentage point.

On winning the election, the ANC had been expected to use its mandate to try to drive through its National Development Plan. This rejected nationalisation and emphasised investment and infrastructure. The business-friendly plan had alarmed South Africa's powerful trades' unions – some of which might break away to form their own party. The Congress of South African Trade Unions (Cosatu) and its affiliate unions were an important political force, traditionally closely linked to the ANC.

New economic aspect?

South African demographics took on a new aspect in 2014 as its black middle class effectively edged out its white counterpart as the economy's mainspring. A report published in the South Africa News suggested that by 2013, 51 per cent of South Africa's middle class were black, only 34 per cent white. Ten years earlier the white component had been 52 per cent and 32 per cent black. The *Four Million and Rising* report estimated the expenditure of the black middle class to be in the order of 400 billion rand (US$27.5 billion).

Citi's Africa economist, David Cowan, described the continental African middle class as a wealthy elite in and a strong consumer group, with, ideally between US$5,000-US$7,000 of disposable income a year. Another study, by the University of Cape Town, estimated South Africa's black middle class to have risen from just under 1.7 million in 2004 to 4.2 million by 2012.

Refugees

By 2015, the dream of the Rainbow Nation, so dear to former President Nelson Mandela had turned into a nightmare. Many Congolese refugees had found their way to Durban, fleeing war and the destruction of their country. However, in South Africa they were subject to more violence, including that meted out by the police. Ironically, those gathering to protest that South Africa was the land of the free found themselves subject to police beatings, from a force that was in principle there to ensure freedom. The other irony was that white middle class demonstrations were not generally assaulted – South Africa's claims to be a fully fledged democracy did not seem to be applicable to those who were either poor, or black, or both. One theory that seemed to be gaining ground was that there was serious support from senior politicians for the xenophobic attacks; it seemed that there were those in the ruling ANC who would rather see their supporters taking it out on defenceless immigrants than complaining about the lack of jobs or inadequate housing. There are many in the ruling party who would rather have the poor divided than united and would rather have the poor turning against their neighbours instead of their real oppressors. There are also people who have their eyes on the businesses and homes of others.

The economy

As June 2015 approached, the South African government could only hope and pray that the credit rating agencies would not downgrade its rating any further. As things stood, the rating was only one notch above junk status, a critical level at which financial institutions would be obliged to sell – or offload, or even dump – the South African debt they held. It was with some relief that they learnt that South Africa's t rating would probably not be downgraded to junk, at least not for the next two years, according to the credit ratings agency Standard & Poor's (S&P). A Director at S&P announced that the outlook was currently stable and that the time horizon was usually 24 months. The S&P decision ran counter to the gloom caused by the electricity cuts that were expected to dampen economic growth. There were also concerns that the continuing public sector wage negotiations might break the budget provisions. There had been particular concern about S&P's ratings, as the agency had last downgraded South Africa's sovereign rating to one notch above junk status.

According to the African Development Bank (AfDB), in 2014 South Africa's growth continued to slow down, recording only 1.5 per cent, its weakest performance since the global financial crisis. The economy was adversely affected by the most protracted industrial action seen since the end of apartheid and significantly weak demand from trading partners. Various infrastructure gaps, notably inadequate electricity supply, weak domestic demand and anaemic investment rates also acted as a drag on growth. Nevertheless, projections based on improvements in the global economy, the successful completion of major government projects (including the Medupi power station) and new investment plans, suggested that growth might rebound to 2.0 per cent in 2015. As one of the BRICS (Brazil, Russia, India, China and South Africa) South Africa is well integrated into the global economy, although collectively the BRICS economic performance had been less than stellar in 2014 and during the first half of 2015.

The strong labour unrest had marked a crack in the tripartite alliance between the ANC, the South African Communist Party (SACP) and Cosatu. Cosatu lost its biggest affiliate union, the National Union of Metalworkers of South Africa (Numsa), as well as its leadership position in the platinum sector to the Association of Miners and Construction Union (AMCU), a new union.

Unemployment continued to pose significant challenges: it had reached 24.3 per cent and youth unemployment had reached 49 per cent at the end of 2014. The service sector had grown in contrast with the manufacturing sector, despite the government's industrialisation plans to combat unemployment. Skills shortages continued to act as a constraint on growth.

The outlook for growth was better for financial services and for the agriculture, forestry and fisheries sectors. The National Development Plan, which aimed to eliminate poverty and reduce inequality by 2030, focussed on creating jobs and improving education.

The South African Reserve Bank (SARB) (central bank) had confirmed its commitment to price and financial stability in 2014, and inflation targeting remained a key monetary policy anchor in South Africa. The depreciation of the rand exchange rate led the SARB twice to increase the base rate, which since July 2014 had been at 5.75 per cent, to 6.25 in November 2015. Rises in interest rates affected investment levels, which were structurally low. South Africa's fiscal position improved with the deficit falling to 3.4 per cent of gross domestic product (GDP), thanks to increased tax revenues, which helped offset increasing government expenditure. High wage demands by public sector unions in 2015 might pose a fiscal risk. Following the 2014 elections the new administration announced a number of measures to consolidate the budget and reduce the growth of expenditure to a real rate of 1.3 per cent over the next two years, mainly by freezing government personnel expenditure and reducing non-essential spending.

In its April 2015 assessment of the South African economy, the International Monetary Fund (IMF) confirmed that South Africa's GDP growth had reached a post-crisis low of 1.5 per cent in 2014, entailing no improvement in per capita income, due to the protracted strikes and electricity constraints. According to the IMF, South Africa continued to under-perform peer Emerging Markets (EMs) and the gap with its trading partners widened. As the electricity crisis deepened, only a muted recovery to 2 per cent growth was expected in 2015–16 mainly due to the anticipation of fewer days lost to strikes. Lower oil prices had improved the terms of trade, but were expected to have a negligible impact on growth as highly-leveraged consumers might not spend much of the extra income and electricity constraints hindered domestic production expansion. Headwinds to growth also arose from the proposed fiscal consolidation, high policy uncertainty and tighter financial conditions. The improvement in growth over the medium term to about 2.8 per cent was predicated on increased energy availability. Unemployment was expected by the IMF to remain above 25 per cent, unless major policy changes were implemented.

The positive terms of trade surprise in 2015 – namely that lower oil prices were more than offsetting softer export commodity prices – was anticipated to reduce the current account deficit to 4.8 per cent of GDP. The projected improvement in the current account balance (of 0.6 percentage point of GDP) was expected to be greater than in most emerging markets and to persist for some years. A lower current account deficit, coupled with the relative resilience of South African balance sheets to dollar appreciation, had translated into somewhat lower relative external vulnerability, as shown by the nominal effective exchange rate being broadly stable since mid-2014. However, the current account was expected to remain weaker than the norm (estimated at about -2 per cent of GDP) throughout the medium term as competitiveness remained weak. Gross external financing requirements were projected to remain elevated and the balance of payments looked likely to rely mainly on non-foreign direct investment (FDI) flows. After declining to 5 per cent in 2015 on lower oil prices, inflation was projected to rebound to 6.1 per cent in 2016.

In the view of the IMF, solving the electricity crisis was of the utmost priority. Severe electricity shortages, the worst since 2008, had become the greatest obstacle to growth, reducing economic activity, sapping confidence and discouraging investment. Moody's and S&P had downgraded Eskom, South Africa's public electricity supplier, to a 'speculative' grade rating. The measures taken, including the establishment of an electricity 'War Room' under the Deputy President to improve co-ordination and remove bottlenecks, the new management strategy and the renewed emphasis on independent power producers and cogeneration were welcomed. Higher electricity tariffs and the government support envisaged were necessary to make Eskom financially sustainable, but needed to be complemented by cost containment (including through improved procurement practices), efficiency enhancements and governance improvements to minimise the impact on consumers and business costs. At the same time, in the opinion of the IMF, consideration needed to be given to further private participation to increase capacity and reduce the cost of generation. Addressing other infrastructure bottlenecks, eg in transport, was important; South Africa's planned rail expansion was a step in the right direction.

The IMF also noted that some recent measures – for example, the new regulation for visas for certain skilled workers and restrictions on temporary employment – risked depressing growth and job creation. Long-standing recommendations for reforms in these areas remained essential for sustainably higher, job-rich growth. Better quality education and training and more liberal immigration policies should, in the longer term, ease the skills mismatch. Reducing the regulatory burden and strengthening competition, including through trade liberalisation, would help reduce the wage-productivity gap by lowering the cost of living and enhancing productivity. Simultaneous labour market reforms – giving more consideration to the unemployed and to small firms in wage setting, exempting small and medium enterprises (SMEs) from the extension of collective bargaining outcomes and reducing laying off costs – would also increase job creation and facilitate new firms' entry. A renewed impetus for reforms in this direction was urgently needed.

The IMF considered that the 2015 budget had been rightly adjusted to lower potential growth, but that further measures and reforms were needed to address risks and make fiscal policy more supportive of long-term growth and jobs. The structural primary balance was projected to improve by one per cent of GDP over three years. This, coupled with GDP rebasing, a better-than-anticipated 2014/15 outcome and lower budgeted transfers to the Southern African Customs Union (SACU) countries, should stabilise South Africa's debt at about 50 per cent of GDP by the 2019/20 fiscal year (which was lower than the 56 per cent of GDP projected). However, the planned sharp deceleration in spending growth in 2016/17 and the use of the contingency reserve to accommodate higher public wages made achieving the authorities' targets a tall order. Additional substantial fiscal risks stemmed from further support to Eskom, lower growth and the fiscal impact of the public sector wage agreement. The planned national health insurance (NHI) could also add to spending pressures and the envisaged nuclear power plants could entail a large public debt increase.

Ongoing efforts to strengthen government procurement, including making smarter use of technology to simplify bidding and increase transparency and standardisation of government contracts to reduce costs, are welcome. While the emphasis on integrating SMEs into the public supply chain should help level the playing field, procurement should remain focused on value for money. In addition, spending reviews and performance-based budgeting would improve the impact of government programmes. While the public sector wage settlement averts a costly strike, it keeps compensation budgets high and could crowd out higher-impact social and capital expenditure, underscoring the importance of the comprehensive review of compensation budgets announced in the 2015 budget. A review of tax expenditures could also help eliminate ineffective spending, creating space for priority programmes. The IMF projected annual inflation to accelerate, breaching the upper end of the target band in the fourth quarter of the 2015 fiscal year and the first quarter of 2016 before easing to 5.5 per cent by the end of 2016.

Risk assessment

Economy	Fair
Politics	Fair
Regional stability	Good

People to watch

Julius Malema, the founder of the Economic Freedom Fighters (EFF) political party.

COUNTRY PROFILE

1652 The Dutch East India Company set up a supply station which became Cape Town, supplying sailing ships to and from the Dutch East Indies (Indonesia).
1795 Britain took control of the Cape.
1806 The Cape Colony became British and settlement began in 1820.
1835 Mass treks by Afrikaners (Boers) moved inland, fighting the Ndebele and Zulus.
1899–1902 After many battles, the Boer War was eventually won by the British. With the signing of the Treaty of Vereeniging on 31 May 1902, all Boers became British subjects.
1910 The Union of South Africa was established from the former British colonies of Cape and Natal and the Boer republics of Transvaal and Orange Free State. South Africa became a self-governing dominion led by former Boer generals.
1912 The Native National Congress, the precursor to the African National Congress (ANC), was founded.
1913 The Land Act was introduced to prevent blacks, except those in Cape Province, from buying land outside reserves. Whites were given 87 per cent of the land, blacks the remaining 13 per cent.
1914 The National Party was founded.
1919 South West Africa (Namibia), formerly a German colony, came under South African administration.
1948 Apartheid (separateness) laws, excluding non-whites from political and economic influence, were applied by successive National Party governments.
1950 The population was classified by race. The Group Areas Act was passed to segregate blacks and whites. The South African Communist Party (SACP) was banned. The ANC responded with a campaign of civil disobedience led by Nelson Mandela.
1960 Apartheid laws were brutally enforced; the most notorious incident was the Sharpeville massacre. The ANC became the main black political organisation opposing the government and consequently was banned.
1961 South Africa was declared a republic and left the Commonwealth. Mandela launched the ANC's military wing which began a campaign of disruption and sabotage.
1964 Nelson Mandela, leader of the ANC, was jailed for life. The UN imposed sanctions against South Africa.
1976 More than 600 people were killed in the Soweto uprising.
1983 An interim constitution established power-sharing of three population groups (whites, Asians and mixed race (coloured)), effectively excluding participation of blacks.
1989 P W Botha (prime minister from 1978–83 and president from 1983–89) was replaced by F W de Klerk; he began a reform programme that started the dismantling of apartheid.
1990 Nelson Mandela was released from prison on 11 February. The ban on the ANC was lifted. Namibia was granted independence.
1991 The last apartheid laws were repealed. Fighting broke out between the ANC and the Zulu Inkatha movement.
1993 A non-racial constitution was formulated through a multi-racial negotiating forum. A transitional Government of National Unity (GNU) was established replacing the three-chamber, racially-based, parliament. Oliver Tambo, long-time anti-apartheid campaigner and former leader of the ANC died.
1994 In the first non-racial, fully democratic elections, the ANC won a majority of seats in parliament and Nelson Mandela became president. South Africa successfully reapplied for Commonwealth membership and took up its seat in the UN General Assembly for the first time in 20 years. South Africa's new flag was unveiled in April.
1996 The new constitution was adopted. A Truth and Reconciliation Commission (TRC) was set up. Those that perpetrated and suffered human rights abuse were allowed to record their experiences for mutual recognition.
1997 Nelson Mandela resigned as president of the ANC.
1998 The TRC branded apartheid a crime against humanity and held the ANC accountable for numerous human rights abuses. South Africa intervened militarily in Lesotho to prevent civil war breaking out in the kingdom.
1999 Nelson Mandela resigned as president and Thabo Mbeki was elected as his successor by the National Assembly. The ANC increased its share of the election vote and formed a coalition government with the mainly Zulu Inkatha Freedom Party (IFP).
2000 The Democratic Party, the New National Party (NNP) and the Federal Alliance merged to form the Democratic Alliance (DA), which won a quarter of the vote in local elections.
2001 South Africa began importing generic HIV/Aids drugs after 39 multi-national pharmaceutical companies stopped legal action. The High Court ruled that pregnant women must be given anti-retroviral drugs to prevent HIV transmission to their infants.
2002 The name of Northern Province was changed to Limpopo Province. The Organisation of African Unity (OAU) became the African Union (AU) with President Mbeki as the first chairman.
2003 Walter Sisulu, a key veteran figure in the anti-apartheid struggle, died.
2004 The ruling ANC won a landslide victory and Thabo Mbeki was elected unopposed for a second term as president. Black economic empowerment (BEE) legislation was enacted; its objectives are to address economic inequalities such as the imbalance in ethnic ownership and lack of black opportunity and aspirations, caused by decades of apartheid. The legislation is binding on all public companies and government entities.
2005 Mbeki dismissed his deputy, Jacob Zuma, who was charged with corruption. Phumzile Mlambo-Ngcuka was named as his successor.
2006 Zuma was acquitted of rape charges and reinstated as ANC deputy president. The corruption charges against him were dismissed. Johannesburg International Airport's name was changed to OR Tambo International Airport.
2007 Jacob Zuma was elected leader of the ANC.
2008 The High Court ruled that Chinese South Africans would be re-classified as 'black' people so that they could benefit from government policies to help those previously disadvantaged under the old apartheid system. The controversial land reform bill was postponed. Following the

statement by the judge in the failed trial of Jacob Zuma for corruption in 2005 that the prosecution had been politically motivated parliament forced President Mbeki to resign. Several senior cabinet members also resigned. Parliament voted for Kgalema Motlanthe (ANC) as president; Motlanthe served the remainder of Mbeki's presidential term. 2009 The High Court ruled that South African citizens living abroad should be allowed to vote in general elections, allowing around two million expatriates to participate in the country's political life. In parliamentary elections, the ANC won 65.9 per cent of the vote, a fall of 33 seats and less than the two-thirds majority needed to change the constitution without parliamentary support. The DA won 16.7 per cent and gained control of the Western Cape Province. The newly created Congress of the People (Cope), led by former president Mbeki, won 7.4 per cent. ANC leader, Jacob Zuma, was elected as president. 2010 The unemployment rate was recorded at over 24 per cent. Eugene Terre Blanche, the ultra-right-wing supremacist, was killed by two of his employees, aged 15 and 21 years old. In a landmark trial, South Africa's former chief of police, Jackie Selebi, was found guilty of corruption and sentenced to 15 years in jail. Nobel peace laureate Archbishop Desmond Tutu retired from public life. In a move that President Zuma said would 'correct the wrongs of the past' the government announced that it planned to abolish six of the 13 traditional rulers' offices, as the incumbents died. A number of traditional leaders had been created during the apartheid era, at the expense of the original monarchs; this was seen as a move to divide the people. They had little real power, but were semi-important cultural figures. The Zulu and Xhosa kings will remain. The Independent Democrats (ID) party announced it would merge with the DA, in preparation of fighting the next general elections (due in 2014). 2011 The special dispensation that allowed Zimbabweans to cross into South Africa during the political disturbances in 2009 to stay in South Africa was due to end in mid-2011. In February, President Zuma was invited to attend the summit of the Bric (Brazil, Russia, India, China) group of emerging economies, to strengthen the African ties to the economic organisation. South Africa became a member of the re-named Brics in April. In September, President Zuma set up a commission to investigate allegations against members of the ANC, including Zuma himself, of corruption during a 1990s multi-billion US$ arms deal to buy European military equipment. A national census was undertaken on 9 October; final results will be published in March 2013. In November, Julius Malema (seen by many as a future leader of the ANC), was suspended from the party until 2016, having been accused of bringing the ANC into disrepute when he proposed the overthrow of the sovereign government of Botswana. In November, parliament passed the Protection of State Information Bill (known as the Secrecy Bill), despite widespread criticism that it would outlaw whistle-blowing and investigative journalism. The government said it would safeguard state secrets and national security. 2012 The ANC celebrated 100 years since its inception on 6 January 1912. The leaders of the Brics countries met in Delhi on 29 March to discuss their position regarding the control the US and Europe has on the World Bank and the IMF. Prime Minister Manmohan Singh (India) said 'The Brics countries have agreed to examine in greater detail a proposal to set up a South-South development bank, funded and managed by the Brics and other developing countries.' On 1 March, Julius Malema was expelled from the ANC for 'sowing divisions' within the party. On 15 July Nkosazana Dlamini-Zuma (former wife of President Zuma) won the 2013 chairmanship of the AU (the first woman to win the position) with 37 votes (out of 54). The first results of the 2011 census recorded a population of 51,770,560, of which 41,000,938 defined themselves as black. Following months of industrial agitation and an ultimatum to disarm, on 16 August the police opened fire on protesting miners, striking at the Marikana platinum mine, killing 46 miners and injuring 78 others. On 27 August the mine was closed and did not reopen until 20 September when a pay rise of 22 per cent was agreed. An inquiry into the violence at the Marikana mine began work on 1 October. On 18 December Jacob Zuma was re-elected to a second five-year term as President of the African National Congress; Kgalema Motlanthe was the only other candidate. 2013 94-year-old Nelson Mandela was taken into a Pretoria hospital on 7 June, suffering from a recurrent lung infection. Although he was initially reported as 'stable' on 23 June the government announced that his condition was 'critical'. A new political party, Agang (Build, in Sepedi language), was launched on 22 June, lead by Mamphela Ramphele, a former World Bank managing director and partner of Steve Biko. Former archbishop Desmon Tutu appealed to the Mandela family not to besmirch the name of Mandela and to end the feud that had escalated between various members. In a cabinet reshuffle on 9 July President Zuma said was a 'strategy to improve the delivery of government services', housing minister Tokyo Sexwale, a veteran of the fight against apartheid, was sacked. He was reportedly behind a move in 2012 to remove Mr Zuma from the presidency. Former ANC Youth League leader, Julius Malema, launched a political group called the Economic Freedom Fighters (EFF) in July. Mr Malema has accused the president of not doing enough to help the poor black voters who had helped to elect him and hopes that disaffected Youth League members will join the EFF. King Buyelekhaya Dalindyebo of Nelson Mandela's Thembu ethnic group defected from the ANC to the DA in July. The king has reportedly said that he would stop smoking marijuana when Mr Zuma stops being corrupt. It is unclear whether he has much support, and since he has a criminal record it is also felt that his membership may backfire on the DA. Nelson Mandela turned 95 on 18 July. He remained 'critical' but stable in hospital until 2 September when he was taken to his home in Johannesburg, where a critical care facility had been arranged. Around 80,000 miners began a strike for higher pay on 3 September. The NUM rejected a 6 per cent offer, asking for 10 per cent. The strike ended on 8 September after the miners accepted a marginally improved offer of 8 per cent. A new political party, the Economic Freedom Fighters, was registered by Julius Mulema in July. He said that he would contest the next elections in 2014, and that his policies would include the redistribution of land and nationalising the mines, as well as provide free, quality education, healthcare and sanitation. Nelson Mandela, South Africa's first black, independently elected president, died on 5 December aged 95. A state funereal was held in his home village of Qunu on 15 December after a memorial service held on 10 December and a-three day lying in state in the Union Buildings in Pretoria. 2014 The general election held on 7 May was won convincingly by the ANC, even though with a reduced majority. The results were ANC 62.15 per cent (249 seats, out of 400); Democratic Alliance (DA) 22.23 per cent (89); Economic Freedom Fighters (the new party lead by Julius Mulema) 6.35 per cent (25). Turnout was 73.50 per cent. Without its two-thirds majority the ANC will nolonger be able to make any changes to the constitution.. Mr Zuma was re-elected as President by parliament on 21 May; he was unopposed. A four-week strike by members of the National Union of Metalworkers of South Africa (Numsa) ended after the union said its 220,000 striking members had 'unanimously' accepted the employers' offer.

The deal agreed at the end of July promised three-year fixed annual wage increases of 10 per cent for Numsa's lowest-paid workers; both sides are said to have compromised heavily. The strike, which had affected some 12,000 companies in the steel and engineering sectors, had, according to the employers, cost R300 million (US$28 million) a day.

South Africa's football captian, Senzo Meyiwa, was shot and killed by a burglar on 26 October.

2015 President Zuma's state of the nation speech on 12 February included proposals banning foreigners from owning land, and set limits on the size of farms locals can own. Mr Zuma's speech was overshadowed by violence in parliament. In May the main opposition party the Democractic Alliance, elected Mmusi Maimane as their first black leader, to succeed Helen Zille who stepped down in February. On 30 September the government announced it would pay compensation to the families of the mineworkers killed in the Marikana wage dispute in 2012. No

Political structure

Constitution

The Constitution was implemented in February 1997.

South Africa consists of a central government and nine provincial governments. The head of a province is called a premier.

The right to regional autonomy is enshrined in the Constitution, subject to the principles of the national constitution.

Electoral system: list-system proportional representation based on universal adult suffrage, aged over 18.

The High Court ruled in February 2009 that South African citizens living abroad should be allowed to vote in general elections. The decision was referred to the Constitutional Court for confirmation, which if passed would allow around two million expatriates to participate in the country's political life.

Independence date

31 May 1961

Form of state

Federal republic

The executive

Executive powers are vested in the president, who is both Head of State and Head of government, and is elected by the National Assembly for no more than two, five-year terms.

The president, must appoint all but two cabinet members from National Assembly members.

National legislature

The bicameral legislature consists of the National Assembly with 400 seats of which members are directly elected in multi-seat constituencies by proportional representation vote. Half of the members are elected proportionally from 9 provincial lists and the remaining half from national lists so as to maintain proportionality.

The National Council of Provinces (NCOP) reviews and aligns national legislation that affects the provinces. Each of the nine provinces has a delegation of 10 members (six permanent and four special) headed by the premier of the province. Permanent delegates are members of parliament (MPs); special delegates are provincial legates, who may be recalled by their provinces at any time. Ten representatives of organised local governments also serve but may not vote.

Both institutions serve for five-year terms.

Legal system

Based on Roman-Dutch law and the constitution.

An anti-prejudice law was passed in 2000.

Last elections

7 May 2014 (presidential); 7 May 2014 (parliamentary)

Results: Presidential: Jacob Zuma (ANC) was elected by the National Assembly unopposed.

Parliamentary: ANC won 62.15 per cent (249 seats, out of up to 400); Democratic Alliance (DA) 22.23 per cent (89); Economic Freedom Fighters 6.35 per cent (25); Inkatha Freedom Party (IFP) 2.45 per cent (10); National Freedom Party 1.57 per cent (6); United Democratic Movement 1.00 per cent (4); seven other parties won less than 1.00 per cent each. Turnout was 73.50 per cent.

Next elections

May 2019 (presidential and parliamentary)

Political parties

Ruling party

African National Congress (ANC) (since 1994; re-elected 7 May 2014)

Main opposition party

Democratic Alliance (DA). In August 2010 the DA announced it would unite with the Independent Democrats (ID). ID municipal officials will join the DA after the 2011 local elections; provincial and national legislators will join after the 2014 general election.

Population

52.98 million (2013)* According to the 2011 census, the racial mix of South Africa was 41,000,938 defined themselves as black, 5,586,838 defined themselves as white and 1,286,930 defined themselves as Indian or Asian. The median age for all South Africans was 25 years, but for black South Africans it was 21 years.

Last census: 9 October 2011: 51,770,560 (preliminary results)

Population density: 35 inhabitants per square km. Urban population 62 per cent (2010 Unicef).

Annual growth rate: 1.5 per cent, 1990–2010 (Unicef).

Ethnic make-up

Black (75 per cent), white (13 per cent), coloured (9 per cent), Asian (3 per cent).

Religions

Christian (68 per cent), Islam (2 per cent), Hindu 1.5 per cent, indigenous beliefs and animist 28.5 per cent.

Education

Public expenditure on education amounts to 5.5 per cent of GDP.

Primary education begins at age six and lasts for six years. Junior secondary school lasts until age 15 when students may choose between an academic programme lasting a further three years at a senior secondary school or a vocational, technical course lasting two years in technical schools.

Government strategy for national schooling includes higher qualified teachers appointed to poorer schools and equalising school expenditure for all racial groups.

Literacy rate: 86 per cent adult rate; 92 per cent youth rate (15–24) (Unesco 2005).

Compulsory years: Six to 15

Enrolment rate: 133 per cent gross primary enrolment of relevant age group (including repeaters); 95 per cent gross secondary enrolment (World Bank).

Pupils per teacher: 45 in primary schools.

Health

There are major national programmes in operation including the Integrated Nutrition Programme, the Polio and Measles Immunisation Campaign and Telemedicine (an interactive medical exchange based on information technology).

A R40 million (US$4.6 million) protocol signed between South Africa, Swaziland and Mozambique to control the spread of malaria lays the basis for a common programme of action in these countries.

HIV/Aids

South Africa has one of the highest HIV/Aids infection rates in the world, an estimated 5.6 million people are HIV positive, which has the largest number of individuals living with the virus in a single country. A study of HIV/Aids infection rates, published in 2009, revealed that the rate had levelled off at 10.9 per cent for those aged two-years and older. Typically, those worst effected are women between the ages of 20–34 at 33 per cent HIV-positive. This trend suggests there will be noticeably fewer mid-adult women than men by 2020. By 2009 deaths by Aids-related illness were expected to exceed all other causes of death. The use of condoms has increased sharply. Government policy was changed from April 2010, following an announcement by President Zuma in 2009 in which he said that all babies less than one year old, if tested HIV positive, would be treated with anti-retroviral (ARV) drugs. Around 59,000 infants are born with HIV each year in South Africa. The level of infection in 2009 did not increase although the level of deaths from Aids is expect to rise up to 2014 as long-term patients succumb to the disease.

With a change in government policy since 2008, the number of people receiving ARV medication has doubled to 1.5 million by 2011; another one million will receive ARVs by 2014. In 2011, 10.6 per cent of the population were living with HIV (5.38 million) and there were 2.1 million Aids orphans. Around one-third of all children, an estimated 5.7 million, may lose one or both parents to Aids by 2015. The treatment to prevent mother-to-child transmission had expanded so that in 2011, 95 per cent of infected pregnant women received ARVs, up from 30 per cent in 2007. Free circumcision, which reduces the risk of transmission by up to 60 per cent, according to state health facilities, coupled with a decrease since 2009 in the number of new infections, may indicate that young people are changing their sexual behaviour.

Former president Nelson Mandela publicly announced that his son had died of Aids, in 2005, saying, 'Let us give publicity to HIV/Aids and not hide it, because the only way of making it appear to be a normal illness, just like TB, like cancer, is always to come out and say somebody has died because of HIV.' In 2004, Inkatha opposition leader, Mangosuthu Buthelezi, had announced that his son had also died of Aids.

South Africa is still in the process of addressing the deprivation wrought on black communities during the apartheid era including, poverty, poor primary healthcare, minimal education and families fractured by migratory work. The South African pharmaceutical company, Aspen, was granted approval by US regulators to manufacture and supply ARV drugs for domestic patients.

HIV prevalence: 21.5 per cent, aged 15–49 years

5.3 million adults and children living with HIV

27.9 per cent pregnant women (attending antenatal services) HIV positive

2.9 million women living with HIV

370,000 Aids deaths (adults and children) in 2003

(UNAids estimates, end 2003)

Life expectancy: 48 years, 2004 (WHO 2006)

Fertility rate/Maternal mortality rate: 2.5 births per woman, 2010 (Unicef)

Birth rate/Death rate: 18.9 births per 1,000 population; 18.4 deaths per 1,000 population (2003).

Population data issued by South Africa's Medical Research Council in March 2004 recorded a 44 per cent increase in adult deaths between 1998–2003, after population growth and improved registration had been factored in; deaths of women 20–49 increased by 168 per cent. It was concluded that this growth was due to Aids.

Child (under 5 years) mortality rate (per 1,000): 45 per 1,000 live births (WHO 2012)

Head of population per physician: 0.77 physicians per 1,000 people, 2004 (WHO 2006)

Welfare

The social assistance programme of the Department of Social Development provides benefits to approximately three million people comprising the elderly, persons with disabilities and children under the age of seven years. The government has emphasised the need to transform expensive institutional services into a more self-reliant approach towards individual and community care. Access to welfare grants is, however, limited. The State Maintenance Grants have been phased out and the availability of services for victims of violence across the country remains equally limited. Lack of an integrated approach towards allocations, capacity to spend and monitor the funds are some of the key problems relating to the distribution of poverty relief funds.

Main cities

Pretoria (Tswane Municipal Municipality is the central area) (capital, estimated population, 1.8 million (m) in 2012), Cape Town (Kaapstad (in Afrikaans) and iKapa (in Xhosa)) (legislative capital, 3.8m), Durban (eThekwini) (3.7m), Johannesburg (financial capital 2.1m), Soweto (1.9m), Port Elizabeth (1.3m), Pietermaritzburg (1.0m), Benoni (667,952), Welkom (667,288), Boemfontein (judicial capital, 664,821).

Languages spoken

Official language/s

Afrikaans, English, Ndebele, Sesotho, Northern Sotho, SiSwati, Tsonga, Tswana, Venda, Xhosa, Zulu.

Media

Two moves in late 2010, a Media Appeals Tribunal being considered by the ANC and a protection of information bill going through parliament, have alarmed the local media. A statement by 37 editors in August 2010 say that the moves will restrict freedom of speech and expression as set out in the constitution. The tribunal will have the power to judge complaints made against print media while the bill would give ministers and officials powers to classify information as secret if they consider it to be 'in the national interest'.

Press

Press freedom is guaranteed by the constitution. The Freedom of Commercial Speech Trust plays an important role in industry self-regulation, forestalling government intervention.

Dailies: Newspapers published in major cities may be available throughout the country as reflect national and local news. News 24 (www.news24.com) is a media organisation that has a number of Afrikaans titles: *Die Burger*, *Volksblad*, *Rapport*, *Jou Geldsaka*, *Sondag*, and *NetAfrikaans* among others.

From Cape Town, in English, *Cape Argus* (www.capeargus.co.za), the *Cape Times* (www.capetimes.co.za), and in Afrikaans *Die Burger* (www.dieburger.com).

From Johannesburg, in English, *The Times* (www.thetimes.co.za), which includes a business section and *Sunday Times*, *Citizen* (www.citizen.co.za), *The Star* (www.thestar.co.za) and *Sowetan* (www.sowetan.co.za). In Chinese *China Express* (www.sa-cnet.com) and *China News* (www.chinanews.co.za).

From Pretoria, in English, *Pretoria News* (www.pretorianews.co.za), *Society News* (www.societynews.co.za) and in Afrikaans *Rekord* (www.rekord.co.za).

From Durban, in English, *Daily News* (www.dailynews.co.za) and *Post* (www.thepost.co.za) (with Indian sections), in Zulu *Isolezwe* (www.isolezwe.co.za) and *Ilanga* (www.ilanganews.co.za).

Weeklies: In English, *Daily Mail & Guardian* (www.mg.co.za), is the leading independent newspaper, *The Sunday Tribune* (ww.sundaytribune.co.za), *Sunday Independent* (www.sunday.co.za), *Sunday World* (www.sundayworld.co.za) and *Weekend Post* (www.weekendpost.co.za). In Afrikaans *Landbou Weekblad* (www.landbou.com).

Business: Publications, in English, include *Business Day* (www.businessday.co.za) *Financial Mail* (http://free.financialmail.co.za), *Cape Business News* (www.cbn.co.za), *Business Report* (www.busrep.co.za), *Guateng Business* www.news24.com/Gauteng_Business/Home) and in Afrikaans *Sake* (www.news24.com/Sake/Home). *Personal Finance* (www.persfin.co.za) covers financial and investment issues. *Destiny* (www.mydestinymag.com) is a business magazine aimed at women

Broadcasting

The South African Broadcasting Corporation (SABC) is the state-owned national broadcaster.

Radio: There are numerous commercial radio stations particularly located around cities and large towns. Services are broadcast in various languages particular to local language spoken in the locale. SABC operates 20 regional and national services in 11 languages and an external radio service broadcasting in short wave to the African continent.

Other major commercial stations include SA FM (www.safm.co.za), East Coast Radio (www.ecr.co.za), Jacaranda FM (www.jacarandafm.com), Cape Talk (www.capetalk.co.za) and Radio Algoa (www.radioalgoa.com).

Television: SABC operates three national channels and two pay-to-view channels. Commercial stations with free-to-air television includes e.tv (www.etv.co.za) and pay-to-view M-Net (www.mnet.co.za) showing many internationally made programmes.

During an election period the media is monitored by the Independent Media Commission.

SAPA (South African Press Association)

National news agency: PO Box 7766, Cotswold House, Greenacres Office Park, Cnr Victory & Rustenburg Roads, Victory Park, Johannesburg, 2000 (tel: 782-1600; fax: 782-1587/8; email: comms@sapa.org.za; internet: www.sapa.org.za).

Economy

The South African economy is modern, diverse and open, with well-developed sectors in mining, agriculture, manufacturing and services. The economy is largely based on the country's abundant mineral and energy resources. Manufacturing is underpinned by the mining sector while gold and diamonds dominate exports.

Foreign investors are attracted by the country's robust infrastructure, with developed transport, water and electricity networks. Dams have been built on the rivers and provide water for irrigation, industrial and household use. The professional services are well developed while the stock exchange is ranked as world class.

However, there is an imbalance in society with the top 20 per cent holding over 65 per cent of the country's wealth, and an underclass of poor, often unemployed people who live in townships, where the bottom 20 per cent hold less than 4.0 per cent of the country's wealth. The GINI index was last reported by the World Bank to be 65 in 2012.

The uneven distribution of wealth in South Africa is a result of its historically segregated society and although there has been a concerted effort to produce a more equitable structure the economy is still split largely between the affluent white minority and the poorer black majority. Whites still own large tracts of fertile land and direct most of the industry and service sectors – the ANC-led government has tried to address this through the Black Economic Empowerment (BEE) law that requires not only black employment but also their fostering and promotion within companies and organisations. The lack of training during the apartheid period has led to a lack of black managers and executives. Many major employers now have courses or back scholarships to redress the situation. Another aspect of BEE is black ownership of shares in companies, which has led to some criticism that only cronies of the ruling ANC are benefiting.

In 2014, the UN Human Development Index (HDI) ranked South Africa 118 (out of 187) for national development in health, education and income. Poverty dropped heavily over the period 2006–12 reaching lows of 20.2 per cent of the population in extreme poverty and 45.5 per cent in moderate poverty. Remittances from migrant workers amounted to US$913 million (0.3 per cent of GDP) in 2014. South Africa is ranked 138th of 149 countries for its ability to turn the wealth of the country into well-being for its population.

The economy of South Africa picked up in 2010, along with global trade, so that GDP growth climbed to 2.9 per cent before increasing to 3.1 per cent in 2011. However in 2012 growth had fallen back to 2.2 per cent and remained at this rate in 2013. This fell to 1.5 per cent in 2014. Only 2 per cent growth is expected in 2015 when the economy needs to expand by at least 5 per cent a year to reduce unemployment.

The weak economy is stoking social unrest and public violence. Foreigners, seen as competition for scarce jobs, were targeted in a recent spate of xenophobic attacks that left at least seven people dead.

Inflation in 2013 had risen to 5.4 per cent before falling to 5.2 per cent in 2014.

Unemployment is pervasive across the economy, reaching 24.9 per cent in 2014 and is forecast to rise to around 27 per cent for 2015.

The service sector constitutes 68 per cent of GDP, agriculture 2.5 per cent and industry 29.5 per cent, of which manufacturing accounts for 13 per cent. South Africa's tourism sector has expanded considerably since the end of the apartheid era but it still has a way to go before reaching its full potential.

The government has many social problems to tackle and has increased spending on public services including a commitment to provide antiretroviral (ARV) treatment to all those who require it. In 2011, 10.6 per cent of the population was living with HIV (5.38 million) and there were 2.1 million Aids orphans. By 2013, 1.5 million HIV-positive people and 95 per cent of infected pregnant women were receiving ARVs. In 2014 it was reported that 18.9 per cent of adults aged 15 to 49 had the disease. 6.8 million have been diagnosed as HIV-positive in South Africa.

In February 2012, De Beers, the world's largest diamond mining company, announced that its trading division had had its second highest ever sales, amounting to US$6.5 billion, a rise of 27 per cent on the 2010 level, due to what it called 'exceptional consumer demand growth'. China was the principal purchaser of De Beer's branded jewellery, with new stores opening up in Beijing, Tianjin, Dalian and a second store in Hong Kong. Sales rose by 3 per cent in 2014 to an all-time high. De Beer reported sales of over US$85 billion in 2014.

External trade

South Africa is a member of the Southern African Development Community (SADC), the objectives of which include reducing trade barriers, achieving regional development and economic growth and evolving common systems and institutions. Its currency, the rand, is also legal tender throughout the Common Monetary Area (CMA) (Swaziland, Lesotho and Namibia).

With its immense mineral wealth, South Africa is the world's leading exporter of gold and platinum. It is also one of the leading world producers of diamonds, wine, railroad rolling stock, mining equipment and synthetic fuels. Exports provide almost 50 per cent of GDP and world commodity prices strongly affect the balance of trade.

Imports

Principal imports are machinery and equipment, vehicles, petroleum and natural gas, chemicals, scientific instruments and foodstuffs.

Main sources: China (15.5 per cent of total in 2014), Germany (10 per cent), Saudi Arabia (7.2 per cent)

Exports

Principal exports are gold (around 20 per cent of total), diamonds, metals and metal products, minerals, machinery and equipment. Other major exports are granite, asbestos, iron, manganese, chrome and titanium ore.

Main destinations: China (9.5 per cent of total in 2014), US (7.1 per cent), Japan (5.3 per cent)

Agriculture

Farming

The original Natives Land Act of 1913 restricted black people from buying or renting land in 'white South Africa', leading to the forced removals of black people. With the end of apartheid in 1994, the ANC government promised to return 30 per cent of this land to its previous owners by 2014. However, by 2013 only 7.5 per cent of the land had been returned. Lack of skill transference and capital to sustain the farms has proven to be a problem.

South African agriculture is open to market forces and farmers take responsibility for production decisions, and pricing and distribution. The country has achieved self-sufficiency in staple grains, such as maize and wheat, and basic foodstuffs such as fresh milk and other dairy products, meat, vegetables and fruit. The sector employs over 10 per cent of the workforce.

LandCare is a key community support programme in the National Department of Agriculture, which aims to promote sustainable land management practices and prevent land degradation in rural areas. The government policy of forging partnerships to stimulate black empowerment is growing within the agricultural sector. Land reforms to enable black farmers' access to quality land has proven to be slow however. The controversial land reform bill was postponed in 2008. Government says that it still wants to redistribute around a third of white owned farmland. South Africa has about 33 per cent of the southern hemisphere's deciduous fruit market in Europe. After minerals and metals, deciduous fruit is the country's largest export industry. The wine industry yields significant indirect benefits for the economy as a major employer and exporter. However, growth and competitiveness in the wine and tobacco industries is likely to be hampered by higher excise duty.

A recent drought has damaged the agricultural performance within the nation.

Fishing

The general policy towards fisheries has been the protection of marine ecology and the promotion and sustained utilisation of the sea and its resources.

South Africa is largely self-sufficient in white fish and has a substantial export surplus and it is self-sufficient in canned fish. Some 10 per cent of the abalone yield and 25 per cent of rock lobster are marketed locally and the rest is exported, mainly to the Far East. Cultivation of oysters and mussels is growing steadily and the possibility of cultivating abalone is being researched.

Of domestic fishmeal demand of 260,000 tonnes per year (tpy), 60,000tpy is locally produced and the rest is imported.

Fishing quotas for foreign vessels are issued in terms of formal bilateral fisheries agreements. Of all the quota fish caught in South Africa's exclusive fishing zone (200 nautical miles offshore), foreign catches make up only 2.4 per cent. The figure does not include non-quota species such as tuna. Foreign boats are allocated quotas for hake, hose mackerel and squid.

Forestry

About 7 per cent of the total land area is forested, with forest cover estimated at 8.9 million hectares (ha). About 27 per cent of the total land area is wooded. The country has extensive forest plantations and a large network of more than 200 protected areas covering nearly 5 per cent of the forest areas, including around 20 national parks. Deforestation accounts for around 1 per cent per annum or the equivalent of 8,000ha of forest cover. Government policy has focussed on making South Africa self-sufficient in wood and wood products, taking into account the country's limited water supply and scarcity of suitable habitats. Industrial roundwood is produced in large quantities. The forestry industry is dependent on resources available from plantations and produces a wide range of wood and paper products. Although it produces and exports pulp and paper, significant volumes of paper are also imported. The forestry sector contributes around 1 per cent of GDP.

Industry and manufacturing

South Africa is one of Africa's most industrialised countries and enjoys a strong resource base. Most of the raw materials and semi-manufactured goods required by industry are available from local sources. Only clothing and textiles, furniture (hardwoods), chemicals and transport equipment (components) still rely to a lesser extent on imports of raw materials or intermediate goods. Engineering and metallic products dominate the output of the country. Leading South African steel companies include Iscor and Highveld Steel.

Other major growth areas are automobile production and the chemical industry. Although food and tobacco processing remain of great importance, their share of total output has fallen significantly. Food products, iron, steel, and transport equipment, account for about a third of the total gross manufacturing output. Other manufactures include paper and paper products, fabricated metal products, electrical and non-electrical machinery.

Industrial policy in the apartheid era had a dual focus: the need to increase value-added manufacturing to reduce dependence on commodity exports and the quest for self-sufficiency to overcome international political isolation.

The slow growth in manufacturing output in the late 1980s was largely attributable to the fall in world demand, low levels of capacity utilisation, reduced investment and disinvestment by foreign companies and labour problems.

Power shortages under Eskom, the failing state utility, have dampened manufacturing. Power cuts are plunging households and businesses into darkness several times a week.

Under President Thabo Mbeki, who was elected in mid-1999, the government has pursued a neo-liberal economic programme — Growth, Employment and Redistribution (Gear) — which is wedded to monetarism, privatisation, free trade and increasing foreign investment. This has involved the restructuring of South African industry, including the rationalisation of the workforce, and increased involvement of the private sector, including foreign investors.

So far the government of President Jacob Zuma has shown little sign of being able to improve matters within the country. The African National Congress, the ruling party, is bogged down in internal political battles, not least over whether to pursue capitalist or socialist economics. The government's National Development Plan, a market-friendly strategy to encourage investment and growth, is largely ignored.

Tourism

South Africa offers a full range of holiday destinations and activities, combining European standards of accommodation with an economic price tag that has encouraged an increasing number of visitors from BRIC and other emerging market countries. There are eight sites included on Unesco's World Heritage List, including a prehistoric site, two cultural landscapes and Robbin Island, as well as several natural sites including the Drakensberg Park.

Travel and tourism contributed 9.4 per cent of GDP in 2014, which is forecast to rise 4.3 per cent per annum to 2025. The industry provides employment to 9.9 per cent of the workforce (1.5 million jobs), and in 2015 this is expected rise 3.6 per cent.

There are four different inter-city rail services, which offer a variety of travel experiences, with sleeping berths for longer journeys, plus suburban trains and rail services to neighbouring countries.

Environment

In February 2008 South Africa announced that for the first time in 13 years it would begin a cull of elephants in a measure to control their numbers and reduce the impact that large herds have on the natural environment, other wildlife and human crops and habitation.

Mining

South Africa is the world's foremost producer and exporter of gold and platinum, and a significant exporter of diamonds, iron ore, asbestos, manganese ore, vanadium, ferro-chromium, chrome ore and granite.

At least 40 per cent of the world's total recoverable gold reserves are in South Africa. Precious metals' producers will also be required to refine more of their output locally to provide more metals for South African design and manufacturing.

The government has begun plans to introduce a state diamond trader company and producers such as UK-based, diamond company De Beers (founded in South Africa and the world's leading diamond trading company) would be required to forward a percentage of rough diamonds intended for export to the new Diamond Exchange and Export Centre (DEEC) for cutting and polishing by local craftsmen.

The mining sector only accounts for 6 per cent of GDP and South Africa sees value added diamond and gold processing as a source of added revenue and employment. The mining sector employs 6 per cent of the country's labour force and contributes up to one-third of the export revenue.

Hydrocarbons

South Africa relies mainly on imports to meet oil demand. Most comes from the Middle East, chiefly Iran and Saudi Arabia. To reduce a dependency on this region South Africa has agreements with Angola, Equatorial Guinea and Nigeria for oil supplies, which are either consumed locally or refined for export to regional southern Africa, East Africa and the Indian sub-continent.

PetroSA is responsible for managing the country's petroleum industry's commercial assets. South Africa has Africa's second largest refinery system (after Egypt), with a capacity of over 500,000bpd, producing high-octane petroleum, distillates, kerosene and alcohols. In 2012 Transnet Pipelines began construction of 19 electric motor-driven pumps and pumping stations along a 712km pipeline to transport diesel, petrol and jet fuel from Durban to the inland Guateng region.

There has been much investment in synthetic fuels and South Africa is the world's largest producer of oil from coal. Around 36 per cent of South Africa's liquid fuels are synthetically produced by the Sasol Company from a mix of low-grade coal and small quantities of natural gas, sourced either locally or from Mozambique.

Coal is South Africa's primary fuel and provides a significant source of foreign exchange. Most of South Africa's reserves are bituminous, with 45 per cent ash content and only one per cent sulphur content. Around 70 per cent of the recoverable reserves are located in three fields – Waterberg, Witbank and Highveld.

Energy

South Africa's energy sector is critical to its economy, as the country relies heavily on its large-scale, energy-intensive coal mining industry. Most of the oil consumed in the country, used mainly in the transportation sector, is imported from Middle East and West African producers in the Organization of the Petroleum Exporting Countries (OPEC) and is locally refined. South Africa's upstream oil and natural gas sectors are dominated by the state-owned company Petroleum Oil and Gas Corporation of South Africa (PetroSA),

Total installed generating capacity was 44.3 gigawatts (GW) in 2014, almost 32 per cent of the total electricity generated on the continent of Africa. Energy provides around 15 per cent of GDP. South Africa exports electricity to Botswana, Lesotho, Mozambique, Namibia, Swaziland and Zimbabwe.

The self-financing state energy company, Eskom, has an installed generating capacity of about 41.2GW and produces around 95 per cent of the country's total electricity with the balance made up by mines, industry and municipalities with their own small stations. It is responsible for generation, distribution and sales of electricity. However only a third of the population has access to the national grid; this has grown since 1990 as 3.5 million homes have been electrified and in 2012 over 85 per cent of the population had access. It operates 17 coal-fired power stations, two hydroelectric, two pumped storage schemes, two gas turbine stations and the country's only nuclear power plant, at Koeberg. The largest generating stations are in Mpumalanga province, adjacent to vast coal reserves.

Eskom is the fourth-largest power company in the world by capacity and is being restructured with a view to eventual privatisation.

Due to severe shortages of electricity, through demand outstripping supply, the government has implemented a rapid programme of expansion of the electricity infrastructure by independent power producers. This included two new coal-fired power stations, which were due to come on-stream in 2013 but as of 2014 had not been built. The 2,000MW nuclear power station is likely to remain the only nuclear facility for some time, but proposals for a new one are under consideration. Three obsolete power stations will be upgraded and re-opened at a cost of US$1.96 billion.

An industry study in 2013 found that in order to supply power plants that are at risk of running short of the fuel as soon as 2015, the country would need to invest as much as US$9 billion. It won't be enough to increase production at existing mines, the majority will need to be met by opening new mines.

Financial markets

Stock exchange

JSE Securities Exchange (JSE)

Banking and insurance

The financial services sector has changed rapidly since South Africa re-entered the global economy in the 1990s. Domestic banks have restructured and foreign banks compete fiercely in the commercial sector.

The South African Reserve Bank (SARB) (central bank) supervises the domestic and international activities of banks, discount houses and building societies. It issues the country's currency and is the custodian of South Africa's gold and foreign exchange reserves. It is responsible for the implementation of monetary policy which it formulates in conjunction with the finance ministry.

In May 2005, the UK's third largest bank, Barclays, purchased a 60 per cent share in South Africa's third largest, Absa. Bought for R33 billion (US$5.2 billion) it was the single largest foreign investment deal since apartheid ended.

Central bank

South African Reserve Bank (SARB)

Main financial centre

Johannesburg

Time

GMT plus two hours

Geography

South Africa occupies the southern extremity of the African continent. It is bordered by Namibia to the north-west, by Botswana and Zimbabwe to the north, by Mozambique to the north-east, and by Swaziland to the east; Lesotho is a 30,000 square km country isolated within South Africa's territory.

South Africa's coastline stretches over 2,500km from the Namibian border on the Atlantic coast in the west, around the Cape of Good Hope to the Mozambique border on the Indian Ocean coast in the east. The land along the coast is low-lying but quickly rises to mountainous escarpments that separate it from the high plateau of the interior. The highest region in South Africa is the Drakensberg Mountains in the east, which also straddle the border with Lesotho. Njesuthi is South Africa's tallest peak at 3,408 metres (m),

although the Drakensberg's highest mountain is Thabana Ntlenyana (3,482m) in Lesotho.
The Kalahari desert in the north-east border region with Namibia and Botswana stretches for 900,000 square km. Much of the central plane is grassland and *veld* (savannah) that stretches to the coast in the east and is flanked in the west by highlands.

Hemisphere
Southern

Climate
There are regional variations due to relative elevations. The Cape coastal area is warm and temperate throughout the year with temperature ranges in Cape Town between 13–20 degrees Celsius (C); inland Pretoria and other high *veld* areas have temperature ranges of 13–22 degrees C and Johannesburg, slightly lower 11–19 degrees C. On the Natal coast humidity can be high during the summer, while the winters are drier with temperatures in Durban 17–24 degrees C. The highest temperatures are recorded in the Kalahari desert and the coldest are recorded in the remote Roggeveld Mountains in the west; the Drakensberg Mountains have snow on their peaks in winter.

Entry requirements
Passports
Required by all and must be valid for 30 days beyond date of departure.
Visa
Are not required by nationals listed at www.southafricahouse.com under *Home Affairs* then *Visa exempt countries* then *foreign citizens* then *Visas*, lastly see *Who needs a visa*. All other nationals must apply to the nearest South African consulate, see www.home-affairs.gov.za/forms.asp for a visa application form; visas must be applied for before arrival. A proposed tourist *univisa* (a single visa to visit all 15-member states of SADC: Angola, Botswana, DRC, Lesotho, Madagascar, Malawi, Mauritius, Mozambique, Namibia, South Africa, Seychelles, Swaziland, Tanzania, Zambia and Zimbabwe) is expected to be in use by 2013. Visitors should check with the appropriate consulates to confirm start of *univisas* and their scope before beginning a tour of southern Africa.
Business travellers should contact a South African consulate for further information.
All visitors must have proof of return/onward passage, and may have to show evidence of sufficient funds for the intended stay.
Currency advice/regulations
Import of local currency is limited to R5,000 and export to R500 per person. Import of foreign currency is unlimited but must be declared; export is limited to the amount declared.
Travellers cheques (in major currencies) are widely accepted.
Customs
Personal items are duty-free.
Prohibited imports
Illegal drugs, pornography, firearms, ammunition, flick-knives and explosives.
Meat, dairy products and processed cheeses.
Plants and plant materials, honey, margarine and vetegable oils require an import permit.

Health (for visitors)
Mandatory precautions
Yellow fever vaccination certificate required if travelling from infected areas, (certificates are not valid until 10 days after immunisation).
Advisable precautions
Vaccinations are necessary for typhoid and hepatitis A and B; vaccination for hepatitis A is advisable. To avoid the risk of bilharzia, only use well-maintained, chlorinated swimming pools. Malaria exists throughout the year in certain areas of northern Transvaal, eastern low veld and northern Natal; prophylaxis should be taken for visits to these areas. Water precautions should be taken in rural areas.
HIV/Aids is prevalent.

Hotels
A wide choice is available in main commercial centres. It is advisable to make reservations well in advance, especially during December and January, March and April.

Credit cards
Major credit and charge cards are widely accepted. ATMs are widely available.

Public holidays (national)
Fixed dates
1 Jan (New Year's Day), 21 Mar (Human Rights Day), 27 Apr (Freedom Day), 1 May (Worker's Day), 16 Jun (Youth Day), 9 Aug (National Women's Day), 24 Sep (Heritage Day), 16 Dec (Reconciliation Day), 25 Dec (Christmas Day), 26 Dec (Day of Goodwill).
Holidays that fall on Sunday are taken on Monday.
Variable dates
Good Friday, Family Day (on Easter Monday) (Mar/Apr)

Working hours
Banking
Mon–Fri: 0830–1530; Sat: 0830–1100. Some banks have extended hours.
Business
Mon–Fri: 0730/0830–1600/1700. Some businesses have extended hours.
Government
Mon–Fri: 0730/0830–1600/1700.
Shops
Mon–Fri: 0830–1700; Sat: 0830–1300. Certain shops are open on Sundays.

Telecommunications
Mobile/cell phones
There are GSM roaming facilities available, with coverage throughout most of the country.

Electricity supply
Usually 220/230V AC, but 220/250V in Port Elizabeth and 250V in Pretoria.

Social customs/useful tips
There are no particular taboos, but visitors should be mindful that in certain parts of the country strong racist attitudes still prevail. It is best not to get involved in political discussions.
Visitors should not photograph security institutions.

Security
Visitors should avoid visiting black townships without guidance from reliable local residents and without a trustworthy companion. Certain townships in the Pretoria-Witwatersrand-Vereeniging region and around the Cape Town, Durban and Pietermaritzburg regions should be avoided unless a visit is absolutely necessary – notably Thokoza, Sebokeng, Alexandra, Boipatong, Katlehong, Langa, Mitchell's Plain, Gugulethu, Khayelitsha, Crossroads, KwaMashu and Mpumulanga.
Periodic attacks on visitors to townships have occurred and the crime rate has soared as unemployment and politically-related violence have increased.
Street crime is less of a problem in major urban areas, though care must be taken in central Johannesburg at night. Care must also be taken when visiting extreme right-wing strongholds such as Ventersdorp in the Western Transvaal. It is advisable not to carry unnecessary valuables, expensive jewellery and large amounts of money.
Crime in Johannesburg continues to escalate. Do not resist if confronted. Avoid walking in the streets alone after shopping. Use taxis at night and only those booked through a reputable hotel or among those listed in the official Johannesburg guide. Keep car doors locked while you are in the vehicle or when it is parked. If you are driving after dark, keep car doors locked and avoid slowing down.

Getting there
Air
National airline: South African Airways
International airport/s: OR Tambo International Airport (name changed from Johannesburg Intenational (JNB) in October 2006), serves as a hub for flights to

other countries in the region. It is 24km from city, duty-free shop, bar, restaurant, bank, post office, shops, car hire; Cape Town International (CPT), 22km east of city, duty-free shop, car hire, bank, bar and restaurant; Durban International (DUR), 16km from city, duty-free shop, car hire, bank, bar and restaurant. Taxis and buses serve all airports.

Other airport/s: Bloemfontein (BFN), 10km east of the city; Port Elizabeth (PLZ), 25km from the city.

Airport tax: None

Surface

Road: Possible from Botswana, Lesotho, Namibia, Swaziland, Zimbabwe and Mozambique. Travellers are generally advised to check regulations and conditions regarding entry by road with the Automobile Association of South Africa.

The Maputo Corridor project includes a link from the Atlantic coast at Namibia's Walvis Bay across the Kalahari desert to join the South African road network, linking the western side of southern Africa with the Indian Ocean at Maputo, Mozambique. There is a toll road between Witbank in South Africa and Maputo.

Rail: There are services from Mozambique, Botswana, Zimbabwe and Namibia.

Water: Cruise ships call at some Indian Ocean islands.

Main port/s: Cape Town, Durban, Port Elizabeth and East London.

Getting about

National transport

Air: All major cities and towns are linked with regular, scheduled services. South African Airways, InterAir and Airlink fly domestic routes.

Road: Extensive network of tarred roads, including 51,000km linking main centres. There is a further 130,000km of untarred roads – some of the remoter sections can become impassable in wet weather.

Buses: Inter-city services are operated by Greyhound, Citiliner and other private companies. Vehicles are a good standard.

Rail: Network of some 24,000km with good services throughout the country. Reservations for express trains should be made well in advance. Two classes available, but visitors are advised to travel first class. Most long distance mainline trains have restaurant cars and all have sleeping accommodation (*couchettes* operated in both first- and second-class).

Named services include: Blue Train, a luxury service, running three times a week (Pretoria-Johannesburg-Cape Town; with sleeping accommodation, restaurant cars, air-conditioning, suites, staterooms available); Trans Orange, once a week (Durban-Cape Town); Trans Natal, daily (Durban-Johannesburg). The O R Tembo International Airport to central Johannesburg section of the Guatrain was opened on 10 June 2010, just in time for the start of the World Cup. The remaining 50km to Pretoria is scheduled for completion in 2011.

City transport

Taxis: Widely available in all towns. Taxis cannot be hailed in the street but must be booked or called from a rank. Fares within a city depend on distance and time, while longer distance fares are lower and should be agreed in advance. A 10 per cent tip is usual.

Buses, trams & metro: There are exstensive bus networks in all main towns. Fares in Cape Town and Johannesburg are zonal, with payment in cash or with ten-ride pre-purchase 'clipcards' from kiosks. In Pretoria there are various pre-purchase ticket systems. In Durban conventional buses vie for passengers with minibuses and combi-taxis (both legal and illegal); also found in other South African towns. Although cheap and very fast, they should be used with care.

Trains: There are frequent local trains in the Cape Town and Pretoria and Johannesburg urban areas. All trains have first- and second-class accommodation.

Car hire

Self-drive and chauffeur-driven cars are widely available. An international driving licence is required unless visitor's national licence carries the photograph and signature of the holder.

Driving is on the left. Speed limits: built-up areas 60kph; country roads 100kph; declared freeways and some main roads 120kph. Heavy fines for speeding.

BUSINESS DIRECTORY

The addresses listed below are a selection only. While World of Information makes every endeavour to check these addresses, we cannot guarantee that changes have not been made, especially to telephone numbers and area codes. We would welcome any corrections.

Telephone area codes

The international dialling code (IDD) for South Africa is +27, followed by area code and subscriber's number:

Bloemfontein	51	Ladysmith	361
Cape Town	21	Pietermaritzburg	331
Durban	31	Port Elizabeth	41
Johannesburg	11	Pretoria	12

Chambers of Commerce

American Chamber of Commerce, 60 Fifth Street, PO Box 1132, Houghton 2041, Johannesburg (tel: 788-0265; fax: 880-1632; e-mail: administrator@amcham.co.za).

Bloemfontein Chamber of Business, 37 Kellner Street, PO Box 87, Bloemfontein 9300 (tel: 447-3368; fax: 447-5064; e-mail:bcci@intekom.co.za).

Cape Town Regional Chamber of Commerce and Industry, 19 Louis Gradner Street, PO Box 204, Cape Town 8000 (tel: 402-4300; fax: 402-4302; e-mail: info@capechamber.co.za).

Durban Chamber of Commerce & Industry, 190 Stanger Street, PO Box 1506, Durban 4000 (tel: 335-1000; fax: 332-1288; e-mail: chamber@durbanchamber.co.za).

Johannesburg Chamber of Commerce and Industry, Private Bag 34, Corner Empire Road and Owl Street, Auckland Park 2006, Johannesburg (tel: 726-5300; fax: 782-2000; e-mail: info@jcci.co.za).

Ladysmith Chamber of Commerce and Industry, PO Box 7, Ladysmith 3370 (tel: 631-0541; fax: 637-4407; e-mail: lcci@futurenet.co.za).

Pietermaritzburg Chamber of Business, Royal Show Grounds, Commercial Road, PO Box 11734, Dorpspruit 3206, Pietermaritzburg (tel: 345-2747; fax: 394-4151; e-mail: pcb@futurenet.co.za).

Port Elizabeth Regional Chamber of Commerce and Industry, 22 Grahamstown Road, PO Box 2221, North End 6056, Port Elizabeth (tel: 484-4430; fax: 487-1851; e-mail: info@pechamber.org.za).

Pretoria Chamber of Commerce and Industry, 852 Park Street, PO Box 40653, Arcadia 0007, Pretoria (tel: 342-3236; fax: 342-1486; e-mail: pcci@mweb.co.za).

South African Chamber of Business, 24 Sturdee Avenue, PO Box 213, Saxonwold 2132, Johannesburg (tel: 446-3800; fax: 446-3847; e-mail: info@sacob.co.za).

Banking

Absa Bank Ltd, 2nd Floor, ABSA Towers North, 180 Commissioner Street, Johannesburg 2001 (tel: 350-4000; fax: 350-3768).

International Bank of Southern Africa Ltd, 3rd Floor, Sunnyside Ridge Bldg, 32 Princess of Wales Terrace, Parktown, Johannesburg 2193 (tel: 644-3300, 643-6740, 643-6743; fax: 643-1122).

Nedcor Bank Ltd, 135 Rivonia Rd, Sandown, Sandton, Johannesburg 2001 (tel: 294-4444; fax: 295-5555).

South African Bank of Athens Ltd, Bank of Athens Building, 116 Marshall Street, Johannesburg 2001 (tel: 832-1211; fax: 838-1001, 833-7976).

Standard Bank of South Africa Ltd, 5 Simmonds Street, Johannesburg 2001 (tel: 636-9111; fax: 636-3544).

Central bank
South African Reserve Bank, 370 Church Street; PO Box 427, Pretoria 0001 (tel: 313-3911; fax: 313-3197; email: www.reservebank.co.za).

Stock exchange
JSE Securities Exchange (JSE), www.jse.co.za

Bond Exchange of South Africa (BESA), www.bondexchange.co.za

Travel information
Airlink, Bonaero Park, Johannesburg (tel: 961-1700; fax: 395-1076; internet: www.flyairlink.com)

Automobile Association of South Africa, Denis Paxton House, Alladale Road, Kyalami Midrand 1685; PO Box 596, Johannesburg 2000 (tel: 799-1000; fax: 799-1960; e-mail: aasa@aasa.co.za).

Blue Train Reservations, PO Box 2671, Joubert Park 2044 (tel: 334-8459; fax: 334-8464; e-mail: bluetrain@transnet.co.za).

Coach Services: Translux Express, PO Box 2383, Johannesburg 2000 (tel: 774-3333; fax: 774-3318); Greyhound Coach Lines, PO Box11229, Johannesburg 2000 (tel: 830-1301; fax: 830-1528); Intercape Mainliner, PO Box 618, Bellville 7535 (tel: 386-4400; fax: 386-2488).

Eastern Cape Tourism Board, PO Box 186, Bisho 5605 (tel: 635-2115; fax: 636-4019; e-mail: info@ectourism.co.za).

Free State Department of Environmental Affairs and Tourism, PO Box 264, Bloemfontein 9300 (tel: 403-3435; fax: 448-8361).

Gauteng Tourism Authority, The Rosebank Mall, Rosebank 2196 (tel: 327-2000; fax: 327-7000; e-mail: tourism@gauteng.net).

Interair South Africa, Private Bag 8, PO JHB Int'nl Airport 1627, Johannesburg (tel: 616-0636; fax: 616-0930; email: info@interair.co.za).

KwaZulu-Natal Tourism Authority, PO Box 2516, Durban 4000 (tel: 304-7144; fax: 305-6693; e-mail: info@tourism-kzn.org).

Mpumalanga TourismAuthority, PO Box 679, Nelspruit 1200 (tel: 752-7001; fax: 759-5441; e-mail: mtanlpsa@cis.co.za).

Northern Cape Tourism Board, Private Bag X5017, Kimberley 8300 (tel: 832-2657; fax: 831-2937; e-mail: tourism@northerncape.org.za).

Northern Province Tourism Board, PO Box 1309, Pietersburg 0700 (tel: 288-0099; fax: 288-0094; e-mail: ceo@greatnorth.co.za).

North-West Parks and Tourism Council, PO Box 4488, Mmabatho 2735 (tel: 386-1225; fax: 386-1158; e-mail: nwptb@iafrica.com).

Rovos Rail Reservations, Victoria Hotel, PO Box 2837, Pretoria 0001 (tel: 323-6052; fax: 323-0843).

South African Airways, Private Bag X13, JHB Int'nl Airport, 1627; Airways Park, 32 Jones Road, Kempton Park, Johannesburg International Airport (tel: 978-1000; fax: 978-3507; internet: www.flysaa.com).

South African National Parks, 643 Leyds Street, Muckleneuk, Pretoria; PO Box 787, Pretoria 0001 (tel: 343-1991; fax: 343-0905; e-mail: reservations@parks-sa.co.za).

Western Cape Tourism Board, Private Bag X9108, Cape Town 8000 (tel: 426-5639; fax: 426-5640; e-mail: info@capetourism.org).

Ministry of tourism
Ministry of Environmental Affairs and Tourism, Fedsure Forum Building, 315 Pretorius Street, Pretoria; Private Bag X447, Pretoria 0001 (tel: 310-3611; fax: 322-0082).

National tourist organisation offices
South African Tourism, Bojanala House, 12 Rivonia Road, Illovo 2196 (tel: 778-8000; fax: 778-8001; e-mail: info@southafrica.net; internet site: http://www.southafrica.net).

Ministries
NB For the following Ministry addresses: Pretoria (administrative), Cape Town (legislative).

Ministry of Agriculture and Land Affairs, Private Bag X250, Pretoria 0001 (tel: 319-6886; fax: 321-8558); Private Bag X9087, Cape Town 8000 (tel: 465-7690; fax: 465-6550).

Ministry of Arts, Culture, Science and Technology, Private Bag X727, Pretoria 0001 (tel: 337-8378; fax: 324-2687); Private Bag X9156, Cape Town 8000; (tel: 465-4850; fax: 461-1425).

Ministry of Communications, Private Bag X882, Pretoria 0001 (tel: 427-8111; fax: 362-6915); Private Bag X9151, Cape Town 8000 (tel: 462-1632; fax: 462-1646).

Ministry of Correctional Services, Private Bag X853, Pretoria 0001 (tel: 323-8803; fax: 323-4111); Private Bag X9131, Cape Town 8000 (tel: 462-2314; fax: 465-4375).

Ministry of Defence, Private Bag X427, Pretoria 0001 (tel: 355-6119; fax: 347-0118); PO Box 47, Cape Town 8000 (tel: 469-6070; fax: 465-5870).

Ministry of Education, Private Bag X603, Pretoria 0001 (tel: 312-5501; fax: 323-5989); Private Bag X9034, Cape Town 8000 (tel: 465-7350; fax: 461-4788).

Ministry of Environmental Affairs and Tourism, Private Bag X447, Pretoria 0001 (tel: 310-3611; fax: 322-0082); Private Bag X9154, Capetown 8000 (tel: 465-7240; fax: 465-3216).

Ministry of Finance, Private Bag X115, Pretoria 0001 (tel: 323-8911; fax: 323-3262); PO Box 29, Cape Town 8000 (tel: 464-6100; fax: 461-2934).

Ministry of Foreign Affairs, Private Bag X152, Pretoria 0001 (tel: 351-0005; fax: 351-0253); 120 Plein St, Cape Town 8001 (tel: 464-3700; fax: 465-6548).

Ministry of Health, Private Bag X399, Pretoria 0001 (tel: 328-4773; fax: 325-5526); Private Bag X9070, Cape Town 8000 (tel: 465-7407; fax: 465-1575).

Ministry of Home Affairs, Private Bag X741, Pretoria 0001 (tel: 326-8081; fax: 321-6491); Private Bag X9102, Cape Town 8000 (tel: 461-5818; fax: 461-2359).

Ministry of Housing, Private Bag X645, Pretoria 0001 (tel: 421-1311; fax: 341-8513); Private Bag X9029, Cape Town 8000 (tel: 465-7295; fax: 465-3610).

Ministry of Intelligence Services, PO Box 56450, Arcadia 0007(tel: 338-1800; fax: 323-0718); PO Box 51278, Waterfront 8002 (tel: 401-1800; fax: 461-4644).

Ministry of Justice and Constitutional Development, Private Bag X276, Pretoria 0001 (tel: 323-8581; fax: 321-1708); Private Bag X256, Cape Town 8000 (tel: 465-7506; fax: 465-2783).

Ministry of Labour, Private Bag X499, Pretoria 0001 (tel: 322-6523; fax: 320-1942); Private Bag X9090, Cape Town 8000 (tel: 461-6030; fax: 462-2832).

Ministry of Minerals and Energy, Private Bag X646, Pretoria 0001 (tel: 322-8695; fax: 322-8699); Private Bag X9111, Cape Town 8000 (tel: 462-2310; fax: 461-0859).

Ministry of Provincial and Local Government, Private Bag X802, Pretoria 0001 (tel: 334-0705; fax: 326-4478); Private Bag X9123, Cape Town 8000 (tel: 462-1441; fax: 461-0851).

Ministry of Public Enterprises, Private Bag X15, Hatfield 0028 (tel: 431-1000; fax: 342-7224); Private Bag X9079, Cape Town 8000 (tel: 461-6376; fax: 465-2381).

Ministry of Public Service and Administration, Private Bag X884, Pretoria 0001 (tel: 314-7911; fax: 328-6529); Private Bag

X9148, Cape Town 8000 (tel: 465-5491; fax: 465-5484).

Ministry of Public Works, Private Bag X890, Pretoria 0001 (tel: 324-1510; fax: 325-6380); Private Bag X9155, Cape Town 8000 (tel: 462-4184; fax: 461-6962).

Ministry of Safety and Security, Private Bag X463, Pretoria 0001 (tel: 339-2800; fax: 339-2819); Private Bag X9080, Cape Town 8000 (tel: 465-7400; fax: 461-2073).

Ministry of Social Development, Private Bag X885, Pretoria 0001 (tel: 312-7637; fax: 321-2658); Private Bag X9153, Cape Town 8000 (tel: 465-4011; fax: 465-4469).

Ministry of Sport and Recreation, Private Bag X869, Pretoria 0001 (tel: 334-3100; fax: 321-8493); Private Bag X9149, Cape Town 8000 (tel: 465-5506; fax: 465-4402).

Ministry of Trade and Industry, Private Bag X274, Pretoria 0001 (tel: 322-7677; fax: 322-7851); Private Bag X9047, Cape Town 8000 (tel: 461-7191; fax: 465-1291).

Ministry of Transport, Private Bag X193, Pretoria 0001 (tel: 309-3131; fax: 328-3194); Private Bag X9129, Cape Town 8000 (tel: 465-7260; fax: 461-6845).

Ministry of Water Affairs and Forestry, Private Bag X313, Pretoria 0001 (tel: 36-8733; fax: 328-4254); Private Bag X9052, Cape Town 8000 (tel: 464-1500; fax: 465-3362).

Office of the President, Private Bag X1000, Pretoria 0001 (tel: 337-5100; fax: 321-8870); Private Bag X1000, Cape Town 8000 (tel: 464-2100; fax: 464-2123).

Other useful addresses

Association of Advertising Agencies (AAA), PO Box 2289, Parklands 2121 (tel: 781-2772; fax: 781-2796; e-mail: aaa@gem.co.za).

Afrikaanse Handelsinstituut (AHI) (Afrikaans Trade Institute), Lynnwood Galleries, 354 Rosemary Street, Lynnwood 0081; PO Box 35100, Menlopark 00101 (tel: 348-5440; fax: 348-8771; e-mail: pta@ahi.co.za).

Association of Marketers (ASOM), 8 Sloane Street, Bryanston, Sandton; PO Box 98859, Sloane Park 2152, Bryanston (tel: 706-1633; fax: 706-4151; e-mail: asom@pixie.co.za).

Board on Tariffs and Trade, Fedlife Forum, Cnr Van der Walt and Pretorius Streets, Private Bag X753, Pretoria 0001 (tel: 322-8244; fax: 322-0149).

British High Commission, 255 Hill Street, Arcadia, Pretoria 0002 (tel: 483-1200; fax: 483-1302); 91 Parliament Street, Cape Town 8001 (tel: 461-7220; fax: 461-0017).

Chamber of Mines of South Africa, PO Box 61809, Marshalltown 2107 (tel: 498-7100; fax: 834-4251).

Chemical & Allied Industries Association, 15th Floor, Metal Box Centre, 25 Owl Street, Auckland Park 2006 (tel: 482-1671; fax: 726-8310).

Clothing Federation of South Africa, 42 van der Linde Street, Bedfordview 2008 (tel: 622-8125; fax: 622-8316).

COEGA Development Corporation, Libra Chambers, Cnr Oakworth Road and Carnarvon Place, Humerail, Port Elizabeth; Private Bag X13130, Humewood, Port Elizabeth 6013 (tel: 507-9111; fax: 585-5445; e-mail: info@coega.co.zu).

Government Communications and Information System (GCIS), 356 Vermeulen Street, Pretoria; Private Bag X745, Pretoria 0001 (tel: 314-2127; 325-2030; e-mail: govcom@gcis.pwv.gov.za; internet site: http://www.gcis.gov.za).

ICC Durban (international convention centre), 45 Ordnance Road, Durban 4001; PO Box 155, Durban 4000 (tel: 360-1000; fax: 360-1005; e-mail: mktg@icc.co.za).

Industrial Development Corporation of South Africa, 19 Fredman Drive, Sandton 2146; PO Box 784055, Sandton 2146 (tel: 269-3000; fax: 269-3116; e-mail: callcentre@idc.co.za).

Iscor Limited, Roger Dyason Road, Pretoria West; PO Box 450, Pretoria 0001 (tel: 307-3000; fax: 307-4721; e-mail: webmaster@iscor.com).

JSE Securities Exchange (stock exchange), 1 Exchange Square, 2 Gwen Lane, Sandown, Sandton 2196; Private Bag X991174, Sandton 2146 (tel: 520-7000; fax: 520-8584; e-mail: miscellaneous@jse.co.za).

South African Association for the Conference Industry (SAACI), PO Box, Kloof 3640 (tel 764-6977; fax: 764-6974; e-mail: sec@saaci.co.za).

South African Business Initiative for Reconstruction and Development, 17th Floor, Metal Box Centre, 25 Owl Street, Auckland Park 2092 (tel: 482-5100; fax: 482-5507).

South African Diamond Board, 5th Floor, SA Diamond Centre, 240 Commissioner Street, Johannesburg 2001 (tel: 334-8980/6; fax: 334-8898; e-mail: mabombol@sadb.co.za).

South African Embassy (USA), 3051 Massachusetts Avenue, NW Washington, DC (tel: (+1-202) 232-4400; fax: (+1-202) 265-1607; e-mail: safrica@southafrica.net).

South African Foreign Trade Organisation (SAFTO), Export House, 71 Maud Street, Sandton; PO Box 782706, Sandton 2146 (tel: 883-3737; fax: 883-6569; e-mail: safto@apollo.is.co.za).

South African Petroleum Industry Association, Trust Bank Centre, Adderley Street, Cape Town 8001; PO Box 7082, Roggebaai 8012 (tel: 419-8054; fax: 419-8058).

Statistics South Africa, Steyn's Building, 274 Schoeman Street, Pretoria 0002; Private Bag X44, Pretoria 0001 (tel: 310-8911; fax: 322-3374; e-mail: info@statssa.pwv.gov.za; internet site: www.statssa.gov.za/).

Trade and Investment South Africa, Rex Welsh House, Maud Street, Sandown, Sandton 2196; PO Box 782084, Sandton 2146 (tel: 884-2206; fax: 884-3236; e-mail: isa@isa.org.za).

US Embassy, 877 Pretorius Street, Pretoria; PO Box 9536, Pretoria 0001(tel: 342-1048; fax: 342-2244).

National news agency: PO Box 7766, Cotswold House, Greenacres Office Park, Cnr Victory & Rustenburg Roads, Victory Park, Johannesburg, 2000 (tel: 782-1600; fax: 782-1587/8; email: comms@sapa.org.za; internet: www.sapa.org.za).

Internet sites

African Development Bank: www.afdb.org

Africa Online: www.africaonline.com

AllAfrica.com: http://allafrica.com

International Finance Corporation: www.ifc.org/abn

Johannesburg Stock Exchange: www.jse.co.za/

Development Bank of South Africa: www.dbsa.org

Mbendi AfroPaedia (information on companies, countries, industries and stock exchanges in Africa): http://mbendi.co.za

Province of the North West Tourist Board: www.tourismnorthwest.co.za/

South African Development Community (SADC): www.sadcreview.com

South African Futures Exchange: www.safex.co.za/

South African yellow pages: www.ipages.co.za/

Trade Web: www.trade.co.za/

South Georgia

COUNTRY PROFILE

1775 Captain Cook landed and took formal possession of South Georgia and the South Sandwich Islands (SGSSI).
1904 A whaling station was established by the Norwegian C A Larsen.
1908 The UK government annexed SGSSI by Letters Patent as part of the Falkland Islands Dependencies and the islands came under UK administration.
1965 Leith Harbour, the last shore-based whaling station in South Georgia, was closed.
1982 Argentine military forces occupied South Georgia for 22 days. South Georgia and the South Sandwich Islands became overseas territories of the UK.
2001 The UK military garrison closed and was replaced by a British Antarctic Survey (BAS) base at King Edward Point. There is a science station for biological study on Bird Island.
2005 A revised version of the 2000 environment management plan was made available on the British Antarctic Survey's website. The new plan was published in 2006 and sets out environmental policies for the next five years.
2006 Alan Huckle became Commissioner.
2009 Doctor Martin Collins was appointed as the new Senior Executive; he is a member of the UK delegation to the scientific committee of the Convention on the Conservation of Antarctic Marine Living Resources (CCAMLR – pronounced 'Kammelar'), which manages marine resources in the Southern Antarctic Ocean.
2010 In the Falkland Islands *Economic Development Strategy* released in July, part of the plans, the bilateral fisheries agreement with South Georgia, will be re-negotiated so that the Falkland Islands fishing interests are better promoted and receive priority in the allocation of fishing rights. Nigel Haywood becamde Governor on 16 October.
2011 In May, a rodent eradication programme was initiated targeted at rats and rabbits (which had been accidentally introduced over the years) that have had a detrimental impact on seabirds and penguin colonies and the habitat in general. In July it was announced that the ashes of Frank Wild were to be disinterred from a chapel in South Africa and buried in Grytviken cemetery on South Georgia in November. Wild had been Earnest Shackleton's second-in-command on the *Endurance* expedition and charged with leading the men left on Elephant Island when Shackleton went for help.
2013 Schedules for the coming 2013/14 summer season showed around 58 cruise ship visits to South Georgia, made by 23 different vessels, an 11 per cent increase in ship visits over 2012. With normal occupancy levels, the number of cruise ship passengers could be as high as 7,000, a 20 per cent increase over last season.
2014 South Georgia Patagonian toothfish longline fishery was again certified as a sustainable and well managed fishery. Marine Stewardship Council (MSC), the world's leading certification and ecolabel programme for wild-caught environmentally sustainable seafood, completed its five-yearly assessment in August. Colin Roberts became Commissioner on 29 April. He resides in Port Stanley, Falkland Islands.

Political structure

South Georgia and the South Sandwich Islands (SGSSI) are British overseas territories, legally distinct from the Falkland Islands but, for convenience, they are administered from the Falkland Islands. With no indigenous or permanent inhabitants, there is no need for representative government, but a separate constitution for the territory was promulgated in 1985. The governor of the Falkland Islands is also the commissioner for the SGSSI; in this capacity he consults the Falklands Executive Council on those matters relating to the territory which might affect the Falkland Islands.
Other administrative posts based in Stanley, Falkland Islands, include the assistant commissioner who is also director of the SGSSI Fisheries, a financial secretary and attorney general. The marine officer, based at King Edward Point, is responsible for customs, immigration, posts and fisheries liaison.
There is no indigenous population. Since 2001, when the British military garrison left, there has been a British Antarctic Survey (BAS) base where a marine officer and 17 staff of the BAS are permanently stationed at King Edward Point.

KEY FACTS

Official name: South Georgia and the South Sandwich Islands (SGSSI)

Head of State: Queen Elizabeth II, represented by Commissioner Colin Roberts (resides in Falkland Islands) (from 29 Apr 2014)

Head of government: Commissioner Colin Roberts (resides in Falkland Islands)

Area: 3,755 square km

Population: 20 (2004) (British Antarctic Survey (BAS) scientists)

Capital: King Edward Point (administrative centre)

Official language: English

Currency: Falkland Islands pound or pound sterling (FI£ or £) = 100 pence

Exchange rate: FI£ or £0.65 per US$ (Nov 2015); (pegged to pound sterling)

Population
20 (2004) (British Antarctic Survey (BAS) scientists)

Main cities
Two British Antarctic Research Stations (Bird Island and King Edward Point) have government officers and museum curators during the summer months. Grytviken, formerly a whaling station on South Georgia, was the garrison town.

Languages spoken
Official language/s
English

Media
Press
Weeklies: The South Atlantic Remote Territories Media Association publishes an online newsletter which includes articles on South Georgia (www.sartma.com).

Economy
Income is derived from fishing licenses, fees for trans-shipping fish catches, tourist landing charges and the sale of postage stamps.
The *South Georgia Environmental Management Plan* (2006–10), outlined the British government's commitment to providing a sustainable policy framework to conserve, manage and protect the rich natural environment, at the same time as permitting some human activities which would lead to the generation of revenue.

Agriculture
Fishing
Large-scale fishing began in 1969/70 by Soviet bloc countries. In 1993, the UK extended its territorial waters around the SGSSI from 19.3km (12 miles) to 321.8km (200 miles) and created the SGSSI Maritime Zone. In 1996, new laws opened fishing grounds with a licensing scheme. Approximately 100–200,000 tonnes of krill are caught around South Georgia each year. The SGSSI government applies conservation measures to the maritime zone, but has the right to impose additional measures if appropriate. There is satellite imagery surveillance of the fishing zone.
The tooth fish total allowable catch (TAC) for the 2006/07 season was increased by 15 per cent by the SGSSI and approved by the Convention for the Conservation of Antarctic Marine Resources

Tourism
Tourism from cruise ships is increasing rapidly, and there is a consequent expected increase in tourist numbers by as much as 20 per cent, assuming normal occupancy rates. Tourism to South Georgia reached record numbers in the 2014/15 season, when 65 cruise ships visited bringing around 8,142 passengers; an increase on the previous record of 8,068 in the 2007/8 season. The islands of South Georgia are primarily sites of scientific research. Tourist visits to South Georgia are strictly controlled according to the tourism management policy (2011). The principal objective of this policy is to protect the island's environment, including its flora, fauna and cultural heritage. All visits must be authorised, by permit from the commissioner (located on the Falkland Islands) prior to arrival, and all visits must be managed (under the leadership of a designated escort) from approved landing sites; no visitors may remain on the islands overnight, unless approved as an 'expedition' and treated accordingly.
The authorities warn that visits to South Georgia carry a greater risk level than many other destinations due to its total lack of medical or emergency facilities, and there are no evacuation services available.

Environment
The South Georgia Environmental Plan 2005 (for the period 2006–10) was published on the British Antarctic website in January 2006.
South Georgia is the breeding ground for some 85 per cent of the world's southern fur seal population, as well as significant populations of elephant seals, albatrosses, petrels and penguins. In 1910, reindeer were introduced by Norwegian whaling companies.
The South Sandwich Islands represent a maritime ecosystem.

Time
GMT minus two hours

Geography
South Georgia is an isolated, mountainous sub-Antarctic island, which lies in the South Atlantic Ocean, 2,150km east of Tierra del Fuego and about 1,390km east-south-east of the Falkland Islands. Surrounded by cold waters originating from the Antarctic, South Georgia has a harsher climate than expected from its latitude. More than 50 per cent of the island is covered by permanent ice with many large glaciers reaching the sea at the head of fjords. The main mountain range is the Allardyce Range, which has its highest point at Mount Paget (2,960m).
The South Sandwich Islands, which comprise a chain of active volcanic islands around 240km long, lie about 750km south-east of South Georgia. The climate is wholly Antarctic and in the late winter, the islands may be surrounded by pack ice.
Hemisphere
Southern

Climate
South Georgia and the South Sandwich Islands are prone to very sudden and unexpected changes of weather brought on by the Antarctic Convergence, where cold waters flowing up from Antarctica meet warm water from the north. The average temperature in summer is -2 degrees Centigrade.

Entry requirements
Only a limited number of visitors are allowed to land each year. All visitors must apply to the Office of the Commissioner, South Georgia and South Sandwich Islands, Government House, Stanley, Falkland Islands (tel: (+500) 27-433, fax: (+500) 27-434; e-mail: gov.house@horizon.co.fk) at least 60 days in advance of their journey for permission to land. Application forms can be obtained from the Commissioner's office or on-line from the official South Georgia government website (www.sgisland.org). Details of all places to be visited must be provided and there is a landing fee. There are no search-and-rescue facilities.
Passports
Passports must be valid for a minimum of six months.
Visa
Not required, but visitors must report to the Marine Officer at King Edward Point, Cumberland Bay East.

Health (for visitors)
Advisable precautions
There are no medical facilities available. Comprehensive medical emergency insurance is necessary as well as sufficient stocks of prescribed medication. Sunburn is a problem in this sub-polar region, sunblock should be applied regularly.
All of the historic buildings in the territory present a safety risk; they are storm damaged and flimsy, causing wind blown asbestos particles. Visitors should not approach within 200 metres of them without permission of the Marine Officer at King Edward Point.

Credit cards
The museum shop accepts VISA and Mastercard, but not American Express.

Working hours
Government
Mon–Fri (winter): 0900–1315, 1430–1730; Mon–Fri (summer): 1100–1315, 1630–1930.

Telecommunications
Postal services
A new post code for the islands has been issued through the Universal Postal Union: SIQQ 1ZZ.

Getting there

Air

There is currently no routine air access, but there are plans for an international airport.

Surface

The only access is by yacht or cruise ships.

Getting about

National transport

Road: There are no road links on the islands.

BUSINESS DIRECTORY

The addresses listed below are a selection only. While World of Information makes every endeavour to check these addresses, we cannot guarantee that changes have not been made, especially to telephone numbers and area codes. We would welcome any corrections.

Telephone area codes

There are no land lines on South Georgia. All communications are by either radio or mobile/cell phones

Travel information

The Office of the Commissioner, Government of South Georgia and the South Sandwich Islands, Government House, Stanley, Falkland Islands, South Atlantic FIQQ 1ZZ (tel: +500 28200; fax: +500 28201; email: info@gov.gs; internet: www.sgisland.gs).

Other useful addresses

British Antarctic Survey, High Cross, Madingley Rd, Cambridge CB3 OET, UK (tel: (+44-1223) 221-400; fax: (+44-1223) 362-616; e-mail: information@bas.ac.uk).

Licensing Officer SGSSI, Fisheries Department, Stanley, Falkland Islands (tel: (+500) 27-260; fax: (+500) 27-265; e-mail: fish.fig@horizon.co.fk).

Office of the Commissioner, South Georgia and South Sandwich Islands, Government House, Stanley, Falkland Islands (tel: (+500) 27-433, fax: (+500) 27-434; e-mail:gov.house@horizon.co.fk).

Project Atlantis (Environmental and educational resource) Dundee University, 23 Springfield, Dundee, Scotland DD1 4JE (tel: (+44) (0)1382 388-159; internet: www.atlantishome.org).

Internet sites

British Antarctic survey: www.antartic.ac.uk

British Geographical Survey: www.bgs.ac.uk

Government website: www.sgisland.org

Information for Yachts visiting South Georgia: www.rccpf.org.uk/ anc click on *Index MAPS showing PUBLICATIONS*.

South Atlantic Remote Territories Media Association: www.sartma.com

South Georgia Heritage Trust: www.sght.org

University of Dundee educational resource: www.atlantishome.org

UK Foreign and Commonwealth Office: www.fco.gov.uk

South Sudan

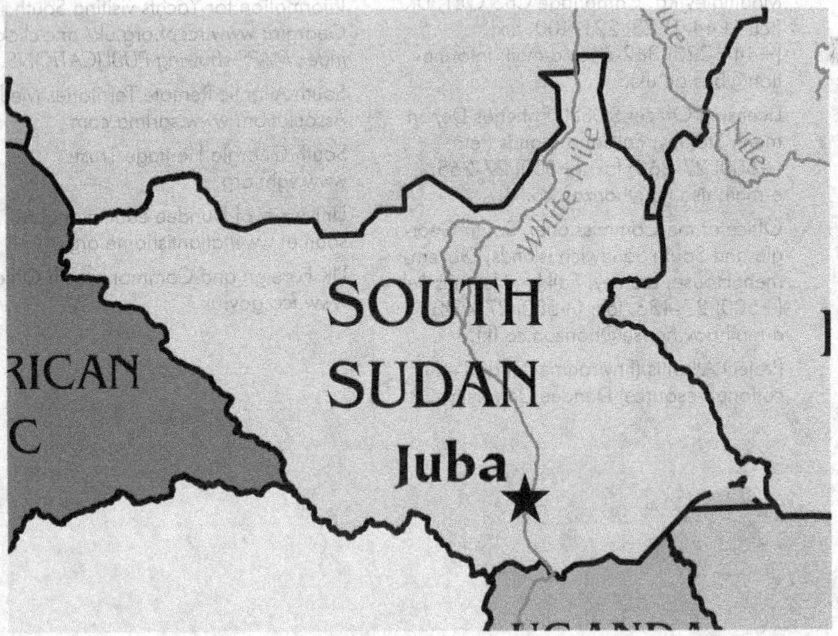

KEY FACTS

Official name: South Sudan (Janub as Sudan)

Head of State: President Salva Kiir Mayardit (SPLA/M) (from 9 Jul 2011)

Head of government: Vice President Riek Machar (SPLA/M) (from 9 Jul 2011)

Ruling party: Sudan People's Liberation Movement (from 9 Jul 2011)

Area: 644,329 square kilometres

Population: 10.88 million (2013)* (8,260,490; 2008 census, disputed)

Capital: Juba (will possibly be moved to Ramshiel)

Official language: English

Currency: South Sudan Pound (SS£) = 100 piasters

Exchange rate: SS£3.05 per US$ Jul 2013

GDP per capita: US$1,262 (2013)*

GDP real growth: 24.00% (2013)*

GDP: US$13.73 billion (2013)*

Oil production: 31,000 bpd (2012)

* estimated figure

In August 2013 South Sudan President Salva Kiir appointed James Wani Igga as his deputy. Mr Igga replaced former vice president Riek Macar who appeared to have been the victim of inter-government feuding that resulted in his dismissal by the president. Mr Igga had been speaker of parliament and a commander in the Sudan People's Liberation Movement (SPLM), the ex-rebel group that now ran the country. After his dismissal, Mr Machar said he planned to challenge Mr Kiir for the leadership of the SPLM so that he can run for president in the 2015 election. The entire cabinet was dismissed at the same time as Mr Machar in July 2013.

Political divisions

Mr Kiir is from the Dinka community, the largest in South Sudan, while Mr Machar was from the second-largest group, the Nuer, some of whom have complained about Dinka domination. It was thought by many that Mr Kiir's choice of vice president might be a way of garnering political support from Mr Igga's large Bari community in South Sudan's Central Equatorial region ahead of the 2015 elections.

Not that the differences between the President and his deputy came as a surprise to anyone. The two men had not been getting along for some time. In April 2013 Mr Kiir had cancelled a national reconciliation programme, a project of Mr Machar, following allegations that the vice president's motivation was to build up his political following. In April 2013 Mr Machar had announced his intention to challenge Mr Kiir for the party leadership. The president had promptly relieved his deputy of some of his powers. The president's decision to dismiss his entire cabinet looked to be rather precipitous. But all was certainly not well within the government. In May 2012 the President had written to a reported 75 government officials politely – or naively? – asking them to return the US$4 billion he alleged had been embezzled since the creation of South Sudan's interim government in 2005.

The cabinet's dismissal was justified as one of replacing corrupt officials with more competent technocrats. The new government, announced at the end of July

2012 when the government decided to shut down oil production following bilateral disagreements with Sudan. Growth fell to an all-time low of -11 per cent in 2012 before rebounding to a healthy rate of 8.8 per cent in 2013 and 30.7 per cent in 2014.

In December 2013, civil war erupted following President Salva Kiir's accusation that his ex-vice-president, Riek Machar was plotting to overthrow him. Much of the fighting has run along ethnic fault lines between Kiir's Dinka and Machar's Nuer people. Rebel factions seized control of several regional towns causing thousands of deaths and many more to flee. Ceasefires were signed but broken several times during the weeks in January, and further talks in February failed to end the violence that displaced more than a million people by April. By November 2015, approximately 2.4 million people had been displaced or driven from the country and 4 million people remained severely food insecure. Furthermore, around 16,000 children have been used by the government and rebel forces as child soldiers. Both sides of South Sudan's conflict have boosted their weapon arsenals and, furthermore, human rights violations including murder and rape have persisted. Seven ceasefires have already been broken since the country spiralled into the bloody conflict in December 2013. Following the ceasefire agreed in August, a 15-member Security Council warned that it was ready to impose an arms embargo if the peace deal were to fail.

In October 2015, the UN reported that some 30,000 people faced death by starvation, and tens of thousands more were on the brink of famine. The government has targeted civilians most notably in the Unity state which is an oil rich northern region. Human rights workers reported more than 50 rapes in just that month. A peace deal was brokered in August 2015 by the Intergovernmental Authority on Development, a bloc of East African nations. Under the accord, Riek Machar is set to return to government as vice-president.

In 17 November 2015 South Sudan's rebels said that government soldiers had launched attacks against their position in Unity State in what they said was a violation of the peace deal signed in August. This unfortunate series of attacks have occurred at a time when the rebels are preparing to visit Juba in order to sensitise the civil population about the signed peace accord between the government and its opposition. Machar is expected in Juba in 19 November 2015 where he is due to meet the South Sudan government leaders at a regional peace conference. It will be his first time back in the capital since the start of the civil war.

South Sudan and Sudan

Sudan's president Omar al-Bashir has met with former president of Botswana Festus Mogae, the new head of the Joint Monitoring and Evaluation Commission (JMEC), which is tasked with overseeing implementation of South Sudan's new peace agreement on 16 November. Al-Bashir described the strong historical ties between the peoples of Sudan and South Sudan, however, he pointed out that Juba is still suspicious that the Khartoum government is harbouring rebels. The Sudanese president said that stability in relations between the two countries is possible, while reiterating his readiness to welcome South Sudanese refugees who are fleeing their country.

Following the forty years of civil year with Sudan, South Sudan's industry and infrastructure is severely underdeveloped and poverty is widespread. Subsistence agriculture provides a living for the vast majority of the population and property rights are insecure because markets are not well organised. After independence, South Sudan's Bank of South Sudan (BoSS) (central bank) issued a new currency, the South Sudanese Pound. South Sudan has only approximately 250 kilometres of paved roads and electricity is produced mostly by costly diesel generators; indoor plumbing and potable water are scarce. South Sudan largely depends on imports for goods, services and capital – predominantly from Uganda, Kenya and Sudan. Despite the dire state in which South Sudan is currently in, it does have abundant natural resources. In 2011, South Sudan produced 75 per cent of former Sudan's total oil output of nearly 500,000 barrels per day (bpd). The government of South Sudan derives 98 per cent of its budget revenues from oil, which is exported through two pipelines that run to Sudanese refineries and shipping facilities at Port Sudan on the Red Sea. The dependency on Sudan for the export of oil will remain until they decide to build another pipeline which will be at great expense. The suspension of oil flows due to transshipment disputes with Sudan in 2012 caused GDP to decline by 48 per cent. Oil production began again in 2013, however, at just 220,000bpd which was 40 per cent lower compared with 2011. Most of South Sudan's proved reserves of oil and natural gas are located in the Muglad and Melut Basins, which extend into both South Sudan and Sudan. National oil companies from Asia dominate the oil sector. The China National Petroleum Corporation, India's Oil and Natural Gas Corporation and Malaysia's Petronas hold large stakes in the leading consortia operating oil fields and pipelines. Total proved reserves of crude oil in South Sudan was 3.8 billion barrels in 2015, the sixth largest in Africa. Nilepet also holds small stakes in operations. Natural gas associated with oil production is flared or re-injected into wells to improve oil output rates. South Sudan neither produces nor consumes dry natural gas. Natural gas reserves were 63.7 billion cubic metres (cum) in 2013. China is by far the leading export destination for crude oil from South Sudan. In 2013, Sudan and South Sudan's crude exports accounted for 2 per cent of China's total crude oil imports, down from 5 per cent in 2011.

The outbreak of conflict in December 2013 caused GDP growth to fall significantly which led to poverty and food insecurity rising, although GDP grew by 30.7 per cent in 2014. South Sudan holds one of the richest agricultural areas in Africa with fertile soils and abundant water supplies; currently the region supports 10–20 million head of cattle. South Sudan is currently burdened by considerable debt, because of increased military spending and rapidly accumulating arears. South Sudan has received approximately US$4 billion in foreign aid since 2005, largely from the UK, the US, Norway, and the Netherlands. Inflation peaked at 80 per cent in May 2012 but has declined to –0.7 per cent in 2014. Long term challenges include diversifying the economy, alleviating poverty, maintaining macroeconomic stability, improving tax collection and financial management and improving the business environment.

The African Development Bank *Economic Outlook* report for 2015 has estimated that 2015 is likely to see negative growth as the ongoing conflict and declines in national oil production and global oil prices devastate the economy. The outlook for economic growth depends on a recovery in global oil prices and a comprehensive resolution of the civil conflict. Oil production accounted for 99 per cent of exports and 50 per cent of GDP in 2014, this is completely unsustainable and, therefore, the economy needs to be diversified. Oil revenue inflows are volatile and unpredictable whilst non-oil revenue is not expected to significantly increase in the short term. It is estimated that GDP will contract by -7.5 per cent in 2015 as the recent conflict and the falling international oil price continue to cast a shadow over economic prospects. Despite the ongoing conflict and low international oil prices, South Sudan has enormous prospects for spatial inclusion. Opportunities exist to develop value chains that create jobs and improve household incomes, including gum acacia (producing gum arabic), shea nuts and significant herds of cattle. Gum acacia is estimated to be available in significant amounts in seven of the ten states, occupying 46 per cent of the land area. The benefits of developing such value chains extend to creating community interdependences and therefore peaceful coexistence. South Sudan was officially accepted as a member of the African Development Bank in May 2012 and it ratified its membership in September 2013.

Risk assessment

Politics	Poor
Economy	Fair
Regional stability	Poor

Muslims in South Sudan

% of population	6.2
Sunni (% of Muslims)	N/A
Shi'a (% of Muslims)	N/A

COUNTRY PROFILE

1821 The vast swamps (Sudd) of southern Sudan continued to discourage outsiders and left the area undisturbed by the Arab-controlled northern regions until the Turkish Ottoman Empire defeated Egypt and conquered northern Sudan. The Ottoman's set up Egypt as its proxy ruler of Sudan.
1839 A slave trade was developed with black male Africans seized for the Egyptian army and black women and children from the south traded in Arab markets.
1869 After the opening of the Suez Canal, the British became involved in Sudan's affairs, through its association with Egyptian governance of Sudan.
1870s Egypt colonised southern Sudan.
1878 Egypt established the province of Equatoria (much of modern-day Darfur, Western Equatoria, Eastern Equatoria, Central Equatoria and part of Somalia), in the southern Sudan and banned slavery, at the behest of Britain.
1881 In northern Sudan, Mohammed Ahmed, who proclaimed himself the long-looked-for Mahdi (the guided one), led his followers, the Muslim Sudanese, in a rebellion against Egyptian rule.
1885 The Mahdi's army massacred the British army, under General Gordon, who had been sent to quash the rebellion. The Mahdi united the tribes in a modern Islamic state and undermined the basis of the province of Equatoria.
1889 The Egyptian province of Equatoria ceased to exist and was split into regions of Sudan.
1898 The Mahdi was defeated by the British and Anglo-Egyptian army.
1899 Sudan was ruled as an Anglo-Egyptian condominium, although north and south Sudan were governed as separate administrative regions.
1947 At the Conference of Juba, held under the auspices of Great Britain and Egypt the end of the Second World War, it was agreed to unify politically northern Sudan and colonial southern Sudan.
1948 A legislative assembly for the unified Sudan was established.
1953 Great Britain and Egypt agreed to grant Sudan independence.
1955 Troops of the Sudan Defence Force (of southern Sudan) mutinied as a southern member of the national assembly was put on trial. The mutiny was suppressed, but a number of troops fled into the countryside and became the core of a poorly armed and ill-organised rebel fighting force (later founding the Anya-Nya guerrilla army).
1956 Sudan gained independence. With the rejection of southern calls for if not secession or even a federation, then more regional autonomy and greater development for the south, a secessionist movement developed led by the surviving mutineers and students from the south, who formed the Anya-Nya guerrilla army. The political and sometimes violent conflict became polarised between the largely Muslim north and the largely Christian/Animist south.
1958 A military coup in the north, led by General Ibrahim Abboud overthrew the civilian government of Prime Minister Abd Allah Khalil. Martial law was declared and Abboud proclaimed himself prime minister of Sudan.
1962 Civil war began in the south, led by the Anya-Nya movement.
1964 The October Revolution overthrew Abboud and a national government for Sudan was established.
1969 Colonel Jaafar Mohammed al Nimieri led the May Revolution military coup, installing a revolutionary council in Sudan.
1971 The Southern Sudan Liberation Movement (SSLM) was founded by former lieutenant Joseph Lagu; it encompassed all southern rebel forces, with a unified command structure and independence as the main objective. It assumed the right to represent the interests of the people of the south.
1972 Nimieri became the first elected president of Sudan and negotiated with Joseph Lagu (SSLM) at the conference on peace in Ethiopia. An estimated 500,000 people had been killed since 1955. The Addis Ababa Agreement ended the first Sudanese civil war, through the creation of the Southern Sudan Autonomous Region (SSAR).
1978 Oil was discovered in southern Sudan.
1983 President Nimieri officially declared Sudan an Islamic State, introduced *Sharia* (Islamic law) and revoked the SSAR agreement. The Sudan People's Liberation Movement (SPLM) was established under the leadership of Colonel John Garang (who was head of the armed Sudan People's Liberation Army (SPLA)) and gained control of much of the south; it campaigned for a united Sudan and blamed the central government for policies leading to Sudan's disintegration.
1985–86 Nimieri was ousted in a bloodless coup and after a brief period of military rule, Sadiq al Mahdi, the great-grandson of the Great Mahdi, became prime minister of Sudan after elections in 1986.
1986 Peace talks began between John Garang (SPLM) and Sadiq al Mahdi in Ethiopia, which culminated in the Koka Dam declaration. It was agreed to abolish *Sharia* in the south and a constitutional conference was proposed. The divided political situation in the north militated against a peaceful solution and fighting continued.
1988 A new agreement was reached, negotiated by a government coalition political party and the SPLM and called the November Accords, but Prime Minister Sadiq al Mahdi was politically weak and was unable to ratify the accords.
1989 Sadiq al Mahdi was replaced following another bloodless coup by the National Salvation Revolution, backed by the fundamentalist Islamic political party, National Islamic Front (NIF) (Al Jabhah al Islamiyah al Qawmiyah); Omar Hassan Ahmad al Bashir became chairman of the Revolutionary Command Council for National Salvation (RCCNS). An informal ceasefire broke down.
1992 The Sudanese pound was replaced as the currency by the Sudanese dinar. The central government mounted a military operation to take all rebel towns in the south, and captured the SPLA's headquarters in Torit. Riek Machar and Lam Akol attempted to overthrow the leadership of John Garang by forming the Nasir Faction. William Nyuon Bany formed a second rebel faction.

1993 Kerubino Kwanyin Bol formed a third rebel faction in the south. The three dissident rebel factions formed a coalition called SPLA-United. However clashes between these rebel factions caused Western powers to overlook their importance. The RCCNS was abolished after Omar al Bashir was appointed president; Sudan returned to civilian rule, although with one political party (Al Muttamar al Watani (National Congress Party) (NCP)) exercising dominance, the country was not strictly a democracy. Non-Muslim judges from the south were transferred to the north and were replaced with Muslim judges. Non-Muslim citizens were subject to arrest and punishment under Islamic religious laws (*Sharia*).
1994 The *Declaration of Principles* (DoP), an initiative sponsored by Eritrea, Ethiopia, Uganda and Kenya setting out objectives for a just and comprehensive peace settlement, was promulgated. Signatories to the DoP included the government of Sudan and the SPLM and SPLA (later reformed into SPLM/A)
1995 Political parties of the north and south formed the National Democratic Alliance. Eritrea, Ethiopia and Uganda increased their military support of SPLA.
1996 Omar al Bashir won the presidential election.
1997 The Khartoum Peace Agreement between the central government and seven southern groups, led by John Garang, was ratified by the National Assembly.
1998–99 Voters in a referendum endorsed a new Sudanese constitution. Sudan began to export oil from southern Sudan. After a power struggle within the ruling NCP between President Bashir and Hassan al Turabi (a hardline Islamist and ideologue), the President imposed a state of emergency and dissolved the National Assembly.
2000 Omar al Bashir and the NCP were re-elected. Most opposition parties boycotted the elections.
2002 After peace talks in Kenya, the government and the SPLA signed the Machakos Protocol: the government accepted the right of the south to seek self-determination after a six-year interim period.
2003 China and the Sudan announced a US$1 billion investment plan to enhance Sudan's oil infrastructure including the construction of a 750-kilometre-long pipeline between Sudan's largest oil deposits in the Kordofan oilfield and the coast.
2004 President Bashir agreed to grant autonomy to the south for six years, split the country's oil revenues with the southern provinces and allow the southerners to vote in a referendum on independence at the end of the six-year period.
2005 The government and the SPLM/A signed the Comprehensive Peace Agreement (CPA), ending the 22-year civil war. Among other things the agreement began a period of transition until 2009, when parliamentary and state legislative elections were scheduled to take place, and provided for an equal sharing of oil revenues between the north and south, with special administrative status given to the oil producing province of Abyei. SPLA leader, John Garang, was appointed vice president of Sudan for the six-year period of reconciliation; the new constitution also gave a large degree of autonomy to the south. John Garang was killed in a helicopter crash; riots broke out in Khartoum, between black southern Sudanese and northern Arabs. Garang's deputy, Salva Kiir, was named his successor as vice president of national Sudan and president of southern Sudan.
2006 UN envoy, Jan Pronk, was expelled for claiming that government troops had suffered defeats in southern Sudan. The Kordofan oilfield was attacked by the SPLA.
2007 The currency was changed from the dinar (in use since 1992), back to the Sudanese pound (S£); the exchange rate was set at S£1 to 100 old dinars. Vice President Kiir accused the national government of supporting militia operating in the south, claiming that they had not been disarmed, and the central government had failed to share the wealth of resources found in the south. The oil producing province of Abyei had been subject to continued armed attacks by the SPLA, so finally the governments in agreement with the SPLM asked the Permanent Court of Arbitration (PCA) (based in The Hague) to rule on the disputed border between the north and south.
2008 The PCA gave its ruling and concluded that Sudan's argument that Abyei only constituted a small sliver of land south of the Kiir/Bahr el Arab River was erroneous and awarded 10,460 square kilometres to South Sudan. It also rejected South Sudan's argument that its demarcation in the eastern and western boundaries was legitimate and awarded those areas, including much of the oil reserves in the area, to Sudan. It also affirmed the right of traditional pastoral herdsmen to continue to use both sides of the border areas in the province of Kordofan (over 18,500 square km) for their flocks
2009 Lam Akol created his own political party – SPLM-Democratic Change – and split from the SPLM, claiming it had failed to fully govern southern Sudan. Both political parties nominated candidates to challenge President Bashir in the next Sudanese presidential election. A delay in completing a census forced the postponement of presidential and parliamentary elections throughout Sudan. The census was criticised by political leaders in the south who said that the southern Sudanese population had been under-recorded.
2010 Almost all of the political parties based in southern Sudan withdrew from the Sudanese presidential elections, due to concerns over fraud and security during voting and what they considered to have been rigging of the electoral process in order to favour the ruling NCP. President Bashir threatened to cancel the referendum on independence in the south in face of the boycotts. In the general elections the NCP won 68.2 per cent of the vote, the SPLM won 22 per cent, Popular Congress 4 per cent. President Bashir was re-elected with 68.24 per cent of the vote. At the same time a presidential election took place in Southern Sudan; Salva Kiir (SPLM) won 92.99 per cent of the vote, Lam Akol (SPLM-Democratic Change) 7.01 per cent. Salva Kiir was sworn in as the first elected president of southern Sudan. The referendum on independence for southern Sudan was set for 9 January 2011. The UN estimated that some 51,000 people travelled south in time to register their vote (14 November–4 December). President Bashir announced on 19 December that if the South broke away the north would adopt an Islamic constitution.
2011 In January, a referendum to determine the future of southern Sudan as either a province of Sudan or as an independent country began. The vote, over nine days, was overwhelmingly in favour of independence. The result was 98.83 per cent of the vote in favour, 1.17 per cent against independence. In February, it was decided by the ruling committee of the SPLM that the official name of the country would be South Sudan when it came into existence on 9 July. [*From now on we will refer to the area of southern Sudan which will become South Sudan on 9 July as South Sudan – Editor*] In March, militia supporting rebel leader General George Athor attacked the town of Malakal, in the oil-rich state of Upper Nile. Official talks with representatives of Sudan were suspended following South Sudan's accusations that President Bashir was plotting to overthrow the future South Sudan government, orchestrated by the Sudanese military intelligence agency. It was claimed that Sudan was 'creating, training, supplying and arming militia groups' in South Sudan, overseen by President Bashir. Fighting between the SPLA and those loyal to rebel-leader, George Athor, killed 70 people in three states in

March. The UN extended its peacekeeping mission in the region until July. It also established a successor mission after independence (Unmiss, on 8 July). The finance minister announced that the new currency, the South Sudan pound, would be issued in July, initially valued on a par with the Sudan pound. In the May gubernatorial elections held in southern Kordofan, Ahmed Haroun (NCP) was declared the winner in what the SPLM declared was a fraudulent election. (The International Criminal Court (ICC) had issued an arrest warrant for Haroun in 2006, charging him with committing war crimes in Darfur (western Sudan)). Adbelaziz al Hilu (SPLM) was elected as deputy governor. In May a group of army personnel from Sudan were ambushed while being escorted out of Abyei by UN peacekeepers and 22 men were killed in what the UN called 'a criminal attack'. The US called on South Sudan to 'account' for the attack. In retaliation, on 22 May northern military 'repelled enemy forces' according to Sudanese state news and occupied Abyei. The UN condemned the escalation in violence and called on Sudan to withdraw its military from the disputed town and region of Abyei, as a UN peacekeeping force was caught in the middle of what South Sudan called an 'invasion'. Around 20,000 people fled from Abyei to South Sudan. Armed men looted and burned buildings in Abyei as the UN warned Sudan that it was 'responsible for maintaining law and order' and that it should 'intervene to stop criminal acts'. In May, President Bashir refused to withdraw troops from Abyei saying the area belonged to Sudan. In June, the UN announced that it would undertake an investigation into the breakdown in order in South Kordofan between Sudan and South Sudan. On 9 July celebrations were held as South Sudan became independent. It become the 193rd member of the United Nations on 14 July, and the 54th member of the African Union (AU) on 15 August. China's foreign minister, Yang Jiechi, arrived in Khartoum on 7 August where he had talks before traveling to South Sudan for talks with President Kiir. China was concerned to maintain its supply of oil, which would in future come from both Sudan and South Sudan. An agreement on border crossings between Sudan and South Sudan was signed in Khartoum in September – 10 border crossings will be opened to ease communications. The agreement was brokered by the AU and is hoped to demonstrate the willingness of the two countries to co-operate. Google maps online became the first mapping service to recognise the new state in September.

2012 On 7 January, the UN launched an emergency programme to aid around 50,000 people, including food distribution for 2,000 people, displaced following attacks by rival ethnic groups, centred on the town of Pibor. The government declared the state of Jonglei a disaster area, as Lou Nuer fighters, who outnumbered the South Sudanese army and UN peacekeepers, attacked in the area. On 27 January, South Sudan began to shut down its oil production following the failure to reach an agreement over oil sharing revenue and oil transit fees with Sudan. On 31 January, South Sudan rejected proposals, backed by the AU, for Sudan to pay US$6.5 billion for oil rights. On 11 February, the chief mediator, former South African president, Thabo Mbeki, announced that South Sudan and Sudan had signed a non-aggression pact, saying that both sides had agreed to respect each other's sovereignty and territorial integrity. On 13 March, Sudan and South Sudan signed an agreement allowing free movement and residence of their nationals in one another's territory. It was agreed that President Bashir would travel to Juba to sign the accord by 1 April. Following President Salva Kiir's official visit to China, on 28 April it was announced that China had agreed to loan South Sudan US$8 billion, to be used on a range of infrastructure projects, including roads, telecommunications, hydroelectric generation and agriculture. Sudan declared a state of emergency (SOE) along its border with South Sudan on 29 April, following weeks of clashes between Sudan and South Sudan forces. On 2 May the UN Security Council warned both Sudan and South Sudan that sanctions would be imposed if they failed to halt the recent violence and that both sides should resume negotiations to resolve their dispute. The UN peacekeeping mission in Abyei confirmed that on 30 May Sudan withdrew its troops from the disputed region, following negotiations undertaken in Ethiopia between officials of Sudan and South Sudan. Presidents Bashir and Kiir signed an agreement on 27 September in Addis Ababa that will finally lead to the resumption of oil production and oil exports. South Sudan agreed to pay US$9.10 per barrel of oil passing through pipelines operated by Dar Petroleum and US$11.00 per barrel through those of Greater Nile Petroleum Operating Company. The National Legislative Assembly approved the agreement on 16 October and on 19 October, the government ordered the resumption of oil production; oil exports will start in around three months.

2013 On 8 June Sudan's President al Bashir ordered the stoppage of oil transfers through its territory from South Sudan to stop from 9 June. Sudanese officials later said the ban would take effect in 60 days. On 10 June South Sudan accused Sudanese troops of crossing into Upper Nile state, as tension between the two states rose. President Kiir sacked the entire cabinet on 24 July, in an apparent power struggle with other senior leaders, particularly Vice President Riek Machar. He appointed a new, smaller, cabinet on 1 August, but no a successor to Mr Macha. James Wani Igga was appointed vice president on 24 August. Mr Igga is a member of the Nuer, South Sudan's second largest group of peoples. Talks between Presidents Bashir and Kiir on 3 September eased tensions between the two; President Bashir withdrew his threat to disrupt oil exports from South Sudan. President Kiir reported on 16 December that an attempted coup the previous day that lead to fighting overnight had been quelled and the government was in full control of Juba. President Kiir said the attack had been carried out 'by a group of soldiers allied to the former vice-president Dr Riek Machar and his group' who had opened fire at a meeting of the ruling SPLM party. Despite the President's assurances, fighting continued for the next two days, with unconfirmed reports that several hundred people had been killed. Dr Machar denied that he had been involved and told the *Sudan Tribune*, a Paris-based news website that 'What took place in Juba was a misunderstanding between presidential guards within their division, it was not a coup attempt.' The French UN ambassador Gerard Araud, UNSC president, told the BBC that there was 'the potential of a civil war' between the two main ethnic groups, the Dinka and the Nuer. This was denied by the governor of Unity State, Simon Kun Pouch, who was quoted on the government website as saying that the conflict had nothing to do with tribes.

2014 Peace talks in Addis Ababa re-started on 11 February. The UN estimates that since the dispute between President Kiir and former vice-president Dr Machar began in mid-December some 868,000 people have fled their homes to elsewhere in the country, and a further 145,000 have fled to Ethiopia and other countries. US President Obama signed an executive order authorising sanctions against anyone aggravating the conflict in South Sudan, including attacking UN peacekeepers.

2015 President Kiir and rebel commander Riek Machar signed a deal on 1 February, agreeing to end the conflict. The ceasefire, which came into effect on 2 February, was signed in Ethiopia; talks continued over the issue of a future government and power-sharing. The conflict has been going on since December 2013. Mr Kiir is expected to continue as president with Mr Machar as vice president. The peace agreement was signed by rebel leader Riek Machar on 17 August, but President Kiir refused. He finally signed on 26 August after intense, closed door talks with the presidents of Ethiopia, Kenya and Tanzania who had come to Juba for the second time to witness the signing. Even so he said he had grave 'reservations', including power-sharing and what he called the ambiguous structure and command of the South Sudan forces once the transitional government takes office. The US had drafted a UN resolution that would have imposed an arms embargo and targeted sanctions unless Mr Kiir signed. Under the agreement a Transitional government of national unity will take office in 90 days and govern for 30 months, with elections to be held 60 days before end of its mandate. A Commission for Truth, Reconciliation and Healing will be commissioned to investigate human rights violations. In October the UN reported that some 30,000 people faced death by starvation, and tens of thousands more were on the brink of famine.

Political structure

Constitution

The interim Constitution for southern Sudan was inaugurated in 2005, as agreed under the Comprehensive Peace Agreement (CPA) with Sudan. It established an autonomous government, headed by a president, who is head of government and commander-in-chief of the Sudan People's Liberation Army (SPLA). A presidential term in office is five-years, with a limit of two terms.

A new, draft Constitution was finalised in March 2011. A version of the constitution was ratified on 7 July 2011 by the South Sudan Legislative Assembly, it replaces the existing 2005 Interim Constitution of Southern Sudan. It establishes a presidential system of government head by a president who is Head of State, Head of Government, and the Commander-in-Chief of the armed forces.

Independence date

9 July 2011

Form of state

Presidential democracy

The executive

The president is elected by simple majority popular vote and is Head of government and appoints a cabinet, approved by parliament. The presidential office is limited to two, four-year terms.

National legislature

The bicameral National Legislature consists of the Council of States and the National Legislative Assembly. The latter is made up of 332 seats of which 170 members were elected in April 2010, 96 members of the former National Assembly, and 66 newly appointed members. The Council of States was established by presidential decree in August 2011, it includes 50 members – 20 former members of the Council of States and 30 appointed representatives.

Legal system

The interim constitution mandated a decentralised institution that is independent of the executive and legislature and with its own budget, so as not to be dependent on the government. Judicial power is derived from the people and exercised in courts in accordance with customs, values, norms and in conformity with the constitution and legislation.

The structure of the judiciary is modelled on the UK judiciary and is headed by a Supreme Court (based in Juba), which is the highest legal institution. Below this court are the Courts of Appeal (based in three state capitals), High Courts (based in all state capitals), County Courts and other courts deemed necessary to establish. The president of the Supreme Court is answerable to the president and parliament for the administration of the judiciary.

Last elections

11–15 April 2010 (presidential first and second rounds); 20 January 2011 (independence referendum). General elections were scheduled to be held in South Sudan by 9 July 2015, however, as a result of continuing conflict in the country, the South Sudan parliament voted in April 2015 to amend the country's transitional 2011 constitution to extend the presidential and parliamentary term until 9 July 2018.

Results: Presidential: Salva Kiir (SPLM) won 92.99 per cent of the vote, Lam Akol (SPLM-(Democratic Congress) DC) 7.01 per cent.

Referendum: 98.83 per cent of the vote in favour, 1.17 per cent against.

Next elections

9 July 2018 (presidential and parliamentary)

Political parties

Ruling party

Sudan People's Liberation Movement (from 9 Jul 2011)

Population

11.38 million (2014)* The result of the 2008 census was disputed by the interim government of Southern Sudan, which claimed that the population of the south should have been around one-third of the total of Sudan (39,154,490). They also claimed that the figure for southerners living in the north (518,000 in the census) was closer to 3.9 million.

The government of Southern Sudan had expected up to 1.5 million people living in northern Sudan and Egypt to return to the south to participate in the January 2011 referendum. However, according the UN Sudan mission, from October 2010– April 2011 288,000 people had made the journey from the north. The majority of these returnees settled in border states and in rural areas.

Last census: 22 April 2008: 8,260,490 million (disputed figure)

Internally Displaced Persons (IDP)

The UN Office for the Co-ordination of Humanitarian Affairs (OCHA) estimated that there were 213,832 returnees to South Sudan (October–February 2010–11) and more people were expected to return from Uganda and Sudan, which would strain food security throughout the country in 2011.

Ethnic make-up

There are over 200 ethnic groups, but the people are socially, culturally and historically related to the peoples of east Africa. The largest group are the Dinka.

Religions

Mainly Christian, animist and traditional beliefs

Education

Only 37 per cent of the population above aged six has attended school.

The Juba National University is based in Khartoum and provides instruction in English for South Sudan students. In 2011 it was in the process of being relocated to South Sudan.

In October 2010, the Dr John Garang International School opened, and in January 2011 it moved to a permanent location in Juba, where it operates a first school, on the UK system. When its intake is complete it will provide education for 350 children, with classes of 25–30 per teacher. It is divided into four stages, kindergarten, pre-school, Key Stage 1 (Years 1 and 2) for children aged five and six and Key Stage 2 (Years 3, 4, 5 and 6) children aged seven–10. The educational year begins in September and finishes in July. Plans for the construction of a high school in 2012 are advancing.

The Southern Sudan Interactive Radio Instruction (SSIRI) provides at-a-distance educational programmes for children (called The Learning Village) and adults (including English), as well as training for teachers, including classroom management. It is funded by US Agency for International Development and administered by the Education Development Centre (EDC). The Association for the Development of Education in Africa (ADEA) in conjunction with educationalists and ministers in Juba, identified the needs of South Sudan to develop educational services for the population.

All statistics on South Sudan were gathered from the National Education Statistical Booklet, Ministry of Education (South Sudan 2009).

Literacy rate: 27 per cent of the population aged above 15 years are literate. Literacy in males is 40 per cent, 16 per cent in females. Urban adult literacy rate: 53 per cent, 22 per cent rural rate. Literacy rate of population aged 15–24 years 40 per cent, of which male rate 55 per cent, 28 per cent female.

Enrolment rate: 72 per cent gross enrolment. Net enrolment in primary school 72 per cent.

Pupils per teacher: 52 students per teacher (average class size 129 students)

Health

In January 2011 there were only 130 doctors in South Sudan as well as a chronic lack of other medical staff.

The senior medical officer at the Juba Teaching Hospital was critical of the health system on the day after independence in July 2011, saying that none of the state-run hospitals or primary care centres available was functioning properly due to a lack of funds, equipment, medical supplies and personnel. Although plans for a new hospital and blood bank, as well as a network of primary care centres were under consideration, the health service could not provide for many patients with traumas and preventable diseases in the meantime.

All statistics gathered from Southern Sudan Centre for Census, Statistics and Evaluation (SSCCSE)

At independence South Sudan had been polio-free for some four years. However, although every child in the country is supposed to be vaccinated against tuberculosis, polio, diphtheria, tetanus, whooping cough and measles by its first birthday, the director of the programme on immunisation (EMI), Anthony Kirbak, said that only happens for about 65 per cent of the country's children due to a scant health infrastructure, poor roads and cyclical violence in some areas of the country. The ministry of health sends thousands of volunteers out across the country four times a year to immunise every child they can find who is under six. Kirbak said they regularly reach more than 90 per cent of the children.

HIV/Aids

HIV prevalence: 1.6 per cent (SSCCSE 2010)

Life expectancy: 42 years (SSCCSE 2010)

Fertility rate/Maternal mortality rate: 2,054 maternal deaths per 100,000 live births

Child (under 5 years) mortality rate (per 1,000): 104 per 1,000 live births (WHO 2012)

Head of population per physician: 80,000 per doctor (2011)

Main cities

Juba (capital, estimated population 508,908 in 2012), Rumbek (81,732), Wau (163,421), Malakal (143,412), Yei (128,880), Yambio (123,673), Kwajok (98,237).

Languages spoken

Colloquial Arabic is widely spoken and Juba Arabic (a pidgin) is spoken in the capital. Native languages include Dinka, Nuer and Ubangian.

Official language/s

English

Media

Press

There are a number of online news outlets, although most are published from abroad.

Weeklies: In English, the *Juba Post* (http://jubapost.org) reports on news, politics, business and other domestic issues. It accepts advertising for both its hardcopy and online editions.

Broadcasting

Radio: Internews operates a community service for the region including South Sudan (www.internews.org), although it is based in the US. The BBC also has services operating (www.bbc.co.uk/worldservice)

The Southern Sudan Interactive Radio Instruction (SSIRI) provides at-a-distance educational programmes for children (called The Learning Village) and adults (including English), as well as training for teachers, including classroom management.

National news agency: South Sudan News Agency (www.southsudannewsagency.com)

Economy

South Sudan has fertile soil suitable for subsistence farmers growing a variety of crops including plantains, sorghum, cassava, millet, groundnuts, maize, okra, millet, rice, sweet potatoes, wheat, sesame and beans. The Ngok Dinka and Misseryia people have traditional use of land for grazing cattle in Abyei, straddling the new border between Sudan and South Sudan. Livestock includes chickens and goats as well as cattle (dairy and beef) in drier, less fertile areas. Mineral deposits include uranium, gold and copper, among others.

There are large petroleum deposits that were initially developed by the central government of Sudan (before the independence of South Sudan), in partnership with foreign, principally Chinese, oil companies. At the end of 2014, South Sudan had proven reserves of 3.5 billion barrels of oil, with production of 159,000 barrels per day (bpd) of oil – a 60.6 per cent increase on 2013. The division of oil production and revenue has been under discussion since the referendum on independence that confirmed South Sudan's future as a sovereign nation. Although the two governments held talks to agree a royalty on previous investment, development and infrastructure costs on the exploitation of the oil fields, an agreement was not reached before independence on 9 July 2011.

The South Sudan government considered an equal division of oil revenue with Sudan as inequitable, given that 70 per cent of total oil production comes from South Sudan. As Sudan refused to negotiate, so in July 2011 South Sudan began discussions with Ethiopia and Kenya to run an oil pipeline through either country to their seaports, thereby circumventing any oil sharing agreement with Sudan. Both projects would take several years to complete.

In January 2012 South Sudan shut down all oil production following the dispute with Sudan over the transit fee for oil piped overland to Sudanese ports. The shutdown resulted in a cut in government revenue, (oil typically provides 98 per cent of government revenue), but the stoppage only lasted until April 2013.

Months of diplomatic negotiations followed and culminated on 23 July 2012, when South Sudan offered compensation of US$3 billion to Sudan for economic losses resulting from revenue loss since South Sudan's independence. South Sudan also offered increased transit fees for oil passing through Sudan amounting to US$9.10 per barrel. The conflict and temporary suspension hit the economy hard, with GDP growth being -47.6 per cent. However, by 2013 growth was positive again at 24.7 per cent.

The World Bank administers the Multi-Donor Trust Fund-South Sudan (MDTF-SS), which has a total of US$232.5 million to invest in capacity building support to the newly formed government of South Sudan. The World Bank advised the new government that anti-corruption measures were essential to ensure good governance when disbursing national revenue derived from petroleum sales.

In early 2011 there were less than 50km of metalled roads in South Sudan, around 80 per cent of the population lived in traditional timber round houses (*tukul*) without electricity or running water, and 90 per cent were living on less than US$1 per day. The UN Food and Agriculture Organisation (FAO) stated that almost 50 per cent of the population were in need of food assistance.

On 20 April 2011 South Sudan formally applied for membership of the International Monetary Fund (IMF), which will allow it to draw on financial technical assistance and loan arrangements in the future. It became a member of both the IMF and World Bank on 18 April 2012.
On 18 July 2011, distribution of the new South Sudan pound (SS£)) began; the first bank notes issued were to the value of SS£50. All Sudanese pounds in circulation in South Sudan were due to be exchanged for the new money at S£1=SS£1, however no deadline for exchange was published. It was estimated that S£2 billion (US$750 million) was in circulation in early 2011.
The South Sudan pound fell in value, losing around 98 per cent of its value in January 2012, due to the shutdown in oil production. Inflation rose sharply, reaching an annual rate of 60.9 per cent in July 2011.
In June 2012, the government struck a loan-deal with the Qatar National Bank (QNB), which agreed to provide a line of credit up to US$100 million in hard currency for imports of food, fuel, medicines and construction materials. At an agreed time, the Bank of South Sudan (BoSS) will buy back the local currency paid to the QNB plus 10 per cent in stamp duties and the interest accrued.
On 15 December 2013 civil war broke out in South Sudan between government forces and rebels led by opposition politicians. The conflict has caused oil production in Unity State, one of the country's two oil areas, to stop completely and other oil fields are also in danger. Two million people have been displaced by the conflict and the disruption to farming means the country is slipping into a famine. Due to the conflict economic data is difficult to collect so the full economic effects of the conflict are not known. In July 2014, the UN Security council described the food crisis in South Sudan as the worst in the world. In August 2015 President Salva Kiir signed an international mediated peace deal following threats of UN sanctions. This deal would lead to rebel leader Riek Machar returning as vice-president.

External trade

South Sudan's future trading will be with traditional partners including all of its neighbours, however in the short term it will need to develop a modern infrastructure to sustain anything but the current, improvised, transportation of goods from anywhere in the region. In early 2011 there were less than 50km of metalled roads, severely hampering private business expansion.
Oil flows north to the Red Sea port of Sudan.

Exports

Petroleum piped through Sudan (for onward delivery to China and other destinations).

Agriculture

Farming

The soil is fertile and crops under cultivation include plantains, sorghum, cassava, millet, groundnuts, maize, okra, millet, rice, sweet potatoes, wheat, sesame and beans. Livestock includes cattle (dairy and beef), chickens and goats.
The civil war that broke out in December 2013 has caused agricultural production to be severely cut, affecting more than 2 million people. Although exact figures and the extent of the problem are not known it is feared that South Sudan is slipping into a state of famine. In June 2014, the UN Security Council described the food crisis in South Sudan as the worst in the world.

Fishing

Artisanal fishermen catch freshwater fish for domestic consumption. The White Nile flows through South Sudan. Together with the associated swamps of the Sudd, the potential fish production could reach 100,000-300,000 tonnes per year.

Forestry

Teak wood is a valuable export.
In 2007, a report by the UN Environment Programme, stated that South Sudan had lost 40 per cent of its forests since 1960s and that desertification was progressing south due to land degradation. It recommended measures to impede the growth of the Sahara, including a reduction in slash-and-burn for agricultural purposes. The need for charcoal was also noted as a potential source of conflict between Sudan and South Sudan, with sufficient supplies for Sudan only being manufactured in South Sudan by 2017.

Industry and manufacturing

In 2008, 53 per cent of the working population were unpaid family members and only 12 per cent of the working population were paid employees. Of the 7,333 formal businesses in the ten state capitals, 84 per cent were retail or restaurants.

Tourism

While the potential for eco-tourism is high, there is little infrastructure to attract any but the most intrepid traveller. South Sudan is the location of the world's largest freshwater swamp (the Sudd), which can increase in size to 130,000sq km during the rainy season and is Africa's largest wetland, and an important habitat for fish, birds and mammals. The civil-war that broke out in December 2013 has had a detrimental effect upon the tourism industry, as many governments warn travellers about visiting the country.

Environment

In June 2010 the African Union backed a proposal to build the 'Great Green Wall' project – a 15km wide, 7,775km long, continuous belt of trees from Senegal in the west to Djibouti in the east (traversing 11 countries, including South Sudan) in an effort to halt the advance of the Sahara Desert. The trees to be used would be drought-adapted, preferably native to the area from a list of 37 possible species, and should help to slow soil erosion and filter rain water.

Mining

There are under-exploited deposits of uranium, iron ore, chromium, zinc, tungsten, mica, gold and copper. However, these are becoming globally more sought after commodities and development is expected in the medium-term.

Hydrocarbons

At the end of 2014, South Sudan had proven reserves of 3.5 billion barrels of oil, with production of 159,000 barrels of oil per day (bpd) – a 60.6 per cent increase on 2013. However, all oil exports had to pass through oil pipelines in Sudan to the Red Sea port of Port Sudan. Sudan entered into negotiations for a royalty on its investment on development and infrastructure costs in the exploitation of this oil. It started at a fee per barrel transported of over US$36, while South Sudan offered less than US$1.
Talks sponsored by the African Union, and mediated by former South Africa president, Thabo Mbeki, were held in Addis Ababa in early 2012. Eventually, an agreement was signed by Presidents Kiir and Bashir on 27 September and South Sudan ordered the resumption of oil production, which had been around 350,000bpd in January. Under the agreement, South Sudan will pay US$9.10 per barrel of oil passing through pipelines operated by Dar Petroleum and US$11.00 per barrel through those of Greater Nile Petroleum Operating Company.
Meanwhile a memorandum of understanding (MOU) had been signed between South Sudan and Kenya on 24 January 2012, to build an oil pipeline to take South Sudanese oil to a Kenyan port for export. The pipeline will be built and owned by South Sudan and the two countries will negotiate transit fees for the oil through Kenya. The pipeline will also include a fibre-optic line giving internet connection to South Sudan. On 2 March construction began on the US$23 billion port and oil refinery project in Lamu District, Kenya. The presidents of Kenya,

South Sudan and Ethiopia were at the launching ceremony, amid tight security in an area close to the border with war-torn Somalia. The project, known as the Lamu Port South Sudan Ethiopia Transit Corridor (Lapsset), is due to be completed by 2016, with initial investment from all three countries, with plans to attract international investment. If it goes ahead, Lapsset will be one of Africa's largest civil engineering projects. It would also obviate the need for oil to pass through Sudan.

Since the completion of the Lapsset MOU in 2012 there have been oil discoveries under Lake Albert (Uganda) and in the Turkana area of Kenya. The Lapsset plans have been redesigned to accommodate oil from these discoveries. Uganda also plans to build a refinery on Lake Albert (60,000bpd).

On 10 February 2012 another MOU, to build another pipeline, this one through Ethiopia to the Port of Djibouti, was signed with Ethiopia. Industry analysts consider that such a pipeline, of 1,000km through rugged terrain, with roving bands of militia, could take up to three years to build at a cost of US$4 billion.

In December 2013 South Sudan entered a civil war, which has meant that oil production and pipeline production had been in part or wholly stopped. However, production figures are on the rise again now.

Energy

South Sudan has very poor energy infrastructure. The majority of the population uses bio-fuel to light their homes and cook their food. South Sudan has the potential to produce a large quantity of hydroelectricity and in 2010 the authorities identified eleven likely sites for hydroelectric power plants. In 2013 South Sudan had an installed capacity of 255.2MW.

In February 2011 the second electricity generation and distribution system was launched in the town of Kapoeta (Eastern Equatoria), with an initial capacity of 894kW and 700 service connections. The US funded the project (US$4 million), to include personnel training along with the infrastructure. The first electricity project was established in Yei (Central Equatoria), in 2008 and the third project with a similar generation and distribution system was launched later in February 2011 in Maridi (Western Equatoria).

In December 2013 the African Development Bank (AfDB) granted South Sudan US$26 million to expand electricity distribution networks. The money was targeted at rehabilitation in Juba where only 1 per cent of the population had access to electricity.

Current figures for energy are not known due to the conflict going on in South Sudan.

Banking and insurance

The Bank of South Sudan (BoSS) was launched in 2006 to provide a financial and banking structure for the newly formed interim government under the Wealth Sharing Agreement with Sudan in 2004.

There were three commercial banks operating in South Sudan in 2010, the Nile Commercial Bank (NCB), the Kenya Commercial Bank (KCB) and the Ivory Bank.

The Qatar National Bank (QNB) began operation in October 2011 and in June 2012, Stanbic Bank (licensed by the Bank of Uganda) began commercial operations in Juba.

The government has called on other foreign banks to increase their quality of operations in South Sudan for business, NGOs and foreign consulates and international organisations.

In 2010, only 1 per cent of the population had access to, or made use of, a bank account.

Central bank

Bank of South Sudan (BoSS)

Main financial centre

Juba

Time

GMT plus three hours (South Sudan does not use daylight saving).

Geography

South Sudan is bounded by Ethiopia in the east, Kenya, Uganda and the Democratic Republic of Congo in the south and the Central African Republic in the west, with Sudan in the north. It has a rainforest environment that includes the 30,000 square kilometres (sq km) Sudd swamp formed by the White Nile. The Sudd is the world's largest freshwater swamp, which can increase in size to 130,000sq km during the rainy season.

The river Kirr (Gurf) (Bahr el Arab) became the border between Sudan and South Sudan, it flows through the province of Kordofan and is a tributary of the Upper (White) Nile. Mount Kinyeti Imatong is the highest peak, situated in the Jebel Marra range located along the border with Uganda. The Nuba Hills, in the centre of north South Sudan, are rugged granite peaks that rise sharply out of the plains with fertile slopes and clay pits between hills.

Southern Sudan is composed of ten states: Western Bahr el Ghazal, Northern Bahr el Ghazal, Unity, Warab, Lakes, Western Equatoria, Eastern Equatoria, Central Equatoria, Jonglei and Upper Nile.

Hemisphere

Northern

Climate

South Sudan has a tropical climate that varies from over 35 degrees Celsius (C) (centigrade) in summer to around 20 degrees C in winter. The rainy season is May–October and the humidity only falls between November–March.

Dress codes

Western business clothing is acceptable.

Entry requirements

Passports

Required by all. Passports must be valid for six months from date of entry.

Currency advice/regulations

Banks exchange the local currency for foreign currency at a fix rate and the US dollars is accepted in all money exchange establishments. Currency exchange bureaus use a flexible rate which may offer a better market rate, however they may not be able to re-convert local currency when a visitor departs. On arrival it is advisable to have plenty of lower denomination bank notes for use in exchange.

Health (for visitors)

Mandatory precautions

Valid yellow fever and cholera certificates are required if travellers are arriving from infected areas, or travellers are intending to visit the south of Sudan.

SUE: I picked this up from our Sudan entry and have now confused myself! Does this now mean all travellers to South Sudan must have a cert or just those moving from South to north?

Advisable precautions

Vaccinations for yellow fever, diphtheria, tetanus, polio, hepatitis A and typhoid are recommended. Other vaccinations that may be recommended are cholera, tuberculosis, hepatitis B and meningitis. There is a risk of rabies. Malaria is prevalent throughout the country. Anti-mosquito measures including repellents, nets and clothing that cover the body should be used (these will also provide protection against hepatitis B and yellow fever). Tap water must be treated as unsafe unless boiled and filtered (bottled water is available in the main cities). Eat only well cooked meals, preferably served hot; vegetables should be cooked and fruit peeled. Dairy products are unpasteurised and should be avoided. Use only well maintained, chlorinated, swimming pools as bilharzia can be contracted from streams and rivers.

Hotels

There are several hotels of differing quality in and around Juba.

Credit cards

Not readily accepted.

Public holidays (national)
Fixed dates

1 Jan (New Year's Day), 9 Jan (signing of the Comprehensive Peace Agreement), 1 May (International Labour Day), 16 May (SPLA Day), 9 July (Independence Day), 30 July (Martyrs Day), 24–26 December (Christmas).

Variable dates

Easter, Eid al Fitr (three days), Eid al Adha (five days).

Islamic year 1437 (15 Oct 2015–2 Oct 2016):: The Islamic year contains 354 or 355 days, with the result that Muslim feasts advance by 10–12 days against the Gregorian calendar. Dates of feasts vary according to the sighting of the new moon, so cannot be forecast exactly.

Working hours
Banking

Sat–Thu: 0830–1200.

Business

Sat–Thu: 0800–1700.

Government

Sat–Thu: 0800/0830–1330/1400.

Shops

Sat–Thu: 0800–1330, 1730–2000.

Telecommunications
Mobile/cell phones

The local operator, Vivacell, extended operations to include more rural areas in 2011.

Sudanese mobile phone operators provide 900/1800 and 3G 2100 services that may operate around urban areas of South Sudan.

Security
There are armed attacks on oil fields and trips outside the capital should be arranged through local contacts. Landmines remain a major hazard in South Sudan, especially south of Juba. Visitors should remain on main roads only. Armed militia loyal to local interests in Upper Nile, Blue Nile and Bahr al Ghazal pose a threat.

Crimes against person and property are frequent in South Sudan and while the police force is fledgling all care should be taken to minimise risk.

Conflict in neighbouring countries occasionally spills over into South Sudan. The armed and lawless militia, the Lord's Resistance Army poses a threat to all along the southern border with Uganda. Banditry is prevalent in South Sudan.

Getting there
Air

National airline: South Sudan does not have a national airline but a number of international carriers land in Juba.

International airport/s: The Juba Airport (JUB), is an airfield located north of Juba. It accepts international flights but has few amenities for travellers.

Surface

Road: A project to pave the 192 kilometres, Juba-Nimule highway to Kampala (Uganda) began in February 2011. When completed (early 2012) an extension to Mombasa (Kenya) will be undertaken. Until the road is metalled, the bus journey between Juba and Kampala is around eight hours.

Water: Rivers provide transport but no scheduled services exist.

Getting about
National transport

There are no paved roads in any directions except north from Juba to Sudan.

BUSINESS DIRECTORY

Telephone area codes
The international direct dialling code (IDD) for South Sudan is +249, followed by area code:

Aweil	844	Malakal	831
Bentiu	861	Torit	322
Juba	811	Wau	841
Kwajok	569	Yei	249

Banking
Central bank

Bank of Southern Sudan (BoSS), PO Box, Juba South Sudan; Juba Town Centre, Between the Ministry of Telecommunications and Postal Services (GOSS) Building and the Central Equatoria Taxation Department (tel: 811-820218, 811-820211; fax 811-820211, 811-823939; internet: www.bankofsouthernsudan.org; email: info@bankofsouthernsudan.org).

Other useful addresses
Southern Sudan Centre for Census, Statistics and Evaluation, PO Box 137, Juda (email: SSCCSE@gmail.com or info@SSCCSE.org).

National news agency: South Sudan News Agency (www.southsudannewsagency.com)

Internet sites
Government of Southern Sudan (GOSS): www.goss-online.org

Southern Sudan Centre for Census, Statistics and Evaluation (SSCCSE): www.SSCCSE.org

Spain

KEY FACTS

Official name: Reino de España (Kingdom of Spain)

Head of State: King Felipe VI (since 19 June 2014)

Head of government: Prime Minister Mariano Rajoy Brey (PP) (from 20 Dec 2011)

Ruling party: Partido Popular (PP) (Popular Party) (from 20 Nov 2011)

Area: 504,782 square km, including the Balearic and Canary Islands, and the Ceuta and Melilla enclaves in North Africa

Population: 46.46 million (2013)

Capital: Madrid

Official language: Castilian Spanish, Catalan (in Catalonia including the Balearics), Basque (in the Basque provinces), Valencian (Province of Valencia), Galician (Galicia).

Currency: Euro (€) = 100 cents

Exchange rate: €0.89 per US$ (Sep 2015)

GDP per capita: US$30,278 (2014)

GDP real growth: 1.39% (2014)

GDP: US$1,406.86 billion (2014)

Labour force: 23.03 million (2014)*

Unemployment: 24.45% (2014)

Inflation: -0.18% (2014)

Balance of trade: -US$28.51 billion (2014)

Annual FDI: US$31.42 billion (2011)

* estimated figure

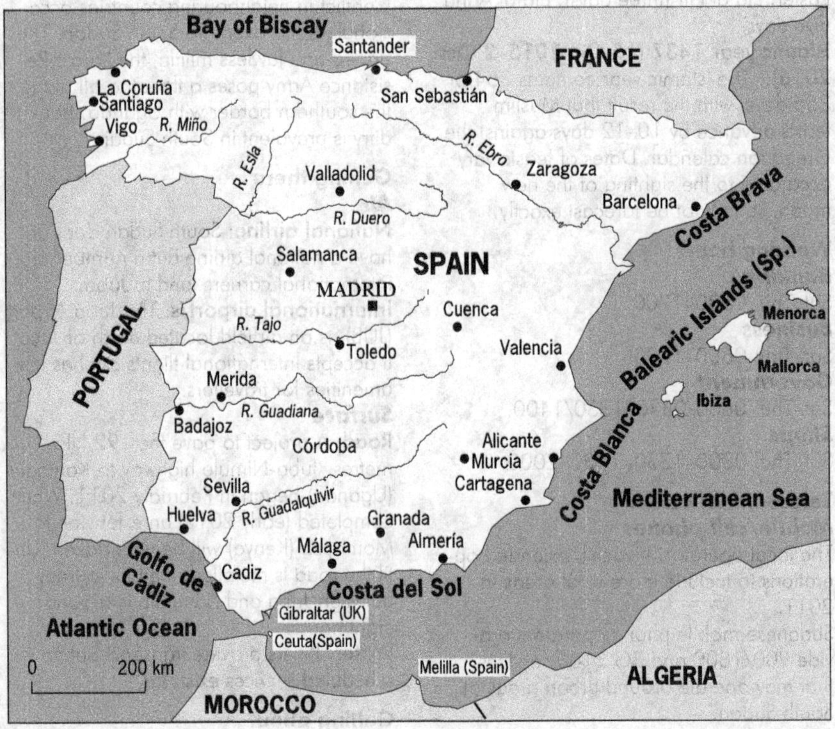

For the long-suffering Spanish electorate, 2015 looked like presenting an even more complicated political mosaic than that seen in the year before. For most of 2014 the unpopular Partido Popular (PP) (Popular Party), led by the uncharismatic Mariano Rajoy, had pinned its hopes of re-election to the incipient recovery of the Spanish economy. That the recovery seemed to be taking hold was certainly the case, as acknowledged by the International Monetary Fund (IMF) in its annual report on the Spanish economy. However, the fruits of the recovery did not seem to be trickling down quite so rapidly, or evenly, as many politicians – not to mention economists – had predicted. The success of Spanish companies such as Ferrovial and Dragados in gaining large civil engineering contracts in countries as far flung as Saudi Arabia, Australia and (closer to home), the UK certainly benefited corporate results; but that success did not generate the levels of employment necessary to create popular confidence in the economic recovery. Small businesses continued to close, unemployment was falling, but slowly, and with a long way to go before Spain could talk of a 'healthy' economy. Spain's youth unemployment figures were such that the emigration of trained and untrained youngsters to Germany, the UK and even the US continued apace in 2015.

'We can'

By late 2014, however, Mr Rajoy found himself with a new political rival. In the opinion polls the Podemos (We Can) party appeared to have overtaken the PSOE (Socialist) Party as the main contender in the election run-up. But Podemos was not the only joker in the electoral pack – in early 2015 a new, centrist party, Ciudadanos emerged, this time threatening to take votes away from the ruling Partido Popular. Podemos was headed by the pony-tailed Pablo Iglesias Turrión, a university lecturer turned firebrand political orator who allegedly saw his party following in the political footsteps of the Greek Syrisa party. Podemos was founded by Mr Iglesias in March 2014. Essentially left wing, to general surprise, in the May 2014 European elections Podemos had obtained almost 8 per cent of the national vote, with 1,200,000 votes cast, electing 5 European Members of Parliament (MEP). Podemos principal platform is one of anti-austerity, placing most of the blame for Spain's high levels of unemployment and social inequality at the feet of the country's membership of the European Union and its adoption of the euro. Mr Iglesias called for the renegotiation of austerity measures and wished to amend the EU's Treaty of Lisbon. Podemos had quickly become a force to be reckoned with. By mid-2015 it was the second largest political party in Spain with 350,000 members (second to the PP).

The more moderate Ciudadanos (Citizens) (Party of the Citizenry), was headed by Albert Rivera, a more moderate academic politician whose party sought its support from the left of centre middle classes who felt let down by the PP. Although its origins were in Catalonia, where in the May 2015 regional elections it won nine seats in the Catalan Parliament, its appeal appeared to have spread to other parts of the peninsula. Controversially, Ciudadanos, despite its Catalan origins, defended the use of Spanish and was opposed to Catalan nationalism. One of the party's slogans was 'Catalonia is my homeland, Spain is my country and the European Union is our future.'

What next?

The run up to the autumn general elections promised to be an unpredictable period, as the opinion polls turned in surprise results, suggesting to a large degree that Spain's post (Franco) dictatorship political pattern, broadly divided between left wing socialism Partido Socialista Obrero Español (PSOE) (Spanish Socialist Workers' Party) and right wing conservatism (PP), had reached its conclusion. What the polls could not so, however, was predict with any accuracy what would happen next.

The election mix had been further complicated by the decision of the Catalan government, headed by the increasingly ineffectual Artur Mas, not to hold an election – which would in effect be a referendum on Catalan independence – until September 2015. The net result was that Catalonia, representing roughly one fifth of the Spanish population and area, found its politicians less interested in properly governing the region than with their likely prospects of assuming post-election power. Over half Catalonia's population was born elsewhere and are not native Catalan speakers. Mr Mas had, in mid-2014, hoped that the Scottish electorate would vote for independence in their September 2014 referendum. As things, turned out, the Scots voted to continue as an autonomous region within the United Kingdom, retaining their allegiance to the British crown. Independent observers noted that in the case of the Scottish referendum, both the preparations and the implementation were better organised than was likely to be the case in Catalonia, where both tempers and feelings ran much higher. In Catalonia the pro-independence regional government headed by Mr Mas had until the regional elections held sway over a large proportion of television stations and newspaper proprietors, denying the region's inhabitants a balanced assessment of the merits and disadvantages of independence. In the aftermath of the elections, Mr Mas found himself quite isolated, as the region's enthusiasm for independence waned.

Corruption

The lacklustre Mr Rajoy also found himself dealing with stridently critical media coverage of what had become an incessant litany of corruption charges. At the top of the social tree was the so called Noos case relating to charitable donations to a Mallorca-based foundation, which appeared to have ended up in the bank accounts of the new King's brother in law, Iñaki Urdangarín, the one time Duke of Palma e Mallorca (he was stripped of his title by his brother in law in early 2015) and, even closer to home, of his wife the new King's sister, the Infanta Cristina. The Infanta's lawyers had resorted to every possible legal ploy, first to have the charges dropped and later to save her from the embarrassing court appearances that inevitably faced her husband. All to no avail.

Other corruption charges had been laid at the door of the ruling PP, whose one-time treasurer and a former senator, José Luis Bárcenas, had been found to own bank accounts in Switzerland with over €50 million (US$56 million) deposited in them. The Bárcenas accusations were followed by further revelations of financial legerdemain by the PP's senior figures. All of which were denied, most of all by the beleaguered Mr Rajoy. However, most neutral Spanish political commentators found it hard to believe that such large sums of money could have been misappropriated without the knowledge of the party's leader. Curiously and in sharp contrast to most Anglo-Saxon democracies, Spanish ministers and senior members of the royal family are granted protection from prosecution while holding office and in certain cases for years afterwards.

No such protection appeared to be forthcoming for the former (PP) minister of finance and one-tine director general of the International Monetary Fund (IMF) Rodrigo Rató. Mr Rató was revered as one of Spain's great post war finance ministers. He was appointed by the overly ambitious PP prime minister, José María

KEY INDICATORS — Spain

	Unit	2011	2012	2013	2014	**2015
Population	m	*46.15	46.77	46.59	46.46	*46.39
Gross domestic product (GDP)	US$bn	1,493.50	1,323.21	1,393.48	1,406.86	*1,230.21
GDP per capita	US$	32,360	28,294	29,907	30,278	*26,517
GDP real growth	%	0.7	-1.6	-1.2	1.4	*2.5
Inflation	%	3.1	2.4	1.5	-0.2	*-0.7
Unemployment	%	21.1	25.0	26.1	24.4	*22.6
Coal output	mtoe	2.5	2.4	1.6	1.6	–
Exports (fob) (goods)	US$m	304,335.0	291,620.0	311,405.0	317,050.0	–
Imports (fob) (goods)	US$m	359,737.0	323,557.0	326,460.0	345,561.0	–
Balance of trade	US$m	-55,402.0	-31,938.0	-15,055.0	-28,511.0	–
Current account	US$m	-51,919.0	-14,814.0	20,033.0	*1,598.0	*3,348.0
Total reserves minus gold	US$m	20,331.8	35,523.0	35,430.0	39,494.0	–
Foreign exchange	US$m	13,803.3	3,180.0	28,168.0	–	–
Exchange rate	per US$	0.75	0.77	0.73	0.82	–

* estimated figure ** forecast figure

Aznar, and was generally credited with improving Spain's public finances. Released on bail, he was the highest ranking political figure to find himself arraigned on charges of corruption.

The lost decade

In its April 2015 assessment of the Spanish economy the IMF noted that it had taken Spain almost 10 years to return to the level of gross domestic product (GDP) last seen before the international financial crisis of 2008. This lost decade placed Spain in the bottom range of countries that had experienced most difficulty in regaining lost economic ground. Setting Greece to one side, only Portugal, Slovenia, Finland and Italy were taking as long. The former Socialist government headed by Mr José Zapatero had first responded by describing the experience as one of economic deceleration rather than a full blown recession. But the Spanish electorate were not that easily fooled. The emperor's new clothes were soon seen through as GDP fell by no less than seven percentage points in a double-dip recession lead by a construction sector that had long thrived on highly geared bank credits. Unemployment soared, abandoned construction sites proliferated. The government's affirmations that the country's banking sector was as strong as ever were soon discredited as one after the other, politically controlled local savings banks hit the buffers.

In the run-up to the 2015 municipal elections the Rajoy government made much of Spain's return to economic growth. The growth figure for 2014 was 1.4 per cent and the IMF forecast for 2015 put the figure at 2.5 per cent, a slightly more cautious figure than the 2.8 per cent estimate of the Banco de España (Bank of Spain) (central bank). The IMF did not take issue with these short term forecasts. But in its view, shared by many economists, the figure for 2016 was clouded with a host of uncertainties, the most important of which was the election's outcome. According to the IMF, the current basis for Spain's economic recovery could not be extended indefinitely. The election apart, the IMF considered that many of Spain's much needed economic reforms had still to be implemented, meaning that the 2015 growth figure might turn out to be no more than a flash in the pan. The longer term IMF forecasts suggested that the growth rate for 2016 might fall to two per cent and still further to an average figure between 1.7 and 1.8 per cent for the period 2017–20.

Quoted by the Washington correspondent of the respected newspaper *El País*, an IMF source stated that 'Complacency would be a disaster, but was the most likely cause for a lack of real growth in the future. Something anyone taking into account the high rate of unemployment cannot fail to appreciate. The blunt truth – again painfully appreciated by the Spanish electorate – was that the growth in Spain's GDP was not being matched by a reduction in unemployment. The chances of the figure of 5 million unemployed falling dramatically by 2020 (which was as far as the IMF forecasts went) were slim. By 2020, according to the IMF, the unemployment rate would still be over 20 per cent, a figure matched only by Greece. According to the Paris-based Organisation for Economic Co-operation and Development (OECD), Spain needed to generate an annual budget surplus of around 2 per cent of GDP if it was to reach a manageable level of national debt, which the OECD considered to be a figure corresponding to less than 70 per cent of GDP and be 'risk-free.' The OECD identified another five countries that needed a budget surplus higher than that of Spain: Japan (almost 6 per cent, Greece (5 per cent) and Italy and Portugal (both above 3 per cent).

The IMF supported the view of the president of the European Central Bank (ECB), Mario Draghi, that Spain needed to return to the drawing board and sort out its labour reforms once and for all, if the problem of its chronic unemployment was to be resolved. The IMF was not impressed by Spain's low levels of productivity, something that whatever educational reforms had been introduced had failed to address. The IMF discounted the likelihood of any significant reforms being introduced during the final months of the current Rajoy (PP) administration. The IMF noted with dismay that even the proposed (and much vaunted) Professional Services legislation which had been proudly paraded at a mid-2014 press conference (and promised to the IMF since 2007) had ended up in a ministerial in-tray. Quixotically and complacently, the Spanish minster of the economy, Luis de Guindos, on a visit to Washington announced that 'the improvement in growth is the consequence of the economic policies of this government. Spain now provides an example.'

The compelling attraction of Mr de Guindos' Spanish example was not immediately apparent. His remarks were clearly designed for consumption outside Spain. Back on the ranch, the Rajoy government steered well clear of calling the Spanish economic situation a recovery. Spanish economic history reveals an interestingly chequered development since the death of General Franco (and the advent of democracy) in 1975. In those 40 years unemployment had passed the 20 per cent mark on three occasions – between 1985 and 1987, from 1993 to 1997 and (indefinitely) since 2009. The average unemployment rate for the 40 years is a staggering 16 per cent, double the European average. The pride of lowering unemployment to 8 per cent in 2007 immediately preceded the crash of the property bubble. At the end of 2014 Spain's unemployment rate was above those of Greece, Portugal, Lithuania, Ireland and Latvia. Ironically, Romania's unemployment rate in 2014 was only 7.4 per cent, questioning the wisdom of those Romanians seeking employment in Spain.

In relative terms, between 2007 and 2011, Spain's GDP fell from being 105 per cent of the EU average to around the 95 per cent mark. Some 3 million jobs simply disappeared and annual per capita income fell from €24,250 to €22,500 (US$27,247–US$25,280). If, by early 2015 there was an economic recovery, it was a slow process. Per capita income had only increased by €262 (US$294.38), well short of the €1,750 (US$1,966.29) that had been lost.

Inequalities

In 2014, according to the OECD, Spain's average annual household income was US$22,799, some US$1,000 less than the OECD average of US$23,938. But the gap between the rich and the poor appeared to be widening. The top 20 per cent earners took home six times the amount earned by the bottom 20 per cent. The number of people surviving on €1,000 (US$1,124) per month has grown. The OECD estimates that around 56 per cent of Spaniards aged between 15 and 64 are in employment; well below the OECD average of 65 per cent. Gender inequality also features prominently – 61 per cent of men have employment, only 51 per cent of women. The casual observer cannot fail to notice how frequently Spain has a national, or a regional holiday. The custom of the *puente* whereby if a public holiday falls on a Thursday or a Tuesday, the intervening weekday (ie the Friday or the Monday) is automatically taken as a holiday. The quantitative effect on productivity of these start-stop shortened weeks is difficult to calculate. But every Spaniard experiences the frustration of delayed appointments and work programmes. Thus, it is hardly surprising that the Spanish work fewer hours per year – 1,686 – than the OECD average of 1,765.

Education levels, which were hardly impressive before the austerity cuts, suffered severely during the austerity period. In Spain only 54 per cent of adults aged between 25 and 64 have a secondary education qualification, well below the OECD average of 75 per cent. Spanish students scored an average of 490 points on the Programme for International Student Assessment (PISA) comparative study, below the OECD average of 497 points. Spain fares badly on other social comparisons – average atmospheric pollution (PM10) is 23.7 microgrammes per cubic metre, higher than the OECD average of 20.1 microgrammes. The percentage of GDP devoted to health provision is a lowly 6.7 per cent (the figure for France is 9.0 per cent and for Germany 8.6 per cent). Health expenditure per head of population is also low, at an annual per capita US$2,059. The figures for France and Germany are US$3,317 and US$3,691 respectively. In the allegedly prosperous region of Catalonia the figure is even lower, at US$1,970.

Elections

What was certain was that the election outcome looked likely to create more, not less, problems. The advent of new political parties offering a fresh start of sorts may be good news for voters fed up with the inadequacies of the old guard. But reaching some sort of a compromise to form a government would probably be easier than agreeing on the selection and implementation of the economic reforms necessary to galvanise the Spanish economy. Compromise of this sort required statesmanship, sacrifice and subtlety – none of which were characteristics normally associated with Spanish political parties or politicians. The commentator Santiago Cabó noted that 'The transformation of the economy is far from finished; perhaps the sober realisation of this is the only guarantee that the economic recovery will continue. It is probably better to assume, in the words of Quevedo, that 'whoever in this life seeks everything to be to his liking, will only find disappointment.'

Perhaps the biggest, overarching, disappointment, mention of which was studiously (but perhaps ill-advisedly) avoided by the IMF, was the elephant in the political room, corruption. In 2015 barely a day went by without either the revelation of a new corruption case such as that involving former finance minister Rodrigo Rató, or new revelations about existing cases such as those involving the PP's former treasurer Luis Bárcenas (in jail) or those of the once respected Catalan politician and father figure Jordi Pujol (discredited) and his extended family. That embezzlement of public funds, money laundering and tax evasion was apparently widespread in senior political circles could only suggest that the same was true of the lower ranks of Spanish politics and its civil service. On Transparency International's 2014 *Corruption Perceptions Index*, Spain ranked an unsatisfactory 37, level with Israel but behind Botswana and Cyprus (31) and Bhutan (30). However poor Spain's 2014 ranking, it was (inexplicably) better than the 2013 ranking of 40.

The notion that the state's money was fair game sadly seemed to pervade all levels of Spanish society. The *paro* (dole, or unemployment pay) was too readily seen as an attractive alternative to work with no stigma attached. Many of Spain's younger generations had decided to emigrate, to the UK, Germany or even the US. Those that remained and were unable to find work, or to find work that paid a respectable wage, were obliged to continue living in the parental home. Those who had married and found work could often only do so with the support of benevolent grandparents, happy (or obliged) to take on the role of unpaid baby-sitters.

Risk assessment

Politics	Fair
Economy	Fair
Regional stability	Good

People to watch

Oriol Junqueras i Vies President of the Republican Left of Catalonia (Esquerra Republicana de Catalunya, ERC)

COUNTRY PROFILE

1492 Spain began colonising much of the Americas, beginning with Hispaniola (Haiti and the Dominican Republic), following Christopher Columbus' landings in the region.

1556 Spain took control of Melilla in Morocco.

1560s Spain colonised the Philippines.

1668 Spain took control of Ceuta in Morocco.

1702–14 The major European powers fought to install a new monarchy in Spain in the War of the Spanish Succession, following the death of Charles II in 1700. France eventually installed the grandson of Louis XIV, Philip of Anjou, as the King of Spain.

1778 Spain took control of Fernando Pó (Bioko, now part of Equatorial Guinea).

1808–13 The Spanish fought against French rule in the War of Independence.

1868 The army revolted against the Spanish monarchy. A military government, led by General Juan Prim, took power. Prim offered the Spanish crown to the son of Italian king Victor Emmanuel II, Amadeo of Savoy.

1873 Prim was assassinated. Amadeo of Savoy left Spain after failing to get installed as the new king. The remnants of the government announced the creation of the First Spanish Republic.

1874 Attempts to introduce constitutional and political reforms to the Republic failed and the monarchy was restored.

1884 Spain took control of the Spanish Sahara (now Western Sahara); it became a province of Spain in 1934.

1885 Spain established the colony of Spanish Guinea in Central Africa, comprising Río Muni and Fernando Pó.

1898 Spain lost control of Cuba, Guam, the Philippines and Puerto Rico, after being defeated in Cuba by the US.

1912 Spain and France partitioned Morocco into protectorates. Spain established the Spanish Morocco protectorate.

1923 The war in Morocco and an economic recession resulted to an authoritarian government in Spain, led by General Miguel Primo de Rivera.

1926 The Spanish and French defeated the Moroccans, bringing the war to an end.

1930 After failing with economic and political reforms, Primo de Rivera resigned from government

1931 Republican parties won the municipal elections, which led the Spanish King, Alfonso XIII, to abdicate. The Second Republic was declared.

1936–39 Civil war broke out when the democratically elected Republican government was attacked in an attempted *coup d'état*. The Nationalist alliance composed of monarchists, right-wing parties and the army, led by Francisco Franco y Bahamonde, fought to take control of Spain. Fascist Germany and Italy, ignoring arms embargoes, supported Franco's forces with men and materials. The government, denied legitimate arms from other European sources, gained the backing of the Soviet Union and welcomed over 56,000 overseas volunteers to fight in the International Brigades.

1939 Nationalist forces won the Civil War. General Franco became Head of State, established a dictatorship, restricted individual liberties and severely repressed all challenges to his power.

1955 An isolated Spain was allowed to join the UN.
1956 Spain granted Morocco independence, but retained control of the Ceuta and Melilla enclaves in northern Morocco.
1958 Spain handed the Tarfaya enclave in West Africa over to Morocco.
1959 The Euskadi ta Azkatasuna (ETA) (Homeland and Freedom) group was formed with the aim of creating an independent Basque region.
1968 Spanish Guinea in West Africa gained independence and was renamed Equatorial Guinea.
1969 Spain withdrew from the Sidi Ifni enclave in West Africa, handing it over to Morocco.
1973 Prime Minister Admiral Luis Carrero Blanco was assassinated by the terriorist group, Euskadi Ta Askatasuna (ETA) (Basque Homeland and Freedom), after the government had executed a number of Basque militants.
1975 General Franco died. Juan Carlos, grandson of the last King, Alfonso XIII, was crowned King Juan Carlos I and became Head of State. Spain withdrew from Western Sahara.
1977 Restrictions on political activity were lifted and free parliamentary elections were held. The Union de Centro Democrático (UCD) (Union of the Democratic Centre) coalition, led by Adolfo Sáurez González, won.
1978 A new constitution confirmed Spain as a parliamentary monarchy with freedom for political parties and enshrined the 'indissoluble unity of the Spanish nation'. It also recognised the right to autonomy of its 'nationalities and regions'.
1980s Referenda on regional autonomy in the Basque region and Catalonia began the process of devolution. Spain was divided into 17 provinces, each with a president and parliament, plus the two self-governing enclaves on the north African coast – Ceuta and Melilla.
1981 The paramilitary *Guardia Civil* (Civil Guard) attempted a *coup d'état*, holding members of the cabinet and parliament hostage. The coup was aborted when King Carlos demanded that the military must remain loyal to the crown and the constitution.
1982 The Partido Socialista Obrero Español (PSOE) (Spanish Socialist Workers' Party), under Felipe González, won the general election. Morocco laid claim to Ceuta, Melilla and the Canary Islands.
1983 A secret death squad known as the Grupo Antiterrorista de Liberacion (GAL) (Anti-Terrorist Group) was set up funded by the Interior Ministry in order to combat ETA. Between 1983 and 1987, 28 people were murdered by the GAL in what became known as Spain's 'dirty war'. Several of those killed later turned out to have no connection with ETA and revelations surrounding the death squads' activities later contributed to the downfall of the PSOE government.
1986 Spain joined the EU.
1986–96 The PSOE won the 1986, 1990 and 1993 parliamentary elections and Felipe González served four terms as prime minister.
1995 José María Aznar, leader of the opposition Partido Popular (PP) (Popular Party) survived an assassination attempt by ETA.
1996 Aznar became prime minister of a PP minority government.
1998 ETA announced a unilateral ceasefire. It was blamed for more than 800 deaths since its campaign of terror began in 1968.
2000 ETA called off its ceasefire. The PP won parliamentary elections.
2001 A new round of talks began between Britain and Spain on the future of Gibraltar.
2002 Euro currency replaced the peseta. An international incident occurred when 12 Moroccan soldiers landed on the disputed tiny uninhabited *Isla del Perejil* (Parsley Island), close to the Spanish-controlled Ceuta enclave in Morocco. Spain re-occupied the island, to which Morocco lays claim and calls *Leila*.
2003 The Batasuna (Unity) party (previously the Herribatasuna party), believed to be the political organisation representing ETA, was banned. Government support for the US-lead coalition invasion of Iraq was opposed by an estimated 85 per cent of the population, causing a further deterioration in support for the PP.
2004 ETA announced a cease-fire. Ten co-ordinated bombs exploded on four commuter trains in Madrid, during the morning rush hour, killing 191 people and injuring over 1,800. ETA denied responsibility; a gang of extremist Islamists, who later committed suicide in a bomb blast during a police raid, were identified as the culprits. The Madrid atrocity had an immediate effect on the electorate, who gave a victory to the opposition party, PSOE, in the general elections. José Luis Rodríguez Zapatero (PSOE) was sworn in as prime minister.
2005 At least 250,000 people marched in Madrid to protest against the government's intention to negotiate with ETA. Spain reinforced fences protecting Ceuta and Melilla, its enclaves in North Africa, after hundreds of would-be immigrants attempted to storm the territories. Spain launched an investigation into allegations that CIA planes made secret stopovers on Spanish territory for purposes of extraordinary rendition, whereby foreign suspects were sent to another country for interrogation under less humane conditions.
2006 Spain agreed to write off most of the debt owed to it by Bolivia. ETA announced a complete cease-fire. In a local referendum residents of Catalonia voted by 73.9 per cent in favour of greater regional autonomy and self-government. The outcome prompted other regions, such as Galicia, Valancia, the Balearic Islands and Andalusia to push for greater autonomy. ETA exploded a car bomb in a Madrid airport car park, killing two people and ending a nine-month cease-fire. However ETA also claimed that its cease-fire was still in effect. Over 31,000 African migrants (six times the numbers arriving in 2005), lacking work permits, made the hazardous ocean journey to the Canary Islands in an attempt to enter the EU for work and a better life.
2007 ETA called off its 15-month cease-fire. Spanish police arrested 23 senior members of Batasuna. Of the 28 defendants on trial for the 2004 Madrid train bombings three were found guilty and sentenced to thousands of years in prison, while seven were acquitted, including the alleged mastermind.
2008 José Zapatero was re-elected as prime minister and named a new cabinet with a majority of women members. The senate voted overwhelmingly to adopt the European Union's Lisbon Treaty. Once King Juan Carlos signed the treaty, Spain became the 23rd EU state to ratify it.
2009 The economy officially entered recession; the unemployment rate reached 17.4 per cent.
2010 After six quarters of falling growth the economy grew by 0.1 per cent for the first three months of 2010; in the same week it was announced that the unemployment rate had reached 20 per cent. The Catalonia parliament voted by 68 to 55 to become the first mainland region in Spain to ban bullfighting, from January 2012. ETA announced a cease-fire, but the Basque and Spanish central government dismissed the declaration as 'meaningless' as ETA had not renounced violence or its dissolution.
2011 A smoking ban in bars and restaurants came into effect in January. In February Spain's number of unemployed was 4.7 million, some 20.5 per cent of the population. In April, Prime Minister Zapatero announced that he would not seek a third term in parliamentary elections due in 2012. An earthquake, of magnitude 5.2 struck Lorca in south eastern Spain in May, killing nine people and leaving over 3,000 people homeless. In May, thousands of young unemployed, including many graduates, protested in Puerta del Sol in Madrid, angry at the government's economic policies that left

so many of them unemployed (44.6 per cent of under 25-year olds). By July the protests had grown into a movement of disaffected called *El Indignado* (The Indignant), which began a 1,500km march to Brussels (headquarters of the EU) to complain about how the EU's financial markets had had a detrimental effect on Spain's economic stability and their future. The prime minister called for elections on 20 November, four months earlier than expected, to 'project political and economic certainty'. A visit by the Pope in August to celebrate mass at the end of World Youth Day was marred by protests against the cost of the visit, and by a violent rain squall that blew off the Pope's skull cap. The last bullfight in Catalonia was held on 25 September. On 20 October, after 40 years of terrorist attacks, Eta announced a 'definitive cessation' to its armed resistance to Spanish rule. Prime Minister Zapatero declared the decision as a 'victory for democracy, law and reason'. In parliamentary elections, the opposition, centre-right, PP won 44.6 per cent of the vote (186 seats out of 350), while the ruling PSOE won 28.7 per cent (110); turnout was 71.7 per cent. Mariano Rajoy Brey took office as prime minister on 20 December.

2012 Spain reported the highest unemployment rate in the EU of 22.9 per cent. Unemployment reached a record 24.4 per cent at the end of March, with 5,639,500 people out of work; in the first quarter 365,900 people lost their jobs. On 17 May the ratings agency Moody's cut the credit ratings of 16 banks, including two of Spain's largest banking institutions, Banco Santander and BBVA; 10 of the 16 were also put on negative credit watch, with further downgrades possible. Moody's cited 'adverse operating conditions' in a renewed recession and the on-going real estate crisis, plus persistent high unemployment, for its decision. The unemployment rate in the second quarter of 2012 reached 24.6 per cent, the highest rate since 1976; Spain's youth unemployment in the second quarter was 53 per cent. On 12 November the Spanish Banking Association declared a two-year moratorium on domestic evictions, following the separate suicide of two people and the public disgust at the loss by 350,000 homeowners of their property (but not the loan). On 26 November, a majority of voters in Catalonia backed pro-independence candidates in local elections. The surprise was that the party of staunchly separatist Catalan President Artur Mas, the CiU, lost 12 seats, although his middle- to right-wing party still maintained the largest bloc of seats – 50 (out of 135). The another left wing pro-Catalan independence party, the ERC, won 21 seats. It is unlikely however that the two parties will be able to work together to win a referendum on independence. On 28 November the European Commission approved the government's plans to restructure and nationalise the top four banks allowing the payment of US$129 billion from the Euro-zone bailout fund.

2013 On 9 July *El Mondo* published documents which it alleges show Prime Minister Mariano Rajoy and other top politicians received illicit payments from a PP 'slush fund'. The PP denies the allegations. On 16 July Rajoy said he would not give in to blackmail, despite calls for his resignation.

In July the South America trade organisation, Mercosur, threatened to withdraw its ambassadors from Spain, Portugal and Italy over their banning from European airspace of President Morales of Bolivia's plane. President Morales was returning from Russia and it was suspected that Edward Snowden, an American accused of leaking secrets about US surveillance schemes, was onboard. Bolivia is an associate member of Mercosur. Official figures published in July showed the unemployment rate for the secon quarter had fallen for the first time in two years, to 26.3 per cent from 27.2 per cent in t he first quarter. The number of unemployed was given at just below six million. On 24 July a high speed train travelling to Santiago de Compostela came off the rails, resulting in 79 deaths. On 1 August Prime Minister Rajoy admitted to MPs that he had made a mistake in trusting disgraced former colleague, Luis Barcenas, but that claims he was corrupt were 'lies and manipulations', and again defied calls for his resignation. Thousands of supporters of the Catalan independence movement formed a 400km chain across the region on 11 September, Catalonia's national day.

2014 King Juan Carlos announced his abdication 2 June. Crown Prince Felipe is expected to succeed him, although special legislation will need to be proposed by the cabinet and confirmed by parliament.

2015 A rally organised by Podemos ('We can do it'), the radical leftists, drew tens of thousands of people to the central Madrid Puerta del Sol square. The party's leader, Pablo Iglesias, told the crowd a 'wind of change' was starting to blow through Europe after the recent victory of its close allies Syriza in Greece. The ruling PP suffered heavy losses in the local and regional elections held on 24 May. Although they remain the largest party with 27 per cent of the vote, they lost control of Barcelona (to Podemos) and Madrid city council to a coalition of Ahora Madrid and Podemos. The solialist PSOE came second with 25 per cent of the votes. Although Spain has officially come out of recession, the level of corruption throughout government was seen as the deciding factor for voters. King Felipe VI removed Princess Cristina's title as Duchess of Palma. His sister is to go on trial charged with tax evasion. In regional elections held on 27 September the Pro-independence parties in Catalonia won an absolute majority, but were short of the 50 per cent necessary to declare independence from Spain within 18 months.

Political structure

Constitution

The Constitution dates from the advent of democracy in 1978. Most laws are debated and passed in Congress first, and then in the Senate, the upper house, which can send back amended bills. In case of emergency, the government may issue decrees. They are called Decree Laws if they require ratification by parliament. All laws require the king's ratification and come into force when published in the Official Bulletin.

There are 17 *comunidades autónomas* (autonomous regions): Andalucia, Aragón, Asturias, Baleares (Balearic Islands), Canarias (Canary Islands), Cantabria, Castilla-La Mancha, Castilla y León, Cataluñya, Comunidad Valencian, Extremadura, Galicia, La Rioja, Madrid, Murcia, Navarra, País Vasco (Basque country). Spain also has sovereignty of five communities on and off the coast of Morocco: the coastal ports of Ceuta and Melilla are administered as autonomous regions; the islands of Chafarinas, Peñon de Alhucemas and Peñon de Velez de la Gomera are under direct Spanish administration.

Autonomous regions have regional parliaments and governments with varying degrees of powers on local affairs. Three regions with a tradition of autonomy and their own language – the Basque country (Euskadi), Cataluñya and Galicia – have these wider powers. The Basque government, for example, raises its own taxes.

The ongoing fight for independence in the Spanish region of Catalonia would result in inevitably devastating consequences for Spain as a whole. After a regional parliamentary election in Catalonia on the 27 September 2015, the 'Together for Yes' group won 62 out of the 135 seats – and has formed an alliance with the smaller CUP party – which won 10 seats. Many in favour of independence believe this results boosts their chances of achieving this dream.

There is universal suffrage from age 18.

Form of state
Federal parliamentary democratic monarchy
The executive
The president of the government (prime minister) appoints the cabinet and has executive power. He is appointed by the Head of State and his appointment must be ratified by the national legislature. The Monarch is hereditary.
National legislature
The bicameral Las Cortes Generales (The General Courts) is composed of the Congreso de los Diputados (Congress of Deputies) (lower house) with 350 members, elected by popular vote on block lists by proportional representation in provincial constituencies, who serve for four-year terms. Two of the members are directly elected from the North African Ceuta and Melilla enclaves by simple majority vote.
In the Senado de España (Senate of Spain) (upper house) has 257-members in total, of which 208 are directly elected and 49 are appointed by regional legislatures. Members serve for four-year terms; appointed members may be recalled by their respective legislatures at any time. Parties need to gain at least 3 per cent of the vote to gain representation in either house.
Legal system
The Spanish legal system is based on civil law. The Supreme Court is at the summit of the judiciary. There are also 16 Division High Courts, 50 Provincial High Courts and, below these, Courts of First Instance, District Courts, Municipal and Peace Courts. Spain does not accept compulsory jurisdiction by the International Court of Justice (ICJ).
Last elections
20 November 2011 (parliamentary)
Results: Parliamentary: the Partido Popular (PP) (Popular Party) won 44.6 per cent of the vote (186 seats out of 350), Partido Socialista Obrero Español (PSOE) (Spanish Socialist Workers' Party) 28.7 per cent (110), Izquierda Unida (IU) (United Left) 6.9 per cent (11), Unión, Progreso y Democracia (UPD) (Union, Progress and Democracy) 4.7 per cent (five), Convergència i Unió (CiU) (Convergence and Union) 4.2 per cent (16), Amaiur (coalition of three parties and independents representing regional homelands) 1.4 per cent (seven), the Eusko Alberdi Jeltzalea-Partido Nacionalista Vasco (EAJ-PNV) (Basque Nationalist Party) 1.3 per cent (five). Turnout was 71.7 per cent.
Next elections
20 December 2015 (parliamentary)

Political parties
Ruling party
Partido Popular (PP) (Popular Party) (from 20 Nov 2011)
Main opposition party
Partido Socialista Obrero Español (PSOE) (Spanish Socialist Workers' Party)

Population
46.46 million (2013). Approximately 15 per cent of children are under 14 years.
Last census: November 2001: 40,847,371 (including offshore territories)
Population density: 79 inhabitants per square km. Urban population 77 per cent (2010 Unicef).
Annual growth rate: 0.8 per cent, 1990–2010 (Unicef).
Ethnic make-up
In addition to Spaniards, there are several minor groups, including Gypsies, Portuguese, Latin Americans and North Africans.
Religions
Roman Catholic (94 per cent), Islam, Protestant and Jewish.

Education
Primary schooling begins at the age of six and lasts for six years. Secondary schooling lasts until aged 16 (both of which are provided free). Final exams allow progression to higher secondary schools which teach either academic or vocational programmes. Teaching may be carried out in Spanish, Catalan, Basque, or Galician.
Private schools are responsible for the education of more than 30 per cent of children.
Higher education is only possible after successfully sitting an entrance exam. There are some 20 state universities, four polytechnics, two independent universities and eight technical universities. The development of alternative forms of higher education have made access to established universities more selective. It has also been proposed that the present five-year university degree courses be reduced to three years.
Public expenditure on education typically amounts to 5 per cent of annual gross national income.
Literacy rate: 97.9 per cent, adult rates (2003)
Compulsory years: Six to 16
Enrolment rate: 109 per cent, gross primary enrolment of relevant age group (including repeaters); 120 per cent, gross secondary enrolment (World Bank).
Pupils per teacher: 15 in primary schools

Health
As Spain's economy has grown, spending on healthcare has risen, reaching 7.5 per cent of GDP, spending just below the Organisation for Economic Co-operation and Development (OECD) average of 7.7 per cent on medical goods and services. Most of this expenditure is in the form of state funding at 71.4 per cent. Efforts are under way to cut the state's pharmaceutical bill, representing 20 per cent of total public health spending. Pre-paid healthcare plans amount to 14.1 per cent of the 28.6 per cent of GDP spent privately on health costs.
The health sector, under the authority of INSALUD, the National Institute of Health, includes hospitals, community health centres and emergency services. The social security health scheme covers all insured persons and their dependants.
HIV/Aids
HIV prevalence: 0.7 per cent aged 15–49 in 2003 (World Bank)
Life expectancy: 80 years, 2004 (WHO 2006)
Fertility rate/Maternal mortality rate: 1.5 births per woman, 2010 (Unicef)
Birth rate/Death rate: 10 births per 1,000 population; 9.5 deaths per 1,000 population (2003).
Child (under 5 years) mortality rate (per 1,000): 5 per 1,000 live births (WHO 2012)
Head of population per physician: 3.30 physicians per 1,000 people, 2003 (WHO 2006)

Welfare
The National Institute of Social Security oversees a national insurance scheme, which is compulsory for all employed and self-employed workers. It provides a range of benefits including those for sickness, maternity, accident insurance, retirement pensions and unemployment benefits. Contributions are paid by employees, employers and the state. The employed are classified in a series of professional and labour categories for the purpose of determining social security taxes. Each category has maximum and minimum contribution bases which are revised annually. The state pays retirement pensions from the age of 65 for men and women. Spain offers a special system of unemployment protection for casual workers in agriculture. The Rural Employment Plan combines employment policy measures and social welfare benefits. The benefit is granted to workers who have paid contributions under the Agricultural Social Security Scheme and is equivalent to 75 per cent of the national minimum wage payable for a maximum period of 180 days.

Main cities
Madrid (capital, estimated population 3.3 million in 2012), Barcelona (capital of Catalonia) (1.6 million), Valencia (831,598), Seville (703,029), Zaragoza (685,963), Málaga (571,731), Murcia

(453,985), Palma (Balearic Islands) (419,285), Las Palmas (Canary Islands) (385,973), Bilbao (capital of Basque region) (351,864).

Languages spoken

Castilian Spanish is the principal language; Catalán, Galician, Euskera (Basque), Aragonese and Asturian are also spoken. English and French are spoken in most business circles.

Official language/s

Castilian Spanish, Catalan (in Catalonia including the Balearics), Basque (in the Basque provinces), Valencian (Province of Valencia), Galician (Galicia).

Media

The constitution enshrines the right to free expression of thoughts, ideas and opinions.

Press

The printed media market is mature with a wide variety of respected titles backed up by a plethora of specialist publications. The media is largely free, although the government has closed down two Basque newspapers, *Egin*, in 1998 and *Euskaldunon Egunkari* in 2003, accusing them of being linked with the terrorist organisation ETA.

Concerns have been raised that media outlets has been unduly influenced by political pressure.

Ownership is largely concentrated in the control of a few large media groups; foreign investment has been redirected to focus on periodicals.

Dailies: There are over 100 newspapers published daily, although most have circulations of less than 100,000. The major dailies are published in Madrid but other cities have their own dailies, particularly in Catalonia and the Basque region. Most publish in Spanish or in regional languages; some are bilingual. Free-issue newspapers account for around 51 per cent of the market.

In Spanish, with the largest circulation *El País* (www.elpais.com) is socialist in character in a tabloid format and has regional and international editions, *ABC* (www.abc.es) is a centre-right paper, *El Mundo* (www.elmundo.es) is a conservative publication. Other newspapers with smaller circulations, from Barcelona *La Vanguardia* (www.lavanguardia.es) and *El Periodico de Catalunya* (www.elperiodico.com) with articles in Catalan; from Bilbao *El Correo* (www.elcorreodigital.com) and *El Diario Montanes* (www.eldiariomontanes.es); from Andalucia *Diario de Cadiz* (www.diariodecadiz.es),*Cordoba* (www.diariocordoba.com) and *Metro* (www.diariometro.es) Seville; from the Balearic Islands *Diario de Ibiza* (www.diariodeibiza.es) and *Mallorca Confidencial* (www.mallorcaconfidencial.com); from Canary Islands *La Provincia* (www.laprovincia.es) and *El Dia* (www.eldia.es); from La Coruna *Xornal* (www.xornal.com) with articles in Galacian; from Andoain *Berria* (www.berria.info) in Basque.

English, French and Germany newspapers are published in areas with large expatriate communities and tourist areas.

Weeklies: There are several general and special interest magazines and news magazines such as *Cambio 16*, *Sábado Gráfico* and *El Tiempo* (www.tiempodehoy.com). *El Mundo* has a Sunday edition called *La Revista*. In the Canary Islands *Canarias 7* reports news items, *Metropolitan* from Barcelona. *Ragazza* (www.ragazza.orange.es) *Inerviú* (www.interviu.es) and *Diez Minutos* (www.diezminutos.orange.es) are tabloid magazines.

Business: In Spanish, *Cinco Días* (www.cincodias.com), *Expansión* (www.expansion.com), *La Gaceta de los Negocios* (www.negocios.com/gaceta), *Agenda de la Empresa Andaluza* (www.agendaempresa.com), *Vigo Empresa* (www.puertodevigo.com), *El Economista* (www.eleconomista.es), *El Mundo Financiero* (www.elmundofinanciero.com) and *Negocio* (www.neg-ocio.com). Weekly financial publications in Spanish include *Su Dinero*, *Levamte-El Mercantil Valencia* (www.levante-emv.com) from Valencia and *Actualidad Económic* (www.actualidad-economica.com) from Madrid.

Periodicals: A number of specialist magazine exist including *Planeta Humano* and *Qué*, bi-monthly covering people and current affairs.

Broadcasting

National public radio and television services are provided by Radiotelevisión Española (RTVE) (www.rne.es), which is funded by state subsidies and advertising.

Radio: The public broadcaster Radio Nacional de España (RNE) (www.rne.es), provides four national services. There are several commercial networks, the largest of which is Cadena SER (www.cadenaser.com) with over 50 regional stations.

There are over 100 radio stations, which have a presence in every region, including overseas territories, providing services over the internet.

Television: Televisión Española (TVE) (www.rtve.es) broadcasts several channels, from popular local programmes such as long-running dramas to international imported shows and special interest programmes. There are another three private terrestrial channels and six regional public broadcasters with 10 channels between them, some in Catalan and Basque. Digital and satellite TV networks have expanded rapidly and the government has plans to discontinue free-to-air analogue signals by 2010. National commercial channels include Tele Cinco (www.telecinco.es), Antena 3 (www.antena3tv.com) and Cuatro (www.cuatro.com).

EFE (government-owned), Espronceda, 32. 28003 Madrid (tel: 346-7519; fax: 346-7173; internet: www.efe.com).

Colpisa (private) (www.colpisa.com).

Europa Press (private) (www.europapress.es with specific sections on regional news).

Economy

Spain has a mixed economy with large agricultural and industrial sectors, as well as important tourism and banking sectors. It is the world's largest olive oil producer, from 2.4 million hectares of olive groves, and a major contributor to the European Union's agricultural production of fruit, vegetables and wine; it also has Europe's largest fishing fleet, which operates in all oceans. It has become an important automotive manufacturer and its tourist industry is one of the most highly developed in Europe.

After the global crisis hit, GDP growth in Spain dropped to 0.9 per cent in 2008 and the trade deficit reached 10 per cent of GDP. This deficit was due to Spain's need to import petroleum, which was at a time of record high prices and also due to collapse of the property market, which was fuelled by unsustainable loans. In 2009 the country went into deep recession, recording a fall in GDP of 3.7 per cent. Speculation of the negative future growth of Spain lead to two international credit rating agencies (Standard & Poor's and Fitch) dropping the country's rating from AAA to AA+. This caused an increase in cost of foreign borrowing. By 2011 Spain's public debt had grown to 68.5 per cent of GDP, and in an attempt to reduce the deficit to 5 per cent of GDP, an austerity budget (which involved cuts of US$35.7 billion) was introduced in March 2012. Unemployment reached a record high since 1997 and reached 24.4 per cent of total labour force in 2012 – 5,639,500 workers were out of jobs. In the same year, prospects of shrinking growth in the future led to further downgrades from rating agencies. Unemployment peaked at a new record in 2013, reaching 26.6 per cent of the labour force without work, despite the fact that the number of unemployed fell by 65,000. This was because the working age population had shrunk due to 260,000 people leaving the country, 40,000 of these were

Spanish nationals and the rest were departing foreign migrants. The number of people without work has decreased in recent years, falling to 22.4 per cent by the second quarter of 2015, however this is still much higher than the EU average of 9.6 per cent.
Spain is battling on two fronts. Domestically it must smooth out the imbalances in the economy and reduce public debt while reducing unemployment, and at the same time manage the international money markets that have lost faith in Spain's liquidity.
The on-going European currency crisis has exposed Spain's weaknesses, although this may be resolved by the European Central Bank (ECB) being allowed to buy Spanish short-term bank bonds, which should cut Spain's borrowing costs and allow time for austerity measures to work.

External trade

As a member of the European Union, Spain operates within a community-wide free trade area, with tariffs set as a whole. Internationally, the EU has free trade agreements with a number of nations and trading blocs world-wide.
While agriculture provides only 2.6 per cent of GDP, Spain never-the-less produces Europe's largest supply of citrus fruits and strawberries and it is the world's leading olive oil producer. It also has Europe's largest fishing fleet. Spain become the world's second largest producer of wine in 2013, producing 6.7 billion bottles which were 41 per cent up on the figures from 2012. Despite dropping back to third in 2014, behind France and Italy, Spain became the world's largest exporter of wine. Manufacturing sources of exports include textiles, food processing, naval engineering, vehicle assembly and machinery; new technology includes information technology and telecommunications.
Exports accounted for around 32 per cent of GDP in 2014, while tourism (Spain is a world-wide top tourist destination) provided most foreign earnings, despite the strength of the euro, which reduced tourist visitor numbers.

Imports

Main imports include machinery and equipment, petroleum and natural gas, chemicals, semi-finished goods, foodstuffs, consumer goods, and medical instruments.
Main sources: Germany (13.2 per cent of total in 2014), France (11.8 per cent), China (6.1 per cent).

Exports

Main exports include machinery, motor vehicles; foodstuffs, pharmaceuticals, medicines and other consumer goods.
Main destinations: France (15.8 per cent of total in 2014), Germany (10.5 per cent), Portugal (7.4 per cent).

Agriculture

Farming

Spain is the world's largest producer of olive oil: the industry has been modernising, although olive groves, mainly located in Andalucía, typically suffer periodic drought and work is usually undertaken by low paid migrant workers. The revised Common Agricultural Policy (CAP) of the EU should benefit the region by limiting unsustainable growth.
Spain is the third largest wine producer in the world, producing 41.6 million hectolitres (hl) in 2014, compared with France and Italy's production of 46.7 and 44.7 million hl respectively. EU restrictions limit the amount of land available for vineyards and, with domestic consumers developing a taste for wines of increased quality, the price of grapes and available vineyards has increased enormously.
Newer regions are producing quality wines to rival those of the long established Rioja and *Penedes denominaciones*.
Cava, the Spanish wine made using the champagne method, is gaining a global reputation for quality and value. Notable among these are Ribera de Duero in Castilla y Leon, where the legendary Vega Sicilia wines are produced, and the *Priorat denominaciones* in Catalonia.

Fishing

As the owner of the largest fishing fleet in the EU, Spain is also the largest consumer of seafood and seafood products in the EU. Spain's total fish catch continues to decline as a result of depleted stocks and lower limits on catches in both EU and non-EU waters. Spain's seafood trade is mainly conducted with other EU countries, Argentina, Morocco and Namibia.

Forestry

Forest and other wooded land accounts for about half the land area, with forest cover estimated at 14.3 million hectares (ha). Most of the forest is available for wood supply. The area of forest has been expanding strongly, at an annual average increase of 0.62 per cent per year. About 80 per cent of forested area is privately owned, while the remaining area is mostly owned by municipalities. Approximately 45 per cent of the forest is available for wood supply. The main species are Scots and Aleppo pine, oak, beech, chestnut, poplars and eucalyptus.
Imported raw materials including eucalyptus pulpwood and hardwood logs are used for all primary forest products. Spain is a net importer of paper and sawnwood, although part of the pulp production is exported.

Industry and manufacturing

The industrial sector contributed approximately 25.3 per cent to GDP in 2014 and employed around 20 per cent of the labour force.
Since joining the EU, Spain's industry and manufacturing sectors have undergone modernisation and restructuring, assisted by large levels of foreign direct investment (FDI). The automotive, telecommunications and chemical industries dominate the sector.

Tourism

The tourist industry has had a long and vital influence on Spain's GDP growth, beginning in the 1970s as mass tourism developed, offering cheap packaged beach holidays with virtually guaranteed sun.
The sector contributed around 18 per cent of GDP in the 1980s, but this fell to as low as 14.5 per cent in 1993 as other sectors within the economy grew and new foreign markets began offering stiff competition. By 2003–05 travel and tourism constituted between 15–16.5 per cent of GDP, but as the global economic crisis struck and visitors from Europe, Spain's prime market, could no longer afford to travel, the industry went into negative growth in 2007. In 2008 all sectors of the industry recorded a fall, including hotel occupation, flights and sea and rail passengers, the only exception was day-trip arrivals, which showed a modest growth of 0.6 per cent. The industry fared even worse in 2009 as the recession deepened and all sections recorded negative growth. In the first quarter of 2009, 5.6 million foreign tourists visited Spain, which was a 16.3 per cent decrease from the same period in 2008.
Spain's economic decline also affected domestic tourism, which added to the industry's malaise so that unemployment for the country in general included a sizable portion of jobs in travel and tourism.
The sector has been streamlined and reorganised at its base to compete for business in a contracted market, and figures in 2013 showed a massive improvement. Figures slightly fell in 2014, however they were still strong, with total contribution to GDP by the travel and tourism industry at EUR161.1 billion (US$218 billion, or 15.2 per cent of GDP) and 2,652,500 people (15.3 per cent of total employment) directly and indirectly employed by the tourism sector. In the first half of 2015, Spain set tourism records with 29.2 million arrivals. This was a 4.2 per cent increase on the same period of the previous year.

Mining

The mining sector contributes 1 per cent to GDP. Spain is the world's second-largest producer of natural stone, which accounts for 15 per cent of the total value of Spanish mining. Marble has become a particularly important source of foreign exchange earnings. Gold, silver and copper mining take place on a small scale. Spain also extracts lignite, iron ore, mercury, pyrites, zinc, lead, copper and tungsten. The traditional production of uranium ore in Spain ceased with the closure of Mina Fé in Salamanca.

In July 2015, it was announced that one of the world's oldest and most historic mining sites – the Rio Tinto Mine in Spain – would be reopened. Operations on the mine that has been mined since 3000BC are expected to begin in 2016.

Hydrocarbons

Oil production is negligible; the largest domestic production comes from the Casablanca complex, in the Mediterranean, which provides around 6,000 barrels per day (bpd). However, consumption is high, making Spain heavily dependent on imported oil, mainly from Mexico and Russia. Spain's multinational conglomerate, Repsol YPF, is a major international oil company, with operations in 29 countries, concerned in both upstream and downstream oil sectors, including exploration, production, transporting and refining of oil, which is then traded on the global market. Repsol YPF also owns networks of petrol stations.

In March 2014 the discovery of two significant offshore oil deposits off the Canaries and the prospects of fracking triggered a black-gold rush. Demand for exploration permits increased by 35 per cent since 2012. This could help pull the country out of economic decline – the new oil industry would create 250,000 jobs.

Despite never having produced liquefied natural gas (LNG), in March 2014, Spain overtook Norway to become Europe's leading exporter of the fuel. The utilities that contracted to buy LNG before the slump have been re-exporting due to six consecutive years of diminishing domestic demand.

Energy

Total installed generating capacity was 101,700MW in 2013, producing 283 billion kilowatt hours. In 2013, Spain became the first country to rely on wind power as its main energy source, helping to reduce emissions by 23 per cent. Hydropower also helped contribute to this drop in emissions. Wind power itself accounted for 21.1 per cent of the country's electricity demand in 2013, which narrowly topped nuclear energy at 21.0 per cent. Wind power is estimated to have generated 53,926,000 megawatt hours (MWh) of electricity, up 12 per cent on 2012. Increased levels of rainfall meant that electricity generated by hydropower was up 16 per cent also, reaching 32,205,000MWh.

There are four major electricity companies operating as regional suppliers. Endesa, is the largest energy company in Spain and is a subsidiary of the Italian energy company Enel, with over 10 million customers at home and the same number abroad. Red Eléctrica de España (REE) is responsible for most of the Spanish national grid and management and co-ordination of the international electricity flows.

Financial markets

Stock exchange

Bolsas y Mercados Españoles (BME)

Banking and insurance

In 2009 the government set up a US$12.7 billion bank fund, which any failing bank in Spain could call on for support through capital injections, mergers or restructuring. The new fund could eventually be subsidised by public finance up to US$103 billion.

In May 2012 the shares of the fourth largest bank, Bankia, were suspended on the Madrid Stock Exchange when Bankia was forced to asked the government for €19 billion (US$24 billion) in financial support, mostly due to bad loans on properties. This bailout was the second following Spain's intervention and purchase of a 45 per cent stake in Bankia in April 2012.

In November 2012 the European Commission approved the government's plans to restructure the top four banks. Bankia, Banco de Valencia, NCG and Catalunya Banc were nationalised, following heavy losses due to toxic loans to homebuyers and property developers. Spain received US$129 billion from the euro-zone bailout fund.

Central bank

Banco de España; European Central Bank (ECB).

Main financial centre

Madrid

Time

Mainland – GMT plus one hour (daylight saving: late March–October, GMT plus two hours) = mainland

Canaries – GMT (daylight saving, GMT plus one hour)

Geography

Spain is situated in south-western Europe. It occupies most of the Iberian peninsula, sharing it with Portugal to the west. The country includes the Balearic Islands in the Mediterranean Sea (200km south-east of Barcelona), the Canary Islands in the Atlantic Ocean and two small enclaves in Morocco. Mainland Spain is bounded to the north by the Cantabrian Sea, the Pyrenees and France, to the east by the Mediterranean, and to the south by the Straits of Gibraltar and Morocco.

Mountains ranges, including the Pyrenees, run from the Atlantic in the north to the Mediterranean coast. Another band runs down the east to the Sierra Nevada in the south, which includes the largest mainland mountain Mulhacén at 3,482 metres (m). Land in the south is dry with many traditional olive groves. The flat central plateau (*meseta*) occupies much of the land around the capital, Madrid. The longest river, the Ebro, is 940km, beginning in the Cantabrian mountains of the north-east and flowing into the Mediterranean. The River Tagus runs for 716km through central Spain and 322km in Portugal.

The Canary Islands are rugged volcanic Atlantic Ocean outcrops. Of the 13 islands six are uninhabited. Pico de Teide, on Tenerife, at 3,718 metres is Spain's tallest mountain.

Hemisphere

Northern

Climate

Most of Spain has a Mediterranean climate with mild winters and hot summers, although the mountainous north is colder and wetter. Temperatures range from 40 degrees centigrade Celsius (C) to minus 15 degrees C.

Dress codes

Particular attention is paid to dress, although dress codes are not rigid. Most businessmen and male officials wear suits and ties during business hours.

Entry requirements

Passports

Are required by all non-EU visitors and must be valid for at least six months beyond the planned stay. EU visitors and nationals of Andorra, Liechtenstein, Malta, Monaco and Switzerland may use valid national ID cards.

Visa

Required by all; except nationals of EU and Schengen Accord signatory countries. Tourists from North America and Australasia may visit, visa-free, for up to 90 days. All other nationals, visiting for business purposes, should contact the nearest Spanish embassy for a visa application form. A Schengen visa application (offered in several languages) can be downloaded from http://europa.eu/abc/travel/ see 'documents you will need'.

Currency advice/regulations

The import of foreign and local currency is unlimited. Export of local currency is unlimited but amounts over eur6,000 must be declared. Export of foreign currencies over the equivalent of eur3,050 in bank

notes and travellers cheques must be declared.
Travellers cheques are widely accepted.

Customs

Personal items are duty-free. There are no duties levied on alcohol and tobacco between EU member states, providing amounts imported are for personal consumption. The Canary Islands are not a member of the EU.

Health (for visitors)

Nationals of the European Economic Area (EEA) countries and Switzerland can access reduced cost and sometimes free medical treatment using a European Health Insurance Card (EHIC) while visiting the EEA. Exceptions include nationals of the 10 countries which joined the EU in 2004 whose EHIC is not valid in Switzerland. Applications for the EHIC should be made before travelling.

Mandatory precautions

None

Advisable precautions

Up-to-date tetanus and polio immunisations are recommended. Long-term visitors should consider hepatitis A immunisation. Tap water may not be safe to drink outside the major cities and visitors are advised to drink bottled mineral water.

Hotels

Hotels are classified from one- to five-star, plus a 'Grand De Luxe' category (pensions/hostels classified from one- to three-star). *Paradores* (national tourist inns) are also increasingly popular. Accommodation should be booked well in advance, especially during holiday season. NB: *Term Residencia* denotes establishments without dining-room facilities.

Credit cards

All major credit and charge cards are accepted. ATMs are widely available.

Public holidays (national)

Fixed dates

1 Jan (New Year's Day), 6 Jan (Epiphany), 1 May (Labour Day), 15 Aug (Assumption Day), 12 Oct (National Day), 1 Nov (All Saints' Day), 6 Dec (Constitution Day), 8 Dec (Immaculate Conception), 25 Dec (Christmas Day).

Variable dates

Good Friday (Mar/Apr).

Working hours

Executives rarely arrive in their offices before 0900. Many then go out for coffee, and again for a snack at 1200 to keep them going until a late lunch. Lunches, no earlier than 1400, and often preceded by a visit to a bar for an aperitivo, are abundant and lengthy. A business lunch, always accompanied by wine, coffee, brandy and cigars, can last from three to five hours. It is considered impolite to get down to business until after dessert. Although many go home for lunch and a brief siesta, an increasing number of companies in big cities are abolishing the long lunch break. In December 2005 the government officially abolished the *siesta* when a law was published decreeing that lunch breaks would be one hour only, thereby allowing civil servants to finish work at 6pm.
In the hot summer months, most ministries and many companies close down for the day at 1400 or 1500. In August, many businesses close down completely.

Banking

Mon–Fri: 0830–1400. In some autonomous regions larger bank branches may open later in the afternoon and on Saturday morning, between Apr–Sep.

Business

Usually open Mon–Fri: 0900–1400 and 1630–1930.

Government

Vary considerably from region to region and according to time of year. In Madrid: Mon–Fri: generally 0900–1330 and 1500–1800; except Jul and Aug, 0830–1430 (1400 on Fri) with only skeleton staff remaining during afternoon.

Shops

Mon–Sat: 0930–1330, 1700–2030; Department stores and malls Mon–Sat: 1000–2200.

Telecommunications

Mobile/cell phones

There are 3G and 900/1800 GSM services.

Electricity supply

220V AC with round, two-pin plugs.

Social customs/useful tips

A ban on smoking in public places was introduced on the 1 January 2006. It was extended to bars and restaurants from 2 January 2011.
Handshaking is the customary form of greeting. Although English is widely spoken, an effort to speak Spanish is appreciated. Business cards are frequently exchanged as a matter of courtesy.
Meals are taken later in Spain than in other European countries which means that people go to bed later and also generally go to work later. Dinner is after 2200 and people rarely go to bed before 2400. Leaving someone's home before 0100 can be taken as a sign of boredom. It is acceptable to telephone someone at home until 2400.
Spaniards generally use two surnames, the last being their mother's surname. When addressing someone, either personally or in correspondence, only the first of the surname is used. *Don* is a widely used title of respect, and is used in conversation with the christian name only. The *tu* (more intimate second person singular) form is today used widely, even on first acquaintance.
Entry into the EU in 1986 has slowly changed customs as Spaniards are keen to be seen as Europeans. However, they remain very attached to an informal and relaxed way of life and enjoyment is an important part of life. Many cities and villages have their annual festivals which would not be complete without dance, songs, wine and a bullfight. Bullfighting remains popular despite a budding animal protection movement, and soccer remains by far the most popular sport.
Family and friendship ties are of major importance and often a source of mutual favours. Regional origins also command loyalties. Spaniards, even children of migrants to big cities, constantly refer to their home province. In Catalonia Catalan is very much, and very proudly, the *lingua franca*, and it helps at least to be able to greet people in Catalan. This is less the case in the Basque country, where fewer people speak Basque, and is not an issue either in Valencia or in Galicia, both of which have their own languages, but where Castilain Spanish is the *lingua franca* for day-to-day purposes.
A ban on clothing that might make identification difficult, such as the burqa, niqab, balaclavas, motorbike helmets and ski masks, is scheduled to come into effect in Barcelona's public installations in the second half of 2010.

Security

A chronic drug problem, coupled with persistent unemployment and frequent amnesties for petty criminals, has caused an increase in petty crime in big cities. Mugging has become frequent, and often violent, in tourist areas. Many insurance companies no longer cover the theft of car radios.

Getting there

Air

National airline: Iberia.
International airport/s: Madrid Barajas (MAD), 13km north-east of Madrid. Facilities include banks, restaurants, duty-free and car hire. There are buses, taxis and a railway service to the city centre.
Continental and regional fights arrive at Alicante (ALC), 12km south-west of city; Barcelona (BCN) 10km south-west of city; Bilbao (BIO), 9km from city; Málaga (AGP) 8km south-west of city; Santiago de Compostela (SCQ), 10km north-east of city; Seville (SVQ), 12km east of city, Valencia (VLC), 10km west of city. Also on Balearic Islands: Palma de Mallorca (PMI), 9km south-east of Palma; on Canary Islands: Gran Canaria (LPA), 19km south of Las Palmas; Tenerife TCI Sur

Reina Sofia (TFS), 61km south-west of Santa Cruz de Tenerife.
Airport tax: In July 2012, the government introduced an additional departure tax of €7 (US$10) for all air passengers.

Surface

Road: There are several good quality toll motorways connecting Spain to France and Portugal.
Rail: Services radiate from the Madrid hub and express services connect to the pan-European network, through France. There are several services connecting Portugal.
Water: The are regular ferry and shipping services from UK (Plymouth-Santander), France (Marseilles-Alicante) and Algeria (Algiers-Alicante).
Main port/s: Barcelona, Valencia, Alicante, Málaga, Algeciras, Cádiz, La Coruña, Bilbao, Vigo.

Getting about

National transport

Air: Frequent services from Madrid to all major urban centres are operated by Iberia.
Road: Roads are based on radial routes centred on Madrid. They are often very busy during the holiday season. Good roads connect all main towns. There is a network of over 150,000km, including 2,000km of motorways (usually toll) mostly confined to coastal regions. As an energy-saving measure, deduction in the motorway speed limit from 120kph to 110kph from 7 March 2011 was announced on 25 February by Deputy Prime Minister Alfredo Pérez Rubalcaba. The measure was reversed in late June 2011 after 'circumstances changed', reported Mr Pérez, and the country had saved Spain 450 million euros (US$320 million) Spain imported some 9 per cent of Libya's oil before the revolt there began; Repsol, the Spanish oil company, was forced to shut down production.
Buses: There are regular bus and coach services between main towns.
Rail: There are approximately 14,410km of track, of which about 11,500km is operated by Red Nacional de Ferrocarriles Españoles (RENFE) (National Network of Spanish Railroads) and the rest (narrow gauge) by Ferrocarriles Españoles de Via Estrecha (FEVE). A high-speed link between Madrid and Barcelona, operated by RENFE, opened in February. The train will take just over two and a half hours over the 550Km (342 miles).
Water: Regular steamer and hydrofoil services operated by Compañía Transmediterránea connect Balearic Islands with Barcelona, Valencia and Alicante. Also weekly ferry service to Las Palmas (Canary Islands) from Barcelona.

City transport

Taxis: Available in most major cities; all metered. Tend to have a distinct colour in each city. Tipping between 5–10 per cent.

Car hire

Available at competitive rates in most large towns. A national driving licence is normally all that is required. Drive on the right. Speed limits are 60kph in towns, 100kph on national highways, 120kph on motorways and 90kph on other roads. Traffic coming from right generally has priority. Seat belts must be worn in front seats. Spanish drivers tend to drive faster than their northern counterparts.

BUSINESS DIRECTORY

The addresses listed below are a selection only. While World of Information makes every endeavour to check these addresses, we cannot guarantee that changes have not been made, especially to telephone numbers and area codes. We would welcome any corrections.

Telephone area codes

The international direct dialling (IDD) code for Spain is +34 followed by area code and subscriber's number:

Alicante	96	León	987
Avilés	98	Madrid	91
Barcelona	93	Málaga	95
Bilbao	94	Salamanca	923
Cádiz	956	Santander	942
Cartagena	968	Seville	95
Castellón de la Plana	964	Tarragona	977
Ceuta	952	Valencia	96
Granada	958	Valladolid	983
Huelva	959	Vigo	986
La Coruña	981	Zaragoza	976

Chambers of Commerce

American Chamber of Commerce in Spain, 8 Tuset, 08006 Barcelona (tel: 415-9963; fax: 415-1198; e-mail: info@amchamspain.com).

Barcelona Cámara de Comercio, 452 Avenguda Diagonal, 08006 Barcelona (tel: 416-9300; fax: 416-9301).

Bilbao Cámara Oficial de Comercio, Industria y Navegación, 50 Almeda Recalde, 48008 Bilbao (tel: 470-6500; fax: 443-6171; e-mail: info@camarabilbao.com).

British Chamber of Commerce in Spain, 21 Calle Bruc, 08010 Barcelona (tel: 317-3220; fax: 302-4896; e-mail: britchamber@britchamber.com).

Cádiz Cámara Oficial de Comercio, Industria y Navegación, 4 Antonio López, 11004 Cádiz (tel: 010-000; fax: 250-710; e-mail: ccincadiz@camerdata.es).

Consejo Superior de Cámaras de Comercio, Industria y Navegación de España, Calle Velazquez 157, 28002 Madrid (tel: 590-6900; fax: 590-6908; e-mail: csc@cscamaras.es).

Córdoba Cámara Oficial de Comercio e Industria, Pérez de Castro 1, 14003 Córdoba (tel: 296-199; fax: 202-106; e-mail: info@camaracordoba.com).

Franco-Spanish Chamber of Commerce and Industry, Calle Ruiz de Alarcon 7, 28014 Madrid (tel: 522-6742; fax: 523-3642; e-mail: lachambre@lachambre.es).

French Chamber of Commerce and Industry in Barcelona, Passeig de Gràcia 2, 08007 Barcelona (tel: 270-2450;fax: 270-2451; e-mail: ccfbcn@ccfbcn,es).

Granada Cámara Oficial de Comercio, Industria y Navegación, Paz 18, 18002 Granada (tel: 536-276; fax: 536-292; e-mail: ccigranada@camaras.org).

Las Palmas de Gran Canaria Cámara Oficial de Comercio, Industria y Navegación , León y Castillo 24, 35003 Las Palmas de Gran Canaria (tel: 391-045; fax: 362-350; e-mail: webmaster@cameraalp.es).

Madrid Cámara Oficial de Comercio e Industria, Calle Huertas 13, 28012 Madrid (tel: 538-3500; fax: 538-3677; e-mail: camaramadrid@camaramadrid.es).

Málaga Cámara Oficial de Comercio, Industria y Navegación, Cortina del Muelle 23, 29015 Málaga (tel: 221-1673; fax: 222-9894; e-mail: info@camaramalaga.com).

Mallorca, Ibiza y Formentera Cámara de Comercio, Estudio General 7, 07001 Palma de Mallorca (tel: 710-188; fax: 726-302; e-mail: ccinmallorca@camaras.org).

Sevilla Cámara Oficial de Comercio, Industria y Navegación, Plaza de la Contratación 8, 41004 Sevilla (tel: 211-005; fax: 225-619; e-mail: ccinsevilla@camaradesevilla.com).

Valencia Cámara de Comercio, Industria y Navegación, Poeta Querol 15, 46002 Valencia (tel: 103-900; fax: 531-742; e-mail: info@camaravalencia.com).

Zaragoza Cámara Oficial de Comercio e Industria, Calle Isabel La Catolica 2, 50071 Zaragoza (tel: 306-161; fax: 357-945; e-mail: cci@camarazaragoza.com).

Banking

Banco Atlántico SA, Diagonal 407 bis, Barcelona (tel: 237-1240).

Banco Bilbao Vizcaya Argentaria, Plaza de San Nicolás 4, 48005 Bilbao (tel: 424-4620).

Banco de la Exportación SA, Barcas 10, Valencia 2 (tel: 351-7862).

Banco de Sabadell, Plaza Sant Roc 20, 08201 Sabadell (tel: 726-2100).

Banco Español de Crédito (Banesto), Paseo de la Castellana 7, Madrid (tel: 338-1000).

Banco Internacional de Comercio, José Ortega y Gasset 56, 28006 Madrid (tel: 402-8362).

Banco Popular Español, Velázquez 34, 28001 Madrid (tel: 435-3620).

Banco Santander Central Hispano (BSCH) (established April 1999), Apartado de Correos 00045, Santander (tel: 221-200).

La Caixa de Catalunya, Avinguda Diagonal 621, Barcelona 08028 (tel 934-045000).

Confederación Española de Cajas de Ahorros (confederation of Spanish savings banks), Alcalá 27 Madrid 14 (tel: 232-7810).

Consejo Superior Bancario (central committee of Spanish banking), José Abascal 57, Madrid 9 (tel: 441-0611).

La Caixa de Barcelona (savings bank), Avinguda Diagonal 530, 08006 Barcelona (tel: 201-6666).

Central bank

Banco de España, Alcalá 48, 28014 Madrid (tel: 338-5000).

European Central Bank (ECB), Kaiserstrasse 29, D-60311 Frankfurt am Main, Germany (tel: (+49-69) 13-440; fax: (+49-69) 1344-6000; email: info@ecb.int).

Stock exchange

Bolsas y Mercados Españoles (BME), www.bolsasymercados.es

Travel information

Federación Española de Hoteles, Orense 32, 28020 Madrid (tel: 556-7112; fax: 556-7361; e-mail: federahoteles@ipf.es).

Iberia, 130 Velazquez Madrid, (tel: 902-400-500 (bookings); www.iberia.com).

Instituto De Turismo De España (Turespaña) 6 Jose Lázaro Galdiano, 28071 Madrid (tel: 343-3500; internet: www.tourspain.es/en).

Ministry of tourism

Ministerio de Industria, Turismo y Comercio, José González de Galdiano 6, Madrid (tel: 343-3621; email: turespaña@turespaña.es

Ministries

Ministry for Development, P de la Castellana 67, 28071 Madrid (tel: 597-7000; fax: 597-8502).

Ministry of Economy, Finance and Trade, Alcalá 9, Madrid 28071 (tel: 595-8000).

Ministry of Education and Culture, Alcalá 34, 28071 Madrid (tel: 532-5089; fax: 532-5873).

Ministry of the Environment, Pza San Juan de la Cruz, 28071 Madrid (tel: 597-7000; fax: 597-6349).

Ministry of Foreign Affairs, Pza de la Provincia 1, 28071 Madrid (tel: 379-9549).

Ministry of Health and Consumer Affairs, P del Prado 18-20, 28071 Madrid (tel: 596-1000; fax: 429-3525).

Ministry of Industry and Energy, Paseo de la Castellana 160, Madrid 16 (tel: 349-4806).

Ministry of the Interior, P de la Castellana 5, 28071 Madrid (tel: 537-1000; fax: 537-1177).

Ministry of Justice, San Bernardo 45, 28071 Madrid (tel: 930-2000).

Ministry of Labour and Social Affairs, Agustín de Bethencourt 4, 28071 Madrid (tel: 553-6000; fax: 554-7528).

Ministry of Public Administrations, P de la Castellana 3, 28071 Madrid (tel: 586-1000; fax: 319-2448).

President's Office, Complejo de la Moncloa, 28071 Madrid (tel: 335-3535).

Other useful addresses

Agencia EFE, SA (news agency), Espronceda 32, Apartado 1112, 28003 Madrid (tel: 441-5599).

Agencia para el Desarrollo, Consejeria de Economia e Innocacion Tecnologica, Comunidad de Madrid (fax: 420-6456, 399-7451; e-mail: agencia.desarrollo@madrid.org).

Bolsa de Comercio de Valencia (stock exchange), Pascual y Genis 19, 46001 Valencia (tel: 352-1487).

Bolsa de Madrid (stock exchange), Palacio de la Bolsa, Plaza de la Lealtad 1 (tel: 232-8484).

Central de Reservas de los Paradores de España, Calle Velázquez 25, 28001 Madrid (tel: 435-9700/9744/9768/9814).

Confederación Española de Organizaciones Empresariales (Spanish confederation of employers' organisations), Diego de León 50, 28006 Madrid (tel: 262-4410).

Fira de Barcelona, Avenida Reina Maria Cristina s/n, 08004 Barcelona (tel: 423-3101; fax: 423-8651).

IFEMA (Feria de Madrid), Parque Ferial Juan Carlos 1, 28042 Madrid (tel: 722-5180/5000; fax: 722-5801; e-mail: infoifema@ifema.es).

Instituto Nacional de Estadística, Paseo de la Castellana 183, E-28071 Madrid (tel: 583-9100; fax: 573-2713).

Instituto Nacional de la Seguridad Social, Subdirección General de Relaciones Internacionales, Padre Damián 4, 28036 Madrid (tel: 450-1900).

Spanish Embassy (USA), 2375 Pennsylvania Avenue, NW, Washington DC 20037 (tel: (+1-202) 452-0100; fax: (tel: (+1-202) 833-5670; e-mail: spain@spainemb.org).

Internet sites

Andalucia: www.andalucia.com

Balearics: www.caib.es

Bank of Spain: www.bde.es

Barcelona: www.bcn.es

Basque Country: www.euskadi.net

Bilbao: www.bilbao.net

Canary Islands: www.gobcan.es

Current affairs: www.sispain.com

El Pais newspaper: www.elpais.es

Galicia: wwwxunta.es

Government spokesman: www.la-moncloa.es

Hotel reservations: www.red2000.com

Iberia: www.iberia.com

Madrid: www.munimadrid.es

Ministry of Tourism: www.tourspain.es

Paradores (hotels): www.parador.es

Renfe (national railways): www.renfe.es

Spain statistics: www.ine.es/welcoing.htm

Spanish Rail Service: www.spanish-rail.co.uk

Spanish Tourism: www.spain.info

Spanish yellow pages (in Spanish): www.paginasamarillas.es

Stock Exchange: www.bolsamadrid.es

Train information: www.renfe.es

Valencia: www.gva.es

Sri Lanka

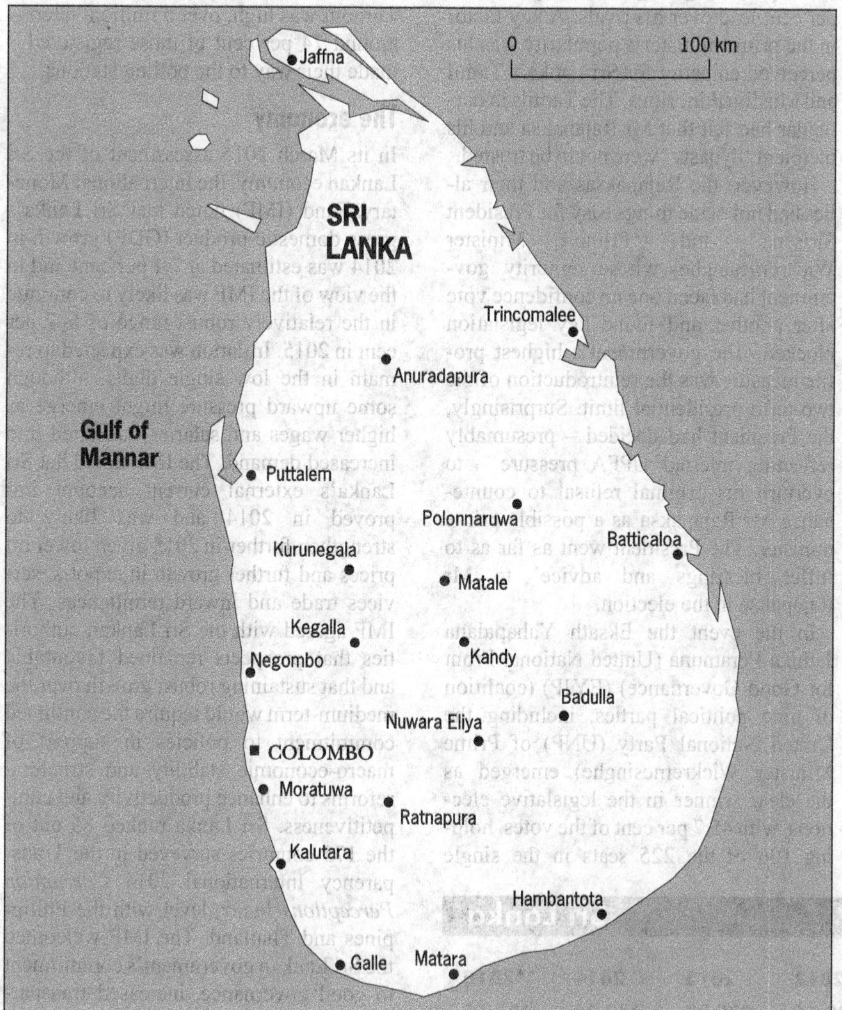

KEY FACTS

Official name: Sri Lanka Prajathanthrika Samajavadi Janarajaya / Llankais Sananayaka socialisak kutiyarasa / Democratic Socialist Republic of Sri Lanka

Head of State: President Maithripala Sirisena (since 9 January 2015)

Head of government: President Maithripala Sirisena, Ranil Wickremesinghe (prime minister) (since 9 January 2015)

Ruling party: Coalition led by the United National Party (UNP), United National Front for Good Governance (UNFGG)

Area: 65,610 square km

Population: 20.96 million (2014)*

Capital: Colombo (official capital); many governmental functions are centred in Sri Jayawardenepura, a suburb of Colombo.

Official language: Sinhala, Tamil, English

Currency: Rupee (Rs) = 100 cents

Exchange rate: Rs138.38 per US$ (Sep 2015)

GDP per capita: US$3,558 (2014)*

GDP real growth: 7.40% (2014)*

GDP: US$74.59 billion (2014)*

Labour force: 7.57 million (2009)

Unemployment: 4.00% (2014)*

Inflation: 3.27% (2014)

Balance of trade: -US$8.29 billion (2014)

Annual FDI: US$955.92 million (2011)

* estimated figure

At the beginning of 2015 Sri Lanka's electorate approached their forthcoming elections with some apprehension. Sri Lankans were grappling with the central decision posed by the election – did they want to see the return of the Rajapaksa family to power? An increasingly bitter election risked becoming an increasingly violent one, risking the resurgence of the ethnic divisions that had torn the country apart for decades.

Rajapaksa's return?

Mr Rajapaksa had come to power in 2005 and in a dramatically violent finale, had secured victory over the Tamil separatists in 2009. The Rajapaksa regime – wielded through the United People's Freedom Party (UPFA) had not been without controversy, much of which was related to the end of the war with the Tamil Tigers (LTTE) in 2009, when it was alleged there had been widespread human rights' violations and the cold-blooded murder of civilians. The pro-China Rajapaksa administration was also accused of corruption and nepotism; its single success was that of economic growth, which reached over seven per cent on the Rajapaksas' watch.

His 2005 election victory had enabled the flamboyant Mr Rajapaksa to ride a wave of popularity among the Sinhalese population, but left many of the issues that had originally led to the civil war unaddressed. Disregarding the obvious structural weaknesses of Sri Lankan society, Mr Rajapaksa wasted no time in appointing his three brothers, a son and nephew to influential government positions while he busied himself with changing the constitution to allow Sri Lanka's presidents to stand for three consecutive terms of office. Then Mr Rajapaksa had miscalculated badly when he called for a snap presidential election for 8 January 2015 hoping to shoe himself into a third term as president. He had appeared to be the odds-on favourite, but his rival in the election, the mild mannered health minister Maithripala Sirisena, struck a chord not only among the Tamil community, but also among disenchanted Sinhalese. So it was that Mr Sirisena confounded the pundits, winning by a margin of six per cent. The electorate at large were also surprised, all the more so by the fact that the Rajapaksas appeared to accept the electorate's verdict on their regime, packing their bags and departing quietly.

So it was that (ex) president Rajapaksa not only failed to gain re-election to parliament and claim the post of prime minister – held for the United People's Freedom Party (UPFA) by Ranil Wickremesinghe, a rival of the Rajapaksas – he also failed to persuade Sri Lankans that his term of office had pointed the country in the right direction. The former president had initially to overcome the resistance of President Sirisena to allow him to stand as a candidate in the 2015 snap general election; at one stage the President had also made it clear that even if Mr Rajapaksa did secure re-election, the President would not allow him to be appointed prime minister. The incumbent Mr Wickremesinghe's poll ratings had steadily risen, giving him a reported 10 per cent lead over his rivals. A key factor in the prime minister's popularity was his perceived empathy for Sri Lanka's Tamil and Muslim minorities. The Tamils in particular had felt that Mr Rajapaksa and his incipient 'dynasty' were not to be trusted.

However, the Rajapaksas and their allies had not made things easy for President Sirisena and Prime Minister Wickremesinghe, whose minority government had faced one no confidence vote after another and found key legislation blocked. The government's highest profile measure was the reintroduction of the two-term presidential limit. Surprisingly, the President had decided – presumably reflecting internal UPFA pressure – to overturn his original refusal to countenance Mr Rajapaksa as a possible prime minister. The President went as far as to 'offer blessings and advice' to Mr Rajapaksa in the election.

In the event the Eksath Yahapalana Jathika Peramuna (United National Front for Good Governance) (EYJP) (coalition of nine political parties, including the United National Party (UNP) of Prime Minister Wickremesinghe) emerged as the clear winner in the legislative elections, with 45.7 per cent of the votes, holding 106 of the 225 seats in the single chamber legislature. However, this still left Mr Wickremesinghe seven seats short of an absolute majority. The swing towards Mr Wickremesinghe's EYJP was just over 16 per cent; by contrast the UPFA vote fell by almost 18 per cent. As the newly appointed leader of the UPFA, Mr Rajapaksa became the leader of the opposition, his party winning 95 seats. Turnout was high, over 5 million voters – around 74 per cent of those registered – made their way to the polling stations.

The economy

In its March 2015 assessment of the Sri Lankan economy, the International Monetary Fund (IMF) noted that Sri Lanka's gross domestic product (GDP) growth in 2014 was estimated at 7.4 per cent and in the view of the IMF was likely to continue in the relatively robust range of 6–7 per cent in 2015. Inflation was expected to remain in the low single digits, although some upward pressure might emerge as higher wages and salaries translated into increased demand. The IMF noted hat Sri Lanka's external current account improved in 2014 and was likely to strengthen further in 2015 given lower oil prices and further growth in exports, services trade and inward remittances. The IMF agreed with the Sri Lankan authorities that prospects remained favourable and that sustaining robust growth over the medium-term would require the continued commitment to policies in support of macro-economic stability and structural reforms to enhance productivity and competitiveness. Sri Lanka ranked 85 out of the 175 countries surveyed in the Transparency International 2014 *Corruption Perceptions Index*, level with the Philippines and Thailand. The IMF welcomed the Sri Lankan government's commitment to good governance, increased transparency and financial discipline. The IMF agreed with the Sri Lankan authorities that medium-term fiscal consolidation should remain a linchpin in the country's macro-economic policy – ensuring a durable reduction in the country's public debt. However, the IMF highlighted a number of concerns with respect to the Sri Lankan Interim Budget. In the view of the IMF, achieving a deficit of 4.4 per cent of GDP would be challenging and therefore the authorities should consider contingency measures should revenues fail to materialise as projected. Furthermore, the one-off tax measures introduced to finance the Interim Budget were not considered by the IMF as a step toward a more effective tax system. The IMF and the authorities

KEY INDICATORS — Sri Lanka

	Unit	2011	2012	2013	2014	**2015
Population	m	*20.54	*20.66	*20.82	*20.96	*21.11
Gross domestic product (GDP)	US$bn	59.10	59.41	67.45	*74.59	*80.59
GDP per capita	US$	2,877	2,876	3,239	*3,558	*3,818
GDP real growth	%	8.2	6.3	7.3	*7.4	*6.5
Inflation	%	6.7	7.5	6.9	3.3	*1.7
Unemployment	%	4.9	4.0	4.0	*4.0	*4.0
Exports (fob) (goods)	US$m	10,558.8	9,773.5	10,394.3	11,130.1	–
Imports (fob) (goods)	US$m	18,241.9	19,190.2	18,002.8	19,416.8	–
Balance of trade	US$m	-7,683.1	-9,416.7	-7,608.5	-8,286.7	–
Current account	US$m	-4,675.1	-3,915.0	-2,606.0	*-2,790.0	*-1,639.0
Total reserves minus gold	US$m	6,707.3	6,378.0	6,611.0	7,316.0	–
Foreign exchange	US$m	5,651.8	6,300.0	6,522.0	–	–
Exchange rate	per US$	110.20	129.26	130.73	131.21	–

* estimated figure ** forecast figure

agreed on the need for more comprehensive reforms to streamline the tax system and reduce or eliminate exemptions to put revenues on a steady upward path. Forthcoming technical assistance from the IMF would focus on these areas.

A succession of steps to ease monetary policy over the 2013–14 period had helped facilitate a recovery of private sector credit late in 2014 and into early 2015. The IMF viewed the authorities monetary policy stance to be appropriate, but the Central Bank of Sri Lanka would need to monitor credit, inflation and liquidity developments closely in the immediate future. The IMF noted the decline in central bank foreign exchange reserves over the previous six months, especially the need to preserve Sri Lanka's cushion of foreign exchange reserves; special attention was drawn to the need for exchange rate flexibility. Intervention here should be limited to dealing with excessive short-term volatility. The Sri Lankan exchange rate did not appear to be out of line with the country's fundamentals, particularly given the projected improvement in the balance of payments.

The ADB view

The Asian Development Bank (ADB) in its annual review of the economy agreed that GDP had grown by 7.4 per cent during 2014, up slightly from the 7.2 per cent seen a year earlier. This continued high growth was driven by faster expansion in industry, which offset the substantially weaker growth in agriculture. Provisional estimates showed that industry had provided the lift to growth as it grew by 11.4 per cent, up from 9.9 per cent a year earlier, reflecting the expansion in construction and a pickup in manufacturing apparel for export. This performance would have been better if not for a temporary slowdown in garment manufacturing and exports in October and November 2014. According to the ADB, the services sector grew by 6.5 per cent in 2014, little changed from a year earlier, driven by continued solid expansion in hotels and restaurants, wholesale and retail trade and post and communication. The improving global economy also contributed to higher tourist arrivals and a better trade performance. Agriculture performance was much weaker than a year earlier, however, expanding by a mere 0.3 per cent because of drought and floods during some months of 2014.

The ADB reported that on the demand side, investment, exports and government consumption were estimated to have recorded higher nominal growth in 2014 than in 2013. Expansion in private consumption slowed, however, to 8.5 per cent from 9.9 per cent in 2013. Government consumption rose by an estimated 15.4 per cent from 11.3 per cent in 2013, reflecting increased salaries and wages for public employees, as well as larger special allowances and the cost-of-living allowance granted during the year.

Fixed capital investment expanded by 15.7 per cent, fuelling robust construction performance. Inflation continued to fall in 2014. Annual average inflation was 3.3 per cent in 2014, the lowest recorded since 1985. Non-food inflation averaged 2.8 per cent, dropping significantly from 6.1 per cent in 2013 with the fading of the base effect from increased energy prices in 2013, as well as with the decreases in fuel prices in September and December 2014. The 2015 budget was revised by the new government to further reduce fuel prices at the end of January 2015. As a result, the non-food index showed deflation featuring since October 2014. Food inflation was on the rise, however, climbing to 12.0 per cent by January 2015 because of earlier adverse weather that reduced harvests, especially of rice, before easing to 9.5 per cent in February.

The central bank had relaxed its monetary policy in December 2012 as inflation eased. Interest rates were further reduced by 50 basis points in October 2013 and again in January 2014. In response, banks' lending rates declined from 9.7 per cent in January 2014 to 6.4 per cent in January 2015. Credit to the private sector nevertheless decelerated until July 2014, when it turned up to reach an annual 8.8 per cent by December 2014. This helped to support a pickup in private sector investment.

The ADB noted that Sri Lanka's fiscal consolidation continued in 2014. The budget deficit was estimated to have dropped to 5.2 per cent of GDP in 2014, compared with 5.9 per cent in 2013. Capital expenditure was estimated at 5.7 per cent of GDP, broadly consistent with the government target of 6–7 per cent. Domestic revenue was estimated to have increased to 14.2 per cent of GDP in 2014 from 13.9 per cent in the previous year. In January and April 2014, the government successfully issued foreign currency denominated debt on international markets for US$1 billion and US$500 million, respectively. Total government debt declined to 74.4 per cent of GDP in 2014 from 78.3 per cent in 2013. Total public debt – including government debt, treasury guarantees and the borrowing of state-owned enterprises from banks and foreign sources – was estimated to have been 88.9 per cent of GDP by the end of 2014.

Exports expanded by 7.0 per cent in 2014, amounting to US$11.1 billion, following growth recovery in the second half of 2013. However, export performance showed some weakness toward the end of 2014, when exports were down by 13.7 per cent year on year in October and 10.7 per cent in November. Imports grew by 7.9 per cent to reach US$19.4 billion in 2014, swiftly recovering from a 6.2 per cent drop in the previous year. Oil imports, which accounted for about a quarter of total imports, started to decline in the second half of 2014 in line with the general trend in global prices. Service industry exports were boosted in 2014 as Sri Lanka's booming tourism ran up a 28.6 per cent increase in earnings and robust remittances expanded by 9.5 per cent.

The current account balance was estimated to have recorded a deficit of 3.5 per cent of GDP in 2014, an improvement on the deficit of 3.9 per cent in 2013. Notwithstanding outflows on account of foreign debt service payments amounting to US$2.1 billion and payments to the IMF amounting to US$704 million, strong financial inflows maintained a surplus in the overall balance of payments for 2014.

Sri Lanka's official foreign currency reserves increased to US$8.2 billion by the end of December 2014, covering 5.1 months of imports. The Sri Lankan rupee held steady against the US dollar in 2014, depreciating marginally by less than one per cent. It appreciated, however, in nominal and real effective terms by nearly 6 per cent over the year, with most of the change occurring after mid-year as the dollar strengthened markedly against other currencies, notably the euro.

Following the election in January 2015 that ousted a powerful incumbent and anticipating the June 2015 parliamentary elections, Sri Lanka found itself experiencing substantial political transition in 2015. The risk to economic growth arose from uncertainties during the transition and a wait-and-see approach adopted by investors. The election manifesto of the new president (Sirisena) set out the broad policies of the new government, which emphasised good governance, inclusive growth and private sector development. The good governance agenda included reviewing some of the previous administration's development projects for possible corruption and waste. The government initially focused on its 100 days programme toward reducing the powers of the executive president and addressing corruption. In addition, relief to low-income groups promised in the campaign was a main focus in the new government's budget, which replaced that of the previous administration. The direction of development strategy and fiscal policy was likely to be clear only after the 17 August general elections.

The revised budget for 2015, which parliament approved in February 2015, featured current expenditure higher than in the original budget and substantially lower capital expenditure, cut to 4.6 per cent of GDP from 6.2 per cent. While the revenue ratio was reduced, the fiscal deficit was lowered slightly to 4.4 per cent of GDP, compared with 4.6 per cent earlier. The revised budget planned to collect more revenue through new one-off taxes from high income groups and large commercial operations in order to finance additional expenditure. Since the increase in recurrent expenditure would continue in the following years, it had been crucial for the government to ensure fiscal revenue increase, so that sufficient public investment was secured to support long-term economic growth.

Recurrent expenditure increased due to higher salaries and pensions for public workers and for transfers and subsidies, which included a 200 per cent increase from April 2015 in the *Samurdhi* (prosperity) monthly social security payment. Capital spending was reduced by removing expenditure considered wasteful, such as allocations for poorly performing state-owned enterprises. The taxes introduced to fund the additional recurrent expenditure included heavy taxes on assets such as large houses and on large profits, as well as the one-off super gain tax, which was levied on companies and on individuals that earned profits over Rs2 billion (US$0.014 billion) in 2013–2014.

Both the IMF and ADB considered that growth in 2015 would be affected by the political transition and the revised priorities of the government. Construction would slow after leading growth in previous years, driven by large government infrastructure projects. Political uncertainty would retard private investment. While investment was likely to lose momentum in 2015, consumption was expected to pick up. Price reductions for food and fuel would encourage private consumption and government consumption would rise with the shift in the budget toward recurrent expenditure.

The expected faster growth in the advanced economies would benefit export industries such as apparel and tourism. How well agriculture performed after its mixed fortunes over the previous 5 years would depend on the weather, but increases in government-guaranteed prices for several agricultural products should boost production. Against this backdrop, assuming that Sri Lanka's politics settled down in the second half of 2015 and that investment rebounded, growth was projected to ease to 7.0 per cent in 2015 and then strengthen to 7.3 per cent in 2016.

Inflation was expected to remain low in 2015, held in check by a series of reductions in fuel prices in September and December 2014 and January 2015 that were expected to restrain other prices. With international oil prices expected to remain low in 2015–16, inflationary pressures were expected to ease. Moreover, the government's revised budget had announced tax reductions for several essential items including flour, bread, milk powder and sugar. Accordingly, inflation was expected to drop to 2.0 per cent in 2015 before rebounding to 5.0 per cent in 2016 on account of the base effect. With inflation remaining low, the central bank had signalled that monetary policy would maintain its current accommodative stance. Policy rates were likely to be kept low in 2015, supporting higher private sector credit.

Exports were expected to continue to improve in 2015 and 2016 as Sri Lanka's partner economies picked up pace. Imports were expected to rise, although imports of investment goods would probably slow down facing more moderate investment. Higher domestic consumption would exert upward pressure on imports and shift the composition of imports away from investment to consumption goods, while low international oil and food prices would help contain total value. Earnings from tourism and remittances were expected to continue their growth trends. This should contain the current account deficit at 1.4 per cent of GDP in 2015. The deficit was projected to widen marginally to 1.5 per cent in 2016 as the economy and domestic investment both picked up.

There are indications, according to the ADB, that Sri Lanka was being viewed more favourably internationally with the change in government and its policies, which should attract higher foreign direct investment (FDI) and cement trade ties, especially with Europe and the US. These factors were expected to strengthen the balance of payments position in the medium term.

With GDP per capita estimated at about US$3,700 in 2014, Sri Lanka was within reach of gaining upper-middle-income status. While the country had been focusing on infrastructure and human capital development, the time had come to adjust strategy to enable it to rise to the next stage of development. Private sector investment should take over the role of driving economic growth. A new focus on human capital development had already started and emphasis should gradually shift to higher skills and tertiary education to meet the market requirements of the knowledge economy.

With upper-middle-income status would come the need for greater gains in efficiency, or total factor productivity, to continue climbing to high-income status. In the view of the ADB Sri Lanka should start by strengthening its technological readiness to accept technology transfer through FDI. At the same time, it should begin innovating. The development of infrastructure and human resources should be adapted to this new policy agenda.

Risk assessment

Economy	Good
Politics	Good
Regional stability	Fair/good

Muslims in Sri Lanka

% of population	8.5
Sunni (% of Muslims)	99
Shi'a (% of Muslims)	1

COUNTRY PROFILE

1815 The British became the first colonial power to win control of the island, which became known as Ceylon. Tamils from India were brought over to work on the plantations.

1931 The right to vote was introduced by the colonial authorities, who also established a system of power-sharing with the people of Ceylon.

1948 Ceylon gained full independence from British rule.

1949 The right to vote was taken away from Indian Tamils.

1951 Solomon Bandaranaike left the ruling Ekshat Jathika Pakshaya (EJP) (United National Party) to form the Sri Lanka Nidahas Pakshaya (Sri Lanka Freedom Party) (SLFP).

1953 A decision by the EJP government to cut the rice ration in the slump following the Korean War saw riots assume insurrectionary proportions.

1956 Bandaranaike became prime minister. Sinhala was made the state language by Bandaranaike's SLFP government, sparking anti-Tamil pogroms.

1959–60 Bandaranaike was assassinated by a Buddhist monk in 1959. His widow, Sirimavo Bandaranaike, was elected SLFP

leader and prime minister the following year. She stepped up the nationalisation programme.
1964 A pact with India forced half a million Indian Tamil plantation workers to return to India.
1965 The EJP won elections and began attempts to reverse the nationalisation programme.
1970 Sirimavo Bandaranaike began what would be her second term as prime minister, which would last until 1977.
1971 A rural uprising led by the Marxist Janatha Vimukthi Peramuna (JVP) (People's United Liberation Front) was crushed.
1972 The country changed its name from Ceylon to Sri Lanka and Buddhism became the country's official religion.
1976 The main Tamil party, the Federal Party, and other Tamil groups, formed the Tamil United Liberation Front (TULF), calling for a separate Tamil state in the northern and eastern parts of the country. The Liberation Tigers of Tamil Eelam (LTTE, also known as the Tamil Tigers) was formed.
1977 A constitutional amendment was passed which established a presidential system of government from the end of the year. In elections, the TULF won all the seats in Tamil areas.
1978 J R Jayewardene became the country's first executive president. Continued violence and pressure from the Tamils led the government to recognise the Tamil language in the new constitution.
1983–84 Tamil terrorist activity and anti-Tamil pogroms broke out in what came to be known as 'Black July'. The latter constituted the worst outbreak of violence for many years, sparking a state of emergency. India began training Tamil guerrillas. Conflicts developed in the north of the island between the army and the Tamil Tigers.
1985 The first attempts at peace talks with the LTTE failed.
1986 Violence continued to convulse the northern and eastern provinces. Sri Lanka's relations with India were severely strained by the violence. India mediated informally between TULF legislators, Tamil leaders and the Sri Lankan government.
1987 Following an accord with India, more than 7,000 Indian troops were sent to Sri Lanka to try to implement a peace accord. The government agreed and signed accords that created new councils for Tamil areas in the north and east.
1989 Ranasinghe Premadasa was sworn in as president. The state of emergency which had been in force since May 1983 was repealed.
1990 Indian troops went home after losing more than 1,000 soldiers and failing to achieve their objectives. The LTTE controlled large parts of northern Sri Lanka.
1991 The LTTE was implicated in the assassination of Indian prime minister Rajiv Gandhi.
1993 President Premadasa was killed in an LTTE bomb attack.
1994 The Bahejana Nidasa Pakhsaya (People's Alliance) (PA), a left-wing nine-party coalition centred on the SLFP, won the legislative elections. The prime minister, Chandrika Bandaranaike Kumaratunga (SLFP), was elected president. She appointed her mother, Sirimavo Bandaranaike, as prime minister.
1996 The LTTE bombed the capital, Colombo, leading to a nationwide state of emergency.
1998 Sri Lanka's fiftieth anniversary celebrations were marred by renewed fighting between the army and separatist LTTE in the north of the country. The Tamil Tigers bombed Sri Lanka's holiest Buddhist site and captured key northern towns in a large offensive.
1999 President Kumaratunga won her second and final term in office; she had been partially blinded in one eye in a terrorist bombing at an election rally.
2000 Government forces lost control of a key military base in the north to Tamil Tiger separatists. Norway began mediation talks between the government and the LTTE. The general elections resulted in a hung parliament, with the PA dependent on two moderate Tamil-linked parties for support. Former prime minister (the world's first female head of government) Sirimavo Bandaranaike died soon after casting her vote.
2001 The LTTE was declared a terrorist organisation by Britain and Canada. The LTTE destroyed half Air Lanka's fleet of airplanes at Colombo's airport. President Kumaratunga announced a snap general election, which were won by the opposition EJP.
2002 It was estimated that 64,000 people had been killed since the LTTE's armed struggle for independence began. A cease-fire, negotiated by Norway, came into effect, ending the civil war. The ruling EJP won local elections, which were also billed as a referendum on peace plans. The ban on the LTTE was lifted as a prelude to peace talks at which the LTTE dropped its demand for independence in favour of regional autonomy with self-government.
2003 The LTTE withdrew from peace talks, as it demanded interim executive powers over the north and east, where the Tamil population is concentrated. Peace talks stalled and fearing the break-up of Sri Lanka, the president suspended parliament and deployed troops in Colombo as a state of emergency was declared.
2004 President Kumaratunga called snap elections, which were won by the United People's Freedom Alliance (UPFA) and Mahinda Rajapaksa became prime minister. An earthquake off the Indonesian island of Sumatra caused a *tsunami* that devastated coastal areas of north and eastern Sri Lanka; the final estimate in Sri Lanka was 35,322 dead or missing and 516,150 people displaced.
2005 Reconstruction of the coastal regions under *de facto* control of the LTTE devastated by the *tsunami* was necessary in many areas. The government planned to give the LTTE separatists a key role in the distribution of international aid that had been received and encourage peace talks in the process. However only reduced aid was provided and anger mounted in the stricken areas. The nationalist JVP pulled out of the government coalition in protest and reduced the government's working majority. The foreign minister, Lakshman Kadirgaamar, was assassinated. Mahinda Rajapaksa (UPFA) won presidential elections; Ratnasiri Wickremanayake was appointed prime minister.
2006 The South Asia Free Trade Agreement (SAFTA) came into effect between Sri Lanka, Bhutan, Bangladesh, India, Maldives, Nepal and Pakistan. The EU added the LTTE to its list of terrorist organisations (a move that followed the US and India), and froze all LTTE financial assets held within the EU. The United Nations Children's Fund (Unicef) accused the LTTE of abducting and recruiting children as soldiers. The number of dead attributed to the conflict since 1972 was estimated at 60,000.
2007 S P Thamilselvan, a leading political member of the LTTE, was killed in a government air raid.
2008 The prime minister announced a formal ending to the 2002 cease-fire with the LTTE.
2009 Government forces over-ran the LTTE's *de facto* capital of Kilinochchi in the north, after more than a decade of being held by the rebels. There was also heavy fighting as government forces took control of the strategic causeway linking the Jaffna Peninsula and strongholds of the LTTE with the mainland, along with the last rebel region of Mullaitivu in the north-east. In the 25-year conflict for a Tamil homeland an estimated 70,000 people had been killed. The LTTE agreed to international calls for a cease-fire but refused to lay down its arms, a prerequisite of the government, which in turn rejected any consideration of a conditional truce. The UN requested another cease-fire, to allow trapped civilians, estimated at 50,000–100,000, in the area to flee; this was rejected. Victory, after 26

years, was declared by President Rajapaksa as government troops over-ran the last enclave of the LTTE and the deaths of its leaders were announced, including its founder Velupillai Prabhakaran. Provincial elections were held for the Jaffna Municipal Council; the governing UPFA won 13 seats (out of 23) and the Illankai Tamil Arasu Kadchi (Tamil National Alliance) eight; of the four other candidates running for office two won seats. The government finally allowed refugees who had been held in camps since the end of the fighting to leave at will. They had previously been prevented from leaving before they had been screened for links with the Tamil Tigers.

2010 The EU withdrew trade benefits because of human rights concerns. As a result exports to the EU faced higher tariffs. In presidential elections, incumbent Mahinda Rajapaksa was re-elected with 57.88 per cent of the vote; his closest rival, Sarath Fonseka (New Democratic Front (NDF)) 40.15 per cent. The Supreme Court decided that as the presidential election had been called two years early, President Rajapaksa's new term in office would begin in November and he could remain in power until 2016. Over 7,000 candidates competed for 225 seats in the unicameral parliament. The ruling UPFA won 144 seats, gaining 39 seats over the 2004 elections. The United National Front, a coalition of three opposition Sinhalese parties led by Ekshat Jathika Pakshaya (EJP) (United National Party) won 60 seats, the Illankai Tamil Arasu Kachchi (Tamil National Alliance) (TNA) won 14, the Democratic National Alliance (DNA) won seven; turnout was 61.3 per cent. President Rajapaksa appointed D M Jayaratne as prime minister. The cabinet, chaired by the President, held a special symbolic meeting in Kilinochchi, the former capital of the Tamil Tigers. It reviewed the progress of reconstruction, which was hampered by deposits of unexploded ordinance (UXO). A commission set up to examine the conduct of the civil war held its first public meeting. Contruction began on a new deep-sea port, funded by US$360 million in Chinese soft loans, in southern Hambantota, including four terminals (two for cargo and two for fuel bunkering); it was completed in 2012. Another phase, equally large, to provide the infrastructure to service the port was completed in 2011. Mahinda Rajapaksa's 30 month sentence for violating military procurement procedures was confirmed by the president. Former presidential candidate and army chief, Sarath Fonseka was convicted in a military court, on charges of making irregular purchases for the military while in charge; he was sentenced to 30 months in prison.

2011 A UN report into the official conduct of the Sri Lankan civil war was published on 25 April. It concluded that there was evidence of the government and military being responsible for war crimes and crimes against humanity. The report dealt with the period from September 2008 to May 2009 and the military assault on the north-eastern coast, the heartland of the LTTE. Although the government had refused all UN interviews with its military personnel the Expert Panel, appointed by the UN Secretary General, had considerable information given to them by credible outside agencies, media and individuals from which to draw their conclusions. The government claimed the findings were 'baseless, biased and unilateral'. President Rajapaksa received a summons, issued by a US federal court in June, linked to three civil cases filed under the Hague Convention, by relatives of Tamil victims of alleged extra-judicial killings during the civil war. In November, Fonseka was given a further three-year jail sentence for lending credence to allegations that the defence secretary ordered the killing of Timil Tiger rebels while they were trying to surrender in 2009. Fonseka claimed the accusation and verdict were politically motivated.

2012 On 21 May Sarath Fonseka was released from prison; the government offered no explanation for his release. On the 14 November an internal report by the UN was released detailing its failure to protect Tamil civilians during the ending of the civil war in 2009. The review concluded that various UN agencies had been intimidated by Sri Lankan authorities. This lead to a reluctance on behalf of the UN to publish casualty figures and as UN staff withdrew from the war zone they failed to report the evidence of widespread government forces shelling civilian areas. The government denied the intimidation. On 23 November parliament began impeachment proceedings against the chief justice, Shirani Bandaranayake, accused of 14 charges of financial and official misconduct.

2013 The newly expanded Colombo Port formally opened for business on 5 August. The Port authorities hope that with the new breakwater, deeper basin, and the first of three modern new terminals now open, Colombo Port will be able to accept the latest generation of 18,000 20-foot equivalent units (TEU) container ships. With these facilities goods can be sent faster and more cost efficiently to other ports in the region. A curfew was imposed on Colombo after violence between Budhists and Muslims on 11 August. The Northern Provincial Council elections held on 21 September were won by the TNA, the main Tamil party, with 30 seats (out of 38). The UPFA led coalition won seven seats and the Sri Lanka Muslim Congress one seat. On 7 October Canadian Prime Minister Stephen Harper confirmed that he would not be attending the Commonwealth Heads of Government meeting in Sri Lanka in protest over alleged human rights abuses. Prime Minister Manmohan of India and Prime Minister Ramgoolam also said they would not be attending.

2014 Floods in central, eastern and northern Sri Lanka in December caused several deaths and displaced some one million people. The floods were the worst since 1956. In early November President Rajapaksa sought the opinion of the Supreme Court on whether he could stand for a third term as president. On 20 November he issued a proclamation calling for a presidential election at which he would seek re-election. The election commissioner confirmed the date as 8 January 2015, some two years ahead of schedule.

2015 The presidential election held on 8 January 2015 was won by Maithripala Sirisena (New Democratic Front (NDF)) with 51.28 per cent of the vote. Former president, since 2005, Mahinda Rajapaksa (47.58 per cent), tweeted that he looked forward to a peaceful transition of power, although there were rumours and accusations of an attempted coup by Mr Rajapaksa as it became clear that the election was running against him.

On 29 April parliament voted to restore the two-term limit for a president, and to rescind some of the extra presidential powers former president, Mahinda Rajapaksa, had given himself, including the power to sack parliament after one year (rather than four and a half years), as well as greater powers over the police, civil service and judiciary (allowing him to appoint all the top judges). President Sirisena had promised to remove the extended powers as part of his campaign for president.

Political structure

Constitution

The Constitution dates from 1978, when a presidential system of government was established. Local authority is represented by 24 district councils in nine provinces and the Pradesiya Sabas (councils based on local administrative divisions). The devolution of power is limited, partly due to non-implementation, and partly due to the fact that Article 2 of the Constitution stipulates a unitary state. Also politically significant is Article 9, which guarantees the 'foremost place' to Buddhism among faiths and stipulates the duty of the state to protect and sustain the religion. Both are obstacles to any scheme for devolution. Article 76 further stipulates that parliament may not 'abdicate or in any manner alienate its legislative power', complicating the creation of an autonomous Tamil entity.

The constitutional situation reflects events in 1987, when a peace accord was signed with India, which had intervened to protect the Tamil population. The Indo-Sri Lankan accord introduced a tier of government at provincial level, with elected provincial councils and certain powers delegated from the central government. Traditionally there are nine provinces, but the accord provided for the temporary merger of the Northern and Eastern Provinces (those regarded by Sri Lankan Tamils as their traditional homelands), pending a referendum for which the political conditions have not yet materialised.

The constitution provides the executive and security forces with sweeping powers on the declaration of a state of war. The Public Security Ordinance grants the armed forces wide powers of arrest and confiscation and allows home entry without a warrant once a war footing is declared. A two-thirds parliamentary majority is required for the removal of the president or amendment of the constitution.

A constitutional amendment was introduced on 28 April 2015 which established the Independent Commissions and limited the term of office of the President to five years while the President would continue to function as the Head of State and Head of Security Forces.

A Twentieth Amendment has been proposed to change the Electoral System.

Independence date

4 February 1948

Form of state

Socialist democratic republic

The executive

The president is directly elected for a five-year term and is Head of State, head of the executive, Head of government and head of the armed forces. No presidential incumbent may serve more than two terms. The president has the power to appoint or dismiss the prime minister (whose powers are relatively limited) and the cabinet and to dissolve parliament. After the election victory of the EJP in December 2001, President Kumaratunga agreed to delegate some of her extensive powers to the cabinet.

National legislature

The unicameral Parliament of Sri Lanka has 225 members elected by proportional representation, off which 196 are elected in 22 multi-seat electoral districts and the remainder by party lists nationally dependent on the share of the vote. All serve for six-year terms.

Legal system

The judiciary is formally independent of the executive. The Supreme Court has sole jurisdiction over interpretation of the constitution. It is also the final arbiter in settling charges against the president. The legal code reflects the system of English law inherited in 1948, with subsequent amendments in line with legal changes in the UK.

Last elections

17 August 2015 (parliamentary); 8 January 2015 (presidential).

Results: Parliamentary: Eksath Yahapalana Jathika Peramuna (United National Front for Good Governance) (EYJP) (coalition of nine political parties) won 45.7 per cent of the vote (106 seats out of 225); the United People's Freedom Alliance (UPFA) (coalition of six parties) won 42.4 per cent (95); Illankai Tamil Arasu Kachchi (Tamil National Alliance) (TNA) 4.6 per cent (16), Janatha Vimukthi Peramuna won 4.9 per cent (6). Turnout was 77.7 per cent.

Presidential: Maithripala Sirisena (New Democratic Front) won 51.3 per cent of the vote, Mahinda Rajapaksa (United People's Freedom Alliance) won 47.6 per cent; the remaining 17 candidates won less than 1 per cent each. Turnout was 81.5 per cent.

Next elections

2021 (parliamentary); January 2021 (presidential)

Political parties

Ruling party

Coalition led by the United National Party (UNP), United National Front for Good Governance (UNFGG)

Main opposition party

United People's Freedom Alliance

Population

20.96 million (2014)*

Last census: July 2001: 16,864,544 (provisional)

Population density: 315 inhabitants per square km (2010). Urban population 14 per cent (2010 Unicef).

Annual growth rate: 0.9 per cent, 1990–2010 (Unicef).

Internally Displaced Persons (IDP)

430,000–500,000 (UNHCR 2004)

Ethnic make-up

Sinhalese (74 per cent), Tamils (18 per cent), Moors (7 per cent), others (1 per cent).

Sri Lankan Tamils form the overwhelming majority in the Northern Province. The Eastern Province is ethnically mixed with three groups in sizeable numbers – Sri Lankan Tamils, mainly Tamil-speaking Moors (Muslims) and Sinhalese. Indian Tamils, descendants of those brought over by the British to work the tea plantations, are concentrated in the plantation districts of the Central Highlands. Elsewhere the Sinhalese are in the majority and make up about three-quarters of the total population.

Religions

Buddhism (69 per cent), Hinduism (15 per cent), Christian (7 per cent), Muslim (9 per cent). Sinhalese are predominantly Theravada Buddhists and Tamils are Hindus, while Arab and Malay descendants are mainly Muslims.

Education

Public investment in education amounts to 1.3 per cent of GDP. Universal primary education and gender parity, at this level, have been achieved.

Primary and junior secondary school are compulsory, lasting until aged 14. Senior secondary and collegiate schools are discretional and last until aged 18. All schooling until this age is provided free. Teaching is provided in English, Sinhala, Tamil and GCE exams at aged 16 must include a language subject in the student's mother tongue of Sinhalese or Tamil.

The education sector faces problems such as declining efficiency and quality of educational institutions and a shortage of teachers, nevertheless, standards are high and the importance allocated to education is evident in the high literacy rates.

Sri Lanka has received assistance from the World Bank, via the International Development Association (IDA). The ongoing Second General Education Project contributed a US$70.3 million for programmes based on improving enrolment, curriculum development and textbook provision. The Asian Development Bank has provided concessional loans to aid the North and East Community Restoration Development project to fund, among other programmes, educational facilities damaged during the internal conflict.

Literacy rate: 92 per cent adult rate; 97 per cent youth rate (15–24) (Unesco 2005).

Compulsory years: Five to 14

Enrolment rate: 110 per cent, gross primary enrolment of relevant age group (including repeaters); 74 per cent, gross secondary enrolment (World Bank).

Pupils per teacher: 28 in primary schools.

Health

World Bank estimates show that the average life expectancy is higher than in most developing countries and the infant mortality rate is relatively low. Sri Lanka's social indicators showed steady improvement during the 1990s including a decline in the maternal mortality rate. There is increased access by the rural population to safe water (from 29 per cent to over 83 per cent) and sanitation (from 39 per cent to over 60 per cent). However, relevant sources indicate increased incidences of malaria and a high malnutrition rate for children under the age of five. The government's *Samurdhi* (Prosperity) Programme is assisting, particularly the most vulnerable groups, to reduce child malnutrition. Adolescent health services, nutrition and geriatric services and institutions are under strain. The use of traditional medicine (*ayurveda*) to supplement public healthcare is widespread.

HIV/Aids

HIV prevalence: 0.1 per cent aged 15–49 in 2003 (World Bank)

Life expectancy: 71 years, 2004 (WHO 2006)

Fertility rate/Maternal mortality rate: 2.3 births per woman, 2010 (Unicef); maternal mortality 30 per 100,000 live births (World Bank).

Birth rate/Death rate: 16 births and 6.5 deaths per 1,000 population (2003)

Child (under 5 years) mortality rate (per 1,000): 10 per 1,000 live births (WHO 2012)

Head of population per physician: 0.55 physicians per 1,000 people, 2004 (WHO 2006)

Welfare

Despite sustained government efforts to introduce various poverty reduction programmes such as direct income transfers and subsidies, about 21 per cent of the country's population are poor. However, estimates on the poverty level exclude the conflict-centered north-east, which has about 2.8 million people, 15 per cent of the total population.

For a number of years poor families have been able to benefit from a food stamps project which provides vouchers for food. A much more ambitious poverty alleviation scheme, the *Janasaviya* programme, begun in the mid-1990s, entitled families to a monthly payment for the purchase of specific consumer goods. The Prosperity Programme is another government sponsored poverty reduction scheme, introduced in 1994, which aims to provide social services and a social safety net to very poor households. Two projects, funded by the Asian Development Bank, are the Emergency Assistance for the Rehabilitation of North and East Sri Lanka, and the Eastern Province Coastal Community Development Project.

Old age, disability and death have been covered since 1958 by a social insurance programme funded from the Employees' Provident Fund (EPF). Employers pay 12 per cent of salaries to the EPF, the country's main social insurance fund, with a further 8 per cent taken from employees. A social assistance programme for the unemployed – arguably the hallmark of a comprehensive welfare system – saw legislation introduced in 1995 in advance of a three-stage phasing in of the programme, aimed at families earning less than Rs1,000 (US$10.41) per month.

Main cities

Colombo (capital, estimated population 752,933 in 2012); Dehiwala-Mount Lavinia (245,974), Moratuwa (207,755), Negombo (127,754), Kandy (110,049), Kalmunai (94,653), Jaffna (88,138).

Many of the governmental functions are located in Jayawardenepura, a suburb of Colombo (135,806).

Languages spoken

The national languages, Sinhala and Tamil, are widely spoken. English is commonly used in government and is spoken by about 10 per cent of the population.

Official language/s

Sinhala, Tamil, English

Media

The human rights watchdog, Amnesty International said that between 2006 and Februray 2008 at least 10 media workers had been killed and others abducted, detained or 'disappeared'. Tamil journalists working in the conflict areas of the north and east of the country were most at risk, while Sinhalese journalists in the south faced official intimidation, especially if they reported on corruption.

Press

The government assumed wide powers to censor the press under a Public Security Ordinance in 2000. Media outlets are divided along language and ethnic lines and offer services in major languages only.

The government reinstated the Press Council in June 2009, in the face of strong opposition from media outlets that claimed self-censorship, introduced in 2003, had been working satisfactorily. The Press Council has the power to charge, fine and imprison journalists who transgress the press code. Campaigner for press freedom claim that Sri Lanka is 'one of the most dangerous places for journalist to operate in'.

Dailies: In Singhala, *Dinamina* is government-owned, *Lankadeepa* (www.lankadeepa.lk) and *Lakbima* (www.lakbima.lk) are private.

In Tamil, *Uthayan* (www.uthayan.com), *Virakesari* (www. Virakesari.lk) and *Thinakkural* (www.thinakural.com) are privately owned.

In English, *Daily News* (www.newslk.com) is government-owned, *The Island* (www.island.lk), and *Daily Mirror* (www.dailymirror.lk) are private. There are a number of English online news outlets including (*http://123srilanka.com*), (*www.lankatruth.com*), (*http://news.onlanka.com*) and (*www.srilankanewsfirst.com*).

Weeklies: The *Sunday Observer The Sunday Leader* (www.thesundayleader.lk), *Sunday Island* and *Sunday Times* (www.sundaytimes.lk), are published weekly, together with Sinhalese and Tamil weeklies such as *Virakesari Illustrated Weekly*.

Business: Several newsletters of specific interest are published by various representative groups including *Ceylon Commerce* by the Ceylon Chamber of Commerce (www.chamber.lk), *Industrial Ceylon* by the Ceylon National Chamber of Industries, *Business Lanka* and *Expo News* by the Ministry of Trade and Shipping Information Service, *Sri Lanka Ports News* by the Sri Lanka Ports Authority, *Clothing* magazine by the Clothing Industry Training Institute and the *Sri Lanka Investment News* by the Greater Colombo Economic Commission. An Indian publication *Business Today* (www.business-today.com) is also widely read.

Periodicals: Some of the popular and useful periodicals include *Explore Srilanka*, *Lanka Monthly Digest* (www.lmd.lk) and the fashion magazine *Satyn*.

Broadcasting

Radio: The state-owned Sri Lanka Broadcasting Corporation (www.slbc.lk) transmits six services with commercial programmes in Sinhala, Tamil and English. ABC Radio is the largest commercial network with five national stations, MBC (www.maharaja.lk) has four radio channels. There are dozens of local, privately operated radio stations, mostly broadcasting in FM including TNL Rocks (www.tnlrocks.com) and Yes FM (www.yesfmonline.com). External services are broadcast, on short wave, by Colombo International Radio in over six languages to central Asia.

Television: The state controlled Sri Lanka Rupavahini Corporation (SLBC) (www.rupavahini.lk), which operates two channels and Independent Television Network (ITN) (www.itn.lk) one. Other private operators include Sirasa TV (www.sirasa.com), MTV (www.capitalmaharaja.com), Swanavahini (www.swarnavahini.lk) in Sinhala and Shakthi TV (www.webtv.lk) in Tamil.

Other news agencies: The Sinhalaya News Agency (www.news.sinhalaya.com).

Economy

In 2014, the composition of the economy was dominated by the service sector with 56.7 per cent; industry accounted for 33.1 per cent and agriculture 10.2 per cent. The tourist industry, which provides vital foreign exchange, fell by 1.1 per cent

in 2009 as the civil war in the north came to a bloody end. However in January 2010, visitor numbers had increased by 31.9 per cent so that the annual rate of tourism grew by 10.7 per cent (over the same period in 2009). In 2013 visitor numbers were still rising, showing an increase of 24.8 per cent on 2012, to 1,275,000 total visitors. In 2014, visitor number increased even further to 1,525,000 tourists, a 19.8 per cent on numbers in 2013.
New industries, such as information technology (IT), software development and communications (call centres) are contributing an increasingly larger share of overall GDP. Traditional industries include garment and leather goods manufacturing, rubber products and food processing. Natural resources include mined sapphires and rubies, which are processed domestically for the tourist trade, limestone and graphite, mineral sands and phosphate. Tealeaf production, rice, coconuts and spices lead agricultural products. Agriculture and industry are located particularly in the southern and western parts of the country.
GDP growth was 6 per cent in 2008, falling to 3.5 per cent in 2009 as the global economic crisis cut world trade. However in 2010 as international trade picked up and the government increased investment in the north as it reintegrated its economy with the world market following the end of the civil war, GDP growth climbed to 8 per cent. By 2013, after a period of continual growth, it had slowed slightly to 7.3 per cent. In 2014, GDP growth had continued to stabilise at a very healthy 7.4 per cent.

External trade

Sri Lanka is a member of South Asia Association for Regional Co-operation, which operates a preferential trading arrangement that covers 6,000 products. In 2004 the South Asia Free Trade Area (Safta) was ratified, implemented between the seven member states (Afghanistan, Bangladesh, Bhutan, India, Maldives, Nepal, Pakistan and Sri Lanka) in 2012. The seven foreign ministers of the region signed a framework agreement on SAFTA to reduce customs duties of all traded goods to zero by the year 2016. In 2014, Safta had a combined population of approximately 1.8 billion people.
Traditional plantation produce (tea, rubber and coconuts) continue to have a significant influence on export earnings, however clothing and leather product manufacturing is now the largest sector accounting for 39 per cent of total output followed by the production of food, beverages and tobacco at 22 per cent. The industrial sector also includes petrochemicals, plastics and processed rubber. There is a growing trade in information technology and software development. The export of precious gems is a modest but important export addition to foreign earnings.

Imports

Major imports are petroleum, textiles, machinery and transportation equipment, building materials, mineral products and foodstuffs.
Main sources: India (20.7 per cent of total in 2014), China (17.8 per cent), UAE (9.1 per cent), Singapore (6.6 per cent) and Japan (4.9 per cent).

Exports

Major exports are textiles and apparel, tea and spices, diamonds, emeralds, rubies, coconut products, rubber manufactures and fish.
Main destinations: US (25 per cent of total in 2014), UK (10.2 per cent), India (5.7 per cent), Italy (5.6 per cent) and Germany (4.6 per cent).

Agriculture

Farming

Sri Lanka's economy is becoming more service-oriented and less dependent on agriculture. The agriculture sector includes mostly large state-owned tea, rubber and coconut plantations and smaller holdings where rice, sugar cane, cassava, sweet potatoes, soya beans, other vegetables, cashew nuts, cocoa, castor, spices, chillies, onions and other crops are produced, sometimes at virtually subsistence level. Other agricultural products include cinnamon and coffee. Sri Lanka is self-sufficient in rice, the main food crop. Livestock raised include buffaloes, goats, pigs, sheep and poultry.
Agricultural productivity on the small farms is low. The sector as a whole is struggling against declining terms of trade, with a general decline in the price of commodities like coconut and rubber coupled with rising costs, particularly transport.
Plantation crops provide export earnings, although output has declined in recent years. Sri Lanka exports 44 per cent of its rubber output, with production increasingly shifting to crepe rubber and latex. Tea is the most important agricultural export and accounts for around 2 per cent of GDP, although there is a lot of room for productivity gains. Smallholdings account for around 65 per cent of total output. The sector is showing signs of improvement. Private tea plantations owned by foreign investors are increasingly common and a number of new tea-blending units have become operational, helping to increase the added value of tea. Over one million labourers are directly or indirectly employed by the industry.
Production has matched the steady increase in world demand for spices. Sri Lanka produces over 85 per cent of the world's demand for cinnamon. Spice production accounts for over 95,000 hectares of land.
The Sri Lankan government has introduced a National Food Production Plan for 2016-18, which aims to grow agricultural products that can be grown in the country in the next three years and restrict food imports. 80 per cent of requirements for chilies, soya, cowpea and green gram are met by imports. In order to accomplish this, President Sirisena plans to use state owned lands that have not been cultivated for food production in the future. The empty lands, which have not been utilized for food production and owned by private sector, will also be taken on a temporary basis for food production.

Fishing

Fishing accounted for 1.8 per cent of GDP in 2013. Production includes prawns, shrimps, lobsters, crabs and sea cucumbers, for export and local consumption. Production of the fishing industry was in the region of 500,000 tonnes in 2013, which was a growth in value of 15.8 per cent on 2012.
New companies engaged in marine fishing qualify for a five-year tax holiday. Fishing activity has been affected both by higher petroleum prices and by the poor security situation.
Sri Lanka will introduce new laws in late 2015 to punish illegal fishing in international waters, as part of efforts to lift a ban on exports to the European Union. Illegal fishing will be fined up to five times the value of the catch.

Forestry

About 30 per cent of the land area (1.86 million hectares) is forested, and forestry accounts for 2 per cent of GDP, providing timber for local demand. Around 15 per cent of land area is subject to national protection. Forests of broad-leaved, deciduous and evergreen trees are adapted to dry and monsoon seasons. Savannah and thorn woodland are found beside coastal areas populated by mangroves.
Plantations account for around 316,000 hectares (ha) of forest cover and are established at a rate of 3,100ha per year. In the 1990s, Sri Lanka lost almost 20 per cent of its natural forest, at an average of 35,000ha per annum, so that only small fragments of tropical rainforest remain, each less than 10,000 hectares in area. Illegal logging has removed timber from unprotected forests, adding to the reduction. Some tropical timber plantations provide teak, eucalyptus, pine and mahogany, which are commercially farmed.

Most paper is imported. Non-wood forest products harvested include bamboo, rattan, gums, resins and medicinal plants, cinnamon, cloves, nutmeg and cardamom.

Industry and manufacturing

Industry contributed around 32 per cent of GDP in 2013. One-third of manufacturing output, which accounts for around 15 per cent of GDP, is based on raw materials from the agricultural sector. There are 10 dedicated Export Processing Zones, mainly employing female labour. A master plan for industrial development, co-ordinated with the Japanese International Co-operation Agency (JICA) and the United Nations Industrial Development Organisation (Unido), identifies electronics, information technology, rubber and plastics, machinery, footwear, textiles and apparel and agro-based industries as target sectors, with policy development responsibilities for these sectors shared between JICA and Unido.

Tourism

Sri Lanka has a long history as a tourist destination with a diverse range of facilities, from beach resorts to highland tea plantations. There are eight sites on Unesco's World Heritage List, including ancient and historic cities and towns as well as the Sinharaja Forest Reserve and a national park and conservation forest. Tourism has benefitted from the end of the civil war as visitor numbers jumped from 448,000 in 2009 to 654,000 in 2010. In 2013 visitor numbers were still rising, showing an increase of 24.8 per cent on 2012, to 1,275,000 total visitors. In 2014, visitor number increased even further to 1,525,000 tourists, a 19.8 per cent on numbers in 2013. The total contribution of travel and tourism to GDP was $US7.6 billion in 2014. Travel and tourism contributed 11.1 per cent to GDP in 2014, an increase from the 9.4 per cent in 2013, and provided employment for 10 per cent of the work force (819,500 jobs) in 2014, a big increase from 8.4 per cent of the workforce (688,500 jobs) in 2013.
Sri Lanka's quarter century long civil war, which ended in May 2009, has left war damage to tourism facilities and infrastructure in the north that are still in need of repairs. However, new hotels have been built and a beach development is under way in Batticaloa.

Mining

Mining and quarrying accounts for around 2 per cent of GDP and employs 1 per cent of the workforce. Sri Lanka is rich in minerals such as ilmenite, plumbago, graphite, dolomite, kaolin, rutile, feldspar, quartz, mica, monazite, apatite, industrial clays and limestone. Precious and semi-precious stones, such as sapphires, rubies, catseyes, alexandrites, aquamarines, garnets, tourmalines, zircons, topaz, spinels, amethysts and moonstones provide increasing export income.
Australian mineral sands miner Iluka Resources Ltd purchased a Sri Lankan company in the business of sand mining and is set to begin operations soon. The company has been given environmental clearance in October 2015 and is set to discuss with the government legal and investment terms. The project will contribute economically and socially to the country, including direct and indirect employment; the introduction of new mining, processing and industrial technology to Sri Lanka, as well as high value export products generating material foreign exchange revenues for the country.

Hydrocarbons

Sri Lanka currently has no known reserves of natural gas or oil. It imports all its needs from nations including the UAE.
Cairn India Ltd relinquished its exploration rights in the South Asian Island in 2015. They will keep Cairn's seismic study worth about US$300 million and won't charge any penalty for pulling out. As a result, Sri Lanka will issue a fresh international tender for offshore oil and gas blocks. There might be potential for significant reserves of oil or natural gas and companies including Reliance Industries Ltd and BP Plc in neighbouring India might be interested.
Any use of coal is commercially insignificant.

Energy

Total installed generating capacity was 3.9 gigawatts (GW) in 2014. The current energy generation is predominantly made up of thermal (diesel and all other fuel sources), hydro and other renewables. Renewable energy capacity accounts for 442MW, dominated by mini-hydro power technology, which contributes 293 MW capacity, while wind energy technology represents 124 MW capacity. Renewable energy capacity has a share of over 11 per cent in installed capacity as well as generation. The Ceylon Electricity Board plans to increase the renewable energy capacity to 972 MW by 2020, which would contribute 20 per cent to the total power generation in the country. Mini-hydro power and wind energy will represent the majority of the mix while biomass-based power and solar power will also have represent a significant percentage. Around 85 per cent of the population had access to electricity in 2012.

Financial markets

Stock exchange

Colombo Stock Exchange (CSE)

Banking and insurance

In 2009 HSBC became the first bank to announce it would open a branch in Jaffna, in 2010. The opening demonstrated the bank's confidence in the economy's emergence after the civil war which ended in 2009.
There are 26 commercial banks, but the sector is dominated by two state banks – Bank of Ceylon and People's Bank — which hold 55 per cent of market share.
The government's deficit financing crowds out the private sector, meaning that banks have traditionally focussed on the public sector and reap high spreads from soaring interest rates. Meanwhile, deposit rates are low thanks to Sri Lanka's closed capital account and lack of competition among banks. This has created a perverse situation, where, although government security yields are higher than those from risky bank deposits, money keeps flowing into the banks.
The dominance of the two state banks is holding back development of the sector. Government-mandated lending policies mean that the two are effectively the industry's interest rate setters. Monopoly yields insulate the public banks from competitive problems that would otherwise be caused by managerial slack, poor asset bases and high costs. Organised resistance from unions and a desire to keep the banks' huge funds within the public sector have so far ruled out privatisation, although there are signs the government is amenable to gradual privatisation and an eventual stock market listing.

Central bank

Central Bank of Sri Lanka

Main financial centre

Colombo

Time

GMT plus 5 hours 30 minutes

Geography

Sri Lanka lies on the same continental shelf as India, from which it is separated by the shallow Palk Strait. The relief is dominated by the central highland massif, with an average elevation of over 1,500 metres, situated in the south central part of the island. This is surrounded by upland ridges and valleys which in the south-west of the island continue to the coast. The eastern region is an undulating plain with isolated hills and the north has flat, low and fertile plains intersected by ridges.

Hemisphere

Southern

Climate

Colombo and the south-west experience monsoon rains May–September; the likely temperature range is 22–31 degrees Celsius (C) with average annual rainfall of

2,240mm. The north-east experiences monsoon rains November–February; lower temperatures (down to 10 degrees C) occur inland at higher altitudes, with average rainfall of 1,000–1,500mm a year.

Dress codes

Men usually wear a lightweight or tropical suit and tie for business meetings, and women mostly dress conventionally. On social occasions, dress as for business meetings unless stipulated otherwise. Rainwear is needed, as are warmer clothes for the hilly areas, especially between November and February. Discreet dress in public places is appreciated.

Entry requirements

Passports

Passports are required by all, and must be valid for at least three months from the date of issue of visa.

Visa

From 1 January 2011 tourists or business travellers will need to apply for their visas in advance, usually online via a new site, www.eta.gov.lk and pay a processing fee of US$50 for tourists, US$60 for business travellers or US$25 for transit passengers. Only those from Singapore or The Maldives will be exempt.

Currency advice/regulations

The import of local currency is limited to Rs1,000; export is limited to Rs250. The import of Indian and Pakistani foreign currency is prohibited, all other foreign currency is unlimited but amounts over US$5,000 (or equivalent) must be declared; export of foreign currency is limited to the amount declared on arrival. Travellers cheques are accepted in banks.

Customs

Personal effects are allowed duty-free, however, valuable items (including jewellery) must be declared and must be re-exported on departure. Tobacco imports are not duty-free.

Prohibited imports

The import of firearms, ammunition, explosives, dangerous weapons, illegal drugs and pornography is strictly prohibited.

The export of antiques, rare books, palm leaf manuscripts, rare anthropological material and any wild animal (including ivory), bird or reptile, tea or rubber is prohibited.

Health (for visitors)

Medical facilities are adequate if limited. Immediate cash payment is often required by doctors and hospitals.

Mandatory precautions

A vaccination certificate for yellow fever is required if travelling from an infected area. Infants under one year are exempt.

Advisable precautions

Vaccinations for diphtheria, tuberculosis, hepatitis A and B, Japanese B encephalitis, polio, tetanus and typhoid are recommended. Malaria, dengue fever and chikungunya fever are caused by mosquitoes; precautions including mosquito repellents, nets and clothing covering the body should be used. There is a rabies risk. Water should be boiled and filtered before drinking. Fruit must be washed in such water and peeled.

Medical insurance, including emergency evacuation, is necessary.

Hotels

A 10 per cent service charge is added to hotel bills.

Credit cards

Major credit cards are widely accepted; charge cards have limited acceptance.

Public holidays (national)

Fixed dates

1 Jan (New Year's Day), 4 Feb (Independence Day), 13–14 Apr (Sinhala and Tamil New Year), 1 May (Labour Day), 17 Dec (Ramazan), 25 Dec (Christmas Day).

Variable dates

Good Friday, Tamil Thai Pongal Day (Jan), Mahasivarathri (Feb), Vesak (Buddha Purnima) (May), Diwali (Hindu, Oct/Nov), Eid al Adha, Birth of the Prophet Mohammed, Eid al Fitr.

Although not official public holidays, Poya holidays are observed on the day of each full moon.

Hindu, Muslim and Buddhist festivals are timed according to local sightings of various phases of the moon.

Working hours

Banking

Mon–Fri: 0900–1500.

Business

Mon–Fri: 0900–1700.

Government

Mon–Fri: 0830–1615.

Shops

Mon–Fri: 0900–1730; Sat: 0900–1300.

Telecommunications

Mobile/cell phones

GSM 900 and 1800 services cover much of the island, particularly in the east and populated areas.

Electricity supply

230–240V AC, 50 cycles

Weights and measures

Metric system (local units also in use)

Social customs/useful tips

Alcoholic drinks are not served in hotels or restaurants on *Poya* (full moon) days. Footwear and headgear should be removed before entering Buddhist shrines; photographing statues of the Buddha is acceptable but not posing beside them; a yellow-robed Buddhist *bhikku* should not be asked to pose for photographs nor should visitors attempt to shake hands with him.

Filming with a video camera and other photography near military and government installations is prohibited.

Appointments should be made in advance. Punctuality is appreciated. Men shake hands on meeting and taking leave. Some people may prefer not to shake hands with those of the opposite sex.

The form of address is Mr or Mrs followed by family or surname, and people with an academic or professional title should be addressed by their full title.

Visitors should take note of local customs and take care to respect religious conventions. It is the convention to use the right and not the left hand when shaking hands and passing or receiving anything.

Restaurants usually add a service charge but further gratuities are optional.

Security

Visitors should avoid areas north of Puttalam, Anuradhapura and Nilaveli as well as the eastern side of the island south of Trincomalee including Batticaloa.

The areas once under conflict were heavily mined and travelling off main roads can be hazardous; warning notices are posted. Visitors must comply with any instruction issued at road blocks and security checks.

Registration with the relevant national embassy on arrival is highly advisable.

Getting there

Air

National airline: SriLankan Airlines

International airport/s: Colombo Bandaranaike International (CMB) in Katunayake, 29km north of Colombo, with duty-free shops, bar, restaurant, bank, post office and car hire. There are taxis, bus and rail links.

Airport tax: Departure tax: Rs1,000

Surface

Water: Ferry services between Colombo and Tuticorin in Tamil Nadu state of India were resumed on 14 June after almost 30 years of having been suspended due to the security situation. There will be two round trips per week initially.

Main port/s: Colombo, Trincomalee, Galle, Kandasanturai. The newly expanded Colombo Port formally opened for business on 5 August 2013.

Getting about

National transport

Air: There are airports in Batticaloa, Gal Oya, Palali and Trincomalee; the airport at Jaffna is currently closed.

Road: The extensive road network has 27,000km of road, 19,000km of which is surfaced. Over 90 per cent of all haulage is transported by roads.

Buses: Express services are available to all main destinations and should be booked in advance. Some services have air-conditioning.

Rail: An intercity express train runs between Colombo and Kandy. There are regular services linking Colombo to other main centres. Some services offer air-conditioning, dining cars and first-class accommodation. The service to Jaffna has been discontinued.

City transport

Taxis: Metered taxis are usually found in large towns, they may have yellow tops and red numbers on a white plate. Air-conditioned taxis cost 10 per cent more. A 10 per cent tip is usual.

Car hire

Self-drive and chauffeur-driven car hire are available although chauffeur-driven cars are generally recommended. If driving, do not ignore 'no parking' signs (in Colombo vehicles parked illegally are destroyed by security forces suspecting a terrorist bomb). It is highly advisable to be aware of all traffic laws and parking restrictions. Driving is on the left.

Traffic is generally congested and the average rate of progress on roads nationwide is 30kph. Many roads are one-way only.

A national or international driving licence must be presented for local endorsement (on weekdays only) at the Automobile Association offices in Colombo.

BUSINESS DIRECTORY

The addresses listed below are a selection only. While World of Information makes every endeavour to check these addresses, we cannot guarantee that changes have not been made, especially to telephone numbers and area codes. We would welcome any corrections.

Telephone area codes

The international direct dialling code (IDD) for Sri Lanka is +94, followed by area code and subscriber's number:

Colombo Central	11	Moratuwa	11
Dehiwela	11	Negombo	31
Galle	91	Nuwara Eliya	52
Jaffna	21	Panadura	34
Kandy	81	Trincomalee	26
Kurunegala	37		

Useful telephone numbers

Police, fire and ambulance: 90
Emergency: 433-333
Accident service: 693-184/185
Directory enquiries: 161
International calls: 100
Speaking clock: 104

Chambers of Commerce

American Chamber of Commerce in Sri Lanka, Colombo Hilton Hotel, Lotus Road, Colombo 1 (tel: 233-6073; fax: 233-6072; e-mail: amcham@itmin.com).

Ceylon Chamber of Commerce, 50 Navam Mawatha, PO Box 274, Colombo 2 (tel: 245-2183; fax: 243-7477; e-mail: info@chamberlk).

Federation of Chambers of Commerce and Industry of Sri Lanka, 29 Gregory's Road, PO Box 2015, Colombo 7 (tel: 698-225; fax: 699-530; e-mail: info@fccisl.org).

National Chamber of Commerce of Sri Lanka, 450 DR Wijewardene Mawatha Street, PO Box 1375, Colombo 10 (tel: 268-9600; fax: 268-9596; e-mail: sg@nccsl.lk).

Banking

Bank of Ceylon, 4 Bank of Ceylon Mawatha, Colombo 1 (tel: 244-8348; fax: 244-8606).

Commercial Bank of Ceylon, 21 Bristol St, Colombo 1 (tel: 244-5010; fax: 244-9889; email: email@combank.net).

DFCC Bank, 73/5 Galle Road, Colombo 3 (tel: 244-0366; fax: 244-0376; email: dfcc@sri.lanka.net).

Hatton National Bank, 10 RA de Mel Mawatha, Colombo 3 (tel: 234-3473; fax: 244-0658).

National Development Bank, 40 Navam Mawatha, Colombo 2 (tel: 243-7701; fax: 244-0262).

Pan Asia Bank, 450 Galle Road, Colombo 3 (tel: 256-5564; fax: 256-5576; email: panasia@pabnk.lk).

People's Bank, 110 Sir James Peiris Mawatha, Colombo 2 (tel: 232-4188; fax: 244-7671).

Sampath Bank, PO Box 997, Sampath Centre Building, 110 Sir James Peiris Mawatha, Colombo 2 (tel: 230-0260; fax: 230-0143).

Seylan Bank, Ceylinco Seylan Towers, 90 Galle Road, Colombo 3 (tel: 243-7901; fax: 243-3072).

Union Bank of Colombo, World Trade Centre, Echelon Square, Colombo 1 (tel: 234-6346; fax: 234-6356).

Central bank

Central Bank of Sri Lanka, PO Box 590, 30 Janadhipathi Mawatha, Colombo 1 (tel: 247-7000; fax: 247-7712; e-mail: cbslgen@sri.lanka.net).

Stock exchange

Colombo Stock Exchange (CSE), www.cse.lk

Travel information

Atlas Lanka (Pvt) Ltd, 86/1. Chatham Street, Colombo 1 (tel: 233-4255/6; fax 243-5292; email: atlaslka@sltnet.com).

Automobile Association of Ceylon, 40 Sir Macan Markar Mawatha, Galle Face, Colombo 3 (tel: 242-1528; fax: 244-6074).

Bandaranayake International Airport, Katunayake (tel: 225-2861; fax: 225-3187).

SriLankan Airlines, Level 22, East Tower, World Trade Centre, Echelon Square, Colombo 1 (tel: 733-5555; fax: 733-5122; internet: www.srilankan.aero).

Ministry of tourism

Ministry of Tourism, 64 Galle road, Colombo 03 (tel: 238-5241; fax: 239-9274; internet: www.slmts.slt.lk).

National tourist organisation offices

Sri Lanka Tourist Board, 80 Galle road, Colombo 03 (tel: 243-7059/60; fax: 244-0001; internet: www. srilankatourism.org).

Ministries

Ministry of Agriculture, Sampathapay, 82 Rajamalwatte Road, Battaramulla (tel: 288-6623).

Ministry of Aviation and Airports Developments, 64 Galle Road, Colombo 3.

Ministry of Buddha Sasana and Religious Affairs, 135 Anagarika Dharmapala Mawatha, Colombo 7 (tel: 232-9064; fax: 243-7992).

Ministry of Constitutional Affairs and Industrial Development, 73/1 Galle Road, Colombo 3 (tel: 232-7553; fax: 244-9402).

Ministry of Co-operative Development, 349 Galle Road, Colombo 3.

Ministry of Cultural Affairs, Sethsiripaya, Battaramulla.

Ministry of Defence, 155 Baladaksha Mawatha, Colombo 3 (tel: 243-0860; fax: 254-1529).

Ministry of Development, Rehabilitation & Reconstruction of the East and Rural Housing Development, 43/89 Bristol Building, York Street, Colombo 1.

Ministry of Development, Rehabilitation & Reconstruction of the North and Tamil Affairs, North and East: 121 Park Road, Colombo 5.

Ministry of Education, Isurupaya, Sri Jayewardenepura Kotte, Battaramulla (tel: 286-5141; fax: 286-5162).

Ministry of Ethnic Affairs and National Integration, 152 Galle Road, Colombo 3.

Ministry of Finance and Planning, Secretariat Building, Colombo 1 (tel: 243-3937; fax: 244-9823; email: minfi@boisrilanka.org).

Ministry of Fisheries and Aquatic Resources Development, Maligawatte, Colombo 10 (tel: 244-6183; fax: 254-1184).

Ministry of Foreign Affairs, Republic Building, Colombo 1 (tel: 232-5371; fax: 244-6091; email: for_min@sri.lanka.net).

Ministry of Forestry and Environment, Unity Plaza Building, Colombo 4 (tel: 258-8274; fax: 258-3290).

Ministry of Health, Suwasiripaya, 385 Wimalawasa Mawatha, Colombo 10 (tel/fax: 269-2694).

Ministry of Higher Education and IT Development, 18 Ward Place, Colombo 8.

Ministry of Highways, Sethsiripaya, Battaramulla.

Ministry of Information and Media, World Trade Centre, Echelon Square, Colombo 1.

Ministry of Internal & International Commerce, Muslim Religious Affairs, and Shipping Development, Insurance Building, Vauxhall Street, Colombo 2.

Ministry of Irrigation and Water Resources Management, 500 TB Jayah Mawatha, Colombo 10 (tel: 268-7491; fax: 269-4968).

Ministry of Justice, Superior Courts Complex Colombo 12 (tel: 232-9044; fax: 232-0785).

Ministry of Labour, Labour Secretariat, Kirula Road, Colombo 5 (tel: 258-8078; fax: 258-2938).

Ministry of Land Development and Minor Export Agriculture, Govijana Mandiraya, Rajamalwatte Road, Battaramulla.

Ministry of Estate Infrastructure and Livestock Developemnt, 45 St Michaels Road, Colombo 3.

Ministry of Mahaweli Development, 500 TB Jayah Mawatha, Colombo 10 (tel: 268-7491; fax: 268-7386).

Ministry of Plan Implementation, Sethsiripaya, Battaramulla (tel: 286-2721; fax: 286-2478).

Ministry of Ports Development and Development of the South, 45 Laden Bastian Road, Colombo 1 (tel: 242-1231; fax: 242-3485).

Ministry of Post and Telecommunications, Sethsiripaya, Battaramulla.

Ministry of Power and Energy, 80 Flower Road, Colombo 7.

Ministry of Provincial Councils and Local Government, 330 Union Place, Colombo 2 (tel: 242-1211; fax: 234-7529).

Ministry of Public Administration, Home Affairs and Plantation Industries, Independence Square, Colombo 7 (tel: 269-6211; fax: 269-5279).

Ministry of Rural Industrial Development, Janakala Kendraya, Pelawatte, Battaramulla.

Ministry of Samurdhi, Rural Development, Parliamentary Affairs and Up-Country Development, 7A Reed Avenue, Colombo 7 (tel: 268-9589; fax: 268-8945).

Ministry of Science and Technology, 320 TB Jaya Mawatha, Colombo 10.

Ministry of Social Services and Housing Development for Fishing Community, Sethsiripaya, Battaramulla.

Ministry of Transport, 1 DR Wijewardana Mawatha, Colombo 10 (tel: 268-7105; fax: 269-4547).

Ministry of Urban Development, Construction and Public Utilities, Sethsiripaya, Battaramulla (tel: 286-2721; fax: 286-4765).

Ministry of Vocational Training, 475/32 Kotta Ropad, Rajagiriya.

Ministry of Womens Affairs, 177 Nawala Road, Colombo 5.

Ministry of Youth Affairs, 7A Reed Avenue, Colombo 7.

Other useful addresses

Board of Investment of Sri Lanka (BOI), World Trade Centre, Echelon Square, Colombo 1 (tel: 243-6639; fax: 244-7994; internet: www.boisrilanka.com/boihome/boi.htm).

British High Commission, 190 Galle Road, Colombo 3 (tel: 243-7336; fax: 243-0308; email: bhc@eureka.lk).

Colombo Plan, 28 St Michael's Road, Colombo 3 (tel: 256-4448; fax: 256-4531; email: cplan@slt.lk).

Colombo Stock Exchange, World Trade Centre, Echelon Square, Colombo 1 (tel: 244-6581; fax: 244-5279; internet: www.lanka.net/cse).

Sri Lanka Embassy (USA), 2148 Wyoming Avenue, NW, Washington DC 20008 (tel: (+1-202) 483-4025; fax: (+1-202) 232-7181; email: slembassy@starpower.net).

Sri Lanka Export Credit Insurance Corporation, Export Guarantee House, Colombo 2 (tel: 271-9410; fax: 271-9400; email: slecic@tradenetsl.lk).

Sri Lanka Export Development Board, 42 Navam Mawatha, Colombo 2 (tel: 230-0675; fax: 230-0715; email: serve@edbtradenetsl.lk).

Sri Lanka Importers', Exporters' and Manufacturers' Association, PO Box 12, Colombo 10 (tel: 269-6321; fax: 252-2524; email: sliema@isplanka).

Sri Lanka Tea Board, 574 Galle Road, Colombo 3 (tel: 258-2236; fax: 258-9132; email: tboard@sri.lanka.net).

US Embassy, 210 Galle Road, Colombo 3 (tel: 244-8007; fax: 243-7345; email: cdscmb@usia.gov).

The Sinhalaya News Agency (www.news.sinhalaya.com).

Internet sites

InfoLanka (gateway site): www.infolanka.com

Sri Lanka Telecom directory: www.slt.lk

Sri Lanka, virtual library: www.lankalibrary.com

Tamilnet: www.tamilnet.com

Sudan

KEY FACTS

Official name: Jamhuryat es Sudan (Republic of Sudan)

Head of State: President Omar Hassan Ahmad al Bashir (from1993; re-elected Apr 2010)

Head of government: President Omar Hassan Ahmad al Bashir

Ruling party: Al Muttamar al Watani (National Congress Party) (NCP) (from 1998; re-elected Apr 2010)

Area: 1,861,484 square km

Population: 34.38 million (2013)*

Capital: Khartoum

Official language: Arabic

Currency: Sudanese pound (S£) = 100 piastre

Exchange rate: S£5.70 per US$ (Jul 2014)

GDP per capita: US$2,040 (2013)*

GDP real growth: 3.35% (2013)*

GDP: US$70.13 billion (2013)*

Unemployment: 10.00% (2013)*

Inflation: 36.52% (2013)*

Oil production: 122,000 bpd (2013)

Balance of trade: -US$4.75 billion (2012)

Foreign debt: US$37.98 billion (Dec 2010)

Annual FDI: US$2.89 billion (2010)

* estimated figure

In 1989, President Omar al Bashir seized power in a military *coup*. Something of the sort had long been expected – Sudan had been described by Jon Lee Anderson, writing in the *New Yorker* as 'a catastrophically failed state.' On independence from Britain in 1956 it had become Africa's biggest state, although Mr Anderson continued by saying that it was 'perhaps its most dysfunctional, a forced union of mismatched parts.'

Omar Hassan Ahmad al Bashir

The direction in which Sudan developed was very much determined by the background of its president. The conflict with what was to become South Sudan saw some two million Sudanese die. Al Bashir is no softy: he had joined the Egyptian army and fought in the 1973 war with Israel. An apparently devout Muslim, with two wives, he was reportedly connected to the Muslim Brotherhood and had allowed the (now dead) leader of al Qaeda, Osama bin Laden, to live in Sudan for some years. He was also the first incumbent head of state to be indicted by the International Criminal Court (ICC) in The Hague (Holland). Mr Anderson described him as 'Africa's Hugo Chávez'. However, after twenty four years in comfortably autocratic power, 2013 saw President al Bashir uncomfortably on the back foot as thousands of Sudanese protesters took to the streets of the capital, Khartoum, bravely calling for the resignation of their President of over two decades. The unprecedented demonstrations followed the killing of dozens of people in a week of protest at the government's austerity measures. The next presidential elections are scheduled for 2015.

Don't panic

The panicky government could only resort to sticking plaster measures, counts indicated majorities of the order of 90 per cent win for the incumbent. The opposition parties boycotted the presidential and parliamentary elections, but the Arab League monitoring mission saw nothing amiss, announcing that the general elections were carried out 'transparently and in accordance with international standards.' Quite which international standards the Arab League had in mind was not clear. On the 2014 Transparency International *Corruption Perceptions Index*, Sudan ranked 173 out of the 175 countries surveyed. Only North Korea and Somalia ranked lower.

Times change

Following the division of the former Sudan into two states, the northern Sudan found times were getting harder, very much harder. The rump country was faced with a treble whammy: it now only garnered transit fees for the oil now produced in South Sudan and the civil war in South Sudan meant that the oil could not always be pumped. And the price of that oil had also fallen through the floor. Times were indeed tough. In the days when there was money to be made from oil, the funds that did not end up in its rulers' pockets were frittered away on grandiose, for the most part unproductive, projects. By 2015 there was little spare cash, even less foreign exchange and inflation was nearing 50 per cent. Cumbersome wheat and fuel subsidies ate into what money there was in the government's coffers. Economic hardship prompted many middle-class Sudanese to join the September 2014 street protests against the ending of subsidies. A worried government panicked, and an estimated 200 people died. Dissent was not confined to the streets. Senior NCP member Ghazi Salahuddin Atabani was sacked after criticising Bashir's handling of the protests. In December 2014 Bashir sacked a number of senior ministers, later announcing plans for reform, including a 'national dialogue' and a new constitution.

In the cabinet reshuffle, Lieutenant-General Bakri Hassan Saleh was made first vice president and was considered a likely successor to Mr Bashir. The army, which Mr Bashir once headed, still underpins the regime. Over 60 per cent of government expenditure goes on defence and security – excluding the cost of new military hardware, which is 'off balance sheet'.

The president will need a close ally to succeed him, essentially to ensure that he does not end up in the International Criminal Court in The Hague, which had accused him of committing atrocities in Darfur.

The economy

Desperately seeking friends with cash, President Bashir had been pitching the Gulf States. As is the case elsewhere in Africa, China is one of Sudan's few big recent investors. Iran is Bashir's main supplier of weapons. According to the African Development Bank (AfDB) growth of Sudan's gross domestic product (GDP) had been estimated at 3.4 per cent in 2014 and is projected at 3.1 per cent and 3.7 per cent in 2015 and 2016, respectively. GDP was expected to be driven by rain-fed agriculture, minerals and oil-transit fees. Domestic services grew by 3.1 per cent and accounted for 45.6 per cent of GDP in 2014. Services, however, typically provide low-productivity jobs. Inflation in Sudan, the highest in Africa and averaging 36.9 per cent in 2013–14, was largely down to exchange-rate devaluations, gold purchases and supply disruptions owing to civil conflicts. Although it was projected to drop to 21.8 per cent in 2015 on the back of a tight policy stance, build-ups of inflationary pressures will increase the already high rates of poverty and unemployment. In the short- and medium-term, growth should be sustained by the revitalisation of agriculture and increased production of mineral and non-mineral exports, in addition to restraining inflation.

A new IMF Staff-Monitored Programme (SMP) and a five-year programme of economic reform (FYPER, 2015–19) were adopted in 2014, aimed at enhancing macro-economic stability and sustaining inclusive growth. However, Sudan's policy makers faced challenges stemming from the structural weaknesses of the economy and limited market penetration. The slow growth of credit to the private sector due to low financial intermediation and the crowding-out effects of fiscal operations had further restrained the formalisation of business and job creation. Refusal, since 2014, of foreign correspondent banks to process transfers to and from Sudan in order to avoid violating US sanctions had tightened the foreign-exchange market and raised the costs of imported inputs. In this respect, effective outreach was needed to remove the US sanctions. Additionally, Sudan's heavy external debt and volatile internal and external political environments could effectively weaken progress towards meeting the World Bank's Millennium Development Goals (MDGs).

Urbanisation in Sudan has been propelled since the 1990s by worsening conditions in the rural areas and protracted civil conflicts. This had led to the development of slums and camps for the internally displaced, housing shortages in many cities and what the AfDB termed 'the proliferation of informality.' The absence of a strategy for co-ordinating land use within the national development planning process has contributed to excessive urban growth lacking in structural transformation and specialisation. A specific spatial strategy was needed to focus on maximising the benefits of existing urban assets in order to spread entrepreneurial opportunity, while reviving the rural

KEY INDICATORS — Sudan

	Unit	2011	2012	2013	2014	**2015
Population	m	*32.66	*33.51	*36.16	*37.29	*38.44
Gross domestic product (GDP)	US$bn	64.80	63.03	66.48	*73.82	*76.20
GDP per capita	US$	1,982	1,881	1,838	*1,980	*1,983
GDP real growth	%	-3.9	-3.0	3.7	*3.4	*3.3
Inflation	%	18.1	35.5	36.5	*36.9	*19.0
Unemployment	%	12.0	10.8	14.8	*13.6	*13.3
Oil output	'000 bpd	453.0	82.0	122.0	109.0	–
Exports (fob) (goods)	US$m	9,655.7	3,367.7	7,086.2	4,350.2	–
Imports (fob) (goods)	US$m	8,127.6	8,122.7	8,727.9	8,105.9	–
Balance of trade	US$m	1,528.1	-4,755.0	-1,641.7	-3,755.7	–
Current account	US$m	-290.0	-6,579.0	-7,570.0	*-3,806.0	*-3,230.0
Total reserves minus gold	US$m	–	192.6	193.0	181.5	–
Exchange rate	per US$	2.66	4.41	5.70	5.82	–

* estimated figure ** forecast figure

economy in order to reduce the potential risks and backlash related to economic clustering.

Hydrocarbons

South Sudan gained independence from Sudan in July 2011. Most of the oil production capacity was now in South Sudan, but the country is landlocked and remained dependent on Sudan because it must use Sudan's export pipelines and port. Disagreements over oil revenue sharing and armed conflict have curtailed oil production from both countries over the past few years. Prior to independence, the unified Sudan fought two civil wars. The second civil war ended with the signing of the Comprehensive Peace Agreement that was put into place from 2005 to 2011. South Sudan gained its independence from Sudan in July 2011. However, there were still unresolved issues that had caused tension between the countries after independence. The border between the two countries was ill-defined and some areas along the border remained contested.

Most of Sudan's and South Sudan's proved reserves of oil and natural gas are located in the Muglad and Melut Basins, which extend into both countries. Natural gas associated with oil production is flared or re-injected into wells to improve oil output rates. Neither country currently produces or consumes dry natural gas.

National oil companies from Asia dominate the oil sectors of both Sudan and South Sudan. The China National Petroleum Corporation, India's Oil and Natural Gas Corporation and Malaysia's Petronas hold large stakes in the leading consortia operating oil fields and pipelines. National oil companies Sudapet (Sudan) and Nilepet (South Sudan) also hold small stakes in operations. South Sudan experienced frequent disruptions to production over the previous few years. In January 2012, the country voluntarily halted its production because of a dispute over transit fees with Sudan. South Sudan's production was partially shut down again at the end of 2013 because of civil conflict.

Risk assessment

Economy	Poor
Politics	Poor
Regional stability	Poor

Muslims in Sudan

% of population	71.4
Sunni (% of Muslims)	99
Shi'a (% of Muslims)	1

People to watch

Lieutenant-General Bakri Hassan Saleh – vice president and thought likely to become President after Bashir.

COUNTRY PROFILE

1821 The swamps of southern Sudan were unaffected by the Arab-controlled northern regions until the Turks defeated Egypt, conquered northern Sudan and opened the south to trade.

1869 After the opening of the Suez Canal, the British became involved in Sudan.

1881–85 Mohammed Ahmed, who proclaimed himself the long-looked-for Mahdi (the guided one), led his followers, the Muslim Sudanese, in a rebellion against Egyptian misrule; General Gordon was sent by Britain to quash the rebellion. In 1885, Gordon and the British army were massacred by the Mahdi's army at Khartoum. Sudan was ruled by the Mahdi for the next 17 years. The Mahdi united the tribes in a modern Islamic state.

1898 The Mahdi was defeated by the British and Anglo-Egyptian army.

1899 Sudan was ruled as an Anglo-Egyptian condominium until it achieved independence as a parliamentary republic in 1956.

1945 At the end of the Second World War, political parties emerged. The Umma Party was created by supporters of the Mahdi while the Ashiqqa Party was established by rivals of the Mahdi and eventually became the National Union Party (NUP).

1956 Sudan gained independence. With southern calls for a federation or even secession rejected, a civil war broke out between the largely Muslim north and the largely Christian/Animist south.

1958 A military coup led by General Ibrahim Abboud overthrew the civilian government of Prime Minister Abd Allah Khalil. Martial law was declared and Abboud proclaimed himself prime minister.

1962 Civil war began in the south, led by the Anya Nya movement.

1964 The 'October Revolution' overthrew Abboud and a national government was established.

1969 Colonel Jaafar Mohammed al Nimieri led the 'May Revolution' military coup, installing a revolutionary council.

1972 Nimieri became the country's first elected president and gave the southern provinces a degree of autonomy under the Addis Ababa agreement between the government and the Anya Nya, reducing the level of fighting.

1978 Oil was discovered in southern Sudan.

1983 The President increased the Islamisation campaign when the autonomy agreement was revoked and *Sharia* (Islamic law) was introduced. In the south the Sudan People's Liberation Movement (SPLM) was established; its armed wing, the Sudan People's Liberation Army (SPLA) gained control of much of the south.

1985–86 Nimieri was ousted in a bloodless coup and after a brief period of military rule, Sadiq al Mahdi, the great-grandson of the Great Mahdi, became prime minister after elections in 1986.

1989 Sadiq al Mahdi was replaced following another bloodless coup by the National Salvation Revolution; Omar Hassan Ahmad al Bashir became chairman of the Revolutionary Command Council for National Salvation (RCCNS).

1992 The Sudanese pound was replaced as the currency by the Sudanese dinar.

1993 The RCCNS was abolished after Omar al Bashir was appointed president; Sudan returned to civilian rule, although with one political party exercising dominance – Al Muttamar al Watani (National Congress Party) (NCP), the country was not strictly a democracy.

1995 Egyptian President Mubarak accused Sudan of being involved in an attempt to assassinate him in Addis Ababa.

1996 The first presidential and legislative elections since the coup in 1989 were held; Omar al Bashir was elected president for a five-year term. Sanctions were imposed against Sudan by the UN for the country's failure to extradite three men suspected of involvement in the 1995 attempted assassination of Mubarak.

1997 The Khartoum Peace Agreement was ratified by the National Assembly. Peace talks between the SPLA and the government resumed in Nairobi.

1998–99 Voters in a referendum endorsed a new constitution. Sudan began to export oil. After a power struggle within the ruling NCP, between Bashir and Hassan al Turabi (a hardline Islamist and ideologue), the President imposed a state of emergency and dissolved the National Assembly.

2000 Omar al Bashir and the NCP were re-elected. Most opposition parties boycotted the elections.

2001 Hassan al Turabi, was arrested and his party, the National Islamic Front (NIF), was banned. The UN Security Council approved the lifting of sanctions imposed in 1996. The UN's World Food Programme estimated that three million people were facing famine.

2002 After peace talks in Kenya, the government and the SPLA signed the Machakos Protocol: the government

accepted the right of the south to seek self-determination after a six-year interim period.
2003 Rebels in the western region of Darfur started an uprising by attacking government targets, claiming the region was being neglected by Khartoum. Hassan al Turabi was released and the ban on the NIF was lifted. China and the Sudan announced a US$1 billion investment plan to enhance Sudan's oil infrastructure, including increased capacity at the Khartoum refinery and construction of a 750-kilometre-long pipeline between the Kordofan oilfield and the coast.
2004 A campaign to quell the insurrection in Darfur began; thousands of people were displaced by the fighting. Army officers and opposition politicians, including al Turabi, were arrested over an alleged coup plot. Bashir agreed to grant autonomy to the south for six years, split the country's oil revenues with the southern provinces and allow the southerners to vote in a referendum on independence at the end of the six-year period. The conflict in the western region of Darfur between nomad Arab militia and black African villagers gained world attention. The government denied that it supported the *Janjaweed* militias, accused of systematic killings of African villagers, and said that there was no evidence of any atrocities.
2005 The government and the Sudan People's Liberation Army (SPLA) signed a peace agreement which ended the 22-year civil war. The agreement began a period of transition to run until 2009, when parliamentary and state legislative elections would take place. SPLA leader, John Garang, was appointed vice president for the six-year period of reconciliation, and a new constitution gave a large degree of autonomy to the south. Security forces arrested many members and top officials of the main opposition Umma Party (UP), because of planned celebrations marking an anti-government uprising in 1986. Sudan said it had found quantities of oil in its western region of Darfur. John Garang was killed in a helicopter crash; riots broke out in Khartoum, between black southern Sudanese and northern Arabs. Garang's deputy, Salva Kiir, was named his successor as vice president of national Sudan and president of southern Sudan. Chad declared 'a state of belligerence' with Sudan. In an effort to ease tensions between the two countries, President Obasanjo of Nigeria, as head of the African Union, attempted mediation between a Sudanese envoy and Chad's President Déby, but with little success.
2006 The AU extended the mandate for its peacekeeping force by a further 10 months. Chad broke-off diplomatic relations with Sudan, following attacks on Chadian towns by Sudanese backed Chad rebels based in the Darfur region. A UN resolution was passed calling for a 20,000 international force of soldiers and police to be admitted to the Darfur region as peace-keepers. President Bashir remained uncompromising in its opposition to intervention. The UN envoy, Jan Pronk, was expelled for claiming that government troops had suffered defeats in southern Sudan.
2007 The currency was changed from the dinar (in use since 1992), back to the Sudanese pound (S£); the exchange rate was set at S£1 to 100 old dinars. Vice President Kiir accused the national government of supporting militia operating in the south, who had not been disarmed, and failing to share the wealth of resources found in the south. An agreement was signed between Sudan, Chad and the Central African Republic whereby no shelter would be given to rebel movements from another country. The minister of humanitarian affairs, Ahmed Haroun and a Janjaweed leader, Ali Mohammed Ali Abd al Rahman (known as Ali Kushayb) were indited by the International Criminal Court for crimes against humanity, committed during attacks on the civilian population of Darfur. The UN voted for a UN peacekeeping force to be sent to Sudan to bolster African Union (AU) troops already deployed in Darfur to protect civilians. An AU base, staffed by mostly Nigerian troops acting as military observers, was attacked by heavily armed rebels; 10 soldiers were killed and the incident sparked international condemnation. Dissident members of the SLA, the Justice and Equality Movement (JEM), were blamed for the attack. Rebels burned down the AU-base town of Haskanita. The UN Mission (Unmis) reported the town was under the control of government troops. The government announced a unilateral ceasefire in Darfur in advance of peace talks, despite two rebel groups boycotting the talks, which were being held in Libya. The SLA-Unity and the JEM groups decided not to attend the talks as other, smaller, rebel groups had also been invited. Representatives approached SLA-Unity and JEM to reconsider their decision. Meanwhile, the northern National Congress Party and southern Sudan People's Liberation Movement finally agreed to implement all provisions of the 2005 peace agreement. The UN-AU Mission in Darfur (Unamid) began operations, replacing the AU forces. The oil producing province of Abyei was subject to continued armed attacks by the SPLA, so finally the government, in agreement with the SPLM asked the Permanent Court of Arbitration (PCA) (based in The Hague) to rule on the disputed border between the north and south.
2008 The International Criminal Court (ICC) accused President al Bashir of genocide in Darfur and formally requested a warrant for his arrest. Sudan does not recognise the ICC and claimed the move was a 'foreign conspiracy'. The AU called on the UN to suspend the war crimes accusation against President Bashir, saying it would jeopardise the on-going peace process. The PCA ruling concluded that the government in Khartoum's argument that Abyei only constituted a small sliver of land south of the Kiir/Bahr el Arab River was erroneous and awarded 10,460 square kilometres to southern Sudan. It also rejected southern Sudan's argument that its demarcation in the eastern and western boundary areas was legitimate and awarded those areas, including much of the oil reserves in the area, to Khartoum. It also affirmed the right of traditional pastoral herdsmen to continue to use both sides of the border areas in the province of Kordofan for their flocks (over 18,500 square km).
2009 The ICC issued a warrant for the arrest of President Bashir on two counts of war crimes and five counts of crimes against humanity. Sudan dismissed the charges and re-affirmed its position of non-co-operation with the ICC. Sudan expelled 10 foreign aid agencies within hours of the issue of the arrest warrant. General elections to be held in 2009 were postponed until 2010; when undertaken, there would be six elections, including national presidential and parliamentary, the south Sudanese presidency and parliament and state gubernatorial and assemblies. The government reversed its earlier decision and invited new aid-NGOs into the country and allowed those already in operation to expand their activities. The ruling SPLM of the autonomous southern region split when Lam Akol created his own political party SPLM-Democratic Change, claiming the SPLM had failed to govern South Sudan. Both parties will nominate a candidate to challenge President Bashir in the next presidential elections. A delay in completing a census forced the postponement of presidential elections. The census was criticised by political leaders in the south who said that the southern Sudanese population had been under-recorded.
2010 The government agreed a ceasefire with the JEM rebels in Dafur. Almost all of the political parties based in southern Sudan threatened to withdraw from the presidential elections, due to fears concerning fraud and security during the voting. They maintained that the electoral process had been rigged to favour the ruling NCP.

President Bashir threatened to cancel a referendum on independence in the south in the face of the boycotts; the elections were duly held. The presidential and parliamentary elections were extended by two days due to organisational problems and high voter turnout. Two election monitoring organisations declared that the elections failed to meet full international standards due to intimidation and harassment, although neither called for a re-election. The announcement of the results was delayed as counting took longer than anticipated. President Bashir (NCP) won 68.24 per cent of the northern presidential vote and his political party NCP won 68.2 per cent. Salva Kiir (SPLM) was sworn in as the first elected president of southern Sudan. Sudan signed an agreement with Egypt, Ethiopia, Uganda, Tanzania and Rwanda to redistribute their relative share of Nile water; negotiations had been taking place since 1977. Opposition leader, Hassan al Turabi, who had been imprisoned by the government was released. The ICC added a second arrest warrant for President Bashir, for genocide. The UN reckoned that some 51,000 people travelled south to register in time. President Bashir announced that if the south broke away, the north would adopt an Islamic constitution.

2011 A seven-day referendum in southern Sudan, which began in January, to determine its future as either a province of Sudan or as an independent country, was overwhelmingly in favour of independence. The result was 98.83 per cent of the vote in favour, 1.17 per cent against independence. In February, it was decided by the ruling committee of the SPLM that South Sudan would be the official name of the country when it comes into existence in July. In May a group of army personnel of Sudan were ambushed while being escorted out of Abyei by UN peacekeepers and 22 men were killed in what the UN called 'a criminal attack', while the US called on South Sudan to 'account' for the attack. In retaliation, northern military 'repelled enemy forces' and occupied Abyei, according to Sudanese state news. The UN condemned the escalation in violence and called on Sudan to withdraw its military from the disputed town and region of Abyei, as a UN peacekeeping force was caught in the middle of what South Sudan called an 'invasion'. Around 20,000 people fled from Abyei to South Sudan. Armed men looted and burned buildings in Abyei as the UN warned Sudan that it was 'responsible for maintaining law and order' and that it should 'intervene to stop criminal acts'. President Bashir refused to withdraw troops from Abyei saying the area belonged to Sudan. In June, the UN announced that it would undertake an investigation into the breakdown in order in South Kordofan between Sudan and South Sudan in May. In a deal mediated by the AU in May, Sudan and South Sudan agreed to set up a demilitarised zone along their 2,100km border, including Abyei. The zone is to be jointly patrolled. In the meantime President Bashir arrived in China, a day late after his plane turned back to Tehran (where he had been attending an anti-terrorism conference) in June. China is not a member of the ICC and does not recognise the arrest warrant for Mr Bashir, issued in 2009. In July, the UN Security Council authorised the deployment of a 4,200-strong Ethiopian force (UN Interim Security Force for Abyei – UNISFA) as the violence continued. Sudan introduced a new set of bank notes in July and only issued them in the north, thus rendering worthless all stocks of Sudanese pounds kept in the south. South Sudan's minister of peace, Pagan Amum, accused Sudan of starting an 'economic war'. China's foreign minister, Yang Jiechi, arrived in Khartoum in August where he had talks before travelling to South Sudan for talks with President Kiir. China was concerned to maintain its supply of oil, which now comes from both Sudan and South Sudan. In September, the government closed the Khartoum offices of the largest opposition political party, SPLM-North, on the grounds that it was not a legally represented political party. There was violence in Blue Nile State, between the army and ex-rebel militia loyal to Governor Malik Agar (chairman of SPLM-North). The president named Adam Youssef, a politician from Darfur, to replace Salva Kiir (who became president of South Sudan in July) as one of two vice presidents. An agreement on border crossings between Sudan and South Sudan was signed in Khartoum in September; 10 border crossings will be opened to ease communications. The agreement was brokered by the AU and is hoped to demonstrate the willingness of the two countries to co-operate.

2012 On 9 February the government established the Darfur Regional Authority (DRA), a new organisation aimed at underpinning a range of support mechanisms. These include regional development, power sharing, wealth creation, security and overseeing the safe return of thousands of people from refugee camps to their homes. On 11 February, the chief mediator, and former South African president, Thabo Mbeki, announced in Ethiopia's capital, Addis Ababa, that Sudan and South Sudan had signed a non-aggression pact, saying that both sides had agreed to respect each other's sovereignty and territorial integrity. The agreement establishes a monitoring mechanism that allows complaints to be lodged if border disputes erupt. On 13 March, Sudan and South Sudan signed an agreement allowing free movement and residence of their nationals in one another's territory. President Bashir will travel to Juba to sign the accord by 1 April. Sudan declared a state of emergency (SOE) along its border with South Sudan on 29 April, following weeks of clashes between Sudan and South Sudan forces. On 2 May the UN Security Council warned both Sudan and South Sudan that sanctions would be imposed if they failed to halt the recent violence and that both sides should resume negotiations and resolve their dispute. The UN peacekeeping mission in Abyei confirmed that on 30 May Sudan withdrew its troops from the disputed region, following negotiations in Ethiopia between officials of Sudan and South Sudan. On 23 September, President Bashir and President Kiir met in Ethiopia, following a UN threat to impose sanctions on both countries if they did not produce a solution to their joint oil production crisis. Although an agreement on trade, oil and security was achieved they failed to resolve their border issues. Sudan accused Israel of an air raid on a weapons factory in Yarmouk, south of Khartoum, on 23–24 October; Israel declined to comment. The factory was thought to have been an Iranian-run plant making weapons for Hamas in Gaza.

2013 On 8 June President al Bashir ordered the stoppage of oil transfers through its territory from South Sudan to stop from 9 June. Officials later said the ban would take effect in 60 days. On 10 June South Sudan accused Sudanese troops of crossing into Upper Nile state, as tension between the two states rose. Wide spread floods, the worst in 25 years, hit Sudan in August. Khartoum was one of the worst hit areas. Talks between Presidents Bashir and Kiir on 3 September eased tensions between the two; President Bashir withdrew his threat to disrupt oil exports from South Sudan. The government reduced fuel subsidies on 23 September, leading to disturbances and attacks on petrol stations. There were reports of over 25 deaths, mostly from gunshot wounds.

2014 In October Omar Bashir was chosen ahead of four other candidates by the ruling NCP's decision-making council to stand in the 2015 presidential election. Mr Bashir had previously said he would not stand again. On 13 December the International Criminal Court announced it was ending its probe into allegations of war crimes in Darfur. The chief prosecutor, Fatou Bensouda, cited lack of action by the UN as the reason. President Bashir claimed the action as a victory.

2015 On 26 January a new presidential palace, built by the Chinese, was officially opened. In the presidential election held on 26 April Omar Bashir was re-elected with 94 per cent of the vote; the election was boycotted by the main opposition parties. Turn-out was officially put at 46 per cent although a number of international observers put it at less. A number of Western countries, including the US, Britain and Norway, criticised the polls for being neither free nor fair.

Political structure

Constitution

A multi-party parliamentary system was introduced in 1986, comprising a five-member Supreme Council and a 360-member Majlis Watani (National Assembly).

In 1994, the government increased the number of states to 26. Each state has a wali (governor), legislative council and council of ministers. In March 2002, the government indicated that it would replace elections for the wali with a system of electoral colleges which would submit six possible candidates, giving the president the final decision on appointments.

A new Constitution was promulgated on 1 January 1999, allowing opposition political associations to register prior to the elections. Eligibility for voting was reduced from 18 to 17 years on 3 January 1999.

On the 4 January 2015, Sudan's parliament approved changes to the country's constitution, giving President Omar Al-Bashir additional powers to appoint and remove senior officials, as well as expanding the role of the intelligence service.

Independence date

1 January 1956

Form of state

Federal republic

The executive

The president has inherited most of the powers of the now disbanded Revolutionary Command Council of National Salvation (RCCNS), which assumed unified powers in the 1989 military coup. These include the right to override constitutional elections to the 26 state governorships. Executive power at the operational level resides with the cabinet, which includes both civilian and military representatives. In 2002, the government scrapped the two-term limitation to the presidency. The president is directly elected by universal suffrage.

National legislature

The national assembly elected in 2000, was suspended by presidential decree a year later. It was superseded by a new, bicameral parliament, established in 2005 following agreement between the Sudanese government and the southern-based Sudan People's Liberation Army (SPLA). The new Majlis Watani (National Assembly) has 450 seats of which 270 members are directly elected in single-seat constituencies by simple majority vote, 112 for women only directly elected by proportional representation vote, and 68 directly elected by proportional representation vote. Members serve six-year terms. The Majlis Welayat (Council of States) has 50 seats of which members are indirectly elected – two each by the 25 state legislatures to serve six year terms.

Legal system

Sharia (Islamic law) with an admixture of English common law operates officially at the federal level, although individual states choose whether or not it should apply at state level. In practice the legal system is split along political lines, with *Sharia* imposed universally in the north, but ineffective in the rebel-held south. The judiciary is in theory politically independent under the constitution introduced at the beginning of 1999. However, military or paramilitary elements influence the judiciary or operate direct extra-judicial military rule throughout the country.

Last elections

13–16 April 2015 (presidential and parliamentary)

Results: Parliamentary: Al Mu'tamar al Watani (National Congress Party) (NCP) won 78.8 per cent of the vote (323 seats out of 426), the Democratic Unionist Party won 5.9 per cent (25), other parties and independents won the remaining seats.

Presidential: Omar Hassan Ahmad al Bashir (NCP) won 94 per cent of the vote, Fadl el-Sayed Shuiab won 1.4 per cent; the other 14 candidates won less than one per cent of the vote.

Next elections

2020 (presidential and parliamentary)

Political parties

Ruling party

Al Mu'tamar al-Watani (National Congress Party) (NCP) (from 1998; re-elected Apr 2015)

Main opposition party

Democratic Unionist Party

Population

37.29 million (2014)* Projections put the population at 50 million by 2030. Around 7 per cent of the population are nomads.

Last census: 22 April 2008: 39,154,490

Internally Displaced Persons (IDP)

4.0 million (UNHCR 2004)

Ethnic make-up

Black (52 per cent), Arab (39 per cent), Beja (6 per cent). In the north and central regions the population consists mainly of Muslim Arabs and Nubians. In the south the people are socially, culturally and historically related to the peoples of east Africa.

Religions

Islam (Sunni Muslim) in the north (70 per cent); in the south traditional beliefs (25 per cent) and Christianity (5 per cent).

Education

Elementary education for those aged six to 12 years is free. Intermediate education starts at the age of 13 and lasts three years. Secondary education starts at 16 years and also lasts for three years. Students completing secondary education are eligible for university. There are five universities, two in Khartoum (one is a branch of Cairo University), an Islamic university at Omdurman and universities at Juba and Wad Medani.

Public expenditure on education typically amounts to 1 per cent of annual gross national income.

Unicef has voiced concerns at the low-level of public spending on education and at low enrolment and high dropout rates, calling for, among other things, significantly increased public spending, stronger teacher training and in particular the attention given to girls' education. Interventions to promote girls' education have resulted in an increase in the enrolment of girls by 5.7 per cent. The percentage of total girls' enrolment increased marginally from 45.3 per cent in 2000–01 to 45.6 per cent in 2001–02. Nationally, enrolment in primary schools increased by 5.8 per cent.

In 2002 Unicef undertook, with BRAC (an international NGO educational organisation specialising in providing schooling in poor rural areas), to provide 100 primary schools under the Village Girls Schools Project, in southern Sudan, within three years.

Literacy rate: 60 per cent adult rate; 79 per cent youth rate (15–24) (Unesco 2005).

Compulsory years: Six to 14.

Enrolment rate: 51 per cent gross primary enrolment of relevant age group (including repeaters); 21 per cent gross secondary enrolment (World Bank).

Pupils per teacher: 29 in primary schools.

Health

Public health services are organised by the ministry of health. Some health care is provided free of charge. Total expenditure on health is about 3.5 per cent of GDP, of which government spending is about 19 per cent.

In 2004 epidemiologists of the Global Polio Eradication Initiative announced that new cases of polio had been confirmed in the Darfur region of Sudan. The infection is believed to have spread from Northern Nigeria.

HIV/Aids

The conflict in southern Sudan has left many destitute; UN peacekeepers are expected to provide a buffer between the warring sides and when this happens UNAids will send in teams to ensure HIV/Aids is not an inevitable consequence of the peace-keepers' arrival and the sex-industry that usually develops in conflict zones.

HIV prevalence: 2.3 per cent aged 15–49 in 2003 (World Bank)

Life expectancy: 58 years, 2004 (WHO 2006)

Fertility rate/Maternal mortality rate: 4.1 births per woman, 2009 (FAO 2012)

Birth rate/Death rate: 36.5 births per 1,000 population; 9.6 deaths per 1,000 population (2003).

Child (under 5 years) mortality rate (per 1,000): 73 per 1,000 live births (WHO 2012)

Head of population per physician: 0.22 physicians per 1,000 people, 2004 (WHO 2006)

Welfare

Social insurance in Sudan is not provided through the government. There is no social security budget.

Main cities

Khartoum (capital, estimated population 2.7 million in 2012), Omdurman (2.8 million), Khartoum North (936,349), Port Sudan (585,090), Kassala (510,165), Kusti (487,982), Nyala (468,955), al Ubayyid (408,357), Wad Medani (369,733), al Qadarif (354,598), al Fasir (256,803).

Languages spoken

Arabic and English are used in business. African languages include Nilotic and Nilo-Hamitic. The government is considering eliminating the official teaching and use of English as part of its Islamisation programme.

Official language/s

Arabic

Media

The broadcast media is tightly constrained by censorship laws and statutory government ownership. There is a military censor permanently stationed in Sudan television to ensure the official line is always adopted. Print media enjoys a less restrictive regime but authorities have mechanism to control and influence items published, which had resulted in an unsurprising amount of self-censorship.

Press

Press restrictions have eased with increasing discussion of some domestic and foreign policy issues. Ownership of publications by individuals or political groups is banned. The board and chairman of a publication must be government-appointed, and 26 per cent of the publisher's equity goes to the government. The National Press and Publications Council (NPPC) has the power to suspend any publication. A wide variety of English and Arabic-language publications operate in the shadow of the government's information policy.

Dailies: Most newspapers are published in Khartoum. In Arabic, national publications include *Al Ayaam* (www.alayaam.net), *Al Rayaam* (www.rayaam.net), a mass circulation private newspaper; regional publications include *Al Sahafah* (www.alsahafa.info), *Akhbar Al Youn* (www.akhbaralyoumsd.net), *Al Mshaheer* (www.almshaheer.com), *Al Sudani* (www.alsudani.info). In English, leading independent include *Khartoum Monitor* and *Sudan Vision*. Online news is published by Sudan Tribune (www.sudantribune.com) and Sudan Online (www.sol-sd.com).

Weeklies: In Arabic, publications include *Al Sudan al Jadid* and *Al Fajr* (bi-weekly).

Periodicals: Periodicals include the Arabic political monthly magazine *Addaraweesh* (published in the UK) and the political newspaper *Mehairah* covering current affairs. *Sudanow* is government owned and *Al Midan* is the monthly organ of the Sudanese Communist party (www.midan.net).

Broadcasting

All broadcasting is controlled by the National Radio and Television Corporation based in Omdurman.

Radio: The government-owned The Sudan National Radio Corporation (www.sudanradio.info) broadcasts daily radio programmes in Amharic, Arabic, English, French, Somali and Tigrinya. The privately owned Mango 96 FM is a music station. The internationally funded Miraya radio station (www.mirayafm.org), is run by the UN, broadcasting in Arabic and English it is based in Juba.

Television: The government-owned Sudan National Broadcasting Corporation (SNBC) (www.srtc.gov.sd) has a monopoly for internal broadcasting. The government-owned Juba TV is based in the semi-autonomous south.

There are restrictions on satellite dish ownership, but satellite services are offered in tandem with domestic. A six-channel pan-Arab cable network offers CNN, Saudi Middle East Broadcasting Corporation (MEBC), Kuwait-TV and Dubai-TV.

Economy

The service sector is the largest component of the economy at 37.7 per cent of GDP in 2014, with industry, particularly the petroleum industry, close behind accounting for 35.6 per cent, of which manufacturing is around 6 per cent including car and truck assembly. Agriculture, predominantly subsistence farming and cash crops such as gum Arabic, sesame and cotton contributed 26.8 per cent in 2014.

GDP growth was 11.5 per cent in 2007, falling sharply to 3.2 per cent in 2008 as world energy and food prices were at a record high. In 2009, GDP growth remained static at 3 per cent, but as global trade picked up in 2010, so growth rose by 4.5 per cent. In 2011 the economy fell into recession due to the political turmoil. Negative growth lasted until 2013 when the economy rebounded with growth of 3.3 per cent, which was maintained in 2014 at 3.1 per cent.

Economic growth has been principally fuelled by oil production, although it resulted in little improvement to living standards for the majority of the population. Oil export revenue accounted for over 70 per cent of Sudan's total export earnings prior to the independence of South Sudan (on 9 July 2011), when a large number of oil wells fell across the border into South Sudan. When the two countries failed to reach agreement on the fees South Sudan should pay to transport oil from the south to Port Sudan for export, South Sudan simply halted production.

The expanding oil and gas reserves have been largely developed with the assistance of China, and China is keen to engage with both sides to achieve a commercially viable outcome.

In January 2012 South Sudan shut down all oil production as the dispute with Sudan over the transit fees for oil piped overland to Sudanese ports continued. Months of diplomatic negotiations followed and culminated on 23 July 2012, when South Sudan offered compensation of US$3 billion to Sudan for economic losses resulting from revenue loss since South Sudan's independence. South Sudan also offered increased transit fees for oil passing through Sudan to its oil terminals and ports. However on 21 August 2012 South Sudanese treasury officials announced that limited oil production was unlikely to resume until December, and full production, using all available pipelines (through Sudan), was not expected to resume until June 2013, even if Sudan accepted South Sudan's offer. After still more delays, in September 2012 the two presidents finally sat down, in Ethiopia, to try and thrash out an agreement.

Annual inflation in January 2012 rose to 19.3 per cent from 18.9 per cent in December 2011, as food costs jumped. In February 2012, Qatar agreed to loan Sudan US$2 billion to help it during a

deepening economic crisis, which was compounded by the secession of South Sudan in 2011 and the loss of around 75 per cent of oil reserves it had previously held. Foreign exchange restrictions were imposed from mid-2011, including purchasing and transferring foreign currencies and an import blacklist. Inflation by 2014 was soaring, as high as 36.9 per cent, which was down from 47 per cent in 2012.
The Sudanese pound hit a record low against the US dollar on the black market, on 6 February 2012. The rate was S£5.2 per US$1 compared to S£3.3 per US$1 in July 2011; the official rate remains S£3.0 per US$1.
Sudan has a strategy for poverty reduction based on macroeconomic development and private sector growth. In 2014, the UN Human Development Index (HDI) ranked Sudan 166 (out of 187) for national development in health, education and income. Received remittances in 2013 were US$424 million, which dropped to US$343 million in 2014.

External trade
In 2005 the Greater Arab Free Trade Area (Gafta) was ratified by 17 members, including Sudan, creating an Arab economic bloc. A customs union was established whereby tariffs within Gafta will be reduced by a percentage each year, until none remain.
Around 70 per cent of total export revenue is generated by crude oil. In 2010, Sudan was in negotiation to join the Organisation of the Petroleum Exporting Countries (Opec).
Industrialisation is limited and although Sudan is considered a major source of minerals, exploration and commercialisation is underdeveloped.

Imports
Principal imports are foodstuffs, manufactured goods, refinery and transport equipment, medicines and chemicals, textiles and wheat.
Main sources: Macau (20.1 per cent of total in 2014), UAE (8 per cent), India (8 per cent)

Exports
Principal exports are crude oil and petroleum products, cotton, sesame, livestock, groundnuts, gum Arabic and sugar.
Main destinations: Macau (30.2 per cent of total in 2014), UAE (30.2 per cent), Saudi Arabia (14.6 per cent)

Agriculture

Farming
Sudan is a semi-arid country and a large part is desert. Irrigated farmland constitutes about one-fifth of the total cultivated area, but produces about 50 per cent of total crop production. The traditional farming areas are semi-arid and used for livestock rearing, while export crops are grown in the irrigated areas, mostly in the Gezira area between the Blue and White Niles. The country is often racked by drought and famine.
Principal export crops are cotton, oil seeds (mainly groundnuts and sesame) and gum arabic (used in soft drinks, baking, cosmetics, pharmaceuticals and other industrial applications), of which Sudan is the world's largest producer. Main food crops include sorghum (dura) and millet.
Cotton is the main cash crop providing 45 per cent of agricultural export earnings, followed by gum arabic and sesame (21 per cent). Livestock raising is of considerable importance, employing about 40 per cent of the population. Sudan is aiming to become self-sufficient in rice and tea production.
Sudan has attempted to tackle the problem of land usage. Government policy aims to increase the area of cultivable land (only about 10 per cent of the potential arable land is under cultivation) through the rehabilitation and expansion of existing irrigation schemes. A planting scheme has given precedence to food crops over land devoted to cotton production and export.
Despite the insecurity and harassing from bandits, a booming trade in livestock has thrived for more than two decades along the borders between Somalia, Ethiopia and Kenya.

Fishing
Sudan possesses vast freshwater and marine fishing potential. The freshwater sources comprise rivers and lakes. The Nile alone has an estimated potential output of 60,000 tonnes of fish a year, but the fisheries are barely exploited. Fishing on the Red Sea coastline is also under-exploited and is being encouraged with government assistance.
Over 95 per cent of the Sudanese catch of fish is obtained from inland fisheries on the Nile, its tributaries and associated swamp lands. Subsistence fishing is widespread, but the commercial sector is under-developed. Marine fishing is mainly carried out by artisanal fishermen in small boats.
Sudan exported around US$1 million of fish per annum before the war, but now exports only a small amount of dried and salted fish.

Forestry
Sudan has 17 per cent forest cover, most of which is located in the mountains and the wooded savannahs. Rapid deforestation occurs and is a result of demand for fuelwood. Sudan produces a large amount of industrial roundwood, mainly for posts and poles, and also produces sawnwood, although not enough to ensure self-sufficiency. Sudan's most important non-wood forest product is gum arabic. Sudan is also one of the world's main producers of olibanum resin.
Industry and manufacturing
The industrial sector contributes 35.6 per cent to GDP and employs around 10 per cent of the workforce.
Activity is centred on the processing of agricultural products, particularly textiles, sugar, oilseeds, flour and footwear. Vehicle assembly plants produce civil and military vehicles.
Inadequate infrastructure, shortages of imported inputs, power cuts and lack of skilled manpower have thwarted government efforts at developing large-scale industries.

Industry and manufacturing
The industrial sector contributed around 28 per cent to GDP in 2004 and employs 10 per cent of the workforce. The main activities are oil refining, agricultural products, textiles and leatherwares.

Tourism
Sudan was the largest country in Africa until 2011 when its southern states became the newly founded South Sudan. The remainder of Sudan is a largely desert Arab state with a coastline long the Red Sea. The coastal city of Port Sudan is a stopover for many Muslim pilgrims on their way to Mecca (Saudi Arabia) for their *Hajj*. The scuba diving along this coast is spectacular. The archaeological sites date back into antiquity, with two – the Island of Meroe (the heartland of the Kingdom of Kush) and Gebel Barkal, in the Nubian Desert with a number of tombs and pyramids – included on Unesco's World Heritage List. Khartoum has a number of national museums that house examples and artefacts of Sudan's history.
Travel and tourism contributed 6.7 per cent of GDP in 2014, although the industry has been subject to negative growth since 2010. Employment in the industry is 5.4 per cent of the workforce (572,000 jobs).
A number of Western governments have warned their citizens to avoid travel to certain areas of Sudan, such as Darfur, the Blue Nile and the southern Kordofan regions. Also in the past, terrorist groups have targeted western visitors in Sudan.

Environment
In June 2010 the African Union backed a proposal to build the 'Great Green Wall' project, of a 15km wide, 7,775km long, continuous belt of trees from Senegal in the west to Djibouti in the east (traversing 11 countries) in an effort to halt the advance of the Sahara Desert. The trees to be used would be drought-adapted, preferably native to the area from a list of 37

possible species, and should help to slow soil erosion and filter rain water.

Mining

The mining sector has played a relatively insignificant role in the country's economic development. Chromite, gypsum, gold, copper and iron ore are exploited on a commercial basis. Other mineral deposits include zinc, lead, talc, coal, nickel and tin, phosphate and uranium, but not in sufficient quantities to develop. If financial and infrastructural problems can be overcome, the sector could make a significant contribution to the economy.
Sudan's first gold refining factory was opened on 20 September 2012, which when fully operational will produce 328 tonnes of gold per year. The export of gold ore was banned from this date and the government expects to sell up to US$3 billion within one year. The factory will refine Sudanese gold and silver, as well as ore from other countries in the region. On 23 September, President Bashir and President Kiir met in Ethiopia, following a UN threat to impose sanctions on both countries if they did not produce a solution to their joint oil production crisis.

Hydrocarbons

At the end of 2014 Sudan had proved reserves of 1.5 billion barrels of oil, with production of 109,000 million barrels of oil per day (bpd). An expected 85 per cent of total production and 75 per cent of total Sudanese revenue went to South Sudan on independence on 9 July 2011. Although most of the oil is in the South, all exports will need to use the pipeline across the north to reach Port Sudan. Sudan entered into negotiations for a royalty on its investment on development and infrastructure costs in the exploitation of this oil. It started at a fee per barrel transported of over US$36, while South Sudan offered less than US$1. Both sides dug in their heels and as a consequence in July 2011 the South began discussions with Ethiopia to run an oil pipeline through Ethiopia and circumvent the oil sharing agreement with Sudan.
By the end of 2011, when there had been no progress in the negotiations – Sudan was still demanding US$36 per barrel, and had seized US$800 million of oil in transit and diverted it to their own refinery – the South said they would shut down all production. In January 2012 South Sudan carried out their threat and stopped all oil production. In March Sudan made a slightly better offer of US$32.20 per barrel, which was again rejected.
Talks sponsored by the African Union, and mediated by former South Africa president, Thabo Mbeki, were held in Addis Ababa in early 2012. Eventually an agreement was signed by Presidents Kiir and Bashir on 27 September and South Sudan ordered the resumption of oil production, which had been around 350,000bpd in January. Under the agreement, South Sudan will pay US$9.10 per barrel of oil passing through pipelines operated by Dar Petroleum and US$11.00 per barrel through those of Greater Nile Petroleum Operating Company.
Meanwhile a memorandum of understanding (MOU) had been signed between South Sudan and Kenya on 24 January 2012, to build an oil pipeline to take South Sudanese oil to a Kenyan port for export. The pipeline will be built and owned by South Sudan and the two countries will negotiate transit fees for the oil through Kenya. The pipeline will also include a fibre-optic line giving internet connection to South Sudan. On 2 March construction began on the US$23 billion port and oil refinery project in Lamu District, Kenya. The presidents of Kenya, South Sudan and Ethiopia were at the launching ceremony, amid tight security in an area close to the border with war-torn Somalia. The project, known as the Lamu Port South Sudan Ethiopia Transit Corridor (Lapsset), is due to be completed by 2016, with initial investment from all three countries, with plans to attract international investment. If it goes ahead, Lapsset will be one of Africa's largest civil engineering projects. It would also obviate the need for oil to pass through Sudan.

Energy

Total installed electricity generation capacity was 2.1GW in 2013. The state-owned National Electricity Corporation is responsible for generation, distribution and transmission of electricity. The energy mix is 60 per cent oil, and 40 per cent hydropower, which is subject to weather conditions.
The Roseires dam on the Blue Nile produces a large proportion of Sudan's electricity, with installed capacity of 274MW. Hydroelectric sources are being expanded and the gross theoretical capability is 48 terrawatt hours. New dams are under construction, including the Merowe dam, inaugurated in March 2009 and the Kajbar dam providing an extra 1,250MW. Both dams were controversial as the water catchment area displaced a number of communities and resulted in forced resettlements and in the case of the Kajbar dam the flooding and destruction of ancient Nubian archaeological sites.

Financial markets

Stock exchange

The first stock exchange opened in January 1995.

Banking and insurance

Central bank

Bank of Sudan

Main financial centre

Khartoum

Time

GMT plus two hours

Geography

Sudan lies in north-eastern Africa. It is the largest country in Africa and the ninth largest in the world. It lies entirely within the tropics and is bordered by Egypt and Libya in the north, Ethiopia, Eritrea and the Red Sea in the east, Kenya, Uganda and the Democratic Republic of Congo in the south and the Central African Republic and Chad in the west.
The River Nile and its tributaries, the White and Blue Niles, are the country's most important physical features. The Blue Nile, in particular, plays a vital economic role, supporting 40 per cent of the current irrigated area and with the potential to support 70 per cent of future irrigated land. The Blue Nile is prone to serious seasonal flooding.
The topographic features are a large, broad plain with mountains to the north-east along the coast of the Red Sea and in the south-eastern border region with Uganda and Kenya. This is the location of Mount Kinyeti (3,187 metres) the country's tallest peak.

Hemisphere

Northern

Climate

Tropical in the south, hot and dry in the north. In Khartoum, the hottest month is May (26–42 degrees Celsius (C)), the coldest is January (16–32 degrees C). The northern zone receives very little rainfall and is mainly desert. The south is mainly tropical while the central zone is semi-arid grassland.
From mid-April to the end of June the climate is extremely hot and dry. Sandstorms (*haboobs*) are frequent in desert areas between April and September. The rainy season extends from July to September. During this period road travel outside the cities is difficult. In Khartoum, the average temperature by day in the summer is 42 degrees C and 32 degrees C in the winter.

Dress codes

Formal clothing should be worn for business and social engagements. Lightweight clothing is essential at all times, although visitors should carry some warmer clothing if travelling to Sudan during the winter months (November to March). A light raincoat is needed during the months of July, August and September. Women should be aware of the fact that the north is predominantly Muslim and are advised to dress modestly.

Entry requirements

Passports

Required by all. Passports must be valid for six months from date of entry.

Visa

Required by all. For information see www.sudanembassy.org and follow the link to *visa/passport*.

Business visas require a letter of invitation from a sponsoring company giving purpose of visit, duration of stay, a commitment to financial responsibility and references, plus copies of commercial correspondence with entities in Sudan.

Visitors are required to register with the Aliens Department within three days of their arrival (hotels will do this). Once registered, they are not required to obtain an exit visa.

Contact the closest consulate for further information.

Prohibited entry

Nationals of Israel and holders of passports with Israeli travel stamps,

Currency advice/regulations

The import and export of local currency is prohibited. Import of foreign currency is unlimited but must be declared; export is limited to the amount declared.

Travellers cheques have limited acceptance.

Customs

Alcohol is strictly forbidden; products from Israel are prohibited.

Health (for visitors)

Mandatory precautions

Valid yellow fever and cholera certificates are required if travellers are arriving from infected areas, or travellers are intending to visit the south of Sudan.

Advisable precautions

Vaccinations for yellow fever, diphtheria, tetanus, polio, hepatitis A and typhoid are recommended. Other vaccinations that may be recommended are cholera, tuberculosis, hepatitis B and meningitis. There is a risk of rabies. Malaria is prevalent throughout the country. Anti-mosquito measures including repellents, nets and clothing that cover the body should be used (these will also provide protection against hepatitis B and yellow fever). Tap water must be treated as unsafe unless boiled and filtered (bottled water is available in the main cities). Eat only well cooked meals, preferably served hot; vegetables should be cooked and fruit peeled. Dairy products are unpasteurised and should be avoided. Use only well maintained, chlorinated, swimming pools as bilharzia can be contracted from streams and rivers.

Medical facilities are scarce outside Khartoum. A first aid kit that includes disposable syringes is a reasonable precaution. Medical insurance is essential, including emergency evacuation, and an adequate supply of personal medicines is necessary.

Hotels

Accommodation can be difficult to obtain outside Khartoum and Port Sudan. Advisable to book in advance. Service charge of 10 per cent is usual. Hotel bills are subject to 10 per cent sales tax.

Credit cards

Credit cards may be accepted but visitors should ensure that they have sufficient hard currency (preferably US dollars) to cover their expenses during their stay.

Public holidays (national)

Fixed dates

1 Jan (Independence Day), 30 Jun (Revolution Day), 25 Dec (Christmas Day).

Variable dates

Eid al Adha, Coptic Christmas (Jan), Islamic New Year, Birth of the Prophet, Coptic Easter (Mar/Apr, two days), Eid al Fitr (three days).

Islamic year 1437 (15 Oct 2015–2 Oct 2016):: The Islamic year contains 354 or 355 days, with the result that Muslim feasts advance by 10–12 days against the Gregorian calendar. Dates of feasts vary according to the sighting of the new moon, so cannot be forecast exactly.

Working hours

Banking

Sat–Thu: 0830–1200.

Business

Sat–Thu: 0800–1430.

Government

Sat–Thu: 0800/0830–1330/1400.

Shops

Sat–Thu: 0800–1330, 1730–2000.

Telecommunications

Mobile/cell phones

There are 900 and 900/1800 GSM services available in large urban areas only.

Electricity supply

240V AC

Social customs/useful tips

Visitors should address Sudanese males using the form *Sayed* (meaning Mr) with the first name only. There are a large number of local traditions and most Muslim customs are observed. Politeness and patience are more important than punctuality. Women are often not present at business or social gatherings. There is a ban on alcohol and gambling in the north.

Some souvenirs, such as cheetah skins, although available in the *souks* (markets) are banned by the Government.

Military establishments should not be photographed, nor should bridges, dams, rail and air transport facilities. Visitors should not attempt to photograph Sudanese people without permission or if they appear reluctant. Photography permits issued by the Tourist Information Office in Khartoum are often ignored by the authorities, who may confiscate film and camera.

Most banks in Sudan are heavily fortified and resemble prisons as much as they do commercial institutions.

The Islamic legal and moral code, *Sharia*, is in operation in the north.

Security

Southern Sudan, the Nuba mountains, the Ethiopian and Eritrean borders and the Kassala area near the Eritrean border are all zones of military activity, (including the laying of anti-personnel landmines), and are insecure. There is banditry in Darfur state. Travel in these areas should be avoided unless work is absolutely essential. In general, no land borders into or out of Sudan can be crossed safely, with the exception of the Wadi Halfa crossing into Egypt. The political situation in Sudan is not stable and foreign nationals should contact their embassy, and keep in contact throughout their stay. Before embarking, visitors are advised to consult their embassy for an up-to-date appraisal of the situation, as well as brief themselves regarding developments in the wider region. Demonstrations should be avoided and British and US citizens may wish to keep a low profile.

Getting there

Air

National airline: Sudan Airways

International airport/s: Khartoum (KRT), 4km from city; duty-free shop and restaurant.

Airport tax: Departure tax: US$20, except transit passengers.

Surface

Road: There are road links, with varing degrees of accessibility, to all surrounding countries. Drivers wishing to enter Sudan by road must apply for permission in Khartoum or from overseas representatives. Applicants must list vehicle and passenger details, with supporting documents from a recognised motoring organisation, or a guarantee from a bank or registered business.

Most border crossings remain dangerous, with the exception of the relatively secure border with Egypt via Wadi Halfa.

Rail: A railway line runs from Cairo to the Aswan High Dam in Egypt; passengers can then take a river boat on to Wadi Halfa just inside the Sudanese border, and train to Khartoum.

Water: The only major harbour is Port Sudan on the Red Sea coast. International shipping lines that maintain contacts with

Sudan may provide passenger services on cargo ships.
Sudan's River Transport Corporation (RTC) operates a Nile ferry from Aswan in Egypt to Wadi Halfa, the service can be is hindered by local conditions and circumstances.
Main port/s: Port Sudan.

Getting about

National transport

Travellers must obtain special permits to travel anywhere outside Khartoum. These are obtainable from the Passport and Immigration Office in Khartoum. Before travelling, it is advisable to check the security situation in the area. Visitors arriving in any town or city in Sudan must register with the police on arrival and show the necessary paperwork.
Permits are required to visit archaeological or historical sites. These can be obtained from the Department of Antiquities in Khartoum.
Air: Sudan Airways operates a regular service between Khartoum, Port Sudan and El Obeid and other larger towns. Small air taxi companies fly from Khartoum to main towns.
Road: Main tarred roads are the 1,186km route from Port Sudan to Khartoum, from Port Sudan to Kassala and on to Shavak, from Khartoum to Sennar and on to Malakal. Another 800km of tarred roads exist, but the rest of the country's 48,000km network is of very variable quality.
Buses: Scheduled coach services include Khartoum-Kosti, Khartoum-Omdurman, Khartoum-El Fasher, Juba-Nimule, Juba-Faradge.
Rail: A network links Khartoum with Port Sudan, Kassala, Wau, Nyala and Wadi Halfa, but not Juba. The condition of the network is very dilapidated and services can be very slow.
There are three-classes offered but only first class is suitable for business travel.
Water: There are ferries operating on the White and Blue Niles but may not offer a complete journey as underinvestment has left waterways in need of repair and redevelopment.

City transport

Taxis: Easily available in Khartoum and can be hailed, or taken from ranks. Fares are negotiatable and should be agreed before start of any journey.

Car hire

Available in main centres. A national or international driving licence is required.

BUSINESS DIRECTORY

The addresses listed below are a selection only. While World of Information makes every endeavour to check these addresses, we cannot guarantee that changes have not been made, especially to telephone numbers and area codes. We would welcome any corrections.

Telephone area codes

The international dialling code (IDD) for Sudan is +249, followed by area code and subscriber's number:

El Obeid	81	Khartoum North	85
Kassala	41	Port Sudan City	31
Khartoum	11		

Chambers of Commerce

Union of Sudanese Chambers of Commerce, Gamhoria Street, PO Box 81, Khartoum (email: chamber@sudanchamber.org).

Banking

Bank of Khartoum, PO Box 1008, Khartoum.

Farmers Commercial Bank, PO Box 1116, Kasr Avenue, Khartoum.

Tadamon Islamic Bank, PO Box 3154, Baladia Avenue, Khartoum.

Al-Baraka Bank, PO Box 3583, Al-Baraka Tower, Khartoum.

El Nilein Industrial Development Bank, PO Box 466, 1722 United Nations Square, Khartoum.

Central bank

Bank of Sudan, Al-Gamaa Avenue, PO Box 313, Khartoum, Sudan (email: sudanbank@sudanmail.net).

Travel information

River Transport Corporation, PO Box 284, Khartoum North.

Sudan Airways, SDC Building, Street 15, New Extension, PO Box 253, Khartoum.

Ministry of tourism

Ministry of Tourism and Wildlife, PO Box 22213, Khartoum (email: postmaster@sudan-tourism.gov.sd; internet: www.sudan-tourism.gov.sd).

Ministries

Ministry of Agriculture and Forests, Khartoum.

Ministry of Animal Welfare, Khartoum.

Ministry of Aviation, Khartoum.

Ministry of Culture and Information, Khartoum.

Ministry of Defence, Khartoum.

Ministry of Education, Khartoum.

Ministry of Energy and Mining, Khartoum.

Ministry of the Environment and Tourism.

Ministry of Finance & National Economy, Khartoum.

Ministry of Foreign Affairs, Khartoum.

Ministry of Health, Khartoum.

Ministry of Higher Education and Scientific Research, Khartoum.

Ministry of the Interior, Khartoum.

Ministry of National Industry, Khartoum.

Ministry of Public Services, Khartoum.

Ministry of Social Planning, Khartoum.

Ministry of Trade, Khartoum.

Ministry of Transport, Khartoum.

Other useful addresses

National Corporation for Antiquities and Museums, PO Box 178, Khartoum.

Sudanese Embassy (USA), 2210 Massachusetts Avenue, NW, Washington DC 20008 (tel: (+1-202) 338-8565; fax: (+1-202) 667-2406; email: info@sudanembassyus.org).

Sudapet, Block 9/10, Resident 22/1, Africa Street, P.O. Box 13188, Al Khartoum 11111 (tel: 156-557777; fax: 156-557799; email: info@sudapet.com.sd; website: www.sudapet.sd

Internet sites

Africa Business Network: www.ifc.org/abn
AllAfrica.com: http://allafrica.com
African Development Bank: www.afdb.org
Africa Online: www.africaonline.com
Mbendi AfroPaedia (information on companies, countries, industries and stock exchanges in Africa): http://mbendi.co.za
The Sudan Page: www.sudan.net

Suriname

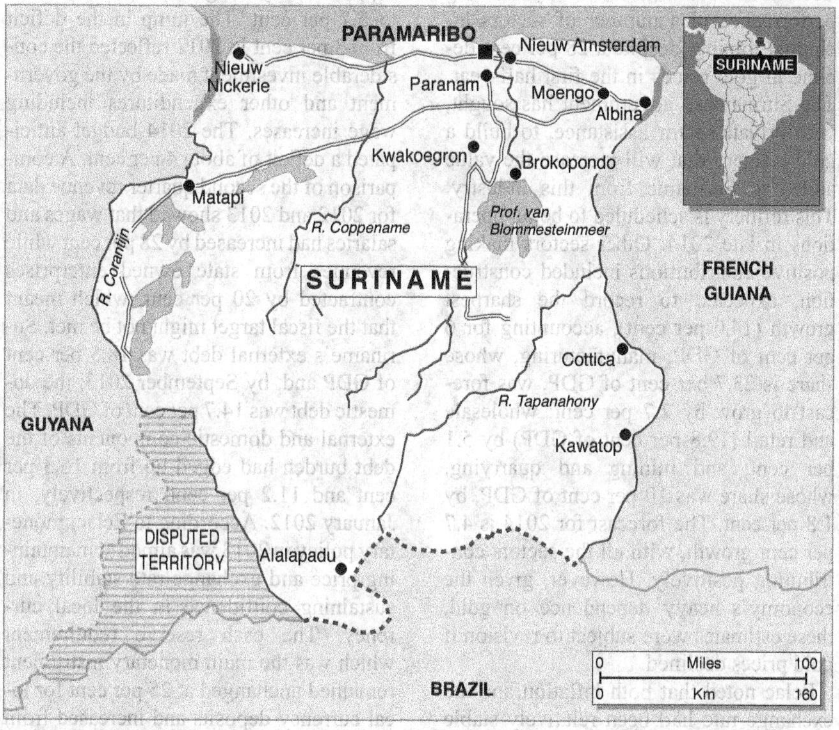

The August 2013 arrest and arraignment by US authorities of Dino Bouterse, the son of Suriname's President Desi (Désiré) Bouterse, did little to improve Suriname's already doubtful image. Bouterse Junior was arrested in Panama and flown to the United States to face charges not only of drugs and weapons trafficking, but even of plotting attacks on the US with the Middle Eastern Hezbollah movement.

Possibly in response to his son's arrest, in early 2014 President Bouterse threatened to have the US ambassador, Jay Anania, expelled from the country if he could not give a satisfactory reason for 'meddling in internal affairs' after the US diplomat had allegedly visited the ministry of home affairs and the Independent Elections Bureau in late February, allegedly inquiring about how the preparations for the elections were progressing. Following a meeting between foreign affairs minister, Winston Lackin, and the US ambassador things seemed to have calmed down. Mr Lackin expressed regret about the stand-off with the ambassador and the fact that it had attracted international attention, which he feared had created the impression that the US was concerned about the outcome of Suriname's 2015 elections.

Low profile

There were a number of reasons why the ruling political alliance – de Mega Combinatie (Mega Combination) – led by the Nationale Democratische Partij (National Democratic Party) (NDP), of which Désiré Bouterse is chairman, were anxious to maintain a low profile. Suriname's President was one of the few, if not the only, of the world's heads of state that has faced charges of murder and a possible 20 year jail sentence. In 1999 Mr Bouterse had been convicted in absentia for importing cocaine from Suriname into the Netherlands. Were he to return to the Netherlands he would spend 11 years in jail. The extradition of Suriname's citizens is not permitted by the country's constitution.

KEY FACTS

Official name: Republiek Suriname (Republic of Suriname)

Head of State: President Desiré Delano Bouterse (since 12 August 2010), re-elected 25 May 2015

Head of government: President Desiré Delano Bouterse (since 12 August 2010), re-elected 25 May 2015

Ruling party: Nationale Democratische (NDP) (National Democratic Party)

Area: 163,265 square km

Population: 553,000 (2014)*

Capital: Paramaribo (Parbo)

Official language: Dutch

Currency: Suriname dollar (Su$) = 100 cents

Exchange rate: Su$3.30 per US$ (Sep 2015)

GDP per capita: US$9,584 (2014)*

GDP real growth: 2.90% (2014)*

GDP: US$5.30 billion (2014)*

Unemployment: 892.80% (2014)*

Inflation: 3.38% (2014)*

Balance of trade: US$183.10 million (2014)

Annual FDI: US$69.80 billion (2011)

* estimated figure

The presidential past

In December 1982, 16 men had been arrested in their houses in Paramaribo and taken to Fort Zeelandia, a former Dutch fort that served as Bouterse's headquarters. The men were journalists, lawyers, professors, businessmen, soldiers and trades union leaders. Mr Bouterse is hardly able to deny his involvement in the torture and death of these people. In April 2011 Suriname's National Assembly passed an amendment to extend an Amnesty Law that virtually brought the trial against President Bouterse, who led a military regime between 1980 and 1987, to a halt. Then in 2012 the Amnesty Act provided the President with a pardon. President Bouterse had called the legislation a 'New beginning, to heal the whole nation.' In 2013 the military court in charge of the case adjourned the trial in order for there to be a review of the new law's constitutionality, which was to be carried out by the Attorney General's Office. Legal experts argued that such a review can only be undertaken by a constitutional court. However, the constitutional court provided for in the 1987 Surinamese constitution was never established.

Referring to President Bouterse's manoeuvrings, the US based Human Rights Watch (HRW) has stated that 'these international crimes are too serious to be forgotten. In protest at the amnesty granted to the President, The Netherlands recalled its ambassador and suspended aid. The amnesty meant that the trial would not proceed

The economy

In 2013, according to the United Nations Economic Commission for Latin America and the Caribbean (Eclac) the Surinamese economy continued to post positive growth and was expected to grow by 3.9 per cent in 2013 and 4.7 per cent in 2014. Growth in 2013 was fuelled by a strong performance in a number of sectors including mining, despite a 28 per cent decline in gold prices in the first half-year. The Surinamese government has sought, with private-sector assistance, to build a gold refinery that will increase the value added to Suriname from this industry. This refinery is scheduled to begin operations in late 2014. Other sectors making positive contributions included construction, expected to record the sharpest growth (14.0 per cent), accounting for 6 per cent of GDP, manufacturing, whose share is 23.7 per cent of GDP, was forecast to grow by 2.7 per cent; wholesale and retail (19.8 per cent of GDP) by 5.1 per cent; and mining and quarrying, whose share was 10 per cent of GDP, by 1.8 per cent. The forecast for 2014 is 4.7 per cent growth, with all the sectors contributing positively. However, given the economy's heavy dependence on gold, these estimates were subject to revision if gold prices declined.

Eclac noted that both inflation and the exchange rate had been relatively stable and are not expected to vary significantly in 2014. The government was also in the process of establishing a sovereign wealth fund in 2013, in recognition of the non-renewable nature of mineral reserves and the volatility of long term commodity prices. In the proposed budget for 2014, there had been an attempt to lower the fiscal deficit, which had expanded to 5.7 per cent of gross domestic product (GDP).

The fiscal deficit had at first been expected to be 3.9 per cent of GDP in 2013, but this figure was revised upwards in a supplementary budget in September 2013 to 5.7 per cent. The jump in the deficit from 3 per cent in 2012 reflected the considerable investment made by the government and other expenditures including wage increases. The 2014 budget anticipated a deficit of about 4 per cent. A comparison of the second quarter revenue data for 2012 and 2013 showed that wages and salaries had increased by 28 per cent while revenues from state owned enterprises contracted by 20 per cent, which meant that the fiscal target might not be met. Suriname's external debt was 18.5 per cent of GDP and, by September 2013, the domestic debt was 14.7 per cent of GDP. The external and domestic components of the debt burden had edged up from 16.3 per cent and 11.2 per cent, respectively, in January 2012. According to Eclac, monetary policy in 2013 was aimed at maintaining price and exchange-rate stability and sustaining confidence in the local currency. The cash reserve requirement which was the main monetary instrument remained unchanged at 25 per cent for local currency deposits and increased from 40 per cent to 45 per cent for foreign-currency deposits, owing to the sharp increase in foreign-currency loans at the beginning of 2013. In terms of money supply, when the first half of 2013 was compared with the same period in 2012, M1 decreased by 3.1 per cent as opposed to a rise of 21 per cent in 2012. During the period August–September 2013, M1 grew by 1.8 per cent. This suggested some dampening in the growth of domestic demand. The exchange rate had been relatively stable at 3.30 Surinamese dollars (Su$) to the US$1 and this looked likely to continue in 2014–15.

In terms of interest rates on Surinamese dollar deposits, between January and September 2013, the average deposit and lending rates inched up slightly to 12.7 per cent and 7.1 per cent from 11.9 and 6.9 per cent, respectively and the interest rate spread remained the same. With respect to domestic credit, between January and September overall credit grew by nearly 18 per cent, while credit to the primary and secondary sectors, which included mining and agriculture, swelled by 26.4 per cent (15 per cent of total credit) and

KEY INDICATORS — Suriname

	Unit	2011	2012	2013	2014	**2015
Population	m	*0.53	*0.54	*0.55	*0.55	*0.56
Gross domestic product (GDP)	US$bn	3.80	4.82	5.04	*5.30	*5.55
GDP per capita	US$	7,096	8,900	9,206	*9,584	*9,950
GDP real growth	%	4.5	4.8	4.1	*2.9	*2.7
Inflation	%	17.7	5.0	1.9	*3.4	*1.9
Unemployment	%	8.0	8.5	8.5	*8.9	*8.9
Exports (fob) (goods)	US$m	2,466.7	2,695.0	2,394.8	2,148.7	–
Imports (fob) (goods)	US$m	1,679.1	1,760.4	2,125.6	1,965.6	–
Balance of trade	US$m	787.6	803.2	269.2	183.1	–
Current account	US$m	251.1	30.0	-198.0	*-386.0	*-433.0
Total reserves minus gold	US$m	735.6	885.1	735.1	573.3	–
Foreign exchange	US$m	597.5	751.8	600.5	–	–
Exchange rate	per US$	2.75	3.30	3.30	3.30	–

* estimated figure ** forecast figure

credit to other sectors grew at a slower pace: by 16.5 per cent.

The first half-year (for 2013) results showed a negative current account balance of US$182 million (5.6 per cent of estimated GDP) and reflected increased imports in the first two quarters relative to the previous year, while exports were about the same for the two periods. This would reduce the trade surplus to about 10 per cent of GDP compared with about 20 per cent in 2012. Foreign direct investment (FDI) soared by 61 per cent in the first half-year relative to 2012. Eclac expected the balance of payments to show some deterioration in 2013 owing mainly to increasing imports. International reserves amounted to US$812 million at the end of June 2013, representing 20 weeks' import cover. Reserves fell to US$770 million by October, which is an adequate import cover for Suriname.

The year-on-year inflation rate, which rose as a consequence of the unification of the official exchange rate and the black market premium in 2011, was 4.4 per cent in 2012 and was projected at 2.0 per cent for 2013. This was likely to hold, given the stable domestic conditions including the increased refining of fuel for domestic energy. The unemployment rate for 2012 was 10 per cent and while there were no unemployment figures for 2013, given that growth would continue to be positive, the unemployment rate was not likely to exceed that of 2012.

Risk assessment

Politics	Fair
Economy	Good
Regional stability	Good

COUNTRY PROFILE

1602 Dutch traders arrived.
1651 British settlers and plantation owners arrived in the region and set up the first community and commercial estates using African slaves.
1652 Britain ceded territory to The Netherlands (later referred to as Dutch Guiana) and gained New Amsterdam (New York) in exchange.
1800s After slavery was abolished, indentured labourers from China, India and Java were brought in to work on plantations.
1916 The mining of bauxite began and gradually become the country's principal export.
1948 The country was renamed Suriname
1954 Suriname gained self-government from The Netherlands, which continued to control defence and foreign affairs.
1975 Full independence was granted. Johan Ferrier became president and Henck Arron of the Nationale Partij Suriname (NPS) (National Party of Suriname) became prime minister. Around 30 per cent of the population emigrated to The Netherlands, fearing an early collapse of the new country.
1980 A military coup, led by Sergeant-Major Desi Bouterse, ousted first Prime Minister Arron and then President Ferrier, who was ultimately replaced by Henk Chin A Sen. Bouterse ruled through the National Military Council, imposing martial law, censorship and banning political parties.
1982 Fiscal aid from The Netherlands and the US was halted following the murder of 15 members of the opposition by the army.
1985 The ban on opposition parties was lifted and a new constitution, which included a strong military role, was devised.
1987 A democratically elected president and a 51-seat National Assembly were re-established. Elections were won by an opposition coalition. A National State Council of politicians and military was established under the constitution, but with an ill-defined 'advisory' role it did not achieve satisfactory government.
1990 Bouterse staged another coup and resumed power.
1991 A civilian government was elected. International aid was resumed. Bouterse retired from the army and founded the Nationale Democratische Partij (NDP) (National Democratic Party). Ronald Venetiaan was elected president.
1996 The nationalistic NDP won a majority of seats in the general elections and joined a coalition government. President Jules Wijdenbosch, an ally of Bouterse, named him special advisor and gave him diplomatic immunity from foreign drug smuggling charges.
1999 A poor economy resulted in widespread strikes, which brought down the government.
2000 Early elections were won by a coalition, Nieuwe Front voor Democratie (NF) (New Front for Democracy); Ronald Venetiaan became president. International relations with Guyana deteriorated over a disputed maritime boundary, including an area rich in oil.
2004 The Suriname guilder (fl) was converted to the Suriname dollar (Su$), at a rate of Su$1.00 per fll,000. The UN attempted to resolve the maritime dispute with Guyana.
2005 The ruling NF coalition narrowly won parliamentary elections. After two unsuccessful presidential elections, Ronald Venetiaan won in the third round.
2006 Major floods devastated homes of around 30,000 people in Upper Suriname. The country's long-term foreign currency, sovereign credit rating was raised from -B to B, as efforts to pay back loans were seen as largely successful. The EU provided eur20 million (US$15.4 million) to upgrade the country's infrastructure and reconstruct the banana industry.
2007 The Japanese agreed to finance the construction of a new fishery centre, meeting international standards and capable of providing modern facilities for the enlarged fishing fleet. The UN ruled that both Suriname and Guyana should share the oil-rich offshore territory.
2008 Desi Bouterse, the former dictator went on trial for the murder of 15 political opponents in 1982. A three-month US humanitarian mission began providing medical treatment and engineering projects in rural areas. Suriname joined the International Criminal Court (ICC).
2009 High school teachers, customs officers, fire fighters and waste collectors went on strike in a dispute with the government over discrepancies within a newly introduced salary scheme for the public sector. The UK-based multinational BHP Billiton sold all of its interest in the bauxite mines it operated in Suriname to domestic mining companies.
2010 In parliamentary elections, the newly established De Mega Combinatie (Mega Combination) coalition of four political parties, led by the NDP, won a total of 23 seats out of 51, enabling it to control the national legislature though a coalition. Desiré Bouterse was elected president by a more than two-thirds majority of parliament.
2011 In July, Suriname re-applied for membership of the Organisation of Islamic Conference (OIC). The Dubai (United Arab Emirates) ports' operators DP World, purchased controlling interests in two Paramaribo ports, Integra Ports Services (IPS) and Suriname Ports Services (SPS).
2012 On the 2 April parliament enacted an amnesty law granting President Bouterse immunity from prosecution for this role in the killing of political opponents during his previous dictatorship in the 1980s. On 11 May a court martial adjourned the trial of President Bouterse and 24 others accused of killing opponents, until a constitutional court reviews the earlier amnesty legislation.
2013 In July the IMF says it expects Suriname's strong growth of recent years to continue for 2013 but decelerate 'somewhat' in 2014. It pointed out that there were, however, 'risks to the outlook, particularly related to gold prices and fiscal pressures'. Dino Bouterse, the son of President Desi Bouterse, was extradited from Panama by the US in August. He was charged on 8 November with attempting

to provide material support to a foreign terrorist organisation. He had allegedly been paid to provide a base and weapons by Hezbollah Shi'a militants who were said to be planning attacks on the US and the Netherlands. In December a dispute was brewing between Suriname and Guyana over

2014 In July the Intermed Group announced it had launched the first Sukuk compliant form of financing for joint venture developments in Suriname. This will allow Muslims to invest in Suriname without being charged, or have to pay, interest.

2015 In January Mr Bouterse announced that elections would be held on 25 May; he is favourite to win a further term. On 10 March President Bouterse's son, Dino Bouterse, was sentenced in federal court in New York City to 195 months in prison for attempting to provide material support and resources to Hezbollah, a designated terrorist organisation, as well as narcotics trafficking and firearms offences. An agreement was signed on 4 May for the Organisation of American States (OAS) to observe the elections. In the general election held on 25 May the ruling NDP won 45.56 per cent of the vote (26 seats, out of 51), the V7 Alliance (formed in January 2015 and consisting of the Progressive Reform Party, the National Party of Suriname, the Surinamese Labour Party, the Democratic Alternative '91, Pertjajah Luhur, the Party for National Unity and Solidarity and the Brotherhood and Unity in Politics) 37.18 per cent (18 seats), the A-Combination 10.53 per cent (5 seats), the Party for Democracy and Development through Unity 4.33 per cent (1 seat) and the Progressive Workers' and Farmers' Union 0.68 per cent (1 seat). President Bouterse is likely to be re-elected by the specially expanded Assembly, although the process could take several months. In a preliminary statement issued on May 30 the CARICOM election observation mission reported that the May 25 process had been transparent, free and fair and that electors had cast their votes without fear. On 14 July parliament elected Mr Bouterse to a second consecutive term as president (without a vote as there was no other contestant). He was sworn in on 12 August. On 13 November Romano Meriba, the foster son of President Desi Bouterse, was arrested in Paramaribo police station for being involved in a robbery in Paramaribo-North.

Political structure

Independence date

25 November 1975 (from The Netherlands)

Form of state

Parliamentary democratic republic

The executive

The presidency is decided by an electoral colleges based in parliament, for a term of five years. The president is Head of State, Head of government and commander-in-chief of the armed forces. During a term in office, the president is accountable to the national assembly. The president has wide executive power to appoint and dismiss ministers, enact laws and declare war (with the assent of the national assembly).

The political system is multi-party and numerous parties must form coalitions to come to power. To win the presidency, a coalition needs a two-thirds majority in the national assembly. Failing three rounds, the vote goes to the United People's Congress, which contains assembly members and local and regional councillors, which elects a president by a simple majority.

National legislature

The unicameral De Nationale Assemblée (commonly referred to as DNA) (National Assembly) has 51 members, sigh members directly elected in multi-seat constituencies by proportional representation, for five-year terms.

Last elections

25 May 2015 (parliamentary); 2015 (presidential, indirect)

Results: Parliamentary: National Democratic Party won 45.5 per cent of the vote (26 seats out of 51), V7 won 37.3 per cent (18 seats) and A-Combination won 10.5 per cent (5 seats); eight other political parties and coalitions failed to win any more than one seat. Turnout was 72.7 per cent.

Presidential: parliament voted for Dési Bouterse to continue his presidential term.

Next elections

May 2020 (parliamentary); 25 May 2020 (presidential, indirect)

Political parties

Ruling party

Nationale Democratische (NDP) (National Democratic Party)

Main opposition party

V7, a political alliance of seven parties; the Progressive Reform party, the National Party of Suriname, the Surinamese Labour Party, the Democratic Alternative '91, Pertjajah Luhur, the Party for National Unity and Solidarity and the Brotherhood and Unity in Politics.

Population

553,000 (2014)*

Last census: August 2004: 492,829

Population density: Three inhabitants per square km. Urban population 69 per cent (2010 Unicef).

Annual growth rate: 1.3 per cent, 1990–2010 (Unicef).

Ethnic make-up

East Indian (37 per cent), Creole (31 per cent), Javanese (15 per cent), Black (10 per cent), Indian (3 per cent), Chinese (2 per cent).

Religions

Hindu (25 per cent), Protestant (25 per cent), Roman Catholic (23 per cent), Islam (20 per cent), traditional beliefs (5 per cent).

Education

Primary schooling begins at age 6 and last until aged 12. An exam deteremines the route either to a general lower secondary, or technical school. Advancement at age 16, following further exams, leads to either an academic, pre-university senior, or upper vocational, school. Teaching may be delivered in either Dutch or English.

Higher education is provided through either a University, Institute, Academy, or Polytechnic College.

Literacy rate: 93 per cent adult rate.

Compulsory years: 7 to 12.

Enrolment rate: 92.18 per cent net primary; 2.93 per cent net secondary enrolments.

Pupils per teacher: 17 in primary schools.

Health

HIV/Aids

HIV prevalence: 1.7 per cent aged 15–49 in 2003 (World Bank)

Life expectancy: 67 years, 2004 (WHO 2006)

Fertility rate/Maternal mortality rate: 2.3 births per woman, 2010 (Unicef)

Birth rate/Death rate: 19.4 births per 1,000 population; 6.8 deaths per 1,000 population (2003).

Child (under 5 years) mortality rate (per 1,000): 21 per 1,000 live births (WHO 2012)

Main cities

Paramaribo (Parbo) (capital, estimated population 246,132 in 2012), Lelydorp (19,991), Nieuw Nickerie (15,109), Moengo (8,252), Meerzorg (7,381), Nieuw Amsterdam (5,579), Marienburg (4,998), Wageningen (4,765).

Languages spoken

Sranan Tongo (Creole) is the *lingua franca*. English, Sarnami (Hindi), Javanese and Chinese are also spoken.

Official language/s

Dutch

Media

Press

Daily newspapers include *De Ware Tijd* (www.dwtonline.com) and *De West* (www.dewestonline.cq-link.sr) and a periodical *Dagblad Suriname* (www.dbsuriname.com).

Broadcasting

Radio: All stations broadcast programmes in Dutch with other local languages. Stichting Radio Omroep Suriname (SRS) is government-owned; commercial stations include Radio Paramaribo, Radio Apintie (www.apintie.fm), Radio Nickerie (RANI), Radio 10 (www.radio10.sr); ABC (www.abcsuriname.com) is a radio and TV broadcasting station.

Television: Government-owned commercial TV services include STVS (www.parbo.com/stvs) and ATV (http://www.atv.sr).

Other news agencies: Caribbean Net News: www.caribbeannetnews.com

Economy

The major economic resource of Suriname is bauxite, which is either exported as aluminium oxide or refined and exported as aluminium. Other primary industries include gold mining, oil production, agriculture (bananas, rice and citrus fruits), fish and shellfish and timber for exports.

GDP is estimated to have grown by 5 per cent in 2013, buoyed by the oil and gold sectors, as well as public investment.

Although Suriname did not suffer directly from the global economic crisis, as its banking sector is considered conservative, it did feel the effects as domestic investors disbursed more funds outside Suriname then foreign investors financed projects in Suriname. The US-based Alcoa's US$65 million expansion of its Paranam alumina refinery, opened in 2005, led to production of 250,000 tonnes per year.

Paranam is the only alumina refinery in operation since the Australian-based BHP Billiton closed its mining operations at the end of 2008, and had ceased all operations in Suriname by 2010. Foreign direct investment in Suriname was negative for most of the 2000s (the exception was in 2005 when FDI was US$27.9 million); it returned to positive FDI in 2011, of US$69.8 million and rose to US$112 million in 2013. The current account balance rose from -3.931 in 2013 to -3.489 in 2014. Macroeconomic conditions have weakened in the years since 2013 as gold and oil prices have declined.

Migrant workers and the remittances they send home constitute an important resource for many families in Suriname. However, as the global economic crisis hit, jobs and wages were cut leading to a reduction in prospects and benefits. According to the World Bank, remittances had been US$140 million in 2007, but this had fallen to US$2 million in 2008 and was still only US$4 million in 2010 (1 per cent of GDP); and was up to some US$8.8 million in 2014.

In 2013, the Rosebel Gold Mines (Suriname's largest gold producer) announced profits were up 7.6 per cent to US$210 million (from US$196 million in 2011). Taxes, royalties and dividends for the treasury amounted to US$156.5 and constituted a 'major contribution' to the Surinamese economy, according to the natural resources minister. The commissioning of the solar farm in 2014 will continue to yield power credits for Rosebel in 2015. Attributable production in 2015 is expected to be in the range of 290,000 to 300,000 ounces. The company expects mining activity in 2015 to be comparable to 2014.

On 15 August 2012, the US Moody's Ratings Agency, Investor Service upgraded Suriname's bond rating from B1 (considered 'junk') to Baa3, which constitutes a grading fit for investment purposes. The grading was granted based on prudent fiscal management and improved debt sustainability, positive short- and medium-term growth prospects, and greater resilience to external shocks. However, weak institutions still remain a key rating constraint on the path to improve their investment climate.

External trade

As a member of the Caribbean Community and Common Market (Caricom), Suriname operates within the single market (Caribbean Single Market and Economy (CSME)), which became operational in 2006. Goods, services, businesses and money are free to move within CSME without barriers and tariffs.

Natural resources include a major world source of bauxite, rainforest timbers, gold, iron ore, seafood and agricultural products.

Imports

Principal imports are capital equipment, petroleum, foodstuffs, cotton and consumer goods.

Main sources: US (31.3 per cent of total in 2014), Netherlands (16.6 per cent), China (10.7 per cent), Trinidad and Tobago (6.9 per cent) and Japan (4.2 per cent).

Exports

Principal exports are aluminium oxide, gold, crude oil, timber, shrimp and fish, rice and bananas.

Main destinations: US (32.1 per cent of total in 2014), UAE (16.8 per cent), Belgium (13.4 per cent), Canada (10 per cent), France (6.2 per cent) and the Netherlands (4.3 per cent).

Agriculture

Farming

Just 0.5 per cent of Suriname's total landmass is accounted for by permanent crop and arable land, concentrated predominantly along the coastal plain. Despite the death of land devoted to agricultural activities, Suriname is self sufficient in most basic foodstuffs and the sector accounts for up to 9 per cent of total GDP. Some 15 per cent of the country's workforce is employed in the agricultural sector.

The staple food crop and most important agricultural export is rice, the farming of which is highly mechanised. Suriname exports 40,000 tonnes of rice annually to the EU. Other major crops include palm oil, coconuts, bananas, sugar, citrus fruits and coffee.

Fishing

The commercial fishing industry accounts for about 7 per cent of Surinam's total export earnings; the sector has grown in importance in recent years. Fishing for shellfish, in particular, has increased. The typical total fish catch is over 19,000 tonnes (t), plus over 7,700t of other seafood, per annum.

Forestry

Suriname has vast forestry resources in relation to its size. Approximately 80 per cent of the country's total landmass is covered by forests and woodland, but just 2 per cent is exploited as access is limited.

Industry and manufacturing

Industrial activities in Suriname centre on the processing of agricultural produce (particularly timber), bauxite mining and timber processing. The sector contributes approximately 36.6 per cent to total GDP and employs one fifth of Suriname's labour force. Industry is largely constituted of mining related activity.

Tourism

Much of the tourist infrastructure is located in the capital and along the coast. The historical inner city of the capital, Paramaribo, and the Central Suriname Nature Reserve are included on Unesco's World Heritage List.

The contribution of travel and tourism to the economy has fallen steadily from 6.9 per cent in 2007 to 2.8 per cent of GDP in 2013, and further to 2.7 per cent in 2014. The sector only accounts for 2.5 per cent of employment (5,000 jobs). Around 12 per cent of Suriname, including a portion of intact, pristine Amazon rainforest is supposed to be protected from logging and mining. The launch of ecotourism may provide the economic incentive to protect the land, although this will need the support of the six native tribes of the interior as well as the Maroons (descendants of escaped slaves who recreated their West African communities). Suriname's involvement in ecotourism has been controversial. Local people have not benefitted from investment or provision of services and have been denied access to traditional hunting locations in favour of foreign revenue.

Mining
In a typical year for the economy of Suriname the mining sector contributes approximately 12 per cent of total GDP. The sector also employs some 5 per cent of the country's total workforce.
Currently, the mining and crude oil industry are the main sectors targeted for large-scale investment. In 2013, parliament approved two gold mining deals with two multinationals. Despite the current decline of world market prices for gold, the government hopes that these investments of approximately US$1.1 billion will continue.
Suriname's reserves of bauxite stand at 600 million tonnes. The US imports 400,000 tonnes of alumina from Suriname each year and it contributes up to 60 per cent of exports and 10–15 per cent of government income.
The deposits in the major mining areas, Moengo and Paranam, are maturing and were expected to reach the end of their life in 2006. Other reserves in the east, west and north of Suriname are expected to last until 2025.
Around 80 per cent of gold production is in the informal sector but in 2011 the government introduced a comprehensive programme to bring order to the sector, which incorporated government policies, security and law enforcement and educating local operators about the impact of gold mining on the environment. The programme will register all informal gold operators (miners), provide improved services to mitigate the damage caused by informal mining and impose proper taxation of the activity.
The Rosebel Gold Mine is jointly owned by IAMGOLD (95 per cent) and the Government of Suriname (5 per cent). The mine is located in the mineral rich Brokopondo District.
Other commercially viable minerals include iron ore, copper, nickel, platinum and kaolin.

Hydrocarbons
Total proven oil reserves were 80 million barrels in 2013. Sustainable production is determined at 15,270 barrels per day (bpd). The state-owned Staatsolie has a monopoly and is responsible for exploration, production and refining crude oil, alone or in conjunction with other oil companies.
While oil exploration was focussed onshore up to 2007, it moved offshore along Suriname's coastal area after a UN tribunal made a decision concerning the disputed oil-rich territory claimed by both Guyana and Suriname. The ruling declared that both countries were entitled to explore the region off the Atlantic coastline with Suriname being granted 17,871 square kilometres. An estimate of the recoverable oil in the area is 2 billion cubic metres (15 billion barrels) and 1.19 trillion cubic metres of gas.
The country's only oil refinery produces 7,000bpd of diesel, fuel oil and bitumen.
In 2005, Suriname, plus a number of other Caribbean states, signed an agreement with Venezuela to establish PetroCaribe, a multi-national oil company, owned by the participating states. PetroCaribe buys low-priced Venezuelan crude oil under long-term payment plans.
Any use of natural gas or coal is commercially insignificant.

Energy
Total installed electricity generation capacity was 410MW in 2013. Around 75 per cent of all electricity was generated by hydropower. One of the world's largest man-made lakes, of around 1,560 square kilometres (depending on rainfall), the Brokopondo Reservoir, provides the water for the dam which generates the energy for the bauxite refinery in Paranam on the Suriname River. It typically allocates 25 per cent of its electricity output to power 75 per cent of the capital Paramaribo's needs.

Banking and insurance
Suriname's banking sector has traditionally been highly indebted and needs reform. The government has equity stakes in six of Suriname's eight banks, including a 10 per cent stake in the largest bank, De Surinaamse Bank. Domestic borrowing is mostly undertaken by the government.
Central bank
Centrale Bank van Suriname
Main financial centre
Paramaribo.

Time
GMT minus three hours

Geography
Suriname is located on the northern coast of South America, facing the Atlantic Ocean. It is bordered by French Guiana to the east, Guyana to the west and Brazil to the south.
The terrain is hilly and most of the country is covered by tropical rain forests, except along a narrow strip of low-lying coastal plain. This area, which is swampy, is 80km at its widest and is home to most of the population. There is a 3,000km network of rivers, most of which flow northwards into the Atlantic Ocean. River travel is the main means of access into the forested interior. The most important rivers are the Corantijn, Suriname, Mariwijne and Coppename. A huge man-made lake, the WJ van Blommestein Meer, one of the largest reservoirs in the world, lies astride the Suriname river in the north-east of the country.

Hemisphere
Northern

Climate
Tropical but cooled by trade winds. Rain throughout the year but heaviest from November–January and from April–July. Average daily temperature remains fairly constant throughout the year at 27 degrees Celsius (C); daily range from 22–35 degrees C from May–October; slightly lower temperatures from November–April.

Entry requirements
Passports
Required by all, valid for six months from date of arrival.
Visa
Required by nationals of most countries; for current list of exceptions, see www.surinameembassy.org. All visitors must have return/onward passage. Business visas require a letter from the employing company explaining the purpose of visit, and the details of all the contacts in Suriname plus an itinerary.
Currency advice/regulations
Import and export of local currency is limited to Su$150. There are no restrictions on the import and export of foreign currencies, subject to declaration of amounts over US$10,000

Health (for visitors)
Mandatory precautions
Yellow fever vaccination certificate required if arriving from an infected area.
Advisable precautions
Yellow fever, typhoid and polio vaccinations. Malaria prophylaxis recommended and water precautions should be taken.

Hotels
Paramaribo and Nieuw Nickerie have a number of modern hotels but beds are limited. Service charge of 10 per cent is usual.

Public holidays (national)
Fixed dates
1 Jan (New Year's Day), 1 May (Labour Day), 1 Jul (Abolition of Slavery Day), 25 Nov (Independence Day), 25–26 Dec (Christmas).
Variable dates
Holi (Hindu, Mar), Good Friday, Easter Monday, Eid al Fitr.
In addition, Chinese, Jewish and Indian businesses will be closed for their own religious holidays.

Working hours
Banking
Mon–Fri: 0800–1500.
Business
Mon–Fri: 0730–1630.
Government
Mon–Fri: 0700–1500.

Shops
Mon–Fri: 0700/0730–1630; Sat: 0730–1300.

Electricity supply
110/127V and/or 220V AC, 60 cycles

Getting there
Air
National airline: Surinam Airways (SLM).
International airport/s:
Paramaribo-Johan Adolf Pengel International Airport (PMB), 46km from city; duty-free shop, bank, cafeterias, car hire.
Airport tax: US$35, payable only in US dollars or euros.
Surface
Road: A coastal road links Paramaribo with Guyana (at Nieuw Nickerie) and French Guiana (at Albina).
Water: There are sea links with the US and Europe. Car ferry services run from French Guiana and Guyana.
Main port/s: Paramaribo.

Getting about
National transport
Most infrastructure has been on the country's narrow coastal plain, with links to the interior weak. Much of the sparsely-populated country is accessible only by air or river.
Air: Domestic flights to towns in the interior are operated from Zorg en Hoop airfield near Paramaribo by Surinam Airways and Gum Air. Charter services are available.
Road: There are over 4,000km of roads, of which around a quarter are paved. Coastal towns are linked by road from Nieuw Nickerie in the west, through Paramaribo, to Albina in the east. Roads in the interior are not surfaced and are poorly maintained.
Bridges over the Coppename and Suriname rivers link the east and west of the country.
Buses: Paramaribo and most towns have a local bus service. Bus routes link coastal towns but service is irregular and tends to be crowded.
Water: River transport is the main means of travel in the interior and in some coastal areas.
City transport
Taxis: Taxis are available, but scarce after 10 pm and on Sundays and holidays. They are not metered and fares should be agreed in advance of journey.
Car hire
Available in Paramaribo at the airport and through main hotels and the Tourist Information Office. International driving licences required.

BUSINESS DIRECTORY

The addresses listed below are a selection only. While World of Information makes every endeavour to check these addresses, we cannot guarantee that changes have not been made, especially to telephone numbers and area codes. We would welcome any corrections.

Telephone area codes
The international dialling code (IDD) for Suriname is +597 followed by subscriber's number.

Chambers of Commerce
Suriname Chamber of Commerce & Industry, PO Box 139, Mr JC de Miranda Straat, Paramaribo (tel: 473-527; fax: 470-802; e-mail: chamber@sr.net).

Banking
De Surinaamse Bank NV, Henck Arronstraat 26-30, Paramaribo (tel: 471-100; fax: 477-835).

Finabank NV, Dr. S. Redmondstraat 55-61, Paramaribo.

Hakrinbank NV, Dr S. Redmondstraat 11-13, Paramaribo (tel: 477-722; fax: 472-066).

Landbouwbank NV, Lim A Postraat 28-30, Paramaribo (tel: 475-945, 475-101; fax: 410-821).

Nationale Ontwikkelingsbank (NOB), Coppenamelaan 160-162, Paramaribo (tel: 465-000; fax: 497-192).

RBTT Bank (Suriname), Kerkplein 1 Paramaribo (tel: 471-555; fax: 411-325).

Surinaamse Postspaarbank (SPSB), Knuffelsgracht 11-13, Paramaribo (tel: 472-256; fax: 472-952).

Surinaamse Volkscrediet Bank (VCB), Steenbakkerijstraat 2, Paramaribo (tel: 472-616; fax: 472-616).

Central bank
Centrale Bank van Suriname, PO Box 1081, Waterkant 16-20, Paramaribo (tel: 473-741; fax: 476-444; e-mail: info@cbvs.sr).

Travel information
Surinam Airways, Jagernath Lachmonstraat 136, PO Box 2029, Paramaribo (tel: 465-700; fax: 491-213; e-mail: publicrelations@slm.firm.sr).

Tourist Information Centre, Waterkant 1, Fort Zeelandia Complex, Paramaribo (tel: 479-200; fax: 477-786; e-mail: stsmktg@sr.net).

Ministry of tourism
Ministry of Transport, Communication and Tourism, Prins Hendrikstraat 26-28, Paramaribo (tel: 420-422; fax: 420-425; e-mail: odc@minctc.sr).

National tourist organisation offices
Suriname Tourism Foundation, Dr JF Nassylaan 2, Paramaribo; PO Box 656, Paramaribo (tel: 410-357; fax: 477-786; email: info@suriname-tourism.org).

Ministries
Ministry of Agriculture, Animal Husbandry and Fisheries, Cultuurtuinlaan, Paramaribo (tel: 474-177; fax: 470-301).

Ministry of Defence, Kwattaweg 29, Paramaribo (tel: 474-244; fax: 420-055).

Ministry of Economic Affairs, Kleine Waterstraat 4, Paramaribo (tel: 75-080).

Ministry of Education, Dr. F. Kaffiludistraat 117-123, Paramaribo (tel: 498-383; fax: 495-083).

Ministry of Finance, Onafhandelijkheidsplein 3, Paramaribo (tel: 472-619; fax: 476-314).

Ministry of Foreign Affairs, Gravenstraat 6-8, Paramaribo (tel: 471-209; fax: 410-851).

Ministry of Justice and Police, Gravenstraat 1, Paramaribo (tel: 473-033; fax: 412-109).

Ministry of Internal Affairs, Onafhankelijkheidsplein 2, Paramaribo (tel: 476-461; fax: 421-170).

Ministry of Labour, Wagenwegstraat 22, Paramaribo (tel: 477-045; fax: 410-465).

Ministry of Natural Resources, Mr. Dr. J.C. de Mirandastraat 13-15, Paramaribo (tel: 473-420; fax: 472-911).

Ministry of Planning and International Co-operation, Dr. S Redmondstraat 118, Paramaribo (tel: 473-628; fax: 421-056).

Ministry of Public Health, Gravenstraat 64, Paramaribo (tel: 474-841; fax: 410-702).

Ministry of Public Works, Verlengde Coppenamestraat 167, Paramaribo (tel: 462-500; fax: 464-901).

Ministry of Regional Development, Van Rooseveltkade 2, Paramaribo (tel: 471-574).

Ministry of Social Affairs and Housing, Waterkant 30-32, Paramaribo (tel: 472-610; fax: 470-516).

Ministry of Trade and Industry, Nieuwe Haven, Paramaribo (tel: 479-886; fax: 477-602).

Ministry of Transportation, Communications and Tourism, Prins Hendrikstraat 26-28, Paramaribo (tel: 420-422; fax: 470-425).

President of the Republic of Suriname, Onafhankelijkheidsplein, Paramaribo (tel: 472-841; fax: 475-266).

Vice President and Council of Ministers, Dr. S. Redmondstraat, 1e Etage, Paramaribo (tel: 474-805; fax: 472-917).

Other useful addresses
Algemene Aannemers Vereniging (AAV), Gravenstraat 73, Paramaribo (tel: 478-419; fax: 474-531).

Associatie van Surinaarns Bedrijfsleven (V.S.B.), Domineestraat 33 boven, Paramaribo (tel: 476-585; fax: 421-160).

Orde van Raadgavende Ingenieursbureaus in Suriname (ORIS), P.O. Box 1864, van Roosmalenstraat no. 30, Paramaribo (tel: 472-275, 474-381; fax: 474-408).

Stichting Planbureau Suriname, PO Box 172, Dr S. Redmondstraat 110, Paramaribo (tel: 473-146).

Suriname Embassy (USA), Suite 108, 4301 Connecticut Avenue, NW, Washington DC 20008 (tel: (+1-202) 244-7488; fax: (+1-202) 244-5878; e-mail: embsur@erols.com).

Vereniging Surinaams Bedrijfsleven (Suriname Trade and Industry Association), Prins Hendrikstraat 18, PO Box 111, Paramaribo (tel: 475-286/7; fax: 472-287).

Caribbean Net News: www.caribbeannetnews.com

Internet sites

De Ware Tijd (English bulletin available): http://www.dwt.net

Economic Commission for Latin America and the Caribbean: http://www.eclac.cl

Inter-American Development Bank: http://www.iadb.org

Organisation of American States: http://www.oas.org

Latin World: http://www.latinworld.com

Latin Trade Online: http://www.latintrade.com

Republic of Suriname homepage: http://www.sr.net.srnet/InfoSurinam

Swaziland

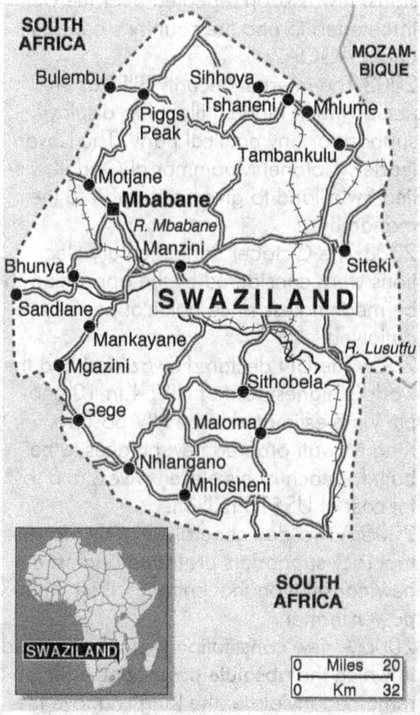

The Kingdom of Swaziland currently faces a dire socio-economic situation. This is in part due to its geographical dependence on South Africa; it has always been said that Swaziland, in the final analysis, can do little that runs counter to the interests of Pretoria. Although it is classified as a lower-middle-income country, income distribution is highly skewed and 700,000 of the 1.1 million people live on less than US$1 a day. A growing fiscal deficit threatens macro-economic stability and increasingly prevalent concerns over governance appear to undermine social harmony within the country. The humanitarian situation is difficult, with persistent high rates of HIV/Aids, unemployment, poverty and food shortages pervasive across much of the nation.

One of Africa's smallest countries, Swaziland covers an area no more than 120 miles north to south and 130 miles east to west. Despite this, its climate and topography is diverse. The Kingdom was established in the mid-eighteenth century under the leadership of Mgwane III. and is one of the World's last remaining monarchies. King Mswati III has sat on the throne since 1986 – showing no signs of enthusiasm for sharing the associated power. Banned opposition parties and trade unions have been vocal in their demands for a constitutional change, thereby limiting the King's power.

The King

The King effectively owns roughly 60 per cent of the land within Swaziland's borders. Under the country's dual land tenure system a form of twenty-first century feudalism is enabled. Antithetical to the vast poverty amongst the residents, King Mswati III has enjoyed great prosperity. A total of 15 wives, 13 palaces, a fleet of expensive cars and a private jet demonstrate the lavish Western consumerism shown by the monarchy. Although much of the country remains proud of their ruling monarch, there is growing unease among Swazis who complain that the King is increasingly out of touch, and a growing network of pro-democracy activists warn that resistance to change will not last for much longer. The failure to respect human rights and the rule of law led to the loss the African Growth and Opportunity Act (AGOA) between the US and Swaziland in 2014. Thousands of jobs were lost, with analysts foreseeing a coming economic crisis that could easily result in widespread unrest. Besides owning most of the land, King Mswati has direct control over a national investment fund called Tibiyo Taka Ngwane with stakes in minerals, real estate, breweries, insurance and agriculture. These assets are worth an estimated US$2 billion.

Economy

According to the African Development Bank (AfDB) economic performance in Swaziland, as indicated by real gross domestic product (GDP) growth, slowed half of a percentage point from 3.0 per cent in 2013 to 2.5 per cent in 2014. Poor prospects in South Africa and various domestic structural constraints have so far proved detrimental to economic recovery and full recovery from the 2011 fiscal crisis has still not been achieved. Nevertheless, declining growth in the secondary sector has largely been counteracted by

KEY FACTS

Official name: Umbuso weSwatini (Kingdom of Swaziland)

Head of State: King Mswati III (since 25 April 1986)

Head of government: Prime Minister Barnabas (Bheki) Sibusiso Dlamini (appointed by the King on 23 Oct 2008)

Ruling party: Political parties are *de facto* banned

Area: 17,363 square km

Population: 1.11 million (2014)*

Capital: Mbabane (administrative capital); Lobamba (legislative capital and the seat of the monarchy)

Official language: English and siSwati

Currency: Lilangeni – plural Emalangeni (E) = 100 cents; at par with the South African Rand

Exchange rate: E13.79 per US$ (Sep 2015)

GDP per capita: US$3,325 (2014)*

GDP real growth: 1.71% (2014)*

GDP: US$3.68 billion (2014)*

Inflation: 5.79% (2014)

Balance of trade: US$169.30 million (2013)

Annual FDI: US$94.75 million (2011)

* estimated figure

growth in the primary sector. Agriculture improved to an estimated 4 per cent, reflecting improvements in the productivity of the sector. Short-term prospects remain subdued with economic growth expected to remain low at around 2.5 per cent per annum through to 2016. The best prospects for growth appear within the export sector, in particular the restoration of the AGOA and the ratification of the Economic Partnership Agreement (EPA) with the European Union (EU) signed in August 2014.

The prevalence of economic issues within the Kingdom of Swaziland reflects associations with a low-income country, rather than the classification of a low middle-income country by the World Bank. A poor business climate, low foreign direct investment (FDI), a high rate of HIV/Aids and an uneven distribution of resources remain major concerns. Wide disparities in income are amongst the highest in the world, with a Gini co-efficient of 0.51. Poverty is also widespread, with 63 per cent of the population living beneath the poverty line. Other challenges include a high unemployment rate of 17.8 per cent. While Swaziland has made some improvements in the past three decades in the fight against the pandemic, the HIV prevalence of 26 per cent among 15–49 year-olds is the highest in the world. This has contributed to plummeting life expectancy to 40.9 years as well as high numbers of orphaned and vulnerable children.

Risk assessment

Economy	Fair
Politics	Poor
Regional stability	Good

COUNTRY PROFILE

1903 After a period of rivalry between the British and the Boers, Swaziland became a British protectorate.
1963 Swaziland's first constitution was introduced.
1964 The first elections resulted in victory for the Imbokodvo National Movement (INM).
1967 Swaziland was granted internal self-government as a protected state. Sobhuza II was recognised as King and head of state; Prince Makhosini Dlamini, leader of the INM, was appointed prime minister.
1968 Independence was granted.
1973 The King revoked the Westminster-based constitution and banned political parties.
1978 The previous constitution was replaced with a system designed to accommodate both western and traditional styles of government but still maintained a ban on Political parties.
1982 King Sobhuza II died.
1986 After a lengthy selection and training period, Crown Prince Makhosetive was chosen to succeed his father and he was crowned King Mswati III.
1992 Parliament was dissolved and Swaziland was governed by a *Liqoqo* (traditional tribal assembly).
1993 Democratic reforms led to the people directly electing some members of the *Liqoqo*.
1996 The King appointed a Constitutional Review Commission (CRC).
2000 The government put five critics of the government under house arrest and banned trade union meetings. The Swaziland Federation of Trade Unions (SFTU) met in South Africa and drew up the Nelspruit Declaration, demanding the formation of an interim government. The government amended the labour laws. Swaziland became eligible for US African Growth and Opportunities Act (AGOA) benefits.
2001 A number of political activists were forced into exile in South Africa. Decree 2 was issued by King Mswati, giving the monarch power to overrule court decisions. It was soon repealed after the US threatened to end the country's benefits under AGOA.
2002 The Internal Security Bill was enacted, which made it illegal to display support for any political party. The Libyan leader, Colonel Muammar al Qadafi, visited Swaziland to give his support to the monarchy.
2003 The October Parliamentary elections were considered by the opposition to be meaningless since political parties are outlawed.
2004 The UN declared Swaziland had the world's highest rate of HIV; 4 in 10 people were estimated to be HIV positive. King Mswati ordered new palaces to be built for each of his eleven wives, at a total cost of US$15 million.
2005 A two-day general strike by pro-democracy supporters protested against a new constitution that entrench the King's power further.
2006 A new constitution was promulgated in which the absolute power of the King remained inviolate; the King is above the law and not accountable to his people, with direct control of all security forces, governmental bodies and government posts. South African police shot at protestors blockading a border crossing into Swaziland; the protestors were demanding political reform.
2007 Six opposition members who took part in the border blockade were charged with sedition. Protests for democratic reforms were held.
2008 The opposition declared it would boycott upcoming elections in protest at the lack of multi-party elections. The King appointed Barnabas (Bheki) Sibusiso Dlamini as prime minister
2010 Swaziland remained the country with the highest prevalence of HIV in the world. The head of UNAids called for greater national response to the disease. Justice minister Ndumiso Mamba resigned after allegations that he was having an affair with King Mswati's 12th (of 13) wives.
2011 Following a pay-freeze of government workers, protesters took to the streets of the capital Mbabane, delivering a petition calling on the government to resign; some blamed it for corruption and were critical of the plans for lavish April anniversary coronation celebrations. Police used tear gas and water cannon to disperse protesters calling for elections.

KEY INDICATORS — Swaziland

	Unit	2011	2012	2013	2014	**2015
Population	m	*1.18	*1.08	*1.09	*1.11	*1.12
Gross domestic product (GDP)	US$bn	3.90	3.86	3.80	*3.68	*3.63
GDP per capita	US$	3,358	3,577	3,474	*3,325	*3,248
GDP real growth	%	0.3	1.9	2.8	*1.7	*1.9
Inflation	%	6.1	8.9	5.6	5.8	*4.6
Exports (fob) (goods)	US$m	2,084.1	1,926.0	1,860.8	–	–
Imports (fob) (goods)	US$m	1,397.9	1,848.0	1,691.5	–	–
Balance of trade	US$m	686.2	78.1	169.3	–	–
Current account	US$m	-341.0	157.0	239.0	*34.0	*14.0
Total reserves minus gold	US$m	678.8	741.0	762.5	690.8	–
Foreign exchange	US$m	597.7	662.4	677.4	–	–
Exchange rate	per US$	6.89	8.69	10.66	11.57	–

* estimated figure ** forecast figure

Swaziland has Africa's last absolute monarchy; political parties were banned 30 years ago. South Africa gave Swaziland an emergency loan of US$355 million in August. The following week the University of Swaziland failed to open for the new academic year; officials gave the reason as non-payment of student fees by the government. An immediate national debate ensued as to whether the money should be spent on repaying loans that had been provided to the government by domestic companies that now needed the money back to ease their cash flow and continue in business, or whether public workers should be paid to continue the business of government. By mid-September, the head of the Swaziland Principals Association confirmed that most schools in Swaziland were shut because of the financial crisis. The emergency loan from South Africa had yet to arrive.

2012 In February, the IMF pressed the government to cut public spending and reduce its workforce. Instead the government imposed a wage freeze. For King Mswati III's birthday on 19 April, 'anonymous sponsors' and 'development partners and friends' presented the king with a DC09 twin-engine jet aeroplane. Opposition activists said that taxpayer's money must have been used to buy it. In June government workers went on strike demanding a pay rise of 4.5 per cent, which the government refused. On 25 July thousands of teachers, who had been on a 'go slow' (reporting to school but not teaching) marched in Siketi and Umhlanga. The government gave them an ultimatum to return to work by 30 July or be sacked. In August all radio stations were banned from broadcasting news and information that did not conform to the government's views (radio broadcasts cannot be 'used for purposes of campaigning by individuals or groups, or to advance an agenda for political, financial popularity gains for individuals or groups'). On 13 November the government banned all members of parliament (MPs) from speaking on the radio (the principal medium for news and comment).

2013 Elections were held on 20 September. Although allowed to register, political parties are not allowed to function as such; there are no policy debates. 43 members standing for re-election to the 55-member House of Assembly (Liqoqo) lost, including six of eight ministers. Leader of the Swaziland Democratic Party (Swadepa) and pro-democracy activist, Jan Sithole, was one of the 55 independent members elected.

2014 Opposition politicians, Mario Masuku (president of the banned People's United Democratic Movement) and Maxwell Dlamini (the general secretary of the Swaziland Youth Congress), were detained after a May Day rally for criticising the King and the government.

2015 Two opposition politicians, arrested in 2014, were freed on bail from a maximum security prison on 14 July. the terrorism chargies against them still stand, and as part of their bail conditions they have been forbidden from addressing rallies.

Political structure

Constitution

The Constitution was promulgated in 1978. The country is run on a dual system. The traditional structure of Swaziland is headed by the Ingwenyama (the lion) (King), the Ndlovukazi (the she-elephant) (Queen Mother), and the more than 300 Chiefs who control the largely rural population. The other is the western-style central government, headed by the King, acting together with parliament, cabinet and civil service. Succession to the throne is governed by Swazi law and custom. The draft of a proposed new Constitution was written in 2003. However, it was available only in English and is also to be published in SiSwati during 2004, after which there is to be a further period of national consultation..

The Kingdom is divided into four regions.

Form of state

Absolute monarchy

The executive

Under the 1978 constitution, considerable executive power is vested in the monarch and exercised through a cabinet of ministers (all appointed by the monarch). Royal decrees carry the full force of law.

National legislature

There is a bi-cameral Libandla (legislature) consisting of the Senate (20 members appointed by the King; additional 10 members elected by the House of Assembly from among its own membership), and the Liqoqo (House of Assembly) (55 elective members, directly elected every five years (the first time in 1993), with voters electing one representative from each of the *tinkhundla* (traditional assemblies); 10 further members appointed by the King). The *Sibaya* is a 'people's parliament' that is supposed to be called annually to allow the people of Swaziland to voice their concerns to the King and his advisors. The last one was held in October 2012.

Legal system

The legal system is based on South African Roman-Dutch law in statutory courts and Swazi traditional law and custom in traditional courts. The Court of Appeal is the highest court in Swaziland. Court decisions are often overruled by the King.

Last elections

20 September 2013

Results: *Parliament*: the elections were considered by the opposition to be meaningless since political parties are outlawed. Only one of the elected MPs has a political affiliation (former prime minister Obed Dlamini, a member of the Ngwane National Liberation Congress). Several other members of outlawed parties contested seats as independent candidates; turnout was low. Of those standing, 43 (out of 55) failed to be re-elected, as did six out of eight ministers.

Next elections

September 2018 (parliamentary)

Political parties

Ruling party

Political parties are *de facto* banned

About 41 per cent of the population is under 14 years.

Population

1.11 million (2014)* About 41 per cent of the population is under 14 years.

Last census: 11 May 2007: 953,524 (provisional)

Population density: 59 inhabitants per square km. Urban population 21 per cent (2010 Unicef).

Annual growth rate: 1.6 per cent, 1990–2010 (Unicef).

Ethnic make-up

Africans (97 per cent), Europeans (3 per cent).

Religions

Christianity (60 per cent), traditional beliefs (40 per cent).

Education

Although education is subsidised by government, free public education remains a distant goal. School drop-out rates for children of vulnerable households are increasing, with more than 10 per cent of school drop-outs in the first term due to families forced to use school fees to pay the rising costs of staple foods.

It is estimated that through the loss of parents, due to HIV/Aids, 10 per cent of households are headed by a child.

The University of Swaziland provides higher education. There is scope for vocational training, including nursing, although there are no training institutes for doctors and dentists.

In June 2012 a strike called by Swaziland's largest teachers' union demanding a below-inflation salary increase spread across the country. The government had refused to entertain any wage demands. The strike led to sporadic clashes and arrests.

Literacy rate: 82 per cent adult rate (2003)

Compulsory years: None.

Enrolment rate: 128 per cent boys, 121 per cent girls gross primary enrolment (including repeaters); 60 per cent gross secondary enrolment (Unicef 2004).

Pupils per teacher: 37 in primary schools; 20 in secondary schools.

Health

HIV/Aids

Swaziland has one of the highest HIV/Aids rate in the world. In a 2005 antenatal survey of pregnant women aged 25–29 the prevalence rate was 56.3 per cent. The number of orphans of Aids is estimated to be between 10–15 per cent of the population in 2010, with the gender imbalance stark as the disease strikes down a disproportionate number of females.

Food security in Swaziland is directly linked to the toll on its young, productive adults, during its longstanding HIV/Aids epidemic. UNAIDS estimates that the annual loss to GDP per capita due to Aids was around 1.2 per cent by 2010. Demographically, urban populations have fallen by 5 per cent as HIV sufferers return to their family farms to receive care.

About 230,000 people are HIV-positive, of whom 65,000 depend on state hospitals to give them free antiretroviral drugs.

HIV prevalence: 42.6 per cent in 2005 (UNAIDS)

Life expectancy: 37 years, 2004 (WHO 2006)

Fertility rate/Maternal mortality rate: 3.4 births per woman, 2010 (Unicef)

Birth rate/Death rate: 29 births and 21 deaths per 1,000 people (2003)

Child (under 5 years) mortality rate (per 1,000): 80 per 1,000 live births (WHO 2012); 10 per cent of children aged under five are malnourished (World Bank).

Head of population per physician: 0.16 physicians per 1,000 people, 2004 (WHO 2006)

Welfare

UN estimates show that 66 per cent of Swaziland's population live below the poverty line. The average unemployment rate is about 40 per cent, although this figure is higher in rural areas.

According to the UN World Food Programme in early 2002, some 144,000 people required food aid after a severe drop in agricultural production. The total food aid amounted to 17,720 tonnes.

Main cities

Mbabane (administrative capital, estimated population 62,630 in 2012), Lobamba (royal compound) (3,793), Manzini (97,934), Malkerns (8,074), Nhlangano (7,161), Mhlume (6,713), Siteki (6,482), Big Bend (6,327), Simunye (5,522).

Languages spoken

Most Swazis are bi-lingual in English and SiSwati. In 2006 concern was expressed that teaching of SiSwati was less than English and that under 25 per cent of students who sat the 2005 Junior Certificate SiSwati examination passed; 92 per cent sitting the English language examination passed.

Official language/s

English and SiSwati

Media

Censorship extends to all radio and television output, excluding the Christian radio station. The print media is also restricted with the only privately owned newspaper reduced to commenting on news trivia while all adverse comments concerning the King are avoided.

Press

Dailies: In English, the privately owned *Times of Swaziland* (www.times.co.sz) is a tabloid style newspaper and *The Swazi Observer* (www.observer.org.sz) is an establishment newspaper.

Weeklies: Both dailies have weekend editions , *Times of Swaziland Sunday*, *The Weekend Observer* (www.observer.org.sz).

Periodicals: The *Dzadze Family Magazine* caters to women and consumer interests.

Broadcasting

Radio: The state-run Swaziland Broadcasting and Information Service operates three channels, the siSwati channel, the English channel and the Information service. The US-owned evangelical Trans World Radio (www.twr.org.za) has transmitters in Swaziland and broadcasts regionally.

Television: The state-run Swaziland Television Authority transmits most services in English with some in siSwati.

Other news agencies: There is no official agency but APA (www.apanews.net) and Panapress (www.panapress.com) report on Swaziland matters.

Economy

Swaziland is heavily dependent on South Africa as a lifeline of its economy as it gets 90 per cent of imports and sends 60 per cent of its exports to its neighbour.

Swaziland's GDP per capita tells a false story as, at US$7,800, it is pegged at a lower middle income country but this is skewed as 20 per cent of the population own 80 per cent of the wealth and 70 per cent rely on subsistence farming.

Swaziland's economy is dominated by industry (47.4 per cent of GDP in 2014), and the service sector (45.4 per cent). Agriculture contributes 7.2 per cent and heavy industry the rest. Manufacturing includes foodstuffs, soft drinks, canned fruit and confectionary, plus forestry products, wood pulp, paper and board products and furniture and others such as soaps and detergents.

The government is heavily dependent on receipts from the Southern African Customs Union (SACU) and personal remittances from broad (which amounted to US$30 million in 2013). By 22 June 2011 the government was unable to pay its employees and King Mswati personally engaged in talks with South African President Jakob Zuma, for financial aid, needed to balance Swaziland's budget and, more immediately, to pay its civil servants. A R2.4 billion (US$355 million) in soft loans was agreed, to be paid in three tranches, beginning in August. In September, a South African treasury spokesman said that no money would be transferred (and had not been) until the paperwork was signed. In August 2012, a first tranche of R800 million (around US$98 million) was due to be paid, but was subject to certain fiscal and technical conditions that had to be met by Swaziland authorities.

The International Monetary Fund refused to bail out the economy, citing the Swazi government's failure to reduce the budget deficit, amend the income tax demand and reduce the bloated bureaucracy.

In April 2012 the head of the IMF mission suspended operations, due to the inability of the government to 'propose a credible reform programme that could by supported by a new IMF Staff Monitored Programme'. All efforts to reduce government spending 2011–12 had failed and the budget 'did not provide sufficient resources to repay all domestic arrears'. Rather, the budget allocated 'an increasing share of resources to some sectors at the expense of education and health'.

GDP growth was 2.8 per cent in 2013, falling to 2.1 per cent in 2014 as investment in the private sector remained low. Foreign investment in Swaziland was very low at US$24 million in 2013, 0.3 per cent of GDP, and investment is unlikely to improve until the nation begins to market itself as a more attractive place to do business, in the 2014 Doing Business Index from the world bank Swaziland ranked 123 out of 189.

Subsistence agriculture provides a livelihood for 70 per cent of the working population. The latest statistics, published in 2012, estimated that over 26.5 per cent of the 15-49 year olds are HIV positive, the highest rate in the world, and that there were over 100,000 orphans. The economic burden of the disease has largely fallen on extended families and non-governmental agencies (NGOs). The UN Food and Agricultural Organisation (FAO) provides funds for Junior Field and Life Schools to offer secure communities for children to grow up in while learning the skills of farming, lost to them through the early deaths of their parents.

According to the 2013 UN Human Development Index (HDI), Swaziland was

ranked 148 (out of 187), for national development in health, education and income, which was marginally above the average for sub-Saharan Africa. In 2013, 25.9 per cent of the population experienced at least one indicator of poverty and 40.63 per cent were living on the equivalent of US$1.25 per day.
The King effectively owns roughly 60 per cent of the land within Swaziland's borders. Under the country's dual land tenure system a form of 21st century feudalism is enabled. Antithetical to the vast poverty amongst the residents, King Mswati III has enjoyed great prosperity. A total of 15 wives, 13 palaces, a fleet of expensive cars and a private jet demonstrate the lavish western consumerism shown by the monarchy. However, much of the country remains proud of the ruling monarch.
Growing unease is starting to appear among Swazis that complain that the King is increasingly out of touch, and a growing network of pro-democracy activists warn that resistance to change will not occur for much longer. The failure to respect human rights and the rule of law led to the loss of a Preferential Trade Agreement between the U.S.A and Swaziland in 2014. Thousands of jobs were lost, with analysts foreseeing a coming economic crisis that could easily result in widespread unrest. Besides owing most of the land, Mswati has direct control over a national investment fund called Tibiyo Taka Ngwane with stakes in minerals, real estate, breweries, insurance and agriculture. These assets are worth an estimated US$2 billion.

External trade

Swaziland is a member of the Common Market for Eastern and Southern Africa (Comesa), and operates within a free trade zone with 13 of the 19 member states. It is a member of the Southern African Development Community (SADC), the objectives of which include reducing trade barriers, achieving regional development and economic growth and evolving common systems and institutions. It is also is a member of the Common Monetary Area (CMA) (South Africa, Lesotho and Namibia) where the South African rand is legal tender throughout.
Sugar and soft drinks concentrate are the leading export earners, with timber and derivatives the next important exports.
Coal and gold mining have declined and their share of exports is no longer significant. Likewise, garment manufacturing no longer plays a leading role in export sales.

Imports

Principal imports are vehicles, machinery, foodstuffs, petroleum and chemicals.
Main sources: South Africa (91.8 per cent of total in 2008), Hong Kong (1 per cent), South Korea (1 per cent).

Exports

Principal exports are soft drinks and concentrates, sugar, wood pulp, citrus and canned fruit and garments.
Main destinations: South Africa (64.7 per cent of total in 2008), US (9.1 per cent), Kenya (5.4 per cent).

Agriculture

Farming

The agricultural sector contributes around 7.6 per cent to GDP and employs 75 per cent of the working population.
Sugar cane is the principal crop. 38,000 hectares of land are given over to it. With yields of 100 tonnes per hectare, Swaziland is one of the world's most efficient sugar producers. All sugar cane is grown under irrigation. The industry is regulated by the Swaziland Sugar Association (SSA). Sugar is Swaziland's highest export earner and accounts for 51 per cent of total agricultural production, 24 per cent of GDP, 13 per cent of total exports and 57 per cent of foreign exchange earnings.
Commercial farming, on the 40 per cent of the land owned by individual (mainly non-Swazi) freeholders, is centred on sugar, citrus, pineapples, tobacco and cotton.
Most maize and cotton is grown by small-scale farmers on Swazi Nation Land (SNL) (60 per cent of the land).
Smallholders own 80 per cent of the livestock. The country's main food crops are maize, beans, groundnuts and sorghum.
In 2012 the International Monetary Fund (IMF) recommended land reform as part of the solution to deepening economic decline in Swaziland, where more than two-thirds of the population lives in poverty.

Forestry

Forests cover 8 per cent of total land area.

Industry and manufacturing

The industrial sector employs over a fifth of the workforce and in 2014 contributed around 47.8 per cent of GDP. It is traditionally centred on the agro-industries: sugar refining, fruit canning and woodpulp processing. The forest products sector is one of the world's main sources of unbleached pulp.
Starting with textile production, the modern industrial sector has grown rapidly, with the South African market its main outlet. The US's African Growth and Opportunities Act (AGOA) enabled Swazi textile producers to access lucrative US markets, although in 2014 the US conducted a review on whether or not to withdraw these benefits unless the government undergoes democratic reform. In particular the US government was said to be 'deeply concerned about the lack of measurable progress on workers' rights issues'. As a result of this review Swaziland was removed from the AGOA due to not paying duties levied by the US. It is yet unclear just what the consequences of this are but it is predicted that the textile industry is likely to take a big hit, with multiple factories facing imminent closure unless the government complies with US duties.
Other activities include brick manufacture and shoe production.

Tourism

Swaziland can offer visitors a range of African experiences, including nature reserves, cultural ceremonies and adventure activities. Most visitors reach Swaziland, by road, through South Africa. Visitor numbers in 2013 were 1.1 million, as in 2012.
Travel and tourism contributed only a total of 4.1 per cent to GDP in 2014, employing 3.7 per cent of the workforce (12,500 jobs) in the same period. Capital investment in the tourist industry, which stood at only 4.9 per cent of total investment in 2014, is needed to improve the tourist infrastructure and provide a greater share of contribution to GDP.

Mining

Mining activity has declined due to the depletion of iron ore, diamonds, gold and tin and the closure of the Bulembu asbestos mine. Coal is mined for export to South Africa. Mineral production accounts for around 2 per cent of GDP.

Hydrocarbons

There are no known oil or natural gas reserves; Swaziland is therefore entirely dependent on imported fuels, which amount to 4,540 barrels of oil per day (2013).
There are substantial reserves of high-quality anthracite coal, which is extracted at the Maloma colliery for export to South Africa. Swaziland produced 489,000 tonnes in 2013.

Energy

Total installed generating capacity was 149MW in 2011 (latest figures), around 85 per cent of electricity is supplied by South Africa and the remainder from Mozambique. A feeder line connecting South Africa and Mozambique crosses Swaziland.
Hydropower supplies 62MW to the country's overall generating capacity. A hydroelectric station at Maguga Dam on the Komati River, has begun operations, contributing a maximum output of 20MW.
Swaziland belongs to the Southern African Development Community (SADC), which has plans to expand hydropower to utilise

the combined potential of 114,000MW available.
In October 2008 the government called for tenders to build and operate a 1,000MW coal-fired power plant at the dormant EmaSwati Colliery, Mpaka, in order to utilise Swaziland's huge reserves. However by 2015 construction had still not begun and it has been speculated that the project has been cancelled.

Financial markets
Stock exchange
Swaziland Stock Exchange (SSE)

Banking and insurance
In a report published in December 2002, the IMF praised Swaziland's 'well-developed banking system' and noted that in 2002 'banks' capitalisation, risk management and provisioning appeared to be sound and their non-performing loans were relatively low.' However, the future of the government-owned Swaziland Development and Savings Bank (SDSB) remains in doubt due to its high level of bad loans. The IMF has urged the government to privatise the bank.
Central bank
Central Bank of Swaziland
Main financial centre
Mbabane

Time
GMT plus two hours

Geography
Swaziland is a landlocked country that is surrounded on three sides by South Africa and on its forth side by Mozambique. It is one of the smallest country in Africa and is located on the eastern flank of the Drakensberg mountains extending to the Lubombo escarpment in the east.
These volcanic mountains produce a landscape of high veld with altitudes of 1,800 meters (m) in the north, south and west dropping down to middle veld of between 400–600m to the lowlands or bush veld at around 300m. There are five major rivers and their tributaries running through the country with large lakes and waterfalls and is a major habitat for rare birds and invertebrates.
Hemisphere
Southern

Climate
Temperatures range from about 7–10 Celsius (C) (with occasional frost) during April–September, to 20–30 C during August–January. The wettest months are December and March.
The mountainous high veld region to the north-west has a temperate climate with hot, wet summers and dry winters when the temperature rises during the day but with cold nights. The adjacent middle veld has a warm temperate climate, while further to the east lies the sub-tropical low veld, including the Lubombo plain and escarpment.

Entry requirements
Passports
Required by all.
Visa
Required by all; except citizens of UK, North America, Australasia and others listed at www.gov.sz, see *Entry requirements* under *Tourism, Environment and Community*. To stay over 60 days requires a visa extension, to be obtained from the immigration department.
A proposed tourist *univisa* (a single visa to visit all 15-member states of SADC: Angola, Botswana, DRC, Lesotho, Madagascar, Malawi, Mauritius, Mozambique, Namibia, South Africa, Seychelles, Swaziland, Tanzania, Zambia and Zimbabwe) is expected to be in use by 2013. Visitors should check with the appropriate consulates to confirm start of *univisas* and their scope before beginning a tour of southern Africa.
Currency advice/regulations
The import and export of local and foreign currency is unlimited. It is advisable to exchange local currency before leaving Swaziland as the lilangeni is not readily accepted elsewhere.
Travellers cheques are widely accepted.

Health (for visitors)
Mandatory precautions
A yellow fever certificate is required if arriving from an infected area.
Advisable precautions
Vaccinations for diphtheria, tetanus, hepatitis A and typhoid are recommended. Other vaccinations that may be advised include tuberculosis, cholera and hepatitis B. There is a risk of rabies.
Anti-malaria prophylaxes are needed in all but the high elevations. There is a very high prevalence of HIV/Aids.
Water precautions are essential. Eat only cooked food, served hot; avoid dairy, pork and salads; all fruits should be peeled. To avoid bilharzia, use only well maintained, chlorinated swimming pools.
Any medicines required by the traveller should be brought into the country and it would be wise to have precautionary antibiotics if going outside major urban centres. A travel kit including a disposable syringe is a reasonable precaution.
Medical insurance is essential, including emergency evacuation.

Hotels
There is no official rating system. Accommodation is fairly scarce, especially during national holidays, so rooms should be booked well in advance. Bills generally include the service charge, but a 10 per cent tip is also usual. A 10 per cent government tax is added to the room rates.

Credit cards
Major credit and charge card are accepted.

Public holidays (national)
Fixed dates
1 Jan (New Year's Day), 19 Apr (King's Birthday), 25 Apr (National Flag Day), 1 May (Labour Day), 22 Jul (Birthday of the late King), 6 Sep (Independence Day), 25–26 Dec (Christmas).
Variable dates
Good Friday, Easter Monday, Ascension, Umhlanga/Reed Dance Day^ (Aug/Sep).
^Dependent on local sightings of the moon.

Working hours
Banking
Mon–Fri: 0830–1300/1430; Sat: 0830–1100.
Business
Mon–Fri: 0800–1300, 1400–1700; Sat: 0815 or 0830–1230.
Government
Mon–Fri: 0800–1300, 1400–1700.

Telecommunications
Mobile/cell phones
There is a 900 GSM service throughout most of the country.

Electricity supply
230V AC, 50 Hz, with round, three-pin plugs.

Security
If you enter Swaziland from South Africa by road, on the N4, via the Oshoek border post, avoid travelling after dark as there is a risk of hijacking.

Getting there
Air
National airline: Royal Swazi National Airways
International airport/s: Matsapha (MTS), 9km south-west of Manzini, 40km from Mbabane; refreshments, currency exchange, car hire. There are no direct intercontinental flights, but regular services operate regionally, particularly from South Africa. Swazi Express provides a regional air service
Airport tax: Departures tax: E20
Surface
Road: There are tarred roads from Johannesburg and Durban and from Mozambique (Siteki-Lomahasha road). All Swazi border posts open daily throughout the year; hours of operation vary. Vehicles are subject to searches.
Rail: There is a rail service between Durban (South Africa) and Maputo (Mozambique) via Mpaka in the central eastern district of Lubombo.

Getting about

National transport

Road: The network is fairly well developed. An ongoing project improved the network with the provision of a dual carriageway and toll road between Manzini-Mbabane, which was opened in October 2003 and completed the Matspha-Mbabane-Ngwenya highway.

Buses: There is a good system that extends throughout the country.

Taxis: Minibus taxis run shorter routes than the buses, at slightly higher prices.

City transport

Taxis: Scarce. Best to order from hotel. A tip is usual.

Car hire

Self-drive cars are available at airport and city centre; a national driving licence is required. Driving is on the left and the maximum speed limit is 80kph.

BUSINESS DIRECTORY

The addresses listed below are a selection only. While World of Information makes every endeavour to check these addresses, we cannot guarantee that changes have not been made, especially to telephone numbers and area codes. We would welcome any corrections.

Telephone area codes

The international direct dialling code (IDD) for Swaziland is +268, followed by subscriber's number.

Chambers of Commerce

Swaziland Chamber of Commerce and Industry, PO Box 72, Mbabane (tel: 404-4408; fax: 404-5442; e-mail: chamber@dial.pipex.sz).

Banking

First National Bank of Swaziland Ltd, 2nd Floor, Sales House Building, Mbabane (tel: 404-5401/2/3; fax: 404-4735).

Nedbank (Swaziland) Limited, PO Box 68, Corner Plaza Mall Street and Bypass Road, Mbabane (tel: 404-3351/5; fax: 404-4060).

Standard Bank Swaziland Ltd, Standard House, Swazi Plaza, Mbabane (tel: 404-6930/1/2, 404-6599, 408-30/4; fax: 404-5899).

Swazibank, PO Box 336, Gwamile Street (tel: 404-2551; fax: 404-1241: email: vinahnkambule@swazibank.sz).

Central bank

Central Bank of Swaziland, PO Box 546, Warner Street, Mbabane (tel: 404-2000; fax: 404-0063; email: info@centralbank.org.sz).

Stock exchange

Swaziland Stock Exchange (SSE), www.ssx.org.sz

Travel information

Hotels and Tourism Association of Swaziland, PO Box 462, Mbabane (tel: 404-2218; fax: 404-4516).

Royal Swazi National Airways, PO Box 939, Matsapa Airport, Manzini.

Swazi Express (charter airline), Matsapha (tel: 518-6840; fax: 518-7160; internet: www.swaziexpress.com).

Ministry of tourism

Ministry of Tourism, Environment and Communications, 2nd Floor, Income Tax Bld, Mhlambanyatsi Road; PO Box 2653, Mbabane (tel: 404-4556; fax: 404-5415).

National tourist organisation offices

Swaziland Tourism Authority, PO Box A1030, Mbabane (tel: 405-7510; internet: www.welcometoswaziland.com).

Ministries

Cabinet Office, PO Box 395, Mbabane (tel: 404-2251; fax: 404-3943).

Ministry of Agriculture and Co-operatives, PO Box 162, Mbabane (tel: 404-2731; fax: 404-4700).

Ministry of Broadcasting, Information and Tourism, PO Box 338, Mbabane (tel: 404-2761/9; fax: 404-2774).

Ministry of Defence, PO Box 1928, Mbabane (tel: 404-2809; fax: 404-2483).

Ministry of Economic Planning and Statistics, PO Box 602, Mbabane (tel: 404-3765; fax: 404-2157).

Ministry of Education, PO Box 39, Mbabane (tel: 404-2491; fax: 404-3880).

Ministry of Enterprise and Employment, PO Box 451, Mbabane (tel: 404-3201; fax: 404-4711); Trade Promotion Unit (tel: 404-5180).

Ministry of Finance, PO Box 443, Mbabane (tel: 404-8148; fax: 404-3187).

Ministry of Foreign Affairs and Trade, PO Box 518, Mbabane (tel: 404-2661; fax: 404-2669).

Ministry of Health and Social Welfare, PO Box 5, Mbabane (tel: 404-2431; fax: 404-2092).

Ministry of Home Affairs, PO Box 432, Mbabane (tel: 404-2941; fax: 404-4303).

Ministry of Housing and Urban Development, PO Box 1832, Mbabane (tel: 404-6035; fax: 404-4085).

Ministry of Justice and Constitutional Development, PO Box 924, Mbabane (tel: 404-3531; fax: 404-4796); Attorney General's Chambers, PO Box 578, Mbabane (tel: 404-2807).

Ministry of Natural Resources and Energy, PO Box 57, Mbabane (tel: 404-6244; fax: 404-2436); Geological Survey & Mines, PO Box 57, Mbabane (tel: 404-2411). Rural Water Supply, PO Box 961, Mbabane (tel: 404-1231).

Ministry of Public Service and Information, PO Box 338, Mbabane (tel: 404-2761; fax: 404-2774).

Ministry of Public Works and Transport, PO Box 58, Mbabane (tel: 404-2321; fax: 4042364); Civil Aviation (tel: 404-2420).

Prime Minister's Office, PO Box 395, Mbabane (tel: 404-2251; fax: 4043943). Deputy Prime Minister's Office, PO Box A33 Swazi Plaza (tel: 404-2723; fax: 404-4085).

Other useful addresses

Central Co-operative Union, PO Box 551, Manzini (tel: 505-2787; fax 505-5313; email: ccu.admin@africaonline.co.sz).

Central Statistics Office, PO Box 456, Mbabane (tel: 404-2151/4; fax: 404-2157).

Central Transport Administration, PO Box 378, Mbabane (tel: 404-2871; fax: 404-3002).

Civil Service Board, PO Box 158, Mbabane (tel: 404-2601).

Cotton Board, PO Box 230, Manzini (tel/fax: 505-2775).

Federation of Swaziland Employers, PO Box 777, Mbabane (tel: 404-0768; fax: 404-6107; email: fse@realnet.co.sz).

National Agricultural Marketing Board, PO Box 1713, Matsapha (tel: 518-5211; fax: 518-4088).

National Maize Corporation, PO Box 158, Manzini (tel: 518-7432; fax: 518-4461).

Parliament, King's Office (tel: 416-1080). Parliament Offices (tel: 416-1286).

Police Headquarters, PO Box 49, Mbabane (tel: 404-2051).

Posts and Telecommunications Corporation, PO Box 125, Mbabane (tel: 404-2341; fax: 404-3130).

Small Enterprise Development Co Ltd, Mbabane Industrial Sites, PO Box A186, Swazi Plaza (tel: 404-2811; fax: 404-0723).

Statistics Department, PO Box 456, Mbabane (tel: 404-2151; fax: 404-2157).

Swazi Business Growth Trust, PO Box 78, Eveni (tel: 404-4705; fax: 404-4783). Swaziland Citrus Board, PO Box 343, Mbabane (tel: 404-3547).

Swaziland Commercial Board, PO Box 509, Mbabane (tel: 404-2930).

Swaziland Cotton Board, PO Box 230, Manzini (tel: 505-2775).

Swaziland Dairy Board, PO Box 2975, Manzini (tel: 505-8262).

Swaziland Electricity Board, PO Box 258, Mbabane (tel: 404-6668; fax: 404-2335).

Swaziland Embassy (USA), 1712 New Hampshire Ave, NW, Washington DC 20009 (tel: (1-202) 234-5002; fax: (1-202) 234-8059; e-mail: embassy@swaziland-usa.com).

Swaziland Industrial Development Company, PO Box 866, Mbabane (tel: 404-3391; fax: 404-5619).

Swaziland International Trade Fair, PO Box 877, Manzini (tel: 505-4242; fax: 505-2314).

Swaziland Investment Promotion Authority, PO Box 4194, Mbabane H100 (tel: 404-0470; fax: 404-3374; email: sipa@business-swaziland.com).

Swaziland National Housing Board, PO Box 798, Mbabane (tel: 404-5610; fax: 404-5224).

Swaziland Railway, PO Box 475, Mbabane (tel: 404-27211; fax: 404-7210).

Swaziland Sugar Association, PO Box 445, Mbabane (tel: 404-2646).

Swaziland Television Authority, PO Box A146, Swazi Plaza (tel: 404-3036; fax: 404-2093).

Tinkhundla Headquarters, PO Box A33, Swazi Plaza, Mbabane (tel: 404-2723; fax: 404-4058).

Water Services Corporation, PO Box 20 Mbabane (tel: 404-5584; fax: 404-5355).

There is no official agency but APA (www.apanews.net) and Panapress (www.panapress.com) report on Swaziland matters.

Internet sites

Africa Business Network: www.ifc.org/abn

AllAfrica.com: http://allafrica.com

African Development Bank: www.afdb.org

Africa Online: www.africaonline.com

Mbendi AfroPaedia (information on companies, countries, industries and stock exchanges in Africa): http://mbendi.co.za

Simunye news service: www.swazis.org.uk/~news/

Swazi news: www.swazinews.co.sz/about.htm

Swazi Observer: www.swaziobserver.sz/

Swaziland Solidarity Campaign: www.swazis.org

Sweden

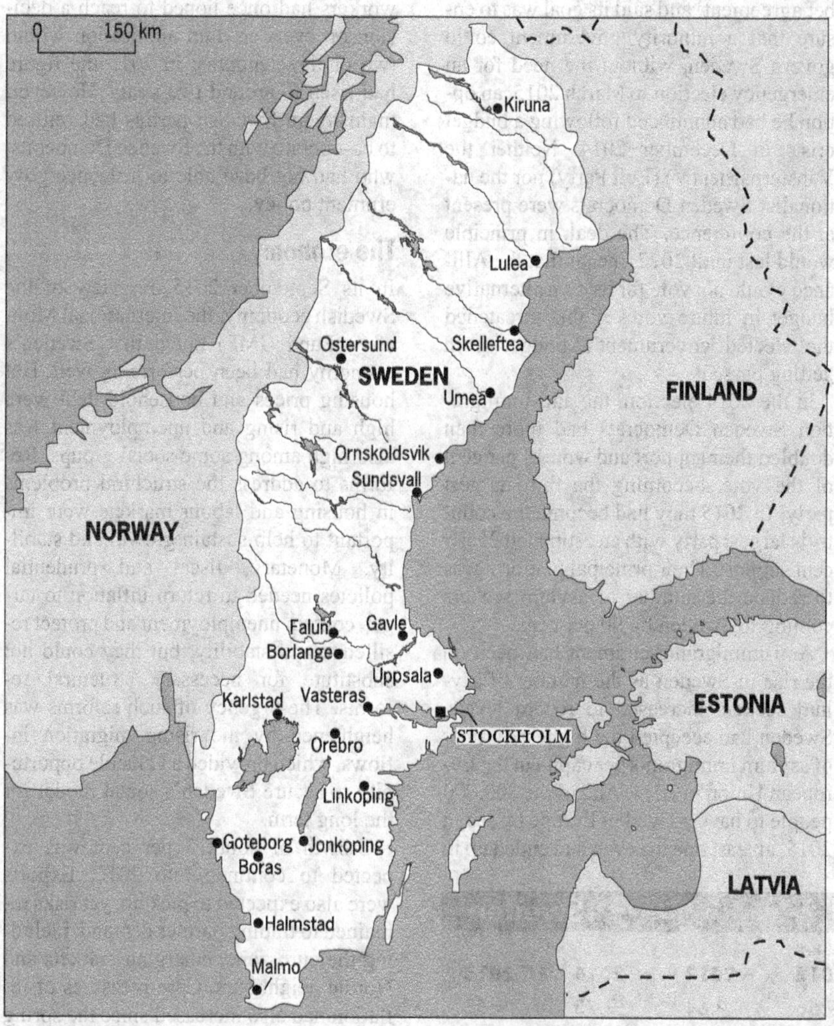

KEY FACTS

Official name: Konungariket Sverige (The Kingdom of Sweden)

Head of State: King Carl XVI Gustaf (crowned 19 Sep 1973)

Head of government: Prime Minister Stefan Lofven (SAP) (since 3 Oct 2014)

Ruling party: Minority government lead by Sveriges Socialdemokratiska Srbetareparti (SAP) (Swedish Social Democrats) with Miljöpartiet de Gröna (MP) (Environmental Party the Greens)

Area: 448,964 square km

Population: 9.75 million (2014)

Capital: Stockholm

Official language: Swedish

Currency: Swedish krona (SKr) = 100 öre

Exchange rate: SKr6.78 per US$ (Sep 2015)

GDP per capita: US$58,491 (2014)

GDP real growth: 2.14% (2014)

GDP: US$570.14 billion (2014)

Labour force: 5.15 million (2014)*

Unemployment: 7.93% (2014)

Inflation: -0.18% (2014)

Balance of trade: US$17.45 billion (2014)

Annual FDI: US$12.30 billion (2011)

* estimated figure

In Sweden's 2014 general elections, Stefan Löfven became prime minister – although his coalition of Sveriges Socialdemokratiska Srbetareparti (SAP) (Swedish Social Democrats) (113 seats out of the 349 in the Riksdag (parliament)) and Miljöpartiet de Gröna (MP) (Environmental Party the Greens) (25 seats) could not gain an absolute majority. The prime minister's Social Democratic Party garnered 31 per cent of the votes. Together with the Green Party's 6.9 per cent, the left-of-centre coalition thereby achieved 37.9 per cent. The centre-right Alliance, which includes the Moderata Samlingspartiet (Moderata) (Moderate Party), the Folkpartiet Liberalerna (FpL) (Liberal People's Party), the Centerpartiet (Cp) (Centre Party) and the Kristdemokraterna (KD) (Christian Democrats), collected 39.4 per cent of the votes. Since Sweden has a system of 'negative parliamentarism', meaning that a government can stay in power as long as it doesn't have a majority against it, the Social Democrats and the Greens could still have formed a government by themselves. In short, the 2014 elections left Sweden in a complicated parliamentary situation. A left-of-centre minority coalition was in government and the far-right Sweden Democrats were in a so-called swing vote position, having gained nearly 13 per cent of the votes.

In the 2010 election there had been a shock when the populist Sverigedemokraterna (SD) (Sweden Democrats) had even ended up with a foothold in parliament. Even more-so, when they did well enough in the 2014 election to topple the conservative-led government. Sweden's parliament works on coalitions, but no party seemed prepared to do any kind of deal with the Sweden Democrats. They were regarded as almost toxic, unacceptable. But in terms of votes cast, according to the polls, they had become the number one party in Sweden. At first it had been argued that the lunatics fringe would peter out, consumed by their own madness. It emerged, however, that they had prepared well for debates in the Swedish Parliament – even those which were not televised. Their stature had grown and the attacks against them risked becoming counterproductive. The pollsters YouGov put their support at 25 per cent ahead of 23 per cent for the governing Social Democrats and 21 per cent for the dethroned conservatives. But it seemed to be part of a pattern across Scandinavia: populist movements arising from the perceived failure to control immigration.

Snap elections?

Plans to hold a snap election in March 2015 were eventually abandoned at the end of 2014 after crisis talks between the Social Democrat Prime Minister Stefan Löfven and the country's four centre-right parties known as the Alliance. The coalition was made up of the Moderate Party – which had led the previous coalition government under Fredrik Reinfeldt – the Centre Party, the Liberal Party and the Christian Democrats. Also present were the co-leaders of the Green Party, which was in coalition with Mr Löfven's centre-left Social Democrats. The prime minister called the new deal the 'December agreement' and said its goal was to ensure that a minority government could govern Sweden, without the need for an emergency election in March 2015, an option he had announced following a budget crisis in December 2014. Neither the Vänsterpartiet (V) (Left Party) nor the nationalist Sweden Democrats were present at the conference. The deal, in principle would last until 2022, meant that the Alliance would not vote for its own alternative budget in future votes if this threatened the elected government's budget from getting passed.

In the 2014 election, the anti-immigration Sweden Democrats had more than doubled their support and won 13 per cent of the vote, becoming the third largest party. In 2015 they had become the country's largest party with an estimated 25 per cent support. Their principal platform was to reduce the number of asylum seekers coming to Sweden by 90 per cent.

Anti-immigrant sentiment had been on the rise in Sweden as the number of asylum seekers increased to record levels. Sweden had accepted the highest number of asylum immigrants per capita in the European Union in 2014. And of the 800,000 people to have arrived in Europe by sea in 2015, at least one in seven had ended up in Sweden, even though the country accounted for just one in 50 EU citizens. In 2015, over 120,000 people had applied for asylum in Sweden. The country's Migrationsverket agency expected the total number of refugees to reach about 170,000 by the end of 2015, with 10,000 people arriving every week, compared with 4,000 during the summer. Case workers had once hoped to reach a decision on every asylum application within two or three months; in 2015 the figure had risen to around two years. However, mainstream Swedish parties had refused to co-operate with the Sweden Democrats, who had not been able to influence government policy.

The economy

In its September 2015 overview of the Swedish economy, the International Monetary Fund (IMF) noted that Sweden's economy had been performing well. But housing prices and household debt were high and rising and unemployment was also high among some social groups. Reforms to address the structural problems in housing and labour markets were important to help sustain growth and stability. Monetary, fiscal and prudential policies needed to return inflation to target, contain unemployment and protect resilience and stability, but they could not substitute for necessary structural reforms. The urgency of such reforms was heightened by the rising migration inflows, which provided a valuable opportunity to secure Sweden's social model for the long term.

Growth of about 3 per cent was expected to continue into 2016. Exports were also expected to pick up, yet risks remained to trading partner demand, including the euro-zone, emerging markets and Nordic neighbours. Core measures of inflation had also increased since the spring of 2014 and rising resource utilisation was expected to progressively raise inflation in future. Sweden's humanitarian migration policy had allowed a significant rise in migrant inflows in 2014–15 and inflows appeared likely to remain relatively high for some years. Ensuring that migrants were integrated into the labour force more rapidly was key to avoiding higher unemployment in the medium term and to maximising their contributions to growth over the longer term. However, structural problems in labour and housing markets were major blocks to fulfilling Sweden's economic potential and they were also causing rising domestic risks. Despite solid overall employment growth,

KEY INDICATORS **Sweden**

	Unit	2011	2012	2013	2014	**2015
Population	m	*9.45	9.56	9.64	9.75	*9.83
Gross domestic product (GDP)	US$bn	538.20	523.94	579.53	570.14	*487.40
GDP per capita	US$	56,956	54,829	60,086	58,491	*49,582
GDP real growth	%	4.0	0.9	1.3	2.1	*2.7
Inflation	%	1.4	0.9	–	-0.2	*0.2
Unemployment	%	8.1	8.0	7.9	7.9	*7.7
Exports (fob) (goods)	US$m	188,640.0	184,827.0	181,289.0	178,849.0	–
Imports (fob) (goods)	US$m	175,972.0	163,264.0	159,578.0	161,397.0	–
Balance of trade	US$m	12,668.0	21,563.0	21,712.0	17,452.0	–
Current account	US$m	32,248.0	31,793.0	42,340.0	35,733.0	*30,759.0
Total reserves minus gold	US$m	44,624.0	45,519.0	60,495.0	57,704.0	–
Foreign exchange	US$m	39,659.8	40,294.0	55,375.0	–	–
Exchange rate	per US$	6.38	6.65	6.49	7.83	–

* estimated figure ** forecast figure

the low-skilled and foreign born represented a rising portion of the unemployed. Housing prices were rising fast from already elevated levels, resulting in households taking on higher debt burdens and making the economy more vulnerable to shocks. The lack of affordable housing in the major cities also undermined labour mobility, further dragging on Sweden's potential.

In the view of the IMF, Sweden's macro-economic policies should continue supporting domestic demand to bring inflation back to target and to contain unemployment. Fiscal, macro-prudential and housing policies should aid the rebalancing of housing supply and demand to moderate the rise in housing prices and debt. Labour market and integration policies should help the low skilled and migrants find work.

Sweden's inflation has picked up, but remained below the 2 per cent target. Underlying (CPIF) inflation excluding energy had risen to 1.4 per cent in August 2015, up from 0.75 per cent in 2014. And inflation expectations were more strongly anchored following the Sveriges Riksbank's (central bank) signal in February of its determination to raise inflation, with the shift to a negative repo rate and quantitative easing (QE).

This would allow a rebuilding of space for monetary policy to cushion external or domestic shocks. It would also protect the credibility of the inflation target as the benchmark for inflation expectations, which facilitates macro-economic stability, including through steady functioning of the wage formation process. Allowing low inflation to persist would also pose greater risks of deflation and would require lower, not higher, interest rates to maintain full employment.

Sweden's firmly stimulatory monetary stance should continue until core inflation was durably close to target. Monetary conditions were highly stimulatory when taking into account the downward shift in the yield curve and exchange rate movements. These stimulatory conditions supported inflation reaching the target within the next two years. Maintaining such conditions would require an extension of QE into 2016, depending on the inflation outlook.

In the view of the IMF, the Riksbank should remain ready to do more. There were some uncertainties around the timing of a rise in inflation. Appropriately, the Riksbank maintained a high level of preparedness to make monetary policy even more expansionary if this were to become necessary. With other instruments still available and given Sweden's strong external position, intervention in the foreign exchange market should be a last resort.

The IMF considered Sweden's fiscal stance in 2016 to be broadly appropriate. Fiscal policy was expected to be neutral over 2015–16, with annual variations mostly reflecting fluctuations in capital gains revenues. Such a stance was appropriate considering the need to avoid impeding monetary policy efforts to raise inflation and to help integrate large migrant inflows.

This was the time to start phasing out mortgage interest deductibility to help rebalance the housing market. Sweden's low level of recurrent property taxes meant that the fiscal environment strongly favoured debt-financed home ownership over renting, with higher income households benefitting disproportionately. A number of European countries had or were in the process of phasing out mortgage interest deductibility. Low interest rates and robust housing demand made this an ideal time to phase out deductibility in a fiscally neutral manner, thereby moderating house prices and household debt over time with limited effects on economic activity. Increasing the threshold for carrying forward capital gains taxes would alleviate 'lock in' effects, facilitating more efficient use of existing dwellings.

Sweden's fiscal framework had enabled a reduction in public debt to a modest level. From this strong position, Sweden needed to allow the full operation of automatic fiscal stabilisers over the cycle and be ready to support the economy in case of adverse developments. The current net lending target of a 1 per cent of GDP surplus over the cycle had served the country well, but a balanced target (excluding variations in the pension balance) could also safeguard Sweden's fiscal buffers.

High house prices and household debt increase the sensitivity of domestic demand and employment to shocks. International experience indicated that household deleveraging and wealth effects can give rise to prolonged recessions. Even if mortgage defaults are limited, significant distressed loans can emerge among firms reliant on the domestic market. It was therefore welcome that the Finansinspektionen (Financial Supervisory Authority (FSA)) was undertaking a review of risk weights on banks' corporate loan books.

Macro-prudential policies needed to protect financial resilience while containing the drag on economic growth. Although they cannot substitute for reforms to address structural imbalances in the housing market, such policies could help contain risks in the medium-term, especially during a period of exceptionally low interest rates.

Regional co-operation on financial stability issues and the resolution framework for large cross-border banks needed to be enhanced. In particular, regarding financial services group, Nordea's planned shift to a branch structure, robust cross-border supervisory co-operation was needed between the Swedish, regional and European authorities, such as information sharing, depositor protection and resolution arrangements.

In the view of the IMF, housing supply was falling behind rising needs. The slow response of new construction to urban population growth partly reflected municipal land acquisition and planning systems that limited competition. Rent controls had greatly reduced the supply of rental apartments by driving conversion to tenant ownership and deterring new construction. Moreover, lock-in effects from these controls hindered mobility and the efficient utilisation of the remaining rental supply. As a result, many young households had to buy rather than rent.

The Swedish labour market has become increasingly polarised. Although overall employment is high, unemployment falls heavily on the low skilled and the foreign-born. These gaps in part reflect high entry-level wages and strict employment protection for regular contracts. Rising migration inflows, with the majority being asylum seekers, would add to these challenges.

Sweden's labour market needs further adaptation to the evolving composition of its labour force. The IMF considered that Sweden's social partners should explore ways to ensure that entry-level wages were not a hurdle for groups with high unemployment to gain work, for example by introducing special wage scales for those needing on-the-job training or by enhancing flexibility. Adequate income could be ensured through social support and tax credits. Partners should also review employment protection for regular contracts so that these exit costs do not deter firms from giving opportunities to new entrants with sufficient skills. Greater emphasis on training that meets employer needs could better assist vulnerable groups gain jobs and early active labour market support should be provided where long-term unemployment risks are high. The effectiveness of public matching services could be increased by expanding contacts with employers and wage subsidies can be made more effective when combined with effective matching.

Faster integration of asylum seekers into the labour market was seen by the IMF as critical. Sweden has a well-developed introduction programme for asylum seekers; avoiding delays was particularly important given the rising numbers. The government was taking welcome steps to accelerate the integration process such as 'fast tracks' and should seek further improvements. Employment programmes for youth – which combined work and training – should be expanded to help newly-arrived refugees gain their first job and build needed skills.

Risk assessment

Economy	Good
Politics	Good
Regional stability	Good

Muslims in Sweden

% of population	70
Sunni (% of Muslims)	95
Shi'a (% of Muslims)	5

COUNTRY PROFILE

1397 Union of Kalmar united Denmark, Sweden and Norway under a single monarch with Denmark the dominant power.
1520 The Massacre of Stockholm occurred when the Danish King Kristian II, in an attempt to assert his supremacy, executed resisting Swedish noblemen, which led to a revolt, headed by Gustav Eriksson Vasa.
1523 King Kristian II was defeated by Vasa, who was crowned Gustav I. Sweden was separated from the Union. Vasa's victory heralded the start of Sweden's ascendancy in Europe.
1611 Gustav II Adolph (Gustavus Adolphus) became King. He engaged in expansionist policies and attempted to gain control of the Baltic trading routes; this brought him into conflict with neighbouring states.
1629 Sweden fought to possess Prussia and Pomerania (now part of Germany) in the Thirty Years War.
1632 Gustav II was killed at the battle of Lutzen (in Saxony, now part of Germany) and was succeeded by his daughter, Kristina.
1654 Kristina abdicated after converting to Catholicism – an act that was unacceptable in Lutheran Sweden.
1700 Start of the Great Nordic War when Russia, Denmark, Norway and Poland formed an alliance against Sweden and its 15-year old King Karl XII in an attempt to retrieve some of their lost lands.
1700–1720 A succession of battles resulted in the loss of all Swedish lands in Germany, the Baltic provinces of Russia and much of Finland. Success against the Danes in Norway allowed Sweden to consolidate into easily defended borders.
1718 The power of the monarchy diminished and was vested in the Council of Aristocrats who depended on parliament for its authority.
1772 King Gustav III began reforms that strengthened the power of the monarchy. These developments resulted in an almost absolute monarchy.
1792 King Gustav III was assassinated by members of the Swedish nobility. Gustav IV Adolf became King.
1808–09 Sweden was defeated by the Russians. Finland, which was then part of Sweden, was ceded to Russia. King Gustav IV Adolf was replaced by Karl XIII in 1809.
1814 Sweden entered a union with Norway.
1905 The emergence of Norwegian nationalism led Norway to declare independence. A parliamentary form of government emerged in Sweden.
1920s The Sveriges Socialdemokratiska Arbetarparti (Swedish Social Democratic Party) first came to power. It typically contested elections under the name Arbetarepartiet-Socialdemokraterna (Labour Party-Social Democrats) but was commonly referred to as the Socialdemokraterna (Social Democrats). Except for a brief period during 1936, the Social Democrats stayed in power from 1932 to 1976.
1939–45 Sweden declared its neutrality during the Second World War, although German troops were transported through its territory to Norway. Sweden also supplied Nazi Germany with iron ore until 1943.
1952 Sweden became a founder member of the Nordic Council.
1959 Sweden became a founder member of the European Free Trade Area (EFTA) with Austria, Denmark, Norway, Portugal, Switzerland and the UK.
1969–71 Olof Palme (prime minister 1969–76 and 1982–86) introduced constitutional reforms. The bicameral legislature was replaced by a unicameral legislature, elected by proportional representation.
1975 A new constitution was promulgated; it reduced the power of the monarchy and limited its role to that of figurehead and ceremonial duties.
1976 A centre-right coalition government, the Centerpartiet (Cp) (Centre Party), and Moderata Samlingspartiet (Moderata) (Moderate Party) won the parliamentary election.
1978 The coalition government collapsed due to disagreement about economic problems and the building of a controversial nuclear power plant. The former coalition partner, Folkpartiet Liberalerna (FpL) (Liberal People's Party) formed a new government.
1979 The Cp won the parliamentary elections by a one seat majority.
1982 The Socialdemokraterna won the parliamentary elections. Olof Palme became prime minister again.
1986 Palme was assassinated in Stockholm by an unknown gunman.
1991 After parliamentary elections, Moderata formed the government with Carl Bildt as prime minister.
1994 The Socialdemokraterna won the general election. Sweden joined Nato's Partnership for Peace (PfP) military co-operation programme.
1995 Sweden joined the EU.
1996 Carlsson stepped down as the leader of the SSA and prime minister. Göran Persson replaced him.
1998 Following parliamentary elections the SSA formed a minority government. The reduced vote for the Socialdemokraterna was believed to be due to widespread anger at social expenditure cuts.
2002 The Socialdemokraterna won the parliamentary elections and continued to lead a minority government that relied on support from the Vänsterpartiet (V) (Left Party) and the Miljöpartiet de Gröna (MP) (Environmental Party the Greens).
2003 Foreign Minister Anna Lindh was stabbed to death in a Stockholm department store. In a referendum voters narrowly defeated the proposal to join the single European currency.
2004 The man who confessed to killing Anna Lindh was convicted of her murder and sentenced to life imprisonment, overturning a previous ruling which consigned him to a psychiatric hospital.
2006 In parliamentary elections the ruling Socialdemokraterna narrowly lost with 46.2 per cent against the opposition coalition, led by Moderata Samlingspartiet (Moderate) (Moderate Coalition Party), which won with 48.1 per cent of the vote (178 seats in the 349 legislative assembly); turnout was 80.4 per cent. Fredrik Reinfeldt (Moderate) became prime minister.
2008 Around 100 countries took part in a conference held outside Stockholm to discuss support and efforts to restore stability and rebuild a functioning economy in Iraq. De rödgröna (Red-Green) coalition was formed by three political parties.
2009 After 17 years of sanctions imposed against Iraq by the UN, the Swedish

airline, Nordic Leisure, flew the first commercial flight between Iraq and Europe, with around 150 passengers, mainly Iraqis.

2010 In parliamentary elections, the ruling Social Democrats won 30.66 per cent of the vote (112 seats out of 349), closely followed by Moderata with 30.06 per cent (107). The right-wing nationalist Sverigedemokraterna (SD) (Sweden Democrats) won 5.7 per cent and its first seats in parliament (20). A coalition of four centre-right parties, formally called the Alliansen (Alliance), consisting of the Moderata, MP, Cp and KD, retained power although as a minority government; Fredrik Reinfeldt remained as prime minister.

2011 In March Haakan Juholt (S) became leader of the oposition Socialdemokratiska (S) (Social Democrats). In July two Swedish reporters were arrested in Ethiopia and charged with terrorism, having crossed the border from Somalia in the company of a separatist rebel group. In December they were sentenced to 11 years in prison. On 19 December 2011, the automotive company Saab was declared bankrupt by its chief executive, and ceased operations.

2012 On 21 January, Haakan Juholt (S) resigned as leader, following nine months of increasing criticism and fall in support for his leadership. On 10 September, the two jailed journalists were freed in Ethiopia, following a presidential pardon. On 16 November, the furniture maker and retailer, Ikea, apologised for the use of political prisoners in Communist East Germany and Cuba for almost 30 years from the 1970s. A spokesperson said that at that time Ikea did not have a well organised control system to prevent the use of prisoners and forced labour.

2014 Elections were held to the Riksdag on 14 September. The results were a win for the Sveriges Socialdemokratiska arbetareparti (SAP) (Swedish Social Democratic Party) with 31.01 per cent (113 seats, out of 349).

2015 A YouGov poll published in *Metro* newspaper on 20 August gave the Sweden Democrats support of 25.2 per cent of voters, ahead of the ruling Social Democrats with 23.4 per cent and the centre-right Moderates with 21 per cent.

Political structure

Constitution

The Constitution consists of four separate documents: the *Regeringsformen* (Instrument of Government) passed in 1974, *Successionsordningen* (Act of Succession) dating from 1810, the *Tryckfrihetsförordningen* (Freedom of the Press Act) of 1949 (originating from 1766), and the *Yttrandefrihetsgrundlagen* (Freedom of Expression Act) of 1991.

There are 288 municipalities throughout the country, each with a popularly elected council. Immigrants, resident for three years, have the right to vote and run for office in local elections.

Universal suffrage is at aged 18. Voter turnout is traditionally high, between 85–90 per cent.

Under proportional representation 310 parliamentary seats are allocated on a constituency basis, in 28 multi-member constituencies; the remaining seats are divided nationally. To win parliamentary representation, a party must poll either 4 per cent overall – to receive a seat from the national allocation – or 12 per cent in any one constituency for a seat from the national remainder.

Form of state

Parliamentary democratic monarchy

The executive

Executive power is exercised by the Regeringen (cabinet) which is led by the prime minister (elected by parliament) and is responsible to parliament. The prime minister appoints members of the cabinet.

National legislature

The unicameral Riksdag (parliament) has 349 members directly elected by proportional representation, for a four-year term. 39 of the members are directly elected in 'at large' seats. In the event of an early dissolution, the new parliament serves only the remainder of the previous parliament's term.

Legal system

The legal system is divided into the general courts and the general administrative courts. The general courts are composed of a Supreme Court (Högsta domstolen), six Courts of Appeal and 95 District Courts which are responsible for criminal cases involving individuals. The Supreme Court is the highest court in the land and is composed of 16 judges appointed by the government. The general administrative courts are responsible for cases involving public authorities and individuals.

Last elections

14 September 2014 (parliamentary).

Results: Parliamentary: the Sveriges Socialdemokratiska Srbetareparti (SAP) (Swedish Social Democrats) won 30.01 per cent of the vote (113 seats out of 349), Moderata Samlingspartiet (Moderata) (Moderate Party) 23.33 per cent (84), Sverigedemokraterna (SD) (Sweden Democrats) 12.86 per cent (49), Miljöpartiet de Gröna (MP) (Environmental Party the Greens) 6.89 per cent (25), Centerpartiet (Cp) (Centre Party) 6.11 per cent (22), Vänsterpartiet (V) (Left Party) 5.72 per cent (21), Folkpartiet Liberalerna (FpL) (Liberal People's Party) 5.42 per cent (19), Kristdemokraterna (KD) (Christian Democrats) 4.57 per cent (16); turnout was 85.81 per cent.

Next elections

9 September 2018 (parliamentary)

Political parties

Ruling party

Minority government lead by Sveriges Socialdemokratiska Srbetareparti (SAP) (Swedish Social Democrats) with Miljöpartiet de Gröna (MP) (Environmental Party the Greens)

Main opposition party

Arbetarepartiet-Socialdemokraterna (Labour Party-Social Democrats, known as Socialdemokratiska (S) (Social Democrats)

Population

9.63 million (2013). Since the 1940s, immigration, mostly from neighbouring Scandinavian countries, has accounted for over 40 per cent of population growth. About 85 per cent of the total population lives in the southern half of the country. From 2014, refugees and asylum seekers from the Middle East, especially Syria, and Africa changed the migrant profile. Some 100,000 arrived in Sweden in 2014 and 120,000 had applied for residence by mid-2015.

Last census: 31 December 2003: 8,975,670

Population density: 20 inhabitants per square km. Urban population 85 per cent (2010 Unicef).

Annual growth rate: 0.5 per cent, 1990–2010 (Unicef).

Ethnic make-up

Native Swedes account for 88 per cent of the population. Around 50 per cent of all foreign nationals are from other Nordic countries (Denmark, Finland, Iceland and Norway).

Sweden has two minority groups of native inhabitants in the north: the Finnish speaking people of the north-east and an estimated 17,000 Sámi (Lapp) people.

Religions

About 90 per cent of the population belong to the Church of Sweden (Lutheran); there are 8 per cent other Protestants and 1 per cent Roman Catholics.

Education

Pre-school classes are offered to any six year old enrolled, the first (and compulsory) school begins at aged seven; both are free of charge and the majority are run by municipalities. In 2001–02 over one million pupils were enrolled (within both); independent schools accounted for 1 per cent of enrolments. The average number of pupils per school was 209, with an average of 108 pupils in independent schools. Many schools are now working with integrated age levels where children of different ages are taught together in the same class. Around

three-quarters of all compulsory schools are connected to the Internet. At aged 16 students who have successfully completed their compulsory schooling progress to upper secondary school. Nearly all pupils continue to the upper secondary school. Each municipality has the right to establish its own upper secondary schools and a national curriculum provides a basis for further studies and basic eligibility for higher education.
Higher education is offered in 13 state-run universities and 23 university colleges. There are also three private universities: Chalmers University of Technology, the University College of Jönköping and the Stockholm School of Economics. Further education for adults (aged 20 years and over) is offered within the public adult education system through municipal adult education.
Literacy rate: 99 per cent, adult rate (2003)
Compulsory years: 7 to 16
Enrolment rate: 107 per cent gross primary enrolment, 140 per cent gross secondary enrolment: of relevant age groups (including repeaters and training for unemployed within the age group) (World Bank 2001).
Pupils per teacher: 12 in primary schools

Health
Sweden has for many years actively worked with health promotion in line with the World Health Organisation's (WHO) European 'Health for All' policy. There is a close collaboration between the government and local and regional providers of public medical and healthcare services.
A governmental body, the National Public Health Committee, is responsible for providing many recommendations to the government, along with wide-ranging consultation, is being used as a basis for the future development of the healthcare system.
The public sector finances health services, through taxation, for the entire population although the Federation of Health Insurance Societies, (established in 1907), helps to promote a national compulsory system of health insurance.

HIV/Aids
HIV prevalence: 0.1 per cent aged 15–49 in 2003 (World Bank)
Life expectancy: 81 years, 2004 (WHO 2006)
Fertility rate/Maternal mortality rate: 1.9 births per woman, 2010 (Unicef)
Birth rate/Death rate: 9.7 births and 10.6 deaths per 1,000 people (2003)
Child (under 5 years) mortality rate (per 1,000): 3 per 1,000 live births (WHO 2012)
Head of population per physician: 3.28 physicians per 1,000 people, 2002 (WHO 2006)

Welfare
The Swedish social insurance system is managed by the state and is compulsory for everyone, providing means-tested and general benefits. The main goal of the social insurance is to provide protection against loss of income and is composed of sickness insurance, early retirement pensions, occupational injury insurance and old age pensions. The Social Services Act of 1982 regulates the welfare benefit system while the National Board of Health and Welfare (Socialstyrelsen) supervises the overall quality of social service provision.
A Social Insurance Act was introduced in 2001, dividing social insurance into two categories: a domicile-based insurance scheme, which provides guaranteed benefits, and a work-related insurance scheme, which safeguards against loss of income. These insurance systems are available to anyone living or working in Sweden. Social insurance is divided into 50 per cent going into pensions, 25 per cent to sickness and disability benefit and 15 per cent to families with children.
The pension system was reformed in 1998 and is composed of various components, including an income-related pension, a premium pension and a guaranteed pension. The premium pension allows a person to invest their own funds into part of the pension scheme. A state pension is guaranteed to all the population on a low income or without any income.

Main cities
Stockholm (capital, estimated population 1.3 million in 2012), Göteborg (528,237), Malmö (269,549), Uppsala (135,367), Västerås (109,092), Örebro (101,614), Linköping (101,031), Helsingborg (95,886).

Languages spoken
Finnish, Skäine and Sámi are spoken. English, and to a lesser extent German, are also widely spoken.

Official language/s
Swedish

Media

Press
Dailies: In Swedish, the most influential nationals are either owned or run by political parties and trade unions. These include *Aftonbladet* (www.aftonbladet.se) (Social Democratic), *Dagens Nyheter* (www.dn.se) (Liberal, independent), *Expressen*(www.expressen.se) (Liberal), *Göteborgs-Posten* (www.gp.se) (Liberal), *Svenska Dagbladet* (www.svd.se) (Conservative) *Sydsvenska Dagbladet* (www.sydsvenskan.se) and *Aktuellt I Politiken* (www.aip.nu). In Finnish *Ruotsin Suomalainen* (www.ruotsinsuomalainen.com).
Regional publications in Swedish, include from Stockholm *Kristdemokraten* (www.kristdemokraten.com) *Metro* (www.metro.se), from *GT* (www.gt.se), from Malmo *Kvallsposten* (www.kvp.se) and *SVT Sydnytt* (www.svt.se/sydnytt) and from Uppsala *Upplands Nyheter* (www.upplandsnyheter.se) and *Uppsalanytt* (www.uppsalanytt.se).
Weeklies: Main Sunday newspapers and weekly publications include for men *Café* (www.cafe.se), *Se och Hör* (TV listings), *Aftonbladet* (www.aftonbladet.se) and *Dagens Nyheter* (www.dn.se).
Business: In Swedish, *Affärsvärlden* (www.affarsvarlden.se) is the oldest and most respected business magazine. Other publications include the weekly *Ekonominyheterna* (http://ekonominyheterna.se) an affiliate of *Veckans Affärer*, the daily *Dagens Industri* (http://di.se) and *Finanstidningen* (owned by the major media organisation Modern Times Group). *Fri Kopenskap* (www.fri-kopenskap.se) and *Privata Affarer* (www.privataaffarer.se) are published in Stockholm.
Periodicals: These include *Galago* (on culture), *Grönköpings Veckoblad* (www.gronkoping.nu) a literary magazine *Moderna*, *Slitz* (www.slitz.se) is a magazine for men. Two major women's magazine include *Amelia* (www.amelia.se), published fortnightly, which is Sweden's most popular and *Vecko Revyn* (www.veckorevyn.com) is a tabloid style publication.

Broadcasting
All broadcasting is overseen by Granskningsnamnden (Swedish Broadcasting Commission). State broadcasting is provided by Sveriges Television and Radio.
Radio: There are four national radio stations provided by Sveriges Radio (www.sr.se), with news broadcasts provided in 14 foreign languages. External services can by accessed via short wave, or on-demand through the internet, which also has archived and live transmissions. There are around commercial 100 radio stations some of which have drawn together to produce near-national networks. The largest stations and networks include Rix FM (www.rixfm.com), NRJ (www.nrj.se), Mix Megapol (www.mixmegapol.com) and Radio Match (www.radiomatch.com).
Television: All Swedish television will be provided by digital signals by 2008. Most homes have cable or satellite reception with dozens of channels on offer.
Sveriges Television (svt.se) has 2 major networks and a 24 hour news channel, as

well as special interest programmes via satellite TV. There are four commercial TV channels including TV3 (www.tv3.se), TV4 (www.tv4.se), Kanal 5 (http://kanal5.se) and ZTV (www.ztv.se).

Other news agencies: TT (Tidnignarnas Telegrambyrå) 105 12 Stockholm, (tel: 692-2600; fax: 692-2855; email: redaktionen@tt.se). TT is a private independent agency.

Economy

Sweden has an advanced economy ranging from primary industries to sophisticated industrial processes to high-end service industries. Its main industries include agriculture, principally timber production due its 41 million hectares of mixed forests. The service industries include tourism and financial services, centred on the Nordic Stock Exchange (OMX), based in Stockholm.

GDP growth declined to -0.8 per cent, as the global economic crisis struck and exports of Swedish consumer durables fell. As credit was severely limited and financial wholesale markets closed, investment dried up so that in 2009 the situation deteriorated further with GDP growth at -4.8 per cent. As global trade recovered in 2010, so too GDP growth rebounded with a high of 5.8 per cent. It fell back in 2011, to an estimated 4 per cent, the weakness due largely to the insecurity caused by the drop in exports. In 2012 it had dropped even further to 0.9 per cent, and improved slightly to 1.5 per cent in 2013. 2.3 per cent represents a large improvement for the Swedish economy in 2014.

As Swedish exports are predominately capital goods and consumer durables the economy is vulnerable to international shocks. It was one of the first economies to go into recession, and did not recover until other countries were able to begin spending again. Income, employment and confidence in Sweden were depressed, which slowed private consumption, and further weakened GDP growth.

External trade

As a member of the European Union (EU), Sweden operates within a community-wide free trade area, with tariffs set as a whole, however it does not belong to the European Monetary Union and retains the krona as its currency. Internationally, the EU has free trade agreements with a number of nations and trading blocs worldwide. Over 50 per cent of all exports are traded with the EU.

Merchandise trade accounts for 57 per cent of GDP, whilst goods exports totalled US$181 billion for 2013.

Imports

Main imports include machinery, petroleum and derivatives, chemicals, vehicles, iron and steel, foodstuffs, consumer goods and clothing.

Main sources: Germany (17.2 per cent of total in 2014), Norway (7.9 per cent), Denmark (7.7 per cent)

Exports

Main exports include machinery (35 per cent), motor vehicles, paper product, pulp and wood, iron and steel products and chemicals.

Main destinations: Norway (10.3 per cent of total in 2014), Germany (9.7 per cent), United Kingdom (7.0 per cent)

Agriculture

Farming

Although Sweden is one of the biggest countries in Europe, its arable land amounts to only 2.8 million hectares (ha) constituting about 7 per cent of the total land area. Grain is harvested on 45 per cent of arable land. Agriculture contributes 2 per cent of GDP and employs less than 2 per cent of the total work force. Dairy products, grains, sugar beets and potatoes are produced. There are 1.7 million cows in the country. Over the past decade, cattle herd numbers have fallen while yields have risen.

Most farms are family concerns, in which members of the family do the work. Part-time farming, with income supplemented by other employment (e.g. forestry), has become a common feature. Restructuring and modernisation of equipment has resulted in fewer but larger farms. Farming is concentrated in the southern regions, where livestock farming predominates.

Sweden's adherence to the EU's Common Agricultural Policy (CAP) has introduced some regulation to agriculture. Agricultural support policies have been adjusted to CAP, including production quotas and increased export subsidies. Import licences are required for certain agricultural commodities.

Fishing

The Swedish market for seafood is typically over 150,000 tonnes annually calculated on the basis of product weight. Estimated output from the domestic seafood processing sector amounts to around 85,000 tonnes per year. About 75 per cent of this amount is for the home market with marinated herring the most important product. Over half of the fishing industry is located in western Sweden. In addition to coastal and deep-sea fishing around the western coast, Sweden has an abundance of natural lakes, which can provide enough fish to meet domestic needs.

Most fish imports are from Norway and Denmark, which together typically account for 75 per cent of total Swedish imports, indicating the importance of the Scandinavian link in its seafood industry.

As the EU presses for radical reform to its Common Fisheries Policy (CFP), Sweden is expected to support its principles based on the ecosystem approach.

Forestry

Forest and other wooded land accounts for nearly 75 per cent of the land area, with forest cover estimated at 27.1 million hectares (ha). Approximately 23 million ha of forest area is available for wood supply. Spruce and pine are the main species of tree in Sweden, and make up 80 per cent of total timber stock.

The forest industry and forestry account for 3 per cent of Sweden's GDP, 12 per cent of industrial employment and 12 per cent of Sweden's exports. Sweden's pulp and paper industry is the third largest in Europe after Germany and Finland. About one-third of Sweden's wood pulp and over half of its paper and board are exported. Sweden accounts for more than 13 per cent of paper demand in the EU. Following large scale divestiture, 50 per cent of forest land is owned privately, 14 per cent is owned by the state (primarily through Sveaskog AB) and 25 per cent through commercial companies.

Industry and manufacturing

The powerful industrial sector accounts for 75 per cent of all exports and has traditionally afforded the Swedish people one of the highest standards of living in the world. Industrial strength was traditionally based on extensive reserves of iron, timber and the rivers and lakes that provided cheap energy, although in recent years hi-tech production has increased in significance. With such a small domestic market, industry has always had to look overseas for survival and it profited from the development of a mature export culture. Industry accounted for 12 per cent of GDP in 2014.

Beyond the diminishing state sector, private ownership is generally concentrated in relatively few hands, including institutional investors and several family dynasties, such as the Wallenbergs (Ericsson, Eletrolux and other major companies) and Bonniers (Bonnier AB media group).

The state is gradually decreasing its ownership in firms under its control. The government is committed to ending state subsidies for inefficient industries. As a result of this policy, traditional sectors, such as shipyards and the textile industry, have virtually ceased to exist. In other traditional industries, there has been drastic rationalisation and concentration on narrow segments of the market.

The industrial sector is based largely on indigenous resources (iron ore, timber and water-power). Major industries include motor vehicles, food processing, chemicals, iron and steel, transportation equipment, electrical and electronic equipment and forestry products. Sweden's industrial structure tends to be centred on large, capital-intensive companies, due to the nature of tax, social security and labour market regulations, which do not favour smaller firms.

Engineering is Sweden's main industrial sector, accounting for around a third of industrial output and for a similar proportion of exports. The country's main engineering companies include Ericsson, Electrolux, Volvo (owned by Ford), SKF, Saab, Scania and Sandvik.

Manufacturing accounts for some 16 per cent of GDP and employs approximately 20 per cent of the workforce.

Information technology (IT) is an important contributor to the economy. Internet companies in Sweden are mostly managing to survive the burst of the 'dotcom' bubble (boo.com was a notable exception in 2001) and the country is at the forefront of the development of mobile telephone internet technology. Sweden is also beginning to lead the way in the biotechnology sector and has more biotech companies per capita than any other country.

Timber production accounts for just over a fifth of industrial output. Sweden has a large forestry sector supplying raw materials to industry and for export.

Ericsson is not Sweden's only well-known company; the furniture retailer, IKEA, has 301 stores in 37 countries. AGA and Electrolux are other well-known brands. Volvo, now owned by Ford Motor Company, and Saab Automotives, owned by General Motors, sell their cars worldwide. Hennes and Mauritz (H&M) is considered one of the world's most profitable fashion retailers.

Tourism

Although Sweden does not offer typical sun-sea-surf holidays, it can provide many water activities, cultural city events plus rural settings for a relaxed stay. Sweden is also an important market for foreign companies.

Sweden has 14 sites included on Unesco's World Heritage List that range from prehistoric, archaeological locations to historic buildings and gardens and natural sites.

Travel and tourism in total contributed 9.5 per cent of GDP in 2014, which is predicted to rise by 4.7 per cent for 2015. The industry provided employment indirectly to 11 per cent of the workforce (527,000 jobs) in the same period. Visitor numbers in 2007 were 5.2 million, which fell steadily to 4.9 million by 2010 and have remained largely the same in 2014. However, visitor exports in the same period rose from US$12.2 billion in 2007 to US$13.3 billion in 2010 and further to US$16.3 billion in 2013 before falling to US$11.8 billion in 2014.

Sweden is a popular destination for shopping trips by its neighbours and those accessing health clinics and wellness facilities.

There is a comprehensive public transport service that can move visitors from Sweden's airports and ferry ports around the country in a degree of comfort, coupled with an active private hire car sector.

Mining

The mining sector typically accounts for 9 per cent of GDP and employs 0.5 per cent of the industrial workforce.

Sweden is rich in mineral deposits, the most important of which are iron ore, zinc, lead, copper, silver and pyrites. There are also large deposits of uranium, exploitation of which has been limited by environmental and political objections.

Swedish companies focus on making high quality speciality iron and steel. Sweden's share of total world iron ore output comes to around 2 per cent, making Sweden one of the largest iron ore exporters in Europe. Sweden's shares of the Western world's production of copper, lead and zinc concentrates amount to 1 per cent, 3.7 per cent and 3.3 per cent, respectively.

The continuous demand on the global mineral and metal markets gives Sweden an extraordinary position with its favorable investment climate and mineral-rich bedrock. The vision of growth suggests that Sweden will triple its mining production by 2025. This would create more than 50,000 new jobs.

The country is a significant ore producer in the EU having accounted for between 80 and 90 percent of the EU's iron ore in 2011. Even with respect to other metals such as copper, zinc and silver, Sweden is among the major producers in the EU.

Hydrocarbons

Sweden is sparse in hydrocarbon resources and has limited reserves. As a result, oil represents a large proportion of total Swedish imports, approximately 300 thousand barrels per day (bpd). Swedish refineries have an annual capacity of 503,000bpd. The largest, Scanraff, north of Göteborg, has a capacity of over 200,000bpd. Natural gas is imported in small quantities through a pipeline from Denmark across the Baltic Straits, for use in southern Sweden. In 2012 consumption of natural gas was 1,129 million cubic metres. Consumption of coal was 2.8 million tonnes in 2012.

As of 2006 the Swedish government has been on a mission to become the world's first oil-free nation by 2020. In 2013, oil consumption was 307,000bpd, which was a 13.3 per cent reduction from 354,000bpd in 2006. Oil in 2013 accounted for under 27 per cent of Sweden's energy, an enormous decrease from 77 per cent in 1970.

Energy

Around 15 per cent of the country's energy supply is obtained from its hydroelectric plants, many of them on the main northern rivers. Over 40 per cent of energy consumed comes from imported oil, 7 per cent from imported coal and coke. Sweden's operational nuclear reactors provide over 15 per cent of total energy (almost 50 per cent of electrical energy). The rest of the energy supply comes from a number of sources, including bio-fuels, peat and waste heat.

Sweden is sparse in hydrocarbon resources and has limited reserves. As a result, oil represents a large proportion of total Swedish imports, approximately 300 thousand barrels per day (bpd). Swedish refineries have an annual capacity of 503,000bpd. The largest, Scanraff, north of Göteborg, has a capacity of over 200,000bpd. Natural gas is imported in small quantities through a pipeline from Denmark across the Baltic Straits, for use in southern Sweden. In 2012 consumption of natural gas was 1,129 million cubic metres. Consumption of coal was 2.8 million tonnes in 2012.

Financial markets

Stock exchange

Stockholmsbörsen (Stockholm Stock Exchange)

Banking and insurance

Liberalisation and increased openness has boosted the competitiveness of the Swedish financial sector. There have been serveral mergers between banking and insurance firms. There is a predominance of large corporations in the sector. More than 70 per cent of people in this sector are employed by firms with a payroll of more than 200.

Central bank

Sveriges Riksbank

Main financial centre

Stockholm

Time

GMT plus one hour (daylight saving, late March to late October, GMT plus two hours)

Geography

Sweden is situated in northern Europe. It occupies about 66 per cent of the Scandinavian peninsula and is bordered by Finland to the north-east and Norway to the west. Sweden has a long coastline, with the Baltic Sea and the Gulf of Bothnia to the east and the Skagerrak and Kattegat to the south-west.

Approximately 15 per cent of Sweden lies north of the Arctic Circle. There are thousands of lakes and islands. Around 54 per cent of the country is covered in coniferous forests. Agricultural land is located in the southern plains, where the population is most concentrated. The central region comprises lowlands. The west bordering Norway is mountainous, from which numerous rivers drain into the Gulf of Bothnia; the highest point in Sweden at 2,111m is Mount Kebnekaise.

Hemisphere

Northern

Climate

Because of the Atlantic gulf stream, Sweden has a milder climate than some other regions in the same latitude. The average winter temperature in the north, where there is always snow from December to March, is minus 13 degrees Celsius (C), in central Sweden minus 3 degrees C and in the south minus 1 degree C. In summer average temperatures are 13 degrees C in the north, 18 degrees C in central Sweden and 17 degrees C in the south.

Dress codes

Clothing to suit the climate is vital because of the extremes. Heavy coats, warm boots, gloves and ear protection are required in winter and light clothing in summer.

Swedes can be informal in business attire, but suits are worn at business meetings and for social events in the evening.

Entry requirements

Passports

Required by all, except nationals of countries which are signatories of the Schengen Accords, which includes most EU/EEA member states, who may visit on national IDs.

Visa

Required by all, except nationals of EU countries, Iceland, Norway, North America, Australasia and Japan, for up to three months. For those requiring a visa, a Schengen visa covers all entry needs; for business trips, an invitation from a business contact in Sweden and proof of occupation and travel funds should be included when applying. A Schengen visa application (offered in several languages) can be downloaded from http://europa.eu/abc/travel/ see 'documents you will need'.

Currency advice/regulations

There are no restrictions on the import and export of local or foreign currencies.

Customs

Personal items are duty-free.There are no duties levied on alcohol and tobacco between EU member states, providing amounts imported are for personal consumption.

Health (for visitors)

Nationals of the European Economic Area (EEA) countries and Switzerland can access reduced cost and sometimes free medical treatment using a European Health Insurance Card (EHIC) while visiting the EEA. Exceptions include nationals of the 10 countries which joined the EU in 2004, whose EHIC is not valid in Switzerland. Applications for the EHIC should be made before travelling.

Mandatory precautions

Vaccination certificates not required unless travelling from an infected area.

Advisable precautions

Up-to-date tetanus and polio immunisations are recommended.

Hotels

There is no official rating system in operation. There is a shortage of accommodation in major cities so reservations should be made well in advance.

Public holidays (national)

Fixed dates

1 Jan (New Year's Day), 6 Jan (Epiphany), 1 May (Labour Day), 6 June (National Day), 24–26 Dec (Christmas).

Variable dates

Good Friday, Easter Monday, Ascension Day, Whit Monday, Midsummer Holiday (fourth Sat in Jun), All Saints' Day (first Sat in Nov).

Working hours

Banking

Mon–Fri: 0930–1500 (larger branches open longer).

Business

Mon–Fri: 0830–1700 (often closed one hour earlier in summer).

Government

Mon–Fri 0900–1700.

Shops

Mon–Fri: 0900–1800 (closed 1400 or 1600 on Sat).

Telecommunications

Mobile/cell phones

There are 3G, 900 and 1800 GSM (including WAP, GPRS, SMS and MMS) services throughout the country.

Electricity supply

220V AC

Social customs/useful tips

Swedes appreciate punctuality. A gift of flowers is usual when visiting a business partner's home for the first time. Guests should not start drinking before their hosts have proposed their health.

Think twice before refusing to go to a sauna with a host, since such an invitation is seen as a gesture of confidence and friendship by your host. Business meetings are sometimes conducted in saunas.

Security

Sweden has very low rates of violent crime, but some districts in the major cities should be avoided, particularly at night and particularly by women. Car burglaries and drugs-related crimes are increasing.

Getting there

Air

National airline: Scandinavian Airlines System (SAS).

International airport/s: Stockholm-Arlanda (ARN), 45km north of capital; Stockholm-Västerås (VST), 5km east of Västerås; Göteborg-Landvetter (GOT), 25km east of Göteborg; Malmö-Sturup (MMX), 30km east of Malmö.

Airport tax: None

Surface

Road: Sweden can be reached by road from Denmark via the Øresund tunnel and bridge link between Copenhagen and Malmö. There is also road access from Norway and Finland.

Rail: Statens Jarnvagar (SJ) (State Railways) is the major rail company in Sweden. It runs international high-speed trains between either Stockholm/Göteborg-Copenhagen (Denmark) – journey time five hours/3.30 hours; Stockholm-Oslo – journey time 4.45 hours. These services offer business class accommodation. Overnight trains with sleeping coaches are available between Berlin (Germany) and Malmö.

Water: There are ferry links with ports in northern and eastern Europe.

Getting about

National transport

Air: There are daily flights connecting all main towns, some by SAS and others by small local airlines.

Road: Sweden has a well-developed and maintained road network totalling about 420,000km, two-thirds of which are privately-managed, including unpaved forestry roads. Most private roads are open to the public. At least 95 per cent of traffic is carried by the national and municipal roads. There are around 20,000km of motorways.

Dipped headlights during the day are mandatory. The roads are snow-bound or icy during the winter months, when appropriate tyres are a requirement.

Buses: Efficient bus service, mainly controlled by the Statens Jarnvagar (SJ) (State Railways). Services integrated with rail service.

Rail: There are good, reliable rail links between most major cities and towns, especially in the south. Seats on express services must be booked in advance.

Water: There is an extensive ferry network in and around Sweden.

City transport
Taxis: Available in all major towns. If you order a taxi in advance there is an extra charge. Some taxi companies offer flat rates for travel within urban areas, and others have special fares for women travelling alone at night.
Gratuities for taxis are around 10 per cent.
Buses, trams & metro: All rail, bus and tram services have a unified ticketing system. Books of 20 travel coupons are available for purchase at Press Agency news-stands.
A city transfer service links Arland and Västerås airports with Stockholm city centre, with a journey time of about 40 minutes. The journey time from Västerås airport is around 75 minutes.
Trams run in the southern parts of Bromma and Lidingö.
Metro: The *Tunnelbana* serves many districts of Stockholm, with 100 stations marked by a blue T sign. The extended rail service includes outlying suburbs.
Car hire
Available at all airports and in most towns and cities.

BUSINESS DIRECTORY

The addresses listed below are a selection only. While World of Information makes every endeavour to check these addresses, we cannot guarantee that changes have not been made, especially to telephone numbers and area codes. We would welcome any corrections.

Telephone area codes
The international direct dialling code (IDD) for Sweden is +46, followed by area code and subscriber's number:

Gävle	26	Malmö	40
Göteborg	31	Norrköping	11
Helsingborg	42	Oxelösund	155
Jönköping	36	Stockholm	8
Karlskrona	455	Sundsvall	60
Karlstad	54	Umeå	90
Luleå	920	Uppsala	18

Useful telephone numbers
Police, fire and ambulance: 112

Chambers of Commerce
American Chamber of Commerce in Sweden, 3 Jakobs Torg, PO Box 16050, 10321 Stockholm (tel: 5061-2610; fax: 5061-2910; e-mail: amcham@chamber.se).

British Swedish Chamber of Commerce, 3 Jakobs Torg, PO Box 16050, 10321 Stockholm (tel: 5061-2617; fax: 5061-2915; e-mail: bscc@chamber.se).

Central Sweden Chamber of Commerce, 1 Linnévägen, PO Box 296, 80104 Gävle (tel: 662-080; fax: 662-099; e-mail: chamber@mhk.cci.se).

East Sweden Chamber of Commerce, 3 Nya Rådstugugatan, 60224 Norrköping (tel: 28-5030; fax: 13-7719; e-mail: info@east.cci.se).

Jönköping Chamber of Commerce, 11 Elmiavägen, 55454 Jönköping (tel: 301-430; fax: 129-579; e-mail: jncci@jn.wtc.se).

Mid Sweden Chamber of Commerce, 26 Kyrkogatan, 85232 Sundsvall (tel: 171-880; fax: 618-640; e-mail: sdl@mid-chamber.cci.se).

Southern Sweden Chamber of Commerce and Industry, 2 Skeppsbron, 21120 Malmö (tel: 690-2400; fax: 690-2490; e-mail: info@handelskammaaren.com).

Stockholm Chamber of Commerce, 9 Västra Trädsgårdsgatan, PO Box 16050, 10321 Stockholm (tel: 5551-0000; fax: 5663-1635; e-mail: info@chamber.se).

Swedish Chambers of Commerce, 9 Västra Trädsgårdsgatan, PO Box 16050, 10321 Stockholm (tel: 5551-0036; fax: 5663-1637; e-mail: info@chamber.se).

Uppsala Chamber of Commerce, Uppsala Science Park, 75183 Uppsala (tel: 502-950; fax: 554-458; e-mail: info@uppsala.chamber.se).

Wermland Chamber of Commerce, 6 Södra Kyrkogatan, 65224 Karlstad (tel: 221-480; fax: 221-490; e-mail: info@wermland.cci.se).

Western Sweden Chamber of Commerce and Industry, 18 Mässens Gata, PO Box 5253, 40225 Göteborg (tel: 835-900; fax: 835-936; e-mail: info@handelskammaren.net).

Banking
Götabanken, Sveavägen 14, 10377 Stockholm (tel: 790-4000) and Hamngatan 16, 40509 Gothenburg (tel: 625-000).

Handelsbanken, 20540 Malmö (tel: 245-000; fax: 236-134).

Nordea, Västra Trädgårdsgatan 17, 5 tr, 10571 Stockholm (tel: 614-8558; fax: 614-7530).

Skandinaviska Enskilda Banken, Kungsträdgårdsgatan 8, 10640 Stockholm (tel: 763-5000; fax: 242-394).

Svenska Bankforeningen (Swedish bankers' association), Regeringsgatan 42, Box 7603, 10394 Stockholm (tel: 243-300).

Svenska Handelsbanken, Kungsträdgårdog 2, 10670 Stockholm (tel: 701-1000; fax: 611-5071).

Svenska Sparbanksforeningen (Swedish savings banks' association), Drottninggatan 29, Box 16426, 10327 Stockholm (tel: 572-000).

SwedBank, Brunkebergstorg 8, 10534 Stockholm (tel: 790-1000).

Central bank
Sveriges Riksbank, Brunkebergstorg 11, SE-103 37 Stockholm (tel: 787-0000; fax: 210-531; e-mail: registratorn@riksbank.se).

Stock exchange
Stockholmsbörsen (Stockholm Stock Exchange)
www.omxnordicexchange.com

NGN-Borsen (Nordic Growth Market) (NGM), www.ngm.se

Travel information
Kungliga Automobil Klubben (KAK), Blasieholmshamnen 6, 11148 Stockholm (tel: 678-0055; fax: 678-0068; e-mail: info@kak.se).

SJ AB (State Railways), 105 50 Stockholm (tel: 762 20 00; fax: 762 24 24; website: www.sj.se); on-line booking at www.swedenbooking.com).

Svenska Turistföreningen (Swedish Tourist Association), Stureplan 4, PO Box 25, 10120 Stockholm (tel: 463-2100; fax: 678-1958; info@stfturist.se).

Svensk Turism AB, Kammakargatan 39, Box 1158, 11181 Stockholm (tel: 762-7400; e-mail: info@svenskturism.se).

Scandinavian Airlines System (SAS), Frösundaviks Allé 1, 19587 Stockholm (tel: 797-0000; fax: 797-1603).

National tourist organisation offices
VisitSweden (The Swedish Travel and Tourism Council), Sveavögen 21, Box 3030, 103 61 Stockholm (tel: 789-1000; fax: 789-1031; e-mail: reception@visitsweden.com).

Ministries
All ministries in Sweden have the same address: S-10333 Stockholm (tel: 405-1000; fax: 723-1171).

Invest in Sweden Agency, S-10338 Stockholm (tel: 676-8876/0; fax: 676-8888).

National Board of Forestry, S-55183 Jönköping (tel: 155-600; fax: 190-740).

National Board of Trade, Box 1209, S-11182 Stockholm (tel: 791-0500; fax: 200-324).

National Electrical Safety Board, Box 1371, S-11193 Stockholm (tel: 453-9700; fax: 453-9710).

National Maritime Administration, S-60178 Norrköping (tel: 191-000; fax: 101-949).

National Post and Telecom Agency, Box 5398, S-10249 Stockholm (tel: 678-5500; fax: 678-5505).

Statistics Sweden, Karlavägen 100, S-11581 Stockholm (tel: 783-4000; fax: 661-5261).

Swedish Board of Agriculture, S-55182 Jönköping (tel: 155-000; fax: 190-546).

Swedish Board of Customs, Box 2267, S-10317 Stockholm (tel: 789-7300; fax: 208-012).

Swedish Civil Aviation Administration, S-60179 Norrköping (tel: 192-000; fax: 192-575).

Swedish Board for Investment and Technical Support, BITS, Box 7837, S-10398 Stockholm (tel: 678-5000; fax: 678-5050).

Swedish National Board of Fisheries, Lilla Bommen 6, S-40126 Göteborg (tel: 630-300; fax: 156-577).

Swedish National Board for Industrial and Technical Development (NUTEK), S-11786 Stockholm (tel: 681-9100; fax: 196-826).

Swedish National Road Administration, S-78187 Borlänge (tel: 75-000; fax: 84-640).

Swedish Nuclear Power Inspectorate, S-10658 Stockholm (tel: 698-8400; fax: 661-9086).

Swedish Patent Office, Box 5055, S-10242 Stockholm (tel: 782-2500; fax: 666-0286).

Swedish Standards Institution, Box 3295, S-10366 Stockholm (tel: 613-5200; fax: 411-7035).

Swedish Trade Council, PO Box 5513, S-11485 Stockholm (tel: 783-8500; fax: 662-9093).

Other useful addresses

British Embassy, Skarpögatan 6-8, Box 27819, 11593 Stockholm (tel: 671-9000; fax: 662-9989 (commercial section).

Federation of Commercial Agents of Sweden, Hantverkargatan 46, 11221 Stockholm (tel: 540-975).

Federation of Commercial Agents of Sweden, Western Division, Box 36059, 40013 Göteborg (tel: 192-045).

Federation of Swedish Industries, Storgatan 19, 11485 Stockholm (tel: 783-8000; fax: 662-3595).

Federation of Swedish Wholesalers and Importers, Grevgatan 34, Box 5512, 11485 Stockholm (tel: 635-280).

Handels Arbetsgivareorg (HAO) (commercial employers' confederation), Box 1720, 11187 Stockholm (tel: 762-7700).

Kungl Automobil Klubben (KAK) (Royal Automobile Club), S. Blasieholmshamnen 6, S-11148 Stockholm (tel: 678-0055; fax: 678- 0068).

Motormännens Riksförbund (Automobile Association), Sturegatan 32, PO Box 5855, 10248 Stockholm 5 (tel: 782-3800; fax: 666-0371).

SACO/SR (confederation of professional associations), Box 2206, 10315 Stockholm (tel: 225-200).

Sollentunamassan (organisers of trade fairs), Box 174, 19123 Sollentuna (tel: 925-900; fax: 929-774).

Stockholmsbörsen, SE-10578 Stockholm (tel: 405-6000; fax: 405-6001).

Stockholm Technical Fair (Stockholmsmassan AB), Alvsjo, 12580 Stockholm (tel: 749-4100; fax: 992-044).

Svenska Arbetsgivareforeningen (employers' confederation), Sodra Blasieholmshammen 4A, 10-330 Stockholm (tel: 762-6000; fax: 762-6290).

Sveriges Exportrad (Swedish Trade Council), PO Box 5513, 11485 Stockholm (tel: 783-8500; fax: 663-6706).

Swedish Embassy (USA), Suite 900, 1501 M Street, NW, Washington DC 20005 (tel: (+1-202) 467-2600; fax: (+1-202) 467-2699; e-mail: ambassaden.washington@foreign.ministry.se).

Swedish Institute, Box 7434, 10391 Stockholm (tel: 789-2000).

Swedish Trade Fair Foundation (Svenska Massan), Skanegatan 26, Box 5222, 40224 Göteborg (tel: 109-100; fax: 160-330).

TCO (central organisation of salaried employees), Box 5252, 10245 Stockholm (tel: 782-9100).

Tidningarnas Telegrambyrå (news agency), Kungsholmstorg 5, 10512 Stockholm (tel: 132-600; fax: 515-377).

TT (Tidnignarnas Telegrambyrå) 105 12 Stockholm, (tel: 692-2600; fax: 692-2855; email: redaktionen@tt.se). TT is a private independent agency.

Internet sites

Export directory: www.swedishtrade.se/sed

Government of Sweden: www.sweden.gov.se

Invest in Sweden Agency: www.isa.se/

Statistics Sweden: www.scb.se/eng/index.asp

Swedish Statistics network: www.svenskstatistik.net

Virtual Sweden: www.sweden.se

Visit Sweden: www.visit-sweden.com

Switzerland

KEY FACTS

Official name: Schweizerische Eidgenossenschaft (German); Confédération Suisse (French); Confederazione Svizzera (Italian) (Swiss Confederation)

Head of State: President Simonetta Sommaruga (since 1 January 2015)

Head of government: President Simonetta Sommaruga (since 1 January 2015)

Ruling party: Coalition led by the Schweizerische Volkspartei (SVP) (Swiss People's Party) (since 1999; re-elected 2011)

Area: 41,293 square km

Population: 8.14 million (2014)

Capital: Bern (German)/Berne (French)

Official language: German, French, Italian and Romansch

Currency: Swiss franc (Swf) = 100 centimes

Exchange rate: Swf1.02 per US$ (Sep 2015)

GDP per capita: US$87,475 (2014)

GDP real growth: 1.99% (2014)

GDP: US$712.05 billion (2014)

Labour force: 5.01 million (2014)*

Unemployment: 3.16% (2014)

Inflation: -0.01% (2014)

Balance of trade: US$55.02 billion (2014)

Annual FDI: US$666.50 million (2011)

* estimated figure

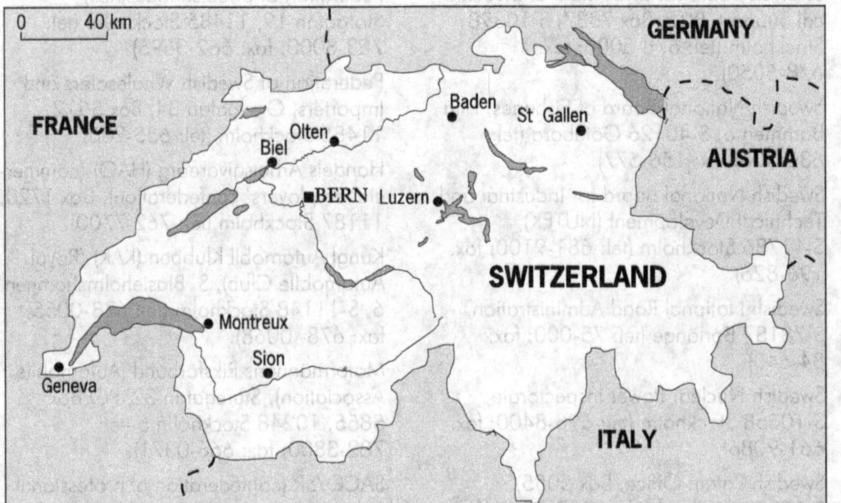

In its third *World Happiness Report* the United Nations rated Switzerland the planet's happiest country. It was followed in the rankings by Iceland, Denmark and Norway, none of which are normally associated with sunshine and smiles. Writing in the London *Financial Times*, John Kay wondered whether the criteria for the report's ratings would be widely shared. In Switzerland's case, a random survey of the faces surrounding your correspondent on a train from Geneva to Martigny was none too promising. No buzz of animated conversation, no laughter. The attractions for most visitors to Switzerland and probably for most of its residents, were summed up by one commentator as 'Mountains and Money'. Generalisations are, of course, always just that – a failure to note the exceptions and the abnormalities.

Contributions

The rather tired jokes have always been that the greatest Swiss contributions to contemporary civilisation have been the cuckoo clock and the Swiss army penknife. Writing to the London *Financial Times* from Canada this argument was well contradicted by a Mr Robert Zimmerman, who added a serious note to the list by pointing out that Calvin was Swiss, as was the little known Ulrich (Huldrych) Zwingli, the founder of the now little known Zwinglianism and a sixteenth century contemporary of both Calvin and Luther. Mr Zimmerman added to his list by including two contemporary theologians who 'are or have been' Swiss, Messrs Karl Barth and Hans Kueng. Great Swiss mathematicians, he notes, have included Euler and the Bernouilli family.

Moving on to perhaps more familiar territory, the psychology pioneer Carl Jung was Swiss, as was Pestalozzi the educational reformer. The name Piaget may be best-known today for upmarket Swiss watches, but Jean Piaget was a leading twentieth century development psychologist. Mr Zimmerman's list continued with the architects Le Corbusier and Honegger, playwrights Duerrenmatt and Frisch and ended with two Swiss inventions – the insecticide DDT and the hallucinogenic LSD. Switzerland ranks fourth in the world in Nobel prises per capita, not first as Mr Zimmerman apologetically chooses to ignore the rankings obtained by the Faroe Islands, St Lucia and even Luxembourg. For the record the Swiss Nobel ranking consulted mysteriously includes Médecins sans Frontières (founded in France) and two laureates who were not, in fact, born in Switzerland.

Switzerland's mountains are a constant; its money has traditionally been strong – if less than competitive in international trade. Towards the end of 2014 the Swiss National Bank (SNB) decided to do something about its overvalued currency. The best laid plans. In January 2015 the SNB took the surprise step of ending its currency peg against the euro in view of the imminent quantitative easing (QE) programme – amounting to as much as €1.1 trillion (US$1.24 trillion) – to be embarked upon by the European Central Bank (ECB). The decision backfired rather, as the Swiss Franc immediately began to appreciate against the euro and other major currencies by as much as 20 per cent and at one stage reaching more or less at par with the US dollar. On the platform of Geneva's railway station your correspondent was invited to pay €5.00 (US$5.61) for a 33ml plastic bottle of mineral water. Ten miles away, in France, the same bottle could be purchased for €1.50 (US$1.69) or even less.

Somehow or other, the gnomes of the SNB had got in a muddle. An expensive muddle: in the second quarter of 2015 the SNB announced losses of US$20 billion. Taking into account the first quarter losses, the decision to float the franc had set the bank back by around SFr50 billion (US$49 billion), or seven per cent of gross domestic product (GDP). At the macro-economic level the decision to float the Franc was bad news leading to the massive losses in Switzerland's foreign currency reserves – not that the country was bust – at the beginning of the year those reserves amounted to a comfortable US$550 billion. However, around US$230 billion was euro denominated. The losses against the euro amounted to almost 95 per cent of the total losses.in the first two quarters of 2015.

Holidaymakers heading for the ski-slopes also felt the pinch as – inflation apart – hotel and restaurant prices in ski resorts soared past the levels of London and Frankfurt. Visitor numbers were down and for those who had already booked, the only alternative was to eat out less and watch the six-nations rugby tournament in the chalet rather than swigging pints of lager at US$10.00 a go in Verbier's bars. Inevitably, the economy started to shrink in the first quarter not only because of the effect on tourism. Swiss exports – watches for example – became more expensive and less price competitive.

So the gnomes had to resort to their slide rules and accept that their currency strategy had crashed. If the Swiss franc was overvalued, restoring it to a more sensible exchange rate was no easy task. Negative interest rates could and were, introduced as the SNB began a catch-up policy of intervening to purchase foreign currencies. The catch-22 situation was that as the euro dropped in value against the Swiss franc, it created losses on the SNB's balance sheet, which in the first place simply did not look good and in the second risked creating political difficulties if there was less funding available for government. In a fortuitously timed study on inflation in Switzerland and other European countries, the International Monetary Fund (IMF) noted that in 2011 to limit the appreciation of the Swiss franc and its impact on inflation, an exchange rate floor had been introduced. During the first three quarters of 2011, strong capital inflows resulted in a substantial appreciation of the Swiss franc against the euro and lowered imported inflation. Despite concerns about the risks related to rising house prices and household debt, the SNB cut its base interest rate to zero in 2011 to stem appreciation pressures and help lift imported inflation. However, as appreciation continued, a floor of Swf1.20 per euro was implemented in September 2011. Although inflation was still close to or below zero after the floor was introduced, in the view of the IMF, inflation probably would have been even lower in the absence of the exchange rate floor. While the floor was effective in stemming further appreciation, substantial exchange rate pressure in late 2014 prompted renewed interventions at a rapid pace. As a result, the size of the SNB's balance sheet expanded substantially, approaching 90 per cent of GDP. In addition, the SNB was concerned that, once the magnitude of its interventions became public, speculation about exit from the floor would mount, fuelling a vicious cycle of rising inflows and a rapidly growing balance sheet. In turn, the SNB made a surprise move to exit from the exchange rate floor on 15 January 2015 and lowered the deposit rate to -0.75 per cent. Even as rates had moved into negative territory, the macro-prudential policies that had been introduced over the previous few tears to limit housing related risks, including a minimum down payment and amortisation requirements, appeared to be having some effect. Meanwhile, Switzerland's fiscal rule had helped it maintain low deficits and debt, requiring the federal government budget to be in structural balance *ex ante* and that any *ex post* over-runs be made up by running structural surpluses.

As noted above, by April 2015, the real effective exchange rate (REER) had appreciated by about 10 per cent relative to its average level in 2014. The appreciated level of the exchange rate could result in new challenges for both growth and inflation by further worsening competitiveness and deepening near-term deflation. In fact, two-year ahead inflation expectations have dropped considerably (by 0.8 percentage points to 0.4 per cent) since the exit from the exchange rate floor. The response of inflation to an expectations shock suggested to the IMF that this could reduce headline inflation by as much as 0.25 percentage points in 2015.

The IMF considered Switzerland's financial sector reform agenda should also

KEY INDICATORS — Switzerland

	Unit	2011	2012	2013	2014	**2015
Population	m	*7.84	*7.96	8.04	8.14	*8.19
Gross domestic product (GDP)	US$bn	636.10	631.18	685.87	712.05	*688.43
GDP per capita	US$	81,161	79,344	85,318	87,475	*84,070
GDP real growth	%	1.9	1.0	1.9	2.0	*0.8
Inflation	%	0.2	-0.7	-0.2	–	*-1.2
Unemployment	%	3.2	2.9	3.2	3.2	*3.4
Exports (fob) (goods)	US$m	345,615.0	332,445.0	378,514.0	327,570.0	–
Imports (fob) (goods)	US$m	320,424.0	295,430.0	321,139.0	272,555.0	–
Balance of trade	US$m	25,191.0	37,015.0	57,375.0	55,015.0	–
Current account	US$m	55,718.0	60,853.0	73,345.0	*49,529.0	*39,711.0
Total reserves minus gold	US$m	234,517.5	475,659.0	495,958.0	505,463.0	–
Foreign exchange	US$m	227,624.7	467,933.0	488,561.0		–
Exchange rate	per US$	0.89	0.93	0.90	0.99	–

* estimated figure ** forecast figure

be completed. The Swiss authorities had, in the organisation's view, made important progress in this regard and further steps were planned. Specific priorities included raising the leverage ratios of the two large international banks, increasing public disclosure of information on risk weights, reforming the Swiss Financial Market Supervisory Authority's (FINMA) use of external auditors, overhauling deposit insurance and containing housing – and mortgage-related risks. Over the medium term, Switzerland faced a number of structural challenges. The priorities included adopting the proposed pension reforms to ensure the sustainability of the system for future generations; completing the continuing reforms of corporate taxation and financial controls in ways that ensured full compliance with international initiatives aimed at limiting money laundering and cross-border tax evasion and avoidance; finally the elimination of uncertainties related to Switzerland's future immigration policies and its relations with the European Union (EU).

Taking a more general look at the Swiss economy, in May 2015 the IMF noted that following the exit from the exchange rate floor in January 2015 and the subsequent appreciation of the franc, the Swiss economy faced exchange rate overvaluation, slower near-term growth and deflation. Both growth and inflation were expected to recover gradually over the medium term – to around two per cent and one per cent, respectively – as the economy adjusted to what the IMF described as the 'shock'. However, in the view of the IMF, this 'relatively benign' scenario was subject to important risks, most notably that operating in a low inflation environment might 'prove more difficult than originally assumed.' Changes to monetary and fiscal policies might be in order to support faster adjustment and reduce risks. As already noted, monetary easing via purchases of foreign assets would help limit the near-term growth slowdown, reduce risks related to low inflation and lessen franc overvaluation. However, the extent to which fiscal policy could still be deployed to support aggregate demand was, in the view of the IMF, limited by Switzerland's fiscal rule and the small, open nature of Switzerland's economy.

Broadly agreeing with the IMF, in its June 2015 *Economic Forecast Summary*, the Paris-based Organisation for Economic Development and Co-operation (OECD) also noted that the Swiss economy had weakened over the first half of 2015, but in the view of the OECD growth was projected to rise gradually into 2016 as the exchange rate appreciation was absorbed. Private consumption was expected to remain constant on the back of rising wages and favourable financial conditions. However, the OECD expected both exports and business investment to suffer. The lower oil prices had combined with the appreciating Swiss franc to bring inflation back into negative territory.

The OECD also expected interest rates to remain negative 'for the foreseeable future.' Should growth slow further, healthy public finances would leave ample room for fiscal support. The OECD considered that increasing funding for childcare and education for migrant children would both boost job opportunities for women and increase growth. Raising competition and efficiency in health care could also free up consumer spending for other items.

In the view of the OECD, investment in Switzerland would be adversely affected by lower business confidence, exchange rate volatility and the continued uncertainty surrounding the implementation of immigration quotas in 2017. In the medium term, as Switzerland phased out its nuclear power plants, investment in other forms of energy would need to increase, which should boost domestic demand. Swiss transport infrastructure was already well developed, but implementing peak-load pricing in motorway and train utilisation could help reduce congestion and boost productivity.

Immigration

Switzerland is normally cautious about introducing new legislation. But as Europe faced a surge in immigration in September 2015, Switzerland was providing something of an example to follow. In early September Germany's Chancellor Merkel declared herself to be inspired by the Swiss asylum policy, suggesting that it was a model to follow. Mrs Merkel and her staff had been taking a look at what other European countries were doing to cope with the problem. However, in Switzerland the immigration problem seemed to be on a different scale: an article in Bern's *Tages Anzeiger* noted that refugees from Kosovo, for example, only accounted for one per cent of Switzerland's total applications, despite the relatively large Kosovar diaspora in Switzerland.

Switzerland's immigration system had introduced in 2015 a new procedure, which meant that would-be immigrants from countries to the west of the Balkans considered to be 'safe', the process took only 48 hours. Since then the number of applicants had fallen dramatically. Applicants were housed in federally run centres, interviewed within two days by a specialist and, in most cases expelled straight away. To ensure that they will be safely welcomed by their countries of origin, Switzerland had signed agreements with Kosovo, Serbia and Bosnia. A similarly accelerated system had been adopted for applicants from African countries considered to be safe.

New immigration legislation was intended to speed things up. Applicants were lodged in federal centres, but only those where it looked likely that they would qualify for acceptance were sent off to different cantons (regions) based on fixed allocation numbers. For those being held in federal centres, the process should not take more than 140 days; for those who had been sent on to their different cantons, a year at most. To ensure the proper treatment of would-be refugees, lawyers were on hand for the applicants.

However, not everyone considered the Swiss system to be perfect. Amnesty International had criticised Switzerland for its treatment of Syrian refugees. Swiss legislation did not recognise as refugees those who could not demonstrate individual persecution. None the less, the majority of Syrian refugees arriving in Switzerland were 'provisionally accepted', but with less rights than those who could demonstrate their status according to the Swiss legal requirements.

Risk assessment

Economy	Good/fair
Politics	Good
Regional stability	Good

COUNTRY PROFILE

Switzerland was part of the Holy Roman Empire until 1499 when it gained independence. Switzerland's Roman connection remains strong. The Pope is still guarded by a some 135-strong Swiss Guard, drawn largely from the Catholic cantons of central Switzerland.

1515 Switzerland declared its neutrality after nearly being defeated by the French and Venetians.

1648 The Peace of Westphalia concluded the Thirty Years' War in Europe and recognised Swiss independence.

1815 The Congress of Vienna restored independence to Switzerland after it had been annexed by France as part of the Napoleonic Empire during 1798–1803. The Congress laid down the principle of the perpetual neutrality of Switzerland.

1874 The modern constitution was inaugurated.
1914–18 Switzerland was neutral during the First World War.
1919–20 The Treaty of Versailles again recognised Switzerland's neutrality. In 1920, the country joined the League of Nations, but did not join its successor, the UN, when it was formed in 1945.
1939–45 Switzerland pursued a policy of neutrality during the Second World War, but refused refuge to Jews trying to escape German-occupied Europe and traded gold with the Nazis. Swiss banks also provided interest free credits to the Axis powers, which enabled Germany to finance its war effort.
1959 Switzerland was a founder member of the European Free Trade Agreement (EFTA).
1971 Women were granted the right to vote.
1986 The Swiss population rejected UN membership in a referendum.
1988 Switzerland's first female minister, Elisabeth Kopp, resigned from her post following accusations that she had violated official secrecy laws by tipping off her husband about an inquiry into his business affairs.
1992 In a referendum on Swiss membership of the European Economic Area (EEA), a free trade agreement between the EU and EFTA, opponents of the pact won with 50.3 per cent of the vote. Switzerland joined the World Bank and IMF.
1998 Swiss banks agreed to a US$1.25 billion settlement with Jewish Holocaust survivors and families.
1999 Ruth Dreifuss became Switzerland's first female president. The Schweizerische Volkspartei (SVP) (Swiss People's Party) won the largest electoral victory for any party in Switzerland for over 80 years.
2001 The national airline, Swissair, went bankrupt.
2002 Switzerland joined the UN. An independent panel of historians concluded Swiss authorities knew of the fate of Jewish refugees turned away in 1942 and that Swiss banking bolstered the economy of Nazi Germany, although not enough to have prolonged the Second World War.
2003 The SVP won the biggest share of the vote in the parliamentary elections at the expense of the Christlich-Demokratische Volkspartei (CVP) (Christian Democratic People's Party).
2004 Swiss banks began to inform EU tax departments on personal accounts held by EU taxpayers. Stem cell research was agreed in a referendum.
2005 New compliance banking laws, introduced to curtail money laundering, and the EU-wide decline in personal tax rates led to a reduction in the flow of money into Switzerland's banks.
2006 Genetically modified crops were banned for five years. Tough new asylum laws were introduced.
2007 Violence erupted in Berne during the election campaign of the ruling, anti-immigration party, SVP, when left-wing protesters began hurling rocks and bottles. The SVP went on to win the highest number of votes (29 per cent) in general elections. however, as there was no clear winner a coalition of four parties was formed. One of the world's largest, and Switzerland's biggest, bank, UBS, was forced to write off US$10 billion in bad US sub-prime mortgage debts.
2008 UBS declared its losses were greater than originally announced, with a total of US$22 billion lost by the end of the first quarter. A referendum, whereby Swiss communes could vote to limit naturalisation of foreigners in individual cases, was rejected. Switzerland joined the Schengen Agreement group of countries allowing free movement for EU citizens and external visitors with a Schengen visa.
2009 Hans-Rudolf Merz (FDP) became federal president. The government eased banking laws to allow the sharing of bank data to crack down on offshore tax evasion and avoid being listed as a non-co-operative tax haven by the Organisation of Economic Co-operation and Development (OECD). The economy officially slipped into recession for the first quarter as UBS reported a further loss of US$1.32 billion.
2010 Doris Leuthard (CVP) became federal president. Drawings and manuscripts of Franz Kafka, which had been secured in a Swiss vault since the 1940s, were finally seen by one academic, after a long legal battle of ownership agreed on this compromise. Israel claims the documents as national treasure, while the daughters of Esther Hoffe, secretary to Kafka's friend Max Brod, who was entrusted with the work, claim they are part of their inheritance. The Swiss franc reached an all-time high against the euro (Swf 1.02 per US$1) as money flowed in from investors worried about sovereign risk elsewhere in the world. The Swiss National Bank (SNB), lost Swf14 billion (US$12.9 billion) in the first half of the year while attempting to hold the currency down against the euro and maintain its global competitiveness.
2011 Micheline Calmy-Rey (SP) became federal president in January. In August, the SNB took action to reduce the value of the Swiss franc by increasing the supply of francs and undertaking foreign exchange swaps. International investors had been buying Swiss francs as other major currencies came under threat. The franc had almost reached parity with the euro and the high value against the US dollar was hurting exports. Federal parliamentary elections were held in October, with modest gains for the centrist political parties and reversing the trend towards polarisation as seen in 1990s and 2000s. The SVP remained as the single largest political party in parliament, having won 26.6 per cent of the vote (54 seats out of 200) and will be the strong centre of a coalition government.
2012 Eveline Widmer-Schlumpf (BDP) became federal president in 1 January. On 18 April parliament voted to re-impose immigration limits on workers of some Eastern European EU member states. The EU condemned the decision. On 26 November the UK's Financial Services Authority fined UBS £29.7 million (US$47.6 million) for its 'seriously defective' systems, controls and management, which failed to stop a trader within its London office, Kweku Adoboli, from committing Britain's biggest bank fraud (£1.4 billion (US$2.3 billion)). The Swiss Financial Market Supervisory Agency (Finma) announced that UBS would be subject to extraordinary eternal supervision. On 5 December, Ueli Maurer (SVP) was elected as federal president for 2013, winning 148 votes (out of 202).
2013 In a national referendum held on 22 September a large majority voted to keep compulsory military service.
2014 In a national referendum held on 9 February a small majority (50.3 per cent, 19,526 votes) voted to limit the number of immigrants through the use of quotas. A further immigration related referendum was held on 30 November. The so-called 'Ecopop' proposal would limit net immigration to 0.2 per cent of the total population. Supporters say restricting immigration will safeguard Switzerland's environment by reducing the need for new transport links and new housing. The European Commission said it regretted the result and will need to examine the implications for the future of EU-Swiss relations.
2015 Federal elections were held on 18 October for the National Council and the first round of elections to the Council of States. The result was a win for the Schweizerische Volkspartei (SVP) (Swiss People's Party) with 29.4 per cent of the votes (65 seats, out of 200), followed by Sozialdemokratische Partei der Schweiz (SP) (Social Democratic Party of Switzerland) with 18.8 per cent (43).

Political structure

Constitution

Switzerland's Constitution dates back to 1874 and has been much amended over the years. It unites more than 3,000 communes and 26 cantons and half-cantons

in a confederation which devolves considerable powers to local bodies.
Responsibility for determining and administering civil, penal and commercial law, foreign and trade issues, defence, communications, social insurance and energy is reserved for the federal government.
The cantons and half-cantons, each of which have their own Constitution and government, are responsible for the administration of federal law as well as their own cantonal laws. The communes have local autonomy over roads, local public utilities and the granting of citizenship.
Major issues are frequently decided by referendum. The constitution, or any of the country's federal laws, may only be amended by the passage of a proposal by national referendum. A national referendum may be called if a petition is signed by 50,000 people (on a legislative matter) or 100,000 people (on a constitutional matter). In some cantons, referenda may be necessary to approve all changes in cantonal legislation. The federal government, or its political opponents, may also initiate a referendum on any issue. Voter turnout averages 40–50 per cent. Since the constitution's inception, voters have been asked to approve over 148 amendments.

Independence date
1 August 1291

Form of state
Federal parliamentary democratic republic

The executive
The chief executive organ in the country is the Federal Council, whose seven members each hold a ministerial portfolio, and whose president and vice president are appointed each calendar year on a rotating basis from among its members.

National legislature
The bicameral Federal Assembly consists of the National Council with 195 members directly elected by proportional representation in constituencies containing around 37,500 electorates and five members in half cantons directly elected by simple majority vote. The Council of States has 46 members who represent cantons (local district administrations) directly elected by simple majority vote. All members of the Federal Assembly serve four-year terms.
The Federal Assembly supervises the army, the civil service and the administration of the law as well as electing the Federal Supreme Court, the Federal Tribunal of Insurance and the Federal Council.

Legal system
Customary law marginally influences the civil law system. Individual cantons elect and maintain their own magistracy. Each canton has justices of the peace, District Courts, Labour Courts, Courts for Tenancy, an Appeal Court, a Cassation Court and, for more important cases under penal law, a Jury Court. Apart from military courts, there are just two federal judicial authorities: the Federal Supreme Court and the Federal Tribunal of Insurance.

Last elections
23 October 2011 (federal assembly)
Results: National Council: the Schweizerische Volkspartei (SVP) (Swiss People's party) won 26.6 per cent of the vote (54 seats out of 200), the Sozialdemokratische Partei (SPS) (Social Democrat Party) 18.7 per cent (46), the Freisinnig-Demokratische Partei (FDP) (Freethinking-Democratic Party) 15.1 per cent (30), the Christlich-Demokratische Volkspartei (CVP) (Christian Democratic People's Party) 12.3 per cent (28), the Grüne Partei (GPS) (Green Party), 8.4 per cent (15), Grünliberale Partei (GLP) (Liberal Green Party) 5.4 per cent (12), Bürgerlich-Demokratische Partei (BDP) (Conservative Democratic Party) 5.4 per cent (nine); three other political parties and one independent each won no more than 2 per cent and shared six seats, four parties won no seats. Turnout was 49.1 per cent.

Next elections
18 October 2015 (parliament)

Political parties

Ruling party
Coalition led by the Schweizerische Volkspartei (SVP) (Swiss People's Party) (since 1999; re-elected 2011)

Main opposition party
Grüne Partei der Schweiz (GPS) (Green Party of Switzerland)

Population

8.14 million (2014)
Last census: December 2000: 7,204,055
Population density: 182 inhabitants per square km. Urban population 74 per cent (2010 Unicef).
Annual growth rate: 0.7 per cent, 1990–2010 (Unicef).

Ethnic make-up
Switzerland is dominated by Germans (65 per cent), French (18 per cent) and Italians (10 per cent). Foreigners comprise 19.7 per cent of the population. In a referendum held in September 2000, the Swiss voted against limiting the proportion of foreigners to 18 per cent.

Religions
Roman Catholic (46 per cent), Protestant (40 per cent).

Education

With no central ministry of education, each of the 26 Swiss cantons (semi-autonomous regions) have overall and exclusive responsibility for education. Private schools exist at the level of vocational secondary school but do not attract federate funding or canton control.
Most cantons set the number of compulsory years for primary schooling at six, some others set it at four or five; for lower secondary school most set the minimum years at three, and some at five or four; whichever cycle is used, overall, compulsory schooling lasts for nine years. Teaching is given in the language of the canton.
At aged 16, students can go into upper level secondary schools (either private or state-run), which offer general or vocational programmes and last for between three and four years. General secondary education (*Matura*), offers academic study, preparing a student for university. Technical high schools provide a range of vocational and training programmes.
Typically 85 per cent of students complete upper secondary school.
Switzerland has 12 universities and higher education colleges. There are also a number of science universities and more than 20 polytechnics (*Fachhochschulen*).
In the 1990s, the cantons began a reform of the educational system to ensure that it provided the best means of maintaining a high degree of educated citizens.
Literacy rate: 99 per cent, adult rate (2003)
Compulsory years: Six to 15.
Enrolment rate: 97 per cent gross primary enrolment of relevant age group (including repeaters); 100 per cent gross secondary enrolment (World Bank).
Pupils per teacher: 19 in primary schools.

Health

Healthcare services are entirely private and individuals are expected and, in some areas, obliged, to cover themselves with private health insurance policies.
Each canton has responsibility for the provision of healthcare. The type of hospital a patient may be admitted to will depend on the level of health insurance the person holds.

HIV/Aids
HIV prevalence: 0.4 per cent aged 15–49 in 2003 (World Bank)
Life expectancy: 81 years, 2004 (WHO 2006)
Fertility rate/Maternal mortality rate: 1.5 births per woman, 2010 (Unicef); maternal mortality five per 100,000 live births (World Bank).
Birth rate/Death rate: 9.6 births and 8.8 deaths per 1,000 people (2003)
Child (under 5 years) mortality rate (per 1,000): 4 per 1,000 live births (WHO 2012)
Head of population per physician: 3.61 physicians per 1,000 people, 2002 (WHO 2006)

Welfare

Switzerland's comprehensive social welfare system is funded by the state, by employer contributions and by employee national insurance contributions. It is a legal requirement that all citizens residing for three months or more in Switzerland must take out minimum healthcare insurance.

Unemployment insurance is compulsory and many employees are also insured against accidents at work. Old age, disability and widow(er)s' pensions are paid out of compulsory contributions. The precise arrangements may differ in each canton.

Over 20 per cent of the federal budget is spent on social welfare. Some social security schemes have their own separate budgets.

Main cities

Bern/Berne/Bienne (capital, estimated population 122,925 in 2012), Zürich (380,723), Geneva/Genève (190,544), Basel/Basle (167,297), Lausanne (129,944), Winterthur (102,654), St Gall (73,637), Lugano (59,922), Sion/Sitten (capital of Valais) (30,390), Chur/Coire (capital of Graubünden) (33,794).

Languages spoken

The national languages are German in central and eastern areas (64 per cent), French in the west (19 per cent) and Italian in the south (8 per cent).

Raeto-Romansch is spoken in the south-east (1 per cent). English is widely spoken.

There are two forms of German spoken. High German, or Hochdeutsch is only spoken in formal situations or used for written work; Swiss-German, or Schwyzertütsch is spoken by all in daily life in German-speaking Switzerland, using different dialects and is incomprehensible to all who speak High German.

Official language/s

German, French, Italian and Romansch

Media

Press

There is a decentralised press owing to regional variations in language and culture, producing a large number of publications with relatively small circulation. There are more than 600 newspapers in total and nearly 2,000 magazines.

Dailies: About 120 regional newspapers (75 per cent printed in German and 20 per cent in French). The most popular includes, *20 Minutten* (www.20min.ch), a free publication with a tabloid style; from Zurich, *Blick* (www.blick.ch) and *Tages Anzeiger* (www.tagesanzeiger.ch); from Genéva, *Le Temps* (www.letemps.ch) and *Tribune de Genéva* (www.tdg.ch); from Lugano *Corriere del Ticino* (www.cdt.ch); from Bern *Berner Zeitung* (www.bauernzeitung.ch); from Lausanne, *Le Matin* (www.lematin.ch) and from Basel *Basler Zeitung* (www.baz.ch).

Weeklies: Many dailies have weekend editions including *Sonntags Blick*, *Le Matin Dimanche* and *Sonntags Zeitung*. A Swiss edition of a French magazine is *l'Hebdo* (www.hebdo.ch) is available in French speaking cantons.

Business: Daily newspapers include *Neue Zürcher Zeitung* (www.nzz.ch) from Zürich and is of international repute; *Cash* (www.cash.ch) for finance and Handelzeitung (www.handelszeitung.ch), *Agefi* (www.agefi.com). Others periodicals include *Finanz und Wirtschaft* (www.fuw.ch) (twice weekly) *Swiss News* (www.swissnews.ch) and *Bilanz* (www.bilanz.ch) (monthlies).

Periodicals: In German, *The Panorama Journal* (www.panoramajournal.ch) reports on events, sport and life in the Bern area; *Der Schweizerische Beobachter* (www.beobachter.ch), is a consumer magazine; *Nebelspalter* (www.nebelspalter.ch), is a satirical magazine; *Pro* (www.pro-helvetia.ch) is a Swiss Arts Council publication,

Broadcasting

A fee for reception of any radio or television signal is levied by Billag AG (www.billag.ch). The Federal Office of Communications (www.bakom.ch) has overall responsibility for broadcast media. Digital Audio Broadcasting (DAB) was underway in 2007 and expected to be fully implemented nationally within a few years. The public broadcaster is SRG SSR Idée Suisse (www.srg-ssr.ch), which operates national radio and television stations, broadcasting in Swiss-German (www.drs.ch), French (www.rsr.ch), Italian (www.rtsi.ch) and Rumansch (www.rtr.ch).

Radio: Apart from the national networks provided by SRG SSR Idée Suisse, independent radio stations are typically exclusive to a city or region, including from Bern, Radio BE1 (www.radiobe1.ch), from Zürich, Energy Züri (www.energyzueri.ch) and Radio 24 (www.radio24.ch), and from Basel, Radio 105 (www.105.ch) and Radio X (www.radiox.ch).

SRG SSR Idée Suisse broadcasts an international service in nine languages.

Most radio stations provide services over the internet.

Television: There are over 80 local and regional TV stations providing services for all linguistic populations. Pay-for-view, satellite and cable television are available.

Other news agencies: SDA+ATS (in German) (www.sda.ch).

Swiss Infor (operated by SRG SSR Idée Suisse in nine languages) (www.swissinfo.org).

Economy

Switzerland is world renowned for its financial services – which together with education, scientific research and tourism accounts for over 75 per cent of its GDP. It has international brand names in watch-making, pharmaceuticals, precision instruments, luxury jewellery and consumer durables. It is one of the wealthiest countries in the world, with a highly skilled labour force and ready access to the European Union (EU). Despite not being a member of the EU, the Swiss economy remains heavily dependent on the economic fortunes of the EU and the euro. Swiss exports are dominated by chemicals and machinery and electronic goods. The EU takes over 65 per cent of Swiss exports (19 per cent to Germany alone) and supplies 76 per cent of imports (over one-third from Germany).

Switzerland's economy has performed relatively well since the global financial crisis, with growth reaching 2 per cent at the end of 2014. The economic environment became more complicated in the later period of 2014, however. Increased capital inflows forced the Swiss National Bank (SNB) to intervene and defend its exchange rate floor of 1.2 franc per euro. The SNB exited the floor in January 2015; this caused substantial appreciations in the exchange rate before eventually stabilising at around 1.05 francs per euro. This strong value of the franc is likely to slow down in the future with economic growth diminishing as the current account suffers due to reductions in net exports. Estimations reflect this, as GDP growth is forecasted to decline to around 0.75 per cent of GDP by the end of 2015.

As its banking system became embroiled in the worldwide credit squeeze and toxic debt scandal of 2008, Swiss banking was badly damaged by significant losses due to bad debts, created by the collapse of the sub-prime market in the US. In 2008 Switzerland's UBS AG, one of the world's top-10 banks, lost over US$39 billion and had to be rescued by the government. Even so, when coupled with Credit Suisse, the country's next largest bank, their combined assets in 2009 of US$900 billion were twice the size of the Swiss economy. In 2010, the Swiss financial regulator called for greater powers to liquidate failing banks. In September 2012, an English court prosecuted a senior UBS trader, accused of a US$2.3 billion fraud (2008–11) and risking a further US$12 billion which could have threatened the future of the bank. Safeguards introduced in 2008 to avoid high-risk trading has been circumvented and this episode undermined the reputation of the bank.

In 2009, the banking sector also had to deal with international pressure to accept concessions on bank secrecy. Swiss banking is well known for its 'numbered accounts' and secrecy laws. But in an effort to avoid joining the Organisation for Economic Co-operation and Development (OECD) blacklist of non-co-operative tax havens, Switzerland eased its banking laws to allow the sharing of bank data. Switzerland agreed in 2015 to start sharing financial information with the European Union, making it much harder for Europeans to hide wealth from tax authorities. The pact means European countries will in the future automatically receive the names, addresses, tax identification numbers and dates of birth of their residents with accounts in Swiss banks. As the global pressure to tackle tax evasion mounted, Switzerland entered a number of bilateral agreements with countries like the U.K. and Australia, and is now negotiating one with the U.S.

External trade

Although Switzerland has consistently rejected EU membership, it is a member of the European Economic Area (EEA), which gives it access to the EU's single market. It has a trade agreement with the EU on a number of measures including trade in processed agricultural goods, customs fraud and taxation.

Foreign trade accounts for almost 80 per cent of all trade with exports providing 45 per cent of GDP, of which industry accounts for around 30 per cent. Over 60 per cent of exports are destined for the EU. Precision tools and equipment, pharmaceuticals and chemicals, electrical and electronic goods are important export items, while banking, insurance and tourism provide the greater part of foreign earnings.

Imports

Main imports are machinery, chemicals, vehicles, metals, agricultural produce and textiles.

Main sources: Germany (28.0 per cent of total in 2014), Italy (9.7 per cent), France (8.1 per cent)

Exports

Main exports are machinery, chemicals, metals, watches and agricultural products.

Main destinations: Germany (18.3 per cent of total in 2014), US (12.9 per cent), France (7.2 per cent)

Agriculture

Farming

The agricultural sector contributes around 1 per cent to GDP and employs four per cent of the workforce, with activity concentrated on dairy farming. Agriculture is a state subsidised sector – approximately 75 per cent of a farmer's income is financed by subsidies. There are around 80,000 peasant farms of less than 20 hectares (ha) remaining, and of these barely half provide full-time occupations for their owners. Holdings of over 20ha number around 13,000. The average farm is less than 16ha in size. Pasture land totals some 8,500 square km, equivalent to a fifth of the total land area. A further 11,700 square km is taken up by arable land, orchards and vineyards. Farming is highly mechanised, with one of the highest tractor densities in the world. Farmers have use of large and expensive equipment through machinery syndicates. Government fixing of minimum prices means that meat, sugar, vegetables and fruit are two or three times more expensive than in neighbouring countries, a situation which international agencies such as the World Trade Organisation are anxious to see rectified. There are protective customs barriers and other duties on imported goods as well as actual import restrictions, so that the domestic market remains highly protected, a significant factor in Switzerland's opposition to EU membership.

Fishing

Switzerland's fish industry, based on 123,000 hectares of lakes, is insignificant and declining. Untreated industrial and agricultural effluents are polluting fisheries, while canalisation, underground channelling of watercourses and the absence of suitable spawning grounds have contributed to the reduction of fish habitats.

There are more than 50 fish species found in Swiss waters, but only a few have been used by the fishing industry for food. Catches consist for the most part of lake herring and perch together with various other types of whitefish. Catches of whitefish and perch have steadily declined.

Only around 5 per cent of the fish and fish products consumed within the country are obtained from domestic sources.

Forestry

Forest and other wooded land accounts for nearly a third of the land area, with forest cover estimated at 1.19 million hectares. 90 per cent of the forest area is available for wood supply. 4.5 million cubic metres of wood is produced annually There has been a steady rise in growing stock with afforestation accounting for an annual average increase of 4,000ha of forest covers between 1990 and 2000. More than two-thirds of the forest area is under public ownership.

Domestic consumption is 6.4 million cubic metres. Sensitivity about preserving the scenic environment is high. In light of acid rain damage, particularly in the north-west, as well as increased competition in the sector, the prospects for further growth in production appear limited.

The forest industry has to cope with high labour costs. Although paper production is sufficient to meet domestic demands, the industry is partly dependent on pulp imports. Per capita consumption of forest products remains above the European average.

Industry and manufacturing

The industrial sector contributes approximately 25 per cent to GDP and employs about 30 per cent of the labour force. The well-developed export-oriented manufacturing sector is centred on the production of finished goods. Traditional industries include machines, tools, pharmaceuticals, textiles, watches, food processing, chemicals and engineering. Among well-known Swiss companies are Nestlé and Novartis. There is an increasing emphasis on specialisation and the development of high technology products. Swiss companies spend 2.9 per cent of GDP on research and development, one of the highest figures in the world. Switzerland is home to the world's biggest clock and watch industry, which produces about 8 per cent of annual export revenues.

Tourism

Switzerland has a long-established tourist industry based on its Alpine scenery and winter sports. Mountaineers still consider climbing Western Europe's highest peak (Mont Blanc) and those in the Bernese Alps (Jungfrau and Finsteraarhorn) as challenging. Visitors, at around 8.5 million per year, are typically older and more affluent than visitors to neighbouring countries.

There are 11 Swiss sites included on Unesco's World Heritage List, such as historic buildings, the old city of Berne, the Rheatian Railway and three natural mountain sites.

Travel and tourism contributed an average of 8.2 per cent of GDP from 2007–11, and contributed 7.4 per cent of GDP in 2014. The industry employed 9.6 per cent of the workforce (471,000 jobs) over the same period. Visitor exports rose from US$14.6 billion in 2007 to US$20.7 billion in 2011, before falling to US$18.7 billion in 2014. Investment in the industry was 1.9 per cent of total investment for 2014.

Switzerland has a fully integrated public transport service and regular, scheduled train services from all surrounding countries, as well as extensive road connections.

China designated Switzerland as an approved destination for its holidaying citizens and their number could swell Switzerland's arrival numbers by millions.

Mining

Switzerland is not richly endowed with mineral deposits. Only rock salt and building materials are mined or quarried in significant quantities.

Switzerland is almost completely dependent on imported raw materials and is, therefore, vulnerable to world economic developments.

Switzerland has no fossil energy resources of its own apart from a small deposit of natural gas at Finsterwald and is, therefore, entirely dependent on imports to meet its energy requirements. Around 1.3 per cent of total energy consumption is of fossil fuels. Oil, gas and coal are all imported. Nor does Switzerland have any minerals.

Hydrocarbons

Switzerland has no fossil energy resources apart from a small deposit of natural gas at Finsterwald, which is not under current production. All hydrocarbon needs are imported which constitutes 238,000 barrels per day (bpd) of oil; domestic oil refinery capacity is 132,000bpd. Coal consumption, which is around 230,000 short tonnes of oil equivalent, has declined in recent years, largely for environmental reasons.

Energy

Total installed generating capacity was 17.5 gigawatts (GW) in 2006. Electricity consumption has been growing at 2 per cent since the 1980s and planners see 2020 as the year of shortage if measures are delayed to expand generation. Hydroelectricity is the only natural energy resource, although expansion has been deemed unfeasible; it supplies 12 per cent of total energy requirements. There are five nuclear reactors with total installed capacity of 3.2GW. In May 2011 the government announced it would be phasing out nuclear power, amid growing public hostility to the industry. The five ageing plants will not be replaced after they reach the end of their lifetimes between 2019 and 2034. They will not, however, be decommissioned early.

Switzerland imports and exports electricity to and from France, Germany and Italy. The energy market was liberalised in 2007, with local energy companies allowed to compete nationally while retaining close links to their cantons. The national electricity grid operator, Swissgrid, is responsible for distributing power generated by the power companies The Swiss Federal Office of Energy (SFOE) is responsible for national policy for the implementation of renewable energies.

Financial markets

Stock exchange

Borse (SWX) (Swiss Exchange)

Banking and insurance

Switzerland is the world's biggest offshore private banking centre, but banking secrecy laws and a favourable taxation regime are coming under increasing scrutiny in the light of the dormant accounts scandal and the possibility of EU membership. In an effort to avoid joining the global list of non-co-operative tax havens, held by the Organisation of Economic Co-operation and Development (OECD), Switzerland eased its banking laws to allow the sharing of bank data that cracks down on offshore tax evasion. The Swiss proviso is that only 'concrete and justified' requests will be acted on.

Switzerland is a signatory of a new EU tax agreement, introduced in 2005 in a number of non-EU countries. Switzerland will impose a withholding tax, up to 35 per cent, to be passed to the tax department of an EU citizen's country, but retaining the anonymity of the saver, instead of informing the relevant EU country about the amount of money in savings accounts and allowing tax to be levied from the home country.

Switzerland has also agreed to supply information on tax fraud, for criminal or civil trials, and notify EU member states about additional malpractices.

Were Switzerland to join the EU its competitive advantage in financial services would almost certainly be reduced. Banking remains the largest sector in the canton of Zürich, but the success of these operations lies increasingly with their non-Swiss business.

New banking rules were introduced in January 2003 requiring proof of identity, nationality and date of birth for the ultimate owners of bank accounts opened by financial intermediaries.

In January 2013 Switzerland's oldest bank, Wigelin & Co, announced that it was closing permanently after pleading guilty in a New York court to helping Americans evade their taxes. It agreed to pay US$57.8 million in fines, after which it it 'will cease to operate as a bank'.

Central bank

Swiss National Bank (SNB)

Time

GMT plus one hour (daylight saving, late March to late October, GMT plus two hours)

Geography

Switzerland is a landlocked country bordered by Germany to the north, Austria to the east, Italy to the south and France to the west.

Located high in the Alpine region of western Europe, most of the country's land area is too mountainous to permit any great density of population, which means that most of the country's population reside in the low-lying urban areas. About half of the country's total land area is covered by rock, water or glaciers, or is forested, and a further quarter is either under grass or cultivation.

Hemisphere

Northern

Climate

Geographic factors mean, inevitably, that Switzerland experiences particularly marked variations in weather. While winters are generally severe, especially at higher altitudes, summers tend to be warmer than in the countries to the north. Low-lying areas are often wet. Zürich is prone to a heavy atmosphere in certain wind conditions. Temperatures range from about minus 1 degrees Celsius (C) to 18 degrees C.

Dress codes

Business attire is formal. Warm clothing is essential from September to May, especially in the higher altitudes.

Entry requirements

Passports

Required by all, valid for three months beyond date of departure.

Visa

Switzerland joined the Schengen Agreement group of countries on 12 December 2008, allowing free movement for EU citizens and external visitors with a Schengen visa. A Schengen visa application (offered in several languages) can be downloaded from http://europa.eu/abc/travel/ see 'documents you will need'.

Currency advice/regulations

There are no restrictions on the import or export of local and foreign currencies.

Customs

Personal effects and gifts up to value of Swf300 are duty-free.

Health (for visitors)

Nationals of the European Economic Area (EEA) countries and Switzerland can access reduced cost and sometimes free medical treatment using a European Health Insurance Card (EHIC) while visiting the EEA. Exceptions include nationals of the 10 countries which joined the EU in 2004 whose EHIC is not valid in Switzerland. Applications for the EHIC should be made before travelling.

Mandatory precautions

Vaccination certificates are not usually required.

Advisable precautions

Medical insurance is advisable as treatment is expensive.

Hotels

Hotels keep a high standard throughout the country, and are classified by the Swiss Hotel Association from one- to five-star. A 15 per cent service is included on bill. Reservations should be made well in advance during the winter holiday season.

Credit cards
All major credit cards are accepted.

Public holidays (national)
Fixed dates
1 Jan (New Year's Day), 1 Aug (National Day), 25 Dec (Christmas).
Variable dates
Good Friday, Easter Monday, Ascension Day, Whit Monday.

Working hours
Banking
Regional variations but generally Mon–Fri: 0830–1630. Money exchange at any airport and larger railway stations daily until 2200.
Business
Mon–Fri: 0800–1200, 1330–1700.
Government
Mon–Fri: 0730–1145, 1330–1800, or 0800–1230, 1315–1730.
Shops
Mon–Fri: 0800–1215, 1330–1830 (in larger cities also during lunch hours but Mon morning often closed); Sat: 0830–1600.

Telecommunications
Mobile/cell phones
There are 3G, 900/1800 GSM services available.

Electricity supply
220V AC, 50Hz

Social customs/useful tips
Appointments should always be made before making visits. If the appointment cannot be kept, this should be communicated.
Hand-shaking is frequent. When invited to dinner in a private house, flowers or chocolates for the hosts are the usual gifts.
When drinks are served, it is customary to wait until all the party has been attended to, and then to raise the glass with a salute to each.
The Swiss are proud of their often colourful cultural traditions. Traditional costume is still worn daily in a few areas of the country, although in most areas, it is restricted to celebrations and tourist-related events.

Security
There are no special problems with security in Switzerland; normal precautions apply, especially in the cities.

Getting there
Air
There are regular flights by all major international airlines.
National airline: Swiss International Airlines (Swiss)
International airport/s: EuroAirport Basle-Mulhouse-Freiburg (BSL), 5km from Basle; Berne-Belp (BRN), 9km from city; Geneva International (GVA), 5km north of city; Zürich (ZRH), 9km north of city.
Zürich and Geneva airports are directly linked to the national rail system.
Airport tax: None.
Surface
There are good road and rail links with all surrounding countries. It is advisable to book for rail travel beforehand.
Road: Major roads and tunnels link Switzerland to all neighbouring countries.
Water: There is limited access by water from France, Germany and Italy.

Getting about
National transport
Air: There are several daily flights linking Zürich, Geneva, Basle, Lugano and Berne.
Road: There is a road network of around 72,000km, including 17,000km of motorways. Roads are of good quality, but travel can be slow due to the terrain and the volume of traffic.
Rail: There are over 5,000km of track, practically all electrified. About 60 per cent is operated by Schweizerische Bundesbahnen (SBB) (Swiss Federal Railways) and the rest by about 120 small private companies. Rail journeys between major towns rarely exceed two or three hours.
In December 2007 the Lötschberg rail tunnel was opened between Bern and Valais cantons. It is estimated that the link will save up to an hour across the Alps. It will allow heavier trains, including 'piggy back' services for lorries.
Water: All the larger lakes are serviced by steamers operated by SBB.
City transport
A train from Zürich airport to the city centre takes about 12 minutes, while a taxi can take more than twice as long.
All local city transport is linked together on the same ticketing system. Tickets should be purchased before boarding from ticket dispensers by the stops.
Taxis: Widely available but they do not ply for hire. Zürich taxis have a higher tariff than elsewhere. A 15 per cent service charge is included; no tip required.
Buses, trams & metro: Good services in major towns. Tickets should be bought in advance from vending machines.
Multi-journey tickets also available. Flat fare up to five stops.
Car hire
Self-drive and chauffeur-driven cars available in all main towns. A valid national or international driving licence is required, and insurance is compulsory. Speed limits are 50kph in built-up areas, 80kph on normal roads and 120kph on motorways.
Further information can be obtained from the Touring Club Suisse (TCS) or the Automobil Club der Schweiz/Automobile Club Suisse (ACS).

BUSINESS DIRECTORY

The addresses listed below are a selection only. While World of Information makes every endeavour to check these addresses, we cannot guarantee that changes have not been made, especially to telephone numbers and area codes. We would welcome any corrections.

Telephone area codes
The international direct dialling (IDD) code for Switzerland is +41, followed by area code and subscriber's number:

Basel	61	Lucerne	41
Bern	31	Neuchâtel	32
Fribourg	26	St Gallen	71
Geneva	22	Winterthur	52
Lausanne	21	Zürich	1

Useful telephone numbers
Police: 117
Fire brigade: 118
Ambulance: 144
Motor breakdown service: 140
Swiss Air Rescue: 47-47-47
Emergency service of Touring Club of Switzerland: 35-80-00

Chambers of Commerce
American Swiss Chamber of Commerce,41 Talacker, 8001 Zurich (tel: 211-2454; fax: 211-9572; e-mail: info@amcham.ch).

Basel Chamber of Commerce, 67 Aeschenvorstadt, 4010 Basel (tel: 270-6060; fax: 270-6005; e-mail: hkbb@hkbb.ch).

Bern Chamber of Commerce and Industry, 1 Gutenbergstrasse, PO Box 5464, 3001 Bern (tel: 388-8787; fax: 382-8788; e-mail: info@bern-cci.ch).

British-Swiss Chamber of Commerce, 155 Freiestrasse, 8032 Zürich (tel: 422-3131; fax: 422-3244; e-mail: bscc@bscc.co.uk).

Fribourg Chamber of Commerce, Industry and Services, 37 Route du Jura, 1706 Fribourg (tel: 347-1220; fax: 347-1239; e-mail: cfcis@cci.ch).

Geneva Chamber of Commerce and Industry, 4 Boulevard du Théâtre, PO Box 5039, 1211 Genève 11 (tel: 819-9111; fax: 819-9100; e-mail: ccig@cci.ch).

St Gallen-Appenzell Chamber of Commerce and Industry, 16 Gallusstrasse, 9001 St Gallen (tel: 224-1010; fax: 224-1060; e-mail: sekretariat@ihk.ch).

Swiss Business Federation, 47 Hegibachstrasse, 8032 Zürich (tel: 421-3535; fax: 421-3434; e-mail: info@economiesuisse.ch).

Swiss Chambers of Commerce and Industry, 47 Avenue d'Ouchy, PO Box 315, 1001 Lausanne (tel: 613-3535; fax: 613-3505 e-mail: info@cci.ch).

Vaud Chamber of Commerce and Industry, 47 Avenue d'Ouchy, 1001 Lausanne (tel: 613-3535; fax: 613-3505; e-mail: cvci@cvci.ch).

Winterthur Chamber of Commerce, 15 Neumarkt, 8401 Winterthur (tel: 213-0763; fax: 213-0729; e-mail: info@haw.ch).

Zürich Chamber of Commerce, 5 BleicherwegPO Box 3058, 8022 Zürich (tel: 217-4050; fax: 217-4051; e-mail: direktion@zurichcci.ch).

Banking

Banque Cantonale de Genève, Quai de l'Ile 17, Case postale, 1211 Genéve 2 (tel: 317-2727; fax: 793-5960).

Banca della Svizzera Italiana, 2 Via Magatti, 6901 Lugano (tel: 587-111).

Bank Leu, Bahnhofstrasse 32, CH-8001 Zürich (tel: 219-1111).

Crédit Suisse, Paradeplatz 8, CH-8021 Zürich (tel: 215-1111).

Crédit Suisse, Pl Bel-Air 2, Case postale, 1211 Genève 70 (tel: 391-2111; fax: 391-2591).

Société de Banque Suisse, rue de la Confédération 2, Case postale, 1211 Genève 2 (tel: 375-7575; fax: 376-5024).

Swiss Bank Corporation, Aeschenvorstadt 1/Gartenstrasse 9, Basel (tel: 202-020).

Swiss Bankers' Association, Aeschenplatz 4, Postfach 4182, CH-4002 Basel (tel: 235-888).

Swiss Volksbank, Weltpoststrasse 5, 3015 Bern (tel: 328-111).

Union de Banques Suisses, Rue Rhone 8, Case postale, 1211 Genève 2 (tel: 388-1111; fax: 388-9652).

Union Bank of Switzerland, Bahnhofstrasse 45, CH-8000 Zürich (tel: 234-1111).

United European Bank, 11 Quai des Bergues, CP 2280, 1211 Genève (tel: 907-2111; fax: 732-3002).

Zürcher Kantonalbank, Bahnhofstrasse, PO Box 4039, 8022 Zürich (fax: 211-1525).

Central bank

Schweizerische Nationalbank, Börsenstrasse 15, 8022 Zürich (tel: 631-3111; fax: 631-3911; e-mail: snb@snb.ch).

Stock exchange

Borse (SWX) (Swiss Exchange), www.swx.com

Berner Börsenverein (BX Berne Exchange), Zürich, www.berne-x.com

Travel information

Automobile Club de Suisse (ACS), Wasserwerkgasse 39, 3000 Bern (tel: 328-3111; fax: 311-0310; e-mail: acszv@acs.ch).

Swiss Travel Centre, Grubenstrasse 12, 8045 Zürich (tel: 210-5500; fax: 210-5501; e-mail: information@stc.ch).

Touring Club Suisse (TCS), Chemin de Blandonnet 4, 1214 Vernier, Geneva (tel: 417-2727; fax: 417-2020; e-mail: info@tcs.ch).

National tourist organisation offices

Switzerland Tourism, Tödistrasse 7, 8002 Zürich (tel: 288-1111; fax: 288-1205; email: info@myswitzerland.com).

Ministries

Bundesamt für Statistik (BFS) (central statistics office), Schwarzftorstrasse 96, CH-3003 Bern (tel: 323-6011; fax: 323-6061).

Federal Department of Finance, Bundesgasse 3, 3003 Bern (tel: 66-111).

Federal Department of Public Economy, Bundeshaus-Ost, 3003 Bern (tel: 612-111).

Federal Office for Industry, Crafts and Labour, Bundesgasse 8, CH-3003 Bern (tel: 612-944).

Swiss Federal Tax Administration, Eidgenössische Steuerverwaltung, Eigerstrasse 65, CH-3003 Bern (tel: 617-112).

Other useful addresses

British Embassy, Thunstrasse 50, CH-3005 Berne 15 (tel: 352-5021/6; fax: 352-0583).

Embassy of the United States of America, Jubilumstrasse 93, CH-3005 Berne (tel: 357-7011; fax: 357-7344).

Fédération Suisse des Agences de Voyages, Postfach, Hardstrasse 316, CH-8027 Zürich (tel: 426-442)

Swiss Embassy (USA), 2900 Cathedral Avenue, NW, Washington DC 20008 (tel: (+1-202) 745-7900; fax: (+1-202) 387-2564; e-mail: vertretung@was.rep.admin.ch).

Swiss Federation of Commerce and Industry, Börsenstrasse 26, CH-8022 Zürich (tel: 221-2707).

Swiss Lawyers' Federation, Lavaterstrasse 83, CH-8027 Zürich (tel: 202-5650).

Swiss News Agency, Langgasstrasse 7, CH-3012 Bern (tel: 244-461).

SWX Swiss Exchange, Selnaustrasse 30, Postfach, CH-8021 Zürich (tel: 229-2111).

Union Suisse d'Agences-Conseils en Publicité (advertising), Kurfürstenstr 80, CH-8002 Zürich (tel: 202-6540).

SDA+ATS (in German) (www.sda.ch).

Swiss Infor (operated by SRG SSR Idée Suisse in nine languages) (www.swissinfo.org).

Internet sites

Details of government departments: www.admin.ch/ch/e/index.html

Index of Swiss business and tourism: www.swissdir.ch

Swiss Federal Statistical office: www.admin.ch/bfs/eindex.htm

Yellow pages Switzerland: www.pages-jaunes.ch/index.html

Syria

KEY FACTS

Official name: Jumhuriya al Arabya as Suriya (Syrian Arab Republic)

Head of State: President Bashar al Assad (since 2000)

Head of government: Prime Minister Wael al-Halki (from 11 Aug 2012)

Ruling party: Al Jabha al Wataniyyah at Wahdwamiyyah (National Progressive Front) (NPF), a coalition of 10 parties led by Hizb al Ba'ath al Arabi al Ishtiraki (Ba'ath Party) (Arab Socialist Rebirth Party) (re-elected Apr 2007)

Area: 185,180 square km (plus 1,295 square km Israeli-controlled Golan Heights)

Population: 20.82 million (2011)*

Capital: Damascus

Official language: Arabic

Currency: Syrian pound (Syr£) = 100 piastres

Exchange rate: Syr£188.82 per US$ (Nov 2015)

GDP per capita: US$2,803 (2010)

GDP real growth: 3.40% (2010)

GDP: US$60.30 billion (2010)

Unemployment: 9.00% (2008)* (Including a percentage of Iraqi refugees)

Inflation: 4.40% (2010)

Oil production: 33,000 bpd (2014)

Natural gas production: 4.40 billion cum (2014)

Balance of trade: -US$3.60 billion (2010)

Annual FDI: US$1.38 billion (2010)

* estimated figure

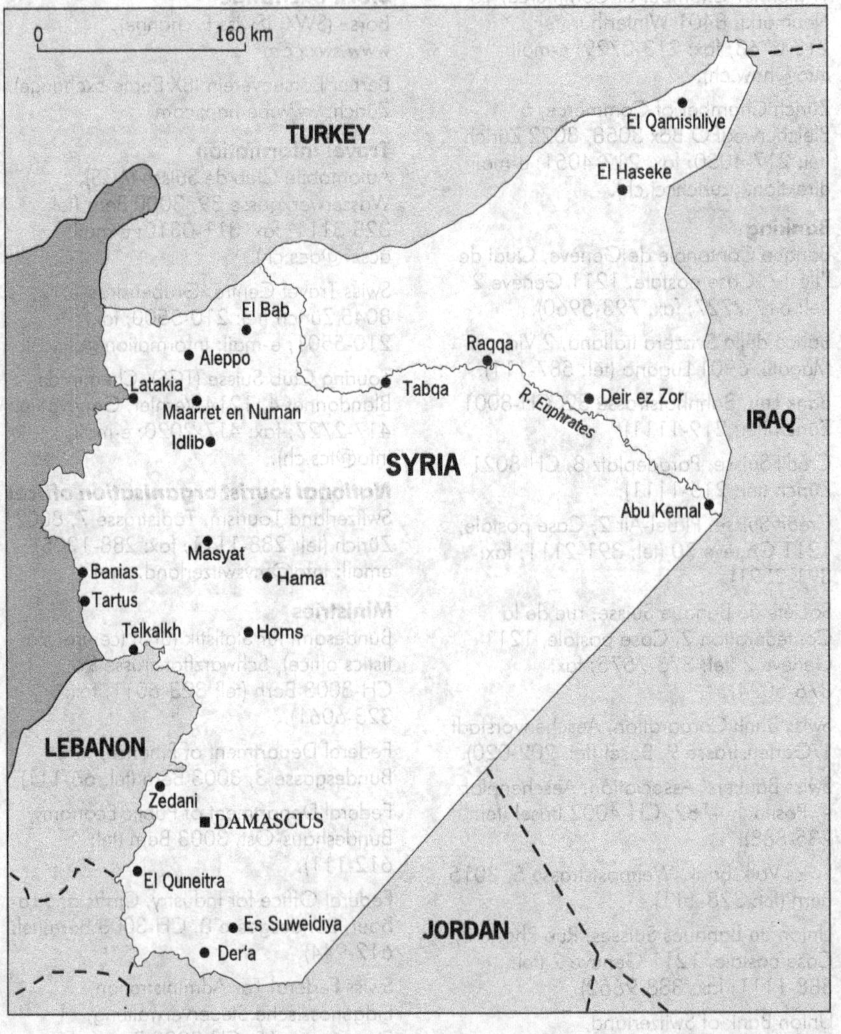

Russia's President Putin, having carved out a niche for himself as the isolated Machiavelli of international politics, surprised virtually everyone in late September 2015 by unilaterally committing Russian troops to engaging in the Syrian civil war, or as the former US General and CIA director David Petraeus famously described it, 'the geopolitical Chernobyl'. However much Mr Putin thought his actions would bolster the Assad regime, he must have reserved one of his frozen smiles for the moment he heard his ally claim that Syria was now part of a coalition made up of Iran, Iraq and… Russia. Russia's strategic position was best summed up by its foreign minister Sergei Lavrov: 'Saddam Hussein is hanged: is Iraq a better place? Qadafi murdered in front of the viewers: is Libya a better place? Now we are demonising Assad. Can we try to draw lessons?'

One thing both the US and Russia shared was a concern over quite how the endgame, if there was ever to be one, might play out. Having seen how events transpired in Iraq, Egypt and Libya above all the US goal was to avoid an uncontrolled collapse of the regime. The objective was to give some thought to how a post-Assad Syria might look. The United States and its coalition allies eventually sought to impose some sort of authority, even if that meant co-operating with a rump Syrian military. The theory might be commendable, but the bad news was that Mr Putin's intervention was probably based on a similar assumption. His late arrival on the scene of conflict might have been designed to support his long-time ally, but at the same time to make sure that if Assad did fail, Russia had a seat at the post-Assad negotiating table.

US intelligence had, on this occasion, served President Obama well. On the CBS television programme *60 Minutes* the president was quite forthcoming, saying that 'We knew that Putin was planning to provide the military assistance that Assad was needing because they were nervous about a potential imminent collapse of the regime.' However, it also emerged that US intelligence suspected the regime was marshalling a significant attack force near Homs, consisting of hundreds of Iranian-backed militia fighters and Hezbollah troops. Both Obama and Putin would have to wait for some time before taking their seats at any post-war negotiating table.

Blood brothers?

Governments may be able to choose their allies, but coalition partners can come to resemble family. Once sufficient time has elapsed and you are able to realise what's going on, it's too late: you're stuck with them. Putin was also stuck, not so much with Bashar al Assad, but with the extended al Assad family and an alliance between their two countries that went back to the days of Leonid Brezhnev. Critically, it was the al Assad family who still held the keys granting access to Russia's only Mediterranean sea base, at Tartus near Latakia in the Alawite heartland. The base, in theory the home of Russia's Black Sea fleet, is officially described as a 'Material-Technical Support Point' rather than a 'base'. Russia, having sat on the side-lines for more than four years, did at least know who its allies – and its enemies – were. By contrast, the Western coalition opposed a number of the groupings opposed to Mr Assad, including Ahrar al Sham and Jabhat al Nusra (an al Qaeda franchise). But hopes of forming some sort of a coherent opposition force had disappeared. What hopes remained of any resolution to the Islamic State (IS) problem probably had to be pinned on the Kurdish Pesh Merga, who could hardly be termed a 'rebel' group. But in mid-2015 no-one seemed to have identified the policy which might unlock what was euphemistically termed a stalemate. The simple truth was that neither side had the strength or the strategy to inflict defeat on the other. If there was anything resembling a trend, it was the reversal of some of the régime's advances. In 2015 the Assad regime had managed to lose Idlib in Syria's north, the IS had taken the ancient city of Palmyra and rebel forces surrounded Syria's second city, Aleppo.

The lines in the sand were however, less than clear. Evidence for the beleaguered city of Aleppo suggested that whatever the régime's vocal opposition to IS, it had continued to focus its attacks on the less well organised and resourced opposition groups on Northern Syria, seemingly avoiding any direct attacks on IS positions and communication lines. Marie Hart, a spokeswoman for the US state department went on record to say that 'We have long seen that the regime avoids ISIL (aka IS) lines, in complete contradiction to its public claims to be fighting ISIL.'

The scale of the Russian intervention – hailed in much of the Western press as 'decisive' – was almost negligible compared to the forces ranged against IS. It comprised a single squadron of fighters and a few combat helicopters deployed at the Hmeimim air base, also near Latakia. The Iranian presence gave Bashar al Assad professional feet on the ground. In June 2015 al Assad had invoked Syria's mutual defence pact with Iran to enlist additional assistance and, where possible, prevent further losses to IS. Syria had signed a defence pact with Iran in 2005 following the US lead invasion of Iraq. Arrangements between the two countries were formalised in May 2015 when Ala al Din Boroujerdi the chair of the Iranian parliamentary national security committee visited Damascus. Following the meetings in Damascus Qassem Soleimani, the commander of Iran's Revolutionary Guards announced that there would be a new approach in the conflict. It was thought that the Iranians had persuaded al Assad that it was preferable to defend and protect those areas under government control than to endeavour to wage battle across the country. According to the Syrian Observatory for Human Rights, the Syrian army had, by mid-2015, fallen to below 200,000 soldiers, half its size before the war broke out. Other independent estimates put the figure as low as 175,000 men. It was estimated that some 68,000 government troops had perished.

Bashar holds on

In March 2015 an article in the Lebanese independent, generally pro-Assad, *As-Safir* daily pointed out that in July 2012 a Friends of Syria conference had concluded that the toppling of Syrian President Bashar al Assad was a *fait accompli*. The defection of Syrian General Manaf Tlass, the commander of the Revolutionary Guards, on the day following the conference, only confirmed the theory. The French foreign minister, Laurent Fabius, was reported as seeing General Tlass as being the next president of Syria. Nor did the Qatari foreign minister Hamad bin Jassem mince his words after the conference, stating that 'President Al Assad will not be at the presidential palace by September.' (2012). The plot thickened when a couple of days later a detonation shattered the building of the Syrian national security in Damascus, wiping out the crisis management cell that had been supporting al Assad in leading the military and security operations. The explosion killed the head of the cell and the vice president for military affairs, General Hassan Turkmani, defence minister Daoud Rajha and his deputy Assef Shawkat (the president's brother in law). The head of the National Security Bureau, Hesham Bakjtyar, was also killed. A telephone call between Russian President Vladimir Putin and American President

KEY INDICATORS **Syria**

	Unit	2011	2012	2013	2014	**2015
Population	m	*21.82	*20.82	–	–	–
Oil output	'000 bpd	332.0	164.0	56.0	33.0	–
Natural gas output	bn cum	8.3	7.6	4.5	4.4	–
Total reserves minus gold	US$m	18,605.0	–	–	–	–
Foreign exchange	US$m	18,162.0	–	–	–	–
Exchange rate	per US$	47.18	70.85	141.30	159.50	–

* estimated figure ** forecast figure

Barack Obama indicated that Russia had abandoned Al Assad and had accepted the coming fall of the regime. Mr Putin – and Mr Lavrov – had apparently experienced a Damascene conversion. They and whoever had organised the events of mid-2012 had simply miscalculated. An expensive miscalculation that, inter alia, led to the creation of the IS. In June 2015 it was the turn of the recently appointed Saudi Arabian minister of foreign affairs, Adel al Jubeir to predict the fall of the Assad regime. This prediction was made following the reverse suffered in north-eastern Syria. There was little doubt that the al Assad forces had suffered and were seriously weakened. The government's position, under Iranian guidance, was to hold on to what it had got. In practical, territorial, terms this was not a lot. It held sway in 25 per cent of Syria's territory, where 60 per cent of the population now found themselves. Independent estimates put at between 10 and 15 per cent the size of the population living under IS control and at between 20 and 25 per cent those living under the control of the al Nusra Front. A further 5 to 15 per cent were thought to be under Kurdish control.

Iran

Whatever Russia may have thought about its relationship with the Assad regime, it faded into insignificance when compared to that of Iran. With the possible exception of the United Arab Emirates (UAE) all the members of the 'Western' coalition perceive Iran to be a negative regional influence, or even threat. The other regional coalition members are all Sunni – Jordan, Turkey, Saudi Arabia and Qatar – and fear that Iranian ambitions will result in regional expansion through Tehran's close links with the region's other Shi'a states, groupings and organisations – in Bahrain, Yemen, Iraq, Lebanon (where Hezbullah call the shots) and the Alawites in Syria. The shorthand description given to this alliance is the 'Shi'ite Crescent'. In terms of strategic planning, the Syrian regime has replaced an unsatisfactory reliance on its own generals with the presence in regime held areas of the Iranian Revolutionary Guards Quds force, headed up by the seasoned General Qassem Soleimani. In early October General Hossein Hamedani, an Iranian military advisor was killed by IS militants outside Aleppo. In January 2015 Iranian General Mohammad Ali Allah-Dadi was killed in an Israeli attack in Quneitra near the Golan heights. Announcing the incident, the Lebanese Hezbollah confirmed that six Iranian soldiers were killed, alongside six from Hezbollah. This was a rare incidence of overt Israeli intervention in the Syrian conflict. Israel claimed that the Syrian régime's convoy posed a threat to its borders.

The figures say it all

In the four years since the Syrian conflict broke out the situation reflected by the statistics had either steadily deteriorated, or become even more confused. In 2015 normally remote words such as epidemics, starvation and malnutrition had become commonplace. The UK defence and warfare analysts *Jane's Report* estimated that some 83 per cent of Syrian territory was held by rebel forces (including IS). The United Nations (UN) put the figure at 65 per cent. Writing in the *New York Review of Books*, the respected commentator Charles Glass (of Syrian ancestry) reported that the population of Damascus had grown five times larger, from 'two million before the war to around ten million in 2015.' In the same report Mr Glass quoted a World Health Organisation (WHO) spokesperson as saying that 'nine out ten people in Damascus Hospitals are not from Damascus. They come from Raqqa and elsewhere.' Figures for the total death toll vary; according to Mr Glass, by September 2015 the figure had risen to 320,000. And the number of refugees continued to rise. Roughly one fifth of Syria's pre-war population of 22 million had managed to leave the country. Lebanon alone had received more than one million; Turkey an estimated two million. Almost half a million were housed in Jordanian refugee camps. In August 2015 the flow of refugees into Europe steadily mounted as Syrians defied the risks of the sea journey and the sharp practices of Turkish people smugglers to reach Greece and then endeavour to thread their way through the unwelcoming Balkan states to Germany and Austria.

According to the World Bank, in 2014, half the Syrian population had been forced to leave their homes including 7.6 million internally displaced persons (IDPs). By September 2015, 4 million Syrians had registered as refugees with the UNHCR. Additionally, according to United Nations Office for the Co-ordination of Human Affairs (UNOCHA), Syrian Centre for Policy Research-SCPR more than 12.2 million people in Syria were in need of humanitarian aid, including 5.6 million children according, The lack of access to health care and the scarcity of medicine had led to a catastrophic health situation. Poor food availability and quality and successive cuts in subsidies on bread had exacerbated nutritional deprivation. An estimated 25 per cent of schools were not operational in 2014. The conflict had also significantly damaged public and private assets including health, education, energy, water and sanitation, agriculture, transportation, housing and infrastructure. The World Bank *Damage and Needs Assessment Report* of July 2015 (conducted in six governorate capitals namely Aleppo, Dar'a, Hama, Homs, Idlib and Latakia) estimated that the total damages for the six cities was between US$3.7 to US$4.5 billion. The major city of Aleppo was the most affected city, accounting for roughly 40 per cent of the estimated damages.

A report published by the respected Syrian Centre for Policy Research (SCPR) published in March 2015 estimated that Syria had lost more than US$119 billion in gross domestic product (GDP) since the outbreak of the civil war up until 2014. The same report put Syria's 'total losses' at US$220 billion when comparing to a scenario without the conflict. For a country whose GDP in 2007 was valued at US$40 billion, this represented an enormous loss in Syria's output. Another report, published by the United Nations Relief and Works Agency for Palestine Refugees in the Near East (UNRWA), made the depressing calculation that 'even if the conflict ceased now and GDP grew at an average rate of five per cent each year, it is estimated that it would take the Syrian economy 30 years to return to the economic level of 2010.' Commenting on the figures Erik Meyersson of the Stockholm Institute of Transition Economics (SITE part of the Stockholm School of Economics) noted that

'These are all striking ways of describing the economic costs of the Syrian conflict. At the same time, neither the UNRWA report nor the SCPR is very specific about how it arrived at these quoted estimates.' Mr Meyersson observes in his paper on the subject that for longer-horizon forecasts, the IMF (at least in published work) appeared to have given up trying to forecast Syria's economy sometime in 2012 due to 'the uncertain political situation.' The SCPR had forecast Syria's GDP growth at 6.6 per cent per year 2010–14, while the IMF's *World Economic Outlook* (WEO) in 2010 was forecasting 5.6 per cent growth per year for the same period.

Concluding his paper, Mr Meyersson considered that the human suffering in a conflict such as that in Syria sometimes gets lost in numbers. None the less, when taken together, the numbers add up to a summary of the massively destructive nature of war. Syria's Civil War, as far as the so-far available data goes, appears to be among the very worst economic contractions in post-war history.

Oil goes, gas gone

Once the eastern Mediterranean's leading oil and natural gas producer, following the outbreak of civil war, Syria has seen its production fall to a fraction of pre-conflict levels. Syria is no longer able to export oil and as a result, government revenues from the energy sector have fallen significantly. It seems a distant memory since the Syrian oil industry was producing 383,000 barrels per day (bpd) of oil and 316 million cubic feet per day (Mmcf/d) of natural gas, As noted above, the oil and gas sector once accounted for approximately one fourth of government revenues.

Syria also faced major challenges in supplying fuel oil to its citizens. Electricity supply in much of the country was sporadic directly as a result of fighting between government, opposition forces and the IS. Further, the exploration and development of the country's oil and natural gas resources had been delayed indefinitely. As the previously noted, even if the fighting were to subside, it would probably take years for the Syrian domestic energy system to return to its pre-conflict operating levels.

According to the United States government Energy Information Administration (EIA), quoting the US based *Oil & Gas Journal* (OGJ), Syria's proved reserves of oil were estimated at 2.5 billion barrels as of 1 January 2015, a total larger than each of Syria's neighbours except for Iraq. Most of Syria's crude oil is heavy (low gravity) and sour (high sulphur content), which requires a specific configuration of refineries to process. Sanctions placed on Syria by the European Union (EU) in particular – whose member countries had previously accounted for the majority of Syrian oil exports – limited the number of markets available to import and process the heavier Syrian crudes. The loss of oil export capabilities severely limited Syrian government revenues, particularly the lost access to European markets, which in 2011 imported over US$3 billion worth of oil from Syria, according to the European Commission (EC). Prior to sanctions, European refineries were the target market for Syrian oil because they were better configured to process heavy, sour oil.

Since the swift advance of IS in 2014, Syrian oil production had, according to the EIA, essentially ceased. The lack of domestic crude oil production caused the country's two main refineries to operate at less than half of normal capacity, resulting in supply shortages for refined petroleum products. Further, sanctions – and the resulting loss of oil export revenues – had made importing petroleum products difficult. It looked as though Iran was continuing to supply Syria with crude oil and refined products. Oil theft was also a problem, with Syrian officials claiming that hundreds of barrels of crude oil were being stolen and shipped to neighbouring countries every day.

In 2015 possession of Syria's largest producing fields including those in the Deir-ez-Zour region – which included Syria's largest field, Omar – had fallen to IS. The exact level of current production from these fields was, unsurprisingly, unknown, but the US-led coalition airstrikes had certainly caused structural damage in the region and had seriously limited its output.

By early 2013, more than 30 of Syria's power stations were inactive and at least 40 per cent of the country's high voltage lines had been attacked, according to Syria's minister of electricity. Syria's electricity generating capacity was 8.9 gigawatts in 2012, although damage to electricity generating facilities, high voltage power lines and other infrastructure has likely reduced the country's effective capacity. Electricity distribution losses, already 17 per cent of total generation in 2012, were likely to have climbed even further.

Risk assessment

Economy	Catastrophic
Politics	What?
Regional stability	What's that?

Muslims in Syria

% of population	92.8
Sunni (% of Muslims)	82
Shi'a (% of Muslims)	18

COUNTRY PROFILE

636 Muslim armies conquered Syria
1516 Syria became part of the Ottoman Empire.
1831–39 Egypt occupied Syria.
1915 Jamal Pasha, determined to tighten the Ottoman Empire's control of the region, hanged 21 Arabs in the city squares of Damascus and Beirut. The Martyrs' Day national holiday in Syria and Lebanon commemorates this event.
1918 End of the Ottoman Empire in Syria. Prince Faisal entered Damascus and assumed control of all Syria except for the area along the Mediterranean coast where the French were garrisoned.
1919 Prince Faisal convened the General Syrian Congress, which declared Syria sovereign and free. Arabic was declared the official language.
1920 France and Britain refused to recognise Syrian independence and under the Sykes-Picot Agreement Syria became a French Mandate, ending Syrian independence.
1925–26 Insurgent action resulted in France bombarding Damascus.
1928 The French allowed the formation of the Al Kutlah al Wataniyah (National Bloc), composed of various nationalist groups centred in Damascus. A constituent assembly drafted a constitution that included the reunification of Syria and denied the authority of France; it was rejected by the French High Commissioner.
1930 A constitution was imposed by the French.
1936 France agreed to Syrian independence, subject to France remaining dominant in military and economic fields.
1941 Allied forces occupied Syria. General de Gaulle promised an end to the French mandate.
1943 The National Bloc Syria won new parliamentary elections. Parliament elected Shukri al Kuwatli as Syria's first president.
1945 Syria became a Charter member of the United Nations (UN) (an indication of its sovereign status) and signed the pact of the League of Arab States (Arab League).
1946 A UN resolution prompted France to relinquish control and the sovereign state of Syria came into being.
1947 The Hizb al Ba'ath al Arabi al Ishtiraki (Ba'ath Party) (Arab Socialist Rebirth Party) was founded by Michel Aflaq.
1948–49 Syria contributed to a pan-Arab military force that failed to occupy the newly-created state of Israel.
1949 President al Kuwatli was overthrown in a military coup.
1953 In a referendum, Syrians approved a new constitution making Syria a presidential republic.
1954 Civilian government was re-installed; Shukri al Kuwatli returned from exile and was elected president. Syria moved towards greater economic and political co-operation with Egypt.
1958–61 A United Arab Republic (UAR) was formed between Syria and Egypt, following a referendum in both countries. Egyptian president, Gamel Abdel Nasser, became president of both states, Cairo was chosen as the capital and a new federal constitution was adopted. Nasser dissolved all political parties.

1961 Discontent at Egyptian domination led to the overthrow of the UAR, by a military *coup*, which dissolved the partnership.
1963 The Ba'ath Party seized control.
1967 Israel launched and won the June Six Day War taking control of the strategic Golan Heights from Syria.
1970 Former air force commander and defence minister, Hafez al-Assad, seized power in a bloodless coup.
1971 Al Assad was elected president. He was re-elected for four successive seven-year terms in 1978, 1985, 1992 and 1999.
1973 A new constitution was adopted. In the 6 October War (also known as the Yom Kippur War), Egypt and Syria invaded Israel to reclaim some of the land lost in the Six Day War, but despite some early strategic gains for Egypt and Syria, Israel counter-attacked and repelled the invasion, re-conquering the Golan Heights.
1974 Diplomatic relations with the US were resumed.
1975 President al Assad offered peace with Israel if it agreed to withdraw from all occupied Arab land. The offer was rejected.
1976 The Syrian army intervened in the Lebanese civil war to ensure the *status quo*; the Maronite leadership remained in power.
1980 Syria backed Iran in the Iran-Iraq War.
1981 Israel formally annexed the Golan Heights.
1982–87 Israel invaded Lebanon and attacked the Syrian army based there. After hostilities ended, Syrian forces remained in Lebanon.
1990 Syria participated in the US-led allied military operations against Iraq.
2000 President Hafez al Assad died. The Ba'ath party amended the constitution, reducing the minimum age for a president from 40 to 34 years, thereby allowing former President Hafez al Assad's son, Bashar al Assad, to become president.
2001 The UN General Assembly voted Syria a two-year seat on the Security Council.
2002 Syria, along with Cuba and Libya, were added to the original list (Iran, Iraq and North Korea) of the US' so-called Axis of Evil states. Syria denied US allegations that it was acquiring weapons of mass destruction.
2003 Muhammed Naji al Otari was appointed prime minister.
2004 The US imposed economic sanctions, citing Syria's support for terrorism and failing to stop militants entering Iraq from Syria. A UN Security Council resolution called for Syrian forces to leave Lebanon; Syria re-deployed some of its troops stationed around Beirut.
2005 Syrian troops were withdrawn from Lebanon following mass anti-Syrian protests in Beirut, and after accusations that Syria was responsible for the car bomb attack that killed former Lebanese prime minister, Rafik Hariri. The ruling Ba'ath party relaxed a number of laws that sanctioned some independent political parties, granted more press freedom and relaxed the state of emergency (that had been in place since 1963). UN investigators were allowed to question Syrian officials about the assassination of Rafik Hariri. Interior minister, Ghazi Kanaan, accused of being involved in the murder of Hariri, was found dead, apparently of suicide. An official UN interim report implicated senior Syrian and Lebanese security officials in the killing of Hariri; Syria rejected the report. Following weeks of pressure, Syria agreed to allow five senior officials to be interviewed by the UN investigator, Detlev Mehlis.
2006 The Danish and Norwegian embassies in Damascus were attacked after worldwide Muslim condemnations of cartoons depicting the Prophet Mohammed were published in a Danish newspaper. Syria and Iraq restored diplomatic relations after a 25-year gap and became an increasingly safe haven for those fleeing the war in Iraq.
2007 The dominant Ba'ath Party-led Al Jabha al Wataniyyah at Wahdwamiyyah (National Progressive Front) (NPF) coalition won parliamentary elections. Bashar al Assad's presidency was endorsed by referendum. Tough visa requirements were imposed on Iraqis, as the influx of refugees grew. Israel bombed and destroyed what it claimed was a secret nuclear reactor.
2008 The US published satellite images of what was called Syria's secret plutonium-producing nuclear reactor, claiming North Korea had helped build it. The site was cleared before UN inspectors from the International Atomic Energy Agency (IAEA) visited the site. The preliminary investigation declared the results inconclusive. An agreement to improve diplomatic relations was reached and a common border to be formally demarcated between Lebanon and Syria agreed. In a move to recognise Lebanon's sovereignty and independence, Syria established full diplomatic relations with Lebanon, and established a new embassy in Beirut.
2009 The first high-level talks since 2005 between the US and Syria took place in Damascus. The Damascus securities exchange began trading stocks for the first time.
2010 A ban on smoking in enclosed public places such as restaurants and cafés was imposed; the ban includes the traditional *nargile* (hubble-bubble). The US renewed its sanctions on Syria, first imposed in 2004, after President Obama said Syria continued to support terrorism and was pursuing development of weapons of mass destruction. A ban on the *niqab* (full face veil worn by Muslim women) was introduced in all Universities, both public and private. The *hijab* (headscarf) was deemed acceptable. Lebanese Prime Minister Hariri visited to discuss bilateral relations and closer ties. Hariri said that his accusation that Syria was responsible for the murder of his father was an error and that it was a 'political accusation'.
2011 Demonstrations against the Assad regime in the southern city of Deraa and the northern port of Latakia in March lead to concerns that they undermined the government's authority. The government resigned as a response to widespread discontent with the political system. Muhammad Naji Otari remained in post as caretaker prime minister.
President Assad announced a new cabinet in April with former agriculture minister Adel Safar as the new prime minister. President Assad issued a decree granting citizenship to tens of thousands of Kurds. The Kurds make up as much as 15 per cent of the population and had long demanded citizenship.
Civil rights groups claimed 560 people had been killed by security forces in Syria since protests began against the Assad regime in March. On Syria's Independence Day (17 April) there were a number of protests in Aleppo, Deraa and Suweida. The army killed 10 people and arrested 499 men in house-to-house raids in Deraa.
In May, the US imposed economic and travel sanctions on President Bashar al Assad, for human rights abuses since the civil unrest began. The US had already imposed sanctions on his brother and cousin in April.
In June, France and the UK sponsored a resolution in the UN Security Council condemning Syria's use of violence to suppress the protestors. The resolution did not include a proposal to use military action if the condemnation was ignored. The army attacked the town of Jisr al Shughour to 'restore security' after 120 security personnel had allegedly been killed. Citizens fled either into the surrounding countryside or across the border into Turkey, where refugee camps were hastily set up; within two weeks over 5,000 people had found sanctuary.
China, Russia and Brazil expressed their concerns over the proposed UN resolution of condemnation. President Assad's television speech gave nothing new in the

way of reforms and was greeted with scepticism by protesters.
In July, the largest anti-government demonstration in the country so far was held in Hama. As a result, the governor was sacked and security forces sent to the city. Amnesty International called for an international investigation into the violence committed by the security forces, including crimes against humanity. The National Salvation Council, a 25-member body, including Islamists, liberals and independents, elected from a group of around 300 opposition activists, met in Istanbul on 17 July. State media reported that the government had adopted a draft law allowing the formation of political parties other than the ruling Ba'ath party, providing they were not based on religious, tribal or regional support. Large anti-government protests in Hama, with barricades thrown up at road entrances to the city, led to the army attacking the city on 31 July and 1 August. Hundreds of protestors were reported to have been killed, following the shelling of the city by tanks.
The government crackdown continued and into August, with an estimated 2,000 people killed by troops. The US, Russia and Turkey warned President Bashar al Assad of the consequences of continued violence towards the people of Syria.
World leaders joined together in August and called on President Assad to step down, as the UN said that the excessive force used to suppress protests 'may amount to crimes against humanity'.
In early September, the EU banned imports of oil. A national council was formed including Kurds, Islamists, secularists and members of grassroots committees. Their intended aims were to 'convey the Syrian people's just problems on the international platform, to form a pluralist and democratic state'.
During a meeting in Istanbul (Turkey) on 1–2 October the newly combined opposition, the Syrian National Council (SNC), agreed its structure and aims. The SNC, led by Chairman Burhan Ghalioun, will challenge the regime of President Bashar al Assad to bring about democracy in Syria. Mishaal al Tammo, a Kurdish member of the opposition national council, was assassinated. The UN estimated that since March the number of people killed had exceeded 3,000 and that the authorities had 'manifestly failed to protect its population'.
In November the newly created Free Syrian Army (FSA) (of defecting soldiers), attacked an air force intelligence base in the suburbs of Damascus, in its most daring assault on government forces and installations to date. The Arab League issued a deadline for the government to 'stop the bloody repression' and begin 'real dialogue toward real reform' by or risk sanctions. The Arab League imposed sanctions against Syria, which included curbs on transactions with the Syrian Central Bank and halting the funding of projects by the Arab League. The sanctions followed the failure of Syria to meet the deadline for allowing Arab League observers into the country to monitor anti-government protests. Syria responded by calling the actions a betrayal of Arab solidarity. Turkey imposed a number of sanctions against Syria including suspension of financial dealing with and a freeze of assets of the Syrian government and a travel ban on the Syrian leadership; an arms ban is already in place.
On 2 December the UN declared that 4,000 people had been killed since mid-March. A delegation of 50 observers from the Arab League arrived in Damascus on 26 December. There was no pause in the violence and disruption during their visit.
2012 On 2 January, an Arab League spokesman defended the role of the observers, saying its presence was placing pressure on the Syrian authorities to comply with Arab peace initiatives and the Syrian army had been withdrawn from a number of cities, almost 3,500 detainees had been released and humanitarian aid delivered to beleaguered cities. Latest UN data reported that over 5,400 people had been killed in the civil war since March 2011. Russian Foreign Minister Sergey Lavrov visited Syria on 7 January and called for reforms. He said President Assad wanted Arab monitored peace efforts and would set a date for a constitutional referendum and that he was 'fully committed' to ending bloodshed and undertaking negotiations with all political forces. The Arab League convened an emergency meeting on 7 January to review its observer mission's work and discuss its future role. A suicide bomber killed 26 and injured over 60 people in the al Midan district of Damascus. The bomber targeted buses carrying riot police, shortly before an anti-government demonstration was about to begin; most casualties were civilians. 13 January was declared 'Friday of Support for the Free Syrian Army' with tens of thousands demonstrating in Homs, Hama, Aleppo and Damascus suburbs. On 21 January the Arab League proposed the transfer of power by President Assad to a deputy and a government of national unity. This was rejected by Assad. On 24 January observers from the Gulf States within the Arab League were pulled out of Syria and called on the UN to 'end the bloody upheaval'. By 27 January the city of Homs was besieged by the Syrian army. The remaining Arab League observers were pulled out on 28 January. On 29 January, the Syrian army, using tanks, launched an assault to retake suburbs of Damascus held by rebel forces.
On 4 February, the UN Security Council (UNSC) voted on a resolution calling for President Assad to resign and institute an Arab League peace plan. Although 13 members of the council voted in favour, Russia and China vetoed the proposal because they perceived it to be a violation of Syria's sovereignty and could allow military intervention and regime change. General Secretary Ban Ki-moon said the result 'undermines the role of the United Nations and the international community in this period when the Syrian authorities must hear a unified voice calling for an immediate end to its violence against the Syrian people'. Anti-Assad activists reported the death of 200 people in Homs since the army offensive began in January. On 7 February, Prime Minister Erdogan of Turkey announced that his government would 'start a new initiative with those countries who stand by the Syrian people, not the regime.' By 8 February, Homs had been under bombardment for five days; Arab Gulf States began to expel Syrian ambassadors and recalling their own, due to what they described as 'mass slaughter' of civilians. Ban Ki-moon said the failure of the UN resolution had encouraged the Syrian regime 'to step up its war on its own people'. As the Syrian army continued to shell Homs, foreign observers considered the government's grip on northern Syria as tenuous, as so much of it was in open revolt. UK-based war correspondent Marie Colvin and French photographic journalist Remi Ochlik were killed on 22 February in Homs. Colvin had been reporting the death of civilians and French President Sarkozy accused the Syrian authorities of assassination by deliberately targeting the house in the Bab Amr suburb of Homs being used as a press centre by foreign journalists. On 28 February, the UN announced that the death toll in Syria had surpassed 7,500. A constitutional referendum was held on 26 February, as violence continued in some areas of the country. New proposals included dropping Article 8, which enshrines the rule of the Ba'ath Party, a proposal for multiparty elections by May and limiting presidential terms to two, of seven years each. Voter turnout was 57.4 per cent and 89.4 per cent voted in favour of the changes. Foreign observers were not permitted to witness the voting. President al Assad signed the new constitution into law on 27 February.
The month-long bombardment of the besieged city of Homs stopped on 2 March. The government denied access by the Red Cross and Red Crescent to the stricken

area for several days, saying the area was too dangerous to enter as it had been mined and booby-trapped. On 12 March, the bodies on 21 women and 26 children were found in Karm el Zaytoun and Al Adawiyeh neighbourhoods, in the devastated city of Homs. The government accused 'armed terrorist gangs' while the opposition (SNC) claimed government security forces (Shabiha militia) were responsible for the massacre. On 16–18 March a UN mission, accompanied by Syrian officials, visited a number of sites, including Homs, Deraa and Hama. However, the UN experts were denied free access and were not allowed to visit Idlib in the north. On 19 March Russia called for a daily two-hour truce for humanitarian relief to be given to the besieged and to evacuate the wounded from battle zones around the country. It also said that the Syrian leadership had made 'a lot of mistakes'. On 27 March, on the same day as the UN revised its estimate of the number of dead due to the conflict to 9,000 people, former UN secretary general Kofi Annan brokered a six-point peace deal, which was endorsed by both the Arab League and by all members of the UNSC. The agreement included addressing the aspirations and concerns of the Syrian people; a UN-supervised cessation of armed violence by all; the provision of humanitarian assistance to all areas affected by the fighting, with a two-hour ceasefire; release of arbitrarily detained persons; freedom assured for journalists and respect of the freedom of peaceful association and the right to demonstrate.

On 8 April, two days before the peace deal was due to be implemented (with a full ceasefire by 6am on 12 April), when troops were to be withdrawn, the Syrian government objected, saying it required a written guarantee by the opposing forces that they would lay down their arms during the pull-out; the demand was rejected by the rebels. Residents of Homs, who had fled across the border into Turkey on 10 April, reported that the government army was continuing to shell the city. Syrian forces also fired into a refugee camp inside the Turkish border in the Gaziantep province. On 12 April, following a day of relative peace, Kofi Annan said that the UN was ready to send in monitors to oversee the implementation of the ceasefire. On 16 April, an advanced team of six monitors arrived in Syria; with the remaining 25 due in the following days. On 22 April, UN-envoy, Kofi Annan said that the UNSC vote to deploy 300 observers was a 'pivotal moment for the stabilisation of the country'. The UN and Arab League also called on the government to withdraw its tanks and weapons from the cities. On 26 April, Ban Ki-moon warned that the Syrian government was 'in contravention' of the international agreed peace plan, with the presence of heavy weapons and troops deployed in cities, as reported by UN monitors.

On 10 May, two car-bombs exploded in Damascus, killing at least 55 people and wounding around 400. Both sides of the conflict accused the other of responsibility and the UNSC 'condemned in the strongest terms the terrorist attacks'. The government was held responsible by the UN for the army shelling of the civilian town of Houla on 25 May. At least 108 people were killed (including 49 children), despite a vigorous denial by an official Syrian spokesman. The army action was called 'indiscriminate and unforgivable' by Major General Robert Mood of the UN's observer mission. It later transpired that most of the Houla civilians killed had been summarily executed, with blame being laid on the pro-Assad militia, the Shabiha. On 31 May Colonel Qassim Saadeddine, a commander of the FSA, pronounced a 48-hour deadline for the Assad government to observe the UN ceasefire or he would consider the FSA 'no longer bound' by the Annan peace plan. However, the threat was dissipated when General Riyad Asaad the FSA head later denied the deadline.

On 5 June the government declared the ambassadors of 17 countries *personae non gratae* following these countries' decision, days earlier, to expel top Syrian diplomats. On 6 June, Riad Farid Hijab (a staunch Assad loyalist) was appointed as prime minister.

On 17 July fighting broke out in Damascus as the FSA launched a campaign, called 'the Damascus Volcano and earthquakes of Syria', to liberate the city. At the same time, Kofi Annan was meeting President Putin (in Russia) where he called for more support for a new UNSC resolution to end the conflict. Putin said Russia's obstacle to acceptance was the West's demand for sanctions, which could eventually lead to military force to end the 'civil war'. On 19 July Russia and China vetoed the UNSC resolution proposing greater sanctions on Syria. Government troops were mobilised to fight rebels who had killed three senior members of the regime and seized parts of Damascus and Aleppo.

On 2 August, Kofi Annan, the UN-Arab League joint special envoy to Syria announced that he was resigning, due to the failure of his six-point peace plan which he said had become a 'mission impossible'. An estimated 20,000 people had been killed in Syria by August. On 6 August prime minister Riad Hijab defected, in support of 'the holy revolution', according to his spokesman who informed the news agency, al Jazeera. Hijab and his family fled into Jordan. Omar Ghalawanji was appointed as acting prime minister until Wael al Halki was appointed prime minister of 9 August. On 11 August Wael al-Halki was sworn into office as prime minister.

On 16 August, the UN observer mission in Syria was ended after its mandate expired. On 18 October, human rights groups in Syria estimate that at least 28,000 people (of all ages, gender and status) had 'disappeared' since the beginning of the conflict, picked up by either the military or militia and had not been seen again. Following meetings in Qatar that began on 8 November, on 11 November an agreement between opposition parties chose Moaz al Khatib as leader of a new coalition, to join the disparate factions against Bashir al Assad's government. On 20 November British foreign minister, William Hague, told parliament that the National Coalition of the Syrian Revolutionary and Opposition Forces was the 'sole legitimate representative' of the Syrian people. On 11 December, US President Obama officially recognised the SNC as the 'sole legitimate representative' body of the Syrian people. The announcement came after recognition of the SNC by France, Germany and the UK, among others. Russia condemned the US move as a violation of earlier accords.

2013 In March Ghassan Hitto was named as prime minister by the National Coalition for Syrian Revolutionary and Opposition Forces and set to forming an interim government to administer so-called 'liberated' zones, co-ordinating the provision of basic services and supplies. Prime Minister Wael al-Halqi survived a car bomb attack in Damascus on 29 April. The UN Disengagement Observer Force (Undof), which monitors the only open border crossing between the Israeli-controlled Golan Heights and Syria, lost a number of international peacekeepers as the violence in Syria spread. Austria began withdrawing its 377 UN soldiers from the mission on 12 June, following the withdrawal of troops by Canada, Croatia and Japan. Troops from the Philippines and India remain.

On 22 June President Assad ordered the salaries of all government employees to be raised. Syrian news agency, SANA, reported that the decree raised monthly salaries by 40 per cent for the first Syr£10,000 (US$50), 20 per cent for the second Syr£10,000 and 10 per cent for the third Syr£10,000. A salary of Syr£30,000 (US$150) would be Syr£37,000 (US$185). The decree also raised the minimum monthly wage for the private, co-operative and joint venture sector to Syr£13,670 (US$70).

On 6 July the National Coalition opposition alliance named Ahmed Jarba as its president. At the same time Saudi-backed candidates defeated those allied with Qatar in several elections. Ghassan Hitto resigned as prime minister of the rebel held areas, saying that he would never-the-less 'continue working for the interests of the revolution'. Mr Jarba has close links to Saudi Arabia, and said he expected advanced weapons supplied by Saudi Arabia. A report by the Liwa al Islam Brigade on 8 August said they had hit President Assad's convoy while he was moving through Damascas. He was later seen attending prayers at his usual mosque. The attack was denied by the government. On 31 July the government finally agreed to the visit of UN inspectors to three sites suspected of being the subject of chemical attacks. A chemical weapons attack that killed hundreds in a suberb of Damascas on 21 August was widely condemned internationally. Although the UN inspectors were stayimng within 10 kilometres they were not allowed to visit the site. Video clips on YouTube showed pictures of the injured and dying. Both sides denied making the attack. The UN's disarmament chief, Angela Kane, arrived in Damascas on 24 August; an agreement between the government rebels was reached to allow inspectors to visit the site on 26 August. A ceasefire will allow the inspectors to collect material for examination. US Vice President Joe Biden said on 27 August that there was 'no doubt' the Syrian government had used chemical weapons on it's people and it must be held accountable. By the beginning of September UN agencies were reporting that the number of Syrian refugees had reached two million. Unexpected discussions between Russia and the US led to a framework document agreed on 14 September that stipulates Syria must provide details of its stockpile of chemical weapons within a week. President Obama said that the US-Russian deal 'represents an important, concrete step toward the goal of moving Syria's chemical weapons under international control so that they may ultimately be destroyed'. At the same time he warned that there would be 'consequences should the Assad regime not comply with the framework'. The report by the UN inspectors into the use of chemical weapons was published on 16 September. It confirmed that sarin-filled rockets had been fired. UN Secretary General Ban Ki-moon called it a 'despicable crime'. The US, UK and France said the technical details showed only the regime could have been responsible for the 21 August attack. However, Russia accused the UN of a biased report and said they had evidence rebels had been responsible. In an interview aired on 18 September (after Syria had acceded to the Chemical Weapons Convention on 14 September) with US Fox News President Assad said that he was committed to getting rid of Syria's chemical weapons, but that it might take a year and cost US$1 billion. He denied that his forces were responsible for the recent attacks, accusing rebels of being responsible. A number of rebel groups announced on 24 September that they do not support groups formed outside the country, including the main opposition group, the National Coalition, which is based in Istanbul. At the same time, UN inspectors retured to Syria to further their investigations of chemical weapons. The UNSC unanimously adopted a binding resolution demanding Syria destroy all its chemical weapons. However a second resolution would be required before force could be used if necessary. The team of international experts from the Organisation for the Prohibition of Chemical Weapons (OPCW), charged with dismantling Syria's chemical weapons, arrived on 1 October. In an interview with *Der Spiegel* in Germany President Assad suggested Germany might be a suitable mediator. On 14 October, leader of the Syrian National Council (SNC), George Sabra, said his group would pull out of the coalition if it took part in talks planned for Geneva in November. He said that conditions on the ground in Syria were not conducive to a satisfactory outcome. Talks with SNC opposition officials were held in London on 22 October to try and persuade them to attend the next round of talks in Geneva. They were urged by the Friends of Syria group of countries 'commit itself fully' to planned peace talks. On 28 October the OPCW announced that all but two chemical weapons sites had been visited. Although this means a deadline has been missed, the OPCW has said it will continue negotiations to ensure the conditions necessary for safe access to the two remaining sites will continue. The WHO annouced in late October that there had been 10 cases of polio confirmed, mostly in children, the first cases in 14 years. It is thought that the disease may have been brought in by foreign fighters from the three countries where polio is still endemic (Nigeria, Pakistan and Afghanistan). Lakhdar Brahimi, the UN-Arab League envoy, met President Assad in Damascus on 30 October to try to win backing for planned peace talks in November. Mr Assad said that the talks would only succeed if foreign powers ended 'support for terrorist groups' fighting his forces. On 30 October Israeli aircraft attacked a site near Latakia, destroying missiles intended for the Lebanese militant group Hezbollah. On 31 October the OPCW confirmed Syria had destroyed all equipment for producing, mixing and filling chemical weapons. The weapons themselves were put under seal. The OPCW and the Syrians must agree a detailed plan by mid-November on destroying the weapons. Lakhdar Brahimi, UN-Arab League envoy on Syria, said on 5 November that the peace talks were being delayed. On 15 November the OPCW said that it had adopted a detailed plan for the destruction of Syria's stockpile by mid-2014, although where exactly remained unclear after Albania refused to allow the destruction to take place in Albania. On 18 November a large bomb on a Syrian government building near Damascus killed 31 people, including four generals, according to the Syrian Observatory for Human Rights. Salim Idriss of the Free Syrian Army (FSA)'s Supreme Military Command fled Syria in early December. He was reported as saying that he would be willing to join government forces against al Qaeda affiliated groups, including Islamic State of Iraq and al-Sham (ISIS)/12/2013.

2014 A three-day humanitarian truce to enable aid to be delivered to the Old Quarter of Homs was agreed in early February. On the third day a convoy was finally able to deliver aid to the area and evacuate as many as 600 women, children and the elderly, despite mortar fire and shooting. On 21 April the government announced that the presidential election would be held on 3 June. For the first time more than one name can appear on the ballot. The result was another win, with 88.7 per cent, for Mr Assad, but this time there had been three contenders: Hassan al-Nouri and Maher Hajjar as well as Bashar al Assa.

2015 The Syrian Observatory for Human Rights reported that a heavy attack with hundreds of rocket and missiles fired at several districts, including government-held areas, was launched by Islamist groups on Aleppo on 2 July. The groups were said to be a new alliance of rebel groups called Ansar Sharia, which includes the jihadist al-Nusra Front. Although control of Aleppo, Syria's largest city and the country's industrial and financial centre, has been divided between government and rebel forces since shortly after fighting began in 2012, with the government by-and-large holding the west of the city and various rebel groups the east, the complete loss of control would be a major set-back for President Assad. Russia began air strikes on IS positions in Syria on 30 September. President Assad paid a surprise visit to Russia for talks with President Putin on 20 October. After IS claimed they had shot down a Russian passenger aircraft returning from Sharm el

Sheikh with holiday makers, Russia increased its bombing operations against IS within Syria.

Political structure

Constitution

The 1973 Constitution was based on five principles: Syrian Arab revolution to achieve unity, freedom and socialism; Arab unity against the threat of imperialism and Zionism; socialism as a fundamental necessity; economic freedom and social liberalisation; Arab revolution towards world liberalisation.

An amended Constitution came into effect on 27 February 2012. It included the ending of the Ba'ath party's monopoly of Syria's political life and the formation of other political parties; presidential elections to take place every seven years, contested by several candidates; Syria will no longer be a planned economy; scientific research, artistic creation, literature and cultural creativity to be protected, while maintaining Islamic jurisprudence; discrimination based on sex, origin, religion and language will be forbidden and military service will remain compulsory.

Independence date

17 April 1946

Form of state

Socialist democratic republic that has been run by a military regime since 1963.

The executive

The president is Head of State, and has almost absolute power as the country is a one-party state with a disproportionate share of power in the hands of the Hizb al Ba'ath al Arabiyah al Ishtiraki (Ba'ath Party) (Socialist Arab Rebirth Party) and minority Alawite community.

Presidential candidates are nominated by parliament and agreed by referendum, for a seven-year term.

The president appoints and dismisses the vice presidents, the prime minister and the Council of Ministers. He holds the posts of commander-in-chief of the armed forces and secretary general of the Ba'ath Party. The Council of Ministers is headed by the prime minister and its members are appointed from the Ruling party.

National legislature

The unicameral Majlis al Shaab (People's Council) has 250 members, directly elected in 15 multi-seat constituencies (in which the NPF is guaranteed 167 seats) by proportional representation vote, for four-your terms. The assembly proposes the presidential candidate but may not initiate laws; it may assess and may occasionally modify those proposed by The executive branch.

Legal system

The judiciary is guaranteed independence under the constitution, however in practice, the minister of justice has the power to appoint, promote and transfer members of the judiciary and has undue influence. The legal system has separate religious and secular courts using *Sharia* (Islamic law) and a civil law code respectively.

Syria has not accepted compulsory International Court of Justice (ICJ) jurisdiction.

Last elections

7 May 2012 (parliamentary); 3 June 2014 (presidential); 27 February 2012 (constitutional referendum)

Results: Parliamentary: Al-Jabha al-Wataniyyah at-Wahdwamiyyah (National Progressive Front) (NPF), a coalition of 10 parties led by Hizb al Ba'ath al Arabi al Ishtiraki (Ba'ath Party) (Arab Socialist Rebirth Party), won 168 seats (out of 250); 77 seats were won by independents.

Presidential: Bashar al Assad received 88.7 per cent of the vote, Hassan al-Nouri 4.3 per cent and Maher Hajjar 3.2 per cent. Turnout was 73.42 per cent.

Constitutional referendum: 89.4 per cent agreed to the amendments, 9 per cent disagreed; turnout was 57.4 per cent.

Next elections

June 2021 (presidential); 2016 (parliamentary).

Political parties

Ruling party

Al Jabha al Wataniyyah at Wahdwamiyyah (National Progressive Front) (NPF), a coalition of 10 parties led by Hizb al Ba'ath al Arabi al Ishtiraki (Ba'ath Party) (Arab Socialist Rebirth Party) (re-elected Apr 2007)

Main opposition party

Most political opposition is severely repressed and leading critics of the government are in exile.

Syria's annual population growth rate is among the highest in the Middle East. About 38 per cent of the population is under 14 years of age; in 2006, 5 per cent of the population were over aged 60. There were an estimated 1.5 million Iraqi refugees resident in Syria in 2007.

Population

20.82 million (2011)*

Last census: September 2004: 17,921,000

Population density: 104 inhabitants per square km.Urban population 56 per cent (2010 Unicef).

Annual growth rate: 2.5 per cent, 1990–2010 (Unicef).

Internally Displaced Persons (IDP)

200,000–500,000 (UNHCR 2004)

Ethnic make-up

Arabs (90 per cent); Kurds, Armenians and Assyrians (10 per cent).

Religions

About 90 per cent of the population are Muslim with those of the Sunni denomination outnumbering Alawi (Shi'a) Muslims by about six to one. The remainder are Christian (8 per cent), Druze and Jewish (2 per cent). Religious freedom is provided by the constitution.

Education

Primary schooling lasts for six years. Secondary education, which begins at the age of 12, also lasts for six years and is divided into two three-year cycles. Students may either enter the general or the technical branches, although entry is selective and is based on the Intermediate Level Diploma (*al Kafa'a*) examination. The first cycle is introductory. Technical secondary education is divided into industrial and commercial tracks. There are agricultural and technical schools and four universities, at Damascus, Aleppo, Tishreen and Homs. All higher education institutions are state-controlled and state-financed.

Literacy rate: 80.8 per cent adult rate; 95 per cent youth rate (15–24) (latest figures WHO 2008, Unesco 2005).

Compulsory years: Six to 12.

Enrolment rate: 101 per cent gross primary enrolment, of relevant age group (including repeaters); 43 per cent gross secondary enrolment (World Bank).

Pupils per teacher: 23 in primary schools.

Health

Per capita total expenditure on health (2005) was US$61; of which per capita government spending was US$31, at the international dollar rate, (WHO 2008).

Improved souces of water are available to 89 per cent of the population.

Medical services are relatively well developed in larger towns and cities, with 14 hospital beds per 10,000 head of population, but there is considerable variation in rural areas.

HIV/Aids

HIV prevalence: 0.1 per cent aged 15–49 in 2003 (World Bank)

Life expectancy: 72 years, 2006 (WHO 2008)

Fertility rate/Maternal mortality rate: 2.9 births per woman, 2010 (Unicef); maternal mortality 130 deaths per 100,000 live births (WHO 2008).

Child (under 5 years) mortality rate (per 1,000): 15 per 1,000 live births (WHO 2012); 8.5 per cent of children aged under five are malnourished (WHO 2008).

Head of population per physician: 5 physicians per 10,000 people, 2006 (WHO 2008)

Welfare

The government maintains a basic range of social welfare provisions, including free healthcare for low-income groups, and is officially committed to improving the quality of state welfare provision as economic conditions allow. The government claims that the expansion of the private sector has led to more young children working. The labour and social affairs minister is responsible for enforcing minimum wage levels in the public and private sectors. The law does not protect temporary workers who are not subject to regulations on minimum wages.

Main cities
Damascus (capital, estimated population 1.9 million (m) in 2012), Aleppo (Halab) (1.9m), Homs (900,492), Hamah (527,429), al Ladiqiyah (402,700), Dayr az Zawr (275,473), ar Raqqah (207,594), Idlib (178,980), Duma (136,665).

Languages spoken
English is widely spoken and French is spoken predominantly by the older generation.
Official language/s
Arabic

Media
Press
Dailies: The state runs four national and many regional newspapers with news contained in them provided by the Syrian Arab News Agency (SANA). In Arabic, *Al Thawra* (www.althawranews.net), has the largest circulation; *Al Baath* (http://albaath.online.fr) (official publication of the Ba'ath Party); *Tishreen* (www.tishreen.info) and in English *Syria Times* (http://syriatimes.tishreen.info). The first private, political daily newspaper to open since 1963 was *Al Watan* (www.al-watan.com).
Weeklies: In Arabic, *Tishreen al Osboi* a political magazine and *Mawkef al Riyadhi* (http://riadi.alwehda.gov.sy) covering sports news are government-run. *Star Syria* (www.star-sy.com) is a youth magazine.
Business: In Arabic, *Al Iqtisad wal Nagl* (www.aliqtisad.com) is a monthly magazine; *Al-Iqtissadiya (www.iqtissadiya.com) for business and political news.*
Periodicals: There are over 140 private magazines and others produced by government departments, state organisations, trade unions, political, professional and religious associations. In Arabic, *Al Arabieh* and *Ayam Al Osrah* (www.ayam-mag.com) are women's magazines; *Al Maaloumatieh* is a consumer magazine. In Arabic and English, *Al Nashra al Ektisadyeh* (www.dcc-sy.com) is published by the Chamber of Commerce. In Arabic and French, *Ougarit* (www.ougarit.org) (quarterly) and *Maaber* (www.maaber.org) for culture and literature. In English, *Syria Today* (www.syria-today.com) for current affairs.
Broadcasting
Radio: The state radio service, Radio Sout Al Sha'ab (www.rtv.gov.sy) broadcasts domestic and external programmes in Arabic, French, English, Russian, German, Spanish, Portuguese, Polish, Turkish and Bulgarian. Private radio stations, all broadcasting from Damascus, include Farah FM (www.farah.fm), Rotana Style FM (www.rotana.net) and Syria Al Ghad (www.syriaalghad.com).
Television: Syrian television (www.rtv.gov.sy) operates two terrestrial channels and a satellite station. Many households subscribe to satellite television providers and the only private station based in Syria, Al Sham, competes for audiences with pan-Arab and Western (generally for expatriate communities) TV satellite stations.
The minster of information plans to license up to a further 24 private satellite television channels.
National news agency: SANA
Other news agencies: All4Syria (www.all4syria.org).

Economy
In 2015 reliable data on the state of Syria's economy was almost impossible to find. Even the International Monetary Fund (IMF) has given up publishing their regular figures. The comments here cover Syria as it was before the civil war, and which might be expected to apply once calm has resumed and Syria is once again a fully functioning country. Despite the lack of reliable data, it is known that in 2014 the economy deteriorated further due to international sanctions, infrastructural damage, lack of domestic consumption and production, high inflation and reduced subsidies.
In January 2011, protest asking for democratic reform lead to the outbreak of a civil war in Syria. This war was still on going in mid-2014 and had many major effects on the economy. A report by the Syrian Centre for Policy Research (SPCR) estimated that by November 2012 the equivalent of 81.7 per cent of the 2010 GDP in economic terms had been lost. The report also noted that almost two decades worth of human development achievements had been lost.
Even before the civil disturbances of 2011 and 2012, the main sectors of the Syrian economy, agriculture and hydrocarbons, had been struggling to emerge from decades of over-centralisation and stagnation. In 2009, the service sector constituted 46.5 per cent of GDP, through the expansion of tourism with around three-quarters of visitors to Syria coming from the Gulf States. The government, recognising the contribution tourism makes to the economy, was seeking to expand the sector and to build infrastructure more suitable to a wider market. Tourism in 2009 was next only to agriculture and oil in importance to the economy. The banking sector, where private banking has been allowed, was subject to reforms and produced an improvement in the economy. Agriculture accounted for 23 per cent of GDP in 2009, with around 25 per cent of the population involved and ensuring self-sufficiency in food. Syria has been dependent on its oil and gas reserves to sustain the economy while the industrial sector constituted 30 per cent of GDP, of which manufacturing was 13.4 per cent in 2009. Hydrocarbons, which typically contribute 20 per cent to GDP, have been responsible for 65 per cent of exports and 50 per cent of government revenue. Production and exports, however, are falling as the existing fields decline. It is forecast that, in the absence of the discovery of significant new deposits in the meantime, Syria will run out of oil by 2020 (in 2012 it became a net importer of oil). Unless other activities are developed and foreign direct investment (FDI) increases, Syria could find itself relegated to the status of a low-income country.
During 2014, as the on going conflict worsened, the number of people living in Syria in need of help from international assistance increased from 9.3 million to 12.2 million, as well as the number of Syrian refugees increasing from 2.2 million to over 3.3 million.

External trade
In 2005 the Greater Arab Free Trade Area (Gafta) was ratified by 17 members, including Syria, creating an Arab economic bloc. A customs union was established whereby tariffs within Gafta will be reduced by a percentage each year, until none remain. It is also a signatory of the Euro-Mediterranean Partnership agreement, which provides for the introduction of free trade between the EU and 10 Mediterranean countries.
Foreign trade provides almost 70 per cent of GDP and over 65 per cent of all exports are oil and its derivatives, and natural gas. As manufacturing provides only around 25 per cent of GDP, its importance to exports is less than that of agriculture, which exports livestock and cereals, and the majority of the annual cotton lint harvest not used domestically for spinning and garment production.
Imports
Major imports are capital machinery and vehicles, food and livestock, appliances, chemicals, plastics, various yarns and paper.

Main sources: Saudi Arabia (24.5 per cent of total in 2014), UAE (12.0 per cent), Turkey (10.0 per cent)

Exports

Main exports are crude oil, petroleum products, cotton, clothing, fruits, vegetables, wheat, meat and live animals.

Main destinations: Iraq (63.8 per cent of total in 2014), Saudi Arabia (11.1 per cent), Kuwait (7.0 per cent)

Agriculture

Farming

Agriculture remains a leading sector of the economy, however has dropped in contribution to GDP over the period 2003–14 from approximately 25 per cent to 16.4 per cent. The sector employs about 14 per cent of the total workforce, which has dropped from 27 per cent over the same period.

Agricultural land is mainly privately owned. Approximately 31 per cent of the total land is cultivated. Much of Syria is mountainous and part of the eastern part of the country is desert or semi-desert. The fertile areas include the coastal strip and the Euphrates and Khabur valleys. Intensification of farming in the rain-fed areas is on going; these areas account for more than 80 per cent of the total crop area. The al Thaura dam on the Euphrates, built with Russian technology, brings irrigation to a vast area.

Main crops are cotton, wheat and barley. Wheat and barley together account for two-thirds of the cultivated area. Extreme fluctuations in grain production from year to year caused by rainfall variability have traditionally caused much hardship for the rural population. Cotton is the main cash crop. Other leading crops include vegetables, citrus fruits, olives, tobacco and sugar beet. Sheep and goats are grazed in many areas. Wool is also an important product.

Fishing

Syria's small annual fish catch is mostly destined for the domestic market.

Forestry

Syria is lightly forested with less than 3 per cent of forest or woodland cover. In ancient times, Syria had extensive mountain forests but these have largely been cleared or degraded and only remnants of mixed coniferous forest remain. The predominant species include *Abies cilicica*, *Pinus halipensis* and *Pinus brutia*. Syria has established a moderately large area of plantations based on cypress, pine and eucalyptus species. The country has a modest network of protected areas – State Forest Protection Zones provide the most substantive forest conservation measures. Syria produces very modest volumes of sawn timber, veneer, plywood and particleboard. The majority of demand for wood and paper products is met by imports.

Industry and manufacturing

The industrial sector as a whole contributed around 33.7 per cent to GDP in 2014 and employs around 16 per cent of the labour force.

In the mid-1960s, the government began a policy of rapid industrialisation, especially in the areas of iron and steel and other heavy industries. Factories turn out a wide range of products, including tractors and television sets.

Many of Syria's industries are agrarian-based, such as food processing and textiles. Sugar processing, an important activity, is mainly conducted by state-owned enterprises. The textile industry is the oldest established, contributing approximately 15 per cent of export earnings. Other industries include cement, soap, glass, footwear, leather goods and brassware.

Industry and manufacturing

The industrial sector as a whole contributed around 33.7 per cent to GDP in 2014 and employs around 16 per cent of the labour force.

In the mid-1960s, the government began a policy of rapid industrialisation, especially in the areas of iron and steel and other heavy industries. Factories turn out a wide range of products, including tractors and television sets.

Many of Syria's industries are agrarian-based, such as food processing and textiles. Sugar processing, an important activity, is mainly conducted by state-owned enterprises. The textile industry is the oldest established, contributing approximately 15 per cent of export earnings. Other industries include cement, soap, glass, footwear, leather goods and brassware.

Tourism

Almost all governments have warned their citizens not to travel to Syria until the conflict has been resolved.

Syria has many important ancient sites dating back into antiquity, a number of which are included on Unesco's World Heritage List, including the ancient cities of Aleppo, Bosra and Damascus. The religious sites attract devotees of both Islam (particularly Iranian pilgrims) and Christianity, as well as those interested in the Greco-Roman occupation. Syria is a member of the Euromed Heritage Programme, a computerisation project, sponsored by the EU, which focuses on cultural tourists of archaeology, arts and history, promoting sites through the internet.

Travel and tourism in total contributed 10.6 per cent of GDP in 2014, which is estimated to drop by 3.4 per cent in 2015. As the conflict intensified throughout 2011 and foreign visitors failed to arrive, by May 2012 hotel occupancy had fallen to less than 15 per cent. The industry used to employ 12.6 per cent of the workforce (691,430 jobs), but by 2014 total employment had dropped to 7.6 per cent of the workforce (490,500 jobs).

Before the conflict, tourism had been a growing industry with visitor numbers rising from 4.2 million in 2007 to 8.5 million in 2010. Tourism is typically geared to the Middle East market and is heavily concentrated in Damascus. Tourists were mainly Lebanese and Jordanian, although Syria was also popular with the French and Russians.

Mining

The mining sector contributes up to 10 per cent to GDP and employs around 5 per cent of the working population. Syria has large phosphate deposits that are used in its growing fertiliser industry. Approximately 76 per cent of phosphate mined is exported, with 10 per cent used at the Homs fertiliser factory. Other mineral resources include gypsum.

Hydrocarbons

The Syrian Petroleum Company (SPC) is responsible for upstream production and development, often in partnership with small to medium sized foreign oil companies. Further oil production will be intensified through enhanced oil recovery measures. The oil industry faces many challenges, as production has dropped continually from 652,000 barrels per day (bpd) in 2003 to 52,000bpd in 2013. This in combination with the rising consumption will see Syria become a net importer of oil by 2020. The drop in output has arisen from technological problems and depletion of oil reserves.

There are two state-owned oil refineries, in Banias and Homs, with a total capacity of 240,000bpd. The construction of three new refineries, with an additional 380,000bpd has been planned since 2005, but without tangible results in 2013. In December 2010, Syria and Venezuela signed a memo of understanding (MOU), for the joint development of the Froklos oil refinery, in eastern Homs. The refinery was originally planned in 2008, to process 140,000bpd, at an estimated cost of US$5 billion to build. The MOU covers the work on planning, construction and operating the plant. The oil refinery had not been built by 2015.

The government plans to increase domestic consumption of natural gas, allowing more oil to be exported, if it can develop local gas resources and secure gas imports from regional sources. However, with fixed and subsidised oil prices,

persuading the population to switch to gas may prove to be a painful process.
In May 2004, significant gas discoveries were made by a Croatian oil and gas company in the northern central part of Syria. The new gas production will allow Syria to export for the first time. The first oil joint venture between China and Syria was set up in July 2004. The joint venture is between the largest oil producer in China, China National Petroleum Corporation (CNPC) and the state-owned Syrian Petroleum Company (SPC). It is hoped that the establishment of the company – the Sino-Syrian Kawkab Oil Company (SSKOC) – will speed up CNPC's development of the Kbeibe oil field in the northeast of Syria.
In order for production levels of oil and gas to increase foreign investment is vital. However following the outbreak of the Syrian civil war, western companies are legally prohibited from working in the country. EU sanctions have caused Shell to halt operations in Syria as of 2011 after a long history of production.

Energy
Total installed generating capacity is approximately 8.9GW (global rank 60) producing over 29 billion kilowatt hours (kWh). The government is promoting the rapid development of gas production for electricity generation and converting oil-fired electrical generating plants to natural gas. The Tishreen Power Plant was expanded, following a contract signed in October 2009 with the Bharat Heavy Electricals Limited (BHEL) of India, to increase generating capacity by 400MW, at a cost of US444.6 million. Two new generators of 200MW were installed in 2012. However, in December 2013 rebels fired mortars at the power plant causing a drop in its power feed.
The state-run Public Establishment for Electricity Generation and Transmission (PEEGT) is responsible for generation and transmission and the Public Establishment for Distribution and Exploitation of Electrical Energy (PEDEEE) deals with sales and distribution. Annual growth in consumption has been 7 per cent and generating capacity must be increased in order to meet domestic demand. However, lack of investment has hampered efforts.
Power failures have been experienced during summer when drought conditions have suspended operation of the three hydroelectric power stations on the Euphrates River. Despite shortcomings in its system, Syria is a net exporter of electricity, being part of an integrated power grid linked to Jordan, Lebanon and Turkey.

Financial markets
Syria's first stock exchange since the 1960s opened for business on 9 March 2009, under the supervision of the Syrian Commission on Financial Markets and Securities, in a crucial step by government to liberalise the state-controlled economy. The Damascus Securities Exchange initially trades in six companies, on the two days a week it operates.
Stock exchange
Damascus Securities Exchange

Banking and insurance
A series of reforms since 2000 has included official approval of private banking, in joint ventures, with foreign equity limited to 49 per cent, to be sited in 'free zones'. The role and status of the central bank was redefined with the establishment of the Conseil Monétaire et de Crédit (CMC) (Monetary and Credit Council) which was established to supervise monetary policy and co-ordinate the activities of private banks. Restrictions on the trading of foreign currency and the need for a majority local partner will be a disincentive to a wider pool of potential participants.
Three Lebanese banks – Fransabank, Banque Européenne pour le Moyen Orient and Société Générale Libano-Européenne de Banque – opened branches in the free zones. Five other non-Syrian banks, including the Jordanian Arab Bank and Housing Bank for Trade and Finance (HBTF) were later given approval to begin trading.
The government has eased the ban on domestic nationals opening foreign currency accounts. Nevertheless this reform has been of limited benefit as it is still technically illegal to hold hard currency and most Syrians continue to channel their funds through Lebanese banks. The lack of domestic credit and the poor quality of Syria's banking sector represent a major hindrance to the development of the country's economy.
Central bank
Central Bank of Syria
Main financial centre
Damascus

Time
GMT plus two hour (daylight saving, April to October, GMT plus three hours)

Geography
Syria is bordered by Turkey to the north; by the Mediterranean Sea and northern Lebanon to the west; by Israel and Jordan to the south; and by Iraq to the east.
Western Syria contains a series of mountain ranges, lying parallel to the Mediterranean. The northern range is separated from Syria's coastline by a narrow plain. The highest peak is Jabal ash Shaykh (Mount Hermon) in the extreme south-west of the country. To the east of the mountains, the Euphrates River crosses partly cultivatable plains in the north, while the central and southern areas consist mainly of desert plains.
Hemisphere
Northern

Climate
Syria has a moderate Mediterranean climate, four distinct seasons, and cloudless blue skies for the greater part of the year. Temperatures in autumn and spring range between 20 and 25 degrees Celsius (C), 30–35 degrees C in summer (May–September) and 5 to 10 degrees C in winter. Winter is generally moderate but wet in the coastal region and cold inland; summer is hot and dry inland, hot and humid on the coast.

Dress codes
Lightweight clothing is needed during the hottest months (May–September). Both men and women should dress discreetly in public. For business meetings men should wear a suit and tie, women a two-piece suit or equivalent. On social occasions dress as for business meetings unless otherwise indicated.

Entry requirements
Passports
Passports are required by all and must be valid for at least a month from the date of visit. Passports that carry an Israeli visa are prohibited.
Visa
Required by all except Arab nationals. All visas should be acquired before travelling. Business visas require a letter of introduction and full itinerary along with the application. Contact the nearest consulate for further details.
Visa extensions are needed for visits over 15 days and can only be obtained from the Syria Immigration and Passport Administration.
Prohibited entry
Nationals of Israel, holders of passports with evidence of travel in Israel.
Currency advice/regulations
The import and export of local and foreign currency is limited to US$5,000 (or equivalent).
Travellers cheques are not widely accepted outside the main cities.
Customs
Personal items are duty-free. Gold jewellery must be declared on arrival.
Prohibited imports
Firearms, ammunition; birds and bird products.

Health (for visitors)
Medical services are well developed and many doctors speak English.
Mandatory precautions
A certificate of vaccination against yellow fever is required if travelling from an infected area.

Advisable precautions

Typhoid, tetanus, hepatitis A and polio immunisations are recommended, and anti-malaria precautions should be taken. There is a risk of rabies.

Hotels

Rooms are in short supply, and it is essential to book in advance. At first-class and international hotels, it will be necessary to pay in foreign currency (Arab nationals and resident foreigners exempted).
Hotels in Damascus are located close to most tourist attractions.

Credit cards

Credit cards are accepted in main business areas – contact the card provider for more details. Charge cards are not accepted.
In 2003, the Real Estate Bank (REB) became the first Syrian bank to accept MasterCard and Visa cards issued abroad.

Public holidays (national)

Fixed dates

1 Jan (New Year's Day), 8 Mar (Revolution Day), 21 Mar (Mothers' Day), 17 Apr (Independence Day), 1 May (Labour Day), 6 May (Martyrs' Day), 6 Oct (Liberation War Day), 25 Dec (Christmas Day).
Holidays that fall at the weekend are taken later *in lieu*.

Variable dates

Eid al Adha (three days), Islamic New Year, Birth of the Prophet, Eid al Fitr (three days).
Islamic year 1437 (15 Oct 2015–2 Oct 2016):: The Islamic year contains 354 or 355 days, with the result that Muslim feasts advance by 10–12 days against the Gregorian calendar. Dates of feasts vary according to the sighting of the new moon, so cannot be forecast exactly.

Working hours

Friday is the weekend break.

Banking

Sat–Thu: 0800–1400; early closing Thu.

Business

Sat–Thu: 0830–1430.

Government

Sat–Thu: 0830/0900–1300/1400, 1600/1700–1900/2000.

Shops

Sat–Thu: 0930–1400, 1630–2100 (summer); Sat–Thu: 0930–1400, 1600–2000 (winter).

Telecommunications

Mobile/cell phones

Two networks exist: GSM 900 and 1800

Electricity supply

220V, 50Hz AC with European, two-pin plugs.

Weights and measures

Metric system (local units also in use).

Social customs/useful tips

Appointments should be made in advance. Punctuality is appreciated. It is conventional to shake hands on meeting and taking leave. Sometimes a conference visit is a way of doing business. The host may hold several conversations with guests at the same time. It is not customary to start talking business immediately. At meetings it is polite to drink coffee or tea, when offered. It is useful for business cards to have Arabic translations on the reverse side. A few words of Arabic will be appreciated.
Smoking in cafes, restaurants and other public places, including educational institutions, health centres, sports halls, cinemas, theatres and public transport, was banned by presidential decree in October 2009. There is a fine of Syr£2,000 (US$46). The ban includes the hubble-bubble pipe.
Do not drink in public during Ramadan. Islamic customs should be respected. Shoes should be removed on entry to mosques. Women should dress modestly. It is the convention to use the right and not the left hand when shaking hands and passing or receiving anything.
Alcohol is available to visitors.
Do not photograph anything remotely connected with the armed forces, including radio transmission aerials, and remember that some Syrians, particularly in rural areas, may regard cameras with suspicion.
It is considered very impolite for men to sit next to women on buses.
The punishment for possession of drugs is life imprisonment. For drug trafficking, the death penalty applies.
Travellers cheques are generally accepted in the main cities although it is advisable to take US dollars as well. Accommodation in all hotels must be paid in hard currency, except one-star hotels. Food, beverages, telephone calls etc can be paid in local currency. It is illegal to change money on the streets. Only change money in recognised exchange shops, banks and hotels.

Security

Visitors should keep in touch with developments in the Middle East as any increase in regional tension might affect travel advice. Visitors are advised to carry identity documents at all times. Avoid driving outside the main cities at night.

Getting there

Air

National airline: Syrianair
International airport/s: Damascus International (DAM), 29km south-east of city, with banking, refreshments and duty-free shop. A bus service operates every 30 mins from 0600-2300, into the city centre.
Aleppo (ALP) 10km from city, with banking, refreshments and duty-free shop.
Taxis are available from both airports, and fares should be negotiated beforehand. Journey time into Damascus city centre is 30 minutes, and 20 minutes into Aleppo.
Airport tax: International departures: Syr£200, excluding transit passengers.

Surface

Road: From Istanbul via Ankara the E5 road runs to Damascus via Aleppo. From the east a road runs from Iran via Iraq, and used to be considered excellent, however border crossings are sometimes suspended. From the south the road from Aqaba, (the terminus of the E5) runs via Amman (Jordan), and includes stretches of motorway. Other roads include those from the Lebanon.
Service taxis are faster than buses and run between Damascus-Amman or Irbid (Jordan).
Rail: Routes link Syria with Istanbul and Ankara (Turkey) and Amman (Jordan). Sleeper-cars are available and all trains are air-conditioned.
There are rail lines running from northern Iraq to the Syrian coast, however services are sometimes suspended.
Water: Car ferries sail from Bodrum (Turkey), Rhodes, Heraklion, Santorini and Piraeus (Greece). Cruise ferries are run by Italian, Greek, Cypriot and Turkish companies, with sailings that vary from year to year. Passage may take up to three days. Ferries from Alexandria (Egypt) dock at the Lebanese port of Beirut – the distance to Damascus is shorter than via any Syrian port; visitors should check the viability of this route before travelling.
Main port/s: Latakia, Tartus and Banias.

Getting about

National transport

Air: There are internal flights by Syrianair between Damascus, Aleppo, Latakia, Qamishli and Deir ez-Zor.
Road: The 30,208km road network has some 22,500km of relatively good surfaced roads linking main centres.
Buses: Luxury couch services operate between major towns. Bus tickets, with assigned seats, should be bought prior to boarding. Qadmous, al Ahliah and al Ryan are private bus companies.
Minibuses serve smaller locations; they have no schedule and leave when full.
Microbuses are modern vans used on short routes between cities and on routes to small towns and villages. They are more comfortable than the minibuses and there is no standing room. Departures are more frequent but they are more

expensive than the minibuses. Fares are usually paid on board.

Taxis: May be used to travel between cities as they are affordable; either negotiate a fare with the driver or check that the meter runs correctly. Long-haul service (shared) taxis are also available on the more popular routes, they cost more than microbuses but less than a personal taxi hire.

Rail: Two classes of rail service are available, with restaurant cars, sleeping carriages and air-conditioning. The railway links all the major cities and has a regular timetable, but it can be slow so it may not suit the business traveller.

City transport

Taxis: Yellow cabs in Damascus are expensive; always check the meter has been set. Fares are mostly by negotiation. Drivers do not expect a tip.

In other cities, fares are set by government departments.

Buses, trams & metro: From airport to city centre.

Car hire

Private cars are rarely available, but taxis are reasonably priced.

BUSINESS DIRECTORY

The addresses listed below are a selection only. While World of Information makes every endeavour to check these addresses, we cannot guarantee that changes have not been made, especially to telephone numbers and area codes. We would welcome any corrections.

Telephone area codes

The international direct dialling (IDD) code for Syria is +963, followed by the area code and subscriber's number:

Aleppo	21	Latakia	41
Damascus	11	Raqqah	22
Hassakah	52	Tartous	43
Homs	31	Zabadani	13

Chambers of Commerce

Federation of Syrian Chambers of Commerce, Mousa bin Nosair Street, PO Box 5909, Damascus (tel: 333-7344; fax: 333-1127; fax: syr-trade@mail.syr; internet: www.fedcommsyr.org).

Aleppo Chamber of Commerce, Amir Palace Hotel Building, Bab Jnein Street, PO Box 1261, Aleppo (tel: 223-8236; fax: 221-3493; e-mail: alepchmb@mail.sy).

Aleppo Chamber of Industry, PO Box 1859, Aleppo (tel: 362-0600; fax: 362-0040; e-mail: alpindus@net.sy).

Damascus Chamber of Commerce, 126 Mouawiah Street, Hariqa, PO Box 1040, Damascus (tel: 221-1339; fax: 222-5874; e-mail: dcc@net.net).

Damascus Chamber of Industry, Mouawiah Street, PO Box 1305, Damascus (tel: 221-5042; fax: 224-5981; e-mail: dci@mail.sy).

Damascus Countryside Chamber of Commerce, Bagdad Street, PO Box 5859, Damascus (tel: 231-5653; fax: 231-3798).

Hasakah Chamber of Commerce and Industry, PO Box 243, Hasakah (tel: 221-645; fax: 313-842).

Homs Chamber of Commerce and Industry, Abulauf Street, PO Box 440, Homs (tel: 469-440; fax: 464-247; e-mail: homschamber@homschamber.org).

Lattakia Chamber of Commerce and Industry, PO Box 124, Latakia (tel: 479-530; fax: 478-526; e-mail: lattakia@chamberlattakia.com).

Tartous Chamber of Commerce and Industry, PO Box 403, Tartous (tel: 329-852; fax: 329-728; e-mail: info@tarcci.com).

Banking

Agricultural Co-operative Bank; PO Box 4325, al Naanaa Garden, Damascus (tel: 221-3462, 222-139).

Commercial Bank of Syria (Banque Commerciale de Syrie) PO Box 933, Yousef Azmeh Square, Damascus (tel: 221-8890, 221-8891).

Industrial Bank; PO Box 7578, Almuhandiseen Building, Maisaloun Street, Damascus (tel: 222-8200).

Popular Credit Bank, PO Box 2841, Maisaloun Street, Damascus (tel: 222-7604, 221-8555).

Real Estate Bank, PO Box 2337, Y al Azme Square, Damascus (tel: 221-8602/3).

Central bank

Central Bank of Syria, PO Box 2254, 29 Ayar Street, Damascus (tel: 221-6581; fax: 245-5576).

Stock exchange

Damascus Securities Exchange, www.dse.gov.sy

Travel information

Silk Road Travel and Tourism, Fardoss Street, PO Box 12958, Damascus (tel: 223-0500/5; fax: 223-1138, 231-5555; email: hanano@silkroad-tours.com).

Syrianair, Syrian Arab Airlines, Youssef al Azmeh Square; PO Box 417, Damascus (tel: 223-1838, 223-2154; fax: 221-4923; internet: www.syriaair.com).

Ministry of tourism

Ministry of Tourism, Kwatli Street, Barada Bank, Damascus (tel: 221-0122/ 223-7940; fax: 224-2636; web: www.syriatourism.org).

Ministries

Ministry of Agriculture and Agrarian Reform, Sa'dallah Al Jaberi Street, Damascus (tel: 221-3613/222-2513; fax: 224-4078/224-4023; web: www.syrianagriculture.org).

Ministry of Al Awkaf, Rukeneddin, Damascus (tel: 441-9079/441-9080; fax: 419-969).

Ministry of Construction and Building, Sa'dallah al-Jaberi Street in Front of the Mail Center, Damascus (tel: 222-3595/222-7966/222-3196/222-3597).

Ministry of Communications, Al Salheyeh, Damascus (tel: 222-7033/34; fax: 224-6403).

Ministry of Culture, Al Rawda, George Haddad Street, Damascus (tel: 333-1556/333-8633/338-600; fax: 332-0804).

Ministry of Defense, Omayad Square, Damascus (tel: 777-0700/880-980/371-0980/372-0936).

Ministry of Economy and Foreign Trade, Maysaloun Street, Damascus (tel: 221-3514/221-3515; fax: 222-5695; web: www.syrecon.org).

Ministry of Education, Al Mazraa, Al Shahbandar Square, Damascus (tel: 444-4703/4/2/444-4800; fax: 442-0435).

Ministry of Electricity, Kwatli Street, Damascus (tel: 222-3086/222-9654; fax: 222-3686).

Ministry of Environment, Al Salheyeh, Damascus (tel: 222-2600/1/2/3/4; fax: 333-5645).

Ministry of Finance, Al Sabee Bahrat Square, Baghdad Street., Damascus (tel: 221-9600/1/2/3; fax: 222-4701).

Ministry of Foreign Affairs, Muhajereen, Shora Avenue, Damascus (tel: 333-1200/4/333-7200; fax: 332-0686).

Ministry of Health, Parliement Street, Damascus (tel: 333-9600/1/2; fax: 222-3085).

Ministry of Higher Education, Al Rawda, Kasem Amin Avenue, Damascus (tel: 333-0700/1/2/3; fax: 333-7719; web: www.syrianeducation.org).

Ministry of Housing and Utilities, Al-Salheyeh, Yousef Azmeh Square, Damascus (tel: 372-2552/221-7571/221-7572/372-2552; fax: 221-7570).

Ministry of Information, Mezzeh Autostrad, Dar al Ba'th Building, Damascus (tel: 666-4600/666-4601; fax: 662-0052).

Ministry of the Interior, Al Bahsah Street, Damascus (tel: 223-8682/223-8683; fax: 224-6921).

Ministry of Justice, El-Nasre Street, Damascus (tel: 221-4105/220-302; fax: 224-6250).

Ministry of Industry, Maysaloun Street, Damascus (tel: 223-1834; fax: 223-1096; web: www.syrianindustry.org).

Ministry of the Interior, Al Shuhadaa Square, Damascus (tel: 221-1001/221-9401; fax: 222-3428).

Ministry of Irrigation, Fardoss Street, Damascus (tel: 221-2741/222-1400; fax: 332-0691).

Ministry of Petroleum and Mineral Resources, Adawi, Insha'at; PO Box 31483, Damascus (tel: 444-5610/445-1624; fax: 445-7786).

Ministry of Social Affairs and Labour, Al Salheyeh, Yousef Azmeh Square, Damascus (tel: 221-0355/222-5948; fax: 224-7499).

Ministry of Supply and Internal Trade, Al Salheyeh, Damascus (tel: 221-9044/221-9241; fax: 221-9803).

Ministry of Transport, Al Jalaa Street, Damascus (tel: 333-6801/2/3; fax: 332-3317; web: www.min-trans.net).

Syrian Cabinet of Ministers, Shahbandar Street, Damascus (tel: 222-600 /222-1000/211-0212).

Other useful addresses

Arab Advertising Organisation, Moutanabbi Street, PO Box 2842, Damascus.

British Embassy, Kotob Building, 11 Mohd Kurd Ali Street, Malki PO Box 37, Damascus (tel: 371-2561/3).

Cotton Marketing Organisation, BP 729, Rue Bab al araj, Aleppo (tel: 238-486).

Director General of the Damascus International Fair, Kouwatli Street, Damascus (tel: 229-853/840/914).

General Organisation for Cement, PO Box 5265, Damascus (tel: 666-7000/3).

General Organisation for Chemicals and Foodstuffs, PO Box 893, Damascus (tel: 222-8521, 222-5421).

General Organisation for Engineering Industries, PO Box 3120, Damascus (tel: 212-1824/5).

General Organisation for Insurance (The Syrian Insurance Company), PO Box 22679, Damascus (tel: 221-8430/1; fax: 222-0494).

General Organisation for Machinery and Equipment, PO Box 3130, Damascus (tel: 221-8223, 221-8156; fax: 221-1118).

General Organisation for Metals and Building Materials, PO Box 3136, Damascus (tel: 442-0941, 442-0944, 442-0948; fax: 442-0947).

General Organisation for Sugar, PO Box 429, Homs.

General Organisation for the Textile Industries, BP 620, Rue Fardoss, Damascus (tel: 221-6200, 222-7158; fax: 221-6201).

General Organisation for Trading and Distribution, PO Box 15, Damascus (tel: 221-0396).

General Organisation of Free Zones, PO Box 2790, Damascus (tel: 219-137).

International Centre for Agricultural Research in the Dry Areas, Box 5466, Aleppo.

Public Establishment for Distribution and Exploitation of Electric Energy, PO Box 35199, Damascus (tel: 224-5926, 222-3086, 222-9654).

Public Establishment for Electricity Generation and Transmission, PO Box 3386, Damascus (tel: 212-9795, 211-9935; fax: 222-9062).

Syrian Embassy (USA), 2215 Wyoming Avenue, NW, Washington DC 20008 (tel: (+1-202) 232-6313; fax: (+1-202) 234-9548; email: info@syrianembassy.org).

Syrian Tourism Investment Forum, Damascus (tel: 223-9383; email: invest-souq@syriatourism.org; www.syriatourism.com).

National news agency: SANA, PO Box 2661, Damascus (tel: 212-9702; fax: 222-4292; internet: www.sana.org).

All4Syria (www.all4syria.org).

Internet sites

Al Thawra newspaper: www.thawra.com

ArabNet: www.arab.net

Arabia Online: www.arabia.com

Ministry of Information: www.moi-syria.com

Museums with no borders www.discoverislamicart.org

Travel Information: www.visit-syria.com

Taiwan

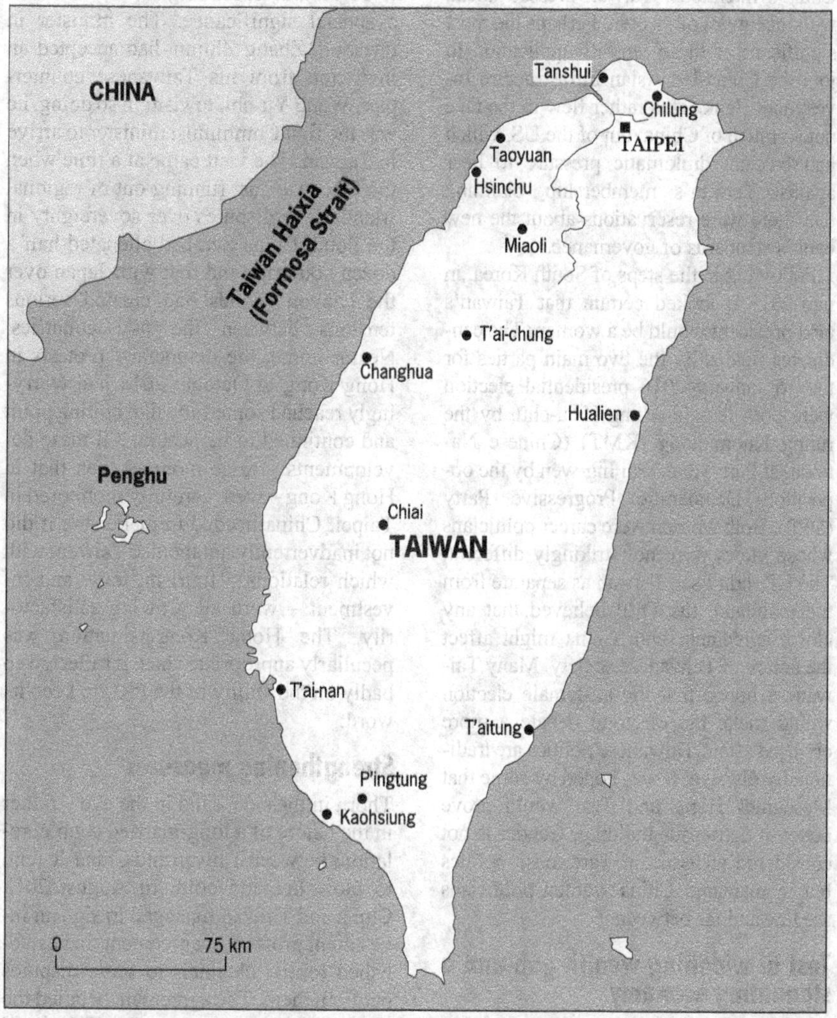

KEY FACTS

Official name: Chung-hua Min-kuo (Republic of China) (known as Taiwan)

Head of State: President Ma Ying-jeou (Kuomintang) (since May 2008; re-elected 14 Jan 2012)

Head of government: Premier Mao Chi-kuo (since 8 December 2014)

Ruling party: Kuomintang (KMT) (Chinese Nationalist Party) (from 12 Jan 2008)

Area: 35,961 square km

Population: 23.43 million (2014)

Capital: Taipei

Official language: Mandarin Chinese

Currency: Taiwanese dollar (T$) = 100 cents

Exchange rate: T$32.70 per US$ (Sep 2015)

GDP per capita: US$22,598 (2014)

GDP real growth: 3.74% (2014)

GDP: US$529.55 billion (2014)

Labour force: 10.92 million (2009)*

Unemployment: 3.96% (2014)

Inflation: 1.20% (2014)

Balance of trade: US$23.36 billion (2010)

Foreign debt: US$79.80 billion (2009)*

* estimated figure

In a rare broadcast interview, the president of Taiwan Ma Ying-jeou told Carrie Gracie, the British Broadcasting Corporation's (BBC) China Editor that in his view political progress in mainland China was unstable. President Ma expressed his disappointment that 'despite improvements in the economic relationship during his two terms as president, there had been no meeting between himself and President Xi Jinping of China.'

Ma, He's Making Eyes at Me

President Ma went on to say that since 'Mainland China was only 100 nautical miles away from Taiwan' it was both an opportunity and risk for Taiwan. 'Any leader here has to learn how to minimise the risks and maximise the opportunity. That's what I've been doing for the past seven years.'

Taiwan's dependence on its trade with China (see Economy below) was, by 2015, overwhelming. Forty per cent of Taiwan's exports go to China. And in 2014 there were almost four million tourist visits by mainlanders. None the less, according to President Ma in his BBC interview, the politics of the People's Republic (PRC) were still a serious stumbling block to good relations. President Ma continued the interview by noting that 'In the past several years I've been constantly reminding the mainland Chinese authorities that the important thing is to close the psychological distance between people across the strait. Taiwan believes in the core values of freedom, democracy, human rights and rule of law. But now we also see that the authorities have arrested some human rights advocates including some lawyers. So that's why people will worry that the human rights situation in China is deteriorating.'

Mr Ma also expressed disappointment that after two terms of working hard to improve relations with the mainland, Beijing was still resisting a face-to-face meeting. 'A meeting of leaders should be a natural development. In the past two years we were hoping to use last November's (2014) Association of Pacific Economies (Apec) summit as an opportunity. However, it was not successful which was, of course, a very great pity.' Interestingly, Mr Ma added that 'Of course we are not clear about the decision-making process, but I believe it was Mr Xi who made the final decision.'

What was certainly the case was that since taking office at the beginning of 2013, China's President Xi Jinping had toughened Chinese policy on many fronts, from national security to internet freedoms and Hong Kong. The issue of Taiwan, he had advised, 'cannot be postponed indefinitely.'

Events, events

The background to virtually every political development and initiative in Taiwan, the prism through which events and statements must be examined, is that the Chinese government continues to claim Taiwan to be part of its sovereign territory, threatening to counter any perceived move to outright independence by military force. Thus, in March 2014, hundreds of young activists, calling themselves the 'Sunflower Movement', had occupied Taiwan's parliament building to protest against a trade pact aimed at forging closer ties with Beijing. Later in the year, the government's perceived pro-China policy led to a substantial defeat for the ruling Kuomintang party in local elections, eventually forcing Mr Ma to step down as the chairman of his own party.

Meanwhile, in addition to worrying about China's intentions, Taiwan pressed ahead with incentives of its own. Perhaps the most significant of these was its application to join the China-led Asian Infrastructure Investment Bank. This rather flew in the face not so much of China, but of the US, which had brought diplomatic pressure to bear against Taiwan's membership, claiming that there were reservations about the new bank's standards of governance.

Following in the steps of South Korea, in mid-2015 it looked certain that Taiwan's next president would be a woman. The candidates fielded by the two main parties for the 16 January 2016 presidential election were both female, Hung Hsiu-chu, by the ruling Kuomintang (KMT) (Chinese Nationalist Party) and Tsai Ing-wen by the opposition Democratic Progressive Party (DPP). Both women were career politicians whose views were not strikingly different. The NP didn't see Taiwan as separate from the mainland; the DPP believed that any closer agreement with China might affect the nature of Taiwanese society. Many Taiwanese hoped that the all-female election would make the electoral debate a more civilised affair. Taiwanese politics are traditionally divisive. It was hoped by some that Mesdames Hung and Tsai would prove better at consensus building. Gender is not considered an issue in Taiwanese politics but in mainland China women politicians are few and far between.

Test of widening wealth gap and a stagnating economy

Given its scant natural resources and international isolation (it only has full diplomatic relations with a handful of countries), since 1949, in no mean achievement Taiwan had transformed itself into one of the world's most powerful and well funded economies. Between most of the world's countries, ministerial visits are no big deal. But that of the PRC's head of its Taiwan Affairs Office to Taipei and Kaoshiung in June 2014 had a special significance. The minister in question, Zhang Zhijun, had accepted an invitation from his Taiwanese counterpart, Wang Yu-chi, to visit; in so doing, he was the first Communist minister to arrive in Taiwan. The visit came at a time when the PRC was fast running out of regional friends. The disputes over sovereignty in the South China Sea had alienated half a dozen countries and that with Japan over the Diayou islands had created serious tensions between the two countries. Nearer home, the democracy protests in Hong Kong in October 2014 had worryingly reached something like boiling point and continued to be heated. All these developments – none more so than that in Hong Kong – were carefully monitored in Taipei. China needed to make sure it did not inadvertently antagonise Taiwan, with which relations – tourism, trade and investment – were all growing satisfactorily. The Hong Kong situation was peculiarly appropriate since it reflected so badly on the ability of the PRC to keep its word.

Strengthening measures

Thorn in the side, sand in the eye – rather in the nature of a long-married couple, relations between Taiwan and China do tend to blow hot and cold. In August 2012 China and Taiwan managed to sign an investment protection agreement that established formal channels to settle disputes between them. The agreement detailed the rights of Taiwanese investors if detained by Chinese authorities and vice versa. The overall context of the agreement was the fact that China is Taiwan's biggest trading partner, with bilateral trade worth a paltry US$110 billion each year.

A year later, amid the formality, ceremony and stage-managed smiles of the fifth Straits Forum in Xiamen, in China's Fujian province, (according to reports published in the Hong Kong based *South China Morning Post*), Beijing announced a long list of measures to strengthen the ties between the countries. An indication of the importance of the meeting was the fact that the Chinese delegation was headed up by President Xi Jinping himself and on the Taiwanese side by Wu

KEY INDICATORS — **Taiwan**

	Unit	2011	2012	2013	2014	**2015
Population	m	*23.23	23.32	23.37	23.43	*23.49
Gross domestic product (GDP)	US$bn	466.80	475.33	511.28	529.55	*527.77
GDP per capita	US$	20,101	20,386	21,874	22,598	*22,464
GDP real growth	%	4.0	1.5	2.2	3.7	*3.8
Inflation	%	1.4	1.9	0.8	1.2	*0.7
Unemployment	%	4.8	4.2	4.2	4.0	*4.0
Current account	US$m	41,600.0	50,672.0	55,257.0	65,335.0	*65,705.0
Exchange rate	per US$	29.03	29.75	29.90	31.61	–

* estimated figure ** forecast figure

Poh-hsiung, the honorary chairman of Taiwan's ruling Kuomintang. Mr Wu, who was thought to act as a proxy for Taiwan's President Ma Ying-jeou, also expressed Taiwan's desire to participate in Asia's Regional Comprehensive Economic Partnership and in other global activities.

The economy

Two factors had for some time represented the major concerns about the Taiwanese economy: the widening wealth gap and the stagnating economy. In its *Asian Development Outlook* assessment of the Taiwanese economy the Asia Development Bank (ADB) noted that at least one of these concerns seemed to have eased: gross domestic product (GDP) expanded in 2014 by 3.7 per cent year on year, the strongest growth in 3 years, fuelled by rising consumption, investment and exports. In the view of the ADB, all the domestic demand components had added to growth. Private consumption expanded by 3.0 per cent, adding 1.6 percentage points to growth as improving consumer confidence boosted private spending. Government consumption grew by 3.4 per cent, adding 0.5 percentage points and total investments rose by 4.4 per cent to contribute 1.0 percentage point as private investment remained strong despite moderating since 2013.

The ADB reported that the exports of goods and services, which provided 70 per cent of the economy's GDP, rebounded by 5.7 per cent in 2014 in response to stronger demand from the US, Japan and the euro-zone for machinery, electronic products and electrical equipment. Exports to other Asian economies were mixed, with those to the PRC almost stable and those to Hong Kong improving by 7.9 per cent. Imports of goods and services also expanded by 5.4 per cent, as demand picked up for capital equipment and consumer goods. In sum, net exports improved by 7.7 per cent, lifting GDP growth in 2014 by 0.6 percentage points.

On the supply side, the industrial production index, which had been almost flat in 2013, rose by 6.1 per cent in 2014 and industrial output grew by 5.7 per cent, contributing 1.9 percentage points to GDP growth. This reflected a rebound in manufacturing by 6.3 per cent as growth in the production of information and communications technology (ICT) products rose by double digits. Mining and quarrying continued to weaken, however, as oil prices declined and growth in construction faltered in the cooling property market. The service sector grew by 2.2 per cent with solid expansion in information and communication, finance and insurance, transport and storage and trade, contributing 1.3 percentage points to GDP growth. According to the ADB, agriculture expanded by 3.5 per cent. Inflation edged up to 1.2 per cent in 2014 as higher food prices outweighed the decline in prices for fuels, lubricants and transportation equipment. Core consumer prices, which exclude energy and fresh food, rose by 1.3 per cent. Looking at government policies, the ADB noted that the Central Bank of China's (sic) (central bank) monetary policy remained accommodative, with no change in the rediscount rate. Money supply (M2) climbed by 6.1 per cent in 2014 as banks' net foreign assets rose by 11.0 per cent and bank credit to the private sector grew by 5.7 per cent. The cooling of the property market eased the concentration of real estate in banks' loan portfolios. The budget deficit had risen from the equivalent of 0.9 per cent of GDP in 2013 to 1.3 per cent in 2014. Central government revenue declined by 1.4 per cent despite the higher business tax rate for banks and insurance companies implemented in the second half of 2014. Meanwhile, expenditure increased by 3.1 per cent as education, culture and defence outlays grew.

The current account surplus reached a record 12.3 per cent of GDP in 2014 on the back of strong exports and net service receipts boosted by tourist arrivals from the PRC. The continued depreciation of the local currency helped boost the current account. Despite increased outflows of US$53.0 billion to finance higher investment in foreign debt securities, the balance of payments registered a surplus equal to 2.5 per cent of GDP, higher than the 2.2 per cent recorded in 2013. However, foreign exchange reserves had declined by 0.9 per cent to US$419 billion by the end of December 2014, mainly on valuation changes as the US dollar appreciated against other major currencies.

Taiwan's GDP growth was forecast to remain stable at 3.7 per cent in 2015, reflecting strong external demand and improving prospects for local consumer demand, as well as the probable stimulus to production caused by the drop in global oil prices and resultant lower costs and higher corporate profits. Export orders rose by 8.1 per cent in January 2015, on top of a double-digit surge in September and October 2014, with those from the US and Europe surpassing those from the PRC and Southeast Asia. The outlook was positive for exports, tourism and repatriated earnings from overseas investments, which were expected to lift the current account surplus to 12.5 per cent of GDP in 2015 and 13.0 per cent in 2016.

The ADB expected consumption to be robust in 2015. Consumer confidence had been rising since October 2014, unemployment was low and real wages would rise with the planned 3.8 per cent increase in the minimum wage by mid-2015.

Consumption was expected to receive further boosts from lower fuel and utilities prices and as tourism expanded due to the expected increase in tourist arrivals from the PRC. The public investment outlook for 2015 and 2016 was somewhat less positive, moderated mainly by the government's continuing efforts to consolidate its budget and uncertainty over energy-related investments. Private investment looked set to expand by the start of 2016 following an announcement from a leading chip manufacturer that it would increase production of 'next generation' computer chips. Meanwhile, the manufacturing industry sentiment index rebounded in December 2014 from a 3-year low and the expectations of rising external demand and tourist arrivals could provide some impetus to investment growth. With the gains from lower oil prices wearing off and as export competition intensified further, growth was projected to slip to 3.6 per cent in 2016.

Inflation was forecast to fall downward in 2015 to average 0.5 per cent before rising again to 1.0 per cent in 2016 as oil prices gradually recovered, employment prospects improved and incomes rose. Monetary policy was expected to remain accommodative, given the low and stable inflation environment in 2015 and 2016. The central bank had ample room to adjust its monetary policy if required by any sudden economic or financial developments at home or abroad.

The ADB reported that the government's fiscal policy would aim to narrow the deficit, mainly by raising government revenue. Following the increase in business tax rates for banks and insurers under the Sound Finance Programme initiated in early 2014, the government was expected to introduce a new top bracket for income tax and a tax on profits from property sales, as well as increase the goods and services tax. Budgetary expenditure might increase as the 2016 election approached, but the budget deficit was expected to fall to 1.0 per cent of GDP in 2015.

The downside risks to the forecasts arose primarily from the slowdown and production re-location in the PRC and the changing political landscape in Taiwan.

Exports could suffer as competition in ICT products heated up following a free trade agreement signed by the PRC and the Republic of Korea in November 2014, as well as Apple's announcement that it would shift to the Republic of Korea a big part of its production of chips and other components hitherto produced in Taiwan. On the other hand, higher-than-expected growth in the US and the euro-zone could provide an upside surprise, enabling stronger demand for electronic products and positive knock-on effects to propel growth.

Risk assessment

Politics	Fair
Economy	Good
Regional stability	Fair

COUNTRY PROFILE

Before the arrival of the Europeans, the island was occupied by indigenous people and immigrants from mainland China.
1590 Portuguese navigators discovered Taiwan and called it *Ilha Formosa*, meaning 'beautiful island' in Portuguese. This is the origin of Taiwan's other name, Formosa.
1624 The Dutch arrived in Taiwan.
1629 The Spaniards, alarmed by growing Dutch control of Taiwan, arrived and occupied the northern part of the island.
1630 The Dutch formally settled on the island.
1630–62 The Dutch and Spanish fought for control of the island. The Spanish were defeated and driven out. The Dutch strengthened their control after the establishment of the Dutch East India Company and Taiwan became an important trading centre. Chinese resistance eventually grew so strong that the Dutch were driven off the island.
1700–1800 Chinese mass migration to the island took place.
1885 Taiwan was officially made a province of China.
1895 China ceded control of Taiwan to Japan following the Sino-Japanese war. The Japanese modernised the country, upgrading infrastructure, restoring the communications network and developing agriculture.
1945 After Japan's defeat in the Second World War, Taiwan became a province of the Republic of China, controlled by the Kuomintang (KMT) (Chinese Nationalist Party).
1949 The KMT was driven out of the mainland by the communist People's Liberation Army (PLA) led by Mao Zedong. President Chiang Kai-shek withdrew his forces to Taiwan. The KMT asserted that it, rather than the new People's Republic of China, constituted the rightful government of mainland China and that it would eventually resume control of all of China.
1954 The US signed a security agreement with the KMT pledging to protect Taiwan.
1971 The People's Republic of China replaced Taiwan as Chinese representatives at the UN.
1975 Chiang Kai-Shek died. His son, Chiang Ching-kuo, became president.
1987 Martial law and one-party rule were dismantled.
1988 After the death of President Chiang Ching-kuo, Taiwan-born Lee Teng-hui became president.
1994 Nationwide local elections were held. The KMT retained its dominance of the political system, although the candidate of the opposition Min-chu Chin-pu Tang (MCT) (Democratic Progressive Party), Chen Shui-bian, was elected mayor of Taipei.
1995 The KMT lost ground to the MCT in the legislative elections.
1996 President Lee Teng-hui comfortably won Taiwan's first direct presidential elections.
1998 The KMT was re-elected, with an increased majority.
1999 Taiwan suffered its worst earthquake for nearly 100 years.
2000 Chen Shui-bian (MCT) became president.
2001 The pro-independence MCT won the parliamentary elections; the KMT lost its majority for the first time in 50 years.
2002 Taiwan joined the World Trade Organisation. Laws were enacted to put the military under the control of the civilian cabinet. President Chen Shui-bian took over the leadership of the MCT.
2004 President Chen Shui-bian (MCT), was re-elected, having survived an assassination attempt on the eve of the elections. Although President Chen's pro-independence Min-chu Chin-pu Tang MCT won the single largest number of seats in the general elections, it narrowly failed to take control of parliament.
2005 Mainland China's National People's Congress passed an anti-secession law, enshrining Beijing's claim of sovereignty and its threat of military force in the event of Taiwan's formal independence; more than one million people took to the streets in Taiwan to express opposition to the law.
2006 Following the defeat of the MCT in local elections, Prime Minister Hsieh resigned and was replaced by Su Tseng-chang. A referendum on the president's suitability for office, following corruption scandals involving the president's family and entourage, led to President Chen devolving some powers to the prime minister's office. The president's wife appeared in court on corruption charges.
2007 Su Tseng-chang resigned and Chang Chun-hsiung was appointed as prime minister. Costa Rica broke diplomatic ties with Taiwan in favour of China and its potential investment in Costa Rica. The UN rejected Taiwan's application for membership.
2008 Electoral reforms were enacted that reduced the number of Legislative Yuan seats. In parliamentary elections the opposition Kuomintang (of the Pan-Blue Coalition) won 81 seats (out of 113), with 72 per cent of the vote. The ruling MCT (Pan-Green Coalition) only managed 27 seats and resulted in President Chen stepping down as leader of the MCT. In presidential elections, Ma Ying-Jeou (Kuomintang) won 58.46 per cent of the vote; Frank Hsieh (MCT) won 41.55 per cent. Ma Ying- Jeou took office as president and appointed Liu Chao-shiuan as prime minister. In formal talks with China (they had been suspended since 1999) an agreement to allow 36 direct flights (18 each) a week between the two countries was signed; a further agreement allowed 3,000 tourists per day to visit each country.
2009 Former president, Chen Shui-bian was sent to trial on embezzlement, bribe-taking and money laundering charges. China and Taiwan agreed to a wide-ranging trade agreement. Typhoon Morakot struck over three days, setting off huge mudslides and leaving around 700 people dead or missing. Premier Liu Chao-shiuan resigned following widespread criticism of his government's response to Typhoon Morakot; Wu Den-yih replaced him.
2010 The Taiwan Strait Tourism Association opened an office in Beijing. Although classified as 'non-governmental' it was the first Taiwanese office to open in mainland China since 1949. A landmark trade deal with China was signed, which sparked a protest that grew into a brawl in parliament and landed two members in hospital with injuries. In local elections, the president's party won three of five mayoral seats, although the opposition won more of the popular vote. The elections were seen as a test for the president's economic policy towards China.
2011 In June, former president Lee Teng-hui was charged with embezzling US$7.79 million of state funds over 1988–2000.
2012 In parliamentary elections held on 14 January the ruling Kuomintang-led coalition won 51.48 per cent of the vote and a total of 69 seats (out of 113); in presidential elections held at the same time, incumbent Ma Ying Jeou (Kuomintang) won another term in office with 51.6 per cent of the vote. Sean Chen became premier on 6 February. On 27

November, Taiwan's most popular newspaper *Apple Daily* was sold by the Hong Kong publisher Jimmy Lai, to a Taiwanese consortia of pro-Beijing businessmen, for US$601 million.
2013 A law that removed powers from the military to prosecute and punish members of the military during peace time came into force in August. Military jails will be closed and courts closed in 2014. Under the law some 350 cases will be transferred to the civilian courts.
2014 Local elections were held on 28 November. The KMT lost heavily across the country, including the mayor's office in Taipei. As a result Prime Minister Jiang Yi-huah resigned the next day. The election had been widely seen as a referendum on relations with China; the KMT supports good relations with the mainland.
2015 President Ma Ying-jeou of the Republic of China and President Xi Jinping of the People's Republic of China met in Singapore on 7 November, the first time leaders of the two countries have met since Chiang Kai-shek and Mao Zedong in 1945.

Political structure

Constitution

The Legislative Yuan, presided over by the prime minister, is the highest government body. It is responsible for passing laws and drafting the budget. It is elected every three years and has the power to dismiss the prime minister.
The 29-member Control Yuan exercises powers of investigation, impeachment and censure over senior officials, including the grand justices of the Judicial Yuan and members of the Examination Yuan, and power of audit over central and local government finances. Its members are appointed by the president with the approval of the legislature.
The Examination Yuan supervises examinations for entry into public office and deals with personnel questions of the civil service.
The Kuo-min Ta-hui (National Assembly) passed a series of Constitutional amendments in April 2000 which reduced itself to an *ad hoc* institution deprived of most of its powers. The powers of initiating Constitutional amendments, changing the national boundaries, impeaching the president or vice president and approving the appointment of senior officials, were transferred to the Legislative Yuan. The Kuo-min Ta-hui retains the functions of ratifying constitutional amendments and impeachment proceedings against the president.
The National Assembly is to convene for a month from no later than 31 May 2005 to vote on whether public referenda could be used to change the constitution, which means the abolition of the Assembly itself. Other constitutional amendments slated to go before the Assembly are plans to streamline the Legislative Yuan by halving the number of seats from 225 to 113, beginning from 2007, and the extension of legislators' terms from three to four years and whether it should hand over to grand justices the rights to impeach the president.

Form of state

Representative democracy

The executive

The president is directly elected for a four-year term. The president nominates a prime minister to head the Executive Yuan (cabinet), which is the highest administrative organ of the nation, and is responsible to the Legislative Yuan. The Executive Yuan consists of the ministries and commissions and 19 subordinate administrative organs of state.

National legislature

The number of seats in the Legislative Yuan were reduced to 113; of which 73 are directly elected by majority votes in single-seat constituencies, 34 by proportional representation from party lists (50 per cent of seats must be allocated to women) and six reserved for indigenous (aboriginal) people. Members serve four-year terms.

Legal system

The Judicial Yuan is the highest judicial organ of state. Justices are appointed by the president with the approval of the Control Yuan. Subordinate organs of the Judicial Yuan include the Supreme Court, the high courts, the district courts, the Administrative Court and the Commission on the Disciplinary Sanctions of Public Functionaries.

Last elections

14 January 2012 (parliamentary and presidential)
Results: Parliamentary: The Pan-Blue coalition won 51.48 per cent of the vote, a total of 69 seats (out of 113). The coalition was led by the Kuomintang, which won 44.55 per cent of the vote (64 seats), with the People First Party (PFP) and Non-Partisan Solidarity Union (NPSU) winning a combined five seats. The Pan-Green coalition won 43.56 per cent, a total of 43 seats, led by the Democratic Progressive Party (DPP) with 34.6 per cent (40) and the Taiwan Solidarity Union (TSU) 8.96 per cent (three).
Presidential: Ma Ying Jeou (Kuomintang) won 51.6 per cent of the vote, Tsai Ing Wen (DPP) 45.63 per cent, James Soong Chu-yu (PFP) 2.77 per cent.

Next elections

16 January 2016 (parliamentary and presidential)

Political parties

Ruling party

Kuomintang (KMT) (Chinese Nationalist Party) (from 12 Jan 2008)

Main opposition party

Min-chu Chin-pu Tang (MCT) (Democratic Progressive Party)

Population

23.43 million (2014). Approximately 22 per cent of the population is aged under 15 years, and 70 per cent aged 15–64. Over 53 per cent of the population lives in urban areas. About 90 per cent of the population live on the flat and fertile western side of the country. Taiwan's fertility rate became the lowest in the world, when it declined to 0.9 children per childbearing woman in 2010, down from 1.03 in 2009. The decline was despite government incentives, including an allowance for giving birth and subsidised childcare services.
Population density: 640 inhabitants per square km (2010)
Annual growth rate: 0.9 per cent (2010)

Ethnic make-up

Taiwan's population is mostly ethnic Han Chinese. A majority of these are local Taiwanese, who have language links to Fujian province across the Taiwan Strait. There is a powerful minority of immigrants that came from the mainland during the 1940s, as well as a Hakka minority.
Taiwan's non-Han aborigines (yuanchumin) are related to the Polynesian and Malay ethnic groups. They comprise dozens of distinct groups, including the Rukai tribe (about 8,000 strong) and the Clouded Leopard People. They have limited rights and may not sell or develop lands. Indigenous rights groups have campaigned to regain political and economic autonomy in the aboriginal territories that were demarcated during the Japanese occupation.

Religions

The majority of people are Buddhist or Taoist with Confucian influence. Most Chinese make no sharp distinction between Buddhism and Taoism in Taiwan, and most practise a hybrid of these two religions. About 2.5 per cent of the population are Christian.

Education

There are 2,600 primary schools with a total enrolment around two million students. Primary school lasts for six years before entry to junior high school, at aged 12, for three years. Dependent on exam results at aged 15, students may move on to either a senior vocational high school or a senior high school (for more academic courses which lead to entrance exams for higher education). There are 986

secondary schools and 188 vocational institutions.
All education is delivered in Chinese however English is a compulsory subject during the secondary cycles. Higher education is offered at colleges and universities from aged 18. The total number of universities and colleges is 150 and the gross enrolment of graduates aged between 18 and 21 years is nearly 70 per cent per cent.
Compulsory years: Six to 15.
Pupils per teacher: 19 in primary school.

Health
Taiwan's public health sector offers a universal health insurance system, the first in Asia to ensure equal access to care for the entire population. Total expenditure on health per capita is approaching developed country standards.
Taiwan has 700 hospitals and 17,000 clinics and an active pharmaceutical industry.
Life expectancy: 77 years (government statistics, 2004).
Fertility rate/Maternal mortality rate: 1.4 births per woman; maternal mortality 7.86 per 100,000 live births (Government statistics).
Birth rate/Death rate: 3.25 per 1,000 (Government statistics).
Child (under 5 years) mortality rate (per 1,000): 6.7 per 1,000 live births (2003)

Welfare
The welfare policy is not universal but is budgeted according to the county or city governments. There is provision for special subsidies and assistance to low-income earners and families, based on variations in regional income distribution for each fiscal year. Some low-income families with children qualify for an additional monthly subsidy.
The elderly comprise a growing proportion of the population. Pensioners (aged from 65 years) of Taipei City and County, Ilan, Hsinchu, Tainan, Chiayi City, Kaohsiung and Penghu counties benefit from organised pension systems. There is serious shortage of housing for elderly people, despite Taiwan's 350 retirement and nursing homes.

Main cities
Taipei (capital, estimated population 2.7 million (m) in 2005), Kaohsiung (1.5m), Taichung (1.1m), Tainan (788,008), Panchiao (549,625), Taoyuan (424,625), Zhonghe (417,685); Magong (largest city on Penghu Island) (57,423).

Languages spoken
The second language spoken is Fukienese, a dialect of Mandarin, but very different to it, that is spoken in the Fujian province in China. Fukienese is also called Taiwanese. Other Chinese dialects spoken are Shanghaiese, Hakka and Cantonese. English is spoken only by the elite.

Official language/s
Mandarin Chinese

Media
Press
Dailies: In Chinese, *United Daily News* (http://udn.com), *China Times* (http://news.chinatimes.com), *Liberty Times* (www.libertytimes.com.tw), *Central Daily News* () and the *Taiwan Daily*. In English, *The China Post* (www.chinapost.com.tw), *Taiwan News* (www.etaiwannews.com) and *Taipei Times* (www.taipeitimes.com). Local newspapers, in Chinese include *Apple Daily* (http://1-apple.com.tw), and *Taiwan Shin Sheng Daily News* (www.tssdnews.com.tw) from Taipei and *Keng Sheng Daily News* (www.ksnews.com.tw), from Hualien.
Business: In Chinese and English, *Taiwan Economic News* (http://cens.com) and *CommonWealth* (www.cw.com.tw) (monthly) specifically deal with business and financial news. Major newspapers have business sections and the government publishes *Taiwan Journal* (http://taiwanjournal.nat.gov.tw) with information on trade and statistics and *Invest in Taiwan* (http://investintaiwan.nat.gov.tw) with information on local industries.
Periodicals: In English and published by the government, *Taiwan Panorama* (www.taiwan-panorama.com) and *Taiwan Review* (http://taiwanreview.nat.gov.tw) are news and general interest monthlies.

Broadcasting
The Central Broadcasting System (CBS) is the national broadcaster for Taiwan.
Radio: The RTI (Radio Taiwan International) broadcasts nationally and to mainland China. External services are relayed worldwide in up to10 languages.
There are over 170 radio stations, which cater for specific musical genres. UFO Network is one of the most popular private radio station, others include Hit FM (www.hitfm.com.tw) and Kiss Radio Taiwan (www.kiss.com.tw). The only English language station is ICRT FM (www.uforadio.com.tw).
Television: There are three state-owned TV networks (www.pts.org.tw) but most households subscribe to cable TV.
National news agency: Central News Agency (www.cna.com.tw).

Economy
Taiwan's economy in based on the service sector, which contributes 64 per cent of GDP. The sector is underpinned by its entrepreneurial businessmen who invest widely in the Asian region, and its manufacturing exports at over 25 per cent of GDP. With a limited amount of agricultural land, available agriculture accounts for less than 2 per cent of GDP. Exports, led by electronics, machinery, and petrochemicals have provided the primary impetus for economic development. This heavy dependence on exports exposes the economy to fluctuations in world demand. Taiwan's diplomatic isolation, low birth rate, and rapidly aging population are other major long-term challenges. The number of people over the age of 65 is expected to account for nearly 20 per cent of the island's total population by 2025. Taiwan's total fertility rate of just over one child per woman is among the lowest in the world, raising the prospect of future labour shortages, falling domestic demand, and declining tax revenues.
Closer economic links with China bring greater opportunities for Taiwan's economy but also pose new challenges as the island becomes more economically dependent on China at a time when political differences remain unresolved. There is public frustration in Taiwan with stagnant wages, skyrocketing house prices, and the difficulty of finding entry-level jobs.
Taiwan is one the world's leading manufacturers of computers and computer components as well as other electronic consumer goods. However, to maintain its manufacturing base Taiwan has to import not only the necessary raw materials for manufacturing but also primary goods such as foodstuffs and fuel for its population.
GDP growth was 6.0 per cent in 2007, falling to 0.7 per cent by 2008 as the global economic crisis hit and bank lending was cut, limiting credit and funds for investment. Taiwan did not officially enter recession until 2009 when GDP growth fell to -1.8 per cent; Taiwanese workers were quickly laid-off and capital spending halted as worldwide trade slowed down and the government had to introduce measures to boost the economy, aiming at an annual average growth of 5 per cent over 2009–12. GDP growth soared to 10.7 per cent in 2010, due to burgeoning sales of computer components to China. Private investment and consumer confidence were also cited as two of the key drivers of growth. GDP growth fell back to an estimated 4 per cent in 2011. The GDP growth rate halved to 2.1 per cent in 2012 before stabilising at 2.2 per cent in 2013. In 2014, GDP growth rebounded at 3.7 per cent.
Political tensions between Taiwan and China have eased since the election of the Koumintang political party in 2008, which undertook to improve their relationship. Taiwan signed a free trade agreement (FTA) with China in 2010, which cut

tariffs on 539 products exported to China (valued at US$13.84 billion), with tariffs on 267 Chinese products exported to Taiwan also cut (valued at US$2.86 billion). The FTA not only has an economic benefit for Taiwan, but politically it eases tension between the two countries.

External trade

Taiwan belongs to the 21-member Asia-Pacific Economic Co-operation (Apec) forum, which is a bloc of countries that border the Pacific with the aim of facilitating trade, economic growth and investment in the region. Taiwan is also a member of the World Trade Organisation (WTO) and an observer member of the Organisation of Economic Co-operation and Development (OECD). Taiwan signed a free trade agreement (FTA) with China on 29 June 2010, which cut tariffs on 539 products exported to China, while tariffs on 267 Chinese products exported to Taiwan were also cut.

The manufacturing sector accounts for over 25 per cent of GDP. Taiwan is a leading global producer of hi-tech goods and the largest supplier of semi-conductors, telecommunication equipment, computers and monitors and optical disks (DVDs). Industrial production includes polycarbonates, refined petroleum and vehicle assembly. With few natural resources it has to import most of its energy needs and raw materials. Nevertheless, the balance of trade is kept level by the high volume of Taiwanese exports.

Imports

Imports are dominated by raw materials, machinery and electrical equipment (around 45 per cent of total), coal, crude oil and natural gas.

Main sources: China (17.6 per cent of total in 2014), Japan (15.3 per cent) and the US (10 per cent).

Exports

Main export commodities are electronics, computers and monitors, textiles, refined oil and derivatives, polycarbonates and vehicles.

Main destinations: China (26.1 per cent of total in 2014), Hong Kong (12.7 per cent) and the US (11.3 per cent).

Agriculture

Farming

The agriculture sector contributes 2 per cent to GDP. Taiwan has refocussed its agricultural objectives by reducing its workforce to 633,000 workers and placing an emphasis on quality of food rather than quantity. Taiwan's farm plots are generally small, hindering cost-efficient management. Estimates show that 76 per cent of all farming households have less than one hectare (ha) of arable land and 80 per cent have members working part- or full-time in other occupations.

Rice is still the principal and most valuable crop (in quantity and cultivated land), followed by betel nuts, pineapples, mangoes, sugar cane, watermelons, tea, bamboo shoots, pears, and peanuts. Industrial crops include cotton, hemp and jute.

Fishing

The fishing industry has gradually developed from small-scale coastal fishing to deep-sea commercial fishing. The deep-water fishing industry is large and expanding, supplemented by aquaculture. Taiwan's fishing production was worth US$3.4 billion in 2013 (0.7 per cent of GDP), it grew by 2.8 per cent in 2014 and it is expected to grow by 4 per cent in 2015. 90 per cent of catches, especially tuna and squid, are for exportation.

Taiwanese fish products could face an import ban in Europe beginning in 2015 after the European commission issued a yellow card on 1 October 2015 over illegal, unreported and unregulated fishing. Taiwan has six months to commit to regulate their fishing industry. Exports to the EU were worth US$15.5 million in 2014. Taiwan has the largest tuna fleet in the Pacific, and with 1200 small boats, mainly fishing on the high seas the fishery sector is out of control.

Eel is an important aquaculture product as are milkfish, tilapia, groupers, tiger prawn and oyster. Intense aquaculture has done some damage to the environment by drawing off huge amounts of water. This has caused land to cave in. The government is tackling the problem by encouraging the recycling of freshwater. The government has been actively engaged in international fishery management and has signed official or private fishery agreements with 29 countries.

Following the annual meeting of the Commission for the Conservation of Southern Bluefin Tuna (CCSBT), held on Cheju Island, South Korea, all members agreed to a 20 per cut in the roughly 17,000 tonnes in 2009 bluefin tuna catches from 2010. Scientists had warned that without a cut fish stocks could crash as numbers had become dangerously low.

Forestry

The timber industry is limited by inaccessibility, the poor quality of much of the forestry resources and by an official policy of conserving supplies. Taiwan's forested area covers around 2.1 million hectares, which is about half the land area. Forestry products include sawn timber, plywood, paper and fuel for local use.

Industry and manufacturing

Taiwan's major strength is its high-tech industry. In recent years, Taiwan has moved away from manufacturing electronic toys, deemed to be unhealthy for children and is focusing on electronic components. The majority of production is exported accounting for an estimated 55 per cent of total exports and 20 per cent of the country's GDP. Taiwan's electronics sector is heavily dependent on US demand. Industry was worth 34 per cent of GDP in 2014 and it employed 36 per cent of the labour force.

The semiconductor industry began in the 1960s and has since grown to provide Taiwan with a leading place in global electronics. Many Taiwanese products have an important share in the global market. Taiwan is also a leading manufacturer of digital cameras, with a 70 per cent share of the global market.

Taiwan's communications industry has been boosted by the liberalisation of the global telecommunications industry. The main focus has been the production of optical communication technology and mobile phone related items. The Taiwanese government is also concentrating on the production of wireless communications techniques.

The main concern for Taiwan's industry is that more and more low-end and mid-range manufacturers are moving to China. To remain competitive, Taiwan needs to focus on developing integrated software design.

Taiwan is the world's second favourite country (after Malaysia) to build new factories, having overtaken China. Lower income and corporation taxes, and easier employee retention levels have made the island nation a more attractive investment prospect than China. Manufacturing is not simply about making things at the lowest possible price, many companies also consider 'market conditions' factoring in political and economic risk to their supply chains as well as branding, which had made a score of highly developed nations increasingly attractive to produce in like Taiwan.

Tourism

Taiwan's west coast is an almost continuous urban conurbation, but the east coast is much less populated and offers sites of natural beauty. The central mountain range is second in height only to the Himalayas in Asia. The tourism bureau offers the visitor choices in city destinations with the attractions of gourmet, health, cultural and heritage, and as well as ecotourism, including coastal-marine based activities.

Tourism is recognised as an important sector in the economy. It provided 5.5 per cent of GDP (US$27 billion) in 2014 and it is expected to increase by 5.4 per cent in 2015. Employment in the industry makes up 6.1 per cent of the workforce

(676,500 jobs). Revenue from foreign visitors constitutes 51 per cent of travel and tourism's overall contribution to GDP while domestic spending was 49 per cent in 2014.
The Taiwan High Speed Rail (THSR) began operations in 2007 and has influenced the growth in tourism. As services grew, THSR stations became regional transport hubs, opening up tourism opportunities previously underdeveloped.
The Taiwan Strait Tourism Association opened an office in Beijing in May. Although classified as 'non-governmental' it was the first Taiwanese office to open in mainland China since 1949.

Mining
Mining accounts for less than 1 per cent of GDP. Taiwan has few exploitable mineral resources. Due to the depletion of local sources, nearly all of the rare earth and metallic mining products are imported. Over 20 types of minerals are mined in Taiwan, mainly marble, limestone, serpentine and gravel. Marble is Taiwan's most important mineral resource with reserves conservatively estimated at over 300 million tonnes. Marble, salt, sand and gravel constitute the most valuable mineral products. Taiwan also produces iron and steel from imported iron ore and iron scrap and processed products such as aluminium, copper, lead, nickel, tin and zinc from imported raw materials.
Taiwan has four gold-bearing mines with metal content estimated at 100 tonnes. Taiwan utilises its large trade surpluses to import gold.

Hydrocarbons
Proven oil reserves were 2.38 million barrels in 2014, with production averaging 1,726 barrels per day (bpd). With consumption at 974,000bpd Taiwan must rely on imports to meets its energy needs. Taiwan has four refineries with a total capacity of 1.3 million bpd; the surplus, after domestic supply is met, is exported.
The state-owned CPC Corporation is responsible for all aspects of surveying, extracting, refining, transporting and selling petroleum, natural gas and petroleum products. However downstream government has deregulated the CPC's monopoly and other, private companies compete for business.
Taiwan, along with Vietnam, China, Brunei, Malaysia and The Philippines, claims the potentially oil-rich Spratly Islands.
Total natural gas reserves were 6.2 billion cubic metres (cum) in 2014, with production at 379.4 million cum. Consumption, primarily in the form of electricity generation, was 16.2 billion cum and imports to meet the shortfall were delivered as liquefied natural gas (LNG) from Asia, Africa and the Middle East.
Proven coal reserves are 1.0 million tonnes, but production has ceased. Taiwan consumes 55 million tonnes of coal per annum, imported mostly from China, Indonesia and Australia. Coal is used for electricity generation, steel production, cement and petrochemical industries.

Energy
Total installed generating capacity was 48.5GW in 2014. The state-owned Taiwan Power Company (Taipower) operates 72 power stations with output at 72 per cent thermally produced, 13 per cent nuclear, 6.3 per cent hydro-power and 8.7 per cent renewable sources.
Independent power producers are allowed to provide up to 20 per cent of Taiwan's electricity with foreign investors allowed to participate in the electricity sector.

Financial markets
A computerised over-the-counter (OTC) market, the Taisdaq, was introduced in 1994. Taiwan's financial markets are regulated by the Securities and Futures Commission.

Stock exchange
Taiwan Stock Exchange

Banking and insurance
Foreign banks have been allowed to compete in the Taiwanese market since 1989. In June 2001, the government passed a package of legislation to reform the financial sector. The most important part of this legislation is the financial holding company law, which allows banks, security houses, insurance companies, investment funds, and futures brokerages to be grouped under one entity.

Central bank
Central Bank of China

Main financial centre
Taipei

Offshore facilities
Offshore banking has also been available since 1984. Foreign banks are permitted to set up offshore banking units (OBUs) without first having established a branch in Taiwan.

Time
GMT plus eight hours

Geography
Taiwan is an island 395km long and 144km across. It has high mountains, rising out of the sea along its eastern shore. The western side is flat and fertile. Taipei is located at the northen end of the island and is the largest city.

Hemisphere
Northern

Climate
Subtropical with temperatures ranging from 33 degrees Celsius (C) in Jul–Aug to 12 degrees C in Jan–Feb. Average rainfall is 2,500mm per year, with typhoons from May–Oct and occasional snow in the mountains in Jan–Feb.

Entry requirements

Passports
Required by all and must be valid for six months from date of visit.

Visa
Required by all, except citizens of EU, North America, Australasia and some Asian countries. Visit www.boca.gov.tw for a full list of nationals from *visa-exempt entry* countries and application forms for those who must apply of a visa. Visa free (tourist) visits are limited to 30 days without extension. All business visits of less than six months may be undertaken on visitors visas. Applications require a business letter of intent and itinerary. All visitors must have return/onward passage.

Currency advice/regulations
All currencies imported must be declared in writing on arrival; re-convertion is allowed on production of exchange receipts. The import and export of foreign currency is unlimited; amounts over US$10,000 (or foreign equivalent) must be declared. Import and export of local currency is limited to T$8,000; permission must be obtain from the Ministry of Finance for export of amounts in excess of this.
Travellers cheques are accepted in banks and tourist venues.

Customs
All baggage must be itemised in writing. Personal effects are duty-free.

Prohibited imports
Illegal drugs, gambling aids (including mahjong sets), firearms and explosives, non-canned meat and fresh fruit. Communist propaganda and items originating from China, Cuba, North Korea and members of the CIS.

Health (for visitors)

Mandatory precautions
Vaccination certificate for either yellow fever or cholera if travelling from an infected area.

Advisable precautions
Inoculations and boosters should be current for diphtheria, tetanus, hepatitis A, polio and typhoid. Other vaccinations that may be recommended are cholera, tuberculosis, and Japanese B encephalitis and hepatitis B. Use malaria prophylaxis (which will also provide protection against dengue fever and hepatitis B) including mosquito repellents, sleeping nets and clothing that cover the body after dark. There is a risk of rabies in rural areas. Use only bottled or boiled water for drinks, washing teeth and making ice. Eat only well cooked meals, preferably served hot; vegetables should be cooked and

fruit peeled. Dairy products are unpasteurised and should be avoided. Avoid pork and salad and food from street vendors. A full first-aid kit would be useful.
Locally manufactured Western proprietary medicines are easily obtainable, but visitors on regular medication should bring their own supplies – amounts for the length of the visit only.
Visitors should have medical insurance, including emergency evacuation.

Hotels
It is advisable to book hotel rooms in advance. Room facilities usually include TVs and refrigerators. Larger hotels will arrange transport to/from the airport. A 10 per cent service charge is added to the bill. Reasonably priced accommodation is available at Japanese-style hot springs resorts in the mountains.

Credit cards
Major credit and charge cards are accepted in most establishments.

Public holidays (national)
Fixed dates
1 Jan (Founding of the Republic of China), 28 Feb Memorial Day.
Holidays that fall on the weekend are taken on the next working days *in lieu*.
Variable dates
Chinese New Year (Jan/Feb, four days), Tomb Sweeping Day (Mar/Apr), Tuen Ng (Dragon Boat) Festival (May/Jun), Mid-Autumn Moon Festival (Sep/Oct).
Religious and cultural festivals are determined by the Buddhist lunar calendar.

Working hours
Banking
Mon–Fri: 0900–1530; Sat: 0900–1200.
Business
Mon–Fri: 0830–1230, 1330–1730; Sat: 0830–1230.
Government
Mon–Fri: 0830–1230, 1330–1730; Sat: 0830–1230.
Shops
Sun–Sat: 0900–2200 (department stores 1100–2130).

Telecommunications
Mobile/cell phones
There are 900 and 1800 GSM service throughout most of the island.

Electricity supply
110V AC, 60 cycles

Weights and measures
Metric system (some Chinese units in use).

Social customs/useful tips
Shaking hands is the normal form of greeting. When addressing Chinese persons, the family or surname comes first. Business cards are usually exchanged and should be in both Chinese and English. They constitute an important part of the business culture, and Taiwanese expect visitors to carry cards. Cards using mainland (simplified) script are not advisable as this could cause offence.
Visitors should remember that Taiwanese of all backgrounds need to maintain 'face', this means that it is important not to embarrass your Taiwanese counterpart either privately or when in company. Rejection of gifts as small as cigarettes may cause offence, as a sign that the offerer is not considered wealthy. In general, however, the social environment in Taiwan is very liberal and visitors need not fear inadvertently causing offence.
When visiting people's homes, removing shoes is mandatory. The subject of death should be avoided in conversation as it is considered a bad omen.

Getting there
Air
An agreement was signed with China on 13 June 2008 to allow 36 direct flights (18 each) a week to start on 4 July. A further agreement will allow 3,000 tourists per day into each country from 18 July.
National airline: China Airlines (CAL). Taiwan's second carrier, Eva Air, is a major international carrier.
International airport/s: Taiwan Taoyuan International Airport (TTY) (formerly called Chiang Kai-Shek International), 40km south-west of Taipei, with duty-free shop, bar, restaurant, bank, post office, hotel reservations and shops; Kaohsiung International (KHH).
There are bus and taxi services to the closest cities.
Airport tax: None
Surface
Water: Regular ferry services run between Keelung and Kaohsiung ports (Taiwan) and Okinawa (Japan). There are also some sea links between Kaohsiung and Macao.
Main port/s: Keelung (including Suao), Hualien, Taichung.

Getting about
National transport
Air: Domestic air services are operated by China Airlines. Far Eastern Air Transport and seven other carriers connect most of the main cities.
Road: The road network covers 20,000km, most of it surfaced. A good highway links the main centres between Keelung and Kaohsiung. Bad terrain and one-way systems can make road travel difficult outside urban centres.
Buses: Extensive bus services cover coastal, cross-island and inland areas. Express coach services link Taipei, Kaohsiung and other main centres. Advance booking is recommended. Destinations are clearly marked in English at urban bus stations.
Rail: The railway extends the whole length of Taiwan, mainly along the west coast, including high-speed intercity trains. These services are good with air-conditioned express trains linking main centres. Urban train stations have destinations marked in English.
A US$17.8 billion high speed 345km rail system linking Taipei with the southern city of Kaohsiung (journey time 80 minutes) is expected to be operational by the end of 2006.
Water: There are ferry services from Kaohsiung and Chiayi to the Pescadores Islands, from Taitung to the Lanyu and Green Islands.
City transport
Rush-hour traffic in Taipei can be chaotic and stressful. Allow plenty of time for getting to and from the airport.
Taxis: Taxis are plentiful. Metered taxis are available in Taipei, and fares are metered by kilometres and delay time. Have the destination (and the return address) written in Chinese for the taxi driver's reference.
Tipping is not an established practice, though it is becoming more usual.
From Taiwan Taoyuan International Airport to city centre the journey time is 45–60 minutes.
Buses, trams & metro: An underground rail system and a Rapid Mass Transit System are under construction in Taipei and Kaohsiung. Construction of the Taipei system is expected to be fully completed by 2009; Kaohsiung in 2007.
Car hire
Self-drive car hire is available, although chauffeur-driven cars are recommended due to traffic conditions. An international driving licence is required. Driving is on the right-hand side of the road.

BUSINESS DIRECTORY
The addresses listed below are a selection only. While World of Information makes every endeavour to check these addresses, we cannot guarantee that changes have not been made, especially to telephone numbers and area codes. We would welcome any corrections.

Telephone area codes
The international direct dialling (IDD) code for Taiwan is +886 followed by the area code and subscriber's number:

Hualien	38	Taichung	4
Kaohsiung	7	Tainan	6
Keelung	32	Taipei	2
Pingtung	8		

Useful telephone numbers
Fire and ambulance: 119.
Police: 110.
English-speaking police: 311-9940, 311-9816 ext 264.
Ambulance: 721-6315.

Women's help-line 581-5469.
International calls: 100.
Directory enquiries: Chinese language 104 (long-distance: 105). English language 311-6796.

Chambers of Commerce

American Chamber of Commerce in Taipei, Chia Hsin Building, 96 Chungshan North Road, Section 2, Taipei 104 (tel: 2581-7089; fax: 2542-3376; e-mail: amcham@amcham.com.tw).

British Chamber of Commerce in Taiwan, Fu Key Building, 99 Ren Ai Road, Section 2, Taipei 106 (tel: 2356-0210; fax: 2356-0211; e-mail: info@bcctaipei.com).

Chinese National Association of Industry and Commerce, 390 Fu Hsing South Road, Taipei 106 (tel: 2707-0111; fax : 2701-7601; e-mail: webmaster@nfict.org).

European Chamber of Commerce Taipei, 285 Zhongxiao East Road, Section 4, Taipei (tel: 2740-0236; fax: 2772-0530; e-mail: ecct@ecct.com.tw).

Taiwan Chamber of Commerce, 158 Sung Chiang Road, Taipei 104 (tel: 2536-5455; fax: 2521-1980; e-mail: tcoc@tcoc.org.tw).

Banking

Bank of Taiwan, 120 Chungking S Road, Sec 2, Taipei (tel: 2314-7377; fax: 2331-5840).

Chang Hwa Commercial Bank, 23-1 Chang An E Rd, Sec 1, Taipei City (tel: 2523-0739; fax: 2523-0172).

Chiao Tung Bank, 91 Heng Yang Road, Taipei (tel: 2361-3000; fax: 2311-3263).

Citibank, PO Box 3343, Citicorp Center, 52 Minsheng E Road, Sec 4, Taipei City 105 (tel: 2715-5931; fax: 2712-7388).

First Commercial Bank, 30 Chungking S Road, Sec 1, Taipei 10036 (tel: 2311-111; fax: 2361-0036).

Hua Nan Commercial Bank, 38 Chungking S Road, Sec 1, Taipei (tel: 2371-3111; fax: 2371-5734).

International Commercial Bank of China, 100 Chi Lin Road, Taipei (tel: 2563-3156; fax: 2561-1216).

Shanghai Commercial & Savings Bank Ltd, 2 Min Chuan East Road, Section 1, Taipei City (tel: 2581-7111; fax: 2567-1921).

Standard Chartered Bank, 168 Tun Hwa North Rd, Taipei City 105 (tel: 2716-2621, 2717-2866; fax: 2716-4068).

Taipeibank, 50 Chungshan North Road, Section 2, Taipei City (tel: 2542-5656; fax: 2542-8870).

Taiwan Co-operative Bank, 77 Kuanchien Road, Taipei (tel: 2311-8811; fax: 2331-6567).

Central bank

Central Bank of China, 2 Roosevelt Road, Section 1, Taipei 100 (tel: 2393-6161; fax: 2357-1974; internet: www.cbc.gov.tw).

Stock exchange

Taiwan Stock Exchange, www.twse.com.tw

Travel information

China Airlines (CAL), 131 Nanking East Road, Section 3, Taipei 104 (tel: 2715-2626; fax: 2717-5120).

Taiwan Taoyuan International Airport, No 9, Hangjan S Rd, Dayuan Shiang, Taoyuan, Taiwan 33758 (tel: 2398-2143, 2398-3274; internet: www.cksairport.gov.tw)

Flight information (24 hours) (tel: 2398-2050).

Sungshan Domestic Airport Travel Information Service Centre (tel: 2349-1580).

Taiwan Visitors' Association, 5th Floor, 9 Ming Chuan East Road, Sec 2, Taipei (tel: 2594-3261; fax: 2594-3265).

Tourist Information Hot Line (tel: 2717-3737).

National tourist organisation offices

Tourism Bureau, 9F Floor, 280 Chung Hsiao East Road, Section 4; PO Box 1490, Taipei (tel: 2721-8541; fax: 2773-5487: internet www.taiwantourism.org).

Ministries

Ministry of Economic Affairs, 15 Foochow Street, Taipei (tel: 2321-2200; fax: 2391-9398).

Ministry of Education (MoE), 5 Chungshan S. Road, Taipei (tel: 2356-6051; fax: 2397-6920).

Ministry of Finance, 2 Aikuo West Road, Taipei (tel: 2322-8000; fax: 2321-1205).

Ministry of Foreign Affairs, 2 Chieh Shou Road, Taipei (tel: 2311-9292; fax: 2314-4972).

Ministry of the Interior (MoI), 5 Hsuchow Road, Taipei (tel: 2356-5000; fax: 2356-6201).

Ministry of Justice (MoJ), 130 Chungking S. Road, Sec. 1, Taipei (tel: 2314-6871; fax: 2389-6239).

Ministry of National Defence, Chiehshou Hall, Chungking S. Road, Taipei (tel: 2311-6117; fax: 2314-4221).

Ministry of Transportation and Communications, 2 Changasha Street, Section 1, Taipei (tel: 2349-2900; fax: 2389-6009).

Monetary Affairs Dept, Ministry of Finance, 2 Aikuo W Road, Taipei (tel: 2321-3836).

President's Office, 122 Chungking South Road, Section 1, Taipei (the First Bureau tel: 2311-3731; fax: 2314-0746; Protocol Section: 2311-5877; Spokesman's Office: 2331-1604).

Other useful addresses

Board of Foreign Trade, 1 Hukou St, Taipei (tel: 2351-0271; fax: 2351-3603).

British Trade and Cultural Office, 9th floor, Fu Key Building, 99 Jen Ali Road, Section 2, Taipei 10625 (tel: 2322-4242; fax: 2394-8673).

China External Trade Development Council (CETRA), 4-8th floor, International Trade Building, 333 Keelung Road, Sec 1, Taipei 10548 (tel: 2725-5200; fax: 2757-6653).

Chinese National Association of Industry & Commerce, 13th floor, 390 Fu Hsing South Rd, Sec 1, Taipei (tel: 2707-0111; fax: 2701-7601).

Chinese National Export Enterprises Association (CNEEA), 6th floor, 285 Nanking E. Road, Sec. 3, Taipei (tel: 2713-8153; fax: 2713-0115).

Chinese National Federation of Industries, 12th floor, 390 Fuhsing South Road, Section 1, Taipei (tel: 2703-3500; fax: 2703-3982).

Chinese Petroleum Corporation, 83 Chung-Hwa Road, Section 1, Taipei 10331 (tel: 2361-0221; fax: 2371-5944).

Council for Economic Planning and Development, 9/F, 87 Nanking East Road, Section 2, Taipei (tel: 2551-3522; fax: 2581-8549).

Directorate-General of Budgets, Accounting & Statistics, Executive Yuan, 1 Chung Hsiao East Road, Section 1, Taipei (internet: www.stat.gov.tw/).

Euro-Asia Trade Organisation, 3rd floor, 9 Roosevelt Road, Sec. 2, Taipei (tel: 2393-2115; fax: 2392-8393).

Government Information Office, Taipei (tel: 2322-8888).

Industrial Development Bureau, MOEA, 41-3 Hsinyi Road, Sec. 3, Taipei (tel: 2754-1255; fax: 2703-0160).

Industrial Development and Investment Centre, MOEA, 4 Chunghsiao W. Road, Sec 1, Taipei (tel: 2389-2111; fax: 2382-0497).

Industry of Free China, 9th Floor, 87 Nanking East Road, Section 2, Taipei (tel: 2543-5988).

International Co-operation Department, MOEA, 15 Foochow St., Taipei (tel: 2321-2200; fax: 2321-3275).

International Economic Co-operation Development Fund, 7th floor, 51

Chung-Ching S. Road, Sec. 2, Taipei (tel: 2396-6316; fax: 2396-9147).

International Telecommunications Administration (ITA), 28 Hangchou S. Rd, Sec. 1, Taipei (tel: 2344-3781).

International Trade Association of the R.O.C., 8th floor, 148 Chunghsiao E. Road, Sec. 4, Taipei (tel: 2772-6252; fax: 2752-2411).

Investment Commission, Ministry of Economic Affairs, 8th Floor, 7 Roosevelt Road, Sec 1, Taipei (tel: 2351-3151; fax: 2396-3970).

Securities and Exchange Commission, 12th Floor, Yangteh Building, 3 Nanhai Road, Taipei (tel: 2341-3191; fax: 2394-8249).

Taipei Economic and Cultural Representative Office (USA), 4201 Wisconsin Avenue, NW, Washington DC 20016 (tel: (+1-202) 895-1800; fax: (+1-202) 363-0999; email: contact@tecro-info.org).

Taipei World Trade Centre Exhibition Hall, 5 Hsinyi Road, Section 5, Taipei (tel: 2886-2725; fax: 2886-1314).

Taiwan Stock Exchange Corp, 85 Yen Ping S Road, Taipei (tel: 2311-4020; fax: 2311-4004).

Taiwan Textile Federation, 22 Ai-Kuo E. Road, Taipei (tel: 2341-7251; fax: 2392-3855).

World Trade Center Taichung, 60 Tienpao St, Taichung (tel: 2254-2271; fax: 2254-2341).

National news agency: Central News Agency (www.cna.com.tw).

Internet sites

Taiwan business directory: www.tbdo.anjes.com.tw

Taiwan business express: www.business.com.tw

Taiwan News, the Voice of Taiwan: www.eTaiwanNews.com

Taiwan Trade Point: www.tradepoint.anjes.com.tw

Tajikistan

KEY FACTS

Official name: Respublika i Tojikiston (Republic of Tajikistan)

Head of State: President Emomali Rahmon (leader since 1992; re-elected 2006)

Head of government: Prime Minister Qohir Rasulzoda (since 23 November 2013)

Ruling party: Hizbi Demokrati Khalkii (HDK) (People's Democratic Party) (elected 2000; re-elected 2010; re-elected 2015)

Area: 143,100 square km

Population: 8.30 million (2014)*

Capital: Dushanbe

Official language: Tajik (Farsi)

Currency: Somoni (Sm) = 100 dirams

Exchange rate: Sm6.71 per US$ (Nov 2015)

GDP per capita: US$1,113 (2014)*

GDP real growth: 6.70% (2014)*

GDP: US$9.24 billion (2014)*

Labour force: 2.10 million (2009)*

Inflation: 6.06% (2014)*

Balance of trade: -US$3.98 billion (2014)

Annual FDI: US$11.14 million (2011)

* estimated figure

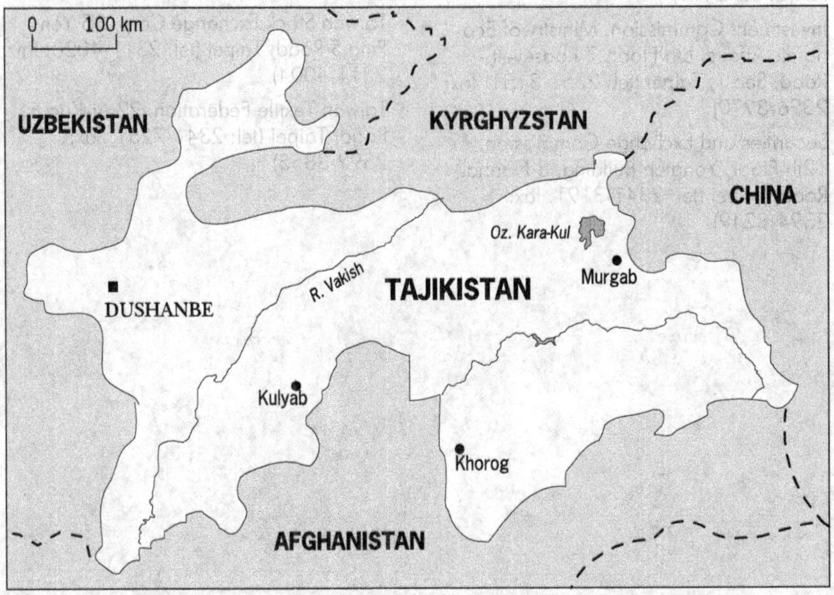

Of the former Soviet states, Tajikistan is the poorest, and this status is set to continue due to the behaviour of President Emomali Rahmon. Rahmon and his peers resist transparency and reform, and according to *The Economist*, remain 'With their gilded palaces and vanity projects.' The President's most recent project was a US$100 million theatre. But despite this obvious corruption in the government's handling of funds, not only has Mr Rahmon held office for 23 years but is also frequently the recipient of financial aid from the West. The reason for this, according to Western diplomats, is due to 'Tajikistan's support of their governments involvement in Afghanistan'.

Those that speak out in public against President Rahmon can expect to be on the receiving end of death threats or be locked up on spurious charges. One example of the danger of being a critic was the assassination of Umarali Kuvatov, a leading detractor, in Istanbul. Kuvatov fled Tajikistan in 2012 following a dispute with the ruling family, reportedly due to a business deal with the president's son-in-law turning saw. After spending nine months in Dubai, held under a Tajik warrant, Kuvatov moved to Turkey where he sought asylum. During his flight, the fugitive took to Facebook to 'declare war on Rahmon's kleptocracy'. However, on 5 March 2015, Rahmon's grasp caught up with Kuvatov, as the tycoon and his family fell ill while dining in Istanbul (potentially from poisoning claim Turkish media), and as he stepped outside to seek medical help he was shot once in the back of the head before the assassin vanished.

(Un)Friendly relations

Tajikistan increasingly took on the aspect of a failed state in 2015. President Emomali Rahmon clung on to the vestiges of power, but in many parts of Tajikistan it was errant warlords who were calling the shots. In mid-2012 Tajikistan had accused neighbouring Uzbekistan of imposing an economic blockade around it to try to trigger a humanitarian catastrophe and destabilise the country, allegations senior Uzbek politicians dismissed as groundless. But it was the fierce rivalry, bordering on armed struggle, that characterised the relationship between Tajikistan and its neighbour.

In a strongly worded statement, Tajikistan had accused the Uzbeks of blocking railway links and cutting gas supplies. The Tajik news agency Asia-Plus, quoted the statement as saying.

'The situation, if it continues, will lead to the further deterioration of the conditions of life of the people of Tajikistan and threatens to turn into a humanitarian catastrophe.' The news agency went on to say that Tajikistan was one of the poorest of the Central Asian states. One of its only natural resources is water which runs off the Pamir mountains into Uzbekistan, where it irrigates the economically important cotton fields.

As if the tensions with Uzbekistan were not enough, in August 2014 Reuters reported that two Tajiks had been killed in a border shootout, this time between Tajikistan and Kyrgyzstan. Although tensions had been rising, the August incident was the bloodiest clash of the year on the frontier between the former Soviet neighbours. The Tajik police claimed that gun fire from Kyrgyzstan had killed a border guard and one civilian and wounded four other civilians. However, the Kyrgyz border force blamed the incident on Tajikistan, accusing Tajik servicemen of trying to erect a border post 'on an un-delimited part of the border' and attempting to destroy a bridge across a river used by Kyrgyz citizens. Each side blamed the other for the incident; there were no reports of any casualties on the Kyrgyz side during the half-hour shootout. Shortly afterwards the Tajik Deputy Prime Minister Murodali Alimardon was due to travel to the Kyrgyz capital Bishkek to try and defuse the tension and the Kyrgyz foreign ministry confirmed that it had handed a note of protest to Tajikistan about the incident. Kyrgyzstan claimed that it had registered a total of 31 incidents on its 970km border with Tajikistan since the beginning of 2014, including three when firearms were used. Border clashes and conflicts in Central Asia are surprisingly common, as villagers often clash over land, water and pastures, confrontations that sometimes result in the use of weapons by border guards.

Of the five former Soviet Central Asian states, only the isolationist Turkmenistan is not a member of the Shanghai Co-operation Organisation (SCO), the group named after the city where it was set up in 2001. In mid-2012 China's state newspaper, the *People's Daily*, reported that Chen Bingde, the highest ranked general in China, had flown to Dushanbe, the Tajik capital, after bilateral visits to Uzbekistan and Turkmenistan. SCO military were due to play out a counter terrorism exercise in Tajikistan, according to media reports. Over the previous decade China has strengthened its interests in Central Asia. As well as playing a major role in the SCO, China has provided cheap loans, developed infrastructure and become a major client for oil and gas.

The economy

According to the Asian Development Bank (ADB) Tajikistan's gross domestic product (GDP) growth slowed to 6.4 per cent in the first half of 2015, due mainly to industrial expansion moderating from 16.8 per cent a year earlier to 14.9 per cent. This reflects a meagre 3.5 per cent growth in aluminium, and cut services growth to 0.8 per cent due to spill over from Russia's recession. The ADB expects retail trade and services to decline further in the second half of 2015, counteracting the growth seen in industry and agriculture.

Auctions of securities by the National Bank of Tajikistan (NBT) (central bank) and of Treasury bills to reduce liquidity have aided the average inflation rate in moderating to 5.5 per cent in the first half of 2015. Simultaneously the Tajik somoni depreciated by about 18 per cent against the US dollar, and by 32 per cent against the ruble, despite currency interventions by the NBT.

In the first half of 2015 remittances dropped by 35 per cent over the same period in the previous year. This drop contributed to a fall in imports of 25 per cent, and exports decreased by 8 per cent.

In the 2015 *Asian Development Outlook* (ADO) update, the growth forecast has been reduced, and slower expansion is expected to carry on over into 2016, despite the predicted recuperation of the Russian Federation's economy. Inflation is expected to be at 7.0 per cent in 2016 in view of projected increasing global food prices and upcoming hikes in part-time salaries in the public sector, reflected in part by increase in utility prices. If the Tajik somoni continues to depreciate then inflation could increase even further, as well as currency controls that are in place to manipulate production and imports.

Risk assessment

Politics	Poor
Economy	Fair
Regional stability	Fair/poor

Muslims in Tajikistan

% of population	99
Sunni (% of Muslims)	93
Shi'a (% of Muslims)	7

COUNTRY PROFILE

1916–17 The Central Asian republics joined in a violent uprising against Russian rule, which was suppressed. After the October Revolution in Russia, the Russian ruler, Lenin, gave the peoples of Central Asia the right of self-determination.

1920s Southern Tajikistan remained under the control of the Khan of Bukhara while northern Tajikistan was incorporated into Soviet-controlled Turkestan, which also included Uzbekistan, Kyrgyzstan, part of northern Turkmenistan and southern Kazakhstan. Soviet nationalities policy, under the direction of Stalin, saw Soviet rule enforced by Red Army troops who put down fierce Muslim resistance in Central Asia after the Russian civil war.

1924 Tajikistan was granted autonomous status in the Socialist Soviet Republic (SSR) of Uzbekistan.

KEY INDICATORS — Tajikistan

	Unit	2011	2012	2013	2014	**2015
Population	m	*7.85	*7.96	*8.13	*8.30	*8.48
Gross domestic product (GDP)	US$bn	6.52	7.59	8.51	*9.24	*8.53
GDP per capita	US$	935	953	1,046	*1,113	*1,007
GDP real growth	%	7.4	7.5	7.4	*6.7	*3.0
Inflation	%	14.4	5.8	5.0	*6.1	*12.8
Exports (fob) (goods)	US$m	592.9	825.9	574.1	5,268.6	–
Imports (fob) (goods)	US$m	4,164.9	4,382.7	4,535.5	4,508.9	–
Balance of trade	US$m	-3,572.0	-3,556.8	-3,961.4	-3,982.0	–
Current account	US$m	-787.0	-151.0	-244.0	*-839.0	*-604.0
Total reserves minus gold	US$m	–	297.9	460.7	169.4	–
Foreign exchange	US$m	–	190.7	353.3	–	–
Exchange rate	per US$	4.61	4.67	4.74	5.02	–

* estimated figure ** forecast figure

1929 Tajikistan was detached from Uzbekistan and became a separate SSR.
1930s–80s The country underwent a period of agricultural collectivisation and industrialisation, which was unpopular with the population.
1989 Tajik became the official state language.
1990 Social and ethnic tensions erupted in violence in Dushanbe and along the Tajikistan-Kyrgyzstan border. A state of emergency was declared and Soviet troops were sent to Dushanbe to suppress pro-democracy protests. President Kahar Mahkamov resigned after being accused of supporting an attempted coup against the Soviet leader Mikhail Gorbachev.
1991 The collapse of the Soviet Union resulted in Tajikistan declaring independence. Rahmon Nabiyev was appointed president after winning Tajikistan's first direct presidential elections. Tajikistan joined the Commonwealth of Independent States (CIS), following the collapse of the Soviet Union.
1992 Anti-government demonstrations in Dushanbe turned into civil war between pro-government forces and Islamist and pro-democracy groups. Nabiyev was forced to resign and the Hizbi Komunistii Tojikiston (HKT) (Communist Party of Tajikistan) government collapsed. Pro-Communists massacred thousands of government supporters in Dushanbe. The HKT regained power and Emomali Rakhmonov became head of state.
1993 The Supreme Court returned the country to one-party rule after banning all political parties other than the ruling HKT. A CIS peace-keeping force was deployed along the Tajikistan-Afghan border to prevent armed incursions by Islamic guerrilla groups.
1994 A cease-fire between the government and the rebels was agreed. A presidential constitution was approved by national referendum. Rakhmonov won the presidential elections, which were deemed by international observers to be neither free nor fair.
1995 Rakhmonov supporters won the legislative elections, which took place without the participation of any of the opposition groups. Fighting erupted on the Afghan border.
1996 A UN-sponsored cease-fire between the government and Islamist rebels came into effect.
1997 Opposition parties were legalised and as part of a peace treaty between the Tajikistan government and the Islamic United Tajik Opposition (UTO), the government agreed to give 30 per cent of its seats to opposition representatives, retaining 50 per cent for itself, and to give the remaining 20 per cent to independents.
1998 The government removed the ban on religious political parties. Rakhmonov pardoned all opposition leaders in exile. Tajikistan joined the CIS Customs Union.
1999 President Rakhmonov was re-elected for a third term. The UTO armed forces were integrated into the state army.
2000 A new bicameral parliament was set up. The elections were won by the Hizbi Demokrati Khalkii (HDK) (People's Democratic Party). The somoni replaced the Tajik rouble as the currency. Belarus, Kazakhstan, Kyrgyzstan, Russia and Tajikistan (formerly the Customs Five) established the Eurasian Economic Community (EEC).
2001 Tajikistan, China, Russia, Kazakhstan, Kyrgyzstan and Uzbekistan formed the Shanghai Co-operation Organisation (SCO). Rahmon Sanginov, a renegade warlord, declared one of the country's most wanted criminals, was killed in a gun battle with security forces.
2002 Tajikistan became the last Central Asian republic to join NATO's Partnership for Peace (PfP) programme. The number of border guards was doubled to prevent al Qaeda members from crossing the border with Afghanistan to escape US forces.
2003 Russian President Vladimir Putin announced an agreement to increase Russian military presence. A referendum extended President Rakhmonov's term in office by two more consecutive seven-year terms.
2004 A moratorium on the death penalty was introduced. Russia regained control of a former Soviet space-monitoring centre at Nurek and opened a military base in Dushanbe.
2005 The ruling HDK was re-elected. However, international observers said the elections had not reached acceptable international standards. Opposition leader, Mahmadruzi Iskandarov (HDK), had been arrested and released in Moscow after an extradition request was dismissed, was kidnapped and transported to Tajikistan to be re-arrested; he was sentenced on terrorism and corruption charges and received a 23-year sentence.
2006 Incumbent Emomali Rakhmonov won 79 per cent of the vote for president; giving him his fourth term in office. The election was neither free nor fair according to international observers.
2007 A bridge across the Pyanj River, built by the US army, was opened, linking the Tajik town of Nizhny Pyanj with Shir Khan Bandar and extending the trans-Afghanistan road (Regional Road Corridor Improvement Project) through Central Asia. The president removed the 'ov' from his name and discouraged Russian-style names from use.
2009 Tajikistan reached an agreement with the US to allow non-military shipments destined for Afghanistan to fly over and through its territory.
2010 In parliamentary elections, the incumbent HDK won an overwhelming majority of 55 seats (out of 63). The Organisation for Security and Co-operation in Europe (OSCE) judged the elections had 'failed on many basic democratic standards' and widespread fraud. The opposition mounted a legal challenge to the results. Russia hosted a regional summit meeting of presidents from Afghanistan, Pakistan, Tajikistan and Russia. Economic and development co-operation was promised between them.
2011 At the beginning of the year Russia began several negotiations towards achieving a security treaty and to return Russian border guards to the joint Tajikistan-Russian border, due to the sharp increase in drugs-trafficking across the border and the risk of regional Islamic violence spilling over into Russia's southern Central Asian states. An agreement was reached between Tajikistan and China, which settled a century-old border dispute, following the Tajik parliament's vote in January to cede 1,000 square kilometres of land in the Pamir mountain range to China. Although this only represented 5.5 per cent of the land claimed, China accepted the land as a resolution to the dispute. In August, as part of the anniversary celebrations, President Rakhmon gave an amnesty to 15,000 prisoners who had fought against his forces during the 1990s civil war.
2012 On 4 April, international relation with Uzbekistan degenerated following Tajikistan's accusation that its neighbour had imposed an 'economic blockade' in an effort to trigger a humanitarian catastrophe and destabilise the government. The complaint was that Uzbekistan had blocked railway links and cut natural gas supplies. In turn, Uzbekistan claimed that the new hydroelectric dam, under construction, would severely reduce water supplies to a patched Uzbekistan with vital cotton fields. On 5 October an agreement was signed with Russia to allow it a 30-year extension on a military base, with a deployed division of 7,000 Russian soldiers, guard the mutual border.
2015 The 1 March general election was convincingly won by the Hizbi Demokrati Khalkii (HDK) (People's Democratic Party) wity 65.4 per cent of the vote (51 seats out of 63). The Organisation for Security and Co-operation in Europe (OSCE) monitoring group reported that as many as half the votes they saw being counted should have been thrown out. They also reported ballot-box stuffing and

intimidation. On 5 June Umarali Kuvatov, leader of the opposition Group 24, was shot and killed in Istanbul.

Political structure

Constitution

A presidential Constitution was approved by national referendum in 1994. The Constitution granted basic economic and political rights and guaranteed religious freedoms. It gave the president powers to appoint the chairs of regions, districts, cities, including Dushanbe, as well as of the Gorno-Badakshan Autonomous Region and the governor of the National Bank of Tajikistan (central bank), subject to the approval of deputies in parliament. The president also has powers of dismissal over these offices. In addition, the president gained the power to declare a state of martial law and issue decrees, as well as immunity from prosecution. Parliament has the power to impeach the president, subject to the findings of the Constitutional Court. If more than two-thirds of deputies vote in favour of impeachment, parliament may dismiss the president from office.

Independence date

9 September 1991

Form of state

Presidential socialist republic

The executive

The president, elected by universal suffrage every seven years, holds executive power. The government consists of the prime minister and cabinet and may present its resignation to the president if it declares it cannot function normally.

In 2003, voters in a referendum favoured allowing President Rakhmonov to run two further consecutive seven-year terms in office after 2006.

National legislature

The bicameral Majlisi Oli (Supreme Assembly) consists of the Majlisi Namoyandogan (Assembly of Representatives) (lower house), with 63 members, of which 22 are elected by proportional representation and 41 in single-seat constituencies; the Majlisi Milliy (National Assembly) (upper house) has 34 seats, of which 25 are elected by subordinate regional assemblies and eight are appointed by the president. One is reserved for the former president. All Assembly members serve for five-year terms.

Legal system

The judiciary is constitutionally independent from the legislature and executive.

Courts include the Supreme Court, Constitutional Court, Military Court and High Economic Court. In addition there are district and city courts, as well as the Dushanbe City Court. Gorno-Badakshan Autonomous Region has its own court.

The president has powers to appoint and dismiss judges of all courts on petition of the minister of justice, except for judges appointed to the Supreme Court, High Economic Court and Constitutional Court. The latter is composed of seven judges elected from the legal profession, one of whom is a representative of Gorno-Badakshan Autonomous Region.

Last elections

1 March 2015 (parliamentary); 6 November 2013 (presidential)

Results: Parliamentary: Hizbi Demokrati Khalkii (HDK) (People's Democratic Party) won 65.4 per cent of the vote (51 seats out of 63), Agrarian Party (APT) 11.7 per cent (five), Party of Economic Reforms, 7.5 per cent (three), Hizbi Kommunistii (Communist Party) (CP) 2.2 per cent (two); the remaining four parties won no more than one seat each. Turnout was 87.7 per cent.

Presidential: Emomali Rakhmonov won with 83.9 per cent of the vote. Turnout was 86.6 per cent

Next elections

November 2020 (presidential); 2020 (parliamentary)

Political parties

Ruling party

Hizbi Demokrati Khalkii (HDK) (People's Democratic Party) (elected 2000; re-elected 2010; re-elected 2015)

Main opposition party

Hizbi Agrarii Tojikiston (APT) (Agrarian Party)

Population

8.30 million (2014)* Approximately 40 per cent of the population is under 14 years and 5 per cent over 65 years of age.

The population is concentrated in valleys covering less than 5 per cent of the country's surface (the terrain is extremely mountainous).

Last census: January 2000: 6,127,000 (provisional)

Population density: 54 inhabitants per square km (2010). Urban population 26 per cent (2010 Unicef).

Annual growth rate: 1.3 per cent, 1990–2010 (Unicef).

Ethnic make-up

Tajik (69.1 per cent), Uzbek (25 per cent), Russian (2.7 per cent), with remaining minorities including Tatar and Kyrgyz groups. Tajikistan is the exception among the Central Asian republics in that its population is predominantly Persian rather than Turkic. The Tajiks are made up of a number of closely related ethnic groups which differ both anthropologically (inhabitants of the Pamir mountains in the north are tall, dark complexioned with light-coloured eyes; those from Kuliab are stocky and dark-skinned; northern Tajiks are fair-complexioned, brown- and black-eyed). Customs and rituals also differ.

Religions

The majority (80 per cent) of ethnic Tajiks and Uzbeks are Sunni Muslims; 5 per cent are Shi'a Muslims. Ethnic Badakhshanis belong to the Ismaili Muslim sect and have the Aga Khan as their spiritual leader. There are also Baptists and Bukhara Jews. There is no official religion.

Education

Public expenditure on education typically amounts to 3 per cent of GDP.

Primary education lasts four years, followed by eight years of secondary schooling which is divided into two cycles of five and three years in either general, technical or vocational education. Successful students may progress to either a university or institute of which there are 29 established.

In 2003, the Asian Development Bank (ADB) approved a US$7.5 million loan for education reforms to give about 90,000 children better access to quality education. About 300 schools, in pilot districts, which were damaged during the civil war and lacked maintenance, received funding for refurbishment and to provide textbooks and learning materials, plus pay for enhancing female teacher training.

The total cost of the project was US$9.38 million, 80 per cent of which was covered by the ADB's loan, while the government provided the balance of US$1.88 million.

Nationwide, the education system is suffering from an exodus of large numbers of qualified teachers to find better paid work. School attendance levels are also falling, as children are pressed into helping their families cope with the widespread poverty and social vulnerability. Gender imbalance is particularly marked at the upper secondary level, with the proportion of girls declining.

Literacy rate: 100 per cent adult rate; 100 per cent youth rate (15–24) (Unesco 2005).

Compulsory years: Seven to 16.

Enrolment rate: 85 per cent gross primary enrolment (ADB); 76 per cent gross secondary enrolment (Unicef).

Pupils per teacher: 24 in primary schools.

Health

The structure of Tajikistan's health system has evolved from the Soviet model of healthcare with few structural changes.

The state funds most of the healthcare services in the country. The health ministry runs national-level healthcare services, while local authorities administer most regional services.

State hospitals have limited supplies of free medicines. People have been increasingly forced to pay for their own healthcare, often buying their own medicines off the street.

The health budget each year has major shortfalls that are partially covered by international aid. The government has introduced more than 11 national and sectoral programmes, including those to combat tuberculosis, prevent HIV/Aids and improve reproductive health. The World Bank began a major rehabilitation project with an estimated expenditure of US$25 million in 2000–03 in the Soghd and Khatlon regions. The project aimed to rehabilitate 300 health posts, rural physician clinics and outpatient facilities.

Tajikistan has the youngest population of any former Soviet states, with 70 per cent aged under 30 years.

Tajikistan has substantial environmental problems that pose risks to human health. There is high risk of communicable disease with the breakdown of public health measures such as mosquito control and immunisation. Less than 50 per cent of the rural population have access to clean water. Tajikistan is one of the primary transfer points for the flow of drugs due to transparent border controls and poor custom regulations.

HIV/Aids

HIV prevalence: 0.1 per cent aged 15–49 in 2003 (World Bank)

Life expectancy: 63 years, 2004 (WHO 2006)

Fertility rate/Maternal mortality rate: 3.3 births per woman, 2010 (Unicef); maternal mortality 66.5 per 100,000 live births (World Bank).

Birth rate/Death rate: 32.8 births and 8.5 deaths per 1,000 people (2003).

Child (under 5 years) mortality rate (per 1,000): 58 per 1,000 live births (WHO 2012)

Head of population per physician: 2.03 physicians per 1,000 people, 2003 (WHO 2006)

Welfare

As the poorest of the CIS countries, a significant proportion of Tajikistan's population now faces severe social hardship, especially with most of the country's social welfare budget being spent on pensions. The country relies heavily on overseas assistance, highlighting the failure of the state to create a self-financing welfare system.

Main cities

Dushanbe (capital, estimated population 747,705 in 2012), Khujand (140,225), Kulob (86,735), Qurgonteppa (65,309), Konibodom (62,127), Uroteppa (58,227), Kofarnihon (45,563), Isfara (40,612).

Languages spoken

The Tajik language is very close to Persian, spoken in Iran, and to Dari, spoken in Afghanistan. Although Tajik is spoken locally, in practice, Russian is widely used in government and business. Uzbek is also spoken. The Badakhshanis speak the Pamir languages, but also speak Tajik or Russian. There are three main groups – the Pamir languages, the southern Kulyab and the northern Khodzent dialects.

A State Language law provides for a transition to the Tajik language with Arabic script.

Official language/s

Tajik (Farsi)

Media

Despite a constitutionally guaranteed free press, the government has a heavy influence on all media outlets and has led to widespread self-censorship. Laws prohibit the dissemination of information containing state secrets, inciting racial discrimination and any form of ethnic or religious hatred.

Press

Tajikistan does not possess any pulp mills or paper making industries and has to import all newsprint paper and printing equipment, which has resulted in significantly higher printing costs and an inability to produce daily newspapers. The UN considers this situation denies citizens access to current news.

Weeklies: The four official weeklies are not popular as they are concerned with published resolutions, government decision and official chronicles and lack any innovation. They have deplorable circulation figures of 700–2,000, of which 75 per cent are secured by subscription and only 25 per cent are sold retail.

Government-owned and published three times per week, *Jumhuriyat* and *Sadio Mardum*in Tajik, *Khalq Ovozi* in Uzbek and *Narodnaya Gazeta* in Russian. Private publications include *Neru-i Sukhan* and *Tajikiston* in Takik. Political parties publish *Minbar-i Khalq* (People's Democratic Party), *Nido-i Ranjbar* in Takik (Communist Party), *Golos Tajikistana* in Russian (Communist Party), *Najot* (Islamic Rebirth Party).

Broadcasting

The broadcasting law prohibits dissemination of information containing state secrets, inciting of racial discrimination and any form of ethnic or religious hatred.

Radio: The Government runs Tajik radio with two national networks and in the capital, Radio Sado i Dushanbe. There are two private stations, Asia Plus (www.asiaplus.tj) and Radio Vatan (www.vatan.tj) in the capital and Radio Tiroz (www.tiroz.tj) in Khujand.

External radios stations can be received including BBC, VOA and Voice of Free Tajikistan (run by national exiles).

Television: The state runs three regional networks, Tajik TV, Soghd TV and Khatlon TV. Safina TV (www.safina.tj) the only private operation.

National news agency: Khovar (in Russian) (www.khovar.tj).

Other news agencies: Avesta news agency (www.avesta.tj/en).

Economy

The economic problems faced by Tajikistan, which has one of the lowest gross domestic products (GDP) of all the Commonwealth of Independent States (CIS), are not insurmountable. Tajikistan's economic situation is weak because of uneven implementation of structural reforms, corruption, weak governance, seasonal power shortages, and its large external debt burden. The 1992-97 civil war severely damaged an already weak economic infrastructure and led to rapid decline in industrial and agricultural production. Because of a lack of employment opportunities, one million Tajik citizens work abroad – roughly 90 per cent in Russia. Remittances accounted for 42 per cent of GDP in 2013. The agriculture sector is underdeveloped and Tajikistan needs to import 60 per cent of its food, mostly by rail. Mineral resources include silver, gold, uranium, and tungsten. Industry consists of mainly small obsolete factories in food processing and light industry, substantial hydropower facilities, and a large aluminium plant – currently operating well below its capacity.

Tajikistan has recently sought to develop its substantial hydroelectricity potential through partnership with Russia and Iranian investors. The government is pinning its drive for energy independence on completion of the Roghun dam, which will take 8-11 years to construct. On its completion, it will be the tallest dam in the world and would significantly expand Tajikistan's electricity output. Unfortunately, this has damaged relations with Uzbekistan (opposed to the project), leading to them closing one of the rail lines into Tajikistan in late 2011, hampering the transit of good to and from the southern part of the country. As a result, food and fuel prices in Tajikistan have increased to the highest levels since 2002.

In 2014, the service sector constituted 51 per cent of GDP, with industry comprising 22 per cent, of which manufacturing was 9.5 per cent and agriculture 27.2 per cent

The country is dependent on remittances, cotton, aluminium sales, and hydroelectricity for its foreign exchange, all of which are subject to external shocks. The country continues to lack investment. Foreign direct investment (FDI) had averaged US$280 million over 2004–08 through growth in light industries and the service sector, as well as Russian investment in the Rogun and Sangtuda hydroelectric plants. However it fell to US$15.8 million in both 2009 and 2010 as the global economic crisis cut the availability of international (particularly Russian) investment. FDI in Tajikistan still remains extremely low at just US$263 million in 2014.

GDP growth was 7.9 per cent in 2008, falling to 3.9 per cent in 2009 as limited FDI cut down on construction and production. However, growth rebounded to 6.4 per cent in 2010 and was estimated to have grown by 7.4 per cent in 2011. GDP growth has remained fairly stable at 7.5 per cent in 2012, 7.4 per cent in 2013 and 6.7 per cent in 2014.

The unemployment rate was just 2.5 per cent in 2013 but it is not reflective of a healthy economy, most of Tajikistan's workers are in Russia and the remaining labour force are paid very little. GDP per capita was an extremely low US$2,700 in 2014. The UN Human Development Index (HDI) ranked Tajikistan 133 (out of 187) in 2013 for national development in health, education and income.

Tajikistan, located at the crossroads of Russia, Iran, Pakistan and China, is reported to have become a narcotics hub and a major transit route for opium produced not only in Afghanistan but also increasingly in Tajikistan itself. It has been estimated by experts that the value of narcotics transiting Tajikistan is equivalent to 30 to 50 per cent of GDP.

External trade

Tajikistan belongs to the Eurasian Economic Community (EAEC), established to promote a customs union between its six member states (Belarus, Kazakhstan, Kyrgyzstan, Russia, Tajikistan, and Uzbekistan), and among other objectives to introduce a standardised currency exchange and rules for trade in goods and services. The EAEC evolved out of the Commonwealth of Independent States (CIS) Customs Union and has begun the process of merging with the Central Asian Co-operation Organisation (CACO). However, by 2010 only three members (Russia, Belarus and Kazakhstan) had instituted a customs union. On 19 October 2011, a free trade agreement (FTA) was signed by Russia with seven of its former Soviet republics: Armenia, Belarus, Kazakhstan, Kyrgyzstan, Moldova and Tajikistan. The FTA must be ratified by all relevant parliaments before its instigation in 2012.

Tajikistan has the potential to mine gold, silver, uranium, antimony and tungsten, which are yet to be exploited commercially. One aluminium smelter, Talco, produces about 75 per cent of all exports. Cotton is another important commodity and accounts for almost 10 per cent of exports. Both of these products are subject to world prices and Talco is an old Soviet era factory, which along with the general infrastructure is in need of re-investment. Remittances are vital to the country's foreign earnings.

Imports

Main imports are petroleum products, aluminium oxide, machinery and equipment and foodstuffs.

Main sources: China (46.6 per cent of total in 2014), Russia (16.8 per cent), Kazakhstan (10.5 per cent) and Turkey (5.2 per cent)

Exports

The main exports are aluminium, electricity, cotton, gold, fruits, vegetable oil and textiles.

Main destinations: Turkey (23.2 per cent of total in 2014), Iran (13 per cent), Afghanistan (10.7 per cent), Kazakhstan (10.5 per cent), Italy (8.5 per cent), Bangladesh (7.4 per cent), China (6.9 per cent) and Russia (5.4 per cent)

Agriculture

Farming

During the Soviet era agriculture was the mainstay of the Tajikistan economy, particularly cotton and wheat. Agriculture accounted for 27 per cent of GDP and employed 47 per cent of the workforce in 2014.

Because of Tajikistan's mountainous nature, only 7 per cent of the land is suitable for farming. Tajikistan is a large net importer of different types of grain. The main agricultural areas are in the lower-lying regions of the southwest and the northwest – part of the Fergana basin. In semi-arid farmland, yield depends on extensive irrigation; aging rural irrigation systems have fallen into serious disrepair after more than a decade of neglect, causing widespread water shortages, silting of irrigation channels, waterlogging, and soil salinity.

Crops constitute about two-thirds, and animal husbandry one-third, of rural production. Cattle, sheep and goats are reared. Important produce is cotton, grain, fruits, grapes, vegetables and tobacco leaves. Lack of processing and packing facilities and inefficient distribution mean that large amounts of the vegetable and fruit crops are wasted and that the country often fails even to meet its domestic needs. Farm machinery has suffered depreciation over the years without replacement, and the quality of seed varieties has fallen.

The International Crisis Group (ICG) has said that while the former Soviet cotton producing countries of Uzbekistan, Tajikistan and Turkmenistan continued to exploit their cotton growers there was little hope of improving economic development and tackling poverty. The cotton industry is vital to the economy of Tajikistan, yet while the industry continues to rely on cheap labour (including children), land ownership is uncertain, state intervention discourages competition and the rule of law is limited, there is little incentive for the powerful vested interests to reform the system.

In addition to the economic and social costs to the rural populations, the environmental costs of the monoculture have been devastating. The degradation of the Aral Sea in particular has led to international concern.

Fishing

Fishing remains important for domestic consumption, but pollution and a lack of investment have reduced fish stocks drastically. Tibet stone loach is a common fish in Tajikistan where it is present up to 4,500 metres altitude, but is of no commercial importance. The typical annual fish catch is over 200 tonnes.

Forestry

The state-owned forestry and wooded land accounts for only 5 per cent of land area with forest cover estimated at over 400,000 hectares (ha). Most of the forests located between 1,000 and 3,000 metre altitude are protected. The main stock of the forests include coniferous and juniper species, which are not available for wood supply.

There are no large-scale primary forest industries and the relatively low per capita consumption of forest products is met mainly by imports from the Russian Federation.

Industry and manufacturing

The industrial sector contributed 27 per cent to GDP in 2014. Industrial production experienced a significant decline throughout the 1990s, although decline slowed with the end of the civil war. The industrial sector is dominated by some 300 large state-owned enterprises in areas such as heavy industry, transport and wholesale trading and is mainly built around inefficient, labour-intensive production.

Cotton yields between 31 per cent and 33 per cent of cotton fibre after processing. There are 19 cotton-processing plants. The domestic textile industry uses more than 20 per cent of total domestic cotton fibre production.

Chemicals, aluminium, manufactured metal goods, power transformers and cables, and agricultural equipment is produced. The aluminium and power industries, plagued by heavy debts, continue to suffer.

Light industry accounts for around 45 per cent of the value of total industrial production. The main sectors are food processing (mainly dairy products, meat, fruit and cooking oil), tobacco, cotton-cleaning, silk, textiles, knitted goods, footwear, tanning, carpet weaving and simple electronics.

Aluminium is Tajikistan's key industrial sector. The country has one of the world's largest aluminium smelters, the state-owned Tadaz aluminium smelter, which has a capacity of 517,000 tonnes a year. Located at Tursunzade in western Tajikistan, the plant is a main source of revenue for the government. However, the smelter has never produced at its planned maximum annual capacity and remains in need of investment. The pace of restructuring at Tadaz is uncertain.

Tourism

Tourist facilities are underdeveloped and travellers to Tajikistan, who may wish to experience outdoor activities such as mountain climbing, skiing and hiking, will have to either undertake the planning and logistics necessary themselves, or join programmed tours. Visitors to the cities can enjoy the culture of the Tajik people that dates back into antiquity, although the Saminid Empire (of the Middle Ages), a Sunni Islamic Persian state, is considered the first Tajik state.

Around 300,000–400,000 people visit per year, the majority of which are from neighbouring countries. The State Museum of Antiquities in Dushanbe has remarkable artefacts displaying Tajikistan as a trading centre and its role as a crossroads for cultures using the historic Silk Road.

Environment

The Aral Sea is drying up due to the overuse of water from the two main rivers which feed into it and has lost 40 per cent of its water, dropping by up to 19 metres. This has resulted in desertification of the surrounding land. A UN study published in 2004 reported that there was no possibility of restoring the water and the need must be on preserving what is left.

The government has endorsed a 2004 joint strategy to resolve the demands of its water requirements with its neighbours.

Hundreds of thousands of people endured the worst winter since the 1960s without heat, electricity or running water before an appeal was made to the UN for aid in 2008. As the first winter snows fell and temperatures dropped to -20 Celsius people began to overload the power system in an attempt to keep warm, while rivers in the mountains that fed the hydroelectric power stations froze and cut off supplies; domestic pipes froze and left millions without drinking water. The UN issued an appeal for US$25 million.

A meeting was held in April 2009 to determine water sharing between Tajikistan, Kyrgyzstan, Uzbekistan, Turkmenistan and Kazakhstan failed, as negotiators were unable to find a trade in water for energy and hydrocarbons. Tajikistan and Kyrgyzstan hold around 80 per cent of the water in the Aral Sea but suffer from lack of electricity during freezing winters, while the remaining three states downstream are semi-arid and need water for their cotton industries and agriculture.

Mining

Tajikistan has an established history of mineral production. In the Soviet era, uranium was mined and processed (amounting to around 500,000 tonnes per year of ore), but with demand falling in the post-Soviet era, uranium production ceased in the 1990s.

Tajikistan holds around 500,000 tonnes of antimony reserves, 6.2 million tonnes of mercury, 60,000 tonnes of silver and 150 tonnes of gold. Lack of modern equipment and techniques means that some resources are not exploited to full capacity. Antimony, bismuth and mercury have been mined, but most deposits are depleted and the mines closing down. Despite large silver reserves, only around one tonne of silver is produced every year. There are significant deposits of world-class marble; also uranium, radium, arsenic, bismuth, mica and small amounts of potassium salts, molybdenum, sulphur, boron, common salt, carbonates, fluorite, quartz sand, asbestos, lead and zinc. Deposits of semi-precious stones include lapis lazuli, rubies, amethyst and ornamental quartz.

Hydrocarbons

There are negligible proven oil reserves (of 12 million barrels in 2014) with production in 2013 of just 206 barrels per day (bpd). Consumption of petroleum products in 2013 was 15,290 bpd of which the majority was imported from Uzbekistan (70 per cent of oil imports). In total, the CIS accounts for over 97 per cent of Tajikistan's oil needs. The state-owned national oil company, Tajikneftegaz, is responsible for all oil exploration, drilling and production.

Proven natural gas reserves were 5.6 billion cubic metres in 2014, with production at 3.9 million cum and consumption at 3.9 million cum meaning that Tajikistan is self-sufficient in natural gas. TajikGas is responsible for distribution of natural and liquefied gas; the state-owned Tajiknefteproduct carries out imports and distribution of petroleum products.

Tajikistan does not export any natural gas or oil.

Tajikistan could have up to six billion tonnes of coal reserves, among of the largest coal deposits in Central Asia, but these are not yet proven. There are six large coalfields, with that at Fan Yagnob estimated to contain two billion tonnes of reserves. Mostly brown coal is mined in Yagnob and Myonadu, with coking coal at Nazarailok in the Karateginsk Valley in the east.

Energy

Total installed generating capacity was 4.5 gigawatts (GW) in 2013, of which 91 per cent was produced by hydropower; 40 per cent is consumed by the aluminium industry and 9 per cent produced from fossil fuels.

Tajikistan is a mountainous country with the potential to produce vast quantities of hydro-electricity. The potential is 300 billion kilowatt hours (kWh), whereas current production is 16.5 billion kWh. However, as one of the poorest countries in central Asia it requires foreign investment to develop its resources. Russia and Iran assisted in the construction of a 670MW Sangtuda-1 hydroelectric power station on the Vakhsh River. There are plans for two more, larger, power stations.

The government is pinning its drive for energy independence on completion of the Roghun dam, which will take 8-11 years to construct. On its completion, it will be the tallest dam in the world and would significantly expand Tajikistan's electricity output. Unfortunately, this has damaged relations with Uzbekistan (opposed to the project) which closed one of the rail lines into Tajikistan in late 2011, hampering the transit of good to and from the southern part of the country. As a result, food and fuel prices in Tajikistan have increased to the highest levels since 2002.

Barqi Tojik is the state-owned joint stock company with responsibility for production, transport and distribution of electricity. Energy generation is extremely variable from year to year, depending on the level of rainfall, especially in the winter period. There are two separate electrical networks, the northern grid in the Leninabad region and the southern grid, both linked to Uzbekistan. Both grids are destined to be linked following further investment.

Financial markets

Stock exchange

The Tajik commodity exchange was inaugurated in March 1996.

Banking and insurance

The banking sector remains extremely weak, with the five largest banks (which account for 85 per cent of total

commercial bank credit and 90 per cent of deposits) handicapped by substantial non-performing loans. A law on Banks and Banking Activity in May 1998 introduced regulations which are close to international standards.
The restructuring of Agroinvestbank, the largest commercial bank, was completed in March 2004.

Central bank
National Bank of Tajikistan

Time
GMT plus five hours

Geography
Tajikistan is situated in the south-east of Central Asia. To the south of Tajikistan lies Afghanistan, Uzbekistan to the north and west, the People's Republic of China to the east and Kyrgyzstan to the north-east.
The terrain is almost entirely mountainous with more than one-half of the country above 3,000 metres. The main mountain ranges are the western Tian Shan in the north, the southern Tian Shan in the central region and the Pamirs in the south-east. The northern Pamirs are the highest mountains of Tajikistan, and of the former Soviet Union – Lenin Peak 7,134 metres and Ismail Samani Peak (formerly Communism Peak) 7,495 metres. There is a dense river network.

Hemisphere
Northern

Climate
Extreme continental; temperatures range between minus 20 degrees Celsius (C) and 0 degrees C in January, and from 0 degrees C to 30 degrees C in June, depending on altitude. From minus 5 degrees C to 35 degrees C in foothills, valleys and Dushanbe; sub-zero temperatures in the Pamir mountains. Rainfall between 150 and 250mm per annum.

Dress codes
Not overly formal but modest, particularly outside Dushanbe.

Entry requirements

Passports
Required by all, valid for at least six months after date of departure.

Visa
Required by all, except nationals of Russia, Belarus, Kazakstan and Kyrghyzstan. Visas may be obtained at Dushanbe airport by air travellers, but land travellers must obtain their visas in advance from the nearest Tajik embassies. All applications must be supported by a letter of invitation endorsed by the Ministry of Foreign Affairs. (For details, see www.traveltajikistan.com/visas).
A business visa requires, in addition to a letter of invitation from a local company or organisation, a business letter undertaking full financial responsibility for expenses incurred by the representative and a full itinerary.
Visitors must obtain special permission to visit Gorno-Badakhshan autonomous region.

Currency advice/regulations
There are no restrictions on the import of local and foreign currencies, but it must be declared on arrival. Export of local currency is prohibited. Foreign currency can be exported up to the amount declared on arrival.
Travellers cheques are not generally accepted. Tajikistan is a cash-only economy, although carrying large amounts of cash can be dangerous. US dollars are widely accepted.

Customs
Most personal effects may be imported duty-free, subject to declaration on arrival.

Health (for visitors)
A reciprocal health agreement for urgent medical treatment exists with the United Kingdom. Proof of UK residence will be required. Standards of healthcare are significantly below Western levels. Although emergency treatment can be very expensive, doctors and hospitals often expect immediate cash payment. Uninsured visitors requiring urgent medical evacuation may face extreme difficulties. Comprehensive travel and medical insurance, including evacuation by air ambulance, is essential.

Mandatory precautions
Vaccination certificates are required for yellow fever if travelling from an infected area. Visitors staying for longer than 90 days may be submitted to an Aids test, which carries the possibility of infection with HIV or other pathogens, given the lack of medical supplies in Tajikistan.

Advisable precautions
Water precautions are recommended: water purification tablets may be useful, or drink bottled water. The risk of water-borne diseases, including cholera, is high.
It is advisable to be in date for the following immunisations: polio and tetanus (both within 10 years), typhoid, hepatitis A, and tuberculosis. Anti-malarial precautions are also advisable. There has been a significant increase in the number of cases of diphtheria and professional advice should be sort to determine a suitable precaution.
Any medicines required should be taken by the visitor, and it would be wise to have precautionary antibiotics if going outside major urban centres. A travel kit including a disposable syringe is a reasonable precaution.

Hotels
Visitors are advised to use well-known travel operators with established contacts in Tajikistan. There is a lack of adequate hotel accommodation and there are very few hotels outside the two main towns, Dushanbe and Khodzhent.

Credit cards
Credit cards are not generally accepted.

Public holidays (national)
The Islamic year contains 354 or 355 days, with the result that Muslim feasts advance by 10–12 days against the Gregorian calendar. Dates of feasts vary according to the sighting of the new moon, so cannot be forecast exactly.
Tajikistan uses the Persian calendar, which differs from the Gregorian calendar: there are 31 days in each of the first six months of the Persian calendar, 30 days in each of the next five months and 29 days in the last month, except in leap year when it has 30 days.

Fixed dates
1 Jan (New Year's Day), 8 Mar (Women's Day), 20–22 Mar (Navruz/Persian New Year), 1 May (Labour Day), 9 May (Victory Day), 9 Sep (Independence Day), 6 Nov (Constitution Day), 9 Nov (National Reconciliation Day).

Variable dates
Eid al Adha, Eid al Fitr.

Working hours

Banking
Mon–Fri: 0800–1700.

Business
Mon–Fri: approximately 0900–1800 (appointments are best made in the morning).

Shops
No formal hours, but generally within 0800–2100.

Telecommunications

Mobile/cell phones
Limited 900/1800 GSM services exist particularly around Dushanbe.

Electricity supply
220V AC

Social customs/useful tips
The increasing influence of Islam is widely evident, particularly in rural areas. The Islamic faith can be traced back to the seventh century in Tajikistan and although religious activity was banned during the Soviet era it has begun to play a more important role in everyday life since the late 1980s. Closer links with Iran (Iranian television is beamed into Tajikistan) have been established since independence, although alcohol (generally vodka) is still freely available and consumed. Gratuities are becoming more customary, particularly in international hotels.

'Dushanbe' – Tajik for Monday – is named after the day when, for centuries, merchants have gathered at Dushanbe's famous oriental bazaar.

Security

The prevalence of light weapons and local warlords throughout the country mean that care should be taken at all times. Visitors should avoid demonstrations, crowds, or congregations of military personnel.

Visitors may have their movements, hotel rooms and correspondence (including telephone and fax) monitored by security personnel. Taking photographs of military or otherwise strategically significant installations is not advised. There are periodic nightly curfews. Travel alone or on foot after dark is highly inadvisable. Car hire with a driver is advised rather than the use of public transport. Visitors are reminded to be vigilant and to dress down.

Getting there

Air

National airline: Tajikistan Airlines

International airport/s: Dushanbe (DYU), 3km south of city; restaurant, post office, chemist and left luggage.

There are bus services (nos 3 and 12), hours 0600–1800, and train services (lines 3 and 4), hours 0600–1900, between the airport and city centre, with a journey time of 20 minutes. Taxis operate between 0800—2000, journey time five minutes; as they are not metered the fare should be agreed in advance.

Airport tax: None.

Surface

There are border crossings with neighbouring countries, but not all of them may be open. It is advisable to check in advance.

Road: There are a few primary roads; secondary roads, particularly in mountain areas, are of poor quality. An all-weather road connects the capital Dushanbe to the Samarkand railhead (in Uzbekistan) to the north-west. Vehicles with Tajik licence plates may be refused entry into Uzbekistan.

On 26 August 2007, a bridge was opened across the Pyanj River, build by the US army (at a cost of US$37 million), linking the Tajik town of Nizhny Pyanj with Shir Khan Bandar in Afghanistan and extended the trans-Afghanistan road (Regional Road Corridor Improvement Project) through Central Asia.

The Regional Road Corridor Improvement Project, estimated at US$18 billion, to improve Central Asian roads, airports, railway lines and seaports and provide a vital transit route between Europe and Asia was agreed, on 3 November 2007. Six new transit corridors, between Afghanistan, Azerbaijan, China, Kazakhstan, Kyrgyzstan, Mongolia, Tajikistan and Uzbekistan, of mainly roads and rail links, will be constructed, or existing resources upgraded, by 2013. Half the costs with be provided by the Asian Development Bank and other multilateral organisations and the other half by participating countries.

Rail: Tajikistan is linked to the rail network of the former Soviet republics, with the main line running south from Dushanbe to the Uzbekistan border town of Termez and on to Samarkand, Tashkent and the Black Sea. A line running from Andizhan to Samarkand, both in Uzbekistan, cuts through the northern tip of Tajikistan.

Getting about

National transport

Air: There are flights between Dushanbe and Khorog, Khojand and Kulyab, but take-off is dependent on weather conditions and fuel availability.

Road: The road network is generally in a poor condition. Roads are often closed due to weather conditions. Road travel, especially in the east, can be impeded by checkpoints, from which soldiers or other armed groups may shoot if vehicles do not stop. Travel by road should only be undertaken during daylight hours, with the appropriate vehicle and with the utmost precautions.

Buses: Buses run between the main centres when weather conditions permit.

Rail: The railway system is not well-developed, with only around 500km of rail track. The north and south of the country are not linked by rail, because of the mountainous terrain. Passengers are advised to safeguard their possessions.

City transport

Taxis: Taxis can be found at prominent places in the cities. They can also be hailed in the street. It is advisable to use only officially-licensed taxis. As they are not metered, the fare should be agreed in advance. Before setting off, the passenger should be satisfied that the driver is clear about the destination.

Minibus taxis (*marshrutkas*) travel on fixed routes and stop on request, but they can be over-crowded.

Car hire

There are no international car hire companies operating in Tajikistan.

BUSINESS DIRECTORY

The addresses listed below are a selection only. While World of Information makes every endeavour to check these addresses, we cannot guarantee that changes have not been made, especially to telephone numbers and area codes. We would welcome any corrections.

Telephone area codes

The international direct dialling (IDD) code for Tajikistan is +992, followed by area code and subscriber's number:

Dushanbe 372

Useful telephone numbers

Police: 02

Fire: 01

Ambulance: 03

Chambers of Commerce

Tajikistan Chamber of Commerce and Industry, 21 Mazayeva Street, 734012 Dushanbe (tel: 279-519; fax: 211-480).

Banking

Agroinvestbank, Prospekt S Sherozi 21, Dushanbe (tel: 210-385; fax: 211-206).

Orienbank, 95/1 Rudaki Ave, Dushanbe (tel: 210-920; fax: 211-662).

Tajikbankbusiness (commercial bank), 29 Shotemur Street, 734025 Dushanbe (tel/fax: 210-634).

Tajikvnesheconombank (Tajikistan Bank for Foreign Economic Affairs), Dushanbe (tel: 233-571, 225-952).

Central bank

National Bank of Tajikistan, Prospekt Rudaki 107A, 734003 Dushanbe (tel: 600-3227; fax: 600-3235; e-mail: info@natbank.tajnet.com).

Stock exchange

The Tajik commodity exchange was inaugurated in March 1996.

Travel information

Tajikistan Airlines, Titova Street 32/1, 734006 Dushanbe (tel: 212-247; fax: 510-041; e-mail: mop_gart@tajnet.com).

Tajikistan Republican Council of Tourism and Excursions, Sherozi Avenue 11, 734018 Dushanbe (tel: 332-770; fax: 334-420).

Travel Tajikistan, Proletarskaya 5/11, 734000 Dushanbe (tel: 247-673; fax: 217-184; e-mail: info@ traveltajikistan.com).

National tourist organisation offices

National Tourism Company SAYOH, Pushkin Street 14, 734095 Dushanbe (tel: 234—233; fax: 217-184)

Ministries

Council of Ministers, Prospekt Rudaki 48, 734025 Dushanbe (tel: 232-903; fax: 228-120).

EU Co-ordinating Unit, c/o Ministry of External Economic Relations, Prospekt Rudaki 42, Dushanbe (tel: 222-403, 227-077; fax: 228-120).

Ministry of Agriculture, 46 Rudaki Ave, Dushanbe 734051 (tel: 276-249).

Ministry of Communications, 57 Rudaki Ave, 734025 Dushanbe (tel: 232-284;

fax: 212-953; International Relations Department (tel: 216-010; fax: 510-277).

Ministry of Construction, 36 Kirova Street, Dushanbe 734025 (tel: 226-143).

Ministry of Economy and External Economic Affairs, 42 Rudaki Ave, 734025 Dushanbe (tel: 232-944).

Ministry of Finance, Prospekt Kuibysheva 3, 734025 Dushanbe (tel: 273-941; fax: 213-329).

Ministry of Foreign Affairs, 40 Rudaki Ave, 734051 Dushanbe (tel: 221-560, 232-971; fax: 227-051).

Ministry of Foreign Economic Relations, 42 Rudaki Ave, Dushanbe (tel: 232-971; fax: 232-964).

Ministry of Grain Products, 42 Rudaki Ave, Dushanbe 734051 (tel: 276-131).

Ministry of Industrial Afairs, 80 Rudaki Avenue, Dushanbe 734023 (tel: 232-249, 231-845; fax: 232-381).

Ministry of Information, Ulitsa Negmata Karabaeva 17, 734018 Dushanbe (tel: 335-851).

Ministry of Justice, 25 Rudaki Ave, 734025 Dushanbe (tel: 214-405; fax: 218-066).

Ministry of Trade and Material Resources, 37 Bokhtar Street, Dushanbe 734002 (tel: 273-434).

Prime Minister's Office, 80 Rudaki Ave, 734023 Dushanbe (tel: 211-871; fax; 215-110).

Other useful addresses

British Embassy, Gulyamov Street 67, Tashkent 700000, Uzbekistan (accredited to Tajikistan) (tel: (+998 71) 120-7852; fax: (+998 71) 120-6549).

State Statistical Committee (SSC), 17 Bokhtar Street, Dushanbe 734025 (tel: 276-882; fax: 275-408).

Tajikistan Embassy (USA), 1005 New Hampshire Avenue, Washington DC 20037 (tel: (+1-202) 223-6090; fax: (+1-202) 223-6091; e-mail: tajikistan@verizon.net).

Tajikistan (TDA) Office, c/o Tajik Bank Business, 23/2 Rudaki Avenue, 734620 Dushanbe (tel: 233-512; fax: 224-844).

Tajikvneshtorg (foreign trade organisation), Prospekt Lenina 41, 734051 Dushanbe (tel: 232-903; fax: 228-120).

National news agency: Khovar (in Russian) (www.khovar.tj).

Avesta news agency (www.avesta.tj/en).

Internet sites

Tajikistan Privatisation Agency: http://privatization.tajikistan.com

Tajikistan Resource Page: http://www.eurasianet.org/resource/tajikistan/index.shtml

National Tourism Company: http://www.tajiktour.tajnet.com

Tanzania

KEY FACTS

Official name: Jamhuri ya Muungano wa Tanzania (United Republic of Tanzania)

Head of State: President John Pombe Magufuli (CCM) (elected 25 Oct 2015)

Head of government: President John Pombe Magufuli (CCM) (elected 25 Oct 2015) (the Prime Minister is nominted by the President but is not head of government)

Ruling party: Chama Cha Mapinduzi (CCM) (Party of the Revolution) (since 1977; last re-elected 25 Oct 2015)

Area: 945,087 square km

Population: 47.66 million (2014)*

Capital: Dodoma (official, legislative centre); Dar es Salaam (the former capital is the largest city and *de facto* commercial capital)

Official language: KiSwahili and English

Currency: Tanzania shilling (Tsh) = 100 senti (convertible with currencies of Kenya and Uganda)

Exchange rate: Tsh2,175.00 per US$ (Sep 2015)

GDP per capita: US$1,006 (2014)*

GDP real growth: 7.24% (2014)*

GDP: US$47.93 billion (2014)*

Labour force: 21.23 million (2009)*

Inflation: 6.13% (2014)*

Balance of trade: -US$5.77 billion (2013)*

Annual FDI: US$1.10 billion (2011)

* estimated figure

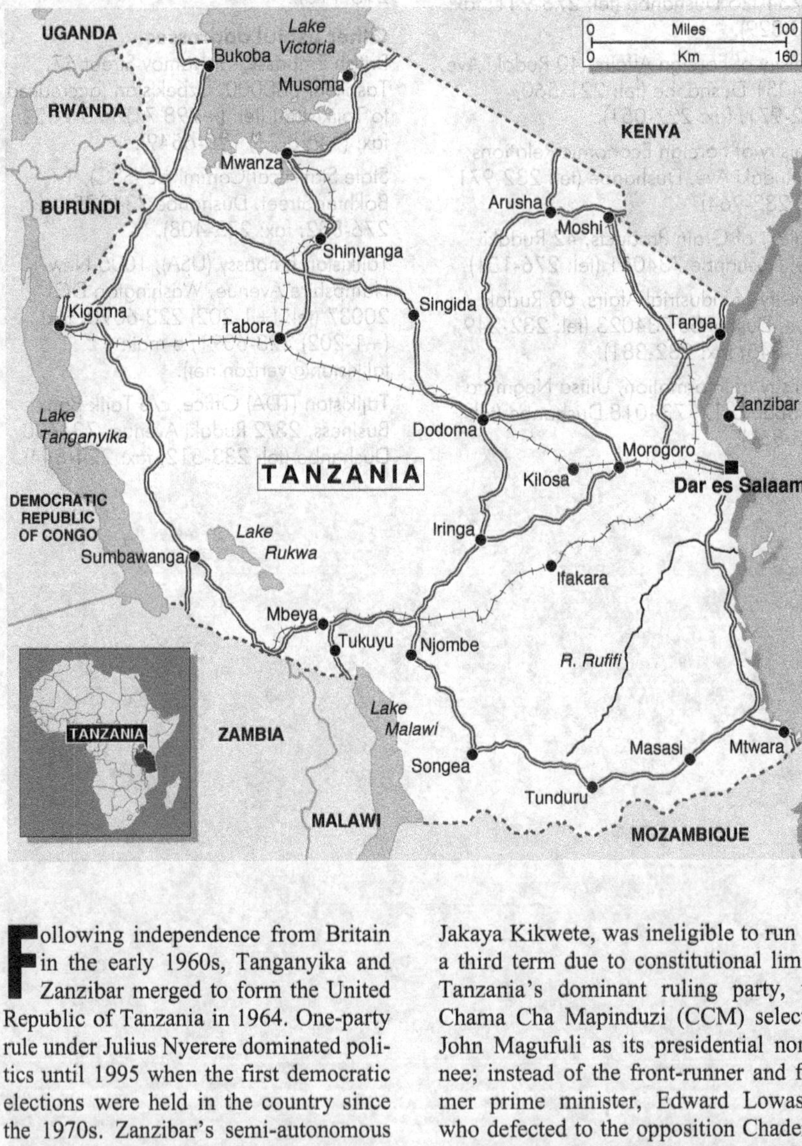

Following independence from Britain in the early 1960s, Tanganyika and Zanzibar merged to form the United Republic of Tanzania in 1964. One-party rule under Julius Nyerere dominated politics until 1995 when the first democratic elections were held in the country since the 1970s. Zanzibar's semi-autonomous status and popular opposition led to two contentious elections since 1995, which the ruling parties won despite international observers' claims of voting irregularities. In the 2010 elections, the formation of a government of national unity between Zanzibar's two leading parties succeeded in minimising electoral tension.

The latest general election was held on 25 October 2015 and it marked the fifth since the restoration of a multi-party system in 1992. The incumbent president, Jakaya Kikwete, was ineligible to run for a third term due to constitutional limits. Tanzania's dominant ruling party, the Chama Cha Mapinduzi (CCM) selected John Magufuli as its presidential nominee; instead of the front-runner and former prime minister, Edward Lowassa, who defected to the opposition Chadema party that once labelled him as one of the most corrupt figures in Tanzanian society. Magufuli won 58.5 per cent of the vote while Edward Lowassa won just 40 per cent of the vote, a clear majority for the CCM nominee.

Prior to the election Mr Kikwete had been accused by many media representatives of attempting to prolong his stay in office by altering the constitution to allow a third term. However, he proved them wrong by stepping down without a fight. Rather than express his disappointment at ending his long reign as president of Tanzania, he seemed very happy to retire saying that the job was thankless and stressful.

During the campaign the government had to warn politicians not to engage in witchcraft because, according to a deputy minister, if there are seen to be reports linking politicians with the killing of people with albinism, however erroneous, this could mean the reports are true as it (the killing) increases during the election period. A ban on witchdoctors was imposed in January 2015 because some of them condone the killings due to superstitious beliefs that the victims' bodies possess powers that bring luck and prosperity.

Zanzibar

Mid-count the Zanzibar Electoral Commission (ZEC) cancelled the results, saying that they were fraught with irregularities. On 19 November 2015 police in Zanzibar launched an investigation into allegations of a political election fraud during the election. The police are collecting evidence and exhibits before filing the case in court against the suspects for sabotaging the election. The ZEC Chairman, Jecha Salim, described the election as having a number of shortfalls in the conduct of the poll that contributed to the delay in the announcement of the results on 28 October. Salim cited a number of irregularities, one of the most notable being in Pemba, where the number of votes cast at some polling stations actually exceeded that of voters registered for the election. The decision by the ZEC chairman to invalidate the election results was highly criticised by local and international election observers. The United States called upon the Commission to reconsider the decision to nullify the results of the Zanzibar presidential elections saying the poll was held in an orderly and peaceful manner as declared by observers. The Tanzania Election Monitoring Committee (Temco), a group made up of more than 700 observers in Zanzibar also criticised the decision and recommended disciplinary action against ZEC staff. The opposition assumed it was cancelled because they were winning.

Constitutional referendum

The government had postponed a referendum on a new constitution after delays in registering voters in April 2015. The new constitution would replace the one passed in 1977, when the state was under one-party rule. The changes were approved in October 2014 by an assembly dominated by the then president, Jakaya Kikwete's CCM party, which has been in power since Tanzania's independence from Britain in 1961. A group of bishops has urged Christian worshippers to vote against the proposed constitution, saying it was written by an inclusive assembly. Kikwete, a moderate Muslim, warned clerics not to meddle in politics and said tensions between Muslims and Christians threatened peace. Tanzania's population of 45 million is roughly evenly split between Muslims and Christians. The proposed constitutional changes would create an Independent Electoral Commission, allow presidential election results to be legally challenged, limit the number of ministers a president can appoint, require that there is a 50/50 split of men and women in the National Assembly and ensure equal land ownership rights for women. The draft constitution would also impact the autonomous government in Tanzania's Zanzibar archipelago by keeping the ties, amid calls by some islanders to end the 50-year union with the mainland. The date for when the referendum on the constitution will be held is still unknown as of November 2015.

The economy

Tanzania is one of the world's poorest economies in terms of per capita income at just US$2,700 in 2014, it is ranked 204 out of 230 countries by International Monetary Fund (IMF). In 2014, Tanzania ranked 159 out of the 182 countries surveyed on the United Nations Development Programme's (UNDP) *Human Development Index* (HDI). Its ease of doing business rating was 139 out of 212 countries in the World Bank *Ease of Doing Business* survey. Tanzania remains as one of the world's poorest countries with 66.4 per cent of its population living in multi-dimensional poverty and 67.9 per cent living under US$1.25 a day. Despite having these negative statistics, Tanzania has achieved high growth rates based on its vast natural resource wealth and tourism. Growth was an impressive 6–7 per cent from 2009–14 and it recorded a rate of 7.2 per cent in 2014. The country has largely completed its transition to a market economy, however, the government retains a presence in sectors such as telecommunications, banking, energy and mining. The economy depends on agriculture which accounts for 27 per cent of GDP, provides 85 per cent of exports, and employs approximately 80 per cent of the workforce. The agricultural sector is plagued by infrastructure gaps and low productivity. The World Bank, the IMF, and bilateral donors have provided funds to improve Tanzania's faltering infrastructure, including rail and ports that provide important trade links for inland countries. The financial sector has expanded with foreign-owned banks accounting for 48 per cent of the banking industry's total assets in 2014. Competition among foreign banks has resulted in significant improvements to the efficiency and quality of financial services in Tanzania, though interest rates are still relatively high, reflecting high fraud risk. In 2014, a highly publicised scandal in the energy sector involving senior Tanzanian officials resulted in international donors freezing nearly US$500 million in direct budget support to the government.

KEY INDICATORS — Tanzania

	Unit	2011	2012	2013	2014	**2015
Population	m	*42.18	44.93	*46.28	*47.66	*49.09
Gross domestic product (GDP)	US$bn	23.30	28.45	43.73	*47.93	*49.97
GDP per capita	US$	553	633	945	*1,006	*1,018
GDP real growth	%	6.7	6.9	7.3	*7.2	*7.2
Inflation	%	7.0	16.0	7.9	*6.1	*4.2
Exports (fob) (goods)	US$m	5,097.7	5,912.3	5,258.1	–	–
Imports (fob) (goods)	US$m	9,827.5	10,324.9	11,029.1	–	–
Balance of trade	US$m	-4,729.8	-4,412.6	-5,771.1	–	–
Current account	US$m	-4,561.1	-4,513.0	-4,515.0	*-4,868.0	*-5,007.0
Total reserves minus gold	US$m	3,666.9	4,053.4	4,673.7	4,389.7	–
Foreign exchange	US$m	3,399.9	3,800.2	4,423.5	–	–
Exchange rate	per US$	1,348.25	1,578.80	1,585.00	1,735.20	–

* estimated figure ** forecast figure

The *African Development Bank Outlook 2015* has suggested that medium-term prospects for the Tanzanian economy are favourable, with growth projected to remain above 7 per cent, supported by public investment in infrastructure, particularly in the transport and energy sectors. Despite Tanzania's impressive macroeconomic achievements driven by information and communications, construction, manufacturing and other services, growth is not sufficiently broad based, and poverty levels remain high. Poverty remains more prevalent in rural than in urban areas. Inflation has stabilised at single digits in 2015 after declining to an annual average of 6.8 per cent in 2014 due to prudent monetary policy, a favourable food situation and declining fuel prices. Export performance remains strong, driven by gold and tourism receipts, however, the import bill has grown mainly due to imports of capital and intermediate goods, particularly oil, keeping the current account deficit wide at around 11 per cent of GDP. The fiscal deficit is projected to be maintained at around 5–6 per cent for the foreseeable future while expenditures and government net lending are projected at around 25 per cent of GDP, in line with targets of the Policy Support Instrument programme. Spatial inclusion remains problematic in Tanzania, mainly due to regional disparities, the poorer regions are predominantly rural and their economies are much less diversified. Agriculture is the main economic sector in these areas, with low productivity and low-paying employment. Consequently, per capita incomes in these regions are less than half that of Dar es Salaam, the wealthiest area, and the poverty rate is eight times higher than in the largest Tanzanian city. The government needs to boost earning opportunities for the rural population, mainly through improved productivity in agriculture supported by rural infrastructure investments, particularly rural roads and improved overall connectivity between rural and urban areas

According to the US government's Energy Information Administration (EIA) Tanzania produces small volumes of natural gas for domestic consumption, but is reported to have the potential to become a liquefied natural gas (LNG) exporter in the future. Tanzania does not produce crude oil and there has not been a commercial oil discovery in the country recently. The BG Group (UK), in partnership with Ophir Energy (UK) and Statoil (Norway), in partnership with ExxonMobil (US), have made several offshore natural gas discoveries since 2010, totalling 6.5 billion cubic metres of recoverable gas resources, according to PFC Energy.

The Tanzanian government, Statoil, ExxonMobil, BG Group and Ophir Energy are all currently working on plans to develop a joint LNG plant, according to Statoil. President Magufuli has promised more urgency in decision-making, one example of this failure has been delays in finalising the site for the multi-billion dollar LNG plant that will exploit huge offshore gas finds. Tanzania could increase growth by a further 2 per cent annually simply by starting work on the huge plant that would bring in billions of dollars of investment. Tanzania had proven reserves of 6.5 billion cubic metres (cum) of natural gas in 2014 with production at 995 million cum, all of which was consumed locally. The country expects to increase natural gas production in the next few years from the Mnazi Bay Concession, located in south-east Tanzania in the Rovuma Basin. A pipeline is being constructed to transport natural gas from Mnazi Bay to Tanzania's commercial centre (and former capital) Dar es Salaam.

On 17 November 2015, five Tanzanian gold miners were rescued after being trapped for 41 days, while twelve others are still missing. The artisanal miners survived by eating roots, soil, frogs and cockroaches and are receiving treatment at hospital. The group had gone underground to save 11 other miners when they became trapped themselves. Many people search for gold in unregulated mines in remote areas of Tanzania in the hope of becoming rich. This is one of the longest periods that miners have remained trapped underground, although not as long as the 69 days Chilean miners were trapped underground in 2010. The eleven miners who were the initial ones to get trapped, and a colleague who went to search for them, are presumed dead.

Risk assessment

Politics	Fair
Economy	Fair
Regional stability	Good

Muslims in Tanzania

% of population	29.9
Sunni (% of Muslims)	65
Shi'a (% of Muslims)	20

COUNTRY PROFILE

1832 The increasing importance of Zanzibar as a spice and slave-trading centre led the Sultan of Oman to transfer his capital there from Muscat. Around this time, Britain signed a number of agreements with Oman to limit the potential threat to Britain's colonies from France. Meanwhile, Germany signed a number of 'friendship' treaties with local chiefs – treaties which formed the basis of the German East Africa Company, which was established to exploit and colonise what became Tanganyika.

1886 The UK and Germany signed an agreement which gave Germany control of mainland Tanzania and the UK control of Zanzibar.

1918 After Germany's defeat in the First World War, the League of Nations mandated the territory to Britain.

1961 Tanganyika gained independence under Julius Nyerere and the Tanganyika Africa National Union (Tanu).

1964 The United Republic of Tanzania was formed following the union of Tanganyika and Zanzibar.

1977 The new constitution established a real one-party state for the whole of Tanzania after the Tanganyika African National Union and Zanzibar's Afro-Shirazi Party merged to create Chama Cha Mapinduzi (CCM) (Party of the Revolution).

1979 Tanzania invaded Uganda, forcing its dictator, Idi Amin, to flee to Saudi Arabia.

1985 Nyerere stepped down as president and was replaced by the president of Zanzibar, Ali Hassan Mwinyi.

1992 The constitution was amended to allow multi-party politics.

1995 The first multi-party elections took place. Benjamin William Mkapa (CCM) was elected president and the CCM was re-elected to government. The Zanzibar opposition Civic United Front (CUF) refused to accept the election results in Zanzibar.

1999 A conciliation agreement was signed between the CCM and the CUF, bringing an end to four years of hostility. Julius Nyerere, the former president and founder figure of modern Tanzania, died.

2000 President Benjamin Mkapa was re-elected for a second term. The CCM was re-elected in the parliamentary elections. Because of unfair elections in Zanzibar, a re-run was held in 16 of its 50 constituencies; it was won by the ruling party, the CCM.

2001 There were clashes in Zanzibar between supporters of CUF and the police. The CCM and the opposition CUF signed a further agreement aimed at ending hostilities on Zanzibar.

2002 The African Development Bank (ADB) signed an agreement with the Deputy Minister for Finance, Alhaj Adbisalaam Issa Khatibu, for a loan of approximately US$47 million to partially finance the Dar

es Salaam water supply and sanitation project.
2004 The presidents of Tanzania, Uganda and Kenya signed a protocol in Arusha over a proposed customs union.
2005 Jakaya Kikwete was elected president. The CCM retained an outright majority of seats in parliamentary elections.
2006 A challenge to the legality of the 1964 Act of Union was dismissed by the Zanzibar high court. The African Development Bank cancelled over US$640 million in debt by Tanzania.
2008 President Jakaya Kikwete was elected chairman of the African Union for one year. Governor of the central bank, Daudi Ballali, was sacked after an international audit found evidence of improper payments to local companies of over US$120 million. A corruption scandal forced the president to dissolve his cabinet and the prime minister to resign. Mizengo Pinda was appointed as prime minister.
2009 China granted US$22 million in aid to Tanzania, during the visit of Chinese President Hu Jintao, who also opened a US$56 million, 60,000 seat sports stadium, funded mainly by the Chinese government. Japan agreed to provide around US$22 million under its poverty support credit scheme.
2010 Around 162,000 Burundi refugees, domiciled since 1972 after some 150,000 Hutus had been killed in Burundi, were granted citizenship. Tanzania along with Uganda and Ethiopia signed an agreement to share the waters of the River Nile. In the new deal the three nations (out of five) that form the source of the river, reserved more of the water for themselves. Egypt and Sudan, which had until then taken the greater share, objected but finally agreed after 13 years of negotiations had failed to resolve the issue earlier. A new micro-finance bank, Access Bank Tanzania, was launched, specifically aimed at women who can open an account with minimal capital and an identity card. Seven candidates took part in presidential elections held and incumbent President Jakaya Kikwete (CCM) won 61.17 per cent of the vote, his closest rival Willibrod Slaa (CDM) won 26.34 per cent. The ruling CCM won 258 seats (out of 343) in parliamentary elections, held on the same day. Mizengo Pinda remained in post as prime minister. In presidential elections in Zanzibar, Ali Mohamed Shein (CCM) won 50.1 per cent of the vote and Seif Sharif Hamad (CUF) 49.1 per cent. President Shein took office on 3 November.
2011 According to government statistics in August the economy was growing by an average 6.7 per cent, despite the chronic shortage of energy, which was having an adverse effect on horticultural cultivation as production of perishable flowers with time-sensitive deliveries were cut. An investigation by the UK's Serious Fraud Office, begun in 2005, which had been investigating alleged bribery by BAE Systems (the defence company) was finally concluded when the company agreed to make an *ex gratia* payment of £29.5 million (US$50 million) to the Tanzanian government. The government agreed to use the money for educational projects. A ferry travelling between the Zanzibar islands of Unguja and Pemba sank on 10 September. Of the some 800 passengers on-board, rescuers managed to save around 620.
2011 On 4 May, President Jakaya Kikwete sacked six government ministers over allegations of graft, following a critical auditor-general report that implicated many officials in cases of bribery and corruption. On 14 June, the Norwegian oil company Statoil announced that it and its partner, the US energy company ExxonMobil, had discovered a second large natural gas field of approximately 84.9 billion cubic metres, called Lavani. On 16 October, the Tanzanian ambassador was ordered to leave Malawi due to the dispute between the two countries over sovereignty of Lake Malawi (also known as Lake Nyasa) and its potential for oil and gas discoveries. On 18 October the government declared that only it had the right to announce to the public any new oil and natural gas discoveries and not investors in the industry. A new commuter train service in Dar es Salaam was launched on 29 October, with two lines operating during peak hours only.
2012 In May President Jakaya Kikwete sacked six senior ministers (of finance, energy, tourism, trade, transport and health) on allegations of government corruption. The inspector of the government's accounts reported the rampant misuse of funds in their ministries.
2013 Two young British women were injured in an acid attack on the island of Zanzibar on 7 August. The Zanzibar government offered a reward of Tsh10 million (US$6,170) for information leading to the capture of attackers. On 13 September a Roman Catholic priest also had acid thrown at him. In November President Kikwete sharply criticised Kenya, Rwanda and Uganda for taking decisions at the East African Community without consulting other members.
2015 Presidential and parliamentary elections were held on 25 October in what were considered to be the most tightly contested since independence in 1961 with the Ukawa coalition of four opposition parties standing against the CCM which had been power for 54 years. John Pombe Magufuli ('The Bulldozer') was the surprise presidential nominee of the CCM, beating Edward Lowassa, who defected to the opposition and became the candidate for the Ukawa coalition. The presidential election was won by John Magufuli with 58.46 per cent to Mr Lowassa with 39.97 per cent. In Zanzibar, the election was annulled by the Zanzibar Electoral Commission (ZEC), who said it had been marred by 'rigging'. They were said to have been 'orderly and peaceful' by the US embassy. Predictably the opposition said it had been cancelled because it had won.

Political structure

Constitution

The Constitution was introduced in 1965 following the union of Zanzibar and Tanganyika in 1964. Zanzibar is partially autonomous, with 50 political constituencies.
The 1977 Constitution established a one-party state for the whole of Tanzania after the two parties merged to create Chama Cha Mapinduzi (CCM) (Party of the Revolution).
A constitutional referendum was planned to be held on 30 April 2015, however, delays to voter registration led it to be postponed. The proposed changes included the creation of an Independent Electoral Commission, allowing presidential election results to be legally challenged, limiting the number of ministers a president can appoint, a requirement that there is a 50/50 split of men and women in the National Assembly and ensuring equal land ownership rights for women.

Independence date

1961

Form of state

Republic

The executive

Executive power rests with the president, who is elected by direct popular vote for a five-year term. The president can serve a maximum of two terms.
The Prime Minister is the leader of government business in the Parliament of Tanzania, but is not the head of government.
One vice president is appointed by the president, as is the cabinet (in consultation with the prime minister), and the second vice president is the directly elected president of Zanzibar.

National legislature

The unicameral National Assembly (Bunge) has 357 seats of which 239 members are directly elected in single-seat constituencies by simple majority vote for a five-year term. The president allocates 102 special seats to women directly elected by proportional representation and five indirectly elected by simple majority vote by the Zanzibar

House of Representatives. Ten members are appointed by the president and one seat is reserved for the attorney general.

Legal system

The legal system is based on English common law, the 1977 Union and 1985 Zanzibari constitutions, as amended. The judiciary is relatively independent. A permanent Commission of Enquiry has wide powers to investigate abuses of power. In Zanzibar, *Kadhis* (Islamic courts) have jurisdiction over certain areas of law.

Last elections

25 October 2015 (presidential and parliamentary)

Results: Presidential (2015): John Magufuli (CCM) won 58.46 per cent of the vote, Edward Lowassa (CDM) 39.97 per cent, no other candidate won more than 1 per cent.

Parliamentary (2010): Chama Cha Mapinduzi (CCM) (Revolutionary Party) won 259 seats (out of 350), Chama Cha Demokrasia Na Maendeleo (Chadema) (Democracy and Progress Party) 48, Chama Cha Wananchi (CCW) (Civic United Front) 36, National Convention for Construction and Reform–Mageuzi (NCCR–Mageuzi); the remaining fifteen parties failed to win any seats. Turnout was 39.7 per cent.

Next elections

25 October 2015 (presidential and parliamentary)

Political parties

Ruling party

Chama Cha Mapinduzi (CCM) (Party of the Revolution) (since 1977; re-elected 30 Oct 2010)

Main opposition party

Chama cha Demokrasia na Maendeleo (Chadema) (Party for Democracy and Progress)

Population

47.66 million (2014)*

Last census: August 2002: 34,443,603 (provisional). Approximately 44 per cent of the total population is under 14 years.

Population density: Urban population 26 per cent (2010 Unicef).

Annual growth rate: 2.8 per cent, 1990–2010 (Unicef).

Ethnic make-up

About 98 per cent of the population is of indigenous African or Arab (Zanzibar) origin, with the remainder mainly from the Indian sub-continent. Those of Indian, Pakistani and Goan descent tend to work in the towns, mainly dominating the trading environment, but also moving into the industrial sector. The small population of Arab descent is mainly engaged in trade. There are about 10,000 Europeans.

Over 120 tribal groups exist in Tanzania, the most important of which are Sukuma (12 per cent of total population), Makonde (4 per cent), Chagga (4 per cent), Haya (3 per cent), Nyamwezi (3 per cent), Ha (3 per cent), Gogo (3 per cent) and Hehe (3 per cent).

Religions

Islam and Christianity are the main organised religions. However, many people adhere to ancient tribal and animist religions. The religious make-up is believed to be Christianity: 33 per cent, Islam: 33 per cent, traditional beliefs: 33 per cent and Hinduism: 1 per cent.

Education

In 2003, three million seven to 13-year-olds were not in school, most enrolled late and intake and transition rates remained very low. This was the a result of the introduction of 'user fees' during the 1990s, when more than two million Tanzanian children were prevented from entering school and the rate of illiteracy began rising at 2 per cent a year. The education system is beset with problems of poor quality and a lack of participation among enrolled students. This reversed the country's early success of the 1960s when the literacy rate was around 91 per cent (the highest in Africa). The root cause of the problem is the government's debt obligations which have forced it to cut back on education. By 2000, the government was spending twice as much per capita on debt repayments than on education.

In 2001, the government announced in 2001 that it would abolish primary school fees, and the World Bank announced US$150 million interest free credit to expand school access and increase school retention at the primary level. During 2001, Tanzania enrolled 1,100,000 pupils in school, a 41 per cent increase over 779,000 in 2000.

The fees for secondary education, however, widened the gap between those participating in primary and secondary education. Parents must pay fees they cannot afford and teachers are under pressure to act as debt collectors to finance their schools. The situation is particularly dire in rural areas where schools are only able to recover around a third of fees. As a result, the education system is beset with problems of poor quality and a lack of participation among enrolled students. Oxfam, the main non-governmental organisation investing in Tanzanian education, estimates that in poorer schools there is only one desk for every 38 pupils and one textbook for every four children. Meanwhile, teachers are trying to cope with crumbling classrooms, falling salaries, worsening conditions and increasing class sizes.

Moreover, gross inequalities have developed between genders and classes, particularly in the fee-paying secondary schools. This has led to a progressive exclusion and marginalisation of adolescents and the most vulnerable children from basic family and community support.

Literacy rate: 77 per cent adult rate; 92 per cent youth rate (15–24) (Unesco 2005).

Compulsory years: Seven to 14.

Enrolment rate: 67 per cent gross primary enrolment; 6 per cent gross secondary enrolment; of relevant age groups (including repeaters) (World Bank).

Pupils per teacher: 37 in primary schools.

Health

The public health sector has been increasingly deprived of funds in recent years due to the government's move towards privatisation of the health service sector. User fees, introduced in the 1990s to ease the government's fiscal problems, have denied pregnant women and the rural poor access to primary healthcare facilities and essential medicines. While the government claims that mothers and children under five years receive free healthcare, in reality it is very different, particularly for those suffering from HIV/Aids, mental health problems and other diseases. Moreover, medicines which are supposed to be free are often in short supply at state-run hospitals and the number of hospital beds per capita has declined since 1990.

HIV/Aids

On top of inadequate health service provision, HIV/Aids is a continuing problem with infection rates estimated at over 25 per cent in urban areas. Like many African countries, Tanzania cannot afford the expensive Western drugs needed to treat the effects of Aids and initiatives aimed at the promotion of safe sex are often poorly designed and ineffective.

In 2007, officials in Zanzibar released figures that showed the HIV/Aids rate had increase from 0.6 per cent in 2002, to 0.9 per cent of the population in 2006.

HIV prevalence: 8.8 per cent aged 15–49 in 2003 (World Bank)

Life expectancy: 48 years, 2004 (WHO 2006)

Fertility rate/Maternal mortality rate: 5.5 births per woman, 2010 (Unicef); maternal mortality 1,100 per 100,000 live births (World Bank)

Birth rate/Death rate: 39.5 births and 17.4 deaths per 1,000 people (2003)

Child (under 5 years) mortality rate (per 1,000): 54 per 1,000 live births (WHO 2012); 29.4 per cent of children aged under five were malnourished (World Bank).

Head of population per physician: 0.02 physicians per 1,000 people, 2002 (WHO 2006)

Welfare

Between 15 million and 18 million of the total population live below the World Bank poverty line. The state does not have the capacity to function as a welfare provider while its ability to increase poor adult literacy rates, especially among women, remains negligible. Rather than building up the capacity and efficiency of state institutions, multilateral and bilateral donors are contracting out welfare services to non-governmental organisations (NGOs), which have little accountability and whose impact is usually localised and short-term.

Main cities

Dodoma (capital, estimated population 190,604 in 2012), Dar es Salaam (former capital and *de facto* commercial capital, estimated population 3.5 million), Arusha (504,178), Mbeya (340,275), Morogoro (298,766), Tanga (225,504), Kigoma (196,180), Tabora (167,636).
Zanzibar City (estimated population 539,882 in 2012), Chake Chake (33,423), Wete (29,267).

Languages spoken

KiSwahili is the predominant language with English spoken by most people, especially in the main towns. English is the language most used in business.

Official language/s

KiSwahili and English

Media

The government allows private newspapers and private radio and television operators, although these organisations exercise a strong degree of self-censorship.
Media policies on Zanzibar are different from the mainland; there are no private broadcasters or newspapers although reception of both is received on the islands.

Press

Dailies: A number of newspapers have English and KiSwahili editions including the government-owned *Daily News* and *Harari Leo* (www.dailynews-tsn.com), *Nipashe* and *The Guardian* (www.ippmedia.com); in KiSwahili, *Majira* (www.majira.co.tz), *Tanzania Daima* (www.freemedia.co.tz); in English *This Day* (www.thisday.co.tz).
Weeklies: Including Sunday papers, are *Sunday News*, *Mzalendo* (KiSwahili), *Daily News on Saturday*, *East African*, *Express*, *Heko*, *Mfanyakazi*, *Shangwe*, *Sunday Mail*, *Sunday News*, *Sunday Observer*, *Sunday Times* and *Taifa Letu*. The *Government Gazette* is a weekly, which lists official announcements.
Business: Publications include the weekly *Business Times* (www.businesstimes.co.tz) and *The Express* (www.theexpress.com).
Periodicals: A wide range is published. They include *The African Review*, published by the Department of Political Science of the University of Dar es Salaam; *Foreign Trade News Bulletin* published twice a year by the Ministry of Industry.
Weeklies
Some daily newspapers have Sunday editions. Other publications include *The Arusha Times* (www.arushatimes.co.tz), the *Government Gazette*, which lists official announcements and *Taifa Letu*.

Broadcasting

Radio: The public service Radio Tanzania Dar es Salaam (RTD) and Parapanda Radio Tanzania (PRT), an FM station geared to younger listeners, are adapting to the increasingly commercial media environment. RTD covers 85 per cent of the country with internal services in KiSwahili and external services in English. The Voice of Tanzania and Zanzibar broadcasts on three wavelengths in KiSwahili. The Voice of Tanzania-Zanzibar operates from Zanzibar.
There are many locally based FM radio stations, including Radio Free Africa (www.radiofreeafrica.co.tz), Radio One (www.ippmedia.com), Kiss FM (www.kissfmtz.net), Clouds FM (www.cloudsfm.co.tz) has a network of nine city stations include Zanzibar.
Television: Public service Televisheni ya Taifa (TVT) does not have complete national coverage. Independent Television (ITV) (www.itv.co.tz) is a popular network, Coastal Television Network and Dar es Salaam Television and Star TV (www.startvtz.com) are private, while TV Zanzibar is state run.
Other news agencies: The Guardian Limited (www.ippmedia.com).

Economy

Tanzania has achieved high growth rates based on its vast natural resource wealth and tourism. GDP growth in 2009-14 was an impressive 6-7 per year. Tanzania has almost fully transitioned into a market-based economy. However, the government still has presence in sectors such as telecommunications, banking, energy and mining. The economy depends heavily on agriculture, which accounts for 25 per cent of GDP while employing approximately 80 per cent of the workforce. The World Bank, the IMF, and bilateral donors have provided funds to rehabilitate Tanzania's aging infrastructure, including rail and ports that provide important trade links for inland countries. The financial sector has expanded in recent years and foreign-owned banks account for around 48 per cent of the banking industry's total assets. Competition among foreign commercial banks has resulted in improvements in the efficiency and quality of financial services although high fraud risk has kept interest rates high. In late 2014, a highly publicized scandal in the energy sector involving senior Tanzanian officials resulted in international donors freezing nearly US$500 million in direct budget support to the government.
Although the service sector constituted 48 per cent of GDP in 2014, agriculture still plays a dominant role in the economy, accounting for 27 per cent in 2014 and around 50 per cent of national income, up to 75 per cent of merchandise exports and providing work for around 80 per cent of the workforce. However it is also characterised by subsistence farming with farm sizes of 0.9–3.0 hectares each and women the mainstay of the agricultural workforce. Around 70 per cent of all crops are hand cultivated and only 10 per cent of primary production is mechanised. Major cash crops include coffee, cotton, cashew nuts, tobacco, tea, sisal and cut flowers.
Industry in 2014 constituted 25 per cent of GDP, dominated by gold mining, which has grown in production and contributes significantly to the mining sector (which constitutes 3 per cent of GDP). Tourism has grown into an important sector of the economy, with the potential for significant growth in both foreign exchange earnings and employment.
Annual GDP growth during the 2000s was an average 6.8 per cent according to the IMF, and was not unduly affected by the global economic crisis; it was 7.3 per cent in 2008, falling to 6.7 per cent in 2009, and remaining constant at 6.5 per cent in 2010 with an estimated growth of 6.7 per cent in 2011. Growth has been underpinned by a rise in global gold prices and fiscal measures introduced by the government to enhance macro-economic policies in public financial management under the terms of an IMF loan of around US$330 million. GDP growth has remained high at 5.1 per cent in 2012 before stabilising at 7.3 per cent in 2012 and 7.2 per cent in 2014.
However, inflation remained high during this period, at 8.4 per cent in 2008, rising to 11.8 in 2009 before falling somewhat to 10.5 per cent in 2010. Inflation was estimated to have fallen to 7 per cent in 2011. The inflation rate increased slightly to 7.9 per cent in 2013 before falling to 6.1 per cent in 2014.
Tanzania is East Africa's third-largest economy (after Kenya and Ethiopia), but it remains an unequal society. In 2014, the UN Human Development Index (HDI) ranked Tanzania 159 (out of 187) for national development in health, education

and income. In 2014, 66.4 per cent of the population lived in multidimensional poverty, while 67.9 per cent lived on the equivalent of less than US$1.25 per day. Migrant worker remittances provided only US$64 million (0.2 per cent of GDP) in 2014, as Tanzania is a destination for migrant workers rather than a source of migrant workers.

In June 2014, proven natural gas reserves were 6.5 billion cubic metres, of which a significant amount is located offshore. Foreign direct investment (FDI) was deemed necessary to exploit the reserves offshore, FDI was US$2.1 billion in 2014 marking a significant increase from the US$1.8 billion in 2012.

External trade

Tanzania is a member of the East African Community (EAC) (with Burundi, Kenya, Rwanda and Uganda). The East African Community Common Market Protocol (EACMP) was launched on 1 July 2010, which will lead to the free movement of labour, capital, goods and services between member states as well as employment opportunities and easier flow of investment capital. The signed protocol now requires that legislation in all states must be harmonised to conform to its jurisdiction. Tanzania is also a member of the Southern African Development Community (SADC), the objectives of which include reducing trade barriers, achieving regional development and economic growth and evolving common systems and institutions.

Foreign earnings provided by tourism ranks second to industrial and manufacturing exports, in particular gold, followed by agricultural exports including coffee, which is the principal cash crop, along with cotton, sisal and tobacco. Cloves are Zanzibar's principal export commodity.

Imports

Principal imports are consumer goods, machinery and transportation equipment, industrial raw materials and crude oil.

Main sources: China (27.6 per cent of total in 2014) and India (24.5 per cent).

Exports

Main exports include gold, coffee, cashew nuts, cotton, sisal, manufactured goods and tobacco.

Main destinations: India (21 per cent of total in 2014), China (9.9 per cent), Japan (5.3 per cent) and Germany (4.7 per cent).

Agriculture

Farming

The agricultural sector is an important component of the economy. It contributes around 27 per cent of GDP and over 50 per cent of export earnings. 80 per cent of the workforce is employed in agriculture. Approximately 70 per cent of the population are peasant farmers. All land in Tanzania is owned by the government, who can lease land for up to 99 years. Proposed reforms to allow for land ownership, particularly foreign land ownership, remain unpopular.

Tanzania has more than 40 million hectares of arable land, but only six million are cultivated. Only 15 per cent of the country has access to water, and the crops are almost totally dependent on the weather. Coffee, cotton, sisal, tobacco, cashew nuts and tea are the most important crops.

There has been a serious decline in production of most crops. Coffee, cotton and sisal are among the crops that have declined and stagnated, although some export crops are showing signs of growth, including tobacco, tea, cashew nuts and horticulture.

The cashew nut sector has benefited from a return to a system where smallholders deal directly with the buyers. Tanzania supplies more than one-quarter of the global market.

Heavy cotton subsidies in the US have affected cotton production in Tanzania, following the liberalisation of the markets. The effects of subsidies are also felt in traditional industries such as beef, wheat and dairy products and also in non-traditional markets like spices.

Fishing

Tanzania has extensive inland as well as marine fisheries, with the freshwater lakes and rivers accounting for over 80 per cent of production. Foreign vessels trawl Tanzania's exclusive economic zones and take their catches elsewhere for processing; the government wishes to attract some of this business to Tanzania. Nile perch and sardines make up over three-quarters of Tanzania's total fish exports. Tanzania exports around US$150 million of Nile perch and related products annually, 80 per cent of which are sold to the EU market. The industry is well organised and gives employment to over 300,000 people. The government is encouraging domestic fish consumption by developing local fish markets.

Forestry

Tanzania has around 33 million hectares of forests and woodlands. The forests have been under intense pressure from population growth and activities such as harvesting of fuelwood, agricultural demands, fires and illegal logging. The government is seeking to create the conditions for private investment in plantation and sustainable management by local communities.

Industry and manufacturing

The industrial and manufacturing sector accounts for 16.7 per cent of GDP and employs 5 per cent of the workforce. Typically, less than a fifth of industrial production is exported.

Most production is geared towards import substitution and the government has traditionally directed public investment towards the sugar and textile industries, tanneries, pulp and paper mills, the fertiliser industry, cement factories, and sisal and cashew nut processing industries. These are engaged in the processing of local minerals and agricultural raw materials for local consumption. Production also includes paper and pulp, cement, textiles and some light engineering.

Growth has been restricted by a lack of foreign exchange needed for the import of raw materials, spare parts and fuel. Foreign aid is aimed at rehabilitating existing industries, but the government is slowly gearing production towards export markets. The high cost of credit inhibits the development of the private sector which is characterised by small enterprises.

Industrial production increased by 8.4 per cent in 2003.

In November 2005, a US$6 billion Mini-Tiger Plan 2020 was launched. Designed to attract foreign direct investment, the scheme aims to expand Tanzania's manufacturing base and increase annual GDP by 2020 to US$40 billion.

Tourism

Tanzania has two of Africa's most spectacular wildlife reserves in the Serengeti National Park and the Ngorongoro Reserve, both included on Unesco's World Heritage List; it also has some of the best African coastal resorts along the Indian Ocean and around the islands of Zanzibar and Mafia.

Tourism has been recognised as not only an integral component of the economy but also a source of growth. Capital investment in the industry was US$844 million in 2014.

Travel and tourism contributed 14 per cent to GDP in 2014 (US$3.7 billion) and provided employment to 12.2 per cent of the workforce (1.3 million jobs) in the same period. International visitor numbers are set to decrease to 1.1 million in 2015 and visitor revenues were US$1.5 billion in 2014.

The government has backed the formation of more cultural tourism sites (rising from three in 1990s to 24 by 2010), where visitors can meet and experience some of the heritage of, for example, the Maasai people and Hadza Bushmen. Local communities are encouraged to show visitors local activities, sacred places, farming and fishing for the benefit of both participants.

A single cross-border tourist visa for Rwanda, Kenya and Uganda was launched on 20 February 2014. The visa costs US$100 and is valid for 90 days (see http://www.visiteastafrica.org/visa/ for details). Tanzania and Burundi are expected to join in the future.

Environment

There is concern about gold mining activities taking place in the Eastern Arc Mountains of Tanzania, which are said to be destroying the Amani nature reserve, a UNESCO-designated biosphere reserve and Balangai forest reserve.

It was revealed in January 2008 that a new genus of monkey, the Rungwecebus kipunji, (known locally as the kipunji) the first to be described since 1925, had been located in two remote forests – Rungwe-Livingstone Forest in the Southern Highlands and the Ndundulu Forest in the Udzungwa Mountains. The kipunji are threatened on two fronts – their habitat is at risk from loggers and they are often trapped and killed by farmers as they raid cultivated crops. It is estimated that there are around 1,000 Kipunji in existence.

The Rungwecebus kipunji is being considered for inclution on the International Union for Conservation of Nature and Natural Resources (IUCN) Red List of Threatened Species.

Mining

Tanzania is well endowed with mineral sources, especially gold, base metals, diamonds and other gemstones. Mining accounted for around 3 per cent of GDP in 2014 and is targeted to increase to 10 per cent by 2025.

Gold mining and production has expanded considerably in recent years. 36 tonnes were produced in 2014, a 1.3 per cent increase on 2013 and ending a two-year decline. Tanzania is the fourth largest gold producer in Africa. Gold has become a major export, mainly to the EU.

There is significant interest in the Kagera nickel-copper-cobalt belt, which runs north and east bordering with Burundi.

There are considerable reserves of iron, tin, gypsum and kaolin. There is a large phosphate mine at Minjingu, supplying a fertiliser plant at Tanga.

Tanzania is also a significant producer of gems, including a diamond mine in Shinyanga and rubies from Longido.

Other gemstones include sapphires and tanzanite, which is unique to Tanzania.

Hydrocarbons

There are no known oil reserves and Tanzania must import all of its domestic needs, which was 52,500 barrels per day of oil in 2013. International oil and gas exploration companies have been operating offshore in territorial waters since 2007 and by 2014 they have still found nothing.

Tanzania's only refinery can process 15,000bpd of crude oil. Vehicles consume more than 50 per cent of imported oil, with industry consuming 25 per cent and the rest used commercially and in homes.

In May 2010, the government in partnership with US-based Noor Oil and Industrial Technologies began construction of a 200,000 barrels per day oil refinery and pipeline. The cost is estimated at US$3.5 billion. The pipeline will connect Dar es Salaam to Mwanza and Kigoma, with plans to expand the pipeline into a network linking neighbouring countries.

Proved natural gas reserves were 6.5 billion cubic metres (cum) in 2014. Offshore reserves have been discovered at Songo Songo Island in the Indian Ocean, Kimbiji and Mnazi Bay near Mtwara. Natural gas is pumped from the offshore Songo Songo field to the Ubungo power station in Dar es Salaam.

Natural gas production was 929 million cum in 2013 with consumption also at 929 million cum, therefore, Tanzania is currently self-sufficient in natural gas and does not need to import any. It does no export any natural gas either.

There are proven coal reserves of 200 million tonnes, with typical production at 30,000 tonnes per annum. The coal is bituminous with low sulphur content, typically used in power stations.

Energy

Total installed generating capacity was 1.6 GW in 2014.

In October 2015 all Tanzania's hydropower plants were switched off as water levels in dams fell below operating levels. Hydropower constitutes 35 per cent to total generating power; natural gas provides 34 per cent and liquid fuel power plants provide 31 per cent. Natural gas from the Songo Songo gas field, supplied through a 200km pipeline to Dar es Salaam, powers the upgraded Ubungo electricity plant and produces 115MW. All power generated is sold to the Tanzania Electric Supply Company (Tanesco) through a 20-year purchase agreement.

Although Tanzania has been implementing a rural electrification programme, progress has been slow due to the very low population density and the high cost of distribution; wood fuel is still the principal energy source for most people in the country. Photovoltaic panels (solar power) are used to supply electricity in rural schools, health and other community centres, providing a total 1.2WM (maximum at peak times), with a growth rate of 20 per cent per annum.

There is a potential to obtain biogas from the 1.4 million tonnes available from sugar cane and other waste material, but technology and infrastructure is not currently available in Tanzania. With the presences of hot springs in Tanzania comes the potential of geothermal power, which has yet to be exploited. Private individuals have utilised wind-turbines to produce electricity with mixed success.

The Tanzanian government has plans to increase installed generating capacity to more than 10 GW over the next 11 years. Nearly 4 GW will be generated from natural gas and 200 MW will be generated from geothermal. The project requires approximately US$1.9 billion per annum, of which 73.5 per cent is for generation. Economists believe that availability of funds could remain a challenge, as the government (the main investor) is still struggling to improve revenue collection in the country. Tanzania is, therefore, looking to the private sector in a shift that will see the financing of power projects move away from government hands and reduce public expenditure on electrical supply projects.

Financial markets

Stock exchange

Dar es Salaam Stock Exchange

Banking and insurance

Central bank

Bank of Tanzania

Main financial centre

Dar es Salaam

Time

GMT plus three hours

Geography

Tanzania consists of Tanganyika, on the African mainland, and the nearby islands of Zanzibar and Pemba. Tanganyika lies on the east coast of Africa, bordered by Uganda and Kenya to the north, by the Democratic Republic of Congo (DRC) to the west, and by Zambia, Malawi and Mozambique to the south. Zanzibar and Pemba are in the Indian Ocean about 40km (25 miles) off the coast of Tanganyika, north of Dar es Salaam.

Tanzania is by far the largest country in east Africa. It is divided into three major regions: the coastal plains and river valleys, the central plateau and basin country, and the southern highlands.

The northern coastal area is humid and rainy, with some of the lushest vegetation in Tanzania. Further south the rainfall decreases and the vegetation develops into a drier savanna woodland. Tanzania's major rivers cut across the coastal plains, creating fertile alluvial fans where cotton, sisal and tropical fruits are grown. A few miles inland from the ocean the vegetation switches to tropical savannah woodland.

The central plateau region occupies the major part of the country, wedged between the two rift valleys. The plateau is bordered by Lake Victoria in the north, the Rukwa Valley in the south, Lake Tanganyika and the Ruwenzori Mountains in the west, and the coastal plains in the east. The famous Serengeti Plains and the Masai Steppe are located in the north-east of this central region.

The southern highlands consist of a variety of mountain and hill formations and are sparsely populated.

The islands of Zanzibar and Pemba are located about 35km from the Tanzanian coast in the Indian Ocean. They are low-lying and coral ringed.

Hemisphere

Southern

Climate

Tropical, with variations according to altitude. Rainy seasons April–May and November–December. Warmer on coast, cooler in upland areas. Temperatures range from 23–30 degrees Celsius (C).

Climatically, Tanzania can be divided into two major zones, the wet and humid lowlands around Lake Victoria and the Indian Ocean, and the semi-arid plateau region. The coastal area is almost always hot and humid with a rainy season that extends for more than 10 months. The most uncomfortable period is December–April when the temperature sometimes exceeds 32 degrees C, with humidity over 90 per cent. The coolest time of the year, and the best time to visit, is June–September when the temperature drops to 15–21 degrees C with relatively low humidity.

The central plateau has distinct wet and dry seasons with great seasonal variations in temperature. Heavy rains fall in March–May and light rains in November–December.

In Dar es Salaam the rainy seasons are usually March–May and November–December, but these can vary from year to year.

Dress codes

Men should wear a lightweight/tropical suit and tie, and women a lightweight suit or formal dress, for business meetings. Women's dress should be modest. On safari it is considered best to avoid bright colours as they may irritate the animals. Visitors to the highlands are advised to take warm clothing. A light raincoat and umbrella are useful during the rainy season.

Entry requirements

Passports

Required by all.

Visa

Required by all; with a few exceptions for citizens of some African states. Details can be found on the visa form, see www.tanzania.go.tz and link to visa. A proposed tourist *univisa* (a single visa to visit all 15-member states of SADC: Angola, Botswana, DRC, Lesotho, Madagascar, Malawi, Mauritius, Mozambique, Namibia, South Africa, Seychelles, Swaziland, Tanzania, Zambia and Zimbabwe) is expected to be in use by 2013. Visitors should check with the appropriate consulates to confirm start of *univisas* and their scope before beginning a tour of southern Africa.

Business travellers should submit an application form with a letter of invitation from a local contact; or introduction by an employing company, detailing nature of business and itinerary.

All visitors must have proof of return/onward passage.

Currency advice/regulations

The import and export of local currency is illegal. The import and export of foreign currency is unlimited. A receipt for all money transactions should be obtained and kept until departure.

Travellers cheques are accepted in banks and *bureaux de change*.

Customs

Personal items are duty-free, however a custom's bond may be demanded for video and filming equipment, radios, tape recorders and musical instruments until re-exported. Firearms require a special permit.

The export of local handcraft must be accompanied by sales receipts on departure.

Visitors have to go through customs travelling to and from Zanzibar.

Health (for visitors)

Mandatory precautions

A yellow fever vaccination certificate if arriving from areas of known infection. Zanzibar authorities require yellow fever vaccination certificate if arriving from Tanzania.

Advisable precautions

Visitors should take precautions against all tropical diseases. Vaccinations for diphtheria, polio, tetanus, hepatitis A, typhoid and Yellow fever are recommended. Other vaccinations that may be recommended are cholera, tuberculosis, hepatitis B and meningitis. There is a risk of rabies. HIV/Aids is prevalent.

Malaria is a countrywide problem, except at altitudes above 1,800 metres. Malaria prophylaxis should be taken.

A reasonable precaution could include a first aid kit with a sterile needle kit and disposable syringes.

All water should be regarded as potentially contaminated, use only bottled water (readily available in Dar es Salaam) or boiled and filtered water for drinking, brushing teeth, washing vegetables and reconstituting powdered milk. Local dairy products should be avoided as milk is unpasteurised; vegetables, meat and fish should be well cooked and eaten hot. Fruit should be peeled. Use only well maintained, chlorinated, swimming pools as bilharzia can be contracted from streams and rivers.

Medical insurance is essential, including emergency evacuation, and an adequate supply of personal medicines is necessary.

Hotels

Accommodation tends to be expensive and can be difficult to obtain, especially in Dar es Salaam, so reservations should be made well in advance and confirmation obtained. Bills must be settled with foreign exchange.

Credit cards

Tanzania has a cash economy and major credit cards are only accepted in larger hotels.

Public holidays (national)

Fixed dates

1 Jan (New Year's Day), 12 Jan (Zanzibar Revolution Day), 26 Apr (Union Day), 1 May (Labour Day), 7 Jul (Saba Saba/Industry Day), 8 Aug (Nane Nane/Farmers' Day), 14 Oct (Nyerere Day), 9 Dec (Independence and Republic Day), 25–26 Dec (Christmas).

Variable dates

Eid El Haj, Good Friday and Easter Monday (Mar/Apr), Maulid Day (Apr/May), Eid al Fitr.

Islamic year 1437 (15 Oct 2015–2 Oct 2016):: The Islamic year contains 354 or 355 days, with the result that Muslim feasts advance by 10–12 days against the Gregorian calendar. Dates of feasts vary according to the sighting of the new moon, so cannot be forecast exactly.

Working hours

Banking

Mon–Fri: 0800–1300; Sat: 0830–1300. In larger town branch opening hours may be extended Mon–Fri: 1400–1800.

Business

Mon–Fri: 0900–1230, 1500–1700.

Government

Mon–Fri: 0800–1230, 1400–1600.

Shops

Mon–Fri: 0800–1800.

Telecommunications

Mobile/cell phones

GSM services 900/1800/400 are available in populated areas only.

Electricity supply

230V AC, 50 cycles; with a variety of round and square three-pin plug sockets.

Weights and measures

The metric system is in use but UK weights and measures are still used in many industries, for example, building.

Social customs/useful tips
Patience is required when doing business in Tanzania. Visitors should use cameras only in private settings and tourist resorts otherwise permission must be sought. Visitors should be aware that bridges, railway stations and public buildings are regarded as security installations and should not be photographed. There are no restrictions on alcohol. Almost all business executives speak English.
Business visitors should address Tanzanians as Mr, Mrs or Ms. The term *Ndugu* is equivalent to comrade in English. The normal greeting when meeting an individual is *Jambo*. Handshaking is normal practice both on meeting and parting. Tanzania has a large number of local traditions, although few will affect the business traveller or tourist. There are no particular taboos, but visitors should be aware of religious customs. Muslims should not be offered pork or ham and many do not drink alcohol. During the Islamic holy month of Ramadan, Muslims do not eat or drink during daylight hours.

Security
Street crime is a serious problem in Tanzania, especially in Dar es Salaam. Be alert at all times. Passports, traveller's cheques, wristwatches and cash are regularly stolen. Use hotel safe deposit boxes and do not carry too much cash.

Getting there
Air
National airline: Air Tanzania.
International airport/s: Dar es Salaam (DAR), 13km from city, duty-free shops, restaurant, bar, bank, shops, post office; Kilimanjaro International (JRO), 50km from Arusha (between Arusha and Moshi), bar, restaurant, post office, shops. Shuttle bus services run to town centres. Zanzibar (ZNZ), 8km from Kisauni. Taxis are available.
Airport tax: Zanzibar only, departure tax: US$25
Surface
Road: The Great North Road runs from Zambia through Tanzania to Kenya; the road is in good condition. Road links from Rwanda, Uganda, Mozambique and Malawi are less reliable.
Rail: The Tanzania-Zambia Railway Authority (Tazara), jointly owned and administered by the Tanzanian and Zambian governments, operates a 1,860km railway link between Dar es Salaam and Kapiri Mposhi (Zambia). Passenger services run twice a week; there are three classes, with sleeper carriages for first- and second-class passengers; bookings are recommended.
Water: Ferry services connect with ports in Burundi, the Democratic Republic of Congo and Zambia (on Lake Tanganyika), Kenya and Uganda (on Lake Victoria) and Malawi (on Lake Malawi).
Main port/s: Dar es Salaam, Mtwara, Tanga and Zanzibar

Getting about
National transport
Air: Air Tanzania operates services between Dar es Salaam, and Zanzibar and other major towns. Precision Air also operates scheduled domestic and regional flights.
ZanAir operates flights from Zanzibar. There are charter companies that operate to isolated airfields, national parks and numerous towns.
Road: All-weather roads connect major centres, but minor roads are liable to be impassable in the rainy season except to four-wheel drive vehicles. There are roads from Songea to Makambako and from Mwanza to Musoma.
Buses: Express services link most centres. Routes include: Dar es Salaam-Songea; Dodoma-Moshi; Lindi-Tunduma; Lindi-Mtwara.
Some services may be unreliable.
Rail: There are seven lines run by the Tanzanian Railway Corportation, mostly radiating out from the Dar es Salaam to all regions in the north and west.
Water: Ferry services run from Dar es Salaam to Zanzibar and Pemba Islands every day. A number of steamer services run during the week on Lakes Tanganyika and Victoria. Two ferries operate on Lake Malawi on the Tanzanian side between Itungi port and Mbamba bay, passing through various small ports.
City transport
Taxis: It is advisable to use only authorised taxis, available in main towns. Taxis from hotels have fixed rates for journeys within Dar es Salaam. Fares in any other taxis are by negotiation and should be agreed before the journey. Taxi drivers do not expect tips.
Buses, trams & metro: Bus services operate within Dar es Salaam; a flat fare system operates but they are generally unreliable and overcrowded and unsuitable for business visitors.
Car hire
Car hire, with or without a driver, can be arranged through hotels or at the airport. It is advisable to get a four-wheel-drive if intending to go off main roads.
An international driving licence is necessary and driving is on the left.

BUSINESS DIRECTORY
The addresses listed below are a selection only. While World of Information makes every endeavour to check these addresses, we cannot guarantee that changes have not been made, especially to telephone numbers and area codes. We would welcome any corrections.

Telephone area codes
The international direct dialling (IDD) code for Tanzania is +255, followed by area code and subscriber's number:

Arusha	27	Mwanza	28
Dar es Salaam	22	Tanga	53
Kilimanjaro	27	Zanzibar	54
Moshi	55		

Chambers of Commerce
Arusha Chamber of Commerce, Industry and Agriculture, PO Box 141, Arusha (tel: 250-8556; fax: 250-4191; e-mail: tccia.arusha@cats-net.com).

Tanzania Chamber of Commerce, Industry and Agriculture, Twiga House, Samora Avenue, PO Box 9713, Dar es Salaam (tel: 212-1421; fax: 211-9437; e-mail: tccia.info@cats-net.com).

Zanzibar National Chamber of Commerce, Industry and Agriculture, Darajani, PO Box 1407, Zanzibar (tel: 223-3083; fax: 223-3349; e-mail: znzchamber@zitec.org).

Banking
Access Bank Tanzania Ltd, PO Box 3167, Bagamoyo Road, Dar es Salaam (tel: 255 22 276-1347, 255 22 277-4355; internet: www.accessbank.co.tz).

Akiba Commercial Bank Limited, PO Box 669, TDFL Bldg (Phase II), Upanga Rd, Dar es Salaam (tel: 211-8340–4; fax: 211-4173).

Azania Bancorp Ltd, PO Box 9271, Samora Ave, Dar es Salaam (tel: 211-8026, 211-7998; fax: 223-6741).

Bank of Tanzania, PO Box 2939, 10 Mirambo Street, Dar es Salaam (tel: 211-0945–7, 211-0950–2; fax: 212-8151; 211-2671, 211-2573, 211-3325, 211-2537; email: info@bot-tz.org).

Citibank (T) Limited, PO Box 71625, Ali Hassan Mwinyi Road, Dar es Salaam (tel: 211-7575, 211-7601; fax: 211-3910, 211-7576).

CRDB Limited, PO Box 268, Maktaba St, Dar es Salaam (tel: 211-7442–7).

Diamond Trust Bank (T) Limited, PO Box 115, Jamhuri/Ali Hassan Mwinyi Rd, Dar es Salaam (tel: 211-4888–4892; fax: 211-4210).

Eurafrican Bank (T) Limited, PO Box 3054, NDC Development House, Kivukoni/Ohio Street, Dar es Salaam (tel: 211-0928, 211-1229, 211-0104; fax: 211-3740).

Exim Bank (T) Limited, PO Box 6649, 9 Samora Avenue, Dar es Salaam (tel: 211-9738; fax: 211-9737).

Habib African Bank Limited, PO Box 70086, India St, Dar es Salaam (tel: 211-1107/9).

International Bank of Malaysia (T) Limited, PO Box 9362, Haidery Plaza, Upanga/Kisutu St, Dar es Salaam (tel: 211-0518, 211-0520, 211-0571; fax: 211-0196).

Kenya Commercial Bank Ltd, PO Box 804, Audit House, 36 Upanga Road, Dar es Salaam (tel: 211-5386–8; fax: 211-5391).

Kenya Commercial Bank (T) Limited, PO Box 804, Peugot Hse, Dar es Salaam (tel: 211-5386–8; fax: 211-5391).

NBC Limited, PO Box 1863, NBC House, Sokoine Drive, Dar es Salaam (tel: 211-3914; fax: 211-2887).

National Microfinance Bank, PO Box 9213, Samora Ave, Dar es Salaam (tel: 225 22 211-8785; 255 22 211-0900; fax: 255 22 211-4058)

Stanbic Bank Tanzania Ltd, PO Box 72647, Sukari House, Ohio Street/Sokoine Drive, Dar es Salaam (tel: 211-2195–2200; fax: 211-3742).

Standard Chartered Bank Tanzania Ltd, PO Box 9011, Ohio/Sokoine Drive, Dar es Salaam (tel: 211-7350–52, 211-3787, 211-7377; fax: 211-3770, 211-3775).

Tanzania Investment Bank, PO Box 9373, Samora Avenue, Dar es Salaam (tel: 2111708–13; fax: 211-3438) .

Tanzania Postal Bank, PO Box 9300, Mkwepu Street, Dar es Salaam (tel: 211-2358–60, 211-2385/9, 211-6409, 211-7748; fax: 223-8212).

Central bank

Bank of Tanzania, 10 Mirambo Street, PO Box 2939, Dar es Salaam (tel: 211-0945/6/7, 211-0951/2; fax: 211-3325; e-mail: info@hq.bot-tz.org).

Stock exchange

Dar es Salaam Stock Exchange, www.darstockexchange.com

Travel information

Air Tanzania, PO Box 543, ATC House; 2nd Floor, 773/40 Ohio Street, Dar es salaam, (tel: 211-8411; fax: 211-3114; email: bookings@airtanzania.com; internet: www.airtanzania.com).

Dar es Salaam International Airport, PO Box 19043, Dar es Salaam (tel: 284-4610/19; fax: 284-4343, 284-3022, 284-4209).

Kilimanjaro International Airport, PO Box 995, Arusha (tel: 222-2941; fax: 222-8553).

www.precisionairtz.com).

Scandinavia Express, Nyerere Road, Vingunguti; PO Box 2414, Dar es Salaam (tel: 286-1947–9; fax: 286-1950; internet: www.scandinaviagroup.com).

Tanzanair, Azikiwe & Samora Ave/Airport International Terminal, PO Box 364, Dar es Salaam (tel: 230-232/4, 246-583; fax: 246-296).

Tanzania National Parks, PO Box 3134, Arusha (tel: 250-1930/1931; fax: 254-8216; email: tanapa@yako.habari.co.tz; internet: www.tanapa.com).

Tanzania Railways Corporation, PO Box 468, Dar es Salaam (tel: 211-0599, 211-0600; fax: 211-6525; internet: www.trctz.com).

Tanzania Zambia Railway Authority, Head Office, Nyerere Road; PO Box 2834, Dar es Salaam (tel: 286-5187; fax: 286-5334; internet: www.tazara.co.tz).

Zanair Ltd, PO Box 2113, Zanzibar (tel: 223-3670; internet: www.zanair.com).

Zanzibar Tourist Corporation, PO Box 216, Zanzibar (tel: 223-2344; fax: 223-3430).

National tourist organisation offices

Tanzania Tourist Board, IPS Building, 3rd Floor, PO Box 2485, Dar es Salaam (tel: 211-1244/5; fax: 211-6420; e-mail: safari@ud.co.tz).

Ministries

Ministry of Agriculture and Food Security, PO Box 9192, Dar es Salaam (tel: 286-2480/1; fax: 286-2077; email: psk@kilimo.go.tz).

Ministry of Energy and Minerals, PO Box 9152, Mkwepu Street, Dar es Salaam (tel: 211-7153–59; fax: 211-6719; email: madini@africaonline.co.tz).

Ministry of Finance, Tancot, PO Box 9111, Dar es Salaam (tel: 211-1174–79; fax: 213-8573).

Ministry of Industries and Trade, PO Box 9503, Lumumba Street, Dar es Salaam (tel: 218-1397, 218-0049/50; fax: 218-2481).

Office of the President, State House, Magogoni Road; PO Box 9120, Dar es Salaam (tel: 211-6679; fax: 211-3425).

Office of the President of Zanzibar (vice president), PO Box 776, Zanzibar (tel: 30-814; fax: 33-722).

Prime Minister's Office, Magogoni Road; PO Box 3021, Dar es Salaam (tel: 213-5076, 211-7249/50/51/52).

Other useful addresses

Board of External Trade, PO Box 5402, Dar es Salaam (tel: 233-524).

Board of Internal Trade, PO Box 883, Dar es Salaam (tel: 228-301).

Cashew Nut Authority of Tanzania, PO Box 533, Mtwara.

Coffee Authority of Tanzania, PO Box 732, Moshi (tel: 275-4190).

National Development Corporation, Development House, Kivukoni Front/Ohio Street, PO Box 2669, Dar es Salaam (tel: 211-2893, 211-1460/3; fax: 211-3618; e-mail: ndc@cats-net.com; internet: www.ndctz.com).

National Insurance Corporation of Tanzania Ltd, PO Box 9264, Dar es Salaam.

Radio Tanzania, PO Box 9191, Dar es Salaam.

State Mining Corporation, PO Box 4958, Dar es Salaam.

Tanzania Electric Supply Company Ltd (TANESCO), PO Box 9024, Dar es Salaam (tel: 211-2891; fax: 211-3836; email: mdtan@intafrica.com).

Tanzania Exporters' Association (TANEXA), c/o Sima International, PO Box 1175, Dar es Salaam.

Tanzania Harbours Authority, PO Box 9184, Dar es Salaam (internet: www.tanzaniaports.com).

Tanzania National Parks, PO Box 3134, Arusha (tel: 250-1930/1931; fax: 254-8216; email: tanapa@yako.habari.co.tz; internet: www.tanapa.com).

Tanzania Petroleum Development Corporation (TPDC), Managing Director, PO Box 2774, Dar es Salaam; Director of Exploration and Production, PO Box 5233, Dar es Salaam; email: tpdcexploration@raha.com); Director of Research & Corporate Services, PO Box 2774, Dar es Salaam.

Tanzania Railways Corporation, PO Box 468, Dar es Salaam.

Tanzania Revenue Authority, PO Bnox 11491, Dar es Salaam (tel: 211-9591/4; fax: 212-8593; email: trais@afsat.com).

Tanzanian Embassy (USA), 2139 R Street, NW, Washington DC 20008 (tel: (+202-1) 939-6129; fax: (+202-1) 797-7408; email: tanz-us@clark.net).

Television Zanzibar, PO Box 314, Zanzibar.

US Embassy, Laibon Road, PO Box 9123, Dar es Salaam.

The Guardian Limited, (www.ippmedia.com).

Internet sites

AllAfrica.com: http://allafrica.com

African Development Bank: www.afdb.org

Africa Online: www.africaonline.com

Official government website: www.tanzania.go.tz

Official Zanzibar Government website: www.zanzibargovernment.org

Terres Australes

COUNTRY PROFILE

1552–59 Saint Paul and Amsterdam Islands were sighted by survivors of a Portuguese expedition led by Ferdinand Magellan.
1772 Captain Marion Dufresne and ship's mate Crozet saw the group of islands, which became known as the Crozet Archipelago. Yves de Kerguelen sighted another archipelago, later named after him.
1840 Terre Adélie, in Antarctica, was sighted and claimed by the French.
1924 A French government decree placed the administration of the islands with the government of Madagascar (then a French colony).
1947 France established observation stations.
1955 Terres Australes et Antarctiques Francaises (TAAF) were accorded the status of an overseas French territory.
1959 The international community signed the Antarctic Treaty, establishing the legal framework for the management of Antarctica, banning any military activity within the Antarctic continent and guaranteeing the protection of its environment and wildlife.
1961 The Antarctic Treaty came into force.
1993 An agreement between the national institutes in charge of polar research in France and Italy agreed to construct a permanent scientific base, Concordia, approximately 1,000km from the French scientific base of Dumont d'Urville.
2000–01 Concordia was built and completed.
2002 Ten countries began working on a glacial project, the European Programme of Glaciology (EPICA), drilling to study the climate in the Antarctic during the last 500,000 years. Drilling reached 2,871 metres and collected ice samples from 520,000 years ago.
2003 The drilling reached the rock base of the Antarctic continent at a depth of 3,300 metres.
2004 The role of the *Administrator-Superior* was undertaken by a *préfet*, based in Saint Pierre on Réunion.
2005 Michel Champon took office as *préfet*. TAAF celebrated its fiftieth anniversary.
2007 Eric Pilloton was appointed *préfet*.
2008 Rollon Mouchel-Blaisot took office as *Administrator-Superior* for the French Southern and Arctic Lands, in Paris.
2007 Eric Pilloton was appointed *préfet*. Nicolas Sarkozy became head of state and president of the French Republic.
2008 Rollon Mouchel-Blaisot took office as *Administrator-Superior* for the French Southern and Arctic Lands, in Paris.
2009 A new advisory committee was established to provide recommendations on how best to administer the largely under-populated region where representative government is unfeasible.
2010 A new plan of action to protect French wetlands within national parks, including Terres Australes, was instigated, with a budget of €20 million (US$27.6 million) for 2010–13. Christian Gaudin took office as *Administrator-Superior* for the French Southern and Arctic Lands, in Paris, on 4 November.
2011 TAAF signed a partnership agreement with Centre National de Documentation Pédogogique (CNDP) (National Centre for Educational Documentation), providing a teaching resource for French schools.
2012 On 29 February, Pascal Bolot was named as *Administrator-Superior*. He took office on 10 April, based in Réunion, for TAAF. The first round of the French presidential elections was held on 22 April, in which 10 candidates took part. Incumbent Nicolas Sarkozy (UMP) won 27.18 per cent of the vote but his chief rival François Hollande (Parti Socialiste (PS) (Socialist Party)) won 28.63 per cent. The runoff was held on 6 May, in which the socialist candidate, François Hollande won 51.63 per cent of the vote and Nicolas Sarkozy 48.37 per cent; turnout was 80.35 per cent. On 15 May François Hollande took office as president and head of state. Jean-Luc Marx was appointed as *Administrator-Superior* on 27 August.
2013 The results of a scientific exhibition to assess the sustainability of fishing in the area were announced on 1 October. The report included an analysis of a new species: the icefish.
2014 The Sea Shepherd Conservation Society announced a new campaign in 2014 to prevent over-fishing of toothfish in the Antarctic.

KEY FACTS

Official name: Le Territoire des Terres Australes et Antarctiques Françaises (TAAF) (French Southern and Antarctic Territories)

Head of State: President of France François Hollande (PS) (from 15 May 2012), represented by *Préfet* Dominique Sorain (appointed 30 July 2014) (based in Saint Pierre, on Réunion)

Head of government: Prime Minister Manuel Valls (PS) (from 31 March 2014)

Area: 439,797 square km consisting of: Kerguelen Archipelago 7,215 square km, Crozet Archipelago 115 square km, Amsterdam Island 54 square km, Saint Paul Islands 7 square km, Terre Adélie (in Antarctica) 432,000 square km

Population: 310 (summer total) (150 winter total)

Capital: Port-aux-Françaises (on Kerguelen)

Official language: French

Currency: Euro (€) = 100 cents

Exchange rate: €0.73 per US$ (Feb 2014)

Political structure

Terres Australes et Antarctiques Françaises (TAAF) (French Southern and Antarctic Territories) is a French Téritoire d'Outre Mer (TOM) (Overseas Territory), but is administered under two different international laws. France exercises full sovereignty over the southern islands, unanimously recognised by all nations. Adélie Land (on mainland Antarctica) is administered according to the 1959 Antarctic Treaty, despite the US not recognising France's claim to the Land. The Antarctic Treaty is an international agreement which provides for broad scientific co-operation and demilitarisation of the Antarctic continent and restrained existing territorial claims without prejudicing the solution to the sovereignty problem.

The fully sovereign area is governed by one law and two main decrees. The law of 6 August 1955 confers administrative and financial autonomy on the TOM. The implementation decree of 13 January 1956 defines the TOM's financial system and the decree of 8 September 1956 provides for the TOM's administrative organisation.

The TOM is under the authority of a chief administrator, whose official residence is in Paris. The administrator is assisted by an advisory council, which meets twice a year and consists of seven members appointed for five-year terms. The council must be consulted on the TOM's draft budget and it is kept informed and consulted on any proposed new scientific missions or applications for concessions and commercial activities.

The TOM is divided into four districts, each under the authority of a district head appointed by the chief administrator:

Saint Paul and Amsterdam Islands – permanent settlement is Martin de Viviés.

Crozet Islands – settlement is Alfred Faure (Possession Island).

Kerguelen Islands – settlement is Port aux Français.

Adélie Land – settlement is Dumont D'Urville.

The population, which comprises members of scientific missions, fluctuates according to season – it is higher in the summer (December–February). Saint Paul Island is uninhabited.

Population

310 (summer total) (150 winter total). The population, which comprises members of scientific missions, fluctuates according to season – it is higher in the summer (December–February). Saint Paul Island is uninhabited.

Annual growth rate: 0.0 per cent (2003)

Languages spoken

Official language/s

French

Media

There are two publications issued by Terres Australes et Antarctiques Francaises (TAAF). A monthly official journal and a quarterly pamphlet of general interest see publications at www.taaf.fr.

Economy

The Terres Australes have no permanent population, but are temporarily inhabited by scientific research groups. Scientific activities are supported and developed by the Institut Français pour la Récherché et la Technologie Polaires (IFRTP) (French Institute for Polar Research and Technology) and the administration of the TOM is in charge of the logistics. Most of the TOM's economic activities centre on supporting the IFRTP. Fishing is the other main economic activity with fish landed by foreign ships exported to France and Réunion; other activities are philately and tourist cruises.

External trade

Crayfish and other fish are exported to France and Réunion.

Agriculture

Farming

Research has indicated the viability of large-scale farming of giant brown macrocystis, a type of seaweed.

Fishing

French vessels fish for crayfish off Amsterdam and Saint Paul. There is an agreement between France and Ukraine to fish for icefish and toothfish.

A research programme which has been carried out since 1970, has shown that trout adapt well to a sub-antarctic environment and the result of sea-ranching salmon was also a biological success. There are estimated to be 60 to 120 million tons of krill in the TOM's coastal waters. Around Saint Paul and Amsterdam Islands, there are plentiful supplies of bull head fish, false cod, crayfish and cape lobster.

Tourism

Much of the Arctic region encompassed by TAAF is protected as a National Nature Reserve. Some tourists are accepted on-board the biannual (Spring and Autumn) supply ship (*Marion Dufresne*) for its 28-day round trip, but without any guarantee of passage if a scientific party needs transport.

Hydrocarbons

No commercial quantities of hydrocarbons have been located.

Energy

There are three diesel generators in operation, in Amsterdam, powered by imported fuel.

Banking and insurance

Central bank

The Paris-based Institut d'Emission d'Outre-Mer (IEOM) provides all central banking services except foreign exchange reserves.

Time

GMT plus five hours

Geography

Terres Australes consists of several groups of islands in the southern Indian Ocean and a sector of Antarctica.

Adélie Land, a narrow segment of mainland Antarctica, is thick continental ice over barren rock. Les Îles Crozet consists of five large and 15 tiny islands, their combined area is over 330 square km. They are volcanic with black basalt geology and treeless terrain. Pic Marion-Dufresne (1,090 metres) is the highest point on Île de l'Est. The main island of Îles Kerguelen, in the southern Indian Ocean, is volcanic, its highest point is the glaciated Mount Ross. It has around 300 smaller islands forming an archipelago, which combined is 7,000 square km in area. Iles Saint-Paul et Amsterdam are small uninhabited volcanic islands.

Hemisphere

Southern

Climate

The climate of Iles Saint-Paul et Amsterdam is oceanic, damp and mild. The temperature averages 15 degrees Celsius (C).

The climate is particularly extreme in the Crozet Archipelago – the islands lie at the centre of an area where tropical and antarctic air masses meet, causing deep depressions and cyclone-forming processes.

The Îles Kerguelen have a cool, humid climate due to the proximity of the Antarctic continent. The summers last from December to March and are similar to those beyond the Arctic Circle. The winters from May to October are comparatively mild. The climate is unstable with constant winds, sometimes at a speed of 160kph. The temperature of the surrounding sea averages 4 degrees C.

Adélie Land's climate is harsh. The temperature of the coastal area never rises above 4 degrees C in summer and can fall to minus 37 degrees C in winter.

Entry requirements

Visa

Required by all, except citizens of EU, North America, Australasia and Japan, for stays up to one month; this includes business trips by representatives of overseas companies or organisations. For further exceptions, full details and a copy of the application form visit www.diplomatie.fr/venir/visas/ index.html. Proof of adequate funds for stay and return/onward ticket are necessary.

Health (for visitors)

Advisable precautions

Protective clothing is essential. Sunscreen should be applied and protective eyewear worn in summer in the Antarctic.

Weights and measures

The metric system is in use.

Getting there

Air

There are no air links to or between the bases.

Surface

Water: Relief ships bring new personnel and supplies. A charter vessel calls five times a year to the Antarctic islands and another calls twice a year to Adélie Land.

BUSINESS DIRECTORY

The addresses listed below are a selection only. While World of Information makes every endeavour to check these addresses, we cannot guarantee that changes have not been made, especially to telephone numbers and area codes. We would welcome any corrections.

Banking

Central bank

Institut d'Emission d'Outre-Mer (IEOM), 5 rue Roland Barthes, 75598 Paris Cedex 12, France (tel: (+33-1) 5344-4141; fax : (+33-1) 4347-5134; email: contact@ieom.fr).

Other useful addresses

Institut Français pour la Recherche et la Technologie Polaires (IFRTP), Technopole Brest Iroise, BP 75, 29280 Plouzane, France (tel: (+33-2) 9805-6500; fax: (+33-2) 9805-6555).

Terres Australes et Antarctiques Françaises (TAAF), 34 Rue des Renaudes, 75017 Paris (tel: (+33-1) 4053-4652; fax: (+33-1) 4766-9123).

Internet sites

French tourism: www.discoverfrance.net/Colonies/Antarctic.shtml

Information about antarctica: www.gdargaud.net/Antarctica/InfoAntarctica.html

Secretariat of the Antarctic Treaty: www.ats.aq

TAAF (in French): www.taaf.fr

Thailand

KEY FACTS

Official name: Prathet Thai; Ratcha Anachak Thai (Kingdom of Thailand)

Head of State: King Bhumibol Adulyadej (Rama IX) (since 1946)

Head of government: Prime Minister General Prayut Chan-o-cha (since 25 August 2014) after launching a military coup against the government and then assuming control of the country.

Ruling party: Following Gen. Prayut Chan-o cha's coup, he issued an interim constitution granting himself sweeping powers and giving himself amnesty for staging the coup. In August 2014, a military dominated national legislature, whose members were handpicked by Prayut, elected him as the new prime minister.

Area: 514,000 square km

Population: 68.66 million (2014) (65,479,453; 2010 census figure)

Capital: Bangkok

Official language: Thai

Currency: Baht (B) = 100 satang

Exchange rate: B36.17 per US$ (Sep 2015)

GDP per capita: US$8,445 (2014)

GDP real growth: 0.71% (2014)

GDP: US$373.80 billion (2014)

Labour force: 385.82 million (2014)*

Unemployment: 0.84% (2014)

Inflation: 1.90% (2014)

Oil production: 453,000 bpd (2014)

Natural gas production: 42.10 billion cum (2014)

Balance of trade: US$24.56 billion (2014)

Annual FDI: US$7.78 billion (2011)

* estimated figure

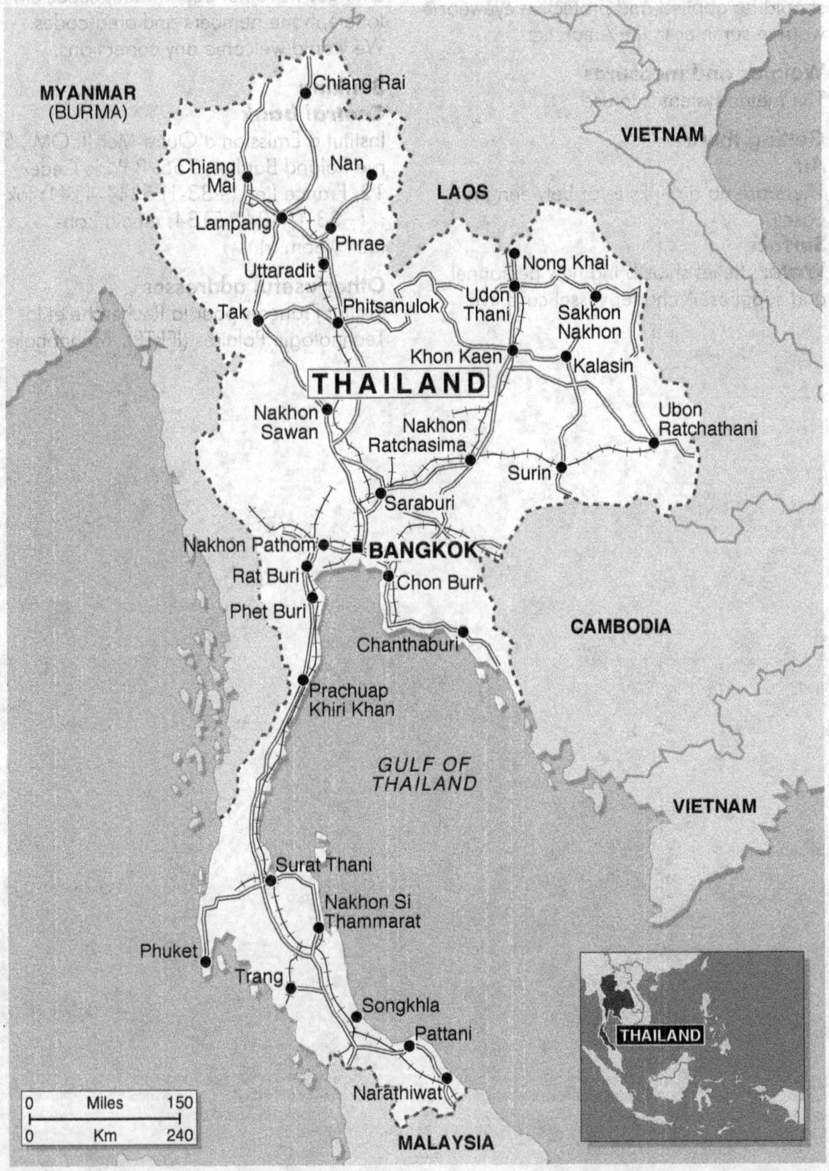

The martial law legislation introduced in late May 2014 remained in place across Thailand after April 2015 when it had been due to be lifted. The only exceptions, originally, were for the Southern provinces of Pattani, Yala and Narathiwat, the Sadao district of Songkhla province and some remoter border areas.

Constitution confusion

Article 44 of the interim constitution continued to grant General Prayut Chan-o-cha (previously spelt Prayuth Chan-ocha), the acting prime minister and head of the National Council for Peace and Order (NCPO), wide powers to take action to enforce law and order. Restrictions also remained on freedom of assembly and expression. This it was hoped, would continue to discourage the demonstrations which, before Martital Law, had regularly taken place on varying scales in Bangkok and other cities.

At the November 2015 summit meeting of the Asia-Pacific Economic Co-operation Organisation (APEC) in Manila, US President Barack Obama acknowledged that Thailand's internal politics were complicated and that the US was ready to co-operate with the Kingdom in its bid to forge a stable democracy. The remarks were made during a side meeting with Prime Minister Prayut. A government spokesman said that Mr Prayut had told Barack Obama that he would do his best to bring full democracy back to Thailand. Obama had added that not only were Thai politics complicated, but that the US was ready to help Thailand return to 'sustainable democracy.'

According to the US Council for Foreign Relations (CFR) the May 2014 *coup* and the related army intervention were caused by the constant bickering of elected politicians, the venality of the former Phak Puea Thai (PPT) (For Thais Party) government and the gridlock created by the long-running stand-off between Puea Thai leaders and the anti-Shinawatra protestors who had paralysed parts of Bangkok for months. Inevitably, as the year wore on, it appeared that contrary to the army's story that it had only considered intervention at the eleventh hour in May, the generals had been planning a *coup* for many months. Former prime minister, Thaksin Shinawatra, and in 2015 Thailand's leading *éminence grise*, who had been quiet for some time, now contended that senior advisors in the royal palace had helped foment the street protests and then mastermind the *coup*, although this story seemed difficult to believe, given the tension between senior palace advisor Prem Tinsulanonda and junta leader Prayut Chan-o-cha.

Whatever the precise origins and timing of the *coup*, at the end of the first year of martial law few of the challenges cited by the *coup*-makers as reasons for their intervention had actually been addressed. Although the military was assiduously trying to remove the Shinawatras and their allies from politics forever, there was no evidence that the unelected government had made inroads against graft. Thailand ranked 85 on the 2014 Transparency International *Corruption Perceptions Index*, level with fellow ASEAN member, the Philippines. In the first six months of the military government, the junta faced numerous scandals over alleged graft in government purchases, which rather deflated any hopes that the army was going to seriously fight corruption.

Meanwhile, Thailand's politics remained in a state of paralysis. Unsurprisingly, General Prayut appeared to have developed a taste for power, indefinitely delaying elections and the day on which he would hand back power to an elected government. The National Reform Council had voted in September 2015 to jettison a proposed new constitution which a tame set of drafters had spent the previous ten months drawing up. This decision meant the beginning of a new drafting process, which would take another seven months or so. Which meant that there was little chance of elections before 2017, at the earliest.

According to the London *Economist*, the generals had at one stage promised to 'bring happiness back to Thailand.' The draft constitutional framework was part of the process. Its authors, doing the junta's bidding, came up with a set of rules which allowed for elections but neutered the victors. The draft seemed designed to produce weak governing coalitions able to be bossed about by higher powers. It would have introduced a largely appointed senate. And it removed a requirement that the prime minister be elected.

Had it been approved, the new constitution would have proceeded to a referendum. It reportedly rendered future Thailand elected governments weaker than their predecessors in the 2000s and 2010s, strengthening the power of unelected parts of the bureaucracy. None the less, the pool of elected would still be dominated by Puea Thai supporters, even under the would-be constitution's system of proportional representation. This elected government looked likely to clash with the elite-dominated unelected bodies set up by the new constitution and possibly even with the military and the palace as well.

The Junta had avoided the creation of institutions to mediate political conflicts – only ones to investigate and possibly punish elected leaders. Thailand needed mediators, conflict resolvers and compromisers based outside the military and the palace, the institutions that have been charged with resolving conflicts for all of Thailand's modern history. The *coup* had not brought the country closer to compromise or created alternatives to solving any future political gridlock other than another *coup*.

Down South

In Thailand's insurgency-battered south, violent clashes between insurgents and the military continued in 2015, despite the imposition of martial law. In the southern provinces of Pattani, Yala and Narathiwat, the Muslim, ethnically Malay majority continued to seek increased autonomy or even independence. The demands were not new; many residents of the three provinces cast their minds back to the days before their homelands were incorporated into the Thai state in the

KEY INDICATORS — Thailand

	Unit	2011	2012	2013	2014	**2015
Population	m	*69.52	67.89	68.30	68.66	*68.84
Gross domestic product (GDP)	US$bn	345.60	366.00	387.25	373.80	*386.29
GDP per capita	US$	5,394	5,390	5,670	8,445	*5,612
GDP real growth	%	0.1	6.5	2.9	0.7	*3.7
Inflation	%	3.8	3.0	2.2	1.9	*0.3
Unemployment	%	0.4	0.7	0.7	0.8	*0.8
Oil output	'000 bpd	345.0	440.0	459.0	453.0	–
Natural gas output	bn cum	37.0	41.4	41.8	42.1	–
Coal output	mtoe	6.0	5.1	5.0	5.0	–
Exports (fob) (goods)	US$m	219,119.3	226,114.2	225,408.2	224,761.7	–
Imports (fob) (goods)	US$m	202,128.5	217,768.2	218,972.3	200,201.0	–
Balance of trade	US$m	16,990.8	8,346.0	6,436.0	24,560.7	–
Current account	US$m	5,917.8	-1,470.0	-2,452.0	14,231.0	*17,085.0
Total reserves minus gold	US$m	177,905.7	173,328.0	161,328.0	151,253.0	–
Foreign exchange	US$m	175,795.9	171,106.0	159,022.0	–	–
Exchange rate	per US$	30.36	30.68	32.96	32.91	–

* estimated figure ** forecast figure

early twentieth century. Economic factors had contributed to the rebellion; the southern provinces had lower incomes than the rest of the country and lower levels of education. The Thai military had allegedly mistreated the Muslim population, seeking to end their distinctive culture and religious observation.

Tourism

Martial Law had little affect on travel and tourism with most businesses, facilities and attractions in the industry continuing as usual. For some travellers, travel insurance may have been invalid depending on their providers policy, but the Tourism Authority of Thailand (TAT) assisted with this and launched Thailand Travel Shield to provide visiting tourists with valid travel insurance options.

The removal of Martial Law was seen as a positive step and did not affect tourists planning a visit to Thailand in 2015. Since Martial Law was imposed, British and Irish tourist arrivals had remained buoyant, with growth year on year in 2014 for British arrivals (0.4 per cent) and a positive start for the Irish market in January 2015 (+2.21 per cent).

The economy

According to the Asian Development Bank (ADB) the contraction in gross domestic product (GDP) in the first quarter of 2014 was followed by a cautious recovery sufficient for the economy to post marginal growth of 0.7 per cent for the year. The political unrest and street protests had disrupted economic activity into the first half of 2014. Indeed, various disruptions since 2007 had confined average growth over this period to 2.9 per cent. Consumption and net exports contributed to the slight GDP increase in 2014, while investment fell sharply. Private consumption recorded meagre growth of 0.3 per cent, weighed down by depressed consumer confidence during the political strife and a decline in farm incomes caused by weaker prices for agricultural products. Government consumption also made a minor contribution to GDP growth.

However, fixed investment fell by 2.8 per cent in 2014, following on from a 2.0 per cent decline in the previous year. Public fixed investment was hampered by political disruptions and legal challenges to the previous administration. Political uncertainty and soft domestic and external demand hurt private investment, which started to recover in the second half. Imports of goods and services shrank in volume terms more than exports did, allowing net external demand to make the biggest contribution to GDP growth.

On the supply side, services grew by 2.2 per cent and agriculture by a modest 1.1 per cent, but industry contracted by 0.9 per cent. Services benefitted from growth in telecommunications and finance, partly offset by weakness in wholesale and retail trade – and in hotels and restaurants as tourist arrivals fell by 6 per cent to 24.8 million, suppressed by street protests and military intervention. Agriculture, hampered by lower prices for rice and natural rubber and a disease in shrimp aquaculture, grew at the weakest pace in four years. The contraction in the industrial sector stemmed mainly from declines in manufacturing and construction. Manufacturing, hit by slack domestic demand and declining export orders, shrank by 1.1 per cent. Construction contracted by 3.8 per cent, mainly the result of a political vacuum in the first part of the year that delayed construction by state-owned enterprises.

Inflation decelerated for a third straight year in 2014, to average 1.9 per cent. Weak domestic demand and lower food and oil prices pulled inflation down to 0.6 per cent year on year by December. Responding to the first-quarter economic contraction, the Bank of Thailand, the central bank, lowered its base interest rate in March 2014 by 25 basis points to 2.0 per cent. Although commercial banks trimmed lending rates, growth in credit to the private sector slowed sharply to 4.5 per cent, reflecting subdued demand for loans and banks' deepening caution toward extending credit to households and small businesses. Government spending through the first half of FY2014 (ended 30 September 2014) was severely limited by legal and political constraints, causing the fall in public fixed investment. Total government spending and revenue fell over the fiscal year and the fiscal deficit widened to 2.5 per cent from 2.0 per cent in the previous year.

In the external accounts, sluggish demand in major markets and falling prices for export commodities, including natural rubber and sugar, pulled merchandise exports down by 0.3 per cent to US$224.8 billion in 2014. Exports to the People's Republic of China fell by a relatively sharp 7.9 per cent. Merchandise imports dropped by 8.5 per cent to US$200.2 billion, a result of lower exports, falling oil prices and weak domestic demand, particularly for capital goods. Consequently, the trade surplus jumped to US$24.6 billion and the current account turned to a surplus of US$14.2 billion, equal to 3.8 per cent of GDP.

Thailand's capital and financial accounts registered net outflows of US$15.3 billion, mainly on outflows of portfolio investment and the balance of payments showed a small deficit. Gross international reserves of US$157.1 billion at the end of 2014 covered 7.4 months of imports. The Thai baht weakened early in 2014 but ended the year little changed against the US dollar. However, it appreciated over the year against the euro, the Japanese yen and most regional currencies. The previous government's costly support programme for rice farmers ended in 2014. After that, farmers faced not only declining rice prices but also drought in many areas. The interim military administration provided support through subsidies for rice farmers' production costs, capped at B15,000 per farm. It paid B1 million to each drought-affected district for community investments and hired farmers temporarily to maintain irrigation canals. Rubber producers also received a subsidy for production costs

The Thai economy was expected to benefit in 2015 from a relatively calm political environment, the restoration of government investment, better prospects for exports to the major industrial economies and lower fuel costs for businesses and consumers. These factors were forecast to lift GDP growth to 3.6 per cent in 2015 and 4.1 per cent in 2016. In particular, public fixed investment was expected to rise in 2015 after last year's decline and was also expected to accelerate in 2016. The interim government had approved an infrastructure programme that included US$95 billion in investments over 8 years in railways, roads, ports, airports and special economic zones. In 2015, public investment would be confined to relatively small projects, with larger-scale construction to start from next year. The government planned to offer contracts for mass transit rail lines in Bangkok and for double-tracking rail lines across the country.

Fiscal policy was expected to support economic recovery. The budget for 2015 provided for a deficit of B250 billion, equivalent to 1.9 per cent of projected GDP. In addition, the government was implementing stimulus measures such as a soft-loan programme through state-owned financial institutions and was drawing on funds carried over from past budgets to help finance public investment. The execution of budget programmes had improved as 42.6 per cent of the budget was disbursed in the first 5 months of 2015. Looking to 2016, the fiscal deficit was expected to widen to B390 billion to accommodate additional spending. Public debt was manageable at 45.8 per cent of GDP, below the 60.0 per cent ceiling set under the fiscal sustainability framework.

Private fixed investment is recovering gradually and was expected to pick up as infrastructure projects got under way and consumption spending strengthens. After approvals for firms' investment privileges ground to a halt in 2014 during the political disruptions, they have resumed. Lower energy costs and the further reduction in interest rates in March 2015 should support investment, though low capacity utilisation hinders expansion in some industries.

The interim government plans to develop five special economic zones along Thailand's borders to attract industries such as logistics, processing agricultural products and labour-intensive manufacturing. Investors in the zones get several tax breaks and privileges, including permission to employ foreign experts and for foreign investors to own land. Under the plan, migrant workers from neighbouring countries can work in the Thai zones and still live at home.

Consumer confidence rallied in the second half of 2014 on the calmer political environment, but waned in early 2015. Household spending was expected to show a modest increase in 2015, supported by higher civil service salaries from January, lower fuel costs and government measures to help farmers. However, data for January 2015 showed that private consumption and private investment remained sluggish.

Risk assessment

Economy	Fair
Politics	Poor
Regional stability	Good/fair

COUNTRY PROFILE

1767 The former capital of Siam, Ayutthaya, fell to Burmese invaders.
1782 King Rama I – first of the Chakri dynasty – was crowned and founded the capital city Bangkok.
1851–68 King Mongkut (Rama IV) began a period of reform and modernisation while adroitly avoiding European colonisation. Treaties were signed with the US, Great Britain, France and Japan, among others. Barriers against traders were eliminated, allowing expansion.
1868–1910 Chulalongkorn, (Rama V) continued his father's programmes by modernising the legal and administrative systems, reforming the political structure and abolishing slavery. He also began construction of a railway network. Some Siam territories in Indochina were ceded to Britain and France.
1910 Vajiravudha (Rama VI) became King. He introduced compulsory education, among other reforms.
1925 Prajadhipok, the brother of Vajiravudha, became King (Rama VII).
1932 A group of students, led by Pibul Songgram and Pridi Phanomyang forced King Prajadhipok to replace the absolute monarchy with a constitutional monarchy and introduce parliamentary government. A new National Assembly was established.
1933 The first general elections were held.
1935 The King abdicated. A council of regency chose his 10-year old brother, Ananda, to be Rama VIII. He was studying in Switzerland at the time.
1938 Pibul Songgram became prime minister
1939 Siam was renamed Thailand on June 24.
1941–1946 Under the leadership of Pibul, Thailand allied itself with Japan and allowed Japanese troops to traverse the country. Thailand declared war on the US and Britain but the Thai ambassador in Washington withheld the official declaration and so technically the country remained neutral. Pridi Phanomyang led an American-backed anti-Japanese movement.
1945 Pridi became prime minister and Pibul was jailed briefly for war crimes.
1946 King Ananda returned for the second time from studying in Switzerland but died shortly after in mysterious circumstances. He was succeeded by his brother, Bhumipol Adulyadej, as King Rama IX, although he was not formally crowned until 1950. Inflation and corruption marred the government's reputation.
1947 Pibul led an army *coup d'état* and instituted a military dictatorship. Pibul was staunchly anti-Communist and under his rule the Chinese community, suspected of being Communist sympathisers, was harassed.
1950 Bhumibol Adulyadej became King and was crowned Rama IX. Thailand aligned itself with the US during the Cold War and sent troops to fight in the Korean War.
1957 Pibul was overthrown in a coup led by Field Marshal Sarit Thanarat.
1958 Sarit deposed his own premier, took power himself and imposed martial law and dissolved all political parties.
1973 Student riots destabilised the military government and free elections were held. The King appointed a civilian, Sanya Thammasak, as premier.
1974 A new constitution was introduced, legalising political parties.
1975 With the ending of the Vietnam War Thailand became the temporary home to many refugees from Indochina.
1976 The military seized power and Admiral Sa'ngad Chaloryoo annulled the 1974 constitution and re-introduced martial law. A new constitution was introduced. Thanin Kraivixien became prime minister, he imposed a harsh rule and kept unions under tight control while he carried out anti-Communist purges of the civil service and educational institutions.
1977 Thanin was overthrown by General Kriangsak Chomanand.
1978 A new constitution was promulgated in which a bicameral National Assembly was established.
1991 Another military coup led by General Suchinda Krapayoon replaced Kriangsak.
1992 General Krapayoon resigned and elections were held. A coalition led by the Phak Prachathipat (PP) (Democrat Party) was victorious.
1995 The Phak Chat Thai Patthana (CP) (Thai Nation Development Party) won the general election and formed a coalition government.
1997 The constitution was amended to allow the direct election of a prime minister. The baht fell sharply during the Asian financial crisis and led to bankruptcies and unemployment. Chuan Leekpai (PP) was elected prime minister; he worked closely with the IMF to reform the badly damaged economy.
2000 Thailand's first senate election was held. Subsequent rulings against the results by the Election Commission necessitated two further elections.
2001 In general elections, Thaksin Shinawatra became prime minister and the Thai Rak Thai (TRT) (Thais Love Thais) formed a coalition government with the Phak Chart Patthana (PCP) (National Development Party).
2002 The PCT and the Phak Khwam Wang Mai (PKWM) (New Aspiration Party) joined the ruling coalition. Supachai Panitchpakdi became director general of the World Trade Organisation (WTO).
2004 A wave of terrorist attacks by separatist Islamic and ethnic Malays from southern provinces killed over 100 people. Over 100 Islamic insurgents were killed while attacking several police bases in the south and 85 Islamic detainees were killed while in custody following violence at a rally in the south. Millions of domesticated birds were slaughtered following an outbreak of avian flu. Six west coast provinces, including the tourist resorts of Phuket and Khao Lak, were devastated by a *tsunami* which swept the whole region following an earthquake off

the coast of Sumatra (Indonesia). The final estimate for Thailand was 8,212 dead or missing and 6,000 people displaced.
2005 The ruling TRT party won the general elections; Thaksin Shinawatra was the first prime minister to win a second term in office.
2006 Amid controversial allegations concerning corruption charges against him, Thaksin Shinawatra called snap general elections which the opposition parties boycotted; they were won by the ruling TRT with 57 per cent of the vote. Despite the victory, the prime minister was forced to step down in favour of his deputy, Chidchai Vanasatidya. But the Supreme Administrative Court ruled that the general elections were invalid and allowed Shinawatra to resume his duties as prime minister. While abroad attending a UN General Assembly meeting Shinawatra was deposed in a bloodless army coup. A ban was placed on all political party activities. Retired ex-army general, Surayud Chulanont was sworn in as prime minister. Shinawatra resigned his leadership of TRT.
2007 Matial law was lifted in Bangkok and 41 (out of 76) provinces two months after its imposition; it continued in border regions and in the north in general. The constitutional court ordered the dissolution of the TRT and barred TRT leader Thaksin Shinawatra from politics for breaking election laws in 2006; the court also barred a further 110 party members from politics for five years. The ban on political party activities was lifted, but the TRT remained dissolved. Former members of TRT agreed to stand as parliamentary candidates for the Palang Prachachon (PPP) (People's Power Party). An arrest warrant was issued for Shinawatra on fraud charges. A referendum agreed constitution changes. King Bhumibol Adulyadej celebrated his eightieth birthday. Although the king has few legal powers, he has been instrumental in calming relations between the military and civilian government and the people. In snap parliamentary elections the PPP won 233 seats (out of 480) and began coalition talks with minor parties.
2008 A coalition government led by the PPP and five minor political parties was formed. Samak Sundaravej (PPP) was elected as prime minister. Thaksin Shinawatra returned from self-imposed exile, to a welcome of thousands of flag-waving supporters. He was arrested and taken to court immediately to face charges of abuse of power during his tenure as prime minister; he was released on bail. He and his wife went on trial on corruption charges related to a Bangkok real estate deal. His wife was found guilty and he fled Thailand into exile in the UK. Shinawatra was found guilty *in absentia* of corruption and sentenced to two years in jail. Prime Minister Samak Sundaravej was sacked from office by the Constitutional Court for violating electoral laws in 2007. Somchai Wongsawat became prime minister, but was banned from political office until 2013 along with his party, the PPP. Most parliamentary members of PPP joined the newly established Phak Puea Thai (PPT) (For Thais Party). Both main Bangkok international airports were closed for over a week in December as anti-government demonstrators besieged the termini, stranding thousands of visitors and crippling the tourist industry. Opposition leader, Abhisit Vejjajiva (PP), became prime minister. A new government coalition was formed, led by the PP with CP.
2009 Mass rallies showed renewed support of Thaksin Shinawatra, while condemning government efforts to manage the economic crisis. The Asean summit, due to be held in Pattaya, was cancelled after demonstrators stormed the venue. Sonthi Boonyaratglin (who had led the 2006 coup that overthrew Shinawatra) became leader of the Matuphum (Motherland) party (mostly comprised of Muslim politicians) and campaigned on bringing unity to Thailand. A new political party Karn Muang Mai (New Politics Party) was formed, to represent the views of the 'yellow shirts'.
2010 The Supreme Court sequestrated US$1.4 billion of Shinawatra wealth, deemed illegally acquired while Mr Shinawatra was prime minister. Thousands of supporters of Shinawatra, known as 'red shirts', took to the capital's streets for weeks of civil disorder and disruption, calling for new elections. A state of emergency was declared, giving the security forces wide powers, including detention for 30 days without charge. Protestors were finally dispersed by security forces leaving 80 people dead and around 1,800 injured. The US put Thailand on a list of countries not doing enough to combat human trafficking, an illegal industry that generates around US$10 billion a year. The state of emergency was lifted after over 400 people had been arrested under the emergency rules, which banned the gathering of more than five people.
2011 Parliament was dissolved in May and a general election was set for July. In May, PPT elected Yingluck Shinawatra, the sister of ousted-prime minister Taksin Shinawatra, as its leader. In the elections, the opposition PPT in its first contested national election won a convincing majority of 265 seats out of 500, including 48.41 per cent of the proportional vote (61 seats out of 125); the former ruling PP won 159 seats. A five-party government coalition was agreed on 4 July, led by PPT, with CP, BJT and two other minor parties. Parliament voted Yingluck Shinawatra into office as prime minister in August. Of the 500 members 296 voted for her, three against and 197 abstained. She became Thailand's first female head of government. Floodwaters that had been building following months of heavy monsoon rains reached Bangkok in October. In the provinces 356 people were killed and 110,000 families displaced from their homes. By November, as floodwaters reached the outskirts of Bangkok, authorities instigated evacuations (estimated at around 16,000 residents) as it diverted run-off floodwater in an attempt to protect the densely populated capital. Nationwide over 562 people had been killed and the floods had effected 22 (out of 77) provinces, while in Bangkok waters in some lower-lying areas were 50cm deep, but in others in general water had begun to recede.
2012 GDP growth in the fourth quarter of 2011 fell by 9 per cent due to the October flooding which caused US$11 billion of damage to just the infrastructure. Manufacturing and agriculture were also adversely affected. On 17 September the Truth for Reconciliation Commission (TRC) published its final report on the 2010 political unrest and the anti-government demonstrations. The TRC held both the military and the Red Shirts responsible for the violence and the deaths of over 90 people. On 5 December thousands gathered in Bangkok to celebrate the 85th birthday of King Bhumibol Adulyadej, the world's longest serving monarch.
2013 A peace talks deal between government forces and Muslim separatists in the south of the country was announced in February. Malaysia would to act as mediator. In July a cease-fire (the Ramadan Peace Initiative) for the month of Ramadan was agreed between the two parties whereby Thai security forces would refrain from 'aggressive actions' and rebel groups, including the Barisan Revolusi Nasional (BRN) (National Revolutionary Front), will not engage in 'armed attacks, bombings and ambushes' against Thai troops. King Bhumibol Adulyadej left hospital on 1 August. He had been admitted in September 2009 with a lung infection. He was reported as going to his sea-side palace with his wife, Queen Sirikit, who has herself been in hospital for a year with 'reduced blood flow to the brain'. There was tight security in early August as parliament prepared to debate a controversial bill that would grant amnesty to those involved in political violence since 2006. There were fears that the bill might allow ex-leader Thaksin Shinawatra to return without serving a prison sentence. Mr Thaksin had been convicted of abuse of

power in 2008 and sentenced *in absentia* to a prison term of two years. On 30 October four opposition members resigned their positions so that they could lead street protests against the amnesty, just days before the bill was approved by the lower house on 31 October. However, as protests grew and tens of thousands of protestors took to the streets, when it came to the Senate the ruling PPT withdrew its support and all 141 Senators present voted against it. Ms Shinawatra had already said she would abide by the Senate's ruling.
2014 The Constitutional Court ruled on 7 May that Prime Minister Yingluck Shinawatra and a number of her ministers should stand down. The Court ruled that the PPT had benefited by Ms Shinawatra's transfer of national security chief, Thawil Pliensri, making the transfer illegal. Since only nine ministers were forced to resign, the cabinet continued to survive in its caretaker role. The cabinet agreed to appoint Niwattumrong Boonsongpaisan as caretaker prime minister. On 22 May the military suspended the constitution and appointed General Prayut Chan-o-cha (previously spelt Prayuth Chan-ocha) as acting prime minister. On 23 May Yingluck Shinawatra and several of her former ministers were summoned to a meeting by the General. In July Yingluck Shinawatra was given permission by the military to travel out of Thailand. General Prayut Chan-ocha was nominated for the post of prime minister by the junta (he had been the only candidate) and was officially appointed prime minister on 26 August after being endorsed by the King. He will remain as interim prime minister until the elections promised by the military for 2015. On 31 August Prime Minister Prayut named a cabinet featuring serving or former generals in more than one-third of positions.
2015 On 25 January the National Legislative Assembly voted to impeach Yingluck Shinawatra and impose a five-year ban from politics, along with a criminal charge that carries a 10-year jail sentence. King Bhumibol Adulyadej was treated for hydrocephalus in August. Authorities say he has been recovering well. In late November the prime minister said that his government would hand over to a new government in July 2017, although he did not say whether this would be an elected government or not.

Political structure

Constitution

A new Constitution was agreed by referendum in 2007. Articles of change included: each province to return at least three members of parliament in multi-seat constituencies; making just over half the senate seats to be elected; limiting the powers and privileges of the prime minister – as no prime minister or cabinet may govern while the House of Representatives is dissolved; restricting the term in office to two; banning a prime minister from owning major holdings in private companies and making it easier to impeach a prime minister. Turnout for the referendum was 60 per cent.
Following the military coup in May 2014, an interim constitution was signed on 22 July 2014, it paves the way for the establishment of a national legislature. Although it recognises Thailand as a democratic state and the people as sovereign, the constitution grants amnesty for all past and future military actions. It has resulted in giving the military enormous power in that the National Council for Peace and Order can issue any order at will for the sake of the reforms or security.

Form of state

Constitutional monarchy

The executive

Executive power lies with the cabinet, headed by a prime minister for a term of four years, who must be an elected member of the House of Representatives. Thai army declared martial law on 20 May 2014 followed by the coup on 22 May 2014. How the executive will be formulated remains in the balance.

National legislature

Following the 2014 military coup, a National Legislative Assembly of no more than 220 members will replace the bicameral National Assembly. Elections for a permanent legislative body are currently unscheduled and may not occur until February 2017.

Legal system

Courts follow the traditional pattern of courts of first instance, a court of appeal and a Supreme Court.

Last elections

2 February (parliamentary), however, voting was disrupted in 69 of 375 constituencies by the opposition that had called for a boycott. The re-run date was on 2 March, but it became invalidated by Thailand's Constitutional Court because it was not completed within one day throughout the nation.

Results: No valid results.

Next elections

Late 2016 (parliamentary)

Political parties

Ruling party

Following Gen. Prayut Chan-ocha's coup, he issued an interim constitution granting himself sweeping powers and giving himself amnesty for staging the coup. In August 2014, a military dominated national legislature, whose members were handpicked by Prayut, elected him as the new prime minister.

Main opposition party

No opposition party exists at present within government.

Population

Over 24 per cent of the population is under 14 years of age.
68.66 million (2014) (65,479,453; 2010 census figure)

Last census: 1 September 2010: 65,479,453

Population density: 131 inhabitants per square km (2010). Urban population 34 per cent (2010 Unicef).

Annual growth rate: 1.0 per cent, 1990–2010 (Unicef).

Ethnic make-up

Approximately 80 per cent of the population are Thais, 10 per cent Chinese and 5 per cent Malays. Other ethnic minorities include Laotian, Vietnamese, Kampuchean and a number of hill tribes.

Religions

Buddhist (85 per cent), Muslim (4 per cent), Christian (0.5 per cent), Hindu and Confucian.

Education

Primary schooling lasts for six years until students are aged 13 when they progress to the lower secondary school. At aged 16 students may either follow a general academic or vocational path in an upper secondary school.
There are 16 universities in Thailand, of which 12 are in Bangkok. There are also 21 recognised private colleges of higher education. Culturally, higher education is biased towards the social sciences and humanities, with science and technology accounting for only 22 per cent of total tertiary enrolment.
The education system in Thailand is undergoing major reforms. The main objective is the eventual decentralisation of education in the country as in 2001, policy was implemented through a central office, regional office, provincial office, then a district office. From August 2002 it will be administered through a central office, a local area education office and the school.
The government hopes to transform the learning process from a teacher-oriented system to a learner-oriented method. There are plans to introduce more technology in education.

Literacy rate: 93 per cent adult rate; 98 per cent youth rate (15–24) (Unesco 2005).

Compulsory years: Six to 16

Enrolment rate: 89 per cent gross primary enrolment; 59 per cent gross secondary enrolment, of relevant age groups (including repeaters), (World Bank).

Pupils per teacher: 21 in primary schools

Health

It is estimated that only 10 per cent of the population have pre-paid health insurance plans. Improve access to healthcare has been promised by the government by implementing a standard B30 (US$0.70) per hospital visit rule across the country. There are fears, however, that the reduced cost will entail a fall in healthcare standards.

The government has as a central objective, the standardisation of healthcare throughout the country. Plans stress the need to reorganise and decentralise public health administration. Private sector healthcare is expanding faster than the public sector, with private healthcare expenditure currently estimated to be running at double the public sector level.

Private hospitals (over 370) account for 25 per cent of all hospital beds.

The ministry of health provides free medical services to the poor in all government hospitals. Thailand has well over 1,000 public hospitals, over 13,000 specialised private clinics, over 8,000 health centres and an estimated 0.23 doctors per 1,000 of the population. The health of the Thai population has improved significantly over the last 20–30 years with life expectancy rising by 17 years, the infant mortality rate dropping by about two-thirds and the proportion of the population with access to safe drinking water more than trebling.

HIV/Aids

In a region where conservative leaders have been reluctant to publicly endorse HIV/Aids prevention programmes, Thailand took the initiative in 1994 and introduced a full scale public education and condom distribution programme, so that by 2004 people newly testing HIV positive fell to 21,260, vastly less than the peak of 142,819 in 1991.

HIV prevalence: 1.5 per cent aged 15–49 in 2003 (World Bank)

Life expectancy: 70 years, 2004 (WHO 2006)

Fertility rate/Maternal mortality rate: 1.6 births per woman, 2010 (Unicef); maternal mortality 44 deaths per 100,000 (World Bank).

Birth rate/Death rate: 16.4 births and 6.9 deaths per 1,000 people (2003)

Child (under 5 years) mortality rate (per 1,000): 13 per 1,000 live births (WHO 2012); 18 per cent of children aged under five were malnourished (World Bank).

Welfare

The social insurance bill provides for cover during illness or accidents unrelated to work, maternity, disability, funeral expenses, child welfare, pensions and unemployment. The welfare system was radically restructured in 1997 with the introduction of a centralised Government Pension Fund (GPF) worth about B71 billion (US$1.57 billion), replacing the old civil service pension scheme with a privately managed autonomous entity.

The labour department of the Ministry of the Interior manages workers' security and welfare and oversees a compensation fund for workers. In 70 out of 73 provinces, employers with more than 20 workers are required by law to contribute to the compensation fund. This fund provides benefits to employees who suffer injury in the workplace, or who fall ill or die as a result of the performance of their work. On average, 60 per cent of the monthly wages will be paid. This amount should not fall below B2,000 (US$46) and should not exceed B9,000 (US$206). Medical expenses are also paid in the case of an injury and in the case of death, the funeral expenses will be covered by the employer.

The public welfare department (PWD) of the Ministry of the Interior provides welfare services to various groups of people such as children and the young, landless farmers, hill tribe minorities, the destitute, the disabled, the handicapped, the aged and those hit by disaster.

Thaksin Shinawatra has ambitious objectives to deal with social problems in Thailand. These include plans to establish family advisory centres and childcare clinics.

Child prostitution in Thailand has received strong international attention. Eradicating the trade in children and women is likely to be a slow process for Thailand, since anti-trafficking laws have been difficult to implement. Female unemployment in Thailand remains high, so many turn to prostitution to earn their living.

Main cities

Bangkok (Krung Thep) (capital, estimated population 5.9 million (m) in 2012), Samut Prakan (465,588), Nonthaburi (435,512), Udon Thani (231,520), Pak Kret (211,977), Chon Buri (205,223), Phra Pradaeng (205,108), Hat Yai (202,587), Nakhon Ratchasima (200,384), Si Racha (199,623).

Languages spoken

Business is conducted in Thai. Chinese (mainly the Zhiu Zhou dialect from southern China) is spoken in major towns. Many senior government officials and businessmen speak some English which, along with French and German, is increasingly being used in tourist areas. Malay and indigenous languages are spoken.

Official language/s

Thai

Media

Much of terrestrial television and radio is controlled and operated by the government and military.

Press

Dailies: In Thai, main newspapers includes the mass-circulation *Daily News* (www.dailynews.co.th) and *Thairath* (www.thairath.co.th); other local and regional publications include *Thai Post* (www.thaipost.net) and *Matichon* (www.matichon.co.th), principal in of a media network. In English, the principal example include *The Bangkok Post* (www.bangkokpost.co.th) and *The Nation* (www.nationmultimedia.com) and Chiang Mai (www.chiangmai-mail.com).

Weeklies: Daily newspapers produce weekend editions including, in Thai, *Matichon*.

The UK-based *The Economist* was banned in January 2009 for what the authorities called 'insulting the King' (*lèse majesté*) in an article that questioned the monarch's role in public life.

Business: In Thai, *Krungthep Turakij* (www.bangkokbiznews.com), *Manager* (www.manager.co.th), *Post Today* (www.posttoday.com), *Prachachat Turakij* (www.matichon.co.th/prachachat), *Siam Turakij* (www.siamturakij.com) and *Than Settikij* (www.thannews.th.com); in English, *Business Day* (http://www.biz-day.com), *Thailand News and Press Releases* (www.thailand4.com) is a business media outlet.

Periodicals: Various international publications such as *New York Times*, *Newsweek*, *The Economist* and *Asiaweek* are sold by newsagents.

Broadcasting

Radio: The National Broadcasting Service of Thailand (NBT) (www.prd.go.th) operates a national network and external service which broadcasts in nine languages, including English. There are many commercial including MCOT (http://radio.mcot.net) and Bangkok FM (www.bangkokfm.com) and non-commercial radio stations, such as KU Radio network (http://radio.ku.ac.th) operated by Kasetsart University and Army Radio (www.tv5.co.th).

Television: NBT operates Channel 11 (www.prd.go.th); Thailand Independent Television (TiTV) and Modernine TV (http://modernine.mcot.net) are government operated; TV5 (www.tv5.co.th) and BBTV (www.ch7.com) are operated by the Royal Thai Army. Thai TV3 (www.becnews.com) is commercial.

National news agency: Thai News Agency (MCOT)

Economy

With an export-led economy, the strength, or otherwise, of global trade has a significant impact on the Thai economy. With full employment, Thailand attracts an estimated 2-4 million migrant workers from neighbouring countries, and faces labour shortages. Following the May 2014 coup d'état, tourism decreased 6-7 per cent but is beginning to recover. In 2013, the Thai government implemented a nation-wide US$10 minimum wage per day policy and deployed new tax reforms designed to lower tax rates on middle-income earners.

The industrial sector constituted 33 per cent of GDP in 2014, of which manufacturing was the largest component, including manufactured items such as computers and electronics, furniture, food stuffs, jewellery and toys and plastic products. The global economic crisis caused trade to weaken in 2009 and industrial annual production fell to -5 per cent, while manufacturing production fell by 6.1 per cent, particularly in capital goods and hi-tech products such as integrated circuits and hard disk drives, vehicles and electrical goods. From 2011 through to 2014, apart from a short spike in 2013, industrial production has shown consistent small negative growth. The industrial production growth rate was -1.1 per cent in 2014.

The service sector constituted 56 per cent of GDP in 2014, of which tourism was the largest component- – in 2014 travel and tourism directly contributed 19.3 per cent to GDP (US$66 billion). Thailand has been subject to a series of external and internal shocks since 2008, including the global pandemic swine flu, the mobbing of the international airport in Bangkok by protestors, the global economic crisis (tourist numbers fell to 6.6 million in the first half of 2009 (7.88 million in the same period in 2008)) and the political turmoil at the beginning of 2010, which was estimated to have cut visitor numbers by 1–2 million and cost the economy over US$4 billion. Following the May 2014 coup d'état, tourism decreased 6-7 per cent but is beginning to recover. Experience has shown that Thailand's popularity with tourists typically allows a quick reversal of such ill fortune – in 2013 the number of tourists hit a record high of 26.7 million, which was a 19.6 per cent increase on 2012. Tourist numbers visiting Thailand fell to 24.7 million in 2014, a 6.6 per cent drop on 2013 figures.

The economy fell into recession at the beginning of 2009 as GDP for the year fell 2.3 per cent. The government introduced a series of stimulus packages from 2008–10, totalling 4.2 per cent of GDP, to help kick-start growth. Measures included tax instruments, capital investment and payments to workers on low incomes. Private and public consumption rose by 5.8 per cent in 2009 and by 2010 as world trade picked up and GDP growth rebounded to 7.8 per cent. However in 2011 devastating floods in and around the capital swamped thousands of factories and disrupted production causing a sharp drop in GDP, with growth estimated at 0.1 per cent. GDP growth rose to about 6.5 per cent as reconstruction stimulated the economy in 2012, however, it slowed to 2.9 per cent in 2013. The economy experienced slow growth and declining exports in 2014, in part due to political turmoil and sluggish global demand. GDP growth fell to 0.7 per cent in 2014.

Agriculture constituted 11.6 per cent of GDP in 2014 – Thailand is the world's leading rice exporter. A new government policy aimed at improving the lives of the rural poor was launched on 7 October 2011, whereby the government buys un-milled paddy rice directly from farmers for 50 per cent above the prevailing market price. This will cut out the independent merchants, who have previously exported some one third of Thailand's rice production. Not only will taxpayers be required to fund this scheme (estimated at US$8 billion per annum), but recent international food shortages have occurred, due in part to hoarding of rice by other Asian countries. This cut in exports by the world's leading rice exporter could exacerbate a shortage of rice on the international market. In February 2014 Indonesia claimed that Thailand had been dumping excess rice from the subsidy scheme – that ended in early 2014 -– in Indonesia.

In 2014, the UN Human Development Index (HDI) ranked Thailand 89 (out of 187), a drop of 14 places from 2013 for national development in health, education and income. In 2014, 1 per cent of the population lived in multidimensional poverty and 0.4 per cent of the population lived under US1.25 per day. Personal remittances in 2014 were US$5.7 billion, (1.3 per cent of GDP).

External trade

Thailand belongs to the Association of Southeast Asian Nations (Asean) Free Trade Area (Afta) and maintains a list of goods that have preferential import duties between members and a programme of tariff reductions due to be introduced in the next few years. It also belongs to the 21-member Asia-Pacific Economic Co-operation (Apec) forum, which is a bloc of countries that border the Pacific with the aim of facilitating trade, economic growth and investment in the region.

A diversified manufacturing sector provides a wide range of export commodities from rice (Thailand is a world producer), rubber, steel, tin, vehicles, hi-tech electronic goods, garments, seafood and processed food and electricity.

Imports

Principal imports are capital goods, intermediate goods and raw materials, consumer goods, petroleum and natural gas.

Main sources: China (16.9 per cent of total in 2014), Japan (15.6 per cent), US (6.4 per cent), Malaysia (5.6 per cent) and the UAE (5.6 per cent).

Exports

Principal exports are vehicles and parts, crude oil, computers and electronic goods and electrical appliances, textiles and footwear, agricultural and fishery products, rice, natural rubber, jewellery.

Main destinations: China (11 per cent of total in 2014), US (10.5 per cent), Japan (9.6 per cent), Malaysia (5.6 per cent) and Hong Kong (5.5 per cent).

Agriculture

Farming

Agriculture accounts for 11.6 per cent of GDP and employs 32.2 per cent of the workforce. The rise of the manufacturing industry has meant that agriculture's share of GDP is declining, although farming still provides income for a significant portion of the population.

About 39 per cent of the total land area is cultivated. Production has generally been increased by expansion of planted acreage, rather than productivity improvements such as irrigation or use of fertilisers. Yield per paddy is one of the lowest in south-east Asia.

Thailand is known as the rice bowl of Asia and is one of the world's leading net exporters of food. The principal rice-growing area is the Chao Phya river basin. Tapioca is mainly produced in the south-east, kenaf in the north-east and maize in the central plain. Thailand is the world's largest exporter of natural rubber. Over 90 per cent of the rubber is produced in the south and most of it is exported through Penang in Malaysia.

Other major crops include sugar, cassava, cotton, jute, tobacco, fruit (especially pineapples), beans, oilseeds and coffee.

Livestock raised includes pigs, cattle, sheep and poultry. Buffaloes, oxen, horses and elephants are used as draught animals.

Crocodiles are farmed for their skins.

Agricultural co-operatives are organised by farmers to help co-ordinate joint farming activities and to provide low interest credits to members. The ministry of agriculture and co-operatives regulates the co-operatives.

A government policy aimed at improving the lives of the rural poor, which was launched on 7 October 2011, was stopped in February 2014. Under the policy the government bought directly from farmers un-milled paddy rice for 50 per cent above the prevailing market price. This cut out the independent merchants, who have previously exported some one third of Thailand's rice production. Not only were taxpayers required to fund this scheme (estimated at US$8 billion per annum), but recent international food shortages have occurred due in part to hoarding of rice by other Asian countries. This cut in exports by the world's leading rice exporter exacerbated this shortage of rice on the international market.

Fishing

Thailand is the world's main exporter of fish and seafood. Exports typically earn US$4 billion per year. Shrimp products account for over half of the export revenue. Canned tuna is another important export item, typically accounting for 15 per cent of export revenue. The government has focussed on upgrading the fishing industry by cutting production and improving product quality. Shrimp exporters are moving to create more ready-to-eat fish-based products.

Forestry

Forests are estimated to cover 17 per cent of total land area, with a further 18 per cent subject of a reforestation programme following a rapid decrease in the 1980s. There has been a ban on logging in natural forests since 1989 and the government has implemented a number of measures to protect the remaining forests and encourage plantation forest management.

Industry and manufacturing

Thailand's major industries are frozen shrimps, processed vegetables and fruit, leather products, automobiles, petrochemicals, textiles and garments, agricultural processing and household electrical appliances.

Thailand produces about 1.0 million tonnes of canned vegetables and fruit per year, most of which is exported. Tinned pineapples make up about 61 per cent of total output. Major competitors in the canned fruit industry include the Philippines, Indonesia, China and Kenya. Thai producers are being encouraged to improve their manufacturing techniques and improve product quality. Diversification would also make Thai products more competitive in the international marketplace. There are only a few well-known Thai items among fruit and vegetable consumers. These are mainly pineapples, longans, lychees, baby corn and bamboo shoots.

The main markets for Thai finished leather are China, Singapore, Indonesia and Vietnam. The Thai leather industry faces severe competition from India and Pakistan.

The slowdown in the global economy has intensified competition in Thailand's textile industry. The US and Japan are Thailand's major markets for textiles and garments. Economic problems in each country meant that demand for these products decreased. The major problem for Thailand is China. In 2001, China was admitted to the World Trade Organisation (WTO). With lower manufacturing costs, higher wages and a wide production base, China is becoming a serious threat in Asia-Pacific. The main challenge for Thailand is to produce individual goods and improve efficiency to cope with the competition. Malaysia and Taiwan have overtaken China as the best countries in the world to open factories in 2014 and, therefore, putting even more pressure on Thailand which will have to adjust its industry sector to keep up with the increasing competition.

The US is also an important market for Thai household appliances and absorbs 20 per cent of total exports in this sector. Japan is another major importer of air conditioners and refrigerators. Thailand is the largest producer of refrigerators in South-east Asia, producing 2 million units per year.

Sony will launch a new smartphone factory in Thailand, setting up a start-to-finish production system, covering chip mounting through assembly. Initial investment is expected to total several billion yen, mass production will begin in fiscal 2016, with initial volume predicted to reach several million units a year. The new Thai factory will be Sony's first plant for the mobile communications segment in 20 years; the last one was built in Beijing through a joint venture with three local partners.

Mazda has started production of engines in Thailand – the 'most important production location outside Japan'. The plant is able to produce 30,000 engines per year. According to the managing executive officer, Thailand is their most important production location outside of Japan because the workforce are capable of comprehensive vehicle manufacture, including engine and transmission production as well as vehicle assembly.

Automotive manufacturing in Thailand grew 13.3 per cent in 2014, compared to figures in 2013 while exports also rose 13.9 per cent. Despite the success in Thailand's automotive manufacturing sector, the production of electronics goods and electrical appliances plunged 25.1 per cent year-on-year. The reason for this is weakening domestic purchasing power and economic slowdown in Thailand's key export markets, including the EU and Japan. A further reason is that a television-manufacturing base in Thailand has relocated to produce in another Southeast Asian country. Competition with Chinese steel producers has also pushed the country's steel production down by 14.9 per cent.

Tourism

Following the May 2014 coup d'état, tourism decreased 6-7 per cent but is beginning to recover. Tourist numbers visiting Thailand fell to 24.7 million in 2014, a 6.6 per cent drop on 2013 figures. Thailand has fallen two spots due to their poor year in 2014 as the fourth most popular destination in Asia, now behind China, Hong Kong and Malaysia.

In 2013, Chinese visitors, for the second year in a row, were the most numerous with 4.7 million tourists followed by Malaysia and Russia. Visitors from the UK, who had been the third most numerous in 2009 (841,425) fell to tenth in 2013 as visitors, among others, from South Korea, Japan and India outnumbered them.

Thailand has many historic sites and its capital, Bangkok, is renowned for its wealth of temples. Its coastline has a range of resorts and hotels, some locally owned and operated and some owned by international chains.

There is a good rail service, with tourist quality comfort that connects the north and south of the country, plus train, ferry and bus services providing access to other areas within Thailand as well as with its neighbours.

In 2014 travel and tourism directly contributed 19.3 per cent to GDP (US$66 billion), providing employment to 14.1 per cent of the workforce (5.4 million jobs). Although the global economic crisis had an adverse effect on the tourist industry in 2010, when it only contributed 14.4 per cent of GDP and employment dropped to 11.2 per cent of the workforce (4.3 million jobs) by 2013 a strong recovery had been made, although that has slightly diminished in 2014.

Although Thailand is a popular destination for Western tourists it has picked up an undesirable reputation as a place for sleaze and sex-tourism.

Environment

In July 2012 Thai customs officials seized almost 500,000 tonnes of Kenyan ivory, worth an estimated US$700,000, being smuggled through Bangkok's airport. The raw elephant tusks, poached in Kenya, were expected to be turned into jewellery or decorative carvings or used in traditional medicines.

Mining

Mining accounts for around 2.5 per cent of GDP and employs three per cent of the workforce.

Mining has been officially designated a priority economic sector eligible for preferential tax and promotional privileges from the Board of Investment. The Bank of Thailand sets guidelines for private commercial banks to extend loans to the sector at prime lending rates.
Although many reserves remain largely unexploited, Thailand has a rich variety of mineral resources, including antimony, fluorite, iron ore, lead, lignite, limestone, manganese, precious stones, tungsten and zinc.
Thailand is the world's second-largest tungsten producer and the third-largest tin producer.
Tin, which is produced in northern, central and southern Thailand, is the most important mining commodity in terms of revenue. It is estimated that only 30 out of 145 tin mines are still active in the country.
Thailand is the world's biggest gem exporter. Low cost labour has helped Thailand remain a leading exporter. China is expected to become a major competitor in gem production and export. While Thailand's gem industry is more developed, China's lower priced stones have already entered the market.

Hydrocarbons
The publicly owned Petroleum Authority of Thailand (PTT) implements the national energy policy and is responsible for exploration, production, transmission and sale of oil and gas through subsidiary companies. It also manages international trade in hydrocarbons.
The government, in the face of oil price surges, encouraged refiners to reduce imports and increase domestic production; total refinery capacity was 1.1 million bpd in 2013. Thai Oil plans to spend US$1.8 million in expansion of some of the major refineries in Thailand. There are a total of seven oil refineries in operation; the three major refineries are Thai Oil Refinery, IRPC Refinery and PTT Global Chemical Refinery.
Proven crude oil reserves were 449 million barrels in 2014 with production at 454,000 bpd. Refined petroleum production amounted to 914,000 bpd while consumption was approximately 1,000,000 bpd. Around 794,000 bpd are imported to make up the difference.
Proven reserves of natural gas was 256 billion cum in 2014 while production was 41.3 billion cum. Consumption was 50.1 billion cum and therefore the difference of 9.6 billion cum needed to be imported.
Thailand relies on imports from Myanmar via an international pipeline to make up its shortfall. Most of the output is used for electricity generation. Bongkot, in the Gulf of Thailand, is the largest gas field supplying up to 35 per cent of national demand.
Thailand is active in the area of gas exploration, particularly in the Malaysian-Thailand Joint Development Area (JDA) in the Gulf of Thailand. By 2013, 238 billion cubic metres (cum) of proved and probable natural gas reserves were found over 22 fields. Chevron is the largest producer of oil and gas in Thailand and supplies around 40 per cent of the country's natural gas. The company has interests in many projects in Thailand and is the operator of the Platong II project, a US$3.1 billion site in the Gulf of Thailand that produces 9.3 million cum of natural gas per day.
A new, US$700 million, 5 million tonne per year, liquefied natural gas (LNG) terminal has been constructed at Rayong, south-east of Bangkok. In 2013, the Rayong LNG Terminal had a capacity of 18.7 million cum per day.
Proven coal reserves were 1.24 billion tonnes in 2011, of less valuable and polluting lignite (brown coal); around 90 per cent of all coal is produced in the north at Mae Moh. Total production was 6.0 million tonnes oil equivalent (mtoe). Thailand imports coal to meet domestic requirements.

Energy
Total installed generating capacity was 32.6GW in 2012 (with a further 11.7GW generated privately for personal consumption). Around 89 per cent of generation is provided by fossil fuel, with natural gas as the principal source, providing around 70 per cent of the total. Around 90 per cent of the country's coal output is used in the Mae Moh power plant in the north of Thailand, providing around 15 per cent of total electricity generation. Hydroelectricity plants provide 11 per cent of electricity production.
Several large hydroelectric projects have been suspended due to environmental and social issues of deforestation and displaced people. Instead over 25 small dams of up to 25MW are planned.
Electricity is imported from Laos and Malaysia. There is a connection with Cambodia under construction, which should become operational by 2016.
Other renewable energy sources include geothermal, biomass gas and wind power.

Financial markets
Stock exchange
The Stock Exchange of Thailand (SET)

Banking and insurance
Thailand set up the Thai Asset Management Corporation (TAMC) in 2001 to take over bad loans in the banking sector. The high level of non-performing loans has prevented Thailand's banks from functioning properly. Banks have been reluctant to lend and this has made economic recovery difficult.
Internal reform also continued in 2001–02 as part of the ongoing restructuring drive. The implementation of risk management systems has been high on the agenda. Siam Commercial Bank, Thailand's most profitable bank is concentrating on upgrading technology and attracting more customers to its internet banking system. Thai Farmers Bank underwent major restructuring, splitting its branches into different departments and making them more customer-oriented.
Central bank
Bank of Thailand
Main financial centre
Bangkok

Time
GMT plus seven hours

Geography
Thailand is situated in the Indo-Chinese peninsula, sharing borders with Myanmar to the west and north, Laos to the east and north, Cambodia to the east and Malaysia to the south.
Thailand can be divided into four regions – the central alluvial plain, the semi-arid plateau of the north-east, the mountainous north and the southern peninsula. It covers an area of 513,115 square km, about the size of France, and measures 1,650km from north to south and 800km from west to east. It has a coastline of 2,400km.
Its narrowest part is the Kra Isthmus, which is about 64km wide, with the Gulf of Thailand to the east and the Andaman Sea to the west.
Hemisphere
Northern

Climate
The climate varies from tropical savannah in the north and tropical monsoon in the south. There are three main seasons: hot (March–May), rainy (June–October) and cool (November–February). In Bangkok temperatures range from 25 degrees Celsius (C) in December to 34 degrees C in April and May.

Dress codes
Light, loose cotton clothing is advisable, although it should be modest. Sweaters may be needed in the evenings and during the cooler season. Businessmen wear shirts and ties, while jackets are worn for official functions or meetings with government officials; jackets and ties may be required for evening wear at larger hotels.
Smart attire is also expected of businesswomen.

Entry requirements

Passports

Required by all and must be valid for six months beyond date of visit.

Visa

Required by all; a list of exceptions for certain nationals visiting as tourists are listed at www.thai-la.net, follow link to visa.

A business visitor must complete a non-immigrant visa application and produce a letter of invitation from a Thai company, printed on a company letterhead. The letter must include the host company's registration, stating the 'capital investment' and documentation of the payment of the last two years' taxes. Proof of visit for business purposes must also be furnished along with a letter of approval by the Thai Labour Department. Business visas are only valid for up to 90 days. Extensions, for either tourist or business visas, may be granted by the Immigration Bureau in Thailand.

Prohibited entry

Entry is refused to nationals of Afghanistan unless in transit within three hours. Entry may be refused to persons of untidy appearance.

Currency advice/regulations

The import and export of foreign currency is unlimited. The import of local currency is unlimited; export of amounts greater than B50,000 require prior authorisation. Travellers cheques are accepted in most banks.

Customs

Personal effects are allowed duty-free. Radio equipment requires a permit and cameras, computers and luxury jewellery must be declared at customs.

Export of images or statues of Buddha, antiques and archaeologically valuable items is only allowed with a certificate from the Department of Fine Arts. Articles exceeding B10,000 in value require a Certificate of Exportation.

Prohibited imports

Illegal drugs, pornographic material, firearms and ammunition. Live animals and meat, plants and plant material require a permit.

Health (for visitors)

Mandatory precautions

A vaccination certificate for yellow fever is required if travelling from an infected area.

Advisable precautions

Inoculations and boosters should be current for diphtheria, tetanus, hepatitis A, polio and typhoid. Other vaccinations that may be recommended are cholera, tuberculosis, and Japanese B encephalitis and hepatitis B. Use malaria prophylaxis (which will also provide protection against dengue fever and hepatitis B) including mosquito repellents, sleeping nets and clothing that cover the body after dark. There is a risk of rabies in rural areas. Use only bottled or boiled water for drinks, washing teeth and making ice. Eat only well cooked meals, preferably served hot; vegetables should be cooked and fruit peeled. Dairy products are unpasteurised and should be avoided. Avoid pork and salad and food from street vendors. A full first-aid kit would be useful.

Locally manufactured Western proprietary medicines are easily obtainable, but visitors on regular medication should bring their own supplies – amounts for the length of the visit only.

Visitors should have medical insurance, including emergency evacuation.

Hotels

Choose a hotel in the district in which you are doing business. Most top hotels have good facilities for meetings and can arrange secretarial services if notified in advance. A 10 per cent service charge and 11 per cent tax are added to hotel bills, and it is customary to give small tips for good service.

Credit cards

Major credit and charge cards are widely accepted.

Public holidays (national)

Fixed dates

1 Jan (New Year), 6 Apr (Chakri Day), 13–16 Apr (Songkran/Thai New Year), 1 May (Labour Day), 5 May (Coronation Day), 9 Aug (Sin National Day), 12 Aug (Queen's Birthday), 23 Oct (Chulalongkorn Day), 5 Dec (King's Birthday), 10 Dec (Constitution Day).

Holidays falling on a weekend are taken on the following Monday/Tuesday.

Variable dates

Chinese New Year (Jan/Feb), Makha Bucha Day (Feb), Visakha Bucha Day (May), Asanha Bucha Day (Jul), Buddhist Lent Day (Jul), Naga Fire Ball (Oct), Loy Kratong (Nov).

Religious festivals are determined by the Buddhist lunar calendar.

Working hours

Banking

Mon–Fri: 0830–1530.

Business

Mon–Fri: 0830–1700. Sat: 0830–1200.

Government

Mon–Fri: 0830–1630.

Shops

Mon–Sun: 0900–1800/1900. Some shops are open 24 hours.

Telecommunications

Mobile/cell phones

There are 900, 1800 and 1900 GSM services throughout most of the country.

Electricity supply

220V AC, 50 cycles for domestic use, with plug fittings having two round or flat pins.

Weights and measures

Metric system (local units also in use).

Social customs/useful tips

Always carry business cards and give them to any new acquaintance when introduced. To show respect, offer and accept business cards with both hands, and always read the cards you receive before putting them down.

To the Thais *face* is very important and losing it can be disastrous, with little chance of social recovery; all dealings should be controlled, polite and respectful.

Thai business relationships, networks and associations can be extensive and visitors should expect to spend much time cultivating contacts.

Both men and women should dress in smart, lightweight casual wear. Shorts, bare shoulders, and sandals would be inappropriate in a business setting. Westerners are expected to shake hands and Thais are willing to accommodate this practice. Thai women, however, may still be reluctant to shake hands, and may prefer simply to exchange smiles on being introduced. Thais address each other and foreign visitors by their forename, prefixed by *khun*.

The head is considered the most esteemed part of the body and the feet the least, so visitors should take care not to touch someone's head (even accidentally) or show the soles of their feet.

Images of Buddha are held sacred and cannot be taken out of Thailand without official permission.

Shoes should be removed when entering a Thai house or Buddhist temple. Women must never touch a Buddhist monk, give things to him, or receive things from him, directly.

It is a criminal offence to make critical or defamatory comments about the King or other members of the Royal family, punishable by a sentence of three to 15 years.

Security

Experienced business visitors should not encounter any problems, particularly in central Bangkok. However, Thailand's position in the world drug trade, puts the gullible traveller at risk. It is advisable to lock all luggage and keep it in sight while travelling. Do not accept anything to be taken through customs on behalf of someone else.

Getting there

Air

National airline: Thai Airways International.

International airport/s: The Suvarnabhumi-Bangkok Airport (BKK) (opened in September 2006), 25km east of the city, is the central hub for Thai Airways and the country's principal commercial airport. Facilities include duty-free shopping, restaurants, entertainment, bank, post office, hotel reservations, car hire and business suites. There are train, bus and metered taxi services; limousines, either luxury or 4WD-SUV, are available. In March 2007 Don Muang, the original Bangkok international airport, was re-opened to ease congestion at Suvarnabhumi, caused mostly by the increase in traffic from low-cost airlines. Suvarnabhumi Airport is the world's second largest (after Hong Kong International Airport) single building and terminal (563,000 square metres), it took six years to build and cost around US$3 billion. Chiang Mai International (CNX); Phuket International (HKT), 35km from Phuket; Hat Yai International (HDY), 9km from Hat Yai.

Other airport/s: Don Muang International, 30km north of Bangkok was decommissioned after the new Suvarnabhumi-Bangkok airport was opened in September 2006. It may re-open for udget airlines to use its facilities.

Airport tax: Departure tax: B700, excluding transit passengers.

Surface

Road: The Asian Highway runs from the northern region through Bangkok and on to southern Thailand, crossing the border with Malaysia and ending in Singapore. The Friendship Bridge in the north links Thailand and Laos.

Rail: There are daily rail services, including the Eastern and Oriental Express, between Singapore, Penang, Kuala Lumpur and Bangkok (including a ferry ride). Trains are air-conditioned with sleeper-coaches (journey time 48 hours). A service runs from Bangkok to Phnom Peng (Cambodia) and through to Saigon (Vietnam). The journey time is over 24 hours and the trains are more basic in facilities.

Water: Passenger liners occasionally visit. International shipping lines that maintain contacts with Thailand may provide passenger services on cargo ships. Limited ferry services are available from Cambodia, Laos and Malaysia.

Main port/s: Bangkok

Getting about

National transport

Considerable investment is earmarked for improving the country's transport facilities. In remote areas conditions are still uncertain, and banditry occurs in the north-west of the country.

Air: Thai Airways and Bangkok Airways operate domestic services to main centres.

Road: There are over 64,000km of national and provincial roads and highways, most of which are paved. Major highways are four-lanes. Toll roads exist around Bangkok.

Buses: Long-distance (air-conditioned) express coaches operate between main centres; local services are not generally recommended.

Rail: Thailand's railway network is controlled by the State Railway of Thailand (SRT), which is responsible for building, operating and maintaining Thailand's 4,600km of railway track.

Rail services are generally recommended: the system is equipped with modern rolling stock, including air-conditioned coaches, sleeping accommodation and restaurant cars on main express services. All main lines originate in Bangkok. Four main routes radiate from Bangkok's main station (Hualompong), with the track to the south extending to the Malaysian border.

Water: There are 1,110–1,600km of navigable inland waterways, depending on the season. Various types of ferries and passenger/cargo boats operate on rivers and in coastal areas.

City transport

Avoid rush-hour travel; hours-long traffic jams are routine in Bangkok, the fastest method of travel is either the metro or a motorbike taxi.

Taxis: Taxis have yellow number plates and, although they are metered, fares should be agreed in advance; a surcharge is imposed during traffic jams. Tipping is not customary.

Taxi drivers rarely understand English and it is best to have the name and address of one's destination written in Thai to show to the driver. There are air-conditioned limousine services provided by main hotels. *Tuk tuks* are motorised trishaws.

Buses, trams & metro: The metro consists of two networks, the underground and the over-ground. Tokens for single trips or cards for frequent travel are not interchangeable between the two networks, however work is underway to unify the system. The metro system is planned to be 91km long with three lines covering major areas of Bangkok by 2009.

Trains: The Bangkok Mass Transit System opened in 1999. The subway, a new mass transit system, opened on 3 July 2004.

Helicopter: Royal Orchid Sheraton jointly operates a helicopter service between the airport and the River City shopping complex next to the hotel, with a flight time of seven minutes. There is a five-minute walk by connecting bridge to the hotel.

Car hire

Chauffeur-driven car hire is available in Bangkok, Pattaya, Hat Yai, Phuket and Chiang Mai. It is not advisable to drive yourself in Bangkok. An international driving licence is required and driving is on the left. A driving licence is required to ride motorcycles.

BUSINESS DIRECTORY

The addresses listed below are a selection only. While World of Information makes every endeavour to check these addresses, we cannot guarantee that changes have not been made, especially to telephone numbers and area codes. We would welcome any corrections.

Telephone area codes

The international direct dialling code for Thailand is +66, followed by area code and subscriber's number:

Bangkok	2	Nakhon Ratchasima	44
Chiang Mai	53	Nakhon Sawan	56
Khon Kaen	43	Phuket	76
Lampang	54	Udon Thani	42

Useful telephone numbers

Metropolitan Mobile Police: 123, 191, 246-1338/42

Tourist Assistance Centre: 195, 281-5051

Capital Security Police: 123

Fire: 199, 246-0199

Ambulance: 252-2171/75

Directory (Bangkok): 13

Directory (provinces): 183

International calls: 100

Rail travel: 223-1431

Chambers of Commerce

American Chamber of Commerce in Thailand, Kian Gwan Building, 140 Wireless Road, Bangkok 10330 (tel: 251-9266; fax: 651-4472; e-mail: service@amchamthailand.com).

British Chamber of Commerce Thailand, 208 Wireless Road, Bangkok (tel: 651-5350; fax: 651-5354; e-mail: info@bccthai.com).

Chiang Mai Chamber of Commerce, Hillside Plaza and Condotel, Huai-Kaew Road, Chiang Mai 50300 (tel: 223-256; fax: 222-482).

Khon Kaen Chamber of Commerce, 359 Mittaphab Road, Khon Kaen 4000 (tel: 224-521; fax: 225-719; e-mail: info@kkchamber.com).

Nakhon Ratchasima Chamber of Commerce, 1818 Suranarai Road, Nakhon Ratchasima 30000 (tel: 296-120; fax: 296-124).

Phuket Chamber of Commerce, 1 Montree Road, Phuket 83000 (tel: 217-567; fax: 232-038; e-mail: cham,ber@phuket.ksc.co.th).

Thai Chamber of Commerce, 150 Rajabophit Road, Bangkok 10200 (tel: 225-0086; fax: 225-4913; e-mail: tcc@tcc.or.th).

Banking

Bangkok Bank PCL, 333 Silom Road, Bangkok (tel: 231-4333; fax: 236-8281/2).

Bangkok Bank of Commerce Ltd, 99 Surasak Road, Silom, Bangrak, Bangkok 10500 (tel: 234-9230, 235-5040/9; fax: 234-2939).

Bangkok Metropolitan Bank Ltd, 2 Chalermkhet 4 Street, Pomrab, Bangkok (tel: 223-0561; fax: 224-3768).

Bank of Agriculture and Agricultural Co-operatives, 469 Nakhon Sawan Road, Dusit, Bangkok 10300 (tel: 280-0180).

Bank of America NT & SA, 2/2 Wireless Road, Bangkok 10500 (tel: 251-6333; fax: 253-1905).

Bank of Asia PCL, 191 South Sathorn Road, Bangkok 10120 (tel: 287-2211/3; fax: 287-2973/4).

Bank of Ayuthaya Ltd, 1222 Rama III Road, Bangkok 10120 (tel: 296-2000, 683-1000; fax: 683-1304).

Bank of Toyko Ltd, 62 Silom Road, Bangkok (tel: 236-0119/9103; fax: 236-9110).

Chase Manhattan Bank, Siam Shopping Centre, 965 Rama I Road, Bangkok 10330 (tel: 252-1141).

Citibank NA, 127 Sathorn Tai Road, Bangkok (tel: 213-2441; fax: 213-2517).

Deutsche Bank, 21 Sathorn Tai Road, Bangkok (tel: 240-9401; fax: 240-9425).

Export-Import Bank of Thailand, Boon Pong Tower, 1193 Thanon Phahonyothin, Bangkok 10400 (tel: 271-3700, 278-0047; fax: 271-3204).

First Bangkok City Bank Ltd, 20 Yukhon Road 2, Pomrab, Bangkok (tel: 223-0501; fax: 225-3036).

Hongkong & Shanghai Banking Corporation, 64 Silom Road, Bangkok (tel: 267-3000; fax: 236-7687).

Import-Export Bank of Japan, 138 Silom Road, Bangkok 10500 (tel: 235-7373).

Industrial Finance Corp of Thailand, 1770 New Petchburi Road, Bangkapi, Bangkok 10320 (tel: 253-7111; fax: 253-9677).

International Commercial Bank of China, 36/12 PS Tower, Asoke, 21 Sukhumvit, Phrakhanong, Bangkok 10110 (tel: 259-2000; fax: 259-1330) .

Krung Thai Bank Ltd, 35 Sukhumvit Road, Bangkok (tel: 255-2222; fax: 255-9391/6).

Nakornthon Bank Ltd, 90 Sathonthanee Building, Sathorn Nua Road, Bangrak, Bangkok (tel: 233-2111; fax: 236-4226).

Siam Commercial Bank, 9 Rachadapisek Road, Bangkok (tel: 344-1111; fax: 937-7454).

Siam City Bank Public Company Limited, 1101 New Petchburi Road, Bangkok 10400 (tel: 208-5000/5043; fax: 253-1240).

Standard Chartered Bank, 990 Rama IV Road, Bangkok (tel: 636-1000; fax: 636-1198/9).

Thai Danu Bank Ltd, 393 Silom Road, Bangkok (tel: 233-9160/9; fax: 236-7939).

Thai Farmers Bank, 1 Thai farmers Lane, Rat Burana Road, Bangkok (tel: 470-1122; fax: 470-1571).

Thai Military Bank Ltd, 3000 Phahonyothin Rd, Bangkok 10900 (tel: 299-1111, 273-7020; fax: 273-7121/7124).

Central bank

Bank of Thailand, 273 Samsen Road, Bangkok 10200 (tel: 283-5353; fax: 280-0449).

Stock exchange

The Stock Exchange of Thailand (SET), www.set.or.th

The Market for Alternative Investment (Mai), www.mai.or.th

Agricultural Futures Exchange of Thailand (AFET), www.afet.or.th

Thailand Futures Exchange (TFEX), www.tfex.co.th

Travel information

Police (Tourist) (to reports a theft for insurance purposes), 29/1 Soi Lang Suan, Ploenchit Road, Lumpini, Bangkok (tel: 255-2964/8).

Royal Automobile Association of Thailand, 151, Soi Aphaisongkram, Phaholyothin, 10900, Bangkok (tel: 511-2230/1).

Thai Airways, 89 Vibhavadi Rangsit Road, Bangkok 9 10900 (tel: 356-1111; fax: 356-2222; internet: www.thaiairways.com).

Thai Hotels Association, 203-209/2 Rajdamnoen Klang Avenue, Bangkok 10200 (tel: 281-9496, 281-9579; fax: 281-4188).

National tourist organisation offices

Tourism Authority of Thailand, Le Concorde Building, 202 Rachadapisek Road, Huai Khwang, Bangkok 10320 (tel: 694-1222; fax: 694-1329, 694-1221; internet: www.tourismthailand.org).

Ministries

Ministry of Agriculture and Co-operatives, Thanon Ratchadamnoen Nok, Bangkok 10200 (tel: 281-5955, 281-5939; fax: 280-1691).

Ministry of Commerce, Thanon Samamchai, Bangkok 10200 (tel: 282-6171/9; fax: 280-0775).

Ministry of Defence, Thanon Samamchai, Bangkok 10200 (tel: 225-0098, 222-1121; fax: 226-3115).

Ministry of Education, Wang Chan Kasem, Thanon Ratchadamnoen Nok, Bangkok 10300 (tel: 280-0306).

Ministry of Finance, Thanon Rama VI, Bangkok 10400 (tel: 273-9021; fax: 293-9408).

Ministry of Foreign Affairs, Sri Ayutthaya Road, Bangkok 10400 (tel: 643-5000; fax: 643-5180).

Ministry of Industry, Thanon Rama VI, Bangkok 10400 (tel: 202-3000; fax: 202-3048).

Ministry of the Interior, Thanon Atsadang, Bangkok 10200 (tel: 222-1141/55; fax: 223-8851).

Ministry of Justice, Thanon Rachadaphisek, Chatuchak, Bangkok 10900 (tel: 541-2284/91; fax: 541-2307).

Ministry of Labour and Social Welfare, Thanon Mitmaitri, Dindaeng, Bangkok 10400 (tel: 245-4782; fax: 246-1520).

Ministry of Public Health, Thanon Tiwanond, Amphoe Muang, Nonthaburi 11000 (tel: 591-8491; fax: 591-8492).

Ministry of Science, Technology and Environment, Thanon Rama VI, Ratchathewi, Bangkok 10400 (tel: 246-0064; fax: 246-5146).

Ministry of Transport and Communications, 38 Thanon Ratchadanoen Nok, Bangkok 10100 (tel: 283-3000; fax: 281-3959).

Ministry of University Affairs, 328 Thanon Si Ayutthaya, Khet Ratchathewi, Bangkok 10400 (tel: 246-0025, 246-1106/14; fax: 245-8636, 245-8930, 246-8883).

Other useful addresses

ASEAN Secretariat, 70 A J1 Sisingamangaraja, Jakarta 12110, Indonesia (tel: 62(21)726-2991, 724-3372; fax: 724-3504, 739-8234; web: www.asean.or.id).

Bangkok Mass Transit Authority, 131 Tiumruammitr Road, Huay Kwang, Bangkok 10310 (tel: 246-0339, 246-0741/4, 246-0750/2).

Chiangmai Province Commercial Office, Chiangmai City Hall, Chotana Road, Muang District, Chiangmai 50300 (tel: 221-217; fax: 221-121).

Communications Authority of Thailand, 99 Chaeng Watthana Road, Bangkok 10002 (tel: 573-0099).

Customs Department, Atnarong Road, Klongtoey, Bangkok 10110 (tel: 249-0431, 671-7555/7).

Department of Export Promotion, 22/77 Rachadapisek Road, Bangkok 10900 (tel: 513-1909/15, 511-5066/77; fax: 512-1079, 513-1917).

Department of Foreign Trade, Samamchai Road, Bangkok 10110 (tel: 225-1315/29; fax: 224-7269, 225-4763).

Deparetment of Industrial Promotion,Thanon Rama VI, Ratchathewi, Bangkok 10400 (tel: 202-4415/6; fax: 246-0031)

Department of Local Administration, Thanon Asadang, Bangkok 10200 (tel: 222-3852, 222-8847; fax: 222-5858).

Department of Mineral Resources, Rama VI Road, Bangkok 10400 (tel: 246-0034, 246-1161/9).

Eastern Trader's Association for Exporting Fruit-Vegetable, 30/31-32 Trirat Road, Muang District, Chanthaburi 22000 (tel: 325-962; fax: 325-962).

Economic and Social Commission for Asia and the Pacific (ESCAP), United Nations Building, Bangkok (tel: 288-1234; fax: 288-1000).

Export Promotion Centre-Chanthaburi, 30/31-32 Trirat Road, Chanthaburi 22000 (tel: 325-962/3; fax: 325-962).

Export Promotion Centre-Chiang Mai, 29/19 Singharaj Road, Chiang Mai 50200 (tel: 216-350/1, 221-376; fax: 215-307).

Export Promotion Centre-Hat Yai, 7-15 Jootee-Uthit 1 Road, Hat Yai, Songkla 90110 (tel: 234-349, 231-744; fax: 234-329).

Export Promotion Centre-Khon Kaen, 68/4 Kiang Muang Road, Khon Kaen 40000 (tel: 221-472; fax: 221-476).

Export Promotion Centre-Surat Thani, 148/59 Surat-Nakornsri Road, Bang Kung, Surat Thani , Bangkok 84000 (tel: 286-916; fax: 288-632).

Export Service Centre, Department of Commercial Relations, Ministry of Commerce, 22–77 Thanon Rachadaphisek–Ladprao, Bangkok 10900 (tel: 513-1905).

Federation of Nakhon Ratchasima Industries, 269 Friendship Highway, Tambon Kokgruad Muang District, Nakhon Ratchasima 30280 (tel: 251-028; fax: 251-033).

Federation of Southern Industries, Songkhla Chapter, 165 Southern Industrial Promotion Center Building, 3rd Floor, Karnchanawanitch, Haadyai District, Songkhla 90110 (tel: 211-905).

Federation of Thai Industries, Queen Sirikit National Convention Center, Zone C 4th Floor, 60 New Rachadapisek Road, Klongtoey, Bangkok 10110 (tel: 229-4255; fax: 229-4941).

Federation of Thai Industries, Chiangmai and Nearby Chapter, Northern Industrial Promotion Centre Building, 1st Floor, 158 Tung Hotel Road, Muang District, Chiangmai 50000 (tel: 304-346; fax: 246-353).

Federation of Thai Industries, Khon Kaen Chapter, 359/2 Mittaphab Road, Muang District, Khon Kaen 40000 (tel: 225-679; fax: 225-678).

Federation of Thai Industries, Surathani Chapter, 160/19 Surat-Punpin Road, Makhamtia, Muang District, Surathani 84000 (tel: 285-722).

Federation of Thai Udon Thani Industries and Nearby Chapter, 83/14 Watana Road, Muang District, Udon Thani 41000 (tel: 242-004; fax: 246-498).

Fishery Association of Thailand, 1575 Charoen Nakom Road, Bangkok 10600 (tel: 437-0158/62; fax: 437-1262).

Foreign Bankers Association, 19th Floor, Sathorn Thani Building 2, 92/55 North Sathorn Road, Silom Bangrak, Bangkok 10500 (tel: 236-4730, 236-7224; fax: 236-4731).

Industrial Estate Authority of Thailand, 618 Nikhom Makkasan Road, Phayathai, Bangkok (tel: 253-0561).

Industrial Finance Corporation, 1770 New Petchaburi Road, Bangkok 10500 (tel: 253-7111, 253-9666; fax: 253-9677, 254-8098).

Lawyers Association, 26 Ratchadamnern Avenue, Bangkok 10220 (tel: 224-1873).

National Statistical Office, Lan Luang Road, Bangkok 10100 (tel: 281-3022; fax: 281-3815, 281-3848).

Northern Industrial Promotion Center, 158 Tung Hotel Road, Muang District, Chiangmai 50000 (tel: 245-361; fax: 248-315).

Northern Investment Promotion Office, 369/1 Charoenrat Road, Watgate, Muang District, Chiangmai 50000 (tel: 248-778; fax: 240-919).

Office of the Board of Investment, 555 Vibhavadi-Rangsit Road, (opposite Central Plaza Hotel), Chatuchak, Bangkok 10900 (tel: 537-8111, 537-8155; fax: 537-8177; email: head@boi.go.th).

Office of Foreign Trade, Sanambin Road, Suthep, Muang District, Chiangmai 50200 (tel: 274-672; fax: 277-901).

Office of the National Culture Commission, Thanon Ratchadapisek, Khet Huay Khwang, Bangkok 10310 (tel: 248-5839, 247-0013/19 (ext 201); fax: 248-5841, 248-5851, 248-5845).

Office of the National Economic and Social Development Board, 962 Krung Kasem, Bangkok 10100 (tel: 282-8434; fax: 282-0891).

Port Authority of Thailand, Thanon Sunthomkosa, (tel: 249-0362).

Prime Minister's Office, Government House, Thanon Nakhon Pathom, Bangkok 10300 (tel: 282-6543, 282-6877; fax: 282-8587, 282-8631).

Religious Affairs Department, Thanon Ratchamnoen Nok, Bangkok 10300 (tel: 281-6080 (ext 43, 74 or 40); fax: 281-5415).

Securities Exchange of Thailand, 32 Sinthon Building, Bangkok 10500 (tel: 250-0001/8).

Southern Industrial Economic Affairs Center, 3rd Floor, Songkhla Industrial Office Building, Karnchanawanitch Road, Muang district, Songkhla 90000 (tel: 321-166; fax: 321-167).

Southern Industrial Promotion Center, Department of Industrial Promotion, 165 Karnchanawanitch, Muang District, Songkhla 90110 (tel: 211-905).

Stock Exchange of Thailand (SET), Sinthon Building, 2nd Floor, 132 Wireless Road, Bangkok 10330 (tel: 254-0960, 254-0969, 256-7100, 256-7109; fax: 254-7120, 256-3040).

Telephone Organisation of Thailand, 89/2 Moo 3 Chaeng Wattana, Bangkok 10002 (tel: 505-1000; fax: 574-9533).

Thai Bankers' Association, 4th Floor, Lake Rachada Office Complex, Building II, Rachadapisek Road, Bangkok 10110 (tel: 264-0883/7; fax: 264-0888).

Thai Mining Association, 79 Prachatipatai Road, Banpanthom, Pranakom, Bangkok 10200 (tel: 282-8947/9; fax: 280-3786, 282-7372).

Thai Petrochemical Industry and Trade Association, 175-177 Surawong Road, Bangkok 10500 (tel: 238-2956/9; fax: 236-3110).

Thai Rice Mill Association, 81 Soi Rong Nam Kheng, Charoenkrung Road, Samphanthawong, Bangkok 10100 (tel: 235-7863, 234-7295; fax: 234-7286).

Trade Statistics Centre, Department of Business Economics, Ratchadamnoen Klang, Bangkok 10200 (tel: 282-6393, 280-1727; fax: 280-0775, 280-0826).

National news agency: Thai News Agency (MCOT)

Timor-Leste

KEY FACTS

Official name: República Democrática de Timor-Leste (Democratic Republic of Timor-Leste)

Head of State: President José Maria Vasconcelos, more popularly known under his *nom de guerre*,Taur Matan Ruak (from 20 May 2012)

Head of government: Prime Minister Rui Maria Araújo (Fretilin) from 16 Feb 2015)

Ruling party: Coalition led by Conselho Nacional de Reconstrução de Timor (CNRT) (National Congress for Timorese Reconstruction), with Partido Democrático (PD) (Democratic Party) and Frente de Reconstrução Nacional de Timor-Leste (Mudança) (Front for National Reconstruction of Timor-Leste (Change)) (from 2007; re-elected 7 Jul 2012)

Area: 19,000 square km

Population: 1.23 million (2014)* (1,066,582; 2010, census figure)

Capital: Díli

Official language: Portuguese and Tetum (Portuguese is the language of documentation).

Currency: US dollar (US$) = 100 cents (adopted as transitional currency, Jan 2000)

Exchange rate: US$1.00 per US$ (Jul 2014)

GDP per capita: US$3,638 (2014)*

GDP real growth: 6.56% (2014)*

GDP: US$4.48 billion (2014)*

Inflation: 2.49% (2014)

Balance of trade: -US$748.80 million (2014)

Foreign debt: US$43.00 million (2012)

Annual FDI: US$47.07 million (2011)

* estimated figure

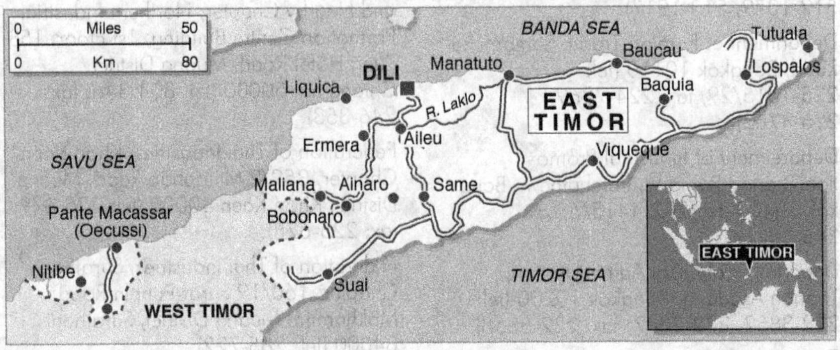

Timor Leste declared itself independent from Portugal on 28 November 1975 and was invaded and occupied by Indonesian forces nine days later. It was incorporated into Indonesia in July 1976 as the province of Timor Timur (East Timor). An unsuccessful campaign of pacification followed over the next two decades, during which an estimated 100,000 to 250,000 people died. In an August 1999 referendum supported by the United Nations (UN), an overwhelming majority of the people of Timor-Leste voted for independence from Indonesia. Subsequently, for the next three weeks anti-independence Timorese militias – organised by the Indonesian military – commenced a large-scale, scorched-earth campaign of retribution. The militias killed approximately 1,400 Timorese and forced 300,000 people into western Timor as refugees. The majority of the country's infrastructure, including homes, irrigation systems, water supply systems, schools and the electricity grid were destroyed. On 20 September 1999, Australian-led peacekeeping troops deployed to the country and brought the violence to an end. On 22 May 2002, Timor Leste was internationally recognised as an independent state. Unfortunately, peace did not last for long and in 2006, internal tensions threatened its security when a military strike led to violence and a breakdown of law and order. An Australian-led International Stabilisation Force (ISF) deployed to Timor-Leste, and the UN Security Council authorised a police presence of over 1,600 personnel under the UN Integrated Mission in Timor-Leste (UNMIT). The combined effort restored stability, allowing for presidential and parliamentary elections in 2007 in a largely peaceful atmosphere. Peaceful elections were held once again in 2012 and later in 2012, the UN Security Council ended its peacekeeping mission in Timor-Leste and both the ISF and UNMIT departed the country.

Timor Leste made a formal request to join the Association of Southeast Asian Nations (Asean) in 2011. It is unsurprising that they have made this bid for membership priority, considering the country's economic and political fragility. It is the only country in the Southeast Asian region not to have joined the regional institution despite it making small steps towards membership. Not all Asean countries have supported its bid for membership, Singapore in particular has been reticent to accept Timor Leste's bid, believing that the country will hinder Asean 's hopes to establish an Asean Economic Community (AEC) in 2015. Asean membership would allow Timor-Leste to benefit from a thriving Asean economy, valued at approximately US$1.5 trillion, while it would also have access to national development funds offered by Asean to reduce disparities between member states. Timor-Leste remains one of Asia's poorest nations, ranking 128 out of 187 countries on the United Nations *Human Development Index* in 2014. Generating economic opportunity and employment are among the government's greatest challenges.

Following the parliamentary elections on 7 July 2012, the incumbent Conselho Nacional de Reconstrução de Timor (CNRT) (National Congress for Timorese Reconstruction) party, led by Prime Minister Xanana Gusmao won the majority. CNRT won 36.7 per cent of the vote and 30 seats (out of 65) while the main opposition party, Frente Revolucionária do Timor-Leste Independente (Fretilin) (Revolutionary Front for Timor-Leste Independence) won just 29.9 per cent of the vote and 25 seats. The election campaign was focussed on economic issues, particularly the question of what should be done with the country's oil fund, worth US$10.5 billion. The CNRT pledged to increase the amount of money the fund contributed to the state budget beyond the 3 per cent limit. It also promised to improve infrastructure and attract foreign investment. Fretilin opposed these changes and instead ran a populist campaign focussed on raising levels of income and education.

As the 2017 elections approached one of the potentially biggest problems Timor Leste faced was that, at the beginning of 2015 Mr Gusmão did not want to stand down. Instead, he chose – in the manner of the Titanic deckchairs – to further reshuffle his cabinet. Per head of population Timor Leste had more cabinet ministers than any country in the world. – 55. Most citizens of Timor Leste have grown up with Xanana Gusmão as their leader. 'Big Brother', as he is commonly referred to, as he led the struggle to free the country from 24 years of brutal Indonesian rule. He became the first elected president in 2002 and he has remained in power, although during the past seven years he has served as prime minister in government. Then, on 6 February Mr Gusmão officially stepped down from office with his resignation accepted by the president, Taur Matan Ruak. This represented an unsettling moment for many because, although Mr Gusmão had failed to fulfil his promise to raise living standards and reduce the desperately poor country's dependence on revenue from oil and gas, he remained popular, especially amongst the poor. He also promised that after his departure, the cabinet would slim down from 55 to 34 ministers and that members of the opposition be included. The president also accepted Mr Gusmão's nomination of 50 year old Rui Araujo as his successor. Mr Araujo is a widely respected senior member of Fretilin, the biggest opposition party, and a former deputy prime minister and minister of health. Reducing the number of cabinet members should help get rid of the ministers who have been accused of corruption, nepotism and mismanagement, such problems have been endemic among politicians since independence. For all the government's faults Mr Gusmão is still seen as a unifying figure who has helped keep the country stable predominantly because he has kept control over the army.

Rebuilding

Timor Leste has faced great challenges in rebuilding its infrastructure, strengthening the civil administration, and generating jobs for young people entering the workforce since gaining its independence in 1999. The development of oil and gas resources in offshore waters has greatly supplemented government revenues. Unfortunately, the hydrocarbons industry has not helped to provide many jobs because there are no production facilities in Timor Leste, gas is currently piped to Australia for processing. The country has, however, expressed interest in developing a domestic processing capacity. Timor Leste has a Petroleum Fund to serve as a repository for all petroleum revenues and to preserve the value of its petroleum wealth for future generations. The Fund held assets of US$16.5 billion, as of December 2014. Oil revenues accounted for 90 per cent of government revenues in 2014, however, the drop in the price of oil in the same year led to concerns about the long-term sustainability of government spending although annual government budget expenditures dropped significantly in 2013 and again in 2014. Historically, the government has failed to spend as much as its budget allowed and it has increasingly focussed resources on basic infrastructure, including electricity and roads. Limited experience in infrastructure building has hampered these projects. gross domestic product (GDP) growth was 7.1 per cent in 2014 having increased significantly from the 5.4 per cent rate in 2013. Growth is expected to slow to 6.2 per cent in 2015 as stimulus from rising public spending eases, then rise to 6.6 per cent in 2016 as major public and private investment projects move forward. Inflation remained low in 2014 at 2.5 per cent having fallen from 3.3 per cent in 2013. Despite a lower growth forecast, encouraging signs have emerged of a more active private sector. Work on a new US$45 million brewery and bottling plant is set to begin 2015, and domestic and foreign investors are considering several other major investment projects. The 2015 public investment programme includes US$66 billion to upgrade national roads and bridges and an additional US$57 million for the electricity system. Work to develop a new international port is expected to start, and the budget anticipates investments in other transport infrastructure to be greatly scaled up in 2016.

The toughest economic challenge the country has is to figure out how best to use wealth procured from hydrocarbons to lift the non-oil economy onto a higher growth path and to reduce poverty. Crude oil production was at 76,490 barrels per day (bpd) in 2014 of which all of it is exported. The processed petroleum that Timor Leste consumes is bought back from Australia but it is only 1,300bpd. Natural gas reserves stood at 200 billion cubic metres (cum) in 2010 of which

KEY INDICATORS — Timor-Leste

	Unit	2011	2012	2013	2014	**2015
Population	m	*1.10	*1.15	*1.19	*1.23	*1.27
Gross domestic product (GDP)	US$bn	4.32	6.31	4.97	*4.48	*6.83
GDP per capita	US$	3,949	5,474	4,164	*3,638	*3,114
GDP real growth	%	10.6	9.3	5.4	*6.6	*6.8
Inflation	%	13.5	13.1	9.5	2.5	*1.8
Exports (fob) (goods)	US$m	34.1	33.3	17.7	15.5	–
Imports (fob) (goods)	US$m	378.0	671.6	696.2	764.2	–
Balance of trade	US$m	-344.0	-638.4	-678.5	-748.8	–
Current account	US$m	2,385.3	2,738.0	2,224.0	*1,167.0	*443.0
Total reserves minus gold	US$m	289.4	883.6	687.0	311.5	–
Foreign exchange	US$m	277.1	871.6	675.1	–	–
Exchange rate	per US$	1.00	1.00	1.00	1.00	–

* estimated figure ** forecast figure

none is being produced and none is being consumed.

An ongoing dispute between Timor Leste and Australia over their maritime borders represents arguably the single biggest issue facing the country's future. The dispute is holding up development of Woodside's Greater Sunrise Field, which is worth tens of billions of dollars in revenue across coming decades. Timor Leste's main source of income, the Bayu-Undan field, is nearing the end of its life. Even if the Australian government decided to give in on a moral basis, the Dili government cannot necessarily be trusted to use the revenues from the oil extracted from the Greater Sunrise Field to directly assist their impoverished people. There are many examples of shiny, new government offices that have sprung up around the country that were built when the government was benefitting from high oil prices and which sit alongside slums. The population living in multidimensional poverty was 64.3 per cent in 2014, with 68.2 per cent of the population living under US$2 a day. In simple terms, this shows that the revenues from oil have been disproportionately divided amongst the population as the vast majority still remains in poverty. Despite the country's many shortcomings, a major success is that it has an 85 per cent primary school enrolment rate. This is especially phenomenal because around nine-tenths of Timor Leste's education infrastructure was in ruins by 1999. There is still a lot to be done because most children do not start school until six or seven, and nearly two-thirds suffer from malnutrition. Furthermore, only 37 per cent go on to secondary school and while the country is home to a host of languages – five Papuan and 22 Austronesian – which is good for diversity, it is not good for schooling. Many children find themselves with teachers who speak another language to them, 40 per cent of students cannot read a single word after two years of primary school.

Risk assessment

Politics	Fair
Economy	Good
Regional stability	Fair/good

COUNTRY PROFILE

Before the arrival of the Portuguese and Dutch, the island of Timor was linked by trade to China and India.

1512 Portuguese navigators landed and established Díli as the colonial capital. Sandalwood, honey, wax and slaves were exported.

1749 The eastern half of Timor became a Portuguese colony (East Timor) and remained so until the mid-1970s, when the Portuguese colonial empire disintegrated. The western half became part of the Dutch East Indies and later Indonesia.

1895 There were several uprisings against Portuguese rule.

1942 The Japanese invaded. Up to 60,000 people were killed during fighting between Australian and Japanese troops.

1945 The end of the Second World War saw the end of Japanese rule.

1974–75 A military coup in Portugal led to a policy of decolonisation. The Portuguese governor and administration withdrew and the capital, Díli, was occupied by the Marxist Frente Revolucionária do Timor-Leste Independente (Fretilin) (Revolutionary Front for Timor-Leste Independence). Indonesian troops occupied the state, setting up a provisional government. An estimated 200,000 people died in the military crackdown and famine that followed.

1976 East Timor was integrated into Indonesia, becoming the 27th Indonesian province, although this act was never officially recognised by the UN.

1985 The rebels suffered a setback when the Australian government recognised Indonesia's incorporation of East Timor. Nevertheless Australia gave shelter to exiled Timorese dissidents.

1991 Portugal took Australia to the International Court of Justice (ICJ), on behalf of East Timor, alleging Australia had failed to observe the rights of the Timorese to national self-determination when it had recognised Indonesia's occupation of Timor-Leste in 1975.

1992 Fretilin leader, Xanana Gusmão, was captured by Indonesian troops and convicted of subversion.

1995 The ICJ ruled it did not have jurisdiction in the matter of Australian actions concerning East Timor.

1996 Bishop Carlos Belo and foreign minister-in-exile, José Ramos Horta, jointly won the Nobel Peace Prize.

1998 President Suharto of Indonesia was forced to step down. President B J Habibie considered offering East Timor 'special status' and wider autonomy, but exiled Timorese leaders and Portugal rejected the idea.

1999 The UN Mission organised a referendum, which had a 98.5 per cent turnout, with 78.5 per cent of the population voting for independence. International military intervention halted Indonesian army atrocities and the Indonesian government agreed to grant East Timor extensive autonomy. The first donor conference was held in Tokyo, Japan.

2000 The Lisbon, Portugal, donor conference was held. The UN Transitional Administration for East Timor (UNTAET) established the East Timor Transitional Administration (ETTA). A donor conference was held in Brussels in Belgium.

2001 Gusmão resigned as head of the interim parliament. East Timor voted for an Assembleia Constituinte (Constituent Assembly) in their first democratic election run by the UN. Fretilin won 55 of the 88 seats in the constituent assembly. The ETTA was transformed into the East Timor Public Administration (ETPA) after the elections and Mari Alkatiri was sworn in as chief minister. The gradual reduction of the UNTAET peace-keeping force began.

2002 East Timor became independent as the Democratic Republic of Timor-Leste on 20 May, with independence hero, Xanana Gusmão, as president and Mari Alkatiri as prime minister. The constituent assembly became the newly inaugurated Parlamento Nacional (National Parliament). Timor-Leste became a member of the World Bank Group and joined the UN.

2003 The former Indonesian military chief in Timor-Leste was sentenced by an Indonesian court to five years in jail for crimes against humanity, due to his failure to prevent attacks on civilians following the 1999 independence vote. The Australian parliament ratified the Timor Sea Treaty, which permitted the development of the Bayu-Undan gas field, the royalties from which will fund the country's economic development.

2004 A UN-backed tribunal issued a warrant for the arrest of the Indonesian presidential candidate, General Wiranto, for human rights abuses in Timor-Leste.

2005 Indonesia and Timor-Leste recognised the location of their shared land border.

2006 Timor-Leste and Australia signed an agreement for the start of oil and gas production in the Greater Sunrise field with an equal share of the proceeds. Prime Minister Alkatiri resigned and was replaced by José Ramos-Horta.

2007 José Ramos-Horta won the presidential elections. General elections did not produce a clear winner but the coalition led by Conselho Nacional de Reconstrução do Timor (CNRT) (National Congress for Timorese Reconstruction), headed by former president Xanana Gusmão, defeated the ruling Fretilin.

2008 The UN troops that had restored peace in 2005 and had since been in control of security began to transfer power to local police forces. President Ramos-Horta was shot and seriously wounded by rebel military forces that attacked his home as parliament extended a state of emergency; he underwent emergency medical treatment in Australia.

2009 The UN voted unanimously to keep its peacekeeping force in Timor-Leste for another year, while the situation remained fragile. The UN formally handed over control of policing for the district of Lautem to local police, thereby beginning the process of devolving domestic security to local forces.
2010 A commissioner was sworn into office, to investigate officials accused of corruption. Following a seven-month trail of 27 men (mostly ex-soldiers) charged with the assassination attempt on President Ramos-Horta in 2008, 24 were sentenced to imprisonment and three acquitted.
2011 The police took over full control from the UN from in March, although a group of 1,280 UN police will remain until after the presidential elections in 2012. In July the government released its Strategic Development Plan (2011–30), with objectives for social, economic and infrastructural goals. In August President Ramos-Horta officially disbanded Forças Armadas para a Liberação Nacional do Timor-Leste (Falintil) (Armed Forces of National Liberation of East Timor), the insurgent army of independence, in a ceremony attended by officials of its former occupiers, Indonesia. Former military leader of Falintil, Major General José Maria Vasconcelos (known as Taur Matan Ruak (Two Sharp Eyes)) announced that he would stand as presidential candidate in the upcoming elections.
2012 Twelve candidates took part in the presidential elections held on 17 March, in which the leading contenders Francisco Guterres (Fretilin) won 28.76 per cent and Taur Matan Ruak (independent but supported by CNRT) 25.71 per cent of the vote. Incumbent President Ramos-Horta (independent) won 17.48 per cent and acknowledged defeat when the results were announced. International observers declared the elections free and fair. As no candidate had won more than the 50 per cent threshold a runoff was held on 16 April. Ruak won 61.2 per cent and Guterres 38.8 per cent; turnout was 73.1 per cent. International observers declared the elections free and fair. Taur Matan Ruak was sworn in as president on 20 May. Parliamentary elections were held on 7 July, in which 21 political parties took part. The CNRT won 36.66 per cent (30 seats out of 65) and Fretilin won 25. Without an overall majority, the CNRT entered talks to form a new coalition. On 15 July demonstrators gathered in Dili to oppose the CNRT announcement that it would not form a coalition government with Fretilin. Instead the CNRT formed a coalition with Partido Democrático (PD) (Democratic Party) and Frente de Reconstrução Nacional de Timor-Leste (Mudança) (Front for National Reconstruction of Timor-Leste (Change)). On 31 October, the UN officially handed over control of policing operations of the Policia Nacional de Timor-Leste (PNTL) (National Police of East Timor) to the civil authorities. Peacekeepers from 40 countries that had provided law and order plus training for the domestic force will leave in stages.
2013 The last Unmit troops left in January. The 2014 budget unveiled at the end of October showed a US$1.5 billion spending plan funded almost exclusively – 95 per cent – by lucrative oil and gas revenues.
2015 Rui Maria Araújo was appointed prime minister on 16 February.

Political structure

Constitution

The constitution, passed in 2001, became valid on 20 May 2002, when Timor-Leste gained independence.

Independence date

20 May 2002

Form of state

Semi-Presidencialist Republic

The executive

The president of the republic is the Head of State and supreme commander of the defence force, and is elected by universal suffrage. The term of office is five years and no president can serve more than two terms. The President can also exercise the right to veto legislation put forth by the government and approved by the National Parliament. Following legislative elections, the presidents appoints the prime minister as the leader of the majority party or majority coalition.
The Government is the Executive body of the State and is responsible for the development and implementation of the Government program for the five-year term. The Head of Government is the Prime Minister.
The Council of State is the political advisory body of the president, headed by the president. It comprises the speaker of the national parliament, the prime minister, five citizens elected by the national parliament and five citizens designated by the president for the period corresponding to the president's term of office.

National legislature

The unicameral Parlamento Nacional (National Parliament) has between 52–65 members. Members are elected by popular vote to a five year term. The parliament elects the prime minister. Some legislation may be vetoed by the president.

Legal system

The legal system is under reform, putting in place structures under the new constitution.
Since 2000, the International Development Law Organisation (IDLO) has delivered practical training programmes to Timor-Leste's judges and prosecutors as part of a USAID-funded project for upgrading the system of justice.
Amnesty International issued a report in March 2003 which claimed that Timor-Leste's legal framework was incomplete and that there was 'a lack of clarity among judicial and other relevant officials about existing applicable law'. Some of the main problems include a lack of public defenders, delayed processing of court cases and legislation that was inconsistent with international human rights law and standards. It said that these problems encouraged vigilante violence and a loss of confidence in the legal system among police officers.

Last elections

7 July 2012 (parliamentary); 17 March and 16 April 2012 (presidential, first round and runoff)
Results: Parliamentary: Conselho Nacional de Reconstrução de Timor (CNRT) (National Congress for Timorese Reconstruction) won 36.66 per cent (30 seats out of 65), Frente Revolucionária do Timor-Leste Independente (Fretilin) (Revolutionary Front for Timor-Leste Independence) 29.87 per cent (25), Partido Democrático (PD) (Democratic Party) 10.31 per cent (eight), Frente de Reconstrução Nacional de Timor-Leste (Mudança) (Front for National Reconstruction of Timor-Leste (Change)) 3.11 per cent (two); 17 other political parties failed to win any seats. Turnout was 74.78 per cent.
Presidential (first round): Francisco Guterres (Fretilin) won 28.76 per cent of the vote, Taur Matan Ruak (independent but supported by CNRT) 25.71 per cent, José Ramos-Horta (independent) 17.48 per cent, Fernando de Araújo (Partido Democrático (PD) (Democratic Party)) 17.3 per cent; eight other candidates each won less than 4 per cent of the vote. Turnout was 78.2 per cent. Runoff: Ruak won 61.2 per cent and Guterres 38.8 per cent; turnout was 73.1 per cent.

Next elections

July 2017 (parliamentary); March 2017 (presidential)

Political parties

Ruling party

Coalition led by Conselho Nacional de Reconstrução de Timor (CNRT) (National Congress for Timorese Reconstruction), with Partido Democrático (PD) (Democratic Party) and Frente de Reconstrução Nacional de Timor-Leste (Mudança) (Front for National Reconstruction of Timor-Leste (Change)) (from 2007; re-elected 7 Jul 2012)

Main opposition party
Frente Revolucionária do Timor-Leste Independente (Fretilin) (Revolutionary Front for Timor-Leste Independence)

Population
1.23 million (2014)* (1,066,582; 2010, census figure)
Last census: 22 July 2010: 1,066,582
Population density: 72 inhabitants per square km (2010). Urban population 28 per cent (2010 Unicef).
Annual growth rate: 2.1 per cent, 1990–2010 (Unicef).
Ethnic make-up
Before the arrival of the Europeans, peoples of Asia and Insulindia, mainly Malays, Makasare and Papuans, migrated to Timor-Leste.
Religions
Roman Catholic (91.4 per cent), Protestant (2.6 per cent), Muslim (1.7 per cent). There are also Buddhist and Hindu communities.

Education
Around 70 per cent of school age population attend primary school and 44 per cent are enrolled at secondary school. There is a shortage of teachers due to the fact that 80 per cent of Timor-Leste's teachers were Indonesian and the vast majority left following Indonesia's withdrawal. More than half the population is illiterate. The Roman Catholic Church is attempting to implement a literacy programme for the schools as the country needs to educate its people to manage the new nation's bureaucracy.

Health
Life expectancy: 63 years, 2004 (WHO 2006)
Fertility rate/Maternal mortality rate: 6.2 births per woman, 2010 (Unicef)
Child (under 5 years) mortality rate (per 1,000): 57 per 1,000 live births (WHO 2012); 42.6 children aged under 5 are malnourished (World Bank).
Head of population per physician: 0.1 physicians per 1,000 people, 2004 (WHO 2006)

Main cities
Díli (capital, estimated population 195,499 in 2012), Dare (22,980), Los Palos (19,727), Baucau (17,322), Ermera (15,762), Maliana (12,909), Suai (7,570).

Languages spoken
Tetum and Bahasa Indonesian/Malayu are the local languages. It is estimated that Portuguese is spoken by only 5 per cent of the population, with Tetum spoken by 82 per cent and Indonesian by 43 per cent. Although Tetum is widely spoken, it is an undeveloped language and only recently achieved a standardised grammar and spelling.
Official language/s
Portuguese and Tetum (Portuguese is the language of documentation).

Media
Press
There are two daily publication based in Timor Leste, *Suara Timor Lorosae* (www.suaratimorlorosae.com) and the *Timor Post*; periodicals include *La'o Hamutuk* (www.laohamutuk.org) a joint government and international organisations publication.
Broadcasting
Radio: Around 90 per cent of the public receive transmissions from the national public service provided by Radio Nacional de Timor Leste (RTL). There are two other radio stations, Radio Falintil/Voz da Esperanca is a community radio and Radio Timor Kmanek (RTK) is operated by the Catholic Church.
Television: Fewer residents have access to Televisão de Timor Leste (TTL), but programmes are broadcast for 24 hours a day in Tetum, Indonesian, English and Portuguese. Rural districts show three-hour videotaped summaries of the week's programming on projection screens.

Economy
Crude oil sales and hydrocarbon extraction has been the single greatest source of economic growth since 2004, when production first began. According to the International Monetary Fund (IMF) since 2010 growth has been achieved through successfully channelling capital from the petroleum fund into the public sector, while sustaining a level of funding to benefit future generations from the profits of the petroleum wealth. The majority of the population is engaged in subsistence farming, with rice as the principal food crop and coffee as the principal export crop; vanilla is being cultivated for future export.
GDP growth was 14.6 per cent in 2008, a year when world oil prices were at an historic high. The economy was not affected by the global economic crisis in 2009 when most Western economies experienced recession and a fall in production cut oil imports. GDP growth was 12.8 per cent, dropping to 9.5 per cent in 2010, and by 2014 growth stood at 6.7 per cent.
The financial assets of the Petroleum Fund were US$14.9 billion at the end of 2013, which helped to underwrite much needed development, such as investment in upgrading Dili airport, the electricity grid, the Comoro power station, roads and a new LNG plant. In 2013 foreign direct investment was US$18.9 million.
Timor-Leste remains, despite the steady growth since independence, one of the poorest countries in the world. In 2014, the UN Human Development Index (HDI) ranked Timor-Leste 128 (out of 187) for national development in health, education and income. Since 2000, Timor-Leste's progress has grown from a level lower than others in East Asia and the Pacific and although by 2014 it still did not match other members' improvements in its peer group, it has shown improvement in its HDI. In 2014, 64.3 per cent of the population experienced at least one indicator of poverty.
Combined unemployment and under-employment are estimated at around 70 per cent, while the country suffers from a serious shortage of skilled workers throughout the economy.
Timor-Leste has been developing its regulatory framework and administrative capacity as well as new investment, insurance and export laws, which should help create a business climate attractive for investors.

External trade
In 2015, Timor Leste did not belong to the World Trade Organisation or any other regional economic block, although plans to join the Association of Southeast Asian Nations (Asean) are underway. The country is the recipient of much foreign aid needed to repair and instigate development of not only the physical infrastructure but social and entrepreneurial structures as well. Production in off-shore oil and natural gas fields have begun and provide the majority of the country's income. Coffee is the principal agricultural product for export and vanilla cultivation for export is being encouraged.
Imports
Principal imports include food, petroleum, building materials, vehicles and machinery.
Main sources: Indonesia (34.3 per cent of total in 2014), Malaysia (15.4 per cent), Singapore (12.8 per cent).
Exports
Principal exports are oil, natural gas and coffee.
Main destinations: Indonesia (34.7 per cent of total in 2014), Germany (14.5 per cent), US (13.8 per cent)

Agriculture
Farming
Livestock has been a traditional source of income for the Timorese and the majority of rural families hold livestock. Livestock has a large social and economic function: it is exchanged in marriage, and can be a source of cash income or a savings account. An IMF-sponsored vaccination programme significantly reduced the incidence of disease among farm animals.

Investment is required to recommence and improve poultry and livestock farming. Timor-Leste's agriculture has very low productivity due to a lack of technology, modern techniques and money. In 2014, agriculture contributed 16.7 per cent to GDP while about half of the workforce is involved in farming.

The World Bank is encouraging diversification into horticultural products. Vegetables and rice could be grown commercially. The higher elevations in Timor-Leste are ideal for growing pineapples, oranges, mangoes, bananas and papaya.

Coffee is the principal agricultural source of foreign exchange. Its production is in the hands of about 45,000 growers with an average of only one-hectare each. There are virtually no large-scale farms. Wet processed Arabica beans fetch the highest price but the processing facilities were put out of action during the fighting. Arabica beans account for about 80 per cent of the annual harvest. All coffee is produced organically. Renewal and maintenance of the road infrastructure is necessary for the rehabilitation of the coffee industry.

Subsistence farming is giving way to a market economy. The government sees the country's farming future in goods with high margins such as cashew nuts, vanilla and cut flowers. The main priority for now, however, should be food security.

Timor-Leste is vulnerable to adverse climate conditions, such as La Niña, which in 2010 caused an unrelenting rainy season which dragged on for months and left farmers without a June harvest and unsure when to plant for the next one.

Fishing

Although there are extensive and rich fishing areas in the seas surrounding Timor-Leste, only traditional coastal fishing is practised as there is no established structure for offshore or deep-sea fishing. The government is contemplating establishing an exclusive economic zone for Timor-Leste and administering fishing and other activities in this area. Domestic fish consumption is very low. There are plans to promote the consumption of dried fish which could be more easily distributed from the coast to inner areas.

Forestry

A quarter of Timor-Leste's forested areas are in danger of degradation. Deforestation has caused landslides, and a worsening in soil and water quality. In recent years, sandalwood, teak, ebony and redwood have been exploited at an unsustainable rate. The forestry sector, if responsibly managed, has potential for good revenue and significant employment opportunities.

Industry and manufacturing

The coffee industry is large and a service sector is developing in urban areas. The manufacturing industry in Timor-Leste is virutally non-existent. Priority areas for investment are industries processing raw materials from forests and marine and agricultural resources, and industries fabricating agricultural machinery, tools and small- and medium-sized fishing boats. In 2013 industry constituted 81.6 per cent of GDP.

The government is promoting the development of native handicrafts for export.

Tourism

The tourist industry is underdeveloped and lacks a range of hotel accommodation, plus other facilities. Transport services are limited and taxis and public services are scarce after dark. Ecotourism will represent an important sector in the development of tourism, although there remains a danger from unexploded ordinance in otherwise pristine rural and forest areas. In 2011, the World Wildlife Fund established the MyCoralTriangle conservation campaign, which encompasses six countries, including Timor-Leste, to offer protection to their contiguous marine environment, and by extension six (out of seven) of the world's species of marine turtles.

Travel advice from Western governments in 2012 has been moderated so that few warnings are in place. Tourist numbers doubled from 22,000 in 2007 to 44,000 in 2009, but fell to 40,000 in 2010 before increasing again in 2012 to 58,000. The new Archive and Museum of the Timorese Resistance was opened in May 2012 in Díli. It concentrates on displays and documents relating to the independence insurgency.

Environment

An Asian Development Bank (ADB) study (*Economics of Climate Change in the Pacific*) published in November 2013 reported that economic losses from climate change could reach as much as 10 per cent of Timor-Leste's annual GDP by 2100, making it one of the worst hit in the Pacific.

Mining

At the moment there is no significant mining activity. There are indications however that there could be economically interesting deposits of marble, granite, limestone and gold. The government is in the process of setting up a fiscal policy and regulatory framework, which would enable surveys and exploration to begin.

Hydrocarbons

Australia and Timor-Leste signed a treaty in 2006 to equitably share revenue generated by oil and gas fields found between their coastlines.

Timor-Leste had a total oil production of 79,260 barrels per day (bpd) in 2013 and consumption was only 1,980 bpd. There is no gas or coal production in Timor-Leste.

Energy

The national power system had been managed by Indonesians who had left during the violence of 1999. This departure left a lack of people technically capable of maintaining power supplies following independence. Generating capacity is around 38.3MW. The government has been investing in electrical infrastructure but rural areas still have very limited access to electricity and prices are high throughout the country.

A reliance on biomass, predominantly wood fuel, has led to deforestation and more sustainable energy resources are a matter of urgency.

Banking and insurance

By 2005, the banking system consisted of four commercial banks, but most bank deposits are invested abroad. The banking sector requires a stronger regulatory framework and more investment opportunities if it is to grow.

The Banking and Payments Authority (BPA) provides currency – US dollars – to the country's banks. It also supervises commercial banking, strives to ensure monetary stability and moderate inflation. In the future the BPA will develop into a central bank.

Central bank

Central Bank of Timor-Leste (formerly the Banking and Payments Authority)

Time

GMT plus eight hours

Geography

The island of Timor is the largest and furthest east of the Lesser Sundar Islands in the Malay Archipelago, between the Indian and Pacific Oceans. Timor-Leste occupies the eastern part of the island, together with the Oecussi-Ambeno enclave in the north-west of the island. The island of Atauro, to the north of Dili, and the small, uninhabited island of Jaco off the eastern tip are also part of the territory. Indonesia, of which the rest of Timor island is a part, lies to the west and north, New Guinea to the east and Australia to the south.

The terrain is mountainous in the interior. The highest point is Mount Ramelau, which rises to 2,963m. A range of mountains runs the length of the country from east to west, dividing the hot northern coastal region from the milder south coastal plain and its rivers and swamps.

Hemisphere
Southern

Climate
The dry season is between July and October when it becomes very hot and dusty with the monsoon winds blowing off the deserts of Australia. Rainy season: Nov–Jun. Temperatures range from 15 degrees Celsius (C) in the mountains to 30 degrees C and above on the north coast. Humidity: 75—85 per cent. There is a risk of tropical cyclones.

Entry requirements
Passports
Required by all, valid for six months beyond date of departure.
Visa
Visas are not required in advance, but are issued to passport-holders on arrival for a fee of US$35 for visits up to 30 days and may be extended.
Currency advice/regulations
The import of currency is permitted, subject to declaration of amounts over US$5,000.

Health (for visitors)
Comprehensive medical and travel insurance is essential as medical services are severely limited. In the event of a medical emergency, evacuation to Australia is probably the only option for treatment, and insurance policies should cover this eventuality. Such treatment carried out locally will require immediate cash payment for doctors' and hospital services.
Advisable precautions
Malaria prophylaxis should be taken. Dengue fever and Japanese encephalitis are common throughout the island and tuberculosis is prevalent, while cholera and rabies may also be present.

Public holidays (national)
Fixed dates
1 Jan (New Year's Day), 1 May (Labour Day), 20 May (Independence Day), 15 Aug (Assumption Day), 30 Aug (Constitution Day), 20 Sep (Liberation Day), 1 Nov (All Saints' Day),12 Nov (Santa Cruz Day), 28 Nov (Independence Manifesto Day), 8 Dec (Immaculate Conception), 25 Dec (Christmas Day).
Variable dates
Good Friday

Working hours
Banking
Mon–Fri: 0930–1530.
Business
Mon–Fri: 0800–1700.
Government
Mon–Fri: 0800–1730.

Social customs/useful tips
Visitors should expect to pay all expenses in hard cash.

Security
The political situation in Timor-Leste is volatile. Visitors should keep away from public demonstrations and public buildings and not venture out after dark.

Getting there
Air
International airport/s: Nicolau Lobato International Airport (DIL), 5km west of Dili. It has limited commercial flights and few gound facilities. There are scheduled services to Western and Northern Australia.
Airport tax: US$10 departure tax.
Surface
The main land route into Timor-Leste from West Timor (Indonesia) is the border crossing at Motaain near the town of Batugede. Entry into the Oecussi-Ambeno enclave is through the border crossing at Oesilo. Travellers entering Timor-Leste from West Timor are issued with Timorese visas on arrival; Indonesian visas for entry into West Timor from Timor-Leste must be obtained in advance.
Water: There are weekly shipping services between Díli and Singapore, and Díli and Darwin, Australia.

Getting about
National transport
Outside the capital, infrastructure is extremely limited.

BUSINESS DIRECTORY

The addresses listed below are a selection only. While World of Information makes every endeavour to check these addresses, we cannot guarantee that changes have not been made, especially to telephone numbers and area codes. We would welcome any corrections.

Telephone area codes
The international direct dialling (IDD) code for Timor-Leste is +670, followed by the subscriber's number.

Banking
Central bank
Banking and Payments Authority of Timor-Leste, Avenida Bispo Medeiros, PO Box 59, Dili (tel: 331-3712; fax: 331-3713; e-mail: info@bancocentral.tl).

Travel information
National tourist organisation offices
Timor-Leste Government Tourism Office, Ministry of Development, Apartado 194, Edificio do Fomento, Rua Dom Aleixo Corte-Real, Dili (tel: 331-0371; fax: 333-9179; e-mail: info@turismotimorleste.com).

Ministries
Ministry of Foreign Affairs and Cooperation, GPA Building 1, Rua Avenida Presidente Nicolau Lobato, PO Box 6, Dili (tel: 333-9600; fax: 333-9025).

Ministry of Health, Edifício dos Serviços Centrais do Ministério da Saúde, Rua de Caicoli, PO Box 374, Dili (tel: 332-2467; fax: 332-5189; e-mail: ministerforhealthtl@yahoo.com).

Ministry of Justice, Avenida Jacinto Candido, Dili (e-mail: moj@mj.gov.tl).

Ministry of Planning and Finance, Building 5, Palaco do Governo, Dili (e-mail: itds@mopf.gov.tl).

Prime Minister's Office, Government Palace, Rua Avenida Presidente Nicolau Lobato, Dili (tel: 723-0140; fax: 332-2026; e-mail: mail@primeministerandcabinet.gov.tp).

Other useful addresses
British Embassy, Deutsche Bank Building, 80 Jalan Imam Bonjol, Jakarta 10310, Indonesia (tel: 331-2652; fax: 331-2652; e-mail: britishembassydili@fco.gov.uk).

Commission for Reception, Truth and Reconciliation in East Timor (CAVR), Comarca Balide, Dalan Balide, PO Box 144, Dili (tel: 331-1263; e-mail: info@cavr-timorleste.org).

Oil, Gas and Energy Directorate, Edificio do Fomento, Rua Dom Aleixo Corte-Real, PO Box 171, Dili (tel: 331-7142; fax: 331-7143; e-mail. emrd@gov.east-timor.org).

US Embassy, Praia de Coquieros, Dili (tel: 332-4684; fax: 331-3206).

Internet sites
East Timor Action Network: http://www.etan.org

Petroleum Transparency: http://www.transparency.gov.tl

Timor Leste government: http://www.timor-leste.gov.tl

Togo

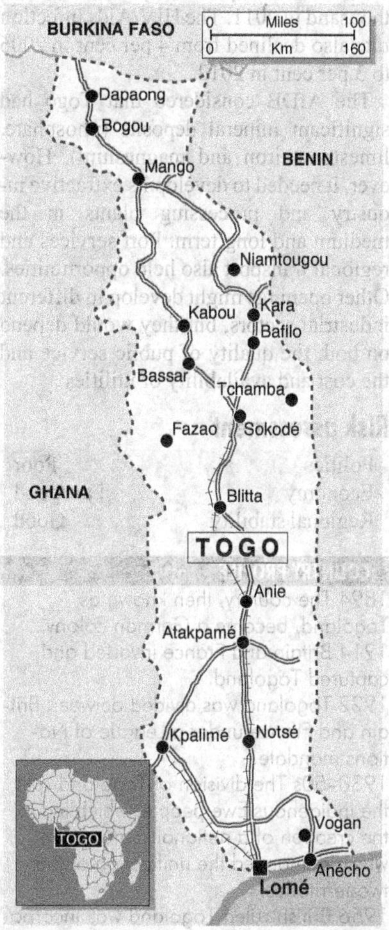

In July 2013, Reuters reported that Togo's ruling party had won more than two-thirds of the seats in the parliamentary elections. The opposition parties had hoped to win the parliamentary majority necessary to secure the reforms required to curb the power of one of Africa's oldest political dynasties. President Faure Gnassingbe's family had ruled Togo for almost five decades. But Mr Gnassingbe's Union Pour la République party (UNIR) (Union for the Republic) won 62 out of the 91 seats (68 per cent) in the single-chamber body. This was a slightly increased majority – before the election UNIR had held 50 of the 81 parliamentary seats (61 per cent). Togo's 10 opposition parties, which had been pushing for a two-term limit on the presidency that would bar Gnassingbe from running for re-election in 2015, together took just 25 seats. Independents and a party currently in Gnassingbe's government took the remaining four seats.

While the election was not marked by the kind of violence that had characterised previous polls, the principal opposition grouping, CST, had denounced what it claimed were irregularities and evidence of fraud. However election observer missions including those from the African Union (AU) and the regional ECOWAS said the process had been acceptable and transparent. The European Union's High Representative for Foreign Affairs, Catherine Ashton, called for any disputes over the results to be settled through the proper legal channels.

Eyadéma succession

President Gnassingbe's father, Gnassingbe Eyadema, had seized power in a 1967 military *coup*. He had finally died in February 2005 and, supported by the military, was succeeded by his son Faure Gnassingbé. The succession, in direct contravention of the nation's constitution, was challenged by popular protest and a threat of sanctions from regional and international leaders. Faure Gnassingbé Eyadéma reluctantly agreed to hold elections in April 2005. He was re-elected and in turn elected Edem Kodjo, the leader of a moderate opposition party, prime minister. Kodjo brought the leaders of two other opposition parties into government, but only remained prime minister for just over a year. The current prime minister, Séléagodji Kwesi Ahoomey-Zunu Arthème was selected by the president in July 2012 and again after the elections in July 2013.

The economy

Togo's economic growth had levelled off in the early 1980s with the fall in world demand for phosphates. Despite this major setback, Togo's relative prosperity was still the envy of many poorer landlocked neighbours in West Africa's Sahel zone. In 2014 Togo's economy was heavily dependent on both commercial and subsistence agriculture, which

KEY FACTS

Official name: République Togolaise (Togolese Republic)

Head of State: President Faure Gnassingbé (RPT) (from 2005; re-elected 25 April 2015)

Head of government: Prime Minister Komi Klassou (since 5 July 2015) (appointed by Gnassingbé after his re-election)

Ruling party: Union Pour la République party (UNIR) (Union for the Republic) (since 25 Jul 2013)

Area: 56,000 square km

Population: 7.00 million (2014)* (5,753,324; census figure Nov 2010)

Capital: Lomé

Official language: French

Currency: CFA franc (CFAf) = 100 centimes (Communauté Financière Africaine (African Financial Community) franc).

Exchange rate: CFAf586.44 per US$ (Sep 2015)

GDP per capita: US$658 (2014)*

GDP real growth: 5.20% (2014)*

GDP: US$4.60 billion (2014)*

Inflation: 0.13% (2014)*

Balance of trade: -US$558.00 million (2012)

Annual FDI: US$53.77 million (2011)

* estimated figure

provided employment for 65 per cent of the labour force, although some basic foodstuffs were still being imported. Cocoa, coffee and cotton generated about 40 per cent of export earnings, with cotton being the most important cash crop. Togo is still the world's fourth-largest producer of phosphate.

The decade-long effort, supported by the World Bank and the International Monetary Fund (IMF), to implement economic reform, encourage foreign investment and bring revenues in line with expenditures had moved slowly. In the view of the IMF, real progress depended on increased openness in government financial operations, progress toward legislative elections and continued support from foreign donors. Togo has been working with donors to draft a poverty reduction paper that could eventually lead to a debt reduction plan. Togo has also come under fire from international organisations for human rights abuses and for its chronic political unrest. European Union, which cut off aid in 1993 over the country's human rights record, initiated a partial resumption of co-operation and development aid in late 2004 based upon commitments by Togo to expand opportunities for political opposition and liberalise portions of the economy.

According to the African Development Bank (AfDB) in its 2014 *Economic Outlook*, the 5.6 per cent growth seen in 2013 was largely due to the primary sector, namely cotton and food crops, plus services such as retail, transport and storage and communications. Continuing public investment and a boost to the cotton and phosphate sectors were expected to sustain growth, projected at 6.0 per cent in 2014 and 6.3 per cent in 2015.

Despite an 11 per cent increase in tax revenue, the tax ratio increased only slightly from 16.4 per cent in 2012 to 16.9 per cent in 2013. The deficit in the overall balance improved from 5.8 per cent of gross domestic product (GDP) to 4.6 per cent. Inflation was 1.8 per cent and would be controlled in the medium term. The 2013 legislative elections were without incident. Peaceful preparation for the 2015 presidential elections would be a key factor in the country's continued progress.

Three-quarters of the Togolese population are under 35 and just 35 per cent are aged 15–35. According to the AfDB, the latter age group had a particularly high rate of unemployment (8.1 per cent) and under-employment (20.5 per cent). The poverty rate decreased by 3 percentage points from 61.7 per cent in 2006 to 58.7 per cent in 2011. While, in the view of the AfDB, these results are positive, they were well under the Millennium Development Goal (MDG) target of 30.9 per cent by 2015. This shortcoming was exacerbated by the extreme poverty rate, which increased from 28.6 per cent to 30.4 per cent over the same period. The rise in extreme poverty was linked to an upturn in inequality, with the Gini coefficient increasing from 0.361 to 0.393.

In education, government measures in recent years had lead to a gross enrolment rate of 114.5 per cent in 2012/13. Nevertheless, students at all levels were not completing their education. As a result, close to 85 per cent of job seekers remained without qualifications. Insufficient resources and governance issues also plagued the health sector. Child mortality increased slightly from 123 per thousand in 2006 to 124 per thousand in 2010, while infant mortality also increased slightly from 76 per thousand to 77 per thousand over the same period. Maternal mortality, on the other hand, dropped from 350 per one hundred thousand births in 2008 to 300 per one hundred thousand in 2011. The HIV/Aids infection rate also declined from 4 per cent in 2006 to 3 per cent in 2012.

The AfDB considered that Togo had significant mineral deposits (phosphate, limestone, iron and magnesium). However, it needed to develop its extractive industry and processing plants in the medium and long term. Port services and regional transport also held opportunities. Other openings might develop in different industrial sectors, but they would depend on both the quality of public service and the cost and availability of utilities.

Risk assessment

Politics	Poor
Economy	Fair/good
Regional stability	Good

KEY INDICATORS — Togo

	Unit	2011	2012	2013	2014	**2015
Population	m	*7.14	*6.64	*6.82	*7.00	*7.18
Gross domestic product (GDP)	US$bn	3.62	3.69	*4.35	*4.60	*4.51
GDP per capita	US$	588	590	*638	*658	*628
GDP real growth	%	4.9	5.9	*5.4	*5.2	*6.0
Inflation	%	3.0	2.6	1.8	*0.1	*1.9
Exports (fob) (goods)	US$m	1,178.8	1,293.3	–	–	–
Imports (fob) (goods)	US$m	2,019.8	1,851.3	–	–	–
Balance of trade	US$m	-841.0	-558.0	–	–	–
Current account	US$m	-258.0	-461.0	*-311.0	*-290.0	*-225.0
Total reserves minus gold	US$m	816.3	441.6	507.1	507.0	–
Foreign exchange	US$m	721.3	349.8	415.0	–	–
Exchange rate	per US$	466.82	505.65	480.26	542.07	–

* estimated figure ** forecast figure

COUNTRY PROFILE

1894 The country, then known as Togoland, became a German colony.

1914 Britain and France invaded and captured Togoland.

1922 Togoland was divided between Britain and France under a League of Nations mandate.

1930–50s The division of Togoland split the indigenous Ewe people, which led to the creation of a nationalist movement which demanded the unification of the two territories.

1956 British-ruled Togoland was incorporated into Ghana.

1960 The French section of Togoland gained independence as a republic under the presidency of Sylvanus Olympio.

1962 A proposed referendum on unification with Ghana was blocked by President Olympio.

1963 Olympio was executed in a coup by Gnassingbé Eyadéma. Nicolas Grunitzky was appointed president.

1967 Grunitzky was in turn ousted by Major General Gnassingbé Eyadéma.

1979 Eyadéma stood and won as the sole candidate in the presidential election.

1985 France intervened militarily to support the Eyadéma regime, following an attempted coup.

1985–1990 Political pressure for democratic rule increased.

1991 A new government headed by Joseph Koffigoh introduced a national conference to pave the way for multi-party

elections. Much of the president's powers were stripped from him. The unrest that followed – orchestrated by the army, which backed Eyadéma – included spontaneous uprisings, a series of attacks on reformers, the prime minister's residence and the bombing of electoral material.
1992 The fragile democratic process of reforms faltered as a series of governments of national unity were imposed, through which much of Eyadéma's powers were re-gained. A new constitution was introduced. Parliamentary elections were postponed and a general strike lasting six months ensued.
1993 Representatives of Germany and France failed to bridge the rift between the government and Eyadéma. The army opened fire on crowds that had gathered at the meeting, killing many and forcing the foreign representatives to depart the country hurriedly. After a series of delays, the country's first multi-party presidential elections were held. Eyadéma, standing for the Rassemblement du Peuple Togolais (RPT) (Rally of the Togolese People), was the only candidate as all other major parties boycotted the election. The EU suspended aid in protest at the abandoned democratic elections.
1994 The RPT won the legislative elections, but needed the support of the Union Togolaise pour la Démocratie (UTD) (Togolese Union for Democracy) to form a majority. The Union des Forces de Changement (UFC) (Union of Forces for Change) boycotted the election.
1996 After winning three delayed by-elections, the RPT no longer required UTD's support.
1998 Opposition parliamentary members were arrested and held in detention. Human rights abuse escalated in the run-up the presidential elections, including extra-judicial executions. Eyadéma won the presidential election; the official results were strongly contested by opposition parties and criticised by the UN.
1999 An independent electoral commission (CENI), was formed, with equal representation of opposition and government. Parliamentary elections were boycotted by all opposition parties after the government unilaterally amended the electoral code and altered the representation on the CENI.
2001 The UN and the Organisation of African Unity (OAU) concluded there were hundreds of summary executions and torture in the run-up to the 1998 presidential election.
2002 The ruling RPT won the parliamentary elections; the main opposition parties boycotted the elections. The constitution was amended allowing unlimited terms in office for a president and required a one-year residency for any candidate – effectively barring the strongest opposition candidate, Gilchrist Olympio (UFC), (exiled son of Sylvanus Olympio, the first president of Togo, executed by Eyadéma).
2003 The opposition parties were unable to agree on a candidate to run against the incumbent Eyadéma, who won the presidential elections; there were allegations of widespread vote rigging.
2004 The French government resumed partial aid to Togo, suspended since 1998.
2005 President Gnassingbé Eyadéma died. Unconstitutionally, the armed forces conferred power on his son, Faure Gnassingbé, but after international pressure he stepped down and later won the presidential elections, against Emmanuel Bob Akitani of the opposition UFC; the opposition disputed the results and there were violent protests in the streets of the capital, Lomé. A clampdown by security forces provoked thousands of opposition supporters to flee to Benin or Ghana. The Constitutional Court confirmed the election of Faure Gnassingbé as president. Edem Kodjo was sworn in as prime minister.
2006 Reconciliation talks – that had been halted on the death of Gnassingbé Eyadéma – were resumed in Burkina Faso between the government and opposition leaders. The EU agreed to re-establish aid and trade if political and economic progress was undertaken. An agreement was reached with opposition parties, excluding Gilchrist Olympio and the UFC, and President Faure Gnassingbé appointed Yawovi Agboyibo, who had helped broker the agreement, to the post of prime minister. Agboyibo's principal undertaking was preparing the country for parliamentary elections in 2007.
2007 Floods that devastated Togo during the summer left 20,000 people homeless at a cost of US$1.1 million. Historic parliamentary elections, which included opposition political parties that had boycotted all elections since 1993, were held. The RTP won 50 seats (out of 81) and the UFC 27. Komlan Mally was appointed prime minister. The EU resumed aid following the successful multi-party elections.
2008 Komlan Mally resigned and Gilbert Houngbo replaced him as prime minister.
2009 The death penalty was abolished. The European Union gave its first grant, of €15 million (US$22.3 million), as budgetary support. There was an attempted coup.
2010 In presidential elections incumbent Faure Gnassingbé won 60.9 per cent of the vote, his closest rival Jean-Pierre Fabre won 33.9 per cent. Opposition parties condemned the result claiming it was fraudulent. A bimonthly Benin newspaper, the *Tribune d'Afrique* was indefinitely banned in Togo by a Togolese court for an article that linked the brother-in-law of President Gnassingbé to drug trafficking. The court also fined the newspaper editor US$113,000 and the chief executive US$3,800. The first census since 1981 was held on 19 November.
2011 In May, France cancelled the entire Togolese debt to France, of €101 million (US$104.1 million), as part of France's commitment to the Paris Club (of creditors) agreement of December 2010. An additional US$102 million of Togolese debt will be cancelled by other Paris Club creditors. The debt cancellation was due to economic reforms undertaken since 2006. The 2010 census results, announced in July, recorded a total population of 5,753,324, composed of 2,799,086 males and 2,954,238 females. President Gnassingbe's half-brother, Kpatcha Gnassingbe, the former defence minister, was convicted and sentenced to 20 years in prison for an attempted coup in 2009.
2012 For three days, from 13 June, protestors rioted in Lomé calling for a reversal of electoral reforms agreed by parliament, which were said to favour the ruling RTP. The protestors were demanding a return to the 1992 constitution which limited the mandate of the Head of State to two terms in office. Parliamentary elections, expected to be held in October, were later postponed until 2013. On 11 July, Gilbert Houngbo resigned as prime minister and on 19 July Kwesi Ahoomey-Zunu was appointed in his stead.
2013 Elections were held on 25 July. The result was a win for President Faure Gnassingbe's Union Pour la République party (UNIR) (Union for the Republic) with 46.7 per cent (62 seats, out of 90), followed by Let's Save Togo Collective 28.9 per cent (19).
2014 A new round of talks, including all political parties represented in parliament, began on 19 May. The ambitious agenda included discussions on Togo's political regime, the selection and powers of the prime minister, presidential eligibility, the creation of a senate, and the electoral code. The talks however, ended without agreement, including, crucially, the presidential term in office.
2015 Komi Sélom Klassou became prime minister on 5 June.

Political structure

Constitution

In 2002 a new, democratic Constitution, formally initiating Togo's fourth republic was instituted.

On the death of the president, the chairman of the National Assembly becomes interim president until elections are held.
The country is divided into *préfectures*, administered by préfects, and supervised by the interior ministry.
In November 2014, several thousand street protesters called for constitutional change that would bar President Faure Gnassingbe from seeking a third term in office ahead of the 2015 presidential election. Evidently, it made little difference as he ran for a third term in office and won to become president for a third successive term.

Independence date
27April 1960

Form of state
Republic

The executive
Executive power is vested in the president, who is elected by simple majority popular vote for a period of five years (no term limits).
The prime minister is the Head of government and is selected by the president from the parliamentary majority. A Council of Ministers is appointed by the president and the prime minister.

National legislature
The unicameral L'Assemblé Nationale (National Assembly) has 91 seats of which members are directly elected in multi-seat constituencies by proportional representation vote. Members serve five-year terms.

Legal system
Togo has a French-based court system.

Last elections
25 April 2015 (presidential),

Results: Presidential: Faure Gnassingbé won 58.8 per cent of the vote, Jean-Pierre Fabre 35.2 per cent, Tchaboure Gogue won 4 per cent; the two remaining candidates each won less than 1.1 per cent of the vote. Turn-out was 60.9 per cent.
Parliamentary (2013): Union Pour la République party (UNIR) (Union for the Republic) 46.7 per cent (62 seats, out of 90), Let's Save Togo Collective 28.9 per cent (19), Rainbow Alliance 10.8 per cent (6), Union des Forces du Changement (Union of Forces for Change) 7.7 per cent (3), Independent (1). Turnout was 66.1 per cent.

Next elections
2018 (parliamentary); 2020 (presidential)

Political parties

Ruling party
Union Pour la République party (UNIR) (Union for the Republic) (since 25 Jul 2013)

Main opposition party
Alliance Nationale pour le Changement (ANC) (National Alliance for Change). The ANC was formed from the collapse of the Union des Forces de Changement (UFC) (Union of Forces for Change) after the 2010 elections.
Approximately 45 per cent of the total population are under 14 years.

Population
7.00 million (2014)* (5,753,324; census figure Nov 2010)
19 November 2010: 5,753,324
The previous census in 1981 recorded a population of 2,719,567.

Population density: 77 inhabitants per square km. Urban population 43 per cent (2010 Unicef).

Annual growth rate: 2.5 per cent, 1990–2010 (Unicef).

Ethnic make-up
African (99 per cent), European (1 per cent).

Religions
Traditional beliefs (50 per cent), Christianity (35 per cent) (mostly Roman Catholic), Islam (15 per cent).

Education
Public expenditure on education is 4–5 per cent of GDP, of which per capita expenditure is 16–17 per cent per student.

Literacy rate: 60 per cent adult rate; 77 per cent youth rate (15–24) (Unesco 2005).

Compulsory years: Six to 15

Enrolment rate: 124 per cent gross primary enrolment, 36 per cent secondary enrolment; of relevant age groups (including repeaters) (World Bank).

Pupils per teacher: 46 in primary schools

Health

HIV/Aids
The impact of HIV/Aids has yet to peak with deaths, orphans and HIV positive pregnant women all showing an increase. By the end of 2003 there were an estimated 10,000 deaths from Aids, although this number could be as high as 16,000; the difference may be due to underreporting or misdiagnosis.
Of the estimated 110,000 people living with HIV/Aids, 9,300, are children (aged 0–14) and 54,000 are women; and 9 per cent of pregnant women tested were positive for HIV in 2003, which bears out the UNAids message that women and children are typically more vulnerable to HIV/Aids in Africa.
Between 2001–03 the number of orphans (aged 0–17) rose from 8,700 to 9,300.

HIV prevalence: 4.1 per cent aged 15–49 in 2003 (World Bank)

Life expectancy: 54 years, 2004 (WHO 2006)

Fertility rate/Maternal mortality rate: 4.1 births per woman, 2010 (Unicef)

Birth rate/Death rate: 35.2 births and 11.5 deaths per 1,000 people (2003)

Child (under 5 years) mortality rate (per 1,000): 96 per 1,000 live births (WHO 2012); 25 per cent of children aged under five are malnourished (World Bank).

Head of population per physician: 0.04 physicians per 1,000 people, 2004 (WHO 2006)

Main cities
Lomé (capital, estimated population 1.8 million in 2012), Sokodé (115,692), Kara (110,623), Atakpamé (85,408), Kpalimé (81,924), Dapaong (55,286), Tsévié (53,831), Notsé (38,973).

Languages spoken
Ewe and Kabyè are widely spoken.

Official language/s
French

Media

Press
There is only one daily newspaper, in French, *Togo Presse* (www.editogo.tg) is national and state-owned. There are several weekly publications including *Nouvelle Combat*, *Carrefour*, *Crocodile*, *Le Regard*, *Le Combat du Peuple*, *Motion d'Information*, *Le Togolais*, *Le Canard*, *Le Changement* and *Le Replublicain*.

Broadcasting

Radio: As the most popular medium, particularly in rural areas, the state-operated Radio Togolaise, broadcasting in French and local languages, runs a national radio network, Radio Lomé (www.radiolome.tg) on FM. Other, external services, are provided by the French service RFI 1 Afrique (www.rfi.fr), VOA and BBC. There are many private commercial radio stations including Zephyr FM (www.zephyr.tg) and Africa No1 (www.africa1.com) from Lomé and Radio Maria Togo (www.radiomaria.tg) operated by the Catholic Church.

Television: All television stations are based in Lomé. The state-owned Télevision Togolaise (TVT) (www.tvt.tg) broadcasts mainly in French, with other local languages. There are several external services broadcasting locally including the French television channel TV5 (www.tv5.org), Euronews (www.euronews.net) and on cable, Media Plus and Canal Plus Horizon.

National news agency: Agence Togolaise de Presse (ATOP)

Other news agencies: République Togolaise (in French and English) (www.republicoftogo.com)
Le Togolais (in French) (www.letogolais.com)

Economy
Although agriculture is a major component of the economy, comprising some 30.8 per cent of GDP in 2014, it is substantially subsistence farming, typically on

farms of 1–3 hectares. Despite this Togo is self-sufficient in wheat, yams, sorghum, millet and groundnuts. Cotton, coffee and cocoa are the principal cash crops. The reliance on primary production means that Togo is vulnerable to climatic problems and external economic shock in world commodity prices. Trade, particularly of agricultural goods and traditional clothes, which are sold both domestically and to neighbouring countries, provides another important component of GDP.
The deep-water harbour and port of Lomé provides significant foreign exchange and underpins the country's role as a trading centre, with goods transiting Togo to landlocked neighbours. The mining industry is centred on Togo's natural resources, which include limestone, marble and phosphates. Manufacturing includes small replacement goods such as shoes, tyres and cloths, plus processed foods and cement.
GDP growth was 3.2 per cent in 2009. As world trade picked up in 2010 it gave a much needed boost to all trading partners and in Togo GDP was estimated to have risen to 3.4 per cent in 2010 and marginally higher by an estimated 3.7 per cent in 2011. In 2013 Togo's GDP growth had risen to 6 per cent, dropping slightly to 5.6 per cent in 2014.
Togo is a poor country and in 2014, the UN Human Development Index (HDI) ranked it 166 (out of 187) for national development in health, education and income. Since 2000, Togo's progress has grown to match the improvement of other countries in sub-Saharan Africa. In 2014, 50.85 per cent of the population experienced at least one indicator of poverty, while 28.22 per cent lived on less than the equivalent of US$1.25 per day.
Remittances are an important source of earnings for households and foreign exchange for the country. Remittances from migrant workers amounted to US$244 million (6.5 per cent of GDP) in 2011 and reached US$345 million in 2012 (8.8 per cent of GDP).
There were no international aid programmes in Togo from 2003, due to the internal political situation and Togo's record on human rights violations and lack of any democratic institutions. Then in 2008 the EU granted €15 million (US$22.3 million), which helped Togo to prepare for its first democratic presidential election, held in 2010. From 16 December 2010, Togo became eligible for debt relief under the IMF's Heavily Indebted Poor Countries (HIPC) initiative, following the country's successful adherence to IMF set criteria, including financial controls, debt management and procurement.
Since then cut to international aid has been met with threats by the Togolese president, Faure Gnassingbe, stating that worsening the situation for the people in Togo could lead to rise in popularity of extremist groups.

External trade

Togo is a member of the Economic Community of West African States (Ecowas), which was set up to promote economic integration among members. It is also a member of the Union Économique et Monétaire Ouest Africaine (UEMOA) (West African Economic and Monetary Union) (WAEMU). As a member of the Communauté financière d'Afrique (CFA) (Financial Community of Africa), it uses the CFA franc currency along with the seven other CFA members.
Cash crops include coffee, cocoa and cotton although phosphates provide the single largest share of foreign exchange. China has become a major export market for Togolese phosphates. There are reserves of limestone and marble yet to be fully exploited. Togo is a regional hub for trading and transit, with re-exports of consumer goods to neighbouring, landlocked countries.
Cotton, coffee, and cocoa are responsible for around 40 per cent of export earnings while gold generates for a further 11 per cent.

Imports

Principal imports are machinery and equipment, foodstuffs and petroleum products.
Main sources: China (26 per cent of total in 2012), TheNetherlands (16 per cent), Belgium (6.2 per cent).

Exports

Principal exports are cotton, phosphates, coffee and cocoa.
Main destinations: Cameroon (10 per cent of total in 2012), India (9.5 per cent), Burkina Faso (8.5 per cent).

Re-exports

Many goods are re-exported and others transhipped to landlocked, neighbouring countries from the port of Lomé.

Agriculture

Farming

The agricultural sector contributes around 30.8 per cent to GDP.
Traditional methods of cultivation still prevail despite attempts at rapid modernisation.
Self-sufficiency in basic foodstuffs is generally maintained except during drought years. The majority of farmers are smallholders who raise stock and grow maize, millet, yams, cassava, sorghum and rice.
Cotton, coffee and cocoa are the principal export earners.

Forestry

The majority of timber production is used in domestic fuel.

Industry and manufacturing

The industrial sector, in 2014, contributed 15.5 per cent to GDP, of which 6 per cent was manufacturing, and employed 5 per cent of the workforce.
Activity is centred on the processing of agricultural commodities and the production of phosphoric acid, fertilisers and cement along with beverages, footwear, textiles and plastics.

Tourism

Togo has several distinct environments to offer the tourist, from Atlantic beach resorts to high savannah game parks and tropical forests. Facilities may be basic but should attract eco-tourists wishing to see some unspoiled African landscapes.
The Koutammakou in the north-eastern region is included on Unesco's World Heritage List, and is a remarkable destination, but difficult for visitors to reach. The distinct, cultural dwellings of the Batammariba and landscape are deeply imbedded to the rituals and beliefs of the local people.
While Togo has the potential to become a top destination for cultural tourism, major capital investment is necessary and in the meantime what leisure tourism there is is attracted to the beaches around Lomé.
In 2014 tourism contributed a total of 6.7 per cent of GDP, 1.9 per cent of total investment, and 5.7 per cent of total employment (around 60,500 jobs).

Mining

The mining sector contributes around 12 per cent to GDP and employs 5 per cent of the workforce. Mining production is concentrated on phosphates, marble and limestone, although the country has potential for commercial extraction of diamonds, gold and base metals. There are also known reserves of iron ore, bauxite, dolomite and chromite.
Phosphate mining is the second principal export earner after cotton. Reserves are estimated at over 60 million tonnes, mainly located around Lake Togo. There are environmental concerns about the high level of cadmium in Togolese phosphate rock. The possible development of safer but lower-grade carbo-phosphates is being explored. There are 200 identified base metal deposits, including the lead zinc prospect at Pagala which is licensed to Anglo American.

Hydrocarbons

There are no known reserves of hydrocarbons. All domestic energy needs are met by imports, which were 12,260 barrels per day of oil in 2013.
The US$260 million West African Gas Pipeline (WAGP) supplies natural gas from Nigeria's Escravos field to Togo. The

1,000km pipeline is managed by Chevron Texaco.
Any use of natural gas or coal is commercially insignificant.

Energy
Total installed generating capacity was 90MW in 2013, producing 13 million kilowatt hours. According to the World Bank, only 26.5 per cent of the population has access to electricity (2011). Biomass accounts for 80 per cent of primary energy, hydrocarbons 16 per cent and hydropower and thermal energy 4 per cent. Around 80 per cent of electricity is imported from Ghana. The Adjaralla dam on the Mono River, downstream from the existing Nangbeto Dam, is planned to produce 94MW, however construction as of 2015 has not yet begun.
Power stations are traditionally thermal fuelled by oil but were converted to natural gas when the West African Gas Pipeline (WAGP) was completed in 2008, bringing Nigerian natural gas to Togo.

Financial markets
Stock exchange
Afribourse (Bourse Régionale des Valeurs Mobilières) (BRVM)

Banking and insurance
Central bank
Banque Centrale des Etats de l'Afrique de l'Ouest (Central Bank of West African States).
Main financial centre
Lomé.

Time
GMT

Geography
Togo lies in West Africa, forming a narrow strip stretching north from a coastline around 50km wide on the Gulf of Guinea. It is bordered by Ghana to the west, by Benin to the east, and by Burkina Faso, to the north.
Togo is 550km long and varies in width from 40 to 130km. Much of the country is savannah, thicker in the south than the north, with deciduous forests in the central part. The terrain varies from the wide, rolling sandstone Oti Plateau in the north to the low, sandy coastal plain facing the ocean in the south. The narrow coastal strip is fringed by extensive inland lagoons and marshes; Lake Togo is in this area. Further inland are the Ouatchi Plateau and the Mono tableland. The Togo mountains straddle the country from the south-west to north-west; the average elevation is 700m. At the southern extremity of the range is Mount Agou, which at 986m is the highest point in Togo. The main rivers are the Mono, which with its tributaries drains the southern part of the country, and the Oti, which drains the northern plains.

Hemisphere
Northern

Climate
Tropical, mean annual temperature 28 degrees Celsius. Drier in the north. Two rainy seasons between April–June and September–October.

Entry requirements
Passports
Required by all, valid for six months beyond date of departure.
Visa
Required by all, except nationals of Benin, Burkina Faso, Côte d'Ivoire and Niger.
Currency advice/regulations
The import of local currency is restricted to CFAf1 million and export to CFAf25,000. Import of foreign currencies is restricted to CFAf1 million, subject to declaration on arrival, and export to the amount declared.

Health (for visitors)
Mandatory precautions
Yellow fever vaccination certificate required by all.
Advisable precautions
Malaria precautions and prophylaxes are essential. Hepatitis A and B, tetanus, typhoid and polio. There is an HIV/Aids risk and a rabies risk.
All water should be regarded as a potential health risk; only bottled or boiled water should be used for drinking, brushing teeth or making ice. Milk is unpasteurised and should be boiled and dairy products should be avoided. Only hot, cooked food and peeled fruit should be eaten. Medical insurance that includes evacuation is advised.

Hotels
High-standard hotels in Lomé, which should be booked well in advance. Ten per cent tip is usual.

Credit cards
Credit cards accepted.

Public holidays (national)
Fixed dates
1 Jan (New Year's Day), 13 Jan (Liberation Day), 27 Apr (Independence Day), 1 May (Labour Day), 21 Jun (Martyrs' Day), 15 Aug (Assumption Day), 1 Nov (All Saints' Day), 25 Dec (Christmas Day).
Variable dates
Easter Monday, Ascension Day, Whit Monday, Eid al Adha, Birth of the Prophet, Eid al Fitr.
Islamic year 1437 (15 Oct 2015–2 Oct 2016):: The Islamic year contains 354 or 355 days, with the result that Muslim feasts advance by 10-12 days against the Gregorian calendar. Dates of feasts vary according to the sighting of the new moon, so cannot be forecast exactly.

Working hours
Banking
Mon–Fri: 0730–1130, 1430–1600.
Business
Mon–Fri: 0700–1200, 1430–1730.
Government
Mon–Fri: 0700–1200, 1430–1730.
Shops
Mon–Fri: 0800–1200, 1430–1730; Sat: 0730–1230.

Telecommunications
Mobile/cell phones
A GSM 900 service is available in populated areas.

Electricity supply
220V AC, 50 cycles.

Social customs/useful tips
Business is conducted in French.

Security
Togo is relatively trouble-free, although visitors should be wary of the occasional car hijacking.

Getting there
Air
International airport/s: Gnassingbé Eyadéma International (LFW), 6km from Lomé; duty-free shop, restaurant, bank, post office, car hire. Taxis operate, from 0600 until the last flight, to the city centre.
Airport tax: None.
Surface
Road: A well-surfaced coastal road, which passes through Lomé, connects Togo with Ghana and Benin and thence to Nigeria. There is a road from Burkina Faso down to Lomé.
Main port/s: Lomé. Kpeme handles phosphate shipments.

Getting about
National transport
Air: Air Togo flies between Lomé, Sokodé, Mango, Lama-Kara, Niamtougou and Dapaong.
Road: Surfaced roads run from Lomé to the borders of neighbouring countries, along the coast west to Ghana and east to Benin, and northwards the length of Togo to Burkina Faso. Other roads may not be passable in the rainy season.
Rail: The main railway lines run from Lomé northwards to Blitta (midway between Atakpamé and Sokodé) and to Kpalimé, and eastwards to Aného.
Water: Ferries serve the ports along the coast.
City transport
Taxis: Readily available in Lomé, while shared taxis ply to other main towns; tipping is not usual.

Car hire

Available, but generally expensive. International driving licence required.

BUSINESS DIRECTORY

The addresses listed below are a selection only. While World of Information makes every endeavour to check these addresses, we cannot guarantee that changes have not been made, especially to telephone numbers and area codes. We would welcome any corrections.

Telephone area codes

The international direct dialling (IDD) code for Togo is +228, followed by subscriber's number.

Chambers of Commerce

Togo Chamber of Commerce, Agriculture and Industry, Angle Avenues de la Présidence et Georges Pompidou, PO Box 360, Lomé (tel: 221-2065; fax: 221-4730; e-mail: ccit@rdd.tg).

Banking

Banque Internationale pour l'Afrique au Togo, BP 346, 13 rue du Commerce, Lomé (tel: 221-3286; fax: 221-1019; e-mail: bia-togo@café.tg).

Banque Togolaise de Développement, BP 65, Place de L'Independance, Angle Avenues des Nîmes et Grunitzky, Lomé (tel 221-3641; fax: 221-4456; e-mail: togo_devbank.btd.tog).

Banque Togolaise pour le Commerce et l'Industrie, BP 363, 169 Boulevard du 13 Janvier, Lomé (tel: 221-4641; fax: 21-3265; e-mail: sda@btci.tg).

Ecobank-Togo, BP 3302, 20 Rue du Commerce, Lomé (tel: 222-6574; fax: 221-4237; e-mail: ecobanktg@ecobank.com).

Société Inter Africaine de Banque, BP 4874, 14 Rue du Commerce, Lomé (tel: 221-1341; fax: 221-5829; e-mail: siab@bibway.com).

Société Nationale d'Investissement et Fonds Annexes BP 2682, 11 Avenue du 24 Janvier, Lomé (tel: 221-6221; fax: 221-6225; e-mail: sni@ids.tg).

Union Togolaise de Banques, BP 359, Boulevard du 13 Janvier, Lomé (tel: 221-6411; fax: 221-2206; utbsdg@café.tg).

Central bank

Banque Centrale des Etats de l'Afrique de l'Ouest, Direction Nationale, BP 120, Rue des Nimes, Lomé (tel: 221-2512; fax: 221-7602).

Stock exchange

Afribourse (Bourse Régionale des Valeurs Moblières) (BRVM), www.brvm.org

Travel information

Ministry of tourism

Ministry of Culture, Tourism and Leisure, BP 3114, Lomé (tel: 221-5400; fax: 221-8927).

National tourist organisation offices

Office national togolais du tourism, BP 1289, Route d'Aného, Lomé, (tel: 221-4313; fax: 221-8927; e-mail: info@togo-tourisme.com).

Other useful addresses

Direction de la Statistique, BP 118, Lomé (tel: 270-662).

Direction des Professions Touristiques, BP 1289, Lomé (tel: 215-662, 214-313).

Kpeme Port Authority, OTP BP 362, Lomé (tel: 213-901; fax: 217-105).

Office des Produits Agricoles du Togo, BP 1334, Lomé (agency dealing with marketing, export, development) (tel: 214-471).

OPTT-Post Office and Telecommunications of Togo, Lomé (tel: 213-737; fax: 210-373).

Togo Embassy (USA), 2208 Massachusetts Avenue, NW, Washington DC 20008 (tel: (+1-202) 234-4212; fax: (+1-202) 232-3190).

National news agency: Agence Togolaise de Presse (ATOP)

République Togolaise (in French and English) (www.republicoftogo.com)

Le Togolais (in French) (www.letogolais.com)

Internet sites

Africa Business Network: http://www.ifc.org/abn

AllAfrica.com: http://allafrica.com

African Development Bank: http://www.afdb.org

Africa Online: http://www.africaonline.com

Mbendi AfroPaedia (information on companies, countries, industries and stock exchanges in Africa): http://mbendi.co.za

Republic of Togolais (in French): http://www.republicoftogo.com

Online Togo news: http://www.togodaily.com

Togo Official website: http://www.afrika.com/togo/html

Tokelau

KEY FACTS

Official name: Tokelau

Head of State: Queen Elizabeth II, represented by Governor General of New Zealand, Anand Satyanand (since 23 Aug 2006) and Administrator Jonathan Kings (since February 2011)

Head of government: Siopili Perez (since 23 February 2015).

Area: 12 square km (three coral atolls: Nukunonu, Fakaofo, Atafu)

Population: 1,353 (2012)*; some 6,000 Tokelauans live in New Zealand.

Capital: Each atoll has its own administrative centre

Official language: Tokelauan (English also spoken)

Currency: New Zealand dollar (NZ$) =100 cents; also Tala or Samoan dollar (S$)

Exchange rate: NZ$1.58 per US$ (Nov 2015)

GDP per capita: US$1,035 (2009)*

Balance of trade: -US$2.35 million (2009)

* estimated figure

Tokelau has a population of less than 1,500 on its three coral atolls – Nukunonu, Fakaofo, Atafu – although another 6,000 or so Tokelauans live in New Zealand. The physical characteristics of the atolls allow limited scope for economic development and the few natural resources are sufficient only to meet the needs of the people. Agricultural products are of a basic subsistence nature. Food crops consist of coconuts, pulaka, breadfruit, taamu, papaya, edible padanus fruit and bananas. Many other seeds have been tested but because of the poverty of the soil very poor results have been achieved. Crops, particularly coconut trees, must be protected from the Polynesian rat and the rhinoceros beetle.

Livestock consists of pigs, poultry and goats. Attempts to improve the local pig stock have achieved some positive results. Exotic breeds have been interbred with local pigs to produce new bloodlines.

Tokalau is heavily dependent on New Zealand for economic support, although it does have its own Trust Fund (standing at US$58 million) and is looking at ways of increasing its own revenue earning capacity in areas such as fisheries licensing, handicrafts, tourism and stamps and coins.

Ocean and lagoon fish and shellfish are readily available and are part of the staple diet. Fisheries licence fees contribute some US$500,000 a year to Tokelau's budget.

Copra production has declined significantly in recent years due to falling international requirements. Tokelauan handicraft, particularly woven items such as mats, hats, bags and fans, are renowned throughout the Pacific for their detail.

Each village has co-operative stores run by village management committees. The public service administration works closely with these committees to assist with management and to reduce the costs of goods arriving in Tokelau.

COUNTRY PROFILE

Tokelau's three atolls are believed to have been settled by people from Samoa, Cook Islands and Tuvalu. Nineteenth-century whalers and missionaries were among the first European visitors to Tokelau, formerly known as the Union Islands.

1765 Atafu was first sighted by Commodore John Byron and named Duke of York's Island.

1889 The Union Islands became a British protectorate.

1916 At the request of the inhabitants, the United Kingdom annexed the islands and included them within the Gilbert and Ellice Islands Colony (now Kiribati and Tuvalu).

1926 The British government transferred administrative control of the islands to New Zealand (NZ).

1946 The islands were renamed Tokelau Islands.

1948 The Tokelau Islands Act made NZ the formal administering authority.

1976 The islands were renamed Tokelau.

1994 Executive and administrative functions were delegated by NZ to the General Fono (or Council of Faipule when the General Fono is not in session).

1996 Subordinate legislative power was granted to the General Fono by the New Zealand Tokelau Amendment Act.

2001 Tokelau became responsible for its own public service.

2003 A new Principles of Partnership document was signed with NZ.

2004 The UN presented a *Special Case Study* on de-colonisation, urging Tokelau to become independent. The NZ premier Helen Clark visited and signed a three-year agreement on economic support. The General Fono agreed to explore an option of self-government in free association with NZ.

2005 A draft constitution was approved by the General Fono, and agreement was reached on the main elements of the Treaty of Free Association.

2006 A referendum on the Treaty of Free Association with NZ failed with less than the necessary two-thirds majority. Tokelau's status remained unchanged. David Payton was appointed administrator. Census results showed that the population on the three tiny atolls had dropped by 20 per cent over five years.

2007 A second referendum on the Treaty of Free Association also failed to reach a two-thirds majority.

2009 The worst health epidemic since the 1970s struck, with one-in-ten locals falling sick with influenza. Village gatherings

were cancelled and schools closed and a New Zealand medical team was dispatched to provide aid.
2010 Kuresa Nasau became head of the on-going government. Tokelau declared that its territorial waters had become a whale sanctuary, of over 300,000 square kilometres.
2011 Tokelau's internet domain name (.tk) became the world's third most used country-code, mainly as a source of *phishing* (sending fraudulent e-mails claiming to be from legitimate concerns in order to persuade recipients to reveal personal information, such as credit-card details). Sir Jerry Mateparae was appointed as Governor General of New Zealand. A state of emergency was declared in October after fresh water ran out and bottled water dwindled to a week's supply. The shortage was caused by a lack of rainfall blamed on the *La Nina* weather pattern. The New Zealand Defence Force and Red Cross responded by delivering personnel and water supplies as well as desalination machines, while Samoa organised a shipment of 100,000 litres of water. A national census was conducted on 18 October, the results of which were published in December. The count was of 1,411 people, which showed a 3.8 per cent decrease in the number recorded in 2006 (1,466). On Thursday 29 December at 11.59.59 Tokelau lost one day, as it moved forward to Saturday 31 December at 00.00 and moved its relative position from east of the International Dateline to the west, so that Tokelau became one of the first countries to begin the daily cycle and not the last to see the sun set; in effect it moved a day ahead in time and came into line with its trading partners in Oceania and Australasia in a move that matched the same move by Samoa.
2012 On 15 February, Aliki Faipule Foua Toloa became *Ulu-o-Tokelau* (titular head). The New Zealand government provided Tokelau with a new 36-seat ferry, leased for two years at a cost of NZ$6 million (US$7.3 million), to replace the existing, aging vessel. On 7 November, all electricity needs were switched from diesel fuel to photovoltaic (solar) power, from panels constructed on the three atolls and provided by New Zealand.
2013 Tokelau became the first nation to be entirely powered by the sun. Three solar photovoltaic systems (one on each island) supply 150 per cent of current electricity needs.
2014 Elections to the Fono were held on 23 January. Only three members retained their seats in the Council of the Ongoing Government. All members are independents.
2015 After a meeting in October to dicuss climate change, the Pacific islands of Fiji, Kiribati, Tuvalu and Tokelau issued a joint statement in which they asked for help in funding the cost of raising buildings above predicted sea level increases and to safeguard water supplies from saltwater intrusion. The low-lying nations said that moving people because of rising sea levels, storms and ruined agriculture was a last resort, but the 'calamity' of climate change required industrialised countries to devise a plan.

Political structure

Constitution

Under the 1948 Tokelau Islands Act (through which New Zealand was the formal administering authority), Tokelau is within the territorial boundaries of New Zealand and Tokelauans are New Zealand citizens. The 1948 Act was amended and subordinate legislative power was granted to the General Fono by the Tokelau Amendment Act in 1996.

Form of state

Self-administering territory of New Zealand.

The executive

The Head of State is the British Monarch, who is represented by an administrator, appointed from New Zealand. The Ulu o Tokelau (head of government) is a position, which is rotated annually among the three Faipule (leaders) and holds executive power and presides over the Council for Ongoing Goverment (cabinet). The Council consists of the Faipule and Pulenuku (mayors) of each atoll. It has a mandate to manage government business but not to pass laws or introduce taxes.

National legislature

Each island atoll has a Council of Elders (Taupulega) which is the source of authority. The Taupulega delegates authority to the General Fono (parliament) on matters of taxes, law, national policy, budget and management. Parliament sits for three–four days, three–four times a year on the atoll which is home to the current Ulu o Tokelau (head of government). When not in session government business is executed through the Council of Ongoing Government. The unicameral parliament comprises 20 members, elected by simple majority vote between the three islands: Nukunonu six seats, Fakaofo and Atafu seven seats, elected by universal suffrage for a term of three years.

Legal system

The villages have the statutory power to enact their own laws covering village affairs.
Civil and criminal jurisdiction is exercised by commissioners and the New Zealand high court.
There is little crime apart from petty theft and there are no prisons. Punishment generally takes the form of public rebukes, fines or labour.

Last elections

23 January 2014 (General Fono)
Results: General Fono: all seats were won by independents, only three members were re-elected.

Next elections

2017 (General Fono).

Political parties

There are no organised political parties. Around 42 per cent of the population are under 14 years. An estimated 8,000 Tokelauans are resident overseas, mainly in New Zealand and Samoa. A national census was conducted on 18 October 2011, the results of which were published in December. The count was of 1,411 people, which showed a 3.8 per cent decrease in the number recorded in 2006 (1,466).
Despite outside influences, the majority of the population adheres to the *Faka Tokelau* (the traditional family and community way of life).

Population

1,353 (2012)*; some 6,000 Tokelauans live in New Zealand.
Last census: 18 October 2011: 1,411
Annual growth rate: -0.6 per cent (2003)

Ethnic make-up

The residents are mainly Polynesians, with close links to Samoa.

Religions

Christianity

Education

Each atoll has its own school with classes beginning at pre-school and carrying through to Year 10. The Year 11 class is hosted on a different atoll every five years and is made up of students combined from each atoll. After graduation from school, the top eight or 10 students are given a scholarship for further study overseas. Staff members are qualified teachers, usually from Samoa, Fiji and New Zealand.

Health

Tokelau has two doctors, one dentist, eight nurses and three midwives. Tokelau collaborates with the World Health Organisation (WHO) in health promotion projects. There are hospitals on Atafu, Fakaofo and Nukunono.
Life expectancy: 69 years (estimate 2003)

Main cities

Fakaofo (estimated population 253 in 2012), Atafu (126), Nukunonu (85).

Languages spoken

Official language/s

Tokelauan (English also spoken)

Media

Press

There are online news outlets including Event Polynesia, with a sub-heading for Tokelau (www.eventpolynesia.com).

Broadcasting

Radio: There is only one radio station which broadcasts to each of the islands in AM and FM. External service include Pacific Island Radio (www.pacificislandsradio.com), Radio Australia (www.radioaustralia.net.au/pacbeat) and from New Zealand (www.accessradio.org.nz), which provides news for expatriate Tokelauns.

Television: There are no television broadcasts.

Other news agencies: ABC Pacific Beat: www.radioaustralia.net.au/pacbeat Pacific Magazine: www.pacificmagazine.net

Economy

The economy is based on communal subsistence, agriculture and fishing. The atolls' size, isolation and lack of land-based resources allow little scope for economic development.

Sales of licences to fish for tuna, postage stamps, souvenir coins, handicrafts and remittances from migrant workers are the principal sources of foreign exchange.

Fees from fishing licences, purchased by foreign companies operating within Tokelau's Exclusive Economic Zone, raise up to US$700,000 annually.

Grants from New Zealand account for about 80 per cent of expenditure. Funding from the New Zealand bilateral aid programme, the UN Development Programme (UNDP), the South Pacific Commission, the ILO and other international agencies has been the main source of development assistance. The International Trust Fund, which was set up in 2004 to provide Tokelau with an independent source of revenue, had reached NZ$78.5 million (US$51.3 million) in 2014. Tokelau is almost entirely dependent on aid from New Zealand to sustain itself, with a GDP per capita of some US$1,000.

Since 1982, the General Fono has collected a tax on the salaries of public servants unavailable for communal service (called the Community Services Levy) in order to subsidise copra and handicrafts producers, provide honoraria to members of island councils and supplement village projects.

At the end of 2011, in order to improve their regional trade links, Tokelau and Samoa skipped a day in order to join the same time zone as main trade partners Australia and New Zealand.

External trade

Tokelau has a close link to New Zealand which provides a framework for international trade. Tokelau's isolation (25–30 hours by sea from its closest neighbour) hampers trade.

Imports

Imports are foodstuffs, building materials and fuel.

Main sources: New Zealand and Australia.

Exports

Modest exports of stamps, copra and handicrafts.

Main destinations: New Zealand and Australia.

Agriculture

Farming

The soil is thin and infertile and the land does not rise more than five metres above sea level. Rainfall is erratic and crops are subject to drought and storm damage. The main subsistence crops are coconut and breadfruit, supplemented by pulaka, ta'amu, pandanus, bananas, pawpaw, with experimental crops of cucumbers, tomatoes, beans, cabbage and watermelon.

Fishing

Fishing for tuna, bonito, trevally and mullet supplies the main source of protein for the inhabitants. The typical annual marine fish catch is 200t.

Industry and manufacturing

Main industries include copra production, woodwork and the manufacture of woven and plaited goods such as hats, mats, bags and fans. The copra industry suffers from volatile world prices.

Tourism

Tokelau is not a tourist destination, but it does attract a small number of visitors. The main accommodation is a small hotel. There is opportunity for swimming and snorkelling.

Access is only via the state-owned MV Tokelau, which carries 65 passengers in total (but lacks berths for all) and cargo in a 6–11 day round trip to and from Tokelau and the Samoan capital Apia. The service is fortnightly.

Although plans for a new ship with added facilities, being built and funded through New Zealand aid, have no published timetable, in 2012, a new 36 seat ferry was leased for two years, to replace the existing one, at a cost of NZ$6 million (US$7.3 million).

There is no commercial air service to Tokelau.

Hydrocarbons

There are no known hydrocarbon reserves and all domestic energy needs are met by imports from New Zealand.

Banking and insurance

The nearest commercial banking services are in Apia, Samoa, although savings facilities under the control of the administrative officer have been set up on each atoll.

Time

GMT plus 13 hours; daylight saving, GMT plus 14 hours (from 31 December 2011).

Geography

Tokelau comprises three atolls (Atafu, Nukunonu and Fakaofo) lying about 480km (300 miles) north of Samoa in the Pacific Ocean.

Hemisphere

Southern

Climate

The average mean temperature is 28 degrees Celsius; warmest in May and coolest in July. Rainfall is heavy but irregular. Severe tropical storms are rare, but possible.

Entry requirements

Tokelau is a dependent territory of New Zealand. Passport and visa requirements are the same as for New Zealand.

Visa

Consent to visit Tokelau should be obtained in advance from the Councils of Elders (*taupulega*). This, together with visas and visitor and cruising permits, can be arranged through the Tokelau Apia Liaison Office in Samoa. Accommodation and a return ticket must be booked before arrival.

Currency advice/regulations

There are no restrictions on the import and export of local or foreign currencies.

Customs

Any firearms must be surrendered until departure.

Prohibited imports

Illegal drugs, plants or plant material, animals or by-products, biological specimens, artifacts made from endangered wildlife and weapons, such as flick knives, are prohibited.

Health (for visitors)

Mandatory precautions

Vaccination certificates required for yellow fever if travelling from infected area.

Advisable precautions

Vaccination for hepatitis A and B, tetanus, typhoid. Rabies is a risk.

Hotels

The Luana Liki Hotel can be found on the atoll of Nukunonu. There are no hotels on Atafu and Fakaofo, although accommodation can be arranged through local families prior to or upon arrival.

Social customs/useful tips
Visitors should be considerate of the island's customs, such as paying due respect to all older persons.
Atafu is officially a dry island. Atafu, Fakaofo and Nukunono have only one co-operative store each. Water is scarce everywhere.

Getting there
Air
There are no air services to Tokelau.
Surface
Water: Tokelau can only be reached by sea. The *MV Tokelau* carries cargo and passengers between Samoa and Tokelau, supplemented by two other vessels (*Samoa Express* and *Lady Naomi*), which ply the route less frequently. Private yachts are the only other means of reaching Tokelau. There are no harbour facilities and only small boats are able to pass through the surrounding reefs; these passages are too shallow for most yachts, which, like the cargo ships, have to anchor outside the reef, although conditions are often unsuitable for such anchorage.

Getting about
National transport
Road: There are no paved roads and few vehicles.
Water: There is a fortnightly catamaran passenger service, which runs between the atolls.

BUSINESS DIRECTORY
The addresses listed below are a selection only. While World of Information makes every endeavour to check these addresses, we cannot guarantee that changes have not been made, especially to telephone numbers and area codes. We would welcome any corrections.

Telephone area codes
The international direct dialling (IDD) code for Tokelau is +690 followed by subscriber's number.

Other useful addresses
Tokelau Apia Liaison Office, PO Box 865, Apia, Samoa (tel: (+685) 20-822; fax: 21-761; e-mail: maka@lesamoa.net).

Tokelau Council of Faipule, PO Box 865, Apia, Samoa (tel: (+685) 20-822; fax: 21-761; e-mail: falani.aukuso@clear.net.nz).

ABC Pacific Beat: www.radioaustralia.net.au/pacbeat

Pacific Magazine: www.pacificmagazine.net

Internet sites
General information on Tokelau: www.dot.tk

Government of Tokelau: www.tokelau.org.nz

Tonga

KEY FACTS

Official name: Kingdom of Tonga

Head of State: King Tupou VI (21 Mar 2012)

Head of government: Prime Minister Samiuela 'Akilisi Pohiva (from 30 Dec 2014)

Ruling party: Democratic Party of the Friendly Islands (DPFI)

Area: 748 square km (170 islands)

Population: 102,000 (2014)*

Capital: Nuku'alofa (on Tongatapu)

Official language: Tongan

Currency: Tongan dollar or Pa'anga (T$) = 100 seniti

Exchange rate: T$2.17 per US$ (Sep 2015)

GDP per capita: US$4,429 (2014)*

GDP real growth: 2.32% (2014)*

GDP: US$454.00 million (2014)*

Inflation: 1.33% (2014)*

Balance of trade: -US$173.00 million (2012)*

Foreign debt: US$166.00 million (2012)

Annual FDI: US$10.41 million (2011)

* estimated figure

COUNTRY PROFILE

Tonga's dynasty goes back to the tenth century.
1616 Dutch explorers were the first Europeans to visit Tonga.
1773–77 Captain James Cook visited Tonga three times
1875 Taufa'ahau Tupou became George Tupou I and established the Tongan monarchy.
1899 Under the Tripartite Treaty, Britain gained control of Germany's rights in Tonga, Niue, and the Solomon Islands in exchange for withdrawing its claim to Samoa.
1918 Queen Salote Tupou III was crowned.
1953 Queen Salote visited Britain for the coronation of Elizabeth II as Queen.
1965 Queen Salote died and her son was crowned King Taufa'ahau Tupou IV.
1970 Tonga ceased to be a British protectorate and became fully independent within the Commonwealth.
1992 A Pro-Democracy Movement (PDM) emerged.
1994 The PDM formed the first political party, the Tonga Democratic Party, later renamed the People's Party (PP).
1996 In the general election, the PP won a majority of those seats open to popular vote.
1999 The Human Rights and Democracy Movement (HRDM) (formerly the Peoples' Party) won five of the popularly elected nine seats in the Legislative Assembly.
2000 Prince 'Ulukalala Lavaka Ata was appointed prime minister by the King (his father).
2001 Tonga was removed from the Organisation for Economic Co-operation and Development (OECD) blacklist of countries acting as unfair tax havens.
2002 In parliamentary elections, the HRDM won seven of the nine elected seats.
2003 Changes to the constitution were made, giving greater powers to the King and increasing state control of the media.
2004 Royal Tongan Airlines (RTA) was declared bankrupt; with debts of over US$8.5 million and a lack of funds RTA had been forced to halt its inter-island services.
2005 In parliamentary elections, the HRDM won seven of the nine seats. The People's Democratic Party (PDP) was formed led by Teisina Fuko.
2006 Prince Ulukalala Lavaka Ata resigned and Feleti Sevele (HRDM) became the first commoner to be prime minister. King Taufa'ahau Tupou IV died after a long illness and was succeeded by his eldest son, Sia'osi Taufa'ahau Manumata'ogo Tuku'aho Tupou (known as Crown Prince Tupouto'a). He was sworn in as King Sia'osi (Tongan for George) Tupou V. A pro-democracy demonstration turned into a riot that killed eight people, injured dozens and led to the arrest of over 100 demonstrators and the destruction of the central business district, including an arson attack on a supermarket owned by the prime minister. The King's formal coronation was postponed.
2007 Tonga became the 151st member of the WTO.
2008 The King announced that he would relinquish the monarchy's traditional near-absolute power, changing the country's form of state to a constitutional monarchy by 2010, through a democratic elected parliament.
2009 The Asian Development Bank (ADB) awarded a US$10 million programme grant to help maintain financial stability during the global economic crisis. The reconstruction of the business district of the capital Nuku'alofa was begun, funded by a US$58.8 million loan from China.
2010 Parliament approved the increase in the number of legislative assembly members from nine to 17, to reflect the new, single seat, parliamentary constituencies. A new political party, the Tongan Democratic Labour Party, was formed in June to contest the November elections. In April, the Tonga Broadcasting Commission (TBC) was required to censor parliamentary candidates' political broadcasts and TBC reporters were prohibited from interviewing candidates on the grounds that they 'lacked the necessary training for objective coverage'. On 6 September, Samiuela 'Akilisi Pohiva, along with Uliti Uata (leader of the pressure group Human Rights and Democracy Movement (HRDM)), founded the Paati Temokalati 'a e 'Otu Motu 'Anga'ofa (PTOMA) (Democratic Party of the Friendly Islands). The King officially relinquished most of his powers following Tonga's first egalitarian

parliamentary elections, held on 25 November, in which four political parties and over 120 independent candidates took part. The PTOMA won 28.49 per cent of the vote (12 seats out of 26) while independents won a total of 67.3 per cent (five); three other political parties failed to win any seats. Nine seats were reserved for representatives of the nobility. Turnout was 89 per cent. As the PTOMA failed to win enough seats to rule independently, coalition talks began immediately. On 21 December, parliament voted by 14 votes for Lord Siale'ataonga Tu'ivakano (elected as a representative by the noblility) as prime minister, by 14 votes against 12 for Samiuela 'Akilisi Pohiva (PTOMA). Prime Minister Lord Tu'ivakano took office on 22 December.

2011 Opposition leader Samiuela 'Akilisi Pohiva (PTOMA) resigned from the government on 14 January. The trial of the operators of the *MV Princess Ashika* ferry that sank in 2008 with the loss of 74 people was concluded on 4 April. Seven men were sentenced for up to five years in jail (although a few had suspended sentences) and the company fined one million pa'anga (around US$506,000), to be paid in compensation to the women and children's crisis centre in recognition of the loss of the women on-board. The King opened the first democratically elected parliament in Tonga's history on 2 June. On 18 August, Tonga requested development assistance from Australia to help it through its debt crisis. Around one-third of Tonga's GDP is owed in its debt to China.

2012 On 18 March, while on a visit to Hong Kong, King Sia'osi (George) Tupou V died, aged 63 years. Crown Prince Tupouto'a Lavaka Ata, (younger brother of King Tupou V), was formally proclaimed as King Tupou VI on 21 March. King George Tupou was buried following a state funeral on 27 March. In April, the Kingdom of Tonga made a bid to host the 2019 Pacific Games, which typically attracts over 5,000 athletes and officials from competing countries.

2013 Chathams Pacific, previously the only airline with scheduled services within Tonga, pulled out in March after local company Real Tonga said it was setting up operations. There was concern within the tourist industry when Chathams stopped flying before Real Tonga was scheduled to begin at the start of the main tourist season. However, at the last minute Real Tonga managed to lease an aircraft from Air Vanuatu. Chathams Pacific was believed to be flying a DC3 understood to be nearly 70 years old and the only DC3 in the world still flying passengers on regularly scheduled commercial services.

2014 The first review of the trade policies and practices of Tonga took place in February. The basis for the review was a report by the WTO Secretariat and a report by the Government of Tonga. Elections were held on 27 November. On 29 December parliament elected Samuela 'Akilisi Pohiva as prime minister by 15 votes to 11, the first commoner to take the post. He was sworn in on 30 December.

2015 In October the prime minister addressed the UN General Assembly, and delivered Tonga's statement during the General Debate sessions on 29 September.

Political structure

Constitution

The constitution dates from 1875. Changes to the constitution were made in October 2003, giving greater powers to the King and increasing state control of the media.

By 2010, pro-democracy activists had succeeded in procuring wide-ranging reforms to the Tongan constitution, which had more or less remained unchanged since its inception. Essentially, power was taken from the monarchy and Tonga's form of state moved from hereditary to constitutional monarchy. The prime minister is now chosen by the legislative assembly and is, in turn, allowed to choose his/her own cabinet – both previously the job of the monarch.

Further changes to the electoral system now mean that the majority of legislative assembly are democratically elected, rather than hereditary nobles appointed by right of birth.

Voting age: 21 years

Form of state

Constitutional monarchy

The executive

Since 2010, the cabinet has become the highest executive authority in Tonga. The cabinet is chosen by the prime minister and then appointed by the king. Cabinet members must come from the legislative assembly.

National legislature

The Fale Alea (Legislative Assembly) is a unicameral chamber, with 26 members. 17 of the members are elected by popular vote. There are plans to make it fully democratic in the near future.

Last elections

27 November 2014 (parliamentary)

Results: Parliamentary: DPFI won 9 seats, Independents won 8 seats; the remaining 9 seats were taken by Noble's representatives

Next elections

2018 (parliamentary)

Political parties

The constitution does not allow political parties to form a government, but at the discretion of the monarch, some representatives may join the cabinet.

Ruling party

Democratic Party of the Friendly Islands (DPFI)

Main opposition party

People's Democratic Party (PDP)

Political situation

The MV *Princess Ashika*, an inter-island ferry, sank in July 2009 six weeks after going into service in Tonga and killed 74 people. It was declared a national tragedy and a Royal Commission was convened to enquired into the details of the sinking. The conclusion of the commission in 2010 was that the Tongan government had not had the *Princess Ashika* surveyed for seaworthiness before purchase and subsequent surveys by the ministry of transport failed to stop the operations of the vessel. Manslaughter charges were later laid against the captains and operator of the ferry.

Approximately 38 per cent of the total population are under 15 years. Most of the 170 islands are uninhabited.

Population

104,000 (2013)*

Last census: 30 November 2006: 101,991

Population density: 138 inhabitants per square km (2010). Urban population 23 per cent (2010 Unicef).

Annual growth rate: 0.4 per cent, 1990–2010 (Unicef).

Ethnic make-up

The population is mainly of Polynesian descent. Only about 300 inhabitants are of European origin.

Religions

The Wesleyan Methodist church is the major denomination.

Education

In June 2005, New Zealand and the World Bank announced their co-operation in a US$10 million project to improve the quality of education in Tonga.

Literacy rate: 98.5 per cent, adult rate (2003)

Compulsory years: 6 to 14.

Health

Figures from the United Nations Children's Fund (UNCF) (formerly Unicef) revealed in January 2010 that 80 per cent of families in the most vulnerable communities were without funds to buy food; more heads of households were losing their jobs due to the global economic crisis, which had resulted in rising food prices and falling remittances. Malnutrition, particularly among children and women, was becoming of increasing concern as governments in the Pacific region were cutting back on social expenditure in the face of recession.

Life expectancy: 71 years, 2004 (WHO 2006)

Fertility rate/Maternal mortality rate: 3.9 births per woman, 2010 (Unicef)

Birth rate/Death rate: 24.5 births and 5.5 deaths per 1,000 people (2003)

Child (under 5 years) mortality rate (per 1,000): 13 per 1,000 live births (WHO 2012)

Head of population per physician: 0.34 physicians per 1,000 people, 2001 (WHO 2006)

Welfare

Statistic by the United Nations Children's Fund (UNCF) (formerly Unicef) revealed in January 2010 that 80 per cent of families in the most vulnerable communities were without funds to buy food, as more heads of households were losing their jobs due to the global economic crisis. Malnutrition, particularly among children and women, was becoming of increasing concern as governments in the Pacific region were cutting back on social expenditure in the face of recession.

Main cities

Nuku'alofa, on Tongatapu (capital, estimated population 24,571 in 2012), Ma'a (5,294), Neiafu (3,954), Havelolоto (3,575), Vaini (3,114), Tofoa-Koloua (2,653), Pangai (1,556), Ohonua (1,270), Hihifo (633).

Languages spoken

English is widely spoken. It is used in education and for administrative purposes.

Official language/s

Tongan

Media

Press

A constitutional amendment increased the power of the state to control the media with licensing laws and ownership rules. Publications in Tongan include *Taimi o Vavau* (The Tonga Times) (www.timesoftonga.com).

Weeklies: Weeklies are available in both English and Tongan covering local political and economic news. These include *Ko e Kalonikali Tonga/Tonga Chronicle* and *Tonga Times* (bi-weekly) in Tongan and English editions.

Taimi o Tonga is a bi-lingual weekly publication – the government banned *Taimi o Tonga* in 2003, following a March 2002 sedition charge which was later dropped; its licence was re-approved by the government in October 2004.

Periodicals: In Tongan and English, *Matangi Tonga* (www.matangitonga.to) and *Eva*, are quarterly magazines, *Tonga Star* (www.tongastar.com), is bi-monthly and provides critical analyses of the economic and political affairs. Others include *Lao & Hia* (fortnightly), *Ofa ki Tonga* (Christian publication, *Ko e Tohi Fanongonongo* and *Taumu'a Lelei* (Catholic publication) monthly.

Broadcasting

The public service broadcaster is the Tonga Broadcasting Commission (TBC) (www.Tonga-broadcasting.com), which does not accept advertising.

Radio: The national network, TBC, has three stations include Radio Tonga 1, Kool 90FM and FM103 (a 24 hour Radio Australia relay), broadcasts are in Tongan and English. Private local radio stations include Milennium Radio (www.tongatapu.net.to), UCB Pacific (Christian service), Radio 2000 and Radio Nuku'alofa.

Television: TBC operates Television Tonga. There are several private TV stations including the Friendly Island Broadcasting Network, based in Vava'u, Tonfon TV, a pay-to-view service and OBN TV7 a popular channel that has it service suspended by the government in November 2006. A new channel, TelevisionTonga 2, was launched in 2008, broadcasting a range of programmes including sports, films and foreign programmes.

Other news agencies: ABC Pacific Beat: www.radioaustralia.net.au/pacbeat
Pacific Magazine:
www.pacificmagazine.net
Pacific Islands New Association (Pina): www.pina.com.fj

Economy

Tonga has a small, open economy, with tourism and agriculture as the main generators of wealth. The service sector accounted for 59.3 per cent of GDP in 2014, of which tourism accounted for 17.2 per cent. Agriculture contributed around 19.2 per cent to GDP, and industry 21.5 per cent. The number of visitors to the islands tops 40,000 per year (45,000 in 2013), the majority of which arrive by air; although a significant minority (over 2,000) arrive by yacht. The greater number are expatriates from New Zealand (over 15,000), and visitors from the US and Australia (around 10,000) constituting the majority of the remainder. Agricultural exports include fish, squash, vanilla, kava, coconuts and their derivatives, and root crops. Farms in Tonga are either small, family-run plots, with farmers combining to form co-operatives to grow crops either for local consumption or for export, or large commercial enterprises. Meat is a staple of the diet, although Tonga's production is unable to meet domestic demand, so large quantities of either live animals or butchered meat are imported annually. Foreign aid and private remittances typically offset Tonga's regular trade deficit. Remittances in 2010 were US$77 million (19.7 per cent of GDP), a figure that had fallen to US$59.6 million by 2012.

GDP growth was 0.5 per cent in 2008, which improved only marginally by 0.9 per cent in 2009, as a result of the global economic recession that depressed world trade in general and cut tourist numbers, which quickly impacted Tongan growth, jobs and foreign exchange. In 2010, GDP growth was 1.6 per cent and in 2013 the economy dropped into recession recording growth of -2.7 per cent before returning to the positive rate of 2.1 per cent in 2014.

One of the main problems facing Tonga is job creation. There are around 2,000 school-leavers per year, but only some 500 find jobs and few can emigrate. Unemployment and under-employment are creating social problems. Areas of possible development include offshore oil, fish and vegetable canneries and coconut-based industries. Offshore banking has had to deal with a global crackdown on international money laundering and Tonga has had to undertake anti-corruption measures as a central part of the economic reform programme.

In November 2011, the World Bank announced a loan that amounted to the equivalent of US$9 million. The grant has been used to strengthen public financial management and fiscal policy, promote structural reform and improve social protection.

External trade

Tonga is a member of the South Pacific Regional Trade and Economic Co-operation Agreement (Sparteca) along with 12 other regional nations, which allows products duty free access by Pacific Island Forum members to Australian and New Zealand markets (subject to the country of origin restrictions). Tonga is a member of the World Trade Organisation

Tourism and remittances contribute the dominant proportions of foreign earnings. Manufacturing is underdeveloped and agriculture is either large-scale enterprises or small co-operative farming units producing principally squash for export. Fishing, either by domestic fishermen or licensed foreign trawlers, is a growing industry.

Imports

Main imports are foodstuffs, dairy, live animals (cattle, sheep and chickens), building materials, machinery and vehicles, fuels and chemicals.

Main sources: Fiji (35 per cent of total in 2014), New Zealand (20.5 per cent), China (10.8 per cent), United States (9.1 per cent) and Japan (5 per cent).

Exports

Main exports are agricultural produce including squash, coconuts, vanilla beans, root crops, tuna, seaweed and sea slugs.

Main destinations: New Zealand (16.7 per cent of total in 2014), United States (15.6 per cent), Fiji (11.2 per cent), Japan (10 per cent), Samoa (9.5 per cent), South Korea and Australia 7.9 per cent).

Agriculture

Farming

Agriculture and fishing accounted for around 19.2 per cent of GDP in 2014 and employed a large chunk of the labour force. The soil is generally fertile, but production can suffer from hurricane damage.

All land is held by the Crown and every adult male Tongan is entitled to a smallholding (alienation of land is forbidden). Two-thirds of the kingdom's families raise their own livestock (pigs and poultry) and subsistence crops of manioc, yams, breadfruit, watermelons, tomatoes, cassava, oranges and capsicum. Coconut, vanilla and bananas are produced for export, as is the tranquiliser ingredient, kava.

Cash crops include squash and vanilla crops and aloe vera, which has become a popular crop among farmers as it has a viable export market and there is a new processing plant in Nuku'alofa.

Fishing

Fishing provides additional food and export revenue. Seaweed is in big demand, particularly from Japanese buyers.

The typical annual marine fish catch is over 4,000 tonnes (t), plus over 300t of other seafood.

Forestry

Old coconut tree trunks fulfil up to 25 per cent of timber needs. Typical annual production is 2,000 cubic metres (cum) industrial roundwood, 2,000cum sawnwood and 90,000cum wood fuel.

Industry and manufacturing

The industrial sector accounts for 21.9 per cent of GDP and employs approximately 7.0 per cent of the workforce.

There is a thriving small-industries centre on a mini-industrial area in Nuku'alofa where most of the more advanced products are made. Annual industrial production is almost US$20 million per annum. Manufacturing accounts for 6 per cent of GDP and employs 5 per cent of the labour force. The wide range of products includes shoes, saddles, footballs, knitwear, wooden toys, corrugated iron, plastic piping, bicycle assembly, wire netting, paper, paint, biscuits and processed milk, pulp and passion fruit processing, dumper truck bodies and mini-excavators.

Tourism

Tourism is an important component of the economy – Tonga has a history for welcoming visitors. Attractions include aquatic and native wildlife, handicrafts and historical features. Activities are largely centred on the ocean, with yachting, fishing and diving being some of the most popular. The industry has been under development and attracted an average 8.2 per cent of total capital investment over 2013.

Travel and tourism contributed 17.2 per cent of GDP over 2014. The sector employed 17.4 per cent of the workforce (6,000 jobs) in the same period.

There has been a growth in development in conference and incentive travel to Tonga and in 2012 the government made a successful bid to hold the 2019 Pacific Games, using existing venues in Nuku'alofa with the main sports events hosted in the new stadium funded by the Chinese government.

Mining

The US Geological Survey has found huge undersea sediment-filled basins that could hold oil deposits near Tonga, the Solomon Islands and Papua New Guinea. German and Russian researchers have discovered copper and zinc deposits off Tonga.

The government signed an agreement in March 2009 with the Australian company, Blue Water Metals, to prospect undersea for gold, silver, copper and zinc, inside its territorial waters.

Hydrocarbons

There are no known hydrocarbon resources; all domestic energy needs must be met by imported petroleum products, typically 1,000 barrels per day of oil, mainly from New Zealand. Tonga does not import gas or coal.

Energy

Tonga's installed generating capacity in 2013 was 12,000MW. Construction began on the Popua solar Farm, the first part of the national 'energy road map' (ERM) in November 2011. The production of 1,880MW per year of electricity (around 4 per cent of total energy requirement for Tongatapu) came on stream in August 2012.

The New Zealand government-funded NZ$12 million (US$15.6 million) project replaces Tonga's reliance on diesel generating energy production. The government developed a realistic plan, based on technical studies, for Tonga to produce 50 per cent of its generating needs from renewable sources by 2020. Feasibility studies are underway to consider other renewable sources to add to the ERM, including wind farms and biofuels.

Banking and insurance

Main financial centre

Nuku'alofa.

Time

GMT plus 13 hours

Geography

Tonga (also known as the Friendly Islands) comprises 172 islands in the south-western Pacific Ocean, about 650km (400 miles) east of Fiji. The Tonga Islands are divided into three main groups – Tongatapu (southern group) Ha'apai (middle group) and Vava'u (northern group). Only 36 of the islands are permanently inhabited.

All are formed from limestone but with two different geological bases, either an uplifted coral foundation or an overlay of a volcanic base. The maximum height of any volcanic range is 1,033 metres, on Kao. Few islands have rivers or lakes and most rely on wells and rainwater for their supply.

Hemisphere

Southern

Climate

From May–November, temperatures are relatively cool and reach between 11–29 degrees Celsius (C). December–April is the wet season, with temperatures reaching 32°C and with high humidity. Average rainfall is 1,700mm per year, but varies from place to place.

Entry requirements

Passports

Required by all, and must be valid six months from date of entry.

Visa

Tourists and business persons listed at www.tongaconsulate.us/visa/visa4tim.htm I may enter for a period not exceeding 31 days providing the visitor holds onward/return passage and proof of adequate funds.

A one month extension is possible if permission is obtained locally from the principal immigration officer; a fee applies.

Currency advice/regulations

No restrictions on import and export of local and foreign currency.

Travellers cheques are accepted in banks and major hotels; Australian dollars and pounds sterling cheques will avoid additional exchange fees.

Customs

Personal items are duty-free. Imports from some countries may require an import licence or be subject to temporary control.

Prohibited imports

Illegal drugs and firearms. Quarantine is required for all imported live animals and plants.

Health (for visitors)

Mandatory precautions

Vaccination certificate for yellow fever if travelling from an infected area.

Advisable precautions

Inoculations and boosters should be current for tetanus, hepatitis A and typhoid. There may be a need for vaccinations for diphtheria, tuberculosis and hepatitis B. Insect repellent should be worn at all times, especially during the early morning and evening. There is a rabies risk.

Hotels

Information regarding various types of tourist accommodation is available in Nuku'alofa and throughout the islands from the Tonga Visitors' Bureau.

Credit cards

Credit and charge cards are accepted.

Public holidays (national)

Fixed dates

1 Jan (New Year's Day), 25 Apr (Anzac Day), 4 May (Crown Prince's Birthday), 4 Jun (Independence Day), 4 Jul (King Taufa'ahau Tupou IV's Birthday), 4 Nov (Constitution Day), 4 Dec (Tupou I Day), 25–26 Dec (Christmas).

Variable dates

Good Friday and Easter Monday (Mar/Apr).

Working hours

Sunday is widely observed as a day of rest, with work, sports and transport services forbidden.

Banking

Mon–Fri: 0930–1530; Sat: 0900–1200.

Business

Mon–Fri: 0800–1700; Sat: 0800–1200.

Government

Mon–Fri: 0830–1630.

Shops

Mon–Fri: 0800–1700; Sat: 0800–1200.

Telecommunications

Telephone/fax

The telephone system is fully automatic with 24-hour international communications.

Mobile/cell phones

There are GSM 900 service available on many inhabited islands.

Electricity supply

240V AC, with Australian style flat three-pin plugs.

Weights and measures

Metric system

Social customs/useful tips

It is customary to shake hands on meeting and taking leave. Business cards are exchanged after introduction. Appointments should be made in advance. Those meeting for the first time are addressed by their title and family name; Tongans address each other by their first name.

Gratuities are not encouraged or customary. Tongans appreciate modesty in dress, casual attire is recommended for most occasions. Beachware is only acceptable at the beach and not in general public. It is an offence to appear in public without a shirt. Drunkenness is frowned upon; alcohol consumption may be restricted.

Getting there

Air

National airline: Air Fiji has provided international access since Royal Tongan Airlines collapsed in 2004.

International airport/s: Fua'amotu International, Tongatapu (TBU), 15km south-east of Nuku'alofa; bank, duty-free shop and car hire. Taxis and buses available to centre.

Airport tax: International departures include a passenger service charge of T$25; not applicable for transit passengers.

Surface

Water: No regular passenger services to the kingdom, but berths may be available on cruise ships visiting Nuku'alofa and Vava'u.

Main port/s: Nuku'alofa (on Tongatapu), Neiafu (on Vava'u), Pangai (on Lifuka), Ha'apai.

Getting about

National transport

No public transport, shipping or air services operate into, out of, or on Tonga on Sundays.

Air: Airlines of Tonga (partly owned by Air Fiji), a new domestic carrier and Peau 'o Vava'u Airways operate inter-island flights.

Road: Total road network of about 400km with 80–90 per cent paved; over 190km are on Tongatapu.

Buses: Buses serve all parts of Tongatapu from Nuku'alofa.

Water: Various shipping lines operate inter-island ferry services. The principal service leaves Nuku'alofa in the afternoon and arrives the following morning in Ha'apia, at Hafeva then Pangia, then goes on to Vava'u; by mid afternoon it retraces its route back to Nuku'alofa. There is no need for advance bookings, schedules may change at short notice due to weather conditions. Charter yachts are available.

City transport

Taxis: Private taxis are for hire. Fares should be agreed before undertaking a journey.

Car hire

Self-drive or chauffeur-driven cars are available. International or national driving licence must be presented to the Police Traffic Department in Nuku'alofa to obtain local driving licence.

Speed limits of 40kph in country areas and slower through towns are enforced. Driving is on the left.

BUSINESS DIRECTORY

The addresses listed below are a selection only. While World of Information makes every endeavour to check these addresses, we cannot guarantee that changes have not been made, especially to telephone numbers and area codes. We would welcome any corrections.

Telephone area codes

The international direct dialling (IDD) code for Tonga is +676 followed by subscriber's number.

Useful telephone numbers

Police: 992

Fire: 999

Ambulance: 933

Chambers of Commerce

Tonga Chamber of Commerce, Tungi Arcade, PO Box 1704, Nuku'alofa (tel: 25-168; email: chamber@kalianet.to).

Banking

Bank of Tonga, PO Box 924, Naku'alofa (tel: 23-933; fax: 23-634).

ANZ Bank, PO Box 910; Cnr Salote and Railway Roads, Nuku'alofa (tel: 24-944; fax: 23-870; email: anztonga@anz.com).

MBf Bank Limited, PO Box 3118; Nuku'alofa, Taufa'ahau Rd, Nuku'alofa (tel: 24-600; fax: 24-662; email: mbfbank@kalianet.to).

Tonga Development Bank; PO Box 126; Nuku'alofa, Fatafehi Rd, Nuku'alofa (tel: 23-333; fax: 23-775; email: tdevbank@tdb.to).

Westpac Bank Tonga, PO Box 924; Taufa'ahau Rd, Nuku'alofa, (tel: 23-933; fax: 23-634; email: westpactonga@westpac.com.au).

Central bank

National Reserve Bank of Tonga, Queen Salote Road, PO Box 25, Nuku'alofa, Tonga (tel: 24-057 fax: 24-201; e-mail: nrbt@reservebank.to).

Travel information

Flight information (0630-1930 hours Mon-Sat) (tel: 32-088).

Fua'amotu International Airport, Ministry of Civil Aviation, PO Box 845, Nuku'alofa (tel: 32-001; fax: 32-003).

Tourist information (tel: 32-060).

Peau Vava'u Limited (domestic airline), Taufa'ahau Road, Nuku'alofa (tel: 878-8896; fax: 28-637; email: administration@peauvavau.to).

National tourist organisation offices

Tonga Visitors' Bureau, PO Box 37, Nuku'alofa (tel: 23-507, 21-733; fax:

22-129; internet: www.vacations.tvb.gov.to).

Ministries

Ministry of Civil Aviation, PO Box 845, Nuku'alofa (tel: 32-001; fax: 32-003).

Ministry of Labour, Commerce and Industries, Salote Road, PO Box 110, Nuku'alofa (tel: 23-688; fax: 23-887).

Office of Prime Minister, Ministry of Agriculture, Fisheries and Forestry, Ministry of Marine, Nuku'alofa (tel: 21-300).

Other useful addresses

Asian Development Bank (ADB), South Pacific Regional Mission, La Casa di Andrea, Lini Highway; PO Box 127, Port Vila, Vanuatu (tel: (+678-2) 23-300; fax: (+678-2) 23-183; adbsprm@adb.org; internet: www.adb.org/SPRM).

Immigration Division, Ministry of Foreign Affairs, Government of Tonga, P O Box 352, Nuku'alofa (tel: 26-970, 26-969; fax: 26-971, 23-360).

Tonga Department of Statistics, PO Box 149, Nuku'alofa (email: dept@stats.gov.to; internet: www.spc.int/prism/country/to/stats).

ABC Pacific Beat: www.radioaustralia.net.au/pacbeat

Pacific Magazine: www.pacificmagazine.net

Pacific Islands New Association (Pina): www.pina.com.fj

Internet sites

Government of Tonga: http://pmo.gov.to

Tonga information website: www.tongatapu.net.to

Trinidad and Tobago

KEY FACTS

Official name: Republic of Trinidad and Tobago

Head of State: President Anthony Carmona (Independent) (since 18 March 2013)

Head of government: Prime Minister Keith Rowley (People's National Movement (PNM)) (since 9 September 2015)

Ruling party: People's National Movement (PNM)

Area: 5,128 square km

Population: 1.35 million (2014)

Capital: Port-of-Spain

Official language: English

Currency: Trinidad and Tobago dollar (TT$) = 100 cents

Exchange rate: TT$6.33 per US$ (Sep 2015)

GDP per capita: US$21,311 (2014)*

GDP real growth: 1.09% (2014)*

GDP: US$28.79 billion (2014)*

Labour force: 621,000 (2009)

Unemployment: 4.00% (2014)

Inflation: 7.04% (2014)*

Oil production: 112,000 bpd (2014)

Natural gas production: 42.10 billion cum (2014)

Balance of trade: US$5.43 million (2011)

Annual FDI: US$574.00 million (2011)

* estimated figure

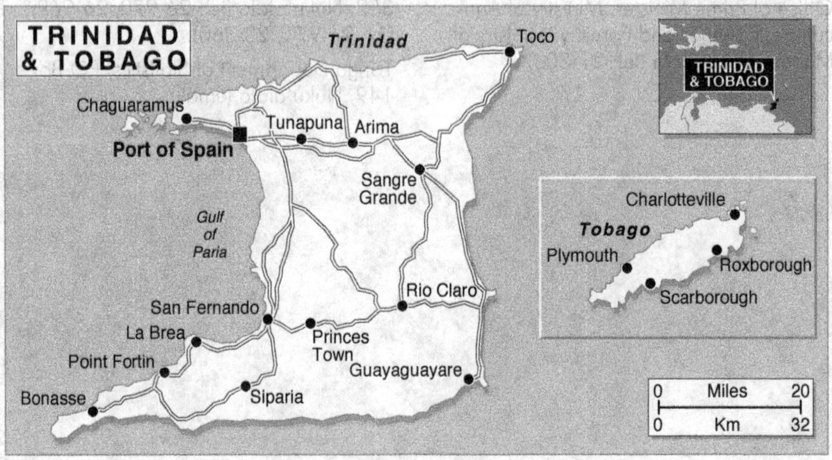

The opposition People's National Movement (PNM), a party led by Keith Rowley, a 65 year-old geologist, won Trinidad and Tobago's general election in September 2015. The PNM managed to secure 23 out of 41 of the constituencies on the oil-rich, twin-island nation. Kamla Persad-Bissessar's incumbent United National Congress party won 18 seats. The Independent Liberal Party (ILP), led by disgraced former Fifa vice-president, Jack Warner, failed to secure a seat in the central region's Chaguanas East constituency.

The resignation in July 2014 of Trinidad and Tobago's sports minister did not come as a huge surprise. Trinidadians were getting used to dismissals from ex-Prime Minister Kamla Persad-Bissessar's cabinet. The minister in question, Anil Roberts, was the twelfth to be sacked by Persad-Bissessar when a government investigation discovered fraudulent goings on in one of the ministers programmes. Like most of those sacked before him, Mr Roberts denied any wrongdoing and attempted to face down calls from opposition parties and the public to resign over the alleged misdemeanours in the 'LifeSport' programme, which was aimed at training youths to keep away… from crime.

Governance

Former Prime Minister Persad-Bissessar had said she was 'disillusioned, disappointed and distressed by the level of deception and dishonesty' allegedly discovered to be going on in the programme, which was reportedly found to harbour a series of irregularities including theft and procurement breaches. She continued: 'The expectation of the public that something will be done when wrongs are committed in public office is now the hallmark of good governance. I have decided to accept the offer of resignation as minister of sport from Mr Roberts.' Persad-Bissessar's four-year-old government had been rocked by a series of scandals. One cabinet minister was accused of slapping a lover, another of grasping an air hostess's breast. In terms of governance Trinidad and Tobago can hardly claim to have progressed much. On the Transparency International 2014 *Corruption Perceptions Index* it ranked a mediocre 85 out of the 177 countries surveyed, well behind other Caribbean states such as Barbados (17), the Bahamas (24), St Vincent (29) and Puerto Rico (31).

Perhaps the highest profile corruption case was that against Trinidadian political veteran Jack Warner, a former Fifa vice president, who was forced to resign as national security minister in 2013 following a damning report by the Confederation of North, Central American and Caribbean Association Football (Concacaf), the confederation responsible for soccer in North and Central America and the Caribbean, which published detailed allegations of financial mismanagement. Worryingly for the people of Trinidad and Tobago, less than a year later he was 're-elected' to parliament.

In September 2015, Jack Warner was 'banned for life' by Fifa's ethics committee following allegations of corruption and involvement in the Fifa scandal. Warner is also facing criminal charges in the US over an alleged US$152 million fraud. This ban coincides with investigations that could lead to suspensions for Sepp Blatter and Michel Platini. The former minister of national security for Trinidad and Tobago has not been involved in football for over four years, and therefore the ban will be merely symbolic as there is very little chance of his return to the sport. And then he lost his seat in parliament again in the September 2015 elections.

A divided nation?

In addition to the contribution made by a booming hydrocarbons sector, Trinidad and Tobago's flourishing private sector has led to a rapid growth of the middle class, an important stabilising factor in what is, in so many respects, a divided nation. Economic and social mobility are distinguishing characteristics of Trinidad and Tobago life, not matched elsewhere in the Caribbean or indeed in most developing oil economies.

In Trinidad and Tobago, political allegiance has long tended to follow ethnic lines. Simmering beneath the surface of Trinidad and Tobago's politics is the nagging question of the racial divide. The 2013 local government elections marked what one journalist described as 'a return to tribal politics'. The results saw the Congress of the People (COP) loose all its seats as voters migrated from the previously ruling coalition People's Partnership to the Independent Liberal Party and the People's National Movement.

The economy

The International Monetary Fund's (IMF) 2015 end-of-mission report of its visit to Trinidad and Tobago named the recent changes in the energy markets as a major economic challenge for the islands, whose exports are heavily dependent on these markets. Despite not knowing how the markets will settle, the drivers of the energy price seem likely to endure. In order to deal with this likely outcome, the government has decided to prepare revised budget plans based on conservative price assumptions.

The case for policy tightening remains intact, as the economy appears to be at full capacity according to the IMF. The authorities' have therefore altered their goal to return to the original 2014/15 target of a fiscal deficit of 2.3 per cent. The IMF's fiscal recommendations for the medium term remain critical to achieving long-term goals of diversification, and saving and investing for the future. Scaling down fuel subsidies at the time of low global energy prices was also suggested.

Trinidad and Tobago's shortage of foreign exchange persists in hampering the economy, as businesses continue to report difficulties in paying suppliers. The IMF stated it was encouraged by the Central Bank of Trinidad and Tobago's intention to increase size and frequency of foreign exchange injections until the backlog of orders is eliminated. This is necessary if foreign exchange demand is to be met and the market's confidence is to be restored.

The report also stated that there had been progress on the structural reform front. The Central Statistical Office's (CSO) provision of data has somewhat improved, but is still not quite acceptable. The IMF suggested it was important that the pace of the CSO's improvement would need to be maintained and encouraged the government in placing the CSO on a well-funded, independent footing. Financial reforms have also shown further progress, and the costs of doing business have improved. Procurement legislation has been passed, and according to the IMF once implemented should help to achieve better expenditure efficiency and dispel worries about corruption. However, critical priorities remain improving the functioning of the civil service and reducing the distortions to the labour market that linger as a result of temporary employment programmes.

Hydrocarbons

According to the US government Energy Information Administration (EIA) Trinidad is the largest oil and natural gas producer in the Caribbean. Trinidad and Tobago's hydrocarbon sector moved from an oil-dominant to a mostly natural gas-based sector in the early 1990s; by 2013, Trinidad and Tobago was the world's sixth-largest LNG exporter, according to the *BP Statistical Review of World Energy* of June 2015 (BP15 Review) Trinidad is also the largest LNG exporter to the United States, accounting for nearly 74 per cent of US LNG imports in 2013.

According to BP, (the largest player in the Trinidad and Tobago oil and gas industry) total primary energy consumption in Trinidad and Tobago was about 872 trillion British Thermal Units (Btu) in 2013. Natural gas consumption accounted for approximately 92 per cent and the consumption of petroleum products was just over 8 per cent. Renewable fuels, in the form of biomass and waste, now represent a negligible share of energy consumption.

In December 2014, Trinidad and Tobago had 12.2 trillion cubic feet (tcf) of proven natural gas reserves, a slow

KEY INDICATORS — Trinidad and Tobago

	Unit	2011	2012	2013	2014	**2015
Population	m	*1.32	*1.34	*1.34	1.35	*1.36
Gross domestic product (GDP)	US$bn	22.70	26.74	27.26	*28.79	*29.21
GDP per capita	US$	17,158	19,993	20,279	*21,311	*21,516
GDP real growth	%	-1.3	1.2	1.7	*1.1	*1.2
Inflation	%	5.1	9.3	5.2	*7.0	*7.3
Unemployment	%	5.0	4.8	3.8	4.0	*4.0
Oil output	'000 bpd	136.0	121.0	118.0	112.0	–
Natural gas output	bn cum	40.7	42.2	42.8	42.1	–
Exports (fob) (goods)	US$m	14,913.1	–	–	–	–
Imports (fob) (goods)	US$m	9,478.3	–	–	–	–
Balance of trade	US$m	5,434.8	–	–	–	–
Current account	US$m	2,623.0	1,323.0	1,829.0	2,379.0	*1,508.0
Total reserves minus gold	US$m	9,638.3	9,794.4	10,600.5	11,896.7	–
Foreign exchange	US$m	9,068.1	9,200.7	9,987.0	–	–
Exchange rate	per US$	6.41	6.36	6.41	6.38	–

* estimated figure ** forecast figure

decline since 2005, according to the *BP Review 2015*. Trinidad and Tobago produced roughly 42.1 billion cubic metres (bcm) of dry natural gas in 2014, according to the ministry of energy and energy affairs. Together, BP Trinidad and Tobago (BPTT), the largest natural gas producer in the country, and British Gas Trinidad and Tobago Limited (BGTT) account for more than three-quarters of total natural gas production, according to IHS Energy. Trinidad and Tobago also houses one of the largest natural gas processing facilities in the Western Hemisphere. The Phoenix Park Gas Processors Limited (PPGPL) natural gas liquids (NGL) complex was the second major acquisition made by the National Gas Company (NGC) in August 2013. It is located in the Port of Savonetta and has a processing capacity of almost 2 billion cubic feet (bcf) per day and an output capacity of 70,000 barrels per day (bpd) of NGL.

Trinidad and Tobago's electricity sector is fuelled almost entirely by natural gas. Gross power generation in 2013 was 7.9 terra watt hours (Twh), a decline from the peak of 8.9Twh in 2011, according to BP. The government commissioned the country's second combined cycle gas-fired power plant with a capacity of 720 megawatts at the end of 2013 to serve both industry and the power grid.

According to the *BP Review 2015*, Trinidad and Tobago had 0.8 thousand million barrels of proven crude oil reserves at the end of 2014. Production was 112,000bpd in 2014. Petroleum and other liquids production in Trinidad and Tobago had peaked at 179,000bpd in 2006. However, since then it has declined overall according to the EIA (quoting IHS Energy), because of maturing oilfields and operational challenges.

With a crude oil distillation capacity of 168,000bpd, Trinidad and Tobago's state-owned Pointe-a-Pierre refinery is the only refinery in the country and in 2014 was being improved for overall profitability and competitiveness. Plans for two new refineries, with an aggregate refining capacity of 278,000bpd, had been proposed in the past, but these projects had not advanced.

Petrotrin, the state-owned oil and gas company and largest crude oil producer in the country, has sought to identify oil and gas deposits for further exploration and had completed a 197 square mile seismic survey in May 2014. A little known fact is that Trinidad and Tobago is the world's largest exporter of ammonia and the second-largest exporter of methanol. It possesses no less than eleven ammonia plants and seven methanol plants, according to the government.

Risk assessment

Politics	Fair
Economy	Good
Regional stability	Good

Muslims in Trinidad

% of population	5.8
Sunni (% of Muslims)	99
Shi'a (% of Muslims)	1

COUNTRY PROFILE

1498 Trinidad was sighted by a Spanish expedition led by Christopher Columbus.
1532 The island was colonised by the Spanish.
1595 Spanish colonisers were defeated by an English fleet under Sir Walter Raleigh.
1630s The Dutch settled on Tobago and created sugar plantations.
1763 Trinidad was occupied by France, with Spanish consent.
1781 The French seized Tobago.
1797 Trinidad was seized by the British during the Napoleonic wars.
1802 Trinidad was officially transferred to British sovereignty.
1814 Tobago became a British colony of the Windward Island group.
1834 Slavery was abolished and indentured workers were brought in from India to work on the sugar plantations.
1889 Tobago was amalgamated with Trinidad and together the islands became a unified British colony.
1945 Universal suffrage was granted.
1956 Eric Williams founded the People's National Movement (PNM).
1958 Trinidad and Tobago became part of the British-sponsored West Indies Federation.
1959 Britain gave Trinidad and Tobago internal self-government with Williams as prime minister.
1962 When Jamaica opted to leave the West Indies Federation, Trinidad and Tobago followed, becoming independent within the Commonwealth.
1967 Trinidad and Tobago joined the Organisation of American States (OAS).
1968 Anglophone Caribbean states, including Trinidad and Tobago, formed the Caribbean Free Trade Area (Carifta), which became the Caribbean Community and Common Market (Caricom) in 1973.
1970 A state of emergency was declared after the army mutinied against the minority East Indian population.
1972 The state of emergency was lifted.
1976 On 1 August, Trinidad and Tobago became a republic within the Commonwealth. The PNM won the parliamentary elections. Ellis Clarke, previously the governor general, was sworn in as the country's first president and Eric Williams became prime minister.
1981 Eric Williams died and George Chambers became prime minister.
1986 The PNM lost power in the general election – its first defeat since 1957. The Tobago-based National Alliance for Reconstruction (NAR), led by Arthur Robinson, won a decisive victory.
1987 Noor Hassanali became president.
1990 More than 100 Islamic extremists staged a *coup détat*, blowing up the police headquarters, seizing parliament and holding Prime Minister Robinson and several senior officials hostage. The uprising was short-lived.
1991 The harsh economic programme lost the NAR the general elections. The PNM took over and Patrick Manning became prime minister.
1995 The Asian-dominated United National Congress (UNC) won most seats in the general election and formed a coalition government with the support of the NAR. Basdeo Panday became prime minister.
1997 Arthur N R Robinson was elected president. As prime minister in 1989, he had proposed to the UN the founding of the International Criminal Court (ICC) to prosecute individuals for genocide, crimes against humanity and war crimes; the ICC was inaugurated in 2002
1999 Trinidad and Tobago restored the death sentence.
2000 The ruling UNC narrowly won the general election with 19 seats (PNM 16 and NAR one). Three UNC members of parliament defected to the opposition and the government fell in December.
2001 The result of the general election was a tie with the UNC and PNM both winning 18 out of 36 seats. President Robinson appointed Patrick Manning as prime minister, despite the UNC garnering a larger percentage of the vote. With a hung parliament little legislation was carried out.
2002 Prime Minister Manning finally called the third general election in three years and his PNM won power with 20 seats.
2003 George Maxwell Richards became president. Caroni, the state-owned sugar company closed, with the loss of over 8,000 jobs.
2005 Trinidad became the home of the Caribbean Court of Justice (CCJ), a final court of appeal intended to replace the UK-based Privy Council.
2006 Former prime minister, Basdeo Panday was convicted of financial impropriety and sentenced to two years in prison. Chief Justice, Satnarine Sharma,

was accused of misconduct by interfering in the outcome of the case and, following a series of court cases, stepped down as chief justice in 2008. New, commercially viable oil and gas deposits were found off Trinidad. BWIA, the national airline, ceased operations.
2007 Caribbean Airlines began operations; it took over routes previously flown by BWIA. The ruling PNM won parliamentary elections. Patrick Manning retained the office of prime minister.
2008 As the only candidate standing, President Maxwell Richards was re-elected president by an electoral college.
2009 A new, draft constitution was proposed, with changes including an executive president and a diminished role for the prime minister as well as an alternative way of appointing a chief justice.
2010 Two years ahead of schedule, the prime minister called a snap general election, following allegations of public corruption and severe criticism of spending on capital works. A coalition was formed to contest the upcoming elections, led by UNC and including the Congress of the People (CP), Tobago Organisation of the People (TOP), National Joint Action Committee (NJAC) and Movement for Social Justice (MSJ); it was called the People's Partnership. The parliamentary election was won by the People's Partnership coalition (led by United National Congress (UNC)). Kamla Persad-Bissessar (UNC) became prime minister. The first president of Trinidad and Tobago, Sir Ellis Clarke died, aged 93 years.
2011 In March, Prime Minister Persad-Bissessar said her government was reluctant to use the CCJ instead of the Privy Council, as the judicial process was working without need for change. In October, the Tobago Assembly considered proposed amendments to reform the constitution concerning the relationship between Tobago and Trinidad. The first act would provide an entrenchment of powers for the Tobago Assembly and the second would enhance the status of the Tobago Assembly to enable it to enact further legislation – in effect legitimacy would be conferred on the assembly and any subsequent legislation issued by the assembly.
2012 On 21 November, BP announced that it had made a further discovery, estimated at 28.3 billion cubic metres, of natural gas in the Savonette gas field off the south-east coast of Trinidad.
2013 On 15 February Anthony Carmona was elected unopposed in indirect presidential elections. He took office on 18 March. On 17 December the first of some 11 oil spills from Petrotrin's Point-a-Pierre facility destroyed beaches and marine habitats in the south-western peninsula. The controversial dispersant, Corexit 9500, used by BP against its spill in the Gulf of Mexico in 2012, was used by Petromin in an effort to clear the spillage.
2014 Minister of the people, Dr Glenn Ramadharsingh, was fired by Prime Minister Persad-Bissessar on 24 March, allegedly for inappropriate behaviour. A week later she also accepted the resignation of Chandresh Sharma, Minister of Tourism. In May Fishermen and Friends of the Sea (FFOS) published its most recent survey of the impact of the December 2013 oil spill by Petrotrin. The survey showed a 'catistrophic' 80 per cent average drop in fish catches from some 850 Trinidad fishermen from over 25 fishing depots in the Gulf of Paria. An opinion poll held in September showed the two main parties running almost neck-and-neck.
2015 On 9 January Prime Minister Persad-Bissessar announced that there would be a shortfall of US$1.16 billion to the 2015 budget as a result of the fall in the oil price. Although the support grants, senior citizens' pensions, new minimum wage and baby grants would not be touched, she did not state where cost-cutting would appear, other than a lower fuel subsidy outlay. The revised budget would be pegged on an oil price of US$45 a barrel, a 44 per cent reduction from the original benchmark of US$80 a barrel. On 17 January the finance and economy minister, Larry Howai, was reported by Trinidad Express Newspapers as saying the government would have to shelve a number of projects following the readjustment of the oil and natural gas prices. They include the new port of Port of Spain, the dry-dock, six economic free zones, the Endeavour Economic Park and downgrading of the extent of work on some of the country's health centres. On 1 February the Prime Minister announced that she had asked for and received the resignations of national security minister Gary Griffith and attorney general Anand Ramlogan. At the same time Ms Persad-Bissessar asked the President to revoke the appontments of five other ministers; these were believed by analysts to be in preparation for the September elections, while the first two resignations are said to be part of an on-going investigation into witness tampering. Opposition leader Dr Keith Rowley was suspended from parliament on 6 May following a motion of no confidence. He will not be allowed to return before the session ends on 17 June. A short-stay visa waiver agreement signed between the EU and a number of ACP countries on 28 May will allow citizens of Trinidad and Tobago to travel visa free to the Schengen area. In early July Prime Minister Persad-Bissessar requested a technical observer team from the Commonwealth for the 7 September general election. In late July the Prime Minister was accused by Jack Warner (under indictment in the US on multiple counts of racketeering, corruption and money laundering) of accepting a bribe of TT$8.3 million (US$1.3 million) from two local businessmen in exchange for legislative protection against extradition. The allegation has been referred to the Anti-Corruption Bureau of the Police Service. In the 7 September general election the ruling People's Partnership Coalition (led by United National Congress (UNC)) lost to the People's National Movement (PNM) by 23 seats to 17. Dr Keith Rowley (PNM) became prime minister. On 21 September it was announced that the Attorney General had signed the US request for the extradition of Jack Warner. Vasant Bharath, resigned as an opposition senator on 11 November, in order to contest the United National Congress (UNC) party leadership post.

Political structure

Constitution

The Constitution was adopted in 1976. In August 12 2014, the House of Representatives in Trinidad and Tobago passed a Constitutional Amendment Bill by a simple majority. The first of the three amendments requires that House candidates be elected with a majority vote. The second gives voters in their electoral district the power to recall their representative. The final amendment acts to limit prime ministerial service to no more than two terms, it limits the president's power as he cannot appoint a prime minister who has reached the ten-year limit.

Form of state

Republic

The executive

Executive power is divided between the president, who is the Head of State, and the prime minister, who is the Head of government.
The president is indirectly elected every five years by an electoral college made up of members of both houses of parliament.
The prime minister, who has a cabinet composed of members of parliament, is usually the leader of the majority party or the majority coalition in the House of Representatives and is appointed by the president.

National legislature

The parliament is bicameral. The House of Representatives has 41 seats of which members are directly elected in single-seat constituencies by simple majority vote for five-year terms.
The Senate consists of 31 seats of which 16 members are appointed by the ruling party, 9 by the president, and 6 by the opposition party. Members also serve five-year terms.

Legal system
An independent judiciary is guaranteed by the constitution. Foreign investors have the same rights as Trinidad and Tobago citizens.
The Supreme Court is the highest legal body. Civil trials are handled by a single judge in the high court without a jury. Decisions made by the high court can be presented for appeal to the three–judge court of appeal. Court of appeal decisions can be appealed to the regional Caribbean Court of Justice (CCJ), which was inaugurated in 2005, replacing the Privy Council in London as the highest court of appeal.
Last elections
15 February 2013 (presidential *indirect*); 7 September 2015 (parliamentary).
Results: Presidential: Maxwell Richards was elected unopposed by the Electoral College comprised of members of both chambers of parliament.
Parliamentary: Parliamentary: the People's National Movement won 51.7 per cent of the vote (23 seats out of 41), United National Congress (UNC) won 39.6 per cent (17 seats) and Congress of the People won 6 per cent (1 seat); no other party won more than one per cent of the vote or any seats. Turnout was 66.8 per cent.
Next elections
2020 (parliamentary); February 2018 (presidential).

Political parties
Ruling party
People's National Movement (PNM)
Main opposition party
United National Congress (UNC)

Population
1.35 million (2014) Over 95 per cent of the population resides on Trinidad and the remainder live on Tobago.
Last census: May 2000: 1,262,366
Population density: 251 inhabitants per square km. Urban population 14 per cent (2010 Unicef).
Annual growth rate: 0.5 per cent, 1990–2010 (Unicef).
Ethnic make-up
Black (43 per cent), East Indian (40 per cent), mixed (14 per cent), white (1 per cent), Chinese (1 per cent).
Religions
Roman Catholics (34 per cent), Hindus (30 per cent), Protestants (19 per cent), Muslims (10 per cent).

Education
Primary schooling lasts for seven years followed by secondary, academic and technical or vocational qualifications. World Bank estimates show that the total primary school enrolment of the relevant age group typically stood at 99 per cent for boys and 98 per cent for girls (including repetition rates) between 1994—2000. The number of pupils per primary school teacher is typically 25. Public expenditure on education typically amounted to 3.6 per cent of annual gross national income between 1994—97.
A new campus of the University of Trinidad and Tobago, costing US$100 million, opened in 2006 including a donation of US$10 million from British Petroleum (BP) towards construction of the university, which was founded as a charitable trust by the government.
Literacy rate: 99 per cent adult rate; 100 per cent youth rate (15–24) (Unesco 2005).
Compulsory years: Five to 11
Pupils per teacher: 25 in primary schools

Health
Improved water sources are available to 86 per cent of the population.
HIV/Aids
The prevalence rate is relatively high, although the number of deaths due to Aids between 2001–03 did not increase significantly, from an estimated 1,500–1,900. There were 29,000 people living with HIV at the end of 2003, of which 700 were children (aged 0–14). Research among young adults (15-24) showed that 95 per cent knew that a healthy–looking person could be HIV positive, and 33 per cent knew of at least two prevention methods and three myths concerning the disease.
HIV prevalence: 0.1 per cent aged 15–49 in 2003 (World Bank)
Life expectancy: 70 years, 2004 (WHO 2006)
Fertility rate/Maternal mortality rate: 1.6 births per woman, 2010 (Unicef)
Birth rate/Death rate: 8 deaths and 13 births per 1,000 people (World Bank)
Child (under 5 years) mortality rate (per 1,000): 21 per 1,000 live births (WHO 2012)

Welfare
Trinidad and Tobago operates social insurance and social assistance systems that were implemented in 1999. The 1999 law ensures state provision for employees, domestic and agricultural workers, but does not cover self-employed workers. Social assistance covers residents aged 65 or older or aged 40 years for those with special needs, based on a means-test.
Old age pensions are available to men aged 60–65 and above with 750 weeks of contribution and compulsory retirement. The state also operates a welfare system for benefits covering sickness, maternity, medical provision for workers and family allowance, including a food subsidy. Medical care is available in public hospitals and health offices and centres for recipients of means tested pensions.
Trinidad and Tobago is experiencing a rise in social problems related to young people, despite the economy's improved performance. Restricted access to the secondary education system and unemployment (which reached 30 per cent for the 15–19 age group in 2001), poverty and reduced family care have contributed to youth involvement in crime and drug abuse.

Main cities
Port of Spain (capital, estimated population 50,405 in 2012), Chaguanas (79,381), San Fernando (centre of the oil industry) (57,605), Arima (39,245), Marabella (26,601), Tunapuna (19,695), Point Fortín (18,646); Scarborough (main town on Tobago, estimated population (4,814).

Languages spoken
Hindi is commonly spoken within the East Indian community.
Official language/s
English

Media
Press
Dailies: There are three national, daily newspapers, including *Daily Express* (www.trinidadexpress.com) and *Trinidad Guardian* (www.guardian.co.tt) and *Newsday* (www.newsday.co.tt); tabloids include *TnT Mirror* an important online news outlet *Trinidad & Tobago News* (www.trinidadandtobagonews.com) and *Tobago News* (www.thetobagonews.com).
Weeklies: Daily newspapers have weekend editions including *Mirror Weekend* and *The Sunday Punch* (politics and satire) plus a magazine *The Bomb* (politics).
Broadcasting
The state-owned Caribbean New Media Group (CNMG) operates radio and television stations.
Radio: Broadcasts may be in English, Hindi and Creole reflecting the islands ethnic diversity with programme contents produced for a variety of listening tastes. The majority of stations are located on Trinidad. CNMG operates four radio stations, Radio 730 AM, Vibe CT 105, Sandeet 106.1 and the most popular 95.1FM City Talk radio. Other private radio stations include i95.5 FM (www.i955fm.com) with news, WeFM (www.96wefm.com) and Power FM (www.power102fm.com).
Television: The commercial channel, TV6, has the largest audiences with a combination of local and foreign (mostly US) programmes. CNMG has two channels. Other channels include Gayelle (www.gayelletv.com) and NCC TV (www.ncctt.org), which are community

TVs. Pay-to-view TV includes Jump TV (www.jumptv.com) and Media Zone (www.mediazone.com).
Other news agencies: Cananews: www.cananews.net

Economy

Trinidad and Tobago is the only significant exporter of oil and gas of the Caribbean islands, thereby affording the population the highest per capita income in the Caribbean and Latin America, with over US$23,000 in 2014 (an increase on previous record high of US$21,298 in 2008). It had proven oil reserves of 800 million barrels at the end of 2014 and oil production of 112,000 barrels per day (bpd). Proven natural gas reserves were 300 billion cubic metres (cum), with annual production of 42.1 billion cubic metres at the end of 2014. Trinidad and Tobago had a strong economy that grew steadily over 1993–2008 at 6 per cent per annum, but it was seriously affected by the global economic crisis in 2009 as energy prices fell dramatically and GDP growth dropped to -3.3 per cent, before stagnating at 0.0 per cent in 2010 and was estimated to have fallen into a double-dip recession with GDP growth of -1.3 per cent in 2011 before returning to positive GDP growth and reaching 3.4 per cent by 2014.

Unemployment, which had fallen to 3.9 per cent in 2008 when oil prices had been at a record high, grew to 5.1 per cent in 2009 and peaked at an estimated 7.8 per cent in 2010 but falling to 3.3 per cent in 2014. A number of workers go overseas for work to provide remittances for their families; in 2010 remittances were at a low of US$109 million (0.4 per cent of GDP), rising to US$131 million in 2014.

Financial services dominate the service sector. The collapse of the insurance conglomerate CL Financial in January 2009 was a severe blow to the economy and led to a government and Central Bank of Trinidad and Tobago bailout of TT$5 billion (US$787 million). Trinidad and Tobago fell into a recession from a position of strength with low debt and large fiscal surpluses.

Another major component of the service sector is the tourist industry. In 2014 tourism contributed a total of 8.7 per cent to GDP and was directly responsible for 4.4 per cent of total employment (27,000 jobs).

Staple crops include wheat, maize and rice, cassava, yams and taro. Cash crops for export include sugarcane, citrus and timber. Livestock is typically tropical breeds including goats and sheep and water buffalo, but also includes poultry and pigs. In 2014, agriculture contributed only 0.6 per cent to GDP.

In January 2015 Prime Minister Persad-Bissessar announced that there would be a shortfall of US$1.16 billion to the 2015 budget as a result of the fall in oil price. Although the support grants, senior citizens' pensions, new minimum wage and baby grants would not be touched, she did not state where cost-cutting would appear, other than through a lower fuel subsidy outlay. The revised budget would be pegged on an oil price of US$45 a barrel, a 44 per cent reduction from the original benchmark of US$80 a barrel. On 17 January the finance and economy minister, Larry Howai, was reported by Trinidad Express Newspapers as saying the government would have to shelve a number of projects following the readjustment of the oil and natural gas prices. They include the new port of Port of Spain, the dry-dock, six economic free zones, the Endeavour Economic Park and downgrading of the extent of work on some of the country's health centres.

External trade

Trinidad and Tobago is a member of the Caribbean Community and Common Market (Caricom) and operates within the single market (Caribbean Single Market and Economy (CSME)), which became operational in 2006.

Natural gas has replaced oil as the principal export earner, mainly in the form of liquefied natural gas (LNG). The petrochemical sector produces oil derivatives including methanol, ammonia and urea. Natural gas would have allowed for aluminium smelting using domestic gas but in September 2010 the government halted plans for a 125,000 tonnes per year plant on environmental grounds. Manufacturing exports are dominated by food processing, tobacco and factory assemblies. Agriculture is losing its importance as the sugar industry has contracted.

Imports

Principal imports include mineral fuels, lubricants, machinery, transportation equipment, manufactured goods, food, chemicals and live animals.

Main sources: US (34.6 per cent of total in 2014), Brazil (7.7 per cent), Gabon (6.2 per cent), China (6.1 per cent), Russia (5 per cent) and Canada (4.1 per cent).

Exports

Principal exports petroleum and petroleum products, liquefied natural gas, methanol, ammonia, urea, steel products, beverages, cereal and cereal products, sugar, cocoa, coffee, citrus fruit, vegetables and flowers.

Main destinations: US (29.1 per cent of total in 2014), Argentina (9.3 per cent), Brazil (6.6 per cent), Chile (5.9 per cent) and Peru (4.5 per cent).

Agriculture

Farming

Agriculture only contributes 0.6 per cent to GDP. About 10.5 per cent of the total land area is farmed. Although there is abundant rainfall, it is unevenly distributed, some areas becoming waterlogged, thereby curtailing production. Only 3 per cent of arable land is irrigated. About 60 per cent of the country's agriculture is in private hands and 40 per cent is controlled by the government.

The farming of major cash crops (sugar, coffee, cocoa and citrus fruits) has slumped due to labour shortages, diseases and falling export demand.

The Agricultural Development Bank (ADB), which is primarily government-owned, provides loans to farmers and finances about 85 per cent of the country's agricultural development.

The Agricultural Development Corporation is charged with developing the agricultural sector. The sector is also the subject of an investment incentive programme, involving tax exemptions for approved projects. Other measures include a US$21 million four-year repair and rehabilitation programme for roads and more funding for water management and flood defence systems.

Fishing

The country does not have a large commercial fishing industry, but relies on small private fishermen whose production does not meet domestic demand. The fishing sector is an important local source of food. In May 2014 Fishermen and Friends of the Sea (FFOS) published its survey of the impact of the December 2013 oil spill by Petrotrin. The survey showed a 'catastrophic' 80 per cent average drop in fish catches from some 850 Trinidad fishermen over 25 fishing depots in the Gulf of Paria.

Forestry

Forests cover around one-third of the total land area. The country has a well-developed commercial forests industry, based primarily on the harvesting of teak and Caribbean pine. Some three-quarters of the wood is used for industrial purposes, and the rest is used for fuel and charcoal. It produces modest quantities of industrial round timber and sawn timber. Much of the domestic demand is met by imports of sawn timber, wood-based panels and paper products.

Industry and manufacturing

Trinidad and Tobago is the most industrialised of the Caribbean islands. The industrial sector typically contributes 57.4

per cent of GDP, of which manufacturing contributes 6 per cent to total GDP. Development since the 1970s has centred on heavy export-oriented industries, which are geared towards maximising the country's energy resources.

The principal manufactured products include refined petroleum, petrochemicals, nitrogenous fertilisers, iron, steel, methanol, plastics, sugar, and various import-substitution products. The growth of the petrochemicals sector has helped offset the effects of a decline in the sugar industry.

Tourism

The islands are a mix of mountains and plains with a tropical climate and palm-lined beaches. They have much to offer visitors, but due to the pre-eminence of hydrocarbons in the economy, tourism in Trinidad is not as heavily promoted as by other Caribbean islands. Tourism in Tobago, however, is important and the government has invested in capital projects to promote the island. Most tourism is concentrated in resort developments in the south-west, where there are many beaches. In November 2011 a new luxury Magdalena Grand Beach Resort was opened, the first new resort since 1991. Apart from the sea-sports available (Tobago is known for its reef diving) the protected forests of the interior offer eco-friendly holidays.

In 2014 tourism contributed a total of 8.7 per cent to GDP and was responsible for 4.4 per cent of total employment (27,000 jobs).

Infrastructure is improving and air routes to Europe and the US are being expanded. The US is the principal market, followed by the Caribbean and the UK.

On 23 September 2011, the minister of transport announced that a private public partnership project was being sought, to provide a new public ferry service between Trinidad and Tobago and other islands of eastern Caribbean. In January 2012 five companies responded and Fast Ferry Caribbean Ltd was announced winner. The company is head quartered in the Port of Spain with the first phase planned to offer trips to Grenada, St Vincent and the Grenadines, St Lucia and Barbados.

Visitor arrivals from the US, which makes up almost 40 per cent of tourists, grew by 20 per cent in the first quarter of 2015.

Mining

Trinidad and Tobago's mining sector revolves around the petroleum industry. Asphalt and pitch sand are extracted. Other minerals quarried include diorite, limestone, argillite clay and porcelainite. The world's largest supply of natural asphalt is found in La Brea on Trinidad.

Hydrocarbons

Proven oil reserves were 800 million barrels at the end of 2014, with oil production of 112,000 barrels per day (bpd).

The majority of oil fields are located offshore between Trinidad and Tobago and Venezuela (another major oil producer), as well as a younger oil field off the north-east coast of Trinidad.

The Pointe-á-Pierre refinery has a capacity of 190,000 barrels per day.

The state-owned Petrotrin is an integrated oil and gas company, which owns many of the offshore fields and the Pointe-á-Pierre refinery. It is responsible for exploration, development and production of hydrocarbons and petroleum products.

The oil and gas sectors account for 40 per cent of GDP and some 70 per cent of the country's export earnings.

Proven natural gas reserves were 300 billion cubic metres (cum) in 2014, with production at 42.1 billion cum, a decrease of 1.6 per cent on the 2013 figure.

Liquefied natural gas (LNG) has increased in significance, following completion of the major facilities by the Atlantic LNG Company (jointly-owned by the National Gas Company, BP, British Gas, Suez and Repsol-YPF). LNG is exported to the Americas, Europe and Asia for use in electricity, industry and petrochemical production. Trinidad and Tobago is the sixth largest exporter of LNG in the world and supplies the US with around 40 per cent of its LNG.

A pipeline from Trinidad and Tobago to Martinique and Guadeloupe, connecting several other Caribbean islands, is set to start construction in late 2014 and as planned will be completed by 2016.

Coal is neither produced nor imported

Energy

Total installed generating capacity was 1,605MW in 2014, of which over 99 per cent of production was generated by fossil fuels, primarily natural gas.

The state-owned Trinidad and Tobago Electricity Commission (T&TEC) is responsible for the overall control of the transmission and distribution network, as well as sales both retail and commercial. It also has a majority shareholding in PowerGen, which is co-owned by US companies Southern Electric International and Amoco, and is responsible for generation, with electricity supplied to the national grid.

Financial markets

Stock exchange

Trinidad and Tobago Stock Exchange (TTSE)

Banking and insurance

The country has a number of international and domestic commercial banks including Citibank, Royal Bank and Scotia Bank.

Central bank

Central Bank of Trinidad and Tobago

Main financial centre

Port of Spain

Time

GMT minus four hours

Geography

Trinidad and Tobago lies in the Caribbean Sea off the eastern coast of Venezuela. Trinidad is the larger of the two islands, Tobago lies 32km north-east of Trinidad. The terrain of Trinidad is principally flat, although three ranges of higher land – peaking at almost 1,000 metres – cross the island from west to east.

Hemisphere

Northern

Climate

The islands have a humid, tropical climate with a rainy season from June to December, and an annual temperature range between 21 and 32 degrees Celsius.

Dress codes

Dress is generally informal and suited to the hot tropical climate. Men generally wear a shirt and tie for business meetings.

Entry requirements

Passports

Required by all, except nationals of Caricom countries, valid for six months beyond date of departure.

Visa

Required by all who are not exempt; a full list can be found at www.visittnt.com/General/things/visa.html. Business travellers should submit an employer's letter stating credentials with the visa application form.

Currency advice/regulations

There are no restrictions on the import of local and foreign currencies, subject to declaration on arrival. Export of local currency is limited to TT$200 and of foreign currency to TT$2,500 per annum.

Prohibited imports

Illegal drugs, weapons and explosives, specific animals (including monkeys and mongoose), animals that have died on transit, products used in relation to certain animals (such as used animal blankets and saddles) as well as dung may not be brought into Trinidad and Tobago.

Health (for visitors)

Mandatory precautions

Yellow fever vaccination certificate if arriving from infected area.

Advisable precautions

Yellow fever, hepatitis A, polio and tetanus vaccinations are advisable. Water precautions should be taken.

Hotels
A range of hotels is available in Trinidad and Tobago. They are generally expensive, although less so in Tobago. A 10 per cent tip is usual. A hotel room tax (in properties of 16 rooms or over) of 10 per cent has replaced value-added tax.

Book well in advance if arriving during Carnival time.

Credit cards
Credit cards are accepted.

Public holidays (national)
Fixed dates

1 Jan (New Year's Day), 30 Mar (Shouter Baptist Liberation Day), 30 May (Indian Arrival Day), 19 Jun (Labour Day), 1 Aug (Emancipation Day), 31 Aug (Independence Day), 24 Sep (Republic Day), 25–26 Dec (Christmas).

Variable dates

Good Friday, Easter Monday, Corpus Christi (May/Jun), Diwali (Hindu, Oct/Nov), Eid al Fitr.

Working hours
Carnival (two-day event immediately preceding Ash Wednesday) is usually taken as an unofficial holiday.

Banking

Mon–Thu: 0800–1400; Fri: 0800–1200, 1500–1700.

Business

Business hours are 0800–1600.

Government

Mon–Fri: 0815–1630.

Shops

Mon–Fri: 0800–1630; Sat: 0800–1200. Supermarkets stay open later in the evenings and are open all day Saturday. Some open on Sunday. Some close on Thursday afternoon.

Telecommunications
Mobile/cell phones

GSM 850/1900 and 1800 services provide cover for most of the islands.

Electricity supply
Domestic: 115 and 230V AC, 60 cycles. Industrial: 400V, 60 cycles three-phase.

Weights and measures
Metric system legally in use since 1981, but many traders continue to use the imperial system.

Social customs/useful tips
Both the social and business environment in Trinidad and Tobago are friendly and informal, and it is common to be on a first-name basis with people whom you have met before.

Security
The last major instance of political violence was in 1990, and the islands are generally a safe place to visit. The usual precautions against pickpockets should be taken in crowded areas.

Getting there
Air

National airline: Caribbean Airlines (replacing BWIA in early 2007 as the national airline). CAL receives a fuel subsidy, sometimes refered to as a 'fuel hedge' from the government, giving it an advantage over regional airline LIAT.

International airport/s: Piarco International, 25km east of Port of Spain, Trinidad; duty-free shop, restaurant, bank, post office, car hire.

Crown Point International, 5km west of Scarborough, Tobago.

Airport tax: TT$100, payable in local currency only.

Surface

Water: There are ferry services to neighbouring islands. Cruise ships call at Port of Spain, Trinidad, and Scarborough, Tobago.

Main port/s: Chaguaramas, Point Lisas, Port of Spain, Point-à-Pierre (Trinidad); Scarborough (Tobago).

Getting about
National transport

Air: Tobago Express flies frequent 'airbridge' services throughout the day between Piarco and Crown Point airports. The journey takes about 25 minutes.

Road: There is an extensive road network of around 8,000km. Major highways run north-south and east-west. Traffic jams are common.

Buses: Cheap and generally crowded.

Water: The two islands are connected by ferries between Port of Spain (Trinidad) and Scarborough (Tobago). There are two fast catamaran ferries, with a journey time of around two hours. A daily car ferry takes over six hours and the passage can be uncomfortable.

City transport

Taxis: Shared, route taxis are widely used. Routes with standard fares operated by passenger cars bearing 'H' registration plates and two-coloured Maxi Taxis (yellow stripe in Port of Spain). Negotiate fares for regular taxis in advance. Limousine service available at airport.

Taxis can be hired by distance, by the hour or by the day.

Car hire

National driving licences of most countries accepted for a period of three months from arrival. Insurance required. Cars drive on left. The maximum speed limit is 80kph on highways.

BUSINESS DIRECTORY
The addresses listed below are a selection only. While World of Information makes every endeavour to check these addresses, we cannot guarantee that changes have not been made, especially to telephone numbers and area codes. We would welcome any corrections.

Telephone area codes
This international direct dialling code for Trinidad and Tobago is +1-868 followed by subscriber's number.

Useful telephone numbers
Police: 999, 623-5191

Fire: 990

Ambulance:990, 625-3222/3

Chambers of Commerce
American Chamber of Commerce of Trinidad and Tobago, Trinidad Hilton Hotel and Conference Centre, Lady Young Road, Port of Spain (tel: 627-8570; fax: 627-7405; e-mail: inbox@amchamtt.com).

British-Caribbean Chamber of Commerce, Chamber Building, Columbus Circle, West Moorings, PO Box 499, Port of Spain (tel: 637-6966; fax: 637-7427; e-mail: info@britishcaribbean.com).

Caribbean Association of Industry and Commerce, Trinidad Hilton Hotel and Conference Centre, Lady Young Road, PO Box 442, Port of Spain (tel: 623-4830; fax: 623-6116; e-mail: caic@trinidad.net).

Greater Chaguanas Chamber of Industry and Commerce, Kibon House, 1 Endevour Road, Chaguanas (tel/fax: 671-5754; e-mail: admin@chaguanaschamber.com).

South Trinidad Chamber of Industry and Commerce, Cross Crossing Shopping Centre, Lady Hailes Avenue, PO Box 80, San Fernando (tel: 657-9077; fax: 652-5613; e-mail: execoffice@southchamber.com).

Trinidad and Tobago Chamber of Industry and Commerce, Chamber House, Columbus Circle, West Moorings, PO Box 499, Port of Spain (tel: 637-6966; fax: 637-7425; e-mail: chamber@chamber.org.tt).

Banking
Agricultural Development Bank of Trinidad and Tobago, PO Box 154, Port of Spain (tel: 623-6261/5, 625-6539; fax: 624-3087).

Bank of Commerce, PO Box 69, Port of Spain (tel: 627-9325/8; fax: 627-0904).

Bank of Nova Scotia, The Scotia Building, 56–58 Richmond Street, Port of Spain (tel: 625-3566/5222; fax: 623-0256).

Citibank, PO Box 1249, 12 Queen's Park East, Port of Spain (tel: 625-6445/9, 625-1046/9; fax: 624-8131; 625-6820).

Citicorp Merchant Bank, 12 Queen's Park East, Port of Spain (tel: 623-3344; fax: 624-8131).

CLICO Investment Bank, 1 Rust Street, St. Clair, Port of Spain (tel: 628-3628; fax 628-3639).

First Citizens Bank, Park & Henry Streets, Port of Spain (tel: 623-2423, 623-2576/8; fax: 627-5956).

Republic Bank Ltd, PO Box 1153, Port of Spain, Trinidad (tel: 625-3611, 623-0371; fax: 623-0371); Corner Wilson and Castries St, Scarborough, Tobago (tel: 639-2561).

Royal Merchant Bank & Finance Company, 7th Floor, 55 Independence Square, Port of Spain (tel: 625-3511, 624-5212).

The Royal Bank of Trinidad and Tobago, Head Office, Royal Court, 19-21 Park Street, Port of Spain (tel: 623-4291, 625-3764; fax: 624-4866).

Central bank

Central Bank of Trinidad and Tobago, Eric Williams Plaza, Independence Square, PO Box 1250, Port of Spain (tel: 625-4835; fax: 627-4696; e-mail: info@central-bank.org.tt).

Stock exchange

Trinidad and Tobago Stock Exchange (TTSE), www.stockex.co.tt

Travel information

Caribbean Airlines, Sunjet House, 30 Edward Street, Port of Spain (tel: 669-3000; fax: 669-1680).

Piarco International Airport, Caroni North Bank Road, Piarco (tel: 669-8047; fax: 669-0228).

Tourist Information Office, Crown Point Airport (tel: 639-0509; fax: 639-3566).

Tourist Information Office, Piarco Airport (tel: 669-5196; fax: 669-6045; e-mail: tourism-info@tdc.co.tt).

Trinidad and Tobago Automobile Association (TAA), 41 Woodford Street, Newtown, Port-of-Spain (tel: 622-7194; fax: 622-9079; e-mail: taa@tstt.net.tt).

Ministry of tourism

Ministry of Tourism, 51-55 Frederick Street, Port of Spain (tel: 624-1403; fax: 625-0437; e-mail: mintourism@tourism.gov.tt).

National tourist organisation offices

Tourism Development Company Ltd, Maritime Centre, 29 Tenth Avenue, Barataria (tel: 675-7034; fax: 675-7432; e-mail : info@tdc.co.tt).

Ministries

Ministry of Communications and Information Technology, Kent House, Long Circular Road, Maraval (tel: 628-1323; fax: 622-4783).

Ministry of Community Empowerment, Autorama Building, El Socorro Road, San Juan (tel: 675-6728; fax: 674-4021).

Ministry of Consumer Affairs, Agostini Compound, 3 Duncan Street, Port of Spain (tel: 623-7741; fax: 625-4737).

Ministry of Culture, Algico Building, Jerningham Avenue, Queen's Park East, Port of Spain (tel: 625-3012; fax: 625-3278).

Ministry of Education, Hayes Street, St Clair (tel: 622-2181; fax: 628-7818).

Ministry of Energy and Energy Industries, Level 9, Riverside Plaza, Corner Besson & Piccadilly Streets, Port of Spain (tel: 623-6708; fax: 623-2726).

Ministry of Enterprise Development, Level 15, Riverside Plaza, Corner Besson & Piccadilly Streets, Port of Spain (tel: 623-2931; fax: 627-8488).

Ministry of the Environment, Level 16, Eric Williams Finance Building, Independence Square, Port of Spain (tel: 627-9700; fax: 625-1585).

Ministry of Finance, Level 8, Eric Williams Finance Building, Independence Square, Port of Spain (tel: 627-9700; 627-6108).

Ministry of Food Production and Marine Resources, PO Box 389, St Clair Circle, St Clair (tel: 622-1221; 622-8202).

Ministry of Foreign Affairs, Knowsley Building, 1 Queen's Park West, Port of Spain (tel: 623-4116; fax: 627-0571).

Ministry of Health, Corner Duncan Street & Independence Square, Port of Spain (tel: 627-0012; fax: 623-9528).

Ministry of Housing and Settlements, NHA Building, Corner George Street & South Quay, Port of Spain (tel: 624-5058; fax: 625-2793).

Ministry of Human Development, Sacred Heart Building, 16-18 Sackville Street, Port of Spain (tel: 624-2000; fax: 625-7003).

Ministry of Infrastructure Development, Corner Richmond & London Streets, Port of Spain (tel: 625-1225; fax: 625-8070).

Ministry of Integrated Planning and Development, Level 14, Eric Williams Finance Building, Independence Square, Port of Spain (tel: 623-4308; fax: 623-8123).

Ministry of Labour, Manpower Development and Industrial Relations, Level 11, Riverside Plaza, Corner Besson & Piccadilly Streets, Port of Spain (tel: 623-4241; fax: 624-4091).

Ministry of Legal Affairs, 72-74 South Quay, Port of Spain (tel: 625-4586; fax: 625-9803).

Ministry of Local Government, Kent House, Long Circular Road, Maraval (tel: 628-1325; fax: 622-7410).

Ministry of National Security, Temple Court, 31-33 Abercromby Street, Port of Spain (tel: 623-2441; fax: 625-3925).

Ministry of Sport, ISSA Nicholas Building, Corner Frederick & Duke Streets, Port of Spain (tel: 625-5622; fax: 623-4507).

Ministry of Transport, Corner Richmond & London Streets, Port of Spain (tel: 625-1225; fax: 627-9886).

Office of The Attorney General, Cabildo Chambers, Corner Sackville & St Vincent Streets, Port of Spain (tel: 623-7010; fax: 625-0470).

Office of The Prime Minister, Whitehall, Maraval Road, Port of Spain (tel: 622-1625; fax: 622-0055).

Other useful addresses

Businessmen's Association of Trinidad and Tobago, PO Box 322, Time Plaza, Room 10, 28 Henry Street, Port of Spain (tel: 623-4568).

Caribbean Employers' Confederation, 43 Dundonald Street, Port of Spain (tel: 625-4723).

Caribbean Industrial Research Institute, O'Meara Industrial Estate, Macoya Road, Trincity, Arima (tel: 662-7161/4; fax: 663-4180).

Export Development Corporation, Export House, 10-14 Phillips Street, PO Box 582, Port of Spain (tel: 623-6022/3; fax: 625-0050).

Industrial Development Corporation, 10-12 Independence Square, PO Box 949, Port of Spain (tel: 623-7291/6, 623-7289).

Management Development Centre, Room 212, Salvatoria Building, PO Box 1301, Port of Spain (tel: 623-4951/3).

National Gas Company of Trinidad and Tobago Limited, Goodrich Bay Road, Point Lisas Industrial Estate, Point Lisas (tel: 636-4662; fax: 679-2384).

Petroleum Company of Trinidad and Tobago Limited (PETROTRIN), Administrative Building, Southern Main Road, Pointe-à-Pierre (tel: 658-4200, 658-4230; fax: 658-1315; e-mail: petroweb@petrotrin.com).

Reinsurance Company of Trinidad and Tobago, Trinre House, 52 Jerningham Avenue, Belmont, PO Box 1087, Port of Spain (tel: 623-6194/6602; fax: 624-4021).

Small Business Association of Trinidad and Tobago, Third Floor, MPU Building, 3 Besson Street, Port of Spain (tel: 624-3666).

Shipping Association of Trinidad and Tobago, Room 12a, 64-66 South Quay, Port of Spain (tel: 623-8570).

Telecommunications Services of Trinidad and Tobago Ltd (TSTT), 54 Frederick Street, PO Box 971, Port of Spain (tel:

624-5756/5703; fax: 625-4585; e-mail: tsttceo@tstt.net.tt).

Tobago House of Assembly, (Foreign Investment Proposals in Tobago), Bacolet Street, Scarborough.

Trinidad and Tobago Development Finance Co Ltd, PO Box 187, 8-10 Cipriani Boulevard, Port of Spain (tel: 623-4665/7, 625-4666/8; fax: 624-3563).

Trinidad and Tobago Embassy (USA), 1708 Massachusetts Avenue, NW, Washington DC (tel: (+1-202) 467-6490; fax: (+1-202) 785-3130; e-mail: embttgo@erols.com).

Trinidad and Tobago Export Trading Company Limited, Level 4 Long Circular Mall, Long Circular Road, St. James (tel: 622-7968; fax: 628-2349).

Trinidad and Tobago Manufacturers' Association, 8 Stanmore Avenue, Port of Spain (tel: 623-1029/31, fax: 623-1031).

Cananews: www.cananews.net

Internet sites

Government website: http://www.gov.tt

Information on economic trends, investment opportunities, infrastructure, news and events: http://www.tidco.co.tt/

Petroleum Company of Trinidad and Tobago Ltd: http://www.petrotrin.com

Prime Minister's Office: http://www.opm.gov.tt

Statistics Office: http://www.cso.gov.tt

Telecommunications Services of Trinidad and Tobago Ltd: http://www.tstt.net.tt

Trinidad and Tobago company database: http://tradepoint.tidco.co.tt/ttcdbase/

Tristan da Cunha

KEY FACTS

Official name: Tristan da Cunha

Head of State: Queen Elizabeth II (since 6 February 1952)

Head of government: Governor Mark Capes (since 29 October 2011)

Area: 98 square km

Population: 263 (2010)

Capital: Edinburgh of the Seven Seas

Official language: English

Currency: Pound sterling (£) = 100 pence

Exchange rate: £0.65 per US$ (Sep 2015)

COUNTRY PROFILE

1506 The island was sighted by the Portuguese admiral, Tristão da Cunha, on his way to the East Indies.
1810 The first settlers arrived but failed to establish a permanent community.
1816 The island was annexed by Britain and a garrison established to provide additional security for Napoleon who was being held in exile on St Helena.
1817 The garrison was withdrawn but Corporal Glass elected to stay on the island with his wife to guard the remaining stores and incidentally founded the community.
The community gradually developed during the nineteenth century and for a time became relatively prosperous with frequent calls by American whalers in the 1850s. The seven families represented four nations – Britain, Holland, US and Italy. With the decline of sail the island became increasingly isolated and impoverished; sometimes several years passed without a ship calling. The only contact with the outside world was provided by an irregular succession of pastors and a very occasional passing ship.
1938 The island became a dependency of St Helena.
1942 A garrison and radio/meteorological station were built.
1949 The island's extreme isolation ended with the establishment of the crawfish industry when the first fish processing factory was opened.
1950s, The British pound was introduced as the official currency.
1961 The volcano erupted and the entire community was evacuated, returning some two years later to re-establish the settlement.
1981 The Nationality Act ended the islanders' British citizenship and right of abode.
1999 The Nationality Act came under review in the UK government's 'Partnership for Prosperity and Progress' White Paper.
2000 Development of the crawfish industry ended Tristan's dependence on the UK and gave the islanders economic confidence.
2001 The island was hit by a hurricane which inflicted considerable damage.
2004 A new, long wheel-based type Land Rover fire engine, provided by the UK government, was delivered. Michael Clancy became governor.
2006 An oilrig ran aground on a reef on the southeast side of the island during a hurricane while being towed from South Africa to South America. It took several months and two attempts to re-float the rig. By 2006 very home on the island had a telephone line, and a new satellite service allowed for broadband internet access and live television broadcasts.
2007 David Morley became the resident administrator and Andrew Gurr became governor.
2008 Plans to repair and refurbish the harbour were announced, with work to be undertaken by UK Royal Engineers and materials supplied through the European Development Fund and UK government.
2009 The FCO announced a new constitution for Tristan da Cunha, which included a bill of rights and limits to the power of the governor. It also proposed an executive Legislative Council with either a single constituency for the whole island or two or more constituencies.
Tristan da Cunha later voted in favour of the proposed changes. A new, larger and modern fish factory replacing the one that had been burned down in 2008 was opened. Work began, under the auspices of the Tristan Conservation Department, to eradicate the alien plant *Sagina apetala* (Pearlwort) from Gough Island, which was displacing native floral. Funding and management was being provided by the Royal Society for the Protection of Birds (RSPB) from the UK's Overseas Territories Environment Programme.
2010 New island councillors were voted into office in March. In November it was announced that Calshot Harbour is to be repaired by the UK Department for International Development (DfID). It was severely damaged by storms earlier in the year and it was feared that unless emergency repairs were made before the 2011 winter storms the islanders would be cut off. Calshot Harbour is essential to the island's economy, which is primarily based on tourism and fishing. Sean Burns became Administrator on 21 September.
2011 On 19 July Tristan da Cunha's rock lobster fishery was awarded Marine Stewardship Council (MSC) accreditation for sustainable and well-managed fisheries. On 23 September, Governor Gurr's term

in office ended and Attorney General Ken Baddon was sworn in as acting governor on 24 September, until Mark Andrew Capes takes up the post in 29 October.
2012 On 3 August, *HMS Dauntless* arrived for the first of its regular visits to the island. It was carrying the doctor who was a replacement for the existing doctor who had become unwell. The *HMS Dauntless'* helicopter flew VHF repeater station equipment to the north-east of the island to close a gap in the communications network. On 15 October the FCO appointed Peter Hayes as director in the Defence and Intelligence Directorate for the UK Overseas Territories.
2013 Governor Mark Capes appointed Mr Alex Mitham as Administrator on 5 October. The 50th Anniversary of the Re-Settlement of Tristan da Cunha was celebrated in Glasgow, Scotland, on 1 November.
2014 The 2014/15 fishing season got under way on the 1 July. Total Allowable Catches (TAC) for the islands of Gough, Inaccessible, Nightingale and Tristan were a total of 399 tonnes, 4 tonnes up on 2013/14.
2015 In March RIBA Competitions launched a Design Ideas Competition on behalf of Tristan da Cunha's government. Thirty-seven 37 entries submitted to the first phase of the competition by architect-led design teams based in Australia, Brazil, Canada, China, Germany, Italy, Japan, New Zealand, Russia, Spain, Switzerland, Turkey, United Kingdom and the United States of America. The anonymous submissions were reviewed in June when the Tristan da Cunha Administrator and Head of Government was in the UK. As well as HH Alex Mitham, the Panel also comprised Laura Benyohai (Tristan da Cunha & Pitcairn Desk Officer, Foreign and Commonwealth Office) Chris Carnegy (Tristan da Cunha, UK representative), Jim Kerr (Tristan da Cunha, UK adviser) and John Whiles (Jestico + Whiles, acting as the RIBA Architect Adviser). The Panel identified a long-list of 15 schemes for further consideration. These were presented by Alex Mitham to the Island Council for their final selection of the shortlist on his return to Tristan in July. The Island Council was delighted by the interest shown in Tristan by design teams from around the globe, together with the myriad ideas contained within the phase one design proposals.

Political structure

Tristan is the only inhabited island, although there is a meteorological station on Gough Island, maintained by the South African navy.
Although technically under the jurisdiction of St Helena, the island effectively administers itself independently. Responsibility for it, as a British Overseas Territories, is divided between the British Foreign and Commonwealth Office (FCO) and the Department for International Development (DfID). The post of Minister for Overseas Territories within the FCO was created and an Overseas Territories Consultative Council set up.
In 2002, full British citizenship was granted to the inhabitants of Tristan da Cunha.

Form of state

As a British Overseas Territory, Tristan da Cunha is a dependency of St Helena.

The executive

The Executive Council consists of the governor, three ex-officio officers and five elected members of the Legislative Council.
The monarch is hereditary and appoints the governor.

National legislature

The unicameral Legislative Council has 15 seats of which 12 members are directly elected in a single countrywide constituency by simple majority vote, three members are ex-officio members (chief secretary, finance secretary and attorney general) for a four-year term.

Last elections

17 July 2013 (Legislative Council)
Results: The 12 elected members of the Legislative Council were elected in a single constituency, with voters having 12 votes to cast. Eight candidates failed to be elected into the Legislative Council. Ian Sebastian Rummery won the most votes with 894.
There are about 80 families living on the island, with eight names between them.
Tristan is the most isolated inhabited island in the world. The settlement of Edinburgh of the Seven Seas in the north-west and is the only inhabited area.

Population

263 (2010)
Last census: December 1988: 296
Population density: 3.0 inhabitants per sq km.

Ethnic make-up

English, Scottish, Irish, Dutch and Italian.

Main cities

Edinburgh of the Seven Seas (capital, estimated population 231 in 2012).

Languages spoken

Official language/s

English

Media

Press

News is published by the online newspaper Tristan Times (www.tristantimes.com) and the South Atlantic Remote Territories Media Association (www.sartma.com).

Broadcasting

The Tristan Broadcasting Service provides local and BBC World Service programmes on 93.5FM.
Radio: Atlantic FM was re-launched on 13 January 2008 providing a limited service with local news and information.

Economy

Tristan's commercial economy is based on crawfish (Tristan Rock Lobster), sheep farming, philatelic sales and to a much lesser extent through tourism by the provision of guides and accommodation to visitors. Hand-knitted garments and other woollen handicrafts and souvenirs are sold, some of which are also sold by mail order. All families work in farming or fishing, including pensioners and children, and adults also have additional salaried jobs working for the government or small domestic services.
Since the opening of the first crawfish cannery and freezing plant in 1949, the economy has been transformed from subsistence, sometimes near starvation level, to self-sufficiency. In the 2013 fishing season, 1 July till 30 September, there were only 10 days suitable for fishing. The annual crawfish catch is limited to 340 tonnes, of which 145 tonnes comes from the main island and the balance from the fisheries around Gough, Nightingale and Inaccessible Islands. An agreement has also been signed with a New Zealand company for catching Patagonian toothfish. Revenue from the industry more than adequately covers the island's running costs and has allowed reserves to be built up. These provided a buffer against the decline in Far Eastern demand. A fire in 2008 burned down the island's only fish processing factory. It was rebuilt to EU standards as a bigger, modern facility able to export lobsters to the EU. The island's oldest inhabitant, Alice Glass (93 years old), opened the new factory in 2009.
Other economic activities are hampered by poor access with only about 60 days per year suitable for landing. A new harbour has improved conditions and allows for more regular visits, particularly by small yachts. Tristan's fresh water is considered to have special properties and there were plans to develop a mineral water export business, but which by early 2014 had not progressed beyond the feasibility planning stage.

External trade

As a UK Overseas Territory, Tristan da Cunha is a member of the European Union's Association of Overseas Countries and Territories (OCT Association), and some EU regulations apply. Foreign earnings are generated by commercial fishing licences, with postage stamps, coins and handicrafts supplied by mail order.

Agriculture
Farming
The cultivated area is estimated at no more than 15 hectares (ha). Potatoes are the main crop. Cattle, sheep and poultry are kept. Each married couple is allowed to graze seven sheep and two cows on settlement land, or any number on the plateau.
Each family grows potatoes on about 0.5ha of ground. Potatoes were first introduced to the island in 1816 when the first settlers arrived and have been grown on the same land each year without rotation; they are easily grown in volcanic soil.
Fishing
Tristan da Cunha's fisheries zone is rich in unique species including rock lobsters, wreckfish, Tristan red scorpion fish, Tristan wrasse and Atlantic amberjack.
The economy is based on crawfish (rock lobster). Fish provide a major source of protein.
A fire in 2008 burned down the island's only fish processing factory. It was rebuilt to EU standards as a bigger, modern facility able to export lobsters to the EU.
Forestry

Tourism
Being 'the most remote island in the world', tourist visits are largely dependent on cruise ship itineraries and personal sailings. When visitors arrive their welcome is personal as the population of the island is too small to be unappreciative of any newcomer. A display of the history and culture is exhibited in the local post office and tourism centre and there are walks to the top of the volcano, led by island guides. Beach fishing and golf are activities on offer to visitors.

Hydrocarbons
There are no known hydrocarbon reserves and all petroleum needs are met by imports.

Time
GMT

Geography
The Tristan da Cunha archipelago comprises the main island as well as Inaccessible and Nightingale Islands. Gough Island, to the south-east, also comes under Tristan administration, combined their surface area is 201 square kilometres.
The main island of Tristan da Cunha is a single, almost circular, volcanic island that lies 2,400km west of Cape Town in the South Atlantic Ocean. It has only one relatively flat area, where the capital is located. Queen Mary's Peak (2,010 metres) is the highest mountain, at the centre of the island.
Inaccessible Island lies 32km west of Tristan; the three Nightingale Islands 35km south; and Gough Island (Diego Alvarez) 350km south, which has a manned weather station with seven personnel.
Hemisphere
Southern

Climate
Tristan da Cunha has a mild, temperate climate. Temperatures range from 3–25 degrees Celsius. The average annual rainfall is 1,700mm.

Entry requirements
Visa
None required, but visitors must have permission of the Island Council and Administrator to land; this is normally granted. All visitors must have onward/return passage, full medical insurance including emergency evacuation and sufficient funds for a visit. A small landing fee is charged.

Hotels
There is no hotel accommodation on the island.

Working hours
Government
Mon–Fri: 0830–1230, 1300–1630.

Telecommunications
Telephone/fax
The Administrator's office and the factory in Tristan have satellite communications by telephone and fax. Faxes are only available to the government.
A public satellite telephone provides an international service through a radio telephone link via Cape Town Radio.
Postal services
The international postal code for Tristan da Cunha is TDCU 1ZZ.

Getting there
Surface
Shipping is the sole means of regular access to the island.
Water: Calshot Harbour, completed in 1967 and named after the Hampshire village where many islanders lived after the volcanic explosion of 1961, is too small for ocean going boats to berth. Passengers are normally ferried to land in small boats and landing is not guaranteed. Cargo is loaded onto barges and off loaded by crane. Improvements and repairs to the harbour, which is vital to the economy, were agreed in 2006 for completion by 2008. The improvements included deepening the harbour. Finance for the work was to come from the British government and from the EU. However, in 2010 the work still had to be agreed and commissioned.
In February 2008 a team of 40 Royal Engineers plus a detachment from the Royal Logistic Corps and a medical support team from the Royal Navy, were transported along with their materials by the RFA *Lyme Bay*, to carry out urgent repairs to the main harbour. Operation Zest was a joint government response involving the foreign and commonwealth office, the department for international development (DfID) (who funded the work) and the ministry of defence. Within months of the successful completion of Operation Zest, the main crane collapsed in April, leaving the islanders with the problem of not only how to bring ashore a new crane, but also the materials to rebuild the fish factory.
The new crane was finally commissioned in January 2009 and further improvements and repairs were finished by April.
The Austral storms of 2010 again damaged the harbour walls and it was feared that unless emergency repairs were made before the winter storms of 2011 the islanders would be cut off. In November island administrator, Sean Burns, announced that DfID had agreed to fund the £6 million (US$3.77 million) needed to fund the fifty 10-tonne concrete 'dolosse' blocks specially designed to protect the most vulnerable part of the harbour from future storms.
Calshot Harbour is essential to the island's economy, which is based on tourism and fishing, as well as enabling supplies to be delivered.
The RMS *St Helena* makes an annual visit. The ship is operated under contract by Andrew Weir Shipping Ltd on behalf of the owners, St Helena Line Ltd.
Premier Fishing operates two fishing boats, the *Kelso* and the *Edinburgh*, which make irregular connections between Tristan and Cape Town.
The South African Navy operates the *Agulhas* to approximate sailing dates, mainly for official personnel.
Yachts call frequently and offer an alternative means of reaching the island, as does the occasional cruise ship.

BUSINESS DIRECTORY

The addresses listed below are a selection only. While World of Information makes every endeavour to check these addresses, we cannot guarantee that changes have not been made, especially to telephone numbers and area codes. We would welcome any corrections.

Telephone area codes
The international direct dialling (IDD) code for Tristan de Cunha is +874 (satellite) followed by subscriber's number.

Travel information
Travel information (for air travel and bookings on the RMS St Helena):
Passenger Services Department, Andrew Weir Shipping Ltd, Dexter House, 2 Royal

Mint Court, London EC N4XX, UK (tel: (+44-207) 575-6480; fax: (+44-207) 575-6200; email: reservations@aws.co.uk; internet site: www.aws.co.uk).

Premier Fishing, PO Box 181, Cape Town 8000, South Africa. (tel: (+27-21) 419-0124).

St Helena Line, Andrew Weir Shipping (SA) Pty Ltd, 3rd Floor, BP Centre, Thibault Square, Cape Town, South Africa (tel: (+27-21) 425-1165; fax: (+27-21) 421-7485; email: sthelenaline@mweb.co.za).

Miss Kerry Yon, Solomon and Co plc, Jamestown, St Helena, South Atlantic (tel: (+290) 2523; fax: (+290) 2423; email: solco.shipping@helanta.sh).

Ministries

Administrator's Office, Edinburgh of the Seven Seas (e-mail: hmg@cunha.demon.co.uk).

Other useful addresses

The Tristan Resource Centre, Michael Swales, Denstone College, Uttoxeter, Staffs, UK (tel: (+44)-(0)1538) 703-322).

St Helena Desk Officer, Foreign and Commonwealth Office, Room, King Charles Street, London SW1A 2AH, UK (tel: (+44-(0)207) 270-2695).

Miles Apart (books, maps, videos on South Atlantic Islands), 5 Harraton House, Exning, Newmarket, Suffolk CB8 7HF, UK (tel: (+44-(0)1638) 577-627; fax: (+44-(0)1638) 577-874); 5929 Avon Drive, Bethesda, Maryland 20814, US (tel/fax: (+1-301) 571-8942; email: familycarter@msn.com).

Internet sites

Sartma (South Atlantic Remote Territories Media Association): www.sartma.com

Tristan Times: www.tristantimes.com

Tunisia

KEY FACTS

Official name: Jumhuriya at Tunisiya (Republic of Tunisia)

Head of State: President Beji Caid Essebsi (since 31 December 2014)

Head of government: Prime Minister Habib Essid (since 6 February 2015)

Ruling party: Coalition led by Nidaa Tounes consisting of Union Patriotique Libre (UPL) (Free Patriotic Union), Afek Tounes (Tunisian Aspiration), Harkat en-Nahda (Ennahda Movement) and independent politicians.

Area: 164,150 square km

Population: 11.00 million (2014)*

Capital: Tunis

Official language: Arabic

Currency: Dinar (D) = 1,000 millimes

Exchange rate: D1.97 per US$ (Sep 2015)

GDP per capita: US$4,415 (2014)*

GDP real growth: 2.30% (2014)*

GDP: US$48.55 billion (2014)

Labour force: 3.77 million (2010)

Unemployment: 15.30% (2014)*

Inflation: 4.92% (2014)

Oil production: 53,000 bpd (2014)

Balance of trade: -US$6.56 billion (2014)

Annual FDI: US$432.67 million (2011)

* estimated figure

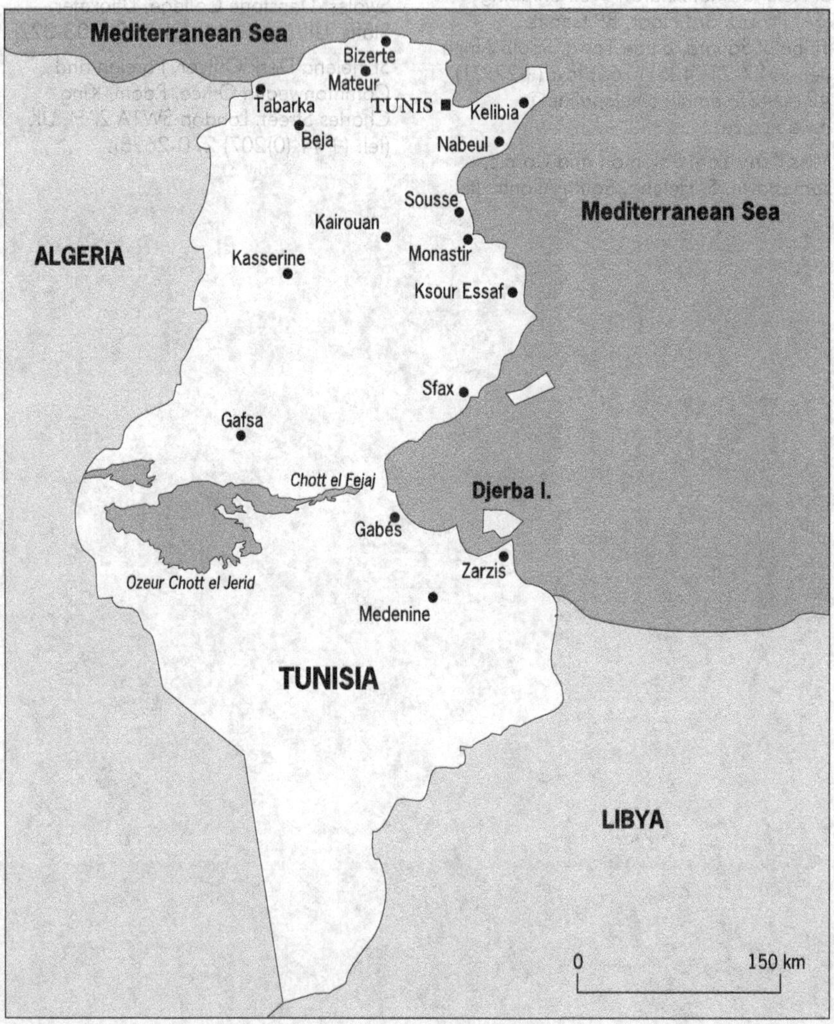

Tunisia was not the happiest of countries in 2015. The terrorist attacks that had left the country's important tourism industry in a state of empty paralysis had one sadly ironic side effect – in late March after the first attack that claimed the lives of 24 tourists visiting the famous Bardo museum, as many as 60,000 demonstrators filled the streets of Tunis to protest at the massacre. The rally was seen as a significant demonstration of solidarity for Tunisia's elected government. Sadly, there was more to come. In late June, a lone terrorist by the name of Seifeddine Rezgui, calmly killed 38 tourists on the beach of the Hotel Imperial Marhaba, in Sousse. If the first attack was dismissed as one of the so called Islamic State (IS)'s random international attacks, the Sousse incident changed that perception. Tunisia, it now seemed, had been singled out by IS for particular attention.

Insurgence

The first mass murder in Tunisia took place in 2002, when al Qaeda operatives killed 22 tourists, most of whom were from Germany. By 2015 al Qaeda had effectively given way to the more grandiose and better resourced, Islamic State (IS).

Since 2014 the IS had been making efforts to set itself up in Tunisia, having established a foothold in Libya. Its skilful use of social media had enabled it both to recruit in Tunisia, but also to establish links with existing terrorist groups operating in the country.

The Bardo and Sousse attacks were thought to have been carried out by the IS Tunisian 'franchise' Okba ibn Nafaa, which accounted for the bulk of the 3,000 Tunisian fighters who had signed up for the Islamic State in Syria and Iraq. Closer to home, Tunisia also had supplied some 2,000 fighters in neighbouring Libya. In September 2014 Okba ibn Nafaa had switched its allegiance from al Qaeda in the Islamic Maghreb to the (so called) Islamic State. In February 2015 the Okba ibn Nafaa Brigade killed four Tunisian police officers in the Kasserine region of the country at a checkpoint on the Algerian border. The Okba Ibn Nafaa Brigade derives its name from Uqba ibn Nafi who was an Arab general in the Umayyad Dynasty that aided in the conquest of the Maghreb. The Brigade had also sought to interfere with the Tunisian elections in 2014.

The Brigade was led by Khaled Chaieb, also known as Lokman Abou Sakhr, until he was killed in an anti-terrorism operation near the Algerian border in March 2015. It operates primarily along the Algerian-Tunisian border. The Islamic State affiliates in Libya very much depended on the influx of Tunisian fighters. The porous border with Libya allowed the easy influx of weapons into Tunisia where there were thought to be a number of clandestine IS training camps. As the fighters crossed back and forth between Libya and Tunisia, it had to be assumed that fighters from the Libyan affiliate of the Islamic State are returning to Tunisia as IS officers, training and supporting the local franchisees, principally the Okba Ibn Nafaa Brigade and Ansar al Sharia Tunisia. The Tunisian government claimed to have prevented an estimated 9,000 Tunisians from attending an IS training camp near the Tunisian-Libyan border.

The Tunisian government could be forgiven for not knowing where to begin. A state of national emergency was declared after the June tragedy, giving the police and the army increased powers of arrest and authority. At the same time the government's freedom to act was increased. Public assemblies and other activities were declared illegal. Following the quiet revolution in 2011 that saw the end of the Zine Ben Ali regime and triggered what became known as the Arab Spring, Tunisia has been confronting the increased jihadist activity, which has been responsible for the deaths of both policemen and members of the armed forces. The IS claimed responsibility for the two attacks on visiting foreigners. President Beji Caid Essebsi announced the closure of some 77 *shaabi* mosques (outside the jurisdiction of the government).

According to Human Rights Watch (HRW), the new counter-terrorism law gave Tunisia's security forces broad monitoring and surveillance powers, while it extended incommunicado detention from six to up to 15 days for terrorism suspects, allowing the courts to close hearings to the public and to allow witnesses to remain anonymous to the defendants. An HRW spokesman noted that 'Terrorism endangers everyone in Tunisia, but so does a law that allows the police to interrogate suspects without a lawyer for 15 days.' The Assembly of the People's Representatives, Tunisia's 217-member parliament, adopted the law late on 25 July 2015, with 174 in favour and 10 abstentions. The government had sent the bill to parliament in late March 2015, following the March attack on the Bardo Museum.

The new law replaced that introduced in 2003 under the rule of the then-President Zine El Abidine Ben Ali. By the time he was ousted in January 2011, the courts had tried about 3,000 people under the legislation. Many suspected opponents were charged under the law in the absence of any credible evidence linking them to terrorism, with convictions based on confessions extracted under torture, according to a United Nations (UN) report. After President Ben Ali's deposition, Tunisia's interim authorities had almost stopped applying the 2003 law, but resumed in May 2013, after a series of armed attacks on security forces in the Chaambi Mountains, near the Algerian border.

Parliament had amended the legislation to promote increased protection of human rights, including a measure to strengthen the right of journalists to shield their sources and another that criminalised unauthorised government surveillance. Tunisian non-governmental organisations (NGOs) were concerned that the definition of terrorism contained in the law was too broad and ambiguous. The law included as terrorist offences the act of 'prejudicing private and public property, vital resources, infrastructures, means of transport and communication, IT systems or public services when they are part of an individual or collective enterprise aiming at intentionally spreading terror among the population or forcing the government or an international organisation to accomplish an act or abstain from so doing.' HRW considered that this definition could allow the repression of certain acts that were not of a terrorist nature as defined by international law. The legislation extended the limit on pre-charge detention in terrorism cases from 6 days under the 2003 law to 15 days, during which time the suspect remained incommunicado and had no access to a lawyer or family members. The Tunisian government had

KEY INDICATORS — Tunisia

	Unit	2011	2012	2013	2014	**2015
Population	m	*10.65	*10.78	*10.89	*11.00	*11.11
Gross domestic product (GDP)	US$bn	45.86	45.42	46.99	48.55	*45.28
GDP per capita	US$	4,351	4,215	4,317	*4,415	*4,075
GDP real growth	%	-1.2	3.6	2.3	*2.3	*3.0
Inflation	%	3.5	5.6	5.8	4.9	*5.0
Unemployment	%	13.0	17.6	15.3	*15.3	*15.0
Oil output	'000 bpd	78.0	–	62.0	53.0	–
Exports (fob) (goods)	US$m	17,876.3	17,071.1	17,145.6	16,841.3	–
Oil	US$m	–	2,832.0	–	–	–
Imports (fob) (goods)	US$m	22,623.0	23,101.9	22,981.1	23,402.8	–
Balance of trade	US$m	-4,746.7	-6,030.8	-5,835.5	-6,561.5	–
Current account	US$m	-3,385.7	-3,705.0	-3,904.0	-4,332.0	*-2,917.0
Total reserves minus gold	US$m	9,055.9	8,357.2	7,287.4	7,235.1	–
Foreign exchange	US$m	8,583.5	7,899.1	6,832.1	–	–
Exchange rate	per US$	1.39	1.57	1.65	1.87	–

recognised that the police response to the Sousse massacre had been both slow and inadequate. A number of senior policemen and civil servants had lost their jobs as a result, including the governor of Sousse.

Elections again

In February 2015 Tunisia's parliament had approved a unity coalition government led by the secular Nidaa Tounes party (rumoured to have maintained links with the deposed President) and including its Islamist rivals. The cabinet headed by the veteran politician and Prime Minister, the 88 year old Habib Essid, included members of the Nidaa Tounes party and the former majority Ennahda party, had won approval with votes from 166 members of the 217-seat parliament in the October 2014 parliamentary elections. The initial results had indicated a surprise gain for the business tycoon Slim Rahi, whose Union Patriotique Libre (UPL) (Free Patriotic Union Party) which won 16 seats, an increase of 14.The principal loser in the elections was the Ennahda Perty, which in the 2011 elections had captured a large popular vote, but had subsequently faced increased insecurity and a failing economy.

Truth and Dignity Commission

Alone among Arab States and based on South Africa's Truth and Reconciliation Commission, Tunisia's first equivalent body was set up shortly after the overthrow of the Ben Ali regime in 2011. While most high profile Arab Spring states subsequently fell back into war or dictatorship, Tunisia had at least made visible efforts to address the question of accountability. These efforts eventually came together with the establishment of the Instance Vérité et Dignité (IVD) (Truth and Dignity Commission) which began work in December 2014, the first resourced and constitutional attempt at a 'truth and reconciliation'-style process. Ironically, the new Commission's arrival on the political scene coincided with the marked increase in insurgent violence.

Sadly, one of the first instances of the new commission's problems came with its efforts to collect the Presidential Archive, a necessary and presumably incriminating, collection of documents listing the goings on during six decades of corruption and oppression. On arriving at the Presidential palace, however, the Commission's convoy, with a military escort, was confronted by a line of armed police. Sihem Bensedrine, the President of the IVD who had chosen to accompany the convoy showed the commanding police officer her signed presidential authority, but the police refused to move. The state may have been on her side, but only partially. There still existed another part of the state that manifestly did not want the archive to be made public. A state of affairs that did not bode well for the Commission's future effectiveness.

The economy

Lower oil prices and their initially positive effect on government fiscal balances, external current accounts and economic growth have required governments to recalibrate their finances. The lower oil prices would be credit positive for the Middle East and North Africa's region's five oil-importing and sub-investment-grade nations, especially Tunisia. Following a September 2015 visit to Tunisia, Christine Lagarde, the Managing Director of the International Monetary Fund (IMF) congratulated the Tunisian authorities for the country's successful and peaceful political transition to democracy. Mrs Lagarde also commended them for the resilience of the Tunisian economy, despite a difficult international economic environment, the knock-on effects of regional conflicts and the challenging domestic situation with its grave security concerns. However, Mrs Lagarde noted that the growth of Tunisia's economy – which had slowed down in 2015 – was insufficient to reduce unemployment and improve Tunisians' standard of living.

Mrs Lagarde went on to say that she was more convinced than ever that Tunisia needed to move forcefully ahead with the next phase of its economic and social transition to broad-based, sustainable growth. A sound banking system, a more efficient government and civil service, a fair and efficient tax system, investment-oriented public spending, a business environment more conducive to investor risk taking and a modern social safety net will all be needed and were key to maintaining growth and creating jobs.

Earlier in the year (in August 2015) the IMF had summarised its annual assessment of the Tunisian economy by noting that after reaching 2.4 per cent gross domestic product (GDP) growth in 2014, the momentum had diminished. Growth was projected by the IMF to slow to one per cent for 2015 as the repercussions of the Bardo and Sousse attacks and persistent social tensions – work stoppages and strikes – undermined the benefits derived from the post-transition confidence boost, lower global oil prices and the euro-zone recovery. External imbalances were expected to remain high, with the current account deficit improving marginally to 8.5 per cent of GDP in 2015 while foreign exchange reserves remained at an appropriate level of four months import coverage, which was necessary to strengthen external buffers and reduce vulnerabilities. Inflationary pressures were expected to remain contained, helped by lower energy and food prices and a prudent monetary policy.

The IMF welcomed the modest loosening of the fiscal stance in 2015 to accommodate the short-term economic fallout of the recent economic slowdown, including through increased security expenditures and transfers to small and medium sized enterprises (SMEs). The mission noted the growing public sector wage bill and called for the need to contain it to make room for priority and productive capital spending, which had reached record lows.

'The recent reduction in energy subsidies, resulting from the decline in global oil prices, is a welcome development. An automatic fuel price formula should be designed urgently to allow for a much needed decline in domestic retail fuel prices, which are currently above international levels for some products. It will also be important for the government to move quickly in adopting the tax reform, whose design followed a long process of consensus building during the national tax consultations and aims at promoting greater transparency, efficiency and equity.

It was hoped that Tunisia's prudent monetary stance would continue containing inflationary pressures while greater exchange rate flexibility – including through continuing to limit foreign exchange interventions to smooth large fluctuations – would contribute to reducing external imbalances and strengthening reserve buffers. In the view of the IMF, the implementation of the Tunisian authorities' broad reform agenda was progressing. However, with unemployment at 15.2 per cent, there was an urgent need to push ahead with structural reforms to boost job creation and help meet the aspirations of the Tunisian population for a more inclusive society.

The IMF considered the reform of the banking sector to be of particular significance. Steps taken to strengthen public banks, such as the initiation of the recapitalisation of public banks and changes in their governance framework, were important. The adoption of a new banking law and further strengthening of the supervisory and regulatory framework would be needed to construct a modern banking sector and facilitate financial sector intermediation.

The IMF concluded its summary by noting that 'Creating a level playing field for investors would require adopting and implementing key legislation, such as bankruptcy and competition laws. Advances in strengthening the social safety net by better identifying and targeting the vulnerable population were also welcome.'

People to watch

Slim Riahi, leader of the Union Patriotique Libre (UPL) (Free Patriotic Union Party)

Risk assessment

Economy	Fair/poor
Politics	Fair
Regional stability	Fair

Muslims in Tunisia

% of population	99.8
Sunni (% of Muslims)	90
Shi'a (% of Muslims)	1

COUNTRY PROFILE

670 The Arabs conquered Carthage.
1207–1574 After the Arab Empire collapsed, Tunisia became part of the Moroccan empire of the Almohads before emerging as the independent Hafsid empire.
1600s The Hafsids were defeated by the Ottomans, who developed a system of rule by a local elite descended from the Turks, the Huseinid beys.
1700s Tunisia became a national monarchy.
1881 France invaded Tunisia from Algeria.
1883 Tunisia was declared a French protectorate.
1930s The Néo-Destour nationalist movement developed under Habib Bourguiba, who was jailed by the French.
1942–43 During the Second World War, German and Italian troops, who came to Tunisia to resist allied forces in Algeria, were driven out by the Allies in 1943.
1956 Tunisia gained independence from France under the leadership of Bourguiba.
1957 The monarchy was abolished and the Republic of Tunisia declared.
1961–63 The Tunisian government demanded the withdrawal of French troops from the strategic port of Bizerte; fighting broke out between French and Tunisian forces. French forces left Bizerte following an agreement between the French and Tunisian governments in 1963.
1974 A constitutional amendment named Bourguiba 'President for Life'.
1981 The first multi-party parliamentary elections since independence were won by President Bourguiba's party in a landslide victory.
1982–85 The headquarters of the Palestinian Liberation Organisation (PLO) relocated from Beirut to Tunis, where it stayed until it moved to the Palestinian autonomous areas (Gaza and Jericho) in 1994. In 1985, Israel raided the headquarters in revenge for a PLO attack on a yacht in Larnaca, Cyprus.
1987 In line with the constitution, Prime Minister Zine al Abidine Ben Ali succeeded President Bourguiba, who was declared by his physicians mentally unfit to rule, due to senility.
1989 President Ben Ali won the presidential election; he was re-elected in 1994; both elections were uncontested.
1999 Ben Ali was re-elected for a third term in the first multi-party presidential elections. Mohamed Ghannouchi was appointed prime minister.
2000 Violence erupted in several towns and cities over increasing levels of poverty and price rises in certain basic commodities.
2002 An al Qaeda terrorist bomb killed 19 people in a synagogue in Djerba. A referendum agreed to abolish the three-term limit for incumbent presidents and to raise the age limit of an incumbent president from 70 to 75.
2004 Incumbent Zine al Abidine Ben Ali won 94.5 per cent of the presidential vote, Mohamed Bouchiha won 3.8 per cent. The ruling, Rassemblement Constitutionnel Démocratique (RCD) (Democratic Constitutional Rally), was re-elected with 91.6 per cent of the popular vote.
2005 A second parliamentary legislative body, the Chamber of Advisors, was inaugurated with 112 members, drawn from professional bodies, local officials and presidential appointees.
2006 A ban on the wearing in public places of the *hijab* (by women) was introduced. The opposition Mouvement des Démocrates Socialistes (MDS) (Movement of Democratic Socialists), elected May Eljeribi as the first female political leader in Tunisia.
2007 The law banning the wearing of the *hijab* was lifted following a ruling by the Administrative Court of Tunis which deemed it unconstitutional.
2009 President Zine al Abidine Ben Ali (RCD) was re-elected to a fifth consecutive five-year term in office. Two prominent opposition candidates boycotted the elections. In parliamentary elections, the ruling RCD won 84.6 per cent of the vote (161 seats out of 214).
2010 The annual cereal harvest was halved following a drought during the time of sowing; around two million tonnes were imported to make up the shortfall. The UN announced that Tunisia was among one of the few African states to have achieved their Millennium Development Goals. On 17 December, a street vendor, Mohamed Bouazizi immolated himself in the town of Sidi Bouzid (central Tunisia), in protest at having his fruit and scales confiscated by municipal inspectors. The next day, his family berated the town's governor by throwing coins over at the office gate, crying 'here is your bribe' and were joined by other protesters complaining about corruption, nepotism and officials taking bribes. As crowds grew, police reacted by beating protesters and firing tear gas. Extra police were drafted into Sidi Bouzid and two more protestors killed themselves. Demonstrations of solidarity with Sidi Bouzid began in Tunis. Independent trade union activists called on people to demonstrate and about 1,000 people demanded work and an end to corruption and, for the first time, the resignation of President Ben Ali. The president visited Mohamed Bouazizi in hospital. Security forces stopped the demonstration in Tunis as other demonstrations began in provincial cities of Sousse, Sfax and Meknassy. Lawyers staged protests and were violently assaulted by security forces, causing various degrees of injury.
2011 Mohamed Bouazizi died on 4 January. Steep rises in food prices and widespread unemployment underlined the angry protests as riots broke out, which were quelled by security forces, at the cost of 21 deaths. Military personnel were deployed in a number of towns nationwide. The interior minister was sacked. A night-time curfew was launched in Tunis, but was largely ignored as the general population joined protestors, concerned by the weak economy and political frustration with the rule of President Ben Ali. In a speech in January the president announced that he would not stand for election again in 2014. While the country was under a state of emergency, President Ben Ali was forced to resign and went into exile in Saudi Arabia. Prime Minister Mohammed Ghannouchi appointed himself acting president, under Article 56 of the constitution. However, the Constitutional Court declared that Ben Ali had permanently vacated the presidency and Fouad Mebazaa was appointed interim president, under Article 57 of the constitution. Ghannouchi tried to form a government of unity that included members of the opposition. International arrest warrants were issued for Ben Ali and his family, accusing them of illegally acquiring property

and other assets and removing state funds aboard. In February, the revised figure of numbers killed during the overthrow of former president Ben Ali was at least 219. The Mebazaa administration decided to suspend and close the offices of the RCD, before a final decision was taken on the future of the party. The lower house of the senate passed legislation to allow President Mebazaa to rule by decree, thereby side-stepping parliament which was still dominated by Ben Ali supporters. A court dissolved the former ruling RCD and thus prevented the party from putting forward any candidates for future elections. Mohammed Ghannouchi resigned as prime minister in February and Béji Caïd Essebsi was appointed in his place. The moderate Islamist political party Ennahda was legalised in March, allowing it to contest presidential and parliamentary elections. President Mebazaa announced that an interim government would stay in power until a new constitution could be written. Elections for members for a council of representatives to rewrite the constitution were scheduled for July. In March round 19,000 Tunisians had fled to the Italian island of Lampedusa, overwhelming local resources and immigration procedures, and prompting Italy to call on the EU for increased funds to deal with the influx. Accusations against ex-president Ben Ali, his family and close associates had, in April, grown to include charges of involuntary manslaughter and drug-trafficking. In June the interim government announced a three month delay to elections originally planned for July. The elections were rescheduled for 23 October. Ben Ali was tried *in abstentia* in June, on charges of possessing illegal drugs and weapons and sentenced to 15 years imprisonment; abroad, he denied all charges of embezzlement and misuse of state funds, nonetheless he was found guilty and he and his wife were sentenced to 35 years imprisonment and fined US$66 million between them. Later, the ex-president, his daughter and son-in-law were also found guilty *in abstentia* of corrupt property dealing and sentenced to 16 years in goal and jointly fined US$100 million. The election for the 217-seat Tunisian Constituent Assembly (TCA) (of which 18 members represent expatriate Tunisians in North America and Europe) was held in October. The TCA has a mandate to draft a new constitution. In November, the winning, moderate, centre-right, Hizb Ennahda (Nahda) (Renaissance Party) formed a coalition with the Congrès pour la République (CPR) (Congress of the Republic) and the Forum Démocratique pour le Travail et les Libertés (Ettakatol) (Democratic Forum for Labour and Liberties). Hamadi Jebali (Nahda) was appointed as prime minister, Moncef Marzouki (CPR) as president and Mustafa Ben Jaafar (Ettakatol) as speaker of the TCA. Interim Prime Minister Béji Caid Essebsi resigned in November. The constituent assembly endorsed Marzouki as president on 14 December with 153 votes (out of 217) in favour. The TCA is a sovereign entity and may set its own timetable for drafting the constitution. It also has the power to either appoint a new government or endorse the current administration until a general election is held.

2012 On 27 March, senior members of Nahda said they would not support moves by the Salafis (ultra-conservative Muslims) to enshrine *Sharia* (Islamic law) into the new constitution, although Nahda itself supported the rule that proclaimed Tunisia as an Islamic state. A series of clashes with the Salafis began on 28 May, when hundreds attacked bars and shops in Jendouba and were stopped by security personnel. The Salafis rioted again in June, August and October. However in August thousands gathered in Tunis to protest at moves by the Islamist-led TCA with plans to reduce women's rights, when details of the draft constitution were made known. On 10 October parliament was told that the draft constitution was almost ready for consideration, but by mid-December no news of its publication was available.

2013 Prominent secular figure, Chokri Belaid, was assassinated on 6 February. His death sparked mass protests and forced Prime Minister Hamadi Jebali to resign on 19 February. Mr Jebali had attempted to form a non-partisan government, but his Ennahda party rejected it. Ali Larayedh became prime minister on 14 March. The opposition MP for Sidi Bouzid, birthplace of Arab Spring, Mohamed Brahmi, was murdered on 24 July, plunging Tunisia into political crisis. There were reports that the same gun was used to kill both Belaid and Brahmi. Opposition legislators called for the Islamist-led government to be replaced by a national unity administration. Several dozen withdrew from the national assembly. On 1 August the minister of education, Salem Labyedh, a secular politician, resigned following the assassination of Mr Brahmi. His decision came amid growing pressure from opposition groups on the Islamist-led government to step down. There were large demonstrations in Tunis on 7 August, held to demand the resignation of the Islamist-led government. The powerful Tunisian General Labour Union (UGTT) had called on its 600,000 members to join the demonstrations. A meeting of political parties and civil society organisations (Workers' Party, Nidaa Tounes, the Ettakatol reforming movement, El Kotb, the Socialist Party, the Farmers' Voice, the Arab Democratic Vanguard Party, The Tunisian Anti-Torture Organisation and the Union of Unemployed Graduates) held on 26 July announced the formation of a National Salvation Front (NSF). The NSF has set itself the task of forming a national higher authority for national salvation. On 25 August thousands of Tunisians rallied outside the National Assembly after the NSF called for protests and the resignation of the Islamic-led government. The Salafist Ansar al-Sharia movement was designated as a 'terrorist group' on 27 August. The government accused the hardline group of being behind the killing of two politicians. Talks between the government and its opponents to negotiate a caretaker government were agreed on 28 September, to start in the week beginning 30 October. The Ennahda government agreed to resign and hand power to an independent transition leadership, and set a date for elections. The UGTT labour union will mediate the talks. On 5 October the deal was signed in Tunis between Ennahda and the opposition; a caretaker cabinet of technocratic, independent figures will be in power until fresh elections can be held. A new prime minister, Mehdi Jomaa, was named on 14 December after members of the opposition and Ennahda came to an agreement on 12 December to end their differences. Mr Jomaa will head a caretaker government until elections to be held in 2014. Also under the agreement Ennahda will hand over power to the caretake government. on 14 December Mehdi Jomaa became prime minister designate and was instructed to form a cabinet.

2014 Ali Laarayedh resigned as prime minister on 9 January. The constitution was approved by the National Constituent Assembly on 26 January by 200 out of 216. Mehdi Jomaa became prime minister on 29 January. Mr Jomaa also announced that he had formed a new caretaker government, mainly consisting of independents and technocrats. It will stay in place until general elections take place later in the year. General elections were held on 4 October and were won by Nidaa Tounes (generally translated as Call for Tunisia) with 37.56 per cent (86 seats, out of 117), followed by Ennahda with 27.79 per cent (69 seats). Although Beji Caid el Sebsi, leader of Nidaa Tounes has the right name a prime minister he said that he would await the presidential election (to be held on 23 November and in which he is a candidate) before deciding on a coalition government.

2015 Gunmen attacked the Bardo Museum in Tunis on 18 March, killing 22 people, mostly foreign tourists. Islamic State (IS) claimed they had committed the attack. The museum reopened on 24 March. On 26 June a lone gunman attached the resort of Sousse, killing 38, mostly British, holiday makers. Islamic State said they were responsible for this attack too. The Tunisian government arrested a number of suspects and declared a state of emergency on 4 July. Tourism is an important sector of the economy and the attack is expected to have an adverse affect on the industry. The Tunisian National Dialogue Quartet won the 2015 Nobel peace prize. The group is formed of four Tunisian organisations from areas such as human rights, public welfare and principles of law and was selected 'for its decisive contribution to the building of a pluralistic democracy in Tunisia in the wake of the Jasmine Revolution of 2011'.

Political structure

Constitution

The constitution was introduced in 1959. Parties must be officially recognised before they can contest elections. Legal opposition parties are guaranteed a minimum of 34 seats in the lower chamber of parliament.

Constitutional amendments in 2002, included unlimited terms of office for the president and a age limit of 75 years and gave the president control over voting procedures and immunity from prosecution for life.

A new second legislative chamber was also agreed.

The Tunisian Constitution of 2014 was adopted on January 26 2014 by the Constituent Assembly. It is the result of a compromise between the Islamist party (Ennahda) and the opposition forces. It devotes a dual executive, gives preference to Islam and, for the first time in legal history of the Arab world, introduced a target parity between men and women in elected bodies.

Independence date

20 March 1956

Form of state

Republic

The executive

Prior to the Jasmine Revolution in 2011, executive power was held by the president, who was also Head of State, elected by universal suffrage for a five-year term. After the October 2011 elections, the Tunisian Constituent Assembly (TCA) was charged with formulating a new constitution.

The president is directly elected by absolute majority popular vote in 2 rounds if needed for a five-year term (eligible for a second term).

The prime minister is selected by the majority party or majority coalition and appointed by the president.

National legislature

The Tunisian Constituent Assembly (TCA) was elected with 217 members (of which 18 members represent expatriate Tunisians in North America and Europe) in October 2011, with a mandate to draft a new constitution. Although the TCA has 12 months to draft a new constitution it also has sovereignty and may set its own timetable. It has the power to appoint a new government or endorse the current administration until a general election is held.

Under the new (2014) constitution seats are elected by party-list proportional representation, using the largest remainder method.

Legal system

The legal system is based on the French civil law system and Islamic law. There is some judicial review of legislative acts in the Supreme Court.

Last elections

26 October 2014 (parliamentary), 23 November and 21 December 2014 (presidential)

Results: Parliamentary: Nidaa Tounes 37.56 per cent (86 seats, out of 217); Ennahda Movement 27.79 per cent (69); Free Patriotic Union 4.13 per cent (16); Popular Front 3.64 per cent (15); Afek Tounes 3.02 per cent (8); Congress for the Republic 2.05 per cent (4); Democratic Current 1.95 per cent (3); People's Movement 1.34 per cent (2); National Destourian Initiative 1.34 per cent (3); Current of Love 1.20 per cent (2); five other small parties won one seat each and there were five independents.

Presidential (first round): Beji Caid Essebsi (Nidaa Tounes) won 39.5 per cent of the vote, Moncef Marzouki (Congress for the Republic) won 33.4 per cent, Hamma Hammami (Popular Front) won 7.8 per cent, Hechmi Hamdi (Current of Love) won 5.8 per cent and Slim Riahi (Free Patriotic Union) won 5.6 per cent; the remaining 22 candidates failed to win more than 1.5 per cent of the vote. Turnout was 64.6 per cent.

Runoff: Behi Caid Essebi won a majority of 55.7 per cent while Moncef Marzouki won 44.3 per cent of the vote. Turnout was 61.5 per cent.

Next elections

2019 (parliamentary and presidential)

Political parties

Ruling party

Coalition led by Nidaa Tounes consisting of Union Patriotique Libre (UPL) (Free Patriotic Union), Afek Tounes (Tunisian Aspiration), Harkat en-Nahda (Ennahda Movement) and independent politicians.

Main opposition party

Front Populaire pour la Réalisation des Objectifs de la Révolution (Popular Front for the Realization of the Objectives of the Revolution).

Approximately 8 per cent of the population live below the national poverty line.

Population

11.00 million (2014)*

Last census: September 2004: 9,932,400

Population density: 60 inhabitants per square km. Urban population 67 per cent (2010 Unicef).

Annual growth rate: 1.2 per cent, 1990–2010 (Unicef).

Ethnic make-up

Arab-Berber (98 per cent), European (1 per cent), other (1 per cent).

Religions

Islam is the state religion – observance is strong (98 per cent); Christianity (1 per cent); Jewish (1 per cent) – there has been a Jewish population on the southern island of Djerba for 2,000 years and there remains a small Jewish population in Tunis which is descended from those who fled Spain in the late fifteenth century.

Education

Education is free up to university level – the government typically spends as much as 20 per cent of its revenues on an extensive education system. Primary education begins aged six, and lasts for six years. Secondary education begins at 12 and lasts seven years. Registration at primary schools is 95 per cent (100 per cent of boys and 89 per cent of girls) – the highest in north Africa and the Middle East. A compulsory schooling period of nine years has been introduced, although some children still leave school at the age of 12, especially in rural areas. A stronger emphasis has been placed on scientific and technical subjects at secondary level.

Literacy rate: 73 per cent adult rate; 94 per cent youth rate (15–24) (Unesco 2005).

Compulsory years: Six to 16.

Pupils per teacher: 24 in primary schools.

Health

State healthcare is provided free of charge to the families of employees paying social security contributions and at least nominal tax. This covers an estimated 70 per cent of the population. Free state healthcare is also available for those with any kind of disability. The discrepancy between urban and rural access to healthcare diminished during the 1990s, with most rural areas having at least basic health clinics.

There is a well-developed private healthcare sector, with private clinics in towns providing substantially better facilities than state hospitals. Many healthcare professionals have carried out at least part of their training abroad, mostly in France.

HIV/Aids

HIV prevalence: 0.1 per cent aged 15–49 in 2003 (World Bank)

Life expectancy: 72 years, 2004 (WHO 2006)

Fertility rate/Maternal mortality rate: 2.0 births per woman, 2010 (Unicef)

Child (under 5 years) mortality rate (per 1,000): 16 per 1,000 live births (WHO 2012); 4 per cent of children under aged five are malnourished (World Bank).

Head of population per physician: 1.34 physicians per 1,000 people, 2004 (WHO 2006)

Welfare

The social security system provides pensions for the elderly and disabled, and welfare for orphans and the needy. A total of 945,500 employees, or 47.7 per cent of the workforce, are insured under the social security system. The scheme is financed by compulsory levies from employers and employees. There are no contributions from the state budget. The main social security institution is the Caisse Nationale de la Sécurité Sociale (CNSS) (National Social Security Organisation), which deals with about 45 per cent of outlay.

There is a graded scheme for contributions. The non-agricultural private sector pays most as a proportion of the employee's salary: 11.5 per cent paid by the employer and 6.25 per cent by the employee. In the public sector, where contributions are made to the Caisse Nationale de Retraite et de Prévoyance Sociale (CNRPS) (National Pension Fund), the employer pays 8 per cent and the employee 7 per cent. State pensions are paid to CNSS and CNRPS contributors.

Main cities

Tunis (capital, estimated population 743,724 in 2012), Ariana (329,396), Sfax (288,745), Ettadhamen (242,050), Sousse (221,388), Qabis (128,358), Kairouan (128,225), Binzart (124,791), al Muruj (99,168), Qafsah (92,804).

Languages spoken

French is the business language. The number of Tunisians speaking English is increasing.

Official language/s

Arabic

Media

The government maintains control of all media reporting by and encourages widespread self-censorship, with fines and imprisonment as ultimate sanctions.

Press

The government uses mandatory pre-screening and controls the advertising revenue to censor 'unacceptable' publications. While the constitution guarantees freedom of expression, the Press Code gives allows wide-ranging powers to ban publications.

There are several independent newspapers and magazines, including two opposition party journals.

Dailies: In Arabic, *Al Horria* (www.tunisieinfo.com/alhorria), published by the RCD political party, *Assabah* (www.assabah.com.tn) and *Essahafa* (www.essahafa.info.tn). Publications from Tunis include *Al Chourouk* (www.alchourouk.com) and *el Wahda* (www.elwahda.org.tn).

In French, *La Presse* (www.lapresse.tn), published by the RCD political party, *Le Renouveau* (www.tunisieinfo.com/LeRenouveau).

Weeklies: In French, *Réalités* (www.realites.com.tn) and *L'Observateur* and *L'Avenir*. In Arabic, *Ar Rai* and *Al Moustaqbal*. Others are *Dialogue*, *Al Tariq al Jadid* and *Al Mauqif*. In English, *Tunisia News* is published in the Maghreb, on Saturdays.

Business: *L'Economiste Maghrebin* (www.leconomiste.com.tn), is published bi-monthly.

Periodicals: There are many magazines published in Arabic, French and one in Italian.

Broadcasting

Radio: Tunisian Radio (www.radiotunis.com), with four stations covering, news, youth, culture and live transmissions. Other private, commercial stations include Radio Mosaique FM (www.mosaiquefm.net), Jawhara FM (www.jawharafm.net) and the religious station Ezzitouna Radio.

Television: La Télévision Tunisienne (http://tunisiatv.com) is the national, state-run TV with two channels, Tunis 7 and Canal 21. The other domestic channel is Hannibal TV (www.hannibaltv.com.tn), with a wide variety of programmes. Pan-Arab channels are readily received.

National news agency: Tunisian News Agency (TAP) (in Arabic, French and English)

Economy

The geography of Tunisia has an important influence on its economy. In the southern half of the country desert conditions limit production, while the fertile northern region is heavily populated, with tourism a major source of foreign exchange. The service sector dominates the economy having constituted 61.9 per cent of GDP in 2014; industry and manufacturing accounted for 29.4 per cent of GDP and agriculture 8.7 per cent. Although agriculture has fallen in its primary significance to the economy it nevertheless employs just under a quarter of the labour force.

At the end of 2014, proven oil reserves were 400 million barrels, with production of 53,000 barrels per day (bpd) (down from a high of 80,000bpd in 2010). As long-term production in oil and gas has fallen the government has attempted to diversify the economy further, into other industries and an expanded manufacturing base, with a programme to enhance productivity in preparation for global competition.

Other industries include mining, (iron ore, phosphates and salt) and manufacturing of, among others items, food processing, clothing and textiles, fabricated and finished products, parts and materials, chemicals, ceramics, glass and crystal, plastics and paper. Tunisia is self-sufficient in seafood, crops, dairy and meat, of which beef and lamb dominates, and it is a leading producer of olive oil, dates and potatoes, as well as other fruits, grains and livestock and seafood, most of which are exported.

GDP growth was 4.5 per cent in 2008, at a time of high world prices for fuel and food. The economy weakened in 2009, falling to 3.1 per cent as the global economic crisis cut trade. Growth was maintained at 3.2 per cent in 2010, at a time when global trade picked up. The Arab Spring revolution tumult began in Tunisia in 2011 and adversely affected the service sector, with visitor numbers dropping dramatically and revenue from tourism cut by 50 per cent causing negative growth of -0.5 per cent. Tourists returned in 2012 and GDP growth climbed to 4.7 per cent before falling to 2.4 per cent by 2014.

In June 2015, two gunmen associated with the Islamic State attacked a tourist resort in Sousse. Thirty-eight were killed as a result of the shootings. Flights from Britain to Tunisia were cancelled in early July and some airlines offered customers the chance to change their destinations if they had tickets to Tunisia. The inevitable decrease in tourist numbers will cause the economy to suffer greatly as a result of the terrorist attack. In August 2015, the head of Tunisia's Union of Agriculture and Fishing Abdelmajid Zar announced that demand for agricultural produce required by the country's tourist resorts had significantly fallen, leading to a 35 per cent decrease in wholesale markets

compared to the previous season. This attack was the second of the year, with 22 killed as a result of a shooting in Tunis in March 2015.
Remittances in 2010 were US$2.1 billion (4.4 per cent of GDP), which dropped to US$1.96 billion in 2011, before recovering back to US$2.2 billion in 2012. Remittances have somewhat stabilised in Tunisia to US$2.3 billion in 2014.
Tunisia is a country where 55 per cent of the population is aged under 25 and where a growing work force has led to an official unemployment rate of around 14 per cent; however with high underemployment this rate may not reflect the true nature of the jobless market. Tunisia has been a closed economy, which severely restricted foreign investment and domestic private enterprise. It was the lack of opportunity and corruption that led to the revolution that toppled the Ben Ali regime in January 2011. Tunisia has to not only address its underlying economic weaknesses and develop its future direction through reform, but also to contend with a foreign debt rating that was cut from Ba2 to Ba3 by the international credit ratings agency Moody's in November 2013.
The Islamic Development Bank (IDB) and the World Bank announced in 2010, that they were setting up a regional initiative of up to US$1 billion to help close the infrastructure gap in the Middle East and North Africa (Mena) and help boost economic growth. The World Bank considers that the Mena region requires US$75–100 billion per year to sustain the growth of recent years and boost economic competitiveness. However private sector investment is limited and the new initiative should address the shortfall in investment through Sharia-compliant and conventional investment. The initiative should benefit Egypt, Morocco, Jordan and Tunisia in particular.

External trade

In 2005 the Greater Arab Free Trade Area (Gafta) was ratified by 17 members, including Tunisia, creating an Arab economic bloc. A customs union was established whereby tariffs within Gafta will be reduced by a percentage each year, until none remain. It is also a signatory of the Euro-Mediterranean Partnership agreement, which provides for the introduction of free trade between the EU and 8 Mediterranean countries by 2014, with five more prospective partners.
Despite natural resources including oil, natural gas, phosphate (of which Tunisia is the world's largest producer) and iron, foreign earnings are dominated by agriculture and tourism.

Imports

Main imports are raw cotton, machinery and electronic equipment, vehicles and hydrocarbons.
Main sources: France (19.9 per cent of total in 2014), Italy (19.5 per cent), Germany (7.6 per cent), China (5.5 per cent), Spain (5.4 per cent) and Turkey (4.1 per cent)

Exports

Main export commodities are foodstuffs, textiles, clothing and footwear, steelwork, phosphate, iron ore, manufactured and leather goods, agricultural products, chemicals and hydrocarbons.
Main destinations: France (29.7 per cent of total in 2014), Italy (17.1 per cent), Germany (11.5 per cent) and Libya (5.4 per cent).

Agriculture

Farming

Total agricultural land is 15.5 million hectares, of which 31 per cent is pasture, 17.4 per cent arable and 14.3 per cent permanent crops. Just under a quarter of the workforce is employed in agriculture.
The government sees agriculture as a principal growth sector, however it is heavily influenced by the climate and rainfall. The principal area of cultivation is in north, along the Mediterranean coast, where ancient oil groves are still located. Major projects to augment irrigation are underway, with a new dam and reservoir supplying the northeast region with waterways being installed. In the desert in the south, oasis crops of dates are famous and exported throughout the region and Europe. In the central area rainfall directly affects crop production, as a wet year will produce a good harvest; conversely, a dry year risks desertification and very little crop production.
The agricultural investment code offers tax and other financial advantages, while the Agence de Promotion des Investissements Agricoles (APIA) (Agency for the Promotion of Agricultural Investment) channels investment into agriculture. The Banque Nationale Agricole (BNA) provides medium- and long-term credit for agricultural development projects. Since all suitable land is already being farmed, government policy centres on improving yields through new farming techniques and making the most of water resources. Rural depopulation, an inequitable land tenure system, drought, soil erosion, overgrazing and low producer prices remain the major constraints to development.
The country's 55 million olive trees occupy one-third of all arable land and olive oil, at over 70 per cent of production is the most important agricultural export. Tunisia is the world's fourth, after Italy, Spain, Greece, largest exporter. Other main products from the sector are flour, sugar, tomato paste, milk, wine and animal feed.
The recent growth in organic food has encouraged over 240 operations, which have attracted international certification accredited to the EU, producing among others, olive oil and dates.
In August 2015, the head of Tunisia's Union of Agriculture and Fishing Abdelmajid Zar announced that demand for agricultural produce required by the country's tourist resorts had significantly fallen as a result of the Sousse attack, leading to a 35 per cent decrease in wholesale markets compared to the previous season.

Fishing

Most seafood production is for domestic consumption and the sector is relatively undeveloped, with extensive small-scale fishing using more traditional methods. The coastal areas around Sfax and the Kerkennah Islands, where the sea is very shallow, are well-known locally for their fishing industry. Total seafood production is typically around 80,000 tonnes, with some 20 per cent of this exported. Catches typically include sardines, pilchards, tuna and whitefish. However, tuna fishing is diminishing as Mediterranean stocks decline.

Forestry

An arid climate, a fast-growing population and animal herds have put Tunisia's already limited woodland areas at serious risk. However efforts to reverse the trend have increased forests by 0.2 per cent or 1,000 hectares.
The oak forests of the country's north provide timber and cork.

Industry and manufacturing

The industrial sector is based primarily on processing domestic raw materials, notably phosphates and agricultural commodities. An industrial restructuring programme launched in the mid-1990s has seen US$1 billion invested by the government in upgrading businesses' competitiveness, in preparation for the liberalisation of markets and European competition. The present strategy is to target specific types of products where relatively cheap labour, proximity to Europe and government incentives can combine to give Tunisia a price and quality advantage over other exporters. The programme has been particularly successful among small- and medium-sized enterprises (SMEs).

Tourism

Tourist numbers slumped from 4.5 million in 2010 to 2.5 million in 2011 as the Tunisian revolution that sparked other uprisings, later known as the Arab Spring, frightened off many visitors. The tourism authorities have launched major

campaigns, not only to bring back previous visitors but also to diversify and target other markets, such as Turkey, Russia and China.
The tourist industry suffered from two terrorist attacks in March and June of 2015 that led to the deaths of 60 people. The second was particularly detrimental as two gunmen associated with the Islamic State attacked a tourist resort in Sousse. Thirty-eight were killed as a result of the shootings. Flights from Britain to Tunisia were cancelled into early July and some airlines offered customers the chance to change their destinations if they had tickets to Tunisia. A few days after the attack almost half of the Britons holidaying in Tunisia had returned home.
There are eight sites included on Unesco's World Heritage List, many of which belong to Tunisia's classical history and the many fine monuments from earlier civilisations. The Ichkeul Lake and wetlands (in the Ichkeul National Park) are a major stopover point for hundreds of thousands of migrating birds. There are traditional habitats of the Matmata of carved stone rooms in a mountainous region (as seen in the Hollywood blockbuster *Star Wars*) and the Bedouin encampments in the south, in the Sahara Desert. While most visitors choose to enjoy the sun and leisure in some of the latest beach resort developments.
Travel and tourism contributed 15.2 per cent of GDP in 2014; it is predicted to grow by 3.7 per cent in 2015. The industry provided employment to 13.9 per cent of the workforce (473,000 jobs) in the same period.
The infrastructure is comprehensive with ferries from Europe, a number of motorways and a rail service that runs from the capital to other major towns.

Mining
The mining sector contributes around 3 per cent of GDP and employs around 4 per cent of the working population. Tunisia is the world's fifth-largest source of phosphates although the quality of the rock mined is poor. Extraction (largely in Metlaoui and Gafsa) is geared increasingly towards local phosphate processing rather than exporting it in a raw state.
Other important minerals mined include iron ore, salt, fluorspar, barytes, lead, zinc, potash and uranium. Foreign investment is being sought by the government for the mining industry.

Hydrocarbons
Total oil reserves stood at 400 million barrels in 2014, with production at 53,000 barrels per day (bpd). Most of the country's oil deposits are located offshore in the Gulf of Gabés.
There is one refinery at Bizerte, with a small capacity of 34,000bpd. The state-owned Societe Tunisienne des Industries de Raffinage (STIR) is overseeing plans for a new 120,000bpd joint Tunisian-Libyan oil refinery, sited in the east at La Skhira.
To replace declining oil reserves, the government is promoting the natural gas sector; local production typically meets 80 per cent of domestic demand. In May 2012 the new government resumed negotiations concerning investment by Qatar Petroleum in the expansion of the existing Skhira oil refinery, in the south-east of Tunisia. The D3 billion (US$4.6 billion) project began work by the end of 2012 and when completed will produce 250,000bpd, however as of 2015 it was not operational.
Proven natural gas reserves were 65.1 billion cubic metres in 2014, with production of 2 billion cubic metres. There is a network of pipelines transporting natural gas from fields offshore and in the south-west as well as a number of planned international natural gas pipelines transiting Tunisia from Algeria and Libya, to supply natural gas to Europe via the Transmed pipeline to Italy.
Tunisia does not produce coal but imports over 100,000 tonnes per annum of coke.

Energy
Total installed generating capacity was 3.65GW in 2013. The state-owned electricity and gas company, Société Tunisienne de l'Electricité et du Gaz (STEG) no longer has a monopoly on power generation, although the company retains its monopoly on distribution.
Demand for electricity is growing by 7 per cent per annum; since 2012, 100 per cent of homes have had access to electricity. The government intends to add around 300MW of generating capacity every 2–3 years.

Financial markets
Stock exchange
Bourse de Tunis (Tunis Stock Exchange)

Banking and insurance
Tunisia aims to become the regional financial centre and is keen to build on its status as an economy with investment grade status. However, the banking sector is overcrowded, plagued by bad debts and dominated by the public sector.
The government is determined to rationalise the sector and the government has engaged in a modernisation programme, including privatisation and mergers in a process of consolidation in the sector. The capital base of many banks has improved with the injection of government funds into state-owned banks and the restructuring of non-performing loans.
By June 2010, the Kuwaiti-owned Burgan Bank had completed the purchase of Tunis International Bank from the United Gulf Bank as part of its regional expansion strategy. The US$725 million purchase will allow the Burgan Bank access to other North African markets, to offer specifically investment banking and asset management.

Central bank
Banque Centrale de Tunisie

Main financial centre
Tunis

Time
GMT plus one hour

Geography
Tunisia is in North Africa, between Algeria to its west and Libya to its south-east. The north and eastern borders are a long, 1,148km Mediterranean coastline. It has two islands off its eastern coast, the larger of which, Ile de Jerba, is connected to the mainland by a 6km causeway, and is the location of Tunisia largest international airport. The other is the island chain of the Iles des Kerkennah.
The mainland has three distinct regions from the fertile north where most of the agricultural crops are grown, and where the Atlas mountains run down to the sea. The middle section is semi-arid desert that is wholly dependent on rainfall for its agricultural produce; the Sahara Desert occupies the southern region, and is largely unproductive. There are no major rivers, irrigation is supplied through rainwater dams and bore-holes.

Hemisphere
Northern

Climate
The northern coastal area has a Mediterranean climate with warm, rainy winters (December–March) and hot summers. The southern and inland area is hot and arid. Temperatures in Tunis range from 6–14 degrees Celsius (C) in January to 21–33 degrees C in August. The wettest month is January and the driest is July.

Dress codes
Formal attire should be worn for business meetings. Women should wear clothes that cover most of the body, including shoulders and legs. In the countryside, western dress and customs are rare and dress should be modest.

Entry requirements
Passports
Required by all, and must be valid for at least six months beyond date of visit.

Visa
Required by all; some exceptions, for visits up to three months, include citizens of US, EU, certain Arab, and many Commonwealth countries. A full list of exceptions

can be found at www.tunisia.or.jp/ (see under visas). Business travellers from these countries may visit as a tourist without further reference. Those visitors, both business and tourist, not included on the list should contact the nearest Tunisian consulate for information and visa application form at least three weeks before departure.

Currency advice/regulations

Local currency may not be imported or exported; there are no restrictions on the import of foreign currency. However, the re-export of foreign cash is limited to the amount imported, and the re-conversion of dinars into foreign exchange may not exceed 30 per cent of any foreign currency converted during the visit, or D100, whichever is the greater. Therefore all currency forms should be retained.

Traveller's cheques are widely accepted, and preferably made up of sterling, euros or US dollars.

Customs

Personal items are duty-free and gifts to the value of D100 are allowed.

Antiques require an exit permit.

Prohibited imports

Firearms (except for hunting), explosives, narcotics, immoral or obscene publications, walkie-talkies and material deemed subversive.

Health (for visitors)

Mandatory precautions

Yellow fever vaccination certificate required if arriving from an infected area.

Advisable precautions

Immunisation is recommended against diphtheria, hepatitis, polio, tetanus and typhoid. Rabies is present. Water precautions should be taken outside main towns: boil tap water or drink mineral water and wash fresh foods carefully.

Hotels

Classified into five categories; a government hotel tax is added to the bill. Hotel and restaurant staff expect 10 per cent tip.

Credit cards

Major credit and charge cards are widely accepted. ATMs are common in town centres.

Public holidays (national)

Fixed dates

1 Jan (New Year's Day), 20 Mar (Independence Day), 21 Mar (Youth Day), 9 Apr (Martyrs' Day), 1 May (Labour Day), 25 Jul (Republic Day), 13 Aug (Women's Day), 7 Nov (New Era Day/Accession of President Ben Ali).

Many businesses close during July/August.

Variable dates

Eid al Adha (*Tabaski*, two days), Islamic New Year, Birth of the Prophet, Eid al Fitr (*Korité*, two days).

Islamic year 1437 (15 Oct 2015–2 Oct 2016):: The Islamic year contains 354 or 355 days, with the result that Muslim feasts advance by 10–12 days against the Gregorian calendar. Dates of feasts vary according to the sighting of the new moon, so canno be forecast exactly.

Working hours

The weekly day of rest is Sunday, not Friday as is usual in the Muslim world. Tunis is virtually closed down during August.

Banking

Mon–Fri (summer): 0730–1130;
Mon–Thu (winter): 0800–1100 and 1400–1615, Fri (winter): 0800–1100 and 1300–1600.

Business

Mon–Sat (summer): 0830–1300; Mon–Fri (winter): 0830–1300, 1500–1745.

Government

Mon–Sat (summer): 0830–1300; Mon–Fri (winter): 0830–1300, 1500–1745. Government offices' opening hours may vary by half an hour.

Shops

Mon–Sat (summer): 0800–1200 and 1600–1900; Mon–Sat (winter): 0900–1300 and 1500–1900.

Telecommunications

Mobile/cell phones

There are 900 GSM services available, with coverage throughout the inhabited part of the country.

Electricity supply

220V AC, with round two-pin plugs.

Social customs/useful tips

The legacy of French rule is considerable in the towns and a rather formal attitude to courtesy prevails. Senior government or company officials should be addressed as *Monsieur* and government ministers as *Monsieur le Ministre*. It is customary to shake hands on meeting and taking leave. Business cards are exchanged after introduction.

Personal relationships are important in business, and time is usually spent in light conversation, over tea or coffee, before embarking on business matters. Regular visits and personal contact are vital in order to establish a relationship of confidence with agents and customers in Tunisia.

Hospitality is important. It is appropriate to present a small gift in appreciation of hospitality.

Islam affects society at every level. A statute passed in the first year of independence enforced equality of the sexes. Nevertheless, gatherings of men and women are usually separate, the sexes are separated in mosques, and only men may enter a cemetery to attend a funeral.

Alcohol is freely available in towns, although less common in rural areas. Strict Muslims will not drink alcohol, but many Tunisian men do, and it is acceptable for non-Muslim visitors to do so. The minimum drinking age is 21 years.

Mint tea or fresh lemon or orange juice are typical non-alcoholic drinks. It is polite to accept a drink when offered.

During Ramadan visitors are advised not to eat, drink or smoke in public during daylight hours.

Getting there

Air

National airline: Tunisair.

International airport/s: The two largest are Tunis-Carthage (TUN), 8km from the city, with flights by national airlines; travel time to the city is 15–30 minutes and Monastir (MIR) 9km from the city, accepting charter flights. Facilities in both include duty-free shopping, bank, restaurant and car hire.

Smaller airports for regional flights include Djerba-Zarzis (DJE), 9km from Houmek Souk; Sfax-el Maou (SFA), 7km west of city; Tozeur-Nefta (TOE), 10km from city; Tabarka (TBJ), 8km from city. All have duty-free shops and bus and taxi services.

Construction of a new international airport in Enfidha, 75km from Tunis, began in March 2005.

Airport tax: None

Surface

Road: Access is possible by road from Algeria and Libya.

Rail: Access by rail from Algeria.

Water: Passenger traffic comes mostly to Tunis-La Goulette. Regular passenger ferry services operate between Tunis and France, Italy and Malta.

Main port/s: Tunis-La Goulette, Sfax, Bizerte, Gabes, Sousse and Zarzis; of which Tunis-Goulette and Sfax are the largest.

Getting about

National transport

Air: Tuninter operates regular domestic services linking Tunis with Djerba, Monastir, Tozeur and Sfax. The air taxi company, Tunisavia, operates executive flights, from Tunis, throughout the country.

Road: The road network extends for around 19,000km, of which main national roads account for 10,800km. About 57 per cent of the network is paved. There is a 143km motorway between Tunis and Sousse.

Buses: Extensive long-distance services connect all major towns and cities.

Taxis: Long distance taxis (*louages*) operate between all main towns; these are considered the fastest method of road transport.

Rail: A 2,200km network links the main towns. There are two classes, some with air-conditioned, first-class accommodation. It is recommended purchasing a ticket in advance; those purchased onboard may be charged at a much higher price. It is an advantage to book in advance especially for air-conditioned trains.

Water: There are regular ferries from Sfax-Iles Kerkenna and Djerba island.

City transport

In 2004 work started on a major new bridge linking the Rades and La Goulette suburbs of Tunis, which is scheduled to be finished in 2007. Its capacity, estimated at 3,000 vehicles a day, will greatly increase traffic between northern and southern suburbs of the capital city.

Taxis: Taxis are available in all main towns and are fairly easy to obtain. *Louage* taxis have fares shared by several passengers. Taxis are metered, a surcharge is added at night.

Buses, trams & metro: The Société Nationale de Transports operates local buses with extensive services operating in all main towns.

The SMLT light-rail metro that runs four lines through Tunis has a focal point for all at Place de la République and connects to national and suburban lines.

Car hire

Cars are easy to hire at airports and hotels but are expensive and the condition of the cars vary. Roads are being improved but local driving is erratic. International driving permit required if national driving licence doesn't include a photograph. Traffic drives on the right; speed limits are 110kph on major highways and 50kph in towns. Permission must be obtained to drive in Saharan areas.

BUSINESS DIRECTORY

The addresses listed below are a selection only. While World of Information makes every endeavour to check these addresses, we cannot guarantee that changes have not been made, especially to telephone numbers and area codes. We would welcome any corrections.

Telephone area codes

The international direct dialling (IDD) code for Tunisia is +216 followed by subscriber's number.

Chambers of Commerce

American-Tunisian Chamber of Commerce and Industry, 10 Avenue Mosbah Jarbou, Rue 7116, El Manar 3, 2092 Tunis (tel: 7188-9780; fax: 7188-9880; e-mail: tacc@tacc.org.tn).

British-Tunisian Chamber of Commerce and Industry, 23 Rue de Jérusalem, 1002 Tunis (tel: 7180-2284; fax: 7180-1535; e-mail: tbcci@gnet.tn).

Cap Bon Chambre de Commerce et d'Industrie, 3 Rue de Fel, Cité Néapolis, PO Box 113, 8000 Nabeul (tel: 7228-7260; fax: 7228-7417; e-mail: cci.capbon@planet.tn).

Central Chambre de Commerce et d'Industrie, Rue Chédly Khaznadar, 4000 Sousse (7322-5044; fax: 7322-4227; e-mail: ccis.sousse@planet.tn).

French-Tunisian Chambre de Commerce et d'Industrie, 39 Rue 8301, 1002 Tunis (tel: 7184-4310; fax: 7184-5962; e-mail: ctfci@planet.tn).

North-Eastern Chambre de Commerce et d'Industrie, 46 Rue Ibn Khaldoun, 7000 Bizerte (tel: 7243-1044; fax: 7243-2379; e-mail: ccine.biz@gnet.tn).

North-Western Chambre de Commerce et d'Industrie, Hedi Chaker Street, 9000 Beja (tel: 7845-6261; fax: 7845-5789; e-mail: ccino.beja@gnet.tn).

Sfar Chambre de Commerce et d'Industrie, 10 Rue Tahar Sfar, PO Box794, 3018 Sfax (tel: 7429-6120; fax: 7429-6121; e-mail:ccis@planet.tn).

South-Eastern Chambre de Commerce et d'Industrie, 202 Avenue Farhat Hached, 6000 Gabes (tel: 7527-4900; fax: 7527-4688; e-mail: csise@gnet.tn).

South-Western Chambre de Commerce et d'Industrie, Rue des Roses, PO Box 46, 2100 Gafsa (tel: 7622-6650; fax: 7622-4150; e-mail: cciso@planet.tn).

Tunis Chambre de Commerce, 1 Rue des Entrepreneurs, 1000 Tunis (tel: 7135-0300; fax:7135-4744; e-mail: ccitunis@planet.tn).

Banking

Alubaf International Bank – Tunis, PO Box 51, Rue 8007 Montplaisir, 1002 Tunis (tel: 7178-3500 fax: 7179-3905, 7178-4343).

Amen Bank, Avenue Mohamed V, 1002 Tunis (tel: 7134-0511; fax: 7134-9909).

Banque Arabe Tuniso–Libyenne de Développment et de Commerce Extérieur, PO Box 102, 25 Avenue Kheireddine Pacha, 1002 Tunis (tel: 7178-1500; fax: 7178-2818).

Banque du Sud, 95 Avenue de la Liberté, 1002 Tunis (tel: 7184-9400, 7179-2400; fax: 7178-2663).

Banque Internationale Arabe de Tunisie SA, PO Box 520, 70-72 Avenue Habib Bourguiba, 1080 Tunis Cedex (tel: 7134-0722/0733, 7125-2655, ; fax: 7134-0680, 7134-7648).

Banque Nationale Agricole, Rue Hedi Nouira, 1001 Tunis (tel: 7183-1000/1200; fax: 7183-5388, 7183-2807).

Société Tunisienne de Banque SA, Rue Hedi Nouira, 1001 Tunis (tel: 7134-0477, 7125-8000; fax: 7134-0009, 7134-8400, 7134-0446).

Tunis International Bank, PO Box 81, 18 Avenue des Etats Unis D'Amerique, 1002 Tunis (tel: 7178-2411; fax: 7178-9970).

Central bank

Banque Centrale de Tunisie, 25 Rue Hédi Nouira, PO Box 777, 1080 Tunis (tel: 7134-0588; fax: 7134-0615; e-mail: boc@bct.gov.tn).

Stock exchange

Bourse de Tunis (Tunis Stock Exchange), www.bvmt.com.tn

Travel information

Tunisair, Customer Service Unit, Boulevard du 7 Novembre 1987, 2035 L'Ariana, Tunis (tel: 7083-7000 ext: 2572/2510; fax: 7083-6839; reservations tel: 7194-1285; email: resaonline@tunisair.com.tn; internet: www.tunisair.com).

Tunisian Airports Office, Ministère des Technologies de la Communication et du Transport, Direction Générale de l'Aviation Civile, 13 Rue 8006 Montplaisir, 1002 Tunis (tel: 7179-4424; fax: 7179-4227).

Tunisavia, Boulvard de l'Environnement 2035, Aéroport Tunis-Carthage, Tunis (tel: 7128-0555, 7128-0521; email: siege@tunisavia.com.tn; internet: www.tunisavia.com.tn).

National tourist organisation offices

Tunisian National Tourism Office (ONTT), 1 Ave Mohamed V, 1001Tunis (tel: 7134-1077; fax: 7135-0997; email: info@tourismtunisia.com; internet: www.tourismtunisia.com).

Ministries

Ministry of Agriculture, 30 rue Alain Savery, 1002 Tunis Belvedere (tel: 7128-7133).

Ministry of Communication Technologies, Cabinet de Monsieur le Ministre, 3 bis, rue d'Angleterre, 1000 Tunis.

Ministry of Communications, Belvedere du 9 Avril 1938, 1030 Tunis (tel: 7133-6409; fax: 7135-4628).

Ministry of Economic Development, Direction Générale de la Privatisation, Place Ali Zouaoui, 1000 Tunis (tel: 7135-4467; fax: 7135-0975).

Ministry of Defence, 1008 Montfleury, Tunis (tel: 7156-0244).

Ministry of Education, Boulevard Bab Bnat, Tunis (tel: 71263850; fax: 7156-9307).

Ministry of Equipment and Housing, Av H Cherita –Cite Jardin, 1002 Tunis (tel: 7168-1802).

Ministry of Higher Education, 28 rue de Sousse, 1030 Tunis (tel: 7178-2947).

Ministry of Public Health, Bab Saadoun, Tunis (tel: 7126-0727).

Ministry of Vocational Training and Employment, 21 rue de Lybie – Lafayette, 1002 Tunis (tel: 7178-2432).

Other useful addresses

Agence de Promotion de L'Industrie, 63 rue de Syrie, 1002 Tunis-Belvédère (tel: 7179-2144; fax: 7178-2482).

Agricultural Investment Promotion Agency, 62 rue Alain Savary, 1003 Tunis Khadra, Tunis (tel: 7128-8400, 7128-8091; fax: 7178-2353).

American Embassy, Zone Nord-Est des Berges du Lac, Nord de Tunis, 2045, La Goulette, Tunisia (tel: 7110-7000; fax: 7196-2115).

American Express, c/o Carthage Tours, 59 avenue Habib Bourguiba, 1001 Tunis (tel: 7125-4304; fax: 7135-2740).

Arab League, avenue Khéreddine Pacha, Tunis.

British Embassy, 5 Place de la Victoire, 1000 Tunis (tel: 7124-5100, 7124-5324, 7134-1444; fax: 7135-1487; email: britishemb@planet.tn; internet: www.brit-ish-emb.intl.tn).

Central Post Office, rue Charles de Gaulle, Tunis.

CEPEX (agency for promotion of Tunisian exports), 28 rue v Gandhi, 1001 Tunis (tel: 7135-0043, 7135-0801; fax: 7135-3683; email: cepexedpuc@attmail.com).

Entreprise Tunisienne D'Activités Petrolières, 27 avenue Khéreddine Pacha, 1002 Tunis (tel: 7178-2288).

Export Promotion Centre, 28 rue Ghandi, 1001 Tunis (tel: 7135-0344; fax: 7135-3683).

Industrial Land Agency, 2 rue Badii Ezzamen, Cité Mahrajéne, 1002 Tunis-Belvédère, El Menza I (tel: 7179-7360, 7180-0616; fax: 7178-2303).

Institut National de Statistique, 27 rue de Liban, Tunis (tel: 7128-2500).

Maghreb Permanent Consultative Committee, 14 rue Yahia ibn Omar, Mutuelleville, Tunis.

National Sanitation Office, 32 rue Hedi Nouira, Tunis (tel: 7170-4000).

National Water Distribution Company, 67 rue Jawarhel ehru, Montfleury (tel: 7149-3700; fax: 7139-0561).

Office du Commerce de Tunisie, avenue Mohammed V, 1002 Tunis (tel: 7128-8673, 7128-8864, 7168-2903; fax: 7178-8974, 7178-4974).

Prime Ministry, Privatisation General Directorate, 4 Rue ibn Nadim Montplaisir, 1002 Tunis (tel: 7128-2467; fax: 7128-1675).

Tunisian Chemical Group, 5–7 rue Khartoum, 1002 Tunis (tel: 7178-4488).

Tunisian Electricity and Gas Company, 38 rue Kemal Ataturk, Tunis (tel: 7134-1311; fax: 7134-9981).

Tunisian Embassy (USA), 1515 Massachusetts Avenue, NW, Washington DC 20005, USA (tel: (+1-202) 862-1850; fax: (+1-202) 862-1858).

Tunisian External Communication Agency, 2 rue d'Algérie, 1001 Tunis (tel: 7165-1999, 7135-0202; fax: 7134-1902).

Union Tunisienne de l'Industrie, du Commerce et de l'Artisanat, 32 rue Charles de Gaulle, Tunis (tel: 7124-3711).

National news agency: Tunisian News Agency (TAP) (in Arabic, French and English), (tel: 7187-0657; fax: 7188-8999; email: desk.national@email.ati.tn; internet: www.tap.info.tn).

Internet sites

Information on Tunisia: www.tunisiaonline.com

www.investintunisia.tn

www.tunisie.com

Africa Business Network: www.ifc.org/abn

AllAfrica.com: http://allafrica.com

African Development Bank: www.afdb.org

Mbendi AfroPaedia (information on companies, countries, industries and stock exchanges in Africa): http://mbendi.co.za

Radio Tunisia: www.radiotunis.com

Turkey

KEY FACTS

Official name: Türkiye Cumhuriyeti (Republic of Turkey)

Head of State: President Recep Tayyip Erdogan (inaugurated 28 August 2014)

Head of government: Prime Minister Ahmet Davutoglu (AKP) (from 28 August 2014)

Ruling party: Adalet ve Kalkinma Partisi (AKP) (Justice and Development Party) (elected 2002; re-elected 12 Jun 2011). AKP has lost its majority in the most recent elections in June 2015. Having failed to form a coalition government, new elections will be held on November 1

Area: 779,452 square km

Population: 76.90 million (2014)*

Capital: Ankara

Official language: Turkish

Currency: Yeni Turk Lirasi (New Turkish Lira) (YTL) = 100 kurus

Exchange rate: YTL3.02 per US$ (Sep 2015)

GDP per capita: US$10,482 (2014)*

GDP real growth: 2.90% (2014)*

GDP: US$806.11 billion (2014)*

Labour force: 28.98 million (2014)*

Unemployment: 9.91% (2014)*

Inflation: 8.86% (2014)

Balance of trade: -US$63.58 billion (2014)

Annual FDI: US$16.04 billion (2011)

* estimated figure

After the June 2015 elections, in which his plans to change the constitution were thwarted, President Erdogan had to reconsider his options. His grand plan to change the constitution had become no more than that, a plan that now seemed impossible to realise. Increasingly umpopular, Erdogan had misjudged events and simply lost touch with the popular mood. His aggressive campaign had been constrained by his position as president, which prevented him from campaigning directly, despite having the entire government security apparatus at his fingertips. Although the result was a win for his Adalet ve Kalkinma Partisi (AKP) (Justice and Development Party), it was by a reduced majority of 40.87 per cent (down from 49.83 per cent in June 2011).

Without a majority, the party was obliged to attempt to form a coalition, first with the Cumhuriyet Halk Partisi (Republican People's Party) and when that didn't work, then with the Milliyetçi Hareket Partisi (Nationalist Movement Party). However, when neither had proved succcessful by the deadline to form a new government on 23 August Mr Erdogan said he would call a snap general election for 1 November.

In a number of respects, President Erdogan was certainly swimming against the political and popular tide. He continued to place obstacles in the path of an accommodation with the Kurds and a raft of corruption scandals threatened to damage further his already weakened credibility. The opposition Cumhuriyet Halk Partisi (CHP) (Republican People's Party) had presented the ruling Adalet ve Kalkinma Partisi (AKP) (Justice and Development Party) with a dossier that allegedly revealed how nepotism had thrived under the AKP, with a list of the names of relatives and friends of AKP members who had by-passed the Public Personnel Selection Exam to obtain public jobs or had climbed the public service promotion ladder with seemingly lighting speed. On top of it all, Erdogan's foreign policy appeared to be in disarray, lacking direction and purpose. Finally, there were murmurs of further devaluation of the lira.

Election gloom – and glory

If it came as a surprise that the AKP could only muster 41 per cent of the vote in the June election, it was also something of a humiliation. The biggest change in the parliamentary make-up was the entry of the pro-Kurdish, left wing Kurdish Peoples Democratic Party (HDP) led by the charismatic Selahattin Demirtas. The AKP's exaggerated response to the HDP backfired completely, generating sympathy rather than hatred and permitting the HDP to sail past the 10 per cent of the vote required to enter parliament. The HDP advent had combined with the desertion of large numbers of once traditional AKP supporters. In May 2015 bomb attacks had been made on the HDP offices in the cities of Adana and Mersin wounding three people. The chairman of the party, Selahattin Demirtas, was about to arrive in the Adana HDP offices when the bomb went off. For President Erdogan Mr Demirtas was something of a raw nerve, having run against Erdogan in the August 2014 presidential elections when he gained 9.8 per cent of the vote.

Game changer

The AKP's failure to secure a parliamentary majority and the arrival of the HDP certainly represented a 'New Turkey'. But not the body politic that Erdogan had hoped for. Quoted in the London *Guardian*, the political scientist Ahmet Insel noted that 'The attempt to block his (Erdogan's) plans for the presidential system in Turkey made voting for the HDP the most rational choice. Erdogan's push for an executive presidency effectively turned the election into a referendum on his plans instead of a choice between political parties. The AKP were not, however, the only party to lose votes. The HDP took at least one million votes from the opposition CHP. Many of those voters opted to change simply in order to stop Erdogan.'

The 2015 parliamentary elections had always promised to provide an element of drama. President Erdogan had mistakenly cast the election as a vote on Turkey's future constitutional arrangements. The President's hidden agenda was to transform the presidency from a largely ceremonial function to one of political power. Before becoming president in 2014, Mr Erdogan had served as the AKP prime minister for over a decade. Choosing to forsake the president's impartial constitutional role, Mr Erdogan had more than simply endorsed the AKP. He had done all he could to secure an AKP majority in parliament; this would enable him to make the constitutional changes that would eventually give Turkey a president with executive powers. President Erdogan had needed to win more than 330 seats in the 550-seat parliament to get his way.

The 're-run' of the election on 1 November was this time won by the AKP with 49.50 per cent (317 seats, out of 550), giving Mr Erdogan a clear majority. Unlike the June election which were considered to be 'fair' by international observers, the Organisation for Security and Co-operarion in Europe (OSCE) and the Parliamentary Assembly of the Council of Europe (PACE) both considered the November voting to be 'unfair'. The OSCE reported concerns over media bias and that voter safety had cast a 'shadow' over the results, and political parties expressed suspicions over a controversial collapse in the Supreme Electoral Council's ballot tracking systems during the counting process.

But what about the Kurds?

Whatever may be thought about Erdogan, the fact remained that in the first two decades of the twenty-first century, he was the towering figure in Turkish politics. He dominated his party and at the same time had managed to marginalise the armed forces. For years Turkish politicians had to look over their backs to make sure they had the tolerance, if not the support, of Turkey's efficiently professional military. If the generals were restless, it boded ill for the government.

In the run up to the 2015 elections, it was ironically clear that the only thing standing in the way of Erdogan was the HDP, representing a significant majority of Turkey's Kurdish population. The electoral barrier was set high; Turkey's electoral system is heavily biased as far as the smaller parties are concerned. Should a party fail to win ten per cent of the votes, the seats where it had obtained a majority were shared out among those which had secured the magic percentage. Which in 2015 meant for the most part that the beneficiary was almost certainly the AKP, which had traditionally come second behind the HDP in the latter's strongholds.

Ironically, although it was Erdogan who had initiated the 'peace' process with Turkey's rebellious Kurdish minority, the electoral system had meant that what was gained in discussion could be lost at the ballot box. The *Al Monitor* website reported that civil disobedience in the Kurdish majority areas, as well as in the major cities where there were large concentrations of Kurds, had been likely to be the outcome if the HDP failed to make the cut. Fortunately for the Kurds and for Turkey, significant numbers of ethnic Turks opposed to Erdogan had voted for the HDP.

Turkey's back-yard is packed with explosive scenarios: Syria, Iraq, Palestine and Egypt for starters. In many of these areas there are both large and small – but always influential – Kurdish communities. In the days when Sykes Picquot still meant something, the Kurds were overwhelmingly fragmented. But post 2003, the Kurds had started to flourish; Erbil, their designated capital had become one of the Middle East's most prosperous cities, often described as the 'New Beirut'.

Problems with Iran?

The Turkish government had for some years been warily conscious of Shi'a Iran's growing presence in the Middle East. Turkey's 2015 support for the Saudi-Arabian military intervention in Yemen had little to do with Yemen itself, much more to do with preventing the perceived Iranian hegemony from spreading.

KEY INDICATORS — Turkey

	Unit	2011	2012	2013	2014	**2015
Population	m	*73.95	74.89	*76.06	*76.90	*77.74
Gross domestic product (GDP)	US$bn	778.10	788.04	821.92	*806.11	*752.51
GDP per capita	US$	10,522	10,523	10,807	*10,482	*9,680
GDP real growth	%	8.5	2.2	4.1	*2.9	*3.1
Inflation	%	6.5	8.9	7.5	8.9	*6.6
Unemployment	%	9.8	9.2	9.0	*9.9	*11.4
Coal output	mtoe	16.6	15.4	13.2	17.8	–
Exports (fob) (goods)	US$m	143,497.0	163,317.0	163,565.0	168,931.0	–
Imports (fob) (goods)	US$m	232,486.0	228,552.0	243,381.0	232,510.0	–
Balance of trade	US$m	-88,989.0	-65,235.0	-79,816.0	-63,579.0	–
Current account	US$m	-77,141.0	-48,497.0	-64,658.0	-45,846.0	*-31,719.0
Total reserves minus gold	US$m	88,799.0	99,430.0	110,927.0	1,069,060.0	–
Foreign exchange	US$m	87,072.6	98,280.0	109,249.0	–	–
Foreign direct investment (FDI)	US$bn	16.0	–	–	–	–
Exchange rate	per US$	1.50	1.79	2.17	2.33	–

There were those in Turkey who resorted to a vague historical argument that Yemen still belonged to the Ottomans. This reflected what was described as the 'New Ottoman' mindset, which naively hoped that Muslims were looking to Sunni Turkey (rather than Shi'a Iran) for leadership. What was an equally tenuous historical argument was that the Zaydis, to which tribe the Houthis in Yemen belonged, had persistently revolted against Ottoman rule in Yemen.

President Erdogan had certainly taken up the verbal cudgels aggressively, waging what *Al Monitor* described as a 'war of words' with Iran. In the view of *Al Monitor*, Turkey's position had more to do with 'strengthening bonds with Gulf states… than with burning the bridges with Iran', which for some decades had been the Middle Eastern country with which Turkey had enjoyed a stable relationship. Mr Erdogan appeared to lay the blame for his failed plans in Syria and Iraq squarely on Iran, repeating the mantra that 'Iran is virtually trying to dominate the region.' Erdogan was also trying to manufacture alliances, saying that 'This has begun to annoy many countries – us as well as Saudi Arabia and the Gulf states.'

Iran responded by making it known that President Erdogan, who was due to make an official visit to Tehran in April 2105, was unwelcome. Senior Iranian politicians criticised Turkey's support for the US lead coalition's actions in Iraq and Syria and one – Mansour Haghighatpour – said that 'Erdogan's visit to Tehran will be of no use. It should be postponed.'

Yemen… and Israel

Quoting a March 2015 message by Erdogan in which he said that 'We cannot accept Iran's efforts to exert its hegemony over the Middle East', *Al Monitor* also reported the Turkish President as continuing: 'Iran is only taking action against the Islamic State to advance its interests in the region and to wrest control of Iraq and Syria.' The Shi'ite Houthis were considered by Turkey and others to be the 'long arm of Tehran'. Mr Erdogan's remarks were curiously identical to those of Israel's Benjamin Netanyahu in his March 2015 speech to the US Congress. 'Your enemy's enemy is your enemy.' As Turkey's relationship with Israel cooled, Erdogan rarely missed an opportunity to attack the Israeli government over its treatment of the Palestinians.

However, in mid-2015 the climate seemed to be changing. It seemed that not only the president, but other Turkish ministers appeared to be avoiding rising to any controversial statements by Netanyahu and his maverick foreign minister Avigdor Liberman. In March 2015 in Edirne, in north-western Turkey, the city's Great Synagogue had been reconsecrated. Once the largest synagogue in the Balkans and the third-largest in Europe, it was no doubt hoped by the Erdogan regime that this would be well received in Israel. However, in November 2014, the governor of Edirne province had caused a controversy when he called for the synagogue to be confiscated from the Jewish community and turned into a museum.

The consecration ceremony was intended to be an expression of Turkey's tolerance and openness toward the Jews, although the Jewish community had long since departed Edirne. Representatives of the Jewish community and senior Turkish officials had been invited to the ceremony. Although Israel's chief rabbis were invited, they diplomatically opted to remain in Jerusalem. Israeli diplomats serving in Turkey, however, did attend the event. Anti-Semitism was considered to be on the rise in Turkey, often linked to provocative statements by politicians.

The economy – the IMF

In its December 2014 assessment of the Turkish economy, the Washington-based International Monetary Fund (IMF) noted that the economy was mostly driven by domestic demand growth. In the view of the IMF, Turkey had managed to rebound strongly after the global financial crisis, growing at 9 per cent per year on average in 2010–11, but it had since been growing more modestly. The authorities' policies and large capital inflows had supported domestic demand. However, average inflation had been 7.9 per cent with an average current account deficit of 7.5 per cent of gross domestic product (GDP) during the period 2010–13. While there had been some rebalancing in 2012, this proved short-lived owing to policy loosening. In 2013 GDP had grown by 4.1 per cent and the current account deficit had widened to 7.9 per cent of GDP, financed mostly by short-term debt-creating inflows, while inflation ended the year at 7.4 per cent, once again above the 5 per cent target.

In the view of the IMF, ample capital inflows, intermediated by the financial sector and what the IMF described as 'financial deepening', eased credit constraints and led to a rapid growth of private sector credit and consumption. Private savings decreased, opening up a large gap between (low) saving and (modest) investment. Hedged external wholesale foreign currency borrowing has become a key feature sustaining loan growth and the loan-to-deposit ratio has risen well above 100 per cent.

Severe turbulence hit Turkey's economy in early 2014. US 'Fed' tapering, loose and opaque monetary policy and domestic political uncertainty led to a 15 per cent exchange rate (FX) depreciation early in the year. The authorities had initially embarked on unsterilised FX intervention, which resulted in a rapid loss of international reserves. Subsequently, the Türkiye Cumhuriyet Merkez Bankasi (TCMB) (Central Bank of the Republic of Turkey) increased the one week repo rate by 550 basis points and adjusted its policy framework. The banks and corporate sector had shown resilience during this short-lived period of turmoil, with corporate FX losses not translating into non-performing loans. Inflation remained too high and the IMF expected that the current account deficit would remain between 5.5–6 per cent of GDP on current policies. Reflecting in part the large share of short-term external debt, gross external financing requirements were expected to exceed a quarter of GDP per year. Turkey's net foreign asset position, which had already deteriorated by about 25 percentage points of GDP since 2008, was also expected to weaken further. The current account deficit remained 2.5–5 per cent of GDP higher than warranted by fundamentals and optimal policy settings. The IMF drew attention to the fact that these trends were not sustainable and if they were not redressed, Turkey could sooner or later suffer a sharp adjustment.

However, Turkey's macro-economic policies had not supported rebalancing by increasing domestic savings, leaving Turkey exposed to shocks. Fiscal and monetary policies had been too loose. Public sector expenditure had grown faster than GDP and Turkey's structural primary balance had deteriorated. The monetary stance had emphasised growth over inflation and thus has been too loose for too long. Negative real policy interest rates had caused high inflation, thereby eroding competitiveness and reducing incentives for private savings.

Over the past five years, according to the IMF, the current account deficit had averaged 6.4 per cent of GDP, with large fluctuations in the recent years. Weaker domestic demand conditions and decreased gold imports in 2014 pointed to another episode of external rebalancing.

The deficit was expected to have narrowed to 5.8 per cent of GDP by the end of 2014. Exports to the Middle East and North Africa (MENA) region had moderated. The share of export to the region fell from 32.2 per cent of the total in 2012, to 27.9 per cent in 2013, partly due to diminished gold re-exporting activities. Iraq remained the most important export market in the region and the second largest export destination for Turkey (after Germany), accounting for 8 per cent of total exports. Conflicts in several MENA countries in 2014 are expected to have negatively impacted Turkey's trade with the region. And although there are signs that exports to traditional European partners were beginning to pick up, the recovery was expected to be slow due to the region's subdued economic recovery.

Low levels of foreign direct investment (FDI) provide an insight into the challenges confronting Turley. In 2013, Turkey saw a total FDI inflow of 1.6 per cent of GDP, below the average of 2.5 per cent of GDP for its G-20 emerging-market peers. The share of FDI in the tradable sector, which had been gaining grounds in previous years, fell back to 47 per cent of the total, on account of the greater FDI going into financial services. The overall low level of FDI into Turkey probably reflected the trend decline in FDI flows into most emerging markets since 2009. None the less, Turkey's high inflation, volatile growth and structural bottlenecks can be assumed to play key roles in impeding FDI. The World Economic Forum's 2014 Global Competitiveness Report gave a low rank to Turkey regarding the reliance on imports (106 out of 144), inflation performance (122) and labour market efficiency (131). Turkey also received a relatively low rankings in the quality of both primary (94) and higher education (89). On the Berlin-based Transparency International *Corruption Perceptions Index*, Turkey ranked an embarrassingly low 64 out of the 175 countries surveyed, the lowest level of any Organisation for Economic Co-operation and Development (OECD) member country.

The European Bank for Reconstruction and Development (EBRD), in its 2014 *Transition Report* reported that progress on improving the business climate had been mixed. In the World Bank *Doing Business 2015* report Turkey had improved its position, ranking 55 out of 189 countries, despite receiving low scores in dealing with construction permits and resolving insolvency procedures. An amendment to the Public Procurement Law, which would enforce a compulsory 15 per cent price advantage for medium and high-tech domestic products, had been criticised by the European Commission. Nevertheless, some steps to improve the business climate had been taken. An omnibus bill, banning the reversal of privatisation transactions five years after the assets had been transferred to the private sector, had been adopted and was expected to increase business confidence among foreign investors

The economy – The Chamber of Commerce

Going into much more 'feet on the ground' detail, the Istanbul Industry Chamber's data on Turkey's 500 largest companies, as published by *Al Monitor*, showed that the companies' debt-equity ratio had climbed to 132.4 per cent, its highest level in a decade. In developed countries, this ratio stood at around 70 per cent. Companies spent YTL19 billion (US$6.3 billion) of their YTL36.5 billion (US$12 billion) profits for financing. The economy had seen serious financial fluctuations since the second half of 2013. The debt stock of the 500 largest companies had increased, climbing to YTL238 billion (US$78.8 billion) in 2013, up 25 per cent from YTL190 billion (US$62.9 billion) in 2012. In 2015, the private sector's total debt stock reached about US$280 billion, which poses a grave risk to the economy given the recent adverse developments in foreign exchange rates. Turkey's external financing need had reached US$220 billion, but with the Fed expected to hike interest rates, the global financing taps are being turned off for emerging economies such as Turkey. In this environment, the Chamber noted, Saudi and Gulf capital was becoming more and more important in meeting Turkey's external financing need and maintaining fiscal stability.

Energy

In the view of the US government Energy Information Administration (EIA), Turkey was well placed to serve as a hub for oil and natural gas supply headed to Europe and other Atlantic markets from Russia, the Caspian region and the Middle East. Turkey had long been a major transit point for oil and was, in the view of the EIA, becoming more important as a transit point for natural gas. Growing volumes of Caspian oil were being sent to Black Sea ports such as Novorossiysk (Russia) and Supsa (Georgia) and then on to Western markets by tanker via the Turkish Straits (the Bosporus and the Dardanelles). Caspian oil and gas from northern Iraq also crossed Turkey by pipeline, through the Ceyhan oil terminal on Turkey's Mediterranean coast.

The EIA considered that Turkey was set to become a significant natural gas pipeline hub. However, in 2015 most of its natural gas pipeline connections only brought natural gas into Turkey, as growing demands had left little natural gas for export. Since 2010, Turkey had experienced some of the fastest growth in total energy demand among countries in the OECD. Unlike several other OECD countries in Europe, Turkey's economy had avoided the post financial crisis stagnation that had characterised much of the continent for the past several years.

In January 2015, the *Oil & Gas Journal* (OGJ) estimated Turkey's proved oil reserves at 296 million barrels, located mostly in the south-east region of the country. Turkey's petroleum and other liquids' production peaked in 1991 at 85,000 barrels per day (bpd), but since then production had declined each year and bottomed out in 2004 at 43,000bpd. Although Turkey's production of liquid fuels had increased since 2004, the EIA noted that it was much less than annual consumption.

Türkiye Petrolleri Anonim Ortakligi (TPAO) is the dominant exploration and production entity in Turkey. As a state-owned firm, TPAO has preferential rights in petroleum exploration and production and any foreign involvement in upstream activities is limited to joint ventures with TPAO. In 2013, TPAO produced 34,000bpd of crude oil accounting for 73 per cent of the total crude oil production in Turkey.

Most of Turkey's 296 million barrels of proved oil reserves are located in the Batman and Adiyaman Provinces in the south-east (where most of Turkey's oil production occurs), with additional deposits found in Thrace in the north-west. In 2014, Turkey produced an estimated 61,000bpd of petroleum and other liquids, accounting for about 9 per cent of Turkey's oil consumption. Offshore and shale reserves may become a future source of Turkey's oil supply. There may also be significant reserves under the Aegean Sea, although this had not been confirmed because of territorial disputes with Greece. The Black Sea may also hold significant oil production potential for Turkey.

The EIA stressed Turkey's increasingly important role in the transit of oil. Turkey is strategically located at the crossroads between the oil-rich former Soviet Union and Middle East countries and European demand centres. It is home to one of the world's busiest chokepoints, the Turkish Straits, through which almost 3 million bpd flowed in 2013. About 70 per cent of this volume was crude oil and the remainder was petroleum products. The Turkish Straits include the Bosporus and the Dardanelles waterways, through which significant volumes of Russian and Caspian oil move by tanker to Western markets.

Turkey also has two crude oil import pipelines, the Baku-Tbilisi-Ceyhan (BTC) pipeline from Azerbaijan and a pipeline from northern Iraq to Ceyhan, Turkey. The Iraq pipeline has two branches. The original line of the Iraq pipeline stretched from the Iraq-Turkey border to Kirkuk, Iraq. However, little oil has flowed on this part of the pipeline since the Islamic State of Iraq and Syria (ISIS, or just IS) began seizing territory in the area in early 2014 and the pipeline was sabotaged. The BTC pipeline has also been targeted. In 2013, the Kurdish Regional government (KRG) completed construction of a second line of the Iraq pipeline, beginning at Taq Taq field near Erbil in the KRG controlled portion of northern Iraq, which joins the existing pipeline to Ceyhan, near the Iraq-Turkey border. Initial flows on the KRG line were low, as the Iraqi central government objected to the KRG selling oil without central government approval or involvement. The two sides reached an agreement and in January 2015 and the KRG began exporting its own oil as well as the central government controlled oil that was produced in northern Iraq.

Natural gas is also of importance; the EIA noted that Turkey has a strategic role in natural gas transit because of its position between the world's second-largest natural gas market, continental Europe, and the substantial natural gas reserves of the Caspian Basin and the Middle East. In January 2015, the OGJ estimated Turkish natural gas reserves at 218 billion cubic feet (bcf). Turkey produces only a small amount of natural gas, with total production amounting to 19bcf in 2013. With 11bcf produced in 2013, TPAO accounted for most of Turkey's natural gas production. Turkey is an important consumer of natural gas and is one of the few countries in Europe where natural gas consumption continues to show strong growth. This growing consumption had helped spur development of multiple pipelines to bring natural gas into the country and while it had left little natural gas available for export, new supplies have been contracted and new pipelines are under construction that would increase both Turkey's imports and exports of natural gas.

Risk assessment

Economy	Fair
Politics	Fair
Regional stability	Fair

Muslims in Turkey

% of population	98.6
Sunni (% of Muslims)	85
Shi'a (% of Muslims)	15

People to watch

Mustafa Sarigul. Principal opposition (CHP) candidate as Mayor of Istanbul. In the March 2014 elections Mr Sarigul narrowly lost to the incumbent Kadir Topbas of the AK Party.

COUNTRY PROFILE

Founded by Constantine the Great in AD330, Turkey (or Asia Minor as it was known) was for more than 1,000 years the heartland of the Eastern Roman (Byzantine) empire. From the eleventh century, invasions from Central Asia led to the Islamic Turkification of the region, headed by the Ottomans, a name derived from their fourteenth century leader Osman Gazi, who had masterminded the comprehensive defeat of the Byzantines at the Battle of Baphaeon in 1301. The modern republic was established in the 1920s by nationalist leader Kemal Atatürk.

1453 The Ottomans gradually expanded their areas of territorial control, creating the Ottoman Empire.

1500s–1800s The Ottoman Empire attempted to widen its territorial control into the Mediterranean and central Europe. This led to conflicts with the major European powers, including the Habsburgs and the Russians. Successive wars eventually undermined the Ottoman Empire.

1914–18 Turkey fought in the First World War on the side of the Germans. The majority of Ottoman possessions came under British or French control after the war.

1920–22 Mustafa Kemal, renamed Atatürk (Father of all the Turks) in 1934, led the country in the War of National Liberation, following the dismemberment of the Ottoman Empire by the *entente* powers at the end of the First World War.

1923 The Republic of Turkey was established; the independence of the Turkish state was recognised by the Treaty of Lausanne. Atatürk was elected as the Republic's first president. Sweeping changes were made in all areas – legal, political, social and economic. The Islamic legal codes were replaced by Western ones. Turkey is the only Muslim country where the principle of secularism is written into the constitution.

1925 Turkey adopted the Gregorian calendar. The fez (a conical, brimless hat), considered to be a sign of Ottoman backwardness, was prohibited.

1928 Islam ceased to be the State religion. The Arabic script was replaced by the Latin alphabet.

1930 Constantinople was officially renamed Istanbul.

1934 Women were given the vote.

1938 Atatürk died and was succeeded by Ismet Inonu.

1945 President Inonu kept Turkey out of the Second World War, except for the last four months, when it fought on the side of the Allies against Germany. Turkey joined the UN.

1950 The first open multi-party elections were won by the Democratic Party.

1952 Turkey joined NATO.

1960 The government was overthrown in a military coup.

1961 A constitution was approved in a referendum; it established a two-chamber parliament. Elections were held and civilian rule was restored.

1963 An agreement was signed with the European Economic Community (EEC).

1965 Süleyman Demirel became prime minister (he went on to occupy this office seven times).

1971 After a wave of strikes and unrest, there was a period of military supervision of government.

1973 Return to civilian rule.

1974 Turkey invaded northern Cyprus and 37 per cent of the island came under Turkish control, enforcing partition between north and south.

1978 The US lifted the trade embargo it had imposed on Turkey after the 1974 invasion.

1980 A military coup followed civil unrest and martial law was declared throughout the country.

1981 All political parties were disbanded.

1982 A new constitution was approved in a referendum. It created a seven-year presidency and reduced parliament to a single chamber.

1983 New political parties were allowed, subject to strict rules. Turgut Ozal became president. Northern Cyprus officially declared its independence as the Kuzey Kýbrýs Türk Cumhuriyeti (KKTC) (Turkish Republic of Northern Cyprus) and introduced its own government and legal system. The independence move was rejected by the international community and only Turkey recognised it as a state.

1984 The Partiya Karkerên Kurdistan (PKK) (Kurdistan Workers' Party) launched

a separatist guerrilla war in the south-east.
1987 Martial law ended, enabling Turkey to become a full and active member of the Organisation of Economic Co-operation and Development (OECD), in addition to becoming an associate member of the EEC.
1990 Turkey allowed the use of its bases for the launch of air strikes against Iraq by the US-led coalition in the war to drive Iraqi forces out of Kuwait.
1992 In an anti-PKK operation, Turkish troops entered Kurdish safe havens in Iraq. Turkey joined the Black Sea alliance.
1993 Following the death of Turgut Ozal, Süleyman Demirel became president. Tansu Ciller was appointed as Turkey's first female prime minister. The PKK declared a unilateral cease-fire in March but by July it had broken down.
1995 Turkey launched a major military offensive against the Kurds in northern Iraq. The Ciller coalition collapsed. Although the pro-Islamist Welfare Party (RP) won the elections, it lacked support to form a government. Two major centre-right parties formed an anti-Islamist coalition. Turkey entered the EU customs union.
1996 The centre-right coalition fell and Necmettin Erbakan was appointed prime minister, heading the first pro-Islamic government since 1923.
1997 The Erbakan coalition government collapsed and Mesut Yilmaz was appointed prime minister.
1998 Corruption allegations forced out the Yilmaz government and Bülent Ecevit was appointed prime minister. The RP was banned.
1999 The PKK leader, Abdullah Öcalan, captured in Kenya, received a death sentence, later commuted to life imprisonment. Two earthquakes in the Izmit region killed over 17,000 people.
2000 After the failure of a move to change the constitution to allow Süleyman Demirel to stay in office, Ahmet Necdet Sezer was elected president.
2001 Parliament voted to change the constitution to bring it closer to the constitutions of EU countries.
2002 To meet EU conditions on opening membership talks, parliament voted for wide reforms. The Islamist Adalet ve Kalkinma Partisi (AKP) (Justice and Development Party) won a landslide victory in parliamentary elections. Abdullah Gül became prime minister. Constitutional changes allowed the AKP leader, Recep Tayyip Erdogan, previously disbarred from public office due to a criminal conviction, to run for parliament.
2003 Recep Tayyip Erdogan was appointed prime minister. Parliament adopted a package of human rights reforms including freedom of speech, giving the Kurdish language some rights and reducing the political role of the military.
2004 EU leaders agreed to open talks towards Turkey's EU accession after Turkey agreed to recognise Cyprus as an EU member. The death penalty was banned.
2005 The new Turkish lira, Yeni Turk Lirasi (YTL), was introduced as six zeroes were dropped from the currency. EU accession negotiations commenced. The Blue Stream gas pipeline under the Black Sea from Russia to the Turkish port of Samsun opened.
2006 The Baku-Tbilisi-Ceyhan oil pipeline opened. Turkey's refusal to open its ports to Cypriot traffic caused deadlock in the EU accession negotiations.
2007 After two rounds in a presidential election, held in parliament, the sole candidate, Abdullah Gül (AKP), failed to win enough votes. Protests against his candidacy due to his Islamist background came from both the public and military, which protested he would challenge the secular constitution. Gül withdrew his candidature. The government was denied the option of reforming the constitution to allow directly elected presidents. To resolve the issue, early general elections were called in which the ruling AKP won 46.76 per cent of the vote (341 seats out of 550). With a majority in parliament the AKP was able to elect Abdullah Gül as the president. The Turkish military launched air strikes against the Kurdish PKK inside Iraq.
2008 Parliament approved a constitutional change to allow women to wear the *hijab* (Islamic headscarf) in universities. The ruling AKP risked a ban on its existence and loss of power when it was accused of undermining the secular constitution by introducing this legislation that was seen by its opponents as creating an Islamic state by stealth. The Constitutional Court overturned the legislation and fined the political party 50 per cent of its treasury funding for one year. An indictment was filed against 86 people for plotting to overthrow the government; they were alleged to belong to the ultra-nationalist and Kemalist group, Ergenekon.
2009 Legislation to allow civilian courts to try military personnel for threats to national security or involvement in organised crime was ratified by the president. An agreement was signed to allow the EU-backed Nabucco gas pipeline to transit Turkey. Turkey agreed 'in principle' to also allow the rival Russian South Stream gas pipeline to transit Turkey. The EU seeks to ensure a supply of energy that is not dependent on Russian oil and gas, and Russia wants to avoid transiting Ukraine, with which it has had several disagreements over payments. Turkey's accession talks (to the EU) were blocked by the Cypriot government when it refused to allow the start of talks in five policy areas unless Turkey changed its position on the Cyprus dispute.
2010 After a four-day marathon parliamentary session all but one of 27 amendments to the constitution were approved. Among the proposed changes were increased power for the government, while reducing the influence of the military, and reform of the judiciary, which critics claim may weaken Turkey's secular society in favour of one more Islamic. A flotilla of six ships, organised by a Turkish human rights organisation, attempted to break the Israeli blockade of the Gaza Strip. It was repelled by the Israeli military, with the deaths of nine Turkish activists. Condemnation of the Israeli military action was voiced by many in the international community. The Constitutional Court annulled the changes that would have reduced the powers of the army and the judiciary. A referendum on constitutional reforms covering economic and social rights, individual freedoms and judicial reforms passed with 58 per cent in favour; the proposal to limit the power of the Supreme Court to dissolve political parties failed. The changes brought the constitution into line with EU standards.
2011 Prime Minister Erdogan announced in April that a new waterway would be built to by-pass the Bosphorus, which has become very crowded. General elections were held in June, in which the ruling AKP won 49.83 per cent of the vote (327 seats out of 550) and the CHP won 25.98 per cent (135). The AKP failed to win the two-thirds majority necessary to allow it to change the constitution in line with its political objectives. Some 30 per cent of the elected members (from the main opposition party (CHP) and minority Kurds) boycotted parliament's swearing in ceremony in June. The CHP later rescinded their boycott but the Baris ve Demokrasi Partisi (BDP) ((Kurdish) Peace and Democracy Party), despite urging by Abdullah Ocalan, leader of the PKK, maintained their boycott. Ironically the constitutional changes proposed by Erdogan, which needed BDP support would benefit the Kurdish community. In June, Syrians refugees fled across the border into Turkey, where refugee camps were hastily set up; within two weeks over 5,000 people had found sanctuary. In July Turkey recognised the rebel Transitional National Council in Benghazi (Libya) as the legitimate representatives of the Libyan people. Angered by the arrest of senior military personnel, accused of plotting to undermine the government, Isik Kosaner, chief of the armed forces, resigned in July, along with the army, navy and air force heads. President Gül appointed General Necdet Ozel as

head of the army. In August, Turkey warned the Syrian government to stop its military operations, aimed at quelling internal civil disorder, 'immediately and unconditionally'. A UN report, published on 2 September, into the deaths of nine Turkish activists on board a convoy of ships attempting to break the naval blockade of the Gaza Strip in May 2010 concluded that Israel had used 'excessive force', but that the naval blockage was legal. Turkey immediately expelled the Israeli ambassador and cut military ties with Israel. While Turkey demanded an apology from Israel for the killings, it rejected the findings of the report and threatened to set it before the International Court of Justice (ICJ) for a judicial ruling. During a meeting in Istanbul on 1–2 October the newly combined opposition, the Syrian National Council (SNC), led by Chairman Burhan Ghalioun agreed its structure and aims. An earthquake of magnitude 7.2 struck the eastern province of Van in October. Initial estimates put the death toll of over 200 people and over 1,000 people injured, as dozens of buildings were destroyed. In November, Turkey imposed a number of sanctions against Syria that included suspension of financial dealing with and a freeze of assets of the Syrian government and a travel ban on the Syrian leadership; an arms ban is already in place.

2012 On 7 February, Prime Minister Erdogan said that the veto of the UN resolution to halt the violence in Syria was a 'licence to kill' for Syrian President Bashir al Assad. He also announced his government would 'start a new (regional) initiative with those countries which stand by the Syrian people, not the regime.' On 30 March, a new controversial education bill was passed that not only extended compulsory education from aged eight to 12 years, but allowed children to switch from state, secular schools to specialist, religious schools as young as 10 years of age. Some members of parliament (MPs) came to blows during the debate, while outside demonstrations in Ankara were broken up by police with tear gas and water cannon. The secular Cumhuriyet Halk Partisi (CHP) (Republican People's Party) accused the prime minister of wanting to impose Islamic values on the country. Prime Minister Erdogan refuted the charge saying he was committed to secularism but not at the expense of those Turks who wish to express their religious beliefs openly. On 12 June public schools were allowed to offer the Kurdish language as an optional course. On 22 June, Syria shot down a Turkish military jet plane; in response Turkey changed its rules of engagement and so that all Syrian troops would be seen as a military threat if they approached the Turkish border. On 3 October Syria fired mortars into a border town, killing five civilians; in retaliation Turkey shelled Syrian targets on 3–4 October. On 6 November a Turkish court began the trial of four senior Israeli military commanders, *in absentia*, for the deaths of nine Turkish activists in 2010. Israel refused to co-operate with the prosecution, but if the military commanders are found guilty of the charges an international warrant of arrest could be issued. On 4 December NATO approved the deployment of the Patriot anti-missile batteries along the Turkish-Syrian border, following news that Syria had been preparing chemical weapons for use.

2013 Murat Karayilan, military leader of the PKK, announced on 25 April that under the terms of a ceasefire, PKK fighters would begin withdrawing from Turkey in May. The move followed lengthy negotiations between the Turkish government and the PKK's imprisoned leader Abdullah Ocalan. Ocalan said that 'the weapons should be silent and ideas should speak. The withdrawal will be in three stages: withdrawal of PKK forces from Turkey; constitutional amendments by the Turkish government; and, once Ocalan and other imprisoned Kurdish militants have been released, the PKK to lay down all arms. On 8 May PKK separists began leaving south-east Turkey for northern Iraq. Five years after their trials began, former armed forces chief, Gen Ilker Basbug, and numerous officers, lawyers, writers and journalists, were convicted of involvement in the so-called Ergenekon plot. General Basbag, lawyer Kemal Kerincsiz and Workers' Party leader Dogu Perincek were sentenced to life imprisonment and there were long sentences for others including 34 years for Mustafa Balbay, a journalist and MP. On 22 October the EU agreed to restart membership talks. Prime Minister Erdogan opened a new railway tunnel under the Bosphorus Strait on 29 October. The 1.4km tunnel was begun in 2004 and cost some US$4 billion. Initially only a limited part will be in operation. After a gap of over three years, negotiations with the EU over Turkey's membership were restarted on 5 November.

2014 Turkey's first election of a president was won by Prime Minister Recep Tayyip Erdogan with 52 per cent. Mr Erdogan had become prime minister in 2003 and under the constitution could not stand for a third term. He was inaugurated on 28 August. The AKP will appoint a party leader and prime minister designate; likely to be a supporter of Mr Erdogan. Pope Francis paid a three-day visit to Turkey at the end of November. His visit was aimed at strengthening interfaith relations and included two meetings with Patriarch Bartholomew I, the spiritual leader of the world's 250 million Orthodox Christians.

2015 The 7 June general election was a win for Mr Erdogan's Adalet ve Kalkinma Partisi (AKP) (Justice and Development Party), but by a reduced majority of 40.87 per cent (down from 49.83 per cent in June 2011). Without a majority, the party was obliged to attempt to form a coalition, first with the Cumhuriyet Halk Partisi (Republican People's Party) and when that didn't work, then with the Milliyetçi Hareket Partisi (Nationalist Movement Party). However, when neither had proved succcessful by the deadline to form a new government of 23 August Mr Erdogan said he would call a snap general election for 1 November. Two suicide bombs went off at a peace rally in Ankara on 10 August. Although not initially clear who was responsible, the following day the Turkish airforce bombed KPP militants in south-east Turkey and Iraq. The 're-run' of the election on 1 November was this time won by the AKP with 49.50 per cent (317 seats, out of 550), giving Mr Erdogan a clear majority. Turkey inadvertantly shot down a Russian SU24 bomber on 24 November.

Political structure

Constitution

A 1982 referendum approved a new Constitution embodying considerable restrictions on personal liberty.

The constitution was amended in 1999 and 2001. The 1999 amendment was undertaken to ease the path of the privatisation programme while an amendment in 2001 was aimed at redefining human rights in view of Turkey's aspirations to join the EU. In 2002, three articles of the constitution were amended, allowing a person with a prison conviction (non-terrorist charge) to stand for parliament. Apart from these additions, the new constitution differs little from the 1926 version, promulgated by Kemal Atatürk, which enshrines Turkey as a secular, democratic and unitary republic.

A referendum will be held in June 2010, following parliamentary proposals, in May, that had failed to gain the necessary two-thirds majority to amend the constitution. Proposals include the prime minister being given increased powers, while reducing the influence of the military on the democratically elected government.

A constitutional referendum was held on 12 September 2010, in which 57.88 per cent of voters agreed to 23 changes to articles within the constitution to bring it into line with European Union standards. Measures included equality of men and women, protection of children and vulnerable adults, personal data protection, increased worker's rights including right of

collective bargaining for government employees. The ban on overseas travel was lifted for business people under investigation and with tax debts. The right of citizens to have disputes with government adjudicated by an ombudsman and the right to petition the constitutional court were granted. The abolition of legal safeguards for the 1980 military coup conspirators was enacted as well as further judicial reforms.
The new constitution will allow parliament to select senior judicial candidates and the removal of existing judges. The judiciary would no longer be able to prohibit political parties.

Independence date
29 August 1923

Form of state
Parliamentary democratic republic

The executive
Executive power rests with the president and council of ministers. The president is the Head of State. The president, who serves a seven-year term, is elected by the parliament and appoints the prime minister, who in turn chooses the Council of Ministers. A National Security Council guides government policy in areas of security and law and order. It is chaired by the president and is composed of government ministers and armed forces commanders.

National legislature
The unicameral Türkiye Büyük Millet Meclisi (TGNA) (Turkish Grand National Assembly) has 550 representatives, elected by proportional representation from party lists, to serve five-year terms. Only political parties with over 10 per cent of the vote are eligible to sit in the TGNA.
Only political parties gaining more than 10 per cent of the national vote are entitled to parliamentary seats
Voting eligibility: universal direct suffrage over 18 years.

Legal system
The legal system is based on European models and the 1982 constitution.
The court system is divided into three areas: civil, penal and administrative. The highest courts are the Appeal Court for civil and penal cases and the State Council for tax and administrative cases.

Last elections
10 August 2014 (presidential); 1 November 2015 (parliamentary)
Results: Presidential: (first, and only, round): Recep Tayyip Erdogan 51.79 per cent, Ekmeleddin Mehmet Ihsanoglu 38.44 per cent; Selahattin Demirtas 9.76 per cent. Turnout was 74.13 per cent.
Parliamentary (Nov 2015): Adalet ve Kalkinma Partisi (AKP) (Justice and Development Party) won 49.50 per cent of the vote (317 seats out of 550), Cumhuriyet Halk Partisi (CHP) (Republican People's Party) 25.32 per cent (134), Milliyetçi Hareket Partisi (MHP) (Nationalist Movement Party) 11.90 per cent (40), Halklarin Demokratik Partisi (HDP) (Peoples' Democratic Party) 10.76 per cent (59). 13 other political parties each won less than 2.5 per cent and failed to win seats. Turnout was 85.23 per cent.

Next elections
2020 (parliamentary). 2019 (Presidential).

Political parties

Ruling party
Adalet ve Kalkinma Partisi (AKP) (Justice and Development Party) (elected 2002; re-elected 12 Jun 2011). AKP has lost its majority in the most recent elections in June 2015. Having failed to form a coalition government, new elections will be held on November 1

Main opposition party
Cumhuriyet Halk Partisi (CHP) (Republican People's Party)

Population
About 31 per cent of the population is under 14 years; 64 per cent 15–64; 5 per cent over 65.
There has been a huge shift of population from the countryside to the towns: in 1945 only 18 per cent of the population lived in towns; by 2005, the urban population was estimated at 67.3 per cent of the total population.
76.90 million (2014)*
Last census: October 2000: 67,803,927
Population density: 84 inhabitants per square km. Urban population 70 per cent (2010 Unicef).
Annual growth rate: 1.5 per cent, 1990–2010 (Unicef).
Internally Displaced Persons (IDP)
Over 1.0 million (UNHCR 2004)

Ethnic make-up
Mainly ethnic Turks, with a large Kurdish minority and small numbers of Armenians, Greeks and Jews.

Religions
Muslim with a small Christian minority. Turkey is a secular state which guarantees complete freedom of worship to non-Muslims.

Education
A new education bill was passed in March 2012 that not only extended compulsory education from aged eight to 12 years, but more controversially allowed children to switch from state, secular schools to specialist, religious schools at as young as 10 years of age (the previous age was set at 15 years).
Although complusory education is free, facilities are extremely limited, forcing a number of students to attend night school or take private tuition to improve their chances of gaining a place at one of Turkey's 29 universities.
Literacy rate: 87 per cent adult rate; 96 per cent youth rate (15–24) (Unesco 2005).
Compulsory years: Six to 14
Enrolment rate: 105 per cent male, 96 per cent female, gross primary enrolment; 67 per cent male, 48 per cent female, gross secondary enrolment, of relevant age groups (including repeaters), (Unicef 2004).
Pupils per teacher: 23 in primary schools.

Health
Healthcare is provided free of charge. Standards are low, leading many to seek medical services in private hospitals and abroad. Major differences exist in the availability and quality of medical care between major urban centres and eastern parts of the country. Family planning was introduced in the 1960s. Due to opposition from religious groups it did not receive strong support and funding.
Life expectancy: 71 years, 2004 (WHO 2006)
Fertility rate/Maternal mortality rate: 2.1 births per woman, 2010 (Unicef)
Birth rate/Death rate: 17.95 births per 1,000 population; 5.95 deaths per 1,000 population (World Bank).
Child (under 5 years) mortality rate (per 1,000): 14 per 1,000 live births (WHO 2012); 8 per cent of children under aged five are malnourished (World Bank).
Head of population per physician: 1.35 physicians per 1,000 people, 2003 (WHO 2006)

Welfare
The social security system is based on three major organisations, the Social Insurance Institution (SSK), the Emekli Sandigi (government employees' retirement fund) and Bag-Kur for the self-employed.
Mass social security began in 1946 with the SSK giving limited benefits and has been gradually expanded. Membership is compulsory for all salaried employees except civil servants, who join Emekli Sandigi. Social insurance law provides for benefits covering work injury and occupational illness, sickness, maternity, old age, disability and death.

Main cities
Ankara (capital, estimated population 4.2 million (m) in 2012), Istanbul (12.9m), Izmir (2.9m), Bursa (1.6m), Adana (1.6m), Gaziantep (1.5m), Konya (942,298), Kayseri (850,442), Antalya (826,145), Mersin (626,918).

Languages spoken
Armenian, Greek and Ladino are used by ethnic minorities. The use of Kurdish was restricted until parliament voted to change the constitution in 2001 and relaxed the restriction. Arabic, Circassian, and Judezmo are also spoken.
Almost all educated Turks have command of a foreign language and English is the dominant language for international business. German and French are also spoken.
Official language/s
Turkish

Media
Press
Dailies: There are several national and regional dailies including in Turkish *Hürriyet* (www.hurriyet.com.tr), *Türkiye* (www.turkiyegazetesi.com.tr) and *Milliyet* (www.milliyet.com.tr), are mass circulation newspapers, *Yeni Asir* (www.yeniasir.com.tr) and *Sabah* (www.sabah.com.tr), *Aksam*(www.aksam.com.tr), *Posta* (www.postagazetesi.net) and *Today's Zaman* (www.todayszaman.com) (with English online articles).
In English, the main publication is *Turkish Daily News* (www.turkishdailynews.com.tr) with *The New Anatolian* (www.thenewanatolian.com).
Weeklies: Some daily newspapers have weekend editions, such as *Sunday's Zaman*. Other magazines, in Turkish, include *Aksiyon* (www.aksiyon.com.tr), *Aydinlik* (www.aydinlik.com.tr), *Yeni Mesaj* (www.yenimesaj.com.tr) and *Yeni Ümit* (www.yeniumit.com.tr). In English *Voices* (www.voicesnewspaper.com) from Altinkum and *Turkish Weekly* (www.turkishweekly.net).
Business: In Turkish, *Dünya Ekonomi Politika* (www.dunyagazetesi.com.tr), (with English online articles), and *Finansal Forum* are important publications; others include *Eko Haber* (www.ekohaber.com.tr) and *Referans* (www.referansgazetesi.com). Ýktisat, Ýpletme ve Finans Dergisi (Journal of Economy, Business and Finance) is a monthly economic publication.
Periodicals: In Turkish, English, and French.*Bizim Anadolu* (www.bizimanadolu.com) is a monthly newspaper. The State Institute of Statistics (www.turkstat.gov.tr) publish yearbooks.
Broadcasting
The national broadcaster is the Türkiye Radyo ve Televizyon Kurumu (TRT) (www.trt.net.tr).
Radio: TRT (www.trt.net.tr) has six stations, providing a national, regional and local network, which includes news, education and cultural programmes, modern and traditional music and programmes for foreign tourists. There are numerous commercial radio stations based in all regions, including Kanal D (www.kanald.com.tr), Radio Sok (www.asyaradyo.com) (Adana), Radyo Marti (www.radyomarti.net) (Antalya), Radyo Net (www.vizeradyonet.com) (Ankara) and Metro FM (www.metrofm.com.tr) (Istanbul).
Television: TRT (www.trt.net.tr) operates four national channels. There are many subscriber cable and satellite television services available with programmes in Turkish, Kurdish and Arabic. Major TV networks include NTV MSNBC (www.ntv.com.tr), Pusula (www.pusula.tv), Samanyolu Haber TV (www.samanyoluhaber.com), Sky Turk (www.skyturk.tv) and Ulusal Kanal (www.ulusalkanal.com.tr).
National news agency: Anadolu Agency
Other news agencies: Anka News Agency (www.ankaajansi.com.tr) Turkish News Agency (www.turkishnewsagency.com)

Economy
Turkey has a mixed economy, dominated by the service sector, which in 2014 contributed 65 per cent to GDP. Industry provided 27 per cent, of which manufacturing constituted 18 per cent of total GDP and agriculture 8.2 per cent. Despite Turkey being increasingly driven by its industry and service sectors, agriculture still employs about 25 per cent of the workforce. An aggressive privatization program has reduced state involvement in light industry, banking, transport, and communication, and an emerging number of middle-class entrepreneurs, which is improving diversification within the economy. The automotive, construction, and electronics industries are rising in importance and have surpassed textiles within Turkey's export mix. FDI in Turkey reached nearly US$195 billion in 2014.
Turkey's economy retains significant weaknesses, specifically Turkey's relatively high current account deficit and domestic political uncertainty. Turkey also remains dependent on often volatile, short-term investment to finance its large deficit.
Several gas pipeline projects are moving forward to help transport Caspian gas to Europe through Turkey, which over the long term will help address Turkey's dependence on imported oil and gas, which currently meets 97 per cent of its energy needs.
The tourist sector has increased in importance for over a decade, so that by 2014 there were 37 million foreign tourists contributing a total of 12 per cent to total GDP. The majority of visitors arrived from the Organisation for Economic Co-Operation and Development (OECD) countries of Europe. The volume of tourists did not fall even though the global economic crisis in 2008 cut into the disposable income of foreign holidaymakers. As the euro rose in value during 2008–09 European-Mediterranean holidays became progressively more expensive and Turkey was seen as a more economical destination.
Industrial production is centred on textile and clothing manufacturing, consumer electronics and electrical goods, vehicle assembly and automotive parts and shipbuilding. Turkey is self-sufficient in food production and is a world leader in production of hazelnuts, cherries, figs, apricots, quinces and pomegranates and is second in producing watermelons, cucumbers and chickpeas with its surplus sold for export. Livestock farming and by-products contribute around 30 per cent of overall output; fishing and aquaculture are also important components of the agricultural sector.
GDP growth in 2007 was 4.7 per cent, falling to 0.7 per cent in 2008 as the economic crisis cut worldwide trade and investment. The economy fell into recession in the first quarter of 2009 with an annual rate of -4.8 per cent. In 2010 as world trade picked up, GDP growth surged to 9 per cent, led by private consumption and investment, before weakening slightly to an 8.5 per cent in 2011 and eventually falling to a more stable 4.4 per cent in 2013. Economic growth has slowed to a mediocre 2.9 per cent in 2014.
In 2009, the currency was renamed the Turkish lira, with the issuing of new banknotes and coins. Since then it has appreciated in value, prompting the Türkiye Cumhuriyet Merkez Bankasi (TCMB) (Central Bank of the Republic of Turkey) to moderate some policy measures and to de-couple the behaviour of the Turkish lira exchange rate from other emerging market currencies. When signs in 2011 indicated deterioration in global markets the TCMB reversed its policies and applied more controls, contributing to the domestic slowdown. Inflation stood at 7.5 per cent in 2013. Inflation has since increased further to 8.9 per cent in 2014.

External trade
Turkey is a member of the regionally based, Islamic, intergovernmental Economic Co-operation Organisation (ECO), comprising 10 regional Central Asian countries that promote economic, technical and cultural development between member countries. Turkey has trade agreements with its neighbours in the Black Sea Economic Co-operation Organisation (BSEC), which promotes trade and investment among the 11 regional member states. Turkey is also a signatory

of the Euro-Mediterranean Partnership agreement, which provides for the introduction of free trade between the EU and 10 Mediterranean countries.

Turkey has been in negotiation for entry to the European Union since 1987, but has yet to resolve the issue of Cyprus and the Turkish Republic of Northern Cyprus (TRNC). In 2014, negotiations were still underway. Turkey has a customs union with the EU, although this is hampered by Turkish refusal to allow Cypriot vessels to dock at its ports.

Manufacturing consists principally of textiles and clothing and consumer electronics and electrical goods, vehicle assembly and automotive parts and shipbuilding.

Turkey exports many agricultural products and is the world's third largest exporter of tobacco.

Turkey is ideally placed to carry oil and natural gas between the Middle East, Central Asia and Europe (including the Baku-Tbilisi-Ceyhan (Btc) pipeline).

Imports

Principal imports include machinery, chemicals, semi-finished goods, fuels and transport equipment.

Main sources: Russia (10.4 per cent of total in 2014), China (10.3 per cent), Germany (9.2 per cent), US (5.3 per cent), Italy (5 per cent) and Iran (4.1 per cent).

Exports

Principal exports are apparel, foodstuffs, textiles, metal manufactures and transport equipment.

Main destinations: Germany (9.6 per cent of total in 2014), Iraq (6.9 per cent), UK (6.3 per cent), Italy (4.5 per cent), France (4.1 per cent) and the US (4 per cent).

Agriculture

Farming

Turkey is self-sufficient in food and agriculture accounted for around 8.5 per cent of GDP in 2014, over 11 per cent of exports and employed about 26 per cent of the labour force.

The mainstays of Turkish agriculture are wheat and sheep, although there has been an increase in fruit and vegetable production as well as growth in regional crops such as tea, tobacco, cotton and hazelnuts. Turkey expects to become a leading cotton producer over the next 10 years.

Turkey is the world's largest producer of hazelnuts (70 per cent of the world supply). Production is dominated by Fiskorbirlik, the state-run hazelnut farmers' co-operative.

The Great Anatolian Project (GAP) irrigation project, although incomplete, has already raised production and productivity considerably: according to official figures, wheat production nationally has jumped 64 per cent since 1985, barley production by 42 per cent and cotton production by almost 500 per cent. Rice, wheat, soybeans and potatoes are now produced in more than minimal amounts for the first time. The project will irrigate some 1.8 million hectares (ha), 25 per cent of which will be given over to cotton production. The main part of the project was completed at the end of 2012. However, date for full competition is not yet known.

Agricultural exports include tobacco, cotton, dried fruit (hazelnuts, seedless raisins, figs, and apricots), pulses (chickpeas and lentils), live sheep, goats, fresh fruits (apples and citrus fruits) and fresh tomatoes. Cereals, especially wheat and barley, are Turkey's most important crops.

Imports, particularly of dairy products and beef, are growing faster than exports. Significant quantities of rice and processed food products are also imported. Liberal trade policies have opened up markets for imports of both cotton and burley tobacco.

Fishing

Salt-water fishing contributes to 77 per cent of the total fishery production, with 62 per cent of the catches obtained from the Black Sea. Anchovies remain the traditional catch with a potential for further processing. Fishery production also thrives on horse mackerel, whiting and bonito. The main production area for inland fisheries is Lake Van, where grey mullets are mainly caught. The Atatürk Dam and other smaller dams, which were constructed under the Southeast Anatolian Project (GAP), have increased the potential for inland fisheries by over 9,000 tonnes.

Trout constitute more than 60 per cent of the total aquaculture production, 25 per cent of which is obtained from the Aegean Sea. Turkey mainly exports large quantities of canned tuna to the EU and other developed countries.

Forestry

Forest and other wooded land accounts for 15 per cent of total land area. Most of the forest is available for wood supply, although it is moderately used for fuel consumption. Only a small area of forest is owned by the state.

Turkey produces a significant quantity of industrial roundwood. Major forest industries rely on local resources for the production of sawnwood, particleboard and plywood. The pulp and paper industry is able to meet domestic demand by imports.

Industry and manufacturing

Industry accounted for 27.1 per cent of GDP in 2013 and employs approximately 26 per cent of the labour force.

There have been high levels of industrial growth since the mid-1970s, despite low levels of capital investment and plant utilisation. There has also been rapid development of light industry, general diversification and growth in exports of manufactured goods.

Main areas of specialisation include textiles, ready-to-wear clothes, ceramics and glass, iron and steel, chrome, chemicals and light consumer goods.

The industrial sector is still dominated by large state-owned industries. These State Economic Enterprises are mainly engaged in textiles, food processing, chemicals, metals and motor vehicle production. The food processing sector is growing rapidly and agricultural products continue to provide a large proportion of export revenue.

Turkey's non-state industrial sector is dominated by a number of family-run conglomerates. Koç Holding is the largest, with 108 companies operating in 10 core sectors. Koç produces one-third of Turkey's cars, most of its fridges and televisions and owns the biggest supermarket chain. Sabanci Holdings, which has 50 operating companies, is active in chemicals, textiles, cars, banking, and supermarkets. The third-largest conglomerate, Çukorova, is active in commercial vehicles, paper and mobile telephones, although it is concentrating its efforts on the finance sector. There are also dozens of smaller conglomerates with up to 33 companies.

The textile sector, once one of the engines of Turkish economic growth, is losing the interest of the major conglomerates that dominate Turkey's industrial structure.

Tourism

Although Turkey is the site of the world's oldest known temple, at Göbekli Tepe, and the ancient city of Troy, as well as the classical city of Byzantium (later renamed Constantinople and then during the Ottoman Empire, Istanbul), tourist activity is concentrated along the coasts of the Aegean and Mediterranean Seas, where the bulk of accommodation is concentrated. There are 10 sites included on Unesco's World Heritage List, which ranges from cultural to mixed cultural and natural sites. There is a growing market of visitors travelling to spars and clinics in Turkey for health and wellness. Turkey is large and diverse enough to offer many activities, in both summer and winter.

Most visitors (37 million in 2014) enjoy competitively priced packaged holiday deals in coastal resorts.

Infrastructure facilities are good with a comprehensive road network, ferries, international and domestic flights, plus a reliable rail network.

Travel and tourism has grown to be an important component of the economy, contributing 12 per cent (2014) to GDP and providing employment for 8.2 per cent of the workforce (2.1 million jobs). The southern and south-eastern regions may not be safe for tourists, due to instability in neighbouring countries and a simmering Kurdish insurgency.

Mining

Substantial mineral reserves exist, including copper, zinc, lead, iron ore, coal and lignite. Deposits of borax, wolfram and chromite are internationally significant. Turkey is the world's second-largest producer of boron and a leading exporter of chrome. Etibank controls 60 per cent of all mining activity.

Hydrocarbons

Proven oil reserves were 295 million barrels in 2014, located mainly in the south-east. Production has fallen by half, from its peak of 85,290 barrels per day (bpd) in 1991 to 47,340 bpd in 2014. Consumption was 728,400 bpd in 2014 so Turkey relies on imported petroleum products, notably from Russia as well as Middle Eastern countries such as Libya and Algeria. The state-owned Turkish Petroleum Corporation (TPAO) is responsible for exploration, distribution, trading, services and storage of oil and gas. There are five oil refineries processing 728,400bpd.

Turkey has a strategic position as a hub and transit country for oil and gas pipelines. The Baku-Tbilisi-Ceyhan (BTC) 1,760km oil pipeline was opened in 2005, it carries oil from Azerbaijan's port of Baku, through Georgia, then across Turkey to its Mediterranean port of Ceyhan. The pipeline has a capacity of one million bpd. The Nabucco natural gas pipeline is planned to follow this and branch off towards Europe at Erzurum in central Turkey. A conference was convened in Prague, in May 2009, for gas exporting countries in Central Asia and the Middle East including Turkey and hosted by the EU. The purpose was to state the EU's seriousness as a buyer of natural gas and its commitment to new gas pipelines and trade between the EU and gas exporters and to end the wrangling that has halted progress on the 3,300km Nabucco pipeline. The pipeline is predicted to be completed by 2018.

Other proposed gas pipelines to transit Turkey originate in Egypt, Iraq, Iran and Saudi Arabia.

Turkey has natural gas reserves of 6.8 billion cubic metres (cum) in 2014, with production at 537 million cum per day and consumption at 45.6 billion cum the balance must be imported. Turkey's domestic gas consumption has quadrupled since 1992, reflecting government policy of increasing use of gas. Gas is cleaner, plentiful in neighbouring countries and allows Turkey to diversify energy sources and increase energy security. Turkey can charge transit fees, as well as bring neighbouring post-Soviet republics into its sphere of influence.

Exploration of gas fields centres on the western Black Sea, off Turkey's coast.

Proven coal reserves were 8.7 billion tonnes in 2013 - mostly sub-bituminous and lignite (brown) coal which is typically used for power generation and which is generally of poor quality and highly polluting. Production stood at 13.5 million tonnes oil equivalent (mtoe), down 13.2 per cent from the 2012 figure, and consumption was 33mtoe.

Energy

Total installed generating capacity was 69.7 GW in 2014, with around 75 per cent coming from thermal sources. Installed power generation capacity is set to increase to 100 GW by 2023.

Turkey is a net energy importer (about 60 per cent of its energy requirements) and is Europe's fastest-growing energy market. Demand still outstrips supply and the country experiences blackouts and industrial losses as a result of the energy bottleneck.

The Ministry of Energy and Natural Resources has responsibility for over viewing the private energy companies that generate, distribute and supply electricity wholesale and retail.

On 3 April 2011, the Kurdistan ministry of electricity signed a US$18 million contract with the Turkish energy company Shar to connect electricity power lines between the provinces of Sulaimaniya (Iraq) and Erbil (Turkey).

Financial markets

Stock exchange

Istanbul Menkul Kiymetler Borsasi (IMKB) (Istanbul Stock Exchange)

Commodity exchange

The Istanbul Gold Exchange (IGE) includes silver and platinum spot trading.

Banking and insurance

Central bank

Türkiye Cumhuriyet Merkez Bankasi (TCMB) (Central Bank of the Republic of Turkey)

Time

GMT plus two hours (daylight saving, late March to late October, GMT plus three hours)

Geography

Turkey is mostly situated in Asia Minor on the Anatolian peninsula, which is bordered to the north-east by Georgia and Armenia, to the east by Iran, and to the south by Iraq and Syria. Part of the country reaches into Europe, occupying eastern Thrace (Trakiya), which is separated from the rest of Turkey by the inland Sea of Marmara and is bordered to the west by Greece and Bulgaria. Turkey has an extensive coastline with the Black Sea to the north, the Mediterranean Sea to the south and the Aegean Sea to the west. The Sea of Marmara links the Black Sea and the Aegean Sea.

Turkey is a mountainous country, over three-quarters of which exceeds 500m elevation and averages 1,130m. The highest point is Mount Ararat (Agri Dagi) in the east, reaching 5,165m. There are two major ranges: the North Anatolian mountains in the north and the Taurus mountains in the south. Many short, fast rivers flow down from the mountains, as well as the great Tigris and Euphrates rivers, which rise in the mountains of eastern Turkey, where practically all the water they carry down to the Persian Gulf is generated. There are numerous lakes, the largest of which is Lake Van to the east near the Iranian border.

Hemisphere

Northern

Climate

Coastal regions have a Mediterranean climate, with mild, moist winters and hot, dry summers. The interior plateau has low and irregular rainfall, cold and snowy winters and hot, almost rainless summers. Ankara: 0–23 degrees Celsius (C) (Jan–Jul); annual rainfall 367mm. Istanbul: 5–23 degrees C (Jan–Jul); annual rainfall 723mm. Ismir: 8–27 degrees C (Jan–Jul); annual rainfall 700mm.

Dress codes

Although the population is predominantly Muslim, Turkey is a secular state and for the visitor daily life in cities and tourist areas is similar to that in Europe. However, in rural areas, standards are much more conservative and women should be cautious in their dress. They should wear clothing which covers most of the body and probably also a headscarf, or at least be able to cover their hair if the need arises. Topless bathing is illegal but tolerated on southern and Aegean tourist beaches.

Dress for formal occasions is conservative and men normally wear a dark business suit or formal dress. Ties are almost always worn for business meetings. Turkish women dress formally for most social occasions.

Entry requirements

Passports

Required by all, valid for at least three months from date of departure, with exception of nationals of Belgium, France,

Germany, Greece, Italy, Luxmbourg, Malta, the Netherlands and Spain.

Visa

Required by all, except nationals of some EU and other European, Latin American, Middle East and Asian countries and New Zealand. Details of requirements for individual countries can be found at www.turkishconsulate.org.uk/en/visa.htm.

Currency advice/regulations

There are no restrictions on the import of local or foreign currencies. Visitors bringing in a large amount of foreign currency should have it recorded in their passports by the Turkish authorities. Export of local and foreign currencies is restricted to US$5,000. Currency exchange slips should be retained.

Travellers cheques can be cashed in banks, but cash in euros or US$ is preferred.

Customs

Personal effects and gifts up to the value of eur255.65 may be brought in duty-free. It is advisable to retain invoices and foreign currency exchange slips to cover value of purchases. Export of antiques is prohibited.

Health (for visitors)

Mandatory precautions

Cholera certificate required if travelling from an infected area.

Advisable precautions

Anti-malaria and anti-cholera precautions are advisable. Hepatitis and rabies are prevalent in all areas, and there have been outbreaks of cholera in eastern Turkey. Malaria tablets should be taken for travel to the Adana area and inoculation against cholera and typhoid for travel to the south-eastern region is advised. A tetanus booster if travelling to central and eastern Anatolia is recommended.

Tap water is unpalatable due to heavy chlorination. Bottled water is easily obtainable in food stores. Medicines are easy to purchase without prescription in local pharmacies. The location of a nearby all-night pharmacy is displayed in any pharmacy window. Medical services are adequate in main city hospitals like Istanbul's American and German hospitals.

Hotels

Classified into five categories – deluxe and first- to fourth-class. Prices vary and many hotels reduce their rates between mid-Oct and mid-Apr. A service charge of 15 per cent usually added and tipping is extra; 18 per cent VAT is also added. Advance reservations are advisable. Tap water is safe in major hotels.

Credit cards

Access, Diners Club, Visa, American Express and Eurocard are accepted in most hotels, restaurants and shops, and can be used to withdraw money from automatic cash dispensers at banks.

Public holidays (national)

Fixed dates

1 Jan (New Year's Day), 23 Apr (National Sovereignty/Children's Day), 19 May (Atatürk Commemoration/Youth and Sports Day), 30 Aug (Victory Day), 29 Oct (Republic Day).

Variable dates

Eid al Adha (four days), Eid al Fitr (three days).

Islamic year 1437 (15 Oct 2015–2 Oct 2016):: The Islamic year contains 354 or 355 days, with the result that Muslim feasts advance by 10–12 days against the Gregorian calendar. Dates of feasts vary according to the sighting of the new moon, so cannot be forecast exactly.

Working hours

Banking

Mon–Fri: 0830–1230; 1330–1700.

Business

Mon–Fri: 0830–1200; 1300–1730.

Government

Mon–Fri: 0830–1230; 1330–1730.

Shops

Mon–Sat: 0900–1300; 1400–1900.

Many flower shops open late. Pharmacies display the location of one opening late. Many food shops open on Sun.

Telecommunications

Mobile/cell phones

GSM 1800 and 900 services are available throughout most of the country.

Electricity supply

220V AC, 50Hz (110V in parts of Istanbul).

Social customs/useful tips

Hospitality is very important. Turkey is a Muslim country and religion plays an important part in Turkish life. Practically all business entertaining is conducted in restaurants and clubs.

Personal contact is the key to doing business. Bureaucracy tends to be the greatest obstacle for foreigners. Information is most easily and efficiently obtained by going directly to the top of any organisation, government or private.

It is polite when visiting the home of a business associate to bring a gift of chocolates, flowers or cake. When entering you may be asked to take off your shoes and put on slippers. Do not be critical of Ataturk, the founder of the Republic, and avoid discussion of Kurds, Armenians and other minorities.

Security

Levels of petty crime in main cities are comparable to those in most Western European cities.

Ultra-leftist and Kurdish terrorists are active in Istanbul and other western cities but do not constitute more than a minor threat. Visitors to south-eastern Turkey are advised to travel only during daylight hours and on major roads. The police monitor checkpoints on roads throughout the south-eastern region. Drivers and all passengers in the vehicle should be prepared to provide identification if stopped at a checkpoint.

Getting there

Air

National airline: Turkish Airlines

International airport/s: Ankara-Esenboga (ESB), 35km north-east of the city; duty-free shop, bank, restaurants and bars.

Istanbul-Atatüürk (IST), 24km west of the city; duty-free shop, bank, restaurant, bar and car hire.

Istanbul-Sabiha Gökçen (SAW), 32km east of the city. With bank, duty-free shop, restaurants and business centre.

Airport tax: None

Surface

Road: Coach services are available from Austria, France, Germany and Switzerland, as well as a number of countries in the Middle East.

There are connecting routes from the CIS, Greece, Bulgaria and Iran. It is possible to select the northern route via Belgium, Germany, Austria or the southern route through Belgium, Austria and Italy with a car-ferry connection to Turkey.

Rail: Express rail services from Munich, Vienna, Budapest and Bucharest. Connections are available from London (Liverpool Street) via the Hook of Holland and Cologne to Istanbul on the Istanbul Express, which also transports cars from other European cities.

Water: Turkish Maritime Lines (TML), the national shipping organisation, and several other cruise lines operate services to Turkey. There are ferry connections with Italy, Cyprus and Greece. For the one-day ferry from the Greek island of Rhodes to Marmaris, a visa is not required.

Getting about

National transport

Air: Turkish Airlines operate regular services between Istanbul, Izmir, Ankara and other major towns. Bodrum regional airport offers internal flights and connections to other nearby Mediterranean destinations. Travelling by air within Turkey is relatively inexpensive.

Road: The Tarsus-Pozanti-Ayrimi-Gaziantep (Tag) motorway connects the southern Antolian region with the rest of Turkey, providing a vital link for the future growth of the region. There has been an extensive road building and maintenance programme in operation since 1999 involving over 1,400km of motorway.

Buses: Many private companies operate day and night services between all cities. Services are generally quicker than trains and prices are competitively low.

Rail: There is 8,542km of rail track. Most major cities and towns are linked by regular rail services. Prime Minister Erdogan opened a new railway tunnel under the Bosphorus Strait on 29 October 2013. The 1.4km tunnel was begun in 2004 and cost some US$4 billion. Initially only a limited part will be in operation.

Water: There are steamship services between Istanbul and most major coastal towns. Car ferries that offer cabins are highly sought-after and should be booked in advance.

City transport

Taxis: Metered taxis available in major towns and cities. Also available are the much cheaper *Dolmus* taxis, which have fixed routes and carry 8–12 passengers. Tipping not customary. For longer journeys the fare should be agreed beforehand. Drivers rarely speak much English and may be new to the city, so advisable to carry a road map.

Buses, trams & metro: Metros run in three of Turkey's main cities — Ankara, Istanbul and Izmir — and are planned for Bursa and Adana.

Car hire

All international companies are represented. Available at main hotels, airports and travel agents but expensive. International driving licence preferred, but most foreign licences accepted. Driving is on the right.

BUSINESS DIRECTORY

The addresses listed below are a selection only. While World of Information makes every endeavour to check these addresses, we cannot guarantee that changes have not been made, especially to telephone numbers and area codes. We would welcome any corrections.

Telephone area codes

The international direct dialling code (IDD) for Turkey is +90, followed by area code and subscriber's number:

Adana	322	Istanbul (Thrace)	212
Ankara	312		
Bursa	224	Izmir	232
Dlyarbakir	412	Kayseri	352
Gaziantep	342	Konya	332
Istanbul (Anatolia)	216	Malatya	422
		Samsun	362

Chambers of Commerce

Adana Chamber of Commerce, 52 Abidinpasa Cadessi, Adana (tel: 352-0052; fax: 351-8009; e-mail: basanlik@adan-to.org.tr).

American-Turkish Business Association, Emlak Kredi Bloklari, Levent, 80620 Istanbul (tel: 270-6718; fax: 279-0031; e-mail: taba@taba.org.tr).

Ankara Chamber of Commerce, 2 Sogutozu Mahallesi, 06530 Ankara (tel: 285-7950; fax: 284-2314; info@atonet.org.tr).

British Chamber of Commerce in Turkey, 18 Mesrutiyet Cadessi, Galatasaray, 34435 Istanbul (tel: 249-0658; fax: 252-5551; e-mail: buscenter@bcct.org.tr).

Istanbul Chamber of Commerce, Resadiye Cadessi, Eminonu, 34378 Istanbul (tel: 455-6000; fax: 513-1565; e-mail: ito@ito.org.tr).

Izmir Chamber of Commerce, 126 Ataturk Cadessi , Pasaport, 35210 Izmir (tel: 441-7777; fax: 446-2251; e-mail: info@izto.org.tr).

Kayseri Chamber of Commerce, 6 Tennuri Sokak, 38040 Kayseri (tel: 222-4528; fax: 232-1069; e-mail: kaytic@kayserito.org.tr).

Konya Chamber of Commerce, 1 Vatan Cadessi, 42040 Konya (tel: 353-4850; fax: 353-0546; e-mail: kto@kto.org.tr).

Samsun Chamber of Commerce and Industry, Hancerli Mahallesi, 8 Abbasasa Sokak, 55020 Samsun (tel: 432-3626; fax: 432-9055; e-mail: samsuntso@samsuntso.org.tr).

Turkey Union of Chambers of Commerce, Industry, Maritime Trade and Commodity Exchanges, 149 Ataturk Bulvari, Bakanlyklar, Ankara (tel: 413-8000; fax: 418-3268; e-mail: info@tobb.org.tr).

Banking

Akbank, Sabanci Center, 80745 4.Levent, Istanbul (tel: 270-2666/0044; fax: 269-7383/8081).

Demirbank, Büyükdere Cadessi 122, 80280 Esentepe, Istanbul (tel: 275-1900; fax: 267-4794/2786).

Esbank, Eskisehir Bankasi, Mesrutiyet Cadessi 141, 80050 Tepebasi, Istanbul (tel: 251-7270; fax: 243-2396).

Garanti Bank, 63 Buyukdere Caddesi, Maslak 80670 Istanbul (tel/fax: 335-3535).

Koçbank, Barbaros Bulvari, Morbasan Sokak, Koza Is Merkezi C Blok, 80692 Besiktas, Istanbul (tel: 274-7777; fax: 267-2987).

Pamukbank, Büyükdere Cadessi 82, 80450 Gayrettepe, Istanbul (tel: 275-2424; fax: 275-8606).

Türkiye Is Bankasi, Atatürk Bulvari 191, 06684 Kavaklidere, Ankara (tel: 428-1140; fax: 425-0750/2).

Yapi ve Kredi Bankasi, Büyükdere Cadessi Yapi Kredi Plaza, A Blok, 80620 Levent, Istanbul (tel: 280-1111; fax: 280-1670/1).

Central bank

Türkiye Cumhuriyet Merkez Bankasy, Ystiklal Cadessi 10 Ulus, 06100 Ankara (tel: 310-3646; fax: 310-7434; e-mail: info@tcmb.gov.tr).

Stock exchange

Istanbul Menkul Kiymetler Borsasi (IMKB) (Istanbul Stock Exchange), www.ise.org

Commodity exchange

The Istanbul Gold Exchange (IGE) includes silver and platinum spot trading.

Travel information

Turkish Airlines, General Administration Building, Ataturk Airport Yesilkoy, Istanbul (tel: 463-6363; fax: 465-2121; e-mail: turkishairlines@thy.com).

Ministry of tourism

Ministry of Culture and Tourism, Atatürk Bulvari 29, 06050 Opera, Ankara (tel: 309-0850; fax: 312-4359; e-mail: kultur@kultur.gov.tr).

National tourist organisation offices

Tourism Information Office, Gazi Mustafa Kemal Bulvari 121, Ankara (tel: 488-7007; fax: 231-5572).

Ministries

President's Office, Cankaya, Ankara (tel: 468-5030; fax: 427-1330; internet site: www.cankaya.gov.tr).

Prime Minister's Office, Bakanliklar, Ankara (tel: 419-5896; fax: 417-0476; internet site: www.basbakanlik.gov.tr).

Ministry of Agriculture and Rural Affairs, Ataturk Bulvari 153, Ankara (tel: 417-6000; fax: 417-7168).

Ministry of Defence, Ankara (tel: 425-4596; fax: 418-1795).

Ministry of Education, Ataturk Bulvari, Ankara (tel: 419-1410; fax: 417-7027).

Ministry of Energy and Natural Resources, Inonu Bulvari 27, Ankara (tel: 212-6915; fax: 212-3816).

Ministry of the Environment, Eskisehir Yolu, Ankara (tel: 287 9965; fax: 285-2742).

Ministry of Finance, Ankara (tel: 425-0080; fax: 425-0058; internet site: www.maliye.gov.tr).

Ministry of Foreign Affairs, Balgat, Ankara (tel: 287-1665; fax: 287-8811).

Ministry of Forestry, Ataturk Bulvari 153, Ankara (tel: 417-6000; fax: 213-2610).

Ministry of Health, Sihhiye, Ankara (tel: 431-4820; fax: 431-4879).

Ministry of Industry and Trade, Eskisehir Yolu, Ankara (tel: 286-0365; fax: 285-4318).

Ministry of the Interior, Ankara (tel: 418-1368; fax: 418-1795).

Ministry of Justice, Ankara (tel: 419-6050; fax: 417-3954).

Ministry of Labour and Social Security, Inonu Bulvari, Ankara (tel: 212-9700; fax: 215-4962).

Ministry of Public Works and Housing, Vekaletler Cad 1, Ankara (tel: 417-9260; fax: 418-5540).

Ministry of Transport, Ankara (tel: 212-4416; fax: 212-4930).

Other useful addresses

Borsa Komiserligi (stock exchange), Menkul Kiymetler ve Kambiyo Borsasi, Rihtim Caddesi 245, 80030 Karakoy, Istanbul (tel: 298-2100; fax: 298-2500; internet site: http://www.ise.org).

British Consulate General Ankara, Merutiyet Caddesi No 34, Tepebasi, Beyoglu PK33, Ankara (tel: 293-7450; fax: 245-4989).

British Embassy, Sehit Ersan Caddesi 46/A, Cankaya, Ankara (tel: 468-6230/42; fax: 468-3214).

Customs Modernisation Project, Gümrük Müstesarligi, Anafartalar Cad No 6 Kat 14, 06100, Ulus, Ankara (tel: 306-8532, 306-8439; fax: 306-8535).

Director General of Mining, Ankara (tel: 287-9750; fax: 287-9152).

Director General of Press and Publications, Ankara (tel: 468-4967; fax: 468-4966).

Director General of State Water Affairs, Ankara (tel: 418-3415; fax: 418-3409).

Director General of Telecommunications, Ankara (tel: 313-1121; fax: 313-1919).

Embassy of the United States of America, 110 Ataturk Blvd, Ankara (tel: 426-5470, 468-6110; fax: 467-0057/19).

Export Promotion Centre (IGEME), Mithatpasa Cad No 60, Kisilay, Ankara (tel: 418-5351; internet site: http://www.igeme.org.tr).

General Directorate of Foreign Investment, Inönü Bulvari, 06510 Emek, Ankara (tel: 212-8914/5; fax: 212-8916).

Housing Development Administration, Project Implementation Unit, Bilkent Plaza, B1 Blok Kat 1, Bilkent 06530, Ankara (tel: 266-7764, 266-7774; fax: 266-7733).

Modern Tercume Burosu (translation service), Karanfil Sokak 21/4, Yenisehir, Ankara (tel: 417-8122).

Privatisation Administration, Ziya Gokalp Street No 80, Kurtulus 06600 Ankara (tel: 430-0194, 430-4560; fax: 430-6930; e-mail: hascili@oib.gov.tr).

State Institute of Statistics, Necatibey Caddesi 114, Ankara (tel: 417-6440; internet site: http://www.die.gov.tr/ENGLISH/index.html).

State Planning Organisation, Necatibey Caddesi 108, Ankara (tel: 417-6440; internet site: http://www.dpt.gov.tr).

Türk Argus Ajansi (translation service), Lamartin Caddesi 32/4 Taksim, Istanbul (tel: 250-5200).

Türk Haberler Ajansi (news agency), Turkocagi Caddesi 1/4, Cagaloglu, Istanbul (tel: 511-4200).

Turkish Embassy (USA), 2525 Massachusetts Avenue, NW, Washington DC 20008 (tel: (+1-202) 612-6700; fax: (+1- 202) 612-6744; e-mail: info@turkey.org).

Turkish International Co-operation Agency, Kizilirmak Cadessi 31, Kocatepe, Ankara (tel: 417-2790).

Türkiye Radyo Televizyon Kurumu, Nevzat Tandogan Caddesi 2, Kavaklidere, Ankara (tel: 428-2230; fax: 414-2767).

Türk Snayicileri ve Isadamlari Dernegi (association of Turkish industrialists and businessmen), Cumhuriyet Caddesi, 233/9-10 Harbiye, Istanbul (tel: 246-2412, 240-1205).

National news agency: Anadolu Agency, Anadolu Ajansi, Genel Müdürlügü, Gazi Mustafa Kemal Bulvari 128/C, Tandogan, Ankara (tel: 231-7000; internet: www.aa.com.tr).

Anka News Agency (www.ankaajansi.com.tr)

Turkish News Agency (www.turkishnewsagency.com)

Internet sites

Foreign Trade Secretariat: http://dtm.gov.tr

Republic of Turkey: http://www.turkey.org

State Institute of Statistics: http://www.die.gov.tr

Treasury Secretariat: http://www.treasury.gov.tr

Turkish Foreign Trade and Tourism Centre: http://www.turkex.com

Turkish highways: http://www.kgm.gov.tr/indexe.htm

Turkmenistan

KEY FACTS

Official name: Türkmenistan Jumhuriyati (Republic of Turkmenistan)

Head of State: President Gurbanguly Berdymukhamedov (TDP) (from 2007; re-elected 12 Feb 2012)

Head of government: President Gurbanguly Berdymukhamedov

Ruling party: Türkmenistanyn Demokratik partiýasy (TDP) (Turkmenistan Democratic Party)

Area: 488,100 square km

Population: 5.80 million (2014)*

Capital: Ashgabat

Official language: Turkmen

Currency: New Manat (M) = 100 tennesi (The new manat was introduced on 1 January 2009, with an exchange rate of 5,000 old manat to one new manat).

Exchange rate: M3.50 per US$ (Sep 2015)

GDP per capita: US$8,271 (2014)*

GDP real growth: 10.32% (2014)*

GDP: US$47.93 billion (2014)*

Inflation: 5.95% (2014)*

Oil production: 239,000 bpd (2014)

Natural gas production: 69.30 billion cum (2014)

Balance of trade: US$875.00 million (2009)

Annual FDI: US$3.19 billion (2011)

* estimated figure

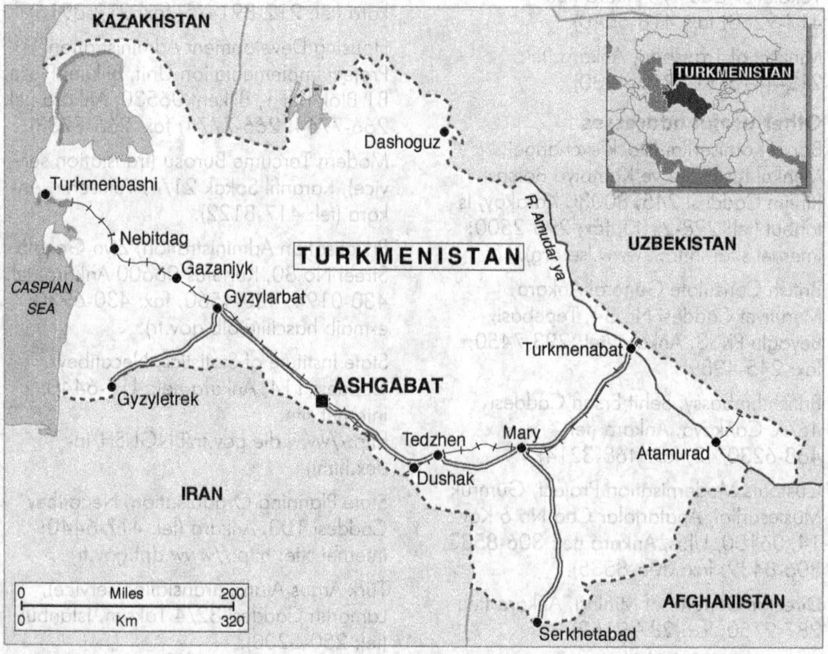

Politics in Turkmenistan offers little by way of security of tenure. In October 2015 the country's leader Gurbanguly Berdymukhamedov decided to sack a number of senior government officials, possibly *pour encourager les autres*, possibly because he could no longer ignore the rumours of extensive corruption and the slow pace of reforms in key sectors of the economy.

Ministers go

That ministers were dismissed on charges of corruption could come as no surprise to most Turkmen citizens. On the 2014 Transparency International *Corruption Perceptions Index* Turkmenistan could hardly rank lower, coming 169 out of the 175 countries surveyed, behind even Libya, Eritrea and Venezuela. President Berdymukhamedov, a 58-year-old former-dentist who had became president in late 2006, sacked his deputy prime minister, Annamukhamed Gochyev, 'for serious drawbacks in his work' not long after Mr Gochyev had reported to a government meeting the good news of the continued growth in the gas-fuelled economy. Mr Berdymukhamedov, a tough leader with something of a personality cult in his Central Asian nation of 5.5 million, said 'cases of bribery are not infrequent' in the economic and finance sector run by Gochyev. Mr Gochyev was the high visibility victim of a wider purge which had seen some 80 banking, tax and financial services workers charged with committing various crimes. President Berdymukhamedov had reportedly attacked his cabinet for the slow development of Turkmenistan's banking sector and the securities market. He added that key ministries had failed to assess the impact of the global crisis on Turkmenistan's economy. 'All this leads to big losses for the state,' he said, also sacking the country's economy and development minister, a deputy prime minister in charge of agriculture and the construction minister. Turkmenistan holds the world's fourth-largest reserves of natural gas, exports of which have fuelled rapid economic growth.

The economy

Just minutes before his sacking, Gochyev had announced that growth in gross domestic product (GDP) had slowed to 9.1 per cent in the first half of 2015 from 10.3 per cent in the same period of last year.

The International Monetary Fund (IMF) expected Turkmenistan's economic growth to decelerate to 9.0 per cent in 2015, down from 10.3 per cent in 2014 on the back of declining natural gas export revenues and lower public investment as a share of GDP.

Rumours in February 2015 that Turkmenistan's currency, the manat, was about to be devalued again saw queues form at exchange offices. At the start of the year, Turkmenistan's Central Bank of Turkmenistan had devalued the manat against the US dollar by 18 per cent and at the same time increased natural gas and gasoline prices. The January move raised the exchange rate to 3.50 manats per dollar, up from the previously fixed rate of 2.85 manats per dollar that had been in place since 2009.

According to the Asian Development Bank (ADB) high growth at 10.3 per cent in 2014 reflected robust public investment and gas exports. Strong foreign direct investment (FDI) nevertheless drove the current account to a deficit of 4.4 per cent of GDP. Growth is projected to slow to 9.7 per cent in 2015 and 9.2 per cent in 2016, and the current account deficit to widen further to 8.4 per cent of GDP before moderating to 6.2 per cent in 2016. Inflation is forecast to reach 7.0 per cent before subsiding to 6.5 per cent.

The government reported growth in 2014 at 10.3 per cent, slightly above 10.2 per cent a year earlier. The large hydrocarbon sector grew by 6.1 per cent, while the rest of the economy expanded twice as fast, by 13.0 per cent. On the supply side, industry and services were the main sources of growth. The government reported that industry expanded by 11.4 per cent in 2014, an improvement from 7.3 per cent in 2013 that reflected faster growth in hydrocarbons, electricity, chemicals, construction materials, textiles, and agro-industrial products. The expansion in the services sector slowed to 10.6 per cent from 12.7 per cent in 2013. Growth in agriculture decelerated to 4.2 per cent from 10.0 per cent in 2013 as unfavourable weather held wheat and livestock production below targets.

On the demand side, strong investment was the main source of growth. Public investment for infrastructure under the National Programme of Socio-Economic Development of Turkmenistan for 2012–16 expanded by 6.7 per cent in 2014, compared with 7.1 per cent in 2013. Despite some declines in prices for food and services in the first half of the year, inflation rose in the second half with the reduction of subsidies and the concomitant rise in charges for public transportation and utilities. Nevertheless, the consumer price index was estimated to have risen by only 6.0 per cent on an annual average basis, versus 6.8 per cent in 2013, as the government continued to administer prices for basic goods and services and maintained a fixed exchange rate through the end of 2014. Tighter monetary policy had helped slow broad money growth to 22.6 per cent from 31.1 per cent in 2013, and expansion in private sector credit is estimated to have slowed marginally to 45 per cent from 50 per cent. The government's fiscal surplus was estimated to have narrowed to 0.8 per cent of GDP from 1.5 per cent in 2013, reflecting higher outlays for social programmes and a 10 per cent increase in pensions, students' stipends, and public wages. Revenue was estimated at 16.4 per cent of GDP, and identified budget expenditure at 15.6 per cent. Public investment was also supported by off-budget resources. The large non-hydrocarbon fiscal deficit suggested that hydrocarbon revenues continued to finance growth in the rest of the economy. Public debt was estimated to have fallen to 16.8 per cent of GDP in 2014 from 21.1 per cent in 2013. Imports financed by FDI for large hydrocarbon projects pushed the current account to a deficit of 4.4 per cent of GDP. Exports were estimated to rise by 3.3 per cent in 2014, while imports grew by 1.8 per cent. FDI rose above US$4 billion to equal 8.7 per cent of GDP.

With hydrocarbons representing more than 90 per cent of exports, the continued decline in energy prices and fluctuating demand for Turkmen gas were likely to reduce export revenues, weakening the current account. However, Turkmenistan has strong external buffers, as the IMF estimated its foreign exchange reserves equal to 22 months of imports in 2014. Moreover, breakeven petroleum prices for the fiscal and external balance are considered to be the lowest in the region, providing some insulation against fluctuating energy prices.

GDP growth is projected to slow to 9.7 per cent in 2015 and 9.2 per cent in 2016, reflecting lower public investment. Growth was set to slow further if external difficulties persisted and required fiscal adjustment. On 1 January 2015, the government, as already mentioned, devalued the manat by 19 per cent to M3.50 per dollar from the previous M2.85, the first such adjustment in 7 years. The move was intended to keep non-energy exports competitive, ease pressure on the currency from falling energy prices, and offset some of the 40 per cent appreciation against the rouble during the second half of 2014.

Along with further price increases for gasoline and public utilities, the devaluation was likely to spur inflation to 7.0 per cent in 2015 before slowing to 6.5 per cent in 2016. To limit inflation, the government would continue its import substitution policies and price administration. The central bank was expected to tighten monetary policy by slowing credit expansion.

Growth in the money supply was forecast to slow to 19.0 per cent in 2015 from 22.6 per cent in 2014. The state budget for 2015 was planned to be broadly balanced and anticipated a 9.5 per cent rise in spending and a 13.0 per cent increase in revenues. Under current projections of low prices for hydrocarbons but some recovery in 2016, the current account deficit was forecast to widen to 8.4 per cent of

KEY INDICATORS — Turkmenistan

	Unit	2011	2012	2013	2014	**2015
Population	m	*5.53	*5.61	*5.70	*5.80	*5.89
Gross domestic product (GDP)	US$bn	24.11	35.16	41.01	*47.93	*44.66
GDP per capita	US$	4,722	6,263	*7,190	*8,271	*7,585
GDP real growth	%	9.9	11.1	10.2	*10.3	*9.0
Inflation	%	9.7	5.3	6.8	*6.0	*7.7
Oil output	'000 bpd	216.0	222.0	231.0	239.0	–
Natural gas output	bn cum	59.5	64.4	62.3	69.3	–
Exports (fob) (goods)	US$m	14,189.0	–	–	–	–
Imports (fob) (goods)	US$m	9,567.0	–	–	–	–
Balance of trade	US$m	4,622.0	–	–	–	–
Current account	US$m	569.0	15.0	*-2,984.0	*-2,852.0	*-4,945.0
Exchange rate	per US$	2.85	2.85	2.85	2.85	–

* estimated figure ** forecast figure

GDP in 2015 before narrowing to 6.2 per cent in 2016. External debt would remain low, decreasing to 18.6 per cent of GDP in 2015 and 16.4 per cent in 2016 as earlier loans were repaid.

Hydrocarbons

Despite Turkmenistan's vast oil and natural gas resource base, the US government Energy Information Administration (EIA) did not consider Turkmenistan as a major player in energy markets because of its lack of infrastructure, which limited its exporting capabilities. In the past few years, the country had increased investments to develop its reserves and export more natural gas to countries such as China. Total primary energy consumption in Turkmenistan was 1.242 quadrillion British thermal units in 2014 and had risen about 60 per cent over the previous decade, according to BP's Statistical Review of World Energy. Natural gas consumption accounted for approximately 80 per cent, and consumption of petroleum products represented the remaining 20 per cent.

Controlled by the Turkmenistan ministry of energy and industry, the electricity sector is fuelled almost entirely by natural gas. Turkmenistan's total installed generation capacity was nearly 4.3 gigawatts in 2014. Domestic electricity consumption fell below the country's gross generation of more than 22 billion kilowatt-hours, allowing the country to export the remaining production. Turkmenistan is linked to the Central Asian electricity grid and exports electricity to Afghanistan, Iran, and Turkey among other Central Asian countries.

In 2013, the government developed a policy of modernising and expanding its electricity sector by increasing transmission infrastructure and constructing 14 natural gas-fired electric power plants between 2013 and 2020. Turkmenistan had an estimated 600 million barrels of proven oil reserves as of January 2015. The country's estimated oil production in 2014 was 238,000 barrels per day (bpd), remaining roughly flat compared with 2013, which averaged 229,000 bpd.

In October 2015 Japan and Turkmenistan signed deals worth over US$18 billion on a package of projects in the chemicals and energy sectors. The occasion was the official visit of Japanese Prime Minister Shinzo Abe. Turkmenistan was reportedly interested in acquiring Japan's experience in creating and using new technologies. Japanese companies were already actively involved in large-scale projects in Turkmenistan, building plants to process natural gas into fertilisers, ethylene, polyethylene and polypropylene, as well as into liquid fuel. China has supplanted Russia as the main buyer of Turkmen gas in recent years, annually importing 30-35 billion cubic metres of the fuel. Moscow had angered Ashgabat with plans to cut its imports to 4 bcm from the 11 bcm of 2014.

Risk assessment

Politics	Poor
Economy	Fair/good
Regional stability	Good

Muslims in Turkministan

% of population	93.3
Sunni (% of Muslims)	99
Shi'a (% of Muslims)	1

COUNTRY PROFILE

Present-day Turkmenistan was divided three ways between Tsarist Russia and the Khanates of Bukhara and Khiva until 1881, when Russian troops captured Ashgabat and incorporated the country into Russian Turkestan. The fierce Turkmen tribes south of the Amu Darya River were subdued in 1885.

1917 Central Asian peoples were given the right of self-determination by Lenin after the October Revolution in Russia.

1916–21 Turkmens joined other Central Asians states in violently opposing a Russian decree conscripting them for non-combatant duties. They fought against the Bolsheviks during the Russian civil war. In 1921, Turkmenistan formed part of the Turkestan Autonomous Soviet Socialist republic (ASSR).

1924 Turkmenistan was given Union Republic status.

1920s–1930s The Soviet programmes of agricultural collectivisation and secularisation saw an upsurge in armed resistance and popular uprisings in Turkmenistan.

1960s The completion of the Kara-Kum canal led to a rapid expansion in cotton production. The canal is around 800km long and carries water from the Amu Darya River westwards to Mary and Ashgabat.

1971 Muhammad Gapusov was appointed head of the Turkmenistan Communist Party.

1985 Saparmurad Niyazov replaced Gapusov.

1989 Agzybirlik (Unity), a democratic front led by Turkmen intellectuals, was formed, but was banned the following year.

1990 Turkmenistan's Supreme Soviet declared economic and political independence from Moscow and elected Niyazov as its chairman (in effect, state president).

1991 Niyazov supported an attempted military coup against Soviet President Mikhail Gorbachev. Turkmenistan declared independence just before the collapse of the Soviet Union and joined the Commonwealth of Independent States (CIS).

1992 Turkmenistan adopted a new constitution, making the president head of government as well as head of state and giving him the option to appoint a prime minister. Niyazov was re-elected in a direct election in which he was the only candidate allowed to stand.

1993 The manat was introduced as the new national currency. The government began opening up the country to limited foreign investment in the country's oil and gas reserves.

1994 In parliamentary elections, all candidates were returned unopposed. In a referendum, President Niyazov's term of office was extended to 2002 without a new election.

1997 The private ownership of land was legalised.

1998 A natural gas pipeline to Iran was opened.

1999 Parliament made President Niyazov president for life. In parliamentary elections, all the elected officials were privately approved by the President.

2002 Turkmenistan became a full member of the Islamic Development Bank (IDB). The President renamed the months of the year after himself, his mother and his spiritual guide, the Ruhnama.

2003 Russian oil producer, Gazprom, agreed to buy 60 billion cubic metres of gas from Turkmenistan annually. The President cancelled a 1993 dual citizenship agreement with Russia, which sparked a diplomatic row with Moscow.

2004 An agreement on water resources was signed by the presidents of Turkmenistan and Uzbekistan. In parliamentary elections all 50 seats were filled by candidates supporting the president.

2006 President Niyazov died. The State Security Council named Deputy Prime Minister Gurbanguly Berdymukhamedov as acting president.

2007 Gurbanguly Berdymukhamedov was elected president with 89.2 per cent of the vote, beating five other candidates; turnout was 98.7 per cent. Turkmenistan Russia and Kazakhstan agreed to build a new gas pipeline north of the Caspian Sea to ensure gas supplies to Russia.

2008 Natural gas supplies to Iran were cut, during one of the coldest winters in many years. Turkmenistan blamed a technical fault but required Iran to pay more for a resumed supply. A new constitution was adopted that abolished the Khalk Maslakhaty (People's Council) and changed the structure of power including

the roles of parliament and the president. The Persian Islamic calendar imposed by the previous president was dropped and the old version re-adopted. The government removed references to the late president Niyazov from the national anthem. Names of months and days, cities, an airport and a meteorite, which were also named after Niyazov and his family, reverted to their original names. In parliamentary elections, 125 seats (out of 125) were won by the Türkmenistanyn Demokratik partiýasy (TDP) (Turkmenistan Democratic Party). They were the first multi-party elections ever held in the country; however due to the lack of time given to register political parties before the elections were called for the newly expanded parliament, opposition parties were unable to field any candidates and the TDP was the only party registered. Opposition groups and Western observers said the elections were a 'sham'; of the 288 candidates running for parliament 90 per cent belonged to the TDP and the rest were state-approved individuals.
2009 The new manat was introduced with an exchange rate of 5,000 old manat to one new manat. President Berdymukhamedov ceremonially began the construction of the latest channel to bring run-off water from the country's cotton fields across thousands of kilometres of desert to create an inland sea. The project, which began in 2000 with two other channels bi-secting the country and hundreds more planned to create feeder funnels, is estimated to cost US$20 billion. The first pipeline to transport Central Asian natural gas to China was opened. The pipeline starts at the Samandepe gas field and crosses Uzbekistan and Kazakhstan on its way to China.
2010 Turkmenistan requested a US$4.1 billion loan from China to develop its untapped South Yolotan natural gas field, which contains proven reserves of 2.8 trillion cubic metres of natural gas, with a further estimated 4–14 trillion cubic metres. The field is one of the world's largest gas fields.
2011 A military arms depot outside Abadan exploded in July, causing many deaths and widespread damage that sparked panic and mass looting. Prolonged power failures in the capital followed. In August it was announced that negotiations between Turkmenistan and the five European partnership countries (Austria, Bulgaria, Hungary, Romania, Turkey) of the Nabucco pipeline were to be held in Poland in September.
2012 Eight candidates took part in presidential elections on 12 February. Incumbent Gurbanguly Berdymukhamedov won 97.1 per cent of the vote; turnout was 96.3 per cent. European election monitoring bodies declined to send observers, saying that Turkmenistan lacked any degree of democracy. The Observers Mission of the CIS declared there were 'equal opportunities' during the campaign and the Russian state news agency RIA-Novosti, declared the elections had been democratic. On 23 May India, Pakistan and Turkmenistan signed an agreement to build a new gas pipeline (as part of the Turkmenistan, Afghanistan, Pakistan India (TAPI) pipeline) and the subsequent supply of natural gas. On 13 August, as part of the celebration of the holy month of Ramadan President Berdymukhamedov pardoned 1,327 convicts (including 14 foreigners). On 14 September the first stage of a national census was undertaken by recording people in remote settlements. The major stage to complete the census will be held on 15 December.
2013 Parliamentary elections were held on 15 December in which the ruling Democratic Party emerged as the largest faction in the Assembly of Turkmenistan with 47 of the 125 seats, losing its parliamentary majority for the first time since independence. The elections were the first multi-party elections in the country's history, however, both contesting parties claimed loyalty to President Gurbanguly Berdimuhamedow. The elections were criticised by Amnesty International and opposition groups such as the Turkmen Initiative for Human Rights because they argued that there was little difference between the two major parties.
2014 The four state gas companies of Turkmenistan, Afghanistan, Pakistan, and India established a company that will begin to build, own and operate the planned 1,800 km Turkmenistan-Afghanistan-Pakistan-India (TAPI) natural gas pipeline.
2015 In January, Turkmenistan devalued its currency by 19 per cent against the US dollar – the first such depreciation in almost seven years – amid a slump in energy prices and a weak Russian rouble.

Political structure

Constitution

Turkmenistan was the first Central Asian state to adopt a Constitution (on 18 May 1992), which upholds political pluralism, separates legislative, executive and judicial powers and guarantees private ownership of property. However, adherence to the principles of the Constitution is rare. A new constitution was adopted on 25 September 2008 that abolished the Khalk Maslakhaty (People's Coucil) and changed the structure of power including the roles of parliament and the president. Turkmenistan is divided into five administrative regions: Ashkhabat, Turkmenbashi (formerly Krasnovodsk), Mary, Tashauz and Chardzhou.

Independence date

27 October 2001

Form of state

Republic

The executive

The president is elected by direct popular vote for a five-year term. All candidates must have lived in the country for 15 years before the elections. The president, as head of the executive branch of government, can dissolve the legislature only if the parliament is deadlocked on the election of the Speaker. Parliament would appoint a deputy prime minister as acting president if the president is unable to perform his duties; an acting president cannot run for office as president.

National legislature

The Majlis (Assembly) (established in 2008) has125 members, elected in multi-seat constituencies by absolute majority vote for five-year terms. Candidates may be nominated by political parties, public organisations, and interest groups. Parliament may pass laws, amend the constitution, approve the state budget, set dates for elections of the president, members of the legislature, and local governing bodies and can ratify or reject international treaties. The parliament delivers binding interpretation of laws and determines the legality of executive branch decisions. It may also terminate a president's term of office for reasons of health.

Legal system

The legal system is based on civil law. Members of the Supreme Court, the highest judicial body, are appointed by the president. There is no judicial review of legislative acts or presidential decrees.

Last elections

15 December 2013 (parliamentary); 12 February 2012 (presidential)

Results: Parliamentary: 47 seats of 125 were won by the Democratic Party, 33 won by the Organisation of Trade Unions of Turkmenistan, 14 won by the Party of Industrialists and Entrepreneurs, 16 won by the Women's Union of Turkmenistan, 8 won by the Magtymguly Youth Organisation and 7 won by Citizen Groups. Turnout was 91.3 per cent.
Presidential: Gurbanguly Berdymukhamedov won 97.1 per cent of the vote, Yarmukhammet Orazgulyev 1.2 per cent; the remaining six candidates shared 1.7 per cent of the vote. Turnout was 96.3 per cent.

Next elections

December 2018 (parliamentary); 2017 (presidential)

Political parties
Ruling party
Türkmenistanyn Demokratik partiýasy (TDP) (Turkmenistan Democratic Party)
Main opposition party
Organisation of Trade Unions of Turkmenistan

Population
5.80 million (2014)*
Last census: January 1995: 4,483,251
Population density: 11 inhabitants per square km (2010). Urban population 50 per cent (2010 Unicef).
Annual growth rate: 1.6 per cent, 1990–2010 (Unicef).
Ethnic make-up
Turkmen (77 per cent), Russian (6.7 per cent), Uzbek (9.2 per cent) and Kazakh (2 per cent).
Religions
The majority of the population are Sunni Muslim (89 per cent). The remainder are predominately Eastern Orthodox Christians (9 per cent).
The government directly controls the hiring, promotion and sacking of Sunni Muslim and Eastern Orthodox clergy.
Turkmenistan has a tradition of Sufism or Islamic mysticism and hosts several important Sufi religious sites.

Education
Secondary specialised education lasts for three to four years. General higher education lasts for four years. The Academy of Sciences in Ashgabat was the Republic's principal college of higher education. However, funding problems meant that by 2000 the Academy was closed. According to the government, 20 per cent of the relevant age group participate in some form of tertiary education. Those doing so are forced to undergo family checks going back three generations, while overseas education is not sanctioned by the government.
Females constitute 53 per cent of students in secondary education, 38 per cent of students in higher education and 29 per cent of students in professional schools. Although there is equal opportunity for females in education, they are often disadvantaged in employment situations.
A series of reforms have taken place since independence, with the aim of reducing the costs of education in general and vocational education in particular. Vocational training schools provide training to general education graduates, or adults who are required to pay fees. Some schools, especially in the bigger cities, are able to make enough income to maintain or even expand their activities. However, as government spending on vocational training in rural areas was reduced in the late 1990s, a number of vocational schools closed.
The quality of education is widely regarded as poor at all levels, and the sector is likely to come under increasing pressures from budgetary cuts and high population growth in the region. In September 2000, President Niyazov announced the axing of 5,000 jobs in the education sector as part of his drive to control the government's budget. Combined with low wages in the sector, this move is likely to undermine morale and reduce Turkmenistan's relatively high education statistics.
Literacy rate: 98 per cent adult rate; 100 per cent youth rate (15–24) (Unesco 2005).
Enrolment rate: 90 per cent gross primary enrolment of relevant age group (including repeaters) (World Bank).

Health
The healthcare system in Turkmenistan has suffered serious under-funding in recent years so that the benefits enjoyed by Turkmenis under the Soviet regime has been lost. Life expectancy has fallen to the lowest of any central Asean state. Free healthcare no longer exists, hospitals outside the capital have been closed, leaving 55 per cent of the population, living in rural areas, forced to travel long distances for treatment.
The availability of prescription drugs is severely limited, although the privatisation of pharmacies has led to an increase in the supply of non-prescription drugs.
There are no private hospitals or clinics in the region although some practitioners offer basic medical services.
Environmental hazards have contributed to widespread respiratory diseases, which prompted the government to ban smoking in public places. Nevertheless government policy on healthcare has ignored the need for Aids awareness, which is thought, by campaigners, to be an heavily underreported.
HIV/Aids
HIV prevalence: 0.1 per cent aged 15–49 in 2003 (World Bank)
Life expectancy: 60 years, 2004 (WHO 2006)
Fertility rate/Maternal mortality rate: 2.4 births per woman, 2010 (Unicef); maternal mortality 65 per 100,000 live births (World Bank).
Child (under 5 years) mortality rate (per 1,000): 53 per 1,000 live births (WHO 2012)
Head of population per physician: 4.18 physicians per 1,000 people, 2002 (WHO 2006)

Welfare
The government has attempted to deliver social services during the transitional period, but significant fiscal constraints continue to impede the progress of universal social transfers in the long-run. Taxes collected by the state tax service go to the state budget and the social security fund. The social security system is partly financed by payroll taxes set at 30 per cent of wages and voluntary contributions, while the government bears the full cost of social pensions and other subsidies as needed.
The state provides for different types of welfare payments, including pensions and several benefits related to disability, child-care, minimum social allowance, workers compensation, unemployment and family allowances. In 2001, the government decided to double public sector salaries.
Pensions are calculated on the number of years employed and the level of income. Pension benefits were doubled in 2003 following a presidential decree.
Maternity leave benefits are paid according to work experience and income. It is usually paid for 112 days. Workers' compensation benefits are paid at the rate of 6 per cent of salary in cases of unhealthy work conditions and 12 per cent of salary for severely harmful work conditions.
Those working in desert areas receive compensation at the rate of 10 per cent of their salary.
The government's human rights record remains extremely poor and it continues to commit serious human rights abuses. Interference with citizens' privacy remains a problem. Domestic violence and discrimination against women are prevalent.

Main cities
Ashgabat (capital, estimated population 1.0 million in 2012), Turkmenabat (Chärjew) (408,906), Dashhowuz (275,278), Mari (208,682), Balkanabat (133,489), Bayramali (131,173).

Languages spoken
There is a 28 per cent population of Russian or Uzbek speakers. English is also spoken.
Official language/s
Turkmen

Media
The Turkmen government has an absolute monopoly of the media.
In 2008 the Paris-based Reporters Without Borders condemned Turkmenistan for isolating its population from the world and subjecting it to 'propaganda worthy of a bygone age'.
Press
It has been reported that Turkmenistan is a very repressive climate for journalists, according to international observers, it controls not only printing presses but it monitors media outlets and imposes editorial policies.

In Turkmen, *Turkmenistan* is published six times a week, *Watan* is published three times a week, *Galkynys* is a weekly and represents the Democratic Party of Turkmenistan, *Turkmen Dunyasi* is a monthly and represents the Ashgabat-based World Turkmens Association. *Edebiyat we Sungat* is a literature and the arts magazine. In Russian the *Neytralnyy Turkmenistan* is published six times a week.

Broadcasting

Radio: Turkmen Radio operated two stations, Watan and Char Tarapdan (also in English) (assess may be by www.intervalsignals.net).

Television: There are four channels operated by Turkmenistan state television including TMT 1-2-3 and 4. TMT4 is multinational, transmitting in Turkmen, Russian, English and French. Imported programmes are routinely edited before public broadcasting.

National news agency: Turkmen State News Service (TSNS): www.turkmenistan.ru

Other news agencies: News Central Asia: www.newscentralasia.net

Economy

Turkmenistan is largely a desert country with intensive agriculture in irrigated oases and significant reserves of natural gas and oil. The two largest crops are cotton, most of which is produced for export, and wheat which is domestically consumed. Although agriculture only accounts for 14 per cent of GDP, it continues to employ nearly half of the country's workforce. Turkmenistan's authoritarian regime has taken a cautious approach to economic reform, hoping to use gas and cotton export revenues to sustain its inefficient and highly corrupt economy. The government introduced a privatization plan in 2012. While some small- and medium-size enterprises have been privatized since 2013, the implementation of the reform has been slow, and privatization goals remain limited. Corruption, a poor educational system and the government's misuse of oil and gas revenues does not bode well for Turkmenistan's future. The majority of Turkmenistan's economic statistics are state secrets, the figures released by the government are subject to wide margins of error. Based on government-provided data, the IMF reported 10.3 per cent economic growth in 2014.

Industry constituted 49 per cent of GDP in 2014 which dominates the economy, the service sector provides over 37 per cent and agriculture constitutes 13 per cent of GDP.

Turkmenistan's wealth is almost entirely derived from hydrocarbons and cotton. Turkmenistan's proven oil reserves were 600 million barrels in 2015, with annual production of 242,900 barrels per day. Proven natural gas reserves were 17.5 trillion cubic metres (cum) in 2014 (the world's fourth largest deposits behind Russia, Iran and Qatar), with annual production of 85 billion cum.

GDP growth was a high of 11.1 per cent in 2007 as world prices for oil were at a peak. GDP grew to 14.7 per cent in 2008, before falling to 6.1 per cent in 2009 as global trade weakened due to worldwide economic crisis. However growth picked up in 2010 with an estimated growth of 9.2 per cent, as global trade began to recover coupled with an increase in gas sales to China and a surge in public investment. GDP growth was 11.1 per cent in 2012, 10.2 per cent in 2013 and 10.3 per cent in 2014. These figures are probably wrong simply because Turkmenistan's government releases untrustworthy data.

In 2010, Turkmenistan announced that it intended to increase exports of natural gas by 700 per cent by 2030. This followed a summit meeting with Russia's then President Medvedev in which negotiations for the sale of natural gas to Europe should be via Russia's state-controlled Gazprom energy company's network of gas pipelines, thereby avoiding the European-backed Nabucco gas pipeline. The Nabucco pipeline in 2011 was not ready to accept Turkmen natural gas; Turkmenistan has to balance this with its experience of Russia's unilateral closure of its Caspian pipeline and the loss of revenue in 2009, against possible greater revenue returns if it sold its gas directly to Europe. Turkmenistan and China have a 30-year agreement for the supply of 30 billion cum per year of natural gas. A second natural gas pipeline was opened between Turkmenistan's Dovletabad gas field to Iran in 2010 and will, when fully operational, double gas exports to Iran to 20 billion cum.

Over 80 per cent of Turkmenistan's land mass is covered by the Kara Kum desert. Even so the majority of the population work in agriculture, principally nomadic cattle raising and intensive agriculture, particularly in cotton cultivation – Turkmenistan is Central Asia's second largest cotton producer and Turkmenistan produced 327 million tonnes (mtoe) of cotton in 2014 which makes it the ninth largest producer in the world.

The economy is dominated by the state, which accounts for around 80 per cent of annual output. A central control system is prevalent, with the state fixing prices, output targets and controlling the distribution, marketing and trade of most products. Investors remain largely wary of Turkmenistan, whose economy is characterised by an inadequate legal framework, often contradictory laws, corruption and excessive bureaucracy. Growth is driven by domestic investment – mostly state-led investments in oil and gas extraction, petrochemicals, electricity generation and transmission, textiles, and luxury housing. About 1.5 per cent of GDP is invested by foreign companies developing oil and gas fields under production-sharing agreements. FDI was US$3.2 billion in 2014, a slight increase on the US$3.1 billion in 2013.

Life remains austere for many in Turkmenistan with over half the population living below the poverty line.

Turkmenistan was ranked 103 (out of 187) in the Human Development Index (2014). Statistics remain unknown with regards to poverty in Turkmenistan but it is likely to be very high.

External trade

Turkmenistan is a member of the Economic Co-operation Organisation (ECO), comprising 10 regional Central Asian countries.

National statistics are not published; exports are chiefly primary products, cotton and hydrocarbons. Manufacturing and the service sector are underdeveloped and therefore most industrial and community requirements are imported.

Imports

Principal imports are machinery and equipment, chemicals, and foodstuffs.

Main sources: Turkey (25.1 per cent of total in 2014), Russia (13 per cent), China (10.7 per cent), UAE (7 per cent), US (5.1 per cent) and the Ukraine (4.9 per cent).

Exports

The main exports are gas, crude oil, petrochemicals, textiles and cotton fibre.

Main destinations: China (69.7 per cent of total in 2014) and Turkey (4.6 per cent).

Agriculture

Farming

Agriculture contributed 13 per cent to GDP in 2014 and employs 48 per cent of the workforce according to outdated data from 2004. The cultivated land area is around 32 million hectares (ha), with arable land accounting for 19 million ha. Cotton, a major export earner, is cultivated on over 750,000ha of arable land. Turkmenistan was the second largest producer of cotton in the former Soviet Union and is the ninth largest global producer.

In a report published in 2005 – *The Curse of Cotton: Central Asia's destructive monoculture* – the International Crisis Group (ICG) said that while the former Soviet cotton producing countries of Uzbekistan, Tajikistan and Turkmenistan continued to exploit their cotton growers there was little hope of improving economic development and tackling poverty. The cotton industry is vital to the economy of Turkmenistan, yet while the industry continues to rely on cheap labour (including children), land ownership is uncertain, state intervention discourages competition and the rule of law is limited, there is little incentive for the powerful vested interests to reform the system.

The government has started to diversify production in the agricultural sector away from the cotton monoculture. This has generated a small export surplus in cereal production and a growth of 18 per cent in wheat production. The 23 per cent rise in agricultural output could possibly signal self-sufficiency in grain production.

Turkmenistan is reliant on an inefficient Soviet irrigation system, which diverts water from the Amu Darya River and has contributed to the drying up of the Aral Sea. The irrigation system suffers from poor management and maintenance, with water losses of about 50 per cent, rising salinity and poor drainage.

An absence of storage and packaging facilities means that up to 30 per cent of the grain and cotton harvests are lost annually. Livestock accounts for around one-quarter of agricultural production, including the famous Karakul sheep.

Fishing

Turkmenistan has considerable fishing resources, with estimated total reserves at 50,000 tonnes of Caspian Sea fish and 8,000 tonnes of inland water fish. Turkmenbashi, on the Caspian Sea, provides an excellent base for accessing marine resources, being located near the main fishing grounds and remaining ice-free throughout the year. The typical annual fish catch is over 12,000 tonnes; the main fish type is kilka, although herring, shad, mullet and crayfish are also harvested.

Forestry

Less than 10 per cent of Turkmenistan has forest cover. All forested land is owned by the state. There is no large-scale forest industry and most wood products are imported from Russia.

Industry and manufacturing

The industrial sector typically contributed 49 per cent of GDP and employed 14 per cent of the workforce in 2014. The industrial production growth rate was estimated at 16.7 per cent in 2014, however, this is not necessarily accurate due to the inaccuracy of the government's statistics. Industry is dominated by the processing of hydrocarbons and other raw materials. The sector is labour-intensive and the use of energy and raw materials is wasteful. There is some light engineering industry, which mainly concentrates on the production of cables. The US-based Coca-Cola has a plant in Turkmenistan. The GAP-Turkmen joint venture was built in the mid-1990s and is now a fully vertically-integrated jeans producer, using locally-produced cotton.

Tourism

The potential for tourism in Turkmenistan, a large part of which is desert, is limited. Attractions include a number of historical and cultural sites. Mountain and coastal resorts are being developed and hotel accommodation is expanding. Visitor numbers are modest at some 8,000 a year, but increasing slowly. Air connections are improving and Ashgabat Airport has been modernised.

The National Tourist Zone of Avaza (Awaza) on the Caspian Sea, 12km west of the capital, was decreed by President Berdymukhamedov in 2008. It has eight multi-storey hotels, with plans for more, and a network of ornamental canals plus a range of tourist facilities. However, with little supporting infrastructure, no international flights to the nearest airport, poor water supply and a petroleum plant close enough to be an annoyance for paying guests, this growing development has been considered as possibly 'the most ill-conceived resort ever built.'

Environment

The Aral Sea is drying up due to the overuse of water from the two main rivers which feed into it and has lost 40 per cent of its water, dropping by up to 19 metres. This has resulted in desertification of the surrounding land. A UN study published in 2004 reported that there was no possibility of restoring the water and the need must be on preserving what was is left. The government has endorsed a 2004 joint strategy to resolve the demands of its water requirements with its neighbours.

An artificial lake (132 cubic metres deep, 3,460 square km in area) in the Kara Kum Desert is planned to be constructed by 2010 at a cost of US$6 billion. It will be situated at the Karashor valley and according to the government will prevent the 4,060 square km large lowlands from being flooded, stop desalinisation of the land and return the area to crop growing. Environmentalists claim it will undermine the agricultural sector and contribute to water loss.

A meeting was held in April 2009 to determine water sharing between Tajikistan, Kyrgyzstan, Uzbekistan, Turkmenistan and Kazakhstan failed, as negotiators were unable to find a trade in water for energy and hydrocarbons. Tajikistan and Kyrgyzstan hold around 80 per cent of the water in the Aral Sea.but suffer from lack of electricity during freezing winters, while the remaining three states downstream are semi-arid and need water for their cotton industries and agriculture.

Mining

There are large deposits of iodine-bromine, sodium sulphate, magnesium, sulphur, potassium and other salts in Turkmenistan. Prime deposits of ore and rock are located in Tourakyr, Bolshoy Balkhan, Kopet Dag, Badkhyz, Govurdak, Kugitang, Cheleken, Turkmenbashi peninsula, central and south-east Garagum and northern Turkmenistan. Of these, the Zulfagar alunite deposit in Badkhyz in the south contains several million tonnes of ore with a 50 per cent alunite content. Turkmenistan has the third largest deposits of sulphur in the world, located in the Kara Kum desert. Deposits of industrial minerals, notably kaolin and building granite, are also exploited. Non-ferrous and rare metals are mined and used for the production of chemicals. Gold and platinum are also present.

Despite Turkmenistan's vast resources, mineral deposits are under-exploited and not used significantly in domestic industry. Turkmenistan has not traditionally extracted or processed any significant amounts of metal ores, although the government has shown interest in attracting foreign investment to build its own metal-producing facilities.

Hydrocarbons

Proven oil reserves were 600 million barrels in 2014, with production at 242,900 barrels per day (bpd), 144.000 bpd are consumed domestically and 60,910 bpd are exported. State-owned Turkmenneft accounts for 90.5 per cent of oil extraction and the rest by foreign companies in production-sharing arrangements.

Turkmenistan's oil reserves remain difficult to estimate as potential oil reserves depend on negotiations to define ownership and prospecting rights in the Caspian Sea.

Turkmenistan has two oil refineries – Turkmenbashi and Chardzhou – with a combined capacity of 237,000bpd.

Proven natural gas reserves were 17.5 trillion cubic metres in 2014 making it the country with the fourth largest reserves in the world; the government claims the actual figure is far higher. Natural gas production was 84.8 billion cubic metres (cum) in 2013. The state-owned Turkmengaz accounts for 85 per cent of production with the remainder produced by foreign companies in production-sharing arrangements.

The 1,818km Turkmenistan-China natural gas pipeline, passing through Uzbekistan and Kazakhstan (both of which have undertaken to build their section of the pipeline) to take advantage of natural gas supplies, began construction in 2008. The 188km Turkmenistan section of a 7,000km natural gas pipeline was completed in 2009, at a cost of US$400 million. Natural gas supplies began flowing from the Caspian Sea, across Central Asia to China in 2009. China has a 30-year agreement for the supply of 30 billion cum per year of natural gas using this pipeline.

Energy
Total installed generating capacity was 4.3 gigawatts (GW) in 2014.
Turkmenistan exported 2.9 billion kWh to Iran and Kazakhstan in 2012. All power stations are fuelled by domestically produced natural gas.
Turkmenistan is connected to Iranian power lines and exchanges electricity during periods of peak energy consumption, usually summer in Turkmenistan and winter in Iran. The government also plans to sell electricity through Iran to other countries of the Economic Co-operation Organisation (ECO), which includes six former Soviet republics.

Financial markets
Stock exchange
Türkmenistanyn Döwlet Haryt – Çig Mal Biržasy (The State Commodity and Raw Materials Exchange of Turkmenistan)
Commodity exchange
The State Commodity and Raw Materials (SC&RM) exchange trades commodities only.

Banking and insurance
The economic crisis of 1997–98 led to all banks in Turkmenistan becoming 'government commercial banks'. Prior to this move, Turkmenistan had 67 banks, two of which were state-owned banks (Vneshekonombank and Sberbank). Vneshekonombank has become one of the largest banks in Central Asia since its creation in 1991. The bank dominates import/export operations and is a key institution for the operation of foreign investment in Turkmenistan. Sberbank holds 95 per cent of all household deposits.
The banking sector is widely viewed as corrupt and inefficient, failing to channel funds effectively, and is constrained by the government's tight control of the credit and foreign exchange markets.
Central bank
Central Bank of Turkmenistan
Main financial centre
Ashgabat

Time
GMT plus five hours

Geography
Turkmenistan is the second largest Central Asian republic and shares lengthy borders with Iran to its south and Uzbekistan to its north and east. The country also borders Kazakhstan to the north-west and Afghanistan to the south-east. The Caspian Sea, where the major port of Turkmenbashi is located, is to the west. The Kara Kum desert comprises over 80 per cent of Turkmenistan's total area. The Kopet Dag mountains extend along Turkmenistan's southern border with Iran and Afghanistan.
Hemisphere
Northern

Climate
Temperatures in Ashgabat range between 0 and 40 degrees Celsius (C).
Turkmenistan can be very hot in the summer, with temperatures of 35 degrees C common and a maximum of up to 50 degrees C in some provinces. Winters in the Ashgabat area tend to be mild and temperatures do not usually fall below freezing. However, in mountainous southern areas it is not uncommon for temperatures as low as minus 33 degrees C to be recorded. Ashgabat is the southernmost capital city of the former Soviet republics, on the same latitude as San Francisco and Cordoba.

Dress codes
Smart clothes are required for business visitors.

Entry requirements
Passports
Required by all. Passports must be valid for six months after date of departure.
Visa
Required by all. Business visitors require a full itinerary and an invitation, certified by the Ministry of Foreign Affairs in Ashgabat, from a local, private individual or company to support their application. The Turkmen Chamber of Commerce can provide new business visitors with such a letter. For tourists, these can be obtained from authorised travel agents in Ashgabat. All visitors must provide evidence of sufficient funds for the visit and return/onwards passage.
For further information visit www.turkmenistanembassy.org.
All visa applications made overseas are referred to Ashgabat for a decision. This can take several weeks. There is an accelerated 24 hours service, but a supplementary fee is levied.
On arrival visitors must complete an immigration card and pay a US$10 immigration fee. The authorities retain one copy and the other must be handed back, by the visitor, on departure.
Visitors must register within three days of their arrival, excluding weekends and holidays, with the Turkmenistan State Registration Service. This is carried out by the inviting organisation or individual, and a registration fee is paid. Tourists should register with the State Committee of Turkmenistan for Tourism and Sports. Registration is for the period of the visa; three days before departure, visitors must de-register with the same authorities. Visitors not staying in Ashgabat should register at the local *velayat* office of their place of residence (there is no need to register both in Ashgabat and regionally).
Visitors transiting the country can be registered at entry and exit points if their stay is not longer than five days and they hold a valid transit visa. Transit visitors cannot change their visas in-country, and need to notify the authorities if they intend to vary their route through the country.
Currency advice/regulations
On 1 January 2008 local currency began to be exchanged for foreign currency at regulated commercial rates. The import of foreign currency is unlimited but must be declared; export is limited to the amount declared. Visitors should check with the central bank for up-to-date regulations.
Ensure you bring enough US dollars to cover all potential needs, Turkmenistan is a cash-only economy. Traveller's cheques and credit cards are not commonly accepted.
Customs
On arrival declare all foreign currency and valuable items such as jewellery, cameras, computers etc.
Prohibited imports
Firearms, illegal drugs and wool carpets.

Health (for visitors)
Mandatory precautions
Vaccination certificate required for yellow fever if travelling from an infected area.
Advisable precautions
Water precautions recommended: water purification tablets may be useful or drink bottled water.
It is advisable to be in date for the following immunisations: polio, diphtheria, tetanus, typhoid, hepatitis A, tuberculosis. Also hepatitis B if you are spending more than 6–8 working weeks in a year in the region.
Anti-malarial precautions are advisable. Inoculation against rabies is advisable if travelling to rural areas. It could be wise to have precautionary antibiotics if going outside major urban centres. A travel kit including a disposable syringe is a reasonable precaution. There is a shortage of routine medications and visitors should take all necessary medicines with them. Medical insurance, including emergency evacuation, is necessary.

Hotels
Rooms are often in short supply and expensive. It is advisable to book in advance through Intourist or other specialist

travel agents. A number of major hotel renovations and new building projects have been undertaken in the centre of Ashgabat.

Credit cards
Credit cards are accepted.

Public holidays (national)

Fixed dates
1 Jan (New Year's Day), 12 Jan (Remembrance Day), 19 Feb (National Flag Day), 20 Mar (Novruz Bairam/Persian New Year), 9 May (Victory Day), 18 May (Constitution Day), 6 Oct (Remembrance Day), 27–28 Oct (Independence celebrations), 17 Nov (Students' Day), 12 Dec (Day of Neutrality).

Variable dates
Eid al Adha (Kurban Bairam), Eid al Fitr (Seker Bairam – three days).

Islamic year 1437 (15 Oct 2015–2 Oct 2016):: The Islamic year contains 354 or 355 days, with the result that Muslim feasts advance by 10–12 days against the Gregorian calendar. Dates of feasts vary according to the sighting of the new moon, so cannot be forecast exactly.

Working hours

Banking
Mon–Fri: 0930–1730.

Business
Mon–Fri: 0900–1800.

Government
Mon–Fri: 0900–1800.

Shops
Mon–Sat: 0900–1800.

Telecommunications

Mobile/cell phones
The usage of mobile phones is extremely limited; a GSM 900 services exist in Ashgabat, Mary and Turkmenabat.

Electricity supply
220V AC 50Hz. Round two-pin continental plugs are standard.

Social customs/useful tips
Gratuities are becoming more customary, particularly in international hotels. Visitors are advised to carry some form of identity at all times.

Security
It is unwise to venture out on the streets alone at night. Visitors should be vigilant and are advised to dress down. Keep expensive jewellery, watches and cameras out of sight.

Getting there

Air
National airline: Turkmenistan Airlines
International airport/s: Ashgabat Airport (ASB), 4km from city centre. The are limited services from UK, Germany, Russia and the Middle East.
Airport tax: Departure tax: US$25; nationals of CIS countries US$15.

Surface
Road: Primary roads are few; secondary roads, particularly in desert areas, are of poor quality.
There are border crossings with Iran, Afghanistan, Kazakhstan and Uzbekistan. A road links Chardhzhou and Mazar-e-Sharif in Afghanistan.
Rail: A railway service operates from Iran. It runs nearly 300km from the Iranian Silk Road city of Mashhad, crosses the Turkmen border at Sarakhs and joins the Soviet-era Turksib railway at Tedzhen. It gives Turkmenistan access to the Iranian Gulf port of Bandar Abbas.
Water: The only coastline is along the Caspian Sea.
Main port/s: Turkmenbashi, has ferry links to Baku (Azerbaijan).

Getting about

National transport
Air: Akhal Air Company (division of Turkmenistan Airlines) operates domestic services. Daily flights between Ashgabad and Mary.
Road: Roads are poorly maintained and sometimes dangerous. However, new highways are under construction.
Buses: Buses serve Turkmenbashi (formerly Krasnovodsk) and Mary.
Rail: There are lines between Ashgabat, Turkmenbashi, Dashgouz and Mary.
Trains to Gushgi are currently prohibited to foreign visitors due to the proximity of the Afghan border.

City transport
Taxis: Volga taxis have a sign on top. Agree a price beforehand. It is safer to use officially marked taxis which should not be shared with strangers.

Car hire
A national licence with authorised translation, or an international driving permit, is required.

BUSINESS DIRECTORY

The addresses listed below are a selection only. While World of Information makes every endeavour to check these addresses, we cannot guarantee that changes have not been made, especially to telephone numbers and area codes. We would welcome any corrections.

Telephone area codes
The international direct dialling (IDD) code for Turkmenistan is +993, followed by area code and subscriber's number:

Ashgabat	12
Mary	522
Turkmenabad (Chardhzhou)	378
Turkmenbashi (Krasnovodsk)	243

Useful telephone numbers
Fire: 01
Police: 02
Ambulance: 03
Gas leak: 04

Chambers of Commerce
Turkmenistan Chamber of Commerce and Industry, 17 Karreyeva Street, Ashgabat 744000 (tel: 355-594; fax: 355-381; e-mail: asccitm@online.tm).

Banking
Daykhanbank, 60 Atabayeva St, Ashgabat (tel: 419-873, 419-875; fax: 419-868).

Garashsyzlyk, 30 A Shevchenko St, Ashgabat (tel: 354-875, 397-393; fax: 397-892).

International Joint-Stock Bank Garaguma, 3 K Kuliyeva St, Ashgabat (tel: 354-062, 475-269; fax: 353-854).

National Bank of Pakistan, Sheraton Turkmen Hotel, 7 Gorogly St, 744000 Ashgabat (tel: 350-465, 512-050; fax: 350-465).

Obabank, 51 Ostrovskogo, Ashgabat (tel: 346-968, 346-558; fax: 246-968).

Prezidentbank, (temporarily at:) 22 Bitarap Turkmenistan Str, Ashgabat (tel: 357-943; fax: 510-812).

The Savings Bank of Turkmenistan, 86 Prospect Mahtumkuly, 744000 Ashgabat (tel: 394-298, 395-4671; fax: 396-553).

Senagat, 42 Turkmenbashy Shayoly Prospect, Ashgabat (tel: 510-305, 350-694; fax: 510-571).

The State Bank for Foreign Economic Affairs of Turkmenistan (Turkmenvnesheconombank), 22 Asudalyk St, 744000 Ashgabat (tel: 235-0252; fax: 239-7982).

Central bank
Central Bank of Turkmenistan, 22 Bitarap Turkmenistan St, 744000, Ashkabad, (tel: 353-442; fax: 356-711; email: cbtmode@cat.glasnet.ru).

Stock exchange
Türkmenistanyn Döwlet Haryt – Çig Mal Biržasy (The State Commodity and Raw Materials Exchange of Turkmenistan), www.exchange.gov.tm

Commodity exchange
The State Commodity and Raw Materials (SC&RM) exchange trades commodities only.

Travel information
Akhal Air Company, Ashgabat Airport, 744088 Ashgabat (tel: 225-6084/1052; fax: 229-0724, 225-4402).
DN Tours, Magtumguly Avenue 48/1, 744000 Ashgabat (tel: 270-438, 270-449; fax: 270-420; email: dntour@online.tm; internet: www.dntours.com).
Intourist, Hotel Ashgabat, Prospekt Makhtumkuli 74, 744023 Ashgabat (tel: 290-026).

Lufthansa Airport Office, Ashgabat Airport (tel: 510-697; fax: 510-728).
Turkmenintour, Ul Makhtumkhuli 74, Ashgabat (tel: 256-932, 255-191; fax: 293-169).
Turkmenistan Airlines, Ashgabat Airport (foreign economic relations) (tel: 290-766; fax: 254-402).

National tourist organisation offices
State Committee of Turkmenistan for Tourism and Sport, 17-1984 Pushkin Street, 744000 Ashgabat, (tel: 354-777, 397-606, 396-740; internet: www.tourism-sport.gov.tm; www.turkmenistan.gov.tm; www.turkmens.com).

Ministries
Ministry of Agriculture, Ulitsa Azadi 63, Ashgabat 744000 (tel: 256-691; fax: 253-557).

Ministry of Automobile Transport, Ulitsa Baba Annanova 2, Ashgabat 744025 (tel: 474-992; fax: 470-391).

Ministry of Communications, Ulitsa Zhitnikova 36, Ashgabat 744000 (tel: 256-665).

Ministry of Construction, Ulitsa Alishera Navoi 56, Ashgabat 744000 (tel: 256-060).

Ministry of Construction Materials Industry, Ulitsa Steklozavodskaya 1, Ashgabat 744000 (tel: 251-560; fax: 251-913).

Ministry of Consumer Goods, Ulitsa Annadurdieva 52, Ashgabat 744000 (tel: 255-442; fax: 254-833).
Ministry of Economy and Finance, Borodinskaya Street no 2, Ashgabat 744000 (tel: 251-653; fax: 256-511).

Ministry of Energy and Industry, Ulitsa N Pomma 6, Ashgabat 744000 (tel: 254-921; fax: 291-670).

Ministry of Foreign Affairs, Prospect Lenina no 11, Ashgabat 744000 (tel: 251-463).

Ministry of Foreign Economic Relations, Ulitsa Kemine 92, Ashgabat 744000 (tel: 297-511; fax: 297-524).

Ministry of Health, Prospect Magtymguly 95, Ashgabat 744000 (tel: 251-063; fax: 255-032).

Ministry of Information, Ulitsa Chekhova 8, Ashgabat (tel: 297-572).

Ministry of Interior Affairs (tel: 251-328).
Ministry of Melioration and Water Resources, Ulitsa Seidi 1, Ashgabat 744000 (tel: 253-032; fax: 298-589).
Ministry of Oil and Gas Industry and Mineral Resources, 28 Gogolia Street, Ashgabat 744000 (tel: 293-827; fax: 510-443).
Ministry of Trade, Pervomayskovo Street no 1, Ashgabat 744000 (tel: 251-047; fax: 295-108).
Office of the President (tel: 254-534).

Other useful addresses
American Business Liaison, Gogol Street no 17, Ashgabat 74000 (tel: 253-386).

British Embassy, 301-308 Office Building, Ak Altin Plaza Hotel, Ashgabat (tel: 251-0861; fax: 632-510).
Central Asia Research Forum, School of Oriental and African Studies, Thornhaugh Street, London WC1H 0XG, UK (tel: (+44-(0)20) 7323-6300; fax: (+44-(0)20) 7436-3844).

Department of Investments, Cabinet of Ministers, Ashgabat (tel: 254-954; fax: 255-112).
EU-TACIS, 92 Kemine Street, Ashgabat (tel: 512-117, 251-020; fax: 511-721).
Kuvyat (state energy corporation), 6 Nurberdi Pomma Street, Ashgabat; Foreign Economic Relations (tel/fax: 254-921).

State Agency for Foreign Investment of Turkmenistan, 53 Azadi Street, Ashgabat 74400 (tel: 350-231; fax: 350-415).

State Committee on Statistics, 72 Magtymgyly Avenue, Ashgabat 744000 (tel: 294-265, 253-596; fax: 254-379).

State Commodity and Raw Materials Exchange, Magtumguly Street 3111, Ashgabat (tel: 254-321; fax: 510-304).

State Customs Office, 7 Stepan Razin, 7440225 Ashgabat (tel: 470-455; fax: 470-221).

State Railway of Turkmenistan, 7 Saparmirat Turkmenbashi Street, 744007 Ashgabat; Engineering Department (tel: 473-936; fax: 473-958); International Services (tel: 473-958; fax: 510-632).

State TV and radio, Prospekt Svobody 89, Ashgabat (tel: 251-515).

Turkmenistan Embassy (USA), 2207 Massachusetts Svenue, NW, Washington DC 20008 (tel: (1-202) 588-1500; fax: (1-202) 588-0697; e-mail: turkmen@earthlink.net).

Turkmenintorg Foreign Trade Organisation, Hivinskaya Str 1, 744000 Ashgabat (tel: 298-774/684/975, 297-521; fax: 298-774/955, 295-987).

National news agency: Turkmen State News Service (TSNS): www.turkmenistan.ru

News Central Asia: www.newscentralasia.net

Internet sites
Turkmenistan Embassy, Washington, US: www.turkmenistanembassy.org

Turkmenistan Information Centre: www.turkmenistan.com

Turks and Caicos Islands

KEY FACTS

Official name: Turks and Caicos Islands

Head of State: Queen Elizabeth II, represented by Governor Peter Beckingham (from 9 Oct 2013)

Head of government: Premier Rufus Washington Ewing (PNP) (from 13 Nov 2012)

Ruling party: Progressive National Party (PNP) (from 2003; re-elected 9 Nov 2012)

Area: 430 square km

Population: 39,184 (2011)*; 31,458 (2012, preliminary census result)

Capital: Cockburn Town (on Grand Turk)

Official language: English

Currency: US dollar (US$) = 100 cents

* estimated figure

Prime Minister Dr Rufus Ewing announced a two-stage reshuffle of ministerial portfolios and responsibilities in early January. The first stage, on 19 January, saw swaps in portfolios between Ewing (who added the health portfolio) and Porsha Stubbs-Smith (who became minister of tourism, culture and heritage) and Amanda Missick (to the ministry of government support services) and George Lightbourne (to the ministry of environment and home affairs). The second stage, planned for 1 April, will see more intricate departmental changes as well as the renaming of actual ministries.

In a move to bring the islands more in line with one of their chief tourist markets, Turks and Caicos Islands stopped changing the clocks from winter to summer time and back on 8 March when they put the clocks forward by one hour for the last time. This puts the islands on Atlantic Standard Time and gives an extra hour of evening sunshine.

The curious case of Michael Misick, first premier of Turks and Caicos, continued in 2015. Mr Misick had taken office in 2003 and masterminded the updated 2006 constitution. He also oversaw rapid growth in the island, especially in the high-end tourist industry.

Despite this, concerns had grown over his premiership after his personal wealth grew from US$50,000 before he entered office to over US$180 million by the time of his resignation six years later. The owner of a US$16 million mansion, and welcoming host to a string of high-profile celebrities, Misick attracted the attention of the British government.

After learning of British intentions to arrest him, Misick fled to Rio de Janeiro in 2009, but was eventually captured. His trial is scheduled to take place in December 2015. Even against the weight of evidence, Misick maintains he is a political prisoner and that the British government has overstepped its jurisdiction. Indeed, in some sections of Turks and Caicos society, Misick's arrest has re-ignited calls for independence.

COUNTRY PROFILE

The first residents of the islands were Amerindians. There are claims that Christopher Columbus actually made his first landing (1492) in the Americas on Grand Turk, and not in the neighbouring Bahamas.

1512 Spanish explorer, Juan Ponce de León, arrived.

1678 British settlers came from Bermuda and set up a salt-panning industry.

1766 Having overridden French and Spanish claims to the islands, Britain appointed a colonial resident.

1799 The islands were annexed to the Bahamas.

1874–1962 The islands were administered from British ruled Jamaica, after which they became a Crown colony and were ruled from the Bahamas.

1972 When the Bahamas gained independence the islands gained their own governor.

1976 A constitution was adopted and the first independent elections were won by the pro-independence People's Democratic Movement (PDM).

1980 The PDM lost the general election to the Progressive National Party (PNP) which was committed to maintaining the status quo.

1982 Plans for independence were reversed.

1985 Chief Minister Norman Saunders, the minister for development and commerce, and a PNP member of the Legislative Council, were arrested and subsequently convicted in the US on drug trafficking charges.

1986 The constitution was suspended following allegations of corruption in local government and a commission of inquiry found the chief minister, Nathaniel Francis, and two of his ministers, unfit to govern. The governor assumed direct control of government and the Executive Council, and ruled through a special Advisory Council.

1988 The constitution was reinstated with revisions.

2002 Jim Poston became governor.

2003 The ruling PDM won the parliamentary election, but in two by-elections, won by the opposition, the PNP gained a majority in parliament. Chief Minister Taylor resigned and Michael Eugene Misick was sworn in on the same day.

2004 The EU's Savings Tax Directive was implemented.

2005 Richard Tauwhare was sworn in as governor.
2006 A new constitution revised the title of the chief minister to premier. A new minimum wage, for all workers, was introduced.
2007 In general elections the ruling PNP won 60 per cent of the vote (13 out of 15 seats); the DPM 40 per cent (two). Michael Misick continued as premier.
2008 Governor Tauwhare resigned and Deputy Governor Mahala Wynns became acting governor. The governor announced he had appointed a Commission of Inquiry (CoI) into allegations of corruption and other serious dishonesty in relation to past and present elected members of the House of Assembly. Gordon Wetherell became governor.
2009 The CoI reported that there were 'clear signs of political amorality and immaturity and of general administrative incompetence' and 'a high probability of systemic corruption or serious dishonesty' in the Turks and Caicos Islands (TCI) government. Prime Minister Misick resigned. The constitution was suspended and power and responsibility for government business reverted to the governor and an advisory council and consultative forum for a minimum period of two years. Galmo Williams and six other members of the House of Assembly were sworn into office as premier and cabinet ministers respectively, although all legislative and executive power remained the responsibility of the governor. The CoI's final report was published and recommended that criminal investigations into the activity of five cabinet ministers, including the former premier, be undertaken by the police.
2010 The Bank of Providenciales was closed down and liquidated by order of the TCI supreme court, at the behest of the official Financial Service Commission (FSC) when it was confirmed that there were insufficient funds to cover withdrawals and the bank was unable to obtain additional financial support. In the first legal actions to be undertaken by the Special Investigative Prosecuting Team, writs of corruption against three businesses that allegedly bribed the former premier Misick and a former cabinet member were filed.
2011 In February, the UK government agreed to provide a financial support package of US$260 million, which included a bridging loan of US$170 million and a five-year loan of US$30 million to shore up the TCI treasury. In March the new, draft TCI constitution was published by the UK Foreign and Commonwealth Office. The final 2008–09 CoI report was published in May, following the last dismissals of legal challenges to the conclusions in the report. It reiterated its initial recommendations that criminal investigations should be undertaken into the activities of former ministers, premier Michael Misick, minister of finance Floyd Hall, minister of natural resources McAllister Hanchell, minister of works Jeffrey Hall and minister of health and education Lillian Boyce. Lack of financial support from the UK government to fund the investigation team delayed prosecution. In July, the UK minister responsible for Overseas Territories announced that as much as US$5 billion was missing from the TCI treasury due to the fraudulent activities of the Misick administration. The draft constitution was negotiated with civic leaders and the UK government in June and an agreement achieved in July. In September, Damian Roderic Todd took office as governor.
2012 An international arrest warrant was issued for former prime minister Michael Misick on 19 March. On 20 March, Misick announced that he would seek asylum in a third country (suspected of being Dominican Republic) due to his claims of political persecution in TCI. On 19 July a new value added tax (VAT) was enacted to come into force on 1 April 2013. Exemptions will include fresh foodstuffs, hurricane supplies, water and electricity and published materials. On 4 September, a new political party was announced, called the People's Progressive Party (PPP). A new constitution came into force on 15 October. In parliamentary elections held on 9 November, the PNP won eight seats out of 15 and the PDM seven; turnout was 84 per cent. Oswald Skipping, the leader of the PDM called for a recount, which was held on 12 November and the outcome did not change. Rufus Ewing (PNP) took office as premier on 13 November.
2013 On 1 May the Turks and Caicos Islands, along with Anguilla, Bermuda, the British Virgin Islands, the Cayman Islands and Montserrat, signed a tax sharing agreement with the tax authorities of France, Germany, Italy, Spain and the UK.
2014 Michael Misick due to be extradicted from Brazil between January 7 and 13. The Turks and Caicos got its first rating when international ratings agency Standard and Poor's (S&P) gave it a BBB+ on 1 July. The rating highlights that the Turks and Caicos is a prosperous country.
2015 Prime Minister Dr Rufus Ewing announced a two-stage reshuffle of ministerial portfolios and responsibilities in early January. The first stage, on 19 January, saw swaps in portfolios between Ewing (who added the Health portfolio) and Porsha Stubbs-Smith (who became Minister of Tourism, Culture and Heritage) and Ministers Amanda Missick (to the Ministry of Government Support Services) and George Lightbourne (to the Ministry of Environment and Home Affairs). The second stage, planned for 1 April, will see more intricate departmental changes as well as the renaming of actual ministries. Turks and Caicos Islands stopped changing the clocks from winter to summer time and back on 8 March when they put the clocks forward by one hour for the last time. This puts the islands on Atlantic Standard Time and gives an extra hour of evening sunshine. Figures reported by the Turks and Caicos Tourist Board Statistics Office in March showed an overall increase in both cruise passenger and stop-over arrivals of 31.6 per cent in 2014 over 2013.

Political structure

Constitution

The 1976 constitution was suspended in 1986, restored and revised in 1988 and amended in 1993. It provided for the exercise of a ministerial type of government, through a governor appointed by the British monarch, an Executive Council (ExCo) which had general control of government, and a Legislative Council (LegCo). A new constitution of August 2006 replaced the legislative council with a unicameral house of assembly of 21 members, 15 of whom are directly elected for a four-year term, four nominated from the cabinet, one ex-officio (the attorney-general) and the speaker. The cabinet consists of two ex-officio members (the financial secretary and the attorney-general), the premier and other ministers. The British monarch continues to be head of state, represented by a governor.

The constitution was suspended on 25 March 2009 with power and responsibility for government reverting to the governor and an advisory council and consultative forum for a minimum period of two years. The present form of the constitution was passed in 2011 and came into effect in October 2012. Following the 2006 version being criticised for permitting excessive discretion to cabinet ministers, the modern one has greater restraints on public office. For example, the Attorney General no longer presides over criminal prosecutions – replaced by a new Director of Public Prosecutions.

Voting: universal suffrage 18 years and over.

Independence date

25 November 1975

Form of state

Caribbean dependency status: overseas territory of the UK.

The executive

The head of state, Queen Elizabeth II, is represented by an appointed governor. The cabinet consists of two ex-officio members (the financial secretary and the attorney-general), the premier and other ministers.

National legislature

21 members, 15 of whom are directly elected for a four-year term, four nominated from the cabinet, one ex-officio and a speaker

The unicameral house of assembly is composed of 19 seats; 15 are directly elected of which 10 are seats elected in single member constituencies and five are 'at large'. In addition four seat are appointed by the governor (including the posts of attorney-general and the speaker), two candidates are nominated by the premier and two by the leader of the opposition

Legal system

The legal system is based on laws of England and Wales, with a small number of laws adopted from Jamaica and The Bahamas.

Last elections

9 November 2012 (parliamentary)

Results: Parliamentary: Progressive National Party (PNP) won 44.87 per cent of the vote and eight seats (out of 15), People's Democratic Movement (PDM) 50.13 per cent and seven seats; turnout was 84 per cent.

Next elections

2016 (parliamentary)

Political parties

Ruling party

Progressive National Party (PNP) (from 2003; re-elected 9 Nov 2012)

Main opposition party

People's Democratic Movement (PDM)

Political situation

Prime Minister Michael Misick resigned in March 2009, perhaps before he could have been sacked, following the critical report by the Commission of Inquiry into allegations of corruption and other serious dishonesty. The commission reported that there were 'clear signs of political amorality and immaturity and of general administrative incompetence' and 'a high probability of systemic corruption or serious dishonesty' in the Turks and Caicos Islands (TCI) government.

While Misick was trenchant in his denouncement of the accusations and declaration of his innocence, the UK government took over control of the government of the TCI, through its governor Gordon Wetherell.

Legal action began against Michael Misick and his brother, and former attorney-at-law, Chalmers (Chal) Misick for corrupt transactions, in 2010

There are approximately 7,000 European expatriates and illegal migrants, mainly from Haiti and the Dominican Republic, living in the Turks and Caicos. Their numbers are increasing as the upmarket tourism sector recruits overseas, and the island's higher living standards and public services attract migrants from more impoverished locales.

The legal population is referred to as 'Belongers'.

About two-thirds of the total population lives on Providenciales island.

Population

39,184 (2011)*; 31,458 (2012, preliminary census result)

Population density: 53 inhabitants per square km.

Annual growth rate: 3.2 per cent (2003)

Ethnic make-up

Afro-Caribbean (95 per cent)

Religions

Baptist (41 per cent), Methodist (19 per cent), Anglican (18 per cent), Seventh-Day Adventist (2 per cent).

Education

The school system is constrained by insufficient infrastructure and is poorly equipped to deal with children of immigrants for whom English is not a first language.

The UK government has a number of projects, which it is working on through the Department for International Development (DFID). By improving teaching methods, the government hopes that around 80 per cent of children will achieve levels in reading and mathematics acceptable to their age.

The primary and secondary curriculum is also under review with plans that it will be standardised.

Compulsory years: Four to 16

Enrolment rate: 94 per cent primary enrollment of relevant age group, 80.2 per cent secondary enrollment.

Health

The UK government has designed an ongoing programme of reforms to improve the health care system. Priorities include human resource development, greater access to financial resources and the prevention and control of HIV/Aids.

The hospital on the island of Grand Turk serves as a referral centre for all of the islands. There are nine community health care clinics throughout the islands.

HIV/Aids

HIV prevalence: Less than 1 per cent in 2004

Life expectancy: 77.7 years (estimate 2003)

Fertility rate/Maternal mortality rate: 4.61 births per woman

Welfare

There is a reciprocal health and welfare agreement with the UK, which entitles nationals of the Turks and Caicos islands to benefits such as income support, housing allowances and child benefits.

Main cities

Cockburn Town (capital, on Grand Turk island, estimated population 1,174 in 2012), Five Cays (4,821), Honda Road (4,322), The Bight (4,165) Wheeland (3,210).

Main islands

Grand Turk (business centre), Providenciales (most tourism facilities), South Caicos (fishing and sailing), Salt Cay, Middle Caicos, North Caicos (natural bird sanctuary), Pine Cay and Parrot Cay.

Eight out of 30 islands are inhabited.

Languages spoken

Official language/s

English

Media

Press

There are no dailies but three weekly newspapers all published in . *Turks and Caicos Weekly News* (www.tcweeklynews.com), *Turks and Caicos Free Press* (www.tcifreepress.com) and the *Turks and Caicos Sun* (www.suntci.com). There is an online community newsletter (http://enews.tc). *Times of the Island* (www.timespub.tc) is a quarterly magazine.

Broadcasting

Radio: Radio Turks and Caicos (RTC) (http://tcimall.tc/rtc) broadcasts three channels. Private stations include the religious Radio Vision Christina (www.radiovision.net) and Power 92.5 (WIV) (www.power925fm.com).

Television: The Turks & Caicos Television, is based in Grand Turk, while WIV-TV is based in Providenciales, both are cable television services. Multi-channel satellite television is received from the US and Canada. WIV Cable TV was bought by Digitel in April 2014.

Economy

The economy is wholly dependent on its service sector, with tourism and financial services providing the major share of foreign exchange and GDP growth. GDP is composed of 1.1 per cent agriculture; 23.3 per cent industry; and 75.7 per cent services (2014), the services large contribution is largely due to tourism.

The UK government became increasingly perturbed at allegations of corruption and mismanagement and launched a Commission of Inquiry. In 2009, the resulting report for the UK Foreign and Commonwealth Office (FCO) into the financial dealing of the Michael Misick administration concluded 'that there was a high probability of systemic corruption in the former Turks and Caicos Islands

Government.' In August 2009 the constitution was suspended and power and responsibility for government business reverted to the UK-appointed governor and a locally drawn advisory council and consultative forum for a minimum period up to 2011.

The first legal actions, to be undertaken by the Special Investigative Prosecuting Team, filed writs of corruption on 30 April 2010 against three businesses that had allegedly bribed former premier Misick and a former cabinet member.

By 2011 the FCO had concluded that the 'fiscal picture in Turks and Caicos Islands represents an unacceptable collapse in the fiscal governance of the Territory', which needed urgently to be addressed. It appointed a chief financial officer tasked with addressing the structural deficit and developing a strategy for putting the economy on a course towards a sustainable fiscal surplus by the financial year 2012/13. On 9 February 2011, the UK government agreed to provide a financial support package of US$260 million, which included a bridging loan of US$170 million and a five-year loan of US$30 million to shore up the TCI treasury.

The Turks and Caicos got its first rating when international ratings agency Standard and Poor's (S&P) gave it a BBB+ on 1 July 2014. The rating highlights that the Turks and Caicos is a prosperous country.

External trade

As a UK Overseas Territory the Turks and Caicos Islands is a member of the European Union's Association of Overseas Countries and Territories (OCT Association). It is also an associate member of the Caribbean Community (Caricom) and Common Market but does not operate within the single market strategy (Caribbean Single Market and Economy (CSME)), which became operational in 2006.

Foreign earnings are derived from the offshore financial sector, tourism and fisheries. All capital goods and foodstuffs are imported.

Imports

Principal imports are food and beverages, tobacco, clothing, consumer goods, manufactures and construction materials.

Main sources: UK and US

Exports

Principal reported exports are lobster, fish, dried and fresh conch, and conch shells.

Main destinations: UK and US

Agriculture

Farming

The agricultural sector is limited to small-scale production for domestic consumption and accounts for around 1 per cent of GDP. The growing tourism sector has encouraged production of fruit and vegetables for hotels and restaurants. Farming is confined to the rearing of livestock and the growing of maize, beans and some fresh fruit. A hydroponics facility has been developed at Providenciales.

Fishing

The fishing industry grew as the salt industry declined. Over-fishing, low prices and better paid jobs in the growing tourism industry in the 1990s led to a decline in fishing. However, as export prices started to improve, particularly for conch, and the government started to improve conservation techniques and encourage value-added processing, so the industry has rebounded.

Fishing for lobster and conch production accounts for just under 2 per cent of GDP. There is a commercial conch farm on Providenciales.

The typical total annual fish catch is over 1,300 tonnes (mt); shellfish, molluscs and cephalopods account for another 1,000mt per annum.

Industry and manufacturing

The industrial sector accounts for 20.8 per cent of GDP. Activity is confined to fish processing (mainly lobsters and conch) and construction work. A rice-milling and packaging plant, supplied with rice from Guyana, is the only significant industrial enterprise.

Construction activity has increased with new tourist and residential developments. The Turks and Caicos Investment Agency is promoting the islands as a location for manufacturing electronic goods.

Tourism

The TCI have all of the Caribbean attributes (even though they lie in the Atlantic Ocean) to offer a visitor, with sun, sea and service. They are closest to the US-Florida coast and receive daily, direct flights from Miami and other US cities, Canada and Europe as well as other Caribbean destinations. The islands are noted for the wildlife on land and offshore in the coral reef. Fishing tournaments and yachting regattas are held regularly during the tourist season (November– May).

In August 2011, the extension to the main runway of the Providenciales International Airport was completed, allowing larger passenger aircraft to land. This work was the first phase in a US$100 million expansion, which will include an enlarged terminal and improved access to the airport.

Tourism is the principal component of GDP. The marked growth in cruise liner business was encouraged by the completion of the Carnival Cruise Centre on Grand Turk, which is a large dock and recreation facilities for cruise ship passengers including a serviced beach, shops and restaurants. Cruise liners began visiting TCI in 2004; before this private yachting accounted for around 20,000 visitors each year, by 2007, around 380,000 passengers disembarked from 185 commercial liners. In 2014, TCI had 1.4 million visitors, a rise of 31.6 per cent on the 2013 figure.

Hydrocarbons

There are no known hydrocarbons reserves, all energy needs are met by imports. The Islands do not import either natural gas or coal.

Banking and insurance

Under an EU tax directive introduced in July 2005 in a number of associate and dependent EU countries, the Turks and Caicos began imposing a withholding tax to be passed to the relevant EU depositor's country but retaining the anonymity of the saver. Withholding taxes began at 15 per cent, and rose to 35 per cent 2011. Turks and Caicos has also agreed to supply information on tax fraud, for criminal or civil trials, and notify EU member states about additional malpractices.

On 1 May 2013 the Turks and Caicos Islands, along with Anguilla, Bermuda, the British Virgin Islands, the Cayman Islands and Montserrat, signed a tax sharing agreement with the tax authorities of France, Germany, Italy, Spain and the UK.

Central bank

There is no central bank.

Main financial centre

Cockburn Town, Grand Turk.

Offshore facilities

The Financial Services Commission is an independent statutory body responsible for licensing and supervising all finance-related entities and registering companies.

Time

GMT minus four hours (Turks and Caicos Islands stopped changing the clocks from winter to summer time and back in 2015 when on 8 March they put the clocks forward by one hour for the last time.)

Geography

The Turks and Caicos Islands (TCI) are a group of around 40 islands in the North Atlantic Ocean, split into two groups by a deep channel, which combined covers 500 square km of land. They are situated in the north of the Caribbean, 48km south of the Bahamas and 145km north of Haiti. The islands are limestone plateaux, no higher that 75 metres, most with lush green vegetation. Off their northern shore, TCI has the world's third largest coral reef system.

Hemisphere

Northern

Climate
Tropical, tempered by trade winds. Winter nights sometimes cool, summers are hot. Mean temperature range from 25–29 degrees Celsius.

Entry requirements
Passports
Required by all except visitors from North America who require birth certificate (or, a notarised copy) and photo ID (all US and Canadian nationals require a passport for re-entry to their country from January 2007). Proof of onward/return passage is required.
Visa
Not required except by citizens not found within the list given in www.turksandcaicostourism.com – *Facts and General Information – Visas and Immigration*. Further local information can be found at www.tcimall.tc/government or from the nearest British consulate.
Currency advice/regulations
The import and export of local and foreign currency is unrestricted.
Prohibited imports
Illegal drugs and pornography; firearms require a permit from the commissioner of police prior to arrival.

Health (for visitors)
Mandatory precautions
Yellow fever vaccination certificate required if arriving from an infected area.
Advisable precautions
Typhoid and polio vaccinations. Water precautions.

Hotels
Accommodation is available on Grand Turk, South, Middle and North Caicos, Salt Cay, Pine Cay, and Providenciales, reservations are necessary. There is an 8 per cent room tax and 10–15 per cent service charge added to bills.

Public holidays (national)
Fixed dates
1 Jan (New Year's Day), 12 Jun (Queen's Birthday), 25–26 Dec (Christmas).
Variable dates
Commonwealth Day (second Mon in Mar), Good Friday and Easter Monday (Mar/Apr), National Heroes' Day (last Mon in May), Emancipation Day (first Mon in Aug), National Youth Day (last Fri in Sep), Columbus Day (second Mon in Oct).

Working hours
Banking
Mon–Thu: 0830–1430; Fri: 0830–1230, 1430–1630.
Business
Mon–Fri: 0830–1600.
Government
Mon–Thu (winter): 0800–1230, 1400–1630; Fri: 0800–1230, 1400–1600.
Mon–Thu (summer): 0700–1130, 1300–1530; Fri: 0700–1130, 1300–1500.

Telecommunications
Mobile/cell phones
A GSM 850 service is available.

Electricity supply
120/240 V, 60 cycles

Getting there
Air
International airport/s: Grand Turk (GDT); South Caicos International (XSC); Providenciales (PDS), duty-free shop, car-hire.
Airport tax: Departure tax: US$35.
Surface
Water: Cruise ships visit regularly.
Main port/s: Cockburn Harbour (South Caicos), Grand Turk, Providenciales.

Getting about
National transport
Air: Air Turks and Caicos serves Providenciales, South, Middle and North Caicos, Salt Cay and Grand Turk. Other scheduled and charter companies operate between the islands.
Road: Main roads on Grand Turk, South Caicos and Providenciales are surfaced.
Taxis: Taxis are unmetered and can be hired for the day, agree a price before travelling.
Water: There are scheduled ferries and island hoppers operating between most of the islands.
Car hire
Available on Grand Turk, Providenciales and South Caicos. National driving licence required, a flat tax of US$10 is levied on all hirings. Driving is on the left.

BUSINESS DIRECTORY

The addresses listed below are a selection only. While World of Information makes every endeavour to check these addresses, we cannot guarantee that changes have not been made, especially to telephone numbers and area codes. We would welcome any corrections.

Telephone area codes
The international direct dialling code (IDD) for Turks and Caicos Islands is +1 649 followed by subscriber's number.

Chambers of Commerce
Grand Turk Chamber of Commerce, PO Box 148, Grand Turk (tel: 946-2324; fax: 946-2504).

Banking
Bordier International Bank and Trust Ltd, PO Box 5, Caribbean Place, Providenciales (tel: 946-4535; fax: 946-4540; email: enquiries@bibt.com).

First Caribbean Bank, PO Box 258, Grand Turk (tel: 946-2831; Fax: 649 946 2695; email: care@firstcaribbeanbank.com).

Scotiabank International, Cherokee Road; PO Box 15, Providenciales (tel: 946-4750; fax: 946-4755; email: bns.turkscaicos@scotiabank.com).

Turks and Caicos Banking Co Ltd (private international banking services), PO Box 123, Harbour House, Front Street, Grand Turk (tel: 946-2368; fax: 946-2365; email: ajbf@turksandcaicosbanking.tc).

Central bank
None

Travel information
Air Turks and Caicos, PO Box 191; 1 Interlsland Plaza, Old Airport Road, Providenciales, (tel: 941-5481; fax: 946-4040; email: fly@airturksandcaicos.com).

SkyKing Airlines, PO Box 398, Providenciales (admin tel: 941-5464 ext 200 / 504; fax: 941-4264; email: cservices@skyking.tc; reservations: 941-3136; fax: 941-5127; email: res@skyking.tc; internet: http://skyking.tc).

Spirit Air (regional flights) 2800 Executive Way, Miramar, Florida 33025, USA (tel: (+1-954) 447-7965; fax: (+1-954) 447-7979; internet: www.spiritair.com).

National tourist organisation offices
Turks and Caicos Tourist Board, Front Street, PO Box 128, Grand Turk (tel: 946-2321/2; fax: 946-2733; email: tci.tourism@tciway.tc; internet: www.turksandcaicostourism.com).

Turks & Caicos Islands Tourist Board, Stubbs Diamond Plaza, Providenciales (tel: 946-4970, 491-5746; fax 941-5494).

Ministries
Governor's Office, Government House, Waterloo, Grand Turk (tel: 946-2309; fax: 946-2903; e-mail: govhouse@tciway.tc).

Main Government Offices, Cockburn Town, Grand Turk (tel: 946-2801).

Ministry of Education, Youth, Sports and Women's Affairs (tel: 946-2801, ext 142; fax: 946-1337; e-mail tci.sports@tciway.tc).

Ministry of Finance, Commerce and Development (tel: 946-2935, 946-2937; fax: 946-2557; e-mail: fsc@tciway.tc).

Ministry of Health and Education (tel: 946-2801; fax: 946-2722).

Other useful addresses

Development Board, PO Box 105, Hibiscus Square, Pond Street, Grand Turk (tel: 946-2058).

Financial Services Commission, Harry Francis Building, Pond Street, Grand Turk (tel: 946-2802; fax: 946-2821).

General Trading Company (Turks & Caicos) Ltd, PMBI, Cockburn Town, Grand Turk (tel: 946-2464).

Government Information Service (GIS), Government Square, Grand Turk (tel: 946-2301 ext 40505/40506; fax: 946-1120).

Immigration And Work Permits, Director Of Immigration, Immigration Department, Southbase, Grand Turk (tel: 946-2939/2700; fax: 946-2924; email: iam@tciway.tc).

TCInvest, Hibiscus Square, Box 105, Grand Turk (tel: 946-2058; fax: 946-1464; email: tcinvest@tciway.tc; internet: www.tcinvest.tc).

Turks & Caicos Hotel Association, Third Turtle Inn, Providenciales (tel: 946-4230).

Turks Islands Importers Ltd (TIMCO), Front Street, PO Box 72, Grand Turk (tel: 946-2480).

Internet sites

Gateway Sites: www.turksandcaicos.tc

Local Information: www.tc/info.htm

KEY FACTS

Official name: Tuvalu

Head of State: Queen Elizabeth II, represented by Governor General Lakoba Italeli (from 16 Apr 2010)

Head of government: Prime Minister Enele Sopoaga (from 4 Aug 2013; re-elected April 2015)

Ruling party: There are no organised political parties, although there are opposing political groupings.

Area: 26 square km (nine islands – five coral atolls and four reef islands)

Population: 11,000 (2014)*

Capital: Vaiaku in Funafuti administrative division

Official language: Tuvaluan, English

Currency: Australian dollar (A$) = 100 cents)

Exchange rate: A$1.43 per US$ (Sep 2015)

GDP per capita: US$3,484 (2014)*

GDP real growth: 2.24% (2014)*

GDP: US$38.00 million (2014)*

Inflation: 3.30% (2014)*

Balance of trade: -US$5.05 billion (2013)

Foreign debt: US$13.00 million (2012)

* estimated figure

Tuvalu

Like many other small Pacific islands, Tuvalu depends largely on remittances from overseas Tuvaluans and grants, particularly from Australia. After two years of contraction, the economy grew by 1.0 per cent in 2011, largely due to higher remittances. The consumer price index increased by 0.5 per cent in 2011 and had reached 1 per cent by 2013, which was still lower than in most other Pacific economies, reflecting the appreciation of the Australian dollar (which Tuvalu uses as its currency) against the US dollar.

The *Asian Development Bank Economic Outlook 2012* reports that total revenues and grants for 2011 were slightly below budget but about 20 per cent higher than in 2010. The increase was mainly due to the grants. Government expenditure fell by more than 7 per cent as subsidies were reduced and spending on capital projects declined. These developments led to a reduction in the fiscal deficit from over 30 per cent of GDP in 2010 to about 8 per cent in 2011. However, weakly controlled spending on the Tuvalu Medical Treatment Scheme remains a heavy drain on the budget with actual expenditure 70 per cent above budget in 2011. Total government debt was estimated at 44.3 per cent of GDP in 2010, and may be higher with the status of contingent liabilities from joint-venture fishing companies to be determined.

The market value of the Tuvalu Trust Fund stood at A$115.1 million as of 30 September 2011. As this was 9.7 per cent below its prescribed maintained value, nothing was distributed from the fund to the Consolidated Investment Fund (CIF – the vehicle through which budget deficits are financed).

Growth is expected to edge up to 1.4 per cent and 1.3 per cent in the next two years, supported by development partner–financed upgrading of the Tuvalu airfield and airport. Increases in remittances are also expected. Total revenue and grants are budgeted at A$24.1 million in 2012, 7 per cent less than actual 2011, due to a projected 3.3 per cent reduction in receipts from fishery licences and lower grant funds. Government expenditure is estimated at A$29.2 million (US$30.4 million) (13 per cent below 2011) as the government tries to control spending. At A$5.1 million (US$5.3 million), the budget deficit is forecast at 14.3 per cent of GDP. The CIF held A$3.1 million (US$3.2 million) in December 2011 and, given the expected deficit, is likely to be exhausted this year. Further distribution from trust fund earnings is not expected until 2014 at the earliest.

COUNTRY PROFILE

1819 The captain of a ship owned by Edward Ellice, an English member of parliament, visited Funafuta and named the island Ellice Island.

1850–75 European diseases, and the kidnapping of islanders for forced labour on plantations in Fiji and Australia (a practice known as 'blackbirding'), reduced the population from 20,000 to 3,000.

1877 The Western Pacific High Commission was set up by Britain, headquartered in Fiji. The Ellice Islands and other island groups come under its jurisdiction.

1892 A British protectorate was declared over the Ellice Islands and the group was linked administratively with the Gilbert Islands to the north.

1916 The UK annexed the protectorate, which was renamed the Gilbert and Ellice Islands colony.

1975 The Ellice Islands, under the old native name of Tuvalu (eight standing together), became a separate British dependency.

1978 Tuvalu became an independent country within the Commonwealth.

1987 The Tuvalu Trust Fund was established; it provides an average 15 per cent of the country's annual budget.

1989 A UN report on the greenhouse effect listed Tuvalu as one of the island groups, which would completely disappear beneath the sea in the twenty-first century unless drastic action was taken.

1996 The 12-member parliament was forced out and Bikenibeu Paeniu became prime minister.

1998 Tomasi Puapua was appointed governor general.

1999 A no-confidence vote forced out Paeniu. Ionatana Ionatana was elected prime minister.

2000 Ionatana Ionatana died suddenly. Tuvalu was formally admitted to the UN.

2001 Parliament elected Faimalaga Luka as prime minister but later lost a no-confidence vote; Koloa Talake was elected as his replacement.
2002 Nine out of 15 MPs were re-elected. Parliament elected Saufatu Sopoanga as prime minister.
2003 The Sopoanga government lost its majority and ruled as a minority government. Faimalaga Luka was sworn in as governor general. The government regained its majority.
2004 During the first six months of the year, there were several very high 'king tides' associated with the new moon. At only four metres above sea level at their highest points, the islands experienced seawater swamping of homes and agricultural land. Prime Minister Sopoanga lost a no-confidence vote; Deputy Prime Minister Maatia Toafa was elected prime minister.
2005 Filoimea Telito was sworn in as governor general. Tuvalu signed the Pacific Islands Air Service Agreement (PIASA), to become the eighth Pacific Islands Forum country to do so. PIASA is designed to ensure open skies policies with more viable routes for airlines in the Pacific.
2006 In general elections, eight out of 15 members of parliament lost their seats, including the entire cabinet. Maatia Toafa retained his seat but lost the premiership when Apisai Ielemia was selected as prime minister.
2008 In a referendum voters agreed to maintain a constitutional monarchy.
2010 The US awarded Tuvalu a grant of US$10,000 to begin a biofuel power generation programme, using copra-bio-diesel, made from the waste of the copra crop (coconut shells and husks). Lakoba Italeli became governor general. Tuvalu became the 187th member of the IMF. In parliamentary elections, of the 26 non-partisan candidates participating, 10 (out of 15) incumbent MPs retained their seats. Maatia Toafa won nine votes (out of 15) to become prime minister again. Prime Minister Toafa's first budget was challenged and Willy Telavi joined with the opposition to topple him. Telavi was elected by parliament as prime minister; he won eight votes Enele Sopoaga won seven.
2011 A two-week state of emergency was declared in January following opposition-led street demonstrations that threatened the residences of the governor general and prime minister. Constituents of the Nukufetau island community demanded that their representative, finance minister Lotoala Metia, should resign. The government introduced a ban on public meetings, lifted in February. In June, the project to supply water to every home in Tuvalu had progressed to installing water tanks and associated plumbing to the seven outer islands. Funding for the work was provided by the UN and EU. A state of emergency was declared in October after fresh water ran out and bottled water dwindled to a week's supply. The US Navy delivered 136,000 litres of bottled water and the New Zealand Red Cross responded by delivering personnel and desalination machines. The shortage was the result of a lack of rainfall blamed on the La Nina weather pattern. Tuvalu had no rainfall for seven months and low rainfall for three years. The lack of rain had an impact on crops giving the island a food shortage problem. There were 30 confirmed cases of water borne diseases, due to the poor quality of drinking water. During the Commonwealth Heads of Government summit, in October, the 16 countries in which the British monarch is Head of State unanimously agreed to change the royal line of succession from that of first born son to the first born child (regardless of its gender). The change will be enacted after the succession of Prince William (currently second in line to the throne, after his father Prince Charles).
2012 In July, the US warned Tuvalu not to register Iranian ships and provide a flag of convenience (allowing owners to obtain insurance and financing of cargo), thereby breaking international sanctions against Iran. On 1 July the Seasonal Workers Programme (SWP) was officially launched. Australia grants special visas to Pacific Island workers on the SWP, on the proviso that they return to their home country when their sponsored work in Australia is completed. Around 150 workers had applied for the SWP by October.
2013 A constitutional crisis developed after the death in December 2012 of Lotoala Metia and the holding of a by-election to elect his successor. The Nukufetau by-election was eventually held on 28 June and was won by opposition candidate Elisala Pita. Governor General Italeli had to intervene to order Parliament to convene on 30 July; Toam Tanukale resigned, in an apparent manoeuvre to allow Prime Minister Televi to suspend parliament and delay a by-election to replace Mr Tanukale. Governor General Italeli exercised his powers and removed Mr Telavi, replacing him with Enele Sopoago as interim prime minister; he was confirmed in office by parliament on 4 August. The by-election was held on 10 September and was won by Leneuoti Maatusi, giving Prime Minister Sopoago a majority of three. Under the Majuro Declaration signed in September after the annual Pacific Forum meeting in the Marshall Islands Tuvalu stated its intention of being 100 per cent powered by renewable energy by 2020.
2014 Speaker Sir Kamuta Latasi was outvoted by the government side in March. He was replaced by Otinielu Tauteleimalae Tausi, who had been elected to parliament in the Nanumaga by-election on 14 January. At a meeting of the Smaller Island States leaders held as part of the Pacific Islands Forum Leaders summit in Palau in August, Prime Minister Sopoaga said small island states will be left adrift unless they focus on working together.
2015 After a meeting in October to dicuss climate change, the Pacific islands of Fiji, Kiribati, Tuvalu and Tokelau issued a joint statement in which they asked for help in funding the cost of raising buildings above predicted sea level increases and to safeguard water supplies from saltwater intrusion. The low-lying nations said that moving people because of rising sea levels, storms and ruined agriculture was a last resort, but the 'calamity' of climate change required industrialised countries to devise a plan.

Political structure

Constitution

The constitution dates from 1978. The British sovereign is head of state, represented by a governor general with limited powers. The governor general's powers to veto government measures were abolished under a constitutional amendment in 1986. Each island is ruled by a traditional council of chiefs which runs services and determines development priorities.
Amendments in December 1999 and August 2007 increased membership of parliament from 12 to 15 and increased the number of ministers from 5 to 7 respectively.
In 2008, Tuvaluans rejected an amendment that proposed replacing Queen Elizabeth with a democratically elected president as head of state.

Independence date

1 October 1978

Form of state

Constitutional monarchy and parliamentary democracy

The executive

The British monarch is titular Head of State, represented by a governor general, whose functions are largely ceremonial. The governor general is appointed on the advice of the prime minister, in consultation with parliament.
Executive power is exercised by a cabinet of five members and is led by the prime minister. The government is collectively accountable to parliament.

National legislature

The unicameral Fale i Fono (parliament) has 15 members, directly elected for

four-year terms. Seven islands send two members each, with one from Nukulaelae (with the smallest population). The parliament has the power to make laws, it can remove the prime minister through a vote of no-confidence and can be dissolved early by the governor general in accordance with the constitution.
Given the lack of party affiliation in Tuvalu, the vote of no confidence is used in a more personal way than in other countries. There are only 15 members of parliament and if the prime minister is seen to sway from the majority's line, a vote of no confidence is occasionally called. Votes have also been called over accusations of corruption and inefficiency. Essentially, the vote is used not so much as a matter of national emergency as it is in other countries but rather as a more ordinary political tool.

Last elections
31 March 2015 (parliamentary)

Results: Parliament: 31 non-partisan candidates stood for election, 15 were chosen, with Prime Minister Enele Sopoaga being re-elected unopposed. Apart from deputy prime minister Vete Sakaio, the government of Sopoaga all returned to office

Next elections
2019 (parliament)

Political parties

Ruling party
There are no organised political parties, although there are opposing political groupings.

Political situation
The politics of Tuvalu are dominated by the very real possibility that this collection of low-lying islands and atolls will disappear as global warming raises sea levels. Progress towards implementation of the Kyoto Protocol on climate change has not been broad or thorough enough and the peoples of all small islands are running out of time. So the action by the representative of Tuvalu, at the UN conference on climate change in Copenhagen (Denmark) in December 2009, when he pleaded with delegates to produce a legally binding agreement before storming out and closing the day's session, could be understood, if not forgiven. Environmental campaigners gave impromptu support for the passionate protest.
The population is projected to reach 14,000 by 2025.
Population density is the highest in the South Pacific. Just over half of the total population is concentrated on Funafuti, which is the only urban centre. The water supply is poor.
In September 2003, Niue invited Tuvaluans to migrate to their island to boost the dwindling population.

Population
11,000 (2013)*

Last census: November 2002: 9,561

Population density: 372 inhabitants per square km (2010). Urban population 50 per cent (2010 Unicef).

Annual growth rate: 0.4 per cent, 1990–2010 (Unicef).

Ethnic make-up
Tuvalu's population is Polynesian in origin.

Religions
Christianity, under which the Church of Tuvalu (Congregationalists) accounts for 97 per cent of the population.

Education
The vast distances between islands make the provision of education harder, as each small community requires a trained teacher. There is only one public, secondary school, located on the island of Vaitupu, where children reside for the academic year.

Compulsory years: Seven to 14.

Pupils per teacher: 19.5 (in primary schools); 12.2 (in secondary schools) (2005)

Health
Tuberculosis has been a long-term problem, which is monitored regularly and remedied under directly observed treatments (Dots), which has notably increased the rate of recoveries.
Figures from the United Nations Children's Fund (UNCF) (formerly Unicef) revealed in January 2010 that 80 per cent of families in the most vulnerable communities were without funds to buy food; more heads of households were losing their jobs due to the global economic crisis, which had resulted in rising food prices and falling remittances. Malnutrition, particularly among children and women, was becoming of increasing concern as governments in the Pacific region were cutting back on social expenditure in the face of recession.

Life expectancy: 61 years, 2004 (WHO 2006)

Fertility rate/Maternal mortality rate: 3.7 births per woman, 2004 (WHO 2006)

Child (under 5 years) mortality rate (per 1,000): 30 per 1,000 live births (WHO 2012)

Head of population per physician: 0.55 physicians per 1,000 people, 2002 (WHO 2006)

Welfare
Statistic by the United Nations Children's Fund (UNCF) (formerly Unicef) revealed in January 2010 that 80 per cent of families in the most vulnerable communities were without funds to buy food, as more heads of households were losing their jobs due to the global economic crisis. Malnutrition, particularly among children and women, was becoming of increasing concern as governments in the Pacific region were cutting back on social expenditure in the face of recession.

Main cities
Vaiaku in Funafuti administrative division (capital, estimated population 5,310 in 2012), Asau (664), Lolua (539) Savave (503), Kua (457).

Languages spoken

Official language/s
Tuvaluan, English

Media

Press
The *Tuvalu Echo* is published fortnightly and the government publishes a newsletter *Sikuleo o Tuvalu*.

Broadcasting
The government operates Radio Tuvalu and the online Tuvalu-News (www.tuvalu-news.tv). Most residents receive foreign television satellite programmes.

Radio: Radio Tuvalu is a government-owned station.

Other news agencies: ABC Pacific Beat: www.radioaustralia.net.au/pacbeat
Pacific Magazine: www.pacificmagazine.net
Pacific Islands New Association (Pina): www.pina.com.fj

Economy
Tuvalu is a mere 26 square kilometres in size and has an economy to match. The small subsistence economy accounts for approximately 30 per cent of GDP. It is supplemented by copra exports and official transfers and investment income from overseas assets. Its smallness means that even a slight change in economic activity will affect GDP. Tuvalu has had to take its revenue where it can and when it was allocated .tv as its country-level domain (CLD) indicator it went into business with a California corporation to take advantage of it. The government sold its share in DotTV Corporation in 2001 for A$20 million (US$10 million) and continues to receive a small royalty.
Other sources of revenue are fishing licences for the exclusive economic zone, which exceeded budget projections by 25 per cent in 2013, and remittances from seafarers (some 20 per cent of GDP). The Tuvalu Maritime Training Institute was upgraded over the period 2005–07. This was an important project as it not only increased economic activity but also ensured the Institute retained its accreditation from the International Maritime Organisation.
The Tuvalu Trust Fund (TTF) invests in equities and is normally an important source

of income. The government invests its budget surpluses in the TTF as a financial stockpile for years when it runs a deficit. A second fund – the Falekaupule Trust Fund – for the outer islands, has been provided with funds by a loan from the Asian Development Bank (ADB).

Tuvalu's growth has been accelerating since 2012 when GDP growth was 0.2 per cent, jumping to 1.3 per cent in 2013 and further to 2.2 per cent in 2014. The Asian Development Bank (ADB) estimates GDP growth to remain at around 2 per cent for 2015--16. A sales tax of 5 per cent exists but the proposals to introduce value added tax (VAT) was introduced in 2009 and raised to 7 per cent in 2013. The introduction of VAT became important when the Pacific Island Countries Trade Agreement was ratified, since Tuvalu was expected to loose customs revenue on imports goods from the region. In October 2015 the ADB approved a US$2 million grant to support a policy reform programme aiming to strengthen Tuvalu's fiscal sustainability.

External trade

Tuvalu is a member of the South Pacific Regional Trade and Economic Co-operation Agreement (Sparteca) along with 12 other regional nations, which allows products duty free access by Pacific Island Forum members to Australian and New Zealand markets (subject to the country of origin restrictions).

Foreign earnings are also provided by sales of stamps and coins by mail order, and remittances.

Imports

Principal imports are food, animals, vehicles, mineral fuels, machinery and manufactured goods.

Main sources: Singapore (34.3 per cent of total in 2013), Fiji (28.3 per cent), Japan (24.2 per cent).

Exports

Copra and fish are the principal export commodities; coconut oil is exported to New Zealand.

Main destinations: Japan (63.2 per cent of total in 2013), South Korea (9.2 per cent), Australia (6.9 per cent).

Agriculture

Farming

About 80 per cent of the population survive through subsistence agriculture.

Much of the soil is infertile, rainfall is variable and crops are liable to cyclone damage. Copra is the only export crop. Family smallholdings produce subsistence crops of pulaka, taro and other vegetables, bananas and coconuts. Agriculture is under threat from salinisation of the soil caused by rising ocean waters.

Fishing

Fishing and exploitation of the sea are important to the economy, serving mainly local consumption. There is potential to increase income by negotiating fisheries agreements with other countries. The typical annual marine fish catch is 500 tonnes.

On 12 April 2011, a summit of the Parties to the Nauru Agreement (PNA) concluded its strategy for a policy of sustainable fishing in the Pacific. The PNA treaty, which was established in 1989 and expired in 2012, was seen as in need of an overhaul. As a collective region, the PNA (FSM, Kiribati, Marshall Islands, Nauru, Palau, PNG, Solomon Islands and Tuvalu) control around 25–30 per cent of world stocks of tuna. Only 5 per cent of sales revenue is returned to the PNA and ministers called for specific changes, including an increased share of profits, PNA crews on-board purse seine vessels (minimum 10 per cent), conservation and management measures including a limit to fish trapping (fish aggregating devices (FADs)), net mesh rules and the establishment of an observer agency and fisheries information management system. The PNA met in May 2012 to discuss even stronger management measures to ensure even more sustainable tuna fisheries and minimise environmental damage. Many of the ideas put forward were implemented in January 2013, for example observation and monitoring of catches and environmental damage by 100 per cent independent bodies.

Industry and manufacturing

A small industry sector (baking, construction, boat building, coconut oil mill, soap making etc) serves local needs, some handicrafts are exported.

Tourism

There is no developed tourist industry owing to Tuvalu's remote location, infrequent flights and lack of amenities. However in 2013 the government was able to invest in the expansion of the airport.

In 2011 (the latest government statistics), there were 1,232 visitor arrivals, a drop of 25 per cent from 2010, most of which were from Fiji (311), followed by Japan (150) and New Zealand (133). However, the majority of Fijian arrivals are expatriates returning home to see family and friends.

Facilities, including the airport, the sole hotel and some guest houses, are concentrated on Funafuti. The other islands are relatively unspoilt, but are not easily accessible.

Environment

The government has publicly acknowledged the problem of the rising sea levels, but feels the situation has been exaggerated by the world media. Claims that the islands will be washed away by 2050 are debateable.

Mining

Tuvalu has no known mineral resources.

Hydrocarbons

There are no known hydrocarbon reserves. All fuel requirements are met by imported petroleum products.

The UN Law of the Sea gives Tuvalu an exclusive economic zone of 12,949 square km for exploration.

Energy

Total installed generating capacity was 2,400kW in 2013. The Energy Department is responsible for policy and planning for the atolls, while the Tuvalu Electricity Corporation supplies energy to customers. Japan agreed to supply three new 600kW diesel-powered generators and upgrade the distribution grid. The government has placed an emphasis on renewable energy in a bid to reduce reliance on imported fuel; there has been a take-up in the supplementary use of solar-photovoltaic (PV) panels on Vaitupu and Niutao. Niulakita is entirely powered by solar-PV home systems.

On the 5th September 2013 the Majuro Declaration was signed between all the members of the Pacific Islands Forum, of which Tuvalu is a member. This agreement looks to highlight the impact of climate change on the low-lying islands of the pacific. It commits the signatories to work towards the 'urgent deduction and phase down of greenhouse gas pollution' and aims to spark a 'new wave of climate leadership'.

Tuvalu aims to become the first country to get 100 per cent of it's energy from renewable sources by 2020.

Banking and insurance

The state-owned National Bank of Tuvalu (NBT) dominates the country's banking sector. Its monopoly position ensures that it remains in profit.

Tuvalu's currency is the Australian dollar and interest rates are determined by the Reserve Bank of Australia (RBA), so the government has little control over monetary policy. The royalty revenues generated by the '.tv' domain name (after the sale of the DotTV Corporation) have been lower than expected and are paid irregularly.

Central bank

National Bank of Tuvalu

Time

GMT plus 12 hours

Geography

Tuvalu is a scattered group of nine small atolls, extending about 560km (350 miles) from north to south in the western Pacific Ocean. Fiji lies to the south, Kiribati to the north and the Solomon Islands to the west. The Tuvalu archipelago consist of six true atolls and three reef islands. The true atolls are Funafuti, Nanumea, Nui, Nukufetau and Nukulaelae, while Nanumaga, Niulakita and Niutao are single islands. The last three have small salt-water ponds, while Nanumea has a fresh water pond, unusual for an atoll.

At their highest point, these islands are only four metres above sea level, and vulnerable to the rise in sea levels caused through global warming.

Hemisphere

Southern

Climate

Hot and humid, temperatures 26–32 degrees Celsius. Rainfall varies considerably, up to 3,000mm in a year, falling most heavily from November–February. Hurricanes possible.

Entry requirements

Passports

Required by all.

Visa

None required, however visitors must have return/onward tickets and sufficient funds for their stay.

Currency advice/regulations

No restrictions on import and export of local and foreign currency.

Customs

Personal effects allowed duty-free. There are quarantine regulations for plants and animals, and it is inadvisable to carry fruit or plant material. Certain goods may be subject to regulation or import licensing, such as arms, fireworks, drugs, motorcycles, jewellery.

Health (for visitors)

Health facilities are basic.

Mandatory precautions

Vaccination certificate for yellow fever required if travelling from an infected zone.

Advisable precautions

There is rabies risk. Vaccinations for diphtheria, tuberculosis, hepatitis A and B, polio, tetanus and typhoid are recommended.

Hotels

There is only one hotel, the government owned Vaiaku Lagi Hotel. Reservations should be made well in advance. Visitors may be asked to share rooms when there are accommodation shortages. Private guest houses are also available.

Tipping is optional and not expected.

Public holidays (national)

Fixed dates

1 Jan (New Year's Day), 15 May (Gospel Day) 12 Jun (Queen's Official Birthday), 5 Aug (National Children's Day), 1–2 Oct (Tuvalu Days, Anniversary of Independence), 25–26 Dec (Christmas).

Holidays that fall at the weekend are taken either on Friday or Monday.

Variable dates

Commonwealth Day (second Mon in Mar), Good Friday, Easter Monday.

Working hours

Banking

Mon–Thu: 0930–1300; Fri: 0830–1200.

Business

Mon–Fri: 0800–1600.

Government

Mon–Thu: 0730–1615; Fri: 0730–1245.

Shops

Mon–Sat: 0630–1730.

Electricity supply

240V AC (on island of Funafuti only)

Weights and measures

Imperial system (metric units allowed in some instances).

Social customs/useful tips

Tipping is not customary. In business an informal attitude prevails. It is customary to shake hands on meeting and taking leave. Sometimes business cards are exchanged after introduction. Business is conducted in English. Visitors should be perceptive to unfamiliar local customs. Alcohol is generally available, but there are some limitations on consumption outside licensed premises. The minimum drinking age is 20 years.

Getting there

Air

International airport/s: Funafuti International (FUN), east of Funafuti.

Airport tax: Departure tax: A$10; not applicable to transit passengers

Surface

Water: There are two government-owned ships that sail infrequently between Suva (Fiji) and Funafuti; sailing time is three days.

Getting about

National transport

Road: The only tar roads are on Funafuti. Elsewhere there are tracks. There is a limited number of vehicles, including some minibuses.

Water: An inter-island service is available which can be interupted by bad weather.

City transport

Taxis: There are a few taxis from the airport to the city centre. Hotels offer an airport pick-up service.

BUSINESS DIRECTORY

The addresses listed below are a selection only. While World of Information makes every endeavour to check these addresses, we cannot guarantee that changes have not been made, especially to telephone numbers and area codes. We would welcome any corrections.

Telephone area codes

The international direct dialling (IDD) code for Tuvalu is +688 followed by subscriber's number.

Useful telephone numbers

Police and fire: 20-726

Ambulance: 20-749

Chambers of Commerce

Tuvalu Chamber of Commerce, PO Box 27, Funafuti (tel: 208-46; fax: 208-29).

Banking

Development Bank of Tuvalu, PO Box 9, Vaiaku, Funafuti (tel: 201-99; fax: 208-50).

Central bank

National Bank of Tuvalu; PO Box 13, Vaiaku, Funafuti (tel: 208-03; fax: 208-02; e-mail: gmbt@tuvalu.tu).

Travel information

Air Fiji, 185 Victoria Parade, Suva, Fiji (tel: (+679) 331-5055; email: suvasales@airfiji.com.fi).

Air Marshall Islands, PO Box 1319, Majuro MH 96960, Republic of the Marshall Islands (tel: (+692) 625-3731; fax: (+692) 625-3730; email: amisales@ntamar.net; internet: www.airmarshallislands.com).

Funafuit International Airport, Vaiaku Funafuti (tel: 20-737, 20-057; email: travel@tuvalu.tv).

Funafuti International Airport, Department of Civil Aviation, Ministry of Works and Communication, Private Mail Bag, Funafuti (tel: 20-737, 20-725, 20-721; fax: 20-722).

South Pacific Tourism Organisation, Level 3, FNPF Place, 343-359 Victoria Parade; PO Box 13119, Suva, Fiji (tel: (+679) 330-4177; internet: www.spto.org).

Tuvalu Marine Department, Vaiaku, Funafuti, (tel: 20-055; fax: 20-722; email: danitaleli@yahoo.co.nz).

National tourist organisation offices

Tuvalu Tourism Office, Private Mail Bag, Vaiaku, Funafuti (tel: 20-184, 20-480; fax: 20-829; lleneuoti@yahoo.com; internet: www.timelesstuvalu.com).

Ministries

Ministry of Commerce and Natural Resources, Vaiaku, Funafuti.

Ministry of Finance, Vaiaku, Funafuti (tel: 20-840).

Statistics Division, c/o Finance Ministry, Vaiaku, Funafuti (tel: 20-839).

Other useful addresses

Asian Development Bank (ADB), South Pacific Regional Mission, La Casa di Andrea, Lini Highway; PO Box 127, Port Vila, Vanuatu (tel: (+678-2) 3300; fax: (+678-2) 3183; email: adbsprm@adb.org; internet: www.adb.org/SPRM).

Broadcasting and Information Office, Vaiaku Funafuti.

Business Development Advisory Board, PO Box 9, Funafuti (tel: 20-850).

Department of Civil Aviation, Ministry of Works and Communications, Private Mail Bag, Funafuti (tel: 20-737, 20-725, 20-721; fax: 20-722).

Department of Commerce, PO Box 33, Funafuti (tel: 20-839).

UN Permanent Mission of Tuvalu, 800 Second Avenue, Suite 400 B, New York, NY 10017 (tel: (+1-212) 490-0534; fax: (+1 212) 808-4975; email: enele@onecommonwealth.org).

ABC Pacific Beat: www.radioaustralia.net.au/pacbeat

Pacific Magazine: www.pacificmagazine.net

Pacific Islands New Association (Pina): www.pina.com.fj

Internet sites

South Pacific Tourism Organisation: www.tuvalu.spto.org

Tuvalu home page: www.tuvaluislands.com

Uganda

KEY FACTS

Official name: Republic of Uganda

Head of State: President Yoweri Kaguta Museveni (NRM) (since 1986; re-elected 18 Feb 2011)

Head of government: President Yoweri Kaguta Museveni (since 1986)

Ruling party: National Resistance Movement (NRM) (from 1999; re-elected 2011)

Area: 236,036 square km

Population: 38.04 million (2014)*

Capital: Kampala

Official language: English

Currency: Ugandan shilling (Ush) = 100 cents

Exchange rate: Ush3,660.00 per US$ (Sep 2015)

GDP per capita: US$726 (2014)*

GDP real growth: 4.90% (2014)*

GDP: US$27.62 billion (2014)*

Inflation: 4.67% (2014)

Balance of trade: -US$2.15 billion (2013)

Annual FDI: US$796.94 million (2011)

* estimated figure

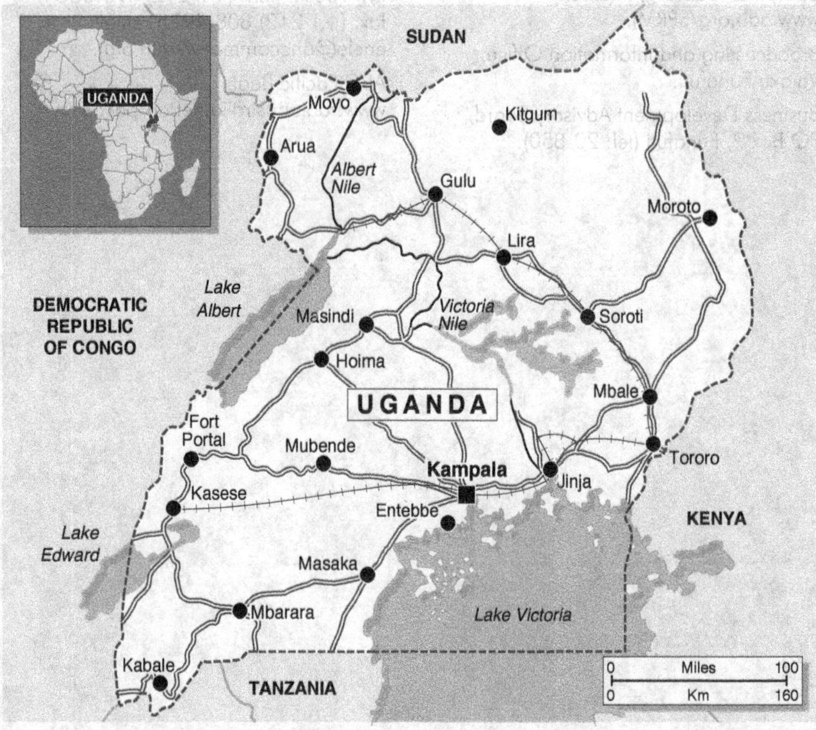

In Uganda's general election on 18 February 2014 President Yoweri Museveni won easily, confirming his position among Africa's geriatric leaders.

Budding rap artist

The president has some interesting methods when it comes to wooing voters in election campaigns. For example, when trying to attract the support from the youth in his country prior to elections, in 2010 Mr Museveni released a rap titled 'Yes Ssebo' – a common nickname for the president. He obviously didn't feel like it was time to end his musical career after this, as in 2015 he released a second rap ahead of his presidential campaigns with the aid of a renowned producer. Only after the elections in 2016 will we know if Museveni is more than a one-hit wonder.

Having assumed power by means of a guerrilla war in 1986, Mr Museveni and his National Revolutionary Movement (NRM) had long been expected to win his elections. The only time he had looked like losing his grip on power was in 2001 when Ugandans voted for Kizza Besigye, a doctor. In 2006, Mr Museveni managed to have Mr Besigye arraigned on doubtful rape charges. Opposition supporters were harassed and, unsurprisingly, Mr Museveni won a flawed election.

Progress, what progress?

Over a quarter of a century is a long time to be in power. Attitudes harden, flexibility diminishes and tolerance vanishes. In February 2014 President Museveni succeeded in bringing Uganda to world attention by signing into law what was generally known as the 'Anti-gay' Bill. The British Broadcasting Corporation (BBC) reported that the new bill tightened up penalties for gay people, but at least no longer contained a draconian clause criminalising those who failed to report them. The bill also provided for life sentences for gay sex and same-sex marriages. A once proposed sentence of up to 14 years for first-time offenders had been removed. Such was the retrogressive nature of the bill that even US President

Barack Obama had cautioned that it would be a backward step. Mr Museveni had at one stage undertaken to place the new legislation on hold pending US scientific advice. The BBC's Africa Correspondent Andrew Harding noted that 'the new law is blunt and uncompromising. Having spelled out its definition of homosexuality – which includes touching another person 'with the intention of committing the act of homosexuality' – the act concludes that convicted offenders will be sentenced 'to imprisonment for life.' The offence of 'aggravated homosexuality' – which includes having sex with 'a person living with HIV' or being 'a serial offender' – will also lead to life imprisonment. Critics of the bill could at least take some comfort from the fact that a death penalty clause had been removed.

Just a few months after the 'anti-gay' law had been introduced, it was annulled in August 2014 as the law was passed without the requisite quorum – not enough MPs were present at the vote. The activist community welcomed the decision with celebrations, however, there is a chance the law will be reconsidered in the future. When talking to *The Guardian* UK newspaper about homosexuality, politician and member of the NRM Medard Bitekyerezo stated that 'I will never believe that homosexuality has something to do with genetics.' He also claimed that homosexuals were recruiting children with the intention of 'teaching them homosexuality'. Bitekyerezo is one among a group of MPs who haven't given up on attempts to further criminalise homosexuality.

According to the respected NGO Human Rights Watch (HRW) in its 2014 report on Uganda, President Museveni and his ruling NRM party, in power for 29 years, continue to curtail freedom of expression, assembly, and association among other basic human rights. Despite the overturning of the Anti-homosexuality Act in August 2014, the government continues to voice outspoken support for its discriminatory provisions. The report also mentions that in some areas police have prevented opposition party's from holding public meetings, relying on the sweeping police powers under the 2013 Public Management Act. Impunity for abuses by the security forces, especially during protests, remains a serious problem.

In August 2014, Meseveni also signed the HIV Prevention and Control Act into law, which is widely considered to be counterproductive in achieving the national HIV goals as it discourages people from seeking treatment. This is because, contrary to international guidelines, the act criminalises intentional HIV transmission, attempted transmission, and behavior that might result in transmission by those who know their HIV status.

The HRW report also mentions the major corruption scandals that have repeatedly surfaced over recent years; however, no high-ranking officials have served prison sentences for corruption-related offences. Scandals have damaged health services, due to the misuse of funds intended for the provision of immunisations and essential medicines to fight HIV, tuberculosis and malaria. On the Transparency International 2014 *Corruption Perceptions Index* Uganda ranked 142 out of the 177 countries surveyed – a fall in two places on the 2013 rank, suggesting that more scandals are becoming apparent.

How to win an election

Although in the run-up to the 2014 election, the persistent Mr Besigye and other opposition candidates were able to campaign freely, they were up against Mr Museveni's effective pork barrel tactics. The London *Economist* reported that the president had personally distributed brown envelopes stuffed with cash to peasants, teachers and officials all over the country. According to the *Economist* the election had turned out to be the most expensive in Ugandan history, helped by the fact that Mr Besigye was also in the business of spending money, much of it from businessmen hedging their bets. His Forum for Democratic Change contested 295 of the 330 parliamentary seats. However, to get rid of Museveni, Uganda probably needed a new opposition candidate. Mr Besigye's campaign was deemed to be less than charismatic, failing to ignite the anger many Ugandans felt towards Mr Museveni.

The *Economist* noted that even if the oil was handled well, there were warning signs. Uganda's population had grown from 15 million in 1986 to 32 million in 2014. Half the population was under 16 years old and youth unemployment was 80 per cent. The NRM's campaign promises in 2006 to support industry had amounted to little. Mr Museveni had managed to keep youth frustration at bay by appealing to national cohesion, especially in the face of an increasing number of suicide bombings by jihadist groups. But the geriatric president's clinging to power and failure to indicate a successor in the face of rumours of a Museveni 'dynasty' have rendered Ugandan politics a busted flush. Were Mr Museveni's son, Lieutenant-Colonel Moohisi Kainerugaba, commander of the presidential guard, not to succeed him, the *Economist* considered Mr Museveni looks set on spending political capital and money his country can ill-afford to buy himself yet another term when 2016 comes around.

The economy

In its *African Economic Outlook* (AEO) report, the African Development Bank (AfDB) stated that in 2014 Uganda saw the consolidation of macroeconomic stability and a gradual return of economic activity. However, economic growth over the 2013/14 financial year only reached 4.5 per cent (significantly less than the

KEY INDICATORS — Uganda

	Unit	2011	2012	2013	2014	**2015
Population	m	*35.20	35.65	*36.82	*38.04	*39.19
Gross domestic product (GDP)	US$bn	16.80	21.24	25.57	*27.62	*26.81
GDP per capita	US$	478	596	694	*726	*684
GDP real growth	%	6.7	2.8	3.9	*4.9	*5.4
Inflation	%	6.5	14.0	4.8	4.7	*4.9
Exports (fob) (goods)	US$m	2,576.2	2,810.5	2,828.7	–	–
Imports (fob) (goods)	US$m	5,254.9	5,186.7	4,974.1	–	–
Balance of trade	US$m	-2,678.6	-2,376.3	-2,145.4	–	–
Current account	US$m	-2,275.8	-2,224.0	-1,625.0	*-2,082.0	*-2,348.0
Total reserves minus gold	US$m	2,614.4	3,167.2	3,337.5	3,316.4	–
Foreign exchange	US$m	2,386.9	2,950.5	3,122.3	–	–
Exchange rate	per US$	2,410.17	2,625.30	2,527.00	2,756.00	–

* estimated figure ** forecast figure

expected 5.7 per cent) largely due to under-execution of externally financed public investment and depressed exports as demand from trading partners stalled. The AfDB predicted that prospects in Uganda would improve in the 2014/15 financial year due to the government's resolve to improve the fiscal space through domestic revenue mobilisation efforts, scaled-up public investment and a recovery in private demand as households and corporations start accessing bank credit.

The outlook mentioned that the Poverty Status Report predicted a mixed future for human development. Positively, poverty as a percentage of population declined by 4.8 percentage points between 2010 and 2013. However, other indicators have exhibited stagnation or reversals, such as universal primary education and health, in particular HIV. Uganda was ranked at 164 out of 187 countries in the 2014 UN *Human Development Index*.

Progress is also concentrated in particular regions; the north and north-east lag behind the rest of the country in development, whilst the central and western regions advance ahead. According to the Uganda National Household Survey (2013) poverty in the central region is 5 per cent, whilst in the north it is at 44 per cent. The AfDB states that these disparities arise from unevenly distributed socio-economic infrastructure such as road networks, good access to markets, health and educational facilities and private sector investments. On a similar note, the rural-urban divide has been widening, and the government's main weapon in combating this has been the 2007 Peace, Recovery and Development Plan (PRDP). Despite the still-present disparities, the PRDP has produced some positive strides such as in infrastructure development.

Oil on the way

Uganda's hopes of energy independence were balanced by the worries of the IMF and others that Uganda's institutions would not be up to the job when the oil started flowing. However, the negotiations with oil companies had gone better than expected and there had been some degree of transparency, but few expected that to last. The all-powerful army would inevitably want its share of the expected bonanza. There was a lurking fear that Uganda, in terms of the distribution of its future oil wealth, would turn out to be another Equatorial Guinea.

In February 2014, the Ugandan government announced that it had reached a memorandum of understanding (MOU) with Tullow, Total and China National Offshore Oil Corporation (CNOOC) on a commercialisation and development plan. The plan included developing fields in the Albertine Graben area, fuelling a 30,000 to 60,000 barrels per day (bpd) refinery and constructing a crude oil export pipeline to the Lamu Port in Kenya. According to Tullow's 2013 annual report, the three companies were targeting gross oil production of more than 200,000bpd. However, the refinery would be authorised first call on production, according to IHS Energy.

According to the UD government's Energy Information Administration (EIA), the Ugandan government was in the process of choosing a lead investor to develop the refinery. The refinery will be located in the Hoima district in western Uganda and is expected to initially process 30,000bpd of crude oil, increasing to 60,000bpd before 2020.

The first commercial oil discovery in Uganda was made in the Lake Albert Rift Basin in 2006. Since then, according to the EIA successful well appraisals had boosted Uganda's proven crude oil reserves from zero in 2010 to 2.5 billion barrels in January 2015. As reported by the *Oil & Gas Journal* (OGJ) January 2014 natural gas reserves were 500 billion cubic feet. In 2014 Uganda had yet to produce any hydrocarbons, but crude oil production was expected to start within five years. Initial oil flows would be used to fuel a 50-megawatt crude-fired electricity plant in the Lake Albert region, according to IHS Energy. Commercial oil production was expected to start in 2018, although the date had been rescheduled several times.

Risk assessment

Politics	Fair/poor
Economy	Fair
Regional stability	Good/fair

Muslims in Uganda

% of population	12
Sunni (% of Muslims)	94
Shi'a (% of Muslims)	5

COUNTRY PROFILE

By the eighteenth century, the territory, now known as Uganda, was occupied by Nilotic peoples in the north – the Acholi and Langi – and by Bantus and Bagandas, from whom the country gets its name, in the south.

1886–1890 The UK colonised Uganda.

1900 Bugunda in western Uganda became an autonomous region with its own constitutional monarchy.

1958 The UK allowed Uganda self-government.

1962 Uganda became an independent state within the Commonwealth.

1963 Uganda became a republic. Sir Edward Mutesa II, the King of Buganda, became Uganda's first president.

1966 Milton Obote, the defence minister, seized power with the help of Colonel Idi Amin, second-in-command of the army. Obote repressed the Baganda and re-integrated Buganda.

1967 The constitutional role of kings was abolished, along with federal system of government.

1971 Obote was ousted by Idi Amin, who expelled the large Asian (mainly Indian) community and carried out purges in which thousands died. Asians had owned 90 per cent of Uganda's businesses and the economy collapsed.

1979 Tanzania invaded Uganda, causing Amin to flee to Saudi Arabia. Yusufu Lule was briefly appointed president before being replaced by Godfrey Binaisa.

1980 Obote won the presidential election and started to pursue liberal economic policies to obtain aid from western donors, and the economy began to improve.

1985 Ethnic feuding resulted in a coup removing Obote from power.

1986 Yoweri Museveni came to power at the head of the National Resistance Movement (NRM), which had waged a guerrilla war since 1981. He banned multi-party politics, saying they led to ethnic fighting.

1996 President Museveni was elected president for a five-year term.

1998 Uganda intervened in the Democratic Republic of Congo (DRC) on behalf of the rebels who were opposed to the Kabila government.

2001 President Museveni was re-elected. In legislative elections, the supporters of the 'No Party' Movement – formerly the NRM – secured a majority, although they lost over 50 MPs, including 10 ministers. President Museveni's cabinet was headed by incumbent Prime Minister Apolo Nsimbabi. A peace agreement was signed by Rwanda and Uganda in London.

2002 Over 400,000 people were evacuated from villages in the northern war-zone at risk of brutal attacks from the Lord's Resistance Army (LRA).

2003 The LRA announced a cease-fire, but as attacks continued an all-out offensive against the rebels was ordered. As Uganda withdrew the last of its troops from eastern DRC tens of thousands of DRC civilians fleeing fighting in their own country sought asylum in Uganda. Idi Amin died in Saudi Arabia.

2004 LRA rebels killed around 200 people at a camp for displaced persons in the north. President Museveni retired from the

army at the rank of general. Faltering peace talks between the government and the LRA began.
2005 The constitution was amended, removing the limit to presidential terms in office, and multi-party politics were restored. The International Criminal Court (ICC) issued arrest warrants for five commanders of the LRA including its leader, Joseph Kony. Opposition presidential candidate, Kizza Besigye, was arrested after he returned from exile and was accused of terrorism and unlawful possession of firearms. Uganda was ordered by the International Court of Justice (ICJ) to pay compensation for rights abuses and plundering the DRC during its occupation in 2003.
2006 Besigye was bailed allowing him to campaign in the presidential election, which was won by Yoweri Museveni. Kizza Besigye was acquitted of the charge against him. A cease-fire was agreed between government forces and the LRA. The UNHCR estimated that there were 1.5 million refugees of the long-running conflict in displacement camps in neighbouring countries; within two months, over 300,000 had returned to their homes.
2007 Racial violence erupted in Kampala, forcing police to protect Asian businesses and a Hindu temple in a conflict over allowing a development within an area of rain forest. Severe flooding caused widespread damage in the north-west.
2008 The LRA signed a permanent cease-fire during talks in Juba, Sudan. However, General Kony refused to sign the peace deal saying he did not understand the workings of the special court to be set up to try rebels. Peace negotiations resumed but broke down within weeks as the government rejected Kony's approach for talks to resume. Interior minister, Ruhaka Rugunda, said that after two years of negotiations there was nothing more to discuss and Kony should have signed the peace agreement earlier. With the peace talks stalled after arrest warrants for Joseph Kony were not withdrawn (by the ICC) as demanded by the LRA, a joint operation against the LRA, based in the Garamba region of the Democratic Republic of Congo (DRC), was launched by the armies of Uganda, Sudan and DRC.
2009 The LRA called for a cease-fire, which was rejected. The government announced that Uganda's army had halted its operations prematurely and had withdrawn from DRC, due to political pressure from DRC, but that the conflict with the LRA continued. Famine in the north-west around Arua district was declared with an appeal for funds to feed the local population. A law banning female genital mutilation (circumcision) was introduced.
2010 Torrential rains on Mount Elgon caused mudslides, near the eastern town of Bududa, which killed at least 100 and made over 5,000 people homeless. A later decision was taken to remove 500,000 people from the area. Traditional tombs of Buganda kings, built mostly of timber and reeds and which were on the list of Unesco World Heritage Sites, were destroyed by fire; a later decision was to rebuild the tombs. Uganda, along with Tanzania and Ethiopia signed an agreement to share the waters of the River Nile. In the new deal the three nations (out of five) that form the source of the river, reserved more of the water for themselves. Egypt and Sudan, which had until then taken the greater share, objected but finally agreed after 13 years of negotiations had failed to resolve the issue earlier. Two bombs exploded in Kampala during the Football World Cup final, killing some 80 people. The Somali Islamist militant group, al Shabab, claimed responsibility. During the 15th AU Summit meeting held in Kampala President Museveni said that the al Shabab should be 'swept out of Africa'. He called for more AU troops to be sent to Mogadishu. Three men who had been resident in Kenya were charged with the bombings and several others were later arrested. The government 'repossessed' the Kingfisher oil field, near Lake Albert Rift Basin, in a dispute with its original developers, Heritage Oil, over its refusal to pay US$283 million in tax before selling its assets to Tullow Oil. Of the people accused of the Kampala bombing, 18 were released, although three were rearrested and state prosecutors said that 17 others would be tried on charges of terrorism, murder and attempted murder. An outbreak of yellow fever was confirmed in the north, the first for some 40 years.
2011 Eight candidates took part in the presidential election held in February. Incumbent, Yoweri Museveni (NRM), won 68.4 per cent of the vote and remained in office for another term. His closest rival Kizza Besigye (FDC) alleged fraud during the election. In parliamentary elections held at the same time, the ruling NRM won an overwhelming majority of 263 seats (out of 375). Dr Besigye was arrested in April as he attempted to join the 'walk-to-work' march protesting against the rising cost of living, was followed by a demonstration broken up by police using tear gas and rubber bullets. Dr Besigye was released and left the country for hospital treatment in Kenya. In a further demonstration, against the manner of Dr Besigye's arrest, two demonstrators were reported to have been killed by police. In May police sprayed a pink liquid on opposition leaders and protesters who were heading towards Constitution Square in Kampala to attend a rally. President Museveni was sworn in for his fourth term in office in May; supporters of opposition leader Kizza Besigye stoned the convoy transporting dignitaries to the ceremony. Police placed Besigye under house arrest to prevent alleged mobilisation of his supporters during the opening of parliament ceremony. President Yoweri Museveni appointed Edward Ssekandi as vice president and Amama Mbabazi as prime minister. The trial of Thomas Kwoyelo on 53 charges including murder and hostage-taking began in July in Uganda's International Crimes Division court in Gulu. He was the first LRA commander to stand trial. Foreign affairs minister, Sam Kutesa, and two other officials resigned in October after being accused of corruption.
2012 The government signed a production agreement with Tullow Oil on 3 February, which will allow a US$10 billion investment in an oil pipeline and refinery. The deal includes Tullow Oil selling two-thirds of its interest in the Lake Albert Rift Basin to the Chinese state oil company CNOOC and the French energy company, Total. The agreement ends the deadlock over future taxes and protects companies from potential future losses if the government alters tax laws. The authorities announced the opening of a third refugee camp to provide aid to those fleeing eastern Democratic Republic of Congo (DRC). Around 100 people per day had been crossing the border to escape the violence that had erupted following the chaotic DRC presidential elections in November 2011. An outbreak of the deadly Ebola virus, which killed 14 people, was reported to have reached Kampala by 31 July. President Museveni advised people to avoid personal contact with one another. The outbreak was brought under control by 1 August. On 16 November, following an audit report into corruption published in October and its own forensic audit, the UK government announced that it had cut all aid to Uganda. Denmark, Ireland, Norway and Sweden had already cut their aid following the audit report. Another outbreak of Ebola was reported on 15 November, killing two members of a family. Uganda was accused of supporting the March 23 Movement (M23) rebellion in the DRC and in response, on 12 November, it threatened to withdraw all of its troops deployed on AU missions.
2013 Sections of legislation granting a blanket amnesty to members of armed groups who surrender under Uganda's Amnesty Act were reinstated in May. The sections will remain in force for two years with only top LRA commanders being

ineligible for amnesty. The sections had been allowed to lapse in May 2012 when internal affairs minister Hilary Onek announced that all rebels would have to go through the courts and legal process with the courts deciding whether or not to proscecute or grant amnesty to indivuals who appeared before them. Erias Lukwago, mayor of Kampala and a critic of President Museven said that he was beaten by police and tear gas was thrown into his car on 20 June. In a separate incident, opposition leader Kizza Besigye was arrested for holding an unsanctioned rally. A bill passed on 6 August will effectively ban all political discussion say critics. Under the bill any Ugandans wanting to talk politics in groups of three or more will have to apply for permission a week in advance.
2014 A single cross-border tourist visa for Burundi, Kenya and Uganda was launched on 20 February. The visa costs US$100 and is valid for 90 days. Tanzania and Rwanda are expected to join in the future.
2015 Rebel commander Dominic Ongwen was arrested in the Central African Republic (CAR) in January. He arrived in The Hague on 21 January to stand trial at the International Criminal Court (ICC) on war crimes charges.

Political structure

Constitution
An elected constituent assembly drafted a constitution which was promulgated on 8 October 1995. It retains the system of non-party government.
In July 2005, the Ugandan parliament voted for a constitutional amendment to allow President Yoweri Museveni to stay longer in office; he should have stood down in 2006. It removed all presidential term limits and legalized a multi-party political system.

Form of state
Unitary republic

The executive
The president is elected by absolute majority popular vote in two rounds if needed for a five-year term (unlimited terms). The president appoints the Cabinet from among elected members of the National Assembly. The prime minister assists the president in supervising the cabinet.

National legislature
The unicameral Parliament of Uganda has 388 seats of which 238 are Constituency Representatives, 112 are District Woman Representatives, 10 Uganda People's Defence Forces (UPDF) representatives, five youth representatives, five representatives of disabled people and five workers' representatives. Members are directly elected in single-seat constituencies by simple majority vote. In addition there are 13 ex officio members appointed by the president. Members serve five-year terms.

Legal system
The legal system is based on English common law and the 1995 constitution.

Last elections
18 February 2011 (parliamentary); 18 February 2011 (presidential)

Results: Parliamentary: National Resistance Movement (NRM) won 263 seats (out of 375), Forum for Democratic Change (FDC) 34, Democratic Party (DP) 12, Uganda People's Party (UPP) 10, Conservative Party (CP) one, Justice Forum (JF) one, Independents 43, representatives of the Uganda People's Defence Force 10.
Presidential: Yoweri Museveni (NRM) won 68.4 per cent of the vote, Kizza Besigye (FDC) 26 per cent, Norbert Mao (DP) 1.9 per cent, and Olara Otunnu (Uganda People's Congress (UPC)) 1.6 per cent. Turnout is 59.3 per cent.

Next elections
2016 (parliamentary); February 2016 (presidential).

Political parties

Ruling party
National Resistance Movement (NRM) (from 1999; re-elected 2011)

Main opposition party
Forum for Democratic Change (FDC).
Approximately 50 per cent of the total population is under 14 years of age.

Population
38.04 million (2014)*

Last census: September 2002: 24,442,084

Population density: 114 inhabitants per square km. Urban population 13 per cent (2010 Unicef).

Annual growth rate: 3.2 per cent, 1990–2010 (Unicef).

Internally Displaced Persons (IDP)
1.6 million (UNHCR 2004)

Ethnic make-up
There are over 20 ethnic groups of which the Baganda, Banyankole and Basoga are the largest. Approximately 99 per cent of the population is of African descent and 1 per cent European or Asian.

Religions
Christianity (71 per cent), traditional beliefs (13 per cent), Islam (5 per cent), others (11 per cent).

Education
Unesco reported that a government's education programme launched in 1997, had successfully increased primary school enrolment from 2.5 million in 1997 to 6.5 million in 2001. The programme provided free primary education to four children including orphaned and disabled children from each household.
Primary school lasts for seven years and, having successfully undertaken exams, students then follow either an acedemic or vocational secondary schooling.

Literacy rate: 69 per cent adult rate; 80 per cent youth rate (15–24) (Unesco 2005).

Compulsory years: None.

Enrolment rate: 74 per cent gross primary; 12 per cent gross secondary; of relevant age groups, (including repeaters) (World Bank).

Pupils per teacher: 35 in primary schools.

Health
The lack of resources and an extreme dependence on foreign aid has resulted in a high infant and maternal mortality rate and low immunisation coverage.
Improved water sources are available to 42 per cent of the population.

HIV/Aids
In 2005 there were an estimated 800,000 people living with HIV/Aids, with 100,000 new infections each year. Even though the prevalence has been falling – down to 6 per cent in 2005 from the high of 30 per cent in the early 1990s – those who are developing Aids is increasing and putting social and economic pressure on the country's resources. The number of people living longer with HIV has been rising due to anti-retroviral (ARV) drugs; there are over 65,000 patients currently receiving ARV medication. Since the beginning of the pandemic in Uganda, an estimated one million people have died of Aids and the government expects another to be treating over 50,000 Aids suffers each year.
Uganda was the first country in sub-Saharan Africa to show a decrease in the number of HIV positive sufferers, due to an extensive, long-term government initiative to combat the spread of the disease (one of the best instituted in Africa). UNAIDS granted US$250 million (2001–06) for government sponsored projects from the Global Fund to fight HIV/Aids, Tuberculosis and Malaria.
Rural areas have been badly hit with productivity and output in the agricultural sector significantly fallen as Aids has taken its toll of workers and those that curtail their time in the fields to care for the sick.
In April 2005, US researchers upheld findings of a 1997 Ugandan study that claimed the Aids drug Nevirapine was safe and effective. The use of the drug, to limit HIV mother-to-child infection, was embroiled in a politicised row in 2004 when it was claimed poor record keeping had invalidated the trial of the drug and that is was unsafe and causing thousands of severe side effects, including deaths.

A factory in Kampala, to open for production by January 2008, will produce three-in-one tablets of HIV/Aids anti-retoviral and anti-malaria medication. Domestic production reduces the need for and cost of imported drugs. Nevertheless, national distribution remains the largest impediment for healthworkers to manage in a country where only 41 per cent of HIV patients receive anti-retroviral drugs. Uganda has cut its HIV/Aids infection rate from 30 per cent in the 1990s to less than 10 per cent in 2007.

HIV prevalence: 4.1 per cent aged 15–49 in 2003 (World Bank)

Life expectancy: 49 years, 2004 (WHO 2006)

Fertility rate/Maternal mortality rate: 6.1 births per woman, 2010 (Unicef); maternal mortality rate 510 per 100,000 live births (World Bank).

Birth rate/Death rate: 46.6 births and 17 deaths per 1,000 people (2003).

Child (under 5 years) mortality rate (per 1,000): 69 per 1,000 live births (WHO 2012); 38 per cent of children aged under five are malnourished (World Bank).

Head of population per physician: 0.08 physicians per 1,000 people, 2004 (WHO 2006)

Welfare

The distribution of income in Uganda is less unequal than most countries in Africa, with the richest 20 per cent of the country owning 44.9 per cent of the national wealth while the bottom 20 per cent earning 7.1 per cent of the country's income. Around 10 per cent of the rural population lives under the national poverty line, while around 40 per cent of the urban population is classified as poor. The informal sector employs over 80 per cent of the urban population, implying a high degree of job insecurity and casual labour.

Main cities

Kampala (capital, estimated population 1.6 million in 2012), Gulu (255,067), Lira (219,126), Kasese (108,328), Kitgum (104,605), Jinja (100,238), Mbarara (98,782), Mbale (83,302).

Languages spoken

KiSwahili, Luganda and Luo are widely spoken.

Official language/s

English

Media

Press

The Media Council (http://mediavisionsite.com) regulates and censors information.

Dailies: The government publishes two newspapers, *Bukedde* (www.bukedde.co.ug) in Luganda and *The New Vision* (www.newvision.co.ug) in English. *The Monitor* (www.monitor.co.ug) and *Red Pepper* (www.redpepper.ug) (a tabloid) are independent and published in English.

Weeklies: The government publishes three regional newspapers, *Orumuri* (www.orumuri.co.ug) *Rupiny* (www.rupiny.co.ug) and *Etop* (www.etop.co.ug) in local languages. All daily newspapers have Sunday editions. *The Observer Weekly* (www.ugandaobserver.com) and *Entatsi* (in Runyakitara) are independent. .

Business: Apart from daily newspaper with business sections *East African Business Week* (http://www.busiweek.com) is based in Kampala.

Periodicals: In Luganda, *Musizi* is a Catholic monthly publication.

Broadcasting

The Uganda Communications Commission (www.ucc.co.ug) is responsible for the communications industry.

Radio: There has been a large expansion of services with many private local radio stations in operation. The public broadcaster is the Uganda Broadcast Corporation (UBC), with a national FM network with channels on Radio Uganda called Blue, Red, Green and Butebo, which provide programmes in English, KiSwahili and 20 local languages. Private stations include 95N9 Touch FM (www.touch.fm) and Arua One FM (www.aruaonefm.com) and the women's community radio Mama FM (http://interconnection.org/umwa/community_radio.html).

Television: There are over a dozen channels broadcasting by terrestrial, cable and satellite. The state-owned UBC television service is a commercial service, broadcastings mainly in English, KiSwahili and Luganda. Most networks are privately-owned, including WBS Television (www.wbs-tv.com), which is centred on Kampala, as well as Multichoice, Nation TV and Pulse TV; Nkabi Broadcasting Services in based in Jinja. There are several Christian channels including Record Television Network, Top TV and Christian Life Ministries. Foreign channels are provided by Digital Satellite Television DSTV

Economy

Uganda has ample fertile land and good rainfall so that agriculture is an important contributor, at 21.9 per cent in 2014, to GDP. Exports include coffee, tea, tobacco, vanilla beans and cut flowers and fish (Nile perch and tilapia) and fish products. Produce for the domestic market includes cassava, potatoes, wheat, vegetables and fruit, while livestock produces beef and dairy, goat and poultry. Industry and manufacturing, which constitutes a further 26.7 per cent of GDP, includes light manufacturing of textiles and clothes and consumer goods as well as processed agricultural products. Heavy industry includes cement production and other building materials and hydroelectricity. The service sector, dominated by government services, constitutes 51.3 per cent of GDP.

GDP growth was consistently high for several years leading up to and including the global economic crisis, when Uganda's growth rate did not fall below 7 per cent (over the period 2007–09). However, after this period the economy decelerated and by 2012 GDP growth had fallen to 2.6 per cent. In 2013 growth increased to 3.9 per cent, and thanks to the consolidation of macroeconomic stability and a recovery of economic activity, Uganda posted a growth in GDP of 4.9 per cent in 2014. High inflation has been a long-term problem, averaging over 5 per cent for most of 2000s. It peaked at 18.7 per cent in 2011, before falling down to 4.3 per cent by 2014.

Remittances are an important resource, not only for the immediate benefit of families but also for the country. Remittances from migrant workers amounted to US$910.3 million in 2012 and reached US$931.6 million in 2013 (3.8 per cent of GDP).

In 2014, the UN Human Development Index (HDI) ranked Uganda 164 (out of 187) for national development in health, education and income. Since 2000, Uganda's progress has grown to match the improvement of other countries in sub-Saharan Africa. In 2014, 70.3 per cent of the population lived in multidimensional poverty, while 38.0 per cent lived on less than the equivalent of US$1.25 per day.

In March 2015, Energy and Minerals Minister announced that Uganda was confident it would source crude oil from the ground in early 2018 and be able to start feeding it into a proposed refinery refining as it seeks to become a regional energy hub. In February 2012, the government signed a production agreement with the UK-based Tullow Oil (after it had sold two-thirds of its interests in Uganda's three oil blocks to Total and CNOOC). The three companies plan to invest up to US$10 billion in an oil development project in the Albertine rift basin around Lake Albert, containing over an estimated 1 billion barrels of oil. Tullow estimated that by 2018 Uganda could be producing 350,000bpd. Uganda has other natural resources such as copper, cobalt, salt, phosphate and limestone.

The first gold refinery in Uganda had been opened in 2010, in Kampala, with a capacity to produce 10kg of gold per day. The US$1.5 million, Russian-owned refinery will process gold from the Democratic Republic of Congo and other countries in the region.

In 2010, following 13 years of failed negotiations over distribution of water rights of the Nile River, a split occurred when Tanzania, Uganda, Ethiopia and Rwanda unilaterally demanded a more equitable share. The original agreements had shared 90 per cent between Egypt and Sudan, leaving just 10 per cent to be shared among the other nine countries of East Africa. Uganda should benefit with more water available for its arid northern region.

External trade

Uganda is a member of the East African Community (EAC) (with Burundi, Kenya, Rwanda and Tanzania). The East African Community Common Market Protocol (EACMP) was launched on 1 July 2010, set up for the free movement of labour, capital, goods and services between member states as well as employment opportunities and easier flow of investment capital. The signed protocol now requires that legislation in all states must be harmonised to conform to its jurisdiction.

Uganda is also a member of the Common Market for Eastern and Southern Africa (Comesa), and operates a free trade area with 13 of the 19 member states.

With ample, fertile land and good rainfalls agriculture provides the opportunity to cultivate a number of cash crops, including coffee (accounting for around 23 per cent of total agricultural exports), tea, tobacco, vanilla, cotton and cut flowers (flown to European markets within hours of preparation). Industrial production is progressively replacing imports of construction materials, foodstuffs and household goods. Remittances are also an important source of foreign exchange.

Uganda is a landlocked country and any heavy or bulky exports must be transport either by road or train to seaports to Tanzania or Kenya, each adding to a time delay and an increase in the cost of freight.

Imports

Principal imports are capital equipment, vehicles, petroleum, chemicals and pharmaceuticals, medical supplies and cereals.

Main sources: India (26.8 per cent of total in 2013), China (10.7 per cent), Kenya (9.7 per cent).

Exports

Principal exports are agricultural products, coffee (typically 23 per cent), tea, cotton, live animals, fish and fish products, horticultural products and, from 2010, petroleum.

Main destinations: Kenya (13.1 per cent of total in 2013), DR of the Congo (11.1 per cent), Sudan (9.9 per cent).

Re-exports

Gold, diamonds, coltan and niobium, mostly from neighbouring DRC.

Agriculture

Farming

Around 80 per cent of the population derive their livelihood from agriculture. The area under cultivation has only increased by one-third over the last 30 years. The situation has been worsened by irregular rainfall and climate change. This has eroded the farmers' confidence in applying improved technology to increase productivity, resulting in crop and livestock yields, which have been ranked among the lowest in the world. Agricultural development is hampered by shortages of vital inputs, damage caused by civil war, low producer prices and corrupt purchasing bodies.

Uganda's varied climate allows the production of a wide range of produce. Around 75 per cent of Uganda's agricultural output is made up of food crop production, two-thirds of which is used for subsistence. Maize is one of the main food crops and is grown around Lake Victoria as a cash crop. The fertility of Ugandan land could make it a breadbasket for East Africa, particularly if the effects of periodic droughts are ameliorated by adequate irrigation techniques.

Coffee is the main cash crop, providing around 70 per cent of agricultural export earnings. Most production is carried out on a small-scale basis. Rehabilitation of coffee holdings has been the main stimulus to economic growth in recent years. The government has encouraged planting of clone coffee which yields in a shorter period of around two years, is more disease resistant and gives higher yields. The private sector controls over 90 per cent of the coffee trade in Uganda. Liberalisation of the coffee market has meant that producers can sell coffee on the open market to the highest bidder, although the dismantling of state marketing boards has meant that they are more vulnerable to price fluctuations and have to deal with often unscrupulous middlemen. The formation of co-operatives has become a basis for reducing the adverse effects of liberalisation. There was concern in 2007 that the economic partnership agreement (EPA) between the EU and Africa, Caribbean and Pacific developing countries would have an adverse affect on coffee growers if the EU did not remove subsidies on its domestic coffee industries. Around 15,000 coffee farmers are certified as organic growers, out of a total number of one million growers. Uganda mostly grows Robusta coffee.

Cotton was once an important cash crop, but due to its labour intensiveness, relatively high cost of production and a poor marketing system, farmers looked towards growing non-traditional cash crops, which have a readily available market. Cotton growing is being revived in some eastern areas, and production has been boosted by reforms in agricultural pricing and marketing regimes introduced in the 1990s. Sugar is grown on several vast estates and production is creeping up after collapsing completely in the early 1980s. Tobacco and tea are also important cash crops.

Fishing

Uganda's fishing industry is important, both for domestic consumption and export. The annual catch is typically around 220,000 tonnes, 40 per cent of which is exported. In 2004, the industry is estimated to have added US$100 million or six per cent to the nation's economy.

The fisheries industry is mostly based on inland capture fisheries from lakes Victoria, Albert, Edward, George and Kyoga. Lake Victoria is Uganda's most important fishery, supplying some 50 per cent of the national catch. Nile perch obtained from Lake Victoria alone amount to 110,000 tonnes and remains the largest fish export item to the markets of Europe, Australia and South-East Asia. Estimates of Lake Kyoga put supplies at 30,000 tonnes, with the nature of the fishery shifting from a prolific Nile perch and tilapia fishery to increased supplies of mukene.

Forestry

Uganda is moderately forested with around 30 per cent forest cover and an additional 48 per cent of other wooded land. The majority of timber production is used in domestic fuel. There is a wide network of protected areas, including 50 parks and nature reserves. A large proportion of household energy needs are met by fuelwood. The sector produces sawnwood from local hardwood species and much of industrial roundwood is used for agricultural purposes. Paper is imported in large quantities.

Industry and manufacturing

The industrial sector's contribution to GDP has grown from around 20 per cent in 2000 to 26.7 per cent in 2014, reflecting a slow but steady process of industrialisation.

The industrial sector is mainly involved in import substitution. It has seen encouraging growth, particularly in food processing, tobacco, beverages, timber/paper and chemicals/soap. Under-utilisation of factory capacity and lack of foreign

exchange continues to inhibit greater progress.
Other industries are textiles, cement, plastics, steel, metal products and brewing. Most of these are operating well below capacity mainly due to shortages of imported materials, spares and fuel, inadequate infrastructure and a lack of skilled manpower.

Tourism
Tourism is a growing sector with the government backing promotions and co-operative developments to provide incentives for the increasing number of visitors. In 2012 there were 1,197,000 international arrivals to Uganda, growing slightly to 1,206,000 in 2013.
The Bwindi Impenetrable National Park, home of exceptional biodiversity, and many endangered species, including the mountain gorilla, and the Rwenzori Mountain National Park are included on Unesco's World Heritage List, along with the Tombs of Buganda Kings (in Kasubi). These tombs were gutted by fire in 2010, and while some restoration of the surrounding buildings had, by 2014, been completed the central mausoleum remained to be rebuilt.
Travel and tourism contributed 9.9 per cent to GDP in 2014, and the industry provided employment to 8.6 per cent of the labour force, the equivalent of 592,500 jobs.
The ministry of tourism, wildlife and heritage runs training schools to provide professional skills for those working in the industry, particularly hoteliers and restaurateurs. There is a full range of hotels and (game) lodges, from luxury to budget.
In a move calculated to encourage tourists, Kenya, Rwanda and Uganda announced in November 2013 a joint visa scheme for tourists to take effect from 1 January 2014. The cost of the joint visa is expected to be US$100; the current cost per visa is US$50 each for Kenya and Uganda and US$30 for Rwanda. The single cross-border tourist visa for Rwanda, Kenya and Uganda was launched on 20 February 2014. The visa costs US$100 and is valid for 90 days (see http://www.visiteastafrica.org/visa/ for details). Tanzania and Burundi are expected to join in the future.

Environment
In 2008 the governments of Democratic Republic of Congo, Rwanda and Uganda agreed to joint measures to protect the mountain gorillas found within their shared border regions. Tourists visiting the area to view the endangered great apes raise a combined US$5 million for the countries concerned. However, poaching and civil strife have dropped the numbers of gorillas to critically endangered levels, so that a 10-year conservation project which focuses of security and encouraging local people to preserve the animals and habitat is seen as the only hope for the gorilla's survival

Mining
Uganda has deposits of copper, cobalt and iron ore, as well as less viable fields of tungsten, beryl, columbo-tantalite, gold, bismuth, tin, limestone and phosphates. Uganda's mineral potential remains untested due to very little exploration to date.
The first gold refinery in Uganda was opened in Kampala in May 2010, with a capacity to produce 10kg of gold per day. The US$1.5 million, Russian-owned refinery will process gold from the Democratic Republic of Congo and other countries in the region.

Hydrocarbons
Up to 20 major discoveries of oil have been made since 2006 so that by 2015 Uganda had some 2.5 billion barrels of proved reserves.
In 2009 UK-based oil companies Tullow and Heritage had announced, in separate statements, that they had located 'world class' oil discoveries in the Lake Albert Rift Basin in western Uganda, which could total over 400 million barrels of oil. The full potential of the oil field may not be known until further exploration.
Both companies announced they would invest in a 500,000bpd oil pipeline to Eldoret and then to Nairobi (Kenya). The 320km, Eldoret-Kampala oil pipeline was scheduled to begin construction in 2009, however by mid-2015 the extension to Kampala had not yet been started. Domestic oil will replace 114,000 tonnes of imported petroleum products that are currently transported by road and rail. However in May, President Museveni, who is against a pipeline that would carry only crude oil (and not refined oil) and thereby limit exports to crude oil, announced that he had signed a co-operation agreement with Iran, which would fund a new refinery. This may lead to changes in the pipeline contract. The Italian energy company Eni bought a 50 per cent share in two Ugandan oil fields in 2009 from the Canadian Heritage oil exploration company. Eni paid US$1.35 billion in cash with a deferred payment of US$150 million. Oil production, by Tullow Oil, starting at 500–1,000bpd had been expected to begin in 2010, rising to 10,000bpd in 2011 and expected to reach 150,000bpd by the end of 2015.

Energy
Total installed generating capacity was 711.4MW in 2014. Uganda relies on imported oil for a large share of its energy needs, the balance being provided by hydroelectricity. Nalubaale (Owen Falls) power station, operating since the mid-1950s, and its Kiira extension supply almost all of the electricity system's capacity. Less than 20 per cent of the population has access to electricity, which due to growing demand of 30–40MW per year, has to be rationed.

Financial markets
Stock exchange
Uganda Securities Exchange

Banking and insurance
Great efforts are being made to improve efficiency in the banking sector, including the placement of local banks under statutory management. However, Uganda's banking sector remains weak. In recent years, the Bank of Uganda's (BoU) (central bank) regulatory powers have been insufficient, with reports that troubled banks have failed to meet their reserve requirements.
In an effort to reverse the situation, the BoU increased the capital requirements of all banks and was granted power to close banks that failed to comply with a number of regulations. As a result, the ratio of non-performing loans to total assets has fallen and banking system profitability has improved. However, the BoU was forced to seize control of the Uganda Commercial Bank (UCB) after its privatisation due to fraudulent behaviour by the buyer. In 2002, an 80 per cent stake in UCB was sold to South Africa's Standard Bank Group.
The government is planning to increase the availability of credit to poor rural areas through micro-finance and a lighter regulatory framework.

Central bank
Bank of Uganda

Main financial centre
Kampala

Time
GMT plus three hours

Geography
Uganda is a landlocked country in East Africa, bordered by Sudan to the north, the Democratic Republic of Congo (DCR) to the west, Kenya to the east and Rwanda, Tanzania and Lake Victoria to the south.
The terrain is mainly plateau, stretching northwards from Lake Victoria and declining gradually from around 1,500m to 900m towards the Sudan border. Mountain ranges and volcanic hills ring the country. The highest point at 5,110m is Marherita Peak on snow-capped Mount Stanley. Lakes, swampland and rivers occupy around 20 per cent of the country. Lake Victoria occupies much of the south-easten corner of Uganda, stradding

the borders with Kenya and Tanzania. In the west the frontier with the DRC passes through lakes Albert and Edward. The White Nile rises in Lake Victoria and travels north through Lakes Kyoga and Albert towards Sudan.
Much of the country is savannah and semi-desert, but there are equatorial forests in the central zone.

Hemisphere

Straddles the equator

Climate

Equatorial, tempered by high altitude. Temperatures are fairly constant throughout the year, hottest months December–February, June–August, with daytime range (in Kampala) of 27–29 degrees Celsius (C) compared with an annual average of 26 degrees C (night-time average 16 degrees C). Heaviest rainfall occurs March–May, October–November; April is wettest month (average fall for month 175 mm).

Dress codes

Lightweight clothing is advisable all year round. Senior officials tend to wear suits, local businessmen and government officials wear suits or safari suits. Light cotton dresses, skirts and blouses or lightweight suits are advised for women. A lightweight raincoat may be needed at any time of the year.

Entry requirements

Passports

Required by all, valid for six months from date of arrival.

Visa

Required by all, except nationals of COMESA and other countries listed on www.ugandaembassy.com/visa.htm (countries with reciprocal visa-free entry).
In a move calculated to encourage tourists, a single cross-border tourist visa for Rwanda, Kenya and Uganda was launched on 20 February 2014. The visa costs US$100 and is valid for 90 days (see http://www.visiteastafrica.org/visa/ for details).

Currency advice/regulations

Import and export of local currency is prohibited. There is no restriction on the import of foreign currency, subject to declaration on arrival, or on the export of foreign currency up to the amount declared on arrival.

Customs

Duty-free allowances are: one litre of spirits or wines, 500ml of perfume or toilet water, 225 grammes of tobacco products.

Prohibited imports

Game trophies require special permit.

Health (for visitors)

Mandatory precautions

A valid international certificate of vaccination against cholera is required for entry into and exit from Uganda. Vaccination must have taken place not less than seven days and no more than six months prior to entering the country. A valid international certificate of vaccination against yellow fever is also required for visitors arriving from infected areas; an outbreak was confirmed in the north in December 2010. The certificate becomes valid 12 days after vaccination and lasts for 10 years.

Advisable precautions

There is a risk of malaria, typhoid is a risk outside main towns. Normal precautions for the tropics with regard to hygiene and drinking water should be taken. Bilharzia risk is present in the lakes and rivers and visitors are advised to swim only in well-maintained swimming pools. A mild form of dysentery is common. Rabies is a risk.
The Aids virus has reached epidemic proportions and precautions should be taken, including a travel kit with disposable syringe and needles. Any medicines required should be brought with the visitor and accompanied by their original packaging.
Medical facilities are limited and visitors should have sufficient insurance to ensure medical evacuation.

Hotels

Private and government-owned, variable standard, but available in all main centres. Should be booked in advance.

Credit cards

Most car hire firms and travel agencies refuse credit cards.

Public holidays (national)

Fixed dates

1 Jan (New Year's Day), 26 Jan (Liberation Day), 8 Mar (Women's Day), 1 May (Labour Day), 3 Jun (Martyrs Day), 9 Jun (National Heroes Day), 9 Oct (Independence Day), 25–26 Dec (Christmas).

Variable dates

Good Friday, Easter Monday, Ascension Day, Eid al Adha, Eid al Fitr.

Working hours

Banking

Mon–Fri: 0900–1400. Some bureaux de change open Sat and Sun.

Business

Mon–Fri: 0830–1245, 1400–1700.

Government

Mon–Fri: 0830–1245, 1400–1700.

Shops

Mon–Fri: 0830–1700; Sat: 0900–1600.

Telecommunications

Postal services

Not very reliable.

Mobile/cell phones

GSM 900 services are available throughout most of the country.

Electricity supply

240V AC, 50 cycles.

Social customs/useful tips

Appointments are essential for business meetings. Ugandans have a less urgent sense of time than Europeans, and appointments often run late, particularly if it is raining.
The customary form of greeting is to shake hands. Exchanging business cards is an established ritual.
Visitors should remember that an increasing number of Hindus and Muslims are engaged in commerce and local advice should be obtained if any entertainment is planned. There are many local traditions, but few will affect business visitors and tourists.

Security

There are still areas of the country that are not under secure government control. Rebel activity occasionally targets tourists, and visitors are advised to check with local embassies if they intend to travel away from the main urban centres or main road and rail routes. The government has stepped up its campaign against lawlessness.
Due to rebel raids, including activity spilling over from neighbouring countries, visitors are warned against travelling to certain destinations, particularly the northern and south-western regions, where the Mountains of the Moon and several game parks are located.

Getting there

Air

National airline: The government holds a 20 per cent in Victoria International Airlines, which has a limited number of southern African routes.

International airport/s: Entebbe (EBB), 35km from Kampala; duty-free shop, restaurant, bank, post office, car hire.

Airport tax: None

Surface

Road: There is road access from neighbouring countries, but the Sudanese border crossing is not open to general traffic. There are daily bus services between Nairobi (Kenya) and Kampala.

Rail: There is a joint Kenyan-Ugandan rail link between Nairobi and Kampala, but it has been out of service for some time. Revival of the line is in prospect following transfer of control to a private company in November 2006.

Water: There are ferry services across Lake Victoria from Mwanza (Tanzania) and Kisumu (Kenya).

Getting about

National transport

Road: Uganda has a road network of around 35,000km. Most of the country is served by dirt roads of varying quality, but there are around 3,000km of surface roads connecting the main towns. Many major roads are in good condition.

Buses: Regular services scheduled include Entebbe-Kampala (journey time: 30–45 minutes). There are services between most main centres but they tend to be crowded. An interstate bus service between Kampala and Kigali (Rwanda) is frequently suspended due to military activity. Akamba Bus regularly travels between Kampala and Nairobi (Kenya).

Rail: Two Uganda-Kenya railway agreements were signed in April 2006. In Uganda a concession agreement covers the freight services of Uganda Railways Corporation (URC), while an Interface agreement covers matters common to the Kenya freight and passenger concession and the Uganda freight concession. The Rift Valley Railways Consortium (RVRC) will invest US$15 million over the first five years and a further US$75 million over the remainder of the agreement in Uganda and US$45 and US$300 million respectively in Kenya.

Water: Some freight and passenger transport is available on Lake Victoria.

City transport

Taxis: Available at airport and in Kampala at hotels, the railway station, main park and near major office blocks. The drive from Entebbe airport to Kampala city centre takes 45 minutes. *Matatus* (public taxis) are available within Kampala, its suburbs and in all major towns.

Car hire

Car hire is expensive. Services are available, mainly with driver, from a number of rental firms, and through independent taxi drivers. Driving is on the left. A valid international driving licence is required.

BUSINESS DIRECTORY

The addresses listed below are a selection only. While World of Information makes every endeavour to check these addresses, we cannot guarantee that changes have not been made, especially to telephone numbers and area codes. We would welcome any corrections.

Telephone area codes

The international direct dialling (IDD) code for Uganda is +256, followed by area code:

Entebbe	42	Lugazi	44
Fort Portal	483	Masaka	481
Jinja	43	Mbale	45
Kampala	41	Mbarara	485
Kasese	483	Tororo	45

Useful telephone numbers

Ambulance, fire, police: 999
Directory enquiries: 901
International hospital: 340-531, 345-768

Chambers of Commerce

Uganda National Chamber of Commerce and Industry, PO Box 3809, Kampala (tel: 225-8791; fax: 225-8793; e-mail: uncci@uol.co.ug).

Banking

Allied Bank International Uganda Ltd, PO Box 2750, 45 Jinja Road, Kampala (tel: 223-6535; fax: 223-0902; e-mail: allied@alliedbank.co.ug).

Bank of Baroda (Uganda) Ltd, PO Box 7197, 18 Kampala Road, Kampala (tel: 223-3680; fax: 225-8263; e-mail: bobho@spacenet.co.ug).

Barclays Bank of Uganda Ltd, PO Box 7101, 16 Kampala Road, Kampala (tel: 223-0972; fax: 225-9467; e-mail: uganda.barclays@barclays.com).

Cairo International Bank Ltd, PO Box 7052, 30 Kampala Road, Kampala (tel: 223-0136; fax: 223-0130; e-mail: cib@spacenetuganda.com).

Centenary Rural Development Bank Ltd, PO Box 1892, 7 Entebbe Road, Kampala (tel: 225-1276; fax: 225-1273; e-mail: info@centenarybank.co.ug).

Citibank Uganda Ltd, PO Box 7505, Centre Court, 4 Ternan Avenue, Nakasero, Kampala (tel: 234-0625; fax: 234-0624).

Crane Bank Ltd, PO Box 22572, 38 Kampala Road, Kampala (tel: 234-5345; fax: 223-1578; e-mail: cranebank@cranebanklimited.com).

Diamond Trust Bank (U) Ltd, PO Box 7155, 17/19 Kampala Rd, Kampala (tel: 225-9331; fax: 324-2286; e-mail: dtbu@spacenetuganda.com).

East African Development Bank, PO Box 7128, 4 Nile Avenue, Kampala (tel: 223-0021; fax: 225-9763; e-mail: dg@eadb.org).

Nile Bank Ltd, PO Box 2834, Spear House, 22 Jinja Road, Kampala (tel: 234-6904; fax: 225-7779; e-mail: comments@nilebank.co.ug).

Orient Bank Limited, PO Box 3072, 6 Kampala Road, Kampala (tel: 223-6012; fax: 234-8039; e-mail: mail@orient-bank.com).

Stanbic Bank Uganda Ltd, PO Box 7131, 45 Kampala Road, Kampala (tel: 223-1151; fax: 223-1116).

Standard Chartered Bank Uganda Ltd, PO Box 7111, 5 Speke Road, Kampala (tel: 225-8211; fax: 223-1473; e-mail: scb.uganda@standardchartered.com).

Tropical Africa Bank Ltd, PO Box 7292, 27 Kampala Road, Kampala (tel: 223-2857; fax: 221-2296; e-mail: admin@trafbank.com).

Central bank

Bank of Uganda, PO Box 7120, 37–43 Kampala Rd, Kampala (tel: 258-441; fax: 230-878; e-mail: info@boa.or.ug).

Stock exchange

Uganda Securities Exchange, www.use.or.ug

Travel information

Automobile Association of Uganda, 39 William Street, PO Box 10542, Kampala (tel: 225-0814; fax: 234-1245; e-mail: aau@africaonline.co.ug).

Eagle Aviation, Adam House, 11 Portal Avenue, PO Box 7392, Kampala (tel: 234-4292; fax: 234-4501;
e-mail: admin@flyeagleuganda.com).

East African Airlines, Pan Africa House, 3 Kimathi Avenue, PO Box 2389, Kampala (tel: 226-0625; fax: 234-9875;
e-mail: info@flyeastafrican.com).

Uganda Wildlife Authority, 7 Kira Road, PO Box 3530, Kampala; (tel: 234-6287; fax: 234-6291; e-mail: uwa@uwa.or.ug).

Ministry of tourism

Ministry of Tourism, Trade and Industry, Farmers House, Parliament Avenue, PO Box 7103, Kampala (tel: 234-3947; fax: 234-7286; e-mail: mintrade@mtti.co.ug).

National tourist organisation offices

Tourism Uganda, 13/15 Kimathi Avenue, Impala House, P.O.Box 7211, Kampala (tel: 234-2196; fax: 234-2188; e-mail: utb@visituganda.com).

Ministries

Ministry of Education and Sports, 17/19 Hannington Rd, PO Box 7063, Kampala (tel: 223-4451; fax: 223-44920; e-mail: pro@education.go.ug).

Ministry of Energy and Mineral Development, Amber House, 29-32 Kampala Road, PO Box 7270, Kampala (tel: 232-3355;fax: 223-0220; e-mail: psmemd@energy.go.ug).

Ministry of Finance, Planning and Economic Development, 2/12 Apollo Kaggwa Road, PO Box 8147, Kampala (tel: 270-7000; fax: 223-0163; e-mail: webmaster@finance.go.ug).

Ministry of Foreign Affairs, Parliament Building, PO Box 7048, Kampala (tel: 225-7525; fax: 225-6722; e-mail: mofa@starcom.co.ug).

Ministry of Gender, Labour and Social Development, Simbamanyo House, 2 Lumumba Avenue, PO Box 7136 , Kampala (tel: 234-7854; fax: 225-6374; e-mail: ps@mglsd.go.ug).

Ministry of Health, 6 Lourdel Road, PO Box 7272, Wandegeya, Kampala (tel: 234-0884; fax: 234-0887; e-mail: info@health.go.ug).

Ministry of Justice and Constitutional Affairs, 1 Parliament Avenue, PO Box 7183, Kampala (tel: 223-0538; fax: 225-4829; e-mail: info@justice.go.ug).

Ministry of Local Government, 1 Pilkington Road, PO Box 7037, Kampala (tel: 234-1224; fax: 225-8127; e-mail: info@molg.go.ug).

Ministry of Public Service, 12 Nakasero Hill Road, PO Box 7003, Kampala (tel: 225-5651; fax: 225-5643; e-mail: ps@publicservice.go.ug).

Ministry of Water, Lands and Environment, Century House, Parliament Avenue, PO Box 7096, Kampala (tel: 234-2931; fax: 223-0891; e-mail: mwle@mwle.go.ug).

Other useful addresses

British High Commission, Commercial Section, 120/12 Parliament Avenue, PO Box 7070, Kampala (tel: 225-7301; fax: 225-7304).

Civil Aviation Authority, PO Box 5536, Kampala (tel: 225-6874; fax: 225-6807).

Export Policy Analysis and Development Unit (EPADU), Impala House, PO Box 10951, Kampala (tel: 223-1390; fax: 223-1329).

Nile International Conference Centre, PO Box 3496, Kampala (tel: 225-8619; fax: 225-9130).

Privatisation Unit, Ministry of Finance and Economic Planning, IPS Building, 6th Floor, 14 Parliament Avenue, PO Box 10944, Kampala (tel: 225-6467; fax: 225-9997; e-mail: pmu@imul.com).

LRA incident tracker http://www.lracrisistracker.com/

Public Enterprise Reform and Divestiture, IPS Building, PO Box 10944, Kampala (tel: 225-6467; fax: 225-9997).

Uganda Development Corporation, UDC Building, Parliament Avenue, PO Box 7042, Kampala (tel: 223-4383; fax: 224-1588).

Uganda Investment Authority, 28 Kampala Road, PO Box 7418, Kampala (tel: 225-1562; fax: 224-2903; e-mail: info@ugandainvest.com).

Uganda Railway Corporation, PO Box 7150, Kampala (tel: 225-8051; fax: 244-405).

Uganda Tea Corporation Ltd, Kasaku Estate, Jinja-Kampala Rd, PO Box 8955, Lugazi (tel: 48-230/45; fax: 223-0698).

Ugandan Embassy (US), 5911 16th Street, NW, Washington DC 20011 (tel: (+1-202) 726-7100; fax: (+1-202) 726-1727; e-mail: ugembassy@aol.com).

Internet sites

Africa Business Network: www.ifc.org/abn

African Development Bank: www.afdb.org

Africa Online: www.africaonline.com

AllAfrica.com: http://allafrica.com

Mbendi AfroPaedia (information on companies, countries, industries and stock exchanges in Africa): http://mbendi.co.za

Ukraine

As the conflict in Ukraine entered its second year in mid-2015, it was hard to see how any sort of satisfactory resolution might be sought. This was not a war for territory, nor was it for ideas. It was a war in which two systems, two ways of running countries and respecting liberties, were set on showing that neither could be deflected from its course. If there was doubt about whether there was any obvious winner, there was no doubt at all as to who was the obvious loser. The people of Ukraine, particularly those living in eastern Ukraine had seen members of their families killed – in the conflict's first year there had been well over 6,000 casualties – and maimed, their houses brought to the ground, their villages destroyed. But no obvious benefits at all. On the contrary: the so called 'leadership' of the pro-Russian separatists was described in the London *Economist* as being 'heavy on guns and light on butter.' After lengthy negotiations between Russian President Vladimir Putin, Ukrainian President Petro Poroshenko, French President Francois Hollande and German Chancellor Angela Merkel, a ceasefire had been agreed in Minsk in mid-February 2015. Initially, the ceasefire was more notable for its failures than its successes. Slowly, it began to hold, however. Known as the 'Minsk II' agreement, it replaced a failed agreement reached in September 2014, which barely lasted a matter of days.

The new agreement provided for the withdrawal of heavy weapons from the front line. It also contained political elements, notably that there would be some degree of decentralisation for the rebel-controlled regions. Western press reports painted Vladimir Putin as the villain of the piece. Meanwhile, in Russia, on the back of the Crimea annexation, the Russian President's popularity ratings continued to climb.

Fault line folly

Russia's unopposed annexation of Crimea in 2014 had given the world the clearest possible indication of its agenda. But military analysts also knew that Russia could ill afford to enter a fully fledged, resource draining conflict with Ukraine. Least of all, enter a conflict that risked involving North Atlantic Treaty Organisation (NATO). However, as the conflict appeared, in mid-2015, to be sputtering towards an unsatisfactory stalemate, Russia's concern to plant a marker in

KEY FACTS

Official name: Ukraina (Ukraine)

Head of State: President Petro Poroshenko (Independent) (elected 25 May, assumed office 7 June 2014)

Head of government: Prime Minister Arseniy Petrovych Yatsenyuk (Batkivshchyna) (All-Ukrainian Union Fatherland) (from 27 Feb 2014)

Ruling party: Petro Poroshenko Bloc

Area: 603,700 square km

Population: 42.77 million (2014)*

Capital: Kiev (Kyiv)

Official language: Ukrainian

Currency: Hryvna (H) = 100 kopiyka (plural hryvni)

Exchange rate: H22.20 per US$ (Sep 2015)

GDP per capita: US$3,055 (2014)*

GDP real growth: -6.83% (2014)

GDP: US$130.66 billion (2014)

Labour force: 19.32 million (2014)*

Unemployment: 10.49% (2014)*

Inflation: 12.10% (2014)

Natural gas production: 18.60 billion cum (2014)

Balance of trade: -US$7.64 billion (2014)

Annual FDI: US$7.21 billion (2011)

* estimated figure

eastern Ukraine did not appear to run to feeding its (literally) beleaguered citizens. Deprived of their former income from Kiev, but receiving nothing from Moscow, an estimated 800,000 people were dependent on charities such as Responsible Citizens and Pomozhem, founded by the Ukrainian oligarch Rinat Akhmetov and busily distributing food parcels to as many as 800,000 people on either side of the geo-political divide that had once been their country. The International Committee of the Red Cross had reportedly opened half a dozen hospitals in eastern Ukraine and Médecins sans Frontieres had supplied a number of doctors.

It's the economy, of course

A year of conflict and uncertainty had taken its toll in a number of ways. Ukraine – and Russia – found themselves sunk in something more than a simple military conflict. For much of the year, the attention of Brussels had been more focussed on Athens than on Kiev, despite the fact that the population of Ukraine is five times greater than that of Greece. Having signed – in June 2014 – a Free Trade and Association Agreement with the European Union (EU) the Kiev government might have expected a little bit more in the way of tender love and care (aka TLC) from Brussels. It certainly needed it: to begin with, the country's financial situation was dire. Kiev needed, somehow, to renegotiate its growing debt – which was simply unserviceable – with its private lenders and creditors (mostly from the US). However, in 2014 Ukraine's foreign currency reserves had fallen through the floor, leaving it with only US$9 billion for repayments due in September, October and December 2015. In March 2015 the International Monetary Fund (IMF – see below) had promised a loan of US$17.5 billion on the condition that further economic reforms were carried out, the issue of corruption addressed and the banking system overhauled. The reforms may have looked rational enough in Washington and in Brussels, but for a government coping with a military conflict that was draining its reserves, there were other fish to fry.

As long as the conflict in eastern Ukraine continued, the government's hands were tied. The economy was languishing. Gross domestic product (GDP) had shrunk by 7.5 per cent in 2014 and forecasts for 2015 anticipated a further shrinkage, this time by some 9 per cent. Ukraine's currency, the hryvnia (H), which had seen a devaluation of 48 per cent against the dollar in 2014, had fallen a further 40 per cent in the first half of 2015. Inflation was expected to reach 50 per cent in 2015. In simply economic terms, the problem was that the Donbass region, which had become a combat zone, accounted for 15 per cent of Ukraine's GDP and 25 per cent of its exports.

The Ukrainian government had set out in a letter addressed to Christine Lagarde, the IMF's managing director, its understanding of the necessary reforms. The letter was signed not only by Ukraine's minister of finance, Natalye Jaresko, but also by President Petro Poroshenko, Prime Minister Arseniy Yatsenyuk and Valeria Gontareva, governor of the National Bank of Ukraine (NBU) (central bank). Offering an interesting insight into government priorities, the four heavyweights noted in the letter that:

'Notwithstanding the exceptionally difficult situation in Ukraine – with the unresolved conflict in the East – we have made steadfast efforts to implement policies under the EFF [Extended Fund Facility]-supported programme reflecting our strong commitment to economic adjustment and reforms. Following the significant economic contraction in the first quarter of 2015, there are signs that economic stability is gradually taking hold. The foreign exchange market has remained broadly stable in the last few months. Our official reserves, although still very low, have increased considerably following disbursements from official creditors and the NBU's foreign currency purchases from the market. We have taken bold measures to advance much needed reforms, including in the energy sector, by adopting a new gas sector law and increased gas and central heating retail prices by 285 per cent and 67 per cent, respectively. These are important first steps toward reaching cost recovery based on international market prices and thus eliminating the large losses in the state-owned gas company Naftogaz, while at the same time increasing significant allocations for social assistance programmes. Budget outturn for the first quarter of 2015 was stronger than expected owing mainly to large value added tax (VAT) revenue driven by the higher than expected exchange rate depreciation and inflation. Banks' local currency deposits are growing again, although the foreign exchange (FX) deposit outflows continue, which remains a key concern.

'Our actions ensured that all performance criteria (PC) for end-March, the continuous PC and most structural benchmarks due through June 2015 were met, albeit some with a delay. We have also met the end-June PCs. We passed the necessary legislation to strengthen collections of Naftogaz receivables prior to the completion of the review. We also passed important legislation that strengthens the NBU independence and governance arrangements. Our efforts now focus on restoring macro-economic stability and

KEY INDICATORS — Ukraine

	Unit	2011	2012	2013	2014	**2015
Population	m	*45.55	45.45	*42.90	*42.77	*42.69
Gross domestic product (GDP)	US$bn	165.00	176.24	179.57	130.66	*85.44
GDP per capita	US$	3,621	3,877	4,185	*3,055	*2,002
GDP real growth	%	5.2	0.2	–	-6.8	*-5.5
Inflation	%	8.0	0.6	-0.3	12.1	*33.5
Unemployment	%	7.9	7.5	7.3	*10.5	*11.5
Natural gas output	bn cum	18.7	18.6	19.3	18.6	–
Coal output	mtoe	45.1	45.9	45.9	31.5	–
Exports (fob) (goods)	US$m	62,383.0	64,003.0	59,097.0	50,552.0	–
Imports (fob) (goods)	US$m	80,414.0	86,834.0	80,854.0	58,197.0	–
Balance of trade	US$m	-18,031.0	-22,831.0	-21,757.0	-7,645.0	–
Current account	US$m	-10,233.0	-14,315.0	-16,478.0	*-5,228.0	*-1,216.0
Total reserves minus gold	US$m	35,817.2	22,655.8	18,775.5	6,622.2	–
Foreign exchange	US$m	35,779.9	22,646.6	18,759.5	–	–
Exchange rate	per US$	7.96	7.99	8.24	15.82	–

* estimated figure ** forecast figure

setting the stage for robust and inclusive growth so critical for the Ukrainian people. This includes actions to improve competitiveness and the business climate through far-reaching structural reforms, rehabilitate the banking system and restore sustainable external and fiscal positions.'

The four signatories went on to report that despite strong efforts, the debt restructuring process was advancing more slowly than expected. Constructive discussions with holders of the state-owned Ukreximbank's US$1.5 billion Eurobonds had lead to the completion of a consensual re-profiling of those notes on 8 July. Separately, state-owned Oschadbank had launched on 6 July a consent solicitation for a re-profiling of its US$1.2 billion Eurobonds with the backing of an ad hoc committee holding a majority of the notes. These re-profiling operations were fully in line with the debt operation targets under the EFF supported programme. There was teady progress on the broader sovereign debt restructuring with the objective of concluding an agreement as soon as possible (as noted in the joint statements with the Ad Hoc Creditor Committee on 1 and 15 July). 'We remain' they said 'determined to complete the debt operation in line with its stated programme objectives…

'…We believe that the policies set forth in the attached Memorandum of Economic and Financial Policies (MEFP) are adequate to achieve the macro-economic and financial objectives of the programme, but we will take any additional measures that may be appropriate for this purpose. We will consult with the IMF on the adoption of these measures and in advance of revisions to the policies contained in the MEFP, in accordance with the IMF's policies on such consultation. We will provide IMF staff with the data and information it requests for the purpose of monitoring implementation. Reaffirming commitment to our policy of transparency, we consent to the IMF's publication of this letter.'

Apart from the brave move of publishing the letter to the IMF, another encouraging innovation in the Kiev government was the appointment of competent foreigners to government positions. Natalie Jaresko, the minister of finance holds an American passport, the rconomy minister, Aivaras Abromavicius, was born in Lithuania and had lived in Estonia, the US and Russia before coming to Kiev. The minister of health is Georgian.

In the view of the IMF, the Ukrainian authorities' commitment to the reform programme remained strong. All the performance criteria for the end of March 2015 had been met and all the 'structural benchmarks' due in the first few months of 2015 were also on course to be met, albeit some with a delay. The IMF was complimentary about the success of the EFF programme implementation, noting that it had been 'achieved notwithstanding an exceptionally difficult environment, in part related to the unresolved conflict in the East,' which took a perhaps predictably heavier toll than expected on the Ukrainian economy in the first quarter of 2015. The mission had revised downwards its growth projections for 2015 to –9.00 per cent and projected end-year inflation of a whopping 46 per cent. However, the IMF noted that this high level of inflation was mostly driven by the one-off knock-on effects of the Ukraine's exchange rate depreciation in February as well as the inevitable energy price increases.

The IMF also considered that there were also signs that economic stability was gradually taking hold. The foreign exchange market had remained broadly stable. Ukraine's international reserves, although still very low, had increased to US$9.6 billion by the end of April 2015. Bank deposits in domestic currency were also recovering. The budget results in the first months of 2015 were also stronger than expected.

The Ukrainian government had recognised that the decisive implementation of economic reforms was indispensable for entrenching financial stability and restoring robust and sustainable growth. According to the IMF, the Ukrainian authorities were 'committed to advancing fiscal consolidation and energy sector reforms, including further energy tariff adjustments to eliminate the large losses of Naftogaz, reduce energy consumption and foster energy independence.' They were also progressing with the rehabilitation of the Ukrainian banking system and the improvement of the business environment to enhance the productive potential of the economy.

Relating to the debt issue (see above) the IMF took the view that the Ukrainian authorities 'were also determined to complete the ongoing debt operation in line with programme objectives.' This would ensure that public debt was sustainable and realistic and that the programme remained fully financed, which were requirements for the completion of the review. 'Continued financial support for Ukraine's reform efforts from official and private creditors was vital for the success of the programme.'

Sitting on the sidelines of the IMF and the debt restructuring discussions, the so-called Group of Seven finance ministers' meeting in late May 2015 gave its support to Ukraine's efforts to restructure its debt. German finance minister, Wolfgang Schäuble, was quoted by the London *Financial Times* (FT) as saying: 'We agreed we must try to support the negotiation of the restructuring of Ukraine's debt, which must be brought to a successful conclusion.'

Any failure to reach agreement on the debt question would jeopardise the next IMF disbursement, as according to the IMF rules, which the FT pointed out stated that 'governments must have at least one year of financing in place to receive such disbursements.' Although Ukraine had managed not to default on any of the 29 bonds and loans included in its restructuring programme, such was the fragility of its fiscal position that an agreement on restructuring had become essential.

Corruption

Surprisingly the Ukraine government's letter to the IMF made no reference at all to the country's endemic corruption. Perhaps it was not so surprising: one report in the US publication *Foreign Policy* (FP) made the observation that Ukraine's leaders 'never miss an opportunity to miss an opportunity.' The FP noted that 'although it's still unclear whether the new government can break this pattern, the opportunity before it now is nothing less than to undo the system of institutionalised corruption that has held Ukraine down since independence and made it vulnerable to aggression and dismemberment.' On the 2014 *Corruption Perceptions Index* published by Berlin based Transparency International, Ukraine ranked 142 out of the 175 countries surveyed. This was the worst ranking of any European country, six places behind Russia and only two places better than its 2013 ranking of 144. In the view of FP, 'If it can change the corruption equation, Ukraine may be able – at long last – to have a political system that mirrors its European neighbours.'

One achievement of the post-Yanukovich governments had been to create greater public awareness of just how serious the problem of corruption actually was. In 2015 there was widespread support to rid the Ukrainian government of corruption. Anger at corruption and the impunity of former regimes, especially that of Viktor Yanukovych, became a higher priority than the expression of pro-EU sentiment. FP maintained that 'nothing would help cement national unity or spur resilience against the aggression in Donbass more than success in the fight against institutionalised corruption.'

In a 2011 Transparency International report, Ukrainians had identified their judiciary as their most corrupt institution, followed by the police and parliament. In a magazine interview Aivaras Abromavicius, the economy minister observed that: 'First and foremost, Ukraine needs a rule of law. So judicial reforms need to be passed. Everybody knows that every single judge in Ukraine is corrupt and most of them need to be changed. Judicial reform comes first.'

Despite the absence of any mention of the corruption problem in their letter to the IMF, both President Petro Poroshenko and Prime Minister Arseniy Yatsenyuk had pledged their commitment to anti-corruption efforts, claiming that the push would come following the election of a reformist parliament; by mid-2015 that parliament was in place. They had also stressed that the conflict in Donbass was no excuse for postponing reform.

Energy

Ukraine's budgetary subsidies for energy – much of them for Naftogaz – amounted to an alarming 7 to 9 per cent of GDP in 2014, several times Ukraine's defence budget. The Ukrainian gas sector had long been a happy hunting ground for Ukrainians for over two decades. With state prices fixed at US$30 per thousand cubic meters of gas, connected individuals could buy at that rate and then sell to the market at over 10 times the price. While presiding over huge losses, the Naftogaz management enriched itself lavishly under President Yanukovych. An analysis of Ukrainian energy policy suggested that the objective was to keep Ukraine dependent on expensive Russian gas, discourage domestic production, enrich oligarchs and encourage wasteful consumption. The solution appeared to be the removal of hugely distorting subsidies for gas consumers and the end of price controls on domestically produced gas.

The US government Energy Information Administration (EIA) reported in early 2015 that more than half of Ukraine's primary energy supply came from its uranium and coal resources, although natural gas also played an important role in its energy mix. Ukraine consumed about 1.5 trillion cubic feet (tcf) of natural gas in 2014, with domestic production accounting for 47 per cent of the total at about 700 billion cubic feet (bcf). The remainder of the supply was made up by Russian natural gas, imported through the Bratstvo and Soyuz pipelines.

According to IHS Energy, coal became the largest component of Ukraine's primary energy consumption in 2013 at 36.4 per cent, followed by natural gas at 36.1 per cent and nuclear (about 18 per cent). Only a relatively small portion of the country's total energy consumption is accounted for by petroleum and other liquid fuels and renewable energy sources. Because of Ukraine's large industrial sector as a proportion of total economic activity, Ukraine's economy is, according to the EIA, one of the most energy-intensive in the world.

In 2013, Ukraine relied on Russian natural gas exports for over 50 per cent of its domestic consumption. Imports from Russia had been lower in 2014 and 2015, with Russia's annexation of Crimea and relations between the two countries remaining contentious. Additionally, Ukraine's natural gas pipeline connections with Poland, Slovakia and Hungary were reconfigured to allow gas to flow into Ukraine from those countries.

Ukraine's geographic position and proximity to Russia explain its importance as a natural gas and petroleum liquids transit country. About 2.2 trillion cubic feet (tcf) of natural gas flowed through Ukraine in 2014 to Austria, Bosnia-Herzegovina, Bulgaria, Croatia, Czech Republic, Germany, Greece, Hungary, Moldova, Poland, Romania, Slovakia and Turkey. This volume represented a decrease of almost 28 per cent from 2013 according to the Ukrainian ministry of energy.

Two major pipeline systems carry Russian gas through Ukraine to Western Europe – the Bratstvo ('Brotherhood') and Soyuz ('Union') pipelines. The Bratstvo pipeline is Russia's largest pipeline to Europe. It crosses from Ukraine to Slovakia and splits into two directions to supply northern and southern European countries. The Soyuz pipeline links Russian pipelines to natural gas networks in Central Asia and supplies additional volumes to central and northern Europe. A third major pipeline through Ukraine delivers Russian natural gas to the Balkan countries and Turkey. In the past, disputes between Russia and Ukraine over natural gas supplies, prices and debts have resulted in interruptions to Russia's natural gas exports through Ukraine, with the latest one occurring in 2014.

Risk assessment

Economy	Poor
Politics	Poor
Regional stability	Very poor

People to watch

Vitali Klitschko elected Mayor of Kiev in May 2014

Petro Oleksiyovych Poroshenko, elected President in May 2014

COUNTRY PROFILE

1917 The Bolsheviks consolidated control over Ukraine, until the incorporation of the republic into the Soviet Union. The Russians retained direct control of eastern Ukraine from 1918 until the country's independence from Russia in 1991. The city of Lviv (formerly Lvov) near the western border was seized from the collapsing Austro-Hungarian Empire.

1920s Russia lost control of parts of western Ukraine to Poland, Czechoslovakia and Romania during the civil war between the Bolsheviks and counter-revolutionary forces supported by Western European armies. Soviet dictator, Josef Stalin, initiated a system of collective agriculture which forced Ukrainian farmers to render fixed quantities of produce to the authorities. These quotas were unrealistic, creating entirely artificial famine conditions during which over five million Ukrainians were estimated to have died.

1932 It is estimated that at least three million, and possibly as many as 10 million, died of starvation in the *Holodomor* or 'famine plague' when the 1932 grain harvest did not meet Kremlin targets and Joseph Stalin sent activists to villages to confiscate all food. The move was part of Stalin's determination to crush the resistance to the collectivisation of farming.

1945 Following the end of the Second World War, the Soviet Union regained control of the lost areas of western Ukraine.

1954 Responsibility for the government of Crimea, an autonomous republic within Ukraine, was transferred from Russia to Ukraine as part of reforms initiated by Nikita Kruschev after Stalin's death.

1986 The Chernobyl nuclear reactor based in Ukraine exploded, causing widespread damage in both Ukraine and neighbouring Belarus.

1991 Under pressure from the opposition parties, in particular Narodniy Rukh Ukrayiny (Rukh) (People's Movement of Ukraine), the government gradually moved towards independence. Political power was transferred from the government of the former Soviet Union to Ukrainian national authorities in Kiev. A majority voted for independence in a referendum, leading to a declaration of

independence and the recognition of Ukraine as an independent state by the international community. Leonid Kravchuk won the presidential elections.
1992 Disagreements over economic policy saw the resignation of Ukraine's first prime minister, Vladimir Fokin, who was replaced by Leonid Kuchma.
1993 Arguments over economic policy and labour strikes led to the resignation of Kuchma and Yukhlym Zvyahilsky assumed the post.
1994 Kuchma returned as the main challenger to Kravchuk in the presidential elections, finally defeating Kravchuk in the run-off. Kuchma's attempts to swing the balance of power from parliament in favour of the presidency, in order to reduce the opposition to his economic programme, achieved mixed success.
1996 A new constitution gave the president the power to appoint a government formed by parliamentary deputies.
1997 Valeriy Pustovoitenko became prime minister.
1998 After elections, the Komunistychna Partiya Ukrainy (KPU) (Communist Party of Ukraine) emerged as the largest single party.
1999 Kuchma was re-elected president. He appointed reformist independent deputy Viktor Yushchenko as prime minister.
2000 Over 80 per cent of voters in a referendum supported President Kuchma's proposals for constitutional reform, designed to increase the powers of the presidency.
2001 Yushchenko's pro-reform government was toppled by the KPU-dominated parliament. Anatoly Kinakh became prime minister.
2002 In parliamentary elections, Viktor Yuschenko's Narodnyi Soyuz Nasha Ukraina (NSNU) (People's Union Our Ukraine) bloc gained the highest percentage of votes at 23.6 per cent. Russia, Ukraine, Kazakhstan and Belarus signed an economic union treaty.
2003 Mass demonstrations in Kiev demanded the resignation of President Kuchma. Ukraine and Russia signed an agreement on the joint use of the Kerch Strait and the status of the Azov Sea.
2004 Russian-backed Viktor Yanukovych won the presidential election and opposition supporters gathered in Kiev to protest against election fraud (the Orange Revolution) and the Supreme Court annulled the result. Viktor Yushchenko won the re-run election.

2005 Yushchenko was sworn in as president and Yulia Tymoshenko was approved as prime minister. Yushchenko dismissed Tymoshenko and replaced her with Yuri Yekhanurov. Russia cut off gas supplies after Ukraine refused to agree to a four-fold price increase. The BJT was disbanded and merged with the Vseukrayins'ke Obyednannya Bat'kivshchyna (Fatherland) (All-Ukrainian Union (Fatherland).
2006 Prime Minister Yekhanurov was sacked by parliament. Yushchenko, unwilling to lose his prime minister refused to nominate another candidate and Yekhanurov remained in office. In general elections (judged free and fair by international observers), the ruling NSNU lost ground to both the Partiya Regioniv (PR) (Party of the Regions) led by Viktor Yanukovich and the party created by the president's erstwhile colleague Yulia Tymoshenko of Blok Yulia Tymoshenko (BJT) (Yulia Tymoshenko Bloc). President Yushchenko was forced to nominate his archrival, Viktor Yanukovych (PR), as prime minister or call another general election. The Yanukovych cabinet was later approved by parliament.
2007 Months of friction between the pro-Western president and the pro-Russian prime minister lead to a political stalemate, resulting in a presidential decree dissolving parliament. Prime Minister Yanukovych refused to obey the decree, but eventually agreed to early elections, won by the PR. Yulia Tymoshenko (BJT) was proposed as prime minister; she lost three rounds of voting but was eventually elected.
2008 Ukraine became a member of the WTO. The Russian state-owned gas producer Gazprom cut supplies of gas by 25 per cent, claiming Ukraine had debts of US$1.5 billion. Gas supplies were resumed when an agreement was reached whereby Gazprom supplied industrial customers directly and cut out a Ukrainian intermediate supply company. The ruling coalition collapsed following the refusal by BJT to back the president's support of Georgia in its dispute with Russia, and the BJT's unwillingness to support the president's veto of several laws aimed at reducing the power of the presidency.
2009 Russia suspended gas supplies to Ukraine again, due to non-payment of Ukraine's debt. Gas supplies to the rest of Europe fell, amid accusations by Russia that Ukraine was 'stealing' gas supplies transiting Ukraine and destined for Europe. Within a week a ten-year gas transit deal was signed. The International Court of Justice settled a 40-year disagreement on the maritime boundary dispute between Romania and Ukraine, with a new border extending a line from the land border over an area of the Black Sea and giving each country an area of what is thought to contain rich fields of hydrocarbons.
2010 Former revolutionary leader, Victor Yushchenko, won fewest votes in the first round of presidential elections; he stepped down as president. In the run-off, Viktor Yanukovych (PR) won 48.95 per cent and Yulia Tymoshenko (Fatherland) 45.47 per cent. However Tymoshenko refused to accept the result and challenged it with accusations of electoral fraud. She eventually withdrew her objections following a legal ruling that denied her permission to scrutinise certain voting papers. Yanukovych was sworn in as president. Prime Minister Tymoshenko and her government lost a vote of no-confidence in parliament and were forced to resign, while President Yanukovych began forming a coalition government. Oleksandr Turchynov was named acting prime minister; however parliament appointed Mykola Azarov (PR) as prime minister. The parliamentary session debating the extension of the lease on a Russian naval base on the Black Sea erupted as politicians brawled and the speaker was pelted with eggs and smoke bombs exploded. After order was restored, the lease was extended to 2045, in return for cheaper supplies of Russian natural gas. Yulia Tymoshenko was arrested and charged with misusing state funds as prime minister. Political blocs (alliances) were banned from forming to contest elections.
2011 During her trial Yulia Tymoshenko accused President Yanukovych of orchestrating her arrest, aimed at destroying the country's opposition, and in June that the judge was a 'puppet'. In August, Tymoshenko was arrested during her trial for systematically disrupting proceedings; her supporters fought with police as she was driven away from court. In October, Tymoshenko was sentence to seven years, for abusing her powers in office and paying too much for Russian natural gas imports. She was also ordered to pay damages to the state-owned energy company, Naftogaz, the sum of H1.5 billion (US$187.4 million). Criticism of the conviction came from the US and EU, which referred to the trial and result as 'politically motivated' and 'selective justice'.
2012 Ukraine had agreed to eliminate its stockpile of weapons-grade nuclear material and the US was confident this would be completed by the end of the year. Yulia Tymoshenko ended her hunger strike in prison after 21 days in protest at her treatment. European leaders expressed their concerns for her welfare. A controversial vote to move the Russian language to the status of 'regional language' was passed in parliament on 5 June (234 votes out of 450). It requires a second reading of the bill, due later in 2012, and the sanction of President Yanukovych. Nine new political parties took part in parliamentary elections held on 28 October, although only three won

seats. The ruling PR won 187 of 450 seats and the right to form a coalition government. The newly formed Ukrainian Democratic Alliance for Reform (UDAR), a party that had once dominated the BJT, led by Yulia Tymoshenko, won 40 seats. International observes of the elections considered the process flawed because they 'were characterised by the lack of a level playing field, caused primarily by the abuse of administrative resources, lack of transparency of campaign and party financing, and lack of balanced media coverage'. On 5 November, opposition parties held a rally in Kiev in protest at the elections results, which they considered as having been rigged in favour of pro-government candidates. Prime Minister Azarov resigned on 28 November; President Yanukovych finally accepted his resignation on 3 December.

2013 On 24 October Vitali Klitschko, leader of the UDAR party, announced that he would stand for the presidency in 2015, despite a recent bill passed by parliament banning candidates who have lived outside the country in the last 10 years. Mr Klitschko has permanent resident status in Germany. President Yanukovych was due to sign an association agreement with the EU at a summit being held in Vilnius, Lithuania on 30 November; however the week before he suspendended preparation for the signing saying there were 'several crucial steps left to be made'. Mr Yanukovych also said he had come under pressure from Russia not to sign. The agreement with the EU In Kiev some 10,000 demonstrators gathered in Independence Square to protest at his refusal to sign. The daughter of jailed opposition leader, Yulia Tymoshenko, was reported as saying her mother had begun a hunger strike in protest.

2014 On 20 February several members of the ruling Party of Regions called for the disintegration of Ukraine and for the country to join the Russian Federation. On 22 February Viktor Yanukovych was ousted by parliament in a move he described as a 'coup'. Oleksandr Turchynov was elected Speaker of the Verkhovna Rada and the following day he was designated interim president; a presidential election was called for 25 May (initially scheduled for March 2015). Yulia Tymoshenko was released from prison just hours after a bill was passed by parliament on 22 February releasing her. On 27 February parliament voted (371in favour, out of 450) for Arseny Yatsenyuk (371) as prime minister of a coalition government of Fatherland, UDAR, All-Ukrainian Union 'Svoboda' ('Svoboda'), and a number of parliamentary factions and one independent. On 6 March the regional government of the Autonomous Republic of Crimea voted to hold a referendum on whether the Crimea should become part of Russia. Neither of the two questions on the ballot paper allowed for the continuing relationship as an autonomous region of the Ukraine. The two questions were first, 'Are you in favour of the Autonomous Republic of Crimea reuniting with Russia as a constituent part of the Russian Federation?' and second 'Do you support the restoration of the 1992 Crimean constitution and the status of Crimea as a part of Ukraine?' This second question would mean Crimea loosing its autonomous status. The 16 March referendum was easily won by the pro-Russians with 96.77 per cent of those who voted. Russia's Duma (lower house of parliament) announced it would pass legislation 'in the very near future' allowing the Crimea region to join Russia. On 27 March former prime minister, Yulia Tymoshenko, announced she would stand in the May presidential election. The UN General Assembly approved a resolution on 27 March describing the Moscow-backed referendum that led to Russia's annexation of Crimea as illegal. On 28 March the IMF confirmed a loan worth some US$14–18 billion for Ukraine. On 29 March Vitaly Klitschko announced he would not be standing in the May presidential election, leaving Yulia Tymoshenko and Petro Poroshenko as the main contenders. On 7 April pro-Russian protesters stormed government buildings in Donetsk, Luhansk and Kharkiv in eastern Ukraine. They hung Russian flags from the buildings and called for a referendum on independence. Acting President Turchynov called a meeting of Ukraine's security chiefs. President Putin said that Russia has the right to protect Russian speakers who are under threat. The presidential election held on 25 May was won by Petro Poroshenko with 9,957,118 votes (54.7 per cent), beating Yulia Tymoshenko who polled 2,309,836 votes (12.81 per cent). Turnout was 50.1 per cent. Prime Minister Arseny Yatsenyuk resigned on 24 July after the breakup of the his coalition government. However, in a vote of 16 for and 109 against, parliament rejected his resignation on 31 July. Some 300 lorries left a military base near Moscow on 12 August said to be carrying aid for eastern Ukraine. It came to a halt around 300km short of the border crossing after Prime Minister Yatsenyuk said they would be refused entry. On 30 October an agreement was reached with Russia to resume gas supplies to Ukraine over the winter. The deal was brokered by the EU and will also ensure continued gas supplies to EU countries via Ukraine. Leadership elections, described by the EU 'illegal' were held by pro-Russian separatists in eastern Ukraine on 2 November. The government in Kiev described them as a 'farce' while Russia said it 'respects the will of the people' in the polls. Alexander Zakharchenko won the vote.

2015 Deposed president Viktor Yanukovych was put on Interpol's wanted list in January, accused by Ukrainian officials of embezzling millions of dollars of public funds. In January Ukraine, Russia, France and Germany issued a joint call to end fighting in the east, including agreeing a line of demarcation between separatists and government forces from which both sides were meant to withdraw their forces. By end-January this had not happened. In the meantime, Ukraine's defence ministry withdrew its troops from the main terminal of Donetsk airport, where there had been bitter fighting. Pro-Russian separatist leader Alexander Zakharchenko, announced he would be recruiting 100,000 men to fight Ukrainian forces. After fighting intensified in the east in early February diplomatic efforts increased with US Secretary of State John Kerry, French President Francois Hollande and German Chancellor Angela Merkel visiting Kiev 5 February to present a new peace initiative. Fighting between Ukrainian forces and pro-Russian rebels is estimated to have killed more than 5,000 people since April 2014. Direct flights between Ukraine and Russia were stopped from 25 October as new sanctions initiated by Kiev come into effect.

Political structure

Constitution

The 1996 constitution defines Ukraine as a sovereign, unitary state answerable to individual citizens, with the protection of citizens' rights as its foremost responsibility. The constitution forbids multiple nationality for Ukrainian citizens. The development and protection of the Ukrainian language is a constitutional obligation, but the constitution also guarantees free use of Russian and other minority languages, and requires the state to promote the study of languages of 'international communication'.

The constitution recognises and guarantees the right to local self-government. Local government is based on 24 *oblasts* (regional divisions) and one autonomous republic (Crimea). The *oblasts* are further divided into *rayons* (districts).

The Autonomous Republic of Crimea is bound by the Ukrainian constitution and by acts of the Verkhovna Rada (Supreme Council). However, it has the power to legislate separately on matters such as transport, planning, land use and healthcare.

Constitutional changes agreed in December 2004, which entered into force in January 2006, have given more power to the parliament at the expense of the office of president. Following the parliamentary elections on 26 March 2006, the parliament now nominates the prime minister who must then be approved by the president, replacing the previous system under which the prime minister was nominated by the president and approved by the parliament.

In 2010, the Constitutional Court of Ukraine overturned the 2004 amendments, reverting back to the original 1996 document.

Independence date

24 August 1991

Form of state

Presidential democratic republic

The executive

The highest executive authority rests with the president, who is directly elected for a five-year term and nominates the prime minister and regional governors, whose appointment are subject to the approval of parliament. The president has the power to appoint the cabinet, although parliament must approve it. Members of the cabinet do not necessarily need to be drawn from parliament. The president may rule by decree and did so in 1998, during deadlock in the legislature. Under normal circumstances, the prime minister shares some executive powers with the president and both can propose and approve legislation. This creates the potential for conflict between the two executive branches.

National legislature

The unicameral Verkhovna Rada (Supreme Council) (commonly called the Rada) has 450 deputies, of which 225 are elected by proportional representation (PR) from party lists and 225 in single-seat constituencies. Only parties that obtain over 4 per cent of the vote are allocated PR seats. All deputies are elected for a five-year term.

The Rada elects a speaker and plays an active role in proposing and enacting legislation.

Legal system

The legal system is based on a civil law code and, since the collapse of communism, has been engaged in an ongoing process of reform. The Constitutional Court is the highest interpreter of the constitution and is permitted to carry out judicial review of legislation. There are 18 Supreme Court judges, six each appointed for a nine-year non-renewable term by the president, parliament and a congress of Ukrainian judges.

The Supreme Court is the court of final appeal for civil and criminal cases originally heard in the lower courts. The Supreme Court's judges are appointed by a plenary session of existing judges. The lower courts are organised according to both geography and legal specialisation. The constitution encourages trial by jury and forbids the creation of emergency courts. Judges are granted legal immunity and can only be dismissed by a verdict of the Supreme or Constitutional Courts, or by an order of parliament.

Last elections

Parliamentary: 26 October 2014, presidential: 25 May 2014

Results: Presidential: Petro Poroshenko (Independent) won 54.7 per cent, Yulia Tymoshenko (Fatherland) 12.8 per cent, Oleg Lyashko (Radical party) 8.32 per cent, Anatoliy Hrytsenko (Our Ukraine), Serhiy Tihipko (Strong Ukraine), the remaining 16 candidates scored at 3 per cent or under; turnout was 50%

Parliamentary: Petro Poroshenko Bloc won 21.8 per cent of the vote and 132 seats (out of 450), People's Front won 22.1 per cent and 82 seats, Self Reliance won 10.9 per cent and 33 seats, Opposition Bloc won 9.4 per cent and 29 seats, Radical won 7.4 per cent and 22 seats and Fatherland won 5.7 per cent and 19 seats.

Next elections

2019 (presidential); 2019 (parliamentary).

Political parties

Ruling party

Petro Poroshenko Bloc

Main opposition party

People's Front

Population

45.37 million (2013)*

Last census: December 2001: 48,457,102

Population density: 87 inhabitants per square km. Urban population 69 per cent (2010 Unicef).

Annual growth rate: -0.6 per cent, 1990–2010 (Unicef).

Ethnic make-up

Ukrainian (72 per cent), Russian (22 per cent), Belarussian, Moldovan, Polish, Romanian and Tatar (in Crimea). Over 10 million ethnic Russians live in eastern Ukraine; Crimea is about 63 per cent Russian.

Religions

The principal religion is Christianity, of various denominations including Ukrainian Orthodox, Autocephalous Orthodox, and Ukrainian Greek Catholic (Uniate) Church. There is a small Jewish minority, and a Muslim minority mostly located in Crimea.

Education

The reversal of the Russian dominated education system is the primary aim of the government.

Literacy is almost universal in Ukraine, reflecting the high level of educational participation and high quality of teaching. Increased emphasis has also been placed on Ukrainian history, culture and literature.

Elementary schooling must begin by aged seven (parents may choose to enrol their children in school at aged six), and lasts until aged 10. This is followed by secondary basic education, which lasts until aged 15 when examinations determine academic upper secondary education until aged 18, or vocational education which lasts until aged 20.

Ukraine has large scientific and educational centres in Kiev, Odessa, Lviv, Kharkiv and Donetzk, with more than 200 higher educational institutes. There are 10 universities.

Literacy rate: 100 per cent adult rate; 100 per cent youth rate (15–24) (Unesco 2005).

Compulsory years: 6/7 to 16.

Enrolment rate: 78 per cent gross primary enrolment; 105 per cent gross secondary enrolment, of relvant age groups (including repeaters), (Unicef 2004)

Pupils per teacher: 21 in primary schools.

Health

The precipitous economic decline since 1991 has significantly lowered living standards in Ukraine and adversely affected health. Although high soil fertility enables most Ukrainians to enjoy a sufficient diet, nutrition levels remain lower than optimum and high alcohol and tobacco consumption does little to improve matters. Moreover, lacking adequate funds, many health facilities have closed or reduced their level of service since independence. Although the number of doctors is well above the Organisation for Economic Co-operation and Development (OECD) average, they lack the training, facilities and medicines to provide adequate preventative or primary healthcare. One result of this has been outbreaks of tuberculosis, which reached epidemic levels in the late 1990s.

HIV/Aids

HIV prevalence: 0.1 per cent aged 15–49 in 2003 (World Bank)

Life expectancy: 67 years, 2004 (WHO 2006)

Fertility rate/Maternal mortality rate: 1.4 births per woman, 2010 (Unicef)

Birth rate/Death rate: 10 births and 16.4 deaths per 1,000 population (2003)

Child (under 5 years) mortality rate (per 1,000): 11 per 1,000 live births (WHO 2012)

Head of population per physician: 2.95 physicians per 1,000 people, 2003 (WHO 2006)

Welfare

As part of its plan to reduce the fiscal deficit and meet IMF spending restrictions, the government has been forced to alter its social security structure.

More targetting of assistance to vulnerable groups is being planned, with reforms to family benefits, sickness benefits and the employment fund. A social insurance system provides benefits for old age pensions, sickness, maternity, work injury, and employee family allowances.

The pension system is being reformed, with preferential pensions being scaled down. The retirement age is 60 and 55 for men and women, with 25 or 20 years contributions, respectively. Reforms being enacted in 2004 intend to raise this and introduce additional voluntary and mandatory savings schemes. There are also plans to increase the pension age gradually.

The insurance scheme is funded by employee earnings of 1 per cent on wages up to H150 and 2 per cent on wages of H150 or more (capped at wage of H1,600 per month); employers pay 37 per cent of payroll and central and local governments provide subsidies as needed. There are an estimated 2.2 million Ukrainians who are eligible for extra social security payments as victims of the 1986 Chernobyl disaster.

Main cities

Kiev (Kyiv) (capital, estimated population 2.7 million (m) in 2012), Kharkiv (Kharkov) (1.5m), Dnepropetrovsk (1.0m), Donetsk (999,975), Odessa (979,263), Zaporizhzhya (776,998), Kryvyy Rih (740,632), Lviv (Lvov) (733,856), Mykolayiv (505,777).

Languages spoken

Ukrainian, Polish and German are widely spoken in western Ukraine, while Russian is widely spoken in the east. Romanian, Bulgarian, Hungarian and Belarusian are also spoken.

Controversial legislation was enacted on 3 July 2012 whereby the Russian language was upgraded to a 'regional language'. This enables it to be used in public services and for teaching in schools in predominately Russian speaking areas, historically in the east of the country.

Official language/s

Ukrainian

Media

Press

Press freedom in the Ukraine has been described as partial, by the UK-based Freedom House, in 2007. Violence and intimidation of journalists is ongoing, perpetrated by politicos and criminals, while the legal system has not succeeded in finding those responsible for the death of prominent journalist Georgiy Gongadze in 2000.

Dailies: In Ukrainian, *Fakty i Kommentarii* (www.facts.kiev.ua), *Segodnya* (www.segodnya.ua) and *Vecherniye Vesti* are mass-circulations newspapers, others include *Silski Visti* (www.silskivisti.kiev.ua) and *Kievshiye Vedomosti* (www.kv.com.ua), *Ukrayina Moloda* (www.umoloda.kiev.ua) and *Holos Ukrayiny* (http://uamedia.visti.net/golos) the parliamentary newspaper.

In English, *Den* (www.day.kiev.ua), and online Ukryinska Pravda (www2.pravda.com.ua/en).

There are also local newspaper in provincial cities, including *Oga* (www.ogo.ua) from Rivne, *Slovo* (www.slovo.odessa.ua) from Odesa and in Russian, *Zik* (www.zik.com.ua) and *Ekspres* (www.expres.ua) from Lviv, and *Gorod* (www.gorod.donbass.com) from Donetsk in Russian.

Weeklies: Magazines in Ukrainian include *Krytyka* (http://krytyka.kiev.ua), *Zerkalo Nedeli* (www.zn.ua) comments on politics, and *Ji* (www.ji-magazine.lviv.ua), a cultural magazine. In English, *The Ukrainian Observer* (www.ukraine-observer.com) and *Kyiv Post* (www.kyivpost.com).

Business: In Ukrainian, *Kontrakty* (www.kontrakty.com.ua) and *Delovaya Stolitsa* (www.dsnews.com.ua) are newspapers. *Finansovaya Ukraina* covers financial news. In English, the *Eastern Economist* is published weekly.

Broadcasting

The Derzhkominform of Ukraine (state committee, for television and radio broadcasting) is responsible for providing transmission frequencies and dissemination of official information.

Radio: The government operated national service is Ukrayinsko Radio One with three stations (www.nrcu.gov.ua), plus Radio Ukraine International, with external transmissions. There are many private, commercial radio stations which are based regionally or in a city including Trand M Radio (www.trans-m-radio.com), from the Crimea, Shanson Radio (www.shanson.ua), from Kharkov, Melodia FM (www.melodia.ua), Planeta FM (http://planetafm.net), and Dovira FM (www.dovira.com.ua), from Kiev, Mama Radio (http://mama.odessa.fm) from Odessa.

Television: The government-operated network, National TV Company of Ukraine (www.1tv.com.ua), (known as UT1) operates three network channels, which broadcasts over 97 per cent of the territory. There are plans that by 2009 UT1 will acquire public broad broadcaster status and the government will forego its control of the network.

There are a number of commercial channels broadcasting via cable, satellite and terrestrial signals with a range in product content from entertainment, news, music, sports and culture. The most popular TV channel is Inter (http://intertv.com.ua) followed by Studio 1+1 (http://1plus1.tv).

National news agency: Ukrinform (Ukranian National News Agency)

Other news agencies: Unian: www.unian.net/eng

Interfax-Ukraine: www.interfax.com.ua/en

Economy

Ukraine's economy has been transformed in many ways since its break with the old Soviet Union in the 1990s. It has always had the potential for strong economic growth with its natural resources of coal, iron ore, mineral deposits, timber and many hectares of fertile agricultural land, coupled with traditional industries such as mining, iron and steel production, light engineering industries such as machinery and transport manufacturing, food-processing, textile and clothing manufacturing as well as modern industries including power generation and communications. However, Ukraine's economic development has been marred by a lack of political consensus on which way to turn to best provide the conditions for a market economy: – west towards the European Union or east towards the Russian Federation.

Ukraine's dependence on Russia for energy supplies and the lack of significant structural reform has made the economy vulnerable to external shocks. Ukraine depends on imports to meet approximately 75 per cent of its annual oil and natural gas requirements and 100 per cent of its nuclear fuel needs. Movement towards an Association Agreement with the EU, which would commit Ukraine to economic reforms in exchange for preferential access to EU markets, was curtailed by a November 2013 decision of President Yanukovych. A month later, Yanukovych and President Putin concluded a financial assistance packaging containing US$15 billion in loans and lower gas prices. However, the end of Yanukovych's government in February 2014 caused Russia to halt further funding. With the formation of an interim government in late February 2014, the international community began efforts to stabilize the Ukrainian economy, including a 27 Match 2014 IMF assistance package of US$14-18 billion. Russia's recent seizure of the Crimean Peninsula and the Ukrainian revolution

together have wrecked economic growth for the Ukraine in 2014.
The political instability since 2004 between the factions that proposed partnerships either west or east undermined Ukraine's ability to focus on economic growth. The global economic crisis was particularly hard for the Ukraine in 2008, as its vulnerability was exposed as a steel exporter and a borrower on international markets. As one of the world's least energy-efficient counties Ukraine is highly dependent on natural gas imports from Russia. When global oil prices were at an all-time high in 2008, imported energy cost the country US$22 billion, up from US$15.3 billion in 2007, and before falling to a still high US$14.5 billion in 2009. This unwelcome drain on the country's balance of payments compounded the government's financial problems. Confidence in the currency and banking sector was eroded causing a system-wide run on deposits, further reducing government revenue. The Ukrainian economy contracted nearly 15 per cent in 2009, among the worst economic performances in the world. Economic growth continued to stall in 2012 and 2013 recording rates of 0.2 per cent and 0.0 per cent respectively before plummeting to a disastrous -6.8 per cent in 2014. GDP per capita has also shrunk from US$9,300 in 2013 to US$8,700 in 2014. Inflation has increased from -0.3 per cent in 2013 to an extremely high figure of 12.1 per cent in 2014. Continuing the unhealthy trend, unemployment has also increased from 7.2 per cent in 2013 to 10.5 per cent in 2014.
In February 2014, following the Ukrainian revolution, a dispute began over control of the Crimean peninsula between Ukraine and Russia. When the interim President Turchynov was appointed in Ukraine, Russia condemned the new government as illegitimate. Beginning on 26 February pro-Russian forces started taking control of the Crimean peninsula, and while these troops occupied Crimea's parliament building, the Crimean parliament dismissed the Crimean government and called for a referendum on Crimea's autonomy. The US and the EU recognised Turchynov's government and therefore the crisis has led to a global dispute. In April 2014, Russia's Gazprom cancelled Ukraine's natural gas discount, which had been agreed in December 2013, as its debt to the company had risen to US$1.7 billion. The Russian government annulled an export-duty exemption for Gazprom leading to a jump in the price to US$485 per 1,000 cubic metres (cum). On the 16 June 2014, Gazprom announced that Ukraine's debt to the company was US$4.5 billion. There were worries that this would disrupt Russian gas exports to the rest of Europe also, seeing as 30 per cent of Europe's gas comes from Russia through pipelines in Ukraine.
The crisis has also affected global grain prices because Ukraine is one of the world's largest exporters of corn, so prices are likely to rise. The EU also banned import of all goods from Crimea to its member states.
The election as president of businessman and pro-European Unionist, Petro Poroshenko, on 25 May is likely to irritate the Russians but lead to closer EU association.

External trade

Following the break-up of the Soviet Union, trade was formalised with former republics through the Commonwealth of Independent States (CIS), and in October 2011 the Commonwealth of Independent States Free Trade Agreement was signed. As the world's fifth largest exporter of cereals, and sixth largest exporter of iron, primary industries are important to the economy. Prior to the Crimean crisis over 30 per cent of all exports are traded to the EU and 25 per cent to Russia. Manufacturing reflects the Ukraine's historic role as an important manufacturing base of the former Soviet Union with production in heavy industry including steel making, shipbuilding, locomotive and aerospace industries, nuclear reactors and boilers, machinery and machine tools. Fees for oil transiting the country from Russia to Europe provide an important source of foreign earnings.
In March 2014 Ukraine signed the political provisions of the EU-Ukraine Association Agreement. The agreement commits Ukraine to economic, judicial and financial reforms but also opens the doors to many markets of free trade.

Imports

Principal imports include energy, machinery and equipment and chemicals. .

Main sources: Russia (23.3 per cent of total in 2014), China (10 per cent), Germany (9.9 per cent), Belarus (7.3 per cent) and Poland (5.6 per cent).

Exports

Principal exports are ferrous and non-ferrous metals, fuel and petroleum products, chemicals, machinery and transport equipment and foodstuffs.

Main destinations: Russia (18.2 per cent of total in 2014), Turkey (6.6 per cent), Egypt (5.3 per cent), China (5 per cent), Poland (4.9 per cent) and Italy (4.6 per cent).

Agriculture

Farming

Historically known as the 'bread basket' of the former Soviet Union, Ukraine used to produce 25 per cent of the total Soviet agricultural output. The agricultural sector, despite Ukraine's rich land resources (with one-third of the world's total acreage of black soil), went into decline for several years as a result of general inefficiency, late payments and a lack of finance for fuel, fertilisers and machinery. Progress of agricultural sector reforms included price and trade reforms, and agriculture-specific institutional reforms will have a significant impact on the future of agricultural production. Economy-wide reforms will allow the sector to absorb technological advances more rapidly.
Despite not being used to full potential the agricultural industry in Ukraine turns 40 to 60 per cent profit. Analysts say profits could be multiplied fourfold however. Agriculture constituted 12 per cent of GDP in 2014 and it employs 5.6 per cent of the labour force.
The main agricultural products are wheat, barley, potatoes, vegetables, beef, milk, sugar beet and flax. Ukraine is the world's largest producer of sugar beet and sunflower oil.

Fishing

The fishery sector is an elaborate organisational complex of oceanic fisheries, pond fish farms, co-operatives, scientific research and education as well as enterprises dealing with processing and the sale of fish products, stock protection and restoration. The sector typically employs more than 60,000 people. The Black Sea fishing industry is concentrated around the ports of Odessa, Mariupol, Berdyansk and Izmail.
Ukraine could harvest and rear between 700,000–800,000 tonnes of fish, with an annual output of food fish products from vessels and coastal enterprises amounting to more than 600,000 tonnes. The country exports over a third of its fish catch and the industry makes a substantial contribution to the country's trade balance.

Forestry

Ukraine has mainly mixed and steppe forests, which account for one-sixth of the land area, with forest cover estimated at 9.5 million hectares (ha). Nearly two-thirds of the forest is available for wood supply, although consumption of forest products per capita is significantly below the European average. The state owns all the forest area.
The Zavarpattska and Polisia regions are the main centres for the forestry and paper industries. Apart from the smaller wood processing enterprises, most of the forest industry is privatised and caters to domestic demand. The industry is being modernised by improving the sawmills and other manufacturing operations. Small quantities of roundwood and half-finished products are exported to the Middle East and European countries.

Wood pulp and paper, mainly from the Russian Federation are imported.

Industry and manufacturing
The industrial sector, which contributed around 27 per cent to GDP in 2013, is essentially divided into two. Most of the sector is concentrated on heavy industry, principally in metallurgy, mining and mechanical engineering. The iron and steel industry is the main earner of hard currency revenues. It is dominated by large companies, such as JSC Zaporozhstal, and the government has been reluctant to introduce privatisation and other reforms. Ukraine has benefited from China's increasing demand for steel.
The high-technology industry, having been located in Ukraine in Soviet times, is modern and internationally competitive.

Tourism
In 2013 the tourism and travel industry contributed in total US$9.6 billion (8.6 per cent of GDP) and employed 1,570,000 workers (indirectly 7.7 per cent of the total workforce). In 2014, the tourism and travel industry contributed US$4.7 billion (7.1 per cent of GDP) and employed 1,270,000 jobs (6 per cent of the total workforce). Therefore, 2014 marked a significant decrease from the role of the tourism sector in the Ukrainian economy in 2013. This can mainly be attributed to the revolution and the Russian annexing of the Crimea. Tourism and travel is expected to increase its contribution to GDP to US$6.7 billion.

Environment
Extensive pollution is one of the more persistent legacies of the Soviet regime when massive industrialisation was pursued at any cost. The most obvious example is the Chernobyl nuclear power explosion which increased rates of thyroid cancer, leukaemia and birth defects in the surrounding areas. All Ukraine's cities suffer from pollution, both in the air as well as rivers and agricultural land. The Lviv region has the most polluted water in the country. Only about 55 per cent of the Ukranian population has access to safe water.

Mining
The mining sector traditionally accounts for 10 per cent of GDP and employs 3 per cent of the workforce.
Ukraine possesses an estimated 5 per cent of the world's mineral reserves. It has one of the world's largest reserves of titanium, the seventh-largest deposit of iron ore (6.5 billion tonnes) in 2015 and 4 per cent of the world's manganese ore. It also has deposits of mercury, uranium and nickel, and a small amount of gold.
The largest iron ore deposits are in the Krivoy Roj area, Kremenchuk and Kerch and Belozerskie in the Donetsk region. The manganese deposits around Nikopol are thought to be the largest in the world. Gold deposits containing an average of between five and six grammes of gold per tonne of ore exist in the Trans-Carpathian region. The area also contains deposits of zinc and lead.
Other natural resources present in Ukraine include salt, lime, limestone, china clay, sulphur (around Lviv) and granite. Phosphorus deposits of about 20 billion tonnes are also present.
Ukraine typically produces 50 million tonnes per year (tpy) of iron, 1,000 tpy of nickel and 500 tpy of uranium.

Hydrocarbons
Proven oil reserves were 395 million barrels in 2014, the majority of which is located in the Dnieper-Donetsk basin in the eastern part of Ukraine. These reserves are under-exploited while Ukraine typically relies on oil imports from Russia. Ukraine and Russia have been in conflict since the latter began charging market rates for its hydrocarbons. Prior to the Crimean crisis, around 900,000 barrels per day (bpd) of Russian oil and gas transited Ukraine, via pipelines, of which around 250,000bpd was reserved for domestic use. There are six oil refineries with total capacity of 880,000bpd. In June 2014, the Russian natural gas company Gazprom announced that Ukraine had a debt of US$4.5 billion to the company. Efforts to reduce dependence on Russian oil have included the construction of an international oil terminal at Odessa port. The price of natural gas from Russia has historically been lower for Ukraine than other European states, however it has been consistently on the rise. After the Crimean crisis in 2014 it was US$485 per 1,000 cum, despite the Ukrainian-Russian action plan of December 2013 that stated the price would not rise above US$268 per 1,000 cum.
Crude oil production was 68,500 bpd in 2014 and consumption was 318,000 bpd, and, therefore the difference had to be imported, primarily from Russia.
Proven natural gas reserves were 1.1 trillion cubic metres in 2014, production was 20 billion cu m while consumption was 53 billion cu m. The difference had to be imported by Russia. There is opportunity for Ukraine to produce more natural gas and become self-sufficient while exporting the excess.
Coal production is minimal and it needs to import most of it.

Energy
Total installed generating capacity was 54.4 gigawatts (GW) in 2014. There are four major thermal power stations and four nuclear power plants. The last working nuclear reactor at the Chernobyl plant was closed in 2000. Thermal power, much of which is gas-fired, accounts for nearly 65 per cent of the electricity produced in Ukraine, while nuclear energy provides 25 per cent and hydroelectric plants supply the remainder.
A state-owned company, Enerhoatom, oversees the nuclear power plants. Lack of funding has meant that safety standards continue to be lax and strike action and power breakdowns are frequent.
After the Crimean crisis of 2014 Gazprom prices for Ukraine rocketed, causing the country to go into serious debt to the Russian company.

Financial markets
Stock exchange
Ukraine Stock Exchange

Banking and insurance
There are seven domestic banks operating in the banking sector, two of which are state-owned and originate from the Soviet era. Foreign investors are permitted to participate in the banking sector, but are only granted a licence after at least a year of running an office in the country.
In February 2004, Ukraine was removed from the OECD Financial Action Task Force (FATF) list of non-co-operative countries on money-laundering after reforms had been implemented.

Central bank
National Bank of Ukraine

Time
GMT plus two hours (daylight saving, late March to late October, GMT plus three hours)

Geography
Ukraine is situated in Eastern Europe. The largest country entirely within Europe, Ukraine covers 603,700 square kilometres, stretching 2,000km from east to west and 1,000km from north to south. The Crimean peninsula in the south juts into the Black Sea, and has the Sea of Azov to the east.
In eastern Ukraine, the country is bordered by Russia to the east and north. In the western part of the country the northern border is with Belarus, and there are western borders with Poland and Slovakia. There are also short borders with Hungary, Romania and Moldova to the south-west, and a small salient of land south of Moldova which borders Bulgaria and has access to the Danube River delta.
The average height above sea level in Ukraine is only 175 metres, and most of the land area is composed of rolling steppes and wooded plains. About two-thirds of the country is covered by a thick layer of humus-rich soil, making it one of the most fertile regions in the world.

The only mountains are in the south on the Crimean peninsula (maximum height 1,545 metres) and the Carpathians in the west (maximum height 2,061 metres). The main rivers are the Dnepr which drains the central regions of the country and flows into the Black Sea near Kherson and the Dnestr which flows through western Ukraine and Moldova before entering the Black Sea near Odessa.

Hemisphere

Northern

Climate

The moderate continental climate varies little across the country. The Black Sea resorts around Odessa and Yalta are usually warmer and drier than the rest of Ukraine. The average rainfall per year is 1,440mm, with the Crimea receiving only 400mm. Average temperatures in Kiev range from 20 degrees Celsius (C) in July to minus 7 degrees C in January. Average temperatures in Lviv in western Ukraine range from 16 degrees C in July, to minus 5 degrees C in January.

Dress codes

Business clothes are appropriate for meetings, including a suit or jacket with a tie for men and formal clothing for women.

Entry requirements

Passports

Required by all, valid for one month beyond departure date.

Visa

Required by all, except nationals of EU/EEA countries, North America, Japan, Switzerland, Andora, Vatican City, Monaco and San Marino. Letters of invitation are not required for either business or tourist visits by nationals of EU countries, US, Canada, Japan, Switzerland, Slovakia, or Turkey.

Currency advice/regulations

Import and export of local currency is restricted to H1,000; up to H5,000 may be exported subject to customs declaration. Import and export of foreign currencies is restricted to US$1,000 or, subject to customs declaration, up to US$10,000.

Customs

Small amount of personal goods, 200 cigarettes, 1 litre spirits, 2 litres wine and 10 litres beer are allowed duty free. There are strict regulations governing the export of antiques and items of historical interest. If in doubt seek prior permission from customs authorities.

Prohibited imports

Weapons, illegal drugs and certain pharmaceutical and communcations products are subject to import restrictions; licences are issued by the relevant government ministries.

Health (for visitors)

Mandatory precautions

Vaccination certificates if travelling from a cholera or yellow fever infected area. An HIV/Aids test is required for long-stay visitors only. A UK-issued certificate is usually accepted. All visitors entering Ukraine are required to purchase health insurance at the airport of entry and prior to passing through immigration control. British passport holders are exempt due to a reciprocal agreement between the Ukrainian and British governments.

Advisable precautions

It is advisable to be in date for the following immunisations: polio (within 10 years), tetanus (within 10 years), typhoid fever and hepatitis A (moderate risk only). There is a rabies risk. Any medicines required by the traveller should be imported and it is advisable to have precautionary antibiotics if travelling outside the major urban centres. However, there are restrictions on the import of some pharmaceuticals and visitors are advised to check with their local Ukrainian embassy prior to travel. A travel kit including a disposable syringe is a reasonable precaution.Water precautions are recommended (water purification tablets may be useful).

Hotels

Kiev has a shortage of hotels. It is worth booking rooms several weeks in advance through the Intourist travel agency.

Credit cards

Credit cards are not widely accepted.

Public holidays (national)

Fixed dates

1 Jan (New Year's Day), 7 Jan (Orthodox Christmas Day), 8 Mar (Women's Day), 1-2 May (Labour/May Days), 9 May (Victory Day), 28 Jun (Constitution Day), 24 Aug (Independence Day).

Variable dates

Orthodox Easter Monday, Orthodox Whit Monday.

Working hours

Banking

Mon–Fri: 0930–1730.
Open 24 hours at Kiev Borispol airport, but only until noon at Odessa.

Business

Mon–Fri: 0900–1800.

Government

Mon–Thu: 0700–1700; Fri: 0900–1200.

Shops

Mon–Sat: 0900–1900.

Telecommunications

Internet/e-mail

Social customs/useful tips

Tips are not expected at most cafes, although at more expensive restaurants a tip of between 5 and 10 per cent is appropriate.

Small gifts for your host are appreciated in the event of personal hospitality. Handshaking is customary on meeting and on leaving. The formal mode of address, *Pan* (Mr) or *Pani* (Mrs) is usual even after several meetings. The use of business cards is widespread. It is important to be on time for meetings and appointments.

Referring to Ukraine as part of the Soviet Union or, even worse, as part of Russia, is a serious insult. The post-independence reaction to decades of 'Russification' led to strong nationalistic feelings, particularly in western Ukraine.

Security

Normal precautions should be taken when visiting Ukraine – avoid displaying large amounts of cash or expensive personal belongings. Avoid travelling alone at night in Kiev, particularly on the metro or in the city's parks.

Getting there

Air

National airline: Ukraine International Airlines

International airport/s: Kiev-Borispol International Airport (KBP), 27km from city centre; bank, post office, duty-free shop, car rental.

Other airport/s: Zhulhany Airport (IEV), 6km from Kiev.

Airport tax: None

Surface

Ukraine is included in the Pan-European Corridor 5 scheme. The project has some 3,270km of railways, linking Kiev in the Ukraine with western Europe via Italy, and 2,850 of new and upgraded roads.

Road: There are roads into Ukraine from all neighbouring countries.

Rail: There are links connecting Kiev and Lviv with all Commonwealth of Independent States member states. Direct rail connections are available to Warsaw in Poland, Budapest in Hungary and Bucharest in Romania.

Water: There are ferry services from Russia to the Crimean ports. Odessa and Yalta on the Black Sea have regular arrivals from Haifa, Istanbul, Limassol, Piraeus and Port Said. Riverboats from Odessa go to a number of Central European cities via the Danube.

Main port/s: The main Crimean ports are Yalta and Sevastopol, with Kerch the main port for the Sea of Azov. Izmail is the main Danube River port, and Odessa is the largest Black Sea port.

Getting about

National transport

Air: The main airports for domestic air traffic are Borispol International and Zhulany, from which there are connections to Chernivitsi, Dniepropetrovsk,

Donetsk, Ivano-Frankivsk, Kharkov, Lugansk, Lviv, Mariupol, Odessa, Simferopol, Uzhgorod and Zaporizhzhya. Services during the winter months are often subject to cancellation or delay.

Road: There is an extensive road network comprising approximately 172,00km of road, with around 29,000km of these being main or national roads. Many roads are poorly surfaced and in need of modernisation.

Buses: Ukraine has an extensive bus network, with routes to every city and most smaller towns.

Taxis: Using taxis for long-distance journeys is an option as they are reasonably cheap. Payment is usually requested in hard currency. Agree a price before setting off.

Rail: The Ukrainian rail network links the major cities, most of which are at least one night's travel apart. There are three types of sleeper carriage: the *spalny vahon* is the first class compartment for two people; the *kupe* or *kupeyny* is the second class compartment for four people; and the *platskart* is the third class open carriage with groups of six bunks in each alcove, with more beds along the aisles – avoid the *platskart* unless absolutely necessary.

It is advisable to pre-book tickets before arriving in Ukraine. Foreigners can usually buy rail tickets from separate offices with English-speaking clerks, although the price will be slightly higher.

Although journey times are slower than air, rail travel is more reliable during the winter months.

Water: Passenger transport is available on the Dnepr and Dnestr rivers, which traverse large areas of the country, but price increases, lack of spare parts and cheaper land-based transport have caused a sharp decline in services.

City transport

Taxis: In most cities there are metered official taxis, unofficial 'gypsy cabs' with negotiated fares and fixed route, fixed price shared taxis and minibus services.

Car hire

International agencies are represented in the main cities, in addition to local agencies, offering a range of vehicles. Car hire is relatively cheap.

Speed limits are 60kph (37mph) in built-up areas, 90kph (55mph) in open areas and 110kph (69mph) on motorways. An international driving permit is required. It is illegal to drive having consumed any amount of alcohol.

BUSINESS DIRECTORY

The addresses listed below are a selection only. While World of Information makes every endeavour to check these addresses, we cannot guarantee that changes have not been made, especially to telephone numbers and area codes. We would welcome any corrections.

Telephone area codes

The international direct dialling code (IDD) for Ukraine is + 380, followed by area code and subscriber's number:

Dnepropetrovsk	56	Odessa	48
Donetsk	62	Sevastopol	69
Kharkov	57	Simferopol	65
Kiev	44	Yalta	65
Lviv	32		

Useful telephone numbers

Fire brigade: 01
Militia (Police): 02
Hospital enquiries: 003
Directory enquiries: 09
Address enquiries: 061
Lost property office: 229-7844
Paid enquiries service: 009
Railway timetable: 09
River port: 416-1268
Taxi: 058
Taxi enquiries: 225-0396
Time: 060

Chambers of Commerce

American Chamber of Commerce in Ukraine, 42 Shovkovychna Street, 01601 Kiev (tel: 490-5800; fax: 490-5801; e-mail: acc@amcham.ua).

British-Ukrainian Chamber of Commerce, 34a Grushevskogo Street, 01021 Kiev (tel: 410-5720; fax: 230-2151; e-mail: administrator@bucc.com.ua).

Crimea Chamber of Commerce and Industry, 45 Sevastopolskaya Street, 95013 Simferopol (e-mail: cci@cci.crimea.ua).

Dnipropetrovsk Chamber of Commerce and Industry, 4 Shevchenko Street, 49044 Dnipropetrovsk (tel: 236-2258; fax: 236-2259; e-mail: miv@dcci.dp.ua).

Donetsk Chamber of Commerce and Industry, 12 Dzerzinskogo Avenue, 83000 Donetsk (e-mail: dcci@dtpp.donetsk.ua).

Kharkov Chamber of Commerce and Industry, 3a Kartsarskaya Street, 61012 Kharkov (e-mail: info@kcci.kharkov.ua).

Kiev Chamber of Commerce and Industry, 55 Bogdana Khmelnitskogo Street, 01054 Kiev (tel: 246-8301; fax: 246-9966; e-mail: info@kiev-chamber.org.ua).

Lviv Chamber of Commerce and Industry, 14 Stryisky Park, 79011 Lviv (e-mail: lcci@cscd.lviv.ua).

Odessa Chamber of Commerce and Industry, 47 Bazarna Street, 65011 Odessa (tel: 728-6610; e-mail: orcci@orcci.odessa.ua).

Sevastopol Chamber of Commerce and Industry, 34 Bolshaya Morskaya Street, 99011 Sevastopol (e-mail: stpp@optima.com.ua).

Ukrainian Chamber of Commerce & Industry, 33 Velyka Zhytomyrska, 01601 Kiev (tel: 272-2911; fax: 272-3353; e-mail: ucci@ucci.org.ua).

Banking

Aggio Joint Stock Bank, 9 Leskova Street, 252011 Kiev (tel: 295-0305; fax 295-3164).

Commercial Bank (Ekspobank), 2-4 Volodarskogo Street, 254025 Kiev (tel: 216-1676; fax: 216-6073).

First Ukrainian International Bank (under full management of Bank Mees and Hpe Pierson NV, ABN/AMRO), 8 Prorizna Street, 252034 Kiev (tel: 224-2187; fax: 224-2055).

Gradobank, 1 Dimitrova Street, 252650 Kiev (tel: 261-9191; fax: 268-1530).

Inki Bank, 10/2 Mechnikova Street, 252023 Kiev (tel: 294-9219; fax: 290-6292).

Legbank Commercial Bank for Light Industry, 8/10 Esplanadna (Kuybysheva) Street, 252601 Kiev (tel: 220-6125; fax: 220-8684).

Ukreximbank, 8 Kreshchatyk Street, Kiev (tel: 226-3363; fax: 229-8082).

Ukrainian Bank for Foreign Economic Affairs, 8 Kreshchatyk Street, 252001 Kiev (tel: 293-1698).

Ukrainian Financial Group Joint Stock Commercial Bank, 7 Vokzalnaya Street, 252032 Kiev (tel: 245-4560; fax: 245-4587).

Central bank

National Bank of Ukraine, 9 Institutska Street, Kiev 01601 (tel: 253-0180; fax: 230-2033; e-mail: info@bank.gov.ua).

Stock exchange

Ukraine Stock Exchange, www.ukrse.kiev.ua

Travel information

Ukraine International Airlines, 63A Bogdana Khmelnytskogo Street, 01054 Kiev (tel: 461-5656 ; fax: 216-7994; e-mail: uia@ps.kiev.ua).

Ukrainian Travel Information System, 29A, Electrikov Street, 04176 Kiev (tel/fax: 537-2727; e-mail: info@utis.com.ua)

Ministry of tourism

Ministry of Culture and Tourism, 19 Ivana Franka Street, 01601 Kiev (tel: 235-2378; fax: 235-3257; e-mail: info@mincult.gov.ua).

National tourist organisation offices

State Tourism Administration of Ukraine, 36 Yaroslaviv Val Street, 01034 Kiev (tel:

212-4215; fax: 212-4277; e-mail: info@tourism.gov.ua).

Ministries

Ministry of Agriculture and Foodstuffs, 24 Kreshchatyk Street, 252001 Kiev (tel: 226-2772; fax: 229-8756).

Ministry of the Coal Industry, 4 Bohdana Khmelnitskoho Street, 252001 Kiev (tel: 226-2273, 228-0372; fax: 228-2131).

Ministry of Communications, 22 Kreshchatyk Street, Kiev (tel: 226-2140; fax: 228-6141).

Ministry of Culture, 19 Ivana Franka Street, 252030 Kiev (tel: 224-4911, 226-2645, 226-2902; fax: 225-3257).

Ministry of Defence, 6 Povitroflotsky Avenue, 252168 Kiev (tel: 224-7152; fax: 226-2015).

Ministry of Education, 10 Peremogy Avenue, 252135 Kiev (tel: 216-7210, 216-7763, 216-1575; fax: 274-1049).

Ministry of Engineering, the Defence Industry and Conversion, 6 Pushkinska Street, 252034 Kiev (tel: 229-0390; fax: 228-7653).

Ministry of Environment Protection, 5 Kreshchatyk Street, 252001 Kiev (tel: 226-2428, 228-0644; fax: 229-8383).

Ministry of Finance, 12/2 Hrushevskoho Street, 252008 Kiev (tel: 226-2044; fax: 293-2178).

Ministry of Foreign Affairs, 1 Mihaylivska Square, 252018 Kiev (tel: 226-3379, 293-1581; fax: 226-3169, 293-3302).

Ministry of Foreign Economic Relations, 8 Lvivska Square, 254655 Kiev (tel: 212-3005; fax: 212-5259).

Ministry of Forestry, 5 Kreshchatyk Street, 252001 Kiev (tel: 226-3253, 226-2735, 228-5666; fax: 228-7794).

Ministry of Health, 7 Hrushevskoho Street, 252021 Kiev (tel: 293-6194; fax: 293-6975).

Ministry of Industry, 34 Kreshchatyk Street, 252001 Kiev (tel: 226-2623; fax: 227-4104).

Ministry of Information, 2 Prorizna Street, 252601 Kiev (tel: 226-2871).

Ministry of Internal Affairs, 10 Bogomoltsa Street, 252021 Kiev (tel: 291-3333, 226-3317; fax: 291-3182).

Ministry of Justice, 13 Karl Marx Street, 252001 Kiev (tel: 226-2416; fax: 226-2416).

Ministry of Labour, 28 Pushkinska Street, 252004 Kiev (tel: 226-2445, 226-2639, 226-3215; fax: 224-5905).

Ministry for Nationalities, Migration and Cults Issues, 21/8 Instytutska Street, 252021 Kiev (tel: 293-5335; fax: 293-3531).

Ministry of Power Engineering and Electrification, 30 Kreschchatyk Street, 252001 Kiev (tel: 224-9388; fax: 224-4021).

Ministry for Protection of the Population against the Consequences of Chernobyl, 8 Lvivska Square, 254655 Kiev (tel: 212-5049; fax: 212-5069).

Ministry of Social Welfare, 26-28 Kudriavka Street, 252053 Kiev (tel: 222-5555, 226-2401; fax: 212-2535).

Ministry of Statistics, 3 Shota Rustaveli Street, 252023 Kiev (tel: 226-2021, 227-7057; fax: 227-0783, 227-4266).

Ministry of Transport, 51 Horkoho Street, 252005 Kiev (tel: 226-2266, 227-1029, 227-7087; fax: 227-7351).

Ministry of Youth and Sports Issues, 42 Esplanadna Street, 252023 Kiev (tel: 220-0200, 220-1461; fax: 220-1294).

Ukrainian Ministry for Economics and Issues of European Integration, 12/2 Hrushevskoho Street, 252008 Kiev (tel: 293-4005, 293-9329; fax: 293-6371).

Other useful addresses

British Embassy, 9 Desyatinna, 01025 Kiev (tel: 462-0011/15; fax: 462-0013; internet: wwwbritemb-ukraine.net).

Cabinet of Ministers, 12/2 Hrushevskoho Street, 252001 Kiev (tel: 226-3263; fax: 293-2093).

Committee for Standardisation, Methodology and Certification, 10 Kypska Street, 252021 Kiev (tel: 226-2971).

EBRD Kiev Office, c/o National Hotel, 5 Lipska Street, 252021 Kiev 21 (tel: 291-8847, 291-8977; fax: 291-6246).

EU Co-ordination Unit – TACIS Programme, Agency for International Co-operation and Investment, 1 Mihailivska Ploscha, 252018 Kiev (tel: 212-8312; fax: 230-2513).

European Centre for Macroeconomic Analysis of Ukraine, Kiev (tel & fax: 228-3283; e-mail: ecman@gv.kiev.va).

Foreign Trade Organisation (UKRIMPEX), 22 Vorovsky Street, 252054 Kiev (tel: 216-2174; fax: 216-1926, 216-2996).

International Finance Corporation Field Office, Suite 7, 28-A Lyuteranska Street, 252024 Kiev (tel: 293-4857, 293-8341; fax: 293-0539).

Kiev City Administration, 36 Khreshchatyk Street, Kiev (tel: 220-8065; fax: 228-4718).

Kiev Universal Commodity Exchange (KUCE), 1 Kudryashova Street, 252035 Kiev (tel: 276-7129, 244-0143, fax: 276-7129).

Soros International Economic Advisory Group, Kiev (tel: 296-9877; fax: 269-5263).

State Ukrainian Property Fund, 18/9 Kutuzova Street, 252133 Kiev (tel: 296-6963; fax: 296-6984).

Ukrainian Association of Industrialists and Entrepreneurs, 34 Kreshchatik Street, 252001 Kiev (tel: 224-3122, 228-3069; fax: 226-3152).

Ukrainian Embassy (USA), Suite 711, 3350 M Street, NW, Washington DC 20007 (tel: (+1-202) 333-0606; fax: (+1-202) 333-0606; e-mail: vmar@aol.com).

Ukrainian Exchange (commodities and stock exchange), 15 Proreznaya Street, 252601 Kiev (tel: 228-6481; fax: 229-6376).

Ukrainian League of Enterprises with Foreign Capital, 19A Lyuteranska Street, 252073 Kiev (tel: 229-3544; fax: 229-8739).

Ukrainian National News Agency (UKRINFORM), 8-16b Khemlnitski Street, 252601 Kiev (tel: 226-2469, 229-0143; fax: 229-2439/8007, 228-1659).

Ukrainian Universal Commodity Exchange, 1 Academika Glushkova Avenue, 252085 Kiev (tel: 261-6333, 261-6375; fax: 261-6362).

UKRINTERENERGO (State Foreign Trade Company), 27 Komintern Street, 252032 Kiev (tel: 291-7296; fax: 220-1885).

World Bank Field Office, Suite 2/3, 26 Shovkovychna Street, 252024 Kiev (tel: 293-1110, 293-4045; fax: 293-4236).

National news agency: Ukrinform (Ukranian National News Agency)

Address: 8/16 Bohdan Khmelnytsky St, Kiev 01001 (tel: 234-8366; fax: 279-8665; email: office@ukrinform.com; internet: http://news.ukrinform.ua).

Unian: www.unian.net/eng

Interfax-Ukraine: www.interfax.com.ua/en

Internet sites

Ukraine gateway site:
http://www.brama.com

Ukraine Embassy, Washington:
http://www.ukremb.com

General information:
http://www.bizukraine.com

Tourism and travel:
http://www.ukraine.com

Ukraine International Airlines:
http://www.ukraine international.com

History and culture:
http://www:uazone.net

News on Ukraine:
http://www.infoukes.com

Travel and tourism:
http://www.travel.kyiv.org

United Arab Emirates

KEY FACTS

Official name: Al Imarat al Arabiyya al Muttahida (United Arab Emirates) (UAE)

Head of State: President Sheikh Khalifa bin Zaid al Nahyan (ruler of Abu Dhabi) (since Nov 2004)

Head of government: Prime Minister Sheikh Mohammed bin Rashed al Maktoum (ruler of Dubai) (from 4 Jan 2006)

Ruling party: There are no official political parties

Area: 83,600 square km

Population: 9.30 million (2014)*

Capital: Abu Dhabi (federal capital); Dubai (commercial capital)

Official language: Arabic

Currency: Dirham (Dh) = 100 fils

Exchange rate: Dh3.67 per US$ (fixed)

GDP per capita: US$43,180 (2014)*

GDP real growth: 3.60% (2014)*

GDP: US$401.65 billion (2014)*

Inflation: 2.35% (2014)

Oil production: 3.71 million bpd (2015)

Natural gas production: 57.80 billion cum (2014)

Balance of trade: US$63.69 billion (2010)

Annual FDI: US$7.68 billion (2011)

* estimated figure

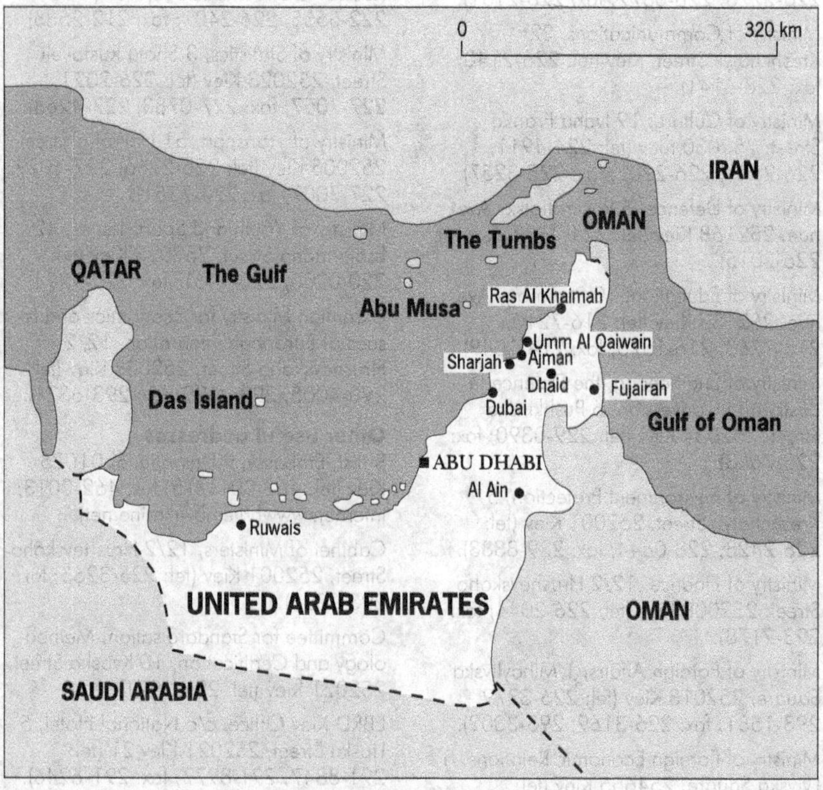

In the heat of the Arabian summer and as the fasting month of Ramadan approached, the government in Abu Dhabi could have done without continued bad news. In August 2015 the United Arab Emirates (UAE) stock markets slid steadily downwards in response to further weakness in oil prices and the decision by Fitch Ratings to cut its outlook for Saudi Arabia's debt, essentially because – as was the case in Abu Dhabi – the oil price continued to fall. The prospect of the region's most important economy going into the red gave cause for concern among all its neighbours. What had traditionally underpinned most of the region's economies was not just abundant oil supplies – and revenues – but also an oil price that had once seemed immovably entrenched around the US$150 per barrel mark.

In mid-August oil was trading even below US$40 a barrel, the first time it had been so low in six years, when the global financial crisis had dragged it south. Bad news comes in threes; in August Fitch lowered its Saudi Arabia outlook to 'negative' from 'stable'. In effect this was a shot across the bows for all the oil dependent Gulf States. As if on cue, the third bit of bad news came from the Dubai exchange. Admittedly the region's most volatile market, in one day in August the Dubai exchange fell by 4.0 per cent, to 3,563 points, a four-month low. Less volatile, Abu Dhabi's index sank by 1.4 per cent. Among the major losers, Dubai's largest property firm, Emaar Properties, fell by 5.9 per cent and Abu Dhabi's biggest developer, Aldar Properties, also dropped, by 4.4 per cent. In theory, with its relatively diversified economy and strong government finances, the UAE was better placed than most Gulf economies to ride out an era of cheap oil. But investors were concerned that a further plunge in the Saudi stock market and slowing growth there could have an impact on asset prices around the region. Riding out a period of low oil prices was one thing; Abu Dhabi was known for its conservative approach to fund management. But 'Bling' Dubai had twice been bailed out by Abu Dhabi and in the view of many investors, might well be heading for another rescue. Dubai's Sheikh Mohammed looked relaxed enough as he strolled over the manicured greensward of the Meydan racecourse; had he subcontracted the worrying to his advisers?

The economy

In its early August assessment of the UAE economy, the International Monetary Fund (IMF) considered that lower oil prices risked eroding the UAE's long-standing fiscal and external surpluses, but that the impact on economic activity in the UAE had been limited owing to large buffers. Real estate prices had declined somewhat since mid-2014, but rents were rising, driving up inflation. Following the fiscal consolidation of 2013, the fiscal stance had been expansionary in 2014.

In the perhaps predictable view of the IMF, the economic outlook was expected to moderate reflecting the lower oil prices. Non-oil growth was projected to slow in 2015, before accelerating in the medium term. Export and revenue losses from lower oil prices would be the most significant concern for the UAE economy. With persistently lower oil prices, gradual fiscal consolidation had become important to strengthen long-term fiscal sustainability while cushioning the negative effects on growth. Achieving sustainability would require what the IMF described as the rationalisation of spending and the further mobilisation of non-hydrocarbon revenues. Efforts on strengthening the medium-term budget frameworks needed to continue. Liquidity management needed to remain supportive of credit growth.

The UAE banking sector was in the view of the IMF, well capitalised, liquid, profitable and with low non-performing loans. The IMF concluded by recommending that the implementation of structural reforms should be pursued to strengthen competitiveness and accelerate private sector-led job creation for nationals. This could focus on further opening up foreign direct investment (FDI), improving selected areas of the business environment and easing access to finance for start-ups and SMEs.

Jig saw make-up

It is impossible to make broad generalisations about the United Arab Emirates (UAE). The country's very make-up brings together emirates of differing sizes, wealth, economies and history. Abu Dhabi is by a long chalk, the largest and most powerful, oil-based traditional emirate. However, what neighbouring Dubai lacks in oil resources it makes up for in bling; it has the altogether different atmosphere to be expected from an emirate which has become a major tourist attraction as well as a banking centre of sorts.

The other five emirates inevitably play something of a subordinate role; to compete with Dubai's national carrier, Emirates, Abu Dhabi now has an airline of its own, Etihad, which is expanding fast. Sharjah has an under-used airport, Ras al Khaimah once had hopes for tourism, Ajman and Umm al Qawain are so small as to barely register on the international map. Fujairah, the only Emirate on the Indian Ocean, has long hoped to become a significant port and tourist resort but those hopes have yet to bear fruit.

Largely thanks to Abu Dhabi's oil revenues, the UAE has managed to build up substantial financial reserves since independence. In 2013 per capita gross domestic product (GDP) was comparable to that of most European countries, although the equal distribution of that wealth left something to be desired. When independence loomed, the two major emirates already had a number of highly competent European and North American advisers in place. The National Bank of Dubai was jokingly referred to locally as the National Bank of Scotland, reflecting its habit of recruiting canny Scotsmen. The then Ruler of Dubai, Sheikh Rashid, was known not just for his accessibility, but also for his simple tastes. One wonders what he would make of the mega-city his sons have built up. Shaikh Rashid also had his Richelieu, a Bahraini adviser by the name of Mahdi Tajir. No signing ceremony, bank opening or official representation was complete without a photograph of Sheikh Rashid with Mahdi Tajir at his side.

Together, the emirates appear to have deployed successful economic policies, creating a relatively diverse and open economy which depends on hydrocarbons for 25 per cent of its GDP. But this very openness made it inevitably vulnerable across the board to the global economic crisis of 2008–09. Financial services, manufacturing, retail, as well as the hospitality and real estate sectors were all severely hit by the downturn in regional and global growth, nowhere more so than Dubai.

Although the UAE authorities have emphasised the importance of other non-oil sectors for the country's future economic growth, the real estate market has remained an important component of the economy. In 2012, the real estate and business services sectors accounted for 10.2 per cent of GDP and construction for 11.4 per cent of GDP. Property market trends will probably continue to play a disproportionately important role in the UAE's economic development.

Hydrocarbons

At the beginning of August 2015, as the temperature steadily rose, the government relaxed the fuel subsidies that had kept the UAE's petrol and diesel prices some 30 per cent below market rates. In 2013 the fuel subsidies had cost the government

KEY INDICATORS — United Arab Emirates

	Unit	2011	2012	2013	2014	**2015
Population	m	*5.38	*8.77	*9.03	*9.30	*9.58
Gross domestic product (GDP)	US$bn	360.10	383.80	402.34	*401.65	*363.71
GDP per capita	US$	67,008	43,774	44,552	*43,180	*37,962
GDP real growth	%	4.9	4.4	5.2	*3.6	*301,540.0
Inflation	%	0.9	0.7	1.1	2.3	*2.1
Oil output	'000 bpd	3,322.0	3,380.0	3,646.0	3,712.0	–
Natural gas output	bn cum	51.7	51.7	56.0	57.8	–
Current account	US$m	33,313.0	66,553.0	64,682.0	*48,453.0	*19,278.0
Total reserves minus gold	US$m	52,553.3	47,035.2	68,202.7	78,424.4	–
Foreign exchange	US$m	51,440.8	45,826.1	66,950.9	–	–
Exchange rate	per US$	3.67	3.67	3.67	3.67	–

* estimated figure ** forecast figure

around US$7 billion. The move reflected the continued fall in oil prices. It had been estimated by the IMF that together, the Arab Gulf states would see export revenues in 2015 drop by around US$380 billion. According to the IMF, only Kuwait and Qatar will avoid a budget deficit.

The relaxation of the subsidies had pushed the price of UAE petrol to the highest level in the Gulf. Oman came next, where petrol was about half as dear. The UAE's prices were not completely free of control. August's price was only 13 US cents below the US retail price. In contrast to most other Gulf States, in the UAE the price increase would largely be met by expatriates, who make up some 90 per cent of the population.

According to a report in the London *Economist*, Arab Youth Survey polls among Middle Eastern and North African youth had named the UAE as the most popular place to work for the previous four years. Perhaps surprisingly, the US consultancy Mercer recently made Dubai the most-searched after international destination for American job-seekers.

UAE nationals, according to the *Economist*, benefited from a generous welfare state that assists them with everything, from education and health care to housing and even the cost of marriage. Generous public-sector wage increases had helped the 80 per cent of nationals employed by the state. It was hoped that the UAE's move on relaxing fuel subsidies would embolden its neighbours. Low oil prices represented a unique opportunity to get rid of fuel subsidies.

Hydrocarbons

According to the US government Energy Information Administration (EIA) the UAE is the sixth-largest petroleum producer in the world. In 2013, hydrocarbon export revenues were US$123 billion, up from approximately US$75 billion in 2010, according to the IMF. In addition to the growing hydrocarbon economy, the UAE has becomie an important financial centre and a major trading centre in the Middle East. Investments in non-energy sectors, such as infrastructure and technology, along with a rapidly recovering real estate sector, continued to provide the UAE with insurance against oil price declines and global economic stagnation. IMF data indicate the UAE's real gross domestic product grew by 5.2 per cent in 2013. However, a sustained decline in oil prices could lead to a reduction in spending in the near future. The likelihood of further major oil discoveries is low, but the UAE uses enhanced oil recovery (EOR) techniques to increase the extraction rates of the country's mature oil fields.

Natural gas use in the UAE has been rising. Although the country is a member of the Gas Exporting Countries Forum (GECF), domestic demand is likely to draw heavily on the UAE's natural gas resources. Currently, the country both imports and exports liquefied natural gas (LNG) and shares international natural gas pipelines with Qatar and Oman. The UAE is also one of the world's leaders in the use of natural gas in enhanced oil recovery (EOR) techniques. With natural gas demand rising, the government plans to expand domestic production using EOR techniques to meet the demand for domestic consumption and exports.

Each of the seven emirates is responsible for regulating the oil industry within its borders, creating a mix of production-sharing arrangements and service contracts. In Abu Dhabi, the Supreme Petroleum Council (SPC) sets Abu Dhabi's petroleum-related objectives and policies. Given Abu Dhabi's status as the central player in the UAE's oil industry, the SPC is the most important entity in the country when it comes to establishing oil policy.

The Abu Dhabi National Oil Company (ADNOC) – which operates 16 subsidiaries throughout the oil, natural gas and petrochemical sector – leads the day-to-day operations and implementation of SPC directives and it is the key shareholder in nearly all upstream activity in Abu Dhabi. ADNOC's subsidiaries engage in oil and natural gas exploration, processing and distribution, among other activities. The Dubai Supreme Council of Energy (DSCE) oversees Dubai's energy-policy development and co-ordination. The DSCE includes representatives from several key entities, including the Emirates National Oil Company (ENOC), the Dubai Petroleum Establishment (DPE) and the Dubai Nuclear Energy Committee (DNEC). The DSCE seeks to ensure that Dubai's economy has adequate and sustainable access to energy resources. The other Emirates have small oil and natural gas sectors, but details on their structures are limited. Natural gas production and regulation are the responsibilities of the individual emirates and are often carried out under the same leadership as their oil sectors.

According to *Oil & Gas Journal* estimates, in January 2015 the UAE held the seventh-largest proved reserves of oil in the world at 97.8 billion barrels, with most of the reserves located in Abu Dhabi (approximately 94 per cent of the UAE's total). The other six Emirates combined accounted for just six per cent of the UAE's crude oil reserves, led by Dubai with approximately 4 billion barrels. The UAE holds approximately 6 per cent of the world's proved oil reserves.

The UAE produced 3.5 million barrels per day (bpd) of petroleum and other liquids in 2014, of which 2.7 million bpd was crude oil and the remainder was non-crude liquids (condensate, natural gas plant liquids and refinery processing gain), ranking them second in petroleum production in Organisation of the Petroleum Exporting Countries (Opec) behind Saudi Arabia. The UAE was the fourth-largest crude oil producer in Opec in 2014, behind Saudi Arabia, Iraq and Iran. The UAE plans to increase crude oil production by 800,000bpd to 3.5 million bpd in 2020. With limited prospects for major discoveries, production increases in the UAE will come almost exclusively by using EOR techniques in Abu Dhabi's existing oil fields. However, EOR projects are typically based on oil prices around US$100 per barrel, which may prove these projects uneconomic at current price levels. The EIA estimates that the UAE exported more than 2.5 million bpd of crude oil in 2014, with most of it going to markets in Asia.

The UAE holds the seventh-largest proved reserves of natural gas in the world, at slightly more than 215 trillion cubic feet (tcf). Despite its large endowment, the UAE became a net importer of natural gas in 2008. This phenomenon is a result of two things: (1) the UAE reinjected approximately 30 per cent of gross natural gas production in 2012 into its oil fields as part of EOR techniques and (2) the country's inefficient and rapidly-expanding electricity grid – already taxed by the swift economic and demographic growth of recent decades – relies on electricity from natural gas-fired facilities.

In 1977, the UAE became the first country in the Middle East to export LNG, sending its first load to the Tokyo Power Company (TEPCO) as part of a long-term supply agreement. The UAE signed a second contract in 1990 to double LNG exports to Japan and in 1994, a third LNG train at Das Island began operations to help fulfil the terms of the agreement.

In 2013, the UAE exported 284bcf of natural gas, mostly in the form of LNG (more than 90 per cent) and the remainder via pipelines. All of the UAE's exported LNG cargoes (260bcf) went to Japan.

With planned expansion at the terminal at Das Island and the country's new focus on developing its vast natural gas reserves, the UAE could experience export growth in the short to medium term.

Risk assessment

Economy	Good
Politics	Poor
Regional stability	Fair

Muslims in United Arab Emirates

% of population	76
Sunni (% of Muslims)	85
Shi'a (% of Muslims)	15

COUNTRY PROFILE

1498 The Portuguese occupied the region.
1633 The Dutch turned the Portuguese out of their trading posts, to be ousted in their turn, by the British.
1820 Britain and a number of rulers in the Gulf signed a treaty to combat piracy. This began a series of agreements which led to the area becoming known as the Trucial Coast, comprising the Trucial states (Abu Dhabi, Dubai, Sharjah, Ras al Khaimah, Umm al Qaiwain, Fujairah and Ajman).
1892 Exclusive Agreements between the Trucial States and Britain were signed, which effectively gave the British control over foreign affairs, while each emirate retained control over internal affairs.
1952 The seven emirates formed a Trucial council to promote increased co-operation.
1958 Oil was discovered off Abu Dhabi.
1962 Oil was exported for the first time from Abu Dhabi.
1966 Oil was discovered off Dubai.
1968 Britain announced its intention to withdraw from the Gulf by 1971. A British plan to form a single state consisting of Bahrain, Qatar and the Trucial States did not take place.
1971 The independence of Bahrain and Qatar was negotiated. Iran occupied the islands of Greater and Lesser Tumb and Abu Musa. Abu Dhabi, Dubai, Sharjah, Fujairah, Umm al Qaiwain and Ajman formed the United Arab Emirates (UAE), a loose federation. Sheikh Zayed bin Sultan al Nahyan (ruler of Abu Dhabi) was elected president of the federation. Ras al Khaimah's ruler did not join at this point since he optimistically hoped that successful oil exploration would enable him to hold out for a better deal.
1972 Ras al Khaimah joined the federation; the Federal National Council (FNC) was created as a 40-member consultative body, appointed by the seven rulers of the UAE.
1980s The UAE supported Iraq during the Iran-Iraq war.
1981 A political and economic union, Co-operation Council for the Arab States of the Gulf (CCASG) (known as the Gulf Co-operation Council (GCC)) was formed by Bahrain, Kuwait, Oman, Qatar, Saudi Arabia and the UAE. The GCC's inaugural meeting was held in Abu Dhabi.
1991 The UAE joined the US-led alliance against Iraq. The Bank of Credit and Commerce International (BCCI), in which the Abu Dhabi royal family owned a 77.4 per cent stake, collapsed.
1992 Iran insisted that visitors to the islands of Abu Musa and Greater and Lesser Tumb must have Iranian visas.
1993 Abu Dhabi sued BCCI's executives for damages.
1994 A court in Abu Dhabi convicted 11 of the 12 former BCCI executives accused of fraud. They were given prison sentences and ordered to pay compensation.
1996 Iran's dispute with the UAE over the islands of Abu Musa and the Tumbs was further fuelled by Iran when it built an airport on Abu Musa and a power station on Greater Tumb. Two BCCI executives were cleared of fraud charges on appeal.
1998 Diplomatic relations with Iraq were restored – the UAE had severed them at the outbreak of the Gulf War.
1999 The GCC reiterated its support for the UAE over the three disputed islands of Greater and Lesser Tumb and Abu Musa.
2001 Six thousand prisoners were pardoned by the President on humanitarian grounds. The government ordered financial institutions to freeze the assets of 62 organisations and individuals suspected of funding terrorist movements.
2002 The UAE and Oman signed a final agreement delineating their entire 1,000km border.
2003 Crown Prince Sheikh Khalid bin Saqr al Qasimi, who had been handling day-to-day affairs of state, was dismissed by his father in favour is his brother (a traditionalist), Sheikh Saud bin Saqr al Qasimi.
2004 President Sheikh Zayed died. Sheikh Khalifa bin Zayed al Nahyan succeeded his father as ruler of Abu Dhabi. The Federal National Council (FNC) elected him president of the UAE.
2005 A new terminal for Abu Dhabi International Airport was opened. Sheikh Zayed announced plans to elect half of the 40 members of the FNC, by a limited number of citizens.
2006 Sheikh Maktoum bin Rashed al Maktoum, ruler of Dubai, vice president and prime minister of the UAE, died. He was succeeded by Sheikh Mohammed bin Rashid al Maktoum. The state-owned company, Dubai Ports, purchased the UK shipping line P&O, which in turn controlled the management-company of six of the largest ports in the US, which sparked a US national controversy concerning border security. Dubai Ports was forced to sell its US assets to American International Group within weeks. The working week was changed to bring it into line with Western nations. The first indirect elections of half the membership of the FNC were held; of the more than 300,000 people eligible to vote, only 6,595 were chosen by the authorities and given the right to vote, and of these 1,163 were women.
2008 A common market was created by Bahrain, Kuwait, Oman, Qatar, Saudi Arabia and UAE, the six wealthiest Gulf States. Citizens of these countries are now allowed to travel between and live in any of the six states, where they may find employment, buy properties and businesses and use the educational and health facilities freely. France was given permission to set up a permanent military base in Abu Dhabi. The Emir of Dubai, Sheikh Mohammed bin Rashid al Maktoum, issued a decree appointing his son Sheikh Hamdan bin Mohammed bin Rashid al Maktoum as crown prince of the Emirate. The entire debt owed to the UAE by Iraq was cancelled. The parliamentary term for the FNC was extended from two years to four.
2009 Sheikh Rashid ibn Ahmad al Mu'alla, the ruler of Umm al Qaiwain, died, his son Sheikh Saud ibn Rashid al Mu'alla succeeded him. The UAE federal government bought US$10 billion of Dubai government bonds to ease its liquidity problems. The money was used to pay off debts, which had accumulated in real estate and tourism projects. The Dubai bonds were for five-year terms at 4 per cent annual interest. The UAE withdrew from the Gulf region monetary union and retained the dirham. The French opened its permanent military base in Abu Dhabi, called the Peace Camp.
2010 The Burj Khalifa, the world's tallest building at 828 metres, with 160 floors, was opened. It was originally called the Burj Dubai but was renamed in honour of the ruler of Abu Dhabi and the UAE after Abu Dhabi had loaned Dubai US$10 billion to help pay off its construction debts. The Hamas leader from Palestine, Mahmoud al Mabhouh was killed in a Dubai hotel, with most observers believing the Israeli secret service, Mossad, responsible. The perpetrators used fake UK, Irish, French and German passports to enter and leave the UAE, prompting international condemnation from the countries involved. The population grew by 65 per cent over 2006–10, according to official statistics, and was 8.26 million, of which only 948,000 were UAE nationals. Sheikh

Saqr bin Muhammad al Qasimi, Emir of Ras al Khaimah, died; he was aged 90 and had been the world's oldest and longest serving monarch. His son Sheikh Saud bin Saqr al Qasian became Emir.
2011 In August the Central Bank announced that the UAE's currency, the dirham, would continue to be pegged to the US dollar 'without change', as bank deposits in June increased by 0.2 per cent from May, and reached Dh1.126 trillion (US$4.134 trillion). UAE became a net lender to the international money markets as its banking system moved from deficit to surplus. A new law was introduced in August that prescribes a jail term of three–five years for anyone spreading rumours using social network media, such as BlackBerry the Internet, Twitter and Facebook. In parliamentary elections held in September, 554 independent candidates took part, including 85 women. Of the 40 members making up the new legislature, 20 were elected and 20 were appointed by the Emirs. Turnout was 27.8 per cent.
2012 The Dubai Electricity and Water Authority (DEWA) began construction of a new water extension pipeline to meet the growing demand for drinking water to the new and heavily populated areas along Emirates Road. On 15 July a new overland oil pipeline became operational from the oil fields in the UAE's western desert to Fujairah, a major oil storage hub in the east. Shipments of up to 1.5 million barrels of crude oil per day can now bypass the Strait of Hormuz (which Iran threatened to blockade in 2012) with direct access to the Indian Ocean. A new visa system (similar to the European Schengen agreement) allowing multiply entry for foreigners to the six Gulf Co-operation Council (GCC) countries was introduced in November.
2013 President Sheikh Khalifa bin Zaid al Nahyan paid a state visit to Britain beginning 30 April. He was greeted by the Queen and taken by horse drawn carriage to Windsor Castle.
2014 The UAE government announced plans to send an unmanned spacecraft to the planet of Mars by 2021 to coincide with the 50th anniversary of the country's founding. This will represent the first space probe by an Arab or Islamic country. As part of the plan, the UAE will set up a new agency to oversee its nascent space industry and to marshal the Mars mission.
2015 The UAE and four other members of the Gulf Cooperation Council (GCC) took part in Saudi-led air strikes on Houthi rebels in Yemen. In September, UAE warplanes launched pre-dawn bombing raids against the rebels in the eastern province of Maarib – where the 60 coalition troops had been killed – and on Yemen's rebel held capital Sana'a, as well as on Houthi strongholds of Saada in the far north and the central city of Ibb.

Political structure

Constitution

A temporary constitution came into effect on 2 December 1971 in an effort to form a political union between the seven Arab states. It was formally accepted in May 1996 after an amendment removed the word "interim", with Abu Dhabi being acknowledged as the permanent capital.
Highest government authority is vested in the Supreme Council of Rulers, which consists of the rulers of the seven emirates — Abu Dhabi, Dubai, Sharjah, Ras al Khaimah, Umm al Qaiwain, Fujairah and Ajman — which comprise the UAE. It is responsible for most internal and external affairs. Abu Dhabi and Dubai hold the power of veto on the Supreme Council. The Supreme Council meets four times a year, and elects the president and vice president (each for terms of five years). The president appoints the prime minister and the Council of Ministers.
The 40 members of the Federal National Council (FNC), drawn proportionately from each emirate, are appointed by the rulers.
The individual emirates have retained a great degree of autonomy and all local powers which are not specifically reserved for the federal government belong to them. Since 1971, the president has been the ruler of Abu Dhabi and the prime minister and vice president the ruler of Dubai, suggesting that elections are a matter of form and that in fact the two emirates with the largest economic and political muscle tend to dominate the federation.

Independence date

2 December 1971

Form of state

Federal monarchy

The executive

The Head of State is president for a term of seven years, chosen by the seven, hereditary rulers of the Emirates who make up the membership of the Federal Supreme Council (FSC).
The president, vice president and FSC comprise the executive branch. The FSC convenes four-times annually to set policies and sanction federal legislation. Within the FSC, Abu Dhabi and Dubai have effective veto power.

National legislature

The UAE parliament, Majlis al Watani al Ittihadi (Federal National Council) (FNC), has 40 members, Abu Dhabi and Dubai appoint eight members each, Sharjah and Ras al Khaimah appoint six members each and Ajman, Fujairah and Umm al Qaiwain appoint four members each. Of these, half the members are chosen by indirect votes through electoral colleges in each Emirate (the size of each college is 100 times the number of FNC members held by each Emirate) and the other half are appointed by each Emir. All FNC members serve for four-year terms.
Under the constitution the FNC is a consultative body with legislative and supervisory roles, with the authority to review and amend proposed federal legislation, although it cannot veto proposed legislation. It may also assess the performance of any minister or ministry.

Legal system

The federal courts, which consist of the Union Supreme Court and primary tribunals, were established by law in 1979. The former primary tribunals in Abu Dhabi, Sharjah, Ajman and Fujairah became federal primary tribunals and the former primary tribunals of other towns became circuits of the federal primary tribunals. The law applied is *Sharia* (Islamic Law).

Last elections

24 September 2011 (parliamentary)
Results: Parliamentary: 20 independent candidates were elected and 20 candidates were appointed. Turnout was 28%, and voters were handpicked by the ruling government.

Next elections

October 2015 (FNC)

Political parties

Party political activity is not officially permitted in the UAE.

Ruling party

There are no official political parties

Population

About 28 per cent of the population is under 14 years of age with 70 per cent between 15–64 years and 2 per cent over 65 years of age.
Abu Dhabi has the highest population (40 per cent of total), Dubai (25 per cent), Sharjah (17 per cent), Ras al Khaimah (7 per cent), Fujairah (4 per cent), Umm al Qaiwain (3 per cent), Ajman (4 per cent).
5.54 million (2012)*
Last census: 5 December 2005: 4,106,427
Population density: 30 inhabitants per square km. Urban population 84 per cent (2010 Unicef).
Annual growth rate: 7.1 per cent, 1990–2010 (Unicef).

Ethnic make-up

UAE nationals make up a fifth of the population. Around 80 per cent of the population are expatriates, with those from the Indian subcontinent accounting for about 40 per cent of the population. The second largest group is Iranians, who make up about 17 per cent. Non-UAE Arabs make up about 13 per cent and Westerners about 5 per cent.

Abu Dhabi is dominated by the Bani Yas tribe of which the al Bu Falasah is the most important section (to which the al Maktoums of Dubai belong).

Religions

The majority are Sunni Muslims; about 20 per cent are Shi'a Muslims. Many expatriates from the Indian subcontinent are Christian. The constitution guarantees full religious rights to all. The Apostolic Vicariate of Arabia is in Abu Dhabi.

Education

Primary education is compulsory and is followed by three years' preparatory education which qualifies students for general or technical secondary education. The language of instruction is English.
General secondary education lasts for three years. It consists of a common first year followed by specialisation in science or the humanities. At aged eighteen, students take an examination for progression to higher education.
Technical secondary education lasts for six years following primary school and comprises three main streams: technical, agricultural and commercial in both preparatory and secondary cycles. At aged eighteen, a Technical Secondary Diploma is awarded.
Secondary education is also offered in religious institutions.
Higher education is offered in public and private universities and Higher Colleges of Technology. These include the United Arab Emirates (UAE) University, and the Dubai University College, (a private college).
Emirate and federal politics can at times threaten academic standards. Education is allocated some 20 per cent of the federal budget.
Literacy rate: 77 per cent adult rate; 91 per cent youth rate (15–24) (Unesco 2005).
Compulsory years: 6 to 12.
Enrolment rate: 89 per cent gross primary enrolment; 80 per cent gross secondary enrolment, of relevant age groups (including repeaters) (World Bank).
Pupils per teacher: 16 in primary schools.

Health

In October 2012, the first phase of the private health insurance scheme for government employees of Sharjah was launched.
Life expectancy: 77 years, 2004 (WHO 2006)
Fertility rate/Maternal mortality rate: 1.7 births per woman, 2010 (Unicef); maternal mortality 3 per 100,000 live births (World Bank).
Child (under 5 years) mortality rate (per 1,000): 8 per 1,000 live births (WHO 2012); 7 per cent of children aged under five are malnourished (World Bank).
Head of population per physician: 2.02 physicians per 1,000 people, 2001 (WHO 2006)

Welfare

In 2008 a mandatory health insurance policy called *Thiqa* (trust) was established, which entitles all UAE nationals to free extensive primary, secondary and tertiary healthcare. Expatriate workers are insured under the National Health Insurance Company (Daman) scheme, established in 2006. In 2012 Daman was the largest health insurance company in the Gulf region, with 2.1 million customers.

Main cities

Abu Dhabi (federal capital estimated population 613,368 in 2012), Dubai (commercial capital, 1.8 million), Sharjah (941,424), al Ayn (502,035), Ajman (255,869), Ras al Khaimah (124,005), al Fujayrah (104,375), Umm al Qaiwain (51,868).

Languages spoken

Languages of the Indian sub-continent are widely spoken among the expatriate community. Persian (Farsi), Urdu and English are also spoken.
Official language/s
Arabic

Media

Dubai is the hub of the UAE's media industry and the dedicated Dubai Media City, which assures clients freedom of speech, is growing as an important regional centre attracting distinguished international media outlets.
Press
While the press is largely independent, in November 2007, Reporters Without Frontiers reported that press freedom in the UAE was bound by widespread self-censorship which eschewed any criticism of the government to avoid prosecution.
Dailies: Most newspapers are published in either Abu Dhabi or Dubai. Newspapers in Arabic that comment on news and politics include *Al-Bayan* (www.albayan.ae), *Akhbar Al Arab* (www.akhbaralarab.co.ae), also has economic and sports editions, *Emarat al Youm* (www.emaratalyoum.com), *Al Khaleej* (www.alkhaleej.co.ae). In English newspaper include *Emirates Today* (www.emiratestodayonline.com), *Gulf News* (www.gulf-news.com), *Khaleej Times* (www.khaleejtimes.com) and *7 Days* (www.7days.ae).
Weeklies: In Arabic, *Al Azmina Al Arabia* (www.alazmina.info), bi-weekly for politics, culture and economics, *Al-Sada* (www.e-sada.com) is a magazine for women. In English, *The Dubai Life* (www.thedubailife.com) and *Time Out Dubai* (ww.timeoutdubai.com/dubai), covers entertainment and consumer items.
Business: In English monthly publications include the monthly *Capital* (www.capital-me.com), and *UAE Banking & Business Review* (www.sterlingp.ae) and *Gulf Business* (www.gulfbusiness.com) monthly magazine. The CPI Financial services published an online newsletter concerning banking and the financial services (www.cpifinancial.net).
Periodicals: There are over 30 magazines in Arabic and English. *Al Shindagah* (www.alshindagah.com), published six times a year and *Review* (www.sterlingp.ae) covers current affairs, *Al Shumookh* (www.alshumookh.net) monthly magazine lists cultural events.
Broadcasting
The state-owned Emirates Media Incorporated (EMI) operates three satellite TV channels and seven radio stations, four publications and five interactive internet websites.
The switchover to digital signals will be completed by 2013, according to the Director General of the Telecoms Regulatory Authority (TRA), on 26 April 2011.
Radio: Each Emirate has its own radio station, although most are located in either Abu Dhabi or Dubai. There are general interest music and news radio stations, broadcasting throughout the Emirates, while some are dedicated to religious texts or programmes for immigrant populations. Apart from EMI (www.emi.co.ae), another national network is the popular commercial Arabian Radio Network (ARN) (www.arnonline.com), including in English, Dubai 92.
A shortwave world service broadcasts to North America, Asia and Europe.
Television: Of the six TV networks based in UAE, three are pan-Arabic. The state-owned, Dubai Media Incorporated (DMI) produces a number of local TV programmes and operates four domestic channels (http://www.dubaitv.gov.ae), which provides programmes of information, entertainment, religion, culture, news and politics. In 2007 tests were undertaken by DMI to evaluate the viability of mobile digital video broadcasting. MBC (http://www.mbc.net) operates a four channels include the Al Arabiya News Channel (www.alarabiya.net). The private and independent satellite broadcaster Showtime Arabia (www.showtimearabia.com), based in Dubai, which operates over 30 channels showing imported programmes, by subscription. Residents also have a choice of hundreds of regional channels broadcasting via foreign satellite or cable TV companies. Many commercial channels

broadcast foreign programmes in English with Arabic subtitles.
Residents have a choice of hundreds of regional channels broadcasting via satellite or cable. Many commercial channels broadcast foreign programmes in English with Arabic subtitles.
There are two local TV stations operating from Ajman (www.ajmantv.com) and Sharjah (www.sharjahtv.ae).
National news agency: Emirates News Agency
Other news agencies: DPM News Agency: www.dpmnewsagency.com

Economy
The UAE is a free-market economy, initially dominated by hydrocarbons. It has a high per capita income and a sizable annual trade surplus, successful efforts at economic diversification has reduced the portion of GDP based on oil and gas output to 25 per cent. Since its transformation to a developed state because of oil, the government has increased spending on job creation, infrastructure expansion and is opening up utilities to greater private sector involvement. The country's free trade zones – offering 100 per cent foreign ownership and zero taxes – are helping to attract foreign investors.
Dependence on oil, a large expatriate workforce, and growing inflation pressures are significant long-term challenges. GDP per capita was US$64,500 in 2014, the thirteenth highest in the world.
Proven oil reserves were 97.8 billion barrels in 2014, with annual production of 3.5 million barrels per day. Proven natural gas reserves were 6 trillion cubic metres in 2014, with annual production of 56.0 billion cubic metres.
The richest Emirates, Abu Dhabi, Dubai and Sharjah, account for approximately 50 per cent, 30 per cent and 8 per cent respectively of overall GDP. They transfer revenue to other emirates to ensure similar standards in basic public goods and services (health, education and transport) are maintained.
GDP growth was 5.3 per cent in 2008, falling to -3.3 per cent in 2009 as the global economic crisis cut demand for oil. In 2009, the credit rating agency Standard and Poor's cut its ratings for six Dubai government-backed entities to A- and Emaar Properties from A- to BBB+.
The Dubai building boom was badly hit by the global recession. Dubai World, including a series of artificial islands built in Dubai's shallow waters, was an ambitious multi-million dollar project that had to be bailed out of near collapse in November 2009 by the Dubai government. Although losses were incurred by Dubai, ultimately international financial pressure on the UAE economy was eased when Abu Dhabi agreed to buy fiduciary bonds in 2010 and allow Dubai to avoid defaulting on an estimated US$87 billion in debt. As the economy declined so imports fell and inflation dropped from 12.3 per cent in 2008 to 1.0 per cent in 2009. The crisis resulted in pressures on the banking sector and a contraction in the availability of credit. In 2010, GDP growth was 0.9 per cent as global trade picked up and increased continually to 5.2 per cent in 2013. GDP growth has shrunk to a modest 3.6 per cent in 2014.
The UAE has developed a range of manufacturing industries, financial services and a tourist industry, and is emerging, because of its favourable tax regime, as an important international diamond centre.
Overseas companies and foreign direct investment have been attracted to the UAE by the creation of a dozen free trade zones, which offer special advantages, while enabling the UAE to expand its non-oil exports. The UAE has made good progress in privatising small agricultural enterprises and has broadened the programme to include larger-scale industrial projects and public utilities. The tourist industry plays a very big part in contributing to the GDP — the UAE has some of the most luxurious hotels in the world. Other important industries include aluminium, fishing, cement, fertilizers, commercial ship repair, construction materials, handicrafts and textiles.
In July 2011, the IMF estimated that the gross national debt of UAE was US$236.1 billion (6.3 per cent of GDP), of which Abu Dhabi owed US$104 billion and Dubai US$112 billion. Around US$33 billion matured in 2011, with US$25.8 billion maturing in 2012 and in 2013 the debt had reduced to US$168.8 billion. In 2014 external debt increased to US$173.3 billion in the UAE.

External trade
The UAE is part of the Greater Arab Free Trade Area (Gafta) along with 16 other members, including Saudi Arabia, which creates an Arab economic bloc. Gafta includes a customs union in which tariffs are reduced by a percentage each year, until none remain. The UAE also belongs to the Gulf Co-operation Council, which negotiates bilateral free trade agreements on behalf of members.
The government has encouraged new manufacturing enterprises in metal processing, furniture and jewellery making and food processing. However, the service sector achieves more foreign earnings than any other except oil and natural gas, through tourism, financial services and banking and transport. The Dubai Ports Authority is one of the largest container handling bodies in the world.
Imports
Main imports are machinery and transport equipment, chemicals and food.
Main sources: China (15.7 per cent of total in 2014), India (13.4 per cent), US (8.9 per cent) and Germany (5.3 per cent).
Exports
Main exports are crude oil, natural gas, pearls and precious stones, electronic equipment and vehicles, re-exports, dried fish and dates.
Main destinations: Japan (14.8 per cent of total in 2014), Iran (11.4 per cent), India (9.6 per cent), South Korea (5.7 per cent), China (5.5 per cent) and Singapore (5.4 per cent).
Re-exports
Rice, dried fish and dates and aluminium.

Agriculture
Farming
Agriculture contributes around 0.6 per cent to GDP and employs 7 per cent of the workforce. A harsh climate and sandy soil make self-sufficiency in food production an unlikely prospect. The northern Emirates of Ras al Khaimah, Fujairah (on the western Gulf of Onan coast) and Ajman supply 25 per cent of local demand. Ajman is the most productive and has been a focal region for agricultural development. Ras al Khaimah and Fujairah produce a more diverse selection of agricultural produce as a result of the higher rainfall they receive. Very few nationals still work on farms, where labour is mostly from Bangladesh and Baluchistan in south-west Pakistan.
Government farm subsidies are generous. Many farms are supported through funding available on easy credit terms, seed allocations and technical advice on fertilisation, irrigation, mechanisation and marketing of crops. Earth-moving and wells are free, and seeds, fertilisers and insecticides are half the market price. Abu Dhabi gives land to its citizens without charge, as well as underwriting other Emirates' grants of land to other UAE citizens via its financing of the federal budget. The main state-funded agricultural research centres and extension services are at al Dhafra, Liwa and Madina Zayed. The Arid Lands Research Centre operates experimental vegetable greenhouses on Saadiyat Island near Abu Dhabi town. The UAE is self-sufficient in various winter vegetables and excess crops of vegetables are sometimes dumped in the desert, due to a lack of processing facilities. The government already buys crops at 'favourable' prices, before selling them at discounted rates in the market.
Fishing
Catches cover over 80 per cent of domestic consumption. The UAE ranks fourth in

the Arab world in the volume of its annual catch. Around 20 fishing ports and 25 repair workshops have been established along the coastline in Dubai, Sharjah and Ras al Khaimah. Over 15,000 tonnes of fish are imported to supplement domestic sources.

High demand for fish and crews whose salaries depend on how much they catch have led to over fishing. In 2014 UAE fish stocks were down by over two thirds in a decade. The UAE consumes fish at a rate of 33 kg per capita annually, the highest of all the Gulf States.

Forestry

The UAE has around 3.8 per cent forest cover, almost all of which is plantation. The government has initiated a long-term programme of afforestation. Abu Dhabi's western region now has about 5,000 hectares of mature tree plantations, including 120 million tamarind, tamarisk, acacia, neem and cork trees, as well as some 30 million date palms.

Industry and manufacturing

The industrial sector accounted for 59 per cent of GDP in 2014 and employed 15 per cent of the workforce. Non-oil industry, particularly manufacturing and re-exports, is centred in free trade zones.

The government is placing increased emphasis on the expansion of non-oil manufacturing. This has centred on producing cement, building materials, aluminium, fertilisers, foodstuffs, garments, furniture, plastics, fiberglass and processed metals.

Most non-oil export production is centred on Dubai. The Dubai government is intensifying its efforts to promote foreign investment and attract regional and global capital. In April 2002, the Dubai Authority for Investment and Development (DAID) was set up to grant concessions, franchises and incentives and to issue licences to large investors. The DAID is authorised to set up, own and develop investment companies on its own or with other organisations.

The UAE has developed a range of manufacturing industries, financial services and a tourist industry, and is emerging, because of its favourable tax regime, as an important international diamond centre.

Overseas companies and foreign direct investment have been attracted to the UAE by the creation of a dozen free trade zones, which offer special advantages, while enabling the UAE to expand its non-oil exports. The UAE has made good progress in privatising small agricultural enterprises and has broadened the programme to include larger-scale industrial projects and public utilities. The tourist industry plays a very big part in contributing to the GDP — the UAE has some of the most luxurious hotels in the world. Other important industries include aluminium, fishing, cement, fertilizers, commercial ship repair, construction materials, handicrafts and textiles.

Tourism

The two largest Emirates, Dubai and Abu Dhabi, have their own strategies for tourism. The UAE has an overarching development strategy, which has identified tourism as a key element and the potential to become an important component of the economy. In 2014, Abu Dhabi had 150 hotels and hotel apartments and the majority of guests were either from Europe or from within the UAE. Abu Dhabi has actively promoted itself as a destination for meeting, incentives, conferences and events (MICE), becoming a top destination for such business occasions.

Dubai is the largest tourist market, attracting both business travellers and an increasing number of leisure tourists. Dubai adopted a competitive strategy that identified its location as its prime attribute, lying as it does between Europe and the Far East – one non-stop flight from almost all major cities in the world.

In 2014 the total contribution of travel and tourism to GDP was US$35.0 billion (8.4 per cent of GDP) and indirectly employed 9.2 per cent of the workforce (518,500 jobs). In 2015 the contribution to GDP is forecast to increase by 5.1 per cent and percentage of total employment in the tourism sector is set to increase to 9.4 per cent.

Visitor numbers are forecast to reach 14.8 million in 2015, a 1.4 per cent increase on 2014. By 2025, international tourist arrivals are forecast to total 37 million.

Tourism

The two largest Emirates, Dubai and Abu Dhabi, have their own strategies for tourism. The UAE has an overarching development strategy, which has identified tourism as a key element and the potential to become an important component of the economy. Dubai is the largest tourist market, attracting both business travellers and an increasing number of leisure tourists.

In 2013 the total contribution of travel and tourism to GDP was US$32.0 billion (8.4 per cent of GDP) and indirectly employed 9.1 per cent of the workforce (496,500 jobs). In 2014 the contribution to GDP is forecast to rise by 4.5 per cent. Visitor numbers in 2013 reached 11 million, a 10 per cent increase from the 10 million in 2012.

Dubai adopted a competitive strategy that identified its location as its prime attribute, lying as it does between Europe and the Far East – one non-stop flight from almost all major cities in the world.

In 2013, Abu Dhabi had 150 hotels and hotel apartments and there were 2.8 million visitors (26 per cent increase on 2012), the majority of which were either from Europe or from within the UAE. Abu Dhabi has actively promoted itself as a destination for meeting, incentives, conferences and events (MICE), becoming a top destination for such business occasions.

Mining

The development of non-hydrocarbon minerals plays a role in the government's policy of diversification away from dependence on the oil sector. Limestone, gypsum and dolerite are exploited. Celestite is known to exist but has not yet been extracted.

Copper is known to exist in Fujairah and Ras al Khaimah. There is also thought to be talc in Fujairah, chromium in Sharjah, Ajman, Fujairah and Ras al Khaimah, and manganese throughout the northern Emirates. Mineral studies are being undertaken in the Madah region of Fujairah, in Al-Siji in Sharjah and in the Masfouyt and Manama areas of Ajman. Ras al Khaimah already has two quarries, four cement companies and further downstream factories, with annual cement production of 2.3 million tonnes.

Hydrocarbons

The UAE is one of the world's largest producers of crude oil and natural gas, which together account for around 25 per cent of GDP. Under the UAE's constitution, each emirate is responsible for its own production and resource development. Abu Dhabi holds approximately 94 per cent of total reserves.

On 15 July 2012, a new overland oil pipeline became operational from the oil fields in the UAE's western desert to Fujairah, a major oil storage hub in the east. Shipments of up to 1.5 million barrels of crude oil per day can now bypass the Strait of Hormuz (which Iran threatened to blockade in 2012) with direct access to the Indian Ocean. The first tanker of oil was shipped to Pakistan for refining. Proven oil reserves were 97.8 billion barrels in 2014, with annual production of 3.5 million barrels per day. Refinery capacity was 1 million bpd in 2014, with production located at Ruwais, Umm al Nar and Jebel Ali.

Abu Dhabi holds 92.5 per cent of the total natural gas reserves, with 5.0 per cent in Sharjah. Domestic consumption has grown, mainly in the production of electricity, particularly during summer. Dubai's consumption has been growing at almost 10 per cent annually, as its industrial sector has expanded. Proven natural gas reserves were 6 trillion cubic metres in 2014, with annual production of 56.0

billion cubic metres. Power consumption is projected to rise to 40GW by 2025 from the current 22GW.

Energy

Total installed generating capacity was 23.3GW in 2014, producing about 84 billion kilowatt hours (kWh). Consumption is among the largest in the region due to expansion of tourism, financial projects and an increased population.

A Gulf Co-operation Council (GCC) project to link the six member states (Saudi Arabia, Qatar, Bahrain, Kuwait, Oman and the United Arab Emirates) to an integrated power-grid began in 2005. The first phase of the GCC power grid was completed in 2009 at a cost of US$1,095 million, linking Saudi Arabia, Bahrain, Kuwait and Qatar through 800km of transmission lines. Kuwait and Saudi Arabia will each receive an extra 1,200MW of power capacity and later, the UAE will receive 900MW, Qatar 750MW, Bahrain 600MW and Oman 400MW. In the first phase, a 400kV overhead line links Kuwait's Al Zour power station with Doha, and a 400kV submarine line to Saudi Arabia with Bahrain. The second phase will link the UAE with Oman. The resulting two mega-grids will be joined in the final phase.

The government is seeking to open up the sector with limited privatisation in order to inject new capital and increase capacity to meet soaring demand. Abu Dhabi is leading the way, with the creation of new independent power and water projects and joint ventures with minority interests held by foreign firms. The Abu Dhabi government has rejected full privatisation of the water and power sector.

The Abu Dhabi Water and Electricity Authority (Adwea) commissioned the building of a 1,500MW power station in October 2011. Other new plants already under construction will supply 2,500MW to the system, (1,600MW by the Shuweihat 3 power plant which became operational in 2013), for ultimate use among GCC member states.

In 2015, the UAE is investing US$35 billion to diversify its energy mix and reduce its dependence on natural gas imports. Over 99 per cent of power generation in the UAE is fuelled by natural gas. The aim was to decrease dependence on natural gas from 100 per cent to 70 per cent by 2021. Those investments are going to be in nuclear and renewable energy projects. The UAE is one of the world's top 20 gas producers, but the country became a net importer of natural gas in 2008. Its natural gas consumption reached a record high of more than 2.4 trillion cubic feet in 2013. The US$20 billion Barahkah project to start building nuclear power plants is expected to provide 24 per cent of the UAE's energy by 2020, when all four reactors come on stream.

Financial markets

Stock exchange

Abu Dhabi Securities Exchange (ADX)

Commodity exchange

Dubai Mercantile Exchange (DME)

Banking and insurance

Financial services constitute a key sector throughout the Emirates, with Dubai at the leading edge and hoping to overtake Bahrain as the Gulf's leading financial centre. The UAE's banking sector has attracted more foreign interest than other Gulf states due to its liberal banking regime and low level of taxation.

Development of the sector is focussed on the Dubai International Financial Sector (DIFC), which was launched in 2001 as a link between the financial markets of Africa, Asia, the Middle East and the West. The DIFC has concentrated on the development of asset management, administration, reinsurance and Islamic finance in an attempt to develop a niche market.

Continuing large-scale infrastructure projects, growing prospects in the tourism industry and the creation of an automated stock exchange all represent considerable opportunities for banks. WTO membership, effective from 2003, obliges the UAE authorities to admit new foreign banks and help to increase competition in the sector. On the downside, the UAE's banking sector lacks transparency, although the OECD's Financial Action Task Force (FATF) declared the UAE's performance in 2002 as 'satisfactory'.

The merger of Emirates Bank International (EBI) and the National Bank of Dubai (NBK) was announced in 2007. The new bank, Emirates NDB, will dominate banking in the UAE and be the largest bank by assets in the Gulf region.

By order of the Emir of Dubai, the failing Dubai Bank was taken over by the Emirate's largest lending institute, NBD on 13 October 2011. In May 2011, the government had to save Dubai Bank as loan losses mounted, brought about by the Dubai property bubble; the bank had remained weak and lacked a diverse business foundation.

Central bank

Central Bank of the United Arab Emirates

Time

GMT plus four hours

Geography

The UAE is bordered by Oman to the east, Saudi Arabia to the west and south, Qatar to the north, and by a coastline of approximately 650km on the southern shore of the Gulf. Much of the land is sand desert or salt flats. Six of the Emirates lie on the Arabian Gulf coast. Fujairah, the seventh, lies on the Gulf of Oman. The region is one of shallow seas and offshore islands and coral reefs. The UAE's two coasts are divided by the Hajjar Mountains stretching through the Musandam Peninsula to the Straits of Hormuz.

Hemisphere

Northern

Climate

Summer temperatures are hot, reaching 49 degrees Celsius (C) in the shade, while January, the coldest winter month, sees temperatures ranging from three to 28 degrees C. Humidity, particularly on the coast, can be extreme. Average annual rainfall is very low, ranging between 100mm and 200mm.

Dress codes

A lightweight suit or lightweight jacket and trousers are advised. A tie is *de rigueur* at business meetings but a jacket need not be worn. Long-sleeved shirts should be worn at business and official meetings. In public places, women should dress discretely and men should wear shirts and long trousers. Bikinis are allowed on certain beaches.

Entry requirements

Passports

Required by all.

Visa

Required by all, except citizens of EU, North America, Australasia, Japan and a few other Asian countries, for visits up to one month. For a full list of exceptions visit www.uae-embassy.org and follow the link from *Travel to UAE* to *consular services* where a visa application form can also be found. All visits for those requiring a visa must be arranged through a sponsor such as tour operator or UAE resident or company. The sponsor organises a visa and will provide a letter of invitation, giving details of the sponsor's residency permit, and a copy of their passport. Visas for business visits are arranged by invitation only. Company credentials must be provided including a trading licence to a sponsor who arranges the visa and will meet the traveller at the airport.

A new visa system (similar to the European Schengen agreement) allowing multiply entry for foreigners to the six Gulf Co-operation Council (GCC) countries was introduced in November.

Prohibited entry

Israeli nationals and holders of passports with Israeli visas stamped in them.

Currency advice/regulations

The import and export of local and foreign currency is limited to Dh40,000 (or equivalent). Amounts in excess of this must be declared on entry.

Travellers cheques are widely accepted.

Customs

Personal effects are duty-free. Small quantities of alcohol are allowed entry (non-Muslims only).

Prohibited imports

Firearms and ammunition require a special permit. Illegal drugs (drug trafficking is a capital offence), poppy seeds in all forms, religious propaganda, commercial loose pearls, raw seafood and fruit and vegetables from cholera infected areas are prohibited.

Health (for visitors)

Mandatory precautions

None.

Advisable precautions

Inoculations and boosters should be current for hepatitis A, polio, tetanus and typhoid. There may be a need for vaccinations for tuberculosis, hepatitis B and diphtheria. Anti-malaria precautions are recommended if travelling to the border with Oman, in the east.

NB Some drugs normally taken under a doctor's supervision are classified as narcotics in the UAE. A doctor's prescription should be carried along with any medication that is brought into the country. If suspected of being under the influence of drugs or alcohol, individuals may be required to submit to blood and/or urine tests and may be subject to prosecution.

Hotels

Excellent standards throughout the UAE, and rooms are generally in adequate supply although advance booking is always advisable.

A 20 per cent tax is included in all bills.

Credit cards

Major credit and charge cards are widely accepted.

Public holidays (national)

The working week was altered in 2006, to bring it into line with Western nations (Saturday and Sunday weekend), although a two-day weekend was not made compulsory for the private sector.

Fixed dates

1 Jan (New Year's Day), 6 Aug (Sheikh Zayed's Accession), 2 Dec (National Day).

Variable dates

Eid al Adha (three days), Islamic New Year, Birth of the Prophet, Ascension of the Prophet, Eid al Fitr (two days).

Islamic year 1437 (15 Oct 2015–2 Oct 2016):: The Islamic year has 354 or 355 days, with the result that Muslim feasts advance by 10–12 days against the Gregorian calendar each year. Dates of the Muslim feasts vary according to sightings of the new moon, so cannot be forecast exactly.

Working hours

Working hours may vary between Emirates and change from summer to winter. The working week was altered in 2006, to bring it into line with Western nations (Saturday and Sunday weekend), although a two-day weekend was not made compulsory for the private sector. During Ramadan, the Muslim holy month of fasting, working hours are reduced with most people working during daylight hours 0900–1300.

Banking

Mon–Thu: 0800–1300, 1500/1600–1800/1900; Fri: 0800–1300.

Business

Mon–Thu: 0800–1300, 1500/1600–1800/1900; Fri: 0830–1300. Some businesses operate on Saturday.

Government

Mon–Fri: 0700–1430.

Shops

Sat–Thu: 0930–1300, 1630–2130; Fri: 1400/1500–2100. Shopping centres general do not close during the day.

Telecommunications

Mobile/cell phones

There is a 900 GSM service operating throughout the territory – there are plans for 3G and 900/1800 services in the future.

The threat to ban some Blackberry functions (such as sending emails and accessing the internet) from October 2010 was lifted after the government held talks with the maker, RIM.

Electricity supply

240/415V AC (Abu Dhabi) and 220/380V AC (Northern Emirates), with three-pin round or flat type plug fittings.

Weights and measures

Metric system (imperial system and local units also used).

Social customs/useful tips

Pork should not be eaten in the presence of Muslims. It is discourteous to eat, drink or smoke in front of Muslims in daylight hours during Ramadan (when it is illegal to do so in public).

Avoid using the term 'Mohammedan'.

Avoid asking personal questions, especially about wives.

Always shake hands on meeting and leaving. You may find the handshake lasts longer than in the West, but this is a sign of friendship. If you have made a good impression, the handshake on departure will be longer than that on arrival.

If coffee is served it is courteous to accept it. Cups will generally be refilled automatically unless the cup is shaken from side to side as it is returned to the server. To take only one cup of coffee is an insult, and to take three or more is considered greedy in some quarters – if in doubt follow the example of your host.

Most restaurants and hotels have bars and licensed restaurants, although a licence, which lays down a monthly quota, is required for purchase for consumption at home. Licences are not issued to Muslims.

Some Blackberry functions (such as sending emails and accessing the internet) have been banned since October 2010.

Security

Visitors should keep in touch with developments in the Middle East as any increase in regional tension might affect travel advice.

The level of street crime has been traditionally far lower than in the West because of the severity of the penalties imposed. The influx of expatriate workers since the early 1970s has encouraged incidents of theft. Murder and violent crimes such as mugging and rape remain rare. Generally speaking the UAE has a very low incidence of crime.

Getting there

Air

Air Arabia, the Middle East's first low-fare airline, is headquartered in Sharjah and flies within the region and to the Indian subcontinent.

National airline: Etihad Airways and the airline Emirates are owned by the governments of Abu Dhabi and Dubai respectively.

International airport/s: Abu Dhabi International Airport (AUH); 35km from city. Expansion with a new terminal has increased facilities with duty-free shop, bar, bank, hotel reservations, post office, shops, car hire.

Dubai International (DXB), 4km from city, with duty-free shop, bar, bank, hotel reservations, post office, shops, car hire.

Sharjah International (SHJ), 10km from city, with duty-free shop, bar, restaurant, bank (restricted hours), hotel reservations.

Ras al Khaimah International (RKT).

The Al Maktoum International Airport (DWC) (Dubai), was opened in June 2010. When fully operational (expected 2011) the airport will be the largest in the world with five runways, through-flow of five million passengers annually and 250,000 tonnes capacity for cargo.

Other airport/s: Al Ain is Abu Dhabi's second airport 23km from the oasis of Al Ain. Fujairah has an airport.

Airport tax: None

Surface

Road: Road links are through Oman and Saudi Arabia. Buses run between Dubai and Muscat.

Water: Passenger services run between Sharjah and Bandar-é Abbas in Iran.

Getting about

National transport

Air: There are several daily services between Dubai and Abu Dhabi. There are numerous airstrips thoughout the region for charter hire flights.

Road: Good, surfaced roads along the coast links of all the Emirates.

City transport

Taxis: Taxis are plentiful and English is widely understood if not spoken.

Metered taxis are available in Abu Dhabi and the rounding-up of the charge is typical for a tip. It is advisable to negotiate fares in advance in other Emirates as taxis are not usually metered.

City traffic in Dubai has become very congested and it is advisable to allow plenty of time to reach a destination. Taxis on stands outside hotels charge more than those flagged in the street. Fixed fares are available for pre-paid journeys from Dubai airport to the city.

Some hotels offer a courtesy pick-up service; others offer the service but charge. A limousine can be booked through the hotel.

Buses, trams & metro: Dubai's new metro system began operations in 2009 along the 52.9km, 29 station, Red Line, which runs both over and under the city, from the airport terminal to the Jebel Ali seaport terminal. Ticket prices are divided into three zones, with payment via different modes including a pre-paid, smart card. Other lines are under construction. The second metro rail network in Dubai became operational on 9 September 2011. The Green Line runs for around 23km from Etisalat to Dubai Health Care City; however, not all stations were completed and opened.

Car hire

Personal and chauffeur-driven car hire is available. International licences are acceptable only for short-term visitors and requirements should be checked on arrival. Driving is on the right, with speed limits of 60kph in towns and 80–100kph elsewhere.

BUSINESS DIRECTORY

The addresses listed below are a selection only. While World of Information makes every endeavour to check these addresses, we cannot guarantee that changes have not been made, especially to telephone numbers and area codes. We would welcome any corrections.

Telephone area codes

The international direct dialling (IDD) code for The United Arab Emirates is +971 followed by the area code:

Abu Dhabi	2	Fujairah	9
Ajman	6	Ras Al-Khaimah	7
Al-Ain	3	Sharjah	6
Dubai	4	Umm Al-Quwain	6

Useful telephone numbers

Directory enquiries: 180

Operator: 100

Call enquiries: 160

Call bookings: 150

Police (Abu Dhabi): 461-461

Chambers of Commerce

Abu Dhabi Chamber of Commerce and Industry, PO Box 662, Abu Dhabi (tel: 621-4000; fax: 621-5867; e-mail: service@adcci-gov.ae).

American Business Council (Dubai and Northern Emirates), PO Box 9281, Dubai (tel: 331-4735; fax: 331-4227; e-mail: amchamdx@emirates.net.ae).

American Business Group (Abu Dhabi), PO Box 43710, Abu Dhabi (tel: 626-2086; fax: 626-2087; e-mail: abgroup@emirates.net.ae).

Ajman Chamber of Commerce and Industry, PO Box 662, Ajman (tel: 742-2177; fax: 742-7591; e-mail: ajmchmbr@emirates.net.ae).

British Business Group (Abu Dhabi), PO Box 43635, Abu Dhabi (tel: 457-234; fax: 450-605; e-mail: bbgauh@emirates.net.ae).

British Business Group (Dubai and Northern Emirates), PO Box 9333, Dubai (tel: 397-0303; fax: 397-0939; e-mail: britbiz@emirates.net.ae).

Dubai Chamber of Commerce and Industry, PO Box 1457, Dubai (tel: 228-1181; fax: 221-1646; e-mail: dcciinfo@dcci.org).

Federation of UAE Chambers of Commerce and Industry, PO Box 3014, Abu Dhabi (tel: 621-4144; fax: 633-9210; e-mail: fcciauh@emirates.net.ae).

Federation of UAE Chambers of Commerce and Industry, PO Box 8886, Dubai (tel: 221-2977; fax: 223-5498; e-mail: fccidxb@emirates.net.ae).

French Business Group (Abu Dhabi), PO Box 73390, Abu Dhabi (tel: 674-1137; fax: 678-6650; e-mail: fbgad@emirates.net.ae).

Fujairah Chamber of Commerce and Industry, PO Box 738, Fujairah (tel: 222-2400; fax: 222-1464; e-mail: fujccia@emirates.net.ae).

Ras Al-Khaimah Chamber of Commerce and Industry, PO Box 87, Ras Al-Khaimah (tel: 233-3511; fax: 233-0233; e-mail: rkchmbr@emirates.net.ae).

Sharjah Chamber of Commerce and Industry, PO Box 580, Sharjah (tel: 568-8888; fax: 568-1119; e-mail:scci@sharjah.gov.ae).

Umm Al-Quwain Chamber of Commerce and Industry, PO Box 436, Umm Al-Quwain (tel: 765-1111; fax: 765-7056; e-mail: uaqcci@emirates.net.ae).

Banking

Abu Dhabi Commercial Bank, Al-Salam Street, PO Box 939, Abu Dhabi.

Arab Bank for Investment & Foreign Trade, PO Box 46733, Abu Dhabi.

Commercial Bank of Dubai Ltd, PO Box 2668, Dubai.

Emirates NDB (result of merger between Emirates Bank International and National Bank of Dubai in 2007), PO Box 2923, Dubai..

HSBC, UAE Omeir bin Yussuf Bld, Airport Road; PO Box 242 Abu Dhabi (tel: 633-2200; fax: 633-1564; internet: www.uae.hsbc.com).

Mashreq Bank, P.O. Box 1250, Omar Ibn Al Khatab Rd, Next to Al Ghurair Retail City, Deira, Dubai.

National Bank of Abu Dhabi, PO Box 4, Abu Dhabi.

National Bank of Fujairah, PO Box 786, Abu Dhabi..

National Bank of Sharjah, PO Box 4, Sharjah.

National Bank of Umm Al-Qawain, PO Box 17888, Al-Ain.

RakBank (National Bank of Ras Al-Khaimah), PO Box 5300, Oman Street, Al-Nakheel, Ras Al-Khaimah (tel: 228-1127; fax: 228-3238; email: nbrakho@emirates.net.ae).

Union National Bank, PO Box 865, Abu Dhabi.

Central bank

Central Bank of the United Arab Emirates, Al Bainunah Street; PO Box 854, Abu Dhabi (tel: 665-2220; fax: 666-7494; internet: www.centralbank.ae).

Stock exchange

Abu Dhabi Securities Exchange (ADX, www.adx.ae

Dubai Financial Market, www.dfm.ae

Nasdaq Dubai, www.nasdaqdubai.com

Commodity exchange

Dubai Mercantile Exchange (DME), www.dubaimerc.com

Dubai Gold and Commodities Exchange (DGCX), www.dgcx.ae

Travel information

Abu Dhabi International Airport, PO Box 28, Abu Dhabi (tel: 575-7500; fax: 575-7285; internet: www.dcaauh.gov.ae).

Abu Dhabi National Hotels Company, PO Box 6806, Abu Dhabi.

Air Arabia, Um Tarafa Area, Al Arouba Street, Rolla, Sharjai (call centre tel: 558-0000; internet: www.airarabia.com)

Dubai Airport (internet: www.dubaiairport.com).

Dubai Tourism P.O.Box 594, Dubai (tel: 223-0000; fax: 223-0022; internet: http://dubaitourism.co.ae).

Emirates Group, Emirates Headquarters, Near Clock Tower, Dubai (tel: 295-1111; internet: www.emirates.com).

Gulf Air, Hamdan St/Airport Road, Abu Dhabi.

Oman Air, PO Box 1058, Central Post Office Seeb International Airport, Muscat, Oman.

Qatar Airways, Almana Tower, Airport Road, PO Box 22550, Doha, Qatar.

Ras Al-Khaimah National Travel Agency, Ras Al-Khaimah.

Ministry of tourism

Department of Tourism and Commerce Marketing, PO Box 594, Dubai (tel: 223-0000; fax: 223-0022; e-mail: info@dubaitourism.co.ae; internet: www.dubaitourism.co.ae).

Ministries

Ministry of Agriculture & Fisheries, PO Box 213, Abu Dhabi.

Ministry of Communication, PO Box 900, Abu Dhabi.

Ministry of Defence, PO Box 2838, Dubai.

Ministry of Economy & Commerce, PO Box 901, Abu Dhabi.

Ministry of Education and Youth, PO Box 295, Abu Dhabi.

Ministry of Electricity & Water, PO Box 629, Abu Dhabi.

Ministry of Finance & Industry, PO Box 433, Abu Dhabi.

Ministry of Foreign Affairs, PO Box 1, Abu Dhabi.

Ministry of Health, PO Box 848, Abu Dhabi.

Ministry of Higher Education & Scientific Research, PO Box 45253, Abu Dhabi.

Ministry of Information & Culture, PO Box 17, Abu Dhabi.

Ministry for the Interior, PO Box 398, Abu Dhabi.

Ministry for Justice and Islamic Affairs & Awqaf, PO Box 2272, Abu Dhabi.

Ministry for Labour & Social Affairs, PO Box 809, Abu Dhabi.

Ministry of Petroleum & Mineral Resources, PO Box 59, Abu Dhabi.

Ministry of Planning, PO Box 904, Abu Dhabi.

Ministry of Public Works & Housing, PO Box 878, Abu Dhabi.

Ministry of State for Cabinet Affairs, PO Box 899, Abu Dhabi..

Minister of State for Supreme Council Affairs, PO Box 545, Abu Dhabi.

Ministry of Youth & Sports, PO Box 539, Abu Dhabi.

Other useful addresses

Abu Dhabi Company for Onshore Oil Operations (ADCO), PO Box 270, Abu Dhabi.

Abu Dhabi Gas Liquifaction Co Ltd, PO Box 3500, Abu Dhabi.

Abu Dhabi National Oil Co (ADNOC), PO Box 898, Abu Dhabi.

Abu Dhabi Water and Electricity Authority, ADWEA Building, Al Falah Street, PO Box 6120, Abu Dhabi.

Ajman Independent Studios, PO Box 442, Ajman.

Arab Monetary Fund (headquarters), PO Box 2818, Abu Dhabi.

British Embassy, Khalid Bin-Walid Street; PO Box 248, Abu Dhabi (tel: 610-1111; fax: 610-1585.

British Embassy, Al-Seef; PO Box 65, Dubai (tel: 309-4445; fax: 309-4302).

Department of Information, Dubai Municipality, PO Box 67, Dubai.

Dubai International Trade Centre, PO Box 9292, Dubai.

Dubai TV, PO Box 1695, Dubai.

Executive Council of Dubai (runs the emirate's political and financial affairs)

Jebel Ali Free Zone Authority, PO Box 3258, Dubai.

Gulf Arab Marketing & Exhibition Co (GAME), PO Box 610, Abu Dhabi.

Ports Authority of Dubai, PO Box 3258, Dubai.

Ports Authority of Sharjah, PO Box 510, Sharjah.

UAE Embassy (USA), 1010 Wisconsin Avenue, NW, Washington DC 20007 (tel: +1-202) 672-1050; fax: (tel: +1-202) 672-1082).

UAE Radio & TV Dubai, PO Box 2765, Dubai.

UAE Television & Broadcasting Corporation, PO Box 17, Abu Dhabi.

UAE TV Sharjah, PO Box 111, Sharjah.

National news agency: Emirates News Agency, 3790 Abu Dhabi, (tel: 445-4545; fax: 445-4695; email: wamnews@eim.ae; internet: www.wam.org.ae).

DPM News Agency: www.dpmnewsagency.com

Internet sites

Arab Net: www.arab.net

Arabia OnLine: www.arabia.com

Dubai Metro: http://dubaimetro.eu

Dubai Tourism: http://dubaitourism.co.ae

Etisalat web portal: http://ecompany.ae

UAE Government: www.government.ae

UAE information: www.uae.org.ae

UAE interact: www.uaeinteract.com

Yellow Pages: www.uae-ypages.com

United Kingdom

KEY FACTS

Official name: The United Kingdom of Great Britain and Northern Ireland (UK)

Head of State: Queen Elizabeth II (crowned 2 Jun 1953)

Head of government: Prime Minister David Cameron (from 12 May 2010)

Ruling party: The Conservative Party

Area: 244,103 square km

Population: 64.51 million (2014)

Capital: London

Official language: English; English and Welsh in Wales; English and Scottish Gaelic in Scotland.

Currency: Pound sterling (£) = 100 pence

Exchange rate: £0.65 per US$ (Sep 2015)

GDP per capita: US$45,653 (2014)

GDP real growth: 2.55% (2014)

GDP: US$2,945.15 billion (2014)

Labour force: 32.78 million (2014)*

Unemployment: 6.20% (2014)

Inflation: 1.46% (2014)

Oil production: 850,000 bpd (2014)

Natural gas production: 36.60 billion cum (2014)

Balance of trade: -US$199.62 billion (2014)*

Annual FDI: US$28.31 billion (2011)

* estimated figure

When election day arrived, on 7 May 2015 at the end of the Conservative/Liberal coalition government's first term, it appeared that the British electorate had opted for the continuation of the known quantity of David Cameron and his treasury minister George Osborne, a team which for better or for worse had at least delivered an annual growth rate of 2.8 per cent in 2014. The alternative seemed to be that of a less than positive Labour government, almost certainly beholden to the Scottish National Party (SNP). The driving force in the election had turned out to be fear – not so much fear of anything in particular, simply the fear of the unknown.

Opinion poll failure

Given the authority attached to them, not to mention the money invested in their results, it was universally surprising that with one solitary exception (an exit poll conducted by the BBC) all the major pollsters failed to predict the result with any accuracy. Eleven opinion polls had predicted that the Conservatives would win by around 20 seats. This might have enabled the Labour Party, in coalition with the SNP, to form a government. However, the Conservatives, with 36.9 per cent of the votes, in the end won enough seats (331) to give them a majority big enough to enable them to form a government without having resort to coalition partners. This was reportedly above the most optimistic expectations of the party's own forecasters. The election victory cleared the way for the next hurdle in the Conservative government's path, that of the so-called 'Brexit' referendum on whether the United Kingdom should continue to be a member if the European Union (EU). In his victory speech, Mr Cameron also made reference to the complexity of the UK's political make-up, especially that presented by the new emergence of parties such as the UK Independence Party (UKIP) – which had failed to win a single new seat in the parliament. The only pundit who called the result with any accuracy was former prime minister, Tony Blair, who had told hi closest colleagues a month earlier that he expected an outright Conservative victory. His reasoning was that he could not detect any real enthusiasm on the part of Labour voters for leader David Miliband's offering.

The Labour vote fell to 30.4 per cent, giving the party 232 seats, 48 less than they had managed in 2010. Proportionately, the biggest losers were the Liberal Party, headed by former deputy prime minister, Nick Clegg, whose vote plummeted to 12.6 per cent as they lost 49 seats, leaving them with only 8. UKIP may have failed to win any seats, but did manage to garner almost 4 million votes. The size of the UKIP vote did give David Cameron cause for concern in that it would almost certainly represent a substantial 'no' vote in any EU membership referendum.

What had changed since the 2010 election was that England and Scotland had become two markedly different entities. Scotland in the north of the country continued to be left-wing and probably now in favour of independence, England, in the south, unionist and right of centre. Although David Cameron was the titular prime minister of both north and south, in reality his writ did not count for a great deal north of the border. Labour's parliamentary presence north of the border also hung by a thread. Although Scottish Labour had won twice the number of votes than the Conservatives in Scotland, it still only had one seat to show for it.

In the May 2015 election one of the most unexpected features was seen in Scotland, where less than a year earlier the 'No' referendum vote to independence had been seen as the reconfirmation of the political *status quo*. But the political map that Scots woke up to represented a radical change. The pro-independence SNP had taken 56 of Scotland's 59 parliamentary seats; the big losers were the Labour Party, whose representation had fallen from 41 to a solitary single seat. The election result appeared to mark the end – temporarily or permanently was difficult to say – of Labour's traditional dominance north of the border. The wave of euphoria that spread over the nationalist camp was tempered by a word of warning from the SNP leader, Nicola Sturgeon, who while second page or by simply ignoring it. The *Sun* considered the fortunes of the new boy-friend of the ex-girl friend of a well known rugby football player to be of greater importance, while the *Daily Mirror* devoted its front page to the death of a race-horse. However, the popular – and populist – *Daily Mail* carried a front page headline: 'Now, Autonomy for England!' It also referred to the Queen's post referendum message that her Kingdom should now heal its wounds. This theme was more than echoed by the *Daily Telegraph*, which ran a front page picture of the Queen in full regalia at her Balmoral (in Scotland) residence with a royal quotation: 'We all have in common a great love for Scotland, which will be one of the things that unites us.'

The two principal Scottish newspapers devoted their front pages to Mr Salmond's resignation. The *Herald*, published in Glasgow where there was a 'Yes' majority, published extracts from the first minister's speech. The *Scotsman*, published in Edinburgh where the 'No' vote prevailed, devoted a special commemorative number on the referendum's outcome. 'What happens to Wales now?' was the front page headline of the *Western Mail*, the principality's major newspaper, reflecting the likely concern of the Welsh Assembly and Welshmen at being left behind or not seated at the negotiating. table. The *Western Mail* was the only British newspaper to suggest that Mr Salmond was perceived to be a victim of the 'Nixon Syndrome' and the one time US President Nixon, asking its readers: 'Would you buy a second-hand car from this man?' In the US, the UK's closest and most important ally, the *Washington Post* ran an evocative photo of a 'Yes' supporter, walking home alone in the rain soaked streets of Edinburgh, soaking wet. The newspaper observed that the 'self-government box' had been opened for all four members of the United Kingdom. The *Wall Street Journal* raised concerns about a possible period of economic uncertainty following David Cameron's 'surprise' announcement of government reforms. In its digital edition, the US newspaper also drew a parallel with the declarations of Quebec's politicians, who insisted that once the referendum process was established, the Scots would wish to use it again.

Had the 'yes' vote won, within 18 months Scotland would have had to decide on its currency arrangements, an area that in all the debates leading up to the referendum Mr Salmond had chosen – or preferred – to ignore. The choice seemed

lessons for everyone in politics.' In a thinly disguised self plaudit, Mr Johnson had said that the other candidates for the Labour leadership were 'anaemic, gelatinous and vacillating opportunists.'

Soon after Mr Corbyn's election as party leader, London's bookmakers were giving odds as to how long he was likely to last. The scenarios were staged – a palace *coup* on the part of MPs worried about their job security might see Mr Corbyn deposed before the end of the parliament – which had almost five years to run. A post election crisis meeting following another election defeat in 2020 would see him go shortly after the next election. The possibility of him staying in power until 2025 offered the longest odds of all. Probably the most suitable definition for Mr Corbyn was that of 'contrarian' (one who opposes or rejects popular opinion), to judge from his admiration of Hugo Chávez, his sympathy for Vladimir Putin's Russia and chumminess with Hamas and Hezbullah. He is avowedly anti-American and anti-North Atlantic Treaty Organisation (NATO) Nato. His support for Greece's Syrisa has won him friends among his own left-wingers.

The economy

The April 2015 visit of the UK Chancellor (finance minister) George Osborne to Washington came as something of a surprise – taking place three weeks before a predicted to be tightly competitive May 2015 general election. But as soon as the International Monetary Fund's (IMF) Chairman Christine Lagarde spoke, it became clear that with the fulsome praise of the then coalition government she was the answer to the prayers of the Conservative Party. Her pro-active endorsement of the government's economic policies and recognition that the UK economy was growing faster than any of the larger European economies was music to a smiling Mr Osborne. As if Mrs Lagarde's praise was not enough, her views on the British economy were endorsed by the normally taciturn German finance minister, Wolfgang Schäuble.

In its July 2014 assessment of the United Kingdom economy the IMF had noted that the economy had rebounded strongly and prospects were promising. Headwinds that had previously held back the economy – including adverse credit conditions and diminished confidence – had eased. There were signs that demand was becoming more balanced, with growth in business investment now ahead of private consumption. Employment growth had also remained strong. Despite this, inflation had been contained.

Nonetheless, sustaining strong growth would depend on a recovery in productivity growth and real wages. In addition, the housing market is becoming buoyant, potentially creating financial stability risks. Further demand rebalancing is needed: net trade has made only a modest contribution to the recovery and the real exchange rate is moderately overvalued.

Policies have been directed toward supporting growth, while strengthening public finances through a mix of revenue and expenditure measures and ensuring financial stability. Monetary policy remains highly accommodative and effective monetary conditions have eased compared with last year. A number of micro-prudential and credit policy measures have been introduced in an effort to take some of the steam out of the housing market, such as modification of the Funding for Lending Scheme and the introduction of tighter underwriting standards for owner-occupier mortgages. The Financial Policy Committee of the Bank of England (central bank) has also recommended the implementation of macro-prudential measures aimed at insuring against excessive household indebtedness. Meanwhile, the 2014 budget implies a half-percentage point tightening in the cyclically-adjusted primary balance. Going forward, fiscal policy aims to eliminate the budget deficit by FY2018 and to put the debt ratio firmly on a downward path while preserving the delivery of quality public services and paying due attention to social equity.

After the overhaul of the UK's financial regulatory architecture in 2013, which saw the establishment of the Prudential Regulation Authority, Financial Conduct Authority and Financial Policy Committee, efforts to strengthen bank balance sheets and implement durable structural reforms to the financial sector continued. These include higher bank capital and provisioning, a robust multi-pronged framework for assessing capital adequacy and stress testing of major banks for large shocks. Liquidity backstops have been strengthened, which should help solvent UK banks ride out temporary funding stresses that could otherwise create domestic and outward credit spillovers. But easier access to liquidity requires commensurately strong supervision of banks and other financial intermediaries.

In a later interim report, the IMF considered that the external position in 2014 was weaker than implied by medium-term fundamentals and desirable policy settings. The real exchange rate appreciation seen in 2015 might further affect the external position. External deficits reflected insufficient public and private saving rates. The UK's external position was influenced by the lack of competitiveness and limited export diversification.

KEY INDICATORS — United Kingdom

	Unit	2011	2012	2013	2014	**2015
Population	m	*62.64	*63.70	*64.09	64.51	*64.94
Gross domestic product (GDP)	US$bn	2,417.60	2,484.45	2,680.12	2,945.15	*2,853.36
GDP per capita	US$	38,592	38,999	41,820	45,653	*43,940
GDP real growth	%	0.7	0.3	1.7	2.6	*2.7
Inflation	%	4.5	2.8	2.6	1.5	*0.1
Unemployment	%	7.7	8.0	7.6	6.2	*5.4
Oil output	'000 bpd	1,100.0	967.0	866.0	850.0	–
Natural gas output	bn cum	45.2	41.0	36.5	36.6	–
Coal output	mtoe	11.2	10.2	7.8	7.0	–
Exports (fob) (goods)	US$m	479,140.0	473,030.0	476,620.0	480,810.0	–
Imports (fob) (goods)	US$m	639,440.0	643,480.0	645,350.0	680,430.0	–
Balance of trade	US$m	-160,300.0	-170,450.0	-168,730.0	-199,620.0	–
Current account	US$m	-46,530.0	-92,687.0	-119,924.0	*-162,210.0	*-135,579.0
Total reserves minus gold	US$m	77,057.1	88,600.0	9,240.0	95,700.0	–
Foreign exchange	US$m	55,644.3	64,950.0	69,550.0	–	–
Exchange rate	per US$	0.61	0.61	0.61	0.64	–

* estimated figure ** forecast figure

In the view of the IMF, sustaining a strong and durable recovery in the UK required rebalancing away from public support toward private-sector led demand, along with greater reliance on external demand. The current fiscal consolidation plan implemented within a medium-term framework and an accommodative monetary policy stance contributed to the goal of external rebalancing. Further structural reforms focussed on broadening the skill base and investing in public infrastructure would boost productivity, improving the competitiveness of the economy.

In its second quarter Inflation Report, the Bank of England noted that the outlook for global growth had weakened since its August Inflation Report. Many emerging market economies had slowed markedly and the Bank had downgraded its assessment of their medium-term growth prospects. While growth in advanced economies had continued and broadened, the Bank nonetheless expected the overall pace of UK-weighted global growth to be more modest than had been expected in August. There remained downside risks to this outlook, including that of a more abrupt slowdown in emerging economies. However, the UK's domestic momentum remained resilient. Consumer confidence was firm, real income growth in 2015 was expected to be the strongest since the financial crisis and investment intentions also remained robust. As a result, domestic demand growth had been solid despite the fiscal consolidation. Although it had moderated, growth was projected to pick up a little towards the middle of 2016, as a tighter labour market and stronger productivity supported real incomes and consumption and as accommodative credit conditions encouraged strong investment and a pickup in the housing market. The Bank judged the risks to domestic demand to be broadly balanced. Robust private domestic demand was expected to produce sufficient momentum to eliminate the margin of spare capacity over the following year. Domestic cost pressures were expected to build up as a result of a pickup in wage growth relative to productivity growth. CPI inflation was nonetheless expected to remain below 1 per cent until the second half of 2016, reflecting the continuing drag from commodity and other imported goods prices. Beyond that, the dampening influence of sterling's past appreciation on inflation is expected to be persistent, diminishing only slowly over the Bank of England's Monetary Policy Committee (MPC)'s forecast period. In this context, the MPC judged it appropriate to return inflation to the target in around two years.

Another referendum?

If the 2014 Scottish referendum had been something of a nail-biter for David Cameron, by mid-2015 the possible referendum on future British EU membership, or on what had become known as the Brexit, was looking like a nightmare. Flush with his May 2015 electoral victory, Mr Cameron had set off for Europe with a view to winning Europe's heads of state and government round to his point of view. With each capital visited, however, the list got shorter. On possible British opt-outs from legislation on EU employment regulations, the Brussels European Commission and the French government both said 'no'. Austria, already trying to cope with a tide of refugees politely suggested that the UK needed to take in more refugees if it wanted a 'trade off' agreement, a request that Mr Cameron knew was politically unacceptable with the right wing of his own Conservative Party, not to mention UKIP.

The rocky start in the corridors of European power was followed by a further hiccough when the UK's Electoral Commission decided that even the question to be asked had not been correctly drafted. Voters were initially to be asked 'Should the United Kingdom remain a member of the European Union?', to which they could answer 'yes' or 'no'. However the Electoral Commission concluded that the subtleties of the language would be better reflected by 'Should the United Kingdom remain a member of the European Union or leave the European Union?' with 'Leave the European Union' or 'Remain a member of the European Union' being the alternatives.

When it came to the less precise aspects of the referendum, Mr Cameron was able to relax. His hope was that come the day, the UK's heads would prevail over their 'little Englander' hearts. In the game of chess that he had started, he hoped that the four million pawns deployed by UKIP would be no match for the Queens and rooks of the Confederation of British Industry (CBI) which had reported that 'the majority of British firms believe that the pros of EU membership outweigh the cons,' or of the foreign secretary who deplored the prospect of a British veto. The governor of the Bank of England, the Canadian Mark Carney had also weighed in, stating that EU membership had made the British economy stronger and more dynamic, adding that Britain had been the leading beneficiary of the EU's four freedoms of movement: goods, people, services and capital.

It had been reported in the British press that Mr Cameron had felt more strongly about the outcome of the Scottish referendum than he did about the EU vote. That might have changed however, with the announcement by the Scottish National party that were Britain to vote to leave, it would immediately request a further referendum on independence simply because the Scots would wish to remain a part of the EU. So Mr Cameron risked ending up with the worst of all possible worlds. A 'Little England' that had lost Scotland and was no longer a member of the EU.

Energy

The United Kingdom is, according to the US government Energy Information Administration (EIA) the largest producer of oil and the second-largest producer of natural gas in the EU. Despite this, following years of exports of both fuels, the UK became a net importer of natural gas and crude oil in 2004 and 2005, respectively. Production from UK oil and natural gas fields peaked around the late 1990s and had subsequently declined steadily as the discovery of new reserves and new production had not kept pace with the maturation of existing fields. The UK became a net importer of petroleum products in 2013, making it a net importer of all fossil fuels for the first time since the early 1970s.

Oil remained important to the UK energy balance and contributed 37 per cent of total energy consumption in 2013. Once a major producer of oil from the North Sea, ageing reservoirs and infrastructure have affected UK's oil production over the past few years with production declines and widespread outages as a result of technical problems. Falling production has made the UK increasingly reliant on imports of both crude oil and petroleum products and the UK became a net importer of petroleum products for the first time in 2013 since 1984.

The UK government does not hold a direct interest in oil production, but the sector remains important to the government because Corporation Tax and Supplementary Tax income from the sector accounts for about 25 per cent of UK corporate tax receipts, according to the offshore industry association Oil & Gas UK. Since 2011, there had been a number of tax changes that affected production (or investment) in the United Kingdom Continental Shelf (UKCS), including the change in the rate of supplementary charge (an addition to the corporate tax) and the capping of relief for decommissioning costs at 20 per cent of the supplementary charge. In addition, the tax rate for fields subject to petroleum revenue tax (PRT) increased to 81 per cent of their profits (from the previous 75 per cent rate) and fields that were not subject to PRT now paid a 62 per cent tax (compared with the 50 per cent rate of the past).

As a result of the significant increases in taxes, the UKCS projects had become even less competitive. Increases in operating costs coupled with higher taxes had resulted in decreased investment in both brownfields and new exploration. Even without the increased taxes, operating costs in the UKCS were prohibitively high, exacerbated by the high decommissioning costs of old facilities, which also discouraged investors.

Almost immediately after the new tax rates were implemented, development on several start-ups had been suspended, including Statoil's Mariner and Chevron's Bressay fields. In addition, Centrica launched a review of all of its exploration activities, as many projects were deemed uneconomical under the new rates. Given a nearly 16 per cent decline in production following the implementation of the new tax rates, the UK government has introduced new incentives for producers to counter some of the increase in taxes.

The EIA expected UK oil production to continue to decline through 2015. The main reason for this decline was the overall maturity of the country's oil fields and diminishing prospects for new substantial discoveries in the future. Although its proximity to major consuming markets made UK exploration attractive, the increases in taxes would continue to affect the attractiveness of the UK fields in the longer term.

According to the *Oil & Gas Journal* (OGJ), the UK had 3.0 billion barrels of proven crude oil reserves at the end of 2014, the most of any EU member country but 4.6 per cent below the January 2013 level. This drop marked a major downward trend in oil reserves in the UKCS because of cost increases (making some projects uneconomic) and re-appraised key projects, according to *Oil & Gas UK*. The major project that could offset some of this decline is the Mariner field, which was discovered in 1981. DECC approved development of the field in February 2013 and Statoil expected production to start in 2017, rising to 55,000 barrels per day (bpd) before 2020.

Once a major exporter of oil, the UK exports have dropped in tandem with decreasing domestic production. However, despite being a net importer of crude oil and petroleum products, the UK is still one of the largest petroleum producers and exporters in Europe and exported 576,000bpd of crude oil in 2012.

UK customs export data show that the vast majority of crude oil exports (over 80 per cent) were destined to EU countries, mainly Germany and the Netherlands – the bulk of the exports to Germany are for refining and consumption there, while the exports to the Netherlands include oil destined for onward trade to other countries. Most of the non-EU export trade was with South Korea and the United States.

The UK government, aware of the country's increasing reliance on imported fuels, has developed key energy policies to address the domestic production declines. These include: using enhanced recovery from current and maturing oil and gas fields, promoting energy efficiency, decreasing the use of fossil fuels and thus reliance on imports, promoting energy trade co-operation with Norway and decarbonising the UK economy by investing heavily in renewable energy. However, for the UK to decarbonise its economy, huge investments in the energy infrastructure are needed.

Renewable energy use, particularly in the electric power sector, had more than tripled between 2000 and 2012. However, petroleum and natural gas continue to account for the vast majority of UK's energy consumption. In 2012, petroleum and natural gas accounted for 37 and 33 per cent, respectively, of total energy consumption. Coal also continues to be a significant part of total energy consumption (16 per cent in 2012). Energy use per unit of gross domestic product (GDP) in the UK is one of the lowest among Western economies. The UK has seen total primary energy consumption decline by 16 per cent between 2004 and 2012. This decline resulted from smaller contribution of energy-intensive industry to the economy, economic contraction and improvements in energy efficiency.

Natural gas

According to the OGJ, the UK held an estimated 8.5 trillion cubic feet (tcf) of proven natural gas reserves as of December 2014. Most of these reserves occur in three distinct areas: 1) associated fields in the UKCS; 2) non-associated fields in the Southern Gas Basin, located adjacent to the Dutch sector of the North Sea; and 3) non-associated fields in the Irish Sea. The United Kingdom has substantial volumes of prospective shale gas and shale oil resources within shale formations distributed broadly in the northern, central and southern portions of the country. The technically recoverable shale resources of the UK are estimated at 26tcf of shale gas and 0.7 billion barrels of shale oil and condensate in the two regions assessed by the 2013 EIA/ARI shale gas and oil report.

Compared with North America, the shale geology of the UK is considerably more complex. Shale testing is still at an early phase in the UK. In a temporary setback, the first shale well triggered a series of minor earthquakes related to a nearby fault. Following an 18-month moratorium, the government concluded that the environmental risks of shale exploration are small and manageable. The government allowed shale drilling to resume in December 2012, albeit with stricter monitoring controls. Current shale operators include Cuadrilla Resources, IGAS, Dart Energy and others.

Risk assessment

Economy	Good
Politics	Good
Regional stability	Good

Muslims in UK

% of population	4.6
Sunni (% of Muslims)	85
Shi'a (% of Muslims)	15

People to watch

Nigel Farage UKIP leader and loosing parliamentary candidate in the 2015 general election

Boris Johnson, mayor of London and successful Conservative candidate in the 2015 general election. Considered by many to be a prospective leader of the Conservative Party

COUNTRY PROFILE

1837–1901 The long reign of Queen Victoria saw the British Empire at the height of its power.

1914–1918 Great Britain called on all its colonies and dominions to help it fight alongside its allies, France and Russia, in the First World War against Germany and its allies.

1916 An uprising in Dublin by Irish republicans was supressed after a few days and its leaders were either executed or interned.

1922 The Irish Free State (Eire) was created in southern Ireland; the six north-eastern counties of Ireland remained part of Great Britain.

1939 Britain declared war on Germany having failed to limit its expansionist policies and after Germany had invaded Poland.
1939–45 In the Second World War, Britain was a major member of the allied forces, along with the US and the Soviet Union, against the Axis powers of Germany, Italy and Japan.
1945 Facing near economic collapse as a result of the war, the UK began to relinquish control of its Empire and its role in the world as its power declined.
1945–51 The Labour Party was elected into government. Led by Prime Minister Clement Attlee, the government implemented reforms to education, healthcare, housing and the social security system.
1953 Queen Elizabeth II was crowned on 2 June.
1969 The start of 'The Troubles' in Northern Ireland. Violence between the Catholic civil rights movement and the Unionists, who perceived it as republicanism, intensified.
1973 The UK joined the European Economic Community.
1979 Following a decade marred by economic stagnation and endemic inflation, the Conservative Party (Tories) won a parliamentary majority in the general election. Margaret Thatcher, leader of the party, became the UK's first woman prime minister.
1979–1990 Thatcher's radical domestic policies, including privatisation and local government reforms, did not prevent her securing two further election victories, in addition to a victory in the 1982 Falklands conflict.
1990 Introduction of the community charge and a loss of party confidence stemming from her vociferous opposition to the European Community finally led to Thatcher being replaced by John Major as leader of the Conservative Party and as prime minister.
1992 The treaty on European Union (the Maastricht Treaty) was signed. The Treaty harmonised legislation in key areas of European Union (EU) social policy, immigration and finance, although the UK successfully opted out of the Social Chapter. The UK was forced out of the European Exchange Rate Mechanism (ERM) after the pound dropped below the permitted parity with the deutschmark. The Conservatives won the general election.
1997 The Labour Party, under the leadership of Tony Blair, won an overwhelming victory in the general election.
1998 The UK and Irish governments attempted to bring to an end the problems in Northern Ireland through the signing of the Good Friday Peace Agreement. The political settlement established a precedent for Ireland's direct involvement in Northern Ireland's affairs, with cross-border co-operation and the decommissioning of paramilitary arms.
1999 Scotland's first legislature for 300 years and Wales' first for 600 years were opened in June. Power and conditional authority were also devolved in Northern Ireland in December.
2000 Nationwide cases of foot and mouth broke out; four million cattle were culled and compensation payments totalled £1.1 billion (US$1.5 billion).
2001 The Labour Party won a second landslide parliamentary victory.
2003 British forces joined a US-led invasion of Iraq, prompted in part by an intelligence report that said President Saddam Hussein of Iraq had a stock of weapons of mass destruction (WMD)
2004 The Iraq Survey Group concluded Iraq did not possess WMD. A UK inquiry into the quality of intelligence used to justify UK participation in the Iraq war found no evidence of 'deliberate distortion or culpable negligence' by the government.
2005 The Labour Party won its third term in office but with a significantly reduced majority. On 7 July four bombs exploded (on three underground trains and a bus) during the morning rush hour in London, killing 52 people and injuring over 700. Four Islamic extremists, including three British-born Muslims, were later convicted for this act of terrorism.
2006 Police investigated allegations of peerages being bought through financial donations to the Labour Party. Aleksandr Litvinenko, former Russian security service officer and outspoken critic of Russia's ruling elite was poisoned by radioactive thallium in London. Police traced the source to Russia but authorities there refused to extradite the prime suspect.
2007 Following Northern Ireland elections the Democratic Unionist Party (DUP) and Sinn Féin agreed to share power, ending direct rule from London. The Scottish National Party (SNP) took office after winning Scotland's general election. Prime Minister Blair resigned and was replaced, unopposed, by Gordon Brown.
2008 The first run on a bank by customers since the early 1860s lead the government to nationalise the Northern Rock Bank. The government had to invest £37 billion (US$74 billion) to partly nationalise another three failing banks and guarantee billions more to support the financial sector. In foreign exchange markets the pound sterling dropped against the US dollar as well as other currencies.
2009 The UK fell into recession in the first quarter and the Bank of England's official bank rate was reduced to 1.5 per cent, the lowest level since it began operations in 1694. Halifax-Bank of Scotland announced the largest corporate loss in British history – of around US$41.3 billion (£28 billion). UK troops began leaving Iraq. An inquiry into the Iraq War was undertaken, to investigate the circumstances, conduct and outcome of the war. The UK climbed out of recession in the last quarter.
2010 Following parliamentary elections in which no party won a majority (326 seats), the Tories, with most seats (306), formed a coalition government with the Liberal Democrats (Lib Dems) (57 seats). David Cameron (Tories) became prime minister. An early budget announced public spending cuts, particularly in welfare. It also included bank levies, a public sector worker's pay freeze, a VAT rise from 17.5 per cent to 20 per cent. In a surprise result, Ed Miliband became leader of the Labour Party. He beat his elder brother, David Miliband, by 50.65 per cent to 49.35 per cent of votes cast.
2011 In March, the UK joined in a five-country coalition (with Canada, France, Italy and the US) to impose a no-fly zone over Libya. A referendum to change the voting system to proportional representation for the UK parliament was defeated by 67.9 per cent to 32.1 per cent. In May the Scottish Parliamentary elections were won by the SNP, who had promised a referendum on independence from the UK's Act of Union. First Minister Alex Salmond (SNP) stated his preference for a referendum on independence in 2014 or 2015. In elections held on 5 May, the Labour Party won leadership the Welsh National Assembly when they gained four seats from the previous election; nationalist Plaid Cymru lost four seats. The Labour Party still required support from other parties to pass legislation. The UK military operations in Iraq ended completely in May. Rioting and looting broke-out in several major English cities over three nights in August. Order was restored with the deployment of 16,000 police officers in London; magistrate courts stayed open for 24 hours to process those arrested. In October the 16 Commonwealth Heads of Government of which the British monarch is Head of State unanimously agreed to change the royal line of succession from that of first born son to the first born child (regardless of its gender). The change will be enacted after the succession of Prince William (currently second in line to the throne, after his father Charles, Prince of Wales). In November, the British embassy in Tehran (Iran) and a British diplomatic compound in northern Tehran were stormed by hundreds of protestors angry at British sanctions against Iran. All UK diplomatic staff and their families were evacuated as all Iranian embassy staff in London were told to leave the UK within 48 hours.

2012 In January, the UK executive challenged Scotland's right to hold a referendum on independence and claimed that only the powers vested in the UK parliament could do so. Moreover, the result of any such referendum would not be legally binding as referenda in the UK are advisory only. Queen Elizabeth II marked her diamond jubilee on 6 February. The economy weakened with GDP growth in the first quarter of 0.2 per cent, following 0.3 per cent in the fourth quarter of 2011. Unemployment in the second quarter fell to 2.47 million (7.8 per cent of total), however there was a record increase in the number of part-time workers at 27 per cent of total (the highest level since records began in 1991). On 30 May the International Criminal Court sentenced former president Charles Taylor (of Liberia) to 50 years in jail for crimes against humanity. Under an agreement, sanctioned by Tony Blair in 2006, Taylor's sentence will be served out in the UK prison system. The Scottish pro-independence campaign began in Scotland on 25 May and a month later, on 25 June the pro-union campaign began. On 12 June, while addressing the UN Committee on Decolonisation, President Fernandez de Kirchner of Argentina demanded that the UK enter negotiations over the sovereignty of the Falkland Islands (Las Malvinas). Prime Minister Cameron responded on 13 June by saying there would be 'absolutely no negotiation' on sovereignty rights. Meanwhile the Falklands Islanders decided to conduct a referendum on its 'political status' in 2013. Results of the 2011 England and Wales national census were published on 16 July, showing a population of 56,075,900 in England and Wales, a rise of 3.7 million on the 2001 census. In Northern Ireland there were 1,810,900 people; Scotland is scheduled to publish its results in December. On 2 August Buenos Aires province, in a largely symbolic move, banned all British merchant ships passing to or from the Falkland Islands from using its ports. The move is to prevent ships flying the British Red Ensign (instead of the Falkland Island flag) from using the ports. In 2011 the trading bloc Mercosur had banned ships flying the Falkland Island flag from all their ports. On 15 October Prime Minister Cameron and First Minister Salmond signed an agreement to hold a referendum on Scottish independence. The vote will be in late 2014, will have a single yes/no question and will allow 16 and 17 year olds to participate. The result of the referendum will be held binding by both sides. The UK placed a ban on all cargo flying in from Yemen in 2010, following the discovery of improvised bombs sent by agents of Al Qaeda; the ban was still in operation in 2012. On 9 November, Justin Welby was appointed as Archbishop of Canterbury (leader of the worldwide Anglian Church), to take over when the incumbent Rowan Williams retires in December. The Leveson Inquiry report into press standards was published on 29 November. It recommended that a new self-regulating body be established, independent of serving editors, politicians and business interests. It also made the contentious recommendation that it be underpinned by statute designed to assess the acceptable behaviour of the press.

2013 Former prime minister, Margared Thatcher, died on 8 April. The annual marching season in Northern Ireland began on Friday 12 July with riots in Belfast. A Parades Commission had ruled that a parade by three Orange Order lodges would not be allowed to march along a stretch of the Crumlin Road that separates loyalist and nationalist communities, on its return journey from the main Belfast demonstration.. The serious rioting on Friday and Saturday night was followed by low level disturbances in several towns for the next few days. The first stage of an audit of EU powers, which Tory MPs hope will be the basis of a future re-negotiation of the UK's membership, was published on 22 July. The 'balance of competences' review examined which powers are delegated to Brussels and which are retained by the UK; Prime Minister Cameron has said that he would like to renegotiate some of the powers and has promised a referendum in 2017 if the Conservatives win the next election. The economy grew by 0.6 per cent in the three months to June, according to official figures. Foreign secretary, William Hague, announced on 8 October that a *charge d'affaires* will be appointed to work with Iran, the first diplomatic appoint since the embassies were closed in November 2011. Iran will in turn appoint a *charge d'affaires* to work with the UK. On his final day of a trade visit to China, George Osborne, the Chancellor, announced that Chinese companies would be allowed to invest in the UK nuclear plant industry.

2015 Parliament was dissolved just after mid-night on 29 March in preparation for the general election on 7 May. the election was won by the Conservative Party with 36.9 per cent of the vote (330 seats out of 650). The Labour Party came second with 30.4 per cent (232), followed by the Scottish National Party 4.7 per cent (56) and Liberal Democrats wity 7.9 per cent (8).

Political structure

Constitution

There is no formal written constitution, instead constitutional law is based on legal precedent and legislation both within the UK and from EU supranational institutions. Power within the UK is partially devolved to Scotland, Wales and Northern Ireland. Local councils operate at the level of metropolitan boroughs, counties, districts and parishes, delivering a number of public services such as education and policing, although their powers, particularly regarding taxation and spending, are circumscribed by central government.

Form of state

Parliamentary democratic monarchy

The executive

The monarch is head of state. The monarchy is governed by convention and may not participate in politics or government affairs. It has, however, by unspoken agreement three rights: to be consulted, to encourage and to warn.

The monarch, in regard to democratic principles, accedes to the results of the popular vote and appoints the winner of any general election, and only in extreme circumstances may a monarch dismiss the government.

While government ministers act nominally in the name of the Crown, almost all power rests with the prime minister as head of government and his cabinet of ministers (part of the executive but drawn from the legislature).

The prime minister chooses and chairs the cabinet, who are members of the political party which typically has most seats in the House of Commons. The cabinet consists of around 20 ministers, although its exact composition is not fixed and there are some ministers without portfolio. Secretaries of state are ministers who head specific government departments. Major figures of importance in the cabinet include the chancellor of the exchequer (responsible for economic management), the foreign secretary (foreign policy) and the home secretary (responsible for law and order). Other ministers deal on a functional basis with trade and industry, health, energy, transport and so on. Cabinet ministers head departments of civil servants and have junior ministers (who do not, as a rule, have a seat in the cabinet) to assist them. These ministries are effectively the executive arm of central government, implementing decisions of the cabinet and parliament.

National legislature

The bicameral parliament consists of the House of Commons (lower house) and House of Lords (upper house). Both are commonly referred to as the Commons and Lords respectively. The Commons has 650 members of parliament (MPs), directly elected in single seat constituencies who serve for up to four-year terms. Legislation may be introduced by both houses; the Lords can suggest amendments to

and, except for financial legislation, it can refuse to pass legislation, but the Commons has ultimate power.
The Lords has 782 seats, including life peers, hereditary peers and Church of England archbishops and bishops who serve for as long as they deem necessary.
Devolution of power to Scotland and Wales took place in 1999 and was Scotland's first legislature for 300 years and Wales' first for 600 years. Elections to the 129-member Scottish Parliament and the 60-member Welsh Assembly are conducted under a system of proportional representation. The Scottish Parliament may raise taxes; however the Welsh Assembly must seek funds from the UK parliament.

Legal system

The judiciary is independent of both the legislature and executive. The legal system in Scotland and Northern Ireland differs from that in England and Wales.
In England and Wales around 300 county courts deal with minor civil cases. Magistrates courts deal with minor criminal cases. Civil and criminal appeals from these courts are heard by crown courts, which sit in about 90 venues. Scotland and Northern Ireland have slightly different judicial systems. The main purpose of a crown court is to try the more important criminal cases. The High Court of Justice is the main civil court, divided into three sections: Chancery Division, Queens Bench Division and the Family Division.
In October the highest court in England, Wales and Northern Ireland, which had been operated by the House of Lords, became the Supreme Court, entirely separate from the legislature.
Since the signing of the Single European Act in 1988, the European Court of Justice (ECJ) has supreme jurisdiction over some aspects of UK law, although this is not often exercised.

Last elections

7 May 2015 (parliamentary); 5 May 2011 (parliamentary Scotland and Wales and UK referendum); 18 September 2014 (Scotland only independence referendum)

Results: Parliamentary: the Conservative Party won 36.9 per cent of the vote (330 seats out of 650), Labour Party 30.4 per cent (232), Scottish National Party 4.7% (56), Liberal Democrats 7.9 per cent (8), Democratic Unionist Party 0.6 per cent (8), Sinn Fein 0.6 per cent (4), Plaid Cymru 0.6 per cent (3) UK Independence Party 12.7 per cent (1). Turnout was 66.1%
Scottish Parliament: the Scottish National Party won 64 seats (out of 129), Labour Party 38, Conservatives 15, Liberal Democrats 5, Green Party 2, various independents 3
Welsh Assembly: the Labour Party won 30 seats (out of 129), Conservatives 14, Plaid Cymru 11, Liberal Democrats five.
Referendum: 67.9 per cent voted against and 32.1 per cent in favour of changing the voting system for the UK parliament, from 'first-past-the-post' to 'alternative voting' (AV), whereby voters rank their choice of candidates.
Scottish independence referendum: to the question, "Should Scotland be an independent country?" 44.7% of the electorate voted "Yes" while 55.3% voted "No". Voter turnout was exceptionally high at 84.59% and Scotland remained in the United Kingdom.

Next elections

May 2020 (parliamentary)

Political parties

Ruling party

The Conservative Party

Main opposition party

The Labour Party

Population

The population is expected to grow to 64.8 million by 2025. In common with much of Western Europe, the UK population is ageing owing to long life expectancy and low birth rates.
64.09 million (2012)*

Last census: March 2011: 63,182,178

Population density: 247 inhabitants per square km. Urban population 80 per cent (2010 Unicef).

Annual growth rate: 0.4 per cent, 1990–2010 (Unicef).

Ethnic make-up

The English, Scots, Welsh and Irish peoples combined make up over 90 per cent of the population of the UK; the largest ethnic minorities are those of Caribbean or African descent (875,000 people). The next largest ethnic groups are Indians (840,255 people) and Pakistani and Bangladeshis (639,390 people). Ethnic minority groups represent just under 6 per cent of the population.

Religions

Church of England (25 million (baptised)), Roman Catholic (4.12 million), Muslim (1.5 million), Presbyterian (1.1 million), Methodist (800,000), Sikh (500,000), Hindu (320,000), Jewish (285,000).

Education

The UK has a devolved education system. Alongside the state system are independent schools, often denominational, which are financed by fees, endowments and the state. Pre-school education is not state-funded; it is available for ages two to five, through playgroups and nursery schools. There is a national curriculum and assessment targets for all primary schools and a minimum attainment is set for all children.
The usual age for transfer to secondary schools is 11 in England, Wales and Northern Ireland and 12 in Scotland.
About 90 per cent of state secondary school pupils in England, Wales and Scotland attend comprehensive schools, which provide a wide range of secondary education for most children of all abilities. In other areas, the grammar school system has been retained alongside the comprehensive system, with admission through some form of testing at the age of 10 or 11.
All children are tested at the ages of 7, 11 and 14 years, and take General Certificate of Secondary Education (GCSE) or Scottish Certificate of Education (SCE) examinations at 15–16 years. Students can then opt to study at further education institutions for a range of academic and vocational qualifications, such as Advanced level (A-level) or the National Vocational Qualification (NVQ).
Tertiary education typically starts at aged 18, when students go on to university or colleges of higher education. UK higher education has expanded so that first degrees and further post-graduate qualifications are taken at over 162 universities and other colleges of higher education.

Compulsory years: 5 to 16 in England, Wales and Scotland; 4 to 16 in Northern Ireland.

Enrolment rate: 101 per cent gross primary enrolment of relevant age group (including repeaters); 158 per cent gross secondary enrolment; 59 per cent tertiary enrolment (World Bank).

Pupils per teacher: 19 in primary schools

Health

The National Health Service (NHS) benefits from major government spending, with UK citizens provided with free treatment. Most people are required to pay an initial fee for some aspects of treatment such as eye tests, dental care and prescriptions.
The NHS accounts for 85 per cent of total healthcare provision in the UK.
The service provided by the NHS is generally of high quality, but delays for many non-urgent operations have encouraged people to take out private health insurance policies. Private health cover is becoming increasingly common as a company benefit.
Latest figures show 83 per cent of children were immunised against measles before aged one year. Many parents have withdrawn their infants from the programme and questioned the efficacy of the triple MMR (measles, mumps and rubella) vaccine, following a hotly contested report that claimed the onset of autism and the MMR vaccination were linked.

The government announced that it would take measures to prohibit visitors or 'health tourists' from accessing NHS services, limiting treatment to accidents and emergency cases only.
Foreign medical providers provide some surgical treatment, outside the administration of local health authorities. This has provided competition for the NHS, to match the provision of treatment at a reduced cost with speedier flow-through.

HIV/Aids

HIV prevalence: 0.2 per cent aged 15–49 in 2003 (World Bank)

Life expectancy: 79 years, 2004 (WHO 2006)

Fertility rate/Maternal mortality rate: 1.9 births per woman, 2010 (Unicef)

Birth rate/Death rate: 12 births and 11 deaths per 1,000 people (World Bank)

Child (under 5 years) mortality rate (per 1,000): 5 per 1,000 live births (WHO 2012)

Welfare

The UK has long-established social security and welfare systems. Jobseekers Allowance is provided to most of those registered as unemployed. Additional benefits are paid to families on low incomes or with special needs, for example through the Family Credit Scheme. There is also a wide range of allowances for disabled people. The Housing Benefit Scheme is administered by local authorities and provides assistance with rent and other payments.

Pensions

The UK has an ageing population, with the number of over 65 year-olds projected to outnumber the numbers below 16 years by 2008. The number of those past retirement age is expected to peak at around 15 million in the 2030s. Bills for healthcare and pensions are set to rise significantly, while revenue from income tax falls. Government policy is to actively encourage private pension schemes for all employees, and most people now entering the labour market do not expect to receive a sufficient state pension on retirement. Private pension schemes allow retirement at any time between age 50 and 75.
The State Retirement Pension is paid to men at age 65 and women at age 60, although for women this age is starting to increase with the state retirement age to be equalised at age 65 by April 2020.
A report published in October 2004 found that state pensions were underfunded, and that 9–12 million people (or 40 per cent of the workforce) were not saving enough for their retirement.
In March 2005 the unfunded public workers' pensions liability was estimated at £690 billion (US$1.2 trillion) or 1.5 times the net public sector debt. The government has begun taking action to alleviate the problem but much more will be required and may include some combination of higher taxes, compulsory savings and/or an increase in the retirement age over 65.
In April 2005 the Pension Protection Fund (PPF) began operation. The fund is aimed at workers who lose their pension when their employer declares bankruptcy. The scheme is an insurance plan, to which all final salary pension schemes must belong. Pension schemes pay fees for each member into a fund and when a business collapses the employees should receive at least 90 per cent of the sum they were due when they retire and retired members should receive 100 per cent of the sum. Critics claim this measure will discourage businesses from running final salary pensions, if they are to shoulder yet another financial burden, and that one large enterprise that collapsed could overwhelm the fund.

Main cities

London (capital of UK and England, estimated population 7.9 million in 2012), Birmingham (935,270), Liverpool (449,063), Leeds (440,055), Sheffield (409,189), Manchester (396,830), Bristol (371,042), Leicester (300,210).
Scotland: Edinburgh (capital) (456,898), Glasgow (579,422), Aberdeen (162,622), Dundee (140,043).
Wales: Cardiff (capital) (322,192), Swansea (175,204), Newport (121,379).
Northern Ireland: Belfast (capital) (254,410), Londonderry (Derry) (92,133), Lisburn (88,473).

Languages spoken

Other communities such as Indian, Pakistani, Jewish and Chinese maintain their languages.
In 2004 the Bòrd na Gàidhlig (the Bòrd) was established, as a statutory body, working to secure the status of Gaelic as an official language of Scotland.

Official language/s

English; English and Welsh in Wales; English and Scottish Gaelic in Scotland.

Media

Alternative proposals for a press regulator put forward by the newspaper industry was said to be 'flawed' by the Privy Council sub-committee set up to look into press regulation. The Privy Council is expected to present its decision on the proposals put forward by politicians and campaigners on 30 October.

Press

The Press Complaints Commission (www.pcc.org.uk) monitors ethical guidelines required by British media.
There are over 2,000 newspapers published in the UK. All major newspapers are in English. The impact of the internet has led all major national news corporations to invest in online editions.

Dailies: Of the 10 daily newspapers published in England, tabloid readership is the greatest, with the most popular, *The Sun* typically selling three million copies. The biggest selling broadsheet is *The Daily Telegraph* with around 900,000 copies sold daily. Broadsheets by popularity include *The Daily Telegraph* (www.telegraph.co.uk), *The Times* (www.timesonline.co.uk), *The Guardian* (www.guardian.co.uk) and *The Independent* (www.independent.co.uk). A free issue newspaper in London *Metro* (www.metro.co.uk) rivals some of the tabloid newspaper circulations.
Influential newspapers in Scotland include the *Daily Record* (www.dailyrecord.co.uk) and *The Herald* (www.theherald.co.uk); in Wales *Western Mail* (http://icwales.icnetwork.co.uk); in Northern Ireland *Belfast Telegraph* (www.belfasttelegraph.co.uk) and *The Irish News* (www.irishnews.com).
There are a number of evening newspapers distributed in major cities including the London *Evening Standard* (www.thisislondon.co.uk), *Manchester Evening News* (www.manchestereveningnews.co.uk), *Bristol Evening Post* (www.epost.co.uk) and *The South Wales Evening Post* (www.thisissouthwales.co.uk). In January 2009, ex-KGB agent Alexander Lebedev bought the ailing *London Evening Standard*, to be run by his son Evgeny Lebedev. An editorial committee will guarantee editorial independence.

Weeklies: Most daily newspapers publish Sunday editions. There are numerous speciality magazines targeting women and men, young and old; the National Magazine Company (www.natmags.co.uk) publishes several of these magazines. Those with serious comment on general interest, with national and international circulation, include *Prospect* (www.prospect-magazine.co.uk), *The Spectator* (www.spectator.co.uk) and *New Statesman* (www.newstatesman.com). Topics can be exclusive, such as *The New Musical Express NME* (www.nme.com), or technology or aimed at ethnic groups, others can be regional and some international. Satirical publications include *Private Eye* (www.private-eye.co.uk) and *Viz* (www.viz.co.uk). There are two tabloid magazines with large circulations *Hello* (www.hellomagazine.com) and *Heat* (www.heatworld.com).
The last edition of the *News of the World* was published on 10 July 2011, following the scandal that a number of staff had

systematically hacked into the mobile phones of celebrities, politicians and the bereaved families of military personnel and murder victims.

Business: There are a large number of publications covering all aspects of business, some with international circulation, the most prestigious are *The Financial Times* (www.ft.com) a daily newspaper and *The Economist* (www.economist.com) a weekly magazine. Others include *The Business* (http://info.thebusiness.co.uk), *Independent Business Today* (www.ibpl.co.uk) is a newsletter published by the Institute of Independent Business, *Financial News* (www.efinancialnews.com), and *Investors Chronicle* (www.investorschronicle.co.uk) (weekly). Other regional publications include *Business Brief Channel Islands*, *London Business Matters*, *Business and Finance in Scotland* and *Business Scotsman* (http://business.scotsman.com). The Bank of England (www.bankofengland.co.uk/publications) regularly publishes news on the British economy. *The Shariah Investor* (www.shariahinvestor.com) has articles concerning Islamic banking.

Periodicals: *Which* (www.which.co.uk) is an influential consumer monthly magazine.

Broadcasting

Public broadcasting is provided by the British Broadcasting Corporation (BBC), a behemoth in the area of worldwide broadcasting. Services are paid for by a licence fee levied against any owner of a television set.

Radio: The BBC operates the largest national network with 11 stations targeting differing audiences, including the World Service, which broadcasts in over 30 languages worldwide. Digital and live online and podcast services are available (www.bbc.co.uk/radio). There is also a BBC local radio network covering the four countries with programmes in English, Welsh and Gaelic.

Private, commercial radio stations thrive throughout the country, although the BBC typically garners the highest listening audiences for both age-related programming and general audience ratings. Popular commercial services include Virgin Radio (www.virgin.com), Classic FM (www.classicfm.co.uk), Talk Sport (www1.talksport.net) and Independent Radio News (IRN) (www.irn.co.uk).

Television: Digital television services are due to be fully implemented by 2012, when all analogue services will be suspended. A number of service providers are transmitting programmes in high definition.

There are five national terrestrial television channels in operation – BBC1 and BBC2 (www.bbc.co.uk), ITV1 (www.itv.com), Channels 4 (www.channel4.com) and 5 (www.channel5.com). All channels commission their own productions and transmit a range of genre programmes.

Free-to-air digital services are provided by all national channels, and some by pay-to-view satellite and cable TV providers. BBC Wales and Channel 4 Wales called S4C provide services in the Welsh language.

Major cable, digital and satellite systems are growing, particularly the Sky network (www.sky.com) and Virgin (www. virgin.com), which includes news and sports channels.

National news agency: PA Group

Economy

The UK is a major financial centre and one of the world's largest exporters of financial services. The economy is large, open and mixed and characterised by an export-oriented manufacturing sector. The UK is the third richest country in Europe and a member of the G8, a bloc of the wealthiest countries worldwide. This status is in no small measure based on its financial and service industries including insurance, banking and financial transaction services and tourism; the London Stock exchange is Europe's oldest and largest trading forum and globally one of the top stock exchanges.

Although proven reserves are falling the UK is still a major European oil producer, with reserves of 3.0 billion barrels at the end of 2013, and production of 866 thousand barrels per day (bpd). However, consumption was 1.5 million bpd. There were 200 billion cubic metres (cum) of proven natural gas supplies at the end of 2013, and production of 36.5 billion cum, against consumption of 73.1 billion cum. All deficits are met by imports.

GDP growth in 2007 was 3.5 per cent, but as the global economic crisis struck in 2008 the economy fell into a recessionary -1.1 per cent, which intensified to -4.4 per cent in 2009. Unemployment had risen to a high of 7.8 per cent in 2009 (youth unemployment was much higher at 19.8 per cent) as inflation fell to 2.1 per cent, down from 3.6 per cent in 2008 (1.6 per cent above the Bank of England's consumer price index target of 2.0 per cent). The Bank of England's official bank rate was reduced to 0.5 per cent in 2009, the lowest level since it began operations in 1694. Sterling fell rapidly and manufacturing contracted by 4.6 per cent, despite the help to exporters of a weak pound.

The global economic crisis hit the UK hard as it is so dependent on its financial services sector for growth. It has high household indebtedness and an unsustainably high housing market. By the third quarter of 2009 insolvencies were at an all-time high as cheap credit became scarce. The government was forced, since the run on the Northern Rock Bank in 2007, to commit public funds to prop up the banking sector and later the economy in general. Stimulus packages amounting to 0.2 per cent and 1.4 per cent of GDP were committed in 2008 and 2009 respectively as the UK, in conjunction with other developed countries, tackled its failing economy, through the mechanism of quantitative easing (injecting money directly into the economy). The money was used by the banking sector to provide liquidity for, among other things, inter-bank lending, asset guarantees and by the government in spending to promote growth.

The credit ratings agency, Standard and Poor's, review of the UK's economy was revised from stable to negative in May 2009, stating its finances were deteriorating faster than expected. Nevertheless, the agency did not change the UK's triple-A rating, as it saw merit in the government's plans to reduce debt as sound. In June 2010 the Fitch Ratings Agency advised that efforts to cut the budget deficit should be speeded up to prevent the UK from losing its triple-A rating.

Global trade picked up in 2010 and the economy returned to growth of 2.1 per cent. A new coalition government was elected in May 2010, which undertook to repay the budget deficit of £163 million (US$239 million) through, among other measures, higher taxes, wage freezes for public workers and social welfare cuts.

Despite austerity measures that cut public spending and controls on public borrowing the economy weakened in 2011, as annual GDP growth fell to 0.7 per cent. GDP growth in the first quarter of 2012 was 0.2 per cent, following 0.3 per cent in the fourth quarter of 2011. Unemployment in the second quarter of 2012 fell to 2.47 million (7.8 per cent of total), however there was a record increase in the number of part-time workers at 27 per cent of total (the highest level since records began in 1991).

In 2013 the economy showed more promising growth than 2012, with increase in GDP being 1.8 per cent as opposed to 0.3 per cent. Inflation has also continued to improve, dropping from 2.8 per cent in 2012 to 2.6 in 2013. In the first and second quarters of 2014, inflation was around 1.6 per cent, which was the lowest since 2009 and below the target of 2.0 per cent. Unemployment rates have also improved, reaching 6.6 per cent in April of 2014.

External trade
As a member of the European Union, the UK operates within a community-wide free trade area, with tariffs set as a whole. Internationally, the EU has free trade agreements with a number of nations and trading blocs worldwide.
The sector that produces the biggest share of export earnings is banking and financial services, with international banking rated as one of the best and most profitable globally. Despite the decline in heavy industry and manufacturing, output has been maintained by hi-tech industries in aerospace and telecommunications, pharmaceuticals and niche manufacturing that account for 25 per cent of GDP. The UK is still a major exporter of hydrocarbons, but is a net importer of oil and natural gas.
In 2007, Scotch whisky was awarded greater protection from foreign copiers by British consumer laws. Scotch whisky exports are worth around US$4 billion to the Scottish economy annually and the regulation is seen as a vital measure to protect the integrity of the product. In 2013 exports reached US$7.4 billion which in volume terms was an increase of 3 per cent from 2012.

Imports
Main imports are vehicles, consumer goods, capital machinery, raw materials, fuels and foodstuffs.
Main sources: Germany (13.6 per cent of total in 2013), China (8.8 per cent), US (8.3 per cent).

Exports
Main exports are manufactured goods, fuels, chemicals and pharmaceuticals, food, beverages and tobacco.
Main destinations: Switzerland (13.0 per cent of total in 2013), US (11.4 per cent), Germany (8.8 per cent).

Agriculture

Farming
Agriculture contributes one per cent to GDP, employs 2 per cent of the workforce and meets over two-thirds of domestic food consumption needs. The sector is highly efficient and is a significant exporter of agricultural produce, fertilisers and foodstuffs. However, the farming industry remains stuck in long-term recession. Agriculture utilises about 70 per cent of the country's land area.
Government policy is to keep the agricultural industry competitive by reducing subsidies and allowing market forces to determine a farm's viability. The National Farmers' Union (NFU), represents around one-third of UK farmers.
UK membership of the EU has created policy disputes between the farmers' organisations, the UK government and the EU. Most of UK agriculture is governed by the EU's Common Agricultural Policy (CAP), which was reformed fundamentally in 2005. The subsidies paid on farm output, which tended to benefit large farms and encourage overproduction, were replaced by single farm payments not conditional on production. This was expected to reward farms that provided and maintain a healthy environment, food safety and animal welfare standards. The changes were also intended to encourage market conscious production and cut the cost of CAP to the EU taxpayer.
Restrictions on upland sheep farms, which were instituted in 1986 following the radioactive fallout from the Chernobyl disaster, were finally lifted in June 2012, allowing free movement of sheep. By 2012 the mandatory radioactivity testing on the original 9,800 UK farms under restriction was lifted.

Fishing
Once an important contribution to the economy, the UK's fishing industry is in decline. The total annual marine catch is typically 750,000 tonnes. Cod stocks in the North Sea, Skagerrak, Irish Sea and waters west of Scotland have been in decline for a number of years.

Forestry
The UK has ideal conditions for tree growth, with mild winters, plentiful rainfall and fertile soil. Hardwood (broadleaved) trees in the British Isles have a growth rate twice that of mainland Europe and softwood (conifers) trees grow three times as fast than in Sweden. Forests cover 24,000 square kilometres, accounting for nearly 10 per cent of total land use. Careful management and replanting programmes mean that forests in the UK are growing by almost 130 square kilometres per annum. Much of the forest plantations have been in the form of non-indigenous coniferous trees, such as the Norwegian Spruce, but in 2005 the government announced a change in policy in favour deciduous woodlands.
In the Independent Panel on Forestry's (IPF) 2012 report it recommended that the portion of England's land area covered in forest should rise to 15 per cent by 2060. The UK typically produces around 7.5 million cubic metres of timber per annum. The UK is far from being self-sufficient in timber or wood products, importing up to 90 per cent of its requirements.
The UK is one of the largest markets for forest products in Europe, with consumption per capita remaining around the European average. Most of the internal demand for pulp and sawnwood is met by imports, although the paper industry depends on the large domestic supply of recovered paper.

Industry and manufacturing
The manufacturing industry is centred in northern England and the Midlands.
Heavy industry and mining have steadily declined since the nineteenth century industrial revolution, but more rapidly in recent decades. Regions where heavy industry and manufacturing were once important typically have lower GDP per capita and higher unemployment than in the south-east. Northern England, the Midlands and Wales were dealt several blows between the late 1990s and 2002 as foreign-owned plants, notably in the vehicle manufacturing sector, closed, causing tens of thousands of redundancies. The sector's contribution to GDP has fallen in the last twenty years from over 40 per cent to around 25 per cent.
The government's involvement in industry has decreased since the 1980s. Policy has focused on small- and medium-sized enterprises (SMEs) and on the development of high-tech industry. The government has reformed its subsidies system to the larger industries, including the phased abolition of subsidies to ship-building operations.
The long-awaited turnaround in manufacturing investment has been delayed by rising oil and commodity prices pushing up costs and putting pressure on profit margins.

Tourism
According to the World Tourism Organisation, the UK ranked eighth for international tourist arrivals in 2013, with 31.2 million visitors (France ranked first with about 86 million); London ranked second for international visitors to cities with 15.9 million (Bangkok 16.0 million).
The distinct countries within the UK (England, Scotland, Wales and Northern Ireland) all have separate strategies for marketing their tourist destinations.
The direct contribution of travel and tourism to the economy fell from a high in 2007 of US$66.6 billion and an indirect contribution of US$193.1 billion, to a low in 2009 of US$52.8 billion of direct and US$157.1 billion of indirect contribution at a time when the global economic crisis was affecting all aspects of the economy.
Direct employment in the tourism industry has increased since 2007, from around 3 per cent of all employment to 5.5 per cent in 2013 (1,765,000 jobs). In the same year the tourism industry indirectly employed 12.5 per cent of the workforce (4,020,000 jobs).
Direct contribution to GDP from tourism and travel in 2013 was US$98.2 billion (3.5 per cent of GDP), and indirect contribution was US$292.3 billion (10.5 per cent of GDP). Total contribution to GDP is forecast to rise by 2.5 per cent in 2014.

The London Olympics in 2012 gave a major boost to the economy, not only for the country but also for local communities that host events and visitors. According to the Office for National Statistics (ONS), each of the 590,000 people who visited for the Olympics spent on average GBP1,290 (US$2,212) compared with GBP650 (US$1,115) of other visitors. So there was an increase in revenue on the same month from the previous year from tourism, despite the fact that there was 5 per cent decrease in actual visitors.

Environment

The Carbon Reduction Commitment (CRC) came into effect on 31 March (2010), requiring around 5,000 big businesses and organisations to cut their carbon emissions, by either buying allowances for their emissions or reducing their emissions by a given amount. Those deemed most efficient will be rewarded and those considered least efficient will be penalised; a league table will be published later.

Mining

The UK is a significant producer of zinc, lead and limestone. There are also deposits of silver, copper, gold, iron ore and potash. Lead and tin production typically reach 2,000 tonnes per annum. Potash production is around 890,000 tonnes, placing UK in the top 10 producers in the world. An estimated 14.6 million tonnes of sandstone, 104.6 million tonnes of sand/gravel and 95.7 million tonnes of limestone are also produced.

Hydrocarbons

Prime Minister David Cameron signed a deal with his Norwegian counterpart in 2012 to ensure that Britain could continue to depend on Norway, the third largest oil exporter in the world, for affordable and secure energy supplies. Energy imports from Norway meet a quarter of all of the UK's energy needs. The Langeled pipeline carries natural gas from Norway to the UK; it was once the largest pipeline in the world.

Massive reserves of oil and gas were discovered in the continental shelf under the North Sea in the 1960s, enabling the UK to become a net exporter of hydrocarbons and making it one of the most oil-rich nations in Europe. There are around 25 offshore oil and gas fields, mostly based in the North Sea, including the large Brent and Forties fields. The domestic oil and gas industry is expected to decline as reserves are depleted in the coming decade.

Output and reserves of natural gas, which plays a major role in the country's energy balance, are both rising. The regulatory body of the gas industry, Ofgem, has been instrumental in assisting the gas industry replace coal as the UK's main source for electricity generation.

The UK and Norwegian governments signed a treaty in April 2005 to supply gas from the Ormen Lange fields, off Norway's west coast, and for the joint exploration of Norwegian- and UK-zone oil and gas fields in the North Sea.

A new oil field, off the west coast of the Shetland Islands, was discovered in 2004 with an estimated 500 million barrels. However, as of 2013 a final decision had not been made to proceed with development of the project.

As the major upstream oil producers are pulling out of production in the North Sea, to concentrate on richer sites in Africa and central Asia, many more smaller companies are drilling for harder to obtain oil. These sites are yielding oil that has only become feasible to produce due to the high global oil prices.

Another pipeline, connecting the east of England to Belgium, was increased in capacity in 2007, to 25.5 billion cum per annum from 20.0. This pipeline is bi-directional; meaning it has the capability to facilitate energy trading in both markets.

Due to natural gas production having decreased since it peaked in 2000, the UK has had to find other cheap reliable energy supplies. This led the government to allow a number of liquefied natural gas (LNG) storage facilities to be built in areas of existing hydrocarbon processing. The majority of these have been built in Wales, with the largest (and largest in Europe) facility being the South Hook LNG terminal in Milford Haven in south Wales. This combined with the smaller near by Dragon LNG terminal can handle up to 25 per cent of the UK's gas requirements.

Coal mining has declined far faster than expected since privatisation in 1994, with the growth of gas-fired power stations reducing demand for coal and the strength of sterling making coal imports cheaper. In 2013 there are only three working deep mines left; Hatfield Colliery and Kellingley Colliery in Yorkshire and Thoresby Colliery in Nottinghamshire and these are operating at near capacity.

Coal only accounts for 28 per cent of electricity production and the likelihood of the industry being revitalised to fill the gap in gas and oil supplies is low. Additional coal reserves would take around 15 years to get into production, as new mines would need to be constructed, at an estimated cost of £400 million (US$723 million). Capital investment for new power stations using 'clean-burn' technology would also need to be found as well as new miners to succeed an ageing or re-deployed workforce.

Energy

Total installed generating capacity was 89.2GW in 2012. Around 75 per cent of electricity is generated by conventional thermal power plants (around 50 per cent natural gas, 40 per cent coal, and 10 per cent oil and others), 17.7 per cent nuclear, 4.5 per cent wind and 1.3 per cent hydropower. Although natural gas power stations are replacing those powered by coal the government announced in April 2009 that four new coal-fired power stations equipped with carbon capture and storage will be built by 2020.

The energy sector is wholly privatised with private companies competing for market share. Government policy required companies to produce 10 per cent of generated electricity by renewable sources by 2010. The integrated national grid is also linked to the French and Netherlands grids and the UK imports electricity during times of peak flow. The National Grid is also linked to Ireland, with plans to link others including Belgium, Norway and Denmark.

The largest single producer of power was British Energy (BE) before it was taken over by Électricité de France (EDF) in 2009. At the time of the acquisition BE operated eight nuclear power stations, the majority of which have been given extensions on their operating time. The most modern is the 1,188MW, pressurised-water reactor, Sizewell B, in eastern England. The inclusion of nuclear power in a trinity of renewable energy and clean coal technology is expected to ensure the UK's future energy security while reducing its CO_2 emissions.

In October 2012, the Japanese engineering company Hitachi signed a £700 million (US$1.1 billion) agreement to build a new nuclear power station, part of the UK's expansion programme.

The UK agreed to reduce its emission of greenhouse gases by 12.5 per cent by 2012, which the government considers could be achieved through the use of new technology and renewable energy.

The UK is reported to have Europe's best wind resources. Onshore wind farms in the UK include the 26-turbines site at Scout Moor in north-western England with a generating capacity of 65MW, which was opened in 2008. Europe's largest onshore wind farm was opened in Whitelee, Scotland, in May 2009, with a 215-turbine site that supplies a total capacity of 539MW. In 2014 eight major renewable energy projects were unveiled by the government. These include several large offshore wind farms; a 23-turbine wind farm in the North Sea along the Aberdeenshire Scottish coast and a 341 turbine wind farm off the Essex (south-east) coast which will, during its first phase, produce

630MW. These are stated to provide up to 4.5GW of electricity by 2020. Government policy allows individuals to erect solar panels and wind turbines where appropriate, for private use, with excess electricity sold to the national grid.
Wave power provides electricity to the national grid, from the Pelamis project off the coast of Orkney (Scotland).

Financial markets
Stock exchange
London Stock Exchange (LSE)
Commodity exchange
Liffe Connect

Banking and insurance
The UK's high street banks have been very profitable since the mid-1990s, despite being the focus of criticism. The UK banking sector is generally regarded as highly concentrated, but the rise of internet and telephone banking has put renewed pressure on high street banks. One consequence has been the decision by several leading banks to reduce the number of small branches in areas of low population density.
It is not yet clear whether a radical switch to internet banking will appeal to customers, or whether the combined (so-called 'clicks and mortar') approach will prove more successful). There is evidence that cost-cutting among British banks has given them a better chance of breaking into European markets. Likewise, to compete in a tighter market, banks are being forced into mergers and take-overs. In 2004 the Banco Santander Central Hispano successful bid for the Abbey National Bank in a £8.5bn (US$15.6 billion) deal that created the world's eighth largest and Europe's fourth largest banking group.
Independent financial centres within the UK, Jersey, Guernsey, and the Isle of Man, are adhering to a new EU tax agreement, which was introduced in 2005. They are imposing a withholding tax, up to 35 per cent, to be passed to the tax department of an EU citizen's country, while retaining the anonymity of the saver, instead of informing the relevant EU country about the amount of money in savings accounts and allowing tax to be levied from the home country.
They also supply information on tax fraud, for criminal or civil trials, and notify EU member states about additional malpractices.
In June 2011 the UK government announced that it will require all commercial banks to separate their retail and investment banking operations, so that bank branches and public savings and loans would not suffer if an investment arm were to become insolvent. Retail banks will also be required to hold more capital to underwrite their operations, greater than the new international 7 per cent minimum.
Central bank
Bank of England. Monetary policy and the Exchange Equalisation Account is managed by the Bank of England. In 1997, the government authorised the Bank of England to set interest rates independently.
Main financial centre
The City of London. Edinburgh is the nation's second largest centre.

Time
GMT (daylight saving, late March to late October, GMT plus one hours)

Geography
The UK consists of a major island (divided into England, Wales and Scotland) together with the northern part of the island of Ireland and a number of other smaller islands, including the Channel Islands, the Isle of Man (both dependencies of the Crown) and other islands which are part of the main countries constituting the UK. There are extensive, though not particularly high, mountain and hill ranges in Wales, Scotland and parts of England. The rest of the country includes flatlands (as in East Anglia) and more gently rolling agricultural land.
Hemisphere
Northern

Climate
The climate is temperate, with a reasonable amount of rainfall. Very hot summers or very cold winters, such as are found on continental Europe, are rare. The temperature rarely goes above 25 degrees Celsius (C), or much below zero, except in mountainous regions such as the Scottish highlands. Rainfall is around 75mm per month on average, although it is higher in Scotland at up to an average of 280mm per month. The wettest month is usually November.

Dress codes
In general, British dress codes follow the conventional North American or European pattern. A suit and tie for men and smart attire for women are advisable at most business occasions.

Entry requirements
Passports
Required by all and must be valid for at least six months after the intended departure date.
Visa
Visas are required by all, except nationals of North America, Australasia, Japan and other EU members. For further exceptions and advice visit www.ukvisas.gov.uk (includes application forms). All visas must be applied for before travelling. In October 2013 it was announced that Chinese visitors would be able to visit without a separate visa if they booked a package to Europe though selected travel agencies.
Currency advice/regulations
The import and export of local and foreign currencies is unlimited.
Travellers cheques are widely accepted.
Customs
Personal items are duty-free. There are no duties levied on alcohol and tobacco between EU member states, providing amounts imported are for personal consumption.
Prohibited imports
Illegal drugs, pornography, offensive weapons, counterfiet goods, meat and dairy products.
Firearms require a permit, to be obtained before arrival.

Health (for visitors)
Nationals of the European Economic Area (EEA) countries and Switzerland can access reduced cost and sometimes free medical treatment using a European Health Insurance Card (EHIC) while visiting the EEA. Exceptions include nationals of the 10 countries which joined the EU in 2004 whose EHIC is not valid in Switzerland. Applications for the EHIC should be made before travelling.
Mandatory precautions
There are no mandatory vaccination certificates required, although evidence of good health may be requested if travelling from areas infected with, for instance, yellow fever.
Advisable precautions
There are no major health hazards for foreign visitors. It is recommended that visitors have up-to-date tetanus immunisation.

Hotels
Classified from one- to five-star by AA and RAC (automobile associations), with five being the best. Rating system in Northern Ireland – A star, A, B star, B, C and D. Prices usually includes a 10–15 per cent service charge, but tipping is also expected.

Credit cards
Major credit and charge cards are widely accepted. ATMs are widely available.

Public holidays (national)
Fixed dates
1 Jan (New Year's Day), 2 Jan (Scotland only), 17 Mar (St Patrick's Day) and 12 Jul (Battle of the Boyne, Northern Ireland only), 25–26 Dec (Christmas).
Holidays that fall on the weekend are taken on the following Monday/Tuesday *in lieu*.

Variable dates
Good Friday, Easter Monday, May Day Bank Holiday (first Mon in May), Spring Bank Holiday (last Mon in May) and Summer Bank Holiday (last Mon in Aug). Scotland has an additional public holiday (first Mon in Aug).

Working hours
Banking
Mon–Fri: 0900–1500/1630. Some banks open Saturday morning and there are variations in hours in Scotland and Northern Ireland.
Business
Mon–Fri: usually 0900–1700.
Government
0900–1700 (Mon–Fri). As flexible working hours are often adopted in government departments, it is advisable to make an appointment before a visit.
Shops
Mon–Sat: generally 0900–1730. An increasing number of shops are also taking advantage of Sunday shopping hours (a maximum of 6 hours) and are open 1000–1600 or 1100–1700.

Telecommunications
Mobile/cell phones
There are 3G, 900 and 1800 GSM (including WAP, GPRS, SMS and MMS) services throughout the country and surrounding islands.

Electricity supply
230V AC with flat three-pin plugs.

Social customs/useful tips
A reasonable degree of punctuality is required by those in business. Business cards are usually exchanged at meetings. Gifts are not usually offered to business acquaintances, although when visiting a private home it may be appropriate to take chocolates or wine.
There are few unusual or particularly strict laws. Alcoholic drinks are not allowed into some sporting fixtures, notably soccer matches. Smoking is banned in Scotland and actively discouraged in the rest of the UK in many public places and is banned on all transport services.

Security
Street crime is still much less prevalent in the UK than, for instance, the USA. The police, with a few exceptions, remain unarmed. The number of firearms used in criminal activity is relatively low, although it has increased in recent years.

Getting there
Air
National airline: There are no state-owned airlines, but BA (British Airways) is internationally recognised.
International airport/s: London Heathrow (LHR), 24km west of London is the principal UK airport.
Other satellite airports serve regional cities that provide short-haul international flights. London City (LCY) 10km east of city; London Gatwick (LGW), 46km south of London; London Stansted (STN), 55km north-east of London.
Channel Islands: Guernsey (GCI), 6km south-west of St Peter Port; Jersey (JER), 8km west of St Helier.
Northern Ireland: Belfast International (BFS), 29km north-west of city.
Scotland: Aberdeen (ABZ), 11km north-west of city; Edinburgh (EDI), 11km west of city; Glasgow (Int) (GLA), 14km west of city.
Wales: Cardiff (Int) (CWL), 19km south-west of city.
The Heathrow Express connects Heathrow Airport to west London's Paddington station. Services run, every 15 minutes, between 05.00 and 23.45. The slower London underground connects, initially via the Piccadilly Line, to all mainline stations and city centre.
An extensive airbus service operates from Heathrow airport to the city, including Victoria coach station, Russell Square and Liverpool Street Station.
Rapid train services are available from other London airports to the city centre.
Other airport/s: London Luton (LTN), 51.2km north-west of London; Birmingham International (Int) (BHX), 13km east of city; Bournemouth Int (BOH), Bristol Int (BRS), East Midlands Int (EMA), Humberside Int (HUY), Leeds Bradford Int (LBA), Liverpool John Lennon (LPL), 11km south of Liverpool; Manchester Int (MAN); Newcastle Int (NCL), 8km north-west of Newcastle; Norwich (NWI), Plymouth City (PLH), Southampton Int (SOU), Teeside Int (MME).
Airport tax: All taxes are generally paid within the price of an airline ticket, however a doubling of an environmental tax on all flights leaving the UK may mean passengers are required to pay before boarding.
Surface
Road: There are major road links to all parts of the UK and from the Republic of Ireland to Northern Ireland.
Rail: The newly restored St Pancras International railway station was opened on 6 November 2007; the station is the London terminus for Eurostar, Britain's first high speed train service to Europ. Eurostar connects Paris and Brussels via the channel tunnel, which carries foot and vehicle passengers and freight. The scheduled service operates everyday except Christmas day.
Water: Regular ferry and hovercraft connections with the continent and Ireland.
Main port/s: The main ports are London, Liverpool, Grimsby, Southampton, Milford Haven, Tees and Hartlepool, Dover, Felixstowe, Larne and Holyhead.

Getting about
National transport
Air: Most major cities are linked by regular flights to 21 main commercial airports. A number of small, 'no-frills' airlines have introduced domestic flights that can be very cheap if booked early enough, including connections to Ireland and Scotland and other regional cities.
Road: There is an extensive network of about 370,000km, including 2,800km of motorway, linking all major cities and towns. The M25 circles London as a hub linking other motorways in a network. Traffic can be heavy on these routes, especially as road haulage (wholly in the private sector) use them extensively. Major towns and cities are connected by trunk roads (A roads). Note that roads in rural areas (B roads) can be slow and winding.
Information on planning motorway journeys can be obtained through: www.trafficengland.com
Buses: Express buses between towns and cities are fully in the private sector. Urban and local buses are often still run by local authorities, although private companies operate some routes. For details of services contact www.traveline.org.uk/.
Rail: There is a network of about 18,400km, with relatively expensive first- and second-class services. All principal towns in the UK are connected by regular inter-city services.
Regional companies operate network services. It is advisable to book tickets in advance. These can be obtained on-line (www.thetrainline.com). For more information on UK train services and fare prices, contact: National Rail Enquiries on 0845 748 4950.
Water: There are public and private ferry and car ferry links between Hampshire and the Isle of Wight. Services also provide links with the isles of Scotland, subject to weather conditions, and Northern Ireland. Inshore and inland waterways, are under the control of the British Waterways Board.
City transport
Taxis: Available in all major cities and towns. Taxis can be hailed in the street, at taxi ranks or contacted by telephone.
Taxis may charge extra – over and above the metered charge – depending on the number of passengers, the size of luggage items, for journeys at night and at weekends and for journeys exceeding 8km. Tipping is usually in the region of 10 per cent.
Buses, trams & metro: Extensive network linking all parts of the capital. Central London buses are the only ones still

formally protected from private competition. Good bus services are also available in all other major towns. London is served by an extensive underground rail (metro) system. The new East London Line train service began in April 2010; it has regular services with connections to the Underground service. Reliable metro services also operate in Glasgow, Liverpool, Manchester (Metrolink Rapid Transit Tram) and Newcastle (Tyne and Wear Metro).

Ferry: There are passenger and car ferry services across the Thames in London and the Mersey in Liverpool.

Car hire

Widely available at airports and in main towns. All major international hire firms are represented. International driving licence or full national licence required. Driving is on the left. Speed limits: motorways/dual carriageways maximum 70mph (113kph), normal roads 40-70mph (64-97kph) (signposted) and built-up areas 30 or 40mph (48 or 64kph) (signposted). Speed cameras are in operation on motorways and other roads and imposed fines are usually forwarded as per car rental agreements.

BUSINESS DIRECTORY

The addresses listed below are a selection only. While World of Information makes every endeavour to check these addresses, we cannot guarantee that changes have not been made, especially to telephone numbers and area codes. We would welcome any corrections.

Telephone area codes

The international direct dialling (IDD) code for United Kingdom is +44, followed by area code and subscriber's number. When dialling from within the UK, add a 0 in front of the area codes below.

Aberdeen	1224	London	20
Belfast	2890 2	Manchester	161
Birmingham	121	Newcastle	191
Cambridge	1223	Nottingham	115
Cardiff	2920	Oxford	1865
Coventry	2476	Perth	1738
Dundee	1382	Plymouth	1752
Edinburgh	131	Portsmouth	2392
Exeter	1392	Sheffield	114
Glasgow	141	Southampton	2380
Liverpool	151	Swansea	1792

Useful telephone numbers

Emergency services999

Directory enquiries (BT, fee service) 118-500

International directory enquiries (BT, fee service)118-505

Chambers of Commerce

Birmingham Chamber of Industry and Commerce, 75 Harbourne Road, Birmingham B15 3DH (tel: 454-6171; fax: 455-8670; email: info@birminghamchamber.org.uk).

British Chambers of Commerce, 50 Broadway, St James Park, London SW1H 0RG (tel: 7152-4046; fax: 7565-2049).

Cardiff Chamber of Commerce, Trade and Industry, St David's House East, Wood Street, Cardiff CF10 1ES (tel: 2034-8280; fax: 2037-7653; email: enquiries@cardiffchamber.co.uk).

Edinburgh Chamber of Commerce, 27 Melville Street, Edinburgh EH3 7JF (tel: 477-7000; fax: 477-7002; email: information@ecce.org).

Leeds Chamber of Commerce, 102 Wellington Street, Leeds LS1 4LT (tel: 0113-247-0000; fax: 0113-247-111; email: info@leedschamber.co.uk).

London Chamber of Commerce and Industry, 33 Queen Street, London EC4R 1AP (tel: 7248-4444; fax: 7489-0391; email: lc@londonchamber.co.uk).

Manchester Chamber of Commerce and Industry, Churchgate House, 56 Oxford Street, Manchester M60 7HJ (tel: 237-4102; fax: 237-3277; email: info@mcci.org.uk).

Sheffield Chamber of Commerce and Industry, Albion House, Savile Street, Sheffield S4 7UD (tel: (0)114-201-8888; fax: (0)114-272-0950; email: info@scci.org.uk).

Banking

Abbey National, 2 Triton Square, Regent's Place, London NW1 3AN (tel: 7612-4000; fax: 7612-4230; email: investor@abbeynational.com).

Bank of Scotland, The Mound, Edinburgh EH1 1YZ (tel: 470-7777; fax: 243-5640).

Barclays Bank, 54 Lombard Street, London EC3P 3AH (tel: 7699-5000; fax: 7699-2680).

British Bankers' Association, Pinners Hall, 105-108 Old Broad Street London EC2N 1EX (tel: 7216-8800; fax: 7216-8811).

Chartered Institute of Bankers in Scotland, Drumsheugh House, 38b Drumsheugh Gardens, Edinburgh EH3 7SW (tel: 473-7777; fax:473-7788; email: info@ciobs.org.uk).

Clydesdale Bank, 30 St Vincent Place, Glasgow G1 2HL (tel: 248-7070; fax: 223-2559).

Halifax Plc, Trinity Road, Halifax HX1 2RG (tel: 01422-333-333; fax: 01422-391-777).

HSBC, 10 Lower Thames Street, London EC3R 6AE (tel: 7260-0500; fax: 7260-0501).

Lloyds TSB, 71 Lombard Street, London EC3P 3BS (tel: 7626-1500; fax: 7356-1731).

National Westminster Bank, 135 Bishopsgate, London EC2M 3UR (tel: 7375-5000; fax: 7375-5050).

Royal Bank of Scotland, 36 St Andrew Square, Edinburgh EH2 2YB (tel: 556-8555; fax: 557-6565).

Central bank

Bank of England, Threadneedle Street, London EC2R 8AH (tel: 7601-4444; fax: 7601-5460; internet: www.bankofengland.co.uk).

Stock exchange

London Stock Exchange (LSE), www.londonstockexchange.com

LIFFE (London International Financial Futures and Options Exchange), www.euronext.com

Commodity exchange

Liffe Connect, www.nyse.com/nyseeuronext

European Climate Exchange (ECX), www.europeanclimateexchange.com, London Metal Exchange, www.lme.co.uk

Travel information

Aberdeen Airport, Dyce, Aberdeen AB21 7DU (tel: 1224-722-331; fax: 1224-775-845; email: glal@baa.com).

Belfast International Airport, Aldergrove, Belfast BT 29 4AB (tel: 448-4848; fax: 448-4849; email: info.desk@bial.co.uk).

Birmingham International Airport, Birmingham B26 3QJ (tel: 767-5511; fax: 782-8802; email: custsrvs@bhx.co.uk).

BA, Waterside, PO Box 365, Harmondsworth, Middlesex (tel: 8738-5100; fax: 8738-9838).

Cardiff International Airport, Rhoose CF62 3BD (tel: 1446-711-111; fax: 1446-711-675; email: info@cial.co.uk).

Edinburgh Airport, Edinburgh EH12 9DN (tel: 333-1000; fax: 344 3470; email: glal@baa.com).

Gatwick Airport, West Sussex RH6 0NP (tel: 0870-000-2468; fax: 1293-503-794; email: gatwick_feedback@baa.com).

Glasgow Airport, Paisley, Renfrewshire PA3 2SW (tel: 887-1111; fax: 848-4769; email: glal@baa.com).

Heathrow Airport, 234 Bath Road, Harlington, Middlesex UB3 5AP (tel: 0870-0000-123; fax: 8745-4290; email: lhr1feedback@baa.com).

London City Airport, Royal Docks, London, E16 2PX (customer services tel: 7646-0088; internet: www.londoncityairport.com).

Manchester Airport, Manchester M90 1QX (tel: 489-3000; fax: 489-3813; email: info@manchesterairport.co.uk).

Northern Ireland Tourist Board, 59 North Street, Belfast BT1 1NB (tel: 231-221; fax: 240-960; email: info@nitb.com).

Passport Office, Globe House, 89 Ecclestone Square, London SW1V 1PN (tel: 0870-521-0410; fax: 7271-8403; email: london@ukpa.gov.uk).

Glasgow Prestwick International Airport, Aviation, Prestwick, Ayrshire KA9m 2PL (tel: 1292-511-000; fax: 1292-511-010; email: info@gpia.co.uk).

Stansted Airport, Essex CM24 1QW (tel: 0870-0000-303; fax: 1279-662-066; email: stansted_feedback@baa.com).

VisitScotland, 23 Ravelston Terrace, Edinburgh EH4 3TP (tel: 332-2433; fax: 343-1513; email: info@visitscotland.com).

Wales Tourist Board, Brunel House, 2 Fitzalan Road, Cardiff CF24 0UY (tel: 499-909; fax: 485-031; email: info@visitwales.com).

Ministry of tourism

Department of Culture, Media and Sport, 2-4 Cockspur Street, London SW1Y 5DH (tel: 7211 6200; email: enquiries@culture.gov.uk)

National tourist organisation offices

VisitBritain, Thames Tower, Blacks Road, Hammersmith, London W6 9EL (tel: 8563-3000; fax: 8563-3234; email: comments@englishtourism.org.uk).

Ministries

Cabinet Office, 70 Whitehall, London SW1A 2AS (tel: 7270-1234).

Department of Culture, Media and Sport, 2-4 Cockspur Street, London SW1Y 5DH (tel: 7211-6000; e-mail: enquiries@culture.gov.uk)

Department of Education and Skills, Sanctuary Building, Great Smith Street, London SW1P 3BT (tel: 0870-000-2288; fax: 01928-79-4248; e-mail: info@dfes.gov.uk).

Department of Environment, Food and Rural Affairs, Nobel House, 17 Smith Square, London SW1P 3JR (tel: 7238-6000; fax: 7238-6591).

Department of Health, Richmond House, 79 Whitehall, London SW1A 2NS (tel: 7210-4850; e-mail: dhmail@doh.gsi.gov.uk).

Department of International Development, 94 Victoria Street, London SW1E 5JL (tel: 7917-7000; fax: 7917-0019; e-mail: enquiry@dfid.gov.uk).

Department of Trade and Industry, 1 Victoria Street, London SW1H OET (tel: 7215-5000; e-mail: dti.enquiries@dti.gsi.gov.uk).

Department of Transport, Local Government and Regions, Eland House, Bressenden Place, London SW1E 5DU (tel: 7944-3000).

Department of Work and Pensions, Richmond House, 79 Whitehall, London SW1A 2NS (tel: 7238-0800; fax: 238-0763; peo@dwp.gsi.gov.uk).

Foreign and Commonwealth Office, King Charles Street, London SW1A 2AH (tel: 7270-1500).

Home Office, 50 Queen Annes Gate, London SW1H 9AT (tel: 7273-4000; fax: 7273-2065; e-mail: public.enquiries@homeoffice.gti.gov.uk).

Lord Chancellor's Department, Selborne House, 54-60 Victoria Street, London SW1E 6QW (tel: 7210-8500; e-mail: general.enquiries.@lcdhq.gsi.gov.uk).

Ministry of Defence, Main Building, Horse Guards Avenue, London SW1A 2HB (tel: 0870-607-4455).

Northern Ireland Office, 11 Millbank, London SW1P 4PN (tel: 7210-3000; fax: 7210-0249; e-mail: press.nio@nics.gov.uk).

Prime Ministers Office, 10 Downing Street, London SW1A 2AA (tel: 7270-3000).

Scotland Office, Dover House, London SW1A 2AU (tel: 7270-6754; fax: 7270-6812; e-mail: scottish.secretary@scotland.gov.uk).

Treasury, Parliament Street, London SW1P 3AG (tel: 7270-4558; fax: 7270-5244; e-mail: public.enquiries@hm-treasury.gov.uk).

Wales Office, Gwydyr House, London SW1A 2ER (e-mail: wales.office@wales.gsi.gov.uk).

Other useful addresses

Aberdeen Exhibition and Conference Centre, Bridge of Don, Aberdeen (tel: 1224-824-824; fax:1224-825-276; email: aecc@aecc.co.uk).

Advertising Standards Authority, 2 Torrington Place, London WC1E 7HW (tel: 7580-5555; fax: 7631-3051; email: inquiries@asa.org.uk).

British Council, 10 Spring Gardens, London SW1A 2BN (tel: 7930-8466; fax: 7389-6347; email: general.enquiries@britishcouncil.org).

British Waterways Board, Willow Grange, Church Road, Watford WD17 4QA (tel: 01923-201-120; email: enquiries.hq@britishwaterways.co.uk).

Confederation of British Industry (CBI), Centre Point, 103 New Oxford Street, London WC1A 1DU (tel: 7395-8247; fax: 7240-1578; email: enquiry.desk@cbi.org.uk).

Crown Estate, 16 Carlton House Terrace, London SW1Y 5AH (tel: 7210-4377; fax: 7210-4236; email: pr@crownestate.co.uk).

Customs and Excise, New King's Beam House, 22 Upper Ground, London SE1 9PJ (tel: 7620-1313; fax: 7865-4975; email: enquiries.lon@hmce.gsi.gov.uk).

Guild of Registered Tourist Guides, The Guild House, 52d Borough High Street, London SE1 1XN (tel: 7403-1115; fax: 7378-1705; email: guild@blue-badge.org.uk).

Institute of Export, Export House, Minerva Business Park, Lynch Wood, Peterborough PE2 6FT (tel: 1733-404-400; fax: 1733-404-444; email: institute@export.org.uk).

Institute of Linguists, Saxon House, 48 Southwark Street, London SE1 1UN (tel: 7940-3100; fax: 7940-3101; email: info@iol.org.uk).

London Stock Exchange, Old Broad Street, London EC2N 1HP (tel: 7797-1000; email: enquiries@londonstockexchange.com).

National Exhibition Centre, Birmingham B40 1NT (tel: 780-4141; fax: 780-2517; email: centre-exhibitions@necgroup.co.uk).

Office for National Statistics, 1 Drummond Gate, London SW1V 2QQ (tel: 7233-9233; fax: 7533-6262; email: info@statistics.gov.uk).

Press Complaints Commission, 1 Salisbury Square, London EC4Y 8JB (tel: 7353-1248; fax: 7353-8355; email: pcc@pcc.org.uk).

Trades Union Congress (TUC), Congress House, 23-28 Great Russell Street, London WC1B 3LS (tel: 7636-4030; fax: 7636-0632; email: info@tuc.org.uk).

National news agency: PA Group, 292 Vauxhall Bridge Road, London SE1V 1AE (tel: 120-3200; fax: 120-3201; internet: www.thepagroup.com).

Internet sites

Bank of England: www.bankofengland.co.uk

British Chambers of Commerce: www.britishchambers.org.uk/internet_home_page.htm

Confederation of British Industry: www.cbi.org.uk

Department of Trade and Industry: www.dti.gov.uk

UK Online (UK government gateway): www.ukonline.gov.uk

UK trade information: www.ukinfo.com

United States of America

KEY FACTS

Official name: United States of America

Head of State: President Barack Hussein Obama (Dem) (from 2009; re-elected 6 Nov 2012)

Head of government: President Barack Obama

Ruling party: Republican Party (in House of Representatives) (from 2010); Democratic Party (in the Senate) (from 2006)

Area: 9,300,000 square km

Population: 319.05 million (2014) (308,745,538; 2010, census figure)

Capital: Washington DC

Official language: There is no official language declared in the constitution. English is the *de facto* working language and Spanish is the second, widely spoken, unofficial language.

Currency: US dollar (US$) = 100 cents

Exchange rate: US$1.00 per US$ US$0.73 per euro (Jul 2014)

GDP per capita: US$54,597 (2014)

GDP real growth: 2.39% (2014)

GDP: US$17,418.93 billion (2014)

Labour force: 156.14 million (2014)*

Unemployment: 6.15% (2014)

Inflation: 1.61% (2014)

Oil production: 11.64 million bpd (2014)

Natural gas production: 728.30 billion cum (2014)

Balance of trade: -US$741.46 billion (2014)

* estimated figure

The one thing that amazes most foreign observers about the US Presidential election process is just how long it goes on. With some eighteen months to go, mid-November 2015 saw no less than eight would-be Republican candidates take the stage in Milwaukee for the fourth Republican televised debate. One also ran from the 2012 primaries – Mike Huckabee – the former governor of Arkansas, had already been taken off the race-card. That left Jeb Bush (brother of one former President and son of another), Cuban American Senator Marco Rubio and Senator Ted Cruz.

The fusion of show business with politics was left to businessman Donald Trump. *Wall Street Journal* editor-in-chief Gerard Baker summed up Mr Trump's debating stance as that of the 'annoyed gambler bluffing through a string of weak hands.'

Checking my e-mails

On the Democratic side of the political spectrum, matters were calmer. Serious politics featured more prominently and the show-business quotient was for the most part provided by the Clinton family. To the relief of the Republican Party, one so-called scandal had emerged following the news that in 2009, when Hillary Clinton was about to become Secretary of State she had installed a private e-mail server at her home. To most neutral observers this seemed innocuous enough, but as Mrs Clinton later observed, 'What was supposed to be convenient turned out to be anything but convenient.' Federal law determined that the e-mail information should be handed over to the State Department, which Mrs Clinton did. But before doing so, with her lawyers, she removed a reported 30,000 e-mails from the server on the grounds that they were private. The opinion polls suggested that most Democratic voters had no problem with this, but for the Republicans it represented a chink, perhaps the only one, in Mrs Clinton's electoral armour. The State Department, following normal practice, had handed the matter over to the Federal Bureau of Investigation (FBI), to ascertain whether Mrs Clinton or the e-mails' recipients could be arraigned for the mishandling of secret government information.

Meanwhile, as in October 2015 the presidential debates got under way, the Democrats (predictably) fielded Mrs Clinton as their front runner, alongside a number of make-weights, of whom the only credible contender was Senator Bernard Sanders of Vermont. For the record, the other contenders were Messrs Martin O'Malley, a former governor of Maryland, Lincoln Chafee and Jim Webb. As a state, Vermont had long been considered something of a leader on environmental issues – it was the first US state to abolish roadside billboard advertising. Surprisingly, as the representative of Vermont, Mr Sanders seemed off course when it came to the issue of gun control. In early December, two individuals with Muslim activist backgrounds killed fourteen in San Bernadino, California. This was one of many similar incidents that had taken place over recent years. The national opinion tide – at least within the Democratic Party – seemed to be inching towards some sort of limitation on the freedom to carry a gun. (An academic acquaintance of your correspondent, on moving to a new position in Colorado was horrified to discover that her students were entitled to carry guns in class or in lectures.) However, in the debate, Mr Sanders had rather feebly to explain why it was that on a number of occasions he had voted against greater gun control. In Vermont tradition, Mr Sanders had wished to appear as the ethical candidate *cum laude*; on the issue of gun control, at least, he appeared to be as opportunistic as any politician. (See: Gun Control, below)

Mrs Clinton also had the simple advantage of experience. Writing in the *New Yorker* Steve Coll described her vulnerabilities as a presidential candidate as 'her conspicuous wealth, a self-protecting style and the baggage accumulated during three decades in public life.' Mr Coll went on to note that Mrs Clinton was a 'formidable campaigner – always on message, gaffe-free in debates and town halls, encyclopaedic on

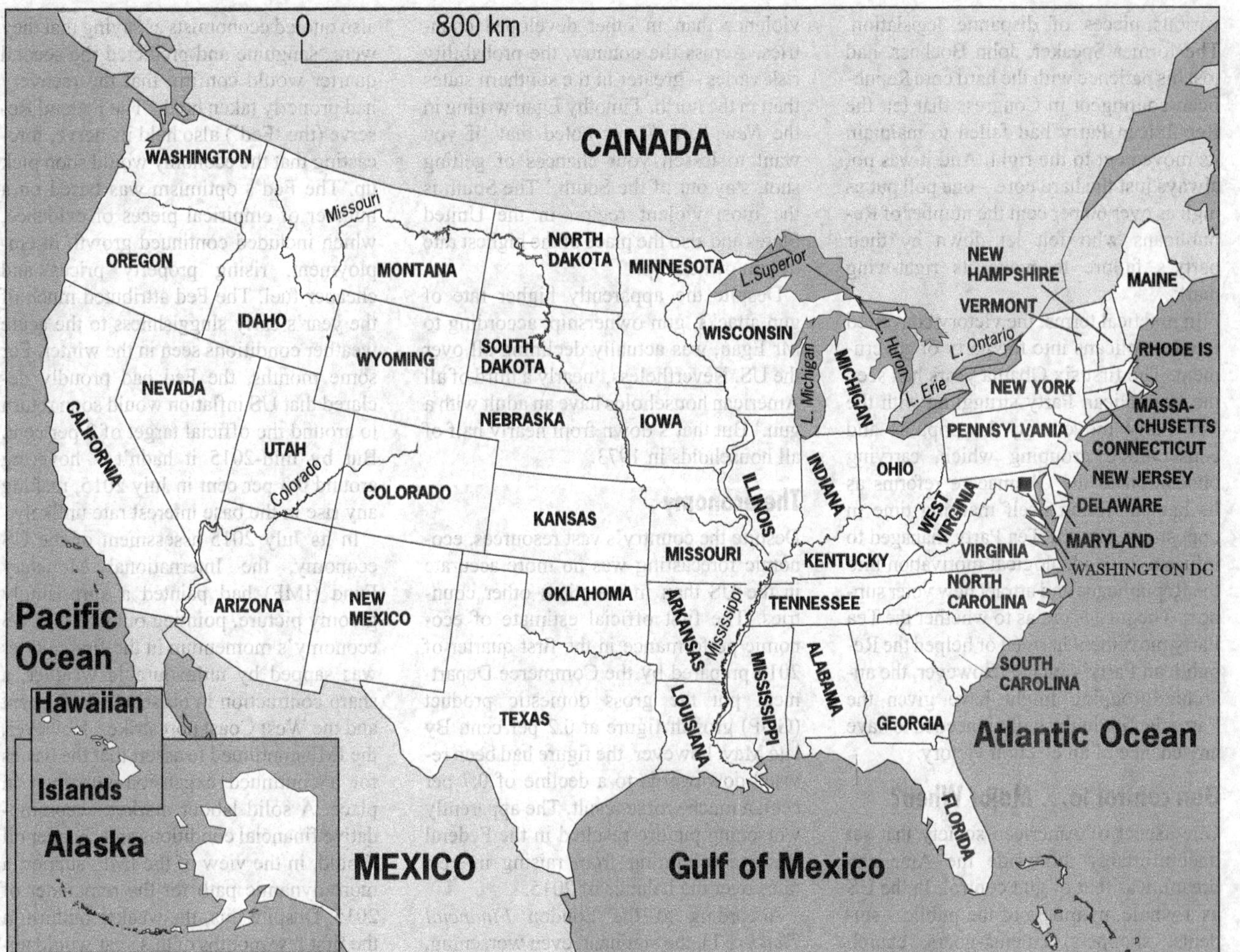

policy and comfortable with confrontation and competition.' She certainly seemed able to dodge the punches on the only issue that weakened her position, that of the use of the alternative server for e-mails, both personal and professional. As the only female 'possible' on both sides of the divide, Mrs Clinton knew which Washington levers to pull and when and how hard. It would be surprising to find out that she was not a die-hard Washington insider. The first Democratic Party presidential debate demonstrated that she was. And how.

In late October Mrs Clinton's candidacy was further strengthened by the decision of the incumbent Vice President, Joe Biden, not to enter the race. Mr Biden had hesitated for some time and finally had to acknowledge that his earlier indecision had effectively made it impossible for him to stand much of a chance. In the interim, Mrs Clinton had lined up most of the obvious major donors and had received the support of most of the Democratic Party's great and good.

Regrets, I've had a few…

President Barack Obama, weakened and seemingly almost semi-retired, had needed to avoid becoming an irrelevancy for the two final years of his term of office, which was due to end in January 2017. In the mid-term elections, the Republicans had conquered the Senate and increased their majority in the House of Representatives. They had also been victorious in a number of states seen as key to the 2016 Presidential Elections. In a press conference, the President in a wise after the event observation, said that 'I have heard you.' He then went on to say that the message of the election was not only important for him, but also for America's right wing. 'The American people expect the people they elect to work as hard as they themselves do, they expect us to heed their ambitions, not our own.'

After the mid-term election defeat, the President, who came to power in 2009 on a wave of optimism, found himself entering what were inevitably limited initiatives. He acknowledged that the game was now with the Republicans. He promised to listen carefully to any proposals put to him by the future Republican majority leader in the Senate, Mitch McConnell, and by Paul Ryan, Speaker of the House of Representatives. Mr Ryan was among those who had originally said they would not be making a bid for the job. Some weeks later, following the change of heart of the House majority leader Kevin McCarthy, the former chairman of the House Budget Committee changed his mind and announced that he would consider the appointment if the party united behind him. It was thought that Mr Ryan's fiscal conservatism may have enabled the hard core Tea Party and the more mainstream wings of the Republican party to agree on his election as speaker. It now fell to Mr Ryan to endeavour to bring them together on various pieces of disparate legislation. The former Speaker, John Boehner, had lost his patience with the hard core Republican contingent in Congress that felt the Republican Party had failed to maintain its movement to the right. And it was not always just the hard core – one poll put as high as over 60 per cent the number of Republicans who felt let down by their party's failure to make its right-wing mark.

In practical terms, the victory converted the Republicans into the party of government. The first six Obama years had seen the Republican Party struggling with the Tea Party movement, the populist and conservative grouping which, carrying opposition to the Obamacare reforms as its banner, found itself marking time in opposition. But the Tea Party managed to infuse a fresh ideological motivation into the Republicans and attract new voter support. The jury is out as to whether the Tea Party movement harmed or helped the Republican Party's image. However, the anarchic grouping might have given the Party the fire in the belly it needed to have any chance of an election victory.

Gun control to… Major When?

One aspect of American society that sat uncomfortably alongside the American dream, was that of gun control. In the US as a whole, members of the public – students, shoppers, cinema-goers, church worshippers, the list is long – are twenty times more likely to be killed by gun violence than in other developed countries. Across the country, the probability risk varies – greater in the southern states than in the north. Timothy Egan writing in the *New York Times* noted that 'if you want to lessen your chances of getting shot, stay out of the South.' The South is the most violent region in the United States and also the place of the highest rate of gun ownership.

Despite the apparently higher rate of gun attacks, gun ownership, according to Mr Egan, was actually declining all over the US. Nevertheless, 'nearly a third of all American households have an adult with a gun.' But that's down from nearly half of all households in 1973.

The economy

Despite the country's vast resources, economic forecasting was no more accurate in the US than in countless other countries. The first official estimate of economic performance in the first quarter of 2015 prepared by the Commerce Department put the gross domestic product (GDP) growth figure at 0.2 per cent. By late May, however, the figure had been revised downwards to a decline of 0.7 per cent, a much worse result. The apparently worsening picture resulted in the Federal Reserve refraining from raising interest rates over the balance of 2015.

According to the London *Financial Times* (FT), the stagnant, even worsening, economic picture also reflected the effect of a still high, overvalued, dollar. The FT also quoted economists as saying that they were 'sanguine and predicted the second quarter would confirm that the recovery had properly taken hold.' The Federal Reserve (the 'Fed') also held its nerve, forecasting that the economy would soon pick up. The Fed's optimism was based on a number of empirical pieces of evidence, which included continued growth in employment, rising property prices and cheaper fuel. The Fed attributed much of the year's early sluggishness to the acute weather conditions seen in the winter. For some months, the Fed had proudly declared that US inflation would soon return to around the official target of 2 per cent. But by mid-2015 it hadn't – hovering around 0.3 per cent in July 2015, making any rise in the base interest rate unlikely.

In its July 2015 assessment of the US economy, the International Monetary Fund (IMF) had painted a surprisingly gloomy picture, pointing out that the 'US economy's momentum in the first quarter was sapped by unfavourable weather, a sharp contraction in oil sector investment and the West Coast port strike.' However, the IMF continued to assert that the basics for a continued expansion remained in place. A solid labour market, accommodative financial conditions and cheaper oil should, in the view of the IMF, support a more dynamic path for the remainder of 2015. Despite this, the weaker outturn in the first few months of this year would unavoidably pull down 2015 growth, which was projected at 2.5 per cent. Stronger growth over the next few years was expected to return output to its potential before it began to decline again, down to two per cent over the medium term.

The IMF noted that Inflation pressures remained muted. In May, the headline and core personal consumption expenditure inflation had declined to 0.2 and 1.2 per cent year over the year, respectively. Long-term unemployment and high levels of part-time work both pointed to continued employment slack and wage indicators for the most part had shown only tepid growth. When combined with the dollar appreciation and cheaper energy costs, inflation was expected by the IMF to rise slowly starting in late 2015 and reaching the Federal Reserve's two per cent medium-term objective by mid-2017.

However, an important risk to growth was any further US dollar appreciation. The appreciation of the currency had been rapid, reflecting cyclical growth divergences, different trajectories for monetary policies among the systemically important economies and a portfolio shift

KEY INDICATORS — United States of America

	Unit	2011	2012	2013	2014	**2015
Population	m	*311.95	314.15	*316.74	*319.05	*321.24
Gross domestic product (GDP)	US$bn	15,094.00	16,244.58	16,768.05	17,418.93	*18,124.73
GDP per capita	US$	48,387	51,709	52,939	54,597	*56,421
GDP real growth	%	1.7	2.8	2.2	2.4	*3.1
Inflation	%	3.1	2.1	1.5	1.6	*0.1
Unemployment	%	8.9	8.1	7.4	6.2	*5.5
Oil output	'000 bpd	7,841.0	8,905.0	10,003.0	11,644.0	–
Natural gas output	bn cum	651.3	681.4	687.6	728.3	–
Coal output	mtoe	556.8	515.9	500.5	507.8	–
Exports (fob) (goods)	US$m	1,500,920	1,561,910	1,590,320	1,632,640	–
Imports (fob) (goods)	US$m	2,235,820	2,302,710	2,293,570	2,734,100	–
Balance of trade	US$m	-734,900	-740,800	-703,260	-741,460	–
Current account	US$m	-465,920	-440,417	-400,255	-410,627	*-410,178
Total reserves minus gold	US$m	131,130.0	139,130.0	133,530.0	119,050.0	–
Foreign exchange	US$m	53,378.6	49,920.0	47,600.0	–	–

* estimated figure ** forecast figure

toward US dollar assets. Lower oil prices and increasing energy independence had contained the US current account deficit, despite the cyclical growth divergence with respect to its main trading partners and the rise in the US dollar. Nevertheless, over the medium term, at current levels of the real exchange rate, the current account deficit was forecast to widen toward 3.5 per cent of GDP.

Despite important policy uncertainties, the near term fiscal outlook had improved and the federal government deficit was likely to move modestly lower in the current fiscal year. Following a temporary improvement, the federal deficit and debt-to-GDP ratios were, however, expected to begin rising again over the medium term as ageing-related pressures asserted themselves and interest rates normalised. In the near-term, the potential for disruption from either a government shutdown or a stand-off linked to the federal debt ceiling represented important (and avoidable) downside risks to growth and job creation that might move to the forefront, once again, later in 2015.

The IMF underlined the importance of the fact that much had been done over the previous several years to strengthen the US financial system. However, the search for yield during the prolonged period of low interest rates, rapid growth in assets in the non-bank sector and signs of stretched valuations across a range of asset markets pointed to one or two emerging pockets of vulnerabilities. The IMF considered that the more serious risks were likely to be linked in the first place to the migration of intermediation to the non-banks; secondly, the potential for insufficient liquidity in a range of fixed income markets that could lead to abrupt moves in market pricing finally, from life-insurance companies that had taken on greater market risk. But several factors mitigated these risks. In particular, the US banking system had strengthened its capital position and appeared resilient to a range of extreme market and economic shocks. In addition, overall leverage did not appear excessive, household and corporate balance sheets looked generally healthy and credit growth had been modest.

Writing in the *New York Times*, Albert H Hunt struck a more positive note, pointing out that if you believed the broader political discussion, you could be forgiven for assuming that the American economy was in dreadful shape. Mr Hunt noted that 'The economy invariably becomes a political target when there was no White House incumbent running for re-election.' In his view, things weren't quite so bad: 'Unemployment was down to 5.3 per cent, from 10 per cent in President Obama's first year in office. GDP was expanding at a clip, a modest pace, but growth nonetheless. The federal deficit was estimated at US$486 billion in 2015, or about a third of what it was in 2008. Despite all the concerns about the affordable care act (aka 'Obamacare') 15 million more Americans are covered than two years ago.'

Mr Hunt rightly noted that when faced with the run-up to an election, it fell upon the opposition party to talk about how bad things were and submit its ideas for change. It was more difficult for the incumbent party, which both had to defend their record while promising something new. However hard they listened to the views of political commentators, as well as to the politicians themselves, most of the electorate almost certainly saw things differently. Most had yet to experience any real recovery from the crisis of seven years earlier; wages remained low and many labour contracts were neither permanent nor full time, creating both insecurity and poverty.

Energy

Dominated by its enormous hydrocarbon reserves, the energy industry has played an important role in the development of the US. In 2014 the US had become the world's largest producer of oil and also, according to the British oil company BP, became the first country ever to increase oil production by more than 1 million barrels per day (bpd) for three consecutive years. In the same year, the US set a new country record for oil production at 11.6 million bpd, passing its previous 1970 record of 11.3 million bpd. US natural gas production also reached a new record high (728.3 billion cubic metres (bcm) for the fourth consecutive year. At the same time and for the second consecutive year, the US recorded above-average domestic energy consumption growth. And despite the naysayers as the price per barrel fell to record lows, in 2015 American oil production had actually risen slightly, reaching 9.6 million bpd in June.

Increasing consumption of natural gas (+2.9 per cent), renewables in power (+10.8 per cent), oil (+0.5 per cent) and nuclear (+1.0 per cent), outweighed declines in hydro (-3.7 per cent) and coal (-0.3 per cent). Oil remained the dominant fuel, accounting for 36 per cent of US energy consumption. Oil consumption in 2014 was 1.8 million bpd lower than the record high set in 2005. Natural gas consumption (30 per cent of US energy consumption) increased for the fifth consecutive year and set a new record high at 759.4bcm. The US remained the world's largest consumer of gas (23 per cent of global consumption). Coal consumption (20 per cent of US energy consumption), declined slightly in 2014 to 453 million tonnes oil equivalent (mtoe). Renewables in power (3 per cent of US consumption) have expanded every year since 2001. Hydro (3 per cent of US consumption) declined for the third consecutive year in 2014. Energy intensity (the amount of energy required per unit of GDP) declined by 1.1 per cent in 2014, slightly slower than the ten-year average of -1.7 per cent.

US production growth of oil (+15.9 per cent), natural gas (+6.1 per cent), coal (+1.4 per cent), renewables in power (+10.8 per cent), nuclear (+1.0 per cent) and biofuels (+5.6 per cent), outweighed declines in hydro (-3.7 per cent). Primary energy production grew by 6.5 per cent (+124mtoe) in 2014, the largest increase in US history, surpassing the previous 1984 record. Domestic production was sufficient to meet 89 per cent of domestic consumption. US oil production increased by 1.6 million bpd in 2014, the largest annual increase in US history and the fourth-largest increase in the history of the world. Natural gas production increased by 39.2bcm in 2014, the largest growth in the world last year and the second largest in US history (after 2011). US net oil imports fell by 1.1 million bpd to 5.1 million bpd, the lowest level since 1985. Natural gas imports fell by 3.5bcm to 33.6bcm, the lowest level since 1986.

Shale on you

In June the price of a barrel of oil, then almost US$115, began to slide; to close to US$70. By mid-December it was US$40. This plunge was thanks partly to the sluggish world economy, which was consuming less oil than markets had anticipated and partly to OPEC itself, which had produced more than markets expected. But the main culprits were the oilmen of North Dakota and Texas. Over the previous four years, as the price hovered around US$110 a barrel, they had set about extracting oil from shale formations previously considered unviable. Their manic drilling – they had completed perhaps 20,000 new wells since 2010, more than ten times Saudi Arabia's tally – had boosted America's oil production by a third, to nearly 9 million bpd. That was just 1 million bpd short of Saudi Arabia's output. The contest between the shalemen and the sheikhs has tipped the world from a shortage of oil to a surplus.

Cheaper oil was expected to act like a shot of adrenalin to global growth. A US$40 price cut shifted some US$1.3 trillion from producers to consumers. The typical American motorist, who spent US$3,000 in 2013 at the pumps, might be US$800 a year better off – equivalent to a two per cent pay rise. Big importing countries such as the euro-zone, India, Japan and Turkey were enjoying especially big windfalls. Since this money was likely to be spent rather than stashed in a sovereign-wealth fund, global GDP should rise. The falling oil price would reduce already-low inflation still further and so might encourage central bankers towards looser monetary policy. The Federal Reserve would put off raising interest rates for longer; the European Central Bank would act more boldly to ward off deflation by buying sovereign bonds.

There would, of course, be losers. Oil-producing countries whose budgets depended on high prices were in particular trouble. The Saudis seemed to be adopting a different tactic: let the price fall and put high-cost producers out of business. That should soon crimp supply, causing prices to rise. There were signs that such a shake-out was already under way. The share prices of firms that specialised in shale oil had been falling. Many of them were deeply endebted. Even before the oil price started falling, most were investing more in new wells than they were making from their existing ones. With their revenues now dropping fast, they would find themselves over-stretched. A rash of bankruptcies was likely. That, in turn, would diminish shale oil's reputation among investors. Even survivors might find the markets closed for some time, forcing them to rein in their expenditure to match the cash they generated from selling oil. Since shale-oil wells were short-lived (output could fall by 60–70 per cent in the first year), any slowdown in investment would quickly translate into falling production.

This shake-out was likely to be painful. But in the long run the shale industry's future seemed assured. Fracking, in which a mixture of water, sand and chemicals was injected into shale formations to release oil, was a relatively young technology and it was still making big gains in efficiency. IHS, a research firm, estimated that the cost of a typical project had fallen from US$70 per barrel produced to US$57 in the previous year, as oilmen had learned how to drill wells faster and to extract more oil from each one. The firms that had weathered the current storm would have masses more shale to exploit. Drilling was just beginning (and might now be cut back) in the Niobrara formation in Colorado, for example and the Mississippian Lime along the border between Oklahoma and Kansas.

The Middle East

The September 2015 arrival of Russian forces in Syria left the US-lead coalition looking less than clever. The *raison d'être* of the coalition had always been the reversal, if not the destruction of the so-called Islamic State (IS) presence in Syria and Iraq. At first sight the Kremlin appeared to share this objective, but it soon emerged that the principal objective was to shore up the government forces of the discredited Bashar al Assad. That the US was nervous of any military engagement in the Middle East went without saying. The first term of the Obama Presidency had focussed on the final withdrawal from Iraq; the second on disengaging from Afghanistan, which electorally was a double edged sword. Some voters perceived withdrawal to be applauded as a common sense initiative, others as a further sign of US military weakness and indecision. President Putin's arrival on the scene risked ending the American hegemony in the Middle East that had prevailed since the former Soviet Union withdrew from Afghanistan and (the then) South Yemen in the 1970s.

In simple terms, the Russian media had described the despatch of the Russian air force to Syria as a ruse to force the US to recognise Russia not as a regional adversary, but as an 'equal partner'. The end-game was to end the US lead isolation of Russia following the annexation of Crimea and its messy attempts to destabilise Ukraine. Quoted in the *Economist*, Alexander Baunov of the Carnegie Moscow Centre described it as 'an attempt to turn the page and achieve reconciliation with the West not by crawling to it on its knees, but by presenting Russia as an influential and indispensable power. '

Despite the grandiose promises made during and following, his inaugurations President Obama did not seem to relish the challenge of international affairs. On a number of key occasions he had shown himself to be hesitant, indecisive and even devious (possibly when seeking to avoid embarrassment). He apparently saw the US armed forces not as something to be deployed at the outset as a deterrent to conflict, but more often as the last ditch solution to a problem that had got out of hand and, crucially, might affect US interests. Much of the blame that was heaped on the President was ill-informed, wrong and plain mistaken. Even where the criticism was not distorted by ideological factors, the President was judged through an unfavourable political and even occasionally racial spectrum. Presidential power might be enormous, but there still existed the checks and balances that were able to thwart any US President, whatever his political allegiance.

Risk assessment

Economy	Good
Politics	Good
Regional stability	Good

COUNTRY PROFILE

1700s As the eighteenth century progressed, an increasing number of European settlers arrived. British attempts to assert authority over its 13 North American colonies led to conflicts with the French and the indigenous population. In order to recoup losses after winning the conflict the British imposed higher taxes (which lead to the slogan 'no taxation without representation'); civil unrest followed and the first stirrings of an independence movement.

1776 Independence from Britain was declared by the colonies.

1781 Rebel states set up a loose confederation, codified in Articles of Confederation, after defeating the British at the Battle of Yorktown.

1783 The British accepted the loss of their colonies under the Treaty of Paris.

1787 The 'founding fathers' drew up the constitution, which created a federal structure for the United States of America.

1788 The constitution came into effect.

1789 George Washington was elected the first US president.

1800s During the nineteenth century, populations expanded across the plains to the west coast. By 1850, a combination of land purchases, war and diplomacy had created much of the modern-day US. After 1850, immigrants began arriving from all over the world, mainly attracted by the industrial jobs in the north. The south remained committed to agriculture and the use of slaves.

1860 When the abolitionist Abraham Lincoln became president, the south seceded from the north and civil war was declared in 1861.

1865 The north won the civil war, but after Lincoln's assassination blacks in the

south remained disenfranchised and segregated.
1898 The US's emergence as a world power was demonstrated when Spain lost control of its colonies in Cuba, Guam, the Philippines and Puerto Rico, after being defeated in Cuba by the US.
1914 The US declared its neutrality at the start of the First World War.
1917 The US declared war on Germany after a torpedo attack on the passenger vessel *Lusitania* a year earlier. Over one million US troops had served on the Allied side by the time the war ended in 1918.
1929 The Wall Street crash resulted in a lengthy economic recession referred to as the 'Great Depression'.
1941 After remaining neutral at the outbreak of the Second World War in 1939, the US declared war on the Axis powers following the Japanese air attack on Pearl Harbour.
1944 The US led the Allied liberation of Nazi-occupied Western Europe.
1945 Following the victory in Europe, the US dropped two atomic bombs on the Japanese cities of Hiroshima and Nagasaki, ending the Pacific War.
1947–50s The US's Marshall Plan was instrumental in the rebuilding of post-war Western Europe and Japan, providing financial aid. The Cold War emerged between the capitalist US and Western Europe and the communist Soviet Union and its Eastern European bloc.
1950–53 The US led a UN military force against communist North Korea after it had invaded South Korea. The Chinese intervened on the side of the North Koreans. A cease-fire was agreed in 1953, but no peace treaty was ever signed.
1962 Tensions between the Soviet Union and the US reached a climax during the Cuban missile crisis.
1963 John F Kennedy, the first Catholic and youngest-ever US president, was assassinated in Dallas, Texas in November. Vice President Lyndon B Johnson became president.
1964–73 The US was embroiled in the Vietnam War. The US government provided South Vietnam with military assistance against communist North Vietnam, but was forced to withdraw in 1973 when the war was lost and there was mounting domestic opposition to the high number of casualties.
1974 President Richard Nixon, who was elected in 1969, was forced to resign over the Watergate scandal involving a break-in at Democrat headquarters; tape recordings made in the White House showed he had sanctioned the burglary and subsequent cover-up. Vice President Gerald Ford became president.
1970s and 1980s was a period of great technological advancement and declining industrialisation when US corporations became worldwide leaders and US brands in computers, fast-food and entertainment became global brands. The collapse of the Soviet Union by 1991 left the US as the world's sole superpower.
1979 Iranian students attacked the US embassy in Tehran and held 63 hostages for 444 days. A failed military rescue mission in 1980 damaged the chances of incumbent Jimmy Carter winning the 1980 presidential election.
1980 Ronald Reagan became president. As a conservative popularist his policies were based on reducing federal services and cutting tax, particularly for high-income earners, later dubbed Reagonomics.
1988 George H W Bush won the presidential election.
1989 US troops invaded Panama to oust General Manuel Noriega from power.
1991 In the first Gulf War, a US-led coalition forced Iraq to withdraw from Kuwait.
1992 The Democratic Party (D) candidate Bill Clinton defeated the Republican Party (R) incumbent, George Bush, in presidential elections.
1995 A bomb in Oklahoma killed over 160 people; it was the worst case involving domestic terrorists in US history.
1996 Clinton was re-elected president.
1999 The US led a NATO military campaign against Yugoslavia in response to Serbian violence towards ethnic Albanians in the Kosovo region.
2000 George W Bush was elected president but only after controversial vote counting was declared valid by Florida's Supreme Court.
2001 On 11 September, two passenger jets were flown into the twin towers of the World Trade Centre in New York, demolishing both towers. A third jet was crashed into the Pentagon in Washington. In all, 3,025 people died in the attacks. President Bush declared a 'war on terrorism'. The US launched military action in Afghanistan against the Taliban and Osama bin Laden's extreme Islamist al Qaeda group, blamed for being behind the terrorist attacks. The giant energy provider Enron declared bankruptcy when massive accountancy frauds were uncovered.
2002 President Bush described Iran, Iraq and North Korea as part of an 'axis of evil'. A multi-billion dollar accounting fraud in WorldCom became the biggest failure in US business history to date. The Department of Homeland Security was formed with a remit to protect the US against terrorist attacks.
2003 The space shuttle Columbia broke-up on re-entry killing its crew of seven astronauts. A US-led coalition invaded Iraq. Within two months President Bush declared that 'major combat operations in Iraq have ended'.
2004 The US restored diplomatic relations with Libya after a break of 24 years. Former president, Ronald Reagan died. A Senate report declared the war on Iraq was based on 'flawed' information. Institutional failings in intelligence agencies and the government were held to be responsible for the failure to prevent the 11 September 2001 attack. George W Bush was re-elected president.
2005 New Orleans was devastated by hurricane Katrina; hundreds of people died and thousands made homeless.
2006 The Supreme Court ruled that it would be unconstitutional for Guantanámo Bay prisoners to be tried by military tribunals. Former president Gerald Ford died.
2007 The collapse of the sub-prime loans market had a knock-on effect on all major US banks with total losses estimated at US$500 billion. A credit squeeze began and spread abroad.
2008 The government was forced to extend lines of credit for Fanny Mae and Freddy Mac (institutions mandated by the US Congress to provide funding to the housing market), to meet their financial obligations. One of the largest independent US banks, Lehman Brothers, filed for bankruptcy with losses of US$3.9 billion, with a further US$138 billion lost in Federal Reserve-backed advances. The financial crisis deepened in domestic and international markets as the House of Representatives (congress) delayed agreement in funding a US$700 billion rescue plan. In presidential elections, Barack Obama (D) won with 52.7 per cent of the vote on a turnout of 64 per cent. The Democrats also won a majority in the Congress and the Senate. The world's leading economies, the Group of 20 (G20), agreed to co-ordinate action to stimulate economic growth.
2009 Barack H Obama was inaugurated as president and quickly moved to approve the American Recovery and Reinvestment Act. The US$787 billion stimulus package (totalling over US$2 trillion since 2008) was designed to stabilise the financial and banking sectors. An additional 17,000 military troops were deployed to Afghanistan; 38,000 personnel were already deployed and expected to remain until at least 2012. President Obama's US$3.6 trillion budget for 2010 was published and approved by Congress. President Obama committed a further 30,000 US troops to Afghanistan, bringing US military strength to 100,000. Other foreign troops totalled around 32,000 at the end of 2009.
2010 The US announced that people travelling from or through 14 countries

(Afghanistan, Algeria, Iraq, Lebanon, Libya, Nigeria, Pakistan, Saudi Arabia, Somalia, Cuba, Iran, Sudan, Syria and Yemen) would be subject to extra screening measures, including pat-downs, scanning and the inspection of hand luggage. The *Patient Protection and Affordable Care Act* (PPACA; commonly referred to as Obamacare) was signed in March, sparking widespread political and public protest. Twenty six states objected to the reforms, in particular the 'individual mandate' that requires all adult Americans must buy healthcare insurance or pay a fine, claiming the act challenged the constitution. The 2010 census took. The US and Russia signed another nuclear disarmament treaty in Prague (Czech Republic). The treaty limits the number of warheads and launchers each country may possess. The signing took place only after the US scrapped previous plans for a 'missile shield' based in Eastern Europe that Russia considered provocative. BP's Deepwater Horizon oil well off the Louisiana coast ruptured creating the largest oil spill in US history. Over 90,000 records compiled by the military concerning their operational involvement in Afghanistan, including previously hidden details, were leaked and published on the internet. The US placed a ban on all cargo from Yemen, following the discovery of improvised bombs sent by agents of al Qaeda. In mid-term elections, the Republicans won 243 seats (out of 435) in congress, while in the senate, despite losing six seats, the Democrats retained a majority of 51 seats (out of 100) and two incumbent independents voting with the Democrats. President Obama signed a landmark law allowing gay people serving in the military to be open about their sexuality.

2011 In March a two year freeze on new military trials for detainees at the Guantanamo Bay prison was lifted. In March, the US joined in a five-country coalition (Canada, France, Italy and the UK) to impose a no-fly zone over Libya. The 2010 census showed that Hispanics outnumbered African Americans for the first time in most metropolitan areas. Osama Bin Laden, the leader of al Qaeda, was shot dead by US military special forces in his fortified hideout on the outskirts of Abbottabad in north-west Pakistan in May. His body was flown first to Afghanistan and then buried at sea. The Nasa Shuttle programme ended in May, when its last shuttle returned from the space-station to earth; it was a victim of government budget cuts. In June the Defence Secretary confirmed that 'preliminary' talks between the US and the Taliban in Afghanistan had taken place. In June President Obama announced the withdrawal of 10,000 US troops from Afghanistan in 2011 and another 23,000 by the end of September 2012. The US Joint Chief of Staff, Admiral Mullens stated to a US Senate inquiry, in September, that the militant Islamist Haqqani Network (allied to the Taliban), for one, acts as a veritable arm of Pakistan's Inter-Services Intelligence Agency' (ISIA). He referred to two terrorist attacks, one on coalition troops and the other on the US embassy, both in Kabul and in September, of which, he said the Haqqani Network had support from the ISIA. Trade agreements with South Korea, Panama and Colombia were agreed by both houses of congress in October. The agreement with South Korea was the biggest deal since the Nafta agreement of 1994. President Obama said the deals would safe-guard American jobs and boost foreign trade. The US military operations in Iraq were formally ended on 18 December, as the last 4,000 soldiers left (200 soldiers remained as advisors). However, 15,000 US personnel remain in the world's largest embassy, the US embassy in Bagdad.

2012 The defence secretary announced on 1 February that the US will seek to wind down combat operations in Afghanistan in 2013. On 16 April, US-citizen Jim Yong Kim was appointed as president of the World Bank. In April the governments of the US and Japan reached an agreement whereby around 9,000 US marines will be relocated outside Japan, leaving a force of 10,000 on the island of Okinawa. The final date of closure of the USAF Futenma airbase on Okinawa remains to be decided. On 28 June the Supreme Court dismissed the challenges of the 26 states to the PPACA and designated the act as constitutional. However, the ruling stated that Congress could place conditions on the use of federal funds to provide Medicaid (a healthcare programme for low-income citizens). US astronaut, Neil Armstrong, the first man to walk on the moon, died on 26 August, aged 82. On 25 September President Obama, in an address to the UN General Council, condemned extremism, saying that is was 'the obligation of all leaders to speak out forcefully against violence and extremism'. The largest ever recorded hurricane (later downgraded to a post-tropical cyclone) struck the east coast of the US, south of Jersey City, on 29 October. It was over 1,600 kilometres in diameter with wind speed up to 120kph. The cyclone caused storm surges of up to 4 metres, which caused extensive damage to low-lying regions along the eastern seaboard. Around one million people were evacuated from all states within its path while electricity to 6.2 million residents and 29 hospitals was cut. Presidential elections took place on 6 November, which was won by incumbent Barack Obama with 50.6 per cent; Mitt Romney (Rep) won 47.9 per cent. Of the 33 seats in the senate elections, the Democrats won 21 seats (for a total of 53 seats, out of 100), Republicans 10 (total 45 seats), independents (voting with Democrats) two. In elections for the House of Representatives, the Republican Party won 243 seats (out of 435), Democratic Party 200 seats. As the year ended the so-called 'fiscal cliff' loomed as Congress debated the relative merits of tax cuts v increased spending.

2013 A financial crisis was narrowly averted as compromise rather than consensus turned out to be the order of the day in Congress. After a number of false starts, the very beginning of the 2013 New Year saw Congress approve a mixture of tax rises and spending cuts, thereby avoiding the dreaded fiscal clff. Two home-made bombs went off near the finish of the Boston Marathon on 15 April. Three people were killed and 264 injured. Two Chechen brothers were identified; one was shot while being arrested and the younger brother was captured and charged with the bombing. The trial of US Army Private Bradley Manning on spying charges ended on 30 July with the judge finding him guilty on 20 charges including theft and computer fraud, but not guilty on the most serious charge of aiding the enemy. On 1 August the American Edward Snowden, who had been sheltering in Moscow's Sheremetyevo Airport since 23 June, was granted a one year passport with permission to stay. The Americans expressed annoyance that asylum was granted to a man who had been charged with leaking documents showing the extent of US government snooping and said they were 'reconsidering' a meeting scheduled for September between President Obama and President Putin at the G20 economic talks to be held in St Petersberg. The meeting was cancelled on 7 August and the Russians expressed 'disappointment.' Intercepted conversations between two senior al Qaeda figures prompted the closure of 19 US embassies and consulates in North Africa and the Middle East for a week from 4 August. On 9 August 'non-emergency' staff were withdrawn from the US consulate general in Lahore, Pakistan, although the move was said not to be connected to the earlier closures. 18 of the embassies were reopened on 12 August; the embassy in Sana'a remained closed. On 24 August thousands of people gathered at the Lincoln Memorial in Washington DC to commemorate 50 years since Martin Luther King's 'I have a dream…' civil rights speech. Vice President Joe Biden said on

27 August that there was 'no doubt' the Syrian government had used chemical weapons on it's people and it must be held accountable. On 31 August President Obama said he would formally ask Congress to authorise military action against Syria. However, it became obvious that despite Mr Obama's efforts Congress would probably not authorise military action. Presidents Obama and Putin held discussions at the G20 meeting in St Petersburg which apparently lead to a Russian proposal that Syria should surrender all its chemical weapons. It appeared that Syria would agree to the proposal. On 10 September President Obama gave a televised speech to the nation confirming he had postponed asking Congress to authorise the use of force, while at the same time setting out a binding set of circumstances that would need to be followed by Syria. In an article published in the *New York Times* on 11 September Russian President Putin made an appeal to the American people over the Syrian crisis the day before a scheduled meeting between Russian and US officials on Syria's chemical weapons. In an 'opinion' article he said that millions of people see the US not as a model of democracy but as relying on brute force. A hand shake between President Rouhani of Iran and President Obama did not materialise during Mr Rouhani's visit to the UN in September, but a 15-minute telephone call was said to be cordial. Part of the US government shut down on 1 October after Congress failed to agree on the new budget; the Republicans were demanding the repeal or delay of the Obamacare law, signed into law in March 2010. President Obama stood his ground, accusing the Republicans of holding the government to ransom. The President initially cancelled the last two stops (Malaysia and the Philippines) on his Asian tour starting 5 October, and later the whole tour. He will nolonger attend an Asia-Pacific Economic Co-operation (Apec) summit meeting in Bali and an East Asian summit in Brunei. Secretary of state, John Kerry said that nevertheless US commitment to Asia remained undiminished. On 8 October the President offered to talk with the Republicans, but not until they agreed to lift 'threats' against the economy; earlier, Republican House Speaker John Boehner had told reporters he was 'disappointed that the president refuses to negotiate'. Talks to avert the debt crisis were held between Presdent Obama and Republican leaders on 10 October. After talks held on 14 October both sides reported they were inching towards a deal. After several more hiccoughs, and with just hours to spare, a deal was passed by 285–144 in the House of Representatives, when the Republican leadership begrudgingly agreed to support the measure. President Obama signed the bill in the early hours of 17 October. Under the bill the treasury's borrowing authority is extended until 7 February, and the government is funded until 15 January 2014, allowing government agencies to reopen and hundreds of thousands of employees to return to work. At the end of October President Putin was named the world's most powerful person by *Forbes* magazine, pushing President Obama into second place. Democrat Bill de Blasio won the New York mayoral election on 5 November. Democrats also won the key governorship of Virginia.

2014 Republicans took control of the Senate in the mid-term elections held on 4 November, increasing their power for the final two years of Barack Obama's presidency. In the mid-terms, so-called because they fall half way between presidential elections, about one-third of the Senate, the entire House of Representatives, 36 of 50 state governors, and countless state and local offices were up for election. On 5 November the Senate's new Republican leader, Mitch McConnell, and President Barack Obama both promised to end the political gridlock and make the ineffective Senate function and pass bills. Mr Obama said he was 'eager to work with the new Congress to make the next two years as productive as possible'.

2015 On 29 January the Senate passed the bill approving the 1,400km (875 mile) Keystone XL pipeline that would carry tar sands oil from Canada to the US; President Obama has said he will veto the bill. On 21 July Cuba once again had an embassy in the US with the raising of the Cuban flag on their on 16th Street building in Washington. On the same day the US embassy in Cuba opened in Havana. On 30 August President Obama announced that Alaska's Mt McKinley, north America's highest mountain at 6,194 metres., would be renamed Denali from 2020. Denali ('the great one' in Athabaskan, the language of Alaska natives) was the name it was known by until officially named after President William McKinley in 1917.

Political structure

Constitution

The constitution of 17 September 1787 came into effect on 4 March 1789. The constitution strictly separates powers between the executive (presidential administration), legislature (Congress – Senate and House of Representatives) and judiciary (Supreme Court).

Independence date

4 July 1776

Form of state

Federal constitutional republic

The executive

The president, elected for a maximum of two terms of four years by an electoral college of representatives elected from each state, wields executive power. The president is both the chief of state and head of government. While at state level, each will elect a respective governor who is granted executive power.

National legislature

The bicameral Congress consisting of the House of Representatives (typically referred to a The House) and Senate, all legislative power is vested in Congress, which must be equally agreed by both houses. Each house has unique powers, as all revenue-raising bills must originate in the lower house, while all treaties and top appointments by the president are sanctioned by the upper house. All House members are appointed for fixed two-year terms, and re-elected at the same time, whereas Senators are elected for fixed six-year terms and around one-third are elected in rotation every two years.

The House has 435 members which are apportioned among the states by population number. The Senate has 100 members, two from each state regardless of its population. It also has non-voting members for US overseas territories.

Legal system

The legal system is based on English common law. There are judicial reviews of legislative acts. The US accepts compulsory International Court of Jurisdiction (ICJ) authority, although only with reservations. The nine justices of the Supreme Court are appointed for life by the president, with confirmation by the Senate.

Last elections

4 November 2014 (Senate, House of Representatives); 6 November 2012 (Presidential)

Results: House of Representatives: Republican Party won 247 seats (out of 435), Democratic Party 188 seats. Senate: Republican Party won 54 seats (out of 100), Democratic Party 44 seats Presidential: Barack Obama won 50.55 per cent of the vote, Mitt Romney 47.86 per cent; five other candidates each won less than 1 per cent.

Next elections

8 November 2016 (Presidential, House of Representatives and 34 Senate seats)

Political parties

Ruling party

Republican Party (in House of Representatives) (from 2010); Democratic Party (in the Senate) (from 2006)

Main opposition party

Republican Party

Population
314.18 million (2012)* (308,745,538; 2010, census figure)
Last census: 1 April 2010: 308,745,538
The 2010 census recorded a 9.7 per cent increase in the population from the 2000 census. The count was of all of residents and included Puerto Rico, American Samoa, Northern Marianas Islands, Guam and the US Virgin Islands. Censuses have taken place every ten years since 1790; the figures are used to allocate congressional seats and federal funds.
The US has the third-largest population in the world (after China and India) and contains a varied social and ethnic mix. The US is not following the trend of an ageing population as seen in many OECD countries.
The growth in population indicates a high rate of immigration rather than a fertility rate no greater than 2.0 per cent. Approximately 22 per cent of the population is under 14 years of age.
Population density: 31 inhabitants per square km. Urban population 82 per cent (2010 Unicef).
Annual growth rate: 1.0 per cent, 1990–2010 (Unicef).
Ethnic make-up
The 2010 census showed that Hispanics (16.7 per cent of the total population in 2010) now outnumber African Americans (13.6 per cent of the total population in 2010) in most metropolitan areas for the first time. Hispanics are expected to be around a third of the population by 2050. Some 12 per cent of the total population claim British ancestry, 16.5 per cent German and 12 per cent Irish ancestry.
Religions
There are some 90 religious organisations in the US with over 50,000 members each. There are approximately 86 million Protestants, 58 million Catholics, six million Jews and over six million members of other faiths. The total number of members of religious groups is estimated to be about 156 million. In the southern United States, the 'bible belt' stretches from California to Florida where the Baptist Church and Evangelism is strong. Numerous protestant sects can be found, each with their own unique outlook.

Education
Under a federal system, each state sets its own educational cycles; each year is a grade, from 1–12. Whichever cycle is adopted it incorporates 12 years. Education is mainly funded at local and state levels with policy set by the local school boards and state education authorities. Some federal funding is available to meet special needs. Schooling is generally compulsory from the age of six (states vary) to 16 years. Pupils at elementary and high schools (up to age 18) generally pay no tuition fees; further education establishments in general charge tuition fees. There is no state assistance for either tuition or living expenses for most university and undergratuate students, although loans are available. Some grant assistance is provided for students from low income and disadvantaged categories and scholarships are available on a competitive and special category basis.
High school graduates who decide to continue their education may enter a technical or vocational institution, a two-year college, or a four-year college or university.
The 2000 census reported that there were over 32 million elementary school children and over 15 million in high school and combined, projected number was expected to exceed 53 million, a figure not reached since the baby boomers swelled numbers in the early 1960s. The majority of high school students go on to college. Altogether, the system caters for over 72 million individuals in education.
Educational expenditure is typically around 7 per cent of the annual GDP. Elementary and secondary schools spent about 60 per cent of this total, and colleges and universities accounted for the remaining 40 per cent.
Compulsory years: 6 to 16
Enrolment rate: 98.5 per cent gross primary enrolment; 94 per cent gross secondary enrolment, of relevant age groups (including repeaters). (Unicef 2012).
Pupils per teacher: 16 in primary schools.

Health
Healthcare is largely a private-sector concern. Exceptions include the extensive Medicare programme for the elderly and the lesser Medicaid programme for those on welfare. Some emergency hospital treatment is free of charge for the poor. Health expenditure of 13 per cent of GDP is greater than the Organisation of Economic Co-operation and Development (OECD) average of 8 per cent.
Most people have private health insurance, either as a job benefit or paid for by themselves and is becoming a major financial burden, both for individuals and for the companies who pay for employee health schemes.
The *Patient Protection and Affordable Care Act* (PPACA; commonly referred to as Obamacare) was signed into law by President Obama on 23 March 2010, introducing reforms to improve access to affordable healthcare coverage for everybody in the US; it also provided protection for consumers from abusive insurance company practices. In 2010, almost 50 million Americans were uninsured for healthcare, of which the groups that lacked insurance were: white 15.4 per cent, Asian 18.1 per cent, black 20.8 per cent, Hispanic 30.7 per cent.
The act was divided into nine titles, with a rolling timetable of implementation, from June 2010 to 1 January 2012.
HIV/Aids
HIV prevalence: 0.6 per cent aged 15–49 in 2003 (World Bank)
Life expectancy: 78 years, 2004 (WHO 2006)
Fertility rate/Maternal mortality rate: 2.1 births per woman, 2010 (Unicef)
Child (under 5 years) mortality rate (per 1,000): 7 per 1,000 live births (WHO 2012); 1 per cent of children aged under five are malnourished (World Bank).

Welfare
Income security programmes are in general a mixture of federal and state funding and vary from state to state. The major programmes are unemployment compensation, housing subsidies for low income families and individuals, food stamps, child nutrition, payments to the disabled and family support payments. While states provide some limited form of income security, federal government policy concentrates on encouraging recipients back to work. In addition, the federal government makes social security payments to one in six Americans, either aged or disabled.
Pensions
Medicare trustees, in 2004, reported that the finance for the programme, set up to pay retirees, was deeply underfunded. Retirement payments are made from current revenue and the US$72 billion obligation (inluding the social security pension), to expected numbers of retirees, will outstrip assets and budgets by 2014, leaving the government to either make up the shortfall with tax increases or cut the pension benefits.
A trend by private companies to convert defined benefit and final salary schemes into defined contribution schemes (with uncertain benefits) has increased, with 75 per cent conversion in two decades, and US underfunding of defined benefit schemes estimated at US$278.6 billion. One of the largest providers of a defined benefit pension – United Airlines – has proposed transfering assets to the Pensions Benefit Guaranty Corporation (PBGC), a federal insurer, and divesting itself of a costly legacy. Worry has been expressed that if this and other businesses do likewise it could bankrupt the PBGC and require a government bail out costing tens of billions of dollars.

Main cities

Washington (capital, estimated population 603,860 in 2012), New York (8.2 million (m)), Los Angeles (3.8), Chicago (2.7m), Houston (2.1m), Philadelphia (1.5m), Phoenix (1.5m), San Antonio (1.4m), San Diego (1.3m), Dallas (1.2m).

Languages spoken

There is no official language declared in the constitution. English is the *de facto* working language and Spanish is the second, widely spoken, unofficial language.

Official language/s

There is no official language declared in the constitution. English is the *de facto* working language and Spanish is the second, widely spoken, unofficial language.

Media

The Constitution guarantees both press and broadcasters freedom of speech, subject to the laws of libel and slander, although even in the latter cases, there are well established public interest defences to these charges.

The law that prevents dual ownership of broadcast and print media outlets was scrapped by the Federal Communications Commission (www.fcc.gov) in December 2007. Media entities will now be able to own both TV channels and newspapers in 20 US cities, but only if there are already eight independently owned media businesses existing in the market concerned, and any TV channel to be purchased is not one of the top four rated stations.

Press

US media organisations since 2000, including the Hearst Corporation, the New York Times Company, the Tribune Company and the Journal Register Company, which all own more than one state- or city-wide publication, have reacted to a downturn in their income (from loss of circulation and a drop in advertising revenue) by either restructuring their newspaper entities or closing them altogether; several major newspapers are under threat of closure.

Dailies: There are over 1,500 daily newspapers, published in either the morning or evening and mostly serving a city, state or region. The majority of newspapers are published in English, while some serve ethnic communities and are published in other languages. The main national dailies include *USA Today* (www.usatoday.com), *New York Times* (www.nytimes.com), *Washington Post* (www.washingtonpost.com), *Los Angeles Times* (www.latimes.com), *Boston Globe* (www.boston.com), distributed nationally in main centres. Other major publications include, the *Philadelphia Enquirer* (www.philly.com), *Baltimore Sun (www.baltimoresun.com)*, *Chicago Sun-Times* (www.suntimes.com), *San Francisco Chronicle* (www.sfgate.com), *Detroit Free Press* (www.freep.com), *Chicago Tribune* (www.chicagotribune.com), *Atlanta Journal* (www.ajc.com) and *Houston Chronicle* (www.chron.com).

Tabloid daily newspapers include the *Daily News* (www.nydailynews.com) and the *New York Post* (www.nypost.com).

Weeklies: There are around 8,000 national magazines, mostly published in English and widely read including *Time* (www.time.com), *Newsweek* (www.newsweek.com) and *US News & World Report* (www.usnews.com). *The Nation* (www.thenation.com), a bi-monthly and *Harvard Political Review* (http://hprsite.squarespace.com) are independent political magazines. Condé Nast (www.condenast.com) publishes over 30 speciality magazines targeting women, men, young and old and special interests. The *Christian Science Monitor* (www.csmonitor.com), became a weekly publication, with a daily website, in 2009. In October 2012, the currents affairs magazine *Newsweek* announced that from 31 December the complete publication will be online, due to revenue loss as traditional advertising has declined.

Business: The *Wall Street Journal* (http://online.wsj.com), the premier financial and business daily, is published in four regional editions. Major business magazines include BarronsWeekly, publicated by the *Wall Street Journal Business Week* (www.businessweek.com), *Forbes* (www.forbes.com) and *Fortune* (http://money.cnn.com with a link to Fortune). Others business news is carried by *Market Watch* (www.marketwatch.com), *Investor's Business Daily* (www.investorsbusinessdaily.com) and *Washington Business Journal* (http://washington.bizjournals.com). Business magazines which target ethnic groups include black entrepreneurs, *Black Enterprise* (www.blackenterprise.com), *Minority Business Entrepreneur* (www.mbemag.com) and Hispanic groups, *Enterprise* (http://hol.hispaniconline.com).

Periodicals: The *Harvard Political Review* (http://hprsite.squarespace.com) is an independent political magazines published four times a year. *The New Yorker* (www.newyorker.com) is an influential literary monthly magazine.

Broadcasting

Radio: Virtually all US households have a radio and there are several national networks with numerous local stations offering a variety of programmes to cater for all tastes. Clear Channel (www.clearchannel.com) is the largest commercial network with over 1,200 stations. CBS Radio (www.cbsradio.com) and ABC Radio Network (http://abcradionetworks.com) provide premium quality radio programmes to its own stations and affiliates (privately-owned stations that broadcast programmes made by others).

Regional networks include Keystone Broadcasting (www.keystonebroadcasting.com), Sheridan Broadcasting Network (SBN), which operates the American Urban Radio Networks (www.aurnol.com), of radio stations and affiliates targeting black American audiences and the non-commercial National Public Radio (www.npr.org), which has member stations broadcasting news, talk and cultural shows. In Spanish, the Hispanic radio network (http://especiales.univision.com), broadcasts in major cities nationwide.

External radio services are provided in over 40 languages to all parts of the world by the Voice of America radio network (www.voanews.com).

Television: Virtually all US households have a television set and 60 per cent have cable TV. In June 2009 all US public television services were switched to digital signals.

With the rapid growth in new technology in digital and satellite broadcasting the dominance of the four major commercial TV broadcasting networks has decreased. New mediums allow a wide variety of programmes to be seen at times dictated by the audience, eroding viewer numbers for the traditional broadcast stations. Cable TV services in their turn are being challenged by wifi services. In the large cities, viewers may have 50 or more channels to choose from, allowing advertisers to target their audience. Since viewer ratings determine success all networks compete fiercely with each other for viewers and advertising revenue. The four major networks are Columbia Broadcasting System (CBS) (www.cbs.com), National Broadcasting Corporation (NBC) (www.nbc.com), Capital Cities/ABC (ABC) (http://abc.go.com) and Fox. In January 2013 the Qatar-based Al Jazeera group bought Current TV, the cable television network founded by former vice president, Al Gore. In August Current TV was re-launched as Al Jazeera America

The national public broadcasting network (PBS) (www.npr.org) is supported by donations from the government and 'pledges' from viewers.

Business television channels include CNBC (www.cnbc.com), Bloomburg (www.bloomberg.com) and Fox Business Network (www.foxbusiness.com), which was launched to challenge CNBC.

Most broadcasting is in English, but there are also TV and radio stations serving local ethnic communities in their own languages. The Hispanic community is

relatively well served in Florida, California and New York City.
Worldwide US government services are provided by VOA, International Broadcasting Bureau (http://ibb7-2.ibb.gov).
Other news agencies: UPI (United Press International):www.upi.com
Associated Press: www.ap.org
Voice of America: www.voanews.com

Economy
The US economy is a balance of two opposites: on one side is the largest economy by GDP worldwide, significantly driving global growth, but the other has an eye-watering budget deficit – US$439 billion in FY 2015. To maintain this balance, the US has both world-class reserves of natural resources including oil, natural gas and minerals, a large mechanised agriculture sector including cotton, wheat and livestock, and a manufacturing sector that produces a wide range of products for its large domestic market and larger foreign markets. It produces a diverse range of goods for export, including hi-tech instruments, electronic, computer and telecommunications equipment, automobiles and aircraft, foods and drinks, iconic and cultural movies, music and literature. If the US does not directly produce manufactured goods it is often the owner of offshore manufacturing processes, which export their international brand names worldwide. The US is also a major centre of financial services, including banking, insurance and investment. It is a world leader in scientific research including medicine, computer sciences, astronomy, oceanography and earth sciences. It also has a large, well-funded and innovative military force. It also spends; its people, institutions and businesses use credit to buy the products that keeps the US economy (and by association, global trade) growing.
Since recovering from recession in 2010 with an expansion in GDP of 2.5 per cent, the United States economy has remained very stable. GDP growth has been largely maintained, averaging 2.3 per cent from 2012–14.
GDP growth was 1.9 per cent in 2007, which, as the global economy crisis began to take hold, fell into recession with an annual rate of -0.3 per cent in 2008. The crisis had been sparked by a downturn in the US property market, which had become inflated by cheap loans that encouraged speculative borrowing, particularly through 'sub-prime' loans. These loans had been re-packaged and sold to banks and other investors worldwide. As the sub-prime market collapsed investors suffered major losses as stock markets fell significantly and lending almost ceased in a credit squeeze that brought commerce to a standstill. What had begun as defaults in a risky market escalated, as financial institutions and banks worldwide were unable to borrow to cover their debts and had to be rescued by governments, causing national economies to fall into full-blown economic recession. The recession deepened in 2009 as GDP growth fell to -3.5 per cent as consumer spending (which had previously driven growth) fell as wages and salaries shrank, before recovering in 2010, as global trade picked up, with growth of 3 per cent.
In 2008 as the economic crisis took a grip of the global financial system, the US bank rate was cut to an historic low of 0.25 per cent in an attempt to stimulate the US economy. A new US$1.5 trillion bank bailout plan was announced in 2009 and President Obama signed a US$787 billion economic stimulus plan that included measures to create jobs, boost consumer spending and rebuild the infrastructure through the use of tax breaks and federal funding. The unemployment rate in October 2009 rose to 10.2 per cent, the highest rate since 1983; 8.2 million workers had lost their jobs since the beginning of the global economic crisis in 2007. The governor of the US Federal Reserve said the world's financial crisis was the worst since the 1930s. Lehman Brothers, a global investment bank, was declared bankrupt in September 2008, with losses of US$613 billion. The biggest quarterly loss in US corporate history was announced in March 2009 by the insurance giant AIG, at US$61.7 billion. In November 2008, the government had given AIG a financial bailout of US$150 billion to save the company from collapse during the economic crisis. On 18 March the Federal Bank announced that it would buy around US$1.2 trillion worth of long-term government debt to help boost lending.
The reputation of the US as a world leader, not only in financial services and as the stimulus for world trade, but also as a prudent and reputable global partner took a severe blow during the economic crisis. The US government began a review of its banking regulations that is on-going, while federal prosecutors investigate allegations of massive fraud perpetrated on investors, corporate and personal.
In September 2011, the government was unable to pass legislation to allow the US$1.56 trillion budget and suffered an embarrassing loss of its triple A rating as Standard and Poor's downgraded the US credit rating, the first in the history of such ratings.
From the 1-16 of October 2013, the US government entered the third largest government shutdown in US history after Congress failed to enact legislation appropriating funds for the fiscal year 2014. This caused 800,000 workers to be furloughed, and a further 1.3 million were required to work without knowing when they would be paid. After the shutdown, the economy showed promise of recovery with a growth of 3.2 per cent in the fourth quarter of 2013, and the biggest burst of consumer spending in three years.
A large contribution to public debt and the budget deficit have been the wars in Iraq and Afghanistan, which required a diversion of resources from civilian to military purposes. In total the direct costs of the wars reached as much as US$1.5 trillion over 2014.
In 2014 unemployment in the US fell to 6.2 per cent, and further still to 5.5 per cent by mid-2015 – the lowest rate since the global economic crisis struck. Inflation also decreased falling to as low as 1.7 per cent, as well as the budget deficit as a percentage of GDP, at 2.8 per cent in 2014.

External trade
The USA is a founding member of the North American Free Trade Agreement (Nafta), under which it has tri-lateral trade agreements with Canada and Mexico. Nafta has FTAs with a number of regional trading blocs. Around 30 per cent of all exports are achieved through Nafta.
The US is the leading global exporter of a number of products including wheat and corn, liquefied natural gas, aluminium, sulphur, phosphates, salt and is the third largest exporter of rice. It is reliant on imported hydrocarbons, but is the world's largest producer of electricity. It has a full range of manufacturing industries, which provide around 20 per cent of GDP, from hi-tech semiconductors and telecommunications to automotive and aerospace assembly fabrication, from pharmaceutical and petrochemical production to metal processing, mineral extraction and foodstuff production including cheese, soya beans and tobacco. The services sector, including financial services, is an important source of foreign earnings. The South Korean parliament did not endorse the FTA until 15 March 2012. Under the FTA, 80 per cent of traded goods have their tariffs removed and a further 15 per cent will be removed by 2017.
The US Congress finally ratified free trade agreements (FTA) with Colombia, Panama and South Korea on 13 October 2011. The South Korean FTA had been in negotiations for 16 years and is expected to increase US exports by up to US$10 billion. However, the South Korean parliament has yet to endorse the agreement.
The Trans-Pacific Partnership (TPP) is a proposed trade agreement between

twelve Pacific Rim countries including the United States. After five years of negotiations, an agreement was reached on 5 October 2015 on a variety of economic policies. The TPP will see the reduction of trade barriers between member states, among other things.

Imports

Principal imports are consumer goods (over 30 per cent of total), oil and natural gas, industrial supplies, agricultural products, capital goods, (over 30 per cent), computers, telecommunications equipment, vehicles and parts, office machines and electric generating and distribution machinery.

Main sources: China (19.9 per cent of total in 2014), Canada (14.8 per cent), Mexico (12.5 per cent)

Exports

Principal exports are agricultural products (soybeans, fruit and corn), industrial supplies, capital goods and consumer goods.

Main destinations: Canada (19.2 per cent of total in 2014), Mexico (14.8 per cent), China (7.6 per cent)

Agriculture

Farming

Agriculture accounted for just 1.6 per cent of total GDP in 2014 and employs approximately 1 per cent of the country's workforce. However, despite its relatively small contribution to total US GDP, the agricultural sector continues to account for half of the world's corn production and over 20 per cent of world grain output. The US is the world's largest agricultural exporter with exports accounting for about 25 per cent of farmers' receipts. There are around 2.2 million farms in the US, which account for an area of 373 million ha.

Capital-intensive farming techniques produce dairy products, potatoes, fruit, vegetables and poultry for urban markets in the north-eastern states; wheat, barley, maize, oats, soya beans, fodder crops, pigs and cattle in the mid-west and central plains; cotton, tobacco, peanuts, citrus fruits, rice and sugar cane in the south; cattle and sheep in the central and western states; apples, berries and nuts in the Pacific north-west; and vines, apples, citrus fruits, peaches, tomatoes, olives, cotton and rice in California.

In 2007, subsidies for cotton growers were declared illegal by the WTO, following an official complaint by Brazil that such payments constituted unfair trade. Brazil reserved the right to impose sanctions against the US, which could amount to US$4 billion. The US carried on providing the subsidies to domestic cotton producers into 2013, making it increasingly difficult for developing countries to compete.

Fishing

Total seafood exports typically amount to over US$3 billion, mainly comprising ground fish (38 per cent), salmon (18 per cent), herring, lobster, shrimps, squid and crab. The top US export markets include Japan (37 per cent), Canada (21 per cent) and the EU (18 per cent). Shrimps account for approximately 36 per cent of total fish and seafood imports.

Forestry

One third of the total land area – 225.9 million hectares (ha) – of the Unites States is covered in forested land. Forests and other wooded areas are mainly concentrated in the east and west of the central plain.

The major part of the forest is classed as semi-natural, with less than a tenth remaining undisturbed, located mainly in Alaska and the west. About nine-tenths of the forest is available for wood supply. The government owns nearly two fifths of forest and other wooded land, while the remainder is shared among private individuals and institutions, forest industries and some by indigenous peoples.

Forestry is widespread and about half of all domestic timber needs are met by Oregon and Washington states, with the south-east producing increasing quantities of softwood for pulp. About 30 per cent of global industrial roundwood comes from the US. The US produces and consumes large quantities of sawn timber, wood-based panels and paper. It is also the largest importer and the second-largest exporter, of forest products.

Industry and manufacturing

The industrial sector remains a relatively significant contributor to the US economy. The sector employs approximately 13 per cent of the total workforce and contributes approximately 20 per cent to total GDP. The manufacturing sector has declined in significance over recent years as the services sectors have expanded.

There has been a shift in the manufacturing sector away from 'smokestack' industries, such as cars, primary metals and heavy machinery, towards high-technology industries, such as aerospace, communications equipment, electronic components and computers. Food, printing and publishing and textiles and clothing are also important.

Tourism

The US has a range of sights, cultures, entertainment, sports, interests and experiences to offer any visitor, of which there were 74.8 million in 2014. However, US travellers visiting foreign destinations in 2014 topped 68 million (31 million overseas). An overwhelming number of foreign visitors either arrive in or visit New York City by at least a ratio of 2:1. Miami, Los Angeles, Orlando and San Francisco each attracted over 3 million visitors annually. At the height of the tourist boom in 2008, before the global economic crisis cut visitor numbers, tourist spending totalled US$767 billion, of which accommodation and food and beverages accounted for the majority of the total at just under US$265 billion. At the same time over US$112 billion was spent on airfares to and within the US.

The USA is ranked second (behind France) among the world's top destinations for arrivals but first for tourist receipts. In 2014, total visitor numbers were 74.8 million, with 23.0 million visitors arriving from Canada and 17.3 million from Mexico, 13.7 million from Europe.

Travel and tourism contributed 8.0 per cent of GDP in 2014, and is forecast to rise 3.1 per cent in 2015.

The tourism industry provided employment to 9.3 per cent of the workforce (13.7 million jobs) in 2014. Although visitor exports topped US$194 billion in 2014, domestic spending on travel and tourism was over US$791 billion, as most US citizens prefer to take holidays in their own country.

In May 2011, travel industry representatives complained that too many potential visitors were being either turned away or troubled by restrictions on foreign tourists and called on the government to ease visa rules and have border controls offer a more welcoming demeanour. An estimated 78 million 'unfamiliar tourists' were denied entry or put off applying between 2000–10; only 36 countries worldwide benefit from visa-free, 90-day, entry to the US.

Environment

The US is not a signatory to the Kyoto Protocol.

Mining

The mining sector contributes approximately 4 per cent to total US GDP and employs approximately 4 per cent of the total US workforce.

While there are economically exploitable reserves of virtually every mineral within the US, these are insufficient to meet the needs of the economy in almost all circumstances. The country is 100 per cent dependent on imports for its consumption of bauxite, graphite and manganese among others. Mineral resources include ores of iron, copper (about 13 per cent of worldwide production), lead (17 per cent of worldwide production), gold (15 per cent), silver (12 per cent) and nickel.

The US accounts for approximately 17 per cent of worldwide aluminium production.

Hydrocarbons

Total proven oil reserves were 48.5 billion barrels at the end of 2014. Around 80 per cent of proven reserves are located in just four states: Texas, Louisiana, Alaska and California. Production in 2014 was 11.6 million barrels per day (bpd), which was an increase of 15.9 per cent on the 10.1 million bpd in 2013. As mature oil fields have declined in production there has been a compensating increase as more deep-water oil wells in the Gulf of Mexico and onshore oil fields in Alaska have come on-stream.

In February 2012, the US and Mexico signed an agreement to co-operate on developing the deep-water oil and gas fields that straddle their mutual border in the Gulf of Mexico.

The US is the world's largest net importer of oil, receiving over 20 per cent of the world's total, with the largest supplies originating from Canada, the Middle East, Mexico and Africa. Consumption was 19.0 million bpd in 2014 a figure that has dropped slightly from 2010 (19.2 million bpd) up to which it remained largely constant, despite fluctuations since 1997.

Refinery capacity was 18.0 million bpd in 2014. Two new refineries began operating in early 2015, a 19,000 bpd facility in North Dakota, and the 42,000 bpd facility in Texas. There are plans to double the Texas facility's capacity by the end of 2015. Despite these new refineries, the US must continue to import refined oil to meet its domestic demand.

Around 45 per cent of US oil imports come from Opec countries. Canada, Saudi Arabia, Mexico and Venezuela are the largest suppliers of oil to the US. The US has an emergency oil stockpile, the strategic petroleum reserve (SPR), with a capacity of 727 million barrels of oil. In July 2015 the SPR contained 695 million barrels of oil. The SPR is intended to cushion the US from the effects of a disruption in foreign oil supply and is the largest strategic stockpile in the world.

In April 2012, the Environmental Protection Agency (EPA) issued its first set of guidelines for hydraulic fracturing (fracking), which releases natural gas from shale rock. Previous tests of fracking had caused earthquakes and pollution of groundwater though the release of many ancillary agents. Energy companies will be required to capture many of these compounds during the drilling process.

The states with the largest coal production include Wyoming, West Virginia and Kentucky. More than 90 per cent of US coal output is consumed by the electricity sector. There is a trend towards consumption of coal with lower sulphur content in order to meet environmental targets for sulphur dioxide emissions. As of 2014, while natural gas was replacing coal as the main source of domestic power, production of coal for export to Asia was increasing.

The US has 26.6 per cent of the world's total coal reserved

The industry is broadly located in three regions: the Appalachian, the Interior and the Western regions. The Western region is the largest and most productive accounting for over half the annual coal mined. Wyoming accounted for 39 per cent of all US coal production, mining 388.3 million tonnes in 2013. The Appalachian, with West Virginia as the second most productive state, mined 165.1 million tonnes or 17 per cent of all US coal.

Over 90 per cent of coal consumption is through electricity power stations. The environmental impact of mining has become an issue for the industry with legal challenges to the New Source Review, which determines the level of review necessary for permitting certain mining practices and power stations. Legal proceedings have halted and slowed the permits for new and renewed mining, particularly in the Appalachian region.

In 2014 US coal production was the second largest in the world – after China – with 507.8 million tonnes of oil equivalent (mtoe). This was an increase of 1.4 per cent on the 2013 level. Consumption of coal fell by 0.3 per cent in 2014, to 453.4 mtoe.

Energy

Total installed generating capacity was 1,039GW in 2013 (the second largest in the world after China), producing around 4.1 trillion kilowatt hours (kWh). Electricity demand is growing by 1.5 per cent per annum. This increase will require a significant addition in generating capacity and the government forecasts that 1,300 new power plants will be needed between 2002 and 2020. In 2013 coal-fired power stations accounted for 39 per cent of all generation, with natural gas at 27 per cent, nuclear at 19 per cent, hydropower at 7 per cent, other renewables 6 per cent and the remainder by others, including petroleum.

The Federal Energy Regulatory Commission (FERC) is responsible for the regulation of the bulk power transmission system and wholesale bulk power markets. Independent utility companies generate and sell electricity in a competitive market with consumers free to choose their suppliers.

Following California's near miss with energy cuts due to a crisis in cost, the state has encouraged the use of renewable power sources. A contract was let in 2009 for the world's largest photovoltaic energy power station producing in total 2,610MW through a series of solar power plants, to be built by 2016.

In 2011 a major milestone in renewable energy was reached in the US – the amount of energy produced via renewable means surpassed the amount produced through nuclear power plants.

The first nuclear reactors to be built since 1978 were approved in February 2012. Two nuclear reactors will be built at an existing power plant in the state of Georgia. The project is expected to cost US$14 billion and be operational by 2016–17.

Financial markets

Stock exchange

American Stock Exchange (AMX)

Commodity exchange

Chicago Board Options Exchange (CBOE)

Banking and insurance

The banking and financial services industry in the US is noted for its complicated regulations, which are overseen by numerous federal and state authorities with overlapping jurisdictions.

Regulatory agencies include the Federal Reserve, the Federal Deposit Insurance Corporation (FDIC), the Securities and Exchange Commission, the Comptroller of the Currency, the Department of Justice and state bank departments. Depositors in banks or savings and loan associations which are members of the FDIC or Federal Savings and Loan Insurance Corporation have their deposits guaranteed to a limit of US$100,000 by the government's system of deposit insurance.

In February 2012 the Bank of America, Chase Manhattan, Citibank, Wells Fargo, JPMorgan Chase and Ally Financial Incorporated agreed to provide US$25 billion in relief to one million beleaguered home owners and state authorities for taking illegal shortcuts during foreclosures proceedings.

Central bank

Federal Reserve System

Time

There are six time zones

Eastern Standard Time – GMT minus five hours (daylight saving, minus four hours)

Central Standard Time – GMT minus six hours (daylight saving, minus five hours)

Mountain Standard Time – GMT minus seven hours (daylight saving, minus six hours)

Pacific Standard Time – GMT minus eight hours (daylight saving, minus seven hours)

Alaska Time – GMT minus eight hours (no daylight saving)

Hawaii Time – GMT minus 10 hours (no daylight saving)

Daylight saving from March (from 2007, previously daylight saving started in April) to November

Geography

The US is about half the size of Russia and covers a total area of about nine million square km. It stretches from the North Atlantic Ocean to the North Pacific Ocean. The US has borders with Canada (8,893km) (including 2,477km Alaska/Canada), Cuba 29km (US Naval Base at Guantanamo Bay) and Mexico (3,326km).

The western part of the country is dominated by the two major mountain ranges, the Rockies and Sierras. In the eastern US, the lower Appalachian and Allegheny mountains provide the western boundary to the coastal plain. The lowest point is Death Valley, -86 metres; the highest point is Mount McKinley (see below) at 6,194 metres. The central part of the country, the mid-west, is a vast plain, much of it flat and featureless with large wheat fields and known as the breadbasket of the US.

Alaska has mountains and broad river valleys. Hawaii is rugged and volcanic. The Everglades in southern Florida comprise the world's largest marsh at 5,659 square kilometres (2,185 square miles), and averages a depth of 150mm.

On 30 August 2015 President Obama announced that Alaska's Mt McKinley, north America's highest mountain, would be renamed Denali from 2020. Denali ('the great one' in Athabaskan, the language of Alaska natives) was the name it was known by until officially named after President William McKinley in 1917.

Hemisphere

Northern

Climate

The size of the land area and the natural mountain barriers give a wide range of climates. It is tropical in Hawaii and Florida, arctic in Alaska, semi-arid in the great plains west of the Mississippi River and arid in the Great Basin of the south-west. California (especially the south) has a Mediterranean-style climate with mild winters and hot summers. The south and Gulf of Mexico areas have a semi-tropical climate. The east coast and the mid-west are invariably very cold in winter and very hot in summer. Snow can be heavy at times, but most cities are equipped for swift snow removal from major streets and the transportation system can cope fairly well in poor weather. Most buildings, cars and public transport are well heated or air-conditioned, according to the season.

Dress codes

There are no overriding dress codes. In the Wall Street financial district of New York and other financial centres, business suits are *de rigueur*, while on the west coast, senior executives might wear anything from suits or sports jackets and trousers to jeans and T-shirts. The more normal business attire would be a business suit, shirt and tie. Despite the reputation US businessmen have for flashy dressing, formal colours are more acceptable, with dark suits, dark socks and sombre ties being the most acceptable form.

Entry requirements

Passports

Required by all.

Extensive information can be gained through http://travel.state.gov.

The US has introduced machine-readable passport (MRP) technology to enhance security measures, screening visitors into and out of the US.

Visitors who do not possess MRP passports are required to apply for a visa for entry.

For Canadian citizens only, under the Nexus programme entry may be achieved using a Nexus photo-identification card.

All arrivals, including US citizens, travelling between Canada, Mexico, Central and South America, the Caribbean and Bermuda through land borders or by sea (including ferries) must have a passport or other biometric, secure documentation as proof of identity since, 23 January 2008.

Visa

Extensive information can be gained through http://travel.state.gov.

Visas are required by all, with some exceptions under the Visa Waiver Program (VWP). This reciprocal programme allows citizens of, among others, most of the EU, Australasia and Japan entry without a visa if they possess a machine readable passport (MRP) and have a return/onward ticket, entry for business and tourist visits up to 90 days.

All citizens of visa-free countries who do not have a MRP must apply for a visa. All other visitors must apply for a visa.

Currency advice/regulations

The import and export of local and foreign currencies is allowed. Amounts over US$10,000 (or foreign equivalent) must be declared.

Gold coins, medals and bullion may be imported unless originating from embargoed countries.

Travellers cheques, in US dollars, are widely accepted.

Customs

Personal items are duty-free. National alcohol allowances may be in excess of state allowances and may result in excess amount being taxed or confiscated.

Certain firearms and ammunition are allowed with a customs permit, obtained in advance.

Prohibited imports

Illegal drugs (personal medication requires a doctor's certificate); soil, plant and animal products (including endangered species); meat, poultry (fresh, dried or canned) and live fish (unless certified disease-free), their eggs (unless canned, pickled or smoked); Cuban cigars (purchased in any country); wildlife and endangered species (including hunting trophies, shells and crafted items); fireworks and hazardous material; some South American pre-Columbian artefacts; merchandise from embargoed countries and counterfeit items.

These prohibitions apply to transit passengers.

Health (for visitors)

Mandatory precautions

No vaccination certificates are required, however, visitors from countries where cholera or yellow fever is rife, or where an outbreak of infectious disease occurred within six months of arrival, will require vaccination certificates.

Advisable precautions

There are no major health hazards for visitors, and no inoculations or vaccinations are necessary.

All personal medicines must have a physician's certificate declaring their prescribed use. As health costs can be extremely high medical insurance, including emergency evacuation, is necessary.

Hotels

Major hotels have toll-free telephone numbers (with an 800 area code) for reservations. Unless a deposit has been paid, a hotel room will often not be held after 1700/1800, even when the hotel is notified of late arrival. Check-out times vary from 1000–1300 and short extensions can be arranged. Visitors may be charged for overstaying check-out time without making arrangements. Most good hotels have restaurant facilities, bars, free parking and swimming pools. Many hotels provide courtesy transport or an airport bus service.

Road-side motels are numerous and relatively inexpensive.

Credit cards

Major credit and charge cards are widely accepted. A credit card is essential for car hire and usually necessary for hotel bookings.

Public holidays (national)

Fixed dates

1 Jan (New Year's Day), 4 Jul (Independence Day), 11 Nov (Veterans' Day), 25 Dec (Christmas Day).

Any holiday falling on Saturday is taken on Friday before; holidays falling on a Sunday are taken on Monday following.

Variable dates

Martin Luther King's Birthday (third Mon in Jan), Washington's Birthday (third Mon in Feb), Memorial Day (last Mon in May), Labour Day (first Mon in Sep), Columbus

Day (second Mon in Oct), Thanksgiving Day (fourth Thu in Nov).
Statutory and public holidays are fixed by state legislation and vary considerably between states.

Working hours
Most offices remain closed on the Friday following Thanksgiving. Working hours vary considerably depending on the industry.

Banking
Mon-Fri: 0900–1500.

Business
Mon-Fri: 0900–1700.

Government
Mon-Fri: 0830–1730.

Shops
Mon-Fri: 0930–1800; Sun: 1200–1700.

Telecommunications
Mobile/cell phones
GSM 850 and 1900 services are available throughout most of the country.

Electricity supply
110–120V AC, 60 cycles single phase, with flat two-point plug fittings.

Weights and measures
Units of measurement used in the US are in general the same as the imperial system. Short ton = hundredweight = 45.4 kilograms, one pound = 0.45 kilogram; one gallon = 3.79 litres, one pint = 0.47 litre. Conversion to metric system is taking place very slowly and on a voluntary basis, with the US Metric Board co-ordinating the process.

Social customs/useful tips
People are likely to use first names in discussions with you. They are also likely to refer to someone else by their surname only. Neither of these usages is considered impolite.
The main cultural role model in the US is that of the pioneer, the isolated man or woman battling against the odds, the story of someone rising from a deprived background to become rich and/or famous. This has led to an admiration for hard work, free enterprise and determination. Gun ownership by civilians is considered, by many, to be a part of American heritage.
San Francisco legislators voted in November 2012 to ban nudity in public places for anyone over the age of five.

Security
The US has a reputation for crime and violence. New York, Baltimore, Chicago, Detroit, Washington and Los Angeles have a high rate of robbery. Washington, Detroit, Baltimore, Dallas, Houston, Philadelphia, Atlanta and Los Angeles have high murder rates.
However, much of the trouble is concentrated in parts of each city and avoiding these neighbourhoods will considerably reduce any risk. Elementary precautions should prevent visitors having too much trouble. Avoid walking in deserted streets, and try to walk on the street-side rather than next to buildings. Always be aware of the kind of neighbourhood it is. At night, except in lively and well-lit areas, call a taxi to collect you rather than walking to look for one.
Although the risk of being mugged is often exaggerated (and crime figures have been falling since the mid-1990s), it is recommended not to resist a robbery attempt. Keep your valuables (especially expensive jewellery) out of sight.

Getting there
Air
International airport/s: The US is accessible by air from all continents and a vast number of countries. Some of the busiest international airports are La Guardia (LGA) (New York), Los Angeles (LAX), Miami International Airport (MIA), O'Hare International Airport (ORD), Hartsfield-Jackson Atlanta Airport (ATL); other important international airports include those in Boston (Logan Airport), Dallas-Fort Worth, Philadelphia, Houston, San Francisco, Washington Dulles International and John F Kennedy Airport (Newark).
Airport tax: Departure taxes are included in the price of a ticket, although local airport departure tax may be charged if the ticket was purchased outside the US.
There is a national programme that allows airports to impose a passenger facility charge of up to US$4.5.

Surface
Road: The US has land borders with Mexico in the south and Canada in the north and there are plenty of efficient overland border crossings between the US and these countries. Border crossings are strictly controlled.
Rail: There are limited passenger services from Mexico, crossing the border at either Yuma, El Paso or Del Rio. Rail links from Canada include Vancouver–Seattle, Toronto–Chicago and Montréal–New York, although these are not all direct and without layovers. Some rail lines run up to the border with Canada, in Michigan.
Water: The US has numerous sea and inland water ports and is well served by the international shipping lines.

Getting about
National transport
Inter-state transport can be variable, however the US is generally perceived to have one of the most advanced transport structures in the world, including metro systems in most major cities and sufficient national bus networks. Transport by ferries and helicopters is also widely available. Nevertheless, the easiest and quickest method of crossing great distances in the US is by air.
Air: A highly developed network of airline services connects most towns of importance. Fare systems have been deregulated, leading to sharp competition.
Road: There is a comprehensive network of highways (interstate) that bisect the country from the east to west coast and from the borders with Canada through to Mexico. During the winter even the interstates can be closed or slowed by snow. There is an extensive secondary road system.
Buses: A wide network of air-conditioned long-distance buses link all major cities, but smaller cities and rural areas are generally not well served by public transport. Greyhound is the main bus system in the US and plays an important transport role in most parts of the country.
Rail: Around 245,000km of grade one railroad links approximately 500 stations. Most long-distance trains are air-conditioned and equipped with dining and sleeper carriages. Amtrak is generally comfortable and runs a popular shuttle service between New York and Washington; the New York to Boston route is also well travelled. Much of the national network is in need of new equipment, however, and in terms of time and cost, rail travel compares poorly to air travel on most inter-city routes.
Water: Ferries supply connections for national Highways across the Mississippi at various places.

City transport
Most cities have a good public transport network including a mixture of buses, suburban trains and subways. At night, taxis are the safer option for travel. Fares vary in different cities. Public transport is woefully inadequate in Los Angeles and the cable cars of San Francisco are a special treat. Commuter rail services throughout the US are usually safe and reliable.
Most cities have severe parking problems in downtown areas and it is more convenient to travel by public transport or taxi.
Taxis: It is wise to confirm the approximate cost when entering a cab.
In Los Angeles, taxis do not cruise streets looking for passengers, but there are taxi stands at airports, major hotels, and train and bus terminals.
Taxi fares in Washington DC are based on the unmetered zone system with a basic fare and each zone charged extra; drivers may stop and pick up several passengers following the same general route. Enquire in advance how many zones you will ride.
Buses, trams & metro: There are bus services in all main cities. Many hotels

have courtesy bus services to and from airports.

In New York City buses are slower than the subway, and especially crowded during rush hours, but the routes are more varied and the stops more frequent, usually every two blocks. The subway is the fastest way to get around. Trains are identified by number or letter which are displayed on the front and sides of the cars. Some are local and some express so be sure the train you board stops where you need to get off. If travelling after 2200, wait for the train in the areas marked for off-peak hours.

A subway connects downtown Chicago and O'Hare International Airport with fast and frequent services from Terminal 2; from the city, the Dearborn Street subway runs to the airport.

Union Station is the transport hub in Washington DC. Connections between Metrorail and Metrobus are available at all Metrorail stations.

Ferry: There are commuter ferries across Boston, San Francisco and New York harbours.

Car hire

Car hire is widely available in major cities. A valid overseas or international driving licence and an international credit card are required. Other methods of payment may not be accepted. Driving is on the right. States are free to set their own speed limits: Montana has no day-time limit but at night the limit is 55mph; 75mph in Kansas, Nevada and Wyoming; 70mph in California, Missouri, Oklahoma, South Dakota and Texas.

For further information on state highways see www.us-highways.com with links to other relevant sites.

BUSINESS DIRECTORY

The addresses listed below are a selection only. While World of Information makes every endeavour to check these addresses, we cannot guarantee that changes have not been made, especially to telephone numbers and area codes. We would welcome any corrections.

Telephone area codes

The international direct dialling code (IDD) for the United States of America is +1, followed by area code and subscriber's number:

Alaska 907 NY, Manhattan 212
Albuquerque 505
Atlanta 404 Newark 201 Austin 512 Montana 406
Boston 617 Oklahoma City 405
Chicago 312
Denver 303 Philadelphia 215
Phoenix 602
Detroit 313 Pittsburgh 412
Hawaii 808 Portland 503
Houston 713 Sacramento 916
Kansas City 816 St Louis 314
Indianapolis 317 St Paul 612
Las Vegas 702 Salt Lake City 801
Los Angeles 213 San Francisco 415
Louisville 502 Seattle 206
Memphis 901 Washington DC 202
Miami 305
New Orleans 504 Wichita 316
New York 718

Useful telephone numbers

Emergency services: 911

Chambers of Commerce

British-American Business Council, 52 Vanderbilt Avenue, 20th Floor, New York NY 10017 (tel: 661-5660; fax: 661-1886; e-mail: info@babc.org).

United States Chamber of Commerce, 1615 H Street, NW, Washington DC 20062 (tel: 659-6000; e-mail: intl@uschambers.com).

Banking

Bank of America, 555 California Street, San Francisco, California, 94104 (tel: 415-622-3456; fax: 510-675-8170).

Bankers Trust, 280 Park Avenue, New York, New York, 10017 (tel: 212-250-2500; fax: 212-250-4029).

Chase Manhattan, 1 Chase Manhattan Plaza, New York, New York, 10081 (tel: 212-552-2222).

Chemical Bank, 270 Park Avenue, New York, New York, 10017 (tel: 212-270-6000; fax: 212-682-3761).

Citibank, 399 Park Avenue, New York, New York, 10043 (tel: 212-559-1000; fax: 212-223-2681).

First National Bank of Chicago, 1 First National Plaza, Chicago, Illinois, 60670 (tel: 312-732-4000; fax: 312-732-5965).

Inter-American Development Bank, 1300 New York Avenue NW, Washington DC 20577 (tel: 202-623-3900; fax: 202-623-2360).

Morgan Guaranty Trust, 60 Wall Street, New York, New York, 10260 (tel: 212-483-2323; fax: 212-233-2623).

Nations Bank, 100 North Tryon Street, Charlotte, North Carolina, 28255 (tel: 704-386-5000; 704-386-0645).

Central bank

Federal Reserve System, 20th Street and Constitution Avenue, NW, Washington DC 20551 (tel: (202) 452-3000; fax: (202) 452-3819).

Stock exchange

American Stock Exchange (AMX), www.amex.com

Nasdaq OMX, www.nasdaqomx.com

National Stock Exchange (NSX), www.nsx.com

International Securities Exchange, www.ise.com

Miami Stock Exchange (WS4X), http://ms4x.com

Commodity exchange

Chicago Board Options Exchange (CBOE) www.cboe.com

Chicago Mercantile Exchange (CME), www.cmegroup.com

Chicago Climate Exchange (CCX), www.chicagoclimatex.com

Intercontinental Exchange (ICE), www.theice.com

Kansas City Board of Trade (KCBT), www.kcbt.com

Minneapolis Grain Exchange (MGEX), www.mgex.com

Travel information

Amtrak (tel: 1-800-872-7245; internet: www.amtrak.com).

California Tourism, PO Box 1499, Sacramento, CA 95812-1499 (1-916-444-4429; internet: www.visitcalifornia.com).

Greyhound Lines Inc, PO Box 660362, MS 470 Dallas, TX 75266- 0362 (tel: 789-7000; internet: www.greyhound.com).

John F Kennedy International Airport, Building 14, Jamaica, New York 11430, (tel: 244-4444; internet: www.kennedyairport.com).

LaGuardia Airport Hangar 7 Center, Third Floor, Flushing, New York 11371 (tel: 533-3400; fax: 533-3421; internet: www.laguardiaairport.com).

Los Angeles International Airport, 1 World Way, Los Angeles, Ca 90045 (tel: 646-5252; internet: www.lawa.org/lax).

Metropolitan Transportation Authority, 347 Madison Avenue, New York, NY 10017-3739 (internet: www.mta.nyc.ny.us).

Miami International Airport, PO Box 592075, Miami, Florida 33159 (tel: 876-7000; fax: 876-7398; internet: www.miami-airport.com).

O'Hare International Airport, PO Box 66142 Chicago, Illinois 60666 (tel: 686-3700, 686-2200; fax: 686-3573; internet: www.ohare.com).

Visit Florida, Welcome Center, The Capitol, West Entrance, Tallahassee FL 32301 (tel: 488-6167; fax: 414-2560; internet: www.visitflorida.com).

Ministries

Department of Agriculture, 1400 Independence Avenue, SW, Washington DC 20250 (tel: 720-3631; internet: www.usda.gov).

Department of Commerce, 1401 Constitution Avenue, NW, Washington DC 20230 (tel: 482-2000; fax: 482-2741; internet: www.commerce.gov).

Department of Defence, The Pentagon, Washington DC 20301-1950 (tel: 692-7100; fax: 428-1982; internet: www.defenselink.mil).

Department of Education, Federal Office Bld 6, 400 Maryland Ave, Washington DC 20202 (tel: 401-3000; fax: 401-0596; internet: www.ed.gov).

Department of Energy, 1000 Independence Avenue, SW, Washington DC 20585 (tel: 586-5000; fax: 586-4403; internet: www.energy.gov).

Department of Health and Human Services, 200 Independence Ave, SW, Room 615F, Washington DC 20201 (tel: 690-7000; fax: 690-7203; internet: www.hhs.gov).

Department of Homeland Security, 3801 Nebraska Avenue, NW, Washington DC 20528 (tel: 282-8000; fax: 282-8401; internet: www.dhs.gov).

Department of Housing and Urban Development, 451 7th Street, SW, Room 10000 Washington DC 20410 (tel: 708-0417; fax: 619-8365; internet: www.hud.gov).

Department of the Interior, 1949 C Street, NW Washington DC 20240 (tel: 208-7351; fax: 208-6956; internet: www.doi.gov).

Department of Justice, 950 Pennsylvania Ave, NW Washington DC 20530-0001 (tel: 514-2001; fax: 307-6777; internet: www.justice.gov).

Department of Labor, 200 Constitution Ave, NW Washington DC 20210 (tel: 693-6000; fax: 693-6111; internet: www.dol.gov).

Department of State, 2201 C Street, NW Washington, DC 20520-0001 (tel: 647-5291; fax: 647-7120; internet: www.state.gov).

Department of Transportation, 400 7th Street, SW Washington DC 20570 (tel: 366-1111; fax: 366-7202; internet: www.dot.gov).

Department of the Treasury, 1500 Pennsylvania Ave, NW Washington DC 20220; (tel: 622-1100; fax: 622-0073; www.untreas.gov).

Office of the President, The White House, 1600 Pennsylvania Ave, Washington DC 20500 (tel: 456-1414; fax: 456-2461; internet: www.whitehouse.gov).

Other useful addresses

British Embassy, 3100 Massachusetts Avenue NW, Washington DC 20008-3600 (tel: 588 6500; fax: 588 7850; internet: www.britainusa.com).

Consumer Product Safety Commission, 4330 East West Highway, Bethseda, MD 20814 (tel: 504-7923; fax: 504-0124; internet: www.cpsc.gov).

Council of Economic Advisers, The White House, 1600 Pennsylvania Avenue NW Washington, DC 20500 (tel: 456-1414).

Environmental Protection Agency, Areil Rios Bld, 1220 Pennsylvania Ave NW, Washington DC 20460 (tel: 814-5000; internet: www.epa.gov).

Federal Trade Commission, 600 Pennsylvania Avenue, NW, Washington DC 20580 (tel: 382-4357; internet: www.ftc.gov).

New York Stock Exchange, 11 Wall Street, New York, NY 10005 (tel: 656-3000; internet: www.nyse.com).

Office of Science and Technology Policy, Executive Office of the President, 725 17th Street, Room 5228 Washington DC 20502 (tel: 456-7116; internet: www.ostp.gov)

Office of the United States Trade Representative, 600 17th Street, NW Washington DC 20508 (tel: 395-7360; internet: www.ustr.gov).

Securities and Exchange Commission, 100 F Street, NE, Washington DC 20549 (tel: 551-6551; internet: www.sec.gov).

United States Information Agency, 301 Fourth Street, SW, Washington DC 20547 (internet: http://usinfo.state.gov).

UPI (United Press International):www.upi.com

Associated Press: www.ap.org

Voice of America: www.voanews.com

Internet sites

Alamo Rent A Car: www.alamo.com

American Airlines: www.aa.com

American Chamber of Commerce: www.amcham.com

American Stock Exchange: www.amex.com

Big Book (information on 16m businesses):www.bigbook.com

Big yellow pages (business and residential information):www.bigyellow.com

Continental Airlines: www.flycontinental.com.

Delta Airlines: www.delta.com

Export and Trade Information: www.stat.usa.gov

Federal Agencies: www.fedworld.gov

Lookup USA (locate addresses and telephone numbers of US businesses): www.infousa.com

Northwest Airlines: www.nwa.com

Southwest Airlines: www.southwest.com

Trade US: www.tradeUS.com

United Airlines: www.ual.com

US Bureau of Census: www.census.gov

US Customs and Border Protection www.cbp.gov

US Department of Commerce: www.commerce.gov

US Government gateway site: firstgov.gov/

US Office of Insular affairs: www.doi.gov/oia

US International Trade Administration: www.ita.doc.gov/ita_home

US Virgin Islands

KEY FACTS

Official name: Virgin Islands of the United States

Head of State: President of the United States of America Barack Obama (from 2009; re-elected 6 Nov 2012)

Head of government: Governor Kenneth Mapp (Democrat) (from 5 Jan 2015 (elected in 28 Nov 2014 run-off election))

Ruling party: Democratic Party of the Virgin Islands (affiliated to the US Democratic Party) (from 2002; re-elected Nov 2008)

Area: 355 square km

Population: 109,666 (2011)*

Capital: Charlotte Amalie (on St Thomas)

Official language: English

Currency: US dollar (US$) = 100 cents

* estimated figure

COUNTRY PROFILE

1493 The islands were first sighted by Columbus.

1494–1670 The indigenous Carib and Arawak Indian population endured various waves of European invasions and settlement, including African slaves who were used on sugar cane plantations.

1670 The islands of St John and St Thomas were colonised by Denmark.

1733 Denmark purchased St Croix from France.

1917 Denmark sold the islands to the US for US$25 million.

1927 US citizenship was granted to the islands' population.

1931 The Virgin Islands were placed under the administration of the US State Department.

1936 Universal suffrage and local government were provided for under the Organic Act of the Virgin Islands.

1954 The United States Virgin Islands (USVI) became an unincorporated territory of the United States, under a revised Organic Act, which introduced a form of constitution, with a governor appointed by the president of the US and an elected 15-member unicameral legislature (senate).

1970 A governor was elected for the first time, following the 1968 Elective Governor Act, which also included an elected government for the islands.

1973 The USVI elected a non-voting delegate to the US House of Representatives for the first time.

1995 Damage to the power system occurred when Hurricane Marilyn hit the islands. The US Federal government transferred control of Water Island to the territorial government.

1998 Governor Charles W Turnbull was elected. Three serious hurricanes (Bonnie, George and Mitch) tore through the West Indies and between them killed over 9,700 people. However there was less damage inflicted in US Virgin territories due to reconstruction after previous hurricanes which required buildings to be built to withstand Category 2 storms.

2002 Charles Turnbull was re-elected governor and the Democrats won a majority in the parliamentary election.

2006 John deJongh (D) won the gubernatorial election with 49 per cent of the vote.

2007 An area along the coastline of St John was reserved by the Trust for Public Land to be included in the US Virgin Islands National Park, giving it its largest expansion ever.

2008 A 30-member Constitutional Convention began work on drafting a new constitution. It was the fourth time since 1965 that a new constitution has been envisaged, with previous work stalled over the lack of federal voting rights. John deJongh and the Democrats were re-elected.

2009 USVI received three different funds from the US: US$20.2 million to improve housing for low income residents, around US$71 million for education and US$1.3 million for coral reef restoration. Governor John deJongh rejected the draft constitution submitted by the Constitutional Convention stating it violated federal law, failed to defer federal sovereignty and disregarded basic civil rights. He refused to submit it for consideration in the US.

2010 In January the US Postal Services assigned specific zip codes to islands within the territory: VI followed by 008xx for the five designated destinations. The resident population of the USVI took part in the United States census on 1 April, which, after personal details, included questions on race, housing and internet and mobile phone access. A successful legal challenge to Governor deJongh's refusal to present the draft constitution forced him to comply. President Obama forwarded the draft proposals to the US Congress in May. The US Justice Department restated the concerns of Governor deJongh when the draft was submitted for consideration; as a result Congress rejected the draft requesting that it be reconsidered by the Constitutional Convention on 30 June. In gubernatorial elections held on 2 November, incumbent John deJongh won 56 per cent; Kenneth Mapp (independent) won 44 per cent.

2011 On 24 June the senate passed an austerity act, which will reduce salaries of public workers and allow possible dismissals to reduce costs. The approval was given to avoid the governor's proposal to dismiss up to 600 government employees before April 2012. In August, preliminary results of the 2010 census showed a drop in the population to 106,405, from 108,612 in 2000. It also recorded an

increase in the population of St John and a decline in St Croix.
2012 In January it was announced that the Hovensa refinery on St Croix would be shutdown, beginning in February. The refinery had been the biggest private employer in USVI and its closure means the loss of 1,018 directly employed workers and an additional, estimated 1,200 workers from refinery contractors. Unemployment on the island, standing at 18.7 per cent, will increase to some 28.7 per cent. The Venezuelan owners of the refinery reported US$1.3 billion in losses from the refinery since 2009. The terminal will be converted to a fuel storage facility.
2013 The Virgin Islands Economic Development Authority (VIEDA) announced in September that it has applied for a Choice Neighborhood Initiative Implementation Grant for US$20 million, a grant made possible by the US Department of Housing and Urban Development (HUD). This grant will provide funding for the VIEDA's Enterprise Zone Commission (EZC).
2014 The US Office of Insular Areas of the Department of the Interior notified Governor de Jongh on 5 September that the annual rum excise tax cover-over of US$165 million for fiscal 2015 had been approved. In September Governor de Jongh met with legislators to report that an agreement in principle had been arrived at between Hovensa and a prospective buyer. In the 4 November gubernatorial election Kenneth Mapp, running as an independent, won 47.47 per cent of the votes, under the 50 per cent + 1 required by the Revised Organic Act of the Virgin Islands. In the run-off held on 18 November, Mr Mapp succeeded over Donna Christian-Christensen with just under 64 per cent.
2015 Kenneth Mapp assumed office on 5 January. In early September the government announced it would be taking action against Hess Corporation for the unlawful closure of the Hovensa refinery in 2012. The law suit, filed on 14 September, is seeking damages of at least US$1.5 billion, a figure that covers at least US$150 million per year in benefits to the people of the USVI over the ten-year period from 2012 to 2022 that Hess was obligated under the law to continue operating the refinery.

Political structure
Constitution
USVI is an unincorporated territory of the United States and only certain parts of the US constitution apply. Power is delegated from the US Congress. The Revised Organic Act of the Virgin Islands functions as a constitution for a territory of the United States. It is a US federal law, passed by the US Congress on 22 July 1954. Citizens are not able to vote in US federal or presidential elections. However US Virgin Islanders are entitled to vote in presidential primary elections and to send one, non-voting, member to the US House of Representatives for a two-year term.
Form of state
Overseas territory of the United States of America
The executive
Executive authority is exercised by the governor (elected for a four-year term by popular vote) who makes other executive appointments with the concurrence of the legislature.
National legislature
The unicameral legislature, the Senate, has 15 members each serving for two-year terms. The islands are divided into two multimember constituencies with seven senators each. St John is its own constituency and has one senator elected from a list of all-comers.
Legal system
The legal system is based on US laws.
Last elections
4 November 2014 (gubernatorial); November 2012 (Senate)
Results: Gubernatorial: Kenneth Mapp, running as an independent, won 47.47 per cent, Donna Christian-Christensen 39.16 per cent. As this was under the 50 per cent + 1 required by the Revised Organic Act of the Virgin Islands, a run-off was held on 18 November. Mr Mapp succeeded over Donna Christian-Christensen by 63.89 per cent to 35.87 per cent.
Senate: The Democratic Party of the Virgin Islands (Dem) won nine seats (out of 15) independents four and the Independent Citizens Movement (ICM) two.
Next elections
2018 (gubernatorial); 2016 (parliamentary)

Political parties
Ruling party
Democratic Party of the Virgin Islands (affiliated to the US Democratic Party) (from 2002; re-elected Nov 2008)
Political situation
The economic downturn in the US has had a knock-on effect on the islands. The undercapitalised Virgin Islands Community Bank was sold to FirstBank Virgin Islands in an emergency deal, before a deadline would have resulted in the Federal Deposit Insurance Corporation taking the bank into receivership.
Since then the US House of Representatives has passed a plan to stimulate the economy, including measures to expand mortgage loan opportunities for families at risk of home repossession. It also has islander taxpayers receiving a tax rebate of between US$300–US$600 per person, plus US$300 per child. The money is expected to strengthen the local economy and encourage consumer spending.
In March 2011, the Republican controlled US-Congress voted to rescind the voting rites of representations of the US Virgin Islands, effectively disenfranchising their electorate in policies that directly affect them.
About 64 per cent of the population is aged between 15 and 64 years.

Population
109,666 (2011)*
Last census: 1 April 2010: 106,405
Population density: 352 inhabitants per square km. Urban population: 46 per cent (1994–2000).
Annual growth rate: 3 per cent (2003)
Ethnic make-up
Descendants of former African slaves form the majority (80 per cent) of the population. Whites make up a further 15 per cent. Almost three-quarters (74 per cent) of inhabitants are West Indians (45 per cent Virgin Islands-born, 29 per cent from elsewhere in the Caribbean). Puerto Ricans make up 5 per cent of the population.
Religions
Various Christian denominations predominate, (Baptist, Roman Catholic and Episcopalian).

Education
Compulsory years: Five to 16 years

Health
Life expectancy: 78.3 years (estimate 2003)
Fertility rate/Maternal mortality rate: 2.2 births per woman (World Bank)
Child (under 5 years) mortality rate (per 1,000): 8.3 per 1,000 live births (World Bank).

Main cities
Charlotte Amalie (on St Thomas, capital, estimated population 9,544 in 2012), Charlotte Amalie East (2,574), Charlotte Amalie West (4,798), Anna's Retreat (7,174).
Frederiksted on St Croix (3,049), Grove Place (2,948), Christiansted (2,714).
The third major island St John is the least populous; Cruz Bay (on St John) (3,037).

Languages spoken
Spanish and Creole are also spoken.
Official language/s
English

Media
Press
Dailies: The two major dailies are *Virgin Islands Daily News* (www.virginislandsdailynews.com) and *St Croix Avis*. Other publications include an

independent community newspaper *St John Times*.
The island is served by on-line news services (www.onepaper.com). The *St Croix Source* provides an alternative news and information source for and about the St Croix community. It is the sister publication of *St Thomas Source* and *St John Source*.
Weeklies: *Tradewinds St John Newspaper* (www.stjohntradewindsnews.com) is published and distributed weekly on St John, as well as to international subscribers. Since 1972, Tradewinds Newspaper has been the island authority. A general tourist publication, *St Thomas This Week Magazine*, is available on-line (www.st-thomas.com/week).
Business: Publications include *Virgin Islands Business Journal*.
Broadcasting
Television services are provided by US commercial broadcasters. WSVI TV 8 (Channel 8) (www.wsvi.tv) is an ABC affiliate and WVGN TV 14 (Channel 11) (www.wvgn.com) is an NBC affiliate; both channels broadcast syndicated US shows. There are several radio stations located on both islands and are identified by their call signs, a few are networked such as VI Radio (www.viradio.com). Most broadcast music while a few are news, talk and religious radio stations.

Economy
The islands have little in the way of natural resources and most industries are dependent on either trade with the US or as an offshore site of the US. Manufacturing includes rum, textiles, electronic assembly of components, pharmaceuticals and wristwatch assembly.
Agricultural production is insufficient to provide for the population and most foods have to be imported.
The service sector constitutes the largest component of GDP (78 per cent in 2012 (latest available)), of which tourism is the single biggest sector accounting for around 29.9 per cent of GDP and 27.0 per cent of employment in 2014. Tourism provides the islands' main economic activity, including employment and investment. The global economic crisis had an adverse effect on the USVI as tourist numbers fell from 2.55 million in 2008 to some 2 million annually since then. However, more recently there has been an improvement as in the first four months of 2015 there were 304,000 stay over visitors – a 6.5 per cent increase on the same period in 2014.
The economy has been in a long-term recession as GDP has been contracting. Growth in GDP was -7.5 per cent in 2011, falling further to -13.8 per cent in 2012 before slightly speeding up to an estimated -5.4 per cent in 2013.
On 25 January 2012, the Hovensa oil refinery on Saint Croix was closed down leaving 1,158 workers unemployed. By May, emergency funds of over US$7.8 million had been provided by the federal government to assist the affected workers. The oil refinery had been not only the largest refinery in the Caribbean; it had also been one of the world's largest oil refineries, capable of producing 495,000 barrels per day (bpd). The owners decided to convert the refinery into an oil storage terminal, which will require a workforce of only 100. However, by mid-2015 the refinery was still shuttered. A proposal to allow the sale of the refinery was put to the senate by Governor de Jongh on 19 December 2014. The senate rejected the proposal on the grounds that they considered it would not financially benefit the territorial government. The Governor regretted the move saying the agreement was a pre-condition to the sale of the refinery to Atlantic Basin Refining (ABR). In September 2015 Hovensa entered a deal for the sale of its St Croix terminal operations for US$184 million to Limetree Bay Holdings LLC (LBH).
Current US federal law requires that any excise tax collected on rum manufactured in the territory and imported into the United States be returned or 'covered-over' to the US Virgin Islands. The government submits an annual estimate of excise tax collections to the Office of Insular Affairs, and generally payments are made in September of each fiscal year. Since 2007 revenue from this has increased from US$68 million to over US$100 million annually. In September 2014 Governor de Jongh was reported as saying 'Our reliance on these receipts to support bonded debt, which has enabled us to mitigate the impact of the worst economic conditions experienced in recent times, cannot be overstated. We have utilised this resource to enable us not only to maintain essential operations in healthcare, education and law enforcement, but also to make critical investments in our current infrastructure, inclusive of our broadband investment, to lay the foundation for future growth opportunities.' The payment for fiscal 2015 was US$165 million.

External trade
As an unincorporated territory of the USA the US Virgin Islands are not part of the American Free Trade Agreement (Nafta), despite its heavy reliance on imports and aid from the US. Trade with the US is either directly by air and sea, or indirect via Puerto Rico.
The principal foreign exchange earner is tourism. There is a growing financial services sector and USVI has become the home to a number of foreign sales offices.
Imports
Main imports are foodstuffs, consumer goods and building materials.
Main sources: US, Puerto Rico
Exports
Main exports rum, clocks and watches.
Main destinations: US and Puerto Rico.

Agriculture
Farming
The agricultural sector contributes around 2 per cent to GDP. The US Virgin Islands are mainly hilly with little flat land. The poor quality of the soil and lack of rain precludes large-scale cultivation. Small quantities of sorghum, fruit and vegetables are produced on St Croix and St Thomas. Cattle are the main agricultural product; a special breed of Senepol cattle hardened to the hot temperatures was developed on St Croix for meat export.
Fishing
There is some commercial fishing, mainly of lobsters, but fishing is mostly for game, not commercial purposes. The typical total fish catch is over 300 tonnes (t), plus over 36t of other seafood, per annum.

Industry and manufacturing
The industrial sector contributes around 17 per cent to GDP. Manufacturing is better developed here than in much of the Caribbean; it is small-scale and export-based (mainly to the US). Manufacturers have the right to stamp 'Made in America' on their products. The main activities are rum distilling (3–4 million gallons per year), watch/clock assembly, ethanol refining, woollen textiles and garments.

Tourism
Tourism plays an important role in the islands' economy, with visitor numbers averaging some 2 million annually. Travel and tourism contributed 29.9 per cent of GDP in 2014 and employed 27.0 per cent of the workforce (12,000 jobs).
The Department of Tourism has actively promoted the islands, particularly in the US, offering affordable packaged holidays and the opportunity of visiting without the need of a passport (which most US citizens do not have).
In May 2012, Royal Caribbean International announced it was adding two cruise liners to its regular schedule to the USVI from the 2013–14 season. Apart from the current port-of-calls in St Thomas, St Croix was reinstated on the itinerary.

Hydrocarbons
There are no known deposits of hydrocarbons; all domestic needs must be met by

imports mainly from Trinidad and Tobago. Consumption of petroleum products was 62,000 barrels per day in 2013. On 25 January 2012, the Hovensa oil refinery on Saint Croix was closed down leaving 1,158 workers unemployed.
Any use of imported natural gas is commercially insignificant; around 288,000 tonnes of coal per annum are imported.

Energy
Total installed generating capacity was 323MW in 2013. In 2012 a 15-year energy initiative was launched to reduce fossil fuel use by 60 per cent. At the moment the Islands' rely 100 per cent on oil to generate electricity.

Banking and insurance
Central bank
Federal Reserve System

Time
GMT minus four hours

Geography
The US Virgin Islands consist of four main inhabited islands (St Croix, St Thomas, St John and Water Island) and about 50 smaller, mostly uninhabited, islands. They are situated at the eastern end of the Greater Antilles, about 64km (40 miles) east of Puerto Rico in the Caribbean Sea. These islands are volcanic in origin and have mountainous interiors.
Hemisphere
Northern

Climate
Sub-tropical with a mean annual temperature of 26 degrees Celsius. Low levels of humidity. Rainy season runs May–November.

Entry requirements
Passports
Required by all.
From 23 January 2007, all travellers arriving by air from Canada, Mexico, Central and South America, the Caribbean and Bermuda must have a biometric passport. For Canadian citizens only, under the Nexus programme entry may be achieved using an Air Nexus Card, which includes a retinal-scan.
From 23 January 2008, all arrivals, including US citizens, travelling between Canada, Mexico, Central and South America, the Caribbean and Bermuda through land borders or by sea (including ferries) must have a passport or other biometric, secure documentation as proof of identity.
Visa
US entry requirements apply; visas required by all with some exceptions under the Visa Waiver Program (VWP). This reciprocal programme allows citizens of, among others, the EU, Australasia and Japan entry without a visa if they possess a MRP and have a return/onward ticket, for business and tourist visits up to 90 days. All citizens of visa-free countries who do not have a MRP must apply for a visa. All other visitors must apply for a visa.
For all information on visas see http://travel.state.gov/visa and follow link to *Visa Types for Temporary Visitors* for specific business visas and extended stays.
Currency advice/regulations
The import of local and foreign currency is unrestricted; amounts over US$10,000 (or equivalent) must be declared.
Customs
Personal items are duty-free. Alcohol and gifts are not duty-free.
Certain firearms and ammunition are allowed with a customs permit, obtained in advance.
Prohibited imports
Illegal drugs (personal medication requires a doctor's certificate); soil, plant and animal products (including endangered species); meat, poultry (fresh, dried or canned) and live fish (unless certified disease-free), their eggs (unless canned, pickled or smoked); Cuban cigars (purchased in any country); wildlife and endangered species (including hunting trophies, shells and crafted items); fireworks and hazardous material; some South American pre-Columbian artefacts; merchandise from embargoed countries and counterfeit items.
These prohibitions apply to transit passengers.

Health (for visitors)
Mandatory precautions
Yellow fever vaccination certificate if arriving from infected area.
Advisable precautions
Health insurance is strongly advised.
Adopt precautions when drinking water in rural areas. There is a bilharzia (schistosomiasis) risk when swimming – chlorinated pools are safe. Visitors should consider immunisation against hepatitis A.

Hotels
Advisable to book in advance, especially in winter months. There is an 8 per cent hotel tax. A 15 per cent tip is usual.

Public holidays (national)
Fixed dates
1 Jan (New Year's Day), 6 Jan (Three Kings' Day), 19 Jan (Martin Luther King Day), 3 Jul (Emancipation Day), 4 Jul (US Independence Day), 25 Jul (Hurricane Supplication Day), 17 Oct (Virgin Islands Thanksgiving Day), 1 Nov (D Hamilton Jackson Day), 11 Nov (Veterans' Day), 25 Dec (Christmas Day).
Variable dates
President's Day (second Mon in Feb), Maundy Thursday, Good Friday, Easter Monday, Memorial Day (fourth Mon in May), Labour Day (first Mon in Sep), Columbus Day (second Mon in Oct), US Thanksgiving Day (fourth Thu in Nov).

Working hours
Banking
Mon–Fri: 0900–1430; Fri: 0900–1400, 1530–1700.
Business
Mon–Fri: 0900–1700
Government
Mon–Fri: 0800–1700.
Shops
Mon–Sat: 0900–1700. Some Sunday opening when cruise ships are in port.

Telecommunications
Mobile/cell phones
There are GSM service available.

Electricity supply
110/120V AC, 60 Hz

Getting there
Air
International airport/s: St Thomas-Cyril E. King (STT), 3km west of Charlotte Amalie, duty-free shop, bar, restaurant, bank, shops, car hire. St Croix-Alexander Hamilton (STX), 14km south-west of Christiansted.
Airport tax: None
Surface
Water: Regular ferry service with the British Virgin Islands.
Main port/s: Charlotte Amalie (St Thomas), Christiansted, Frederiksted, South Shore cargo port (St Croix).

Getting about
National transport
Air: There are frequent services between St Thomas and St Croix (by Sunaire Express).
Road: Throughout the islands there are around 800km of well maintained roads.
Buses: Public service on all main routes and group tours available.
Water: Regular ferry service between St Thomas and St John and the British Virgin Islands.
City transport
Taxis: Widely available; fixed-rate system applies but is not always strictly adhered to.
Higher charges are made for extra passengers, luggage and at night. Taxi vans usually carry multiple passengers; private taxis can be arranged for extra cost.
Car hire
A wide selection of cars is available. National licences are accepted and required. Traffic drives on the left. Speed limit is 35kph in towns and 55kph elsewhere.

BUSINESS DIRECTORY
The addresses listed below are a selection only. While World of Information makes every endeavour to check these

addresses, we cannot guarantee that changes have not been made, especially to telephone numbers and area codes. We would welcome any corrections.

Telephone area codes

The international direct dialling code (IDD) for the US Virgin Islands is +1 340 followed by the subscriber's number.

Chambers of Commerce

St Croix Chamber of Commerce, PO Box 4369, Kingshill, St Croix 00851 (tel: 773-1435; fax: 773-8172; e-mail: stcroixchamber@vipowernet.net; internet: www.stxchamber.org).

St Thomas-St John Chamber of Commerce, 6 Main Street, PO Box 324, Charlotte Amalie, St Thomas 00804 (tel: 776-0100; fax: 776-0588; e-mail: chamber@islands.vi).

Banking

Banco Popular de Puerto Rico, Church St, Christiansted, St Croix, VI 00820.

First Virgin Islands Federal Savings Bank, 50 Kronprindesens Gade, Charlotte Amalie, St Thomas, VII 00803 (tel: 776-9494).

Central bank

Federal Reserve System, 20th Street and Constitution Avenue, NW, Washington DC 20551 (tel: (202) 452-3000; fax: (202) 452-3819).

Travel information

National tourist organisation offices

USVI Department of Tourism, PO Box 6400, St Thomas, VI 00804 (tel: 800-372; internet: www.usvitourism.vi).

Other useful addresses

Department of Economic Development and Agriculture (responsible for promotion and development of tourism), PO Box 6400, St Thomas 00804 (tel: 774-8784).

Industrial Development Commission, PO Box 3499, St Croix (tel: 773-6499); PO Box 6400, St Thomas (tel: 774-8784).

Office of the Governor, Government House, 21–22 Kongens Gade, Charlotte Amalie, St Thomas, VI 00801 (tel: 774-0001).

St Croix Hotel and Tourism Association, PO Box 24238, Gallows Bay, St Croix, USVI 00824 (tel: 773-7117; fax: 773-5883, e-mail: hax@noc.usvi.net).

St Thomas and St John Hotel Association, 4-D Contant, St Thomas, USVI 00803 (tel: 774-6835).

US Virgin Islands Economic Develoment Agency, 8000 Nisky Shopping Center, Suite 620, St Thomas, VI 00802 (tel: (340) 714-1700; www.usvida.org)

Virgin Islands Port Authority, Cyril E King Airport, St Thomas, VI 00801 (tel: 774-1629).

Internet sites

Tourist information: www.here.vi

US Office of Insular Affairs: www.doi.gov/oia

US Virgin Islands Guide: www.usvi.net/

Uruguay

KEY FACTS

Official name: República Oriental del Uruguay (Oriental Republic of Uruguay)

Head of State: President Tabare Vazquez (Broad Front) (since 1 March 2015)

Head of government: President Tabare Vazquez

Ruling party: Frente Amplio (FA) (Broad Front) coalition (since 2004)

Area: 176,215 square km

Population: 3.40 million (2014)

Capital: Montevideo

Official language: Spanish

Currency: Peso Uruguayo (Ur$) = 100 centavos

Exchange rate: Ur$28.70 per US$ (Sep 2015)

GDP per capita: US$16,199 (2014)

GDP real growth: 3.32% (2014)

GDP: US$55.14 billion (2014)

Unemployment: 6.49% (2014)

Inflation: 8.88% (2014)

Balance of trade: -US$924.90 million (2014)

Annual FDI: US$2.18 billion (2011)

In Uruguay's 2014 Presidential Election runoff Tabaré Vázquez found himself back in his old job as president. In the run-off Sr Vázquez won comfortably with 52.8 per cent support, well ahead of his centre-right challenger, Luis Lacalle Pou, who gained 40.5 per cent of the vote. The Vázquez victory was very much a vote for continuity, extending the decade-long rule of a leftist coalition and famously allowing it to roll out the legislation that legalised the production and sale of marijuana.

Mr Lacalle had conceded defeat after counts showed an easy victory for Vazquez. No ordinary politician, Uruguay's new president, aged 74, was a respected oncologist who had helped mend the splits within the Frente Amplio (FA) (Broad Front) coalition in the late 1990s and led it to power in 2005, ending the two decades of conservative rule that had followed Uruguay's military dictatorship.

During his earlier presidency from 2005 to 2010, his mixture of welfare programmes and pro-business policies had begun a decade of solid growth and had reduced poverty. He succeeded President José Mujica, a hard act to follow and a political associate whose no-nonsense, folksy style had won him popular affection

Of concern to the Uruguayan electorate were the country's rising crime levels and faltering education performance. Sr Vázquez had promised to increase spending on schools and cut wasteful government spending.

President Vázquez, endorsed the cannabis law, but was less enthusiastic about it than the outgoing president and had reserved the right to modify the legislation depending upon its impact. Losing candidate Lacalle had threatened to repeal much of the legislation if he was elected president, but he had struggled to connect with working-class and rural voters. In earlier Congressional elections the Broad Front had narrowly won a majority, enabling Mr Vázquez to be well in charge when his term as president began in March 2015.

The economy

According to the United Nations Economic Commission for Latin America and the Caribbean (ECLAC), although the international context was not as favourable as in previous years, Uruguay's economy was set to grow by 3.5 per cent in 2014 as it continues to cool. Even so, growth had outperformed the country's historical averages. The labour market had remained strong, with real wages expected to rise by more than two per cent on average and unemployment at a minimum. One of the main concerns of the government had been to fight persistent inflation, which was expected to come in slightly below previous years. The fiscal deficit had widened, to more than 3 per cent of gross domestic product (GDP).

In the 12 months to June 2014 the primary balance fell to post a deficit equivalent to 0.8 per cent of GDP, which was 0.2 per cent larger than for the same period in 2013. The overall public sector deficit widened, too, to the equivalent of 3.6 per cent of GDP at the end of June compared with 1.7 per cent of GDP in the same period of 2013. Fiscal policy could, in ECLAC's view, be regarded as expansionary, especially in view of the increased investment in the non-financial public sector and the tax cuts implemented in 2014 in order to contain inflation. In October 2014 annual inflation was running at 8.11 per cent, down from more than 9 per cent in early 2014 following the government's price containment policy that included the removal of VAT on certain goods and public tariff services and suspending it on specific foods, such as some vegetables.

In mid-2013 the Banco Central del Uruguay (central bank) had begun to implement its monetary policy by managing the monetary aggregates. It had set targets for the trajectories of monetary aggregates, monitoring the broad M1 indicator (cash in circulation, demand deposits and savings accounts). After this change, the central bank had pursued a contractionary monetary policy, which had resulted in a gradual moderation of year-on-year increases in broad M1. In fact, the target ranges for year-on-year variations of the benchmark indicator fell steadily while actual variations were within the ranges – or even below the thresholds set, as had been the case for much of 2014. The contractionary trend could also be seen in local-currency interest rates. For example, in the first five months of 2014, monetary regulation instrument rates had been kept above 14 per cent for all maturities.

The gross public sector debt at the end of June topped US$34 billion, equivalent to 62.8 per cent of GDP. But net debt had held at relatively low levels throughout 2014, showing that the economy's payment capacity had grown. At the end of June it stood at 21.7 per cent of GDP – slightly less than the previous year. After closing 2013 below 21.5 Uruguayan pesos per dollar, the price of the dollar rose steadily during the first half of 2014 to stand at 23 Uruguayan pesos in April and hold at around that level over the following months. Overall, the real effective exchange rate index edged up, driven by improved price competitiveness compared with non-regional trading partners in the first quarter and with respect to other countries within the region in the second quarter.

Between January and September 2014 goods exports (mainly meat, rice and leather) rose by 5 per cent, more than offsetting the decline in agricultural product exports. Although exports of these products increased in volume, prices were down from the previous year. The opposite happened with agro-industrial products, where export volume did not increase but export prices did, especially for dairy products and tanned leather. Service exports jumped 10 per cent because of a bad tourist season. Demand in Brazil and China (the main destinations for Uruguay's goods exports) dropped off but the share going to Mexico and the Middle East almost doubled. As for the trade balance, the current account deficit in goods narrowed, but the historical balance-of-services surplus has disappeared and 2014 could well turn out to be the first year of the twenty-first century to close with a deficit. This had helped worsen the current account trade balance, which posted a 2.5 per cent deficit in the 12 months to June 2014. This deterioration was somewhat more pronounced than in the previous floating year, when the deficit was 1.9 per cent.

Imports of goods increased by 1.5 per cent between January and September 2014. The sector that saw the greatest increase was machinery and equipment (19.2 per cent), fuelled by massive public and private investments. Purchases of consumer goods grew by 6.4 per cent, with particularly sharp rises in durable goods other than automobiles. Oil imports, which have a major impact on total imports, fell 13 per cent in the first three quarters of the year. In services there was a sharp increase in foreign travel.

Foreign direct investment (FDI) climbed 9 per cent in the first half of 2014, but the increase was expected to drop back

KEY INDICATORS — Uruguay

	Unit	2011	2012	2013	2014	**2015
Population	m	*3.37	*3.38	*3.39	3.40	*3.42
Gross domestic product (GDP)	US$bn	46.90	49.92	55.71	55.14	*56.84
GDP per capita	US$	13,914	14,767	16,421	16,199	*16,642
GDP real growth	%	5.7	3.9	4.4	3.3	*2.8
Inflation	%	8.1	8.1	8.6	8.9	*7.9
Unemployment	%	5.9	6.0	6.5	6.5	*6.8
Exports (fob) (goods)	US$m	9,306.9	9,906.6	10,317.4	10,376.2	–
Imports (fob) (goods)	US$m	10,690.4	12,217.0	11,591.0	11,301.1	–
Balance of trade	US$m	-1,383.5	-2,310.4	-1,273.6	-924.9	–
Current account	US$m	-1,442.0	-2,708.0	-2,920.0	-2,615.0	*-2,184.0
Total reserves minus gold	US$m	8,534.4	13,591.0	16,271.0	17,545.0	–
Foreign exchange	US$m	8,013.6	13,058.0	15,721.0	–	–
Exchange rate	per US$	19.09	19.74	21.50	24.32	–

* estimated figure ** forecast figure

slightly by year's end. Manufacturing, real estate investment and land purchases were the top three destinations for foreign investment. Cumulative GDP growth was not expected to top 3.5 per cent in 2014, according to the survey of economic expectations published by the central bank. The information available for the first half of the year points to 3.3 per cent expansion of GDP. The two sectors driving growth were power generation (thanks to heavy rains) and a steadily-growing telecommunications sector. Primary activities and manufacturing remained relatively stable, although some areas saw expansions and contractions. Construction sector activity was down.

As part of Uruguay's long term plan to promote investment in infrastructure and finance investment in electric power plants using renewable energy resources, essentially wind and solar so as to diversify the country energy mix and cut CO2 emissions, the country will be receiving a US$250 million credit line from the Inter American Development Bank (IDB). The plan, known as the Financial Programme for Productive Development, also included financing agriculture investment in irrigation projects and upgrading the citrus growing sector. The programme was to be implemented by Uruguay's development bank, the Banco de la República Oriental del Uruguay (BROU), which has a long and recognised experience in this sort of investment programme.

The initiative strengthened the BROU's position as the financial arm of energy and agricultural investments that contribute to sustainable growth, based on productivity and the competitive position of the Uruguayan agricultural sector. The programme would provide the BROU with resources to finance companies that develop wind power farms. It was estimated that the plan would help finance a series of projects that would generate up to 120MW of clean energy and help alleviate the problems associated with the weakness of the Uruguayan energy mix during years of little rainfall. It would also finance around 2MW in small, distributed-generation solar energy plants so as to demonstrate the viability of this technology.

Risk assessment

Economy	Good
Politics	Good
Regional stability	Good

COUNTRY PROFILE

1516 Spanish explorer Juan Díaz de Solis was killed by indigenous people while he was navigating the Rio de la Plata. His death discouraged European exploration for more than a century.

1700s The Portuguese began colonising Uruguay.

1726 The Spanish founded Montevideo and took over Uruguay.

1776 Uruguay became part of the vice royalty of La Plata, which was run from Buenos Aires in Argentina.

1808 The defeat of the Spanish monarchy by Napoleon weakened La Plata, leading to a rebellion in Uruguay which overthrew the vice royalty. The Uruguay resisted Argentine and Brazilian invaders.

1825 Uruguay achieved formal independence from Spain.

1830 A constitution was approved.

1838–65 Uruguay became embroiled in civil war between the conservative Colorados (reds) and the liberal Blancos (whites).

1865–70 Uruguay joined Argentina and Brazil and fought a war against Paraguay, which was eventually defeated.

1904 The Colorados and Blancos fought their last civil war. The Blancos became the Partido Nacional (PN) (National Party) and the Colorados the Partido Colorado (PC).

1903–07 and 1911–16 President José Batlle y Ordonez (PC), introduced the welfare state, extended the right to vote to women, disestablished the Roman Catholic Church and abolished the death penalty.

1933 A military coup led to the abolition of opposition parties.

1951 A new constitution replaced the post of president with a nine-member council.

1962–73 The Tupamaros guerrillas engaged in a campaign of insurgency.

1973–85 A military dictatorship took power, unleashing a campaign of harsh repression.

1984 Violent protests erupted against military rule. The military dictatorship agreed to step down and return the country to constitutional government.

1985 Julio María Sanguinetti (PC) was elected president.

1989 Luis Alberto Lacalle Herrera (PN) (known as Cuqui) was elected president. A referendum agreed to an amnesty for human rights abusers.

1994 Julio María Sanguinetti was elected president.

1999 Jorge Batlle Ibañez (PC) was elected president.

2000 A commission was set up to investigate 'disappearances' under the military regime.

2002 The financial crisis that weakened many economies in Latin America prompted Batlle to introduce fiscal measures including tax increases, while banks were closed to stop the mass withdrawal of savings; a general strike was called.

2003 The government managed to restructure almost half of its US$11 billion foreign debt, pushing the repayment dates back five years. A referendum rejected proposals for the sale of state oil assets to foreign investment.

2004 The World Bank approved a US$6.80 million grant to promote energy efficient goods and service. Left-wing, Tabaré Vázquez (Frente Amplio) won the presidential election and the Frente Amplio (FA) (Broad Front) coalition party won the parliamentary elections.

2006 International Court of Justice (ICJ) rejected the claim by Argentina that the building of two US$1 billion-plus pulp mills, by Finnish company, Botnia, on its border with Uruguay, would pollute the river ecosystem. Uruguay paid back its US$1.1 billion debt to the International Monetary Fund.

2007 Montevideo became the home of the new parliament of Mercosur, South America's leading trading bloc.

2008 The industry minister announced a natural gas field had been found offshore in Uruguayan waters.

2009 In the first general elections with compulsory voting, the incumbent FA won 60 seats out of 99 in the chamber of deputies and 16 seats out of 30 in the Senate. José Mujica (FA) won the run-off presidential election with 54.8 per cent of the vote; his rival, Luis Alberto Lacalle (PN), won 45.2 per cent.

2010 President José Mujica was sworn into office. A co-operation agreement was signed by the presidents of Uruguay and Brazil, aimed at increasing political and economic integration between the two neighbours. Uruguay denied entry to *HMS Gloucester*, the British frigate charged with guarding the Falklands Islands, which had been *en route* to the Falklands when the captain had requested permission to take on fuel and provisions in Montevideo.

2011 In March, Uruguay recognised the Palestinian State, with borders that existed before the (Arab-Israeli) Six-Day War, in 1967. In August, the Inter-American Development Bank (IADB) approved a US$1.8 billion loan to Uruguay to invest in infrastructure projects.

2012 On 17 October the government approved a new law that legalised abortions (in the first 12 weeks of pregnancy) for all women. On 12 December the lower house of parliament approved a new bill to allow marriage between homosexuals.

2013 Members of the House of Representatives passed a bill to legalise marijuana on 31 July. If passed by the Senate it will make Uruguay the first country to regulate

the production, distribution and sale of marijuana. Regulations will ensure that only the state can sell marijuana, to registered buyers over 18 and not to foreigners. A law permitting same sex marriages came into force on 5 August.
2014 Just months before the Fifa World Cup in Brazil, the entire board of football mad Uruguay's national Football Association resigned on 31 March over the level of violence at football matches.
On 22 November, history was made in Uruguay with the first ever ordination of women to the Anglican priesthood in the country. The ordinations came a day after the synod of the Anglican Church of Uruguay had passed a motion approving the ordination of women to priesthood. The motion was unanimously approved by all three houses of the church's synod. Uruguay is the second country in South America to ordain women to the priesthood after Bolivia, which did so earlier in 2015. The Rev Audrey Gonzalez, the Rev Cynthia Dickin and the Rev Susana Lerena were all ordained priests on the Feast of the Reign of Christ at Holy Trinity Cathedral in Montevideo. All three had been deacons since the late 1990s.

Political structure

Constitution

The constitution dates from 1967, with a period of suspension during military rule between 1973 and 1985. Voting is by secret ballot and is obligatory for all citizens aged 18 and over. The electorate has to vote in support of a single party list for president, mayors and legislators. A reform to permit cross-party voting for the different positions was defeated at a referendum in 1994. In 1997 a major amendment stipulated that in the year leading up to general elections, political parties must hold primary elections in order to choose a presidential candidate to put forward. A smaller 2004 amendment dealt with public ownership of the water supply.

Form of state

Presidential democratic republic

The executive

Executive power is vested in the president, who is directly elected every five years, usually in October or November. The president is assisted by a vice president and an appointed council of ministers. The president has the power to veto parliamentary resolutions, but the veto can be overturned by a three-fifths majority of Congress. The president cannot be elected for consecutive terms.

National legislature

The bicameral Asamblea General (General Assembly) comprises the Cámara de Diputados (Chamber of Deputies) with 99 members and the Cámara de Senadores (Chamber of Senators (Senate)) with 30 members, plus the vice president. Both chambers are elected by proportional representation and members of both serve for five-year terms. Compulsory voting was introduced from October 2009 for the parliamentary and presidential elections.

Legal system

The legal system is based on Spanish civil law. Written law is passed by parliament and promulgated by the president. The ultimate source of the law is the constitution.
Judicial power is exercised by the Supreme Court of Justice which has five members elected by Congress. The Court nominates all other judges and officials.

Last elections

26 October 2014 (parliamentary), 26 October–30 November 2014 (presidential and runoff).
Results: Parliamentary: Broad Front won 49.5 per cent, 50 seats in the chamber (out of 99) and 15 (out of 30); National Party won 31.9 per cent, 32 seats in the chamber and 10 in the senate; Colorado Party won 13.3 per cent, 13 chamber seats and 4 senate seats; Independent Party won 3.2 per cent, 3 chamber seats and 1 senate seat; Popular Assembly 1.2 per cent, 1 chamber seat and 0 senate seat. Two other parties won less than 1 per cent of the popular vote and failed to win seats in either parliament. Turnout was 90.51 per cent.
Presidential (first round): Tabare Vazquez (FA) won 49.5 per cent, Luis Alberto Lacalle Pou (PN) won 31.9 per cent, Pedro Bordaberry (Colorado Party) won 13.3 per cent. (Runoff): Tabare Vazquez won 56.6 per cent, Luis Alberto Lacalle Pou won 43.4 per cent. Turnout for the runoff was 88.57 per cent.

Next elections

October 2019 (presidential and parliamentary)

Political parties

Ruling party

Frente Amplio (FA) (Broad Front) coalition (since 2004)

Main opposition party

Partido Nacional (PN) (National Party)

Population

3.39 million (2013)*
Last census: 30 September 2011: 3,251,526
Population density: 19 inhabitants per square km. Urban population 92 per cent (2010 Unicef).
Annual growth rate: 0.4 per cent, 1990–2010 (Unicef).

Ethnic make-up

Around 90 per cent are of European descent, with approximately one-quarter of the population of Italian origin. Minorities are black and *mestizo* (mixed race), but there are no pure Indian groups.

Religions

The majority of Uruguayans are Roman Catholic (66 per cent) with a small minority of Protestants (2 per cent) and Jews (1 per cent). Secular traditions are strong and a third of the population have no professed religious faith.

Education

All education, including university tuition, is provided free of charge. The curriculum is the same in both public and private schools. Secondary education is available from aged 12 and divided into two three-year courses. Technical studies are offered in technical schools and last between two and seven years. There are five universities and enrolment in tertiary education is typically 30 per cent.
Literacy rate: 98 per cent adult rate; 99 per cent youth rate (15–24) (Unesco 2005).
Compulsory years: Six to 14
Enrolment rate: 109.5 per cent gross primary enrolment; 98.5 per cent gross seconday enrolment, of relevant age groups (including repeaters) (Unicef 2004).
Pupils per teacher: 20 in primary schools

Health

HIV/Aids

HIV prevalence: 0.3 per cent aged 15–49 in 2003 (World Bank)
Life expectancy: 75 years, 2004 (WHO 2006)
Fertility rate/Maternal mortality rate: 2.1 births per woman, 2010 (Unicef); maternal mortality 26 per 100,000 live births (World Bank).
Child (under 5 years) mortality rate (per 1,000): 7 per 1,000 live births (WHO 2012)
Head of population per physician: 3.65 physicians per 1,000 people, 2002 (WHO 2006)

Welfare

Uruguay maintains one of the most comprehensive systems of social security in Latin America, including free education, state medical care, pensions and unemployment benefits. Social security spending accounts for around 15 per cent of GDP.
The largest welfare expenditure is the payment of old age pensions. The long tradition of healthcare provision and a relatively low mortality rate have produced an ageing population. The pension age is low (with sometimes less than 30 years' service required). There are some 800,000 old-age pensioners out of a total population of three million and compared to a workforce of only one million, producing one of the highest ratios of pensioners to workers in the world.

There is widespread and vociferous opposition to any modification of the social security system. Many of the welfare benefits, including a workers' charter stipulating maximum hours, minimum wages and paid holidays, date from the beginning of the twentieth century.
Social security is covered by the state budget with about 50 per cent of contributions coming from tax revenues. Despite attempts by the government to raise the percentage derived from taxes, the remaining 50 per cent is still split roughly equally between contributions from workers and employers. Almost 90 per cent of the population is covered for all benefits. Housewives, who are ineligible for retirement benefit, only receive separate pensions after their husbands have died.
Benefits include: a retirement pension at 60 for men, 55 for women or after 30 years of recognised service; an invalidity pension after 10 years of recognised service; an early retirement pension for citizens fulfilling political duties; free maternity care for working women and workers' wives; and sick pay of up to three months for all workers. Unemployment pay of up to six months is provided for all workers who have paid contributions for a year or more. This can reach up to 75 per cent of nominal salary. All medical costs are met by the state during the six-month period.

Main cities

Montevideo (capital, estimated population 1.3 million in 2012), Salto (108,197), Ciudad de la Costa (107,154), Las Piedras (80,052), Paysandú (78,868), Rivera (71,222), Maldonado (65,865), Tacuarembó (54,994), Melo (54,674), Artigas (44,905).

Languages spoken

Business languages: English and Portuguese. French and Italian are also widely spoken.

Official language/s

Spanish

Media

Press

Dailies: In Spanish, national newspapers, mostly published in Montevideo, include *El País* (www.elpais.com.uy), *Diario Cambio* (www.diariocambio.com.uy), *El Telégrafo* (www.eltelegrafo.com), *La República* (www.larepublica.com.uy), and *Ultimas Noticias* (www.ultimasnoticias.com.uy) an evening newspaper.
Weeklies: In Spanish, there are many magazines, the biggest of which is *Brecha* (www.brecha.com.uy), *Juventud* (www.chasque.apc.org/juventud) is a youth magazine, *Guambia* (www.guambia.com.uy) is a satirical weekly.
In English, the *Uruguay Daily News* (www.uruguaydailynews.com) has an online news digest.
Business: In Spanish, the leading weekly publications are *Crónicas Económicas* (www.cronicas.com.uy) and *Búsqueda (Search)*, while *El Observador* (www.observador.com.uy) is a business-oriented newspaper. *Económico* (www.redtercermundo.org.uy/tm_economico/) is a monthly publication.
Periodicals: There are numerous periodicals and a few trade publications. The government's official journal *Diario Oficial* (www.impo.com.uy) is a monthly publication.

Broadcasting

The government-owned, national broadcaster is Servicio Oficial de Defusión Radiotelevisión y Espectáculos (SODRE) (www.sodre.gub.uy).
Radio: The public radio network has four stations broadcasting cultural, news, educational and entertainment programmes. There are more than 100 private, commercial radio stations, all broadcasting in Spanish, located throughout the country. From Montevideo, Radio Monte Carlo (www.radiomontecarlo.com.uy), Radio El Espectador (/www.espectador.com), Radio Sarandí (www.radiosarandi.com.uy) and 1410 AM Libre (www.1410amlibre.com.uy) transmit news and entertainment programmes.
Television: Over 70 per cent of households own television sets.
The public television channel TV Nacional Uruguay known as TNU (www.tnu.com.uy) broadcasts news, documentaries and cultural programmes nationally. Commercial TV stations include Teledoce (www.teledoce.com), Saeta TV Canal 10 (www.canal10.com.uy) and Monte Carlo TV canal 4 (www.canal4.com.uy) broadcasts foreign Spanish language shows, as well as dubbed US TV shows, and TV Ciudad (www.teveciudad.org.uy) broadcasting cultural shows.
There are pay-for-view television services available through (www.paysandu.com).
Other news agencies: Mercopress (in English): www.mercopress.com

Economy

The wealth of Uruguay is generated by agriculture and manufacturing, including food processing using domestic products. Its natural resources include fertile farmland, plentiful water for hydroelectricity generation and minerals including granite and marble. Its service sector, which constituted 64 per cent of GDP in 2014, includes a healthy tourist industry as well as ancillary and support industries for agriculture and manufacturing. Agricultural products include wheat, rice, barley and wine. However its single most important component is its cattle production. Uruguay suffered a period of severe draught between 2008 and 2009 which affected its cattle production capabilities. By 2014 cattle production was showing signs of recovery, with 580,000 tonnes carcass weight equivalent (cwe) forecast. Increasing calf prices have encouraged cattle slaughter, which in 2013 was 2.1 million head. As well as meat, exports include dairy and leather products plus live animals. Its large flocks of sheep produce lambs' meat and wool for export (around 80 per cent of wool production). In 2013 China became the main destination for Uruguayan meat exports (26 per cent of all meat exports went to China), overtaking Russia and Europe.

The total volume of exported beef for the year ending April 2015 was 115,731 tons, whereas in 2014 the number stood at 102,154 tons. The change in revenue and the change in volume of beef exports therefore both amount to increases of 13 per cent, compared with the same period in 2014.
Uruguay's exported meat, meat products and by-products were worth US$550 million in the year up to April 2015, 8 per cent more than the same period of 2014. Beef exports totalled 454 million in the first months of the year, with the main buyers including China, member countries of the North American Free Trade Agreement (NAFTA), the European Union and Israel.
The financial sector is an important component of the economy. Following the international financial crisis, the Banco Central del Uruguay (central bank) approved US$4 million to strengthen institutional supervision of the sector in December 2009. This aided the country in avoiding recession and maintaining positive growth rates.
GDP growth was 3 per cent in 2014; down from 5 per cent in 2013. Inflation rose from 7 per cent in 2013 to 10 per cent in 2014.
Uruguay's per capita income is one of the highest in Latin America. It is growing steadily — in recent years from US$14,767 in 2012 to an estimated US$16,810.9 in 2014, reflecting the general growth in the economy as a whole. Remittances in 2013 were US$122.7 million (0.2 per cent of GDP), dropping slightly to US$122 million in 2014. Unemployment in Uruguay has been slowly reducing since 2009 and was at 6.49 per cent in 2014.

External trade

As a member of Mercosur, the world's fourth largest free-trade zone, Uruguay (along with Argentina, Brazil, Venezuela and Paraguay), has access to a market of over 200 million consumers. The EU and Mercosur have been in negotiations to create a mutual free trade zone since 2004 and in 2015 these were still ongoing. Uruguay is also an associate member of the Andean Community (AC), with which Mercosur has negotiated a free trade area.

Foreign trade accounts for around 50 per cent of GDP. Almost 90 per cent of productive land is used for animal husbandry with agriculture the largest exporting sector. Processed meat (fresh, canned and frozen) and animal products account for around 50 per cent of manufactured activity.

Imports

Main imports are fuels, capital machinery, chemicals and plastics, vehicles, electrical and electronic equipment.

Main sources: China (18.5 per cent of total in 2014), Brazil (17 per cent), Argentina (12.9 per cent).

Exports

Main exports are meat (particularly beef), rice, wine, raw hides and skins, wool, fish and dairy products.

Main destinations: Brazil (17.6 per cent of total in 2014), China (13.3 per cent), Argentina (4.8 per cent).

Agriculture

Farming

Though agricultural production accounts for approximately 6 per cent of total GDP, agricultural-related products make up more than half of the country's exports. The sector also employs around 11 per cent of the Uruguayan workforce.

Traditional exports have been hit by protectionism and tough competition from the EU.

The sector is also an important supplier of raw materials (sugar, oilseeds, etc) to industry. It is expanding more rapidly than industry.

Livestock rearing forms the basis of the sector with cattle and sheep being produced for domestic consumption and for export (as meat, wool, hides and skins). Poultry and pigs are largely produced for the home market but exports of dairy products are increasing in importance. Exports of butter and cheese to Mercosur countries are substantial. A severe drought in 2008–09 caused a fall in cow herd numbers, which affected the amount of beef available for export; numbers have since increased so that 580'000 tonnes carcass weight equivalent was forecast. However, pasture available has been reduced and passed over to soybean cultivation whilst livestock production has become more intense, with an emphasis on maintaining its bovine spongiform encephalopathy-free (BSE) status and improving herd management. Uruguay has been systematically vaccinating its national herd against foot-and-mouth disease (FMD) to avoid foreign import restrictions.

There is virtual self-sufficiency in food, although imports of wheat are required at times of low harvests.

Principal crops are wheat (mainly grown on mixed farms), rice (the main export crop, grown almost entirely in the north-east), sugar (cane and beet), maize, barley, sorghum, linseed, sunflower seed, vegetables (mainly grown by smallholders) and citrus fruits (mainly oranges and tangerines).

Fishing

The fishing industry typically generates US$80 million in exports per annum. Uruguay suffers from water pollution from its meat and leather industries, which has hit the fishing sector over the years. If this problem can be permanently eradicated the prospects for the fishing industry will improve markedly.

In 2013, Nigeria's ban on fish imports caused Uruguay's volume of fish exports to reduce by 20 per cent. Before this, Nigeria was the main importer of fish from Uruguay.

Forestry

Uruguay has approximately 1.2 million hectares of forested land, which constitutes 5 per cent of the country's total landmass.

Assisted by fiscal incentives, forestry has become a dynamic sector, attracting both foreign and domestic investment. Local forest resources produce modest quantities of sawn timber and pulp with most of paper products imported.

It is estimated that 1.7 million tonnes of timber per year could be exported, but improvements and remodelling of existing facilities and infrastructure would be needed in order to transport the timber.

Industry and manufacturing

The industrial sector contributes around 20 per cent to GDP in 2014, and employs around 19 per cent of the workforce. However, the sector has been in recession since 1999 and is suffering large reductions in investment. However, investment rose to 7.3 per cent of total investment in 2014 and is expected to rise by 2.1 per cent per annum for the next 10 years. Government industrial policy has promoted export operations, based mainly on agricultural processing and related labour-intensive industries. Although traditional key sectors such as meat processing and packing, the wool industry and fisheries still have priority, attention has turned to other sectors such as textiles and leather. The penetration of new markets has been a key feature of plans to stimulate manufacturing industry and exports.

Despite a number of new trade agreements with Mercosur, the US and Mexico, industry has still suffered from deep-seated structural problems. These have included high levels of internal debt, obsolete machinery and poor investment. The recent and sharp depreciation of the Uruguay peso has pushed up the cost of imported capital and intermediate goods, thereby preventing a restocking of capital.

Tourism

Uruguay is a popular destination for foreign travellers due to its small population, its old-world charm and diverse landscape, ranging from the Atlantic shore to the interior countryside, well-liked by active holiday makers. The historic quarter of the city of Colonia del Sacramento is included on Unesco's World Heritage List, for its mix of Portuguese, Spanish and post-colonial architecture.

Travel and tourism contributed 8.8 per cent of GDP in 2014 providing employment for 8.3 per cent of the workforce (132,000 jobs). Visitor exports in the 2014 was US$43.1 billion and forecast to grow by 2 per cent in 2015.

The new passenger terminal at Carrasco International Airport (Montevideo) opened in 2009 and catered for 1.7 million arrivals in 2013.

The flag carrier airline of Uruguay, Pluna announced that it might collapse in 2012 after experiencing financial distress that led to an US$18 million loss over the eight month period ending in February of that year. Later on the government announced that Pluna's fleets and routes would be auctioned.

Uruguay made tax reforms in 2009 that allowed visitors to reclaim value added tax (VAT) on Uruguayan made (including food and beverage) purchases when leaving the country. VAT is not charged by hotels, thus boosting Uruguay as a tourist destination, with a competitive edge over neighbouring countries.

Mining

Mining and quarrying combined make up less than 1 per cent of Uruguay's total GDP. The country has few known mineral reserves and is wholly dependent on imports for raw materials ranging from oil to aluminium.

There are known deposits of iron ore, gold, manganese, copper, zinc and lead. Regulations in 1990 opened up the sector to foreign investment but very few foreign companies are active. Argentina has been the main purchaser of sand from Uruguay

while Spain, South Africa and the US have purchased semi-precious stones and granite. Japan and Argentina are also important markets for granite exports. However, most mine production is consumed domestically.
A US$3 billion Valentines open-pit iron ore project, known as Aratarí, will go ahead according to the Uruguayan President, Jose Mujica. The proposal by London-based Zamin Ferrous has been met with great opposition. Despite this, the project will begin construction in the next year.

Hydrocarbons
The state oil company, the Administration Nacional de Combustibles Alcohol y Portland (National Administration of Fuel, Alcohol and Portland Cement) (ANCAP) has a monopoly on oil importing and refining. Capacity at the country's only refinery at La Teja near Montevideo is 50,000 barrels per day (bpd). La Teja is relatively efficient, making Uruguayan refined oil sufficiently competitive to allow ANCAP to re-export small quantities of refined products when production exceeds domestic demand, typically around 7,000 barrels per day. Uruguay is a member of Asistencia Recíproca Petrolera Empresarial Latinoamericana (Reciprocal State Assistance for Petroleum in Latin America) (ARPEL), grouping all countries in the region. Despite efforts for privatisation, ANCAP still operates a monopoly.
There is a natural gas pipeline connecting the Argentine gas fields to Uruguayan power plants runs from Entre Rios, Argentina to Paysandu, Uruguay. This pipeline system is being managed by the state oil company ANCAP. A second larger pipeline including the US$170 million Cruz del Sur (Southern Cross) line enhances natural gas trade between Argentina, Brazil and Uruguay. Substantial work on the pipeline began in March 2001. The main market will initially be Montevideo. This pipeline was developed by Gasoducto Cruz del Sur, a consortium comprising British Gas (40 per cent), Pan American Energy (40 per cent) and ANCAP (20 per cent). Other investments totalling approximately US$961 million will be used to extend the gas network throughout Uruguay.
The importance of natural gas in the country's energy sector will increase with the construction of new pipelines and distribution systems. The first pipeline in production carries natural gas from Argentina to western Uruguay, with a capacity of 138,000bpd. There are plans for an extensive pipeline network as the government encourages an increase in gas usage to 30 per cent of primary energy consumption; however the country's economic problems have hindered this target. Currently only negligible quantities are imported.
There are some known deposits of low-grade coal although no coal is produced and imports are less than two million tonnes per annum.
Significant offshore explorations have been occurring since 2012. Investments of US$3 billion is estimated to have contributed to the explorations from 2012–2015.

Energy
Total installed generating capacity was 2.59 gigawatts (GW) in 2013. Production was 9.5 billion kilowatt hours (kWh) in 2011, and consumption was 7.96kWh. Uruguay's electricity mainly comes from hydropower but also relies heavily on imports, predominantly from Argentina and Brazil.
The 1.9GW hydropower plant at Salto Grande (built with Argentina), the 300MW Palmar plant, and two plants on the Rio Negro, provide the majority of energy consumed.Total installed generating capacity was 2.59 gigawatts (GW) in 2013. Production was 9.5 billion kilowatt hours (kWh) in 2011, and consumption was 7.96kWh. Uruguay's electricity mainly comes from hydropower but also relies heavily on imports, predominantly from Argentina and Brazil.
The 1.9GW hydropower plant at Salto Grande (built with Argentina), the 300MW Palmar plant, and two plants on the Rio Negro, provide the majority of energy consumed.
2015: Uruguay is in the process of modifying its energy mix with the aim of achieving carbon neutrality by 2030, by means of a strategy that bolsters non-conventional clean energy sources through public-private partnerships and new investment. By the end of 2014, Uruguay's energy mix was made up of 55 per cent renewable sources, compared to a global average of just 12 per cent. A Energy Efficiency Plan was adopted on 3 August 2015 which aims to reduce energy consumption in all industries and sectors of the economy, but especially in residential areas and transportation, which will be responsible for 75 per cent of the total accumulated reduction by 2024.

Financial markets
Stock exchange
Bolsa de Valores de Montevideo (BVM) (Montevideo Stock Exchange)

Banking and insurance
Uruguay's banking and financial services sector continues to be dominated by three public banks. The Banco Central del Uruguay (BCU), which does not offer private credit, the Banco de la República Oriental de Uruguay (BROU) and the Banco Hipotecario de Uruguay (BHU) are the kingpins of the financial system.
The BROU is multi-purpose and is the largest credit provider, offering 40 per cent of overall private credit in Uruguay and receiving 33 per cent of deposits. The Banco Hipotecario specialises in mortgage lending.
In 2003, the Banco Comercial, the Banco de Montevideo and the Banco la Caja Obrera merged into a new institution, the Nuevo Banco Comercial.
A new Bank of the South, with a headquarters in Venezuela, will be launched in 2008 to provide an alternative source of development funding for the participating countries. Assets of US$7 billion will underpin its operations.
Central bank
Banco Central del Uruguay
Main financial centre
Montevideo

Time
GMT minus three hours (daylight saving, GMT minus two hours, is determined by presidential decree)

Geography
Uruguay has an area of 176,215 square km and is bordered by Argentina to the west, by Brazil in the north and by the Atlantic and the wide River Plate estuary to the south-east. The largest river, the Uruguay, runs along the border with Argentina.
About 95 per cent of the country is rolling grassland, with few hills above 300 metres. The highest point is the Cerro Catedral at 514 metres. Only about 6 per cent of the land is naturally forested.
The River Negro (Río Negro), the main tributary of the River Uruguay, cuts across the centre of the country, separating the two main ranges of hills, the Cuchilla de Haedo and the Cuchilla Grande. Artificial lakes on the Rio Negro cover 1,199 square km.
Hemisphere
Southern

Climate
The climate is temperate and rainfall is abundant, with an average of about 100 days of rain a year. In January, the hottest summer month, average temperatures range between 21 degrees Celsius (C) on the coast and 26 degrees C inland. In July the average temperatures are between 11 degrees C on the coast and 13 degrees C in the interior, with temperatures occasionally falling to freezing point at night.

Dress codes
Clothing is mostly informal, but jackets and ties or suits for men and skirts for

women are usual for business. Uruguayans generally wear more conservative colours than their neighbours in Brazil and Argentina.

Entry requirements

Passports

Required by all except nationals of Argentina, Bolivia, Brazil, Chile, Colombia, Costa Rica, Dominican Republic, Ecuador, Guatemala, Honduras, Paraguay, Peru and the US. Nationals from these countries need a national identity card.

Visa

Required by all except nationals of EU, US, Canada, Japan, Norway, Switzerland, most Latin American countries and certain others for visits up to three months. A Tourist Card will be issued when travellers enter the country (usually given to airline passengers before landing), and must be kept until departure.

Business travellers from the countries mentioned above do not require visas. All other business visitors must have a letter of authorisation from their company or organisation.

The visitor is advised to check with the nearest consulate to determine the validity of their status before travelling.

Currency advice/regulations

The import and export of local and foreign currency is unrestricted.

Travellers cheques, in US dollars (US$50 and US$100 denominations only) are readily accepted. All other currency cheques have very limited acceptance.

Customs

Personal effects are allowed in duty-free, precious jewels and gold (worth more than US$500) must be declared.

Prohibited imports

Precious jewels, gold, firearms, pornography, subversive literature, inflammable articles, acids, illegal drugs, plants, seeds, and foodstuffs as well as some antiquities and business equipment must be declared.

Health (for visitors)

Mandatory precautions

None

Advisable precautions

A typhoid vaccination may be necessary. Water precautions should be taken outside Montevideo.

Excellent health care is available but foreign visitors must pay the full cost.

Hotels

Graded into four classes by the National Tourism Bureau – de luxe, 1, 2A and 2B. There is a 20 per cent value added tax on hotel bills. Service charge is normally included – if not, usually 10 per cent tip.

Credit cards

Major credit and charge cards are readily accepted. ATMs may not accepted foreign cards.

Public holidays (national)

Fixed dates

1 Jan (New Year's Day), 6 Jan (Epiphany), 1 May (Labour Day), 19 Jun (Birth of General Artigas), 18 Jul (Constitution Day), 25 Aug (Independence Day), 12 Oct (Discovery of America Day), 2 Nov (All Souls' Day), 25 Dec (Christmas Day).

Variable dates

Carnival (two days, Feb), Holy Wednesday–Good Friday (Easter–three days, Mar/Apr), Landing of the 33 Patriots (third Mon Apr), Battle of Las Piedras (third Mon May),

Working hours

Banking

Mon–Fri: 1000–1400; summer variations may apply in certain areas.

Business

Mon–Fri: 0830–1200, 1430–1830.

Government

From mid-Mar to mid-Dec: Mon–Fri: 0900–1600. From mid-Dec to mid-Mar: Mon–Fri: 0730–1330.

Shops

Mon–Sat: 0830–1230/1300, 1530/1600–1900/2000; Sun 0830–1200 food shops only.

Telecommunications

Mobile/cell phones

There are 850/1900, 1900 and 1800 GSM services available throughout most of the country.

Electricity supply

220V AC, 50 cycles

Social customs/useful tips

Punctuality is expected and business cards are essential. Uruguay's population is mostly of Italian or Spanish descent, and maintains many European customs, ranging from diet to dress. There is a long tradition of liberal legislation in contrast to many South American countries. Divorce and gambling, for example, are both legal. There is provision in the law for duels in matters of honour, something which much of the population considers an anachronism but which is nevertheless invoked from time to time.

Same sex marriage became legal from 5 August 2013.

Security

Residents consider the capital relatively safe to walk around at night compared with other South American cities.

Getting there

Air

National airline: Former national airline Pluna was closed down in 2012.

International airport/s: Montevideo-Carrasco International (MVD), 19km from city; duty-free shops, bar, restaurant, bank, post office and car hire.

Airport tax: Departure tax: US$26; Buenos Aires only US$14. Not applicable to transit passengers.

Surface

Road: There are a number of border crossings from Brazil, the crossing from Argentina is preferable by car-ferry. A US$176 million programme to improve primary highways is under way.

Water: There are high-speed ferries and a night-ferry service from Buenos Aires–Montevideo (internet: www.buquebus.com). There are also services from Colonia (160km west of Montevideo) to Buenos Aires by ferry and a hydrofoil service (three times daily). A port departure tax may be levied.

Main port/s: Montevideo River Plate (Rio Plate) harbour includes all the country's main port facilities, served by worldwide cargo lines.

Getting about

National transport

Air: The only internal destinations currently offered are domestic legs of international flights.

Road: Ninety per cent of roads are paved and while urban roads are good, rural roads are only fair. The highway network radiates from Montevideo towards the borders of Brazil and Argentina.

Buses: ONDA, CITA and COT run fast and frequent lines, connecting most towns across the country (routes include: Montevideo-Punta del Este and Montevideo-Paysandú).

Rail: The slow rail system only connects a few villages and is under threat of closure.

Water: Scheduled river services do not exist.

City transport

Taxis: Taxis are widely available in towns and from airports. They can be hailed in the street. Fares are metered, with higher charges for extra passengers and between 0000–0600. They can be hired on a time basis, in which case fares should be negotiated in advance. A 10 per cent tip is usual.

Buses, trams & metro: An extensive bus service links all the capital's suburbs. There is an airport bus to the city centre, travelling time 35 minutes.

Car hire

International driving licence must be accompanied by two photographs; traffic conditions within Montevideo can be difficult and chauffeur-driven cars are recommended. A driving permit for 90 days can be obtained from Montevideo town hall.

BUSINESS DIRECTORY

The addresses listed below are a selection only. While World of Information makes every endeavour to check these addresses, we cannot guarantee that changes have not been made, especially to telephone numbers and area codes. We would welcome any corrections.

Telephone area codes

The international dialling code (IDD) for Uruguay is +598 followed by area code and subscriber's number:

Canelones	33	Minas	44
Florida	352	Montevideo	2
Las Piedras	2	Paysandú	72
Maldonado	42	Punta del Este	42
Mercedes	53	San José de Carrasco	2

Useful telephone numbers

Emergency: 911
Emergency, outside Montevideo: 02911
Roadside assistance: 1707

Chambers of Commerce

American-Uruguayan Chamber of Commerce, Plaza Independencia 831, Edificio Plaza Mayor, 11100 Montevideo (tel: 908-9186; fax: 908-9187; email: info@ccuruguayusa.com).

British-Uruguayan Cámara de Comercio, Avenida Libertador Brigadier General Lavalleja 1641, Piso2, Oficina 201, CP 11.100 Montevideo (tel: 908-0349; fax: 908-0936; email: camurbri@netgate.com.uy).

Uruguay Cámara Nacional de Comercio y Servicios, Rincón 454, 11000 Montevideo (tel: 916-1277; fax: 916-1243; email: info@cncs.com.ny).

Banking

Banco de la República Oriental del Uruguay, Cerrito No. 351 Casa Central, Montevideo.

Banco Exterior, Sarandi No. 402, 11000 Montevideo.

Banco Holandés Unido, Sucursal Montevideo, 25 de Mayo No. 501, 11000 Montevideo.

Banco Pan de Azucar, Rincón No. 518/528, 11000 Montevideo .

Banco Santander, Cerrito No. 449, 11000 Montevideo.

Banco Sudameris, Rincón No. 500, Montevideo.

Banco Surinvest, Rincón No. 530, Montevideo.

Banesto-Banco Uruguay, 25 de Mayo No. 401, 11000 Montevideo.

Citibank, Cerrito No. 455, Montevideo.
Discount Bank (Latin America), Rincón No. 390, Montevideo.

The First National Bank of Boston, Zabala No. 1463, 11000 Montevideo.

ING Bank S.A., Misiones No. 352/60, Montevideo.

Lloyds Bank (BOLSA), Zabala No. 1500, Montevideo.

Nuevo Banco Comercial (NBC), Cerrito No. 400, 11100 Montevideo.

Central bank

Banco Central del Uruguay, Diagonal Fabini 777, 11100 Montevideo. (tel/fax: 1967; e-mail: info@bcu.gub.uy).

Stock exchange

Bolsa de Valores de Montevideo (BVM) (Montevideo Stock Exchange), www.bolsademontevideo.com.uy

Bolsa Electronica de Valores de Uruguay (BEVSA), www.bevsa.com.uy

Travel information

Pluna Airlines, Administration Head Offices, Miraflores 1445, Carrasco (tel: 604-2244; fax: 604-2260; email: info@pluna.aero; internet: www.pluna.com.uy).

Ministry of tourism

Ministerio de Turismo del Uruguay (Ministry of Tourism), Rambla 25 de Agosto de 1825 esq, Yacaré, S/N (plano), Montevideo (tel: 188-5100; internet: www.turismo.gub.uy).

Ministries

Ministerio de Defensa Nacional (National Defence), Edificio 'Gral.Artigas', Avda. 8 de Octubre 2628, Montevideo.

Ministerio de Economía y Finanzas (Economy and Finance), Colonia 1089, P3, Montevideo.

Ministerio de Educación y Cultura (Education and Culture), Reconquista 535, Montevideo.

Ministerio de Ganadería, Agricultura y Pesca (Livestock, Agriculture and Fisheries), Constituyente 1476 Montevideo.

Ministerio de Industria, Energía y Minería (Industry, Energy and Mines), Rincón 747, Montevideo.

Ministerio del Interior (Home Office), Mercedes 993, Montevideo.

Ministerio de Relaciónes Exteriores (Foreign Affairs), Av 18 de Julio 1205, Montevideo.

Ministerio de Salud Pública (Public Health), Av 18 De Julio 1892, Montevideo. Ministerio de Trabajo y Seguridad Social (Labour and Social Security), Juncal 1511, Montevideo.

Ministerio de Transporte y Obras Públicas (Transport and Public Works), Rincón 561, Montevideo.

Ministerio de Vivienda, Ordenamiento Territorial y Medio Ambiente (Housing, Territorial Regulation and Environment), Zabala 1427, Montevideo.

Oficina de Planeamiento y Presupuesto (OPP) (Planning and Budget Office), Dr Luis A de Herrera 3350, Montevideo.

Other useful addresses

Aero Consultora Uruguaya, Florida 1280-202, Montevideo.

Asociación de Importadores y Mayoristas de Almacén, Ed de la Bolsa de Comercio, Rincón 454, Montevideo.

British Embassy, Calle Marco Bruto 1073, Montevideo (tel: 622-3630; fax: 622-7815; email: bemonte@internet.com.uy).

Comisión Para el Desarrollo de la Inversión (Committee for Investment Development), Plaza Independencia 776, P1 11100 Montevideo.

Cenci (Centro de Estadísticas Naciónales y Comercio Internacional del Uruguay) Misiones 136, 1 Montevideo.

Comisión Sectorial para el Mercosur, Paysandú esq, Florida, Montevideo.

Compañía Uruguaya de Exportaciónes S.A. (Comurex), Misiones 1372 Oficina 303, Montevideo.

Dirección General de Comercio Exterior (Bureau of Foreign Affairs), Cuareim 1384, P2 11100 Montevideo.

Dirección General de Estadísticas y Censos (DGEC), Cuareim 2052, Montevideo.

Dirección Nacional de Aduanas, Rbla. 25 de Agosto esq. Yacaré, Montevideo.

Laboratorio Tecnológico del Uruguay, Av Italia 6201, Montevideo.

Latin American Integration Association, Cebollati 1461, Casilla de Correo 577, Montevideo.

Unidad Asesora de Promoción Industrial, Rincón 723, P.2, Montevideo.

Unión de Exportadores, Rincón 454, P.2, Montevideo.

Uruguayan Embassy (USA), 1913 'I' Street, NW, Washington DC 20006 (tel: (1-202) 331-1313; fax: (1-202) 331-8142; e-mail: uruwashi@uruwashi. org).

Mercopress (in English): www.mercopress.com

Internet sites

El Observador Económico (Spanish): http://www.observador.com.uy

El Pais digital edition (Spanish): http://www.diarioelpais.com.edicion

Crónicas Económicas: http://www.cronicas.com.uy

Montevideo Free Zone (Zona France de Montevideo): http://www.zfm.com

Uzbekistan

According to the Asian Development Bank (ADB), in 2014 Uzbekistan's growth rose marginally to 8.1 per cent as increased lending and public outlays offset the impact of the weakening economy in the Russian Federation. Recession in Russia and sluggish external demand were projected to slow growth to 7.0 per cent in 2015 before it edging back up to 7.2 per cent in 2016 as the external outlook improves. Inflation is projected to reach 9.5 per cent in 2015 and 10.0 per cent in 2016, with the current account showing surpluses of 0.9 per cent and then 1.1 per cent of GDP.

Growth

The government had also reported growth at 8.1 per cent in 2014, slightly above 8.0 per cent in the previous year. Lower growth was expected because of the economic slowdown in Russia, Uzbekistan's largest trade partner and its major source of remittances. The slowdown there reduced bilateral trade and remittances, while lower export earnings accelerated the depreciation of the Uzbek sum against the US dollar. In response, the government had expanded public spending and commercial lending to sustain domestic demand. On the supply side, industry and services were the main contributors to growth, as industry, excluding construction, expanded by 8.3 per cent, versus 8.8 per cent in 2013 and services expanded by 15.4 per cent, up from 13.7 per cent in 2013. In industry, the ongoing state modernisation programme, backed by substantial public investment, boosted the production of machinery, metals and chemicals, which expanded by 10.2 per cent and contributed almost 40 per cent of total industrial output. In services, strong performers were information and communication technology (up by 24.1 per cent) and finance (up by 33.9 per cent), supported by robust demand and domestic lending. Another important service sub-sector – trade and catering – grew by 17.5 per cent. Despite unfavourable weather, agriculture grew by 6.9 per cent, faster than in 2013, on healthy vegetable harvests and expanded livestock production.

On the demand side, increases in wages and pensions, public investment and commercial lending were the main sources of growth. Public sector wages rose by 19.1 per cent in 2014, sustaining private consumption. Gross fixed capital formation was reported rising by 10.9 per cent. Capital investment reached US$14.6 billion, or 24 per cent of GDP, including more than US$3.0 billion in foreign investment. Notable projects completed in 2014 included the expansion of the General Motors

KEY FACTS

Official name: Ozbekiston Respublikasy (Republic of Uzbekistan)

Head of State: President Islam Abduganievich Karimov (since 1991; last re-elected 29 Mar 2015)

Head of government: Technically it is Prime Minister Shavkat Mirziyayev (appointed 11 Dec 2003), but in reality Karimov rules as an autocratic dictator

Ruling party: Coalition of Uzbekistan Liberal Democratic Party, People's Democratic Party of Uzbekistan, Uzbekistan National Revival Democratic Party and Justice Social Democratic Party

Area: 447,400 square km

Population: 30.60 million (2014)*

Capital: Tashkent

Official language: Uzbek

Currency: Sum (Sum) = tiyin

Exchange rate: Sum2,605.83 per US$ (Sep 2015)

GDP per capita: US$2,046 (2014)*

GDP real growth: 8.10% (2014)*

GDP: US$62.62 billion (2014)*

Inflation: 8.42% (2014)*

Oil production: 67,000 bpd (2014)

Natural gas production: 57.30 billion cum (2014)

Balance of trade: -US$162.00 million (2010)

* estimated figure

Uzbekistan automobile manufacturing plant and the completion of a key branch of the gas pipeline linking Central Asia to the People's Republic of China. Commercial bank lending raised credit to the economy by 31.2 per cent.

The government reported average annual inflation at 6.1 per cent in 2014. Official consumer price index data showed that inflation slowed primarily because food prices fell in line with global trends. The International Monetary Fund (IMF) estimated, using the same data as the government but a different methodology, that inflation had slowed to 8.4 per cent from 11.2 per cent in 2013. Inflation was nevertheless believed to have risen in the fourth quarter because of rapid currency depreciation against the US dollar. Unofficial street market rates showed the sum, losing approximately 20 per cent of its value in 2014 and the pace of depreciation accelerated in the last quarter along with rouble depreciation and falling global fuel prices. In response to slowing exports and the currency depreciation on the curb market, the National Bank of Uzbekistan (NBU) (central bank) accelerated its official depreciation of the sum against the US dollar and tightened import controls.

Broad money was estimated to have grown by 26 per cent in 2014, about the same as in 2013, reflecting higher domestic credit. Monetary survey data were not available, but net foreign assets in the banking system might have decreased as domestic credit grew more quickly than broad money. The government reported a budget surplus of 0.2 per cent of GDP in 2014.

Factoring in the surplus of the Uzbekistan Fund for Reconstruction and Development, the country's sovereign wealth fund, the augmented budget balance was estimated to have shown a surplus equal to 2.4 per cent of GDP, down from 2.7 per cent in 2013. Budget revenues are estimated to have slipped from 36.2 per cent of GDP in 2013 to 36.1 per cent in 2014, in line with declining international prices for key export commodities. Higher government spending – notably for wages, pensions, health care and education – raised budget expenditures from 33.5 per cent of GDP in 2013 to 33.7 per cent in 2014. Total government debt edged up from 8.5 per cent of GDP in 2013 to 8.7 per cent in 2014 as foreign lending for infrastructure increased.

The current account surplus was estimated to have narrowed to 1.2 per cent of GDP from 1.6 per cent in 2013, reflecting a smaller trade surplus and lower remittances. External demand remained weak and international prices for Uzbekistan's key export commodities declined from historic highs. Much of the narrowing in the trade surplus reflected lower earnings from energy, which accounts for about 30 per cent of all exports. Earnings from energy exports have been declining since the third quarter of 2014 in line with retreating global oil prices. Total exports are estimated to have declined by 2.0 per cent. Developments in the economy of the Russian Federation during late 2014 profoundly affected Uzbekistan's exports and remittances. Weak consumer demand there, coupled with rapid nominal appreciation of the sum against the rouble, hurt bilateral trade. Diminished labour demand in construction and logistics – the main employers of Uzbek migrants – helped cut remittances from the Russian Federation by an estimated 10 per cent to about US$5.0 billion. Quarter by quarter, bilateral trade and remittances were both lower than in 2013. Imports of goods and services rose by 1.1 per cent, driven mainly by imports of consumer goods and chemicals. Despite declining by about 10 per cent from 2013, machinery and equipment remained the largest import items, accounting for 40 per cent of imports. This reflected continued but moderating demand for capital goods from state-led infrastructure development and industrial modernisation programmes scheduled to end in 2015. With the decline in exports, the trade balance was estimated to have moved into deficit by the end of 2014. Public and private external debt estimated to have increased to 13.4 per cent of GDP in 2014.

KEY INDICATORS — Uzbekistan

	Unit	2011	2012	2013	2014	**2015
Population	m	*28.84	*29.75	*30.24	*30.60	*30.97
Gross domestic product (GDP)	US$bn	45.40	51.19	*57.17	*62.62	*68.19
GDP per capita	US$	1,572	1,721	*1,890	*2,046	*2,202
GDP real growth	%	8.3	8.2	*8.0	*8.1	*6.2
Inflation	%	12.8	12.1	*11.2	*8.4	*9.5
Unemployment	%	0.2	–	–	–	–
Oil output	'000 bpd	86.0	68.0	63.0	67.0	–
Natural gas output	bn cum	57.0	56.9	55.2	57.3	–
Coal output	mtoe	–	–	–	1.4	–
Current account	US$m	2,612.0	600.0	*-963.0	*73.0	*169.0
Exchange rate	per US$	1,706.83	1,984.00	2,202.20	2,422.00	–

* estimated figure ** forecast figure

Asia's sick man?

President Islam Abduganievich Karimov has led the country since before its independence, becoming the head of the Communist Party in Soviet Uzbekistan in 1989. Two subsequent referendums allowed Karimov to extend his rule. He was last elected to office in March 2015, in a vote opponents dismissed as a sham. Mr Karimov takes a ruthlessly authoritarian approach to all forms of opposition, using the danger of Islamic militancy to justify the absence of civil rights.

However, in 2014 President Karimov was known to have been unwell. He had suffered from a heart attack in 2013. There was a time when the likelihood of Mr Karimov being succeeded by his flamboyant daughter, Gulnara, was strong. But by 2014, lines were being drawn up for a succession battle outside the President's family. The two camps were that of Prime Minister Shavkat Mirziyoyev and that of Vice President Rustan Azimov, who is also finance minister. Mr Mirziyoyev was backed by Russia and seemed to be in a strong financial position, largely due to his daughter's marriage to a Russian oligarch. Mr Azimov's clash with Gulnara Karimova in 2013 (when she accused him of corruption) had provided him with significant popular support.

Were Mr Azimov to win the day, there would be some consternation in Moscow. Russia might try to prevent Azimov, an advocate of closer ties with the United States, from distancing Uzbekistan from Russia. President Vladimir Putin will have drawn up his game plan. As was already happening in Ukraine, an assertive President Putin could well decide that the time was right to restore Russian primacy in the region.

Gulnara

The lack of any obvious pattern of succession had also opened up the possibility of a *coup d'état* in Uzbekistan as the President's faithful coterie of advisors and supporters do their best to undermine the chances of the President's glamorous, but unpopular, daughter Gulnara of taking over the reins of state. In a report filed from Moscow, the London *Economist* alleged that Gulnara's charity network – known to be the mainspring of her extremely effective personality network and suspected to be a source of her income – was under investigation. A parallel investigation into the affairs of one of her media companies also resulted in their bank accounts being frozen. Gulnara is reported to have amassed a fortune worth an estimated US$600 million under her father's nose. In October 2013 Ms Karimova's cousin, one Akbarali Abdulayev, (aka 'the purse') was arrested following allegations of an involvement with organised crime. Meanwhile, Swedish prosecutors had been investigating Gulnara on suspicion of taking bribes to let Nordic telecoms company TeliaSonera enter the country's market. The prosecutors were looking into allegations that when TeliaSonera paid 2.3 billion Swedish crowns (US$358 million) for a 3G licence in Uzbekistan in 2007 to a Gibraltar-registered firm called Takilant, 'it knew the company was a front for Ms Karimova.' The allegations had resulted in the resignations of virtually the entire TeliaSonera board of directors, including its chief executive and several senior employees. The case is also being investigated by Dutch and US authorities. The prosecutors said that they suspected that representatives for TeliaSonera had bribed members of Uzbekistan's 'political elite', affirming that 'there is now a concrete basis, including information on control over assets, which gives reason to suspect that Gulnara Karimova, who also served as a public official during the time period relevant for the case, was the one who orchestrated, controlled and also was the one who primarily benefited from the procedure.'

Human rights

Gulnara's activities did little to enhance Uzbekistan's wobbly record on human rights. Human Rights Watch (HRW) published, in September 2014, a report, entitled *Until the Very End: Politically Motivated Imprisonment in Uzbekistan*, which cited the cases of 34 prominent political prisoners as evidence that torture, kidnapping, incommunicado detention, solitary confinement and extension of sentences were all widespread. The HRW Uzbek office, which had been ordered to shut in 2011, claimed that its findings were based on more than 150 interviews with detainees' relatives, former prisoners, human rights activists and a former prison official. The researcher responsible for HRW in Uzbekistan reported that 'Whether behind bars for 20 years or a shorter time, these people have been wrongfully imprisoned and shouldn't spend even one more day behind bars.' HRW also reported that local human rights bodies believed the number of political prisoners in Uzbekistan was in the thousands.

In its 2013 assessment of the state of affairs in Uzbekistan HRW had reported that: 'Uzbekistan's human rights record is atrocious. Torture is endemic in the criminal justice system. Authorities intensified their crackdown on civil society activists, opposition members and journalists. Muslims and Christians who practice their religion outside strict state controls are persecuted and freedom of expression is severely limited. The government forces more than one million adults and children to harvest cotton under abusive conditions. Authorities still deny justice for the 2005 Andijan massacre, in which government forces shot and killed hundreds of protesters, most of them unarmed.' Heady stuff.

On its 2013 *Corruption Perceptions Index* Transparency International ranked Uzbekistan 168 out of the 174 countries surveyed, level with Syria and Turkmenistan and an improvement of two places over the 2012 ranking of 170.

Regional shifts

In 2012 Uzbekistan had decided to withdraw from a Russian-lead military alliance, prompting speculation that it was seeking closer ties with the US. Strategically located on the southern fringe of Central Asia, Uzbekistan had been an important, if uncomfortable partner for a North Atlantic Treaty Organisation (NATO) alliance looking for practical ways of repatriating vast amounts of military equipment from neighbouring Afghanistan.

Unsurprisingly, the Collective Security Treaty Organisation (CSTO) avoided giving any reasons for Uzbekistan's withdrawal from the alliance, but most observers described it as a move towards the US. A Moscow based think tank, PIR-Centre was quoted: 'The United States will make Uzbekistan its strategic ally, will provide financial and military assistance, assume some security guarantees, close its eyes to human rights violations.' The Uzbekistan solution was seen as a replacement for the southern exit route from Afghanistan through Pakistan; Washington's deteriorating relations with Islamabad had forced the US into the arms of Uzbekistan, which boasts the best railway network links in the region.

Risk assessment

Politics	Poor
Economy	Fair
Regional stability	Good

Muslims in Uzbekistan

% of population	96.5
Sunni (% of Muslims)	99
Shi'a (% of Muslims)	1

COUNTRY PROFILE

1865–1876 The Russians took Tashkent and made it the capital of Turkestan, incorporating vast areas of Central Asia. They annexed the emirate of Bukhara and the khanates of Samarkand, Khiva and Kokand

1917 Following the October Revolution in Russia, the Tashkent Soviet was established.

1920 The Tashkent Soviet ousted the emir of Bukhara and the other khans.

1921 Uzbekistan became part of the Turkestan Autonomous Soviet Socialist Republic (ASSR).

1924 The Uzbek Soviet Socialist Republic (SSR) was formed from the Turkestan ASSR, the Bukharan People's Soviet Republic and the Khorezmian People's Soviet Republic; it was given Union Republic status in the Union of Soviet Socialist Republics (USSR).

1930s The Uzbek capital was transferred from Samarkand to Tashkent.

1944 The Soviet leader, Stalin, deported 160,000 Meskhetian Turks from Georgia to Uzbekistan.

1950s–80s Cotton production was boosted as the government undertook major irrigation projects on Uzbekistan's rivers and lakes. The country's water levels fell drastically.

1984 Thousands of Uzbek officials were arrested on corruption charges over the 'cotton affair' when millions of roubles went missing as a result of invented crop yields.

1989 Islam Karimov became the leader of the Communist Party of Uzbekistan. Ethnic violence broke out against the Meskhetian Turks and other minorities in the Ferghana Valley. Birlik (Unity), a nationalist movement, was founded.

1990 The Communist Party of Uzbekistan declared economic and political sovereignty and Islam Karimov became president.

1991 Independence from the USSR was declared. Uzbekistan joined the Commonwealth of Independent States (CIS). The first presidential elections were won by Islam Karimov; only a few opposition groups were allowed to field candidates.
1992 President Karimov banned the political parties Birlik and Erk (Freedom) Democratic Party and members of the opposition were arrested.
1994 Uzbekistan signed an economic integration treaty with Russia and an economic, military and social co-operation treaty with Kazakhstan and Kyrgyzstan.
1995 The ruling Chalk Demokratik Partijasi (CDP) (People's Democratic Party), formerly the Communist Party of Uzbekistan, won the elections. A referendum extended President Karimov's term of office until the year 2000.
1996 Uzbekistan, Kazakhstan and Kyrgyzstan agreed to create a single economic market.
1998 The Islamic Movement of Uzbekistan (IMU), based in Afghanistan and Tajikistan, was formed. It is said to pose a genuine armed threat to Uzbekistan. The activity of the IMU, which aims to overthrow Uzbekistan and establish a separate Islamic polity in the Ferghana valley, has made the Tajikistan-Uzbekistan border a zone of continual near-war. The government severely represses those it suspects of Islamic extremism.
1999 The president blamed bomb blasts in Tashkent on the IMU. A declaration of *jihad* was broadcast by the IMU from a radio station in Iran, demanding the resignation of the Uzbek leadership. The IMU, operating from mountain hideouts, attacked government forces (the first of many future cross-border incursions).
2000 President Karimov was re-elected. Uzbekistan was accused of widespread torture by US-based Human Rights Watch.
2001 The Shanghai Co-operation Organisation (SCO) was formed between Tajikistan, China, Russia, Kazakhstan, Kyrgyzstan and Uzbekistan. The US military were allowed to use bases in Uzbekistan for its troops, and to use Uzbekistan airspace for the US-led military operations in Afghanistan.
2002 Uzbeks voted by referendum to increase the unicameral parliament to two chambers and the presidential term in office from five to seven years. A long-standing border dispute with Kazakhstan was resolved.
2003 The Birlik movement and the opposition Erk party were allowed to hold official meetings; other political parties were denied registration. President Karimov dismissed Prime Minister Otkir Sultanov after the worst cotton harvest ever and appointed Shavkat Mirziyayev to replace him.
2004 The European Bank for Reconstruction and Development (EBRD) cut aid due to the country's poor record on economic reform and human rights. Trading practices were restricted and sparked violent street protests in the eastern city of Kokland. An agreement with Turkmenistan on water resources was signed. Opposition parties were barred from taking part in parliamentary elections.
2005 CDP and independents formed a government. Violence erupted in Andijan after gunmen released inmates from prison and troops opened fire on demonstrators. The death toll was disputed – eyewitnesses said hundreds had been killed and the government only 180. Fifteen men were convicted of organising the violence and sentenced to 14–20 years in jail.
2006 Two opposition leaders were jailed for eight years for 'economic crimes' by criticising the crackdown in Andijan. Russia agreed to help in the development of Uzbekistan's gas and oil resources.
2007 President Islam Karimov was elected for a third term in office. The result was heavily criticised by international human rights observers as an election that was not considered free or fair.
2008 Igor Vorontsov, the representative of US-based Human Rights Watch, was expelled. Construction of a 525km gas pipeline between Uzbekistan and China began; when completed it is expected to carry 30 billion cubic metres per year.
2009 The president confirmed that non-military supplies bound for Afghanistan could be transported through Uzbekistan, with the use of rail and road links. The EU agreed to lift an embargo on arms sales that had been in place for four years. The EU said there had been 'positive steps' towards improving human rights issues.
2010 Following the second round of parliamentary elections, O'zbekiston Liberal Demokratik Partiyasi (O'zLiDEp) (Uzbekistan Liberal Democratic Party) won a total of 53 seats (out of 135) and became the single largest party in the national assembly. However, all political parties were supporters of the president and unable to provide an opposition to the administration. Around 400,000 Uzbek refugees fled ethnic violence in Osh, Kyrgyzstan; while many remained in Uzbekistan for two weeks before returning home a significant number preferred to stay.
2011 In March constitutional amendments were implemented by parliament. The new measures strengthened parliamentary democracy. They are also intended to diminish the role of cliques and the ruling elite. In May, a Kyrgyzstan Inquiry Commission (KIC) published its report into the ethnic violence in Osh in 2010. It concluded that political fanaticism mixed with ethno-nationalism had resulted in violence and that the minority Uzbek community was the overwhelming victim of attack. The report also said that there was evidence of official Kyrgyz complicity. In May, the 153 Kyrgyz families (over 1,000 people) living in Barak, Uzbekistan, used a petition to call on the Kyrgyzstan authorities to relocate them to Kyrgyzstan.
2012 On 15 August, Prime Minister Mirziyayev banned the use of children in the cotton harvest. As a result, office workers and medical staff were drafted into the fields without exception.
2013 In September the Asian Development Bank pledged US$220 million to help Uzbekistan modernise its irrigation system. The practice of forcing some one million people, including students, teachers and doctors, to work at picking cotton, Uzbekistan's 'white gold' for two months at the end of each year continues, despite objections by international organisations such as Unicef.
2014 The first round of the general election was held on 21 December, with 113 seats (out of 125) elected. The second round is due in January 2015.
2015 The second round of the general election was held on 4 January. The final, complete result was a win for the Demokratik Partiyasi, O'zlidep (Uzbekistan Liberal Democratic Party) with 52 seats (out of 150) followed by O'zbekiston Milliy Tiklanish Demokratik Partiyasi (Uzbekistan National Revival Democratic Party) with 36 seats, O'zbekistan Xalq Demokratik Partiyasi (O'zXDP) People's Democratic Party of Uzbekistan 27 seats, Adolat Sotsial Demokratik Partiyasi (Justice Social Democratic Party) 20 seats and the O'zbekiston Ekologik Harakati (Ecological Movement) finished with 15 seats. Turnout was 88.94 per cent for the first round and 76.93 per cent for the second.

Political structure

Constitution

The constitution was adopted in December 1992. It guarantees respect for all citizens, regardless of language, custom or tradition, and forbids any group or individual to exercise power on behalf of the people of Uzbekistan except for the elected president and legislature. The creation of a state ideology and censorship of the media are also contrary to the constitution; however, media censorship is still practised.

The autonomous region of Karakalpakstan has its own constitution,

but is subject to the laws of Uzbekistan. Karakalpakstan has the right to withdraw from Uzbekistan depending on support via a referendum.
On 8 December 1992, Uzbekistan became the second Central Asian state to adopt a post-independence constitution. The already considerable powers of the president were increased, giving him the right to appoint regional governors who report directly to him. The constitution also included guarantees of freedom, of conscience and of travel, and a statement that the country should be a secular democracy. President Karimov has pointed to the Turkish state as his country's model. On 27 January 2002, a nationwide referendum agreed with the extension of the president's constitutional term in office from five to seven years and authorised the election of a bicameral parliament. 2002 amendments also stipulated that the president should be restricted to two-terms. Karimov was allowed to run again, however, on the premise that since the changes were adopted in 2002 his two terms before the date did not count.

Independence date

1 September 1991

Form of state

Secular, (theoretically) democratic and presidential republic.

The executive

The president is head of state, holds supreme executive power and is directly elected for no more than two consecutive terms. A January 2002 referendum approved a two-year extension of the president's constitutional term of office from five to seven years (it was originally due to expire in 2005 and has been extended to 2007).
The president appoints the prime minister and ministers, subject to confirmation by the legislature, appoints the judges of the lower courts and the governors of the regions.
The Cabinet of Ministers is the government of the country; it is subordinate to the president.

National legislature

The bicameral Oliy Majlis (National Assembly) comprises the Legislative Chamber with 120 members, directly elected in a two-round voting system, for five-year terms, and the Senate with 100 members of which 84 are elected by subordinate assemblies and 16 are appointed by the president.
The minimum voting age used to be 25 years (the highest in the world), but has recently been reduced to 18.

Legal system

Judicial power is nominally independent of government, but as the judges of the higher courts are selected from among lower court judges, who are themselves appointed by the president, there is in practice significant political control over the system.
The three highest courts are the Constitutional Court, the Supreme Court and the High Commercial Court. The first rules on the validity of legislation and on disputes between the government of Uzbekistan and the Karakalpakstan autonomous region. The second is the highest court of appeal for criminal and civil cases initiated in the lower courts. The third is the highest court of arbitration for civil cases initiated in the lower courts.

Last elections

21 December 2014 / 4 January 2015 (parliamentary); 29 March 2015 (presidential).
Results: Parliamentary: After two rounds of voting the complete results were: O'zbekiston Liberal Demokratik Partiyasi, O'zlidep (Uzbekistan Liberal Democratic Party) won 52 seats (out of 150), O'zbekiston Milliy Tiklanish Demokratik Partiyasi (Uzbekistan National Revival Democratic Party) won 36 seats, O'zbekiston Xalq Demokratik Partiyasi (O'zXDP or PDPU) People's Democratic Party of Uzbekistan won 27 seats, Adolat Sotsial Demokratik Partiyasi (Justice Social Democratic Party) won 20 seats and the O'zbekiston Ekologik Harakati (Ecological Movement) finished with 15 seats. Turnout was 88.94 per cent for the first round and 76.93 per cent for the second.
Presidential: Islam Karimov won 90.39 per cent of the vote, no other candidate won more than 3.08 per cent. Turnout was 91.08 per cent.

Next elections

December 2022 (presidential); December 2022 (parliamentary)

Political parties

In 1997, legislation came into force prohibiting parties based on ethnic or religious lines, or those advocating war or subversion of the constitutional order.
As a result of amendments to the Law on Elections in August 2003, only registered political parties and voters' initiative groups have the right to field candidates for election.

Ruling party

Coalition of Uzbekistan Liberal Democratic Party, People's Democratic Party of Uzbekistan, Uzbekistan National Revival Democratic Party and Justice Social Democratic Party

Main opposition party

All parties in the Supreme Assembly are loyal to the president. The banned O'zbekiston Erk Demokratik Partiyasi (OEDP) (Erk Democratic Party) is considered to be the main opposition party to the Karimov regime. The *Guardian* has quoted leader, Atanazar Arif, arguing that [Uzbekistan is] not democratic. Karimov is a neo-communist dictator. He's a bit like Mugabe...He has no intention of giving up power.'

Population

30.60 million (2014)*
Last census: January 1989: 19,810,077
Population density: 64 inhabitants per square km (2010). Urban population 36 per cent (2010 Unicef).
Annual growth rate: 1.5 per cent, 1990–2010 (Unicef).

Internally Displaced Persons (IDP)

3,000 (UNHCR 2004)

Ethnic make-up

Uzbek (72 per cent), Russian (8 per cent), Tajik (7 per cent), Kazakh (4 per cent), others (9 per cent). There is a Korean minority estimated at 7 per cent. The Uzbeks are the second most numerous Turkic people in the world after the Turks themselves.

Religions

Muslim (88 per cent, mostly Sunni); Christian Eastern Orthodox (9 per cent).

Education

Although Uzbekistan's overall literacy rate is high, the government is implementing a long-term programme of transition from Cyrillic to Latin script, and in the short-term there are likely to be some changes in the literacy rate.
Primary education begins at aged six and last until aged 10. General secondary education lasts until aged 15, when students may choose between a technical, vocational or academic course for two years. From aged 17, specialised secondary schools offer advanced vocational or academic two-year courses.
There are 16 universities and 42 research institutes in the country, including the state-run Tashkent Islamic University.
The government initiated a National Programme for Personnel Training, giving high priority to introducing new educational technologies and attracting international donors. The reform programme replaced existing schools and it is estimated that seven million pupils will enrol in these new schools, and in sharp contrast with the past, 90 per cent (an unprecedented amount in the New Independent States) of these pupils are expected to enrol in vocational education and training.
In February 2005 a report by the International Crisis Group alleged that thousands of children are forced out of school to work in cotton fields. Uzbekistan is the world's fifth largest cotton producer and during the harvest season children of all ages are used to pick the cotton. Pay for this work may be denied and refusal to work may lead to expulsion from school.

Literacy rate: 99 per cent adult rate; 100 per cent youth rate (15–24) (Unesco 2005).
Compulsory years: Six to 15
Enrolment rate: 100 per cent gross primary school enrolment rate in 2000, 94 per cent at secondary level and 36 per cent at tertiary level.
Pupils per teacher: 21 in primary schools.

Health

Healthcare standards were fairly uniform across the former Soviet Union, but the breakdown in trade and economic crises have brought about a severe shortage of medicines and equipment.
According to a presidential decree in 1999, private healthcare institutions, were exempted from tax in order to facilitate investment in medical equipment; it also included a programme for the development of medical treatment centres in villages over 2001–05. The government also plans to make premises and funds available for private healthcare institutions.

HIV/Aids

HIV prevalence: 0.1 per cent aged 15–49 in 2003 (World Bank)
Life expectancy: 66 years, 2004 (WHO 2006)
Fertility rate/Maternal mortality rate: 2.4 births per woman, 2010 (Unicef); maternal mortality 21 per 100,000 live births (World Bank).
Birth rate/Death rate: 23 births and 6 death per 1,000 people (World Bank)
Child (under 5 years) mortality rate (per 1,000): 40 per 1,000 live births (WHO 2012); 7.9 per cent of children aged under five are malnourished (World Bank).
Head of population per physician: 2.74 physicians per 1,000 people, 2003 (WHO 2006)

Welfare

Social spending is relatively high compared to most other transitional countries. Social assistance is channelled through traditional local structures using the national Malhalla foundation, which is responsible for meeting the needs of the poor. The Malhalla collects information on the claimants' needs independently of the state. Wages in the agricultural sector have tended to fall behind the national average as a result of high taxes, contributing to increased risks of civil unrest. Expenditure on the social safety net continues to account for 3.5 per cent of GDP and benefits are usually increased in line with wages rather than with official inflation.
There is a comprehensive system of benefits for sickness, disability, maternity and unemployment, as well as a combined state and private pension scheme.
However, many of these payments are linked to the declining minimum wage, with the result that those depending on benefits are likely to drop below the poverty line.
There are special payments to veterans of the Soviet war in Afghanistan. The government also provides benefits through budget subsidies for housing maintenance and public utilities.

Main cities

Tashkent (capital, estimated population 2.2 million in 2012), Namangan (437,119), Andijon (376,159), Samarkand (348,070), Nukus (246,348), Karshi (230,772), Bukhara (230,336), Kukon (210,794), Margilon (172,227), Fergana (167,367).

Languages spoken

Uzbek is of Turkic origin and is the most commonly used language, although Russian remains the language of inter-ethnic communication and business. Turkish and Arabic are also spoken. English and other Western languages are increasingly common, particularly in Tashkent and other urban areas.

Official language/s

Uzbek

Media

Although the Uzbek Constitution guarantees press freedom, the state maintains tight control of the media with routine harassment of journalists. The government has control of much of the printing and distribution infrastructure. A law, pass in 2007, holds all media outlets responsible for the objectivity of their output and, as such, self-censorship is widespread.

Press

Dailies: In Uzbek, *Hurriyat* (www.hurriyat.uz), a government-owned publication, *Khalq Sozi* has a Russian editionNarodnoe Slovo (www.narodnoeslovo.uz), *Uzbekistan Ovozi* and *Tashkent Hakikati*. In Russian, *Pravda Vostoka*, *Zerkalo XXI* (www.zerkalo21.uz). In English, *Good Morning* and *Ovozi Times*.
Weeklies: In Uzbek, *Mohiyat*.
Business: Russian language publications include *Review* (www.review.uz), *Business Partner Uzbekistana* and *Business-vestnik Vostoka)* (Bvv) (Business News of the East) and *Kommercheskij Vestnik* (Commercial News). In English, publications include *Business Partner* and *Business Review*.

Broadcasting

The National Television and Radio Company (MTRK) (www.mtrk.uz) has a network of four TV channels and five radio stations.
Radio: MTRK national stations include radios' Uzbekistan, Yoshlar (the youth station), Mashal, Tashkent and Oltin Zamin. Private, commercial radio stations include Oriat FM (www.oriat.uz), Uzbegim Taronasi (www.fm101.uz), Radio Grand (www.grand.uz) and Radio Sezam FM.
Television: MTRK operates four channels, Uzbekistan, Yoshlar, Sport and Tashkent. There are two national and four, privately run TV stations, located in cities around the country including Bagdad TV and Muloqot from the Fergana region, Bekabad from the Tashket region, Aloqa AK from the Syrdarya region and Samarkand TV and Orbita TV.
National news agency: Jahon Information Agency
Other news agencies: UzA (Uzbekistan National News Agency): www.uza.uz/en

Economy

Uzbekistan is a landlocked country of which more than 60 per cent of the population lives in densely populated rural communities. Exports of gold, natural gas and cotton provide a significant share of foreign exchange earnings. Despite attempts to diversify crops, Uzbekistani agriculture remains largely centred around cotton; it is the world's fifth largest exporter and sixth largest producer.
Uzbekistan's economic growth has been driven primarily by state-led investments and a favourable export environment, however, it has had a history of rocky relations with the United States because foreign companies have abused Uzbekistani laws. Low foreign investment and difficulties transporting goods across borders further challenge its economy. Uzbekistan has recently intensified economic relations with China, Tashkent began exporting natural gas to China and Chinese investments in the country have substantially increased. FDI in 2014 was US$751 million.
Uzbekistan had 594 million barrels of proved oil reserves in 2014, with production of 100,000 barrels per day. It also had 1.8 trillion cubic metres (cum) of proved natural gas reserves in 2014, with production of 63 billion cum in 2012. Hydrocarbon extraction is the single most dominant component of the economy.
Other industrial production includes mining of uranium, gold and other non-ferrous and rare metals such as molybdenum, zinc, wolfram, lithium and lead. Other mineral reserves include kaolin, quartz spar, phosphorus and bentonite clay. Textiles, food processing, machine building, metallurgy, and chemicals are other notable industries providing for Uzbekistan's economy. The service sector constitutes 50 per cent of GDP and agriculture around 19 per cent. Industry represented 32 per cent of GDP in 2014 of which manufacturing, particularly the automotive industry has grown to

constitute around 10 per cent of GDP, with products assembled for export and aimed at Russia.
Agriculture has fallen in importance in the economy, although cotton production and trade is the third largest source of Uzbekistan's wealth; it is the world's fifth largest producer of cotton. Cotton cultivation alone constitutes over 10 per cent.
An Oxfam-Australia report in 2010 stated that cotton production in Uzbekistan was 'one of the most exploitative enterprises in the world' as it relies on forced labour, including mandatory employment by school children, students and civil workers, working in poor conditions for very little pay. In 2014 and 2015, the country is beginning to enforce a ban on the use of child labour in its cotton harvest and is trying to address international criticism for its previous use of this practice. Other crops include silk, livestock, wheat, fruit and vegetables. Farming is typically either large agri-business enterprises or small family-run concerns that provide poor incomes.
GDP growth has remained strong for several years, reaching a high of 9.5 per cent in 2007 as global prices for oil reached a record level. Growth did not fall significantly during the global economic crisis of 2008–09 when growth was 9.0 per cent and 8.1 per cent respectively, principally because Uzbekistan is self-sufficient in food and energy, the two commodities that help increase costs for other countries. In 2010, GDP growth was 8.5 per cent and remained constant at an estimated 8.3 per cent in 2011. GDP growth has remained stable at 8.2 per cent in 2012, 8 per cent in 2013 and 8.1 per cent in 2014.
While the government has gradually redirected the economy towards an open free-market system, the number of state-owned enterprises, and government influence in their business, remains high. Unemployment and underemployment are long-term problems, for a workforce that is generally well educated. However corruption in the education system has begun to erode the status of Uzbekistan qualifications in the region at a time of high migrant numbers. Estimates of Uzbeks working aboard range from 3–5 million, mostly in Russia, the Middle East and south-east Asia.
GDP per capita was US$5,600 in 2014, a small increase from the US$5,200 figure in 2013. In 2014 the UN Human Development Index (HDI) ranked Uzbekistan 116 (out of 187) for national development in health, education and income, whilst 3.6 per cent of the population live in multidimensional poverty.
Uzbekistan is both an importer and exporter of electricity between its neighbouring countries. It is in disagreement with Tajikistan over their country's building of the Rohgan hydroelectric dam, which it says was planned in the 1970s and based on defunct technology, while the loss of water to be trapped in the dam could cause long-term damage to Uzbekistan's agricultural production.

External trade

Uzbekistan is a member of the Economic Co-operation Organization (ECO), comprising 10 regional Central Asian countries. It belongs to the Eurasian Economic Community (EAEC), which was established to promote a customs union between its six member states (Belarus, Kazakhstan, Kyrgyzstan, Russia, Tajikistan, and Uzbekistan), and among other objectives, to introduce standardised currency exchange and rules for trade in goods and services. The EAEC evolved out of the Commonwealth of Independent States (CIS) Customs Union and has begun the process of merging with the Central Asian Co-operation Organisation (CACO). By mid-2015 negotiations for Uzbekistan's membership of the World Trade Organisation were still ongoing.
Natural gas has become the principal export and foreign currency earner, supplanting cotton as the primary export. Other important export products include gold, rare minerals, food, electricity and manufactured goods.

Imports

Principal imports are machinery and equipment, foodstuffs, chemicals and metals.
Main sources: Russia (22.8 per cent of total in 2014), China (19.6 per cent), South Korea (14.9 per cent), Kazakhstan (10.2 per cent), Germany (4.8 per cent) and Turkey (4.4 per cent).

Exports

Principal exports are natural gas, oil, cotton, gold and precious stones, mineral fertilisers, ferrous metals, textiles, food products and vehicles.
Main destinations: China (26.8 per cent of total in 2014), Russia (14.7 per cent), Kazakhstan (14.6 per cent), Turkey (13.1 per cent) and Bangladesh (10.2 per cent).

Agriculture

Farming

Agriculture represented 19 per cent of GDP in 2014 and it employed approximately 26 per cent of the labour force. Only 9 per cent of the land is suitable for cultivation. Over 1,500 farms operate on a co-operative basis. Family farms dominate 99 per cent of the cotton sector and 93 per cent of the corn sector.
Cotton is the main crop, around a million tonnes a year being produced, three-quarters of it for export. In a report published in 2005 – *The Curse of Cotton: Central Asia's destructive monoculture* – the International Crisis Group (ICG) said that while the former Soviet cotton producing countries of Uzbekistan, Tajikistan and Turkmenistan continued to exploit their cotton growers there was little hope of improving economic development and tackling poverty. The cotton industry is vital to the economy of Uzbekistan, yet while the industry continues to rely on cheap labour (including children), land ownership is uncertain, state intervention discourages competition and the rule of law is limited, there is little incentive for the powerful vested interests to reform the system. In 2013 the practice of forcing some one million people, including students, teachers and doctors, to work at picking cotton, Uzbekistan's 'white gold' for two months at the end of each year was continuing, despite objections by international organisations such as Unicef. In 2014 and 2015, the country was beginning to enforce a ban on the use of child labour in its cotton harvest and is trying to address international criticism for its previous use of this practice.
In addition to the economic and social costs to the rural populations, the environmental costs of the monoculture have been devastating. The degradation of the Aral Sea in particular has lead to international concern.

Forestry

Only 8 per cent of Uzbekistan is forested and commercial exploitation is for domestic purposes only as fuel. There is low production of industrial roundwood, because the government has placed restrictions on harvesting due to the poor condition of forests.

Industry and manufacturing

The industrial sector contributed approximately 32 per cent to GDP and employed 13 per cent of the working population in 2014.
Main industries include chemical and gas production, heavy engineering, specialising in machinery for the cotton-growing and textile industries, aircraft construction, metal works, textiles and cotton derivatives, canned foods and nitrogenised fertilisers.

Tourism

Uzbekistan is a landlocked country in Central Asia that relies on air and overland access for visitors, which somewhat limits numbers. However, in 2015 tourist arrivals are predicted to reach 1,924,000, a 3.8 per cent decrease on numbers in 2014. The government strategy has been to concentrate its focus on tourism from the region and the greater Asian market. Through public-private initiatives the infrastructure is improving as wealthier visitors provide the stimulus for investment.

Travel and tourism contributed 3 per cent to GDP (US$1.6 billion) in 2014 and it employed 2.5 per cent of the workforce (395,000 jobs).

The ancient Silk Road runs through Uzbekistan (and continues into Turkmenistan and Kyrgyzstan) and this resource alone provides 30 per cent of all visitor receipts and 20 per cent of total tourism income. Organised groups offer visitors the chance to travel along its route, from Tashkent in the east to Khiva in the west, taking in some major sites, such as Samarkand. The historic centre of Bukhara (home to a style of handmade oriental carpets), Shakhrisyabz, and Itchan Kala are all included on Unesco's World Heritage List.

Environment

The Aral Sea had been drying up due to the overuse of water from the two main rivers which feed into it, with the loss of up to 50 per cent of its water. This resulted in desertification of the surrounding land. However, by 2006, a World Bank funded project had begun a reversal, as building works on the river Syr Darya, in Kazakhstan, increased the level of water in the northern section of the Aral Sea. Work continues to allow more water into the southern section and directly benefit Uzbekistan.

Uzbekistan has numerous environmental problems, more than half of its irrigated land is heavily salinated and eroded. Surface and underground water sources used for human consumption in parts of the country have also been polluted by industrial and communal discharges.

A meeting was held in April 2009 to determine water sharing between Tajikistan, Kyrgyzstan, Uzbekistan, Turkmenistan and Kazakhstan failed, as negotiators were unable to find a trade in water for energy and hydrocarbons. Tajikistan and Kyrgyzstan hold around 80 per cent of the water in the Aral Sea but suffer from lack of electricity during freezing winters, while the remaining three states downstream are semi-arid and need water for their cotton industries and agriculture.

Mining

Uzbekistan is rich in unexplored mineral deposits – its potential mineral wealth amounts to a value of US$3,000 billion. There are around 100 deposits of various metals, including gold, silver, uranium, zinc, copper and tungsten, which need developing. Uzbekistan is the seventh-largest uranium producer in the world with a rate of 2400 tonnes in 2014. However, it only has 2 per cent of the known recoverable resources of uranium in the world.

In 2014, Uzbekistan was the twelfth-largest gold producer in the world. Its commercial reserves are associated with opencast mines of the Muruntau field in the Kyzylkum desert in central Uzbekistan, which have been developed by the main state gold producer Kyzylkumredmetzoloto (Navoi Integrated Mining and Metallurgical Plant) since 1967. Its annual output amounts to 55–60 tonnes, producing the majority of Uzbekistan's total gold production. Uzbekistan's total gold production was 85 tonnes in 2014.

The Zarafshan-Newmont joint venture between Uzbekistan and the US mining company Newmont, set up in 1995, processes about 200 million tonnes of low-grade ore, previously regarded as waste, from the Muruntau open gold pit. The project is due to end in 2012.

Dzhetymtau, located in the Kyzylkum desert is estimated to hold reserves of 400 tonnes of gold and 350,000 tonnes of tungsten ores.

There are silver deposits in the central Kyzylkum region, which also contain gold, platinum group metals, cobalt and nickel, which can be recovered as by-products.

Uzbekistan is the only producer of enriched uranium in the former Soviet Union. All output is exported, since Uzbekistan has no nuclear reactors. Uzbekistan's proven uranium reserves were around 91,300 tonnes in 2014. Sugraly is one of Central Asia's biggest uranium fields and holds an estimated 38,000 tonnes of uranium.

Kyzylkumredmetzoloto (Kyzylkum Precious Metals and Gold) is Uzbekistan's only uranium producer and exporter.

Uzbekistan possesses considerable reserves of lead and zinc.

Copper production in Uzbekistan averages 80,000 tonnes per year. The copper is principally from the Kalmakir open mine, with the remainder mined at the Sari Checku open pit. The ore is processed at the Almalyk concentrator.

Uzbekistan produces over 100,000 tonnes per year of feldspar, about one-third of the output of the former Soviet Union. The non-ferrous metal industry includes the mining of bismuth, tungsten and molybdenum. Other natural resources include rock salt, potassium salts, anthracite, graphite, ozokerite, sulphur, quartz, limestone, gypsum, bentonites and semi-precious stones.

Hydrocarbons

Proven oil reserves were 594 million barrels in 2014, with production at 100,000 barrels per day (bpd). Consumption was 105,600bpd in 2013, with the balance met by imports.

There are three refineries – at Fergana, Alty-Arik and Bukhara with total capacity of 222,000bpd.

Proven natural gas reserves were 1.8 trillion cubic metres (cum) in 2014 and Uzbekistan has one of the largest reserves of natural gas in the world, but the country lacks the infrastructure to exploit it.

Natural gas production was 63 billion cum in 2012, of which 53 billion cum was consumed domestically.

The industry is almost entirely state-controlled, with 14 companies grouped around Uzbekneftegaz (Uzbek Oil and Gas), which is responsible for all aspects of exploration, production, distribution and processing in the hydrocarbons sector. Principal oil and gas fields include Kuanish, Shakhpakthy and Chembar. Other fields have been discovered in the Mamangan and Ferghana regions.

Proven reserves of recoverable coal are 3 billion tonnes, about one-third of which is highly valued anthracite, for which production has increased, while production of less valued bitumen has remained negligible. The industry is in need of modernisation, but production meets all domestic needs of around one million tonnes per annum of which over 80 per cent is used in power stations.

Energy

Total installed generating capacity was 11.6 gigawatts (GW) in 2013. Natural gas provides most of the necessary energy for local electricity generation. Uzbekistan is the largest energy producer among the Central Asian republics and a net exporter. The energy sector is almost entirely state-controlled by the joint stock company UzbekEnergo. 86 per cent of the energy mix comes from fossil fuels while 14 per cent comes from hydroelectric plants. Uzbekistan is part of the Central Asian power distribution system, it has 37 electric power plants including the hydroelectric power plants on the Syr Darya, Narin and Chirchik rivers, and thermal power stations at Syr Darya, Tashkent, Novo-Angren, Tachiatasch and Ferghana.

Financial markets

Stock exchange

Republican Stock Exchange

Banking and insurance

Three state-owned banks dominate the banking sector: Bank Asaka, National Bank of Uzbekistan (NBU) and Narodny Bank.

Central bank

National Bank of Uzbekistan (NBU)

Main financial centre

Tashkent

Time

GMT plus five hours

Geography

Uzbekistan is located in the heart of Central Asia. The fourth-largest republic in the former Soviet Union, Uzbekistan measures approximately 925km from north to south and 1,400km from west to east at its widest points. The republic has a short border with Afghanistan to the south, Kazakhstan lies to the north, Kyrgyzstan and Tajikistan to the east and south-east and Turkmenistan to the south-west.

The western region, including the Karakalpakstan oblast, marks the eastern fringe of the Turkmen desert. The Kyzylkum desert covers most of the area between Tashkent and the Aral Sea. The western reaches of the Tien Shan mountain range protrude from Kyrgyzstan and Tajikistan into south-eastern Uzbekistan. The fertile Ferghana Valley runs from the north-eastern finger of Uzbekistan, east of Tashkent, across the border into Kyrgyzstan. Half of the Aral Sea lies within Uzbekistan, the other half in Kazakhstan. There are two main rivers. The Amu Darya, which enters from Afghanistan at Termez and runs along the border with Turkmenistan before turning north at Khiva and flowing into the southern end of the Aral Sea. The Syr Darya flows from the Tien Shan mountains northwards, east of Tashkent and into Kazakhstan, eventually reaching the northern end of the Aral Sea.

Hemisphere

Northern

Climate

Uzbekistan comprises mostly desert and semi-desert, with extreme continental temperatures: the average stands at minus 8 degrees Celsius (C) in January and 26 degrees C in June. Temperatures in Tashkent vary from minus 1 degree C in January to 29–40 degrees C or more in summer. Rainfall averages between 80 and 90mm per annum on the plains and 890 to 1,000mm per annum in the mountains.

Dress codes

Smart clothes are required for business visitors. Otherwise dress is not overly formal but modest, particularly outside Tashkent.

Entry requirements

Passports

Passports are required by all and must be valid for at least six months after the intended date of departure.

Visa

Required by all. Business travellers must obtain an invitation from a local company or organisation. Exceptions include nationals of the US, UK, Austria, Belgium, France, Germany, Italy, Japan, Spain and Switzerland who may apply directly. The Uzbek contact should submit a visa support letter to the Ministry of Foreign Affairs in Tashkent before the visitor applies for a visa. When an approval to visit has been agreed a confirmation is sent by the ministry to the embassy and the visitor should contact a consular section to ensure that a visa issuance confirmation of the Ministry of Foreign Affairs is in place before submitting their application.

To download a visa application see www.uzbekembassy.org and *consular section*, see *visa information* for further details.

Travellers on visitor's visas whose stay in Uzbekistan exceeds three days are required to register with the Local Department of the Ministry of Internal Affairs within three working days of arrival. Hotel administration should take care of such registration automatically.

Transit visas issued in other CIS countries are no longer recognised.

Currency advice/regulations

The import and export of local currency is unlimited. The import of foreign currency is unlimited but must be declared on arrival; export is limited to the amount declared. However, proof of legal exchange to local currency must be provided for re-export for imported sums of over US$2,000; retain all currency exchange receipts.

Travellers cheques have limited acceptance.

Customs

Personal items are duty-free, goods to the value of US$10,000 can be imported for personal use; valuable items such as jewellery, cameras, computers must be declared.

The export of antiques and art objects is subject to duty and a special permit from the Ministry of Culture, a certificate stating the age of the item(s) should be obtained when purchased.

Prohibited imports

Firearms, ammunition, illegal drugs, anti-Uzbek propaganda, fruit or vegetables, precious metals, gem stones and furs.

Health (for visitors)

Mandatory precautions

Vaccination certificates are required for yellow fever if travelling from an infected area.

Advisable precautions

Vaccinations for diphtheria, tetanus, hepatitis A and typhoid are recommended. Other vaccinations that may be advised include tuberculosis and hepatitis B. A non-malignant malaria occasionally occurs in the border area of Afghanistan and Tajikistan, visitors should avoid being bitten by using anti-mosquito sprays and long clothing. There is a risk of rabies.

Water precautions are recommended using water purification tablets or drinking bottled water.

Any medicines required by the traveller should be brought into the country and it would be wise to have precautionary antibiotics if going outside major urban centres. A travel kit including a disposable syringe is a reasonable precaution.

Medical insurance is essential, including emergency evacuation.

Hotels

Advisable to book in advance through Uzbektourism or other specialist travel agents.

Credit cards

Credit cards are not widely accepted outside Tashkent's top hotels and restaurants.

Public holidays (national)

Fixed dates

1 Jan (New Year's Day), 8 Mar (Women's Day), 20–22 Mar (Nawruz/Persian New Year), 1 May (Labour Day), 9 May (Victory Day), 1 Sep (Independence Day), 18 Nov (Flag Day), 8 Dec (Constitution Day).

Variable dates

Eid al Adha, Persian New Year, Birth of the Prophet, Eid al Fitr.

Islamic year 1437 (15 Oct 2015–2 Oct 2016):: The Islamic year contains 354 or 355 days, with the result that Muslim feasts advance by 10–12 days against the Gregorian calendar. Dates of feasts vary according to the sighting of the new moon, so cannot be forecast exactly.

Working hours

Banking

Mon–Fri: 0900–1800; Sat: 0900–1500. Banks at Tashkent airport are open only at arrival of international flights.

Business

Mon–Fri: 0800–1300, 1400–1700. Business hours generally include Saturday mornings.

Government

Mon–Fri: 0800–1300, 1400–1700. Some government offices are open Saturday mornings.

Shops

Mon–Fri: 0800–2000/2100. Shops are closed for lunch for one hour at any time between 1100 and 1500.

Telecommunications

Mobile/cell phones

There are 900 and 900/1800 GSM services located in highly populated areas only.

Electricity supply

220V AC, with round two-pin plugs.

Social customs/useful tips

Business is conducted formally. Appointments are essential when business cards are exchanged.

Personal relationships are the key to doing business in Uzbekistan, with the hierarchy confined to a small group of influential families. Establishing contact within that group can be vital.
Gratuities are illegal.
The giving of small gifts is widely practised, not as bribes but as social niceties. Uzbek hospitality is renowned. It may be regarded as insulting to decline an invitation to a private function. Offering basic food is considered insulting. It is polite to see a visitor off at a train station. If travelling on public transport, make sure to give up your seat to the old, parents with children and the disabled. Superstitions are taken somewhat seriously: for example, do not give an even number of flowers, as this is funereal; do not greet people in a doorway – this is considered unlucky.
Local customs of note are ram butting and wrestling, and wedding ceremonies in September which take place in the street.
Alcohol is available and smoking is widespread.

Security
Terrorist bombings in Tashkent have prompted many Western governments to advise their citizens not to visit Uzbekistan unless absolutely necessary. Visitors should alert their presence to their own embassies on arrival and take all precautions and advice given regarding safety measures.
It is unwise to venture out on the streets alone at night. Dress inconspicuously, as wealthy-looking foreigners can be a target for muggers. Identification should be carried at all times, and visitors should avoid photographing official buildings. If taking photographs in the vicinity of police or soldiers, it is best to ask their permission first.
Since 1999, there has been an increasing terrorist and kidnapping threat in the north-east of the country, especially in the Ferghana Valley and mountainous regions on the Kyrgyz and Tajik borders. Visitors should register with the Uzbek authorities before entering these areas. Outbreaks of violence can lead to strong reactions from the Uzbekistani army, including widespread road blocks and the closure of some destinations. If stopped by police, visitors should remain calm and polite.

Getting there

Air
National airline: Uzbekistan Airlines
International airport/s: Tashkent International airport (TAS), 11km from city centre. Facilities include duty-free shops, bureau de change, left luggage, restaurants and bar. There are taxis, trains and trolley buses to the city (journey time 10–20 minutes).
Airport tax: Departure tax: US$10

Surface
There are border crossings with Afghanistan, Kazakhstan, Kyrgyzstan, Tajikistan and Turkmenistan, however not all are open and available to international travellers. Check with local authorities before making an abortive trip.
Road: Primary roads along trade routes are being upgraded to increase access for freight. Secondary roads are in poor condition especially in desert areas such as the borders with Turkmenistan and the western borders with Kazakhstan.
The Regional Road Corridor Improvement Project, estimated at US$18 billion, to improve Central Asian roads, airports, railway lines and seaports and provide a vital transit route between Europe and Asia was agreed, on 3 November 2007. Six new transit corridors, between Afghanistan, Azerbaijan, China, Kazakhstan, Kyrgyzstan, Mongolia, Tajikistan and Uzbekistan, of mainly roads and rail links, will be constructed, or existing resources upgraded, by 2013. Half the costs with be provided by the Asian Development Bank and other multilateral organisations and the other half by participating countries.
Rail: Tashkent is the hub of rail services in Central Asia. Lines run west to Ashgabat (Turkmenistan), south to Samarkand and on to Dushanbe (Tajikistan), east to Bishkek (Kyrgyzstan) and Almaty (Kazakhstan) and north to Moscow (Russia). The distances involved do not make this the most convenient means of travel, services are few and slow, and tickets must be purchased with hard currency, preferably US dollars.

Getting about

National transport
Air: Uzbekistan Airways has scheduled flights to many cities and towns around the country providing a realistically quick method of getting around the country. Tashkent, Bukhara, Samarkand and Urgench are all served by internal flights.
Road: The road network is deteriorating and many published statistics on paved and unpaved roads are often a decade out-of-date. Driving can be hazardous for the visitor and it is recommended that arrangements should be made to use a local driver and a four-wheel drive vehicle, particularly if travelling to the Tien Shan mountain ranges. Tashkent roads are relatively well maintained with street lighting. Outside the city however the risks of driving, especially at night, include livestock and farm vehicles (often animal-drawn). There are security checkpoints at the city limits of Tashkent and other towns throughout the country. A permit is necessary if travelling to Termez and other areas of the Surkhandarya region. The permit can be applied for in Tashkent and usually takes five days to process.
Uzbekistan has a large highway police force, and drivers are frequently stopped for minor infractions or document checks.
Buses: Routes between the main cities are served by modern air-conditioned coach services which are reliable but infrequent. Other regional services are irregular and often used for transporting goods and livestock.
Rail: Tashkent, Samarkand and Bukhara are all connected by an electrified network. Some other routes are in varying states of disrepair, and long-distance travel by train should be avoided.

City transport
Taxis: In each city there are official taxis (with sign on top) and unofficial taxis. Agree rates in advance when using the official taxis. A few dollars are sufficient for a local journey in an unofficial taxi. In Tashkent it is safer to use official taxis or hire cars. Taxis can be hired for an hour, a day or a week.
Buses, trams & metro: An underground railway, trolleybus service and buses provide a comprehensive network in Tashkent.

Car hire
The are very few car hire facilities; a national licence with authorised translation or international driving permit is required.

BUSINESS DIRECTORY

The addresses listed below are a selection only. While World of Information makes every endeavour to check these addresses, we cannot guarantee that changes have not been made, especially to telephone numbers and area codes. We would welcome any corrections.

Telephone area codes

International direct dialling code (IDD) for Uzbekistan is +998, followed by area code and subscriber's number:

Andijan	74	Bukara	65
Ferghana	73	Samarkand	66
Tashkent	71		

Useful telephone numbers

Police: 02
Fire: 01
Ambulance: 03

Chambers of Commerce

American Chamber of Commerce in Uzbekistan, 41 Buyok Turon Street, Tashkent 700000 (tel: 120-6077; fax: 120-7077; e-mail: office@amcham-uzbekistan.org).

Uzbekistan Chamber of Commodity Producers and Entrepreneurs, 6 Bukhoro Street, Tashkent 700047 (tel: 133-0699; fax: 133-3799; e-mail: root@ptp.co.uz).

Banking
Agrobank, 43 Muqimiy Street, Tashkent 100096. (tel:: 150-5369, 120-8833).

Bank Asaka (specialised state joint stock commercial), 67 Nukus Str, 700015 Tashkent (tel: 120-8111; fax: 120-8173).

Hamkorbank, Avenue Bobur 85, Andijan (tel: 244-73-33; 244-77-18).

Narodny Bank (People's Bank), Tashkent.

National Bank for Foreign Economic Activity of the Republic of Uzbekistan, 101 Amir Temur St, 700084 Tashkent (tel: 137-6077; fax: 133-3200).

Pakhta Bank, 79A Nukus St, Apar 1–2, Tashkent 700015 (tel: 120-5855; fax: 120-7712).

Ravnak Bank, 2 Furkat St, Tashkent 700021 (tel: 144-0753; fax: 144-1091).

Tadbirkorbank, 52 S Azimov St, Tashkent (133-1875; fax: 133-8100).

Uzbekistan-Turkish Bank, No.15/B Drujba Naradov Street, Tashkent (tel: 173-8323, 173-8324; fax: 120-6362).

Uzpromstroybank, 3 Shahrisabzskaya St, Tashkent 700000 (tel: 120-4528; 120-4520).

Central bank
Central Bank of Uzbekistan (CBU), Prospekt Uzbekistana 6, Tashkent 700001 (tel: 133-6829; fax: 136-7704).

Stock exchange
Republican Stock Exchange, www.uzse.uz

Travel information
Sairam Tourism, 13A Movarounnahr St, Tashkent 700060 (tel: 133-7411; fax: 120-6937; internet: www.sairamtour.com).

Tashkent Intourist, 69A Navoi St, Tashkent (tel: 144-1294, 144-0278, fax: 144-0776).

Uzbekistan Airways, 41 Movaraunnakhr Street, Tashkent 700060 (tel: 255-1850; fax: 255-6822; internet: www.uzairways.com).

National tourist organisation offices
Uzbektourism, 47 Khorezm St, 700047 Tashkent (tel: 133-3854; fax: 136-7948; internet: www.uzbektourism.uz).

Ministries
Ministry of Agriculture, 4 Navoi St, 700004 Tashkent (tel: 114-1353, 141-0020; fax: 141-0053).

Ministry of Communication, 1 Alexei Tolstoi St, 700000 Tashkent (tel: 133-8503; fax: 133-1695).

Ministry for Cultural Affairs, 30 Navoi St, 700129 Tashkent (tel: 139-4957).

Ministry of Defence, 100 Academician Abdullaev St, 700000 Tashkent (tel: 133-6667).

Ministry of Energy and Electrification, 6 Horezm St, 700000 Tashkent (tel: 133-6128; fax: 136-2700).

Ministry of Finance, 5 Mustaqillik Sq, 700078 Tashkent (tel: 1391943; fax: 144-5643).

Ministry of Foreign Affairs, 9 Uzbekistan Ave, 700029 Tashkent (tel: 133-6475; fax: 139-4348; internet: http://jahon.mfa.uz).

Ministry of Foreign Economic Relations, Elyor Madjidovich Ganiev, 75 Buyuk Ipak Yuli St, 700077 Tashkent (tel: 1670734, 168-9256, 134-4480; fax: 168-7231, 168-7477).

Ministry of Health, 12 Navoi St, 700012 Tashkent (tel: 141-1680; fax: 141-1641).

Ministry of Higher and Special Secondary Education, 6 Mustaqillik Sq, 700078 Tashkent (tel: 139-4808; fax: 139-4329).

Ministry of Internal Affairs, 1 Herman Lopatin St, 700029 Tashkent (tel: 158-3614; fax: 133-8934).

Ministry of Justice, 5 Hamza St, 700047 Tashkent (tel: 133-5039; fax: 133-5176).

Ministry of Labour, 4 Abai St, 700195 Tashkent (tel: 141-7628; fax: 139-7821).

Ministry of Land Improvement and Water Economy, 5a Abdulla Qodiri St, 700128 Tashkent (tel: 141-1353; fax: 141-4924).

Ministry of Public Education, 5 Mustaqillik Sq, 700078 Tashkent (tel: 139-4214; fax: 139-1173).

Ministry of Social Security, 20a Abdulla Avioni St, 700100 Tashkent (tel: 153-5371).

Other useful addresses
British Embassy, 67 Gulyamov St, Tashkent 700000 (tel: 120-6574; fax: 120-6430; email: brit@emb.uz).

Business-Vestnik Vostoka (BVV) (English newspaper) (32 Matbuotchilar St, Tashkent (tel: 133-9593; email: bvv@bvv.bcc.com.uz).

Cabinet of Ministers, 5 Mustakillik Maidoni, Tashkent (tel: 139-8188; fax: 139-8121).

Central Asia Research Forum, School of Oriental and African Studies, Thornhaugh St, London WC1H 0XG, UK (tel: (+44) 171-323-6300; fax: (+44) 171-436-3844).

EU Co-ordinating Unit, Tarasa Chevchenka St Dom 4, 700029 Tashkent (tel: 138-4018, 156-3479, 156-0417; fax: 132-0652).

Foreign Investment Agency, 4th Floor, 16A Navoi Street, Tashkent (tel: 141-5541, 141-5752; fax: 189-1201).

Government House, 700008 Tashkent (tel: 139-8295; fax: 139-8601).

National Agency for Telecommunications and Postal Services, 1 Tolstoy Street, Tashkent (tel: 133-6503, 133-6645; fax: 139-8732).

National Association of Gold Mining and Diamond Processing Companies, 26 Turaqorghan Thoroughfare, 700019 Tashkent (tel: 148-0720; fax: 144-2603).

National Joint Stock Corporation for Construction in the City of Tashkent, 16a Uzbekistan Ave, 700027 Tashkent (tel: 133-9033; fax: 136-4788).

SME Development Agency, 89 Gargarin St. Samarkand, PO Box 703029 (tel: 124-2966; fax: 131-0107; email: ravshan@samarkand.silk.glas.apc.org).

State Company for Television and Radio Broadcasting, 69 Navoi St, 700011 Tashkent (tel: 133-8106; fax: 144-0021).

State Committee on Agriculture and Construction of the Republic of Uzbekistan, 6 Abai St, 700011 Tashkent (tel: 144-0084/5).

State Committee on Forecasting and Statistics of the Cabinet of Ministers, 45a Uzbekistanskii Ave, 700008 Tashkent (tel: 139-8216, 139-8669; fax: 167-2509, 167-7816).

State Committee on Forests, 49a Uzbekistan Ave, 700017 Tashkent (tel: 145-9180).

State Committee on Geology and Mineral Resources, 11 Taras Shevchenko St, 700060 Tashkent (tel: 133-7206; fax: 156-0283).

State Committee on Precious Metals, 26 Turk-Kurganskiy Proezd, 700019 Tashkent (tel: 148-0720, 148-0663; fax: 144-2603, 148-0481).

State Committee for Privatisation (GKI), Mustaqillik Maydoni 6, Tashkent (tel: 139-8768; fax: 139-8548).

State Committee on the Protection of Nature, 5a Abdulla Qodyri St, 700000 Tashkent (tel: 141-0442; fax: 141-3990).

State Committee on Science and Technology, 29 Hadicha Syleimonova St, 700017 Tashkent (tel: 139-1843; fax: 139-1243).

State Committee for Television and Radio, Ulitsa Khoremzskaya 49, Tashkent (tel: 144-3287).

State Corporation on Industrial and Civil Engineering Construction, 17 Proletar St, 700060 Tashkent (tel: 133-7725; fax: 133-1041).

State Corporation of Local Industries, 5 Mustaqillik Sq, 700078 Tashkent (tel: 139-1058; fax: 139-4853).

State Joint-Stock Association on Trade, 6 Mustaqillik Sq, 700078 Tashkent (tel: 139-4971; fax: 139-1282).

State Property Committee of the Republic of Uzbekistan, Prospekt Uzbekistanskij 55, 700003 Tashkent (fax: 113-94617; 139-2236).

Embassy of Uzbekistan (USA) 1746 Massachusetts Avenue, NW Washington 20036-1903 (tel: (+1-202) 887-5300; fax: (+1-202) 293-6804; internet: www.uzbekistan.org).

Uzbek Information Agency (state news agency), Ulitsa Khamza 2, Tashkent (tel: 139-4982, 133-1622).

Uzbekinvest, 5 Mustaqillik Sq, 700078 Tashkent (tel: 139-1989; fax: 189-1538, 144-5186).

Uzbekiston Ovozi Times (English newspaper), 32 Matbuotchilar St, Tashkent (tel: 133-2036, 133-3855; fax: 133-7914).

Uzbekneftgas (national corporation of the oil and gas industry), 21 Akhunbabaev St, 700047 Tashkent (tel: 133-5757; fax: 132-1062).

Uzbek Post Office, 1 Tolstoy Street, Tashkent (tel: 133-5747; fax: 136-0921).

National news agency: Jahon Information Agency, 9 Uzbekistan Street, Tashkent, 700029 (tel: 133-6591, 153-8682; fax: 120-6443; email: aajohon@mfa.uz; internet: http://jahon.mfa.uz)

UzA (Uzbekistan National News Agency): www.uza.uz/en

Internet sites

The Times of Central Asia: www.times.kg

News and commercial information: www.uzreport.com

General and government information: www.uzland.uz

Regional news and links: www.eurasianet.org

Vanuatu

COUNTRY PROFILE

Human settlement dates back to around 4,000 BC.
1606 Portuguese explorers, Luis Váez de Torres and Pedro Ferdinand de Queirós, arrived on the island they called Espiritu Santo, at Big Bay.
1792 Captain Cook explored the islands in 1792, calling the group the New Hebrides.
1887 The islands were administered as a joint French-British naval commission.
1906 An Anglo-French Condominium was established. Over half the male population was conscripted as indentured workers into Australia. The native population dropped dramatically, falling to 45,000 by 1935.
1938 A new religion emerged called the John Frum Cargo cult.
1956 The John Frum Cargo religious cult was recognised by the authorities.
1960s An independence movement, NaGriamel, grew; it advocated the return of land to the native Ni-Vanuatu.
1971 With over 36 per cent of the land owned by foreigners, NaGriamel petitioned the United Nations to prevent further sales to non-indigenous people.
1977 The UK, France and local representatives agreed independence plans.
1980 The leader of NaGriamel attempted to gain independence for Espiritu Santo, but the insurrection was put down and the entire state of New Hebrides gained independence on 30 July, under the new name of Vanuatu. The first prime minister was Walter Lini, an Anglican priest.
1981 Vanuatu joined the United Nations. Vanuatu was divided into six provinces, the English names of which are formed from the initials of the islands which constitute each province.
1995 A coalition government of the Union des Partis Moderés (UPM) (Union of Moderate Parties) (Francophone) and the National United Party (NUP) (Anglophone) took office and Serge Vohor became prime minister.
1998 Donald Kalpokas formed a coalition government, comprising his Vanua'atu Party (VP) (Party of Our Land) and the NUP.
1999 John Bernard Bani was elected president. Parliament elected Barak Sopé prime minister, ousting Donald Kalpokas.
2001 Sopé and his government were ousted following a no-confidence vote. A new government was formed with a coalition of the UPM and the VP; Edward Natapei became prime minister.
2002 An earthquake struck Vanuatu, causing US$700,000 of damage. The UPM won the parliamentary elections.
2004 Cyclone Ivy caused flooding in many areas and some 1,000 people were evacuated to temporary shelters in Port Vila. In snap elections no clear majority was achieved, the VP, NUP, Vanuatu Republican Party (VRP), National Community Association (NCA) and People's Progressive Party (PPP) formed a coalition government. Alfred Masing Nalo was elected president by an electoral college, but the Supreme Court removed him and after several attempts to resolve the matter, Kalkot Mataskelekele finally became president. Serge Vohor became prime minister and formed a government of national unity. Vohor was ousted in a no-confidence motion and Ham Lini Vanuaroroa was elected prime minister.
2008 Vanuatu completed the domestic requirements of the Pacific Island Countries Trade Agreement (PICTA). In parliamentary elections, the ruling VP and NUP won most seats (11 and eight respectively); Edward Natapei (VP) became prime minister.
2009 Iolu Abil, supported by Natapei and VT, won the presidential election in parliament. Prime Minister Natapei was expelled from parliament, although a legal challenge led to the decision to bar him being ruled as unconstitutional.
2010 While out of the country, Prime Minister Natapei was ousted in a parliamentary vote of no-confidence; he was replaced by the deputy prime minister, Sato Kilman.
2011 Prime Minister Kilman lost a parliamentary vote of no-confidence and Serge Vohor was elected prime minister in April. Kilman and his supporters lost a legal appeal against the procedure of his ousting. In May, the Court of Appeal ruled that the appointment of Serge Vohor as prime minister was unconstitutional and that the decision of the Speaker of the House of Parliament when he ruled to remove Sato Kilman from office as prime minister was 'not in existence'. Kilman was reinstated. On 16 June the Supreme Court

KEY FACTS

Official name: Ripablik blong Vanuatu (Republic of Vanuatu)

Head of State: President Baldwin Lonsdale (from 22 Sep 2014)

Head of government: Prime Minister Sato Kilman (from 11 June 2015)

Ruling party: A coalition led by Vanua'aku Pati (VP) with National Unity Party (NUP), Union des Partis Moderés (UPM) (Union of Moderate Parties), Leba Pati (Vanuatu Labour Party) (VLP) and independents (since 2004; re-elected 30 Oct 2012)

Area: 11,880 square km (82 islands)

Population: 263,000 (2014)*

Capital: Port Vila (on Efate)

Official language: Bislama (Ni-Vanuatu Pidgin), English, French

Currency: Vatu (V) = 100 centimes

Exchange rate: V111.91 per US$ (Sep 2015)

GDP per capita: US$3,092 (2014)*

GDP real growth: 2.90% (2014)*

GDP: US$812.00 million (2014)*

Inflation: 1.02% (2014)

Balance of trade: -US$242.84 million (2011)

Foreign debt: US$111.00 million (2010)

* estimated figure

invalidated the December 2010 election of Sato Kilman as prime minister, since the parliamentary speaker had failed to hold a secret ballot. In the interim Edward Natapei was reinstated. However, Mr Natapei he would not stand for re-election. On 26 June, Sato Kilman stood for the post of prime minister and was re-elected by parliament. Vanuatu became the 120th country to adopt the Rome Statute System of the International Criminal Court (ICC).

2012 On 1 February, legislation to endorse the ICC system became operational. In May parliamentary elections were announced for 30 October. On 14 October the first independent FM radio station in Vanuatu was launched. Parliamentary elections were held on 30 October, in which the VP won eight seats (out of 52), the PPP won six, UPM five, NUP four, Graon mo Jastis Pati (GJP) (Land and Justice Party) (a political party launched in 2010) four; 11 other political parties and four independence won the remaining 25 seats. On 19 November parliament re-elected Sato Kilman as prime minister by 29 votes, defeating Edward Natapei with 23 votes.

2013 Eight MPs crossed the floor and joined the opposition on 20 March. Prime Minister Kilman resigned and on 23 March Moana Carcasses Kalosil was elected prime minister by parliament. He became the first nationalised citizen (he was born in French Polynesia) to lead the country. During his first 100 days he revoked 'about ten' diplomatic passports, tore up a defence co-operation agreement with Indonesia, and told China to relocate a major aid project. On 29 July the Prime Minister lead a parade celebrating 150 years since the ending of 'blackbirding', the practice whereby Pacific Islanders were kidnapped for forced labour in Australia. He later called on the Australian government to apologise for the treatment of people taken from the islands.

2014 Prime Minister Kalosil lost a vote of no-confidence on 15 May by 35 votes in favour, 11 against and 4 abstensions. He was immediately succeeded by Joe Natuman with 40 out of the 52 votes cast. Vanuatu and New Zealand signed a Tourism Partnership Arrangement in July. The Arrangement sets out their responsibilities for a five year programme of tourism co-operation, leading to a 'buoyant, resilient and sustainable tourism sector that provides greater economic returns for the people of Vanuatu'. After eight rounds of voting Baldwin Lonsdale won the presidential election on 22 September with 46 votes of the 58 possible.

2015 Cyclone Pam hit Vanuatu on 13 March. President Baldwin Lonsdale described it as a 'monster' and declared a state of emergency. Many buildings were destroyed, power lines felled and water supplies cut, Aid from Australia and New Zealand started to arrive on 15 March.

Political structure

Constitution

The constitution created a republic, headed by a president with ceremonial powers only. The president is elected by a two-thirds majority in an electoral college from members of parliament and presidents of regional councils including Shefa, Sanma, Penama, Tafea, Malampa and Torba. The president serves a five-year term.

A Malvatumauri (National Council of Chiefs) advises the government on matters of custom, land tenure and the preservation of Vanuatu's traditions. Members of the council are hereditary peers and may not sit in parliament unless given leave to and elected by their peers.

Independence date

30 July 1980

Form of state

Republic

The executive

The executive consists of a Council of Ministers headed by the prime minister who is elected by parliament from among its members. The prime minister and the 12 co-members of the Council of Ministers oversee the administration of the 13 government ministries.

The president, who is head of state, is elected for a five-year term by an electoral college made up of the members of parliament and the presidents of the six provincial governments. A two-thirds majority is required.

National legislature

The 52-member parliament is elected by universal adult suffrage for a four-year term in multi-seat constituencies.

Legal system

Based on English law.

Last elections

30 October 2012 (parliamentary); 22 September 2014 (presidential)

Results: Parliamentary: the Vanua'aku Pati (VP) (Party of Our Land) won eight seats (out of 52), Parti Progressiste Popula (PPP) (People's Progressive Party) six, Union des Partis Moderés (UPM) (Union of Moderate Parties) five, National United Party (NUP) four, Graon mo Jastis Pati (GJP) (Land and Justice Party) four; 11 other political parties and four independence won the remaining 25 seats.

Presidential: After 8 rounds of voting (the longest in Vanuatu history) Baldwin Lonsdale defeated 12 opponents with 46 votes (out of a possible 58).

Next elections

30 October 2016 (parliamentary); 2019 (presidential indirect)

Political parties

Ruling party

A coalition led by Vanua'aku Pati (VP) with National Unity Party (NUP), Union des Partis Moderés (UPM) (Union of Moderate Parties), Leba Pati (Vanuatu Labour Party) (VLP) and independents (since 2004; re-elected 30 Oct 2012)

Political situation

Who owns and who has the right to determine the fate of either tribal or public land has created problems for the government. On the one hand the government wishes to take up partnerships with foreign companies and provide land for commercial endeavours to develop the islands. On the other hand, local people consider traditional lands to be in the ownership of all

KEY INDICATORS — Vanuatu

	Unit	2011	2012	2013	2014	**2015
Population	m	*0.25	*0.25	*0.26	*0.26	*0.27
Gross domestic product (GDP)	US$bn	0.74	0.79	0.80	*0.81	*0.75
GDP per capita	US$	3,036	3,142	3,124	*3,092	*2,775
GDP real growth	%	3.3	1.8	2.0	*2.9	*-4.0
Inflation	%	1.2	1.4	1.3	1.0	*2.0
Exports (fob) (goods)	US$m	67.4	54.7	44.6	–	–
Imports (fob) (goods)	US$m	310.2	253.3	267.5	–	–
Balance of trade	US$m	-242.8	-198.5	-222.8	–	–
Current account	US$m	-126.9	-51.0	-26.0	*-11.0	*-107.0
Total reserves minus gold	US$m	164.1	–	–	184.0	–
Foreign exchange	US$m	161.9	–	–	–	–
Exchange rate	per US$	87.03	91.83	99.13	99.93	–

* estimated figure ** forecast figure

the community and are not in the government's purvue to sell or lease.
Vanuatu came top of the World Bank's *Ease of Doing Business* in the Pacific in 2010, as well as the *Lonely Planet*'s best destination. At the same time Australia condemned Vanuatu as an offshore tax haven that allowed its citizens to evade tax and criminals to launder money.
To improve the reliability of official records, a new scheme was introduced in November 2009, whereby births and deaths in rural areas can be registered via text-messages using mobile phones provided at schools and health clinics.

Population
266,000 (2013)*
Last census: 2009: 234,023
Population density: 20 inhabitants per square km (2010). Urban population 26 per cent (2010 Unicef).
Annual growth rate: 2.5 per cent, 1990–2010 (Unicef).

Ethnic make-up
The great majority of the population is Melanesian in origin, with around 5 per cent of European descent.

Religions
About 80 per cent of the population is Christian, although animism is still in evidence, and the cargo cult remains on Tanna Island. There have been localised secessionist movements in Santo, Malekula, Ambrym, Aoba, Pentecost and Maewo.

Education
In 2003, the EU awarded a grant of eur8 million to 14 pacific countries to be used to enhance basic education, and in the case of Vanuatu, to extend compulsory schooling to eight years. The government has backed the 'one laptop per child' programme (OLPC).
Literacy rate: 53 per cent adult rate in 2004
Compulsory years: Six to 12.
Enrolment rate: 117 per cent gross primary enrolment; 28.5 per cent gross secondary enrolment, of relevant age groups (including repeaters) (Unicef 2004).

Health
HIV/Aids
In August 2004, Vanuatu had two confirmed HIV/Aids cases.
Life expectancy: 68 years, 2004 (WHO 2006)
Fertility rate/Maternal mortality rate: 3.9 births per woman, 2010 (Unicef)
Child (under 5 years) mortality rate (per 1,000): 18 per 1,000 live births (WHO 2012)

Main cities
Port Vila, on Efate (capital, estimated population 51,319 in 2012), Luganville (Santo) (14,427), Port Olry (3,042), Mele (2,667), Norsup 2,428), Isangel (1,734).

Languages spoken
English is spoken by 60 per cent of the population and French by 40 per cent. There are 115 indigenous languages.

Official language/s
Bislama (Ni-Vanuatu Pidgin), English, French

Media
Press
In English, the only daily is *Vanuatu Daily Post* (www.dailypost.com.vu), other weeklies are *Port Vila Presse* (www.news.vu/en), *The Vanuatu Independent* (www.independent.vu), *Nasara*, and in Bislama *Ni-Vanuatu*.

Broadcasting
The state-owned Vanuatu Broadcasting and Television Corporation (VBTC) is responsible for public transmissions.
Radio: The VBTC operates Radio Vanuatu AM and Nambawan FM, in Bislama, English and French. External services by RFI Radio France, BBC and Radio Australia are received. Laef FM is a religious radio station.
On 15 October 2012, the first independent FM radio station, Buzz FM 96, in Vanuatu was launched.
Television: VBTC operates Television Blong Vanuatu, the only public service. Cable and satellite services are available including Vanuatu TV (http://vanuatu.tv).
Other news agencies: ABC Pacific Beat: www.radioaustralia.net.au/pacbeat
Pacific Magazine:
www.pacificmagazine.net
Pacific Islands New Association (Pina): www.pina.com.fj

Economy
The economy of Vanuatu is dominated by its service sector, which constitutes 64.1 per cent of GDP; agriculture, comprising 25.1 per cent, is the other major component with industry and manufacturing contributing less than 10.8 per cent of GDP (2014).
The majority of the population is engaged in subsistence agriculture, with copra as the principal export crop, followed by cocoa, with timber, beef and fish providing smaller earnings. Tourism and the tax-free financial centre offset the recurring trade deficit, while providing greater employment. Tourism contributed 18.6 per cent of GDP directly in 2014, and when indirect contribution is taken into account tourism contributed a total of 48.8 per cent to GDP. Vanuatu is the oldest offshore financial centre and tax haven in the Pacific, opened in 1971, it has around 2,000 registered financial institutions and trust-fund services, providing an important source of foreign exchange.
The economy's progress has slowed down since the global economic crisis struck, reducing the amount of arrivals, in 2008 when growth in GDP was 6.2 per cent. By 2012 the annual expansion in GDP had fallen to 1.8 per cent. However, in 2013 it started to accelerate again recording a growth of 2.0 per cent and then 2.9 per cent in 2014.
The traditional herb kava has been used in the Pacific for generations to alleviate stress and strains. It is typically chewed but can also be brewed; most Western countries banned its use due to the risk of liver damage. Luckily for Vanuatu, international trade talks managed to get this ban lifted and in 2010 a new kava bottling plant (LAV Vanuatu Kava) opened in Rentepau on Efate. However, in 2015 the EU and US were again considering banning the imports of kava products due to the health concerns associated with it.
The tourism sector is recognised by the government as a key sector in its economic development to provide employment opportunities for its young and rapidly growing population, tourism directly employs 14.6 per cent (10,500 jobs) of all those in employment. Although bureaucracy is one of the issues facing new investment, there have been some successful investment proposals approved by the Vanuatu Foreign Investment Board, which have centred on the tourism, international finance and agricultural sectors.
Vanuatu's beef industry has been a success, mainly due to access to export markets, since domestic demand for beef is not sufficient to keep the enterprise going. It is marketed as being 'grass-fed and antibiotic and hormone free'.
In March 2015 Cyclone Pam hit Vanuatu and was considered one of the worst natural disasters in the history of Vanuatu. Sixteen people lost their lives directly or indirectly due to the storm. The damage wrought by the cyclone has weighed heavily on the tourism and agriculture industries. In June, arrivals by air were down 24 per cent on the figures from June 2014 and arrivals by cruise ship were down by 56 per cent.

External trade
Vanuatu is a member of the South Pacific Regional Trade and Economic Co-operation Agreement (Sparteca) along with 12 other regional nations, which allows products duty free access by Pacific Island Forum members to Australian and New Zealand markets (subject to the country of origin restrictions). It is also a member of the Melanesian Spearhead Group (with Fiji, Papua New Guinea and the Solomon Islands) as a sub-regional trade group, whereby customs tariffs have been

harmonised under the Melanesian free trade agreement (MFTA).
Agriculture provides over 85 per cent of commodity exports, however tourism is the largest export earner.

Imports
Principal imports are machinery and equipment, live animals and foodstuffs, vehicles and fuels.
Main sources: China (20.2 per cent of total in 2012), Singapore (28.8 per cent), US (15.0 per cent).

Exports
Main exports are copra, beef, timber, kava and tuna.
Main destinations: Thailand (41.7 per cent of total in 2012), CÔte d'Ivoire (30.3 per cent), Japan (14.7 per cent).

Agriculture

Farming
The agricultural sector accounts for around 25.1 per cent of GDP (2014), employs some 60 per cent of the workforce and provides up to 85 per cent of the country's exports. Agricultural production and livestock rearing is mainly carried out by smallholding farmers. More than 90 per cent of all the fruit and vegetables consumed in Vanuatu are imported.
Around 41 per cent of the land area is cultivatable, although only half is utilised. The soil is generally fertile and rainfall adequate, although crops can be subject to cyclone damage. The sector is hampered by a general lack of capital and investment, technical skills as well as the isolation of farmers.
Copra is Vanuatu's main export crop, accounting for approximately one-third of total export earnings and 6 per cent of GDP. A mechanised coconut-desiccating factory opened, in the northern region, capable of processing 24,000 coconuts per day. It is projected that this plant will produce 44 tonnes of coconut oil and 118 tonnes of coconut meat per day expanding export markets.
Kava, used for manufacturing tranquilliser drugs, has become an important export commodity, although production was scaled back due to plant disease and medical concerns over the substance's effects on the liver. In 2015 Vanuatu's kava industry was under serious threat as the EU and the US were considering banning the imports of kava due to health reasons.

Cattle rearing and forestry are becoming increasingly important foreign exchange earners.
Despite the detrimental affects on agriculture from Cyclone Pam that hit Vanuatu in March 2015, there was a large but temporary increase in coconut oil exports in the second quarter of the year. However, exports of other major commodities fell significantly compared to the same period in 2014.

Fishing
An experimental project to seed reefs with trochus raised in hatcheries has been under way since the 1990s (the shells are collected and sold as buttons). Investment project permits have been issued for fish farming.
The typical annual fish catch is over 27,000t, with 850t other seafood and 100,000 units pearls and shells.

Forestry
Access only by sea to exploitable forests has limited timber production. The government is working to achieve certification by the International Tropical Timber Organisation (ITTO) to prove that the country's forests are being sustainably managed. This would increase the added value of timber products. However, in 2014 Vanuatu was still having trouble to protect its forests and maintain a state of sustainability.

Industry and manufacturing
The industrial sector accounts for approximately 10.7 per cent of GDP and employs some 7 per cent of the workforce. Manufacturing contributes about 5 per cent of GDP.
Main industries include copra processing, meat canning, fish processing, soft drinks bottling, furniture making, timber production, metalwork and handicrafts for the growing tourist market.
Japan has played an important part in helping to improve regional commercial centres for transporting and distributing agricultural products and other goods, providing investment for wharves on Tanna and Malekula Islands.

Tourism
The Pacific islands that constitute Vanuatu offer a range of tropical resorts, which are most popular with Australian visitors. Chief Roi Mata's Domain is included on Unesco's World Heritage List and is the historic home of Vanuatu's last paramount chief and moral leader.
Travel and tourism plays a vital role in GDP, by contributing an average 18.6 per cent directly (2014) and contributing 48.8 per cent when all related industries and contributions are included. Tourism also provided employment for 14.6 per cent of the workforce directly (10,500 jobs) in the same period, and the total contribution to employment was 41.8 per cent (29,500 jobs). To maintain the health of the industry travel and tourism attracted 15.7 per cent of total capital investment in 2014.
In March 2015 Cyclone Pam hit Vanuatu and was considered one of the worst natural disasters in the history of Vanuatu. Sixteen people lost their lives directly or indirectly due to the storm. The damage wrought by the cyclone has weighed heavily on the tourism industry. In June, arrivals by air were down 24 per cent on the figures from June 2014 and arrivals by cruise ship were down by 56 per cent.

Environment
An Asian Development Bank (ADB) study (*Economics of Climate Change in the Pacific*) published in November 2013 that looks at the effects of climate change in the Pacific region shows that a substantial rise in temperatures on the larger Vanuatu islands of Malampa, Penama and Sanma is highly probable, bringing with it a detrimental impact on agriculture, with spillover effects on the broader economy. As a result it projects that Vanuatu's economic losses could exceed 6.2 per cent of GDP by 2100.

Mining
While Vanuatu has mineral resources, including precious metals, these have yet to be exploited. In 2006, the government signed an agreement with a Swiss-American company to exploit the manganese spoil left over at an abandoned mine on Efate. Hundreds of jobs are expected to be created.

Hydrocarbons
There are no known hydrocarbon reserves. All domestic energy needs must be met by imported petroleum products, which was 1,140 barrels per day of oil in 2013.

Energy
Total installed generating capacity was around 28MW in 2013, including 4.4MW of renewable energy. The rest is provided by imported diesel oil. Unelco Vanuatu Limited (Unelco) is responsible for generation and supply of electricity.
An Asian Development Bank project at the end of 2012 reported that around 33 per cent per the population had access to electricity, with 82 per cent in urban areas and 17 per cent in rural areas.
The government is encouraging renewable energy companies to invest in Vanuatu, as it became the first country in the Asia-Pacific region to attempt to base its entire economy on renewable energy. It plans to reach that goal by 2020, with electricity generated by geothermal heat, wind and solar power and locally manufactured hydrogen-based fuels, which could also be exported.
In 2009 the Australian company KUTh Energy was awarded two licences to undertake a study into the feasibility of using the hot springs on Efate Island for geothermal energy. As a result geothermal energy is planned to provide electricity for Efate by 2017, following the successful

connection of the preliminary power plant, near the hot pools by Takara village, to the grid on 7 July 2011.

Banking and insurance

The introduction in 1983 of the International Companies Act helped Vanuatu to develop as an offshore banking centre, attracting some 100 banks. Following the 11 September 2001 terrorist attacks in the US, the US cut off all direct financial dealing with Vanuatu. The aim was to block all financial transactions that could be linked to terrorists, although Vanuatu was not considered to be a haven for terrorist assets. Vanuatu complied with the requirements of the OECD and was removed from the list of nations with 'tax havens' in 2003.

Central bank

Reserve Bank of Vanuatu

Main financial centre

Port Vila

Time

GMT plus 11 hours

Geography

Vanuatu comprises an irregular archipelago of about 80 islands in the south-west Pacific Ocean, spread over a distance of about 900km (560 miles) from north to south. The islands lie about 1,000km (600 miles) west of Fiji and 400km (250 miles) north-east of New Caledonia.

Most islands are mountainous and volcanic in origin. The capital and second largest town are on the islands if Efate and Espiritu Santo, respectively. Mount Tabwemasana, on Espiritu Santo, (height 1,877 metres) is the highest peak in the archipelago.

Hemisphere

Southern

Climate

Temperatures can range from 16–33 degrees Celsius and rainfall varies from 1,000–2,000mm per annum. Cyclones may occur from December to April.

Entry requirements

Passports

Required by all and must be valid for six months from date of arrival.

Visa

Required by all except citizens of the Commonwealth, EU, and the US for stays of up to 30 days. For a full list of exceptions see www.vanuatu.discoverparadise.org and follow link to *resources* to *travel tips* then to *Visa Requirements*. All travellers must hold onward/return tickets and sufficient funds for their stay.

A visa application can be downloaded from the above internet address (and follow links) and must be forwarded to the Principal Immigration Officer, The Immigration Department, Port Vila, Vanuatu, PMB 014 and must be approved before entry.

Prohibited entry

Anyone whose demeanour is not considered acceptable is prohibited entry.

Currency advice/regulations

The import and export of local and foreign currency is unrestricted.

Travellers cheques are widely accepted.

Customs

Personal items are duty-free. All goods of commercial value must be declared.

Prohibited imports

Firearms, ammunitions, illegal drugs, animals, plants and goods carried on behalf of other persons.

Health (for visitors)

Mandatory precautions

Vaccination certificate for yellow fever if travelling from an infected area.

Advisable precautions

Vaccinations for diphtheria, tetanus, hepatitis A and typhoid are recommended. Other vaccinations that may be advised include tuberculosis and hepatitis B. Malaria prophylaxes are required including mosquito nets, insect sprays and long clothing at night. Sunscreen is highly recommended, even in winter.

Any medicines required by the traveller should be brought into the country. Medical insurance is essential, including emergency evacuation.

Hotels

A 10 per cent tax is added to hotel bills.

Credit cards

Major credit cards are widely accepted. ATMs are available in most banks.

Public holidays (national)

Fixed dates

1 Jan (New Year's Day), 21 Feb (Father Lini Day), 5 Mar (Custom Chief's Day), 1 May (Labour Day), 24 Jul (Children's Day), 30 Jul (Independence Day), 15 Aug (Assumption Day), 5 Oct (Constitution Day), 29 Nov (Unity Day), 25–26 Dec (Christmas).

Variable dates

Good Friday, Easter Monday, Ascension Day.

Working hours

Banking

Mon–Fri: 0830–1500.

Business

Mon–Fri: 0800–1100, 1300–1700.

Government

Mon–Fri: 0730–1700.

Shops

Mon–Fri: 0730–1630/1700 (large supermarkets open until 1930). Sat: 0800–1200. Some shops open Sun morning.

Telecommunications

Telephone/fax

Domestic and international telecommunications are operated by Telecom Vanuatu. Formed in 1989, this is jointly owned by the government of Vanuatu and British and French telecommunications companies. A domestic firm, Communication Services (Vanuatu) Ltd, was granted a telecommunications licence in 1999.

Mobile/cell phones

There is a 900 GSM service in operation.

Electricity supply

220V AC, 50 Hz with flat, three-pin plugs.

Weights and measures

Metric system

Social customs/useful tips

Tipping and bartering are not considered polite behaviour. It is customary to shake hands on meeting and taking leave.

An informal attitude prevails in business. Sometimes business cards are exchanged after introduction. Business is often conducted in Pidgin, English or French.

Getting there

Air

National airline: Air Vanuatu

International airport/s: Port Vila-Bauerfield (VLI), 6km from Port Vila (on Efate); duty-free shop, currency exchange, hotel reservations, post office, car hire and business lounge.

Airport tax: Departure tax: V2,500, included in ticket price.

Surface

Main port/s: Port Vila and Luganville (Santo)

Getting about

National transport

Air: VanAir operates inter-island services to 16 destinations from Port Vila-Bauerfield airport. A V400 service charge is imposed at every airport for any domestic flight.

Road: There are some 150km of surfaced road on Efate, and 100km on Espiritu Santo, which are passable in dry weather.

Buses: Privately run minivans operate unscheduled and unspecified routes around the islands.

Water: Inter-island sea links are unscheduled but generally good.

City transport

Taxis: Taxi services are plentiful and metered. Journey time from the airport to the city centre is about 10 minutes.

Buses, trams & metro: Buses serve the whole of Port Vila. Journey time from airport to city centre is 10 minutes.

Car hire

Car hire is available in Port Vila and Luganville. International, French and UK licences are acceptable.

BUSINESS DIRECTORY

The addresses listed below are a selection only. While World of Information makes every endeavour to check these addresses, we cannot guarantee that changes have not been made, especially to telephone numbers and area codes. We would welcome any corrections.

Telephone area codes

The international direct dialling code (IDD) for Vanuatu is +678 followed by subscriber's number.

Useful telephone numbers

Police: 22-222
Fire: 22-333
Ambulance: 22-100

Chambers of Commerce

Vanuatu Chamber of Commerce and Industry, PO Box 189, Port Vila (tel: 27-543; fax: 27-542; e-mail: vancci@vanuatu.com.vu).

Banking

ANZ Bank (Vanuatu) Ltd, Private Mail Bag 003, Port Vila (tel: 22-536; fax: 22-814).

Banque d'Hawaii (Vanuatu) Ltd, PO Box 29, Lini Highway, Port Vila (tel: 22-412; fax: 23-579).

European Bank Ltd, PO Box 65, International Bldg, Kumul Highway, Port Vila (tel: 27-700; fax: 22-884).

National Bank of Vanuatu, PO Box 249, Air Vanuatu House, Rue de Paris, Port Vila (tel: 22-201; fax: 22-761).

Central bank

Reserve Bank of Vanuatu, PMB 62, Port Vila, Vanuatu (tel: 23-333; fax: 24-231).

Travel information

Air Vanuatu, Air Vanuatu House, Rue de Paris, Port Vila (tel: 23-838; 23-878; fax: 23-250, 26-591; internet: www.airvanuatu.com).

Bauerfield Port Vila International Airport, Civil Aviation Department, PMB 068, Port Vila (tel: 22-993, 22-819; fax: 23-783).

The Principal Immigration Officer, PMB 014, Port Vila.

Tour Vanuatu, PO Box 409, Port Vila (tel: 22-733; fax: 23-442).

National tourist organisation offices

National Tourism Office of Vanuatu, PO Box 209, Port Vila (tel: 22-515, 22-685; fax: 23-889; internet site: http://www.vanuatutourism.com).

Ministries

Ministry of Finance and Housing, PO Box 31, Port Vila (tel: 22-951).

Ministry of Postal Services, Telecommunications and Meteorology, Private mail Bag 011, Port Vila (tel: 25-059; fax: 23-142).

Ministry of Trade, Co-operatives, Energy and Industry, Port Vila (tel: 23-979).

Prime Minister's Office, Private Mail Bag 053, Port Vila (tel: 22-413).

Other useful addresses

Asian Development Bank (ADB), South Pacific Regional Mission, La Casa di Andrea, Fr Dr W H Lini Highway; PO Box 127, Port Vila (tel: 23-300; fax: 23-183; email: adbsprm@adb.org; internet: http://www.adb.org/SPRM).

Department for Foreign Affairs, Port Vila (tel: 22-913, 22-347; fax: 23-142).

The Immigration Department, Port Vila, PMB 014, (tel: 22-354; fax: 25-492).

ABC Pacific Beat: www.radioaustralia.net.au/pacbeat

Pacific Magazine: www.pacificmagazine.net

Pacific Islands New Association (Pina): www.pina.com.fj

Internet sites

Investment promotion authority: www.investinvanuatu.com

Telephone directory (worldwide): www.teldir.com

Vanuatu government: www.vanuatu.gov.vu

Vanuatu online: www.vol.com.vu

Vanuatu portal: Vatu.com

Vanuatu Broadcasting and Television Corporation: www.vbtc.com.vu

Vatican City (The Holy See)

For Rome's conservative Curia, the appointment of Pope Francis in 2014 had not been good news. Instead of blindly following the opinions and advice of his advisers, Francis was often prepared to launch out on his own. A pattern had emerged: the Pope would often depart from the text prepared for him either to announce a new departure for the Vatican, or to clarify existing policy.

Revolutionary...

Surprising a congregation of thousands (including Ecuador's President Rafael Correa) in Quito, Pope Francis echoed the cries of the country's founders, announcing that their cry 'was born of an awareness of lost liberties, of exploitation and plunder, often at the hands of those who happened to be in power at the time.' Having identified the Roman Catholic Church as a revolutionary body, 'Our faith is revolutionary. That is our most heartfelt and constant cry.' President Correa would not have found the Pope's address comforting. The Pope went on to say 'that revolutionary cry made over 200 years ago was not lacking in conviction or in strength. But history has taught us that it only carried force when it ignored personalities, when it dismissed the concentration of power in one person, the failure to understand or appreciate political systems that were different, but not necessarily antagonistic, from our own.'

Pope Francis' use of concepts such as 'revolution' and 'civil rights' sent waves of concern rippling through the Vatican. The Curia were not comfortable with what one commentator described as a 'subversive dressed as the Pope.' But confronted with the Pope's obvious popularity, when the Pope was on the road, the Curia were rendered ineffective. The Pope was well aware that by visiting three Latin American countries and harnessing the enthusiasm of the millions who came to hear him, he was defining a Catholicism that no longer focussed on fear and hellfire, but on the happiness of sharing Christ's teachings. 'We are aware every day that we live in a world wounded by war and violence. It would be a mistake to think that division and hatred are the preserve of countries and social groups.'

... and rich

In November 2015 two books were about to be published in Italy revealing further details of the Vatican's finances. Not long after Francis' appointment it was reported that the Pope was trying to begin reforms but had encountered 'a lot of difficulties and entrenched resistance.' A highlight of one of the books was the transcript of an illicit recording of the Pope at a meeting in July 2013 – four months after his election – in which he complained to senior Vatican officials about its murky finances. According to the transcript, the Pope said that 'We have to better clarify the finances of the Holy See and make them more transparent.' The Pope continued: 'Clarity. That is what's done in the most humble companies and we have to do it, too. It is no exaggeration to say most of our costs are out of control.'

In each case the studies' weakness seemed to be that it was based on leaked information. The *glasnost* process initiated by Pope Francis of not only making matters more transparent, but also of reforming them, *perestroika*. the manner in which the Catholic Church managed its financial affairs had got off to an unsatisfactory start. The Church was also endeavouring to comply with international regulations on money-laundering and the funding of terrorism, potential measures which ran counter to traditional Curia thinking.

Days before publication, according to a report in the London *Economist*, a papal spokesman revealed that detectives of the Vatican Gendarmerie had traced the origin of the leaks and locked up two former members of a committee established by Francis to advise him on restructuring his financial bureaucracy. Neither of the whistle-blowers had Vatican citizenship. But the Pope's prosecutor had claimed jurisdiction over their alleged offences. The books' revelations sat uncomfortably alongside the 'revolutionary' church of the poor that was central to Pope Francis' teachings. One of the books claimed the Holy See's (Vatican) real-estate holdings,

KEY FACTS

Official name: Stato della Cittá del Vaticano (Vatican City State). Santa Sede (The Holy See) – the head organisation of the Roman Catholic Church – operates from the territory of the Vatican City State.

Head of State: Pope Francis (elected 13 Mar 2013, inaugurated 19 Mar 2014)

Head of government: President of the Pontifical Commission for Vatican City State (since 1 June 2013) and President of the Governorate of Vatican City State (since 1 Oct 2011) Cardinal Giuseppe Bertello

Area: 0 square km

Population: 460 (2010; census figure)

Capital: Vatican City

Official language: Latin; Italian is most commonly spoken.

Currency: Vatican City Lira and Euro (VCL and €)

Exchange rate: VCL and €0.89 per US$ (Feb 2014); (the Vatican City State has its own currency which, by agreement with the Italian state, is also legal tender in Italy; its value is pegged to that of the euro).

excluding church properties, were worth at least €4 billion (US$4.4 billion). It was also alleged that a fund for the care of sick children had paid €200,000 (US$) towards the conversion of a cardinal's penthouse apartment and €23,800 to charter a helicopter for him.

According to a leaked auditors' report, the Vatican earned a tidy €60 million (US$) a year selling petrol, cigarettes and other products at below Italian market prices. These items were, in theory, only available to the city-state's citizens. Allegedly, some 40,000 Italians hold cards giving them access to the Vatican's shops.

Synod

Pope Francis had pinned his reformist hopes on persuading the October 2015 Synod meeting to get in line. The theme of the gathering was 'The Family'. However, he discovered that in the Curia he faced stronger opposition than he had imagined. After three weeks of debate, the Synod closed without fulfilling the Pope's expectations. Even re-marrying divorcees were not as a rule to be allowed communion; instead their cases were to be analysed more carefully 'without creating a scandal'. This ran directly counter to the Pope's exhortations. In his closing speech the Pope openly accused the cardinals and bishops of using methods that were 'not altogether benevolent' to make their points. The Pope concluded by adding that 'The true defenders of doctrine are not those who defend the letter, but those who defend its spirit. Not the ideas, but the man.' The Synod's outcome demonstrated the fissure that had opened up between the Curia and the Pope. Seen in the context of the orthodoxy of the Synod's closing document, the pope's final address could be seen as a correction, or simply as a warning.

Risk assessment

Economy	Fair
Politics	Improving
Regional stability	Fair

COUNTRY PROFILE

1917 The Code of Canon Law was devised. The Law provides codified information and rules on the operations of the Catholic Church.
1922 Achilles Ratti became Pope Pius XI.
1929 The Pope was instrumental in defining the Vatican's position within Italy, which was confirmed by the signing of the Lateran Treaty, when the Vatican City State was formed as a separate state.
1939 When Pius XI died, Eugenio Pacelli became Pope Pius XII, the 261st Pope.
1958 After Pius XII died, Pope John XXIII was elected.
1963 Second Vatican Council assembled (the first council sat in 325 AD), to debate the role of the Church in the modern world, particularly regarding church administration, doctrine and discipline. Foremost in the 16 decrees issued were the reforms in the format of the mass and the liturgy, adoption of local languages instead of Latin for services, and the promotion of ecumenicalism within Christian churches.
1964 Paul VI, appointed Pope in 1963, made the first-ever papal visit to Israel.
1965 Paul VI made the first papal trip to the Western hemisphere, with a visit to the UN headquarters in New York. The Vatican published a document that proclaimed the Jews were not to blame for the death of Jesus Christ.
1967 The Apostolic Constitution was ratified.
1974 The Vatican intervened in Italian politics by urging voters to vote in favour of a referendum to repeal a recently passed law (1971) that made divorce legal. The referendum failed and divorce remained legal.
1978 John Paul I was elected Pope, but died one month later, which made his the shortest reign as Pope. A Polish national, Karol Jozef Wojtyla, succeeded him as John Paul II.
1981 There was an assassination attempt on Pope John Paul II. The Vatican intervened in Italian politics by urging voters to support a referendum to repeal a recently passed law that made abortion legal. The proposal was rejected by almost 68 per cent.
1983 A new and revised Code of Canon Law was introduced.
1993 The Vatican officially recognised Israel as an independent state.
1998 The commandant of the Pope's Swiss Guard, Alois Estermann, and his wife were murdered by a fellow Guardsman. It was the first murder case in the Holy See within living memory.
1999 The Istituto per le Opere di Religione (IOR) (the Institute for Religious Works, otherwise known as the Bank of the Holy See or the Vatican Bank) was sued in the US for helping to conceal in 1945 Nazi-era assets looted from Holocaust survivors and Nazi sympathisers from Croatia.
2000 Pope John Paul II apologised for anti-Semitism by Christians throughout the ages and called for the formation of an independent Palestinian state.
2001 Pope John Paul II appointed 44 new cardinals. The Pope issued a worldwide apology to victims of sexual abuse by Roman Catholic priests and other officers of the Church.
2003 The Vatican hosted a closed-door seminar of top officials and international medical experts on the problem of paedophilia within the Church
2004 The Vatican library, which housed nearly two million books and manuscripts, adopted radio frequency identification (RFID) tags.
2005 Pope John Paul II died aged 84. Joseph Cardinal Ratzinger was elected Pope and chose the name Benedictus XVI. The Pope intervened in Italian politics by successfully urging a boycott of a referendum on Italy's fertility laws. A diplomatic row between the Vatican and Israel broke out when Israel demanded to know why the Pope did not mention Israeli victims during a speech deploring terrorism. The Vatican published a new policy document on homosexuality and the clergy, sparking controversy among liberal and conservative Catholics alike.
2006 The Vatican joined the European Union Schengen area, whereby all travellers may cross borders without a passport or visa. The Vatican excommunicated two bishops consecrated by the breakaway Chinese Catholic Church in an act considered illegal by the authorities. In a speech given at the University of Regensburg in Germany, the Pope quoted a fourteenth century Byzantine emperor who seemed to say that the teachings of the Prophet Mohammed were 'spread by the sword' and were 'evil and inhuman'. This caused a serious international storm of controversy among Muslims. It took a number of apologies by the Vatican and the Pope to lessen the tension, explaining that this was not necessarily the Pope's belief but was a quotation.
2007 A meeting was held between Pope Benedict and the monarch of Saudi Arabia, King Abdullah. The meeting was the first between the two leaders and concerned Middle East conflict and inter-faith dialogue.
2008 A three-day summit was held between 48 Christian and Muslim officials and scholars to develop an inter-faith, theological dialogue which could diffuse any future religious and political tensions.
2010 In March, in the his Easter address, the Pope condemned media reporting of the child sexual abuse scandal and paedophile priests that had besmirched the reputation of the religious body and said he would not be intimidated by what he described as 'petty gossip'.
2011 A new law of citizenship was enacted on 1 March. The Vatican City now has five categories of inhabitant: the pope; cardinals residing in the city; active members of the Holy See's diplomatic corps; other directors of Vatican offices and services; and official Vatican 'residents' (those that live in the city but are

not citizens). In a book published in March, Pope Benedict rejected the idea of Jewish 'collective guilt' for the death of Jesus Christ, arguing there was no basis in scripture for blame of the Jewish people. The Catholic Church had repudiated Jewish 'collective guilt' in 1965. The late Pope John Paul II was beatified (the last stage before sainthood) by Pope Benedict XVI on 1 May. In July the Vatican and Malaysia agreed to establish diplomatic ties. The Vatican's special envoy in Ireland, Papal Nuncio Giuseppe Leanza, was recalled on 25 July after a damning report on the Catholic Church's handling of child abuse by priests.
2012 The Vatican initiated an exceptional criminal investigation into unauthorised release of news items to the Italian media, described as 'grave acts of disloyalty'. The leaks described not only alleged mismanagement and internal conflicts among top officials but also corruption. The head of the Istituto per le Opere di Riligione (Institute for Works of Religion), commonly known as the Vatican bank, Ettore Gotti Tedeschi, was sacked on 24 May for 'dereliction of duty'. His removal followed police investigations into alleged money-laundering at the bank. On 26 May the butler to the pontiff, Paolo Gabriele, was arrested for leaking private papers to Italian journalists. On 30 May the Pope denounced the coverage of the scandals within the Holy See, saying they were 'exaggerated' and 'gratuitous'. On 31 August, Cardinal Carlo Maria Martini died and left an interview that was published posthumously, which called the Catholic Church 'old' and 'tired' and called for a 'radical transformation, beginning with the Pope and his bishops'. Cardinal Martini was a senior member of the establishment, a distinguished scholar, but dissenting voice within the church. On 6 October Gabriele was convicted and sentenced to 18 monthes in jail for theft and transmission of Vatican papers.
2013 On 11 Feb 2013 Pope Benedict announced his resignation, because of 'lack of strength of mind and body'. He stepped down on 28 Feb becoming the first pope to resign since Pope Gregory XII in 1415. He became known as Pope Emeritus, and continues to live in the Vatican compound, spending his life in prayer and contemplation. Jorge Mario Bergoglio of Argentina was elected Pope Francis on 13 March and inaugurated on 19 March. On 5 July the Vatican announced that Pope John Paul II (from 1978–2005) and Pope John XXIII (1958–63), are to become saints. The canonisations are expected to take place in late 2013. In August Pope Francis made what turned out to be a contoversial appointment to the commission to enquire into the Vatican's financial administration. Francesca Chaouqui will be the only woman on the commission; she has been criticised for making a number of tweets including one that appeared to accuse a cardinal of corruption. In his first public comment since retiring the former Pope, Benedict XVI, denied having any role in covering up child sex abuse by priests. He made the comments in a letter to a prominent atheist in September. Also in September, Pope Francis gave an interview to the Jesuit magazine *Civilta Cattolica* in which he seemed to suggest a less authoritarian Church government and tone at the Vatican in future and criticised 'small-minded' Catholic rules. On 1 October the Pope met for the first time with the group of eight cardinals (the G8) from around the world he has appointed to look into the administration of the Catholic Church. Also on 1 October the Institute for Religious Works (IOR) (the Vatican's bank) published its annual report for the first time; it showed a net profit in 2012 of €86.6 million (US$115.5 million), €54.7 million (US$73 million) of which was allocated to the Pope to use for the Church's mission abroad. In October sale of 6,000 new papal medals was stopped after it was noticed that 'Jesus' was miss-spelled as 'Lesus'. The sale of coins is a useful revenue earner for the Vatican and new coins are struck after the election of every Pope. The Vatican has withdrawn from sale 6,000 copies of a new papal medal on which the name of Jesus was misspelt.
2014 Pope Francis visited South Korea in August to attend a Catholic Youth Festival. He also celebrated a large open-air Mass to beatify 124 of South Korea's first Catholics at a ceremony in the capital Seoul on 16 August.
2015 In an interview with Mexican television in March Pope Francis hinted that, like his predecessor, he might resign when he said 'I have the feeling that my pontificate will be brief. Four or five years; I do not know, even two or three.' Although the Vatican traditionally opposes military intervention, in March it said force could be necessary to stop attacks on Christians and other Middle East minorities by Islamic State (IS) if no political solution could be found. The Vatican's top diplomat at the UN in Geneva, Archbishop Silvano Tomasi, said jihadists were committing 'genocide' and must be stopped.

Political structure

The Vatican City and the Holy See are two different entities: the Vatican is the physical state, while the Holy See is a non-geographical sovereign entity. The Holy See participates in a number of international organisations, such as the UN, as an observer. Italy is in charge of defending the city state, although the Pope's personal guards, the Swiss Guards, belong to the Vatican City.
The Vatican City State employs 1,534 people. It is a sovereign country recognised as a separate subject under international law. The Pope is its absolute monarch and chief of state, but its general administration is overseen by an executive called the Pontifical Commission, appointed by the Pope and headed by a president. The Pope plays little part in the Commission's administration. The Commission runs a police force and post office, has a railway station and issues car licence plates. The term 'Vatican' is commonly used to describe the residence of the Pope – the Apostolic Palace.
The Holy See is exclusively made up of ecclesiastical dignitaries, being the head organisation of the Roman Catholic Church and consisting of the Pope and the Roman Curia. It operates from the territory of the Vatican City State and constitutes a sovereign institution with the status of a subject of international law. The Curia is headed by the Secretariat of State which is presided over by a Cardinal who assumes the title of Secretary of State. The Cardinal Secretary of State is the person primarily responsible for the diplomatic and political activity of The Holy See, in some circumstances representing the person of the Supreme Pontiff himself.
Central offices of The Holy See are: Secretariat of State (two sections), nine congregations, three tribunals, 11 pontifical councils, the Apostolic Chamber, the Administration of the Patrimony of the Apostolic See (APSA) (sometimes referred to as the Vatican Bank), Prefecture of the Economic Affairs of The Holy See, Prefecture of the Papal Household, Office of the Liturgical Celebrations of the Supreme Pontiff, The Holy See Press Office, Vatican Information Service, Central Office of Church Statistics, five pontifical commissions and committees, nine institutions linked to The Holy See, the Synod of Bishops and six pontifical academies. In addition to these central offices, there are 118 pontifical representations to nations and to international organisations. There are 2,674 people working in the Roman Curia: 755 ecclesiastics, 344 religious and 1,575 lay people. There are about 1,000 retired persons.
The Pope is elected for life by a Conclave composed of members of the College of Cardinals. Pope John Paul II changed the rules to make a simple majority sufficient to elect a Pope if no-one has the traditional two-thirds majority after 30 rounds of voting. The College of Cardinals consists of 183 cardinals, of which 117 are

electors. Suffrage is limited to cardinals less than 80 years old.
After the Pope's death, the chamberlain becomes acting head of state. An official nine-day mourning period, known as the *novemdiales*, follows the death of the Pope. The Pope's body lies in state in St Peter's Basilica in the Clementine Chapel until the funeral, which takes place between four and six days following the Pope's death. A Conclave, consisting of all the Cardinals under 80 years, meets to elect the next pope no less than 15 days, and no more than 20 days, after the death of the Pope.

Constitution

In 2001, a new basic law, incorporating constitutional amendments adopted since the creation of the Vatican City State under the 1929 Lateran Treaty with Italy, entered into force. It replaced the 1967 document *Regimini Ecclesiae Universae* as the Vatican's constitutional text. It distinguishes between the legislative, executive and judicial branches, continuing to vest absolute authority over all three branches in the Pope as supreme pontiff and sovereign.

Form of state

Theocratic state, non-hereditary, elected monarchy (Bishop of Rome and Pope)

The executive

The Pope is the *ex officio* Head of the State and head of government of Vatican City. He has absolute monarchy powers with total control of legislative, executive and judicial power. He appoints his own advisors. The appointments include president of the Pontifical Commission for the State of Vatican City (head of government).
When a Pope is unable to perform his duties important decisions on the confirmation of bishops, doctrinal issues and the promulgation of laws within the Catholic Church are left in abeyance.
The Roman Curia is the administrative organisation that oversees the Roman Catholic Church, together with the Pope, providing the necessary organisation and objectives of the church.

Population

A new law of citizenship was enacted on 1 March (2011). The Vatican City now has five categories of inhabitant: the pope; cardinals residing in the city; active members of the Holy See's diplomatic corps; other directors of Vatican offices and services; and official Vatican 'residents' (those that live in the city but are not citizens).
572 citizens (of which 220 were living in the city on 1 March 2011)
352 Holy See's diplomatic corps
Over 600 official Vatican 'residents'
460 (2010; census figure)

Last census: 26 February 2010: 460
Population density: 1,595 inhabitants per square km. Urban population 100 per cent (2010 Unicef).
Annual growth rate: -2.6 per cent, 1990–2010 (Unicef).

Ethnic make-up

Predominantly Italian and Swiss.

Religions

Roman Catholic

Main cities

Vatican City (capital)

Languages spoken

Mainly Italian and Latin.

Official language/s

Latin; Italian is most commonly spoken.

Media

Quite apart from the hundreds of publications worldwide, which proclaim the policies and pronouncements of the Catholic Church, there are powerful transmitters that broadcast directly to a global audience.

Press

The only daily newspaper is *L'Osservatore Romano* (www.vatican.va see news services), with weekly editions published in several languages.
The official bulletin of the Holy See is *Acta Apostolicae Sedis*, which is published periodically and on papal pronouncements.

Broadcasting

Radio: Vatican Radio (www.radiovaticana.org) broadcasts in over 40 languages, with modern facilities for podcasts and interactive blogs. It broadcasts from a centre at Santa Maria di Galeria, which has diplomatic privileges similar to a foreign embassy.
Vatican Radio began broadcasting advertising in July 2009, in an effort to offset rising annual costs of US$30 million. Advertisements are vetted to ensure they are in keeping with the Catholic Church's moral standards and ethos.
Television: Centro Televisivo Vaticano (CTV) (www.vatican.va) provides live broadcasts of religious and papal matters, with footage for foreign news broadcasters; it acts as a press centre for broadcast journalists.
National news agency: Agenzia Internazionale Fides

Economy

The economy of Vatican City is separate from the Roman Catholic Church (The Holy See), which is a separate entity although headquartered in Vatican City.
Vatican City produces very little and what is manufactured is typically for local consumption only and without commercial value (market gardening, artwork and manuscripts for church purposes and so forth), income is generated through trade of tourist mementoes (made elsewhere) and services to tourists, plus the sale of postage stamps and publications, and fees for admission to museums as well as donations from its religious followers, all within its territory. The Vatican City posted a budget deficit of €24 million (US$27 million) in 2014.
The Holy See is financed from real estate and an internationally diversified portfolio of stocks and bonds, plus donations from Catholic dioceses, institutions and individuals.
The Holy See funds the ecclesiastical Roman Curia (bureaucracy, diplomatic missions and other international Catholic bodies). A fundraising collection (usually collected on the 29th June or the nearest Sunday), used and directed by the Pope for charitable purposes, is the annual *Obolo di San Pietro* (Peter's Pence), which was US$78 million in 2013, compared to US$65.9 million in 2012.
The Istituto per le Opere di Religione (IOR) (Institute for Works of Religion), commonly known as the Vatican Bank collects money from residents. On 24 May 2012, the head of the IOR, Ettore Gotti Tedeschi was sacked for 'dereliction of duty'. His removal followed police investigations into alleged money-laundering at the bank. By 18 July 2012, the IOR had passed a key European financial transparency test (required by the Council of Europe), although it still received poor reviews of the effectiveness of its new financial watchdog agency and its ability to ensure that its customers and transactions were clean. The IOR announced it was endeavouring to comply with all banking regulations. In June 2013, Monsignor Nunzio Scarano who was a priest and former banker at the Vatican Bank, was charged with fraud and corruption for attempting to embezzle €20 million (US$27.2 million) of the Vatican's money by officially moving it through businessmen in Naples and then removing a chunk of it for himself. Scarano was charged along side two others, a secret agent and a financial broker.

Tourism

Tourism and tourist numbers for the Vatican City are difficult to ascertain, as there is no practical border between it and Italy; however, it is estimated that there are some 18 million visitors each year.
Around 100,000 people congregate in St Peter's Square to listen to the Pope's Christmas and Easter messages. The Vatican Museums attracted more than 5 million visitors for the first time in 2011. In 2013 visitor numbers were forecast to exceed 5.5 million.

Banking and insurance

The Vatican's banking sector has been embroiled in a number of trans-national

controversies over the past three decades. The IOR acknowledged 'moral involvement' in the collapse of the Italian private bank, the Banco Ambrosiano, in 1982 and paid US$241million to creditors. Roberto Calvi, who headed the Banco Ambrosiano, fled Italy pending a trial for corruption and was found dead in London in June 1982. Five people, all alleged to have Mafia ties, were charged in Rome with Calvi's murder in April 2005.
In 1999, survivors of Nazi-run concentration camps filed a law suit claiming that the IOR helped conceal assets looted from camp victims by the then pro-Nazi Croatian government.

Central bank
Istituto per le Opere di Religione (IOR) (Bank of The Holy See); European Central Bank (ECB).

Time
GMT plus one hour (daylight saving, late March to late October, GMT plus two hours)

Geography
The State of the Vatican City (The Holy See) is situated entirely within the city of Rome, Italy.

Hemisphere
Northern

Climate
Mediterranean, with hot summers and mild winters. Temperatures range from 4–30 Celsius (C).

Dress codes
Dress should be modest — no shorts or sundresses. Lightweight clothing for summer; medium-weight and light topcoat for winter.

Entry requirements
No formal regulations exist, however visitors must adhere to Italian entry requirements before entry to the city.
Italy: no visa requirements for citizens of Europe, the Americas, Australasia and some Asian countries, visiting for up to 90 days. For a full list, and further information for those citizens not included on the list of visa-free travel, see www.ambwashingtondc.esteri.it and see consular services. A Schengen visa application (offered in several languages) can be downloaded from www.eurovisa.info/ApplicationForm.htm.

Currency advice/regulations
The euro is legal tender alongside the Vatican City Lira.

Health (for visitors)
As for Italy, where no special immunisations are needed.

Public holidays (national)

Fixed dates
1 Jan (New Year's Day), 6 Jan (Epiphany), 25 April (Liberation Day), 1 May (Labour Day), 2 Jun (National Day), 15 Aug (Assumption Day), 1 Nov (All Saints' Day), 8 Dec (Immaculate Conception), 25–26 Dec (Christmas).

Variable dates
Easter Monday

Working hours

Business
Mon–Fri: 0830–1245 and 1630–2000.

Getting there

Air
A heliport is used by Vatican City officials and visiting dignitaries.
A low-cost charter airline was launched 27 August 2007 to carry pilgrims from Rome to Lourdes and other holy sites including the Holy Land, Santiago di Compostela, Fatima and places in Poland and Mexico.
International airport/s: Rome, served by Leonardo da Vinci (Fiumicino) (FCO), 35km from the Vatican City.

Surface
By road or rail through Rome. There is a speed limit of 30kph in the Vatican City.

Getting about

National transport
Rail: The Vatican City has its own small railway which runs into Italy. It covers 862 metres before leaving the City.

BUSINESS DIRECTORY

The addresses listed below are a selection only. While World of Information makes every endeavour to check these addresses, we cannot guarantee that changes have not been made, especially to telephone numbers and area codes. We would welcome any corrections.

Telephone area codes
The international direct dialling (IDD) code for Vatican City is +39 followed by the area code 066982; this is complete in itself, giving access to a central switchboard/operator.

Banking

Central bank
Istituto per le Opere di Religione (IOR), 00120 Città del Vaticano, Rome (tel: 83-354; fax: 85-195); European Central Bank (ECB), Kaiserstrasse 29, D-60311 Frankfurt am Main, Germany (tel: +49(69)13-440; fax: +49(69)1344-6000).

Other useful addresses
Annuario Pontificio, Palazzo Apostolico, 00120 Città del Vaticano (tel: 698-3064); Press Room, Via della Conciciazione, 54, 00193 Roma (tel: 698-3466).

Apostolic Nunciature (UK), 54 Parkside, Wimbledon, London SW19 5NE, UK (tel: (+44-20) 8946-1410; fax: (+44-20) 8947-2494; email: gb nuntius@eaglenet.co.uk).

Apostolic Nunciature (USA), 3339 Massachusetts Ave, NW, Washington, DC 20008, (+1-202) 333-7121; fax: (+1-202) 337-4036).

British Embassy, Via dei Condotti 91, 00187 Rome (tel: 6992-3561; fax: 6994-0684).

Centro Televisivo Vaticano, Palazzo Belvedere, 00120 Vatican City (tel: 698-5467).

Prefecture of the Economic Affairs of the Holy See, Palazzo delle Congregazioni, Largo del Colonnato 3, 00193 Rome (tel: 84-263; fax: 85-011).

Radio Vaticana, Palazzo Pio, Piazza Pia 3, 00120 Roma (tel: 6988-3551; fax: 6988-3237).

Secretariat of State, Palazzo Apostolico, 00120 Vatican City (tel: 6982).

National news agency: Agenzia Internazionale Fides, Palazzo de Propaganda Fide, 00120 Città del Vaticano (tel: 6988-0115; fax: 6988-0107; email: fides@fides.va; internet: www.fides.org).

Internet sites
Vatican City: www.vatican.va
Vatican Facts: www.vaticanfacts.com

Venezuela

KEY FACTS

Official name: República Bolivariana de Venezuela (Bolivarian Republic of Venezuela)

Head of State: President Nicolas Maduro (elected 14 April 2013 (following the death of Hugo Chávez))

Head of government: President Nicolas Maduro (PSUV) (elected 14 Apr 2013)

Ruling party: Partido Socialista Unido de Venezuela (PSUV) (United Socialist Party of Venezeula) (replaced the defunct Movimiento V República (Quinta) (Fifth Republic Movement) which had won the 2005 election) (from 2007; re-elected 26 Sep 2010)

Area: 916,490 square km

Population: 30.46 million (2014)*

Capital: Caracas

Official language: Spanish

Currency: Bolívar fuerte (Bf) = 100 céntimos (new currency was introduced 1 Jan 2008)

Exchange rate: Bf6.31 per US$ (Sep 2015)

GDP per capita: US$6,757 (2014)*

GDP real growth: -4.00% (2014)*

GDP: US$205.79 billion (2014)*

Labour force: 11.94 million (2011)*

Unemployment: 7.99% (2014)*

Inflation: 62.17% (2014)*

Oil production: 2.72 million bpd (2014)

Natural gas production: 28.60 billion cum (2014)

Balance of trade: US$35.97 billion (2013)

* estimated figure

At a public appearance in early 2015 President Nicolás Maduro appeared to be wearing a cross between a strait- jacket and the national flag, more appropriate to Dolly Parton than to a head of sate. His attire gave him the aspect of a sad faced clown rather than an authoritative president, causing one commentator to ask if he had mistakenly donned his former bus driver's uniform.

If President Chávez had been seen as charismatic but incompetent, then Mr Maduro simply lacked the charisma. In fairness to the lumbering President, the consequences of many of the ill-considered (and worse implemented), Chávez initiatives had come home to roost with President Maduro, often undermined or rendered impossible by the fall in the oil price. As that tide went out, so began to disappear much of the once substantial support for the regime.

The economy struggles

Most forecasts suggested that Venezuela's economy was likely to contract by some 7 per cent in 2015, with inflation possibly ending the year around 100 per cent. Frightening figures for an oil-rich country. The jokes about Venezuelans in the 1960s were that they purchased a new car when the old one's ash trays were full. But by 2015 the exchange rate made even the purchase of a car prohibitive for most Venezuelans. In early 2015 a new government foreign exchange auction had failed to dent the escalating black market rate, which – almost in Weimar Republic style – was running at some Bf250 to the US dollar. This was no less than forty times the official exchange rate of Bf6.3 to the US dollar used by official bodies to pay for imports of food and medicines and to calculate the country's minimum wage.

Venezuela was in a classic inflationary bind – the empty shops, the lack of vital medicines and medical equipment were slowly choking the economy and triggering increased social unrest. For Mr Maduro and his political intimates the biggest single irritation (and weakness) behind all their 'anti-Yanqui' political statements was the embarrassingly blunt fact that Venezuela's economic relationship with the United States is too important to be imperilled.

Shortages of basic foodstuffs, medicines and spare parts had simply crippled the economy. President Maduro announced on 7 March 2015 that the government would begin to ration food at 20,000 supermarkets throughout Venezuela. The objective was to set weekly limits on purchases and require shoppers to have their fingerprints scanned before being allowed to buy their goods – a lot of which would normally be imported from the US. However, when the Venezuelan president taunts and mocks the US, the US State Department doesn't bat an eyelid. Mr Maduro has improbably attributed Venezuela's tribulations to the 'economic war' carried out against his government by Venezuelan expatriates in Miami working with the US government. Seasoned observers of Venezuelan affairs will inevitably opt for the chaos theory against that of conspiracy. The unprecedented fall in oil prices had coincided with the government's hopelessly inept economic management to bring Venezuela to its knees.

Little optimism

By the beginning of 2015 reliable economic data on Venezuela had become precious. According to the United Nations Economic Commission for Latin America and the Caribbean (ECLAC/CEPAL), in 2014 Venezuela's Banco Central de Venezuela (BCV) (central bank) did not actually publish official data on gross domestic product (GDP). However, based on partial, unofficial data, ECLAC estimated that private consumption, gross fixed capital formation and exports and imports had all shrunk, resulting in an estimated 3.0 per cent contraction in GDP in 2014, (compared with 1.3 per cent growth in 2013). Annual inflation had surged to 63.4 per cent in August 2014, compared with a year-on-year variation of 45.4 per cent in August 2013.

Central government expenditure and income is channelled through the Fondo Nacional para el Desarrollo Nacional (FONDEN) (National Development Fund) – which in turn is financed with contributions from Petróleos de Venezuela SA (PdVSA) and the BCV joint Chinese-Venezuelan funds (financed with loans from China that are repaid with oil exports) and central bank lending to PdVSA. PdVSA contributions to FONDEN (equivalent to 2.6 per cent of GDP in 2013) were expected by ECLAC to have fallen during 2014, as oil prices slumped in the second half of the year. According to its own data, the central bank increased its lending to state-owned enterprises by the equivalent of 5.9 percentage points of GDP (from 17.3 per cent of GDP in October 2013 to 23.2 per cent of GDP in October 2014).

ECLAC also noted that monetary policy was expansionary during the first nine months of 2014. The M1 and M2 monetary aggregates posted average year-on-year growth of 73 per cent and 72 per cent respectively, outstripping the average year-on-year inflation rate of 61 per cent. The increase in liquidity was attributable to public spending and the funding of state-owned enterprises via loans from the central bank. In an attempt to rein in monetary base growth, between October 2013 and April 2014 the BCV gradually raised the legal reserve requirement from 17 per cent to 21.5 per cent for existing net liabilities and ceded investments and to 31 per cent for new ones.

The more complex the exchange rate, the less productive the economy; so goes the dictum and the received wisdom. When your correspondent first visited South America in 1967, there hardly existed a country that enjoyed a free exchange market. In 2014, that was still the case for Venezuela. The new exchange rate legislation introduced in early 2014 stipulated that the rate for most private-sector transactions would be set using the so-called Complementary System for Foreign Currency Administration (SICAD). According to ECLAC the exchange rate for most categories of imported goods and services (food and medicine were unaffected) was thus raised from Bf6.3 to the dollar to Bf11.3 to the dollar. In November 2014, the SICAD exchange rate stood at Bf12 to the.

In March 2014, as if the exchange rate legislation was not already complex enough, the government introduced a third foreign-exchange system, the Alternative Foreign Currency System (SICAD II); since its inception the exchange rate under this system had remained stable at almost Bf50 to the dollar (seven times the 6.3 bolívares per dollar rate). SICAD II was helped by the repeal of the Illegal Currency Transactions Act and the entry into force of the new Currency Administration System and Illegal Currency Transactions Act, which means that state-owned public companies, including PdVSA, the central bank, private companies and individuals could bid for dollars in cash or bonds. Following the introduction of SICAD II, use of the two pre-existing systems was confined to specific priority areas. The official exchange rate (Bf6.3 to the dollar) covered only basic necessities (notably food and medicine). According to ECLAC, there were no permanently pre-defined priority areas for SICAD I, which meant that the

KEY INDICATORS — **Venezuela**

	Unit	2011	2012	2013	2014	**2015
Population	m	*29.77	*29.52	*29.98	*30.46	*30.93
Gross domestic product (GDP)	US$bn	315.80	381.29	218.43	*205.79	*169.67
GDP per capita	US$	10,610	12,918	7,285	*6,757	*5,485
GDP real growth	%	4.2	5.5	1.3	*-4.0	*-7.0
Inflation	%	26.1	21.1	40.6	*62.2	*96.8
Unemployment	%	9.3	7.8	7.5	*8.0	*12.8
Oil output	'000 bpd	2,720.0	2,725.0	2,623.0	2,719.0	–
Natural gas output	bn cum	31.2	32.8	28.4	28.6	–
Coal output	mtoe	6.3	1.2	1.7	1.8	–
Exports (fob) (goods)	US$m	92,649.0	97,336.0	88,958.0	–	–
Imports (fob) (goods)	US$m	46,197.0	59,305.0	52,991.0	–	–
Balance of trade	US$m	46,452.0	38,031.0	35,967.0	–	–
Current account	US$m	27,325.0	11,016.0	5,327.0	*8,865.0	*-7,943.0
Total reserves minus gold	US$m	11,095.0	9,900.0	6,038.0	–	–
Foreign exchange	US$m	7,021.3	5,964.0	2,064.0	–	–
Exchange rate	per US$	4.29	4.29	6.29	6.35	–

* estimated figure ** forecast figure

government could change the sectors to which it applied according to its requirements. The remaining segments of the economy and individuals still needed to resort to SICAD II or the parallel market, where rates had soared.

Never short of ideas, in September 2014, the government issued Exchange Rate Agreement No 30 which stipulated that the sale of foreign currency by PdVSA to the BCV in order to provide bolívares to FONDEN for special contributions – triggered when oil prices rise above US$60 per barrel – could be settled at any of the official exchange rates. These preferential contributions had previously been made at the rate of Bf6.30 to the dollar, but could now be transacted at the SICAD II exchange rate (Bf50 to the dollar), resulting in a degree of greater liquidity for projects financed by FONDEN.

Between January and November 2014, according to ECLAC figures, Venezuela's international reserves averaged US$21.030 billion, down 14 per cent on the average for the same period in 2013. About 70 per cent of reserves were held in gold (non-liquid reserves). In November, President Maduro announced that reserves would be bolstered by US$4 billion with proceeds from Chinese fund loans.

The lack of official figures for quarterly or annual GDP rates in 2014 meant that ECLAC had to base its estimates on partial, unofficial data. ECLAC estimated that private consumption, gross fixed capital formation and exports and imports (including the inputs required for domestic production) had all diminished, resulting in a 3.0 per cent contraction in GDP for the year. Year-on-year inflation was estimated by ECLAC to have quickened to 63.4 per cent in August 2014, with a 91.1 per cent rise in the basic necessity category of food and beverages. The consumer price index methodology was changed in July 2014. The rate of inflation snowballed, despite continued efforts by the government to control prices. Data on the lack of commercially available products (that is, the shortage index) were last published in January 2014, when the index stood at 28 per cent.

During the first nine months of 2014, the average urban unemployment rate fell by 0.6 percentage points against the 2013 average and stood at 7.3 per cent. The participation rate gained 0.7 percentage points to stand at 65.0 per cent. Since January 2014 the minimum wage has risen twice (in May and December 2014), resulting in a nominal increase of 50 per cent, or a 6 per cent fall in real terms. Armed forces personnel pay was raised by 45 per cent in November 2014.

No (notional) quarterly balance of payments data were published by the Venezuelan government, either for the fourth quarter of 2013 or for 2014. ECLAC estimated that the value of goods exports (mainly oil) slid by 8 per cent, almost exclusively due to an estimated 8.2 per cent drop in the price of the Venezuelan export basket. According to data from the National Institute of Statistics (INE), imports declined by 21.8 per cent in the first half of 2014, compared with the same period in 2013. In November 2014, ahead of the expiry of the special powers granted under an enabling act, President Maduro passed no less than 28 laws, mostly in economic matters. Among other things, they aimed to regulate production and agriculture, encourage foreign investment, increase certain taxes and customs duties and change the way international reserves are accounted for.

That obsessive neighbour to the North

Through 2014 and into 2015 President Maduro's criticism of the United States had grown stronger and shriller, culminating in accusations of support from Washington for an alleged *coup* attempt by junior Venezuelan Air Force officers who, in the realms of fantasy, planned to bomb the presidential palace and other targets with one propeller-driven aircraft. The President didn't pull his punches, suggesting that the avuncular US Vice President Joe Biden was behind the plot. With that accusation under his belt, Mr Maduro went on, making a handful of *coup* accusations and at the end of February, ordering that the size of the United States embassy in Caracas be reduced by some 80 per cent to 17 diplomats, which he said was the size of the Venezuelan presence in Washington. To top the list, the President also decreed that American citizens would henceforth need to apply in advance for visas to visit Venezuela; he also barred a number of prominent US citizens, including former President George W Bush, from entering.

Predictably enough, the Obama administration denied Mr Maduro's *coup* charges before itself taking action on sanctions. White House spokesman Earnest simply went on record that 'Venezuelan who violate the human rights of Venezuelan citizens and engage in acts of public corruption will not be welcome here. Mr Earnest called on President Maduro to release the régimes's political prisoners, including opposition leaders Leopoldo López and Caracas Mayor Antonio Ledezma. Mr López had been jailed for a year awaiting the conclusion of a trial on charges of arson and inciting riots. Mr Ledezma was arrested on 20 February 2015 for being part of the alleged *coup* plot.

While it would probably be far-fetched to attribute any Russian military guidance to Maduro's decision to order his country's armed forces to start exercises in mid-March to improve their preparations for no less than a US invasion, there was something strangely theatrical about the initiative, clearly playing to the populous gallery. As probably, for parallel political reasons, a number of Venezuelan opposition figures were surprisingly in favour, to the extent that senior members of the Primero Justicia party of former vice president Henrique Capriles, as well as the opposition Copei party gave their support. But in his coat of many colours, Mr Maduro knows he is fighting with one hand tied behind his back. In Venezuela's dire economic and political straits, Mr Maduro has leant over backwards not to push Washington too far.

It's all about energy, or at least ...the money

Venezuela's abundant crude oil, which is heavy in sulphur, coke and other minerals, can only be processed by a small number of refineries in the world, the majority of which happen to be located in the United States. Thus the US oil purchases, already diminished following US shale gas discoveries, remain a vital source of foreign exchange for Venezuela. Given the overwhelming political uncertainty and the travails of the bolivar in world markets, levels of foreign direct investment (FDI) have also slumped to almost zero, meaning that the possibility of corruption ridden Venezuela attracting the necessary investment funds had evaporated.

Caracas is doubly dependent on its US exports for much-needed foreign currency since not all the recipients of Venezuelan crude actually pay hard currency. Many are bound into offset arrangements where payment is offset against cash loans. Nowhere is that more the case than with China. Exports to China may be growing, but as no cash is received, the government ends up little better off.

According to the US government Energy Information Administration (EIA) in 2014 Venezuela held some of the largest oil and natural gas proven reserves in the world. In 2013, Venezuela was the third-largest exporter of crude oil to the United States and for decades had steadily ranked as one of its top suppliers of crude oil. Venezuela was, in simple terms, a major 'player' in the international oil markets, hardly surprising as in 2013 it was the world's nineth largest exporter and its twelveth largest producer of petroleum and other liquids in 2013.

Much of Venezuela's oil deposits are found in the Orinoco Belt and, according to the EIA, may contain more than 513 billion barrels of crude oil. However, much of this proven resource is heavy and requires additional capital to bring it to market. As noted above, investment capital is currently scarce in Venezuela and foreign investments into the highly politicised oil industry are unrealistic for the immediate future.

As indicated above, Venezuela has a close commercial relationship with the US, was the fourth-largest supplier of imported crude oil and petroleum products to the United States in 2013. However, Venezuela's exports to the United States have been declining while US exports of (refined) petroleum products to Venezuela have been increasing.

Venezuela maintained 2.8 million barrels per day (bpd) of total global refining capacity in assets throughout the United States, the Caribbean, Europe and domestically in Venezuela in 2013. Also in 2013, domestic natural gas production accounted for just over a third of Venezuela's natural gas supply.

Venezuela has the second-largest natural gas reserves in the Americas, behind only the United States. Much of that natural gas is used to bolster production in its mature oil fields. About 90 per cent of Venezuela's natural gas is found associated with oil but Venezuela is looking to locate and produce more natural gas from non-associated fields.

Venezuela depends on hydroelectricity for the bulk of its electricity needs, accounting for 60 per cent or more in the past decade.

Fair weather friends

The Obama administration had announced in 2014 that it did not plan to curtail oil purchases from Venezuela, but any possible threat of a cutback is enough to make sure that Maduro doesn't push his luck too far. Although the Venezuelan president may have friends in the region, they are political rather than economic friends. Venezuela may feel peeved that its earlier largesse has not been reciprocated, but neither Nicaragua nor Ecuador, Argentina or Bolivia look likely to come to the rescue. The heady early days of the Bolivarian Alliance for the Peoples of Our America (ALBA), seemed long gone. The balance sheet was doubtful; the same was the case with the Caribbean Petrocaribe, which shipped thousands of subsidised barrels of Venezuelan oil on favourable trade terms to no less than 16 'sympathetic' Caribbean and Central American countries, and had certainly not produced the expected political never mind economic benefits. To many observers it appeared to be a question of regional cupboard love. Happily signed, easily dropped.

Outlook

In the twenty-first century, forecasting likely events in Venezuela had become something of a challenge. The moveebles in the equation are varied, ranging from national bankruptcy, to a *coup d'état* , civil war or a popular uprising. Much will depend on the level of oil prices, but even a dramatic rise in the price of oil would do little to rein in the soaring rate of inflation – estimated officially at 64 per cent, unofficially at over 120 per cent. The government's ostrich answer to poor economic statistics has been simply not to publish them. Alice would have been proud of this economic wonderland.

What could not be hidden, easily disguised or simply dismissed were the massive interest payments that Venezuela had to make during the course of 2015. This was particularly the case in the second half of the year, which added up to US$5.8 billion. With oil hovering around the US$50 a barrel mark, the going was inevitably going to get tough. Total debt payments for the year were estimated at US$11.00 billion. One report noted that the nationalised steel company Sidetur had already defaulted on its debt payments.

Energy – the odd couple

In 2015 it rather looked as though Venezuela's oil – the industry and the reserves – had become as much a liability as an asset. If the global oil price was low, the Venezuelan price per barrel was even lower. Because of its relative heaviness, Venezuelan oil trades at some US$5.00 per barrel cheaper. Expensive subsidies have meant that domestic oil prices are the cheapest in the world, losing Venezuela's treasury money on each of the 800,000bpd sold at the national pumps. And as years without serious investment accumulated, production had dropped to around a forlorn 2.5 million bpd. Thus, most of Venezuela's cash income from oil exports is derived from... the US. And that cash income had, in 2015, shrivelled to around US$27 billion annually. And that simply isn't enough to keep the economy, never mind the show, on the road.

The United States remains Venezuela's leading supplier of goods by a large margin and the largest export market for its oil, positions it has held for most of the last 100 years. That had lead President Maduro's critics to question the president's current round of US-bashing, which had left governmental relations at their lowest point since 1999 when the late Hugo Chávez was sworn in as president. Even a passing handshake and brief conversation at the Organisation of American States (OAS) summit in Panama failed to generate anything of a thaw.

'If this government is so anti-imperialist, why do they continue selling oil to the US?' opposition leader and Miranda state governor, Henrique Capriles Radonski, was reported as asking in a March 2015 speech. But Mr Capriles was aware, as were most educated Venezuelans, that despite the huffing and puffing, Mr Maduro dare not antagonise Washington too much because he knows he simply can't afford to do so.

Like his predecessor, the late Hugo Chávez, Maduro uses the United States as a scapegoat when his popularity begins to plummet. But at the beginning of 2015 he had refrained from applying any restrictions on the two countries' commercial relations. Venezuela continued to export a little less than 800,000 barrels of crude oil to the United States per day. That has steadily decreased from a peak of 1.5 million barrels per day in the 1990s, but the amount is enough to make Venezuela the United States' fourth- or fifth-largest supplier of crude. (That number changes on a monthly basis.) Last year, the value of those oil exports totalled close to US$30.2 billion, according to the US Census Bureau. Meanwhile, US exports to Venezuela came to US$11.3 billion in 2014 – more than a quarter of the country's total imports. And Venezuelans import upwards of 70 per cent of what they consume, including agricultural commodities, processed foods and manufactured goods. Although some US companies have closed or cut back operations in Venezuela, the majority have taken a wait-and-see attitude while holding fire on new investments.

Many doubted that Sr Maduro was seeking any serious rupture with Washington, despite the rhetoric. Instead, according to most reports, he was looking for a distraction from Venezuela's dire economic situation. In March 2015, the Obama administration may have unwittingly handed him such a distraction in declaring Venezuela a 'threat to US national interests', at the same time sanctioning seven Venezuelan officials for human rights violations. Mr Maduro, whose support had fallen to 22 per cent in the latest Datanalis poll, called the sanctions an 'interference in his country's national affairs' and requested that the National Assembly grant him special powers 'sufficient to defend the peace, the sovereignty and integrated development of Venezuela' against the US government.

Los Soles – allegations

Compounding Venezuela's US obsessed paranoia concerning US attitudes and motivations were the allegations, made in mid-May 2015 by the *Wall Street Journal* that the President of the Venezuelan Parliament, Diosdado Cabello – once an intimate of the late President Chávez – was closely involved with the Los Soles drug cartel. As drug smuggling organisations go, Los Soles is thought to be something of a world leader, holding a virtual monopoly on contraband activities between Colombia's eastern border with Venezuela. Its strength is attributed to its close links with the army. Mr Cabello was not only the powerful leader of parliament, he was also the vice president of the Venezuelan Partido Socialista Unido de Venezuela (PSUV) (United Socialist Party of Venezeula). He had earned his military credentials with Chávez by participating in the failed military *coup* of 1992. After the *coup* attempt he was kicked out of the army, but maintained close links with his then military contemporaries. Earlier reports of his connections to Los Soles had been published by the Madrid ABC; in response, Mr Cabello had obliged a tame Venezuelan law court to issue an edict banning from leaving Venezuela no less than 22 directors of the three media outlets that had reproduced the ABC story. Faced with the *Wall Street Journal* report, he described it as 'an attack on the Patria', saying that 'those who are organising this campaign are committing a fundamental error; they don't know their adversary. I will never give in, not today, not tomorrow, never. I am undefeatable.'

Venezuelans had long been intrigued by press reports of successful army and air-force operations against foreign – for the most part Mexican – aircraft caught illegally crossing the border. Press photographs showed downed aircraft but no information concerning their crews or their cargoes was ever supplied. *Sic transit Gloria marijuana*.

Risk assessment

Politics	Catastrophic
Economy	Disastrous
Regional stability	Fair

People to watch

Henrique Capriles Radonski: opposition leader and Miranda state Governor

Leopoldo López: jailed for a year in 2014 on charges of arson and inciting riots.

Antonio Ledezma: erstwhile Caracas Mayor. Arrested in February 2015 for being part of an alleged *coup* plot.

COUNTRY PROFILE

1498 Christopher Columbus landed at the mouth of the Orinoco River on 2 August.

1499 Alonso de Ojeda first saw Lake Maracaibo and called the area 'little Venice', or Venezuela, after the houses the local inhabitants built on stilts.

1520s Spanish colonisation began. The most exploitable resource was cocoa.

1567 Caracas was founded.

1620 By this time cocoa had become the principal export. Production attracted many Spanish immigrants.

1749 First rebellion against Spanish rule.

1810–21 Simón Bolívar defeated the Spanish army in a long war and created Greater Colombia out of Venezuela, Colombia, Ecuador, Bolivia and Peru.

1823 The last battles for independence gained Venezuela its freedom from Spanish control.

1830 Bolívar died, José Antonio Paez assumed the presidency.

1859–63 A civil war erupted between conservative centralists and liberal federalists forces, which was won by the latter.

1908–1935 The dictator, Juan Vicente Gómez, ruled the country, instituting a harsh policy of repression while developing Venezuela into an oil-based, technocratic economy. Direct foreign investment in the oil sector also brought interest and influences on domestic policies.

1945–48 Rómulo Ernesto Betancourt Bello (Acción Democrática (AD) (Democratic Action)), set up a new government committed to democracy and social and land reforms. Foreign powers were suspicious of the government's left-wing credentials until Betancourt announced prompt elections would be held, acceptable reforms implemented and no radical action would be taken against foreign oil interests.

1947 A new constitution that provided for a popular vote, by secret ballot, to elect a president was promulgated. Romulo Gallegos Freire (AD) became the first Venezuelan president to be elected by democratic vote.

1948 The government was overthrown in a military *coup d'état* backed by conservative elements opposed to the reforms. A succession of *juntas* formed governments.

1952 Marcos Evangelista Pérez Jiménez seized power and became the next presidential dictator.

1953 The United States of Venezuela was renamed the Bolivian Republic of Venezuela.

1958 Pérez Jiménez was deposed by the military and a governing council allowed free elections, in which Betancourt (AD) was elected president. A pact between the main parties, including the AD and the Partido Demócrata Cristiano de Venezuela (Copei) (Christian Democrat Party of Venezuela), agreed to share power and maintain a pluralistic democracy. Moderate economic reforms, with regard for US interests, were slowly introduced.

1969 Rafael Caldera Rodríguez became Venezuela's first Copei president and managed to achieve a degree of political and economic stability.

1973 Venezuela joined the Andean Community, which also included Ecuador, Colombia, Peru and Bolivia.

1974–79 Carlos Andrés Pérez Rodríguez (AD) held presidential office and used massive oil revenues to nationalise industries and diversify the economy.

1979–84 The election of President Herrera (Copei) coincided with a downturn in global oil prices which led to a series of problems, including rising corruption, capital flight, economic stagnation and high levels of external debt.

1988 Presidential and legislative elections were held in December. Pérez became the first former president to be re-elected.

1989 Public protests against the government's austerity programme, which involved drastic government spending cutbacks in order to stabilise the economy, broke out around the country. The first-ever direct elections of state governors were held.

1992 Lieutenant Colonel Hugo Rafael Chávez Frías led an unsuccessful coup attempt against President Pérez.

1993 Ramon Jose Velasquez became interim president as Pérez was prosecuted on charges of corruption.

1995 Rafael Caldera was elected president.

1996 Ex-president Pérez was convicted of embezzlement and corruption.

1998 Hugo Chávez (Movimiento V República (Quinta) (Fifth Republic

Movement)), became president with over 56 per cent of the vote.
1999 President Chávez announced his 'Bolívarian Revolution' that included a unicameral national assembly, a new constitution, reduced civilian control of the military and an increased control by government of the economy. A referendum approved all the amendments. Torrential rains and severe flooding killed around 30,000 people.
2000 Chávez was re-elected president under the new constitutional rules. His coalition won 99 out of 165 assembly seats, not enough to pass laws without support from elsewhere. The assembly granted him the right to legislate by decree.
2001 Chávez passed 49 laws by decree, mostly regarding land redistribution and the oil sector.
2002 Civil unrest interrupted oil exports. A failed *coup d'état* briefly ousted President Chávez, but his supporters forced his reinstatement. Nearly one-half of state-owned oil company PdVSA's employees walked off the job in protest against the rule of Chávez. The strike severely affected PdVSA, practically bringing the company's operations to a halt. PdVSA fired 18,000 workers following the strike, draining the company of technical knowledge and expertise.
2003 The government imported petrol from Brazil as oil facilities were strike-bound.
2004 The electoral authority ruled that opponents of Chávez had collected enough signatures for a referendum on whether President Chávez should serve his remaining term in office. Chávez won 58 per cent of the vote.
2005 Land reforms, including land distribution, were introduced. The Petrocaribe Alliance was created to supply directly 13 Caribbean states, including Cuba, with cheaper Venezuelan oil. Not only was it intended to cut the energy bills of the small island economies, but also to reduce US influence in the region. National assembly elections were boycotted by the opposition and Chávez loyalists made big gains. Quinta won 60 per cent of the vote (116 out of 167 seats).
2006 Parliament approved a new flag, with an eighth star for the province of Guayana Esequiba (a disputed border region with Guyana). Venezuela signed a US$3 billion arms deal with Russia for jet fighters and helicopters. Venezuela became a trading partner of Mercosur, which has a market of around 250 million people and accounts for almost 75 per cent of South America's GDP. Foreign owned oil companies were required to give the state-owned PdVSA, 60 per cent of their Venezuelan operations. Hugo Chávez won a third term in office, with 62 per cent of the vote; his opponent, Manuel Rosales, won 38 per cent.
2007 Nationalisation of electricity and telecommunications companies began. The national assembly granted Chávez the right to legislate by decree until mid-2008. Although Exxon Mobil and ConocoPhilips initially rejected the Venezuelan offer to relinquish majority control of their oil operations, eventually they agreed. A referendum rejected constitutional reforms by 51 to 49 per cent. Hugo Chávez founded a new political party, Partido Socialista Unido de Venezuela (PSUV) (United Socialist Party of Venezeula).
2008 The new Bolívar fuerte (Bf) was introduced at a rate of Bf1 to old B1,000. President Chávez was instrumental in the release of six hostages held by the Colombian Fuerzas Armadas Revolucionarias de Colombia-Ejército del Pueblo (Farc) (Revolutionary Armed Forces of Colombia-Peoples' Army). He also advised Colombian President Uribe that Farc should be considered insurgents instead of terrorists. Colombia took pre-emptive, cross-border strikes against Farc terrorists hiding out in Venezuela and Ecuador, killing over a dozen including the senior Farc leader Raul Reyes. Following the incursion troops were mobilised along the border and Venezuela expelled Colombian diplomats. Relations improved later after Ingrid Betancourt was freed from her Farc captors and President Uribe visited Venezuela for talks. The coalition Mesa de la Unidad Democrática (MUD) (Coalition for Democratic Unity) was formed to provide an opposition to President Hugo Chávez.
2009 A constitutional amendment to remove the limit on times a president and all other elected officials may occupy an office was ratified by 54 per cent. Extensive power cuts were imposed on industry and businesses in an effort to avoid mass power cuts, as electricity output of the country's principal Guri hydroelectric power station began falling due to severely low water levels caused by prolonged drought.
2010 The bolívar was devalued; two official exchange rates were established, the first pegged at Bf2.6 per US dollar for all transactions not related to petroleum, the second pegged at Bf4.3 per US dollar for all petroleum related transactions and imports deemed non-essential. President Chávez severed diplomatic ties with Colombia as he objected to claims by Colombia that Venezuela was harbouring Farc guerrillas. Diplomatic relations were restored after a meeting with the new president of Colombia, Juan Manuel Santos. In parliamentary elections the PSUV won 48.2 per cent (96 seats out of 167), MUD 47.2 per cent (64), Patria para Todos (PT) (Fatherland for All) 3.1 per cent (two), others 1.4 per cent (three). The new congress granted the president powers to pass laws by decree, until the middle of 2012.
2011 In April, President Chávez ordered a tax increase from 60 to 95 per cent on oil revenues at prices over US$100 per barrel, which alarmed foreign investors. The oil minister said that companies investing in new developments would pay the higher rate only after they had recouped their original expenditure. In 19 of the country's 23 states, electricity services were rationed from May, following failures in transmission lines and the on-going drop in electricity output from the country's principal hydroelectric power station on the Guri Dam. Critics claim the government's failure to invest in the country's energy infrastructure was the reason for the on-going rationing. President Chávez appeared on television from Cuba on 30 June to announce that he had had a cancerous growth removed, but that he was now on the way to 'full recovery'. There had been speculation about his health after he underwent an operation for a pelvic abscess, but had not been seen for some three weeks. He returned to Caracas in July, in time to celebrate Venezuela's 200th anniversary of independence from Spain on the following day. He went back to Cuba for further treatment after delegating a number of presidential powers to vice president Elias Jaua and finance minister Jorge Giordani; the powers included budgetary transfers. In September President Chávez confirmed he would seek re-election in the next presidential election. The Gran Polo Patriótico (GPP) (Great Patriotic Pole), an alliance of political parties and movements, was formed to support Mr Chávez in his re-election bid. Also in September opposition politician Leopoldo Lopez began his campaign to challenge President Chávez after the Inter-American Court of Human Rights (IACHR) ruled that he should be allowed to stand in the 2012 presidential election. In October, President Chávez announced that he was free of cancer, following four cycles of chemotherapy.
2012 On 1 June the private ownership of firearms was banned with only the army, police and designated groups, such as security companies, allowed to buy weapons and ammunition. On 30 June Venezuela's membership of the trade organisation Mercosur was approved. In the 7 October presidential elections, incumbent, Hugo Chávez (PSUV) won a decisive 55.25 per cent of the vote, Henrique Capriles Radonski (MUD), his closest rival

won 44.13 per cent; none of the four other candidates won more than 1 per cent of the vote. President Chávez returned to Cuba for further treatment and was reported to be suffering a severe lung infection after an operation. In early December it seemed that he was beginning to accept that his health would not permit him to remain in office for a full term and he named Vice President Nicolas Maduro as his prefered successor.

2013 On 9 January the Supreme Court ruled that there was a clear distinction between taking the oath and the beginning of a new mandate so that although the swearing-in ceremony was an important formality, it was not indispensible for the start of a new presidential term. The ruling allowed for the postponement of Hugo Chávez' inauguration ceremony, although no time limit was given. Hugo Chávez died on 5 March. Diosdado Cabello had earlier been re-elected as leader of the National Assembly and became caretaker president. In the 14 April presidential election to replace Mr Chávez, Nicolas Maduro narrowly defeated Henrique Capriles. 25 April Nicolas Maduro was formally declared the winner of the presidential election by 50.7 per cent of votes to 49.1 per cent for Henrique Capriles. Fistfights over the disputed election result broke out in parliament on 30 April. Henrique Capriles formally challenged the result of the presidential election on 2 May. His lawyers filed a complaint at the Supreme Court, alleging a number of irregularities and calling for the result to be annulled. On 12 June Venezuela's electoral body confirmed the victory of President Nicolas Maduro in the April election, after carrying out an audit on millions of votes. Mr Capriles' complaint was rejected by the Supreme Court of Justice on 7 August, describing the appeal as 'inadmissible'. Mr Capriles tweeted that there was a 'lack of justice' in Venezuela. Finance minister, Nelson Merentes, said (on 1 September) that Venezuela was still suffering from the economic policies of former President Chávez and the current government had yet to succeed in improving living standards. A power failure hit some 70 per cent of the country, including parts of Caracas, on 3 September. On 8 October the President asked parliament to give him special powers to fight corruption and 'economic sabotage'. The move would allow the President to govern by decree for a set period. Hugo Chávez had previously used the move on four occasions. The first reading of a bill that will pave the way to granting special powers that will enable President Maduro to govern by decree for 12 months was approved on 14 November. Mr Maduro has said he will the powers to tackle corruption and the economic crisis. Critics fear he may use it to silence opposition.

2014 By mid-May both Air Canada and Alitalia had suspended flights to Caracas due to the currency situation which was making payments difficult. On 4 November the President said he would be raising wages by 15 per cent in December. This will be the third rise in 2014 and will take the minimum monthly wage to 4,889 bolivars (US$776).

2015 Venezuela's government bond ratings were downgraded by Moody's Investors Service on 12 January to Caa3 from Caa1.

Political structure

Venezuela sends 12 deputies to the Latin American Parliament and five to the Andean Parliament.

Constitution

A new constitution was promulgated in 1999 which set out to strengthen civil and human rights. It extended a presidential term from five to six years, with one consecutive re-election, revised impeachment mechanism and limited emergency powers. The bicameral parliament was replaced with a single chamber when the senate was abolished, but popular participation by the people was to be encouraged through referenda. A stronger government involvement in the economy included a ban on the privatisation of the country's oil reserves.

A constitutional referendum, held in February 2009, voted by 54.85 per cent in favour of proposed amendments to limit the consecutive number of terms in office served by deputies in the national assembly to two. The presidency was increased to two consecutive five-year terms of office, with the date of the next election re-aligned to the same date as the national assembly.

Independence date

5 July 1811

Form of state

Federal presidential republic

The executive

Executive power rests with the president who is elected by popular, direct, universal suffrage for a six-year term, with one consecutive, renewable term.

National legislature

The unicameral, Asamblea Nacional (National Assembly) has 165 deputies elected through a combination of directly elected and proportional representation through party lists. An additional three deputy seats are reserved for representatives of indigenous peoples. Since 2009 deputies may only serve for two consecutive, five-year terms.

Legal system

The Supreme Court appoints judges in consultation with civil society groups.

Last elections

15 February 2009 (constitutional referendum); 26 September 2010 (parliamentary); 14 April 2013 (presidential, following the death of Hugo Chávez)

Results: Constitutional referendum: 54.85 per cent of the electorate voted in favour and 45.15 against the proposed amendments; turnout was 70.33 per cent. Parliament: Partido Socialista Unido de Venezuela (PSUV) (United Socialist Party of Venezeula) won 48.2 per cent (96 seats out of 165 elected seats), Mesa de la Unidad Democrática (MUD) (Coalition for Democratic Unity) 47.2 per cent (64), Patria para Todos (PT) (Fatherland for All) 3.1 per cent (two), others 1.4 per cent (three).

Presidential: Hugo Chávez (PSUV) won 55.25 per cent of the vote, Henrique Capriles Radonski (MUD) 44.13 per cent; four other candidates each won less than 1 per cent of the vote. Turnout was 80.67 per cent.

Next elections

September 2015 (parliamentary); October 2018 (presidential)

Political parties

Ruling party

Partido Socialista Unido de Venezuela (PSUV) (United Socialist Party of Venezeula) (replaced the defunct Movimiento V República (Quinta) (Fifth Republic Movement) which had won the 2005 election) (from 2007; re-elected 26 Sep 2010)

Main opposition party

Mesa de la Unidad Democrática (MUD) (Coalition for Democratic Unity)

Population

29.52 million (2012)*

Last census: 30 November 2011: 27,051,095

Population density: 28 inhabitants per square km. Urban population 93 per cent (2010 Unicef).

Annual growth rate: 1.9 per cent, 1990–2010 (Unicef).

Ethnic make-up

Mestizo (67 per cent), White (21 per cent), Black (10 per cent), Indian (2 per cent).

Religions

Roman Catholic (96 per cent), Protestant (2 per cent).

Education

Pre-primary (one year) and basic education lasts until aged 15. Exams then determine whether students progress onto an academic course for two years or a vocational course for three years. Many institutes of higher education have a selection procedure and often run preparatory courses as part of the admission process.

Professional courses last for three years, catering for the industrial, farming, commercial and health sectors.
Universities, institutes, two ecclesiastic university institutes and three military institutes, provide higher education. Institutes and University Colleges generally provide for short courses of study lasting between two and three years. Long courses lasting for five to six years are also available. The universities are both public and private. National public universities are both autonomous and experimental institutions.
Literacy rate: 93 per cent adult rate; 98 per cent youth rate (15–24) (Unesco 2005).
Compulsory years: Five to 17
Enrolment rate: 91 per cent gross primary enrolment; 40 per cent gross seconday enrolment of relevant age groups (including repeaters).
Pupils per teacher: 21 in primary schools

Health

Venezuela has achieved significant long-term advances with regard to health in hospital care but preventive and primary health care remains on a very small scale. Venezuela is vulnerable to natural disasters, the most frequent of which are floods with concurrent landslides, and there is also a risk of earthquakes. The Ministry of Family has assisted non-governmental organisations (NGOs) and community-based groups to participate in social programmes at a household level.

HIV/Aids

HIV prevalence: 0.7 per cent aged 15–49 in 2003 (World Bank)
Life expectancy: 75 years, 2004 (WHO 2006)
Fertility rate/Maternal mortality rate: 2.5 births per woman, 2010 (Unicef); maternal mortality 60 per 100,000 live births (World Bank).
Birth rate/Death rate: 4 deaths per 24 births per 1,000 people; infant mortality 19 per 1,000 live births (World Bank).
Child (under 5 years) mortality rate (per 1,000): 15 per 1,000 live births (WHO 2012); 4 per cent of children under aged five are malnourished (World Bank).
Head of population per physician: 1.94 physicians per 1,000 people, 2001 (WHO 2006)

Welfare

Venezuela operates a social insurance system covering employees in private and public employment, unemployed and family members.
The welfare system of benefits covers sickness, maternity, work injury, unemployment and family allowances. Pensioners are also covered for medical benefits.
Sickness benefits are covered for up to 52 weeks. Maternity benefit is payable up to six months before and after confinement. Workers' medical benefits include free general and specialist care and hospitalisation. Unemployment benefit covers 60 per cent of the average weekly salary of the last 50 weeks and is paid for up to 13 weeks after waiting for one month following loss of employment. Unemployed persons are entitled to transportation subsidy, training and guidance services.

Pensions

A new system of private pensions was introduced in 1998. In 1999, Venezuela moved away from a pay-as-you-go pension system to one based on 'individual capitalisation funds', along the lines of the Chilean model. Under the mandatory pay-as-you-go system all participants receive pensions in proportion to their contributions, amounting to 12–13 per cent of base salary, and on the basis of the accumulation of the individual fund. The government pays for any deficiency between the accumulated value of the individual capitalised fund and the minimum amount of pension.
Full pensions are paid at aged 60, provided 240 months of contributions have been paid. At the age of 60, the employee has the option of either buying a life annuity from an insurance company, or withdrawing fixed monthly amounts from their individual capitalisation account.
A disability pension is available with 250 weeks of contribution, plus 30 per cent of workers' average earnings, payable after six months of disability.

Main cities

Caracas (capital, estimated population 2.0 million (m) in 2012), Maracaibo (2.4m), Valencia (1.7m), Barquisimeto (1.1m), Ciudad Guayana (884,657), Maracay (637,372), Petare (564,946), Maturin (506,382), Barcelona (479,387), Ciudad Bolívar (440,018).

Languages spoken

Spanish is spoken by the majority of the population. Indian dialects are spoken by about 200,000 Amerindians in the remote interior.

Official language/s

Spanish

Media

Press

Dailies: In Spanish, *El Nacional* (www.el-nacional.com), *Ultimas Noticias* (www.ultimasnoticias.com.ve), *2001* (www.2001.com.ve) is a tabloid, *El Mundo* (www.elmundo.com.ve) is an evening edition, *El Universal* (www.eluniversal.com), which has an English language edition called *Daily News* (http://english.eluniversal.com).
Weeklies: There are also numerous periodicals including *El Carabobeño* (www.el-carabobeno.com) with supplements and the monthly *Producto* (www.producto.com.ve).
Business: The magazine *Dinero* (www.dinero.com.ve) is a national publication; *Reporte* is a newspaper from Caracas.

Broadcasting

The president broadcasts a weekly programme on the public radio and TV services.
Radio: There are over 280 radio stations and all broadcast in Spanish. The state broadcaster, *Radio Nacional de Venezuela* (www.rnv.gov.ve) operates 15 radio stations in a nationwide network. Private commercial stations include Union Radio Noticias (www.unionradio.com.ve) and Fama FM (www.fama.fm).
The news agency ABN has recordings of National Assembly sessions online, (www.abn.info.ve), in Spanish.
Television: Venezolana de Television (www.vtv.gob.ve) is government run while all others are private and commercial and all broadcast in Spanish. Around 96 per cent of households have a TV set.
Private TV networks include Televen (www.televen.com), Venevision (www.venevision.net) with imported programmes and Telsur (www.telesurtv.net) a pan-Latin station. Radio Caracas Television (RCTV) had its licence withdrawn in May 2007.
The owner of Globovision (www.globovision.com), a 24-hour news channel, fled the country in July 2010, to avoid prosecution for supposed business irregularities. President Chávez said that the government may consequently own just under 50 per cent of the company and that he planned to have a government representative on the board. The station had been critical of the president in the past.
National news agency: ABN (Agencia Bolicariana de Noticias)

Economy

Venezuela is an economy dominated by one commodity – albeit a much prized commodity –petroleum. Oil revenues account for 96 per cent of export earnings, 40 per cent of government revenues and 11 per cent of GDP. Venezuela ended 2014 with an estimated 4 per cent contraction in its GDP, 68.4 per cent inflation, widespread shortages of consumer goods, and declining central bank international reserves. The IMF forecasts that GDP will shrink a further 7 per cent in 2015 and inflation may reach 80 per cent. The government's response to the economic crisis was to increase state control over the economy and blame the private sector. It has also maintained strict currency controls since 2003, which has presented significant obstacles to trade with Venezuela because importers cannot obtain sufficient dollars to purchase goods needed to maintain their operations. President Maduro has not made any plans to move the economy in the other direction and state control will continue to dominate the economy with businesses continuing to flounder. Due to Venezuela's unattractive economic environment, some US and multinational firms have chosen to reduce or shutdown Venezuelan operations. Falling oil prices since 2014 have aggravated Venezuela's economic crisis. Investment in the petroleum sector has also slowed, resulting in a decline in oil production. FDI has been cut from a healthy US$6 billion in 2012 to US$2.7 billion in 2013 and US$320 million in 2014.

In 2014, proven oil reserves were 298 billion barrels with production at 2.5 million barrels per day (bpd); natural gas reserves were 5.6 trillion cubic metres (cum) with production of 28 billion cum; coal reserves were 479 million tonnes, with production at 6.3 million tonnes of oil equivalent (mtoe) per year. Generation of hydroelectricity was 19.5mtoe, some of which was exported. There is a thriving manufacturing sector that contributes around 15 per cent of GDP, which could grow further if it was unhindered by the lack of private investment. Manufactured goods include clothing, textiles, foodstuffs and beverages, cement, fertilisers, paper, steel, aluminium, and vehicles. Venezuela cannot sustain its own food requirements and must import around 60 per cent of its food needs, which leaves it vulnerable to external shocks.

Hugo Chavez set up PetroCaribe in 2005 when Venezuela was flush with money from oil revenues and he was eager to buy influence for his country and the 'Chavista' brand of authoritarian populism he sought to export to the region. PetroCaribe gave 18 Caribbean nations access to subsidized petroleum loans. Venezuela promised to finance up to 50 per cent of the cost of the oil over a 25-year period. In 2014, PetroCaribe was dismissed because Venezuela is on the verge of bankruptcy. The reason for this is because of Venezuela being hard-pressed by low oil prices and the consequences of Chavez's long, corrupt, and disastrous mismanagement of Venezuela's economy. The current president, Maduro is working with Wall Street to offer incentives to those PetroCaribe beneficiaries to repay their debts now – decades before they are legally due.

GDP growth in 2008 was 5.3 per cent, but as the global economic crisis cut international trade, and oil prices that had been at a record high fell markedly, the economy fell into recession and growth was a negative -3.2 per cent in 2009. GDP growth rebounded in 2012 to 5.6 per cent before decreasing to 1.3 per cent in 2013 and plummeting to -4 per cent in 2014.

Inflation has been a long term problem and when global prices for food and fuel were at their highest in 2007, the rate was 31.2 per cent, which fell only marginally, to 30.8 per cent, in 2008, before falling back to 18.2 per cent in 2009 as domestic spending weakened. Although global trade picked up in 2010, in January 2010 the bolívar was devalued and two official exchange rates established, the first pegged at Bf2.6 per US dollar for all transactions not related to petroleum, the second at Bf4.3 per US dollar for all petroleum related transactions and imports deemed non-essential. This was expected to allow the government to regulate foreign currency exchange, kick-start growth in the private sector and stimulate government and domestic spending. However, the economy remained in recession in 2010 with growth staying at a negative -1.5 per cent, before a strong recovery in 2011 recorded an estimated 4.2 per cent. On 1 January 2011 the government weakened the official exchange rate on 'essential' goods to Bf4.3 per US dollar, in essence abolishing the two fixed exchange rates. Inflation, stimulated by the reduced spending power of the bolivar, picked up rising to 22.9 per cent in 2010, and higher still to an estimated 30 per cent in 2011. The inflation rate has since increased exponentially to 41 per cent in 2013 and 68 per cent in 2014.

In January 2012, the government announced that it would pay US energy company ExxonMobil only US$255 million in compensation for nationalising its assets in 2007, despite an International Chamber of Commerce (ICC) tribunal that judged the compensation should be US$908 million.

External trade

As a trading partner of Mercosur, the world's fourth largest free-trade zone, Venezuela has access to a market of over 200 million consumers. Venezuela has been a member of Mercosur since 2012. In 2004, twelve South American countries signed an agreement to launch the South American Community of Nations (CSN), modelled on the European Union. In 2007 the name was changed to Union of South American Nations (Unasur). Unasur seeks to integrate with the Andean Community of Nations and Mercosur in a single market by 2014, when tariffs on non-sensitive products are abolished with the remainder eliminated by 2019. However political tensions within the region have hampered the ongoing process.

The export of petroleum plays an overwhelming influence on the economy and provides a trade surplus. Other commodities include heavy industrial products, energy, manufactured goods and agricultural products.

Imports

Principal imports are agricultural products, livestock, raw materials, machinery and equipment, transport equipment, construction materials, medical equipment, petroleum products, pharmaceuticals, chemicals and iron and steel products.

Main sources: US (24.2 per cent of total in 2014), China (12.1 per cent), Brazil (9.9 per cent), Colombia (4.3 per cent) and Argentina (4.1 per cent).

Exports

Principal exports are petroleum and petroleum products, bauxite and aluminium, minerals, chemicals and agricultural products.

Main destinations: US (34.6 per cent of total in 2014), India (15.1 per cent), China (12.9 per cent), Cuba (5.3 per cent) and Singapore (4.8 per cent).

Agriculture

Farming

Land use is divided between arable land (3 per cent), permanent crops cultivation (1 per cent), meadows and pastures (20 per cent), forest and woodland (50 per cent) and other use (26 per cent). The country is subject to periodic droughts. Venezuela's main arable centres are Acarigua, El Tigre, Maracay, Valencia and Barquisimeto.

The agricultural sector is not hugely important to the economy of Venezuela, having constituted just 4 per cent of total GDP in 2014. The agricultural sector also constituted 7 per cent of the workforce. There has been little investment in modern farm technology. Inefficient marketing, poor farm management and scant irrigation are all features of the Venezuelan agricultural industry.

The major crops are rice, maize, sorghum, sugar cane, coffee (the main export crop), cocoa and cotton. Tropical fruits, cassava, beans, groundnuts and other vegetables are staple crops for small farmers. Poultry and pig farming are of growing importance with small quantities of meat exported. Beef production has, however, slumped due to the smuggling of cattle to Colombia (where prices are higher), and cheap imports. Bananas, milk, eggs and fish are other agricultural products.

Throughout the 1990s, the government liberalised agricultural imports through lowering tariffs and removing quantitative restrictions in the form of import licences. The overall aim was to boost agricultural efficiency and to refocus production on areas where the country has a comparative advantage.

An agricultural programme is under way, involving the improvement and irrigation of 350,000 hectares of existing agricultural land and the use of about one million new hectares for cultivation. The programme aims to increase output of cereals, sugar and oilseeds (to reduce dependence on imports), and promote crop diversification.

Fishing

Since coming to power President Chávez has passed legislation that regulates the activities of large trawlers in order to protect small fishing communities.

Generally, the fishing industry has seen good growth, owing to an increase in the tuna catch. The overall typical fish catch is in the region of 435,000mt, including 318,000mt marine fish and 79,000mt shellfish.

Forestry

Approximately half of Venezuela's total landmass is covered with forests and woodland, the majority of which are in the south and east of the country. The forestry sector remains undeveloped and around half the country's wood-derived products are imported.

Industry and manufacturing

The industrial sector as a whole contributed 35 per cent to GDP in 2014 of which manufacturing contributed 14.9 per cent. The sector also employed 22 per cent of the workforce.

Industrial development since the 1960s has been based on the utilisation of the country's natural resources, particularly iron ore, bauxite, natural gas and oil. Heavy industries that have arisen with the intention of using local materials as inputs include refining of aluminium (an increasingly significant export), petrochemicals (ammonia, sulphuric acid, fertilisers, plastics etc), cement and steel production. Import-dependent industries include motor vehicle assembly, tyres, rubber, pharmaceuticals, electrical goods and machinery. The traditional home market industries are beverages, textiles, food processing, ceramics and paper/pulp. Major state enterprises include Sidor (steel), Venalum and Alcasa (aluminium) and Pequiven (petrochemicals). Manufacturing production is highly concentrated, with around 10 per cent of all firms accounting for 75 per cent of output.

Tourism

Venezuela has traditionally been a popular destination for foreign visitors but since the introduction of a *de facto* dual currency exchange rate the number of visitors has fallen. Due to the devaluation of the new Bolívar fuerte in 2010, low- and middle-income domestic tourists have limited their holidays to Venezuela. The north of the country offers city and urban facilities, as well as Caribbean coastal resorts, while further south there are national parks and rural settings that attract eco-visitors.

The historic old towns of Caracas and Coro and its port (containing the only remaining mix of Spanish Mudéjar and Dutch architectural techniques, as well as the Canaima National Parks, which includes the world's highest sheer cliff waterfall (over 1,000 metres), are included on Unesco's World Heritage List.

Travel and tourism contributed 8.6 per cent to GDP (US$53.2 billion) in 2014 and provided employment to 7.4 per cent of the workforce (967,000 jobs). Foreign visitor spending was US$62.2 million in 2014 constituting 4.1 per cent of travel and tourism's contribution to GDP.

Mining

At present, the mining industry contributes just 1 per cent of the country's total GDP. Venezuela is endowed with a significant range of mineral resources. However, these deposits remain largely undeveloped. The sectors of the industry retaining the most importance include iron ore, bauxite, gold, diamond and nickel laterites. Other sources include zinc, copper, lead, silver, manganese, titanium, nickel, marble, sulphur, phosphates, mercury and uranium.

Venezuela produced 23 tonnes (mtoe) of gold in 2014. It has the sixteenth largest reserves of gold in the world with proven reserves of 386 tonnes (mtoe).

Several foreign investment and joint ventures have propped up the sector. Venezuelan, Canadian and US companies have combined to exploit the extensive kimberlite sills in the region of Guaniamo and aid in the marketing of diamonds.

Nickel is mined at Loma de Niquel. The main mineral exploited is iron ore; reserves are estimated at 2,800 million tonnes, 80 per cent high-grade. The largest deposits are located at Cerro Bolívar and San Isidro. Estimated reserves of bauxite at Los Pijiguaos typically amount to some four billion tonnes of high-grade ore.

Hydrocarbons

Venezuela was one of the founding members of the Organisation of Petroleum Exporting Countries (Opec) and continues to be one of the world's most important oil exporters. The country is endowed with the most extensive proven oil reserves in South America. The petroleum industry is the mainstay of the economy.

Total proven oil reserves were 298 billion barrels in 2014. Production in 2013 was 2.5 million barrels per day (bpd); supplies and production are restricted by Venezuela's OPEC quota.

The oil industry has been radicalised since Hugo Chavez became president as he used oil as an extension of his political ideology. He has agreed to oil sales, on preferential terms, in countries in the region to strengthen ties between South America and the Caribbean in an effort to counter US influence. Private oil fields were nationalised in 2007, and in 2009, President Chavez announced that companies that provide services to the oil industry would also be nationalised. In January 2012, the government announced that it would only pay US energy company ExxonMobil US$255 million in compensation for nationalising its assets in 2007; the International Chamber of Commerce tribunal had judged the compensation should be US$908 million.

Hugo Chavez set up PetroCaribe in 2005 when Venezuela was flush with money from oil revenues and he was eager to buy influence for his country and the 'Chavista' brand of authoritarian populism he sought to export to the region. PetroCaribe gave 18 Caribbean nations access to subsidized petroleum loans. Venezuela promised to finance up to 50 per cent of the cost of the oil over a 25-year period. In 2014, PetroCaribe was dismissed because Venezuela was on the verge of bankruptcy - hard-pressed by low oil prices and the consequences of Chavez's long, corrupt, and disastrous mismanagement of Venezuela's economy. The current president, Maduro is working with Wall Street to offer incentives to those PetroCaribe beneficiaries to repay their debts now – decades before they are legally due.

1.1 million bpd of refined petroleum is produced in Venezuela and 638,000 bpd is exported while 784,000 bpd is consumed. 1.6 million bpd of crude oil is exported.

Venezuela has become one of China's largest oil and gas suppliers. Venezuela plans to export up to 700,000bpd to China in 2016.

Total proven natural gas reserves were 5.6 trillion cubic metres in 2014, the second largest in the Americas, behind the US. Production was 28.4 billion cubic metres in 2014. Exploitation of gas reserves is a priority, since the majority of Venezuela's energy is produced by natural gas.

The government agency Enagas regulates the natural gas sector. Around 70 per cent of gas production is consumed by the oil industry, the majority of which is used as re-injection to aid crude oil extraction.

There are natural gas explorations of the country's north coast ongoing, in areas leased by PdVSA.
The natural gas pipeline network has been enhanced to allow greater domestic access. The international gas pipeline began operation in 2008, supplying 2–4 billion cum per day of Colombian natural gas to western Venezuela. In 2012 a reverse flow came into fruition with exports to Colombia of 4 billion cum per day.
Plans for the export of liquefied natural gas (LNG) from 2013 were agreed between PdVSA and three international consortia. Total exports of LNG are expected to be in excess of 10 million tonnes per year.
Venezuela is the second largest producer of coal in Latin America, after Colombia, and has 479 million tonnes of coal reserves (2014). PdVSA operates, through joint ventures between its subsidiary Carbozulia and foreign companies, four mines with production at 6.3 million tonnes of oil equivalent (2014). Domestic consumption is only around 20,000 tonnes per annum and most of Venezuela's bituminous coal is exported to markets in North and South America and Europe.

Energy

Total installed generating capacity was 27.5 gigawatts (GW) in 2013.
Hydropower produces over 64 per cent of total electricity generated, with traditional thermal sources constituting the remainder. Construction of more hydroelectric power stations - with capacity of 2,250MW - are underway with an additional 2,964MW planned.
Almost half of Venezuela's electricity generating capacity is provided by the 10GW Raul Leoni hydroelectric dam on the Caroní River. Another renewable source of electricity includes a small geothermal energy plant producing 1MW.
Venezuela's grid is connected to that of Colombia, enabling the country to export surplus electricity. However, there have been serious electricity shortages in recent years due to low rainfall and electricity theft, which is estimated to account for a quarter of Venezuelan energy consumption.
The electricity sector is dominated by the state-owned Electrificación de Caroni (EDELCA). Cadafe, which includes Cadela, Elecentro, Eleoriente, Eleoccidente, Desurca, and Semda, is the world's second-largest state-owned electricity company.

Financial markets

Stock exchange

Bolsa de Valores de Caracas (BCV) (Caracas Stock Exchange)

Banking and insurance

With the bankruptcy of the second biggest bank in the country, Banco Latino, in 1994, the Venezuelan banking and financial services system went into meltdown. About a third of Venezuela's banks subsequently went into insolvency as depositors panicked, closing accounts and forcing under-capitalised banks to close. Since then, the financial sector in Venezuela has undergone a vigorous restructuring, ensuring that the banks of today are well capitalised with relatively clean balance sheets.
The government has been able to recuperate its losses through the privatisation of several leading banks, and Venezuela's financial system is largely controlled by foreign interests. Foreign participation in Venezuela's banking system rose to around 70 per cent of total banking assets. As elsewhere in Latin America, it was the Spanish banks which had the most influence in the banking system, with Spanish Grupo Santander taking the lead in buying indigenous banks.
Venezuela's banking superintendent privately told several of the country's large banks that President Chávez intended to place official government representatives on their governing boards. In 2008, President Chávez began plans to nationalise the Commercial Bank of Venezuela, owned by the Spanish Grupo Santander. The bank was nationalised in May 2009 and Venezuela paid US$1.05 billion to Grupo Santander. The government closed four banks in December 2009, following suspicions of regulatory violations and the arrest of their owners for misappropriating funds. Of the four, Provivienda and Canarias will be liquidated and Bolivar and Confederado may be rescued; together these banks accounted for around 6 per cent of the banking sector.
A new Bank of the South, (South America) with a headquarters in Venezuela, was to be launched in 2008, to provide an alternative source of development funding for the participating countries, with assets of US$7 billion to underpin its operations. However as the global economic crisis intensified it undermined the intentions of the new bank so that by 2009 countries in the region were again turning to the IMF and World Bank for assistance.

Central bank

Banco Central de Venezuela

Main financial centre

Caracas

Time

GMT minus four and a half hours (from 9 December 2007)

Geography

Venezuela is on the north coast of South America, bordered by Colombia to the west, Guyana to the east and Brazil to the south.
Venezuela is a mountainous country. A spur of the Andes reaches into the north-west and is home to Pico Bolivar, at 5,007m the highest point in Venezuela. In the south-east, bordering on Brazil, are the densely-forested Guiana Highlands, which make up around half of the country's terrain. The Angel Falls, the highest waterfall in world, is in the Guiana Highlands. The centre of the country, between the mountain ranges and opening to the Caribbean Sea, are plains (*llanos*) and coastal lowlands. The Orinoco, Venezuela's biggest river, rises in the Guiana Highlands, draining most of the country on its way to the north-eastern coast and culminating in an extensive delta, which is marshy and thickly wooded.

Hemisphere

Northern

Climate

Tropical, hot and humid, with more moderate temperatures in highlands.
Dry season from December–April, with mean temperature in Caracas 19 degrees Celsius (C), rising to 28 degrees C during the day; nights are cool. Rainy season from May–November, with mean daytime temperature in Caracas 23 degrees C.

Entry requirements

Passports

Required by all, valid for six months from date of arrival.

Visa

Required by all, except nationals of EU/EEA countries, North America, Australasia, Japan, some South American, Asian and other countries for up to 90 days. For a full list of exemptions and other details, visit www.embavenez-us.org

Currency advice/regulations

There are no restrictions on the import and export of local or foreign currencies

Health (for visitors)

Mandatory precautions

None (yellow fever vaccination certificates may be required by visitor leaving for other countries).

Advisable precautions

Yellow fever, cholera, typhoid, polio vaccinations. Malaria prophylaxis recommended for visits to some rural areas. Rabies is present and dengue fever is becoming more common. There are occasional outbreaks of viral encephalitis. In north-central regions, to avoid the risk of Bilharzia use only chlorinated swimming pools for bathing.
Bottled water is advisable for new visitors. Unwashed raw foods and undercooked meats are not safe to eat.

Healthcare facilities are good in main cities, but the cost is high and therefore medical insurance is recommended.

Hotels

The selection of first-rate hotels is rather limited. Good standard in Caracas and main centres. Graded into classes by Tourism Department on a one- to five-star basis. Booking in advance is essential. There are some seasonal variations of rates. There is a 10 per cent tourist tax.

Public holidays (national)

Fixed dates

1 Jan (New Year's Day), 19 Apr (Emancipation Day), 1 May (Labour Day), 24 Jun (Battle of Carabobo), 5 Jul (Independence Day), 24 Jul (Simon Bolívar Day), 15 Aug (Assumption Day), 12 Oct (Spanishness Day), 1 Nov (All Saints' Day), 25 Dec (Christmas Day).

Variable dates

Epiphany (first Mon in Jan), Carnival (Feb), Maundy Thursday, Good Friday, Immaculate Conception (Dec).

Working hours

Banking

Mon–Fri: 0830–1130, 1400–1630.

Business

Mon–Fri: 0800–1800 (with long lunch break from noon to 1430).

Government

Mon–Fri: range from 0730–1530 to 0930–1730; long lunch break from noon to 1430.

Shops

Mon–Sat: 0900–1300, 1500–1900.

Telecommunications

Postal services

There is an efficient service to Europe and the US.

Mobile/cell phones

A GSM 900 network is limited to coverage in Caracas and main towns.

Electricity supply

110V AC, 60 cycles

Social customs/useful tips

The normal form of greeting is a handshake or an *abrazo*, a cross between a handshake and a hug. Luncheons are frequently heavy. Wine in restaurants tends to be expensive.

Public services are inefficient and it is advisable to hire professional help to carry out official transactions.

Punctuality is not a strong point and the traffic is often blamed for delays. Business meetings may be cancelled or rescheduled at the last moment.

There is no numbering system for streets in Caracas, and many street names are not marked. Directions are given by building or residence name and the neighbourhood or *urbanización*.

Security

Carry identification at all times as police make spot checks and a person without identification may be detained.

Beware of pickpockets. If unlucky enough to be robbed, do not argue as criminals can quickly become violent. Many Caracas residents carry handguns for personal defence and are prepared to use them.

Getting there

Air

National airline: Aeropostal.

International airport/s: Caracas-Maiquetía International (MQV), 22km north of city, duty-free shopping, bank, restaurants, post office and car hire. Journey time to city by bus 45 minutes running every hour. Taxis are located at a rank.

Other airport/s: Maracaibo-La Chinita (MAR), 17km from city, restaurant, car hire.

Airport tax: US$16.

Surface

Road: It is possible to cross from Colombia by the Caribbean Coastal Highway, or by the Pan-American Highway via San Cristobal. The only road from Brazil (via Santa Elena de Uairen) is very rough and is difficult in the rainy season. There is no direct access from Guyana.

Main port/s: Guanta, La Guaira, Maracaibo, Puerto Cabello.

Getting about

National transport

Air: Several carriers operate services to many destinations in Venezuela. Overbooking is common and it is advisable to arrive at the airport well before minimum check-in time. Cancellations and schedule changes are also likely to occur. Unlimited travel tickets are available.

Road: Roads between main cities are of a high standard, but there are maintenance problems. The road from Caracas to Maiquetía International Airport is closed indefinitely due a collapsed bridge. There are around 36,000km of surfaced roads, including 17,000km motorways and 13,000km highways. The Pan-American Highway runs from Caracas, via Valencia and Barquisimeto, to the Colombian border. Other main highways include: Valencia-Puerto Cabello; Coro-La Ceiba; Caracas-Ciudad Bolívar.

Buses: There are frequent services between major cities. It is advisable to book in advance. Buses are overcrowded, tend to break down and traffic jams are a problem.

Rail: A very limited service available (Barquisimeto-Puerto Cabello; around four trains per day). The first new line since 1937, connecting Caracas and Cua, was inaugurated in October 2006.

City transport

Taxis: Taxis are not metered and it is advisable to agree the fare before travelling. Higher fares are charged for late night journeys. Outside Caracas fares can be expensive for long trips. Licensed taxis are white with yellow number plates and can be hailed in the street. A fleet of black Ford Explorers operates from Caracas airport. Visitors should avoid taxi touts and unlicensed taxis, especially at the airport. Taxis from reliable companies can be booked through the hotels, some of which run their own limousine services. Shared taxis (*por puestos*) are widely used.

Buses, trams & metro: The metro reaches main points all along the Valley of Caracas. It is fast, cheap, clean, comfortable and safe, although pickpockets abound. It links with the metrobus services.

Car hire

Most international rental car companies are available in main towns and at airports. National or international licence accepted. A credit card is required. Insurance cover is recommended.

BUSINESS DIRECTORY

The addresses listed below are a selection only. While World of Information makes every endeavour to check these addresses, we cannot guarantee that changes have not been made, especially to telephone numbers and area codes. We would welcome any corrections.

Telephone area codes

The international direct dialling (IDD) code for Venezuela is +58, followed by area code and subscriber's number:

Barquisimeto	251	Maturin	291
Caracas	212	Merida	274
Ciudad Bolivar	285	Puerto Cabello	242
Cumana	293	San Cristobal	276
Maracaibo	261	Valencia	241
Maracay	243		

Chambers of Commerce

American-Venezuelan Cámara de Comercio, Torre Credival, 2da Avenida de Campo Alegre, Caracas (tel: 263-0833; fax: 263-1829; e-mail: vanamcham@venamcham.org).

British-Venezuelan Chamber of Commerce, Avenida Francisco de Miranda, Multicentro Empresarial del Este, Caracas (tel: 267-3112; fax: 263-0362; e-mail: britcham@ven.net).

Caracas Cámara de Comercio, Calle Andrés Eloy Blanco 215, Los Caobos, Caracas (tel: 571-3222; fax: 571-0050; e-mail: comercioccs@cantv.net).

Valencia Cámara de Comercio, Avenida Bolivar Norte, Edificio Cámara de Comercio, Valencia (tel: 857-5109; fax:

857-5147; e-mail: camaracomercio@cantv.net).

Venezualan Federación de Cámaras y Asociaciones de Comercio y Producción, Avenida El Empalme, Urbanizacion El Bosque, PO Box 2568, Caracas (tel: 731-1711, 731-0246; e-mail: direje@fedecamaras.org.ve).

Banking
Banco Industrial de Venezuela, Av Universidad Esquina de Traposos, Zona postal 1010, Apartado postal 2054, Caracas (tel: 545-9222/541-8622; fax: 545-8315).

Banco Mercantil, Av Andrés Bello No 1, Edif Mercantil, Aportado postal 789, Caracas 1010-A (tel: 541-4320, 541-6666; fax: 507-1239, 574-3216; e-mail: mercan24@bancomercantil.com; internet site: http://www.bancomercantil.com).

Banco Provincial, Av Este 'O', San Bernardo, Zona postal 1010-A, Apartado postal 1269, Caracas (tel: 574-5611, 574-6611; fax: 574-9408, 574-2065).

Central bank
Banco Central de Venezuela, Avenida Urdaneta esq Las Carmelitas, Apartado 2017, Caracas 1010 (tel: 801-5111; fax: 861-1649; e-mail: biblio@bcv.org.ve).

Stock exchange
Bolsa de Valores de Caracas (BCV) (Caracas Stock Exchange), www.bolsadecaracas.com

Travel information
Caracas-Maiquetía Airport, Ed Vargas, Maiquetia 1161 (tel: 303-1329; fax: 355-1224; e-mail: consejo_admin@iaaim.com.ve).

Ministry of tourism
Ministry of Tourism, Edificio Mintur, Avda Francisco de Miranda con Avda Principal de La Floresta, Caracas (tel: 208-4511; e-mail: webmaster@mintur.gob.ve).

National tourist organisation offices
Inatur (National Institute of Tourism), Edificio Mintur, Avda Francisco de Miranda con Avda Principal de La Floresta, Caracas (tel/fax: 286-3016; fax: 286-3016; e-mail: gpminatur@gmail.com).

Ministries
Ministry of Agriculture and Livestock, Torre Este, Piso 14, Caracas (tel: 509-0445; fax: 574-2432).

Ministry of Defence, Fuerta Tiuna, Conejo Blanco, Caracas 1090 (tel: 622-2745).

Ministry of Education, Esquina de Salas, Edificio Sede Del Ministerio de Educación, Caracas (tel: 564-0672).

Ministry of Energy, Torre Oeste, Parque Central, Piso 16, Caracas (tel: 507-6604; fax: 571-3953).

Ministry of the Environment, Torre Sur, Centro Simon Bolivar, Piso 25, Caracas (tel: 481-6275; fax: 483-1148).

Ministry of Family Affairs, Torre Oeste, Parque Central, Piso 51, Caracas (tel: 575-3690; fax: 573-7481).

Ministry of Finance, Edif Banco la Guaira, Piso 12, Av Mexico, Caracas (tel: 509-8281; fax: 509-7831).

Ministry of Foreign Affairs, Conde a Carmelitas, Torre M.R.E., Piso 2, Caracas 1010 (tel: 862-4484; fax: 861-0894).

Ministry of Foreign Trade, Centro Comercial los Cedros, Mezzanina 3, Avda Libertador, Caracas (tel: 762-2777; fax: 762-3883).

Ministry of Health and Social Security, Edif, Sur, Centro Simón Bolívar, Caracas (tel: 483-1566).

Ministry of Home Affairs, Esquina de Carmelitas, Caracas 1010 (tel: 483-4334; fax: 861-1967).

Ministry of Housing (tel: 509-8676; fax: 509-8437).

Ministry of Industrial Development, Edif Sur, Piso 9, Centro Simón Bolívar, Caracas (tel: 419-296; fax: 483-2607).

Ministry of Justice, Torre Norte, Centro Simón Bolívar, Piso 25 (tel: 483-1170; fax: 483-7515).

Ministry of Labour, Torre Sur, Piso 5, Centro Simón Bolívar, Caracas (tel: 483-1881; fax: 483-5940).

Ministry of Planning, Parque Central, Torre Oeste, Piso 26, Caracas (tel: 507-7902; fax: 573-2834).

Ministry of Public Works and Commercial Affairs, Centro Simón Bolívar, Torre Sur, Piso 6, Caracas (tel: 483-2124-; fax: 412-553).

Ministry of Trade and Industry, Av Libertador Centro Comercial Los Cedros, Piso 2, Caracas (tel: 531-0026; fax: 762-9869).

Ministry of Transport and Communications, Torre Este, Parque Central, Piso 50, Caracas (tel: 509-10761; fax: 509-1769).

Ministry of Urban Development, Torre Oeste, Parque Central, Piso 51, Caracas (tel: 574-5349; fax: 571-1767).

President's Office, Palacio de Miraflores, Avenida Urdeneta, Caracas 1010 (tel: 861-0811; fax: 861-1101).

Other useful addresses
Asociación Nacional de Comerciantes e Industriales, Plaza Panteón Norte 1, Apdo 33, Caracas.

CVG Bauxita de Venezuela S.A. (Raw Material for Aluminun), Av. La Estancia, Edif, Diamen, Piso 2, Chuao, Caracas (tel: 922-311, 916-187, 916-487).

British Embassy, Edificio Torre Las Mercedes, 3 Piso, Avenida La Estancia, Chuao, Caracas 1060 (tel: 911-255, 993-4111, 926-542, 914-253).

Central Information Office (OCI), Parque Central, Torre Oeste, Piso 18, Caracas (tel: 572-7110; fax: 572-2675).

Conapri (National Council for Investment Promotion), Centro Banavén, PB, Local 4, Chuao, Caracas (tel: 923-801; fax: 926-498).

Consejo Venezolana de la Industria, Edif Cámara de Industriales, Esq de Puente Anauco, Caracas.

Corporación Venezolana de Guayana (CVG) (Main Company), Edif. de Administración, Via Caracas, Puerto Ordaz, Ciudad Guayana, C.P. 80915, Edo. Bolivar (tel: 303-333; fax: 226-300, 225-311).

CVG Ferrominera del Orinoco AA (Iron), Av La Estancia, Chuao, Edif, Torre Las Mercedes, Piso 9, Caracas 1070-A (tel: 911-166; fax: 911-639).

Fondo de Inversiones de Venezuela (Privatisation Programme Information), Torre Financiera del Banco Central de Venezuela, Piso 20, Esq de Santa Capilla, Avda Urdaneta, Caracas (tel: 806-5974; fax: 819-169).

PdVSA (Petróleos de Venezuela), Avda Liberator, La Campina, Apdo 169, Caracas 1010-A (tel: 708-1111; fax: 708-4661).

CVG Siderúrgica del Orinoco CA SIDOR. (Aluminium, Iron and Steel), Av La Estancia, Chuao, Edif. General de Seguros, Caracas, 1070-A (tel: 912-333, 911-462).

Superintendencia de Inversiones Extranjeras (SIEX – Superintendency of Foreign Investment), Apdo 213, Edif La Perla, Piso 3, Bolsa a Mercaderes, Caracas (tel: 483-6666; fax: 484-4368, 481-7919).

Unión Patronal Venezolana de Comercio, Edif General Urdaneta, Piso 2, Marrón a Pelota, Apdo 6578, Caracas.

US Embassy, Avda Principal de la Floresta, Esq Francisco de Miranda, La Floresta, Caracas (tel: 285-3111; fax: 285-0336).

National news agency: ABN (Agencia Bolicariana de Noticias), (internet: www.abn.info.ve).

Internet sites
Venezuela Export Directory: http://www.ddex.com/

Venezuela trade: http://www.trade-venezuela.com

Vietnam

Some things just don't change in Vietnam. One of them is the human rights situation in Vietnam, which reportedly remained critical in 2014. In a political time warp, the Dang Cong San Viet Nam (DCSV) (Communist Party of Vietnam) continued its one-party rule, in place since 1975. However, maintaining such an all-embracing monopoly on power has its price; the ruling party faces growing public discontent with the lack of what in other countries would be considered basic freedoms. Although fewer political activists were arrested than in 2013, the security forces increased various forms of harassment and intimidation of critics.

Still no rights

The Australian Human Rights Watch (HRW) chapter reported that Vietnam's human rights record 'remained dire', noting that the one-party communist state suppresses virtually all forms of political dissent, using what HRW describes as a broad array of repressive measures. Freedom of expression, association and assembly are tightly restricted. The police routinely use torture and beatings to extract confessions and punish detainees. Vietnam's religious minorities and activists are harassed, intimidated and imprisoned. The criminal justice system lacks independence and operates under the direction of the government and party. State-run drug rehabilitation centres exploite detainees as forced labourers in the manufacture of goods for local markets and for export. Yet, despite the pressure, increasing numbers of bloggers and activists are vocal in calling for genuine democracy and greater freedoms.

HRW noted that over 2014 a few political prisoners had been released and there were indications that the pace of political arrests had slowed. But the releases appeared to be little more than a cosmetic exercise and it appeared that the government was replacing arrests with what HRW described as 'orchestrated thuggery'. The number of known political prisoners in Vietnam had dropped by about 50 since 2013, but few of these had been released as a result of any reforms. In many cases, released detainees had simply completed their sentences and were now out on probation, effectively silenced. Any further political or dissident activity would see them back in prison. HRW had documented well over 200 such prisoners in 2013 and put the current total number of political prisoners now at at least 135.

However difficult the Vietnamese government found it to control criticism of the regime, it was quite happy to allow anti-China sentiment to flourish on social media and elsewhere. Tension between the countries had continued to grow as the maritime dispute between Vietnam and China worsened. In May 2014, violent protests against China had erupted in Binh Duong and Ha Tinh provinces, causing the death of four Chinese nationals and, rather unfortunately, the destruction of facilities of many foreign-owned companies, not only those belonging to Chinese interests, but also to Taiwanese, South Korean and Japanese businesses.

Vietnam has in fact accepted 182 of the 227 recommendations made by the United Nations Human Rights Council (HRC) in its June 2014 review of Vietnam's human rights record, but rejected a number of crucial and, more important, recommendations such as the release of political prisoners and people detained without charge or trial, legal reform to end the politically motivated imprisonment of people for their peaceful exercise of fundamental human rights, the creation of an independent national human rights institution and other steps to promote public political participation. In November 2014, Vietnam's National Assembly ratified the UN Convention against Torture and the Convention on the Rights of Persons with Disabilities (CRPD).

Other points raised, but not addressed by the Vietnamese authorities, included the question of political prisoners and the government's perceived misuse of the criminal justice system. Vietnamese courts were seen to lack independence and continued to be used as political tools of the CPV against critics. During the September 2014 trial of land rights activists charged with 'fighting against those on public duty', the court refused to summon witnesses who

KEY FACTS

Official name: Cong Hoa Xa Hoi Chu Nghia Viet Nam (The Socialist Republic of Vietnam) (SRV)

Head of State: President Truong Tan Sang (from 25 Jul 2011)

Head of government: Prime Minister Nguyen Tan Dung (from 2006; re-elected 26 Jul 2011)

Ruling party: Dang Cong San Viet Nam (DCSV) (Communist Party of Vietnam)

Area: 329,556 square km

Population: 90.63 million (2014)*

Capital: Hanoi

Official language: Vietnamese

Currency: Dong (D) = 100 xu

Exchange rate: D22,482.50 per US$ (Sep 2015)

GDP per capita: US$2,053 (2014)*

GDP real growth: 5.98% (2014)*

GDP: US$186.05 billion (2014)*

Labour force: 48.26 million (2009)*

Unemployment: 2.45% (2014)*

Inflation: 4.10% (2014)*

Oil production: 365,000 bpd (2014)

Natural gas production: 10.20 billion cum (2014)

Balance of trade: US$8.73 billion (2014)

* estimated figure

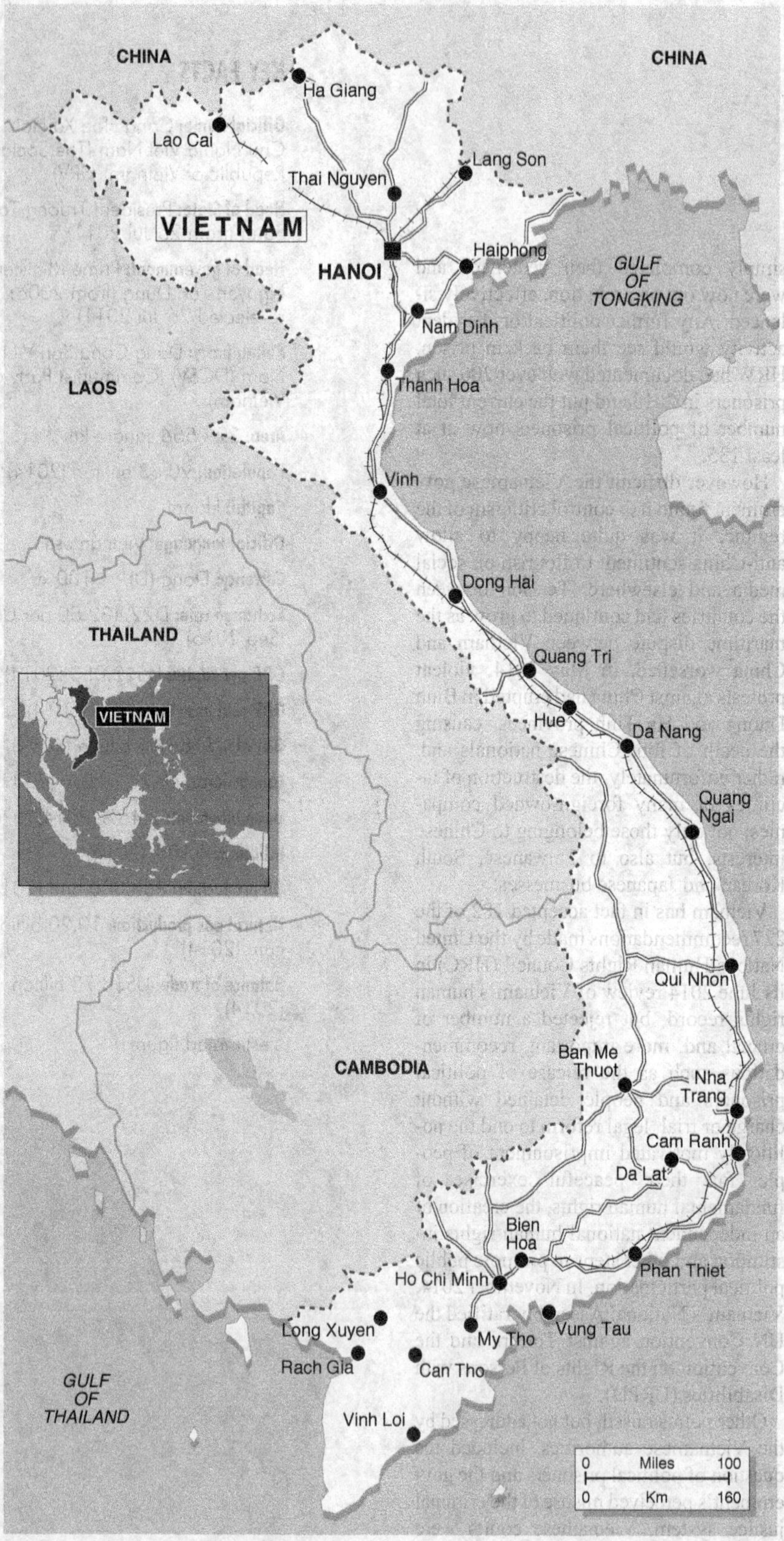

might have provided statements in favour of the accused and actually prevented the defence lawyer presenting his defence. In February 2014, three activists were arrested on their way to visit a fellow activist on charges of 'causing traffic jams', and were sentenced to between two and three years in prison. Bloggers were persistently arrested on various spurious charges. If not arrested, campaigners often faced physical assaults.

Vietnam, reported HRW, banned all independent political parties, labour unions and human rights organisations. Authorities required official approval for public gatherings and refused to grant permission for meetings, marches, or protests they deemed politically or otherwise unacceptable. Domestic restriction of movement is used to prevent bloggers and activists from participating in public events, such as anti-China protests, human rights discussions, or attending trials of fellow activists. The government has also prevented many critics from making trips outside Vietnam, citing 'national security'. The Vietnamese government also monitors any religious groups that operate outside official, government-registered and government-controlled religious institutions.

Police brutality, including deaths in police custody, are an increasing source of public concern. In many cases, those killed in police custody were being held for minor infractions. Police frequently engage in cover-ups, including by alleging the detainee's suicide. There was one positive development when in September 2014 the National Assembly Judicial Committee held its first public hearing on forced confessions, torture and other misconduct by police. Vietnamese who are dependent on drugs, including children, continue to be held in government detention centres where they are forced to perform menial work in the name of 'labour therapy'. In 2014, the government belatedly developed a plan to 'reform' the system that would not do away with forced labour and, despite promises to close some centres and reduce the overall number of detainees, would still leave more than 10,000 detainees held in the system in 2020. For Vietnam, 2015 promised to be a significant political year. The Communist Party's Twelfth Congress is due to convene in January 2016 to renew the nation's leadership. All the aspirants to senior positions had begun to canvas support at all party levels.

The economy

As long ago as 1986, the 6th Party Congress had abandoned efforts to run a command economy broadly modelled on the Soviet Union, opting instead for what was described as 'market socialism', a compromise that allowed private entrepreneurial activity to exist alongside state-owned – and managed – enterprises.

The 7th Congress five years later (in 1991) went for *doi moi* (renewal) reforms, designed to harness entrepreneurial energy. This appeared to work, as Vietnam's gross domestic product (GDP) grew by 7 or 8 per cent annually for some 20 years.

In 2007 Vietnam was admitted to the World Trade Organisation and foreign banks began to lend. However, as the 2008 recession took hold, the government preferred to limit funds to domestic borrowers. Sadly, the result was not further growth but instead a period of inflationary speculation in the real estate markets. It was not until 2014 that inflation appeared to be under control, Vietnam had returned to surplus and international companies considered Vietnam as a competitive manufacturing base. Significantly Vietnam's credit ratings were also improving.

But not all was well. On the Transparency International 2014 *Corruption Perceptions Index* Vietnam ranked 119 out of the 175 countries surveyed, level with Belarus and Sierra Leone. An official anti-corruption campaign had achieved some improvement, but crony capitalism was, in the view of neutral observers, still the order of the day. Economic choices and how to deal with corruption are of course the subject of political debate and discussion.

Midway through 2014, Chinese moves to establish Beijing's hegemony in the South China Sea was bad news for those in Vietnam's regime who sought closer ties with China.

Vietnam began 2015 on a fairly sound economic footing. The national economy had largely recovered from Hanoi's ill-advised efforts to mitigate the impact of the 2009 Great Recession. That sobering experience exposed structural weaknesses which, left unfixed, could condemn Vietnam to languish in a middle-income trap, unable to realise the potential of its relatively young and well-educated population.

According to the Asian Development Bank (ADB) the Vietnamese economy grew by 6.0 per cent in 2014, the strongest rate of growth since 2011. Industry expanded by 7.1 per cent, against 5.4 per cent in 2013, benefitting from foreign direct investment (FDI) that boosted growth in manufacturing to 8.5 per cent. The recovery in demand for property lifted growth in construction to 7.1 per cent. Agriculture picked up to grow by 3.5 per cent, supported by higher exports of fish and shrimp.

According to the ADB, the growth in the services sector eased from the previous year to 6.0 per cent, partly a result of fewer visitors from China, which hurt tourism. Total visitor arrivals increased by 4.0 per cent in 2014 – a deceleration from 10.6 per cent in 2013. On the demand side, private consumption accelerated by almost a percentage point to 6.1 per cent, reflecting improved consumer sentiment. Growth in public consumption eased to 7.0 per cent as the government reduced capital expenditure and contained increases in public sector wages.

Investment strengthened in 2014 as gross capital formation rose by 8.9 per cent, spurred by an estimated 16 per cent increase in FDI disbursements and lower domestic interest rates. However, net external demand reduced GDP growth because imports of goods and services rose in volume terms at a faster pace than exports.

Inflation decelerated to average 4.1 per cent in 2014, the lowest in 10 years, owing to better food production and lower global prices for oil and commodities. By the end of 2014, inflation was just 1.8 per cent year-on-year. Moderating inflation paved the way for the State Bank of Vietnam (central bank) to reduce base interest rates by a further 50 basis points, to 6.5 per cent for the refinancing rate and to 4.5 per cent for the discount rate. Commercial banks lowered lending rates, which helped to stimulate credit growth to an estimated 12.6 per cent, meeting the central bank's 12–14 per cent target for 2014. M2 money supply grew by an estimated 16 per cent, also in line with the official target.

The ADB noted that international reserves recovered by the end of 2014 to an estimated 3 months of import cover. Merchandise exports rose by an estimated 13.7 per cent on a balance-of-payments basis and in US dollars, supported by further gains in shipments of manufactured products such as mobile phones from foreign-invested factories. Measured the same way, imports rose by 12.1 per cent, so that the trade surplus increased to an estimated US$11.9 billion. Exports benefitted from a 1 per cent devaluation of the dong against the US dollar in June 2014, which followed a similar devaluation in mid-2013.

The current account recorded its fourth consecutive surplus, estimated at US$8.1 billion or 4.4 per cent of GDP. On the capital account, the 16 per cent increase in FDI disbursements to US$8.1 billion more than offset a drop in portfolio inflows. Fiscal policy was moderately expansionary in 2014. The fiscal deficit, excluding off-budget and 'onlending' items, widened to 4.4 per cent of GDP from 3.9 per cent in 2013. Preliminary figures showed that budget expenditure remained at the equivalent of 25.9 per cent of GDP, but revenue and grants fell to 21.5 per cent of GDP, mostly a result of weak growth in tax collection.

Encouragingly, Moody's Investors Service raised Vietnam's sovereign credit

KEY INDICATORS — Vietnam

	Unit	2011	2012	2013	2014	**2015
Population	m	*89.32	*88.76	*89.69	*90.63	*91.58
Gross domestic product (GDP)	US$bn	122.70	155.57	170.57	*186.05	*204.49
GDP per capita	US$	1,374	1,753	1,902	*2,053	*2,233
GDP real growth	%	5.9	5.2	5.4	*6.0	*6.0
Inflation	%	18.7	9.1	6.6	*4.1	*2.5
Unemployment	%	4.5	4.5	2.8	*2.5	*2.5
Oil output	'000 bpd	328.0	348.0	350.0	365.0	–
Natural gas output	bn cum	8.5	9.4	9.8	10.2	–
Coal output	mtoe	24.9	23.5	23.1	23.1	–
Exports (fob) (goods)	US$m	96,906.0	114,573.0	132,135.0	–	–
Imports (fob) (goods)	US$m	97,356.0	104,688.0	123,405.0	–	–
Balance of trade	US$m	-450.0	9,885.0	8,730.0	–	–
Current account	US$m	236.0	9,061.0	9,471.0	*10,074.0	*9,816.0
Total reserves minus gold	US$m	12,220.3	25,573.3	25,893.5	34,189.4	–
Foreign exchange	US$m	11,795.6	25,161.3	25,480.7	–	–
Exchange rate	per US$	19,974.00	20,828.00	21,110.00	21,387.50	–

* estimated figure ** forecast figure

rating by one notch to B1 and Fitch upgraded its rating to BB–, citing improved macro-economic stability and stronger external accounts. These actions supported the government's sale of US$1 billion in 10-year bonds at an annual coupon rate of 4.8 per cent, the lowest rate of its three issuances of offshore debt denominated in US dollars since 2005. The Vietnam Asset Management Company acquired from banks an estimated US$5.7 billion in non-performing loans by the end of 2014, a key part of the government's efforts to mend a banking system handicapped by impaired balance sheets and insufficient capital.

However, the ADB considered that the government had still to outline a clear strategy to resolve the question of non-performing loans. Further, the extent of bad loans remaining with the banks was unclear. Cross holdings between banks, as well as between banks and non-banks, posed risks to the financial sector. The central bank introduced new prudential regulations to address this issue which, if effectively implemented, would improve financial stability.

GDP growth was forecast by the ADB to edge up to 6.1 per cent in 2015 and 6.2 per cent in 2016, with FDI an important driver. The ADB reported that data from the Foreign Investment Agency showed that new FDI commitments rose to US$15.6 billion in 2014, while an additional US$4.6 billion was committed to existing foreign-funded projects.

Better economic performance in the major industrial economies – particularly the US, Vietnam's biggest export market – were expected to spur exports, but this positive effect would be partly offset by slowing growth in China. Exports of manufactured products would continue to expand, given that 76 per cent of 2014's disbursed FDI was directed into manufacturing. Factors bolstering private consumption were expected to expand employment, low inflation and growth in remittances, which reached almost US$10 billion in 2014. In January 2015, ahead of the lunar new year, retail sales jumped by 13 per cent in nominal terms. Lower interest rates, ratings upgrades and brighter prospects for manufactured exports had improved the outlook for investment.

The central bank targeted credit growth of 13–15 per cent for 2015, slightly above 2014's estimated outcome. Restrictions on foreign investment in real estate would be eased from July 2015, which should support other measures taken by the government to revive the property market. The drop in global oil prices from 2014 was a positive development for the Vietnamese economy. Although Vietnam produces about 350,000 barrels of oil per day and is a net exporter of crude oil, it is a net importer of refined petroleum products. Lower fuel prices boost household disposable income, stimulate consumption and reduce costs for many businesses, supporting profits and investment. The National Financial Supervisory Commission estimated that savings on domestic production costs could reach 3 per cent in 2015. The fall in oil prices would dent government revenue, but fiscal policy was still likely to promote economic growth.

Risk assessment

Economy	Fair/good
Politics	Poor
Regional stability	Good/fair

COUNTRY PROFILE

1428 After a long period of rule by successive Chinese rulers, Vietnam gained independence from the Ming dynasty's control. The Le dynasty ruled until 1527.
1680 The Portuguese, Dutch, English and French established trading posts in Vietnam.
1771–1802 The Tai Son Rebellion years. The Tai Son brothers wrested control from the ruling Nguyen family. They aimed to seize the wealth of the rich and aid the poor. Most of the members of the Nguyen family were killed, except for Nguyen Anh, the nephew of a Nguyen lord.
1802 Vietnam was unified under the leadership of Nguyen Anh who recaptured much of Vietnam from the Tai Son brothers.
1830–40 The Nguyen dynasty tried to rid Vietnam of French missionaries by forcing the Christian movement underground and executing priests. In response, the missionaries appealed to the French government for military intervention in Vietnam.
1859 The French began their attack on the region, capturing the city of Danang.
1861 The French captured Saigon (now Ho Chi Minh city).
1862 Vietnam agreed to the Treaty of Saigon that gave the French control of three provinces and the island of Poulo Condore, free passage of French ships and freedom for the missionaries.
1883 French rule began over the whole country as part of the Indochina territory that included Cambodia. Under colonial rule, transportation and communications improved but the standard of living among the Vietnamese people remained low. Their suffering contributed to rising nationalist sentiment.
1930 A revolutionary, Ho Chi Minh, formed the Indochinese Communist Party (ICP) to fight against French rule.
1940 The French administration was replaced by Japanese occupation during the war.
1945 The Japanese were expelled by the ICP and French forces. A war of independence against France began.
1954 At a peace conference in Geneva, Vietnam was divided at the seventeenth parallel into communist Democratic Republic of Vietnam (north) and American-backed Republic of Vietnam (south). North Vietnam sponsored a growing guerrilla movement (Viet Cong) in the south, which aimed to re-unite Vietnam.
1964 US armed forces began their official intervention in support of South Vietnam after the US Gulf of Tonkin resolution. The US was committed to South Vietnam.
1967 The US military presence totalled nearly 500,000 troops.
1968 The Communists launched an attack on South Vietnam. This 'Tet Offensive' targeted five major cities. The Communists were forced to retreat within weeks. The US bombing campaign against North Vietnam ended and US troops in South Vietnam were reduced.
1973 The Paris peace accords were signed, temporarily ending hostilities between the US and North Vietnam.
1975 US troops withdrew.
1976 North and South Vietnam were combined to form the Socialist Republic of Vietnam. Saigon was renamed Ho Chi Minh City.
1979 Vietnamese troops invaded Cambodia overthrowing the Pol Pot regime and instituting their own puppet government; Chinese troops invaded Vietnam but were defeated. During this time Vietnam established close relationships with the Soviet Union, which was necessary for its economic development.
1986 Economic reform began with the adoption of the *doi moi* (renovation) reforms.
1992 The state constitution was introduced, which allowed for some liberalisation of the Vietnamese economy.
1993 Full Western aid resumed.
1995 Vietnamese and American rapprochement began. Vietnam joined the Association of Southeast Asian Nations (Asean).
1997 Tran Duc Luong was elected president by the National Assembly, and Phan Van Khai was appointed prime minister.
2000 Vietnam and the US signed an agreement enabling normal trading relations between the two countries.
2001 Nong Duc Manh was appointed secretary general of the Dang Cong San Viet Nam (DCSV) (Communist Party of Vietnam).

2002 Russia closed its naval base in Cam Ranh. Vietnam signed an accord with Russia to construct a US$100 million hydroelectric power station in Vietnam's central highlands. DCSV members won most seats in the National Assembly elections.
2004 The first US commercial flight since 1973 landed in Ho Chi Minh City.
2005 Prime Minister Phan Van Khai visited the US as the first Vietnamese leader since the end of the Vietnam War.
2006 Nguyen Minh Triet and Nguyen Tan Dung replaced Tran Duc Luong and Phan Van Khai as president and prime minister in what was seen as a move towards a younger leadership. A trade agreement with the US was concluded.
2007 Vietnam joined the World Trade Organisation (WTO) after a 12-year accession process. In elections for the National Assembly, the coalition Vietnamese Fatherland Front (led by the Communist Party) won 492 seats (out of 493). The US agreed to fund a study into eliminating the high levels of Agent Orange (a highly toxic defoliant used by the US military during the Vietnam War) from storage sites. Prime Minister Dung was re-appointed and promised to implement economic reforms.
2008 Petrol prices were increased by 31 per cent as the government moved to cut back on subsidies. A two-child limit for families was re-introduced, in an effort to limit population growth. An agreement resolved a 30-year border dispute with China.
2009 Petrovietnam began operating a natural gas pipeline from the offshore Su Tu Vang gas field to electricity power plants in the south-east region with an initial 500,000 cubic metres per day. Tropical storm Mirinae caused the deaths of around 90 people during severe flooding in the central provinces. A deal was signed between the Vietnam and Russian central banks allowing payments for bilateral trade to be made in the dong and the rouble. The currency was devalued by 5 per cent.
2010 In March, the two-child per family limit was relaxed to allow a third, not only to accommodate children of a previous marriage and any that may be handicapped, but also to redress a growing gender imbalance due to abortions following ultrasound scans. The government ordered all online gold trading floors to close by the end of March until new credit institution laws were enacted. The online trading was thought to have been turning over some US$1 billion per day, but was becoming unstable due to lax regulations. On 18 August, the Pepsi Cola Company announced plans to invest US$250 million in a variety of projects around the country. In September, the Coca-Cola Company said it would double its investment to US$400 million in Vietnam.
2011 Nguyen Phu Trong was elected general secretary of the DCSV on 19 January. The dong was devalued by 8.5 per cent in February, leading to an inflation rate of 13.9 per cent year-on-year in March. Fuel prices were increased for the second time in five weeks on 30 March. Public sector wages were increased by 14 per cent in May, in an attempt to shield workers from the high rate of inflation. A decision, by the four-country Mekong River Commission, to implement plans to build the controversial, Mekong Xayaburi dam in Laos was due to be taken on 19 April, but following ecologically and socially adverse reports the decision was postponed. The Mekong River is a food source for millions of people along its length; the dam would reduce food production in favour of electricity production. In parliamentary elections held on 22 May the DCSV won 496 of 500 seats; self-nominated candidates four. Turnout was 99.99 per cent. On 25 July, parliament elected Truong Tan Sang as president, with 487 votes (out of 500). President Troung nominated Prime Minister Nguyen for another term in office. Widespread flooding along the Mekong Delta caused the death of 78 people; over 125,000 homes were inundated, and 4,000 hectares of rice fields submerged. The International Red Cross appealed for US$1 million in assistance for the tens of thousands affected by the rising waters, in the worst flood for over a decade.
2013 On 11 June Prime Minister Nguyen Tan Dung secured the full support of less than half of parliament in an unprecedented confidence vote. A number of bloggers were arrested on 13 June. After the DCSV put forward suggestions for reforms to the constitution there was a lively debate from the public. A number of bloggers expressing opposition to the DCSV were detained in August – questioning the party's monopoly on power is considered a serious crime. Activists, including members of the ruling DCSV, were said to be considering forming a new political party. General Vo Nguyen Giap, who defeated French forces at Dien Bien Phu in 1954, effectively ending French colonial rule in the region, died on 4 October aged 102. He was North Vietnam's defence minister at the time of the Tet Offensive against US forces in 1968, considered to be the beginning of the end for the US in then South Vietnam. After causing havoc in parts of the Philippines, Tropical Storm Haiyan made landfall in north Vietnam on 12 November, leaving at least 13 people dead and 81 injured. Just a few days later a tropical depression lead to flooding and landslides in central Vietnam which left at least 28 people dead, nine missing and some 80,000 homeless.
2014 In August, the chairman of the US Joint Chiefs of Staff, Martin Dempsey, held talks with Vietnamese leaders, in the highest level visit by an American military officer since the Vietnam War. Following the high profile visit, the US said that it would partially lift its embargo on arms sales to Vietnam, which had been in place for three decades. Washington said that the move applied to weapons for maritime purposes only.
2015 The Vietnamese government revoked the licence of an outspoken newspaper *Nguoi Cao Tuoi website – 'Elderly' in Vietnamese – after it published articles which allegedly 'abuse freedom and democratic rights'. According to the information and communications ministry, the newspaper had published some articles that revealed confidential information related to national security and abused democratic rights to undermine the nation's legal benefits. The online newspaper had allegedly published articles aimed at insulting and making false accusations against some organisations and individuals.*

Political structure

Constitution

Vietnam has adopted, in broad terms, a Marxist-Leninist political ideology. A number of its political systems are derived from those of China and the former USSR. The political structure is dominated throughout by the Dang Cong San Viet Nam (DCSV) (Communist Party of Vietnam).

Under the 1992 state constitution, the DCSV continues to be ultimately responsible for policy, but the government assumed greater administrative and executive responsibility.

Twenty-four amendments to the 1992 constitution were passed in December 2001. The most important gave equality to the private sector of the economy.

Local government is vested in elected provincial, municipal and district councils.

Independence date

2 September 1945

Form of state

Socialist republic

The executive

Executive power is officially exercised by a Western-style council of ministers under a prime minister. However, in practice, there is a two-way balance with the presidency and party. The president is elected by the National Assembly for a five-year term. Between sessions of the National Assembly, affairs of state are dealt with by the president and the National Assembly's

standing committee, the council of state. In any case, membership of the Council of Ministers generally coincides with that of the Politburo and Secretariat of the DCSV, and executive decisions may, *de facto*, be taken by the DCSV even without the co-operation of the government.
The DCSV's 166-member Central Committee meets once or twice a year and is responsible for selecting the Politburo, which has 17 members. The Politburo oversees the DCSV's daily functions and has the power and authority to issue directives to the government. It is the highest policy-making body.

National legislature

The Council of Ministers is responsible to and appointed by the legislative Quoc Hoi (National Assembly), itself elected to a five-year term by universal adult suffrage (voting is mandatory).
The Quoc Hoi is the highest representative and legislative body and the only institution with the authority to enact the constitution, codes and laws and elect the president and vice president, prime minister, president of the supreme people's court and procurator general, among other high officials.
The National Assembly, which is dominated by the ruling DCSV, meets twice a year in plenary session for about two to three weeks at a time. The Assembly's principal purpose is the (generally automatic) approval of Politburo decisions and DCSV-inspired legislation.

Legal system

Vietnam applied French law in the colonial period, but assumed a legal system based on the Soviet mould after the communist takeover. The country has a civil law system, but much of the law is underdeveloped and in the process of being innovated, for example in the case of foreign investment. Civil cases involving such matters as family law are distinguished from 'economic' cases, which include disputes arising from trade, investment and payments involving foreign entities. 'Economic' cases are dealt with by a separate arbitration system, in which the Vietnam International Arbitration Centre (VIAC) is a prominent body.
The People's Supreme Court is Vietnam's highest court. Under it are People's Courts for each province, municipality and district.
The legal system is in the process of being reformed.

Last elections

22 May 2011 (parliamentary); 24 July 2011 (presidential, indirect)
Results: Parliamentary: Dang Cong San Viet Nam (DCSV) (Communist Party of Vietnam) won 496 of 500 seats; self-nominated candidates four. Turnout was 99.99 per cent.
Presidential: Presidential: Truong Tan Sang won 487 votes (out of 500).

Next elections

No date set (presidential); 2016 (parliamentary)

Political parties

Ruling party

Dang Cong San Viet Nam (DCSV) (Communist Party of Vietnam)

Main opposition party

There are no opposition parties.

Population

The total population is expected to reach 94 million by 2015. About 20 per cent of the population is under 14 years of age. About 37 per cent of the total population live in poverty. The worst poverty occurs in the mountainous regions bordering China, Laos and Cambodia. The floods in the Mekong delta in 2000 worsened the poverty situation, affecting over one million families.
The south contains less than one-third of Vietnam's population.
90.39 million (2012)*
Last census: April 2009: 85,846,997
Population density: 262 inhabitants per square km (2010). Urban population 30 per cent (2010 Unicef).
Annual growth rate: 1.3 per cent, 1990–2010 (Unicef).

Ethnic make-up

Vietnamese (84 per cent) and Chinese (2 per cent). The remainder are Khmers, Chams and members of some 51 ethnic groups.

Religions

Although the country is officially atheist, many Vietnamese profess to being Buddhists. Christians are a significant minority (five million, mostly Catholics), followed by Caodaists, Hoa Hao Buddhists, Muslims and Hindus. There is a religious revival in Vietnam.

Education

Primary school lasts until age 11. Secondary school education is divided into lower secondary and upper secondary school lasting for four and three years, respectively. There is also provision for technical and vocational secondary education. Universities, specialised colleges, community and junior colleges provide higher education. There are currently over 100 higher education institutions. Distance education is offered in two open universities and other provincial centres.
The Ministry of Labour, Invalids and Social Affairs is expected to build a vocational training school in each province and a job training centre in each district by 2005. Since 1998, the state has invested US$12 million to upgrade infrastructure in job training centres and set up 39 new vocational schools. Trainees at vocational schools have annually increased by 20 per cent. Vietnam will provide vocational training to 1.3 million people annually, including 200,000 technicians, until 2010. As a result, the number of untrained workers will be reduced by 1.6 per cent by that year.
In December 2011, PetroVietnam announced that it was prepared to set up its own, purpose built university on the outskirts of Hanoi, with a campus for 55,000 students.
Public expenditure on education typically amounts to 3 per cent of annual gross national income.
Literacy rate: 90 per cent, adult rate (Unesco 2005)
Compulsory years: Six to 14.
Enrolment rate: 105.6 per cent gross primary enrolment; 67.1 per cent gross secondary enrolment, of relevant age groups (including repeaters) (World Bank 2004).
Pupils per teacher: 28, in primary schools.

Health

The government has sought to improve the country's deteriorating healthcare system, which suffers from chronic underfunding and resultant shortages of medicine and equipment, recruitment problems and low staff morale. In 2001, an agreement was signed by the International Finance Corporation to invest US$8 million to establish a foreign-owned, Western-style hospital in Ho Chi Minh City. The new hospital will have modern equipment and advanced medical facilities. It is the first hospital project to be partly funded by private investors and reflects the government's promotion of investment in Vietnam's healthcare system.
The parlous state of Vietnam's healthcare system today dates back to the end of the war in 1975. Although on paper the results are impressive, including the establishment of 9,000 communal clinics and the training of an additional 23,000 doctors to give a ratio of approximately 40 doctors per 10,000 population, the reality is that many clinics are not equipped or stocked and are given inadequate budgets. Many doctors prefer to concentrate their efforts on the more remunerative private treatment of better-off patients.
This difference between private and public expenses partly reflects the system of health fees introduced in the 1990s to supplement the health budget. The new charges (from which civil servants and war veterans are exempt) backfired, resulting in lower bed-occupancy rates – in some cases drops of 40 per cent were registered.

HIV/Aids
The official number of HIV/Aids cases by March 2006 was 104,000, however, some estimates put the real figure at three times this number. Young people, between 15–24 years, account for 40 per cent of the overall infection rate. The government has allocated US$6.7 million and the Asian Development Bank (ADB) allocated US$20 million for a programme, implemented over a five-year period, targetted specifically at the young. In 2004 the US included Vietnam in a list of 15 countries to benefit from a US$15 billion fund, at the beginning of in a five-year aid programme.
HIV prevalence: 0.4 per cent aged 15–49 in 2003 (World Bank)
Life expectancy: 71 years, 2004 (WHO 2006)
Fertility rate/Maternal mortality rate: 1.8 births per woman, 2010 (Unicef)
Birth rate/Death rate: 12.7 births and six deaths per 1,000 people (2003).
Child (under 5 years) mortality rate (per 1,000): 23 per 1,000 live births (WHO 2012); 37 per cent of children aged under five are malnourished (World Bank).
Head of population per physician: 0.53 physicians per 1,000 people, 2001 (WHO 2006)

Welfare
Vietnam's transition to a market economy has increased problems of unemployment and the availability of social security benefits. The country has about 46.6 million people of working age, accounting for 59 per cent of the total population. Vietnam aims to create 1.4 million jobs annually in the period between 2001–05. The country also plans to reduce unemployment to 5 per cent and increase working time in rural areas.
Although there are social security systems for the victims of war, the collapse of the co-operative system has affected benefits in rural areas. With the introduction of a new Labour Code in 1994, and the Law on Co-operatives in 1996, the Vietnamese government declared its willingness to provide social insurance to workers in all economic sectors. The Vietnam Social Security Organisation, founded in 1995, has a social insurance scheme covering both state and private employees for benefits including retirement, survivorship, sickness, maternity and compensation for work related injuries. The pension scheme is supported by 10 per cent and 5 per cent contributions from the employer and the employee, respectively.
The Ministry of Public Security has undertaken education programmes aimed at halting the increase in the traffic, to China each year, estimated at thousands of women, and young girls aged under 18 – who account for one in six cases.

Main cities
Hanoi (capital, estimated population 1.5 million (m) in 2012), Ho Chi Minh City (formerly Saigon) (3.4m), Hai Phong City (651,057), Da Nang City (498,562), Bien Hoa (462,938), Hue (313,922), Nha Trang (312,050), Rach Gia (282,550).

Languages spoken
The Vietnamese alphabet is an adaptation from the Roman, using tonal marks. French is spoken in official circles and some English is spoken in business circles, especially in the south. Business is usually conducted in Vietnamese or English, although many executives speak French and Russian, and a few speak Chinese.
English and French are officially taught in secondary schools.

Official language/s
Vietnamese

Media
The Ministry of Culture and Information retains firm control of press and broadcasting and laws circumscribe journalists' ability to report freely.

Press
Dailies: In Vietnamese and most with English versions, *Nhân Dân* (www.nhandan.com.vn), is the Communist Party newspaper, *Tuoi Tre* (www.tuoitre.com.vn) has a wide circulation among the young, *Quân doi Nhân Dân* (www.qdnd.vn/qdnd), is the army's newpaper.
In English, *Viet Nam News* (vietnamnews.vnanet.vn), *Saigon Giai Phong* (www.saigon-gpdaily.com.vn), is the communist newspaper in Ho Chi Minh City. In French *Le Courrier du Vietnam* (http://lecourrier.vnagency.com.vn).
Weeklies: In English the *Vietnam Courier* is a communist publication and *Doanh Nghiep* is published by the Union of Co-operatives.
Business: In Vietnamese *Tin Nhanh Chúng Khoán* (www.tinnhanhchungkhoan.vn), with stock exchange details, *Nghien Cuu Kinh Te* (www.ie.netnam.vn) a bi-monthly, academic, Economic Studies Review publication.
In English, the *Vietnam Investment Review* (www.vir.com.vn), is a weekly circulated in Vietnam, and distributed throughout Asia, Europe and the US, coupled to the online business news outlet (http://english.vietnamnet.vn). *The Saigon Times Weekly* (www.saigontimesweekly.saigonnet.vn) is another weekly. Monthlies include *Vietnam Economic Times* (www.vneconomy.com.vn/eng) with analysis and business tips, and *Vietnam Business Forum* (http://vibforum.vcci.com.vn), a Chamber of Trade and Commerce publication.
Periodicals: Several commercial periodicals that have recently begun publishing, in Vietnamese, to an international standard include *Nha Dep* a women's magazine, *Dinh Cao* (Sports and Fitness), *M* (Fashion) and *Phu Nu The Gioi* (Woman's World). Other popular publications include *Tuoi Tre* (youth), and *Lao Dong* (Labour).

Broadcasting
Radio: The national radio service, Voice of Vietnam (VOV) (www.vov.org.un) has two networks with six channels broadcasting a wide variety of show including news, current affairs culture and music and an external service with programmes in many languages including English, French and Russian. There are other radio stations, some commercial, operating regionally including Hanoi Radio (www.htv.org.vn), The Voice of Ho Chi Minh (www.voh.com.vn) and Lamp Dong Radio (www.lamdong.gov.vn).
Television: The national broadcaster is Vietnam Television (VTV) (www.vtv.org.vn) with nine channels and is available via satellite. VTV also operates the country's largest cable network VCTV (www.vctv.com.vn) and a direct-to-home (DTH) satellite service which supplies the nine free-to-air channels, nine subscription channels and around 40 international channels. Ho Chi Minh city also has a TV station (HTV) (www.htv.com.vn) with domestic and foreign programmes.
National news agency: VNA (Vietnam News Agency)

Economy
Vietnam is a densely populated that has been transitioning from the rigidities of a centrally planned economy since 1986. Agriculture's share of GDP has shrunk from 25 per cent in 2000 to 18 per cent in 2014, while industry's share increased slightly from 36 per cent to 38 per cent in the same period. The services sector constituted 44 per cent of GDP in 2014. State-owned enterprises now account for just 40 per cent of GDP. Vietnam joined the WTO in January 2007 highlighting its commitment to economic modernization. Poverty has declined significantly in recent years, and Vietnam is working to create jobs to meet the challenge of a labour force that is growing by more than one million people every year. Despite the positives, Vietnam's economy continues to face challenges from an undercapitalized banking sector and non-performing loans weighing heavily on banks and businesses.
Industrial production is centred on mineral extraction, including petroleum. Proven oil

reserves were 4.4 billion barrels in 2014, with production of 349,200 barrels per day (bpd); natural gas reserves were 699 million cubic metres with production of 9.3 billion cubic metres of which 8.4 billion cum is consumed domestically. Other minerals include coal, antimony, chromium, gold, zinc, tin and iron. Numerous gem stone deposits include rubies and sapphires. Domestically mined bauxite is used in locally produced aluminium for export. Agriculture is diverse with high productivity, so that Vietnam is a net exporter of food and one of the world largest exporters of rice.

Agriculture is based on subsistence farming, coupled with some commercial agriculture. Vietnam is the world's fifth largest producer of rice estimated at 44 million tonnes in 2013. Other cash crops include coffee, spices, tobacco and rubber. Much of the logged forests are being reforested (five million hectares) to provide timber for future exports. Vietnam also has a large fishing fleet that fishes not only in the seas of south-east Asia but also in the fresh waters of the huge network of tributaries and lakes along the Mekong River. Many varieties of fish and crustaceans are important export products as well as the pearls found in harvested oysters. Manufacturing comprises around 20 per cent of the industrial share of GDP, of which food processing, tobacco and chemicals are major industries. Textiles and clothing manufacturing are also important in the economy, but have been adversely affected by the slowdown in global trade.

The economy remained strong throughout the period of the global economic crisis, as Vietnam is not fully integrated into the global financial markets. GDP growth was 6.3 per cent in 2008, falling to 5.3 per cent in 2009, before growing to 6.8 per cent in 2010; growth in 2011 was estimated to be 5.9 per cent. GDP growth was 5.2 per cent in 2012 stabilising at 5.4 per cent in 2013. In 2014, GDP growth increased slightly to 6 per cent.

Inflation in 2008 peaked at 23.1 per cent in a year of record high fuel and food prices, before falling sharply to 6.7 per cent in 2009, which better reflected not only the decrease in global trade that cut exports and the high price of food imports, but also the ambitious stimulus package implemented by the government. Inflation was 6.6 per cent in 2013 before decreasing to 4.1 per cent in 2014.

Despite the strong growth and healthy economy, the informal economy is still estimated to be 10 per cent of official GDP, but as an entrepreneurial reaction to unemployment rather than tax evasion.

In 2014, the UN Human Development Index (HDI) ranked Vietnam 121 (out of 187) for national development in health, education and income. In 2014, 6.5 per cent of the population was living in multidimensional poverty, while 16.9 per cent lived on less than the equivalent of US$1.25 per day.

Remittances from migrant workers amounted to US$12 billion in 2014 and it forecast to increase to between US$13 billion and US$14 billion in 2015.

Vietnam has benefited from sustained high levels of foreign direct investment (FDI). In 2008 FDI was US$9.6 billion but as the global economic crisis hit investment, it fell to US$7.6 billion in 2009, before recovering marginally to US$8 billion in 2010. FDI increased slightly to US$8.4 billion in 2012 and US$8.9 billion in 2013. FDI was US$9.2 billion in 2014.

External trade

Vietnam belongs to the Association of Southeast Asian Nations (Asean) Free Trade Area (Afta) and maintains a list of goods that have preferential import duties between members. There is a programme of tariff reductions being introduced. It is a member of the World Trade Organisation and has an FTA with the US. Vietnam joined the WTO in January 2007 highlighting its commitment to economic modernization.

Rice is a key exporter while other exports include coffee, tea and rubber, as well as manufactured goods such as textiles, clothes and footwear. The growing hydrocarbon sector is providing increasing foreign exchange.

Imports

Principal imports include machinery and equipment, petroleum products, steel products, raw materials for the clothing and shoe industries, electronics, plastics and automobiles.

Main sources: China (30.4 per cent of total in 2014), South Korea (15 per cent), Japan (8.9 per cent), Thailand (4.9 per cent), Singapore (4.7 per cent) and the US (4.4 per cent).

Exports

Principal exports include clothes, shoes, electronics, seafood, crude oil, rice, coffee, wooden products and machinery.

Main destinations: US (20 per cent of total in 2014), China (10.4 per cent), Japan (10.3 per cent) and South Korea (5 per cent).

Agriculture

Farming

Agriculture accounted for around 18 per cent of GDP and employs 48 per cent of the workforce. Agricultural goods including forestry and fishery products, account for more than 50 per cent of total export revenues.

About 15–18 per cent of the total land area is cultivated arable. In the south especially, climate and soils are ideal for rice production. Considerable losses can be sustained from typhoons, flooding and drought.

In the south, 60 per cent of the land is privately farmed; in the north, 95 per cent of farms have been turned into substantial collectives. A contract system on the land spurred a marked improvement in agricultural production.

Ambitious plans include increased use of fertilisers, development of irrigation systems and resettlement of small farmers. Farmers have boosted rice production by planting high-yield varieties and using more modern farming techniques; government credit of about US$100 million was used mainly in the Mekong Delta. Half of Vietnam's rice is grown along the Mekong Delta.

Other main food crops include sugar cane, coconut, soya beans, silk, rubber, coffee, tea, tobacco and jute. Livestock raised includes pigs, buffaloes, cattle, sheep, goats, horses and poultry.

The Vietnam National Rubber Corporation (VNRC) development plans for the rubber industry will increase the area under cultivation from 250,000 hectares (ha) to 700,000ha. The VNRC estimates 1.7 million ha of natural land are available for rubber cultivation. The private sector is expected to take a 30–50 per cent share in the development of the industry.

The Vietnam National Coffee Corporation (Vinacaphe) has increased the total area of coffee cultivation to around 200,000ha, principally in the central highlands. Much cultivation in the coffee-growing highlands is under-reported due to a special tax regime.

Fishing

Fishing has traditionally been an important source of export earnings. The sector is facing severe depletion of inshore stocks. Coastal waters were typically overfished by the poorly equipped Vietnamese fleet, whose boats could only stay at sea for short periods of time. Poor infrastructure and processing technology is compounded by a lack of skills required for deep-water fishing on the part of fishermen.

Main fish products are shrimp, freshwater fish, catfish, dried squid and tuna.

Forestry

About 50 per cent of the total land area is forested. Forestry is developing, with 12–15 per cent of the removed volume of timber classified as industrial wood.

Legal exploitation from around one million hectares (ha) of plantations produces a domestic supply of approximately three million cubic metres of wood annually, but insufficient for the processing industry. The industry is estimated to have the potential to approach a turnover of US$1 billion annually, especially following the relaxation of import licences and quotas for domestic processors importing wood. The domestic industry is likely to remain dependent on felled and imported wood of dubious legal status at least over the medium-term.

Industry and manufacturing

Industry contributed 38 per cent to GDP in 2014 and employed 21 per cent of the workforce. The heavy industrial base is located mostly in the north, and in the past was adversely affected by conflicts with China. The economy's leading industries were incorporated into the state sector following the communist take-over and most remain in state hands. They include oil and gas, food and foodstuff processing, synthetic yarns and fabrics, textiles and engineering, cement, fertilisers, glass, rubber products, tobacco, chemicals, paper and steel.

In the steel sector, for example, there have historically been four state owned steel production groups in Vietnam, each with production ranging from 200,000 to 400,000 tonnes per annum. Of some 6,000 state-owned enterprises, only 400 have been equitized, while 2,000 have been organised into 'general corporations' (akin to conglomerates) and 77 'special corporations' tending to reinforce monopoly conditions.

With increasing FDI flow into its manufacturing sector, Vietnam stands a great chance of leaping ahead and replace China as the new production centre along with Malaysia and Thailand in 2015. Foreign investors registered US$11.4 billion for manufacturing projects. Although FDI is not as high in Vietnam as China, Indonesia or Thailand, Vietnam has a good location and boasts a source of labour, which is plentiful and cheap. Vietnam's pending opportunities comes from international producers' recent shifts to South-east Asian countries from China, which is losing its appeal with slowing economic growth and surging labour costs. In order to achieve these predictions, Vietnam needs to develop its supporting industries, only 36 per cent of local manufactures take part in the global production network, compared to nearly 60 per cent in Thailand and Malaysia.

Tourism

Vietnam relies on its natural beauty and rich cultural sites as its principal tourist attractions, since 2009 it has also chosen one province to promote vigorously each year, not only overseas but also domestically, emphasising local cuisine, tours and festivals. It has also joined the Asean Tourism Strategic Plan to develop unified strategies that enhance tourist industries and boost visitor numbers to the region.

There are seven sites included on Unesco's World Heritage List, ranging from ancient and historic monuments, towns and the Imperial Citadel of Thang Long (Hanoi) as well as the Phong Nha-Ke Bang National park and spectacular Ha Long Bay. These are among Vietnam's most popular and revered tourist, cultural and religious sites.

Travel and tourism contributed 9.3 per cent to GDP (US$16.4 billion) and provided employment to 7.7 per cent of the workforce (4,088,500 jobs) in the same period. Vietnam is predicted to attract 5,941,000 international tourists in 2015, a 7.4 per cent increase on 2014. The majority of tourists arrived from China, South Korea, Japan and then the United States.

Mining

Vietnam is believed to possess a wide range of minerals. The sector is relatively undeveloped, owing to lack of investment and a discouraging legislative environment.

Mining is largely concentrated in the north. Commercially significant quantities of iron ore, apatite, chromite, rubies and gold exist. There are reserves of manganese, titanium ore, bauxite, tin, copper, zinc, lead, nickel, graphite and mica. Other minerals include phosphates, salt, tin, chromium, wolfram, silver, antimony, pirit, kaolin and limestone.

Vietnam imports a number of metals, including steel.

Hydrocarbons

Proven oil reserves were 4.4 billion barrels in 2014 and production was 349,200 barrels per day (bpd). Vietnam is the third largest oil producer in south-east Asia (after Indonesia and Malaysia).

The largest oil fields are Back Ho, Rang Dong, Hang Ngoc and Dai Hung. The country's first refinery, a 148,000 barrels per day (bpd) plant, was opened in 2009 and will provide over 30 per cent of Vietnam's fuel demand. The state-owned PetroVietnam Exploration Production Corporation (PVEP) had to take over the US$3 billion project when foreign companies pulled out claiming political interests were compromising its economic efficiency. The refinery is sited in Dung Quat Bay in the central province of Quang Ngai, where unemployment is high but is hundreds of kilometres from either industrial hubs or offshore oil fields. PVEP has begun offshore surveys of the country's central costal region. The Russian energy company Lukoil purchased a 50 per cent interest in Vietnam's Hanoi Trough-02 offshore block, which has already identified several prospects.

PetroVietnam largely controls upstream activities in the oil sector as the only firm licensed to conduct petroleum activities; foreign investors must conduct their activities in co-operation with it.

Vietnam, along with China, Taiwan, Brunei, Malaysia and The Philippines, claims the potentially oil-rich Spratly Islands.

Proven natural gas reserves were 699 billion cubic metres (cum) in 2014 with production of 9.3 billion cum. In 2009 PVEP announced it had located its largest gas field off the northern coast, in the Hac Long field, with a flow rate of 400,000 cum per day.

Vietnam had coal reserves of 150 million tonnes in 2012, all of which is the valuable anthracite, located in Quang Ninh province. Coal is the principal source of commercial energy, meeting about half of Vietnam's annual primary energy needs. Production totalled 24.9 million tonnes oil equivalent in 2011. Vietnam exports around five million tonnes of coal, mainly to China and Japan.

Energy

Total installed electricity generating capacity was 26.3GW in 2012. The single largest contributor in the energy mix was hydropower with 45 per cent; conventional thermal power stations provided over 55 per cent, of which coal provided most. Natural gas-fired power plants are beginning to be introduced. Although domestic demand is increasing Vietnam still has one of the lowest per capita energy consumption in south-east Asia.

The Asian Development Bank (ADB) has been involved in promoting the Greater Mekong Sub-region (GMS) electricity market to form a regional electricity grid, which incorporates the uneven load demands and different resource bases. By 2008 a regional energy trading and sustainable development scheme was in place and bilateral arrangements included electricity from Laos being exported to Vietnam, which in turn exports electricity to China. Future expansion plans of the GMS network include two other power lines, from Cambodia and Laos. Vietnam has huge potential for hydropower and with growing regional demand for energy should allow expansion of this resource at the same time as natural gas power stations become operational.

Financial markets

The State Capital Investment Corporation (SCIC) and the US-based Morgan Stanley Investment Bank agreed in 2007, to form a securities joint venture; the first in Vietnam's Communist-ruled economy.

Stock exchange

Hochiminh Stock Exchange (HSE)

Banking and insurance

VietcomBank regulates matters relating to exchange control and is responsible for all transactions involving foreign exchange, including bills of exchange, foreign remittances, traveller's cheques and foreign currencies.

In 2005 the government decided that VietcomBank was to be the first state bank to be offered for partial privatisation and ostensibly to operate on purely commercial principles. In preparation for public ownership VietcomBank reduced its portfolio of state enterprised down to 50 per cent and reported a first-half year gross profit of US$82 million in 2005, up by 41 per cent on the previous year. The decision to part-privatise was based on the government's need to sustain economic growth.

There are four large state banks, which account for around 70 per cent of total lending, of which 60 per cent of loans are awarded to state entities and some are of dubious financial viability. Official figures for bad debt levels do not exist but officials in the state bank estimate it could be as high as 20 per cent.

Central bank

State Bank of Vietnam

Main financial centre

Hanoi

Time

GMT plus seven hours

Geography

Vietnam is bordered to the north by the People's Republic of China, to the west and south-west by Laos and Cambodia and to the east by the South China Sea. The country has 3,200km of coastline, 1,150km of land border with China and 1,650km of land border with Laos.

The country is broad in the north and south and narrow in its central region. There are two main cultivated areas, the Red River Delta (15,000 square km) in the north and the Mekong Delta (60,000 square km) in the south. Three-quarters of the country consists of mountains and hills, the highest point being Phan Si Pan mountain in the Hoang Lien Son range in the far north-west of Vietnam.

Hemisphere

Northern

Climate

Located in the tropical monsoon zone, Vietnam's climate is hot and humid with abundant seasonal rainfall.

In the north, climatic changes occur in four seasons: spring (January–April) brings light rain and constant humidity; summer (May to July) is very hot, humid and rainy; autumn (August–October) brings drier weather but sometimes includes storms; winter (October–early January) is cooler.

In the centre and the south it is hot year round and there are only two seasons: a rainy season (May–October) and a dry season (October–April).

Average annual temperatures in Hanoi are 29 degrees Celsius (C) in the hot season and 17 degrees C in the cold season; Hue in central Vietnam: 29 degrees C and 21 degrees C; Ho Chi Minh City: 30 degrees C and 24 degrees C.

The average annual rainfall in Hanoi is 1,680mm; Hue: 2,890mm; Ho Chi Minh City: 1979mm.

Dress codes

In Hanoi in the summer (officially from 15 April to 15 October), no jackets are required even for the most formal occasions. In winter, a jacket is more usual but a bush jacket is acceptable even when the weather is warm.

In the south, informal tropical-weight clothing is all that is needed at any time of the year. A jacket and tie is not necessary. In the highlands, where it is cooler, a bush jacket is acceptable any time.

Entry requirements

Passports

Required by all and must be valid for one month beyond the date of departure.

Visa

Required by all. Tourist visas are issued for visits up to one month long and can be extend when in Vietnam.

Business visas are issued only after authorities in Vietnam have approved sponsorship by a local company or organisation. If the business visitor does not have a local sponsor, assistance can be obtained from the embassy.

For a list of embassies worldwide where applications may be obtained see www.mofa.gov.vn/en, see *Countries and Regions*.

All visitors must retain the yellow portion of the immigration arrival-departure card, to be surrendered to authorities when leaving.

Currency advice/regulations

The import and export of local currency is prohibited. The import of foreign currency is unlimited, but amounts over US$3,000 (or equivalent) should be declared on arrival; export is limited to the amount declared.

Major hard currency may be freely traded however outside cities and main towns they are less likely to be accepted.

Travellers cheques (in US dollars) are widely accepted in banks and hotels.

Customs

Personal items are duty-free.

Antiques cannot be exported. Caution is advised when purchasing souvenirs made of ivory, silver, gold and stone, as you may require a permit from customs to take them out of Vietnam.

Prohibited imports

Firearms, anti-government propaganda, pornography and illegal drugs; drug smuggling is a capital offence.

Health (for visitors)

Mandatory precautions

Vaccination certificate required for yellow fever if travelling from an infected area.

Advisable precautions

Vaccinations for diphtheria, tetanus, hepatitis A, cholera and typhoid are recommended. Other vaccinations that may be advised include tuberculosis, hepatitis B, and Japanese encephalitis. Malaria prophylaxes are required including mosquito nets, insect sprays and long clothing at night.

Use only bottled or boiled water for drinks, washing teeth and making ice. Eat only well cooked meals, preferably served hot; vegetables should be cooked and fruit peeled. Avoid pork and salad and food from street vendors. A full first-aid kit, including disposable syringes, would be useful. Any medicines required by the traveller should be brought into the country. Medical insurance is essential, including emergency evacuation.

Hotels

Redevelopment and expansion has increased hotel accommodation in both Ho Chi Minh City and Hanoi where the standard of hotel accommodation is equal to Western hotels. Provincial town also have adequate facilities.

Tipping is discretionary; it is not a Vietnamese tradition although staff in restaurants and hotels may expect to be tipped.

Credit cards

Are accepted in more outlets but only in main towns and cities; where ATMs can be found.

Public holidays (national)

Fixed dates

1 Jan (New Year's Day), 30 Apr (Liberation of Ho Chi Minh City/Saigon), 1 May (May Day), 2 Sep (National Day).

Variable dates

Tet Nguyen Dan (Vietnamese New Year) (Jan/Feb – three days)

Working hours

Banking

Mon–Fri: 0730/0800–1130, 1300–1600.

Business

Mon–Sat: 0730–1130, 1230–1630 in summer (15 Apr to 15 Oct); 0800–1200, 1230–1630 in winter (16 Oct to 14 Apr).

Government

Mon–Sat: 0730–1130, 1230–1630 in summer; 0800–1200, 1230–1630 in winter.

Shops
Many small privately owned shops stay open seven days a week, often until late at night.

Telecommunications
Mobile/cell phones
There are 900 and 900/1800 GSM services available throughout most of the country.

Electricity supply
Electric current is 220V, 50Hz with round two-pin plug. Electricity supplies can be problematic, laptop computers should be protected by a surge suppressor.

Social customs/useful tips
Business is conducted slowly with many familiarisation meetings. Be patient with language difficulties and red tape. The combination of Confucian interaction norms and communist bureaucracy may create large amounts of the latter.

Most Vietnamese names consist of a family name, a middle name and a given name, in that order. The given name is used in address but to do so without a title is considered as expressing either great intimacy between friends or arrogance of the sort a superior would use with his or her inferior. The titles, *Bac* or *Ong* (Mr) (in increasing seniority), *Ba* (Mrs), *Co* or *Chi* (Miss) precedes a Vietnamese given name (sometimes full name). Wives may retain their own names and children take their father's family name. The middle name may be common to all the male members of a family.

It is rude to show the soles of the feet/shoes. Do not touch anyone's head, not even that of a child. When handing over or receiving anything, the right hand should generally be used. On formal occasions it is considered polite to use both hands. Etiquette for male visitors is to shake hands with a man but not with a woman, unless she offers her hand.

Shoes must be removed before entering any religious building. It is also customary to remove shoes before entering a Vietnamese home, but in modern residences the requirement is no longer observed.

Security
Most visits to Vietnam are trouble-free and serious or violent crimes against foreigners are rare. There have been some reports of aggravated theft and assault in areas frequented by tourists in Ho Chi Minh City, prompting the city police chief, Nguyen Chi Dung, to say that tourists who were robbed would receive an apology from the police.

Outside Hanoi and Ho Chi Minh City, the provision of prompt consular assistance is difficult because of poorly developed infrastructure throughout Vietnam, meaning travel and health insurance are well advised. Travel is restricted near military installations and in some border areas. Unexploded mines, bombs and shells are a hazard in former battlefield areas.

Getting there
Air
National airline: Vietnam Airlines (formerly Hang Khong Vietnam and the General Civil Aviation Administration of Vietnam).

International airport/s: Tan Son Nhat (SGN), 7km from Ho Chi Minh City, facilities include a café, duty-free shopping, VIP services, business lounge, currency exchange, limousine service and car rental with driver.

A new terminal, to handle up to 15 million passengers a year and at cost of US$240 million, was begun in 2004. The first phase of construction is expected to be completed by 2007.

Noi Bai (HAN), 38km from Hanoi, facilities include a café, duty-free shopping and currency exchange.

Danang International Airport, five-minutes drive to Danang City.

Metered taxis are available at all airports.

Airport tax: International departures US$14, excluding transit passengers.

Surface
Road: There is overland access to Vietnam via China (Quang Ninh and Lang Son border crossings in the north), Cambodia (Moc Bai) and Laos (Lao Bao). Status of overland routes should be checked, as passage has not always been practicable.

Rail: Hanoi and Nanning, in China's Guangxi province, are linked by rail. China and Vietnam have also started a second cross-border rail service. The 761km rail link between Hanoi and Kunming, the capital of Yunnan (south-west China), and which runs through the northern Vietnamese border town of Lao Cai, is being upgraded with work expected to be completed by 2008. There is rail connection linking Hanoi with Pingxiang in China's Guangxi province via the Dong Dang border point in Lang Son province, 200km north of Hanoi. Construction of a new line linking Phnom Penh and Ho Chi Minh City is underway. This project is part of the Asian Development Bank's (ADB) Greater Mekong sub-regional co-operation scheme as part of the Trans-Asia railway.

Services include air-conditioned day and overnight sleeping carriages and restaurant cars.

Water: There are daily and weekly ferry services along the Mekong River from Phnom Penh (Cambodia) to Chau Doc and Can Tho.

Main port/s: Ho Chi Minh City, Haiphong, and Danang.

Getting about
National transport
Air: Vietnam Airlines, provides regular scheduled services between Hanoi, Hue, Danang and Ho Chi Minh City. Flights should be booked well in advance.

Road: There is a 88,000km road network in relatively good condition; roads are better in the south. The coastal Route 1 between Hanoi and Ho Chi Minh City can become impassable in heavy rain. A four-wheel drive vehicle is advisable outside the major centres.

Rail: There is over 2,650km rail network in various degrees of maintenance. The main line between Hanoi-Ho Chi Minh City (travel time 30 hrs minimum) is efficient with first class accommodation with air-conditioning, sleeper carriages and restaurant cars. Long-distance trains are more reliable and comfortable, as well as offering a faster service. Fares for foreigners are comparable to internal air fares.

Water: There are several local ferry services including hydrofoils between Mong Cai and Cat Ba and motorboats between Phu Quoc and Rach Gia.

City transport
Taxis: Taxis serving the hour-long route between downtown Hanoi and the city's airport will typically be ancient and non-air-conditioned vehicles. In Ho Chi Minh City, taxis are modern. Tipping is discretionary; taxi drivers do not expect to be tipped. Taxis and motorbikes are a faster form of hired transport. When travelling by taxi it may be advisable to note down the registration number of the driver (displayed on the rear side of the vehicle), for security reasons.

In Hanoi, cycle-rickshaws (the famous *cyclo*) are available, but slow and best for sightseeing.

Car hire
Personal car hire is not allowed, all hire vehicles come with a driver; hiring can be from half a day to over a week. A four-wheel-drive vehicle is required outside major cities.

BUSINESS DIRECTORY
The addresses listed below are a selection only. While World of Information makes every endeavour to check these addresses, we cannot guarantee that changes have not been made, especially to telephone numbers and area codes. We would welcome any corrections.

Telephone area codes
The international direct dialling code (IDD) for Vietnam is +84, followed by area code and subscriber's number:

Da Nang	51	Ho Chi Minh City	8
Haiphong	31	Lang Son	25
Hanoi	4	Lao Cai	20

Useful telephone numbers
English-language directory enquiries: 108
Police: 113
Fire: 114
Ambulance: 115

Chambers of Commerce

American Chamber of Commerce in Vietnam - Hanoi, Press Club, 59A Ly Thai To Street, Hanoi (tel: 934-2790; fax 934-2787; e-mail: info@amchamhanoi.com).

American Chamber of Commerce in Vietnam - Ho Chi Minh City, New World Hotel, 76 Le Lai Street, Ho Chi Minh City (tel: 824-3562; fax: 824-3572; e-mail: amcham@hcm.vnn.vn).

British Business Group Vietnam - Hanoi, Metropole Hotel, 56 Ly Thai To Street, Hanoi (tel: 936-2420; fax: 936-2419; e-mail: eurochamhanoi@hn.vnn.vn).

British Business Group Vietnam - Ho Chi Minh City, 25 Le Duan Boulevard, Ho Chi Minh City (tel: 829-8430; fax: 822-5172; e-mail: bbgv.hcmc@hcm.fpt.vn).

Vietnam Chamber of Commerce and Industry, 9 Dao Duy Anh Street, Hanoi (tel: 574-3084; fax: 574-2020; e-mail: vcci@hn.vnn.vn).

Banking

ANZ International Merchant Banking Division, 14 Le Thai To Street, Hanoi (tel: 825-8190; fax: 825-8188/9).

Bank of America, 27 Ly Thuong Kiet St, Hanoi (tel: 824-9316; fax: 824-9322).

Crédit Lyonnais, Han Man Officetel, 65 Nguyen du St., Quan 1, Ho Chi Minh City (tel: 299-226; fax: 296-465).

Indovina Bank Ltd (first joint-venture bank), 36 Ton That Dam, D1, Ho Chi Minh City (tel: 822-4995, 823-0130; fax: 823-0131).

Thai Military Bank, Unit 113, 1 Floor, Saigon Trade Center, No. 37 Ton Due Thang Street, Ben Nghe Ward, District 1, Ho Chi Minh City (tel: 910-0606, 910-1388/90; fax: 910-0505).

Industrial and Commercial Bank of Vietnam, 108 Tran Hung Dao, Hanoi (tel: 942-1066, 942-1186; fax: 942-1143).

Central bank

State Bank of Vietnam, 49 Ly Thai To Street, Hoan Kiem District, Hanoi (tel: 825-8388; fax: 825-8385; internet: www.sbv.gov.vn).

Stock exchange

Hochiminh Stock Exchange (HSE), http://hose.vse.vn

Hanoi Securities Trading Centre (HSTC), http://en.hastc.org.vn

Travel information

Ben Thanh Tourist Service, 165 Pham Ngui Lao Street, 1st District, Ho Chi Minh City (tel: 886-0635; fax: 836-1953).

Cathay Pacific Airways, 58 Dong Khoi Road, District 1, Ho Chi Minh City (tel: 822-3203; fax: 822-2679); also at 27 Ly Thuong Kiet Street, Hanoi (tel: 824-9427; fax: 822-2679).

Quang Nam-Da Nang Tourist Company (Da Nang Tourism), 68 Bach Dang Street, Da Nang (tel: 822-112, 821-423, 822-213).

Thua Thien-Hue Tourist Company, No. 9 Ngo Quyen Street, Hue City (tel: 83-288, 82-369).

Sasco Travel (for limousine service), Sasco Building, Tan Son Nhat Airport, Ho Chi Minh City (tel: 848-7142; fax: 848-7141; internet: www.sascotravel.com.vn).

Viet Value Travel Ltd (for car hire), 4th Floor ILU Building, 18 Yen Phu, Ba Dinh, Hanoi (tel: 715-0753; fax: 715-0754; email: vietvaluetravel@yahoo.com; internet: http://vietvaluetravel.com).

Vietnamtourism, 30A Ly Thuong Kiet Street, Hanoi (tel: 825-5552, 826-4148; fax: 855-7583).

Vietnam Airlines (formerly Hang Khong Vietnam and the General Civil Aviation Administration of Vietnam), Gailem Airport, Hanoi (tel: 827-2643; fax: 827-2291).

National tourist organisation offices

Vinatour, 54 Nguyen Du, Hanoi (tel: 942-4490; 942-3997; fax: 942-2707; internet: www.vinatour.com.vn).

Vinatour, 28 Le Thi Hong Gam, District 1, Ho Chi Minh City, (tel: 217- 925, 297-026; fax: 299-868; email: vinatour-saigonoffice@saigonnet.vn).

Ministries

Ministry of Agriculture and Rural Development, 6 Ngoc Ha Street, Hanoi; International Relations Department (tel: 845-9670/71/72; fax: 845-4319).

Ministry of Construction, 37 Le Dai Hanh Street, Hanoi; International Relations Department (tel: 825-5497; fax: 825-2153).

Ministry of Culture and Information, 51-53 Ngo Quyen, Hanoi.

Ministry of Education & Training, 49 Dai Co Viet Street, Hanoi; International Relations Department (tel: 869-4961; fax: 826-3243).

Ministry of Energy, 18 Tran Nguyen Han, Hanoi.

Ministry of Finance, 8 Phgan Huy Chu Street, Hanoi; International Relations Section (tel: 826-2061, 824-0437; fax: 826-2266).

Ministry of Fisheries, 57 Ngoc Khanh, Hanoi.

Ministry of Foreign Affairs, 1 Ton That Dam Street, Hanoi; International Organisation Department (tel: 845-6525, 845-5900; fax: 845-9205).

Ministry of Forestry, 123 Lo Duc, Hanoi.

Ministry of Health, 138 Duong Giang Vo, Hanoi.

Ministry of Industry, 7 Trang Thi Street, Hanoi (fax: 826-9033); International Relations Department (tel: 826-7988, 825-9887).

Ministry of Justice, 25a Cat Linh Street, Hanoi; Internatinal Relations Department (tel: 843-0931; fax: 825-4835).

Ministry of Labour, War Invalids and Social Affairs, 2 Dinh Le Street, Hanoi; International Relations Department (tel: 826-9534; fax: 824-8036).

Ministry of Marine Products, 57 Ngoc Khanh Street, Hanoi; International Relations Department (tel: 832-5607; fax: 832-6702).

Ministry of National Defence, 28A Dien Bien Phy Street, Hanoi (tel: 826-8101; fax: 845-7195); International Relations Department, 33 A Pham Ngu Lao Street, Hanoi (tel: 825-3646).

Ministry of Planning and Investment (background information on aid-financed projects), 2 Hoang Van Thu, Hanoi; External Economic Relations Department (tel: 845-8241 (ext 3505); fax: 823-0161).

Ministry of Public Health, 138 A Giango Vo, Hanoi; International Relations Department (tel: 844-2463, 846-4050; fax: 846-4051).

Ministry of Sciences, Technology and Environment, 39 Tran Hung Dao Street, Hanoi; International Relations Department (tel: 826-3388; fax: 825-2733).

Ministry of Trade, 31 Trang Tien Street, Hanoi; (tel: 826-2522; fax: 826-4696).

Ministry of Transport, 80 Tran Hung Dao Street, Hanoi; International Relations Department (tel: 825-3301; fax: 825-5851).

Office of the National Assembly, 35 Ngo Quyen, Hanoi (tel: 252-861).

Other useful addresses

ASEAN Investment Promotion Agency, Ministry of Planning and Investment, c/o ASEAN Vietnam, 7 Chu Van An Street, Hanoi (fax: 843-5758).

ASEAN Secretariat, 70 A Jl Sisingamangaraja, Jakarta 12110, Indonesia (tel: (+62-21) 726-2991, 724-3372; fax: (+62-21) 724-3504, 739-8234).

Asian Development Bank, Vietnam Resident Mission, c/o State Bank of Vietnam, Room 401, 16 Tong Dan Street, Hanoi (tel: 824-5908; fax: 824-6171).

British Consulate General, 25 Le Duan, District 1, Ho Chi Minh City (tel: 829-2433; fax: 822-5740).

British Embassy, 31 Hai Ba Trung, Hanoi (tel: 825-2510; fax: 826-5762).

British Embassy Commercial Office, 100 Tue Tinh Street, Hanoi (tel: 822-6875, 822-9455, 822-9457; fax: 822-9457).

Commerical and Tourist Services Centre, 1 Ba Trieu Street, Hanoi (tel: 826-8499; fax: 826-5388).

Department General for Post and Telecomunication, 18 Nguyen Du Street, Hanoi; International Relations Department (tel: 822-6622; fax: 822-6590).

Electricity of Vietnam (EVN), 18 Tran Nguyen Han Street, Hanoi (tel: 826-3725; fax: 824-9462).

Foreign Trade & Investment Development Centre, 92-96 Nguyen Hue Ave, District 1, Ho Chi Minh City (tel: 822-2982; fax: 822-2983).

Investip (will provide business contacts), 1 bis Yet Kieu Street, Hanoi (tel: 826-4707; fax: 826-6185).

The National Oil Service Company of Vietnam, 2 Le Loi Street, Vung Tau Srv, Ho Chi Minh City (tel: 897-562; fax: 897-664).

Petrovietnam, 22 Ngo Quyen Street, Hanoi; International Relations Department (tel: 825-2526; fax: 826-5942).

Saigon Shipping Company (Saigonship), 9 Nguyen Cong Tru Street, District 1, Ho Chi Minh City (tel: 896-316, 896-302; fax: 825-067).

State Committee for Co-operation and Investment Consultancy Service Centre (will provide business contacts), 56 Quoc Tu Giam Street, Hanoi (tel: 825-4970; fax: 825-9271).

Tea Estate Agencies Ltd, 31 Nguyen Gia Thieu Street, Hanoi (tel: 822-8556; fax: 822-7923).

US Embassy, 7 Lang Ha, Dong Da District, Hanoi (tel: 843-1500).

Vietnam Civil Aviation, Gia Lam Airport, Hanoi; International Relations Department (tel: 827-2241).

Vietnam Fund Management Co Ltd (investment into Vietnamese companies and projects), 3 Trieu Viet Vuong Street, Hanoi (tel: 822-8632, 826-6315; fax: 822-8648); 4 Dong Khoi, District 1, Ho Chi Minh City (tel: 829-1074, 829-7206; fax: 823-0685).

Vietnam National Foreign Trade Corporation (TRANSAF), 46 Ngo Quyen, Hanoi.

Vietnamese Embassy (US), Suite 400, 1233 20th Street, NW, Washington DC 20036 (tel: (+1-202) 861-0737; fax: (+1-202) 202-861-0917; email: info@vietnamembassy-usa.org).

National news agency: VNA (Vietnam News Agency), 5 Ly Thuong Kiet Street, Hoan Kiem District, Hanoi (tel: 933-2418; fax: 933-0970; internet: www.vnagency.com.vn).

Internet sites

Asian Development Bank: www.adb.org/vrm

General Statistics Office (GSO): www.gso.gov.vn

Vietnam Access (trade fairs and business opportunities): http://vietnamaccess.com

Vietnam Business Journal: www.viam.com

VietnamNet.vn (news website)

Wallis and Futuna

KEY FACTS

Official name: Wallis and Futuna

Head of State: President of France François Hollande (PS) (from 15 May 2012), represented by *Administrateur Supérieur* Michel Jeanjean (from June 2010)

Head of government: President of the Territorial Assembly Mikaele Kulimoetoke (from 26 November 2014)

Ruling party: Coalition of various political parties and independent members, usually categorised into those that are 'left-leaning' and those that are 'right-leaning'. Currently the collated right holds more seats in the assembly.

Area: 144 square km – Wallis (or Uvea): 77.6km; Futuna: 64.4km

Population: 15,507 (July 2012)*

Capital: Mata Utu (on Wallis)

Official language: Wallisian, Futunian, French

Currency: Change Franc Pacifique franc (CFPf) = 100 centimes

Exchange rate: CFPf106.68 per US$ (Sept 2015); (pegged CFPf119.25 per euro)

* estimated figure

COUNTRY PROFILE

Around 1400 AD Polynesian navigators from Tonga landed on Uvea and Samoans on Futuna and Alofi.

Historical profile

1616 The islands of Futuna and Alofi were sighted by two Dutch navigators, Willem Cornelius van Schouten and Jacob le Maire, who re-named them the Hoorn Islands.

1767 Samuel Wallis, the English navigator, sighted the island of Uvea, and renamed it Wallis.

1820 The Takumasiva royal dynasty was restored in the kingdom of Uvea (Wallis).

1837 The first European settlers were French, led by missionaries.

1842 Wallis was granted French protection following a local rebellion.

1887 Queen Amelia of Uvea signed a treaty, establishing an official French protectorate.

1888, The Kings of Alo and Sigave (Futuna and Alofi) signed a treaty establishing an official French protectorate.

1924 The protectorates were annexed and became an official French colony

1942 US forces used Wallis as a strategic air base during the Second World War.

1959 Following a referendum, Wallis and Fortuna voted to become a Térritoire d'Outre-Mer (TOM) (Overseas Territory).

1959 Tomasi Kulimoetoke II became the Lavelua (King of Uvea), ending a period of instability within the royal family.

1961 Wallis and Futuna became a TOM and adopted the French constitution.

1999 Sagato Alofi became the the Tuiagaifo (King of Alo); Pasilio Keletaona became the Keletaona (King of Sigave).

2002 The ruling right-wing Rassemblement pour la République (RPR) (Rally for the Republic) and its affiliates retained a majority in the Territorial Assembly elections. Christian Job was appointed *administrateur supérieur*, replacing Alain Waquet. Wallis and Futuna's only newspaper, the weekly *Te Fenua Fo'ou*, closed down after being subjected to threats and raids from the local (traditional) authorities.

2003 Through a constitutional change, Wallis and Fortuna became a collectivités d'outre-mer (COM) (overseas collectivity). A limited census was undertaken.

2004 Xavier de Furst was appointed *administrateur supérieur*.

2006 Richard Didier was appointed *administrateur supérieur, Préfet*.

2007 Following parliamentary elections Pesamino Teputai became president of the territorial assembly. Tomasi Kulimoetoke II, the King of Uvea, died.

2008 Kapiliele (Gabriel) Faupala was chosen by members of the traditional council of ministers to succeed the late King Tomasi, who had designated him to follow him as king. Philippe Paolantoni was appointed *administrateur supérieur*. A census was undertaken recording a population of 13,484.

2009 The results of the 2008 census were published, which showed a decrease in the population (down by 1,460 since 2003), and an ageing population, with 11 per cent over 60 years (up from 7 per cent in 1996).

2010 In June, Micheal Jeanjean was appointed *administrateur supérieur*.

2011 In July, the Minister for Overseas Territories, Marie-Luce Penchard, joined the islands' ceremony in celebration of the fifty years since Wallis and Futuna became a French territory.

2012 The French presidential elections, held in April and May, were won by the socialist candidate, François Hollande, with 51.63 per cent of the vote; incumbent Nicolas Sarkozy had 48.37 per cent; turnout was 80.35 per cent. On 15 May François Hollande took office as president and head of state. David Vergé was elected as Wallis and Futuna's representive

2013 The 2013 Pacific Mini Games were held in Mata-Utu from 2–12 September. Athletes from 22 Pacific countries and territories participated.

2014 Wallis and Futuna suffered a moderate, 4.5 magnitude, earthquake on 21 August.

2015 Wallis and Futuna competed in the Pacific Games held in Papua New Guinea from 4 to 18 July.

Political structure

Constitution

28 September 1958 (French Fifth Republic)

In 1961, Wallis and Futuna became a Térritoire d'Outre-Mer (TOM) (Overseas Territory) of France.

Wallis and Futuna is administered by an administrator (administrateur supérieur) appointed by France and is represented in

the French parliament by a deputy and a senator.
The islands are divided into three administrative districts based on the ancient kingdoms: *Uvea* (Wallis), *Alo* (Futuna) and *Sigave* (Futuna).
Wallis and Futuna is the only French territory where a native system of monarchy has been allowed to survive. There are three traditional kings: the Lavelua (King of Uvea), the Tuiagaifo (King of Alo) and the Keletaona (the title of King of Sigave depends on family heritage, and therefore, he has the title of Tui Sigave, Tamolevai or Keletaona).
In *Uvea*, there is a kivalu, the equivalent of a prime minister, who is appointed by the King.

Form of state

Térritoire d'Outre-Mer (TOM) (Overseas Territory) of France

The executive

The President of the French Republic is the head of state, represented by an appointed *administrateur supérieur, Préfet* (supreme administrator) who exercises executive power with the right of veto over some of the territorial assembly decisions.

National legislature

The Assemblée Territoriale (Territorial Assembly) has 20 members, elected by popular vote for five-year terms, (13 from Wallis and seven from Futuna). The assembly deals with local affairs although the administrator has the right of veto over many of the Assembly's decisions. Once the Territorial Assembly is elected, the members then vote for the President.
As Collectivités d'Outre-mer (COM) (overseas collectivity) Wallis and Fortuna is a first-order administrative division of France and citizens vote in French elections for president and return a representative for Wallis and Fortuna to both the French National Assembly and Senate. It is divided into three districts that exactly match the traditional chiefdoms, Uvea, Sigave and Alo.

Legal system

French law is applied while the traditional kings deal with customary law.

Last elections

17 and 24 March 2013. The 2012 elections were annulled after financial irregularities were found with David Verge's victory, necessitating a by-election one year later.
Results: Parliamentary: Napole Polutélé, standing as an independent candidate but allied to the broader right-leaning parties, garnered 37.4% in the first round and 37.5% in the second round. Mikaele Kulimoetoke of the left-leaning alliance won 33.1% and 32.3% respectively, whilst Laurianne Verge of the Socialist Party took 29.5% and 30.2%. Despite being elected on a right-wing ticket, within 6 months Polutélé had joined the Socialist Party in order to "lobby" more effectively.

Next elections

2017 (territorial assembly)

Political parties

Ruling party

Coalition of various political parties and independent members, usually categorised into those that are 'left-leaning' and those that are 'right-leaning'. Currently the collated right holds more seats in the assembly.
Many people emigrate to New Caledonia for work.

Population

15,507 (July 2012)*
According to the 2008 census the population was 13,445, a decrease of 1,460 since 2003. It also showed an ageing population with 11 per cent over 60 years (a growth from 7 per cent in 1996), due in large part to the many young workers who leave to search for employment in New Caledonia.
Population density: 55 inhabitants per square km.
Annual growth rate: 1 per cent (2003)

Ethnic make-up

Polynesian

Religions

Roman Catholic

Education

Compulsory education is provided free-of-charge. Primary education is either provided by public funds or by Roman Catholic missionaries. Secondary education is pubically provided.
Compulsory years: Five to 14

Health

Healthcare is publically funded. There is a 60-bed hospital on Wallis and a 23-bed hospital on Futuna; severe emergency medical cases are evacuation to New Caledonia or Australia.
Life expectancy: 73 (estimate 2003)
Child (under 5 years) mortality rate (per 1,000): 21 per 1,000 live births.

Welfare

While there is no social security benefits offered to the general community, the state assist in the care of old aged pensioners.

Main cities

Mata Utu, on Wallis (capital, estimated population 1,400 in 2012), Alele (1,144), Toloke (810), Aka'aka (804); Kolia (on Futuna) (455).

Languages spoken

Official language/s

Wallisian, Futunian, French

Media

The islands maintain international and local contacts for news and information through electronic media.

Broadcasting

Radio: The French RFO (http://wallisfutuna.rfo.fr) service provides overseas radio programmes for broadcasting.

Economy

The economy is based on subsistence agriculture and fishing and it has been estimated that up to 25 per cent of the economy is based on the barter system. Public administration (through grants from France) is the single largest source of economic activity, followed by licensing of fishing rights, import taxes and remittances from migrant workers.
Although tourism could be an important source of foreign exchange, it is an under-developed sector due to the isolation of the islands and the distances for visitors plus the lack of amenities on the islands. In October 2015 some of the leaders of the islands claimed they were unhappy with the French administration and raised the question of independence.

External trade

As a Térritoire d'Outre-Mer (TOM) of France, Wallis and Futuna is integrated as an outermost region of the European Union and EU trade agreements may apply.

Imports

Principal imports are chemicals, machinery, vehicles and consumer goods.
Main sources: France (typically 97 per cent of total), Australia (2 per cent), New Zealand (1 per cent).

Exports

Exports are copra, chemicals and construction materials.
Main destinations: Italy (typically 40 per cent of total), Croatia (15 per cent), US (14 per cent), Denmark (13 per cent)

Agriculture

Farming

Approximately 80 per cent of the labour force depend on agriculture for their livelihood. The soil of the main islands is volcanic and rainfall is adequate.

Fishing

Tuna is fished for local consumption. Licensing of fishing rights to Japan and South Korea provide an important source of revenue.
The typical annual fish catch, for local consumption, is 300 tonnes (t) with 4t other seafood.

Forestry

Timber is logged for local consumption and some pine reforestation has been undertaken.

Industry and manufacturing

Industrial activity is limited to handicrafts.

Tourism
Tourism is under-developed, as the islands are difficult to get to and lack many amenities. There are four hotels and three private lettings on Wallis, plus a few restaurants in Mata Utu; there are two hotels on Futuna. However there is only one bank in the territory, which is a subsidiary of BNP Paribas; the branch on Futuna is only opened on two days per month. Activities such as tennis, scuba diving and fishing are available through local associations.

Hydrocarbons
There are no known hydrocarbon reserves; all needs are met by imports.

Energy
Total installed generating capacity is around 6KW.

Banking and insurance
The only bank is Banque de Wallis et Futuna (a subsidiary of BNP, the French multinational bank).

Central bank
The Paris-based Institut d'Emission d'Outre-Mer (IEOM) provides all central banking services except foreign exchange reserves.

Time
GMT plus twelve hours

Geography
Wallis and Futuna consists of two islands groups – Wallis Island (also known as Uvea) and 22 islets on the surrounding reef, and, to the south-east, Futuna (or Hooru), comprising the two small islands of Futuna and Alofi. Combined, the area of the islands is 274 square kilometres and are 230km apart. They are north-east of Fiji and west of Samoa.
The islands are volcanic with the tallest peak, Mont Singavi (on Futuna) at 765 metres. The main islands had lush rain forests covering them but have been seriously denuded since wood is the major source of fuel. Deforestation has resulted in soil erosion particularly on Futuna. Alofi has no source of fresh water and does not have any permanent settlements.

Hemisphere
Southern

Climate
Hot and humid, although May–October can be dry and cooler. Rainy season from November to April. Average temperature 27 degrees Celsius.

Entry requirements

Passports
Required by all except certain French nationals.

Visa
Required by all, except citizens of EU, North America, Australasia and Japan, for stays up to one month; this includes business trips by representatives of foreign entities with an invitation from a local company or organisation. Proof of adequate funds for stay, an itinerary, a guarantee of repatriation if necessary and return/onward ticket are also required. For further exceptions, full details and a copy of the application form visit www.diplomatie.gouv.fr and follow the link *Getting to France* to *Getting a Visa*.

Currency advice/regulations
As there are only two banks in the country (none at the airport), it is advisable to enter the country with cash, the most practical being the local currency, Comptoirs Français du Pacifique franc (CFPf). Travellers cheques can be exchanged at the banks, but each transaction is accompanied by a large commission; the banks will give advances on Visa or MasterCard.

Health (for visitors)

Mandatory precautions
Vaccination certificates required for yellow fever if travelling from an infected area.

Advisable precautions
Vaccinations for diphtheria, tuberculosis, hepatitis A and B, polio, tetanus and typhoid are recommended. Rabies risk.

Hotels
There are only four hotels with 26 rooms available, all located in Mata Utu on Wallis. Holiday residences are available.

Public holidays (national)

Fixed dates
1 Jan (New Years Day), 28 Apr (Saint Pierre Chanel), 1 May (Labour Day), 8 May (Victory Day 1945), 14 Jul (National Day), 29 Jul (Territory Day), 1 Nov (All Saints Day), 11 Nov (Armistice Day), 25 Dec (Christmas).
Holidays that fall at the weekend are not taken *in lieu*.

Variable dates
Good Friday (Mar/Apr), Ascension (Apr/May) Assumption (Aug).

Working hours

Banking
Mon–Fri: 0730–1545.

Business
Mon–Fri: 0730–1130, 1330–1730. Sat: 0730–1130.

Government
Mon–Fri: 0730–1130, 1215–1600.

Shops
Mon–Fri: 0730–1100, 1400–1800. Half-day Sat and Sun.

Telecommunications

Telephone/fax
Communications are by satellite, although a limited radio link is maintained.

Electricity supply
220V, 50 Hz with round, either two or three pin-plugs.

Weights and measures
Metric system

Getting there

Air
Scheduled but only weekly flights are via either New Caledonia or Fiji, provided by Aircalin. Book well in advance.
National airline: Wallis and Futuna is planning to set up its own airline.
International airport/s: Wallis Hihifo Airport (WLS), 6km from Mata Utu; *bureau de change*, bars, VIP lounge, duty-free, pharmacy, tourist help desk.

Surface
Water: There are no regular passengership services to the islands.
Main port/s: Mata Utu; Leava

Getting about

National transport
There is no public transport or taxis.
Road: There are surfaced roads in Mata Utu and a road network links the main towns on Wallis.
Buses: Minibus services operate on Wallis.

Car hire
Car hire is available on Wallis.

BUSINESS DIRECTORY

The addresses listed below are a selection only. While World of Information makes every endeavour to check these addresses, we cannot guarantee that changes have not been made, especially to telephone numbers and area codes. We would welcome any corrections.

Telephone area codes
The international direct dialling (IDD) code for Wallis and Futuna is +681 followed by the subscriber's number .

Banking
Banque de Wallis et Futuna, PO Box 59, Mata Utu (tel: 722-124; fax: 722-156; internet: www.bnpparibas.com).

Central bank
Institut d'Emission d'Outre-Mer (IEOM), 5 rue Roland Barthes, 75598 Paris Cedex 12, France (tel : (+33 1) 5344-4141; fax : (+33 1) 4347-5134; e-mail: contact@ieom.fr).

Travel information
Aircalin, 8 Rue Frédéric Surleau, BP 3736, Noumea 98846 New Caledonia (tel: (+687) 265-500; fax: (+687) 265-561)..

Wallis Hihifo Airport, BP 1, Mata Utu 98600 (tel: 721-200; fax: 721-203; email: aviation.sna@wallis.co.nc).

Other useful addresses
Service des Postes et Télécommunications, BP 00 98600, Mata Utu (tel: 720-700; fax: 722-500; e-mail: spt.get@wallis.co.nc).

Yemen

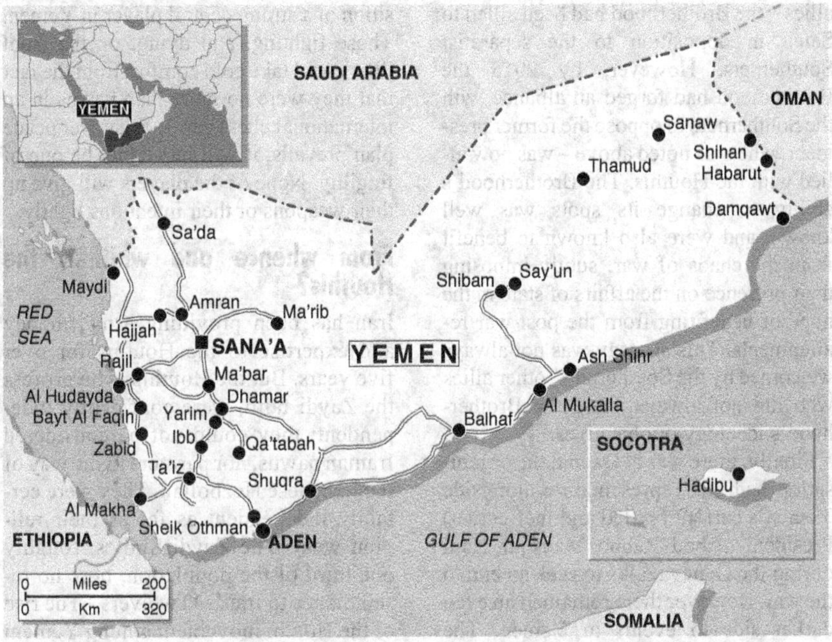

Yemen has long been one of the poorest countries in the Middle East, with high rates of unemployment and illiteracy and an absence of basic services; an estimated 20 million people are currently in need of humanitarian assistance, including an estimated 9.4 million Yemeni children, more than 250,000 refugees and 335,000 internally displaced persons. In March 2015 a Saudi-led coalition, Operation Decisive Storm, which included Gulf Co-operation Council (GCC) members Bahrain, Kuwait, Qatar and the UAE, as well as Egypt, Jordan, Morocco and Sudan, launched a military operation in Yemen against Houthi rebels, at the request of Yemen's President Abd-Rabbu Mansour Hadi. The military offensive against the Houthis attracted immediate criticism for reportedly using internationally banned cluster bombs. In addition to air strikes, Saudi Arabia had imposed a naval blockade of Yemen which has had dramatic effects on the civilian population.

A complex mosaic

The mosaic of forces at play in 2015 Yemen was as complex as it was changeable. For a decade or so the Shi'a Houthis had been taking shots at the central government, steadily weakening it and aggravating the ethnic and religious weaknesses already present – if not always obvious – in Yemeni society. The 2011 revolution and its rejection of then president, Ali Abdullah Saleh's rule created the conditions in which much of the Yemeni population felt justified in and capable of, challenging an authoritarian political system. Saleh's ousting and the revolution's promise of a truly democratic state under President Abed Rabbo Mansour Hadi gave Yemenis of all walks of life – not only the traditional political elite – a sense of ownership of and expectation from, their political system. It created a critical opportunity for a break from the *status quo* for the better. But the post-revolutionary period saw the remnants of Saleh's regime – including Saudi Arabia's proxies – manage a transitional process that intentionally obstructed the goals of the revolution and reinforced the power structures of the *ancien régime*. It is not surprising then that the Houthis, among

KEY FACTS

Official name: Jamhuriya al Yamaniya (Republic of Yemen)

Head of State: President Abed Rabbo Mansour Hadi (from 27 Feb 2012) (Resigned 22 Jan 2015 and fled to Aden.)

Head of government: Prime Minister Khaled Baha (from 9 Nov 2014) (Resigned 22 Jan 2015 and left country after being released from house arrest in March 2015.)

Ruling party: Ansar Allah (known as Houthis)

Area: 527,968 square km

Population: 27.46 million (2014)*

Capital: Sana'a

Official language: Arabic

Currency: Rial (YR) = 100 fils

Exchange rate: YR215.10 per US$ (Sep 2015)

GDP per capita: US$1,574 (2014)*

GDP real growth: -0.19% (2014)*

GDP: US$43.23 billion (2014)*

Labour force: 6.64 million (2009)

Unemployment: 35.00% (2009)

Inflation: 8.16% (2014)*

Oil production: 145,000 bpd (2014)

Natural gas production: 9.60 billion cum (2014)

Balance of trade: -US$2.91 billion (2013)

* estimated figure

others, proclaimed the transitional process, the Hadi presidency and his government, illegitimate

Sometimes in theory, sometimes in practice, the Houthis had been seen as the principal enemy of former President Saleh (1978–2012); in 2015 that enmity appeared to have faded, as the Houthis joined forces with their former enemy. The later collapse of President Hadi's government, which for the previous couple of years had openly supported US drone strikes in Yemen against al Qaeda in the Arabian Peninsula (AQAP), made the Houthis, a pro-Iranian, anti-American, Shi'ite militia an important player in this desperately poor but strategically important country. The Houthis all-embracing slogan was: 'Death to America, death to Israel, curses to the Jews and victory to Islam.'

Comprehending the conflict in Yemen was not simply a case of understanding what the Houthis were about. There was also the Southern secessionist movement. The motive force here was the constant disappointment and disaffection that had resulted from the 1990 unification of North and South Yemen. The latter had once been the Marxist independent state known as PDRY, the People's Democratic Republic of the Yemen. The Southern Yemenis desire for separation from the North had a lot, but not everything, to do with the growing domination of the Houthis, who were from Yemen's North. There were other social, cultural and political reasons. Those from the South were not seeking a return to the *status quo ante*, which meant the continued control from Sana'a, which they perceived as Northern control. Many southerners saw their country's confused, complex conflict as an opportunity to establish a *de-facto* independence.

The role played by the Muslim Brotherhood was one of utter confusion. Before the conflict got seriously under way – with the involvement of Saudi Arabia and its allies – the Brotherhood had been allied to Saleh in opposition to the separatist Southerners. However, by 2015 the Brotherhood had forged an alliance with the Southerners to oppose the former president, who – as noted above – was now allied with the Houthis. The Brotherhood's ability to change its spots was well known, and were also known to benefit from the chaos of war, subtly imposing their presence on the affairs of state in the hope of benefiting from the post war realignments. This strategy was not always welcomed by the Southerners' other allies who did not always share the Brotherhood's ideology or objectives.

Finally, there was al Qaeda; the organisation had one representative alongside Yemen's current (exiled and ineffectual) President Abed Rabbo Mansour Hadi during the Geneva talks to seek an end to the war. However there remained an even darker side to events in Yemen. The forces of IS in Yemen were born from a union of al Qaeda and the Brotherhood. The movement's long-term objective was somewhere akin to that of the Afghanistan Taliban: strict adherence to the Sharia and a violently hierarchical, misogynistic society.

KEY INDICATORS — Yemen

	Unit	2011	2012	2013	2014	**2015
Population	m	*24.84	*25.88	*26.66	*27.46	*28.28
Gross domestic product (GDP)	US$bn	33.70	35.05	40.41	*43.23	*43.14
GDP per capita	US$	1,340	1,354	1,516	*1,574	*1,525
GDP real growth	%	-10.5	2.4	4.8	*-0.2	*-2.2
Inflation	%	17.6	9.9	11.0	*8.2	*8.1
Oil output	'000 bpd	228.0	180.0	161.0	145.0	–
Natural gas output	bn cum	9.4	7.6	10.3	9.6	–
Exports (fob) (goods)	US$m	8,662.2	7,808.3	7,841.6	–	–
Imports (fob) (goods)	US$m	8,248.4	11,354.5	10,755.9	–	–
Balance of trade	US$m	413.7	-3,546.2	-2,914.3	–	–
Current account	US$m	-1,663.1	-443.0	-1,242.0	*-681.0	*-966.0
Total reserves minus gold	US$m	5,274.1	6,067.7	5,284.1	–	–
Foreign exchange	US$m	4,988.5	5,813.8	5,032.7	–	–
Exchange rate	per US$	213.80	214.89	214.90	215.00	–

* estimated figure ** forecast figure

The Yemeni conflict involved not only national players, but also and to one degree or another, international players such as Sunni Saudi Arabia and Shi'a Iran. Tribal, religious, regional and secessionist interests all merged, fell apart and regrouped continuously. Perhaps the only thing that this diversity of interests had in common was the wish to thwart the imposition of a strong central player in Yemen. Those fighting, and dying, on the front lines could take cold comfort from the fact that they were no more than pawns in an international chess game. Whatever peace plan prevails, it will inevitably be one of fragility. None of the players will give up their weapons or their intentions lightly.

From whence and whither, the Houthis?

Iran has been providing arms, money and expertise to the Houthis for over five years. But the Houthis, who profess the Zaydi faith, were confidently independent; they could not be considered Iranian pawns, nor partners in the way of the Lebanese Hezbollah. They were certainly independent as far as their religion went. The Zaydi Shiites, roughly one third of the population, bore no resemblance to Iran's 'Twelvers.' The rise of the Houthi movement among Yemeni Zaydis was initially a rural, tribal revolt against an authoritarian nationalist government and against attempts by Saudi Arabia to proselytise Zaydis and make them into hard-line Sunnis, called Salafis. The Houthis' Zaydi faith was considered by some Iranian clerics as a disguised form of Sunni Islam. It was thought that by 2015 their goal was to restore the Zaydi Imamate that had ruled North Yemen until the 1962 revolution. In the civil war that followed the revolution, the Saudis had backed the Zaydi royalists against the Egyptian-backed republic. After 2004, however, the Saudis fought a series of border wars with the Houthis. The death of Saudi Arabia's King Abdullah in January 2015 and the return of Yemen's President Abdu Rabbu Mansour Hadi had made Yemen the first priority for Saudi Arabia's new King Salman. The Saudis had reportedly spent over US$4 billion in endeavouring to prop up Hadi. Other Gulf Co-operation Council (GCC) member states had allegedly provided billions more. The government of former president for life Ali Abdullah Saleh received this crucial foreign aid from the Saudis in return for a lame acceptance of Saudi influence on Yemeni religious culture towards the Saudi form of Sunnism.

Decisive Storm

The nationalist government also neglected the Zaydi Saada region in the north with regard to services and development projects. Yemeni tribes in any case do not necessarily folly their religion when making alliances; many Sunni tribes have joined the Houthis politically. While Israeli president, Benjamin Netanyahu, and the Saudis, along with President Hadi, accuse Iran of fomenting the Houthis, they are a local movement with local roots and there is no reason to think that that their successes owe anything to Iran. Indeed, most of their success since last summer apparently derives from a decision by former president Saleh to ally with them and direct elements of the Yemeni army to support them or stand down in the face of their advances. To turn around and blame these developments on distant Iran is absurd.

By mid-2015 the conflict in Yemen had spread to 20 of the country's 22 governorates. By early May an estimated (by the World Health Organisation (WHO)) over 4,439 people had been killed and almost 6,000 injured since the outbreak of hostilities. In July 2015 the UN declared Yemen a level 3 emergency, the highest on the scale; the country's health system was facing 'imminent collapse'. According to the WHO, 15.9 million people in Yemen were in need of humanitarian assistance. According to UNICEF, 9.9 million children had been severely affected by the conflict, with 279 children killed and 402 injured since March 2015. At least 1.8 million children had lost access to education, which placed them at increased risk of recruitment or use by armed groups and of other forms of abuse. According to UNICEF, children comprised up to one third of all fighters in Yemen, at least 140 having been recruited between 26 March and 24 April 2015 alone. Over 150 children were confirmed to have been recruited and used by armed groups in 2014 and that figure had already doubled in 2015. UNICEF estimated that more than half a million children under the age of five were at risk of developing severe acute malnutrition and 1.2 million children under the age of five were at risk of moderate acute malnutrition

In April 2015, the Saudi-led coalition announced that Operation Decisive Storm was changing to a new, more peaceful phase, code named – in a rather limp public relations exercise, Operation Restore Hope. The bombing resumed within hours of the coalition's announcement and to most Yemenis it appeared that little had changed except for the branding of the war. Saudi Arabia had used Operation Decisive Storm (and then Operation Restore Hope) to mark a new chapter in its own history as a military and political power. It was clear that Saudi Arabia had modelled itself and its military persona on that of the United States. From the formation of the coalition King Salman and his son Mohammad, the twenty-eight year old minister of defence and deputy crown prince, had deployed the vague language of 'legitimacy' to justify their military action in Yemen. The questionable extent of Iran's involvement in Yemen in general and its influence on the Houthis, had been the subject of much debate. The Saudi government had depended on the Houthi-Iran axis as a justification for their military intervention. However, a number of other governments, including the United States, had expressed doubts on the Iranian participation. Protests against the Saudi attacks on Yemen had been widespread and vociferous. A range of anti-war groups and liberals in the US, Britain and a number of Arab countries expressed their opposition. The London-based Saudi scholar Madawi al Rashid described it as the latest stage in Saudi Arabia's aggressive military interventionist policy in the Arabian Peninsula.

Saudi Arabia had meddled incessantly in Yemeni politics since at least the 1960s. All the Gulf monarchies opposed the revolutionary movement then against British colonialism and the sultans it supported in what was then South Yemen. The Saudis financially backed restoration of the Zaydi imam, who had been overthrown in 1962 by republican officers backed by forces from Gamal Abdel Nasser's Egypt. When revolutionaries came to power in what became the People's Democratic Republic in the South and secular republican officers prevailed in the North, the Saudi government and various princes paid stipends to friendly clients in both parts of Yemen as a way of influencing domestic politics. The radically anti-Socialist Islamist party known as Islah was founded in North Yemen with Saudi encouragement by two of the country's most prominent conservatives, both known for close ties with the Saudi Kingdom: the fanatical Salafi preacher Abd al Majid al Zindani and the late sheikh of the Hashid tribal confederation and long-time Speaker of Parliament, Abdullah bin Hussein al Ahmar.

It's the History, Boys

Approximately fifty years had passed since Saudi Arabia and Egypt had invaded Yemen to (re)install a regime of their choice. That war, in the 1960s, had culminated with the defeat of the Saudi-backed Zaydi imamate, the triumph of a republican regime in North Yemen and the re-affirmation of the political and military supremacy of Nasserist Arab nationalism. Power and alliances may have shifted the motivation for Saudi intervention remained the same. After decades of doggedly fuelling political Islam as a bulwark against Nasserist Arab nationalism and other ideologies of the left, Saudi Arabia has emerged the powerful victor. Instead of secretly hatching political deals behind closed doors, bankrolling local proxies, or dispatching armies of religious and cultural missionaries and emissaries, today Saudi Arabia tells the world that it asserts its power unequivocally and with an authority that only 'legitimacy' can confer. The Kingdom had long set out to subordinate and weaken the Yemeni state; in mid-2015 it remained to be seen if this objective was to be achieved.

The economy

Confirming the views of other observers, in its September 2014 assessment of the Yemeni economy, the International Monetary Fund (IMF) noted that Yemen was a strategically important country in the Arabian Peninsula, overlooking the Mandab Strait, with great economic potential with its large labour force, long shoreline and agricultural and hydrocarbon resources. None the less, Yemen in 2015 remained one of the poorest and most fragile countries in the world. Poverty, malnutrition and unemployment were widespread and water resources very scarce. The poor social indicators added to social tensions, complicated the management of the economy and contributed to security challenges. Furthermore, a high dependence on hydrocarbon resources exposed the economy to external shocks.

Over the previous few years, Yemen had, according to the IMF, faced multiple severe shocks which imposed a heavy toll on economic activity. In particular, oil production declined sharply and the social unrest and widespread sabotage activities affected investment and resulted in frequent damage to oil pipelines and infrastructure. The 2011 political crisis aggravated an already difficult economic situation. Private sector activity suffered, public finances and official reserves came under pressure and inflation surged. The economy eventually stabilised and started to recover in 2012 thanks in part to sizeable external grants from Saudi Arabia and some reform implementation in the context of the IMF Rapid Credit Facility. The recovery, however, was short lived and pressures emerged in early 2014 due to frequent attacks on oil facilities, which reduced fiscal and export revenues and delays in implementing fundamental reforms necessary for diversification. The resulting threats to macro-economic stability prompted a new round of reforms in September 2014.

Yemen's overarching (if in 2015 impossible) economic challenge was to achieve high and inclusive growth and create adequate job opportunities in a stable economic environment. This necessitated sustained efforts to overcome policy and structural impediments to achieving the full potential of the economy. In particular, it was essential to tackle the weak structure of public finances, reduce pervasive fuel subsidies, address corruption, (Yemen ranked 161 out of the 175 countries surveyed in the 2014 Transparency International *Corruption Perceptions Index*) improve public service delivery and efficiency, enhance the business environment, promote human capital, facilitate access to finance and strengthen assistance to poor. The Yemeni authorities had launched a bold home-grown reform agenda to address these challenges and to enhance the resilience of the economy to shocks. The strength and pro-poor orientation of the reforms undertaken by the authorities had encouraged disbursements of donor support.

Preliminary information, in the view of the IMF, pointed to the large economic cost of the crisis, in addition to the human losses. The impact on the poor was of particular concern. Early data for 2015 indicated that economic activity, exports and reserves were all on a declining path, while inflation and exchange rate pressures had started to emerge. The IMF closed by stating that the international community needed to be ready to move quickly to support economic recovery and resumption of reforms once the political and security uncertainty clarifies.

Energy

The US government Energy Information Administration (EIA) in a September 2014 overview of Yemen's energy sector noted that although Yemen was not a major hydrocarbon producer when compared to several other countries in the Middle East, the country had sufficient oil and natural gas resources for both domestic demand and exports. However, according to the EIA, Yemen's difficult security environment hindered the production and transport of those resources.

Yemen's energy sector, said the EIA, was in a state of flux. Declining oil production and frequent attacks on Yemen's energy infrastructure had offset the positive developments in the country's natural gas sector since 2009. Yemen's difficult security environment complicated the exploration, production and transport of energy resources in the country and was undermining the country's emerging liquefied natural gas (LNG) export sector.

Yemen was clearly not a major energy producer or exporter compared with a number of other countries in the Middle East. However, its location at the Bab el-Mandab, a key checkpoint in international shipping, made Yemen important in terms of international energy trade. More than 3.4 million barrels of oil per day (bpd) passed through Bab el-Mandab in 2013, on their way to the Suez Canal and the Mediterranean. Closure of the two-mile strait would force tankers to sail around the southern tip of Africa to reach European, North American and South American markets.

Yemen's government coffers depend on its country's hydrocarbons sector. Even with the earnings from natural gas exports, the IMF estimates that Yemen needs an oil export price of approximately US$215 per barrel to balance its budget. IMF figures also show that 63 per cent of government revenues came from the hydrocarbons sector between 2010–12 and that hydrocarbons accounted for 89 per cent of total export revenues. Yemen, as a member of the Extractive Industries Transparency Initiative (EITI), reported in July 2013 that government revenues from the oil and natural gas sector in 2011 were more than US$5 billion. Oil production in Yemen had declined steadily after peaking in 2001, but beginning in 2009, the country began producing commercial quantities of natural gas for domestic use and for exports as LNG. This development could help the country stabilise its economy even without an extremely high oil export price. However, replacing oil export revenues with LNG export revenues would not reduce the country's dependence on its hydrocarbons sector.

Risk assessment

Economy	Poor
Politics	Poor
Regional stability	Poor

Muslims in Yemen

% of population	99
Sunni (% of Muslims)	55
Shi'a (% of Muslims)	45

COUNTRY PROFILE

1500s–1600s The Ottomans controlled most of Yemen.

1839 Aden came under British rule, serving as a major refuelling port after the opening of the Suez Canal in 1869.

1918–62 The Ottoman Empire broke up and north Yemen gained independence under Imam Yahya. His son, Imam Ahmad succeeded him in 1948 and ruled until his death in 1962. A *coup d'état* overthrew his son and the Yemen Arab Republic (YAR) was established by the military. A civil war between royalists, supported by Saudi Arabia, and republicans, backed by Egypt, ensued.

1967 British withdrew from Aden as local resistance to their presence grew steadily more violent. A communist state in the south was established, comprising Aden and the former protectorate of South Arabia. It was officially known as the People's Democratic Republic of Yemen (PDRY). A nationalisation programme began.

1970s–80s The YAR and the PDRY were in conflict. Ali Abdullah Saleh became president of the YAR in 1978. President Ali Nasser Mohammed of the PDRY fled the country in 1986, after thousands died in political conflict.

1990 The YAR and the PDRY were unified and became the Republic of Yemen, with Ali Abdullah Saleh as president.

1991 A constitution was adopted. Yemen's support for Iraq in the Gulf War led to around a million migrant workers from other gulf states being evicted and returning home.

1993 Democratic elections (the first in the Arabian Peninsula) led to a three-party coalition comprising the former ruling party of the YAR, General People's Congress (GPC), led by Ali Abdullah Saleh, the former ruling party of the PDRY, Yemeni Socialist Party (YSP), led by al Beedh, and a mainly northern Islamic tribal grouping, the Congregation for Reform (Islah). Disputes within the coalition resulted in an escalating political crisis.

1994 The constitution was amended. In spite of the signing of a conciliation agreement, a series of military confrontations broke out, leading to a full-scale civil war between northern and southern forces. Unity was restored and President Saleh was re-elected by parliament. A

coalition government was formed, comprising the GPC and Islah, with the YSP and other smaller parties in opposition.
1995 Yemen and Eritrea clashed over the Hanish islands in the Red Sea.
1997 The ruling GPC won the first election since the 1994 civil war.
1998 Eritrea and Yemen accepted the ruling of the Permanent Court of Arbitration in The Hague that Yemen should have the island of Greater Hanish.
2000 Yemen and Saudi Arabia signed a treaty resolving a 65-year dispute over land and sea boundaries. The US naval vessel, *USS Cole*, was damaged in a suicide attack in Aden; a bomb exploded at the British Embassy.
2001 A referendum approved the extension of the president's term of office by two years to seven years and the parliamentary term by two years to six years. In response to the attack on the Twin Towers in New York, President Saleh told US President Bush that Yemen would join the fight against terrorism.
2002 Jarallah Omar, secretary general of the opposition party, YSP, was assassinated by an Islamic militant. Yemen expelled more than 100 foreign Islamic scholars, suspected of being al Qaeda members. The supertanker *Limburg* was badly damaged in an explosion off the coast of Yemen.
2003 The ruling GPC was re-elected. The 10 chief suspects in the bombing of the *USS Cole* escaped from custody in Aden.
2004 Government troops fought with followers of Hussein al Houthi, the leader of an insurrection in the north. Fifteen men were sentenced on terror charges, some for bombing the supertanker *Limburg*, and two more for bombing the *USS Cole*. Government troops killed Hussein al Houthi
2005 More fighting between government forces and al Houthi supporters caused over 200 deaths. The World Health Organisation confirmed 83 cases of polio; Yemen had been free of the disease. An agreement with the northern insurgents was reached.
2006 Over 625 supporters of the al Houthi uprising were freed from prison under an amnesty. In presidential elections Ali Abdullah Saleh was re-elected.
2007 Dozens of followers of al Houthi were killed in clashes with government troops. Ali Mohamed Mujawar was appointed prime minister. Abdul Malik al Houthi agreed to a ceasefire. Citizens were banned from carrying firearms in the capital and demonstrations without permits were banned.
2008 More violence broke out between supporters loyal to Abdul Malik al Houthi and security forces. Bomb attacks were carried out against local police and official buildings as well as foreign businesses, embassies and tourist targets.
2009 Parliament approved a once-only election postponement to 27 April 2011, allowing further discussions on electoral reforms.
2010 The government stopped issuing visas at international airports. A military official was quoted in the defence ministry newspaper *September 26* as saying that 'granting visas to foreigners will take place only through the embassies of Yemen, and after consulting security authorities to verify the identities of travellers'. He went on to say that the move was 'to prevent the infiltration of any suspected terrorist elements' after it was revealed that the Nigerian who had attempted to blow-up an aircraft over Detroit in 2009 had been trained by al Qaeda elements in Yemen. In a siege of the southern Shabwa Province an estimated 8,000–12,000 civilians fled the town of Huta as a military offensive against al Qaeda got underway. The US, UK, Germany and France placed a ban on all cargo from Yemen following the discovery of improvised bombs sent by agents of al Qaeda; in 2012 the ban remained in place.
2011 In January the overthrow of President Ben Ali of Tunisia by a popular uprising caused similar street protests in Yemen. President Saleh pledged not to extend his presidency in 2013, or pass on the presidency to his son. Protests continued unabated and police snipers killed over 50 demonstrators, in March. Senior military personnel and then some politicians began to back the protestors. A proposal including the issue of the transfer of the president's power, negotiated between opposition parties, tribal leaders and religious scholars was presented to President Saleh. Initial reports were that it had been positively received. President Saleh announced that there would be a referendum later in 2011 on measures to change the constitution, including an election law to move towards a parliamentary system. A 30 day emergency law was passed. In an effort to mediate between the president and demonstrators demanding he resign, a Gulf Arab initiative, led by Saudi Arabia, proposed a transfer of power away from President Saleh. Security forces fired live-rounds into protesting crowds in Sana'a in April, following President Saleh's earlier comment that protestor's behaviour was 'un-Islamic'. From February–April, over 100 people died in civil disturbances as the president said he would step down and hand over power, but only into 'safe hands'. In May the US ordered all non-essential diplomatic staff to leave Yemen. Hundreds of armed members of the Hashid tribe (one of the two main tribal groupings in Yemen), fought with government troops as they marched on Sana'a in June to join forces with other of their tribe already in the capital. Sheikh Sadeq al Ahmar, head of the Hashid tribe, and son of the founder of the opposition party Islamist Islah. President Saleh was injured by shrapnel in the chest during an attack on his Sana'a palace compound. On 4 June, Abdu Rabu Mansour Hadi became acting prime minister. Saleh left Yemen to receive medical treatment in Saudi Arabia. President Saleh appeared on Yemen state television on 7 July, the first time since he was injured. Both hands were bandaged and he did not appear to move his arms. He said that dialogue was needed to resolve Yemen's problems, although any resolution had to be 'within the framework of the constitution and in the framework of the law'. In August President Saleh left hospital, chosing to remain in Saudi Arabia, but vowing to return to Yemen and remain in office until 2013. On 22 August, former prime minister Abdul Aziz Abdul Ghani died of his injuries sustained during the attack on the Sana'a presidential palace on 3 June. Demonstrations for and against the regime continued in Sana'a.
A series of demonstrations resulted in counteraction by security forces that involved the elite republican guard, led by President Salah's son Ahmed in the second city Taiz opened fire and killing at least 10 people, and security forces firing on demonstrators in Sana'a using automatic weapons and killing at least 20 people, while snipers fired from rooftops into a protest camp. President Saleh returned in September and took back the Presidency on 23 September. Tawakkul Karman was announced as one of three women to win the 2011 Nobel Peace Prize in October. The three women were honoured for 'their non-violent struggle for the safety of women and for women's rights to full participation in peace-building work'. The UN Security Council called on President Saleh to resign immediately, following weeks of excessive violence meted out by security forces on demonstrators against his regime. In November, President Saleh signed an agreement, brokered by the GCC, to transfer his powers to Vice President Abdrabuh Mansur Hadi who became Acting President again on 23 November. In return Saleh retained the honorary title of president, with immunity from prosecution. Year-long demonstrators condemned the deal; five were killed and 33 injured by security forces. Vice President Hadi designated Muhammed Salim Basindwa, an opposition politician, as prime minister on 27 November.

2012 Ali Abdullah Saleh left the country on 22 January. A presidential election was held on 21 February with one candidate – former Vice President Abd Rabbuh Mansur al Hadi. He won 99.8 per cent of the vote, on a turnout of 65 per cent, and took office on 25 February. On 23 May, a group of aid agencies warned that the political instability had left 10 million Yemenis (around 44 per cent of the population) undernourished, of which five million required emergency aid. On 6 May Fahd Mohammed Ahmed al Quso (also known by eight other names) (leader of al Qaeda in Yemen) was killed by a US, CIA drone missile. On 14 June the army took control of three towns overrun by al Qaeda, after a month of fierce fighting. On 13 September the US Embassy in Sana'a was mobbed by protestors angry at the uploading on the internet in the US of an amateur film that insulted the Prophet Mohammed, forcing security forces to open fire with tear gas, water cannon and bullets.

2013 The British and US governments closed their embassies and consulates on 4 August and withdrew their diplomats. On 7 August Yemen said it had foiled a major al Qaeda plot to blow up oil pipelines and seize two of the country's main ports. On the night of 7 August US drone strikes are said to have killed a number of senior al Qaeda leaders in Zinjibar in southern Yemen; innocent civilians also died, raising tensions. The US reopened all its embassies throughout the Middle East and North Africa on 12 August, except the Sana'a embassy. The UK re-opened its embassy on 18 August. Prime Minister Basindwa survived an assassination attempt on 31 August. Two bomb attacks in southern Yemen by suspected al Qaeda militants killed at least 40 persons on 20 September. On 5 December a suicide car bomb followed up by an armed assault on the Yemen ministry of defence left over 50 people dead and injured more than 160. Al Qaeda were suspected.

2014 The National Dialogue Conference (NDC) ended on 25 January. It had agreed a constitutional referendum to be held in September, and parliamentary elections would be held in April 2015. Khaled Baha became prime minister on 9 November. On 6 December the US failed in an attempt to rescue two hostages held by al-Qaeda in the Arabian Peninsula (AQAP) in the east of the country. Both hostages (US journalist Luke Somers and South African teacher Pierre Korkie) were killed.

2015 On 15 January it was announced that the President had been given the draft constitution on 6 January. He had previously rejected the two-region federal state demanded by southern separatists and the Zaidi-Shia 'Ansar Allah' Houthi Movement, claiming that the proposal would lead to Yemen's fragmentation. The six-region division as agreed as a basis for drafting the constitution is reported to have been rejected by rival armed political factions. On 22 January Yemen was left without a government, after President Hadi and Prime Minister Bahah resigned and the cabinet dissolved. Although Mr Bahah was ordered by the Houthis to return to work, he refused. President Abdrabbuh Mansour Hadi was ousted in February by the Houthis; he fled to Aden where he established a rival power base. The UN Security Council unanimously approved Resolution 2201 on 15 February. The Resolution called on the rebels to surrender their military gains and everyone to get behind the 2011 Gulf Co-operation Council (GCC) initiative and the draft constitution. Taiz was seized by the Houthis on 22 March, as they moved south towards Aden. Foreign minister, Riad Yassin, called for Gulf Arab states to intervene to prevent the advance of Shia Houthi rebels. On 26 March Saudi Arabian jets targeted Houthi positions in Sana'a. The government said they were part of a coalition including UAE, Bahrain, Kuwait, Qatar, Jordan, Morocco and Sudan, who were sending aircraft, and Egypt, Jordan, Sudan and Pakistan who were ready to take part in any ground offensive. The Saudi Arabian Ambassador to the US announced the formation of the coalition on 25 March and said they were 'defending the legitimate government' of President Hadi. President Hadi himself was said to have gone into hiding. Despite the coalition's actions Houthi rebels continued their advance on Aden where a three-way battle between supprters of the president, the Houthi and the Saudi Arabians continued. President Hadi returned to Yemen November.

Political structure

Constitution

The constitution was adopted in 1991 and was amended in 1994 and 2001. A 2001 referendum approved the extension of the president's and parliament's terms of office from five to seven years, and from four to six years, respectively. A new constitution was drafted (2012-14) but both the GPC and the Houthis have refused to vote on it. Thus the referendum on its introduction has been suspended and, with it, parliamentary and presidential elections.

Voting eligibility: 18 years.

Independence date

1918 North Yemen; 1967 South Yemen. 22 May 1990 unification.

Form of state

Republic

The executive

Power is vested in the post of president, who is the Head of State. The president is elected by popular vote from at least two candidates, endorsed by parliament. He sets a national agenda and is empowered to rule by decree in the case of parliament's absence, call for parliamentary elections, appoint a prime minister to form a government, call for general referenda and form the National Defence Council.

The president can serve a maximum of two, seven-year terms.

The prime minister, in consultation with the president, selects the cabinet to assist in the duties of the executive branch. However, given the Houthis current control of office, presidential powers have been transferred to a five member revolutionary committee.

National legislature

The bicameral parliament consists of the Majlis al Nuwaab (Assembly of Representatives) with 301 members, elected by popular vote to serve six-year terms and the Shura (Consultative Council) with 111 members, appointed by the president, and serving as advisory body.

Legal system

An independent judiciary was established under the constitution. It is based on *Sharia* (Islamic law), Turkish law, English common law and local tribal customary law. The Supreme Court is based in the capital.

Last elections

27 April 2003 (parliamentary); 21 February 2012 (presidential)

Results: Parliamentary: GPC won 58.01 per cent of the votes (238 seats out of 301); Islah won 22.55 per cent (46 seats); Yemen Socialist Party 3.84 per cent (eight seats). Turnout was 75.98 per cent.

Presidential: Abd Rabbuh Mansur al Hadi won 99.8 per cent of the vote; turnout 65 per cent.

Next elections

Given the current situation, it is impossible to accurately predict the dates of new elections. Parliamentary elections have been consistently delayed since 2009, whilst the presidential equivalents were due for 2015, but will almost certainly be postponed given the existing political landscape.

Political parties

Ruling party

Ansar Allah (known as Houthis)

Main opposition party

General People's Congress (GPC)

Population

26.66 million (2013)*

About 48 per cent of the population is under 14 years of age; 50 per cent 15–64; 2 per cent over 65.
Yemen is the most densely populated country in the Arabian Peninsula.
Last census: 16 December 2004: 19,685,161
Population density: 30 inhabitants per square km. Urban population 32 per cent (2010 Unicef).
Annual growth rate: 3.5 per cent, 1990–2010 (Unicef).

Ethnic make-up
Arabs form 96 per cent of the population. There are ethnic tensions between Arabs and Afro-Arab and South Asian minorities. European communities are concentrated in the major metropolitan areas.

Religions
Muslim (more than 99 per cent), including Shi'ite, Sunni and Zaydi (members of a Shi'ite subsect). Small number of Jews.

Education
Primary education begins at the age of six and lasts for nine years.
Secondary education is provided for academic and vocational courses both lasting three years. The first year comprises a common curriculum, with the option to choose either the scientific or literary subjects for the remaining two years. There are some technical secondary schools, three vocational training centres, a Veterinary Training School and several agricultural secondary schools. There are also religious institutions, which concentrate on Islamic education. Higher education is provided by the University of Sana'a (1970), the University of Aden (1973) and the University of Science and Technology, Sana'a.
Literacy rate: 49 per cent adult rate; 68 per cent youth rate (15–24) (Unesco 2005).
Compulsory years: Six to 15.
Enrolment rate: 70 per cent gross primary enrolment; 34 per cent gross secondary enrolment, of relevant age groups (including repeaters) (World Bank).
Pupils per teacher: 30 in primary schools.

Health
There were cases of polio reported to the World Health Organisation – Global Polio Eradication Initiative in 2006; the country had previously been free of the disease and its re-emergence was due to infected travellers.

HIV/Aids
HIV prevalence: 0.1 per cent aged 15–49 in 2003 (World Bank)
Life expectancy: 59 years, 2004 (WHO 2006)
Fertility rate/Maternal mortality rate: 5.2 births per woman, 2010 (Unicef); maternal mortality 350 per 100,000 live births (World Bank).
Child (under 5 years) mortality rate (per 1,000): 60 per 1,000 live births (WHO 2012); 46 per cent of children under aged five are malnourished (World Bank).
Head of population per physician: 0.33 physicians per 1,000 people, 2004 (WHO 2006)

Welfare
On 23 May 2012, a group of aid agencies warned that the yearlong political instability had left 10 million Yemenis (around 44 per cent of the population) undernourished, of which five million require emergency aid. Since 2009, malnutrition rates have doubled, due to a surge in food and fuel prices and the displacement of almost 500,000 people because of the internal conflict.

Main cities
Sana'a (San'a) (capital, estimated population 2.3 million in 2012), Aden (737,811), Ta'iz (591,543), Hodeida (494,619), Ibb (331,146), al Mukalla (222,024), ar Rawdah (211,726), Damar (192,391), Amran (90,792).

Languages spoken
English is the second language and is often understood in business circles.

Official language/s
Arabic

Media

Press
Dailies: In Arabic, the government-owned national newspaper is *Al Thawra* (www.althawranews.net), other regional private publications include *Al Ayyam* (www.al-ayyam.info) and *14 October* (www.14october.com), from Aden,, *Al Thaqafiah* (www.y.net.ye/althaqafiah) and *Al Shoura* from Sanna.
In English, the *Yemen Times* (http://yementimes.com) is a widely read newspaper, *Yemen Observer* (www.yobserver.com) is an independent English online newspaper covering current events.
Weeklies: In Arabic, publications include *26 September* (www.26september.info), *Al Ray News* (www.raynews.net), and *Ektissad ws Aswaq* (www.ekwas.net) on economics, news and analysis.

Broadcasting
High rates of illiteracy has effectively left radio and television as primary sources of news and information for the domestic population.
Radio: The state-run Yemen Radio (www.yemenradio.net) has two networks, from the capital and Aden.
Television: The only terrestrial TV network is Yemen Television with two channels. There is satellite TV with nine international and pan-Arab networks available, including the government-owned Yemen Satellite Channel, offering a wide variety of programmes.
National news agency: Saba (Yemen News Agency)

Economy
Yemen is a low-income country that is highly dependent on declining oil resources for revenue. Oil and gas revenues account for 25 per cent of GDP and 65 per cent of government revenue. The Yemeni government has attempted to diversify the economy and one successful example has been the exportation of LNG, however, the economy is still heavily dependent on the hydrocarbons market. Progress towards achieving stability since the unrest that began in 2011 has been slow and uneven and Yemen continues to face difficult long-term challenges. They include declining water resources, high unemployment, severe food scarcity, and a high population growth rate. In July 2014, the government eliminated some fuel subsidies that accounted for approximately 25 per cent of government spending in 2013; and in August 2014, the IMF approved a three-year, US$570 million Extended Credit Facility for Yemen.
Yemen had 3 billion barrels of oil in 2014 and produced 125,100 barrels per day (bpd), of which 43,000 bpd was exported. There are also 479 billion cubic metres (cum) of proven natural gas reserves, with production of 10.3 million cum. Production of liquefied natural gas (LNG) began in 2009 and by 2014 9.6 million cum was being exported to the US, Asia and Europe. Stocks of oil are falling, however, without any new discoveries, and the non-oil economy is not strong enough to replace its importance to GDP.
Agriculture and herding is an important component of GDP constituting 9.2 per cent and providing the primary occupation for the majority of the workforce. Services, construction, industry, and commerce account for less than 25 per cent of the labour force. The industry suffers from a number of environmental problems including deforestation that has led to soil erosion and desertification and above all a scarcity of water. Through an increased use of irrigation, farmers have switched production from lesser valued, rain-fed cereals to the more valuable, irrigated fruit and vegetables. However, this use of groundwater is depleting the resource as the water-table falls by around two metres per year. The cultivation and use of the mildly narcotic *qat* has increased, so much so that the World Bank estimates that trade and consumption of the plant accounts for over 6 per cent of GDP, while its cultivation alone accounts

for 10 per cent of GDP. Farmland used for its cultivation has denied its use for other cash crops necessary for export. The fishing industry is underinvested and caters for local needs only. Other agricultural products include pulses, coffee, cotton; dairy products, livestock (sheep, goats, cattle and camels) and poultry.

Tourism could provide a greater component of GDP but the threatening security situation and danger experienced by tourists in the recent past has kept visitor numbers to a minimum.

GDP growth averaged 3.5 per cent over 2006–09, before it jumped to 7.7 per cent in 2010 following an International Monetary Fund (IMF) programme, in which Yemen received US$370 million, disbursed over three years, in exchange for various economic reforms in revenue diversification and its tax system, subsidy reforms and government spending. However in 2011, the IMF warned that socially sensitive reforms and weak institutional capacity were at a higher risk of faltering from the political unrest that ultimately toppled the president and caused widespread civil disobedience. The IMF programme was suspended and the economy fell into a deep recession, with GDP growth estimated at -10.5 per cent. GDP growth improved to reach 2.4 per cent in 2012 before increasing significantly to 4.8 per cent in 2013. In 2014, GDP growth has plummeted to a dismal rate of -0.2 per cent.

In 2008 inflation peaked at 19 per cent at a time of high fuel and food prices, falling to 3.7 per cent in 2009 as consumer spending fell. Inflation was 11 per cent in 2013 before decreasing slightly to 8.2 per cent in 2014.

In 2014, the UN Human Development Index (HDI) ranked Yemen 154 (out of 187) for national development in health, education and income, remaining in the same position since 2011. Since 2000, Yemen's progress has matched the growth of other economies designated as low HDI, but has not matched the improvement of other Gulf Arab States. In 2014, 37 per cent of the population lived in multidimensional poverty, while 17.5 per cent lived on less than the equivalent of US$1.25 per day. 18.4 per cent of the population was living in severe multidimensional poverty in 2014.

Remittances from migrant workers amounted to US$1.5 billion (3.9 per cent of GDP) in 2010 and was estimated to have reached US$1.6 billion in 2011. Remittances from migrant workers increased to US$3.5 billion in 2014 (9.7 per cent of GDP). Remittances provide a significant portion of GDP to Yemen and it is likely to become even more important as skilled, young people choose to work elsewhere.

International economic aid is essential to Yemen's short- to medium-term development, not only to provide a more prosperous future for the population but also to nullify the adverse influence of the terrorist group, al Qaeda. The Arab Spring unrest in 2011–12 has given al Qaeda further means to undermine Yemen's economic prospects, by sowing mistrust with its democratic partners and donors. On 5 September 2012, the World Bank announced that Yemen would benefit from an aid package of US$6.4 billion, to help it stabilise its economy at a time of food shortages and security risk. The IMF has provided a loan worth US$48.8 million in 2014 while the World Bank has pledged to add US$400 million to its ongoing US$700 million program of support for Yemen. The project will focus on improving the education system, supporting Yemen's own Social Welfare Fund and improving infrastructure like roads to boost internal trade.

External trade

The Greater Arab Free Trade Area (Gafta) has been ratified by 17 members, including Yemen, creating an Arab economic bloc. A customs union has been established whereby tariffs within Gafta are reduced by a percentage each year, until none remain.

Crude oil dominates the export market but reserves are diminishing. A liquefied natural gas (LNG) plant began production in 2009, with exports destined for the US, Europe and South Korea.

The coffee harvest was replaced in prominence by the cultivation of *qat* (a highly addictive, mild hallucinogen), used openly in Yemen but trafficked illegally to the Horn of Africa.

Imports

Main imports are food and live animals, machinery and equipment and chemicals.

Main sources: China (15.9 per cent of total in 2014), UAE (14 per cent), India (9.6 per cent), Saudi Arabia (6.6 per cent), Kuwait (5 per cent) and Turkey (4.6 per cent).

Exports

Main exports include crude oil, coffee, dried and salted fish and liquefied natural gas.

Main destinations: China (28.3 per cent of total in 2014), South Korea (23 per cent), Thailand (11.2 per cent), Japan (8.1 per cent) and the UAE (5.3 per cent).

Agriculture

Farming

With its fertile soil and relatively high levels of rainfall, Yemen possesses the best climatic conditions for agriculture on the Arabian Peninsula. Due to its mountainous terrain, terrace agriculture is common practice. In the east and north, herding is the chief activity. In southern Yemen, fertile areas are severely limited and confined to the wadis, comprising only 1 per cent of the total land area. The Marib Dam provides irrigation and for a region adjacent to the desert (Empty Quarter).

Agriculture and herding is an important component of GDP constituting 9.2 per cent and providing the primary occupation for the majority of the workforce. Services, construction, industry, and commerce account for less than 25 per cent of the labour force. The industry suffers from a number of environmental problems including deforestation that has led to soil erosion and desertification and above all a scarcity of water. Through an increased use of irrigation, farmers have switched production from lesser valued, rain-fed cereals to the more valuable, irrigated fruit and vegetables. However, this use of groundwater is depleting the resource as the water-table falls by around two metres per year.

The cultivation and use of the mildly narcotic *qat* has increased, so much so that the World Bank estimates that trade and consumption of the plant accounts for over 6 per cent of GDP, while its cultivation alone accounts for 10 per cent of GDP. 25 per cent of irrigated land is used for cultivating qat. Farmland used for its cultivation has denied its use for other cash crops necessary for export. The fishing industry is underinvested and caters for local needs only. Other agricultural products include grains, pulses, coffee, cotton; dairy products, livestock (sheep, goats, cattle and camels), fish and poultry.

Cereals, fruit and vegetables account for 75 per cent of output, but annual imports of grain are still required. Cereal yields are low and the climate is more suitable for fruit production. Private sector trading companies have invested in agriculture in Tihama and Marib, concentrating on bananas and citrus fruits.

Fishing

Fisheries are one of Yemen's greatest potential sources of wealth after oil. There are some fish exports to Europe and the Middle East.

Industry and manufacturing

The industrial sector contributed 37.5 per cent of GDP, of which manufacturing was 4.9 per cent in 2004. The sector employs around 10 per cent of the working population. Excluding the petroleum sector, industry accounts for only 4 per cent of GDP.

Heavy industry is mostly government-owned while the private sector is encouraged to participate in joint ventures and light industries including food processing, clothing, textiles, leather goods,

jewellery, cosmetics, mineral water, fertilisers and cigarettes.
Fish processing is a growth area.
Industrial production increased by 5.0 per cent, and manufacturing by 5.3 per cent, in 2004.

Tourism
Yemen has a rich history; not only did its own traders travel far overseas, but it has had contact with all of the great sea-faring nations of the world, reaching back into antiquity. As such its cultural heritage is reflected in its contribution to Unesco's World Heritage List including the historic town of Zabid (a flourishing, fortified town and former capital, dating from the birth of Islam) and the cities of Sana'a (established in biblical times and later a major religious centre of Islamic learning) and Shibam (a traditional, high-rise city, nicknamed 'the Manhattan of the desert').
The majority of visitors to Yemen were from Arab countries in the region, (often 50 per cent of the total are from Saudi Arabia); a very small number of visitors come from Europe, of the ones that do go, German visitors were the most numerous (over 5,000).
Travel and tourism contributed 8.5 per cent to GDP in 2014 (US$3.5 billion) and provided employment to 8.1 per cent of the workforce (499,500 jobs) in the same period. The political turmoil in Yemen in 2011 affected the industry badly as it experienced negative GDP growth of -8.1 per cent and employment growth was down by 5.1 per cent. Travel and tourism's contribution to GDP is set to increase by 2.5 per cent per annum and reach US$4.7 billion by 2025.

Environment
Yemen has water shortages, especially in the increasingly urbanised areas around Sana'a and other cities.

Mining
Mining accounted for less than 1 per cent of GDP in 2014. Salt is mined at Salif, where deposits total 25 million tonnes. Gypsum and marble are extracted. There are also deposits of zinc, lead, iron, sulphur, gold, silver, copper and nickel.

Hydrocarbons
Proven oil reserves were 3 billion barrels in 2014, with production at 125,100 barrels per day (bpd), which has fallen steadily since the 457,000 in 2002. Typically, 34.4 per cent of total oil production is exported. The government is attempting to secure foreign investment to expand production, but political instability and poor security have deterred many major oil companies. Consumption of oil was 134,000 bpd in 2013, Yemen imported 110,600 bpd of refined petroleum.
Downstream, Yemen has a refining capacity of 143,000bpd with two ageing refineries at Aden (120,000bpd) and Marib (10,000bpd). The government has plans to upgrade these facilities by 150,000bpd and 25,000bpd respectively. A new 50,000bpd refinery at Ras Issa has been planned since but is yet to be completed. There is an integrated network of 900km of pipelines, which transport crude oil and natural gas from production sites to either domestic users or terminals for export.
Proven natural gas reserves were estimated at 479 billion cubic metres (cum) in 2014. Production of natural gas began in 2009 and in 2014 production was 10.3 billion cum, of which 9.6 billion cum was converted into liquefied natural gas (LNG) for export worldwide. The French energy company GDF Suez has a long-term contract to buy 2.54 million tonnes of LNG per year and the oil companies Total and the Korea Gas Corporation 2.03 million tonnes.
Any use of coal is commercially insignificant.

Energy
Total installed electricity generating capacity was 1.3 gigawatts in 2013, 99.9 per cent of which was produced in conventional thermal power stations, 0.1 per cent being produced from renewable sources. Only an estimated 35 per cent of the urban and 5 per cent of the rural population has access to the national grid.
The state-owned Public Electricity Corporation (PEC) is responsible for generation and distribution and has organised international development aid to improve electricity supplies. However, to access such investment energy subsidies will have to be terminated – a previous attempt at price increases resulted in riots, leaving the government with a hard choice. The inadequacies of the distribution network are under review with an upgrade in the network expected to follow.

Banking and insurance
Domestic banks are burdened by red tape and private sector credit is crowded out by the state, although the government has announced a reform programme to develop the financial sector.

Central bank
Central Bank of Yemen

Main financial centre
Sana'a

Time
GMT plus three hours

Geography
Yemen is situated in the south of the Arabian peninsula, bordered to the north by Saudi Arabia, to the east by Oman, to the south by the Gulf of Aden, and to the west by the Red Sea. The islands of Perim and Kamaran at the southern end of the Red Sea and the island of Socotra at the entrance to the Gulf of Aden are also part of the Republic.

Hemisphere
Northern

Climate
The semi-desert coastal plain known as the Tihama is hot, humid and dusty. The highlands, which are agreeable in summer but cold in winter, enjoy most of the unreliable rainfall (March–April and July–September).

Entry requirements

Passports
Required by all, valid for six months from date of departure.

Visa
Required by all, except nationals of Iraq, Jordan and Syria.
The government stopped issuing visas at international airports in January 2010. A military official was quoted in the defence ministry newspaper *September 26* as saying that 'granting visas to foreigners will take place only through the embassies of Yemen, and after consulting security authorities to verify the identities of travellers'. He went on to say that the move was 'to prevent the infiltration of any suspected terrorist elements' after it was revealed that the Nigerian who had attempted to blow-up an aircraft over Detroit in December 2009 had been trained by al Qaeda elements in Yemen.
All visitors should start by contacting the nearest Yemeni embassy; the following information was valid in early 2010, but is subject to change. Tourist visas, valid for visits up to two months, require a confirmation letter from a tour company and proof of return/onward passage. Business visas, valid for visits up to two months, require a letter from the applicant's company explaining the purpose of the visit and the nature of business and proof of return/onward passage. Visas valid for six months may be issued to business travellers proposing to make several jouneys, in which case a letter of invitation from a Yemeni company is also required.

Prohibited entry
Israeli nationals or holders of passports with Israeli visas or other indication of a visit to Israel are denied entry or transit facilities.

Currency advice/regulations
The import and export of local currency by non-residents is prohibited. There are no restrictions on the import of foreign currencies, subject to declaration of amounts over US$3,000; export of foreign currencies is restricted to the amount imported and declared.

Customs
600 cigarettes, 60 cigars or 450g of tobacco; two bottles of alcohol; one bottle of perfume, perfumed water or eau de cologne; gifts to a value of YR100,000; and gold ornaments up to 350 grams are allowed duty-free.

Prohibited imports
Firearms, illegal drugs, pornographic literature and all products of Israeli origin are prohibited.

Health (for visitors)

Mandatory precautions
Certificate of vaccination against yellow fever if travelling from infected area.

Advisable precautions
Vaccinations against typhoid and polio are recommended, also anti-malaria precautions (malaria has been endemic in Tihama).

Water precautions are essential; water and milk should be boiled. Local dairy products should be avoided as milk is unpasteurised; vegetables, meat and fish should be well cooked and eaten hot. Use only well maintained, chlorinated swimming pools as bilharzia can be contracted from streams and rivers. Gastric upsets common.

Hotels
Sana'a has several first-class hotels. It is advisable to book in advance. The major hotels have good restaurants.

Credit cards
Major credit cards are acceptable.

Public holidays (national)

Fixed dates
1 May (Labour Day), 22 May (Unity Day), 26 Sep (Revolution Day), 14 Oct (National Day), 30 Nov (Independence Day).

Variable dates
Eid al Adha (four days), Eid al Fitr (four days), Islamic New Year, Birth of the Prophet.

Islamic year 1437 (15 Oct 2015–2 Oct 2016):: The Islamic year contains 354 or 355 days, with the result that Muslim feasts advance by 10–12 days against the Gregorian calendar. Dates of feasts vary according to the sighting of the new moon, so cannot be forecast exactly.

Working hours

Banking
Sat–Wed: 0800–1200, Thu: 0800–1130 (closed Fri); in summer: Sat–Wed: 0730–1130, Thu: 0730–1100 (closed Fri).

Business
Sat–Wed: 0800–1230, 1600–1900; Thu: 0800–1200 (closed Fri).

Government
Sat–Thu: 0900–1300.

Shops
Sun-Thu: 0800-1300, 1600-2100.

Telecommunications

Telephone/fax
The telephone directory is in Arabic. For help, ask the telephone operator at your hotel or ring 18 (English spoken).

Mobile/cell phones
There are GSM 900 services available in the south and west of the country.

Electricity supply
Generally 220V AC, with two-pin plug fittings.

Weights and measures
Metric system

Social customs/useful tips
Islamic culture and customs are strictly observed, but visitors are allowed to drink alcohol in hotels or private homes.

Security
Visitors should keep in touch with developments in the Middle East as any increase in regional tension might affect travel advice.

Getting there

Air
National airline: Yemenia (Yemen Airways)
International airport/s: Sana'a International (SAH), 13km north of Sana'a, with duty-free shop, restaurant, bank, car hire; Aden International (ADE), 11km north-east of Aden.
Airport tax: None.

Surface
There are road connections from Saudi Arabia and Oman, but driving to Yemen is advised against.
Main port/s: Aden, Hodeidah and Mukalla

Getting about

National transport
Internal travel may be affected by local night-time curfews and military check points.
Air: Regular scheduled services link Sana'a, Aden, Hodeida, Ta'iz and Marib.
Road: There are metalled roads between main centres.
Buses: There are scheduled services between all main centres.

City transport
Most hosts will send a car to the airport to meet guests.
Taxis: Taxis have yellow licence plates and wait on ranks outside the major hotels and terminals.
Fare is by negotiation and there is a minimum charge system in cities. Always agree the fare before setting off; the hotel will advise what the price should be as the starting point for negotiation. A fixed fare is charged between Sana'a airport and the city centre.
Dahabs (shared taxis) are minibuses which ply set routes in the city. Prices are fixed between destinations and are reasonably cheap.
Buses, trams & metro: Buses wait outside the airport.

Car hire
Available in Sana'a and other main centres.

BUSINESS DIRECTORY

The addresses listed below are a selection only. While World of Information makes every endeavour to check these addresses, we cannot guarantee that changes have not been made, especially to telephone numbers and area codes. We would welcome any corrections.

Telephone area codes
The international direct dialling (IDD) code for Yemen is +967, followed by the area code and subscriber's number:

Aden	2	Sana'a	1
Almahra	5	Taiz	4
Amran	7	Yarim	4
Hodeidah	3	Zabid	3

Chambers of Commerce
Aden Chamber of Commerce, Queen Arwa Road, PO Box 473, Crater, Aden (tel: 221-176; fax: 255-660; e-mail: cciaden@y.net.ye).

Federation of Yemen Chambers of Commerce and Industry, Al-Qiyadah Road, PO Box 16992, Sana'a (tel: 265-038; fax: 261-269; e-mail: fucci@y.net.ye).

Hadhramout Chamber of Commerce and Industry, Mukalla Main Street, PO Box 8302, Mukalla (tel: 353-258; fax: 303-437; e-mail: hdramoutchamber@y.net.ye).

Hodeidah Chamber of Commerce and Industry, Liberty Squaret, PO Box 3370, Hodeidah (tel: 217-401; fax: 211-528; e-mail: hodcii@y.net.ye).

National Chamber of Commerce and Industry, PO Box 5029, Crater, Aden (tel: 51203; fax: 232-412).

Sana'a Chamber of Commerce and Industry, Airport Road, PO Box 195, Sana'a (tel: 232-361; fax: 232-412; e-mail: sanaacomyemen@y.net.ye).

Ta'iz Chamber of Commerce and Industry, Chamber Street, PO Box 5029, Taiz (tel: 210-581; fax: 212-335; e-mail: taizchamber@y.net.ye).

Banking
Arab Bank Plc, PO Box 5130, Madram Street, Maala, Aden (tel: 242-099, 240-043; fax: 242-098).

Credit Agricole Indosuez, PO Box 651, Al Ma'ala Main St, Aden (tel: 247-4024; fax: 247-282).

International Bank of Yemen YSC, PO Box 819, al Maidan - Crater, Off Queen

Arwa Rd, Crater, Aden (tel: 255-795; fax: 252-016).

National Bank of Yemen, PO Box 5, Crater, Aden (tel: 252-875, 253-327; fax: 252-875).

Watani Bank for Trade and Investment, PO Box 4424, Queen Arwa St, Agaba, Aden (tel: 2506-1017; fax: 250-618).

Yemen Bank for Reconstruction and Development, PO Box 239, Aden (tel: 252-104, 254-046; fax: 252-141).

Yemen Commercial Bank, PO Box 4230, Aden (tel: 255-813, 253-384; fax: 255-428).

Central bank

Central Bank of Yemen, PO Box 59, Ali Abdulmoghni Street, Sana'a (tel: 274-310 fax: 274-057; e-mail: info@centralbank.gov.ye).

Travel information

Sana'a International Airport, PO Box 1438, Sana'a (tel/fax: 250-819).

Yemenia (Yemen Airways), PO Box 1183, Sana'a (tel: 201-822; fax: 201-821; e-mail: info@yemenia.com).

Ministry of tourism

Ministry of Culture and Tourism, Al-Hasabah, PO Box 129, Sana'a (tel: 235-112; fax: 235-113; e-mail: yementpb@y.net.ye).

National tourist organisation offices

General Tourism Development Authority, Al-Hasabah, PO Box 129, Sana'a (tel: 252-319; fax: 252-316; e-mail: gtda@gtda.gov.ye).

Tourism Promotion Board, Al-Hasabah, PO Box 5607, Sana'a (tel: 251-033; fax: 251-034; e-mail: ytpb@yementourism.com).

Ministries

Ministry of Agriculture and Water Resources, PO Box 2805 (tel: 200-999; fax: 209-509).

Ministry of Civil Service and Administration Reform, PO Box 1992, Sana'a (tel: 200-404; fax: 274-456).

Ministry of Communications, PO Box 17045, Sana's (tel: 271-100; fax: 251-150).

Ministry of Construction, PO Box 1180, Sana'a (tel: 202-288; fax: 274-145).

Ministry of Culture and Tourism (tel: 200-002; fax: 252-316).

Ministry of Defence (tel: 250-330; fax: 251-559).

Ministry of Economy, Supply & Trade, PO Box 1704, Sana'a (tel: 202-471).

Ministry of Education (tel: 274-548; fax: 274-558).

Ministry of Electricity and Water, PO Box 11422, Sana'a (tel: 250-143; fax: 251-554).

Ministry of Finance, PO Box 190, Sana'a (tel: 260-375; fax: 263-040).

Ministry of Fishery Wealth, PO Box 19179, Sana'a (tel: 262-866; fax: 263-165).

Ministry of Foreign Affairs, PO Box 1994, Sana'a (tel: 202-555; fax: 209-540).

Ministry of Higher Education and Scientific Research, PO Box 11327, Sana'a (tel: 200-463; fax: 262-001).

Ministry of Housing and Urban Planning, PO Box 1445, Sana'a (tel: 262-614; fax: 215-613).

Ministry of Immigrants Affairs, PO Box 1299, Sana'a (tel: 215-666; fax: 263-027).

Ministry of Industry, PO Box 607, Sana'a (tel: 252-339; fax: 252-366).

Ministry of Information (tel: 200-050; fax: 282-050).

Ministry of the Interior and Security (tel: 252-701; fax: 251-529).

Ministry of Justice (tel: 252-158; fax: 252-138).

Ministry of Labour and Vocational Training, PO Box 60, Sana'a (tel: 274-922; fax: 274-107).

Ministry of Legal Affairs, PO Box 1292, Sana'a (tel: 262-047; fax: 262-047).

Ministry of Local Government, PO Box 2198, Sana'a (tel: 250-626; fax: 251-513).

Ministry of Oil and Mineral Resources, PO Box 81, Sana'a (tel: 202-312; fax: 202-314).

Ministry of Planning and Development, PO Box 175, Sana'a (tel: 250-118; fax: 251-503).

Ministry of Provision and Trade, PO Box 804, Sana'a (tel: 252-337; fax: 251-366).

Ministry of Public Health, PO Box 274160, Sana'a (tel: 252-222; fax: 244-143).

Ministry of Securities and Social Affairs (tel: 262-809; fax: 209-547).

Ministry of State for Cabinet Affairs (tel: 200-677; fax: 209-518).

Ministry of State for Foreign Affairs, PO Box L994, Sana'a (tel: 202-544; fax: 209-540).

Ministry of State for House of Deputies Affairs (tel: 200-671; fax: 209-518).

Ministry of Transport, PO Box 2781 (tel: 260-904; fax: 263-169).

Ministry of Tourism, PO Box 129, Sana'a (tel: 252-319; fax: 260-186).

Ministry of WAQF and Guidance (tel: 274-438; fax: 274-17).

Ministry of Youth and Sport, PO Box 2701, Sana'a (tel: 215-653; fax: 263-181).

Other useful addresses

British Consulate-General, PO Box 6304, Khormaksar, Aden (tel: 232-712; fax: 231-256).

British Embassy, PO Box 1287, Sana'a (tel: 264-081; fax: 263-059).

Central Planning Organisation, PO Box 175, Sana'a (tel: 250-1018).

Foreign Trade Corporation, PO Box 77, Sana'a (tel: 72-058).

General Post Office, Liberation (Tahreer) Square, (tel: 71-401/2).

Ports and Marine Affairs Corporation, PO Box 3183, Hodeidah.

Republic of Yemen Embassy (USA), Suite 705, 2600 Virginia Avenue, NW, Washington DC 20037 (tel: (+1-202) 965-4760; fax: (+1-202) 337-2017; e-mail: information@yemenembassy.org).

United Nations Development Programme, PO Box 551 Sana'a (tel: 70-593/70-596).

National news agency: Saba (Yemen News Agency), (internet: www.sabanews.net/en)

Internet sites

ArabNet: http://www.arab.net/welcome.html

Arabia.On.Line: http://www.arabia.com

Embassy of the Republic Yemen, Washington DC: http://www.yemenembassy.org

Yemen gateway site: http://www.al-bab.com/yemen/Default.htm

Yemen Times On-line: http://www.yementimes.com

KEY FACTS

Official name: Republic of Zambia

Head of State: President Edgar Lungu (PF) (from 20 Jan 2015)

Head of government: President Edgar Lungu (PF) (from 20 Jan 2015)

Ruling party: Patriotic Front

Area: 752,614 square km

Population: 15.02 million (2014)* (13,046,508; 2010, census figure)

Capital: Lusaka

Official language: English

Currency: Kwacha (K) = 100 ngwee

Exchange rate: K9.94 per US$ (Sep 2015) Zambia re-based the kwacha on 31 Dec 2012, dropping three zeros

GDP per capita: US$1,781 (2014)*

GDP real growth: 5.42% (2014)*

GDP: US$26.76 billion (2014)*

Inflation: 7.94% (2014)*

Balance of trade: US$1.63 billion (2014)

* estimated figure

Zambia

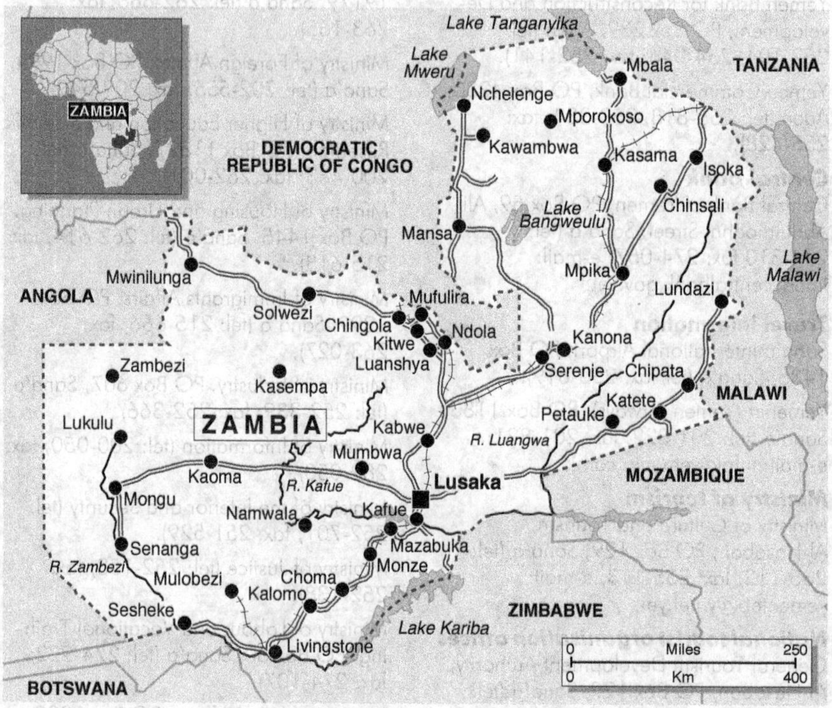

The territory of Northern Rhodesia came under direct rule of the United Kingdom in 1923 and during the 1920s and 1930s, advances in mining spurred development and immigration. The country's name was changed to Zambia upon independence in 1964. During the 1980s and 1990s, declining copper prices, economic mismanagement, and a prolonged drought devastated the economy. Multiparty elections in 1991 brought an end to one-party rule and propelled the Movement for Multiparty Democracy (MMD) to government. The subsequent vote in 1996, however, saw increasing harassment of opposition parties and exploitation of state media and other resources. The election in 2001 was marked by administrative problems, with three parties filing a legal petition challenging the election of ruling party candidate Levy Mwanawasa although Mwanawasa was re-elected in 2006 in an election that was deemed free and fair. Upon his death in August 2008, he was succeeded by his vice president, Rupiah Banda, who won a special presidential by-election later than year. The MMD and Rupiah Banda lost to the Patriotic Front (PF) and Michael Sata in the 2011 general elections. Sata presided over a period of haphazard economic management and attempted to silence opposition to PF policies. He died in October 2014 and was succeeded by his vice president, Guy Scott, who served as interim president until special elections were held in January 2015. Edgar Lungu won the presidential by-election and will complete Sata's term, which expires in late 2016. Lungu won a narrow victory with 48.3 per cent of the vote while his main challenger, Hakainde Hichilema won 47.7 per cent of the vote. Following the elections results, Hichilema denounced the election as a sham, but urged his supporters to remain calm. Zambia thereby successfully achieved yet another peaceful change of president, not something the African continent is necessarily noted for.

Zambia has had one of the world's fastest growing economies for the past decade, with real GDP growth averaging 6.7 per cent per annum. GDP growth was 5.6

per cent in 2014 down slightly from 6.7 per cent in 2013. Privatisation of the government-owned copper mines in the 1990s relieved the government from covering enormous losses generated by the industry and greatly increased copper mining output and profitability, spurring economic growth. Copper output has increased steadily from 2004, due to higher commodity prices and foreign investment, however, it weakened in 2014 when Zambia was overtaken by the Democratic Republic of Congo as Africa's largest copper producer. And has since suffered as the futures price of copper has fallen to US$2.0485 per pound, a drop of some 27 per cent over 10 months in 2015.

Foreign direct investment (FDI) was US$2.4 billion in 2014, a significant increase on the US$1.8 billion in 2013. Zambia's dependency on copper has made it vulnerable to depressed commodity prices, although record high copper prices and a bumper maize crop in 2010 helped Zambia to recover quickly from the world economic slowdown that began in 2008. Despite strong economic growth and its status as a middle-income country, widespread and extreme rural poverty and high unemployment levels remain significant problems, made worse by a high birth rate, a relatively high HIV/Aids burden, and by market-distorting agricultural policies. Over 60 per cent of people remained in multi-dimensional poverty in 2014 while 74.5 per cent of people lived on under US$1.25 a day.

The economy

Economic policy inconsistency and poor budget management has hindered the economy and contributed to weakness in the kwacha, which was Africa's worst performing currency during 2014. On 1 January 2015, a new mineral royalty tax regime dramatically increased mining taxes, and has led to an economic impasse between the government and mines. If left intact, the new tax could result in the closure of less profitable mines, the loss of thousands of jobs, and the loss of additional foreign investment.

Glencore's Zambia copper mining unit laid off 4,300 workers, union and company sources reported on 24 November 2015. Around 5,000 employees working for contractors would also lose their jobs as Mopani Copper Mines would only maintain two contractors specialised in the sinking of shafts. Mopani said that the firm was losing millions of dollars and had to take action to secure its long-term future. The company was expected to pay the 4,300 workers a total of US$33 million. Swiss-based Glencore has pledged to cut its net debt to US$20 billion by the end of 2016 to regain the trust of investors after its shares tumbled to record lows in 2015.

According to the African Development Bank's *African Economic Outlook 2015* (AEO), economic growth in Zambia is expected to remain strong and increase to 6 per cent in 2015. Furthermore, inflation is expected to fall from 7.8 per cent in 2014 to below 7 per cent by 2017. Governance and democratic processes continue to gather strength, with the recent presidential by-election evidence of Zambia's status as a peaceful and stable country. The slower growth in 2014 can be attributed to lower production in the mining sector as well as lack of growth in manufacturing and public services. Despite these short fallings, agriculture put in a strong performance growing at over 6 per cent as a result of a bumper maize harvest. Economic performance is expected to remain strong in the medium term driven by large investments in infrastructure and a growing public administration and defence. Diversifying the economy away from dependence on copper and the creation of good jobs remains the overarching challenge for the government. Improving accountability and strengthening the fight against corruption also remains firmly on the government's agenda. In 2014, the fiscal deficit fell by approximately 1 per cent compared to 2013 and this is expected to continue in the medium term with slower expenditure growth and improved cash management. Productivity in the private sector needs to increase in order to improve competitiveness given the pressure for higher wages. One way to achieve this will be to expand skills and education which the government aims to do along with accelerating interventions in health, water and sanitation in 2015. The government has aimed to deal with spatial inclusion within its Sixth National Development Plan with its improved transport links already helping to provide impetus for growth in parts of the country outside of the capital city and the Copperbelt. The main transport corridors that connect the copper mines in the north with Livingston in the south through the capital city, Lusaka, have benefitted both Central and Eastern Provinces where there has been an influx of investments, creating a basis for further development. An added benefit of industrial policy is the creation of multi-facility economic zones aimed at creating opportunities in the main urban agglomerations and attracting foreign investment.

Risk assessment

Economy	Fair/poor
Politics	Good
Regional stability	Good/fair

COUNTRY PROFILE

1851 British missionary David Livingstone visited central Africa.

1880s British settlers followed Livingstone and the British South Africa Company, headed by British imperialist and financier, Cecil John Rhodes, opened its first copper mine at Broken Hill (later Kabwe) in 1908.

1924 The colony was put under direct British rule.

KEY INDICATORS — Zambia

	Unit	2011	2012	2013	2014	**2015
Population	m	*13.59	*14.07	*14.54	*15.02	*15.52
Gross domestic product (GDP)	US$bn	19.20	20.59	26.83	*26.76	*28.45
GDP per capita	US$	1,414	1,463	1,845	*1,781	*1,833
GDP real growth	%	6.6	7.2	6.7	*5.4	*6.7
Inflation	%	8.7	6.6	7.0	*7.9	*7.7
Exports (fob) (goods)	US$m	8,671.8	9,143.5	10,843.4	10,220.2	–
Imports (fob) (goods)	US$m	6,454.2	7,960.8	9,195.4	8,594.8	–
Balance of trade	US$m	2,217.6	1,452.7	1,648.0	1,625.4	–
Current account	US$m	69.1	789.0	-2.0	*-61.0	*78.0
Total reserves minus gold	US$m	2,347.0	3,042.2	2,683.8	3,078.4	–
Foreign exchange	US$m	1,701.3	2,435.7	2,094.2	–	–
Exchange rate	per US$	5,165.00	5.24	5.52	6.40	–

* estimated figure ** forecast figure

1953–63 Northern Rhodesia (later Zambia) was part of the British-sponsored Federation of Rhodesia and Nyasaland.
1960 The United National Independence Party (UNIP) was formed by Kenneth Kaunda to campaign for independence and the dissolution of white minority rule.
1964 On 18 May the Barotseland Agreement was signed, amalgamating the two British protectorates of Northern Rhodesia and Barotseland (roughly Western Province) into Zambia. Under the Agreement Barotseland and the Litunga (King) retained authority over a number of local matters. (After independence the Kaunda government distroyed the agreement, leading to discontent amoungst hardliners who wanted to see a full secession of Barotseland.) Zambia gained independence under the presidency of Kenneth Kaunda. The government supported Marxist rebels in Mozambique, independence movements in Rhodesia (later Zimbabwe) and the African National Congress (ANC) in South Africa. This led to internal security problems and financial difficulties as Zambia's colonial neighbours attempted to destabilise the country.
1964–1970s Key enterprises and land were nationalised.
1972 Zambia became a one-party state with UNIP as the only legal party.
1975 The Tanzania-Zambia Railway Authority (Tazara) open the rail line linking the Zambian Copperbelt to the Tanzanian port of Dar es Salaam, reducing the country's dependence on Rhodesia and South Africa for port access.
1976 Zambia gave support to Rhodesia's bid for independence and its eventual transformation from white minority rule into Zimbabwe.
1989 Zambia began a programme of austerity measures to stabilise the economy, following a long-term fall in the price of Zambia's chief export, copper.
1990 Food riots heightened calls for an end to one-party rule.
1991 Multi-party elections were held in which Kaunda was defeated by Frederick Chiluba and the Movement for Multi-party Democracy (MMD).
1996 The MMD and President Chiluba were re-elected in a landslide victory.
1999 Angolan terrorists attacked sites in Lusaka and the Indeni Oil Refinery in Ndola was sabotaged.
2000 Kaunda resigned as leader of UNIP.
2001 The MMD was re-elected although the opposition said the elections were flawed.
2002 Levy Mwanawasa (MMD) was inaugurated as president. The government excluded genetically modified (GM) maize from its accepted imported foodstuffs.
2003 Former president Frederick Chiluba's immunity from prosecution was removed and he was arrested and charged on 59 counts, including corruption and abuse of office.
2004 The court case against Chiluba was dropped but he was quickly re-arrested and charged with embezzling US$488,000 from state funds.
2005 The World Bank approved a US$3.8 billion debt relief package, which wrote off over 50 per cent of Zambia's debt. The International Monetary Fund (IMF) and Japanese government also cancelled outstanding debt worth around US$577 million and US$692 million respectively. President Mwanawasa appealed for food for millions of Zambian citizens as drought caused widespread hunger.
2006 The government announced that as a result of the US$4 billion of debt relief, healthcare for people living in the rural areas would be provided free of charge. In presidential elections incumbent Levy Mwanawasa (MMD) won with 43.0 per cent of the vote. In parliamentary elections, the MMD won 72 out of 150 directly elected seats. It was announced that the first deposits of oil and gas had been found in the border region with Angola (Africa's second largest oil producer).
2007 A large mining investment zone was inaugurated by Chinese President Hu Jintao. The UK High Court ruled that former president Chiluba had conspired, along with four aides, to defraud Zambia of around US$46 million.
2008 President Mwanawasa died in France, following specialist treatment for a stroke. Vice President Rupiah Banda became interim president until elections could take place. There was no obvious successor; Mwanawasa was reported to have said that the next president should come from a different province from previous presidents Kaunda (Northern), Chiluba (Luapula) and himself (Central), although his wife, Maureen, was said to be 'considering her position'. In the presidential elections, Rupiah Banda (MMD) won with 40.1 per cent of the vote, while Michael Sata (PF), the closest contender won 38.1 per cent. President Banda was sworn into office (on 3 November) until 2011, when former President Mwanawasa's term would have ended.
2009 The government began to liquidate the dept owed to the Co-operative Bank (closed in the 1990s) of US$23 million, of which around US$11.5 million had been paid to the Zambia Co-operative Federation supporting farming investment. Ten Chinese companies committed US$600 million in the Chambishi economic and trade co-operation zone (particularly in mining, construction and steel production). The ministry of finance released US$31.4 million to build sealed roads, mainly from Leopards Hill to Chainda and Ibex Hill. Former president Frederick Chiluba was acquitted of all charges of corruption. The IMF agreed to the immediate disbursement of US$81.2 million as part of the Poverty Reduction and Growth Facility (PRGF) arrangement; the total amount of disbursement approved was US$329.7 million.
2010 Around 30,000 small-scale farming households, mostly headed by women, were eligible for a US$20 million loan from the International Fund for Agricultural Development (Ifad). The programme focused on stimulating rural economic development through small-scale production. The Global Fund to Fight Aids, Tuberculosis and Malaria (Global Fund) suspended operations in Zambia due to fraud and the Zambian authorities failure to take appropriate action to safeguard Global Fund grant programmes. A railway line between Zambia and Malawi was inaugurated; the Chipata-Mchinji railway line will be extended to Mozambique.
2011 Reuters reported in January that Chinese investment in 2010 exceeded US$1 billion and created over 15,000 jobs. Zambia's first democratically elected president, Frederick Chiluba, died in June at the age of 68. Presidential elections were held in September in which three candidates took part. Michael Sata (Patriotic Front) (PF) won 43 per cent of the vote; incumbent, Rupiah Banda (MMD) won 36.1 per cent and Hakainde Hichilema (UPND) 18 per cent. In a move to reassure foreign investors, President Sata's first official appointment after being sworn in was with the Chinese ambassador. He warned that while he welcomed Chinese companies, they must comply with Zambian law. In parliamentary elections also held September, the opposition PF won 38.25 per cent of the vote, (60 seats out of 150), ousting the MMD from its 20-years in office. President Sato's administration appointed Guy Scott, a white parliamentarian, as vice president.
2012 On 12 March MMD was stripped of its legal status for not paying fees for the past 20 years. On 5 August rioting miners killed a Chinese manager and injured a second, during protests at the delay in implementing a new minimum wage. On 10 October, the Global Fund signed an agreement with the Churches Health Association of Zambia to provide US$102 million to support the national response to HIV infections. The activities are to include prevention of mother to child transmission, promoting male circumcision, reducing new infections and maintaining a high coverage of impact mitigation. On 21

November the government granted environmental approval to the Canada-based First Quantum Minerals, for a planned US$640 million, 300,000 tonnes per year copper smelting operation at its existing Kansanshi mine. By 29 November around 580 (Democratic Republic) Congolese refugees, including 409 children had found sanctuary in Luapula Province.

2013 Tourism minister, Sylvia Masebo, announced in January the banning of hunting of lions and leopards. The ban comes as conservationists warned that wildlife populations now face a greater threat from poaching than at any time since the 1980s. Former President Rupiah Banda pleaded not guilty on 5 November to a charge of corruption alleged to have occurred during the 2011 election campaign.

2014 In May Zambia Railways re-started operations on the Nacala Corridor to Nacala in Mozambique. Zambia Railways also announced that it had signed an agreement in July with DRC's state-owned Société Nationale des Chemins de Fer du Congo (Congo National Railway) to transport some 15,000 tonnes per month of copper from Ndola to Lumbumbashi. The government announced screening of travellers from Tanzania and the DRC after there was a suspected death from Ebola virus in Tanzania in July. The 14 August by-election in Mangango, Western Province, was won by the ruling PF candidate, Rogers Lingweshi, giving the party a total of 79 seats in the 158-seat parliament, just one short of an outright majority. Wynter Kabimba was fired as justice minister and as Secretary General of the ruling PF party in late August. The government declared the Ebola virus to be a notifiable disease in August. At the same time Botswana banned trucks that had passed through DRC from entering the country, resulting in some 90 trucks stranded on the Zambian side of the border at Kazungula by the end of August. In September Fitch Ratings agency upgraded its economic outlook from 'stable' to 'positive'. Justice minister, Edgar Lungu, released the final draft of the new constitution in October. It will be put to the people in a referendum, possible in 2016. President Sato died on 28 October in hospital in London. Vice President Guy Scott became interim president on 29 October. Under the contitution residential elections have to be held within 90 days.

2015 Presidential elections were held on 20 January; heavy rains caused some polling stations to remain open later and others to be opened the following day. Edgar Lungu (PF) secured a narrow victory with 807,925 votes (48.33 per cent) over Hakainde Hichilema (UPND) with 780,168 (46.67 per cent). Turnout was low at 32.4 per cent. Mr Lungu will serve as president until what would have been the end of President Sata's term in 2016. The first parliament under President Lungu opened on 24 February. President Lungu collapsed on 9 March and was flown to hospital in South Africa. He was discharged from the hospital on 14 March after undergoing surgery to correct a narrowing of the oesophagus. Although the 2011 election results gave the PF victory over the MMD with 60 seats to 55, by April 2015 the balance had swung to 76 to 34 after a number of bye-elections. The UNDP had also increased its seats, by four. The ban on hunting lions and leopards imposed in January 2013 was lifted in May. Conservationists are concerned that the lion population is not enough to allow for hunting. Inonge Wina was appointed vice president in May. In September the Electoral Commission of Zambia (ECZ) launched a voter registration exercise ahead of the 2016 general and presidential elections. In late September Moody's Investors Service, downgraded its sovereign credit rating for Zambia from B1 to B2, but changed its economic outlook from 'negative' to 'stable'. Inflation almost doubled between September and October, from 7.7 per cent to 14.3 per cent, mostly due to price increases in both food and non-food items.

Political structure

Constitution

In November 1991, Zambia's one-party state was replaced by a multi-party democratic system based on a new constitution. In 1995 the ruling Movement for Multi-party Democracy (MMD) revised the constitution. The Zambia Law Association criticised the new constitution on the grounds that it allows parliament to make retrospective laws and that a president could be elected on receiving the highest number of votes cast even if these amounted to less than 50 per cent. It also condemned amendments to the Bill of Rights of the 1991 Constitution without a referendum. A controversial Bill passed by President Chiluba on 28 May 1996 made further amendments to the constitution: future presidential candidates must be second-generation Zambians.

Independence date

24 October 1964 (from UK)

Form of state

Republic

The executive

Executive power is held by the president elected by universal suffrage for a five-year term. The constitution provides for a cabinet appointed from within parliament and gives it extra powers. The president does not have the right to declare martial law. The president must obtain parliamentary approval to impose a state of emergency longer than seven days.

Presidents serve for five years and are limited to two terms. The vice-president is personally appointed by the president.

National legislature

The unicameral National Assembly has 158 members in total; 150 are elected by popular vote in single seat constituencies and eight members are appointed by the president, all serve for five-year terms.

Legal system

The president appoints judges and nominates the chief justice. Courts include the Supreme Court of Zambia and the High Court.

Last elections

20 January 2015 (presidential); 23 September 2011 (parliamentary)

Results: Presidential: Elections were bought forward 18 months following the death of incumbent president Michael Sata, who died in office on 28 October 2014. Edgar Lungu, of the ruling PF party won 48.33% of the vote, while challenger Hakainde Hichilema garnered 46.67%.

Parliamentary: the Patriotic Front (PF) won 38.25 per cent of the vote, (60 seats out of 150), Movement for Multi-party Democracy (MMD) 33.56 per cent (55), United Party for National Development (UPND) 16.99 per cent (28), Alliance for Democracy and Development (ADD) 1.18 per cent (one), Forum for Democracy and Development (FDD) 0.75 per cent (one); three independent candidates each won a seat and 15 other political parties failed to win any seats. Turnout was 53.98 per cent. Two seats remained vacant, pending by-elections.

Eight additional parliamentary members were appointed by the president, to make a total of 158 members of parliament (MP).

Next elections

2016 (presidential and general plus a referendum on the Bill of Rights)

Political parties

Ruling party

Patriotic Front

Main opposition party

Movement for Multi-party Democracy (MMD)

Population

14.54 million (2013)*

Around 58 per cent of the total population is under 15 years of age. The majority of people live in the northern Copperbelt towns and Lusaka.

Last census: 16 October 2010: 13,046,508

Population density: 13 inhabitants per square km. Urban population 36 per cent (2010 Unicef).

Annual growth rate: 2.5 per cent, 1990–2010 (Unicef).

Ethnic make-up

There are 73 ethnic groups in Zambia. The largest single group, comprising 34 per cent of the population, is the Bemba (north-east and Copperbelt areas). Other important groups include the Tonga of the southern province with 16 per cent of the population; the Nyanja of the eastern provinces (14 per cent) who are well represented in the capital, Lusaka; and the Lozi (9 per cent) of the west.

The European population live and work mostly in the urban areas, or on the farmlands along the railway lines. A high proportion of the Asian community is to be found on the Copperbelt and other urban centres.

Religions

Christian, Muslim and indigenous beliefs. Approximately 70 per cent of the population is Christian (mainly Roman Catholic and Protestant).

Education

The HIV/Aids crisis in sub-Saharan Africa has not only undermined public investment in education but has also contributed to the shortage of trained teachers, in 2001 815 primary school teachers, or 45 per cent of teachers trained that year, died of Aids. This has resulted in declining literacy rates and low levels of school enrolment. Enrolment rates for the richest households are more than one-third higher than for the poorest households.

A first cycle primary education begins at age seven, lasting until age 11, then three years in a second cycle primary school prepares children for exams to determine progression to a junior secondary school for two years until aged 16 when successfully completed exams allow progression into senior secondary school for the last two years. There are two universities that provide higher education and several specialist institutions providing professional and vocational training.

The government has developed a strong education sector reform through the Basic Education Sub-sector Investment Programme (Bessip), which has set a target of universal primary school enrolment for just under half a million children by 2005. Annual government expenditure during the first phase of the reform amounted to US$56 million, excluding contributions from international donors for the projects. The scheme aims to construct 2,000 additional classrooms and improve training in rural schools. Zambia spends typically less than 3 per cent of GDP on education.

Literacy rate: 80 per cent adult rate; 89 per cent youth rate (15–24) (Unesco 2005).

Compulsory years: Seven to 13.

Enrolment rate: 89 per cent gross primary enrolment; 27 per cent gross secondary enrolment, of relevant age groups (including repeaters) (World Bank).

Pupils per teacher: 39 in primary schools.

Health

Healthcare is provided free in state-funded hospitals and commercially in private sector clinics. Rural health care is rudimentary and frequently provided only by missionary hospitals and clinics. State funding cut-backs have led to severe shortages of medical equipment and staff. Many medical posts are unfilled for lack of funds. The government is keen to encourage private investment in hospitals and believes foreign investment provides the key to the redevelopment of the health sector.

TB incidence in Zambia fell from 716 to 410 per 100,000 people from 1990 to 2013.

Improved water sources are available to 64 per cent of the population.

HIV/Aids

Zambia has one of the highest rates of HIV in Africa. It is estimated that 42 per cent of hospital beds are occupied by HIV/Aids sufferers.

The impact on households is severe, with children often kept from attending school in order to help with harvesting of subsistence crops. Studies show that around 55 per cent of households affected by HIV/Aids are unable to pay school fees. Households affected by HIV/Aids have on average 30–35 per cent less income than those who are not affected. Around 60 per cent of families of Aids sufferers endure food shortages and malnutrition as a direct result of the disease.

Zambia, as one of the poorest countries in the world, has been identified as in need of international aid to fight the disease.

On 10 October 2012, the Global Fund signed an agreement with the Churches Health Association of Zambia to provide US$102 million to support the national response to HIV infections. The activities are to include prevention of mother to child transmission, promoting male circumcision, reducing new infections and maintaining a high coverage of impact mitigation

HIV prevalence: 15.6 per cent aged 15–49 in 2003 (World Bank)

Life expectancy: 40 years, 2004 (WHO 2006)

Fertility rate/Maternal mortality rate: 6.3 births per woman, 2010 (Unicef); maternal mortality 6.5 per l,000 (World Bank).

Child (under 5 years) mortality rate (per 1,000): 89 per 1,000 live births (WHO 2012); 28.1 per cent of children aged under 5 arre malnourished (World Bank).

Head of population per physician: 0.12 physicians per 1,000 people, 2004 (WHO 2006)

Welfare

Zambia is one of the poorest countries in the world, with an estimated 80 per cent of its 11 million people living in desperate poverty. In December 2003 the statistics office stated that 'the food basket... was K528,529 for a family of six. The same family on average was expected to live on K758,961 for all their basic needs'.

The government provides some basic welfare for pensioners, children and people affected by disasters.

The Pension Scheme Regulation Act of 1996 provides a regulatory framework for private pension schemes. The Zambia National Provident Fund (ZNPF) was successfully transformed into the National Pension Scheme Authority (Napsa) in early 2000. The weaknesses of ZNPF, which included poor benefits, delays in payment and ineffective record keeping were critically examined to overcome similar problems for the Napsa. The economic difficulties in Zambia and the low retirement age of 55 made it necessary for Napsa to begin with modest benefits. The scheme offers three principal benefits namely retirement, invalidity and survivors' benefits. Additionally, it provides a funeral grant.

The scheme is based on the principle of social insurance and requires compulsory financial contributions from both employees and their employers at a rate of 5 per cent each. Retirement benefit is paid on the basis of a minimum contributory period of 15 years. The scheme is basic to allow the development of private occupational pension schemes.

Main cities

Lusaka (capital, estimated population 1.5 million in 2012), Kitwe (561,524), Ndola (517,975), Kabwe (220,784), Chingola (182,946), Mufulira (143,516), Livingstone (141,195), Luanshya (134,180), Kasama (120,041), Chipata (117,839).

Languages spoken

English is the usual medium for business. Until 1975 Zambia was said to have an estimated 73 identified African languages, all Bantu, of which seven are recognised as official vernaculars – Chitumbuka-Chisenga, Tonga, Silozi, IciBemba, Kaonde, Luvale, Lunda and Chinyanja. However in 2015 researchers concluded that although there are at least 73 different people groups in Zambia,

there are only 33 indigenous languages, and 18 cross-border languages with a hub in a neighbouring country. A number of indigenous languages, including Luyana (about 220,000 users) and Sala (about 39,000 users) are considered likely to be absorbed by larger language groups. The research was undertaken by Status of Bible Translation Needs in Zambia (2014) by Kenneth S Sawka and Josephat Daka (zambiapibt@gmail.com).
Zambian traders usually have a working knowledge of English.

Official language/s

English

Media

Freedom of the press is constrained by legal provisions, which have led to self-censorship.

Press

Since 1996 readership has been falling and prices have risen by 500 per cent so that newspapers have become a luxury item for most Zambians. Most newspapers are distributed in the capital and Copperbelt towns, while the rest of the country receives copies 1–3 days after publication.

Dailies: The government owns two newspapers, *Times of Zambia* (www.times.co.zm) and *Zambia Daily Mail* (www.daily-mail.co.zm); *The Post* (www.postzambia.com) is privately owned.

Weeklies: Dailies publish Sunday papers including *Sunday Mail* and *Sunday Times*; independent publications include *The Monitor* and *National Mirror* (church owned).

Business: Publications include *The Lusaka Times* (www.lusakatimes.com) and the *Zambia Daily Mail* have sections on business and the economy. Periodicals include *The Zambian Marketer* and *Development Zambia* published by (www.langmead.com).

Periodicals: Langmead and Baker (www.langmead.com) publishes several magazines aimed at various special interest groups.

Broadcasting

The state-run Zambia National Broadcasting Corporation (ZNBC) is the dominant organisation in broadcasting.

Radio: ZNBC has four networks with two broadcasting in English, one in local languages and the fourth which carries commercials.

Radio Phoenix (www.radiophoenix.co.zm) is a national commercial radio network; there are a number of local commercial radio stations in operation including Q-FM and Mazabuka Community Radio and Breeze FM (www.breezefm.makeni.net). There are several religious content radio stations.

Television: ZNBC operates the only public terrestrial network with one channel. There is no Zambian based satellite operation, although the MultiChoice Zambia services can be received from South Africa.

National news agency: Zambia News Agency

Economy

Zambia's wealth is generated by the primary industries of agriculture and mining. Industry constituted 37.3 per cent of GDP in 2014, the service sector constituted 45.1 per cent and agriculture 17.7 per cent. The country has experienced strong growth since 2005, peaking at 10.3 per cent in 2010 before slowing to 6.0 per cent in 2014, and Zambia has reached lower middle income status. However, high inflation has been a long-term problem, averaging 12.2 per cent from 2007-09. Record high world food and fuel prices were the main causes. Inflation has decreased overall since 2009 and has averaged 7.3 per cent from 2010–14.

Its main economic zone follows the line of rail southwards from the Copperbelt around Ndola and Kitwe, through Lusaka, the capital, to Livingstone on the border with Zimbabwe. This area has been subject to urbanisation, although the rest of the country is relatively sparsely inhabited. Of the US$11.07 billion of total exports in 2014, US$8.05 billion was earned through refined and raw copper exports. Steep rises in the price of copper helped to encourage investment in the industry and related infrastructure. This contributed to the average annual GDP growth of 7.7 per cent over the ten-year period ending in 2014. Zambia's copper production accounts for around 70 per cent of Africa's total.

Around 50 per cent of the country's population are concentrated in urban areas, however the largest employer is still the agriculture sector, which makes up for around 70 per cent of the work force. The majority of farms are small-scale with low productivity, leading to food insecurity. Maize is the staple diet and when weather provides the optimum rainfall bumper harvests are attainable. However Zambia is subject to droughts and flooding. Cash crops include coffee, tea, cotton, rice, groundnuts, tobacco, sugarcane and cut flowers. The government is investing in the agricultural sector to improve soil, seeds and equipment to increase productivity.

In the medium-term GDP growth is expected to be led by copper production. The Luanshya Copper Mine reopened in 2011 and Zambia's total copper production is projected to reach 850,000 tonnes. In 2013 the Zambian Environmental Management Agency (ZEMA) approved 27 new exploration and mining licences. Other investment projects include infrastructure and increased electricity generation to provide greater capacity.

The government began economic reforms in 2005, including diversification, to reduce the country's reliance on copper, as the International Monetary Fund (IMF) and World Bank provided large debt relief financing to Zambia. However, despite these efforts the mining industry still dominates the economy.

Full donor support and free market reform have had little impact on poverty and per capita income remains low, having only risen from US$947 in 2006 to US$1,844.8 by 2013 showing that the strong growth of the economy has not translated to significant poverty reduction. However, in 2014 income per capita had dropped to US$1,801.9.

In 2014, the UN Human Development Index (HDI) ranked Zambia 141 (out of 187) for national development in health, education and income. Since 2000, Zambia's progress has improved but has not matched the growth of other countries in sub-Saharan Africa. 63 per cent of the population live in multidimensional poverty conditions; this poverty is heavily concentrated in rural areas where poverty rates are greater than 70.0 per cent, whereas poverty incidence in urban areas such as the Copperbelt and Lusaka regions are relatively low (22.0 and 34.0 per cent).

Unemployment and underemployment are a significant problem, with around half the population falling into one of these categories. Remittances in 2010 were US$68 million, which reached a peak of US$96 million in 2012, before falling to US$81 million by 2014.

In late September 2015 Moody's Investors Service, downgraded its sovereign credit rating for Zambia from B1 to B2, but changed its economic outlook from 'negative' to 'stable'.

External trade

Zambia is a member of the Common Market for Eastern and Southern Africa (Comesa), and operates in a free trade area with 13 of the 19 member states. It is also a member of the Southern African Development Community (SADC), the objectives of which include reducing trade barriers, achieving regional development and economic growth and evolving common systems and institutions. In 2009 international donors pledged US$1 billion to upgrade transport links across eastern and southern Africa, in an initiative to carry goods to market cheaper and faster. Not only have roads and rail links been

improved, but also time-consuming official procedures have been streamlined for efficiency.
There are valuable reserves in minerals including copper, lead, zinc, cobalt and gemstones. Agricultural products are also important exports along with electricity.

Imports

Principal imports are petroleum and derivatives, capital machinery, electricity, fertiliser, foodstuffs and clothing.

Main sources: South Africa (32.4 per cent of total in 2014), DR Congo (15.3 per cent), China (9.0 per cent)

Exports

Principal exports are copper, cobalt, electricity, maize, tea, cotton, rice, groundnuts, tobacco, sugarcane, vegetables, flowers and cotton.

Main destinations: Switzerland (44.7 per cent of total in 2014), China (18.5 per cent), DR Congo (8.3 per cent)

Agriculture

Farming

About 10 per cent of Zambia's 600 million hectares is arable land but only around 30 million hectares are under cultivation. There are more than 300,000 smallholders, mostly subsistence farmers, earning cash from growing mainly cotton and tobacco. About 500 highly mechanised commercial farms and estates account for 40 per cent of marketed crops and animal produce. The country has abundant perennial and underground water resources. Power generated by hydroelectric installations has been extended to some farming areas. In the wetter northern part of the country, tea and coffee thrive at the higher altitudes, with maize and millet at lower levels. The climate of the central province suits maize, soya beans, cotton and tobacco. The south and west are drier and suit sorghum, tobacco, cotton and groundnuts.
Agriculture accounts for approximately 17.7 per cent of GDP. Most state-run farms have been privatised. One problem that the industry faces is that much of the land is under tribal authority and difficult to access. In order to tackle this problem, the government has set up areas of virgin land, such as the Tazara Corridor Services (Tazcor), which are open for investment.
Government policy has long been to achieve self-sufficiency in food production, increase exports and improve the supply of inputs to peasant farmers. Measures have included a wide range of production incentives, comprising preferential tax and loan rates, the encouragement of foreign investment and improvements in producer prices.
Official policy has also encouraged new crops for export, which includes coffee, flowers and exotic vegetables for European markets. In contrast to these successful new crops, cashew nut production has failed to penetrate European markets.
Regional integration means that farmers are finding foreign competition difficult as high production costs, high taxation levels and cheap imports continue to undermine their competitiveness. The country is marginally self-sufficient in food with maize surpluses in times of good weather.
Zambia is susceptible to worldwide events - the shutdown of air travel in Europe in April 2010 for instance, caused by the Icelandic volcanic ash cloud, resulted in the horticultural sector losing around US$150,000 per day over the six-day period of closure, as flowers and vegetables had to be discarded.
By May 2015 the government estimated the maize harvest to be 2,618,221 tonnes for the 2014/15 season, 22 per cent down from the bumper 3,350,671 tonnes of 2013/14. Zambia needs some two million tonnes of maize per annum to feed its people and livestock. The Food Reserve Agency is already sitting on carry-over stock of 1,345,401 tonnes of maize from 2013/14, and is therefore busy selling last year's maize to millers and exporters, at subsidised prices.

Fishing

Annual commercial fish production is estimated at 70,000 tonnes. The sector suffers due to infrastructural difficulties, including lack of input supply, such as nets and boats, poor transport and storage facilities. The private sector has stepped up investment in fish marketing and distribution, fish farming and manufacturing of nets and boats.
The Department of Fisheries in Zambia and the Department of National Parks and Wildlife Management in Zimbabwe, with the co-operation of Norway and Denmark, have undertaken a project to facilitate the sustainable utilisation of the shared fisheries resources on Lake Kariba.
In 2013 Agriculture and Livestock permanent secretary Dr Shamulenge assured that 100 fish ponds would be restocked with 25,000 fingerlings in response to Ikeleng'i Fish Farmers Association chairperson Benwa Lukama stating that 500 fish ponds had been closed down due to lack of fingerlings.
Following a statement saying his 'heart bled' when he found out that Zambia imports 45,000 tonnes of fish every year when it has 20 million hectors of water covered land, President Edgar Lungu announced his government had acquired a US$50 million loan from the African Development Bank (AfDB) in order to revamp aquaculture in the country and eventually become an exporter of fish.

Forestry

Forest and other wooded land accounts for 42 per cent and 37 per cent of the total land area respectively. Although nearly half of Zambia's land area is covered by forest, there are only a few commercially exploitable tree species. It is estimated that forests cover some 31.2 million hectares (ha), with most being open savannah woodlands and *miombo* woodland comprising around 80 per cent of the country's vegetation. There are large networks of protected areas constituting 32 per cent of the forests with around 20 national parks and more than 30 game management areas.
Charcoal is a significant cooking and heating fuel in rural areas but, in some regions, woodland has been ravaged and a severe shortage of charcoal is expected unless there is government sponsored replanting. There is some export of sawn timber, while most of the demand for paper products is met by imports.

Industry and manufacturing

The industrial sector contributed around 37.3 per cent to GDP in 2014 and employs around 10 per cent of the labour force.
Macroeconomic stabilisation and divestiture of state assets has led to a severe contraction in these sectors of the economy. The government is no longer willing to subsidise the industrial and manufacturing sector. This change contrasts vividly with policy in the 1960s and 1970s whereby vast copper profits were used to establish one of the largest parastatal economies in Africa.
Targeted sectors for development include agriculture derived processed products and non-traditional exports such as textiles, chemicals and engineering products.

Tourism

One of the world's most spectacular waterfalls, the Victoria Falls, is located in the Mosi-oa-Tunya National Park and is included on Unesco's World Heritage List. The site is a major tourist resort with facilities for visitors built around the shores of the Zambezi River, at the head of the falls.
The collapse of neighbouring Zimbabwe's tourist industry benefitted Zambian tourism, as visitors discovered that the Victoria Falls could be viewed from the Zambian side. However as Zimbabwe's political situation improves this advantage fades.
Other tourist attractions include safari tours (Zambia pioneered walking safaris in the Luangwa national parks), Lake Kariba for its house-boating excursions and various animal reserves and sanctuaries. Activities include many extreme sports, plus more leisurely cultural tours.
In January 2013 the hunting of big cats (lions and leopards) was banned.

Although hunting brought in US$3 million in 2012, the ministry of tourism considers that it is more important to promote game viewing for the longer term. A report in August 2014 said that the ban on hunting elephants and big cats was later denied by the Zambia Wildlife Authority (ZAWA).
In 2014 Zambia placed third in a study of upcoming tourism and travel destinations based on statistics from the World Travel and Tourism Council (WTTC), though it is under debate whether it has the infrastructure to support this tourism.
The government recognises the sector's importance and although it was aiming to attract a million visitors annually by 2010, the number only reached 815,000 as the global economic crisis had depressed the market in general.
Travel and tourism contributed US$1.65 billion to the economy in total, which was 6.1 per cent of GDP in 2014 and provided employment to 4.2 per cent of the workforce (83,500 jobs) including jobs indirectly supported by the industry.

Mining

Zambia has enormous mineral wealth, with major deposits of copper, cobalt, lead, zinc, emeralds, aquamarine, amethyst and tourmaline. It also has small reserves of selenium, manganese, tin, nickel, iron, gold, silver and diamonds.
The mining sector contributes around a fifth of GDP, is Zambia's paramount employer, directly employing 50,000 workers (around 10 per cent of the workforce).
Copper and its by-products, mostly cobalt, account for around 90 per cent of mining production and mining exports. Zambia is also the second largest producer of cobalt after the Democratic Republic of Congo (DRC) and has one of the world's largest reserves. Substantial amounts of cobalt can be recovered from the copper slag heaps, for which Canada's Colossus Resources obtained a 25-year contract with the Zambia Consolidated Copper Mines (ZCCM) ending in 2025. The Nkana and Mufulira cobalt mines and refineries produce 1,800 tonnes per year (tpy) of cobalt. The Nkana and Nchanga mines produce more than half of Zambia's copper and 70 per cent of its cobalt.
There is very little mining activity outside the Copperbelt although base metal exploration has continued in other regions. Zambia is prospecting for chromium, nickel, tin, tantalite and iron ore. The government allows private sector purchase and export of gemstones. Mining companies can retain 50 per cent of foreign exchange earnings.
Zambia contains approximately a quarter of the world's gem emeralds and accounts for an estimated 20 per cent of output of rough emeralds. Other gemstones mined on a smaller scale include amethysts in the Southern Province near Lake Kariba and Kalomo. Deposits of aquamarine and tourmaline are mined for the jewellery trade. Production of gemstones is estimated to be worth US$200 million annually.
In October 2015 Mopani Copper Mines (owned by Glencore Plc) were reported to be planning to lay off over 4,000 of its 7,000 unionised workers.

Hydrocarbons

There are no known oil or gas reserves and Zambia is dependent on imported fuel supplies. Total oil imports in 2010 were 12,500 barrels per day (bpd). The 1,710km Tazama pipeline from Dar es Salaam, Tanzania, supplies oil to the Indeni refinery at Ndola, which has a capacity of 24,000bpd. The Indeni oil refinery is Zambia's sole refinery, and one of Africa's biggest inland refining sites. In 2013 Zambia sold a 49 per cent stake in the refinery in order to re-capitalise the ageing plant.
The country imports refined petroleum from other countries such as South Africa.
Zambia does not import natural gas.
Zambia's major coal supplier, Maamba Collieries, used to produce 600,000 tonnes per annum in the 1980s but output has been severely cut due to undercapitalisation. However, despite delays due to the transmission line link to the Zesco grid, a 300MW Maamba plant is projected to be completed in 2016. Zambia uses coal in the mining transformation process. All coal produced is consumed and fulfils all domestic demand.
Probable coal reserves are in Luangwa North, Luano, Lukusashi in the Luangwa Valley and Kahare, Chunga and Lubaba in the Western Province, estimated to have in the region of 700 million tonnes.

Energy

Total installed generating capacity was 1.68 gigawatts (GW) in 2013, producing around 11.4 billion kilowatt hours. Two new generators have been commissioned at Kariba North Bank Power Station, the first in December 2013 and the second in August 2014, bringing the generating capacity to 1,080MW.
Hydropower provides virtually all domestic energy, mostly from plants at Kafue Gorge, Kariba North and Livingstone.
The parastatal, Zambian Electricity Supply Company (Zesco), generates, transmits and distributes electricity, with continued responsibility of connecting districts to the national grid. The Kariba North Bank Extension (360MW) and the Kafue Gorge Lower Hydro Project (750MW) are two Zesco projects finished in 2015. Another Zesco project, the Lunzua Hydroelectric plant was upgraded from 0.75MW to 14.8MW in 2015.
The mining industry consumes around 70 per cent of all energy generated; only 10 per cent of the population have access to electricity. New owners of the Maamba Collieries are contracted to build a new 350MW thermal power station.
Zambia also owns the Central African Power Corporation (CAPC) with Zimbabwe. CAPC operates the two Kariba power stations. The country exports energy under the Southern African Development Community (SADC) agreement to Zimbabwe, Botswana, Namibia and Tanzania and is connected to the Democratic Republic of Congo (DRC) (from which Zambia also imports electricity) and South Africa.
The World Bank has agreed to lend Zambia US$75.5 million to boost generation. Contracts for the planned Itezhi-tezhi hydropower plant, on the Kafue River in the southern province, which will have a capacity of 120 megawatts, were let in 2008. The plant is due to be commissioned in 2015/16. A 300MW thermal coal station in Maamba is also due for commissioning in 2016
Construction of the much delayed dam for the 2,400MW Batoka Gorge Hydropower Project is expected to begin in January 2016. Originally planned for 1992, the project was put on hold until Zimbabwe settled its debt from the construction of the Kariba Dam. The World Bank's Co-operation in International Waters in Africa Fund stated that 'the missed opportunity amounted to an estimated US$7 billion in foregone electricity sales and an overall economic loss of over US$45 billion.' The project will cost some US$3 billion and take six years to complete.
Rolling 'power shedding' (planned power cuts) has been in operation throughout most of the country in 2015. In October Zesco announced an increase in rates of up to 250 per cent in some sectors. ZESCO justified its increases by explaining that the new tariffs are intended to attract a US$4.3 billion portfolio of diversified generation projects, including renewable energy, coal and bagasse (waste from sugarcane). The current tariffs are simply not high enough to attract investors. In addition, the new tariffs will mean that ZESCO will no longer have to subsidise power bought from independent power producers. Zambia has the lowest rates at US$0.6 in the SADC region where the average is US$0.10. The 2015 rate rise will bring Zambia more into line with its neighbours.

Financial markets

Stock exchange

Lusaka Stock Exchange (LuSE)

Banking and insurance

Zambia's banking sector has undergone a period of crisis and change. The liberalisation of the economy during the 1990s gave rise to the launch of a number of banks. Poor management and over-banking led to the closure of a number of these banks, prompting a wave of concern among investors and depositors who lost money.

In March 2003 the government first directed the Zambia Privatisation Agency (ZPA) to privatise the main state owned commercial bank, Zambia National Commercial Bank. 49 per cent of its shares were to be sold to a qualified investor with management rights, 25.8 per cent were to be offered to the Zambian public through the Zambia Privatisation Trust Fund (ZPTF), 25 per cent were to be retained by the government and the existing minority shareholders, who held 0.2 per cent, were to retain their shares. The ZPA called for tenders to be received by September 2005.

The largest commercial banks, Barclays Bank of Zambia and Standard Chartered Bank Zambia, are foreign-owned. However, since January 1972 all foreign-owned banks have been required to incorporate locally.

There are several state-owned development banks and other private financial institutions. The Development Bank of Zambia offers medium- and long-term loans and business consultancy services.The Agricultural Finance Company and Zambia Agricultural Development Bank were merged and renamed the Lima Bank. The government-owned Zambia State Insurance Corporation (ZSIC) is the major insurance company in Zambia. Other development banks include the state-owned Zambia National Building Society.

Central bank

Bank of Zambia

Main financial centre

Lusaka

Time

GMT plus two hours

Geography

Zambia is landlocked, bordered to the south by Zimbabwe and the Caprivi Strip (an extension of Namibia); to the south-east by Mozambique; to the east by Malawi; to the north-east by Tanzania; to the north and north-west by the Democratic Republic of Congo (DRC); and to the west by Angola.

About nine-tenths of the country is a high rolling plateau (900–1,200 metres above sea level) covered by savannah bush and woodland. The only relief from the monotony of the plateau is the Zambezi and Luangwa rift system. The Luapula River, part of the Congo River system, cuts into the northern part of the plateau.

Zambia takes its name from the Zambezi River. At 2,655km long, this is the third longest river in Africa.

Hemisphere

Southern

Climate

Altitude governs Zambia's climate and it is generally cooler than its neighbours. There are three distinct seasons: cool and dry from May to August; hot and dry from September to October; and rainy from November to April. Rainfall varies widely across the country. The average temperature is 16 degrees Celsius (C) in the winter and 24 degrees C in summer.

The Zambezi and Luangwa river valleys can remain hot and humid all year, typical of tropical lowlands. They are particularly uncomfortable in the rainy season.

Dress codes

The contrast between morning, midday and evening temperatures means that a sweater is often required in the early morning and after sunset between April and September. A light raincoat or umbrella is useful during the wet season from November to April.

Dress is generally informal. Lightweight suits can be worn for most of the year; during the hot season tropical suits are preferable. Tailored safari suits are popular. A hat and sunglasses are useful for protection against the sun.

Most women wear cotton or other lightweight dresses during the day and evening. Warm dresses and lightweight coats are needed during the coldest season, June to August.

Entry requirements

Passports

Required by all; it must be valid for six months beyond the date of stay and with sufficient space for a visa.

Visa

Required by all, exceptions include those listed on the *Visa Application Instructions* (items 4 and 5) and for tourist visits only, see www.zambiaembassy.org. Tourist visas can be obtained at all border crossings, fees will be levied in cash, usually sterling or dollars (exact amounts as change may not be available).

A proposed tourist *univisa* (a single visa to visit all 15-member states of SADC: Angola, Botswana, DRC, Lesotho, Madagascar, Malawi, Mauritius, Mozambique, Namibia, South Africa, Seychelles, Swaziland, Tanzania, Zambia and Zimbabwe) is expected to be in use by 2013. Visitors should check with the appropriate consulates to confirm start of *univisas* and their scope before beginning a tour of southern Africa.

All business visits require a visa, obtained in advance. Applications should include an invitation from a local company or organisation giving brief details of the nature of business, a full itinerary and proof of onward/return passage.

Currency advice/regulations

The import and export of local currency is limited to K100. The import of foreign currency is unlimited but must be declared, and bank notes with denominations over US$5,000 (or equivalent) must be recorded with customs; export is limited to the amount declared. Retain all official currency exchange forms and receipts (they are also necessary for purchase of domestic airline tickets). Use only authorised banks and *bureaux de change* for currency conversions.

Travellers cheques, in major currencies, are widely accepted.

Health (for visitors)

Mandatory precautions

A yellow fever vacination required. A cholera vaccination certificate is required if arriving from an infected area.

Advisable precautions

Vaccinations for diphtheria, tetanus, polio, hepatitis A and typhoid are recommended. Other vaccinations that may be appropriate are tuberculosis, hepatitis B, meningitis, cholera and yellow fever (if travelling to the remote border region with DRC and Angola).

A malignant malaria is present (*falciparum*, which is resistant to chloroquine) from November to May throughout the country and all year in the Zambezi valley. Use malaria prophylaxis including mosquito repellents, sleeping nets and clothing that fully cover the body after dark. Rabies is a risk. Bilharzia is present, use only well-maintained and chlorinated swimming pools. HIV/Aids is prevalent.

All water for drinking, brushing teeth or making ice should be sterilised when outside of the main cities. Bottled water is available. Milk is pasteurised and therefore safe. Vegetables should be cooked and fruit peeled.

Take all prescription medicines; ensure that medical insurance includes evacuation.

Hotels

Several good quality hotels are available. Hotels are graded from one to five stars by the Hotels Board. A service charge of 10 per cent, plus 10 per cent sales tax are added to all bills. Room charges must be settled in foreign currency. Some hotels require a deposit to cover the room rate and an element for food and drink to be converted to Kwacha on arrival. Tipping is not customary in Zambia but is acceptable.

Credit cards
Major credit cards are accepted in most hotels and tourist facilities. ATMs exist in larger branches in city centres only.

Public holidays (national)
Fixed dates
1 Jan (New Year's Day), 12 Mar (Youth Day), 1 May (Labour Day), 25 May (African Day), 24 Oct (Independence Day), 25 Dec (Christmas Day).
Holidays that fall on the weekend are taken on Monday.
Variable dates
Good Friday and Easter Monday (Mar/Apr), Heroes' Day and Unity Day (first Mon and Tue of Jul), Farmers' Day (first Mon of Aug).

Working hours
Banking
Mon–Fri: 0815–1430. Some larger branches open 0816–1030 on first and last Sat of month.
Business
Mon–Fri: 0800–1230, 1400–1630.
Government
Mon–Fri: 0800–1300, 1400–1700.
Shops
Privately owned: Mon–Fri: 0800–1700, Sat: 0800–1300; state-owned: Mon–Sat: 0800–1800, Sun: 0800–1200.
Note: There are wide variations outside city centres.

Telecommunications
Mobile/cell phones
Some73 per cent of Zambia was connected to a mobile phone network in 2015; there are government plans to increase the coverage to 100 per cent by 2016.

Electricity supply
230V AC

Social customs/useful tips
Visitors normally entertain business guests in hotels or restaurants, while residents prefer to entertain informally at home or at their clubs. Temporary membership of clubs can normally be obtained on an introduction from friends.

Security
The stealing of cheques has become a problem in Zambia. Visitors are advised to carry travellers' cheques in small denominations and to cash only sufficient for current needs. There has also been a rise in violent crime due to the economic decline and care must be taken when travelling after dark. It is not regarded as advisable to travel by car between Lusaka and the Copperbelt after dark.

Getting there
Air
International airport/s: Lusaka International (LUN), 26km from city; duty-free shop, bar, restaurant, bank, shops, car hire; Livingstone International Airport (LVI).
Airport tax: International departures: US$25, in cash, excluding transit passengers. Domestic departures: K12,000.
Surface
Road: There are tarred roads from Zimbabwe, Botswana, Namibia (Caprivi Strip), Democratic Republic of Congo (DRC), Tanzania and Malawi; motorists should check border post hours, and regulations concerning their vehicles. A customs bond may be required for the import of cars.
During the rainy season many rural roads are impassable. It is not advisable to travel by car between Lusaka and the Copperbelt after dark.
The long-planned road bridge between Zambia and Botswana at Kazungula ran into funding difficulties in 2014. Construction of the bridge component was awarded to South Korean constructor Daewoo, even though China Major Bridge Building Corporation had submitted a lower price. The official reason given was that Daewoo was closest to the engineer's assessment, unofficially it was said that Botswana had previously had bad experiences with Chinese companies. As a result the Japanese International Co-operation Agency (JICA) (the main lender with 57.5 per cent) withdrew their funding. The balance of the funding was coming from the African Development Bank (31.5 per cent), EU-Africa Infrastructure Trust Fund (1.8 per cent), Botswana (4.0 per cent) and Zambia (5.2 per cent). As of October 2014 the funding was still unresolved – whether JICA would find a way round their rules that dictate that the cheapest contractor should be chosen, or whether the AfDB would find extra funds. The bridge would replace the current unreliable pontoons and reduce the transit time from as much as six days to six hours.
A road bridge across the River Zambezi between Namibia and Zambia opened in May 2004.
Rail: The Tanzania Zambia Railway Authority (Tazara) railway links Zambia to Tanzania – the connection is at Kapiri Mposhi.
Zambia Railways Limited (ZRL) connects with Democratic Republic Congo and Zimbabwe where lines run on to Mozambique, South Africa and Botswana. Tazara announced the cessation of cross-border passenger services so that from 26 August 2014 trains from Lusaka travelling north and from Dar es Salaam travelling south will terminate at Nakonde where passengers will have to change trains to complete their journeys. Schedules will be designed to allow for passengers to swap.
Zambia Railways also announced that it has signed an agreement in July 2014 with DRC's state-owned Société Nationale des Chemins de Fer du Congo (Congo National Railway) to transport some 15,000 tonnes per month of copper from Ndola to Lumbumbashi.
Water: Services include ferries across the Zambezi river from Botswana (Kazungula) and across Lake Tanganyika from Burundi (Bujumbura) and from Tanzania (Kigoma).

Getting about
National transport
Air: There are regular flights from Lusaka, south to Livingstone and to the Copperbelt in the north. There are several flights a week from Lusaka to other centres including Mfuwe in the Luangwa valley. Charter companies also operate and are in heavy demand. There is a total of around 150 airfields and airstrips.
Road: The total network is almost 40,000km, of which about 6,500km are main roads. Surfaced roads link main centres. During the rainy season many rural roads are impassable.
Buses: Eagle Travel runs regular coach services to numerous locations including tourist sites. Non-tourist services can be irregular and crowded.
Rail: There are three main lines running from Livingstone-Lusaka, Lusaka-Copperbelt and Kapiri Mposhi to the northern border with Tanzania.
There is an overnight train from Livingstone-Lusaka with sleeping carriages, running three time a week. And day-time services that take many more hours, as they stop at more stations along the line. All lengthy trips should be booked at least one week in advance.
The total network is over 2,000km and in need of investment, which through joint ventures, was agreed in 2006 between the governments of Zambia and China. New and refurbished lines, and rolling stock will provide more access to the Indian Ocean through Tanzania and Mozambique.
City transport
Taxis: These are available between airports and hotels and within town centres. They are generally unmetered.
Buses, trams & metro: A number of privately-owned companies run domestic services over a number of routes. Buses are irregular and crowded, especially during the rush hour.
Car hire
Car hire usually comes with a driver; on special request, firms may offer self-drive vehicles. The Zambia Tourist Board has authorised over 16 car-hire firms serving mainly Lusaka, Livingstone and the Copperbelt which are the major urban and tourist centres.

BUSINESS DIRECTORY

The addresses listed below are a selection only. While World of Information makes every endeavour to check these addresses, we cannot guarantee that changes have not been made, especially to telephone numbers and area codes. We would welcome any corrections.

Telephone area codes

The international direct dialling (IDD) code for Zambia is +260, followed by the area code and subscriber's number:

Chingola	2	Livingstone	3
Chipata	6	Luanshya	2
Choma	3	Lusaka	1
Kabwe	2	Mongu	7
Kasama	4	Ndola	2
Kitwe	2	Solwezi	8

Chambers of Commerce

Livingstone Chamber of Commerce and Industry, 29 Airport Road, PO Box 60648, Livingstone (tel/fax: 323-656; email: denmar@zamtel.zm).

Lusaka Chamber of Commerce and Industry, Farmers House, Cairo Rod, PO Box 37997, Lusaka (tel: 221-266; fax: 224-114; email: luschamb@zamnet.zm).

Zambia Association of Chambers of Commerceand Industry, Showgrounds, Great East Road, PO Box 30844, Lusaka (tel: 255-046; fax: 253-007; email: zacci@zamnet.zm).

Banking

Barclays Bank of Zambia, Cairo Rd, PO Box 31936, Lusaka (tel: 228-858/66; fax: 222-519, 226-185).

Cavmont Merchant Bank Ltd, Fourth Floor, Tazara House, Independence Avenue, PO Box 38474, Lusaka (tel: 224 280; fax: 221 643; e-mail: info@cavmont.com.zm).

Citibank, Citibank House, PO Box 30037, Lusaka (tel: 229-025/6/7/8; fax: 226-264).

Indo Zambia Bank, 686 Cairo Rd, PO Box 35411, Lusaka (tel: 225-080, 222-622; fax: 225-090).

Investrust Bank Plc, Investrust House, Plot 4527/8, Freedom Way, PO Box 32344, Lusaka (tel: 238-733; fax: 237 060; e-mail: inquiries@investrustbank.co.zm).

Stanbic Bank, Cairo Rd, Woodgate House, PO Box 31955, Lusaka (tel: 229-071/3, 229-285/6; fax: 221-152, 225-380).

Standard Chartered Bank, PO Box 32238, Lusaka (tel: 229-242; fax: 222-092).

Union Bank, Zimco House, PO Box 34940, Lusaka (tel: 229-397/8; fax: 221-866).

Zambia National Commercial Bank, Cairo Rd, PO Box 33611, Lusaka (tel: 228-979, 221-355; fax: 224-006).

Central bank

Bank of Zambia, Bank Square, Cairo Road, PO Box 30080, Lusaka 10101 (tel: 228-888 fax: 221-722; internet: www.boz.zm).

Stock exchange

Lusaka Stock Exchange (LuSE) www.luse.co.zm

Travel information

Lusaka International Airport, National Airports Corporation Limited, PO Box 30175, Lusaka (tel/fax: 271-359; email: naclaps@zamnet.zm; internet: www.lun.aero).

Tourism Council of Zambia, PO Box 36561, Lusaka (tel: 251-666; fax: 251-501; e-mail: tcz@zamnet.zm; internet: www.zambiatourism.com).

Zambian Airways, Head Office, Lusaka International Airport; PO Box 34777, Lusaka, (tel: 271-230; fax: 271-054; internet: www.zambianairways.com).

Zambian Express, Lusaka (tel: 222-060, 238-162/65; fax: 238-166; e-mail: zamex@zamnet.zm).

Ministry of tourism

Ministry of Tourism, Environment and Natural Resources, PO Box 34011; Cairo Road, Kwacha House, Lusaka 10101 (tel: 021 223-931; fax: 0211 223-930; email: infor@mtenr.gov.zm; internet: www.mtenr.gov.zm).

National tourist organisation offices

Zambia National Tourist Board (ZNTB), Tourist Centre, Mosi-oa-Tunya Road, PO Box 60342, Livingstone (tel: 321-404/5; fax: 321-487; e-mail: zntblive@zamnet.zm); Century House, Cairo Road, Lusaka Square, PO Box 30017, Lusaka (tel: 229-087/90; fax: 225-174; e-mail: zntb@zamnet.zm).

Ministries

Ministry of Agriculture, Food and Fisheries, Mulungushi House, Box RW 50291, Lusaka (tel: 251-537/233; fax: 252-029).

Ministry of Commerce, Trade and Industry, Kwacha House Annex, PO Box 31968/34473, Lusaka (tel: 228-301, 221-184; fax: 226-673).

Ministry of Communication and Transport, PO Box 50065, Lusaka (tel: 251-444/938/740/759; fax: 002-601, 253-260).

Ministry of Community Development and Social Services, Fidelity House, PO Box 31958, Lusaka (tel: 227-840, 228-321; fax: 225-327).

Ministry of Defence, PO Box RW 17X, Lusaka (tel: 251-211, 254-667; fax: 254-670, 221-339, 253-875).

Ministry of Education, PO Box 50093, Lusaka (tel: 227-636; fax: 222-396).

Ministry of Energy and Water Development, Ministerial Headquarters, Lusaka (tel: 263-870; fax: 252-339).

Ministry of Environment and Natural Resources, Mulungushi House, PO Box 30055, Lusaka (tel: 252-711, 250-186; fax: 252-952).

Ministry of Finance, PO Box RW 50062, Lusaka (tel: 250-544, 227-668; fax: 250-501).

Ministry of Foreign Affairs, PO Box 50069, Lusaka (tel: 262-666; fax: 250-634/240, 252-867).

Ministry of Health, PO Box 30205, Lusaka (tel: 227-745, 223-435; fax: 223-435).

Ministry of Home Affairs, PO Box 50997, Lusaka (tel: 254-261/362; fax: 224-656, 254-669).

Ministry of Information and Broadcasting Services, PO Box 50200, Lusaka (tel: 251-766, 253-965; fax: 254-013, 252-391, 250-524).

Ministry of Labour and Social Security, PO Box 32186, Lusaka (tel: 227-640).

Ministry of Lands, Mulungushi House, PO Box 30069, Lusaka (tel: 252-288; fax: 250-130).

Ministry of Legal Affairs, PO Box 50106, Lusaka (tel: 251-588; fax: 253-695).

Ministry of Local Government and Housing, PO Box 34204, Lusaka (tel: 253-077; fax: 252-680).

Ministry of Mines and Minerals Development, PO Box 31969, Lusaka (tel: 252-990; fax: 251-224).

Ministry of Science, Technical Education and Vocational Training, PO Box 50464, Lusaka (tel: 229-673; fax: 252-951).

Ministry of Sports, Youth and Child Development, 4th Floor, Memaco House, Sapele Rd, Lusaka (tel: 227-168; fax: 223-996).

Ministry of Works and Supply, PO Box 50236, Lusaka (tel: 253-266; fax: 222-360).

Other useful addresses

British High Commission, 5210 Independence Avenue; PO Box 50050, 15101 Ridgeway, Lusaka (tel: 251-133; fax: 253-798; email: BHC-lusaka@fco.gov.uk).

Central Statistics Office, PO Box 31908, Lusaka (internet: www.zamstats.gov.zm).

Chilanga Cement plc, Kafue Road, PO Box 32639, Lusaka (tel: 225-2853, 701-297; fax: 252-853, 252-655).

Export Board of Zambia, PO Box 30064, Third Floor, State Lottery Building, Cairo Road, North End, Lusaka (tel: 228-106/7; fax: 222-509).

Lusaka Stock Exchange Ltd, Lusaka (tel: 228-594, 228-391; fax: 228-608, 225-969; e-mail: luse@zamnet.zm).

Metal Marketing Corp of Zambia, PO Box 35570, 10101 Lusaka (tel: 228-131/140).

National Air Charters, PO Box 33650, 10101 Lusaka (tel: 229-154, 228-274).

National Commission for Development Planning, PO Box 50268, Lusaka.

National Import & Export Corporation, PO Box 30282, 10101 Lusaka (tel: 228-018).

Nitrogen Chemicals, PO Box 360226, Kafue (tel: 311-531/5; fax: 311-313).

Zambia Consolidated Copper Mines Ltd (ZCCM), 5309 Dedan Kimathi Road, PO Box 30048, Lusaka (tel: 229-115; fax: 221-057).

Zambia Electricity Supply Corporation Ltd (Zesco), PO Box 33304, Stand 6949 Great East Road, Lusaka 10101 (tel: 223-970, 239-343, 225-074; fax: 223-971, 237-601, 239-343, 222-753).

Zambian Embassy (USA), 2419 Massachusetts Avenue, NW, Washington DC 20008 (tel: (+1-202) 265-9717; fax: (+1-202) 332-0826; e-mail: info@zambiainfo.org).

Zambia Industrial & Commercial Copper Industry Service Bureau, PO Box 22100, Kitwe.

Zambia Investment Centre, 5th Floor, Ndeke House, Haile Selassie Avenue, PO Box 34580, Lusaka (tel: 252-130, 252-152; fax: 252-150; e-mail: invest@zamnet.zm).

Zambia National Broadcasting Corporation, PO Box 50015, 10101 Lusaka (tel: 229-648).

Zambia National Oil Company Limited (ZNOC), Lusaka (tel: 222-135; fax: 220-144, 221-265).

Zambia Privatisation Agency (ZPA), Privatisation House, Nasser Road, PO Box 30819, Lusaka (tel: 227-851, 223-859, 227-791; fax: 225-270; e-mail: zpa@zamnet.zm).

Zambia Railways Ltd (ZRL), PO Box 80935, Kabwe (tel: 223-822, 222-201/209; fax: 228-023/025).

Zambia Telecommunications Co Ltd, Lusaka (tel: 611-111, 612-399; fax: 613-055, 615-855).

National news agency: Zambia News Agency (internet: www.zana.gov.zm).

Internet sites

Africa Business Network: www.ifc.org/abn

African Development Bank: www.afdb.org

Africa Online: www.africaonline.com

AllAfrica.com: http://allafrica.com

Mbendi AfroPaedia (information on companies, countries, industries and stock exchanges in Africa): http://mbendi.co.za

Office of the President: www.statehouse.gov.zm

Zambian Express: www.africa-insites.com

Zambian gateway website: www.zamnet.zm

Zimbabwe

KEY FACTS

Official name: Republic of Zimbabwe

Head of State: President Robert Gabriel Mugabe (Zanu-PF) (since 1980; re-elected 2013)

Head of government: Position was abolished by 2013 constitutional amendment

Ruling party: Zimbabwe African National Union-Patriotic Front (Zanu-PF) (from 28 Jul 2013)

Area: 391,109 square km

Population: 13.26 million (2014)*

Capital: Harare

Official language: English, Shona and Ndebele

Currency: Zimbabwe dollar (Z$) = 100 cents

Exchange rate: Z$361.90 per US$ (Sep 2015) (US dollar, South African rand, Chinese renmimbi, Indian rupee, Australian dollar, and Japanese yen also legal tender) (since 2014)

GDP per capita: US$1,031 (2014)*

GDP real growth: 3.17% (2014)*

GDP: US$13.67 billion (2014)*

Labour force: 3.84 million (2013)*

Inflation: -0.21% (2014)*

* estimated figure

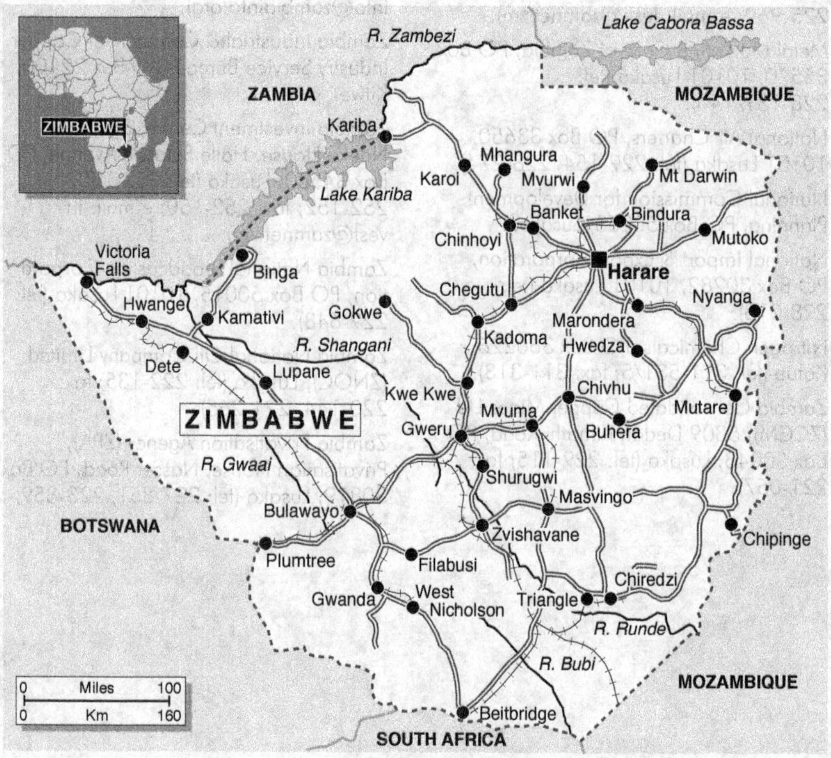

In 1965, the government unilaterally declared its independence from the United Kingdom, however, the UK did not recognise the act and demanded more complete voting rights for the black majority in the country (then called Rhodesia). UN sanctions and a guerrilla uprising finally led to free elections in 1979 and independence (as Zimbabwe) in 1980. Robert Mugabe, the nation's first prime minister, has been the country's only ruler (as president since 1987) and has dominated the country's political system since independence. Mugabe's chaotic land redistribution campaign, which began in 1997 and intensified after 2000, caused an exodus of white farmers, crippled the economy, and brought about widespread shortages of basic commodities. Ignoring international condemnation, Mugabe rigged the 2002 presidential election to ensure his re-election. In April 2005, the capital city of Harare embarked on Operation Restore Order, an urban rationalisation programme, which resulted in the destruction of homes or businesses of 700,000 mostly poor supporters of the opposition.

The last general election in Zimbabwe was held on 31 July 2013 in which Robert Mugabe was re-elected, whilst his Zimbabwe African National Union-Patriotic Front (Zanu-PF) party won a two-thirds majority in the House of Assembly. In the presidential election held at the same time Mugabe won 61.1 per cent of the vote whilst his main challenger, Morgan Tsvangirai, won 34.9 per cent. This was the first election held under the new constitution which was approved in a referendum in March 2013. Under the new constitution, the winner of the presidential election – which Mugabe made sure occurred as soon as possible after the referendum – would serve a five-year term. This represented an obvious attempt to prolong his presidency for as long as possible, having been in this position of power for 26 years prior to the general election. It is clear, therefore, that

Zimbabwe is not a democracy because its governance is closer to authoritarian than anything else. Mugabe's position as president and strength in parliament – through Zanu-PF – has meant that he has had the power to do anything. Allegations were made in 2013, that a third of registered voters were dead or aged 120 (in a country with a life expectancy of 44) and that a considerable number of young voters had not been registered. The Zimbabwe Election Support Network (ZESN), a local observer group with 7,000 monitors, listed a series of offences, including state media bias, a campaign of intimidation in rural areas, and the rushed electoral process before key reforms to the security services were in place. The most effective measure was tampering with the electoral rolls – the roll revealed an estimated one million invalid names, including many deceased voters and it excluded up to one million real ones, mostly in urban areas where support for the opposition party – Movement for Democratic Change (MDC) – is strongest. The Electoral Commission later reported that approximately 305,000 voters were turned away from polls, with an additional 207,000 voters being 'assisted' on casting their ballots. On 9 August 2013, the MDC sought to have the results declared null and void. A week later, they withdrew their petition with the Supreme Court of Zimbabwe ruling that the election was free, fair and credible.

As Robert Mugabe is getting older, he is beginning to require assistance to ensure his continued reign. Zimbabwe's first lady, Grace Mugabe told supporters at a political rally on the 20 November 2015 that she plans to get a special wheelchair for her 91-year-old husband so that he can continue to rule. This statement is a deliberate swipe against critics who say that her husband is too old to govern, Mugabe told supporters that she would ensure her husband remains in power as long as he can still speak. These outcries have occurred on the back of significant mistakes that Mugabe has been making including several stumbles at public events and reading the wrong speech in parliament.

The economy

Zimbabwe's economy depends heavily on its mining and agricultural sectors. Following a decade of contraction from 1998 to 2008, the economy recorded real growth of more than 10 per cent from 2010–13, before slowing to 3.3 per cent in 2014, attributed to poor harvests, low diamond revenues, and decreased investment. Appalling infrastructure and regulatory deficiencies, a terrible investment climate, a large public and external debt burden, and disproportionately high government wage expenses impede the country's overall economic performance. Foreign direct investment (FDI) was US$2.5 billion in 2014, up from a measly US$1.8 billion in 2013. Until the beginning of 2009, the Reserve Bank of Zimbabwe (RBZ) routinely printed money to fund the budget deficit, causing hyperinflation. Dollarization in early 2009 allowed currencies such as the Botswana pula, the South Africa rand, and the US dollar to be used locally, thereby ending hyperinflation. Inflation reduced to below 10 per cent per year, but exposed structural weaknesses that inhibited broad-based growth. Inflation was 0.1 per cent in 2014. In January 2014, as part of the government's effort to boost trade and attract foreign investment, the RBZ announced that Chinese renmimbi, Indian rupee, Australian dollar, and Japanese yen would be accepted as legal tender in Zimbabwe. Zimbabwe's government entered a second Staff Monitored Programme with the International Monetary Fund (IMF) in 2014 and undertook other measures to re-engage with international financial institutions. Foreign and domestic investment continues to be hindered by the lack of clarity regarding the country's Indigenisation and Economic Empowerment Act.

The African Development Bank's *African Economic Outlook 2015* (AEO) has suggested that economic growth is expected to improve only slightly in 2015 and 2016, with persistent de-industrialisation and a growing informal economy acting as the predominant hindrances. There is a need to continue implementation of structural reforms to improve the business environment, achieve a sustainable current account balance, reform public enterprises and make growth more inclusive. Gross domestic product (GDP) growth is expected to improve to 3.2 per cent in 2015, on the back of planned investments in agriculture, mining, communications, and other infrastructure projects, including in the water and energy sectors. The negative inflation in 2014 caused by weak domestic demand, tight liquidity conditions and the appreciation of the US dollar against the South African rand in 2014 should be eased once the use of the Chinese renmimbi, Indian rupee, Australian dollar, and Japanese yen take affect in 2015. Industrial capacity utilisation continues to decline, and is estimated at 36.3 per cent owing to underproduction and lack of competitiveness. The real exchange rate over-valuation relative to the South African rand had caused a loss in external competitiveness, as it has made imports cheaper than domestically produced goods and exports more expensive. The external sector is under severe pressure as a result of increasing demand for imports and dwindling exports, it had an estimated current account deficit of around 23.1 per cent in 2014. Zimbabwe is at high risk of debt distress, with an unsustainable external debt estimated at US$8.4 billion at the end of 2014.

Zimbabwe hosted a 'Mister Ugly' contest for the fourth year in succession in Harare on 20 November 2015. The results upset supporters of the crowd favourite who called the winner too handsome which prompted riots at the event. Judges chose 42-year-old Mison Sere who was proudly showing off his numerous

KEY INDICATORS — **Zimbabwe**

	Unit	2011	2012	2013	2014	**2015
Population	m	*12.57	*12.97	*13.12	*13.26	*13.41
Gross domestic product (GDP)	US$bn	9.30	12.47	13.67	*13.67	*13.97
GDP per capita	US$	741	961	1,028	*1,031	*1,042
GDP real growth	%	9.3	10.6	4.5	*3.2	*2.8
Inflation	%	3.5	3.7	1.6	*-0.2	*-0.1
Coal output	mtoe	1.6	1.7	1.0	2.7	–
Current account	US$m	-3,427.0	-2,508.0	-3,432.0	*-3,044.0	*-3,021.0
Total reserves minus gold	US$m	–	574.4	474.5	363.3	–
Foreign exchange	US$m	–	430.9	330.9	–	–
Exchange rate	per US$	378.20	378.00	378.00	361.90	–

* estimated figure ** forecast figure

missing front teeth using a wide range of grotesque facial expressions. Sere's victory knocked his challenger – William Masvinu – off his perch, having held the title since 2012. Masvinu and his supporters mobbed the judges following the decision claiming that Sere was far too handsome to win and his ugliness was not natural since it was based on missing teeth. Masvinu argued that while he is naturally ugly, Sere was only ugly when he opened his mouth. While no one was injured, there was a lot of pushing and shoving as the results were announced and insults were hurled at the judges. Beauty pageants are popular in Zimbabwe and even though they are typically for women, scandal is not unusual. In May 2015, Miss Zimbabwe winner Emily Kachote faced a backlash on social media, with Zimbabweans calling her ugly and undeserving of the crown. She was later forced to step down when just two weeks into her reign because images surfaced of her posing nude – which coincidentally also brought down her predecessor. Mison Sere dismissed the critics as sore losers and walked away with his US$500 winnings.

Risk assessment

Politics	Poor
Economy	Poor
Regional stability	Fair

COUNTRY PROFILE

1830s The Ndebele people fled Zulu violence in the south. They moved north and settled in Matabeleland.

1830–1890 European adventurers and missionaries explored much of southern Africa.

1889 Cecil John Rhodes was given a British mandate to colonise what became Southern Rhodesia. He founded the British South Africa Company (BSA) and became wealthy from the diamonds found in the area.

1890 White migration began as settlers arrived and named their first settlement Salisbury, which became the capital of Southern Rhodesia (renamed Harare, after independence).

1893 The BSA crushed an Ndebele uprising.

1922 The white minority voted to become a self-governing British dominion, ending BSA administration.

1930 The Land Apportionment Act restricted black access to land, forcing many into waged labour, and setting the ground for what was to become one of modern Zimbabwe's greatest difficulties, that of white owned farms. Opposition to colonial rule began to grow.

1953 The Central African Federation (CAF) was created, merging Southern Rhodesia (Zimbabwe), Northern Rhodesia (Zambia) and Nyasaland (Malawi).

1960s The Zimbabwe African People's Union (Zapu, mainly Ndebele) and the Zimbabwe African National Union (Zanu mainly Shona) were formed.

1963 The CAF collapsed after Zambia and Malawi elected to become separate independent states.

1964 Ian Smith of the Rhodesian Front (RF) became prime minister. He tried to negotiate independence from Britain with an electoral system that would preserve white minority rule.

1965 The RF made a unilateral declaration of independence (UDI) on 11 November. Despite international sanctions, Smith managed to keep his regime intact until 1980 with the support of apartheid South Africa and Portugal's colonialist regime in Mozambique. Zapu and Zanu began a campaign of guerrilla warfare, operating out of Zambia and Mozambique.

1976 Although Zanu and Zapu formed the Patriotic Front (PF) alliance, co-operation between the two remained limited. The civil war continued and intensified towards the end of the 1970s.

1978 Smith was forced to agree a negotiated settlement. Elections for a transitional legislature were boycotted by the PF. The government of Zimbabwe-Rhodesia, led by Bishop Abel Muzorewa of the United African National Council as prime minister and Canaan Banana as president, failed to gain international recognition. The civil war continued.

1979 A new constitution, favourable to the PF but guaranteeing minority rights, was drawn up at Lancaster House in the UK.

1980 Robert Mugabe's Zanu party won the general election and Zimbabwe gained independence from Britain on 18 April. Mugabe became prime minister. Opposition leader Joshua Nkomo was appointed to the cabinet.

1982 Nkomo was sacked after Mugabe accused him of plotting to overthrow the government. Zapu was largely destroyed by the North Korean-trained Fifth Brigade which Mugabe sent into Matabeleland. According to the Catholic Church a systematic campaign of terror was carried out against the rural population.

1987 Zanu and Zapu put their differences behind them and merged to form the Zimbabwe African National Union-Patriotic Front (Zanu-PF). Mugabe changed the constitution and became executive president.

1997 Concerns over compensation payments to former guerrillas and the consequences of seizing 1,480 of mostly white-owned farms lead to economic crisis. Violent demonstrations ensued.

1998 A general strike due to soaring food prices was supported by 80 per cent of workers. Mugabe decided, without consulting parliament, to intervene in the war in Democratic Republic of Congo (DRC) by sending troops and compounding Zimbabwe's economic crisis.

2000 So-called 'squatters' seized hundreds of white-owned farms in a campaign of intimidation. Mugabe lost a referendum vote for constitutional amendments. Zanu-PF won parliamentary elections by a narrow majority. Protests in Harare, against rises in food prices and demanding Mugabe's resignation, turned into riots.

2001 The finance minister declared that foreign reserves were depleted. The World Bank and IMF cut aid due to the ongoing land seizure programme. A list of 2,030 white-owned farms, required to be handed over under the new land-acquisition law, was published.

2002 Criticism of the president was outlawed and sweeping powers were given to the police to maintain public order. The European Union (EU) imposed sanctions on 20 members of the Zimbabwean government, including the president. Robert Mugabe was re-elected in controversial circumstances. His opponent, Morgan Tsvangirai (Movement for Democratic Change (MDC)), was arrested on charges of treason. Zimbabwe was suspended from the Commonwealth. Media freedom was curtailed.

2003 The currency was devalued by 93 per cent. The US imposed economic sanctions on President Mugabe and 76 other high-ranking government officials, freezing their assets and barring Americans from conducting business with them. The Commonwealth refused to end Zimbabwe's suspension, citing election rigging and persecution of dissidents.

2004 After their plane was impounded in Harare, 70 mercenaries planning a coup in Equatorial Guinea were detained and charged. Canaan Banana, Zimbabwe's first black president, died.

2005 The ruling Zanu-PF was re-elected; the opposition MDC claimed the elections were rigged. Thousands of shanty homes and businesses were demolished by the government, and around 200,000 people made homeless. The government passed a number of constitutional amendments, including the re-introduction of a 66-seat upper house (Senate). Treason charges against Morgan Tsvangirai were dropped. Elections to the upper house resulted, as expected, in the ruling Zanu-PF winning a majority. The Consumer Council reported that the cost of buying groceries increased

almost 10-fold during the year; bread rose by some 1,157 per cent.
2006 The Zimbabwe dollar was devalued by 60 per cent; at the same time the central bank dropped three zeros from the currency as new bank notes were issued. The annual inflation rate reached 1,204.6 per cent.
2007 The annual inflation rate jumped by 45.4 per cent in one month to 1,593.6 per cent. By mid-year the inflation rate was estimated to be 15,000 per cent. A new Z$200,000 bank note was introduced in an attempt to tackle Zimbabwe's hyperinflation. Unemployment was estimated at 80 per cent. A Constitutional Amendment Bill, a compromise between the ruling Zanu-PF and the opposition MDC, agreed a redrawing of electoral boundaries and an increased number of parliamentary members. The amendment also agreed that the next presidential election would be held in 2008 to coincide with parliamentary elections, and that parliament would choose Mugabe's successor should he retire mid-term. British Airways, the last foreign long-haul airline flying to Zimbabwe, ended flights to Harare. The RBZ raised the maximum limit on cheques accepted for clearing to Z$500 million. Former prime minister Ian Smith died. The official statistician declared that with the lack of goods in the shops it was impossible to determine an accurate inflation rate.
2008 A new Z$10 million note was introduced valued at around US$3.90 on the black market. The new notes, officially called bearer cheques, were introduced in yet another attempt to stabilise the economy. The official inflation rate was 100,000 per cent; the black-market exchange rate was Z$7.5 million to US$1. It was estimated that around three million people had left the country in search of work abroad while about 80 per cent of the population lived in poverty. The unofficial exchange grew to Z$30–35 million per US$ dollar (compared to the official rate of around Z$31,250 per US$1). In parliamentary elections the opposition MDC won 51.3 per cent (109 seats out of 210), the ruling Zanu-PF won 45.9 per cent (97), independents 2.25 per cent (one). The RBZ introduced a Z$50 million note and increased the maximum withdrawal limit to Z$5 billion per day. A re-count of 23 parliamentary seats confirmed an overall win for the MDC. The result of the presidential election was withheld until a 'verification and collation' process was completed by the electoral commission. While President Mugabe was out of the country attending a UN summit on the on-going global food crisis he banned international aid groups and non-governmental organisations (NGO) from distributing food until they had re-applied for permits. Mugabe forced a rerun of the presidential elections. International observers from Human Rights Watch stated there was a 'campaign of violence' which had 'extinguished any hope of free and fair run-off presidential elections'. Senior officials loyal to Mugabe were linked to violent incidents and with torture camps run by Zanu-PF. African criticism of the violence during the presidential election was voiced by a troika of observer states from the Southern African Development Community (SADC) – Tanzania, Angola and Swaziland – which was monitoring the hustings, and reported that violence was 'escalating throughout Zimbabwe'. The official rebuttal claimed the statement was biased. Morgan Tsvangirai pulled out of the presidential election, citing the violence perpetrated against his supporters. The US announced that it would not recognise the result of the run-off presidential election. Nelson Mandela, condemned the violence and criticised the situation in Zimbabwe as a 'failure of leadership'. Mugabe claimed victory and a sixth term in office. Morgan Tsvangirai refused to attend talks on power-sharing. The central bank issued a Z$500 million banknote to ease cash shortage. The official inflation rate grew to just over 11,250,000 per cent. A new, Z$100 billion note was introduced as the official inflation rate reached 231 million per cent. Mugabe and Tsvangirai signed a Memorandum of Understanding (MoU) that led to an uneasy political settlement. Following the breakdown in the negotiated power-sharing settlement, Prime Minister Tsvangirai was unable to get a passport to travel to Swaziland to take part in regionally sponsored talks with President Mugabe, to resolve the allocation of ministries between Zanu-PF and the MDC. The talks were postponed and later collapsed altogether.
2009 As the economy continued to fail, the use of US dollars spread, with market traders refusing to take local currency. A new Z$100 trillion note was introduced, valued at US$30 on that day. Other denominations in trillions were also released. Morgan Tsvangirai returned to the country. Further power sharing talks began but immediately stalled. The Zimbabwe dollar was finally officially abandoned in January when it was announced that all commercial transactions may be performed in foreign currencies; at the same time, a licence was granted to the stock exchange for trading to be conducted in foreign currencies. The Zimbabwe dollar had 12 zeros removed from the currency in a revaluation effort to stave off economic collapse; Z$1 trillion was reduced to Z$1. A summit of Southern African leaders urged Mugabe to appoint Morgan Tsvangirai as prime minister; he was sworn in on 11 February. The new coalition government began paying the military, teachers and civil servants in foreign currency, in an attempt to re-start the economy and get people back to work. Prime Minister Tsvangirai estimated that it would take US$5 billion to rebuild the country's economy. The UK offered to pay for re-settlement of an estimated 750 households of aged British residents in Zimbabwe. For the first time since 2000, the World Bank agreed to assist Zimbabwe in rebuilding its economy by offering technical assistance and giving it a token US$22 million as 'a first step' to encourage Zimbabwe to adhere to international fiscal commitments and begin to clear its arrears. Zimbabwe owed the World Bank and the African Development Bank over US$1 billion. Retail prices fell for the first time in years. The Organ of National Healing, Reconciliation and Integration (ONHRI) was inaugurated by the unity government to allow a platform to debate 'national healing' following years of violence and oppression. Vice President Joseph Msika, 85, died. Msika was also deputy president of Zanu-PF and the position is normally seen as a stepping stone to the Zimbabwean presidency. His death is likely to lead to intense lobbying over who succeeds Mugabe. Prime Minister Tsvangirai said the MDC would 'disengage' from working with Zanu-PF after the arrest of Roy Bennett (MDC treasurer-general and deputy agriculture minister designate) in October.
2010 Bishop Abel Muzorewa died, aged 85. He had been one of the most prominent politicians before independence and was briefly prime minister, in 1979, of the interim government of Zimbabwe-Rhodesia. After the Lancaster House Agreement was signed and inclusive elections were held in 1980 he lost out to Robert Mugabe in the general elections. Roy Bennett, was acquitted by the High Court on charges of treason, easing relations between Tsvangirai and Mugabe.
2011 Agreement on a US$700 million loan from China was signed in March. In return, the Chinese government urged Zimbabwe to protect Chinese companies from nationalisation plans. According to a report in June by the respected South African Institute of Race Relations, on the newly created Zimbabwean voters' roll, said the roll contained 2.6 million bogus entries, including under-aged voters, the registration of 13,396 new voters added to the roll in one constituency (that did not in any way change boundaries) and 14,000 people aged over 100 years. The authors of the report concluded this number of additional votes could determine

the results of next elections. In Wikileaks, released online in September, a US diplomatic cable dated June 2008 reported that President Mugabe had prostate cancer. Doctors reportedly said that the illness could cause his death in 'three to five years'.
2012 On 23 July the European Union (EU) lifted its curbs on aid to Zimbabwe; however further prospects of removing travel and economic sanctions on all but President Mugabe and his inner circle were dependent on a credible referendum on a new constitution. On 3 July, a Zanu-PF minister declared that all foreign-owned banks, hotels and telecommunications companies should turn over a controlling stake to a black Zimbabwean before the end of 2012. This sparked a row between Prime Minister Tsvangirai and his Zanu-PF coalition minister. The prime minister condemned the proposal and said that it had not been discussed in cabinet, nor agreed. The minister referred to the 2007 law requiring all banks to have 51 per cent of all shares in the hands of local Zimbabweans by 2012.
2013 A referendum on a new constitution was held on 16 and 17 March. It was approved by a resounding 94.49 per cent. Under the new constitution presidents are limited to two five year terms. President Mugabe flew to Singapore on 25 June for a medical check up. A remark by South Africa's envoy, Lindiwe Zulu, that electoral preparations were 'not looking good' after a shortage of ballot papers was reported, lead to a request from Mr Mugabe to President Zuma to stop 'this woman' from commenting. Two days before the 1 August election southern Africa's chief observer to Zimbabwe, Bernard Membe, said he was gravely concerned that a voters' roll had still not been released. Despite reports from various civil society organisations of isolated cases of intimidation and violence, particularly in rural areas, the general consensus is that the run-up to the general elections was peaceful. The election was held on 31 July. Mr Mugabe won a seventh term in office with an apparently convincing margin of 61 per cent to Mr Tsvangirai's 34 per cent. The parliamentary vote was a similar victory of 160 elected seats (out of 210) plus 37 women (out of 60) for ZANU-PF to 49 seats + 21 for the MDC. With over two-thirds of the seats in parliament President Mugabe can, if he wishes, make changes to the constitution. The results were greeted in a subdued manner and without the usual loud celebrations in the street. Shortly after the results were announced members of the opposition MDC party say they were attacked by followers of President Robert Mugabe. On 8 August the electoral commission reported that some 305,000 voters had been turned away. The MDC said the figure was nearer 900,000. On 9 August the MDC filed a legal challenge to Robert Mugabe's victory in the presidential elections. The petition calls for the election to be declared null and void and a new election to be called within 60 days. The MDC cites 15 reasons, including manipulation of the electoral roll, alleged bribery and abuse of 'assisted voting'. The court has to rule within 14 days. On 11 August the ministry of mines denied a report that Zimbabwe had agreed to sell uranium to Iran. In his annual Heroes Day address to the nation (12 August) President Mugabe rejected Mr Tsvangirai's claims that the vote had been stolen, saying that those against him could 'go hang'. The following day, Defence Forces Day, he told a rally that he would be continuing with his policy of 'indiginisation' to empower Zimbabweans. Under the policy all foreign owned companies have to hand over 51 per cent of the company to black Zimbabweans. On 16 August the MDC dropped its challenge to the election results, saying they could not get a fair hearing without information such as the number of people not on the voters' roll who voted. Robert Mugabe was sworn in as President for the seventh time on 22 August. On 31 October Zimbabwe's highest court declared unconstitutional a law which makes it a crime to insult the president. On 14 December Emmerson Dambudzo Mnangagwa was announced as Zanu-PF vice president, in effect making him heir apparent to Mr Mugabe.
2014 On 28 April the opposition MDC suspended Morgan Tsvangirai as leader after he was accused of a 'remarkable failure of leadership'. In May President Mugabe was rumoured to have told a number of his closest allies that he would not stand in the December election for presidency of his party. Although he attended the inauguration of President Zuma of South Africa, he was looking frail. Contenders to succeeded him include Gideon Gono, former Central Bank governor, Emmerson Mnangagwa (known as 'The Crocodile') and Joice Mujuru (current party vice president and known as 'Spill Blood'). Oppah Muchinguri, head of Zanu-PF's women's league, is also thought to be in the running. In August, Grace Mugabe, wife of the President was elected as the national secretary of the women's league during its elective congress. She will take over from Mrs Muchinguri in December; the position means that she will sit on Zanu-PF's powerful politburo, just as tension is rising over who will succeed her husband. Accusations against Vice President Joice Mujuru for corruption and plotting to assassinate the President were rejected by Mrs Mujuru as 'unfounded' and 'ridiculous' on 6 December.
2015 Robert Mugabe was elected as AU chairman for the coming year on 30 January. On 15 September Mr Mugabe read the same state of the nation address he had given in August. Vice President Emmerson Mnangagwa submited the correct speech two hours later and a special session of parliament had to be called the following day to officially record the speech. In June the central bank finally withdrew the Zimbabwean dollar. Zimbabweans were able to exchange their local currency savings for US dollars at a rate of 175 quadrillion Zimbabwe dollars to US$5.

Political structure

Constitution

The constitution was first instigated in 1979, based on articles agreed in the Lancaster House accord. An amendment in 1987 resulted in the appointment of an executive president as Head of State.
The election laws were amended in January 2002 to ban independent election monitors and deny voting rights to Zimbabweans living abroad.
Further amendments to the constitution, in 2005, included the re-introduction of an upper house – the Senate. The Senate has 66 members – 50 members elected for five-year terms (five from each of the 10 provinces), 10 traditional chiefs and six members appointed by the president.
Constitutional Amendment Bill number 18 became law on 30 October 2007. Under the Bill the next presidential election would be brought forward to 2008 so as to coincide with the parliamentary elections. Seats in the lower house were increased from 150 to 210, and in the Senate from 84 to 93. The most controversial admendment was to allow Mugabe to choose his successor, which would be voted on by the then Zanu-PF-dominated parliament.
A constitutional amendment was passed in 2013 by 95% majority, which limits future presidents to a maximum of two five-year terms and abolishes the position of Prime Minister.

Independence date

18 April 1980

Form of state

Presidential Republic

The executive

Executive power is vested in the president (elected by universal suffrage every five years), vice presidents and cabinet. Both the vice presidents and cabinet are appointed by the president. Mugabe has served as president since 31 December 1987.

National legislature

Legislative power is vested in the parliament, comprising 210 elected-members plus 60 women in the House of Assembly (lower house) and a 80-member Senate (upper house), both elected for five years.

Legal system

Based on the constitution and English common law.

Last elections

31 July 2013 (presidential first round and parliamentary) (no second round necessary)

Results: Presidential: Robert Mugabe (Zanu-PF) 61 per cent), Morgan Tsvangirai (MDC) won 34 per cent
Parliamentary: Zanu-PF 160 (out of 210) elected seats + 37 (out of 60) women (total 197), MDC 49 + 21 seats (total 70).

Next elections

March 2018 (presidential, parliamentary)

Political parties

Ruling party

Zimbabwe African National Union-Patriotic Front (Zanu-PF) (from 28 Jul 2013)

Main opposition party

None as such

Population

13.12 million (2013)*

Around 45 per cent of the total population is under 15 years of age.

Last census: August 2012: 13,061,239

Population density: 29 inhabitants per square km. Urban population 38 per cent (2010 Unicef).

Annual growth rate: 0.9 per cent, 1990–2010 (Unicef).

Internally Displaced Persons (IDP)

100,000–200,000 (UNHCR 2004)

Ethnic make-up

Shona (75 per cent) (including the Zezuru clan (18 per cent) and the Karanga clan (22 per cent)); Ndebele (18 per cent); white (1 per cent). There are several minor ethnic groups, and a small number of inhabitants of Asian or mixed racial descent.

Religions

Dual Christian/indigenous beliefs (50 per cent), Christian (25 per cent), indigenous beliefs (24 per cent).

Education

The educational system was one of the best in the region with universal primary school enrolment and secondary education reaching about 50 per cent of those eligible.

The worsening public finances has put the country's education facilities at risk as the government rationalises non-military expenditure. With increases in education levies of between 400 per cent and 2,000 per cent in 2003–04, impoverished families are increasingly unable to find the money to send their children to school. Primary enrolment has declined from 93 per cent in 2000 to 65 per cent in 2003. When schools reassembled for the winter term 2004, they were forced to turn away 800,000 orphans because President Mugabe's government has run out of money to pay their fees.

Literacy rate: 90 per cent adult rate; 98 per cent youth rate (15–24) (Unesco 2005).

Compulsory years: Five to 12.

Enrolment rate: 95.0 per cent gross primary enrolment; 44.5 per cent gross secondary enrolment, of relevant age groups (including repeaters) (World Bank).

Pupils per teacher: 37 in primary schools.

Health

The state of Zimbabwe's healthcare was mixed in the 1990s. Spending on private healthcare (such as private household expenditure and insurance) averaged 3.7 per cent of GDP.

In 2005 the UK gave over US$17.9 million to UN and non-governmental agencies (NGO) to provide food for five million people affected by food shortages. Around US$1 million was allocated to help those who had returned to their rural homes after being evicted under the government's Operation Murambatsvina.

HIV/Aids

The UN stated, in 2005, that one million children have been made orphans and another 160,000 would lose a parent. Unicef called on donor countries to look beyond the political administration of Zimbabwe and focus on the victims of the disease. Only US$14 is contributed for each Zimbabwean compared to US$68 for citizens of neighbouring Namibia or US$111 in Mozambique. With one of the highest infection rates in the region, with an estimated 1.8 million people HIV positive in 2003 Zimbabwe's sick can ill-afford international neglect. Poor governance, profligacy and the politicisation of relief by President Mugabe has left donors averse to giving more.

The HIV prevalence rate for females aged 15–24 years is 33 per cent and the incidence of mother-to-child transmission of HIV/Aids is 12 per cent, and these pose another serious impediment to Zimbabwe's embattled population.

In June 2012 at least 10 members of parliament and 13 other men were circumcised as part in a campaign to reduce HIV infection by encouraging circumcision. The men undertook the procedure (which WHO studies have shown reduces the spread of HIV infection acquired through heterosexual intercourse by up to 60 per cent) to show support for and the simplicity of the operation.

HIV prevalence: 24.65 per cent aged 15–49 in 2003 (World Bank)

Life expectancy: 36 years, 2004 (WHO 2006)

Fertility rate/Maternal mortality rate: 3.3 births per woman, 2010 (Unicef); maternal mortality 400 per 100,000 live births (World Bank).

Child (under 5 years) mortality rate (per 1,000): 90 per 1,000 live births (WHO 2012); 13 per cent of children under aged five are malnourished (World Bank).

Head of population per physician: 0.16 physicians per 1,000 people, 2004 (WHO 2006)

Welfare

Many companies operated some form of social security plan for their employees, which usually included medical aid but the deteriorating economy has curtailed welfare measures. Workers may individually contribute to private insurance and medical aid funds.

Main cities

Harare (capital, estimated population 1.8 million in 2012), Bulawayo (766,500), Chitungwiza (365,026), Mutare (188,753), Epworth (148,157), Gweru (141,872), Kwekwe (101,282), Kadoma (77,749).

Languages spoken

Local languages, Shona and Ndebele spoken by the majority of the population, are written languages and are taught in schools.

Official language/s

English, Shona and Ndebele

Media

The Ministry of Information and Publicity exerts tight control of the media. The *Access to Information* law makes it an offence to report on Zimbabwe unless a state-registered journalist; only Zimbabwean citizens or residents of the country are eligible for registration. Foreign journalists are only allowed into the country to cover specific, usually non-political, events. Through these measures press freedom has been seriously curtailed. Not only are there repressive laws, but violence by either supporters or members of Zanu-PF, have effectively silenced reporters and distorted news and views. In 2007, the Freedom House annual survey showed Zimbabwe had earned the lowest possible score for political rights and civil liberties including, press freedom.

The Zimbabwe Media Commission (ZMC), set up in December 2009, is to spearhead media reforms, including licensing new press, radio and TV outlets. In May 2010 four private newspapers, including the *Daily News* which had been banned in 2003, were granted licences by the ZMC.

Press

Spiralling costs have pushed up the price of production and publications and caused serious falls in circulation numbers.

Dailies: Government-owned newspapers include *The Herald* (www.herald.co.zw) and *The Chronicle* (www.chronicle.co.zw), published in Bulawayo. *The Daily Mirror* (www.zimmirror.co.zw) is independent. *The Daily News* and its weekend edition, critical of the Mugabe government, was suspended in 2003. The ban on *The Daily News* was lifted and began full-time operations on 25 March 2011.

Weeklies: There are more newspapers published at the weekend than daily, including *The Zimbabwe Independent* (www.thezimbabweindependent.com), *The Standard* (www.thezimbabwestandard.com), *The Saturday Mirror* and *The Sunday Mirror* (www.zimmirror.co.zw).

Business: The privately owned *The Financial Gazette* (www.fingaz.co.zw) is a weekly newspaper, published in Harare. Daily newspapers have sections given over to business and economics. *The Farmer* a weekly covers agricultural matters.

Broadcasting

The national, Zimbabwe Broadcasting Corporation (ZBC) is state-run.

Radio: For most Zimbabweans radio is the only source of information and news. ZBC operates four services – Radio 1 (in English), 2 (in Shona and Ndebele) 4 (an educational channel) and Radio 3 is a commercial station aimed at the young. There are no private radio stations although Zimbabwe is targeted by a number of overseas broadcasts. The Voice of the People (VOP) (www.vopradio.co.zw), operated by former staff of ZBC, broadcasts from Madagascar.

Television: ZBC operates one TV channel. Satellite TV is available from South Africa.

Other news agencies: ZimOnline (from South Africa): www.zimonline.co.za
Zimbabwe Daily News online (from UK): www.zimdaily.com
The Zimbabwe Times (from US): www.thezimbabwetimes.com
Jeune Afrique (in French): www.jeuneafrique.com

Economy

Zimbabwe is extremely rich in natural resources, it is home to over 40 different minerals including diamonds, gold, silver, platinum, copper, ferrochrome, coal, lithium and nickel. Zimbabwe also has rich soil which is perfect for crop cultivation including maize, wheat, coffee, tobacco, cotton, tea and sugarcane. Furthermore, it has millions of hectares of forest for timber exploitation and pastures for cattle, pigs, sheep and goats. Despite the seemingly enormous advantages Zimbabwe has had, the country has only recently been reduced from being known as the 'breadbasket of Africa' to a bankrupt and economically pariah state caused by political and ideologically divisive leadership. International financial institutions had either declined to, or been barred from, engaging with their Zimbabwean counterparts as the political regime of President Mugabe instituted greater and more oppressive measures to mould the economy into its ideals of 'Africa for Africans'. In the 2013 elections Robert Mugabe was re-elected whilst his ZANU-PF party won a two-thirds majority in the House of Assembly.

The economy was already in recession in 2007, with GDP growth of -3.6 per cent, which dropped further to -17.6 per cent in 2008 as the economy collapsed and the global economic crisis cut any hope of external funding. By July 2008 inflation had reached the astronomic height of 231,000,000 per cent and larger and larger bank notes were issued to keep pace, ending with a Z$100 trillion note in January 2009. The Zimbabwe dollar was finally officially abandoned and in a revaluation move in February 2009, 12 zeros were removed – Z$1 trillion became Z$1. The official statistician said that with the lack of goods to purchase it was impossible to determine an accurate inflation rate.

Since late 2008 when the opposition Movement for Democratic Change (MDC) entered into a power-sharing government with the ZANU-PF and Morgan Tsvangirai (MDC) became prime minister, efforts to restore some resemblance to a rational economic policy have lifted the economy. In 2009 Tsvangirai began by pleading with world economic institutions to support his efforts for reform. Some US$10 billion was estimated as being needed to rebuild the country and its economy. Individual countries made pledges totalling US$500 million, and for the first time since 2000, in May 2009 the World Bank agreed to offer technical assistance and give a token US$22 million as 'a first step' to encourage Zimbabwe to adhere to international fiscal commitments and begin to clear its arrears (Zimbabwe owed the World Bank and the African Development Bank over US$1 billion).

The economy picked up in 2009 as some foreign direct investment, particularly in mining, stimulated growth to 5.8 per cent and higher still to 11.4 per cent in 2010. Growth continued rising and in 2011 was 11.9 per cent but dropped to 10.6 per cent in 2012. Following this the economy decelerated even further dropping to 3.2 per cent by 2014. This slowdown is a reflection of manufacturing being undercapitalised and capital machinery in need of refurbishment, while being constrained by unreliable power supplies, increased labour costs and regulatory burdens. In the 2010 budget, corporate tax was cut to 25 per cent (from 30 per cent), income tax was reduced to 35 per cent (from 37.5 per cent) and tax rates for the mining industry rose. In the 2014 budget the tax threshold was raised from US$250 a month to US$300 a month.

Agricultural production in 2012 consisted of US$244 million of meat, US$183 million of tobacco and US$136 million amongst many other goods. President Mugabe's act of seizing most of Zimbabwe's white owned land in 2000 had led to a drop in agriculture by 70 per cent according to Commercial Farmers Union (CFU) head Dean Theron. The manufacturing industry has been in a dire state in recent years and continued so in 2014.

Mineral production decreased in 2014 following a period of positive growth, with the value of the industry declining to US$1.46 billion from US$1.50 billion in the previous year.

While improvements have allowed the government to make realistic fiscal plans and submit a budget for approval, the external position of Zimbabwe remains precarious and sustainable economic growth is impeded by a lack of domestic liquidity with very high interest rates, an ailing infrastructure and low domestic demand.

The World Bank estimated in 2011 that at Zimbabwe's current pace a recovery to pre-2000 levels would take until around 2020.

In January 2014, the World Bank ruled out Zimbabwe from its aid scheme, banning the country from accessing loans from international lenders unless the country first clears its arrears.

In the 2014, the UN Human Development Index ranked Zimbabwe 156 (out of 187) for lack of national development in health, education and income, and well below the average for sub-Saharan Africa. In 2014, 41.0 per cent of the population were living in multidimensional poverty.

In September 2013, the EU agreed to lift sanctions on the Zimbabwe Mining Development Corporation (ZMDC) diamond-mining firm. This act will allow the sale of ZMDC's diamonds in Europe, potentially raising tax revenues by US$400 million a year. Global Witness, the anti-corruption watchdog has alleged that state diamond revenues were directly used to fund Mugabe's re-election by citing links between mining companies and insiders at the ZANU-PF.

External trade

Zimbabwe is a member of the Common Market for Eastern and Southern Africa (Comesa), but does not operate a free trade area with the other member states as the economy is too weak to maintain the union. It is also a member of the Southern African Development Community (SADC), the objectives of which include reducing trade barriers, achieving regional development and economic growth and evolving common systems and institutions.

Zimbabwe has some of the world's largest reserves in minerals including coal and asbestos, platinum, copper, nickel, gold, iron and chromite. However, the political situation has discouraged virtually all direct foreign investment and mining production has not been maintained or grown. Traditional exports in tobacco dropped dramatically since 2000, from 237,000 tonnes to 50,000 tonnes in 2006 but have made a comeback in 2012 with 150,000 tonnes, however in 2014 figures fell from the previous year earning 13.5 per cent less from exports. Cotton is the primary agricultural export.

A lack of foreign exchange led to a critical shortage of imported fuel and electricity. A grey economy, with trade in black market goods, has replaced much of the legitimate economy.

Tourism had been a vital foreign exchange earner, but the sector has contracted due to the poor image of Zimbabwe abroad. Remittances, especially in US dollars, have become a necessity for trade within the country. Exports still exist, both primary and manufactured, but intermittent energy supplies hamper production.

Imports

Main imports are food, machinery, fertiliser and general manufactured products.

Main sources: South Africa (42.9 per cent of total in 2014), Singapore (18.3 per cent), China (6.3 per cent)

Exports

Main exports are cotton, timber, tobacco, chrome alloy, gold, diamonds, ferroalloys and asbestos.

Main destinations: South Africa (67.0 per cent of total in 2014), Mozambique (18.8 per cent), Belgium (4.1 per cent)

Agriculture

Farming

Zimbabwe is a rich agricultural country with mainly good rainfall where agriculture used to be the dominant sector of the economy. It was almost self-sufficient in food with annual exports of around US$70 million. In 1999 government policy was to appropriate white-owned farm property with little or no compensation. Over 200,000 black agricultural workers lost their jobs when corporate and white-owned farms were confiscated and the land given to 124,000 black families. The government did not seek to combine land transfers with the necessary capital and expertise to run the farms and this resulted in the virtual destruction of the commercial farming sector. It took over a decade for the sector to recover, it is predicted that it will take to 2020 before the sector can fully recover.

Before the turbulence of the farm take-overs, Zimbabwe was the second biggest exporter of the top quality variety of the tobacco crop known as flue-cured, exporting 236.7 million kg in 2000. By 2008 this had dropped to 48.3 million kg but the production of the crop has recently began a recovery, despite dropping from 216 million kg in 2013 to 167 million kg in 2014.

By 2014 smallholder farmers were the main suppliers of Zimbabwe's beef industry, with around 60 per cent of the total national herd of 5 million cattle.

Fishing

Despite the existence of five major flood plains, the country has little fishery potential. There are no natural lakes of any significant size and large man-made reservoirs are primarily used for hydroelectric and farming purposes.

Lake Kariba (between Zambia and Zimbabwe) accounts for approximately 80 per cent of the country's total fish production. The industrial fishery thrives on fresh water sardines (kapenta) which were introduced to the lake from Lake Tanganyika. Lake Kariba also supports an artisanal gillnet fishery, which is based on 40 indigenous species near the lake's shores. This type of activity is important for the local economy, as most of the land available along the shore is unsuitable for crop cultivation.

The catch from reservoirs other than Lake Kariba is typically estimated at 2,000 tonnes per year. The bulk of the catch from these small reservoirs is not usually marketed but kept for domestic consumption. The catch from small dams typically constitutes another 2,000 tonnes, while rivers and fish farms are estimated to yield 1,000 tonnes of fish.

The Department of Fisheries in Zambia and the Department of National Parks and Wildlife Management in Zimbabwe, with the co-operation of Norway and Denmark, have undertaken a project to facilitate the sustainable utilisation of the shared fisheries resources on Lake Kariba.

Forestry

Various woodland types account for 66 per cent of the country's land area, compared to the 27 per cent covered with cultivation.

Timber production is primarily used for fuelwood (charcoal), which provides three-quarters of domestic energy supplies. The country's main exported forest product is sandalwood.

Industry and manufacturing

Zimbabwe's industrial sector was once one of the most advanced and diversified in sub-Saharan Africa. By 2014 the country's capacity utilisation was only at 30 per cent, and manufacturing accounted for only 12 per cent of GDP, down from 20 per cent ten years prior.

The sector has been undermined by capital flight, a lack of foreign exchange, an overvalued exchange rate, severe fuel shortages and the constant threat of forced nationalisation. Investment has been hit by take-overs of firms by members of the government and their relatives. The largely liberalised textile sector is also struggling against competition from countries such as South Africa where subsidies and tariffs operate as barriers to free trade.

Other problems include a lack of capacity, which can only be improved with increased foreign investment. With supporters of the Zanu-PF beginning to attack foreign companies operating in Zimbabwe, prospects for industrial expansion look dim.

Zimbabwe's heavy industries are also facing hard times, despite being targeted by the government as essential to developing import substitutes, which would reduce the loss in foreign exchange. In recent years, the country has experienced an expansion in the chemicals and cement sectors.

Tourism

The prospects for tourism in Zimbabwe have improved along with the political situation and tourist numbers rose from a low of less than 500,000 in 2000 to 2.3 million in 2010. However from a high in 2011 of 2.4 million tourist arrivals, it decreased to 1.8 million total arrivals in 2012. This figure was maintained in 2013. The Victoria Falls remains the single most popular tourist destination, although safari tours are also very popular. There are ancient ruined cities (most famously Great Zimbabwe in Masingo), a legacy of the Monomotapa Empire, and other natural wonders, including the Victoria Falls which are included on Unesco's World Heritage List.

Travel and tourism contributed US$1,444.3 million in total, which was 10.4 per cent of GDP in 2014 and provided employment to 7.3 per cent of the workforce (426,000 jobs) including jobs indirectly supported by the industry.

The infrastructure, which has been neglected in the recent past, is in need of refurbishment and upgrading before greater growth can be expected. Peripheral investment due to industrial production is keeping major roads and air links open. Zimbabwe belongs to the Regional Tourism Organisation of Southern Africa (Retosa), an association of 15 countries, which works to produce integrated measures at a governmental level to promote best domestic practices and policies in tourism. The UN World Travel Organisation held a meeting at Victoria Falls in 2013.

Mining

The mining sector accounts for around 8 per cent of GDP and employs 5 per cent of the workforce. Many minerals, including chromite, copper and nickel ores, iron ore, tin ore, gold ore, phosphate rock, limestone and iron pyrites are converted to downstream products. The main exceptions are coal, phosphate rock, pyrites and limestone, which, along with a substantial proportion of iron, steel, copper and asbestos production are sold on the domestic market. Import substitution is encouraged. However, high fuel prices have increased costs markedly.

The government's policy on land and assets tenure has left foreign companies concerned that their assets could be seized without cause or warning. The 'economic empowerment provisions' require companies to sell a 20 per cent stake to local black investors and 30 per cent by the end of 2015.

A meeting of the international diamond trade organisation that implements the Kimberly Process Certification Scheme (KPCS) whereby exported diamonds are not part of the 'blood diamond' trade, held in June 2010, became deadlocked over whether Zimbabwe should be allowed to resume legitimate trade in diamonds. Exports could amount to over US$1.7 billion per year. Human rights organisations claim miners are subject to forced labour, harassment, torture and killings by security forces. The government stated it would sell its diamonds on the world market, regardless of the KPCS deliberation. In July, the operators of the KPCS allowed partial trade in stockpiles of Zimbabwe diamonds, with full export in September 2010 dependent on a review of conditions. The ban on the exports of diamonds under the Kimberley process from the Marange mines was lifted on 2 November 2011.

In January 2014, 'massive' diamond fields were found in the Umkondo Basin stretching over 10,000 square km. These fields are expected to bring the country much needed billions of dollars in export earnings.

Hydrocarbons

The National Oil Company of Zimbabwe (Noczim) is responsible for supplying the country with petroleum products; supplies are unreliable due to high fuel prices and Noczim's inability to pay its bills.

Zimbabwe has no proven oil reserves and, therefore it relies heavily on imports for liquid fuel. In order to reduce imports, petrol is being blended with ethanol to create fuel. In 2013 this cut the fuel bill by US$20 million, however motor companies have claimed this fuel will cause malfunctions in the engines of some vehicles.

Due to Zimbabwe's complete dependency on imports for liquid fuels, a project has been started in Chipinge, Manicaland to produce ethanol from cane. The project plans to provide 20 per cent of the country's liquid fuel and create 8,000 jobs.

Any use of natural gas is commercially insignificant.

There is some potential for coal-bed methane gas production. An estimated 500 billion cubic metres of sulphur-free methane gas exists in a 177 square km basin near Lupane in western Matabeleland. Deposits have also been discovered in Manicaland, which in combination with the deposits of diamonds could see the province becoming the richest in terms of minerals.

Zimbabwe's coal primarily comes from Karoo sediments in the north-west, where the Hwange Coalfield is situated. Coal is exclusively used for domestic purposes with around 60 per cent of production used in electricity generation.

Energy

Total installed generating capacity was 2.035GW in 2013. Coal provides 60 per cent of local electricity generating capacity with wood, oil and hydroelectric power providing the rest. Zimbabwe faces problems relating to the rising cost of oil and electricity imports. This resulted in severe debts within the electricity sector and extensive power cuts.

The Zimbabwe Electricity Supply Authority (Zesa), which oversees generation, transmission and distribution of electricity, has plans for a number of projects aimed at rehabilitating existing power generators, as well as creating new ones. There is a project from Zesa to build a hydroelectric power plant in Batoka Gorge, between Victoria Falls and Lake Kariba. Kariba Dam itself already supplies 1,319MW to both Zambia and Zimbabwe. On the Zimbabwe side there are 6 generators producing a total of 750MW. In 2013 Zimbabwe's Finance Minister Patrick Chinamasa stated that the capacity of the Kariba power station would be increased by 300MW for which China will give Zimbabwe US$319 million.

Financial markets

Stock exchange

Zimbabwe Stock Exchange (ZSE)

Banking and insurance

Before the economic crisis that began in 2000, Zimbabwe had a sophisticated banking system. Performance has been adversely affected by the macroeconomic environment, including the government's foreign exchange regime, negative interest rates and the high level of domestic borrowing.

The banking sector comprises the Reserve Bank of Zimbabwe (RBZ) (central bank), five commercial banks, four merchant banks, five finance houses (mainly engaged in hire purchase), two discount houses serving the money market, three building societies and the Post Office Savings Bank. In addition, state-owned corporations invest and lend for specific development purposes.

Central bank

Reserve Bank of Zimbabwe

Main financial centre

Harare

Time

GMT plus two hours

Geography

Zimbabwe is a landlocked country in southern central Africa. It is bounded by the Limpopo river and South Africa to the south, by the Zambezi river and Zambia to the north, by Mozambique to the east and by Botswana to the west.

The country falls into three geographical areas: the high veld, the low veld and the Eastern Highlands. The high veld comprises the major part of the country extending across the central area and rising gradually from the south-west to the north-east, with an average altitude of 1,200 metres. The two main cities, Harare (altitude 1,472 metres) and Bulawayo (altitude 1,343 metres) lie in this area. The low veld comprises the Sabi-Limpopo valleys in the south and the Zambezi valley in the north including the spectacular Victoria Falls that form the border with Zambia. Further east the Zambezi is dammed for electricity generation at Kariba, forming a 250km long lake. The Eastern Highlands borders Mozambique and contains two ranges, the Chimanimani Mountains, with peaks reaching 2,436 metres, and the Inyanga Mountains, with peaks up to 2,595 metres.

Hemisphere

Southern

Climate

Most of the country is semi-tropical with day temperatures of 30 degrees Celsius

(C), or slightly above on hot days in the rainy season, but falling as low as 0 degrees C at night in the dry winter season. Rainfall is largely confined to the months November to March and is subject to wide annual variations with considerable influence on agricultural production. Heavier rain falls in the Eastern Highlands.

Dress codes

Business dress is generally formal, suits or jacket with a tie and trousers for men. Many hotels and restaurants require smart casual attire, particularly in the evening, with some insisting on jacket and tie, thus excluding denim jeans. Women normally dress conservatively in European style.

Entry requirements

Passports

Required by all.

Visa

Are required by all, except citizens of countries with reciprocal visa-free entry, see www.zimbabweembassy-uk.com and follow link to *Consular*, then *Visa Requirements* then *Category A, B* or *C* for further information. A proposed tourist *univisa* (a single visa to visit all 15-member states of SADC: Angola, Botswana, DRC, Lesotho, Madagascar, Malawi, Mauritius, Mozambique, Namibia, South Africa, Seychelles, Swaziland, Tanzania, Zambia and Zimbabwe) is expected to be in use by 2013. Visitors should check with the appropriate consulates to confirm start of *univisas* and their scope before beginning a tour of southern Africa.

Contact the consular section of the nearest embassy for further advice and requirements for a visa, and confirmation the visitor requires a visa. All visitors must have an onward/return ticket and sufficient money for their stay.

Currency advice/regulations

The import and export of local currency is limited to Z$15,000. The import of foreign currency is unlimited but must be declared in writing; export is limited to the amount declared.

The new Zimbabwe dollar went into circulation on 21 August 2006, whereby three zeros were dropped (Z$1,000,000 became Z$1,000). The new notes are now the only legal tender.

Travellers cheques are accepted in banks and major hotels.

Customs

Personal items are duty-free.

Agricultural plant material including seeds and bulbs and fresh meat require an import licence.

Prohibited imports

Illegal drugs, honey, pornographic literature, assault knives and imitation firearms.

Health (for visitors)

Mandatory precautions

Yellow fever vaccination certificate if travelling from an infected area.

Advisable precautions

Vaccinations for diphtheria, tetanus, polio, hepatitis A and typhoid are recommended. Other vaccinations that may be advised include tuberculosis and hepatitis B and cholera. HIV/Aids is prevalent.

Anti-malarial prophylaxis is necessary for the Zambezi valley throughout the year and elsewhere from November–June. Bilharzia is endemic, to avoid the risk, only use well maintained, chlorinated swimming pools. Water precautions are necessary, use only boiled or bottled water. Local dairy products should be avoided as milk is unpasteurised; vegetables, meat and fish should be well cooked and eaten hot. Fruit should be peeled. Sun-screen should be used regularly.

Medical services are poor throughout the country and the services of private doctors may be charged in full before treatment begins. Medical insurance is essential, including emergency evacuation, and an adequate supply of personal medicines is necessary.

A reasonable precaution could include a first aid kit with a sterile needle kit and disposable syringes.

Hotels

Several hotels of various standards are available in the main cities, rated from one to five stars by the Tourist Board. Most of the larger ones are air-conditioned. The government imposes a bed tax per person per night, and it is usual to tip 10 per cent.

Credit cards

Major credit and charge cards are widely accepted. Hyperinflation has led to long queues while clients make several withdrawals at ATMs that were designed to issue a maximum of 40 bank notes.

Public holidays (national)

Fixed dates

1 Jan (New Year's Day), 18 Apr (Independence Day), 1 May (Labour Day), 25 May (Africa Day), 22 Dec (Unity Day), 25–26 Dec (Christmas).

Holidays that fall on the weekend are given *in lieu*.

Variable dates

Good Friday, Easter Monday, Heroes' Day and Defence Force's Day (third Mon and Tue Aug)

Working hours

Banking

Mon–Fri: 0830–1500, (Wed) 0830–1300; Sat: 0830–1130.

Business

Mon–Fri: 0745/0830–1600/1700.

Government

Mon–Fri: 0745/0830–1600/1700.

Shops

Mon–Fri: 0800–1300, 1400–1700; Wed half day. Sat: 0800–1200.

Telecommunications

Mobile/cell phones

There are 900 GSM services available in main towns and cities.

Electricity supply

220V 50Hz with either UK style flat, or round, three-pin plugs.

Social customs/useful tips

Zimbabweans generally rise early and go to bed early, particularly on weekdays. Punctuality is generally appreciated in business circles. Hospitality, particularly for meals, is widely offered and may be freely reciprocated. The formal address (Mr, Mrs or Miss with surname) is usual and a given-name terms are only adopted on closer acquaintance. The giving or receiving of gifts, other than between personal friends, is not customary. No particular proscriptions apply to eating, drinking or smoking and there are no particular religious observances or taboos. Tipping (for example, 10 per cent of a restaurant bill) is common.

It is unwise to photograph major government buildings, military personnel or equipment without prior official permission. Photographers should bring their own film as it is not generally available locally.

Security

Physical attacks, car-jacking and credit card fraud are increasing problems. Foreign nationals who are perceived to be wealthy could be targetted by criminals operating in the vicinity of hotels, restaurants and shopping malls in Harare and other major tourist areas. Caution should be exercised at all times.

Visitors should make two photocopies of the biographic page of their passport; one copy should be retained at home and the other carried at all times for identification purposes.

Getting there

Air

National airline: Air Zimbabwe

International airport/s: Harare International Airport (HRE), 12km from city; post office, restaurant, duty-free shop and bank/bureau de change.

Bulawayo Airport (BUQ), 24km from city.

Other airport/s: Victoria Falls Airport (VFA); Kariba Airport (KAB).

Airport tax: Departure tax varies depending on the destination; all taxes have to be paid in US dollars. To and from UK US$52, to South Africa US$31, to China US$11, to Dubai US$8.

Surface

Road: Direct routes from Zambia via Victoria Falls, Kariba and Chirundu. Entry from South Africa at Beitbridge and from Botswana at Plumtree. There are three main routes from Mozambique in the east. Most of the border posts are closed from 1800 to 0600 hours every day although specific hours vary.

Rail: There are regular services to Zambia via the Victoria Falls and from Botswana via Bulawayo. There is a rail connection from Beira and Maputo (Mozambique). Rail travel from South Africa was suspended in 1999.

Getting about

National transport

Air: Regular inexpensive daily flights to all major destinations.

Road: Network of over 85,000km, of which about one-quarter are classed as main or secondary roads and half are surfaced with gravel. Good roads connect major towns. Nationwide petrol shortages may impede travel.

Buses: Good inter-city network operated by Express Motorways Africa Ltd, Zimbabwe Omnibus Company, plus numerous local operators. Express coach services from Harare to Bulawayo, Mutare, Kariba, Chipinge, Masvingo. Advisable to book in advance.

Rail: National Railways of Zimbabwe operate services between Harare and Gweru, Bulawayo, Victoria Falls, Mutare, Masvingo, Chinhoyi and intermediate towns (there are also certain places served by branch lines). Two classes – some trains carry restaurant cars and couchette sleeping accommodation. (NB Bedding is charged). Advisable to book tickets (and bedding) in advance. The system is badly rundown and lacks investment.

Water: Ferries cross Lake Kariba.

City transport

Taxis: These are not usually hailed in the street, they are available at ranks near main hotels. A 10 per cent tip is usual.

Buses, trams & metro: Urban services in some centres can be sporadic.

Car hire

Self-drive cars are available in main cities and at Harare airport, although their condition may not be well maintained. However, they are a useful method of transport as most main intercity roads tend to be of good quality, always maintain an adequate supply of fuel as shortages may leave a traveller stranded. Traffic drives on the left and a foreign or international driving licence is acceptable during short visits.

BUSINESS DIRECTORY

The addresses listed below are a selection only. While World of Information makes every endeavour to check these addresses, we cannot guarantee that changes have not been made, especially to telephone numbers and area codes. We would welcome any corrections.

Telephone area codes

The international direct dialling code (IDD) for Zimbabwe is + 263, followed by area code and subscriber's number:

Bulawayo	9	Harare	4
Chiredze	31	Mutare	20

Chambers of Commerce

Zimbabwe National Chamber of Commerce, 115 Nelson Mandela Avenue, PO Box 1934, Harare (tel: 799-692; fax: 799-695; e-mail: info@zncc.co.zw).

Banking

Barclays Bank of Zimbabwe Ltd, PO Box 1279, Barclay House, Jason Moyo Avenue/First Street, Harare (tel: 758-280/1/2/3; fax: 752-913).

First Merchant Bank of Zimbabwe, PO Box 2786, FMB House, 67 Samora Machel Avenue, Harare (tel: 703-071, 727-294; fax: 250-682).

Merchant Bank of Central Africa, PO Box 3200, 14th Floor, Old Mutual Centre, Third Street, Jason Moyo Avenue, Harare (tel: 738-081; fax: 708-005).

NMB Bank, PO Box 2564, 1st Floor, Unity Court, Corner 1st Street/Union Avenue, Harare (tel: 759-651/9, 759-601/6; fax: 759-648).

Stanbic Bank Zimbabwe Ltd, PO Box 300, Stanbic Bank Centre, 59 Samora Machel Avenue, Harare (tel: 759-480/3, 759-471/9, 759-479; fax: 749-030).

Standard Chartered Bank Zimbabwe Ltd, PO Box 373, John Boyne House, 38 Speke Ave, Harare (tel: 752-864; fax: 758-076).

Zimbabwe Banking Corporation Ltd, PO Box 3198, Zimbank House, 46 Speke Avenue, Harare (tel: 757-471/94; fax: 757-497, 751-741).

Central bank

Reserve Bank of Zimbabwe, PO Box 1283, 80 Samora Machel Avenue, Harare (tel: 703-000; fax: 707-800; e-mail: rbzmail@rbz.co.zw).

Stock exchange

Zimbabwe Stock Exchange (ZSE), www.zse.co.zw

Travel information

Air Zimbabwe, PO Box AP1, Harare Airport, Harare (tel: 575-111; fax: 575-068).

National tourist organisation offices

Zimbabwe Tourism Authority, 9th Floor, Kopje Plaza, 1 Jason Moyo Avenue, Cnr Jason Moyo/Rotten Row, PO Box CY286, Causeway, Harare (tel: 758-730/34, 752-570, 758-712/14; fax: 758-726/28; e-mail: mktg@ztazim.org; zta@africaonline.co.zw; internet site: http://www.tourismzimbabwe.co.zw).

Ministries

Ministry of Agriculture, Ngungunyana Building 1, Borrowdale Road, P Bag 7701, Causeway, Harare (tel: 706-081, 700-596; fax: 734-646).

Ministry of Defence, Munhumutapa Building, Samora Machel Avenue, P Bag 7713, Causeway, Harare (tel: 700-155, 728-271).

Ministry of Education, Ambassador House, Union Avenue, PO Box CY121, Causeway, Harare (tel: 734-051, 734-067; fax: 734-075).

Ministry of Environment and Tourism, 14th Floor Karigamombe Centre, 53 Samora Machel Avenue, P Bag, 7753, Causeway, Harare (tel: 794-455, 704-701; fax: 794-450).

Ministry of Finance, Munhumutapa Building, Samora Machel Avenue, P Bag, 7705, Causeway, Harare (tel: 794-571, 796-191; fax: 792-750).

Ministry of Foreign Affairs, Munhumutapa Building, Samora Machel Avenue, PO Box 4240, Harare (tel: 727-005, 794-681; fax: 706-293).

Ministry of Health and Child Welfare, Kaguvi Building, 4th Street, PO Box CY198, Causeway, Harare (tel: 730-011, 794-411; fax: 793-634).

Ministry of Higher Education: Old Mutual Centre, 1st Floor, 3rd Street/J Moyo Avenue, PO Box UA 275, Union Avenue, Harare (tel: 702-361, 796-441; fax: 790-923, 728-730).

Ministry of Home Affairs, 11th Floor, Mukwati Building, P Bag 505D, Harare (tel: 723-653, 703-642; fax: 728-768).

Ministry of Industry and International Trade, 13th Floor, Mukwati Building, 4th Street/Livingston Avenue, P Bag 7708, Causeway, Harare (tel: 702-731, 729-801).

Ministry of Information, Posts and Telecommunications, 8th-11th Floor, Linquenda House, Baker Avenue, PO Box CY1276 & CY825, Causeway, Harare (tel: 703-891, 706-891; fax: 735-640).

Ministry of Justice, Legal and Parliamentary Affairs, Corner House, Leopold Takawira Street, P Bag 7704, Causeway, Harare (tel: 790-902, 790-905; fax: 790-901).

Ministry of Lands and Water Development, Ngungunyana Building, 1 Borrowdale Road, P Bag 7701, Causeway, Harare (tel: 706-081, 700-596).

Ministry of Local Government, Rural and Urgan Development, 16th-20th Floors, Mukwati Building, P Bag 7706, Causeway, Harare (tel: 790-601, 728-601).

Ministry of Mines, Zimre Centre, L Takawira Street/Union Avenue, P Bag 7709, Causeway, Harare (tel: 732-881, 732-885; fax: 790-704).

Ministry of National Affairs, Employment Creation and Co-operatives, Zanu PF Building, Rotten Row/Samora Machel Avenue, PO Box 4530, Harare (tel: 734-691, 730-893; fax: 735-338).

Ministry of National Security, Chaminuka Building, 5th Street, Causeway, Harare (tel: 795-965).

Ministry of Public Construction and National Housing, Corner L Takawira Street & H Chitepo Avenue, PO Box CY441, Causeway, Harare (tel: 704-561, 704-021; fax: 702-271).

Ministry of Public Service, Labour and Social Welfare, 12th Floor Compensation House, Central Avenue/4th Street, P Bag 7707, Causeway, Harare (tel: 790-871, 796-451).

Ministry of Sports Recreation and Culture, Pax House, 89 Union Avenue, Harare (tel: 707-411, 794-450; fax: 707-580).

Ministry of Transport and Energy, 4th Floor Atlas House, 62 Robert Mugabe Road, Private Bag 7742, Causeway, Harare (tel: 706-446, 706-161; fax: 708-225, 752-923).

Office of the President and Cabinet, Munhumutapa Building, Samora Machel Avenue/3rd Street, Private Bag 7700, Causeway, Harare (tel: 707-091, 707-098; fax: 734-644, 792-044).

Parliament of Zimbabwe, Baker Avenue Box 8055, Causeway, Harare (tel: 729-722, 795-548).

Other useful addresses

Agricultural Marketing Authority (AMA), Royal Mutual House, 45 Baker Avenue, PO Box 8094, Harare (tel: 730-944).

Attorney-General's Office, Corner House, Leopold Takawira Street, P.Bag 7704, Causeway, Harare (tel: 790-902, 790-905).

British Embassy, 7th Floor, Corner House, Cnr Samora Machel Avenue-Leopold Takawira Street; PO Box 4490, Harare (tel: 772-990, 774-700; fax: 774-605; email: consular.harare@fco.gov.uk).

Chamber of Mines of Zimbabwe, 4 Central Avenue, PO Box 712, Harare (tel: 702-843; fax: 707-983).

Cold Storage Commission (CSC), Josiah Chinamano Road, Bulawayo (tel: 68-961; fax: 67-522).

Commercial Farmers' Union, Agriculture House, PO Box 1241, Leopold Takawira Street, Harare (tel: 791-881).

Confederation of Zimbabwe Industries, Industry House, 109 Rotten Row, PO Box 3794, Harare (tel: 739-833; fax: 702-873).

Cotton Marketing Board (CMB), Kurima House, 89 Baker Avenua, Harare (tel: 739-061; fax: 66-429).

Dairy Marketing Board (DMB), Dolphin House, Leopold Takawira Street, Harare (tel: 705-700).

Grain Marketing Board (GMB), Kurima House, 89 Baker Avenue, Harare (tel: 732-011; fax: 732-019).

Minerals Marketing Corporation of Zimbabwe, Globe House, 51 Jason Moyo Avenue, PO Box 2628, Harare (tel: 703-402, 705-862; fax: 722-441).

Parliament of Zimbabwe, Baker Avenue Box 8055, Causeway, Harare (tel: 729-722, 795-548).

Zimbabwe Broadcasting Corporation (ZBC), Broadcasting Centre, Pockets Hill, PO Box HG444, Highlands, Harare (tel: 486-670, 481-252/9; fax: 498-613).

Zimbabwean Embassy (USA), 1608 New Hampshire Avenue, NW, Washington DC 20009 (tel: (+1-202) 332-7100; fax: (+1-202) 483-9326; e-mail: zimemb@erols.com).

Zimbabwe International Trade Fair, Zift, PO Famona, Bulawayo (tel: 64-911).

Zimbabwe Investment Centre, 109 Rotten Row, PO Box 5950, Harare (tel: 757-931/5; fax: 757-937).

Zimbabwe State Trading Corporation, Globe House, 51 Jason Moyo Avenue, Harare (tel: 729-353).

Zimbabwe Stock Exchange, PO Box UA234, 8th Floor, Southampton House, Union Avenue, Harare (tel: 736-861; fax: 791-045).

Zimbabwe Tourist Development Corporation, PO Box 8052, Causeway, Harare (tel: 793-666).

ZimOnline (from South Africa): www.zimonline.co.za

Zimbabwe Daily News online (from UK): www.zimdaily.com

The Zimbabwe Times (from US): www.thezimbabwetimes.com

Jeune Afrique (in French): www.jeuneafrique.com

Internet sites

Africa Business Network: www.ifc.org/abn

AllAfrica.com: www.allafrica.com

African Development Bank: www.afdb.org

Africa Online: www.africaonline.com

Mbendi AfroPaedia (information on companies, countries, industries and stock exchanges in Africa): http://mbendi.co.za

The World in 2015

Policemen still needed

In 2015 to have a drink in a Parisian bar, attend a football match or simply stroll down a Parisian boulevard had never, even through the years of the occupation seventy years earlier, been considered particularly dangerous occupations. Ten years earlier, the same was the case when taking a London bus, or a Madrid commuter train. Fifteen years earlier going to work in New York had become life threatening. In order to prevent atrocities of this sort, the forces charged with maintaining the world's security needed to be 'lucky' all the time; terrorists, however, needed to be 'lucky' only once.

The apparent collapse of so many aspects of a world order that, for better or worse, had functioned since the end of the Second World War was a painful reminder that governments could still fail to serve their citizens adequately. Heart-rending television images of ill-clad refugees risking their lives aboard inadequate seacraft, or trudging virtually barefoot through mud and rain to reach the promised lands of Northern Europe were an embarrassing indictment of human failings. Angela Merkel's response to the television images of a dead Syrian boy on a Turkish beach was understandable and laudable but – even in the view of many Germans – ill thought through. A German response to a Middle East crisis had served to encourage the flow of human traffic across Southern Europe. A German solution became an enormous European problem. Sweden, long respected for its generously humane immigrant policies looked likely to take in as many as 200,000 refugees in 2015. The social stresses that this was creating succeeded in putting the extreme right-wing Sveriges Socialdemokratiska Srbetareparti (SAP) (Swedish Social Democrats) at the top of the opinion polls.

'Like it or not, the World still needs policemen. And like it or not, the responsibility for being that policeman still falls on the United States.'

The decisions of the German and Swedish governments represented the *de facto* winding up of the Schengen Agreement, which enshrined the free movement of people across most European national frontiers. In mid-2015 borders and frontier posts were being re-erected across Europe: between France and the Netherlands, between Germany and Austria even between Sweden and Denmark. As barbed wire fences were erected in vain efforts to control the flow of desperate people across Europe, the European Union's leaders squabbled in an unpleasant international blame game. The news that the mastermind of the Paris attacks had returned to Europe as a Syrian refugee at least prompted European governments to begin addressing the practicalities, the symptoms of the problem rather than its cause.

Tracing the crisis faultline back to its origins, many researchers' reached the same conclusion. The United States was the only world power that had been able to underpin some sort of world order in the post-war years. Seventy years of *Pax Americana* had, for better or worse, guaranteed some degree of peaceful stability. The faultline suggested that the consequences of the rushed withdrawal from the Middle East by the US, and its initial reluctance to an involvement in Syria had contributed to the Daesh (ISIS) insurgency. In Washington, and in London, little thought, and even less experience, had been devoted to rebuilding the post Saddam Hussein Iraq. The resultant power vacuum had easily linked up with that in Syria.

Like it or not, the World still needs policemen. And like it or not, the responsibility for being that policeman still falls on the United States. No other country has the resources, few other countries have the moral fibre. In the run up to the 2008 US Presidential election, Hillary Clinton had used her famous – or infamous – '3 a m telephone call' television advertisement to question Mr Obama's potential competence as a crisis manager in what was already an increasingly dangerous world. While her methods might be questioned, the question of leadership was totally valid. The perceived withdrawal of the United States from the word's stage reflected not so much US decline, but the decision of the Obama administration to opt for withdrawal rather than involvement.

In his book *Superpower* the US foreign policy commentator Ian Bremner defined America's role as the global policeman as one in which the US not only enforced the rules, but often defined them in the first place. Other countries, North Atlantic Treaty Organisation (NATO) allies, Japan and even China were happy to allow this state of affairs to continue if, at the same time the US protected international free trade and stability, allowing economic growth to flourish. Mr Bremner summed up the situation thus:

'We (*viz* the USA) can't renounce important international commitments overnight. Our allies need time to transition to a world in which they must assume greater responsibility for their own security... Germany and Japan are wealthy countries that can take responsibility for their own security... It will be easier for them to shake their citizens out of their complacency if America makes it clear it will do less in years to come.'

It remains to be seen a) whether the rest of the world would ever be able to step into the US policeman's shoes, and b) whether a putative Clinton would endorse this perceived withdrawal.

Africa

Growing, but still 'Y'en a marre'

Africa's regional growth rate by 2015 had hovered around 4.5 per cent for two or three years. Not stellar, but better than that of Brazil, once the El Dorado of investment fund managers. And Africa's share of the world economy was also rising, expected to double and reach over US$2.6 trillion by 2020, or more than five per cent of the world economy. All of which added up to excellent news for the continent's 50 plus member states.

But good news doesn't always bring more good news. In the case of Africa, the allure of the fatter pork barrel increased the temptation to dive in. The temptation brought with it the obvious requirement to be around, spoon at the ready, when the barrel began to brim over. And so, across Africa, Presidents began to plot stay on, supported by aides who also not only wanted to stay on in their fancy houses, but who feared for their futures (and lives) if their protectors were to go. In his 27 years as President of Burkina Faso, Blaise Campaoré had almost certainly lined his pockets here and there. But when, in late 2014, he proposed hanging around for a further term of office, despite what the constitution said, little did he expect the violent street protests that ended up with his abrupt deposition as head of state at the hands of a popular uprising. Nor was he the first to so seriously mis-calculate; four years earlier, in 2010 something similar had taken place in Niger. And in 2012, in Senegal. In 2009 Niger's President Mamadou Tandja had suspended the constitution and had submitted proposals to parliament whereby he would be able to stand again after ten years in power. However, the scheme was objected to by a young soldier Saliou Djibo who launched a *coup d'etat* with the support of most of the population. Less than a year later, a new government was installed, headed up not by Mr Saliou, but by the country's longtime opposition leader, Mahamadou Issoufou.

> '... an invitation to every African citizen to reconsider his place in society, because for a long time we have been marginalised from decisions.'

In 2011 Senegal had erupted into flames. There had been no obvious single reason for the tired government of President Abdoulaye Wade not to remain in office, other than a thinly veiled whiff of corruption. The list of complaints was long: a prolonged energy crisis which had plunged Dakar into darkness. Corruption, public embezzlement and soaring unemployment had produced a disaffected electorate, which did not take kindly to the President's plans, terminating in the *Y'en a marre* (Fed up) generation's protests inspired by the Arab Spring and the songs of home grown rap artists relayed on YouTube.

Social media of one sort or another were beginning to play an increasingly important role in pan-African politics. One catalyst in this process had been the formation of the African League of Bloggers and Cyberactivists for Democracy (www.africtivistes.org) created by Cheikh Fall. In 2013 two young singers from Burkina Faso, (one rapper, one reggae) started another movement, the Citizens' Broom. The movement's charter was an 'invitation to every African citizen to reconsider his place in society, because for a long time we have been marginalised from decisions.' As in the case of the *Y'en a marre* movement, the singers and their many followers had been instrumental in the deposition of Burkina Faso's President Campaoré.

In Equatorial Guinea (where President Teodoro Obiang had been in power for 35 years) and in Angola where José Eduardo Dos Santos had ruled for the same length of time, satirical blogs had sprung up. In Angola the best known was that of the 'Brigadier'. In Togo, President Faure Gnassingbé had simply inherited 'the throne' from his father, the infamous General Eyadema. The popsongs of Africa were now disseminated on social media, their lyrics no longer about girl friends, clothes or cars, but about corruption and fraud. Their listeners in their countries' schools and universities, garrisons, hospitals and newspaper offices. Time for another shift in opinions? And if so, who will tell the Presidents?

Currencies (units per US$) – Africa

	Unit	Jan 2011	Jan 2012	Jan 2013	Jan 2014	Jan 2015
Algeria	Algerian dinar	74.05	79.04	79.74	78.15	106.11
Angola	Readjusted kwanza	92.85	95.71	96.00	97.62	126.00
Benin	CFA franc	505.26	504.35	495.02	480.26	655.96
Botswana	Pula	6.62	7.99	8.50	8.78	10.52
Burkina Faso	CFA franc	505.26	504.35	495.02	480.26	655.96
Burundi	Burundi franc	1,233.00	1,236.86	1,537.47	1,552.00	1,559.15
Cameroon	CFA franc	505.26	504.35	495.02	480.26	655.96
Cape Verde	Cape Verde escudo	82.78	84.35	81.87	79.42	99.05
Central African Republic	CFA franc	505.26	504.35	495.02	480.26	655.96
Chad	CFA franc	505.26	504.35	495.02	480.26	655.96
Comoros	Comoros franc	378.95	378.26	371.27	360.19	439.83
Congo	CFA franc	505.26	504.35	495.02	480.26	655.96
Democratic Republic of Congo	Congolese franc	916.50	504.35	923.50	917.00	925.00
Côte d'Ivoire	CFA franc	505.26	504.35	495.02	480.26	655.96
Djibouti	Djibouti franc	175.75	175.55	174.70	175.05	177.72
Egypt	Egyptian pound	5.80	6.11	7.00	6.96	7.83
Equatorial Guinea	CFA franc	505.26	504.35	495.02	480.26	655.96
Eritrea	Nakfa	15.00	15.00	15.00	14.85	15.00
Ethiopia	Ethiopian birr	16.64	18.20	18.20	19.16	20.87
Gabon	CFA franc	505.26	504.35	495.02	480.26	655.96
Gambia	Dalasi	28.00	30.28	32.60	38.10	39.63
Ghana	Ghana Cedi	1.48	1.90	2.08	2.34	3.85
Guinea	Guinean franc	6,940.00	69,993.00	7,000.00	7,030.00	7,699.00
Guinea-Bissau	CFA franc	505.26	504.35	495.02	480.26	655.96
Kenya	Kenya shilling	81.00	85.63	87.40	86.85	105.45
Lesotho	Maloti	6.77	8.88	9.81	10.66	13.77
Liberia	Liberian dollar	71.00	73.50	74.01	79.03	87.00
Libya	Libyan dinar	1.26	1.26	1.26	1.24	1.38
Madagascar	Franc Malgache	2,127.50	2,253.00	2,188.34	2,242.45	3,150.00
Malawi	Kwacha	150.77	328.60	330.00	430.00	586.44
Mali	CFA franc	505.26	504.35	495.02	480.26	655.96
Mauritania	Ouguiya	282.00	298.50	300.50	292.50	318.00
Mauritius	Mauritius rupee	30.55	30.90	30.75	30.10	35.17
Morocco	Moroccan dirham	8.56	8.55	8.43	8.22	9.73
Mozambique	Metical	32.40	29.95	29.95	29.95	9.73
Namibia	Namibian dollar	6.77	8.88	9.81	10.66	13.79
Niger	CFA franc	505.26	504.35	495.02	480.26	655.96
Nigeria	Naira	152.25	157.35	160.78	158.53	199.05
Réunion	Euro	0.75	0.77	0.75	0.73	0.89
Rwanda	Rwanda franc	595.23	629.73	650.50	675.00	729.08
São Tomé and Príncipe	Dobra	1,861.40	18,270.00	97,914.00	17,378.00	21,900.00
Senegal	CFA franc	505.26	504.35	495.02	480.26	655.96
Seychelles	Seychelles rupee	12.24	13.15	11.99	12.06	13.17
Sierra Leone	Leone	4,218.36	4,336.74	4,324.80	4,328.00	4,638.00
Somalia	Somali shilling	1,550.00	1,565.00	1,318.00	1,103.00	614.00
South Africa	Rand	6.77	8.88	9.81	10.66	13.79
South Sudan	South Sudan pound	n/a	3.05	3.05	3.05	2.42
Sudan	Sudanese dinar	2.51	4.42	4.41	5.70	6.10
Swaziland	Lilangeni	6.77	8.88	9.81	10.66	13.79
Tanzania	Tanzania shilling	1,475.00	1,601.00	1,620.00	1,585.00	2,175.00
Togo	CFA franc	505.26	504.35	495.02	480.26	655.96
Tunisia	Tunisian dinar	1.46	1.57	1.66	1.65	1.98
Uganda	Ugandan shilling	2,335.00	2,680.00	2,583.00	2,527.00	3,660.00
Zambia	Kwacha	4,750.00	5,210.00	5.47	5.52	9.94
Zimbabwe	Zimbabwe dollar	378.20	378.00	378.00	378.00	361.90

(a) Ghana cedi re-denominated 3 Jul 2007; (b) Sudanese pound (S£) replaced dinar at rate of S£1 to 100 dinar, Jan 2007; (c) Zimbabwe dollar devalued by 99.9 per cent 6 Sep 2007

Key indicators 2014

	Population (m)	Area ('000 sq km)	GDP per capita (US$)	Inflation (%)	GDP real growth (%)	Balance of trade (US$m)
Algeria	*38.7	2,381.70	*5,532	*2.9	*4.1	*945
Angola	*24.38	1,246.70	*5,273	*7.3	*4.2	(c) *419
Benin	*10.59	112.60	*822	*1.0	*5.5	*-2645
Botswana	*2.1	582.00	*7,505	*3.9	*4.9	(c)*241
Burkina Faso	*17.43	274.00	*717	*-0.3	*4.0	(f)*-132
Burundi	*9.2	27.80	*336	*4.4	*4.7	*-531
Cameroon	*22.54	475.40	*1,405	*1.9	*5.1	*-2401
Cape Verde	*0.52	4.03	*3,663	*-0.2	*1.0	*-609
Central African Republic	*4.7	623.00	*380	*15.0	*101.0	*-81
Chad	*11.28	1,284.00	*1,236	*1.7	*6.9	(g)*781
Comoros	*0.78	2.20	*923	*2.9	*3.4	(d)*-198
Congo	*4.27	342.00	*3,159	*0.9	*6.0	(c)*2,080
Democratic Republic of Congo	*79.3	2,345.40	*437	*1.0	*9.1	*1,000
Côte d'Ivoire	*22.72	322.50	*1,495	*0.5	*7.5	*2,990
Djibouti	*0.94	23.20	*1,692	*2.9	*6.0	(c)*-606
Egypt	*86.7	1,001.50	*3,304	*10.1	*2.2	*-30,830
Equatorial Guinea	*0.78	28.10	*18,389	*3.0	*-3.1	(f)*-5,940
Eritrea	*6.36	125.00	*590	*12.3	*1.7	n/a
Ethiopia	*90.1	1,251.30	*575	*7.4	*10.4	(d)*-7,290
Gabon	*1.6	267.70	*10,836	*4.5	*5.1	(e)*5,210
Gambia	*1.9	11.30	*428	*6.3	*-0.2	(d)*-176
Ghana	*26.22	239.50	*1,474	*15.5	*4.2	*-3,850
Guinea	*11.4	245.90	*573	*9.7	*0.4	(c)*-250
Guinea-Bissau	*1.74	36.10	*589	*-1.0	*2.5	(f)*-50
Kenya	*45.54	582.70	*1,416	*6.9	*5.3	*-11,440
Lesotho	*1.91	30.40	*1,130	*3.9	*2.2	(c)*-1,040
Liberia	*4.19	111.40	*484	*9.9	*0.5	(c)*-395
Libya	*6.21	1,775.50	*6,623	*2.8	*-2,403.1	(c)*11,970
Madagascar	*23.57	592.00	*449	*6.1	*3.0	(c)*-851
Malawi	*17.6	118.50	*242	*23.8	*5.7	(d)*-1,020
Mali	*15.79	1,241.20	*755	*0.9	*6.8	(c)*-248
Mauritania	*3.62	1,030.70	*1,403	*3.5	*6.4	(c)*-392
Mauritius	*1.26	1.90	*10,517	*3.0	*3.2	*-2,250
Morocco	*33.18	711.00	*3,291	*0.4	*2.9	(e)*-21,590
Mozambique	*26.49	799.40	*630	*2.3	*7.4	(c)*-4,360
Namibia	*2.19	824.30	*6,095	*5.4	*5.3	(c)*-2,150
Niger	*17.12	1,267.00	*469	*-0.9	*6.9	(d)*-549
Nigeria	*173.94	923.80	*3,298	*8.1	*6.3	(d)*42,320
Réunion	(f)*0.77	2.50	–	–	–	–
Rwanda	*11.10	26.30	*722	*1.8	*7.0	(c)*-1,150
São Tomé and Príncipe	*0.2	0.90	*1,725	*7.0	*4.5	*-128
Senegal	*14.54	196.20	*1,072	*-0.5	*4.5	(e)*-2,510
Seychelles	*0.09	0.50	*15,115	*1.4	*2.9	*-541
Sierra Leone	*6.23	72.30	*808	*8.3	*6.0	(c)*-2,900
Somalia	(d)*51.2	738.00	(g)*600	–	(c)*6.0	
South Africa	*54.00	1,127.20	*6,483	*6.1	*1.5	*-6,370
South Sudan	*11.38	644.33	*1,127	*-0.8	*5.5	–
Sudan	*37.29	1,861.50	*1,980	*36.9	*3.4	*-3,760
Swaziland	*1.1	17.40	*3,325	*5.8	*1.7	(c)*169
Tanzania	*47.66	945.10	*1,006	*6.1	*7.2	(c)*-5,770
Terres Australes	(a) 0.00	439.80	–	–	–	–
Togo	*6.82	56.00	*640	*2.0	*5.6	(e) *-448
Tunisia	*10.92	164.20	*4,345	*6.1	*2.7	(c) *-6,030
Uganda	*38.04	236.00	*726	*4.7	*4.9	(c)*-2,150
Zambia	*15.02	752.60	*1,781	*7.9	*5.4	*1,630
Zimbabwe	*13.26	391.10	*1,031	*-0.2	*3.2	

* Estimated figure; (a) 310 people total; 150 winter only; (c) 2012; (d) 2011; (e) 2010; (f) 2009; (g) 2008; (h) 2007; (i)2006

AFRICA

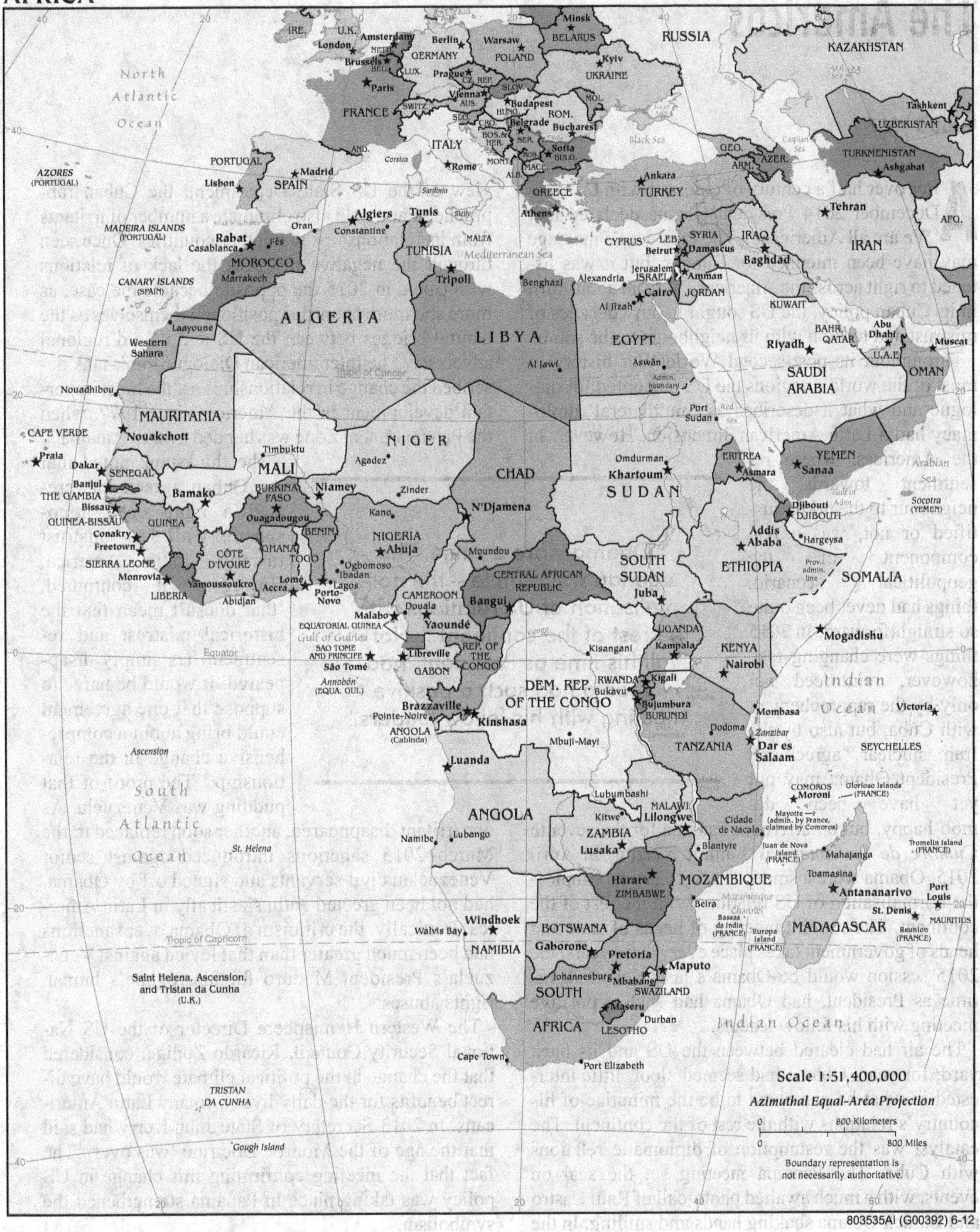

803535AI (G00392) 6-12

The Americas

Cuba's year

After over half a century of cold war with Cuba, in December 2014 President Obama declared that 'We are all Americans'. The President's message may have been intended for Cubans, but it was listened to right across the Americas. With an about-turn in its Cuban policy, the US sought to bury decades of mistrust and tension with its neighbours to the south.

Throughout its post-second World War history in most of the world's regions the US had opted for dialogue and what it described as 'multilateral' diplomacy had a Latin American dimension. However, in the Americas, where resentment towards the neighbour to the north, justified or not, was a real component of the geopolitical scenario, things had never been quite so straightforward. In 2015 things were changing fast, however, reinforced not only by the rapprochement with Cuba, but also by the Iran nuclear agreement. President Obama may not yet have been demob-happy, but on arrival in Panama for the seventh *Cumbre de las Americas* summit meeting in April 2015, Obama wore a smile. The agenda was simple – the normalisation of US relations with the rest of the continent. The summit meeting of heads of state and heads of government takes place every three years; the 2015 session would be Obama's last. Not in all his time as President, had Obama had such a positive meeting with his fellow leaders.

> 'Obama wore a smile. The agenda was simple – the normalisation of US relations with the rest of the continent... Not in all his time as President, had Obama had such a positive meeting with his fellow leaders.'

The air had cleared between the US and its back yard; for years Obama had seemed aloof, little interested in what he perceived to be the minutiae of his country's relations with the rest of the continent. The catalyst was the resumption of diplomatic relations with Cuba. The Panama meeting set the seal on events, with a much awaited photo-call of Raul Castro and Barack Obama shaking hands and smiling. In the view of the US State Department, the Cuban rapprochement would also eliminate a number of irritants from its relationships with other countries. Once seen through the negative prism of the lack of relations with Cuba, in 2015 the opposite became the case, as more and more countries positioned themselves as the natural bridges between the US and its old regional adversary. The Interamerican Dialogue think-tank described the change in relationships as 'the most important development in the Americas since 1977, when the Panama Canal Zone was handed over to Panama.'

The think-tank noted that the Cuban agreement 'created a more open atmosphere, with less mistrust towards Latin America. However,' it continued, 'that doesn't mean that the historical mistrust and resentment has simply disappeared. It would be naïve to suppose that one agreement could bring about a comprehensive change in the relationship.' The proof of that pudding was Venezuela. As one irritant disappeared, another soon replaced it: the March 2015 sanctions introduced against senior Venezuelan civil servants and signed off by Obama, had not been greeted enthusiastically in Latin America. Ironically, the criticism of Obama over sanctions had been much greater than that levied against Venezuela's President Maduro for his régime's human rights abuses.

The Western Hemisphere Director of the US National Security Council, Ricardo Zuñiga, considered that the change in the political climate would have direct benefits for the daily lives of many Latin Americans. In 2013 Secretary of State John Kerry had said that the age of the Monroe Doctrine 'was over;. The fact that the meeting confirming this change in US policy was taking place in Panama strengthened the symbolism.

Currencies (units per US$) – Americas

	Unit	Jan 2011	Jan 2012	Jan 2013	Jan 2014	Jan 2015
Argentina	Peso	3.97	4.83	5.50	6.55	9.33
Belize	Belize dollar	1.95	1.95	1.99	1.95	2.00
Bolivia	Peso Boliviano	6.99	6.91	6.91	6.91	6.90
Brazil	Real	1.68	2.11	2.27	2.40	3.80
Chile	Chilean peso	497.55	480.85	515.10	529.10	689.04
Colombia	Colombian peso	1,856.60	1,814.33	1,891.50	1,938.15	3,148.30
Costa Rica	Colón	511.15	497.99	499.15	501.41	536.50
Ecuador	US dollar	1.00	1.00	1.00	1.00	1.00
El Salvador	Colón	1.00	1.00	1.00	8.75	8.75
French Guiana	Euro	0.75	0.77	0.77	0.73	0.89
Guatemala	Quetzal	8.01	7.89	7.84	7.86	7.73
Guyana	Guyana dollar	203.24	200.95	200.45	202.95	206.12
Honduras	Lempira	18.90	18.90	20.40	20.23	21.94
Mexico	Mexican peso	12.22	12.92	12.76	13.09	16.82
Nicaragua	Gold Cordóba	21.90	24.03	24.82	25.34	27.51
Panama	Balboa	1.00	1.00	1.00	1.00	1.00
Paraguay	Guarani	4,555.00	4,420.00	4,425.00	4,605.21	5,401.66
Peru	New sol	2.80	2.58	2.78	2.80	3.23
Suriname	Suriname dollar	2.75	3.30	3.30	3.30	3.30
Uruguay	Peso Uruguayo	19.95	19.62	21.27	21.50	28.70
Venezuela	Bolívar fuerte	4.29	4.29	6.29	6.29	6.31
NORTH AMERICA						
Canada	Canadian dollar	0.99	0.99	1.03	1.06	1.32
United States of America	US dollar	1.00	1.00	1.00	1.00	1.00
CARIBBEAN						
Anguilla	EC dollar	2.70	2.70	2.70	2.70	2.70
Antigua	EC dollar	2.70	2.70	2.70	2.70	2.70
Aruba	Aruba guilder	1.79	1.79	1.79	1.79	1.79
Bahamas	Bahamian dollar	1.00	1.00	1.00	1.00	1.00
Barbados	Barbados dollar	2.00	2.00	2.00	2.00	2.00
Bermuda	Bermuda dollar	1.00	1.00	1.00	1.00	1.00
British Virgin Islands	US dollar	1.00	1.00	1.00	1.00	1.00
Cayman Islands	Cayman Islands dollar	0.82	0.82	0.82	0.82	0.82
Curaçao	Netherlands Antilles guilder	1.79	1.79	1.79	1.79	1.00
Cuba	Cuban peso	0.82	0.82	1.00	1.00	1.00
Dominica	EC dollar	2.70	2.70	2.70	2.70	2.70
Dominican Republic	Dominican Republic peso	37.91	39.77	41.95	42.55	45.10
Grenada	EC dollar	2.70	2.70	2.70	2.70	2.70
Guadeloupe	Euro	0.75	0.77	0.77	0.77	0.89
Haiti	Gourde	39.75	42.15	43.35	43.88	51.68
Jamaica	Jamaican dollar	85.38	91.28	101.28	106.05	117.74
Martinique	Euro	0.75	0.77	0.77	0.77	0.89
Montserrat	EC dollar	2.70	2.70	2.70	2.70	2.70
Puerto Rico	US dollar	1.00	1.00	1.00	1.00	1.00
St Kitts Nevis	EC dollar	2.70	2.70	2.70	2.70	2.70
St Lucia	EC dollar	2.70	2.70	2.70	2.70	2.70
St Maartins	Netherlands Antilles guilder	1.79	1.79	1.79	1.79	1.79
St Vincent	EC dollar	2.70	2.70	2.70	2.70	2.70
Trinidad and Tobago	Trinidad and Tobago dollar	6.41	6.40	6.41	6.41	6.33
Turks and Caicos Islands	US dollar	1.00	1.00	1.00	1.00	1.00
US Virgin Islands	US dollar	1.00	1.00	1.00	1.00	1.00

(a) Cuban dollar converts to US dollar

Key indicators 2014

	Population (m)	Area ('000 sq km)	GDP per capita (US$)	Inflation (%)	GDP real growth (%)	Balance of trade (US$m)
Argentina	*41.96	2,766.90	*12873	(c) *10.6	*0.5	*9,480
Belize	*0.36	23.00	*4745	*0.9	*3.4	*-336
Bolivia	*11.25	1,098.60	*3061	*5.8	*5.4	*2,210
Brazil	*202.77	8,512.00	*11604	*6.3	*0.1	*-6,250
Chile	*17.82	756.60	*14477	*4.9	*1.8	*7,770
Colombia	*47.66	1,138.90	*8076	*2.9	*4.6	*-4,690
Costa Rica	*4.78	51.10	*10083	*3.2	*3.5	*-5,680
Ecuador	*16.0	270.70	*6286	*3.6	*3.6	(c)*-637
El Salvador	*6.35	21.40	*3988	*1.1	*2.0	*-5,210
French Guiana	(c) *0.25	91.00	–	–	–	
Guatemala	*15.87	108.90	*3807	*3.4	*4.0	*-6,060
Guyana	*0.80	215.00	*3748	*1.0	*3.8	(c)*-471
Honduras	*8.26	112.10	*2361	*6.1	*3.1	(e)*-4,480
Mexico	*119.72	1,958.20	*10715	*4.0	*2.1	*-2,570
Nicaragua	*6.22	148.00	*1881	*6.0	*4.5	*-2,400
Panama	*3.93	77.10	*11147	*2.6	*6.2	*-8,130
Paraguay	*6.90	407.00	*4305	*5.0	*4.4	(c)*1,580
Peru	*31.42	1,285.20	*6458	*3.3	*2.4	(c)*612
Suriname	*0.55	164.00	*9584	*3.4	*2.9	*183
Uruguay	*3.40	176.20	*16199	*8.9	*3.3	*-924
Venezuela	*30.46	916.50	*6757	*62.2	*-4.0	(c)*35,970
NORTH AMERICA						
Canada	*35.49	9,976.10	*50398	*1.9	*2.5	*4,560
United States of America	*319.05	9,300.00	*54597	*1.6	*2.4	*-741,460
CARIBBEAN						
Anguilla	0.01 (14,000)	0.01	(g) *15230	(d) *2.5	(d) *-5.1	(c) *-123
Antigua	*0.09 (88,000)	0.04	*14061	*1.1	*2.4	(c) *-430
Aruba	(e) 0.11	0.02	(d) *25538	(d) *2.3	(d) *7.1	(c) *-1,080
Bahamas	*0.36	13.90	*24034	*1.2	*1.3	*-2,420
Barbados	*0.28	0.40	*15579	*1.9	(c)*-0.7	(f)*-1,080
Bermuda	*0.07	0.01	(c)*85700	(c)*2,7	(c)*-2.5	(e) *487
British Virgin Islands	(e)*0.03	0.15	-	-	-	
' Cayman Islands	*0.05	0.30				
Cuba	(e)*11.1	110.90	(e)*5410	(e)*4.7	(e)*2.7	
Curaçao	(e)0.01			(e)*3.1	(e)*0.1	(c)*1,270
Dominica	*0.07	0.80	*7436	*0.7	*1.1	(c)*-1,376
Dominican Republic	*10.6	48.40	*6044	*4.8	*7.3	*-7,310
Grenada	*0.11	0.34	*8125	*-0.9	*1.5	(c)*-41
Guadeloupe	(e)*0.5	1.80	–	–	–	–
Haiti	*10.32	27.80	*833	*4.0	*2.8	(c)*-2,030
Jamaica	*2.8	11.00	*4926	*7.1	*0.5	*-3,720
Martinique	(f)*0.41	1.10	–	–	–	–
Montserrat	(e)*0.005	0.01	–	–	–	(d)*-30
Puerto Rico	(e)*3.71	8.90	(e) *17687	(e)*3.6	(e)*-1.7	(g)*20,160
St Kitts Nevis	*0.06	0.30	*14102	*1.0	*-2.8	(c)*-193
St Lucia	*0.17	0.60	*7978	*2.5	*-1.1	(c)*-291
St Maarten	(f)*0.04	0.03	–	(e)*3.7	(e)*-0.1	(c)*-747
St Vincent	*0.11	0.40	*6694	*0.2	*1.1	(c)*-280
Trinidad and Tobago	*1.35	5.10	*21311	*7.0	*1.1	(e)*5
Turks and Caicos Islands	(e)*0.04	0.43	–	–	–	–
US Virgin Islands	(c) *0.11	0.40	–	–	–	–

*Estimated Figure (c) 2012; (d) 2011; (e) 2010; (f) 2009; (g) 2008; (h) 2007 (i) 2006; (j) 2005

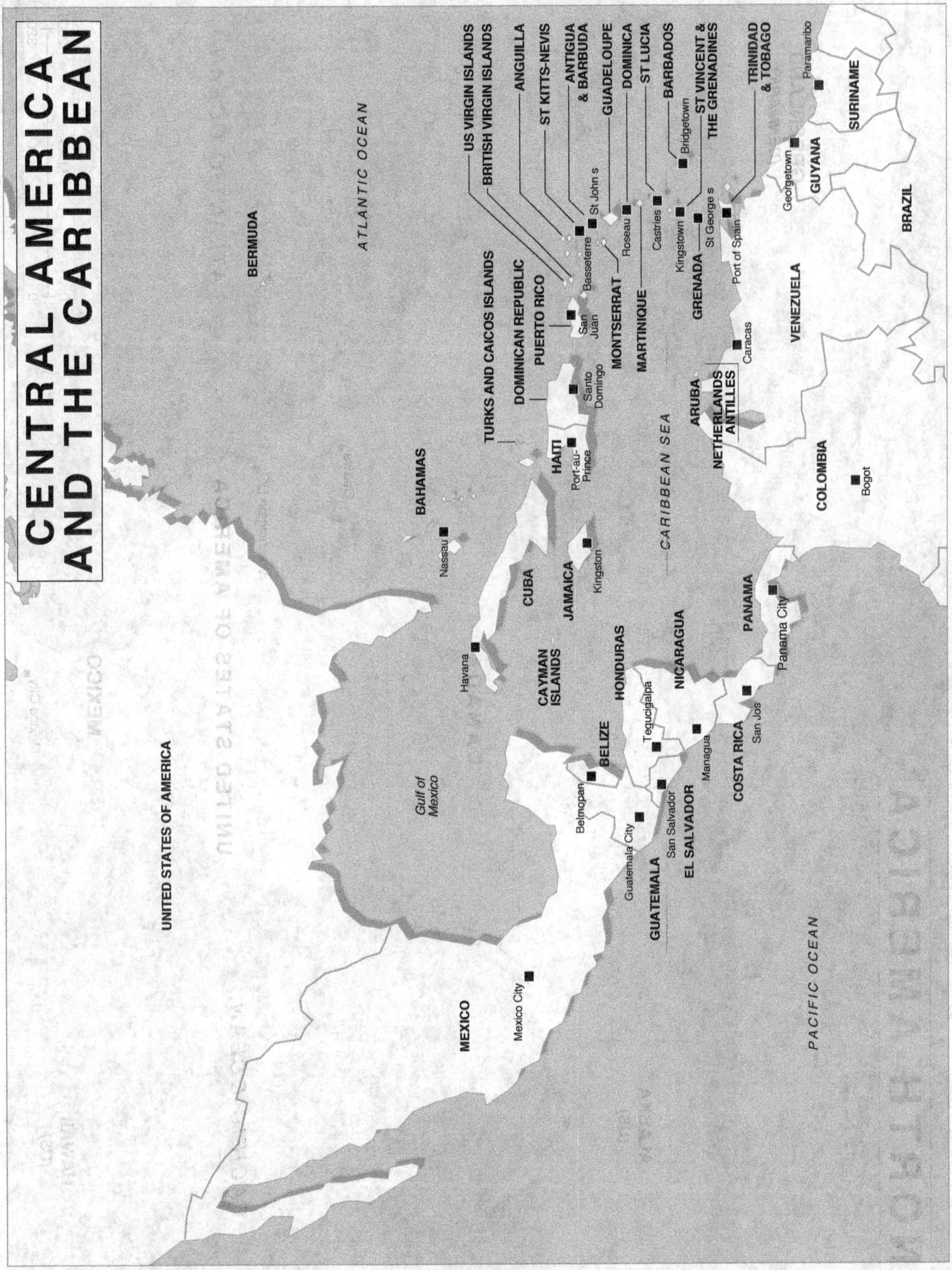
CENTRAL AMERICA AND THE CARIBBEAN
ATLANTIC OCEAN
BERMUDA
UNITED STATES OF AMERICA
Gulf of Mexico
MEXICO
Mexico City
BAHAMAS
Nassau
CUBA
Havana
CAYMAN ISLANDS
JAMAICA
Kingston
HAITI
Port-au-Prince
TURKS AND CAICOS ISLANDS
DOMINICAN REPUBLIC
Santo Domingo
PUERTO RICO
San Juan
US VIRGIN ISLANDS
BRITISH VIRGIN ISLANDS
ANGUILLA
ST KITTS-NEVIS
Basseterre
ANTIGUA & BARBUDA
St John's
MONTSERRAT
GUADELOUPE
DOMINICA
Roseau
MARTINIQUE
ST LUCIA
Castries
BARBADOS
Bridgetown
ST VINCENT & THE GRENADINES
Kingstown
GRENADA
St George's
TRINIDAD & TOBAGO
Port of Spain
CARIBBEAN SEA
ARUBA
NETHERLANDS ANTILLES
BELIZE
Belmopan
GUATEMALA
Guatemala City
HONDURAS
Tegucigalpa
EL SALVADOR
San Salvador
NICARAGUA
Managua
COSTA RICA
San Jos
PANAMA
Panama City
PACIFIC OCEAN
COLOMBIA
Bogot
VENEZUELA
Caracas
GUYANA
Georgetown
SURINAME
Paramaribo
BRAZIL

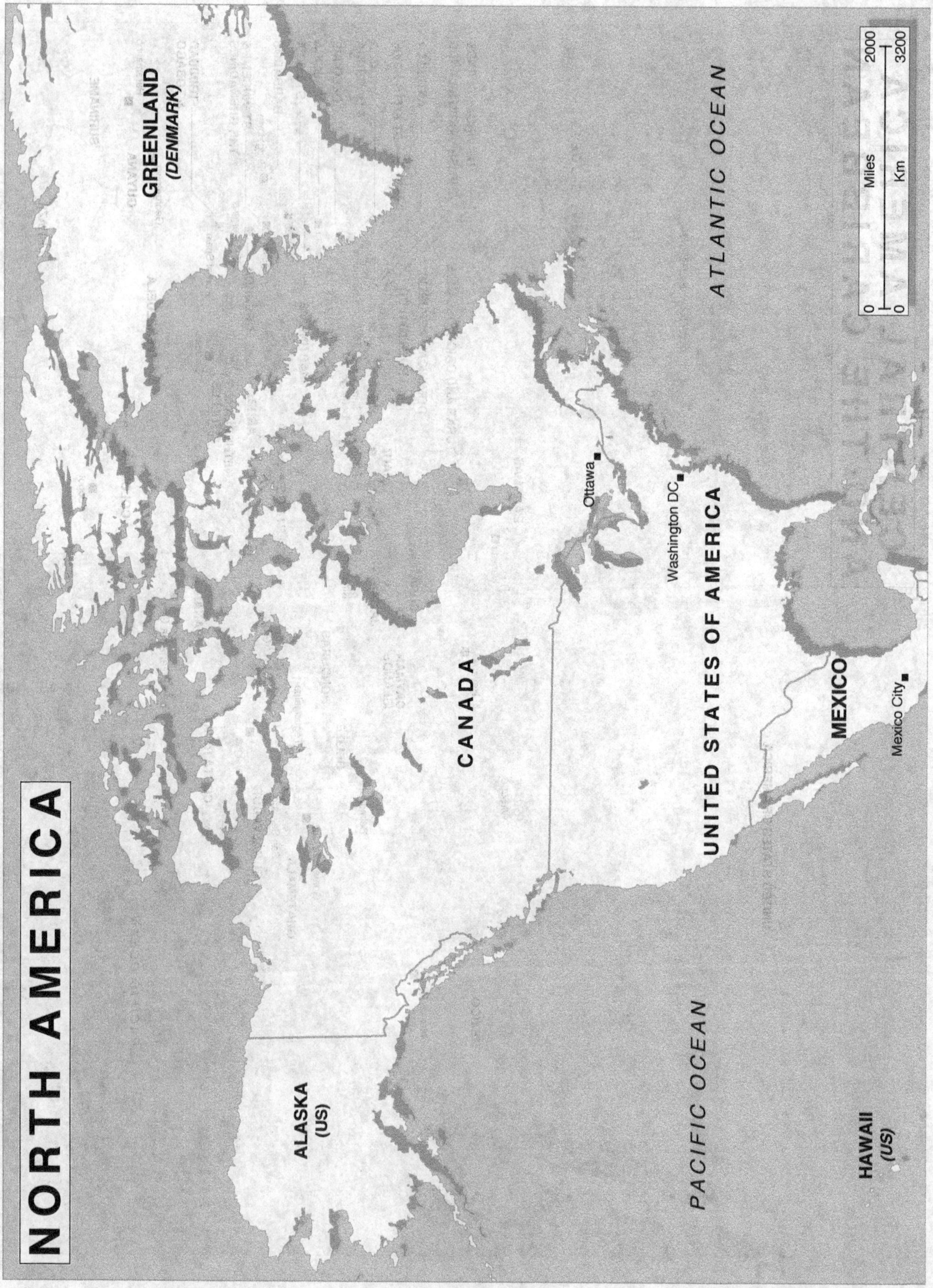
NORTH AMERICA
GREENLAND
(DENMARK)
CANADA
Ottawa
Washington DC
UNITED STATES OF AMERICA
MEXICO
Mexico City
ALASKA
(US)
HAWAII
(US)
PACIFIC OCEAN
ATLANTIC OCEAN
0
2000
Miles
0
3200
Km

SOUTH AMERICA
Caracas
VENEZUELA
GUYANA
Georgetown
Paramaribo
Cayenne
FRENCH GUIANA
Bogot
COLOMBIA
SURINAME
Quito
ECUADOR
PERU
BRAZIL
Lima
Bras lia
BOLIVIA
La Paz
PACIFIC OCEAN
PARAGUAY
Asunci n
CHILE
ATLANTIC OCEAN
ARGENTINA
URUGUAY
Santiago
Buenos Aires
Montevideo
Islas Malvinas (Argentina)
Claimed by UK as Falkland Islands
0 Miles 1000
0 Km 1600

Asia

Growing pains

The decision of the Asian Development Bank (ABD) to mark down the 2015 growth prospects for Asia's two largest markets would have surprised no-one. The Chinese economy was expected by the ADB to grow by 6.8 per cent, India by 7.4 per cent. The cushion provided to the global economy by its emerging markets continued to shrink. One-time hopefuls such as Brazil and South Africa could no longer be relied on. Lower growth than expected for both China and India threatened to drag the whole Asian region down.

Despite the fact that the fall in crude petroleum prices had benefited virtually every country in the region with the possible exceptions of Indonesia and Brunei. However, the seemingly inexorable grip of a new Chinese macro-economic 'normality', coupled with India's delays in introducing economic reforms would inevitably impact on the region that in 2014 had accounted for one third of global economic growth.

The ABD projected Asia's growth for 2015 at 5.8 per cent, rising modestly to 6 per cent in 2016, below the 6.3 per cent that the ABD had originally forecast. Even at lower growth rates – between 0.3 and 0.4 per cent less – China and India's growth rates would be well above the regional average. Following the lower growth rate expected in 2015, the ADB forecast a slightly slower rate for 2016 – 6.7 per cent for China, the world's second most important economy. The ADB expected Beijing to consolidate and prepare for a steady fall in future growth rates. India was expected to do better, the 7.4 per cent of 2015 being followed by a 7.8 per cent figure in 2016 based on the expectation that by then some of Mr Modi's reforms would begin to bear fruit.

If it was the case that after the global financial crisis emerging markets – especially in Asia – became safe havens for international investors seeking to avoid the risks posed by the more developed economies, by 2015 the regional panorama had lost some of its shine. Lower growth had joined forces with the perceived volatility of China – the principal trading partner of so many Asian economies, from Australia to Korea, Pakistan to the Philippines. Improved prospects in the USA and the occasional prospect of a rise in US interest rates had re-ignited interest in capital flows; a number of currencies had faltered when faced with the vagaries of the yuan.

None the less, the ADB's chief economist, Shang-Jin Wei struck a mildly optimistic note: 'We hope that Asia's emerging markets continue to be the major contributors to global growth in future, despite corrections to growth prospects. However, there are strong headwinds. If fluctuations in interest rates on international markets are to be avoided, it will be important to introduce measures to manage international capital flows, and to limit the dependency on foreign currency loans.' India, despite its slowness in implementing economic reforms, appeared to be one of the region's most promising markets – not least – and rather ironically – because of its relatively low level of trade with China.

'We hope that Asia's emerging markets continue to be the major contributors to global growth in future, despite corrections to growth prospects. However, there are strong headwinds.'

The ADB was not the only international body to downgrade its expectations for China for the foreseeable future. The World Bank remained alone in expecting Chinese growth to top the seven per cent mark – projecting 7.1 per cent growth. The International Monetary Fund (IMF) saw growth of 6.8 per cent for 2015 followed by 6.3 per cent in 2016 as China sought to move to a more sustainable economy in which domestic demand replaced stock market speculation as the principal driver. The ADB's Mr Wei noted that 'As long as China continues with its reform programme, there is a good chance that productivity increases and that relatively strong growth is restored.' In fact, China had managed to notch up growth of 7 per cent in the first half of 2015, but after the stock market implosion and the drop in foreign trade, most analysts considered it impossible for China to maintain that level of growth.

Currencies (units per US$) – Asia

	Unit	Jan 2011	Jan 2012	Jan 2013	Jan 2014	Jan 2015
Afghanistan	Afghani	43.00	52.31	56.23	55.56	64.21
Australia	Australian dollar	1.00	0.96	1.10	1.12	1.43
Bangladesh	Taka	70.95	81.33	77.76	77.68	77.80
Bhutan	Ngultrum	45.39	54.40	60.36	62.21	66.55
Brunei	Brunei dollar	1.29	1.22	1.27	1.27	1.41
Cambodia	Riel	4,040.00	3,996.00	4,089.00	3,971.00	4,115.00
China	Renminbi yuan	6.63	6.23	6.13	6.05	6.37
Fiji	Fijian dollar	1.84	1.78	1.88	1.90	2.19
Hong Kong	Hong Kong dollar	7.77	7.78	7.76	7.75	7.75
India	Rupee	45.38	54.40	30.36	62.21	66.55
Indonesia	Rupiah	9,015.50	9,593.50	10,272.50	12,160.00	14,280.00
Japan	Yen	82.98	82.47	98.06	105.03	119.75
Kazakhstan	Tenge	147.10	150.46	153.36	154.35	245.05
North Korea	Won	1.30	1.30	1.30	1.30	1.30
South Korea	Won	1,122.30	1,082.85	1,113.80	1,050.30	1,148.99
Kyrgyzstan	Som	47.17	47.26	48.84	39.19	66.15
Laos	New kip	8,000.00	7,949.00	7,785.00	8,000.00	8,160.00
Macao	Pataca	8.00	7.98	7.99	7.99	7.98
Malaysia	Ringgit	3.07	3.04	3.23	3.29	4.34
Maldives	Rufiyaa	12.80	15.38	15.40	15.41	15.25
Marshall Islands	US dollar	1.00	1.00	1.00	1.00	1.00
Federated States of Micronesia	US dollar	1.00	1.00	1.00	1.00	1.00
Mongolia	Tugrik	1,276.00	1,401.00	1,506.00	1,668.50	1,993.00
Myanmar	Kyat	6.41	(a) 852	(a) 852	982.00	1,297.40
Nepal	Rupee	72.62	87.03	96.58	99.53	106.47
New Zealand	New Zealand dollar	1.31	1.21	1.25	1.23	1.58
Pakistan	Rupee	85.80	96.51	101.76	105.51	104.28
Papua New Guinea	Kina	2.65	2.07	2.31	2.52	2.80
Philippines	Peso	44.15	40.89	43.41	44.45	46.96
Samoa	Tala	2.38	2.28	2.35	2.34	2.60
Singapore	Singapore dollar	1.29	1.22	1.27	1.27	1.42
Sri Lanka	Rupee	110.85	130.15	131.65	130.72	138.38
Taiwan	Taiwanese dollar	29.37	29.05	29.93	29.90	32.70
Tajikistan	Tajik rouble	4.40	4.75	4.77	4.74	6.71
Thailand	Baht	30.39	30.69	31.27	32.96	36.17
Timor-Leste	US dollar	1.00	1.00	1.00	1.00	1.00
Turkmenistan	New Manat	2.85	2.85	2.85	2.84	3.50
Uzbekistan	Sum	1,640.55	1,969.43	2,104.62	2,202.20	2,605.83
Vietnam	New dong	19,499.00	20,850.00	21,180.00	21,110.00	22,482.50

(a) 2 April 2012 the kyat became a managed floating currency starting at K818 per US dollar; (b) Won revalued 2009; (c) New Manat from 1 Jan 2009, pegged to US dollar

Key indicators 2014

	Population (m)	Area ('000 sq km)	GDP per capita (US$)	Inflation (%)	GDP real growth (%)	Balance of trade (US$m)
Afghanistan	*30.55	647.50	*679	*7.4	*3.6	(c) *-8772
Australia	*23.59	7,682.30	*61219	*2.5	*2.7	*323
Bangladesh	*158.22	144.00	*1172	*7.0	*6.1	*-10170
Bhutan	*0.77	47.00	*2730	*7.7	*6.4	*-365
Brunei	*0.41	5.80	*36607	*-0.2	*-0.7	(d)*8770
Cambodia	*15.31	181.00	*1081	*3.9	*7.0	(c)*-2960
China	*1370	9,597.00	*7589	*2.0	*7.4	*384320
Fiji	*0.89	18.30	*4757	*0.5	*4.1	(c)*-1330
Hong Kong	*7.26	1.10	*39871	*4.4	*2.3	*-30140
India	*1260.00	3,287.60	*1627	*6.0	*7.2	*-74490
Indonesia	*251.49	1,919.40	*3534	*6.4	*5.0	*6980
Japan	*127.06	377.70	*36332	*2.7	*-0.1	*-99200
Kazakhstan	*17.42	2,717.30	*12184	*6.7	*4.3	(c)*33690
North Korea	(e)*24.45	122.40	(f)*508	–	(e)*2.5	
South Korea	*50.42	99.10	*28101	*1.3	*3.3	*92690
Kyrgyzstan	*5.64	198.50	*1280	*6.6	*10.5	*-3565
Laos	*6.90	236.80	*1693	*4.1	*7.4	(c)-755
Macao	(d)*0.57	0.03	(e)*60667	(c)*5.3	(e)*20.7	*-10180
Malaysia	*30.26	330.40	*10804	*3.1	*6.0	(c)*32490
Maldives	*0.34	0.30	*8342	*2.5	*5.0	*-1660
Federated States of Micronesia	*0.10	0.70	*3041	*0.7	*0.1	(c)*-131
Mongolia	*2.92	1,565.00	*4096	*12.9	*7.8	(e)*4710
Myanmar	*51.42	676.60	*1221	*5.9	*7.7	(c)*-439
Nepal	*28.11	147.20	*699	*9.0	*5.5	(c)*-5510
New Zealand	*4.52	268.70	*43837	*1.2	*3.2	*960
Pakistan	*182.59	803.90	*1308	*7.4	*3.6	*-15815
Papua New Guinea	*7.53	462.80	*2133	*5.3	*5.8	(c)*1570
Philippines	*99.43	300.40	*2865	*4.2	*6.1	*-15850
Samoa	*0.19	2.80	*4308	*-1.2	*1.9	(c)*-301
Singapore	*5.47	0.60	*56310	*1.0	*2.9	*74500
Sri Lanka	*20.96	65.60	*3558	*3.3	*7.4	*-8290
Solomon Islands	*0.58	27.50	*2009	*5.1	*1.5	(c)*-16
Taiwan	*23.43	36.00	*22598	*1.2	*3.7	(f)*23360
Tajikistan	*8.30	143.10	*1113	*6.1	*6.7	*-3980
Thailand	*68.66	514.00	*8445	*1.9	*0.7	*24560
Timor-Leste	*1.23	19.00	*3638	*2.5	*6.6	*-748
Turkmenistan	*5.80	488.10	*8271	*6.0	*10.3	(g)*875
Uzbekistan	*30.60	447.40	*2046	*8.4	*8.1	*(f)*-162
Vietnam	*90.63	329.60	*2053	*4.1	*6.0	*8730

* Estimated figure; (c) 2012; (d) 2011; (e) 2010; (f) 2009; (g) 2008 (h) 2007.

SOUTHEAST ASIA

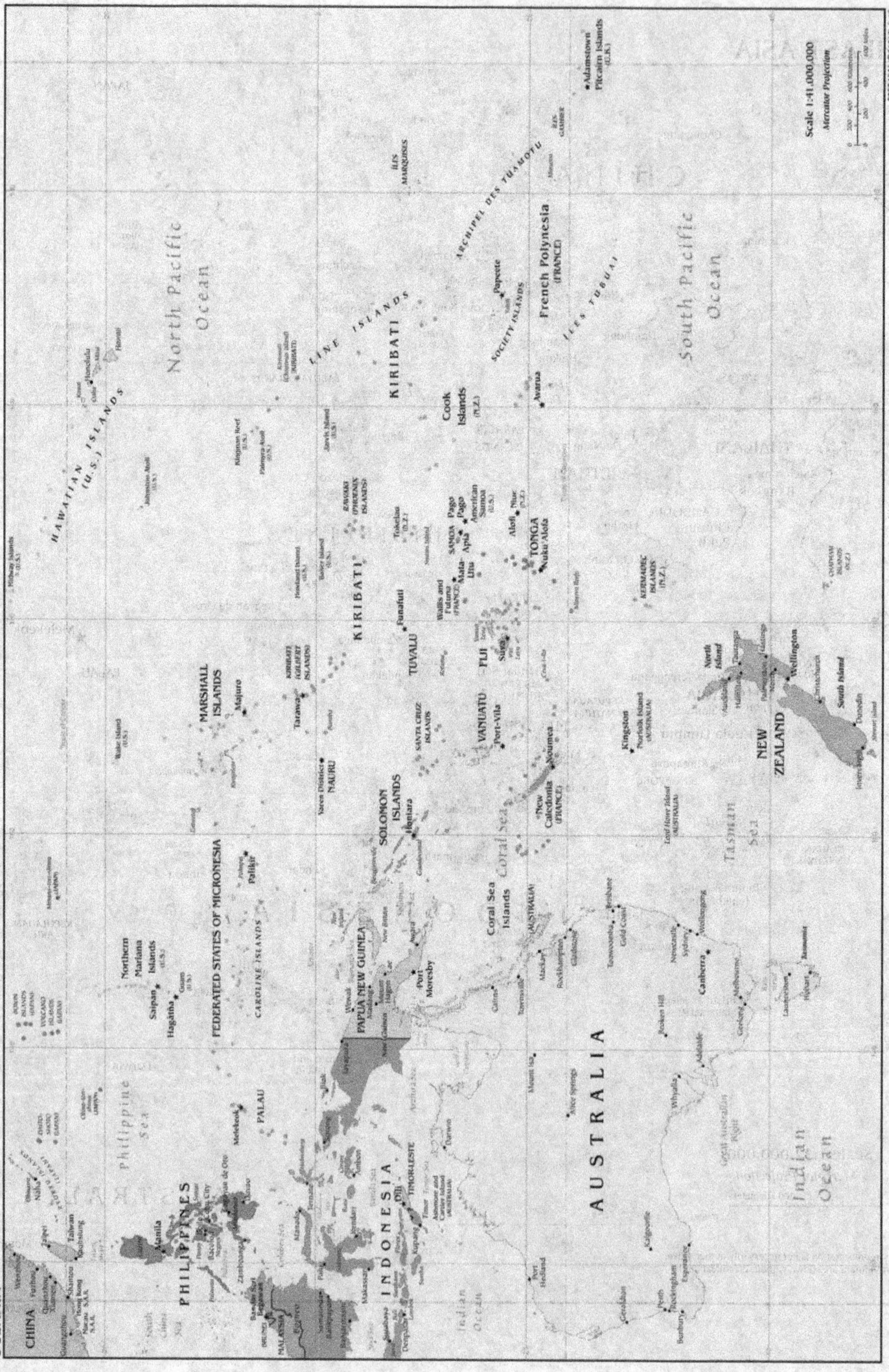
OCEANIA
North Pacific Ocean
South Pacific Ocean
Philippine Sea
Coral Sea
Tasman Sea
Indian Ocean
CHINA
PHILIPPINES
INDONESIA
PALAU
FEDERATED STATES OF MICRONESIA
MARSHALL ISLANDS
PAPUA NEW GUINEA
SOLOMON ISLANDS
NAURU
KIRIBATI
TUVALU
VANUATU
FIJI
TONGA
AUSTRALIA
NEW ZEALAND
French Polynesia (FRANCE)
Cook Islands (N.Z.)
HAWAIIAN ISLANDS (U.S.)
LINE ISLANDS
Scale 1:41,000,000
Mercator Projection

Europe

Migrants, asylum seekers or refugees?

The queue of refugees (whether immigrants of asylum seekers) along Frankfurt's Kennedy Allee was over one kilometre long, four or five wide. No bright clothing, no smiles, no laughter – just muted conversation. Arabic conversation. It was 17.00 on a chilly October Sunday evening; virtually all those still waiting to be processed would have to come back the next day. Or the day after. Meanwhile, they could only depend on handouts, on food parcels provided by charities, on blankets to keep them warm in church halls and schoolrooms.

In 2015 Germany was expecting 800,000 refugees. Those who had got this far could hardly express their relief and thankfulness. Their journey had probably already taken them through three, four or more European Union member states. One by one, Europe's frontiers were closing, bit by bit the welcome mats were being rolled up, to be replaced by the barbed wire fences that flew in the face of the EU Schengen Agreement's lofty principles. When the *Titanic* sank, 1,500 people drowned. By August 2015 it was estimated that in the year to date some 2,400 refugees had drowned in the Mediterranean. That figure was 600 more than in all of 2014. In 2014, one *Titanic*. In 2015 three *Titanics*.

That the immigrant crisis risked destroying the Schengen Agreement was a real likelihood. As country after country sought to place the blame on one or more of its neighbours, so it looked more and more likely that domestic political considerations were beginning to prevail over pan-European ideals. In Germany, Bavarians complained that Mrs Merkel, from the North, had been irresponsibly optimistic in calculating the number of refugees that Germany could actually cope with. Bavaria had long resented Northern hegemony – but it also accused Austria to the South of not pulling its weight, preferring instead to send refugees over the border into a more welcoming Germany. Angela Merkel had already insisted that other EU members raise their game, seeking agreement from countries such as the Czech Republic, Hungary and Slovakia that they too take their fair share of the 120,000 to be allocated across the EU.

In September alone over 200,000 migrants were estimated to have arrived in Germany. Germany's largest tabloid newspaper, *Bild*, had predicted the number rising to 1.5 million by the end of the year. Although Germany was the biggest recipient country in absolute terms, Sweden was taking in a disproportionately larger quota. In part, this was due to a 2013 undertaking to provide permanent residency to almost any Syrian who reached Swedish soil. Of the 800,000 people to have arrived in Europe by sea in 2015 (up to September), at least one in seven had ended up in Sweden, even though the country accounted for just one in 50 EU citizens. In 2015, over 120,000 people had applied for asylum in Sweden. The country's Migrationsverket agency expected the total number of refugees to reach about 170,000 by the end of 2015, with 10,000 people arriving every week, compared with 4,000 during the summer. Case workers had once hoped to reach a decision on every sylum application within two or three months; in 2015 the figure had risen to around two years.

'Of the 800,000 people to have arrived in Europe by sea in 2015 (up to September), at least one in seven had ended up in Sweden, even though the country accounted for just one in 50 EU citizens.'

In 2015 Europe was only just beginning to appreciate that there was no quick fix to the migrant crisis, if there was any fix at all.

Currencies (units per US$) – Europe

	Unit	Jan 2011	Jan 2012	Jan 2013	Jan 2014	Jan 2015
Albania	Lek	106.41	107.52	105.81	102.22	124.91
Andorra	Euro	0.75	0.77	0.75	0.73	0.89
Armenia	Dram	357.00	405.50	408.25	401.47	485.18
Austria	Euro	0.75	0.77	0.75	0.73	0.89
Azerbaijan	New manat	0.80	0.78	0.78	0.78	1.05
Belarus	Belarus rouble	3,008.00	8,595.00	8,890.00	9,540.00	17,822.50
Belgium	Euro	0.75	0.77	0.75	0.73	0.89
Bosnia-Herzegovina	Bosnian marka	1.51	1.50	1.48	1.43	1.74
Bulgaria	Lev	1.51	1.50	1.48	1.43	1.75
Croatia	Kuna	5.68	5.78	5.66	5.58	6.76
Cyprus	Euro	0.75	0.77	0.75	0.73	0.89
Czech Republic	Czech koruna	18.88	19.43	19.47	20.14	24.19
Denmark	Danish krone	5.74	5.74	5.63	55.46	6.67
Estonia	Kroon	(b) 0.75	0.77	0.75	0.73	1.37
Faroe Islands	Faroese krone	5.74	5.74	5.63	55.46	6.67
Finland	Euro	0.75	0.77	0.75	0.73	0.89
France	Euro	0.75	0.77	0.75	0.73	0.89
Georgia	Lari	1.77	1.66	1.65	1.74	2.38
Germany	Euro	0.75	0.77	0.75	0.73	0.89
Gibraltar	Gibraltar pound	0.64	0.62	0.62	0.62	0.62
Greece	Euro	0.75	0.77	0.75	0.73	0.89
Greenland	Danish krone	5.74	5.74	5.63	55.46	6.67
Hungary	Forint	212.86	216.21	225.95	218.21	280.34
Iceland	Icelandic krona	117.58	125.72	119.28	115.62	128.67
Ireland	Euro	0.75	0.77	0.75	0.73	0.89
Italy	Euro	0.75	0.77	0.75	0.73	0.89
Kosovo	Euro	0.75	0.77	0.75	0.73	0.89
Latvia	Lat	0.54	0.53	0.53	0.73	0.89
Liechtenstein	Swiss franc	0.96	0.93	0.93	0.93	0.93
Lithuania	Lit	2.66	2.65	2.61	2.53	0.89
Luxembourg	Euro	0.75	0.77	0.75	0.73	0.89
Macedonia	Macedonian denar	46.80	47.35	46.45	45.05	55.23
Malta	Euro	0.75	0.77	0.75	0.73	0.89
Moldova	Moldovan leu	12.34	12.32	12.70	13.02	19.25
Monaco	Euro	0.75	0.77	0.75	0.73	0.89
Montenegro	Euro	0.75	0.77	0.75	0.73	0.89
The Netherlands	Euro	0.75	0.77	0.75	0.73	0.89
Norway	Norwegian krone	5.95	5.66	5.94	6.13	8.25
Poland	Zloty	2.98	3.16	4.87	3.05	4.03
Portugal	Euro	0.75	0.77	0.75	0.73	0.89
Romania	New leu	3.28	3.47	3.32	3.29	3.96
Russia	Rouble	30.77	30.91	32.94	33.11	68.26
San Marino	Euro	0.75	0.77	0.75	0.73	0.89
Serbia	Dinar	81.64	87.03	85.90	83.78	107.64
Slovakia	Euro	0.75	0.77	0.75	0.73	0.89
Slovenia	**Euro**	**0.75**	**0.77**	**0.75**	**0.73**	**0.89**
Spain	Euro	0.75	0.77	0.75	0.73	0.89
Sweden	Swedish krone	6.89	6.66	6.55	6.49	6.78
Switzerland	Swiss franc	0.96	0.93	0.93	0.9	1.02
Turkey	New Turkish lira	1.56	1.79	1.92	2.17	3.02
Ukraine	Hryvna	7.97	8.19	8.13	8.24	22.20
United Kingdom	UK pound	0.64	0.62	0.66	0.61	0.65
The Holy See	Euro	0.75	0.77	0.75	0.73	0.89

(a) euro adopted 1 Jan 2008; (b) euro adopted 1 Jan 2010.

Key indicators 2014

	Population (m)	Area ('000 sq km)	GDP per capita (US$)	Inflation (%)	GDP real growth (%)	Balance of trade (US$m)
Albania	*2.77	28.8	*4,781	*1.6	*2.2	*-2,520
Andorra	(c) *0.08	0.73	–	–	–	–
Armenia	*3.29	29.8	*3,121	*3.1	*3.4	*2,060
Austria	*8.52	83.9	*51,307	*1.5	*0.3	*-3,180
Azerbaijan	*9.38	86.6	*7,902	*1.4	*2.8	*18,930
Belarus	*9.47	208	*8,042	*18.1	*1.6	*-259
Belgium	*11.20	30.5	*47,722	*0.5	*1.0	*-4,780
Bosnia and Hercegovina	*3.87	51.1	*4,644	*-0.1	*0.8	*-5,490
Bulgaria	*7.20	111	*7,753	*-1.6	*1.7	*-4,560
Croatia	*4.24	56.5	*13,494	*-0.2	*-0.4	(c)-*8,350
Cyprus	*0.89	9.3	*26,115	*-0.03	*-2.3	*-3,540
Czech Republic	*10.51	78.9	*19,563	*0.4	*2.0	*11,630
Denmark	*5.63	43.1	*60,564	*0.6	*1.0	*10,130
Estonia	*1.32	45.2	*19,671	*0.5	*2.1	*-1,340
Faroe Islands	(e)*0.05	1.4	(g)*45,206	(f)*2.3	(f)*2.9	–
Finland	*5.48	338.1	*49,497	*1.2	*-0.1	(c)*4,800
France	*63.92	544	*44,538	*0.6	*0.4	*-48
Georgia	*4.47	69.7	*3,699	*3.1	*4.7	*-4,240
Germany	*81.10	357	*47,590	*0.8	*1.6	*304,150
Gibraltar	*0.03	0.007				
Greece	*10.99	132	*21,653	*-1.4	*0.8	*-23,730
Greenland	(e)*0.06	2,166.10	(e)*37,517	(g)*-19.0	(g)*-5.4	–
Hungary	*9.88	93	*13,881	*-0.3	*3.6	*3,590
Iceland	*0.33	103.1	*51,262	*2.0	*1.8	*-105
Ireland	*4.61	70.3	*53,462	*0.3	*4.8	(c)*5,000
Italy	*59.69	301.3	*35,823	*0.2	*-0.4	*65,310
' Kosovo	(e) *1.73	10.88	(e)3,690	*0.4	*2.7	*-2,730
Latvia	*2.03	64.6	*15,729	*0.7	*2.4	*-3,240
Liechtenstein	(e)*0.04	0.2	(g)134,915	(g)-0.5	(g)-1.2	–
Lithuania	*2.94	65.2	*16,386	*0.2	*2.9	*-1,990
Luxembourg	*0.59	2.6	*111,716	*0.7	*2.9	*-574
Macedonia	*2.07	25.7	*5,481	*-0.1	*3.8	*-2,470
Malta	*0.43	0.3	*24,876	*0.8	*3.6	*-1,450
Moldova	*3.56	34	*2,233	*5.1	*4.6	*-3,100
Monaco	(e)*0.04	0.002	(g)*172,676	(g)*0.5	(g)*-2.6	–
Montenegro	*0.62	14	*7,149	*-0.7	*1.1	*-1,830
Netherlands	*16.86	41.5	*51,373	*0.3	*0.9	*105,250
Norway	*5.16	324	*97,013	*2.0	*2.2	(c)*-60,510
Poland	*38.02	312.7	*14,379	*0.0	*3.3	(d)*-6,870
Portugal	*10.39	92.1	*22,130	*-0.2	*0.9	*-11,890
Romania	*19.93	237.5	*10,035	*1.1	*2.9	*-7,140
Russia	*143.70	17,075.00	*12,926	*7.8	*0.6	*189,740
San Marino	*0.03	0.01	*56,820	*1.1	*-1.0	–
Serbia	*7.16	77.47	*6,123	*2.1	*-1.8	(c)*-5,520
Slovakia	*5.42	49	*18,454	*-0.1	*2.4	*4,510
Slovenia	*2.06	20.3	*24,019	*0.2	*2.6	*1,730
Spain	*46.46	504.8	*30,278	*-0.2	*1.4	*-28,510
Sweden	*9.75	449	*58,491	*-0.2	*2.1	*17,450
Switzerland	*8.14	41.3	*87,475	*0.0	*2.0	*55,020
Turkey	*76.90	779.5	*10,482	*8.9	*2.9	*-63,580
Ukraine	*42.77	603.7	*3,055	*12.1	*-6.8	*-7,640
United Kingdom	*64.51	244.1	*45,653	*1.5	*2.6	*-199,620

* Estimated figure; (c) 2012; (d) 2011; (e) 2010; (f) 2009; (g) 2008; (h) 2007.
(+) area 5.8 square km; (++) area 1.8 square km

EUROPE

Greenland
(DENMARK)
Jan Mayen
(NORWAY)
Greenland
Sea
Denmark
Strait
Barents
Sea
Hammerfest
Tromsø
Murmansk
Norwegian Sea
Kiruna
White Sea
Arkhangel'sk
Reykjavík
ICELAND
Arctic Circle
NORWAY
Luleå
Oulu
Umeå
FINLAND
Lake
Onega
Trondheim
Tórshavn
Faroe Islands
(DENMARK)
SWEDEN
Gulf
of
Bothnia
Lake
Ladoga
Tampere
SHETLAND
ISLANDS
Gävle
Turku
Helsinki
Saint Petersburg
Gulf of Finland
Bergen
RUSSIA
Rockall
(U.K.)
ORKNEY
ISLANDS
Oslo
Stockholm
ÅLAND
ISLANDS
Tallinn
ESTONIA
HEBRIDES
Stavanger
Moscow
North
Atlantic
Ocean
Aberdeen
Skagerrak
Göteborg
Gotland
LATVIA
Riga
Kattegat
Glasgow
Edinburgh
North
Sea
Baltic Sea
Smolensk
LITHUANIA
Vitsyebsk
Öland
UNITED
DENMARK
Copenhagen
Malmö
Vilnius
Mahilyow
Minsk
Belfast
Isle
of
Man
(U.K.)
Kaliningrad
RUSSIA
Dublin
Irish
Sea
Leeds
Bornholm
BELARUS
Gdańsk
IRELAND
Liverpool
Manchester
Hrodna
Homyel'
Chernihiv
KINGDOM
Hamburg
Birmingham
Amsterdam
Bremen
Berlin
Poznań
Warsaw
Brest
Kyiv
Cardiff
NETH.
POLAND
Celtic
Sea
London
Rotterdam
Essen
Leipzig
Łódź
Zhytomyr
Cologne
Wrocław
UKRAINE
English
Channel
Brussels
Lille
BEL.
Bonn
GERMANY
Prague
L'viv
Vinnytsya
Guernsey (U.K.)
Jersey (U.K.)
Frankfurt
Kraków
Luxembourg
CZECH REPUBLIC
Chernivtsi
Mykolayiv
Paris
LUX.
Brno
SLOVAKIA
Chişinău
Stuttgart
Strasbourg
Bratislava
Iaşi
Odesa
Munich
Vienna
Budapest
Cluj-
Napoca
MOLDOVA
Nantes
LIECH.
AUSTRIA
HUNGARY
Zürich
Bern
Vaduz
SWITZ.
Bay of
Biscay
FRANCE
ROMANIA
Geneva
SLOVENIA
Ljubljana
Zagreb
Bucharest
Constanţa
Lyon
Milan
Venice
Black
Sea
A Coruña
Turin
Bordeaux
BOSNIA AND
HERZEGOVINA
Belgrade
CROATIA
Varna
Danube
Genoa
SAN
MARINO
SERBIA
Sarajevo
BULGARIA
Toulouse
MONACO
Florence
Bilbao
Pristina
Sofia
Andorra
la Vella
Marseille
Ligurian
Sea
MONT.
KOS.
Istanbul
Porto
ANDORRA
ITALY
Adriatic
Sea
Podgorica
Skopje
Zaragoza
MACE.
Corsica
Rome
Tirana
Bursa
PORTUGAL
Madrid
VATICAN
CITY
ALB.
Thessaloníki
Barcelona
TURKEY
Naples
Lisbon
Balearic
Sea
SPAIN
Valencia
Sardinia
Tyrrhenian
Sea
GREECE
Aegean
Sea
İzmir
BALEARIC
ISLANDS
Cagliari
Athens
Sevilla
Ionian
Sea
Mediterranean Sea
Palermo
Gibraltar
(U.K.)
Málaga
Sicily
Rhodes
Strait of Gibraltar
Alborán
Sea
Ceuta
(SPAIN)
Algiers
Tunis
Melilla
(SPAIN)
Oran
Crete
Rabat
Casablanca
Valletta
MALTA
TUNISIA
MOROCCO
ALGERIA
Scale 1:19,300,000
Lambert Conformal Conic Projection,
standard parallels 40°N and 68°N
300 Kilometers
300 Miles
803539AI (G00772) 6-12

Middle East

The Arab Spring falters

Whatever problems the rest of the world may face, they pale into insignificance when compared to those of the Middle East. Since the end of the Second World War moments of optimism have come – and gone. In the 1970s Egypt under the moderately nationalist regime of Anwar Sadat had turned conservative and sought alliances with the United States and Saudi Arabia, promoting a politicised Islam alongside the concept of unregulated markets economically. This introduced a form of *status quo*, in which Arab nationalist presidents became entrenched, the oil states happy to see their petroleum revenues safely mounting, those without oil happy to take the West's dollars and promising to widen the distribution of wealth and to reject any advances that the Soviet Union might make.

A pattern of sorts emerged; opposition to Israeli expansionism became muted, resistance left to the ill-equipped, ill-prepared and ill-resourced Palestinians. Anything resembling communist or labour movements was swiftly quashed, oil money was used to bribe or torture the public into quiescence, rather than investing in education and social infrastructure. Local TV and radio were censored – a measure that by 2015 had become ineffective with the growth of the internet and satellite broadcasting. Outside the region not a lot of thought was given to the fact that the emergent ruling status quo was primarily Sunni, in that most of the region's ruling élites were drawn from that branch of Islam, including the president of Iraq, the prime minister of Lebanon and the ruling family of Bahrain – none of which were Sunni-majority societies.

'... once called the Arab Spring: a new generation of Arab youth, frustrated academics and would be politicians combined with nascent working-class movements.'

Ironically coinciding with the election of President Obama, since 2008 the established 'order' began to crumble. Academics have been at pains to identify the causes and trends of what was once called the Arab Spring: a new generation of Arab youth, frustrated academics and would be politicians combined with nascent working-class movements. With the exception of one or two states there was a common denominator of Sunni disenchantment. In its early days few anticipated the likelihood of the tide of disillusion eventually synthesising into a movement as powerful and effective as the Islamic State (IS). Sunni disillusion had combined with the perceived growth and threat from a Shi'a Iran and a (*de facto*) Shi'a Iraq to persuade many Sunni that the IS was their only hope. IS propaganda projected terror – against non-Muslims and non-Sunni Muslims, promising a Utopian Caliphate to those who signed up and celestial bliss for those unlucky enough to encounter Kurdish Pesh Merga units or to be targeted by drones directed by a US led coalition. But within Sunni states the old order risked collapsing for other reasons. Sunni nationalists were increasingly suspicious of the Saudi attachment to Salafi fundamentalism. Algerian and Egyptian officers were a lot less enthusiastic about the rebellion in Syria than were the ruling sheikhs of the Arabian Gulf. In 2015 the signature of the Iranian nuclear agreement represented another shift on the Obama watch. As relations between President Obama and Prime Minister Netanyahu steadily worsened, the perceived wisdom was that Washington and Tehran would forge a new friendship. Israel and the Palestinian question, had simply been placed on the State Department's back burner. If Iran's regional influence was increasing, the blame could be placed at a number of feet. Negligent Sunni despots, corrupt governments, a lack of understanding of the region's tensions and preoccupations – not only in Washington, but also in London, Brussels, Paris and Bonn. President Obama had probably come to regret his original assessment of IS in which he had dismissed its importance, comparing it to a junior university basketball team. In January 2014 the President had declared that 'the analogy we use around here sometimes and I think it is accurate, is if a junior varsity team puts on Lakers uniforms, it doesn't make them Kobe Bryant.' In mid-2015 the President had probably come to regret this judgement. Of greater concern to the world outside was that at the time it this must have been the official line of US national security staff. Underrating the strength of ISIS was the third of three great mistakes made by the US and its Western allies in Syria since 2011, errors that had certainly helped the growth of ISIS. Between 2011 and 2013 the Western allies were convinced that Assad would fall in much the same way as Muammar al Qadafi had in Libya. *Sic transit gloria Arabica*.

Currencies (units per US$) – Middle East

	Unit	Jan 2010	Jan 2011	Jan 2012	Jan 2013	Jan 2014
Afghanistan	Afghani	45.36	43.00	52.31	56.23	55.56
Algeria	Algerian dinar	71.76	74.05	79.04	79.74	78.15
Bahrain	Bahraini dinar	0.37	0.38	0.38	0.38	0.38
Cyprus	Euro	0.69	0.77	0.77	0.75	0.73
Djibouti	Djibouti franc	160.50	175.75	175.55	174.70	175.05
Egypt	Egyptian pound	5.42	5.80	6.11	7.00	6.96
Iran	Rial	9,900.00	1,035.00	12,305.00	12,394.00	12,386.50
Iraq	New Iraqi dinar	1,150.00	1,166.40	1,163.00	1,162.20	1,163.20
Israel	New Shekel	3.68	3.58	3.81	3.57	3.49
Jordan	Jordanian dinar	0.71	0.71	0.71	0.71	0.71
Kazakhstan	Tenge	148.05	147.10	150.46	153.36	154.35
Kuwait	Kuwaiti dinar	0.29	0.28	0.28	0.28	0.28
Kyrgyzstan	Som	44.22	47.17	47.26	48.84	39.19
Lebanon	Lebanese pound	1,502.50	1,501.00	1,505.00	1,511.50	1,503.00
Libya	Libyan dinar	1.22	1.26	1.26	1.26	1.24
Mauritania	Ouguiya	261.50	282.00	298.50	300.50	292.50
Morocco	Moroccan dirham	7.88	8.56	8.55	8.43	8.22
Oman	Rial	0.38	0.38	0.39	0.39	0.39
Pakistan	Rupee	84.20	85.80	96.51	101.76	105.51
Palestine	Dinar (Jordanian)	0.71	0.71	0.71	0.71	0.71
	New shekel (Israeli)	3.68	3.58	3.81	3.81	3.49
Qatar	Riyal	3.64	3.64	3.64	3.64	3.64
Saudi Arabia	Riyal	3.75	3.75	3.75	3.75	3.75
Somalia	Somali shilling	1,457.00	1,550.00	1,565.00	1,318.00	1,103.00
South Sudan	South Sudan pound	–	–	3.05	3.05	3.05
Sudan	Sudanese pound	2.31	2.51	4.42	4.41	5.70
Syria	Syrian pound	45.40	46.85	70.85	104.90	141.30
Tajikistan	Tajik rouble	4.37	4.40	4.75	4.77	4.74
Tunisia	Tunisian dinar	1.31	1.46	1.57	1.66	1.65
Turkey	New Turkish lira	1.45	1.57	1.79	1.92	2.17
Turkmenistan	New Manat	2.85	2.85	2.85	2.85	2.84
United Arab Emirates	Dirham	3.67	3.67	3.67	3.67	3.67
Uzbekistan	Sum	1,516.89	1,640.55	1,969.43	2,104.62	2,202.20
Yemen	Rial	208.62	213.80	214.83	215.03	214.90

(a) Sudanese pound (S£) replaced dinar at rate of S£1 to 100 dinar, Jan 2007; (b) euro adopted 1 Jan 2008; (c) New Manat from 1 Jan 2009, pegged to US dollar

Key indicators 2014

	Population (m)	Area ('000 sq km)	GDP per capita (US$)	Inflation (%)	GDP real growth (%)	Balance of trade (US$m)
Afghanistan	*31.28	647.50	*649	*4.6	*1.5	(c) *-8,772
Algeria	*38.70	2,381.70	*5,532	*2.9	*4.1	*945
Bahrain	*1.20	0.70	*28,272	*2.5	*4.8	(c) *7,270
Cyprus	*0.89	9.30	*26,115	*-0.03	*-2.3	*-3,540
Djibouti	*0.94	23.20	*1,692	*2.9	*6.0	(c)*-606
Egypt	*86.70	1,001.50	*3,304	*10.1	*2.2	*-30,830
Iran	*77.97	1,648.20	*5,183	*15.6	*3.0	(e)*55
Iraq	*35.87	434.90	*6,165	*2.2	*-2.4	(d)*4,410
Israel	*8.21	20.70	*36,991	*0.5	*2.8	*-7,860
Jordan	*6.67	91.90	*5,358	*2.9	*3.1	(c)*-11,470
Kazakhstan	*17.42	2,717.30	*12,184	*6.7	*4.3	(c)*33,690
Kuwait	*4.00	17.80	*43,103	*2.9	*1.3	*77,410
Kyrgyzstan	*5.70	198.50	*1,299	*7.5	*3.6	*-3,040
Lebanon	*4.51	10.50	*11,068	*1.9	*2.0	(c)*-15,170
Libya	*6.21	1,775.50	*6,623	*2.8	*-2,403.1	(c)*11,970
Mauritania	*3.62	1,030.70	*1,403	*3.5	*6.4	(c)*-392
Morocco	*33.18	711.00	*3,291	*0.4	*2.9	(e)*-21,590
Oman	*4.09	320.00	*19,002	*1.0	*3.0	(c)*24,590
Pakistan	*186.29	803.90	*1,343	*7.4	*4.1	*-17,770
Palestine	(e)*4.17	6.30	(f)*2,186	(f)*3.8	–	(e)*4,630
Qatar	*2.23	11.40	*93,965	*3.0	*6.1	*100,570
Saudi Arabia	*30.77	2,149.70	*24,454	*2.2	*3.6	*183,860
Somalia	(d)*51.20	738.00	–	–	(c)*6.0	–
Sudan	*37.29	1,861.50	*1,980	*36.9	*3.4	*-3,760
Syria	(c) *20.82	185.20	(e) *2,823	(e) *4.4	(e) *3.4	(e) *-3,603
Tajikistan	*8.30	143.10	*1,113	*6.1	*6.7	*-3,980
Tunisia	*10.92	164.20	*4,345	*6.1	*2.7	(c) *-6,030
Turkey	*8.14	41.30	*87,475	*0.0	*2.0	*55,020
Turkmenistan	*5.80	488.10	*8,271	*6.0	*10.3	(g)*875
United Arab Emirates	*9.30	83.60	*43,180	*2.4	*3.6	(f)*63,690
Uzbekistan	*30.60	447.40	*2,046	*8.4	*8.1	*(f)*-162
Yemen	*27.46	528.00	*1,574	*8.2	*-0.2	(c)*-2,910

* Estimated figure; (a) 310 people total; (c) 2012; (d) 2011; (e) 2010; (f) 2009; (g) 2008; (h) 2007; (i) 2006.

No current figurework for Palestine and Somalia

MIDDLE EAST

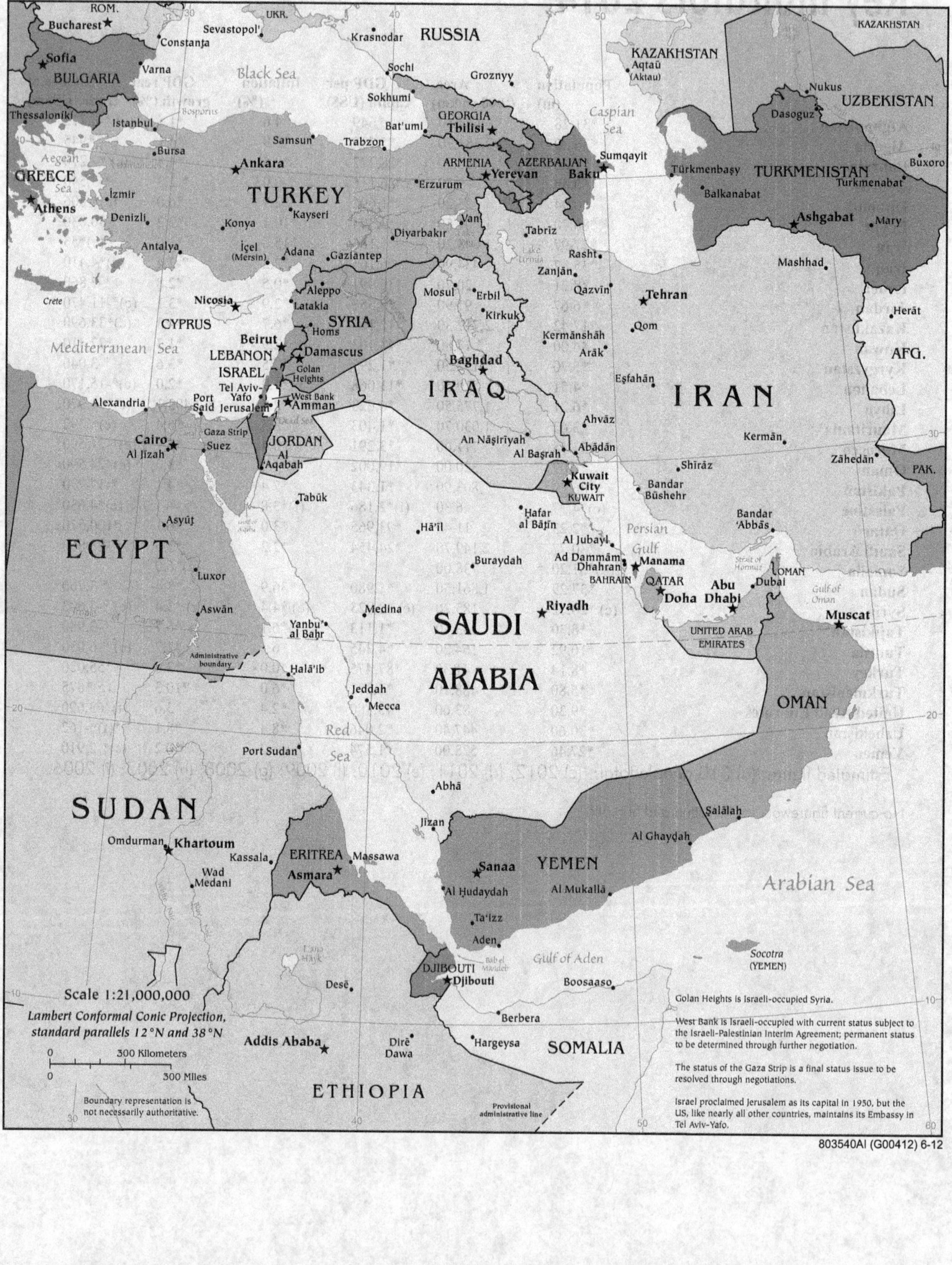

803540AI (G00412) 6-12

2016 Title List

Visit www.GreyHouse.com for Product Information, Table of Contents, and Sample Pages.

General Reference

An African Biographical Dictionary
America's College Museums
American Environmental Leaders: From Colonial Times to the Present
Encyclopedia of African-American Writing
Encyclopedia of Constitutional Amendments
Encyclopedia of Gun Control & Gun Rights
An Encyclopedia of Human Rights in the United States
Encyclopedia of Invasions & Conquests
Encyclopedia of Prisoners of War & Internment
Encyclopedia of Religion & Law in America
Encyclopedia of Rural America
Encyclopedia of the Continental Congress
Encyclopedia of the United States Cabinet, 1789-2010
Encyclopedia of War Journalism
Encyclopedia of Warrior Peoples & Fighting Groups
The Environmental Debate: A Documentary History
The Evolution Wars: A Guide to the Debates
From Suffrage to the Senate: America's Political Women
Global Terror & Political Risk Assessment
Nations of the World
Political Corruption in America
Privacy Rights in the Digital Era
The Religious Right: A Reference Handbook
Speakers of the House of Representatives, 1789-2009
This is Who We Were: 1880-1900
This is Who We Were: A Companion to the 1940 Census
This is Who We Were: In the 1910s
This is Who We Were: In the 1920s
This is Who We Were: In the 1940s
This is Who We Were: In the 1950s
This is Who We Were: In the 1960s
This is Who We Were: In the 1970s
U.S. Land & Natural Resource Policy
The Value of a Dollar 1600-1865: Colonial Era to the Civil War
The Value of a Dollar: 1860-2014
Working Americans 1770-1869 Vol. IX: Revolutionary War to the Civil War
Working Americans 1880-1999 Vol. I: The Working Class
Working Americans 1880-1999 Vol. II: The Middle Class
Working Americans 1880-1999 Vol. III: The Upper Class
Working Americans 1880-1999 Vol. IV: Their Children
Working Americans 1880-2015 Vol. V: Americans At War
Working Americans 1880-2005 Vol. VI: Women at Work
Working Americans 1880-2006 Vol. VII: Social Movements
Working Americans 1880-2007 Vol. VIII: Immigrants
Working Americans 1880-2009 Vol. X: Sports & Recreation
Working Americans 1880-2010 Vol. XI: Inventors & Entrepreneurs
Working Americans 1880-2011 Vol. XII: Our History through Music
Working Americans 1880-2012 Vol. XIII: Education & Educators
World Cultural Leaders of the 20th & 21st Centuries

Education Information

Charter School Movement
Comparative Guide to American Elementary & Secondary Schools
Complete Learning Disabilities Directory
Educators Resource Directory
Special Education: A Reference Book for Policy and Curriculum Development

Health Information

Comparative Guide to American Hospitals
Complete Directory for Pediatric Disorders
Complete Directory for People with Chronic Illness
Complete Directory for People with Disabilities
Complete Mental Health Directory
Diabetes in America: Analysis of an Epidemic
Directory of Drug & Alcohol Residential Rehab Facilities
Directory of Health Care Group Purchasing Organizations
Directory of Hospital Personnel
HMO/PPO Directory
Medical Device Register
Older Americans Information Directory

Business Information

Complete Television, Radio & Cable Industry Directory
Directory of Business Information Resources
Directory of Mail Order Catalogs
Directory of Venture Capital & Private Equity Firms
Environmental Resource Handbook
Food & Beverage Market Place
Grey House Homeland Security Directory
Grey House Performing Arts Directory
Grey House Safety & Security Directory
Grey House Transportation Security Directory
Hudson's Washington News Media Contacts Directory
New York State Directory
Rauch Market Research Guides
Sports Market Place Directory

Statistics & Demographics

American Tally
America's Top-Rated Cities
America's Top-Rated Smaller Cities
America's Top-Rated Small Towns & Cities
Ancestry & Ethnicity in America
The Asian Databook
Comparative Guide to American Suburbs
The Hispanic Databook
Profiles of America
"Profiles of" Series - State Handbooks
Weather America

Financial Ratings Series

TheStreet Ratings' Guide to Bond & Money Market Mutual Funds
TheStreet Ratings' Guide to Common Stocks
TheStreet Ratings' Guide to Exchange-Traded Funds
TheStreet Ratings' Guide to Stock Mutual Funds
TheStreet Ratings' Ultimate Guided Tour of Stock Investing
Weiss Ratings' Consumer Guides
Weiss Ratings' Guide to Banks
Weiss Ratings' Guide to Credit Unions
Weiss Ratings' Guide to Health Insurers
Weiss Ratings' Guide to Life & Annuity Insurers
Weiss Ratings' Guide to Property & Casualty Insurers

Bowker's Books In Print® Titles

American Book Publishing Record® Annual
American Book Publishing Record® Monthly
Books In Print®
Books In Print® Supplement
Books Out Loud™
Bowker's Complete Video Directory™
Children's Books In Print®
El-Hi Textbooks & Serials In Print®
Forthcoming Books®
Large Print Books & Serials™
Law Books & Serials In Print™
Medical & Health Care Books In Print™
Publishers, Distributors & Wholesalers of the US™
Subject Guide to Books In Print®
Subject Guide to Children's Books In Print®

Canadian General Reference

Associations Canada
Canadian Almanac & Directory
Canadian Environmental Resource Guide
Canadian Parliamentary Guide
Canadian Venture Capital & Private Equity Firms
Financial Post Directory of Directors
Financial Services Canada
Governments Canada
Health Guide Canada
The History of Canada
Libraries Canada
Major Canadian Cities

SALEM PRESS

2016 Title List

Visit www.SalemPress.com for Product Information, Table of Contents, and Sample Pages.

Science, Careers & Mathematics

Ancient Creatures
Applied Science
Applied Science: Engineering & Mathematics
Applied Science: Science & Medicine
Applied Science: Technology
Biomes and Ecosystems
Careers in Building Construction
Careers in Business
Careers in Chemistry
Careers in Communications & Media
Careers in Environment & Conservation
Careers in Healthcare
Careers in Hospitality & Tourism
Careers in Human Services
Careers in Law, Criminal Justice & Emergency Services
Careers in Manufacturing
Careers in Physics
Careers in Sales, Insurance & Real Estate
Careers in Science & Engineering
Careers in Technology Services & Repair
Computer Technology Innovators
Contemporary Biographies in Business
Contemporary Biographies in Chemistry
Contemporary Biographies in Communications & Media
Contemporary Biographies in Environment & Conservation
Contemporary Biographies in Healthcare
Contemporary Biographies in Hospitality & Tourism
Contemporary Biographies in Law & Criminal Justice
Contemporary Biographies in Physics
Earth Science
Earth Science: Earth Materials & Resources
Earth Science: Earth's Surface and History
Earth Science: Physics & Chemistry of the Earth
Earth Science: Weather, Water & Atmosphere
Encyclopedia of Energy
Encyclopedia of Environmental Issues
Encyclopedia of Environmental Issues: Atmosphere and Air Pollution
Encyclopedia of Environmental Issues: Ecology and Ecosystems
Encyclopedia of Environmental Issues: Energy and Energy Use
Encyclopedia of Environmental Issues: Policy and Activism
Encyclopedia of Environmental Issues: Preservation/Wilderness Issues
Encyclopedia of Environmental Issues: Water and Water Pollution
Encyclopedia of Global Resources
Encyclopedia of Global Warming
Encyclopedia of Mathematics & Society
Encyclopedia of Mathematics & Society: Engineering, Tech, Medicine
Encyclopedia of Mathematics & Society: Great Mathematicians
Encyclopedia of Mathematics & Society: Math & Social Sciences
Encyclopedia of Mathematics & Society: Math Development/Concepts
Encyclopedia of Mathematics & Society: Math in Culture & Society
Encyclopedia of Mathematics & Society: Space, Science, Environment
Encyclopedia of the Ancient World
Forensic Science
Geography Basics
Internet Innovators
Inventions and Inventors
Magill's Encyclopedia of Science: Animal Life
Magill's Encyclopedia of Science: Plant life
Notable Natural Disasters
Principles of Astronomy
Principles of Chemistry
Principles of Physics
Science and Scientists
Solar System
Solar System: Great Astronomers
Solar System: Study of the Universe
Solar System: The Inner Planets
Solar System: The Moon and Other Small Bodies
Solar System: The Outer Planets
Solar System: The Sun and Other Stars
World Geography

Literature

American Ethnic Writers
Classics of Science Fiction & Fantasy Literature
Critical Insights: Authors
Critical Insights: Film
Critical Insights: Literary Collection Bundles
Critical Insights: Themes
Critical Insights: Works
Critical Survey of Drama
Critical Survey of Graphic Novels: Heroes & Super Heroes
Critical Survey of Graphic Novels: History, Theme & Technique
Critical Survey of Graphic Novels: Independents/Underground Classics
Critical Survey of Graphic Novels: Manga
Critical Survey of Long Fiction
Critical Survey of Mystery & Detective Fiction
Critical Survey of Mythology and Folklore: Heroes and Heroines
Critical Survey of Mythology and Folklore: Love, Sexuality & Desire
Critical Survey of Mythology and Folklore: World Mythology
Critical Survey of Poetry
Critical Survey of Poetry: American Poets
Critical Survey of Poetry: British, Irish & Commonwealth Poets
Critical Survey of Poetry: Cumulative Index
Critical Survey of Poetry: European Poets
Critical Survey of Poetry: Topical Essays
Critical Survey of Poetry: World Poets
Critical Survey of Shakespeare's Plays
Critical Survey of Shakespeare's Sonnets
Critical Survey of Short Fiction
Critical Survey of Short Fiction: American Writers
Critical Survey of Short Fiction: British, Irish, Commonwealth Writers
Critical Survey of Short Fiction: Cumulative Index
Critical Survey of Short Fiction: European Writers
Critical Survey of Short Fiction: Topical Essays
Critical Survey of Short Fiction: World Writers
Critical Survey of Young Adult Literature
Cyclopedia of Literary Characters
Cyclopedia of Literary Places
Holocaust Literature
Introduction to Literary Context: American Poetry of the 20th Century
Introduction to Literary Context: American Post-Modernist Novels
Introduction to Literary Context: American Short Fiction
Introduction to Literary Context: English Literature
Introduction to Literary Context: Plays
Introduction to Literary Context: World Literature
Magill's Literary Annual 2015
Magill's Survey of American Literature
Magill's Survey of World Literature
Masterplots
Masterplots II: African American Literature
Masterplots II: American Fiction Series
Masterplots II: British & Commonwealth Fiction Series
Masterplots II: Christian Literature
Masterplots II: Drama Series
Masterplots II: Juvenile & Young Adult Literature, Supplement
Masterplots II: Nonfiction Series
Masterplots II: Poetry Series
Masterplots II: Short Story Series
Masterplots II: Women's Literature Series
Notable African American Writers
Notable American Novelists
Notable Playwrights
Notable Poets
Recommended Reading: 600 Classics Reviewed
Short Story Writers

2016 Title List

Visit www.SalemPress.com for Product Information, Table of Contents, and Sample Pages.

History and Social Science

The 2000s in America
50 States
African American History
Agriculture in History
American First Ladies
American Heroes
American Indian Culture
American Indian History
American Indian Tribes
American Presidents
American Villains
America's Historic Sites
Ancient Greece
The Bill of Rights
The Civil Rights Movement
The Cold War
Countries, Peoples & Cultures
Countries, Peoples & Cultures: Central & South America
Countries, Peoples & Cultures: Central, South & Southeast Asia
Countries, Peoples & Cultures: East & South Africa
Countries, Peoples & Cultures: East Asia & the Pacific
Countries, Peoples & Cultures: Eastern Europe
Countries, Peoples & Cultures: Middle East & North Africa
Countries, Peoples & Cultures: North America & the Caribbean
Countries, Peoples & Cultures: West & Central Africa
Countries, Peoples & Cultures: Western Europe
Defining Documents: American Revolution
Defining Documents: Civil Rights
Defining Documents: Civil War
Defining Documents: Emergence of Modern America
Defining Documents: Exploration & Colonial America
Defining Documents: Manifest Destiny
Defining Documents: Postwar 1940s
Defining Documents: Reconstruction
Defining Documents: 1920s
Defining Documents: 1930s
Defining Documents: 1950s
Defining Documents: 1960s
Defining Documents: 1970s
Defining Documents: American West
Defining Documents: Ancient World
Defining Documents: Middle Ages
Defining Documents: Vietnam War
Defining Documents: World War I
Defining Documents: World War II
The Eighties in America
Encyclopedia of American Immigration
Encyclopedia of Flight
Encyclopedia of the Ancient World
Fashion Innovators
The Fifties in America
The Forties in America
Great Athletes
Great Athletes: Baseball
Great Athletes: Basketball
Great Athletes: Boxing & Soccer
Great Athletes: Cumulative Index
Great Athletes: Football
Great Athletes: Golf & Tennis
Great Athletes: Olympics
Great Athletes: Racing & Individual Sports
Great Events from History: 17th Century
Great Events from History: 18th Century
Great Events from History: 19th Century
Great Events from History: 20th Century (1901-1940)
Great Events from History: 20th Century (1941-1970)
Great Events from History: 20th Century (1971-2000)
Great Events from History: Ancient World
Great Events from History: Cumulative Indexes
Great Events from History: Gay, Lesbian, Bisexual, Transgender Events
Great Events from History: Middle Ages
Great Events from History: Modern Scandals
Great Events from History: Renaissance & Early Modern Era
Great Lives from History: 17th Century
Great Lives from History: 18th Century
Great Lives from History: 19th Century
Great Lives from History: 20th Century
Great Lives from History: African Americans
Great Lives from History: American Women
Great Lives from History: Ancient World
Great Lives from History: Asian & Pacific Islander Americans
Great Lives from History: Cumulative Indexes
Great Lives from History: Incredibly Wealthy
Great Lives from History: Inventors & Inventions
Great Lives from History: Jewish Americans
Great Lives from History: Latinos
Great Lives from History: Middle Ages
Great Lives from History: Notorious Lives
Great Lives from History: Renaissance & Early Modern Era
Great Lives from History: Scientists & Science
Historical Encyclopedia of American Business
Issues in U.S. Immigration
Magill's Guide to Military History
Milestone Documents in African American History
Milestone Documents in American History
Milestone Documents in World History
Milestone Documents of American Leaders
Milestone Documents of World Religions
Music Innovators
Musicians & Composers 20th Century
The Nineties in America
The Seventies in America
The Sixties in America
Survey of American Industry and Careers
The Thirties in America
The Twenties in America
United States at War
U.S.A. in Space
U.S. Court Cases
U.S. Government Leaders
U.S. Laws, Acts, and Treaties
U.S. Legal System
U.S. Supreme Court
Weapons and Warfare
World Conflicts: Asia and the Middle East
World Political Yearbook

Health

Addictions & Substance Abuse
Adolescent Health & Wellness
Cancer
Complementary & Alternative Medicine
Genetics & Inherited Conditions
Health Issues
Infectious Diseases & Conditions
Magill's Medical Guide
Psychology & Behavioral Health
Psychology Basics

H·W WILSON

H·W WILSON

2016 Title List

Visit www.HWWilsonInPrint.com for Product Information, Table of Contents and Sample Pages

Current Biography

Current Biography Cumulative Index 1946-2013
Current Biography Monthly Magazine
Current Biography Yearbook: 2003
Current Biography Yearbook: 2004
Current Biography Yearbook: 2005
Current Biography Yearbook: 2006
Current Biography Yearbook: 2007
Current Biography Yearbook: 2008
Current Biography Yearbook: 2009
Current Biography Yearbook: 2010
Current Biography Yearbook: 2011
Current Biography Yearbook: 2012
Current Biography Yearbook: 2013
Current Biography Yearbook: 2014
Current Biography Yearbook: 2015

Core Collections

Children's Core Collection
Fiction Core Collection
Graphic Novels Core Collection
Middle & Junior High School Core
Public Library Core Collection: Nonfiction
Senior High Core Collection
Young Adult Fiction Core Collection

The Reference Shelf

Aging in America
American Military Presence Overseas
The Arab Spring
The Brain
The Business of Food
Campaign Trends & Election Law
Conspiracy Theories
The Digital Age
Dinosaurs
Embracing New Paradigms in Education
Faith & Science
Families: Traditional and New Structures
The Future of U.S. Economic Relations: Mexico, Cuba, and Venezuela
Global Climate Change
Graphic Novels and Comic Books
Immigration
Immigration in the U.S.
Internet Safety
Marijuana Reform
The News and its Future
The Paranormal
Politics of the Ocean
Racial Tension in a "Postracial" Age
Reality Television
Representative American Speeches: 2008-2009
Representative American Speeches: 2009-2010
Representative American Speeches: 2010-2011
Representative American Speeches: 2011-2012
Representative American Speeches: 2012-2013
Representative American Speeches: 2013-2014
Representative American Speeches: 2014-2015
Representative American Speeches: 2015-2016
Rethinking Work
Revisiting Gender
Robotics
Russia
Social Networking
Social Services for the Poor
Space Exploration & Development
Sports in America
The Supreme Court
The Transformation of American Cities
U.S. Infrastructure
U.S. National Debate Topic: Surveillance
U.S. National Debate Topic: The Ocean
U.S. National Debate Topic: Transportation Infrastructure
Whistleblowers

Readers' Guide

Abridged Readers' Guide to Periodical Literature
Readers' Guide to Periodical Literature

Indexes

Index to Legal Periodicals & Books
Short Story Index
Book Review Digest

Sears List

Sears List of Subject Headings
Sears: Lista de Encabezamientos de Materia

Facts About Series

Facts About American Immigration
Facts About China
Facts About the 20th Century
Facts About the Presidents
Facts About the World's Languages

Nobel Prize Winners

Nobel Prize Winners: 1901-1986
Nobel Prize Winners: 1987-1991
Nobel Prize Winners: 1992-1996
Nobel Prize Winners: 1997-2001

World Authors

World Authors: 1995-2000
World Authors: 2000-2005

Famous First Facts

Famous First Facts
Famous First Facts About American Politics
Famous First Facts About Sports
Famous First Facts About the Environment
Famous First Facts: International Edition

American Book of Days

The American Book of Days
The International Book of Days

Junior Authors & Illustrators

Eleventh Book of Junior Authors & Illustrations

Monographs

The Barnhart Dictionary of Etymology
Celebrate the World
Guide to the Ancient World
Indexing from A to Z
The Poetry Break
Radical Change: Books for Youth in a Digital Age

Wilson Chronology

Wilson Chronology of Asia and the Pacific
Wilson Chronology of Human Rights
Wilson Chronology of Ideas
Wilson Chronology of the Arts
Wilson Chronology of the World's Religions
Wilson Chronology of Women's Achievements